DATE DUE

DEMCO 38-296

THE COLUMBIA
GRANGER'S®
INDEX TO POETRY

IN ANTHOLOGIES

OTHER COLUMBIA UNIVERSITY PRESS PUBLICATIONS

The Columbia Granger's® Index to Poetry in Collected and Selected Works.
Nicholas Frankovich, ed. (1996)

The Columbia Granger's® World of Poetry 1995 (CD-ROM).

The Columbia Granger's® Dictionary of Poetry Quotations.
Edith P. Hazen, ed. (1992)

The Columbia Granger's® Guide to Poetry Anthologies, Second Edition.
William Katz, Linda Sternberg Katz, and Esther Crain, eds. (1994)

THE COLUMBIA GRANGER'S® INDEX TO POETRY IN ANTHOLOGIES

ELEVENTH EDITION, COMPLETELY REVISED
INDEXING ANTHOLOGIES
PUBLISHED THROUGH JANUARY 31, 1997

EDITED BY

NICHOLAS FRANKOVICH

COLUMBIA UNIVERSITY PRESS
NEW YORK

GRANGER'S® INDEX TO POETRY
ANTHOLOGIES

COPYRIGHT 1904, 1918, 1929, 1940, 1945, 1953, 1957, 1962,
1973, 1978, 1982, 1986, 1990, 1994, 1996, 1997

BY COLUMBIA UNIVERSITY PRESS

ELEVENTH EDITION COMPLETELY REVISED

LIBRARY OF CONGRESS CATALOGING-IN-PUBLICATION DATA

Frankovich, Nicholas.
  The Columbia Granger's index to poetry in anthologies. 11th ed.,
completely rev., indexing anthologies published through January 31,
1997 / edited by Nicholas Frankovich.
  p. cm.
ISBN 0-231-10130-9
  1. Poetry—Indexes.   2. English poetry—Indexes.
I. Granger, Edith. Index to poetry.   II. Title.
  PN1022.H39   1997
  016.80881—dc21   97-18668
                                                       CIP

CASEBOUND EDITIONS OF COLUMBIA UNIVERSITY PRESS BOOKS ARE
PRINTED ON PERMANENT AND DURABLE ACID-FREE PAPER.

PRINTED IN THE UNITED STATES OF AMERICA

c 10 9 8 7 6 5 4 3 2 1

PREFACE

Granger's, one of the oldest continuously published reference works in the United States, undergoes a slight but significant change in title with this, the eleventh edition. Since the fourth edition in 1953, the book has been in fact, if not in name, *The Columbia Granger's Index to Poetry in Anthologies*.

The words "in Anthologies" are new. They distinguish this volume from its companion, *The Columbia Granger's Index to Poetry in Collected and Selected Works*, which was published in 1996. With the publication of that volume, Granger's effectively became a two-volume work, indexing the two types of poetry book most frequently shelved by libraries — anthologies and collections of the work of individual authors.

In this volume we return to anthologies. The eleventh edition locates more than 75,000 poems. It locates by title, first line, author, and subject all the poetry in 379 anthologies (in 395 volumes) that the Press, together with the five members of our Board of Consultants, identified as those whose high editorial and design standards mark them as likely to be found on library shelves. Of these anthologies, 145 are new.

This edition indexes 11,000 authors writing from all parts of the world, and from remotest antiquity to the present. They write on more than 4,000 subjects, ranging from Aardvarks to Zulus.

We have continued the practice, inaugurated in the seventh edition, of singling out 40 anthologies — 30 of which we recommend, and 10 of which we recommend highly.

We provide last-line indexing for 10,000 of the most frequently anthologized poems.

And in the Subject Index we have arranged citations alphabetically by authors' names, enabling users to focus their searches.

HOW TO USE THE INDEXES

This volume is divided into three sections:
—Title, First Line, and Last Line Index
—Author Index
—Subject Index

Each section is arranged alphabetically.

Every poem covered here is cited at least once in each of the three sections (except for those not in the Author Index because their author is unknown, or not in the Subject Index because they are too abstract to be assigned to any heading there). Every poem cited here appears in at least one anthology listed on pages xv–xxviii.

See also the explanatory notes at the beginning of each of the three sections, on pages 1, 1537, and 1837.

Title, First Line, and Last Line Index

The clearest way to explain the Title, First Line, and Last Line Index is to begin by showing how it answers specific questions brought to it.

Where can I find a poem called "To a Chameleon"? Go to the Title, First Line, and Last Line Index. The citation for "To a Chameleon" is followed by the name of the poem's author, Marianne Moore, and by the letter code APo. Look up APo in the List of Anthologies, where the codes, not the titles of the anthologies, are arranged alphabetically. There you learn that you can read "To a Chameleon" in *Animal Poems*, edited by John Hollander and published by Knopf in 1994.

What is the title of the poem that begins "I ne'er was struck before that hour"? The first-line citation is followed by the title, "First Love," and then by the author, John Clare, and nine letter codes, including NOBVV and PoPoPo, which stand for anthologies. The List of Anthologies shows that they are *The New Oxford Book of Victorian Verse* (Christopher Ricks, editor; Oxford, 1987) and *Poems, Poets, Poetry; an Introduction and Anthology* (Helen Vendler, editor; Bedford Books, 1997).

What poem ends with the line "He slept like a rock or a man that's dead"? The last-line citation is followed by the title, "The Weary Blues," and then by the author, Langston Hughes, and ten letter codes. The List of Anthologies indicates that the title of the anthology coded ISC is *In Search of Color Everywhere; a Collection of African-American Poetry* (E. Ethelbert Miller, editor; Stewart, Tabori & Chang, 1994).

First Lines and Last Lines.   First-line and last-line citations are followed by the title (except where the poem has no title). The sign (LL) following last-line citations distinguishes them from first lines.

You know, for example, that "They also serve who only stand and wait" is not a title because the title, "On His Blindness," follows it, and because the initial letters of all the words (except the first one) are lower-case. You know that the citation is a last line and not a first line because it is followed by (LL).

When the first line or the last line of a poem is the same as or slightly longer than the title, only one of them is listed. The poem with the first line "And did those feet in ancient time," for example, has no listing for title because the title is the same.

Brackets.   Brackets usually show variant spellings. For example, see the first-line citation "Whan that Aprille [*or* April *or* Aprill] with his[e] shoures [*or* showres] so[o]te." In the several anthologies in which that first line appears, the spelling may vary as indicated in brackets.

Capitalization.   The first letter of the first word in every citation is capitalized, even when in its published form it appears as lower-case.

Initial Articles.   An article — "a," "an," or "the" — that begins a title or a line is transposed to the end of the citation. "The Seder" by Enid Dame, for example, is listed as "Seder, The."

Titles.   Initial capitals in the important words usually indicate that the citation is the title of the poem. "After Getting Drunk, Becoming Sober in the Night," for example, by Po Chü-i, is a title.

Parentheses.   When an entire citation is enclosed by parentheses, it usually means that it is a variant title, variant first line, or variant last line. Parentheses are used instead of brackets when it is necessary to indicate a version that varies widely from the standard version, with the result that, in this alphabetized index, it can also be found in a place far from where the standard version is listed.

See, for example, "Virtue" by Nicholas Grimald.

> Virtue. Nicholas Grimald.   SCGP
> (Description of Virtue.)   NoSiC

In the anthology indicated by the code NoSiC the poem can be found under the title "Description of Virtue." This information is especially useful when looking for a poem in the table of contents or the title index of the anthology being indicated.

Indentation.   Indentation of a citation indicates that it is a selection. See, for example, "Canterbury Tales, The."

> Canterbury Tales, The. Geoffrey Chaucer, *Middle English.*
> Canon Assistant's Tale, The. OxBoV, *tr. by* David Wright

"Canon Assistant's Tale, The" is indented because it is a selection from The Canterbury Tales.

Author Index

Under each author's name, poems are listed alphabetically by title or, where the poem has no title, by first line.
What poems can I find by Daniel Berrigan? The Author Index lists six poems.

Subject Index

Under each subject heading, poems are listed alphabetically by author's name.
What poems can I find about marriage? The subject index shows that there are 590 poems about marriage, by 410 different poets, including Gwendolyn Brooks and John Donne. Citations for all these poems can be found in the Title, First Line, and Last Line Index, where

the letter codes, which refer to the List of Anthologies, indicate in which books the poems are published.

    Did John Dryden write poems about religion? Go to the heading for "Religion" and locate "Dryden" in the list of poems alphabetized by author.

The Columbia Granger's® Index to Poetry
in Anthologies

ELEVENTH EDITION

PUBLISHER
JOHN D. MOORE

PROJECT DIRECTOR
JAMES RAIMES

DIRECTOR OF DESIGN AND PRODUCTION
AUDREY SMITH

EDITORIAL MANAGER
ADAM TIBBS

EDITOR
NICHOLAS FRANKOVICH

ASSISTANT EDITOR
DAVID LARZELERE

STAFF

CHANITA BAUMHAFT
BRUCE ALEXANDER ANDREW DAUSCH
DANIEL HUGHES DAVID RANDALL

CONTENTS

LIST OF ANTHOLOGIES

Anthologies marked with two asterisks (**) are recommended for priority acquisition by small libraries, one asterisk (*) for further acquisition. Anthologies marked with a dagger (†) have been translated into English. See PREFACE *for fuller explanation.*

AAP   African-American Poetry of the Nineteenth Century; an Anthology. *Joan R. Sherman, ed.* (1992) University of Illinois Press. 506p., pap.

AAS   The Anchor Anthology of Sixteenth Century Verse. *Richard Sylvester, ed.* (1974) Doubleday / Anchor Books; also published 1984 by W. W. Norton with title English Sixteenth-Century Verse. 623p.

ACTP   A Child's Treasury of Poems. *Mark Daniel, ed.* (1986) Dial / Penguin Books. 153p.

ADE   Aesthetes and Decadents of the 1890's. *Karl Beckson, ed.* (1981) Academy Chicago Publishers. 337p., pap.

AEP   An Anthology of Elizabethan Poetry. *Sukanta Chaudhuri, ed.* (1992) Oxford University Press. 170p., pap.

AF   *Against Forgetting; Twentieth–Century Poetry of Witness. *Carolyn Forché, ed.* (1993) W. W. Norton. 812p., pap.

AFr   After Frost; an Anthology of Poetry from New England. *Henry Lyman, ed.* (1995) University of Massachussetts Press. 243p., pap.

AH   American Hymns Old and New. Vols. I–II. *Albert Christ-Janer, Charles W. Hughes, and Carleton Sprague Smith, eds.* (1980) Columbia University Press.

AiP   America in Poetry. *Charles Sullivan, ed.* (1988) Harry N. Abrams. 207p.

AmFP   American Folk Poetry; an Anthology. *Duncan Emrich, ed.* (1974) Little, Brown. 831p.

AmPA   The American Poetry Anthology. *Daniel Halpern, ed.* (1975) Avon Books. 506p., pap.

AmPP   American Poetry and Prose. *Norman Foerster, Norman S. Grabo, Russel B. Nye, E. Fred Carlisle, and Robert Falk, eds.* (5th ed., 1970) Houghton Mifflin. 3 vols., pap.

AnOE   †An Anthology of Old English Poetry. *Charles W. Kennedy, tr.* (1960) Oxford University Press. 174p., pap.

APAD   A Poem a Day. *Karen McCosker and Nicholas Albery, eds.* (1996) Steer Forth Press. 484p., pap.

APN-1   *American Poetry; the Nineteenth Century. Vol. 1. *John Hollander, ed.* (1993) The Library of America. 1,099p.

APN-2   *American Poetry; the Nineteenth Century. Vol. 2. *John Hollander, ed.* (1993) The Library of America. 1,050p.

APo   Animal Poems. *John Hollander, ed.* (1994) Alfred A. Knopf. 256p.

APSN   American Poetry since 1950; Innovators and Outsiders. *Eliot Weinberger, ed.* (1993) Marsilio. 433p.

ArPe   †Arabic & Persian Poems. *Omar S. Pound, ed. and tr.* (1970) New Directions Books. 80p.

AS   The American Songbag. *Carl Sandburg, comp.* (1927) Harcourt, Brace. 495p., pap.

ASW   †The Anglo-Saxon World; an Anthology. *Kevin Crossley-Holland, ed.* (1982) Oxford University Press. 308p.

AVP   †An Anthology of Vietnamese Poetry. *Huynh Sanh Thong, ed.* (1996) Yale University Press. 429p.

AWP   An Anthology of World Poetry. *Mark Van Doren, ed.* (Rev. and enl. ed., 1936) Reynal & Hitchcock. 1,468p.

AYFP   A Year Full of Poems. *Michael Harrison and Christopher Stuart-Clark, eds.* (1991) Oxford University Press. 141p.

BAP-93   Best American Poetry, 1993. *Louise Glück, ed.* (1993) Macmillan. 277p., pap.

BAP-94   Best American Poetry, 1994. *A. R. Ammons, ed.* (1995) Simon & Schuster. 275p., pap.

BAP-95   Best American Poetry, 1995. *David Lehman, ed.* (1995) Simon & Schuster. 303p., pap.

PS614 B33 1996	⊘BAP-96 →BB	Best American Poetry, 1996. *Adrienne Rich, ed.* (1996) Scribner. 318p., pap. The Beat Book; Poems and Fiction of the Beat Generation. *Anne Waldman, ed.* (1996) Shambhala. 351p., pap.

BeJo — Ben Jonson and the Cavalier Poets. *Hugh MacLean, ed.* (1974) W. W. Norton. 591p., pap.

BiHa — Bitter Harvest; an Anthology of Contemporary Irish Verse. *John Montague, ed.* (1989) Scribner's. 211p.

PR8851 MG 1976 →**BIrV** — The Book of Irish Verse; an Anthology of Irish Poetry from the Sixth Century to the Present. *John Montague, ed.* (1974) Macmillan; also published as The Faber Book of Irish Verse. 400p.

BkSV — Black Southern Voices; an Anthology of Fiction, Poetry, Drama, Nonficiton, and Critical Essays. *John Oliver Killens and Jerry W. Ward, eds.* (1992) Meridian. 608p., pap.

PR1175 FH →**BLPA** — *Best Loved Poems of the American People, The. *Hazel Felleman, ed.* (1936) Doubleday. 670p., pap.

BlSi — Black Sister; Poetry by Black American Women, 1746–1980. *Erlene Stetson, ed.* (1981) Indiana University Press. 312p., pap.

BLT — A Book of Luminous Things; an International Anthology of Poetry. *Czeslaw Milosz, ed.* (1996) Harcourt Brace. 320p.

BMAP — The Bloodaxe Book of Moderan Australian Poetry. *John Tranter and Philip Mead, eds.* (1991, 1994) Bloodaxe Books. 474p., pap.

BoLoP — A Book of Love Poetry. *Jon Stallworthy, ed.* (1974) Oxford University Press; also published in Great Britain as The Penguin Book of Love Poetry. 393p.

PNG109.9 B6 →**BoTP** — The Book of a Thousand Poems; a Family Treasury. *J. Murray Macbain, ed.* (1983) Peter Bedrick Books. 630p.

PS153 B6 →**BoWoP** — *A Book of Women Poets from Antiquity to Now. *Aliki Barnstone and Willis Barnstone, eds.* (1980) Schocken Books. 613p.

→**BPo** — *The Black Poets. *Dudley Randall, ed.* (1971) Bantam Books. 355p., pap.

BrRo — Bread and Roses; an Anthology of Nineteenth- and Twentieth-Century Poetry by Women Writers. *Diana Scott, comp.* (1982) Virago Press. 282p., pap.

BWW — British Women Writers. *Dale Spender and Janet Todd, eds.* (1989) Peter Bedrick Books. 921p.

BXAP — The Brand-X Anthology of Poetry. *William Zaranka, ed.* (1981) Apple-Wood Books. 358p.

CA — Celebrating America; a Collection of Poems and Images of the American Spirit. *Laura Whipple, ed.* (1994) Philomel Books. 79p.

PR1175 .C6416 1995 →**CABP** — *The Columbia Anthology of British Poetry. *Carl Woodring and James Shapiro, eds.* (1995) Columbia University Press. 891p.

CaPo — Cavalier Poets; Selected Poems. *Thomas Clayton, ed.* (1978) Oxford University Press. 364p., pap.

PS613 PG8 1975 →**CAPP-1** — Contemporary American Poetry. *A. Poulin, Jr., ed.* (1971) Houghton Mifflin Company

CavPo — The Cavalier Poets; an Anthology. *Thomas Crofts, ed.* (1995) Dover. 92p., pap.

CBAP — The Collins Book of Australian Poetry. *Rodney Hall, comp.* (1981, 1984) Fontana / Collins. 460p.

PS595 C55C65 1994 **CBCWP** — The Columbia Book of Civil War Poetry. *Richard Marius, ed.* (1994) Columbia University Press. 543p.

CBLP — The Chatto Book of Love Poetry. *John Fuller, ed.* (1990) Chatto & Windus. 374p.

CBNP — The Chatto Book of Nonsense Poetry. *Hugh Haughton, ed.* (1988) Chatto & Windus. 530p.

CBWP-1 — Collected Black Women's Poetry. Vol. I. *Joan R. Sherman, ed.* (1988) Oxford University Press.

CBWP 2 — Collected Black Women's Poetry. Vol. II. *Joan R. Sherman, ed.* (1988) Oxford University Press.

CBWP-3 — Collected Black Women's Poetry. Vol. III. *Joan R. Sherman, ed.* (1988) Oxford University Press.

CBWP-4 — Collected Black Women's Poetry. Vol. IV. *Joan R. Sherman, ed.* (1988) Oxford University Press.

CDa — Carrying the Darkness; the Poetrty of the Vietnam War. *W. D. Ehrhart, ed.* (1989) Texas Tech University Press. 288p.

LIST OF ANTHOLOGIES

CDW Carriers of the Dream Wheel; Contemporary Native American Poetry. *Duane Niatum, ed.* (1975) Harper & Row. 300p.

CEEP †Contemporary East European Poetry. *Emery George, ed.* (1983) Oxford University Press. 490p.

CH *Come Hither. *Walter de la Mare, comp.* (3rd ed., 1957) Knopf. 777p.

ChAP A Child's Anthology of Poetry. *Elizabeth Hauge Sword and Victoria Flournoy McCarthy, eds.* (1995) Ecco Press. 323p.

ChiP †Chinese Poems. *Arthur Waley, ed.* (1946) Unwin Paperbacks. 181p., pap.

ChiPo †Chinese Poetry; Through the Words of the People. *Bonnie McCandless, ed.* (1991) Ballantine Books. 130p., pap.

ChIV-1 Chapters into Verse. Vol. I: Genesis to Malachi. *Robert Atwan and Laurance Wieder, eds.* (1993) Oxford University Press. 481p.

ChIV-2 Chapters into Verse. Vol. II: Gospels to Revelation. *Robert Atwan and Laurance Wieder, eds.* (1993) Oxford University Press. 391p.

CIP-2 Contemporary Irish Poetry; an Anthology. *Anthony Bradley, ed.* (New and rev. ed., 1988) University of California Press. 526p.

CKP †Contemporary Korean Poetry. *Kim Jaihuin* (1994) Mosaic Press. 139p., pap.

ClHu The Classic Hundred; All-Time Favorite Poems. *William Harmon, ed.* (1990) Columbia University Press. 250p., pap.

CLPP City Lights Pocket Poets Anthology. *Lawrence Ferlinghetti, ed.* (1995) City Lights Books

CMAP The Carnegie Mellon Anthology of Poetry. *Gerald Costanzo and Jim Daniels, eds.* (1993) Carnegie Mellon University Press. 308p., pap.

CMoP *Chief Modern Poets of Britain and America. *Gerald DeWitt Sanders, John Herbert Nelson, and M. L. Rosenthal, eds.* (5th ed., 1970) Macmillan. 962p.

CoAmPo Contemporary American Poetry. *Donald Hall, ed.* (2d ed., 1972) Penguin Books. 280p., pap.

CoAP The Contemporary American Poets; American Poetry since 1940. *Mark Strand, ed.* (1969) World. 390p., pap.

CoBCP †The Columbia Book of Chinese Poetry; from Early Times to the Thirteenth Century. *Burton Watson, ed. and tr.* (1984) Columbia University Press. 385p., pap.

CoBLCP †The Columbia Book of Later Chinese Poetry. *Jonathan Chaves, ed. and tr.* (1986) Columbia University Press. 490p., pap.

ColAP *The Columbia Anthology of American Poetry. *Jay Parini, ed.* (1995) Columbia University Press. 757p.

CPO Chloe Plus Olivia; an Anthology of Lesbian Literature from the Seventeenth Century to the Present. *Lillian Faderman, ed.* (1994) Viking Penguin. 812p.

CrDW Crossing the Danger Water. *Deirdre Mullane, ed.* (1993) Doubleday. 769p., pap.

CRP Contemporary Religious Poetry. *Paul Ramsey, ed.* (1987) Paulist Press. 227p., pap.

CrSp Cries of the Spirit; a Celebration of Women's Spiritualities. *Marilyn Sewell, ed.* (1991) Boston Beacon Press. 311p., pap.

CTAV A Child's Treasury of Animal Verse. *Mark Daniel, ed.* (1989) Dial / Penguin Books. 153p.

CTC Confucius to Cummings; an Anthology of Poetry. *Ezra Pound and Marcella Spann, eds.* (1964) New Directions. 353p., pap.

CTV A Child's Treasury of Verse. *Eleanor Doan, ed.* (1977) Zondervan. 207p.

DeD Deep Down; The New Sensual Writing by Women. *Laura Chester, ed.* (1989) Faber and Faber. 330p., pap.

DiPo The Direction of Poetry; an Anthology of Rhymed and Metered Verse Written in the English Language since 1975. *Robert Richman, ed.* (1988) Houghton Mifflin. 168p.

EBEV Everyman's Book of English Verse. *John Wain, ed.* (1981) J. M. Dent. 672p.

EBEvV Everyman's Book of Evergreen Verse. *David Herbert, ed.* (1984) J. M. Dent. 387p., pap.

EBNV The Everyman Book of Narrative Verse. *David Herbert, ed.* (1990) J. M. Dent. 315p.

EBVV Everyman's Book of Victorian Verse. *J. R. Watson, ed.* (1982) J. M. Dent. 373p.

EBVVPR The Everyman Book of Victorian Verse; the Post-Romantics. *Donald Thomas, ed.* (1992) J. M. Dent. 284p., pap.

EC2	Editor's Choice II; Fiction, Poetry & Art from the U.S. Small Press. *Morty Sklar and Mary Biggs* (1987) The Spirit That Moves Us Press. 336p., pap.
EC3	Editor's Choice III. *Morty Sklar, ed.* (1991) The Spirit That Moves Us Press. 336p., pap.
ECEV	Eighteenth-Century English Verse. *Dennis Davison, ed.* (1988) Penguin Books. 321p., pap.
ECWP	Eighteenth Century Women Poets; an Oxford Anthology. *Roger Lonsdale, ed.* (1989) Oxford University Press. 555p.
EEP	†The Earliest English Poems. *Michael Alexander, ed.* (1977) Penguin Books. 160p., pap.
EnlH	The Enlightened Heart; an Anthology of Sacred Poetry. *Stephen Mitchell, ed.* (1989) Harper & Row. 171p.
EnLoPo	English Love Poems. *John Betjeman and Geoffrey Taylor, comps.* (1957; paperback ed., 1964) Faber and Faber. 220p., pap.
EnSB	English and Scottish Ballads. *Robert Graves, ed.* (1957) William Heinemann. 163p., pap.
EnVB	English Verse, 1300–1500; Longman Annotated Anthologies of English Verse. Vol. I. *John Burrow, ed.* (1977) Longman. 397p., pap.
EnVR	English Verse 1830-1890. *Bernard Richards, ed.* (1980) Longman. 543p., pap.
EOEF	Ecstatic Occasions, Expedient Forms; 65 Leading Contemporary Poets Select and Comment on Their Poems. *David Lehman, ed.* (1987) Collier Books / Macmillan. 256p.
EP	Erotic Poems. *Peter Washington, ed.* (1994) Alfred A. Knopf. 285p.
EPCY	English Poetry; a Poetic Record, from Chaucer to Yeats. *David Hopkins, ed.* (1990) Routledge. 269p., pap.
ESCV	English Seventeenth-Century Verse; Vol. 1. *Louis L. Martz. ed.* (1963, 1969) W. W. Norton. 525p., pap.
ESPB	English and Scottish Popular Ballads. *Helen Child Sargent and George Lyman Kittredge, eds., from the collection of Francis James Child.* (1904, 1932; reissued 1947) Houghton Mifflin. 730p.
FaBoA	The Faber Book of America. *Christopher Ricks and William L. Vance, eds.* (1992) Faber and Faber. 467p.
FaBoBe	The Family Book of Best Loved Poems. *David L. George, ed.* (1952) Doubleday. 485p., pap.
FaBoCh	The Faber Book of Children's Verse. *Janet Adam Smith, comp.* (1953) Faber and Faber. 412p., pap.
FaBoEE	The Faber Book of Epigrams and Epitaphs. *Geoffrey Grigson, ed.* (1977) Faber and Faber. 291p.
FaBoMo	The Faber Book of Modern Verse. *Michael Roberts, ed.* (4th ed., rev. by Peter Porter, 1982) Faber and Faber. 416p., pap.
FaBoPv	The Faber Book of Political Verse. *Tom Paulin, ed.* (1986) Faber and Faber. 482p., pap.
FaBoSe	The Faber Book of Seductions. *Jenny Newman, ed.* (1988) Faber and Faber. 366p.
FaBoTC	Faber Book of Twentieth-Century Scottish Poetry. *Douglas Dunn, ed.* (1992) Faber and Faber. 424p.
FaBoTw	The Faber Book of Twentieth Century Verse. *John Heath-Stubbs and David Wright, eds.* (3d ed., 1975) Faber and Faber. 348p.
FaBoVe	The Faber Book of Vernacular Verse. *Tom Paulin, ed.* (1990) Faber and Faber. 407p.
FaBoWP	The Faber Book of 20th Century Women's Poetry. *Fleur Adcock, ed.* (1987) Faber and Faber. 330p.
FaPoR	The Faber Popular Reciter. *Kingsley Amis, ed.* (1978) Faber and Faber. 256p.
FFC	A Formal Feeling Comes; Poems in Form by Contemporary Women. *Annie Finch, ed.* (1994) Story Line Press. 308p., pap.
FHYEP	Five Hundred Years of English Poetry; Chaucer to Arnold. *Barbara Lloyd-Evans, ed.* (1989) Peter Bedrick Books. 1200p., pap.
FiLi	First Light; Mother and Son Poems. *Jason Shinder, ed.* (1992) Harcourt Brace Jovanovich. 153p., pap.
FLP	†French Love Poems. *Alistair Eliot, ed.* (1991) Bloodaxe Books. 96p., pap.
FMP	Four Metaphysical Poets. *Richard Willmott, ed.* (1985) Cambridge University Press. 184p., pap.
FP	Friendship Poems. *Peter Washington, ed.* (1995) Alfred A. Knopf. 256p.

LIST OF ANTHOLOGIES

FPC   Favorite Poems of Childhood. *Philip Smith, ed.* (1992) Dover Publications. 90p., pap.

FSCP   Five Seventeenth-Century Poets; Donne, Herbert, Crashaw, Marvell, Vaughan. *Brirjraj Singh, ed.* (1992) Oxford University Press. 297p., pap.

FTOS   From the Other Side of the Century; a New American Poetry 1960–1990. *Douglas Messerli, ed.* (1994) Sun & Moon Press. 1,136p., pap.

FuFo   Funny Folk; Poems about People. *Robert Fisher, ed.* (1986) Faber and Faber. 79p.

FuPo   The Fugitive Poets; Modern Southern Poetry in Perspective. *William Pratt, ed.* (1991) J. S. Sanders & Company. 159p., pap.

FYAP   Fifty Years of American Poetry; Anniversary Volume for the Academy of American Poets. *American Academy of Poets; introduction by Robert Penn Warren* (1984) Harry N. Abrams. 260p.

GaP   Garden Poems. *John Hollander, ed.* (1996) Alfred A. Knopf. 256p.

GBL   The Gambit Book of Love Poems. *Geoffrey Grigson, ed.* (1973) Gambit; originally published in Great Britain by Faber and Faber as The Faber Book of Love Poems. 407p.

GEA   The Golden Ecco Anthology; 100 Great Poems of the English Language. *Mark Strand, ed.* (1994) The Ecco Press. 181p., pap.

GeHe   George Herbert and the Seventeenth-Century Religious Poets. *Marie A. Di Ceare, ed.* (1978) W. W. Norton. 401p., pap.

GePo   †German Poetry; from the Beginnings to 1750. *Ingrid Walsë–Engel, ed.* (1992) Continuum. 338p., pap.

GI   The Gospels in Our Image; an Anthology of Twentieth-Century Poetry Based on Biblical Texts. *David Curzon, ed.* (1995) Harcourt Brace. 279p.

GLoP   Great Love Poems. *Shane Weller, ed.* (1992) Dover. 120p., pap.

GLP   Gay & Lesbian Poetry in Our Time; an Anthology. *Carl Morse and Joan Larkin, eds.* (1988) St. Martin's Press. 463p.

GM   The Great Machines; Poems and Songs of the American Railroad. *Robert Hedin, ed.* (1996) University of Iowa Press. 251p., pap.

GoJo-1   The Golden Journey; Poems for Young People. *Louise Bogan and William Jay Smith, eds.* (1965) Reilly & Lee. 275p.

GrAn   †The Greek Anthology and Other Ancient Epigrams. *Peter Jay, ed.* (1981) Penguin Books. 447p., pap.

GrIP   Greece in Poetry. *Simoni Zafiropoulos, ed.* (1993) Harry N. Abrams. 176p.

GS   The Gazer's Spirit; Poems Speaking to Silent Works of Art. *John Hollander, ed.* (1995) The University of Chicago Press. 380p.

GSo   Great Sonnets. *Paul Negri, ed.* (1994) Dover. 96p., pap.

GT   The Garden Thrives; Twentieth-Century African-American Poetry. *Clarence Major, ed.* (1996) HarperCollins. 470p., pap.

GTBS-P   **Golden Treasury of the Best Songs & Lyrical Poems in the English Language. *Francis Turner Palgrave, comp. With a fifth book selected by John Press.* (Updated ed., by Christopher Ricks, 1991) Oxford University Press. 526p., pap.

HA   The Haiku Anthology. *Cor Van Den Heuvel, ed.* (1986) Simon & Schuster. 367p., pap.

HAP   *The Harper Anthology of Poetry. *John Frederick Nims, ed.* (1981) Harper & Row. 842p.

HATNAP   *Harper's Anthology of 20th Century Native American Poetry. *Duane Niatum, ed.* (1988) Harper & Row. 396p.

HBAPE   The Heinemann Book of African Poetry in English. *Adewale Maja-Pearce, ed.* (1990) Heinemann. 224p., pap.

HCAP   **The Harvard Book of Contemporary American Poetry. *Helen Vendler, ed.* (1985) Belknap Press. 440p.

HCP   The Heinemann Book of Caribbean Poetry. *Stewart Brown and Ian McDonald, eds.* (1992) Heinemann. 236p., pap. *(For second ed., see* Caribbean Poetry Now)

HeIP-4   The Heath Introduction to Poetry. *Joseph DeRoche, ed.* (4th ed., 1992) D. C. Heath. 561p., pap.

HePo   †Hellenistic Poetry; an Anthology. *Barbara Hughes Fowler, ed.* (1990) University of Wisconsin Press. 357p.

PS586
C53
1975 → HoPM   How Does a Poem Mean? *John Ciardi and Miller Williams, eds.* (2d ed., 1975) Houghton Mifflin. 408p.

&HP   Holocaust Poetry. *Hilda Schiff, ed.* (1995) HarperCollins. 234p.

&HSix   †The Horse Has Six Legs; an Anthology of Serbian Poetry. *Charles Simic, ed.* (1992) Graywolf Press. 222p., pap.

&IBB   The Illustrated Border Ballads. *John Marden, ed.* (1990) University of Texas Press. 192p.

&IFJA   I Feel a Little Jumpy around You. *Naomi Shihab Nye and Paul B. Janeczko, eds.* (1996) Simon & Schuster. 256p.

&IIP   Ireland in Poetry. *Charles Sullivan, ed.* (1990) Harry N. Abrams. 208p.

ImGa   Imaginary Gardens; American Poetry and Art for Young People. *Charles Sullivan, ed.* (1989) Harry N. Abrams. 111p.

&ImPo   Immortal Poems of the English Language. *Oscar Williams, ed.* (1952) Simon & Schuster. 637p., pap.

PN6071
D415 → IMW   In the Midst of Winter; Selections from the Literature of Mourning. *Mary Jane Moffat, ed.*
1992   (1992) Vintage Books. 274p., pap.

&InMo   †The Infinite Moment; Poems from the Ancient Greek. *Sam Hamill, ed.* (1992) New Directions. 108p.

PN1042
K36 → InPK-6   *An Introduction to Poetry. *X. J. Kennedy, ed.* (6th ed., 1986) Little, Brown. 480p., pap.
1986 &InPS-3   An Introduction to Poetry. *Louis Simpson, ed.* (3d ed., 1986) St. Martin's Press. 640p.

&IP   †Israeli Poetry; a Contemporary Anthology. *Warren Bargad and Stanley F. Chyet, eds. and trs.* (1986) Indiana University Press. 273p.

&ISC   In Search of Color Everywhere; a Collection of African–American Poetry. *E. Ethelbert Miller, ed.* (1994) Stewart, Tabori & Chang. 256p., pap.

&ITG   Into the Garden; a Wedding Anthology; Poetry and Prose on Love and Marriage. *Robert Haas and Stephen Mitchell, eds.* (1993) HarperCollins. 193p.

&ItIP   †Introduction to Italian Poetry. *Luciano Rebay, ed.* (1969) Dover. 148p., pap.

&KaS   Knock at a Star; a Child's Introduction to Poetry. *X. J. Kennedy and Dorothy M. Kennedy, eds.* (1982) Little, Brown. 148p., pap.

&KSG   King Solomon's Garden; Poems and Art Inspired by the Old Testament. *Laurance Weider, ed.* (1994) Harry N. Abrams. 152p.

&KTR   Kissing the Rod; an Anthology of Seventeenth-Century Women's Verse. *Germaine Greer, Susan Hastings, Jeslyn Medoff, and Melinda Sansone, eds.* (1988) Farrar Straus Giroux. 477p., pap.

PZ8.3
L62 &LaPo   The Lakeland Poets. *Jenny Wilson, ed.* (1991) Weidenfield and Nicholson. 112p.
Lav → LB   Lavender's Blue. *Kathleen Lines, ed.; Harold Jones, illus.* (1989) Oxford University Press.
1962   180p., pap.

&LBC   A Little Book of Comfort. *Anthony Guest, ed.* (1993) HarperCollins. 160p.

&LCAP-2   The Longman Anthology of Contemporary American Poetry. *Stuart Friebert and David Young, eds.* (2d ed., 1989) Longman. 629p., pap.

&LiLi   Lifelines; a Poetry Patterned on the Stages of Life. *Leonard S. Marcus, ed.* (1994) Dutton. 116p.

LiTM   A Little Treasury of Modern Poetry; English and American. *Oscar Williams, ed.* (3d ed., 1970) Scribner's. 937p.

&LoHo   Looking for Home; Women Writing about Exile. *Deborah Keenan and Roseann Lloyd, eds.* (1990) Milkweed Editions. 288p., pap.

&LoL   The Language of Life; a Festival of Poets. *Bill Moyers, ed.* (1995) Doubleday. 450p., pap.

&LoP   Love Poems. *Peter Washington, ed.* (1993) Alfred A. Knopf. 256p.

&LTA   Letters to America; Contemporary American Poetry on Race. *Jim Daniels, ed.* (1995) Wayne State University Press. 230p., pap.

&LW   Love's Witness; Five Centuries of Love Poetry by Women. *Jill Hollis, ed.* (1993) Carroll and Graf. 334p., pap.

PS591
N4A29 MBE   My Black Me; a Beginning Anthology of Black Poetry. *Arnold Adoff* (1974) Dutton. 83p.

&MDDM   Mother to Daughter, Daughter to Mother; Mothers on Mothering. *Tillie Olsen, ed.* (1984) The Feminist Press. 296p., pap.

LIST OF ANTHOLOGIES

MeLP — Metaphysical Lyrics & Poems of the Seventeenth Century; Donne to Butler. *Herbert J. Grierson, ed.* (1921) Oxford University Press. 302p.

MeMAP — The Mentor Book of Major American Poets. *Oscar Williams and Edwin Honig, eds.* (1962) New American Library. 535p.

MFP — †Modern French Poetry. *Martin Sorrell, ed.* (1992) Forest Books. 242p., pap.

MHP — †Modern Hebrew Poetry; a Bilingual Anthology. *Ruth Finer Mintz, ed.* (1966) University of California Press. 371p.

MiEL — †Middle English Lyrics, Authoritative Texts, Critical and Historical Backgrounds, Perspectives on Six Poems *Maxwell S. Luria, ed.* (1974) W. W. Norton. 360p., pap.

MJT — †Modern Japanese Tanka. *Makoto Ueda, ed.* (1996) Columbia University Press. 265p., pap.

MLL — †More Latin Lyrics; from Virgil to Milton. *Dame Felicitas Corrigan, ed.; Helen Waddell, tr.* (1977) W. W. Norton. 392p.

MoAmPo — Modern American Poetry. *Louis Untermeyer, ed.* (8th rev. ed., 1962) Harcourt, Brace. 701p.

MoBrPo — Modern British Poetry. *Louis Untermeyer, ed.* (7th rev. ed., 1962) Harcourt, Brace. 500p.

MoBS — Modern Ballads and Story Poems. *Charles Causley, ed.* (1965) Franklin Watts, 128p. (*Also published in Great Britain as* Rising Early by Brockhampton Press [1964].)

MoCV — Modern Canadian Verse. *A. J. M. Smith, ed.* (1967) Oxford University Press. 426p.

MoLi — More Light: Father & Daughter Poems; a Twentieth-Century American Selection. *Jason Shinder, ed.* (1993) Harcourt Brace & Company. 172p., pap.

MoNo — Moment's Notice; Jazz in Poetry and Prose. *Art Lange and Nathaniel Mackey, eds.* (1993) Coffee House Press. 373p., pap.

MoP — Modern Poems; an Introduction to Poetry. *Richard Ellmann and Robert O'Clair, eds.* (1976) W. W. Norton. 526p., pap.

MT — The Made Thing; an Anthology of Contemporary Southern Poetry. *Leon Stokesbury, ed.* (1987) University of Arkansas Press. 326p.

NAAAL — **The Norton Anthology of African American Literature. *Henry Louis Gates, et al., eds.* (1997) W.W. Norton. 2,655p.

NAAL-1 — *The Norton Anthology of American Literature. Vol. 1. *Nina Baym and others, eds.* (2d ed., 1985) W. W. Norton. 2,535p., pap.

NAAL-2 — *The Norton Anthology of American Literature. Vol. 2. *Nina Baym and others, eds.* (2d ed., 1985) W. W. Norton. 2,652p., pap.

NAAL-3 — *The Norton Anthology of American Literature. *Nina Baym et al., eds.* (3rd ed., 1989) W. W. Norton. 2,459p., pap.

NAEL-1 — *The Norton Anthology of English Literature. Vol. I. *M. H. Abrams, general ed.* (5th ed., 1986) W. W. Norton.

NAEL-2 — *The Norton Anthology of English Literature. Vol. II. *M. H. Abrams, general ed.* (5th ed., 1986) W. W. Norton.

NALW — **The Norton Anthology of Literature by Women; the Tradition in English. *Sandra M. Gilbert and Susan Guber, eds.* (1985) W. W. Norton. 2,457p.

NAmP90 — New American Poets of the '90s. *Jack Myers and Roger Weingarten, eds.* (1991) David R. Godine. 443p.

NAWM-1 — The Norton Anthology of World Masterpieces. Vol. I. *Maynard Mack, general ed.* (5th ed., 1985) W. W. Norton. 2,052p.

NAWM-2 — The Norton Anthology of World Masterpieces. Vol. II. *Maynard Mack, general ed.* (5th ed., 1985) W. W. Norton. 2,165p.

NBLV — The Norton Book of Light Verse. *Russell Baker, ed.* (1986) W. W. Norton. 447p.

NBrP — The New British Poetry, 1968–88. *Gillian Allnutt, Fred D'Aguiar, Ken Edwards, and Eric Mottram, eds.* (1989) Grafton Books. 361p., pap.

NBV — New Black Voices; an Anthology of Contemporary Afro-American Literature. *Abraham Chapman, ed.* (1972) Mentor. 606p., pap.

NCAP — Nineteenth Century American Poetry. *William C. Spengemann and Jessica F. Roberts, eds.* (1996) Penguin Books. 447p., pap.

NeAP — The New American Poetry, 1945–1960. *Donald M. Allen, ed.* (1960) Grove Press. 454p.

NegPo · The Negritude Poets; an Anthology of Translations from the French. *Ellen Conroy Kennedy, ed.* (1989) Thunder's Mouth Press. 284p., pap.

NeIt · †New Italian Poets. *Dana Gioia and Michael Palma, eds.* (1991) Story Line Press. 385p., pap.

NIP-4 · The Norton Introduction to Poetry. *J. Paul Hunter, ed.* (4th ed., 1991) W. W. Norton. 578 p. (*For first ed., see* The Norton Introduction to Literature: Poetry).

NMM-2 · No More Masks. *Florence Howe, ed.* (2d ed., 1993) HarperCollins Publishers. 488p., pap.

NNaP · The New Naked Poetry; Recent American Poetry in Open Forms. *Stephen Berg and Robert Mesey, eds.* (1976) Bobbs-Merrill. 478p.

NNPT · †Ninety–Nine Poems in Translation. *Harold Pinter, Anthony Astbury, and Geoffrey Godbert, eds.* (1994) Grove Press. 149p.

NoAM · *The Norton Anthology of Modern Poetry. *Richard Ellmann and Robert O'Clair, eds.* (2d ed., 1988) W. W. Norton. 1,863p., pap.

PS584
N4 — NOBA · *The New Oxford Book of American Verse. *Richard Ellmann, ed.* (1976) Oxford University Press. 1,076p.

NOBAu · The New Oxford Book of Australian Verse. *Les A. Murray, ed.* (Enl. ed., 1991) Oxford University Press. 399p., pap.

NOBC · The New Oxford Book of Canadian Verse in English. *Margaret Atwood, comp.* (1982) Oxford University Press. 477p.

PR1174
G3 — NOBE · **The New Oxford Book of English Verse, 1250–1950. *Helen Gardner, ed.* (1972) Oxford University Press. 974p.

PR1175
N37 — NOBL · *The New Oxford Book of English Light Verse. *Kingsley Amis, ed.* (1978) Oxford University Press. 347p.

NOBRP · *The New Oxford Book of Romantic Period Verse. *Jerome J. McGann, ed.* (1993) Oxford University Press. 832p.

NOBVV · *The New Oxford Book of Victorian Verse. *Christopher Ricks, ed.* (1987) Oxford University Press. 654p.

NOCV · The New Oxford Book of Christian Verse. *Donald Davie, ed.* (1981) Oxford University Press. 320p.

PR1215
N48 — NOEC · **The New Oxford Book of Eighteenth Century Verse. *Roger Lonsdale, ed.* (1984) Oxford University Press. 870p.
1984

NOIV · *The New Oxford Book of Irish Verse. *Thomas Kinsella, ed. and tr.* (1986) Oxford University Press. 422p.

NoP-4 · **The Norton Anthology of Poetry. *Margaret Ferguson, Mary Jo Salter, and Jon Stallworthy, eds.* (1996) W. W. Norton. 1,998p., pap.

NOSC · **The New Oxford Book of Seventeenth Century Verse. *Alistair Fowler, ed.* (1991) Oxford University Press. 831p.

NoSic · *The New Oxford Book of Sixteenth Century Verse. *Emrys Jones, ed.* (1991) Oxford University Press. 769p.

NOxBChV · The New Oxford Book of Children's Verse. *Neil Philip, ed.* (1996) Oxford University Press. 371p.

NSI · Never Such Innocence; a New Anthology of Great War Verse. *Martin Stephen, ed.* (1988) Buchan and Enright. 358p., pap.

NTCP · A New Treasury of Children's Poetry; Old Favorites and New Discoveries. *Joanna Cole, comp.* (1984) Doubleday. 224p., pap.

PR1175.3
N48
1990 → NTP · A New Treasury of Poetry. *Neil Philip, ed.* (1990) Stewart, Tabori & Chang. 256p.

PS613 NYBP · The New Yorker Book of Poems. *The New Yorker editors, comps.* (1969) Viking Press. 835p.
N4 (*Pap. ed. of 1974 published by William Morrow*).
1969

OAEL-1 · The Oxford Anthology of English Literature. Vol. I. *Frank Kermode and John Hollander, general eds.* (1973) Oxford University Press.

PR1109
OAEL-2 · The Oxford Anthology of English Literature. Vol. II. *Frank Kermode and John Hollander, general eds.* (1973) Oxford University Press.
(*OAEL-1 and OAEL-2 also published as six paperback vols:* Medieval English Literature, *J. B. Trapp, ed.;* The Literature of Renaissance England, *John Hollander and Frank Kermode, eds.;* The Restoration and the Eighteenth Century, *Martin Price, ed.;* Romantic Poetry and Prose,

Harold Bloom and Lionel Trilling, eds.; Victorian Prose and Poetry, Lionel Trilling and Harold Bloom, ed.; Modern British Literature, Frank Kermode and John Hollander, eds.)

OBAL   Oxford Book of American Light Verse, The. *William Harmon, ed.* (1979) Oxford University Press. 540p.

OBCA   The Oxford Book of Children's Verse in America. *Donald Hall, ed.* (1985) Oxford University Press. 319p.

OBCoV   The Oxford Book of Comic Verse. *John Gross, ed.* (1994) Oxford University Press. 512p.

OBCP   The Oxford Book of Christmas Poems. *Michael Harrison and Christopher Stuart-Clark, eds.* (1983) Oxford University Press. 160p.

OBCVT   *†The Oxford Book of Classical Verse in Translation. *Adrian Poole and Jeremy Maule, eds.* (1995) Oxford University Press. 606p.

OBEV   The Oxford Book of English Verse, 1250–1918. *Sir Arthur Quiller-Couch, ed.* (New ed., rev. and enl., 1939) Oxford University Press. 1,083p.

OBGa   The Oxford Book of Garden Verse. *John Dixon Hunt, ed.* (1993) Oxford University Press. 341p.

OBMV   The Oxford Book of Modern Verse, 1892–1935. *William Butler Yeats, ed.* (1936) Oxford University Press. 454p.

OBNC   The Oxford Book of Nineteenth-Century English Verse. *John Hayward, ed.* (1964; reprinted, with corrections, 1965) Oxford University Press. 970p.

OBNV   The Oxford Book of Narrative Verse. *Iona Opie and Peter Opie, eds.* (1983) Oxford University Press. 407p.

OBSP   The Oxford Book of Story Poems. *Michael Harrison and Christopher Stuart-Clark, eds.* (1990) Oxford University Press. 175p.

OBSV   The Oxford Book of Satirical Verse. *Geoffrey Grigson, comp.* (1980) Oxford University Press. 454p., pap.

OBVE   †The Oxford Book of Verse in English Translation. *Charles Tomlinson, ed.* (1980) Oxford University Press. 608p., pap.

OBWP   The Oxford Book of War Poetry. *Jon Stallworthy, ed.* (1984) Oxford University Press. 358p.

OBWVE   †The Oxford Book of Welsh Verse in English. *Gwyn Jones, ed.* (1977) Oxford University Press, 313p.

OHMPC   †One Hundred More Poems from the Chinese; Love and the Turning Year. *Kenneth Rexroth, ed.* (1970) New Directions. 140p.

OHMPJ   †One Hundred More Poems from the Japanese. *Kenneth Rexroth, ed.* (1974) New Directions. 120p., pap.

OHPC   †One Hundred Poems from the Chinese. *Kenneth Rexroth, ed.* (1971) New Directions. 148p., pap.

OHPJ   †One Hundred Poems from the Japanese. *Kenneth Rexroth, ed.* (1964) New Directions. 140p.

OMIP   †The Oxford Anthology of Modern Indian Poetry. *Vinay Dharwadker and A. K. Ramanujan, eds.* (1994) Oxford University Press. 265p.

OpBo   The Open Boat; Poems from Asian America. *Garrett Hongo, ed.* (1993) Doubleday. 303p.

OPOU   100 Poems on the Underground. *Gerald Benson, Judith Chernaik, and Cicely Herbert, eds.* (1991) Cassell. 144p., pap.

OTCP   The Oxford Treasury of Children's Poems. *Michael Harrison and Christopher Stuart-Clark, eds.* (1988) Oxford University Press. 174p.

OxAEP-1   The Oxford Anthology of English Poetry. Vol. I: Spenser to Crabbe. *John Wain, ed.* (1990) Oxford University Press. 659p., pap.

OxAEP-2   The Oxford Anthology of English Poetry. Vol. II: Blake to Heaney. *John Wain, ed.* (1990) Oxford University Press. 770p., pap.

OxBA   The Oxford Book of American Verse. *F. O. Matthiessen, ed.* (1950) Oxford University Press. 1,130p.

OxBB   *The Oxford Book of Ballads. *James Kinsley, ed.* (1969) Oxford University Press. 711p., pap.

OxBC   The Oxford Book of Contemporary Verse, 1945–1980. *D. J. Enright, comp.* (1980) Oxford University Press. 299p.

OxBChV   The Oxford Book of Children's Verse. *Iona Opie and Peter Opie, eds.* (1973) Oxford University Press. 407p.

OxBM   The Oxford Book of Marriage. *Helge Rubinstein, ed.* (1990) Oxford University Press. 383p.

OxBoLi   The Oxford Book of Light Verse. *W. H. Auden, ed.* (1938) Oxford University Press. 552p., pap.

OxBoS   The Oxford Book of the Sea. *Jonathan Raban, ed.* (1992) Oxford University Press. 522p.

OxBoV   The Oxford Book of Villains. *John Mortimer, ed.* (1992) Oxford University Press. 431p.

OxBS   The Oxford Book of Scottish Verse. *John MacQueen and Tom Scott, comps.* (1966) Oxford University Press. 633p.

OxBSn   The Oxford Book of the Supernatural. *D. J. Enright, ed.* (1994) Oxford University Press. 555p.

OxBSP   The Oxford Book of Short Poems. *P. J. Kavanagh and James Michie, eds.* (1985) Oxford University Press. 307p., pap.

OxBTC   *The Oxford Book of Twentieth-Century English Verse. *Philip Larkin, ed.* (1973) Oxford University Press. 641p.

OxNR   The Oxford Nursery Rhyme Book. *Iona Opie and Peter Opie, comps.* (1955) Oxford University Press. 224p.

OxWW   The Oxford Book of Women's Writing in the United States. *Linda Wagner-Martin and Cathy N. Davidson, eds.* (1995) Oxford University Press. 596p.

PAR   Poetry of the American Renaissance; a Diverse Anthology from the Romantic Period. *Paul Kane, ed.* (1995) George Braziller, Inc. 383p., pap.

PaTW   Poetry of the American West. *Alison Hawthorne Deming, ed.* (1996) Columbia University Press. 328p.

PBA   Poems from Black Africa. *Langston Hughes, ed.* (1963) Indiana University Press. 160p.

PBCAP   The Pittsburgh Book of Contemporary American Poetry. *Ed Ochester and Peter Oresick, eds.* (1993) University of Pittsburgh Press. 397p., pap.

PBCIP   The Penguin Book of Contemporary Irish Poetry. *Peter Fallon and Derek Mahon, eds.* (1990) Penguin Books. 462p., pap.

PBCV   The Penguin Book of Caribbean Verse in English. *Paula Burnett, ed.* (1986) Penguin Books. 446p., pap.

PBMAP   The Penguin Book of Modern African Poetry. *Gerald Moore and Ulli Beier, eds.* (1984) Penguin Books. 315p., pap.

PBMP   The Premier Book of Major Poets. *Anita Dore, ed.* (1970) Fawcett Publications. 336p., pap.

PBRV   *The Penguin Book of Renaissance Verse 1509-1659. *David Norbrook, ed.* (1992) Penguin Books. 920p., pap.

PBWP   The Penguin Book of Women Poets. *Carol Cosman, Joan Keefe, and Kathleen Weaver, eds.* (1978) Penguin Books. 399p., pap.

PC   The Poetical Cat; an Anthology. *Felicity Bast* (1995) Farrar Straus Giroux. 144p.

PChr   Poems of Christmas. *Myra Cohn Livingston, ed.* (1980) Atheneum. 172p.

PeECV   The Penguin Book of English Christian Verse. *Peter Levi, ed.* (1984) Penguin Books. 379p.

PeFWW   The Penguin Book of First World War Poetry. *Jon Silkin, ed.* (1979) Penguin Books. 258p., pap.

PeLi   The Penguin Book of Limericks. *E. O. Parrott, ed.* (1983) Penguin Books. 304p., pap.

PeLV   The Penguin Book of Light Verse. *Gavin Ewart, ed.* (1980) Penguin Books. 639p., pap.

PeNZ   The Penguin Book of New Zealand Verse. *Ian Wedde and Harvey McQueen, eds.* (1985) Penguin Books. 575p., pap.

PeP   Pet Poems. *Robert Fisher, ed.* (1989) Faber and Faber. 85p., pap.

PeSA   The Penguin Book of South African Verse. *Jack Cope and Uys Krige, eds.* (1968) Penguin Books. 332p.

PeSAV   The Penguin Book of Southern African Verse. *Stephen Gray, ed.* (1989) Penguin Books. 402p.

PeVV   Victorian Verse. *George MacBeth, ed.* (1986) Penguin Books; first published 1969 as The Penguin Book of Victorian Verse. 440p., pap.

PEW   Poetry by English Women; Elizabethan to Victorian. *R. E. Pritchard, ed.* (1990) Continuum. 272p., pap.

PFE   Poems–Fourth Edition; the Wadsworth Handbook and Anthology. *C. F. Main and Peter J. Seng, eds.* (1978) Wadsworth Publishing Company. 490p., pap.

LIST OF ANTHOLOGIES

PFTM — Poems for the Millennium; the University of California Press Book of Modern & Postmodern Poetry. *Jerome Rothenberg and Pierre Joris, eds.* (1995) University of California Press. 811p., pap.

PGA — †Poems from the Greek Anthology. *Kenneth Rexroth, ed.* (1962) University of Michigan Press. 111p.

PiM — Poetry in Motion; 100 Poems from the Subways and Buses. *Molly Peacock, Elise Paschen, and Neil Neches, eds.* (1996) W. W. Norton. 157p., pap.

PLT — †Poems of the Late T'ang. *Arthur Charles Graham, ed. and tr.* (1977) Penguin Books. 173p., pap.

PLW — Poems of Love and War; from the Eight Anthologies and the Ten Long Poems of Classical Tamil. *A. K. Ramanujan, ed. and tr.* (1985) Columbia University Press. 335p.

PmAP — Postmodern American Poetry; a Norton Anthology. *Paul Hoover* (1994) W. W. Norton. 701p., pap.

PNI — Poets from the North of Ireland. *Frank Ormsby, ed.* (Rev. ed., 1990) The Blackstaff Press. 336p., pap.

PoA — The Poetry Anthology, 1912–1977. *Daryl Hine and Joseph Parisi, eds.* (1978) Houghton Mifflin. 555p.

PoBA — The Poetry of Black America; Anthology of the 20th Century. *Arnold Adoff, ed.* (1973) Harper & Row. 552p.

PoE — Poetry in English; an Anthology. *M. L. Rosenthal, general ed.* (1987) Oxford University Press. 1196p., pap.

PoEL-1 — Poets of the English Language. Vol. I. *W. H. Auden and Norman Holmes Pearson, eds.* (1950) Viking Press. 619p.

PoEL-2 — Poets of the English Language. Vol. II. *W. H. Auden and Norman Holmes Pearson, eds.* (1950) Viking Press. 556p.

PoEL-3 — Poets of the English Language. Vol. III. *W. H. Auden and Norman Holmes Pearson, eds.* (1950) Viking Press. 622p.

PoEL-4 — Poets of the English Language. Vol. IV. *W. H. Auden and Norman Holmes Pearson, eds.* (1950) Viking Press. 535p.

PoEL-5 — Poets of the English Language. Vol. V. *W. H. Auden and Norman Holmes Pearson, eds.* (1950) Viking Press. 624p.

Poetr — Poetry. *Jill P. Baumgaertner, ed.* (1990) Harcourt, Brace, Jovanovich. 703p., pap.

Poetsp — Poetspeak, in Their Work, about Their Work. *Paul B. Janeczko, ed.* (1991) Macmillan. 238p., pap.

PoFWW — Poetry of the First World War. *Edward Hudson, ed.* (1988) Wayland. 128p.

PoLF — Poems That Live Forever. *Hazel Felleman, ed.* (1965) Doubleday. 454p., pap.

PoM — The Postmoderns; the New American Poetry Revised. *Donald Allen and George F. Butterick, eds.* (1982) Grove Press. 436p., pap.

PoPoPo — Poems, Poets, Poetry; an Introduction and Anthology. *Helen Vendler, ed.* (1997) Bedford Books. 656p., pap.

PoRA — Poems to Read Aloud. *Edward Hodnett, ed.* (Rev. ed., 1967) W. W. Norton. 390p.

PoSu — †The Poetry of Survival; Post-War Poets of Central and Eastern Europe. *Daniel Weissbort, ed.* (1991) Anvil Press. 384p.

PoToHe — Poems that Touch the Heart. *A. L. Alexander, ed.* (1956) Doubleday. 403p.

PoWW — Poetry of the World Wars. *Michael Foss, ed.* (1990) Peter Bedrick Books. 192p.

PT — Primary Trouble; an Anthology of Contemporary American Poetry. *Leonard Schwartz, Joseph Donahue, and Edward Foster, eds.* (1996) Talisman House, Publishers. 473p., pap.

PuP-14 — The Puschart Prize XIV; Best of the Small Presses. *Bill Henderson et al.* (1989) Pushcart Press. 534p.

PuP-15 — The Pushcart Prize, XV; Best of the Small Presses. *Bill Henderson et al.* (1990) Simon & Schuster / Pushcart Press. 581p., pap.

PuP-16 — The Pushcart Prize, XVI; Best of the Small Presses. *Bill Henderson et al.* (1991) Simon & Schuster / Pushcart Press. 574p., pap.

PuP-17   The Puschart Prize, XVII; Best of the Small Presses. *Bill Henderson et al.* (1992) Puschart Press. 570p.

PuP-18   The Pushcart Prize XVIII; Best of the Small Presses. *Bill Henderson et al.* (1993) Pushcart Press. 574p.

PuP-19   The Puschart Prize XIX; Best of the Small Presses. *Bill Henderson et al.* (1994, 1995) Puschart Press. 630p., pap.

PuP-20   The Puschart Prize XX; Best of the Small Presses. *Bill Henderson et al.* (1995) Puschart Press. 570p., pap.

PWR   Poetry Worth Remembering; an Anthology of Poetry. *Roy W. Watson, comp.* (1986) Brunswick. 274p.

RA   Rebel Angels; 25 Poets of the New Formalism. *Mark Jarman and David Mason, eds.* (1996) Story Line Press. 259p., pap.

RaBo   The Rag and Bone Shop of the Heart; Poems for Men. *Robert Bly, James Hillman, and Michael Meade, eds.* (1992) Harper Collins. 536p.

RACG   The Routledge Anthology of Cross-Gendered Verse. *Alan Michael Parker and Mark Willhardt, eds.* (1996) Routledge. 216p., pap.

RB   The Rattle Bag; an Anthology of Poetry. *Seamus Heaney and Ted Hughes, comps.* (1982) Faber and Faber. 498p., pap.

ReMoGo   *The Real Mother Goose. *Blanche Fisher Wright, Illust.* (1944) Checkerboard Press. 128p.

Ro   Romanticism. *Duncan Wu, ed.* (1994) Blackwell. 1142p., pap.

SAGP   The Seashell Anthology of Great Poetry. *Christopher Burns, ed.* (1996) Park Lane Press. 349p.

SAmP   Six American Poets; an Anthology. *Joel Conarroe, ed.* (1991) Random House. 281p.

SCAP   Seventeenth-Century American Poetry. *Harrison T. Meserole, ed.* (1968) Doubleday. 540p.

SCGP   Six Centuries of Great Poetry. *Robert Penn Warren and Albert Erskine, eds.* (1955) Dell. 544p., pap.

SCV   Six Centuries of Verse. *Anthony Thwaite, ed.* (1984) Thames Methuen. 290p., pap.

SDW   Sound the Deep Waters; Women's Romantic Poetry in the Victorian Age. *Pamela Norris, ed.* (1991) Little, Brown. 120p.

SeCP   Seventeenth Century Poetry; the Schools of Donne and Jonson. *Hugh Kenner, ed.* (1964) Holt, Rinehart and Winston. 460p.

SeSe   The Second Set; the Jazz Poetry Anthology; Volume II. *Sascha Feinstein and Yusef Komunyakaa, eds.* (1996) Indiana University Press. 250p., pap.

SiPS   Silver Poets of the Sixteenth Century. *Gerald Bullett, ed.* (1947) J. M. Dent. 428p.

Son   The Sonnet; an Anthology. *Robert M. Bender and Charles L. Squier, eds.* (1987) Washington Square Press. 428p., pap.

SoSe-8   Sound and Sense; an Introduction to Poetry. *Laurence Perrine and Thomas R. Arp, eds.* (8th ed., 1992) Harcourt Brace Jovanovich. 342p., pap.

SPE   Surrealist Poetry in English. *Edward B. Germain, ed.* (1978) Penguin Books. 348p., pap.

Spl   Splinters; a Book of Very Short Poems. *Michael Harrison, ed.* (1989) Oxford University Press. 121p.

SpW   Spacways; an Anthology of Space Poems. *John Foster, ed.* (1986) Oxford University Press. 127p.

SSCS   Sky Scrape / City Scape. *Jane Yolen, ed.* (1996) Boyds Mills Press. 32p.

SSLK   Shimmy Shimmy Shimmy like My Sister Kate. *Nikki Giovanni, ed.* (1996) Henry Holt and Company. 188p.

STP   †Shaking the Pumpkin; Traditional Poetry of the Indian NorthAmericans. *Jerome Rothenberg, ed.* (Rev. ed., 1986) Alfred van der Marck Editions. 424p.

StPo   Story Poems, New and Old. *William Cole, ed.* (1957) World. 255p.

STV   *†Sappho to Valéry; Poems in Translation. *John Frederick Nims, ed.* (Rev. and enl. ed., 1990) University of Arkansas Press. 415p., pap.

SuSp   *†Sunflower Splendor; Three Thousand Years of Chinese Poetry. *Wu-chi Liu and Irving Yucheng Lo, eds.* (1975) Indiana University Press. 635p., pap.

TAL   †A Treasury of Asian Literature. *John D. Yohannan, ed.* (1984) Mentor Books. 432p., pap.

TAP   The Treasury of American Poetry. *Nancy Sullivan, ed.* (1978) Doubleday. 838p.

LIST OF ANTHOLOGIES

TCRP †Twentieth Century Russian Poetry; Silver and Steel, an Anthology. *Yevgeny Yevtushenko, Albert C. Todd, Max Hayward, eds.* (1993) Doubleday. 1,078p.

TFi **The Top 500 Poems. *William Harmon, ed.* (1992) Columbia University Press. 1,132p.

TIRV Treasury of Irish Religious Verse. *Patrick Murray, ed.* (1986) Crossroad. 295p.

TLR Talking like the Rain; a First Book of Poems. *X. J. Kennedy and Dorothy M. Kennedy, eds.* (1992) Little, Brown. 96p.

TOF Tongues of Fire; an Anthology of Religious and Poetic Experience. *Karen Armstrong, ed.* (1987) Penguin Books. 352p., pap.

TrCP The Treasury of Christian Poetry. *Lorraine Eitel, comp., with others.* (1982) Fleming H. Revell. 182p.

TrJP A Treasury of Jewish Poetry. *Nathan Ausubel and Maryann Ausubel, eds.* (1957) Crown. 471p.

TRP To Read a Poem. *Donald Hall, ed.* (2d ed, 1992) Harcourt, Brace, Jovanovich. 411p., pap.

TTTS Talking to the Sun; an Illustrated Anthology of Poems for YoungPeople. *Kenneth Koch and Kate Farrell, eds.* (1985) Metropolitan Museum of Art/Henry Holt. 112p.

TTY 3000 Years of Black Poetry. *Alan Lomax and Raoul Abdul, eds.* (1970) Dodd, Mead. 263p., pap.

TwCP Twentieth-Century Poetry; American and British (1900–1970). *John Malcolm Brinnin and Bill Read, eds.* (Rev. ed., 1970) McGraw Hill. 515p. (*Text ed. entitled* The Modern Poets)

UnPo Understanding Poetry. *Cleanth Brooks and Robert Penn Warren, eds.* (4th ed., 1976) Holt, Rinehart and Winston. 602p.

UnSA Unsettling America; an Anthology of Contemporary Multicultural Poetry. *Maria Mazziotti Gillan and Jennifer Gillan, eds.* (1994) Penguin Books. 406p., pap.

UV Unauthorized Versions; Poems and Their Parodies. *Kenneth Baker, ed.* (1990) Faber and Faber. 446p.

VCAP The Vintage Book of Contemporary American Poetry. *J. D. McClatchy, ed.* (1990) Vintage Books. 560p.

VCWP The Vintage Book of Contemporary World Poetry. *J. D. McClatchy, ed.* (1996) Vintage Books. 655p., pap.

VGW The Voice That Is Great Within Us; American Poetry of theTwentieth Century. *Hayden Carruth, ed.* (1970) Bantam Books. 722p., pap.

VoR Voices of the Rainbow; Contemporary Poetry by American Indians. *Kenneth Rosen, ed.* (1975) Viking Press. 232p., pap.

VWP Victorian Women Poets; an Anthology. *Angela Leighton and Margaret Reynolds, eds.* (1991) Blackwell. 691p., pap.

WeT The Wesleyan Tradition; Four Decades of American Poetry. *Michael Collier, ed.* (1993) Wesleyan University Press. 276p.

WeW-3 **Western Wind; an Introduction to Poetry. *John Frederick Nims, ed.* (3d ed., 1992) Random House. 639p., pap.

WHSW Who Has Seen the Wind? an Illustrated Collection of Poetry for Young People. *Kathryn Sky-Peck, ed.* (1991) Museum of Fine Arts, Boston. 63p.

WoRP Women Romantic Poets, 1785-1832; an Anthology. *Jennifer Breen, ed.* (1992) J. M. Dent. 182p.

WPE The Women Poets in English; an Anthology. *Ann Stanford, ed.* (1972) McGraw-Hill. 374p.

WPJ †Women Poets of Japan. *Kenneth Rexroth and Ikuko Atsumi, eds.* (1977) New Directions Books; also published 1977 by The Seabury Press as The Burning Heart. 184p., pap.

WPN Women's Poetry of the 1930's; a Critical Anthology. *Jane Dowson, ed.* (1996) Routledge. 192p., pap.

WPoS Women in Praise of the Sacred; 43 Centuries of Spiritual Poetry by Women. *Jane Hirshfield, ed.* (1994) HarperCollins. 259p., pap.

WPOW *Women Poets of the World. *Joanna Bankier and Deirdre Lashgari, eds.* (1983) Macmillan. 442p.

WWSi Walk on the Wild Side; Urban American Poetry since 1975. *Nicholas Christopher, ed.* (1994) Macmillan. 230p., pap.

ABBREVIATIONS

abr.	abridged		*mod.*	modernized *or* modern
ad.	adapted		*N.T.*	New Testament
add.	additional		*O.T.*	Old Testament
arr.	arranged		*orig.*	original
at.	attributed		*par.*	paraphrase *or* paraphrased
bk.	book		*pr.*	prose
br.	brief		*pt.*	part
ch.	chapter		*rev.*	revised
comp.	compiled *or* compiler		*sc.*	scene
comps.	compilers		*sec.*	section
cond.	condensed		*sel.*	selection
diff.	different		*sels.*	selections
fr.	from		*sl.*	slightly
frag.	fragment		*st.*	stanza
incl.	included *or* including		*sts.*	stanzas
introd.	introduction *or* introductory		*tr.*	translator, translation, *or* translated
ll.	lines		*trs.*	translators *or* translations
LL	last line		*var.*	various
med.	medieval		*vers.*	version *or* versions
misc.	miscellaneous		*wr.*	wrong *or* wrongly

TITLE, FIRST LINE, AND LAST LINE INDEX

Titles, first lines, and last lines are arranged in one alphabetical listing in the Title, First Line, and Last Line Index. Titles are distinguished by initial capital letters on the important words. All first-line entries are followed by the title of the poem, if there is a title. When the title and the first line of a poem are identical, or nearly so, only one of them is listed, although occasionally, for purposes of clarity, the first line has been added in quotation marks and in parentheses to the title entry.

Anthology codes are listed after titles, first lines, and last lines. Last lines are distinguished from first lines by the symbol (LL). However, more complete information as to translators, acts and scenes, abridgments, and various titles is given in the title entry.

An indented citation indicates that the poem is a selection from the work listed one level above. A citation indented and inside parentheses indicates a variant title, variant first line, or variant last line as used in the anthologies that follow.

Generic title entries, such as Ode, Song, Sonnet, are followed by the first line in quotation marks for easy identification. Such entries, of course, may also be located by first-line listing.

Numerals in citations of poems by Horace refer to the Odes; in citations of poems by Ovid, to the Elegies; and in citations of poems by Tennyson, to In Memoriam A.H.H.

Titles and first lines beginning with "O" and "Oh" are filed separately, with cross-refrences where necessary. Names beginning "Mac," "Mc," and "M'" are filed in alphabetical order.

A

"A." Louis Zukofsky.
  "A"-4 ("Giant sparkler, / Lights of the river"). VGW
  "A"-11 ("River That Must Turn Full After I Stop Dying"). APSN; ColAP; VGW
  "A"-12 ("Like Grandpa Paul / The water is all of my mind"). ChIV-1
A, a, a. *Unknown.* MiEL
A, a, a, Domine Deus. David Jones. FaBoTw; NOCV
A B C. Charles Stuart Calverley. OBCoV
A, B, C, and D, / Pray, playmates, agree. The Alphabet. *Unknown.* ReMoGo
A B C D. *Unknown.* OxNR
A, B, C, D, E, F, G, Little Robin Redbreast. *Unknown.* OxNR
A B C D Goldfish. *Unknown.* NTCP
A-bide a- a-. Monk. John Taggart. FTOS
A celuy que pluys eyme en mounde. *Unknown. Fr.* Lines from Love Letters. OBEV
A could be anything. A is unknown. (LL) Zewhyexary. Thomas M. Disch. OBCoV
A, dere God, what I am fayn. Unknown. MiEL
A. E. F. Carl Sandburg. CMoP; MoAmPo
A. E. H. Kingsley Amis. PFE
A. E. Housman. W. H. Auden. OxAEP-2
A. E. Housman and a Few Friends. Humbert Wolfe. BXAP; UV
A.E.I.O.U. Friedrich von Logau, *German.* CBNP
A for 'orses. An English Alphabet. *Unknown.* CBNP
A! [*or* Ah!] fredome [*or* freedom] is a noble thing!, A. Freedom [*or* Fredome]. John Barbour. FaBoCh; OBEV; OxBS *Fr.* The Bruce.
A ha ha ha! this world doth passe. Idle Fyno. *Unknown.* PoEL-2
A-Hunting. Jennie Dunbar. BoTP
A. "I was a Have." B. "I was a 'Have-not.' ." Equality of Sacrifice. Rudyard Kipling. FaBoTw *Fr.* Epitaphs of the War [1914–1918]. OBWP
A is an angel of blushing eighteen. A B C. Charles Stuart Calverley. OBCoV
A is an Apple, as everyone knows. Abecedary. Thomas M. Disch. OBCoV
A is for apron in plastic or cloth. Edna's Alphabet. Barry Humphries. OBCoV
A is for axes, you very well know. The Lumberman's Alphabet. *Unknown.* AmFP
A is the aftermost part of the ship. The Sailors' Alphabet. *Unknown.* AmFP
A is the one that won't. A.E.I.O.U. Friedrich von Logau, *German.* CBNP
À l'Ange Avantgardien. Francis Reginald. MoCV
"A l'usage de M. et Mme. van Gramberen." Eiléan Ní Chuilleanáin. *Fr.* The Rose-Geranium. CIP-2
A.M.: The Hopeful Monster. Alice Fulton. PUP-18
A! Mercy, Fortune; have pitee on me. *Unknown.* MiEL
A mezzo-litro. Grazie, professore. (LL) The Mind-Reader. Richard Wilbur. LCAP-2; NAAL-2; NoAM
A-morwe, whan that day bigan to springe. Chaucer. *Fr.* The General Prologue. FHYEP; NAEL-1; NAWM-1; OAEL-1; PoE *Fr.* The Canterbury Tales.
A, my dere, a, my dere Son. Mary Weeps for Her Child. *Unknown.* OxBoLi
A peels an apple, while B kneels to God. A Primer of the Daily Round. Howard Nemerov. NYBP; NoP-4; WeW-3
À Quoi Bon Dire. Charlotte Mew. OxBTC
  (While Over There.) LBC
A. R. U. *Unknown.* AS
A Says "You're right. He's brilliant but not sound." In the Bistro. Gwen Harwood. FaBoWP
A-sitting on a gate. (LL) The White Knight's Song. "Lewis Carroll." BXAP; CBNP; FaBoCh; HAP; InPS-3; NAEL-2; NOBE; NOBL; NoAM; NoP-4; OAEL-2; OxBChV; PeLV; PoRA; TFi; UV
A soun tres chere et special. *Unknown. Fr.* Lines from Love Letters. OBEV
A. Stands for Absolutely Anything. Noël Coward. NBLV *Fr.* The Little Ones' A. B. C.
A stands for Archibald who told no lies. Hilaire Belloc. NoAM *Fr.* A Moral Alphabet.

A-swell within her billowed skirts. The Mad Woman of Punnet's Town. Leonard Alfred George Strong. MoBrPo

A-traipsin' from a shindig, I unsaddles. Agamemnon before Troy. John Frederick Nims. Son

A was an apple pie, B bit it, C cut it. The Tragical Death of A, Apple Pie. Mother Goose. LB; OxNR

A was an archer, who [or and] shot at a frog. Unknown. LB; OxBChV; OxNR

("Who looked a great fool.") (LL) ACTP

A was once an apple-pie. An Alphabet. Edward Lear. OxBChV

A-way-up out of the way. (LL) The Signifying Monkey. Unknown. CrDW; NAAAL

A-zellen meat-weare I shall get noo meat. Shop o' Meat-Weare. William Barnes. NOBVV

Aa my life, my leman said. Sydney Goodsir Smith. FaBoTC

Aa the skippers of bonny Lothen. Young Allan. Unknown. ESPB

Aa this while, Peter wis doun ablò i the yaird. Bible, N.T., Par. by William Laughton Lorimer. FaBoVe Fr. St. Mark.

Aardvark. Julia Fields. MBE

Aardvark. Kenneth Rexroth. Fr. A Bestiary. OBAL

Aaron. George Herbert. ChIV-1; FSCP; GeHe; MeLP; NOSC; OAEL-1; PeECV

Aaron is a man of mystery. Man of Mystery. Dahlia Ravikovitch, Hebrew. IP, tr. by Warren Bargad and Stanley F. Chyet

Aaron Nicholas, Almost Ten. Janet Campbell Hale. VoR

Aaron Stark. Edwin Arlington Robinson. APN-2; MeMAP; MoAmPo; NCAP; Son

("Withal a meagre man was Aaron Stark.") NCAP

Aa's a broken-hairted keelman and Aa's ower heid in love. Cushie Butterfield. George Ridley. FaBoVe

Ab no, not these! Parentage. Alice Thompson Meynell. PeVV

Abalone. Unknown. AS

Abalone, like inkfish. The Relaxed Abalone. Rosemarie Waldrop. InPK 6

Abandon'd Day, why dost thou now appear? On My Wedding Day. Sarah Fyge Egerton. KTR

Abandoned, The. Nathan Alterman, Hebrew. MHP, tr. by Ruth Finer Mintz

Abandoned, The. Zbigniew Herbert, Polish. PoSu, tr. by Michael March and Jaroslaw Anders

Abandoned camps / pineapple breasts untouched. The Rake. Abu Nuwas, Arabic. ArPe, tr. by Omar S. Pound

Abandoned Churches. Lyubomir Levchev, Bulgarian. CEEP, tr. by Ewald Osers

Abandoned corpses. Evidence. Toki Zenmaro, Japanese. MJT, tr. by Makoto Ueda

Abandoned earthworks nobody tends. Su Tung-p'o, Chinese. CoBCP, tr. by Burton Watson Fr. Eastern Slope.

Abandoned Farmhouse. Ted Kooser. WeW-3

Abandoning the Plans of Visiting West Lake. Hsü Wei, Chinese. SuSp, tr. by Irving Y. Lo

Abandoning Your Car in a Snowstorm: Rosslyn, Virginia. Michael C. Blumenthal. NoAM

Abandonment of Autos. Bruce Dawe. CBAP

Abate, fair fugitive, abate thy speed. Daphne and Apollo. Ovid. NOEC, tr. by Matthew Prior Fr. Metamorphoses.

Abattoir, The. Ania Walwicz. BMAP

Abbey Church at Bath, The. Henry Harington. FaBoEE

Abbot John, in stature small, The. Fulbert of Chartres, Latin. MLL, tr. by Helen Waddell

Abbot of Inisfalen, The. William Allingham. TIRV

ABC, An. Unknown. Fr. The New England Primer.

Abdelazer. Aphra Behn.
 Song: Love Armed. NOSC; Poetr; WeW-3
  (Love Armed.) NALW
  ("Love in fantastic triumph sat.") NoP-4; PEW
  (Song: "Love in fantastic triumph sate.") OBEV; OxAEP-1
  ("While thine the victor is and free.") (LL) LW

Abduction, The. Stanley Kunitz. WeW-3

Abdul. Unknown. NSI

Abdul, the Bulbul Ameer. Unknown. AS

Abecedary. Thomas M. Disch. OBCoV

Abecedary of slaughter. Europa. Anatol Stern, Polish. PFTM, tr. by Stefan Themerson and Michael Horowitz

Abel. Demetrios Capetanakis. GTBS-P

Abel. John Wheelwright. ChIV-1

Abelard to Eloisa. Judith Madan. RACG

Abelard was: God is. Sic et Non. Sir Herbert Read. FaBoTw

Abel's Blood. Henry Vaughan. KSG; OBWVE

Abel's Bride. Denise Levertov. FaBoWP; NALW; VGW

Abenamar, Abenamar. Unknown, Spanish. AWP, tr. by Robert Southey

Aberdarcy: The Chaucer Road. Kingsley Amis. NOBL Fr. The Evans Country.

Aberdarcy: The Main Square. Kingsley Amis. NOBL; NoAM; OxBTC Fr. The Evans Country.

Aberdare, Llanwynno through. Glyn Cynon Wood. Unknown, Welsh. OBWVE, tr. by Gwyn Williams

Abhor[re], and spew out all neutralities. (LL) Neutrality Loathsome. Robert Herrick. ChIV-1

Abhorring a Vacuum. Chris Wallace-Crabbe. BMAP

Abide, gud men, and hald your pays. Unknown. MiEL

Abide in me, O Lord, and I in thee. Harriet Beecher Stowe. AH

Abide not in the realm of dreams. William Henry Burleigh. AH

Abide with me[; fast falls the eventide]. Henry Francis Lyte. EBVV; FaBoBe; FaPoR; LBC; NOCV; PWR; TIRV

("Help of the helpless, O, abide with me.") (LL) LBC

Abiding Love, The. John White Chadwick. BLPA; FaBoBe

Abiku. J. P. Clark Bekederemo. HBAPE; PBMAP Fr. A Reed in the Tide.

Abiku. Wole Soyinka. PBA; PBMAP

Ability to Make a Face Like a Spider While Singing Blues: Junior Wells, The. Sandra McPherson. SeSe

Abishag. Jacob Fichman, Hebrew. TrJP, tr. by Sholom J. Kahn

Abishag. Shirley Kaufman. CrSp

Abishag. Rilke, German. AWP, tr. by Jethro Bithell

Abishag. André Spire, French. TrJP, tr. by Emanuel Eisenberg

Abla. Antar. AWP, tr. by E. Powys Mathers Fr. The Mu'allaqat.

Abnegation. Adrienne Rich. WPE

Abner Silver's "Pu-leeze! Mr. Hemingway!" Ring Lardner. OBAL

Abnormal Is Not Courage, The. Jack Gilbert. CoAP

Aboard a Boat at Night, Drinking with My Wife. Mei Yao Ch'en, Chinese. CoBCP, tr. by Burton Watson

Aboard a Boat, Reading Yüan Chen's Poems. Po Chü-i, Chinese. CoBCP, tr. by Burton Watson

Aboard at a ship's helm. Walt Whitman. APN-1; NOBA; OxBA

Abode of the nightingale is bare, The. Alone. Walter De la Mare. CBLP; EnLoPo

Abolished, and its weeks spent walking aimlessly. Where When Was. Reginald Shepherd. GT

Abomination Of Evil, The. "Angelus Silesius." GePo, tr. by George C. Schoolfield Fr. The Cherubical Wanderer.

Abominations break above the river. Customize the Grass. Peter Finch. NBrP

Aborigine Sound Poem. Unknown. PFTM

Abortion. Ai. BoWoP

Abortion, An. Liz Lochhead. NBrP

Abortion, An. Frank O'Hara. TAP

Abortion, The. Anne Sexton. LCAP-2; Poetr; NMM-2; VGW

Abortions will not let you forget. The Mother. Gwendolyn Brooks. CrDW; CrSp; ISC; MDDM; NAAAL; NALW; NMM-2; PoPoPo Fr. A Street in Bronzeville. BPo; BlSi; FaBoWP

Abou Ben Adhem (may his tribe increase!). Leigh Hunt. APAD; BLPA; ChAP; EBEvV; FaBoBe; FaPoR; NOBE; NTP; OBEV; OxAEP-2; PWR; TFi

About a fly. The Story. Charles Simic. NNaP

About a Hat. Alexander Ilyich Bezymensky, Russian. TCRP, tr. by Daniel Weissbort

About a quarter to ten the door softly opened. Listening to Beethoven on the Oregon Coast. Henry Carlile. Poetsp

About a Year After He Got Married He Would Sit Alone in an Abandoned Shack in a Cotton Field Enjoying Himself. James Whitehead. MT

About a year has passed. I've returned to the place of battle. Elegy. Joseph Brodsky, Russian. AF

About all these I write freely. Other Life, The. Nina Cassian, Romanian. PoSu, tr. by Cristian Andrei and Daniel Weissbort

About an excavation. Charles Reznikoff. NTCP; VGW

About Atlanta. Ntozake Shange. ISC

About beef, for instance? Christmas. Leigh Hunt. ODCP

About Children. Phyllis McGinley. OBAL

About Death and Other Things. Aleksandar Ristovic, Serbo-Croatian. HSix, tr. by Charles Simic

About eight of us were nailing up forts. Words for My Daughter. John Balaban. RaBo

About four, a few flakes. Robert Bly. Fr. Six Winter Privacy Poems. LCAP-2

About Geese. Li Shang-yin, Chinese. SuSp, tr. by Eugene Eoyang and Irving Y. Lo

About him, and lies down to pleasant dreams. (LL) Thanatopsis. William Cullen Bryant. APN-1; AWP; AmPP; ColAP; FaBoBe; NAAL-1;

NAAL-3; NCAP; NOBA; OBEV; OxBA; PAR; PWR; PoToHe; TAP; TFi

About holiday rooms there can be. Inscriptions. Eavan Boland. PuP-17

About Horse. Li Ho, *Chinese.*
   "Last month of the year, grass roots taste sweet." SuSp, *tr.* by Irving Y. Lo
   "Master dragon-tamer has fled the world, The." SuSp, *tr.* by Irving Y. Lo

About Marriage. Denise Levertov. NALW

About Menophila's morals there are strange rumours. Argentarius, *Greek.* GrAn, *tr.* by Fleur Adcock

About my crevice and burrow. (LL) A Drumlin Woodchuck. Robert Frost. NOBA; NoAM

About My Father. Irena Klepfisz. NMM-2

About My Poems. Donald Justice. PoA

About run. (LL) Analysis of Baseball. May Swenson. KaS

About suffering they were never wrong. Musée des Beaux Arts. W. H. Auden. CABP; CMoP; ClHu; GS; GTBS-P; HAP; HeIP-4; ImPo; InPK-6; InPS-3; LiTM; MeMAP; MoP; NAEL-2; NOBE; NoAM; NoP-4; OxAEP-2; PBMP; PFE; PoE; PoPoPo; PoRA; Poetr; RaBo; SCV; SoSe-8; TFi; TRP; TrCP; TwCP

About ten million years ago. A Speck Speaks. Adrian Mitchell. OBSP

About that hour. The Maenads on Cithaeron. Euripides, *Greek.* OBCVT, *tr.* by William Arrowsmith

About the bush, Willie. *Unknown.* ReMoGo

About the cool water. Sappho, *Greek.* OBVE; PGA, *tr.* by Kenneth Rexroth

About the Emperor Hadrian. The New Purpose of Hadrian's Army. Volker Braun, *German.* CEEP, *tr.* by Edward Mackinnon and A. M. Elliott

About the Fairies. Jean Ingelow. BoTP

About the glimmering weirs. (LL) Far in a western brookland. A. E. Housman. AWP; PoEL-5

About the house a multitude of moths. Sunflower. Leonid Nikolaevich Martynov, *Russian.* TCRP, *tr.* by J. R. Rowland

About the little chambers of my heart. Gone. Mary Elizabeth Coleridge. OBEV; OBNC; VWP

About the Phoenix. James Merrill. NoAM

About the Shark, phlegmatical one. The Maldive Shark. Herman Melville. APN-2; APo; AmPP; ColAP; GEA; NAAL-1; NAAL-3; NCAP; NOBA; NoP-4; OxBA; PAR; PFE; PoE; PoEL-5; RB; TAP

About the size of an old-style dollar bill. Poem. Elizabeth Bishop. FYAP; HCAP; NoAM; PoPoPo; VCAP

About the skull of the beloved, filled. Presentation Piece. Marilyn Hacker. AmPA

About the Teeth of Sharks. John Ciardi. OBCA

About the tow'r an' churchyard wall. The Echo. William Barnes. SCGP

About the year of one B.C. Jonah and the Whale. *Unknown.* BLPA

About them. (LL) Hymn To a Woman Under Interrogation. Reiner Kunze, *German.* CEEP; PoSu, *tr.* by Ewald Osers

About This Course. David Shapiro. PoA

About this lady many fruitful trees. The Lady with the Unicorn. Vernon Watkins. TwCP

About this Woman. Judith Rodriguez. BMAP

About to leave, yet by the lamplight she lingers. Chou Pang-yen. SuSp, *tr.* by Irving Y. Lo *Fr.* Tune: "Beautiful Lady Yü, The."

About twenty years ago. Wild Oats. Philip Larkin. InPS-3

About twilight we came to the whitewashed pub. East Coast Journey. James Keir Baxter. NoP-4; PeNZ

About two miles east of here. The King Cobra as Political Assassin. Ray A. Young Bear. HATNAP

About us. Rest shall we. (LL) The Impercipient. Thomas Hardy. EBVV; NAEL-2

About women no one can know. There are some. Mary Magdalene. Saunders Lewis, *Welsh.* OBWVE, *tr.* by Gwyn Morgan

About Writing Poetry. Sophie Slingeland. LoHo

About Yule, when [*or* quhen] the wind blew cule. Young Waters. *Unknown.* ESPB; OxBB

Above, a mountain ten thousand feet high. Alarm at First Entering the Yang-tze Gorges. Po Chü-i, *Chinese.* ChiP, *tr.* by Arthur Waley

Above all, define standards. Neocolonialism. Felix Mnthali. PeSAV

Above all flattery, all thirst of gain. Walter Harte. EPCY *Fr.* An Essay on Satire, Particularly on The Dunciad.

Above all gifts we most should prize. Walter Savage Landor. FaBoEE

Above all rivers thy river hath renown. William Dunbar. *See* To the City of London [*or* In Honour of the City of London].

Above an empty heart. (LL) He Resigns. John Berryman. LBC; OxBSP; WeW-3

Above, below, in sky and sod. The Over-Heart. John Greenleaf Whittier. ChIV-2; NOCV

Above his dreamy abstract stare. (LL) The Ex-Queen Among the Astronomers. Fleur Adcock. NoP-4

Above It All. Philip Levine. NOBA

Above me the abbey, grey arches on the cliff. Caedmon. Norman Nicholson. FaBoTw

Above my desk, whirring and self-important. Angel. James Merrill. CoAmPo; PoA

Above my head, as I sleep, are. Limpopo. Walter Battiss. PeSAV

Above my table three magnolia flowers. At Lemmons. C. Day Lewis. FP

Above Pate Valley. Gary Snyder. CoAP; CoAmPo; LCAP-2; NoP-4; TRP

Above the Arno. May Swenson. NYBP

Above the ash and spittle croaks and leans. (LL) Aubade for Hope. Robert Penn Warren. FuPo

Above the baby powder clouds. Spring Evening. Frederick Turner. RA

Above the boat. Kikaku, *Japanese.* BLT, *tr.* by Lucien Stryk and Takashi Ikemoto

Above the Boca del Arno the sky. Outside Pisa. Chitra Divakaruni. OpBo

Above the Bright Blue Sky. Albert Midlane.
   "There's a Friend for little children." OxBChV

Above the Circus of the World she sat. Rome. Madison Cawein. APN-2

Above the city of White Emperor the clouds leave by the city gate. The City of White Emperor. Tu Fu, *Chinese.* SuSp, *tr.* by Wu-Chi Liu

Above the Crags that fade and gloom. From a Window in Princes Street. William Ernest Henley. EBVV

Above the creek dallies a bright moon. Quatrain. Yüan Hao-wen, *Chinese.* SuSp, *tr.* by Irving Y. Lo

Above the Dock. Thomas Ernest Hulme. FaBoMo; GTBS-P; NTP

Above the fence-flowers, like a bloody thumb. Variations on Southern Themes. Donald Justice. MT

Above the field drowses the kite. The Kite. Aleksandr Blok, *Russian.* PeFWW, *tr.* by David McDuff and Jon Silkin

Above the freeway, over the music. Jazz Station. Michael S. Harper. NoAM

Above the fresh ruffles of the surf. Hart Crane. AmPP; ColAP; MoP; NAAL-2; OxBA; PoE; VGW *Fr.* Voyages. CMoP; MeMAP; NOBA; NoAM; TAP

Above the giant city dying in spastic convulsions. Hallesches Tor: Communion. Henrikas Nagys, *Lithuanian.* CEEP, *tr.* by Jonas Zdanys

Above the gorges, one thread of sky. Meng Chiao. PLT, *tr.* by A. C. Graham *Fr.* Sadness of the Gorges.

Above the grey down. Invalid Dawn. Elizabeth Daryush. WPN

Above the High. Geoffrey Grigson. EnLoPo

Above the Lake. Aleksandr Blok, *Russian.* TCRP, *tr.* by Geoffrey Thurley

Above the meadow of pain, the pins of Queen Anne's lace. What Is Beyond Us. Karen Fish. PuP-15

Above the place where children play. A Sussex Legend. Charles Dalmon. BoTP

Above the Pool. John Montague. NOIV

Above the pools, above the valley of fears. Élévation. Charles Baudelaire, *French.* AWP, *tr.* by Arthur Symons

Above the quiet dock in midnight. Above the Dock. Thomas Ernest Hulme. FaBoMo; GTBS-P; NTP

Above the river, heavy on the heart, thousandfold hills. Written on a Painting Entitled "Misty Yangtze and Folded Hills." Su Tung-p'o, *Chinese.* CoBCP, *tr.* by Burton Watson

Above the rocking heads of the mothers. Nelly Sachs, *German.* PBWP, *tr.* by Ruth *and* Matthew Mead

Above the town a monstrous wheel is turning. Sunset in the City. Richard Le Gallienne. ADE

Above the Tree Line. Kathy Mangan. PuP-15

Above the twelve mountains autumn grasses fade. Bamboo Branch Song. Ho Ching-ming, *Chinese.* CoBLCP, *tr.* by Jonathan Chaves

Above the violent park. A Star. George MacBeth. NYBP

Above the voiceful windings of a river. At the Grave of Henry Vaughan. Siegfried Sassoon. CMoP; GTBS-P

Above the walls the west light hangs, until. Walled Garden. Dorothy, Duchess of Wellington Wellesley. OBGa

Above the whispering sea. Air Raid Across the Bay at Plymouth. Stephen Spender. AF

Above the white pond. Downfall. Georg Trakl, *German.* AF, *tr.* by Daniel Simko

Above the yellow Offices of State. Petersburg Strophes. Osip Emilevich Mandelstam, *Russian.* TCRP, *tr.* by Bernard Meares

Above these cares my spirit in calm abiding. Edna St. Vincent Millay. SAGP

Above this bramble-overarched long lane. The Clearing. Robert Graves. NYBP

Above, through lunar woods a goddess flees. The Lovers. William Jay Smith. MoAmPo

Above through many a bowery turn. An Arabian Night Garden. Tennyson. GaP

Above Tweed Green levels. Young Harper. Valerie Gillies. FaBoTC

Above Us. Julia Hartwig, *Polish*. BLT, *tr. by* Stanislaw Baranczak and Clare Cavanagh

Above us, stars. Beneath us, constellations. Flying at Night. Ted Kooser. InPK-6; PBCAP

Above yon sombre swell of land. The Plough. Richard Henry Horne. OBEV

Above you, idols. Who Knows Something About Women? Sylva Fischerova, *Czech and Slovak*. CEEP, *tr. by* Vera Orac, Stuart Friebert *and* Sylva Fischerova

Above, you paint the sky. How to Paint a Perfect Christmas. Miroslav Holub, *Czech*. OBCP, *tr. by* George Theiner *and* Ian Milner

Abraham. Edwin Muir. ChIV-1

Abraham. Delmore Schwartz. ChIV-1

Abraham built a town of sod. Abraham and Isaac. Else Lasker-Schüler, *German*. BoWoP, *tr. by* Rosemarie Waldrop

Abraham Davenport. John Greenleaf Whittier. AmPP; NoP-4

Abraham Lincoln. William Cullen Bryant. *See* The Death of Lincoln.

Abraham Lincoln. Mildred Plew Meigs. CA

Abraham Lincoln. Richard Henry Stoddard. FaBoBe

Abraham Lincoln Walks at Midnight. Vachel Lindsay. AmPP; CBCWP; CMoP; MeMAP; MoAmPo; NOBA; OxBA; TAP; TFi; VGW

Abraham Lincoln's Creed. *Unknown*. CTV, *tr. by* William E. Barton

Abraham to kill him. Emily Dickinson. ChIV-1; SoSe-8

Abraham's children played with shells. Hagar and Ishmael. Else Lasker-Schüler, *German*. BoWoP, *tr. by* Rosemarie Waldrop

Abraham's Madness. Bink Noll. ChIV-1

Abraham's Sacrifice of Isaac. Sir John Stradling. NOSC

Abram Bailey he'd three sons. Sir Lionel. *Unknown*. AmFP

Abram Brown. *Unknown*. OxNR

Abroad in the meadows to see the young lambs. Innocent Play. Isaac Watts. NOEC

Abroad Thoughts. Edward Blishen. NODL

Abruptly all the palm trees rose like parasols. William Jay Smith. PoA

Absalom. Yona Wallach, *Hebrew*. IP, *tr. by* Warren Bargad and Stanley F. Chyet

Absalom and Achitophel, Pt. I. Dryden.
　Achitophel: The Earl of Shaftsbury. NOBE
　　(Achitophel.) AWP
　"In pious times ere [*or* e'r] priest-craft did begin." EBEvV; FHYEP; FaBoPV; HAP; NOSC; OAEL-1; PoE
　"Some by their friends, more by themselves thought wise." ChIV-1; OBSV
　"With all these loads of injuries oppress." EBEV
　Zimri: "Some of their chiefs were princes of the land." AWP
　Zimri: The Duke of Buckingham. NOBE; OBSV
　　(Zimri: "Numerous host of dreaming saints succeed.") AWP

Absalom and Achitophel, Pt. II. John Dryden *and* Nahum Tate.
　"Doeg, though without knowing how or why." FHYEP; PoEL-3
　Og [and Doeg]. AWP
　"To make quick way I'll leap o'er heavy blocks." OBSV

Absence. Matthew Arnold. EnVR; GLoP *Fr.* Switzerland.

Absence. Richard Jago. OBEV

Absence. Frances Anne Kemble.
　"What shall I do with all the days and hours." PoToHe

Absence. Walter Savage Landor. *Fr.* Ianthe.

Absence. Charlotte Mew. CPO; MoBrPo

Absence. Vita Sackville-West. WPN

Absence. Shakespeare. *See* Sonnet 57.

Absence. Sir Philip Sidney. SiPS

Absence, The. Sylvia Townsend Warner. MoBrPo

Absence! Absenting causeth me to complain. Sir Thomas Wyatt. SiPS

Absence and Presence. Greville Fulke. *Fr.* Caelica.
　("*Absence is paine.*") (LL) PBRV; PoEL-1

Absence / Can you imagine. Can You Imagine. Artur Miedzyrzecki, *Polish*. PoSu, *tr. by* Stanislaw Baranczak *and* Clare Cavanagh

Absence, hear[e] [thou] my protestation. Present in Absence. John Hoskyns, *sometimes at. to* Donne. GTBS-P; MeLP; SCGP

Absence is pain. (LL) Absence and Presence. Greville Fulke. PoEL-1

Absence of heart—as in public buildings. The Chimaeras. W. H. Auden. MeMAP

Absent, The. Edwin Muir. NoAM

Absent Daughter. Barend Toerien, *Afrikaans*. PeSA, *tr. by the author*

Absent from thee, I languish still. Song. John Wilmot, 2d Earl of Rochester. BoLoP; EnLoPo; GBL; GLoP; NOBE; OBEV

Absent Lover. *Unknown, Xhosa*. PBA, *tr. by* A. C. Jordan

Absent-Minded Professor. Howard Nemerov. *Fr.* Epigrams. OBAL

Absent, this morning. Aube Provençale. Marilyn Hacker. AmPA

Absentia Animi. Gunnar Ekelof, *Swedish*. PFTM, *tr. by* Muriel Rukeyser *and* Leif Sjoberg

Absentmindedly. 529 1983. Gerda Mayer. Spl

Absinthe-Drinker, The. Arthur Symons. FaBoTw; NOBVV

Absolute Solitude, The. Hyonsung Kim, *Korean*. CKP, *tr. by* Jaihiun Kim

Absolute zero: the locust sings. Summer. Conrad Potter Aiken. NoAM; Poetr

Absolutely. David Ignatow. BAP-93

Absolutely Abstemious Ass, The. Twenty-Six Nonsense Rhymes. Edward Lear. CBNP; RB

Absolutely nothing / will have been undone. (LL) Boomerang: A Blatantly Political Poem. Quincy Troupe. AF

Absolutely Ordinary Rainbow, An. Les A. Murray. CBAP

Absolution. Diane Ward. FTOS

Absolving You. Colette Inez. NMM-2

Absorbed in the work, final touches. Revision. Linda McCarriston. NMM-2

Absorption of Rock. Maxine Hong Kingston. OpBo

Abstinence. Kenneth Rosen. AmPA

Abstinence sows sand all over. William Blake. EBEV; FaBoEE; GBL; OxBM; PFE *Fr.* Gnomic Verses.

Abstracted by silence from the age of seven. On Himself. David Wright. OPOU

Abstracted, sour, as he reaches across a dish. Scylla and Charybdis. Thomas Kinsella. OxBTC

Abstracts hover like dull angels, The. Magi. Sylvia Plath. GI

Abstruse Buddhahood and Taoist immortality are both unattainable. Mixed Emotions. Huang Ching-jen, *Chinese*. SuSp, *tr. by* Chang Yin-nan *and* Lewis C. Walmsley

Abt Vogler. Robert Browning. FHYEP; NAEL-2; OAEL-2; TOF

Abu Nowas for the Barmacides. *Unknown*. AWP *Fr.* The Thousand and One Nights

Abu / 's a stone black revolutionary. Dudley Randall. BPo

Abukbo. Jim Barnes. *Fr.* Four Things Choctaw. HATNAP

Abundance. John Cage. APSN *Fr.* Diary: How to Improve the World (You Will Only Make Matters Worse).

Abundance and Satisfaction. Pattiann Rogers. BAP-96

Abundant Catch (Luke 5:4–10). Czeslaw Milosz, *Polish*. GI, *tr. by* Czeslaw Milosz *and* Lillian Vallee

Abundantly. In His Name / Phillis. (LL) A Letter from Phillis Wheatley. Robert Earl Hayden. NAAAL; NoAM

Abuse, but the girl's. Case Study. Gayle Kaune. LoHo

Abysmal corners will dis (be) located. Vitality. Maria Amalia Fonte Boa, *Portuguese*. BoWoP, *tr. by* Willis Barnstone *and* Nelson Cerqueira

Abyss. Diane Di Prima. BB

Academia; or The Humours of the University of Oxford. Alicia D'Anvers.
　"I ask'd a young Youth what it mean'd." KTR
　"Next, who 'as leave to domineer, The." KTR
　"Now being arrived at his Colledge." KTR
　"There's some are fat, and some are lean." KTR
　To the University. KTR; NOSC

Academic. Theodore Roethke. FaBoEE; OBAL

Academic Graffiti. W. H. Auden.
　"Henry Adams / Was mortally afraid of Madams." OBAL

Academics? Politics? I've nothing to do with them! Liu E. *Fr.* On the Twenty-fourth: Improvisations. CoBLCP, *tr. by* Jonathan Chaves

Accept from me not silence. Edouard J. Maunick. NegPo, *tr. by* Ellen Conroy Kennedy *Fr.* As Far as Yoruba Land.

Accept, much honoured shade! the artless lays. On the Death of Mrs. Rowe. Elizabeth Carter. ECWP

Accept My Full Heart's Thanks. Ella Wheeler Wilcox. PoToHe

Accept, my God, the praises which I bring. The Offering: Part One. Mary Lee, Lady Chudleigh. WPE

Accept, my love, as true a heart. Les Estreines. Matthew Prior. OxBSP

Accept the university of death. (LL) The Children of the Poor. Gwendolyn Brooks. WPE, *sect.* I, *pt.* 1-2; PoA, *sect.* I, *pt.* 1-3

Accept this indent, Sweet, from me. Chloe. Sir Edward De Stein. NSI

Acceptance. Robert Frost. CMoP; GSo; OxBA

Acceptance. John Wieners. FTOS

Acceptance Speech. Marvin Bell. AmPA

Accepting. Motion of the Cypher. Ray DiPalma. FTOS

Accepts the life given him, long or short. (LL) After Eating. Po Chü-i, *Chinese*. CoBCP, *tr. by* Burton Watson

Accessories shop, The. Pierre McOrlan, *French*. MFP, *tr. by* Martin Sorrell

Accident, An. Frank A. Cross Jr. CDa

Accident, The. Liz Rosenberg. PBCAP

Accident in Art. Richard Hovey. APN-2

"Accident" is what he calls the time, The. Dancing with Poets. Ellen Bryant Voigt. CrSp

Accident or the gods. Subplot. Jack Butler. MT

Accidental Meeting with an Old Friend While Traveling at Night, An. Tai Shu-lun, *Chinese.* SuSp, *tr. by* William H. Nienhauser

Accidentally. Tanka. Ishikawa Takuboku, *Japanese.* MJT, *tr. by* Makoto Ueda

Accidents of Birth. William Meredith. APAD

Accidents will happen—still, in time. If I Should Die Before I Wake. Robert Mezey. NYBP

Acclaim the dawn of Mother's Day! Mother's Day. Edwin Becker. PWR

Accommodating Lion, An. Tudor Jenks. OBCA

Accomodating love with "something still." Agreement with Sir Charles Sedley. Richard Howard. WeT

Accompani'd with thine. (LL) The Soldier Going to the Field. Sir William Davenant. NOBE; OBWP

Accompanying a Gift ("From thy patient, who while here"). Lizelia Augusta Jenkins Moorer. CBWP-3

Accompanying a Gift ("One whose love will never end"). Lizelia Augusta Jenkins Moorer. CBWP-3

Accomplices, The. Conrad Potter Aiken. NOBA

Accomplices. Bei Dao, *Chinese.* AF, *tr. by* Bonnie S. McDougall

Accomplices. Zhao Zhenkai, *Chinese.* VCWP, *tr. by* Donald Finkel

Accordian Player, The. W. R. Rodriguez. EC3

According as his will is. (LL) Christ, My Beloved. William Baldwin. NOCV; OxBSP

According to Breughel. William Carlos Williams. *See* Landscape with the Fall of Icarus.

According to Brueghel. Landscape with the Fall of Icarus. William Carlos Williams. LCAP-2; NAAL-2; NoAM *Fr.* Pictures from Brueghel.

According to Einstein. A Special Theory of Relativity. Alan Bold. FaBoTC

According to my Mood. Benjamin Zephaniah. NOxBChV

According to old Sigmund Freud. Limerick. *Unknown.* PeLi

According to some learn'd opinions. Irish Antiquities. Thomas Moore. FaBoEE

According to the Mighty Working. Thomas Hardy. CMoP

According to the silence, winter has arrived. Shepherd. William Stafford. PoA

According to the word of the Eternal Being. L'Imprévisibilité. Zinaida Hippius, *Russian.* PBWP, *tr. by* Temira Pachmuss

Accordingly, on weighty business bound. Robert Browning. EBVVPR *Fr.* Red Cotton Night-Cap Country. EBVVPR

Accordionist, The. Vasily Vasilevich Kazin, *Russian.* TCRP, *tr. by* Daniel Weissbort

Account of the Cruelty of the Papists, An. Benjamin Harris. SCAP

Account of the Greatest English Poets, An. Joseph Addison.
"But Milton next, with high and haughty stalks." EPCY
"Great Cowley then, a mighty genius, wrote." EPCY

Accountability. Paul Laurence Dunbar. APN-2; PoLF

Accountability. William Stafford. LCAP-2

Accountant dried his imperfect back, The. The Accountant in His Bath. Adrian Mitchell. NYBP

Accountant in His Bath, The. Adrian Mitchell. NYBP

ACCOUNTED our commodities. A Quiet Neighbour. John Heywood. NoSic

Accounting Cat, The. John Clarke. UV

Accoutrement. "Marnia". LW

Across the fallow clods at early morn. Pewits Nest. John Clare. FaBoVe

Accumulation of reefs, The. The Distances. Jim Carroll. PoA

Accursed power which stands on Privilege, The. On a General Election. Hilaire Belloc. FaBoEE; NOBE; NOBL; OBSV; OxBTC; OxBoLi

Accurst [or accursed], and in a cursed [or cursed] hour he hies. (LL) Book II. Milton. FHYEP; NAEL-1; OxAEP-1

Accusation of the Inward Man, The. Edward Taylor. MeMAP

Accused though I be without desert. Sir Thomas Wyatt. SiPS

Ach sun / jiss keepyir chin up. The Miracle of the Burd and the Fishes. Tom Leonard. FaBoTC

Achaian Invasion of Sparta, The. *Unknown, Greek.* GrAn, *tr. by* Peter Jay

Achaians Have Got Troy, upon This Very Day, The. Aeschylus. *Fr.* Agamemnon. NAWM-1, *tr. by* Robert Fagles

Acharnians, The. Aristophanes, *Greek.*
"Since first to exhibit his Plays he began." OBCVT, *tr. by* Rogers, Benjamin Bickley

Ache / drawn border's arousal. Frammenti Romani. Kathleen Fraser. PT

Ache of love! (LL) On the Beach at Fontana. James Joyce. MoBrPo; OBMV; PoA; RB; RaBo

Ache of marriage, The. Denise Levertov. ColAP; ITG; InPK-6; NALW; NOBA; NoAM; PmAP; PoM; PoPoPo; Poetr; SAGP; TAP; VCAP

("Two by two in the ark of / the ache of it.") (LL) ITG

Achieving Perspective. Pattiann Rogers. MT

Achill. Derek Mahon. BiHa; PBCIP; PNI

Achill Woman, The. Eavan Boland. BiHa

Achilleid, The. Publius Papinius Statius, *Latin.*
"This Land, where quarrels no disturbance wrought." OBCVT, *tr. by* Sir Robert Howard *and* John Dryden

Achilles. John Gay.
"Soldier, think before you marry." PeLV
Song: "Think of dress in every light." OxBSP

Achilles and the Tortoise. Miroslav Holub, *Czech.* PoSu, *tr. by* Stuart Friebert *and* Dana Hábová

Achilles kills Lycaon. Homer. OBCVT, *tr. by* Alexander Pope *Fr.* The Iliad.

Achilles Over the Trench. Homer, *Greek.* OBCVT, *tr. by* Alfred Tennyson, 1st Baron Tennyson; OBVE, *tr. by* Tennyson *Fr.* The Iliad.

("So saying, light-foot Iris pass'd away.") OBCVT, *tr. by* Alfred Tennyson, 1st Baron Tennyson

Achilles sets out ("Now issued from the ships the warrior Twain"). Homer. OBCVT, *tr. by* Alexander Pope *Fr.* The Iliad.

Achilles sets out ("Now I shall ask you to imagine how"). Homer. OBCVT, *tr. by* Christopher Logue *Fr.* The Iliad.

Achilles' Song. Robert Duncan. FTOS

Achilles with wild fury in his heart. Homer. OBWP, *tr. by* Robert Fitzgerald *Fr.* The Iliad.

Aching nostalgia—. *Unknown, Japanese.* OHMPJ, *tr. by* Kenneth Rexroth

Aching. Speech / is a mouth. (LL) The Language. Robert Creeley. PmAP; TAP

Achitophel: The Earl of Shaftsbury. Dryden. NOBE *Fr.* Absalom and Achitophel, Pt. I. EBEvV; FHYEP; FaBoPV; HAP; NOSC; OAEL-1; PoE

(Achitophel.) AWP

Achtung. Thomas Hardy. *See* Sapphic Fragment.

Achziv. Yehuda Amichai, *Hebrew.* IP, *tr. by* Warren Bargad *and* Stanley F. Chyet
"And this is how it begins now, my late."
"Clouds have come up from the south, the Nile's." IP, *tr. by* Bargad, Warren *and* Stanley Chyet
"Time after time you're placed at the imagined."

Acid a way very despair I'm her uneasy love. Catullus. *See* Carmen 92 ("Lesbia loads me night & day with her curses").

Acid today / is trendy entertainment. Why I Choose Black Men for My Lovers. La Loca. CLPP

Acis and Galatea. John Gay.
Air: "O ruddier than the cherry!" CBLP; EBEvV; NAEL-1; NOEC
(Song: "O ruddier than the cherry.") NOBE
"I rage, I melt, I burn." NAEL-1

Acknowledge, but own? (LL) Slave Quarters. James Dickey. CAPP-1; NYBP

Acknowledgement. Keorapetse Kgositsile. SeSe

Acme and Septimius; or, The Happy Union Celebrated at the Crown and Anchor Tavern. Catullus. OBCVT, *tr. by* Ellis, George

Acme, Septimius, sighs so amorous. Catullus. *See* Carmen 45 ("Phyllis Corydon clutched to him").

Acne blossoms scarlet on their cheeks. Porirua Friday Night. Sam Hunt. PeNZ

Acolyte, The. Denise Levertov. CrSp

Acoma. William Oandasan. HATNAP

Acon. Hilda Doolittle. VGW

Aconite, The. A. M. Graham. BoTP

Acorn, The. *Unknown.* BoTP

Acorn Song, The. *Unknown.* APN-2, *tr. by* Stephen Powers *Fr.* Sacred Songs of the Konkau.

Acquaint thyself with God, if thou wouldst taste. William Cowper. OxAEP-1 *Fr.* The Winter Morning Walk.

Acquainted with the Night. Robert Frost. CMoP; GSo; HAP; LiTM; MeMAP; MoAmPo; MoP; NOBA; NoAM; NoP-4; PoE; PoLF; Poetr; SAGP; SAmP; Son; TAP; TFi; TRP; TwCP; VGW; WeW-3

Acre of Grass, An. W. B. Yeats. CMoP; NoAM

Acre of performance is worth a, An. Thomas Howell. CTV

Acrid / smell of gasoline, An. Elizabeth Bishop. *See* The Moose.

Acrobatics. Dan Pagis, *Hebrew.* IP, *tr. by* Warren Bargad *and* Stanley F. Chyet

Acropolis. Lawrence Durrell. OxAEP-2

Across a city from you, I'm with you. Adrienne Rich. *Fr.* Twenty-one Love Poems. GLP

Across a limpid stream white birds aslant. On the River. Ku K'uang, *Chinese.* SuSp, *tr. by* Irving Y. Lo

Across a room. Blood or Color. Marjorie Welish. FTOS

Across an autumn freezing everywhere. (LL) What shall I give my children? who are poor. Gwendolyn Brooks. BPo; PoA; WPE

Across daubed rock evacuates its dead. (LL) Requiem for the Plantagenet Kings. Geoffrey Hill. CABP; NAEL-2; NoAM

Across from Chang's Green Emporium. Lala: The Dressmaker. Honor Ford-Smith. HCP

Across Grandmother's knees. Glory, Glory. . . . Raymond R. Patterson. MBE

Across North Wales. Dafydd ap Gwilym Resents the Winter. Rolfe Humphries. NYBP

Across old peach cans and old jelly jars. (LL) The Birth in a Narrow Room. Gwendolyn Brooks. NoP-4

Across our backs. Etheridge Knight. *See* Hard Rock Returns to Prison from the Hospital for the Criminal Insane.

Across Roblin Lake, two shores away. Wilderness Gothic. Alfred Wellington Purdy. HeIP-4; MoCV; NOBC; NoP-4

Across Space and Time. Charles Olson. PoM

Across the ages they come thundering. Say This of Horses. Minnie Hite Moody. PoLF

Across the Bay. Donald Davie. CABP; NoAM

Across the bridge, where in the morning blow. Sunday Chimes in the City. Louise Imogen Guiney. APN-2

Across the brook of Time man leaping goes. Laus Mariae. Sidney Lanier. Son

Across the channel, Mare Island welders cut. Bird-Watching. Dennis Schmitz. LCAP-2

Across the correct perspective to the painted sky. Landscape. David Gascoyne. FaBoMo

Across the dim frozen fields of night. Night Train. Robert Francis. GM

Across the expedient and wicked stones. (LL) Auto Wreck. Karl Shapiro. CMoP; LiTM; NIP-4; RB; VGW

Across the flesh and feeling of soledad. Orisha. Jayne Cortez. BlSi

Across the floor flits the mechanical toy. Cirque d'Hiver. Elizabeth Bishop. ChAP; InPS-3

Across the footpath (tidy. Mercy. Andrew Lansdown. NOBAu

Across the lake the small houses appear. For Two Children. David Malouf. BMAP

Across the lonely beach we flit. The Sandpiper. Celia Laighton Thaxter. CTAV; ImGa

Across the millstream below the bridge. The Blue Swallows. Howard Nemerov. NoP-4; Poetr

Across the mist flowers and grass appear far and hazy. Gathering Lotus. Chu Ch'ing-yü, *Chinese.* SuSp, *tr. by* Irving Y. Lo

Across the narrow beach we flit. The Sandpiper. Celia Laighton Thaxter. CTV; FaBoBe; OBCA; OxBChV; PWR

Across the night. From Creature to Ghost. Pauline Hanson. TAP

Across the open countryside. The Unsettled Motorcyclist's Vision of His Death. Thom Gunn. PoA

Across the Prairie's silent waste I stray. Richard Henry Wilde. APN-1 *Fr.* Hesperia.

Across the road. Flock. Lance Henson. VoR

Across the round field, under the dark male tower. The Lovers. Alex Comfort. PoA

Across the sand I saw a black man stride. Jamaican Fisherman. Philip Sherlock. PBCV

Across the sands. Michael McClintock. HA

Across the sea, along the shore. Arthur Hugh Clough. ChIV-2

Across the sea will come Adze-head. Adze-Head. *Unknown, Irish.* BIrV, *tr. by* James Carney

Across the sky / a lonely requiem of clouds. Love Song. Antonin Bartusek, *German.* CEEP, *tr. by* Ewald Osers

Across the sky run streaks of white light, aching. Before Olympus. John Gould Fletcher. MoAmPo

Across the sky the daylight crept. Coventry Patmore. GBL *Fr.* The Angel in the House.

Across the snout. Ars Poetica. Robert Desnos, *French.* AF, *tr. by* Carolyn Forché

Across the snow the silver bells. Silver Bells. Hamish Hendry. BoTP

Across the snowy pastures of the estate. The Fox Who Watched for the Midnight Sun. Norman Dubie. LCAP-2

Across the still lake. O. Mabson Southard. HA

Across the street—the freeway. Beneath the Shadow of the Freeway. Lorna Dee Cervantes. NMM-2; PBCAP

Across the Swamp. Olav H. Hauge, *Norwegian.* RaBo, *tr. by* Robert Bly

Across the swamps and marshlands of the hours. A Sea-Change: For Harold. Joseph Langland. LiTM

Across the tracks in Cheyenne, behind the biggest billboard. A Long Way Outside Yellowstone. Thomas McGrath. VGW

Across the Victorian mustache / and monocle. Martín Espada. *See* Bully.

Across the Western Ocean *or* Leave Her, Bullies, Leave Her. *Unknown.* AS

Across this dream of seas blue mountains fall. Between Seasons. Anne Welsh. PeSA

Across those plains where once there roamed the Indian and the Scout. The Mid-West. *Unknown.* OBCoV

Across to the Peloponnese. James Welch. CDW

Across upon this undulated board of verdure chequered bright. David Jones. NoAM *Fr.* The Five Unmistakable Marks. NAEL-2 *Fr.* In Parenthesis.

Acrostic on Wharton, An. *Unknown.* OBSV

Acrostick on Mrs. Elizabeth Hull, An. John Saffin. SCAP

Acrostick on Mrs. Winifret Griffin, An. John Saffin. SCAP

Acrostics. George Moses Horton. AAP

Act, An. Kenneth Rosen. AmPA

Act, The. William Carlos Williams. SAmP; VGW

Act #2. John Weiners. BB

Act I / Orlando hails. The Five-Minute Orlando Macbeth. George MacBeth. NOBL; PeLV

Act I, Scene ix, Air XI—"A Soldier and a Sailor." John Gay. *See* Air: "A Fox may steal your hens, sir."

Act II - Crossing At the Tracks. Fiona Templeton. FTOS *Fr.* You: The City.

Act like a crazy dog. Wear sashes & other fine clothes, carry a. Crazy Dog Events. Jerome Rothenberg. RaBo

Act of Love, The. Robert Creeley. HAP

Act of Love. Vernon Scannell. EP

Act of love seemed a dead metaphor, The. The Metaphor. Robert Graves. EP

Act six begins. Peter Goldsworthy. NOBAu

Actaeon. Rayner Heppenstall. FaBoTw

Acteon. Ovid. CTC, *tr. by* Arthur Golding *Fr.* Metamorphoses.

Acting, dear Thornton, its perfection draws. Robert Lloyd. ECEV *Fr.* The Actor.

Action. James Oppenheim. TrJP

Action Rhyme. E. H. Adams. BoTP

Action runs left to right, The. Movies, Left to Right. Robert Sward. NYBP

Action Would Kill It / A Gamble. Robert Adamson. BMAP; CBAP

Actions. Marcel Schwob, *French.* TrJP, *tr. by* William Brown Meloney

"Active balls?" said an old man of Stoneham. Limerick. C. D. Cudmore. PeLi

Acton Town Manufacturing. New York Map Company (1). John Yau. WWSi

Actor, The. Robert Lloyd.
"Acting, dear Thornton, its perfection draws." ECEV

Actor, The. Thomas Snapp. NYBP

Actor lived in the East Ward, An. The Comedian Gets a Curtain Lecture. Nguyễn Khuyến, *Vietnamese.* AVP, *tr. by* Huỳnh Sanh Thông

Actors. Rudyard Kipling. *Fr.* Epitaphs of the War [1914–1918]. OBWP

Actors. Trần Tế Xương, *Vietnamese.* AVP, *tr. by* Huỳnh Sanh Thông

Actors in the theatre. Written at Hsiang-kuo Temple on the Occasion of Watching Actors in the Hsing-hsiang Garden of the T'ung-t'ien-chieh Tao-ch'ang. Wang An-shih, *Chinese.* SuSp, *tr. by* Jan W. Walls

Acts of my life swarm down the street like Puerto Rican kids, The. My Acts. William Meredith. VCAP *Fr.* Consequences.

Acts of Youth, The. John Weiners. BB

Acts passed beyond the boundary of mere wishing. Stephen Spender. OxBTC

Actually: it's the balls I look for, always. Balls. Anne McNaughton. RaBo

Actually Swallowed. Douglas Messerli. FTOS

Ad Amicam. Francis Thompson. Son

Ad Coelum. William Pattison. OxBSP

Ad Coelum. Harry Romaine. BLPA; FaBoBe

Ad Finem. Heinrich Heine, *German.* AWP, *tr. by* Elizabeth Barrett Browning

Ad Finem. Ella Wheeler Wilcox. BLPA

Ad Flaccum. Martial, *Latin.* OBCVT, *tr. by* R. Fletcher

Ad Henricum Wottonem. Thomas Bastard. FaBoEE

Ad Infinitum. Joan Aronsten. NOBAu

Ad Johannuelem Leporem, Lepidissimum, Carmen Heroicum. *Unknown.* CBNP

Ad Leuconoen. Horace. *See* 1.11.

Ad Librum. Samuel Danforth Jr. SCAP

Ad Limina. Joseph Campbell. BIrV

Ad Ministram. Horace, *Latin.* OBCVT, *tr. by* William Makepeace Thackeray

Ad Sabellum. Martial, *Latin.* OBCVT, *tr. by* R. Fletcher

Adage: "Gardener's rule applies to youth and age, The." Henry James byron. NBLV

Adagio. Gerald William Barrax. GT

Adam, a brown old vulture in the rain. Ancient History. Siegfried Sassoon. ChIV-1

Adam and Eve. Itsik Manger, *Yiddish*. TrJP, *tr. by* Jacob Sonntag

Adam and Eve. Milton. *Fr.* Book IV. OAEL-1 *Fr.* Paradise Lost.

Adam and Eve. Karl Shapiro.
   Exile. CRP
   Recognition of Eve, The. ChIV-1
   Sickness of Adam, The. CRP

Adam and Eve. Charles Hubert Sisson. FaBoTw

Adam and Eve in the Garden. Milton. ITG, *tr. by* Robert Hass *Fr.* Book IX. FHYEP; NAEL-1; NAWM-1; OAEL-1 *Fr.* Paradise Lost.
   ("Both turned, and under open sky adored.") ITG, *tr. by* Robert Hass

Adam and Eve, like us. A Circle. Theodore Spencer. NYBP

Adam and God. Anne Wilkinson. MoCV

Adam Bell, Clim of the Clough, and William of Cloudesly. *Unknown.* ESPB
   (Adam Bel, Clym of the Cloughe, and Wyllyam of Cloudesle.) OxBB

Adam Birkett took his gun. Birkett's Eagle. Dorothy S. Howard. MoBS

Adam / Had 'em. On the Antiquity of Microbes. Strickland W. Gillilan. NBLV

Adam / Had 'em. Poem to Answer the Question: How Old Are Fleas? *Unknown.* Spl

Adam, indignant, would not eat with Eve. Paradise Saved. Alec Derwent Hope. OxBC

Adam Lay Bound. *Unknown.* CTC; ChIV-2; EnVB; HAP; InPS-3; MiEL; NAEL-1; NOBE; NOCV; OAEL-1; OxBoLi; PeLV; PoE; PoEL-1; TFi; TOF; TRP; WeW-3
   (Adam.) CH
   (Adam Lay I-bounden.) NoP-4
   (Adam Lay Y-Bounden.) PeLV
   ("Therefore we may singen, 'Deo gracias!'") (LL) NoP-4

Adam paced the footpaths of paradise in a. Martin Sorescu, *Romanian.* CEEP, *tr. by* Stavros Deligiorgis

Adam Posed. Anne Finch, Countess of Winchilsea. ChIV-1; ECWP
   ("Could our first father, at his toilsome plow.") NoP-4
   ("T'have hit the wav'ring form, or giv'n this thing a name.") (LL) NoP-4

Adam Says See. Julia Randall.
   "How shall we walk naked when." CrSp

Adam scriveyn [*or* scrivain *or* scrivein], if ever it thee bifalle. To His Scribe Adam. Chaucer. CABP; NAEL-1; NoP-4; OAEL-1; OxBSP

Adam Speaks. Milton. *Fr.* Book X. FHYEP *Fr.* Paradise Lost.

Adam was my grandfather. For All Blasphemers. Stephen Vincent Benét. OxBA

Adam was no fool. He knew that at his age. A Family Matter. Allen Curnow. *Fr.* Trees, Effigies, Moving Objects. PeNZ

Adam's Complaint. Denise Levertov. BoWoP; NNaP

Adam's Curse. W. B. Yeats. BIrV; CMoP; NAEL-2; NoAM; NoP-4; OAEL-2; PFE; WeW-3

Adam's Dream. David Ferry. PFE

Adam's Dream. Edwin Muir. NoP-4

Adam's Dying. Frederic Ridgely Torrence. FYAP

Adam's Footprint. Vassar Miller. MT; WeT

Adam's Song to Heaven, *'You will be as God, knowing good and evil'.* Edgar Bowers. CoAmPo

Adam's Task. John Hollander. APo; NIP-4; NoP-4

Adapt thyself to time and circumstance. Shem-Tob ben Joseph Palquera, *Hebrew.* TrJP, *tr. by* Rabbi Ettelson

Adder's Epigrams. Colin Ellis. FaBoEE

Addiction to the exceptional event. Barbarossa. Hubert Witheford. PeNZ

Adding father's name. Nicholas Virgilio. HA

Addition to Kipling's "The Dead King (Edward VII), 1910." Max Beerbohm. FaBoEE; OBCoV

Addition to the Opposition. Aleksandr Yeryomenko, *Russian.* TCRP, *tr. by* Albert C. Todd

Additional Poem, An. John Ashbery. FaBoMo

Address. Andrew Geddes Bain. PeSAV

Address. Lynda Hull. PUP-19

Address. Bruce Smith. Son *Fr.* In My Father's House.

Address by an Ex-Confederate Soldier to the Grand Army of the Republic, An. Maurice Thompson. CBCW

Address of my house has changed, The. Prison. Mahmoud Darwish, *Arabic.* AF, *tr. by* Denys Johnson-Davies

Address to a Bachelor on a Delicate Occasion. Priscilla Pointon. ECWP

Address to a Child during a Boisterous Winter Evening. Dorothy Wordsworth. NOxBChV; NTP; OxBChV; WoRP

("Here's a cosy warm house for Edward and me.") (LL) NOxBChV

(Wind, The.) BoTP

Address to Ethiopia. Priscilla Jane Thompson. CBWP-2

Address to Her Husband. Mehetabel Wright. ECWP
   (Disappointed Wife, The.) LW

Address to Lady——, Who Asked What the Passion of Love Was? Charles Morris. NOEC

Address to Miss Phillis Wheatley, An. Jupiter Hammon.
   "O come you pious youth! adore." AmPP

Address to My Soul. Elinor Wylie. AWP; LiTM; OxBA

Address to Nature on its Cruelty, An. Ellen Johnston. VWP

Address to Poetry, An. Helen Maria Williams.
   "Blest Poesy! Oh sent to calm." NOBRP

Address to the Deil. Robert Burns. NOEC; OAEL-1; OxBS; PoEL-4

Address to the Muses, An. Joanna Baillie.
   "Ye are the spirits who preside." ECWP

Address to the Plebeians, An. John Learmont.
   "Poor crawlin' bodies, sair neglectit." NOEC

Address to the Scholars of New England. John Crowe Ransom. LiTM; MeMAP

Address to the Soul Occasioned by a Rain, An. Edward Taylor. MeMAP; NAAL-1; NOBA; OxBA; PoEL-3
   (Let by Rain.) ColAP; NAAL-3
   ("Ye Flippering Soule.") ColAP

Address to the Unco Guid, or the Rigidly Righteous. Robert Burns. ChIV-1; NOBE; NOCV; OxBS

Address to the Vacationers at Cape Lookout, An. William Stafford. NYBP

Address to Venus. Lucretius, *Latin.* AWP, *tr. by* Spencer *Fr.* De Rerum Natura (On the Nature of Things).
   ("And quiet to the weary World restore.") (LL) EP, *tr. by* John Dryden
   ("Great *Venus,* Queene of beautie and of grace.") OBCVT, *tr. by* Edmund Spenser
   (Prayer to Venus.)

Addressed to ——. Lady Mary Wortley Montagu. ECWP

Addressed to a Beech Tree. Christian Carstairs. ECWP

Addressed to a Koto-player. Su Man-shu, *Chinese.* SuSp, *tr. by* Wu-chi Liu

Addressed to Haydon. Keats. OBNC; Ro

Addressing the Comet. Ivan V. Lalic, *Serbo-Croatian.* HSix, *tr. by* Charles Simic

Addressing the readers of a well-run newspaper, that is, one abounding. The Silent World Is Our Only Homeland. Francis Ponge, *French.* AF, *tr. by* Beth Archer

Adela, Adela, Adela Chart. To Henry James. Robert Louis Stevenson. OBCoV

Adelaide's Dream. Christopher Middleton. PeLV

Adelina Patti. Adah Isaacs Menken. CBWP-1

Adelita's name of the lady, *Spanish vers. Unknown, Spanish.* AS, *tr. by* F. S. Curtis, Jr.

Adequate of Hell, The. (LL) Remorse—is Memory—awake. Emily Dickinson. NAAL-1; NAAL-3; NOBA; NOCV; NoP-4; PAR; SAmP

Adew, my King, court, cuntrey, and my kin. To Henry Constable and Henry Keir. Alexander Montgomerie. OxBS

Adhesion to this body. Squeeze. Abigail Child. FTOS

Adhesive Autopsy of Walt Whitman, The. Jonathan Williams. PoM

Adhiambo. Gabriel Okara. See To Adhiambo.

Adieu. Mary E. Tucker. CBWP-1

"Adieu, adieu" for evermore. (LL) Peace; come away: the song of woe. Tennyson. EBVV; EBVVPR; EnVR; FHYEP; IMW

Adieu, Adieu, Forever. Priscilla Jane Thompson. CBWP-2

Adieu and Recall to Love, The. Robert Merry. NOBRP

Adieu, blind fortune, with thy miserable purse. Adieu, to Fortune. Henry Francis Fynn. PeSAV

Adieu Contentment, Safety, Peace and Quiet! (LL) Instructions, Supposed to Be Written in Paris, for the Mob in England. Mary Alcock. ECWP; Ro

Adieu, dear life! here am I left alone. On My Late Dear Wife. Jonathan Richardson. NOEC

Adieu, dear name which birth and nature gave. An Elegy on a Maiden Name. Jane Cave. CABP; ECWP

Adieu, fair isle! I love thy bowers. Composed at the Request of a Lady, and Descriptive of Her Feelings. Maria Gowen Brooks. APN-1; PAR

Adieu, farewell, earth's bliss[e]. A Litany in Time of Plague. Thomas Nashe. CH; ClHu; EBEV; FaBoCh; FaPoR; HAP; HeIP-4; HoPM; NAEL-1; NIP-4; NOBE; NoSic; OAEL-1; OBEV; PoEL-2; PoRA; SCV; TFi; TRP *Fr.* Summer's Last Will and Testament.

Adieu, farewell earth's bliss. Thomas Nashe. *See* A Litany in Time of Plague.

Adieu, New-England's smiling meads. A Farewell to America. To Mrs. S. W. Phillis Wheatley. NoP-4

"Adieu!" she cries; and waved [or waves] her lily hand. (LL) Sweet William's Farewell to Black-Eyed [or Black-Ey'd] Susan. John Gay. AmFP; BoLoP; CBLP; GTBS-P; NOEC

Adieu, sweet Angus, Maeve and Fand. The Passing of the Shee. John Millington Synge. BIrV; FaBoEE

Adieu the woods and waters' side. Lines on Leaving a Scene in Bavaria. Thomas Campbell. OBNC

Adieu, the years are a broken song. *Unknown.* NOBAu

Adieu, to Fortune. Henry Francis Fynn. PeSAV

Adieu to My Landlady, An. George Farewell. NOEC

Adieu, you haughty maiden! Adieu, Adieu, Forever. Priscilla Jane Thompson. CBWP-2

"Adiew, madam my mother dear." Lord Maxwell's Last Goodnight. *Unknown.* ESPB

Adina. Harold Milton Telemaque. TTY

Adjectives. Moishe Nadir, *Yiddish.* TrJP, *tr. by* Joseph Leftwich

Adlatts parke is wyde and broad. Will Stewart and John. *Unknown.* ESPB

Adlestrop. Edward Thomas. APAD; AYFP; CH; EBEvV; HAP; NAEL-2; NOBE; NoP-4; OBEV; OxBTC; UV

("Yes.") APAD; NoP-4

Administrator, The. Marilyn Chin. LoHo

Administrator, An. Geoffrey Grigson. FaBoEE

Admiral Benbow. *Unknown.* EnSB

Admiral Dugout. Cicely Fox- Smith. NSI

Admiral Hosier's Ghost. Richard Glover. NOEC

Admiral, the prisoner of your giant's. John Alexander Allen. NYBP

Admirals All. Sir Henry John Newbolt. FaPoR

Admiral's Caravan, The. Charles Edward Carryl.

Camel's Complaint, The. NOxBChV; OBCA; OxBChV

(Song of the Camel, The.) OTCP

Admiration. Josephine D. Henderson Heard. CBWP-4

Admirations—and Contempts—of time, The. Emily Dickinson. APN-2

Admire Cranmer! Stevie Smith. NoAM

Admire the face of plastered stone. Quebec Farmhouse. John Glassco. NOBC

Admire the old man, admire him, admire him. Admire Cranmer! Stevie Smith. NoAM

Admire the watered silky gap. Anointed Vessel. Paul Verlaine, *French.* EP, *tr. by* Alistair Elliot

Admire thy wreath? And wherefore should I not. To a Plagiarist. Moses ibn Ezra, *Hebrew.* TrJP, *tr. by* Solomon Solis-Cohen

Admire, when you come here, the glimmering hair. Vuillard: "The Mother and Sister of the Artist." W. D. Snodgrass. CoAP

Admirer's Lament of Chaucer, An. Thomas Hoccleve. EPCY *Fr.* Regement of Princes.

Admirers of the Little Box, The. Vasco [or Vasko] Popa, *Serbo-Croatian.* HSix, *tr. by* Charles Simic

Admiring it and adding noughts in vain. (LL) Star-Gazer. Louis MacNeice. NAEL-2; NoP-4

Admission. Henry Vaughan. ESCV

Admit them, admit them. (LL) Song of a Man Who Has Come Through. D. H. Lawrence. CMoP; FaBoMo; GTBS-P; InPS-3; LiTM; OxBTC; PeFWW; PoE; RaBo; TRP

Admit then and be glad. Poem for an Anniversary. C. Day Lewis. CABP

Admonition. Philip Stack. BLPA

Admonition by the Auctor to all yong Gentilwomen: And to al other Maids being in Love, The. Isabella Whitney.

"Ye virgins that from Cupid's tents." PEW

Admonition to a Traveller. Wordsworth. GTBS-P

Admonition to Montgomerie. James I, King of England. GTBS-P; OxBS

Admonition to Myself, An. Chao Meng-fu, *Chinese.* CoBLCP, *tr. by* Jonathan Chaves

Admonition to the Muse. Geoffrey Taylor. FaBoEE

Admonitions. Lucille Clifton. BPo; NALW; NMM-2

Adolescence. W H Auden. MoP; NoAM

Adolescence. Gregory Orr. Poetsp

Adolescence—I. Rita Dove. ISC; NoAM; PiM

Adolescence—II. Rita Dove. AmPA; HCAP; ISC; NoAM; PoPoPo; VCAP

Adolescence—III. Rita Dove. ISC; NoAM

Adolescent. Joyce Peseroff. CMAP

Adolescent night, breath of the town, The. Midsummer. Robert Fitzgerald. PoA

Adolescents on the Sea. Nichita Stanescu, *Romanian.* CEEP, *tr. by* Mariana Carpinisan *and* Mark Irwin

Adolicus; that's a creeper rug, its small. "Robin Hyde." PeNZ *Fr.* The Houses.

Adonais; An Elegy on the Death of Keats. Shelley. EBEV; FHYEP; HoPM; ImPo; NOBRP; OAEL-2; OxAEP-2; PoEL-4; TFi

(Adonais: An Elegy on the Death of John Keats, author of Endymion, Hyperion, etc.) Ro

Cancelled Passages of the Poem.

Elegy on the Death of John Keats, An. OBNC

("I weep for Adonais—he is dead!") CABP

(Mourn Not for Adonais.) NOBE

Go Thou to Rome.

Made One With Nature. LBC

("Sustains it from beneath, and kindles it above.") (LL) LBC

"Most musical of mourners, weep again!" EPCY

"One remains, the many change and pass, The." SCV

Adonis. Hilda Doolittle. AWP

Adonis. Theocritus, *Greek.* NoSic

Adonis, Dying. Praxilla, *Greek.* PBWP; WPOW, *tr. by* Richard Lattimore

Adonis Theater. Mark Doty. NAmP90

Adoramus Te, Christe. David O'Bruadair, *Irish.* NOIV, *tr. by* Thomas Kinsella

Adoration of the Anchor. Laura Jensen. LCAP-2

Adoration of the Disk by King Akhnaten and Princess Nefer Neferiu Aten. *Unknown.* AWP *Fr.* Book of the Dead.

"Cattle roam again across the field, The."

Adoration of the Magi, The. Christopher Pilling. OBCP

Adore the lifted standard of the Cross. On the Cross. Alcuin, *Latin.* MLL, *tr. by* Helen Waddell

Adore the Roses; nor delay. Rosary Beads. Herman Melville. NCAP

Adore we the Lord. *Unknown.* NOIV

Adorning the head that destiny never worried. (LL) O Golden Fleece ("O Golden Fleece she is where she lies tonight"). George Barker. EP; LiTM; MoBrPo

Adown the heights of Ages. Priscilla Jane Thompson. CBWP-2

Adrian Henri's Talking after Christmas Blues. Adrian Henri. PeLV

Adriani Morientis ad Animam Suam. Emperor Hadrian, *Latin.* OBVE; OxBSP, *tr. by* Matthew Prior

(Adriani Morientis Ad Animam Suam. . . Imitated.) OBCVT, *tr. by* Matthew Prior

("Poor little, pretty, fluttering thing.") OBCVT, *tr. by* Matthew Prior

Adriano; or, The First of June. James Hurdis. ECEV

Student, The.

Adrian's Address to His Soul When Dying. Emperor Hadrian. OBCVT, *tr. by* Byron *Fr.* Hadrian's Address to His Soul When Dying. OBVE, *tr. by* Byron

Adrift on an oil-drum raft. Michael Anania. *Fr.* The Riversongs of Arion. NoAM

Adult. Linda Gregg. BLT

Adulterers and customers of whores. Womanisers. John Press. BoLoP

Adulterers and whoremongers / were there, with all unchaste. Michael Wigglesworth. ColAP *Fr.* The Day of Doom.

Adulteries, murthers, robberies, thefts. Roger Williams. SCAP

Adultery. James Dickey. MT; TAP

Adultery. Alan Dugan. CAPP-1

Adulthood. Nikki Giovanni. CrSp; NMM-2

Advanc'd her height, and sparkl'd in her eye. Anne Killigrew. *See* Upon the Saying That My Verses Were Made by Another.

Advance of Education, The. Josephine D. Henderson Heard. CBWP-4

Advance was catlike, The. Cirrhosis. A. L. Hendriks. HCP

Advanced out toward the external from. Celestial Evening, October 1967. Charles Olson. PoM *Fr.* The Maximus Poems.

Advent. Brian Coffey.

"Awakening like return to Earth from Moon." CIP-2

"'My son my son' the Blakean figure mourns and affirms." BiHa

"What have they done to Klio have they done to our Muse." BiHa

Advent. William Everson. NeAP; TrCP

Advent. Anne Hartigan. CIP-2

Advent. Patrick Kavanagh. IIP; TIRV

Advent. Kathleen Norris. CrSp

Advent. Christina Rossetti. TrCP

Advent; a Carol. Patric Dickinson. OBCP

Advent Lyrics. *Unknown, Anglo-Saxon. Fr.* Christ 1. AnOE, *tr. by* Charles W. Kennedy

"'O my Joseph, Jacob's son.'" ASW, *tr. by* Kevin Crossley-Holland

"You govern the locks, You open life." ASW, *tr. by* Kevin Crossley-Holland

Advent 1955. John Betjeman. OBCP

Advent 1966. Denise Levertov. APSN; NNaP

Advent wind begins to stir, The. Advent 1955. John Betjeman. OBCP

Adventure is all in a three-wheel pushchair. It lives in, The. Produce from the colonies. Pierre McOrlan, *French.* MFP, *tr. by* Martin Sorrell

Adventure of the Quartz Pebble, The. Vasco [*or* Vasko] Popa. PoSu, *tr. by* Anne Pennington *Fr.* The Quartz Pebble.

(Adventure of the Pebble.) CEEP, *tr. by* Charles Simic

("Fed up with the circle.") CEEP, *tr. by* Charles Simic

("Hid in its own shadow.") (LL) CEEP, *tr. by* Charles Simic

Adventures in Bronze. Leon Stokesbury. MT

Adventures of Huckleberry Finn, The. "Mark Twain."

Emmeline Grangerford's "Ode to Stephen Dowling Bots, Dec'd." NBLV; OBAL

(Ode to Stephen Dowling Bots, Dec'd.) APN-2; Poetr

Adventures of Id, The. Morris Gilbert Bishop. OBCoV

Adventures of Isabel. Ogden Nash. ChAP; MoAmPo; NOxBChV; NTCP; OBAL; OBCA

Adventures of Master F. I, The. George Gascoigne.

Farewell, A. NOBE; SCGP

Adventures of Simon Swaugum, a Village Merchant, The. Philip Freneau. PoEL-4

Adventurous mariner! in whose gray skiff. Sonnet 18. Amos Bronson Alcott. APN-1

Adventurous Muse, The. Isaac Watts. NOEC

"Give me the Muse whose generous force." EPCY

Adversaries of the Lord shall be broken to pieces; out of heaven shall he thunder upon them: the Lord shall judge the ends of the earth; and he shall give strength unto his king, and exalt the horn of his anointed, The. (LL) Hannah's Song of Thanksgiving. Bible, *O.T.* TrCP, *ad. by* Michael Drayton; AWP

Adversary, The. Phyllis McGinley. FaBoEE; OBCA; OxBSP; SoSe-8

Advertisement for Finnegans Wake, An. James Joyce. CBNP

(Blurb for *Haveth Childers Everywhere*, A.) OBCoV

Advertising Agency Song, The. *Unknown.* NBLV

Advertising Rhymes. *Unknown.*

Burma-Shave Roadside Signs. OBCoV

Force. OBCoV

"There was a little man." OBCoV

Waverly Pen, The.

Advice. Gwendolyn B. Bennett. BlSi

Advice. Lee Cataldi. BMAP

Advice. Bill Holm. RaBo

Advice. Langston Hughes. GEA; NBLV; SAmP

("In between.") (LL) GEA

Advice, The. Sir Walter Ralegh. AAS; SiPS

Advice. Ntozake Shange. NMM-2

Advice. Ruth Stone. CrSp; MDDM; NMM-2

Advice for a Journey. Sidney Keyes. PoWW

Advice from Euterpe. Carter Revard. VoR

Advice from Poor Robin's Almanack. *Unknown.* OBCP

Advice Gratis to Certain Women. Phoebe Cary. APN-2; PAR

Advice of an Efficiency Expert, The. Augustus Young. CIP-2

Advice of Housewives. Thomas Tusser. NoSic *Fr.* Five Hundred Points of Good Husbandry.

Advice to a Child. Eleanor Farjeon. AYFP; OTCP

Advice to a Discarded Lover. Fleur Adcock. PeNZ

Advice to a Forest. Maxwell Bodenheim. TrJP

Advice to a Girl. Thomas Campion. SAGP

Advice to a Lover. Thomas Yalden. ECEV

Advice to a Neighbour Girl. Yü Hsüan-chi, *Chinese.* PBWP, *tr. by* Kenneth Rexroth *and* Ling Chung

(For a Neighbor Girl.) BoWoP, *tr. by* Geoffrey Waters

Advice to a Prophet. Richard Wilbur. AFr; AmPP; FYAP; GEA; MoAmPo; NYBP; NoP-4; OBWP; OxBC; PoE; Poetr; TwCP; VCAP

Advice to a Raven in Russia [December, 1812]. Joel Barlow. APN-1; AmPP; NAAL-1; NAAL-3; NOBA; OBWP; OxBA

(Advice to a Raven in Russia.) ColAP

Advice to a Young Lady Lately Married. Esther Lewis. ECWP

"Advice" to a Young Poet. Raymond Mazisi Kunene, *Zulu.* PeSAV, *tr. by the author*

Advice to Bores. Abraham ibn Chasdai, *Hebrew.* TrJP, *tr. by* J. Chotzner

Advice to Colonel Valentine. Robert Graves. NYBP

Advice to Hotheads. Samuel ben Elhanan Isaac, of Padua Archevolti, *Hebrew.* TrJP, *tr. by* A. B. Rhine

Advice to Lovers. John Armstrong. NOEC *Fr.* The Oeconomy of Love; a Poetical Essay.

Advice to My Best Brother, Colonel Francis Lovelace. Richard Lovelace. BeJo

Advice to My Son. Peter Meinke. Poetsp

Advice to Sophronia. Mary Leapor. ECWP

Advice to Students. Phùng Khắc Khoan, *Vietnamese.* AVP, *tr. by* Huỳnh Sanh Thông

Advice to the Orchestra. David Wagoner. NoAM

Advice to the Same. Sir Philip Sidney. SiPS *Fr.* Arcadia.

Advice to the Young. Miriam Waddington. NIP-4; NOBC

Advice to Travelers. Walker Gibson. NBLV

(Before Starting.) KaS

Advice to Young Ladies. Alec Derwent Hope. NoAM; NoP-4

Advice to Young Ladies. Ann Plato. AAP

Advice to Young Writers. Ron Padgett. BAP-93

Advice was good—not to look back, The. Lot's Wife. Cherra S. Ransom. CrSp

Adze-Head. *Unknown, Irish.* BIrV, *tr. by* James Carney

Ae fond kiss, and then we sever. Song. Robert Burns. BoLoP; EBEvV; NAEL-2; NOBRP; NOEC; OAEL-1; OBEV; PoEL-4

Ae time as Cupy sweet tuith'd Fairy. The 19th Idyllium of Theocritus attempted in the Cumberland Dialect. Theocritus, *Greek.* OBCVT, *tr. by* Josiah Relph

Ae weet forenicht i' the yow-trummle. The Watergaw. "Hugh MacDiarmid." FaBoVe; NAEL-2

Aedh Tells of the Rose in His Heart. W. B. Yeats. *See* The Lover Tells of the Rose in His Heart.

Aedh Wishes for the Cloths of Heaven. W. B. Yeats. *See* He Wishes for the Cloths of Heaven.

Aegean. Louis Simpson. NYBP

Aegean, The. Maria Luisa Spaziani, *Italian.* NeIt, *tr. by* Beverly Allen

Aegean Melancholy. Odysseus Elytis, *Greek.* VCWP, *tr. by* Edmund Keeley *and* Philip Sherrard

Aeglamour's Lament. Ben Jonson. *See* Here She Was Wont to Go.

Aelf-Scin, the shining scimmer the gleam, the shining, The. Michael McClure. PoM

Aella; a Tragycal Enterlude. Thomas Chatterton.

Mynstrelles Songe ("Angelles bee wrogte to bee of neidher kynde"). EnLoPo

Mynstrelle's Songe ("O! synge untoe mie roundelaie"). EnLoPo; NOEC; OxAEP-1

(Minstrel's Song.) HAP; SCGP

(Mynstrelles Songe.) CABP

("Thos the damfelle epake, and dyed.") (LL) CABP

There Lackethe Somethynge Style. OxAEP-1

("Boddynge flourettes bloshes atte the lyghte.")

(Minstrels' Marriage-Song.)

(Mynstrelles Songe.)

Aeneas at Washington. Allen Tate. FYAP; FuPo; NOBA; NoAM; OxBA

Aeneas' firmness. Virgil, *Latin.* OBCVT, *tr. by* John Dryden

Aeneas' Image of War. Virgil. OBVE, *tr. by* Gawin Douglas *Fr.* The Aeneid [*or* Eneados, *Aeneis*].

Aeneas sees his wife. Virgil, *Latin.* OBCVT, *tr. by* John Dryden

Aeneas' story. Virgil, *Latin.* OBCVT, *tr. by* Sir John Denham

Aeneas (with Achates) Meets His Mother, Venus. Virgil. OBVE, *tr. by* Gawin Douglas *Fr.* The Aeneid [*or* Eneados, *Aeneis*].

Aeneid [*or* Eneados, *Aeneis*], The. Virgil, *Latin.*

Aeneas' Image of War. OBVE, *tr. by* Gawin Douglas

Aeneas (with Achates) Meets His Mother, Venus. OBVE, *tr. by* Gawin Douglas

Anchises to Aeneas. OBCVT, *tr. by* Sir Walter Alexander Raleigh

"And now Aeneas charges straight at Turnus." OBWP, *tr. by* Allen Mandelbaum

Building of Carthage, The. OBVE, *tr. by* Gawin Douglas

Building of Carthage, The. OBVE, *tr. by* John Dryden

Charon. OBVE, *tr. by* Gawin Douglas

Charon. OBVE, *tr. by* John Dryden

"Come is the ending day, Troy's hour is come." MLL, *tr. by* Helen Waddell

Creusa. NoSic

"Dear Sister, my resentment had not been." OBVE, *tr. by* Sir John Denham

Death of Priam, The. OBVE, *tr. by* Sir John Denham

Defeat of Turnus, The. OBVE, *tr. by* Gawin Douglas

Dido by Night. OBVE, *tr. by* Henry Howard, Earl of Surrey

Dido in the Elysian Fields. OBCVT, *tr. by* John Dryden

Dido to Her Sister Anna. OBVE, *tr. by* Henry Howard, Earl of Surrey

Dido's Suicide. OBVE, *tr. by* Gawin Douglas

Diomede Mourns His Fate and That of His Friends to the Latian Ambassador Who Seeks His Alliance against Aeneas. OBVE, *tr. by* John Dryden

Euryalus and Nisus Meet Their Deaths. NoSic, *tr. by* Thomas Phaer

Fame. OBVE, *tr.* by John Dryden

"Heaven, the earth, and all the liquid main [*or* mayne], The." OBVE, *tr.* by Sir Walter Ralegh

House of Fame, The. OBCVT, *tr.* by Geoffrey Chaucer

"How hard a fate enthrals the wretched maid." ECWP, *tr.* by Elizabeth Tollet

"I sing of warfare and a man at war." NAWM-1, *tr.* by Robert Fitzgerald, *abr. vers.*

Invocation. OBCVT, *tr.* by John Dryden

Night-Piece, The. OAEL-1

"Now manhood and garbroyls I chaunt, and martial horror." BIrV; OBVE, *tr.* by Richard Stanyhurst

"O boys, O strong of heart in vain." MLL, *tr.* by Helen Waddell

Polyphemus. NoSic, *tr.* by Richard Stanyhurst

Prologue to [*or* of] Book VII, The. OxBS, *tr.* by Gawin Douglas

Rubric, The. OBVE, *tr.* by Gawin Douglas

Second Book of Virgil's *Aeneid*, The. SiPS, *tr.* by Henry Howard, Earl of Surrey

   "And now we gan draw near unto the gate."

   "But lo, Polites, one of Priam's sons."

   "It was the time when, granted from the gods." NAEL-1, *tr.* by Henry Howard, Earl of Surrey

   Laocoön. OBVE, *tr.* by Henry Howard, Earl of Surrey

   "They whisted all, with fixèd face attent."

   Trojan Horse, The. OAEL-1, *tr.* by Henry Howard, Earl of Surrey

   "Whom when I saw assembled in such wise." PoE, *tr.* by Henry Howard, Earl of Surrey

Sybil, The. OBVE, *tr.* by Gawin Douglas

Turnus and the Courser. OBVE, *tr.* by Gawin Douglas

Turnus and the Stone. OBVE, *tr.* by John Dryden

Turnus and the Wanton Courser. OBVE, *tr.* by John Dryden

Turnus Summons His Allies, Aeneas Is "Perturbit wyth Gret Thochtis." OBVE, *tr.* by Gawin Douglas

"Wee leave Creete Country; and our sayls unwrapped uphoysing." BIrV; OBVE, *tr.* by Richard Stanyhurst

Wooden Horse Is Brought into Troy, The. OBVE, *tr.* by Gawin Douglas

Aeolian Harp, The. Coleridge. *See* The Eolian Harp.

Aeolian Harp, The. Herman Melville. AmPP; NCAP

Aeolus looses the winds. Virgil, *Latin.* OBCVT, *tr.* by Gawin Douglas

Aequam Memento. Horace, *Latin.* OBCVT, *tr.* by Louis MacNeice *Fr.* Three Odes of Horace.

Aerial, The. Reiner Kunze, *German.* PoSu, *tr.* by Ewald Osers

Aerialist Narratives, Chapter Three, The. Ed Roberson. PT

Aerin 4. Chi-ha Kim, *Korean.* CKP, *tr.* by Jaihiun Kim

Aerin I. Chi-ha Kim, *Korean.* CKP, *tr.* by Jaihiun Kim

Aerogrammes. Russell Leong. OpBo

Aerophorion. Henry James Pye.

   Air Balloon, The. NOEC

Aeroplane, The. Jeannie Kirby. BoTP

Aeroplane. Pudjipangu, *Aborigine.* NOBAu, *tr.* by Georg von Brandenstein

Aeschyleans, The. Bernadette Mayer. FTOS

Aesop at Play. Phaedrus, *Latin.* AWP, *tr.* by Christopher Smart

Aesop, mine author, makis mention. The Tale of the Upland Mouse and the Burgess Mouse. Robert Henryson. OBNV

Aesop's Fable of the Frogs. Jean de La Fontaine, *French.* OBVE, *tr.* by John Hookham Frere

Aestas. Joshua Sylvester. NOSC

Aesthete, The. Sir William Schwenck Gilbert. *See* Bunthorne's Song.

Aesthete to the Rose, The. *Unknown.* BXAP

Aesthetic. Norman Rosten. PoA

Aesthetic Point of View, The. W. H. Auden. NBLV; OBAL; OBCoV *Fr.* Shorts [1948–1957].

   (Limerick.) PeLi

Aestivation [an Unpublished Poem, by My Late Latin Tutor]. Oliver Wendell Holmes. NOBL; OBAL *Fr.* The Autocrat of the Breakfast Table.

   (Intramural Aestivation, or Summer in Town, by a Teacher of Latin.)

Aestuary, An. George Croly. NOBRP

Aeterna Poetae Memoria. Archibald MacLeish. Son

Æthelstan King, lord of eorls. Battle of Brunanburh. *Unknown, Anglo-Saxon.* AnOE, *tr.* by Charles Kennedy

Æthelstan the King, ruler of earls. Battle of Brunanburh. *Unknown, Anglo-Saxon.* ASW, *tr.* by Kevin Crossley-Holland

Aetna. *Unknown, Latin.*

   Lava-flow. OBCVT, *tr.* by Jabez Hughes

Afar in the desert I love to ride. A War (?) in the Desert. *Unknown.* PeSAV

Afar though near the silence waxes. The Cloak. Norman Henry, II Pritchard. GT

Afay in de ewigkeit! (LL) Hans Breitmann's Party [*or* Barty]. Charles Godfrey Leland. NOBL; OBAL; OBCoV

Affable Irregular, An. The Road at My Door. W. B. Yeats. BIrV; NOBE; PoE *Fr.* Meditations in Time of Civil War.

Affair of Honour. George Whalley. MoCV

Affair of the Heart. Peter Porter. BMAP

Affectionate. Else Von Freytag-Loringhoven. PFTM

Affectionate Shepherd, The. Richard Barnfield. NoSic

   Affectionate Shepherd, The. OBGa

   (Daphnis to Ganymede.)

   ("If thou wilt come and dwell with me at home.")

   Philomel. CH; NOBE; OBEV

   (Nightingale, The.) AWP; GTBS-P

   (Tears of an Affectionate Shepherd Sick for Love, The.) CABP

Affections Must Not. Denise Riley. NBrP

Affinity, The. Anna Wickham. NALW

Affirming it a Soul. (LL) Props assist the House, The. Emily Dickinson. APN-2; WPoS

Affliction. Bible, *O.T.* TrJP *Fr.* Lamentations.

Affliction. Sir John Davies. NOBE *Fr.* Nosce Teipsum. NoSic; SiPS

Affliction. George Herbert. *See* Affliction (1).

Affliction: "Kill me not every [*or* ev'ry] day." George Herbert. NOSC

Affliction (4). George Herbert. ESCV; GeHe; NOSC

   (Affliction (IV).) CABP

   ("Till I reach heav'n, and much more, thee.") (LL) CABP

Affliction of Margaret—The The. Wordsworth. GTBS-P; OxBSn; PoEL-4; RACG

   ("With love and longings infinite.") (LL) OxBSn

Affliction (1). George Herbert. ESCV; FHYEP; FSCP; GeHe; MeLP; NAEL 1; NOBE; NOSC; SoCP

   (Affliction.) FMP

Affliction shall advance the flight in me. (LL) Easter-Wings. George Herbert. CABP; ChIV-1; ESCV; FHYEP; FMP; FSCP; GeHe; HAP; HeIP-4; InPK-6; InPS-3; MeLP; NAEL-1; NIP-4; NOSC; NoP-4; OAEL-1; PBRV; PFE; PoE; PoEL-2; PoPoPo; Poetr; SeCP; TFi; TOF; TRP; TrCP; WeW-3

Affliction so general you find no name, An. Dog Days 1978. Jim Barnes. EC2

Affliction (3). George Herbert. NOSC

Affrayit, I glistnyt of sleip, and stert on feit. Aeneas' Image of War. Virgil. OBVE, *tr.* by Gawin Douglas *Fr.* The Aeneid [*or* Eneados, Aeneis].

Afoot and light-hearted I take to the open road. Walt Whitman. *Fr.* Song of the Open Road. NOBA

Afraid of the sun [*or* sunlight]. Advice to a Neighbour Girl. Yü Hsüan-chi, *Chinese.* BoWoP, *tr.* by Geoffrey Waters; PBWP, *tr.* by Kenneth Rexroth *and* Ling Chung

Afraid of the void I filled with lying. (LL) What Goes Around Comes Around, or The Proof is in the Pudding. Cheryl Clarke. CPO; FFC

Afraid! Of whom am I afraid? Emily Dickinson. PoE

Afreeka Brass. Mwatabu Okantah. SeSe

Afresh'd with paint the shop had glare. New Storefront. Russell Atkins. GT

Africa. Maya Angelou. NIP-4

Africa. Change Is Not Always Progress. Don L. Lee. TAP

Africa. Claude McKay. NAAAL; Son

Africa. Joaquin Miller. APN-2

Africa. Lizelia Augusta Jenkins Moorer. CBWP-3

Africa. Adèle Naudé. PeSA

Africa, Music and Show Business. Abdullah Ibrahim. MoNo

Africa my Africa. David Diop, *French.* NegPo, *tr.* by Ellen Conroy Kennedy; PBA; TTY, *tr.* by Ulli Beier

Africa Says. Carl Phillips. PoPoPo

Africa Sky. Kojo Laing. HBAPE

Africa Thing, The. Adam David Miller. NBV

Africa, you were once just a name to me. The Meaning of Africa. Abioseh Nicol. PBA

African. Peter Tosh. PBCV

African Affair, The. Bruce McM. Wright. PoBA

African Chief, The. William Cullen Bryant. BLPA; ColAP

African China. Melvin Beaunearus Tolson. ColAP; PoBA

African Christmas. John Press. OBCP

African Day. Gloria de Sant'Ana, *Portuguese.* PBWP, *tr.* by Allan Francovich *and* Kathleen Weaver

African Dirge. M. J. Chapman. PBCV

African Dream. Bob Kaufman. GT; PoBA

African Easter. Abioseh Nicol. PBA

African Elegy, An. Robert Duncan. NoAM

"African Image Is Not An Image by Equation. . . , The." Léopold Sédar Senghor, *French.* PFTM, *tr. by* John Reed *and* Clive Wake

African Images, Glimpses from a Tiger's Back. Alice Walker. InPS-3

African in Louisiana. Kojo Gyinaye Kyei. PBA

African Lion, The. A. E. Housman. CBNP; NOxBChV

African Poem. Agostinho Neto. PBMAP

African Poems. Don L. Lee.
    "WE'RE an Africanpeople." MBE

African Sleeping Sickness. Wanda Coleman. PmAP

African Student. Noel H. Brettell. PeSAV

African Sunday. Maureen Owen. PmAP

African Thunderstorm, An. James David Rubadiri. PBMAP

African Trader's Complaint, The. Dennis C. Osadebay. PBA

African Tramp, The. Geoffrey Haresnape. PeSA

Africa's Plea. Roland Tombekai Dempster. TTY

Afro-American Beats III: An American Memory of Africa. Kofi Awoonor. *See* An American Memory of Africa.

Afro-American Fragment. Langston Hughes. PBMP

Aft' them white trash any mo'. (LL) Mrs. Johnson Objects. Clara Ann Thompson. BlSi; CBWP-2

Aften hae I played at the cards and the dice. The Rantin Laddie. Robert Burns. ESPB

After. Ralph Hodgson. MoBrPo

After. Philip Bourke Marston. NOBVV

After. May Probyn. VWP

After. David Shapiro. PT

After a Bath. Aileen Fisher. OTCP

After a black day, I play Haydn. Allegro. Tomas Tranströmer, *Swedish.* SPE, *tr. by* Robert Bly

After a Class in Seaweed. Ingrid Wendt. NMM-2

After a Death. Sandra M. Gilbert. IMW

After a Death. Edwin Morgan. FaBoTC *Fr.* Sonnets from Scotland.

After a Death. Tomas Tranströmer, *Swedish.* VCWP, *tr. by* Robert Bly

After a dozen years of death. Poem to My Grandmother in Her Death. Michele Murray. CrSp; IMW

After a dream in which your love's fullness. The Sapphire. W. S. Merwin. PoA

After a fearful maze where doubt. Chimera. Barbara Howes. TwCP

After a friend has gone I like the feel of it. Nocturne. Eavan Boland. NBrP

After a hundred years. Emily Dickinson. APN-2; AWP; OxBA

After a Journey. Thomas Hardy. CBLP; CMoP; EBEV; EnLoPo; GBL; GTBS-P; LoP; OBNC; OxAEP-2; OxBSn; OxBTC; PoE; PoEL-5

After a little I could not have told—. The Song of the Tortured Girl. John Berryman. CoAP

After a long summer of silence comes this windblown morning: Now I'll. Words. Dan Pagis, *Hebrew.* IP, *tr. by* Warren Bargad *and* Stanley F. Chyet

After a long winter, giving / each other nothing. Chiyojo, *Japanese.* BoWoP, *tr. by* David Ray

After a month and a half without rain. August Rain. Robert Bly. LCAP-2

After a night of languor without rest. The Sea-Breeze at Matanzas. Epes Sargent. APN-1

After a night of rage. Love Poem for a Wife, 2. A. K. Ramanujan. OMIP

After a night of rain. In a Japanese Moss Garden. Brad Leithauser. OBGa

After a night of wind we are surprised. On the Island. Lawrence Raab. CMAP

After a Parting. Alice Thompson Meynell. NOBVV

After a Passage in Baudelaire. Robert Duncan. CMoP; PoA; PoE

After a pretty amorous discourse. The Imperfect Enjoyment. William Walsh *and* Sir George Etherege (1653–91). NOSC

After a Spring meeting in their nineteenth-century fastness at. Irish Hierarchy Bans Colour Photography. Paul Durcan. BiHa; PBCIP

After a Stoic, a Peripatetic, a Pythagorean. John Berryman. *Fr.* Eleven Addresses to the Lord. OxBC

After a Storm, Going a Hawking. George Daniel. NOSC

After a Sultry Morning. Rodney Hall. *Fr.* The Owner of My Face. CBAP

After a Tempest. William Cullen Bryant. APN-1

After a throbbing night, the house still dark, pull. Those of Pure Origin. Roy Fuller. FaBoMo

After a Train Journey. May Sarton. GM

After a Visit to the Natural History Museum. Laura Elizabeth Richards. ImGa

After a week / In the town's brothel. The Husband. Cyril Dabydeen. HCP

After a week of physical anguish. An Evening Lull. Walt Whitman. NAAL-1; NAAL-3

After a while it dawns on us. Historical Museum, Manitoulin Island. Lisel Mueller. PoA

After a wife's death a man may talk. The Possibilities. Beckian Fritz Goldberg. NAmP90

After all, Charlie, we shall see them go. Longshore Intellectual. Sean Lucy. CIP-2

After all, I still have each other. (LL) Limerick. *Unknown.* OBCoV; PeLi

After all the drive-in theaters have closed. Translated from the American. Sherman Alexie. UnSA

After all the late suppers of that faraway. Nineteen Fifty-five. Sherod Santos. NAmP90

After all those years. Accomplices. Zhao Zhenkai, *Chinese.* VCWP, *tr. by* Donald Finkel

After all, what have I become? Anna Hajnal, *Hungarian.* CEEP, *tr. by* Juliette Victor-Rood

After all, you are my rather tedious hero. To Myself. Kenneth Slessor. BMAP

After an age when thunderbolts and hail. Sonnet XVI. Louise Labé, *French.* BoWoP, *tr. by* Willis Barnstone

After an hundred and thirty years' nap. On the Erection of Shakespeare's Statue in Westminster Abbey. Alexander Pope. FaBoEE

After Anacreon. Lew Welch. BB; NeAP; *PoM* *Fr.* Taxi Suite.
    ("When I drive cab / I am moved by strange whistles and wear a hat.") BB

After Annunciation. Anna Wickham. MoBrPo

After Apple-Picking. Robert Frost. AmPP; CMoP; InPS-3; MeMAP; MoAmPo; MoP; NAAL-2; NOBA; NTP; NoAM; OxBA; PoE; Poetr; SAGP; SAmP; SoSe-8; TAP; TFi; TRP; UnPo

After Arguing against the Contention That Art Must Come from Discontent. William Stafford. NoAM

After Asia. Michael Stephens. CDa

After, at sea a tall ship did appear. Petrarch. *Fr.* Visions. AWP

After Aughrim. Emily Lawless. OBEV

After Auschwitz. Anne Sexton. HP

After Babel. Peter Goldsworthy. NOBAu

After Beethoven. Raymond Roseliep. HA

After Bitahatini. *Unknown.* PFTM, *tr. by* Washington Matthews *Fr.* The Night Chant.

After Blenheim. Robert Southey. *See* The Battle of Blenheim.

After Christmas. John Corben. AYFP

After Christmas. Michael Richards. OBCP

After Christopher Wood. John James. NBrP

After Church. Samuel Alfred Beadle. AAP

After Collecting the Autumn Taxes. Po Chü-i, *Chinese.* BLT; ChiP, *tr. by* Arthur Waley

After Communion. Christina Rossetti. WPoS

After Dark. Allison Funk. BAP-94

After Dark. Adrienne Rich. LCAP-2; LiTM; MoLi; VGW

After dark / Near the South Dakota border. Having Lost My Sons, I Confront the Wreckage of the Moon: Christmas, 1960. James Wright. CoAP; HCAP; NAAL-2

After dark vapours have oppressed our plains. Sonnet: "After dark vapours have oppress'd our plains." OBNC

After David Samuilow. Lutz Rathenow, *German.* CEEP, *tr. by* Boria Sax

After Death. Fanny Parnell. IIP

After Death. Christina Rossetti. GBL; NAEL-2; NALW
    ("To know he still is warm though I am cold.") (LL) GSo; LoP

After Death. Swinburne. NOBVV; OxBSn; PeVV

After death. Tanka. Tsukamoto Kunio, *Japanese.* MJT, *tr. by* Makoto Ueda

After death, and clean as a finishing line. (LL) The Crafty Butcher. Susan Hampton. BMAP; NOBAu

After Death Nothing is, and Nothing Death. Seneca's Troas, Act 2. Chorus. Seneca, *Latin.* OBCVT, *tr. by* John Wilmot, 2d Earl of Rochester; PFE, *tr. by* John Wilmot, 2d Earl of Rochester; EBEV; OBVE *Fr.* Troades.

After death, suppose we were judged by animals. The Tribunal. Chris Wallace-Crabbe. ChIV-2

After Dilettante Concetti. Henry Duff Traill. BXAP

After dinner Erasmus. Edmund Clerihew Bentley. OBCoV *Fr.* Clerihews.

After dreaming some hours of the land of Cockaigne. Thomas Moore. BIrV *Fr.* The Fudge Family in Paris.

After Drinking All Night with a Friend, We Go Out in a Boat at Dawn to See Who Can Write the Best Poem. Robert Bly. WeT

After driving all night, trying to reach. The Business of Fancydancing. Sherman Alexie. PaTW

After each quake. Crack in the Wall Holds Flowers. Adam David Miller. PoBA

After Eating. Po Chü-i, *Chinese.*
    ("Accepts the life given him, long or short.") (LL) CoBCP, *tr. by* Burton Watson

("After lunch—one short nap.") ChiP, *tr.* by Arthur Waley

After Eden. James Simmons. PNI

After Elegies. Jean Valentine. LCAP-2

After 11 years. The Most Beautiful Woman at My Highschool Reunion. Ellen Marie Bissert. GLP

After enduring. Tanka. Shaku Chōkū, *Japanese.* MJT, *tr.* by Makoto Ueda

After Ever Happily [*or* , The Princess and the Woodcutter]. Ian Serraillier. OBSP

After every war. The End and the Beginning. Wislawa Szymborska, *Polish.* VCWP, *tr.* by Stanislaw Baranczak *and* Clare Cavanagh

After experience taught me that all the ordinary. W. D. Snodgrass. CoAP; OBWP

After explanations and regulations, he. A WASP Woman Visits a Black Junkie in Prison. Etheridge Knight. LTA; NBV

After father's wake. Nicholas Virgilio. HA

After fifteen months you fly in. Visitation Rights. Heather Wishik. GLP

After fifty years, nearly, I remember. The King's Horses. John Hewitt. IIP

After Five Years. Augustus Young. BIrV

After Floods on the Wharfe. Andrew Marvell. *Fr.* Upon Appleton House [To My Lord Fairfax]. FaBoPV; GeHe; SeCP

After Frost. Brian Patten. EBEV

After fruition ne're to be concern'd. (LL) To Alexis in Answer to his Poem against Fruition. Aphra Behn. KTR; NOSC

After Galen. Oliver St. John Gogarty. FaBoEE; OBMV; PoRA

After gazing at stars. Tom Tico. HA

After Getting Drunk, Becoming Sober in the Night. Po Chü-i, *Chinese.* BLT; ChiP, *tr.* by Arthur Waley

After Getting Drunk, I Scribble Songs and Poems. Lu Yu, *Chinese.* CoBCP, *tr.* by Burton Watson

(After Getting Drunk, I Scribble Songs and Poems in Grass Script—Written as a Joke.) CoBCP, *tr.* by Burton Watson

After-Glow, The. Mathilde Blind. OBNC

After-Glow of Pain, The. Clara Ann Thompson. CBWP-2

After Going Off the Road During the Snowstorm. William Meissner. CMAP

After Goliath. Kingsley Amis. NOBL; OxBTC

After Grave Deliberation. Elizabeth Flynn. NBLV

After great pain a formal feeling comes—. Emily Dickinson. APN-2; AmPP; BoWoP; HAP; HeIP-4; IMW; InPS-3; MoAmPo; NAAL-1; NAAL-3; NALW; NAWM-2; NIP-4; NOBA; NoP-4; OxWW; PAR; PFE; PoE; PoPoPo; Poetr; SAGP; SAmP; TAP; TFi; TRP; UnPo

After great storms the calm returns. Sir Thomas Wyatt. SiPS

After Greece. James Merrill. CoAmPo; ColAP; NOBA; NYBP; TRP

After Grief. Stanley Plumly. AmPA; LCAP-2

After half a minute of conversation. Yüan Mei. *Fr.* Miscellaneous Poems on Growing Old. CoBLCP, *tr.* by Jonathan Chaves

After hangin' Danny Deever in the mornin'! (LL) Danny Deever. Rudyard Kipling. EBEvV; EBVV; FaPoR; GTBS-P; InPS-3; MoBrPo; NAEL-2; NOBE; NOBVV; NoAM; OxBTC; OxBoLi; PBMP; PeVV; PoLF; SCGP; SCV; TFi; UnPo

After having loved we lie close together. Sailing. Henrik Nordbrandt, *Danish.* VCWP, *tr.* by Nordbrandt, Henrik and Alexander Taylor

After having slain very many beasts. Sonnet XIX. Louise Labé, *French.* BoWoP, *tr.* by Willis Barnstone

After he died. She Lived. Lucille Clifton. LoL

After he had gone the wind rose. Sylvia Townsend Warner. MoBrPo; SAGP

After he had several adventures, the potato boy took the. Potchikoo Marries. Louise Erdrich. *Fr.* Old Man Potchikoo. HATNAP

After he leaves. Alexis Rotella. HA

After he stripped off my clothes. Villana, *Sanskrit.* BoWoP, *tr.* by Willis Barnstone

After her husband died, Zita decided to get the face-lift she had. Distance from Loved Ones. James Tate. FiLi

After Her Man Had Left Her for the Sixth Time That Year / (An Uncommon Occurrence). Haki R. Madhubuti. GT

After her pills the girl slept and counted. Tally. Josephine Miles. NoAM

After Hilaire Belloc. Max Beerbohm. OBCuV; UV

After His Death. Norman MacCaig. CBNP

After his ham & cheese in the drape factory cafeteria. Torque. David Rivard. PBCAP

After his stroke, he would walk into the woods. Walt Whitman Bathing. David Wagoner. BAP-95

After his talking destroyed her. Antarctica. Ronald Albert Simpson. CBAP

After Horace. Alfred Denis Godley. NOBL

After hot loveless nights, when cold winds stream. The Sisters. Roy Campbell. BoLoP; EP; FaBoTw; NoP-4; OBMV

After Hours. Nicholas Christopher. WWSi

After I died I could not close my eyes. Departure. Van K. Brock. MT

After I had cut off my hands. Intrusion. Denise Levertov. VCAP

After I Had Worked All Day. Charles Reznikoff. VGW *Fr.* Five Groups of Verse.

After I Have Voted. Laura Jensen. AmPA

After I step. George Swede. HA

After it all the hunchbacked village remained. Needless Return. Dan Pagis, *Hebrew.* IP, *tr.* by Warren Bargad and Stanley F. Chyet

After Jack paces in circles, head down, decides to say something to his wife, says nothing. Prayer. Jason Shinder. WWSi

After Jericho. Ronald Stuart Thomas. OxBC

After Jill died they remembered how she liked this chair. Jill's Death. George Buchanan. PNI

After Johnny wear mi clothes. Johnny Tek Away Mi Wife. "Slim" Beckford and Sam Blackwood. PBCV

After kicking on the swing. Tune: Crimson Lips Adorned. Li Ch'ing-chao, *Chinese.* PBWP, *tr.* by C. H. Kwock and Vincent McHugh; BoWoP, *tr.* by Kenneth Rexroth and Ling Chung

After Lalon. Allen Ginsberg. BB

After late evenings. After Touch. Jan Clausen. GLP

After letting my wife. Tanka. Kitahara Hakushū, *Japanese.* MJT, *tr.* by Makoto Ueda

After Listening to Jack Teagarden. . . . James McKean. SeSe

After Long Busyness. Robert Bly. PoA

After Long Rain. Wang Wei, *Chinese.* TAL, *tr.* by Robert Payne

After Long Silence. W. B. Yeats. BoLoP; CMoP; EnLoPo; HeIP-4; HoPM; LiTM; NAEL-2; OAEL-2; OBMV; UnPo

After long storms and tempests sad assay. Sonnet 63. Edmund Spenser. OAEL-1 *Fr.* Amoretti. AAS

After long trouble in a taedious way. Louis MacNeice. KTR *Fr.* Dark Age Glosses.

After long trouble in a taedious way. Sonnet 31. Mary Sidney, Countess of Montgomery Wroth. KTR *Fr.* Pamphilia to Amphilanthus.

After long wars when comes release. Herba Santa. Herman Melville. NCAP

After Longfellow. *Unknown.* NOBL

After Lorca. Robert Creeley. CoAmPo; InPS-3; LCAP-2; PmAP

After Lorca. Ted Hughes. PoA

After Love. Maxine W. Kumin. CrSp; NMM-2; TAP

After Love. John A. Stone. MT

After lunch. Tanka. Kitahara Hakushū, *Japanese.* MJT, *tr.* by Makoto Ueda

After lunch—one short nap. Po Chü-i. *See* After Eating.

After lunch the old Duchess of Teck. Limerick. *Unknown.* PeLi

After Making Love We Hear Footsteps. Galway Kinnell. ColAP; InPS-3; NIP-4; NoAM; NoP-4; RaBo; SAGP; VCAP

After many scorns [*or* scornes] like these. What He[e] Suffered. Ben Jonson. *Fr.* A Celebration of Charis in Ten Lyric[k] Pieces [*or* Peeces]. BeJo; OxAEP-1; SeCP

After Margrave died, nothing. History of a Literary Movement. Howard Nemerov. PoE

After Mass. "Michael Field." WPE

After Midnight. Louis Simpson. BLT; NoAM

After Midnight. Charles Vildrac, *French.* AWP, *tr.* by Jethro Bithell

After midnight I heard a scream. By Night. Robert Francis. VGW

After midnight they load up. Boat People. Yusef Komunyakaa. AF; CDa; PoPoPo

After Midsummer. Edith Jay Scovell. OxBTC

After much driving. 1974—The Sounds. Christina Beer. PeNZ

After my bath. After a Bath. Aileen Fisher. OTCP

After my illness, so hard to be a traveler. Yang Chi. CoBLCP, *tr.* by Jonathan Chaves *Fr.* From Sand River to Ts'ai Rock.

After Night Flight Son Reaches Bedside of Already Unconscious Father, Whose Right Hand Lifts in a Spasmodic Gesture, as Though Trying to Make Contact: 1955. Robert Penn Warren. NOBA *Fr.* Mortmain.

(After Night Flight.)

After night, the waking knowledge. Awaking. Stephen Spender. NYBP

After Nightfall. William Renton. NOBVV

After night's thunder far away had rolled. Haymaking. Edward Thomas. MoBrPo

After one moment when I bowed my head. The Convert. G. K. Chesterton. ChIV-2

After One Year. Martin Carter. HCP

After our damp skins slid apart. Definition. Lauren Shakely. FYAP

After our Epilogue this crowd dismisses. Epilogue. William Congreve. *Fr.* The Way of the World. NAEL-1

After our fierce loving. The Profile on the Pillow. Dudley Randall. BPo; PoBA; TAP

After our war, the dismembered bits. John Balaban. CDa

After Paradise. Czeslaw Milosz, *Polish*. EP
  (Two of You, The.) ITG, tr. by Czeslaw Milosz *and* Robert Hass
After Passing the Examination. Meng Chiao, *Chinese*. SuSp, tr. by Irving Y. Lo
After Passing the Examination. Po Chü-i, *Chinese*. ChiP, tr. by Arthur Waley
After Picasso. Franz Wright.
  Depiction of Childhood. BLT
After Plotinus. William Stafford. PoA
After Publication of Under the Volcano. Malcolm Lowry. FaBoTw
  ("And had been left in darkness forever to founder and fail.") (LL) CLPP
After rain. Mountain Study. Peter Van Toorn. NOBC
After Rain. Patricia K. Page. NOBC; PoE
After rain a bright moon appears. Written beneath Hui Mountain, When Tsou Liu-yi Comes by for a Visit. Wang Shih-chieng, *Chinese*. SuSp, tr. by Richard John Lynn
After rain, through afterglow, the unfolding fan. Train Ride. John Wheelwright. VGW
After Rain, Visiting the Temple of Heavenly Peace. Wang Shih-chieng, *Chinese*. CoBLCP, tr. by Jonathan Chaves
After rainfall. Tanka. Miya Shūji, *Japanese*. MJT, tr. by Makoto Ueda
After Reading a Child's Guide to Modern Physics. W. H. Auden. NYBP
After Reading in a Letter Proposals for Building a Cottage. John Clare. OxAEP-2
After Reading *Mickey in the Night Kitchen* for the Third Time Before Bed. Rita Dove. LoL; NMM-2
After Reading Nelly Sachs. Linda Pastan. NMM-2
After Reading Shakspere. Edwin Markham. APN-2
After Reading St. John the Divine. Gene Derwood. ImPo; LiTM; WPE
After Reading "The Country of the Pointed Firs." Jean Garrigue. VCAP
After Reading the Life of Mrs. Catherine Stubbs in Isaac Ambrose's "War with the Devils." Isaac Hann. NOCV
After Reading the Poems of Master Han Shan. Wang Chiu-ssu, *Chinese*. CoBLCP, tr. by Jonathan Chaves
  "Floating, floating, the river waters."
  "This crazy man has escaped the world."
After-recollection at Sight of the Same Cottage. Dorothy Wordsworth. Ro
After Rishikesh. The Key of Water. Octavio Paz, *Spanish*. VCWP, tr. by Elizabeth Bishop
After scanning its face again and again. John Muir on Mt. Ritter. Gary Snyder. NOBA *Fr.* Burning. NeAP; PoM *Fr.* Myths and Texts.
After Seeing Paintings in a Small Book by T. C. Cannon (1946-1978). Alice Sadongei. HATNAP
After shaking paws with his dog / (Whose bark would tell the world that he is always kind). W. H. Auden. Terce. CMoP; PoE *Fr.* Horae Canonicae
After sharp words from the fine mind. The Flowering Bars. Charles Donnelly. CIP-2
After she drives her younger daughter to school, struggling. The Woman with the Wild-Grown Hair Relaxes after Another Long Day. Nita Penfold. CrSp
After Snow—Impromptu. Yü Chi, *Chinese*. CoBLCP, tr. by Jonathan Chaves
After so long a race as I have run. 80. Edmund Spenser. CABP *Fr.* Amorette.
After so long an absence. The Meeting. Henry Wadsworth Longfellow. FP
After so many decades of. . . of what? To Whom It May Concern. James Vincent Cunningham. FYAP
After so many years. Hand Mirror. Daisy Zamora, *Spanish*. LoL, tr. by Barbara Paschke
After so much battering of fire and steel. Butchers and Tombs. Ivor Gurney. PeFWW
After some years Bohemian came to this. Epigram. James Vincent Cunningham. VGW
After Soufrière. "Michael Field." VWP
After Stroke. Bill Griffiths. NBrP
After stumbling around for months. Blue Tango. Michael Van Walleghen. NAmP90
After such years of dissension and strife. Dust to Dust. Thomas Hood. NBLV
After sudden rain, a clear autumn night. Stars and Moon on the Yangtse. Tu Fu, *Chinese*. PLT, tr. by A. C. Graham
After sundown the clouds start to burn. Thunderstorm. Sam Mitchell, *Aborigine*. NOBAu, tr. by Georg von Brandenstein
After Tempest. Percy MacKaye. FYAP
After ten days I come here again. On the Sixteenth Day I Visit the Temple Again. Pien Kung, *Chinese*. CoBLCP, tr. by Jonathan Chaves
After that day we hadden never debaat. (LL) Experience, though noon auctoritee. Chaucer. OxBoLi; PeLV

After that hervest inned had his sheves. Thomas Hoccleve. EnVB *Fr.* Hoccleve's Complaint.
After that war, when death had gone away. Joan Miró. Ruthven Todd. SPE
After the act of stabbing and. Stone Wall and Celebration. János Pilinszky, *Hungarian*. PoSu, tr. by Peter Jay
After the air of summer. (LL) Roman Fountain. Louise Bogan. NoP-4; WPOW
After the all been done and i. Island Mary. Lucille Clifton. NALW
After the Anonymous Swedish. James Harrison. VGW
After the Anti-Semitic Calls on a Local Talk Station. Lyn Lifshin. UnSA
After the Ball. Imamu Amiri Baraka. NAAL-2
After the baths and bowel-work, he was dead. Old Relative. Gwendolyn Brooks. ColAP *Fr.* Notes from the Childhood and the Girlhood. LCAP-2
After the Battle. Sir Alan Patrick Herbert. NSI
After the Battle. Audrey Herbert. PoFWW
After the blast of lightning from the east. The End. Wilfred Owen. CH; ChIV-1
After the brief bivouac of Sunday. The Stenographers. Patricia K. Page. HeIP-4; LiTM; NALW; NoAM
After the Broken Arm. Ron Padgett. CoAmPo; SPE
After the bronzed, heroic traveller. The Mapmaker on His Art. Howard Nemerov. NYBP
After the Burial. James Russell Lowell. UnPo
After the burial-parties leave. The Hyænas [or Hyenas]. Rudyard Kipling. NAEL-2; OBSV
After the Chinese. Tess Gallagher. NAmP90
After the cloud came to a dead stop. Genoa. Dino Campana, *Italian*. PFTM, tr. by Charles Wright
After the cloud embankments. Reconnaissance. Arna Bontemps. BPo
After the Convention. Robert Lowell. NoAM
After the Cries of the Birds. Lawrence Ferlinghetti. CAPP-1
After the Dance. Reuben Jackson. GT
After the day's great sun. (LL) At Nightfall. Charles Hanson Towne. BLPA; FaBoBe; PoToHe
After the Death of an Elder Klallam. Duane Niatum. CDW
After the Death of Her Daughter in Child-birth. Lady Izumi, *Japanese*. PBWP, tr. by Edwin A. Cranston
After the Defeat. Yannis Ritsos, *Greek*. AF, tr. by Edmund Keeley
After the Deluge. Wole Soyinka. HBAPE
After the doctor checked to see. First Practice. Gary Gildner. AmPA
After the door shuts and the footsteps die. A Hunt in the Black Forest. Randall Jarrell. CoAP; LCAP-2
After the dread tales and red yarns of the Line. First Time In. Ivor Gurney. FaBoVe; NoP-4
After the dreadful Flood was past. The Tower of Babel. Nathaniel Crouch. OxBChV
After the end of the world. In the Midst of Life. Tadeusz Rózewicz, *Polish*. HP; PoSu, tr. by Adam Czerniawski
After the End of the World. David Jauss. SeSe
After the end, they'll bring you. Remembering San Zeno. Charles Wright. WeT
After the event the rockslide. Clarity. A. R. Ammons. HCAP; TAP
After the explosion or cataclysm, that big. The Eternal City. A. R. Ammons. HCAP
After the eyes that looked, the lips that spake. Gettysburg Ode. Bayard Taylor. CBCWP
After the eyes that looked, the lips that spake. Lincoln at Gettysburg. Bayard Taylor. *Fr.* Gettysburg Ode. CBCWP
After the Fair. Thomas Hardy. CMoP; HAP *Fr.* At Casterbridge Fair.
After the Fall. Gloria Escoffery. HCP; PBCV
After the fall drive, the last. Montana Eclogue. William Stafford. NYBP; PaTW
After the Fall of Saigon. Yusef Komunyakaa. AF; CDa
After the fallen sun the wind was sad. Moonrise Over Battlefield. Edgell Rickword. NSI; PoWW
After the feast, my Shapcott, see. Oberon's Palace. Robert Herrick. CaPo
After the fierce midsummer all ablaze. Friendship After Love. Ella Wheeler Wilcox. APAD; APN-2; LW
After the fiercest pangs of hot desire. A Song. Richard Duke. BoLoP; ECEV
After the First Communion. Sunday Afternoon. Denise Levertov. CoAmPo
After the first death, there is no other. (LL) A Refusal to Mourn the Death, by Fire, of a Child in London. Dylan Thomas. AF; CMoP; EBEV; FaBoMo; GTBS-P; HeIP-4; HoPM; ImPo; LiTM; MoBrPo; MoP; NOBE; NoAM; NoP-4; OAEL-2; OBWVE; OxAEP-2; OxBTC; PoE; PoWW; TFi; TwCP; UnPo
After the First Frost. Lew Blockcolski. VoR

After the First Night. Creation Myth Haiku. Gavin Ewart. APAD

After the first powerful plain manifesto. The Express. Stephen Spender. CMoP; HeIP-4; LiTM; MoBrPo; MoP; NoAM; TwCP

After the first shallows have dropped away. Daily the Ocean between Us. Patricia Goedicke. TAP

After the Flight of the Earls. Fearflatha O'Gnive. NOIV

After the Flood. John Foulcher. NOBAu

After the Flood. Sir David Lindsay. ChIV-1; OxBS *Fr.* The Monarche.

After the full moon. Alexis Rotella. HA

After the funeral, mule praises, brays. Dylan Thomas. CMoP; FaBoMo; ImPo; NAEL-2; NoP-4; OAEL-2; OBWVE; OxAEP-2

After the Funeral of Assam Hamady. Sam Hamod. UnSA

After the Ghanaian dancing, we fought. Grief. Maureen Seaton. LoHo

After the Golden Wedding. James Kenneth Stephen.
"She's not a faultless woman; no!" EBVV; NOBVV; OxBM

After the heavy losses that the Athenians suffered at Aegospotami, / and a little later. After the Defeat. Yannis Ritsos, *Greek.* AF, *tr. by* Edmund Keeley

After the horrors of Heathrow. 747 (London–Chicago). Robert Conquest. OxBC

After the Hunt. Detlev von Liliencron, *German.* AWP, *tr. by* Ludwig Lewisohn

After the Industrial Revolution, All Things Happen at Once. Robert Bly. CoAP; CoAmPo

After the Inscription on a Greek Stele of a Woman Holding Her Grandchild on Her Knees. *Unknown, Greek.* GrAn, *tr. by* Stephen Spender

After the Interrogation. Lawrence Kearney. WeT

After the Irish of Egan O'Rahilly. Egan O'Rahilly. *See* A Time of Change.

After the last bulletins the windows darken. Richard Wilbur. CoAP; CoAmPo; MoAmPo; NYBP

After the Last Dynasty. Stanley Kunitz. TAP

After the Last Practice. Edward Hirsch. NAmP90

After the leaves have fallen, we return. The Plain Sense of Things. Wallace Stevens. HCAP; NoAM

After the leg is lost, the pain remains as an emblem. Phantom Pain. Maxine Chernoff. EOEF

After the legshows and the brandies. Night Club. Louis MacNeice. OxBSP *Fr.* Entered in the Minutes.

After the light has set. The Return. George MacBeth. NYBP

After the long and portentous eclipse of the patient sun. Green Song. Dame Edith Sitwell. BWW

After the love-making. Harvey Shapiro. WeT

After the Massacre. Musaemura Bonus Zimunya. PeSAV

After the midnight unfolding of the White Rose. The Feast of Stephen. Kevin Nichols. OBCP

After the midwinter marriages—the bride of snow. John Hollander. VCAP *Fr.* Powers of Thirteen.

After the milk-white hounds of the moon. (LL) Madman's Song. Elinor Wylie. MoAmPo; PoRA

After / the Moratorium Reading. Nigel Roberts. NOBAu

After the murder. The Last Quatrain of the Ballad of Emmett Till. Gwendolyn Brooks. LCAP-2; PoBA; WPE

After the Night Hunt. James Dickey. PoA

After the noose, and the black diary deeds. Casement's Funeral. Richard Murphy. NOIV; PBCIP *Fr.* The Battle of Aughrim.

After the Pangs of a Desperate Lover. Dryden. PeLV *Fr.* An Evening's Love.
(Love's Fancy.)

After the paradiso and the milky way and the kosmos, seeming. Yolanda Meets the Wild Boys. Jessica Hagedorn. OpBo

After the Party. Luigi Fontanella, *Italian.* NeIt, *tr. by* W. S. Di Piero

After the people and the flowers. Leaving Town after the Funeral. Richard Jones. NAmP90

After the Persian. Louise Bogan. NYBP; PoA

After the planes unloaded, we fell down. The Dead in Europe. Robert Lowell. LiTM; OxBA; OxBC

After the Pleasure Party. Herman Melville. APN-2; NAAL-1; NAAL-3; PAR; PoEL-5
("Fear me, virgin whosoever.") NCAP

After the poem the coastline took. Sydney Clouts. PeSAV

After the Quarrel. Priscilla Jane Thompson. CBWP-2

After the rain of stars. At the Gate of the Valley. Zbigniew Herbert, *Polish.* PoSu, *tr. by* Czeslaw Milosz

After the rain, the vegetables from your garden. Yang Shih-ch'i. CoBLCP, *tr. by* Jonathan Chaves *Fr.* Libationer Hu Became Ill from Eating Sunflowers. These Poems Are Playfully Presented to Him and Are Also Intended to Thank Him for the Vegetables He Sent Me.

After the rapture comes, and everyone goes away. March Journal. Charles Wright. LCAP-2

After the rare arch-poet Jonson died. Upon M. Ben Jo[h]nson: Epigram. Robert Herrick. BeJo; CaPo

After the red leaf and the gold have gone. A Spell before Winter. Howard Nemerov. LiTM

After the red-rose-bordered hem. (LL) To Ireland in the Coming Times. W. B. Yeats. NOIV; NoAM

After the Revolution. Marilyn Hacker. AmPA

After the Revolution for Jesus the Associate Professor [or a Secular Man] Prepares His Final Remarks. Miller Williams. MT

After the ribboning fever of interstate. Frugal Repasts. Lynda Hull. NAmP90

After the rooster falls from the hen. Final Soliloquy on a Randy Rooster (in a Key of Yellow). Robert Peters. BXAP

After the rushing waters had subsided the Lenape of the turtle were close together, in hollow houses, living together there. *Unknown.* APN-2, *tr. by* Daniel Garrison Brinton *Fr.* Walam Olum; or, The Red Score [of the Lenâpé], The [or The Wallam Olum; The Red Score or Painted History of the Lenni Lenape].

After the sagittal and lateral cuts. Threshold. Dean Young. NAmP90

After the satyr's twilight in the park. Homecoming—Massachusetts. John Ciardi. NYBP

After the sea-ship, after the whistling winds. Walt Whitman. APN-1; OxBoS

After the search for meaning bills in the mail. George Swede. HA

After the second book. Poet at Work. Richard Tipping. BMAP

After the Second Operation. Patricia Goedicke. TAP

After the Seizer there were ten chiefs, and there was much warfare south and east. *Unknown.* OBVE, *tr. by* Daniel G. Brinton *Fr.* Walam Olum; or, Red Score [of the Lenâpé], The [or The Wallam Olum; The Red Score or Painted History of the Lenni Lenape].

After the sentence. Letters to Martha. Dennis Brutus. PeSAV

After the shower. Cor Van den Heuvel. HA

After the silence of the centuries? (LL) The Man with the Hoe. Edwin Markham. APN-2; BLPA; GS; MoAmPo; TFi

After the Small Pox. Mary Jones. PEW

After the snowfall. Lorraine Ellis Harr. HA

After the stars were all hung separately [out]. The Book of How. Merrill Moore. FuPo; MoAmPo

After the Storm. Edmond Yi-teh Chang. OpBo

After the storm. City Rain. Kit Wright. AYFP

After the Storm. Henrietta Cordelia Ray. CBWP-3

After the storm, after the rain stopped pounding. Song of Napalm. Bruce Weigl. CDa

After the storm at sunset. The Hotel Sander. Donald Revell. CMAP

After the storm / On Mount Mimuro. Noin, *Japanese.* OHPJ, *tr. by* Kenneth Rexroth

After the streets fall silent. To Those Who Have Gone Home Tired. William Daniel Ehrhart. CDa

After the sudden rain. Old Currawong. Jennifer Rankin. BMAP

After the sun's eclipse. Teresa. Richard Wilbur. NoAM

After the supper and talk—after the day is done. Walt Whitman. MoAmPo; NAAL-1; NAAL-3

After the supper dishes, let us start. Future Conditional. Marilyn Hacker. CPO; DeD *Fr.* Love, Death and the Changing of the Seasons.

After the Surprising Conversions. Robert Lowell. AmPP; CoAmPo; HAP; NAAL-2; NoAM; TRP

After the sweat of swathes and the sinking madder sun. A Drink of Spring. John Ennis. CIP-2; PBCIP

After the test they sent an expert. School Days. William Stafford. LCAP-2

After the third day it began to be familiar. The Week the Dirigible Came. Jay Meek. CMAP

After the third evening roud. Be Seeing You. Vasco [or Vasko] Popa, *Serbian.* PoSu, *tr. by* Anne Pennington *Fr.* Raw Flesh.

After the third evening round. Vasco [or Vasko] Popa. *See* Be Seeing You.

After the throne I came to the first page. The Sleeping Beauty: Variation of the Prince. Randall Jarrell. PoA

After the tiff there was stiff silence, till. The Lovers. William Robert Rodgers. BIrV; OxBSP; PNI

After the tumult and the blood. At Vshchizh. Fyodor Ivanovich Tyutchev, *Russian.* OBWP, *tr. by* Charles Tomlinson

After the uprising of the 17th June. The Solution. Bertolt Brecht, *German.* PoSu, *tr. by* Dereck Bowman

After the Vietnam War. Steven Ford Brown. CDa

After the Visit. Thomas Hardy. NOBE; OBNC

After the War. Douglas Dunn. OxBC

After the war, the terror people underwent produced profound if not irrevocable. Hazardous Waste. James Sherry. FTOS

'After the war,' they used to say, and pictured. Freda C. Bond. WPN

After the War; When Coltrane Only Wanted to Play Dance Tunes. Matthew Graham. SeSe

After the whey-faced anonymity. South Country. Kenneth Slessor. BMAP; CBAP

After the whoosh of doors slid shut. At Lansdowne Bridge. Arthur Nortje. HBAPE

After the Wilderness. Andrew Hudgins. CBCWP

After the Winter. Claude McKay. PoBA

After the words of the magnificence and doom. Country Burial. Janet Lewis. CRP

After these things should be. (LL) The New House. Edward Thomas. EBEV; MoBrPo; NOBE; OBEV; OBWVE

After these words the Weather-Geat prince. Beowulf's Fight with Grendel's Mother. *Unknown*. *Fr.* Beowulf. OAEL-1, *tr. by* Charles W. Kennedy; ASW, *tr. by* Kevin Crossley-Holland

After these years of lectures heard. To a Friend, on Her Examination for the Doctorate in English. James Vincent Cunningham. VGW

After they all leave. Surely You Remember. Dahlia Ravikovitch, *Hebrew*. VCWP, *tr. by* Chana Bloch *and* Ariel Bloch

After they had not made love. Happy Ending. Fleur Adcock. LW

After They Have Tired of the Brilliance of Cities. Stephen Spender. FaBoMo; LiTM

After they passed I climbed. A Story. William Stafford. NNaP

After They Put Down Their Overalls. Lenrie Peters. TTY

After they've gone. Surely You Remember. Dahlia Ravikovitch, *Hebrew*. IP, *tr. by* Warren Bargad *and* Stanley F. Chyet

After 37 Years My Mother Apologizes for My Childhood. Sharon Olds. Poetr

After thirty years. Romance. Gerald Stern. IFJA

After this day's hope—see how the Somme, the Seine, and the wild Slav. Léopold Sédar Senghor. NegPo, *tr. by* Ellen Conroy Kennedy *Fr.* Ode for Three Koras and Balaphong.

After this life here, we're to be awakened one day. Vladimir Holan. *See* Resurrection.

After this opened Job his mouth, and cursed his day. Job Complaineth of Life. Bible, *O.T. Fr.* Job. NAWM-1

After this oracle there will be no more oracles. Last Statement for a Last Oracle. Alan Dugan. NoAM

After those reverend papers, whose soul[e] is. To Sir H. W. at His Going Ambassador to Venice. Donne. MeLP

After-Thought, The. Stevie Smith. OxBC

After-Thought. Wordsworth. OBNC *Fr.* The River Duddon [A Series of Sonnets].
(Valediction to the River Duddon.) NOBE

After three days and nights of rich food. Back from the City. Jane Kenyon. AFr

After three months of autumn chill. To a Discarded Fan. Nguyễn Khuyến, *Chinese*. AVP, *tr. by* Huỳnh Sanh Thông

After thy labour take thine ease. The Mount of the Muses. Robert Herrick. CaPo

After today, how shall I speak with you? After One Year. Martin Carter. HCP

After Tonight. Gary Soto. NoAM

After Tosca. Raymond Roseliep. HA

After Touch. Jan Clausen. GLP

After Treblinka. How We See. Edward Bond. HP

After Trinity. John Meade Falkner. OxBTC

After Twenty Years. Adrienne Rich. TRP

After Twenty Years. Fadwa Tuqan, *Arabic*. AF, *tr. by* Unknown; PBWP

After twenty years I want to call it that, but was it? Rape. Joan Larkin. GLP

After two sittings, now our Lady State. The Last Instructions to a Painter. Andrew Marvell.

After two sittings, now our Lady State. Andrew Marvell. OBSV *Fr.* The Last Instructions to a Painter.

After Two Years. Richard Aldington. MoBrPo

After us there will be. Scrap. Tomasz Jastrun, *Polish*. AF, *tr. by* Daniel Bourne

After W. B. Yeats. G. K. Chesterton. NOBL

After wandering for so many hours up and down. Reminiscence. Vladimir Holan, *Czech*. PoSu, *tr. by* George Theiner

After War. Ivor Gurney. OxBSP

After we got suckered and lost the war. War Hope. William Hathaway. NAmP90

After we had loved each other intently. Listening to the Köln Concert. Robert Bly. RaBo

After we knew that we were dead we sat down and cried a little. The Dead. Louis Dudek. NOBC

After we make love, I teach you. In Language. Eugene Gloria. OpBo

After weeks of watching the roof leak. Gary Snyder. InPK-6; KaS *Fr.* Hitch Haiku. LCAP-2

After what felt like a lifetime of rent. Writing. Andrew Motion. DiPo

After what had / to be said. Drunk. Carroll Arnett. VoR

After Whistler. Stanley Plumly. LCAP-2

After Winter. Sterling Brown. GT; PoBA

After Wiriyamu Village Massacre by Portuguese. Jack A. Mapanje. AF; PeSAV

After Work. Gary Snyder. HoPM; NNaP; PFE

After working the midtown ambulance night slot. One Too Many Mornings. David Rivard. PBCAP

After years of bickerings. Spite Fence. Richard Eberhart. AFr

After years of relative clumsiness. Arachne. Judith Kazantzis. BrRo

After years the reunion. Brushed the dogs. Party. Eddy Van Vliet, *Flemish*. VCWP, *tr. by* John Van Tiel

After Yeats. Allen Ginsberg. FTOS; PFE

After you brought her home with your first child. Roof-Tree. Richard Murphy. BiHa

After you finish your work. Ballad of Orange and Grape. Muriel Rukeyser. ChAP; NoAM; NoP-4

After you have enriched your soul. Jonathan Swift Somers. Edgar Lee Masters. OBAL *Fr.* Spoon River Anthology.

After you left me forever. Semele Recycled. Carolyn Kizer. InPS-3; NALW; Poetr

After your death. Poem. Bill Knott. SPE

After your visit. Marlene Mountain. HA

After you've been to bed together for the first time. Life Story. Tennessee Williams. GLP

Aftereffects of a mother's neglects, The. Mother, Mother, Are You All There? Felicia Lamport. NBLV

Afterglow. Jorge Luis Borges, *Spanish*. NYBP, *tr. by* Norman Thomas Di Giovanni

Afterglow. Jack Butler. MT

Afterglow, The. Henrietta Cordelia Ray. CBWP-3

Afterglow goldens the. The Mountain Afterglow. James Laughlin. VGW

Aftergrowth. "Rachel," *Hebrew*. MHP, *tr. by* Ruth Finer Mintz

Afterimages. Audre Lorde. LTA; VCAP

Afterlife, The. Ted Kooser. CMAP

Afterlife in Elysium. Pindar, *Greek*. OBCVT, *tr. by* Willis Barnstone

Afterlives. Derek Mahon. CIP-2
"I am going home by sea." IIP
"I wake in a dark flat."

Aftermath. Henry Wadsworth Longfellow. APN-1; NAAL-1; NAAL-3; NOBA; PAR; PoPoPo; TAP

Aftermath. Siegfried Sassoon. MoBrPo; NSI; PoFWW; PoWW; TrJP
("Look up, and swear by the green of the spring that you'll never forget.") (LL) PoFWW

Afternoon. Louisa Sarah Bevington. PEW

Afternoon. Louisa S. Guggenberger. NOBVV

Afternoon. Across the garden, in Green Hall. Love in the Classroom. Al Zolynas. BLT; EC3; LTA

Afternoon: Amagansett Beach. John Hall Wheelock. PoRA

Afternoon and two men. In the Woods. Heinz Piontek, *German*. CLPP, *tr. by* Jerome Rothenberg

Afternoon at the Beach, An. Edgar Bowers. MT; VCAP

Afternoon cooking in the fall sun. Song. Robert Hass. AmPA; LoL

Afternoon Gossip, An. Priscilla Jane Thompson. CBWP-2

Afternoon Happiness. Carolyn Kizer. Poetr

Afternoon Hours. Rossana Ombres. PeFWW *Fr.* Excursion to Ravenna of A Young Girl with Her Parents.

Afternoon in February. Henry Wadsworth Longfellow. APN-1; ColAP

Afternoon in the Garden. Ethel Louisa Mason Anderson. NOBAu

Afternoon is all fallen plaster, black stones, dry thorns, The. Yannis Ritsos, *Greek*. AF, *tr. by* Edmund Keeley

Afternoon is invading my eyes. Drunken Poem. David Helwig. NOBC

Afternoon is the snack's own seasoning. Little Pudding. Mary M. Roberts. BXAP

Afternoon, its lazy ways, The. Girl. Octavio Paz, *Spanish*. STV, *tr. by* John Frederick Nims

Afternoon Light. Jacob Fichman, *Hebrew*. MHP, *tr. by* Ruth Finer Mintz

Afternoon light. Who Art Thou, O Great Mountain. Dahlia Ravikovitch, *Hebrew*. IP, *tr. by* Warren Bargad *and* Stanley F. Chyet

Afternoon on a Hill. Edna St. Vincent Millay. BoTP; ChAP; ImGa; NTCP; OBCA; OxBA; TTTS

Afternoon Service at Mellstock. Thomas Hardy. PeECV

Afternoon spreads its fingers on the lawn, The. The Visit. Ellen Bryant Voigt. WeT

Afternoon storm has hit, An. After the Fall of Saigon. Yusef Komunyakaa. AF; CDa

Afternoon sun is on their faces, The. Women in Dutch Painting. Eunice De Souza. OMIP

Afternoon Tea. Charlotte Mew. NTP

Afternoon. / Teacher and nun, bleak refugee, a stone. Street Scene. Robert Mezey. LiTM

Afternoon 3. Saburoh Kuroda. SPE

Afternoon turned dark early, The. During December's Death. Delmore Schwartz. NYBP

Afternoon wears on, The. Pastoral. David Wright. NYBP

Afternoon with heavy hours, The. The Traveller. Allen Tate. LiTM

Afternoons with Baedeker. Osbert Lancaster.

    Eireann. NOBL; PeLV

    English. NOBL; PeLV

    French. NOBL; PeLV

    Manhattan. NOBL; PeLV

Afterthought. Elizabeth Jennings. NOxBChV; OBCP

Afterwake, The. Adrienne Rich. NOBA

Afterward. Herman Melville. APN-2; NCAP Fr. Clarel: A Poem and Pilgrimage in the Holy Land.

    ("Saturnian Age, the Golden!") (LL) NCAP

    ("Seedsmen of old Saturn's land.") NCAP

Afterwards. H. B. K. Allpass. NSI

Afterwards. Thomas Hardy. CH; CMoP; EBEV; GEA; GTBS-P; InPS-3; LiTM; MoBrPo; NOBE; NoP-4; OAEL-2; OBNC; OxAEP-2; PoEL-5; PoPoPo; TFi; TOF

Afterwards. Robert Penn Warren. Fr. Fall Comes in Back-Country Vermont. NYBP; VGW

Afterwards, the compromise. After Love. Maxine W. Kumin. CrSp; NMM-2; TAP

Afterwards, They Shall Dance. Bob Kaufman. TWCP; VGW

Afterwards when he is finished with her. Lisa's Ritual, Age 10. Grace Caroline Bridges. LoHo

Afterwards, when we have slept, paradise-. The Knowing. Sharon Olds. BAP-94; ITG

Afterword. János Pilinszky, Hungarian. CEEP, tr. by Emery E. George

Aga Khan, The. Steve Orlen. Poetsp

Again. Thomas Brush. CDa

Again. Robert Creeley. VCAP

Again. Glyn Jones. OBWVE

Again. Charlotte Mew. MoBrPo

Again. Lenard D. Moore. GT

Again. Jon Stallworthy. OxBC

Again again again again again. Paul-Eerik Rummo, Estonian. CEEP, tr. by Ivar Ivask

Again and again and oooooh. Carolyn M. Rodgers. See We Dance Like Ella Riffs.

Again and again I go away from you. J. Michael Yates. HoPM Fr. The Great Bear Lake Meditations.

Again and again I kiss thy gates at departing. Roma. Namatianus, Latin. CTC, tr. by Ezra Pound OBCVT, tr. by Ezra Pound

Again and then again. . . the year is born. New Year's Day. Robert Lowell. AmPP; CoAmPo; LiTM; TRP

Again as evening's shadow falls. Samuel Longfellow. AH

Again at Christmas did we weave. Tennyson. EBVV; IMW; OAEL-2; PChr; PeECV Fr. In Memoriam A. H. H.

    ("And calmly fell our Christmas-eve.") (LL) PChr

Again, day and night sit balanced. Autumn Equinox. Peter Blue Cloud. Fr. Within the Seasons. HATNAP

Again for Hephaistos, the Last Time. Richard Howard. GLP

Again, his friend's death made the man sit still. John Berryman. NOBA

Again I find myself alone, and ever. Charlotte Brontë. PEW; VWP

Again I promise to try. (LL) Manuelzinho. Elizabeth Bishop. FaBoWP; NYBP

Again I reply to the triple winds. January. William Carlos Williams. MoAmPo

Again I see my bliss at hand. The Lake. Matthew Arnold. EnVR Fr. Switzerland.

Again I see you, ah my queen. Juana. Alfred de Musset, French. AWP, tr. by Andrew Lang

Again I'm caught staring. Pleasures of the Imagination. Peter McDonald. PNI

Again in the mirrored dusk the paddles sank. Downstream. Thomas Kinsella. PBCIP

Again last night I dreamed the dream called Laundry. The Mad Scene. James Merrill. CoAP; NOBA; PoA; PoE; TAP

Again let me do a lot of extraordinary talking. The Song of the Militant Romance. Percy Wyndham Lewis. FaBoTw; OxBTC

Again? new Tumults in my Breast? The First Ode of the Fourth Book of Horace. Horace, Latin. OBCVT, tr. by Alexander Pope

Again on the morrow morning doth Sigurd the Volsung ride. Sigurd Rideth to the Glittering Heath. William Morris. PoEL-5 Fr. The Story of Sigurd the Volsung.

Again retreated—and a second time faced the screen. (LL) The Silent One. Ivor Gurney. NoP-4

Again September, like the swarm of seasons past. Bella Akhatovna Akhmadulina, Russian. TCRP, tr. by Albert C. Todd

Again she Arms prepares: One Captain may. Silius Italicus. OBCVT, tr. by Thomas Ross Fr. The Punica.

Again stands superb as a temple. (LL) An Incident. Douglas Le Pan. NoP-4

Again the call of the winter birds. Poem for Carroll, Descendant of Chiefs. Lance Henson. VoR

Again the Cousin's whistle! Go, my Love. (LL) Andrea del Sarto. Robert Browning. CTC; EnVR; NAEL-2; NOBVV; NoP-4; OAEL-2; PoE; PoEL-5

Again the day. If the Stars Should Fall. Samuel Allen. PoBA

Again the flutter of desert. Negev. David Rokeah, Hebrew. MHP, tr. by Ruth Finer Mintz

Again the glory of the days! The Battle Summers. Herman Melville. APN-2

Again the greyish khaki light descends. (LL) "Elegies By the Senses." Meir Wieseltier, Hebrew. IP, tr. by Bargad, Warren and Stanley Chyet

Again the last ebb. Dieppe. Samuel Beckett. NOIV

Again the light of. Epitaph: Snake River. Lance Henson. VoR

Again the native hour lets down the locks. Allen Tate. Fr. More Sonnets at Christmas. LiTM

Again the shells were falling. Fresco Come to Life. Boris Pasternak, Russian. AF, tr. by Jon Stallworthy and Peter France

Again the snow-clogged pillars. On the Islands. Aleksandr Blok, Russian. TCRP, tr. by Geoffrey Thurley

Again the spiked signal. Red Moon High in the Sky. Husein Tahmisic, Serbian. CEEP, tr. by Ewald Osers

Again the time and blood consuming sun crosses its corner. The Dawn Horse. William Harmon. FYAP

Again the veld revives. Namaqualand after Rain. William Plomer. PeSAV

Again the violet bent double has arrived beside the. What the Flowers Said. Jelaluddin Rumi, Persian. GaP, tr. by A. J. Arberry

Again the violet of our early days. Spring. Ebenezer Elliot. OxAEP-2

Again the wood, and long-withdrawing vale. To Spring. Charlotte Smith. BWW; WPE

"Again they come," and muttered [or mutter'd] as he died. (LL) Peter Grimes. George Crabbe. EBNV; ECEV; FHYEP; OBNV; PoEL-4

Again this morning trembles on the swift stream the image of the sun. Images. Kathleen Jessie Raine. NYBP

Again this procession of the speechless. Daybreak. W. S. Merwin. NAAL-2

Again, this time from the chorus. Larry Neal. See Don't say goodbye to the Porkpie Hat that rolled.

Again to your Naucratis and the Nile. (LL) Doricha. Poseidippus, Greek. AWP; FaBoEE; OBVE, tr. by E. A. Robinson

Again today it is. Self-Portrait Approaching Promontory, Utah. Michael Pettit. GM

Again, traveller, you have come a long way led by that star. Epitaph. Thomas McGrath. RaBo

Again very queer but I'll go on looking. (LL) Wodwo. Ted Hughes. CBNP; MoP; NoAM

Again we have lasted till the snowtime. Snow. Vladimir Nikolaevich Kornilov, Russian. TCRP, tr. by Daniel Weissbort

Again when all the radiant sons of light. George Sandys. NOSC Fr. A Paraphrase Upon Job.

Again your kindly, smiling face I see. Mother. Max Ehrmann. PoToHe

Againe, see also Upon Julia's Voice. Robert Herrick. SeCP

Against a backdrop of Pennsylvania hills. Such a Boat of Land. Lamont B. Steptoe. UnSA

Against a feathery sky. (LL) Adolescence—I. Rita Dove. ISC; NoAM; PiM

Against a Rich Man Despising Poverty. Phineas Fletcher. NOSC

Against a Sickness: To the Female Double Principle God. Alan Dugan. NoAM

Against a somber background, blue as midnight. The Offering of the Heart Tapestry from Arras, XV Century. Rolfe Humphries. FYAP

Against a Wen. Unknown, Anglo-Saxon. ASW, tr. by Kevin Crossley-Holland

Against Absence. Sir John Suckling. CaPo; CavPo

Against an elm a sheep was tied [*or* ty'd]. The Wild Boar and the Ram. John Gay. NOEC *Fr*. Fables.

Against an Old Lecher. Sir John Harington. FaBoEE

Against Augusta, Montana: prairie dovetailed. Silos. Paul Zarzyski. PaTW

Against Blame of Woman. Gerald Fitzgerald, 4th Earl of Desmond. BIrV, *tr. by* the Earl of Longford

Against both bar and tower the black sea runs. (LL) Point Shirley. Sylvia Plath. NIP-4; Poetr

Against Botticelli. Robert Hass. AmPA

Against Broccoli. Roy Blount Jr. NBLV; OBAL

Against compulsory military service: a *"deferment"* of each limb. Deferment. Marcel Duchamp. PFTM

Against Constancy. John Wilmot, 2d Earl of Rochester. CABP; GBL; NOSC; OxAEP-1

  ("And fate change me for worms.") (LL) CABP

Against Coupling. Fleur Adcock. CBLP; LW; NALW

  ("That gap between the Sunday papers and lunch.") (LL) LW

Against Cupid. Sir Philip Sidney. *See* Cupid.

Against Dark's Harm. Anne Halley. NMM-2

Against far off snow mountains. Murakami Kijo, *Japanese*. OHMPJ, *tr. by* Kenneth Rexroth

Against Formal Gardens. William Mason. GaP

Against Fruition. Abraham Cowley. BeJo; NOSC *Fr*. The Mistress.

Against Fruition ("Fie upon hearts that burn with mutual fire[!]"). Sir John Suckling. BeJo; CaPo

Against Fruition ("Stay here, fond youth, and ask no more"). Sir John Suckling. BeJo; CaPo; CavPo; NOSC

Against Gaudy-Bragging-Undoughty Daccus. John, of Hereford Davies. FaBoEE

Against him, die, and find death good. (LL) Love On the Farm. D. H. Lawrence. CABP; CBLP; CMoP; MoBrPo; NAEL-2; NoAM; NoP-4; SAGP; SCGP

Against his coat. Alexis Rotella. HA

Against his forearm, leaning up against the barn. (LL) Land of Little Sticks, 1945. James Tate. LCAP-2; WeT

Against Homosexuality. Thomas Gilbert. NOEC *Fr*. View of the Town, A. In an Epistle to a Friend.

Against Hope. Richard Crashaw. MeLP; NOSC *Fr*. The Mistress.

  ("Hope, whose weak being ruin'd is.") CABP

  (On Hope.) CABP; NOBE

Against Idleness. *Unknown*. ACTP

Against Indifference. Charles Webbe. OBEV

Against its own best time. (LL) Sex without Love. Sharon Olds. DeD; HeIP-4; NIP-4; Poetr; TRP

Against Jealousy [*or* Jealousie]. Ben Jonson. CBLP

Against Love. Katherine Philips. BoWoP; WPE

Against Meaning. Andrei Codrescu. PmAP

Against Minoan sunlight. Wishes for Her. Denis Devlin. CIP-2; NOIV

Against my will. Footprints. Dan Pagis, *Hebrew*. VCWP, *tr. by* Stephen Mitchell

Against Paradise. Jonathan Holden. NAmP90

Against Parting. Natan Zach, *Hebrew*. HP, *tr. by* Everwine, Peter and Shulamit Yasny-Starkman; PoSu, *tr. by* Peter Everwine *and* Shulamit Yasny-Starkman

Against Proud Poor Phryna. John, of Hereford Davies. FaBoEE

Against Romanticism. Kingsley Amis. NoAM

Against Sadness. Natan Zach, *Hebrew*. IP, *tr. by* Warren Bargad *and* Stanley F. Chyet

Against Seasons. Robert Mezey. NYBP

Against Silence. Marilyn Hacker. PuP-14

Against Simple Reading. Meredith Stricker. LoHo

Against sloth. Hesiod, *Greek*. OBCVT, *tr. by* George Chapman

Against Sodomy. Charles Churchill. ECEV *Fr*. The Times.

Against Still Life. Margaret Atwood. MoCV

Against Te Rauparaha. Alistair Campbell. PeNZ *Fr*. Sanctuary of Spirits.

Against that time, if ever that time come. Sonnet 49. Shakespeare. OxAEP-1 *Fr*. Sonnets.

Against the bolts and welder's bloom of rhetoric. Adam Thorpe. APAD

Against the burly air I strode. Genesis. Geoffrey Hill. ChIV-1; HAP; OAEL-2; OxBC; PeECV; TOF

Against the Evidence. David Ignatow. NNaP

Against the Fear of Death. Lucretius, *Latin*. AWP; OAEL-1; OBVE, *tr. by* Dryden *Fr*. De Rerum Natura (On the Nature of Things).

  "What has this Bugbear death to frighten Man." OBCVT, *tr. by* John Dryden

Against the guide of Truth. Epigram V. *Unknown*. *Fr*. Duel with Verses over a Great Man. TrJP

Against the king, sir, now why would ye fight? William Drummond, of Hawthornden. NOSC

Against the lamp I sit by the south window. Sitting at Night. Po Chü-i, *Chinese*. TAL, *tr. by* Robert Payne

Against the Literal. Janet Holmes. BAP-95

Against the Love of Great Ones. Richard Lovelace. CBLP

Against the poet and the legislator. (LL) They wondered why the fruit had been forbidden. W. H. Auden. CMoP; ChIV-1; Son

Against the potent poison of your hate. (LL) The White House. Claude McKay. AmPP; ISC; NAAAL; NIP-4; PoBA

Against the rubber tongues of cows and the hoeing hands of men. Thistles. Ted Hughes. APAD; FaBoVe; NoAM; OxBSP; OxBTC; SoSe-8

Against the Silences to Come. Ron Loewinsohn. PoM

Against the stranger. Lawrence Joseph. *See* Sand Nigger.

Against the Text "Art Is Immortal." Alan Dugan. PuP-16

Against the Transcendentalists. Muriel Spark. FaBoTC

Against the Wind. Amir Gilbo'a, *Hebrew*. MHP, *tr. by* Ruth Finer Mintz

Against the window pane. Summer Rain. Sir Herbert Read. LiTM

Against the wittie gifte of shotinge in a bowe. Euripides. OBCVT, *tr. by* Roger Ascham *Fr*. Heracles.

Against Them Who Lay Unchastity to the Sex of Women. William Habington. BeJo; SeCP *Fr*. Castara.

Against these turbid turquoise skies. Les Ballons. Oscar Wilde. NOBVV

Against Tunes in a Minor Key. Nam Trân, *Vietnamese*. AVP, *tr. by* Huỳnh Sanh Thông

Against what light. Black Dada Nihilismus. Imamu Amiri Baraka. PoM

Against Whatever It Is That's Encroaching. Charles Simic. ColAP

Against Women. *Unknown, Welsh*.

  "Woman is by aptitude." OBWVE, *tr. by* Gwyn Williams

Against your ear. (LL) The Distant Drum. Calvin C. Hernton. GT; TTY

Agamemnon. Aeschylus, *Greek*. NAWM-1, *tr. by* Robert Fagles

  "And then the old leader of the Achaian fleet." OBCVT, *tr. by* Robert Browning

  Chorus: "Great Fortune is an hungry thing." AWP, *tr. by* Gilbert Murray

  "For me, the tears that welled." GrIP, *tr. by* Robert Fagles

  Signal Fire, The. CTC, *tr. by* Dallam Simpson

  "There is the sea." GrIP, *tr. by* Robert Fagles

Agamemnon before Troy. John Frederick Nims. Son

Agamemnon struggles to avert the sacrifice of his daughter Iphigeneia]. Euripides, *Greek*. OBCVT, *tr. by* Charles Gildon

Agamemnon's Tomb. Sacheverell Sitwell. OBMV

  "One by one, as harvesters, all heavy laden." MoBrPo

Agami Beach. Gregory Djanikian. CMAP

Agape the sooty collier stands. John Dalton. NOEC *Fr*. A Descriptive Poem, Addressed to Two Ladies at Their Return from Viewing the Mines, near Whitehaven.

Agatha Christie to. Said. George Starbuck. OBAL

Agbor Dancer. J. P. Clark Bekederemo. PBA

Age. Anacreon, *Greek*. OBCVT, *tr. by* James Bristow

Age. Abraham Cowley. AWP

Age. Robert Creeley. FTOS; PmAP

  ("Most explicit—.") FTOS

Age, An. Laura Jensen. LCAP-2

Age. Rae Desmond Jones. CBAP

Age. Walter Savage Landor. FaBoEE; NOBVV; PoEL-4

Age. Philip Larkin. CMoP

Age after age, the uninstructing dead. (LL) The Gulf. Derek Walcott. NoP-4; PoPoPo

Age and Death. Emma Lazarus. SDW

Age, and the deaths, and the ghosts. He Resigns. John Berryman. LBC; OxBSP; WeW-3

Age and Youth. Shakespeare. *See* A Madrigal: "Crabbed age and youth cannot live together."

Age cannot reach me where the veils of God. Immortality. Susan Langstaff Mitchell. TIRV

Age cannot wither her, nor custom stale. Shakespeare. ImPo *Fr*. Antony and Cleopatra.

Age demanded an image, The. Ezra Pound. HAP; MoAmPo; VGW *Fr*. Hugh Selwyn Mauberley. (Life and Contacts). AmPP; CMoP; InPS-3; LiTM; NOBA; NoAM; TAP

Age grips the body and the heart stays young. Love Is Bitter. *Unknown*. PeSA

Age in her embraces passed [*or* pass'd, *or* past], An. Mistress, The: A Song. John Wilmot, 2d Earl of Rochester. EBEV; NOBE; NOSC; OxAEP-1; PFE

Age in Prospect. Robinson Jeffers. MoAmPo

Age in Youth. Trumbull Stickney. ColAP

Age is a quality of mind. How Old Are You? H. S. Fritsch. PoLF; PoToHe

Age is dull and mean, The. Men creep. For Righteousness' Sake. John Greenleaf Whittier. PoEL-4

Age is ended, another kingdom's ended, An. Haim Guri, *Hebrew*. IP, *tr. by* Warren Bargad *and* Stanley F. Chyet

Age is when to a man. Song. Samuel Beckett. BIrV *Fr.* Words and Music.

Age Looks Back at Youth. Thomas, 2d Baron Vaux of Harrowden Vaux. NoSic

Age of a Dream, The. Lionel Pigot Johnson. OBMV

Age of Benevolence, The. Carlos Wilcox.
  "Sultry noon, not in the summer's prime, A." APN-1

Age of Bronze, The. Byron.
  "Alas, the country! how shall tongue or pen." OBSV

Age of Bronze awoke now in brutality, The. John Heath-Stubbs. *Fr.* Artorius. EBEV

Age of Gold. Pietro Metastasio, *Italian*. CTC, *tr. by* Ezra Pound

Age of Innocence. Graham Hough. PoRA

Age of Plastic, The. John Forbes. BMAP

Age of Reason, The, *mod. by* Donald Attwater. William Langland. NOCV *Fr.* The Vision of Piers Plowman.

Age of Reason, The. Mary Jo Salter. BAP-95

Age of Reason, The. Michael Van Walleghen. NAmP90

Age of seventy is gone, The. I Know Inside. Yüan Mei, *Chinese*. CoBLCP, *tr. by* Jonathan Chaves

Age of Sheen, The. Dorothy Hughes. NYBP

Age of unhappiness has arrived, or is it, The. Antonio Porta, *Italian*. CLPP, *tr. by* Molino, Anthony

Age of War, The. *Unknown*. NOBRP

Age / requires this task, The. A Different Image. Dudley Randall. BPo; TAP

Aged, Aged Man, The. "Lewis Carroll." *See* The White Knight's Song.

Aged, bittersweet, in salt crusted, the pink meat. Smithfield Ham. Dave Jeddie Smith. HCAP

Aged Lover Discourses in the Flat Style, The. James Vincent Cunningham. NoAM

Aged Lover Renounceth Love, The. Thomas, 2d Baron Vaux of Harrowden Vaux. NoSic; OAEL-1; PoEL-1; SCGP

Aged man, that mowes [*or* mows] these fields. A Dialogue betwixt Time and a Pilgrim[e]. Aurelian Townshend. NOBE; OAEL-1; PoEL-2; SeCP

Aged Pilot Man, The. "Mark Twain." OBAL

Aged Sophocles, the light of life has dimmed. Sophocles. *Unknown*, *Greek*. GrAn, *tr. by* Lee T. Pearcy

Aged twenty-six. Birthdays. C. J. Driver. PeSA

Agelaus was kind to Acestorides. Nicarchus of Alexandria, *Greek*. GrAn, *tr. by* Peter Porter

Agent of Love. A. K. Redwing. VoR

Agents, The. Robert Conquest. SPE

Ages, The. William Cullen Bryant. APN-1

Ages of Man, The. Abraham ibn Ezra, *Hebrew*. TrJP, *tr. by* Nina Davis Salaman

Aghast at first, and stupid with Surprize. (LL) The Goddess intervenes between Achilles and Agamemnon. Homer, *Greek*. OBVE, *tr. by* Dryden

Agincourt. Michael Drayton. FaBoBe; FaBoCh; OBEV; OxAEP-1
  (Ballad of Agincourt, The.) NTP

Agincourt Carol, The. *Unknown*. OAEL-1
  (Carol of Agincourt, A.) NoP-4
  (Deo Gracias, Anglia.) EBEV

Aging. Randall Jarrell. PoA

Aging. Erica Jong. CrSp

Aging Actress Sees Herself a Starlet on the Late Show, The. Miller Williams. MT

Aging pederast my friend, The. Dozing on the Porch with an Oriental Lap-Rug. Richard Tillinghast. WeT

Aging Poet, on a Reading Trip to Dayton, Visits the Air Force Museum and Discovers There a Plane He Once Flew, The. Richard Snyder. Poetsp

Aging woman helps her mother up from the table, The. Two Poems on the Fear of Love. Thomas R. Smith. EC2

Agitation of the air, An. End of Summer. Stanley Kunitz. LoL; MoAmPo; Poetsp; SAGP; VGW

Agitato Ma Non Troppo ("I have a grief"). John Crowe Ransom. OxBA *Fr.* Sixteen Poems in Eight Pairings.

Aglaura. Sir John Suckling.
  Song: "No, no, fair heretic[k], it needs must be." BeJo; CaPo; CavPo

Song: "Why so pale and wan, fond lover?" BeJo; BoLoP; CaPo; CavPo; ClHu; EBEvV; EnLoPo; HeIP-4; InPS-3; NAEL-1; NBLV; NIP-4; NoP-4; OxAEP-1; PoEL-3; SeCP; TFi
  (Encouragements to a Lover.) GTBS-P; PBMP

Agnes De Castro. Catherine Trotter.
  "Ah! She who told me of my Husband's Heart." KTR

Agnosco Veteris Vestigia Flammae. James Vincent Cunningham. VGW

Agon. Branko Miljkovic, *Serbo-Croatian*. HSix, *tr. by* Charles Simic

Agonies confirm His hour. Bahá'u'lláh in the Garden of Ridwan. Robert Earl Hayden. PoBA

Agonising pincer-jaws of Heaven, The. (LL) Sanctity. Patrick Kavanagh. NoP-4

Agonizing beyond words. Tanka. Akiko Yosano, *Japanese*. MJT, *tr. by* Ueda, Makoto

Agony [*or* Agonie], The. George Herbert. ESCV; GeHe
  ("Philosophers have measur'd mountains.") CABP; FSCP
  ("Which my God feels as blood; but I, as wine.") (LL) CABP; FMP; FSCP

Agony, The. George Herbert. *See* The Agony [*or* Agonie].

Agony. Giuseppe Ungaretti, *Italian*. PeFWW, *tr. by* Charles Tomlinson

Agony. As Now, An. Imamu Amiri Baraka. AmPP; BPo; LiTM; NAAL-2; PoE
  ("And that thing / screams.") (LL) NoP-4; UnSA

Agony in the Garden, The. Felicia Dorothea Hemans. TrCP

Agora. Aaron Shurin. PT

Agosu if you go tell them. Kofi Awoonor. HBAPE

Agreed that all these birds. All These Birds. Richard Wilbur. NOBA

Agreement with Sir Charles Sedley. Richard Howard. WeT

Agricultural labourer, one has, An. Common Sense. Alan Brownjohn. NOxBChV *Fr.* Pitman's Common Sense Arithmetic, 1917.

Agricultural Show, Flemington, Victoria, The. Suzanne Gardinier. CBAP

Agriculture. Robert Dodsley.
  Rustic Courtship. ECEV

Agrippina, well aware of Claudius' greed. Of Moulds and Mushrooms. Ruthven Todd. FaBoTC

Ah. Robin Blaser. FTOS

Ah. The Shepherd's Wife's Song. Robert Greene. HAP; NoSic; RACG *Fr.* Greene's Mourning Garment.

Ah, ah, ah. Moses and the Princess. Peter Dickinson. NOxBChV

Ah, all the sands of the earth lead unto heaven. Persian Miniature. William Jay Smith. CoAP

Ah, all those scores of years! Love's labor lost! A Retired Mandarin's Wife Complains. U'ng Binh, *Vietnamese*. AVP, *tr. by* Huỳnh Sanh Thông

Ah, are you digging on my grave. Thomas Hardy. MoBrPo; NAEL-2

Ah bar arkh. Fox's Song. Barbara Angell. ImGa

Ah bed, the field where joy's peace some do see. Sonnet 98. Sir Philip Sidney. EnLoPo *Fr.* Astrophil and Stella. AAS; SiPS

Ah Ben! / Say how, or when. An Ode for Ben Jonson. Robert Herrick. AWP; BeJo; CaPo; EPCY; FP; NOSC; SCGP; SeCP

Ah blackbird, giving thanks. *Unknown*. NOIV

Ah blessed absence of God. God's Absence. Mechthild von Magdeburg, *German*. WPoS, *tr. by* Oliver Davies

Ah blow! thou art the last, the last! Broken Heart. Henrietta Cordelia Ray. CBWP-3

Ah, broken is the golden bowl!—the spirit flown forever! Lenore. Edgar Allan Poe. APN-1; AmPP; PAR

Ah, cannot the curled shoots of the larkspur that you. Spring in the Garden. Edna St. Vincent Millay. GaP

Ah certainty of love in the hand. Janine Pommy-Vega. CLPP

Ah! changed and cold, how changed and very cold! Dead before Death. Christina Rossetti. NAEL-2; NALW

Ah, Chloris! could I now but sit. Child and Maiden. Sir Charles Sedley. GTBS-P; OBEV *Fr.* The Mulberry Garden.

Ah, Christ, I love you rings to the wild sky. Allen Tate. Son *Fr.* Sonnets at Christmas. HAP; LiTM; NOBA; OxBA; VGW

Ah, comic officer and gentleman. Elegy. E. W. Louis Edward Sissman. NYBP

Ah! County Guy, the hour is nigh. A Serenade. Sir Walter Scott. CH; GTBS-P *Fr.* Quentin Durward.

Ah! curst Ambition, to thy lures we owe. Thomas Tickell. ECEV *Fr.* On the Prospect of Peace.

Ah Dalmatia, if only I could send word of your dear sons. Ante Kosovic, *Maori*. PeNZ, *tr. by* Amelia Batistich *and* Ian Wedde

Ah Dangerous Swain, tell me no more. A Song. Delariviere Manley. KTR; LW *Fr.* The Lost Lover.

Ah, Dangerous Swain, tell me no more. Song. Delariviere Manley. LW

Ah Dearest, let us haste us. Martin Opitz, *German*. GePo, *tr. by* F. Warnke

Ah dearest limbs, my life's best joy and stay. Robert Sidney. NoSic

Ah dextrous Chirurgeons, mitigate your plan. On Having Piles. Sir Walter Scott. FaBoEE

Ah, did you once see Shelley plain. Memorabilia. Robert Browning. FHYEP; GEA; NAEL-2; NOBVV; NoP-4; OAEL-2; OBNC; PoE; PoPoPo; RB

Ah! didst *thou* tempt my mother? Byron. OxBSn *Fr.* Cain: a Mystery.

Ah, Doctor Faustus, that I might prevail. Marlowe. FaBoSe *Fr.* Doctor Faustus.

Ah, Douglass, we have fall'n on evil days. Douglass. Paul Laurence Dunbar. AAP; CBCWP; GSo; NAAAL; Son

Ah Eros doth not always smite. "Michael Field." VWP

Ah face, young face, sweet with unpassionate joy. Faded. Augusta Davies Webster. VWP

Ah fading joy, how quickly art thou past! Song from The Indian Emperor. Dryden. NoP-4 *Fr.* The Indian Emperor.

Ah! fair and lovely bloom the flowers of youth. Youth and Age. Mimnermus, *Greek.* AWP, *tr. by* John Addington Symonds

Ah! fair face gone from sight. Lionel Pigot Johnson. OBNC; PoEL-5 *Fr.* In Memory.

Ah, fair Zenocrate, divine Zenocrate. Fair Is Too Foul an Epithet. Marlowe. EBEV; PoEL-2 *Fr.* Tamburlaine the Great.

Ah false Amyntas, can that hour. Song. Aphra Behn. WPE *Fr.* The Dutch Lover.

Ah, Faustus,/ Now hast thou but one bare hour [*or* hower] to live. The End of Doctor Faustus. Marlowe. FaBoVe; HeIP-4; PeECV; PoEL-2 *Fr.* Doctor Faustus. NAEL-1; OAEL-1

Ah, flow on, flow on. Sail Peacefully Home. Simeon Grigoryevich Frug, *Yiddish.* TrJP

Ah, flowers that we wear! And Yet the Earth Remains Unchanged. *Unknown.* CA

Ah for the throes of a heart sorely wounded! The Damsel. Omar ben Abi Rabi'a, *Arabic.* AWP, *tr. by* W. G. Palgrave

Ah! Friend, the posting years how fast they fly? The Fourteenth Ode of the Second Book of Horace. Horace, *Latin.* OBCVT, *tr. by* John Potenger

Ah friend! 'tis true—this truth you lovers know—. To Mr. Gay, Who Wrote Him a Congratulatory Letter on the Finishing His House. Alexander Pope. NOEC; OBGa

Ah, friend you have changed; neckless. Friend, Ah You Have Changed! Frank Mkalawile Chipasula. HBAPE

Ah, gaze not on those eyes! forbear. The Vain Advice. Catherine Cockburn. LW

Ah! gentle, fleeting, wav'ring sprite. Adrian's Address to His Soul When Dying. Emperor Hadrian. OBCVT, *tr. by* Byron *Fr.* Hadrian's Address to His Soul When Dying. OBVE, *tr. by* Byron

Ah gentle shepherd, thine the lot to tend. John Dyer. PoEL-3 *Fr.* The Fleece.

Ah glaum lik a clood amang Munros, turnin thi / dwang. The Herr-Knit Bunnet. Robert Crawford. FaBoTC

Ah God, ah God, that day should be so soon. (LL) In The Orchard. Swinburne. BoLoP; LoP

Ah, God, the way your little finger moved. Stephen Crane. APN-2 *Fr.* War Is Kind.

Ah! Grandmother weaves! Grandmother Sleeps. Liz Sohappy Bahe. CDW

Ah-ha, I'm bound away 'cross the wide Missouri. *Unknown. See* Shenandoah.

Ah! Hannah, why should'st thou despair. Hope. Christopher Smart. ChIV-1 *Fr.* Hymns for the Amusement of Children.

Ah hapless sex! who bear no charms. To Alexis in Answer to his Poem against Fruition. Aphra Behn. KTR; NOSC; PEW

Ah, happy, happy boughs! that cannot shed. Keats. *Fr.* Ode on a Grecian Urn. AWP; CABP; ChAP; ClHu; EBEV; FaBoBe; HAP; HeIP-4; HoPM; ImPo; InPS-3; NAEL-2; NAWM-2; NIP-4; NOBE; NOBRP; NoP-4; OAEL-2; OBEV; OBNC; PBMP; PFE; PoE; PoEL-4; PoPoPo; Ro; SCGP; TFi; TOF; UnPo

Ah, happy youths, ah, happy maid. On a Picture by Poussin Representing Shepherds in Arcadia. John Addington Symonds. FaBoBe

Ah! he is fled! The British [*or* Brittish] Church. Henry Vaughan. ESCV; PeECV

Ah, he was a grand man. Tullynoe: Tête-à-Tête in the Parish Priest's Parlour. Paul Durcan. OBCoV

Ah heaven!—what *truth* to him. (LL) The College Colonel. Herman Melville. CBCWP; LiLi; NCAP; OBWP

Ah, hills beloved!—where once, an happy child. Sonnet V. To the South Downs. Charlotte Smith. Ro

Ah, how poets sing and die! Dunbar. Anne Spencer. NAAAL

Ah, how sweet it is to love! Dryden. HoPM *Fr.* Tyrannic Love.

Ah! Hoyland, empress of my heart. Ode to Miss Hoyland. Thomas Chatterton. BXAP

Ah! I could curse them in my woe. Revenge. Mary E. Tucker. CBWP-1

Ah, I still remember well that pain! The Blood. Nina Cassian, *Romanian.* CEEP, *tr. by* Marguerite Dorian *and* Elliott B. Urdang

Ah, in the past, towards rare individuals. Desire. D. H. Lawrence. CBLP

Ah in the thunder air. Trees in the Garden. D. H. Lawrence. CMoP; GaP; MoBrPo; NoP-4

Ah, is there no, no place on earth. Weariness. Mary E. Tucker. CBWP-1

Ah, it is so! Women's Rondo. *Unknown, Aborigine.* NOBAu

Ah—it's the skeleton of a lady's sunshade. The Sunshade. Thomas Hardy. OxBTC

Ah, Jesu Kri. María Sabina. STP, *tr. by* Henry Munn *Fr.* The Chants.

Ah, Lenin, you were richt. But I'm a poet. "Hugh MacDiarmid." OAEL-2 *Fr.* Second Hymn to Lenin.
   "Are my poems spoken in the factories and fields."

Ah, let me, far in some sequestered dell. Lines written at Bridgwater in Somersetshire, on 27 July 1797, during a Long Excursion in Quest of a Peaceful Retreat. John Thelwall. Ro *Fr.* Poems Written Chiefly in Retirement.

Ah, let me look, let me watch, let me wait, unhurried, unprompted! Claude to Eustace. Arthur Hugh Clough. EnVR *Fr.* Amours de Voyage. NOBVV

Ah, let your arms about me in the bed. The Frozen Boy. Brian W. Aldiss. OxBM

Ah! light lovely lady with delicate lips aglow. At Mass. *Unknown, Irish.* BIrV, *tr. by* Robin Flower

Ah! little fly, alighting fitfully. Calvus to a Fly. Charles Tennyson Turner. NOBVV

Ah little recks the laborer. Song of the Exposition. Walt Whitman.

Ah, little road, all whirry in the breeze. The Road. Helene Johnson. BlSi

Ah, London! London! our delight. A Ballad of London. Richard Le Gallienne. ADE

Ah, look, / How sucking their last sweetness from the air. The Divers. Peter Quennell. MoBrPo

Ah Love! could you and I with Him conspire. Omar Khayyám. *Fr.* The Rubáiyát of Omar Khayyám [*of* Naishápúr]. AWP; EBVV; FaBoBe; FaPoR; HAP; NAEL-2; PoEL-5

Ah! Love, my Master, hear me swear. Of His Death. Meleager, *Greek.* AWP, *tr. by* Andrew Lang

Ah, love, the teacher we decried. A Pure Hypothesis. May Kendall. VWP

Ah! lovely appearance of death. Charles Wesley. AH

Ah, Lucasta, why so bright. To Lucasta. Richard Lovelace. CaPo; CavPo

Ah, lute, how well I know each tone of thee. George Henry Boker. APN-2 *Fr.* Sonnets: A Sequence on Profane Love.

Ah Mater, quo te deplorem fonte? Dolores. George Herbert. PBRV *Fr.* Memoriae Matris Sacrum.

Ah me! conceiv'd in sin, and born in sorrow. Childhood. Anne Bradstreet. KTR *Fr.* The Four Ages of Man.

Ah me! How differently th'untutor'd slave. John Singleton. *Fr.* A General Description of the West Indian Islands. PBCV

Ah me, if I grew sweet to man. The Tragic Mary Queen of Scots. "Michael Field." EnLoPo; LW; OBMV

Ah me, my friend! it will not, will not last! Elegy 11. William Shenstone. NOEC

Ah me, the aspidistra grows dusty behind the window pane. In North Great George's Street. "Seumas O'Sullivan." BIrV

Ah me! those old familiar bounds! Ode on a Distant Prospect of Clapham Academy. Thomas Hood. BXAP

Ah, Melissa, where's your famous golden beauty. Rufinus Domesticus, *Greek.* InMo, *tr. by* Sam Hamill

Ah, more than any priest, O soul, we too believe in God. Walt Whitman. *Fr.* Passage to India. APN-1; AmPP; NAAL-1; NCAP; PoEL-5

Ah my Anthea! must my heart still break? To Anthea. Robert Herrick. CaPo

Ah my daughter, my grandchild! All You Others, Eat. Djurberaui, *Aborigine.* NOBAu, *tr. by* Catherine H. Berndt

Ah my dear[e] angry [*or* angrie] Lord. Bitter-Sweet. George Herbert. FHYEP; FMP; GeHe; NOBE; NoP-4; OxBSP

Ah, my dear friend and brother. Keats. FHYEP *Fr.* Epistle to George Keats.

Ah! my heart, ah! what aileth thee. To His Heart. Sir Thomas Wyatt. SiPS

Ah my Perilla! do'st thou grieve to see. To Perilla. Robert Herrick. BeJo; CaPo; NOSC; SCGP; SeCP

Ah, my subject, the rose, I know. In A Queen's Domain. Sarah Morgan Bryan Piatt. NCAP

Ah, Necromancy Sweet! Emily Dickinson. NOBA

Ah no. Parentage. Alice Thompson Meynell. NALW; VWP

Ah no, ah no, they weren't all gross and slow. Michael Foley. PNI *Fr.* True Life Love Stories.

Ah! no! / You are not a soldierly upright row! Upon a Row of Old Books and Shoes in a Pawnbroker's Window. Suzanne Gardinier. CBAP

Ah, nobody knows. Frost. Stella Benson. OxBTC

Ah, not to be cut off. Rilke, *German*. EnlH, *tr. by* Stephen Mitchell

Ah nuts! It's boring reading French newspapers. Les Luths. Frank O'Hara. NOBA; NoAM

Ah, old lady, are you still alive? Letter to My Mother. Sergey Aleksandrovich Yesenin, *Russian*. TCRP, *tr. by* Geoffrey Thurley

Ah! on Thanksgiving Day, when from East and from West. The Pumpkin. John Greenleaf Whittier. ImGa

Ah, pirates, pirates, pirates! Fernando Pessoa. PFTM *Fr.* Maritime Ode.

Ah, pity love where'er it grows! The Old Man's Complaint. *Unknown.* OxBSP

Ah! poor intoxicated little knave. To a Fly, Taken out of a Bowl of Punch. "Peter Pindar." NOEC

Ah poor Olinda never boast. Ode. Elizabeth Taylor. KTR

Ah Posthumus! our year[e]s hence fly[e]. His Age, Dedicated to His Peculiar Friend, Master John Wickes, under the Name of Posthumus. Robert Herrick. CaPo; SeCP

Ah poverties, wincings, and sulky retreats. Walt Whitman. OxBSP

Ah, Psyche, from the regions which / Are Holy-Land! (LL) To Helen. Edgar Allan Poe. APN-1; AWP; AmPP; BoLoP; CH; ClHu; ColAP; FaBoBe; GBL; HAP; HeIP-4; HoPM; ImPo; InPS-3; MeMAP; NAAL-1; NAAL-3; NIP-4; NOBA; NOBE; OBEV; OxBA; PAR; PBMP; PoE; PoEL-4; PoLF; PoRA; TAP; TFi; WeW-3

Ah, ra, chickera. *Unknown.* OxNR

Ah, Robin, / Jolly Robin. Sir Thomas Wyatt. SiPS

Ah! sad wer we as we did peace. The Turnstile. William Barnes. CH; NOBVV

Ah, see the fair chivalry come, the companions of Christ! Te Martyrum Candidatus. Lionel Pigot Johnson. OBMV; TIRV

Ah! She who told me of my Husband's Heart. Catherine Trotter. KTR *Fr.* Agnes De Castro.

Ah silly pugg wert thou so sore afraid. *at. to* Elizabeth I, Queen of England. NoP-4; NoSic

Ah, Sleep, to me thou com'st not in the guise. To Sleep. Lord Alfred Bruce Douglas. GSo

Ah, Spain, already your tragic landscapes. The Spanish War. "Hugh MacDiarmid." CMoP; NOBC

Ah, stay thy treacherous hand, forbear to trace. Verses on Sir Joshua Reynolds's Painted Window at New College, Oxford. Thomas, the Younger Warton. NOEC; PoEL-3

Ah Sun-flower. Ah Sun-flower. William Blake. AWP; EBEV; FHYEP; HAP; ImPo; NIP-4; NOBRP; NOEC; OAEL-2; OBNC; PoE; PoEL-4; PoPoPo; RB; SCGP; TFi; TOF; UnPo; WeW-3 *Fr.* Songs of Experience.

Ah Sun-flower. William Blake. NoP-4; PoPoPo *Fr.* Songs of Experience. ("Ah, sunflower! weary of time.") Ro (Sunflower, The.) ("Where my sunflower wishes to go.") (LL) Ro

Ah, sweet Content! where is thy mylde abode? Content. Barnabe Barnes. AAS *Fr.* Parthenophil and Parthenophe.

Ah, take these lips away; no more. Deadly Kisses. Pierre de Ronsard, *French*. AWP, *tr. by* Andrew Lang

Ah! tell me why, deluded Sex, thus we. Emulation, The: A Pindarick Ode. *Unknown.* KTR

Ah, Teneriffe! Emily Dickinson. InPS-3

Ah, That I Were Far Away. Arthur Hugh Clough. OBNC *Fr.* Amours de Voyage. NOBVV (Upon Apennine Slope.)

Ah! that I were once more a careless Child! (LL) Sonnet to the River Otter. Coleridge. OAEL-2; Son

Ah, that once more I were a careless child! Coleridge. *See* Sonnet to the River Otter.

Ah, the blowfly is whining there, its maggots are eating the flesh. The Blowflies Buzz. *Unknown, Aborigine.* NOBAu, *tr. by* Catherine H. Berndt

Ah, the cold, cold days. A Grandmother Remembers. Janet Lewis. PaTW

Ah the company of the birds. The Company of the Birds. Sasha Moorsom. APAD

Ah! the morning is grey. Chimney-Tops. *Unknown.* BoTP

Ah! the roofs. *Ambo Oral Tradition. Fr.* Five Ghost Songs. TTTS

Ah! the year is slowly dying. Passing of the Old Year. Mary Weston Fordham. CBWP-2

Ah! there's a house that I do know. Slow to Come, Quick a-Gone. William Barnes. NOBVV

Ah! think'st thou, Laura, then, that wealth. Stanzas. Charlotte Smith. NoP-4

Ah! Thomas, wherefore wouldst thou doubt. St. Thomas. Christopher Smart. ChIV-2 *Fr.* Hymns and Spiritual Songs for the Fasts and Festivals of the Church of England.

Ah, through the open door. Spring Morning. D. H. Lawrence. CMoP; MoBrPo

Ah to be alone and uninhibited! American against Solitude. Alan Dugan. CAPP-1

Ah, 'twas a glorious autumn night. The Two Meetings. Eugene Field. PWR

Ah, vale of woe, of gloom and darkness moulded. Song. Rachel Morpurgo, *Hebrew*. TrJP, *tr. by* Nina Davis Salaman

Ah! we've had many horses, but never a horse like her! (LL) Kentucky Belle. Constance Fenimore Woolson. BLPA; CBCWP; FaBoBe

Ah, what a redoubtable god! (LL) A God in Wrath. Stephen Crane. MeMAP; OxBSP; TAP

Ah! what a weary race my feet have run. Sonnet: To the River Lodon. Thomas, the Younger Warton. NOEC; Ro

Ah what avails the sceptred [or sceptered] race[!]. Rose Aylmer. Walter Savage Landor. AWP; BoLoP; CABP; CH; EnLoPo; GBL; GLoP; HAP; HoPM; NAEL-2; NOBE; NOBRP; NoP-4; OAEL-2; OBEV; OBNC; OxAEP-2; PoEL-4; Poetr; Ro; SCGP; TFi; UnPo; WeW-3

Ah, what can be more stately. Walt Whitman. *Fr.* Crossing Brooklyn Ferry. APN-1; AmPP; ColAP; FaBoA; InPS-3; MoP; NAAL-1; NAAL-3; NCAP; NOBA; NoAM; NoP-4; PAR; PiM; TAP

Ah, what is love? It is a pretty thing. Robert Greene. *See* The Shepherd's Wife's Song.

Ah! what pleasant visions haunt me. The Galley of Count Arnaldos. Henry Wadsworth Longfellow. OBEV

Ah, what sagacity perished here! (LL) Safe in their Alabaster Chambers. Emily Dickinson. NAAL-3; NoP-4; PoPoPo

Ah, what shall I be at fifty. Tennyson. NAEL-2 *Fr.* Morning arises stormy and pale. EBVVPR *Fr.* Maud [A Monodrama]. EnVR

Ah! what time wilt thou come? when shall that cry. The Dawning. Henry Vaughan. GeHe; NOCV

Ah! what unthinking, heedless things are men. The Horatian Canons of Friendship. Horace. OBCVT, *tr. by* Christopher Smart *Fr.* The Satires.

Ah! when the mallow in the croft dies down. Moschus. OBCVT, *tr. by* Walter Savage Landor *Fr.* Lament for Bion.

Ah when you drift hover before you kiss. John Berryman. EP *Fr.* Sonnets to Chris.

Ah! where the hedge athirt the hill. When We That Now Ha' Childern Wer Childern. William Barnes. NOBVV

Ah, wherefore, lonely, to and fro. To. Herman Melville. NCAP

Ah! wherefore with infection should he live. Sonnet 67. Shakespeare. SCGP *Fr.* Sonnets.

Ah, who can look on that celestial face. On the Statue of an Angel, by Bienaimé, in the Possession of J.S. Copley Greene, Esq. Washington Allston. APN-1

Ah! why, because the dazzling sun. Stars. Emily Jane Brontë. BrRo; NAEL-2; NALW; VWP

Ah! why from me art thou for ever flown. Jane Cave. ECWP *Fr.* Head-Ache, The; An Ode to Health.

Ah, will no soul give ear unto my moan? An Echo. Sir William Alexander, Earl of Stirling. NOSC

Ah! with no careless pen would I report. Lilian's Second Letter. Bessie Rayner Parkes. VWP *Fr.* Summer Sketches.

Ah, with the grape my fading life provide. Omar Khayyám. EBEV; GTBS-P *Fr.* The Rubáiyát of Omar Khayyám [of Naishápúr]. AWP; EBVV; FaBoBe; FaPoR; HAP; NAEL-2; PoEL-5

Ah, with what longing once again I turn! (LL) Desire. "Æ." OBMV; TIRV

Ah woe is me, of passion naught I knew. Propertius. AWP, *tr. by* F. A. Wright *Fr.* Elegies. AWP

Ah! woman still. Frances Sargent Osgood. ColAP; PAR

Ah, would swift ships had never been, for then we ne'er had found. V.A.D. (Mediterranean). Rudyard Kipling. *Fr.* Epitaphs of the War [1914–1918]. OBWP

Ah Wretch! thou cry'st, ah! miserable me. Against the Fear of Death. Lucretius. AWP; OAEL-1; OBVE, *tr. by* Dryden *Fr.* De Rerum Natura (On the Nature of Things).

Ah yah, tair um bam, boo wah. Jungle Mammy Song. *Unknown.* AS

Ah, yes, I wrote the "Purple Cow." Cinq Ans Après. Frank Gelett Burgess. APN-2; NBLV; OBAL; OBCoV; TFi

Ah, yes, to your misfortune. Patrizia Cavalli, *Italian*. NeIt; VCWP, *tr. by* Judith Baumel

Ah yes, when love allows. Hadewijch, *Dutch*. PBWP, *tr. by* Frans van Rosevelt

Ah! yesterday, d'ye know, I voun'. Polly Be-en Upzides wi' Tom. William Barnes. NOBVV

Ah, you beast of love. Hayden Carruth. VGW

Ah, you have always been a friend to me. Gordon Bottomley. NSI *Fr.* King Lear's Wife.

Ah, you have much to learn, we can't know all things at twenty. Arthur Hugh Clough. FaBoPV *Fr.* Bothie of Tober-na-Vuolich, The [A Long-Vacation Pastoral].

Ah, you Russians, how often I feel like you. How Often I Feel Like You. Iain Crichton Smith. FaBoTC

Ah (you say), this is Holy Wisdom. Hilda Doolittle. NALW; NoAM *Fr.* Tribute to the Angels.

Ah—you thought I'd be the type. "Anna Akhmatova," *Russian.* LoP; SAGP, *tr. by* Judith Hemschemeyer

Ahab's gaily clad fisherfriends. Evil Is No Black Thing. Sarah Webster Fabio. PoBA

Ahead I bear; the Eagle of Gál. The Lament for Urien. *Unknown.* OBMV, *tr. by* Ernest Rhys *Fr.* The Red Book of Hergest.

Ahead of me, the dog reared on its rope. Seventeen. Andrew Hudgins. BAP-95

Ahead, the sun's face in a flaring hood. First Walk on the Moon. May Swenson. RACG

Ah'm goin' whah nobody knows mah name, Lawd, Lawd! Levee Moan. *Unknown.* AS

Ah'm gonna build mahself a raft. Blues Ain' Nothin', De. *Unknown.* AS

Aholibah. Swinburne. ChIV-1; KSG

Ahv drank / thi speshlz. Jist Ti Let Yi No. Tom Leonard. FaBoTC

Aid me Bellona, while the dreadful fight. Edmund Waller. BeJo *Fr.* The Battle [*or* Battel] of the Summer-Islands.

Aideen's Grave. Sir Samuel Ferguson. NOIV

AIDS, Among Other Things. Peter Kocan. ChIV-2

Aiken Drum. *Unknown.* FaBoCh; OxNR

Ailill the king is vanished. The Downfall of Heathendom. *Unknown, Irish.* IIP, *tr. by* Frank O'Connor

Ailing bird over the desert made its agony, An. Our Life. Mbella Sonne Dipoko. PBMAP

Ailing child, An. Tanka. Kitahara Hakushū, *Japanese.* MJT, *tr. by* Makoto Ueda

Ailing Japanese Monk, The. Hsiang Ssu, *Chinese.* CoBCP, *tr. by* Burton Watson

Aim get your sights and its sound. Canto 7: First Thesis. Tom Weatherly. PoBA

Aim Was Song, The. Robert Frost. SoSe-8

Aimed across Delos at a star. (LL) Delos. Lawrence Durrell. GrIP; OxAEP-2

Aimless. Louis Palagyi, *Hungarian.* TrJP, *tr. by* Watson Kirkconnell

Ain' Go'n' to Study War No Mo'. *Unknown.* AS

Ain't been on Market Street for nothing. Ballad of the Hoppy-Toad. Margaret Abigail Walker. BlSi; HoPM; NBV

Ain't gonna let nobody, Lordy, turn me 'round. Ain't Gonna Let Nobody Turn Me Round. *Unknown.* CrDW

Ain't Gonna Let Nobody Turn Me Round. *Unknown.* CrDW

Ain't Gonna Rain. *Unknown.* AS

Ain't I a Woman? Sojourner Truth. BlSi

Ain't it all a bleeding shame. (LL) Poor But Honest. *Unknown.* OxBoV

Ain't It [*or* It's] Fine Today. Douglas Malloch. BLPA

Ain't No Grave Can Hold My Body Down. *Unknown.* AmFP

Ain't you 'shamed, you sleepy- / head! (LL) Time to Rise. Robert Louis Stevenson. ACTP; CTV; OxBChV

Air. Philip Dow. BXAP

Air. John Godfrey. FTOS

Air. Jennifer Maiden. BMAP

Air. Kathleen Jessie Raine. MoBrPo

Air. Ann Taylor. NOxBChV

Air: "Arise, arise, arise!" Henry Brooke. *Fr.* Jack the Giant Queller; an Antique History. NOEC

Air: "Flaxen-headed cow-boy, as simple as may be, A." John O'Keefe. NOEC

Air: "For often my mammy has told." Henry Brooke. *Fr.* Jack the Giant Queller; an Antique History. NOEC

Air: "Fox may steal your hens, sir, A." John Gay. NOEC *Fr.* The Beggar's Opera. OAEL-1

(Act I, Scene ix, Air XI—"A Soldier and a Sailor.") NoP-4

Air: "I ne'er could any lustre see." Richard Brinsley Sheridan. NOEC *Fr.* The Duenna.

Air: "O ruddier than the cherry!" John Gay. CBLP; EBEvV; NAEL-1; NOEC *Fr.* Acis and Galatea.

(Song: "O ruddier than the cherry.") NOBE

Air: "Since laws were made for ev'ry degree." John Gay. NOEC *Fr.* The Beggar's Opera. OAEL-1

Air: "So full of courtly reverence." Dudley North. OxBSP

Air: "Sportsmen keep hawks, and their quarry they gain, The." John Gay. NOEC *Fr.* Polly; an Opera.

Air: "The Love of a Woman." Robert Creeley. VCAP; VGW

Air a-gittin' cool an' coolah. Signs of the Times. Paul Laurence Dunbar. APN-2

Air already smells like snow, my lover, The. Sarah Kirsch, *German.* CEEP, *tr. by* Wayne Kvam

Air[e] and Angels. Donne. CBLP; ESCV; MeLP; NAEL-1; OAEL-1; SeCP ("'Twixt women's love, and men's will ever be.") (LL) FMP

Air and Angels. Charles North. FTOS

Air as the fuel of owls. Snow. Iowa. Michael Dennis Browne. NYBP

Air Balloon, The. Henry James Pye. NOEC *Fr.* Aerophorion.

Air Base at Châteauroux, France, The. Sherod Santos. NAmP90

Air between us is like glass, The. The Air between Us (for an Expatriate). Kendel Hippolyte. HCP

Air-borne ants attacked softer parts of the cyclist, measuring. Race on Gathering Bites. Kojo Laing. HBAPE

(Air commented in a whisper, The). Keith Douglas. *See* Gallantry.

Air commented in a whisper, The. (LL) Gallantry. Keith Douglas. NAEL-2; NoAM; OBWP

Air-Conditioned Air. Debora Greger. WWSi

Air, earth and water meet at the sea's edge. A Naked Girl Swimming. Arthur Rex Dugard Fairburn. PeNZ

Air Force called it Quadrant Bombing, The. Intersection in the Sky. Mcavoy Layne. CDa

Air grows thin. The men are less bewitched, The. Courtesan. Angela Shaw. BAP-94

Air hazed by seed and bug, arms heavy. Eye Blade. George Evans. AF

Air heaves at matter. Night Wind in Fall. William Robert Moses. WeT

Air, I hear, The. Keorapetse Kgositsile. PBMAP

Air in Newfound-land [*or* Aire in Newfoundland-land] is wholesome, good, The. The Pleasant Life in Newfoundland. Robert Hayman. NOBC

Air in the room is dark and greasy, The. A Concise History of the Vietnam War: 1965–1968. Ron Weber. CDa

Air is a mill of hooks, The. Mystic. Sylvia Plath. NYBP

Air is a smoke-tree, the wind, The. Reviewing Past Lives while Leaf-Burning. Anita Endrezze-Danielson. HATNAP

Air is cool. Coming, The. Open Window. Janet Hamill. DeD

Air is filled with apple blossoms and rain, The. This Is English and I Am Speaking It No Matter What. Rosalind Pace. CMAP

Air is full of flying stars, The. Snow-Stars. Frances Mary Frost. CTV

Air is quiet, The. The Coming of Teddy Bears. Dennis Lee. TLR

Air is / Sucked clear of dross, The. January. Hoffman Reynolds Hays. SPE

Air is thick with nerves and smoke, The. University Examinations in Egypt. D. J. Enright. OxBTC; TwCP

Air mass / Puts pressure on the playground, The. Theory of Climate. Geoffrey O'Brien. PT

Air New Zealand. Christian Karlson Stead. PeNZ *Fr.* Clodian Songbook.

Air of June Sings, The. Edward Dorn. NeAP; PoM

Air of the museum, The. The Frozen Hero. Thomas H. Vance. NYBP

Air Plant, The. Hart Crane. MoAmPo

Air Raid. Peter Wild. Poetsp

Air Raid Across the Bay at Plymouth. Stephen Spender. AF

Air: Sentir avec Ardeur. Marie-Françoise-Catherine de, Marquise de Boufflers Beauveau, *French.* CTC; WPOW, *tr. by* Ezra Pound

Air stiffens to a crust, The. The Wound. Louise Glück. NoAM

Air that holds the world that was my world. (LL) Easter Morning. A. R. Ammons. HCAP; NAAL-2; NoAM

Air, the dream-inspiring air, The. An Idyl of Spring. Henrietta Cordelia Ray. CBWP-3

Air was soft, the ground still cold, The. April 5, 1974. Richard Wilbur. HCAP

Air which thy smooth voice doth break, The. Speaking and Kissing. Thomas Stanley. BeJo

Air without has taken fever, The. July. Alexander L. Posey. APAD; APN-2

Airborne dragonfly, An. Hunter's Moon. Stephen Sandy. NYBP

Aircraft. Rita Dove. EC3

Airing clothes and belongings in the courtyard. Sentimental Poem. Po Chü-i, *Chinese.* CoBCP, *tr. by* Burton Watson

Airing Painful Memories. Yüan Chen, *Chinese.* CoBCP, *tr. by* Burton Watson

Airing the Chapel. Sylvia Kantaris. LW

Airliner. Francis Webb. CBAP; NOBAu

Airlock swings open—, The. The Eagle has Landed. Adrian Rumble. SpW

Airly Beacon, Airly Beacon. Charles Kingsley. EBVV; OBEV

Airman. Stephen Spender. *See* Icarus.

Airman's Breastplate, The. Oliver St. John Gogarty. TIRV

Airport. Martin Johnston. CBAP

Airport coffee tastes less of America, The. The Gulf. Derek Walcott. NoP-4; PoPoPo

Air's advice is all, The. Prelude to Commencement. Marie De L. Welch. NYBP

Airs and Graces. Peter Fallon. PBCIP

Airs from the sea blown back. Ovid on the Dacian Coast. Dunstan Thompson. NYBP

Air's heaviness in the dark room, as if a vague bloodlike, The. The Dark Room. Enrique Lihn, *Spanish*. VCWP, *tr. by* David Unger

Airs of Palestine. John Pierpont.
    "Here let us pause:—the opening prospect view." APN-1
    "In what rich harmony, what polished lays." APN-1
    "Now, he recalls the lamentable wail." APN-1
    "On Arno's bosom, as he calmly flows." APN-1

Airs of Pei. Confucius, *Chinese*.
    Efficient Wife's Complaint, The. CTC, *tr. by* Ezra Pound

Airs! that wander and murmur round. The Siesta. *Unknown, Spanish.* AWP, *tr. by* Bryant

Airstrip in Essex, 1960, An. Donald Hall. LCAP-2; LiTM

Airy Christ, The. Stevie Smith. ChIV-2; NOCV

Airy Hall's Exits. Fred D'Aguiar. HCP

Airy spirits, you who love. Inscription in a Beautiful Retreat Called Fairy Bower. Hannah More. ECWP; NoP-4

Aishah Schechinah. Robert Stephen Hawker. OBNC

Aisle of a Temple, The. William Congreve. OxAEP-1

Aisle of Dogs. Chase Twichell. BAP-96

Aisles and abysses; leagues no man explores. Caverns. Madison Cawein. APN-2

Aisling. Paul Muldoon. PNI

Aja, I am joyful; this is good! Utitia′q′s Song. *Unknown, Eskimo.* APN-2, *tr. by* Franz Boas

Ajanta. Muriel Rukeyser. LiTM; MoAmPo; NNaP

Ajax. Sophocles, *Greek*.
    Chorus: "Fair Salamis, the billow's roar." AWP, *tr. by* Winthrop Mackworth Praed
    "Happiest life consists in ignorance, The." IMW
    "Think on thy father in the vale of years." OBCVT, *tr. by* Thomas Francklin

Ajax and his Brother. Homer. OBVE, *tr. by* Alexander Pope *Fr.* The Iliad.

Ajax' Conclusion. Frank Barbour Coffin. AAP

Ajax Samples, The. Laura Jensen. LCAP-2

Ajax the swift swerv'd never from the side. Homer. OBVE, *tr. by* William Cowper *Fr.* The Iliad.

Akat'ani / x'aax'. Tlingit Concrete Poem. Nora Dauenhauer. NIP-4

Akathistos Hymn. *Unknown, Greek.* GrIP, *tr. by* Constantine A. Trypanis

A[h]kond of Swat, The, *limerick.* Edward Lear. CBNP; FaBoCh; PeLi

Al Aaraaf. Edgar Allan Poe. APN-1
    Song: "Young flowers were whispering in melody." NOBA
    Song: "'Neath blue-bell or streamer." AmPP; OxBA

Al this sentence me liketh every deel. Chaucer. *See* Experience, though noon auctoritee.

Al were he mytre, crowne [*or* croune], or diademe. (LL) Gentilesse. Chaucer. AWP; MiEL; NAEL-1; OAEL-1

Ala, mala, mink, monk. *Unknown.* OxNR

Alabama. Julia Fields. PoBA

Alabama Bus. William Hairston. FaBoPV

Alabama Centennial. Naomi Long Madgett. BPo

Alabama Poem. Nikki Giovanni. BkSV

Alabama Song. Bertolt Brecht. PFTM

Alabaster legs of the lonely woman, The. The Merry Window. Francis Scarfe. SPE

Alabushevo. Viktor Aleksandrovich Nekipelov, *Russian.* TCRP, *tr. by* Albert C. Todd

Alack! 'tis melancholy theme to think. The Irish Schoolmaster. Thomas Hood. BXAP

Alakanak Break-Up. Mei-Mei Berssenbrugge. PmAP

Alaric / At Danzig / Saw Pegasus. Three Amphigouris. Jean-Joseph Vade, *French.* CBNP

Alarm, The. Hildebrand Jacob. NOEC

Alarm and time clock still intrude too early. And on This Shore. M. Carl Holman. PoBA

Alarm at First Entering the Yang-tze Gorges. Po Chü-i, *Chinese.* ChiP, *tr. by* Arthur Waley

Alarm Clock, The. Phan Bội Châu, *Vietnamese.* AVP, *tr. by* Huỳnh Sanh Thông

Alarmclock is ringing. (LL) My Alba. Allen Ginsberg. CLPP; NOBA

Alarmed Skipper, The. James Thomas Fields. NBLV

Alarming New Development, An. Ron Schreiber. GLP

Alarum. Urszula Koziol, *Polish.* WPOW, *tr. by* Czeslaw Milosz

Alarum, The. Sylvia Townsend Warner. MoBrPo

Alas. Peter Grimes at Aldeburgh. George Crabbe. NoP-4 *Fr.* Peter Grimes. EBNV; ECEV; FHYEP; OBNV; PoEL-4; Ro *Fr.* The Borough.

Alas! Sadi. AWP, *tr. by* L. Cranmer-Byng *Fr.* The Gulistan.

Alas, Alack! Walter De la Mare. OPOU; OxBChV

Alas! alas! the while. *Unknown.* MiEL

Alas! alas! thou turn'st in vain. Claim to Love. Giovanni Battista Guarini, *Italian.* AWP, *tr. by* Thomas Stanley

Alas, alas, well evil I sped! Undo! *Unknown.* NOCV

Alas, all my years, where have they disappeared? Walther von der Vogelweide, *German.* GePo, *tr. by* Frederick Goldin

Alas! and am I born for this. On Liberty and Slavery. George Moses Horton. AAP; APN-1; PAR

Alas! behold! how steep! how high! The Road to Shu Is Hard. Li Po, *Chinese.* SuSp, *tr. by* Irving Y. Lo

Alas! Carolina! J. Gordon Coogler. OBAL

Alas, dear Clio, every day. To Clio, from Rome. John Dyer. NOEC

Alas, dear mother, fairest queen and best. A Dialogue between Old England and New. Anne Bradstreet.

Alas, departing is ground of wo! *Unknown.* MiEL

Alas, eheu, one question that sorely vexes. Ezra Pound. *Fr.* L'Homme Moyen Sensuel. OBSV

Alas! for all the pretty women who marry dull men. Meditation at Kew. Anna Wickham. FaBoTw; MoBrPo; NALW; SAGP

Alas for me, who loved a falcon well! A Lady Laments for Her Lost Lover, by Similitude of a Falcon. *Unknown, Italian.* AWP, *tr. by* D. G. Rossetti

Alas, for the blight of my fancies! Love Versus Learning. Constance Naden. VWP

Alas! for the South. J. Gordon Coogler. OBAL

Alas for the voyage, O High King of Heaven. Farewell to Ireland. Saint Columcille. AWP, *tr. by* Douglas Hyde

Alas for this unhappy night! A Song of Instruction. Te Kooti Rikirangi, *Maori.* PeNZ, *tr. by* Margaret Orbell

Alas, for us, who need beware. On Worldly Prelates. Charles Wesley. ChIV-2

Alas for Youth. Firdausi, *Persian.* AWP, *tr. by* R. A. Nicholson

Alas, good friend, what profit can you see. Lines to a Reviewer. Shelley. OxBSP

Alas, have I not pain enough, my friend. Sonnet 14. Sir Philip Sidney. NoP-4; NoSic; OAEL-1 *Fr.* Astrophil and Stella. AAS; SiPS

Alas, his mind is sunk. "Heu Quam Praecipih Mersa Profundo." Boethius, *Latin.* MLL, *tr. by* Helen Waddell *Fr.* Consolation of Philosophy, The ("De Consolacione Philosophie").

Alas how barbarous are we. Upon the graving of her Name upon a Tree in Barnelmes Walks. Katherine Philips. PBRV

Alas, how easily things go wrong! Sweet Peril. George Macdonald. BLPA; FaBoBe

Alas! How should I sing? *Unknown.* NOIV

Alas, how soon the hours are over. Plays. Walter Savage Landor. NBLV; OxBSP; OxBoLi; PeLV

Alas, I am so faint I may not stand. The Desertion of Beauty and Strength. *Unknown. Fr.* Everyman. NAEL-1; NAWM-1; OAEL-1; PoEL-1

Alas, I draw breath heavily. An Old Woman's Song. Akjartoq, *Eskimo into Danish.* WPOW, *tr. by* Knud Rasmussen; *English vers. by* Tom Lowenstein

Alas! I have lost my God. Rejected. Lord Alfred Bruce Douglas. ADE; PeVV

Alas! in every aspiration bold. Richard Polwhele. NOBRP *Fr.* The Unsex'd Females.

Alas, is wiser far [*or* farre] than I. (LL) The Bait[e]. Donne. CBLP; HoPM; InPK-6; InPS-3; NAEL-1; NOSC; OAEL-1; PFE; PoRA; RB

Alas, madam[e], for stealing [*or* stelying] of a kiss [*or* kysse]. Sir Thomas Wyatt. BoLoP; CBLP

Alas, my brothers. Hilda Doolittle. NOBA *Fr.* Helen in Egypt.

Alas, my God, I know not what. (LL) The Thanksgiving. George Herbert. ESCV; GeHe

Alas! my love, you [*or* ye] do me wrong. Lady Greensleeves. *Unknown.* EBEvV; GBL; NoSic; OxAEP-1; PBRV; PoEL-2

Alas! my Posthumus, the years. To Posthumus. Horace, *Latin.* OBCVT, *tr. by* Anna Seward

Alas, my Purse! how can lean and low! Soliloquy on an Empty Purse. Mary Jones. ECWP

Alas our good kaspar is dead. Kaspar Is Dead. Hans Arp, *German.* PFTM, *tr. by* Jerome Rothenberg

Alas! our pleasant moments fly. On Parting. Edward Coote Pinkney. APN-1

Alas poor Death, where does thy great strength lye? Meditations for July 25, 1666. Philip Pain. SCAP

Alas! poor Fanny! wretched girl, alas! Fanny's Removal in 1714. John Winstanley. NOEC

Alas, poor heart, I pity thee. *Unknown. Fr.* Medieval Norman Song. AWP, *tr.* by John Addington Symonds

Alas, poor man, what hap have I. Sir Thomas Wyatt. SiPS

Alas! Poor Queen. Marion Angus. FaBoTC

Alas, poor widow, I shall be too hard for thee! Women Beware Women. Thomas Middleton. FaBoSe *Fr.* Women Beware Women.

Alas poore Scholler, whither wilt thou goe. Robert Wild. "In a melancholly studdy." PBRV

Alas, shall I not see again. Heinrich von Morungen, *German.* GePo, *tr.* by Frederick Goldin

Alas, So All Things Now. Petrarch. *Fr.* Sonnets to Laura. ("Alas, so all things now do hold their peace.") NoSic, *sect.* CIX, *tr.* by the Earl of Surrey

Alas, so all things now do hold [*or* thinges nowe doe holde] their peace. A Complaint by Night of the Lover Not Beloved. Henry Howard, Earl of Surrey, *after* Petrarch. AAS; AEP; AWP; EBEV; NAEL-1; OAEL-1; OBVE; SCGP; SiPS; Son

Alas, so all things now do hold their peace. Petrarch. *See* Alas, So All Things Now.

Alas, that earth's mere measure strains our blood. Words for My Daughter from the Asylum. Hayden Carruth. MoLi *Fr.* The Bloomingdale Papers.

Alas, that ever that speche was spoken. *Unknown.* EnLoPo

Alas, that I ne had English, rhyme or prose. Chaucer. EPCY *Fr.* The Legend of Good Women.

Alas, that I should be. To My Infant Daughter. Yvor Winters. VGW

Alas, that I should die. Song of a Woman Abandoned by the Tribe. *Unknown, Shoshone Indian.* WPE, *tr.* by Mary Austin

Alas! that such a soul should taste of death. In Memory of Arthur Clement Williams. Eloise Bibb. CBWP-4

Alas, that wisdom, and youth. Walther von der Vogelweide, *German.* GePo, *tr.* by Frederick Goldin

Alas, the country! how shall tongue or pen. Byron. OBSV *Fr.* The Age of Bronze.

Alas, the grief and deadly wo[e]ful smart[!]. Sir Thomas Wyatt. SiPS

Alas, the ignorance of unhappy men. Boethius, *Latin.* MLL, *tr.* by Helen Waddell *Fr.* Consolation of Philosophy, The ("De Consolacione Philosophie").

Alas, the moon should ever beam. The Water Lady. Thomas Hood. CH; Ro

Alas! the time has come, old dress. Lines to an Old Dress. Mary E. Tucker. CBWP-1

Alas the while! (LL) There was never nothing more me pained [*or* payned]. Sir Thomas Wyatt. AAS; GBL; SiPS

Alas, then, for the homeless beggar old! (LL) Summer and Winter. Shelley. OxAEP-2; SCGP

Alas! they had been friends in youth. The Scars Remaining. Coleridge. OBNC *Fr.* Christabel. FHYEP; NAEL-2; NOBRP; OAEL-2; Ro

Alas, 'tis true I have gone here and there. Sonnet 110. Shakespeare. AEP; EBEV; NoSic; OxAEP-1 *Fr.* Sonnets.

Alas! 'tis very sad to hear. Walter Savage Landor. GTBS-P; WeW-3

Alas, to be / Mortal, and know our sad mortality! Echo. George Santayana. APN-2

Alas, what is the world? a sea of glass. Meditation 10. Philip Pain. NOBA

Alas, whence came this change of looks? If I. Sonnet 86. Sir Philip Sidney. *Fr.* Astrophil and Stella. AAS; SiPS

Alas, why say you I am rich? when I. Robert Sidney. NoSic

Alas! you son of her who is short-eared. Lion. *Unknown, Hottentot.* PeSA

Alas, young man! your days are ne'er be long;. Alexander Pope. EPCY *Fr.* The First Satire of the Second Book of Horace [Imitated]. OAEL-1

Alas! young men, come, make lament. The Dirge of St. Malo. George Washington Cable. APAD; APN-2

Alaska. Mary Weston Fordham. CBWP-2

Alaskan Drinking Song. Dave Morice. EOEF

Alaskan Fragments June 1981—Summer Solstice. Wendy Rose. HATNAP

Alaskan Mountain Poem #1. Leslie Marmon Silko. VoR

Alastor; or, The Spirit of Solitude. Shelley. OAEL-2; Ro

"As an eagle grasped."

Invocation: "Earth, ocean, air, belovèd brotherhood!" NAEL-2

"Startled by his own thoughts, he looked around." OxBoS

"There was a poet whose untimely tomb." FHYEP; TOF

"Wildly he wandered on." TOF

Alba ("As cool as the pale wet leaves"). Ezra Pound. GBL; HAP; WeW-3

Alba. Imamu Amiri Baraka. FTOS

Alba. Samuel Beckett. BIrV

Alba. Confucius. CTC, *tr.* by Ezra Pound *Fr.* Songs of T'ang.

Alba Innominata. *Unknown, French.* AWP, *tr.* by Ezra Pound

Alba ("When the nightingale to his mate"). Ezra Pound. OBVE; VGW; WeW-3 *Fr.* Langue d'Oc.

Albacete knives, magnificent, The. The Quarrel. Federico García Lorca, *Spanish.* AF, *tr.* by Robert Bly

Albany in a time of khaki. The Gathering Place. Alan Alexander. NOBAu

Albeit the Venice girls get praise. Ballad of the Women of Paris. François Villon, *French.* AWP, *tr.* by Swinburne

Albert Ayler: Eulogy for a Decomposed Saxophone Player. Stanley Crouch. PoBA

Albert Einstein's the man we must credit. Limerick. Stanley J. Sharpless. PeLi

Albert is haranguing his mother about his name. In the Heat of the Morning. Anne Szumigalski. FaBoWP

Albert james was black long before me. Reuben Jackson. UnSA

Albert Sidney Johnston. Kate Brownlee Sherwood. CBCWP

Albert Speer. W. D. Snodgrass. NoAM

Alberta, lovely little dame. Priscilla Jane Thompson. CBWP-2

Albion Battleship Calamity, The. William McGonagall. BXAP

Albion's England. William Warner. Tale of the Beginning of Friars and Cloisterers, A. NoSic

Albion's most lovely daughter sat on the banks of the. Mrs. Albion You've Got a Lovely Daughter. Adrian Henri. OxBTC

Album, The. C. Day Lewis. EnLoPo; OxBTC

Album. Haim Gouri, *Hebrew.* IP, *tr.* by Warren Bargad *and* Stanley F. Chyet

Album. Josephine Miles. ColAP; FaBoWP

Album—A Runthru. Clark Coolidge. FTOS

Album Leaf. Stéphane Mallarmé, *French.* OBVE, *tr.* by Keith Bosley

Album Leaves. Arthur Rex Dugard Fairburn. Back Street. PeNZ

Conversation in the Bush. PeNZ

Possessor, The. PeNZ

Alcaics; to H. F. B. Robert Louis Stevenson. OBEV

Alcander's Flower Garden. William Mason. OBGa *Fr.* The English Garden.

Alceste in the Wilderness, *Non, je ne puis souffrir cette lâche méthode / Qu'affectent la plupart de vos gens à la mode. . . .* Anthony Hecht. CoAmPo; PoA

Alceste is here, that al may desteyne. (LL) Balade: "Hide [*or* Hyd], Absalon, thy gilte tresses clere." Chaucer. AWP; EBEV; EnVB; GBL; HAP; ImPo; NOBE; OAEL-1; OBEV; SCGP

Alcestis. Euripides, *Greek.* "Friends, I account the fortune of my wife." OBCVT, *tr.* by Robert Browning

Strength of Fate, The. AWP

Alcestis on the Poetry Circuit. Erica Jong. AmPA; NALW

Alchemical. Paul Celan, *German.* VCWP, *tr.* by Michael Hamburger

Alchemical Ingredients. Ben Jonson. *Fr.* The Alchemist. FaBoSe

Alchemist, The. Louise Bogan. AWP; MoAmPo

Alchemist, The. Richard Church. OxBTC

Alchemist, The. Ben Jonson. FaBoSe "Come on, sir. Now, you set your foot on shore." PoEL-2

"Have you provided for her grace's servants?"

"I will have all my beds blown up, not stuft." EBEV

Alchemist, The. Ezra Pound. CMoP

Alchemists say the Stone turns lead to gold. David Foster. NOBAu *Fr.* The Fleeing Atalanta.

Alchemy of Day, The. Anne Hébert, *French.* BoWoP, *tr.* by A. Poulin, Jr.

Alcheringa Definitions. Orpingalik, *Danish.* PFTM, *tr.* by W. E. H. Stanner

Alciphron and Leucippe. Walter Savage Landor. OBEV

Alcohol. Louis MacNeice. LiTM

Alcohol. Franz Wright. LCAP-2

Alcoholic. John Berryman. NOCV

Alcoholic. F. D. Reeve. NYBP

Alcoholic's Son at Ten, The. Kathleen Peirce. PBCAP

Alcyna met them at the outer gate. Ludovico Ariosto. OBVE, *tr.* by Sir John Harington *Fr.* Orlando Furioso.

Alderman. Marilyn Nelson Waniek. LTA

Aldport (Mystery Tour). Kingsley Amis. NOBL *Fr.* The Evans Country. (Terrible Beauty.)

Aldrin Collins and Armstrong. Michael Rosen. SpW

Ale they drink in Giggleswick, The. Wyndham Lewis. UV *Fr.* A Downland Crisis.

Aleph Poem. Jerome Rothenberg. FTOS

Aleutian Islands. Blaise Cendrars, *French*. BLT, *tr. by* Monique Chefdor

Alex at the Barber's. John Fuller. PeLV

Alex, perhaps a colour of which neither of us had dreamt. Letter to Alex Comfort. Dannie Abse. FaBoTw; TwCP

Alexander and Campaspe. John Lyly.

   Cards and Kisses. GLoP; HoPM; NOBE; OBEV; PBMP

   ("Cupid and my Campaspe play'd.") GLoP

   Serving Men's Song, A. NOBE

   ("Oh, for a bowl of fat Canary.") NoP-4

   Trico's Song. NoSic

   (Spring's Welcome.) OBEV

   (Welcome to Spring.) NOBE

Alexander Jannai. Constantine P. Cavafy, *Greek*. TrJP, *tr. by* Simon Chasen

Alexander the Great. *Unknown*. CH

Alexander's Feast; or, The Power of Music [*or* Musique]. Dryden. FaPoR; GTBS-P; NAEL-1; NOBE; OAEL-1; PeECV; TFi

Alexander's Song. *Unknown*. CBNP

   (Man of Thessaly, [The].) OxNR

Alexandreis. Anne Killigrew. NoP-4

Alexis. Plato, *Greek*. GrAn

Alexis, here she stayed; among these pines. Sonnet. William Drummond, of Hawthornden. NOSC; OBEV

Alfenus Varus / buttonholes me. Catullus. *See* Carmen 10 ("Varus, whom I chanced to meet").

Alfonso was his name; his sad cantina. Skin Diving in the Virgins. John Malcolm Brinnin. NYBP; TAP

Alfonzo Prepares to Go Over the Top. Rita Dove. LoL

Alfred: A Masque. James Thomson *and* David Mallet.

   Rule, Britannia! EBEvV; FaPoR; GTBS-P; NOEC; OBWP

   (Ode: Rule, Brittania!) NAEL-1

Alfred Corning Clark. Robert Lowell. RB

Alfred de Musset. Maurice Evan Hare. OBCoV

Alfred, Lord Tennyson. Dorothy Parker. NALW *Fr.* A Pig's-Eye View of Literature.

Alfrid's Itinerary through Ireland. *Unknown*, *Irish*. TIRV, *tr. by* James Clarence Mangan

Algernon Charles Swinburne. Joseph Seamon Cotter, Sr. AAP

Algy met a bear. *Unknown*. CTV; KaS

Ali. Lloyd M. Corbin Jr. PoBA

Ali Ben Shufti. Anthony Thwaite. OxBTC

Ali / Is our prince. Lloyd M. Corbin Jr. MBE

Alibazan. Laura Elizabeth Richards. OBCA

Alibi. Arthur Guiterman. BXAP

Alicante. Jacques Prévert, *French*. BoLoP, *tr. by* Lawrence Ferlinghetti

Alice. Michael S. Harper. ISC

Alice B. *Unknown*. AS

Alice Brand. Sir Walter Scott. *See* Ballad: Alice Brand.

Alice Corbin is gone. Carl Sandburg. PoA

Alice, dear, what ails you. A Frosty Night. Robert Graves. CH; MoBS; MoBrPo; OxBTC

Alice Fell; or, Poverty. Wordsworth. OBNV

Alice grown lazy, mammoth but not fat. Last Days of Alice. Allen Tate. FuPo; NAAL-2; NOBA; OxBA; UnPo

Alice is gone and I'm alone. W. H. Auden. CBNP

Alice is tall and upright as a pine. Two Rural Sisters. Charles Cotton. BoLoP; EnLoPo *Fr.* Resolution in Four Sonnets, of a Poetical Question Put to Me by a Friend, Concerning Four Rural Sisters. PoEL-3; Son

Alice of Daphne, 1799. John Ennis. PBCIP

Alice Ordered Me to be Made. Alice Notley. FTOS

Alice's Adventures in Wonderland, *sels*. "Lewis Carroll."

   Crocodile, The. CTAV; ChAP; HoPM

   Duchess's Lullaby, The. CBNP

   (Lullaby, A.) NOxBChV

   Evidence Read at the Trial of the Knave of Hearts. GTBS-P; NOBVV; OxBoLi; PBMP; PeLV

   (Verses from the Trials of the Knave of Hearts.) CBNP

   Father William. BXAP; CBNP; ChAP; HoPM; NOBL; NOBVV; OBCoV; OxBChV; PeLV; PoLF; PoRA; TFi; UV; UnPo

   "'You are old,' said the youth, "and your jaws are too weak."'" OxBM

   Lobster, The. OxBChV

   ("So, when *he* lost his temper, the Owl lost its life.") (LL)

   "'Tis the voice of the Lobster: I heard him declare."

   Lobster Quadrille, A. BoTP; CTAV; OxBChV; UV

   (Mock Turtle's Song, The.) CBNP

   ("'Will you walk a little faster?' said a whiting to a snail.") APAD; CTAV

   ("Will you, won't you, will you, won't you, will you / join the dance?")

   (LL) CTAV

   Long Tale, A. NoAM; OBCoV

   ("con- / demn / you to / death.") (LL) NOxBChV

   ("Fury said to / a mouse.") NOxBChV

   (Mouse's Tale, The.) CBNP; NOxBChV

   Mad Hatter's Song, The. NOBL

   ("Like a tea-tray in the sky.") (LL) CTV

   (Mad Hatter's Concert Song, The.) CBNP

   Song of the Mock Turtle, The. UV

Alice's Evidence. "Lewis Carroll." *See* Evidence Read at the Trial of the Knave of Hearts.

Alice's Recitation, *sl. diff. vers*. "Lewis Carroll." *See* The Lobster.

Alien. Gillian Allnutt. NBrP

Alien. Nancy Paddock. LoHo

Alien. William Price Turner. OxBS

Alien at the Zoo. Pamela Gillilan. SpW

Alien goes Shopping. Pamela Gillilan. SpW

Alike he thwarts the hospitable end. Homer, *Greek*. *Fr.* Odyssey. NAWM-1, *tr. by* Robert Fitzgerald

Alison ("In March and April, thereabout"). *Unknown*. HAP

Alison. *Unknown*. CBLP; MiEL; NAEL-1; NoP-4; OAEL-1; OBEV; PeLV

   ("Hendy hap ichabbe yhent, An.") (LL) NoP-4

Alison and Willie. *Unknown*. ESPB

Alison [*or* Allison] Gross. *Unknown*. CH; ESPB; FaBoCh; OxBB

Aliter. Confucius. *Fr.* Songs of Ch'en. CTC, *tr. by* Ezra Pound

Alive for an Instant. Kenneth Koch. PmAP

Alive, in a slippery grave. (LL) Weed Puller. Theodore Roethke. AmPP; HCAP; NAAL-2

Alive, ne'er parted be. (LL) Song: "Sweetest love, I do not go[e]." Donne. AWP; BoLoP; ESCV; FHYEP; FMP; FSCP; GLoP; HeIP-4; InPS-3; LoP; MeLP; NOBE; NoP-4; NoSic; OAEL-1; PoEL-2; SeCP; TFi

Alive or Not. Alfred Wellington Purdy. NOBC

Alive, this man was Manes, a common slave. Anyte, *Greek*. BoWoP, *tr. by* Willis Barnstone

   ("When this man, Manes, lived, he was a slave.") GrAn, *tr. by* Sally Purcell

Alive with expectation. (LL) Soul Music: The Derry Air. Eamon Grennan. BiHa; PBCIP

Alive, you caught the hares and made them cry. To a Dead Dog in the River. Nguyễn Văn Lạc, *Vietnamese*. AVP, *tr. by* Huỳnh Sanh Thông

Alkinoos' Garden, *see also* Gardens of Alcinous, the. Homer, *Greek*. GrIP, *tr. by* Robert Fitzgerald *Fr.* Odyssey. NAWM-1, *tr. by* Robert Fitzgerald

Alkinoos, king and admiration of men. New Coasts and Poseidon's Son. Homer. *Fr.* Odyssey. NAWM-1, *tr. by* Robert Fitzgerald

Alkman's Supper. Alcman, *Greek*. OBCVT, *tr. by* Willis Barnstone

All. Gwendolyn Brooks. *See* The Mother.

All. Antoni Slonimski, *Polish*. TrJP, *tr. by* Wanda Dynowska

All a-tremble she awoke. The Annunciation. Amrita Pritam, *Punjabi*. WPOW, *tr. by* Khushwant Singh *and* Krishna Gorowara

All Abdéra mourned at the funeral pyre. Anacreon, *Greek*. GrAn, *tr. by* Peter Jay

All about. All about all with a word seeming across the world. Time Travel. Nick Piombino. FTOS

All about Boys and Girls. John Ciardi. NOxBChV

All about Carrowmore the lambs. Carrowmore. Lucie Brock-Broido. PoPoPo

All about it. (LL) In Praise of My Sister. Wislawa Szymborska, *Polish*. PoSu, *tr. by* Adam Czerniawski

All after pleasures as I rid one day. Christmas. George Herbert. GeHe; NOSC; PeECV; TOF; TrCP

All afternoon cutting bramble blackberries off a tottering / brown fence. A Strange New Cottage in Berkeley. Allen Ginsberg. BLT

All afternoon you worked at cutting them down. Tent Caterpillars. Susan Mitchell. WeT

All, All a-Lonely. *Unknown*. OxBoLi

All, all are gone, the old familiar faces. (LL) The Old Familiar Faces. Charles Lamb. AWP; BLPA; FP; FaBoBe; FaPoR; GTBS-P; NOBE; NOBRP; OBEV; OxAEP-2; RB; Ro

All, all of a piece throughout. Song: "All, all of a piece throughout." Dryden. HAP; ImPo; InPS-3; OxBSP; WeW-3 *Fr.* The Secular Masque. NAEL-1; OxAEP-1; PoE; PoEL-3; SCGP

All Alone. Mary E. Tucker. CBWP-1

All alone in my little cell. *Unknown*. NOIV

All along the backwater. Duck''s Ditty. Kenneth Grahame. BoTP; CTAV; FPC; NOxBChV; NTCP; OTCP; OxBChV; WHSW *Fr.* The Wind in the Willows.

All along the rail[road]. In Texas Grass. Quincy Troupe. GT; NAAAL; PoBA; UnSA

All along the valley, stream that flashest white. In the Valley of Cauteretz. Tennyson. BoLoP; LBC; NAEL-2; NOBE

All Americans are ambiguous. Shorter American Memory of the American Character According to Santayana. Rosemarie Waldrop. EOEF

All Arcadia hath not seen. (LL) Song: "O're [or O'er] the smooth enamel'd [or enameled or enamelled] green." Milton. OBEV; OxBSP

All are architects of fate. The Builders. Henry Wadsworth Longfellow. PWR

All are but parts of one stupendous whole. Alexander Pope. FHYEP Fr. An Essay on Man.

All are ghosts beside. (LL) Voluntaries. Ralph Waldo Emerson. APN-1; CBCWP

All are not born to soar—and ah! how few. On Imitation. Coleridge. OxBSP

All arms combined magnificently together. (LL) The Persian Version. Robert Graves. CMoP; LiTM; MoP; NOBL; NoAM; NoP-4; OBWP; WeW-3

All around I heard the whispering larches. Forest Song. Sir Shane Leslie. TIRV

All around my house at midnight: rain. Dawn: Clear Skies. Yang Shih-ch'i, *Chinese.* CoBLCP, tr. by Jonathan Chaves

All around old Chattanooga. Freedom at McNealy's. Priscilla Jane Thompson. CBWP-2

All around, shards of a lost tradition. A Lost Tradition. John Montague. CIP-2; PBCIP

All around the altar, huge lianas. Reading the Bible Backwards. Eleanor Wilner. NoP-4

All around the Town. Phyllis McGinley.
  "J's the jumping Jay-walker." SSCS

All Around Us. Constance Urdang. PBCAP

All art is temporal. All art is lost. Against the Text "Art Is Immortal." Alan Dugan. PuP-16

All ashes, all ashes again. (LL) On Neal's Ashes. Allen Ginsberg. PmAP; PoM

All attempts to remove. Mr. Cogito Meditates on Suffering. Zbigniew Herbert, *Polish.* VCWP, tr. by John Carpenter and Bogdana Carpenter

All beauty, and without a spot! (LL) A Vision of Beauty. Ben Jonson. BeJo; NOSC

All beauty, resonance, integrity. Le Livre Est sur la Table. John Ashbery. SPE

All because I think of you. Silhouette. Marc Cohen. EOEF

All beginnings start right here. The Move Continuing. Al Young. PoBA

All Being Well. Wilfrid Wilson Gibson. OxBTC

All beneath the white-rose tree. The Three Captains. *Unknown, French.* AWP, tr. by Andrew Lang

All Bibles or sacred codes have been the causes of the following Errors. William Blake. *See* The Voice of the Devil.

All Bibles or sacred codes. have been the causes of the following Errors. The Voice of the Devil. William Blake. *Fr.* The Marriage of Heaven and Hell. NAEL-2; NOBRP; OAEL-2

All birds love to babble where a man wants quiet. In the Mountains. Ssu-k'ung Shu, *Chinese.* SuSp, tr. by Edward H. Schafer

All birds that swim are mine. My Birds. Solomon Mutswairo, *Shona.* PeSAV, tr. by Solomon Mutswairo and Donald E. Herdeck

"All-bounteous Heaven," Castalio cries. An Unanswerable Apology for the Rich. Mary Barber. ECWP

All Britain knows of this noble city. Durham. *Unknown, Anglo-Saxon.* ASW, tr. by Kevin Crossley-Holland

All busy punching tickets. Crickets. David McCord. NTCP

All but blind. Walter De la Mare. MoBrPo; WeW-3

All but the blithe / Hexameters. (LL) Verse: "What should we know." Oliver St. John Gogarty. FaBoCh; OBMV; PoRA

All Christian men in my behalf. On Sir John Calf. *Unknown.* FaBoEE

All Clear. Roger Woddis. PeLV

All clowns are masked and all *personae.* Delmore Schwartz. OxBA *Fr.* The Repetitive Heart.

All colors come from the sun. And it does not have. The Sun. Czeslaw Milosz. ChAP

All Come to Me. Nguyễn Chí Thiện, *Vietnamese.* AVP, tr. by Huỳnh Sanh Thông

All covered with debt. (LL) Songs of Sorrow. Kofi Awoonor. HBAPE

All craftsmen share a knowledge. They have held. Craftsmen. Vita Sackville-West. OxBTC

All end and say, You can have it. (LL) You Can Have It. Philip Levine. NoP-4; VCAP

All creatures, each has a home. In Praise of Poor Scholars. T'ao Ch'ien, *Chinese.* SuSp, tr. by Eugene Eoyang

All dat English you used to know. Don't Know No English. Nicolás Guillén, *Spanish.* PFTM, tr. by Langston Hughes

All day. James Tipton. HA

All day, a small mild Negro man with a broom. The Sweeper of Ways. Howard Nemerov. HCAP

All day a strong wind blew. A Strong Wind. Austin Clarke. RB

All Day and All October. Laurence David Lerner. PeSA

All day and every day the sea shone, steeped in its blueness. When I Was Young. Alun Llywelyn-Williams, *Welsh.* OBWVE, tr. by Gwyn Williams

All day and night, music. Jelaluddin Rumi, *Persian.* EnlH, tr. by Coleman Barks *and* John Moyne

All day and night, save winter, every weather. Aspens. Edward Thomas. FaBoVe; InPS-3

All day beside the shattered tank he'd lain. Reconciliation. C. Day Lewis. PoWW; TwCP

All-Day Bird, the artist, The. Claritas. Denise Levertov. VGW

All day, day after day, they're bringing them home. Homecoming. Bruce Dawe. BMAP; CBAP

All day he had felt her stirring. The Mermaid. Lisel Mueller. CrSp

All day he slept, his mouth on pennyroyal. The Soldier in the Park. Elizabeth Riddell. CBAP

All day I always want to know. When I Am 19 I Was a Medic. D. F. Brown. CDa

All day I did the little things. The Blue Bowl. Blanche Bane Kuder. BLPA; FaBoBe

All day I have been closed up. Of Rain and Air. Wayne Dodd. BLT

All day I hear the noise of waters. James Joyce. SCGP

All day I heard a humming in my ears. The Awaking of the Poetic Faculty. George Henry Boker. Son

All day I hoe weeds. *Unknown, Japanese.* OHMPJ, tr. by Kenneth Rexroth

All day I tried to distinguish. Elms. Louise Glück. NoAM

All day it has rained, and we on the edge of the moors. Alun Lewis. GTBS-P; NAEL-2; NOBE; NoP-4; OBWP; OBWVE; OxBTC

All day, knowing you dead. The Hours. John Peale Bishop. OxBA

All day long. (LL) Counting the Mad. Donald Justice. CoAmPo; NIP-4; NoP-4; TRP; UnPo

All day long, at Scott's or Menzies', I await the gorging crowd. The Wail of the Waiter. Marcus Clarke. NOBAu

All day long, Bones hasn't been seen. Bad Dog. Brian Lee. PeP

All day long having / buried himself. Kanoko Okamoto, *Japanese.* WPJ, tr. by Kenneth Rexroth *and* Ikuko Atsumi

All day long I have been working. Madonna of the Evening Flowers. Amy Lowell. CPO; NALW

All day long, prismatic dazzle. Midnight. Mary Ursula Bethell. PeNZ

All day long / The sun shines bright. The Night Sky. *Unknown.* BoTP

All day long to the judgement-seat. Gallio's Song. Rudyard Kipling. ChIV-2

All day my sheep have mingled with yours. Shepherdess. Norman Cameron. GBL; OxBS *Fr.* Three Love Poems. FaBoTw; GTBS-P

All day pinecones drop like shot birds. Late November. Sherod Santos. Son

All day she hurried to get through. Mis' Smith. Albert Bigelow Paine. PoLF

All day subdued, polite. Negro Servant. Langston Hughes. VGW

All day the air got harder and harder. Resolutions. Robin Fulton. FaBoTC

All day the bicycles come and go. Nicholas Hasluck. NOBAu *Fr.* Rottnest Island.

All day the bird-song here has seemed. Random Reflections on a Summer Evening. John Hall Wheelock. NYBP

All day the fitful rain. Vermont Ballad: Change of Season. Robert Penn Warren. ColAP

All day the light wind blew on the house. Day on Kind Continent. Robert David Cohen. NYBP

All day the mirrors kindle their brilliance. The Mirrors. Sophia de Mello Breyner Andresen, *Portuguese.* PBWP, tr. by Allan Francovich

All day the opposite house. The Opposite House. Robert Lowell. CMoP

All day the red spit of the chain-shot tore. Evil. Rimbaud. OBWP, tr. by Robert Lowell *Fr.* Eighteen-Seventy.

All day the sound of chopping axes. Campfireburners. Anatoly Zhigulin, *Russian.* TCRP, tr. by Vladimir Lunis *and* Albert C. Todd

All day the unnatural barking of dogs. The Dog. Valentin Iremonger. BIrV

All day the waves assailed the rock. Waves. Ralph Waldo Emerson. AmPP

All day the wind has made love. On Lake Pend Oreille. Richard Shelton. NYBP

All day to the loose tile behind the parapet. The Wasps' Nest. George MacBeth. OxBTC

All day today the sea gulls cried. Out in the Cold. George Starbuck. NYBP

All day under acrobat. Galway Kinnell. *Fr.* Ruins under the Stars. LCAP-2

All day we had ridden through scarred, tawny hills. Spain, 1809. Frank Lawrence Lucas. EBNV

All day we walked the streets. The Fifties. Ira Sadoff. AmPA

All Day We've Longed for Night. Sarah Webster Fabio. BlSi

All day working happily down near the stream bed. What is a Garden. W. S. Merwin. GaP

All do not seek the exalted fire. Earth and Fire. Vernon Watkins. NYBP

All dressed alike in white silk skirts and kerchiefs. Flowering Plums. Han Yü, *Chinese.* GaP, *tr. by* Hans H. Frankel

All dripping in tangles green. The Tuft of Kelp. Herman Melville. APN-2; FaBoEE

All Dull, my Lord, my Spirits flat, and dead. Edward Taylor. NOSC *Fr.* Preparatory Meditations Before My Approach to the Lord's Supper.

All during a night. Shune, *Japanese.* OHPJ, *tr. by* Kenneth Rexroth

All early, when the day. The Spouse of Jesus Laments Her Heart's Flame. Friedrich Spee, *German.* GePo, *tr. by* George C. Schoolfield

All earth is a poet. Swinburne. Joseph Cotter, Sr.. AAP

All endeavor to be beautiful. Primer of Plato. Jean Garrigue. NOBA

All-enlight'ning, all-beholding. Pindar on the Eclipse of the Sun. Pindar, *Greek.* OBCVT, *tr. by* Thomas Love Peacock

All Erdly Joy Returns in Pane. William Dunbar. EnVB

All eyes were on Enceladus's face. Hyperion and Saturn. Keats. *Fr.* Hyperion. OAEL-2; Ro

All (Facts, Stories, Chance). C. S. Giscombe. BAP-96

All fathers in Western civilization must have. The Father of My Country. Diane Wakoski. NoAM; TAP

All feeling hearts must feel for him. The Coming Storm. Herman Melville. APN-2

All filthy facts, and secret acts. Michael Wigglesworth. NAAL-3 *Fr.* The Day of Doom. NAAL-1; SCAP

All fixed: early arrival at the flat. Nothing to Fear. Kingsley Amis. EP; OxBC; OxBoV

All Flesh Is Grass. Bible, *O.T.* TrJP *Fr.* Isaiah.

All flesh is grass, and so are feathers too. Epitaphs [*or* Epitaph] on Two Piping-Bullfinches of Lady Ossory's, Buried under a Rose-Bush in Her Garden. Horace, 4th Earl of Orford Walpole. FaBoEE; NOEC

All flesh waxeth old as a garment. Bible, Apocrypha. OBVE *Fr.* Ecclesiasticus.

All flock together, revel, celebrate! The Fourteenth of July. *Unknown, Vietnamese.* AVP, *tr. by* Huỳnh Sanh Thông

All folks who pretend to religion and grace. The Place of the Damned [*or* Damn'd]. Jonathan Swift. ChIV-2; FaBoEE; OBSV

All Fools' Day. *Unknown.* BoTP

(April Fool's Day.) CTV

All for her sake must the maiden die! (LL) Marriage. Mary Elizabeth Coleridge. LW; PEW; VWP

All for Love. Byron. *See* Stanzas Written on the Road between Florence and Pisa.

All freight, the sudden trains that uncouple my passage home. Freight Train, Freight Train. Alvin Greenberg. GM

All Friends Together. Ronald Albert Simpson. NOBAu

All gates were closed to him. What Bothered Him. David Avidan. *Fr.* Samson, Our Hero. IP, *tr. by* Warren Bargad *and* Stanley F. Chyet

All gentlemen and yeomen good. Robin Hood and the Shepherd. *Unknown.* ESPB

All glory cannot vanish from the hills. The Passing of the Forest. William Pember Reeves. PeNZ

All God's spades wear dark shades. Its Curtains. Ted Joans. PoBA

All goes onward and outward, nothing collapses. Walt Whitman. IMW *Fr.* Song of Myself. AmPP; MoAmPo; NAAL-3; NOBA; OxBA

All gone, / the silver-green silk of time. Immigrant Daughter's Song. Mary Ann Larkin. IIP

All grave old men, and souldiers they had bene, but for age. Homer. OBVE, *tr. by* George Chapman *Fr.* The Iliad.

All great events have harbingers. Nicarchus of Alexandria, *Greek.* GrAn, *tr. by* Peter Porter

All great men were ground to powder. Ivar Grunthal, *Estonian.* CEEP, *tr. by* Ivar Ivask

All great things crush themselves. Lucan, *Latin.* OBCVT, *tr. by* Marlowe

All great things crush themselves; such end the gods. Lucan, *Latin.* NoSic, *tr. by* Marlowe *Fr.* Pharsalia.

All Greece hates. Helen. Hilda Doolittle. BoWoP; ColAP; FaBoWP; LiTM; MoAmPo; NAAL-2; NALW; NMM-2; NOBA; NoAM; NoP-4; PoPoPo; TAP

All hail! Holy Mary, our hope and our joy! Irish Reaper's Harvest Hymn. John Keegan. TIRV

All hail, once pleasing, once inspiring shade. A Hymn Written in Windsor Forest. Alexander Pope. EBEV; NOEC; OxBSP

All hail the Power of Jesus' name! Edward Perronet. NOCV

All hail! thou gorgeous sunset. Sunset. Mary Weston Fordham. CBWP-2

All hail! thou noble Land. America to Great Britain. Washington Allston. APN-1

All hallelujahs, Oh ye heav'nly quires. A Poem upon the Triumphant Translation of. . . Mrs. Anne Eliot. John Danforth. SCAP

All Hallows. Louise Glück. AmPA; HCAP; PoPoPo

"All hands unmoor!" proclaims a boisterous cry. William Falconer. OxBoS *Fr.* The Shipwreck.

All has stilled, Magician Sleep having cast his spell. Those Last, Late Hours of Christmas Eve. Lou Ann Welte. PChr

All he owns is. Squirrel near Library. Genevieve Taggard. WPE

All heavy minds. Sir Thomas Wyatt. SiPS

All Hellas is his monument, though his bones. Euripides. Thucydides, *Greek.* GrAn, *tr. by* Peter Jay

All his children in the same house. Job the Father. Richard Shelton. PBCAP

All his hopes were hands, his ventures hands. The Hands. Tony Harrison. FaBoTw

All his life, Mr. George Bernard Shaw. Limerick. Audrey Herbert. PeLi

All histories commissioned by the winners. (LL) The Historical Judas. Howard Nemerov. NoP-4

All holy influences dwell within. The Children Band. Sir Aubrey De Vere. OBEV

"All honor to him, who shall win the fight." For Those Who Fail. Joaquin Miller. PoToHe

All honour to the persevering toil. The Press. Thomas Phipson. PeSAV

All houses wherein men have lived and died. Haunted Houses. Henry Wadsworth Longfellow. OxBSn; PWR

All how silent and how still. Noon. John Clare. OxAEP-2

All human kind on earth. Boethius, *Latin.* NoSic, *tr. by* Queen Elizabeth I *Fr.* Consolation of Philosophy, The ("De Consolacione Philosophie").

All human race would fain be wits. On Poetry: a Rhapsody. Jonathan Swift. OBSV

All human race would fain be wits. Jonathan Swift. HAP; OBSV; PoEL-3 *Fr.* On Poetry: a Rhapsody. OBSV

All Human Things. Peter Schroeder. BXAP

All human things are subject to decay. Approaching a Significant Birthday, He Peruses The Norton Anthology of Poetry. R. S. Gwynn. RA

All human[e] things are subject to decay. The Crown Prince of Dullness. Dryden. NOBE; NOSC; OBCoV; SCV *Fr.* MacFlecknoe; or, A Satire [*or* Satyr] upon the True-Blue [*or* -Blew] Protestant Poet T. S. CBNP; FHYEP; HAP; OAEL-1; OBSV; OxBoLi; PeLV; Poetr; TFi

All human things are subject to decay. MacFlecknoe; or, A Satire [*or* Satyr] upon the True-Blue [*or* -Blew] Protestant Poet T. S. Dryden. CABP; CBNP; FHYEP; HAP; NAEL-1; NoP-4; OAEL-1; OBSV; OxAEP-1; OxBoLi; PeLV; PoE; Poetr; TFi

(All hung with stars!), there still would be no bear. (LL) The Great Bear. John Hollander. ColAP; LiTM; NYBP; NoAM; TwCP

All hurts. Dear friends. Still Trees. Momcilo Nastasijevic, *Serbo-Croatian.* HSix, *tr. by* Charles Simic

All hushed and still within the house. Emily Jane Brontë. FaBoCh; NOBVV

All I can do is curse, complain. Cassandra's Answer. John Montague. BiHa

All I can do is to offer my testimony. (LL) Rattlesnake Country. Robert Penn Warren. NAAL-2; VCAP

All I can give you is broken-face gargoyles. Broken-Face Gargoyles. Carl Sandburg. AmPP; MoAmPo; OxBA

All I could see from where I stood. Edna St. Vincent Millay. MoAmPo *Fr.* Renascence. ColAP; MoAmPo

All I could see from where I stood. Renascence. Edna St. Vincent Millay. ColAP; MoAmPo

All I know is a door into the dark. The Forge. Seamus Heaney. NAEL-2; NoP-4; OxAEP-2

All I want in this creation's. Black-eyed Susie. *Unknown.* AmFP

All I want is the bread to turn out like hers just once. Luci Tapahonso. UnSA

All I want to say is that I do not know. Valediction—To My Father. Eddy Van Vliet, *Flemish.* VCWP, *tr. by* John Van Tiel

All I wanted was to brew him rhubarb wine. My First Forty Years. Kevin Ireland. PeNZ

All I wanted / was your / love. To Mother and Steve. Mari E. Evans. BPo; PoBA

All I Was Doing Was Breathing. Mirabai, *Rajasthani.* WPoS, *tr. by* Robert Bly

All ignorance toboggans into know. E. E. Cummings. MeMAP; NAAL-2; NOBA; OxBA

All Impelled Onward Alike. Robert Blair. OxAEP-1 *Fr.* The Grave.

All in a Garden Green. William Ernest Henley. OBMV

All-in-All seems here a Greek, The. (LL) The Attic Landscape. Herman Melville. NCAP; NOBA; OBAL

All, in Christ, his saints and heirs. Bible, *O.T. See* Psalm 148.

All in Due Time. James Vincent Cunningham. NIP-4

All in green went my love riding. E. E. Cummings. CMoP; HeIP-4; LiTM; MoP; NoAM; NoP-4; OxBA; PoRA

All in June. W. H. Davies. OxBSP

All in Red. Eileen Mathias. BoTP

All in the April evening [morning]. Sheep and Lambs. Katharine Tynan. BoTP; OBEV; TIRV

All in the diffidence that faltered. (LL) Canto 81. Ezra Pound. CMoP; FaBoMo; FaBoTw; HAP; MoP; NAAL-2; NOBA; NOBE; NoAM; OxBA; PoE; RaBo; VGW

All in the Downs the fleet was moored [or moor'd]. Sweet William's Farewell to Black-Eyed [or Black-Ey'd] Susan. John Gay. AmFP; BoLoP; CBLP; GLoP; GTBS-P; NOEC

All in the drowse of life I saw a shape. The Master-Mistress. Rose Cecil O'Neill. CPO

All in the merry month of May. Barbara Allen's Cruelty. *Unknown.* FaBoBe

All in this pleasant evening, together come are we. Old May Song. *Unknown.* BoTP; CH

All–intellectual eye, our solar round. James Thomson. NOEC *Fr.* To the Memory of Sir Isaac Newton.

All Intents. Larry Eigner. VGW

All Ireland's now one vessel's company. Fearghal Og MacWard. BIrV *Fr.* Flight of the Earls, The, 1607.

All Is Best. Milton. NOBE; NOSC; OBEV *Fr.* Samson Agonistes. FHYEP; OAEL-1; PoEL-3

All is closed in. Jane Cooper. *Fr.* The Weather of Six Mornings. NYBP

ALL IS COOL AND BOUNDLESS AS A ROLLING. For Monk. Michael McClure. SeSe

All is Emptiness, and I Must Spin. Thomas Kinsella. PBCIP

All is lithogenesis–or lochia. On a Raised Beach. "Hugh MacDiarmid." FaBoTC

All Is Not So Simple. Shin Shalom, *Hebrew.* MHP, *tr.* by Ruth Finer Mintz

All is nothing, nothing all. Robert Penn Warren. NOBA *Fr.* Tiberius on Capri.

All is One for Monk. Imamu Amiri Baraka. ISC

All is the same still. Earth and heaven locked in. Emily Brontë. C. Day Lewis. GTBS-P

All Is Vanity. Andreas Gryphius, *German.* GePo, *tr.* by George C. Schoolfield

'All Is Vanity, Saith the Preacher'. Byron. ChIV-1; KSG; TrCP

All its indifference is a different rage. (LL) Codicil. Derek Walcott. MoP; NoAM

All joy to mortals, joy and mirth. Song. Aphra Behn. WPE *Fr.* Emperor of the Moon.

All kings, and all their favo[u]rites. The Anniversary [or Anniversarie]. Donne. BoLoP; ESCV; FHYEP; FSCP; HAP; HoPM; ITG; LoP; MeLP; NOBE; NoP-4; NoSic; OAEL-1; OxBM; SCGP; SeCP; TFi; WeW-3

All-knowing God, 'tis thine to know. *Unknown.* AH

All last night I had quiet. Lascelles Abercrombie. FaBoTw

All Legendary Obstacles lay between. John Montague. BIrV; CIP-2; NOIV; NoP-4; PBCIP; PNI

All look or [or and] likeness caught from earth. Phantom. Samuel Taylor Coleridge, *Unknown, sometimes at. to.* NAEL-2; OAEL-2; OxBSP; PoEL-4

All looking down for the love of me. (LL) The Mermaid. Tennyson. BoTP

All looks be pale, hearts [or harts] cold as stone. A Lamentation. Thomas Campion. CH

All losses are restored and sorrows end. (LL) Sonnet 30. Shakespeare. CABP; NoP-4; PFE; PoPoPo

All love, all beauty. (LL) Dublinesque. Philip Larkin. NoAM; OxBC

All love is sacred, and the marriage-tie. Friendship. Katherine Philips. FP *Fr.* Friendship.

All Lovely Things. Conrad Potter Aiken. PoRA

All matronly in her stoop, her wings canted. The Black Angel. Henri Coulette. NYBP

All meet here with us, finally. Ostriches and Grandmothers! Imamu Amiri Baraka. NeAP

All men are bad and in their badness reign. (LL) Sonnet 121. Shakespeare. NoSic; OAEL-1; OxAEP-1; PoEL-2; SCGP

All men are brothers and each people is my own. My Song to the Jewish People. Leib Olitski, *Yiddish.* TrJP, *tr.* by Jacob Sonntag

All men are locked in their cells. Fall Down. Calvin C. Hernton. GT; PoBA

All men are worms [or wormes]: but this no man. In silk[e]. On Court-Worm[e]. Ben Jonson. SeCP

All men from all lands. Inscription for a Wayside Spring. Frances Darwin Cornford. BrRo

All men may hasty-gone happiness find. Shepherd-Song. Sigmund von Birken, *German.* GePo, *tr.* by George C. Schoolfield

All Men throughout the peopled Earth, *see also* "There is no race of men" *tr.* by Helen Waddell *and* "All human kind on earth" *tr.* by Elizabeth I. Book III. Metre 6. Boethius, *Latin.* OBCVT, *tr.* by Johnson, Samuel and Hester Thrale [later Piozzi] *Fr.* Consolation of Philosophy, The ("De Consolacione Philosophie").

All men wait for battle and when it comes. An Apple Tree and a Pig. Emyr Humphreys. OBWVE

All month a smell of burning, of dry peat. July 1914. "Anna Akhmatova," *Russian.* PeFWW, *tr.* by Stanley Kunitz and Max Hayward; WPOW, *tr.* by Stanley Kunitz, (Pt. I *only*)

All Morning. Terry Stokes. AmPA

All morning & early afternoon clouds swell the sky. Miller Canyon Trail No. 106. Michael Bowden. PuP-15

All morning, as I sit thinking of you. Monarchs. Sharon Olds. LoHo

All morning, I watch him. Sunday. Carl Phillips. GT

All morning long. The Next Story. Pattiann Rogers. NAmP90

All morning long I correct my books, changing "lu" to "yü". Li K'ai-hsien. *Fr.* Impromptu Poems. CoBLCP, *tr.* by Jonathan Chaves

All morning the dream lingers. Gregory Orr. TRP

All morning we saw flames in the distance. The Last Still Days in a Bunker. Walter McDonald. AF

All moves within the visual frame. A Monument. Charles Madge. FaBoMo

All music, sauces, feasts, delights and pleasures. Thomas Traherne. OxBSP *Fr.* Christian Ethics.

All must be used. Barracks Apt. 14. Theodore Weiss. CoAP; TAP

All my dead people. Over the Edge. Fleur Adcock. PeNZ

All my favourite characters have been. Mythology. Lawrence Durrell. OxBTC

All my friends can write them. Li K'ai-hsien. *Fr.* When I Recovered from an Illness After Returning Home To Live in Retirement, I Was Invited by My Friends to Join a Song-Lyric Club. CoBLCP, *tr.* by Jonathan Chaves

All my friends will come shouldering salvation. Morning-Selah. Amir Gilbo'a, *Hebrew.* IP, *tr.* by Warren Bargad *and* Stanley F. Chyet

All my future plans, dear. The Blue Room. Lorenz Hart. OBAL

All my girlfriends were talking about sex. Have You Ever Faked an Orgasm? Molly Peacock. BAP-95

All my life I have struggled from gentleness. Finale. Sue Lenier. LW

All my life/ they have told me. To You. Frank Horne. BPo *Fr.* Letters [or Notes] Found near a Suicide. PoBA

All my neckties. Sooner or Later. John Digby. SPE

All my other lives. (LL) Waxwings. Robert Francis. BLT; LCAP-2; RaBo

All my past life is mine no more. Love And Life. John Wilmot, 2d Earl of Rochester. BoLoP; EnLoPo; GBL; HAP; LoP; NOBE; NoP-4; NOSC; OBEV; PoEL-3

All My Pretty Ones. Anne Sexton. MoLi; NAAL-2; NoAM

All my pwoblems. Maybe Dats Your Pwoblem Too. Jim Hall. CMAP; MT

All my senses, like beacon's flame. 56. Greville Fulke *and* Sir Edward Dyer. CABP *Fr.* Caelica.

All my senses, like beacon's flame. Sonnet ("All my senses, like beacon's flame"). Greville Fulke. NOSC; NoSic; PoEL-1 *Fr.* Caelica.

All my sheep / Gather in a heap. Last Words before Winter. Louis Untermeyer. MoAmPo

All my shortcomings, in this year of grace. Dear Uncle Stranger. Conrad Potter Aiken. ColAP; NOBA; NoAM

All my stars forsake me. Song of the Night at Daybreak. Alice Thompson Meynell. CH

All my thoughts always speak to me of love. Sonnet. Dante. AWP *Fr.* La Vita Nuova.

All Nashville is a chill. And everywhere. A January Dandelion. George Marion McClellan. AAP

All Nature is a temple where the alive. Correspondences. Charles Baudelaire, *French.* AWP, *tr.* by Allen Tate

All Nature is but art, unknown to thee. Alexander Pope. ECEV *Fr.* An Essay on Man.

All Nature seems at work. Slugs leave their lair—. Work Without Hope. Coleridge. BoTP; GSo; LaPo; NAEL-2; NOBE; OBEV; OxAEP-2; Son

All Nature's Incense rise! (LL) The Universal Prayer [Deo Opt. Max.] Alexander Pope. BLPA; FaBoBe; NoP-4

All nearness pauses,while a star can grow. E. E. Cummings. NoAM

All night a noise of leaping fish. The Fisher. Roderic Quinn. CBAP

All night, all night. Interrogations of the Sparrow. Elizabeth Spires. FFC

All night by the rose, rose. *Unknown, Middle English.* GBL; HeIP-4; MiEL ("Alnight by the rose, rose.") EnVB

All night eerily! (LL) Voices from Things Growing in a Churchyard. Thomas Hardy. FaBoVe; OxBTC

All night fell hammers, shock on shock. A London Fete. Coventry Patmore. EBVV; EnVR; HAP; PeVV

All night had shout of men and cry. Easter Night. Alice Thompson Meynell. BrRo; ChIV-2

All night he craned with an unbending neck. Bateleur. Douglas Livingstone. PeSAV

All night I am the doe, breathing. The Strange People. Louise Erdrich. PoPoPo

All night I could not sleep. *Unknown.* BoWoP, *tr. by* Arthur Waley *Fr.* Tzu Yeh Songs.

   ("Nights are long and I cannot sleep.") CoBCP, *tr. by* Burton Watson

All night I could not sleep. Zi Ye. WPoS

All night I sat reading a book. The Reader. Wallace Stevens. SAmP

All night I walked among your spirits, Richard. A Mourning Letter from Paris. Conrad Kent Rivers. BPo

All night I weep[e], all day I cry, Ay me[e]. Song 2. Mary Sidney, Countess of Montgomery Wroth. NOSC *Fr.* Pamphilia to Amphilanthus.

All night it humps the air. Cannery Town in August. Lorna Dee Cervantes. NoAM

All Night Long. *Unknown.* AS

All Night Long, and every night. Young Night Thought. Robert Louis Stevenson. OTCP; PWR

All Night Long Fooling Me. *Unknown.* AmFP

All night long, I couldn't fall asleep. Listening to the Rain. K'ang Hai, *Chinese.* CoBLCP, *tr. by* Jonathan Chaves

All night long into my sleeping bag's head pad the blood. The Far Side of Introspection. Alfred M. Lee. CoAP

All night long the hockey pictures. To a Sad Daughter. Michael Ondaatje. NoAM

All night our room was outer-walled with rain. Summer Rain. Amy Lowell. CPO

All-night Taxi Stand, The. Kenneth Slessor. BMAP

All night the blind entrance of the children. Barren Poem. Michael Ryan. AmPA

All night, the camel-back saddle-cloth was invisible. The Next Day the Fog Was Even Worse. Yüan Mei, *Chinese.* CoBLCP, *tr. by* Jonathan Chaves

"All night the cicada chirps." Bible, *O.T., Hebrew.* ITG, *tr. by* Arthur Waley

All night the expensive Sthenelais I laid. Sthenelais. *Unknown, Greek.* GrAn, *tr. by* Guy Davenport

All night the sound had. The Rain. Robert Creeley. CoAP; CoAmPo; ColAP; PmAP; PoE; RaBo; TRP; VGW

All night the tall young man. Merlin and the Snake's Egg. Leslie Norris. OBSP

All night, the west wind blows over the capital. Snowstorm: At a Gathering at Chang Chu-fu's House, with Tzu-yeh Attending, We All Wrote Poems on This Subject—I Got the Ryhme-Word, "Hu." Tsung Ch'en, *Chinese.* CoBLCP, *tr. by* Jonathan Chaves

All night the west wind cuts the banana leaves. Tune: "Remembering the Prince." Na-lan Hsing-te, *Chinese.* SuSP, *tr. by* William Golightly

All night they marched, the infantrymen under pack. 1935. Stephen Vincent Benét. MoAmPo

All night they whine upon their ropes and boom. Nocturne of the Wharves. Arna Bontemps. BPo; ColAP; GT

All night, this headland. Sleepless at Crown Point. Richard Wilbur. InPK-6; WeW-3

All night vigil. Always Running. Luis J. Rodriguez. UnSA

All night waiting, in an empty house. The Streets of Air. Malcolm Cowley. PoA *Fr.* Blue Juniata.

All-Night Waitress, The. Maura Stanton. AmPA

All of a Sudden. Teresa de Jesús, *Spanish.* WPOW, *tr. by* Maria A. Proser, Arlene Scully *and* James Scully

All of a sudden the big nasturtiums. The Big Nasturtiums. Robert Beverly Hale. NYBP

All of a summer's day. (LL) Milton by Firelight. Gary Snyder. BB; CoAP; CoAmPo; InPS-3; NAAL-2; SAGP

All of her, but voice, is here. (LL) The Picture. Anacreon, *Greek.* AWP; GrIP, *tr. by* Thomas Stanley

All of the clothes she owns. The Onion Woman. Ted Kooser. IFJA

All of them are sitting. A Screened Porch in the Country. James Dickey. WeT

All of them the wind took, all of them the light lured. Alone. Hayyim Nahman Bialik, *Hebrew.* TrJP, *tr. by* Jessie Sampter

All of These. Denis Glover. PeNZ

All of those, ah go inciting those, all of *those.* Catullus. *See* Attis.

All of those sensuous bodies. Landscape with Nymphs and Satyrs. Norman Henry, II Pritchard. GT

All of us always turning away for solace. Delmore Schwartz. OxBA

All of us are sick, Sir. Family. Nissim Ezekiel. OBCoV *Fr.* Songs for Nandu Bhende.

All of us come from a village. From a Village. Ana Blandiana, *Romanian.* CEEP, *tr. by* Irina Livezeanu

All of Us Here. Irving Feldman.

   "Of course, we would wish them angelic lookouts." VCAP

   "Simple outlines, human shapes, daily acts, plain poses." VCAP

   "Surely they're just so large as their burdens allow." VCAP

All of us were there. Kaleidoscope. Maria Elena Cruz Varela, *Spanish.* VCWP, *tr. by* Mairym Cruz-Bernal *and* Deborah Digges

All of you are seeing me off, east of the Emperor's city. Wen Cheng-ming. CoBLCP, *tr. by* Jonathan Chaves *Fr.* Improvised on Horseback to Say Good-bye to Those Who Are Seeing Me Off.

All of you that pour the bath for Pallas. On the Bath of Pallas. Callimachus. HePo, *tr. by* Barbara Hughes Fowler *Fr.* Hymns.

All of your ideas. Andrew Crozier. NBrP *Fr.* High Zero.

All old women sometimes come to this. Old Women of Toronto. Miriam Waddington. NOBC

All on a frosty morning. (LL) The Mulberry Bush. *Unknown.* ACTP; LB

All on the road to Alibazan. Alibazan. Laura Elizabeth Richards. OBCA

All on the threshold, yet all short of life. (LL) A Triad. Christina Rossetti. NAEL-2; NALW; PBWP

All or Nothing. Bayard Taylor. BXAP

All other fair, like flowers, untimely fade. (LL) Sonnet 79: "Men call you fair [or fayre], and you do[e] credit it." Edmund Spenser. AWP; FaBoBe; NAEL-1; Son

All other joys I shall contemn, / Calling to mind Jerusalem. Bible, *O.T. See* Psalm 137.

All other joys of life he strove to warm. George Meredith. EnVR *Fr.* Modern Love.

All other love is like the mone. *Unknown.* MiEL

All other things, to their destruction draw. Our Love Hath No Decay. Donne. LBC

All others talked as if. Caedmon. Denise Levertov. NoAM; NoP-4

"All our French poets can turn an inspired line." The Nihilist as Hero. Robert Lowell. VCAP

All Our Joy Is Enough. Geoffrey Scott. OBMV

All our lives. Tall Buildings. Munib-ur-Rahman, *Urdu.* OMIP, *tr. by* Kathleen Grant Jaeger *and* Baidar Bakht

All our roads go nowhere. On Inhabiting an Orange. Josephine Miles. NoAM; PoA

All our stones like as much sun as possible. Forecast. Josephine Miles. NoAM

All out for Illinois Central. Calling Trains. *Unknown.* AmFP

All out-of-doors looked darkly in at him. An Old Man's Winter Night. Robert Frost. AFr; AWP; HAP; MoAmPo; NAAL-2; NoAM; OxBA; VGW

All over America women are burning dinners. What's That Smell in the Kitchen? Marge Piercy. NBLV; NIP-4

All over the plain of the world lovers are being hurt. Christian Karlson Stead. PeNZ *Fr.* Quesada.

All over the world, Little Bees, Star Scouts. Feminism. Denise Duhamel. BAP-93; IFJA

All passes. Art alone. Austin Dobson. CTC *Fr.* Ars Victrix.

All Paths Lead to You. Blanche Shoemaker Wagstaff. BLPA; FaBoBe

All people that on earth do dwell, *metrical vers. by* William Kethe. Bible, *O.T. See* Psalm 100.

All people that on earth do dwell. Old Hundredth. William Kethe. FaPoR; NOCV; PeECV

All perished—brides and infants. Song of a Jewish Boy. "M. J.," *Polish.* TrJP, *tr. by* A. Glanz-Leyeles

All plants and flowers yearn for their east wind. Waiting for the East Wind. Nguyễn Đình Chiểu, *Vietnamese.* AVP, *tr. by* Huỳnh Sanh Thông

All plants grow here; the most minute. The Garden of the Gods. Thom Gunn. GaP

All Possession Is Theft. Lauris Edmond. PeNZ

All power is saved, having no end. The Dam. Muriel Rukeyser. PFTM

All praise to thee, for thou, O king divine. F. Bland Tucker. AH

All praise to Thee, my God, this night. An Evening Hymn. Thomas Ken. OxBChV

All praise to thee, O Ra! The Body of the Great Cat. Felicity Bast. PC

All praise your face, your verses none abuse. Horace, 4th Earl of Orford Walpole. FaBoEE

All profits disappear: the gain. The Reckoning. Theodore Roethke. PoA

All projects failed, in the August afternoon. Henry's Fate. John Berryman. ColAP

All Quiet, (For Robert Bly) Written at the start of one of our bombing pauses over North Vietnam. David Ignatow. CoAmPo

All quiet along the Potomac tonight. Ethel Lynn Beers, *sometimes at. to* Lamar Fontaine. CBCWP; FaBoBe

All right, gentlemen who cry blue murder as always. Draft of a Reparations Agreement. Dan Pagis, *Hebrew.* AF; HP; PoSu, *tr. by* Stephen Mitchell

All right, I may have lied to you, and about you. Love, 20 Cents the First Quarter Mile. Kenneth Fearing. HAP

All right, I'll die, my spirit is strong. Fear. Vittoria Aganoor Pompili, *Italian.* PBWP, *tr. by* Brenda Webster

All right. Let's hear it. Family Reunion. Anne S. Perlman. CMAP

All right now, listen to me right good. Unloading Rails. *Unknown.* AmFP

All right. Try this. Northern Pike. James Wright. NAAL-2

All right with me, / You are. (LL) Poem: "Little brown boy." Helene Johnson. PoBA

All rites pertaining to his maried state. (LL) New light gives new directions, Fortunes new. George Chapman. PBRV

All round the Browns stretched forty acres of potatoes. The Brown Family. Colleen Thibaudeau. NOBC

All round the horizon black clouds appear. On a Sea-Storm nigh the Coast. Richard Steere. SCAP

All round us / Lies the promised land. Limbo. Husein Tahmisic, *Serbian.* CEEP, *tr. by* Ewald Osers

All Saints' Day. Margherita Guidacci, *Italian.*

"All Saints' Day; November sky." PBWP, *tr. by* Ruth Feldman *and* Brian Swann (b. 1940)

All saints revile her, and all sober men. The White Goddess. Robert Graves. MoBrPo; NAEL-2; NoP-4; OAEL-2

All sea is sea. How mad it is to blame. Antipater of Thessalonica, *Greek.* GrAn, *tr. by* Alistair Elliot

All seas, all ships. (LL) Song for All Seas, All Ships. Walt Whitman. APN-1; CH; FaBoBe

All Seasons in One. *Unknown.* GBL; HeIP-4

All Seasons Shall Be Sweet. Coleridge. BoTP

All seasons shall be sweet to thee. Coleridge. *See* The Silent Icicles.

All shiny in your mind! (LL) Some People. Rachel Lyman Field. ChAP; NTCP

All silence keep, both goats and sheep. Michael Wigglesworth. NAAL-3 *Fr.* The Day of Doom. NAAL-1; SCAP

All silence says music will follow. Onion Bucket. Lorenzo Thomas. GT; PoBA

All songs / are tattoos. The Singer. Diane Wakoski. HeIP-4

All sorts of men through various labours presse. Verses Written by Mrs. Hutchinson. Lucy Hutchinson. KTR; NOSC

All Souls. May Sarton. CrSp; IMW

All Soul''s Day. D. H. Lawrence. LBC

All Souls' Night. Frances Darwin Cornford. EnLoPo; LBC; OxBSP; OxBTC

("Nor I, him.") (LL) LBC

All Souls' Night. W. B. Yeats. OxAEP-2 *Fr.* A Vision.

All Splendor on Earth. Karin Kiwus, *German.* BoWoP, *tr. by* Almut McAuley

All Still. William Barnes. NOBVV

All strangest things the multitudinous years. Speech of Ajax. Sophocles, *Greek.* OBCVT, *tr. by* Charles Stuart Calverley

All such proclivities are tabulated. The Quiet Glades of Eden. Robert Graves. BoLoP; EP

All suddenly a stormy whirlwind blew. The Mask of Cupid. Edmund Spenser. *Fr.* Wood Of Error. AEP

All summer I heard them / rustling in the shrubbery. The Snakes of September. Stanley Kunitz. AFr; ColAP

All summer long the smartypants. A Poem in Response to Doom. William Hathaway. NAmP90

All that blazing day, swift-breasted swallows, envious crows, grackles in trees. Thunderstorm in South Dakota. Kay Boyle. WPE

All that blesses the step of the antelope. Else a great Prince in prison lies. Denise Levertov. VGW

All that Friday. An Ulster Unionist Walks the Streets of London. Tom Paulin. PNI

All That Glisters Is Not Gold. Shakespeare. CTC *Fr.* The Merchant of Venice.

All That Glitters. Maureen Owen. PmAP

All that he is. . . does. . . is attractive. Meleager, *Greek.* GrAn, *tr. by* Peter Whigham

All that I am. Verna Arvey. AH

All that I am hangs by a thread tonight. The Muse. "Anna Akhmatova," *Russian.* TCRP, *tr. by* Stanley Kunitz *with* Max Hayward

All that I do is clumsy and ill timed. The Double-Goer. Daryl Hine. MoCV

All that I had I brought. Exchanges. Ernest Christopher Dowson. OBMV

All that I have. Handfuls of Wind. Yekhi'el [*or* Yehiel] Mar, *Hebrew.* MHP, *tr. by* Ruth Finer Mintz

All that I may swynk or swet. Care Away. *Unknown.* OxBoLi

All that I ran from. The Mood. Quandra Prettyman. PoBA

All that I saw was China, China, China. (LL) Digging for China. Richard Wilbur. ImGa; TwCP

All that I was, became really—my past. Home. Ivan Zhdanov, *Russian.* TCRP, *tr. by* John High

All that I wrote in love, for love of art. (LL) A Plea to Boys and Girls. Robert Graves. GTBS-P; NAEL-2

All That Is Left. Basho, *Japanese.* AWP, *tr. by* Curtis Hidden Page

All that is left and definite. Michael Hartnett. NOIV

All that is left me. Elektra's Keening. Sophocles, *Greek.* OBCVT, *tr. by* Ezra Pound and Rudd Fleming

All That Is Lovely in Men. Robert Creeley. RaBo

All that is moulded of iron. Woodworker's Ballad. Herbert Edward Palmer. OBEV

All that it should be. Andrew Crozier. NBrP *Fr.* High Zero.

All that I've never thought of—think of me! (LL) A Sick Child. Randall Jarrell. InPK-6; NoP-4; OxBC; VGW

All that matters is to be at one with the living God. Pax. D. H. Lawrence. EnlH; PeECV; TrCP

All that past life. Tanka. Saitō Mokichi, *Japanese.* MJT, *tr. by* Makoto Ueda

All that running water outside. The Marshes. Jane Mayhall. TAP

All that was promis'd by the Spring. (LL) To a Very Young Lady. Edmund Waller. SCGP; SeCP

. . . All that winter, in the black cold, the buzz-saw screamed and whistled. Thomas McGrath. PaTW *Fr.* Letter to an Imaginary Friend.

All That You Have Given Me, Africa. Anoma Kanié, *French.* PBWP, *tr. by* Kathleen Weaver

All that you lost, they told me, is yours. Boundaries. José Emilio Pacheco, *Spanish.* STV, *tr. by* John Frederick Nims

All that you send: the unexpected disaster. My Country. Olga Fiodorovna Berggolts, *Russian.* TCRP, *tr. by* Daniel Weissbort

All that you've danced they take from you. Last Waltz in Santiago. Ariel Dorfman, *Spanish.* AF, *tr. by* Ariel Dorfman *and* Edith Grossman

All That's Past. Walter De la Mare. NOBE; OAEL-2; OBMV; OxBTC

All the afternoon there has been a chirping of birds. Free Fantasia on Japanese Themes. Amy Lowell. MoAmPo

All the air quivers, and the east sky glows. (LL) A Front. Randall Jarrell. NoP-4; OBWP; OxBC; PoWW; VGW

All the bells of heaven may ring. A Child's Laughter. Swinburne. NTP; PoLF

All the black same I dance my blue head off! (LL) King David Dances. John Berryman. ChIV-1; KSG; OxBC; OxBSP

All the blue flowers open. (LL) Resurrection of the Right Side. Muriel Rukeyser. LCAP-2; NMM-2

All the boys always wanted her, so. Leda's Sister and the Geese. Katharyn Machan Aal. SoSe-8

All the cages are empty. The Two Selves. Margaret Avison. MoP

All the cattle are resting in the fields. Poem to the Sun. *Ancient Egyptian Oral Tradition.* TTTS, *tr. by* Christopher Wertz

All the children on this ward are dying of AIDS. The Sacrament of Poverty. Marilyn Nelson Waniek. GT

All the Cilicians are bad. Demodocus, *Greek.* GrAn, *tr. by* Alistair Elliot

All the day I worked and played. A Labourer's Wife. John Davidson. EBVV *Fr.* To the Street Piano.

All the Dead Dears. Sylvia Plath. CAPP-1

All the death-room needs. Michael Hartnett. CIP-2

All the dreary Sunday morning. Ted Hughes. HAP, *sect.* 6 *Fr.* Skylarks.

All the earth where she could open at it. XX. P. Inman. FTOS

All the family dogs are dead. Transfer. Ingrid De Kok. BAP-96

All the flies are reading microscopic books. Serious Readers. Peter Redgrove. OxBC

All the flowers of the spring. Vanitas Vanitatum. John Webster. CH; ImPo; NOBE; NOSC; OBEV; PoEL-2; PoRA; SCGP *Fr.* The Devil's Law Case.

All the forms are fugitive. Ralph Waldo Emerson. *Fr.* Woodnotes II ("As sunbeams stream through liberal space"). NOBA

All the full-moon night in the coomb. In the Night of the Full Moon. Carl Busse, *German.* AWP, tr. by Jethro Bithell

All the generations before me. Yehuda Amichai, *Hebrew.* PoSu, tr. by Harold Schimmel

All the here and all the there. Our Two Worthies. John Crowe Ransom. OBAL

All the Hills and Vales Along. Charles Hamilton Sorley. EBEV; FaBoCh; MoBrPo; NSI; OBWP; OxAEP-2; PeFWW; PoWW

All the Hosts of Heaven speak the mighty word. Simeon ben, of Mainz Isaac ben Abun, *Hebrew.* TrJP, tr. by Nina Davis Salaman

All the hot night. Masaoka Shiki, *Japanese.* OHMPJ, tr. by Kenneth Rexroth

All the lights in the house are burning. Blue Elliptic. Joy Harjo. NAmP90

All the Little Animals. Muriel Rukeyser. FiLi

All the lizards are asleep. Nature Study. Craig Raine. NoAM

All the long evening. Automedon, *Greek.* InMo, tr. by Sam Hamill

All the long night we talked of your long hair. Ode 173. Hafiz, *Persian.* EP, tr. by Richard Le Gallienne

All the Maenads had. Haiku: After The Orgies. Gavin Ewart. APAD

All the male poets write of orpheus. Euridice. "Alta." NMM-2

All the materials of a poem. Lumber of Spring. Anne Ridler. NYBP

All the mill-horses of Europe. The Discovery of America. James Logie Robertson. NOBVV

All the more. Tanka. Tawara Machi, *Japanese.* MJT, tr. by Makoto Ueda

All the morning I have lain snugly in bed. Rising Late, and Playing with A-ts'ui, Aged Two. Po Chü-i, *Chinese.* ChiP, tr. by Arthur Waley

All the new thinking is about loss. Meditation at Lagunitas. Robert Hass. ColAP; NoP-4; VCAP

All the night / And all day long. Blacksmith. B. K. Pyke. BoTP

All the night in woe. The Little Girl Found. William Blake. FHYEP; NOBRP; Ro *Fr.* Songs of Innocence.

All the night in woe. The Little Girl Found. William Blake. FHYEP; NOBRP *Fr.* Songs of Experience.

All the night sleep came not upon my eyelids. Sapphics. Sappho, *Greek.* PoEL-5; OBCVT, tr. by Algernon Charles Swinburne

All, the Nothing, The. Yves Bonnefoy, *French.* VCWP, tr. by Lisa Sapinkopf

All the opportunities we miss by being born too soon! Born Too Soon. John Fuller *and* James Fentonr. OBCoV

All the others translate: the painter sketches. The Composer. W. H. Auden. MeMAP

All the pages inside me are blank. Letter. Wayne Dodd. CMAP

All the Past We Leave Behind. Walt Whitman. AH

All the perversions of the soul. A Small Farm. Michael Hartnett. CIP-2; PBCIP

All the pink-coloured horses are coming in. Horses. Mahadai Das. HCP

All the planets in heaven, all the stars. Gaspara Stampa, *Italian.* NNPT, tr. by Sally Purcell

All the Pretty Little Horses. *Unknown.* AmFP; OxBoLi; TTTS

All the promises of the world are lies. The Promises of the World. Moses ibn Ezra. *Fr.* The World's Illusion. TrJP, tr. by Solomon Solis-Cohen

All the Roary Night. Kenneth Patchen. LiTM

All the sailors on deck have mended their many years. (LL) Snowfall in the Afternoon. Robert Bly. NOBA; SPE

All the same, it would make you laugh. Michael Hartnett, *Irish.* CIP-2, tr. by Michael Hartnett

All the sexually active people in Westport. The Chaste Stranger. James Tate. NoAM

All the silly threatening things. Yona Wallach, *Hebrew.* IP, tr. by Warren Bargod *and* Stanley F. Chyet

All the Sioux were defeated. Our clan. Report to Crazy Horse. William Stafford. NoAM

All the sisters of mercy. Canto Llano. Anita Endrezze-Danielson. CDW

All the skippers o Scarsburgh. Young Allan. *Unknown.* ESPB

All the soldiers marching along. Remembering Day. Mary Wright Saunders. CTV

All the Spirit Powers Went to Their Dancing Place. Gary Snyder. UnPo

All the stars turn away their faces. Sappho, *Greek.* InMo, tr. by Sam Hamill

All the summer night / Threading dances light? (LL) Angel spirits of sleep. Robert Bridges. CH; OBEV

All the sweets of life in love. Catullus. *See* Carmen 5 ("My sweetest Lesbia, let us live and love").

All the things. The objects. Cold Term. Imamu Amiri Baraka. BPo

All the time they were praying. The Death Bed. Waring Cuney. PFE

All the toys of the world would break. (LL) Love Poem: "My clumsiest dear, whose hands shipwreck vases." John Frederick Nims. HoPM; InPK-6; SAGP

All the trees they are so high. The Trees So High. *Unknown.* OxBoLi

All the voices of the wood called "Muriel!" Then I Saw What the Calling Was. Muriel Rukeyser. ColAP; FaBoWP

All the way. Tanka. Tsukamoto Kunio, *Japanese.* MJT, tr. by Makoto Ueda

All the way across the Bay Bridge I sang. Buying and Selling. Philip Levine. WWSi

All the Way Back. Laura Riding Jackson. *Fr.* Forgotten Girlhood. RB

All the way home the ground. Like Deer Our Bodies. Wayne Dodd. CMAP

All the way to the hospital. The Almond Tree. Jon Stallworthy. NoAM

All the while among. Fragrance of Life, Odor of Death. Denise Levertov. AF

All the while, believe me, I prayed. Sappho, *Greek.* BoWoP, tr. by Willis Barnstone

All the while I was quite happy. (LL) Nikki-Rosa. Nikki Giovanni. BlSi; CrSp; FaBoA; GT; HeIP-4; ISC; MoP; NAAAL; PBMP; PoBA; SSLK; TAP; UnSA

All the whole world is living without war. Canzone: He Speaks of His Condition through Love. Folcachiero de' Folcachieri, *Italian.* AWP, tr. by D. G. Rossetti

All the wives of my father. Song of the Initiate. Patrice Kayo. PBMAP

All the Women Caught in Flaring Light. Minnie Bruce Pratt. CPO

All the women who leave tell me they're happy. Streamers. Sandra McPherson. VCAP

All the words that I utter. Where My Books Go. W. B. Yeats. OBEV

All the world for love may die. (LL) His Excuse for Loving. Ben Jonson. NOSC; PoEL-2

All the world moved next to me strange. June Jordan. GT; PoBA

All the world shall come to serve Thee. *Unknown, Hebrew.* TrJP, tr. by Israel Zangwill

All the world's a school. Schoolmaster. George Rostrevor Hamilton. FaBoEE

"All the World's a Stage," *ballad, with music.* Victor Gray. NBLV; PeLi

All the world's a stage. The Seven Ages of Man. Shakespeare. APAD; EBEvV; FaPoR; ImPo; PoLF; RB; SAGP; UV *Fr.* As You Like It.

All the years waiting, the whole, barren, young. Sex. Jean Valentine. FaBoWP

All the young men I know. Tanka. Toki Zenmaro, *Japanese.* MJT, tr. by Makoto Ueda

All their clothes. (LL) August. John Updike. AYFP

All their lives in a box! What generations. The Silkworms. Douglas Stewart. CBAP

All their names were Vincent, Ernie, Paul. Miriam Kessler. IFJA

All their pipes were still. Praise of Spenser. William Browne. OxAEP-1

All There Is to Know about Adolph Eichmann. Leonard Cohen. InPK-6

All These Are Vile. Keats. OBCoV

All These Birds. Richard Wilbur. NOBA

All these [*or* those] heads these ears these eyes. Song of the Old Woman. *Unknown, Eskimo in French.* BoWoP, tr. by Paul-Emile Victor; *English vers* by Armand Schwerner

All these illegitimate babies. Valuable. Stevie Smith. OxBTC

All these journeys. Ferry Me Across. B. P. Nichol. FTOS

All these maneuverings to avoid. Love's Stratagems. Donald Justice. NYBP

All these stones, all this sadness, all. Yehuda Amichai. *Fr.* Songs of the Land of Zion Jerusalem. IP, tr. by Warren Bargod *and* Stanley F. Chyet

All these years behind windows. The Animals. W. S. Merwin. VCAP

All things. Hadewijch II, *Flemish.* WPoS, tr. by Jane Hirshfield

All things are doubly fair. Art. Théophile Gautier, *French.* AWP, tr. by George Santayana

All things are people, or were, or will be. Paper Clip, Historian, Coathanger. Frank Murphy. EC3

All things are real. Letter to a Friend: Who Is Nancy Daum? James Schuyler. PmAP

"All things become thee, being thine," I think sometimes. Woman. Randall Jarrell. CBLP; NOBA

All things bright and beauteous. Cecil Frances Alexander. FaPoR; OxBchV; TIRV; UV

  ("Who doeth all things well.") (LL) CTV

  ("Who has made all things well!") (LL) ACTP; ChAP; VWP

All things can tempt me from this craft of verse. W. B. Yeats. CMoP; OxBSP

All things come to pass. My Name Is Afrika. Keorapetse Kgositsile. PoBA

All Things Confine. Hadewijch, *Dutch.* PBWP, tr. by Frans van Rosevelt

All Things Decay and Die. Robert Herrick. CaPo

All Things Drink. Thomas Stanley, *after the Greek of* Anacreon. AWP

All things dull and ugly. "Monty Python." UV

All things felt sweet were felt sweet overmuch. The Two Dreams. Giovanni Boccaccio, *Italian*. OBGa, *tr. by* Algernon Charles Swinburne

All things I can endure, save one. Magdalen. Amy Levy. VWP

All things in nature are beautiful types to the soul that can read them. Correspondences. Christopher Pearse Cranch. APN-1; PAR

All things in this life that he could. (LL) The Performance. James Dickey. CoAP; CoAmPo; LiTM; MoP; PoE; SAGP; WeT

All things innocent, hapless, forsaken. (LL) The Meadow Mouse. Theodore Roethke. ChAP; HeIP-2; RB; TRP

All things pass. Lao Tzu, *Chinese*. APAD, *tr. by* Timothy Leary

All things remain in God. (LL) Crazy Jane on God. W. B. Yeats. CMoP; EBEV; OxBTC; RACG

All things save Beauty alone. (LL) Envoi (1919). Ezra Pound. HAP; MoAmPo; MoP; OxBA; UnPo; VGW

All things that go deep enough. The Ice Skin. James Dickey. NYBP

All things that pass / Are woman's looking-glass. Passing and Glassing. Christina Rossetti. OBNC

All things that Peter saw and felt. Shelley. EPCY *Fr.* Peter Bell the Third.

All things that wake enjoy the sun. Laura Riding Jackson. ColAP

All things uncomely and broken, all things worn out and old. The Lover Tells of the Rose in His Heart. W. B. Yeats. CMoP; MoBrPo

All things within this fading world hath [*or* have] end. Before the Birth of One of Her Children. Anne Bradstreet. BoWoP; ColAP; KTR; NAAL-1; NAAL-3; NOBA; NoP-4; OxBM; PEW; PeECV; WPE; WPOW

All this indigo, nonviolent light will triumph. Sunday Evenings. John Hollander. NYBP

All this is my time. No time to seek disguise. There'll be. Ory Bernstein, *Hebrew*. IP, *tr. by* Warren Bargad *and* Stanley F. Chyet

All this is pretty, it could not be prettier. Stevie Smith. *See* Pretty.

All this is true without deceit. (LL) Every lady in this land. Mother Goose. OxNR; ReMoGo

All this she told with some confusion and. Byron. OxBSn *Fr.* Don Juan.

All this time I had forgotten. Girl at the Chu Lai Laundry. Bruce Weigl. CDa

All, this will be about all. (LL) Balloon Faces. Carl Sandburg. CMoP; PoE

All those buffalos have green horns. A Song of the Red & Green Buffalo. *Unknown, Oto Indian*. STP, *tr. by* William Whitman

All those sleep shapes, crystalline. Paul Celan, *German*. VCWP, *tr. by* Michael Hamburger

All those summers, waiting. Waiting for You to Come By. Simon J. Ortiz. CDW

All those times I was bored. Bored. Margaret Atwood. BAP-95

All those treasures that lie in the little bolted box whose tiny space is. Slow Movement. William Carlos Williams. PoA

All those who, over the sorrows of strangers, led their spirits to dance and *to* delight. From All Sides Laughter Shall Strike Them. Amir Gilbo'a, *Hebrew*. MHP, *tr. by* Ruth Finer Mintz

All those women working. Working. Maxine Scates. PBCAP

All those years that you ate and changed. Peasant. W. S. Merwin. NYBP

All thoughts, all passions, all delights. Love. Coleridge. GTBS-P; OBEV

All Thoughts and Eyes were fix'd upon the Queen. Death of Camilla. Virgil, *Latin*. OBCVT, *tr. by* Nicholas Brady

All three Christs in a locked room for a year—sharing meals. The First Six Seals. David Wojahn. PUP-18

All thro' the breathing night there seemed to flow. A Venetian Night. Hugo von Hofmannsthal, *German*. AWP, *tr. by* Ludwig Lewisohn

All through spring, nothing but wind and rain. Tune: "Bean Leaves Yellow." Lu Yu, *Chinese*. SuSp, *tr. by* James J. Y. Liu

All through that summer at ease we lay. The Castle. Edwin Muir. FaBoTC

All through the day, little peach blossoms in the garden. Little Peach Blossoms in the Garden. Li Shang-yin, *Chinese*. SuSp, *tr. by* Eugene Eoyang *and* Irving Y. Lo

All through the march, besides bag and blanket. Crazed Man in Concentration Camp. Agnes Gergely, *Hungarian*. BoWoP, *tr. by* Edwin Morgan

All through the moonlight sighs an autumn wind. A Song of Sorrow Inside the Royal Harem. Nguyễn Gia Thiều, *Vietnamese*. AVP, *tr. by* Huỳnh Sanh Thông

All Through the Night. *Unknown*. ACTP

All through the night among the unseen hills. Trains in France. Winifred Holtby. WPN

All through the night the happy. The Happy Sheep. Wilfrid Thorley. CTV

All through the Rains. Gary Snyder. CoAmPo

All through the stranger's wood I strolled. Isaac Leibush Peretz, *Yiddish*. TrJP, *tr. by* Joseph Leftwich

All through the valley, the people are whispering. Return of the Wolves. Anita Endrezze-Danielson. HATNAP

All through the windless night the clipper rolled. John Masefield. CMoP *Fr.* Dauber.

All to Myself. Wilbur Dick Nesbit. BLPA

All today I lie in the bottom of the wardrobe. Yoko. Thom Gunn. NoAM

All tongues speak of him, and the bleared sights. Shakespeare. FaBoPV *Fr.* Coriolanus.

All Too Late. *Unknown*. EBEV; OAEL-1

All travellers [*or* travelers] at first incline. Stella's Birthday, 1721. Jonathan Swift. NAEL-1; OxAEP-1; PoEL-3

All trembling in my arms Aminta lay. The Dream. Aphra Behn. PBWP; RACG *Fr.* A Voyage to the Isle of Love.

All tropic places smell of mold. Karl Shapiro. VGW

All truths wait in all things. Walt Whitman. ColAP *Fr.* Song of Myself.

All under the leaves, the leaves of life. The Seven Virgins. *Unknown*. CH; OBEV

All Virgil's idylls end in sunsets; pale. The Voice. Edmund Wilson. NYBP

All walking leans to the left. Pencilled by the Rain. Peter Hooper. PeNZ

All was as it is, before the beginning began, before. Jacob. Delmore Schwartz. ChIV-1

All was in flight. The Wind Was There. Bravig Imbs. SPE

All was quiet in this park. Pain. Mbella Sonne Dipoko. PBMAP

All was taken away from you: white dresses. On Angels. Czeslaw Milosz, *Polish*. AF, *tr. by* Czeslaw Milosz

All was winter and chill. Christmas Star. Boris Pasternak, *Russian*. TCRP, *tr. by* Yakov Hornstein

All waters as the shore. . (LL) Ave atque Vale. Swinburne. NAEL-2; NOBE; OAEL-2; OBEV; OBNC

All We Ask Is Justice. Mrs. Henry Linden. CBWP-4

All we can hope to leave them now is money. (LL) Homage to a Government. Philip Larkin. EBEV; FaBoPV; NoAM

All we make is enough. All Our Joy Is Enough. Geoffrey Scott. OBMV

All we were going strong last night this time. Sonnet 115. John Berryman. APAD; FaBoMo *Fr.* Sonnets to Chris.

All week she watched. The Silos. Nancy Paddock. LoHo

All were to[o] little for the merchant's [*or* merchauntes] hand[e]. George Gascoigne. AAS; Son *Fr.* Gascoigne's Memories.

All which isn't singing is mere talking. E. E. Cummings. VGW

All who are sick at heart and cry in bitterness. The Garden of Song. Moses ibn Ezra, *Hebrew*. TOF, *tr. by* David Goldstein

All who have loved, be sure of this from me. Richard Watson Dixon. OBNC *Fr.* Love's Consolation.

All Wild Animals Were Once Called Deer. Brigit Pegeen Kelly. BAP-95

All winds died this hot day. *Unknown. Fr.* Summer. SuSp, *tr. by* Michael E. Workman *Fr.* Tzu-yeh Songs of the Four Seasons.

All winter long you listened for the boom. The Stoic: for Laura von Courten. Edgar Bowers. CoAP; MT

All winter through I bow my head. The Scarecrow. Walter De la Mare. MoBrPo; OxBTC

All winter your brute shoulders strained against collars, padding. Names of Horses. Donald Hall. AFr; HAP; InPK-6; SoSe-8; TRP

All wished for a piece in hand. (LL) The Tragical Death of A, Apple Pie. Mother Goose. LB; OxNR

All women are beautiful as they rise. Poem for Easter. Robert Kelly. VGW

All women loved dance in a dying light. They Sing. Theodore Roethke. NYBP

All words forgotten— / Thou, Lord, and I. (LL) The Scribe. Walter De la Mare. CMoP; EBEvV; FaBoCh; OBMV; TrCP

All work and no play makes Jack a dull boy. *Unknown*. OxNR

All worldly shapes shall melt in gloom. The Last Man. Thomas Campbell. NOBRP

All Writing Is Garbage. Antonin Artaud, *French*. PFTM, *tr. by* Helen Weaver

All wrong. Charles Olson. NoAM *Fr.* Songs of Maximus. NeAP *Fr.* The Maximus Poems.

All ye nations, pause a moment! listen to the Negro's voice. The Voice of the Negro. Lizelia Augusta Jenkins Moorer. CBWP-3

All ye poets of the age. Namby-Pamby. Henry Carey. CBNP; NOEC; OBSV; UV

All Ye That Go Astray. Moses ibn Ezra. *Fr.* The World's Illusion. TrJP, *tr. by* Solomon Solis-Cohen

All ye that handle harp and viol. Chorus. Moses Hayyim, of Padua Luzzatto. TrJP, *tr. by* Nina Davis Salaman *Fr.* Unto the Upright Praise.

All ye that pass along Love's trodden way. Dante. AWP *Fr.* La Vita Nuova.

All ye that passe be [*or* by] this holy place. *Unknown*. MiEL

All ye who, far from town, in rural hall. On a Wet Summer. John Codrington Bampfylde. NOEC

All ye woods, and trees, and bowers. The God of Sheep. John Fletcher. FaBoCh *Fr.* The Faithful Shepherdess.

All Year Long. *Unknown, Chinese.* OHMPC, *tr. by* Kenneth Rexroth

All year long, he never visits his mine. The Merchant's Joy. Chang Yü, *Chinese.* CoBLCP, *tr. by* Jonathan Chaves

All year, Mozart went under. To a Daughter at Fourteen Forsaking the Violin. Carole Oles. WeW-3

All year the flax-dam festered in the heart. Death of a Naturalist. Seamus Heaney. HAP; NoAM; OxBC; WeW-3

All you are doing and saying is to America dangled mirages. To a President. Walt Whitman. NAAL-1; NAAL-3

All you can about animals as persons. What You Should Know to Be a Poet. Gary Snyder. APSN; NNaP; PoM

All you lords of Scotland ffaire. Tom Potts. *Unknown.* ESPB

All You Others, Eat. Djurberaui, *Aborigine.* NOBAu, *tr. by* Catherine H. Berndt

All you that are single and wild in your ways. Old Maids. *Unknown.* AmFP

All you that delight to spend some time. Little John a Begging. *Unknown.* ESPB

All you that desire to here of a jest. The Unfortunate Miller; or, The Country Lasses Witty Invention. *Unknown.* OxBB

All you violated ones with gentle hearts. For Malcolm X. Margaret Abigail Walker. BPo; NAAAL; PoBA; Son

All you who sleep tonight. Vikram Seth. APAD

All you who would, of your whole life. All Come to Me. Nguyễn Chí Thiện, *Vietnamese.* AVP, *tr. by* Huỳnh Sanh Thông

All young men dream. The Bind. Wayne Brown. PBCV

All your days are holy days. Lullaby for Rachael. James Simmons. PNI

Allace departing, gruid of wo. Fairweill. *Unknown.* OxBS

Allace! So Sobir Is the Micht. Mersar. OxBS

Allah gives light in darkness. Siegfried August Mahlmann, *German.* AWP, *tr. by* Longfellow

Allan Ian Og Macleod of Raasay. Macleod's Lament. Neil Munro. NSI

Allansford Pursuit, The. Robert Graves. RB

"Allas," sche seide, "how that this manis mynde." Heu Quam Precipiti. Boethius. OBMV, *tr. by* John Walton *Fr.* Consolation of Philosophy, The ("De Consolacione Philosophie").

Allegiance is assigned. Choice. James Vincent Cunningham. VGW

Allegiances. William Stafford. PaTW

Allegory, An. Barcroft Henry Boake. CBAP

Allegory. Rafael Campo. RA

Allegory. Carla Harryman. FTOS

Allegory, An. David Ignatow. VGW

Allegory. Jenny Mueller. BAP-94

Allegory of Death and Night. Frank Stanford. MT

Allegory of the Wolf Boy, The. Thom Gunn. OxBC

Allegro. Tomas Tranströmer, *Swedish.* SPE, *tr. by* Robert Bly

Alleluia, alleluia, / Alleluia, now sing we. *Unknown.* MiEL

Alleluia! Christ is risen today. John Henry Hopkins Jr. AH

Alleluia-verse for the Virgin. Hildegard von Bingen, *German.* WPoS, *tr. by* Barbara Newman

Alleluya. "Rubén Dario," *Spanish.* TTY, *tr. by* Lysander Kemp

Allen Ginsberg. Toi Derricotte. PBCAP

Allen said, *I am searching for the true cadence.* Gray. Helicon. John Hollander. Poetr

Allenby. Meir Wieseltier, *Hebrew.* IP, *tr. by* Warren Bargad *and* Stanley F. Chyet

Alley; an Imitation of Spenser, The. Alexander Pope. NOEC

Alley Cat. Esther Valck Georges. OTCP; Spl

Alley of granite arkite pillars, The. Stones: Avesbury. Daisy Aldan. PoA

Alley once, I dragged my idleness, An. The Country Road. Tế Hanh, *Vietnamese.* AVP, *tr. by* Huỳnh Sanh Thông

Allie, call the birds in. Robert Graves. NTP; PeLV

Alligator, The. Beatrice Witte Ravenel. WPE

Alligator Bride, The. Donald Hall. CoAmPo; SPE

Alligator, hippopotamus, fox, rhinoceros. The Ruler. Robin Blaser. FTOS

Alligator's Struggles with the 400 sons. *Unknown. Fr.* The Popol Vuh. STP, *tr. by* Munro Edmonson

Allow me to speak of the great tits. Report. Hollis Spurgeon Summers. PFE

Alloy. Robin Boody Galguera. IFJA

Alloy. Muriel Rukeyser. NoAM

All's a scatteing, / A shining. (LL) Meditation at Oyster River. Theodore Roethke. CMoP; MoAmPo; NYBP

All's Not That Simple. All Is Not So Simple. Shin Shalom, *Hebrew.* MHP, *tr. by* Ruth Finer Mintz

All's over, then: does truth sound bitter. The Lost Mistress. Robert Browning. BoLoP; LoP; NOBE; OBEV; OBNC; SAGP

All's Right with the World. Gerald Massey. EBVV

All's right with the world! (LL) Pippa's Song. Robert Browning. BLPA; BoTP; CTV; EBEvV; FHYEP; FaBoBe; ImPo; NTCP; OBEV; PoToHe; TFi; TrCP; UnPo

All's Vast. Francis Thompson. MoBrPo; Son *Fr.* The Heart. (Correlated Greatness.) GTBS-P

All's Well. John Greenleaf Whittier. OxBSP

All's Well That Ends Well. Shakespeare.
  "O Lord, sir, let me live, or let me see my death!" OxAEP-1

Allthough the most do with officious heat. On the Death of the Queen of Bohemia. Katherine Philips. KTR

Alluding to the One-armed Bandit. David Chapman Berry. BXAP

Allusion to Horace, An. John Wilmot, 2d Earl of Rochester.
  "Sedley has that prevailing, gentle art." EPCY
  "Should I be troubled when the purblind knight." EPCY
  "Waller, by nature for the bays designed." EPCY

Allusion to Martial, An. Martial, *Latin.* OBCVT, *tr. by* John Oldham

Alma. Tom Lehrer. NBLV

Alma; or, The Progress of the Mind. Matthew Prior.
  "In Britain's isles, as Heylyn notes." NOEC

Alma Perdida. Valery Larbaud, *French.* NNPT, *tr. by* Ron Padgett *and* Bill Zavatsky

Alma, te quiero que tú no eres ni gringa. Santos and Stones. J. Delayne Barber. LoHo

Almagest, Last Letter to Zakarias. Siv Cedering Fox. PBCAP

Almanac. May Swenson. NYBP

Almanac Verse. Samuel Danforth. SCAP

Almanac Verse. *Unknown.* SCAP

Almanack for the Year of Our Lord, 1657, An. Samuel Bradstreet. SCAP

Almighty and everlasting God, we thank Thee. Prayer for Every Day. *Unknown, Fanti.* PBA, *tr. by* Kweku Martin

Almighty creator and ruler as well. Hymn to the Creator. John Clare. NOBVV

Almighty God. (LL) Caedmon's Hymn. Caedmon, *Anglo-Saxon.* EBEV, *tr. by* Sally Purcell; OAEL-1, *tr. by* Walter Kendrick

Almighty God in being was. Silas Ballou. AH

Almighty God, into His own Kingdom. (LL) The Dream of the Rood. *Unknown, Anglo-Saxon.* EEP, *tr. by* Michael Alexander

Almighty God, thy constant care. Henry Stevenson Washburn. AH

Almighty God, who fillest the recesses of the heavens. Invocation. Bishop Patrick, *Latin.* NOIV, *tr. by* Thomas Kinsella

Almighty [or Almightie] Judge, how shall poor[e] wretches brook. Judgement. George Herbert. ESCV; GeHe; SeCP

Almighty Lord, with one accord. Melancthon Woolsey Stryker. AH

Almighty Sovereign of the skies! Nathan Strong. AH

Almighty spake, and Gabriel sped, Th'. George Richards. AH

Almighty! what is man? Solomon ibn Gabirol, *Hebrew.* TrJP, *tr. by* Emma Lazarus

Almond flourisheth, the birch trees flow, The. Signs of Spring. Sir Thomas Browne. NOSC

Almond Tree, The. Jon Stallworthy. NoAM

Almoner, An. "Michael Field." VWP

Almora Spring. Sumitranandan Pant, *Hindi.* OMIP, *tr. by* David Rubin

Almost a child again. In the Formal Garden. Peter Jones. OBGa

Almost a Love Poem. Yehuda Amichai, *Hebrew.* HP, *tr. by* Abramson, Glenda

Almost a Spring Poem. Reiner Kunze, *German.* CEEP, *tr. by* Ewald Osers

Almost Aubade. Marilyn Hacker. NoAM

Almost believed in. Paul Brown. NBrP *Fr.* De Rebus.

Almost blind he takes the soft dying. The Copperhead. Linda Gregg. AFr

Almost Blue. Mark Doty. SeSe

Almost Casanova Electricity. Jackson Mac Low. FTOS

Almost delivered, almost airborne. (LL) Hauling Over Wolf Creek Pass in Winter. Walter McDonald. CDa

Almost four years, and, though I merely guess. Elegy, An: December, 1970. Edgar Bowers. MT

Almost Going. David Huddle. PBCAP

Almost happy now, he looked at his estate. Voltaire at Ferney. W. H. Auden. LiTM

Almost Human. C. Day Lewis. NoAM

Almost I, yes, I hear. W. S. Graham. *Fr.* The Dark Dialogues. OxBS

Almost invisible. Tanka. Kitahara Hakushū, *Japanese.* MJT, *tr. by* Makoto Ueda

Almost midnight, and the aunties. Chinese Fireworks Banned in Hawaii. Eric Chock. PuP-16

Almost naked like the children of the sea. (LL) Portrait. Antonio Machado Ruiz, *Spanish.* RaBo; STV, *tr. by* Robert Bly

"Almost persuaded," / Now to believe. Philip Paul Bliss. AH

Almost reluctant, we approach the block. Thumbprint. Celeste Turner Wright. Poetsp

Almost sheer fatigue. Early Pregnancy. Penelope Shuttle. BrRo

Almost singing, she stares past the crowd and flies. Old Woman Awaiting the Greyhound Bus. Duane Niatum. CDW

Almost twenty years. Drinking Cold Water. Peter Everwine. NNaP

Almost two years now I've been sleeping. After Elegies. Jean Valentine. LCAP-2

Almost without a way to bud it creases the netting. Ornamental Syllable. Geoffrey O'Brien. PT

Almswomen. Edmund Blunden. OBMV; OxBTC

Alnight by the rose, rose. *Unknown. See* All night by the rose, rose.

Alnwick Castle. Fitz-Greene Halleck. APN-1

Aloe, agave, portulaca, prickly pear. The Life of Ideas. Chris Wallace-Crabbe. OBGa

Aloe Plant, The. Henry Harbaugh. BLPA

Aloft in Heavenly Mansions, Doubleyou One. The Playboy of the Demi-World[: 1938]. William Plomer. OxBTC; UV

Aloha Oe. Don Blanding. PoToHe

Alone. "Anna Akhmatova," *Russian.* BoWoP, *tr. by* Stephen Berg

Alone. Hayyim Nahman Bialik, *Hebrew.* TrJP, *tr. by* Jessie Sampter

Alone. Chu Shu-chen, *Chinese.* BoWoP; OHPC, *tr. by* Kenneth Rexroth

Alone. Walter De la Mare. CBLP; EnLoPo

Alone. Michael S. Harper. ISC

"Alone." Edgar Allan Poe. APAD; APN-1; MeMAP; NAAL-1; NAAL-3; NTP; PAR

Alone. Sappho, *Greek.* AWP, *tr. by* William Ellery Leonard

Alone. Edith Jay Scovell. GBL

Alone. Richard Shelton. NYBP

Alone. Carolyn Wells. PoToHe

Alone am I, and alone I wish to be. Christine de Pisan, *French.* BoWoP, *tr. by* Julie Allen

Alone and Godless, stopped by the sudden edge. Patrick MacDonogh. BIrV *Fr.* Escape to Love.

Alone and pensive, the most deserted fields. Petrarch. ItIP

Alone and strong in my peace, I look upon you in yours. (LL) The Sleeping Fury. Louise Bogan. LiTM; NALW

Alone at last in my room. By the Looking-Glass. Augusta Davies Webster. VWP

Alone at night. 1951. Frank O'Hara. LCAP-2

Alone, at night, with all the world. Evil Nigger Waits for Lightnin'. Imamu Amiri Baraka. NOBA

Alone at the end of green *allées* alone. The Statues in the Public Gardens. Howard Nemerov. CoAmPo

ALONE/december/night. Victor Hernandez Cruz. PBMP

Alone far in the wilds and mountains I hunt. Walt Whitman. SAmP *Fr.* Song of Myself. AmPP; MoAmPo; NAAL-3; NOBA; OxBA

Alone for a Week. Dolores Kendrick. FFC

Alone for the evening. Bringing Flowers. Roberta Spear. AmPA

Alone God sufficeth. (LL) Bookmark. Saint, of Avila Theresa, *Spanish.* AWP, *tr. by* Longfellow

Alone, I live alone. *Unknown.* MiEL

Alone I sat; the summer day. Emily Jane Brontë. NALW

Alone I sit in dark bamboo. Bamboo Mile Lodge. Wang Wei. *Fr.* Twenty Views of Wang-ch'uan. CoBCP, *tr. by* Burton Watson

Alone I stand, facing the flowers' shade. Ho Ching-ming, *Chinese.* CoBLCP, *tr. by* Jonathan Chaves

Alone I stand in autumn cold. "Spring in Ch'in's Garden." Mao Tse-tung, *Chinese.* SuSp, *tr. by* Eugene Eoyang

Alone I tiptoe through the stars. Star Journey. Naomi Long Madgett. BPo

Alone I tow my death along. (LL) Hidesong. Aig Higo. PBMAP

Alone in a cold autumn I stood. Midstream. Mao Tse-tung, *Chinese.* MoCV, *tr. by* Earle Birney

Alone in an Inn at Southampton, April the 25th, 1737. Aaron Hill. NOEC

Alone in my sorrow, where do my thoughts go? Thinking of My Wife. P'an Yüeh, *Chinese.* CoBCP, *tr. by* Burton Watson

Alone in the atoning belfry how I grieve. Giotto's Campanile. Guy Butler. PeSA

Alone in the Grange. Gregory Harrison. FuFo

Alone in the great storm. (LL) Presaging. Rilke, *German.* AWP; TrJP, *tr. by* Jessie Lemont

Alone in the Night. Li Ch'ing-chao, *Chinese.* OHPC, *tr. by* Kenneth Rexroth

Alone in this desert under the cold moon. If I Forget Thee. Emanuel Litvinoff. TrJP

Alone is delicious. Jonathan Holden. Poetsp

Alone is the hunter. Harold Littlebird. VoR

Alone it stands in Poesy's fair land. The Sonnet. Ella Wheeler Wilcox. APN-2

Alone on Lykaion since man hath been. Mount Lykaion. Trumbull Stickney. OxBA; Son *Fr.* Sonnets from Greece. APN-1

Alone on the empty beach. Puberty. Nina Cassian, *Romanian.* CEEP, *tr. by* Brian Swann *and* Michael Impey

Alone on the hill of storms. Battle of the Stars. Adah Isaacs Menken. CBWP-1

Alone on the lawn. The Dancing Cabman. John Bingham Morton. NOBL

Alone on the road. Nicholas Virgilio. HA

Alone on the tower. Diver. Ronald Albert Simpson. CBAP

Alone one noon on a sheet of igneous rock. Myths. Guy Butler. PeSA

Alone she feeds the white swans. The Swans of Vadstena. Ralph Gustafson. MoCV

Alone the pallid cuckoo now. Pallid Cuckoo. David Campbell. CBAP

Alone tonight one fish ripples the lake. Matsuo Allard. HA

Alone up here on the mountain. *Unknown.* NOIV

Alone with the Sea. Marie Under, *Estonian.* CEEP, *tr. by* Ivar Ivask

Along a street. Tanka. Kondō Yoshimi, *Japanese.* MJT, *tr. by* Makoto Ueda

Along a tarn a delator entangled a dragline. Antic Quatrains. Jackson MacLow. PmAP

Along Ancona's hills the shimmering heat. Poppies on the Wheat. Helen Hunt Jackson. APN-2; ColAP; PAR; SDW

Along Cape Cod, salt crannies of white harbors. Midsummer: XXXI. Derek Walcott. AFr

Along come that F.F.V., the swiftest on the line. George Allen. *Unknown.* AmFP

Along East River and the Bronx. Ode for Walt Whitman. Federico García Lorca, *Spanish.* PFTM, *tr. by* Jack Spicer

Along Galeana Street. Octavio Paz, *Spanish.* VCWP, *tr. by* Elizabeth Bishop

Along grey crowded outskirts of the town. A Peaceful Step. Gane Todorovski, *Macedonian.* CEEP, *tr. by* Dragan Milivojevic

Along history, forever. Muriel Rukeyser. NALW; NNaP

Along how many Main Streets have I walked. The Eternal Return. Robert Silliman Hillyer. AiP; NYBP

Along Lenox Avenue folk said. Old Pettigrew. Melvin B. Tolson. GT

Along that footpath, shepherd, past the oaks. Theocritus, *Greek.* GrAn, *tr. by* Anthony Holden

Along the avenue of cypresses. Giorno dei Morti. D. H. Lawrence. NOBE

Along the banks where Babel's current flows. Joel Barlow. AH; ChIV-1

Along the cement walkway I pick up. Markings. Frank Steele. Poetsp

Along the dark, and silent night. The Bell-Man. Robert Herrick. BeJo

Along the dark bank of the river. After the Night Hunt. James Dickey. PoA

Along the field as we came by. A. E. Housman. GLoP; HAP; MoBrPo; WeW-3

Along the garden terrace, under which. George Meredith. NOBVV *Fr.* Modern Love.

Along the Grand Canal. Ch'in Kuan, *Chinese.* BLT, *tr. by* Kenneth Rexroth

Along the great coast south of Bordeaux. The Bunkers. Michael O'Loughlin. PBCIP *Fr.* The Shards.

Along the hallways of my thought. The Cat. Charles Baudelaire, *French.* PC, *tr. by* William H. Crosby

Along the hard crest of the snowdrift. "Anna Akhmatova," *Russian.* PiM, *tr. by* Jane Kenyon

Along the lake the bugle rings. Echo Reverie. Henrietta Cordelia Ray. CBWP-3

Along the line of smoky hills. Indian Summer. Wilfred Campbell. NOBC

Along the Mekong. John Balaban. CDa

Along the narrow street with a hero's name. The Outing. Marina Kudimova, *Russian.* TCRP, *tr. by* Albert C. Todd

Along the path of ghosts, the ashen path. Package for Another World. Jemal Sharah. NOBAu

Along the path that skirts the wood. The Three Musicians. Aubrey Beardsley. NOBVV; PeVV

Along the precipice, above the chasm, on the very brink. Unruly Horses. Vladimir Semionovich Vysotsky, *Russian.* TCRP, *tr. by* Albert C. Todd

Along the river most homes here. Quatrain at Chen-chou. Wang Shih-chieng, *Chinese.* CoBLCP, *tr. by* Jonathan Chaves

Along the River, Seeing the Home of Absconded Farmers. Kao Ch'i, *Chinese.* CoBLCP, *tr. by* Jonathan Chaves

Along the Road. Robert Browning Hamilton. BLPA

Along the road all shapes must travel by. Prolonged Sonnet: In the Last Days of the Emperor Henry VII. Simone dall' Antela, *Italian.* AWP, *tr. by* D. G. Rossetti

Along the Road to Stone Lake. Su Tung-p'o, *Chinese.*

Tune: Sand of Silk-washing Stream ("Flutter, flutter, on clothes and cap, jujube flowers fall"). CoBCP

Tune: Sand of Silk-washing Stream ("Layer on layer of hemp leaves, jute leaves shining"). CoBCP

Tune: Sand of Silk-washing Stream ("Soft grasses, a plain of sedge fresh with passing rain"). CoBCP

Tune: Sand of Silk-washing Stream ("Throw on rouge and powder, watch the governor pass!"). CoBCP

Along the roadside, like the flowers of gold. Prelude. John Greenleaf Whittier. APN-1; NAAL-1; NAAL-3; OxBA; PoEL-4 *Fr.* Among the Hills.

Along the row of small white houses. Lovely Leda. Yaroslav Vasilevich Smelyakov, *Russian.* TCRP, *tr. by* Simon Franklin *and* Albert C. Todd

Along the sprawled body of the derailed [Great Northern freight car]. Outside Fargo, North Dakota. James Wright. GM; LCAP-2; NNaP; WeT

Along the Strand. Alfred Mombert, *German.* TrJP, *tr. by* Jethro Bithell

Along the street noon, flying unchecked. The Betrothed. Aleksandr Andreievich Prokofiev, *Russian.* TCRP, *tr. by* Lubov Yakovleva

Along those roads we cannot hear him bark. (LL) A Maltese Dog. Tymnes, *Greek.* OBCVT, *tr. by* Edmund Blunden

Along thy dead indifference of walls. (LL) The Berg. Herman Melville. AmPP; ColAP; NCAP; NOBA; NoP-4; PFE; PoEL-5; PoPoPo; TAP

Along with the wraggle taggle gipsies, O! (LL) The Wraggle Taggle Gipsies. *Unknown.* BoTP; CH

Along Without: A Fiction in Film for Poetry. Douglas Messerli.

"NARRATOR: Suddenly someone wakes me. Still half asleep, I see standing in front." FTOS

Alons au bois le may cueillir. Charles, Duc d' Orléans, *French.* AWP, *tr. by* W. E. Henley

Alonzo the Brave and the Fair Imogine. Matthew Gregory Lewis. NOBRP

Aloof. Christina Rossetti. OBEV *Fr.* The Thread of Life.

(Verse I.) PEW

Aloof, as if a thing of mood and whim. The Schreckhorn. Thomas Hardy. OAEL-2

Aloofe, aloofe, and come no neare. Sea Marke. John Smith. SCAP

Alpaca pictures of the previous past. Confounded Nonsense. Thomas Hood Jr. CBNP

aa, ay, ay!. . . stutterer Demosthenes. Them and [uz]. Tony Harrison. NoP-4

Alpha and Omega, God, my God! Prayer to God the Father. Hildebert, *Latin.* MLL, *tr. by* Helen Waddell

Alpha-B375-Earth Visitors' Guide. . . Section, 789/43912399845623A**D. John Cunliffe. SpW

Alphabet ("Great A was alarmed at B's bad behavior"). *Unknown.* OxNR

Alphabet, The. Jejuri Arun Kolatkar, *Marathi.* OMIP, *tr. by* Vinay Dharwadker

Alphabet, An. Edward Lear. OxBChV

Alphabet, The. Karl Shapiro. NoAM; PoA

Alphabet, The. *Unknown.* ReMoGo

Alphabet by the Pool on a Sunday Afternoon, The. Lusia Slomkowska. LoHo

Alphabet Calendar of Amergin, The. *Unknown, Irish.* BIrV, *tr. by* Robert Graves

Alphabet Murders, The. John Tranter. BMAP

Alphabet of, The. The Botticellian Trees. William Carlos Williams. AmPP

Alphabet of Ahtt. Nathaniel Mackey. FTOS

Alphabet of Fishes. Bob Cobbing. NBrP

Alphabet of Love, The. *Unknown, Greek.* GrIP, *tr. by* Theodore Stephanides

Alphabet war-makers. Zangezi: R, K, L, G—. Velemir Khlebnikov, *Russian.* PFTM, *tr. by* Paul Schmidt

Alphabetical Song on the Corn Law Bill. *Unknown.* OxBoLi

Alphabets. Seamus Heaney. NoAM

Alpheus. Bring water foorth, and bind with filets soft there altars round. A Love-charm. Virgil, *Latin.* OBCVT, *tr. by* Abraham Fleming

Alphonso of Castile. Ralph Waldo Emerson. NOBA

Alpine Spirit's Song. Thomas Lovell Beddoes. OBNC

Alps on Alps. Alexander Pope. *Fr.* An Essay on Criticism. NAEL-1; PoEL-3; TFi

("Whole at once is bold, and regular, The.") (LL) ImPo

Already Autumn, and from the belt of Boötes. To Epicles. Antipater of Thessalonica, *Greek.* GrAn, *tr. by* Tony Harrison

Already autumn begins here in the mossy rocks. Thinking of "The Autumn Fields." Robert Bly. NNaP

Already blushes on thy cheek. Nemesis. Ralph Waldo Emerson. NOBA

Already embraced by the arm of heavenly solace. Nelly Sachs, *German.* HP; PoSu, *tr. by* Michael Roloff

Already fallen plum-bloom stars the green. The Poor Man's Pig. Edmund Blunden. MoBrPo

Already I am no longer looked at with lechery or love. A Sunset of the City. Gwendolyn Brooks. FaBoWP; GT; LCAP-2; PBWP

Already in midsummer. To a Butterfly. James Merrill. APo

Already it's late summer. Sunbathers go. The Divine Insect. John Hall Wheelock. NYBP

Already, no more dreams of going to the capital. Living in Retirement at Te-ch'ing. Chao Meng-fu, *Chinese.* CoBLCP, *tr. by* Jonathan Chaves

Already past mid-June. Out of Work, Out of Touch, Out of Sorts. Catherine Davis. FFC

Already prepared in the golden chamber. Antipater of Sidon, *Greek.* GrAn, *tr. by* Tony Harrison

Already she seems bone thin. A Poem about Breasts. James Wright. TAP

Already swallows build their homes of mud. Thyillos, *Greek.* GrAn, *tr. by* Adrian Wright

Already the field, fair with leaves, in her fruitful bringing to birth. Theaitetus, *Greek.* GrAn, *tr. by* John Heath-Stubbs *and* Carol A. Whiteside

Already to mine eyelids' shore. "Michael Field." VWP

Also an old image has a moment's birth. Moon. Nathan Alterman, *Hebrew.* MHP, *tr. by* Ruth Finer Mintz

Also for little ones, just like. The Blade of Grass Sings to the Stream. Leah Goldberg. MHP, *tr. by* Ruth Finer Mintz *Fr.* Songs of the Stream.

Also I love him: me he's done no wrong. John Berryman. NoP-4

Also in sleep I see you, comprehend. The Fire in the Stone. Tuvia Rivner, *Hebrew.* MHP, *tr. by* Ruth Finer Mintz

Also survive its meanings, and my own. (LL) After Greece. James Merrill. CoAmPo; ColAP; NOBA; NYBP; TRP

Also Ulysses once—that other war. Kilroy. Peter Viereck. MoAmPo; PoRA

Altar. Marilyn Chin. PoPoPo

Altar, The. George Herbert. CABP; ChIV-1; ESCV; GeHe; HoPM; InPS-3; NAEL-1; NOSC; NoP-4; OAEL-1; Poetr; SeCP; TrCP

Altar boy marches up the altar steps, The. Soldiers. Padraic Fiacc. PNI

Altar of Mercy, The. Publius Papinius Statius, *Latin.* OBCVT, *tr. by* William S. Lewis

Altar of the Fatherland, The. Andreas Kalvos, *Greek.* GrIP, *tr. by* Philip Sherrard

Altar, 'tis of death! for there are laid, The. The Marriage Vow. Letitia Elizabeth Landon. VWP

Altarwise by owl-light in the half-way house. Dylan Thomas. LiTM;
"Altarwise by owl-light in the half-way house." CMoP; FaBoMo; Son
"Death is all metaphors, shape in one history." CMoP; Son
"First there was the lamb on knocking knees." CMop
"From the oracular archives and the parchment." CMoP
"Let the tale's sailor from a Christian voyage." CMop; FaBoMo; OAEL-2
"Now stamp the Lord's Prayer on a grain of rice." FaBoMo
"This was the crucifixion on the mountain." CMoP
"What is the metre of the dictionary?" CMoP; FaBoMo

Altazor. Sels. Vincente Huidobro, *Spanish.* PFTM, *tr. by* Eliot Weinberger

Alter or mend eternal fact. (LL) The Past. Ralph Waldo Emerson. FaBoCh; MeMAP; PoEL-4; TAP

Alter! When the Hills do—. Emily Dickinson. AmPP; CBLP; FaBoBe; ITG; SoSe-8

Altered look about the hills, An. Emily Dickinson. OxBA; SoSe-8

Altermann, sipping wine, reads with a look. Dom Moraes. NoP-4 *Fr.* Two from Israel.

Alternately in Anecdotes go on. A Town Eclogue. "Peter Pindar." OBCoV *Fr.* Bozzy and Piozzi.

Alternative Endings to an Unwritten Ballad. Paul Dehn. OBCoV

Alternatives. Kingsley Amis. OxBC

Alternatives. Peter Cooley. AmPA

Altho' a slave me is born and bred. Ballad. J. B. Moreton. PBCV

Although. Tanka. Tawara Machi, *Japanese.* MJT, *tr. by* Makoto Ueda

Although a poor blind boy[!]. (LL) The Blind Boy. Colley Cibber. GTBS-P; NOEC; OxBChV

Although accustomed to picking them, it always. The Woman and the Aloe. Perseus Adams. PeSA

Although art is autonomous. On This Day I Complete My Fortieth Year. Peter Porter. BMAP

Although art is, in the end, anonymous. Having Completed My Fortieth Year. John Tranter. BMAP

Although blooming. Tanka. Nakajō Fumiko, *Japanese.* MJT, *tr. by* Makoto Ueda

Although crowds gathered once if she but showed her face. Fallen Majesty. W. B. Yeats. PoA

Although entangled in prolonged grief. Catullus. *See* Carmen 65 ("Grief reached across the world to get me").

Although great in passing, although suddenly enlarged. Death. Sherod Santos. WeT

Although, great Queen, thou now in silence lie. In Honour of That High and Mighty Princess Queen Elizabeth of Happy Memory. Anne Bradstreet. NALW; NoP-4

Although he has no form. Mukta Bai, *Marathi.* BoWoP, *tr. by* Willis Barnstone

Although [*or* Altho'] I be the basest of mankind. St. Simeon Stylites. Tennyson. NOBVV; OAEL-2

Although I can see him still. The Fisherman. W. B. Yeats. CMoP; HAP; NoAM

Although I come to you constantly. Ono no Komachi, *Japanese.* WPJ, *tr. by* Kenneth Rexroth *and* Ikuko Atsumi

Although I conquer all the earth. *Unknown.* TTTS

Although I cry and though my eyes still shed. Sonnet XIV. Louise Labé, *French.* BoWoP, *tr. by* Willis Barnstone

Although I do not hope to turn again. T. S. Eliot. *Fr.* Ash Wednesday [*or* Ash-Wednesday]. MoAmPo; OxBA; VGW

Although I do not know. Saigyo, *Japanese.* AWP, *tr. by* Arthur Waley

Although I had a check. Henry Howard, Earl of Surrey. SiPS

Although I hide it. Kanemori, *Japanese.* OHPJ, *tr. by* Kenneth Rexroth

Although I mean it, and project the meaning. The Ice-Cream Wars. John Ashbery. PoA

Although I put away his life. Emily Dickinson. MoAmPo

Although I shelter from the rain. The Lamentation of the Old Pensioner. W. B. Yeats. HAP; LiLi; PeVV; TRP; WeW-3

Although I try. In the Autumn, on Retreat at a Mountain Temple. Lady Izumi, *Japanese.* WPoS, *tr. by* Jane Hirshfield *and* Mariko Aratani

Although I was her pupil, / even I reproach Myrtis. Korinna, *Greek.* BoWoP, *tr. by* Willis Barnstone

Although it is a cold evening. At the Fishhouses. Elizabeth Bishop. CoAP; FaBoWP; GEA; HAP; HCAP; LCAP-2; LiTM; NAAL-2; NALW; NYBP; PoPoPo; PoRA; Poetr; VCAP

Although it is night, I sit in the bathroom, waiting. Adolescence—II. Rita Dove. AmPA; HCAP; ISC; NoAM; PoPoPo; VCAP

Although it is not plainly visible to the eye. Toshiyuki. AWP, *tr. by* Arthur Waley *Fr.* Kokin Shu.

Although it is not yet evening. The Persistence of Song. Howard Moss. NoP-4

Although lamps burn along the silent streets. James Thomson. EBVV *Fr.* The City of Dreadful Night. OBNC

Although Michaelmas Daisies bloom for a very long time. Gather Ye Rosebuds. Laurence Fowler. BXAP

Although my claws weaken. Sweetness. *Unknown, Irish.* BIrV, *tr. by* John Montague

Although only a fool would mock. Queen Mother to New Queen. Robert Graves. OBSV

Although propriety be crossed. A New Year's Gift. William Cartwright. BeJo

Although she feeds me bread of bitterness. America. Claude McKay. MoP; NAAAL; NIP-4; NoAM; PoBA; TAP; TTY

Although she's a girl, Dorkion. Asclepiades, *Greek.* GrAn; PGA, *tr. by* Kenneth Rexroth

Although some are afraid that to speak of a spade as a spade is a social mistake. Rigoletto. Newman Levy. OBAL

Although the aepyornis. He "Digesteth Harde Yron." Marianne Moore. CMoP; NoAM

Although the cricket's song has no words. Cricket Heard. Lady Izumi, *Japanese.* APo, *tr. by* Jane Hirshfield

Although the field lay cut in swaths. Timothy. Timothy Steele. InPK-6; RA

Although the sign says. The Wild Horses of Assateague Island. John Bensko. MT

Although the snow still lingers. Last Snow. Andrew Young. OxBTC

Although the wind. Lady Izumi, *Japanese.* WPoS, *tr. by* Jane Hirshfield *and* Mariko Aratani

Although their hair is turning gray. A Meeting of Friends. Phillis Levin. RA

Although, those years, we squandered. A Plaint of Flowers. Ernest Sandeen. CRP

Although thou see th'outrageous climb aloft. Bible, *O.T. See* Psalm 37: "Fret not thyself because of evildoers."

Although thy blood be frozen, and thy scalp. To a Covetous Churl. Edward May. FaBoEE

Although thy hand and faith, and good work[e]s too. Change. Donne. CBLP; EBEV *Fr.* Elegies.

Although thy heart with fire like Ætna flame. Defensive measures. Ovid, *Latin.* OBCVT, *tr. by* Overbury, Sir Thomas

Although tormented and ill-treated. Kalonymos ben Judah, *Hebrew.* TrJP

Although we do not all the good we love. John Davies, of Hereford. Son *Fr.* The Holy Rood.

Although your ears must be plentifully occupied. Julius Polyaenus, *Greek.* GrAn, *tr. by* John Heath-Stubbs *and* Carol A. Whiteside

Although your white bones waste in. On a Hound. Simonides, *Greek.* PGA, *tr. by* Kenneth Rexroth

Altitudes. Richard Wilbur. CMoP

Altogether spoilt my game. (LL) The Englishman's Home. Harry Graham. CBNP; PeLV

Alton Locke. Charles Kingsley.
  Sands of Dee, The. CH; EBEvV; EBVV; FaPoR; OxAEP-2

Alumnus Football. Grantland Rice. PoLF

Aluqa, the demon who swims underwater in streams. Meadow Bug. Rossana Ombres, *Italian.* NeIt, *tr. by* Ruth Feldman

Alvin Cash/Keep on Dancin', *to the children of intermediate school 55, ocean hill-brownsville.* David Henderson. GT

Always a cupola. Winter Ritual. Nichita Stanescu, *Romanian.* CEEP, *tr. by* Mariana Carpinisan *and* Mark Irwin

Always a third one's there. The Uninvited. Dorothy Livesay. NOBC; NoP-4

Always afraid to say more than it meant. (LL) The Letter. W. H. Auden. FaBoTw; MoP; NoAM

Always at night I found them. The Children of Saigon. Walter McDonald. AF

Always before, we sped in the same direction. The Queen. Kenneth Pitchford. NYBP

Always before your voice my soul. E. E. Cummings. MoAmPo

Always Begin Where You Are. Thomas Hornsby Ferril. VGW

Always dear to me was this lonely hill. The Infinite. Giacomo Leopardi, *Italian.* ItIP

Always driven, always in the bite of the blast. And Yet We Are Here! Karl Wolfskehl, *German.* TrJP, *tr. by* Carol North Valhope *and* Ernst Morowitz

Always expecting the winter. In Dream: The Privacy of Sequence. Ray A. Young Bear. CDW

Always Finish. *Unknown.* BLPA; CTV; FaBoBe

Always for thirty years now. Fish Peddler and Cobbler. Kenneth Rexroth. NNaP

Always for your never named sake. (LL) The Lost Baby Poem. Lucille Clifton. FiLi; ISC

Always, from My First Boyhood. John Peale Bishop. VGW

Always homing now soul toward light. Lorna Goodison. VCWP

Always I have meant to write of Apollo Café. Apollo Café. Stephen Gray. PeSAV

Always I have searched for the mislaid tin spoon. One Fine Day. János Pilinszky, *Hungarian.* PoSu, *tr. by* Peter Jay

Always I lay upon the brink of love. Judas. Vassar Miller. ChIV-2; MoAmPo

Always I recall the river arbor at twilight. Tune: "As in a Dream: Song." Li Ch'ing-chao, *Chinese.* CoBCP, *tr. by* Burton Watson

Always—I tell you this they learned. House Fear. Robert Frost. NTP; VGW *Fr.* The Hill Wife. CMoP; HAP; InPS-3; LiTM; NoP-4; RACG

Always, In March. Ion Caraion, *Romanian.* CEEP, *tr. by* Marguerite Dorian *and* Elliott B. Urdang

Always / in the middle. Love, Maybe. Audre Lorde. Poetr

Always in the parting year. Else Lasker-Schüler, *German.* TrJP, *tr. by* Ralph Manheim

Always it was a summer afternoon. The House of Broughton Street. Mary Ann Larkin. AiP

Always it was going on. Today Is Friday. Ramon Guthrie. PoE

Always it's moments glimpsed while journeying past. Moments. Jane King. HCP

Always just one demon in the attic. Interferon. Miroslav Holub, *Czech.* VCWP, *tr. by* David Young *and* Dana Hábová

Always long afternoon shadows. The Taxidermist's Daughter. Nancy Schoenberger. MoLi

Always loving. Tanka. Sasaki Yukitsuna, *Japanese.* MJT, *tr. by* Makoto Ueda

Always on Monday, God's name is in the morning papers. The Day after Sunday. Phyllis McGinley. MoAmPo; OBSV; UnPo

Always on time, like the waves. (LL) The Impossible Pictures. Tom Paulin. CABP

Always pruning, always cropping? Matthew 9.12. Francis Quarles. ChIV-2

Always Running. Luis J. Rodriguez. UnSA

Always shade in the cool dry barns. My Son and I Go See Horses. Marianne Boruch. WeT

Always she goes like a captured wild bird. Sappho. Jack Cope. PeSA

Always She Moves from Me. Shirley Kaufman. WPE

Always so late in the day. Mark Strand. NoP-4; Poetr; TRP

Always the arriving winds of words. Words. William Robert Rodgers. OxBSP; PNI

Always the children are included. Mourning the Death, by Hemorrhage, of a Child from Honai. Basil T. Paquet. CDa

Always the Following Wind. W. H. Auden. MoBrPo

Always the heavy air. The Lion-House. John Hall Wheelock. PFE

Always the same, sweet hurt. Why Do So Few Blacks Study Creative Writing? Cornelius Eady. GT; LTA

Always the same, when on a fated night. The Onset. Robert Frost. CMoP; MoAmPo; OxBA; PBMP; PFE

Always the setting forth was the same. Odysseus. W. S. Merwin. NOBA; NoP-4

Always to want to. The Tortoise. Cid Corman. InPK-6; VGW

Always too eager for the future, we. Next, Please. Philip Larkin. CABP; MoBrPo

Always True to You in My Fashion. Cole Porter.
  "If a custom-tailored vet." NBLV

Always, / We hear at night approaching steps. Steps in the Night. Mahmoud Darwish, *Arabic.* VCWP, *tr. by* Denys Johnson-Davies

Always with love, with love. (LL) The Letter. Elizabeth Riddell. LW; NOBAu

Always you are there--standing. The Anima Has a Predilection. Michael Harlow. PeNZ *Fr.* Poem Then, for Love.

Alzheimer's: The Wife. Charles Kenneth Williams. SAGP; VCAP

Am back, with what a tale! (LL) A Visit to the Dead. Norman Cameron. FaBoTC; OxBSn

Am, by being dead, immortal; Can ghosts die? (LL) The Computation. Donne. CBNP; FMP; NoSic; OxBSP; SoSe-8

Am I a dead man? Am I a dead man? John Berryman Listening to Robert Johnson's "King of the Delta Blues," January 1972. David Wojahn. SeSe

Am I a king, that I should call my own. From My Arm-Chair. Henry Wadsworth Longfellow. BLPA

Am I a stone and not a sheep. Good Friday. Christina Rossetti. ChIV-2; PoEL-5

Am I alone,/ And unobserved? I am! If You're Anxious for to Shine in the High Aesthetic Line. Sir William Schwenck Gilbert. NAEL-2; NBLV *Fr.* Patience.

Am I despised because you say. To a Gentlewoman Objecting to Him His Grey Hairs. Robert Herrick. BeJo; CaPo

Am I failing? For no longer can I cast. Sonnet 29. George Meredith. EnVR; GBL; PFE; SCGP *Fr.* Modern Love.

Am I mad, O noble Festus. The Distracted Puritan. Richard Corbet. BeJo; OBCoV; OxBoLi

Am I right to see myself introduced. The Hand Further. Clark Coolidge. PmAP

Am I sadly cast aside. The Slave's Complaint. George Moses Horton. AAP; CrDW

Am I the slave they say. Soggarth Aroon. John Banim. TIRV

Am I thus conquer'd? Have I lost the powers. Mary Sidney, Countess of Montgomery Wroth. *See* Sonnet 14: "Am I thus conquered [*or* conquer'd]? have I lost the powers."

Am I thus conquered [*or* conquer'd]? have I lost the powers. Sonnet 14. Mary Sidney, Countess of Montgomery Wroth. NAEL-1; NOSC *Fr.* Pamphilia to Amphilanthus.

Am I thy gold? Or purse, Lord, for thy wealth. Edward Taylor. MeMAP; NOSC; OxBA; TAP *Fr.* Preparatory Meditations Before My Approach to the Lord's Supper.

Am I to be blamed for the state of it now?—Surely not. Clio's. Mick Imlah. CBLP

Am I to become profligate as if I were a blonde? Meditations in an Emergency. Frank O'Hara. PmAP; TAP; VCAP

Am I to blame the drink or the downpour? Antipater of Thessalonica, *Greek.* GrAn, *tr. by* Tony Harrison

Am I to die? I feel atrocious pain. I Shall Not Die. Nguyễn Văn Năng, *Vietnamese.* AVP, *tr. by* Huỳnh Sanh Thông

"Am I to Lose You?" Louisa S. Guggenberger. NOBVV

Am I too dangerous, that no man can let. Wyndham Lewis. *Fr.* If So the Man You Are. OBSV

Am I your only love—in the whole world—now? Tell Me Again. Nigâr Hanim, *Turkish.* PBWP, *tr. by* Tâlat S. Halman

Am not a Goop—are you? (LL) Table Manners. Frank Gelett Burgess. CTV

Am quite myself again. (LL) Oh, when I was in love with you. A. E. Housman. BoLoP; CBLP; GLoP; LoP; MoBrPo; SAGP; TTTS

Am/Trak. Imamu Amiri Baraka. PmAP

Am was. are leaves few this. is these a or. E. E. Cummings. AF

Amadu I live alone inside four walls of books. Letter to a Tormented Playwright. Syl Cheney-Coker. HBAPE; PBMAP

Amagansett Beach Revisited. John Hall Wheelock. NYBP

Amalkanti is a friend of mine. Nirendranath Chakrabarti, *Bengali.* OMIP, *tr. by* Sujit Mukherjee *and* Meenakshi Mukherjee

Amanda! Robin Klein. OTCP

Amanda Barker. Edgar Lee Masters. NoAM *Fr.* Spoon River Anthology.

Amang the holtis hair. (LL) Robin [*or* Robene] and Makyne. Robert Henryson. BoLoP; MiEL; OBEV; PeLV; PoE; PoEL-1

Amang the lily flower. (LL) The Birth of Robin Hood. *Unknown.* ESPB; OAEL-1; OxBB

Amang the rigs o' barley. (LL) Song: "It was upon a Lammas night." Robert Burns. BoLoP; NOBRP; OxBS; PeLV

Amantium Irae Amoris Redintegratio. Richard Edwards. OBEV (Amantium Irae.) SCGP

Amaranth and Moly. Amy Clampitt. WWSi

Amarantha sweet and fair[e]. To Amarantha, That She Would Dishevel[l] Her Hair[e]. Richard Lovelace. BeJo; CABP; CaPo; CavPo; HoPM; NOSC; NoP-4; OBEV; PoE; SeCP

Amateur, The. Russell Edson. LCAP-2

Amateur and muddled, as their sex goes. The Professionals. Geoffrey Grigson. PoA

Amateur Flute, The. *Unknown.* BXAP

Amateurs of Heaven, The. Howard Nemerov. SoSe-8

Amateurs, we gathered mushrooms. Fall. Robert Hass. AmPA

Amaze then tooke him. Musaeus. OBCVT, *tr. by* George Chapman *Fr.* Hero and Leander.

Amazed we read of Nature's early throes. Man the Monarch. Mary Leapor. ECWP

Amazing Grace. Anselm Hollo. PoM

Amazing Grace in the Back Country. Robert Penn Warren. ColAP

Amazing, how the young man who empties Wing Road. Eamon Grennan. PBCIP

Amazing monster! that, for aught I know. A Fish Answers. Leigh Hunt. NBLV; PeLV; SCGP *Fr.* The Fish, the Man, and the Spirit. HAP; NOBL; NTP; OBEV; PoEL-4

Amazing Sight! The Saviour Stands. Henry Alline. AH *Fr.* Christ Inviting Sinners to His Grace.

Amazon Club. Kenward Elmslie. PmAP

Amazon Twins. Olga Broumas. CPO

Amazone. Mary Jo Bona. UnSA

Amazons. Louise Glück. NAmP90

Ambassador, The. Bruce Weigl. CDa

Ambassador Puser the ambassador. Memorial Rain. Archibald MacLeish. AmPP; CMoP; MeMAP; MoAmPo; OBWP

Amber. Shirley Toulson. PeP

Amber Bead, The. Robert Herrick. BeJo; CaPo

Amber husk / fluted with gold. Sea Poppies. Hilda Doolittle. NALW

Ambition. Mary Astell. KTR

Ambition. W. H. Davies. MoBrPo

Ambition, The. Robert Harris. BMAP

Ambition ("In man, ambition is the common'st thing"). Robert Herrick. CaPo

Ambition. Maggie Pogue Johnson. CBWP-4

Ambition. Henrietta Cordelia Ray. CBWP-3

Ambition. Nathaniel Parker Willis. OBCA

Ambitious ant would a-travelling go, The. Amos Russel Wells. OBCA; OBSP

Amble. Maxine Chernoff. *Fr.* Japan. PmAP

Amboyna; or, The Cruelties of the Dutch to the English Merchants. Dryden. Prologue: "As needy gallants in the scriv'ners' hands." OBSV

Ambrose is an Old Etonian and he. Fiction: The House Party. Gavin Ewart. PeLV

Ambrosia, brought safe. Leonidas of Tarentum, *Greek.* GrAn, *tr. by* Kenneth Rexroth

Ambrosia of Dionysus and Semele, The. Robert Graves. NYBP

Ambulance. Karl Kirchwey. WWSi

Ambulance men touched her cold, The. The Death of Marilyn Monroe. Sharon Olds. HeIP-4

Ambulance Train. Wilfred Wilson Gibson. NSI

Ambulances. Philip Larkin. FaBoTw; NAEL-2; NoP-4; OxBC

Ambulando. Charles Brasch. PeNZ

Ambush of the Fourth Platoon, The. David Hall.
  "There is no place to hide." CDa

Ambushed myself discovered. Humility. Marie Luise Kaschnitz, *German.* WPOW, *tr. by* Michael Hamburger

Amelia Earhart Series. Maureen Owen.
  "'Assholes!' her eyes seem grey in this soup the hangars." DeD

Amelia Erhardt. Amelia Erhardt, *Romanian.* CEEP, tr. by Stavros Deligiorgis

Amelia was just fourteen and out of the orphan asylum. Charles Reznikoff. ColAP *Fr.* Testimony.

Amen. Hilda Doolittle. WPoS *Fr.* The Walls Do Not Fall.

Amen. Christina Rossetti. WPoS

Amen. Richard W. Thomas. PoBA

AMEN. (LL) Tribute to Wyatt. Henry Howard, Earl of Surrey. AAS; EPCY; NAEL-1; NoSic; PeECV

Amen, Amen! Robert Burns. *See* Holy Willie's Prayer.

Amen. Amen. James Weldon Johnson. *See* The Creation.

Amen. The casket like a spaceship bears her. Annie Hill's Grave. James Merrill. WeW-3

Amen, who scared off my girl. (LL) The Rattle Bag. Dafydd ap Gwilym, *Welsh.* NBLV; NNPT; RB, tr. by Joseph Clancy

Amendis to the Telyouris and Sowtaris for the Turnament Maid on Thame, The. William Dunbar. OBSV

Amends. Adrienne Rich. *Fr.* Not Somewhere Else, But Here. BAP-93

Amergin's Charm. Amergin, *Irish.* NNPT, tr. by Robert Ranke Graves

Amergin's Songs. Amergin. NOIV

America. Kofi Awoonor. HBAPE

America. Lucretia Davidson. ColAP

America. Henry Dumas. ChAP; PoBA

America. Claude McKay. MoP; NAAAL; NIP-4; NoAM; PoBA; TAP; TTY

America. Herman Melville. APN-2

America. John Newlove. NOBC

America. Wendy Rose. CDW

America. Samuel Francis Smith. AiP; CTV; EBEvV; FaBoBe; PoLF

America. Walt Whitman. FaBoA

America; a Prophecy. William Blake. OAEL-2

America, America. K. Nisar Ahmad, *Kannada.* OMIP, tr. by A. K. Ramanujan

America Bleeds. Angelo Lewis. PoBA

America calling. Haki R. Madhubuti. NAAAL

America for Me. Henry Van Dyke. BLPA; ChAP

America, I do not call your name without hope. Pablo Neruda, *Spanish.* AF, tr. by Robert Bly

America Is Hard to See. Robert Frost. AiP; FaBoA

America is West and the wind blowing. Archibald MacLeish. *Fr.* American Letter. AmPP; OxBA

America, it is to thee. James M. Whitfield. BPo, *ll.* 1–14 *Fr.* America, it is to thee. NAAAL; PoBA

America I've given you all and now I'm nothing. Allen Ginsberg. CoAP; HCAP; InPS-3; NoAM; PmAP; PoE; PoM; PoPoPo; Poetr; TRP

America, O Power benign, great hearts revere your name. Land of the Free. Arthur Nicholas Hosking. BLPA

America the Beautiful. Katharine Lee Bates. APN-2; BLPA; CTV; EBEvV; FaBoA; FaBoBe; TAP

America / The tongues of your rivers burn with thirst. Lackawanna Elegy. Iwan Goll, *German.* AF, tr. by Galway Kinnell

America to Great Britain. Washington Allston. APN-1

America, you are luckier. The United States. Goethe, *German.* AiP; FaBoA, tr. by Robert Bly

America, you ode for reality! Robert Creeley. UnSA

American against Solitude. Alan Dugan. CAPP-1

American Boyhood, An. Jonathan Holden. Poetsp

American Change. Allen Ginsberg. HCAP

(American Crisis, The). Thomas Paine.
  "These are the times that try men's." CTV

American Dream. Vern Rutsala. CMAP

American Dream: First Report. Joseph Papaleo. UnSA

American Eagle, The. D. H. Lawrence. OAEL-2

American Experiment has entered, The. My Friends the Pigeons. Richard Katrovas. NAmP90

American Farm, 1934. Genevieve Taggard. VGW

American Flag, The. Henry Ward Beecher. CTV

American Flag, The. Joseph Rodman Drake. APN-1; FaBoBe

American frigate, a frigate of fame, An. Paul Jones's Victory. *Unknown.* AmFP

American girl in Versailles, An. "C. K. B." PeLi

American Heartbreak. Langston Hughes. AmPP; BPo; LiTM

American Heritage. Robert Sward. OBAL

American hero must triumph over, The. Eisenhower's Visit to Franco, 1959. James Wright. CAPP-1

American History. Michael S. Harper. BPo; HCAP; NoAM; PoPoPo

American Indian, The. *Unknown.* NBLV

American Indian Art: Form and Tradition. Diane Di Prima. BB

American Innocents, Oberlin, Ohio, 1954. Barry Goldensohn. NAmP90

American Journal. Robert Earl Hayden. ISC

American jump, American jump. *Unknown.* OxNR

American Letter. Archibald MacLeish. AmPP; OxBA

American Lights, Seen from Off Abroad. John Berryman. LCAP-2; OBAL; OBCoV

American Lunch. Bruce Smith. FiLi

American Memory of Africa, An. Kofi Awoonor. HBAPE
  (Afro-American Beats III: An American Memory of Africa.) PBMAP

American Names. Stephen Vincent Benét. FaBoA; OBAL; OxBA

American Poetry. Louis Simpson. FaBoA; MoP; NOBA; NoAM; TAP; WeT

American Portrait: Old Style. Robert Penn Warren. FYAP; Poetr

American Primitive. William Jay Smith. InPK-6; MoAmPo; OxBSP; RaBo; TwCP

American Rain. Marilyn Chin. OpBo

American Rhapsody. Kenneth Fearing. MoAmPo

American Scenes (1904). Donald Justice. MT

American Soldier, The. Philip Freneau. TAP

American Son. Mitsuye Yamada. UnSA

American Sonnet (10). Wanda Coleman. NAAAL

American Sonnet (35). Wanda Coleman. BAP-96

American Sonnets for My Father. Daniela Gioseffi. UnSA

American Spirit speaks, The. Rudyard Kipling. FaBoA

American Sublime, The. Wallace Stevens. FaBoA

American Tourist. B. C. Ramachandra Sharma, *Kannada.* OMIP, tr. by A. K. Ramanujan

American Trains. Reginald Gibbons. GM

American Traveller, The. "Orpheus C. Kerr." OBAL

American Twilights, 1957. James Wright. CoAP

American who would have preferred / to be merely an Indian. (LL) Mr. Brodsky. Charles Tomlinson. MoP; NoAM; OxBC

Americana IX. *Unknown.* InPS-3

Americanized. Bruce Dawe. CBAP

American's a hustler, for he says so, The. A Ballad of Abbreviations. G. K. Chesterton. NOBL

American's Apostrophe to Boz, The. William Edmonstoune Aytoun *and* Sir Theodore Martin.
  "We received thee warmly—kindly—though we knew thou wert a quiz." OBCoV

Americans in 1933–4–5–6–7–8–, Etc. Merrill Moore. FaBoA

America's Answer. R. W. Lilliard. BLPA

America's Welcome Home. Henry Van Dyke. AiP

America's Wounded Knee. Phillip William George. VoR

Amerigo has his finger on the pulse of China. Composed Near the Bay Bridge (after a wild party). Marilyn Chin. WWSi

Ametas and Thestylis Making Hay-Ropes. Andrew Marvell. SeCP

Amherst. Amy Clampitt. NMM-2

Amhrán na mBréag. Pearse Hutchinson. PBCIP

Amid my bale I bathe in bliss. A Straunge [*or* Strange] Passion of a Lover. George Gascoigne. AAS

Amid tall hills and stretches of white sand. A Down-and-Out Fighter and the Spring Nymph. Trần Huy Liệu, *Vietnamese.* AVP, tr. by Huỳnh Sanh Thông

Amid the bitterness of things occult. (LL) For "Our Lady of the Rocks." D. G. Rossetti. EBEV; GS

Amid the cares of married strife. Tell Her So. *Unknown.* PoToHe

Amid the dawn's scaffolding, lines of ink and lead. Plans. Dan Pagis, *Hebrew.* IP, tr. by Warren Bargad *and* Stanley F. Chyet

Amid the derringers I ride. Edward Blishen. NTP

Amid the desolation of a city. The Tower of Famine. Shelley. Poetr

Amid the hush of the distant hills which house. Gettysburg. Edgar Lee Masters. CBCWP

Amid the medley of ironic things. The Cage. Rosamund Marriott Watson. VWP

Amid the sunny farms of Killingworth. (LL) Birds of Killingworth, The (The Poet's Tale). Henry Wadsworth Longfellow. MeMAP; OxBA

Amid the turbulent waters. The Turbulent Water. *Unknown, Chinese.* TAL, tr. by Robert Payne

Amid the waves of time. Tanka. Sasaki Yukitsuna, *Japanese.* MJT, tr. by Makoto Ueda

Amid these fragments of heroic days. Sonnet. James Russell Lowell. NCAP

Amid this fearful trance, a thundering sound. William Falconer. ECEV *Fr.* The Shipwreck.

Amid this hot green glowing gloom. Interlude. Dame Edith Sitwell. MoBrPo

Amid Tibetan snows the ancient lama. What Hath Man Wrought Exclamation Point. Morris Gilbert Bishop. NYBP

Amidst a smoking desolation. Vladislav Felitsianovich Khodasevich, *Russian*. TCRP, *tr. by* Michael Frayn.

Amidst bamboo, gate pulled shut. Nodding Off. Kao Ch'i, *Chinese*. CoBLCP, *tr. by* Jonathan Chaves

Amidst the notes. Akiko Yosano, *Japanese*. OHMPJ, *tr. by* Kenneth Rexroth

Amiel's Leg. Thomas Lux. CMAP

Amien's Song. Shakespeare. *See* Song: "What shall he have that kill'd the dear?"

Amiens's Song. Shakespeare. *See* Song: "Blow, blow, thou winter wind."

Amiens's Song. Shakespeare. *See* Song: "Under the greenwood tree."

Aminta. Torquato Tasso, *Italian*.

  Pastoral[1], A: "Oh [*or* O] happy golden age." OAEL-1; PoEL-2, *tr. by* Samuel Daniel

  (Golden Age, The.) AWP, *tr. by* Leigh Hunt

Amish are a surly sect, The. John Updike. OBAL

Amish Rug, An. Michael Longley. CIP-2; PNI

Amitabha's Vow. Gary Snyder. *Fr.* Burning. NeAP; PoM *Fr.* Myths and Texts.

Ammonite, The. Peter Huchel, *German*. CEEP, *tr. by* Michael Hamburger

Amnesia. David Lehman. EOEF

Amnesia. Bruce Weigl. CDa

Amnesiac. Mark Osaki. CDa

Amnesiac. Sylvia Plath. NYBP

Amnesty. "Ivan Venediktovich Elagin," *Russian*. TCRP, *tr. by* Bertram D. Wolfe

Amo, Amas. John O'Keefe. GBL

Amoeba named Sam, and his brother, An. Limerick. *Unknown*. PeLi

Among all lovely things my Love had been. Wordsworth. GBL

Among bloody candles I welcomed winter 1254. Notation in Gold. Ljubomir Simovic, *Serbo-Croatian*. HSix, *tr. by* Charles Simic

Among branches. Gray Glove. Roo Borson. NOBC

Among green shades and flowering ghosts, the remembrances of love. The Two Fires. Judith Wright. MoBrPo

Among Hawks. Lance Henson. VoR

Among His Books. Edith Nesbit. NOBVV

  ("Silent room—grey with a dusty blight, A.") PEW

Among His Books. Robert Southey. *See* The Scholar.

Among immortal things not made with hands. Nihilism. Lionel Pigot Johnson. ADE

Among left trucks, mailbags, churns. Homing Pigeons. Ted Walker. NYBP

Among men of plain clothes. Ma Chih-yüan. *Fr.* Two Poems to the Tune "Po pu tuan." CoBLCP, *tr. by* Jonathan Chaves

Among mortal petals-and-leaves / light. (LL) Iris. Muriel Rukeyser. APSN; ColAP

Among mosquitoes. Mary Kinzie. FFC

Among my friends love is a great sorrow. Robert Duncan. CLPP

Among / of / green. The Locust Tree in Flower. William Carlos Williams. PFTM; Spl; TTTS

Among pelagian travellers [*or* travelers]. On the Circuit. W. H. Auden. FaBoA; NOBL; OxBTC

Among Philistines. R. S. Gwynn. MT; RA

Among red leaves and green mountains, white clouds fly. T'ang Yin. *Fr.* Poems Inscribed on Paintings. CoBLCP, *tr. by* Jonathan Chaves

Among scattered Christ stones. Ruined Chapel. George Mackay Brown. FaBoTC *Fr.* Runes from a Holy Island.

Among School Children. W. B. Yeats. CABP; CMoP; GTBS-P; HAP; ImPo; InPS-3; LiTM; MoBrPo; MoP; NAEL-2; NAWM-2; NIP-4; NOBE; NoAM; NoP-4; OAEL-2; OxBTC; PoE; PoPoPo; Poetr; SCGP; TFi; TRP

Among Sharks. Alfred M. Lee. AmPA

Among snake-patterned swords Weland tasted sorrow. Deor. *Unknown, Anglo-Saxon*. EBEV, *tr. by* John Wain

Among some hills there dwelt in parody. The Song of Absinthe Granny. Ruth Stone. NALW

Among Strangers. William Stafford. NNaP

Among the ancient tombs both high and low. On an Ancient Tomb East of the Village. Po Chü-i, *Chinese*. TAL, *tr. by* Robert Payne

Among the beautiful pictures. Alice Cary. BLPA

Among the Berkshire Hills. Henrietta Cordelia Ray. CBWP-3

Among the blest [*or* blessed] in endless joys remain. (LL) On My Dear Grandchild Simon Bradstreet, [Who Died on 16TH November, 1669, Being But A Month And One Day Old]. Anne Bradstreet. ColAP; KTR; NAAL-1; NAAL-3; SCAP

Among the blue pine-woods! (LL) Field Manoeuvres. Richard Aldington. PeFWW; PoFWW

Among the busy streets. The Flowers in Town. Stanley Cook. AYFP

Among the dead we come. *Unknown, Greek*. PGA, *tr. by* Kenneth Rexroth

Among the dear old friends we people cherish. Memory of Lincoln and the Yankees. James Ephriam McGirt. AAP

Among the deepening shades. (LL) The Tower. W. B. Yeats. CMoP; LiTM; NoAM; PoE; SCGP

Among the drinking doves, Galla Placidia. Afternoon Hours. Rossana Ombres. PeFWW *Fr.* Excursion to Ravenna of A Young Girl with Her Parents.

Among the Firs. Eugene Lee-Hamilton. NOBVV

Among the first to wake. What wakes with me? A Study. Alice Thompson Meynell. VWP

Among the glittering stars your voices named. (LL) Post-Script: for Gweno. Alun Lewis. BoLoP; GTBS-P

Among the great, no smooth and open world. Nguyễn Trãi, *Vietnamese*. AVP, *tr. by* Huỳnh Sanh Thông.

Among the greatest plagues, one is the third day ague. Of Scolding Wives and the Third Day Ague. Henricus Selyns. AiP; SCAP

Among the high-branching, leafless boughs. The View from an Attic Window. Howard Nemerov. CoAP; CoAmPo

Among the Hills. John Greenleaf Whittier.

  Prelude: "Along the roadside, like the flowers of gold." APN-1; NAAL-1; OxBA; PoEL-4

  (Prelude to *Among the Hills*.) NAAL-3

Among the hundreds. Tanka. Shaku Chōkū, *Japanese*. MJT, *tr. by* Makoto Ueda

Among the iodoform, in twilight-sleep. The Leg. Karl Shapiro. HAP; MoAmPo; UnPo; WeW-3

Among the later dinosaurs. Pachycephalosaurus. Richard Armour. ChAP

Among the leaves the small birds sing. Lauds. W. H. Auden. TrCP *Fr.* Horae Canonicae.

Among the lilies, and forgetting them. (LL) The Obscure Night of the Soul. Saint John of the Cross. AWP, OBMV, *tr. by* Arthur Symons.

Among the men and women the multitude. Among the Multitude. Walt Whitman. APN-1

Among the Missing. Richard Howard. WWSi

Among the Multitude. Walt Whitman. APN-1

Among the Narcissi. Sylvia Plath. FaBoMo; RB; SCV

Among the Nuts. *Unknown*. BoTP

Among the orchard weeds, from every search. Hen's Nest. John Clare. Son

Among the other children playing. The Ugly Girl. Nikolai Alekseievich Zabolotsky, *Russian*. TCRP, *tr. by* Daniel Weissbort

Among the oxen (like an ox I'm slow). The Nativity. C. S. Lewis. ChIV-2; TrCP

Among the pickled foetuses and bottled bones. Siena Mi Fe'; Disfecemi Maremma. Ezra Pound. MoAmPo *Fr.* Hugh Selwyn Mauberley. (Life and Contacts). AmPP; CMoP; InPS-3; LiTM; NOBA; NoAM; TAP

Among the pines—mdash;White Stone Slope. White Stone Slope. Yang Shih-ch'i. CoBLCP, *tr. by* Jonathan Chaves *Fr.* The Intendant Yao Shan Has Requested Six Poems on Living in the Mountains.

Among the plovers and the stonechats. Of Difference Does It Make. Tom Paulin. BiHa

Among the poems I wrote with many pictures spread out before me[2]. Masaoka Shiki, *Japanese*. MJT, *tr. by* Ueda, Makoto

Among the primary rocks. The Forest. Miroslav Holub, *Czech*. PoSu, *tr. by* George Theiner

Among the provisions they carried. Michael Anania. *Fr.* The Riversongs of Arion. NoAM

Among the rain. The Great Figure. William Carlos Williams. AiP; HeIP-4; InPK-6; MoP; NoAM; SAmP; TTTS

Among the red words that drink his voice. (LL) Yuba City School. Chitra Divakaruni. LTA; LoHo; OpBo

Among the rocks. At the Cemetery, Walnut Grove Plantation, South Carolina, 1989. Lucille Clifton. LoL

Among the Rocks. Robert Browning. OxBSP *Fr.* James Lee's Wife.

Among the Roman love-poets, possession. Note on Propertius I.5. Fleur Adcock. BoLoP; EP; PeNZ

Among the sayings of our race. We Are Rising. George Clinton Rowe. AAP

Among the signs of autumn I perceive. Tall Ambrosia. Henry David Thoreau. PoEL-4

Among the smoke and fog of a December afternoon. Portrait of a Lady. T. S. Eliot. TwCP

Among the smooth hills of Manika. Magwere, Who Waits Wondering. Kingsley Fairbridge. PeSAV

Among the splendour of torches of darkness, shedding darkness on the lost bride and her groom. (LL) Bavarian Gentians. D. H. Lawrence. CMoP; FaBoCh; FaBoMo; GTBS-P; HAP; ImPo; InPK-6; InPS-3; MoP; NAEL-2; NOBE; NoAM; OAEL-2; PoE; Poetr; TFi; TRP; TTTS

Among the springs which flow from Ida's head. *Unknown, formerly at. to* Homer. OBVE, *tr. by* Congreve *Fr.* The Hymn to Venus.

Among the swells, the storm past, surfers sit. At Will Robers Beach. Timothy Steele. WeW-3

Among the taller wood with ivy hung. The Vixen. John Clare. RB

Among the white walls we read quietly. House-Rules I: Reading. Alistair Elliot. CBLP

Among the worlds a world. (LL) The Dream of the Quartz Pebble. Vasco [*or* Vasko] Popa. PoSu, *tr. by* Anne Pennington; CEEP, *tr. by* Charles Simic

Among the worst of men that ever lived. Henry David Thoreau. PoEL-4

Among their spears and chariots. (LL) Achilles Over the Trench. Homer, *Greek.* OBCVT; OBVE, *tr. by* Tennyson

Among them marble where the man may lie. A Thurn. John Berryman. NOBA

Among these mountains, do you know. For Allan, Who Wanted to See How I Wrote a Poem. Robert Frost. PChr

Among these othre of Slouthes kinde. John Gower. EnVB, *sect.* IV *Fr.* Confessio Amantis.

Among these tempests great and manifold. His Hope or Sheet-Anchor. Robert Herrick. CaPo

Among These Troopes of Christs Souldiers, Came. . . Mr. Roger Harlackenden. Edward Johnson. SCAP

Among these turf-stacks graze no iron horses. Turf-Stacks. Louis MacNeice. ImPo; LiTM; OBMV

Among these joys, 'tis one at eve to sail. Sailing upon the River. George Crabbe. OBNC *Fr.* The Borough.

Among Those Killed in the Dawn Raid Was a Man Aged a Hundred. Dylan Thomas. Son

Among trees / my father was a spruce. Family Photograph. Gerald Vizenor. VoR

Among twenty snowy mountains. Thirteen Ways of Looking at a Blackbird. Wallace Stevens. CMoP; ChAP; ColAP; HCAP; HeIP-4; InPK-5; InPS-3; LiTM; MoP; NAAL-2; NOBA; NoAM; NoP-4; PiM; PoE; PoPoPo; Poetr; RB; SAmP; TAP; TFi

Among us are those who apply. Kiss Tomorrow Goodbye. Marjorie Welish. FTOS

Among Women. Marie Ponsot. NMM-2

Amongest many kings. Desire of Dominion. Timothy Kendall. NoSic

Amongst the Cliffs. Han Yü, *Chinese.* OHMPC, *tr. by* Kenneth Rexroth

Amongst the highly placed. From a German War Primer. Bertolt Brecht, *German.* AF, *tr. by* John Willett, Ralph Manheim *and* Erich Fried

Amongst the leaves so green. (LL) Robin Hood and Allen [*or* Allin] -a-Dale. *Unknown.* ESPB; FaBoBe; OxAEP-1

Amongst the poets Dacus numbered is. Sir John Davies. NoSic *Fr.* Epigrams.

Amongst the princely paragons. A Princely Ditty in Praise of the English Rose. Thomas Deloney. BoTP

Amongst these graves where good men lie. In an Irish Churchyard. "Violet Fane." VWP

Amongst us there's a canon regular. The Canon Assistant's Tale. Chaucer. OxBoV, *tr. by* David Wright *Fr.* The Canterbury Tale.

Amor Loci. W. H. Auden. NOCV

Amor Mundi. Christina Rossetti. NoP-4; PEW; RACG
    ("Oh where are you going with your lovelocks flowing.") PoEL-5; Poetr

Amor Mysticus. Sister Marcela de Carpio de San Felix, *Spanish.* AWP, *tr. by* John Hay

Amor Vincit Omnia. Edgar Bowers. VCAP

Amores. Ovid, *Latin.*
    Complaisant Swain, The. AWP, *tr. by* F. A. Wright

Amoret. Mark Akenside. OBEV

Amorette. Edmund Spenser.
    18. CABP
    80. CABP

Amoretti. Edmund Spenser. AAS
    Sonnet 1: "Happy ye leaves! whenas those lily hands." EBEV; NAEL-1; OAEL-1; PoE; Son
        ("Happy ye leaves when as those lilly hands.") NoP-4
    Sonnet 3: "Soverayne beauty which I doo admire, The." PoEL-1
        ("Sovereign beauty which I do admire, The.") AEP
    Sonnet 4: "New year, forth looking out of Janus' gate." NoSic
    Sonnet 8: "More than most fair [*or* fayre], full of the living fire [*or* fyre]." PoE; Son
        ("More then most faire, full of the living fire.") NoP-4
        ("Well is he borne, that may behold you ever.") (LL) NoP-4
    Sonnet 10: 'Unrighteous Lord of Love'. AEP
        ("As she doth laugh at me and makes my pain her sport.") (LL) NoP-4
    Sonnet 13: "In That proud port, which her so goodly graceth." Son

Sonnet 15: "Ye tradeful merchants that, with weary toil." HeIP-4; NIP-4; OAEL-1; Son
    ("Her mind adornd with vertues manifold.") (LL) NoP-4
    ("Ye tradefull Merchants that with weary toyle.") NoP-4
Sonnet 16: "One day as I unwarily did gaze." OAEL-1
Sonnet 22: "This holy season, fit to fast and pray." PoE
Sonnet 25: "How long shall this like dying life endure." AAS
Sonnet 27: "Fair proud, now tell me, why should fair be proud." Son
Sonnet 30: "My love is like to ice, and I to fire." ImPo
Sonnet 34: "Like as a ship, that through the ocean wide." NAEL-1; PoE
Sonnet 37: "What guile [*or* guyle] is this, that those her golden tresses." NAEL-1; Son
    ("What guyle is this, that those her golden tresses.") NoP-4
Sonnet 44: "When those renowned noble peers of Greece." PoE
Sonnet 54: "Of this world's Theatre in which we stay." NAEL-1; OAEL-1
    (54.) CABP
    ("She is no woman, but a senseless stone.") (LL) CABP
Sonnet 55: "So oft as I her beauty do behold." Son
Sonnet 56: "Fair ye be sure, but cruel and unkind." Son
Sonnet 61: "Glorious image of the Maker's beauty, The." Son
Sonnet 63: "After long storms and tempests sad assay." OAEL-1
Sonnet 64: "Coming [*or* Comming] to kiss[e] her lips [*or* lyps], (such grace I found)." EBEV; NAEL-1; OAEL-1; PBRV; Son
    ("But her sweet odour did them all excell.") (LL) PBRV
Sonnet 65.": "Doubt which ye misdeeme, fayre love, is vaine, The." NAEL-1
    ("Doubt which ye misdeem, fair love, is vain, The.") AEP
Sonnet 67: "Like a huntsman after weary chase." GBL; HeIP-4; NAEL-1; PoE; PoEL-1; Son
    (67.) CABP
    ("Lyke as a huntsman after weary chace.") NoP-4; PBRV
    ("So goodly won, with her own will beguil'd.") (LL) CABP
Sonnet 68: "Most glorious Lord of Life that on this day." ChIV-2; HAP; InPS-3; NAEL-1; NOCV; NoSic; PoE; Son
    (Easter.) NOBE; OBEV; PeECV
    ("Most Glorious Lord of lyfe that on this day.") NoP-4; PeECV
Sonnet 70: "Fresh Spring the herald of love's mighty king." AWP; HAP; InPS-3; OBEV; PoE; Son
    ("For none can call againe the passèd time.") (LL) NoP-4; PBRV
Sonnet 71: "I joy to see how in your drawen work." PoE
Sonnet 72: "Oft when my spirit doth spread her bolder wings." Son
Sonnet 74: "Most happy letters framed by skilfull trade." NAEL-1
Sonnet 75: "One day I wrote her name upon the strand." AWP; BoLoP; CBLP; EBEV; EPCY; GBL; HAP; HeIP-4; ImPo; InPS-3; NAEL-1; NoSic; OAEL-1; PBMP; PoE; PoPoPo; Son; TFi; WeW-3
    (75.) CABP
Sonnet 75: "Was it a dream, or did I see it plain?" CBLP; NIP-4
Sonnet 76: "Fair bosom! fraught with virtue's richest treasure." NIP-4
Sonnet 78: "Lacking my love, I go from place to place." NoSic
Sonnet 79: "Men call you fair [*or* fayre], and you do[e] credit it." AWP; FaBoBe; NAEL-1; Son
    ("All other fayre lyke flowres untymely fade.") (LL) NoP-4
    ("Men call you fayre, and you doe credit it.") NoP-4
Sonnet 81: "Fair [*or* Fayre] is my love, when her fair [*or* fayre] golden heares." Son
    ("But this the worke of harts astonishment.") (LL) NoP-4
    ("Fair is my love, when her fair golden hairs.") GSo
Sonnet 82: "Joy of my life, full oft for loving you." HeIP-4
Sonnet 89: "Like as the culver on the bared bough." GBL; PoE
    ("And dead my life that wants such lively blis.") (LL) NoP-4
    ("Lyke as the Culver on the barèd bough.") NoP-4

Amorgos. Nikos Gatsos, *Greek.*
    "How very much I loved you only I know." GrIP
Amoris Victima. Arthur Symons.
    "And yet, there was a hunger in your eyes." PeVV
Amorix Exsul. Arthur Symons.
    In the Bay. OBNC
Amorous Leander, beautiful and young. Marlowe. *Fr.* Hero and Leander. AAS
Amorous maiden antique, An. Limerick. *Unknown.* PeLi
Amorous Neptune. Marlowe. NOBE *Fr.* Hero and Leander. AAS
Amorous Temper, An. John Trumbull. *Fr.* The Progress of Dulness. AmPP
Amos. Bible, *O.T.*
    O Ye That Would Swallow the Needy. TrJP
Among the blight–killed eucalypts, amoung. In California During the Gulf War. Denise Levertov. BAP-93

Amount, not wearisome and bare and steep. To a Young Friend, [on His Proposing to Domesticate with the Author]. Coleridge. LaPo

Amours de Voyage. Arthur Hugh Clough. NOBVV

Ah, That I Were Far Away. OBNC

Claude to Eustace. PeLV

Claude to Eustace: "Ah, let me look, let me watch, let me wait, unhurried, unprompted!" EnVR

Claude to Eustace: "I am in love, meantime, you think; no doubt you would think so." EnVR; FaBoVe

Claude to Eustace: "Juxtaposition is great,—but, you tell me, affinity greater." CBLP

Claude to Eustace: "No, the Christian faith, as at any rate I understood it." EnVR

Claude to Eustace: "Shall we come out of it all, some day, as one does from a tunnel?" EBVVPR

Claude to Eustace: "These are the facts. The uncle, the elder brother, the squire." FaBoVe

Claude to Eustace: "Yes, we are fighting at last, it appears. This morning, as usual." EBVV; OxAEP-2; PeVV

Claude to Eustace—*from Bellagio*. FaBoVe

"Dear Eustatio, I write that you may write me an answer." EBVV; EBVVPR; FaBoVe; OxAEP-2

"Dulce it is, and *decorum*, no doubt, for the country to fall, to." EBVV; EnVR; FaBoPV; OxAEP-2

"Farewell, politics, utterly! What can I do? I can not." FaBoPV

Georgina Trevellyn to Luisa: "At last, dearest Louisa, I take up my pen to address you." EBVVPR

Georgina Trevellyn to Luisa: "Dearest Louisa, Enquire if you please about Mr. Claude." FaBoVe

Juxtaposition. OBNC

(Claude to Eustace.) CBLP

"Luther, they say, was unwise; he didn't see how things were going." FaBoVe

Mary Trevellyn to Miss Roper. FaBoVe

"Oh, 'tisn't manly, of course, 'tisin't manly, this method of / wooing;." EBVVPR, *canto* 2, 14

"Only think, dearest Louisa, what fearful scenes we have witnessed!" EBVV

"Rome disappoints me still; but I shrink and adapt myself to it." EBVV; EBVVPR; OxAEP-2

"Rome will not suit me, Eustace; the priests and soldiers possess / it;." EBVVPR, *canto* 5, 10

"So, I have seen a man killed!" EBVV; PeVV

Spirit from Perfecter Ages. OBNC

"To-morrow we're starting for Florence." EBVVPR, *canto* 2, 15

"When God makes a great Man he intends all others to crush him." OBSV

"Wherefore and how I am certain, I can hardly tell; but it [*or* is so]." EBVVPR, *canto* 2, 13

"You have heard nothing; of course I know you can have heard / nothing." EBVVPR, *canto* 5, 11

Amphibious Crocodile. John Crowe Ransom. FuPo; OBAL

Amphitryon. Dryden.

Mercury's Song [to Phaedra]. NOSC; OxBSP; PBMP; PoEL-3

(Song.) AWP

Amphora, The. Fyodor Kuz'mich Sologub, *Russian*. AWP, *tr. by* Babette Deutsch *and* Avrahm Yarmolinsky

Amphora / as an emotion. Luchezar Elenkov, *Bulgarian*. CEEP, *tr. by* Ewald Osers

Ample heaven of fabrik sure, The. A Summer's Day. Alexander Hume. CH

Ample make this Bed. Emily Dickinson. MoAmPo; NAAL-1; NAAL-3; OxBA; PoEL-5

Ample the air above the western peaks. After Nightfall. William Renton. NOBVV

Ampoo is intensely neat, The. The Utter Zoo Alphabet. Edward Gorey. CBNP

Amsterdam. Jean Garrigue. TAP

Amsterdam. Francis Jammes, *French*. AWP, *tr. by* Jethro Bithell

Amsterdam Letter. Jean Garrigue. NYBP; VCAP

Amulet. Ted Hughes. NOxBChV

Amulet, The. Isaac Rosenberg.

"Slime clung, The." PeFWW

Amurrika! Philip Appleman. BXAP

Amusement. Laurie Schorr. CMAP

Amusing myself with rocks, I sit peering into the valley. The Temple of Bequeathed Love. Po Chü-i, *Chinese*. CoBCP, *tr. by* Burton Watson

Amusing Our Daughters. Carolyn Kizer. VCAP; VGW

Amy Elizabeth Ermyntrude Annie. Queenie Scott-Hopper. BoTP

Amy Lowell. Lola Ridge. NMM-2

Amyd the wod his modir met thame tway. Aeneas (with Achates) Meets His Mother, Venus. Virgil. OBVE, *tr. by* Gawin Douglas *Fr.* The Aeneid [*or* Eneados, *Aeneis*].

Amyir gaffirz Gaffir. Hark. Feed Ma Lamz. Tom Leonard. FaBoTC

Amymone. Rufinus, *Greek*. GrAn, *tr. by* Alan Marshfield

Amyntas Led Me to a Grove. The Willing Mistriss. Aphra Behn. FaBoSe; LW; NALW; PEW *Fr.* The Dutch Lover.

An Phurgóid. Michael Hartnett. *See* The Purge.

Ana Historic. Daphne Marlatt.

"Trying. a trying child. trying it on for size. the role." DeD

Ana(Mary-Army)gram. George Herbert. ChIV-2; GeHe; OAEL-1

Anabasis. "St.-John Perse," *French*. PFTM, *tr. by* T. S. Eliot

Anachronism. Oliver St. John Gogarty. FYAP

Anaconda, The. Dennis Sampson. PUP-20

Anacreon. Friedrich von Hagedorn, *German*. GePo, *tr. by* George C. Schoolfield

Anacreon, my teacher. Johann Wilhelm Ludwig Gleim, *German*. GePo, *tr. by* George C. Schoolfield

Anacreon's Dove. Samuel Johnson. AWP

Anacreon's Grave. Goethe, *German*. STV, *tr. by* John Frederick Nims

Anacreon's Portrait of His Mistress. Anacreon, *Greek*. OBCVT, *tr. by* Leigh Hunt

Anacreontic. Austin Clarke. NOIV

Anacreontic. R. S. Gwynn. RA

Anacreontic. Robert Herrick. CaPo; CavPo; OxBoLi

Anacreontic. John Thelwall. NOBRP

Anacreontic, on Parting with a Little Child. Samuel Wesley. NOEC

Anacreontic to Flip. Royall Tyler. OBAL

Anacreontic[k] Verse. Robert Herrick. PeLV

Anacreontique on Love, An. Anacreon, *Greek*. OBCVT, *tr. by* Allan Ramsay

Anactoria. Swinburne. LoP; RACG

Anadarko John. Carroll Arnett. VoR

Anaerobics: Elaine Powers, Wheeling, West Virginia. Linda Mizejewski. CMAP

Anaesthesia. Jean Valentine. TAP

Anagrammic scramble. Scourge / of sound. Alphabet of Ahtt. Nathaniel Mackey. FTOS

Anahorish. Seamus Heaney. PBCIP

Analogue. Marie Ponsot. CLPP

Analogue of Unity in Multeity. Richard Eberhart. Poetr

Analogy. Brian Higgins. FaBoTw

Analysands. Dudley Randall. BPo

Analysis of Baseball. May Swenson. ImGa; KaS

Anaphora. Elizabeth Bishop. AFr

Anarchy and grow your own. Durham. Tony Harrison. NoAM

Anasazi drink from underground rivers, The. David Ferry. FaBoA

Anastasia McLaughlin. Tom Paulin. PBCIP

Anastasia, the Graces blossom and you were their flower. Julianus of Egypt, *Greek*. GrAn, *tr. by* W. S. Merwin

Anathemata, The. David Jones.

Angle-Land. NoAM

"Did he meet Lud at the Fleet Gate? did count the top." EBEV

"Ship's master:/ before him, in the waist and before it." FaBoTw

"We already and first of all discern him making this thing other." PeECV

Anatomy of Happiness, The. Ogden Nash. TAP

Anatomy of Humor, The. Morris Gilbert Bishop. NBLV

Anatomy of Melancholy, The. Robert Burton.

Authors [*or* Author's] Abstract of Melancholy, The. NOSC

Anatomy [*or* Anatomie] of the World, An[: The First Anniversary], *sels.* Donne.

First Anniversary [*or* Anniversarie], The. NAEL-1

"And new philosophy calls all in doubt." NOSC

Anatomy of Winter, The. Hesiod, *Greek*. OBCVT, *tr. by* Robert Garioch

Ancestor. Thomas Kinsella. BIrV; NOIV; PBCIP; PoE

("I was going up to say something.") NoP-4

Ancestors, The. John Peale Bishop. PoA

Ancestors. Edward Kamau Brathwaite. NoP-4

Ancestors. Rowley Habib. PeNZ

Ancestors. Dudley Randall. BPo

Ancestral Faces. Kwesi Brew. PBA

Ancestral Houses. W. B. Yeats. OAEL-2; OBGa *Fr.* Meditations in Time of Civil War.

Ancestral Messengers/Composition 13. Ntozake Shange. GT

Ancestral pearls so deep, so blue. Baptism. Alvin Aubert. BkSV

Ancestral Poem. Olive Senior. PBCV

Ancestral Weight. Alfonsina Storni, *Spanish.* WPOW, *tr.* by Marti Moody

Anchises, Paris, and Adonis too. Spoken by Venus on Seeing Her Statue Done by Praxiteles. *Unknown, Greek.* FaBoEE

Anchises to Aeneas. Virgil, *Latin.* OBCVT, *tr.* by Sir Walter Alexander Raleigh *Fr.* The Aeneid [*or* Eneados, *Aeneis*].

Anchor, The. John Blight. BMAP

Anchor at Hampton Roads we lay, An. The Cumberland. Henry Wadsworth Longfellow. CBCWP

Anchor: I must fight with the waves whipped up by the wind. Cynewulf. ASW, *tr.* by Kevin Crossley-Holland *Fr.* Riddles (Exeter Book).

Anchor: "Oft I must strive with wind and wave." Cynewulf. AnOE, *tr.* by Charles W. Kennedy *Fr.* Riddles (Exeter Book).

Anchorage. Joy Harjo. HATNAP; NMM-2; UnSA

("To survive?") (LL) LTA

Anchored now to Neptune's temple floor, this. A Dedication. Macedonius, *Greek.* GrAn, *tr.* by Adrian Wright

Anchored on the Chin-huai River, the rain has vanished. Tune: "Magnolia Blossoms, Slow"—Traveling on the Yangtze. Chiang Ch'un-lin, *Chinese.* SuSp, *tr.* by Bruce Carpenter

Anchors aweigh! O boat, please let the waves. Far Away. Vū Hoàng Chu'o'ng, *Vietnamese.* AVP, *tr.* by Huỳnh Sanh Thông

Anchorsmiths, The. Charles Dibdin. NOEC

Ancient Airs. Li Po, *Chinese.* SuSp, *tr.* by Joseph J. Lee

(Ancient Air.) BLT, *tr.* by J. P. Seaton

("Westward over Lotus Mountain.") BLT, *tr.* by J. P. Seaton

("Wolves, with men's hats on their heads.") (LL) BLT, *tr.* by J. P. Seaton

Ancient annals strewn left and right. Occasional Poem. Han Yü, *Chinese.* SuSp, *tr.* by Charles Hartman

Ancient Autumn. Charles Simic. ColAP

Ancient Barbarossa, the Kaiser Frederick old, The. Barbarossa. Friedrich Rückert, *German.* AWP, *tr.* by Elizabeth Craigmyle

Ancient biologist, Heine, An. Limerick. Carol Rumens. PeLi

Ancient Castle, The. William Morris. *Fr.* Golden Wings. OBNC

Ancient chestnut's blossoms threw, An. Alciphron and Leucippe. Walter Savage Landor. OBEV

Ancient Christmas Carol. *Unknown.* PChr

Ancient Couple on Lu Mountain, The. Mark Van Doren. VGW

Ancient Feeling. Wu Wei-yeh, *Chinese.* CoBLCP, *tr.* by Jonathan Chaves

Ancient Gesture, An. Edna St. Vincent Millay. NALW; NMM-2

Ancient History. Arthur Guiterman. KaS; OBCA

Ancient History. Siegfried Sassoon. ChIV-1

Ancient Lights. Austin Clarke. BIrV; CMoP

Ancient Masters were profound and subtle, The. Lao Tzu. EnlH *Fr.* Tao Te Ching.

Ancient Monuments. John Ormond. OBWVE

Ancient Music, *par. of* Sumer Is Icumen In. Ezra Pound. BXAP; HeIP-4; LiTM; NBLV; OBAL; OBCoV; OxBA; PBMP; PeLV; UV

Ancient nomadic snowman has rolled around. The Snowman. Patricia K. Page. NOBC

Ancient of Days, old friend, no one believes you'll come back. Stone Canyon Nocturne. Charles Wright. ColAP; HCAP; LCAP-2; VCAP; WeT

Ancient of Days, who sittest throned in glory. William Croswell Doane. AH

Ancient, outworn, Puritanic traditions of Right and Wrong, The. (LL) The Woman and the Angel. Robert W. Service. ChIV-1

Ancient pages of the Talmud. The Talmud. Simeon Grigoryevich Frug, *Yiddish.* TrJP, *tr.* by Alice Stone Blackwell

Ancient Person, for whom I. A Song of a Young Lady to Her Ancient Lover. John Wilmot, 2d Earl of Rochester. APAD; BoLoP; EBEV; GBL; GLoP; NoP-4; NOSC; OxAEP-1

Ancient Person of my Heart. (LL) A Song of a Young Lady to Her Ancient Lover. John Wilmot, 2d Earl of Rochester. APAD; BoLoP; EBEV; GBL; GLoP; NOSC; OxAEP-1

Ancient Pistol, peacock Payne. Tennyson. FaBoEE

Ancient pool. Sound. Basho, *Japanese.* KaS, *tr.* by Olivia Gray

Ancient Prayer, An. Thomas Henry Basil Webb. BLPA; CTV; FaBoBe

(Prayer Found in Chester Cathedral, A.) PoToHe

Ancient Rites of the Condoling Council. *Unknown, Iroquois.*

"TEHKARIHHOKEN! / Continue to listen!" APN-2, *tr.* by Horatio Hale

Ancient saga tells us how, An. Dead Cow Farm. Robert Graves. PoWW

Ancient Song. Amir Gilbo'a, *Hebrew.* IP, *tr.* by Warren Bargad *and* Stanley F. Chyet

Ancient Song of a Woman of Fez, An. *Unknown, Arabic.* BoWoP, *tr.* by Willis Barnstone

Ancient spring year after year abides. Temple of the Orchid Fragrance Goddess. Li Ho, *Chinese.* SuSp, *tr.* by Michael Fish

Ancient story I'll tell you anon, An. King John and the Abbot of Canterbury. *Unknown.* BoTP; EnSB

Ancient to Ancients, An. Thomas Hardy. CMoP; GTBS-P; LiTM; OxBTC; SCGP

Ancient Virgin, An. George Crabbe. OBNC *Fr.* Burials. OAEL-1 *Fr.* The Parish Register.

Ancient Winter. Salvatore Quasimodo. ItIP

Ancient Wisdom, Rather Cosmic. Ezra Pound. NOBA

Ancientest of cats, truest. Hoppy. Reginald Gibbons. DiPo

Ancientness surrounds me. Death. Patty L. Harjo. VoR

Ancients argued that friendship could never last, The. Quarreling. Lyall Tao Tschung Yu. FP

Ancients happily could sing, The. Our Naughty Time. Friedrich von Logau, *German.* GePo, *tr.* by George C. Schoolfield

Ancients lie buried under barren hills, The. A Occasional Poem. Lu Yu, *Chinese.* SuSp, *tr.* by Chiang Yee

Ancients of the World, The. Ronald Stuart Thomas. OPOU; RB

Ancre at Hamel: Afterwards, The. Edmund Blunden. PeFWW

And. Robert Creeley. LCAP-2

And. Desire. Kurt Schwitters, *German.* PFTM, *tr.* by Jerome Rothenberg

And a blind seed all. (LL) The Road. Edwin Muir. CMoP; ImPo; LiTM

And a child I slept. (LL) The View from an Attic Window. Howard Nemerov. CoAP; CoAmPo

And a cruel wind blows. (LL) End of Summer. Stanley Kunitz. LoL; MoAmPo; Poetsp; SAGP; VGW

And a faggot of useless memories. (LL) Nightmare leaves fatigue. Louis MacNeice. BIrV; CIP-2; PNI

And a father's love add up to silence. (LL) A Story. Li-Young Lee. IFJA; LoL; RaBo

And a glass of brandy neat. (LL) Sweeney Erect. T. S. Eliot. OxBTC; VGW

And a good little child will not play with him. (LL) Lion, the Lion, he dwells in the waste, The. Hilaire Belloc. CTAV

And a green coat covers me all. (LL) A Walnut. Mother Goose. LB; OxNR; ReMoGo

And a green gown. (LL) Daffadowndilly. Mother Goose. CTV; NTCP; OxNR

And a Happy New Year. *Unknown.* See Christmas Carol: "God bless the master of this house."

And a little fame. (LL) Since. W. H. Auden. CBLP; InPS-3

And a little shrunken. (LL) Tanka: "Palm of the hand, The, / is not aware of dying." Fumi Saito, *Japanese.* MJT, *tr.* by Makoto Ueda

And a man with his back to the East. (LL) Unwelcome. Mary Elizabeth Coleridge. CH; OBEV; OBNC; VWP; WPE

And a mouse is miracle enough to stagger sextillions of infidels. (LL) I believe a leaf of grass is no less than the journey-work of the stars. Walt Whitman. SAmP

And a pond edged with grayish leaves. (LL) Neutral Tones. Thomas Hardy. CABP; CMoP; EBVV; EnVR; HAP; HeIP-4; InPK-6; InPS-3; MoBrPo; MoP; NAEL-2; NOBVV; NoAM; OAEL-2; TFi; UnPo

An' a rogue is married to, etc. (LL) The Sergeant's Weddin'. Rudyard Kipling. OBCoV; OxBTC

And a singe runs through lace and feather. (LL) A Utilitarian View of the Monitor's Fight. Herman Melville. APN-2; AmPP; ColAP; NAAL-1; NAAL-3; NCAP; PAR; UnPo

And a singer who sings no more. (LL) Ode: "We are the music-makers." Arthur William Edgar O'Shaughnessy. CABP

And a single fishing boat. (LL) Seeking a Mooring. Wang Wei, *Chinese.* ChiPo, *tr.* by Kenneth Rexroth *and* Ling Chung

An a so de rain a-fall. A Song for England. Andrew Salkey. HCP; PBCV

And a soft berth and a smooth course till the long trip ended. (LL) Sea-Chill. Arthur Guiterman. BXAP; UV

And a Star Fell. Marie Under, *Estonian.* CEEP, *tr.* by Ivar Ivask

And a tall tree sprouted from his father's grave. (LL) The Truisms. Louis MacNeice. IIP; NOBE; OBSV; PNI

And a tenth part of Okeanos is given to dark night. Styx. Robert Duncan. VCAP

And a' the glory shall be thine! / AMEN! AMEN! (LL) Holy Willie's Prayer. Robert Burns. CABP

And a' they hoped and wondered. (LL) Farewell to Dostoevski. "Hugh MacDiarmid." FaBoTC

And a thread too bright for the eye. (LL) Shroud. George Mackay Brown. NoP-4

And a time to hate; a time of war, and a time / of peace. Bible, *O.T. See* A Time for Everything.

And a wasted town. (LL) War Poet. Sidney Keyes. NoP-4; PoWW

And a whore and a rogue may part when they please. (LL) Oaths. Thomas Brown. FaBoEE; OBCoV

And a wig-wag. (LL) Four stiff-standers. *Unknown.* LB; OxNR

And abortions are hidden. (LL) Editor Whedon. Edgar Lee Masters. CMoP; FaBoEE; NOBA; OBSV; OxBA; PoE

And about go we, and about go we! (LL) By the Moon ("By the moon we sport and play"). John Lyly *and* Thomas Ravenscroft. BoTP; CH

And Adam knew Eve his wife; and she conceived, and bare Cain. The First Murderer. Bible, *O.T.* OxBoV *Fr.* Genesis.

And adieu for evermore. (LL) The Rover's Adieu [*or* Farewell]. Sir Walter Scott. CH; EnLoPo; GTBS-P; NOBE; OBEV; OBNC

And adieu to you, my darlings. (LL) Three Knights from Spain. *Unknown.* CH; OxNR

And adjust, no one to drive the car. (LL) To Elsie. William Carlos Williams. CMoP; InPS-3; MeMAP; NAAL-2; NOBA; OxBA; PoE; PoPoPo

And after a Long While. Ory Bernstein, *Hebrew.* IP, *tr. by* Warren Bargad *and* Stanley F. Chyet

And after all a slave sits out the centuries. Ghosts II. Lauris Edmond. PeNZ

And, after all, it is to them we return. Quaint Mazes. Geoffrey Hill. NoAM *Fr.* An Apology for the Revival of Christian Architecture in England.

And after all your trapesings, child, lie still! (LL) A St. Helena Lullaby. Rudyard Kipling. EBEV; FaBoCh; OBMV; PoEL-5

And after, *Amor vincit omnia.* (LL) Madame Eglantine. Chaucer. CTC; NOBE

And after singing Psalm the Twelfth. Rochester Extempore. John Wilmot, 2d Earl of Rochester. ChIV-1

And after these the Sea Nymphs marched all. The Sea Nymphs. Edmund Spenser. *Fr.* Wood Of Error. AEP

And after this quick bash in the dark. Portrait of a Young Girl Raped at a Suburban Party. Brian Patten. OxBTC

And afterwards, after the shedding of mucus. A Talk with My Cousin Alone. Hone Tuwhare. PeNZ

And Again. Humphrey Evans. BXAP

And Again. Alison Fell. LW

And again I see the long pouring headland. The Return. Alistair Campbell. PeNZ

And again I was like one of those little girls. Time Caught in a Net. Dahlia Ravikovitch, *Hebrew.* IP, *tr. by* Warren Bargad *and* Stanley F. Chyet

And again Jesus spoke to them in parables, saying. Matthew 22:1–14; And again Jesus spoke to them. Edwin Arlington Robinson. GI *Fr.* St. Matthew.

And again the Spirit of Pity whispered, "Why?" (LL) And There Was a Great Calm. Thomas Hardy. CMoP; LiTM; OAEL-2

And ages drop in it like rain. (LL) Two Rivers. Ralph Waldo Emerson. APN-1; AmPP; NCAP; NOBA; OxBA; PoE

And ages long of troubles end. (LL) At Harper's Ferry Just before the Attack. Edward W. Williams. AAP; CBCWP

And aim a telescope at the inviolate Sun. (LL) Dear brother, would you know the life. Ralph Waldo Emerson. APN-1; OxBA

And al is thorugh [*or* thrugh] thy negligence and rape. (LL) To His Scribe Adam. Chaucer. NAEL-1; OAEL-1; OxBSP

And all beset with flowers. (LL) To the Western Wind. Robert Herrick. CaPo; OBEV

And all deceive. (LL) Tomorrow. Anna Laetitia Barbauld. ECWP; PEW

And all description is a blasphemy. (LL) Tabernacle. D. H. Lawrence. ChIV-1; KSG

And all did wishfully expect the silver–throned morne. (LL) Night Piece: the Trojans outside Troy. Homer, *Greek.* OBVE, *tr. by* George Chapman

And all dishevelled wandering stars. (LL) Who Goes with Fergus? W. B. Yeats. CMoP; FaBoCh; InPK-6; MoP; NAEL-2; NOBE; NOBVV; NoAM; PeVV; PoE; PoRA; TRP

And all for the sake of my little nut-tree. Mother Goose. *See* A Nut Tree.

And all for the want of a horseshoe nail. Mother Goose. *See* For want of a nail[, the shoe was lost].

And all her silken flanks with garlands drest. Vlamertinghe. Edmund Blunden. NoP-4; OBWP; PeFWW

And all his Pictures Faded. (LL) Sir Joshua Reynolds. William Blake. FaBoEE; OxBoLi; PeLV

And all his sences were with deadly fit opprest. (LL) The Cave of Mammon. Edmund Spenser. PoEL-1

And all is done as I have told. (LL) The Mental Traveller. William Blake. ChIV-2; NAEL-2; OAEL-2; PoE; PoEL-4; Ro

And all is hushed at Shiloh. (LL) Shiloh [A Requiem]. Herman Melville. APAD; APN-2; CBCWP; ColAP; NOBA; NoP-4; OBWP; OxBA; SCV

And all is rolled back in the book of days. (LL) The Alphabet. Karl Shapiro. NoAM; PoA

And all is well, though [*or* tho'] faith and form. Tennyson. EBVVPR; OAEL-2 *Fr.* In Memoriam A. H. H.

And all my hearts in unison strike twelve. (LL) The Science of the Night. Stanley Kunitz. ColAP; MoAmPo; TwCP

And all my troubles too. (LL) On Himselfe ("I will no longer kiss"). Robert Herrick. CaPo; CavPo

And all night long we lie in sleep. Boyish sleep. Hamlin Garland. APN-2

And all of Jerusalem is the explanation for his death. Yehuda Amichai. *See* I have nothing to say about the war.

And all of them are near. John Betjeman. *See* House of Rest.

And all of wood. Watch it closely. (LL) The Monument. Elizabeth Bishop. HCAP; NOBA; NoAM; Poetr; TRP

And all our mourning should be to rejoice. (LL) Elegy: "When in the mirror of a permanent tear." Gene Derwood. ImPo; LiTM

And all preparation is for it—and identity is for it—and life and materials are altogether for it! (LL) To think of time—of all that retrospection. Walt Whitman. ImPo; MeMAP

And all so long ago. (LL) Now we are back to normal, now the mind is. Louis MacNeice. CMoP; OxAEP-2

And all such beautiful / sweet things. (LL) Problems With Hurricanes. Victor Hernandez Cruz. PmAP

And all that mighty heart is lying still! (LL) Composed upon Westminster Bridge[, September 3, 1802]. Wordsworth. APAD; AWP; CABP; CH; ChAP; ClHu; FaBoCh; GSo; GTBS-P; HAP; HeIP-4; ImPo; InPK-6; InPS-3; NAEL-2; NAWM-2; NOBRP; NoP-4; OAEL-2; OBNC; OPOU; PBMP; PFE; PoE; PoEL-4; PoLF; PoPoPo; Ro; SCGP; Son; TFi; UnPo

And all that was taken away! (LL) How I Got That Name. Marilyn Chin. LoL; PaTW

And all the birds fly out of my scene. (LL) The Meeting. Muriel Rukeyser. MoAmPo; TrJP

And all the birds in the air couldn't catch me. (LL) A Nut Tree. *Unknown.* ACTP

And all the birds in the air couldn't catch me. (LL) A Nut Tree. Mother Goose. BoTP; CH; NTP; OxBoLi; OxNR; TTTS

And all the bloom we owe. (LL) Piping Peace. James Shirley. NOBE; PoEL-2

And all the blossoms of a pear tree fall in the evening breeze. (LL) Egrets. Tu Mu, *Chinese.* SuSp, *tr. by* Irving Y. Lo; APo, *tr. by* Irving Yucheng Lo

And all the great conclusions coming near. (LL) Answers. Elizabeth Jennings. OxBSP; OxBTC

And all the hills echoed [*or* ecchoed]. (LL) Nurse's Song ("When the voices of children are heard on the green / And laughing is heard on the hill"). William Blake. AWP; CH; FHYEP; FaBoBe; NAEL-2; OxBChV; PeLV; SCGP

And all the little schoolchildren sat down. (LL) Slightly before the middle of Congressman Pudd. E. E. Cummings. FaBoEE; OBAL

And all the rest but vanity we find. (LL) The Vanity of All Worldly Things. Anne Bradstreet. ChIV-1; SCAP

And all the stars looked down. (LL) Christmas Carol: "The Christ child lay on Mary's lap." G. K. Chesterton. BoTP; OBCP

And all the summer through the water saunter. (LL) On This Island. W. H. Auden. CMoP; GTBS-P; MoBrPo; NAEL-2; PoE

And all the terror doubled in their breast. (LL) An Answer to a Love-Letter in Verse. Lady Mary Wortley Montagu. ECWP; LW

And all the while *Duessa* wept full bitterly. (LL) The Fight of the Red Cross Knight and the Heathen Sansjoy. Edmund Spenser. FHYEP; NoSic

And all the while, he knew there was no river. (LL) Eli, Eli. Judith Wright. BMAP; GI

And all the wickedness in this world that man might work or think. God's Mercy. William Langland. NOCV *Fr.* The Vision of Piers Plowman.

And all these through her eyes, have stopped [*or* stopt] her ears [*or* eares]. (LL) My Picture Left in Scotland. Ben Jonson. BeJo; CBLP; FMP; NAEL-1; PBRV; PoEL-2; SeCP

And all this happened to us. Elegy. *Nahuatl Oral Tradition, Spanish.* PaTW, *tr. by* Miguel Léon-Portilla *and* Grace Lobanov

And all this is folly to the world. (LL) A Girl. Ezra Pound. NOxBChV

And all those horses. What She Said. Kapilar, *Tamil.* PLW, *tr. by* A. K. Ramanujan

And all thy sons, O Nature, learn my tale. (LL) Ode to Simplicity. William Collins. NOBE; OBEV; OxAEP-1

And all to one loved folly sacrifice. (LL) 'Tis hard to say, if greater want of skill. Alexander Pope. OAEL-1, *ll.* 1–266

And all we flow from, soul in soul. (LL) The Prayer: "O living will that shalt endure." Tennyson. EBVV; EBVVPR; FaBoBe; OAEL-2

And all we need of hell. (LL) Parting. Emily Dickinson. APAD; APN-2; AmPP; BoLoP; BoWoP; ColAP; EBEvV; GBL; GLoP; HeIP-4; ImGa; LW; MeMAP; MoAmPo; MoP; NAAL-1; NAAL-3; NIP-4; NOBA; NoAM; OxBA; OxBSP; PAR; PFE; Poetr; SAGP; SAmP; SCV; TFi

And all were in the wrong! (LL) The Blind Men and the Elephant. John Godfrey Saxe. BLPA; BoTP; FaBoBe; OBCA; OTCP; PoToHe

And all you folk will die. (LL) I Counsel You Beware. A. E. Housman. PFE; PeVV

And also a city with quiet pockets. The Rumored Conversation with Oneself Continues in Pittsburgh. Diane Ackerman. WWSi

And also many other things. (LL) Sporting Goods. Philippe Soupault, *French*. TTTS, *tr. by* Rosemarie Waldrop

And although we were both grown men / We had just been born. Guillaume Apollinaire. *See* The Little Car.

"And am no more"--she cried. (LL) Silver Wedding. Ralph Hodgson. CBLP; OxBTC

And ample rectory. (LL) House of Rest. John Betjeman. OxAEP-2

And another child. (LL) Once in a Lifetime, Snow. Les A. Murray. NoP-4

And answer, echoes, answer, dying, dying, dying. (LL) Blow, Bugle, Blow. Tennyson. AWP; CH; ChAP; ClHu; EBEvV; EBVV; FHYEP; FaBoCh; GTBS-P; HeIP-4; ImPo; InPK-6; NAEL-2; NOBE; NoP-4; OAEL-2; OBEV; OBNC; PFE; PeVV; PoEL-5; TFi; UnPo

And answer made King Arthur, breathing hard. Tennyson. PeECV, *ll.* 330–440; EBEV *Fr.* The Passing of Arthur. FHYEP; NAEL-2; OBNC *Fr.* Idylls of the King.

("Before the eyes of ladies and of kings.") (LL) EBEV

And answered—"Happy those for whom the fod / Of." Shelley. *See* The Triumph of Life.

And answered thunder with his thunder back. (LL) Frederick Douglass. Paul Laurence Dunbar. CBCWP; PoBA

And anthems in new tongues I hear saluting me. (LL) Prayer of Columbus. Walt Whitman. AmPP; NCAP

And Apollo will none of me. (LL) Rejected. Lord Alfred Bruce Douglas. ADE; PeVV

And are gone. (LL) Emplumada. Lorna Dee Cervantes. NoAM; PBCAP

And are strong. Etheridge Knight. *See* Cell Song.

And are the Gods of Loves Artillery. (LL) In Imitation of Horace. Aphra Behn. KTR; NOSC

And are they dancing: or gazing at the earth. (LL) Are They Dancing. Edward Dorn. NeAP; PoM

And are ye sure the news is true? There's Nae Luck about the House. William Julius Mickle, *also at. to* Jean Adam. GTBS-P; NOEC; OxAEP-1

And art, mine own unrivalled Fair! Catullus. *See* Carmen 31 ("Apple of islands, Sirmio, & bright peninsulas, set").

And art thou dead? Thou very sweetest bird. Sonnet on the Death of the Poet J. Keats. John Taylor. Ro *Fr.* London Magazine, 3 526.

And art thou grieved, sweet and sacred Dove. Grieve Not the Holy Spirit, etc. George Herbert. ESCV

And art thou he, now "fallen on evil days." In Age. William Lisle Bowles. *Fr.* Milton: On the Busts of Milton, in Youth and Age. Son

And as at first still lodge him in the manger. (LL) Preparations. *Unknown*. CH; FaBoCh; NOBE; NoP-4; OBEV; PBRV; PoRA; TrCP

And as for his judgments, they have not known them. Praise ye the Lord. Bible, O.T. *See* Psalm 147.

And as for Man. Loren C. Eiseley. GM

And as for me, though that I konne [*or* can] but [*or* my wit be] lyte. Chaucer. CH; HeIP-4 *Fr.* The Legend of Good Women.

And as He shuts, close up to Maids again. (LL) To Marygolds. Robert Herrick. CavPo; NAEL-1

And as I rise slapping my feet. I Wake Thinking of Myself as a Man. Susan Griffin. GLP

And as I stood and cast aside mine eye. The Lady of the Arbour. *See* And at the last I cast my mine eye aside.

And as I talked, I swam. (LL) With Kit, Age Seven, at the Beach. William Stafford. LiLi; RaBo

And as I walk along, thinking of this. The Pleasure Dome. Shrikant Verma, *Hindi*. OMIP, *tr. by* Vinay Dahrwadker *and* Aparna Dharwadker (b. 1956)

And, as in well-growne woods, on trees, cold spinie Grasshoppers. Helen and the elders. Homer. OBCVT, *tr. by* George Chapman *Fr.* The Iliad.

And as in winter time when Jove his cold-sharpe javelines throwes. Homer. OBVE, *tr. by* George Chapman *Fr.* The Iliad.

And as life is to the living, so death is to the dead. (LL) The Two Mysteries. Mary Mapes Dodge. PWR; TrCP

And as Ovid has sweetly in parables told, / We harden like trees, and like rivers are cold. Lady Mary Wortley Montagu. *See* Lover, The; a Ballad.

And as they led him away, they seized one Simon of Cyre'ne. Luke 23:26–38; And as they led him away. W. H. Auden. GI *Fr.* St. Luke.

And as to the meaning, it's what you please. (LL) Ballad: "The Auld wife sat at her ivied door." Charles Stuart Calverley. BXAP; CABP; NBLV; OBCoV; OxAEP-2; UV

And as to you Death, and you bitter hug of mortality, it is idle to try to alarm. Walt Whitman. ColAP *Fr.* Song of Myself.

And as we came down the staircase. Valse Oubliée. John Heath-Stubbs. OxBTC

And as when with the West-wind's flawes the sea thrusts up her waves. Homer. OBVE, *tr. by* George Chapman *Fr.* The Iliad.

And ask the gods to pardon this clear flame. (LL) Smoke. Henry David Thoreau. APN-1; AWP; ColAP; NOBA; NoP-4; OxBA; TAP

And ask them for your name again. (LL) 'Mystery Boy' Looks for Kin in Nashville. Robert Earl Hayden. LCAP-2; NoAM; NoP-4; PoE

And Assemble the engine again'. (LL) The Dying Airman. *Unknown*. AS; OxBoLi; PeLV; RB

And at the door of the eye. In the Mourning. Keorapetse Kgositsile. PBMAP *Fr.* The Present is a Dangerous Place to Live.

And at the end of eight days. T. S. Eliot. GI *Fr.* St. Luke.

And at the last I cast my mine eye aside. The Lady of the Arbour. WPE *Fr.* The Flower and the Leaf.

("And as I stood and cast aside mine eye.")

And at times I hoped to shape your better world. (LL) Robben Island Sequence. Dennis Brutus. HBAPE

And auld Robin Forbes hes gien tem a dance. Auld Robin Forbes. Susanna Blamire. ECWP; LW

And autumn's best of cheer, *shorter vers*. Helen Hunt Jackson. *See* September [Days Are Here].

And away goes the mare. (LL) One to make ready. *Unknown*. LB; OxNR

And away the vapour flew. (LL) The Little Boy Lost ("Father, father, where are you going?"). William Blake. FHYEP; Ro

And azure water hoisting out of wells. (LL) In the Elegy Season. Richard Wilbur. InPK-6; NYBP

And B, A. Charles Hubert Sisson. OxBC

And baby crows, without being a cock. (LL) Pin has a head, but has no hair, A. Christina Rossetti. CTV; VWP

And Back. Rodney Bennett. BoTP

And back it in care of the Birmingham Jail. (LL) Down in the valley, valley so low. *Unknown*. APN-2

And barely can not hear them calling, "Here's one." (LL) Memorial Service for the Invasion Beach Where the Vacation in the Flesh Is Over. Alan Dugan. AF

And basked and battened in the woods. (LL) In Memoriam A.H.H., 35. Tennyson. OAEL-2

And be a friend to man. (LL) The House by the Side of the Road. Sam Walter Foss. BLPA; FaBoBe

And be among her cloudy trophies hung. (LL) Ode on Melancholy. Keats. CABP; FHYEP; HAP; ImPo; InPK-6; InPS-3; NAEL-2; NAWM-2; NOBE; NoP-4; OAEL-2; OBEV; OBNC; OxAEP-2; PoE; PoEL-4; PoRA; Poetr; Ro; SCGP; TFi

And be buried in the dust of marching feet. (LL) For Black Poets Who Think of Suicide. Etheridge Knight. HeIP-4; InPK-6; LTA; NAAAL; PoBA; SAGP

And be it said of thee. Michael Drayton. EPCY *Fr.* To Henry Reynolds, of Poets and Poesy.

And be like him and he will then love me. (LL) The Little Black Boy. William Blake. AWP; CABP; CH; ChAP; FHYEP; HeIP-4; NAEL-2; NAWM-2; NOBRP; NOEC; NoP-4; OAEL-2; OBEV; OBNC; OxBChV; PeECV; PoE; PoEL-4; PoPoPo; Ro; SCGP; TFi

And be my night, my warmth, my wife. (LL) The Passionate Shepherd to His Love. Delmore Schwartz. PFE

And be the mistress of Mankind! (LL) Upon [His] Leaving His Mistress. John Wilmot, 2d Earl of Rochester. EnLoPo; GBL; NBLV; NOSC

And Beale Street's done gone dry. (LL) Beale Street Blues. William Christopher Handy. CrDW

And bearing brilliant an dnobel human beings. (LL) To the Tune "The River Is Red." Ch'iu Chin, *Chinese*. AiP; BoWoP; PBWP, *tr. by* Kenneth Rexroth *and* Ling Chung

And bears the blazing Present through the Skies. Homer. *See* Vulcan Forges the Shield of Achilles.

And beat him today. (LL) Jack. Charles Henry Ross. ACTP; NOxBChV; OxBChV; Spl

And beat the Buckler's Verge, and bound the whole. (LL) Vulcan Forges the Shield of Achilles. Homer, *Greek*. OBVE, *tr. by* Alexander Pope

And beauty must be fee'd into our arms. (LL) 'Tis woman that seduces all mankind! John Gay. OxBoV; PeLV

AND BECAUSE IT IS MY HEART. (LL) The Heart. Stephen Crane. APAD; APN-2; ColAP; FaBoEE; HoPM; LiTM; MeMAP; MoAmPo; NOBA; NoP-4; OxBSP; TAP

And *becoming* light. (LL) Let There Be Light! D. H. Lawrence. ChIV-1; KSG

And be'est thou worst, yet must I love thee still. Catullus. *See* Carmen 75 ("Reason blinded by sin, Lesbia").

And begin to crow. (LL) Poland / 1931 "The Wedding." Jerome Rothenberg. PoM

And begin to crow. Jerome Rothenberg. *See* Poland / 1931 "The Wedding."

And behold, a lawyer stood up to put him to the test. Luke 10:25–37; And behold, a lawyer. Stephen Mitchell. GI *Fr.* St. Luke.

And behold, one came up to him, saying. Matthew 19:16–24; And behold, one came up to him. Anna Kamienska. GI *Fr.* St. Matthew.

And being good for nothing else, be wise. (LL) The Disabled Debauchee. John Wilmot, 2d Earl of Rochester. BoLoP; HAP; NAEL-1; NOBL; OBSV; OxBoV; PoEL-3; SCGP

And believing she was a maid. The Faithless Wife. Federico García Lorca, *Spanish.* BoLoP, *tr. by* A. L. Lloyd

And bend and touch you on the cheek. (LL) A Confession. Robert Mezey. PFE

And Betty's praised for labours not her own. (LL) What dire offence from am'rous causes springs. Alexander Pope. EBNV; NOEC; Poetr

And bid them seek the morn the hills and fields once more. (LL) The New Man. Jones Very. APN-1; NOBA

And bided my time. (LL) The Ballad of Nat Turner. Robert Earl Hayden. BPo; VGW

And bids my hair stand up? (LL) The Mother of God. W. B. Yeats. ChIV-2; GI

And binding with briars my joys and desires. (LL) The Garden of Love. William Blake. APAD; AWP; EnLoPo; FHYEP; GBL; GLoP; GaP; HAP; NAEL-2; NoP-4; OBGa; OxAEP-2; PoE; PoPoPo; RB; Ro; SCGP; TFi; TOF; TRP

And bite us again! (LL) Octopus. Arthur Clement Hilton. BXAP; UV

And black Fate took these stubborn spearmen. On the Thessalians Who Fought at Marathon. Aeschylus, *Greek.* GrAn, *tr. by* Edwin Morgan

And blessed be the women who get you through. Robin Morgan. GLP *Fr.* The Hallowing of Hell.

And blew. *"Childe Roland to the Dark Tower came".* (LL) Childe Roland to the Dark Tower Came. Robert Browning. EnVR; NAEL-2; NOBVV; NoP-4; OAEL-2; OBNV; PeVV; PoE; PoPoPo

And blights my plagues the Marriage hearse. (LL) London ("I wander through [*or* thro'] each chartered [*or* charter'd] street"). William Blake. APAD; AWP; CABP; ClHu; FHYEP; FaBoPV; HAP; HeIP-4; InPK-6; InPS-3; NAEL-2; NAWM-2; NIP-4; NOBE; NOBRP; NOEC; NoP-4; OAEL-2; OBNC; OxAEP-2; PBMP; PFE; PoE; PoEL-4; PoPoPo; Poetr; RB; Ro; SAGP; SCGP; SCV; TFi; TRP; UnPo; WeW-3

And blood hangs in the pine-soaked air. (LL) Adolescence—III. Rita Dove. ISC; NoAM

And blossom in purple and red. (LL) Song: "Come into the garden, Maud." Tennyson. AWP; EBEvV; EBVV; EBVVPR; EnVR; FHYEP; NOBE; NOBVV; OAEL-2; OBGa; OxAEP-2; PoE; UV

And blow the candle out. (LL) Prophecy. Elinor Wylie. APAD; BoWoP; FaBoWP; NTP; SAGP; VGW

And blow you all a kiss from the tomb. (LL) A New England Bachelor. Richard Eberhart. MoAmPo; NoAM

And boding not knowing to what. W. S. Merwin. *See* For the Anniversary of My Death.

And both thy servants be. (LL) Man. George Herbert. ESCV; FSCP; GeHe; ImPo; NAEL-1; NoP-4; PoEL-2; SeCP

And bowing not knowing to what. (LL) For the Anniversary of My Death. W. S. Merwin. CAPP-1; CoAP; ColAP; HCAP; InPK-6; LiLi; NAAL-2; NOBA; PoPoPo; Poetr; VCAP

And braves as he may the night Of darkness and tears. (LL) Winter Nightfall. Robert Bridges. MoBrPo; OBEV; SCGP

And break[e] before thee. (LL) On the Name of Jesus. Richard Crashaw. ESCV

And break the hidden snare. (LL) The Mouse's Petition. Anna Laetitia Barbauld. ECWP; OxBChV

And break the jam on Gerry's Rocks with their foreman, young Monroe. (LL) The Jam on Gerry's Rock. *Unknown.* AS; AmFP

And brick upon grey brick. (LL) Dublin. Louis MacNeice. CIP-2; IIP; OxBTC

And brighter hope when hope despairs. (LL) When weary with the long day's care. Emily Jane Brontë. EnVR; VWP

And bring about the collapse of the whole empire. (LL) Shame. Richard Wilbur. CoAmPo; FaBoMo; OBCoV; OxBC

And bring her up as mine. (LL) If no one ever marries me—. Laurence Alma-Tadema. ACTP

And bring the most to pass. (LL) Gardener. Robert Graves. GaP; OBGa

And bring to my baby a fresh penny roll. (LL) The Mouse's Lullaby. Palmer Cox. NOxBChV

And bring us into holy bliss. Amen, *mod. vers. by* Frank Ernest Hill. Chaucer. *See* The Nun's Priest's Tale.

And bring us to your holy bliss! Amen. Chaucer. *See* The Nun's Priest's Tale.

And bringe [*or* brynge] us to his heighe [*or* hye, *or* highe] blisse [*or* blisss]! Amen. (LL) The Nun's Priest's Tale. Chaucer. FHYEP; NAEL-1; OAEL-1; OBNV

And broad old cesspools glittered in the sun. (LL) Mouse's Nest. John Clare. InPK-6; NAEL-2; RB

And broken hedge-flowers sweet, mark his impetuous way. (LL) A Reverie. Joanna Baillie. ECWP; WoRP

And, brother, for all time, hail and farewell! (LL) On the Burial of His Brother. Catullus, *Latin.* AWP; IMW; OBCVT, *tr. by* Aubrey Beardsley; LBC

And brothers give you back the sword. (LL) Message to Siberia. Aleksandr Sergeyevich Pushkin, *Russian.* AWP; TTY, *tr. by* Max Eastman

And buds and blossoms like the rest. Tennyson. EBVV; FHYEP; GTBS-P; NOBE; OBNC *Fr.* In Memoriam A. H. H.

"And builds a Hell in Heaven's despite." (LL) The Clod and [*or* &] the Pebble. William Blake. APAD; EnLoPo; FHYEP; GLoP; InPS-3; NAEL-2; NOBE; NoP-4; OBNC; OxAEP-2; OxBSP; PoE; RB; Ro; SCGP; SCV; TFi

And built a braver Palace than before. (LL) The World. George Herbert. GeHe; NOSC

And Burgh under Stanemuir there dwels Dickie. (LL) Dick o' the Cow. *Unknown.* ESPB; IBB; OxBB

And bursten figs won't keep? (LL) Figs. D. H. Lawrence. EP; OAEL-2

And but a chair. (LL) The Pilgrimage. George Herbert. ESCV; GeHe; NAEL-1; NOSC; PoE

And but in darkness is she visible. (LL) To an Old Lady. William Empson. FaBoTw; GTBS-P; NOBE; NoAM; OxAEP-2

And buzzings of the honied hours. (LL) In Memoriam. Tennyson. EBVV; OBNC

And by a river forth I gan costey. The Complaint of the Black Knight. John Lydgate. OBGa *Fr.* The Complaint of the Black Knight.

And, by one o'clock, is gone. (LL) V. B. Nimble, V. B. Quick. John Updike. NYBP; NoP-4; OBCoV

And by what way shall I go back? (LL) L'An Trentiesme de Mon Eage. Archibald MacLeish. LiTM; MoAmPo; MoP; NOBA

And call her crazed with wrong. (LL) Night and Sleep. Coventry Patmore. CH; EBVV

And call ye this to utter what is just, *par. by* Countess of Pembroke, Mary Sidney Herbert. Psalm 58. Bible, *O.T.* BoWoP; NAEL-1; NOCV; NoSic; WPE *Fr.* Psalms.

And call ye this to utter what is just. Psalm 58: Si Vere Utique. Mary Sidney Herbert, Countess of Pembroke. NoP-4; PEW

And called their friend, my Father, God. (LL) The Cottage. Jones Very. APN-1; OxBA

And calling Justice, all things burn. (LL) Decay. George Herbert. ESCV; SCGP; SeCP

And calm of mind all passion spent. (LL) All Is Best. Milton. NOBE; NOSC; OBEV

And calmly fell our Christmas-eve. Tennyson. *See* Again at Christmas did we weave.

And Camelot, and starlit Stonehenge. (LL) Channel Firing. Thomas Hardy. CABP; CMoP; EBEV; EBVV; HAP; HeIP-4; ImPo; MoP; NAEL-2; NIP-4; NoAM; NoP-4; OAEL-2; OxAEP-2; OxBTC; PeECV; PeFWW; PoE; PoEL-5; PoPoPo; PoRA; PoWW; Poetr; RB; SoSe-8; TFi; UnPo

And can I ever bid these joys farewell? Keats. TOF *Fr.* Sleep and Poetry.

And can it be, that I should gain. Free Grace. Charles Wesley. NOCV

And can return no more. (LL) First Love. John Clare. BoLoP; EnLoPo; GBL; GLoP; HAP; NOBVV; NoP-4; PoPoPo; Ro

And can the muse reflect her tear-stain'd eye. *Unknown.* PBCV *Fr.* Jamaica, a Poem in Three Parts, Written in That Island in the Year 1776.

And cannot say it. (LL) Anniversary Poem. George Oppen. APSN; NNaP

And canst thou, sinner slight. Abby Bradley Hyde. AH

And can't explode? (LL) Sherbet. Cornelius Eady. CMAP; GT; LTA

And caressed by the rain. (LL) Scotland. Sir Alexander Gray. FaBoTC; OxBS

And carry you away. (LL) For the Courtesan Ch'ing Lin. Wu Tsao, *Chinese.* BoWoP; WPOW, *tr. by* Kenneth Rexroth *and* Ling Chung

And, cast by conscience out, spendsavour salt? (LL) The Candle Indoors. Gerard Manley Hopkins. ChIV-2; ImPo; LiTM; OxAEP-2; PoEL-5

And ceases, in his heart, to be. Rilke. *See* The Panther.

And certainly they say, for fine behaving. John Hookham Frere. OBCoV *Fr.* Whistlecraft.

And change[,] with hurried hand, has swept these scenes. Frederick Goddard Tuckerman. APN-2; HAP; NOBA; TAP *Fr.* Sonnets.

And cheat the cruel day! (LL) And on My Eyes Dark Sleep by Night. "Michael Field." LW

And Christ comes with a January flower. (LL) Advent. Patrick Kavanagh. IIP; TIRV

And Christe receive thy saule. (LL) Lyke-Wake Dirge, The [*or* A]. *Unknown.* CH; EBEvV; EnSB; FaBoCh; HAP; HoPM; NOBE; NTP; OBEV; PeECV; PoEL-1; TFi; WeW-3

And classic bronze of Benin. (LL) A Different Image. Dudley Randall. BPo; TAP

And clearly I recall the second day's end. The Perfect Disc of the Moon. Richard Kenney. Son

(And close your eyes). (LL) For prodigal read generous. E. E. Cummings. FaBoEE; PBMP

And closed her up, as in a tomb[e]. (LL) The Funeral[l] Rites of the Rose. Robert Herrick. CaPo; NOSC; OBEV

And cluck your children in about your knee? (LL) Sonnet to Gath. Edna St. Vincent Millay. BoWoP; CMoP; MoAmPo

And Coffers heaped with Tears! (LL) For each ecstatic instant. Emily Dickinson. NAAL-1; NAAL-3

And coin [or coyne] to keep [or kepe], as water in a sieve [or syve]. (LL) To Sir Francis Brian. Sir Thomas Wyatt. AAS; NoSic; SiPS

And cold as any icicle. (LL) Parting, without a Sequel. John Crowe Ransom. MeMAP; MoAmPo; NoP-4; PFE; SoSe-8

And cold, on the pillow's dark side. (LL) The Night Mirror. John Hollander. NYBP; VCAP

And collars of his keen-nosed pups. (LL) For that goatfucker, goatfooted. Leonidas, Greek. GrAn; PGA, tr. by Kenneth Rexroth

And come unto my courtship as my prayer. (LL) A Devout Lover. Thomas Randolph. HoPM; OBEV

And coming the proud over all o' the birds o' the sea.'. (LL) Sea Change. John Masefield. FaBoTw; OBMV; RB

And confident thou'lt raise me with the just. (LL) His Metrical Prayer. James Graham, Marquess of Montrose. ChIV-2; FaBoEE; NOSC; OxBS

And confirmation of the old despair. (LL) The City's Queen. James Thomson. EnVR; GTBS-P; NOBE

And Consciousness—is Noon. (LL) There is a Zone whose even Years. Emily Dickinson. APN-2; NCAP

And consummation comes, and jars two hemispheres. (LL) The Convergence of the Twain. Thomas Hardy. CABP; FaBoTw; HeIP-4; InPK-6; InPS-3; LiTM; MoBrPo; MoP; NAEL-2; NIP-4; NoAM; NoP-4; OAEL-2; OxBS; PBMP; PFE; PeVV; PoPoPo; Poetr; SCGP; TFi

And continue special friends. (LL) Twelve Articles. Jonathan Swift. NBLV; OBCoV

And continued to knock him about. (LL) Limerick: "There was an old man who screamed out." Edward Lear. CBNP; EBEV; NOBVV; OxAEP-2

And copper and worn my farthing. Elizaveta Kuzmina-Karavayeva, Russian. TCRP, tr. by Albert C. Todd

And couldn't get up in the morning! (LL) It's raining, it's pouring. Unknown. ACTP; OxNR

And couldn't write. (LL) A Bookshop Idyll. Kingsley Amis. OxBTC; PeLV

And covered up—our names—. (LL) I died for Beauty—but was scarce. Emily Dickinson. APN-2; AWP; BoWoP; ImPo; LiTM; MeMAP; MoAmPo; NAAL-2; NAAL-3; NAWM-2; NOBA; PBMP; SAmP; SDW

And crash a grunting cheat that's young. (LL) The Maunder's Praise of His Strowling Mort. Unknown. CBNP; OxBoLi; PeLV

And crowd to Stella's at fourscore. (LL) Stella's Birthday, 1721. Jonathan Swift. NAEL-1; OxAEP-1; PoEL-3

And crown with love my ever-during night. (LL) Carmen 5 ("My sweetest Lesbia, let us live and love"). Catullus, Latin. AAS; AWP; EBEV; GBL; HAP; HeIP-4; InPS-3; NAEL-1; NoSic; OAEL-1; OBVE; PoE; PoRA; SCGP; TFi; WeW-3, tr. by Thomas Campion

And crowned with the may. (LL) The Elephant. Herbert Asquith. CTAV

And cruell maid, because I see. The Cruell Maid. Robert Herrick. CaPo

And curl forever in some far-off farmyard flower. (LL) Beehive. Jean Toomer. GT; PoBA; TTY

And cursed th' access[e] of that celestial[l] thief. (LL) A Vision upon This Concei[p]t of the Faerie [or Faery] Queen[e]. Sir Walter Ralegh. NAEL-1; NoSic; SCGP; SiPS; Son

And cursing, stumble out like ghosts into the frozen dark. (LL) Epilogue: " 'O where are you going?' said reader to rider." W. H. Auden. FaBoCh; LiTM

And custom for the spreading laurel tree. (LL) A Prayer for My Daughter. W. B. Yeats. CMoP; HAP; LiTM; MoP; NAEL-2; NoAM; NoP-4; OxBTC; PFE; PoA; PoLF; PoRA; RaBo; TFi

And cut them and gave them to me / in my hand. (LL) The Act. William Carlos Williams. SAmP; VGW

And Damaballah, kind father, / sew up / her bleeding hole. (LL) Crow Jane. Imamu Amiri Baraka. BB

And dance and sing all the night. Unknown. See Harry Parry.

And dance like a wave of the sea. (LL) The Fiddler of Dooney. W. B. Yeats. EBVV; FaBoCh; NBLV; OxAEP-2

And da[u]nce to th' music[k] of your chain[e]s. (LL) The Vintage to the Dungeon. Richard Lovelace. BeJo; CaPo

And dances with the Daffodils. (LL) Daffodils. Wordsworth. APAD; BLPA; CABP; CTV; ChAP; ClHu; FaBoBe; GTBS-P; ImPo; InPK-6; InPS-3; LaPo; NAEL-2; NOBE; NOBRP; NoP-4; OAEL-2; OBEV; OBNC; PFE; PWR; PoPoPo; PoRA; Ro; SAGP; SCGP; SCV; SoSe-8; TFi; TTTS; UnPo

And dandelion-seed under the ground. (LL) The Moon in Your Hands. Hilda Doolittle. BoWoP; FaBoWP; NYBP

And dare all Heat but that of Cælia's Eyes. (LL) 1.22. Horace. AWP, tr. by John Quincy Adams; OBVE, tr. by the Earl of Roscommon

And dart from world to world. (LL) George Moses Horton, Myself. George Moses Horton. AAP; NAAAL

And day and night yield one delight once more? (LL) Sudden Light. D. G. Rossetti. BoLoP; CABP; CTC; EBEvV; GLoP; NOBE; NOBVV; NoP-4; OAEL-2; OBNC; PoLF

An de beat well red. Reflection in Red. Onuora Oku. PBCV

And dead. Palladas. See Women all / cause rue.

And dead. (LL) Women all / cause rue. Palladas, Greek. GrAn, tr. by Tony Harrison

And dead my life, that wants such lively bliss. (LL) Sonnet 89: "Like as the culver on the bared bough." Edmund Spenser. GBL; PoE

And death, after all, was only "another room." (LL) Resurrection of Arp. Arthur James Marshall Smith. MoCV; NOBC

And death brooded over the pride of the Plain! (LL) The Cities of the Plain. John Greenleaf Whittier. ChIV-1; NCAP

And death instead of life have sucked from our Nurse. Edmund Spenser. See Mutability.

And death is no evil. (LL) Night. Robinson Jeffers. AWP; ColAP; MoAmPo; NOBA; OxBA

And Death must dig the level where these agree. (LL) Sonnet: "Unlike are we, unlike, O princely Heart!" Elizabeth Barrett Browning. BWW; CABP; EnVR; OBEV; OxAEP-2

And Death once dead, there's no more dying then. (LL) Sonnet 146. Shakespeare. AWP; GTBS-P; HAP; HeIP-4; ImPo; InPS-3; NAEL-1; NOBE; NOCV; NoP-4; OAEL-1; OBEV; OxAEP-1; PoE; PoEL-2; SCGP; Son; TFi

And death shall be no more: Death, thou shalt die. (LL) John Donne. EBEvV; FHYEP; HAP; HeIP-4; ImPo; InPK-6; InPS-3; MeLP; NAEL-1; NAWM-1; NIP-4; NOBE; NOSC; OAEL-1; OPOU; OxAEP-1; PBMP; PoE; PoEL-2; PoRA; Poetr; SCGP; SCV; SeCP; SoSe-8; TRP; TrCP; WeW-3 Fr. Holy Sonnets.

And death shall have no dominion. Dylan Thomas. APAD; CMoP; ChIV-2; EBEvV; LiTM; MoBrPo; NoAM; Poetr; RB; SAGP

And deck the broken stones like saxifrage. (LL) She. Richard Wilbur. AmPP; CoAmPo

And deep-eyed children cannot long be children. Ballad of the Outer Life. Hugo von Hofmannsthal, German. AWP; TrJP, tr. by Jethro Bithell

And defecar on those goddam guidebook. (LL) Sinalóa. Earle Birney. MoCV; OxBC; PeLV

And dense with happy blood, dark rainbow bliss in the sea. (LL) Whales Weep Not! D. H. Lawrence. CMoP; NoAM

And despairs day, but for thy volume's light. (LL) To the Memory of My Beloved, the Author Mr [or Master] William Shakespeare[: And What He Hath Left Us]. Ben Jonson. BeJo; EPCY; HAP; HeIP-4; NOSC; NoP-4; OAEL-1; OxAEP-1; PoEL-2; PoPoPo; SeCP

And did ever a man go black with sun in a Belgian swamp. Nigger. Karl Shapiro. OxBA

And did not burn me. (LL) The Latvian Autumn. Johannes Bobrowski, German. PoSu, tr. by Ruth and Matthew Mead; CEEP, tr. by Ruth Mead and Matthew Mead

And did the animals in Noah's ark. Mark Van Doren. VGW

And did these feet, in pre-war days. The New Jerusalem. Allan M. Laing. UV

And did those feet in ancient time. Jerusalem. William Blake. APAD; AWP; BoTP; CABP; ChIV-1; ClHu; EBEvV; FHYEP; FaBoCh; FaBoPV; FaPoR; HAP; HeIP-4; ImPo; InPS-3; NAEL-2; NAWM-2; NOBE; NOBRP; NOCV; NoP-4; OAEL-2; OBEV; OBNC; OxAEP-2; PeECV; PoE; PoEL-4; PoRA; RB; Ro; SAGP; SCGP; TFi; UV Fr. Milton.

And did we come into our own. Letter to Derek Mahon. Michael Longley. CABP; CIP-2; IIP

And did what doing. (LL) Different. Clere Parsons. APAD

And did you get what. Late Fragment. Raymond Carver. APAD; LBC

And did you know. Snowflakes. Clive Sansom. OBCP

And did you not hear of a jolly young waterman. The Jolly Young Waterman. Charles Dibdin. NOEC; OxAEP-1

And did young Stephen sicken. Emmeline Grangerford's "Ode to Stephen Dowling Bots, Dec'd." "Mark Twain." APN-2; NBLV; OBAL; Poetr Fr. The Adventures of Huckleberry Finn.

And didn't come back for a year and a day. (LL) Finger Play. Unknown. CTAV

And died, content. (LL) A Youth. Stephen Crane. APN-2; MeMAP; MoAmPo; NAAL-2

And died with a toothache in his heel. (LL) Sam, Sam, the butcher man. Unknown. ACTP

And dies between three cannibals. (LL) The Fly. Karl Shapiro. LiTM; MoP; NoAM; PBMP; PFE; SoSe-8

And dinner waiting, and the sun not yet gone down. (LL) The 5:32. Phyllis McGinley. NMM-2

And dinner will be cold. (LL)　Farewell to barn and stack and tree. A. E. Housman. CMoP; MoBrPo; UnPo

And disembodied bones. (LL)　The Eagle and the Mole. Elinor Wylie. AWP; BoWoP; LiTM; MoAmPo; NALW; UnPo

—and disgust. William Carlos Williams. *See* The Raper from Passenack.

And dish water gives back no images. (LL)　No Images. Waring Cuney. NIP-4; PFE; SSLK; TTY

And dismal[l] darkness[e] then doth smutch the face. (LL)　Life is the body's [*or* Bodies] light, which once declining. Robert Herrick. BeJo

And distant from our eyes. (LL)　Cartography. Louise Bogan. PiM; TRP

And do I see some cause a hope to feed. Sonnet 66. Sir Philip Sidney. *Fr.* Astrophil and Stella. AAS; SiPS

And do not even own clothing. (LL)　Salutation. Ezra Pound. HeIP-4; MeMAP; MoAmPo; NOBA; OxBA; TAP; VGW

And do not flow over like you or like me. (LL)　The Jugs. Paul Celan, *German.* HP, *tr. by* Christopher Middleton

And do they so? have they a Sense. Rom. Cap. 8 Ver. 19. Henry Vaughan. ESCV; GeHe; MeLP

And does another thousand start again? (LL)　The Mahratta Ghats. Alun Lewis. OBWVE; PoWW

And does not drift away. (LL)　Medusa. Louise Bogan. AWP; BoWoP; HoPM; MoAmPo; NALW; NMM-2; NoAM; NoP-4; Poetr; WPE

And does the heart grow old? You know. To My Wife. James Vincent Cunningham. SAGP; VCAP

And Don't Be Deaf to the Singing Beyond. Carter Revard. HATNAP

And don't blubber like lubbers when I turn up my keel. (LL)　Tom Deadlight. Herman Melville. APN-2; NCAP

And don't bother telling me anything. César Vallejo, *Spanish.* SPE, *tr. by* Robert Bly

And don't have any kids yourself. (LL)　This Be The Verse. Philip Larkin. NoAM; PoPoPo

And don't wait until you are dead. (LL)　Advice. Ruth Stone. NMM-2

And dost thou faithlessly abandon me? The Unrealities. Johann Christoph Friedrich von Schiller, *German.* AWP, *tr. by* James Clarence Mangan

And dost thou still, thou mass of breathing stone. To the Fragment of a Statue of Hercules, Commonly Called the Torso. Samuel Rogers. GS

And down came the years one after another. Certain Years. Otto Orban, *Hungarian.* CEEP, *tr. by* Jascha Kessler

And down his querulous challenge sent. John Greenleaf Whittier. *See* Snow-Bound [*or* Snow-Bound; a Winter Idyl].

And down to make a bed for you. (LL)　Cackle, cackle, Mother Goose. *Unknown.* CTAV; OxNR

And drank the milk of paradise. Coleridge. *See* Kubla Khan; or, A Vision in a Dream.

And dream my time away. (LL)　Expostulation and Reply. Wordsworth. FHYEP; NAEL-2; NOBRP; OAEL-2; Ro

And dreaming he's dead, he'll forget to awake. (LL)　Willie the Weeper. *Unknown.* BLPA; OBAL

And dreamt of crumbly, currant bread. (LL)　Three Mice. Charlotte Druitt Cole. CTAV

And drew her backward home. (LL)　The Subverted Flower. Robert Frost. CMoP; ColAP; HAP; MeMAP; MoP; NOBA; NoAM; OxBA; PoE; Poetr

And drink them both into the grave. (LL)　Twins. Robert Graves. FaBoEE; OBCoV

And drink thy fill of pure immortal stream[e]s. (LL)　Sonnet: On the Religious Memorie of Mrs. Catherine Thomason My Christian Freind Deca's'd Decem. 1646. Milton. ChIV-2; OxAEP-1

And drinking too much from the town well. (LL)　Incident at Imuris. Alberto A. Ríos. NIP-4; PuP-14

And drinks, and stares, diversified with boggles? (LL)　To a Fish. Leigh Hunt. NBLV; PeLV; SCGP

And driven away the longe nyghtes blake [*or* black]! (LL)　Roundel: "Now welcom[e], Somer [*or* Summer] with thy sunne soft." Chaucer. CTC; EnLoPo; HAP; OAEL-1; OPOU; OxBSP

And drives like she is living. She Drives. Sophie Cabot Black. LoHo

And Dromio's denouement of tragic mirth. (LL)　The Twins. Karl Shapiro. MoAmPo; TrJP

And drove [*or* drave] the first dart deeper more and more. (LL)　Enemy [*or* en'my] of life, decayer of all kind, The [*or* Th']. Sir Thomas Wyatt. OxBSP; SiPS

And drummed them out of town. Mother Goose. *See* The Lion and the unicorn.

And drunk the milk of Paradise. (LL)　Kubla Khan; or, A Vision in a Dream. Coleridge. APAD; AWP; CABP; CH; EBEvV; FHYEP; FaBoBe; FaBoCh; GEA; HAP; HeIP-4; HoPM; ImPo; InPK-6; InPS-3; NAEL-2; NAWM-2; NIP-4; NOBE; NOBRP; NoP-4; OAEL-2; OBEV; OBGa; OBNC; OxAEP-2; PBMP; PoE; PoEL-4; PoPoPo; PoRA; Poetr; Ro; SAGP; SCGP; SCV; SoSe-8; TFi; TOF; TRP; WeW-3

And dulls to distance all we are. (LL)　Ambulances. Philip Larkin. FaBoTw; NAEL-2; NoP-4; OxBC

And dust is for a time. (LL)　In Distrust of Merits. Marianne Moore. ColAP; LiTM; MeMAP; MoAmPo; NAAL-2; OBWP; OxBA

And dying in black and white we fight for what we love, not are. (LL)　Ode: Salute to the French Negro Poets. Frank O'Hara. GLP; NNaP; NeAP; PoM

And each anointed sense will see. (LL)　Extreme Unction. Ernest Christopher Dowson. ADE; MoBrPo; OAEL-2; OBMV; PeECV; PeVV

And each as silent as a man being shaved. (LL)　Prolonged Sonnet: When the Troops Were Returning from Milan. Niccolò degli Albizzi, *Italian.* AWP; OBVE, *tr. by* D. G. Rossetti

And each slow dusk a drawing-down of blinds. (LL)　Anthem for Doomed Youth. Wilfred Owen. AF; APAD; CABP; CMoP; ClHu; EBEV; FaBoMo; GEA; GSo; GTBS-P; HAP; HeIP-4; HoPM; ImPo; InPK-6; InPS-3; LiTM; MoBrPo; MoP; NAEL-2; NOBE; NoAM; NoP-4; OAEL-2; OBEV; OBWP; OxBTC; PoE; PoFWW; PoPoPo; SAGP; SCV; SoSe-8; Son; TFi; WeW-3

And earth and heaven be one. (LL)　This Is My Father's World. Maltbie Davenport Babcock. CTV

And Earth is but a star, that once had shone. (LL)　Prologue: "We Who with Songs Beguile your Pilgrimage." James Elroy Flecker. FaPoR; OBMV; OxBTC; UV

And earth, sea, man, are all in each. (LL)　The Sea-Limits. D. G. Rossetti. EnVR; NAEL-2; OAEL-2

And eat our pot of honey on the grave. (LL)　Sonnet 29: "Am I failing? For no longer can I cast." George Meredith. EnVR; GBL; PFE; SCGP

And eats its dead-dog off a golden dish. (LL)　Arbor Vitae. Coventry Patmore. OBNC; PeVV

And eats the meadow flowers. (LL)　The Cow. Robert Louis Stevenson. CTAV; CTV; FPC; NTCP; OxBChV; PWR; TLR; WHSW

And eek the false empoysoner also. Chaucer. *See* The Pardoner's Tale.

And eke men shal nat [*or* nought] make[n] ernest of game. (LL)　The Miller's Prologue. Chaucer. NAEL-1; OAEL-1

And elder and mullen and pokeweed. Walt Whitman. *See* I believe in you my soul, the other I am must not abase itself to you.

And empty grows every bed. (LL)　Huffy Henry hid the day. John Berryman. CBNP; ColAP; HCAP; NAAL-2; NoP-4; PoE; VCAP

And engines / that devour America. (LL)　In Goya's greatest scenes we seem to see. Lawrence Ferlinghetti. HeIP-4; LiTM; NeAP; NoAM; PBMP; PmAP; PoM; TAP

And engraved in rapid waters. Catullus. *See* Carmen 70 ("Lesbia says she'ld rather marry me").

And escaped from the people of Basing. (LL)　Limerick: "There was an old person of Basing." Edward Lear. CBNP; EBEV; OBCoV; OxAEP-2; PeLi

And Ettrick mourns with her their Poet dead. (LL)　Extempore Effusion upon the Death of James Hogg. Wordsworth. EBEV; NOBE; OAEL-2; SCV

And Ettrick mourns with her their Shepherd dead! Wordsworth. *See* Extempore Effusion upon the Death of James Hogg.

"And even our women," lastly grumbles Ben. The Girl of All Periods: An Idyll. Coventry Patmore. EnVR

And even this is only half a revenge. (LL)　Autobiography. Dan Pagis, *Hebrew.* AF; VCWP, *tr. by* Stephen Mitchell

And eventually sent a telegram. (LL)　How I Brought the Good News from Aix to Ghent (or Vice Versa). R. J. Yeatman *and* W. C. Sellar. BXAP; UV

And ever as he went he swept a lyre. Cancelled Passages of the Poem. Shelley. *Fr.* Adonais; An Elegy on the Death of Keats. EBEV; FHYEP; HoPM; ImPo; NOBRP; OAEL-2; OxAEP-2; PoEL-4; TFi

And ever changing avenues of song. (LL)　Bury the Great Duke. Tennyson. EBVVPR

And Ever is Now. (LL)　A Pavane for the Nursery. William Jay Smith. ITG; MoAmPo

And ever more shall be-O. (LL)　Carol of the Numbers. *Unknown.* AmFP; OxBoLi

And every five minutes he assured his public that he would take up very little of their time. (LL)　The God of War. Bertolt Brecht, *German.* AF, *tr. by* Michael Hamburger

And every fourth year, one day / more. Mother Goose. *See* Thirty days hath September.

And every house a folly. (LL)　For though the eaves were rabbeted. Henry David Thoreau. NCAP; OxBSP; PoEL-4

And every memory you have—will begin / at Genesis. (LL)　Temptation. Nina Cassian, *Romanian.* AF; CEEP, *tr. by* Brenda Walker *and* Andrea Deletant

And every sheaf a golden tree. (LL)　The Voice from the Well [of Life Speaks to the Maiden]. George Peele. InPS-3; NOBE; NoSic; PoEL-2; RB

And every sheave a golden tree. (LL)　A Voice [Speaks] from the Well. George Peele. CBNP; FaBoCh; NOBE; OxBoLi

And every Space that a Man views around his dwelling-place. William Blake. BLT. *Fr.* "Milton."

And every wave is charmed. (LL) Terminus ("It is time to be old"). Ralph Waldo Emerson. APN-1; AWP; AmPP; MeMAP; NCAP; NOBA; OxBA; PoEL-4; PoLF; SAGP; TAP

And every year a world my will did deem. George Gascoigne. Son *Fr.* Gascoigne's Memories.

And every yeare a worlde my will did deeme. George Gascoigne. AAS

And everyone. Carlos Drummond de Andrade. *See* Motionless Faces.

And everyone, everyone pointing up and shouting! (LL) Child on Top of a Greenhouse. Theodore Roethke. KaS; LCAP-2; NOxBChV; NoP-4; VGW

And everyone simply dances away. (LL) Slow Dance. David St. John. AmPA; LCAP-2

And everything he'd touched, an exposed nerve. (LL) Empty House. Stephen Spender. NYBP; PCP

And ev'n Devotion! Robert Burns. *See* To a Louse [On Seeing One on a Lady's Bonnet at Church].

And ev'ry thing, save her, who all should grace. (LL) Invocation: "Pheobus, arise! / And paint the sable skies." William Drummond, of Hawthornden. GTBS-P; OBEV

And exchange names and addresses. (LL) Truce. Paul Muldoon. PBCIP; PNI

And fades away like morning dew. (LL) Waly, Waly ("When cockle shells turn silver bells"). *Unknown.* AS; AmFP

And fading in the most important place we have yet devised. (LL) The Shopping-Bag Lady. Linda Gregg. WWSi

And faintly trust the larger hope. (LL) Wish, that of the living whole, The. Tennyson. EBVV; EBVVPR; EnVR; FHYEP; HAP; OAEL-2; OBNC; TOF

And fall. (LL) November Night. Adelaide Crapsey. FPC

And fall in blood: we bring him even now. (LL) Six o'Clock. Trumbull Stickney. APN-2; OxBA

And falls on the other. (LL) Vaulting Ambition. Shakespeare. EBEvV; OxAEP-1; OAEL-1

And fashions men with true nobility. (LL) Fair Is Too Foul an Epithet. Marlowe. EBEV; PoEL-2

And fastened it in Dawn. (LL) It was a quiet way—. Emily Dickinson. ITG; NCAP

And fat old elephumpasses. (LL) Circles. Harry Behn. CA; CTV

And fate change me to worms. (LL) Against Constancy. John Wilmot, 2d Earl of Rochester. GBL; NOSC; OxAEP-1

And fear lit by the breadth of such calmly turns to praise. (LL) The City Limits. A. R. Ammons. HCAP; MoP; NAAL-2; NOBA; NoAM; NoP-4; PoPoPo; Poetr; VCAP

And fears not portly Azcan nor his hoos. (LL) Bantams in Pine-Woods. Wallace Stevens. CMoP; InPS-3; MeMAP; NOBA; NoAM; OxBA; PFE; SAmP; UnPo

And feel, and die. (LL) War Memoir: Jazz, Don't Listen to It at Your Own Risk. Bob Kaufman. MoNo

And feel like flowers that fade. (LL) Elena's Song. Sir Henry Taylor. OBEV; RACG

And feel with torment that 'tis so. Catullus. *See* Carmen 85.

And feels a temporary death. Catullus. *See* Sappho.

And feels like temporary death. Catullus. *See* Sappho.

And fell asleep by a fire. (LL) Redwings. James Wright. NNaP; WeT

And fell it on the start. (LL) Dream Song 384. John Berryman. PoPoPo

And fetched her to his lair. (LL) The Two Magicians. *Unknown.* OAEL-1; OxBoLi

And fight with honest men to shield a knave. (LL) Time was, ere yet in these degenerate days. Byron. EPCY; FHYEP

And fill your heads with crotchets. (LL) The Distracted Puritan. Richard Corbet. BeJo; OBCoV; OxBoLi

And filled the unclean leper's house. Oscar Wilde. *See* The Ballad of Reading Gaol.

And find Ianthe's name agen. (LL) Well I Remember [How You Smiled]. Walter Savage Landor. HAP; OBNC

And find, in your wife, a Companion and Friend'. (LL) The Conclusion of a Letter to the Rev. Mr. C——. Mary Barber. CABP; ECWP

And find th'effect, for I do burn in love. (LL) Sonnet 25: "The Wisest scholar of the wight most wise." Sir Philip Sidney. NoP-4; OAEL-1

And find your way to the parlour of Government House. (LL) Invitation to Hsiao Ch'u-shih. Po Chü-i, *Chinese.* ChiP, *tr. by* Arthur Waley

And fire their only future. (LL) The Asians Dying. W. S. Merwin. CAPP-1; CoAP; HCAP; NOBA; NYBP; PoPoPo; VCAP

And firesides buried under fallen thatch. (LL) The Eviction. William Allingham. BIrV; NOIV

And first, a sip of wine. It comes from Spain. Giuseppe Giacosa *and* Luigi Illica. OxBoV, *tr. by* Edmund Tracey *Fr.* Tosca.

And flang 't in St. Mary's Loch. (LL) Earl Brand (The Douglas Tragedy). *Unknown.* NoP-4

And fled with every one—. (LL) Cat. Emily Dickinson. APo; SAmP

And flies with the cloud. (LL) Chimes. Alice Thompson Meynell. BoTP; CH; MoBrPo; WPE

And flourished in the open field. (LL) Timothy. Timothy Steele. RA

And for Alice, his wife, pray too. (LL) Shameful Death. William Morris. GTBS-P; PeVV

And for her glory, *Garlands* of fresh *Bayes*. (LL) The Poetresses Petition. Margaret Lucas Cavendish, Duchess of Newcastle. KTR

And for her sake trip up Death. (LL) Little Elegy. X. J. Kennedy. APAD; CoAP; CoAmPo; HoPM

And for His Mother. John Wheelwright. FiLi

And for his sin atones. Bible, *O.T. See* Psalm 137.

And for hours used no hot words. (LL) A WASP Woman Visits a Black Junkie in Prison. Etheridge Knight. NBV

And, for our tongue, that still is so empayr'd. George Chapman. PBRV *Fr.* Homer's Iliad, To the Reader.

And for short time an endless[e] monument [*or* moniment]. (LL) Epithalamion: "Ye learned sisters which have oftentimes." Edmund Spenser. AAS; BoLoP; FHYEP; InPS-3; NOBE; NoSic; OAEL-1; OBEV; OxAEP-1; PoEL-1

And for special things. The Grim Sisters. Liz Lochhead. CABP; FaBoTC

And for the penny in your purse / I'll ferry you. (LL) Ferry me across the water, / Do, boatman, do. Christina Rossetti. BoTP; NTP; OxBChV; TLR

And for those who return. Birago Diop. *See* Diptych.

And for what, except for you, do I feel love? Notes toward a Supreme Fiction. Wallace Stevens.

And for what, except for you, do I feel love? To Henry Church. Wallace Stevens. ColAP; NOBA *Fr.* Notes toward a Supreme Fiction.

And for what purpose? Why go to the cross? For the Last Time on My Native Estate. Ilya Iankelevich Gabai, *Russian.* TCRP, *tr. by* Albert C. Todd

And forced the underbrush—and that was all. (LL) The Most of It. Robert Frost. BLT; HAP; NAAL-2; NoP-4; TOF; TRP; WeW-3

And Forgive Us Our Trespasses. Aphra Behn. EBEV

And form to his, the relish of their souls. (LL) Nature's Influence on Man. Mark Akenside. NOEC

An' forward, tho' I canna see, / I guess an' fear! Robert Burns. *See* To a Mouse[, On Turning Her Up in Her Nest, with the Plough, November, 1785].

And found it of some interest. (LL) Le Jazz Hot. Anselm Hollo. SeSe

And found it was perfectly true. (LL) Limerick: "There was an old man of [*or* from] Peru / Who dreamt [*or* dreamed] he was eating his shoe." *Unknown.* NTCP; SoSe-8

And found Life stepping on my feet! (LL) Esthete in Harlem. Langston Hughes. ColAP

And foxes stunk and littered in St. Paul's'. (LL) On Lord Holland's Seat near Margate, Kent. Thomas Gray. NOEC; OAEL-1

And fractions drive me mad. *Unknown. See* Arithmetic.

And frame from thinking and is realized. (LL) To an Old Philosopher in Rome. Wallace Stevens. ColAP; EnlH; MeMAP; MoP; NOBA; NoAM; Poetr

And freed [*or* free'd] his soul the nearest way. (LL) On the Death of Dr [*or* Mr] Robert Levet [a Practiser in Physic]. Samuel Johnson. ChIV-2; EBEV; InPS-3; NAEL-1; NOBE; NOEC; NoP-4; OAEL-1; OBEV; OxAEP-1; PFE; PeECV; PoE; PoEL-3; SCGP; SCV; TFi

And Freedom's banner streaming o'er us! [*or* ?]. (LL) The American Flag. Joseph Rodman Drake. APN-1; FaBoBe

And freedoms birthright from the weak devours. (LL) The Fallen Elm. John Clare. FHYEP; FaBoPV

And friendship by her are dissolved, / suffered unspoken. Mary Sidney, Countess of Montgomery Wroth. *See* The Duke's Song.

And frightened Miss Muffet away. (LL) Little Miss Muffet / Sat on a tuffet. Mother Goose. FaBoBe; LB; OxNR; ReMoGo

And from louts to run away. (LL) Eleventh Song. Sir Philip Sidney. NAEL-1; NOBE; NoSic; OBEV; OxAEP-1; PoE; PoEL-1; SCGP

And from lowts to run away. Sir Philip Sidney. *See* Eleventh Song.

And from my bosom find a surer rest. (LL) The Earth. Jones Very. APN-1; OxBA

And from that village, steaming with mist, riddled with rain. Listening. David Mura. PuP-15

And from the Citie Tegea there came the Paragone. Ovid. OBVE, *tr. by* Arthur Golding *Fr.* Metamorphoses.

And from the house his mother called his name. (LL) Childhood. Edwin Muir. CMoP; FaBoTC; HeIP-4; NoP-4

And from the veiny flint command / The fountain and the well. Bible, *O.T. See* Psalm 114.

And from the windy West came two-gunned Gabriel. Dylan Thomas. *Fr.* A Sequence of Sonnets.

And from their gibbets take thy dead. (LL) The Study of a Spider. John Byrne Leicester Warren, 3d Baron De Tabley. APo

And frowzy pores that taint the ambient air. (LL) On Jacob Tonson, His Publisher. Dryden. FaBoEE; OBSV

And fuddled by my drunkness forget / —Monangambeeee. (LL) Monangamba. Antonio Jacinto, *Portuguese*. TTY, *tr. by* Alan Ryder

And full of Argus eyes their tailes dispredden wide. (LL) So forth she comes, and to her coche does clyme. Edmund Spenser. NAEL-1; OAEL-1

And futile as regret. (LL) Bewick Finzer. Edwin Arlington Robinson. CMoP; MeMAP; MoAmPo; NAAL-2

And gained her maidenhead. (LL) The Twa Magicians. *Unknown*. ESPB; OAEL-1; OxBB; OxBoLi

And gained in service of our fair / And universal Queen. (LL) Pangloss's Song: A Comic-Opera Lyric. Richard Wilbur. MoP; NBLV; NoAM

And gallop terribly against each other's bodies. (LL) Autumn Begins in Martins Ferry, Ohio. James Wright. ColAP; HCAP; HeIP-4; InPK-6; InPS-3; NoAM; SAGP; VCAP; WeT; WeW-3

And gather roses, while 'tis called to-day. (LL) Of His Lady's Old Age. Pierre de Ronsard, *French*. AWP; CTC, *tr. by* Andrew Lang

And gathering swallows twitter in the skies. (LL) To Autumn. Keats. APAD; AWP; BoTP; CABP; CH; ClHu; EBEV; EBEvV; FHYEP; GTBS-P; HAP; HeIP-4; ImPo; InPK-6; InPS-3; LaPo; NAEL-2; NAWM-2; NIP-4; NOBE; NOBRP; NTP; NoP-4; OAEL-2; OBEV; OBNC; OxAEP-2; PBMP; PFE; PoE; PoEL-4; PoLF; PoPoPo; Poetr; RB; RaBo; Ro; SCGP; SCV; SoSe-8; TFi; TRP; UnPo; WeW-3

And gave away her heart. (LL) The Ballad of Aunt Geneva. Marilyn Nelson Waniek. FFC; GT

And gave me back my beauty. (LL) The Fired Pot. Anna Wickham. LW

And gave the discourse a definitive blow. (LL) A Poem on the Supposition of the Book Having Been Published and Read. Elizabeth Hands. ECWP; WoRP

And gazing, died. (LL) The White Women. Mary Elizabeth Coleridge. PEW; VWP

And gently lay us on the spicy shore. (LL) The New London. Dryden. FaBoCh; NOBE

And gently rhyming rats to death. (LL) Soliloquy on an Empty Purse. Mary Jones. ECWP; PEW

An' get hame my rantin laddie. (LL) The Baron o [*or of*] Leys. *Unknown*. ESPB; OxBB

And gete gold with here glee giltles, I trowe. (LL) Prologue: "In a summer season, when soft was the sun." William Langland. EBVV; NAEL-1; OAEL-1; PoE; PoEL-1

And ghosts then keep their distance; and I know some liberty. (LL) Wessex Heights. Thomas Hardy. CMoP; EBVV; OAEL-2; OBNC; PoEL-5; SCGP

And give her no scouts doing their one good deed. Elderly Lady Crossing on Green. Wyatt Prunty. RA

And give resounding grace to all Heav'ns Harmonies. (LL) Echo. Milton. NOBE; OBEV

And give thanks it was not I, nor yet one close to I. (LL) The Open Sea. William Meredith. CoAP; TAP; UnPo

And give thee peace. (LL) Benediction. Bible, *O.T.* OBVE, *tr. by* William Tyndale; TrJP

And give to February twenty-nine. (LL) Thirty days hath September. Mother Goose. FaBoBe; OxNR; ReMoGo

And glittering eyelids of my soul's desire. Love And Sleep. Swinburne. APAD; BoLoP; CBLP; GLoP; GSo; LoP

And glorious is thy name through all the earth, *par. by* Milton. Bible, *O.T.* *See* Psalm 8.

And go to the moon. (LL) Bean Spasms. Ted Berrigan. PmAP

And go to the tenis! (LL) Haylle, Comly and Clene. *Unknown*. OBEV; OxBoLi

And God—at every Gate. (LL) Our journey had advanced. Emily Dickinson. APN-2; LiTM; NOCV; PAR; PoEL-5; SoSe-8

And God bring all of us to Kingdom Come, *mod. vers. by* Nevill Coghill. Chaucer. *See* The Miller's [*or* Milleres] Tale.

And God looked down at God that day. My God, My God, Look upon Me. Chad Walsh. *Fr.* The Psalm of Christ. TrCP

And God said to the soul. God Speaks to the Soul. Mechthild von Magdeburg, *German*. WPoS, *tr. by* Oliver Davies

And God saw that the wickedness of man was great. Bible, *O.T.* NAWM-1 *Fr.* Genesis.

And God shall bless you from above. (LL) To My Dear Children. Anne Bradstreet. MDDM; NAAL-3

And God shall wipe away all tears from their eyes. An End To Tears. Bible, *N.T.* LBC *Fr.* The Revelation of St John The Divine.

And God stepped out on space. The Creation. James Weldon Johnson. ChIV-1; ISC; KSG; MoAmPo; NAAAL; PBMP; PoBA; PoRA; SAGP; SSLK; TrCP

And God will save the Queen. (LL) 1887. A. E. Housman. FaPoR; NIP-4; NOBVV; SCGP; UnPo

And gods disgusting.—You and I, Cassandra. (LL) Cassandra. Robinson Jeffers. HeIP-4; LiTM

And going to the office in the train. (LL) Dreamers. Siegfried Sassoon. GSo; MoBrPo; NoAM; Son

And gold on my neck the sun. (LL) The Collier. Vernon Watkins. FaBoTw; OBWVE

And gone all trace of me! (LL) Tess's Lament. Thomas Hardy. FaBoTw; FaBoVe

And—good grief! it was perfectly true! *Unknown*. *See* Limerick: "There was an old man of [*or* from] Peru / Who dreamt [*or* dreamed] he was eating his shoe."

And grant his reign over the entire building. (LL) Homage to the British Museum. William Empson. CMoP; FaBoMo; LiTM; MoBrPo; PoE

And grass in the green field. Wordsworth. *See* A Change in the Year.

And grave by grave we civilize the ground. (LL) To the Western World. Louis Simpson. CoAP; CoAmPo; LiTM; NOBA; PFE; TAP; TRP

And great souls, at one stroke, may do and dote. (LL) Sonnet: "The First time that the sun rose on thine oath." Elizabeth Barrett Browning. EnVR; NAEL-2; WPE

And great thy wisdom, Vander Brüin. (LL) A Dutch Proverb. Matthew Prior. FaBoEE; NOEC; OBCoV

And grey hairs were on my head. (LL) The Angel. William Blake. CH; FHYEP; RACG; Ro

And grow incorporate into thee. (LL) Old yew, which graspest at the stones. Tennyson. EBVV; EBVVPR; EnVR; GTBS-P; NOBE; OAEL-2; OBNC; PoEL-5; UnPo

And gulp from them the dailiness of life. (LL) Well Water. Randall Jarrell. InPK-6; NAAL-2; NOBA; OxBSP; VCAP; VGW

And ha I'm bound away, 'cross the wide Missouri. (LL) Shenandoah. *Unknown*. APN-2.

And habit builds the bridge at last! (LL) A Builder's Lesson. John Boyle O'Reilly. PWR; PoLF; PoToHe

And had been left in darkness forever to work and fail. (LL) After Publication of Under the Volcano. Malcolm Lowry. FaBoTw

And half the heaven of the blest! (LL) Song: "Oh! Love, that stronger art than wine." Aphra Behn. LW; WPE; WPOW

And half the seed of Europe, one by one. (LL) The Parable of the Old Man and the Young. Wilfred Owen. ChIV-1; PoFWW

And hang it in the junior college. (LL) Digging for Indians. Gary Gildner. AmPA; PBCAP

And Hannah prayed, and said. Hannah's Thanksgiving. Bible, *O.T.* BoWoP *Fr.* First Samuel.

And haply, bason'd in some unsunn'd cleft. Coleridge. *Fr.* To a Young Friend, on His Proposing to Domesticate with the Author. LaPo

And happy each at home enjoys his love. (LL) Cymon and Iphigenia. Dryden. EPCY; OBNV

And hardly safe from brother traitors there. (LL) To Sir Toby. Philip Freneau. NAAL-1; NAAL-3; NoP-4; TAP

And has the remnant of my life. Thoughts on my sick-bed. Dorothy Wordsworth. PEW; Ro

And hast crowned him with glory and honour, *sel., vv. 3–5*. Bible, *O.T.* *See* Psalm 8.

And hate the idle pleasures of these days. (LL) Hate the Idle Pleasures. Shakespeare. EBEvV; PoE

And haunt the places where their Honour dy'd. . (LL) Epigram: "When other Ladies to the Shades go down." Alexander Pope. FaBoEE; OxBSP; PoEL-3

And have forgotten since their beauty passed. (LL) Tears. Edward Thomas. GTBS-P; NAEL-2

And have His bliss and blessedness for ever! (LL) The Whale. *Unknown*. AnOE, *tr. by* Charles Kennedy; ASW, *tr. by* Kevin Crossley-Holland

And have I strove in vain to move. To Anna Matilda. Robert Merry. NOBRP

And have one Titan at a time. (LL) The Master. Edwin Arlington Robinson. CBCWP; LiTM; MoAmPo

And have the bright immensities. Howard Chandler Robbins. AH

And have we done with War at last? Two Fusiliers. Robert Graves. PoFWW

And having no need to let myself be robbed / a second time. (LL) Nomen. Naomi Long Madgett. BlSi; MoLi

And having nothing, yet hath all. (LL) The Character of a Happy Life. Sir Henry Wotton. EBEvV; GTBS-P; NOBE; NOSC; NTP; OBEV

And haze and vista, and the far horizon fading away. (LL) A Farm Picture. Walt Whitman. BLT; InPS-3; TRP

And He Answered Them Nothing. Richard Crashaw. ChIV-2

And he arose and came to his father. Luke 15:20–32; And he arose and came. Edwin Arlington Robinson. GI *Fr.* St. Luke.

And he bought a wedding Ring-o! (LL) Bingo. *Unknown*. CH; TTTS

And he did—nine soliloquies later. (LL) Hamlet. Stanley J. Sharpless. BXAP; NBLV; PeLi

And he drops, and turns, and goes. (LL) In the Servants' Quarters. Thomas Hardy. FaBoVe; MoBrPo

And he had lived enough when he had dried her tear. (LL) For an Epitaph at Fiesole. Walter Savage Landor. FaBoEE; OBNC

And he has remained alone. Pier Paolo Pasolini. *See* The Day of My Death.

And He hath not forgotten my age. (LL) The Old Man's Comforts and How He Gained Them. Robert Southey. APAD; EBEvV; HoPM; OxBChV; UV; UnPo

And he is risen? Well, be it so. A Drizzling Easter Morning. Thomas Hardy. CMoP

And he lived over nine hundred years. (LL) Methuselah ("Methuselah ate what he found on his plate"). Unknown. BLPA; FaBoBe

And he returns at last to the empty void. (LL) Returning to My Home in the Country ("So long since I've enjoyed the hills and ponds"). T'ao Ch'ien, *Chinese.* CoBCP, *tr. by* Burton Watson

And he said, So is the kingdome of God. Bible, *N.T.* OBVE *Fr.* St. Mark.

And he said, So soule doth magnifie the Lord. Bible, *N.T.* OBVE *Fr.* St. Mark.

And he said, "There was a man who had two sons;.." Luke 15:11–19; And he said, "There was a man." Rilke. GI *Fr.* St. Luke.

And He Shall Judge Among Nations. Bible, *O.T.* PBMP *Fr.* Isaiah.

And he shall judge among the nations, and shall rebuke. And He Shall Judge Among Nations. Bible, *O.T.* PBMP *Fr.* Isaiah.

And he shall [*or* will] redeem Israel from all his iniquities. (LL) Psalm 130. Bible, *O.T.* NoSic; OBVE; TrJP

And he, "To begin with a swelled head and end with swelled feet." (LL) Ezra Pound. Robert Lowell. MoP; NAAL-2; NOBA; NoAM

And he took her hand. Aphrodite reveals herself. *Unknown, Greek.* OBCVT, *tr. by* John D. Niles

And he was left lamenting. (LL) Lord Ullin's Daughter. Thomas Campbell. BoTP; FaPoR; GTBS-P; NOBRP

And he went unto Ramah. There he met. The Dance of Saul with the Prophets. Saul Tchernichovsky, *Hebrew.* TrJP, *tr. by* I. M. Lask

And he will make it plain. (LL) Light Shining out of Darkness. William Cowper. CABP; EBEV; EBEvV; ECEV; FHYEP; FaBoCh; ImPo; NOBE; NOCV; NOEC; NoP-4; PWR; PoEL-3; SCGP; TFi; TOF

And he wondered. Keats. *See* The Naughty Boy.

And heal my troubled breast which cries [*or* cryes], / Which dies [*or* dyes]. (LL) Longing. George Herbert. ESCV; UV

And hear the wild roar of their thunder today! (LL) Lines Composed in a Wood on a Windy Day. Anne Brontë. VWP

And heard the sound of rushing wind. (LL) The Coming of the Plague. Weldon Kees. ChIV-1; VGW

And hears an unintelligible prayer. (LL) The Feast of Stephen. Anthony Hecht. HAP; NoAM; VCAP

And hears, far off, her muted children cry. (LL) Milkmaid. Laurie Lee. APAD

And heartier loves; that lamp is from the tomb. (LL) The Leaders of the Crowd. W. B. Yeats. EBEV; MoBrPo; OxAEP-2

And he'd go and fetch her the drake, drake, drake. (LL) Sam, The Sportsman. Mother Goose. LB; OxNR

And heed not them that warn or chide thee. Hark! The Rosy Days Are Numbered. Moses ibn Ezra. TrJP, *tr. by* Solomon Solis-Cohen

And heel and toe forever and ever. (LL) Two Stories. Charles Wright. FYAP; LCAP-2

And held her in my arms! (LL) Politics. W. B. Yeats. CBLP; CMoP; HeIP-4; InPS-3; OxBTC; PoE; SAGP; SCV

And hemlock-headed in the wood of weathers. (LL) Death is all metaphors, shape in one history. Dylan Thomas. CMoP; Son

An hendy hap etc. (LL) Alison. *Unknown.* CBLP; MiEL; NAEL-1; OAEL-1; OBEV; PeLV

And her amazing linen. (LL) Deaf Girl Playing. James Tate. CMAP; LCAP-2

And her eyes lightnings and her shoulders wings. (LL) In Progress. Christina Rossetti. BoWoP; NAEL-2; WPE

And her groom. D. H. Lawrence. *See* Bavarian Gentians.

And her long robe trails all about the south. (LL) Peace, Be at Peace, O Thou My Heaviness. Charles Baudelaire, *French.* InPK-6, *tr. by* Lord Alfred Douglas

And Her Mother Came Too. Dion Titherage. OBCoV

And her quietus is to render thee. (LL) Sonnet 126. Shakespeare. HeIP-4; NAEL-1

And her right home and her right passion. (LL) Lady Lost. John Crowe Ransom. MoAmPo; NoP-4; UnPo

And her shoes were full of feet. . (LL) In the Night. *Unknown.* FPC; NBLV

And her thorns were my only delight. (LL) My Pretty Rose-Tree. William Blake. BoLoP; FHYEP; NAEL-2; NOBRP; Ro

And here a line in memory of his name and death. (LL) Osceola. Walt Whitman. NAAL-1; NAAL-3

And here comes a chopper to chop off your head. *Unknown. See* The Bells of London.

And here face down beneath the sun. You, Andrew Marvell. Archibald MacLeish. AWP; CMoP; ColAP; FYAP; GEA; HAP; HeIP-4; HoPM; LiTM; MeMAP; MoAmPo; MoP; NAAL-2; NOBA; NoAM; NoP-4; OxBA; PoRA; Poetr; SAGP; SoSe-8; TFi; TRP; TwCP

And here fair freedom shall forever reign. Leander. Hugh Henry Brackenridge *and* Philip Freneau. *Fr.* The Rising Glory of America. AiP

And here I wish my soul died with my breath. Ovid. OBVE, *tr. by* Henry Vaughan *Fr.* Tristium.

And here stand I, a suppliant at the door. (LL) At the Grave of Henry Vaughan. Siegfried Sassoon. CMoP; GTBS-P

And here the precious dust is laid [*or* layd]. Maria Wentworth. Thomas Carew. BeJo; CaPo; CavPo; MeLP; PeECV; SCGP

And here we are back. Going Back Patiently. Frank Mkalawile Chipasula. HBAPE

And here's the child's Dad. *Unknown.* OxNR

And hide its face / for shame. (LL) Death. William Carlos Williams. NAAL-2; OxBA; VGW

And hide the shame! (LL) Ichabod[!]. John Greenleaf Whittier. APN-1; NAAL-1; NAAL-3; NOBA; OxBA; PAR; PBMP; PoEL-4; TAP

And hide thy shame beneath the ground. (LL) Risest thou thus, dim dawn, again. Tennyson. OBNC; PeECV; PoEL-5

And hiding their tossing manes and their tumultuous / feet. (LL) Michael Robartes Bids His Beloved Be at Peace. W. B. Yeats. MoP; NoAM

And Him. Emily Dickinson. *See* A Clock stopped.

And himself, in grateful thanks. (LL) To Venus. Joachim Du Bellay, *French.* FLP; LoP, *tr. by* Alistair Elliot

And, Hinges. Ted Greenwald. FTOS

And his bed father after him. (LL) The Sad Boy. Laura Riding Jackson. CBNP; RB

And his black whiskers and his little dancing feet. (LL) Behaving Like a Jew. Gerald Stern. LoL

And his bleeding body beside the wound of morning. Psalm To Cheer Up. Tadeusz Nowak, *Polish.* CEEP, *tr. by* Leonard Kress

And his deep love endures forever. Bible, *O.T. See* Psalm 100.

And his first minute, after noon[e], is night. (LL) A Lecture upon the Shadow. Donne. AWP; ESCV; ImPo; NAEL-1; NoSic; SCGP; SeCP; UnPo

And his forsworn life. (LL) I am forgotten now. Lady Ukon, *Japanese.* WPJ, *tr. by* Kenneth Rexroth *and* Ikuko Atsumi

And his Georgian chest is broad. (LL) Poem No. 286 (On Stalin). Osip Emilevich Mandelstam, *Russian.* TCRP, *tr. by* Albert C. Todd

And his message easy? (LL) Prognosis. Louis MacNeice. CMoP; NOBE

and his name was Willy Wood. (LL) Aiken Drum. *Unknown.* FaBoCh; OxNR

And his overthrow, our chorus. Thomas Love Peacock. *See* The War Song of Dinas Vawr.

And His own face to see. (LL) The Mystery. Ralph Hodgson. CH; MoBrPo

And his sepulchre shall not be whicted. (LL) Orthography. Ambrose Bierce. APN-2; OBAL; PeLi

And his slow strut moves him on again. (LL) Harlem Freeze Frame. Lebert Bethune. GT

And his son Judas, who was called Maccabeus. Judas Maccabeus. Bible, Apocrypha. TrJP *Fr.* First Maccabees.

And his truth endureth to all / generations. Bible, *O.T. See* Psalm 100.

And ho but I love thee dearly! (LL) The Orphan's Song. Sydney Thompson Dobell. CH; OBNC

And hold love in. (LL) Prayer for This House. Louis Untermeyer. PoLF; PoToHe

And home shall never come. (LL) The Twa Brothers. *Unknown.* CH; EBEV; ESPB; OxBB; PBMP

And hope felt strong and life itself not weak. (LL) Aloof. Christina Rossetti. NOBE; OBEV; OBNC; PEW

And hope was false, but love was true. (LL) Newark Abbey. Thomas Love Peacock. NOBE; OBNC

And Hope without an object cannot live. (LL) Work Without Hope. Coleridge. GSo; LaPo; NAEL-2; NOBE; OBEV; OxAEP-2; Son

And hoping a little, a little, that either may be. (LL) Blackberry Winter ("If the lady hath any loveliness, let it die"). John Crowe Ransom. OxBA; PoRA

And how beguile you? Death has no repose. James Elroy Flecker. OxBTC *Fr.* The Golden Journey to Samarkand.

And how do you do again? (LL) One misty, moisty morning. Mother Goose. BoTP; FaBoBe; LB; OxNR; ReMoGo

And how do you do again. (LL) Song: "Before the barn-door crowing." John Gay. CTAV; OxBSP; PoEL-3

And hurl me to the shark, I shall not die! (LL) The Leg. Karl Shapiro. HAP; MoAmPo; UnPo; WeW-3

And hurls for him, O half hurls earth for him off under his feet. (LL) Hurrahing in Harvest. Gerard Manley Hopkins. APAD; CMoP; MoBrPo; NAEL-2; PeECV; PoE; TOF

And hurry along, Van Winkle—it's getting late! (LL) Van Winkle. Hart Crane. AmPP; MoAmPo

And hymn thy favourite [*or* favorite] name! (LL) Ode to Evening. William Collins. AWP; CABP; EBEV; ECEV; FaBoBe; GTBS-P; HAP; ImPo; NAEL-1; NOBE; NOEC; NoP-4; OAEL-1; OBEV; OxAEP-1; PoE; PoEL-3; SCGP; TFi

And I a beginner. Answer to Yo / Question. Sonia Sanchez. BPo

And I always plaints that pass thorough my throat. (LL) Like to these unme[a]surable mountains [*or* mountayns]. Jacopo Sannazaro, *Italian.* AAS; PoE, *tr. by* Sir Thomas Wyatt

And I am an unhappy stranger. Mexican Loneliness. Jack Kerouac. CLPP

And I am in the wilderness alone. (LL) The Prairies. William Cullen Bryant. APN-1; AmPP; ColAP; NAAL-1; NAAL-3; NCAP; NOBA; OxBA; PAR; PaTW; PoEL-4; TAP

And I am lost in the beautiful white ruins / of America. (LL) Having Lost My Sons, I Confront the Wreckage of the Moon: Christmas, 1960. James Wright. CoAP; HCAP; NAAL-2

And I am Marie of Roumania. (LL) Comment. Dorothy Parker. NBLV; NIP-4; OBAL; OBCoV

And I Am Old to Know. Pauline Hanson. TAP

And I am wild[e] and wanton like to him. (LL) The Vision. Robert Herrick. CaPo; NOSC

And I and I / must admit. Belly Song. Etheridge Knight. BkSV

And I and silence some strange race, / Wrecked, solitary, here. Emily Dickinson. *See* I felt a Funeral in my Brain.

And I became alone. (LL) Wind—tapped like a tired man, The. Emily Dickinson. FaBoVe; MoAmPo; TOF

And I became alone. (LL) The Wind's Visit. Emily Dickinson. APN-2; MeMAP

And I betray the loch for a white coin. (LL) Trout Fisher. George Mackay Brown. FaBoTC

And I [*or* ich] bowed[e] my body and beheld all about [*or* bihelde al aboute]. A Vision of Nature. William Langland. CTC; PoEL-1 *Fr.* The Vision of Piers Plowman.

And I—can I go on like this much longer? (LL) Song: "I watered my horse at the Long Wall caves." Susan Ch'en Lin, *Chinese.* CoBCP, *tr. by* Burton Watson

And I can speak a little then. (LL) The Hushing of the Wye. Tennyson. EBVV; EBVVPR; EnVR; GTBS-P

And I can write no more. (LL) Stanzas on the Death of Mrs Hemans. Letitia Elizabeth Landon. FP; VWP

And I can't sleep for thinking on't. (LL) We're A'[ll] Dry wi' the Drinkin' O't. *Unknown.* NOBL; OxNR

And I captive am again. (LL) Sonnet 45. Mary Sidney, Countess of Montgomery Wroth. LW; PEW

And I choose—just a Crown. (LL) I'm ceded—I've stopped being Theirs. Emily Dickinson. APN-2; NALW; PAR; TRP; WPOW; WPoS

And I content me with my hire. (LL) The Lover Rejoiceth the Enjoying of His Love. Sir Thomas Wyatt. AAS; BoLoP; SiPS

And i could do for many days / Without eggs. (LL) Egg Thoughts. Russell Hoban. NTCP; OTCP

And I could fashion it no more! (LL) Sculpture. *Unknown.* PoLF; PoToHe

And I don't care a dam. Innes Randolph. *See* The Rebel.

And I don't feel so well myself. (LL) On the Vanity of Earthly Greatness. Arthur Guiterman. APAD; BXAP; HeIP-4; HoPM; OBCA; TrJP

And I don't want no Bail. (LL) Girl Held without Bail. Margaret Abigail Walker. BPo; PoBA

And I dream / of embroidering / new skin. (LL) Dreams in Harrison Railroad Park. Nellie Wong. OpBo

And I eat men like air. (LL) Lady Lazarus. Sylvia Plath. ChIV-2; CoAmPo; FaBoWP; HCAP; MoP; NAAL-2; NALW; NIP-4; NOBA; NoAM; NoP-4; OxWW; PoPoPo; Poetr; SAGP; TAP; TRP; VCAP; VGW

"And I fare you well, Lady Ouncebell." Lord Lovel. *Unknown.* ESPB

And I fell in love with a woman so tall that. From the Travels of Gulliver. Suniti Namjoshi. GLP

And i guess nobody ever does. (LL) Legacies. Nikki Giovanni. CrSp; NMM-2

And I hadn't been. (LL) Come In. Robert Frost. AmPP; LiTM; MoAmPo; NOBA; NoP-4; PFE; RaBo; TRP

And I half bent to throw me down withall. (LL) When Windsor Walls. Henry Howard, Earl of Surrey. AAS; CABP; SiPS; Son

And I hated myself. (LL) I, the Survivor. Bertolt Brecht, *German.* PoSu, *tr. by* John Willett; HP, *tr. by* Willet, John

And I have broken down before the wind. (LL) Nocturne of the Wharves. Arna Bontemps. BPo; ColAP; GT

And I have chosen the sea as no man's land. Edouard J. Maunick. NegPo, *tr. by* Ellen Conroy Kennedy *Fr.* As Far as Yoruba Land.

And I have come upon this place. L'An Trentiesme de Mon Eage. Archibald MacLeish. LiTM; MoAmPo; MoP; NOBA

And I have learned how diving's done. Fantasia. Dorothy Livesay. MoCV

And I have loved thee, Ocean! and my joy. Byron. OxBoS *Fr.* The Ocean. PoEL-4 *Fr.* Childe Harold's Pilgrimage.

And I have no children / to float in the space between. Etheridge Knight. *See* The Idea of Ancestry.

And I have tried to keep them from falling. (LL) Canto 13. Ezra Pound. CMoP; FaBoMo; PoE

And I hear the pad of feet to the union hall. Thomas McGrath. *Fr.* Letter to an Imaginary Friend, Part One. NNaP

And I hear the pad of feet to the union hall. Thomas McGrath. *Fr.* Letter to an Imaginary Friend, Part Two. NNaP

And I, I was a good child on the whole. Elizabeth Barrett Browning. BrRo *Fr.* Aurora Leigh. VWP

And I in my bed again! (LL) The Lover in Winter Plaineth for the Spring. *Unknown.* BoLoP; CTC; ClHu; EBEV; EnLoPo; FaBoCh; FaBoVe; GBL; HAP; HeIP-4; InPK-6; KaS; NAEL-1; NIP-4; NOBE; NoP-4; NoSic; OAEL-1; OBEV; OPOU; OxBSP; PFE; PiM; PoE; PoEL-1; PoPoPo; Poetr; SCGP; SoSe-8; TFi; UnPo; WeW-3

And I know the amplitude of time. (LL) Who goes there! hankering, gross, mystical, nude? Walt Whitman. ColAP

And I know where sleeps Holofernes. (LL) Judith. Adah Isaacs Menken. APN-2; CBWP-1; PAR

And I lean toward mine. (LL) Beginning. James Wright. ColAP; SAGP; VCAP

And I let the fish go. (LL) The Fish. Elizabeth Bishop. ChAP; FaBoWP; HAP; HeIP-4; HoPM; InPK-6; LiTM; MoAmPo; MoP; NAAL-2; NALW; NOBA; NTP; NoAM; NoP-4; PoE; PoPoPo; Poetr; RB; TFi; TRP

And I lie listening awake? (LL) Fragment 36: "I know not what to do." Hilda Doolittle. CMoP; CPO; NALW; OxBA; VGW

And I lie silent—but my body shakes. (LL) The Black Panther. John Hall Wheelock. LiTM; PFE

And I Lounged and Lay on Their Beds. Constantine P. Cavafy, *Greek.* PFTM, *tr. by* Edmund Keeley *and* George Savidis

And I love my Daddy like he loves his Dollar. (LL) American Primitive. William Jay Smith. InPK-6; MoAmPo; OxBSP; RaBo; TwCP

And I love the rain. (LL) April Rain Song. Langston Hughes. AYFP; ImGa; NOxBChV; NTCP; OBCA

And I made myself a surrogate wedding-day. The Sisters. Nicki Jackowska. BrRo

And I may be, some time. (LL) Snake. Theodore Roethke. NOBA; NYBP

And I more pleasure in your praise. (LL) To E. Fitzgerald. Tennyson. FP; NOBVV; PoEL-5

And I nae mair maun toddle about the tree. (LL) Alison [*or* Allison] Gross. *Unknown.* CH; ESPB; FaBoCh; OxBB

And I, O Fear, will dwell with thee! (LL) Ode to Fear. William Collins. NOEC; SCGP

And I remain despairing of the port. (LL) The Galley. Petrarch. AAS; HAP; OAEL-1; OBVE; SCGP; SiPS; Son; WeW-3, *tr. by* Sir Thomas Wyatt

And I remember Spain. Louis MacNeice. OBWP; OxAEP-2 *Fr.* Autumn Journal.

And I remembered the cry of the peacocks. (LL) Domination of Black ("At night, by the fire"). Wallace Stevens. AmPP; MoAmPo; OxBA

And I replied, *My Lord.* (LL) The Collar. George Herbert. AWP; CABP; ClHu; EBEV; FMP; FaBoVe; GeHe; HAP; HeIP-4; ImPo; InPS-3; McLP; NAEL-2; NIP-4; NOBF; NOCV; NOSC; NoP-4; OAEL-1; OBWVE; PoE; PoEL-2; PoPoPo; PoRA; SCGP; SCV; SeCP; TFi; TOF; WeW-3

And I rode the Greyhound down to Brooklyn. Wild Strawberry. Maurice Kenny. HATNAP

And I sailing, sailing swiftly from the county of Mayo. (LL) The County of Mayo. Thomas Flavell, *Irish.* BIrV; IIP; OBEV, *tr. by* George Fox

And I say, "Cousin Harriet, here is the *Boston Evening Transcript.*" (LL) The *Boston Evening Transcript.* T. S. Eliot. InPK-6; PFE

And I set forth upon the southern road. (LL) The Southern Road. Dudley Randall. GM; PoBA

And I shall die an old Parisian. (LL) Four Sheets to the Wind and a One-Way Ticket to France. Conrad Kent Rivers. BPo; PoBA

And I shall love you when your own is grey. (LL) Sonnet For Helen. Pierre de Ronsard, *French.* FLP; LoP, *tr. by* Alistair Elliot

And I shall traverse old love's domain / Never again. (LL) At Castle Boterel. Thomas Hardy. EBEV; GTBS-P; NOBE; OBNC; OxAEP-2; PeVV; PoE; SCV

And I shout at Iva, whine at you. Easily. Marilyn Hacker. VCAP *Fr.* Taking Notice.

And I sped to succour thee. (LL) The Poet's Dream. Shelley. GTBS-P, *ll.* 737–749; EPCY; TOF, *ll.* 737–751

And I standing in the shade. Petition. Ronald Stuart Thomas. FaBoMo

And i' th' morning steal all to bed. (LL) Stand! Who goes there? John Lyly. NoSic; OBCoV

And I to my wife or mistress flee. (LL) The Poet's Shuffle. Calvin Forbes. GT; LTA

And I took myself for a walk in the woods that day. Family Outing—a Celebration. Nicki Jackowska. BrRo

And I took twopence home to my wife. Mother Goose. *See* I love sixpence, jolly [*or* pretty] little sixpence.

And I touch you again as you tick in the silence and settle in sleep. (LL) Buick. Karl Shapiro. CMoP; HoPM; Poetr

And I wake saved.—And yet it will not be! (LL) Any Wife to Any Husband. Robert Browning. OBNC; RACG

And I was born with you, wasn't I, Blues? The Blues Don't Change. Al Young. GT

And I was unaware. (LL) The Darkling Thrush. Thomas Hardy. APo; CABP; CMoP; ClHu; EBVV; HAP; Impo; InPS-3; LiTM; MoBrPo; MoP; NAEL-2; NIP-4; NOBE; NOBVV; NoAM; NoP-4; OAEL-2; OBEV; OBNC; PFE; PoE; PoPoPo; Poetr; RB; SoSe-8; TFi; TOF; UnPo

And I went up to that chandeliered place. Poem. Calvin C. Hernton. GT

And I were king of pain. (LL) A Match. Swinburne. CBLP; NOBVV

And I will come out to meet you. Li Po. *See* River Merchant's Wife, The; a Letter.

And I will [*or* shall] dwell in the house of the Lord for ever [*or* forever]. (LL) Psalm 23. Bible, *O.T.* AH; AWP; ChIV-1; FaBoBe; NAWM-1; NIP-4; OBVE; PoLF; TFi; TRP; TrJP

And I will wait on thy name: for it is good before thy saints. (LL) Psalm 52. Bible, *O.T.* NoSic; OBVE

And I wish I did not / feel like your mother. Edna St. Vincent Millay. *See* Rendezvous.

And I with thee will choose to live. (LL) Il Penseroso. Milton. AWP; FHYEP; GTBS-P; HAP; HoPM; ImPo; NOSC; NoP-4; OAEL-1; OBEV; TFi

And I, woman, cloaked in blues. I, Woman. Irma McClaurin. BlSi

And ice below, and above—I toil somewhere in between. Vladimir Semionovich Vysotsky, *Russian.* TCRP, *tr. by* Albert C. Todd

And if a juggler arrives in town. When Tomorrow Is Too Long. Tanure Ojaide. HBAPE

And if an eye may save or slay. Sir Thomas Wyatt. SiPS

And if any man should ask me. Deliverance. Frances Ellen Watkins Harper. WPOW

And if at 80. George Oppen. APSN *Fr.* Route.

And if he ever should come back. The Last Words. Maurice Maeterlinck, *French.* AWP, *tr. by* Frederick York Powell

And If He Had Been Wrong for Me. Robert Duncan. RaBo

An if he will come to me. (LL) Song: "Under the greenwood tree." Shakespeare. AWP; BoTP; CH; CTC; EBEvV; FaBoBe; GTBS-P; HoPM; ImPo; InPS-3; NAEL-1; NoSic; OAEL-1; OBEV; SCGP; TTTS; UnPo

And if I did what then? A Farewell. George Gascoigne. CBLP; EBEV; GBL; HAP; NOBE; NoP-4; PoEL-1; SCGP *Fr.* The Adventures of Master F. I.

And if I dye, who will saye: *This was Immerito?*. (LL) Iambicum Trimetrum. Edmund Spenser. BoLoP; EBEV; OBEV; OxBoLi; PoEL-1

And if I loved you Wednesday. Thursday. Edna St. Vincent Millay. PoA

And if it snowed and snow covered the drive. Poem. Simon Armitage. APAD

And if men ask you why you fled, and what. Refugees. Donald Davidson. FuPo

And, if not shot or hang'd, you'll get knighted. (LL) Stanzas: "When a man hath no freedom to fight for at home." Byron. FaBoEE; NAEL-2; NBLV; OxAEP-2; PoLF; Poetr; TRP

And If the Angel Should Ask. Hayyim Nahman Bialik, *Hebrew.* MHP, *tr. by* Ruth Finer Mintz

And if the dead, and the dead. The Conspirators. Frederic Prokosch. LiTM

And if the soul. George Seferis. GrIP *Fr.* Mythistorima.

And if the wine leaves him witless. Alcaeus, *Greek.* InMo, *tr. by* Sam Hamill

And if tonight my soul may find her peace. Shadows. D. H. Lawrence. LBC; OxBTC

And if ye stand in doubt. John Skelton. NAEL-1; OAEL-1 *Fr.* Colin Clout.

And if you cannot make your life as you want it. Constantine P. Cavafy. *See* As Much As You Can.

And if you sleep, and if the sheets are clean. Aleksandr Semionovich Kushner, *Russian.* TCRP, *tr. by* Paul Graves *and* Carol Ueland

And I'll be true to my love if my love'll be true to me. (LL) The Two Sisters. *Unknown.* AmFP; OxBB

And I'll be with you by-and-by. Mother Goose. *See* Old Woman, Old Woman.

And I'll forgive Thy great big one on me. (LL) Forgive, O Lord, my little jokes on Thee. Robert Frost. LiTM; Poetr; SAmP

And I'm here, sizing the dark, saving my mother's seat. (LL) Sitting at Night on the Front Porch. Charles Wright. ColAP

And I'm your servant, J.M. Synge. (LL) The Curse. John Millington Synge. FaBoEE; NOIV; OBCoV

And imagined her. She Had Known Brothers. Sherley Anne Williams. GT

And, in Africa, a carcass quick with flies. (LL) Black Tambourine. Hart Crane. InPK-6; InPS-3; MeMAP; NoAM; OxBA; OxBSP; TAP

And in August the barley grew up out of the grave. (LL) Requiem for the Croppies. Seamus Heaney. BlrV; CIP-2; FaBoMo; OBWP

And in blue skies the Orb is manifest to Sight. (LL) Epi-Strauss-ium. Arthur Hugh Clough. EnVR; NAEL-2

And in conclusion I'll say. Goodbye. Bella Akhatovna Akhmadulina, *Russian.* BoWoP, *tr. by* Barbara Einzig

And in God's house are many scansions. (LL) Poetry. Mary Elizabeth Fullerton. GI; NOBAu

And in God's house forever more / My dwelling-place shall be. Bible, *O.T.* *See* Psalm 23.

And in immense perdition sinks the soul. (LL) To the University of Cambridge, in New-England. Phillis Wheatley. AmPP; NAAAL; NAAL-1; NAAL-3; TAP

And in its ashes plant the tree of peace! (LL) Worship. John Greenleaf Whittier. ChIV-2; NOCV

And in our faults by lies we flatter'd be. (LL) Sonnet 138. Shakespeare. AWP; EBEV; HeIP-4; NAEL-1; NoSic; OAEL-1; OxAEP-1; PoEL-2; Poetr; SoSe-8

And in praying do not heap up empty phrases as the Gentiles do. Matthew 6:7–15; "And in praying do not heap up empty." D. H. Lawrence. GI *Fr.* St. Matthew.

And in retirement, I can bless the shade. (LL) On Myself. Anne Finch, Countess of Winchilsea. NoP-4; OxBSP

And in September, O what keen delight! Sonnets of the Months: September. Folgore da San Gemignano, *Italian.* AWP, *tr. by* D. G. Rossetti

And in short measures life may perfect be. (LL) The Noble Nature. Ben Jonson. GTBS-P; ImPo; OBEV

And in spite of it all I must. Yehuda Amichai. *Fr.* Songs of the Land of Zion Jerusalem. IP, *tr. by* Warren Bargod *and* Stanley F. Chyet

And in that land dwells a king. Sir Cawline. *Unknown.* ESPB

And in that region there were shepherds out in the field. Luke 2:8–20; And in that region there were shepherds. Bertolt Brecht. GI *Fr.* St. Luke.

And in the deep valleys of the hand. (LL) Taking the hands of someone you love. Robert Bly. IFJA; TRP

And in the ear[e], not conscience ring. (LL) The Windows. George Herbert. ESCV; FMP; GeHe; MeLP; NAEL-1; NOCV; NoP-4; PFE; PeECV; PoE; SeCP; TrCP

And in the end go back to Master Pan's hut. (LL) On Being Assigned as Military Adviser to the Garrison Army. T'ao Ch'ien, *Chinese.* CoBCP, *tr. by* Burton Watson

And in the evening there was light. (LL) What the Birds Said. John Greenleaf Whittier. APN-1; NOBA; PAR

And in the 51st Year of That Century, While My Brother Cried in the Trench, While My Enemy Glared from the Cave. Hyam Plutzik. RB

And in the garden, cries and colors. (LL) Last Month. John Ashbery. CAPP-1; CoAP

And in the hanging gardens there is rain. Conrad Potter Aiken. MoAmPo

And in the herte, there is the hevede–and the heigh welle. (LL) The Incarnation. William Langland. OBEV; PoEL-1

And in the Human Heart. Conrad Potter Aiken. Son

Bend as the Bow Bends. CMoP

Green, Green, and Green Again.

And in the Item loved the Whole. (LL) Herman Melville. Conrad Potter Aiken. NoAM; TAP

And in the light of truth thy Bondman let me live! (LL) Ode to Duty. Wordsworth. AWP; FHYEP; GTBS-P; ImPo; NAEL-2; NOBRP; OAEL-2; OBEV

And in the Lord's house I shall dwell so long as days shall be, *fr.* Bay Psalm Book. Bible, *O.T.* *See* Psalm 23.

And in the midst of all, a fountain stood. Edmund Spenser. CH *Fr.* The Bower of Bliss. PoEL-1 *Fr.* Wood Of Error. AEP

And in the morning the king loved you most. Arcanum One. Gwendolyn MacEwen. MoCV

And in the river the nameless body sifts. Solitaire. Conrad Potter Aiken. ColAP

And in the suburbs Can't sat down and cried. (LL) Kilroy. Peter Viereck. MoAmPo; PoRA

And in their holiness made power. Winkte. Maurice Kenny. GLP

And in this carnival you offer me. Arnold H. Itwaru. HCP

And in this faith I choose to live and die. (LL) His Mother's Service to Our Lady. François Villon, *French.* AWP; CTC, tr. by D. G. Rossetti

And in this swyving there nas noon hir pere. The Continuation of *The Cook's Tale.* William Zaranka. BXAP

And in your fragrant bosom[e] dies [*or* dyes]. (LL) Song, [A]: "Ask me no more where Jove bestows." Thomas Carew. AWP; BeJo; CBLP; CH; CaPo; CavPo; ClHu; EnLoPo; GBL; GLoP; HAP; HoPM; ImPo; InPS-3; LoP; MeLP; NAEL-1; NOBE; NOSC; NoP-4; OBEV; PoE; PoEL-3; PoRA; SCGP; SeCP; TFi

And indeed I shall anchor, one day—some summer morning. Landfall. Randolph Stow. BMAP

And inflict / pain. (LL) Adulthood. Nikki Giovanni. NMM-2

And into his dead mouth slip the set of teeth. (LL) The Linen Workers. Michael Longley. BiHa; CIP-2

And is almost afraid that I / will commit that indiscretion. (LL) The Garden. Ezra Pound. AWP; HeIP-4; MoAmPo; NIP-4; OxBSP; TwCP

And Is It Night? Are they thine eyes that shine? *Unknown.* CBLP; GBL

And is it true that I must go from Troy? Shakespeare. OxAEP-1 *Fr.* Troilus and Cressida.

And is not ours a noble creed. Sinn Fein: Ourselves Alone. Isobel Marchbank. NSI

And is our life, a life wherein we borrow. Matthew X. 28. Roger Wolcott. SCAP

And is the best known, not defining Him. (LL) What God Is. Robert Herrick. BeJo; NOSC

And is the water come? Sure' cannot be. Upon Sir John Lawrence's Bringing Water over the Hills [to My L. Middlesex His House at Witten]. Sir John Suckling. CaPo

And is there care in heauen [*or* heaven]? and is there loue [*or* love]. Guardian Angels. Edmund Spenser. NOCV; NoSic; OAEL-1 *Fr.* Wood Of Error. AEP

And is there glory from the heavens departed? The Lost Pleiad. Felicia Dorothea Hemans. NOBRP

And is there honey still for tea? (LL) The Old Vicarage, Grantchester. Rupert Brooke. EBEvV; MoBrPo; NoP-4; OxBTC; PoRA

And is there sadness in *thy* dreams, my boy? The Dreaming Child. Felicia Dorothea Hemans. NOBRP

And is there then no earthly place. Thomas Moore. OBSV *Fr.* Rhymes on the Road.

And is thine everlasting Store. (LL) A Dialogue Between The Resolved Soul and Created Pleasure. Andrew Marvell. ESCV; FSCP; GeHe; MeLP; OAEL-1; SeCP

And is this—Yarrow?—This the Stream. Yarrow Visited [September, 1814]. Wordsworth. GTBS-P

And is thy glass run out? Is that oil spent. Upon the Poet of His Time, Ben Jonson: His Honoured Friend and Father. James Howell. NOSC

And Isaac brought her / to his mother's tent. Arthur Hugh Clough. *See* Genesis XXIV.

And Isabel calmly cured the doctor. (LL) Adventures of Isabel. Ogden Nash. ChAP; MoAmPo; NOxBChV; NTCP; OBAL; OBCA

And Ishmael crouch'd beside a crackling briar. Ishmael. Herbert Edward Palmer. OBEV

And it all died down. From My Lai the Thunder Went West. Richard Ryan. CIP-2

And it came to pass, after the year was expired. Bible, *O.T.* OxBoV *Fr.* 2 Samuel.

And It Came to Pass at Midnight. Yannai, *Hebrew.* TrJP

And it came to pass in those days, that there went out a decree from Caesar Augustus. Bible, *N.T.* NAWM-1 *Fr.* St. Luke.

And it came to pass just as they had foretold. Adam Cornford. CLPP *Fr.* The Rapture.

And it doesn't hurt / so much / anymore. (LL) Solea. Jessica Hagedorn. MoNo; WWSi

And it ends at half past five. (LL) Office Friendships. Gavin Ewart. FP; PeLV

And it is hard to tell one. To a Friend Who Wouldn't Bother to Strain His Noodleboard Because Even So It Is Hard to Go Hunting When Your Rifle Is Blunt and Love Is Soft as an Old Blanket. Jacob Glatshteyn, *Yiddish.* PFTM, tr. by Benjamin Harshav *and* Barbara Harshav

And it is in dying that we are born to eternal life. (LL) Prayer of St. Francis of Assisi for Peace. Saint Francis of Assisi, *Latin.* PoLF; PoToHe

And it is not much. (LL) Annihilation. Conrad Potter Aiken. GBL; GEA; MoAmPo

And it seemed, while we waited, he began to walk towards us. Geoffrey Hill. NoAM; NoP-4 *Fr.* Mercian Hymns.

And it shall come to pass in that day, that the Lord shall set his hand again the second time to recover the remnant of his people, which shall be left, from Assyria, and from Egypt, and from Path'ros, and from Cush, and from E'lam, and from Shi'nar, and from Ha'math, and from the islands of the sea. (LL) The Rod of Jesse. Bible, *O.T.* AWP; OBVE; TrJP

And it shall come to pass in the end of days. In the End of Days. Bible, *O.T.* TrJP *Fr.* Isaiah.

And it shall come to pass when the days shall grow long. When the Days Shall Grow Long. Hayyim Nahman Bialik, *Hebrew.* TrJP, tr. by A. M. Klein

And it was at that age. . . Poetry arrived. Poetry. Pablo Neruda, *Spanish.* VCWP, tr. by Alastair Reid

And it was still the fifth / of February, 1918. Elizabeth Bishop. *See* In the Waiting Room.

And it's easy to pretend you're screwing her brother. (LL) Epigram: "Hetero-sex is best for the man of a serious turn of mind." Argentarius, *Greek.* OBCVT

And it's forty miles to Nicut Hill. Prince Robert. *Unknown.* AmFP

And it's hard to see the mountains. Can I Say. Dolly Bird. WPOW

And its hero the Conqueror Worm. (LL) The Conqueror Worm. Edgar Allan Poe. APN-1; AWP; ImPo; MeMAP; NCAP; NOBA

And Jack from Joan, and they shall never marry. (LL) Another Song. Donald Justice. CoAmPo; NYBP; VGW

And jest upon their blind forefathers' eyes. (LL) Ignotum per Ignotius, or a Furious Hodge-Podge of Nonsense; a Pindaric. *Unknown.* CBNP; NOEC

And Jesus said to him, "Foxes have holes." Matthew 8:20; And Jesus said to him. Karl Kirchwey. GI *Fr.* St. Matthew.

And Joseph was brought down to Egypt. Bible, *O.T.* NAWM-1 *Fr.* Genesis.

And joy the poet's eye. (LL) The Grave of a Poetess. Felicia Dorothea Hemans. Ro; VWP

And Jude, now you're married, will stretch on the floor. (LL) On an Island. John Millington Synge. BIrV; FaBoVe; MoBrPo; OxBSP; PeVV

And *Juno* lay unheeded by his Side. (LL) Thetis Asks Jove to Revenge Her Son Achilles. Homer, *Greek.* OBCVT; OBVE, tr. by John Dryden

And just by crossing the short sea. Channel Crossing. George Barker. GTBS-P

And just what the fuck else were we supposed to do. (LL) Rape. Jayne Cortez. GT; NMM-2; PmAP

And keep them all like gentlemen! (LL) The Dove and the Wren. Mother Goose. BoTP; CTAV; OxNR; ReMoGo

And keep us from the sin of gluttony. (LL) Monk of Casal-Maggiore, The (The Sicilian's Tale). Henry Wadsworth Longfellow. AmPP; OxBA

And kep't my spirit with the free. (LL) A Vision. John Clare. EBVV; GTBS-P; NAEL-1; NOBVV; NTP; OAEL-2; OBNC; PoE; Ro

And kept the Moon reflected there. (LL) The Witches' Wood. Mary Elizabeth Coleridge. VWP

And killed the mice in his father's barn. (LL) Ding, dong, bell, / Pussy's in the well. Mother Goose. OxNR; ReMoGo

And kindle with thy own productive fire. (LL) Address to Venus. Lucretius, *Latin.* OBVE, tr. by Dryden

And kiss him into slumbers like a bride. (LL) Sleep Song. John Fletcher. NOSC; OxBSP; OxBoLi; PoEL-2; PoRA; SCGP

And kissed my sister instead of me. (LL) Trip upon trenchers, and dance upon dishes. Mother Goose. NOBL; OxNR; ReMoGo

And knit again the knot that should not slide. (LL) Face that should content me wonders [*or* wondrous] well, A. Sir Thomas Wyatt. CTC; EnLoPo

And knock them all down like so many weeds. (LL) Returning to My Home in the Country ("Out here in the fields, few social affairs"). T'ao Ch'ien, *Chinese.* CoBCP, tr. by Burton Watson

And knocked it right off his head, head, head. Mother Goose. *See* Sam, The Sportsman.

And know that I'll be hard put to discover a single blossom. Li Ch'ing-chao. *See* Tune: "Pure Serene Music."

And knows herself in death. (LL) The Great Breath. "Æ." MoBrPo; OBEV; OBMV

And knows no bound, but makes his power his / shores. (LL) Cooper's Hill. Sir John Denham. CABP; PBRV

And knows not whether he be first or last. (LL) Time, Real and Imaginary. Coleridge. NOBE; OBEV; OxBSP; PBMP

And laid my land upon thy mane,—as I do here. (LL) The Ocean. Byron. OBNC; PoEL-4

And land beside a bracelet's fire. (LL) Another Fan. Stéphane Mallarmé, *French.* FLP; LoP, tr. by Alistair Elliot

And landing upon their heads. (LL) Between Ourselves. Audre Lorde. ISC

And landscape, into which the traveler might set out. (LL) The Parachutist. Jon Anderson. AmPA; NYBP

And lapsing waves on quiet shores. John Greenleaf Whittier. *See* Snow-Bound [*or* Snow-Bound; a Winter Idyl].

And last night a man came in. Spring Street Bar. Mei-Mei Berssenbrugge. WPOW

And last, when Words are into Clouds devolv'd. (LL) Love's Witness. Aphra Behn. LW

And lat me tellen al my tale, I preye. (LL) The Tale of Sir Thopas. Chaucer. BXAP, *ll.* 1–248; NAEL-1, *ll.* 1–252

And Later by Myself. Ory Bernstein, *Hebrew.* IP, *tr. by* Warren Bargad *and* Stanley F. Chyet. LW

And, laterally / to Adam's pulsing eye. The Cloud. Derek Walcott. ChIV-1

And laugh—but smile no more. (LL) The Haunted Palace. Edgar Allan Poe. APN-1; CH; MeMAP; NAAL-3; NOBA; OxBA; PoEL-4; TAP; TFi

And laugh—No more have I. (LL) They shut me up in Prose. Emily Dickinson. APN-2; FaBoVe; InPS-3; NALW; NCAP; NOBA; NoP-4; PAR

And lead us not into temptation, but deliver us from evil: For thine is the kingdom, and the power, and the glory, for ever. Amen. (LL) Prayer of-Lord. Bible, *N.T.* PeSAV; PoLF

And leaf-shadow are lost. (LL) Evening. Hilda Doolittle. CMoP; FaBoMo; VGW; WPE

And leans on the air that is hers and here. (LL) Hourglass. Josephine Jacobsen. BAP-93; NoP-4

And leaps from dreams to hail the coming day. (LL) The South. Emma Lazarus. APN-2; ColAP

And learn O voyager to walk. Seafarer. Archibald MacLeish. Poetr

And learn, with joy, the gulf, the vast, the deep. (LL) Putting to Sea. Louise Bogan. LiTM; PoA

And leave dull verse to the dull peaceful time. (LL) The Soldier Addresses his Body. Edgell Rickword. PeFWW; PoWW

And leave her dreaming in the silent land. (LL) The Old House. Amy Levy. PEW; VWP

And leave him then, being made a ready horse? (LL) Elegie: "Nature's lay ideot, I taught thee to love." Donne. CBLP; FMP; NoP-4; OxAEP-1; PeLV; SeCP

And leave our desert to its peace! (LL) Stanzas from the Grande Chartreuse. Matthew Arnold. EBVV; EnVR; NAEL-2; OAEL-2; PoE; PoEL-5

And leave th' earth to their food. (LL) The H[oly] Communion. George Herbert. ChIV-1; ESCV

And leave the house. (LL) Childhood Is the Kingdom Where Nobody Dies. Edna St. Vincent Millay. FaBoWP; NALW

And leave the old and ugly for others. (LL) Sonnet: Of All He Would Do. Cecco Angiolieri, da Siena, *Italian.* ItIP

And leave to thee thy true integrity. (LL) To Dante [*or* Sonnet: Guido Cavalcanti to Dante]. Guido Cavalcanti, *Italian.* AWP; OBVE, *tr. by* Shelley

And leave you with them empty bed blues. (LL) Empty Bed Blues. Bessie Smith. OBAL; UnPo

And leaves his hold and cackles, groans, and dies. (LL) Badger ("When midnight comes a host of dogs and men"). John Clare. FHYEP; GEA; HAP; OAEL-2; PoEL-4; Poetr; SCGP

And leaves thrust violently upon the pane. (LL) Autumn Chapter in a Novel. Thom Gunn. FaBoMo; OxBTC

And led the flock away. (LL) I'll tell you how the Sun rose. Emily Dickinson. APN-2; AmPP; PoEL-5; TAP

And left it to us! (LL) Ancient History. Arthur Guiterman. KaS

And left me old, and cold, and grey. (LL) May. Christina Rossetti. GBL; GLoP; NOBVV

And left the thorn wi' me. Robert Burns. *See* The Banks o'Doon: "Ye flowery banks o' bonie Doon."

And left the vivid air signed with their honour. (LL) I think continually of those who were truly great. Stephen Spender. CABP; CMoP; EBEvV; HAP; HeIP-4; ImPo; LiTM; MoBrPo; NOBE; NoP-4; OAEL-2; OxBTC; PoRA; RaBo; TFi

And left with a debt to another white man. (LL) St. Peter Claver. Toi Derricotte. LTA; PBCAP

And let five o'clock come / if we're to go on living. (LL) Four in the Morning. Wislawa Szymborska, *Polish.* BLT, *tr. by* Magnus J. Krynski *and* Robert A. Maguire

And let him hate you through the glass. Edmund Blunden. *See* The Midnight Skaters.

And let me die before my death!. (LL) Regeneration. Henry Vaughan. ChIV-1; ESCV; FMP; GeHe; MeLP; NAEL-1; NoP-4; PoE

And let the ape and tiger die. (LL) Contemplate all this work of Time. Tennyson. EBVV; EnVR; OAEL-2

And let the woman live. (LL) Women's Locker Room. Marilyn Nelson Waniek. LTA

And let thy patriarchs' [*or* Patriarches] desire. The Patriarchs. Donne. *Fr.* The Litanie. PoEL-2

And let us have a lark instead. (LL) To Minerva. Thomas Hood. NBLV; NOBL; OxBoLi; PeLV

And let you go. (LL) To a Squirrel at Kyle-Na-No. W. B. Yeats. APo; CTAV; ChAP

And let your full lips laugh at Fate! (LL) To a Dark Girl. Gwendolyn B. Bennett. BlSi; ColAP; NAAAL; PoBA; SAGP

And letting them out again. (LL) The Vacant Lot. Gwendolyn Brooks. NAAAL; NAAL-2; NOBA; NoAM

And liars in public places. Ezra Pound. *See* These fought in any case.

And Libye land likewise wyth warlick victorye conquoure. (LL) Now manhood and garbroyls I chaunt, and martial horror, *see also* "Arms, and the Man I sing, who, forc'd by Fate" *tr. by* John Dryden, "I sing of warfare and a man at war" *tr. by* Robert Fitgerald, "Arms, and the Man I sing, the first who bore" *tr. by* William Wordsworth, *and* "Battellis and the man I will descrive, The" *tr. by* Gavin Douglas. Virgil. BIrV; OBVE, *tr. by* Richard Stanyhurst

And lie thou there. Matthew Arnold. EnVR *Fr.* Empedocles on Etna.

And lie with your bride all night. (LL) Harry Parry. *Unknown.* OxNR

And lies down, who was my moon or more. (LL) Complaint. James Wright. NOBA; TAP; VGW

And life be nothing, it shall not stop kissing. (LL) Thy fingers make early flowers of. E. E. Cummings. MoAmPo; NAAL-2

And life for me ain't been no crystal stair. (LL) Mother to Son. Langston Hughes. ChAP; FiLi; ISC; NAAAL; NAAL-2; NTCP; OBCA; SAmP; TTY

And life, some think, is worthy of the Muse. (LL) You like not that French novel? Tell me why. George Meredith. EnVR; NOBVV

And lifts them back in with warm spoons. (LL) Lady Lowbodice. *Unknown.* PeLV; PeLi

And lightly, like the flowers. Pierre de Ronsard, *French.* AWP, *tr. by* W. E. Henley

And, like a bird at rest. National Anthem. Egbert Martin. PBCV

And like a dying lady, lean and pale. The Waning Moon. Shelley. CH; FHYEP; FaBoCh; OBEV; OxBSP; SAGP

And like a finer light in light. (LL) When rosy plumelets tuft the larch. Tennyson. FHYEP; OBNC

And, like a flock of wild geese, sweeps its flowing tail. (LL) The Kite. Adelaide O'Keeffe. NOxBChV

And like a thunderbolt he falls. (LL) The Eagle. Tennyson. APAD; APo; BoTP; CH; CTAV; CTV; ChAP; ClHu; FHYEP; FPC; FaBoCh; GTBS-P; HeIP-4; InPK-6; NAEL-2; NOBVV; NTCP; NTP; NoP-4; OAEL-2; OxBSP; PFE; Poetr; SAGP; SCGP; TFi; TRP; UnPo

And like thy father sing in tunefulness. A Barren Soul. Joseph Ezobi. TrJP, *tr. by* D. I. Friedmann *Fr.* The Silver Bowl.

And, like thy shadow, follow thee. (LL) Compensation ("The Wings of Time are black and white"). Ralph Waldo Emerson. APN-1; AmPP; NOBA; PAR

And listened longer than I did. (LL) A Green Cornfield. Christina Rossetti. ACTP; BoTP

And little Ariadne sleep. (LL) Birthright. John Drinkwater. CH; OxBTC

And little hunted hares. (LL) The Bells of Heaven. Ralph Hodgson. BoTP; LiTM; MoBrPo; NOBE; OBEV; OxBSP

And live forever, like the dust. (LL) Poem in Three Parts. Robert Bly. CoAmPo; NOBA

And live I still to see relations gone? To the Memory of My Dear Daughter in Law, Mrs. Mercy Bradstreet. Anne Bradstreet. KTR

And live on corn dodgers the rest of my life. (LL) Starving to Death on a Government Claim. *Unknown.* AS; AmFP; OBAL

And lived with her. (LL) A Marriage. Robert Creeley. LiTM; NeAP; PoPoPo; RaBo

And lives to-day in Bread and Wine. (LL) Christmas. John Betjeman. OBCP; OxBTC

And lo! on the ground Rose Mary lay. D. G. Rossetti. Poetr *Fr.* Rose Mary.

And lonesome, very lonesome, is my strand. (LL) Autumn. Christina Rossetti. BrRo; VWP

And longed for returning. (LL) Home Coming. Lenrie Peters. HBAPE; PBMAP

—And looked and looked our infant sight away. (LL) Over 2000 Illustrations and a Complete Concordance. Elizabeth Bishop. HCAP; LCAP-2; NAAL-2; NoAM; VCAP

And Loplop, Bird-Superior, has transformed himself into flesh. The Hundred Headless Woman. Max Ernst. PFTM, *tr. by* Dorothea Tanning *Fr.* The Hundred Headless Woman.

And Lords whose parents were the Lord knows who. (LL) Wherever God erects a house of prayer. Daniel Defoe. NOBL; OBSV *Fr.* The True Born Englishman.

And Los and Enitharmon builded Jerusalem weeping. Vala, Night the Ninth Being the Last Judgment. William Blake. OAEL-2 *Fr.* Vala; or The Four Zoas.

And lose my everlasting rest. (LL) Song: "Absent from thee, I languish still." John Wilmot, 2d Earl of Rochester. BoLoP; EnLoPo; GBL; GLoP; NOBE; OBEV

And love, and man's unconquerable mind. (LL) To Toussaint L'Ouverture. Wordsworth. FaBoPV; InPK-6; NOBE; OBNC; PBMP; PoRA; Ro

And love arrived may find us somewhere else. (LL) Delay. Elizabeth Jennings. NIP-4; OPOU; OxBTC

And Love doth hold my hand, and makes me write. (LL) Sonnet 90: "Stella, think not that I by verse seek fame." Sir Philip Sidney. NoP-4; NoSic

And love goes too. . .but goes the last. (LL) O fond, but fickle and untrue. Walter Savage Landor. CBLP; GBL

And love her as hard as you can. (LL) The Way. Robert Creeley. APAD; BoLoP; LiLi; LiTM; NeAP

And love hung still as crystal over the bed. Louis MacNeice. CIP-2; GBL; MoBrPo Fr. Trilogy for X.

And love is where yesterday is at. (LL) That Day. Anne Sexton. BoWoP; CoAmPo; SAGP

And love like anger in the night. (LL) To My Wife. James Vincent Cunningham. SAGP; VCAP

And love the brightest eyes, but love in vain!' (LL) A Hymn Written in Windsor Forest. Alexander Pope. EBEV; NOEC; OxBSP

And love thy favorite name! William Collins. See Ode to Evening.

And love with old familiar love. (LL) The Convent Threshold. Christina Rossetti. NALW; NoP-4; VWP

And love you so much. (LL) Steps. Frank O'Hara. CoAmPo; PmAP

And loved to course with tempests through the night. (LL) Horses on the Camargue. Roy Campbell. GTBS-P; PeSA

And lovers float down from the cliffs like rain. (LL) Salvador Dali. David Gascoyne. FaBoMo; OxBTC; SPE

And Lowells speak only to God. (LL) Boston. John Collins Bossidy, also at. to Samuel C. Bushnell. FaBoEE; NBLV; OBAL; OBCoV; OxBoLi; PeLV

And lust is there, and nights not spent alone. (LL) I too beneath your moon, almighty Sex. Edna St. Vincent Millay. NAAL-2; NALW

And maddening--it's all by someone else! Mirabell's Books of Number. James Merrill. Fr. The Changing Light at Sandover. NAAL-2

And made much within her. (LL) Song of Fixed Accord. Wallace Stevens. InPS-3; SAmP

And made their dove-wings tremble. On he flared. (LL) The Fall of Hyperion. Keats. OAEL-2; Ro

And made ye white. (LL) How Lillies Came White. Robert Herrick. BeJo; CaPo

And Maelstrom in the Sky. (LL) Behind Me—dips Eternity. Emily Dickinson. APN-2; PBWP

And make a dust of their seraphic song. (LL) On Some Shells Found Inland. Trumbull Stickney. APN-2; Son

And make her a saint. (LL) Alcestis on the Poetry Circuit. Erica Jong. AmPA; NALW

And make one mighty Dunciad of the land! Alexander Pope. See Idle Pursuits.

And make the wild fern for a bed do? (LL) Dawlish Fair. Keats. NTP; PeLV

And make us blest at last. (LL) Mistress, The: A Song. John Wilmot, 2d Earl of Rochester. EBEV; NOBE; NOSC; OxAEP-1; PFE

And makes a constant sacrament of praise. (LL) Peter Quince at the Clavier. Wallace Stevens. AmPP; CMoP; HeIP-4; InPK-6; InPS-3; LiTM; MeMAP; NAWM-2; NOBA; NoAM; NoP-4; OxBA; PoE; SAmP; TAP; TFi; TwCP

And makes him bring back one leg. (LL) Riddle: "Two legs sat upon three legs." Mother Goose. LB; NTCP; OxNR

And makes me end[,] where I begun [or begunne]. (LL) Valediction, A: Forbidding Mourning. Donne. CBLP; ESCV; FHYEP; HAP; HeIP-4; HoPM; ImPo; InPS-3; MeLP; NAEL-1; NOBE; NOSC; OAEL-1; PoE; PoEL-2; Poetr; SCGP; SeCP; SoSe-8; TFi; UnPo; WeW-3

And makes the Happiness she does not find. (LL) The Vanity of Human Wishes [The Tenth Satire of Juvenal Imitated]. Samuel Johnson. CABP; EBEV; ECEV; NOEC; NoP-4; OAEL-1; OxAEP-1; PoEL-3; TFi

And making Death a Victory. (LL) Prometheus. Byron. InPS-3; NOBE; OAEL-2; OxAEP-2; Poetr; Ro

And mama complains. Muddy Kid Comes Home. Sandra Cisneros. FFC

And man became a living soul. / Amen. (LL) The Creation. James Weldon Johnson. ChIV-1; MoAmPo; NAAAL; PBMP; PoBA; PoRA; TrCP

And man's religion be complete. (LL) On the Religion of Nature. Philip Freneau. AmPP; NAAL-1; NAAL-3

And many are amazed and many doubt. (LL) Divina Commedia. Henry Wadsworth Longfellow. APN-1; OxBA; TAP

And many voices marshalled in one hymn. Hymn. Thomas Lovell Beddoes. NOBVV

And marching Time drew on, and wore me numb. Thomas Hardy. See A Broken Appointment.

And Marie Carmichael, and me. (LL) Mary Hamilton. Unknown. AmFP; ESPB; NoP-4; SCGP

And Marie said, My soule doth magnifie the Lord. Bible, N.T. See The Magnificat.

And mark it with his name forevermore? (LL) Sonnet: "Oh for a poet—for a beacon bright." Edwin Arlington Robinson. APN-2; NCAP; OxBA

And marries either's Dust. (LL) La Belle Confidente. Thomas Stanley. BeJo; MeLP

And me happiest when I compose poems. The Birth of Tragedy. Irving Layton. MoCV; NoAM; NoP-4

And Melancholy marked him for her own. Thomas Gray. See The Curfew tolls the knell of parting day.

And melt the icicles from off his chin. (LL) A Meditation on Rhode Island Coal. William Cullen Bryant. NCAP

And melt to pity the annalist's iron tongue. (LL) Scotland 1941. Edwin Muir. CABP; FaBoTC

And (Memmius) least you thinke I false grounds lay. The Dissolution of the world proovd from the mortality of every part. Lucretius, Latin. OBCVT, tr. by Lucy Hutchinson

And Memory, that over Time himself prevails! (LL) Moses in Infancy. Jones Very. ChIV-1; KSG

And men, coming and going on the earth. (LL) Clouds. Rupert Brooke. OBEV; OBMV; OxBTC

And mend my rhyme. (LL) Denial[l]. George Herbert. ESCV; FMP; GeHe; NAEL-1; NOBE; NoP-4; OAEL-1; PoEL-2; TOF

And 'midst the stars inscribe Belinda's name. (LL) The Rape of the Lock[, an Heroi-Comical Poem]. Alexander Pope. CABP; FHYEP; HAP; ImPo; NoP-4; OAEL-1; OBNV; OxAEP-1; PeLV; PoEL-3

And miles to go before I sleep. (LL) Stopping by Woods on a Snowy Evening. Robert Frost. AmPP; CMoP; ChAP; ClHu; ColAP; FaBoCh; HAP; HeIP-4; HoPM; ImGa; ImPo; InPK-6; InPS-3; LiTM; MeMAP; MoAmPo; MoP; NAAL-2; NIP-4; NOBA; NTCP; NTP; NoAM; NoP-4; OBCA; OxBA; PFE; PoE; PoPoPo; PoRA; Poetr; RB; SAGP; SAmP; SCV; SoSe-8; TAP; TFi; TOF; TRP; TTT3

And mingle all the world with thee. (LL) Dear friend, far off, my lost desire. Tennyson. EBVVPR; FHYEP; OAEL-2

And mirth was bounty with a humbler name. (LL) Prologue to Hugh Kelly's A Word to the Wise. Samuel Johnson. EBEV; FaPoR; OxAEP-1

And mock you with me after I am gone. (LL) Sonnet 71. Shakespeare. AWP; EBEV; GBL; GTBS-P; HAP; HeIP-4; IMW; ImPo; LBC; NAEL-1; NoSic; OxAEP-1; PoRA; SCGP; Son; TFi

And Monelle said: I will speak to you of actions. Actions. Marcel Schwob, French. TrJP, tr. by William Brown Meloney

And Monelle said: I will speak to you of moments. Moments. Marcel Schwob, French. TrJP, tr. by William Brown Meloney

And Monelle said: I will speak to you of things dead. Things Dead. Marcel Schwob, French. TrJP, tr. by William Brown Meloney

And monocle. (LL) Bully. Martín Espada. LTA

And—more—is Nature's Roman, never to be scourged. (LL) The House-Top. Herman Melville. APN-2; CBCWP; NAAL-1; NAAL-3; NCAP; NOBA

And more pictures gone to pay taxes. Ezra Pound. See Canto 80.

And mossy scabs of the worm fence, heap'd stones, elder, mullein and poke- weed. (LL) I believe in you my soul, the other I am must not abase itself to you. Walt Whitman. APAD; ColAP

And / mother why did you tell me. Stephanie Markman. MDDM

And moulder in dust away! (LL) The Children's Hour. Henry Wadsworth Longfellow. APN-1; CTV; ChAP; FPC; FaBoBe; ImGa; OBAL; OBCA; PoEL-5; PoLF; WHSW

And mourn'd till Pity's self be dead. (LL) Dirge in "Cymbeline." William Collins. CABP; NOBE; NOEC; OBEV; SCGP

And move to space beneath our sky. (LL) M., Singing. Louise Bogan. ColAP; NoAM

And moved again and flashed again, time flashed again. (LL) Martial Cadenza. Wallace Stevens. AFr; MeMAP; OxBA; VGW

And moved his brush to write a new song. (LL) Sailing Homeward. Chan Fang sheng, Chinese. ChiP, tr. by Arthur Waley

And Mr. Ferritt. Judith Wright. MoBrPo

And much good love, without a feather-bed. (LL) In Saturn's reign, at Nature's early birth. Juvenal. OAEL-1; OBSV; OBVE, tr. by Dryden

And murmuring of innumerable bees. Tennyson. See Blow, Bugle, Blow.

And music[k] shall untune the sky. (LL) A Song for St Cecilia's Day [1687]. Dryden. AWP; FHYEP; FaBoTw; GTBS-P; HAP; ImPo; InPS- 3; NOSC; OAEL-1; OBEV; OxAEP-1; PoEL-3; SCGP; TFi

And must have it. (LL) Mother's Voice. Robert Creeley. FiLi; Poetr

And must I lose a soul's inheritance? (LL) Hélas! Oscar Wilde. ADE; GSo; MoBrPo; NAEL-2; Son; TIRV

And must I sing? What subject shall I choose? Ben Jonson. BeJo

And mute as any fish. (LL) A New Song of New Similies . John Gay. CBNP; NOBL

And mutton rained around. (LL) Carol: "While shepherds watched their flocks by night." "Saki." NSI; UV

And my blood which weaves oxygen and time. (LL) In Praise of Plants. Branko Miljkovic, *Serbian.* HSix, *tr.* by Charles Simic

And———my bloody life away. *Unknown. See* I don't want to be a soldier.

And my buffalo have found me. (LL) The Ballad of William Sycamore. Stephen Vincent Benét. SAGP

And my delight is causer of this strife. (LL) Description of the Contrarious Passions in a Lover. Petrarch. AAS; OAEL-1; OBVE; Poetr; SiPS, *tr.* by Sir Thomas Wyatt

And my fear is great that you have taken God from me! (LL) Donal[l] Oge [*or* Og]: Grief of a Girl's Heart. *Unknown, Modern Irish.* GBL; PBWP; RB, *tr.* by Lady Augusta Gregory

And my lively spirit drinketh immortality. (LL) From the Greek. Ptolemy, *Greek.* OBCVT, *tr.* by Bridges, Robert; GrAn, *tr.* by Robert Bridges

And my love loves me. Coleridge. *See* Answer to a Child's Question.

And my neck from the gallows-tree. (LL) The Maid Freed from the Gallows. *Unknown.* AWP; ESPB

And my nineteen years weigh heavily on my feet. (LL) October. Patrick Kavanagh. CIP-2; GTBS-P

And my prayer unto the God of my life, *vv. 1–5, 7–8.* Bible, *O.T. See* Psalm 42.

And my *Pyramides.* (LL) His Poetry His Pillar. Robert Herrick. BeJo; CaPo; NOSC; SeCP

And my silly old collarbone's bust. (LL) Hunter Trials. John Betjeman. EBEvV; OBCoV

And my soul from out that shadow that lies floating on the floor / Shall be lifted—never more! Edgar Allan Poe. *See* The Raven.

And my soul is swept up in joy. Uvavnuk. *See* The Great sea has set me in motion.

And my tears flow without end. (LL) On the Death of His Wife. Mei Yao Ch'en, *Chinese.* OHPC, *tr.* by Kenneth Rexroth; OxBM

And my young sweetheart sat at board with me. Idyl. Alfred Mombert, *German.* AWP, *tr.* by Ludwig Lewisohn

And myself. Edward Thomas. *See* Lights Out.

And nailed a small wing over the corn. (LL) The Hawk. George Mackay Brown. NoP-4; RB

And naked seemed, to stand each lifeless tree. (LL) The Vision of the Night. Philip Freneau. NAAL-1; NAAL-3

And naked was my pastime in between. (LL) Epitaph for Someone or Other. James Vincent Cunningham. OBAL; PFE; TRP; VGW

And Naomi said/ Unto her two daughters-in-law. Naomi and Ruth. Bible, *O.T.* TrJP *Fr.* Ruth.

And Nature's self did vanish, whither no man wist. Edmund Spenser. *See* Dame Nature.

And ne'er the first assault to proffer. (LL) Of Scolding Wives and the Third Day Ague. Henricus Selyns. AiP; SCAP

And neither awful Voice be heard by thee! (LL) Thought[s] of a Briton on the Subjugation of Switzerland. Wordsworth. CABP; GTBS-P; PBMP; UV

And never come back again. (LL) Rain, rain, go to Spain. Mother Goose. FaBoVe; ReMoGo

And never for a moment suppose that they understand. (LL) The Ram's Horn. John Hewitt. BIrV; PNI

And never get up at all? (LL) Skyscrapers. Rachel Lyman Field. ChAP; NOxBChV; SSCS

And never more will be. (LL) The Education of Nature. Wordsworth. GTBS-P; HAP; PoEL-4

And never, never, never / Come back again. Mother Goose. *See* Rain, rain, go to Spain.

And never scent the ground where they must lie. (LL) Simple Autumnal. Louise Bogan. MoAmPo; Son

And never stain a cheek for it. (LL) To His Book[e]. Martial, *Latin.* AWP; OBVE, *tr.* by Robert Herrick

And never wake to feel the day's disdain. (LL) Sonnet: "Care-charmer Sleep[e], son[ne] of the sable night." Samuel Daniel. AAS; CABP; CTC; GSo; GTBS-P; ImPo; InPS-3; NAEL-1; NIP-4; NOBE; NoP-4; NoSic; OAEL-1; OxAEP-1; PoEL-2; SCGP; Son; TFi

And never went there again. (LL) Doctor Foster went to Gloucester [*or* Glo'ster]. Mother Goose. LB; OxBoLi; OxNR; ReMoGo

And new philosophy calls all in doubt. Donne. NOSC *Fr.* The First Anniversary [*or* Anniversarie]. NAEL-1 *Fr.* Anatomy [*or* Anatomie] of the World, An[: The First Anniversary].

And next morning, at the medical center. One More Time. Patricia Goedicke. CMAP

And night and distant travel; for the train. Last Evening. Rilke, *German.* OBWP, *tr.* by J. B. Leishman

And night is pierced with stars. (LL) Round the Year. Coventry Patmore. BoTP; EBVV

And Night shall fold him in soft wings. (LL) Into Battle. Julian Grenfell. FaPoR; OBEV; OBMV; OBWP; OxBTC; PeFWW; PoFWW

And night's trees stood up. (LL) Sarolla's women in their picture hats. Lawrence Ferlinghetti. NeAP; PoM

And no birds sing—. . . . (LL) La Belle Dame Sans Merci. Keats. APAD; AWP; BLPA; CABP; CH; ClHu; EBEvV; FHYEP; FaBoBe; FaBoCh; FaBoSe; GTBS-P; HAP; HeIP-4; ImPo; InPS-3; LaPo; NAEL-2; NAWM-2; NOBE; NOBRP; NTP; NoP-4; OAEL-2; OBEV; OBNC; OBSP; OxAEP-2; OxBSn; PBMP; PFE; PoE; PoEL-4; PoPoPo; PoRA; Poetr; RB; Ro; SAGP; SCGP; SCV; SoSe-8; TFi; TRP; UV; UnPo

And no bread in his pocket. (LL) The Brother. Peter Everwine. FYAP; NNaP

And No Help Came. Peter Porter. BMAP

And no more love: Gone is the heart of Man. (LL) Dirge for the New Sunrise. Dame Edith Sitwell. CMoP; MoBrPo

And no one has warned me that freedom. February 8, 1980: And No One Has Warned Me. Stanislaw Baranczak, *Polish.* AF, *tr.* by Magnus J. Krynski

And No Regrets. Lex Banning. NOBAu

And Noah was six hundred years old when the flood of waters. Bible, *O.T.* NAWM-1 *Fr.* Genesis.

And nobody cares for me. (LL) There was a jolly miller once. Isaac Bickerstaffe. EBEvV; LB; OxNR

And nobody shouts halt. Auschwitz, 1987. Adam Zych, *Polish.* HP, *tr.* by Hilda Schiff

And Nod. Eugene Field. *See* Wynken, Blynken and Nod one night.

And none but thee. (LL) The British Church. George Herbert. ESCV; PeECV

And none but thou shalt be my paramour. (LL) Helen. Marlowe. EBEV; EBEvV; GBL; ImPo

And none has quite escaped my smile. (LL) Let No Charitable Hope. Elinor Wylie. ColAP; LiLi; LiTM; MoAmPo; NAAL-2; NALW; NMM-2; OxBA; OxBSP; PiM; VGW

And none shall speak his name. (LL) Poet. Karl Shapiro. CMoP; LiTM; MoAmPo; NoAM

An noo he's king ower a' his ain. (LL) King Orfeo. *Unknown.* ESPB; OxBB; OxBoLi

And nor knows nor cares for Beeny, and will laugh there nevermore. (LL) Beeny Cliff. Thomas Hardy. CABP; OBNC; OxAEP-2; RB

And not a wave shall trouble thee. (LL) The River[-]God's Song. John Fletcher. ITG; NOSC; SCGP

And not be afraid. (LL) To Turn Back. John Haines. CoAmPo; TRP

And not be ashamed. (LL) April Fool Birthday Poem for Grandpa. Diane Di Prima. CLPP; NMM-2

And not be / one. (LL) From the House of Yemanjá. Audre Lorde. NoP-4

And, not crying in vain. Marina Tsvetayeva, *Russian.* GI, *tr.* by Nancy Pollak

And not one of them all seemed to know the name of care. (LL) The Idlers. Edmund Blunden. BoTP; CH

—and not simply by the fact that this shading of. That the Science of Cartography Is Limited. Eavan Boland. NoP-4

And not the knees. (LL) This dirty—little—Heart. Emily Dickinson. NCAP; PoEL-5

And not waving but drowning. (LL) Not Waving But Drowning. Stevie Smith. APAD; CABP; FaBoWP; GTBS-P; HAP; HeIP-4; MoP; NAEL-2; NALW; NOBE; NoAM; NoP-4; OAEL-2; OxAEP-2; OxBTC; PoE; PoPoPo; Poetr; TFi; UV; WeW-3

And not your yellow hair. (LL) For Anne Gregory. W. B. Yeats. CMoP; ImPo; LiTM; NAEL-2; OxAEP-2; Poetr

And nothing more to give. (LL) I Want to Die While You Love Me. Georgia Douglas Johnson. OxWW

And nothing permanent on earth. (LL) "Nox Nocti Indicat Scientiam." William Habington. BeJo; MeLP; NOBE; OBEV; SCGP

And nothing to do but to pocket my gold! (LL) The Laureate. William Edmonstoune Aytoun. BXAP; UV

And nothing to say or do? (LL) Gloucester Moors. William Vaughn Moody. APN-2; NOBA; OxBA

And nothing wanting is, save She, alas!, *sl. diff. vers.* William Drummond, of Hawthornden. *See* Invocation: "Pheobus, arise! / And paint the sable skies."

And nought beyond, oh, earth! (LL) The Graves of a Household. Felicia Dorothea Hemans. FaPoR; NOBRP; WPE

And nought, when old, enjoy'd, denied the pow'r. (LL) On Late-acquired Wealth *or* Riches. *Unknown, Greek.* OBVE, *tr.* by William Cowper

And Now. Alan Bold. AYFP

And now a fig for the lower house. A Fig for the Lower House. Patrick Carey. NOSC

And now a garden pland with nicest care. The Wish. John Clare. OBGa *Fr.* The Wish.

And now abideth faith, hope, charity, these three; but the greatest of these is charity. (LL) The Greatest of These. Bible, *N.T.* OAEL-1; PBMP

And now Aeneas charges straight at Turnus. Virgil. OBWP, *tr.* by Allen Mandelbaum *Fr.* The Aeneid [*or* Eneados, *Aeneis*].

And now all Nature seem'd [*or* seemed] in love. On a Bank [*or* Banck] asl I Sat [*or* Sate] a-Fishing; a Description of the Spring. Sir Henry Wotton. CH; NOSC; SeCP

And now: And now: here begins Our Voyage, hunters and naturalists of indefatigable enthusiasm. Adolf Wolfli. PFTM, *tr.* by Aaron H. Esman. *Fr.* From the Cradle to the Grave, or, through working and sweating, suffering and hardship, even through prayyer into damnation.

And now, at last, all proud deeds done. Old Mythologies. John Montague. NoP-4

And now begin to weep when they have done. (LL) On the Death of Sir Philip Sidney. Henry Constable. NoSic; OBEV

And now Eurynome had bath'd the king. Ulysses Reunited with Penelope. Homer. NOSC, *sect.* XXIV; OBVE, *tr.* by George Chapman *Fr.* Odyssey. NAWM-1, *tr.* by Robert Fitzgerald

And now gentlemen. The Base of All Metaphysics. Walt Whitman. APN-1

And, now gives Time, her states description. George Chapman. PoEL-2 *Fr.* Euthymiae Raptus; or, The Teares of Peace.

And now good morrow to our waking souls. Donne. ITG

And now his well-known bow the Master bore. The Suitors watch Ulysses string the bow. Homer, *Greek.* OBCVT, *tr.* by Alexander Pope; OBVE, *tr.* by Pope *Fr.* Odyssey. NAWM-1, *tr.* by Robert Fitzgerald

And now I appear on the doorstep. . . . The Prophet. Yevgeny Mikhailovich Vinokurov, *Russian.* TCRP, *tr.* by Daniel Weissbort

And now I, Meleager, am among them. Epigram. Meleager, *Greek.* GrAn, *tr.* by Peter Whigham

And now I see you once. Bajan. Anthony Kellman. HCP

And now I too must wrestle with a brother. On the Pains of Translating Miklós Radnóti. Frederick Turner. RA

And now I will convey thee to thy world. Byron. NOBRP *Fr.* Cain: A Mystery.

And now I'm engaged to Miss Joan Hunter Dunn. (LL) A Subaltern's Love-Song. John Betjeman. APAD; BoLoP; EBEvV; HAP; NOBL; NoAM; OxAEP-2; OxBTC; TwCP

And now, in accents deep and low. Washington Allston. APN-1 *Fr.* The Sylphs of the Seasons.

And now in turn see Swinburne bent. Lines on Swinburne. Robert Browning. EPCY

And now, lash'd on by destiny severe. The Ship Is Lost. William Falconer. OxAEP-1 *Fr.* The Shipwreck.

And now let mee dispose such things. Isabella Whitney. BWW *Fr.* The Manner of Her Will and What She Left to London and to All Those in It, at Her Departing. NoSic

And now let pass a week. Once more behold. Robert Browning. EBVVPR, *sect.* III *Fr.* Red Cotton Night-Cap Country. EBVVPR

And now lies down, who was my moon or more. James Wright. *See* Complaint.

And now, like a posy, a pretty one plump in his hands. (LL) Catch. Robert Francis. InPK-6; RaBo

And now love sang: but his was such a song. Willowwood ("And now love sang: but his was such a song"). D. G. Rossetti. NAEL-1; OAEL-2 *Fr.* The House of Life.

And now man-slaughtering Pallas took in hand. The End of the Suitors. Homer. OBVE, *tr.* by George Chapman *Fr.* Odyssey. NAWM-1, *tr.* by Robert Fitzgerald

And now my pampered beast. Epitaph for My Cat. Jean Garrigue. TAP

And now my story's [*or* is] done. (LL) I'll tell you a story / About Jack a Nory. Mother Goose. LB; OxNR; ReMoGo

And now one prayer. *Unknown.* OBVE *Fr.* The Lay [*or* Short Lay] of Sigurd. AWP, *tr.* by William Morris *and* Eirikr Magnusson *Fr.* The Elder Edda.

And now she cleans her teeth into the lake. Camping Out. William Empson. CMoP; FaBoMo; OxBTC

And now she goes on the trapeze. (LL) The Man on the Flying Trapeze. George Leybourne. BLPA; FaBoBe

And now she knows: The big fist shattering her face. The Female and the Silence of a Man. June Jordan. NAAAL; NMM-2

And now take thought, my sonnet, who is he. Sonnets of the Months: Conclusion. Folgore da San Geminiano. AWP, *tr.* by D. G. Rossetti

And now th'art set wide ope, the Speare's sad art. I Am the Doore. Richard Crashaw. GeHe; NAEL-1

& Now the book is closed. Anne Waldman *and* Ted Berrigan. SPE *Fr.* Merorial Day: a Collaboration.

And now the dark comes on, all full of chitter noise. The Sound of Night. Maxine W. Kumin. SoSe-8; WPE

And now the Queene of women had intent. Homer. OBVE, *tr.* by George Chapman *Fr.* Odyssey. NAWM-1, *tr.* by Robert Fitzgerald

And now the riverbank. For the last time. Marina Ivanovna Tsvetaeva. *Fr.* The Daughter of Jairus. BoWoP, *tr.* by Paul Schmidt

And now the riverbank. I cling. Marina Ivanovna Tsvetaeva. *Fr.* The Daughter of Jairus. BoWoP, *tr.* by Paul Schmidt

And now the sun that through the horizon peeps. Marlowe. OAEL-1 *Fr.* Hero and Leander. AAS

And now the trembling light. Shoreham: Twilight Time. Samuel Palmer. NTP; OAEL-2

And now the words. Mourning Song. Robert Pearl, *Tsimshian Indian.* STP, *tr.* by Armand Schwerner

And now their hour is come. (LL) Compensation ("Why should I keep holiday"). Ralph Waldo Emerson. APN-1; MeMAP; TAP

And now there is nothing left to celebrate. George Barker. LiTM *Fr.* Pacific Sonnets.

And now there rolls in, as on casters, a character. Fame. Vladimir Nabokov, *Russian.* TCRP, *tr.* by Vladimir Nabokov

And now they lien in helle ifere. (LL) Ubi Sunt Qui ante Nos Fuerunt? [*or* Contempt of the World]. *Unknown.* EBEV; HAP; WeW-3

And now they nigh approachèd to the stead. The Mermaids. Edmund Spenser. *Fr.* Wood Of Error. AEP

And now, 'tis silent all!—Enchantress, fare thee well! (LL) Farewell Thou Minstrel Harp. Sir Walter Scott. OBNC; OxAEP-2

"And now to God the Father," he ends. In Church. Thomas Hardy. InPK-6; MoBrPo; SCV *Fr.* Satires of Circumstance in Fifteen Glimpses.

And now to the abyss I pass. Andrew Marvell. OAEL-1 *Fr.* Upon Appleton House [To My Lord Fairfax]. FaBoPV; GeHe; SeCP

("And now to the Abbyss I pass.") PBRV

("As *Constellations* do above.") (LL) PBRV

And now, unveiled, the toilet stands displayed. The Toilet. Alexander Pope. ECEV; NOBE; OxAEP-1 *Fr.* The Rape of the Lock[, an Heroi-Comical Poem]. FHYEP; HAP; ImPo; OAEL-1; OBNV; PeLV; PoEL-3

"And now, *Vexilla regis prodeunt / Inferni.*" Dante's Inferno, Canto XXXIV (The Final Canto). Robert Pinsky. PUP-20

And now was Paris come / From his high towres. Homer. OBVE, *tr.* by George Chapman *Fr.* The Iliad.

And now we gan draw near unto the gate. Creusa. Virgil. *Fr.* The Aeneid [*or* Eneados, *Aeneis*].

And now we gan draw near unto the gate. Virgil. *Fr.* The Second Book of Virgil's *Aeneid.* SiPS, *tr.* by Henry Howard, Earl of Surrey *Fr.* The Aeneid [*or* Eneados, *Aeneis*].

And now we three in Euston waiting-room. (LL) Parting in Wartime. Frances Darwin Cornford. APAD; FaBoWP; NIP-4

And now we walked along the solid mire. Dante. OBVE, *tr.* by Robert Lowell *Fr.* Inferno. NAWM-1, *tr.* by John Ciardi *Fr.* Divina Commedia.

And now what monarch would not gardener be. To Amanda Walking in the Garden. N. Hookes. NOSC; OBGa

And now when sheering of the flocks are done. June. John Clare. Ro

And now with him she sleeps in Yarrow. (LL) The Braes of Yarrow. John Logan. GTBS-P; SCGP

And now you comb and braid your hair. Paulus Silentiarius, *Greek.* InMo, *tr.* by Sam Hamill

And now you're ready who while she was here. Epigram. James Vincent Cunningham. OBVE *Fr.* Five Epigrams.

And now you're ready who while she was here. Scythinus, *Greek.* GrAn, *tr.* by J. V. Cunningham

And nowe I live, and nowe my life is donn. (LL) Tichborne's Elegy. Chidiock Tichborne. PBRV

And nuzzling each other in the smelly fold. (LL) Magnificat. Michele Roberts. APAD; BrRo; NBrP

And O and O. Song of Spring. Keats. BoTP

And, O, pray too for me! (LL) The Maid's Lament. Walter Savage Landor. OBEV; OBNC

And O she was the Sunday / In every week. (LL) The Planter's Daughter. Austin Clarke. CIP-2; OxBTC

And O, ye Fountains, Meadows, Hills, and Groves. Wordsworth. *Fr.* Ode: Intimations of Immortality [from Recollections of Early Childhood]. AWP; FHYEP; HAP; HeIP-4; NOBE; NOBRP; OAEL-2; OBEV; OBNC; PBMP; PoE; PoEL-4

And occasional herring and mouse. (LL) An Old Cat's Confessions. Christopher Pearse Cranch. APN-1; OBCA

And of all that was theirs only the letters were left. Haim Guri, *Hebrew.* IP, *tr.* by Warren Bargad *and* Stanley F. Chyet

And, of its one movement, the depth. (LL) The Movement of Fish. James Dickey. NYBP; VGW

And of new love that they would learn. (LL) A Wife in London. Thomas Hardy. NOBVV; OBWP

And of the Azazmeh too, it would seem. Of the Azazmeh Too. Haim Guri, *Hebrew.* IP, *tr.* by Warren Bargad *and* Stanley F. Chyet

And of the curveship lend a myth to God. (LL) To Brooklyn Bridge. Hart Crane. AiP; AmFP; AmPP; CMoP; ChIV-1; ClHu; ColAP; FaBoA;

HAP; HeIP-4; ImPo; InPS-3; KSG; LiTM; MeMAP; MoAmPo; NOBA; NoAM; NoP-4; OxBA; PoE; PoPoFo; TAP; TFi; TRP; WeW-3

And of thir [*or* their] vain contest appeer'd [*or* appeared] no end. (LL) Book IX. Milton. FHYEP; NAEL-1; NAWM-1; OAEL-1

And oft the owle with ruffull song complaind. Dido by Night. Virgil. OBVE, *tr. by* Henry Howard, Earl of Surrey *Fr.* The Aeneid [*or* Eneados, *Aeneis*].

And often spoken but no longer heard. (LL) The Mixer. Louis MacNeice. FP; FaBoTw

And, oh, may no other maiden know such reproach as I! (LL) Cashel of Munster. William English, *Irish.* BIrV; GBL; OBEV, *tr. by* Sir Samuel Ferguson

And, oh! pray too for me! Walter Savage Landor. *See* The Maid's Lament.

And, oh! 'tis delicious to hate you! (LL) When I loved you, I can't but allow. Thomas Moore. EnLoPo; OxBSP

And old men shall drop by the wayside. (LL) Shaka, King of the Zulus. *Unknown, Zulu.* PBA; TTY, *tr. by* A. C. Jordan

And on My Eyes Dark Sleep by Night. "Michael Field." LW; OBMV

And on that day, upon the heavenly scarp. Upon the Heavenly Scarp. Abraham Moses Klein. PoA *Fr.* The Psalter of Avram Haktani.

And on the beach undid his corded bales. (LL) The Scholar-Gipsy. Matthew Arnold. EBEV; EBVV; EBVVPR; EnVR; FHYEP; HAP; ImPo; NAEL-2; NOBE; NOBVV; NoP-4; OAEL-2; OBEV; OBNC; OxAEP-1; PoE; PoEL-5; SCGP; TFi

And on the fifth day, he was—dead! (LL) The Story of Augustus Who Would Not Have Any Soup. Heinrich Hoffmann, *German.* NBLV; OxBChV

And on the mere the wailing died away. (LL) Morte d'Arthur. Tennyson. EBNV; EBVVPR; FaBoBe; NIP-4; NOBVV; OAEL-2; OBNC; OxAEP-2; PeECV; PoEL-5

And on the porch, across the upturned chair. The Poet at Seven. Donald Justice. MT; WeT; WeW-3

And on the right the slogan Born To Lose. (LL) Black Jackets. Thom Gunn. HeIP-4; NAEL-2; NoP-4; TwCP

And on the wall was limned a mouldering corse. On the Wall. Immanuel di Roma, *Hebrew.* TrJP, *tr. by* Solomon Solis-Cohen

And on this day, which poets unto thee. Ovid. OBVE, *tr. by* Henry Vaughan *Fr.* Tristium.

And on This Shore. M. Carl Holman. PoBA

And on / through the leaves. (LL) Pound at Spoleto. Lawrence Ferlinghetti. PoM

And on to Wakefield take your way. (LL) Dirge: "Weep, weep, ye woodmen, wail." Anthony Munday. CH; CTC

And once again I was within that house. The Dream. John Peale Bishop. LiTM

And once again the angel of Death came. A Poem of Death. George MacBeth. HP *Fr.* The Rumanian of Maria Banus.

And One for My Dame. Anne Sexton. NoP-4

And one for the little boy that [*or* who] lives in the lane. (LL) Baa, baa, black sheep, have you any wool? Mother Goose. FaBoBe; LB; OxNR; ReMoGo

And one is One, free in the tearing wind. (LL) In a dark time, the eye begins to see. Theodore Roethke. NoP-4; PBMP; PaTW

And one morning while in the woods I stumbled suddenly upon the / thing thing. Between the World and Me. Richard Wright. AF; ISC; LiTM; MoP; PoBA; SSLK

And one there was, a dreamer born. Tent on the Beach: The Dreamer. John Greenleaf Whittier. NCAP

And only bitter land was washed away. (LL) Childhood. Margaret Abigail Walker. NoP-4; PBWP; PoBA; Son; WPOW

And only know I should drown if you laid not your hand on me. (LL) Stillness. James Elroy Flecker. CH; MoBrPo

And only then the eye begins to see. (LL) The Counterpart. Elizabeth Jennings. LiTM; TOF

And Opposition of the Stars. (LL) The Definition Of Love. Andrew Marvell. BoLoP; CBLP; EBEV; ESCV; FHYEP; FMP; FSCP; GBL; GLoP; GeHe; HoPM; ImPo; InPS-3; LoP; MeLP; NAEL-1; NOBE; NOSC; NoP-4; OAEL-1; OBEV; PBRV; PoEL-2; SCGP; SeCP; TFi; UnPo

And other wond'rous works were done. The Ascension of Our Lord Jesus Christ. Christopher Smart. NOCV *Fr.* Hymns and Spiritual Songs for the Fasts and Festivals of the Church of England.

And others doth offend when 'tis let loose. (LL) Love's Offence. Sir John Suckling. CaPo; NOSC

And others to shriek and collapse. (LL) Limerick: "As tourists inspected the apse." Edward Gorey. PeLV; PeLi

And our hearts, like thy waters, be mingled in peace. (LL) The Meeting of the Waters. Thomas Moore. IIP; NOIV; OxBoLi; PoEL-4

And our hems crooked forever? (LL) House Guest. Elizabeth Bishop. NYBP; TAP

And our ordinary garments decent in the dead one's eyes. (LL) Journey to the Place of Ghosts. Jay Wright. GT; VCAP

And our skin shall see far off, as it does under water. (LL) Surprised by Evening. Robert Bly. VGW; WeT

And our wheels grazed his dead face. (LL) Dead Man's Dump. Isaac Rosenberg. FaBoMo; GTBS-P; LiTM; NAEL-2; NSI; NoAM; OBWP; PeFWW; PoWW; TrJP

And out; a pause, a long sigh. (LL) In and Out. Jane Kenyon. BAP-93; LoL

And out of his eyes two great tears rolled, like stones, and he died. (LL) Death of a Son. Jon Silkin. GTBS-P; MoP; OxBTC

And out of the swing of the sea. (LL) Heaven-Haven. Gerard Manley Hopkins. APAD; EBEvV; HeIP-4; MoBrPo; MoP; NOBE; NOCV; NoAM; OBEV; OBNC; OxAEP-2; OxBSP; PeECV; RB; SoSe-8; TFi; TOF

And out on the plaza, there were more people. A Filial Republic. Susan Wheeler. BAP-93

And out they sally'd at the Gate. (LL) The Argument. Samuel Butler. EBEV; NAEL-1; OAEL-1

And over all the sky—the sky! far, far out of reach, studded, breaking out, the eternal stars. (LL) Bivouac on a Mountain Side. Walt Whitman. AiP; CBCWP; OxBA; PoLF

And over their city stands the pinnacled corn. (LL) Merlin. Geoffrey Hill. InPK-6; TRP

And Pablo Neruda / that Chilean omnivore of poetry. Lawrence Ferlinghetti. BB *Fr.* Work-in-Progress.

And packing sketches, ink, knife, and quills. Piranesi in L.A. Debora Greger. WWSi

And palms before my feet! (LL) The Donkey. G. K. Chesterton. ACTP; APo; CTAV; ChIV-2; EBEvV; FaPoR; GI; InPK-6; MoBrPo; OBEV; PFE; PoLF; RB

And Paradise does come. Joy. Gavin Bantock. OxBTC

And pardon this one. (LL) Hotel Paradiso e Commerciale. John Malcolm Brinnin. NYBP; TwCP

And Paris be it or Helen dying. A Fragment on Death. François Villon, *French.* CTC; PeVV, *tr. by* Swinburne

And passes into gloom again. (LL) Old warder of these buried bones. Tennyson. PeECV; PoEL-5

And passionate as the dawn. (LL) The Fisherman. W. B. Yeats. CMoP; HAP; NoAM

And Peace, and Art, and Labour joined her train. (LL) Visit of Hope to Sydney Cove, near Botany-Bay. Erasmus Darwin. ECEV; NOEC

And peace on earth for men. (LL) Afterthought. Elizabeth Jennings. NOxBChV

And people will think this like. "Anna Akhmatova," *Russian.* TCRP, *tr. by* Daniel Weissbort

And Pergamos, / City of the Phrygians. Euripides. AWP; OBVE, *tr. by* Hilda Doolittle *Fr.* Iphigenia [*or* Iphigeneia] in Aulis.

And perhaps as well some tasteless specks of salt. (LL) Here is. Jean-Joseph Rabéarivelo, *French.* NegPo, *tr. by* Ellen Conroy Kennedy

And perhaps some tasteless grains of salt. Jean-Joseph Rabéarivelo. *See* Here is.

And perish at the last. (LL) Upon the Troublesome Times. Robert Herrick. CaPo; CavPo

And perish in our own. (LL) Daisy. Francis Thompson. AWP; MoBrPo; OBEV; OBNC

And Phyllis [*or* Phyllis] is some forty-three. (LL) Phillis's Age. Matthew Prior. EnLoPo; FaBoEE

And pierced with a bewilderment of birds. (LL) Learning by Doing. Howard Nemerov. HAP; Poetr; TwCP; WeW-3

And pillared the blue firmament with light? Edwin Markham. *See* The Man with the Hoe.

And Pity pour her healing tear. (LL) Lines, / Written on Seeing My Husband's Picture, painted when he was young: "Those are the features, those the smiles." Anna Sawyer. ECWP; LW

And Place was where the Presence was / Circumference between. (LL) At Half past Three, a single Bird. Emily Dickinson. APN-2; MoAmPo; NAWM-2; OxBA

And plain old Margaret Fuller died as well. (LL) Ballad of Ladies Lost and Found. Marilyn Hacker. FFC; NMM-2; VCAP

And please my self, if pardon'd first by you. (LL) To the University. Alicia D'Anvers. KTR; NOSC

And ploughs down palaces, and thrones, and towers. (LL) The Serf. Roy Campbell. GTBS-P; MoBrPo; OBMV

And plucking / the fruit. Denise Levertov. *See* O Taste and See.

And plung'd all noiseless into the deep night. Keats. OxAEP-2, *book* I–III; FHYEP; NOBRP; OBNC; PoEL-4

And point with taper spire to Heaven. (LL) A Wish. Samuel Rogers. FaPoR; GTBS-P; NOBE; OBEV; OxAEP-2

And points us to a better time than ours. (LL) West London. Matthew Arnold. FP; GSo; SCGP; Son

And polished by the Master's hand. (LL) Taste. Christopher Smart. ChIV-1; NOCV

And poplars stand there still as death. (LL) Southern Mansion. Arna Bontemps. AiP; GT; LiTM; NAAAL; PoBA; TTY

And popped it on again. Mother Goose. *See* Sing a song of sixpence.

And powerful passion bears him to your feet. (LL) The Art of Coquetry. Charlotte Lennox. ECWP; LW

And practice drives me mad. (LL) Arithmetic. *Unknown.* ReMoGo

And praise him who did make and mend our eies. (LL) Love. George Herbert. ESCV; GeHe; HoPM; Son

And pray for Kharma under the holy mountain. (LL) Chard Whitlow. Henry Reed. BXAP; LiTM; MoBrPo; NBLV; NOBL; NoP-4; OBCoV; OxBTC; PeLV; UV; UnPo

And pretty maids all in [*or* of] a row. (LL) Mary, Mary, quite contrary. Mother Goose. LB; OxNR; ReMoGo

And prompt and glad to do the / things I've heard. Howard Arnold Walter. *See* I would be true, for there are those [who trust me].

And prove that death but routs life into victory. (LL) Epilogue: "If Luther's day expand to Darwin's year." Herman Melville. APN-2; NCAP

And pulled my voice / into the ring of the dance. (LL) Caedmon. Denise Levertov. NoP-4

And pure religion breathing household laws. (LL) Written in London, September, 1802. Wordsworth. FaBoPV; GTBS-P; OBEV

And purpose of our being here? (LL) To spend uncounted years of pain. Arthur Hugh Clough. EnVV; NOBVV; OBNC; OxBSP

And Pussy soon had them all dead on the floor. (LL) Six little mice sat down to spin;. Mother Goose. PC

"And put a bullet through his head." (LL) Richard Cory. Paul Simon. PFE

And put him into bed? Why don't they come? (LL) Disabled. Wilfred Owen. CMoP; InPS-3; LiTM; MoP; NAEL-2; NSI; NoAM; OBWVE; OxBTC; PeFWW; PoFWW; PoPoPo; SCGP

And put in twa een o' tree. (LL) Tam Lin. *Unknown.* ESPB; NOBE; OBEV; OBNV; OxBB; OxBS

And Pykes, the Tyrants of the watry Plains. (LL) Hunting and Fishing. Alexander Pope. ECEV; FHYEP; PoEL-3

And quiet sleep and a sweet dream when the long trick's over. (LL) Sea-Fever. John Masefield. CABP; CTV; ChAP; EBEvV; FaBoBe; FaPoR; MoBrPo; NTP; OxAEP-2; OxBTC; OxBoS; PoLF; SAGP; UV

And quiet to the weary World restore. Lucretius. *See* Address to Venus.

And quite invisible but for the end of his nose. (LL) Amphibious Crocodile. John Crowe Ransom. FuPo; OBAL

An' raise dat rucus to-night. (LL) Raise a "Rucus" To-Night. *Unknown.* BPo; TAP

And rattle the door in its chains. (LL) Leningrad. Osip E. Mandelstam, *Russian.* AF; FaBoPV, *tr. by* W. S. Merwin *and* Clarence Brown

And rattles her crutch, which may put forth a small bloom, / perhaps white. (LL) Pursuit. Robert Penn Warren. FuPo; HAP; MoAmPo; TwCP

And raving, distracted, he died the next night. (LL) The Gosport Tragedy. *Unknown.* AmFP

And ravished the daughters, and drove the fathers mad. (LL) So an age ended, and its last deliverer died. W. H. Auden. CMoP; PoE; Son

And read that moderate man Voltaire. (LL) The Respectable Burgher. Thomas Hardy. CMoP; ChIV-2; NoAM

And read your Bible, sir, and mind your purse. (LL) Growing Old. Byron. NOBE; SCV

And receipts and dolls and clothes, tobacco crumbs, vases and / fringes. Gwendolyn Brooks. *See* The Bean Eaters.

And reconciles man to his lot. (LL) Verses Supposed to Be Written by Alexander Selkirk during His Solitary Abode on the Island of Juan Fernandez. William Cowper. EBEvV; GTBS-P; NOEC; PoEL-3; PoLF

And rejoice, honoring You. (LL) Antipsalm. Novica Tadic, *Serbo-Croatian.* HSix; VCWP, *tr. by* Charles Simic

And renownèd thy grave! (LL) Song: "Fear no more the heat o' the Sun." Shakespeare. APAD; AWP; CH; CTC; ClHu; EBEV; EBEvV; FaBoCh; GBL; GTBS-P; HAP; ImPo; InPS-3; NAEL-1; NOBE; NOSC; NoP-4; NoSic; OAEL-1; OBEV; OxAEP-1; PBMP; PoE; PoEL-2; PoPoPo; PoRA; RB; SCGP; SCV; SoSe-8; TFi

And replaced them with golden flowers. Jean-Joseph Rabéarivelo. *See* Cactus.

And rested on a drying hill. (LL) Sir Gawaine and the Green Knight. Yvor Winters. MoP; NoAM; PoRA; VGW

And retreating, always retreating, behind it. (LL) Brazil, January 1, 1502. Elizabeth Bishop. BLT; FaBoWP; NoAM; OxBoP; VCAP

And returned on the previous night. (LL) Limerick: "There was a young lady named [*or* called] Bright." Arthur Buller. NOBL; OxBoLi; PeLV; PeLi

And right perfection wrongfully disgraced. Shakespeare. *See* Sonnet 66.

And ring out, all ye laughter-peals of home. Catullus. *See* Carmen 31 ("Apple of islands, Sirmio, & bright peninsulas, set").

And ringeth faintly in the grassy stones. (LL) Under the mountain, as when first I knew. Frederick Goddard Tuckerman. APN-2; HAP; TAP

And rise the model of the world! (LL) On the Expected General Rising of the French Nation. Anna Laetitia Barbauld. CABP; ECWP

And roll up the windows and drive away. (LL) At Cove on the Crooked River ("At Cove at our camp in the open canyon"). William Stafford. CoAmPo

And rooted in Romance remain. (LL) Old Susan. Walter De la Mare. CMoP; MoBrPo

And round his heart one strangling golden hair. (LL) Body's Beauty. D. G. Rossetti. OAEL-2; PoEL-5; Son

And rubies in her hair. (LL) A Chanted Calendar. Sydney Thompson Dobell. BoTP; OBEV

And rural mirth and manners are no more. (LL) The Deserted Village. Oliver Goldsmith. OBSV; UV

And sae this ends my sang. (LL) Lord Livingston. *Unknown.* ESPB; OxBB

An sae was pu'd or noon! (LL) Ye flowery banks o' bonie Doon, *see also* "Ye banks and braes o' bonie Doon." Robert Burns. BoLoP; NAEL-2; OBEV; PoEL-4; TFi; UnPo

And safe in heaven dead. (LL) 211th Chorus. Jack Kerouac. NeAP; PmAP; PoM

And said: "He had n't very far to fall." (LL) Corporal. Ambrose Bierce. APN-2; OBAL

And said I that my limbs were old. Love. Sir Walter Scott. OxAEP-2 *Fr.* The Lay of the Last Minstrel.

And said, 'Nay, we are seven!'. (LL) We Are Seven. Wordsworth. BLPA; NAEL-2; NOBRP; OxBChV; Ro

And said, "Not yet! in quiet lie." (LL) Daybreak. Henry Wadsworth Longfellow. BoTP; PWR; PoLF

And said, What a good boy am I! (LL) Little Jack Horner/ Sat in a corner. Mother Goose. LB; OxNR; ReMoGo; SoSe-8

And salvage mostly / The leaning. (LL) In These Dissenting Times. Alice Walker. InPS-3; PoBA

And sanctify this ALTAR to be thine. (LL) The Altar. George Herbert. CABP; ChIV-1; ESCV; GeHe; HoPM; InPS-3; NAEL-1; NOSC; NoP-4; OAEL-1; Poetr; SeCP; TrCP

And sank beneath thy chain to a lamented grave. (LL) The Spleen. Anne Finch, Countess of Winchilsea. NALW; NOSC

And sank her in the sea. (LL) The Demon Lover. *Unknown.* AS; AmFP; ESPB; EnSB; HAP; OAEL-1; OxBB; PBMP; SCGP; TFi; UnPo; WeW-3

And sank him back. (LL) Alas, Alack! Walter De la Mare. OPOU; OxBChV

And sat down at his desk and wrote a story. (LL) Herman Melville. W. H. Auden. MeMAP; OxBA

And Satan's self had thoughts of taking orders. (LL) Tophet. Thomas Gray. ChIV-1; FaBoEE; NOEC; OxBSP

And save ourselves unaided. (LL) Storm Fear. Robert Frost. CMoP; ColAP; OxBA; SAGP

And save the serpent in their midst. (LL) In Memory of My Feelings. Frank O'Hara. APSN; ColAP; NAAL-2; NeAP; PoM

And saved a great cause that heroic day. (LL) Opportunity. Edward Rowland Sill. APN-2; BLPA; PFE; PoToHe

And saved the sum of things for pay. (LL) Epitaph on an Army of Mercenaries. A. E. Housman. EBEvV; NSI; NoP-4; SCGP; SoSe-8

And say His name. (LL) A Canticle to the Waterbirds. William Everson. APSN; NeAP; PoM

And, say! how does it seem to you? (LL) Far from the Madding Crowd. Nixon Waterman. BLPA; FaBoBe

And say my glory was I had such friends. (LL) The Municipal Gallery Revisited. W. B. Yeats. GTBS-P; OxBTC

And schoolboys lag with satchels in their hands. (LL) A Description of the Morning. Jonathan Swift. EBEV; ECEV; HAP; HeIP-4; InPS-3; NOBE; NOEC; NoP-4; OAEL-1; OxAEP-1; PoPoPo; Poetr; SoSe-8; TFi

And scorning say, "See what it is to love." (LL) Sonnet 107: "Stella, since thou so right a Princess art." Sir Philip Sidney. NoP-4; OxAEP-1

And scratched [th]'em in again. (LL) Alexander's Song. *Unknown.* CBNP; LB; OxNR

And Sea. Amryl Johnson. HCP

And seal her to the Stranger for his castle in the gloom. (LL) Emily Hardcastle, Spinster. John Crowe Ransom. CMoP; MeMAP; OxBSP

And seal the hushèd casket of my soul. (LL) To Sleep. Keats. EBEvV; LaPo; NAEL-2; NIP-4; OBEV; PoEL-4; Son

And seasons, changeless since the day she died. (LL) The Cross of Snow. Henry Wadsworth Longfellow. APN-1; ColAP; GSo; HeIP-4; MeMAP; NOBA; NoP-4; OxBA; TAP

And see his chariot triumph 'bove his wain. (LL) Ode to Himself. Ben Jonson. BeJo; EPCY; NAEL-1; OAEL-1; SeCP

And see if there be any wicked way in me, and lead me in the way everlasting. Bible, *O.T.* *See* Psalm 139.

And see th' expected hour is on the wing. Prospect of the Future Glory of America. John Trumbull. AmPP

And see the men at play. (LL)   Golf Links [lie so near the mill], The. Sarah Norcliffe Cleghorn. ImPo; InPK-6; KaS; NIP-4; PoLF

And see the rivers how they run. Prospects. John Dyer. GaP *Fr.* Grongar Hill. CABP; NOEC; NoP-4; OxAEP-1; PoEL-3

And see the storm ashore. (LL)   To Maecenas. Horace. AWP, *tr. by* Dryden; FaPoR; OBVE

And see thy blood warm when thou feel'st it cold. (LL)   Sonnet 2. Shakespeare. HeIP-4; ImPo; NoSic; SCGP; Son

And see you safely through diminished fields. (LL)   Riding a One-eyed Horse. Henry Taylor. HeIP-4; InPK-6

And seeing the multitudes, he went up. Bible, *N.T.* NAWM-1 *Fr.* St. Matthew.

And sees within my eyes the tears of two. (LL)   Sonnet: "Go from me. Yet I feel that I shall stand." Elizabeth Barrett Browning. BWW; CBLP; LW; OBEV; OxAEP-2

And send it a thousand miles, thinking. (LL)   Exile's Letter. Li Po, *Chinese.* CTC; FaBoMo; OxBA, *tr. by* Ezra Pound

And send it from above! (LL)   My spirit longeth for Thee. John Byrom. NOBE; OxAEP-1

And sent them out of town. (LL)   Lion and the unicorn, The. Mother Goose. BoTP; CTAV; ReMoGo

And serve but Him alone. (LL)   The Nut-brown Maid. *Unknown.* NoSic; OBEV

And set *me* there—I am so fair as that. (LL)   Beauty Accurst. Richard Le Gallienne. ADE; RACG

And set our billie Archie free'. (LL)   Archie o [*or of*] Cawfield. *Unknown.* AmFP; ESPB; OxBS

And settle Satan's kingdom ev'rywhere. (LL)   The Extravagant Drunkard's Wish. Edward Ward. CBNP; NOEC

And settled upon his eyes in a black soot. (LL)   'More Light! More Light!'. Anthony Hecht. AF; CoAP; CoAmPo; HAP; HP; NOBA; NoAM; NoP-4; OBWP; Poetr; RB; TwCP; UnPo; VCAP; VGW

And several strengths from drowsiness campaigned. The Sermon on the Warpland. Gwendolyn Brooks. BPo; LiTM; NOBA; PoBA

And shake his head at Doctor Swift. (LL)   The Happy Life of a Country Parson. Alexander Pope. BXAP; UV

& shake the shit out of them. (LL)   A Dance for Militant Dilettantes. Al Young. NBV; PoBA

And shall from age to age endure, *metrical vers. by* William Kethe. Bible, *O.T. See* Psalm 100.

And shall I prime my children, pray, to pray? Gwendolyn Brooks. *Fr.* The Children of the Poor. WPE, *sect.* I, *pt.* 1-2; PoA, *sect.* I, *pt.* 1-3; NAAAL *Fr.* The Womanhood.

And shall it ever be again—the joy. Late. Benjamin Paul Blood. APN-2

And shall sing forth thy praise over this meat. (LL)   Meditation 150 (Second Series). Edward Taylor. ColAP

And Shall Trelawny Die? Robert Stephen Hawker. *See* The Song of the Western Men.

And shall we ever seek in vain. All Alone. Mary E. Tucker. CBWP-1

And shall we view these miracles and more. John Rollin Ridge. APN-2 *Fr.* California.

And share my bed with Capricorn and Cancer. (LL)   Altarwise by owl-light in the half-way house. Dylan Thomas. CMoP; FaBoMo; Son

And sharp-edorn / Dinner plates. (LL)   Tinker's Wife. Patrick Kavanagh. CIP-2; InPS-3; MoP; NoAM

And shatter your virginity. (LL)   Corinna In Vendome. Pierre de Ronsard, *French.* LoP, *tr. by* Alistair Elliot; BoLoP, *tr. by* Robert Mezey

And she aloof to laughter—till I don't know. Big, Fat Summer—and the Lean and Hard. Frederick Bock. NYBP

And she, being old, fed from a mashed plate. Old Woman. Iain Crichton Smith. FaBoTw; OxBTC

And she beside another lad. (LL)   Along the field as we came by. A. E. Housman. GLoP; HAP; MoBrPo; WeW-3

And she can't see me. (LL)   Pancake Day. Mother Goose. CBNP; LB; OxNR; ReMoGo

And she compliant to his every wish. (LL)   Note on Propertius I.5. Fleur Adcock. BoLoP; EP; PeNZ

And she [*has*] crept under / [T]he warming pan [*or* frying pan]. (LL)   Ladybird, ladybird fly away home. Mother Goose. FaBoVe; LB; OxNR; ReMoGo

And she dropt me a curtsey. (LL)   As I was going up Pippen Hill. Mother Goose. OxNR; ReMoGo

And she is beautiful, our daughter. To Our Daughter. Jennifer Armitage. BrRo

And she may unlock it without any key. (LL)   I will give my love an apple without e'er a core. *Unknown.* ITG

And she must have looked. Lady Northcote. Mark McWatt. HCP

And she was a Jersey Cow. (LL)   A Farmer's Boy. *Unknown.* CTAV; PeP

And She Washed His Feet with Her Tear[e]s, and Wiped Them with the Hairs of Her Head. Sir Edward Sherburne, *after the Italian of* Giambattista Marina. MeLP; NOSC

And she who slays is she who bears, who bears. (LL)   Parentage. Alice Thompson Meynell. NALW; VWP

And shone that smile on us and sang. (LL)   Homage to the Empress of the Blues. Robert Earl Hayden. HCAP; LCAP-2; NAAAL; PoBA

And shook my head. (LL)   A Moment Please. Samuel Allen. SSLK

And shores and strands and naked piers. Henry James at Newport. Weldon Kees. PoA

And shoved in, and driven away. (LL)   A Note to Olga (1966). Denise Levertov. CAPP-1; NALW

And shun at once the censure and the crime. (LL)   The Repulse to Alcander. Sarah Fyge Egerton. CABP; ECWP

And shuts his eyes. (LL)   Darwin in 1881. Gjertrud Schnackenberg. NoP-4

And sick for home. (LL)   Outside Fargo, North Dakota. James Wright. GM; LCAP-2; NNaP; WeT

And sighs for the bucket that hung in the well. (LL)   The Old Oaken Bucket. Samuel Woodworth. BLPA; FaBoBe

And signifies the same with none. (LL)   What makes a knave a child of God. Samuel Butler. NOBL; OBSV

And silver her streams. (LL)   The Heavenly City. Stevie Smith. APAD; FaBoTw

And Sin is the consort of Woe. (LL)   An Appeal to My Countrywomen. Frances Ellen Watkins Harper. NAAAL

And since this life our nonage is. The Angels. Donne. *Fr.* The Litanie. PoEL-2

And since thou own'st that praise, I spare thee mine. (LL)   To Mary Unwin. William Cowper. GTBS-P; OBEV

And since thou so desirously. The Martyrs. Donne. *Fr.* The Litanie. PoEL-2

And sing the songs he loved to hear. (LL)   It is the day when he was born. Tennyson. EBVV; FHYEP

And singleness: we salute you / season of no bungling. (LL)   Variations Done for Gerald Van De Wiele. Charles Olson. NOBA; NeAP; NoAM

And sink into the marsh near them. (LL)   The Widow's Lament in Springtime. William Carlos Williams. CMoP; GaP; HAP; IMW; LiTM; MoP; NAAL-2; NOBA; NoAM; PoE; SAGP; SAmP; SoSe-8; TAP

And sink off the Lowlands low. (LL)   The Golden Vanity. *Unknown.* CH; ESPB; FaBoCh

And sits by your bed, and brings her knitting. (LL)   Good Luck and Bad ("Good luck is the gayest of all gay girls"). John Milton Hay, *after the German of* Heine. FaBoEE; NBLV; OBAL

And six I'll gie to thee. (LL)   Fair Annie. *Unknown.* CH; ESPB; OxBB

And slander everywhere attended me. Slander. "Anna Akhmatova," *Russian.* TCRP, *tr. by* Daniel Weissbort

And sleep. Nikki Giovanni. *See* Knoxville, Tennessee.

And sleepy winter, like the sleep of death. Elinor Wylie. *See* Wild Peaches.

And slow cascading of the paddle wheel. (LL)   A Simile for Her Smile. Richard Wilbur. HoPM; InPK-6; SAGP

And slowly answered Arthur from the barge. Tennyson. *Fr.* The Passing of Arthur. FHYEP; NAEL-2; OBNC *Fr.* Idylls of the King.

And smelled the clinging blood upon the stones. (LL)   A Visit to Castletown House. Michael Hartnett. BiHa; PBCIP

And smilest, knowing all is well. (LL)   And all is well, though [*or* tho'] faith and form. Tennyson. EBVVPR; OAEL-2

And smiling, entered the pit, ran laughing down its side. (LL)   Sand-Quarry with Moving Figures. Muriel Rukeyser. MoLi; NoP-4

And smite a rock. (LL)   Good Friday. Christina Rossetti. ChIV-2; PoEL-5

And snow collects in the blind eyes of statues. (LL)   For Zbigniew Herbert, Summer, 1971, Los Angeles. Larry Levis. CMAP; FYAP

And so an easier life our Cyclops drew. Cyclops, The ("And so an easier life"). Theocritus. OBVE, *tr. by* Elizabeth Barrett Browning *Fr.* Idylls.

And so, as this great sphere (now turning slow). Sonnet. Frederick Goddard Tuckerman. ColAP

And so cold. (LL)   This Is Just to Say. William Carlos Williams. ChAP; HeIP-4; HoPM; InPK-6; InPS-3; KaS; NAAL-2; NIP-4; NOBA; NTP; NoAM; NoP-4; OPOU; PBMP; PoPoPo; Poetr; TAP; TRP

And so Death took him. Yet be comforted. Publius Papinius Statius. OBCVT, *tr. by* Heathcote William Garrod *Fr.* Silvae.

And so depart into dark. Homage. Gilbert Highet. BXAP

And so, despite the whisperings. Vocation. John Robert Lee. HCP

And so Diana visited a tavern called Diana. Two Canadian Landscapes. August Kleinzahler. BAP-96

And so do I. (LL)   Weathers [*or* Weather]. Thomas Hardy. ACTP; BoTP; CH; EBEvV; FaBoCh; MoBrPo; NTP; OBMV; RB

And so enjoy her, and none miss her. (LL)   Present in Absence. John Hoskyns, *sometimes at. to* Donne. GTBS-P; MeLP; SCGP

And so—for God's sake— hock and soda-water! (LL)   Fragment: "I would to heaven that I were so much clay." Byron. CTC; NAEL-2; NOBL; OAEL-2; OxBSP

And so for nights. The Night-Blooming Cereus. Robert Earl Hayden. NoP-4

And so, here happily we meet, fair friend! Red Cotton Night-Cap Country. Robert Browning. EBVVPR

And so I both enjoy and miss her. John Hoskyns. *See* Ode: "Absence, hear[e] [thou] my protestation."

And so I cross into another world. New Heaven and Earth. D. H. Lawrence. CMoP

And so I lost my Clementine. Percy Montross. *See* Oh, My Darling Clementine.

And so I love no more. (LL) Farewell to Love. Sir John Suckling. CaPo; CavPo

And so I remain in a civil way, your servant to command, Mary. (LL) Mary the Cook-Maid's Letter to Dr. Sheridan. Jonathan Swift. OxBoLi; PeLV

And so I rest your constant friend. (LL) A Letter to the Honourable Lady Miss Margaret Cavendish Holles-Harley. Matthew Prior. NOBE; NOEC; NoAM; OBEV; OxBC; OxBChV; OxBSP

And so I speak/ in place of that primordial cry. Monique Laederach. *Fr.* Penelope. BoWoP, *tr.* by Charles Guenther

And so I went forth, exhilarated. Robyn Selman. PUP-19

And so I went forth in uniform. Robyn Selman. PUP-19

And so I went singing along. (LL) As I was going along, long, long. Mother Goose. OxNR; ReMoGo

And so I woke and knew that he was dead. (LL) The Dead Poet. Lord Alfred Bruce Douglas. ADE; GSo

And so it begins in play. War. Gregory Orfalea. IFJA

And so it comes. Train in the Desert—1916. Christopher Buckley. GM

An' so it seems it is reported. A Young Lass's Soliloquy. Rebekah Carmichael. ECWP

And so, Jesus, I see your feet again. Pietà. Rilke, *German.* GI, *tr.* by David Curzon *and* Will Alexander Washburn

And so live ever—or else swoon to death. (LL) Bright star[, would I were stedfast as thou art—]. Keats. CABP; CBLP; EnLoPo; GBL; GLoP; GSo; GTBS-P; HAP; ImPo; InPK-6; InPS-3; NAEL-2; NAWM-2; NIP-4; NoP-4; OAEL-2; PFE; PoE; Ro; SCV; Son; TFi

And so make a *City* here. (LL) The Wish. Abraham Cowley. NOBE; NOSC; NoP-4; OBEV; OxAEP-1; PBRV

And so, making clear in advance. Praise to the Rich. Marina Tsvetayeva, *Russian.* TCRP, *tr.* by Elaine Feinstein *and* Angela Livingstone

And so must I lose her whose mind. Prothalamium. Donagh MacDonagh. BIrV

And so my deare friend, for this time adue. Michael Drayton. *See* First Steps Up Parnassus.

And so night after night, God, you come to me. Israel. Yitzhak Lamdan, *Hebrew.* MHP, *tr.* by Ruth Finer Mintz

An' so ole Tho'nton bounced you. The Turncoat. Priscilla Jane Thompson. CBWP-2

And so Rome's soldier settles down. The 3.5: Carthaginian Peace. Horace. MLL, *tr.* by Helen Waddell *Fr.* Odes.

And so she makes music wherever she goes. (LL) Ride a cock-horse [or a-cock horse] to Banbury Cross, / To see a fine lady upon a white horse. Mother Goose. BoTP; FaBoBe; OxBoLi; OxNR

And so the castles of world trade. Velemir Khlebnikov. TCRP, *tr.* by Gary Kern *Fr.* Good World.

And so the day beginning. A. J. Seymour. *Fr.* For Christopher Columbus. PBCV

And so the hogs streamed out of the theater crying, only hogs, only hogs. (LL) A Performance at Hog Theater. Russell Edson. AmPA; PmAP

And so the others were the first to leave. After the Party. Luigi Fontanella, *Italian.* NeIt, *tr.* by W. S. Di Piero

And so these daughters fair of Pandarus. The Daughters of Pandarus. Homer. *Fr.* Odyssey. NAWM-1, *tr.* by Robert Fitzgerald

And so they found that the gold of the olive root had dripped in the / recesses of his heart. The Autopsy. Odysseas Elytis, *Greek.* AF, *tr.* by Edmund Keeley *and* Philip Sherrard

And so they had their way; or nearly so. (LL) See where Capella with her golden kids. Edna St. Vincent Millay. CMoP, MoAmPo

And so they kissed, and rode along their way. Chaucer. *See* The Pardoner's Tale.

And so they lived; and so they died. (LL) An Epitaph: "Interred [or Interr'd] beneath this marble stone." Matthew Prior. FaBoEE; NAEL-1; OAEL-1; OBCoV; OBSV; PoEL-3

And so they went back home again. (LL) Robin and a robin's son, A. Unknown. ACTP

And so to a chambre full solacious. Dame Music. Stephen Hawes. PoEL-1 *Fr.* The Pastime of Pleasure. OBGa

And so to bed. My heart is full of poems. Back Trouble. Emily Grosholz. RA

And so was lost in the forest. Track. Norman Finkelstein. PT *Fr.* Track.

And so we too [or two] came where the rest have come. The Question. Frank Templeton Prince. BoLoP; GTBS-P; PeSA

And so when he reached my bed. Grand-Père. Robert W. Service. NSI

And so you found that poor room dull. Appearances. Robert Browning. OxBSP

And so you said, "Well, which goddess then?" Was It Quite Like That? Suniti Namjoshi *and* Gillian Hanscombe. CPO

And Socks of sullennes excedinge sweete. (LL) Sacred muse that first[e] made love divine [or devine]. Sir John Davies. PBRV

And some blue cheese, and crackers, and some fine / Ruddy-skinned pears. (LL) A Late Aubade. Richard Wilbur. Poetr; SoSe-8

And some chose trade they fared the better. The Entertainment Industry. William Langland. NOCV *Fr.* The Vision of Piers Plowman.

And some in velvet gowns. (LL) Hark, hark, the dogs do bark. Mother Goose. LB

And something that. . . that is theirs—no longer ours. The Dispossessed. John Berryman. VGW

And sometimes I am sorry when the grass. Peace. Patrick Kavanagh. IIP

And sometimes I bring her a bottle of *Nuit d'Amour.* (LL) The Dover Bitch. Anthony Hecht. BXAP; NBLV; NIP-4; NOBA; NOBL; OBAL; PeLV; Poetr; TRP; UnPo; VGW

And sometimes in the cool night I see you are an animal. Ode for Soft Voice. Michael Cleure. NeAP

And sometimes you are afraid. A Light, Late Song for Solo Voice Without Piano. Olafs Stumbrs. CEEP

And songs that sing forever. (LL) Recollections of "Lalla Rookh." John Townsend Trowbridge. APN-2; OBAL

And soon I shall know I was talking to·my own soul. (LL) That conversation we were always on the edge. Adrienne Rich. BoWoP; NoAM

And soon may give my dust their funeral shade. (LL) Awed I behold once more. Ralph Waldo Emerson. ColAP; PAR

And sound is, is, his / conjecture. (LL) The Moon Is the Number 18. Charles Olson. CMoP; PoE

And sound will be my sleep. (LL) Sir Hugh; or, The Jew's Daughter. *Unknown.* AmFP; ESPB

And space is as solid as the bronze statue of St. Francis, the fox breaking through the lilacs, my invention of this story, the wind blowing. Joy Harjo. *See* Santa Fe.

And spit out the teeth. (LL) Watermelons. Charles Simic. OBAL; VCAP

And spit whenever we wanted to. (LL) Mrs. Trollope in America. Helen Smith Bevington. NBLV; OBAL

And Splendour borrows all her rays from Sense. Alexander Pope. *See* Timon's Villa.

And split the tomb. (LL) Advent. William Everson. NeAP; TrCP

And spoke the feeling for them, which was what they had lacked. (LL) Large Red Man Reading. Wallace Stevens. HAP; LCAP-2

And spotless Pleasure builds her sacred bower. (LL) Sonnet 65.: "The Doubt which ye misdeeme, fayre love, is vaine." Edmund Spenser. AEP

And, spread in solemn state, supinely reign. (LL) The Crown Prince of Dullness. Dryden. NOBE; OBCoV; SCV

And spread their limbs abroad. Bible, *O.T. See* Psalm 137.

And 'squires resort—to guzzle Beer. (LL) To a New England Poet. Philip Freneau. NAAL-1; NAAL-3

And stab my spirit broad awake. Robert Louis Stevenson. *See* The Celestial Surgeon.

. . . And Stalin lay down in the earth. Poet and Tsar. Grigory Mikhailovich Pozhenyan, *Russian.* TCRP, *tr.* by John Glad

And stamps his black marsh-feet on their white and marshy flesh. (LL) Swan. D. H. Lawrence. CMoP; PoE

And Stands There Sighing. Elizabeth Jane Coatsworth. KaS

And, star and system rolling past. Tennyson. *Fr.* O true and tried, so well and long. OAEL-2 *Fr.* In Memoriam A. H. H.

And started a worm farm. (LL) Nobody loses all the time. E. E. Cummings. CMoP; LiTM; NAAL-2; NBLV; NOBA; RB; TwCP

And started away in surprise. (LL) Limerick: "There was a young lady whose eyes." Edward Lear. EBEV; NOBVV

And stayed His hand! What Thomas an Buile Said in a Pub. James Stephens. CMoP; MoBrPo; MoP; NoAM; PoRA

And step for step they followed dancing. (LL) Into the street the Piper stept. Robert Browning. BoTP; OxAEP-2

And stiffen, and remain. (LL) Winter Holding off the Coast of North America. N. Scott Momaday. ColAP

And still, at sea all night, we had a sense. Samos. James Merrill. HCAP *Fr.* Scripts for the Pageant.

And still Love sang, and what he sang was this:—. (LL) Willowwood ("And now love sang: but his was such a song"). D. G. Rossetti. NAEL-2; OAEL-2

And still my feelings sprout richest. Uphold Me. Karen Gershon. LW

And still no stronger. Swathed in rugs he lingered. A Day in August. Frank Ormsby. IIP; PBCIP; PNI

And still nothing happens. I am not arrested. Entry in an Unknown Hand. Franz Wright. CMAP; NAmP90

And still our horses rustle like the rain. (LL) The Youth Dreams. Rilke, *German.* AWP; TrJP, *tr. by* Ludwig Lewisohn

And still the sun rosies the fronts of houses. Evening of the Whirlwind. Amir Gilbo'a, *Hebrew.* MHP, *tr. by* Ruth Finer Mintz

And still they come and go: and this is all I know. Picture-Show. Siegfried Sassoon. CMoP; NSI

And still, this is the God Hermes, sitting by my hearth. (LL) Maximus. D. H. Lawrence. BLT; TOF

And stood in his grandson's shape. James Dickey. *See* Hunting Civil War Relics at Nimblewill Creek.

And straight he was aware. Hylas and the Water Nymphs. Theocritus, *Greek.* OBCVT, *tr. by* Leigh Hunt

And straight I callèd unto mind [*or* mynde] that it was Christmas Day[e]. (LL) The Burning Babe. Robert Southwell. CH; ESCV; FaBoCh; HAP; HeIP-4; InPS-3; NAEL-1; NOBE; NOCV; NoSiC; OAEL-1; OBCP; OBEV; OxAEP-1; PoEL-2; RB; SCGP; TFi; TOF; TRP; TrCP

And strangely happy with myself. (LL) The Bagel. David Ignatow. CoAmPo; PiM

And strangers walk over our portion. Kofi Awoonor. *See* Songs of Sorrow.

And strangle it, and with it, rhetoric. (LL) Prelude LVI: "Rimbaud and Verlaine, precious pair of poets." Conrad Potter Aiken. FaBoMo; LiTM; NoAM; TwCP

And strives to utter what it feels, in vain. (LL) To Dr. Moore, in Anser to a Poetical Epistle Written by Him in Wales. Helen Maria Williams. ECWP; WoRP

And stroked all night, with a black wing, my wings. (LL) The Black Swan. Randall Jarrell. CMoP; PoE

And strut down the streets with paint on my face. (LL) A Song in the Front Yard. Gwendolyn Brooks. NAAAL; NAAL-2; NOBA; NOxBChV; NoAM; PoBA

And studied his last chapter of Saint John. (LL) Bishop Blougram's Apology. Robert Browning. EBVVPR; OBNC; PoEL-5

And such as it is to be of these more or less I am. (LL) Song of Myself. Walt Whitman. FaBoA

And such beginnings touch their END. (LL) Paradise. George Herbert. GaP; GeHe; ImPo; NOSC; OAEL-1; SeCP

And suddenly. Anesthesia. Veronica Porumbacu, *Romanian.* CEEP, *tr. by* Dorian, Marguerite and Elliott Urdang

And suddenly, again. Of Gravity & Angels. Jane Hirshfield. DeD

And suddenly, all turns gray. Gray Moment. Momcilo Nastasijevic, *Serbo-Croatian.* HSix, *tr. by* Charles Simic

And suddenly, and all at once, the rain! (LL) Memorial Rain. Archibald MacLeish. AmPP; CMoP; MeMAP; MoAmPo; OBWP

And sues for no Compassion. (LL) Sir Walter Ralegh to the Queen. Sir Walter Ralegh. NoSiC; SiPS

And Summer mornings the mute child, rebellious. Eleven. Archibald MacLeish. HAP; MeMAP; WeW-3

And summer turns her head with its dark tangle. Ralegh's Prizes. Robert Pinsky. DiPo; VCAP

And summons read, the great consult began. (LL) Book I. Milton. FHYEP; NAEL-1; OAEL-1; OxAEP-1 *Fr.* Paradise Lost

And sunk beneath thy chain to a lamented grave. Anne Finch, Countess of Winchilsea. *See* The Spleen.

And swear no day was ever passed so ill. (LL) Timon's Villa. Alexander Pope. OBSV

And swinges the scaly horror of his folded tail. (LL) Lizards and Snakes. Anthony Hecht. FaBoMo; TwCP

And sword upon parched veldt and fields of rain-swept gorse. (LL) Courtyards in Delft. Derek Mahon. CIP-2; PBCIP; PNI

And take a lesson from this tale of the Spider and the Fly. (LL) The Spider and the Fly. Mary Howitt. OTCP; OxBChV; PWR; UV

And take a life immortal from my Verse. (LL) To the Reverend Shade of His Religious Father. Robert Herrick. CavPo; PBRV

And take my flight / For Heaven. (LL) To Music, to Becalm His Fever. Robert Herrick. BeJo; CaPo; OBEV

And take short views. (LL) Under Which Lyre, a Reactionary Tract for the Times. W. H. Auden. MoBrPo; NOBL; PeLV

And take thy Rest[!]. (LL) On This Day I Complete My Thirty-sixth Year. Byron. FHYEP; NOBRP; OAEL-2; OBWP; PoE

And take up his cold hands. (LL) The Legend. Garrett Kaoru Hongo. LoL; NAmP90; OpBo; TRP; WWSi

And take your wounds from it gladly. (LL) Ité. Ezra Pound. HAP; MoAmPo

And taking stock of this and that. (LL) Brock. Paul Muldoon. NoP-4

And taking the moon and leaving the paper dark. (LL) The Prediction. Mark Strand. LCAP-2; NoP-4; SPE; VCAP

And tangled dry. It Sounded. Larry Eigner. FTOS

And taught his gorgon destinies to sing. (LL) Luis de Camões. Roy Campbell. FaBoTw; OxAEP-2; PeSA

And tell it as I saw it on the spot. (LL) My Dream. Christina Rossetti. BrRo; VWP

And tell the ages what we are! (LL) The Children of the Night. Edwin Arlington Robinson. APN-2; OxBA

And tell thy soul their roots are left in mine. (LL) Sonnet: "Belovèd, thou hast brought me many flowers." Elizabeth Barrett Browning. EBVV; EnVR; LW; OBNC; WPE

And tell why I have chosen thee! (LL) O thy bright eyes must answer now. Emily Jane Brontë. BrRo; PEW; PoEL-5; VWP

And tells the jest without the smile. (LL) Youth and Age. Coleridge. GTBS-P; LaPo; OBEV; OBNC; PoLF

And thank him than. (LL) Pleasure It Is. William Cornish. CH; CTC

And thank our gracious laws that give such liberty. (LL) On Sir J—— S—— — Saying in a Sarcastic Manner, My Books Would Make Me Mad; an Ode. Elizabeth Thomas. CABP; ECWP

And thank you for the evening of the night on which I fell off my horse in the shadows. That was really useful. (LL) Thank You. Kenneth Koch. NeAP; PoM

And thankfully, / For joy. Edward Taylor. *See* Upon a Spider Catching a Fly.

And that drums had to be rolling, rolling, rolling. (LL) Dry Loaf. Wallace Stevens. MeMAP; NOBA; OxBA; PoRA; RaBo

And that has made all the difference. (LL) The Road Not Taken. Robert Frost. APAD; AiP; AmPP; CMoP; ChAP; EBEvV; FaBoCh; HAP; HeIP-4; ImPo; LiTM; MeMAP; MoAmPo; MoP; NAAL-2; NIP-4; NTP; NoAM; NoP-4; OxBA; PFE; PoLF; PoPoPo; Poetr; SAGP; SAmP; SoSe-8; TAP; TFi; TRP; TwCP

And that inverted Bowl they call the Sky. 72. Edward Fitzgerald. CABP

And that is flitting, doth abide and stay. (LL) Antiquitez de Rome. Joachim Du Bellay, *French.* NNPT, *tr. by* Edmund Spenser

And that is how I came to know. (LL) The Duel. Eugene Field. APN-2; CTV; FPC; FaBoBe; NOxBChV; OBAL; OBCA; PoLF; PoRA; TFi

And that is how we had an accident. (LL) The Murderer. Stevie Smith. FaBoWP; OxBSP

And that is how you die. And that is how you die. (LL) Protocols. Randall Jarrell. LCAP-2; OxBC; VGW

And that is this, and this with thee remains. (LL) Sonnet 74. Shakespeare. NAEL-1; OxAEP-1; Son

And That Is Why. . . . Magda Bartošová, *Czech and Slovak.* CEEP, *tr. by* Magda Bartošová

And that night I was / happy. (LL) When I heard at the close of the day how my name had been receiv'd with plaudits in the capitol, still it was not a happy night for me that follow'd. Walt Whitman. GLoP

And that stands all awry. (LL) Peter White will ne'er go right. Mother Goose. OxBoLi; OxNR

And that the same last eddy swallows up. (LL) The Orchard-Pit. D. G. Rossetti. EnLoPo; GLoP; NAEL-2; OAEL-2; PeVV; PoEL-5; SCV

And that thing / screams. Imamu Amiri Baraka. *See* Agony, An. As Now.

And that was all his travel's story. (LL) The Idiot Boy. Wordsworth. NOBRP; OBNV; Ro

And that was how he brought us out of town. Chaucer. *See* The Miller's [*or* Milleres] Tale.

And that was the end of the monk. (LL) Animal Fair. *Unknown.* AS; BLPA; FaBoBe; NTCP

And that water these words what can they do what can they do / prince. (LL) Elegy of Fortinbras. Zbigniew Herbert, *Polish.* FaBoPV; PoSu, *tr. by* Czeslaw Milosz; VCWP, *tr. by* Czeslaw Milosz and Peter Dale Scott

And that what is less than they must sooner or later lift off from these States. (LL) To a President. Walt Whitman. NAAL-1; NAAL-3

And that White Sustenance—/ Despair. (LL) I cannot live with You. Emily Dickinson. APN-2; AmPP; MoAmPo; NAAL-1; NAAL-3; NOBA; OxBA; PAR; PoEL-5; TRP

And that will be the best. (LL) When smoke stood up from Ludlow. A. E. Housman. MoBrPo; SCGP

And that will never be! *Unknown. See* The Twa Brothers.

And that's all that you'll be underground. (LL) God, A Poem. James Fenton. DiPo; NoAM; NoP-4; OBCoV

—And that's my earliest recollection. (LL) A Terrible Infant. Frederick Locker-Lampson. NOxBChV; OBCoV

And that's my situation, Folks—. (LL) This Form of Life Needs Sex. Allen Ginsberg. CLPP; NNaP

And that's the best cure for a little pussy cat. D'Arcy Wentworth Thompson. *See* That Little Black Cat.

And that's the end of my song. (LL) The Monkey's Wedding. *Unknown.* AS; BLPA

And that's what parents were created for. (LL) The Parent. Ogden Nash. LiLi; Spl

"And that's why He made you a cripple." (LL) Limerick: "To his club-footed child said Lord Stipple." Edward Gorey. OBCoV; PeLi

And that's why I'm going to Tilbury Town. (LL) John Evereldown. Edwin Arlington Robinson. APN-2; CMoP; ColAP; MeMAP; NCAP; OxBA

And the age ended, and the last deliverer died. W. H. Auden. *See* So an age ended, and its last deliverer died.

And the Americans put Pound in a cage. The Cage. John Berryman. PoA

And the angel of numbers. Mathematics. Hanns Cibulka, *German.* CEEP, *tr. by* Ewald Osers

And the angel, taking some pains, told. Joseph's Suspicion. Rilke, *German.* TrCP, *tr. by* J. B. Leishman

And the apple-blossom is allowed to wither on the bough. (LL) Swineherd. Eiléan Ní Chuilleanáin. BIrV; CIP-2; FaBoWP; WPOW

And the barber kept on shaving. (LL) The Owl-Critic. James Thomas Fields. BLPA; OBAL

And the Beatles' first LP. (LL) Annus Mirabilis. Philip Larkin. NBLV; NIP-4; NOBL; OBAL

And the best will come back to you. (LL) Life's Mirror. "Madeline Bridges." BLPA; FaBoBe; PWR; PoToHe

And the bewildered [*or* bewilder'd] chimes. (LL) The Fountain. Wordsworth. GTBS-P; OxAEP-2

And the birds, when in autumn they abandon. Open Door. Vesna Parun, *Croatian.* CEEP, *tr. by* Peter Kastmiler

And the Bishop said: "The ways of God are strange!" (LL) "They." Siegfried Sassoon. CMoP; NAEL-2; NoP-4; OBSV; OBWP

And the bitter storm augments; the wild winds wage. John Josselyn. SCAP

And the body underneath it says: *I am.* (LL) The Knight, Death, and the Devil. Randall Jarrell. GS; WeW-3

And the Bow was gone. (LL) The Rainbow. Walter De la Mare. CTV; NTP

And the buffaloes are gone. (LL) Buffalo Dusk. Carl Sandburg. ChAP; OBCA

And the bugles that do shine. (LL) A New Year Carol. *Unknown.* BoTP; CH; OBCP; OxBoLi

And the cats / wicked on the wall. Alison Fell. *See* Freeze-Frame.

And the child draws another inscrutable house. (LL) Sestina: "September rain falls on the house." Elizabeth Bishop. InPK-6; LCAP-2; NoP-4; PoE; PoPoPo; Poetr

And the Cock Begins to Crow. Richard K. Avery. AH

And the colours have all passed [*or* pass'd] away from her eyes! (LL) The Reverie of Poor Susan. Wordsworth. GTBS-P; OxBoLi

And the Communists have nothing to offer but fat cheeks and [eyeglasses and lying policemen]. Kral Majales. Allen Ginsberg. BB; PoM

And the compass / idea / being / city / interim. Compass Poem. Bill Griffiths. NBrP

And the condemned man ate a hearty meal. The Runner. Louis Simpson. AF

And the congregation telleth out their praise. (LL) Our Fathers. Bible, Apocrypha. OBVE; TrJP

And the crash of loud lyres. (LL) Song of the Clouds. Aristophanes. OBCVT, *tr. by* Oscar Wilde

A*nd* the crew of the captain's gig! (LL) The Yarn of the *Nancy Bell.* Sir William Schwenck Gilbert. BLPA; CABP; EBEvV; EBNV; FaBoBe; FaBoCh; HoPM; NOBL; TFi; UV

An' the Crucified maun bleed. (LL) The Innumerable Christ. "Hugh MacDiarmid." EBEV; OxAEP-2; OxBS

And the Cycles wheel! (LL) Called Back. Emily Dickinson. AmPP; MoAmPo; NOBA; NOCV

And the dark green of grass. A lake. (LL) Storm. Agnes Nemes Nagy, *Hungarian.* CEEP, *tr. by* Laura Schiff

An' the dawn comes up like thunder outer China 'crost the Bay! (LL) Mandalay. Rudyard Kipling. EBEvV; MoBrPo; NOBE; OxAEP-2; PBMP

And the day it's well return'd again. (LL) The Fire of Frendraught. *Unknown.* ESPB; OxBB

And the days are not full enough. Ezra Pound. RB; Spl

And the dead begin from their dark to sing in my sleep. (LL) Journey to the Interior. Theodore Roethke. LCAP-2; NYBP; TRP; VGW

And the dead nations never rise again. (LL) The Jewish Cemetery at Newport. Henry Wadsworth Longfellow. APN-1; AmPP; ChIV-1; ColAP; FaBoA; HAP; HeIP-4; HoPM; MeMAP; NCAP; NOBA; NoP-4; OxBA; PAR; PoPoPo; TAP

And the deep river ran on. (LL) As I walked out one evening. W. H. Auden. CBNP; HeIP-4; InPK-6; LiTM; MoBrPo; NOBE; NoAM; NoP-4; OAEL-2; OxAEP-2; PBMP; PoPoPo; RB; TwCP; UnPo

And the dish ran away with the spoon. (LL) High Diddle Diddle. Mother Goose. CBNP; FaBoBe; HoPM; LB; OxBoLi; OxNR; ReMoGo

And the drake flew away with a quack, quack, quack. Mother Goose. *See* Sam, The Sportsman.

And the drowned and the shipwrecked have happy graves. (LL) Dirge: "We do lie beneath the grass." Thomas Lovell Beddoes. NOBE; NOBVV; OBNC

And the dumb shall speak. (LL) When the Dumb Speak. Robert Bly. CAPP-1; NOBA

And the Earth grow young again. (LL) Lines Written among the Euganean Hills. Shelley. GTBS-P; PoEL-4; Ro

And the Earth Rebelled. Yuri Suhl, *Yiddish.* TrJP, *tr. by* Max Rosenfeld

And "the earth under our feet." At Kenneth Burke's Place. William Carlos Williams. NOBA

And the euphoria. December 1974: a Lament. Abdur-Rahman Slade Hopkinson. PBCV

And the fall to doom a long way. (LL) Should the wide world roll away. Stephen Crane. APN-2; AmPP

And the fire and the rose are one. (LL) Little Gidding. T. S. Eliot. CABP; FaBoMo; FaBoPV; FaBoTw; GTBS-P; MoP; NAEL-2; NAWM-2; NOBA; NOBE; NoAM; OAEL-2; OxAEP-2; OxBTC; PeECV; TAP; TFi

And the first grey of morning filled the east. Sohrab and Rustum. Matthew Arnold. EBNV; OBNV

And the flower weeps. Passion Flower. Christopher Okigbo. PBMAP *Fr.* Heavensgate (1961).

And the foundering shriek of the gale. (LL) Wild Iron. Allen Curnow. NTP; RB

And the fresh-severed head of it, my head. (LL) The Show. Wilfred Owen. ImPo; LiTM; MoBrPo; NSI; OBWVE; OxBTC; PeFWW

And the fret lies on me. (LL) The Lamentation of the Old Pensioner. W. B. Yeats. HAP; InPK-6; NoAM; TRP; WeW-3

And the general view. (LL) Lady "Rogue" Singleton. Stevie Smith. FaBoWP; OPOU; OxBSP

And the girls as sweet as candy. (LL) My Pretty [Little] Pink. *Unknown.* ACTP; AS; AmFP

And the gods shook, they knew not why. (LL) Uriel. Ralph Waldo Emerson. APN-1; NAAL-1; NAAL-3; NOBA; OxBA; PAR

And the good that I can do. (LL) What I Live For. George Linnaeus Banks. BLPA; FaBoBe; PWR; PoToHe

And the graduates can't stand the college-trained staff. Lucky Eugene. Michael Foley. PNI

And the green grass growing over me. (LL) The King's Dochter Lady Jean. *Unknown.* AmFP; ESPB

And the green grass growing over me! *Unknown. See* Waly, Waly [Love Be Bonny].

And the green leaves they grow rarely. (LL) The Cruel Mother. *Unknown.* AmFP; ESPB; InPK-6; OxBB

And the ground spinning beneath us / goes on talking. (LL) For Alva Benson, and for Those Who Have Learned to Speak. Joy Harjo. UnSA

And the ground spoke when she was born. For Alva Benson, and for Those Who Have Learned to Speak. Joy Harjo. HATNAP; UnSA

And the Haggards Ride no more. (LL) To R. K. James Kenneth Stephen. BXAP; FaBoEE; NBLV; NOBL; PeLV; UV

And the harbor's eyes. (LL) Lost. Carl Sandburg. AmPP; CMoP

And the hill of Babylon. (LL) The Burglar of Babylon. Elizabeth Bishop. InPS-3; NYBP; RB

And the hills of Ise. (LL) The Snow Party. Derek Mahon. CIP-2; FaBoPV; OxBC; PBCIP; PNI

And the hoarse nation croaked, "God save King Log!" Alexander Pope. *See* To Dr. Jonathan Swift.

AND THE HORN may now paw the air howling goodbye. . . . Elegy for Alto. Christopher Okigbo. HBAPE; VCWP

And the houses, Egypt, the great houses, had an end. (LL) The Icehouse in Summer. Howard Nemerov. MoP; NoAM

And the hunter home from the hill. (LL) Requiem: "Under the wide and starry sky." Robert Louis Stevenson. APAD; EBEvV; EBVV; FaPoR; MoBrPo; NBLV; NOBE; NOBVV; NTP; OBEV; OBNC; PoLF; PoRA; SAGP; SCGP; TFi

And the king o' England's brither. (LL) The Knight and Shepherd's Daughter. *Unknown.* ESPB; OxBB

And the knob turns. (LL) Meditations in an Emergency. Frank O'Hara. PmAP; TAP; VCAP

And the lake was a dark spot. A Night Without Stars. Nancy Eimers. BAP-96

And the last beam of hope was almost gone. (LL) On Hearing of the Intention of a Gentleman to Purchase the Poet's Freedom. George Moses Horton. AAP; APN-1; NAAAL; PAR

And the last day being come, Man stood alone. Trumbull Stickney. APN-2; NoP-4

And the leaves of the Judgement / Book unfold! (LL) Bedouin Song. Bayard Taylor. APN-2; FaBoBe

And the light, a wakened heyday of air. November Sunday Morning. Alvin Feinman. CoAP

And the lightning laughs at the clouds. The Lightning. Judah Al-Harizi, *Hebrew.* BLT, *tr. by* T. Carmi

And the lily whispers, "I wait." Tennyson. *See* Song: "Come into the garden, Maud."

And the little ones picked the bones, O! *Unknown. See* A Visit from Mr. Fox.

And the living were made of cardboard. (LL) From 115. Ezra Pound. APSN; FaBoMo

And the long stem of connection. (LL) Williams: An Essay. Denise Levertov. InPS-3; PmAP

And the looking-glass in her hands! (LL) A Sea-Song from the Shore. James Whitcomb Riley. FPC

And the Lord discomfited Sisera, and all his chariots, and all his host. Bible, *O.T.* OxBoV *Fr.* Judges.

And the Lord God planted a garden eastward in Eden. Bible, *O.T.* OAEL-1 *Fr.* Genesis.

And the Lord God planted a garden eastward in Eden. Genesis. Bible, *O.T.* OBGa *Fr.* Genesis.

And the love between them kept them warm. (LL) Human Affection. Stevie Smith. LiLi; NALW

And the love, whatever it was, an infection. (LL) Wanting to Die. Anne Sexton. CoAmPo; ColAP; MoP; NoAM; TAP; TRP; VCAP

And the luck of our husbands and lovers, who keep free women. (LL) Two. Carolyn Kizer. FFC

And the luckier lot betide you. (LL) The Faery Beam upon You. Ben Jonson. BeJo; EBEV; FaBoCh; OxBSP

And the message of the yew tree is blackness—blackness and silence. (LL) The Moon and the Yew Tree. Sylvia Plath. CoAP; FaBoMo; FaBoWP; NYBP; VGW; WPE; WPOW

And the midnight message of Paul / Revere. (LL) Paul Revere's Ride (The Landlord's Tale). Henry Wadsworth Longfellow. APN-1; AiP; BLPA; CA; CTV; EBEvV; EBNV; FaBoBe; FaBoTw; FaPoR; ImGa; OBAL; OBCA; OBNV; PWR; TFi

And the mighty Twins? (LL) Leda and the Swan. Oliver St. John Gogarty. PFE

And the mist: and the rain in the west: and the wind steady. The Omelet of A MacLeish. Edmund Wilson. NYBP

And the mist rising from the water has hidden the hills. (LL) Fisherman. Ou-yang Hsiu, *Chinese.* BLT; OHPC, *tr.* by Kenneth Rexroth

And the mole crept along the garden. Terraces of Rain. David St. John. NAmP90

And the mome raths outgrabe. (LL) Jabberwocky. "Lewis Carroll." APAD; CABP; CBNP; CTV; ChAP; ClHu; EBEV; EBEvV; EBVV; FPC; FaBoBe; HeIP-4; HoPM; ImPo; InPK-6; InPS-3; NAEL-2; NBLV; NOBE; NOBL; NOBVV; NOxBChV; NTCP; NoAM; NoP-4; OAEL-2; OBSP; OxAEP-2; OxBChV; PFE; PeLV; PeVV; PoRA; Poetr; RB; SAGP; TFi; TRP; TTTS; UV

And the moss on the shore burning red. (LL) In the Home of the Scholar Wu Su-chiang. Wu Tsao, *Chinese.* BoWoP; WPOW, *tr.* by Kenneth Rexroth *and* Ling Chung

And the music[k] shall be praise. (LL) Doomsday. George Herbert. GeHe; SeCP

And the need of a world of men for me. (LL) Parting at Morning. Robert Browning. AWP; CABP; EBEvV; EnVR; HeIP-4; ImPo; InPS-3; NAEL-2; NOBE; OBEV; OBNC; OxBSP; PFE; SAGP; SCGP; SoSe-8; TFi; UnPo

And the new sun rose bringing the new year. (LL) The Passing of Arthur. Tennyson. FHYEP; NAEL-2; OBNC

And the news inhuman. Wislawa Szymborska. *See* View with a Grain of Sand.

And the North Sea is redly reeking! (LL) North Sea. Jeffery Day. NSI; PoWW

And the notion I cannot endure! (LL) The Baker's Tale. "Lewis Carroll." EBEV; NAEL-2; OxAEP-2

And the old river rolls on, slowly to the gulf. (LL) Foreclosure. Sterling Brown. PoBA

And the Old Women Gathered. Mari E. Evans. BlSi; PoBA

And the ones that got tough. The Inheritors. William Peskett. PNI

And the only windows were the windows they drew. (LL) Ghetto. Michael Longley. NoP-4; PNI

And the other He clapped across the moon. (LL) I Vision God [standing]. *Unknown.* NAAAL

And the pain you are causing to me? (LL) Red River Valley. *Unknown.* AS; FaBoBe

And the past. (LL) So you have swept me back. Hilda Doolittle. NALW; VGW

And the pig got up and slowly walked away. (LL) Judged by the Company One Keeps. *Unknown.* BLPA; NBLV

And the pig got up and slowly walked away. (LL) The Pig. *Unknown.* FaBoEE; OBCoV

And the pink's in us. (LL) After Reading *Mickey in the Night Kitchen* for the Third Time Before Bed. Rita Dove. LoL; NMM-2

And the place of their waiting a long burrow. David Jones. FaBoMo *Fr.* In Parenthesis.

And the place was water. Paean to Place. Lorine Niedecker. APSN

And the point in the spectrum. Hilda Doolittle. NALW *Fr.* Tribute to the Angels.

And the poor stars. At the Poorhouse. Federico García Lorca. PFTM

And the poor, when they're old, have little of peace! (LL) To the Four Courts, Please. James Stephens. BIrV; MoBrPo; UnPo

"And the pump has frozen tonight." (LL) Star-Talk. Robert Graves. MoBrPo; OxBTC

And the quiet of love in her feet. (LL) The Cap and Bells. W. B. Yeats. MoBrPo; NoAM; RB

And the rain will continue. (LL) Monsoon Girl. Harry Clifton. BiHa; PBCIP

And the reconstruction of the mind. (LL) Planetarium. Adrienne Rich. FaBoWP; HCAP; MoP; NAAL-2; NALW; NIP-4; NOBA; NoAM; Poetr; VCAP

And the red glare on Skiddaw rouse the burghers of Carlisle. (LL) The Armada. Thomas Babington Macaulay. FaBoCh; FaPoR

"And the rich He hath sent empty away". (LL) Our Lady. Mary Elizabeth Coleridge. OBEV; OBMV; WPE

And the right one with its white foot. (LL) The Truth Is. Linda Hogan. LTA; NMM-2

And the roads deep in snow? (LL) First Death in Nova Scotia. Elizabeth Bishop. CoAP; FaBoWP; LCAP-2; NOBA; NYBP

And the salt ocean rolled englob'd. (LL) The Book of Urizen [*or* First Book of Urizen]. William Blake. NOBRP

And the Same Words. David Ignatow. NNaP

And the satyrs shall dance, and the bitterns shall cry! (LL) Babylon. Tennyson. ChIV-1; KSG

And the sawbones will say 'Old One-Finger's dead'. (LL) Hallelujah, I'm a Bum. *Unknown.* AS

And the Scream. Stephen Berg. NAmP90

And the sea where it goes. (LL) The Buried Life. Matthew Arnold. CBLP; EnVR; FHYEP; NAEL-2; OAEL-2

And the secret names. I Learned That Her Name Was Proverb. Denise Levertov. CrSp

And the Seventh Dream Is the Dream of Isis. David Gascoyne. SPE

And the shadow of mountains will not fall on your heart. (LL) Water-Lilies. Sara Teasdale. NMM-2

And the shocked father tear for tear return. (LL) On the Death of an Infant of Five Days Old. Elizabeth Boyd. ECWP

And the short quick quench of the sea. (LL) The Raid. William Everson. MoP; NoAM

And the silence off on the hills might be an echo. "Prodigal Son," The. W. S. Merwin. GI *Fr.* "Prodigal Son," The.

And the skies are not cloudy all day. (LL) A Home on the Range. *Unknown, sometimes att. to* Brewster Higley. APN-2; FaBoBe

And the soldier of time lies calm beneath that stroke. (LL) The Soldier's Wound. Wallace Stevens. CMoP; NOBA

And the soldiers with their guns. (LL) Carrickfergus. Louis MacNeice. NAEL-2; NOIV; NoAM; PNI

And the soul creeps out of the tree. (LL) All Hallows. Louise Glück. AmPA; HCAP; PoPoPo

And the spinners backward go. (LL) The Ropewalk. Henry Wadsworth Longfellow. MeMAP; NCAP

And the spring wind blows each of them into my hands. (LL) A Lady Picking Flowers. Shen Chou, *Chinese.* ChiPo; CoBLCP, *tr.* by Jonathan Chaves

And the Squire, and Lady Susan, murmur mildly to me now. (LL) Friends Beyond. Thomas Hardy. EBVV; FaBoVe; GTBS-P; NOBVV; OBEV

And the stars going round in my / head. (LL) Escape at Bedtime. Robert Louis Stevenson. CTV; OTCP

And the startled blood may stop. Isaac Rosenberg. *See* Dead Man's Dump.

And the storm reestablished itself. Morning Jitters. John Ashbery. FTOS

And the strutting fern lay seeds on the black sill. (LL) After the funeral, mule praises, brays. Dylan Thomas. CMoP; FaBoMo; ImPo; NAEL-2; NoP-4; OAEL-2; OBWVE; OxAEP-2

And the style of your prose growing limper and limper. (LL) Academic. Theodore Roethke. FaBoEE; OBAL

And the sun rose dripping, a bucketful of gold. Edna St. Vincent Millay. *See* Recuerdo.

And the sweet name to my mouth. (LL) Italia, Io Ti Saluto! Christina Rossetti. VWP; WPE

And the tall pine-trees tower above. Dorothy Wordsworth. *See* A Cottage in Grasmere Vale.

And the telephone comes to mean. Lollies Noir. Dorothy Porter. BMAP

And the things we have seen and have known and have heard of fail us. (LL) On a Dead Child. Robert Bridges. CMoP; EBEV; LiTM; NOBE; NOBVV; NoAM; OBMV; OBNC; OxAEP-2; SCGP

And the thoughts of youth are long, long thoughts. (LL) My Lost Youth. Henry Wadsworth Longfellow. APN-1; AWP; AmPP; FaBoBe; FaPoR; ImGa; MeMAP; NAAL-1; NAAL-3; NOBA; OBEV; OxBA; PAR; PoEL-5; PoLF; PoRA; TAP; TFi

And the tither a bonny brier. (LL) Fair Janet. *Unknown.* ESPB; OxBB

And the tooth that bruises. (LL) Pisces. Ronald Stuart Thomas. CABP; OxBC

And the Trains Go On. Philip Levine. GM

And the trains that go from Rouen at the ending of the day. (LL) Rouen. May Wedderburn Cannan. NAEL-2; OBWP; OxBTC

And the traveller hopes: let me be far from any. Journey to Iceland. W. H. Auden. PoA

And the tribe to show you its tongue. It has only one. Michael Palmer. *See* Fifth Prose.

And the trunk: "So sweet those words to me that I." Pier delle Vigne. Dante. HoPM, *tr. by* John Ciardi *Fr.* Inferno. NAWM-1, *tr. by* John Ciardi *Fr.* Divina Commedia.

And the Vietnamese boat-people of Portadown. (LL) Home. Frank Ormsby. PBCIP; PNI

And the voice in my dreaming ear melted away. (LL) The Soldier's Dream. Thomas Campbell. FaPoR; GTBS-P; OxAEP-2

And the voice said: Walk. Little Falls. Robert Hogg. MoCV

And the water-palnts with their graceful flat heads, all became part of him. Walt Whitman. *See* There was a child went forth every.

And the way goes on in the worn earth. Prologue. Archibald MacLeish. NoAM *Fr.* Conquistador.

And the way they feels. Ogden Nash. *See* The Eel.

And the Whiskey Boys are drunk outside Philadelphia. (LL) After the Industrial Revolution, All Things Happen at Once. Robert Bly. CoAmPo

And the whole deck put on its leaves again. (LL) The Old Ships. James Elroy Flecker. CH; MoBrPo; OBMV; PoRA

And the whole earth was of one language, and of one speech. Bible, *O.T.* NAWM-1 *Fr.* Genesis.

And the whole garden will bow. E. E. Cummings. *See* If there are any heavens my mother will (all by herself) have.

& the whole garden will bow. (LL) If there are any heavens my mother will (all by herself) have. E. E. Cummings. MeMAP; MoAmPo; NAAL-2

And the wind drove a cloud to seaward, and the sun began to /shine shine. (LL) The Revenge of Hamish. Sidney Lanier. APN-2; EBNV; NCAP; PoEL-5

And the woman calling. (LL) The Voice. Thomas Hardy. APAD; BoLoP; CBLP; CMoP; EnLoPo; GBL; GTBS-P; HAP; InPS-3; LoP; MoP; NAEL-2; NoAM; NoP-4; OAEL-2; OBNC; OxAEP-2; PoE; PoEL-5; Poetr; TFi

And the women warbled: Nothing like us ever was. (LL) Four Preludes on Playthings of the Wind. Carl Sandburg. CMoP; MoAmPo; NOBA

And the Word became flesh and dwelt among us. John 1:14; And the Word became flesh and dwelt among us. Bible, *N.T.* GI *Fr.* St. John.

And the world changed. Survival: Infantry. George Oppen. FTOS

And the World was Calm. Chris Wallace-Crabbe. BMAP

And the worst friend and enemy is but Death. (LL) Peace. Rupert Brooke. OBWP; PoA; PoFWW

And the young ones picked the bones, oh. (LL) A Visit from Mr. Fox. *Unknown.* BLPA; OxNR

And them returning on thy silver wheels. (LL) Tithonus. Tennyson. CABP; EnVR; GEA; HAP; InPS-3; NAWM-2; NOBE; NOBVV; NoP-4; OAEL-2; OBNC; PoE; PoEL-5; SCGP

And theekit it o'er wi' rashes. (LL) Bessy [*or* Bessie] Bell and Mary Gray. *Unknown.* ESPB; OxBB

And their brood perish everlastingly. (LL) The Pity of It. Thomas Hardy. CMoP; LiTM

And their Earth to Earth again. (LL) Epitaph of Pyramus and Thisbe. Abraham Cowley. EnLoPo; FaBoEE

And their experience count as mine. (LL) On an Invitation to the United States. Thomas Hardy. AWP; AiP; FaBoA

And their eyes are burning. (LL) Ballad: "O what is that sound [which so thrills the ear]." W. H. Auden. CMoP; FaBoPV; MeMAP; MoBrPo; PoE

And their judges spoke with one dialect. Tom Leonard. NBrP *Fr.* Situations Theoretical and Contemporary.

And their lives. (LL) "Negro" Hero. Gwendolyn Brooks. ColAP; RACG

And their snuff-laden breath blowing lightly over me in my first sleep. (LL) Frau Bauman, Frau Schmidt, and Frau Schwartze. Theodore Roethke. CoAP; MoP; NAAL-2; NOBA; NYBP; NoAM; TAP

And their tongues are teasing oil from whales. (LL) The Lady in Kicking Horse Reservoir. Richard Hugo. CoAP; LCAP-2; NAAL-2; NoAM; NoP-4; VCAP

And Their Winter and Night in Disguise. George Oppen. APSN; NNaP *Fr.* Some San Francisco Poems.

And their words to the end of the world, *sel., vv. 1–4.* Bible, *O.T. See* Psalm 19.

And Then. Ōkuma Nobuyuki, *Japanese.* MJT, *tr. by* Makoto Ueda

And Then. Ōshima Ryōta, *Japanese.* GaP, *tr. by* Geoffrey Bownas *and* Anthony Thwaite

And then all that has divided us will merge. Judy Chicago. CrSp

And then (and only then) did Aaron laugh. (LL) Aaron Stark. Edwin Arlington Robinson. APN-2; MeMAP; MoAmPo; NCAP; Son

And then, at least, my heart can ne'er be moved. (LL) Stanzas to the Po. Byron. OAEL-2

And then forever to be gone. (LL) The Falling Star. Sara Teasdale. ChAP; OBCA

And then he entered the city: in the old stories. The Return. Laurie Sheck. WWSi

And then he loved her very well. (LL) The Pumpkin-Eater. Mother Goose. LB; OxNR; ReMoGo

And then he would lift this finest. Out-of-the-Body Travel. Stanley Plumly. AmPA; LCAP-2

And then I arrived at the powerful green hill. (LL) Then I Saw What the Calling Was. Muriel Rukeyser. ColAP; FaBoWP

And then I pressed the shell. The Shell. James Stephens. BoTP; CH; CMoP; MoBrPo

And then I said, That's what it means. Skin Trade. Reginald Shepherd. BAP-96

And then I sat me down, and gave the rein. Sonnet. Gustav Rosenhane, *Swedish.* AWP, *tr. by* Sir Edmund Gosse

And then i see the cattle of my own town. My Dream About the Cows. Lucille Clifton. TRP

And then I start getting this feeling of exaltation. (LL) A Blessing in Disguise. John Ashbery. ColAP; PoM

And then I told about the red soil of Oklahoma. Ivar Ivask, *Estonian.* CEEP, *tr. by* Ivar Ivask

And then I tried to pass the buck. Pilate. Mervyn Morris. HCP

And then in mid-May the first morning of steady heat. Late Spring. Robert Hass. BLT

And then I've got to send my boy some money for his school. (LL) Fr. "Ten Poems Recording Things that Happened at the Year's End." Liu K'o-chuang. CoBCP, *tr. by* Watson, Burton (b. 1925)

And then meet here. (LL) His Winding-Sheet. Robert Herrick. CaPo; OBEV

And then my country spoke to me. Osip Emilevich Mandelstam. TCRP, *tr. by* Bernard Meares *Fr.* Stanzas.

And Then No More. Friedrich Rückert, *German.* BIrV; BLPA, *tr. by* James Clarence Mangan

And then one day Hershey played by the door. You Are a Jew! Delmore Schwartz. TrJP *Fr.* Genesis.

And then one or more dies. And we think of this as love. The Sequence. C. S. Lewis. LBC

And then / our lives full of streetcar clamor. Dream Orpheum Balcony. Tom Dent. BkSV

And then she died and became. Survivors. Chana Bloch. CrSp

An' then she made the lasses, O. (LL) Green grow the rashes, O; / Green grow the rashes, O; / The sweetest hours that e'er I spend. Robert Burns. AWP; CTC; ImPo; NAEL-2; OAEL-1; OxAEP-2; PBMP; PeLV; SCGP

And then start down! (LL) Afternoon on a Hill. Edna St. Vincent Millay. BoTP; ChAP; ImGa; NTCP; OBCA; OxBA; TTTS

And then, the Curtain. (LL) He Abjures Love. Thomas Hardy. CBLP; OBNC

And then the dark fell and "there has never." The Journey. Eavan Boland. BiHa

And then the knife. Song of the Hanged. Eléni Vakaló, *Modern Greek.* PBWP, *tr. by* James Damaskos

And then the lighting of the lamps. (LL) Preludes. T. S. Eliot. OPOU; PFE

And then the old inhabitants, so kind. Fishing Village. Louis Dudek. *Fr.* Provincetown. MoCV

And then the old leader of the Achaian fleet. Aeschylus. OBCVT, *tr. by* Robert Browning *Fr.* Agamemnon.

And Then the Water. Milo De Angelis, *Italian.* NeIt, *tr. by* Lawrence Venuti

And then they have their answer home. (LL) The Quip. George Herbert. GeHe; NOSC; OxAEP-1; SeCP

And then to love again. (LL) Upon Drinking in a Bowl. John Wilmot, 2d Earl of Rochester. OxAEP-1; OxBoLi

And then, we'll have that drink. (LL) An Idle Visitation. Edward Dorn. NOBA; PmAP

And then went down to the ship. Canto 1. Ezra Pound. AmPP; CMoP; ColAP; MeMAP; MoAmPo; MoP; NoAM; NoP-4; OBVE; PFTM; PoE; VGW *Fr.* Cantos.

And thEn with bronZe lance heads beaRing yet Arms. Writing through the Cantos. John Cage. PmAP

And then, without his knowing, sweet sleep descended down. The Marriage in Eden. William Williams. OBWVE, *tr. by* Lewis Saunders *and* Gwyn Jones *Fr.* A View of Christ's Kingdom.

And then you do. (LL) Like musical instruments. Tom Clark. CoAmPo; PmAP

—And then you suddenly cried, and turned away. (LL) The Hill. Rupert Brooke. SAGP

And there a clump of houses with a church. (LL) The Onset. Robert Frost. CMoP; MoAmPo; OxBA; PBMP; PFE

And there are lots of other things, too. Philippe Soupault. *See* Sporting Goods.

And there are times truly. An Underdeveloped Country. D. J. Enright. NOBL

And there, beyond the barbed wire, the view—. Natzweiler. Rutger Kopland, *Dutch.* VCWP, *tr. by* James Brockway

And there came two angels to Sodom at even. Bible, *O.T.* HoPM *Fr.* Genesis.

And there goes Miss Bell with her fusty old Nut. (LL) Long John Brown & Little Mary Bell. William Blake. ECEV; RB

"And there goes the bell for the third month." The Fight of the Year. Robert McGough. OBCP

And there he kept her very well. Mother Goose. *See* The Pumpkin-Eater.

And there I found a gray and ancient ass. Pegasus Lost. Elinor Wylie. MoAmPo

And there I found myself more truly and more strange. (LL) Tea at the Palaz of Hoon. Wallace Stevens. FaBoMo; PoA

And there I was. Not a dictionary. Northwest Airlines. Fred Chappell. HoPM

"And there is dying in an hospital." (LL) An Old Man [Travelling]. Wordsworth. OBWP; Ro

And there is nothing at all—neither fear. Natalya Gorbanevskaya, *Russian.* BoWoP, *tr. by* Daniel Weissbort

And there is nothing else. (LL) The Black Angel. Henri Coulette. CoAP; NYBP

And there is nothing hid from the / heat thereof. Bible, *O.T. See* Psalm 19.

And there shall come forth a rod out of the stem of Jesse. The Rod of Jesse. Bible, *O.T.* AWP; OBVE; TrJP *Fr.* Isaiah.

And there shall I stay the rest of my life. *Unknown. See* Starving to Death on a Government Claim.

And there she's leand her back to a thorn. The Cruel Mother. *Unknown.* ESPB

And there the island lay, the waves around. The Enchanted Island. Letitia Elizabeth Landon. CABP; NOBRP

And there the king is but as the beggar. (LL) Running to Paradise. W. B. Yeats. NTP; OxBoLi

And There Was a Great Calm. Thomas Hardy. CMoP; LiTM; OAEL-2

And there was great mourning in Israel in every place. Great Mourning. Bible, Apocrypha. TrJP *Fr.* First Maccabees.

And there were in the same country shepherds abiding in the field. Bible, *N.T.* PChr *Fr.* St. Luke.

And there were spring-faced cherubs that did sleep. The Sea of Death. *Unknown.* CH

And therefore as a stranger give it welcome. Shakespeare. *Fr.* Hamlet. NAWM-1

And there's no date set for my return. (LL) Poem in the Form of a Coffin-Puller's Song ("In the old days I had no wine to drink"). T'ao Ch'ien, *Chinese.* CoBCP, *tr. by* Burton Watson

An' there's no discharge in the war! (LL) Boots. Rudyard Kipling. BLPA; FaPoR; MoBrPo

And therfore is his evyn on Crystes owyn day. (LL) Seynt Stevyn and Herowdes. *Unknown.* ESPB; OxBoLi

And these become of him or her that peruses them now. (LL) There was a child went forth every. Walt Whitman. PAR

And these become of him or her that peruses them now. Walt Whitman. *See* Leaves of Grass (1855).

And these mountains which my eyes have seen. Seven Metal Mountains. Bible, Pseudepigrapha. TrJP *Fr.* Enoch. TrJP

And these prounounced *POOH*! (LL) Pooh! Walter De la Mare. HAP; OBCoV; PeLV

And these the last verses that I write for her. (LL) Tonight I can write the saddest lines. Pablo Neruda, *Spanish.* LoP, *tr. by* W. S. Merwin

And these / these are scavengers birds. In the Zoo. A. K. Ramanujan. VCWP

And they all lived together in a little crooked house. (LL) There was a crooked man, and he went [*or* walked] a crooked mile. Mother Goose. BoTP; CBNP; FaBoBe; LB; OxBoLi; OxNR; PeLV; ReMoGo

And they are better for her praise. (LL) My November Guest. Robert Frost. OxBA; PoLF

And they are rich and ransom all ill deeds. (LL) Sonnet 34. Shakespeare. HeIP-4; OxAEP-1

And they both lived happily ever after. After Ever Happily [*or* , The Princess and the Woodcutter]. Ian Serraillier. OBSP

And they freed their own bold men. (LL) Robin Hood Rescuing Three Squires. *Unknown.* ESPB; EnSB

And they gave me this jolly red nose. (LL) Nose, nose, jolly red nose. Francis Beaumont *and* John Fletcher. FaBoCh; OxNR

And they have said there is a man in the moon. The Man in the Moon. Margaret Stanley-Wrench. WPN *Fr.* The Newdigate Prize Poem 1937.

And they have to get it right. We just need. A Love Poem. John Ashbery. HCAP

And they still control the world, and you are not in my arms. (LL) I come home from you through the early light of spring. Adrienne Rich. BoWoP; CPO

And they stopped before that bad sculpture of a fisherman. Maximus, to Gloucester, Sunday, July 19. Charles Olson. NAAL-2; TRP *Fr.* The Maximus Poems.

And they sunk him in the Lowlands low. (LL) The Golden Vanity. *Unknown.* CH; FaBoCh

And they went to sea in a sieve. (LL) The Jumblies. Edward Lear. CABP; CBNP; CTV; EBEV; EBEvV; FaBoBe; ImPo; NAEL-2; NOxBChV; OxBChV; OxBoLi; PeLV; PeVV; PoRA; TFi; UV

And They were there in the City of Fire, enflamed. JuJu. Askia Muhammad Touré. PoBA; SeSe

And they weren't even / sisters. Audre Lorde. *See* For the Record.

And they will likewise all have places. (LL) Oh No. Robert Creeley. HeIP-4; InPK-6

And they'll all kowtow. (LL) Brush Up Your Shakespeare. Cole Porter. OBAL; OBCoV

And things that are yet to be done. Open the door! (LL) On a Night of Snow. Elizabeth Jane Coatsworth. AYFP; MoAmPo; OBCA

And think it's crazy. (LL) After Lorca. Robert Creeley. CoAmPo; InPS-3; LCAP-2; PmAP

And thinks 'em the best he has tasted this season. (LL) Emerson. James Russell Lowell. APN-1; NOBA; OxBA; PAR; TAP

And thinning sheaf of days. (LL) Bridge. A. R. Ammons. CoAP; NAAL-2

And this bright moon—whose house is it setting on? (LL) Thinking of East Mountain. Li Po, *Chinese.* CoBCP; TTTS, *tr. by* Burton Watson

And this goes down for union. (LL) A Parody. Frederick Douglass. NAAL-1; NAAL-3; NAWM-2

And This Happened. Haim Guri, *Hebrew.* IP, *tr. by* Warren Bargad *and* Stanley F. Chyet

And this happened in Prague many years ago, on a cold grey day. At the Train Station. Haim Guri, *Hebrew.* IP, *tr. by* Warren Bargad *and* Stanley F. Chyet

And this is England! June's undarkened green. This Is England. Laurence Binyon. BoTP

And this is good old Boston. A Boston Toast. John Collins Bossidy. BLPA

And this is how it begins now, my late. Yehuda Amichai. *Fr.* Achziv. IP, *tr. by* Warren Bargad *and* Stanley F. Chyet

And this is how you live: a woman, children. A Primary Ground. Adrienne Rich. NNaP

And this is law, &c. *Unknown. See* The Vicar of Bray.

And this is LOVE. (LL) To Amoret, of the Difference 'twixt Him and Other Lovers, and What True Love Is. Henry Vaughan. BeJo; FMP

And this is the fragrance, almost forgotten. Robin Morgan. CrSp *Fr.* The Network of the Imaginary Mother.

And this is the oppressor's language. (LL) The Burning of Paper instead of Children. Adrienne Rich. LCAP-2; NAAL-2; VCAP

And this is the way they ring. Ringing the Bells. Anne Sexton. CAPP-1; HCAP; PoE; SAGP; TAP; VGW

And this is where. Ian Wedde. PeNZ *Fr.* Angel.

And this our life, exempt from public haunt. Good in Everything. Shakespeare. PoToHe *Fr.* As You Like It.

And this place our forefathers made for man! The Dungeon. Coleridge. Ro

And this rest house is that the which he built. The House That Jack Built. Coleridge. CBNP *Fr.* Sonnets Attempted in the Manner of Contemporary Writers. Son

And this should be the wise man's pattern. (LL) The Scholar in the Narrow Street. Tso Ssu, *Chinese.* ChiP, *tr. by* Arthur Waley

And this was once the realm of Nature, where. America. Lucretia Davidson. ColAP

And those appear that are hateful to me and mock me. (LL) As if a phantom caress'd me. Walt Whitman. GBL; GLoP; SAmP

And those black rocks which overhung the stream. Black Rocks. Charles Hubert Sisson. DiPo

And those of sorrows yet to come. (LL) The Shrubbery. William Cowper. NOBE; OBGa

And those who are very well hung. (LL) The Aesthetic Point of View. W. H. Auden. NBLV; OBAL; OBCoV; PeLi

And thou, all they, hast all the all of me. (LL) Sonnet 31. Shakespeare. NOBE; OBEV; PoEL-2

And thou art dead, as young and fair. Stanzas. Byron. GTBS-P; PoEL-4; Ro

And thou art gone, most loved, most honored [*or* honor'd] friend! Coleridge. Washington Allston. APN-1

And thou art now no longer near! To the Parted One. Goethe, *German.* AWP, *tr.* by Christopher Pearse Cranch

And thou like Adamant draw mine iron heart. (LL) From Holy Sonnets. Donne. EBEV; GSo; MeLP; NAEL-1; NOBE; NOCV; NOSC; NoP-4; OxAEP-1; PoEL-2; SCGP; SeCP; Son

And thou shalt be my Ruling Star! (LL) To the Evening Star. Thomas Campbell. GTBS-P; OBNC

And thou shouldst smile no more. (LL) To Mary. Charles Wolfe. LBC

An thou were my ain thing. An Thou Were My Ain Thing. Allan Ramsay. OxAEP-1

And thou wert sad—yet I was not with thee. Lines on Hearing That Lady Byron Was Ill. Byron. EBEV; OxAEP-2

And thou! whose sense, whose humour, and whose rage. Inscriptio. Alexander Pope. OxBSP

And (though I am perswade) that I. Isabella Whitney. BWW *Fr.* The Manner of Her Will and What She Left to London and to All Those in It, at Her Departing. NoSic

And thought of him I love. Walt Whitman. *See* Spring.

And thought on the Lamb of God. (LL) Sheep and Lambs. Katharine Tynan. BoTP; OBEV; TIRV

And threw him down the stairs. (LL) Goosey, goosey, gander[, where *or* whither shall I wander? shall I wander?]. Mother Goose. CTAV; LB; OxNR; ReMoGo

And through that bitter agony [*or* agonie]. Donne. *Fr.* The Litanie. PoEL-2

And through the Caribbean Sea. Margaret Danner. BPo

And through the wire and home, and got our rum. (LL) The Night Patrol. Arthur Graeme West. NSI; PoFWW

And thus a monologue keeps flowing. Ivar Grunthal, *Estonian.* CEEP, *tr.* by Ivar Ivask

And thus as we were talking to and fro. The Compleynt of the Comoun Weill of Scotland. Sir David Lindsay. OxBS *Fr.* The Dreme.

And thus begins the suit of his pretence. Bible, *O.T. See* Psalm 130.

And thus declared that Arab lady. Solomon and the Witch. W. B. Yeats. ChIV-1; NoAM

And thus, I bid you, live again! (LL) On Observing a Large Red-Streak Apple. Philip Freneau. NAAL-1; NAAL-3

And thus I'll take my pilgrimage. Sir Walter Ralegh. *See* The Passionate Man[']s Pilgrimage.

And Thus in Nineveh. Ezra Pound. VGW

And thus the people every year. Attack of the Squash People. Marge Piercy. NBLV

And thus they grew like giggling fir trees. (LL) Blocks. Frank O'Hara. HCAP; LCAP-2; SPE

And thus they wandered forth, and hand in hand. Byron. EP *Fr.* Don Juan.

And thus went out this lamp of light. An Account of the Cruelty of the Papists. Benjamin Harris. SCAP

And thy illustrious zodiac[ke]. The Apostles. Donne. *Fr.* The Litanie. PoEL-2

And Thymodês also, lamenting a death unforeseen. Epitaph of a Sailor. Damagetus, *Greek.* GrAn, *tr.* by Dudley Fitts

And time to begin a new. (LL) The Secular Masque. Dryden. NAEL-1; OxAEP-1; PoE; PoEL-3; SCGP

And tint her life on Yarrow. (LL) The Braes of Yarrow. *Unknown.* ESPB; OxBB

And to begin again, the night was dark and dreary, and. Sister Water. Robert Penn Warren. MI

And to die is different from what any one supposed, and luckier. (LL) Grass. Walt Whitman. ColAP; ImPo; NoP-4; PAR; SAmP

And to do that to birds was why she came. (LL) Never Again Would Birds' Song Be The Same. Robert Frost. FYAP; HAP; InPK-6; LoP; NIP-4; NoAM; NoP-4; SoSe-8; Son; VGW

And to endurance. Ralph Waldo Emerson. *See* Illusions.

And to Her-Without-Bounds I send. Tribal Memories. Robert Duncan. APSN; NOBA *Fr.* Passages.

And to my dead heart run them in! (LL) The Celestial Surgeon. Robert Louis Stevenson. EBVV; MoBrPo; PoToHe

And to my whole is *JESU*. (LL) JESU is in my heart, his sacred name. George Herbert. GeHe; MeLP

And to possess them, Honour['] d *Margaret.* (LL) To the Lady Margaret Ley. Milton. GTBS-P; OBEV

And to Private Ball it came. David Jones. OBWVE *Fr.* In Parenthesis.

And to 'scape stormy days, I choose / An everlasting night. (LL) A Hymn[e] to Christ, at the Author's Last Going into Germany. Donne. EBEV; MeLP

And to see the city again and to see it again. Patrizia Cavalli, *Italian.* NeIt, *tr.* by Judith Baumel

And to sink by the Low-lands low. (LL) The *Golden Vanity. Unknown.* OxBoV

And to the Ile the name of him then buried in it gave. (LL) Daedalus. Ovid. CTC; OBVE, *tr.* by Arthur Golding

And to the immense, illiterate, consoling angels. (LL) Privilege of Being. Robert Hass. NAmP90; NIP-3

And to the Young Men. Merrill Moore. MoAmPo

And to those who will return. (LL) Diptych. Birago Diop, *French.* NegPo, *tr.* by Ellen Conroy Kennedy

And toll your voyage out again again. (LL) Frontispiece. May Swenson. CoAP; WPE

And tombstones rewrite names on dead men's graves. (LL) Culbin Sands. Andrew Young. GTBS-P; OxBS; OxBTC

An' Tommy ain't a bloomin' fool—you bet that Tommy sees! (LL) Tommy. Rudyard Kipling. CABP; EBEV; FaPoR; MoBrPo; NoP-4; OBWP; OxAEP-2; OxBTC; PeVV; UV

And toss it in the oven for baby and me. (LL) Pat-a-cake, pat-a-cake, baker's man. Mother Goose. LB; OxNR; ReMoGo

And, touched with love like mine, preserve my absent friend. (LL) An Ode on the Popular Superstitions of the Highlands of Scotland. William Collins. NOEC; OAEL-1; OxAEP-1

And trackless, like the Sea—of Tranquillity. (LL) Staying at Ed's Place. May Swenson. SAGP; VCAP

And treat some rescued Breton as a comrade and a guest. (LL) A Ballad for a Boy. William Johnson Cory. FaPoR; OxBChV

And tribal, intimate revenge. (LL) Punishment. Seamus Heaney. FaBoPV; InPS-3; NAEL-2; NoAM; NoP-4; OxAEP-2; PBCIP; PoPoPo; SAGP

And trod as if on the loud winds. (LL) The Nymph and Her Fawn. Andrew Marvell. BoTP; CTAV; FaBoCh

And trodden out the Mills. (LL) Brain, within its Groove, The. Emily Dickinson. NCAP; NOBA; NoAM; SAmP

And trotted home behind the lad. (LL) Recreation. Jane Taylor. OBCoV; OxBoLi; PEW; WoRP

And trouble him; then Death's his Epilogue. (LL) De Morte. Sir Henry Wotton. NOSC; OxBSP

And trouthe thee shall delivere, it is no drede. (LL) Truth. Chaucer. AWP; EnVB; NAEL-1; OAEL-1; SCGP

And Truly It Is a Most Glorious Thing. William Bradford. AH

And trumpet of your resurrection. (LL) Black Rock of Kiltearn. Andrew Young. FaBoTw; RB

And trust the unknown for the known. (LL) The Over-Heart. John Greenleaf Whittier. ChIV-2; NOCV

And Truth diffuse her Radiance from the Stage. (LL) Prologue Spoken by Mr[.] Garrick at the Opening of the Theatre in Drury Lane, 1747. Samuel Johnson. EBEV; NAEL-1; NOEC; NoP-4; OxAEP-1

And Truth reveal herself to you! (LL) An Insincere Wish Addressed to a Beggar. Mary Elizabeth Coleridge. NOBVV; PEW; VWP

And Truthe shall deliver, it is no dread. Chaucer. *See* Truth.

And *try* if we cannot feel forsaken. (LL) In Neglect. Robert Frost. OxBSP; VGW

And try to stack them in a better load. (LL) The Armful. Robert Frost. CMoP; OxBSP; PiM

An' tryin' to be good. (LL) The Favorite Slave's Story. Priscilla Jane Thompson. RACG

And turn once more our *Water* into *Wine*! (LL) Religion. Henry Vaughan. ESCV; NOCV; OAEL-1; OxAEP-1; PeECV; TOF

And turns my sad bone face to the light. (LL) On the Turning Up of Unidentified Black Female Corpses. Toi Derricotte. NAmP90; NMM-2

And Turnus than, quhar he at erth dyd ly. The Defeat of Turnus. Virgil. OBVE, *tr. by* Gawin Douglas *Fr.* The Aeneid [*or* Eneados, *Aeneis*].

And twenty-nine in each leap-year. Mother Goose. *See* Thirty days hath September.

And two blankets embroidered with smallpox. (LL) Meeting the British. Paul Muldoon. BiHa; CIP-2; FaBoPV; NoAM; NoP-4; PNI

And two I knew, an old man and a boy. Frederick Goddard Tuckerman. APN-2 *Fr.* Sonnets.

And two to bear my soul away. (LL) Before Sleeping. *Unknown.* CH; FaBoCh; NTP; OxBoLi; OxNR

And understand our wistful speech! (LL) A Caged Bird. Sarah Orne Jewett. APN-2; ColAP

And Universal Darkness buries all. (LL) Idle Pursuits. Alexander Pope. ECEV, *book* IV, *ll.* 565–604; OBSV

And Universal Darkness buries all. (LL) The Reign of Chaos. Alexander Pope. EBEV; FaBoPV; NOBE; NoP-4; SCV

And Universal Darkness buries all. (LL) Yet, yet a moment, one dim ray of light. Alexander Pope. NAEL-1; OAEL-1; PoEL-3

And universals / are not that world. Ron Welburn. NBV

And unresisted Passion storm'd the Breast. Samuel Johnson. *See* Prologue Spoken by Mr[.] Garrick at the Opening of the Theatre in Drury Lane, 1747.

And unto me no second friend. (LL) One writes, that "Other friends remain." Tennyson. EnVR; PoEL-5

And unto miserly merchant hulks converted. (LL) Good Ships. John Crowe Ransom. MeMAP; WeW-3

And upon the harp will I praise thee, O God, my God, *comprises* Psalms 42 *and* 43. Bible, *O.T. See* Psalm 42.

And "Ut Pictura Poesis" Is Her Name. John Ashbery. InPS-3; VCAP

And vanishes along the level of the roofs. (LL) Morning at the Window. T. S. Eliot. AWP; PoA

And verse is one of them—this most of all. (LL) Washing-Day. Anna Laetitia Barbauld. ECWP; PEW; WoRP

And vindicates its cause. (LL) In Love For Long. Edwin Muir. LoP

And vowed he'd steal no more. (LL) The Tarts. Mother Goose. FaBoBe; LB; OxNR; ReMoGo

And wait, and tend our agonizing seeds. (LL) From the Dark Tower. Countee Cullen. BPo; ColAP; CrDW; LiTM; NAAAL; NAAL-2; PoBA; Son

And waits an hour sometimes for such a will. (LL) Will. Ella Wheeler Wilcox. BLPA; PoToHe

And wake when it is Day! (LL) The Cottager to Her Infant, (By My Sister). Dorothy Wordsworth, *Third and fourth stanzas by* Wordsworth. CABP; CH; NTP; OxBChV; TTTS

And walk the rest of the way. (LL) The Draft Horse. Robert Frost. CMoP; HeIP-4; HoPM; PFE; PoE; SAmP; TRP

And war began next Wednesday [*or* Monday] on the Danes. (LL) Scyros. Karl Shapiro. HoPM; ImPo; LiTM

And warmth and chill of wedded life and death. (LL) Pontoosuce. Herman Melville. APN-2; NOBA

And was helped to a hansom outside. (LL) The Arrest of Oscar Wilde at the Cadogan Hotel. John Betjeman. CMoP; EBEV; MoBrPo; MoP; NoAM; NoP-4; OxBTC

And was it not a worthy sight. Song Sung by Egistus and Clytemnestra. John Pickering. NoSic *Fr.* Horestes.

And was not afraid / Mister? (LL) Music Swims Back to Me. Anne Sexton. ColAP; VCAP

And Was Not Improved. Lerone Bennett Jr. PoBA

And was the day of my delight. Tennyson. OAEL-2 *Fr.* In Memoriam A. H. H.

And wasna he a roguey. The Piper o' Dundee. *Unknown.* OxBS

And wasnt there ever a time when flies. Flies. Jack Kerouac. CLPP

And watch the moon through the clear autumn. (LL) The Jewel Stairs' Grievance. Li Po, *Chinese.* NOBA; OBVE, *tr. by* Ezra Pound

And watch the product coming up. (LL) A Garden Song. George R. Sims. NOBVV; OBCoV; OBGa

And watch thy friends' ways ever! (LL) Counsels of Sigrdrifa. *Unknown.* AWP; OBVE

And waters wide and fleet. William Blake. *See* The Tyger.

And waters wide and fleet. (LL) Song: "If thou art sleeping, maiden." Gil Vicente, *Spanish.* AWP; CTC, *tr. by* Longfellow

And Wayland's work / Is worn away. (LL) Junk. Richard Wilbur. HAP; NoP-4; WeW-3

And we all sing. (LL) Summer Words of [*or* for] a Sistuh [*or* Sister] Addict. Sonia Sanchez. BPo; BlSi; NAAAL; UnPo

And we, are birds beak to beak. Wishful Thinking Is the Master of Reality. Duoduo, *Chinese.* AF, *tr. by* Gregory Lee *and* John Cayley

And we call it wisdom. It is pain. (LL) 90 North. Randall Jarrell. CoAP; FYAP; MT; NAAL-2; NOBA; NoAM; TAP; VCAP

And we clap hands together. (LL) Green Grass. *Unknown.* BoTP; CH; OxBoLi; OxNR

And We Conquered. Rob Penny. PoBA

And we could see exactly what we'd done. (LL) Burial Detail. Andrew Hudgins. CBCWP; MT

And we cry, There dies an *Adonis!.* (LL) Song: "If any wench Venus's girdle wear." John Gay. PeLV; PoEL-3

And we fall, face forward, fighting, on the deck. (LL) Thirty Bob a Week. John Davidson. CABP; EBEV; EBVV; FaBoPV; FaBoTw; ImPo; NOBE; NOBVV; OAEL-2; OBNC; OxBS; OxBTC

And we feel / And live. Bob Kaufman. *See* War Memoir: Jazz, Don't Listen to It at Your Own Risk.

And we gave her all our money but our subway fares. (LL) Recuerdo. Edna St. Vincent Millay. ChAP; ImPo; LiTM; MeMAP; NAAL-2; NoAM; OxBA; PoA; Poetr; TAP

And we guardsmen fed to the tigers. (LL) Lament of the Frontier Guard. Li Po, *Chinese.* OBVE; OBWP; VGW, *tr. by* Ezra Pound

And we had focused back on the furniture of the air. (LL) Melodic Trains. John Ashbery. GM; NoP-4

And we kill blood. Aleksandr Trubin, *Russian.* TCRP, *tr. by* Albert C. Todd

And we live outside his garden in our tempestuous rights. (LL) In Favor of One's Time. Frank O'Hara. NeAP; PoA

And we love Art for Art's sake. Art for Art's Sake. Marc Blitzstein. TrJP *Fr.* The Cradle Will Rock.

And we missed it, lost it for ever. (LL) Youth and Art. Robert Browning. CTC; NAEL-2; NOBVV

And we own / the night. (LL) We Own the Night. Imamu Amiri Baraka. CrDW; PoBA

And we rebuild our cities, not dream of islands. (LL) Paysage Moralisé. W. H. Auden. MoBrPo; OAEL-2; UnPo

And we sing. (LL) The Chicago Picasso. Gwendolyn Brooks. NAAAL

And we take him in. (LL) Snow in the Suburbs. Thomas Hardy. CMoP; EBEvV; MoBrPo; OAEL-2; OBMV; OxBTC

"And we were black," three shades reply, "but kings." (LL) Black Majesty. Countee Cullen. PoBA; VGW

And we were speaking easily and all the light stayed low. In Judgment of the Leaf. Kenneth Patchen. CLPP; VGW

And we, who are going to live after all. Convalescence. Lynne McMahon. NAmP90

And we will lace the. God Send Easter. Lucille Clifton. CrSp

And weave but nets to catch the wind. (LL) Vanitas Vanitatum. John Webster. CH; ImPo; NOBE; NOSC; OBEV; PoEL-2; PoRA; SCGP

And weel paid shall thy cowte foal be. (LL) The Lochmaben Harper. *Unknown.* ESPB; OxBB

And weep the more because I weep in vain. (LL) Sonnet [on the Death of Mr. Richard West]. Thomas Gray. GSo; NOBE; NOEC; NoP-4; PoE; PoEL-3; Son

And weeping anarchic Aphrodite. (LL) In Memory of Sigmund Freud. W. H. Auden. HAP; NoAM; OAEL-2; OxBA

And welcom[e] thee, and wish thee long. (LL) Song: on [*or* of] May Morning. Milton. CH; PBRV

And we'll float melons on the water, dunk crimson plums. (LL) In the hottest time, when all is still and windless. *Unknown.* CoBCP, *tr. by* Watson, Burton (b. 1925)

And we'll strive to please you every day. (LL) Song: "When that I was and a little tiny boy." Shakespeare. CBNP; CH; EBEV; EBEvV; FaBoCh; ImPo; NBLV; NOBE; NoP-4; NoSic; OAEL-1; OxAEP-1; OxBoLi; PFE; PoEL-2; PoRA; SCGP; TFi

And went to bed at noon. (LL) The Last War. Kingsley Amis. OBSV; OxBC; SAGP

And went walloping, walloping, walloping home! (LL) Doggies went to the mill, The. *Unknown.* BoTP; OxNR

And were I not, as a man may say, cautious. Robert Browning. OBCoV *Fr.* The Flight of the Duchess.

And were it for thy profit, to obtain. On Change of Weathers. Francis Quarles. OxBSP

And were killed in the minds of the dead. (LL) The Unreturning Spring. Laurence Binyon. CABP; NSI

And what a charm is in the rich hot scent. Among the Firs. Eugene Lee-Hamilton. NOBVV

And what a cremation that was. Step One. Albert Mobilio. PT

And what a jaded tide will find for us / to play with when this game begins to pall. (LL) Epiderm. Michael Dransfield. BMAP

And what a time a reel of tape can play! (LL) I Was Fair Beat. Robert Garioch. OBCoV; OxBTC

And What About the Children. Audre Lorde. PoBA

And what are you that, wanting you. The Philosopher. Edna St. Vincent Millay. CMoP

And what concern[e]s it not, shalt straight forget. (LL) The Soules Ignorance in This Life and Knowledge in the Next. Donne. NOSC, *ll.* 281–300; OAEL-1

And What Do You Get. Heather McHugh. BAP-95

And what I have learned. Duncan Spoke of a Process. Imamu Amiri Baraka. CAPP-1

And what I was is no affair of yours. (LL) In Peterborough Churchyard. Paulus Silentiarius, *Greek.* FaBoEE; NOBL

And what if after so many words. César Vallejo, *Spanish.* RaBo, *tr. by* Douglas Lawder *and* Robert Bly

And what if all Nature ratify this merciless outrage? Robert Bridges. *Fr.* The Power of Ridicule. NOBE

And what if God had been watching, when my mother. What If God. Sharon Olds. NMM-2

And what if Heraclitus and Parmenides. Lava. Adam Zagajewski. PuP-16

And what if now I told you this, let's say. At a Reading. J. D. McClatchy. DiPo

And what if someone comes and says: Here's the harp. Play for me on this harp. I've Come to the Simplest Words. Amir Gilbo'a, *Hebrew*. IP, *tr. by* Warren Bargad *and* Stanley F. Chyet

And what is left for the others? What Is Left? István Vas, *Hungarian*. CEEP, *tr. by* Emery E. George

And what is life? A Primer for Schoolchildren. Richard Weber. CIP-2

And what is love? It is a doll dress'd [*or* dressed] up. Modern Love. Keats. CBLP; OBNC; SCGP

And what is love? Misunderstanding, pain. Epigram. James Vincent Cunningham. CRP; HAP; HoPM; PoA

And what is reason? and what is love? and what is life? Walt Whitman. *See* The Torch.

And what is so rare as a day in June? What [*or* And what] Is So Rare as a Day in June? James Russell Lowell. CTV *Fr.* The Vision of Sir Launfal.

And what miraculous escapes! (LL) Houses. Donald Justice. PoA; WeT

And what of afterlife? I comfort. Then. Diane Glancy. LoHo

And What of Me? Liz Sohappy Bahe. CDW

And what Oh what would the neighbours say! (LL) My Brother Bert. Ted Hughes. FuFo

And What Shall You Say? Joseph Cotter, Sr.. PoBA

And what this is all about. (LL) Companions. Charles Stuart Calverley. NOBL; PeLV

And what thou art may never be destroyed. (LL) No coward soul is mine. Emily Jane Brontë. APAD; BWW; BrRo; CABP; EBEvV; EBVV; EnVR; NALW; NoP-4; OBNC; OxAEP-2; PEW; PoEL-5; PoPoPo; TRP; TrCP; VWP; WPoS

And what Timotheus was, is DRYDEN now. (LL) An Essay on Criticism. Alexander Pope. InPK-6, *ll.* 362–383

And what Timotheus was, is DRYDEN now. (LL) Poetical Numbers. Alexander Pope. NIP-4, *ll.* 337–383; ECEV; FHYEP; Poetr

And what was the big room he walked in? Before a Fall. Geoffrey Grigson. SPE

And what you best like. (LL) Love's Clock. Sir John Suckling. CaPo; NOSC; PoEL-3

And whelm'd in deeper gulphs than he. (LL) The Castaway. William Cowper. NAEL-1; NOBE; NOBRP; NOEC; OAEL-1; OxBoS; PoE; PoEL-3; TRP

And, when God sends a cheerful hour, refrains. (LL) To Cyriack Skinner. Milton. NoP-4

And when he came to the other side. Matthew 8:28–34; And when he came to the other side. Richard Wilbur. GI *Fr.* St. Matthew.

And when he cried the little children died in the streets. (LL) Epitaph on a Tyrant. W. H. Auden. AF; HeIP-4; MeMAP; NoAM; OxBSP; OxBoV; RB

And when he returned to his birthplace he found sea. Odysseus. Haim Guri, *Hebrew*. MHP, *tr. by* Ruth Finer Mintz

And when i die. Last Instructions. Garth Tate. ISC

And when I go up as a pilgrim in winter, to recover. 1980. Abraham Sutskever, *Yiddish*. HP, *tr. by* Cynthia Ozick *Fr.* Poems from a Diary.

And When I Lamented. Heinrich Heine. TrJP, *tr. by* Emma Lazarus *Fr.* Homeward Bound.

And when I lie between the standing walls. What She Didn't Say. Ory Bernstein, *Hebrew*. IP, *tr. by* Warren Bargad *and* Stanley F. Chyet

And when I pay death's duty. Poem. Robin Blaser. NeAP

And when I rose, I found myself in prayer. (LL) To Wordsworth. Coleridge. EPCY; FHYEP; NAEL-2; OAEL-2

And when I say eyes right I want to hear. Weapons Training. Bruce Dawe. OBCoV

And when I went to the woods. King Solomon's Magnetic Quiz. John Wieners. FTOS

And when, in the city in which I love you. The City in Which I Love You. Li-Young Lee. ChIV-1

And when it does, we lie back in our watery hair and rock. (LL) Spider Crystal Ascension. Charles Wright. HCAP; LCAP-2; VCAP

And when Jesus had crossed again in the boat to the other side. Mark 5:21–43; And when Jesus had crossed. Czeslaw Milosz. GI *Fr.* St. Mark.

And when like her, oh Sákí, you shall pass. Omar Khayyám. TRP *Fr.* The Rubáiyát of Omar Khayyám [of Naishápúr]. AWP; EBVV; FaBoBe; FaPoR; HAP; NAEL-2; PoEL-5

And when my legs had already grown numb. Yevgeny Mikhailovich Vinokurov, *Russian*. TCRP, *tr. by* Daniel Weissbort

And when our ears fill up with sand. Crossing the Desert in a Pram. Selima Hill. NBrP

And when our streets are green again. Song. John McGrath. APAD

And when she wakes she will not think it long. (LL) Rest. Christina Rossetti. GSo; NOBE; OAEL-2; OBEV; OBNC

And when she was bad, she was horrid. (LL) There Was a Little Girl. Mother Goose, *st.* 1; *sts.* 2 *and* 3, *Unknown, at. to* Longfellow. BLPA; FaBoCh; OxBChV; OxNR; ReMoGo

And when suddenly it hit me. Just Looking, Thank You. Leonard Nathan. EC2

And when that ballad lady went. A Road in Kentucky. Robert Earl Hayden. ColAP

And when / the cold white ness. Query. Ebon Dooley. PoBA

And When the Green Man Comes. John Haines. CoAmPo

And when the hectic. John Ashbery. BAP-93 *Fr.* Baked Alaska. BAP-93

And when the star that comes at the set of the sun. The Mousetrap. Callimachus, *Greek*. HePo, *tr. by* Barbara Hughes Fowler

And when the sun puts out his lamp. To the Mountains. Henry David Thoreau. PoEL-4

And when the winter wind rushed straight into my heart. Untitled. Georgi Borisov, *Bulgarian*. CEEP, *tr. by* Lisa Sapinkopf *and* Georgi Belev

And when they asked her what she wanted to be. Vocation. Judith Herzberg, *Dutch*. WPOW, *tr. by* Manfred Wolf

And when they came together in one place. Battle. Homer, *Greek*. OBCVT, *tr. by* Alfred Tennyson, 1st Baron Tennyson; OBVE, *tr. by* Tennyson *Fr.* The Iliad.

And when they drew near to Jerusalem. Matthew 21:1–11. Boris Pasternak. GI *Fr.* St. Matthew.

And when they had sung a hymn, they went out to the Mount of Olives. Mark 14:26–42; And when they had sung. Boris Pasternak. GI *Fr.* St. Mark.

And when we die at last. Heaven and Hell. Nalungiaq, *Eskimo*. STP, *tr. by* Edward Field

And when you have forgotten the bright bedclothes [on a]. When You Have Forgotten Sunday: The Love Story. Gwendolyn Brooks. BPo; NAAAL; WPOW

And when you showed me Brooklyn Bridge. Hymn. Jack Kerouac. CLPP

And when you sleep you remind me of the dead. (LL) The Dug-Out. Siegfried Sassoon. CH; MoBrPo; NSI; PoFWW

And where. Sunday Brunch. Reuben Jackson. ISC

And where am I from? From an anecdote. Natalya Gorbanevskaya, *Russian*. TCRP, *tr. by* Albert C. Todd

And Where Do You Stand on the National Question. Tom Paulin. CIP-2

And where is sleep? (LL) Where is my ruined life, and where the fame. Hafiz. AWP; TAL, *tr. by* Gertrude Lowthian Bell

And where thou mad'st an end, there I'le begin. (LL) The Lamp[e]. Henry Vaughan. ChIV-2; ESCV

And while above Tsarskoye Selo. The Lone Performer. Velemir Khlebnikov, *Russian*. TCRP, *tr. by* Gary Kern

An' while I went 'ithin a train. William Barnes. EnVR *Fr.* The Railroad.

And while it lasts, we cannot wholly end. (LL) Palladium. Matthew Arnold. GTBS-P; OAEL-2; OBNC

And whilst [*or* whil'st] this universal choir [*or* universall Quire]. Donne. *Fr.* The Litanie. PoEL-2

And whip him down the street, but gently, home. (LL) The Poet at Seven. Donald Justice. MT; WeT; WeW-3

And whipped them all soundly and sent them to bed. (LL) There was an old woman who lived in a shoe. Mother Goose. LB

And whistle and I'll come soon. (LL) Eppie Morrie. *Unknown*. ESPB; OxBB

And white owl's feather! (LL) The Fairies. William Allingham. CH; FPC; FaBoCh; NOBE; NOBVV; NOxBChV; OBEV; OTCP; OxBChV; TFi

And who but Lady Greensleeves. (LL) Lady Greensleeves. *Unknown*. FaBoCh; GBL; PoEL-2; TTTS

And who has seen the moon, who has not seen. Moonrise. D. H. Lawrence. LiTM; PoA

And who is He that, sculptured in huge stone. The "Moses" of Michael Angelo. Robert Browning. GS

And who now will wake the dead. Repentance: The Devil's Blossom. Sigitas Geda, *Lithuanian*. CEEP, *tr. by* Jonas Zdanys

And who shall separate the dust. Common Dust. Georgia Douglas Johnson. PoBA; TTY

And whoever forces himself to love anybody. Retort to Jesus. D. H. Lawrence. PeECV

And whoever's asleep let him sleep more soundly. (LL) Dialectics. Edvard Kocbek, *Slovenian*. PoSu, *tr. by* Michael Scammell *and* Veno Taufer; CEEP, *tr. by* Veno Taufer *and* Michael Scammell

And whom I love, I love indeed. (LL) The Pains of Sleep. Coleridge. FHYEP; NAEL-2; OBNC; Ro

And why. Anacreon, *Greek*. InMo, *tr. by* Sam Hamill

And why an honoured [*or* honour'd] ragged shirt, that shows. To a Lady with Child that Asked [*or* Ask'd] an Old Shirt. Richard Lovelace. NOSC

And why are you pointing upwards? (LL) The Black Finger. Angelina Weld Grimké. NAAAL

And why do I feel no shame kicking the loose gravel home? (LL) White Center. Richard Hugo. FiLi; NAAL-2

And why does Gratt teach English? Why, because. Professor Gratt. Donald Hall. OBAL

An' why not every man? (LL) Didn't my Lord Deliver Daniel. *Unknown.* NAAAL

An' why not every man? *Unknown. See* Didn't my Lord Deliver Daniel.

And why on me? why should the envious world. Thomas Dekker, John Ford, *and* William Rowley. OxBSn *Fr.* The Witch of Edmonton.

And why this vault and tomb? Alike we must. Wiston Vault. Katherine Philips. NOSC

And why to me this, thou lame lord of fire. An Execration upon Vulcan. Ben Jonson. BeJo; SeCP

And wild for to hold, though I seem tame. *Unknown. See* Tom o'Bedlam.

And will be to the day that ye dee. (LL) Lizie Lindsay. *Unknown.* ESPB; OxBB

And will emigrate / to the sky. Dan Pagis. *See* Draft of a Reparations Agreement.

And will he [*or* a'] not come again? Ophelia's Songs, 2 ("And will he not come again"). Shakespeare. ImPo; NoSic; PoEL-2 *Fr.* Hamlet. NAWM-1

And will not scare. (LL) Skunk Hour. Robert Lowell. AmPP; CMoP; CoAP; CoAmPo; ColAP; FaBoMo; HAP; HCAP; HeIP-4; InPK-6; InPS-3; LCAP-2; MoAmPo; MoP; NAAL-2; NIP-4; NOBA; NoAM; NoP-4; OxBC; PoE; PoPoPo; Poetr; SAGP; SCV; TAP; TFi; TRP; VCAP

And will they always be so tender, her. Swift Love, Sweet Motor. Hildegarde Flanner. WPE

And will they cast the altars down. In Portugal, 1912. Alice Thompson Meynell. NOCV

And will, while such a lane remain. (LL) Beyond the Last Lamp. Thomas Hardy. NOBE; OBNC

"And will you cut a stone for him." The Stone. Wilfrid Wilson Gibson. MoBrPo

And willing Nations knew their Lawful Lord. (LL) Absalom and Achitophel, Pt. I. Dryden. EBEvV; FHYEP; FaBoPV; HAP; NOSC; OAEL-1; PoE

And willing Nations knew their Lawful Lord. (LL) In pious times ere [*or* e'r] priest-craft did begin. Dryden. EBEvV; FHYEP; FaBoPV; HAP; NOSC; OAEL-1; PoE

And willing to oblige. (LL) Sweet Rain. Tony Hoagland. NAmP90; PuP-16

And willows could not hold more steady sound. (LL) Repose of Rivers. Hart Crane. AWP; CMoP; ColAP; GEA; LiTM; MeMAP; MoAmPo; NOBA; OxBA; PoE

And wilt thou have me fashion into speech. Sonnet. Elizabeth Barrett Browning. BWW; BrRo; CABP; EnVR; VWP *Fr.* Sonnets from the Portuguese.

And wilt [*or* wylt] thou le[a]ve me thus? The Lover's Appeal. Sir Thomas Wyatt. AAS; EBEvV; EnLoPo; GLoP; GTBS-P; NAEL-1; NoSic; SCGP; SiPS

And wilt thou, love, my soul display. The Lover's Farewell. George Moses Horton. NAAAL

And win us both to May. (LL) The Gardens of the Villa D'Este. Anthony Hecht. ColAP; OBGa

And wine can of their wits the wise beguile. Blotto Motto. Homer. *Fr.* Odyssey. NAWM-1, *tr. by* Robert Fitzgerald

And winter pulled a sheet over his head. (LL) The Sleeping Giant. Donald Hall. NYBP; Poetsp; TwCP

And Winter's Coolness spite of Summer's rays. (LL) The Garden. Alexander Pope. GaP; OBGa

And wish not for, nor fear thine end. (LL) A Happy Life. Mildmay Fane, 2d Earl of Westmorland. BeJo; NOSC

And wish to lead others when they should be led. (LL) The Voice of the Ancient Bard. William Blake. FHYEP; Ro

And with damp rags she bathes him, brings him. Anna's Grace. Bruce Weigl. NAmP90

And with each motion she ensnared a heart. (LL) On Lydia Distracted. Philip Ayres. EnLoPo; Son

And with God be the rest! (LL) Prospice. Robert Browning. APAD; FHYEP; ImPo; NAEL-2; PFE; PoLF; PoRA; SAGP; TrCP

And with great fear I inhabit the middle of the night. The Acts of Youth. John Weiners. BB

And with her own fool's colours [*or* colors] gilds them all. (LL) To Dr. Jonathan Swift. Alexander Pope. CBNP; OBSV

And with March a Decade in Bolinas. Joanne Kyger. BLT

And with memory I was there. (LL) Thoughts on my sick-bed. Dorothy Wordsworth. PEW; Ro

And with new light salute our longing eyes. (LL) The Golden Age. Sir Richard Fanshawe. NOSC; OAEL-1; OBVE

And with no language but a cry. (LL) 54. Tennyson. CABP; EBVV; EBVVPR; EnVR; FHYEP; ImPo; OAEL-2; OBNC; PeECV

And with no morning the day is sold. (LL) Blasting from Heaven. Philip Levine. CoAP; WeT

And with soft grateful tears / Ascends the sky. (LL) Morning. William Blake. FaBoCh; OAEL-2

And with that the singer was content. (LL) There Was a Man with a Tongue of Wood. Stephen Crane. MeMAP; MoAmPo

"And with the Ape thou art alone / Do, / Do." (LL) Lullaby: "Though the world has slipped and gone." Dame Edith Sitwell. CMoP; LiTM; NALW

And with the self-same weapon, too! . (LL) Jack and Roger. Benjamin Franklin. FaBoEE; NOBL

And with those virtues which are like the Stars. (LL) Walden. William Ellery Channing. APN-1; PAR

And within the indestructable night I am alone. (LL) Passage Over Water. Robert Duncan. NOBA; NoAM

And without pity heare their dying grones. Bible, *O.T. See* Psalm 137.

And woke far on. I did not know the place. (LL) The Labyrinth. Edwin Muir. FaBoTC

And wonders what's to pay. (LL) Fairies break their dances, The. A. E. Housman. OxBSP; PeVV

And woodthrush calling through the fog / My daughter. (LL) Marina. T. S. Eliot. CABP; CMoP; FaBoMo; GTBS-P; HeIP-4; MoLi; NAEL-2; NOBE; NOCV; PoE; TOF

And word—wrote never more. (LL) Dr. Johnson's Ghost. Elizabeth Moody. ECWP; OxBSn

And Wordsworth! Ah, pale ghosts, rejoice! Matthew Arnold. EPCY *Fr.* Memorial Verses. CABP; NAEL-2; OAEL-2

And would it have been worth it, after all. T. S. Eliot. *Fr.* The Love Song of J. Alfred Prufrock. AWP; AmPP; ClHu; ColAP; EBEV; EBEvV; HAP; HeIP-4; HoPM; InPK-6; InPS-3; LiTM; MoAmPo; MoP; NAAL-2; NAEL-2; NAWM-2; NOBA; NOBE; NoAM; NoP-4; OAEL-2; OxAEP-2; OxBTC; PFE; PiM; PoA; PoE; PoPoPo; PoRA; Poetr; SAGP; SoSe-8; TAP; TFi; TRP; TwCP; WeW-3

And would love more, could I but love thee less. (LL) Song: "No, no, fair heretic[k], it needs must be." Sir John Suckling. BeJo; CaPo; CavPo

And would suffice. (LL) Fire and Ice. Robert Frost. AmPP; CMoP; EBEvV; FaBoEE; HeIP-4; HoPM; InPK-6; LiTM; MoAmPo; MoP; NAAL-2; NOBA; NoAM; OxBA; PFE; Poetr; RaBo; SoSe-8; TAP; TFi

And would you gather turds. A History of Love. William Carlos Williams. VGW

"And would you sign my copy sir?" "A Scotch?" The Poet at Fifty. Laurence David Lerner. PeSA

And wound with flaming ropes of hair. (LL) The Licorice Fields at Pontefract. John Betjeman. CABP; CMoP

And wow gin I were but young for thee. (LL) Werena My Heart Licht I Wad Dee. Lady Grisel Baillie. CABP; LW

And, wow! Tam saw an unco sight! Robert Burns. OxBSn *Fr.* Tam o' Shanter.

And wring his bosom—is—to die. (LL) Song: "When lovely woman stoops to folly." Oliver Goldsmith. AWP; BoLoP; CABP; EBEvV; FHYEP; FaBoSe; GTBS-P; HAP; ImPo; NOBE; NOEC; NoP-4; OBEV; OxAEP-1; SCGP; TFi; UnPo

And write this poem for money, rage, and love. (LL) The Thief. Stanley Kunitz. MoAmPo; PoRA

And write Thy Epitaph in Blood and Wounds! (LL) His Metrical Vow. James Graham, Marquess of Montrose. NOBE; OxBS

And writing novels with her broom. (LL) On the Same. Roy Campbell. OBCoV; OxBTC

And ye can't catch a bowl full. (LL) Riddle: "House full, [a] yard full, [A]." *Unknown.* LB; NTCP

And ye shall walk in silk attire. The Siller Croun. Susanna Blamire. ECWP; LW

And, yeah, brothers. Dark Prophecy: I Sing of Shine. Etheridge Knight. BPo; LTA; PBCAP

And yet a kiss (like blubber)'d blur and slip. Love and Death. John Frederick Nims. HoPM

And yet abide the World! (LL) There came a Wind like a Bugle. Emily Dickinson. APN-2; CMoP; MeMAP; NAAL-1; NAAL-3; NAWM-2; NOBA; OxBA; PAR; RB; SAmP

And yet, and yet, these days are incomplete. (LL) Friendship After Love. Ella Wheeler Wilcox. APAD; APN-2; LW

And yet God has not said a word! (LL) Porphyria's Lover. Robert Browning. AWP; CBLP; EP; EnVR; FHYEP; HAP; NAEL-2; OBEV; OxBoV

And yet hath prayer, the heav'n-breathing foliage of faith. Ethick. Robert Bridges. OxBTC *Fr.* The Testament of Beauty.

And yet I cannot reprehend the flight. Samuel Daniel. OBEV *Fr.* To Delia.

And yet I, too, shall someday die, alas. Nothingness. Xuân Diệu, *Vietnamese.* AVP, *tr. by* Huỳnh Sanh Thông

And yet in some very subtle way. Hilda Doolittle. NALW *Fr.* Tribute to the Angels.

And yet in washing one, she washèd both. (LL) Mary [*or* Marie] Magdalene. George Herbert. ESCV; FMP

And yet not long ago. *Unknown. Fr.* Vox Populi, Vox Dei. FaBoPV

And yet sometimes. Inscribed in the Silver of the Sea. Ivan V. Lalic, *Serbian.* CEEP, *tr. by* C. W. Truesdale

And yet the books will be there on the shelves, separate beings. Czeslaw Milosz, *Polish.* OPOU, *tr. by* Czeslaw Milosz *and* Robert Hass (b. 1941)

And yet the driving mirror shows me plain. To His Coy Mistress. W. J. Webster. BXAP

And Yet the Earth Remains Unchanged. *Unknown.* CA

And yet the southern whale does some time come. The Whales. Marguerite Young. WPE

And yet, there was a hunger in your eyes. Arthur Symons. PeVV *Fr.* Amoris Victima.

—And yet this great wink of eternity. Hart Crane. AmPP; ColAP; HAP; ImPo; LiTM; MoAmPo; OxBA; PoE; RaBo; TRP; UnPo; VGW *Fr.* Voyages. CMoP; MeMAP; NOBA; NoAM; TAP

And Yet We Are Here! Karl Wolfskehl, *German.* TrJP, *tr. by* Carol North Valhope *and* Ernst Morowitz

And yet, where would we be without the American culture. Goodbye Nkrumah. Diane Di Prima. PoM

And yet white[ness]. Draft of a Modern Love Poem. Tadeusz Rózewicz, *Polish.* BLT, *tr. by* Czeslaw Milosz; PoSu, *tr. by* Magnus J. Krynski; VCWP, *tr. by* Magnus J. Krynski *and* Robert A. Maguire

And yet who—did not! (LL) Did Not. Thomas Moore. APAD; BoLoP; EnLoPo; GLoP; PeLV

And yet you experienced the flames of Hell. Proof. Czeslaw Milosz, *Polish.* TOF, *tr. by the author*

And you above them, wounded and dominant. (LL) Messengers. Louise Glück. ColAP; HCAP; VCAP

And you / and / you. (LL) Latin Music in New York. Jessica Hagedorn. PmAP; WWSi

And you as well must die, belovèd dust. Edna St. Vincent Millay. MeMAP; PoLF; PoRA; TAP

And you came back. Samar Attar. PBWP *Fr.* The Return of the Dead.

And you could leave me now. At Parting. Edith Nesbit. OBGa

And you have failed, O Poet? Sad! Failures. May Kendall. VWP

And You, Helen. Edward Thomas. BoLoP; OBWVE

And you just *know* he knows he knows. (LL) The Sloth. Theodore Roethke. ChAP; OBAL; OBCA; PiM; TRP

And you know, I believe him. (LL) Creation. Simon J. Ortiz. ColAP

And you look like hell when they're through with you. (LL) The Hearse Song. *Unknown.* AS; OxBoLi; RB

And you, my sister Moscow, are at ease. Osip Emilevich Mandelstam. TCRP, *tr. by* Bernard Meares *Fr.* Stanzas.

And you my spent heart's treasure. Geoffrey Hill. HAP *Fr.* The Pentecost Castle.

And you (O *Delian* Virgins) doe me grace. *Unknown.* OBCVT, *tr. by* George Chapman *Fr.* An Hymne to Apollo.

And you play the safe game / the orphan game. Margaret Atwood. *Fr.* The Circle Game. MoCV

And you remain. David St. John. *See* Iris.

And you shan't wake up till you're clean plum dead! (LL) The Nine Little Goblins. James Whitcomb Riley. NOxBChV

And you smile up at us—eternally. (LL) In Memory of My Mother. Patrick Kavanagh. BIrV; CIP-2; LBC; MoP; NoAM; RaBo

And you stalwart loins. (LL) From pent-up aching rivers. Walt Whitman. APN-1; BoLoP; GLoP; NAAL-1; NAAL-3; NOBA; OxBM

And you too perished long ago, by a bush with matted roots. Anyte, *Greek.* GrAn, *tr. by* John Heath-Stubbs *and* Carol A. Whiteside

And you, Vanya. Yury Pavlovich Odarchenko, *Russian.* TCRP, *tr. by* Nina Kossman

And you will understand / My hatred. (LL) Hatred. Gwendolyn B. Bennett. BlSi; PoBA; RaBo

And you, you. . . you, you utter / You wait! (LL) Beyond Words. Robert Frost. Spl; WeW-3

. . . And you'll have the strength again. The Ordeal. Olga Fiodorovna Berggolts, *Russian.* TCRP, *tr. by* Daniel Weissbort

And you'll say a nation totters. George Douglas Howard Cole. OxBTC *Fr.* Civil Riot.

And your better best. (LL) Comparatives. *Unknown.* ACTP

And your cool palm smoothes down stern Pluto's cheek. (LL) Ternissa. Walter Savage Landor. NOBE; OBNC; PoEL-4

And your eyes peel to red mud. (LL) Babylon Revisited. Imamu Amiri Baraka. BPo; MoP; NoAM

And your house will be my home as long as I live. Bible, *O.T. See* Psalm 23.

And your letter melts into melody. (LL) The New Cecilia. Thomas Lovell Beddoes. CBNP; OAEL-2

And your little job is done. (LL) To W. R. William Ernest Henley. APAD; EBVV; MoBrPo; NAEL-2; NOBVV; PeVV

And your money, too. (LL) 50—50. Langston Hughes. NOBA; NoAM; PoE; SAGP

And your true name is Mistress Betty. (LL) On A Romantic Lady. Mary Monck. ECWP; NOEC; RACG

Andalusian merchant, that returns, The. *Unknown.* FaBoCh *Fr.* Thule, The Period of Cosmography. HAP

Andirons were the dragons, The. The Castle in the Fire. Mary Jane Carr. ChAP

Andonis, My Daughter. Thomas Love Peacock. VoR

Andraitx—Pomegranate Flowers. D. H. Lawrence. NoP-4

André Chäenier. Marina Tsvetayeva, *Russian.* FaBoPV, *tr. by* Tom Paulin

André who was killed in Riga. Constellation of Dead Brothers. Victor Serge, *Russian.* AF, *tr. by* James Brook

Andrea del Sarto. Robert Browning. CTC; EnVR; NAEL-2; NOBVV; NoP-4; OAEL-2; PoE; PoEL-5

Andreas. *Unknown, Anglo-Saxon.*

St. Andrew's Voyage to Mermedonia. AnOE, *tr. by* Charles W. Kennedy

Andrée Rexroth. Kenneth Rexroth. APSN; VGW

Kings River Canyon.

Andrew Jackson & Martin Van Buren. 1841 (I). Jackson MacLow. APSN *Fr.* The Presidents of the United States of America.

Andrew Jackson was eight feet tall. The Statue of Old Andrew Jackson. Vachel Lindsay. CA

Andrew Jackson's last name's the same as my first. 1829. Jackson MacLow. APSN *Fr.* The Presidents of the United States of America.

Andrew Jackson's Speech, *Dido to Aeneas: 'I have broke faith with the ashes of Sichaeus.'.* Robert Bly. CoAmPo

Andrew Lammle. *Unknown. See* The Trumpeter of Fyvie.

Androgeny is the universe. Yaedi Ignatow. IFJA

Androgynous child whose hair curls into flowers. The Sun. Marge Piercy. WPOW *Fr.* Laying Down the Tower.

Andromache Captive. Ennius, Quintus, *Latin.*

"O father, frendes, my countrey eke, and Priams house farewell." OBCVT, *tr. by* John Dolman

Andromache's Lament for Hector. Homer. OxBM *Fr.* The Iliad.

Andromache's lament is still in our ears. Alpheios, *Greek.* GrAn, *tr. by* Edwin Morgan

Andromache's Lamentation. Homer. OBVE, *tr. by* Congreve *Fr.* The Iliad.

Andromache's Wedding. Sappho, *Greek.* BoWoP, *tr. by* Willis Barnstone

Andromeda. Gerard Manley Hopkins. EBEV; FaBoMo; OxAEP-2; SCGP

Andromeda. Charles Kingsley.

"Whelming the dwellings of men, and the toils of the slow-/ footed oxen." PeVV

Andromeda. Judith Nicholls. SpW

Andromeda, by Perseus saved and wed. Aspecta Medusa. D. G. Rossetti. OxBSP

Andromeda / forgot. Sappho, *Greek.* BoWoP, *tr. by* Willis Barnstone

Andy-Diana DNA Letter. Andrew Weiman. HAP

Ane Ballat of Our Lady. William Dunbar. OxBS

(Ballad of Our Lady.)

"Empryce of prys, imperatrice." EBEV

Ane Godlie Dreame. Elizabeth, Lady Culross Melvill. KTR

Ane Godly Dream. Elizabeth, Lady Culross Melvill.

"Upon one day as I did mourn full sore." ChIV-1

Ane Satire [*or* Satyre] of the Three [*or* Thrie] Estaitis. Sir David Lindsay. *"Bona dies, Bona dies."* SeCP

"My patent pardouns ye may see." OBSV

Anear the centre of that northern crest. The City's Queen. James Thomson. EnVR; GTBS-P; NOBE *Fr.* The City of Dreadful Night. OBNC

Anecdote for Fathers, Showing how the Art of Lying may be Taught. Wordsworth. Ro

Anecdote from William IV Street. D. J. Enright. OxBC

Anecdote of Love, An. John Clare. NOBVV

Anecdote of the Jar. Wallace Stevens. AmPP; CMoP; ColAP; FaBoA; HCAP; HeIP-4; HoPM; InPK-6; MeMAP; MoAmPo; MoP; NAAL-2; NAWM-2; NOBA; NoAM; NoP-4; OxBA; OxBSP; PoA; PoPoPo; Poetr; SAmP; TAP; TFi; UnPo

Anecdotes of the Late War. Charles Olson. CBCWP

Anesthesia. Veronica Porumbacu, *Romanian.* CEEP, *tr. by* Dorian, Marguerite *and* Elliott Urdang

Anesthetist is singing, The. In the Operating Room. Alden Nowlan. NOBC

Angel, The. William Blake. CH; FHYEP; RACG; Ro *Fr.* Songs of Experience.
Angel, The. William Blake. ImPo
Angel. Andrew Elliott. PNI
Angel. John Forbes. NOBAu
Angel, The. Alfred Hayes. TrJP
Angel, The. Galway Kinnell. LCAP-2; NoAM
Angel. Brad Leithauser. DiPo; FYAP
Angel. James Merrill. CoAmPo; PoA
 ("He does not want even these few lines written.") (LL)
Angel. Maxine Scates. PBCAP
Angel. Ian Wedde.
 "And this is where." PeNZ
Angel and Stone. Howard Nemerov. NYBP
Angel and the girl are met, The. The Annunciation. Edwin Muir. CMoP; CRP; ChIV-2; NOCV
Angel asked, as his shoulders were pressed into the stone, The. Statue. Tom Clark. BAP-93
Angel Atrapado VIII. John Yau. PT
Angel Boley. Stevie Smith. EBNV
Angel Butcher. Philip Levine. ColAP
Angel came to me, An. O Simplicitas. Madeleine L'Engle. OBCP; PChr *Fr.* Three Songs of Mary.
Angel came to me and said, An. A Memorable Fancy. William Blake. *Fr.* The Marriage of Heaven and Hell. NAEL-2; NOBRP; OAEL-2
Angel Eye of Memory. John Malcolm Brinnin. PoA
Angel in Blythburgh Church, An. Peter Porter. NoP-4
Angel in the Deluge. Rosario Murillo, *Spanish.* CLPP, *tr. by* Alejandro Murguía
Angel in the House, The. Coventry Patmore.
 "Across the sky the daylight crept." GBL
 Attainment, The. FaBoEE
 Cathedral Close, The. EBVV
 (Salisbury; the Cathedral Close.) EBVV
 Constancy Rewarded. OxBSP
 County Ball, The. EBVV
 Going to Church. PeVV
 Kiss, The. BoLoP; EnLoPo; NOBVV
 Love at Large. EBVV; NOBVV
 Love Serviceable. EnLoPo
 Lover, The. OxAEP-2
 Love's Perversity. EnVR
 Married Lover, The. OBEV; OxAEP-2
 Perspective. FaBoEE; GBL
 Rainbow, The. GTBS-P
 Revelation, The. EnLoPo; GBL; GLoP; GTBS-P; HAP; LoP; OBNC; OxBSP
 Sahara. EBVV
 Spirit's Epochs, The. EBEV; GBL; OxBSP
 Tribute, The. EBEV; OBNC
 "'Twas when the spousal time of May." GBL; OxAEP-2
 "Whirl'd off at last, for speech I sought." GBL
Angel, king of streaming morn. Sun. Henry Rowe. OBEV
Angel of Death, The. *Unknown.* AmFP
Angel of death flies, The. Night. Louise Glück. MoLi *Fr.* Metamorphosis. MoLi
Angel of Dread, The. Miklós Radnóti, *Hungarian.* PFTM, *tr. by* Clayton Eshleman *and* Gyula Kodolanyi
Angel of Peace, Thou Hast Wandered Too Long. Oliver Wendell Holmes. AH
Angel of Rome was a male soprano, The. Castrato. Kenneth Rosen. PuP-15
Angel, robed in spotless white, An. Dawn. Paul Laurence Dunbar. PoLF
Angel said to me: "Why are you laughing?," The. Sarah. Delmore Schwartz. ChIV-1; KSG
Angel [or Angell] saith to Joseph mild, The. For Innocents' Day. Luke Wadding. NOIV; TIRV
Angel slide your hand. A Poem in Yellow after Tristan Tzara. Jerome Rothenberg. PoM
Angel spirits of sleep. Robert Bridges. CH; OBEV
Angel Surrounded by Paysans. Wallace Stevens. HCAP; LCAP-2
Angel that presided o'er my birth, The. William Blake. InPK-6; OxBSP; RB *Fr.* Gnomic Verses.
Angel told Mary, An. Christmas Carol. Harry Behn. PChr
Angel was tired of heaven, as he lounged in the golden street. The Woman and the Angel. Robert W. Service. ChIV-1; KSG

Angel with a voice like summer show'rs, An. Repose. Henrietta Cordelia Ray. CBWP-3
Angela Davis. Alice S. Cobb. BlSi
Angela Honey (she wrote) I would it were not so. From Lois in London. Angela McCabe. AmPA
Angelic, lonely, autochthonous, one white. Timeless, Twinned. Robert Penn Warren. AFr
Angelica has gain'd the dell. Robert Dunbar. PBCV *Fr.* The Caraguin.
Angelica the Doorkeeper. *Unknown, Serbian.* RB, *tr. by* Anne Pennington
Angelical whites of your eyes, The. Susan. Robin Magowan. SPE
Angelles bee wrogte to bee of neidher kynde. Mynstrelles Songe: "Angelles bee wrogte to bee of neidher kynde." Thomas Chatterton. EnLoPo *Fr.* Aella; a Tragycal Enterlude.
Angellica's Lament. Aphra Behn. LW
Angelo Orders His Dinner. Bayard Taylor. BXAP
Angels. Dannie Abse. PoA
Angels, The. Donne. *Fr.* The Litanie. PoEL-2
Angels. Anne Szumigalski. NOBC
Angels, The. Marguerite Young. WPE
Angels alone that sore above / Enjoy [*or* Injoy] such liberty. (LL) To Althea, from Prison. Richard Lovelace. AWP; BLPA; BeJo; CaPo; EBEvV; FaBoBe; GBL; GTBS-P; HAP; ImPo; InPS-3; MeLP; NAEL-1; NOBE; NOSC; OBEV; PoE; PoRA; SCGP; SeCP; TFi
Angels and ministers of grace defend us! Shakespeare. EBEV; OxAEP-1; OxBSn *Fr.* Hamlet. NAWM-1
 ("Say, why is this? wherefore? what should we do?") (LL) OxBSn
Angels are bending, The. Cradle Song. W. B. Yeats. NOBVV
Angels are stooping, The. A Cradle Song. W. B. Yeats. NOxBChV
Angels, as well as birds, on silent wing. On Angels. W. W. Eustace Ross. MoCV
Angels Came a-Mustering, The. *Unknown, Hebrew.* TrJP, *tr. by* Israel Zangwill
Angels' eyes, whom veils cannot deceive, The. Of the Blessed Sacrament of the Altar. Robert Southwell. OBEV
Angel's Flight. Maxine Scates. PBCAP
Angels, from the realms of glory. Nativity. James Montgomery. NOCV
Angels Grieving over the Dead Christ. Gjertrud Schnackenberg. BAP-93
Angels in Heav'n, as we may say. A Poem upon the Caelestial Embassy. Richard Steere. SCAP
Angels in Winter. Nancy Willard. ColAP; LCAP-2
"Angel's like a flea, The." Coleridge. CBNP
Angel's Message, The. Clara Ann Thompson. CBWP-2
Angels / might fall that way. Snowfall: Four Variations. George Amabile. NYBP
Angels of 1912 and 1972, The. Richard Jackson. NAmP90
Angels of the Ruins, The. Rafael Alberti, *Spanish.* AF, *tr. by* Geoffrey Connell
Angel's Song. Charles Causley. OBCP
Angels Sung a Carol, The. Edward Taylor. AH
Angels take approaches, The. Some enter by root. Paul Ramsey. CRP
Angel's Visit, The. Eugene Field. PWR
Angel's Visit, The. Charlotte L. Forten Grimke. AAP
Angels walking under the palm trees. A Little Carol of the Virgin. Félix Lope de Vega Carpio. PChr
Angels' Weather. Bruce Beaver. BMAP
Anger. After Auschwitz. Anne Sexton. HP
Anger Against Children. Robert Bly. LoL *Fr.* Anger Against Children.
Anger, and the vow are the same. (LL) The Bad Old Days. Kenneth Rexroth. NNaP; NoAM
Anger in its time and place. Charles Lamb *and* Mary Lamb (1764–1847). FaBoBe
 ("Vile snake will *always sting you*, The.") (LL) NOxBChV
Anger Lay by Me All Night Long. Elizabeth Daryush. RB
Anger rises with metal filings, The. A Man All Grown Up Is Supposed To. Terry Stokes. AmPA
Anger shines through me. A Just Anger. Marge Piercy. CrSp
Anger Sweetened. Molly Peacock. FFC
Anger that Breaks the Man into Chidren, The. César Vallejo, *Spanish.* RaBo
Anger's Freeing Power. Stevie Smith. NTP; OxBC
Anghiari is medieval, a sleeve sloping down. The Journey. James Wright. NoAM; PoE; WeT
Angilbert's Prayer. Angilbert, *Latin.* MLL, *tr. by* Helen Waddell
Angina. David Campbell. *See* I Starting from Central Station.
Angina Pectoris. Nazim Hikmet, *Turkish.* VCWP, *tr. by* Randy Blasing *and* Mutlu Konuk
Anglais Mort à Florence. Wallace Stevens. SAmP

Angle but only one lime to make / a Margarita, An. (LL) Of Time and the Line. Charles Bernstein. PmAP

Angle-Land. David Jones. NoAM *Fr.* The Anathemata.

Angle of Geese. N. Scott Momaday. CDW; HATNAP

Angle of Vision. Robert Rendall. OxBTC

Angler rose, he took his rod, The. Epitaph. Robert Louis Stevenson. OBCoV

Anglers Song, The, *in* The Compleat Angler *by* Izaak Walton. William Basse.

    Angler's Song, The. NOSC

Angler's Story, The. John Hollander. AFr

Angleworms. Marie Louise Allen. CTV

Anglican curate in want, An. Ronald Arbuthnott Knox. OBCoV

Anglican firelight. The Other Voice. Tom Paulin. PNI

Anglo-American Chainpoem. *Unknown.* SPE

Anglo-Saxon Comedy. Peter Rose. BMAP

Anglo Saxon Street. Earle Birney. HeIP-4; NOBC

Anglorum Feriae. George Peele.

    "Write write yow Croniclers of Tyme and Fame." PBRV

Angola Question Mark. Langston Hughes. BPo; TTY

Angrier than my now occasional. A Preface to the Memoirs. James Merrill. NOBA

Angry Dusk. Jack Lindsay. NOBAu

Angry Poet, The. Frank O'Connor, *Irish.* CIP-2

Angry Samson. Robert Graves. ChIV-1

Angry with China. Douglas Messerli. FTOS

Angry word is like a boomerang, An. Margaret E. Bruner. PoToHe

Angry young husband called Bicket, An. Limerick. John Galsworthy. PeLi

Angst, poetry, urbanized fret. Limerick. Sydney Bernard Smith. PeLi

Angst-ridden amorist, Fred, An. The Love Song of J. Alfred Prufrock. J. Walker. BXAP; PeLi

Anguish. Stéphane Mallarmé, *French.* AWP, *tr. by* Arthur Symons

Anguish. Henry Vaughan. FMP; OxAEP-1

Anguish, a door, Le Portel, body bent over jagged rock. Placements I. Clayton Eshleman. PFTM

Anguish is always there, next door to pleasure. (LL) Elegy 19 (A Kiss): "Without a soul, a mind, a breath, or pulse." Pierre de Ronsard, *French.* EP; FLP, *tr. by* Alistair Elliot

Anguish of a naked body is more terrible, The. A Prayer to the Lord Ramakrishna. James Wright. NNaP

Anguish of Ants, The. David Campbell. BMAP

Ani Maamin, A Song Lost and Found Again. Elie Wiesel.

    "Behold, God of Abraham, God of mercy." HP

Anight the murmuring of the sea. (LL) A Garden By The Sea. William Morris. CH; EBEvV; NOBE; OAEL-2; OBEV; OBNC; PoEL-5

Anima Has a Predilection, The. Michael Harlow. PeNZ *Fr.* Poem Then, for Love.

Anima quodammodo omnia. Translation. Howard Nemerov. CRP

Animal. Max Eastman. FYAP

Animal. Bill Griffiths. NBrP

Animal Acts. Charles Simic. LCAP-2

Animal bones and some mossy tent rings. Lament for the Dorsets. Alfred Wellington Purdy. NoAM

Animal crackers, and cocoa to drink. Christopher Darlington Morley. ChAP ("More for tea!") (LL) CTV

Animal Days. Lee Harwood. NBrP

Animal Fair. *Unknown.* AS; BLPA; FaBoBe; NTCP

Animal Howl, The. "M. J.," *Polish.* TrJP, *tr. by* A. Glanz-Leyeles

Animal I wanted, The. Kenneth Patchen. VGW

Animal Kingdom. Sydney Clouts. PeSA

Animal Magnetism; the Pseudo-Philosopher Baffled. Laurence Hynes Halloran. NOEC

Animal Mimicry. Robert Polito. WWSi

Animal runs, it passes, it dies, The. And it is the great cold. Death Rites II. *Unknown.* TTY, *tr. by* C. M. Bowra

Animal That Drank Up Sound, The. William Stafford. VGW

Animal Weather-Forecasting. Thomas Lodge. NoSic

Animal willows of November. The Willows of Massachusetts. Denise Levertov. NAAL-2

Animals, The. W. S. Merwin. VCAP

Animals, The. Edwin Muir. CMoP; CRP; ChIV-1; EBEV; HeIP-4; KSG; MoBrPo

Animals. Walt Whitman. ImPo *Fr.* Song of Myself. AmPP; MoAmPo; NAAL-3; NOBA; OxBA ("I think I could turn and live with animals, they're so placid and self- / contain'd.") PFE

Animals are coming, The. Songs to Welcome the Society of the Mystic Animals. *Unknown, Seneca Indian.* STP, *tr. by* Jerome Rothenberg *and* Richard Johnny John

Animals Are Passing from Our Lives. Philip Levine. CoAP; ColAP; NOBA; Poetr; RaBo; TAP; WeT

Animals' Arrival, The. Elizabeth Jennings. PBWP

Animals do not sleep. At night. The Face of the Horse. Nikolai Alekseievich Zabolotsky, *Russian.* RB; TCRP, *tr. by* Daniel Weissbort

Animals Enjoying Life. William Cowper. APo *Fr.* The Task.

Animals have no names. A Walk. Nikolai Alekseievich Zabolotsky, *Russian.* RB, *tr. by* Daniel Weissbort

Animals' Houses. James Reeves. OTCP

Animals in That Country, The. Margaret Atwood. NALW; NoAM

Animals live in darkness, The. World of Darkness. Robert Chatain. PoA

Animals Sick of the Plague, The. Marianne Moore, *ad. fr.* La Fontaine. InPS-3

Animals we have seen, all marvelous creatures, The. The Park in Milan. William Jay Smith. CoAP

Animals were, The. Ode to the Cat. Pablo Neruda, *Spanish.* VCWP, *tr. by* John Hollander

Animism. Birago Diop, *French.* NegPo, *tr. by* Ellen Conroy Kennedy

Animula. T. S. Eliot. CRP; GEA

Animula. George Oppen. FTOS

Animula vagula blandula. Conrad Potter Aiken. OBAL; OBCoV

Animula, vagula, blandula: The Emperor Hadrian to his soul. Emperor Hadrian, *Latin.* OBCVT; OBVE, *tr. by* Stevie Smith

Anishinabe children sing songs of sleep. For the Children. Thomas Love Peacock. VoR

Anishinabe Grandmothers. Gerald Vizenor. VoR

Anita and Giovanni. Henrietta Cordelia Ray. CBWP-3

Ank'hor Vat. Denis Devlin. BIrV; CIP-2; NOIV

Ankle's chief end is exposiery, The. Limerick. Anthony Euwer. PeLi

Ankotarinya. *Unknown, Aranda.* CBAP, *tr. by* T. G. H. Strehlow

Ann, Ann! / Come! quick as you can! Alas, Alack! Walter De la Mare. OPOU; OxBChV

Ann Griffith. Ronald Stuart Thomas. PeECV

Ann Lee. Lynne McMahon. NAmP90

Anna Blossom Has Wheels. Kurt Schwitters, *German.* PFTM, *tr. by* Kurt Schwitters

Anna Elise. *Unknown.* OxNR

Anna Grasa. Bruce Weigl. CDa

Anna had been singing there since early morning. Pestel, the Poet, and Anna. "David Samuilovich Samoylov," *Russian.* TCRP, *tr. by* Lubov Yakovleva

Anna Liffey. Eavan Boland. PUP-20

Anna Playing in a Graveyard. Caroline Gilman. OBCA

Anna Speaks of the Childhood of Mary Her Daughter. Lucille Clifton. NALW

Annabel Lee. Edgar Allan Poe. AWP; AiP; BLPA; CH; ChAP; EBEvV; GEA; GLoP; HeIP-4; ImPo; NAAL-1; NAAL-3; NCAP; OBCA; OBSP; TFi

    ("In her tomb by the side of the sea.") (LL) APN-1; AmPP; ColAP; MeMAP; NOBA; NoP-4; OxBA; PAR; PoPoPo; TAP

Annabell and the Witches. Mick Gowar. OBSP

Annan's Water's waiding deep. Annan Water. *Unknown.* CH

Anna's Grace. Bruce Weigl. NAmP90

Anne and the Field-Mouse. Ian Serraillier. NOxBChV

Anne Boleyn. Eloise Bibb. CBWP-4

Anne Rutledge. Edgar Lee Masters. CBCWP; CMoP; HAP; ImPo; LiTM; MoAmPo; MoP; NOBA; NoAM; OxBA; TFi *Fr.* Spoon River Anthology.

Anne, who are dead—and whom I loved in a rather asinine fashion. Wonderful Things. Ron Padgett. PmAP

Annette came through the meadows. Pastoral. Henrietta Cordelia Ray. CBWP-3

Annette Myers. *Unknown.* OxBoLi; OxBoV

Anniad, The. Gwendolyn Brooks. BlSi

Annie and Rhoda, sisters twain. The Sisters. John Greenleaf Whittier. AWP

Annie and Willie's Prayer. Sophia P. Snow. BLPA

Annie Green. The Family. William Freedman. IFJA

Annie Hill's Grave. James Merrill. WeW-3

Annie Laurie. William Douglas, *rev. by* Lady Jane Scott. FaBoBe; ImPo

Annie, my first-born, gentle child. To Annie. Mary E. Tucker. CBWP-1

Annie of Tharaw, my true love of old. *Unknown, German.* GePo, *tr. by* Henry Wadsworth Longfellow

Annie Pearl Smith Discovers Moonlight. Patricia Smith. GT

Annihilation. Conrad Potter Aiken. GBL; GEA; MoAmPo

Anniversaries. May Probyn. VWP

Anniversaries of War. Yehuda Amichai, *Hebrew.* VCWP, *tr.* by Benjamin Harshav *and* Barbara Harshav

Anniversary [*or* Anniversarie], The. Donne. BoLoP; ESCV; FHYEP; HAP; HoPM; MeLP; NOBE; NoSic; OAEL-1; OxBM; SCGP; SeCP; TFi; WeW-3

(Anniversary, The.) FSCP; LoP; NoP-4

("But truly keeps its first, last, everlasting day.") (LL) ITG

("To write threescore.") (LL) NoP-4

("To write threescore.") (LL) FSCP; LoP

Anniversary. Odysseus Elytis, *Greek.* AF; GrIP, *tr.* by Edmund Keeley *and* Philip Sherrard

Anniversary, An. Thomas Hardy. OxBTC

Anniversary. Dorothy Hewett. BMAP

Anniversary. Richmond Lattimore. NYBP

Anniversary. John Wain. TwCP

Anniversary of Death, An. John Wieners. PoM

Anniversary of Samansa's Death, The. Kazuko Shiraishi, *Japanese.* WPJ, *tr.* by Kenneth Rexroth *and* Ikuko Atsumi

Anniversary on the Hymeneals of My Noble Kinsman, Thomas Stanley, Esquire, An. Richard Lovelace. CaPo

Anniversary Poem. George Oppen. APSN; NNaP *Fr.* Some San Francisco Poems

Anniversary Poem Entitled the Progress of Liberty, An. James Madison Bell. "Bondsman's gloomy night has passed, The." AAP

Anniversary Poem for the Cheyennes Who Fell at Sand Creek. Lance Henson. VoR

Anno Domini. Lucian Blaga, *Romanian.* CEEP, *tr.* by Peter Jay *and* Virgil Nemoianu

Anno Domini MCMXLVII. Salvatore Quasimodo, *Italian.* GI, *tr.* by Jack Bevan

Anno 1829. Heinrich Heine, *German.* AWP; OBVE, *tr.* by Charles Stuart Calverley

Annotations of Auschwitz. Peter Porter. HP

"London is full of chickens, on electric spits." OxBTC

Annotations Tropes and Lacunae of the Itoku Master. Ray DiPalma. FTOS

Annotators agree Composer X. St Cecilia's Day Epigram. Peter Porter. PeLV

Announced by all the trumpets of the sky. The Snow-Storm. Ralph Waldo Emerson. APN-1; AmPP; FaBoBe; MeMAP; NAAL-1; NAAL-3; NCAP; NOBA; NoP-4; OxBA; PAR; PoE; PoEL-4; PoLF; PoPoPo; TAP; TFi; UnPo

Announcement of a New Grand Acceleration Company for the Promotion of the Speed of Literature. Thomas Moore. OBCoV

Announcer, The. Vladimir Nikolaevich Kornilov, *Russian.* TCRP, *tr.* by Daniel Weissbort

Annual Gaiety. Wallace Stevens. MoAmPo

Annual Legend. Winfield Townley Scott. CoAP; LiTM

Annual Returns. Greg Williamson. RA

Annuity, The. George Outram. PeVV

Annul. Simon Pettet. PT

Annul Wars. Rabbi Nahman of Bratzlav, *Hebrew.* TrJP, *tr.* by Jacob Sloan

Annulment of a species is as keen, An. The Last Passenger Pigeon in the Cincinnati Zoo. Lucie Brock-Broido. WWSi

Annunciation. Donne. TrCP *Fr.* La Corona. ChIV-2; ESCV; Son *Fr.* Holy Sonnets.

Annunciation. Anna Kamienska, *Polish.* GI, *tr.* by Curzon, David and Grażyna Drabik

Annunciation. Primo Levi, *Hebrew.* AF, *tr.* by Ruth Feldman; GI, *tr.* by Ruth Feldman *and* Brian Swann (b. 1940)

Annunciation, The. Samuel Menashe. GI

Annunciation, The. Douglas Messerli. FTOS

Annunciation, The. Stephen Mitchell. GI

Annunciation, The. Edwin Muir. CMoP; CRP; ChIV-2; NOCV

Annunciation, The. Amrita Pritam, *Punjabi.* WPOW, *tr.* by Khushwant Singh *and* Krishna Gorowara

Annunciation. Rilke, *German.* OBVE, *tr.* by James Blair Leishman

Annunciation. Kay Smith. NIP-4

Annunciation over the Shepherds. Rilke, *German.*

"Look up, you men. Men there at the fire." PChr, *tr.* by M. D. Herter Norton

Annus Mirabilis. Dryden.

"By viewing Nature, Natures hand-maid, Art." OxBoS

New London, The. FaBoCh

(London after the Great Fire, 1666.) NOBE

"Now on their coasts our conquering navy rides." OxAEP-1

"Now van to van the foremost squadrons meet." OBWP

"Swell'd with our late successes on the foe." EBEV

"Yet London, empress of the northern clime." NAEL-1; PeECV

Annus Mirabilis. Philip Larkin. NBLV; NIP-4; NOBL; OBAL

Annus Mirabilis 1989. Elaine Feinstein. HP

Anodda year of love. Give T'anks. Mervyn Morris. HCP

Anointed stone, the coruscated crown—The The. The Circumstance. Hart Crane. PFTM

Anointed Vessel. Paul Verlaine, *French.* EP, *tr.* by Alistair Elliot

Anointing, An. Thylias Moss. GT

Anon out of the earth a fabric huge, *sels.* Milton. *Fr.* Book I. FHYEP; NAEL-1; OAEL-1; OxAEP-1 *Fr.* Paradise Lost.

An[o]on they kiste, and riden [*or* ryden] forth hir weye [*or* waye]. (LL) The Pardoner's Tale. Chaucer. FHYEP; NAEL-1; OAEL-1; PoE

Anonymous as cherubs. Two Voices in a Meadow. Richard Wilbur. PBMP

Anonymous Drawing. Donald Justice. CoAP; HeIP-4

Anonymous handsome, The. The Rejoicing That Attend the Murder of Famous Men. Robley Wilson Jr. PBCAP

Anorexia. Peter Hollenbeck. CDa

Anorexia. Jennifer Maiden. BMAP

Another. Thomas Lovell Beddoes. Son

Another, *see* Letter to Her Husband, Absent upon Public[k] Employment. Anne Bradstreet. NAAL-3; OxBA; SCAP; WPE

(Letter to Her Husband, Absent Upon Publick Employment, A.) LW

Another. Abraham Cowley. *See* Epicure ("Underneath this myrtle shade, The").

Another [Epigram]. Alexander Pope. FaBoEE

("Knock as you please, there's no body at home.") (LL) PFE

(To a Blockhead.) NBLV

Another [Epitaph]: "Here lies John Trot, the Friend of all mankind." William Blake. FaBoEE

Another [Epitaph on Lady Mary Villiers] ("This little vault, this narrow room"). Thomas Carew. BeJo; CaPo

(Epitaph on the Lady Mary Villiers, An.) SeCP

Another [Epitaph on Lady Mary Villiers] ("Purest soul that e'er was sent, The"). Thomas Carew. BeJo; CaPo

Another [Madrigal]. Edward Herbert, 1st Baron Herbert of Cherbury. NOSC

Another [On the Duke of Buckingham]. Thomas Carew. NOSC

Another [To His Booke], *see also* To His Booke ["While thou didst keep thy candor undefil'd"]. Robert Herrick. NOSC

Another ("As I beheld a winters evening air"), *see also* Black Patch on Lucasta's Face, A. Richard Lovelace. SeCP

Another ("Centaur, siren [*or* syren], I forgo[e], The"), *see also* Snail [*or* Snayl], The. Richard Lovelace. CaPo; PoEL-3

Another ("Let the superstitious wife"). Robert Herrick. BeJo

Another Alexandra. Mongane Wally Serote. PeSAV

Another and Another and. Theodore Weiss. DiPo

Another and another and another. James Henry. NOBVV

Another and the Same. Samuel Rogers. OBNC *Fr.* Human Life.

Another armored animal—scale. The Pangolin. Marianne Moore. HAP; NOBA; NoAM; PBWP; Poetr

Another autumn. Nicholas Virgilio. HA

Another bend. John Wills. HA

Another buddy dead. Still Later There Are War Stories. D. F. Brown. CDa

Another Canto. John Bingham Morton. UV

Another Catalogue Item. David Avidan. *Fr.* Traveling in the City. IP, *tr.* by Warren Bargad *and* Stanley F. Chyet

Another Charme for Stables. Robert Herrick. BeJo

("Hang up Hooks and Sheers to scare.") OxBSn

Another Charme (variant). Robert Herrick. OxBSn

Another conference year has passed. To the Conference. Mrs. Henry Linden. CBWP-4

Another cove of shale. On the Marginal Way. Richard Wilbur. CAPP-1; CoAP; NOBA

Another cruel letter today. Lady Izumi, *Japanese.* WPJ, *tr.* by Kenneth Rexroth *and* Ikuko Atsumi

Another Dark Lady. Edwin Arlington Robinson. MeMAP

Another day. Morning Becomes Electric. Bruce Dawe. BMAP

Another day let slip! Its hours have run. The Wasted Day. Robert Fuller Murray. EBVV

Another Day on the Pilgrimage. Peter Gizzi. BAP-95

Another dish of tea. Samuel Johnson. *See* Ballad: "I therefore pray thee, Renny dear."

Another doctor story. Our G.P., Marcus. Nicarchus of Alexandria, *Greek.* GrAn, *tr.* by Peter Porter

Another dreadful tale of woe as I will here unfold. Annette Myers. *Unknown.* OxBoLi; OxBoV

Another Elegy. Donald Hall. BAP-94

Another Epitaph on an Army of Mercenaries, *see also* Housman, "Epitaph on an Army of Mercenaries." "Hugh MacDiarmid." InPK-6; MoP; NAEL-2; NSI; NoAM; NoP-4; OBWP; RB

Another evening we sprawled about discussing. Charles on Fire. James Merrill. HeIP-4

Another Face. Ray A. Young Bear. CDW

Another Fan. Stéphane Mallarmé, *French*. FLP; LoP, *tr. by* Alistair Elliot

Another Fools' Day touches down, another homecoming. Another Fools' Day Touches Down: Shush. Jack A. Mapanje. HBAPE

Another for the Briar Rose. William Morris. NOBVV

Another four I've left yet to bring on. The Four Seasons of the Year. Anne Bradstreet. SCAP

Another Full Moon. Ruth Fainlight. BrRo

Another Grace for a Child. Robert Herrick. *See* Grace for a Child.

Another guest that winter night. Prophetess. John Greenleaf Whittier. *Fr.* Snow-Bound [*or* Snow-Bound; a Winter Idyl]. APN-1; AiP; AmPP; NAAL-3; NOBA; OxBA; TAP; TFi

Another hill town. Hotel Paradiso e Commerciale. John Malcolm Brinnin. NYBP; TwCP

Another holiday. Letter to Breyten Breytenbach from Hong Kong. C. J. Driver. PeSAV

Another. In Defense of Their Inconstancy [*or* Inconstancie]. A Song. Ben Jonson. BeJo; SeCP

(In the Person of Womankind (In Defense of Their Inconstancy).) NAEL-1

Another Kimono. Nancy Eimers. WeT

Another Kind of Burning. Ruth Fox. NYBP

Another Kind of Country. Charles Sullivan. IIP

Another Lady's [*or* Ladyes] Exception, Present at the Hearing. Ben Jonson. *Fr.* A Celebration of Charis in Ten Lyric[k] Pieces [*or* Peeces]. BeJo; OxAEP-1, SeCP

Another land, another age, another self. Covered Bridge. Robert Penn Warren. AiP

Another Life. Frank Bidart. HCAP; VCAP

Another Life. Taslima Nasrin, *Bengali*. VCWP, *tr. by* Carolyne Wright

Another Life. Derek Walcott.
   "Fishermen, like thieves, shake out their silver." PBCV
   "Rain falls like knives, The." PBCV
   "Well, there you have your seasons, prodigy!" PBCV

Another Little Boy. *Unknown*. NOxBChV

Another Love Affair/Another Poem. E. Ethelbert Miller. ISC

Another Man Done Gone. *Unknown*. NAAAL

Another Me. Api, *Tamil*. OMIP, *tr. by* A. K. Ramanujan

Another morn than ours. (LL) The Death-Bed. Thomas Hood. GTBS-P; NOBE; OBEV; OBNC

Another mule kicking. Sterling Plumpp. GT

Another nickel in the slot. A Hero in the Land of Dough. Robert Clairmont. KaS

Another night coats the nose and ears. Night Patrol. William Daniel Ehrhart. CDa

Another Night in the Ruins. Galway Kinnell. AF; CoAP

Another of the placid beauties! Natalya Nikolayevna Goncharov. Don Coles. NOBC

Another of the Same. Sir Walter Ralegh *and* George Clifford. SiPS *Fr.* Commendatory Verses to Edmund Spenser's Fairy Queen.

Another one was coming toward me. So I Lost My Temper. Rose Romano. UnSA

Another Planet. Boris Iulianovich Poplavsky, *Russian*. TCRP, *tr. by* Emmet Jarrett *and* Richard Lourie

Another Poem about the Madness of Women. Tom Wayman. NOBC

Another Poem for Me (after Recovering from an O.D.) Etheridge Knight. NNaP

Another Reply to "In Flanders Fields." J. A. Armstrong. BLPA

Another Rhythm. Akasha (Gloria) Hull. ISC

Another road. It seems sometimes. The Idiot. Keith Wilson. Poetsp

Another Sarah. Anne Porter. KSG; TTTS

Another season centers on this place. The Gourd Dancer. N. Scott Momaday. CDW

Another September. Thomas Kinsella. BIrV; CABP; CIP-2; NoP-4

Another shall hang from the gallows' height. *Unknown. Fr.* The Fortunes of Men. ASW, *tr. by* Kevin Crossley-Holland

Another shout from the wharves. Hilda Doolittle. NOBA *Fr.* Helen in Egypt.

Another side, umbrageous Grots and Caves. Paradise. Milton. *Fr.* Book IV. OAEL-1 *Fr.* Paradise Lost.

Another snapp'd the cherry. (LL) Chop-Cherry. Robert Herrick. CavPo; GLoP

Another Song. Anne Collins. KTR

("Can e'er define.") (LL) PEW

Another Song. Donald Justice. CoAmPo; VGW

(Tune for a Lonesome Fife.) NYBP

Another Song about That Same Dead Person or Mole—Whichever it Was. *Unknown, Seneca Indian*. STP, *tr. by* Jerome Rothenberg *and* Richard Johnny John

Another Song of the Same Woman, to Some Partridges, Sent to Her Alive. Florencia del Pinar, *Spanish*. BoWoP, *tr. by* Julie Allen

Another Spirit Advances. Jules Romains, *French*. AWP, *tr. by* Joseph T. Shipley

Another Spring. Tu Fu, *Chinese*. BLT; OHPC, *tr. by* Kenneth Rexroth

Another summer! Our Independence. Fourth of July in Maine. Robert Lowell. CAPP-1

Another Sunday. Marilyn Hacker. DeD *Fr.* Love, Death and the Changing of the Seasons.

("Sometimes, when you're asleep, I want to do.")

Another Sunday Morning. Derek Mahon. CIP-2

Another Sunday Morning. Carter Revard. VoR

Another sunset of scrambled eggs. Ménage à Trois. Howard Moss. GEA; VCAP

Another Testimony. Dan Pagis, *Hebrew*. IP, *tr. by* Warren Bargad *and* Stanley F. Chyet

Another Time. W. H. Auden. MeMAP; OxBA

Another time has other lives to live. (LL) Another Time. W. H. Auden. MeMAP; OxBA

Another Time Track. Ilze Mueller. LoHo

Another to Bring in the Witch. Robert Herrick. BeJo

Another to the River Ankor. Michael Drayton. NOSC *Fr.* Idea.

Another to Urania. Benjamin Colman. ChIV-1; SCAP

Another Trail of Tears. Return to Mankiller Flats, Oklahoma. Mary Crescenzo Simons. LoHo

Another Tribute to Wyatt. Henry Howard, Earl of Surrey. SiPS

Another True Maid. Matthew Prior. FaBoEE

Another way—to see. (LL) Tint I cannot take—is best, The. Emily Dickinson. APN-2; MoAmPo

Another wedding & Aunt Cherry. Cherry. Stuart Dybek. PBCAP

Another While. Morris Jacob Rosenfeld, *Yiddish*. TrJP

Another Word for Blue. John Engman. NAmP90

Another year! Anita Virgil. HA

Another year! another deadly blow! November, 1806. Wordsworth. OBWP

Another Year Come. W. S. Merwin. NYBP

Another year it may betide. *Unknown*. HAP

Another year like a frail flower is bound. Written in Autumn. Thomas Cole. AiP

Another youthful advocate of truth and right has gone. To the Memory of J. Horace Kimball. "Ada." BlSi

Another's gone, and who comes next. The Pass of Death. George Darley. NOBRP

Ans[wer]. Kiss[e] ye, to kill ye. (LL) Upon Love, by Way of Question and Answer. Robert Herrick. CBLP; CaPo

Anseo. Paul Muldoon. CIP-2; FaBoPV; PNI

Anster Fair. William Tennant.
   "Upon a little dappled nag, whose mane." NOBRP

Answeare to my Lady Alice Edgertons Songe, Of I prethy send mee back my Hart, An. Lady Jane Cavendish. KTR

Answer, The. Sir Robert Ayton. NOSC

Answer, The. Stephen Berg. IMW

Answer, The. Bei Dao, *Chinese*. AF, *tr. by* Bonnie S. McDougall

Answer, An. Robert Frost. OBCoV

Answer, An. Perceval Gibbon. PeSAV

Answer, The. George Herbert. FaBoVe

Answer, The. Robinson Jeffers. CMoP

Answer, The. (LL) Man and Wife. Mitchell Goodman. SAGP

Answer, The. John Montague. CIP-2; TIRV

Answer, The. Sara Teasdale. PoA

Answer, The. Anne Finch, Countess of Winchilsea. NALW; NoP-4

Answer. Zhao Zhenkai, *Chinese* VCWP, *tr. by* Donald Finkel

Answer for Hope. Richard Crashaw. MeLP

(M. [*or* Mr.] Crashaw's Answer for Hope.) NOSC

Answer Me. Adah Isaacs Menken. CBWP-1

Answer me, friends. The Pupil. Veronica Porumbacu, *Romanian*. CEEP, *tr. by* Dorian, Marguerite and Elliott Urdang

Answer of Sorts, An. Leonard Nathan. WeT

Answer that ye made to me, my dear, The [*or* Th']. Sir Thomas Wyatt. SiPS

Answer to a Child's Question. Coleridge. FaBoBe; NOxBChV; NTP; OxBChV

("And my love loves me.") (LL) CTAV

(Birds, The.) BoTP; CTAV

Answer to a Kind Enquiry. Mary Holtby. UV

Answer to a Love-Letter, An. Lady Mary Wortley Montagu. *See* An Answer to a Love-Letter in Verse.

Answer to a Love-Letter in Verse, An. Lady Mary Wortley Montagu. ECWP

(Answer to a Love-Letter, An.) LW

Answer to a Man's Question, "What Can I Do About Women's Liberation?," An. Susan Griffin. GLP; NMM-2

Answer to Another Persuading a Lady to Marriage, An. Katherine Philips. HAP; WeW-3

("More bright and large than his.") (LL) PBRV; PEW

(To One Persuading a Lady to Marriage.) LW; OBEV

Answer to Cloe [*or* Chloe] Jealous. Matthew Prior. *See* A Better Answer to Cloe [*or* Chloe] Jealous.

Answer to Dunbar's "After a Visit." Joseph Cotter, Sr.. AAP

Answer to Marlowe. Sir Walter Ralegh. *See* The Nimphs [*or* Nymph's] Reply to the Sheepheard [*or* Shepherd].

Answer to Mr. Ben Jonson's Ode, to Persuade Him Not to Leave the Stage, An. Thomas Randolph. BeJo

Answer to ——'s Professions of Affection. Byron. OxBSP

Answer to the Parson, An. William Blake. FaBoEE; NBLV; OxBoLi

Answer to Thomas Barry, An. Pierce Fitzgerald, *Irish.* TIRV, *tr. by* Joan Keefe

Answer to Ting Yuan Ch'en, An. Ou-yang Hsiu, *Chinese.* OHPC, *tr. by* Kenneth Rexroth

Answer to Voznesensky and Evtushenko. Frank O'Hara. LCAP-2; NNaP; PoM

Answer to Yo / Question. Sonia Sanchez. BPo

Answer Yes or No. Robert Penn Warren. *Fr.* Tale of Time. LCAP-2

Answered Prayers. Ella Wheeler Wilcox. PWR

Answering A Child. Sarah Morgan Bryan Piatt. NCAP

Answering Li Ying Who Showed Me His Poems about Summer Fishing. Yü Hsüan-chi, *Chinese.* BoWoP, *tr. by* Geoffrey Waters

Answering Machine, The. Philip Schultz. NAmP90

Answers. The. Robert Clairmont. OTCP

Answers. Elizabeth Jennings. OxBSP; OxBTC

Ant, The. Richard Flecknoe. NOSC

Ant, The. Richard Lovelace. CaPo

Ant climbs up a trunk, The. A Short Story. David Escobar Galindo, *Spanish.* ChAP, *tr. by* Piche, Jorge D.

Ant Dodger. Bill Knott. PBCAP

Ant-Heap, The. Arthur Christopher Benson. EBVV

Ant Hill, The. Cynthia Zarin. NoP-4

Ant-Hills. "Marian Douglas." OBCA

Ant on the tablecloth, An. Departmental. Robert Frost. HeIP-4; HoPM; MoAmPo; NAAL-2; NOBA; NOBL; OBAL; PeLV; SAGP; SoSe-8

Ant-seething city, city full of dreams. The Seven Old Men. Charles Baudelaire, *French.* OBVE, *tr. by* Roy Campbell

Ant Trap, The. Joe Rosenblatt. NOBC

Ant wyht in wode be fleme. (LL) Lenten Is Come with Love to Toune. *Unknown.* EBEV; HAP; MiEL; OBEV

Antarctica. Derek Mahon. PBCIP

Antarctica. Ronald Albert Simpson. CBAP

Ante-bellum Negro prayed, The. Must Be Freed. Lizelia Augusta Jenkins Moorer. CBWP-3

Ante-Bellum Sermon, An. Paul Laurence Dunbar. AAP; APN-2; BPo; NAAAL

Ante Mortem. Robinson Jeffers. MoAmPo

Antelope, An. At the zoo (two poems). Sasaki Yukitsuna, *Japanese.* MJT, *tr. by* Makoto Ueda

Antemasque, The: Witches the Nomber Beinge Five. Lady Jane Cavendish. KTR *Fr.* A Pastorall.

Anteroom: Geneva. Denis Devlin. CIP-2

Anthea bade me tie [*or* tye] her sho[o]e. The Sho[o]e Tying. Robert Herrick. CaPo

Anthem: "Let us praise our Maker, with true passion extol Him." W. H. Auden. NOCV

Anthem, An. Sonia Sanchez. UnSA

Anthem for Doomed Youth. Wilfred Owen. AF; APAD; CABP; CMoP; ClHu; EBEV; FaBoMo; GEA; GSo; GTBS-P; HAP; HeIP-4; HoPM; ImPo; InPK-6; InPS-3; LiTM; MoBrPo; MoP; NAEL-2; NOBE; NoAM; NoP-4; OAEL-2; OBEV; OBWP; OxBTC; PoE; PoFWW; PoPoPo; SAGP; SCV; SoSe-8; Son; TFi; WeW-3

Anthem for St. Cecilia's Day. W. H. Auden.

"In a garden shady this holy lady." FaBoTw; TwCP

Anthologistics. Arthur Guiterman. NBLV

Anthology of Nouns. Parker Tyler. PoA

Anthology Poem. Petra von Morstein. BoWoP, *tr. by* Rosemarie Waldrop

Anthropophagites See a Sign on NC Highway 177 That Looks like Heaven, The. Jonathan Williams. OBAL

Anti-aircraft seen from a certain distance. Dam Neck, Virginia. Richard Eberhart. PoWW

Anti-Father. Rita Dove. IFJA

Anti-Lazarus, The. Nicanor Parra, *Spanish.* GI, *tr. by* Edith Grossman

Anti-Love Poems. Elizabeth Brewster. NOBC

Anti-mnemonic self-vaccination. Joyce Mansour, *French.* MFP, *tr. by* Martin Sorrell

Anti-Semanticist, The. Everett Hoagland. BPo; NBV

Antic Hay. Aldous Leonard Huxley.

"Christlike is my behaviour." OBCoV

Antic Quatrains. Jackson MacLow. PmAP

Antichrist, or the Reunion of Christendom; an Ode. G. K. Chesterton. NOBE; NOBL; OBSV; OxAEP-2

Antichrist, playing his lissome flute and merry. Armageddon. John Crowe Ransom. ChIV-2; MeMAP

Anticipating life, to hasten death! (LL) A Rose. Sir Richard Fanshawe. AWP; OBEV; PoEL-2

Anticipation. Emily Jane Brontë. OBNC

Anticipation. Sheila Richter. LoHo

Antico Inverno. Salvatore Quasimodo, *Italian.* NNPT, *tr. by* W. C. Fitzgerald

Antidoted Fanfreluches: or, a Galimatia of Extravagant Conceits Found in an Ancient Monument, The. François Rabelais, *French.* CBNP, *tr. by* Sir Thomas Urquhart

Antiginides' two daughters, Melo. Leonidas of Tarentum, *Greek.* GrAn, *tr. by* Alan Marshfield

Antigone. Sophocles, *Greek.* NAWM-1, *tr. by* Robert Fagles

Chorus. PiM, *tr. by* Robert Fagles

"Many marvels walk through the world." OBCVT, *tr. by* Richard Emil Braun

"Numberless wonders / terrible wonders walk the world but none the match for man—." GrIP

"Over come—O bitter sweetness." OBCVT, *tr. by* W. B. Yeats

Antigone I. Herbert Martin. PoBA

Antigone VI. Herbert Martin. PoBA

Antigone and Oedipus. Henrietta Cordelia Ray. AAP; BlSi; CBWP-3

Antigonish. Hughes Mearns. FPC; NBLV; PoLF

("As I was walking up the stair.") NOxBChV

(Little Man Who Wasn't There, The.) CTV

Antikrates knew the stars. Philodemus, *Greek.* PGA, *tr. by* Kenneth Rexroth

Antiodemis, Aphrodite's pet cherub, from a baby. Antipater of Sidon, *Greek.* GrAn, *tr. by* Tony Harrison

Antipastoral Memory of One Summer, An. Dave Jeddie Smith. MT

Antipathy. Martial, *Latin.* OBCVT, *tr. by* Rowland Watkyns

Antipathy. Rowland Watkyns, *after the Latin of* Martial. FaBoEE

Antiphanes, son of the same, to Hermes. Dedication of a Torch. Crinagoras, *Greek.* GrAn, *tr. by* Alistair Elliot

Antiphon: "Let all the world in ev'ry corner sing / My God and King." George Herbert. PeECV

Antiphon for Divine Wisdom. Hildegard von Bingen, *German.* WPoS, *tr. by* Barbara Newman

Antiphon for the Angels. Hildegard von Bingen, *German.* WPoS, *tr. by* Barbara Newman

Antiphon for the Holy Spirit. Hildegard von Bingen, *German.* WPoS, *tr. by* Barbara Newman

Antiphonal Hymn in Praise of Inanna. Enheduanna, *Sumerian.* BoWoP, *ad. by* Aliki *and* Willis Barnstone

Antiplatonic[k], The. John Cleveland. CBLP; NOSC; PBRV; SeCP

Antipsalm. Novica Tadic, *Serbo-Croatian.* HSix; VCWP, *tr. by* Charles Simic

Antiquary, The. Joseph Campbell. OxBTC

Antiquary. Donne. EBEV; NOSC

Antiquary, The. Sir Walter Scott.

Oyster, The. FaBoCh; NTP

Red Harlaw. OxBB

Antique Father. Carolyn Kizer. MoLi

Antique Harvesters. John Crowe Ransom. FuPo; MoAmPo; OxBA

("Why, the ribs of the earth subsist frail as a breath / If but God wearieth.") (LL) FuPo

Antique Shop. Tina Barr. EC3

Antiques. Walter De la Mare. PoA

Antiquitez de Rome. Joachim Du Bellay, *French.* NNPT, *tr. by* Edmund Spenser *Fr.* Ruins of Rome.

Antiseptic Baby and the Prophylactic Pup, The. Strictly Germ-proof. Arthur Guiterman. BLPA; TrJP

Antlered forests, The. Ank'hor Vat. Denis Devlin. BIrV; CIP-2; NOIV

Antlered scarab rolled a dungball, The. Near Damascus. W. S. Di Piero. ChIV-2

Anton Mikhailovich spat, said "Ugh," spat again, said "Ugh" again, spat. Symphony No. 2. Daniil Kharms, *Russian*. AF, *tr. by* George Gibian

Antonio, Antonio. Laura Elizabeth Richards. CTV; OBCA

Antonio Ce De Baca. Mu Tío Baca el Poeta de Socorro. Jimmy Santiago Baca. PmAP

Antony and Cleopatra. José-Maria de Heredia, *Spanish*. EP; FLP, *tr. by* Alistair Elliot

Antony and Cleopatra. William Haines Lytle. BLPA

Antony and Cleopatra. Shakespeare.
 "Age cannot wither her, nor custom stale." ImPo
 Cleopatra's Lament. UnPo
 Drinking Song, A. NoSic
 "Enobarbus, Antony." OxAEP-1
 "Eros, thou yet behold'st me?" EBEV; OxAEP-1
 "How now! is he dead?" OxAEP-1
 "Miserable change now at my end, The." EBEV
 "Most noble empress, you have heard of me?" OxAEP-1
 "Noblest of men, woo't die?" IMW, *act* V, *scene* 1; OxAEP-1, *sect.* IV, xiii
 "O! bear me witness, night." OxAEP-1
 "Thou hast a sister by the mother's side." OxAEP-1
 "Welcome from Egypt, sir." FaBoSe
 "Welcome from Egypt, sir." FaBoSe

Antony's Oration [over Caesar's Body]. Shakespeare. *See* Mark Antony Addresses the Mob.

Antrim. Robinson Jeffers. BIrV; IIP; NOBA; VGW
 ("Plot the agony of resurrection.") (LL) SAGP

Ants and Others. Adrien Stoutenburg. FYAP; NYBP

Ants are walking under the ground, The. The People. Elizabeth Madox Roberts. NOxBChV

Ants look up as I trot by. Dog's Song. Robert Wallace. TLR

Antwerp. Ford Madox Ford.
 "This is Charing Cross." PeFWW

Antwerp: Musée Des Beaux-Arts. Alan Ross. NYBP

Antwerp to Ghent. D. G. Rossetti. PeVV, *sect.* V *Fr.* A Trip to Paris and Belgium.

Anvil arrow bow box and brahmin. The Alphabet. Jejuri Arun Kolatkar, *Marathi*. OMIP, *tr. by* Vinay Dharwadker

Anvil—God's Word, The. John Clifford. BLPA; PoToHe

Anxiety about Dying. Alicia Ostriker. CrSp

Anxious and trembling for the birth of Fate. (LL) The Voyage on the Thames. Alexander Pope. EBEV; EBNV; ECEV; NOBE; NOEC; OxAEP-1

Any clear thing that blinds us with surprise. Fishnet. Robert Lowell. HCAP; VCAP

Any cold night I am hiding. Some people. Runaway Teen. William Stafford. LiLi

Any color, so long as it's red. Red. Eugene Field. CA

Any Complaints? Vernon Scannell. OxBTC

Any country is only a way of failing. Considerations. David Helwig. NOBC

Any dogsbody can sit up all night. Power Cut. Seamus Deane. PBCIP

Any fool knows a Br'er in a rocker. Br'er Sterling and the Rocker. Michael S. Harper. NAAAL

Any Husband or Wife. Carol Haynes. *See* Any Wife or Husband.

Any Husband to Many a Wife. Emily Jane Pfeiffer. VWP

Any longer, only its stilled shapes. Galway Kinnell. *See* The Last Hiding Places of Snow.

Any Man's Advice to His Son. Kenneth Fearing. CMoP

Any messages, messages, any word? Written in London after a Protest Parade. Jean Garrigue. NMM 2

Any movement kills something. Roberto Juarroz, *Spanish*. VCWP, *tr. by* Mary Crow

Any niche is my college. A Hedge Schoolmaster. Padraic Fallon. CIP-2

Any of the several names. Eulogy for Populations. Ron Welburn. PoBA

Any Part of Piggy. Noël Coward. NBLV; PeLV

Any Saint. Francis Thompson. MoBrPo

A*ny shape* does for me!" (LL) The Camel's Complaint. Charles Edward Carryl. CTAV; NOxBChV; OBCA; OTCP; OxBChV

Any Soul to Any Body. Cosmo Monkhouse. NOBVV

Any thing to me. Hark[e], Despair away. (LL) The Bag. George Herbert. ESCV; GeHe; SeCP

Any thing to me. Harke, Despair away. George Herbert. *See* The Bag.

Any Wife or Husband. Carol Haynes. BLPA
 (Any Husband or Wife.) PoToHe

Any Wife to Any Husband. Robert Browning. OBNC; RACG

Any woman who can give birth to God deserves, I think, a pretty lively. So Let's Look at It Another Way. John Godfrey. PmAP

Any woman's death diminishes me. (LL) From an Old House in America. Adrienne Rich. NNaP; TRP

Anyone, Lifting. Alberta Turner. CMAP

Anyone lived in a pretty how town. E. E. Cummings. CMoP; ChAP; ColAP; EBEvV; HAP; InPK-6; LiTM; MeMAP; MoAmPo; NAAL-2; NOBA; NoP-4; PoA; PoPoPo; Poetr; RB; TAP; TFi; TwCP; VGW

Anyone who has waded. Love's Constancy. Hadewijch, *Flemish*. WPoS, *tr. by* Oliver Davies

Anyone with quiet pace who. Walking West. William Stafford. RB

Anys for my saik. (LL) The Ballad of Kynd Kittok. William Dunbar. OxBoLi; PeLV

Anything at all. Gwendolyn Brooks. *See* Narcissa.

Anything beyond / the nothing when. That Land (3). Stephen Sartarelli. PT

Anything empty as death? Empty as Death. Pyong-hwa Cho, *Korean*. CKP, *tr. by* Jaihiun Kim

Anything Goes. Cole Porter. OBAL

Anyway the time has come to explain. Poem. Jack Kerouac. CLPP

Anyway we are always waking. Souvenirs. Jane Cooper. *Fr.* Dispossessions. FaBoWP

Anywhere, anywhere, out of this room! (LL) A Scherzo. Dora Greenwell. PEW; SDW

Anywhere Out of the World. Charles Baudelaire, *French*. PT, *tr. by* David Rosenberg

Anywoman cannot see his dream. Anywoman's Lyric. Janet Rodney. PT *Fr.* Anywoman's Lyric.

Aodh Ruadh O'Domhnaill. Thomas MacGreevy. CIP-2; OBMV

Aoibhinn, A Leabhráin, Do Thriall. *Unknown, Irish*. BIrV, *tr. by* Flann O'Brien

Apart, and on the sacred hill retired. William Hayley. EPCY *Fr.* An Essay on Epic Poetry.

Apart from my sisters, estranged. Cinderella. Olga Broumas. InPK-6

Apart possibly from waving hands to the cliff-divers. Johnny Weissmuller Dead in Acapulco. Clive James. NOBAu

Apart, thank Heaven, from all to do. The Owl. Walter De la Mare. OxBSP

Apartment Cats. Thom Gunn. PC

Ape. Russell Edson. PmAP; RaBo

Apeneck Sweeney spreads his knees. Sweeney Among the Nightingales. T. S. Eliot. AmPP; CMoP; FaBoMo; HAP; HeIP-4; LiTM; MoP; NAAL-2; NAEL-2; NOBA; NOBE; NoAM; NoP-4; OBMV; OxBA; PoPoPo; Poetr; TFi; WeW-3

Apes in Avernus. (LL) Hark, All You Ladies [That Do Sleep]. Thomas Campion. AAS; EBEV; NoSic; PoEL-2

Apes yawn and adore their fleas in the sun, The. The Jaguar. Ted Hughes. LiTM

Apex. Nate Salsbury. NBLV

Aphorisms. Joel Chandler Harris. CrDW *Fr.* Uncle Remus: His Songs and His Sayings.

Aphrodisiac, The. Medbh McGuckian. PBCIP

Aphrodite! / Aphrodite of the blue sleep. Blue Sleep. Winifred Bryher. PoA

Aphrodite reveals herself. *Unknown, Greek*. OBCVT, *tr. by* John D. Niles

Apis Mellifica. Roger McDonald. NOBAu

APO 96225. Larry Rottman. CDa

Apocalypse. D. J. Enright. OBSV

Apocalypse, The. Ilsong Kwon, *Korean*. CKP, *tr. by* Jaihiun Kim

Apocalypse. Francis Ernest Kobina Parkes. PBA

Apocalypse and Resurrection. John Clifford Bayliss. SPE

Apocalypse Dub. Dennis Scott. HCP

Apocatastasis Foretold in the Shape of a Canvas of Smoke. T. R. Hummer. BAP-95

Apocrypha. János Pilinszky, *Hungarian*. PoSu, *tr. by* Ted Hughes

Apocrypha of Jacques Derrida, The. Norman Dubie. NAmP90

Apocryphal Gospel, An. Jorge Luis Borges, *Spanish*.
 From an Apocryphal Gospel. GI, *tr. by* Norman Thomas Di Giovanni

Apointed in the newe Mone. Medea rejuvenates Aeson. Ovid, *Latin*. OBCVT, *tr. by* John Gower

Apolitical Intellectuals. Otto René Castillo, *Spanish*. AF, *tr. by* Margaret Randall

APOLLINAIRE. Unhistorical Events. Bob Kaufman. CLPP

Apollinaire said. *Unknown*. APAD

Apollo. Thomas Holley Chivers. APN-1

APOLLO. Stanley Cook. SpW

Apollo and Daphne. Paul Whitehead.
  Hunting Song. OxBoLi

Apollo and Daphne. Yvor Winters. Son

Apollo and Marsyas. Zbigniew Herbert, *Polish.* PoSu, *tr.* by John *and* Bogdana Capenter

Apollo as lately a circuit he made. The Circuit of Apollo. Anne Finch, Countess of Winchilsea. CABP; NALW

Apollo Café. Stephen Gray. PeSAV

Apollo Defeats Patroclus. Homer, *Greek.* OBVE, *tr.* by Christopher Logue *Fr.* The Iliad.
  (Apollo hits Patroclus.) OBCVT, *tr.* by Christopher Logue
  ("His hand came from the east.") OBCVT, *tr.* by Christopher Logue
  ("Perhaps.") (LL) OBCVT, *tr.* by Christopher Logue

Apollo Hits Patroclus. Homer. *See* Apollo Defeats Patroclus.

Apollo kept my father's sheep. A Daughter of Admetus. Thomas Sturge Moore. FaBoTw

Apollo now, Sol's carman, drives his stud. Evening; an Elegy. Horace Smith. BXAP

Apollo shrieked—and lo! from all his limbs / Celestial. (LL) Hyperion. Keats. OAEL-2

Apollo Takes Charge of His Muses. A. E. Stallings. BAP-94

Apollophanes married for an alibi. Lucilius, *Greek.* GrAn, *tr.* by Peter Porter

Apollo's first, at last the true God's Priest. (LL) An Elegie upon the Death of the Deane of Pauls, Dr. Donne. Thomas Carew. BeJo; CABP; CaPo; CavPo; EPCY; MeLP; NoP-4; OAEL-1; PBRV; SeCP

Apologia. Lord Alfred Bruce Douglas. ADE

Apologia (Nkomati). Wole Soyinka. HBAPE

Apologia Pro Poemate Meo. Wilfred Owen. LiTM; MoBrPo; NAEL-2; NSI; PeFWW; PoFWW

Apologia pro Vita Sua. A. R. Ammons. HCAP; NOBA

Apologia pro Vita Sua. Coleridge. OxBSP

Apologia pro Vita Sua. Alexander Pope. NOBE *Fr.* Epistle to Dr. Arbuthnot. FHYEP; InPS-3; NoP-4; OAEL-1; OxAEP-1; PoE; PoEL-3; TFi

Apologia pro Vita Sua. Sedulius Scottus, *Latin.* BIrV, *tr.* by Helen Waddell

Apologie for Having Loved Before, An. Edmund Waller. CBLP

Apologie for the Precedent Hymnes on Tereas, An. Richard Crashaw. ESCV

Apologies, dear Aphrodite. I. Philodemos the Epicurean, *Greek.* InMo, *tr.* by Sam Hamill

Apologist's Evening Prayer, The. C. S. Lewis. TrCP

Apologue. Tony Connor. BoLoP

Apologues of Winter Light. Christopher Buckley. PuP-15

Apology, An. Anne Bradstreet. KTR

Apology. Anthony Cronin. CIP-2

Apology, The. Ralph Waldo Emerson. AmPP

Apology, An. William Morris. AWP; EBVV; EnVR; NAEL-2; OAEL-2; OBNC *Fr.* The Earthly Paradise.
  (Earthly Paradise, The.) NoP-4

Apology. Duane Niatum. HATNAP

Apology. Elizabeth Spires. FFC

Apology. Anne Stevenson. WeT

Apology, An. Diane Wakoski. TAP

Apology. William Carlos Williams. OxBA; SAmP

Apology and Explanation. John Sparrow. OBCoV

Apology for Actors, An. Thomas Heywood.
  Author to His Book[e], The. NOSC

Apology for Bad Dreams. Robinson Jeffers. AmPP; MoAmPo; NOBA; OxBA

Apology for Domitian. Robert Penn Warren. NOBA

Apology for the Revival of Christian Architecture in England, An. Geoffrey Hill.
  Idylls of the King. NoAM; PoE
  Laurel Axe, The. NAEL-2; NoAM; PoE
  ("Crystals kissed / in cabinets of amethyst and frost.") (LL) NoP-4
  Quaint Mazes. NoAM

Apology for Understatement. John Wain. OxBTC; PFE

Apon the midsummer evin, mirriest of nichtis. William Dunbar. EnVB, *ll.* 1–149 *Fr.* The Tretis of the Tua Mariit Wemen and the Wedo. OxBS

Apostasy. Aus of Kuraiza, *Arabic.* TrJP, *tr.* by Hartwig Hirschfeld

Apostasy of One and But One Lady, The. Richard Lovelace. CaPo

Apostate, The. Alfred Edgar Coppard. OBMV

Apostates and run-aways. Michael Wigglesworth. ColAP *Fr.* The Day of Doom.

Apostles, The. Donne. *Fr.* The Litanie. PoEL-2

Apostles' Creed, The. *Unknown.* CTV

Apostles of the hidden sun. The Last Supper. Oscar Williams. ImPo; LiTM

Apostrophe to Man. Edna St. Vincent Millay. NALW; PBMP

Apothegms and Counsels. Colette Inez. EOEF

Apotheosis of the Kitchen Goddess II. Teresa Noelle Roberts. CrSp

Appalachian Convalescence. Robert Conquest. OxBC

Appalachian Front. Robert Lewis Weeks. NYBP

Appaloosa, The. Michael S. Weaver. GT

Apparatus is right, The. Note to the Ophthalmologist. Dolores Kendrick. FFC

Apparel of green woods and meadows gay. On Revisiting Cintra after the Death of Catarina. Luis de Camões, *Spanish.* AWP, *tr.* by Richard Garnett

Apparent Failure. Robert Browning. EBVVPR; NAEL-2; NOBE

Apparently in the real past tough men dazzled the illiterate tribes. Kelvin Corcoran. NBrP

Apparently with no surprise. Emily Dickinson. AmPP; NAAL-1; NAAL-3; PFE; Poetr; SAmP; SoSe-8

Apparently / You hate most of the people. Longterm Hatred. David Avidan, *Hebrew.* IP, *tr.* by Warren Bargad *and* Stanley F. Chyet

Apparition, The. Donne. ESCV; EnLoPo; FSCP; GBL; GLoP; HeIP-4; NAEL-1; NAWM-1; NOBE; NOBL; NoSic; OAEL-1; OBEV; OxBSn; PoE; SCGP; SCV; SeCP; SoSe-8; TFi

Apparition, The. Herman Melville. APN-2; NCAP

Apparition, The. Bernard O'Donoghue. NoP-4

Apparition, The. Stephen Phillips. OBEV
  (As Of Old.) LBC

Apparition of a salsa band, The. Latin Night at the Pawnshop. Martín Espada. TRP; WWSi

Apparition of His Mistress[e] Calling Him to Elizium [*or* Elysium], The. Robert Herrick. CaPo; SeCP

Apparition of these faces in the crowd, The. In A Station of the Metro. Ezra Pound. AmPP; ChAP; ColAP; HAP; HeIP-4; InPK-6; MeMAP; MoAmPo; MoP; NAAL-2; NIP-4; NOBA; NoAM; NoP-4; OxBA; PFE; PoE; PoPoPo; Poetr; TAP; TFi; UnPo; VGW; WeW-3

Apparitions, The. W. B. Yeats. CMoP; LiTM; OxBSn; TRP

Appassionato. Lyubomir Levchev, *Bulgarian.* CEEP, *tr.* by Jascha Kessler *and* Aleksandar Shurbanov

Appeal. Edith Nesbit. LW

Appeal. Noémia da Sousa, *Portuguese.* WPOW, *tr.* by Alan Ryder; TTY, *tr.* by Dorothy Guedes *and* Philippa Rumsey; PBMAP

Appeal, An. *Unknown.* NSI

Appeal, The. Sir Thomas Wyatt. *See* The Lover's Appeal.

Appeal to Cats in the Business of Love, An. Thomas Flatman. APAD; EnLoPo; GBL; HAP; OBCoV; PC

Appeal to My Country Women, An. Frances Ellen Watkins Harper. *See* An Appeal to My Countrywomen.

Appeal to My Countrywomen, An. Frances Ellen Watkins Harper. BlSi
  (Appeal to My Country Women, An.) NAAAL

Appeal to the Moongod Nanna-Suen to Throw Out Lugalanne. Enheduanna, *Sumerian.* BoWoP, *tr.* by Aliki *and* Willis Barnstone

Appear, O Mother, was the perpetual cry. Invocation. Wilfred Watson. MoCV

Appearance, An. Sylvia Plath. CAPP-1

Appearance and Reality. John Hollander. OBAL

Appearances. Robert Browning. OxBSP

Appeared to me just now. Ezra Pound's Eye. Anne Hussey. WeT

Appeas'd, the Nymph recover'd her first looke. Io recovers her shape. Ovid, *Latin.* OBCVT, *tr.* by George Sandys

Appendix to the Anniad. Gwendolyn Brooks. BlSi

Appendix to the Vision of Peace, An. Yehuda Amichai, *Hebrew.* PoSu, *tr.* by Glenda Abramson *and* Tudor Parfitt

Appetizers'. Bruce Andrews. FTOS *Fr.* Tizzy Boost.

Applauding youths laughed with young prostitutes. The Harlem Dancer. Claude McKay. BPo; CrDW; ISC; NIP-4; NoAM; SAGP; Son; TAP

Apple, The. Plato, *Greek.* WeW-3

Apple, The. Ray Smith. TrCP

Apple-Barrel of Johnny Appleseed, The. Vachel Lindsay. OxBA

Apple Blight. Paul Zimmer. VGW

Apple Blossom. Louis MacNeice. NTP; PeECV; RB

Apple-blossom, a great spread of it. And Where Do You Stand on the National Question. Tom Paulin. CIP-2

Apple Blossoms. Henry Adams Parker. BoTP

Apple blossoms look like snow. A Comparison. John Chipman Farrar. WHSW

Apple Core. Clarence Major. GT

Apple-Culture. John Philips. OxAEP-1 *Fr.* Cyder.

Apple Dumplings. Mary E. Tucker. CBWP-1

Apple Dumplings and a King, The. "Peter Pindar." OBSV

Apple-Eater, The. Linda Curtis Meyers. IFJA

Apple falls, falling in the quiet night, The. (LL) History among the Rocks. Robert Penn Warren. CBCWP; MoAmPo

Apple from the cupboard rolled to the floor, The. Miroslav Valek, *German*. CEEP, *tr. by* Ewald Osers

Apple Gathering, An. Christina Rossetti. NAEL-2; OBNC

Apple Harvest. Helen Leuty. BoTP

Apple Hell. Mark Van Doren. PoA

Apple of islands, Sirmio, & bright peninsulas, set. Carmen 31. Catullus. OBVE, *tr. by* Thomas Hardy *Fr*. Carmina.

Apple of My Eye. Rosalie Sorrels.
 "What can I say, but that it's not easy?" MDDM

Apple on its bough is her desire, The. Garden Abstract. Hart Crane. GaP; MeMAP; OBGa

Apple Orchard in the Spring, An. William Martin. PWR

Apple Peeler. Robert Francis. LCAP-2

Apple-pie, apple-pie. *Unknown*. OxNR

Apple-raid, The. Vernon Scannell. NOxBChV

Apple Rhyme, The. Madeleine Nightingale. BoTP

Apple Rind. Carol Frost. PuP-17

Apple Tree, The. James Keir Baxter. OxBC

Apple Tree and a Pig, An. Emyr Humphreys. OBWVE

Apple-Tree Man, The. Charles Causley. OBSP

Apple Trees, The. Louise Glück. HCAP

Apple unbitten in the palm, The. (LL) As Bad as a Mile. Philip Larkin. InPK-6; OxBC; OxBSP

Apple Valley School has closed its books, The. Country School. Ted Kooser. KaS

Apples. Donald Hall. LCAP-2

Apples. Shirley Kaufman. CrSp; MDDM; NMM-2

Apples, bright on the leafless bough. Apple Hell. Mark Van Doren. PoA

Apples, Normandy, 1944. Frank Ormsby. PNI *Fr*. A Northern Spring.

Apples of gold, in silver pictures shrined. Meditation 42. Edward Taylor. NAAL-1; NAAL-3 *Fr*. Preparatory Meditations Before My Approach to the Lord's Supper.

Apples on Champlain. Richard Kenney. NoP-4

Apples, swallowing her life. (LL) Apples. Shirley Kaufman. NMM-2

Applicant, The. Sylvia Plath. NAAL-2; NOBA; PoPoPo; TwCP

Appoggiatura. Donald Jeffrey Hayes. PoBA

Appointed Rounds. Louis Jenkins. RaBo

Appointed winners in a long-stretch'd game, The. To-day and Thee. Walt Whitman. PFE

Appointment, The. Leonard Alfred George Strong. OxBTC

Appraisal. Sara Teasdale. MoAmPo

Apprehension. Phillip McCaffrey. EC2

Apprehension this spring. . . the leaves, the leaves. Homage and Lament for Ezra Pound in Captivity. Robert Duncan. NOBA

Apprentice Painter, The. Jack Myers. AmPA

Approach of the Storm, The. *Unknown, Chippewa*. OBVE; TTTS, *tr. by* Frances Densmore

Approach to a City. William Carlos Williams. PoRA

Approach to Thebes, The. Stanley Kunitz. PoA

Approaches, The. W. S. Merwin. NOBA

Approaching a Significant Birthday, He Peruses The Norton Anthology of Poetry. R. S. Gwynn. RA

Approaching Dance, The. *Unknown*. APN-2 *Fr*. War Dance. APN-2, *tr. by* George Catlin

Approaching death. William Carlos Williams. FaBoMo *Fr*. Asphodel, That Greeny Flower.

Approaching night her mantle flings. To ———. James M. Whitfield. AAP

Approaching Storm. Slavko Mihalic, *Croatian*. CEEP, *tr. by* Peter Kastmiler

Approves all forms of competition. Arthur Hugh Clough. *See* The Latest Decalogue.

Approximate Man, The. Tristan Tzara, *French*.
 Part One. PFTM, *tr. by* Jerome Rothenberg

Approximately. Diane Ward. FTOS

Après le Bain. William Carlos Williams. OBAL

Après-midi d'un Faune, L'. Stéphane Mallarmé, *French*. AWP, *tr. by* Aldous Huxley

Apricot about to fade, raindrops quiet now. Things Seen. Yüan Mei, *Chinese*. CoBLCP, *tr. by* Jonathan Chaves

Apricot Garden. Yüan Chen, *Chinese*. SuSp, *tr. by* Angela Jung Palandri

Apricot Tree. Magda Isanos, *Rumanian*. BoWoP, *tr. by* Willis Barnstone *and* Matei Calinescu

Apricot trees form a grove. Pien Kung. *Fr*. Mooring at K'ou-ch'üeh—Sent to Dr. Lin. CoBLCP, *tr. by* Jonathan Chaves

Apricots Die Young. Meng Chiao, *Chinese*.
 "Don't let freezing hands play with these pearls." SuSp, *tr. by* Stephen Owen
 "In vain I gather up these stars from the ground." SuSp, *tr. by* Stephen Owen
 "It must have been a single thread of tears." SuSp, *tr. by* Stephen Owen
 "Nipping chill, the frost killed spring." SuSp, *tr. by* Stephen Owen
 "When I tread the earth, I fear to hurt the ground." SuSp, *tr. by* Stephen Owen
 "When my son was born, the moon was not bright." SuSp, *tr. by* Stephen Owen

April. Vidame de Chartres, *French*. AWP, *tr. by* Swinburne

April. Amy Lowell. CPO

April. Howard Nemerov. *Fr*. Epigrams. OBAL

April. Mogwol Park, *Korean*. CKP, *tr. by* Jaihiun Kim

April. Linda Pastan. Poetsp

April. Ezra Pound. CMoP

April. Henrietta Cordelia Ray. CBWP-3

April. Folgore da San Geminiano. *Fr*. Sonnets of the Months. AWP, *tr. by* D. G. Rossetti

April. Samuel Thompson. BIrV

April. Jean Valentine. TAP

April. Charles Wright. MT

April 30, 1975. John Balaban. CDa

April again, and it is a year again. Elegy. Sidney Keyes. NoP-4

April, and a fool's good day. April Notebook. Christian Karlson Stead. PeNZ

April, and the last of the plum blossoms. A Sleepless Night. Philip Levine. BLT

April, April, / Laugh thy girlish laughter. Song. Sir William Watson. BoTP; OBEV

April at last wakes up. Spring. Kirim Kim, *Korean*. CKP, *tr. by* Jaihiun Kim

April. Bad month. Visit spa. Limerick. Stanley J. Sharpless. PeLi

April, 1885. Robert Bridges. OxBSP; OxBTC

April 5, 1974. Richard Wilbur. HCAP

April Fool, The. Eugene Field. PWR

April Fool. Hal Summers. AYFP

April Fool Birthday Poem for Grandpa. Diane Di Prima. CLPP
 ("They may look on earth / and not be ashamed.") (LL) UnSA
 ("Today is your / birthday and I have tried.") NMM-2

April Fools' Day. Yusef Komunyakaa. GT

April Fool's Day. *Unknown*. *See* All Fools' Day.

April Fool's Day, Mount Pleasant Cemetery. A. F. Moritz. BAP-93

April Fool's Day, or St. Mary Egypt. John Berryman. ChIV-2 *Fr*. Dream Songs.

April Gale. Ivor Gurney. Spl

April Hill, The. Janet Lewis. CRP

April. I have wheeled you to the park. Oradour-sur-Glane. Silence. Lucia Cordell Getsi. LoHo

April in New York. Nicholas Christopher. WWSi

April in Town. Lizette Woodworth Reese. AYFP

April in Town. Yury Ryashentsev, *Russian*. TCRP, *tr. by* Daniel Weissbort

April Inventory. W. D. Snodgrass. CoAP; ColAP; HAP; LiTM; NoAM; NoP-4; Poetr; TAP; TRP; TwCP; VCAP

April is in my mistress' face. All Seasons in One. *Unknown*. GBL; HeIP-4

April is on the way! Alice Moore Dunbar-Nelson. NAAAL

April is the cruellest month, breeding. The Waste Land. T. S. Eliot. AmPP; CABP; CMoP; FaBoMo; HAP; LiTM; MoAmPo; MoP; NAAL-2; NAEL-2; NAWM-2; NOBA; NOBE; NoAM; NoP-4; OAEL-2; OxAEP-2; OxBA; OxBTC; PoE; TAP; TFi; UnPo

April Mortality. Léonie Adams. MoAmPo

April 1939. Dorothy, Duchess of Wellington Wellesley. WPN

April 1962. Paul Goodman. VGW

April Notebook. Christian Karlson Stead. PeNZ

April plunges the classroom into light. Remembering the Ardèche. Emily Grosholz. RA

April Poem. Gerda Mayer. AYFP

April, pride of woodland ways. Remy Belleau, *French*. AWP, *tr. by* Andrew Lang

(April Rain). Robert Loveman. BoTP; CTV; TrJP

April Rain Song. Langston Hughes. AYFP; ImGa; NOxBChV; NTCP; OBCA

April Rape. Marilyn Nelson. IFJA

April this year, not otherwise. Song of a Second April. Edna St. Vincent Millay. CMoP; OxBA

April Wind. Frederick Turner. RA

April. You hearken, my fellow. Earth's Lyric. Bliss Carman *and* Richard Hovey (1864–1900). APN-2

Aprill. Edmund Spenser. NAEL-1 *Fr.* The Shepheardes [*or* Shepeards *or* Shepherd's] Calender.

   ("Tell me, good Hobbinoll, what garres thee greete?") OBEV; PoEL-1

Ditty, A: In Praise of Eliza, Queen of the Shepherds. OBEV

   (Ditty, A: "See where she sits upon the grassy green.") FaBoCh

Lay to Eliza, The. NOBE

Aprille is of al the months moste dyr. Burialle of the Dede. Martin Fagg. BXAP

Aprilly. Bert Leston Taylor. OBAL

Apron of Flowers, The. Robert Herrick. CaPo

Apron Strings. Marge Piercy. TAP

Aprons of Silence. Carl Sandburg. NOBA

Apropos of Garden Statuary: A Disquisition upon a Minor Genre. Robert Druce. OBGa

Apropos of garden statuary, sir. Apropos of Garden Statuary: A Disquisition upon a Minor Genre. Robert Druce. OBGa

Aquarium, The. Thom Gunn. NOxBChV *Fr.* Three for Children.

Aquarium. George T. Wright. NYBP

Ar(chibald')s Poetica. Alan Ribback. BXAP

Arab and His Donkey, An. *Unknown.* NBLV

Arab came to the river side, An. An Arab and His Donkey. *Unknown.* NBLV

Arab Chieftain to His Young Wife, An. Abid ibn al-Abras, *Arabic.* ArPe, tr. by Omar S. Pound

Arab in a bloodied turban on a tall mangy camel, An. War. "Georgy Avdeievich Rayevsky," *Russian.* TCRP, tr. by Albert C. Todd

Arab Love-Song, An. Francis Thompson. AWP; MoBrPo

Arabesque. Fred Johnson. PoBA

Arabia. John Meade Falkner. OxBTC

Arabian Night Garden, An. Tennyson. GaP

Arabs complain—or so I have been told. For the Rain It Raineth Every Day. Robert Graves. NYBP

Arab's Farewell to His Horse, The. Caroline Elizabeth Norton. BLPA

Arachne. Rose Terry Cooke. APN-2; APo

Arachne. William Empson. OBMV

Arachne. Judith Kazantzis. BrRo

Aranda Song. *Unknown, Aranda.* CBAP, tr. by T. G. H. Strehlow

Ararat. Peter Cooley. CMAP

Ararat. Dan Pagis, *Hebrew.* IP, tr. by Warren Bargad *and* Stanley F. Chyet

Ararat. Charles Tomlinson. NoP-4

Arawak Prologue. Basil McFarlane. PBCV

Arawata Bill. Denis Glover.

   Camp Site. PeNZ

   River Crossing, The. PeNZ

   "With his weapon a shovel." PeNZ

Arbor. Nancy Willard. LiLi

Arbor Amoris. François Villon, *French.* AWP, tr. by Andrew Lang

Arbor Vitae. Coventry Patmore. OBNC; PeVV *Fr.* The Unknown Eros.

Arbour, The. Anne Brontë. EBVV

Arc Inside and Out, The. A. R. Ammons. NoAM; NoP-4

Arc-lamped thrown back upon the cutting floor. (LL) What is the metre of the dictionary? Dylan Thomas. CMoP; FaBoMo

Arc of an egg, The. Nothing So Wise. Jeanne Lohmann. CrSp

Arcades. Milton.

   Song: "O're [*or* O'er] the smooth enamel'd [*or* enameled *or* enamelled] green." OxBSP

Arcades Ambo. Charles Stuart Calverley. BXAP

Arcadia. Sir Philip Sidney.

   Advice to the Same. SiPS

   Bargain, The. GLoP; NOBE; OBEV; OxAEP-1

      (Ditty, A.) AWP; GTBS-P

      ("My true love hath my heart, and I have his.") (LL) APAD; GLoP; LBC

      ("My true love hath my heart, and I have his.") APAD; GLoP; LBC

   Complaint of Love. PoEL-1; SiPS

   Country Song, A. SiPS

   Cupid. SiPS

   Double Sestine [*or* Sestina]. ImPo; PoEL-1

      ("Our morning hymne this is, and song at evening.") (LL) PBRV

      ("*Strephon.* Ye Goat-herd gods, that love the grassy.") GEA

      ("Ye goatherd gods, that love the grassy mountains.") NoP-4

   Echo. SiPS

Geron and Histor. SiPS

Get Hence Foule Griefe. PoEL-1

   (Contentment.) SiPS

Graven Thoughts. SiPS

"In vain, mine eyes, you labour to amend." SiPS

Long Their Coupled Joys Maintain. ITG, *tr. by* Robert Hass

   ("O, long their coupled joys maintain!") (LL) ITG, *tr. by* Robert Hass

Love and Jealousy. SiPS

Love and Reason. SiPS

Madrigal. SiPS

"My sheep are thoughts, which I both guide and serve." NoSic; SiPS

Night. SiPS

Old Age. SiPS

Sapphics. SiPS

Shepherd Song. SiPS

Shepherd's Tale, A. SiPS

Sleep. SiPS

   (Sonnet.)

Solitariness. SCGP; SiPS

   (Delight of Solitariness, The.)

   Sweetly Empty Woods.

Sweeter Saint I Serve, A. SiPS

Tale for Husbands, A. SiPS

"What tongue can her perfections tell." SiPS

"When two suns do appear." SiPS

Why Fear to Die? SiPS

Wronged Lover, The. SiPS

Arcanum One. Gwendolyn MacEwen. MoCV

Arch, The. Herman Melville. NCAP

Archaeological Picnic, The. John Betjeman. EnLoPo

Archæologist, The. James Simmons. PBCIP

Archaeology. George Ella Lyon. IFJA

Archaeology of Divorce, The. Patricia Storace. FFC

Archaeology of Love, The. Richard Murphy. EnLoPo

Archaic Hippocamp. Ion Caraion, *Romanian.* CEEP, tr. by Marguerite Dorian *and* Elliott B. Urdang

Archaic Song of Dr. Tom the Shaman. *Unknown, Nootka Indian.* STP, *tr. by* Jerome Rothenberg

Archaic Torso of Apollo, *see also* "We have no idea what his fantastic head." Rilke, *German.* NAWM-2, *tr. by* Stephen Mitchell; RaBo

Archaic Torso of My Uncle Phil. Mark Cox. NAmP90

Archaic Torsos. David Shapiro. PT

Archangel. Ai. SeSe

Archbishop is away, The. The church is gray. Gray Stones and Gray Pigeons. Wallace Stevens. SAmP

Archibald MacLeish Suspends the Five Little Pigs. Louis Untermeyer. MoAmPo *Fr.* Mother Goose Up-to-Date.

Archie o [*or* of] Cawfield. *Unknown.* AmFP; ESPB; OxBS

Archimedes, the early truth-seeker. Limerick. Stanley J. Sharpless. PeLi

Archin' here and arrachin there. Water Music. "Hugh MacDiarmid." FaBoTC *Fr.* Water Music.

Archinos, this retsina bottle contains. Rhianus, *Greek.* GrAn, *tr. by* Peter Jay

Archipelago, The. Herman Melville. APN-2

Archive Film Material. Ruth Fainlight. HP

Archivist in us shudders at such cold, The. Love-Letter-Burning. Daniel Hall. NoP-4

Archy and Mehitabel. Don Marquis.

   Archy at the Zoo. NBLV; OBAL

   Archy Interviews a Pharoah. OBCoV

   Song of Mehitabel, The. OBCoV

Archy at the Zoo. Don Marquis. NBLV; OBAL *Fr.* Archy and Mehitabel.

Archy Interviews a Pharoah. Don Marquis. OBCoV *Fr.* Archy and Mehitabel.

Archy, the Cockroach, Speaks. Don Marquis. *Fr.* Certain Maxims of Archy. OBAL

ARCS above OXUS. Colin Simms. NBrP

Arctic Convoy. James King Annand. OxBS

Arctic honey blabbed over the report causing darkness, The. Leaving the Atocha Station. John Ashbery. PmAP

Arctic Ox, The. Marianne Moore. NYBP

"Arcturus" is his other name. Emily Dickinson. NOBA

Arcturus, the bear driver. Night Sky. Louise Erdrich. HATNAP

Ardan Mór. Francis Ledwidge. AWP

Arden is not Eden, but Eden's rhyme. In Arden. Charles Tomlinson. OxBC

Ardent in love and cold in charity. A Man's [a] Sliding Mood. Mary Elizabeth Fullerton. CBAP; NOBAu

Ardent lover cannot find, The. Address to Her Husband. Mehetabel Wright. ECWP; LW

Ardour and Memory. D. G. Rossetti. OAEL-2 *Fr.* The House of Life.

Are added unto them that have plenty of water. (LL) Green, Green Is El Aghir. Norman Cameron. FaBoTC; FaBoTw; MoBS; OBWP; OxBTC

Are all such off'rings, as are crusht, and bruis'd. Francis Quarles. FaBoEE

Are *all* the dragons fled? Concerning Dragons. H. D. C. Pepler. NOxBChV

Are all these stones. Close-up. A. R. Ammons. PoA

Are all with thee,—are all with thee! (LL) The Ship of State. Henry Wadsworth Longfellow. FaBoBe; PWR

Are all with thee,—are all with thee! (LL) Then the Master. Henry Wadsworth Longfellow. NAAL-1; NAAL-3

Are blue. The top of the sky / is too. (LL) Vaquero. Edward Dorn. NeAP; PoM

Are blurred into one face: a child's set face. (LL) A Hunt in the Black Forest. Randall Jarrell. CoAP; LCAP-2

Are born of like / elements. (LL) The Ring of. Charles Olson. NOBA; VGW

Are by the sunbeams tickled by degrees. (LL) The Coming of Good Luck. Robert Herrick. FaBoEE; OxBSP; Spl

Are casually sitting down to eat. (LL) Divine Love. Michael Benedikt. CoAmPo

Are cat and dog, and rogue and whore. (LL) Phyllis [or Phillis] [or Progress of Love, The]. Jonathan Swift. EBNV; OAEL-1; OBCoV; OBSV; PoE; PoEL-3

Are dark windows? (LL) The World Outside. Denise Levertov. CoAmPo; TRP

Are Friends Delight or Pain? Emily Dickinson. FP

Are frosted like a wedding-cake. (LL) Winter Time [or Winter-Time]. Robert Louis Stevenson. ACTP; EBVV; MoBrPo; OxBChV

Are high-propped on a pillow of blue cloud. (LL) To Tan-Ch'iu. Li Po, *Chinese.* ChiP, *tr. by* Arthur Waley

Are Holy-Land! Edgar Allan Poe. *See* To Helen ("Helen, thy beauty is to me").

Are hot as any hottentot and not the goods for me! (LL) Hornpipe. Dame Edith Sitwell. FaBoMo; GTBS-P; OAEL-2

Are kept alive in the snow. (LL) November. Alice Cary. AYFP

Are like the sun, dazzling, yet plain to all eyes, *shorter vers.* Donne. *See* Satire 3.

Are melodiously mingled in my warm New England breast. (LL) Longfellow's Visit to Venice. John Betjeman. NOBL; OBCoV

Are Miss Beale and Miss Buss. *Unknown. See* Miss Buss and Miss Beale.

Are my poems spoken in the factories and fields. "Hugh MacDiarmid." *Fr.* Ah, Lenin, you were richt. But I'm a poet. OAEL-2 *Fr.* Second Hymn to Lenin.

Are naked as a line of poetry in a war. (LL) The Song of the Borderguard. Robert Duncan. NeAP; PoM

Are Nature still, but Nature methodized. Alexander Pope. *See* First follow Nature, and your judgment frame.

Are nice. Rose Fyleman. *See* (Mice).

Are of bones. The Pause of Joe. Imamu Amiri Baraka. FTOS

Are on your face. (LL) The Troop ship. Isaac Rosenberg. NSI; PoWW

Are paying duty calls. (LL) Song for a Little House. Christopher Darlington Morley. CTV

ARE quiet unquiet between cap and nose. The Murderers. Paul Van Ostaijen, *Dutch.* PFTM, *tr. by* Hidde van Ameyden Van Duym

Are shaken with earth's old and weary cry. (LL) The Sorrow of Love ("The Quarrel of the sparrows in the eaves"). W. B. Yeats. MoBrPo; NOBVV; NoAM; OAEL-2; PoEL-5

Are sisters under their skins! (LL) The Ladies. Rudyard Kipling. MoBrPo; NAEL-2

Are sorrows hard to bear,—the ruin. Burdens. Edward Dowden. NOBVV

Are still allow'd to fiddle with the case. (LL) Flinda's [or Ellinda's] Glove. Richard Lovelace. CBLP; CaPo; CavPo; NOSC

Are still the same, and Life and Death are neighbours nigh. (LL) Nature's Questioning. Thomas Hardy. EnVR; PBMP

Are such things done on Albion's shore? (LL) A Little Boy Lost ("Nought loves another as itself"). William Blake. FHYEP; PeECV; Ro

Are sung—but never more beautiful than there under the guns' noise. Ivor Gurney. *See* First Time In.

Are sweet like wanton loves because I hate. (LL) The White City. Claude McKay. BPo; CrDW; NoAM; RaBo; TAP

Are the children all in bed, for now it's eight o'clock? William Miller. *See* Willie Winkie.

Are the dark seeds, and they end. (LL) It Is This Way with Men. Charles Kenneth Williams. RaBo; SAGP; VCAP

Are the desolate, dark weeks. William Carlos Williams. GEA; MoAmPo; MoP; NOBA; OxBA; PBMP

("These / are the desolate, dark weeks.") MeMAP

Are the horns of the hall on fire? The Battle of Finnsburg. *Unknown, Anglo-Saxon.* AnOE, *tr. by* Charles W. Kennedy

Are the sure signs of a fine day. (LL) Evening red and morning gray. *Unknown.* FaBoBe; FaBoVe; OxNR

Are there not twelve whole hours in every day. The Day of Denial. Jones Very. NOBA

Are there others too. What She Said. Venkorran, *Tamil.* PLW, *tr. by* A. K. Ramanujan

Are These Moods of Mine Memory. Yona Wallach, *Hebrew.* IP, *tr. by* Warren Bargad *and* Stanley F. Chyet

Are these the strings that poets say. The Cat and the Lute. Thomas Master. PC

Are they blind, the lords of Gaza. Angry Samson. Robert Graves. ChIV-1

Are they clinging to their crosses. Antichrist, or the Reunion of Christendom; an Ode. G. K. Chesterton. NOBE; NOBL; OBSV; OxAEP-2

Are They Dancing. Edward Dorn. NeAP; PoM

Are they exiles here from the rest of the world? What Do the Birds Think? Alfred Wellington Purdy. MoCV

Are They Not All Ministering Spirits? Robert Stephen Hawker. OxAEP-2

Are they shadows that we see? Shadows. Samuel Daniel. CH; NOBE; NOSC; NoP-4; PoEL-2 *Fr.* Tethy's Festival.

Are thine eyes weary? is thy heart too sick. November. William Morris. EnVR *Fr.* The Earthly Paradise.

Are those two stars, her eyes, my life's light gone. Giles, the Elder Fletcher. Son *Fr.* Licia.

Are tone. Shelley. *See* To Jane ("The Keen stars were twinkling").

Are vanity and woe. (LL) Ode to Wisdom. Elizabeth Carter. ECWP

Are We Not the People. Al-Samau'al ibn Adiya, *Arabic.*

"Now listen to boasting which leaves the heart dazed." TrJP, *tr. by* Hartwig Hirschfeld

Are we to keep Christ writhing on the cross! (LL) Calvary. Edwin Arlington Robinson. GI; MoAmPo; Son

Are you a trailor, or are you a trolley? Are You You? Edmund Vance Cooke. PWR

Are you alive? The Pool. Hilda Doolittle. CMoP

Are you almost disgusted with life, little man? How to Be Happy. *Unknown.* BLPA

Are you an ethnic poet? After the Dance. Reuben Jackson. GT

"Are you awake, Gemelli." Star-Talk. Robert Graves. MoBrPo; OxBTC

Are You Content. W. B. Yeats. IIP

Are you dead, Pyrrho? Epitaph in Dialogue on the Sceptic Philosopher Pyrrho. Julianus of Egypt, *Greek.* GrAn, *tr. by* Lee T. Pearcy

Are you he who would assume a place to teach or be a poet here in the States? Walt Whitman. FaBoPV *Fr.* By blue Ontario's shore. APN-1

Are you looking for me? Mathenge. Marjorie Oludhe Macgoye. HBAPE

Are you looking for me? I am in the next seat! NOTL. Robert Bly. EnlH *Fr.* Two Translations from Kabir.

Are you out, woman of the lean pelt. Ire. Ronald Stuart Thomas. OxBSP

Are You Ready? Wes Magee. AYFP

Are you ready? soul said again. Two Trinities. Kenneth Mackenzie. CBAP

Are you the new person drawn toward me? Walt Whitman. APN-1; OxBSP

"Are You There?" Strickland W. Gillilan. PoToHe

Are you very weary? Rest a little bit. Rest. *Unknown.* PoToHe

Are you washed in the blood of the Lamb? (LL) General William Booth Enters into Heaven. Vachel Lindsay. AmPP; CMoP; ChIV-2; ColAP; ImPo; LiTM; MeMAP; MoAmPo; NOBA; OxBA; PoA; PoE; TAP

Are you what your faire lookes expresse? Thomas Campion. AAS

Are You You? Edmund Vance Cooke. PWR

Are you You or Me or It? Hello Up There. Marge Piercy. NBLV

Are your rocks shelter for ships. The Shrine. Hilda Doolittle. ColAP

Are your sorrows hard to bear? The Length of Life. Amos Russel Wells. PWR

Aren't lightning flashes the same shape in other countries too? 1914. Max Jacob. PFTM

Aren't You Glad. Charlotte Zolotow. CTV

Ares. Albert Ehrenstein, *German.* TrJP, *tr. by* Babette Deutsch *and* Avrahm Yarmolinsky

Ares at last has quit the field. Under Which Lyre, a Reactionary Tract for the Times. W. H. Auden. MoBrPo; NOBL; PeLV

Arethusa Saved. Ovid, *Latin.* OBCVT, *tr. by* Thom Gunn

Arethusa, The. Prince Hoare. FaPoR

Areyto. Victor Hernandez Cruz. PmAP

Argalus and Parthenia. Francis Quarles.

Hos Ego Versiculos. NOSC

Argent Solipsism. Howard Blake. PoA

Argenteuil County. Peter Dale Scott. MoCV

Argentina in one swing of the bell skirt. The Beautiful Train. William Empson. OxAEP-2

Argentine gaucho named Bruno, An. Limerick. *Unknown.* NOBL

Argoed. T. Gwynn Jones, *Welsh.* OBWVE, *tr. by* Anthony Conran

Argonautica, The. Apollonius Rhodius, *Greek.* HePo, *tr. by* Barbara Hughes Fowler
   "Now rising shades a solemn scene display." OBCVT, *tr. by* Francis Fawkes

Argonautica, The. Gaius Valerius Flaccus, *Greek.*
   "Now as Medea walks, dark echoes fill." OBCVT, *tr. by* Frederic Raphael *and* Kenneth McLeish

Argonauts, The. D. H. Lawrence. GrIP; NoAM

Arguement, The. Anna Hume. KTR *Fr.* Triumphs of Death.

Argument, The. William Blake. *See* The Marriage of Heaven and Hell.

Argument, The. Samuel Butler. EBEV; NAEL-1; OAEL-1 *Fr.* Hudibras.

Argument. René Char, *French.* AF, *tr. by* Mary Ann Caws

Argument. Daniel Halpern. BAP-93

Argument, An. Thomas Moore. BoLoP; EnLoPo; GLoP; OxBSP

Argument. Persius. OBCVT, *tr. by* Barten Holyday *Fr.* The Third Satyre.

Argument ended. Hal Roth. HA

Argument for Resurrection. Virginia Hooper. PT

Argument of His Book, The. Robert Herrick. AWP; BeJo; CaPo; CavPo; EBEV; HAP; ImPo; NAEL-1; NOSC; NoP-4; OAEL-1; OxAEP-1; PeECV; PoE; PoEL-3; PoPoPo; PoRA; SeCP; TFi; TTTS

Argument of the Fourth Booke, The. Lucretius, *Latin.* KTR, *tr. by* Lucy Hutchinson *Fr.* De Rerum Natura (On the Nature of Things).

Argument: on 1942, An. David Mura. LoL

Argument: On 1942, An. David Mura. PoPoPo

Argument Resumed; Or, Up Through Tribeca, The. Thomas M. Disch. WWSi

Argus. Alexander Pope. FP

Aria. Rolfe Humphries. NYBP

Aria. Delmore Schwartz. EP *Fr.* Two Lyrics from Kilroy's Carnival: A Masque.

Aria Senza da Capo. Robert Finch. MoCV

Ariake, Japanese friend, I regard. To Ariake Kambara. Norman Rosten. NYBP

Arid Husband, The. E. L. T. Mesens. SPE

Arid that country and high, anger of sun on the mountains, but. Rattlesnake Country. Robert Penn Warren. NAAL-2; VCAP

Aridity. "Michael Field." OBMV

Ariel. David Campbell. CBAP

Ariel. Sylvia Plath. CMoP; HCAP; HeIP-4; LCAP-2; MoP; NAAL-2; NALW; NOBA; NoAM; NoP-4; PBWP; PoE; Poetr; VCAP
   ("And I eat men like air.") (LL) ColAP

Ariel to Miranda:—Take. With a Guitar, to Jane. Shelley. FHYEP; GTBS-P; OAEL-2

Ariel was glad he had written his poems. The Planet on the Table. Wallace Stevens. HAP; HCAP; PoPoPo; SAmP

Ariel's Dirge. Shakespeare. *See* Ariel's Song ("Full fathom [*or* fadom] five thy father lies").

Ariel's Song ("Full fathom [*or* fadom] five thy father lies"). Shakespeare. EBEvV; NOBE; NOSC; NTP; OPOU *Fr.* The Tempest. OAEL-1
   (Ariel's Dirge.)
   ("Ding, dong, bell.") (LL)
   ("Full fathom five thy father lies.") APAD; NoP-4; PoPoPo
   (Sea Dirge, A.) GTBS-P

Ariel's Song: "Come unto these yellow sands." Shakespeare. CTC; FaBoCh; NOBE *Fr.* The Tempest. OAEL-1
   (Song: "Come unto these yellow sands.") EBEvV; PoEL-2

Ariel's Song: "Where the bee sucks, there suck I." Shakespeare. EBEvV; NOBE *Fr.* The Tempest. OAEL-1

Ariosto. Osip Emilevich Mandelstam, *Russian.* OBVE, *tr. by* W. S. Merwin *and* Clarence Brown

Ariosto's Orlando Furioso Book 34. Sir John Harington.
   "Thus all that day, they spent in divers talke." PBRV

Arise and go now to the city of slaughter. The City of Slaughter. Hayyim Nahman Bialik, *Hebrew.* TrJP, *tr. by* A. M. Klein

Arise and see the glorious sun. Francis Hopkinson. AH

Arise, arise! (LL) Song: "Hark! hark! the lark at heaven's gate sings." Shakespeare. AWP; BoTP; CH; EBEvV; FaBoCh; ImPo; NIP-4; NOSC; NoSic; OBEV; PFE; TFi; UV

Arise, arise, arise! Air. Henry Brooke. *Fr.* Jack the Giant Queller; an Antique History. NOEC

Arise, arise, / Dull fancy, from the bed of earth. My Carol. Mildmay Fane, 2d Earl of Westmorland. BeJo

Arise faint Muse bring one heart-melting verse. An Elegie on the Deplorable Departure of the Honered and Truely Religious Chieftain John Hull. John Saffin. SCAP

Arise, my soul, on wings enraptured [*or* enraptur'd], rise. Thoughts on the Works of Providence. Phillis Wheatley. ColAP; NAAL-1; NAAL-3

Arise, my soul! With rapture rise! Samuel J. Smith. AH

Arise, O glorious Zion. William G. Mills. AH

Arise!—the Sea-god's groaning shell. The Rebellion of the Waters. George Darley. NOBRP

Arise, then women of this day! Mother's Day Proclamation of 1870. Julia Ward Howe. CrSp

"Arise! thrust in Thy sickle"? (LL) Corruption. Henry Vaughan. ESCV; GEA; GeHe; NAEL-1; NOCV; NOSC; OAEL-1; SeCP

Arise up on thy feet, O Quiet Heart! He Biddeth Osiris to Arise from the Dead. *Unknown.* AWP *Fr.* Book of the Dead.

Arise ye daughters of a land. The Women's Marseillaise. F. E. M. Macaulay. BrRo

Arise, ye saints of latter days. *Unknown.* AH

Aristeides. Antipater of Sidon, *Greek.* AWP, *tr. by* Charles Whibley

Aristocrat, The. G. K. Chesterton. OBCoV

Aristocrateia, / You've crossed the dark stream. Mnasalcas, *Greek.* GrAn, *tr. by* Edward Lucie-Smith

Aristocrats. Keith Douglas. FaBoMo; NAEL-2; NoAM; NoP-4; OBWP

Aristomache loved a drink:/ The old chatterbox was fonder. Argentarius, *Greek.* GrAn, *tr. by* Fleur Adcock

Aristophanes. Plato, *Greek.* GrAn, *tr. by* Peter Jay

Aristotle was a little man with / eyes like a lizard. Humanities Lecture. William Stafford. NNaP; NoAM

Aristotle's Story. Mother Goose. CBNP; ReMoGo

Arithmetic. *Unknown.* ACTP; ReMoGo
   ("And fractions drive me mad.") (LL) ACTP

Arithmetic on the Frontier. Rudyard Kipling. OBWP

Arithmetique [*or* Arithmetic] nine digits, and no more. Upon the Loss[e] of His Little Finger. Thomas Randolph. BeJo; NOSC

Arizona. *Unknown.* AmFP

Arizona Highways. James Welch. CDW; NoAM

Arizona Nature Myth. James Michie. FaBoA; NOBL

Ark, The. Noah Calwell Cannon. AAP

Ark, The. Stanley Cook. SpW

Ark. Gu Cheng, *Chinese.* VCWP, *tr. by* Donald Finkel

Ark. Ronald Johnson.
   ARK 37, Prospero's Songs to Ariel. APSN
   Beam 4. APSN
   Beam 7. APSN; PT
      ("May move, in time, the stones themselves to sing.") (LL) PT
      ("Sound is sea: pattern lapping pattern.") PT
   Beam 25, A Bicentennial Hymn. APSN

Ark, The. Jay Macpherson.
   Ark Anatomical. NOBC
   Ark Apprehensive. NOBC
   Ark Artefact. NOBC
   Ark Articulate. NOBC
   Ark Astonished. NOBC
   Ark Overwhelmed. NOBC
   Ark Parting. NOBC
   Ark to Noah. NOBC; PoA

Ark 34, Spire on the Death of L.Z. Ronald Johnson. FTOS

ARK 37, Prospero's Songs to Ariel. Ronald Johnson. APSN *Fr.* Ark.

Ark 44, The Rod of Aaron. Ronald Johnson. FTOS

Ark Anatomical. Jay Macpherson. NOBC *Fr.* The Ark.

Ark Apprehensive. Jay Macpherson. NOBC *Fr.* The Ark.

Ark Artefact. Jay Macpherson. NOBC *Fr.* The Ark.

Ark Articulate. Jay Macpherson. NOBC *Fr.* The Ark.

Ark Astonished. Jay Macpherson. NOBC *Fr.* The Ark.

Ark for Lawrence Durrell, An. Robert Duncan. RaBo

Ark Overwhelmed. Jay Macpherson. NOBC *Fr.* The Ark.

Ark Parting. Jay Macpherson. NOBC *Fr.* The Ark.

Ark to Noah. Jay Macpherson. NOBC; PoA *Fr.* The Ark.

Arkansas Testament, The. Derek Walcott. CBCWP

Arkansas Traveller. Charles Wright. MT

Arkestra glitters in their Saturn gowns, The. After the End of the World. David Jauss. SeSe

Arkheanassa. Asclepiades, *Greek.* GrAn, *tr. by* Peter Jay

Arlo Will. Edgar Lee Masters. PBMP *Fr.* Spoon River Anthology.

Arm in Arm. Louis Simpson. PBCV

Arm in Arm. Virgil Teodorescu, *Romanian.* CEEP, tr. by Donald Eulert *and* Stefan Avadanei

Arm of bronze outstretched against all evil!, The. (LL) Dance of the Macabre Mice. Wallace Stevens. CMoP; NOBA; OxBA; PFTM

Arm thee with thunder, heavenly muse. The Law Given at Sinai. Isaac Watts. ChIV-1

Armada, The. Thomas Babington Macaulay, 1st Baron Macaulay. FaBoCh; FaPoR

"Night sank upon the dusky beach, and on the purple sea." EBEvV; OBNC; PeVV

Armada, 1588, The. John Wilson. OxBChV

Armadillo, The. Elizabeth Bishop. ColAP; HCAP; MoP; NAAL-2; NOBA; NYBP; NoAM; NoP-4; Poetr; TAP; VCAP; VGW

Armageddon. John Crowe Ransom. ChIV-2; MeMAP

Armageddon in Albyn. Sydney Goodsir Smith.

El Alamein. FaBoTC

War in Fife, The. FaBoTC

Armageddon: Private Gabriel Calvin Wojahn 1900–18. David Wojahn. PuP-15

Armchairs. Dan Pagis, *Hebrew.* IP, tr. by Warren Bargad *and* Stanley F. Chyet

("Slowest beasts are the, The.") IP, tr. by Warren Bargad *and* Stanley F. Chyet

Arme, Arme, Arme, Arme, great Neptune rowze, awake. John Smith of His Friend Master John Taylor. John Smith. SCAP

Armed Forces. Lucy Lakides. CDa

Armed Forces Day. Steve Hassett. CDa

Armed Vision. N. P. van Wyk Louw, *Afrikaans.* PeSA, tr. by Jack Cope *and* Uys Krige

Armed with a measuring-rod. (LL) His Shield. Marianne Moore. LiTM; NALW

Armed with his crutches, the thief, wolf-like. The Outsider. Syl Cheney-Coker. HBAPE

Armenian Language Is the Home of the Armenian, The. Moushegh Ishkhan, *Armenian.* BLT, tr. by Diana Der Hovanessian

Armenonville. Edna St. Vincent Millay. NoP-4

Armful, The. Robert Frost. CMoP; OxBSP; PiM

Armgart. "George Eliot."

"Armgart, to many minds the first success." VWP

Armies and lemmings do not go. The New from Ethiopia and the Sudan. J. P. Clark Bekederemo. HBAPE

Armies Enter Cuailnge, The. *Unknown. Fr.* The Táin. NOIV, tr. by Thomas Kinsella

Armies in the Fire. Robert Louis Stevenson. EBVV; FPC

Arminius. Daniel Casper von Lohenstein.

Sonnet: "Here lies the noble flesh of Spartacus the knave." GePo

Sonnet: "Light-spring, oh sun, in light our wedding joys immure." GePo

Sonnet: "Wisest of all men lies buried on this spot, The." GePo

Armistice. Paul Dehn. OxBTC

Armistice Day. Charles Causley. NAEL-2; NoP-4; OBWP

Armitage Street. David Hernandez. UnSA

Armor. James Dickey. CoAP

Armor. Sharon Olds. InPS-3

Armorial. Ralph Gustafson. MoCV

Arms and the Boy. Wilfred Owen. CMoP; HAP; ImPo; LiTM; MoBrPo; OAEL-1; OAEL-2; OxBSP; PBMP; PFE; PoE; Poetr; SAGP; WeW-3

Arms and the Man. Samuel Butler. NOSC *Fr.* Hudibras.

Arms, and the Man I sing, who, forc'd by Fate, *see also* "Now manhood and garbroyls I chaunt, and martial horror" *tr. by* Richard Stanyhurst, "I sing of warfare and a man at war" *tr. by* Robert Fitgerald, "Arms, and the Man I sing, the first who bore" *tr. by* William Wordsworth, *and* "Battellis and the man I will descrive, The" *tr. by* Gavin Douglas. Invocation. Virgil, *Latin.* OBCVT; OBVE, tr. by John Dryden *Fr.* The Aeneid [*or* Eneados, *Aeneis*].

Arms and the Woman. Dorothea MacKellar. NOBAu

Arms at my side like some inadequate sign. Mountain Town—Mexico. Eldon Grier. NOBC

Arms finned-out across the water. The Drowned. David Bottoms. MT

Arms folded. Jack Kerouac. HA

Arms reversed and banners craped. A Dirge for McPherson. Herman Melville. CBCWP; PoEL-5

Arms seem clumsy at first, The. The Fever Toy. Charles Wright. AmPA

Army. Ciaran Carson. BiHa; PBCIP

Army Beach with Trumpets. Jack Spicer. APSN

Army Corps on the March, An. Walt Whitman. AiP; CBCWP; InPS-3; PoLF; SAGP

Army horses, gangs and droves. Meeting the Herdsmen. Mei Yao Ch'en, *Chinese.* SuSP, tr. by Jonathan Chaves

Army. I cannot even dream, The. Clinton. Sterling Plumpp. BkSV *Fr.* Clinton.

Army, Navy. *Unknown.* OxNR

Army of Occupation. Sarah Morgan Bryan Piatt. NCAP

Army of the Dead, The. Barry Pain. NSI

Army of the Lord. I'm a Soldier in the Army of the Lord. *Unknown.* AmFP

Army of unalterable law, The. (LL) Cousin Nancy. T. S. Eliot. OBAL; OxBSP

Army of unalterable law, The. (LL) Lucifer in Starlight. George Meredith. AWP; CABP; CH; ChIV-1; EBVV; EnVR; GSo; HAP; ImPo; InPK-6; NAEL-2; NOBE; NOBVV; NoP-4; OAEL-2; OBEV; OBNC; PBMP; PFE; PoE; PoEL-5; SCGP; Son; TFi; UnPo

Army returned home wet with sunlight, The. One Night Away from Day. John Digby. SPE

Arnolfinis both sat to Van Eyck. Limerick. Sir Robert Witt. PeLi

Around, above my bed, the pitch-dark fly. Truth. Howard Nemerov. HoPM; LiTM

Around, around the sun we go. Mother Goose's Garland. Archibald MacLeish. OBAL

Around Costessey. Francis Webb.

Art. BMAP

Around existence twine. Basho, *Japanese.* TAL, tr. by Harold G. Henderson

Around five in the next garden, a rooster. Likelihood of Snow, The/ The Danger of Fire. Gerald Dawe. PNI

Around her shrine no earthly blossoms blow. La Madonna dell' Acqua. John Ruskin. NOBVV

Around islands of jade and malachite. The Wave Symphony. Arthur Davison Ficke. PoA *Fr.* Four Japanese Paintings.

Around it the furze-clad hills arise. The Mountain Altar. Brian O'Higgins. TIRV

Around me roar and crash the pagan isms. The Pagan Isms. Claude McKay. BPo

Around me the images of thirty years. The Municipal Gallery Revisited. W. B. Yeats. GTBS-P; OxBTC

Around my courtyard the little wall is low. Po Chü-i. *See* Losing a Slave-Girl.

Around my garden the little wall is low. Losing a Slave-Girl. Po Chü-i, *Chinese.* AWP, tr. by Arthur Waley

Around My Room. William Jay Smith. TLR

Around stones called precious. Black Meat. Jean Follain, *French.* BLT, tr. by W. S. Merwin

Around the battlements go by. War on the Periphery. George Johnston. NOBC

Around the bend / that tried to loop me home. Stanley Kunitz. *Fr.* The Testing-Tree. FYAP; UnPo

Around the campfire we sang hymns. Andrew Hudgins. CBCWP; MT

Around the cold pool in the metal light. The Hotel Normandie Pool. Derek Walcott. HCP; VCWP

Around the Corner ("Around the corner I have a friend"). Charles Hanson Towne. PoLF; PoToHe

Around the Corner. Laura Riding Jackson. *Fr.* Forgotten Girlhood. RB

Around the corner from Francis Bacon. Paul Durcan. BiHa

Around the corner I have a friend. Around the Corner. Charles Hanson Towne. PoLF; PoToHe

Around the fire addressed its evening hours. (LL) Say not of me that weakly I declined. Robert Louis Stevenson. OBNC; PeVV

Around the fire one wintry night. The Beggar Man. Lucy Aikin. OxBChV

Around the fireplace, pointing at the fire. On Falling Asleep by Firelight. William Meredith. ChIV-1; KSG; NYBP; NoAM

Around the gleaming map of Europe. Autobahnmotorwayautoroute. Adrian Mitchell. RB

Around the green gravel the grass grows green. *Unknown.* ReMoGo

Around the house. (LL) The Routine Things Around the House. Stephen Dunn. CMAP; NAmP90

Around the house stood an. Grandmothers Land. William Oandasan. HATNAP

Around the house the flakes fly faster. Birds at Winter Nightfall. Thomas Hardy. MoBrPo

Around the pole, in the great room of the sun. (LL) The May Day Dancing. Howard Nemerov. NYBP; Poetr

Around the quays, kicked off in twos. Fishing Boats in Martigues. Roy Campbell. FaBoEE; OxBSP

Around the rick, around the rick. *Unknown.* OxNR

Around the Rough and Rugged Rocks the Ragged Rascal Rudely Ran. John Ashbery. InPS-3

Around the temple, pines and cedars. Wen Cheng-ming. CoBLCP, tr. by Jonathan Chaves *Fr.* The Chung-i Temple.

Around the time when the honeysuckle. Ballad of the Deceived Flowers. Vesna Parun, *Croatian*. CEEP, *tr. by* Peter Kastmiler

Around the Year. Sara Coleridge. *See* The Garden Year.

Around us speeches of birds. I tremble. Lines to a Tree. Judah Leib Teller, *Yiddish*. CEEP, *tr. by* Gabriel Preil *and* Howard Schwartz

Around were all the roses red. Spleen. Paul Verlaine, *French*. AWP, *tr. by* Ernest Dowson

Arp and the barbered arbor. Maison Aragon. Tristan Tzara, *French*. PFTM, *tr. by* Jerome Rothenberg

Arraigned by silence, I recall. The Brethren. Seamus Deane. PNI

Arraignment of a Lover, The. George Gascoigne. AAS

Arraignment of Paris, The. George Peele.

　Fair and Fair. OBEV

　(Oenone and Paris.) NOBE

Arran. *Unknown, Old Irish*. FaBoCh, *tr. by* Kuno Meyer

Arrange the scene with only a shade of difference. An Incident. Douglas Le Pan. MoCV; NoP-4

Arranged by two's as peaches are. Nine Nectarines and Other Porcelain. Marianne Moore. OxBA

Arranged on the opposite porch is a male. Hilaire Kirkland. *Fr.* Observations. PeNZ

Arrangement preserves. The way a calm tureen. The House Destroyed by Fire. Don Bogen. WeT

Arrangements with Earth for Three Dead Friends. James Wright. NIP-4

Arras. Patricia K. Page. MoCV

Arrest of Oscar Wilde at the Cadogan Hotel, The. John Betjeman. CMoP; EBEV; MoBrPo; MoP; NoAM; NoP-4; OxBTC

Arria to Poetus. Mary E. Tucker. CBWP-1

Arrival. Gerald McCarthy. CDa

Arrival, The. Alexander McLachlan. NOBC *Fr.* The Emigrant.

Arrival, The. Daniel S. Simko. CEEP

Arrival. John Wain. EBEV

Arrival and Departure. Charles Eglington. PeSA

Arrival at Kennedy. David Lehman. WWSi

Arrival at Santos. Elizabeth Bishop. FaBoWP; OxBC

Arrival at the Waldorf. Wallace Stevens. HCAP

Arrival in Hell. Ricarda Huch, *German*. PBWP, *tr. by* Susan C. Strong

Arrival of the Bee Box, The. Sylvia Plath. FaBoMo; FaBoWP; HCAP; NALW

Arrival of the Titanic, The. William Dickey. BAP-96

Arrivals at a Watering-Place. Winthrop Mackworth Praed. NOBL; NOBRP; PeLV

Arrivals, Departures. Philip Larkin. MoBrPo

Arrivants. Musaemura Bonus Zimunya. HBAPE

Arrivants: A New World Trilogy, The. Edward Kamau Brathwaite.

　New World A-Comin'. NoP-4

Arrive sluggish, arrive weary horses of space. Mateja Matevski. CEEP, *tr. by* Charles Simic *Fr.* Rains.

Arrive. The Ladies from the Ladies' Betterment League. The Lovers of the Poor. Gwendolyn Brooks. LCAP-2; LTA; MoP; NAAAL; NAAL-2; NOBA; NoAM; Poetr; SSLK

Arrived from scattered cities, several lands. Shipment to Maidanek. Ephim G. Fogel. OBWP; TrJP

Arrived from scattered cities, several lands. Shipment to Maidanek. Ephraim Fogel. HP

Arrived now at our ship, we launched and set. Ulysses Invokes the Dead. Homer. NOSC, *tr. by* George Chapman *Fr.* Odyssey. NAWM-1, *tr. by* Robert Fitzgerald

Arrived upon the downs of asphodel. Classic Encounter. "Christopher Caudwell." OxBTC

Arrives like a jinn, instantly. Resuscitation Team. U. A. Fanthorpe. FaBoWP

Arriving. Daniel Halpern. HoPM

Arriving. Tanka. Tawara Machi, *Japanese*. MJT, *tr. by* Makoto Ueda

Arriving after Rain at the Temple of Heavenly Peace. Wang Shih-chieng, *Chinese*. SuSp, *tr. by* Richard John Lynn

Arriving at Hangchou. Yüan Mei, *Chinese*. CoBLCP, *tr. by* Jonathan Chaves

Arriving at Hsün-yang. Po Chü-i, *Chinese*. ChiP, *tr. by* Arthur Waley

Arriving at North Pond by Stupid Brook on a Morning Walk after the Rain. Liu Tsung-yüan, *Chinese*. SuSp, *tr. by* Jan W. Walls

Arriving in Lo-yang Again. Shao Yung, *Chinese*. CoBCP, *tr. by* Burton Watson

Arrogance. Walter De la Mare. OxBSP

Arrow. Rita Dove. NMM-2

Arrow and the Song, The. Henry Wadsworth Longfellow. CTV; ColAP; MeMAP; PWR; PoToHe; UV

Arrow in the Sky. Henrikas Radauskas, *Lithuanian*. CEEP, *tr. by* Jonas Zdanys

Arrowhead from the Ancient Battlefield of Ch'ang-p'ing, An. Li Ho, *Chinese*. PLT, *tr. by* A. C. Graham

Arrowroot flowers. Tanka. Shaku Chōkū, *Japanese*. MJT, *tr. by* Makoto Ueda

Arrows of the narrow moon flock down direct, The. Communion of Saints: The Poor Bastard under the Bridge. Marie Ponsot. VGW

Arroyo. Tom Weatherly. PoBA

Ars. Marina Tsvetayeva, *Russian*. BoWoP, *tr. by* Willis Barnstone *and* Edward Brown

Ars Poetica. Claribel Alegría, *Spanish*. LoL, *tr. by* D. J. Flakoll

Ars Poetica. Robert Desnos, *French*. AF, *tr. by* Carolyn Forché

Ars Poetica. James ("Jim") Grabill. EC2

Ars Poetica. Vincente Huidobro, *Spanish*. PFTM, *tr. by* David Guss

Ars Poetica. Archibald MacLeish. APAD; AWP; AmPP; CMoP; ColAP; HAP; HeIP-4; HoPM; InPK-6; LiTM; MeMAP; MoAmPo; NAAL-2; NIP-4; NOBA; NoP-4; OxBA; PFE; PoA; PoPoPo; PoRA; Poetr; SAGP; TAP; TFi; WeW-3

　("But be.") (LL) APAD; NoP-4; PoPoPo; SAGP

Ars Poetica. Linda Pastan. NIP-4

Ars Poetica. Victor Van Vriesland, *Dutch*. TrJP, *tr. by* Adriaan J. Barnouw

Ars Poetica about Ultimates. Tram Combs. TwCP

Ars Victrix. Austin Dobson, *after the French of* Théophile Gautier. "All passes. Art alone." CTC

Arsenal at Springfield, The. Henry Wadsworth Longfellow. AmPP

Arsenic. Howard Moss. CoAP; NYBP

"Arsenio" (she writes to me), "I, breathing gently here." Thrust and Riposte. Eugenio Montale, *Italian*. PeFWW, *tr. by* Gavin Ewart

Art. Washington Allston. APN-1

Art. Ralph Waldo Emerson. APN-1

Art. Théophile Gautier, *French*. AWP, *tr. by* George Santayana

Art. Denise Levertov. CAPP-1

Art. Herman Melville. APN-2; ColAP; NCAP; PAR

Art. Herman Melville. AmPP; NAAL-1; NAAL-3; NOBA

Art. James Thomson.

　"Singing is sweet; but be sure of this." NOBVV

Art. *Unknown*. BLPA; NBLV

Art, Section 4. Francis Webb. BMAP *Fr.* Around Costessey.

Art above Nature, to Julia. Robert Herrick. BeJo; CABP; NOSC

Art and Life. Agnes Mary Frances Robinson. VWP

Art for Art's Sake. Marc Blitzstein. TrJP *Fr.* The Cradle Will Rock.

Art, I. Alfred Noyes. OBEV

Art, II. Alfred Noyes. OBEV

Art is the true and happy science of the soul. Robert Bridges. GS *Fr.* The Testament of Beauty, Book III.

Art McCooey. Patrick Kavanagh. CIP-2

Art of Biography, The. Edmund Clerihew Bentley. NOBL; NTP; PeLV *Fr.* Clerihews.

Art of Biography, The. Edmund Clerihew Bentley. *See* George III.

Art of Clay, The. Duane Niatum. HATNAP

Art of Cookery, The. William King.

　"Far from the parlour have your kitchen placed." ECEV

Art of Cookery, In Imitation of Horace's Art of Poetry. To Dr. Lister, The. Horace, *Latin*.

　"Ingenious L———were a Picture drawn." OBCVT, *tr. by* William King

Art of Coquetry, The. Charlotte Lennox. LW *Fr.* The Art of Coquetry.

Art of Coquetry, The. LW

Art of Dancing, The. Soame Jenyns.

　"But let me now my lovely charge remind." ECEV

　"Dare I in such momentous points advise." ECEV

　"Let each fair maid, who fears to be disgraced." ECEV

　"Now haste, my Muse, pursue thy destined way." ECEV

Art of Disappearing, The. Naomi Shihab Nye. LoL

Art of losing isn't hard to master, The. One Art. Elizabeth Bishop. APAD; DiPo; HAP; NAAL-2; NALW; NoAM; NoP-4; PoE; PoPoPo; SAGP; SoSe-8; VCAP

Art of Love, The. Kenneth Koch.

　"To win the love of women one should first discover." NNaP

Art of Love, The. Ovid, *Latin*.

　"If in this Town an unflusht Puny be." OBCVT, *tr. by* Hoy, Thomas

Art of Picasso, The. Salvador Dali, *Spanish*. SPE, *tr. by* David Gascoyne

Art of Poetry, The. Horace, *Latin*.

　"As woods whose change appeares." OBVE, *tr. by* Ben Jonson

　"Paynter if he shoulde adjoyne, A." OBCVT, *tr. by* Thomas Drant

　"Should some ill Painter in a wild design." OBCVT; OBVE, *tr. by* John Oldham

Art of Poetry, An. James Philip McAuley. NOCV

Art of Poetry, The. Alexander Pope. ECEV *Fr.* An Essay on Criticism. NAEL-1; PoEL-3; TFi

Art of Politics, The. James Bramston.
  Time's Changes. NOEC

Art of Preserving Health, The. John Armstrong. OBGa
  Causes of Old Age. ECEV
  Madness. NOEC
  Transience. NOEC
  Urban Pollution. ECEV; NOEC

Art of Satire, The. Alexander Pope. ECEV *Fr.* Epilogue to the Satires, in Two Dialogues. OAEL-1
  (Power of Ridicule, The.) NOBE

Art of the Sonnet. Gil Orlovitz.
  "Night comes. Day runs for its life into my eyes." PoA

Art of War, The. Joseph Fawcett.
  Feast of Blood, The. NOEC

Art of Wenching, The. *Unknown.*
  "Be punctual then to know." NOEC

Art Pepper. Edward Hirsch. NAmP90; SeSe

Art photographer alone, The. Quantum. Martin Johnston. CBAP

Art Poétique. Paul Verlaine, *French.* AWP, *tr. by* Arthur Symons

Art thou afraid the adorer's prayer. Walter Savage Landor. GBL

Art Thou Gone in Haste? John Webster *and* William Rowley. OxBoLi *Fr.* The Thracian Wonder.
  (Chase, The.) CH

Art thou gone so far. Ode: The Spirit Wooed. Richard Watson Dixon. OBNC

Art thou lonely, O my brother? John Oxenham. PoToHe

Art thou not hungry for thy children, Zion. To Zion. Judah Halevi, *Hebrew.* AWP, *tr. by* Maurice Samuel

Art thou pale for weariness. To the Moon. Shelley. GTBS-P; OxAEP-2; PBMP; TTTS

Art thou poor, yet hast thou golden slumbers? The Happy Heart. Thomas Dekker *and others.* APAD; CH; GTBS-P; HAP; InPS-3; NoSic; OBEV; RB; SCGP; UnPo *Fr.* The Pleasant Comedy of Patient Grissell [*or* Grissel *or* Grissill].

Art thou poore yet hast thou golden Slumbers. Thomas Dekker. PBRV

Art thou that she than whom none fairer is. *Unknown.* OxBSP

Art Thou, Time, Way, and Wayfarer. (LL) "I Am the Way." Alice Thompson Meynell. NOBVV; OBMV; OxBSP

Art was a palace once, things great and fair. To the Reader. Richard Le Gallienne. ADE

Artegall and Radigund. Edmund Spenser. *Fr.* Wood Of Error. AEP

Artemeias, surely when you from the nether world's bark. Antipater of Sidon. HePo, *tr. by* Barbara Hughes Fowler *Fr.* Epigrams.

Artemidora! Gods invisible. The Death of Artemidora. Walter Savage Landor. OBNC *Fr.* Pericles and Aspasia.

Artemis. Perses, *Greek.* GrAn, *tr. by* Peter Whigham

Artemisia Tiger, The. Chang Yü. *Fr.* Four Poems On the Ch'ung-wu Festival. CoBLCP, *tr. by* Jonathan Chaves

Artemon once traveled in shadows. Anacreon, *Greek.* InMo, *tr. by* Sam Hamill

Arthritic farmer and a calf watch Dr. Graves, The. These Obituaries of Rattlesnakes Being Eaten by the Hogs. Roger Weingarten. AmPA

Arthur. Ogden Nash. NoP-4; PeLi

Arthur O'Bower has broken his bands [*or* band]. The Wind. *Unknown.* FaBoCh; OxNR

Arthur Ridgewood, M.D. Frank Marshall Davis. BPo

Arthur wes forwunded, wunder ane swithe. The Passing of Arthur. Layamon. PoE *Fr.* The Brut.

Arthur's Anthology of English Poetry. Laurence David Lerner. PeLV

Arthur's Fight with Orgoglio and Duessa. Edmund Spenser. EBNV *Fr.* Wood Of Error. AEP

Arthur's Seat. Thomas Mercer.
  "Where is the gallant race that rose." OxBS

Artichoke. Henry Taylor. MT

Artichokes. Georges Ribemont-Dessaignes, *French.* PFTM, *tr. by* Pierre Joris

Artificer. X. J. Kennedy. TwCP

Artificial Beauty. Lucianus, *Greek.* AWP, *tr. by* William Cowper

Artillery [*or* Artillerie]. George Herbert. GeHe; InPS-3; PoEL-2
  (Artillery.) NoP-4

Artillery. George Herbert. *See* Artillery [*or* Artillerie].

Artillery was burying us. Konstantin Levin, *Russian.* TCRP, *tr. by* Albert C. Todd

Artilleryman's Vision, The. Walt Whitman. CBCWP

Artist, An. Robinson Jeffers. VGW

Artist, The. Amy Lowell. CPO

Artist, The. William Carlos Williams. InPS-3; LCAP-2; NYBP; RB; SAGP; SAmP

Artist has to be enslaved, An. Vladimir Nikolaevich Sokolov, *Russian.* TCRP, *tr. by* Simon Franklin

Artist is the creator of beautiful things, The. Preface. Oscar Wilde. NAEL-2 *Fr.* The Picture of Dorian Gray.

Artist must leave these woods now, The. The Departure. Reed Whittemore. TAP

Artist on Penmaenmawr, The. Charles Tennyson Turner. OBNC

Artist, that underneath my table. The Spider. Edward Littleton. NOEC

Artist, the: disciple, abundant, multiple, restless. *Unknown, Aztec Indian.* STP, *tr. by* Denise Levertov

Artist who lived in St. Ives, An. Limerick. A. G. Prys-Jones. PeLi

Artist who lived near Montmartre, An. Limerick. Sir John Waller. PeLi

Artists' Letters. Thomas Kinsella. BiHa

Artorius. John Heath-Stubbs. EBEV
  "Age of Bronze awoke now in brutality, The."
  "It was the virgin Zennora, who dwelt."
  "Raft drifted, The." PeECV

Arturo. Maria Gillan. UnSA

Arundel Tomb, An. Philip Larkin. NoP-4; OxAEP-2; OxBM

As a bathtub lined with white porcelain. The Bathtub [*or* Bath Tub]. Ezra Pound. NIP-4; PFE; TRP; WeW-3

As a boy with a richness of needs I wandered. Clifford Dyment. OxBTC

As a brave man faces the foe. At Sea. Richard Hovey. APN-2

As a carp ascends to heaven. The Carp. Michael Stevens. CDa

As a child. In This Motherless Geography. Elaine Orr. CrSp

As a child before she knew. Experiments with God. Karen Gershon. HP

As a child holds a pet. Port Bou. Stephen Spender. TwCP

As a child / I bought a red scarf. Four Sheets to the Wind and a One-Way Ticket to France. Conrad Kent Rivers. BPo; PoBA

As a child I came upon a grasshopper. Bulat Shalvovich Okudzhava, *Russian.* TCRP, *tr. by* Deming Brown

As a child I got up. Lost Songs. Vladimir Alekseievich Soloukhin, *Russian.* TCRP, *tr. by* Daniel Weissbort

As a child I was. Woman. Elouise Loftin. PoBA

As a child, I was a fussy eater. Notes for a Poem on Being Asian American. Dwight Okita. UnSA

As a child (in Australia). Strange Adventure. Rossana Ombres, *Italian.* NeIt, *tr. by* Ruth Feldman

As a child of cedar, hemlock, and the sea. No One Remembers [Abandoning] the Village of White Fir. Duane Niatum. CDW

As a child running loose. Learning to Speak. Peter Everwine. NNaP

As a child she planted. Arbor. Nancy Willard. LiLi

As a critic the poet Buchanan. On Robert Buchanan, Who Attacked Him under the Pseudonym of "Thomas Maitland." D. G. Rossetti. FaBoEE

As a dare-gale skylark scanted in a dull cage. The Caged Skylark. Gerard Manley Hopkins. CMoP; LiTM; MoBrPo; OBMV; SoSe-8; Son

As a fond mother, when the day is o'er. Nature. Henry Wadsworth Longfellow. FaBoBe; PoLF; TAP

As a friend to the children commend me the Yak. The Yak. Hilaire Belloc. CTAV; MoBrPo; NBLV; NOBL; NoAM; OxBChV; PeP

As a gift to the east wind, winter's friend. (LL) 1.25: Ribald Romeos Less and Less Berattle ("Parcius iunctas quatiunt fenestras"). Horace, *Latin.* LoP

As a god self-slain on his own strange altar, / Death lies dead. Swinburne. *See* A Forsaken Garden.

As a gray hawk's eyes. Hawk's Eyes. Yvor Winters. PoA

As a hungry fledgling, who sees and hears. Vittoria da Colonna, Marchesa di Pescara, *Italian.* WPOW, *tr. by* Brenda Webster
  ("As a starved little bird, who sees and hears.") WPoS, *tr. by* Laura Anna Stortoni *and* Mary Prentice Lillie

As a little fat man of Bombay. *Unknown.* OxBChV

As a little white snake. What He Said. Catti Natanar, *Tamil.* PLW, *tr. by* A. K. Ramanujan

As a man and woman make. The White Lilies. Louise Glück. PoPoPo

As a man turns to face on-coming snow. (LL) The Decision. Theodore Roethke. CRP; VGW

As a man who soon must be without. Hunger. Gaspara Stampa, *Italian.* WPOW, *tr. by* Brenda Webster

As a naked man I go. In Waste Places. James Stephens. MoBrPo; SCGP

As a people favoured by the Almighty. Eden Says No. Robert Johnstone. PNI

As a Plane Tree by the Water. Robert Lowell. CMoP; CoAP; LiTM; MoAmPo; NOBA; OxBA

As a poet put it once, an ant / may seem 'a monstrous elephant'. Lucilius, *Greek.* GrAn, *tr. by* Peter Porter

As a poplar feels the sun's enfolding kiss. Trumbull Stickney. *Fr.* Pandora's Songs. APN-2 *Fr.* Prometheus Pyrphoros.

As a queen sits down, knowing that a chair will be there. Walking to Sleep. Richard Wilbur. NYBP; VCAP

As a rattlesnake. Judy Grahn. *See* Ella, in a Square Apron, Along Highway 80.

As a reed with the reeds in the river. (LL) A Musical Instrument. Elizabeth Barrett Browning. CABP; EBEvV; EBVV; FaBoBe; NAEL-2; NoP-4; OAEL-2; OBEV; PEW; PoE; PoPoPo; Poetr; VWP; WPE

As a rule all servants dress in their masters' livery. French Dress. Friedrich von Logau, *German.* GePo, tr. by George C. Schoolfield

As a rule, the patients I know do not pace. Their Patients. Robert Pinsky. NoAM *Fr.* Essay on Psychiatrists.

As a sad man, when evenings grayer grow. Trumbull Stickney. APN-2

As a Seal upon Thy Heart. Bible, O.T. TrJP *Fr.* The Song of Songs. AWP

("Set me as a seal on your heart.") BoWoP, tr. by Willis Barnstone

As a short before the main feature. Experiment. Wislawa Szymborska, *Polish.* PoSu, tr. by Magnus F. Krynski

As a signet of carbuncle in a setting of gold. Music. Bible, Apocrypha. TrJP *Fr.* Ecclesiasticus.

As a sloop with a sweep of immaculate wing on her delicate spine. Buick. Karl Shapiro. CMoP; HoPM; Poetr

As a starved little bird, who sees and hears. Vittoria da Colonna, Marchesa di Pescara. *See* As a hungry fledgling, who sees and hears.

As a symbol. Sabina Lampadius, *Greek.* WPoS, tr. by Maarten J. Vermaseren *and* A. M. H. Lemmers

As a teen-ager I was very shy. Norma. Sonia Sanchez. UnSA

As a teenager I would drive Father's. Running on Empty. Robert Phillips. InPK-6

As a torn paper might seal up its side. The Pruned Tree. Howard Moss. NYBP; VCAP

As a tree tilts heavenward. Watching the Stars. No Ch'&obrev;n-my&obrev;ng, *Korean.* CKP, tr. by Jaihiun Kim

As a violet's gentle eye. Variation of the Song of the Moon. Shelley. *Fr.* Prometheus Unbound. NOBRP; OAEL-2

As a voice in a vision that's vanished. From Lines of Swinburne. Charles Bernstein. FTOS

As a whip maps the countries of the air. (LL) Transit. Richard Wilbur. DiPo; LCAP-2; PiM

As a white candle. The Old Woman. Joseph Campbell. AWP; MoBrPo; OxBTC; PoToHe

As a white stone draws down the fish. Behaviour of Fish in an Egyptian Tea Garden. Keith Douglas. FaBoMo; RB

As a wind-mill turns in the wind on an empty sky. (LL) A Tune. Arthur Symons. BoLoP; LBC; OBNC

As a young man, Potchikoo sometimes embarrassed his. How Potchikoo Got Old. Louise Erdrich. *Fr.* Old Man Potchikoo. HATNAP

As Adam early in the morning. Walt Whitman. APN-1; ChIV-1; ColAP; OxBA; SAmP

As Aesop was with boys at play. Aesop at Play. Phaedrus, *Latin.* AWP, tr. by Christopher Smart

As Ah walked oot, yah Sunday morn. Bleeberrying. Jonathan Denwood. MoBS

As an American traveler I have. Internal Migration: On Being on Tour. Alan Dugan. NoAM

As an eagle grasped. Shelley. *Fr.* Alastor; or, The Spirit of Solitude. OAEL-2; Ro

As an egg, when broken, never. Thomas Holley Chivers. BXAP *Fr.* To Allegra Florence in Heaven.

As an immortal nightingale. Trumbull Stickney. *Fr.* Pandora's Songs. APN-2 *Fr.* Prometheus Pyrphoros.

As an intruder I trudged with careful innocence. Old Mansion. John Crowe Ransom. FuPo; HeIP-4; MeMAP; NOBA; OxBA

As an unperfect actor on the stage. Sonnet 23. Shakespeare. CABP; NoSic; Son *Fr.* Sonnets.

As Ann came in one summer's day. The Sleeper. Walter De la Mare. MoBrPo

As Anne, long barren, mother did become. To St John Baptist. Henry Constable. ChIV-2; NoSic

As any of these, with as much or as little reason. (LL) Barnsley and District. Donald Davie. NoAM; OxBC

As any she belied with false compare. (LL) Sonnet 130. Shakespeare. AEP; AWP; BoLoP; CABP; EBEV; GLoP; HAP; HeIP-4; HoPM; ImPo; InPK-6; InPS-3; NAEL-1; NIP-4; NoSic; OAEL-1; OxAEP-1; PBMP; PFE; PoE; PoPoPo; Poetr; SoSe-8; Son; TFi; WeW-3

'As anybody seen Bill 'Awkins? Bill 'Awkins. Rudyard Kipling. CBLP

As anyone ever sat! (LL) Narcissa. Gwendolyn Brooks. NTCP

As anything else, to ease your pain! (LL) In the Cemetery. Thomas Hardy. InPK-6; Son

As Artemis was, when (so imprudently). Jealousy. Tristan l'Hermite, *French.* FLP, tr. by Alistair Elliot

As, at a railway junction, men. Sic Itur. Arthur Hugh Clough. EBVV

As at return of tide the total weight of ocean. Arthur Hugh Clough. FaBoPV *Fr.* Bothie of Tober-na-Vuolich, The [A Long-Vacation Pastoral].

As Bad as a Mile. Philip Larkin. InPK-6; OxBC; OxBSP

As Befits a Man. Langston Hughes. PFE

As best I can, I write His praises down. (LL) As a hungry fledgling, who sees and hears. Vittoria da Colonna, Marchesa di Pescara, *Italian.* WPoS, tr. by Laura Anna Stortoni *and* Mary Prentice Lillie

As birds are fitted to the boughs. Louis Simpson. BoLoP; LBC

As black as death, emitting a strange odor. (LL) The Inner Part. Louis Simpson. PBCV; PBMP; RaBo

As black as ink and isn't ink. *Unknown.* OxNR

As bodies perish through excess of blood. Alexander Pope. *See* Some to Conceit alone their taste confine.

As bold Mirmillo the grey dawn descries. Sir Samuel Garth. ECEV *Fr.* The Dispensary. OBSV

As bryght Phebus, scheyn soverane hevynnys e. The Prologue to [*or of*] Book VII. Virgil. OxBS, tr. by Gawin Douglas *Fr.* The Aeneid [*or* Eneados, Aeneis].

As by the wood drifts thistle-down. Concerning Hebrews. Herman Melville. APN-2 *Fr.* Clarel: A Poem and Pilgrimage in the Holy Land.

As cages, think of department stores and certain zoos. Cages. Marvin Solomon. NYBP

As careful mothers do to sleeping lay. On the Deputy of Ireland's Child. Sir John Davies. FaBoEE

As carefully as your honor. (LL) Meeting a Bear. David Wagoner. PaTW

As certain as color. Ono no Komachi, *Japanese.* OHPJ, tr. by Kenneth Rexroth

As Children Together. Carolyn Forché. NoAM; OxWW

As chorus to their tragic scene. Shakespeare. *See* The Phoenix and the Turtle.

As Christ intact before the infidel. (LL) Constancy. "Michael Field." CPO; VWP

As clever Tom Clinch, while the rabble was bawling. Clever Tom Clinch Going to Be Hanged. Jonathan Swift. NOIV

As close as you your weding kept. I.W. To her unconstant Lover. Isabella Whitney. PBRV

As cold as ice, but just as set on me. (LL) Nothing to Fear. Kingsley Amis. EP; OxBC; OxBoV

As Concerning Man. Alexander Radcliffe. NOSC; OBSV

As *Constellations* do above. Andrew Marvell. *See* And now to the abyss I pass.

As cool as the pale wet leaves. Alba. Ezra Pound. GBL; HAP; WeW-3

As Cortez on the Aztecs made. (LL) America Is Hard to See. Robert Frost. AiP; FaBoA

As Corydon went shiv'ring by. Fire Us with Ice, Burn Us with Snow. Mary Monk. LW

As cruel as a Turk: Whence came. On Mammon. Herman Melville. OxBA *Fr.* Clarel: A Poem and Pilgrimage in the Holy Land.

As custome was, the pepill far and neir. The Assembly of the Gods. Robert Henryson. PoEL-1 *Fr.* The Testament of Cresseid. OxBS

As day did darken on the dewless grass. The Wind at the Door. William Barnes. EnVR; GBL; GTBS-P; LBC; OxAEP-2; PoEL-4

As day new opening fills the hemisphere. The City Morning. Sir William Davenant. NOSC *Fr.* Gondibert.

As Dick and I. Lines Left at Mr Theodore Hook's House in June, 1834. "Thomas Ingoldsby." OBCoV

As did the Outlaw Murray of the forest frie? (LL) The Outlaw Murray. *Unknown.* ESPB; OxBB

As Difference Blends into Identity. Josephine Miles. NoAM; Poetr

As divided. Trip to Berlin. Kondō Yoshimi, *Japanese.* MJT, tr. by Makoto Ueda

As doctors give physic by way of prevention. For My Own Monument. Matthew Prior. FaBoEE; OBEV

As down a lone valley with cedars o'erspread. Timothy Dwight. AH

As down the garden walks we go. (LL) Henry and Mary. Robert Graves. NOxBChV; NTP

As down through Cupid's garden for pleasure I did walk. The 'Prentice Boy. *Unknown.* AmFP

As down through Moore's field one evening I went. The Silk Weaver's Daughter. *Unknown.* AmFP

As down thru Sally's garden one evening as I chanced to stray. Sally's Garden. *Unknown.* AmFP

As Drones, oppressive Habitants of Hives. Hesiod. OBCVT, tr. by Thomas Cooke *Fr.* Theogony.

As due by many titles I resign[e]. Donne. *Fr.* Holy Sonnets. ESCV *Fr.* Holy Sonnets.

As dull as the life of the cloister. Limerick. *Unknown.* PeLi

As Dungeons are for Criminals prepar'd. A Satyr. Elizabeth Tipper. KTR *Fr.* Pilgrim's Viaticum; or, The Destitute, But Not Forlorn.

As each year might assign. (LL) He Never Expected Much. Thomas Hardy. NAEL-2; NoAM; OxBTC; SCV

As, even today, the airman, feeling the plane sweat. Icarus. Valentin Iremonger. BIrV; CIP-2

As evening fell the day's oppression lifted;. Embassy. W. H. Auden. LiLi *Fr.* Sonnets from China.

As evening splendors fade. Nightfall. Alexander L. Posey. APN-2

As ever in my great Task-Ma[i]ster[']s eye. (LL) Sonnet: "How soon hath Time the suttle [*or* subtle] theef [*or* thief] of youth." Milton. APAD; GSo; HeIP-4; InPS-3; NAEL-1; NOSC; NoP-4; PBMP; PFE; PoE; SCGP; Son

As Expected. Thom Gunn. GLP

As fair as morn, as fresh as May. *Unknown.* GBL

As far as Cho-fu-Sa. (LL) River Merchant's Wife, The; a Letter. Li Po, *Chinese.* LiLi; LoP, *tr. by* Ezra Pound; AWP; AmPP; BoLoP; ClHu; FYAP; GEA; GLoP; HAP; HeIP-4; InPK-6; InPS-3; MeMAP; MoAmPo; MoP; NAAL-2; NIP-4; NOBA; NOBE; NoAM; NoP-4; OBMV; OBVE; OxBA; Poetr; PoPoPo; RACG; RB; RaBo; TAP; TFi; TRP; TTTS; TwCP; UnPo; WeW-3

As far as statues go, so far there's not. From Trollope's Journal. Elizabeth Bishop. CBCWP; FaBoPV

As Far as Yoruba Land. Edouard J. Maunick, *French.*

  "Accept from me not silence." NegPo, *tr. by* Ellen Conroy Kennedy

  "And I have chosen the sea as no man's land." NegPo, *tr. by* Ellen Conroy Kennedy

  "Enter in the circle." NegPo, *tr. by* Ellen Conroy Kennedy

  "For there is an African virtue of the tree." NegPo, *tr. by* Ellen Conroy Kennedy

  "I am from everywhere." NegPo, *tr. by* Ellen Conroy Kennedy

  "I have mentioned it by name." NegPo, *tr. by* Ellen Conroy Kennedy

  "I have understood nothing." NegPo, *tr. by* Ellen Conroy Kennedy

  "I made the motions of the sacred place." NegPo, *tr. by* Ellen Conroy Kennedy

  "Ofatedo / seek it out upon the skin of Africa." NegPo, *tr. by* Ellen Conroy Kennedy

  "Point no scornful finger at Yoruba Land." NegPo, *tr. by* Ellen Conroy Kennedy

  "Speaking of Gethsemane in Yoruba Land." NegPo, *tr. by* Ellen Conroy Kennedy

  "This is where the warrior from Ibokun came." NegPo, *tr. by* Ellen Conroy Kennedy

  "Trees were forbidden me, The." NegPo, *tr. by* Ellen Conroy Kennedy

  "Where does this poem come from?" NegPo, *tr. by* Ellen Conroy Kennedy

As fine a piece of furniture. Central. Ted Kooser. Poetsp

As first a various, uniformed hint we find. Music and Poetry. Abraham Cowley. EPCY *Fr.* Davideis.

As flies to wanton boys are we to the gods. Shakespeare. PFE *Fr.* King Lear.

As flowers fall at the river city, memories come to me. Wen Cheng-ming, *Chinese.* CoBLCP, *tr. by* Jonathan Chaves

As flows the rapid river. Samuel Francis Smith. AH

As for him who. Fragment. William Carlos Williams. Spl

As for me, I am a watercolor. / I wash off. Anne Sexton. *See* For My Lover, Returning to His Wife.

As for me, I delight in the everyday Way. *Unknown, Chinese.* CoBCP, *tr. by* Burton Watson

As for me / I have seen Llywelyn. A Day Which Endures Not. A. G. Prys-Jones, *Welsh.* OBWVE, *tr. by* Anthony Conran

As for me, my Nanna ignores me. Condemning the Moongod Nanna. Enheduanna, *ad. by* Aliki *and* Willis Barnstone, *Sumerian.* BoWoP

As for my life, I've led it. A Placid Man's Epitaph. Thomas Hardy. MoBrPo

As for Poets. Gary Snyder. BB; PmAP

A's for the anchor that swings at our bow. The Sailors' Alphabet. *Unknown.* AmFP

As for the Quince. Nuala Ni Dhomhnaill, *Irish.* BiHa; CIP-2; PBCIP, *tr. by* Paul Muldoon

As Fowlers Lie in Wait. Bible, *O.T.* TrJP *Fr.* Jeremiah.

As freedom is a breakfastfood. E. E. Cummings. CMoP; LiTM; NOBA; OxBA; TAP; VGW

As From a Quiver of Arrows. Carl Phillips. BAP-96

As from an [*or* their] ancestral oak. Similes for Two Political Characters of 1819. Shelley. FaBoPV; NAEL-2; OxBoV; RB

As from my own he swept you far away. (LL) Do This Favour For Me. Luis de Camões, *Portuguese.* LBC, *tr. by* Roy Campbell

As from the Dorset shore I travell'd home. The White Horse of Westbury. Charles Tennyson Turner. EBEV; PeVV

As funny as I can. (LL) The Height of the Ridiculous. Oliver Wendell Holmes. OBAL; OBCA

As G-5 put it, Bac Ha hamlet was a good. Bac Ha. David Huddle. CDa

As gentle dews distill. George Rogers. AH

As glad to have my body[,] as my mind. (LL) The Blossom [*or* Blossome]. Donne. AWP; ESCV; ImPo; MeLP; NAEL-1; SCGP; SeCP; UnPo

As Gold is better that's in fire tride. John Taylor. PBRV *Fr.* The Sculler.

As good to write as for to lie and groan. Sonnet 40. Sir Philip Sidney. NoSic *Fr.* Astrophil and Stella. AAS; SiPS

As graceful as the Babylonian willow. To Isa Sleeping. Thomas Holley Chivers. APN-1

As greeted our love's first acknowledgement. (LL) Pure Death. Robert Graves. GTBS-P; LBC

As grit swirls in the wind the word spreads. The Center of Attention. Daniel Gerard Hoffman. FYAP; UnPo

As guns pounded on the shore. (LL) Europe and America. David Ignatow. NNaP; PBMP; UnPo

As hath been, lo, these many generations. John Crowe Ransom. *See* First Travels of Max.

As he came near death things grew shallower for us. Roy Fisher. FaBoMo

As he climbs down our hill, my kestrel rises. Esyllt. Glyn Jones. OBWVE

As he filled up his order book pp. Limerick. *Unknown.* PeLi

As he glowed like a ruddy shield on the Lion's breast. (LL) My life has crept so long on a broken wing. Tennyson. OAEL-2; OBWP

As he knelt by the grave of his mother and father. Milkweed and Monarch. Paul Muldoon. NoP-4

As he left the ship he saw this, only this. The Descent of the Vulture. Marya Alexandrovna Zaturenska. WPE

As he moves the mine-detector. Hunting Civil War Relics at Nimblewill Creek. James Dickey. CBCWP; CoAmPo; WeT

As he said vanity, so vain say I. The Vanity of All Worldly Things. Anne Bradstreet. ChIV-1; SCAP

As he sang upon a tree! (LL) The Rivals. James Stephens. BoTP; OBEV; OBMV

As he sinks two into the chains. (LL) Makin' Jump Shots. Michael S. Harper. ISC; PoE

As he spake to our fathers, to Abraham, and to his seed for ever. (LL) The Magnificat. Bible, *N.T.* BoWoP; OBVE

As he stood against the fretted hedge, which was like white lace. (LL) To a Conscript of 1940. Sir Herbert Read. LiTM; NSI; OBWP; PoWW

As he stood in their shop, Mr. Boosey. Jimmy Pearse. PeLi

As he takes from you, I engraft you new. (LL) Sonnet 15. Shakespeare. AWP; NAEL-1; NoSic; SCGP; Son

As he that sees a dark and shady grove. Holy Baptism (1). George Herbert. GeHe

As He, the maker of this Song. (LL) A Meditation for His Mistress[e]. Robert Herrick. CaPo; NOBE; NOSC; OBEV; SeCP

As he trudged along to school. The Story of Johnny Head-in-Air. Heinrich Hoffmann, *German.* OxBChV

As he was a poet sublimer than me. (LL) A Better Answer to Cloe [*or* Chloe] Jealous. Matthew Prior. AWP; NAEL-1; NOBE; NOEC; OxAEP-1; PoEL-3

As he went on fishing his way. (LL) The Lady and the Bear. Theodore Roethke. ChAP; NBLV

As he would burn or better far his book. (LL) To Elizabeth, Countess of Rutland. Ben Jonson. BeJo; NoP-4

As Hermes once took to his feathers light. A Dream, after Reading Dante's Episode of Paolo and Francesca. Keats. NOBRP

As his own Arthur fared across the mere. The Passing of Tennyson. Ernest Christopher Dowson. EPCY

As his pink feet cling to the granite ledge of the State Building. The Suicide. Kathleen de Azevedo. WWSi

As his when Eden held his virgin heart. (LL) November. John Keble. OBEV; OBNC

As honest Jacob on a night. The Patriarch. Robert Burns. ChIV-1

As honey in wine / wine, honey. Epigram. Meleager, *Greek.* GrAn, *tr. by* Peter Whigham

As I am a Rhymer. On My Joyful Departure from the Same City. Coleridge. NBLV

As I am unhappy. Akiko Yosano, *Japanese.* WPOW, *tr. by* Glenn Hughes *and* Yozan T. Iwasaki

As I approach / The mountain village. Noin, *Japanese.* OHPJ, *tr. by* Kenneth Rexroth

As I beheld a winters evening air. Another. Richard Lovelace. SeCP

As I believe that thou and I should be. (LL) Sonnet: To Guido Cavalcanti. Dante, *Italian.* NNPT, *tr. by* Shelley; AWP, *tr. by* Shelley

"As I cam in by boney Glasgow town." Glasgow Peggie. *Unknown.* ESPB

As I cam in by Dunidier. The Battle of Harlaw. *Unknown.* ESPB

As I cam thro the Garrioch land. The Battle of Harlaw. *Unknown.* ESPB

As I came down from Lebanon. Clinton Scollard. APN-2

As I came from the. Kenneth Rexroth. APSN *Fr.* The Love Poems of Marichiko.

As I came home through Drury's woods. Cold Fear. Elizabeth Madox Roberts. WPE

As I Came in by Fiddich-Side. *Unknown.* RB
(Willie Macintosh.) ESPB

As I came in from Fiddich-side. As I Came in by Fiddich-Side. *Unknown.* ESPB; RB

As I came out of the New York Public Library. Nuns in the Wind. Muriel Rukeyser. NNaP

As I came over Windy Gap. Running to Paradise. W. B. Yeats. NTP; OxBoLi

As I came round the harbo[u]r buoy. The Long White Seam. Jean Ingelow. NOBVV; SDW

As I came through the desert thus it was. James Thomson. *Fr.* The City of Dreadful Night. OBNC

As I came to the edge of the woods. Come In. Robert Frost. AmPP; LiTM; MoAmPo; NOBA; NoP-4; PFE; RaBo; TRP

As I can gulp it down. (LL) Ballad: "I therefore pray thee, Renny dear." Samuel Johnson. OBCoV

As I did the washing one day. The Shirt of a Lad. *Unknown, Welsh.* OBWVE, *tr. by* Anthony Conran

As I did walke my selfe alone. King James and Brown. *Unknown.* ESPB

As I dig for wild orchids. Lady Izumi, *Japanese.* ITG, *tr. by* Jane Hirshfield *and* Mariko Aratani

As I do now? (LL) The One Furrow. Ronald Stuart Thomas. HoPM; OxBC

As I do now, before the advancing day. (LL) Since of no creature living the last breath. Edna St. Vincent Millay. HeIP-4; VGW

As I do zew, wi' nimble hand. Lwonesomeness. William Barnes. NOBVV

As I dressed for dinner tonight. The Belt. Eric Chock. IFJA

As I drive my parents home through the snow. Driving My Parents Home at Christmas. Robert Bly. IFJA

As I drive to the junction of lane and highway. At Castle Boterel. Thomas Hardy. EBEV; GTBS-P; NOBE; OBNC; OxAEP-2; PeVV; PoE; SCV

As I ebb'd with the ocean of life. Walt Whitman. APN-1; AmPP; NAAL-1; NAAL-3; NOBA; PAR; TAP

As I gaed down to Collistown. The Cunning Clerk. *Unknown.* OxBB

As I gaed in by the Duke o' Athole's gates. The Duke o' Athole's Nurse. *Unknown.* OxBB

As I gaze upon. Tanka. Kanoko Okamoto, *Japanese.* MJT, *tr. by* Makoto Ueda

As I get older, I like quiet sitting. Quiet Sitting. Wang Chiu-ssu, *Chinese.* CoBLCP, *tr. by* Jonathan Chaves

As I Gird on for Fighting. A. E. Housman. CMoP

As I glance through a few thin pages and switch off the light. (LL) Achill. Derek Mahon. BiHa; PBCIP; PNI

As I go up to Heaven. (LL) Woman. Valente Goenha Malangatana, *Portuguese.* PBMAP

As I Grew Older. Langston Hughes. AmPP; ColAP
("Of sun!") (LL) ColAP

As I grow more and more each day. My Aim. A. J. Seymour. CTV

As I grow old, and weaker grow my eyes. Yüan Mei. *Fr.* Moments of Fullfillment—mdash;Writing Down Miscellaneous. CoBLCP, *tr. by* Jonathan Chaves

As I guard o'er the fold. (LL) Night. William Blake. BoTP; CH; FHYEP; FaBoBe; OBEV; OxBChV; PoLF; Ro

As I have said, I floated to the earth. Shelley. FHYEP *Fr.* Prometheus Unbound. NOBRP; OAEL-2

As I in *baden-zuyt* was entreating stop-and-go Pushkin here. A Rune. Caroline Knox. BAP-94

As I in hoary [*or* hoarie] Winters [*or* Winter's] night stood[e] shivering[e] in the snow[e]. The Burning Babe. Robert Southwell. AEP; CH; ESCV; FMP; FaBoCh; GEA; HAP; HeIP-4; InPS-3; NAEL-1; NOBE; NOCV; NoP-4; NoSic; OAEL-1; OBCP; OBEV; OxAEP-1; OxBSn; PBRV; PoEL-2; PoPoPo; RB; SCGP; TFi; TOF; TRP; TrCP

As I kissed Agathon my soul swelled to my lips. Sokrates to his Lover. Plato, *Greek.* OBCVT, *tr. by* Willis Barnstone

As I lay asleep in Italy. The Mask [*or* Masque] of Anarchy. Shelley. FHYEP; OBSV; OxAEP-2; RB; Ro; SCV

As I lay dreaming, open-eyed. Her Mouth and Mine. W. H. Davies. CBLP

As I lay, fullness of praise. The Rattle Bag. Dafydd ap Gwilym, *Welsh.* NBLV; NNPT; RB, *tr. by* Joseph Clancy

As I lay musing all alone. The Friar in the Well. *Unknown.* ESPB

As I lay upon a night. *Unknown.* MiEL

As I lay with my head in your lap camerado. Walt Whitman. CBCWP; NAAL-1; NAAL-3; NCAP; OxBA

("Or whether we shall victorious, or utterly quell'd and / defeated.") (LL) NCAP

As I leaned at my window. The Song of Samuel Sweet. Charles Causley. OBNV

As I lie here in the sun. Jonah. Randall Jarrell. ChIV-1

As I lie now. (LL) Man Alone. Louise Bogan. NYBP; NoP-4

As I listened from a beach-chair in the shade. Their Lonely Betters. W. H. Auden. NAEL-2; NoAM; OBGa

As I Looked at a Lake, My Thoughts Turned to a Certain Friend. Chu Yün-ming, *Chinese.* CoBLCP, *tr. by* Jonathan Chaves

As I me rod this ender day. *Unknown.* MiEL

As I my little flock on Ister Bank. Shepherd Song. Sir Philip Sidney. SiPS *Fr.* Arcadia.

As I one evening [*or* ev'ning] sat before my cell. Artillery [*or* Artillerie]. George Herbert. GeHe; InPS-3; NoP-4; PoEL-2

As I pass through my incarnations in every age and race. The Gods of the Copybook Headings. Rudyard Kipling. FaPoR; NoAM; OBSV; OxBTC

As I pass'd [*or* passed] by a river side [*or* riverside]. The Carnal and the Crane. *Unknown.* ESPB

As I reach to close each book. Against the Evidence. David Ignatow. NNaP

As I remember, barracks still stand. Aleksandr Lavrin, *Russian.* TCRP, *tr. by* Vera Dunham

As I remember, I was that kind of girl. I was. Bridget. Lisa Lewis. BAP-95

As I rode in to Burrumbeet. The Traveller. C. J. Dennis. NOBAu

As I roved out impatiently. In the Ringwood. Thomas Kinsella. CMoP; PBCIP

As I roved out on a May morning. Johnny's the Lad I Love. *Unknown.* OxBoLi

As I roved out one summer's morning, speculating most curiously. Colleen Rue. *Unknown.* BIrV

As I row over the plain. Tadamichi, *Japanese.* OHPJ, *tr. by* Kenneth Rexroth

As I rummaged thro' the attic. My Trundle Bed. J. G. Baker. BLPA; FaBoBe

As I sat at the Café I said to myself. How Pleasant It Is to Have Money. Arthur Hugh Clough. GTBS-P; NBLV; NOBE; OAEL-2; OBCoV; OxBoLi *Fr.* Spectator ab Extra. OBCoV; OxBoLi; PeLV; PeVV

As I sat at the café, I said to myself. How Pleasant It Is to Have Money. Arthur Hugh Clough. EnVP; FaBoPV; NOBE; NOBVV; OAEL-2; OxBoLi *Fr.* Dipsychus [and the Spirit].

As I sat by my window last evening. Miss Foggerty's Cake. *Unknown.* BLPA; NBLV

As I sat down one evening. The Frozen Logger. *Unknown.* OBAL

As I sat down to breakfast in state. The Country Clergyman's Trip to Cambridge. Thomas Babington Macaulay, 1st Baron Macaulay. OBSV; OxBoLi; PeLV

As I sat in a lonesome grove. The Little Dove. *Unknown.* AmFP

As I Sat in the Armchair of the Tsar. Bulat Shalvovich Okudzhava, *Russian.* TCRP, *tr. by* Deming Brown

As I sat on a Sunny Bank. *Unknown.* OxBoLi; OxNR

As I sat one evening in sweet meditation. The Twilight Hour. Joshua McCarter Simpson. AAP

As I sate *Musing*, by my selfe alone. A Dialogue between Melancholy and Mirth. Margaret Lucas Cavendish, Duchess of Newcastle. BWW

As I sate Musing by my selfe alone. Thoughts Several Are. Margaret Lucas Cavendish, Duchess of Newcastle. *Fr.* A Dialogue between Melancholy and Mirth. BWW

As I sd to my / friend, because I am. I Know a Man. Robert Creeley. CoAmPo; InPS-3; NIP-4; NOBA; NoP-4; OxBSP; PoM; VCAP

As I see it, T'ao Yüan-ming. The Supervisor, Han Chün-mei, Has Shown Me Five Poems He Has Written Called, The Trees Flourish in Early Summer. I Have Therefore Written Down My Own Ignoble Feelings and Sent Them Via Inspector Juan. At This Time, Chün-mei Is Lecturing to the Various Scholars on the I-ching. Tai Piao-yüan, *Chinese.* CoBLCP, *tr. by* Jonathan Chaves

As I should lay alone. (LL) Whistle, Daughter, Whistle. *Unknown.* AmFP; OxNR; ReMoGo

As I sit by the ruddy oak fire. Nestle-down Cottage. Mary Weston Fordham. CBWP-2

As I sit looking out of a window of the building. The Instruction Manual. John Ashbery. HAP; InPS-3; NOBA; NeAP; NoAM; PoM; Poetr

As I sit writing here, sick and grown old. Walt Whitman. NAAL-1; NAAL-3

As I stepped out the doorway it was ten o'clock. Peace, Horror. Miklós Radnóti, *Hungarian.* AF, *tr. by* Emery E. George

As I stood / Ling'ring upon the threshold, half-concealed. Xantippe. Amy Levy. BrRo

As I strole the city, oft I. Jonathan Swift. BIrV *Fr.* The Legion Club.

As I strolled out one evening just as the sun went down. The Farmer and the Shanty Boy. *Unknown.* AmFP

As I talk with learned people. A Spade Is Just a Spade. Walter Everette Hawkins. PoBA

As I therein no other's face but yours can view. (LL) These verses weare made By Michaell Drayton Esquier Poett Lawreatt the night before hee dyed. Michael Drayton. GBL; NOBE

As I therin noe others face but yours can Veiwe. Michael Drayton. *See* These verses weare made By Michaell Drayton Esquier Poett Lawreatt the night before hee dyed.

As I those other women? (LL) The Portrait. Robert Graves. CMoP; LoP; PBMP

As I travel, there are no flowers. No Flowers. Ch'ien Ch'ien-i, *Chinese.* CoBLCP, *tr. by* Jonathan Chaves

As I walk'd thinking through a little grove. Catch: On a Wet Day. Franco Sacchetti, *Italian.* AWP, *tr. by* D. G. Rossetti

As I Walked by Myself. *Unknown.* CBNP; FaBoEE; OxBSP; OxNR; ReMoGo

As I walked down by the river. A Ballad for Katharine of Aragon. Charles Causley. FaBoTw

As I walked fforth one morninge. Christopher White. *Unknown.* ESPB

As I walked out early. Thomas A. Clark. NBrP *Fr.* Sixteen Sonnets.

As I walked out in the streets of Laredo. The Cowboy's Lament. *Unknown.* APN-2; AS; AmFP; ChAP; FaBoA; RB

As I walked out one evening. W. H. Auden. CBNP; HeIP-4; InPK-6; LiTM; MoBrPo; NOBE; NoAM; NoP-4; OAEL-2; OxAEP-2; PBMP; PoPoPo; RB; TwCP; UnPo

As I walked out one evening, all in the month of May. The Banks of Claudy. *Unknown.* AmFP

As I walked out one evening down by the Strawberry Lane. Captain Wedderburn's Courtship. *Unknown.* AmFP; ESPB

As I walked out one May morninge, / When the small birds sang so sweet. The Lover Proved False. *Unknown.* AmFP

As I walked out one morning for pleasure. *Unknown. See* Whoopee Ti Yi Yo, Git Along Little Dogies.

As I walked out one morning in May. Archie o Cawfield. *Unknown.* AmFP

As I walked out one morning, just as day was dawning. *Unknown.* AmFP

As I Walked Out One Night. The Sailor's Return. *Unknown.* OxBoLi

As I walked out that sultry night. Full Moon. Robert Graves. NOBE

As I walked over the western plain. Legend. Charles Causley. TOF

As I wandered in the forest. The Wild Flower's Song. William Blake. BoTP

As I wandered on the beach. The Great Blue Heron. Carolyn Kizer. CoAP; IMW; WPE

As I wandered over the city through the night. John Gould Fletcher. *Fr.* Irradiations. MoAmPo

As I wandered round the homestead. My Mother's Prayer. T. C. O'Kane. BLPA; FaBoBe

As I wandrede her by weste. *Unknown.* MiEL

As I was a-gwine down the road. Turkey in the Straw. *Unknown.* AS

As I was a-roaming for pleasure one day. The Little Mohea. *Unknown.* AmFP

As I was a-roving one morning in spring. The Mantle So Green. *Unknown.* AmFP

As I was a-walkin' down Paradise Street. Blow the Man Down. *Unknown.* AS

As I was a-walking on Westminster Bridge. *Unknown.* OxNR

As I was a-walking [*or* walked out] one morning for pleasure. Whoopee Ti Yi Yo, Git Along Little Dogies. *Unknown.* AS; ImGa

As I was a-walking to Nottingham Fair. Nottingham Fair. *Unknown.* AmFP

As I was cast in my ffirst sleepe. Young [*or* Younge] Andrew. *Unknown.* ESPB; OxBB

As I was climbing Ardán Mór. Ardan Mór. Francis Ledwidge. AWP

As I was fishing off Pondy Point. Jim Desterland. Hyam Plutzik. RB; VGW; WeT

As I was going along, long, long. Mother Goose. OxNR; ReMoGo

As I was going by Charing Cross. *Unknown.* CH; FaBoCh; OxNR

As I was going o'er Tipple Tine. *Unknown.* OxNR

As I was going over Mulberry Mountain. Mulberry Mountain. *Unknown.* AmFP

As I was going through Windy Gap. Windy Gap. David Campbell. NTP

As I was going to Banbury. *Unknown.* OxNR

As I was going to Derby. The [Wonderful] Derby Ram. *Unknown.* BoTP; CBNP; NTP; OxNR; ReMoGo

As I Was Going to Saint Ives. Daniel Gerard Hoffman. NYBP

As I was going to sell my eggs. Bandy Legs. Mother Goose. OxNR; ReMoGo

As I was going to sell my eggs. *Unknown.* ACTP

As I was going to St. Ives. Mother Goose. LB; NTCP; OxNR; ReMoGo

As I was going up Pippen Hill. Mother Goose. OxNR; ReMoGo

As I was going up the hill. *Unknown.* OxNR

As I was going up the stair. Antigonish. Hughes Mearns. CTV; FPC; NBLV; PoLF

As I was helplessly young. (LL) Childhood. Frances Darwin Cornford. KaS

As I was hiking past the woods, the cool and sleepy summer woods. Out There Somewhere. Henry Herbert Knibbs. BLPA

As I was lumb'ring down de street. Buffalo Gals. *Unknown, sometimes att. to* Cool White. APN-2

As I was musing by myself alone. Mirth and Melancholy. Margaret Lucas Cavendish, Duchess of Newcastle. WPE

As I was putting away the groceries. Bali Hai Calls Mama. Marilyn Nelson Waniek. ISC; IFJA

As I was sitting in my chair. The Perfect Reactionary. Hughes Mearns. NTCP

As I Was Standing in the Street. *Unknown.* NTCP

As I was strolling lonely in the Backs. In the Backs. James Kenneth Stephen. NOBVV

As I was waiting for the bus. Sight Unseen. Kingsley Amis. NoAM

As I Was Walkin' down Wexford Street. *Unknown.* AS

As I was walkin' the jungle round, a-killin' of tigers an' time. Ballad. Guy Wetmore Carryl. BXAP; NBLV

As I was walking. Kore. Robert Creeley. CoAmPo; InPS-3; RaBo

As I was walking all alane [*or* alone]. The Twa Corbies. *Unknown.* AWP; CH; EBEvV; ESPB; EnSB; FaBoCh; GTBS-P; HAP; InPK-6; OBEV; OxBS; PBMP; PFE; RB; SCGP; SoSe-8; UnPo

As I was walking [*or* wa'king] all alone [*or* alane]. The Wee Wee Man. *Unknown.* CH; EBEV; ESPB; FaBoCh; OAEL-1; OxBB

As I was walking among the fires of hell. A Memorable Fancy. William Blake. *Fr.* The Marriage of Heaven and Hell. NAEL-2; NOBRP; OAEL-2

As I was walking down by the seashore. The Lover's Lament for Her Sailor. *Unknown.* AmFP

As I was walking down the lake. *Unknown.* ACTP

As I was walking in a field of wheat. *Unknown.* OxNR

As I was walking in the fields last Tuesday of all days. The Slender Lad. *Unknown, Welsh.* OBWVE, *tr. by* Kenneth Hurlstone Jackson

As I was walking in the *Mall* of late. Horace. OBCVT, *tr. by* John Oldham *Fr.* An Imitation of Horace. Book I, Satyr IX, Written in June, 1681.

As I was walking mine alane. Archie o [*or* of] Cawfield. *Unknown.* AmFP; ESPB; OxBS

As I was walking pensively through a little wood. Franco Sacchetti. *See* Catch: On a Wet Day.

As I was walking up the stair. Hughes Mearns. *See* Antigonish.

As I watch the moon. Ōe no Chisato, *Japanese.* OHPJ, *tr. by* Kenneth Rexroth

As I went a-walking one fine summer's morning. The Shoofly. Felix O'Hare. AmFP

As I went by a dyer's door. The Dyer. *Unknown.* OxNR

As I went down that yella bank. Riddle. *Unknown.* FaBoVe

As I went down the hill along the wall. Meeting and Passing. Robert Frost. GLoP; OxBA

As I went down the village green. Ducks. Norman Ault. BoTP

As I went down to David's town. George Craig Stewart. AH

As I went down to Dymchurch Wall. In Romney Marsh. John Davidson. EBVV; OxBTC

As I went down to the huckleberry picnic. The Kicking Mule. *Unknown.* AmFP

As I went down to the mowin' field. Fod. *Unknown.* AmFP

As I went out a Crow. The Last Word of a Bluebird. Robert Frost. NOxBChV

As I went out a-walking to breathe the pleasant air. Rolly Trudum. *Unknown* AmFP

As I went out one May morning. Bird in a Cage. *Unknown.* AS

As I went out this May morning I found. Hal Summers. AYFP

As I went out walking for pleasure one day. The Little Mohea. *Unknown.* AmFP

As I went over the water. *Unknown.* OxNR

As I went through a guttery gap / I met a wee man with a red cap. Riddle. *Unknown.* FaBoVe

As I went through the garden gap. A Cherry. *Unknown.* ReMoGo

As I went through the marshes. A Doe at Evening. D. H. Lawrence. APo

As I went through yon guttery gap / I met my Uncle Davy. Riddle. *Unknown.* FaBoVe

As I Went to Bonner. *Unknown.* CBNP; OxBoLi; OxNR; ReMoGo

As I went up by Ovillers. Ballad of the Three Spectres. Ivor Gurney. OBWP; PoFWW

As I went up the Brandy hill. *Unknown.* OxNR

As I went up the garden. *Unknown.* BoTP

As I wer readen ov a stwone. Readen ov a Head-Stwone. William Barnes. CH

As idle as a German ship. The Surrender of the Hun Fleet. *Unknown.* NSI

As if a cast of grain leapt back to the hand. An Event. Richard Wilbur. AFr

As if a one-room schoolhouse were all we knew. An Amish Rug. Michael Longley. CIP-2; PNI

As if a phantom caress'd me. Walt Whitman. GBL; GLoP; SAmP

As if all language were rooted in the silent grammar of an implication. Premises. Gustaf Sobin. PT

As if by late light shaped of its. Slipped Quadrant. Nathaniel Mackey. FTOS

As if crouching, springs / to life. (LL) A Little Language. Robert Duncan. FTOS

As if dead the buried text. III. Danielle Collobert, *French.* MFP, *tr. by* Martin Sorrell

As If Ending. James Richardson. MoLi

As if God were an old man. The Task. Denise Levertov. CrSp

As if I didn't have enough. Small Aircraft. Bella Akhatovna Akhmadulina, *Russian.* BoWoP, *tr. by* Daniel Halpern

As if I had committed, against the whole scheme of life, a /desecration desecration. (LL) Moss-Gathering. Theodore Roethke. BLT; VGW

As if in a presence of an intelligence. The Cold. Charles Simic. HCAP

As if in snow you walked. And you walked in snow. A Song of Blue and Red. Amir Gilbo'a, *Hebrew.* MHP, *tr. by* Ruth Finer Mintz

As if in water. Tanka. Ishikawa Takuboku, *Japanese.* MJT, *tr. by* Makoto Ueda

As if it came. Tanka. Miya Shūji, *Japanese.* MJT, *tr. by* Makoto Ueda

As if it had not been. (LL) A Moment. Mary Elizabeth Coleridge. LW; PEW

As if it resembled your hair. Jure Kastelan, *Croatian.* CEEP, *tr. by* Peter Kastmiler

As if it were a scene made-up by the mind. Often I Am Permitted to Return to a Meadow. Robert Duncan. CMoP; ColAP; NOBA; PmAP

As if it were / forever that they move, that we. Merritt Parkway. Denise Levertov. AmPP; NeAP; PoM

As if it's as if it's part of the whole endeavor to get back the finger beclouding what's. Methodology. Bruce Andrews. FTOS

As if my answering machine were a rejection. Phonic. Gail Mazur. NAmP90

As if our sneakers froze to the ground. . . . The Call of the Lake. Andrey Andreievich Voznesensky, *Russian.* TCRP; VCWP, *tr. by* Stanley Kunitz

As if posed for a picture called "Restless Youth." Brooklyn Bound. Barbara Elovic. WWSi

As if some irremediable poison. London. J. R. Rowland. CBAP

As if some little Arctic flower. Emily Dickinson. APN-2

As if somebody ordered it. Tashkent Breaks into Bloom. "Anna Akhmatova," *Russian.* BoWoP, *tr. by* Richard McKane

As if that night. Troubling the Water. Yusef Komunyakaa. BAP-95

As if the chart were given. Emily Dickinson. *See* I never saw a Moor.

As if the Checks were even. (LL) I never saw a Moor. Emily Dickinson. CTV; HeIP-4; ImGa; ImPo; LiTM; MeMAP; MoAmPo; PoLF; SAmP; TAP; TFi; WPoS

As if the sky broke up. On the Origin of the Contrary. Miroslav Holub, *Czech.* VCWP, *tr. by* Stuart Friebert *and* Dana Hábová

As if the trees were not indifferent. Gathered at the River. Denise Levertov. CrSp

As if they were his ripe prize vegetables. (LL) My Father's Garden. David Wagoner. DiPo; NIP-4

As if thou hadst sealed my pardon, with thy blood. (LL) Blow Your Trumpets. Donne. ChIV-2; ClHu; EBEV; FHYEP; HAP; HeIP-4; ImPo; InPS-3; MeLP; NAEL-1; NAWM-1; NOBE; NOSC; OAEL-1; OxAEP-1; PeECV; PoE; PoEL-2; SCGP; SeCP; Son; TFi; TOF

As imperceptibly as Grief. Emily Dickinson. APN-2; CMoP; GEA; NAAL-1; NOBA; NoP-4; PBWP; PoE; PoEL-5; SoSe-8

As in a Dream. Li Ch'ing-chao, *Chinese.* CoBCP, *tr. by* Burton Watson

As in a dream of flood from which we rose intact but alone. The Break. Elizabeth Nancy Sargent. NYBP

As in a duskie [*or* dusky] and tempestuous night. Sonnet. William Drummond, of Hawthornden. NOSC; OxAEP-1

As in a Rose-Jar. Thomas Samuel Jones Jr. PoLF

As in a Watteau fete of rose and silver blue. The Tempest. Marya Alexandrovna Zaturenska. MoAmPo

As in Frank O'Hara's best known poem, "The Day Lady Died." I Was on a Golf Course the Day John Cage Died of a Stroke. Stephen Paul Miller. BAP-94

As in Frege's luminous counter-example. The Counter-Example. David Shapiro. PmAP

As in his burning throne he sits emparadised. (LL) The Celestial City. Giles Fletcher, the Younger. ChIV-2, *stanzas* 30–44; NOSC

As in that twilight, superstitious age. On Rembrant; Occasioned by His Picture of Jacob's Dream. Washington Allston. APN-1

As in the age of shepherd king and queen. L'Allée. Paul Verlaine, *French.* AWP; GaP; OBGa, *tr. by* Arthur Symons

As in the cool-air'd road I come by. My Love's Guardian Angel. William Barnes. GBL; PoEL-4

As in the gardens, all through May, the rose. His Lady's Tomb. Pierre de Ronsard, *French.* AWP, *tr. by* Andrew Lang

As in the house I sate [*or* sat]. Poverty. Thomas Traherne. TrCP

As in the inward suspicious mind. (LL) Written in Her French Psalter. Elizabeth I, Queen of England. PBWP; WPE

As in the midst of battle there is room. Sonnet XXV. George Santayana. APN-2; AWP *Fr.* Sonnets.

As innocent as now thou art. (LL) To His Son [*or* Sonne], Vincent Corbet[t]. Richard Corbet. BeJo; FaBoCh; NOSC; OxAEP-1; OxBChV

As into the Garden Elizabeth Ran. A. E. Housman. NBLV

As into the green cool of the sea. Don't Move Away. Nino Nikolov, *Bulgarian.* CEEP, *tr. by* Ewald Osers

As inward love breeds outward talk. The Angler's Song. William Basse. NOSC *Fr.* The Anglers Song.

As is a face, the throat crushed. Sour-Cherry Trees. Gyula Illyés, *Hungarian.* CEEP, *tr. by* Emery E. George

As is the inward suspicious mind. Elizabeth I, Queen of England. *See* Written in Her French Psalter.

As is the sand upon the ocean's shore. One Generation Passeth Away. Jones Very. ChIV-2

As Israel's king kept his in shepherd's weed. (LL) To St John Baptist. Henry Constable. ChIV-2; NoSic

As it[t] befel[l] in midsum[m]ertime [*or* midsumer-time]. Sir Andrew Bart[t]on. *Unknown.* AmFP; ESPB; EnSB; OxBB

As it befell upon one time. Hughie Grame. *Unknown.* ESPB; OxBB

As it blossoms Aaron's rod. The Rod. Georgy Nikolaevich Obolduyev, *Russian.* TCRP, *tr. by* Vera Dunham

As it comes back, brick by smoky brick. In the Lost Province. Tom Paulin. PBCIP

As it fell on a holy day. John Dory. *Unknown.* ESPB

As it fell one holy-day [*or* on a light holyday *or* high holyday]. Little Musgrave and Lady Barnard. *Unknown.* ESPB; OxBB

As it fell out in a long summer's day. Fair Margaret and Sweet William. *Unknown.* ESPB; OxBB

As it fell out on a holy day [*or* upon a bright holiday *or* upon one day]. The Bitter Withy. *Unknown.* NOCV; NoP-4

As it fell out one May morning. The Holy Well. *Unknown.* FaBoCh; NOCV

As it fell out upon a day [*or* one day]. Dives and Lazarus. *Unknown.* ESPB; OxBB

As it fell upon a day. Philomel. Richard Barnfield. AWP; CH; GBL; GTBS-P; NOBE; OBEV *Fr.* The Affectionate Shepherd. *Also appears as a section in* The Passionate Pilgrim.

As it fell upon a day. A Vision of Truth. Sir John Collings Squire. NOBL

As it grows dark / drinking wine. (LL) After Work. Gary Snyder. HoPM; NNaP; PFE

As It Is. Ralph Angel. WeT

As It Looked Then. Edwin Arlington Robinson. CMoP; MeMAP

As it was doomed to be. Ticonderoga: A Legend of the West Highlands. Robert Louis Stevenson. EBNV; OBNV

As it was in the beginning. Robin Morgan. CrSp *Fr.* The Network of the Imaginary Mother.

As it was the eve of the 14th of July. A Phantom of Clouds. Guillaume Apollinaire, *French.* PFTM, *tr. by* Ron Padgett

As itt beffell in midsumer-time. Sir Andrew Barton. *Unknown.* ESPB; OxBB

As Jack, the jolly plowboy, was plowing of his land. The Jolly Plowboy. *Unknown.* AmFP

As Jack walked out of London city. Jack the Jolly Tar. *Unknown.* AmFP

As Jock the Leg and the merry merchant. Jock the Leg and the Merry Merchant. *Unknown.* ESPB

As Joseph Was a-Walking. *Unknown.* BoTP; PChr

As Julia once a-slumbering lay. The Captived Bee; or, The Little Filcher. Robert Herrick. CaPo

As kingfishers catch fire, dragonflies dráw fláme. What I Do Is Me. Gerard Manley Hopkins. APAD; CMoP; EBEV; EBVV; EnlH; FaBoMo; LiTM; MoBrPo; NAEL-2; NOBVV; NOCV; NoP-4; OxAEP-2; PoE; RB

As kythed in that wild auld carline that day! (LL) Old Wife in High Spirits. "Hugh MacDiarmid." CMoP; OxBTC; PoE

As Lambs into the Pen. Dorothy, Duchess of Wellington Wellesley. FaBoTw

As lamps burn silent, with unconscious light. Modesty. Aaron Hill. OxBSP

As landscapes richen after rain, the eye. Foliage of Vision. James Merrill. VGW

As lark ascending. Praying. P. J. Kavanagh. OxBSP

As *Lesbias* Sparrow, *Tricksy* wanton is. Martial, *Latin*. OBCVT, tr. by Charles Cotton

As life improved, their poems. Postscript. Ronald Stuart Thomas. FaBoMo; OxBC

As life runs on, the road grows strange. Sixty-Eighth Birthday. James Russell Lowell. OxBSP; PFE; PoEL-5

As Life What Is So Sweet? *Unknown.* OxBSP

As little Jenny Wren / Was sitting by the shed. Jenny Wren. Mother Goose. OxNR

As Lob among his cows one day. Lob's Courtship. Elizabeth Hands. ECWP

As long ago they raced. A Dream of Trains. Mark Van Doren. GM

As long ago we carried to your knees. Mother. *Unknown.* PoToHe

As long as Fame's imperious music rings. Three Quatrains. Edwin Arlington Robinson. NCAP

As long as I continue weeping. Sonnet. Louise Labé, *French*. PBWP, tr. by Joan Keefe *and* Richard Terdiman

As long as I live. Me. Walter De la Mare. CTV

As long as I was living in the village. *Unknown, Chinese*. CoBCP, tr. by Burton Watson

As long as it was still noon and the earth. Callimachus, *Greek*. HePo, tr. by Barbara Hughes Fowler *Fr.* Hecale.

As long as it watched me. (LL) February Twilight. Sara Teasdale. AYFP; OBCA

As long as the cat comes home. Love Poem. August Kleinzahler. MoNo

As long as there is anything whatever. (LL) He. Vasco [*or* Vasko] Popa, *Serbian*. NNPT, tr. by Pennington, Anne

As long as we feel another's pain. Andrey Dmitrievich Dementyev, *Russian*. TCRP, tr. by Albert C. Todd

As long as we look forward, all seems free. The Western Approaches. Howard Nemerov. ColAP; HCAP; TAP

As Lords. Milton. *Fr.* Samson Agonistes. FHYEP; OAEL-1; PoEL-3

As Love and I, late harboured in one inn. Michael Drayton. GBL; NoSic *Fr.* Idea.
("As Love and I, late harbour'd in one inn.") LoP

As loving Hind that (Hartless) wants her Deer. Another. Anne Bradstreet. LW; NAAL-3; OxBA; SCAP; WPE

As Lucy went a-walking one morning cold and fine. Walter De la Mare. OBSP

As mad sexton's bell, tolling. Song on the Water. Thomas Lovell Beddoes. FaBoCh *Fr.* Death's Jest Book.

As Magical Mr Mistoffelees! (LL) Mr Mistoffelees. T. S. Eliot. CBNP; NOxBChV

As makes her seem nor fair, nor rich, nor young. (LL) Fair, Rich, and Young. Sir John Harington, *after the Latin of* Martial. FaBoEE; NIP-4

As many red herrings as grow [*or* grew] in the wood. (LL) Man in the wilderness asked [of] me [*or* said to me], The [*or* A]. Mother Goose. BoTP; CBNP; FaBoCh; LB; OxNR; ReMoGo; Spl

As martyrs gridirons, when God calls the roll. (LL) Rolling the Lawn. William Empson. OBGa

As May was opening the rosebuds. Birth of the Foal. Ferenc Juhász, *Hungarian*. RB, tr. by David Wevill

As melting quietly by his boots it fell. (LL) Innocence. Thom Gunn. HP; LiTM

As men, for fear the stars should sleep and nod. Divinity. George Herbert. NOSC

As Moreau painted him, Jason is a youth with brilliant silk to hide his / loins. Poetry and Joy. Edward Foster. PT

As Mozart composed a sonata. Limerick. *Unknown.* PeLi

As Much As You Can. Constantine P. Cavafy, *Greek*. PiM, tr. by Edmund Keeley; GrIP; RB, tr. by Edmund Keeley *and* Philip Sherrard
("And if you cannot make your life as you want it.") PiM
("Till it becomes like an alien burdensome life.") (LL) PiM

As my black hair. (LL) Will he always love me? Lady Horikawa, *Japanese*. OHPJ, tr. by Kenneth Rexroth

As my eyes search the prairie. Spring Song. *Unknown, Chippewa Indian*. OBVE, tr. by Frances Densmore

As my father's breathing. The Stone at the Bottom. Manuel Ulacia, *Spanish*. VCWP, tr. by Reginald Gibbons

As my imagination rises. Beyond Imagination. David Rokeah, *Hebrew*. MHP, tr. by Ruth Finer Mintz

As my master doth set by me. (LL) The Jolly Pinder of Wakefield. *Unknown.* PBRV

As my mind in fancy wanders. The Negro Has a Chance. Maggie Pogue Johnson. CBWP-4

As my mind's leaves. Two Movements Which Begin at the Head and End at the Feet. Richard Caddel. NBrP

As my mother ages and becaomes. My Mother in Old Age. Eric Ormsby. NIP-4

As my new life begins, I start smiling at the people around me. Farewell to Kurdistan. Rosemary Tonks. OxBTC

As my sweet lovely Jean! Robert Burns. *See* Of a' the airts the wind can blaw.

As my sweet lovely Jean! (LL) Of a' the airts the wind can blaw. Robert Burns. GTBS-P

As My Way Passed Through T'ung-ch'uan, I Wished to Visit the Policy Critic of the Right, Mei, but Did Not Know Where to Find Him. Tai Piao-yüan, *Chinese*. CoBLCP, tr. by Jonathan Chaves

As "Name of individual, partnership, or corporation to whom paid." Royalties. D. J. Enright. NOBL; PeLV

As Nature H——'s clay was blending. On a Certain Effeminate Peer. John Winstanley. FaBoEE

As near Portobello lying. Admiral Hosier's Ghost. Richard Glover. NOEC

As needy gallants in the scriv'ners' hands. Prologue. Dryden. OBSV *Fr.* Amboyna; or, The Cruelties of the Dutch to the English Merchants.

As New and as Old. Martin Carter. PBCV

As newer comers crowd the fore. The Superseded. Thomas Hardy. LiLi

As night drew on, and, from the crest. Winter Night. John Greenleaf Whittier. *Fr.* Snow-Bound [*or* Snow-Bound; a Winter Idyl]. APN-1; AiP; AmPP; NAAL-3; NOBA; OxBA; TAP; TFi

As night falls. Tanka. Tsukamoto Kunio, *Japanese*. MJT, tr. by Makoto Ueda

As night was falling slowly on city, town and bush. The Bastard from the Bush. *Unknown.* NOBAu

As Nilus' sudden ebbing here. A Dream Broke. William Cartwright. NOSC

As none at all can perfect passage find. (LL) Cosmus hath more discoursing in his head. Sir John Davies. NoSic; PBRV

As now they do, to hear a boy's heart break. (LL) An Incident in the Early Life of Ebenezer Jones, Poet, 1828. John Betjeman. CMoP; MoP; NoAM

As Ocean's Stream. Fyodor Ivanovich Tyutchev, *Russian*. AWP, tr. by Babette Deutsch *and* Avrahm Yarmolinsky

As o'er my latest book I pored. Printer's Error. P. G. Wodehouse. OBCoV

As o'er thy loved one now in grief ye bendeth. Solace. Josephine D. Henderson Heard. CBWP-4

As Of Old. Stephen Phillips. *See* The Apparition.

As oft as I behold and see. Henry Howard, Earl of Surrey. SiPS

As oft I do record. Jinny. *Unknown.* NOSC

As oft, Sir Tradewel, as we meet. An Allusion to Martial. Martial, *Latin*. OBCVT, tr. by John Oldham

As often as some where before my feet. Francis Daniel Pastorius. SCAP

As old age approaches. Yün Shou-p'ing. CoBLCP, tr. by Jonathan Chaves *Fr.* A Lament for Myself.

As on a Darkling Plain. Henry Taylor. MT; Poetr

As on a window late I cast mine eye. Love-Joy. George Herbert. OAEL-1

As on Euphrates shady banks we lay. Bible, *O.T. See* Psalm 137.

As on the Cross, the Saviour hung. Deep Spring. *Unknown.* AmFP

As on the Heather. Reinmar von Hagenau, *German*. AWP, tr. by Jethro Bithell

As on the highway's quiet edge. Coast, The: Norfolk. Frances Darwin Cornford. CV

As on the very first day. (LL) What She Said to Her Friend ("The Colors on the elephant's body"). Kapilar, *Tamil*. PLW, tr. by A. K. Ramanujan

As once grave Pluto drove his royal wheels. Proserpine's Ragout. Mary Leapor. ECWP

As once, if not with light regard. Ode on the Poetical Character. William Collins. NAEL-1; NOEC; NoP-4; OAEL-1; PoE; PoEL-3

As once in black I disrespected walked. On a Maid of Honour Seen by a Scholar in Somerset Garden. Thomas Randolph. OBGa

As once in heaven Dante looked back down. The Backward Look. Howard Nemerov. OxBC

As once the winged energy of delight. Rilke. EnIH, tr. by Stephen Mitchell *Fr.* Sonnets to Orpheus.

As one, at midnight, wakened by the call. Prelude. Wilfrid Wilson Gibson. MoBrPo

As one grows older and Caesar, Hitler. The Walk Home. Reed Whittemore. CoAmPo

As One Non-Combatant to Another. George Orwell. OxBTC

As One Put Drunk into the Packet-Boat. John Ashbery. HAP; HCAP; VCAP

As one that for a weary space has lain. The Odyssey. Andrew Lang. OBEV; OBNC; PoLF; PoRA

As one that strives, being sick, and sick to death. To Celia, upon Love's Ubiquity. Thomas Carew. CavPo

As one who after long and far-spent years. To Hampstead. Leigh Hunt. Ro *Fr.* The Examiner, no. 385 316.

As One Who Bears beneath His Neighbor's Roof. Robert Silliman Hillyer. MoAmPo

As one who goes between high garden walls. Personality. Agnes Mary Frances Robinson. VWP

As one who goes from holding converse sweet. Lowlands. William Reed Huntington. APN-2

As one who has sailed across an unknown sea. The Solitary. Rilke, *German.* TrJP, *tr.* by C. F. MacIntyre

As one who held herself a part. Sister. John Greenleaf Whittier. *Fr.* Snow-Bound [*or* Snow-Bound; a Winter Idyl]. APN-1; AiP; AmPP; NAAL-3; NOBA; OxBA; TAP; TFi

As One Who Wanders into Old Workings. C. Day Lewis. FaBoMo; LiTM

As other men, so I myself do muse. Michael Drayton. NOSC; NoSic; Son *Fr.* Idea.

As our good manners required. (LL) Manners. Elizabeth Bishop. NOxBChV; OxBC; RB

As our king lay musing on his bed. King Henry Fifth's Conquest of France. *Unknown.* ESPB

As over muddy shores a dragon flock. The Fear. Lascelles Abercrombie. OBMV

As Pants the Hart. Nahum Tate. TIRV

As Parmigianino did it, the right hand. Self-Portrait in a Convex Mirror. John Ashbery. HCAP; NAAL-2

As Phyllis the gay, at the break of the day. Song 3. Edward Moore. ECEV

As pilot well expert in perilous wave. The Cave of Mammon. Edmund Spenser. OAEL-1; PoEL-1 *Fr.* Wood Of Error. AEP

As played by the phantoms of Shrule. Limerick. Tony Butler. PeLi

As pools beneath stone arches take. Invocation. John Drinkwater. PoA

As Porcelain. (LL) Death is the supple Suitor. Emily Dickinson. NALW; NCAP

As power and wit will me assist. Sir Thomas Wyatt. SiPS

As praiseworthy / the power of breathing. Lorine Niedecker. VGW

As proper mode of quenching legal lust. Gerald Massey. NOBVV

As puffed up. First Robin. Jane Yolen. NOxBChV

As pure at ninety-four as any babe. Aunt Lucy. Jane Gentry. CrSp

As Pyramus did on Thisbe's breast bewail. (LL) The Death of Wyatt. Henry Howard, Earl of Surrey. AAS; SiPS

As quiet and chaste as the author's own life. (LL) Poe and Longfellow. James Russell Lowell. APN-1; AmPP; OxBA; PAR; TAP

As riper years approach us. Glimpses of Infancy. Priscilla Jane Thompson. CBWP-2

As Rochefoucauld his maxims drew. Verses on the Death of Dr. Swift, D.S.P.D. Jonathan Swift.

As Rochefoucauld his maxims drew. Verses on the Death of Dr. Swift, D.S.P.D., Occasioned by Reading a Maxim in Rochefoucauld. Jonathan Swift. NOEC; PoEL-3

As rocks resist the billows and the sky. (LL) The Deserted Village. Oliver Goldsmith. CABP; ECEV; FHYEP; ImPo; NOBE; NoP-4; OxAEP-1; TFi

As round as an apple, as deep as a cup. The Well. Mother Goose. OxNR; ReMoGo

As round as an apple, as deep as a pail. *Unknown.* OxNR

As round the rose's heart the golden threads. Soul Incense. Henrietta Cordelia Ray. CBWP-3

As round their dying father's bed. The Father and His Children. *Unknown.* OxBChV

As Sam crumbles lumps of tofu on her tray. Gardens We Have Left. David Mura. OpBo

As sea-foam blown of the winds, as blossom of brine that is drifted. "Home, Sweet Home," with Variations ("As sea-foam blown of the winds, as blossom of brine that is drifted"). Henry Cuyler Bunner. OBAL *Fr.* Home.

As, searing, the twin picks hissed in his eyes. (LL) Among Philistines. R. S. Gwynn. RA

As seventh sign, the antique heavens show. Feast of the Ram's Horn. Harvey Shapiro. VGW

As Shadows Cast by Cloud and Sun. William Cullen Bryant. AH

As shakes the canvass of a thousand ships. The Journalist. Cornelius Mathews. APN-1 *Fr.* Poems on Man in His Various Aspects under the American Republic.

As shall mocke the envious eye. Catullus. *See* Carmen 5 ("My sweetest Lesbia, let us live and love").

As she doth laugh at me and makes my pain her sport. Edmund Spenser. *See* Sonnet 10: 'Unrighteous Lord of Love'.

As she grabbed for me, already screaming. (LL) A Suburban Childhood. Liz Rosenberg. IFJA; PBCAP

As she had sowed them with her odoruos foot. (LL) Here She Was Wont to Go. Ben Jonson. BeJo; CH; OxBSP

As she is showering, I wake to see. An Aubade. Timothy Steele. RA

As she liv'd peerless. Shakespeare. OxAEP-1 *Fr.* The Winter's Tale.

As she passes over them. (LL) Wind and Silver. Amy Lowell. BoWoP; HeIP-4; MoAmPo; Spl

As she shook her little fist. The Death of the Novel. David Young. AmPA

As shine by fountains, bubbles, flowers, or snow? (LL) A Palinode. Edmund Bolton. NoSic; PoEL-2

As shines the sunbeam through dark clouds. Hope. Mary E. Tucker. CBWP-1

As ships, becalmed at eve, that lay. Qua Cursum Ventus. Arthur Hugh Clough. EBVVPR; OBEV

As shows [*or* shews] the air[e], when with a rainbow graced. Upon Julia's Ribband. Robert Herrick. CaPo

As silent as a mirror is believed. Legend. Hart Crane. InPS-3; OxBA

As simple an act. Way Out West. Imamu Amiri Baraka. NeAP; PoBA

As since he dares not come within my sight. (LL) The Dream[e]. Ben Jonson. BeJo; CBLP; NOBE; NOSC; PoEL-2

As sincerely as possible. Steve Benson. FTOS *Fr.* Reverse Order.

As sinewy as biltong, as narrow. My Grandmother. Perseus Adams. PeSA

As Sisyphus against the infernal steep. Byron. OBSV *Fr.* English Bards and Scotch Reviewers.

As slow I climb the cliff's ascending side. At Tynemouth Priory, after a Tempestuous Voyage. William Lisle Bowles. Son

As slow our ship her foamy track. The Journey Onwards. Thomas Moore. GTBS-P; OxAEP-2

As slowly and sadly I strayed by the river. Lost Jimmie Whalen. *Unknown.* AmFP

As soft as silk, as white as milk. A Walnut. Mother Goose. LB; OxNR; ReMoGo

As some brave Admiral in former War. The Disabled Debauchee. John Wilmot, 2d Earl of Rochester. BoLoP; HAP; NAEL-1; NOBL; NoP-4; OBSV; OxBoV; PoEL-3; SCGP

As some fond virgin, whom her mother's care. Epistle to Miss [*or* Miss Teresa] Blount, on Her Leaving the Town after the Coronation. Alexander Pope. BoLoP; EBEV; FHYEP; LoP; NAEL-1; NOBE; NOEC; NoP-4; PoEL-3

As someone on his back for months of illness. Ausiàs March, *Catalan.* STV, *tr.* by John Frederick Nims

As sometimes in a dead man's face. Tennyson. ImPo *Fr.* In Memoriam A. H. H.

As sometimes in a grove at morning chime. Frederick Goddard Tuckerman. NCAP

As Sonata in Praes o Molli. Jonathan Swift. CBLP

As soon as April pierces to the root. Chaucer. *See* The General Prologue.

As soon as he came home, straightway Pygmalion did repair. Pygmalion's Statue Comes to Life. Ovid. OAEL-1, *tr.* by Arthur Golding *Fr.* Metamorphoses.

As soon as I lie down in my soft bed. Sonnet 9. Louise Labé, *French.* BoWoP, *tr.* by Willis Barnstone

As soon as I saw I was naked. Will the Real Me Please Stand Up? A. L. Hendriks. PBCV

As soon as I walked out I felt the mistake in the weather. Divided Touch, Divided Color. Kathleen Peirce. BAP-94

As soon as I'm in bed at night. Mrs. Brown. Rose Fyleman. BoTP; OxBChV

As soon as my sister and I got out of our. The Sisters of Sexual Treasure. Sharon Olds. PBCAP

As soon as night descends, we meet. Mary Magdalene (I). Boris Pasternak, *Russian.* AF, *tr.* by Lydia Pasternak Slater

As soon as the night turns into dawn. In Re Conferences. Vladimir Mayakovsky, *Russian.* TCRP, *tr.* by Albert C. Todd

As soon as you wake they come blundering in. 6 A.M. Thoughts. Dick Davis. APAD

As soon it must, from the mountain. (LL) Here in Katmandu. Donald Justice. CoAP; CoAmPo; HeIP-4; WeT

As soon they will be happy to desert. (LL) Cat Goddesses. Robert Graves. NYBP; OxBSP

As space is disappearing and your singularity. (LL) Sleeping on the Wing. Frank O'Hara. InPS-3; NAAL-2

As Spring the Winter Doth Succeed. Anne Bradstreet. AH

As stands a statue on its pedestal. George Henry Boker. APN-2 *Fr.* Sonnets: A Sequence on Profane Love.

As still as a brooding dove. Shelley. *See* The Cloud.

As still he envied me, so fair she was! (LL) The Bishop Orders His Tomb at Saint Praxed's Church. Robert Browning. CABP; EBVV; EBVVPR; EnVR; FHYEP; HAP; HeIP-4; NAEL-2; NAWM-2; NOBVV; NoP-4; OAEL-2; OBAL; PoE; Poetr; SCGP; TFi

As structures go, it wasn't such a bad one. The Old Complex. John Ashbery. FTOS

As, sum tyme, dois the curser stert and ryn. Turnus and the Courser. Virgil. OBVE, *tr. by* Gawin Douglas *Fr.* The Aeneid [*or* Eneados, *Aeneis*].

As sunbeams stream through liberal space. Ralph Waldo Emerson. *Fr.* Woodnotes II. NOBA

As sure as shooting. From the Brothers Grimm to Sister Sexton to Mother Goose; One Transmogrification. David Cummings. BXAP

As surely as I hold your hand in mine. Brown Boy to Brown Girl. Countee Cullen. PoBA

As sweet as jackfruit, cool like coconut juice. Ode to the Watermelon. *Unknown, Vietnamese.* AVP, *tr. by* Huỳnh Sanh Thông

As swelled from nothing, doth dissolve in nought. (LL) Madrigal: "Like the Idalian Queen." William Drummond, of Hawthornden. CH; GTBS-P; NOSC; OAEL-1

As that Arabian bird (whom all admire). William Browne. OAEL-1 *Fr.* Britannia's Pastorals.

As the Allied tanks trod Germany to shard. May, 1945. Peter Porter. HP; OxBC

As the April fool came over the hill. April Fool. Hal Summers. AYFP

As the army corps advances. (LL) An Army Corps on the March. Walt Whitman. AiP; CBCWP; InPS-3; PoLF; SAGP

As the basket comes in procession, greet it, women. Hymn to Demeter. Callimachus. HePo, *tr. by* Barbara Hughes Fowler *Fr.* Hymns.

As the black curtain of the night. Reveille Matin, or Good Morrow to a Friend. Mildmay Fane, 2d Earl of Westmorland. NOSC

As the blind Milton's memory of light. City Visions. Emma Lazarus. APN-2

As the body denies the means to look. Epigram. Pernette De Guillet, *French.* PBWP, *tr. by* Joan Keefe *and* Richard Terdiman

As the broad mountain where the shadows flit. Thomas Cole. APN-1 *Fr.* The Voyage of Life.

As the cassias blossom. What Her Girl Friend Said. Peyanar. PLW *Fr.* Nine on Happy Reunion. PLW, *tr. by* A. K. Ramanujan

As the cat / climbed over. Poem. William Carlos Williams. ChAP; InPS-3; KaS; NoP-4; PC; PFE; PoPoPo; SoSe-8; TTTS

As the chameleon, who is known. The Chameleon. Matthew Prior. OBSV

As the churches have killed their Christ. Tennyson. *See* Dead, long dead.

As the clouds that are so light. The Clouds That Are So Light. Edward Thomas. FaBoTw

As the crescent moon is born from the Western Sea. Ch'en Tzu-ang. SuSp, *tr. by* William H. Nienhauser *Fr.* Impressions of Things Encountered.

As the Crow Flies, Let Him Fly. Samuel Hoffenstein.
"Early bird may catch the worm, The." NBLV

As the days grow longer. Lengthening Days. *Unknown.* ReMoGo

As the dead prey upon us. Charles Olson. NeAP

As the deer begin to hide. What He Said. Peyanar. PLW *Fr.* Nine on Happy Reunion. PLW, *tr. by* A. K. Ramanujan

As the despair of warmth in January. Conjunction. Semyon Izrailevich Lipkin, *Russian.* TCRP, *tr. by* Albert C. Todd

As the dew flies over the green vallee. (LL) The Wife Wrapt in Wether's Skin. *Unknown.* AmFP; ESPB

As the divorced [*or* divorc'd] soul from her body parts. (LL) The Surrender. Henry King, Bishop of Chichester. BoLoP; CBLP; EBEV; NOSC

As the dove flies over the mulberry-tree. (LL) The Riddling Knight. *Unknown.* FaBoCh; PBMP; PoEL-1

As the dust from the wet dream of a nation. Written in Unbridled Repugnance near Sioux Falls, Alabama—April 30, 1974. A. K. Redwing. VoR

As the earth. Elizabeth Barrett Browning. EPCY *Fr.* Aurora Leigh. VWP

As the elevator car left our floor. Limerick. *Unknown.* PeLi

As the first spring mists appear. Lady Ise, *Japanese.* WPJ, *tr. by* Kenneth Rexroth *and* Ikuko Atsumi

As the Flower of the Grass. May Probyn. VWP

As the flu goes on, I get thinner and thinner. The Pull. Sharon Olds. PuP-17

As the full moon slowly rose. Sappho, *Greek.* InMo, *tr. by* Sam Hamill

As the gods began one world, and man another. Snakecharmer. Sylvia Plath. PFE

As the gook woman howls. In the Mourning Time. Robert Earl Hayden. BPo

As the green grass glows upwards, strangers in the silent garden. (LL) Trees in the Garden. D. H. Lawrence. CMoP; MoBrPo

As the guests arrive at my son's party. Rites of Passage. Sharon Olds. FiLi

As the hart panteth after the water brooks. Psalm 42. Bible, *O.T.* AWP; TrJP *Fr.* Psalms.

As the heroes of Marathon their renown we know. (LL) Towards Lillers. Ivor Gurney. NoP-4

As the holly [*or* holy] groweth [*or* grouth] green [*or* grene]. Green Groweth the Holly. *Unknown.* NoSic

As the image of the sun. Estuary. Ted Walker. NYBP

As the immense dew of Florida. Nomad Exquisite. Wallace Stevens. ColAP

As the late night passes. Hirose Izen, *Japanese.* OHMPJ, *tr. by* Kenneth Rexroth

As the leaf-man rises and stumbles to them. (LL) For the Missing in Action. John Balaban. AF; PuP-15

As the lean tree burst into grief. (LL) The Mad Scene. James Merrill. CoAP; NOBA; PoE; PoE; TAP

As the lovely new flowers. What She Said. Allur Nanmullai, *Tamil.* PLW, *tr. by* A. K. Ramanujan

As the mists rise in the dawn. Fujiwara no Sadayori, *Japanese.* OHPJ, *tr. by* Kenneth Rexroth

As the mute nightingale in closest groves. To the Blessed Virgin Mary. Gerald Griffin. TIRV

As the natives got ready to serve. Limerick. Ed Cunningham. PeLi

As the observer wills. (LL) Study of Two Pears. Wallace Stevens. BLT; InPS-3; NAAL 2; NoAM; OxBA

As the phobic said: it is torture. Suspension: Junior Wells on a Small Stage in a Converted Barn. Sandra McPherson. SeSe

As the player's breath warms the fipple the tone clears. Basil Bunting. *Fr.* Grass caught in willow tells the flood's height that has subsided. FaBoMo *Fr.* Briggflatts [An Autobiography].

As the poets have mournfully sung. The Aesthetic Point of View. W. H. Auden. NBLV; OBAL; OBCoV; PeLi *Fr.* Shorts [1948–1957].

As the poor end of each dead day drew near. He Liked the Dead. Malcolm Lowry. OxBTC

As the primrose spreads so sweetly. (LL) The Cruel Brother. *Unknown.* AmFP; ESPB; OxBB

As the queen upon her throne. (LL) Learning to Read. Frances Ellen Watkins Harper. NAAL

As the rain is lagging, wayward, in the river. On the Fragile Labyrinth. José Emilio Pacheco, *Spanish.* STV, *tr. by* John Frederick Nims

As the rains of spring. Lady Izumi, *Japanese.* PBWP, *tr. by* Edwin A. Cranston

As the rock and ocean that we were made from. (LL) Carmel Point. Robinson Jeffers. BLT; NAAL-2; NoAM; NoP-4

As the season changes. The daughter of Shunzei, *Japanese.* WPJ, *tr. by* Kenneth Rexroth *and* Ikuko Atsumi

As the seed waits eagerly watching for its flower and fruit. Night VIII (The Eternal Man). William Blake. PoE *Fr.* Vala; or The Four Zoas.

As the ships sail softly down the flowing Neva. (LL) Requiem: "No foreign sky protected me." "Anna Akhmatova," *Russian.* AF; TCRP, *tr. by* Stanley Kunitz *with* Max Hayward

As the slanting sun drowsed lazily. Cape Coloured Batman. Guy Butler. PeSA

As the stores close, a winter light. February Evening in New York. Denise Levertov. NoAM

As the sun declined the snow at our feet reflected the most delicate / peach-blossom. Prose Poem. Humphrey Jennings. SPE

As the sun sets, the mountain air becomes cool. Sailing along the Tai Stream from Stone Bridge to the Foot of Mo-ho Peak. Wang Shih-chieng, *Chinese.* SuSp, *tr. by* Chang Yin-nan *and* Lewis C. Walmsley

As the sun that lights creation. Africa. Lizelia Augusta Jenkins Moorer. CBWP-3

As the surgical knife. Tanka. Nakajō Fumiko, *Japanese.* MJT, *tr. by* Makoto Ueda

As the swamp cooler breathes. A Sale of Smoke. Roberta Spear. AmPA

As the sweet sweat of roses in a still. The Comparison. Donne. PeLV *Fr.* Elegies.

As the team's head-brass flashed out on the turn. Edward Thomas. CABP; GTBS-P; NAEL-2; NSI; NoP-4; OBWP; OxAEP-2; OxBTC; PeFWW; PoE; PoFWW; RB

As the train approaches the tunnel, the kids. The Children's Train. Dorianne Laux. GM

As the true stars at daybreak. (LL) Daybreak. Galway Kinnell. BLT; ChAP

"As the twig is bent, the tree's inclined." Her Precious Leg. Thomas Hood. NOBVV *Fr.* Miss Kilmansegg and Her Precious Leg.

As the used anger drips from his hands like blood. The Murderer. Paul Petrie. NYBP

As the war-trumpet drowns the rustic flute. Pindar. Antipater of Sidon, *Greek*. AWP, *tr. by* John Addington Symonds

As the wheel follows the hoof. Kenneth Rexroth. APSN *Fr.* The Love Poems of Marichiko.

As the wind scuds across the green grass. A Landscape. Chaesam Park, *Korean*. CKP, *tr. by* Jaihiun Kim

As the Window Darkens. Laura Jensen. LCAP-2

As the wise men of old brought gifts / guided by a star. The Gift. William Carlos Williams. ChIV-2; GI

As the Word came to prophets of old. Prophets for a New Day. Margaret Abigail Walker. BPo; NAAAL

As the years pass. Humans Bought and Sold (two poems). Ōkuma Nobuyuki, *Japanese*. MJT, *tr. by* Makoto Ueda

As the youthful morning's light. On S. John the Baptist. Thomas Stanley. ChIV-2

As their names occurred. (LL) Anseo. Paul Muldoon. CIP-2; FaBoPV; PNI

As theirs, I lay, like them, my best gifts on thy shrine! (LL) Proem: "I love the old melodious lays." John Greenleaf Whittier. APN-1; OxBA; TAP

As then in death, so now in love. (LL) C[h]aritas Nimia; or, The Dear[e] Bargain. Richard Crashaw. ESCV; NOCV; NOSC

As there, along the elmy hedge, I go. Troubles of the Day. William Barnes. GTBS-P

As there is no doubt. Dubious Foreigner. Cyril Dabydeen. HCP

As These Letters—humid, sunless. The writing occurs on their walls. (LL) Sun. Michael Palmer. APSN

As they came from the East. Kings and Stars. John Erskine. TrCP

As they came in by the Eden side. The Slaughter of the Laird of Mellerstain. *Unknown*. ESPB

As they carry the white paddy of their land. What Her Girl Friend Said to Him, Trying to Dissuade Him from His Long Journey. *Unknown*, *Tamil*. PLW, *tr. by* A. K. Ramanujan

As they sat and talked beneath the boundary trees. Married Love. Sherod Santos. Son; WeT

As they wave their tounges. (LL) Song: I Want a Witness. Michael S. Harper. LTA

As they were saying this. Luke 24:36–49; As they were saying this, Jesus. Alec Derwent Hope. GI *Fr.* St. Luke.

As thin little Proclus was fanning the fire. Lucilius, *Greek*. GrAn, *tr. by* Peter Porter

As things be / come. Word Poem (Perhaps Worth Considering). Nikki Giovanni. PoBA

As this convine and ordinance was mayd. Turnus Summons His Allies, Aeneas Is "Perturbit wyth Gret Thochtis." Virgil. OBVE, *tr. by* Gawin Douglas *Fr.* The Aeneid [*or* Eneados, *Aeneis*].

As this in Kew thirst for the Red Dawn. (LL) Note on Local Flora. William Empson. EBEV; FaBoMo; OxAEP-2

As Thomas was cudgelled [*or* cudgell'd *or* cudgel'd] one day by his wife. Three Epigrams. Jonathan Swift. FaBoEE; NBLV

As those we love decay, we die in part. On the Death of a Particular Friend. James Thomson. OBEV; SCGP *Fr.* On the Death of Mr. William Aikman the Painter.

As those who are not athletic at breakfast day by day. Nature Morte. Louis MacNeice. NoAM

As those who pass the Alps do say. To the Queen. Anne Killigrew. KTR

As thou would'st fly for very eagerness, *sl. diff. 1798 vers.* Coleridge. *See* Frost at Midnight.

As though a bare bulb hung. Billy. Linda McCarriston. LoL

As though an aged person were to wear. Elegy for the Monastery Barn. Thomas Merton. VGW

As though forever, his appointed pigeon. (LL) Pigeons. Alastair Reid. NYBP; TwCP

As though his subject had decided to remain a prayer. (LL) The Painter. John Ashbery. HCAP; NOBA; NoP-4; PoE; PoPoPo

As though I walked the wood with sagamore George. (LL) Here, where the red man swept the leaves away. Frederick Goddard Tuckerman. NOBA; TAP

As though it soared suchwise through heaven too. (LL) Royal Palm. Hart Crane. CMoP; MoAmPo; MoP; NoAM

As though something knew Bly was coming. Despair. Tom Wayman. CDa

As though they did not care. (LL) Old Black Men. Georgia Douglas Johnson. NMM-2; PoBA

As though to let loose. Tanka. Tawara Machi, *Japanese*. MJT, *tr. by* Makoto Ueda

As thou'rt a man. Shakespeare. *Fr.* Hamlet. NAWM-1

As through a mist, the pious prosperous ghosts. (LL) Indian Reservation: Caughnawaga. Abraham Moses Klein. LiTM; NOBC; NoP-4

As through a neighb'ring grove, where ancient beech. Alcander's Flower Garden. William Mason. OBGa *Fr.* The English Garden.

As through earth's garden once I strayed. The Crushed Flower. Mary E. Tucker. CBWP-1

As through the land at eve we went. We Kiss'd Again with Tears. Tennyson. ImPo; PoToHe; SCGP *Fr.* The Princess.

As through the trellis peers the sudden Bridegroom. (LL) At the Indian Killer's Grave. Robert Lowell. NOBA; VGW

As through the wild green hills of Wyre. A. E. Housman. FP

As thumb is genius of the hand. Objects in Mirror are Closer Than They Appear. Jeffrey Skinner. PBCAP

As Time had never known ye. (LL) To a Bed of Tulips. Robert Herrick. CaPo; GaP

As time one day by me did pass. Henry Vaughan. ESCV; GeHe; MeLP

As to Being Alone. James Oppenheim. TrJP

As To His Choice of Her. Wilfrid Scawen Blunt. GSo; Son *Fr.* The Love Sonnets of Proteus.

As to my own concerns, it seems odd, given. Peroration, Concerning Genius. Robert Pinsky. NoAM *Fr.* Essay on Psychiatrists.

As to the blooming prime. Edmund Bolton. NoSic

As to thy greater light a sacrifice. (LL) The Glowworm. Thomas Stanley. BeJo; NOSC

As toilsome I wander'd Virginia's woods. Walt Whitman. APN-1; BLT; NAAL-1; NAAL-3

As Tom the porter went up Ludgate Hill. Tom the Porter. John Byrom. NOEC

As Tommy Snooks and Bessy Brooks. Mother Goose. LB; OxNR; ReMoGo

As tongueless Echo in the pastoral vale. To the Greek Anthologists. George Rostrevor Hamilton, *after the Greek of* Satyros. FaBoEE

As tourists inspected the apse. Limerick. Edward Gorey. PeLV; PeLi

As Tranquil Streams. Marion Franklin Ham. AH

As travellours [*or* travellers] when the twilight's come. The Pilgrimage. Henry Vaughan. ChIV-2; ESCV

As tree and wheat rise green. Nile the Hermit. *Unknown, Greek*. GrAn, *tr. by* Guy Davenport

As twenty days are now. (LL) To a Butterfly. Wordsworth. ACTP; NTP

As two fair vessels side by side. "Michael Field." VWP

As unpredictable as picnic weather, blue. Guide to the Perplexed. David Malouf. NOBAu

As unto the bow the cord is. Hiawatha's Wooing. Henry Wadsworth Longfellow. EBNV *Fr.* The Song of Hiawatha.

As usual I'm up before the sun. Sonnet 115. John Berryman. SAGP *Fr.* Sonnets to Chris.

As usual, the clock in The Clock Bar was a good few minutes. Hamlet. Ciaran Carson. FaBoVe; PNI

As usual, the first gate was modest. It is dilapidated. She can't tell. Tan Tien. Mei-Mei Berssenbrugge. OpBo

As usual / this day is pushed into my room. Reading Matter. Martin Sorescu, *Rumanian*. CBNP

As Venus one day, at her toilet affairs. Venus Attiring the Graces. William Whitehead. ECEV

As virtuous men pass [*or* passe] mildly away. Valediction, A: Forbidding Mourning. Donne. CABP; CBLP; ESCV; FHYEP; FMP; FSCP; HAP; HeIP-4; HoPM; ImPo; InPS-3; MeLP; NAEL-1; NOBE; NOSC; NoP-4; OAEL-1; PBRV; PFE; PoE; PoEL-2; PoPoPo; Poetr; SCGP; SeCP; SoSe-8; TFi; UnPo; WeW-3

As water, silk. On Sitting Down to Write, I Decide Instead to Go to Fred Herko's Concert. Diane Di Prima. PmAP

As we babble about the sky and the weather and the forests of change. (LL) Mixed Feelings. John Ashbery. HAP; WeW-3

As we came through the gate to look at the few new lambs. Ravens. Ted Hughes. InPS-3

As we crossed the field, I told her. (LL) The Centaur. May Swenson. FaBoWP; NMM-2; NOxBChV; NTP; TwCP

As We Dance Round. *Unknown*. CH

As we drink the giddy victory in Tea. (LL) A Pot of Tea. Robert W. Service. NSI; PoWW

As we drove back, crossing the hill. A Locked House. W. D. Snodgrass. VCAP

As We Forgive Those. Eric Pankey. GI

As we get older we do not get any younger. Chard Whitlow. Henry Reed. BXAP; LiTM; MoBrPo; NBLV; NOBL; NoP-4; OBCoV; OxBTC; PeLV; UV; UnPo

As we go about the toils of life. As We Sow We Shall Reap. Maggie Pogue Johnson. CBWP-4

As We Grow Older. Rollin J. Wells. *See* Growing Old [*or* Growing Older].

As we have to be. (LL) Hymn to Priapus. D. H. Lawrence. CMoP; OBMV; PoE; SCGP

As we lay musing in our beds. The Mermaid. *Unknown*. ESPB

As we left the garden-party. Leaving. Richard Wilbur. FP

As we live, we are transmitters of life. We Are Transmitters. D. H. Lawrence. OxBTC

As we pass through the field of purple herbs. Princess Nukada, *Japanese*. WPJ, *tr. by* Kenneth Rexroth *and* Ikuko Atsumi

As we rise above it, row after row. In Praise of New York. Thomas M. Disch. WWSi

As we rowed from our ships and set foot on the shore. The Savages. Josephine Miles. LiTM

As we rush, as we rush in the train. In the Train. James Thomson. BoTP; OBEV *Fr.* Sunday at Hampstead.

As we sailed on the water blue. Whisky Johnny. *Unknown.* AS

As we say farewell to autumn. Yün Shou-p'ing. CoBLCP, *tr. by* Jonathan Chaves *Fr.* Chyrsanthemums.

As We Sow We Shall Reap. Maggie Pogue Johnson. CBWP-4

As we speed out of youth's sunny station. Life's Journey. Ella Wheeler Wilcox. PWR

As we stood on the [edge of the crag] *or* cliff's edge. Against the Wind. Amir Gilbo'a, *Hebrew*. MHP, *tr. by* Ruth Finer Mintz

As we were marching to Quebec. Marching to Quebec. *Unknown.* AmFP

As wearied pilgrims, once possessed. His Own Epitaph. Robert Herrick. CaPo

As weary-hearted as that hollow moon. (LL) Adam's Curse. W. B. Yeats. BlrV; CMoP; NAEL-2; NoAM; NoP-4; OAEL-2; PFE; WeW-3

As weary pilgrim, now at rest. Anne Bradstreet. ColAP; NAAL-1; NAAL-3; PoEL-3; SCAP

("Then come, dear Bridegroom, come away.") (LL) ColAP

As well as if a manor of thy friend's. (LL) Ruins of a Great House. Derek Walcott. PoPoPo; TwCP

As well as these poor poems. The Black Box. Gavin Ewart. OBCoV

As well as things (LL) Riprap. Gary Snyder. HCAP; NAAL-2; NOBA; NeAP; NoAM; PmAP; PoM; PoPoPo; VCAP

As well, maybe, that you cannot read our minds. The Enemy. Randolph Stow. NOBAu

As what he loves may never like too much. (LL) On My First Son [*or* Sonne]. Ben Jonson. AWP; BeJo; CABP; ClHu; EBEV; FaBoEE; HAP; HoPM; IMW; InPK-6; InPS-3; NAEL-1; NIP-4; NOBE; NOSC; NoP-4; OAEL-1; OxBSP; PBMP; PBRV; PFE; PoE; PoEL-2; PoPoPo; Poetr; RB; RaBo; SCGP; SeCP; TFi; TRP; WeW-3

As, when a beauteous nymph decays. Stella's Birthday, 1725. Jonathan Swift. CABP; NOEC

As When a Child. Charles Lamb. Son

As when a Conqu'rour does in Triumph come. To My Lady Morland at Tunbridge. Aphra Behn. CPO

As when a Fragment, from a Mountain torn. Turnus and the Stone. Virgil. OBVE, *tr. by* John Dryden *Fr.* The Aeneid [*or* Eneados, *Aeneis*].

As when a ship, that flyes faire under saile. Edmund Spenser. FHYEP *Fr.* Wood Of Error. AEP

As when an architect some palace wall. Homer. OBVE, *tr. by* William Cowper *Fr.* The Iliad.

As when desire, long darkling, dawns, and first. Bridal Birth. D. G. Rossetti. Son *Fr.* The House of Life.

As when devouring flames some forest seize. Homer. OBVE, *tr. by* William Cowper *Fr.* The Iliad.

As when, down some broad River dropping,we. Frederick Goddard Tuckerman. APN-2 *Fr.* Sonnets.

As when from dreams awaking. Caroline Elizabeth Norton. Ro

As when 'gainst murmuring shores a Western Breese. Battle. Homer. OBCVT, *tr. by* Ogilby, John *Fr.* The Iliad.

As when I fell a-sleeping. (LL) Beauty Bathing. Anthony Munday. EBEvV; GTBS-P; NOBE; OBEV

As when into the garden paths by night. Old Age. Frederick Tennyson. NOBVV

As when it hapneth that some lovely Towne. Content and Resolute. William Drummond of Hawthornden. PBRV

As when of frequent bees. Homer. OBVE, *tr. by* George Chapman *Fr.* The Iliad.

As when of old some orator renowed. Milton. ChIV-1 *Fr.* Book IX. FHYEP; NAEL-1; NAWM-1; OAEL-1 *Fr.* Paradise Lost.

As when rooting in a bin. Dick, a Maggot. Jonathan Swift. NBLV

As When Some Hungry Fledgling Hears and Sees. Vittoria da Colonna, Marchesa di Pescara, *Italian*. BoWoP, *tr. by* Barbara Howes; PBWP, *tr. by* Lynne Lawner

As when some mighty Hero first appears. To Mrs. Manley, upon Her Tragedy Call'd The Royal Mischief. Mary Pix. KTR

As, when some treasurer lays down the stick. Dryden. NOSC *Fr.* Love Triumphant.

As when the bright[e] Crulean firmament. Sir John Davies. NoSic *Fr.* The Gulling[e] Sonnets. Son

As when the cheerfull Sunne, elamping wide. Giles Fletcher, the Younger. PBRV *Fr.* Christs Victorie, and Triumph in Heaven, and Earth, over, and after death.

As when the glorious Magazine of Light. On the 3. of September, 1651. Katherine Philips. PBRV

As, when the squire and tinker, Wood. Prometheus. Jonathan Swift. FaBoPV

As when the water reddened at the feast. (LL) Cana Revisited. Seamus Heaney. GI

As when the winds, ascending by degrees. Homer. OBVE, *tr. by* Alexander Pope *Fr.* The Iliad.

As when, to one who long hath watched, the morn. Sonnet. John Codrington Bampfylde. NOEC

As when two men have loved a woman well. Lost on Both Sides. D. G. Rossetti. EnVR; NoP-4 *Fr.* The House of Life.

As when two monarchs of the brindled breed. Paul Whitehead. NOEC *Fr.* Gymnasiad, The, or Boxing Match.

As when we grope amid the gloom of night. (LL) The Clouded Morning. Jones Very. GSo

As Whistler heard colors like a stretch of music. For the Sake of Retrieval. Linda Bierds. NAmP90

As white their bark, so white this lady's hours. (LL) A Virginal. Ezra Pound. CMoP; ColAP; MeMAP; MoAmPo; NAAL-2; NIP-4; NOBA; OxBA; Poetr; Son; TAP

As who was not, in laughter, pain, and love. (LL) Days of 1964. James Merrill. CoAP; HCAP; NAAL-2; PoE; VCAP

As wild oxen bellowed. What He Said. Peyanar. PLW *Fr.* Nine on Happy Reunion. PLW, *tr. by* A. K. Ramanujan

As William and Mary stood by the seaside. William and Mary. *Unknown.* AmFP

As Winter, fleeing. The Fearless. Mortimer J. Adler. PoA

As with Gladness Men of Old. William Chatterton Dix. FaPoR

As with heaped bees at hiving time. Robert Louis Stevenson. NOBVV *Fr.* Rivers and winds among the twisted hills.

As withereth the primrose by the river. A Palinode. Edmund Bolton. NoSic; PoEL-2

As women do. (LL) Snow White and the Seven Dwarfs. Anne Sexton. HCAP; PoPoPo

As Women of Our Race. Mrs. Henry Linden. CBWP-4

As woods whose change appeares. Horace. OBVE, *tr. by* Ben Jonson *Fr.* The Art of Poetry.

As Wulfstan said on another occasion. Speech for the Repeal of the McCarran Act. Richard Wilbur. CPO

'As ye came from the holy land'. Sir Walter Ralegh. GLoP

As ye go through these palm-trees. A Song of the Virgin Mother. Félix Lope de Vega Carpio, *Spanish*. AWP, *tr. by* Ezra Pound

As ye said, it shall be sae. . . (LL) The Earl of Mar's Daughter. *Unknown.* CH; ESPB

As ye see, a mountain[e] lion fare. Sarpedon's Speech. Homer, *Greek*. NOSC, *tr. by* George Chapman *Fr.* The Iliad.

. . . as ye see a mountaine Lion fare. Homer. *See* Sarpedon's Speech.

As years advance, the abated soul, in most. Jabez Hughes. EPCY

As yonder lamp in my vacated room. The Lamp. Charles Whitehead. OBEV

As you advance in years you long. Of Change of Opinions. Victor Gustave Plarr. NOBVV

As you all know, tonight is the night of the full. 12 O'Clock News. Elizabeth Bishop. OxBC

As you are big for you! (LL) The Little Elf. John Kendrick Bangs. CTV; FPC; FaBoBe; NTCP; OBCA

As You Came from the Holy Land. John Ashbery. GEA

As you came from the holy land. The Holy Land of Walsingham[e]. *Unknown, sometimes at. to* Sir Walter Ralegh. AAS; BoLoP; CBLP; EnLoPo; EnSB; FaBoCh; GBL; HAP; InPS-3; LoP; NOBE; NTP; NoSic; OBEV; OxAEP-2; PBRV; PoEL-2; RB; SCGP; TFi

As You Come In. Anne Marriott. NOBC

As you haven't asked me for advice. Plug. Edmund Vance Cooke. PWR

As you lay in sleep. Cartography. Louise Bogan. PiM; TRP

As You Leave Me. Etheridge Knight. MT; NNaP

("To whistle and to smile at the johns.") (LL) CoAmPo; ISC

As You Like It. Shakespeare.
   Good in Everything. PoToHe
   Motley's the Only Wear. OBCoV
   Orlando's Rhymes. CTC
   Seven Ages of Man, The. ImPo
   Song: "Blow, blow, thou winter wind." CTC; EBEvV; OxAEP-1; PoEL-2
   Song: "If the scorn of your bright eyne." CTC
   Song: "It was a lover and his lass." CTC; EBEvV; OxAEP-1
   (From As You Like It.) APAD

Song: "Under the greenwood tree." CTC; EBEvV
(Amiens's Song.)
("But winter and rough weather.") (LL) APAD; CTV; NoP-4
Song: "What shall he have that kill'd the deer?" CTC
"What would you have? Your gentleness shall force." OxAEP-1

As You Like It. Theodore Weiss. TAP

As you may see on t'other side. Mother Goose. *See* The Tragical Death of A, Apple Pie.

As you plaited the harvest bow. The Harvest Bow. Seamus Heaney. BiHa; NoAM; PBCIP; PNI

As you read, a white bear leisurely. To the Reader. Denise Levertov. AmPP; PFE; PoM; SAGP; VGW

As you set out for Ithaka. Ithaka. Constantine P. Cavafy, *Greek*. GrIP, *tr. by* Edmund Keeley *and* Philip Sherrard

As you walk on your way thinking of other things. Epitaph from Athens. *Unknown, Greek*. GrAn, *tr. by* Peter Jay

As you work, and sleep, and talk, and laugh, and die. (LL) Resurrection. Kenneth Fearing. CMoP; PoE

As you would wish it done. (LL) A Woman Mourned by Daughters. Adrienne Rich. IMW; Poetr

As your eyes are blue. Lee Harwood. NBrP

Asante Sana, Te Te. Thadious M. Davis. BlSi

Ascend my shoulders, firmly keep thy seat. Homer. OBVE, *tr. by* Thomas Parnell *Fr.* The Battle of the Frogs and Mice.

Ascending pile, The. Mulciber. Milton. NOSC *Fr.* Book I. FHYEP; NAEL-1; OAEL-1; OxAEP-1 *Fr.* Paradise Lost.

Ascending Red Cedar Moon. Duane Niatum. CDW

Ascension. Denis Devlin. BIrV; ChIV-2

Ascension [*or* Ascention]. Donne. *Fr.* La Corona. ChIV-2; ESCV; Son *Fr.* Holy Sonnets.

Ascension-Day. Henry Vaughan. ESCV

Ascension Hymn ("Dust and clay"). Henry Vaughan. ESCV; GeHe; NOSC; TrCP

Ascension: 1925, The. John Malcolm Brinnin. InPK-6

Ascension of Our Lord Jesus Christ, The. Christopher Smart. NOCV *Fr.* Hymns and Spiritual Songs for the Fasts and Festivals of the Church of England.

Ascension on Fire Island. Henri Cole. PuP-15

Ascension Thursday. Saunders Lewis, *Welsh*. OBWVE, *tr. by* Gwyn Morgan

Ascensions, The. William Pillen. RaBo

Ascent, The. Stefan Aug. Doinas, *Romanian*. CEEP, *tr. by* Peter Jay *and* Virgil Nemoianu

Ascent of Man, The. Mathilde Blind.
Chaunts of Life. VWP

Ascent of Vasco da Gama, The. Fernando Pessoa, *Portuguese*. PeSAV, *tr. by* F.E.G. Quintanilha

Ascent to the Sierras. Robinson Jeffers. OxBA

Ascetic art student named Josh, An. Limerick. D. H. Cudmore. PeLi

Ascetic, unbelieving, refusing her, demanding nothing not its own. (LL) Austerity in Vermont. Terry Hummer. NAmP90; PuP-15

Asclepiad that greedie Carle. Of a covetous Niggard, and a needie Mouse. Lucilius, *Greek*. OBCVT, *tr. by* George Turberville

Asclepiades the Miser was horrified. Lucilius, *Greek*. GrAn, *tr. by* Peter Porter

Asclepias who loves to love. Meleager, *Greek*. GrAn, *tr. by* Peter Whigham

Asclepius cured the body: to make men whole. On Plato's Grave. *Unknown, Greek*. GrAn, *tr. by* William J. Philbin

Ascot Waistcoat. David McCord. NBLV
(Sportif.) NYBP

Asenath. Diana Hume George. ChIV-1

Ash. Jayanta Mahapatra. VCWP

Ash and the Oak, The. Louis Simpson. CoAmPo

Ash Keys. Michael Longley. PBCIP

Ash on an old man's sleeve. T. S. Eliot. FaBoTw *Fr.* Little Gidding. FaBoMo; FaBoPV; FaBoTw; GTBS-P; MoP; NAEL-2; NAWM-2; NOBA; NOBE; NoAM; OAEL-2; OxAEP-2; OxBTC; PeECV; TAP; TFi *Fr.* Four Quartets.

Ash Plant, The. Seamus Heaney. BiHa

Ash Range, The. Laurie Duggan.
Five. One. BMAP
One. One. BMAP

Ash Wednesday [*or* Ash-Wednesday]. T. S. Eliot. MoAmPo; OxBA; VGW
"At the first turning of the second stair." NOBA
"If the lost word is lost, if the spent word is spent." UV

Ash Wednesday. Christina Rossetti. TrCP

Ashamed and angry to be undeceived! (LL) The Dream. Aphra Behn. PBWP; RACG

Ashen feelers of the frigid morrow, The. The Specter. Ernst Hardt, *German*. AWP, *tr. by* Jethro Bithell

Ashes. Vasco [*or* Vasko] Popa. HSix, *tr. by* Charles Simic *Fr.* Games. RB, *tr. by* Anne Pennington

Ashes of Life. Edna St. Vincent Millay. FaBoBe

Ashes to ashes. *Unknown*. CTV

Ashkelon is not cut off with the remnant of a valley. Judith. Adah Isaacs Menken. APN-2; CBWP-1; PAR

Ashland Tragedy, The. Elijah Adams. AmFP

Ashleaves froze without an ashleaf sound, The. (LL) Sonnet: "I saw magic on a green country road." Michael Hartnett. BIrV; PBCIP

Ashtabula Disaster, The. Julia A. Moore. OBAL

Ashtray (two poems). Ōkuma Nobuyuki, *Japanese*. MJT, *tr. by* Makoto Ueda

Asian Desert. Dorothy Wellesley, Duchess of Wellington. OBMV

Asian Peace Offers Rejected without Publication. Robert Bly. CAPP-1

Asians Dying, The. W. S. Merwin. CAPP-1; CoAP; HCAP; NOBA; NYBP; PoPoPo; VCAP

Aside. Alan Dugan. PoA

Aside. Ronald Stuart Thomas. OxBC

Asides on the Oboe. Wallace Stevens. FaBoMo; MoAmPo

Ask in one life no more. Word by Night. Charles Brasch. PeNZ

Ask, is it well, O thou consumed of fire. The Burning of the Law. Meïr of Rothenburg, *Hebrew*. TrJP, *tr. by* Nina Davis Salaman

Ask Me. William Stafford. LoL

Ask me no more, my truth to prove. Winter Song. Elizabeth Tollet. ECWP; NOEC

Ask me no more: the moon may draw the sea. Tennyson. CBLP; GBL; ImPo; NAEL-2; OBNC; PoEL-5 *Fr.* The Princess.

Ask me no more where Jove bestows. Song, [A]. Thomas Carew. AWP; BeJo; CBLP; CH; CaPo; CavPo; ClHu; EnLoPo; GBL; GEA; GLoP; HAP; HoPM; ImPo; InPS-3; LoP; MeLP; NAEL-1; NOBE; NOSC; NoP-4; OBEV; PoE; PoEL-3; PoRA; SCGP; SeCP; TFi

Ask me not for the semblance of my loue. She Dwelt among the Untrodden Ways. Sir John Collings Squire. BXAP

Ask[e] me why I send you here. The Primrose. Robert Herrick. CBLP; OBEV

Ask Mummy Ask Daddy. John Agard. OTCP

Ask no return for love that's given. Horace Gregory. MoAmPo; VGW *Fr.* Chorus for Survival.

Ask not overmuch for fair. He That Loves a Rosy Cheek. Heinrich von Rugge, *German*. AWP, *tr. by* Jethro Bithell

Ask not the cause why sullen Spring. Song to a Fair Young Lady, Going Out of the Town in the Spring. Dryden. OBEV

Ask not to know this man. If fame should speak. A Little Shrub Growing By. Ben Jonson. BeJo; PFE

Ask not ungainly askings of the end. Horace, *Latin*. OBCVT, *tr. by* Ezra Pound

Ask not why hearts turn magazines of passions. A Funeral Elegy Upon that Pattern and Patron of Virtue. John Norton. SCAP

Ask not why sorrow shades my brow. Song: Montrose. Charles Cotton. NOSC

Ask the Empresse of the night. The Magnet. Thomas Stanley. NOBE

Ask the Lord of the East, "Where lie the ends of the earth?" Tune: "Song of the Lunar Palace"—Sending Off Spring. Kuan Yün-shih, *Chinese*. ChiPo; SuSp, *tr. by* Richard John Lynn

Ask the old men in Chinatown. Not Translation, Not Poetry. Daryl Ngee Chinn. LTA

Ask This of a Mother Whose Daughter Has Been Tortured. Barbara Jamison. EC3

Ask to be put in charge of streams and hills! Nguyễn Trãi, *Vietnamese*. AVP, *tr. by* Huỳnh Sanh Thông

Ask what is human life—the sage replies. Hope. William Cowper.

Ask you what provocation I have had? The Art of Satire. Alexander Pope. ECEV; EPCY; NOBE; NOEC; OBSV *Fr.* Epilogue to the Satires, in Two Dialogues. OAEL-1

Askal barfas canker dranick. Alphabet of Fishes. Bob Cobbing. NBrP

Asked, Don't you dream, do you ever. Erolog. Michael Palmer. FTOS

Asked me for a kiss. (LL) Suicide's Note. Langston Hughes. PoPoPo; SAmP

Asked nothing else, if she had you. (LL) Miss Loo. Walter De la Mare. CMoP; OxBTC

Asked to explain his suicide after a brief creative flurry, the shade replied. The Shade. Tom Mandel. PT

Askest, 'How long thou shalt stay'. The Visit. Ralph Waldo Emerson. APN-1; NOBA; PAR

Asking again: Where did that blood come from? (LL) Osawatomie. Carl Sandburg. CMoP; OxBA

Asking what, asking what?—all a boy's afternoon. Debate: Question, Quarry, Dream. Robert Penn Warren. VGW

Asleap / sleap. Bride's Day. Susan Howe. FTOS *Fr.* Defenestration of Prague.

Asleep he wheezes at his ease. Roger the Dog. Ted Hughes. ChAP; PeP

Asleep in bed. Robert Louis Stevenson. *See* My Shadow.

Asleep in the City. Michael Smith. PBCIP

Asleep, My Love? Shakespeare. CTC *Fr.* A Midsummer Night's Dream.

Asleep on the sand, dozing on the water, they form a flock. About Geese. Li Shang-yin, *Chinese.* SuSp, *tr. by* Eugene Eoyang *and* Irving Y. Lo

Asleep upon a chair. (LL) The Ballad of Father Gilligan. W. B. Yeats. EBVV; MoBrPo; PoRA

Asleep while the children howl and the house burns. Goddess. Judith Johnson Sherwin. BoWoP

Asleep, you turn. Hot Bath in an Old Hotel. Paula Rankin. MT

Asmodeus. Geoffrey Hill. FaBoTw

Asparagus. Jody Gladding. BAP-95

Asparagus bed. Robert Spiess. HA

Asparagus I bite off their heads. Alexis Rotella. HA

Aspatia's Song. Francis Beaumont *and* John Fletcher. AWP; HAP; NOBE; OBEV *Fr.* The Maid's Tragedy.

(I Died True.) CH

Aspect of Love, Alive in the Ice and Fire, An. Gwendolyn Brooks. BPo; CAPP-1; TAP

Aspecta Medusa. D. G. Rossetti. OxBSP

Aspects. Norman MacCaig. OxBS

Aspects of Christianity in America—Continued. Wordsworth. *See* The Pilgrim Fathers.

Aspects of Christianity in America—the Pilgrim Fathers. Wordsworth. *See* The Pilgrim Fathers.

Aspects of Eve. Linda Pastan. CRP; PiM

Aspects of Love. Ruth Miller. LW

Aspects of Now. Gwyn Williams.

"Today has it all, sunshine." OBWVE

Aspects of Robinson. Weldon Kees. CoAP; NYBP

Aspects of Spring in Greater Boston. George Starbuck. NYBP *Fr.* Poems from a First Year in Boston.

Aspects of the World like Coral Reefs. William Bronk. VGW

Aspen. Erin Mouré. DeD

Aspen and the Stream, The. Richard Wilbur. NYBP

Aspen-blue mist sneaks across fields. The Trees Walk Farther Away. Bernard Kangro, *Estonian.* CEEP, *tr. by* Ivar Ivask

Aspen tree, your leaves glance white into the dark. Paul Celan, *German.* PoSu, *tr. by* Michael Hamburger

Aspens. Edward Thomas. FaBoVe; InPS-3

Asphalt memory of blood and pain. (LL) Harlem Gallery: From the Inside. Larry Neal. MoNo

Asphodel. David Malouf. CBAP

Asphodel, That Greeny Flower. William Carlos Williams.

"Approaching death." FaBoMo

"Of asphodel, that greeny flower." CMoP

Asphyxiated Man, The. Victor Serge, *Russian.* AF, *tr. by* James Brook

Aspiration. Mário de Andrade, *Portuguese.* TTY, *tr. by* John Nist

Aspiration. Adah Isaacs Menken. AAP; CBWP-1; PAR

Aspiration. Henrietta Cordelia Ray. CBWP-3

Aspiration. Tanka. Saitō Mokichi, *Japanese.* MJT, *tr. by* Ueda, Makoto

Aspire, in its last act, / to walk on air. Amy Clampitt. *See* Beethoven, Opus 111.

Aspiring Man, by learned pens. Brief Essay on Man. Arthur Guiterman. OBAL

Ass[e], The. Robert Herrick. ChIV-1

Ass, The. Moses Mendes. *Fr.* The Chaplet. TrJP

Ass-Face. Dame Edith Sitwell. OBMV

Ass in the Lion's Skin, The ("Ass put on a lion's skin and went, An"). Aesop, *Greek.* AWP, *tr. by* William Ellery Leonard

Ass put on a lion's skin and went, An. The Ass in the Lion's Skin. Aesop, *Greek.* AWP, *tr. by* William Ellery Leonard

Ass, that for her slowness, was forbid, The. On Balaam's Ass. Francis Quarles. ChIV-1

Ass will with his long ears fray, An. Samuel Butler. FaBoEE

Assailant. John Raven. BPo

Assassination, The. Robert Silliman Hillyer. MoAmPo

Assassination, The. Donald Justice. VCAP

Assassination. Don L. Lee. PoBA

Assassination. Haki R. Madhubuti. GT

Assassination of Charlie Parker, The. Arthur Brown. SeSe

Assassination of John Lennon as Depicted by the Madame Tussaud Wax Museum, Niagara Falls, Ontario, 1987, The. David Wojahn. NAmP90; PBCAP *Fr.* Mystery Train: A Sequence.

Assassination Raga. Lawrence Ferlinghetti. CAPP-1

Assassins. Robert Browning. OxBoV *Fr.* Waring.

Assassin's Fatal Error, The. Lawrence Raab. AmPA

Assemble, all ye maidens, at the door. Elegy on a Lady, Whom Grief for the Death of Her Betrothed Killed. Robert Bridges. OBEV

Assembler. Debra Allbery. PBCAP

Assembly Line. "Shu Ting," *Chinese.* VCWP, *tr. by* Carolyn Kizer

Assembly of Ladies, The. The Lady of the Assembly. OBGa

Palace of Pleasant Regard, The. WPE

Assembly of the Gods, The. Robert Henryson. PoEL-1 *Fr.* The Testament of Cresseid. OxBS

Assents by eternally voting 'I'. (LL) Egotist. Ambrose Bierce. APAD; APN-2; OBAL

Asseverations. Arthur Nortje. HBAPE

Asshole anneal'd to silken skin / all ashes, all ashes again. Allen Ginsberg. *See* On Neal's Ashes.

"Assholes!" her eyes seem grey in this soup the hangars. Maureen Owen. DeD *Fr.* Amelia Earhart Series.

Assignation, The. Juana de Ibarbourou, *Spanish.* PBWP, *tr. by* Brian Swann

Assignation with a Somnambulist. John Streeter Manifold. CBAP

Assist me while I wander here. Caroline Codling. FaBoVe

Assistance, The. Paul Blackburn. NeAP; PoM

Assorted needles and coloured threads. The Sewing Lesson. Kate Lilley. BMAP

Assumption. Padraic Fallon. BIrV; NOIV

Assumption about the Harlem Brown Baby. Salih Michael Fisher. GLP

Assumption of Miriam from the Street in the Winter of 1942, The. Jerzy Ficowski, *Polish.*

Assumption of Miriam from the Street in the Winter of 1942, The. Jerzy Ficowski. HP, *tr. by* Keith Bosley

Assurance, An. Nicholas Breton. CBLP; SCGP

Assurance. Josephine D. Henderson Heard. CBWP-4

Assuredly, a lively scene! The Public Garden. Arthur Hugh Clough. PeLV *Fr.* Dipsychus [and the Spirit].

Assyrian came down like the [or a] wolf on the fold, The. The Destruction of Sennacherib. Byron. APAD; BLPA; CABP; CTV; ChAP; ChIV-1; EBEvV; FHYEP; FaBoBe; FaBoCh; FaPoR; HAP; HeIP-4; InPS-3; NoP-4; OBWP; OxAEP-2; PBMP; PoLF; RB; SCGP; TFi; TrCP; WeW-3

Assyrian [or Assyrians'] King in peace, with foul desire, The [or Th']. Sardanapalus. Henry Howard, Earl of Surrey. NoSic; SiPS

Aster. Plato, *Greek.* GrAn *tr. by* Peter Jay

("My star, star-gazing?—If only I could be.") OBCVT, *tr. by* Peter Jay

Aster, The. Tanka. Akiko Yosano, *Japanese.* MJT, *tr. by* Ueda, Makoto

Astonish me beyond words. (LL) Pastoral: "The Little sparrows." William Carlos Williams. SAmP; TwCP

Astonished Muse finds thousands at her side, The. (LL) Ode, Inscribed to W. H. Channing. Ralph Waldo Emerson. APN-1; AmPP; ColAP; HAP; MeMAP; NAAL-1; NAAL-3; NCAP; NOBA; NoP-4; OxBA; PAR; TAP

Astonishment. Anna Swir, *Polish.* IFJA, *tr. by* Czeslaw Milosz *and* Leonard Nathan

Astræa. Ralph Waldo Emerson. APN-1

Astræa. John Greenleaf Whittier. APN-1

Astral blue of old mountains, ridge after rising ridge. Austerity in Vermont. Terry Hummer. NAmP90; PuP-15

Astrea in this time. Madrigal. William Drummond, of Hawthornden. NOSC *Fr.* Urania, or Spiritual Poems.

Astride a mount pawing misty sedge grass. A Spring Day in the Countryside. Wen T'ing-yün, *Chinese.* SuSp, *tr. by* William R. Schultz

Astride an ox, you pass the village far in the distance. Buffalo Boy. Huang T'ing-chien, *Chinese.* SuSp, *tr. by* Michael E. Workman

Astrologer, The. Agathias, *Greek.* GrAn, *tr. by* Guy Davenport

Astrologer Predicts at Mary's Birth, The. Lucille Clifton. NALW

Astrologer's Song, An. Rudyard Kipling. MoBrPo

Astronaut, The. James Kirkup. SpW

Astronauts. John Travers Moore. SpW

Astronomer, / I strike my gong for you. The Mirror of a Day Chiming Marigold. Diane Wakoski. NALW

Astronomer with patient, searching gaze, The. The Slowness of Belief in a Spiritual World. Jones Very. NCAP

Astronomer's Journal, An. Jane Shore. PoA

Astronomers of Mont Blanc, The. Edgar Bowers. PoA

Astronomica, The. Manilius Marcus, *Latin.*

"From whose large mouth for verse all that since live." OBCVT, *tr. by* John Florio *and* Matthew Gwinne

Astronomy. A. E. Housman. NoP-4; OBWP

Astrophel. Edmund Spenser.

"Such skill, matcht with such courage as he had." OBWP

Astrophil and Stella, *often wr. titled* Astrophel and Stella. Sir Philip Sidney. AAS; SiPS

First Song. OxAEP-1

Second Song. NoSic

Third Song. PoEL-1

Fourth Song. GBL; HAP; NAEL-1; NoP-4; NoSic

Fifth Song.

Sixth Song.

Seventh Song. NoP-4

Eighth Song. NoSic

Ninth Song. NoSic

Tenth Song.

Eleventh Song. NoSic; OxAEP-1

   ("And from lowts to run away.") (LL) PBRV

   (Voices at the Window.) NOBE; OBEV

   ("Who is it that this darke night.") PBRV

Sonnet 1: "Loving in truth, and fain[e] in verse my love to show." AWP; EBEV; EPCY; GBL; HAP; ImPo; InPS-3; NAEL-1; NoSic; OAEL-1; OxAEP-1; PoE; Poetr; SCGP; Son; TFi

   (1.) CABP

   (Astrophil and Stella.) GLoP

   ("'Fool,' said my Muse to me, "look in thy heart and write."") (LL) CABP; NoP-4

   ("Foole, said my Muse to me, looke in thy heart and write.") (LL) PBRV

   ("Loving in truth, and fain in verse my love to show.") CABP; GLoP; GSo; LoP; NoP-4

Sonnet 2: "Not at [the] first sight, nor with a dribbed shot." NAEL-1; OAEL-1

   ("Not at first sight, nor with a dribbed shot.") PBRV

Sonnet 3: "Let dainty wits cry on the sisters nine." NoSic; OAEL-1; Son

Sonnet 4: "Virtue, alas, now let me take some rest."

Sonnet 5: "It is most true that eyes are formed to serve." NAEL-1; NoSic; OAEL-1; Son

Sonnet 6: "Some lovers speak, when they their Muses entertain." NAEL-1; NoSic; Son

   (Sonnet 6: 'some lovers speak'.) AEP

Sonnet 7: "When Nature made her chief work, Stella's eyes." NAEL-1; NIP-4; Son

Sonnet 8: "Love, born in Greece, of late fled from his native place."

Sonnet 9: "Queen Virtue's court, which some call Stella's face." NAEL-1

   ("Of touch they are, and poore I am their straw.") (LL) PBRV

   ("Queene *Vertues* court, which some call *Stellas* face.") PBRV

Sonnet 10: "Reason, in faith thou art well served, that still." NAEL-1

Sonnet 11: "In truth, O Love, with what a boyish kind." CBLP; PoE

Sonnet 12: "Cupid, because thou shin'st in Stella's eyes."

Sonnet 13: "Phoebus was judge between Jove, Mars, and Love."

Sonnet 14: "Alas, have I not pain enough, my friend." NoSic; OAEL-1

Sonnet 15: "You that do search for every purling spring." NAEL-1; NoSic; OAEL-1; OxAEP-1; Son

   (15.) CABP

   ("Stella behold, and then begin to endite.") (LL) CABP

Sonnet 16: "In nature apt to like when I did see." NAEL-1

Sonnet 17: "His mother dear Cupid offended late."

Sonnet 18: "With what sharp checks I in myself am shent." NAEL-1; NoSic

Sonnet 19: "On Cupid's bow how are my heart-strings bent." NoSic

Sonnet 20: "Fly, fly, my friends." NoSic; OAEL-1

   ("But ere I could fly thence, it pierc'd my heart.") (LL) AEP

   (Sonnet 20: 'Fly, fly, my friends'.) AEP

Sonnet 21: "Your words my friend (right healthful caustics) blame." NAEL-1; NoSic; PoE

   ("Hath this world ought so fair as Stella is?") (LL) NoP-4

Sonnet 22: "In highest way of heav'n the sun did ride." Son

Sonnet 223: "Curious wits, seeing dull pensiveness, The."

Sonnet 24: "Rich fools there be, whose base and filthy heart."

Sonnet 25: "Wisest scholar of the wight most wise, The." OAEL-1

Sonnet 26: "Though dusty wits dare scorn astrology." OAEL-1; Son

Sonnet 27: "Because I oft, in dark abstracted guise." NoSic

   (27.) CABP

Sonnet 28: "You that with allegory's curious frame." NoSic; OAEL-1

Sonnet 29: "Like some weak lords, neighboured by mighty kings."

Sonnet 30: "Whether the Turkish new moon minded be." NoSic; PoE

Sonnet 31: "With how sad steps, O Moon, thou climb'st the skies!" AWP; BoLoP; CH; EnLoPo; GBL; HAP; HeIP-4; InPS-3; NAEL-1; NoSic; OxAEP-1; PBMP; PoE; PoRA; SCGP; Son; TFi; TRP

   ("Do they call virtue there ungratefullness?") (LL) NoP-4

   (His Lady's Cruelty.) OBEV

   (Languishing Moon, The.)

   (Sonnet 31: 'With how sad steps'.) AEP

   ("With how sad steps, Oh Moon, thou climb'st the skies.") NoP-4

Sonnet 32: "Morpheus, the lively son of deadly sleep."

Sonnet 33: "I might, unhappy word, O me, I might." OAEL-1

Sonnet 34: "Come, let me write. 'And to what end?' To ease."

Sonnet 35: "What may words say, or what may words not say."

Sonnet 36: "Stella, whence doth this new assault arise."

Sonnet 37: "My mouth doth water, and my breast doth swell." NAEL-1; Son

Sonnet 38: "This night, while sleep begins with heavy wings."

Sonnet 39: "Come Sleep, O Sleep." NAEL-1; NoSic; OxAEP-1; PoE; PoRA; SCGP; SCV; Son; TFi

   ("Come sleep, Oh sleep, the certain knot of peace.") NoP-4

   (Sleep.) OBEV; SAGP

Sonnet 40: "As good to write as for to lie and groan." NoSic

Sonnet 41: "Having this day my horse, my hand, my lance." HAP; NAEL-1; PoE; Son

   (Sonnet 41: 'Having this day my horse, my lance'.) AEP

Sonnet 42: "O eyes, which do the spheres of beauty move."

Sonnet 43: "Fair eyes, sweet lips, dear heart, that foolish I."

Sonnet 44: "My words I know do well set forth my mind."

Sonnet 45: "Stella oft sees the very face of woe." InPS-3; NAEL-1; NoSic; PoE

Sonnet 46: "I cursed thee oft, I pity now thy case."

Sonnet 47: "What, have I thus betrayed my liberty?" GBL; NAEL-1; PoEL-1

   (Yoke of Tyranny, The.)

Sonnet 48: "Soul's joy, bend not those morning stars from me."

Sonnet 49: "I on my horse, and Love on me doth try." NAEL-1; OAEL-1; PoE

Sonnet 50: "Stella, the fullness of my thoughts of thee."

Sonnet 51: "Pardon mine ears; both I and they do pray."

Sonnet 52: "Strife is grown between Virtue and Love, A." NAEL-1

Sonnet 53: "In martial sports I had my cunning tried." NAEL-1; NoSic

Sonnet 54: "Because I breathe not love to every one." ImGa; InPS-3; NoSic

   (54.) CABP

   ("Because I breathe not love to ev'ry one.") CABP

Sonnet 55: "Muses, I oft invoked your holy aid."

Sonnet 56: "Fie, school of Patience, fie; your lesson is." NAEL-1

Sonnet 57: "Woe, having made with many fights his own."

Sonnet 58: "Doubt there hath been, when with his golden chain."

Sonnet 59: "Dear, why make you more of a dog than me?" GBL

Sonnet 60: "When my good angel guides me to the place."

Sonnet 61: "Oft with true sighs, oft with uncalled tears." NAEL-1

Sonnet 62: "Late tired with woe, e'en ready for to pine."

Sonnet 63: "O Grammer rules, ô now your virtues show."

   (Grammar-Rules.)

   ("O grammar rules, O now your virtues show.")

Sonnet 64: "No more, my dear, no more these counsels try." SCGP

Sonnet 65: "Love, by sure proof I may call thee unkind." Son

Sonnet 66: "And do I see some cause a hope to feed."

Sonnet 67: "Hope, art thou true, or dost thou flatter me?"

Sonnet 68: "Stella, the only planet of my light."

Sonnet 69: "O joy, too high for my low style to show." NAEL-1; OxAEP-1

Sonnet 70: "My Muse may well grudge at my heav'nly joy."

Sonnet 71: "Who will in fairest book of Nature know." InPS-3; NAEL-1; NoSic; OAEL-1; PoE; Poetr

Sonnet 72: "Desire, though thou my old companion art." NAEL-1

   ("Now banish'd art—but yet, alas, how shall?") (LL) AEP

   ("Now banisht art, but yet alas how shall?") (LL) PBRV

   (Sonnet 72: 'Desire, though thou my old companion art'.) AEP

Sonnet 74: "I never drank of Aganippe well." NAEL-1; NoSic; Son

Sonnet 74: "Love still a boy, and oft a wanton is." Son

Sonnet 75: "Of all the kings that ever here did reign." NoSic

Sonnet 76: "She comes, and straight therewith her shining twins do move."

Sonnet 77: "Those looks, whose beams be joy, whose motion is delight."

Sonnet 78: "O how the pleasant airs of true love be."

Sonnet 80: "Sweet swelling lip, well mayst thou swell in pride."

Sonnet 81: "O kiss, which dost those ruddy gems impart." NAEL-1; Son

("O kisse, which doest those ruddie gemmes impart.") PBRV
Sonnet 82: "Nymph of the garden where all beauties be." PoE
Sonnet 83: "Good brother *Philip*, I have borne you long."
Sonnet 84: "Highway, since you my chief Parnassus be." SCGP
Sonnet 85: "I see the house; my heart thyself contain."
Sonnet 86: "Alas, whence came this change of looks? If I."
Sonnet 87: "When I was forced from Stella ever dear." NAEL-1
Sonnet 88: "Out, traitor absence: dar'st thou counsel me."
Sonnet 89: "Now that of absence the most irksome night." NAEL-1
Sonnet 90: "Stella, think not that I by verse seek fame." NoSic
Sonnet 91: "Stella, while now by honour's cruel might." NAEL-1; PoE
Sonnet 92: "Be your words made (good sir) of Indian ware." NoSic
Sonnet 93: "O fate, O fault, O curse, child of my bliss."
Sonnet 94: "Grief, find the words, for thou hast made my brain."
Sonnet 95: "Yet sighs, dear sighs, indeed true friends you are."
Sonnet 96: "Thought, with good cause thou lik'st so well the night."
Sonnet 97: "Dian, that fain would cheer her friend the Night."
Sonnet 98: "Ah bed, the field where joy's peace some do see." EnLoPo
Sonnet 99: "When far-spent night persuades each mortal eye." NoSic; PoE; Son
Sonnet 100: "O tears, no tears, but rain from beauty's skies." Son
Sonnet 101: "Stella is sick, and in that sick-bed lies."
Sonnet 102: "Where be those roses gone, which sweetened so our eyes?"
Sonnet 103: "O happy Thames, that didst my Stella bear." OxAEP-1
Sonnet 104: "Envious wits, what hath been mine offence." PoE; Son
Sonnet 105: "Unhappy sight, and hath she vanished by."
Sonnet 106: "O absent presence, Stella is not here."
Sonnet 107: "Stella, since you so right a Princess art." OxAEP-1
Sonnet 108: "When sorrow (using mine own fire's might)."
    Stella's Kiss. NoSic
    (Sonnet 79.)
Astute Melanesians on Munda. Limerick. *Unknown.* PeLi
Aswelay. Norman Henry, II Pritchard. PoBA
Asyde, with faire Adonis playes his wanton partes. (LL) The Garden of Adonis. Edmund Spenser. NOBE; PoEL-1
Asylum. Breyten Breytenbach, *Afrikaans.* VCWP, *tr. by* Stephen Gray *and* A. J. Coetzee
Asylum. Ciaran Carson. PNI
Asylum. John Freeman. OBMV
Asylum under my tread all this day. Samuel Beckett. *Fr.* Echo's Bones. NoAM
Asymmetry of the Universe. Fabio Doplicher, *Italian.* NeIt, *tr. by* Stephen Sartarelli
At 12 O'clock. Meleager. *See* Epigram: "At 12 o'clock in the afternoon."
At 29. Speculations on the Present through the Prism of the Past. June Jordan. GT
At 7 p.m. in a saloon downtown Seoul. The Apocalypse. Ilsong Kwon, *Korean.* CKP, *tr. by* Jaihiun Kim
At a Bach Concert. Adrienne Rich. NIP-4
At a Calvary near the Ancre. Wilfred Owen. ChIV-2; GI
At a Concert of Music. Conrad Potter Aiken. MoAmPo
At a corner. Tanka. Miya Shūji, *Japanese.* MJT, *tr. by* Makoto Ueda
At a Country Hotel. Howard Nemerov. PoRA
At a Danse Macabre. Charles Spear. PeNZ
At a Friends' Meeting. Mary Elizabeth Coleridge. WPE
At a Funeral, *(for Valencia Majombozi, who died shortly after qualifying as a doctor).* Dennis Brutus. PBMAP
At a hospital in Tokyo during the summer of 1911. Kitahara Hakushū, *Japanese.* MJT, *tr. by* Makoto Ueda
At a Low Mass for Two Hot-Rodders. X. J. Kennedy. Poetsp
At a March against the Vietnam War. Robert Bly. CDa; SPE
At a Motel. Brenda Hillman. PuP-14
At a party I spy a handsome psychiatrist. Afternoon Happiness. Carolyn Kizer. Poetr
At a place in the mountains. The Savior Is Abducted in Puerto Rico. Martín Espada. TRP
At a pleasant evening party I had taken down to supper. Ferdinando and Elvira; or, The Gentle Pieman. Sir William Schwenck Gilbert. OBCoV
At a Potato Digging. Seamus Heaney. CIP-2
At a Reading. Thomas Bailey Aldrich. OBAL
At a Reading. J. D. McClatchy. DiPo
At a Reception. Karen Gershon. LW
At a sale of Cupids. A hawk looks at them. (LL) The Token. Frank Templeton Prince. FaBoTw; OxBTC
At a Solemn Music[k]. Milton. EPCY; GTBS-P; HeIP-4; NOBE; OBEV; PoEL-3; SCGP
At a springe-well [*or* springe wel] under a thorn. *Unknown.* MiEL

At a summer home in Ningpo, near Shanghai. A Picture of my Mother's Family. Wing Tek Lum. OpBo
At a Sunlit Window. Ondra Lysohorsky, *Lachian.* AF, *tr. by* Ewald Osers
At a Symphony. Louise Imogen Guiney. APN-2
At a Watering-Place. Thomas Hardy. CMoP *Fr.* Satires of Circumstance in Fifteen Glimpses.
At a Window. Carl Sandburg. FaBoBe; PoToHe
At alarming bell daybreak, before. Eiléan Ní Chuilleanáin. CIP-2 *Fr.* Site of Ambush.
At Algezir, and will in overplus. Two Centos. William Empson. CBNP
All all that he is: the heart of heartlessness. (LL) The Snow-Leopard. Randall Jarrell. APo; LiTM; TwCP
At all times I see them. Harbach 1944. János Pilinszky, *Hungarian.* PoSu, *tr. by* Janos Csokits *and* Ted Hughes; HP, *tr. by* Ted Hughes; AF, *tr. by* Ted Hughes *and* Janos Csokits
At an acute. Thunderstorm. Pavel Davydovich Kogan, *Russian.* TCRP, *tr. by* Daniel Weissbort
At an Exhibition of Historical Paintings, Hobart. Vivian Smith. CBAP; NOBAu
At an Exposition. Nguyễn Khuyến, *Vietnamese.* AVP, *tr. by* Huỳnh Sanh Thông
At an Inn. Thomas Hardy. NOBVV
At an Inn in Yü-kan. Liu Ch'ang-ch'ing, *Chinese.* SuSp, *tr. by* William H. Nienhauser
At an open window sitting. Written on Whitsun-Monday, 1795. Matilda Barbara Betham-Edwards. ECWP
At Annika's Place. Siv Widerberg, *Swedish.* NTCP, *tr. by* Verne Moberg
At any hand but hers? (LL) Symptoms Of Love. Robert Graves. BoLoP; LoP
At Apollinaire's Grave. Allen Ginsberg. BB
At April. Angelina Weld Grimké. BlSi; GT; NMM-2
At Arrow Rapids, the water splashes foam. Wang T'ing-hsiang. CoBLCP, *tr. by* Jonathan Chaves *Fr.* Traveling by Boat.
At Autumn Cove, so many white monkeys. Autumn Cove. Li Po, *Chinese.* CoBCP; TTTS, *tr. by* Burton Watson
At Baia. Hilda Doolittle. ColAP; NAAL-2; NOBA
("No bracelet—accept this.") (LL) CPO
At Ballyshannon, Co. Donegal. William Allingham. NOBVV
At Barstow. Charles Tomlinson. MoP; NoAM; TwCP
At Beautyes barre as I dyd stande. The Arraignment of a Lover. George Gascoigne. AAS
At behest of usura. (LL) Canto 45. Ezra Pound. CMoP; LiTM; MeMAP; NAAL-2; NOBA; PoE
At bend of bay. Old Sailor Looking at a Container Ship. Robert Carson. AiP
At Birth. Anthony Thwaite. PFE
At birth. I was not born. Only you were. (LL) Helen Todd: My Birthname. Sandra McPherson. LoL
At Blackwater Pond the tossed waters have settled. Mary Oliver. CMAP
At Bon Odori. Jim Mitsui. OpBo
At break of day from frightful dreams. Ellenore. William Taylor. NOBRP
At break of day we leave the western gate. After Rain, Visiting the Temple of Heavenly Peace. Wang Shih-chieng, *Chinese.* CoBLCP, *tr. by* Jonathan Chaves
At Breakfast. Ida M. Mills. BoTP
At Brill on the hill. *Unknown.* OxNR
At Candlemas. Charles Causley. OBCP
At Carmel Highlands. Janet Lewis. PoA
At Casterbridge Fair. Thomas Hardy.
    After the Fair. CMoP; HAP
    Ballad-Singer, The. BoLoP
    Former Beauties. CBLP; NoAM; OBMV; OBNC
    Wife Waits, A. SAGP
At Castle Boterel. Thomas Hardy. EBEV; GTBS-P; NOBE; OBNC; OxAEP-2; PeVV; PoE; SCV
At Castor Bay. Sam Hunt. PeNZ
At Chadwicks Bar and Grill. Lance Henson. HATNAP
At Chancellorsville. Andrew Hudgins. CBCWP
At Ch'ang-an—a full foot of snow;. An Early Levée. Po Chü-i, *Chinese.* ChiP, *tr. by* Arthur Waley
At Ch'ang-ku, Reading: To Show to My Man Pa. Li Ho, *Chinese.* CoBCP, *tr. by* Burton Watson
At Ch'en Ch'u. Wang Shih-chieng, *Chinese.* OHMPC, *tr. by* Kenneth Rexroth
At Christmas. Anne Ridler. WPN
At Christmas-Tide. Henrietta Cordelia Ray. CBWP-3
At Christmas time so long ago. The Little Fir Tree. Margaret Rose. BoTP

At Christmas, when old friends are meeting. Good Will to Men—Christmas Greetings in Six Languages. Dorothy Brown Thompson. OBCP

At Clear Brook in Ch'ih-chou. Tu Mu, *Chinese*. PLT, *tr. by* A. C. Graham

At Cock-crow. Prudentius, *Latin*. MLL, *tr. by* Helen Waddell

At Common Dawn. Vivian Locke Ellis. CH

At Communion. Madeleine L'Engle. TrCP

At Condore Port. Đào Duy Kỳ, *Vietnamese*. AVP, *tr. by* Huỳnh Sanh Thông

At Cooloolah. Judith Wright. MoBrPo
  (At Cooloola.) BMAP

At Coueron. My First Gun. Pamela Alexander. WeT

At counters where I eat my lunch. Marble-Top. Elwyn Brooks White. OBAL

At court I met it, in clothes brave enough. On Something, That Walks [*or* Walkes] Somewhere. Ben Jonson. BeJo; NAEL-1; OxBSP; PoE; SCGP; SeCP

At Cove at our camp in the open canyon. At Cove on the Crooked River. William Stafford. CoAmPo; LiTM

At Cove on the Crooked River ("At Cove at our camp in the open canyon"). William Stafford. CoAmPo; LiTM

At Dawn. Michael Patrick Hearn. CA

At Dawn. Arthur Symons. OBNC

At dawn. Tanka. Miyazawa Kenji, *Japanese*. MJT, *tr. by* Makoto Ueda

At Dawn, Climbing the Heavenly Pillar Peak of Mysterious Mountain. Hsü Chung-hsing, *Chinese*.
  "I shake my robe—and mists disperse, leaving clear autumn sky." CoBLCP, *tr. by* Jonathan Chaves

At dawn I hasten toward the Purple Hall. Thoughts While Studying at Hanlin Academy Sent to My Colleagues at the Chi-hsien Academy. Li Po, *Chinese*. SuSp, *tr. by* Joseph J. Lee

At dawn I plucked orchids in the park. Spending the Night on Stone Gate Mountain. Hsieh Ling-yün, *Chinese*. SuSp, *tr. by* Francis Westbrook

At dawn I rode to escort the Doctors of Art;. Escorting Candidates to the Examination Hall. Po Chü-i, *Chinese*. ChiP, *tr. by* Arthur Waley

At dawn I sighed to see my hairs fall. On his Baldness. Po Chü-i, *Chinese*. ChiP, *tr. by* Arthur Waley

At dawn I squat on the garage. Summer. James Harrison. VGW

At dawn I stand on cool roof garden. *Unknown*. *Fr.* Summer. SuSp, *tr. by* Michael E. Workman *Fr.* Tzu-yeh Songs of the Four Seasons.

At dawn of day I saw a man stand by a grog saloon. The Drunkard's Doom. *Unknown*. AS

At dawn of the day the Creator. Gaspara Stampa, *Italian*. BoWoP, *tr. by* J. Vitiello

At dawn remembering her bad grammar. George Swede. HA

At dawn setting out from a cassia and orchid shore. Picking Rushes. *Unknown*, *Chinese*. CoBCP, *tr. by* Burton Watson

At dawn she lay with her profile at that angle. Daybreak. Stephen Spender. BoLoP

At dawn she unmasked. Masquerading. May Probyn. VWP

At dawn the cornering taxis cast. New York. William Logan. EOEF

At dawn the dove croons. California Spring. Charles Wright. ColAP

At Dawn the Light Will Come. N. P. van Wyk Louw, *Afrikaans*. PeSA, *tr. by* Uys Krige *and* Jack Cope

At dawn the ridge emerges massed and dun. Attack. Siegfried Sassoon. MoBrPo; NOBE; OxBTC; PoFWW

At Dawn the Virgin Is Born. Félix Lope de Vega Carpio, *Spanish*. PChr, *tr. by* W. S. Merwin

At dawn to-morrow. After Hilaire Belloc. Max Beerbohm. OBCoV

At dawn tomorrow, time of whitening fields. Victor Hugo, *French*. FLP, *tr. by* Alistair Elliot

At dawn we buried Melanippus. At sunset. Callimachus, *Greek*. HePo, *tr. by* Barbara Hughes Fowler. *Fr.* Epigrams.

At Daybreak. Siegfried Sassoon. LBC

At Daybreak. Adam Zagajewski, *Polish*. VCWP, *tr. by* Renata Gorczynski, Benjamin Ivry, *and* C. K. Williams

At daybreak, when the falcon claps his wings. Ballad Written for a Bridegroom. François Villon, *French*. AWP, *tr. by* Swinburne

At daylight on St. John's, the day after Epiphany, we got our orders. The March toward the Front. Odysseus Elytis, *Greek*. AF, *tr. by* Edmund Keeley *and* George Savidis

At Day's End. Hayyim Nahman Bialik, *Hebrew*. MHP, *tr. by* Ruth Finer Mintz

At day's light. In Autumn. Jon Anderson. AmPA

At dead of night, the sailors sprawled on deck. Nearing La Guaira. Derek Walcott. TTY

At Delft. Charles Tomlinson. NYBP

At Delphos shrine one did a doubt propound. Upon Master Edmund Spenser. Francis Beaumont. FaBoEE

At Devlin's Siding. Barcroft Henry Boake. CBAP

At Dieppe. Arthur Symons.
  Grey and Green. NOBVV; PeVV
  Rain on the Down. OBNC

At dinner, she is hostess, I am host. George Meredith. EnVR; NOBVV; PoE; Son *Fr.* Modern Love.

At distance far approaching to the tomb. Philip Freneau. NAAL-1; NAAL-3 *Fr.* The House of Night.

At Dryhope lived a lady fair. The Dowie Dens of Yarrow. *Unknown*. IBB

At Dunbar, Castle or Arcade. Double Feature. Robert Earl Hayden. NoAM

At Dunwich. Anthony Thwaite. MoBS

At dusk every day, our cattle leave the river. The River and Under the River. Davis McCombs. BAP-96

At dusk / from the island in the river. If the Owl Calls Again. John Haines. CoAP; CoAmPo; HeIP-4

At dusk heavy clouds grieve the long day. Poem to the Tune of "Tsui hua yin." Li Ch'ing-chao, *Chinese*. WPOW, *tr. by* Marsha Wagner

At dusk hot water from the hose. Marlene Mountain. HA

At dusk I sought lodging at Shih-hao village. Recruiting Officer of Shih-hao. Tu Fu, *Chinese*. SuSp, *tr. by* Irving Y. Lo

At dusk they'd ask. Site. Meir Wieseltier, *Hebrew*. IP, *tr. by* Warren Bargad *and* Stanley F. Chyet

At Eagle Farm I stand at the passenger gate. Flights. Roger McDonald. CBAP

At early morning, clear and cold. The Troopship. Lionel Pigot Johnson. EBVV

At Ease. Walter De la Mare. GTBS-P

At Egypt. Clark Coolidge.
  "I came here. I don't know you here." PmAP
  "Morning muezzin in orange and a mosquito." FTOS
  "New hunt / the morning bent, A." APSN

At eight I was brilliant with my body. Black Hair. Gary Soto. UnSA

At 8:00 he rises, bathes, and dresses. Mr. Eliot's Day. Robert Francis. NYBP

At eight stealing a mirror glance. Li Shang-yin, *Chinese*. CoBCP, *tr. by* Burton Watson

At End. Louise Chandler Moulton. PWR

At entrance cried out but not. The Lying Dear. W. S. Graham. FaBoTC

At Eton with Orwell, at Oxford with Waugh. On Himself. Cyril Connolly. OBCoV

At Eutaw springs the valiant died. To the Memory of the Brave Americans. Philip Freneau. AiP; AmPP; PoLF

At evening, sitting on this terrace. Bat. D. H. Lawrence. APo; GTBS-P; HAP; OAEL-1; OAEL-2

At evening the horse comes down unled. The Shadow of Himself. William Renton. NOBVV

At evening, the sound of the cuckoo. Summer. Georg Trakl, *German*. NNPT, *tr. by* Robert Genier

At evening when flicker. Shin Shalom, *Hebrew*. MHP, *tr. by* Ruth Finer Mintz

At evening when I go to bed. Daisies. Frank Dempster Sherman. CTV

At evening when the lamp is lit. The Land of Story-Books. Robert Louis Stevenson. ACTP; CTV; ChAP; FaBoBe; PWR

At Famine's Feast, ye ken, man. (LL) Drone *v.* Worker. Ebenezer Elliot. FaBoPV; OBSV

At Farringford. Tennyson. *Fr.* To the Rev. F. D. Maurice. GTBS-P; NOBVV; PeECV

At fifteen I joined the army. Home. *Unknown*, *Chinese*. OHMPC, *tr. by* Kenneth Rexroth

At Fifteen I Went Off to the Army;. *Unknown*, *Chinese*. CoBCP, *tr. by* Burton Watson

At fifteen I'd buy bottles. White Port and Lemon Juice. Yusef Komunyakaa. ISC

At fifteen Jean Calvin made a list. Preposterous. Jim Hall. MT

At fifty, I approach myself. In a Dream. David Ignatow. PoA

At Fifty in the Crystal-Dead Eye of the Center. Anne S. Perlman. CMAP

At First. Charles Hubert Sisson. OxBC

At first blush, discomfiting. Diehard. Judith Moffett. PoA

At first from your verse. To Dennis Brutus. Kofi Awoonor. HBAPE

At first he refused to deliver junk mail because it was stupid, all. Appointed Rounds. Louis Jenkins. RaBo

At first her grief was a grey. The Passing of Sorrow. Mary Jane Moffat. IMW

At first I thought I would feel. Nothing Could Take Away the Bear-King's Image. Ray A. Young Bear. HATNAP

At first I thought there was a superfine. Fleming Helphenstine. Edwin Arlington Robinson. MeMAP

At first I used to read headlines. The Grocery Store. Maura Stanton. NAmP90

At first I was given centuries. Margaret Atwood. HAP; WPOW

At first I was worried about you. When I Held You to My Chest, You Fit. Jack Myers. AmPA

At first in that place, at all times, above the earth, *see also* On the Creation and Ontogony *for var. translation. Unknown.* APN-2, *tr. by* Daniel Garrison Brinton. *Fr.* Walam Olum; or, Red Score [of the Lenâpé], The [or The Wallam Olum; The Red Score or Painted History of the Lenni Lenape].

At first it seemed a swaying field of flowers. Archive Film Material. Ruth Fainlight. HP

At first it was as though you had passed. Many Wagons Ago. John Ashbery. HCAP

At first it was only an imperceptible quivering of. Hans Magnus Enzensberger. See The Divorce.

At first my mother would be shy. In the Ocean. Patricia Goedicke. NMM-2

At first nobody could bear the heat, like. In Andrea's Garden. Susan Hampton. BMAP

At first nothing is. Nothing Is. Sun-Ra. PoBA

At first she led them out onto the floor. The Dance. Irene McKinney. PBCAP

At first she turned the whole thing to a joke. Aleksandr Blok, *Russian.* TCRP, *tr. by* Geoffrey Thurley

At first, shy, he coiled himself around. The Young Vampire. Nina Cassian, *Romanian.* CEEP, *tr. by* Dorian, Marguerite and Elliott Urdang

At First Sight. Robert Graves. FaBoEE; OxBSP

At first the pig is as tiny as a walnut. Loneliness. Mekeel McBride. CMAP

At first the river's very small. The Growing River. Rodney Bennett. BoTP

At first the surprise. Dancing with God. Stephen Dunn. NIP-4

At first there was nothing. Then a closed space. Endymion. Thomas Kinsella. PBCIP

"At first there were men, all sorts of men, and not one at a time." Her Words from the Corner. Ory Bernstein, *Hebrew.* IP, *tr. by* Warren Bargad *and* Stanley F. Chyet

At first, there's a thin, bright Rider. Apocalypse Dub. Dennis Scott. HCP

At first those closest to you shot holes in you. Asylum. Breyten Breytenbach, *Afrikaans.* VCWP, *tr. by* Stephen Gray *and* A. J. Coetzee

At first we heard the jingling of her ornaments. Egyptian Dancer at Shubra. Bernard Spencer. NoAM

At first we see the tiny leaves. The Strawberry. Maggie Pogue Johnson. CBWP-4

At first when I heard the old song. I Heard the Old Song. B. W. Vilakazi, *Zulu.* PeSA

At five I knew at twelve. Cherry Bombs. Alice Fulton. NAmP90

At five in the afternoon. Lament for Ignacio Sánchez Mejías. Federico García Lorca, *Spanish.* OBVE, *tr. by* A. L. Lloyd; NAWM-2, *tr. by* Stephen Spender *and* J. L. Gili

At five in the morning. A Conversation Through the Door. Anna Swirszczynska, *Polish.* AF, *tr. by* Czeslaw Milosz

At five in the morning, as jolly as any. The Miner's Doom. *Unknown.* AmFP

At five this morn, when Phoebus raised his head. Tunbridge Wells. John Wilmot, 2d Earl of Rochester. OBSV

At Flores in the Azores Sir Richard Grenville lay. Tennyson. EBEvV; EBNV; OBWP *Fr.* The Revenge. EBVV; FaBoCh; FaPoR; PoRA

At Forty. A. K. Ramanujan. VCWP

At forty, a man's not yet old. Inscribed on the Arbor of the Old Drunkard (Tsui-weng-t'ing) at Ch'u-chou. Ou-yang Hsiu, *Chinese.* SuSp, *tr. by* Irving Y. Lo

At forty-six I am still the baby. Late Arrivals. Sybil Kollar. FFC

At Fotheringay. Robert Southwell. PoEL-2

(Decease, Release.) NoSic

At four in the morning the smoke of the forded river. While We Slept. David Wolff. TrJP

At four o'clock. Roosters. Elizabeth Bishop. ChIV-2; LiTM; NALW

At 4:30 AM/ she rose. Ntozake Shange. BoWoP *Fr.* For Colored Girls Who Have Considered Suicide When the Rainbow Is Enuf.

At four years Nature is mountainous. A Young Child and His Pregnant Mother. Delmore Schwartz. FiLi

At 14th Street and First Avenue. Strawberries in Mexico. Ron Padgett. SPE

At Francis Allen's on the Christmas Eve. Epic, The [Morte d'Arthur]. Tennyson. NAEL-2 *Fr.* Morte d'Arthur. EnVR

At Frank 'n' Helen's. Constance Urdang. PBCAP

At Fyvie's yetts there grows a flower. The Trumpeter of Fyvie. *Unknown.* ESPB; OxBB

At Galway Races. W. B. Yeats. IIP

At Gettysburg full anonymity. Yugoslav Cemetery. Celeste Turner Wright. WPE

At Glastonbury. Henry Kingsley. PoRA

At Gold Hill Monastery. Su Tung-p'o, *Chinese.* OHPC, *tr. by* Kenneth Rexroth

At Golgotha I stood alone. Edwin John Ellis. OBMV *Fr.* Himself.

At Graceland with a Six Year Old, 1985. David Wojahn. PBCAP *Fr.* Mystery Train: A Sequence.

At Grandfather's. Clara Doty Bates. OBCA

At Grass. Philip Larkin. HAP; OxBTC; RB; WeW-3

At Great Torrington, Devon. *Unknown.* FaBoEE

At Guaracara Park. Eric Roach. PBCV

At Gull Lake; August, 1810. Duncan Campbell Scott. NOBC

At half-past five—the earth cooling. Bachelor Farmer. Roger McDonald. CBAP

At Half past Three, a single Bird. Emily Dickinson. APN-2; MoAmPo; NAWM-2; OxBA

At Half Past Three in the Afternoon. Jon Stallworthy. EOEF

At Hallowmas, whan nights grow lang. Hallow-Fair. Robert Fergusson. OxBS

At hame it's hard to feel. (LL) Parley of Beasts. "Hugh MacDiarmid." ChIV-1; MoBrPo; MoP; NoAM; OBMV

At Harper's Ferry Just before the Attack. Edward W. Williams. AAP; CBCWP

At Harvard a randy old Dean. Limerick. *Unknown.* PeLi

At Henry's bier let some thing fall out well. John Berryman. NoP-4 *Fr.* Dream Songs.

At her departure his disdain return'd. Homer, *Greek.* OBVE, *tr. by* Dryden *Fr.* The Iliad.

At her doorway Mrs. Mayle. The Lavender Bush. Elizabeth Fleming. BoTP

At Her Fair Hands   Ode: "At her fair hands how have I grace entreated." Walter Davison. BoLoP

At Her Grave. Kuthaiyir, *Arabic.* ArPe, *tr. by* Omar S. Pound

At his cramped desk. Star-Fix. Marilyn Nelson Waniek. LTA; NAmP90

At His Execution. Rudyard Kipling. ChIV-2

At His Father's Grave. John Ormond. FaBoTw; OBWVE

At his last gig in horrid Amsterdam. Hayden Carruth. BAP-93

At home. Home. Kyudong Kim, *Korean.* CKP, *tr. by* Jaihiun Kim

At Home. Linda Pastan. CMAP

At Home. Christina Rossetti. VWP

At home, abroad, and everywhere. (LL) Another. Anne Bradstreet. LW; NAAL-3; OxBA; SCAP; WPE

At home alone, O Nomades. Home, Sweet Home, with Variations, III. Henry Cuyler Bunner. OBAL

At home at Annika's place. At Annika's Place. Siv Widerberg, *Swedish.* NTCP, *tr. by* Verne Moberg

At Home from Church. Sarah Orne Jewett. APAD; APN-2; ColAP

("But only of voice that sings.") (LL) ColAP

At home I loved to wear old clothes. Wang Chien. SuSp, *tr. by* William H. Nienhauser. *Fr.* Palace Poems.

At Home in Dakar. Margaret Danner. BlSi

At Home in Heaven. Robert Southwell. ESCV; EnVR

At home, in my flannel gown, like a bear to its floe. 90 North. Randall Jarrell. CoAP; FYAP; MT; NAAL-2; NOBA; NoAM; TAP; VCAP

At home in the damp hills of Champagne. M. François le Vaillant Recalls His Travels to the Interior Parts of Africa. Patrick Cullinan. PeSAV

At Home in the Summer Mountains. Yu Xuanji, *Chinese.* WPoS, *tr. by* Jane Hirshfield

At Home the Green Remains. John Figueroa. PBCV

At home the sea is in the town. The Sea Eats the Land at Home. Kofi Awoonor. PBMAP

At home we pray every morning, we. Religion. Gwendolyn Brooks. OxWW *Fr.* Ulysses.

At Horizon's End, Thinking of Li Po. Tu Fu, *Chinese.* SuSp, *tr. by* Eugene Eoyang

At Hsin-fêng an old man—four-score and eight;. The Old Man with the Broken Arm. Po Chü-i, *Chinese.* ChiP, *tr. by* Arthur Waley

At Hung-tung Mountain, the war-drums sounded. To the Filial Son, Ts'ui. Hsü Pen, *Chinese.* CoBLCP, *tr. by* Jonathan Chaves

At Ichiyiama / Boating on Lake Niu. Matsumoto Koyu-Ni, *Japanese.* WPJ, *tr. by* Kenneth Rexroth *and* Ikuko Atsumi

At It. Ronald Stuart Thomas. OxBC

At Ithaca. Hilda Doolittle. ColAP; VGW

At its fullest the moon. Moon. Alan Bold. SpW

At Jad Gate Pass mountain ridges several thousand-fold. Wang Ch'ang-ling. SuSp, *tr. by* Ronald C. Miao *Fr.* Following the Army on Campaign.

At Jonestown. Lucille Clifton. NAAAL

At Kenneth Burke's Place. William Carlos Williams. NOBA

At Kfar Kana. Charles Causley. TOF

At Kino Viejo, Mexico. Alberto A. Ríos. NoAM

At Kisheneff two wicked men. Russia's Resentment. Lizelia Augusta Jenkins Moorer. CBWP-3

At Lai Family Village, the spring is beautiful. Walking Outside the City Walls on the Day of the Cold Food Festival. Pien Kung, *Chinese*. CoBLCP, *tr. by* Jonathan Chaves

At lang last, sal I make bydan, *par. by* P. Hately Waddell. Bible, *O.T. See* Psalm 23.

At Lansdowne Bridge. Arthur Nortje. HBAPE

At Last. John Montague. PBCIP

At Last. Elizabeth Siddal. VWP

At last. Tanka. Miyazawa Kenji, *Japanese*. MJT, *tr. by* Makoto Ueda

At last a juggler is led out under the stars. The Initiate. W. S. Merwin. NNaP

At last, at last, unite them there! (LL) Qua Cursum Ventus. Arthur Hugh Clough. EBVVPR; OBEV

At last, by chance and guardian fancy led. Philip Freneau. NAAL-1; NAAL-3 *Fr.* The House of Night.

At last, dearest Louisa, I take up my pen to address you. Georgina Trevellyn to Luisa. Arthur Hugh Clough. EBVVPR *Fr.* Amours de Voyage. NOBVV

At last earnest sternness is transformed to sweet. Hatred Surely Does Not Kiss. Kaspar Stieler, *German*. GePo, *tr. by* George C. Schoolfield

At last free. Sumangalamata. WPoS

At last I can figure out the nature of that whisking sound. Fate in Incognito. Michael Benedikt. OBAL

At last I found the monastery. A young. Abstinence. Kenneth Rosen. AmPA

At last I put off love. He Abjures Love. Thomas Hardy. CBLP; OBNC

At last into opera on somebody's sandbar. Son, when you / clam, / Clam. (LL) Clamming. Reed Whittemore. NYBP; TAP

At last it came into her mind, the answer. The Precipice. Judith Wright. BMAP

At last I've seduced the *au pair*. Limerick. Cyril Ray. PeLi

At last love has come. I would be more ashamed. Sulpicia, *Latin*. BoWoP, *tr. by* Aliki *and* Willis Barnstone

At last, my old, inveterate foe. To Melancholy. Anne Finch, Countess of Winchilsea. WPE

At last, O thou serene retreat. To Retirement. Luís De León, *Spanish*. TrJP, *tr. by* Thomas Walsh

At last, on delicate feet. Sappho, *Greek*. InMo, *tr. by* Sam Hamill

At last she calls to mind where hangs a piece. Shakespeare. *See* Troy Depicted.

At last shee cals to mind where hangs a peece. Troy Depicted. Shakespeare. PBRV *Fr.* The Rape of Lucrece.

At last, so faire a ladie did I spie. Petrarch. *Fr.* Visions. AWP

At last that night the pounding. Clock. Edward Kamau Brathwaite. MoNo

At last the beef appears in sight. Edward Chicken. NOEC *Fr.* The Collier's Wedding.

At last the critic Toynbee wrote with ease. Auden in Old Age. Agnes Gergely, *Hungarian*. CEEP, *tr. by* Emery E. George

At last the dead man walked no more. Oscar Wilde. *See* The Ballad of Reading Gaol.

At Last the Secret Is Out. W. H. Auden. InPS-3

At last, the senses sharpen. All around. Postscript. R. L. Barth. CDa

At Last the Women are Moving. Genevieve Taggard. NMM-2

At last there came. Indian Summer. Hamlin Garland. APN-2

At last, there, when it turns out to be here. (LL) Crude Foyer. Wallace Stevens. LiTM; MeMAP

At last Wayman gets the girl into bed. Wayman in Love. Tom Wayman. NIP-4; NOBC

At last withdraw your cruelty. Sir Thomas Wyatt. SiPS

At last you yielded up the album, which. Lines on a Young Lady's Photograph Album. Philip Larkin. EnLoPo; HAP; OAEL-2

At least 100 seabirds attended my grandmother's funeral. My Grandmother's Funeral. Thomas Lux. WeW-3

At least a hundred times. For Edward Hicks. David Helwig. NOBC

At least as far as he is able. (LL) Whole Duty of Children. Robert Louis Stevenson. CTV; NBLV; OxBChV

At least I broke and stole that branch with love. (LL) For C. Philip Whalen. NeAP; VGW

At least I can offer that. / Com'mere, boy! (LL) Brass Spittoons. Langston Hughes. MoAmPo; NoAM; Poetr

At least I have the flowers of myself. Hilda Doolittle. NMM-2 *Fr.* Eurydice.

At least, my dear. Edna St. Vincent Millay. SAGP

At least the mechanics are honest. Ode to My Car. Gig Ryan. BMAP

At least they died of smoke and age and not some awful, active form. James Wright, Richard Hugo, the Vanishing Forests of the Pacific Northwest. Campbell McGrath. PaTW

At least—to pray—is left—is left. Emily Dickinson. APN-2; NCAP

At least we shall have descendants. (LL) To Pi Ssu Yao. Tu Fu, *Chinese*. BLT; OHPC, *tr. by* Kenneth Rexroth

At Lemmons. C. Day Lewis. FP

At length, by flight, I over-went the Pack. Francis Quarles. ESCV *Fr.* Emblems.

At length by so much importunity pressed. Lover, The; a Ballad. Lady Mary Wortley Montagu. ECWP; LW; NAEL-1; NoP-4; PEW

At length, my Lord, I have the bliss. Thomas Moore. OBSV *Fr.* The Fudge Family in Paris.

At length my soul the fatal union finds. Octavia Walsh. ECWP

At length nigh to the sea they drew. Edmund Spenser. *Fr.* Wood Of Error. AEP

At Length the Busy Day Is Done. Francis Hopkinson. AH

At length the finished garden to the view. Late Spring. James Thomson. GaP

At length the long-expected morning came. The Voyage. Denis Florence MacCarthy. TIRV *Fr.* The Voyage of St. Brendan.

At length the soft nocturnal minutes fly. The Bricklayer's Labours. Robert Tatersal. NOEC

At length the sucking jewels freeze. (LL) The Octopus. James Merrill. APo; CoAP

At length their long kiss severed, with sweet. D. G. Rossetti. *See* Nuptial Sleep.

At length their long kiss severed, with sweet smart. Nuptial Sleep. D. G. Rossetti. EBVV; EnVR; NAEL-2; NOBVV *Fr.* The House of Life.

At Length There Dawns the Glorious Day. Ozora Stearns Davis. AH

At length they came into a larger space. Edmund Spenser. *Fr.* The Cave of Mammon. PoEL-1 *Fr.* Wood Of Error. AEP

At length we have settled a pastor. Wanted, a Minister's Wife. *Unknown*. BLPA

At length with jostling, elbowing, and the aid. Byron. OBSV *Fr.* The Vision of Judgment. OAEL-2

At Les Deux Magots. Maura Dooley. LW

At Lindos. May Sarton. WPE

At Lord's. Francis Thompson. EBVV; OPOU; OxBSP; PeLV

At Loschwitz above the city. The Birch-Tree at Loschwitz. Amy Levy. TrJP

At low tide like this how sheer the water is. The Bight. Elizabeth Bishop. FaBoWP; HCAP; NAAL-2; NYBP; RB; VCAP

At Luca Signorelli's Resurrection of the Body. Jorie Graham. HCAP

At Ma-re Mount shall be kept holiday. (LL) The Poem: "Rise Oedipus, and if thou canst unfold." Thomas Morton. NAAL-3; SCAP

At Martian dawn. Sci-fi Horrorscopes. Geoffrey Summerfield. SpW

At Mass. Vachel Lindsay. VGW

At Mass. *Unknown, Irish*. BIrV, *tr. by* Robin Flower

At Matyne houre in midis of the nicht. Honour with Age. Walter Kennedy. OxBS

At Melville's Tomb. Hart Crane. HAP; MoAmPo; MoP; NAAL-2; NoAM; NoP-4; PoA; TAP; UnPo; VGW

At Memphis the horn'd bull told our friend. Tauromancy at Memphis. Diogenes Laertius, *Greek*. GrAn, *tr. by* Dudley Fitts

At midday like a diamond. Harbor. Henrikas Radauskas, *Lithuanian*. CEEP, *tr. by* Jonas Zdanys

At midday they looked up and saw their death. George Barker. ImPo; LiTM *Fr.* Pacific Sonnets.

At midnight, coming home, I passed a tiger. Coming Home Late at Night. Tu Fu, *Chinese*. BLT, *tr. by* J. P. Seaton

At midnight[,] Death dismissed the chancellor. Lines on the Death of Bismarck. John Jay Chapman. APN-2; PoEL-5

At midnight, flaking down like chromium. Closing Time. David Wagoner. NYBP

At midnight I noticed on my sheet a. Aleksei Eliseievich Kruchyonykh, *Russian*. TCRP, *tr. by* Albert C. Todd

At midnight, I wake to a breeze. Armed Forces. Lucy Lakides. CDa

At midnight I woke up [or awoke]. Clams. Rin Ishigaki, *Japanese*. PBWP, *tr. by* Hiroaki Sato

At midnight, in his guarded tent. Fitz-Greene Halleck. APN-1; HoPM *Fr.* Marco Bozzaris.

At midnight in the alley. The Tom-Cat. Don Marquis. PC; PoRA

At midnight, in the month of June. The Sleeper. Edgar Allan Poe. AmPP; MeMAP; NAAL-1; NAAL-3; NCAP; NOBA; OxBA; PAR; PoEL-4; TAP

At Midnight's Hour I Raised My Head. Henry David Thoreau. PoEL-4

At Midsummer. Norman Dubie. NoAM

At minus tide the music. Poke-Pole Fishing. Dennis Schmitz. AmPA

At Monday dawn, I climbed into my skin. Diary. David Wagoner. CoAP

At morning light the ark lay grounded fast. A Problem in History. Robert Wallace. CRP

At morning we all look out. Hedge Life. James Dickey. LCAP-2

At mo[o]st mischief. Sir Thomas Wyatt. SiPS

At Mother's After Many Years. Vladimir Holan. CEEP

At Mt. Auburn Cemetery. Diana Der Hovanessian. LoHo

At My Country Home in Chung-nan. Wang Wei, *Chinese*. CoBCP, *tr. by* Burton Watson

At my dear Land of Story-Books. (LL) The Land of Story-Books. Robert Louis Stevenson. ACTV; CTV; ChAP; FaBoBe; PWR

At my father's. George Swede. HA

At My Father's Grave. "Hugh MacDiarmid." GTBS-P

At My Father's House. Nancy Travis. ISC

At my father's wake. Desmet, Idaho, March 1969. Janet Campbell Hale. VoR

At my memory's uncertain dawn. The Turkey. Nikolai Stepanovich Gumilyov, *Russian*. TCRP, *tr. by* Simon Franklin

At My Mother's Bedside. Marcia Lee Masters. WPE

At My Nativity. Shakespeare. *Fr.* King Henry IV, Pt. I. NAEL-1

At my nativity / The front of heaven was full of fiery shapes. Henry IV. Shakespeare. OxBSn *Fr.* Henry IV.

At my touch the wild / braid of creation / trembles. (LL) The Snakes of September. Stanley Kunitz. AFr

At my windowpane a bird. That Is All I Heard. "Yehoash," *Yiddish*. TrJP, *tr. by* Isidore Goldstick

At Nature's Shrine. Henrietta Cordelia Ray. CBWP-3

At new moon on the crater / This summer. (LL) Burning Island. Gary Snyder. APSN; VCAP

At Night. Bella Akhatovna Akhmadulina, *Russian*. BoWoP, *tr. by* Daniel Halpern *and* Albert Todd

At night. Dennis Brutus. VCWP

At Night. Frances Darwin Cornford. MoBrPo

At Night. Elizabeth Jennings. OTCP

At Night. Alice Thompson Meynell. CII, OxAEP 2

At night and in the wind and the rain. Chaim Grade, *Yiddish*. HP

At night, as drough the mead I took my way. To Me. William Barnes. PoEL-4

At night at the hairdresser's. At the Hairdresser. Novica Tadic, *Serbo-Croatian*. CEEP; HSix, *tr. by* Charles Simic

At night atop Shou-hsiang Citadel, Hearing Tartar Flutes. Li Yi, *Chinese*. SuSp, *tr. by* Paul Kroll

At night, by the fire. Domination of Black. Wallace Stevens. AmPP; MoAmPo; OxBA

At night Chinamen jump. Poem. Frank O'Hara. CBNP; NOBA; NoAM; PmAP

At night, circling weightless, we dreamed of roses. Roses. Geoffrey Lehmann. BMAP *Fr.* Roses.

At Night, Hearing Someone Singing in the House Next Door. Harry Mathews, *Chinese*. CoBCP, *tr. by* Burton Watson

At night / he'd lie in bed. Louis B. Russell. Bruce Guernsey. InPK-6

At night I always think of Mickey. Dear Mickey. Dahlia Ravikovitch, *Hebrew*. IP, *tr. by* Warren Bargad *and* Stanley F. Chyet

At night I dreamt I was back in Ch'ang-an. Dreaming that I Went with Li and Yü to Visit Yüan Chên. Po Chü-i, *Chinese*. ChiP; FP, *tr. by* Arthur Waley

At night I follow bell and chant. Staying Overnight at Spirit-Source Temple. Wen Cheng-ming, *Chinese*. CoBLCP, *tr. by* Jonathan Chaves

At night I sit, uneasy and unhappy. To Yung-erh—Imitating a Work by Master Jade Stream. Li Tung-yang, *Chinese*. CoBLCP, *tr. by* Jonathan Chaves

At night, in my dream, I stoutly climbed a mountain. A Dream of Mountaineering. Po Chü-i, *Chinese*. BLT; ChiP, *tr. by* Arthur Waley

At night, in New York's Central Park. New York Elegy. Yevtushenko, *Russian*. TCRP, *tr. by* John Updike *and* Albert C. Todd

At night, in the fish-light of the moon, the dead wear our white shirts. Charles Wright. *Fr.* Homage to Paul Cézanne. VCAP

At Night in the Wood. Nancy M. Hayes. BoTP

At night in Vinton County a Satanic cult. Offering. Debra Allbery. PBCAP

At night, in west wind. Ma Chih-yüan. *Fr.* Two Poems to the Tune "Chin-tzu ching" The Sutra in Gold Characters. CoBLCP, *tr. by* Jonathan Chaves

At night, late, the men I loved began. Mauve. Leslie Ullman. NAmP90

At night / my mother opened a chest and took out. White Wedding Slippers. Anna Swirszczynska, *Polish*. AF, *tr. by* Czeslaw Milosz

At night, my Uncle Rufus. Night Starvation or The Biter Bit. Carey Blyton. FuFo

At night on my bed I longed for. Song. Bible, *O.T.* WPoS, *tr. by* Chana Bloch *and* Ariel Bloch *Fr.* The Song of Solomon.

At night somebody puts on my door. Carbon Paper. Martin Sorescu, *Romanian*. CEEP, *tr. by* Irina Livezeanu

At night the azure columns of the temple turn pale. Columns of the Temple of Olympian Zeus. Nicolas Calas, *Greek*. GrIP, *tr. by* Kimon Friar

At night the day is constantly woken up. Work. Andrei Codrescu. PmAP; SPE

At night the dead come down to the river to drink. The Dead. Susan Mitchell. WeT

At night the factories / struggle awake. Varick Street. Elizabeth Bishop. AFr

At Night the Jellyfish Unfold Their Veils. Virgil Teodorescu, *Romanian*. CEEP, *tr. by* Donald Eulert *and* Stefan Avadanei

At night the suburban boulevards are full of snow; the bandits are. War. Max Jacob, *French*. AF, *tr. by* Michael Brownstein

At night the wallpaper shakes. Margherita Guidacci, *Italian*. WPOW, *tr. by* Marina La Palma

At night they pound the vermilion newt. Painting Her Nails. Yang Wei-chen, *Chinese*. CoBLCP, *tr. by* Jonathan Chaves

At night to the blind man. Eyes. Vladimir Dmitrievich Tsybin, *Russian*. TCRP, *tr. by* Lubov Yakovleva

At night when Ale is in. Of Dronkennesse. Antimedon, *Greek*. OBCVT, *tr. by* George Turberville

At night when ale is in. Of Drunkenness. George Turberville. NBLV

At night when dying proceeds to sever all seams. Landscape of Screams. Nelly Sachs, *German*. NNPT; NYBP, *tr. by* Michael Roloff

At night while. Black Warrior. Norman Jordan. PoBA

At night you came and took my hand and we wandered together in. Dreaming of Yüan Chên. Po Chü-i, *Chinese*. ChiP, *tr. by* Arthur Waley

At Nightfall. Charles Hanson Towne. BLPA; FaBoBe

(Nightfall.) PoTolIc

At nightfall the autumn woods cry out. Grodek. Georg Trakl, *German*. PeFWW, *tr. by* Michael Hamburger

At nightfall, when the inquisitive elves in elf-pants. The Lunatic of Lindley Meadow. August Kleinzahler. PmAP

At Nigitazu we wait for the moon. Princess Nukada, *Japanese*. WPJ, *tr. by* Kenneth Rexroth *and* Ikuko Atsumi

At nine I knew what Jesus would do. Uncle. Julia Kasdorf. PBCAP

At nine in the morning there passed a church. Faintheart in a Railway Train. Thomas Hardy. CBLP; CTC; EnLoPo

At Nine Rivers, in the tenth year, in winter—heavy snow. Releasing a Migrant 'Yen' (Wild Goose). Po Chü-i, *Chinese*. ChiP, *tr. by* Arthur Waley

At noon, I leave my clothes out to dry. Drying Clothes. Yang Wan-li, *Chinese*. SuSp, *tr. by* Jonathan Chaves

At noon, in the dead centre of a faith. Desertmartin. Tom Paulin. CIP-2; PBCIP; PNI

At noon in the desert a panting lizard. At the Bomb Testing Site. William Stafford. CoAP; ColAP; LiTM; NIP-4; NoAM; OBWP; Poetr; RB

At noon in the garden on a throne of wood. Royal Progress. Antonin Bartusek, *German*. CEEP, *tr. by* Ewald Osers

At noon sneaky. Cold Lunch. William Corbett. PmAP

At noon they talk of evening and at evening. Cypresses. Robert Francis. LCAP-2

At noon, Tithonus, withered by his singing. The Wedding. Conrad Potter Aiken. CMoP; TAP

At noon today, I woke from a nightmare. Mexico, 1940. Ai. NoAM

At North Farm. John Ashbery. ColAP; HCAP; PoE; Poetr

At once, and he died looking towards my face. (LL) Dream. Richard Watson Dixon. EBEV; NOBVV; PeVV; SCGP

At once mammalian and reptilian. (LL) For An Amorous Lady. Theodore Roethke. LoP; NBLV

At once whatever happened starts receding. Whatever Happened? Philip Larkin. Son

At once with him they rose. Hell. Milton. *Fr.* Book II. FHYEP; NAEL-1; OxAEP-1 *Fr.* Paradise Lost.

At once with resolution held. John Trumbull. AmPP *Fr.* M'Fingal.

At one glance / I loved you. Mihri Hatun, *Turkish*. PBWP, *tr. by* Tâlat S. Halman

At 100 Mile House the cowboys ride in rolling. The Cariboo Horses. Alfred Wellington Purdy. HeIP-4; NOBC

At one the wind rose. Night-Music. Philip Larkin. InPS-3

At our gate he groaneth, groaneth. At Our Golden Gate. Joaquin Miller. APN-2

At Our Golden Gate. Joaquin Miller. APN-2

At our hearts? (LL) At April. Angelina Weld Grimké. GT; NMM-2

At Pakiri Beach. David Mitchell. PeNZ

At Paris it was, at the Opera there. Aux Italiens. "Owen Meredith." BLPA; FaBoBe

At Parting. Duoduo, *Chinese*. AF, *tr. by* Gregory Lee *and* John Cayley

At Parting. Ho Sun, *Chinese*. CoBCP, *tr. by* Burton Watson

At Parting. Edith Nesbit. OBGa

At Parting. Anne Ridler. APAD; LW

At Peach Blossom Bank is Peach Blossom Retreat. Song of Peach Blossom Retreat. T'ang Yin, *Chinese*. CoBLCP, *tr. by* Jonathan Chaves

At Pei-mang how they rise to Heaven. The Desecration of the Han Tombs. Chang Tsai, *Chinese*. ChiP, *tr. by* Arthur Waley

At Penshurst [Another]. Edmund Waller. BeJo; OAEL-1

   ("Had *Dorothea* liv'd when mortals made.") PBRV

   ("Then for a pardon that he dares admire.") (LL) PBRV

At Penshurst ("While in the park I sing, the listning deer"). Edmund Waller. BeJo

At Perigord near to the wall. A Perigord pres del muralh. Bertrans de Born, *Provençal*. CTC, *tr. by* Ezra Pound

At Piccadilly Circus. Vivian de Sola Pinto. OBMV

At Polwart on the Green. Polwart on the Green. Allan Ramsay. NOEC

At present / soup dishes serve us as mess tins. From the War. Aleksandr Petrovich Mezhirov, *Russian*. TCRP, *tr. by* Deming Brown

At Puri, the crows. Taste for Tomorrow. Jayanta Mahapatra. VCWP

At Quincey's moat the squandering village ends. Almswomen. Edmund Blunden. OBMV; OxBTC

At rest among my dearest dead. (LL) The Palanquin. Charles Marie René Leconte de Lisle, *French*. FLP; LoP, *tr. by* Alistair Elliot

At Rest from the Grim Place. Arthur Nortje. PBMAP

At Rest in the Blast. Marianne Moore. MoAmPo

At Robert Fergusson's Grave[, October 1962]. Robert Garioch. FaBoTC; OxBS

At Rochecoart / Where the hills part. Provincia Deserta. Ezra Pound. OxBA

At Saint Patrick's Purgatory. Donnchadh Mor O'Dala, *Irish*. TIRV, *tr. by* Sean O'Faolain

At Sainte-Marguerite. Trumbull Stickney. APN-2; OxBA

At Saxman, the totems slash down. The Circle of Totems. Peggy Shumaker. PBCAP

At Scot Gas, Darnestown Road. Rednecks. Martín Espada. BAP-96

At Sea. Richard Hovey. APN-2

At Sea. Yona Wallach, *Hebrew*. IP, *tr. by* Warren Bargad *and* Stanley F. Chyet

At Set of Sun. "George Eliot." PoToHe

At 7 a.m. you tilt your face to a shaft. The Wildebeest of Carmine Street. Edmund Pennant. EC3

At seven I dreamed again and again. On Alabama Ave., Paterson, NJ, 1954. Rachel De Vries. UnSA

At seven, when I go to bed. A Child's Thought. Robert Louis Stevenson. BoTP

At seven you just nick it. A Public Dinner. Thomas Hood. OBCoV

At seventeen I've come to read a poem. Twelve O'Clock. Carolyn Kizer. PuP-17

At Shagger's funeral there wasn't much to say. Bruce Dawe. NOBAu

At sight of sparkling Bowls or beauteous Dames. Verses in Baretti's Commonplace Book. Samuel Johnson. OxAEP-1

At silo filling time the air was similarly wet. Silo Treading. Bruce Beaver. BMAP

At six A.M. the log cabins. Moose in the Morning, Northern Maine. Mona Van Duyn. ColAP

At six o'clock, most people. Stay with Me. Garrett Kaoru Hongo. WeT

At six years old I had before mine eyes. Old Man. James Henry. NOBVV

At Sixteen. Ann Darr. DeD; LW

At sixteen I came West, riding. A Living Pearl. Kenneth Rexroth. LiTM

At sixty I, Dionysios of Tarsos, lie here. *Unknown, Greek*. GrAn, *tr. by* Peter Jay

At sixty, it might be well to start. The Collector. Desiré Flynn. BrRo

At slammed door and smoker's cough in the hall. (LL) Docker. Seamus Heaney. HeIP-4; IIP; MoP; NOIV; Poetr

At so grotesque a blunder. (LL) George III. Edmund Clerihew Bentley. CBNP; NOBL; OxBoLi; PeLV

At some late day Unto himself again. (LL) Music. Henry David Thoreau. APN-1; PAR

At Some Lone Alehouse. Matthew Arnold. *Fr.* The Scholar-Gipsy. EBEV; EBVV; EBVVPR; EnVR; FHYEP; HAP; ImPo; NAEL-2; NOBE; NOBVV; OAEL-2; OBEV; OBNC; OxAEP-1; PoE; PoEL-5; SCGP; TFi

At spirit séances in Queen's. Limerick. Morris Gilbert Bishop. PeLi

At stated .ic times. Composed in the Composing Room. Franklin Pierce Adams. NIP-4; OBAL

At Su Terrace Viewing the Past. Li Po, *Chinese*. CoBCP, *tr. by* Burton Watson

At sun up I am up. Angel Butcher. Philip Levine. ColAP

At Sunrise. Rosa Zagnoni Marinoni. PoToHe

At Sunset. Ivy O. Eastwick. BoTP

At Sunset. Henrietta Cordelia Ray. CBWP-3

At Sunset. Margaret Elizabeth Munson Sangster. *See* The Sin of Omission.

At sunset from the top of the stair watching. Otranto. Barbara Guest. FTOS

At Tauba's death I swore. Lamenting Tauba. Laila Akhyaliyya, *Arabic*. BoWoP, *tr. by* Willis Barnstone

At tea in cocktail weather. Publisher's Party. Phyllis McGinley. OBAL

At ten a clock, when I the fire rake. Epigram. Francis Daniel Pastorius. SCAP

At ten A.M. the young housewife. The Young Housewife. William Carlos Williams. ColAP; HeIP-4; NAAL-2; TAP

At ten I wanted fame. I had a comb. Behind Grandma's House. Gary Soto. UnSA

At th' utter Porch and evn in Orcus Jaws. Hell's gate. Virgil, *Latin*. OBCVT, *tr. by* Sir John Harington

At That Moment. Raymond R. Patterson. PoBA

At that time. David Diop. *See* The Vultures.

At th'Calends, puts all out againe. Horace. *See* The Praises of a Country Life.

At The Abbey Theatre. W. B. Yeats. Son

At the alder-darkened brink. Hamlen Brook. Richard Wilbur. VCAP; WeW-3

At the Algonquin. Howard Moss. Poetsp

At the Altar. Robert Lowell. InPK-6 *Fr.* Between the Porch and the Altar.

At the Altar-Rail. Thomas Hardy. MoBrPo *Fr.* Satires of Circumstance in Fifteen Glimpses.

At the "Atlantic" Dinner, December 15, 1874. Oliver Wendell Holmes. OBCoV

At the Back of Progress. . . . Taslima Nasrin, *Bengali*. VCWP, *tr. by* Carolyne Wright *and* Mohammad Nurul Huda

At the back of the bookshop a Karate expert. Enzensberger at 'Exiles'. John Tranter. BMAP

At the back of the houses there is the wood. The House in the Wood. Randall Jarrell. LCAP-2

At the Back of the North Wind. George Macdonald.

   Where did You Come From, Baby Dear? ACTP

   ("God thought about you, and so I am here.") (LL) ACTP

At the backyard fence. Michael Dudley. HA

At the Badr Trench. Safiya bint Musafir, *Arabic*. WPOW, *tr. by* Bridget Connelly *and* Deirdre Lashgari

At the Ball! Charles Henry Webb. OBAL

At the Ball Game. William Carlos Williams. CMoP; MoP; NOBA; NoAM; OxBA; PoE

At the Band Concert. John Malcolm Brinnin. PoA

At the beginning. Akiko Yosano, *Japanese*. OHMPJ, *tr. by* Kenneth Rexroth

At the beginning I noticed. A Stone Diary. Pat Lowther. NOBC

At the beginning of winter a cold spirit comes. *Unknown, Chinese*. ChiP, *tr. by* Arthur Waley; BoWoP, *tr. by* Arthur Waley

At the big trumpet, we must all put on. Rise and Shine. Richmond Lattimore. NYBP; Poetr

At the black canvas of estrangement. The Jewish Bride. Paul Durcan. BiHa

At the blackboard I had missed. Zimmer's Head Thudding against the Blackboard. Paul Zimmer. PBCAP

At the Bomb Testing Site. William Stafford. CoAP; ColAP; LiTM; NIP-4; NoAM; OBWP; Poetr; RB

   ("Under a sky that never cared less.") (LL) ColAP

At the bottom. David Lloyd. HA

At the break of day I come to an old temple. A Visit to the Broken Hill Temple. Ch'ang Chien, *Chinese*. SuSp, *tr. by* Joseph J. Lee

At the bridal bed of star-crossed Petalê. The Lost Bride. Antiphanes, *Greek*. GrAn, *tr. by* Dudley Fitts

At the brim, at the lip. Close. Robert Duncan. PmAP

At the British Museum. Richard Aldington. MoBrPo

At the British War Cemetery, Bayeux. Charles Causley. NAEL-2; NoP-4; OBWP; OxBC; PoWW

At the brow of a hill a fair shepherdess dwelt. The Lass of the Hill. Mary Jones. ECWP

At the calends [*or* th'calends], puts all out again. (LL) The Praises of a Country Life. Horace, *Latin*. OBVE; SeCP, *tr. by* Ben Jonson

At the Carnival. Anne Spencer. BlSi; NAAAL

   ("I implore Neptune to claim his child today!") (LL) NAAAL

At the Cascade. Henrietta Cordelia Ray. CBWP-3

At the Castle. Jerome Rothenberg. FTOS

At the Cave. Artur Miedzyrzecki, *Polish*. PoSu, *tr. by* Stanislaw Baranczak *and* Clare Cavanagh

At the Cavour. Arthur Symons. NOBVV; OxBSP

At the Cedars. Duncan Campbell Scott. NOBC

At the Cemetery, Walnut Grove Plantation, South Carolina, 1989. Lucille Clifton. LoL

At the center of the earth. Song. *Unknown, Chippewa Indian.* STP, *tr. by* Jerome Rothenberg

At the ceremony of *Emobo.* Ceremony. Kattie M. Cumbo. BlSi

At the Chiang-ning River Mouth. Wang An-shih, *Chinese.* SuSp, *tr. by* Jan W. Walls

At the Closed Gate of Justice. James David Corrothers. NAAAL

At the Convent Gate. Charlotte Mew. VWP

At the Corner of the World. Tu Fu, *Chinese.* PLT, *tr. by* A. C. Graham

At the corner of Wood Street, when daylight appears. The Reverie of Poor Susan. Wordsworth. GTBS-P; OxBoLi

At the country inn, thousands of peach trees. Inscribed on a Painting. T'ang Yin, *Chinese.* CoBLCP, *tr. by* Jonathan Chaves

At the crack of dawn, Monday stands beside you. Monday. Vijaya Mukhopadhyay, *Bengali.* OMIP, *tr. by* Sunil B. Ray *and* Carolyne Wright *and* Vijaya Mukhopadhyay

At the crest of the arch of the timbrel. Chrysoberyl: The Eye of the Cat. Felicity Bast. PC

At the Crossroads. Harvey Gross. PFE

At the Crossroads. Thomas Kinsella. NoAM

At the Crossroads. Bill Knott. PBCAP

At the cry of the first bird. The Crucifixion. *Unknown, Irish.* TIRV, *tr. by* Kuno Meyer

At the Dark Hour. Paul Dehn. BoLoP

At the dark street corner. Guilt, Desire and Love. James Baldwin. GLP

At the dawn I seek Thee. Morning Song. Solomon ibn Gabirol, *Hebrew.* TrJP, *tr. by* Nina Davis Salaman

At the dawn of your life, you ate gruel. Cheng Hsieh. *Fr.* Mourning for My Son Jun-erh. CoBLCP, *tr. by* Jonathan Chaves

At the dawning of our youth. Poetograd. Nikolai Ivanovich Glazkov, *Russian.* TCRP, *tr. by* Daniel Weissbort

At the day camp years ago where we drove. Dawn. Betsy Sholl. LTA

At the dead of night by the side of the Sea. The Sea-Side Cave. Alice Cary. APN-2; ColAP

At the demolishing, this seat. To My Lord Fairfax. Andrew Marvell. NOSC *Fr.* Upon Appleton House [To My Lord Fairfax]. FaBoPV; GeHe; SeCP

At the Discharge of Cannon Rise the Drowned. Hubert Witheford. PeNZ

At the Door. Lillie Fuller Merriam. PoToHe

At the door of Mercy Sighing. Thomas Mackellar. AH

At the Door of the Native Studies Director. Robert H. Davis. HATNAP

At the Doors. "Der Nistor," *Yiddish.* TrJP, *tr. by* Joseph Leftwich

At the Draper's. Thomas Hardy. MoBrPo; OxBM *Fr.* Satires of Circumstance in Fifteen Glimpses.

At the earliest ending of winter. Not Ideas about the Thing but the Thing Itself. Wallace Stevens. HAP; HCAP; LCAP-2; MeMAP; SAmP; TAP

At the Edge. Denise Levertov. NAAL-2

At the edge. Alexis Rotella. HA

At the edge of all the ages. The Song of Finis. Walter De la Mare. MoBrPo

At the Edge of the Jungle. Patrick Lane. NOBC

At the edge of the page the pen. Houses. Dan Pagis, *Hebrew.* IP, *tr. by* Warren Bargad *and* Stanley F. Chyet

At the edge of the precipice I become logical. George Swede. HA

At the edge of the woods where people. At Woods' Edge. Ory Bernstein, *Hebrew.* IP, *tr. by* Warren Bargad *and* Stanley F. Chyet

At the edge of the world, a traveler long used to grief. My Boat Moored on a River. Yen Yü, *Chinese.* SuSp, *tr. by* Irving Y. Lo

At the Edge of Town. William Stafford. NNaP

At the Edge of Winter. Ellen Bryant Voigt. WeT

At the Electronic Frontier. Miguel Algarin. UnSA

At the End. Richard Ryan. PBCIP

At the end. Alice Walker. *See* Good Night, Willie Lee, I'll See You in the Morning.

At the end a / "The Prisoner of Zenda." The Prisoner of Zenda. Richard Wilbur. NBLV; OBCoV

At the end of a crazy-moon night. Lal Ded, *Kashmiri.* WPoS, *tr. by* Coleman Barks

At the end of a day that's rubble around me. A Letter. Albert Goldbarth. PuP-15

At the end of a freight train rolling away. Late Lights in Minnesota. Ted Kooser. BLT

At the end of a melancholy world. The End of the World. João Cabral de Melo Neto, *Portuguese.* VCWP, *tr. by* James Wright

At the end of delight, one. Limit. Diane Ward. FTOS

At the end of his act. Road Show. Geoff Page. BMAP

At the end of January you will see again. Starting 1973: What to Do Now that Peace Has Been Announced. Joseph Cady. CDa

At the end of life paralysis or those creeping teeth. Bog and Candle. Robert David Fitzgerald. CBAP

At the end of my suffering. The Wild Iris. Louise Glück. ColAP

At the end of myself pencil tip. George Swede. HA

At the End of Spring. Po Chü-i, *Chinese.* ChiP, *tr. by* Arthur Waley

At the End of Spring. Yü Hsüan-chi, *Chinese.* BoWoP, *tr. by* Geoffrey Waters

At the end of Tarriers' Lane, which was the street. Wm. Brazier. Robert Graves. NOBL

At the End of the Affair. Maxine W. Kumin. TAP

At the end of the bough! Sweet Apple. James Stephens. CMoP

At the end of the garden walk. The Cold Green Element. Irving Layton. NOBC; NoP-4

At the end of the journey we built. Journeys. Meg Campbell. PeNZ

At the end of the road, in a drab chapel. Mother Tongue. Jon Stallworthy. NoAM

At the end of the row. The Objection to Being Stepped On. Robert Frost. NBLV; OBCoV

At the end of the war I arose. The Driver. James Dickey. VGW

At the End of the Weekend. Ted Kooser. PBCAP

At the Entrance. Douglas Stewart. CBAP

At the equinox when the earth was veiled in a late rain, wreathed with wet poppies, waiting spring. Continent's End. Robinson Jeffers. AWP

At the Executed Murderer's Grave. James Wright. HCAP; VCAP

At the exhausted lovers where they sleep. (LL) But That Is Another Story. Donald Justice. NoP-4

At the factory I worked. Mexicans Begin Jogging. Gary Soto. LTA

At the family sacrifice don't forget to let your father know. (LL) To Show My Sons. Lu Yu, *Chinese.* CoBCP, *tr. by* Burton Watson

At the feast of Belshazzar and a thousand of his lords. The Handwriting on the Wall. Knowles Shaw. BLPA

At the feet o' Jesus. Feet O' Jesus. Langston Hughes. I3C

At the Ferry. U. A. Fanthorpe. FaBoWP

At the field's edge. The White Hare. Lilian Bowes-Lyon. OxBTC

At the Fillmore. Philip Levine. NNaP

At the first turning of the second stair. T. S. Eliot. NOBA *Fr.* Ash Wednesday [or Ash-Wednesday]. MoAmPo; OxBA; VGW

At the Fishhouses. Elizabeth Bishop. CoAP; FaBoWP; GEA; HAP; HCAP; LCAP-2; LiTM; NAAL-2; NALW; NYBP; PoPoPo; PoRA; Poetr; VCAP

At the Flyfisher's Shack. Sydney Lea. RA

At the font the black marble. Baroque. Marie-Claire Bancquart, *French.* MFP, *tr. by* Martin Sorrell

At the foot of the Cathedral of Burgos. Autobiography. Gloria Fuertes, *Spanish.* PBWP, *tr. by* Philip Levine

At the foot of yonder mountain where the fountains do flow. The Green Briar Shore. *Unknown.* AmFP

At the Fountain. Marcabrun, *French.* AWP, *tr. by* Harriet Waters Preston

At the Frick. Anthony Hecht. GS

At the frontier the long train slows to a stop. The Frontier. John Hewitt. BlrV

At the full face of the forest lies our little town. To the Red Lory. John Shaw Neilson. NOBAu

At the Gate. Chaucer. *Fr.* Troilus and Criseyde [or Criseide]. EnVB

At the gate of old Granada, when all its bolts are barred. The Lamentation for Celin. *Unknown, Spanish.* AWP, *tr. by* John Gibson Lockhart

At the Gate of the Valley. Zbigniew Herbert, *Polish.* PoSu, *tr. by* Czeslaw Milosz

At the Gates. Kofi Awoonor. PBMAP; VCWP *Fr.* Night of My Blood (1971).

At the gates of Zion, over Kedron. Ivan Alekseievich Bunin, *Russian.* TCRP, *tr. by* Simon Franklin

At the gathered ends of rooty paths. The Island in the Evening. Fairfield Porter. PoA

At the Grave of Hazel Hall. Sandra McPherson. NMM-2

At the Grave of Henry Vaughan. Siegfried Sassoon. CMoP; GTBS-P

At the Great Wall of China. Edmund Blunden. GTBS-P

At the Grey Round of the Hill. W. B. Yeats. RB

At the Hairdresser. Novica Tadic, *Serbo-Croatian.* CEEP; HSix, *tr. by* Charles Simic

At the Half-Note Café. Ira Sadoff. NAmP90

At the Hammersmith Palais. Alan Riddell. NOBAu

At the head of a march to the last new Jerusalem. (LL) Lowell. James Russell Lowell. AmPP; NOBA; OxBA; TAP

At the heart of all creation. The Emperor of China Speaks. Hugo von Hofmannsthal, *German.* GaP, *tr. by* Michael Hamburger

At the heart Write: how silent. / Yes. (LL) Starvation Camp near Jaslo. Wislawa Szymborska, *Polish.* AF, *tr. by* Grazyna Drabik *and* Austin Flint

At the Heng-ts'ui Pavilion of Fa-hui Monastery. Su Shih, *Chinese*. SuSp, *tr*. by Irving Y. Lo

At the Holi festival of color. Mirabai, *Hindi*. BoWoP, *tr*. by Willis Barnstone *and* Usha Nilsson

At the hour shaped for him Scyld departed. The Funeral of Scyld Shefing. *Unknown*. EEP, *tr*. by Alexander, Michael *Fr*. Beowulf. OAEL-1, *tr*. by Charles W. Kennedy; ASW, *tr*. by Kevin Crossley-Holland

At the Iga: Franklin, New Hampshire. Jane Kenyon. PuP-15

At the Indian Killer's Grave. Robert Lowell. NOBA; VGW

At the instant of drowning he invoked the three sisters. The Three Fates. Rosemary Dobson. BMAP; BoWoP

At the Jaffé Memorial Fountain, Botanic Gardens. Frank Ormsby. CIP-2

At the Keyhole. Walter De la Mare. MoBrPo

At the Klamath Berry Festival. William Stafford. InPK-6

At the lacquered table—my recent calligraphy. Wen Cheng-ming. CoBLCP, *tr*. by Jonathan Chaves *Fr*. The Chung-i Temple.

At the Lake—Remembering My Dead Son, Yü. Pien Kung, *Chinese*. CoBLCP, *tr*. by Jonathan Chaves

At the Lakehouse. Brighde Mullins. BAP-94

At the large foot of a fair hollow tree. The Country-Mouse. Abraham Cowley, *after the Latin of* Horace. OBVE; SeCP

At the last, tenderly. The Last Invocation. Walt Whitman. MoAmPo; OBEV; OxBA; PAR; PoEL-5; SAGP

At the last, your hand feels steady. (LL) After Dark. Adrienne Rich. LCAP-2; LiTM; MoLi; VGW

At the lectern. Toki Zenmaro, *Japanese*. MJT, *tr*. by Makoto Ueda

At the left edge of the field of vision, a stooped woman dumps. Apocatastasis Foretold in the Shape of a Canvas of Smoke. T. R. Hummer. BAP-95

At the long tables of time. The Jugs. Paul Celan, *German*. HP; OBVE, *tr*. by Christopher Middleton

At the Loom. Robert Duncan. VGW *Fr*. Passages.

At the Mass Graveyard. Eve Shelnutt. CMAP

At the Metro: Old Irrelevant Images, *(for Blaise)*. Jack A. Mapanje. PBMAP

At the Metropolitan Zoo. Shame. Sang Ku, *Korean*. CKP, *tr*. by Jaihiun Kim

At the mid hour of night, when stars are weeping, I fly. Echo. Thomas Moore. GLoP; GTBS-P; LBC; NOBE; OBEV; OBNC; PoEL-4

At the midnight in the silence of the sleep-time. Epilogue. Robert Browning. EnVR; NAEL-1; NOBE; OBNC

At the Moated Grange. Shakespeare. NOBE *Fr*. Measure for Measure. (Seals of Love.)

(Song.) PoEL-2

At the Monument to Pierre Louÿs. Richard Howard. EOEF; VCAP

At the Mountain of the Mysterious Tomb Visiting Master P'ou. Wu Wei-yeh, *Chinese*. CoBLCP, *tr*. by Jonathan Chaves

At the mouth of Wu-ling Stream. Riding a Boat on Wu-ling Stream. Tao-chi, *Chinese*. CoBLCP, *tr*. by Jonathan Chaves

At the Movie: Virginia, 1956. Ellen Bryant Voigt. LTA; NoAM

At the movies i always love the look. Sunday Matinee. Sybil Kollar. FFC

At the muezzin's call for prayer. Ad Coelum. Harry Romaine. BLPA; FaBoBe

At the Nature-Strip. Judith Rodriguez. CBAP

At the New Year. Kenneth Patchen. LiTM *Fr*. Eight Early Poems.

At the news from Fal's high plain I cannot sleep. Geoffrey Keating, *Irish*. NOIV, *tr*. by Thomas Kinsella

At the ninth month, our imperial soldiers ford distant waters. A Song of Distant Waters. Wen T'ing-yün, *Chinese*. SuSp, *tr*. by William R. Schultz

At the northe ende of Selver White. *Unknown*. MiEL

At the Nuclear Rally. Laura Boss. UnSA

At the Office Early. Ted Kooser. PBCAP

At the officers' table, for half an hour afterwards, port. Class Incident from Graves. Alan Brownjohn. OxBTC

At the old concert hall on the Bowery. She Is More to Be Pitied than Censured. William B. Gray. BLPA

At the onset of its sprint, the blazing circle climbs straight ahead. Brush Fire. Fily-Dabo Sissoko, *French*. NegPo, *tr*. by Ellen Conroy Kennedy

At the open grave. Nicholas Virgilio. HA

At the orgy I humped twenty-two. Limerick. *Unknown*. PeLi

At the outset she still carried it quite well. Mary's Visitation. Rilke, *German*. GI, *tr*. by David Curzon *and* Will Alexander Washburn

At the palace of rocks, spring clouds white. Palace of Rocks, The. Yüan Chieh, *Chinese*. SuSp, *tr*. by William H. Nienhauser

At the park. Returned from California. Simon J. Ortiz. HATNAP

At the Party. W. H. Auden. OxBSP

At the Pauwels. Diane Glancy. CRP

At the place of light. Prophetic Powers. *Unknown*, *Ojibwa Native American*. APN-2, *tr*. by Henry Rowe Schoolcraft

At the Place of the Sea. Annie Johnson Flint. BLPA

At the Planning Commission. Barbara Meyn. EC3

At the Playground. William Stafford. TLR

At the Poem Society a black-haired man stands up to say. Fresh Air. Kenneth Koch. CAPP-1; NNaP; NeAP

At the Poem Society a black-haired man stands up to say. Kenneth Koch. *Fr*. Fresh Air. CAPP-1; NNaP; NeAP

At the point of shining feathers. The Night a Sailor Came to Me in a Dream. Diane Wakoski. TAP; VGW

At the Polo-Ground. Sir Samuel Ferguson. NOIV

At the Poorhouse. Federico García Lorca. PFTM

At the Portals of the Future. Lines. Frances Ellen Watkins Harper. APN-2; PAR

At the post house lodge, plum flowers scattering. Tune: Treading on Grass. Ou-yang Hsiu, *Chinese*. CoBCP, *tr*. by Burton Watson

At the Protestant Museum. Hugh Maxton. CIP-2

At the quarry's edge. King Lear. Peter Huchel, *German*. PoSu, *tr*. by Michael Hamburger

At the Record Hop. Wanda Coleman. NAAAL

At the Red Rock House it grows. Last Tsĕ' ni Gisĭ' n, or Song in the Rock. *Unknown*. *Fr*. The Night Chant. APN-2, *tr*. by Washington Matthews

At the rest stop on the way to Mississippi. The Love of Travellers. Angela Jackson. PuP-14

At the rise of summer a hundred beasts and trees. The Beginning of Summer. Po Chü-i, *Chinese*. ChiP, *tr*. by Arthur Waley

At the river-bend. Larry Gates. HA

At the River Tower Parting from My Younger Brother, Fu-ling. Wu Wei-yeh, *Chinese*. CoBLCP, *tr*. by Jonathan Chaves

At the roots of clouds a cutworm hollowing. Five Dawn Skies in November. David Wagoner. VCAP

At the round earth's imagined corners, blow. Blow Your Trumpets. Donne. ChIV-2; ClHu; EBEV; FHYEP; HAP; HeIP-4; ImPo; InPS-3; MeLP; NAEL-1; NAWM-1; NOBE; NOSC; OAEL-1; OxAEP-1; PeECV; PoE; PoEL-2; SCGP; SeCP; Son; TFi; TOF *Fr*. Holy Sonnets. ESCV *Fr*. Holy Sonnets.

At the same time. (LL) Prodigy. Charles Simic. VCAP

At the same time, a cause for sorrow and pain. (LL) Imitating the Old Poems. T'ao Ch'ien, *Chinese*. CoBCP, *tr*. by Burton Watson

At the San Francisco Airport. Yvor Winters. AiP; HeIP-4; InPK-6; NIP-4; NOBA

At the Sea's Edge. Gwen Harwood. CBAP

At the Seaside [*or* Sea-Side]. Robert Louis Stevenson. NTCP; OxBChV; TLR; WHSW

(At the Seaside.) CTV

At the Seaside. Robert Louis Stevenson. *See* At the Seaside [*or* Sea-Side].

At the siege of Belle Isle. (LL) At the siege of Belle Isle. Mother Goose. OxNR; ReMoGo

At the siege of Belle Isle. Mother Goose. OxNR; ReMoGo

At the sight of the beauty that greets them, for the charm they have broken. (LL) London Snow. Robert Bridges. CH; CMoP; EBEV; EBEvV; EBVV; GTBS-P; LiTM; MoBrPo; MoP; NOBE; NOBVV; NoAM; OAEL-2; OBNC; OxAEP-2; OxBTC; PoEL-5; TFi

At the Sign-Painter's. Jared Carter. FYAP

At the Slackening of the Tide. James Wright. UnPo; VGW

At the Smithville Methodist Church. Stephen Dunn. NAmP90

At the song's beginning. Violet. John Hollander. FYAP

At the sorrow of my sweet pipings. (LL) Hymn of Pan. Shelley. FaBoCh; OBEV; PoEL-4

At the spraygun stands large heroic Ted. Portrait of a Gentleman. Ruth Pitter. WPN

At the spring. To Light. Linda Hogan. HATNAP

At the stormy moment of dawn. Swifts. Philippe Jaccottet, *French*. VCWP, *tr*. by Derek Mahon

At the street bookstall in Karlsruhe, my father. Homage to Ferd. Holthausen. Gwen Harwood. NOBAu

At the summit of perception. Prince Henry the Navigator. Sydney Clouts. PeSA

At the Sutra Chanting of Her Dead Daughter. Lady Izumi, *Japanese*. WPJ, *tr*. by Kenneth Rexroth *and* Ikuko Atsumi

At the Swings. Henry Taylor. MT

At the Telephone Club. Henri Coulette. CoAP

At the third hour always. Rain. Paul Murray. BIrV

At the time it seemed unimportant: he was lying. The Day. Roy Fuller. OxBTC

At the time of Matines, Lord, thu were itake. *Unknown*. MiEL

At the time of the White Dawn. Song of the Fallen Deer. *Unknown, Pima.* NNPT; OBVE, *tr. by* Frank Russell

At the time when blossoms. *Unknown.* BoWoP, *tr. by* Arthur Waley *Fr.* Tzu Yeh Songs.

At the time when blossoms fall from the cherry-tree. Summer Song. Emperor Wu of Han, *Chinese.* ChiP, *tr. by* Arthur Waley

At the Tomb of Rachel. "Yehoash," *Yiddish.* TrJP, *tr. by* Isidore Goldstick

At the Tomb of Sophokles. Simmias [*or* Simias] of Rhodes, *Greek.* GrAn, *tr. by* Dudley Fitts

At the Top of My Voice. Vladimir Mayakovsky, *Russian.* TCRP, *tr. by* Max Hayward *and* George Reavey

　"My most respected / comrades of posterity!" AF, *tr. by* George Reavey

At the top of the house the apples are laid in rows. Moonlit Apples. John Drinkwater. BoTP; EBEvV; OBMV; OxBTC; PoRA

At the top of the stairs is a room. The Easiest Room in Hell. Peter Porter. BMAP

At the top of this ridge I could whistle happily. Descending the Ridge of Flying Clouds. T'ang Hsien-tsu, *Chinese.* CoBLCP, *tr. by* Jonathan Chaves

At the topmost peak, one thatch hut. Visiting a Recluse on West Mountain and Not Finding Him In. Ch'iu Wei, *Chinese.* CoBCP, *tr. by* Burton Watson

At the Tourist Center in Boston. Margaret Atwood. *See* At the Tourist Centre in Boston.

At the Tourist Centre in Boston. Margaret Atwood. Poetr
　(At the Tourist Center in Boston.) NoP-4

At the Train Museum. Linda Pastan. GM

At the Train Station. Haim Guri, *Hebrew.* IP, *tr. by* Warren Bargad *and* Stanley F. Chyet

At the Un-National Monument along the Canadian Border. William Stafford. HAP; HeIP-4

At the undulating head he aims. Emu Shot. Tjinapirrgarri, *Aborigine.* NOBAu, *tr. by* Georg von Brandenstein

At the Van Gogh exibition. Toki Zenmaro, *Japanese.* MJT, *tr. by* Makoto Ueda

At the Vietnam War Memorial, Washington, D. C. Robert Dana. CDa

At the Wailing Wall. Aidan Carl Mathews. BiHa; CIP-2

At the Waldron Court Apartments. Adventures in Bronze. Leon Stokesbury. MT

At the Washing of My Son. David Ray. RaBo

At the Washing of My Son. Su Tung-p'o, *Chinese.* OHPC, *tr. by* Kenneth Rexroth

At the Wedding March. Gerard Manley Hopkins. ITG

At the Well. Paul Blackburn. APSN

At the Well. Leonard Nathan. PBCAP

At the western window I paused from writing rescripts;. Being on Duty all Night in the Palace and Dreaming of the Hsien-yu Temple. Po Chü-i, *Chinese.* ChiP, *tr. by* Arthur Waley

At the window, sleet. O. Mabson Southard. HA

At the windows, you look out. Synthesizing Several Abstruse Concepts with an Experience. Carol Poster. BXAP

At the wood's mouth. The Gibber. Theodore Roethke. NAAL-2 *Fr.* The Lost Son. HAP; HCAP; LiTM; VGW

At the Wrong Door. Christopher Reid. CBLP

At the "Ye That Do Truly." Charles Williams. NOCV

At the Zoo. William Makepeace Thackeray. NTCP; OxBChV
　("Then I saw the monkeys—mercy, how unpleasantly / they—smelt!") (LL) CTAV

At the Zoo. Israel Zangwill. TrJP

At the zoo (two poems). Sasaki Yukitsuna, *Japanese.* MJT, *tr. by* Makoto Ueda

At thee the Mocker sneers in cold derision. The Maid of Orleans. Johann Christoph Friedrich von Schiller, *German.* AWP, *tr. by* James Clarence Mangan

At thieves I bark; at lovers wag my tail. *Unknown, after the Latin of* Joachim du Bellay. FaBoEE

At thirteen I was reading Oedipus Rex. The Women I Knew. Lois Roma-Deeley. LoHo

At Thirty-three. Hans Magnus Enzensberger, *German.* VCWP, *tr. by* Enzensberger, Hans Magnus and Michael Hamburger

At Thirty Years. Byron. *Fr.* Canto the First. NAEL-2; OAEL-2; PoE *Fr.* Don Juan.

At this Adonis smiles as in disdain. Shakespeare. EBEV *Fr.* Venus and Adonis.

At this hour of nightfall. Havdala. Amir Gilbo'a, *Hebrew.* IP, *tr. by* Warren Bargad *and* Stanley F. Chyet

At this moment in time. They Flee from Me That Sometime Did Me Seek. Gavin Ewart. OxBC

At this remote village, I have no neighbors. Quatrain. Chang Yü, *Chinese.* CoBLCP, *tr. by* Jonathan Chaves

At this th' Impatient Hero sowrly smil'd. The Goddess intervenes between Achilles and Agamemnon. Homer, *Greek.* OBVE, *tr. by* Dryden; OBCVT, *tr. by* John Dryden *Fr.* The Iliad.

At this time I find the bed very arid. The Reason for Poetry. Nancy Morejón, *Spanish.* WPOW, *tr. by* Anita Whitney

At Thomas Hardy's Birthplace, 1953. James Wright. CoAmPo; WeT

At three A.M., alone, not sleepy. Richard's Blues. Richard Cecil. SeSe

At 3 A.M. Wendy Cope. LW

At 3 a.m. I run my tongue. Death's Head. Phyllis Gotlieb. NOBC

At 3 a.m. the first trilobites swim out. Cambrian Night. James Solheim. PuP-15

At 3 o'clock in the afternoon. Nones. Donald Davie. *Fr.* Horae Canonicae. CRP

At thy approach, my cheek with blushes glows. Chapter II. Elizabeth Singer Rowe. PEW *Fr.* A Paraphrase on the Canticles.

At Tikal. William Bronk. APSN

At times each poet imagines himself. Poetry's Buried. Meir Wieseltier, *Hebrew.* IP, *tr. by* Warren Bargad *and* Stanley F. Chyet

At times I resort, beyond man's discerning. Wind: "At times I resort, beyond man's discerning." Cynewulf. AnOE *Fr.* Riddles (Exeter Book).

At times I see it, present. A Bright Day. John Montague. CIP-2

At times it is like watching a face you have just met. The Way It Sometimes Is. Henry Taylor. MT; Poetr

At times it seemed the country itself was a cloud. England. Mary Jo Salter. DiPo

At times spirit surges up from bodies' prison. David Shimoni, *Hebrew.* MHP, *tr. by* Ruth Finer Mintz

At times the heart looks toward open fields. Near Twelve Mile Point. Lance Henson. HATNAP

At times the real / seems no more than events passing. Opiate Phobia. Joseph Donahue. PT

At times the success of a mission. Man and Height. John Rice. SpW

At times this light comes to me again. For My Godmother. Astride Ivaska, *Latvian.* CEEP, *tr. by* Inara Cedrins

At Timon's villa let us pass a day. Timon's Villa. Alexander Pope. OBSV, *ll.* 99–168; PoE, *ll.* 99–180; ECEV; NOEC *Fr.* Epistle IV, to Richard Boyle, Earl of Burlington. OAEL-1; PoEL-3

At Toriwon. Chi-hun Cho, *Korean.* CKP, *tr. by* Jaihiun Kim

At Tripod Lake on that day His Majesty quit this world. Ballad of Yüan-yüan. Wu Wei-yeh, *Chinese.* CoBLCP, *tr. by* Jonathan Chaves

At Tripolis. Constance Carrier. WPE

At 12 o'clock in the afternoon. Epigram. Meleager, *Greek.* EP; GrAn; OBCVT, *tr. by* Peter Whigham

At twenty, I loved Lise. She was frail and white. Oswald Durand. *See* The Black Man's Son.

At twilight. Virginia Brady Young. HA

At twilight I went into the street. Descending Figure. Louise Glück. FaBoWP

At two a.m. a thing, jumping out of a manhole. News Report. David Ignatow. TwCP

At two / my upper lip split open. For the Color of my Mother. Cherríe Moraga. NMM-2

At Tynemouth Priory, after a Tempestuous Voyage. William Lisle Bowles. Son

At Upton-on-Severn. *Unknown.* FaBoEE

At Viscount Nelson's lavish funeral. 1805. Robert Graves. FaBoCh; OBCoV; OBSV; PeLV

At Vshchizh. Fyodor Ivanovich Tyutchev, *Russian.* OBWP, *tr. by* Charles Tomlinson

At War. Charles Madge. FaBoMo

At water's edge, clouds float up. Night of the Fourteenth. Ho Ching-ming, *Chinese.* CoBLCP, *tr. by* Jonathan Chaves

At wauking of the fauld. (LL) The Wawking of the Fauld. Allan Ramsay. OBEV; OxBS; SCGP

At Wednesbury there was a cocking. The Wednesbury Cocking. *Unknown.* EnSB

At westward window of a palace gray. My Lighthouses. Helen Hunt Jackson. APN-2; ColAP

At whiles (yea oftentimes) I muse over. Dante. AWP *Fr.* La Vita Nuova.

At Will Robers Beach. Timothy Steele. WeW-3

At winter's end. Snowman Sniffles. N. M. Bodecker. TLR

At Woodlawn I heard the dead cry. The Flight. Theodore Roethke. NAAL-2; NoP-4; RB; TRP *Fr.* The Lost Son. HAP; HCAP; LiTM; VGW

At Woods' Edge. Ory Bernstein, *Hebrew.* IP, *tr. by* Warren Bargad *and* Stanley F. Chyet

At Woodward's Gardens. Robert Frost. PoA

At words poetic, I'm so pathetic. You're the Top. Cole Porter. OBAL; UnPo

At Work. Artur Miedzyrzecki, *Polish*. PoSu, *tr. by* Artur Miedzyrzecki *and* John Batki

At work his arms wave like a windmill. The Secretary. Peter Redgrove. OxBTC

At Worthing, an exile from Geraldine G———. My Life Is a———. Frederick Locker-Lampson. OBCoV

At Year's End. Richard Wilbur. *See* Year's End.

At Yellow Crane Tower Taking Leave of Meng Hao-jan. Li Po, *Chinese*. CoBCP, *tr. by* Burton Watson

At your entreaty [*or* Intreaty], I at last have writ. Maidenhead. "Ephelia." KTR; NOSC; PEW; WPE

At Your Feet, Jerusalem. Uri Zvi Greenberg, *Hebrew*. MHP, *tr. by* Ruth Finer Mintz

At your light side trees shy. Poem. Bill Knott. SPE

At your silver wedding in '64 we gave. Psycho. Peter Olds. PeNZ

At your sweet smile the heavens gleam and hills and vallleys bloom;. The Alphabet of Love. *Unknown, Greek*. GrIP, *tr. by* Theodore Stephanides

At Yuen Yang Lake. Wu Wei-yeh, *Chinese*. OHMPC, *tr. by* Kenneth Rexroth

Atalanta in Calydon. Swinburne.
  Chorus: "Before the beginning of years." EBVV; EBVVPR; OBEV (Man.)
  Hounds of Spring, The. AWP; CTC; FaBoBe; HAP; NAEL-2; NOBE; OBEV; PoE; SCGP; TFi; WeW-3
    (Chorus.) EBVVPR; EnVR; GTBS-P
  "Maiden, and mistress of the months and stars." PoEL-5
  "Who hath given man speech? or what hath set therein." OAEL-2

Atameros. John Beevers. SPE

Atavism. Elinor Wylie. NALW; PoA

Atheling Grange; or, The Apotheosis of Lotte Nussbaum. William Plomer. OBNV

Athelstan King. *Unknown*. *See* Battle of Brunanburh.

Athelstan King / Lord among Earls. Battle of Brunanburh. *Unknown, Anglo-Saxon*. OBVE; OBWP; PeVV, *tr. by* Tennyson

Athelstan the king, captain of earls. Brunanburg. *Unknown, Anglo-Saxon*. PoE, *tr. by* Kemp Malone

Athelstane. Priscilla Jane Thompson. CBWP-2

Athenagoras begot Eubulus—. Epitaph. Chairemon, *Greek*. GrAn, *tr. by* Richard Evans

Athenian Garden, An. Trumbull Stickney. APN-2; GaP; NoP-4

Athens. Pindar, *Greek*. OBCVT, *tr. by* Richmond Lattimore

Athens rose: a city such as vision. Shelley. GrIP *Fr*. Ode to Liberty.

Athirst in spirit, through the gloom. Aleksandr Sergeyevich Pushkin. AWP, *tr. by* Babette Deutsch *and* Avrahm Yarmolinsky

Athlete, one vacation, An. An Accommodating Lion. Tudor Jenks. OBCA

Athwart the sky a lowly sigh. London. John Davidson. NOBE; OBNC

Atlanta Exposition Ode. Mary Weston Fordham. AAP; CBWP-2

Atlantic, The. Charles Tomlinson. OxBoS

Atlantic is a stormy moat; and the Mediterranean, The. The Eye. Robinson Jeffers. ImPo; LiTM; NOBA; NoAM; OxBA

Atlantis. W. H. Auden. OxAEP-2

Atlantis. Hart Crane. LiTM *Fr*. The Bridge. NAAL-2

Atlantis. Louis Dudek.
  Marine Aquarium, The. MoCV

Atlantis. John Engman. NAmP90

Atlantis. Slavko Mihalic. PoSu, *tr. by* Charles Simic

Atman. George Campbell Hay. FaBoTC

Atoll in the Mind, The. Alex Comfort. LiTM

Atomic Fairy Tale. Yury Kuznetsov, *Russian*. TCRP, *tr. by* Anatoly Liberman

Atomic Pantoum. Peter Meinke. WeW-3

Atonement. Margaret E. Bruner. PoToHe

Atop a tower I pitched a silken thing. Parachuting Thoor Ballylee. William Zaranka. BXAP

Atropos. Hilaire Kirkland. *Fr*. Clotho, Lachesis, Atropos. PeNZ

Atsá'lei Song. *Unknown*. *Fr*. The Night Chant. APN-2, *tr. by* Washington Matthews

Atta boy! Atta boy! (LL) To Greet a Letter-Carrier. William Carlos Williams. OBAL; SAmP

Attack. Siegfried Sassoon. MoBrPo; NOBE; OxBTC; PoFWW

Attack of the Crab Monsters. The Prophet. Lawrence Raab. AmPA

Attack of the Squash People. Marge Piercy. NBLV

Attainment, The. Coventry Patmore. FaBoEE *Fr*. The Angel in the House.

Attempt at Jealousy, An. Craig Raine. NoAM

Attempt at Jealousy, An. Marina Tsvetaeva, *Russian*. TCRP, *tr. by* Elaine Feinstein

Attempt at Jealousy, An. Marina Tsvetaeva, *Russian*. WPOW, *tr. by* Robert Perelman *and* Aleksandar Petrov

Attempt was brave, how happy our success, Th'. To Mrs. Manley. Catherine Trotter. KTR

Attend, all ye who list to hear our noble England's praise. The Armada. Thomas Babington Macaulay, 1st Baron Macaulay. FaBoCh; FaPoR

Attend my fable if your ears be clean. Roy Campbell. OBSV; PeSAV *Fr*. The Wayzgoose.

Attend my lays, ye ever honour'd nine. An Hymn to the Morning. Phillis Wheatley. TAP

Attend us, but old age and poverty. (LL) The Washerwoman. Mary Collier. ECWP; NOEC

Attend, ye mournful Parents, while. Another to Urania. Benjamin Colman. ChIV-1; SCAP

Attend, Young Friends, While I Relate. *Unknown*. AmFP

Attended only by the loveless moon. (LL) Stars and Planets. Norman MacCaig. OPOU; OxBSP

Attention. Rae Armantrout. PmAP

Attention. Adrienne Rich. TAP

Attention was commanded through a simple, unadorned, unexplained, often decentered presence. Jealousy. Mei-Mei Berssenbrugge. OpBo; PmAP

Attentive eyes, fantastic heed. A Poet. Thomas Hardy. NoAM

Attentively he heard us, while we spoke. Diomede Mourns His Fate and That of His Friends to the Latian Ambassador Who Seeks His Alliance against Aeneas. Virgil. OBVE, *tr. by* John Dryden *Fr*. The Aeneid [*or* Eneados, *Aeneis*].

Atthis hung up the belt with the pompoms. Leonidas of Tarentum, *Greek*. GrAn, *tr. by* Peter Levi

Attibon Legba. René Depestre. NegPo, *tr. by* Ellen Conroy Kennedy *Fr*. Epiphanies of the Voodoo Gods.

Attic, The. Henri Coulette. PoRA

Attic Landscape, The. Herman Melville. NCAP; NOBA; OBAL

Attic maid! with honey fed. To the Swallow. Euenus, *Greek*. OBCVT; OBVE, *tr. by* William Cowper

Attic room and window my ice skates on the wall. My Legs Señor. William S. Burroughs. BB

Atticus ("How did they fume, and stamp, and roar, and chafe"). Alexander Pope. *Fr*. Epistle to Dr. Arbuthnot. FHYEP; InPS-3; NoP-4; OAEL-1; OxAEP-1; PoE; PoEL-3; TFi

Atticus ("Peace to all such! but were there one whose fires"). Alexander Pope. AWP; InPK-6; NOBE; TRP *Fr*. Epistle to Dr. Arbuthnot. FHYEP; InPS-3; NoP-4; OAEL-1; OxAEP-1; PoE; PoEL-3; TFi
  (On Addison.)

Attila József. Attila József, *Hungarian*. AF, *tr. by* John Batki

Attis. Catullus, *Latin*. OBVE; STV, *tr. by* Peter Whigham *Fr*. Carmina.
  "But when the sun within the eastern house." OBCVT, *tr. by* Robert Clayton Casto
  (Carmen 63.) STV, *tr. by* Peter Whigham
  ("Over oceans sped he, Attis, in the speediest of ships.") STV, *tr. by* John Frederick Nims
  ("Spur the others to fey elation; no mad dogs in the house for me.") (LL) STV, *tr. by* John Frederick Nims

Attraction. Ella Wheeler Wilcox. LW

Atween the world o' licht. Scotland. William Soutar. OxBS

Au Champ d'Honneur. Charles Kenneth Michael Scott Moncrieff. NSI

Au Jardin des Plantes. John Wain. OxBTC

Au Tombeau de Mon Père. Ronald McCuaig. NOBAu

Aubade, An. Timothy Steele. RA

Aubade: "Cold snap. Five o'clock." Richard Kenney. NoP-4

Aubade: "Hark! hark! the lark at heaven's gate sings." Shakespeare. *See* Song: "Hark! hark! the lark at heaven's gate sings."

Aubade: "Hours before dawn we were woken by the quake." William Empson. FaBoMo; FaBoTw; OxAEP-2; OxBTC

Aubade: "I press against the emptiness." Vassar Miller. WeT

Aubade: "I work all day, and get half-drunk at night." Philip Larkin. CABP; GEA; NoP-4; SoSe; TRP

Aubade: "It's all the same to morning what it dawns on." Nuala Ni Dhomhnaill, *Irish*. BiHa; PBCIP, *tr. by* Michael Longley

Aubade: "Jane, Jane, / Tall as a crane." Dame Edith Sitwell. BWW; CMoP; MoBrPo; MoP; NALW; NoAM; PoRA; Poetr

Aubade: "Lark now leaves his watery [*or* wat'ry] nest, The." Sir William Davenant. NOBE; OBEV

Aubade: "O, Lady, awake! The azure moon." *Unknown*. PFE

Aubade: "Stay, O sweet, and do not rise." *Unknown, at. to* John Donne. BoLoP; NOBE
  (Daybreak.) OBEV

Aubade: "Waking is this easy." Marilyn Chin. NIP-4

Aubade: "What dawn is it?" Karl Shapiro. VGW

Aubade: Donna Anna to Juan, Still Asleep. Richard Howard. PoA

Aubade for Hope. Robert Penn Warren. FuPo; MoAmPo

Aubade: Lake Erie. Thomas Merton. NYBP

Aubade: N.Y.C. Robert Wallace. HoPM

Aubade: The Desert. Frederick Bock. PoA

Aubade Triste. Agnes Mary Frances Robinson. NOBVV

Aube Provençale. Marilyn Hacker. AmPA

Aubrey, you splashed the sun in my face. The Dreamtime Lives Again. Jan Carew. HCP

Auburn. Oliver Goldsmith. *See* The Deserted Village.

A.U.C. 334: about this date. Advice to Young Ladies. Alec Derwent Hope. NoAM; NoP-4

Aucassin and Nicolette. *Unknown, French.*
   Who Would List. CTC, *tr. by* Andrew Lang

"Auchanachie Gordon is bonny and braw." Lord Saltoun and Auchanachie. *Unknown.* ESPB

Aucthour Maketh Her Wyll and Testament, The. Isabella Whitney. BWW
   ("No longer can I tarry.") (LL) PEW
   ("Of that I leave them till.") (LL) NoP-4
   ("Time is come I must departe, The.") BWW
   (Wyll and Testament.) PEW

Auction Sale, The. Henry Reed. MoBrPo

Auction Sale—Household Furnishings. Adele DeLeeuw. PoToHe

Auction; Saturday 2:00. Donald D. Olsen. EC2

Auctioneer. Carl Sandburg. NOxBChV

Auctioneer of Parting, The. Emily Dickinson. PoEL-5

Auden at Milwaukee. Stephen Spender. AiP

Auden in Old Age. Agnes Gergely, *Hungarian.* CEEP, *tr. by* Emery E. George

Auden, MacNeice, Day Lewis, I have read them all. British Leftish Poetry, 1930-40. "Hugh MacDiarmid." CMoP; FaBoTw; NoAM

Audible and Inaudible. Yannis Ritsos, *Greek.* AF, *tr. by* Minas Savas

Audible trout. Girls on the Bridge. Derek Mahon. NoP-4

Audience with the emperor, Hall of Inherited Brilliance. Presented to Piao, the Prince of Pai-ma. Ts'ao Chih, *Chinese.* CoBCP, *tr. by* Burton Watson

Auditor Thinks about Female Nature, An. Jamie Grant. NOBAu

Audley Court. Tennyson. NOBVV; PeVV
   "Sleep, Ellen Aubrey, sleep, and dream of me." CBLP

Audrey Hepburn moons big-eyed on the cover. A Guide to Holland. Peter Sirr. PBCIP

Audubon. Robert Penn Warren.
   Tell Me a Story. FuPo; MT

Audubon, Drafted. Imamu Amiri Baraka. TTY

Audubon *Enfant.* Pamela Alexander. WeT

Auf dem Wasser zu Singen. Stephen Spender. EnLoPo

Auf meiner Herzliebsten Äugelein. Heinrich Heine, *German.* AWP, *tr. by* Richard Garnett

Augher Clogher Fivemiletown. Omagh Post Office Rhyme. *Unknown.* FaBoVe

Augsburg Adoration, The. Randall Jarrell. NYBP

Auguries of Innocence. William Blake. EBEV; FaBoCh; FaPoR; ImPo; OAEL-1; OBNC; OxAEP-2; OxBoLi; PeECV; PoEL-4; TFi
   "Bat that flits at close of eve, The." UV
   "God appears, and God is Light."
   Three Things to Remember.
   "To see a World in a Grain of Sand." EnlH; InPK-6; NTP, *ll.* 1-4

Augury. W. H. Oliver. PeNZ

August. Eunice Fallon. BoTP

August. Robert Frost. BXAP

August. Michael Lewis. AYFP

August. Louis MacNeice. LiTM

August. Katharine Pyle. OBCA

August. Henrietta Cordelia Ray. CBWP-3

August. Adrienne Rich. NNaP; PBWP

August. Folgore da San Geminiano. CTC *Fr.* Sonnets of the Months. AWP, *tr. by* D. G. Rossetti

August. Edmund Spenser. *Fr.* Wood Of Error. AEP

August. Celia Laighton Thaxter. CTV; FPC; ImGa
   ("Mellow.") (LL) FPC

August. John Updike. AYFP; OBCA *Fr.* A Child's Calendar.

August. Elinor Wylie. MoAmPo

August 17, 1970. Don Receveur. CDa

August 8. Norman Jordan. MBE

August a haze amniotic our dream aether and lens of distance. Tree sentinels in. Christopher Dewdney. FTOS *Fr.* Spring Trances in the Control Emerald Night.

August and the drive-in picture is packed. Dear John Wayne. Louise Erdrich. UnSA

August at the Lake. David Young. AmPA

August Bank Holiday. Jacques Prévert, *French.* MFP, *tr. by* Martin Sorrell

August comes. Poem for August—or for My Birthday. Geraldine Monk. NBrP

August 18. Joanne Kyger. PoM

August Ends. Leonard Clark. AYFP

August/Fresno 1973. Roberta Spear. AmPA

August heat. Haiku. Gerald Vizenor. VoR

August heat. Emily Romano. HA

August Heaven has failed in its divine ministration. A Lament for Ying. Ch'u Yüan, *Chinese.* SuSp, *tr. by* Wu-Chi Liu

August is a dreamless month. Tanikawa Shuntaro, *Japanese.* IFJA, *tr. by* Harold Wright

August is nearly over, the people. Louis MacNeice. CMoP *Fr.* Autumn Journal.

August, Los Angeles, Lullaby. Carol Muske. PBCAP

August Midnight, An. Thomas Hardy. NOBVV

August Moon. Cesare Pavese, *Italian.* AF, *tr. by* William Arrowsmith

August Night. Sara Teasdale. MoAmPo

August 1914. Isaac Rosenberg. EBEV; NOBE; OBWP; OxBTC; PeFWW

August 1968. W. H. Auden. OxBSP

August on Sourdough, a Visit from Dick Brewer. Gary Snyder. LoL

August, on the Rented Farm. Dave Jeddie Smith. ColAP

August Rain. Robert Bly. LCAP-2

August Rain, after Haying. Jane Kenyon. AFr

August 6, 1945. Alison Fell. NBrP

August sky, The. George Swede. HA

August Sleepwalker, The. Zhao Zhenkai, *Chinese.* VCWP, *tr. by* Donald Finkel

August the First; Court Martial. The Mother Speaks. Marjorie Oludhe Macgoye. HBAPE

August the First: The Shadow. Patel Speaks. Marjorie Oludhe Macgoye. HBAPE

August the First: The Watchman Speaks. Marjorie Oludhe Macgoye. HBAPE

August 'twas the twenty-fifth. Bar[']s Fight[, August 28, 1746]. Lucy Terry. BPo; BiSi; CrDW; NAAAL

August 2. Norman Jordan. PoBA

August Was Foggy. Gary Snyder. NNaP

August wind rides Spain tonight in a fierce saddle, The. Casa de Pollos. Kathleen Fraser. AmPA

Augustus was a chubby lad. The Story of Augustus Who Would Not Have Any Soup. Heinrich Hoffmann, *German.* NBLV; OxBChV

Auld Daddy Darkness creeps frae his hole. James Ferguson. OxBChV

Auld Deil cam to the man at the pleugh, The. The Farmer's Curst Wife. *Unknown.* AmFP; ESPB

Auld freen and helper up the hill. Poetical Epistle tae Cullybackey Auld Nummer. Thomas Given. FaBoVe

Auld House, The. William Soutar. OxBS

Auld Lang Syne. Robert Burns. APAD; AWP; EBEvV; ImPo; NAEL-2; NOBE; OBEV; OxAEP-2; OxBS; PoLF; SCGP

Auld Lang Syne. *Unknown.* NOSC

Auld Matrons. *Unknown.* ESPB

Auld mune on her back, The. Leander Stormbound. Sydney Goodsir Smith. OxBS

Auld Noah was at hame wi' them a'. Parley of Beasts. "Hugh MacDiarmid." ChIV-1; MoBrPo; MoP; NoAM; OBMV

Auld Robin Forbes. Susanna Blamire. ECWP
   ("Is the turf that has cover'd my Willy frae me!") (LL) LW

Auld Robin Gray. Lady Anne Lindsay. CH; ECWP; GTBS-P; LW; NOEC; OBEV; PeSAV; WPE

Auld Sang. William Soutar. OxBS

Auld Symie, The. Alan Bold. FaBoTC

Auld wife sat at her ivied door, The. Ballad. Charles Stuart Calverley. BXAP; CABP; NBLV; OBCoV; OxAEP-2; UV

Auld wumman cam' in, a mere rickle o' banes, in a faded black dress, An. Old Wife in High Spirits. "Hugh MacDiarmid." CMoP; OxBTC; PoE

Aulus / is childless. Lucilius, *Greek.* GrAn, *tr. by* Peter Porter

AUM MANI. Mani-Mani Gatha. Jackson Mac Low. PFTM

Auncient Acquaintance, Madam, The. John Skelton. AAS; PoEL-1

Aunt Annie said, "When I turned seventeen. Legacies. Emily Grosholz. FFC

Aunt Chloe's Lullaby. Daniel Webster Davis. AAP

Aunt Chloe's Politics. Frances Ellen Watkins Harper. NAAAL; NALW

Aunt Eliza. Harry Graham. FPC

Aunt Helen. T. S. Eliot. OBAL; PoA

Aunt Ida Pieces a Quilt. Melvin Dixon. EC3

Aunt Jane Allen. Fenton Johnson. PoBA

Aunt Janet's Museum. Kathleen Jamie. FaBoTC

Aunt Jemima of the Ocean Waves. Robert Earl Hayden. LCAP-2; PoBA

Aunt Jennifer's tigers prance across a screen. Adrienne Rich. ColAP; FaBoWP; HeIP-4; InPK-6; NALW; NIP-4; NoAM; NoP-4; OPOU; Poetr; TRP

Aunt Jessie. Wanda Coleman. GT

Aunt Julia. Norman MacCaig. RB

Aunt Laura Moves toward the Open Grave of Her Father. Joseph De Roche. HeIP-4

Aunt Lily stood / behind her candy counter / passing out Mary Janes, Hersheys, and advice. The Candy Lady. Laura Boss. UnSA

Aunt Liza/ Yes? Me, Colored. Peter Abrahams. PBA *Fr.* Tell Freedom.

Aunt Lucy. Jane Gentry. CrSp

Aunt Martha bustles. Old Houses. Melvin B. Tolson. GT

Aunt Pearlie draped her rug across. Ghosts in the Carpet. Robert Morgan. WeT

Aunt Rose—now—might I see you. To Aunt Rose. Allen Ginsberg. CLPP; ColAP; LiTM; NAAL-2; NoAM; NoP-4; PmAP; PoE; VGW

Aunt Sue has a head full of stories. Aunt Sue's Stories. Langston Hughes. SAmP

Aunt Sue's Stories. Langston Hughes. SAmP

Aunt Toni's Heart. Rafael Campo. RA

Aunt Zillah Speaks. Herbert Edward Palmer. FaBoTw

Auntie Bridge and Uncle Pat. Geoffrey Lehmann. *Fr.* Ross's Poems. CBAP

Auntie's Skirts. Robert Louis Stevenson. WHSW

Aunts and Nieces or Time and Space. A. E. Housman. CBNP

Aura Amara, L'. Arnaut Daniel, *Provençal.* CTC, *tr. by* Ezra Pound

Aurelia. Robert Malise Bowyer Nichols. OBMV

Aurelia, when your zeal makes known. The Headache. Mary Leapor. ECWP; PEW

Aurelius, I'm entrusting you with all. Catullus, *Latin.* EP, *tr. by* James Michie

Aureng-Zebe. Dryden.
  Prologue: "Our author by experience finds it true." OxBoLi

Aurora. Timothy Steele. DiPo

Aurora. Sir William Alexander, Earl of Stirling.
  I Envy Not Endymion. Son
    (Sonnet: "I envy not Endymion now no more.")
  I Hope, I Fear. Son
  "O happy Tithon! if thou know'st thy harp." OBEV
  Sonnet: "Cleare moving cristall, pure as the Sunne beames." OxBS
  Sonnet: "I dreamed the nymph that o'er my fancy reigns." NOSC
  Sonnet: "Ile give thee leave my love, in beauties field." OxBS
  To Aurora. GTBS-P
    (Sonnet.)

Aurora and Tithonus. *Unknown, Greek.* OBCVT, *tr. by* William Congreve

Aurora Borealis. Edouard Roditi. SPE

Aurora gazed from out her shell-pink bower. Sunrise Thought. Henrietta Cordelia Ray. *Fr.* A Group of Musings. CBWP-3

Aurora, lady grey. A Simple Pastoral. George Alexander Stevens. NOEC

Aurora Leigh. Elizabeth Barrett Browning. VWP
  "And I, I was a good child on the whole." BrRo
  "As the earth." EPCY
  "Books, books, books!" WPOW
  "By Keats's soul, the man who never stepped." EPCY
  First Book: Young Aurora's Fostermother.
    ("Bring the clean water, give out the new seed.") (LL) PEW
  From Book 5. NoP-4
  "I had a little chamber in the house."
  "I just knew it when we swept above the old roofs of Dijon." PeVV
  "I learnt the collects and the catechism." EnVR
  "I mused/ Up and down, up and down, the terraced streets."
  "My mother was a Florentine." NALW
  "Of writing many books there is no end!" NOBVV
  Olives and Mountains.
  Reading.
  Sweetness of England, The. OxAEP-2
  "Then, land!--then, England! oh, the frosty cliffs." NAEL-2
  "'Then, must it be'." NALW
  "'There it is!/ You play beside a death-bed like a child'." BrRo
  "Truth, so far, in my book; the truth which draws."
  Tuscan Life.
  "Without considering whether they were fit."

Auroras of Autumn, The. Wallace Stevens.

"Farewell to an idea. . . A cabin stands." CMoP; HCAP; PoE

"Farewell to an idea. . . The mother's face." HCAP; PoE

"Is there an imagination that sits enthroned." HCAP

"It is a theatre floating through the clouds." HCAP

"This is where the serpent lives, the bodiless." CMoP; PoE

"Unhappy people in a happy world, An." CMoP; PoE

Auschwitz. Salvatore Quasimodo, *Italian.* AF, *tr. by* Jack Bevan

Auschwitz, 1987. Adam Zych, *Polish.* HP, *tr. by* Hilda Schiff

Auspex. James Russell Lowell. PoEL-5; TAP

Auspice. Brooks Haxton. CMAP

Auspicious night. / The stars balance on poles. Courtesan with Fan. Elizabeth Spires. WeT

Austere the Music of My Songs. Fyodor Kuz'mich Sologub, *Russian.* AWP, *tr. by* Babette Deutsch *and* Avrahm Yarmolinsky

Austerity in Vermont. Terry Hummer. NAmP90; PuP-15

Austerity of Poetry [*or* Jacopone da Todi]. Matthew Arnold. EPCY

Australia. Gary Catalano. NOBAu

Australia. Alec Derwent Hope. BMAP; NoAM; NoP-4

Australia. Bernard O'Dowd. APAD

Australia 1970. Judith Wright. CBAP; NoAM

Australian Dream, The. David Campbell. CBAP

Australian Emigrant, The. Francis Fisher Browne. VWP *Fr.* The Australian Emigrant.

Australian Garden, An. Peter Porter. OBGa

Australorp. Edith Speers. NOBAu

Austrian Army, An. Alaric Alexander Watts. BLPA; NOBL; PeLV

Autant En Emporte le Vent. Marguerite de Navarre, *French.* PBWP, *tr. by* Aline Allard

Autet e bas. Arnaut Daniel, *Provençal.* CTC, *tr. by* Ezra Pound

Authentic! Shadows of it, The. Matins. Denise Levertov. AmPP; FaBoWP; MoP; NOBA; NoAM; Poetr

Author, The. Charles Churchill.
  "Gods! with what pride I see the titled slave." OBSV
  "When with much pains this boasted learning's got." OBSV

Author Apologizes to a Lady, for His Being a Little Man, The. Christopher Smart. BoLoP; CBLP

Author Consults a Critic and Sells His Manuscript, The. Francis Hawling. NOEC *Fr.* The Signal; or, A Satire against Modesty.

Author Loving These Homely Meats, The. John, of Hereford Davies. CBLP; CBNP; OBCoV; Son *Fr.* The Scourge of Folly.
  (Homely Meats.) FaBoCh

Author of American Ornithology Sketches a Bird, Now Extinct, The. David Wagoner. BLT

Author of *Christine,* The. Richard Howard. CoAP

Author, of His Own Fortune, The. Sir John Harington. FaBoEE

Author of light, revive my dying spright. Thomas Campion. AAS

Author to Her Book, The. Anne Bradstreet. AmPP; InPK-6; NAAL-1; NAAL-3; NALW; NOBA; OxBA; PoE; Poetr; SCAP; TAP
  ("Which caused her thus to send thee out of door.") (LL) APAD; ColAP; NoP-4

Author to His Body on Their Fifteenth Birthday, 29.ii.80, The. Howard Nemerov. NoAM

Author to His Book, The. George Alsop. SCAP

Author to His Book[e], The. Thomas Heywood. NOSC *Fr.* An Apology for Actors.

Author to His Wife, of a Woman's Eloquence, The. Sir John Harington. BoLoP; OxBM

Author to the Reader, The. Randall Jarrell. OxBC

Author Unknown. William Montgomerie. OxBS

Authoress, armed with a skewer, An. Limerick. *Unknown.* PeLi

Authority is a disease, and cure. Samuel Butler. FaBoEE

Authors [*or* Author's] Abstract of Melancholy, The. Robert Burton. NOSC *Fr.* The Anatomy of Melancholy.

Authors and actors and artists and such. Bohemia. Dorothy Parker. NBLV

Author's Apology for His Book, The. John Bunyan.
  "When at the first I took my pen in hand." FaBoVe

Author's Epitaph, Made By Himself, The. Sir Walter Ralegh. *See* Verses Made the Night before He Died [*or* Dyed].

Author's Epitaph, Written by Himself, An. Abel Evans. FaBoEE

Authors of Confession, The. Elizabeth Major. KTR *Fr.* Honey on the Rod.

Authors of the Town, The. Richard Savage.
  "First, let me view what noxious nonsense reigns." OBSV

Author's Prologue. Dylan Thomas. ChIV-1

Author's Quietus, The. Henry Carey. FaBoVe

Author's Resolution, The. George Wither. AWP; OBEV *Fr.* Fair Virtue, the Mistress of Philarete.

(Lover's Resolution, A.) BoLoP; NOBE
(Sonnet.)
Authorship. James Ball Naylor. NBLV
Auto-erotic. *Unknown*. PeLi
Auto Mirror. Adam Zagajewski, *Polish*. BLT, *tr. by* Czeslaw Milosz *and* Robert Hass (b. 1941)
Auto Mobile. A. R. Ammons. OBAL
Auto Wreck. Karl Shapiro. CMoP; LiTM; NIP-4; RB; VGW
Autobahnmotorwayautoroute. Adrian Mitchell. RB
Autobiographia Literaria. Frank O'Hara. NNaP; NOBA; TTTS
Autobiographical. Abraham Moses Klein. MoCV; NoAM
Autobiographical Fragment. Kingsley Amis. OBCoV
Autobiography. Sonja [dA]kesson, *Swedish*. BoWoP, *tr. by* Ingrid Claréus
Autobiography. Charles Causley. LiTM; Son
Autobiography. Mbella Sonne Dipoko. TTY
Autobiography. Janet Dubé. BrRo
Autobiography. Gloria Fuertes, *Spanish*. PBWP, *tr. by* Philip Levine
Autobiography. Thom Gunn. NoAM
Autobiography. Joy Harjo. LTA
Autobiography. Louis MacNeice. NOIV; PNI; RB
Autobiography. Tommy Olofsson, *Swedish*. IFJA, *tr. by* Jean Pearson
Autobiography. Dan Pagis, *Hebrew*. AF; PoSu; VCWP, *tr. by* Stephen Mitchell
("Though it's only a sour revenge.") (LL) IP, *tr. by* Warren Bargad *and* Stanley F. Chyet
Autobiography, An. Ernest Rhys. OBEV; OBWVE
Autobiography. Robert Viscusi. UnSA
Autobiography. Tom Weatherly. NBV
Autobiography, Chapter XLII: Three Days in Louisville. Jim Barnes. HATNAP
Autobiography, Chapter XVII: Floating the Big Piney. Jim Barnes. HATNAP
Autobiography: Last Chapter. Jim Barnes. CDW
Autobiography of a Lungworm. Roy Fuller. MoP; NoAM; OxBC
Autocrat of the Breakfast Table, The. Oliver Wendell Holmes.
Aestivation [an Unpublished Poem, by My Late Latin Tutor]. NOBL; OBAL
Chambered Nautilus, The. APN-1; APo; AmPP; ColAP; FaBoBe; HoPM; ImPo; NAAL-3; NCAP; NOBA; NoP-4; PAR; PoEL-5; PoLF; TFi
Contentment. APN-1; AmPP; OxBA; PWR
Deacon's Masterpiece; or, The Wonderful "One-Hoss Shay," The. APN-1; AmPP; NAAL-3; NOBA; OBAL; OBCA; OxBA; PoLF; PoRA; TAP; TFi
(Wonderful "One-Hoss Shay," The.) FaBoBe
Living Temple, The. APN-1
Voiceless, The. APN-1
Autograph on the Soul, The. Adah Isaacs Menken. CBWP-1
Autolycus as Peddler. Shakespeare. OAEL-1 *Fr.* The Winter's Tale.
(Pedlar's Song, The.) CH
Autolycus's Song ("When daffodils begin to peer"). Shakespeare. *See* The Pedlar's Song.
Automatic fingers write, The. Séance. Francis King. PoA
Automobile, The. Russell Edson. LCAP-2; RaBo
Automobiles of the Asylum. Philip Hammial. BMAP
Autopsy, The. Odysseas Elytis, *Greek*. AF, *tr. by* Edmund Keeley *and* Philip Sherrard
Autopsy. Arthur Nortje. HBAPE
Autumn. Bella Akhatovna Akhmadulina, *Russian*. BoWoP, *tr. by* Barbara Einzig
Autumn. Douglas Ridley Beeton. PeSA
Autumn. Roy Campbell. GTBS-P; MoBrPo; OBMV; OxBTC
Autumn. William Carpenter. Poetsp
Autumn. Alice Cary. APN-2
Autumn. Chang Yü. *Fr.* The Four Seasons in the Mountains. CoBLCP, *tr. by* Jonathan Chaves
Autumn. Walter De la Mare. OxBTC
Autumn. Georgi Djagarov, *Bulgarian*. CEEP, *tr. by* Jascha Kessler *and* Aleksandar Shurbanov
Autumn. Fan Ch'eng-ta. SuSp, *tr. by* Irving Y. Lo *Fr.* Seasonal Poems on Fields and Gardens.
Autumn. Florence Hoatson. BoTP
Autumn. Thomas Hood. *See* Ode: Autumn.
Autumn. Thomas Ernest Hulme. FaBoMo; NTP
Autumn ("I at my window sit, and see"). *Unknown*. NOEC
Autumn ("I love the fitful gust that shakes"). John Clare. BoTP
Autumn. Walter Savage Landor. *Fr.* Ianthe.
Autumn. Philip Levine. NNaP

Autumn. Detlev von Liliencron, *German*. AWP, *tr. by* Ludwig Lewisohn
Autumn ("List to the sad wind, drearily moaning"). Priscilla Jane Thompson. CBWP-2
Autumn. Henry Wadsworth Longfellow. APN-1
Autumn. Amy Lowell. NMM-2
Autumn. Itsik Manger, *Yiddish*. CEEP; TrJP, *tr. by* Ruth Whitman *and* Joseph Leftwich
Autumn. Slavko Mihalic, *Croatian*. CEEP, *tr. by* Peter Kastmiler
Autumn. Edna St. Vincent Millay. LBC
Autumn. Yunna Petrovna Moritz, *Russian*. TCRP, *tr. by* J. R. Rowland *with* Odile Taliani
Autumn. Boris Pasternak, *Russian*. TCRP, *tr. by* Henry Kamen
Autumn. Alexander L. Posey. APN-2
Autumn. Aleksandr Sergeyevich Pushkin, *Russian*. AWP, *tr. by* Max Eastman
Autumn. Helen G. Quigless. BkSV *Fr.* Childhood Scenes in Four Seasons.
Autumn. Rilke, *German*. TrJP, *tr. by* C. F. MacIntyre
Autumn. Christina Rossetti. BrRo; VWP
Autumn. Vernon Scannell. OxBTC
Autumn. Thomas William Shapcott. CBAP
Autumn. Princess Shikishi, *Japanese*. PBWP, *tr. by* Hiroaki Sato
Autumn. Stevie Smith. FaBoWP; LW
Autumn. Edmund Spenser. *Fr.* Wood Of Error. AEP
Autumn. Su Tung-p'o, *Chinese*. OHPC, *tr. by* Kenneth Rexroth
Autumn ("Sun shines bright, but sadly, The"). Priscilla Jane Thompson. CBWP-2
Autumn ("Thistledown's flying / Though the winds are all still, The"). John Clare. EnVR; HAP; PoEL-4; WeW-3
Autumn. *Unknown*, *Irish*. OBMV
Autumn. Jean Starr Untermeyer. MoAmPo
Autumn. Andrey Andreievich Voznesensky, *Russian*. TCRP, *tr. by* Stanley Kunitz
Autumn. Wang Wei, *Chinese*. OHMPC, *tr. by* Kenneth Rexroth
Autumn. Charlotte Zolotow. AYFP
Autumn: A Dirge. Shelley. CH
Autumn already!—But why regret an eternal sun if we are embarked on. Farewell. Rimbaud, *French*. PFTM, *tr. by* Louise Varese
Autumn, and the lake is down from its spring thaw fill. The Healing. Shelley White. EC2
Autumn, and we're still like the will-o'-the wisp. To Li Po. 'Aisha bint Ahmad al-Qurtubiyya, *Chinese*. SuSp, *tr. by* Eugene Eoyang
Autumn Begins in Martins Ferry, Ohio. James Wright. ColAP; HCAP; HeIP-4; InPK-6; InPS-3; NoAM; SAGP; VCAP; WeT; WeW-3
Autumn bellflower. Tanka. Kitahara Hakushū, *Japanese*. MJT, *tr. by* Makoto Ueda
Autumn burgeons, sounds rise everywhere. Autumn Night—Sleepless. Wu Wei-yeh, *Chinese*. CoBLCP, *tr. by* Jonathan Chaves
Autumn Chapter in a Novel. Thom Gunn. FaBoMo; OxBTC
Autumn chrysanthemums have beautiful color. T'ao Ch'ien. SuSp, *tr. by* Wu-chi Liu *Fr.* Drinking Wine. CoBCP, *tr. by* Burton Watson
Autumn cicada, The. Naito Joso, *Japanese*. OHMPJ, *tr. by* Kenneth Rexroth
Autumn, cloud blades on the horizon. Clear After Rain. Tu Fu, *Chinese*. BLT; OHPC, *tr. by* Kenneth Rexroth
Autumn colors / on the leaves. Autumn Plants, Flowers, Bamboo, Rocks. Yün Shou-p'ing, *Chinese*. CoBLCP, *tr. by* Jonathan Chaves
Autumn colors trickle through the gauze curtains. A Woman's Room in Autumn. Yüan Hung-tao, *Chinese*. CoBLCP, *tr. by* Jonathan Chaves
Autumn Comes. Li Ho, *Chinese*. PLT, *tr. by* A. C. Graham
Autumn constellations, The. Moon Festival. Tu Fu, *Chinese*. OHPC, *tr. by* Kenneth Rexroth
Autumn Cove. Li Po, *Chinese*. CoBCP; TTTS, *tr. by* Burton Watson
Autumn, Crystal Eye. Margot Ruddock. OBMV
Autumn Day. Rilke, *German*. TrJP, *tr. by* C. F. MacIntyre
Autumn Day, An. Clara Ann Thompson. CBWP-2
Autumn Day, An—Leisurely Boating on West Lake. Liu Pu, *Chinese*. SuSp, *tr. by* Jonathan Chaves
Autumn day its course has run—The Autumn evening falls, The. Charlotte Brontë. NOBVV; SDW
Autumn eats its leaf out of my hand: we are friends. Corona. Paul Celan. PoSu, *tr. by* Michael Hamburger
Autumn Equinox. Peter Blue Cloud. *Fr.* Within the Seasons. HATNAP
Autumn Evening. George Anthony. SPE
Autumn evening. Basho, *Japanese*. OHPJ, *tr. by* Kenneth Rexroth
Autumn evening. Rosamond Haas. HA
Autumn Evening. Robinson Jeffers. ChAP
Autumn Evening. Tu Mu, *Chinese*. PLT, *tr. by* A. C. Graham

Autumn Evening Beside the Lake. Li Ch'ing-chao, *Chinese*. OHPC, *tr. by* Kenneth Rexroth

Autumn feels slowed down, The. Paula Becker to Clara Westhoff. Adrienne Rich. NAAL-2; VCAP

Autumn finds me old and poorer. Meng Chiao. SuSp, *tr. by* Irving Y. Lo *Fr.* Autumn Meditations.

Autumn Fires. Robert Louis Stevenson. NOxBChV; NTP

Autumn Flowers. Jones Very. APN-1

Autumn Garden. Dino Campana, *Italian*. GaP; STV, *tr. by* John Frederick Nims

Autumn has come invisibly. Toshiyuki, *Japanese*. OHPJ, *tr. by* Kenneth Rexroth

Autumn has come / To the lonely cottage. Eikei, *Japanese*. OHPJ, *tr. by* Kenneth Rexroth

Autumn has turned the dark trees toward the hill. Quail in Autumn. William Jay Smith. Poetsp

Autumn hath all the summer's fruitful treasure. Autumn Hath All the Summer's Fruitful Treasure. Thomas Nashe. NoSic; OAEL-1; SCGP *Fr.* Summer's Last Will and Testament.

Autumn Hath All the Summer's Fruitful Treasure. Thomas Nashe. *Fr.* Summer's Last Will and Testament.

Autumn Idleness. D. G. Rossetti. GBL; OAEL-2 *Fr.* The House of Life.

Autumn Imagined. Donald Davie. PoA

Autumn in Sigulda. Andrey Andreievich Voznesensky, *Russian*. TCRP, *tr. by* W. H. Auden

Autumn in the Cascade Mountains. Astride Ivaska, *Latvian*.

"Wild ducks had flown, and early this year." CEEP, *tr. by* Inara Cedrins

Autumn is unquiet everywhere. The Green Side. Jennifer Maiden. BMAP

Autumn is weary, halt, and old. The October Redbreast. Alice Thompson Meynell. MoBrPo

Autumn Journal. Louis MacNeice.

"And I remember Spain." OBWP; OxAEP-2

"August is nearly over, the people." CMoP

"Conferences, adjournments, ultimatums." FaBoPV; OxBTC

"Nightmare leaves fatigue." BIrV; CIP-2; PNI

"Now we are back to normal, now the mind is." CMoP; OxAEP-2

"September has come and I wake." NoP-4

"Shelley and jazz and lieder and love and hymn-tunes." NOBL

"These days are misty, insulated, mute." CMoP

Autumn Leaves. Marilyn Chin. PiM; PoPoPo

Autumn Leaves. James Cushing. SeSe

Autumn Leaves. Clara Ann Thompson. CBWP-2

Autumn Leaves. Jones Very. APN-1; PAR

Autumn Leaves. Charles Henry Webb. OBAL

Autumn light. Tadashi Kondo. HA

Autumn made colors burn, The. Venus Khoury-Gata, *French*. BoWoP, *tr. by* Willis Barnstone

Autumn Meditation. Tu Fu, *Chinese*. PLT, *tr. by* A. C. Graham

Autumn Meditations. Meng Chiao, *Chinese*.

"Autumn finds me old and poorer." SuSp, *tr. by* Irving Y. Lo

"Bones of the lonely-wretched spend no quiet nights." SuSp, *tr. by* Irving Y. Lo

"In autumn moonlight the face turns icy." SuSp, *tr. by* Stephen Owen

"Old and sick, many strange broodings." SuSp, *tr. by* Stephen Owen

Autumn met me today as I walked over Castle Hill. The Stand-To. C. Day Lewis. NoP-4; OBWP

Autumn Morning, An. *Unknown*. BoTP

Autumn Morning. Adeline White. BoTP

Autumn Morning at Cambridge. Frances Darwin Cornford. PoRA

Autumn Morning in Shokoku-ji, An. Gary Snyder. HAP; VGW; WeW-3 *Fr.* Four Poems for Robin. MoP; NNaP; NOBA; NoAM

Autumn Mushrooms. Kenneth Mackenzie. CBAP

Autumn nears. The branches yellow. Aleksey Eisner, *Russian*. TCRP, *tr. by* Bradley Jordan *and* Katya Zubritskaya

Autumn night, in a hotel, the two, An. Georgy Adamovich, *Russian*. TCRP, *tr. by* Yakov Hornstein

Autumn night is clear, The. Tu Fu. *See* Stars and Moon on the Yangtse.

Autumn Night—Sleepless. Wu Wei-yeh, *Chinese*. CoBLCP, *tr. by* Jonathan Chaves

Autumn 1942. Roy Fuller. PoWW

Autumn, 1939. Alun Lewis. PoWW

Autumn Plants, Flowers, Bamboo, Rocks. Yün Shou-p'ing, *Chinese*. CoBLCP, *tr. by* Jonathan Chaves

Autumn rain—. Chuck Brickley. HA

Autumn resumes the land, ruffles the woods. The Laurel Axe. Geoffrey Hill. NAEL-2; NoAM; NoP-4; PoE *Fr.* An Apology for the Revival of Christian Architecture in England.

Autumn River. T'ang Hsien-tsu, *Chinese*. CoBLCP, *tr. by* Jonathan Chaves

Autumn Robin, The. John Clare. BoTP

Autumn season comes to the country, The. Yang Chi. *Fr.* Living in Master Fang's Garden. CoBLCP, *tr. by* Jonathan Chaves

Autumn Sentiments. Yüan Hao-wen, *Chinese*. SuSp, *tr. by* Irving Y. Lo

Autumn Sequel. Louis MacNeice.

Fanfare for the Makers, A. NOBE

Autumn Sequence. Jan Freeman.

Fifteen. OxWW

Autumn Sequence. Adrienne Rich. VGW

Autumn Shade. Edgar Bowers.

"Autumn shade is thin, The. Grey leaves lie faint." MT

"Awakened by some fear, I watch the sky." VCAP

"I drive home with the books that I will read." VCAP

"In nameless warmth, sun light in every corner." VCAP

"Snow and then rain. The roads are wet. A car." VCAP

Autumn Song. Margaret Rose. BoTP

Autumn Song. Johann Ludwig Tieck, *German*. AWP, *tr. by* James Clarence Mangan

Autumn Sonnets, The. May Sarton.

"If I could let you go as trees let go." PoSu

Autumn Spring. Hsüeh T'ao, *Chinese*. SuSp, *tr. by* Eric W. Johnson

Autumn sun over the *t'ung* tree. Wang An-shih, *Chinese*. SuSp, *tr. by* Jan W. Walls

Autumn Sunset, An. Edith Wharton. APN-2

Autumn Supper. Dimitris Tsaloumas. BMAP

Autumn Testament. James Keir Baxter.

"Rata blooms explode, the bow-legged tomcat, The." PeNZ

"Spider crouching on the ledge above the sink, The." PeNZ

"To wish to climb a ladder to the loft." PeNZ

Autumn: the ninth year of Yüan Ho. The Temple. Po Chü-i, *Chinese*. ChiP; OBMV, *tr. by* Arthur Waley

Autumn Thoughts. Han Yü, *Chinese*.

"Frosty wind harries the *wu-t'ung*, A." PLT, *tr. by* A. C. Graham

"Leaves fall turning turning to the ground." CoBCP, *tr. by* Burton Watson

"This morning I can't seem to get out of bed." CoBCP, *tr. by* Burton Watson

"When white dew descends on the hundred grasses." CoBCP, *tr. by* Burton Watson

Autumn Thoughts. Lu Yu, *Chinese*. OHPC, *tr. by* Kenneth Rexroth

Autumn Thoughts. Ma Chih-yüan. CoBLCP, *tr. by* Jonathan Chaves *Fr.* To the Tune "T'ien ching sha."

Autumn Thoughts. Meng Chiao, *Chinese*.

"Face of the autumn moon freezes, The." PLT, *tr. by* A. C. Graham

"Wind and bamboos strum and speak to each other." PLT, *tr. by* A. C. Graham

Autumn Thoughts ("Mornings up before the rooster calls"). Lu Yu, *Chinese*. CoBCP, *tr. by* Burton Watson

Autumn Thoughts ("Sumac showing faint traces of red"). Lu Yu, *Chinese*. SuSp, *tr. by* Burton Watson

Autumn Thoughts. Ts'en Shen, *Chinese*. SuSp, *tr. by* C. H. Wang

Autumn Thoughts. Tu Fu, *Chinese*.

"I have heard the affairs in Ch'ang-an are like a game of chess." SuSp, *tr. by* Wu-chi Liu

"Jade dews deeply wilt and wound the maple woods." SuSp, *tr. by* Wu-chi Liu

"Waters of K'un-ming Pool recalled the achievements of Han times, The." SuSp, *tr. by* Wu-chi Liu

Autumn Thoughts. Mary E. Tucker. CBWP-1

Autumn-time has come, The. My Triumph. John Greenleaf Whittier. APN-1; NOBA

Autumn twilight. Cor Van den Heuvel. HA

Autumn twilight. Nicholas Virgilio. HA

Autumn Twilight in the Mountains. Wang Wei, *Chinese*. OHMPC, *tr. by* Kenneth Rexroth

Autumn upon us was rushing, The. Ravings. Thomas Hood Jr. BXAP

Autumn Vista. Li Meng-yang, *Chinese*. CoBLCP, *tr. by* Jonathan Chaves

Autumn Warrior. Barney Bush. HATNAP

Autumn wastes are each day wilder, The. Tu Fu, *Chinese*. PLT, *tr. by* A. C. Graham

Autumn wheat turns green and lush as spring wheat yellows. Reeling Silk. Fan Ch'eng-ta. SuSp, *tr. by* Wu-chi Liu *Fr.* Four Songs in Imitation of Wang Chien.

Autumn Wind. Ruth Dallas. PeNZ *Fr.* Letter to a Chinese Poet.

Autumn wind, The. Nicholas Virgilio. HA

Autumn wind blows across the sea in the deepening twilight, An. Inscribed on Byron's Poetic Works. Su Man-shu, *Chinese*. SuSp, *tr. by* Wu-chi Liu

Autumn wind blows white clouds, The. Emperor Wu of Han, *Chinese.* OHMPC, *tr. by* Kenneth Rexroth

Autumn wind came stealing. The Thief. Irene F. Pawsey. BoTP

Autumn wind rises. Song of the Autumn Wind. Emperor Wu of Han, *Chinese.* CoBCP, *tr. by* Burton Watson

Autumn wind rises; white clouds fly. Emperor Wu of Han, *Chinese.* ChiP; FaBoCh, *tr. by* Arthur Waley

Autumn wind soughs and sighs, the setting sun is red. Tune: "Song of River Goddess"—Moorinig My Boat at Fen-shui at Night. Huang Shu, *Chinese.* SuSp, *tr. by* James J. Y. Liu

Autumn wind: ten thousand trees wither. The Stone on the Hilltop. Lu Yu, *Chinese.* CoBCP, *tr. by* Burton Watson

Autumn winds blow along the river. The Grain-Barge Wife. Wu Chia-chi, *Chinese.* CoBLCP, *tr. by* Jonathan Chaves

Autumn winds blow in from Chieh-shih Mountain. Sadness in the Autumn Chambers. Yün Shou-p'ing, *Chinese.* CoBLCP, *tr. by* Jonathan Chaves

Autumn winds rise. Emperor Wu of Han, *Chinese.* SuSp, *tr. by* Ronald C. Miao

Autumn winds whistle sadly, the air grows chill. Song of Yen. Ts'ao P'i, *Chinese.* SuSp, *tr. by* Ronald C. Miao

Autumn Woods. William Cullen Bryant. APN-1

Autumnal[1], The. Donne. FSCP; InPS-3; NOSC; PoEL-2 *Fr.* Elegies.

Autumnal. Ernest Christopher Dowson. EBVV; OBNC

Autumnal Ode. Aubrey Thomas De Vere. OBNC

Autumnal Sketch, An. August Kleinzahler. PmAP

Autumnal skies. Vespers. Emile Ologoudou. PBMAP

Autumnal Song. Walter Savage Landor. OAEL-2

Autumnal Work. Lucius Junius Moderatus Columella, *Latin.* GaP, *tr. by Unknown*

Autumn's bright moon. Haiku. Chiyojo, *Japanese.* PBWP, *tr. by* R. H. Blyth

Autumn's done, they have the golden corn in, The. Trumbull Stickney. APN-2

Autumn's onset means cooling breezes. Juan Chi. SuSp, *tr. by* Charles Hartman *Fr.* Poems Expressing My Feelings.

Aux Italiens. "Owen Meredith." BLPA; FaBoBe

Aux Leon. . . Women. Honor Ford-Smith. HCP

Avalanche. Adrien Stoutenburg. NYBP

Avalon. Thomas Holley Chivers. APN-1

Avant-Dernières Pensées. Dionisio D. Martinez. BAP-94

Avant Garde. Louis Dudek. *Fr.* Provincetown. MoCV

Avarice. Anthony Hecht. OxBSP

Avatars. V. Indira Bhavani, *Tamil.* OMIP, *tr. by* Martha Ann Selby

Ave. Diane Di Prima. BB *Fr.* Loba.
    ("O lost moon sisters.")

Ave atque Vale. Swinburne. NAEL-2; NOBE; OAEL-2; OBEV; OBNC

Ave atque Vale. Rosamund Marriott Watson. NOBE; OAEL-2; OBEV; OBNC

Ave Caesar. Robinson Jeffers. FaBoPV; MoP; NOBA; NoAM; OxBA; OxBSP

Ave Imperatrix! Oscar Wilde. PeVV

Ave Maria. Hart Crane. NOBA; NoAM *Fr.* The Bridge. NAAL-2

Ave Maria. Barbara Ferland. PBCV

Ave Maria. Frank O'Hara. CLPP; HCAP; LiLi; NAAL-2; NNaP; NoP-4; PmAP; PoM; PoPoPo; VCAP
    ("Seeing / movies you wouldn't let them see when they were young.") (LL) CLPP

Ave Maria, Gratia Plena. Oscar Wilde. ChIV-2

Ave maris stella, the star of the sea. *Unknown.* CTC

Ave, Virgo! Gr-r-r—you swine! (LL) Soliloquy of the Spanish Cloister. Robert Browning. FHYEP; FaBoVe; ImPo; InPK-6; NAEL-2; NIP-4; NOBL; NOBVV; NoP-4; OAEL-2; OxBoV; PeVV; TOF; UV

'Ave you 'eard o' the Widow at Windsor. The Widow at Windsor. Rudyard Kipling. NAEL-2; NoAM

Avebury. Dorothy Wellesley, Duchess of Wellington. WPN

Avec Amour, *There never was a war that was inward.* Robyn Selman. BAP-95

Avenge O Lord thy slaughtered [or slaughter'd] Saints, whose bones. On the Late Massacre [or Massacher] in Piedmont [or Piemont]. Milton. AWP; CABP; GSo; GTBS-P; HAP; HeIP-4; NAEL-1; NOBE; NOCV; NoP-4; OAEL-1; OBWP; PFE; PoEL-3; PoPoPo; Poetr; SCGP; Son; TFi; TRP; UnPo; WeW-3

Avengers, The. Edwin Markham. MoAmPo

Avenue. Frances Darwin Cornford. LW

Avenue, The. Paul Muldoon. PBCIP

Avenue Bearing the Initial of Christ into the New World, The. Galway Kinnell.
    "Fishmarket closed, the fishes gone into flesh, The." CoAmPo
    "In sunlight on the Avenue." LiTM

"Pcheek pcheek pcheek pcheek pcheek." LiTM

Avenue / defined, The. The Deserted House. Johannes Bobrowski, *German.* CEEP, *tr. by* Ruth Mead *and* Matthew Mead

Avenue of tombs! I stand before, An. In Père La Chaise. Joaquin Miller. APN-2

Avenue was green and long, and green, The. A Visit to Castletown House. Michael Hartnett. BiHa; PBCIP

Avenues, The. David St. John. WWSi

Average man was Private Flynn, An. The Vision. Katharine Tynan. NSI

Avid of life and love, insatiate vagabond. Verlaine. Richard Hovey. APN-2

Avocado. Gary Snyder. PmAP

Avoid extremes; and shun the fault of such. Alexander Pope. FHYEP *Fr.* An Essay on Criticism. NAEL-1; PoEL-3; TFi

Avoid the reeking herd. The Eagle and the Mole. Elinor Wylie. AWP; BoWoP; LiTM; MoAmPo; NALW; UnPo

Avoidances. Ron Welburn. PoBA

Avondale Mine Disaster, The. *Unknown.* AmFP

Aw wish my lover she was a cherry. A Pitman's Lovesong. *Unknown.* FaBoVe

Await us, weighing the unstripped bough. (LL) Farewell to Van Gogh. Charles Tomlinson. CMoP; GTBS-P; NoP-4; PoE

Awaji Island—. Kanemasa, *Japanese.* OHMPJ, *tr. by* Kenneth Rexroth

Awake. Mary Elizabeth Coleridge. OBNC

Awake! William Robert Rodgers. LiTM

Awake, Aeolian lyre, awake. The Progress of Poesy. Thomas Gray. AWP; GTBS-P; NOEC; OBEV

Awake, Aeolian lyre, awake. The Progress of Poesy. Thomas Gray. AWP; GTBS-P; NOEC; OBEV

Awake all night till the. *Unknown, Greek.* PGA, *tr. by* Kenneth Rexroth

Awake, alone, aware. Insomniac Poem. Ron Loewinsohn. NeAP

Awake, and with attention hear. The 34. Chapter of the Prophet Isaiah. Abraham Cowley. ChIV-1

Awake! arise! Oh, men of my race. Daybreak. George Marion McClellan. AAP

Awake, arise, / Pull out your eyes. Mother Goose. OxNR

Awake, arise, the hour is come. A Radical War Song. Thomas Babington Macaulay, 1st Baron Macaulay. OBSV

Awake, Arise, You Drowsy Sleeper. *Unknown.* AmFP

Awake at midnight on the factory side of town. A History of Navigation. Nancy Eimers. BAP-96

Awake, awake, my little Boy! The Land of Dreams. William Blake. CH

Awake, awake, my Lyre! A Supplication. Abraham Cowley. GTBS-P; OxAEP-1 *Fr.* Davideis.

Awake, awake, thou heavy sprite [or spright]. Thomas Campion. ChIV-1

Awake! for morning in the bowl of night. Omar Khayyám. PeVV, *sect.* I–XII; EBEvV; NOBVV; OxAEP-2; TAL; UV *Fr.* The Rubáiyát of Omar Khayyám [of Naishápúr]. AWP; EBVV; FaBoBe; FaPoR; HAP; NAEL-2; PoEL-5

Awake! for Morning in the Bowl of Night. The Rubáiyát of Omar Khayyám [of Naishápúr]. Omar Khayyám, *Persian.* AWP; EBVV; FaBoBe; FaPoR; HAP; NAEL-2; PoEL-5

Awake! for Morning on the Pitch of Night. Strugnell's Rubáiyát. Wendy Cope. UV

Awake! For Sweeney in pyjamas bright. Jack Black. BXAP

Awake, glad heart! get up, and sing. Christ's Nativity. Henry Vaughan. ESCV

Awake I steal what they dream. Sleepers. Branko Miljkovic, *Serbo-Croatian.* HSix, *tr. by* Charles Simic

Awake, like a hippopotamus with eyes bulged. Monday. William Stafford. NYBP

Awake, My Fair. Judah Halevi, *Hebrew.* TrJP, *tr. by* Alice Lucas

Awake, my heart, to be loved, awake, awake! Robert Bridges. GTBS-P; MoBrPo; NOBE; OBEV

Awake, my heart's delight, awake. A Fair Melody: To Be Sung by Good Christians. Hans Sachs, *German.* GePo, *tr. by* Catherine Winkworth

Awake my Lute, daughters of Musick come. Mary Astell. KTR

Awake, My Soul. Moses ibn Ezra. *Fr.* Wine-Songs. TrJP, *tr. by* Solomon Solis-Cohen

Awake, my soul, and with the sun. Morning Hymn. Thomas Ken. NOSC

Awake My Soul, Betimes Awake. Isaac Chanler. AH

Awake, My Soul! In Grateful Songs. Andrew Fowler. AH

Awake, my St. John! leave all meaner things. Alexander Pope. NAEL-1; PoEL-3 *Fr.* An Essay on Man.

Awake, my St. John! leave all meaner things. The Wild Garden. Alexander Pope. *Fr.* Awake, my St. John! leave all meaner things. NAEL-1; PoEL-3 *Fr.* An Essay on Man.

Awake! Oh, north wind. Bible, *O.T.* *Fr.* The Song of Songs. AWP

Awake or sleeping (for I know not which). An Old-World Thicket. Christina Rossetti. VWP

Awake sad heart, whom sorrow ever drowns. The Dawning. George Herbert. ESCV; NOSC

Awake sound sleeper! hark, what dismal knells. Upon the Death of His Much Esteemed Friend Mr. Jno Saffin Junr. Grindall Rawson. SCAP

Awake! The day is coming now. Walther von der Vogelweide, *German.* AWP, *tr. by* Jethro Bithell

Awake, thou best of sense. Upon the Times. Mildmay Fane, 2d Earl of Westmorland. BeJo

Awake, [*or* Awake!] ye forms of verse divine! The National Painting [*or* Paintings]. Fitz-Greene Halleck *and* Joseph Rodman Drake. APN-1 *Fr.* The Croaker Papers.

Awake, ye forms of verse divine! The National Painting. Joseph Rodman Drake. GS

Awake yee westerne nymphs, arise and sing. Samuel Danforth. SCAP

Awaken them; they are knobs of sound. Sanskrit. Jayanta Mahapatra. VCWP

Awakened by love, your body's animals want to get out. Clavicles for a Great Poetic Game. René Daumal. PFTM, *tr. by* Pierre Joris *Fr.* Clavicles for a Great Poetic Game.

Awakened by some fear, I watch the sky. Edgar Bowers. VCAP *Fr.* Autumn Shade.

Awakened to this other bleakness. Falcon Drinking. Dimitris Tsaloumas. BMAP

Awakening. Robert Bly. CoAmPo

Awakening, The. Robert Creeley. NeAP

Awakening. John Haines. SPE

Awakening. Henrietta Cordelia Ray. CBWP-3

Awakening. Anita Virgil. HA

Awakening from Drunkenness on a Spring Day. Li Po, *Chinese.* TAL, *tr. by* Robert Payne

Awakening like return to Earth from Moon. Brian Coffey. CIP-2 *Fr.* Advent.

Awakening spring: how many leaves! Willow. Li Shang-yin, *Chinese.* LoP; SuSp, *tr. by* Eugene Eoyang *and* Irving Y. Lo

Awakening to Snow. Sylvia Kantaris. AYFP

Awakening transports of an inner view of things. (LL) Roots and Branches. Robert Duncan. FTOS; VGW

Awakening— / Voices of birds. Nelly Sachs, *German.* PBWP, *tr. by* Ruth *and* Matthew Mead

Awaking. Stephen Spender. NYBP

Awaking of the Poetic Faculty, The. George Henry Boker. Son

Award. Ray Durem. BPo; PoBA; TTY

Aware. D. H. Lawrence. MoBrPo; NoAM

Aware Aware. Tram Combs. TwCP

Aware that summer baked the water clear. Skykomish River Running. Richard Hugo. PoA

Aware to the dry throat of the wide hell in the world. King David Dances. John Berryman. ChIV-1; KSG; OxBC; OxBSP

Awareness. Don L. Lee. MBE; PoBA

Away. Max Ehrmann. PoToHe

Away! Robert Frost. NOBA

Away. Andrew Salkey. HCP

Away above a harborful. Lawrence Ferlinghetti. BoLoP; PoM *Fr.* Pictures of a Gone World.

Away and away I sail in my light boat. Boating in Autumn. Lu Yu, *Chinese.* ChiP, *tr. by* Arthur Waley

Away, away. (LL) This Is the Key. *Unknown.* BoTP; CBNP; CH; FaBoCh; NTP; OTCP; OxBoLi; OxNR

Away, away in the Northland. A Legend of the Northland. Phoebe Cary. OBCA; OBSP

Away! away! / Tempt me no more, insidious Love. The Complaint. Mark Akenside. OBEV

Away, away! You are safer in the tomb. (LL) To a Shade. W. B. Yeats. NAEL-2; PoEL-5

Away, birds, away! The Bird Scarer. *Unknown.* ReMoGo

Away, Delights. Francis Beaumont *and* John Fletcher. NOBE; OBEV *Fr.* The Captain.

(Sad Song.) GBL

Away despair; my gracious Lord doth hear[e]. The Bag. George Herbert. ESCV; FSCP; GeHe; SeCP

Away down deep and away up high. At the Playground. William Stafford. TLR

Away down East, away down West. *Unknown.* TLR

Away down into the shadowy depths of the Real I once lived. Myself. Adah Isaacs Menken. CBWP-1

AWAY, fear, with thy projects, no false fire. William Alabaster. NoSic

Away, for we are ready to a man! Epilogue. James Elroy Flecker. NOBE *Fr.* The Golden Journey to Samarkand.

Away from earth and its cares set free. Eternity. Josephine D. Henderson Heard. CBWP-4

Away from eyes. Rod Willmot. HA

Away from Home. *Unknown.* PWR

Away from you. Roger McGough. OBCoV *Fr.* Summer with Monika.

Away from you three or four years. Back from Green Dragon. Mei Yao Ch'en, *Chinese.* CoBCP, *tr. by* Burton Watson

Away from you three or four years. Back from Green Dragon, Presented to Hsieh Shih-chih. Harry Mathews, *Chinese.* CoBCP, *tr. by* Burton Watson

Away he goes, the hour's delightful hero. She and the Muse. Denise Levertov. CrSp

Away in a manger[, no crib for a bed]. Cradle Hymn. Martin Luther. AH; BoTP; CTV

Away; let nought to Love displeasing. Winifreda. *Unknown.* OBEV

Away loose-reined careers of poetry! Urian Oakes. NOCV *Fr.* An Elegie upon The Death of the Reverend. . . Mr. Thomas Shepard. SCAP

Away, melancholy, / Away with it, let it go. Stevie Smith. CABP; OxBTC; PBWP

Away mine ashes, then thy fire doth glow. (LL) The Ebb and Flow. Edward Taylor. AmPP; SCAP

Away shall not cast his hand. (LL) Someone told me, Heracleitus. Callimachus, *Greek.* HePo

Away the horde rode, in a storm of hail. The Uncertain Battle. David Gascoyne. PoWW

Away! the moor is dark beneath the moon. Stanzas—April, 1814. Shelley. OBEV; OBNC; SCGP

Away thou fondling motley humourist. A London Street. Donne. NoSic *Fr.* Satires.

Away to Canada. Joshua McCarter Simpson. AAP

Away Vane World. Alexander Montgomerie. NOCV

Away with all whimsical bubbles of air. Botany Bay. John Freeth. NOEC

Away with silks, away with lawn. Clothes Do But Cheat and Cozen [*or* Cousen] Us. Robert Herrick. CaPo

"Away with you, away with you, James de Grant!" James Grant. *Unknown.* ESPB

Away, ye gay landscapes, ye gardens of roses! Lachin y Gair. Byron. OxBS

Aweary Am I. Abu 'l-Ala al-Ma'Arri, *Arabic.* AWP, *tr. by* R. A. Nicholson

Awed I behold once more. Ralph Waldo Emerson. APN-1; ColAP; PAR

Awesome are the works of God. The Works of God. Moses ibn Ezra, *Hebrew.* TrJP, *tr. by* Solomon Solis-Cohen

Awful but cheerful. (LL) The Bight. Elizabeth Bishop. FaBoWP; HCAP; NAAL-2; NYBP; RB; VCAP

Awful Mother, The. Susan Griffin. MDDM

Awful shadow of some unseen Power, The. Hymn to Intellectual Beauty. Shelley. FHYEP; HAP; HeIP-4; ImPo; LaPo; NAEL-2; NOBRP; NoP-4; OAEL-2; OBNC; PoE; Ro; TOF

Awhile in the dead of the winter. Seasons and Times. William Barnes. NOBVV

Awkward first audible / called language, An. (LL) Solo Native. Thomas Lux. CMAP; LCAP-2

Awkward on a hillock of grass. Forever the Snake. Jennifer Rankin. BMAP

Awkward was she yesterday. The Maiden. Peter Hille, *German.* AWP, *tr. by* Jethro Bithell

Awoke in this. Perugia. Art Lange. PmAP

Axe angles / from my neighbor's ashcan, An. Junk. Richard Wilbur. HAP; WeW-3

Axe-fall, echo and silence. Noonday silence. Noonday Axeman. Les A. Murray. NoP-4

Axe Handles. Gary Snyder. ColAP; LoL; NoAM; PmAP; PoPoPo; VCAP

Axe-Helve, The. Robert Frost. OxBA

Axe rings in the wood, The. Remembered Morning. Janet Lewis. SoSe-8; WPE

Axes / After whose stroke the wood rings. Words. Sylvia Plath. APAD; CoAmPo; HCAP; NAAL-2; NALW; PoE; Poetr; VCAP

Axes lie next to the river, The. Lyubomir Nikolov, *Bulgarian.* CEEP, *tr. by* Roland Flint

Axion Esti, The. Odysseus Elytis, *Greek.* VCWP, *tr. by* Edmund Keeley *and* Philip Sherrard

("Praised be the wooden table.") VCWP, *tr. by* Edmund Keeley *and* Philip Sherrard

"In the beginning the light And the first hour." GrIP, *tr. by* Edmund Keeley *and* George Savidis

"Intelligible sun of Justice and you, glorifying myrtle." GrIP, *tr. by* Edmund Keeley *and* George Savidis

Axle Song. Mairtin O Direain. BiHa

Axolotl / looks a littl, The. David McCord. OBAL

Āy: A Gift of Elephants. Mutamociyar, *Tamil*. PLW, *tr. by* A. K. Ramanujan

Ay! and a world of pikes pass through. Robert Herrick. *See* His Cavalier.

Ay [*or* Aye], besherewe yow [*or* beshrew you!] be [*or* by] my fay. Mannerly Margery Mylk and Ale. John Skelton. AAS; NAEL-1; NoP-4

Ay[e], but to die, and go we know not where. Shakespeare. RB   *Fr.* Measure for Measure.

Ay, buzz and buzz away. Dost thou suppose. Luther to a Bluebottle Fly. Eugene Lee-Hamilton. Son   *Fr.* Imaginary Sonnets.

Ay, gaze upon her rose-wreath'd hair. Revenge. Letitia Elizabeth Landon. NOBRP

Āy: His Hill. Mutamociyar, *Tamil*. PLW, *tr. by* A. K. Ramanujan

Ay, his mother was a mad one. The Sad Boy. Laura Riding Jackson. CBNP; RB

Ay, marry, is 't. Shakespeare. *Fr.* Hamlet. NAWM-1

Ay me, alas, heigh ho, heigh ho! Madrigal. Thomas Weelkes. FaBoCh; OxBoLi

Ay me, alas! the beautiful bright hair. Canzone: His Lament for Selvaggia. Cino da Pistoia, *Italian*. AWP, *tr. by* D. G. Rossetti

Ay me, how many perils doe unfold [*or* enfold]. Edmund Spenser. FHYEP; OAEL-1   *Fr.* Wood Of Error. AEP

Ay me! whilst thee the shores and sounding seas. Milton. *Fr.* Lycidas. AWP; CABP; ClHu; EBEV; EBEvV; FHYEP; GTBS-P; HAP; ImPo; InPS-3; NOBE; NOSC; NoP-4; OAEL-1; OBEV; OxAEP-1; PBRV; PFE; PoEL-3; PoPoPo; Poetr; SCGP; TFi; UnPo

Ay, note that Potter's wheel. Why Time Spins Fast. Robert Browning. *Fr.* Rabbi Ben Ezra. NAEL-2; OBNC

Ay, Oliver! I was but seven, and he was eleven. Echo and the Ferry. Jean Ingelow. EBVV

Ay or Nay? Ralph Schomberg. *Fr.* The Judgment of Paris. TrJP

'Ay!' said Creep. (LL) Old Shellover. Walter De la Mare. BoTP; OxBChV

Ay, screen thy favourite dove, fair child. A Child Screening a Dove from a Hawk. Letitia Elizabeth Landon. NOBRP

Ay so, God be wi' ye! Now I am alone. Shakespeare. OxAEP-1   *Fr.* Hamlet. NAWM-1

Ay, so it is in every brain. To a Young Brother. Maria Jane Jewsbury. OxBChV

Ay, tear her tattered ensign down! Old Ironsides. Oliver Wendell Holmes. APAD; APN-1; AiP; BLPA; CTV; EBEvV; FaBoBe; NAAL-1; NAAL-3; NCAP; PAR; PWR; TAP; TFi

Ay, that incestuous, that adulterate beast. Shakespeare. *Fr.* Hamlet. NAWM-1

Ay, 'Tis Thus. *Unknown*, *Hebrew*. TrJP, *tr. by* Israel Zangwill

Ay, workman, make me a dream. Stephen Crane. MeMAP

Aya! / Ayaya, it is beautiful, beautiful it is out-doors when the summer comes at last. Summer Song. *Unknown*, *Eskimo*. APN-2, *tr. by* Franz Boas

Aye, at that time our days wer but vew. Childhood. William Barnes. NOBVV

Aye, but to die, and go we know not where. Shakespeare. *See* Ay[e], but to die, and go we know not where.

"Aye! I am a poet and upon my tomb." And Thus in Nineveh. Ezra Pound. VGW

"Aye, squire," said Stevens, "they back him at evens." How We Beat the Favourite. Adam Lindsay Gordon. CBAP; PeVV

Aye, there it is! It wakes to-night. Emily Jane Brontë. NALW

("Aye there it is! It wakes tonight.") VWP

Aye, thou art welcome, heaven's delicious breath! October. William Cullen Bryant. APN-1

Aye up at the feast, by Melhill's brow. Melhill Feast. William Barnes. OBNC

Aye, well I know 'tis ghastly to descend that valley. On the Same Picture. Walt Whitman. GS

Aye! What a thing is the passing of Cronos, the angular-minded. John Cowper Powys. OBWVE   *Fr.* The Ridge.

Ayee! Ai! This is heavy earth on our shoulders. Burying Ground by the Ties. Archibald MacLeish. GM

Ayres that Were Sung and Played, at *Brougham Castle* in *Westmerland*, in the Kings Entertainment, The. Thomas Campion.

    Dance, The. FaBoCh

Azalea, The. Coventry Patmore. GBL; GLoP   *Fr.* The Unknown Eros.

Azaleas, The. Sowol Kim, *Korean*. CKP, *tr. by* Jaihiun Kim

Azimuth. *Unknown*. NBrP

Aziola, The. Shelley. EBEV

Azouou! Evening Breeze! What a perfect name! Mririda n'Ait Attik, *Berber into French*. WPOW, *tr. by* René Euloge; *English vers. by* Daniel Halpern *and* Paula Paley

Azra, The. Heinrich Heine, *German*. AWP, *tr. by* John Hay

Azure, I come! from the caves of death withdrawn. Helen, the Sad Queen. Paul Valéry, *French*. AWP, *tr. by* Joseph T. Shipley

Azure, or green, or purple when the sun. William Plomer. PeSAV

Azure sky, An. Christmas. Mary I. Osborn. BoTP

Azure striation swirls beyond the stones. Marilyn Hacker. Son   *Fr.* La Fontaine de Vaucluse.

B

B. Larry Eigner. NeAP

B. A Trellis for R. May Swenson. CPO

B C D Goldfish, A. *Unknown*. NTCP

B kw rm. Euenus, *Greek*. GrAn, *tr. by* Alistair Elliot

B Negative, M / 60 / 5 FT 4 / W PROT. X. J. Kennedy. CoAmPo

B stands for Bear. When bears are seen. Hilaire Belloc. NoAM   *Fr.* A Moral Alphabet.

B, taught by Pope to do his good by stealth. A Misconception. James Russell Lowell. OBAL

Ba Cottage. Andrew Young. OxBSP

Baa baa black sheeep. Tom Leonard. NBrP   *Fr.* Ghostie Men.

Baa, baa, black sheep, have you any wool? Mother Goose. FaBoBe; LB; OxNR; ReMoGo

Baa, baa, black sheep, where'd you leave your lamb? *Unknown*. AmFP

Baal Shem Tov. Abraham Moses Klein. TrJP

Babbitt and the Bromide, The. Ira Gershwin. OBCoV

Babbitt met a Bromide on the avenue one day, A. The Babbitt and the Bromide. Ira Gershwin. OBCoV

Babe insures the teat, The. A Child's Guide to Welfare. D. J. Enright. CBNP

Babe was laid in the Manger, The. A Nativity. Rudyard Kipling. GI

Babe, with a cry brief and dismal, The. Limerick. Edward Gorey. OBAL; PeLi

Babel. Giuseppe Ungaretti. PFTM

Babes in the Wood, The ("My dear, do you know"). *Unknown*. OxBChV

Babes in the Wood, The ("Now ponder well, you parents dear"). *Unknown*. OBNV; OxAEP-1

(Children in the Wood, The.) EnSB

Babiaantje, The. Frank Templeton Prince. MoBrPo

Babies, The. Mark Strand. NYBP

Babies Haven't Any Hair. Samuel Hoffenstein. NBLV

Babies twist in their mothers' arms. The men. When a Beautiful Woman Gets on the Jutiapa Bus. Belle Waring. NAmP90; PBCAP

Babii Yar. Yevtushenko, *Russian*. HP; TCRP; VCWP, *tr. by* George Reavey

Babling Nymph that *Echo* hight: who hearing others talke, A. Echo. Ovid, *Latin*. OBCVT, *tr. by* Arthur Golding

Baboon. *Unknown*, *Hottentot*. PeSA

Baboon. *Unknown*. *Fr.* Hunter Poems of the Yoruba. RB, *tr. by* Ulli Beier

Baboon, The. Rhydwen Williams, *Welsh*. OBWVE, *tr. by* R. Gerallt Jones

Baboon 2. *Unknown*, *Hottentot*. PeSA

Babouchka. Sophie Slingeland. LoHo

Babur. Dom Moraes. OMIP

Baby, The. George Macdonald. *See* Where did You Come From, Baby Dear?

Baby and I. *Unknown*. OxNR

Baby at my breast, The. Against Dark's Harm. Anne Halley. NMM-2

Baby, baby. *Unknown*. LiLi

Baby, baby, naughty baby. Mother Goose. NOBL; OxNR

Baby Beds. *Unknown*. BoTP

Baby bird, with drooping wings, A. Orphans. Tô Hũ'u, *Vietnamese*. AVP, *tr. by* Huỳnh Sanh Thông

Baby brother can't wait. Barbershop Ritual. Sharan Strange. ISC

Baby darling, wake and see. Morning Song. Edith Nesbit. SDW

Baby Dolly. *Unknown*. ReMoGo

Baby Hilary, Sir Edmund, the. Kathleen Leland Baker. NBLV

Baby I hold in my arms is a black baby, The. Black Baby. Anita Scott Coleman. FiLi

Baby, / I just want you to. Shades of Pharoah Sanders Blues for My Baby. John O'Neal. NBV

Baby, if you love me. Down and Out. Langston Hughes. PoE

Baby I'm sick. I need. Night Thoughts: Baby & Demon. Gwen Harwood. CBAP

Baby in the House, A. Patrick Williams. PNI

Baby is born [*or* borne], us bliss [*or* blis] to bring, A. Dear Son, Leave Thy Weeping. *Unknown.* CTC

Baby-Land. George Cooper. BoTP

Baby Lazarus. Jackie Kay. NBrP

Baby lies so fast asleep. Christina Rossetti. VWP

Baby loves to play with me. Hide and Seek. Phyllis Drayson. BoTP

Baby Random. Belle Waring. NAmP90; PBCAP

Baby Seeds. *Unknown.* CTV

Baby-Sermon, A. George Macdonald. NOxBChV; NTP; OxBChV; Spl

Baby-Sitting. Gillian Clarke. FaBoWP; NTP

Baby Song. Thom Gunn. RB *Fr.* Three Songs.

Baby Ten Months Old Looks at the Public Domain, A. William Stafford. NYBP

Baby Tortoise. D. H. Lawrence. CMoP

("Tiny bright-eye, / Slow one.") (LL) PeP

Baby Vallejo. David Rivard. SeSe

Baby Verse, A. *Unknown.* BoTP

Baby Villon. Philip Levine. CoAP; WeT

Baby wades alone across the lawn, The. Errantry. Robert Fitzgerald. NYBP

Baby watched a ford, whereto, A. Wagtail and Baby. Thomas Hardy. PeLV

Baby, / You shall be free. Kadia the Young Mother Speaks. Jessie E. Sampter. TrJP

Babylon. Tennyson. ChIV-1; KSG

Babylon and Sion (Goa and Lisbon). Luis de Camões, *Portuguese.* AWP, *tr. by* Richard Garnett

Babylon: 539 B.C.E. Charles Reznikoff. ChIV-1

Babylon, I did not come to you for the sake of coming. Chorus. Matsemela Manaka. PeSAV *Fr.* Pula.

Babylon; or, The Bonnie Banks o' Fordie. *Unknown.* AmFP; ESPB; OxBB

Babylon Revisited. Imamu Amiri Baraka. BPo; MoP; NoAM

Babylon that was beautiful is Nothing now. Siegfried Sassoon. ChIV-1

Baby's Dance, The. Mother Goose, *at. to* Mother Goose. OxBChV; OxNR

Baby's Drinking Song. James Kirkup. NTCP; OTCP

Baby's feet, like sea-shells pink, A. Swinburne. WeW-3 *Fr.* Étude Réaliste.

Baby's Pantoum. Anne Waldman. FFC

Baby's pee, The. Ruth Yarrow. HA

Bac Ha. David Huddle. CDa

Baccalaureate. David McCord. BXAP; NBLV; OBAL

Bacchae. Euripides, *Greek.*

Home of Aphrodite, The. AWP, *tr. by* Gilbert Murray

"Then listen Thebes, nurse of Semele." OBCVT, *tr. by* Wole Soyinka

"What is wisdom: What gift of the gods." GrIP, *tr. by* William Arrowsmith

Bacchanal. Peter De Vries. BXAP; NBLV; NOBL; OBAL

Bacchanalia; or, The New Age. Matthew Arnold.

"Epoch ends, the world is still, The." OAEL-2

Bacchus. Ralph Waldo Emerson. APN-1; AWP; AmPP; NOBA; OBEV; OxBA; PAR; PoEL-4

Bacchus. William Empson. NoAM

"God who fled down with a standard yard, The." PoA

"Herm whose length measured degrees of heat, The." PoA

Bacchus in Tuscany. Francesco Redi, *Italian.*

Bacchus's Opinion of Wine, and Other Beverages. AWP; OBVE

Bacchus must now his power resign. A Drinking-Song. Henry Carey. OBEV

Bacchus, or the Pirates. *Unknown, Latin.* OBCVT, *tr. by* Leigh Hunt

Bacchus, receive my offering, not. Eratosthenes, *Greek.* GrAn, *tr. by* Alistair Elliot

Bacchus that drunken God from Hell comes forth. Alice Sutcliffe. KTR *Fr.* Meditations of Man's Mortalitie; or, A Way to True Blessedness.

Bacchus, that first from out the purple grape. Milton. *Fr.* Comus; a Masque Presented at Ludlow Castle. FHYEP; OAEL-1

Bach. Lisa Zeidner. CMAP

Bạch-đằng River, The. *Unknown, Vietnamese.* AVP, *tr. by* Huỳnh Sanh Thông

Bachelor, The. William Barnes. PeVV

Bachelor, The. Sandor Csoori, *Hungarian.* CEEP, *tr. by* Nicholas Kolumban

Bachelor. William Meredith. NoAM

Bachelor Bold and Young. *Unknown.* AmFP

Bachelor Farmer. Roger McDonald. CBAP

Bachelor Hall. Eugene Field. BLPA

Bachelors' Buttons. Maud Morin. BoTP

Bachelor's-Buttons. William Jay Smith. DiPo

Bachelor's Complaint, The. *Unknown.* AmFP

Bachelor's Song, The. Thomas Flatman. *See* On Marriage.

Back. Wilfred Wilson Gibson. PoFWW

Back. Angela McCabe. AmPA

Back. Robert Mezey. AmPA

Back again. Day one. Fingers blue with cold. I joined the lengthening queue. Slate Street School. Ciaran Carson. CABP

Back Again, Home. Don L. Lee. BPo

Back Again, Home. Haki R. Madhubuti. NAAAL

Back and forth. As in a swing. When there's. Amir Gilbo'a, *Hebrew.* IP, *tr. by* Warren Bargad *and* Stanley F. Chyet

Back and forth, back and forth. Fall 1961. Robert Lowell. GEA; OBWP; VGW

Back and Side Go Bare, Go Bare. William Stevenson *and* John Still. HeIP-4; NAEL-1 *Fr.* Gammer Gurton's Needle.

(Song of Ale, A.) SCGP

Jolly Good Ale and Old. OBEV

Back arched like a bow. Rachel Blau DuPlessis. DeD *Fr.* Eurydice.

Back down the stair. (LL) At Thomas Hardy's Birthplace, 1953. James Wright. CoAmPo; WeT

Back Far Enough, Down Deep Enough. Constance Urdang. PBCAP

Back from Green Dragon. Mei Yao Ch'en, *Chinese.* CoBCP, *tr. by* Burton Watson

Back from Green Dragon, Presented to Hsieh Shih-chih. Harry Mathews, *Chinese.* CoBCP, *tr. by* Burton Watson

Back from the City. Jane Kenyon. AFr

Back from the palace of a famous king. The Larkin Automatic Car Wash. Gavin Ewart. NoAM

Back from the west, back from the war, Marcellus. Crinagoras, *Greek.* GrAn, *tr. by* Alistair Elliot

Back from the Word-Processing Course, I Say to My Old Typewriter. Michael C. Blumenthal. NoAM

Back-Green Odyssey. Alastair MacKie.

"Streekit ahint the winbreak I let." FaBoTC

"Sun's oot. I sit, my pipe alunt and puff, The." FaBoTC

Back here the fall, spreading down the hills. Ember Week, Reseda. Stephen Yenser. EOEF

Back home the black women are all beautiful. W. W. Imamu Amiri Baraka. HeIP-4; NOBA; PoBA

Back in Black Mountain / a child will smack your face. Black Mountain Blues. Bessie Smith. PFTM

Back in our young days whenever. Farewell to Fan Yun at An Ch'eng. Shen Yüeh, *Chinese.* OHMPC, *tr. by* Kenneth Rexroth

Back In Prison. Nguyễn Đình Kiên, *Vietnamese.* AVP, *tr. by* Huỳnh Sanh Thông

Back in *tachanka* days, when Red and Green. Makhno's Philosophers. John Streeter Manifold. CBAP; NOBAu

Back in the caveman days business was fair. The Oxford Hysteria of English Poetry. Adrian Mitchell. PeLV

Back in the dear old thirties' days. The Poet of Bray. John Heath-Stubbs. NOBL

Back in the iron tower he said, "When I left the tower." Two Tongues in a Tower. John Wheelwright. KSG

Back in the painted pavilion, again in late spring. Tune: "Butterflies Lingering over Flowers." Ou-yang Hsiu, *Chinese.* SuSp, *tr. by* Eugene Eoyang

Back in the Return. Huw Menai.

"Where shall the eyes a darkness find." OBWVE

Back in the States. Louis Simpson. PBCV

Back in the years when Phlagstaff, the Dane, was monarch. "Orpheus C. Kerr." *Fr.* The Rejected "National Hymns." OBAL

Back into the Garden. Sarah Webster Fabio. BlSi

Back of Chicago the open fields—were you ever there? Evening Song. Sherwood Anderson. GM

Back of the beating hammer. The Thinker. Berton Braley. BLPA

Back of the dam, under. The Town of Hill. Donald Hall. TAP

Back of the door the child is playing that. Resolution. W. S. Merwin. NYBP

'Back on Times Square, Dreaming of Times Square'. Allen Ginsberg. CLPP; PiM; PoE

("With his music.") (LL) PiM

Back out of all this now too much for us. Directive. Robert Frost. AFr; AmPP; CMoP; ColAP; HAP; ImPo; InPS-3; LiTM; MeMAP; MoAmPo; NAAL-2; NOBA; NoAM; NoP-4; PoE; SAGP; SAmP; TFi

Back path, steeped in musk and mint, A. Flower-Patterned Snake. So Chong-Ju, *Korean.* VCWP, *tr. by* David R. McCann

Back Steps Lookout. Rhyll McMaster. BMAP

Back Street. Arthur Rex Dugard Fairburn. PeNZ *Fr.* Album Leaves.

Back, the yoke, the yardage. Lapped seams, The. Shirt. Robert Pinsky. ColAP; NAmP90

Back Then. Yusef Komunyakaa. GT

Back then I cut off a lock. Semyon Isaakovich Kirsanov. TCRP, tr. by Lubov Yakovleva *Fr.* Your Poem.

Back then I was still young. Blaise Cendrars. PFTM, tr. by Ron Padgett *Fr.* The Prose of the Trans-Siberian and of Little Jeanne of France.

Back then it seemed that wherever a girl took off her clothes. Skin. Lucia Maria Perillo. BAP-93

Back then when so much was clear. Tenderness. Stephen Dunn. NIP-4

Back there where fishermen can't swim. Where Fishermen Can't Swim. Matthew Sweeney. BiHa

Back through clouds. Train Tune. Louise Bogan. GM

Back through the Looking Glass to This Side. John Ciardi. NBLV

Back to a shadow in the night. (LL) La Mélinite: Moulin-Rouge. Arthur Symons. ADE; PeVV

Back To Africa, Miss Mattie? Louise Bennett. PBCV

Back to back, stud poker & an open / pot. Twin Aces. Keith Wilson. Poetsp

Back to back, tonight and every night. (LL) Sex and the Over Forties. Peter Porter. BMAP; CBLP

Back to Base. Jenny Joseph. BrRo

Back to Catfish. Belle Waring. NAmP90

Back to Dublin. Robert Arthur Douglas Ford. MoCV

Back to Griggsby's Station. James Whitcomb Riley. BLPA

Back to him. Tune: "Partridge Sky"—Parting Sorrows. Na-lan Hsing-te, *Chinese.* SuSp, tr. by William Golightly

Back to Hometown Kingston. James Berry. PBCV

Back to it. Larry Eigner. FTOS

Back to Rest. William Noel Hodgson. PoFWW

Back to silent big soap flakes. Don't Hope to Gain by What Has Preceded. Joanne Kyger. PoM

Back to the cold transparent ham again! (LL) Sonnet to Vauxhall. Thomas Hood. OBCoV; PoEL-4

Back to the flower-town, side by side. In Memory of Walter Savage Landor. Swinburne. PoEL-5

Back to the Ghetto. Jacob Glatstein, *Yiddish.* TrJP, tr. by Joseph Leftwich

Back to the green deeps of the outer bay. The Herring Weir. Sir Charles G. D. Roberts. NOBC *Fr.* Songs of the Common Day.

Back to the instruction manual which has made me dream of Guadalajara. (LL) The Instruction Manual. John Ashbery. HAP; InPS-3; NOBA; NeAP; NoAM; PoM; Poetr

Back to the Land. Charles Larcom Graves. NSI

Back to the ordinary. (LL) Roe-Deer. Ted Hughes. NOxBChV; NoAM; OxAEP-2

Back to Town. John Hollander. NoAM

Back to work happy at the thought possibly so. (LL) Personal Poem. Frank O'Hara. CAPP-1; CLPP; PmAP

Back Trouble. Emily Grosholz. RA

Back when it took all day to come up. Hearing. W. S. Merwin. NoAM

Back will go the head with the dark curls. Castanets. Bernard Spencer. WeW-3

Back wings, The. Between Walls. William Carlos Williams. HoPM; TAP; VGW

Back Yard, July Night. William Cole. KaS

Backdrop: The dining room at Stonington. James Merrill. NoAM *Fr.* The Book of Ephraim.

Background, dark vine at the edge of the porch, The. (LL) Forties Flick. John Ashbery. FTOS; NoAM

Background is instrumental. Eating the Forest. D. F. Brown. CDa

Backgrounds to Italian Paintings: Fifteenth Century. Anne Ridler. WPE

Backlash Blues, The. Langston Hughes. BPo

Backra one fo go a hebben? Query. Michael McTurk. PBCV

Backroad leafmold stonewall chipmunk. Silent Poem. Robert Francis. CRP; LCAP-2

Backside to the Wind. Paul Durcan. PBCIP

Backup, The. Wing Tek Lum. IFJA

Backward & down into inbetween as Vicki says. Mean Drunk Poem. Sharon Thesen. NOBC

Backward—as if retentive. The Company. Robert Creeley. FTOS

Backward Look, The. Howard Nemerov. OxBC

Backward, turn backward, O time, in your flight. Rock Me to Sleep[, Mother]. Elizabeth Akers Allen. APN-2; BLPA; FaBoBe; MDDM; OBCA

Backwater Blues. Bessie Smith. NAAAL

Backwoodsman, The. James Kirke Paulding.

    "Here lay dark Pittsburgh, from whose site there broke." APN-1

    "In truth it was a landscape wildly gay." APN-1

    "Neglected Muse! of this our western clime." APN-1

    "'Tis true—yet 'tis no pity that 'tis true." APN-1

"'Twas sunset's hallow'd time—and such an eve." APN-1

Backyard. Diane Di Prima. PmAP

Backyard. John Tranter. BMAP

Backyards and barnlots. The Book of Galahad. Jack Spicer. FTOS

Bacon-smell. Geranium-smell. The Hangman's Room. János Pilinszky, *Hungarian.* PoSu, tr. by Peter Jay

Bacon's Epitaph, Made by His Man. John Cotton. SCAP

Bad actors love to play great villains. Lucilius, *Greek.* GrAn, tr. by Peter Porter

Bad and Good. Alexander Resnikoff. NTCP

Bad Blood. U Tam'si Tchicaya, *French.* NegPo, tr. by Ellen Conroy Kennedy

Bad Break!, A. W. T. Goodge. NOBAu

Bad breed of the natives with their hates, The. D. C. Karl Shapiro. NYBP

Bad company is a disease. Rowland Watkyns. FaBoEE

Bad day at the market for Canobie Dick, A. The Story of Canobie Dick. Libby Houston. OBSP

Bad Dog. Brian Lee. PeP

Bad Dream. Louis MacNeice. NoAM

Bad Dreams. Robert Browning. GLoP

Bad Dreams III. Robert Browning. OAEL-2

Bad for You. Diane Averill. CMAP

Bad Habit, The. Charles Henri Ford. SPE

Bad Kittens, The. Elizabeth Jane Coatsworth. OBCA

Bad Landlord, The. William Chamberlayne. NOSC *Fr.* Pharonnida.

Bad Luck Card. Langston Hughes. NoP-4; SAmP; TRP

Bad luck to this marching. Benjamin Hall Kennedy. OBCoV

Bad luck you'll have all day! (LL) Pins. *Unknown.* FaBoBe; LB; ReMoGo

Bad Man. Langston Hughes. NAAAL

Bad Man Ballad. *Unknown.* AmFP

Bad money drives out good. What Do You Want: A Meaningful Dialogue, or a Satisfactory Talk? Ogden Nash. OBCoV

Bad Morning. Langston Hughes. OBAL

Bad Mother, The. Susan Griffin. CrSp

Bad Mother, The. Beatrice Hawley. FiLi

Bad news has come to town, bad news is carried. Montcalm and Wolfe. *Unknown.* AmFP

Bad Old Days, The. Kenneth Rexroth. NNaP; NoAM

Bad quartos were my first love. Bibliographer. Josephine Miles. FaBoWP

Bad Report—Good Manners. Spike Milligan. NOxBChV

Bad Run at King's Rest. Douglas Livingstone. PeSAV

Bad Season Makes the Poet Sad, The. Robert Herrick. BeJo; CaPo; CavPo; NAEL-1; SCGP

Bad (she said) was. Hymn To a Woman Under Interrogation. Reiner Kunze, *German.* PoSu, tr. by Ewald Osers

Bad (she said) was / the moment of. Reiner Kunze. *See* Hymn To a Woman Under Interrogation.

Bad Sir Brian Botany. A. A. Milne. NOxBChV

Bad Sleeper, A. Paul Verlaine, *French.* EP, tr. by François Pirou

Bad-tempered, I got back. And Then. Ōshima Ryōta, *Japanese.* GaP, tr. by Geoffrey Bownas *and* Anthony Thwaite

Bad Time for Poetry. Bertolt Brecht, *German.* PoSu, tr. by John Willett *and* Ralph Manheim

Bad town, I see a white-faced bull. Clinton. Sterling Plumpp. BkSV *Fr.* Clinton.

Badger ("When midnight comes a host of dogs and men"). John Clare. FHYEP; HAP; OAEL-2; PoEL-4; Poetr; SCGP

    ("And leaves his hold and crackles, groans, and dies.") (LL) NoP-4; PoPoPo

Badger and the hare, The. (LL) The Passing of the Shee. John Millington Synge. BIrV; FaBoEE

Badger grunting on his woodland track, The. John Clare. FaBoVe; InPS-3

    ("And leaves his hold and cackles, groans and dies.") (LL) GEA

Badger grunting on his woodland track, The. Untitled. John Clare. *Fr.* The Badger grunting on his woodland track. FaBoVe; GEA; InPS-3

Badgers, The. Eden Phillpotts. BoTP

Badman of the Guest Professor. Ishmael Reed. BPo; SSLK

Badminton. Sir Alfred Comyn Lyall. PeVV *Fr.* Studies at Delhi, 1876.

Baedeker for Metaphysicians. Brian Higgins. FaBoTw

Baffled Knight, The. *Unknown.* ESPB

    (Courteous Knight, The.) OxBB

Bag, The. George Herbert. ESCV; FSCP; GeHe; SeCP

    ("Any thing to me. Harke, Despair away.") (LL) FSCP

Bag of Tools, A. R. L. Sharpe. BLPA; PoToHe

Bag-Snatching in Dublin. Stevie Smith. OxBoV

Bag Woman. Dudley Randall. NoAM

Bagel, The. David Ignatow. CoAmPo; PiM; TwCP

Baggot Street Deserta. Thomas Kinsella. CIP-2; CMoP; NoAM

Bagpipe Music. "Hugh MacDiarmid." OAEL-2

Bagpipe Music. Louis MacNeice. CABP; CMoP; EBEvV; GTBS-P; ImPo; LiTM; MoP; NAEL-2; NBLV; NOBE; NOBL; NoAM; NoP-4; OAEL-2; OBSV; OxBTC; PeLV; RB; TFi; UV

Bagpipe sear to meadows, the flute to highways dry, The. Timbre. Ion Barbu, *Romanian*. CEEP, *tr. by* Dan Duescu

Bagpipes at the Biltmore. Robert Conquest. OBCoV

Bags of Meat. Thomas Hardy. RB

Bags Packed and We Expected This. Ramona Wilson. VoR

Bah! I have sung women in three cities. Cino. Ezra Pound. VGW

Bahamas. George Oppen. NYBP

Bahá'u'lláh in the Garden of Ridwan. Robert Earl Hayden. PoBA

Baii. Jim Barnes. *Fr.* Four Things Choctaw. HATNAP

Bailey Beareth the Bell Away, The. *Unknown.* CBNP

Bailey Gatzert: The First Grade, 1945. Lonny Kaneko. LTA

Bailiff's Daughter of Islington, The. *Unknown.* AmFP; ESPB; OxBB; OxBoLi; PBMP

Bait, The. Eric Chock. OpBo

Bait[e], The. Donne. CBLP; HoPM; InPK-6; InPS-3; NAEL-1; NOSC; OAEL-1; PFE; PoRA; RB

Baith Gud[e] and Fair and Womanlie [*or* Womanly]. *Unknown.* OxBS

Bajan. Anthony Kellman. HCP

Bajan Litany. Bruce St. John. PBCV

Bakchos the wine-god / dissolver of limbs. *Unknown, Greek.* GrAn, *tr. by* Peter Jay

Baked Alaska. John Ashbery. BAP-93

  "And when the hectic." BAP-93

  "It will do. It's not." BAP-93

  "Some time later, in Provence." BAP-93

Baked and cleaned. Grandmother. Siv Cedering Fox. PBCAP

Baked the day she suddenly dropped dead. Book Ends. Tony Harrison. DiPo; NAEL-2 *Fr.* The School of Eloquence. NAEL-2; NoAM

Baker hadn't yet unfastened the iron shutters of his shop when the, The. Leaves of Hypnos No. 128. René Char, *French.* AF, *tr. by* Cid Corman

Baker is dead, The. *Unknown. See* Hallelujah, I'm a Bum.

Baker's Dozen of Wild Beasts, A. Carolyn Wells. OBCA

  Bath-Bunny, The.

  Corn-Pone-y, The.

  Cream-Puffin, The.

  Mince-Python, The.

Baker's Duzzen uv Wize Sawz, A. Edward Rowland Sill. FaBoBe

Baker's prayer. Sasaki Yukitsuna, *Japanese.* MJT, *tr. by* Makoto Ueda

Baker's Tale, The. "Lewis Carroll." EBEV; NAEL-2; OxAEP-2 *Fr.* The Hunting of the Snark. CBNP; OBNC; OBNV; PoEL-5

Balaam. Charles Causley. EBNV

Balaam. John Keble. OBNC

Balaam's Blessing. Bible, *O.T.* OBVE, *tr. by* William Tyndale *Fr.* Numbers.

Balade: "Hide [*or* Hyd], Absalon, thy gilte tresses clere." Chaucer. AWP; EBEV; EnVB; GBL; HAP; ImPo; NOBE; OAEL-1; OBEV; SCGP *Fr.* The Legend of Good Women.

Balade of Bon Conseill. Chaucer. *See* Truth.

Balade Simple. John Lydgate. GBL

Balade whych Anne Askewe made and sange whan she was in Newgate, The. Anne Askewe. *See* The Ballad Which Anne Askew[e] Made and Sang When She Was in Newgate.

Balalaika. Norman Dubie. AmPA

Balance. Marilyn Nelson Waniek. FFC; NAmP90; RA

Balance and Beauty. Clarence Major. FTOS

Balancing. Austere. Life. Keith Waldrop. PmAP *Fr.* A Shipwreck in Haven.

Balancing / its weight on the horizon's balustrade. The Knot. Vinda Karandikar, *Marathi.* OMIP, *tr. by* Vinay Dharwadker

Balancing on Oriental spike heels. Three Gypsies. Shalin Hai-Jew. UnSA

Balankin was as gude a mason. Lamkin. *Unknown.* ESPB

Balboa, the Entertainer. Imamu Amiri Baraka. AF; NoAM

Bald-bare, bone-bare, and ivory yellow: skull. The U. S. Sailor with the Japanese Skull. Winfield Townley Scott. LiTM

Bald Cavalier, The. *Unknown.* OxBChV

Bald heads forgetful of their sins. The Scholars. W. B. Yeats. APAD; CMoP; NoP-4; OAEL-2; PoA

Bald Mountain Zaum-Poems. *Unknown.* PFTM

Balder. Sydney Thompson Dobell.

  Chanted Calendar, A. BoTP; OBEV

  (Procession of the Flowers, The.)

Balder Dead. Matthew Arnold.

  "But when the Gods and Heroes heard, they brought." PeVV

  "Forth from the east, up the ascent of Heaven." PeVV

Baldpate Pond. E. F. Weisslitz. NYBP

Baldy Bane. W. S. Graham. FaBoTC

Baleful phantoms underground, The. (LL) Low Barometer. Robert Bridges. CABP; CMoP; MoP; NOCV; NoAM; OBNC; Poetr; SCGP

Balgu Song. *Unknown, Balgu.* CBAP, *tr. by* Clancy McKenna

Bali Hai Calls Mama. Marilyn Nelson Waniek. IFJA; ISC

Balkis was in her marble town. Song. Lascelles Abercrombie. MoBrPo *Fr.* Judith.

Ball. Birago Diop. PBMAP

Ball, almost, The. Basketball. Ronald Wallace. PBCAP

Ball no question makes of Ayes and Noes, The. 70. Edward Fitzgerald. CABP

Ball Poem, The. John Berryman. ChAP; CoAP; MoAmPo; NOBA; NoAM; Poetr

Ball will bounce, but less and less. It's not, A. Juggler. Richard Wilbur. CMoP; LiTM; NYBP; Poetr

Ballad: "Altho' a slave men is born and bred." J. B. Moreton. PBCV

Ballad: "As I was walkin' the jungle round, a-killin' of tigers an' time." Guy Wetmore Carryl. BXAP; NBLV

Ballad: "Auld wife sat at her ivied door, The." Charles Stuart Calverley. CABP; OBCoV

Ballad: "Der noble Ritter Hugo." Charles Godfrey Leland. APN-2

Ballad: "I put my hat upon my head." Samuel Johnson. CBNP; KaS; NOBL; OxAEP-1; UV

  ("Whose hat was in his hand.") (LL) KaS

Ballad: "I therefore pray thee, Renny dear." Samuel Johnson. OxAEP-1

  ("Another dish of tea.") (LL) OxAEP-1

  (Parody of Bishop Percy.) OBCoV

Ballad: "If the man who turnips cries." Samuel Johnson. OxAEP-1

Ballad: "I'll tell you a story / concerning John and Joan." Peter Reading. PeLV

Ballad: "Knight went down to the river's rim, A." Gerda Mayer. OBSP

Ballad: "O what is that sound [which so thrills the ear]." W. H. Auden. MoBrPo

Ballad: "Oh, quietly mad I'd like to be." Vladislav Felitsianovich Khodasevich, *Russian.* TCRP, *tr. by* Michael Frayn

Ballad: "Tender infant, meek and mild, The." Samuel Johnson. CBNP; OxAEP-1

Ballad: "They were a man's words, a ballad of an old time." James Still. MT

Ballad: "What's that approaching like dust like poverty." Charles Simic. LCAP-2

Ballad About a Smoke-Filled Railway Carriage. Aleksandr Kochetkov, *Russian.* TCRP, *tr. by* Lubov Yakovleva

Ballad about Friendship, A. Semyon Petrovich Gudzenko, *Russian.* TCRP, *tr. by* Gordon McVay

Ballad about the Circus. Aleksandr Petrovich Mezhirov, *Russian.* TCRP, *tr. by* Deming Brown

Ballad about the German Censor, The. "David Samuilovich Samoylov," *Russian.* TCRP, *tr. by* Lubov Yakovleva

Ballad against the Enemies of France. François Villon, *French.* AWP, *tr. by* Swinburne

Ballad: Alice Brand. Sir Walter Scott. OxAEP-2 *Fr.* The Lady of the Lake.

Ballad: Between the Boxcars. Robert Penn Warren. GM

  "I can't even remember the name of the one who fell." CRP

Ballad by Hans Breitmann. Charles Godfrey Leland. BXAP; NOBL

Ballad for a Boy, A. William Johnson Cory. OxBChV

  (Two Captains, The.) FaPoR

Ballad for Gloom. Ezra Pound. LiTM; MoAmPo

Ballad for Katharine of Aragon, A. Charles Causley. FaBoTw

Ballad in "G," A. Eugene Fitch Ware. PoLF

Ballad of a Barber, The. Aubrey Beardsley. ADE; NOBVV

Ballad of a Bun, A. Sir Owen Seaman. UV

Ballad of a Ferocious Tiger. Kao Ch'i, *Chinese.* SuSp, *tr. by* Irving Y. Lo

Ballad of a Little Lamp. René Depestre, *French.* NegPo, *tr. by* Ellen Conroy Kennedy

Ballad of a Mine, A. Robin Skelton. MoBS

Ballad of a Nun, A. John Davidson. MoBrPo; UV

Ballad of a Strange Thing. Howard Phelps Putnam. OxBA

Ballad of a Thin Man. "Bob Dylan." CBNP

Ballad of Abbreviations, A. G. K. Chesterton. NOBL

Ballad of Agincourt, The. Michael Drayton. *See* Agincourt.

Ballad of an Old Woman. Frank A. Collymore. NOxBChV; NTP; PBCV

Ballad of Aunt Geneva, The. Marilyn Nelson Waniek. FFC; GT; RA

Ballad of Banners (1944), The. John Lehmann. MoBS

Ballad of Barnaby, The. W. H. Auden. OBNV

Ballad of "Beau Brocade," The. Austin Dobson. OxAEP-2

Ballad of Biddy Early, The. Nancy Willard. FFC

Ballad of Billie Potts, The. Robert Penn Warren. FuPo; NOBA; OxBA

Ballad of Billy Rose, The. Leslie Norris. MoBS

Ballad of Birmingham. Dudley Randall. BPo; HeIP-4; ISC; InPK-6; MoP; NIP-4; NoAM; NoP-4; Poetr; SoSe-8

Ballad of Black Grief. Federico García Lorca, *Spanish*. STV, *tr. by* John Frederick Nims.

Ballad of Blossom, The. Mona Van Duyn. EOEF

Ballad of Bouillabaisse, The. William Makepeace Thackeray. APAD; OBEV; OxAEP-2

"This Bouillabaisse a noble dish is."

Ballad of Ching Mountain. Meng Chiao, *Chinese*. SuSp, *tr. by* Stephen Owen

Ballad of Chocolate Mabbie, The. Gwendolyn Brooks. CAPP-1 *Fr. A Street in Bronzeville*. BPo; BlSi; FaBoWP

Ballad of Christmas, A. Walter De la Mare. OBCP

Ballad[e] of Dead Ladies. François Villon, *French*. AWP; CTC; OBVE; PoRA, *tr. by* D. G. Rossetti

(Ballad of Dead Ladies, The.) NNPT, *tr. by* D. G. Rossetti

Ballad of Dead Yankees, The. Donald Petersen. WeT

Ballad of Don and Dave and Di, The. John Heath-Stubbs. EBNV

Ballad of Don Juan Tenorio and the Statue of the Comendador. Roy Campbell. PeSA

Ballad of East and West, The. Rudyard Kipling. EDNV; FaBoBe; FaPoR; OBNV

Ballad of Edie Barrow, The. Gwendolyn Brooks. PFE

Ballad of Faith. William Carlos Williams. OBAL

Ballad of Fat Margot. Augustus Young. CIP-2

Ballad of Fate. Vadim Nikolaevich Delone, *Russian*. TCRP, *tr. by* Nina Kossman

Ballad of Father Gilligan, The. W. B. Yeats. EBVV; MoBrPo; PoRA

Ballad of Fisher's Boardinghouse, The. Rudyard Kipling. PoRA

Ballad of François Villon, A. Swinburne. PoEL-5; PoRA

Ballad of George R. Sims, The. John Betjeman. OBCoV; UV

Ballad of Going Down to the Store, A. Miron Bialoszewski, *Polish*. BLT, *tr. by* Czeslaw Milosz

Ballad of Hampstead Heath, The. James Elroy Flecker. MoBrPo

Ballad of Hector in Hades. Edwin Muir. MoP; NOBE; NoAM

Ballad of Hell, A. John Davidson. HoPM; MoBrPo

(Christmas Eve.) EBVV

Ballad of Hiram Hover, The. Bayard Taylor. BXAP; OBAL

Ballad of Hunters, A. C. J. Driver. PeSAV

Ballad of Immoral Earnings. Bertolt Brechtm *German*. OxBoV, *tr. by* Ralph Manheim *and* John Willett *Fr. The Threepenny Opera*.

Ballad of Jan Palach, Student and Heretic. Ondra Lysohorsky, *Lachian*. AF, *tr. by* Ewald Osers

Ballad of John Cable and Three Gentlemen. W. S. Merwin. CoAP; NOBA

Ballad of Johnny Appleseed, A. Helmer O. Oleson. CTV

Ballad of Joking Jesus, The. James Joyce. ChIV-2

Ballad of Keith of Ravelston, The. Sydney Thompson Dobell. CH; OBEV *Fr. A Nuptial Eve*. OBNC

(Keith of Ravelston.) CH

Ballad of Kynd Kittok, The. William Dunbar. OxBoLi; PeLV

Ballad of Ladies Lost and Found. Marilyn Hacker. FFC; NMM-2; VCAP

Ballad of Lager Bier, The. Edmund Clarence Stedman. OBAL

Ballad of Late Annie, The. Gwendolyn Brooks. ColAP *Fr. Notes from the Childhood and the Girlhood*. LCAP-2

Ballad of London, A. Richard Le Gallienne. ADE

Ballad of Longwood Glen, The. Vladimir Nabokov. NYBP

Ballad of Mrs. Noah, The. Robert Duncan. MoP; NOBA; NoAM

Ballad of Morgan the Moon, The. Max Boyce. SpW

Ballad of Mulan, The. *Unknown, Chinese*. SuSp, *tr. by* William H. Nienhauser

Ballad of Nat Turner, The. Robert Earl Hayden. BPo; VGW

Ballad of Noah's Daughter. Rossana Ombres, *Italian*. NeIt, *tr. by* Ruth Feldman

Ballad of O'Bruadir, The. Frederick Robert Higgins. OBMV

Ballad of Old Women & of How They Are Constrained To Simulate Youth In Order To Avoid Shocking the Young. Norman Talbot. NOBAu

Ballad of Orange and Grape. Muriel Rukeyser. ChAP; NoAM; NoP-4

Ballad of Our Lady. William Dunbar. *See* Ane Ballat of Our Lady.

Ballad of Past Meridian, A. George Meredith. OAEL-2; PeVV

Ballad of Peach Blossom Spring. Yüan Mei, *Chinese*. CoBLCP, *tr. by* Jonathan Chaves

Ballad of Persse O'Reilly, The. James Joyce. CBNP; PeLV *Fr. Finnegans Wake.*

Ballad of Reading Gaol, The. Oscar Fingall O'Flahertie Wills Wilde. CABP; OBNV; OxAEP-2

("And filled the unclean leper's house.") ADE

("At last the dead man walked no more.")

Condemned Man, The. EBNV

"In Debtor's Yard the stones are hard." NOBVV

Ballad of Religion and Marriage, A. Amy Levy. VWP

Ballad of Remembrance, A. Robert Earl Hayden. BPo; NAAAL; PoBA

("Poem of rembrance, a gift, a souvenir for you, A.") (LL) NAAAL

Ballad of Rudolph Reed, The. Gwendolyn Brooks. PFE; RB

Ballad of Sally in Our Alley, The. Henry Carey. *See* Sally in Our Alley.

Ballad of Selling a Child. Wang Chiu-ssu, *Chinese*. CoBLCP, *tr. by* Jonathan Chaves

Ballad of Sue Ellen Westerfield, The. Robert Earl Hayden. AmPP; NoAM

Ballad of the Basking Shark, The. Thomas Hood Jr. CBNP

Ballad of the Bird-Bride. Rosamund Marriott Watson. VWP

Ballad of the Blue Envelope, The. Nikolai Semionovich Tikhonov, *Russian*. TCRP, *tr. by* Michael Frayn

Ballad of the Bread Man. Charles Causley. RB

Ballad of the Bushman. Eileen Duggan. PeNZ

Ballad of the Cool Fountain. *Unknown, Spanish*. BoWoP, *tr. by* Edwin Honig

Ballad of the Days of the Messiah. Abraham Moses Klein. TrJP

Ballad of the Deceived Flowers. Vesna Parun, *Croatian*. CEEP, *tr. by* Peter Kastmiler

Ballad of the Deserted Mansion. Kao Ch'i, *Chinese*. CoBLCP, *tr. by* Jonathan Chaves

Ballad of the Despairing Husband. Robert Creeley. NeAP; OBAL; RaBo

Ballad of the Drinker in His Pub. N. P. van Wyk Louw, *Afrikaans*. PeSA, *tr. by* Uys Krige, Jack Cope, *and* Ruth Miller

Ballad of the Electric Eel. Wayne Brown. PBCV

Ballad of the Emeu, The. Bret Harte. NBLV

Ballad of the Fatherless Boy. Wang Chiu-ssu, *Chinese*. CoBLCP, *tr. by* Jonathan Chaves

Ballad of the Ferocious Tiger. Hsü Pen, *Chinese*. CoBLCP, *tr. by* Jonathan Chaves

Ballad of the Flood. Edwin Muir. MoBS

Ballad of the Frozen Field, The. Dabney Stuart. MT

Ballad of the Gibbet. François Villon, *French*. AWP, *tr. by* Andrew Lang

Ballad of the Girl Whose Name Is Mud. Langston Hughes. SAmP

Ballad of the Good Lord Nelson. Lawrence Durrell. ImPo; LiTM; PeLV

Ballad of the Goodly Fere. Ezra Pound. CMoP; ChIV-2; ImPo; LiTM; MeMAP; MoAmPo; MoBS; PoRA; TrCP

Ballad of the Government Granary Clerk. Ho Ching-ming, *Chinese*. CoBLCP, *tr. by* Jonathan Chaves

Ballad of the Harp-Weaver, The. Edna St. Vincent Millay. PBMP

Ballad of the Hoppy-Toad. Margaret Abigail Walker. BlSi; HoPM; NBV

Ballad of the Icondic. John Ciardi. OBAL

Ballad of the Landlord. Langston Hughes. HCAP; NAAAL; NOBA

Ballad of the Late Annie, The. Gwendolyn Brooks. *See* The Ballad of Late Annie.

Ballad of the Little Cart, A. Ch'en Tzu-lung, *Chinese*. SuSp, *tr. by* Wu-chi Liu

Ballad of the Londoner. James Elroy Flecker. EnLoPo

Ballad of the Lords of Old Time. François Villon, *French*. AWP; PeVV, *tr. by* Swinburne

Ballad of the Magic Glasses. Maura Stanton. FFC

Ballad of the Man Who's Gone. Langston Hughes. SAmP

Ballad of the Merchant. Hsü Pen, *Chinese*. CoBLCP, *tr. by* Jonathan Chaves

Ballad of the Morning Streets. Imamu Amiri Baraka. TTTS

Ballad of the Mouse. Robert Wallace. NYBP

Ballad of the Nails, The. Nikolai Semionovich Tikhonov, *Russian*. TCRP, *tr. by* Michael Frayn

Ballad of the Neighborhood Shaman. Kao Ch'i, *Chinese*. CoBLCP, *tr. by* Jonathan Chaves

Ballad of the Oedipus Complex. Lawrence Durrell. OBCoV

Ballad of the Orioles in the Fields. Ts'ao Chih, *Chinese*. SuSp, *tr. by* Hans H. Frankel

Ballad of the Outer Life. Hugo von Hofmannsthal, *German*. AWP; TrJP, *tr. by* Jethro Bithell

Ballad of the Sad Astronaut. Judith Nicholls. SpW

Ballad of the Scarecrow Christ. Elder Olson. ChIV-2

Ballad of the Shot Heart. Nikolai Vasil'evich Panchenko, *Russian.* TCRP, tr. by Daniel Weissbort

Ballad of the Stonegut Sugar Works. James Keir Baxter. PeNZ

Ballad of the Swimming Angel. Jeffrey Skinner. WeT

Ballad of the Tempest. James Thomas Fields. FaBoBe; PoLF

Ballad of the Ten Casino Dancers. Cecília Meireles, *Portuguese.* BoWoP, tr. by James Merrill

Ballad of the Three Spectres. Ivor Gurney. OBWP; PoFWW

Ballad of the Tinker's Wife, The. Sigerson Clifford. IIP

Ballad of the Two Tapsters. Vernon Watkins. MoBS

Ballad of the Werewolf. Graham R. Tomson.
"Gudewife sits i' the chimney-neuk, The." OxBSn; VWP, at. to Rosamund Marriott Watson.

Ballad of the Western Island in the North Country. *Unknown, Chinese.* ChiP, tr. by Arthur Waley

Ballad of the Women of Paris. François Villon, *French.* AWP, tr. by Swinburne

Ballad of the Wondrous Moment. Pavel Grigoryevich Antokolsky, *Russian.* TCRP, tr. by Bernard Meares

Ballad of the Yorkshire Ripper, The. Blake Morrison.
"Ower t'ills o Bingley." FaBoVe

Ballad of Trees and the Master, A. Sidney Lanier. APAD; APN-2; ChIV-2; ColAP; NOBA; OxBA; PoEL-5; PoLF

Ballad of Villon and Fat Madge, The. François Villon, *French.* OBVE, tr. by Swinburne
("What though the beauty I love and serve be cheap.") EP, tr. by Swinburne

Ballad of William Bloat, The. *Unknown.* NOBL; PeLV

Ballad of William Sycamore, The. Stephen Vincent Benét. MoAmPo; PoRA; SAGP

Ballad of Yi River. Ho Ching-ming, *Chinese.* CoBLCP, tr. by Jonathan Chaves

Ballad of Yüan-yüan. Wu Wei-yeh, *Chinese.* CoBLCP, tr. by Jonathan Chaves

Ballad of Yukon Jake, The. Edward E. Paramore Jr. BLPA

Ballad on the Marriage of Philip and Mary, A. John Heywood.
"Egles byrde hath spred his wings, The." PBRV

Ballad on the Taxes, A. Edward Ward. OxBoLi

Ballad-Singer, The. Thomas Hardy. BoLoP *Fr.* At Casterbridge Fair.

Ballad: The Sun Had Grown on Lessening Day. John Clare. EnVR

Ballad: Time of Roses. Thomas Hood. CH; OBEV; OxAEP-2
(It Was the Time of Roses.) CH

Ballad to a Traditional Refrain. Maurice James Craig. BIrV; TIRV

Ballad to Mrs. Catherine Fleming in London from Malshanger Farm in Hampshire, A. Anne Finch, Countess of Winchilsea. ECWP

Ballad[e] [upon a Wedding], A. Sir John Suckling. BeJo; CaPo; EBEV; EBNV; NoP-4; OxBM; SeCP

Ballad Which Anne Askew[e] Made and Sang When She Was in Newgate, The. Anne Askew. CABP; NoP-4; NoSic; WPE
(Balade Whych Anne Askewe Made and Sange Whan She Was in Newgate, The.) PBRV
("Lyke as the armed knyght.") PBRV
("Of their inyquyte.") (LL) PBRV

Ballad Written for a Bridegroom. François Villon, *French.* AWP, tr. by Swinburne

Ballade: "Pretty maid she died, she died, in love-bed as she lay, The." Paul Fort, *French.* AWP, tr. by Frederick York Powell

Ballade: "Tell me where, in what country, where." François Villon, *French.* STV, tr. by John Frederick Nims

Ballade: "Wisdom, innocently the sun rises." Branko Miljkovic, *Serbo-Croatian.* HSix, tr. by Charles Simic

Ballade de Marguerite. *Unknown, French.* AWP, tr. by Oscar Wilde

Ballade des Belles Milatraisses. Rosalie Jonas. BlSi

Ballade D'une Grande Dame. G. K. Chesterton. OxBoLi; OxBoV

Ballade Made in the Hot Weather. William Ernest Henley. MoBrPo

Ballade of Broken Flutes. Edwin Arlington Robinson. APN-2

Ballade of Dead Actors. William Ernest Henley. EBVV; OBMV

Ballade of Dead Gentlemen. C. S. Lewis. OBCoV

Ballade of England. Louis MacNeice. NYBP

Ballade of Evolution, A. Grant Allen. EBVV

Ballade of Genuine Concern. Hilaire Belloc. EBEvV

Ballade of Lost Objects. Phyllis McGinley. CRP; NBLV; PoRA

Ballade of Lovers. May Probyn. VWP

Ballade of Sayings. W. S. Merwin. NNaP

Ballade of Suicide, A. G. K. Chesterton. NBLV; OBCoV

Ballade of the Armada, A. Austin Dobson. FaPoR

Ballade of the Chinese Lover. Stuart Merrill. APN-2

Ballade of the New God. Thomas M. Disch. RA

Ballade of the Outcasts. Stuart Merrill. APN-2

Ballade of the Poetic Life. Sir John Collings Squire. OBMV

Ballade to His Mistress. François Villon, *French.* WeW-3, tr. by Norman Cameron

Ballade Tragique à Double Refrain. Max Beerbohm. OBSV

Ballade un Peu Banale. Arthur James Marshall Smith. MoCV

Ballade which Villon Made. Donagh MacDonagh. TIRV

Ballat o the Hingit. François Villon, *French.* OBVE, tr. by Tom Scott

Ballat o the Leddies o Langsyne. François Villon, *French.* OBVE, tr. by Tom Scott

Ballata 5: "Light do I see within my Lady's eyes." Guido Cavalcanti, *Italian.* CTC, tr. by Ezra Pound

Ballata: Concerning a Shepherd-Maid. Guido Cavalcanti, *Italian.* AWP, tr. by D. G. Rossetti
("In a small grove I met a little shepherdess.") ItIP
("That the god of love—I seemed to see.") (LL) ItIP

Ballata: He Reveals, in a Dialogue, His Increasing Love for Mandetta. Guido Cavalcanti, *Italian.* AWP, tr. by D. G. Rossetti

Ballata: He Will Gaze upon Beatrice. Dante, *Italian.* AWP, tr. by D. G. Rossetti

Ballata: His Talk with Certain Peasant Girls. Franco Sacchetti, *Italian.* AWP, tr. by D. G. Rossetti

Ballata: In Exile at Sarzana. Guido Cavalcanti, *Italian.* AWP, tr. by D. G. Rossetti

Ballata: Of a Continual Death in Love. Guido Cavalcanti, *Italian.* AWP, tr. by D. G. Rossetti

Ballata: Of His Lady among Other Ladies. Guido Cavalcanti, *Italian.* AWP, tr. by D. G. Rossetti

Ballata: Of True and False Singing. *Unknown, Italian.* AWP, tr. by D. G. Rossetti

Ballata: One Speaks of the Beginning of His Love. *Unknown, Italian.* AWP, tr. by D. G. Rossetti

Ballatetta. Ezra Pound. VGW

Ballet [or Ballit] of de Boll Weevil, De. *Unknown.* AS; NOBA

Ballet of Happiness, The. James Seay. WeT

Ballet of the Fifth Year, The. Delmore Schwartz. OxBA; TwCP

Ballet of the Twelve Dancing Princesses, The. Stevie Smith. WPN

Balliol Rhymes. Various authors.
"First come I. My name is Jowett." FaBoEE; NOBL; PeLV
"I am Branson; Nature's laws." FaBoEE
"I am featly-tripping Lee." FaBoEE
"I am rather tall and stately." FaBoEE; NOBL
"I am the Dean, and this is Mrs. Liddell." FaBoEE
"I am the Dean of Christ Church, Sir." FaBoEE; NOBL
"I'm the great Sir William Anson." FaBoEE
On the Hon. George Nathaniel Curzon, Commoner of Balliol. OBCoV
"Positivists ever talk in s-/Uch an epic style as Dawkins." FaBoEE

Ballistical student named Raffity, A. Limerick. D. H. Cudmore. PeLi

Ballit of de Boll Weevil, De. *Unknown.* NOBA

Balloon, The. Mother Goose. ReMoGo

Balloon Faces. Carl Sandburg. CMoP; PoE

Balloon Man, The. Rose Fyleman. BoTP

Balloon Man, The. E. Herbert. BoTP

Balloon Seller, The. Elizabeth Fleming. BoTP

BalloonMan whistles / far / and / wee. E. E. Cummings. *See* In Just- / spring when the world is mud-.

BalloonMan whistles /whistles /far /far /and /and /wee wee. (LL) In Just- / spring when the world is mud-. E. E. Cummings. AmPP; ChAP; FaBoVe; HeIP-4; InPK-6; MoAmPo; NAAL-2; NIP-4; Poetr; SoSe-8; WeW-3

Balloons. Sylvia Plath. FaBoWP; PoE

Balloons hang on wires in the Marigold Gardens, The. Balloon Faces. Carl Sandburg. CMoP; PoE

Ballot, The. John Pierpont. *Fr.* Word from a Petitioner.

Ballot and the Bullet, The. Chris Van Wyk. PeSAV

Ballot / This means voting, The. The Ballot and the Bullet. Chris Van Wyk. PeSAV

Balls. Anne McNaughton. RaBo

Ball's Bluff. Herman Melville. CBCWP; OBWP

Ballydavid Pier. Thomas Kinsella. BIrV

Ballyshannon foundered off the coast of Cariboo, The. Etiquette. Sir William Schwenck Gilbert. FaBoCh

Balme. Edmund Spenser. CH *Fr.* Wood Of Error. AEP

Balmy as summer. It won't last. Sunday Morning Through Binoculars. Eamon Grennan. PBCIP

Balsham Bells. Kenrick Prescot. NOEC

Balthasar's Song. Shakespeare. *See* Song: "Sigh no more, ladies, sigh no more."

Baltic, The. Violet Jacob. FaBoTC

Baltic Summer. Yunna Petrovna Moritz, *Russian*. TCRP, *tr. by* Bernard Meares

Baltimore evening I saw, The. Soul Music. Baron Wormser. LTA

Balulalow. John James *and* Robert Wedderburn. OBEV

Bambini picking daisies in the new spring grass. Daisies of Florence. Kathleen Jessie Raine. NYBP

Bamboo. William Plomer. PeSA

Bamboo. Eric Rolls. NOBAu

Bamboo bed, rattan pillow, A. Chu Yün-ming. *Fr.* Miscellaneous Poems Written in My Studio on an Autumn Day. CoBLCP, *tr. by* Jonathan Chaves

Bamboo Branch Song. Ho Ching-ming, *Chinese*. CoBLCP, *tr. by* Jonathan Chaves

Bamboo Branch Song. Liu Yu Hsi, *Chinese*. CoBCP, *tr. by* Burton Watson

"Gorges of Wu are hoary and dim in the season of mist and rain, The." SuSp, *tr. by* Daniel Bryant

"Up in the hills are bank on bank of blossoming peach and plum trees." SuSp, *tr. by* Daniel Bryant

Bamboo Branch Song of Han-chia. Wang Shih-chieng, *Chinese*. CoBLCP, *tr. by* Jonathan Chaves

Bamboo Branch Song of the Seacoast. Yang Wei-chen, *Chinese*. CoBLCP, *tr. by* Jonathan Chaves

Bamboo Branch Song of West Lake. Yang Wei-chen, *Chinese*. CoBLCP, *tr. by* Jonathan Chaves

Bamboo by Li Ch'e Yun's Window, The. Po Chü-i, *Chinese*. OHMPC, *tr. by* Kenneth Rexroth

Bamboo Elegy: Two. Edmond Yi-teh Chang. OpBo

Bamboo fishing coat, purple official gown. Feelings in Nature ("Bamboo fishing coat, purple official gown"). Ma Chih-yüan. *Fr.* Four Poems to the Tune "Ch'ing-chiang yin." CoBLCP, *tr. by* Jonathan Chaves

Bamboo hedgerow cut a dark-green swath, The. Nam Xuyên, *Vietnamese*. AVP, *tr. by* Huỳnh Sanh Thông

Bamboo Mile Lodge. Wang Wei. *Fr.* Twenty Views of Wang-ch'uan. CoBCP, *tr. by* Burton Watson

Bamboo Villa, The. Shen Chou, *Chinese*. CoBLCP, *tr. by* Jonathan Chaves

Bamboo's chill creeps into the chamber. A Tired Night. Tu Fu, *Chinese*. SuSp, *tr. by* Jan W. Walls

Bamboos of Vietnam. Nguyễn Duy Nhuệ, *Vietnamese*. AVP, *tr. by* Huỳnh Sanh Thông

Bamboos rustle, the wind in battle array. Written While Lying on My Pillow in the Morning on the Twelfth Day of the Eleventh Month. Fan Ch'eng-ta, *Chinese*. SuSp, *tr. by* Wu-chi Liu

Banal Sojourn. Wallace Stevens. GaP

Banana leaves are burning. Containing Communism. Charlie Cobb. PoBA

Banana Plant, The. Tongmyong Kim, *Korean*. CKP, *tr. by* Jaihiun Kim

Bananas down at the Safeway, The. The High-Class Bananas. Gary Gildner. PBCAP

Bananas ripe and green, and ginger-root. The Tropics in New York. Claude McKay. CrDW; GT; NoAM; PBMP; PFE; PoBA; TTY

Banbury Fair. Edith G. Millard. BoTP

Band of the bold were gathered together, The. The Parting of the Red Sea. *Unknown*. AnOE, *tr. by* Charles W. Kennedy *Fr.* Exodus.

Band Played On, The. John F. Palmer. OBAL

Band plays an intro. Lady's Way. Reuben Jackson. GT

Banded Cobra, The. C. Louis Leipoldt, *Afrikaans*. PeSA, *tr. by* Uys Krige, Jack Cope, *and* Ruth Miller

Bandit, The. Vladimir Aleksandrovich Lugovskoy, *Russian*. TCRP, *tr. by* Gordon McVay

Bandstand. Michael S. Harper. SeSe

Bandy Legs. Mother Goose. ReMoGo

Bang Bang Bang. The History of the Flood. John Heath-Stubbs. MoBS; NOxBChV; NTP; OxBTC

Bang! the starter's gun—. Dorthi Charles. KaS

Bangkok. Francis Reginald Scott. MoCV

Baning Summer. Thomas Nashe. OxBSP; SCGP *Fr.* Summer's Last Will and Testament.

Banish Air from Air. Emily Dickinson. NCAP

Banished, dispossessed dead, The. Litany of the Rooms of the Dead. Franz Werfel, *German*. TrJP, *tr. by* Edith Abercrombie Snow

Banished Duke of Grantham, The. *Unknown*. EnSB

Banished Gods, The. Derek Mahon. OxBC

Banishment from Ur. Enheduanna, *Sumerian*. BoWoP, *tr. by* W. W. Hallo *and* J. J. A. van Dijk

Bank-manager's rapid signature, A. At the Wrong Door. Christopher Reid. CBLP

Bank of fine grass and light breeze, A. Night Thoughts aboard a Boat. Tu Fu, *Chinese*. SuSp, *tr. by* James J. Y. Liu *and* Irving Y. Lo

Bank of spring clouds, rain swelling the stream, A. Going Out to the Country on a Boat Trip, Sheltering from Rain Beneath a Tree. Kao Ch'i, *Chinese*. CoBLCP, *tr. by* Jonathan Chaves

Bank Thief, The. J. R. Farrell. BLPA

Bank to bank, the stream is wide. T'ao Ch'ien. SuSp, *tr. by* Eugene Eoyang *Fr.* The Seasons Come and Go.

Banker, The. Raymond Roseliep. HA

Bankers at war. Continuity. Stella Gibbons. WPN

Banking Potatoes. Herbert Asquith. NAAAL

Banking Potatoes. Yusef Komunyakaa. NoP-4

Bankis of Helicon, The. *Unknown*.
"Declair, ye bankis of Helicon." OxBS

Bankrupt. Cortlandt W. Sayres. PoLF; PoToHe

Banks O' Doon, The. Robert Burns. NOBE; NOEC

Banks of a River, The. Abraham Sutskever, *Yiddish*. CEEP, *tr. by* Ruth Whitman

Banks of Champlain, The. *Unknown*. AmFP

Banks of Claudy, The. *Unknown*. AmFP

Banks of Dee, The. *Unknown*. AmFP

Banks of reed. Christopher Okigbo. PBMAP *Fr.* Limits (1962).

Banks of Sacramento, The. *Unknown*. AS

Banks of Sweet Dundee, The. *Unknown*. AmFP

Banks of the Condamine, The. *Unknown*. NOBAu

Banks of the Gaspereaux, The. *Unknown*. AmFP

Banks of Wye, The. Robert Bloomfield. OBNC
Coracle Fishers, The.
Meandering Wye.

Banneker. Rita Dove. LCAP-2; NoAM

Banner of the Jew, The. Emma Lazarus. TrJP

Banners! Bunting! The engine throbs. A Special Train. Daniel Gerard Hoffman. CD9

Banquet, The. George Herbert. ESCV; GeHe

Banquet, The. Keats. *Fr.* Lamia. FHYEP

Banquet at the Tso Family Manor. Tu Fu, *Chinese*. OHPC, *tr. by* Kenneth Rexroth

Banquet was a bonza, a rare recherché feed, The. Thank you, Mr Rason, for the Apples. E. G. Murphy. OBCoV

Bantam Rooster, A. Kikaku, *Japanese*. KaS, *tr. by* Harry Behn

Bantams in Pine-Woods. Wallace Stevens. CMoP; InPS-3; MeMAP; NOBA; NoAM; OxBA; PFE; SAmP; UnPo

Baobab Fruit Picking; or, Development in Monkey Bay. Jack A. Mapanje. PeSAV

Baptism. Alvin Aubert. BkSV

Baptism. Claude McKay. PBCV

Baptism. Dale Zieroth. NOBC

Bar. Langston Hughes. APSN

Bar, The. *Unknown*. PoToHe

Bar[re] close as you can, and bolt fast too your door[e]. No Lock against Lechery. Robert Herrick. CaPo

Bar Giamaica, 1959-60. Charles Wright. EOEF

Bar is closed and I come, The. Night on Clinton. Robert Mezey. AmPA

Bar Kochba. Emma Lazarus. TrJP

Bar of steel—it is only, A. Carl Sandburg. AiP *Fr.* Smoke and Steel.

Bar on the Piccola Marina, A. Noël Coward. NBLV

Bar-Room Conversation. James Keir Baxter. PeLV *Fr.* Cressida.

Bar-Room Matins. Louis MacNeice. NYBP

Barabbas, Judas Iscariot. The Morning After. Dorothy, Duchess of Wellington Wellesley. OBMV

Barbadoes. M. J. Chapman. PBCV
"Still sparkles here the glory of the west."
"While the noon-lustre o'er the land is spread."

Barbados. Nathaniel Weekes. PBCV
"Virtues of the cane must now be sung, The."
"When frequent rains, and gentle show'rs descend."

Barbara. Jacques Prévert, *French*. AF, *tr. by* Harriet Zinnes

Barbara Allan ("It was about the Martinmas time"). *Unknown*. EnSB
(Bonny Barbara Allan.) NoP-4
("It was in and about the Martinmas time.") NoP-4

Barbara Allen. *Unknown*. EBEvV; EBNV
(Barbara Allen's Cruelty.) OBEV

Barbara Allen's Cruelty ("All in the merry month of May"). *Unknown*. FaBoBe

Barbara Frietchie. John Greenleaf Whittier. APN-1; AiP; BoTP; CBCWP; CTC; ChAP; ColAP; EBNV; FaBoBe; FaPoR; NCAP; NOBA; OBAL; OBCA; PAR; PoLF; TFi
("On the stars below in Frederick town!") (LL) ChAP

Barbara remember. Jacques Prévert, *French*. MFP, *tr. by* Martin Sorrell

Barbarian Suite. Marilyn Chin. OpBo

Barbarians. Jovan Hristic, *Serbo-Croatian.* HSix, *tr. by* Charles Simic

Barbarians Are Coming, The. Marilyn Chin. PUP-20

Barbarians! growled Attila. No Interims in History. Norman MacCaig. FaBoTC

Barbarians in a garden, softness does. In the Grounds. Douglas Dunn. NoP-4

Barbarossa. Friedrich Rückert, *German.* AWP, *tr. by* Elizabeth Craigmyle

Barbarossa. Hubert Witheford. PeNZ

Barb'd blossoms of the guarded gorse. A Song of Winter. Emily Jane Pfeiffer. OBWVE

Barbecue Service. James Applewhite. MT

Barbed Wire Fence Meditates upon the Goldfinch, A. Don McKay. NOBC

Barbed-wire / is the cloak of saints. Our Ashes. Horst Bienek, *German.* AF, *tr. by* Matthew Mead

Barbed wire looks incredibly evil still, The. Hartmanswillerkopf. Naomi Mitchison. WPN

Barber, The. John Gray. ADE; NOBVV

Barber, The. T(tilde;a)n Đà, *Vietnamese.* AVP, *tr. by* Huỳnh Sanh Thông

Barber, barber, shave a pig. Mother Goose. LB; OxNR; ReMoGo

Barber is cutting the hair, A. Self-Portrait at Thirty-Nine. Ted Kooser. PBCAP

Barber shaved the mason, The. *Unknown.* OxNR

Barberry-Bush, The. Jones Very. PAR

Barbershop. Martin Gardner. FPC

Barbershop Ritual. Sharan Strange. ISC

Barbie Doll. Marge Piercy. NIP-4; Poetr

Barbie's Ferrari. Lynne McMahon. NAmP90

Barbra Allen. *Unknown.* AS

Barbury Camp. Charles Hamilton Sorley. NSI

Barcan, its urging windslope in motion. ARCS above OXUS. Colin Simms. NBrP

Barcarolle. May Probyn. VWP

Bard. Gavin Bantock. FaBoTw

Bard is buried here, not strong, but sweet, A. The Epitaph of Eusthenes. Edward Cracroft Lefroy. AWP *Fr.* Echoes from Theocritus.

Bard may draw his parting groan, The. Sir Walter Scott. *See* Caledonia.

Bard of the Fleece, whose skilful genius made. To the Poet, John Dyer. Wordsworth. EPCY

Bard, The. William Blake. *See* Introduction: "Hear the voice of the Bard!"

Bard, The [A Pindaric Ode]. Thomas Gray. GTBS-P; NOBE; NOEC; OAEL-1; OxAEP-1

"Ruin seize thee, ruthless King!"

Bard whom pilf'red pastorals reknown, The. Alexander Pope. OBSV *Fr.* Epistle to Dr. Arbuthnot. FHYEP; InPS-3; NoP-4; OAEL-1; OxAEP-1; PoE; PoEL-3; TFi

Bards, The. Walter De la Mare. NOBL

Bard's Family, A. Peruncittiranar, *Tamil.* PLW, *tr. by* A. K. Ramanujan

Bards of passion and of mirth. Ode. Keats. FHYEP; GTBS-P; OBEV; OxAEP-2

Bare Almond-Trees. D. H. Lawrence. FaBoVe

Bare Arms of Trees, The. John Tagliabue. Poetsp

Bare branches tremble, The. Tzu Yeh, *Chinese.* WPOW, *tr. by* Kenneth Rexroth *and* Ling Chung

Bare bulb, a scatter of nails, The. An Ulster Twilight. Seamus Heaney. CIP-2; PBCIP

Bare earth it is, the way to my love. The Hour's Late. Abba Kovner, *Hebrew.* IP, *tr. by* Warren Bargad *and* Stanley F. Chyet

Bare Fig-trees. D. H. Lawrence. FaBoVe

Bare-handed, I hand the combs. Stings. Sylvia Plath. NALW

Bare hill. Above it, the early evening sky, a flat, A. The Dream. William Matthews. PuP-16

Bare oaks rock and snowcrust tumbles down, The. Thoughts Before Dawn. John Balaban. CDa

Bare root of the bean is pink, The. What She Said. Allur Nanmullai, *Tamil.* PLW, *tr. by* A. K. Ramanujan

Bare skin is my wrinkled sack. The Shrouded Stranger. Allen Ginsberg. NeAP

Bare trees / alternate, The. Larry Eigner. PoM

Barefoot and ragged, with neglected hair. On a Fair Beggar. Philip Ayres. EnLoPo

Barefoot Boy, The. John Greenleaf Whittier. APN-1; CTV; FaBoBe; OBAL; OBCA; PoLF

"Blessings on thee, little man."

"Oh for boyhood's painless play." AiP

Barefoot I went and made no sound. The Viper. Ruth Pitter. FaBoTw

Barefoot, in unaccustomed clouts or skirts of raw muslin. The New Saddhus. Robert Pinsky. NAmP90

Barefoot through clover. Alexis Rotella. HA

Barefoot through the bazaar. Sindhi Woman. Jon Stallworthy. OxBC

Barefoot without a stitch she walks. Dance with Banderillas. Richard Duerden. NeAP

Barely a twelvemonth after. The Horses. Edwin Muir. CABP; CMoP; FaBoTC; GEA; HAP; HeIP-4; MoBrPo; MoP; NOBE; NoAM; OAEL-2; OxBTC; PoE; Poetr; RB; TRP; WeW-3

Barely affluent, we always had maids. Birmingham, 1962. Diann Blakely Shoaf. PUP-19

Barely, rarely, comest thou. Shelley. *See* Song: "Rarely, rarely, comest thou."

Barely There. Dara Wier. CMAP

Barely through. For Thurman Thomas. Reuben Jackson. ISC

Barely tolerated, living on the margin. Soonest Mended. John Ashbery. HCAP; NAAL-2; VCAP

Barely twelve years old. In Memory of My Arab Grandmother. Evelyn Arcad Zerbe. WPOW

Bargain, The. Sir Philip Sidney. GLoP; NOBE; OBEV; OxAEP-1 *Fr.* Arcadia.

(Ditty, A.) AWP; GTBS-P

("My true love hath my heart, and I have his.") (LL) APAD; GLoP; LBC

Bargain Sale, A. Samuel Ellsworth Kiser. PoToHe

Barge glided, The. Vision. Israel Zangwill. TrJP

Barge she sat in, like a burnish'd throne, The. Cleopatra. Shakespeare. EBEvV; SCV *Fr.* Antony and Cleopatra.

Barges on the Hudson. Babette Deutsch. WPE

Baring the Device. Andrew Joron. PT

Bark leaps love-fraught from the land, The. The Thousand Islands. Charles Sangster. NOBC *Fr.* St. Lawrence and the Saguenay.

Bark of the rubgub [*or* rubagub] tree, The. (LL) The *Walloping Window-Blind.* Charles Edward Carryl. APN-2; NBLV; OBAL; OBCA

Bark went forth, with the morning's smile, A. The Australian Emigrant. Francis Fisher Browne. VWP *Fr.* The Australian Emigrant.

Barks the melancholy dog. Wakeful in the Township. Elizabeth Riddell. NOBAu

Barley-Break , A. Sir John Suckling. CaPo

Barley-Break; or, Last in Hell. Robert Herrick. CaPo

Barman vaulted the counter, The. A True Story Ending in False Hope. Pearse Hutchinson. PBCIP

Barn, The. Edmund Blunden. MoBrPo

Barn, The. Elizabeth Jane Coatsworth. OBCP

Barn, The. Seamus Heaney. HAP

Barn, The. Stephen Spender. CMoP

Barn / blazing in darkness, all they wish to see, The. Louise Glück. *See* The Magi.

Barn Fire. Thomas Lux. CMAP; LCAP-2

Barn owl / daughter of snow. Meeting. Peter Huchel, *German.* CEEP, *tr. by* Michael Hamburger

Barn-yard, The. Sheila Cussons, *Afrikaans.* PeSAV, *tr. by* Johann de Lange

Barney Bigard. Suzanne Noguere. FFC

Barney Bodkin broke his nose. *Unknown.* OxNR

Barney Google. Billy Rose. OBAL

Barney McGee. Richard Hovey. OBAL

Barns huddle over the horns. November Harvest. Anita Endrezze-Danielson. HATNAP

Barns like scarlet lungs are breathing in, The. Landscape with Barns. Louis Simpson. WeT

Barnsley and District. Donald Davie. NoAM; OxBC

Barnyard, The. *Unknown.* AmFP

Barnyard Melodies. Fred Emerson Brooks. OBAL

Baron has decided to meet the monster, The. The Bride of Frankenstein. Edward Field. CoAP; HeIP-4

Baron o [*or* of] Leys, The. *Unknown.* ESPB; OxBB

Baron of Brackley, The. *Unknown.* ESPB

Baron of Braikley, The. *Unknown.* OxBB

Baron of Smalho'me rose with day, The. The Eve of Saint John. Sir Walter Scott. PoEL-4

Baron of the sea, the great tropic, A. The Marvel. Keith Douglas. RB

Barones an burgeises and bondemen als. William Langland. FaBoVe *Fr.* The Vision of Piers Plowman.

Baroness Mu Impeded in Her Wish to Help Famine Victims in Wei. Confucius. *Fr.* Yung Wind. CTC, *tr. by* Ezra Pound

Baroque. Marie-Claire Bancquart, *French.* MFP, *tr. by* Martin Sorrell

Baroque Exterior. "Ern Malley." BMAP

Baroque Sunburst, A. Amy Clampitt. ColAP

Baroque Wall-Fountain in the Villa Sciarra, A. Richard Wilbur. AmPP; ColAP; GS; NAAL-2; NYBP; NoP-4; OBGa; Poetr; TwCP; VCAP

Barques we ride on over the sea. The Trees. Bill Manhire. PeNZ

Barracks Apt. 14. Theodore Weiss. CoAP; TAP

Barracks-square, washed clean with rain, The. In Barracks. Siegfried Sassoon. FaBoTw

Barred owls scream in the black pines, The. Owls. Louise Erdrich. TRP

Barrel Organ, The. Daniel Mark Epstein. DiPo *Fr.* Homage to Mallarmé.

Barrel-Organ, The. Alfred Noyes. BoTP; MoBrPo; PoRA

Barrel-Organ, The. Arthur Symons. NOBVV

Barrels of blue potato-spray, The. Spraying the Potatoes. Patrick Kavanagh. BIrV; CABP; IIP

Barrels of the rifles turned, The. On Reconnaissance. Mikhail Arkadyevich Svetlov, *Russian.* TCRP, *tr. by* Daniel Weissbort

Barren. "Rachel," *Hebrew.* TrJP, *tr. by* L. V. Snowman

Barren Moors, The. William Ellery Channing. APN-1

Barren Poem. Michael Ryan. AmPA

Barren Shore, The. Coventry Patmore. GBL

Barren soil, the evil men, the slag and hideous rot, The. (LL) The Rounded Catalogue Divine Complete. Walt Whitman. NAAL-1; NAAL-3

Barren Soul, A. Joseph Ezobi. TrJP, *tr. by* D. I. Friedmann *Fr.* The Silver Bowl.

Barren Spring. D. G. Rossetti. EBVV; IMW; OAEL-2; OBNC; PoEL-5 *Fr.* The House of Life.

(83. Barren Spring.) NoP-4

Barren Tree, The. Llewelyn Wyn Griffith.

"From his own solitude to the world unheeding." OBWVE

Barren Woman. Sylvia Plath. OxBSP

Barricade—a wall—a stronghold, A. The Breech. Michael McClure. NeAP

Barricades. Michael S. Harper. PoBA

Barrier, The. Louis Lavater. NOBAu

Barrio Beateo. Jesse F. García. UnSA

Bar[']s Fight[, August 28, 1746]. Lucy Terry. BPo; BlSi; CrDW; NAAAL

Bars on Eighth Avenue in Harlem, The. Harlem Gallery: From the Inside. Larry Neal. BPo; MoNo; NBV

Bartender, make it straight and make it two—. An Ex-Judge at the Bar. Melvin Beaunearus Tolson. NAAAL

Barter. Marie Blake. PoToHe

Barter. Sara Teasdale. SoSe-8

Bartholdi Statue, The. John Greenleaf Whittier. GS

Bartleme Fair. George Alexander Stevens. NOEC

Bartley Costello, eighty years old. Gaeltacht. Pearse Hutchinson. BIrV; PBCIP

Bartow Black. Timothy Thomas Fortune. AAP

Baruch. Bible, Apocrypha.

Path of Wisdom, The. TrJP

Baruch Spinoza of Amsterdam / was seized by a desire to reach God. Mr. Cogito Tells about the Temptation of Spinoza. Zbigniew Herbert, *Polish.* GI, *tr. by* John Carpenter *and* Bogdana Carpenter

Bas Bleu; Or, Conversation, The. Hannah More.

"Long was Society o'er-run." PEW

Bas Bleu, The; or, Conversation. Hannah More.

Cold Ceremony. ECWP

Bas-Relief. Carl Sandburg. ColAP

Basalt wolves are howling now, The. Gypsy Christmas. Otto Orban, *Hungarian.* CEEP, *tr. by* Emery E. George

Base Details. Siegfried Sassoon. MoBrPo; OxBSP; OxBoV; PeFWW; PoFWW; SAGP

Base metal hanger by your master's thigh! One Writing against His Prick. *Unknown.* NOSC

Base of All Metaphysics, The. Walt Whitman. APN-1

Base Stealer, The. Robert Francis. NTCP

Base words are uttered only by the base. Words. W. H. Auden. OxBSP; PeLV *Fr.* Shorts [1939–1947].

Baseball. Paul Hoover. BAP-94

Baseball. Frank Dempster Sherman. OBCA

Baseball and Classicism. Tom Clark. PmAP

Baseball and Writing. Marianne Moore. BoWoP; FaBoA

Baseball Canto. Lawrence Ferlinghetti. BB

Based on a volume of / Japanese prints. (LL) From the Grove Press. Anthony Hecht. OBAL; OBCoV

Bashert. Irena Klepfisz. AF

Bashful young fellow of Brighton, A. Limerick. E. O. Parrott. PeLi

Bashō, A Departure. Robert Hass. LoL

Bashō, coming / To the city of Nagoya. The Snow Party. Derek Mahon. CIP-2; FaBoPV; OxBC; PBCIP; PNI

Basia. Johannes Secundus, *Latin.*

"Not always give a melting kiss." OBVE, *tr. by* Thomas Stanley

Basil. Gibbons Ruark. MT

Basis then, of belief: base 10? base alphabet? base, The. St. Anzas IX. B. P. Nichol. FTOS

Basket Case. Basil T. Paquet. CDa

Basket of dirty clothes, A. Repetition of Words and Weather. Ruth Stone. BoWoP

Basket Of Summer Fruit, A. Charles Harpur. NOBAu

Basketball. Nikki Giovanni. NOxBChV

Basketball. Ronald Wallace. PBCAP

Baskets of ripe fruit in air. Gardener Janus Catches a Naiad. Dame Edith Sitwell. MoBrPo; OBGa

Basking close to the sun as they are able. Goldfish in the Garden Pond. Valerie Worth. NOxBChV

Basking Shark. Norman MacCaig. FaBoTC

Bass Culture. Linton Kwesi Johnson. PBCV

(Bass drum beaten loudly). Vachel Lindsay. *See* General William Booth Enters into Heaven.

Bast shoe idly on the road, A. Nikolai Ivanovich Glazkov, *Russian.* TCRP, *tr. by* Daniel Weissbort

Basta! D. H. Lawrence. CBLP

Bastard, The. Richard Savage.

"In gayer hours, when high my fancy ran." NOEC; OBSV

Bastard from the Bush, The. *Unknown.* NOBAu

Bastard God!, A. (LL) To the Christians. Francis Lauderdale Adams. ChIV-2; OxBS

Bat, The. Jane Kenyon. CrSp; LoL

Bat. D. H. Lawrence. APo, GTBS-P; IIAP; OAEL-1; OΛEL 2

Bat, The. Theodore Roethke. ChAP; OBCA

Bat, The. Dame Edith Sitwell. FaBoMo

Bat, The. Roberta Spear. AmPA

Bat Angels. Larry Levis. AmPA

Bat, bat, come under my hat. Mother Goose. OxNR; ReMoGo

Bat is born, A. Bats. Randall Jarrell. ChAP; NTCP; OBCA

Bat is dun with wrinkled Wings, The. Emily Dickinson. NAAL-1; NAAL-3 ("His Eccentricities.") (LL) APo; NCAP

Bat on the Road, A. Seamus Heaney. PoE

Bat that blocks at close of play, The. Joyce Johnson. UV

Bat that flits at close of eve, The. William Blake. UV *Fr.* Auguries of Innocence. EBEV; FaBoCh; FaPoR; ImPo; OAEL-1; OBNC; OxAEP-2; OxBoLi; PeECV; PoEL-4; TFi

Batalis and the Man, The, *see* "I sing of warfare and a man at war" *tr. by* Robert Fitzgerald *and* "Arms, and the Man I sing, who, forc'd by Fate" *tr. by* Dryden. Virgil. *See* The Rubric.

Batchelor's Song, The. Thomas Flatman. OxBM

Bateleur. Douglas Livingstone. PeSAV

Batellis [or Batalis] and the man I will descrive. The Rubric. Virgil, *Latin.* OBVE, *tr. by* Gawin Douglas *Fr.* The Aeneid [or Eneados, Aeneis].

Bath, The. Robin Becker. PBCAP

Bath. John Godfrey. FTOS

Bath, The. Joel Oppenheimer. NeAP

Bath, The. Ira Sadoff. NAmP90

Bath, The. Gary Snyder. NNaP; PmAP; TAP; VCAP

Bath after Sailing. John Updike. OxBoS

Bath-Bunny, The. Carolyn Wells. *Fr.* A Baker's Dozen of Wild Beasts. OBCA

Bath-house bench pinched Graphicus' bottom, The. Strato, *Greek.* GrAn, *tr. by* W. G. Shepherd

Bath; or, The Western Lass, The. Thomas D'Urfey.

Dialogue, between Crab and Gillian. NOEC

Bathe me O god in thee, mounting to thee. Walt Whitman. *Fr.* Passage to India. APN-1; AmPP; NAAL-1; NCAP; PoEL-5

Bather whose clothing was strewed, A. Limerick. *Unknown.* PeLi

Bathers, The. W. S. Merwin. PoE

Bathhouse, The. Boris Abramovich Slutsky, *Russian.* TCRP, *tr. by* J. R. Rowland

Bathing. Kate Daniels. NAmP90

Bathing in the roaring white waterfall. A Hunter Once, Now an Ascetic. Marippittiyar, *Tamil.* PLW, *tr. by* A. K. Ramanujan

Bathing Song. Anne Ridler. NYBP

Bathing the Aged. Paul Monette. AmPA

Bathing the Infant. Su Shih, *Chinese.* SuSp, *tr. by* Irving Y. Lo

Bathos, The. Richard Porson. FaBoEE

Bathroom, The. Group Therapy. Carolyn M. Rodgers. ISC

Bathroom tiles are very pink and new, The. Sonnet for Iva. Marilyn Hacker. NMM-2

Bathsheba in mourning. Angie Gilligan. NBrP

Bathsheba's Song. George Peele. *See* Bethsabe's Song.

Bathtub [*or* Bath Tub], The. Ezra Pound. NIP-4; PFE; TRP; WeW-3

Bathtub is white and full of strips, The. The Stones of Time. Kenneth Koch. NoAM *Fr.* Days and Nights.

Bathtubs. Richmond Lattimore. NYBP

Batrachomyomachia (The Battle of the Frogs and Mice). *Unknown, Greek.*

Battle in the balance, The. OBCVT, *tr. by* Thomas Parnell

Cause of War, The. OBCVT, *tr. by* Thomas Parnell

Mice prepare for battle, The. OBCVT, *tr. by* William Cowper

Bats. Randall Jarrell. ChAP; NTCP; OBCA

Bats. Mary Oliver. HeIP-4

Bats. Dave Jeddie Smith. NoAM

Batt he gets children, not for love to reare 'em. Upon Batt. Robert Herrick. FaBoEE

"Batter my heart, three-person'd God; for you." Donne. GSo *Fr.* Holy Sonnets. ESCV *Fr.* Holy Sonnets.

("Batter my heart, three-personed God.") FMP; FSCP; PFE; PoPoPo

("Batter my heart, three-personed God for You.") NoP-4

(Holy Sonnet 14.) PoPoPo

("Nor ever chast, except you ravish mee.") (LL) PBRV

Batter my heart, three-personed God. Donne. *See* "Batter my heart, three-person'd God; for you."

Batter my heart, three-personed [*or* three person'd] God; for you. "Batter my heart, three-person'd God; for you." Donne. ClHu; EBEV; EBEvV; FHYEP; HAP; HeIP-4; HoPM; ImPo; InPK-6; InPS-3; MeLP; NAEL-1; NIP-4; NOSC; OAEL-1; OxAEP-1; PeECV; PoE; PoEL-2; Poetr; SeCP; SoSe-8; Son; TFi; TOF; TrCP *Fr.* Holy Sonnets. ESCV *Fr.* Holy Sonnets.

Batter my heart, three-personed God for You. Donne. *See* "Batter my heart, three-person'd God; for you."

Batter'd, wreck'd old man, A. Walt Whitman. *See* Prayer of Columbus.

Batter'd, wrecked old man, A. Prayer of Columbus. Walt Whitman. AmPP

Battered and shiny like the moon. (LL) The Shampoo. Elizabeth Bishop. FaBoWP; OxBC; VCAP

Batteries Out of Ammunition. Rudyard Kipling. *Fr.* Epitaphs of the War [1914–1918]. OBWP

Battery woman. Pierre McOrlan, *French.* MFP, *tr. by* Martin Sorrell

Battle, A. Isabella Valancy Crawford. NOBC

Battle. John Davidson. CABP

Battle. Homer, *Greek.* OBCVT, *tr. by* Alfred Tennyson, 1st Baron Tennyson *Fr.* The Iliad.

Battle. Robinson Jeffers. *See* May-June, 1940.

Battle, The. Louis Simpson. InPS-3; OBWP; PBCV; PoWW

Battle Autumn of 1862, The. John Greenleaf Whittier. CBCWP

Battle Cry [*or* Battle-Cry] of Freedom, The. George Frederick Root. CBCWP; FaBoBe

Battle-Field, The. William Cullen Bryant. PoLF

Battle Hymn of the Republic, The. Rafael Campo. BAP-95

Battle Hymn [*or* Battle-Hymn] of the Republic, The. Julia Ward Howe. AH; APAD; APN-1; BLPA; CBCWP; CH; ColAP; EBEvV; FaBoA; FaBoBe; FaPoR; ImPo; NOBA; NOCV; NoP-4; OBWP; PAR; PWR; SAGP; SCV; TAP; TFi; WPE

("Our God is marching on.") (LL) CTV

Battle in the balance, The. *Unknown, Greek.* OBCVT, *tr. by* Thomas Parnell *Fr.* Batrachomyomachia (The Battle of the Frogs and Mice).

Battle Lines. John C. Schafer. CDa

Battle News. Samuel Hazo. CDa

Battle of Antietam Creek, The. *Unknown.* AmFP

Battle of Argoed Llwyfain, The. Taliesin, *Welsh.* OBWVE, *tr. by* Anthony Conran

Battle of Aughrim, The. Richard Murphy.

Casement's Funeral. NOIV; PBCIP

"Deep red bogs divided." CIP-2

Green Martyrs. NOIV

"Luttrell, Master of Luttrellstown." PBCIP

Orange March. NOIV

Planter. BIrV

Rapparees. BIrV; NOIV; PBCIP

"Slate I picked from a nettlebed." PBCIP

Wolfhound. NOIV

Battle of Blenheim, The. Robert Southey. CABP; FaBoPV; FaPoR; GTBS-P; OBNC; OBWP; OxAEP-2; PBMP; PoLF; Ro; TFi; UV

(After Blenheim.) GTBS-P; OxAEP-2; UV

("'Twas a summer evening.") UV

Battle of Bothwell Bridge, The. *Unknown.* OxBB

(Bothwell Bridge.) ESPB

Battle of Brunanburh, *see trs.* Brunanburg *and* Battle of Brunanburh. *Unknown, Anglo-Saxon.* AnOE, *tr. by* Charles Kennedy; ASW, *tr. by* Kevin Crossley-Holland; OBVE; OBWP; PeVV, *tr. by* Tennyson ("Athelstan King.") CABP, *tr. by* Tennyson

Battle of Bull Run, The. *Unknown.* AmFP

Battle of Finnsburg, The. *Unknown, Anglo-Saxon.* AnOE, *tr. by* Charles W. Kennedy

Battle of Flodden, The. *Unknown.* NoSic *Fr.* Scot[t]ish Field[e].

Battle of Gettysburg, The. Edgar Lee Masters. CBCWP

Battle of Harlaw, The. *Unknown.* ESPB

Battle of India and Europe. Aleksei Eliseievich Kruchyonykh, *Russian.* CBNP, *tr. by* Vladimir Markov

Battle of Maldon, The. *Unknown, Anglo-Saxon.* AnOE; ASW, *tr. by* Kevin Crossley-Holland; OAEL-1, *tr. by* Charles W. Kennedy ("He humbled and hewed down until at last he fell himself.") (LL) OBWP, *tr. by* Kevin Crossley-Holland

("It was shattered.") OBWP, *tr. by* Kevin Crossley-Holland

Battle of Murfreesboro. Allen Tate. FaBoA

Battle of Naseby, The. Thomas Babington Macaulay, 1st Baron Macaulay. OxAEP-2

Battle of New Orleans, The. *Unknown.* AmFP

Battle of Niagara, The. John Neal.

"Fresher and fresher comes the air. The blue." APN-1

"It is that hour when listening ones will weep." APN-1

"O save thy children blue Ontario!" APN-1

"There's a fierce gray Bird, with a bending beak." APN-1

Battle of Otterburn [*or* Oterborne], The. *Unknown.* ESPB; IBB; OxBS

Battle of Philiphaugh, The. *Unknown.* ESPB

Battle of Shiloh, The. *Unknown.* AmFP

Battle of the Baltic. Thomas Campbell. FaPoR; GTBS-P; OBEV

Battle of the *Bonhomme Richard* and the *Serapis.* Walt Whitman. RB; UnPo, *sect.* XXXV-XXXVI *Fr.* Song of Myself. AmPP; MoAmPo; NAAL-3; NOBA; OxBA

(Old-Time Sea-Fight, An.)

("Stretch'd and still lies the midnight.") ColAP

Battle of the Falkland Isles. "I. C." NSI

Battle of the Frogs and Mice, The. at. to Homer, *Greek.*

"Ascend my shoulders, firmly keep thy seat." OBVE, *tr. by* Thomas Parnell

Battle of the Kegs, The. Francis Hopkinson. OBAL

Battle of the Stars. Adah Isaacs Menken. CBWP-1

Battle [*or* Battel] of the Summer-Islands, The. Edmund Waller.

"Aid me Bellona, while the dreadful fight." BeJo

Battle of Waun Gaseg, The. Llywelyn ab y Moel, *Welsh.* OBWVE, *tr. by* H. Idris Bell

Battle of Wills Disguised, A. Marge Piercy. HeIP-4

Battle on the Blackbird's Field, The. Vasco [*or* Vasko] Popa. PoSu, *tr. by* Anne Pennington

Battle, Over and Over Again, The. Safiya Henderson-Holmes. UnSA

Battle Problem. William Meredith. NYBP

Battle rent a cobweb diamond-strung, The. Range-finding. Robert Frost. MoP; NIP-4; NoAM; OBWP; Poetr; RB

Battle Report. Bob Kaufman. ISC; MoNo; TTY

Battle Scene. Aricil Kiḷār, *Tamil.* PLW, *tr. by* A. K. Ramanujan

Battle Song. Ebenezer Elliot. OxAEP-2

Battle Song. Macuilxochitl, *Nahuatl Indian.* WPOW, *tr. by* Catherine Rodriguez-Nieto

Battle Song. Shaka, King of the Zulus, *Zulu.* PeSAV, *tr. by* Henry Francis Fynn

Battle Songs of the King Tshaka. *Unknown, Zulu.* PeSA

Battle Summers, The. Herman Melville. APN-2

Battle, The ("By this, though deep the evening fell"). Sir Walter Scott. PoEL-4 *Fr.* Marmion.

Battle waged strong, The. The Release. Adah Isaacs Menken. CBWP-1

Battledore. John Gray. NOBVV

Battlefield. Richard Aldington. OBWP

Battlefield. Lilian Bowes-Lyon. WPN

Battlefield. August Stramm, *German.* PeFWW, *tr. by* Michael Hamburger ("Child's gaze.") (LL) PFTM, *tr. by* Pierre Joris

("Clods' friability lulls iron to sleep.") PFTM, *tr. by* Pierre Joris

Battling to the death for what is his. (LL) Gamecock. James Dickey. HoPM; UnPo

Battue of Berlin, The. Harry Graham.

"It was a winter's morning." UV

Batyushkov. Osip Emilevich Mandelstam, *Russian.* OBVE, *tr. by* W. S. Merwin *and* Clarence Brown

Baucis. Erinna, *Greek.* AWP, *tr. by* Richard Garnett

Baucis and Philemon. Katherine Hoskins. PoA

Baucis and Philemon. Ovid, *Latin*. NOSC, *tr. by* Dryden *Fr.* Metamorphoses.

Baucis and Philemon. Ovid. *Fr.* Philemon and Baucis. CTC, *tr. by* Arthur Golding *Fr.* Metamorphoses.

Baucis and Philemon, *ad. fr.* Ovid, Metamorphoses, 8.626–724. Jonathan Swift. NOEC; OAEL-1

Baucis and Philemon, Imitated, From the Eighth Book of Ovid's Metamorphose. Ovid, *Latin.*
   "From lofty Roofs the Gods repuls'd before." OBCVT, *tr. by* Dryden
   "In antient Times, as Story tells." OBCVT, *tr. by* Swift

Baudelaire. Delmore Schwartz. SAGP; TwCP; VGW

Baudelaire in Brussels. Anthony Cronin. BIrV

Baudelaire Series. Michael Palmer.
   "Here the image of a child on a hill." APSN

Baudelaire took the train. Radiant Silhouette III. John Yau. OpBo

Bavarian Gentians. D. H. Lawrence. CMoP; FaBoCh; FaBoMo; GTBS-P; HAP; ImPo; InPK-6; InPS-3; MoP; NAEL-2; NOBE; NoAM; OAEL-2; PoE; Poetr; TFi; TRP; TTTS
   ("And her groom.") (LL) CABP
   ("Lost bride and her groom, The.") (LL) NoP-4; PoPoPo

Baviad, The. William Gifford.
   "Lo, Della Crusca! In his closet pent." NOBRP

Bawl of a steer, The. The Cowboy's Life. James Barton Adams. CTV

Baxter Bickerbone of Burlington. On Learning to Adjust to Things. John Ciardi. KaS; OBCA

Bay, The. James Keir Baxter. PeNZ

Bay breeze, The. Salt. George Barlow. GT

Bay is cold, heavy under a north wind, The. Whitecaps. Betsy Sholl. CrSp

Bay is not blue but sombre yellow, The. Self-Criticism in February. Robinson Jeffers. AmPP

Bay of Biscay, The. *Unknown.* AmFP

Bay of Tsunu, The. Hitomaro, *Japanese.* OHPJ, *tr. by* Kenneth Rexroth

Bay Poem. Lance Henson. VoR

Bay Psalm Book, The. *Unknown.*
   Psalm 1: "O Blessed man, that in th'advice." SCAP
   Psalm 19: "Heavens doe declare/ The majesty of God, The." SCAP
   Psalm 23: "Lord to me a shepherd is, The." OBCA
   Psalm 103: "O Thou my soule, Jehovah blesse." SCAP
   Psalm 107: "O Give yee thanks unto the Lord." SCAP
   Psalm 121: "I to the hills lift up mine eyes." OBCA

Bay steed of your stable could not be caught in a portrait, The. A Song of the Bay Steed of Governor Wei. Ts'en Shen, *Chinese.* SuSp, *tr. by* Daniel Bryant

Bay the color of steel, of a warship, The. Rain. Roo Borson. NoP-4

Bay undz is es geven andersh. I knew nothing. My Mother's Sabbath Days. Irena Klepfisz. NMM-2

Bayliff's Daughter of Islington, The. *Unknown. See* The Bailiff's Daughter of Islington.

Bayonne Turnpike to Tuscarora. Allen Ginsberg. NNaP

BC:AD. U. A. Fanthorpe. OBCP

Be a loafer / Wash off the dust of fame and gain in the vast waves. Lu Chih. SuSp, *tr. by* Sherwin S. S. Fu *Fr.* Tune: "Pleasure in Front of the Hall."

Be against all sorts of mortmain. (LL) Commission. Ezra Pound. BoLoP; TwCP

Be ahead of all parting, as though it already were. Rilke. EnlH *Fr.* Sonnets to Orpheus.

Be always in time. *Unknown.* OxNR

Be an unlikely treasure hoard. (LL) The Seafarer. Ezra Pound. CTC; FaBoTw; HeIP-4; NoP-4; OxBA; OxBoS

Be assured, the Dragon is not dead. Vanity. Robert Graves. GTBS-P

Be attentive to this trembling shade. Natan Zach, *Hebrew.* PoSu, *tr. by* Peter Everwine *and* Shulamit Yasny-Starkman

Be be / tween them. (LL) 40—Love. Roger McGough. OBCoV; Poetr

Be-Bop Boys. Langston Hughes. APSN; MoNo; OBAL

Be born a saint; or keep. Pearse Hutchinson. PBCIP

Be Careful. *Unknown.* NBLV

Be careful! Be careful! Ome Shushiki, *Japanese.* WPJ, *tr. by* Kenneth Rexroth *and* Ikuko Atsumi

Be careful. Open your life. Natan Zach. PoSu

Be careful, then, and be gentle about death. All Soul''s Day. D. H. Lawrence. LBC

Be careful what / You say or do. Zoo Manners. Eileen Mathias. BoTP

Be cheerful, sir. Shakespeare. APAD; EnlH *Fr.* The Tempest. OAEL-1

Be composed—be at ease with me—I am Walt Whitman, liberal and lusty as Nature. To a Common Prostitute. Walt Whitman. MoAmPo

Be Cool, Baby. Rob Penny. PoBA

Be Daedalus. Nanina Alba. PoBA

Be dark enough thy shades, and be thou there content. (LL) The Introduction: "Did I, my lines intend for public[k] view." Anne Finch, Countess of Winchilsea. BWW; NAEL-1; NALW; NoP-4; WPOW

Be dumb ye infant chimes, thump not the metal. Great Tom. Richard Corbet. OxBoLi

Be easy, October. No cackle hen, horse neigh, tree sough, duck quack. (LL) Clay is the word and clay is the flesh. Patrick Kavanagh. NoP-4

Be ever meek and humble, nor essay. The Meek and the Proud. Abraham ibn Chasdai, *Hebrew.* TrJP, *tr. by* J. Chotzner

Be extra careful by this door. The Whisperer. Mark Van Doren. MoAmPo

Be Frugal. Richard Church. OxBSP; OxBTC

Be glad, of all maidens floure. *Unknown.* MiEL

Be glaid, al ye that luvaris bene. Four May Poems: "Be glaid, al ye that luvaris bene." *Unknown.* OxBS

Be Glorified Eternally. Balthasar Hoffman, *German.* AH, *tr. by* Sheema Z. Buehne

Be good. For Starters. Victoria McCabe. CRP

Be governour baith guid and gratious. To the Queen. Henry Stuart, Lord Darnley. OxBS

Be happy, be happy again. Song of Delight. Shao Yung, *Chinese.* CoBCP, *tr. by* Burton Watson

Be happy for me, girls, / my mother-in-law is dead! Traditional Women's Song of Algeria. *Unknown, Arabic.* BoWoP, *tr. by* Willis Barnstone

Be helpful. Courtesy Tips. *Unknown.* CTV

Be his memory forever green and rich. Baal Shem Tov. Abraham Moses Klein. TrJP

Be hopeful, friend, when clouds are dark and days are. Strickland W Gillilan. PoToHe

Be hushed, all voices and untimely laughter. A Dead March. Mary C. Gillington. PeVV

Be in me as the eternal moods. Doria. Ezra Pound. MoAmPo

Be in my mind [or mynde] without[e] recure? / What no, perdy [or perdye or perdie]! (LL) What no, Perdy [or Perdie or perdie][!] ye may be sure[!]. Sir Thomas Wyatt. AAS; PoEL-1

Be it not mine to steal the cultured flower. Simple Nature. George John Romanes. PFE

Be it right or wrong, these men among. The Nut-brown Maid. *Unknown.* NoSic; OBEV

Be it so, for I submit; his doom is fair. Milton. NAWM-1 *Fr.* Paradise Lost.

Be Judge your self, I'll bring it to the test. On Man. John Wilmot, 2d Earl of Rochester. *Fr.* A Satire [or Satyre] against [Reason and] Mankind. NOSC; OAEL-1; OBSV; PoEL-3; SCV

Be just (domestick monarchs) unto them. George Alsop. SCAP

Be kept with us perpetuall Holy day! (LL) To the Excellent Mrs A. O. upon her receiving the name of Lucasia. Katherine Philips. KTR; NOSC

Be kind and tender to the Frog. The Frog. Hilaire Belloc. CTAV; CTV; ChAP; FaBoBe; NOxBChV; NTCP; OxBChV

Be kind / Be iron—. Leonid Nikolaevich Martynov, *Russian.* TCRP, *tr. by* J. R. Rowland

Be kind, good sir, and I'll lift my sark. Confucius. *Fr.* Songs of Cheng. CTC, *tr. by* Ezra Pound

Be kind to her. To End Her Fear. John Freeman. OBMV

Be kind to the three babes I've born to thee. (LL) Jamie Douglas. *Unknown.* ESPB; OxBB

Be kind to thy father: for when thou were young. Margaret Courtney. PoToHe

Be kind to yourself, it is only one. Who Be Kind To. Allen Ginsberg. NNaP

Be kindly affectioned one to. Bible, *N.T.* CTV *Fr.* The Bible, Romans 12:10,11.

Be land ready. Be Ready. Carl Sandburg. NOxBChV

Be lesse anothers Laurell, then thy praise. (LL) To His Honoured and Most Ingenious Friend Mr. Charles Cotton. Robert Herrick. CaPo; NOSC

Be life what it has been, and let us hold. To His Wife. Ausonius, *Latin.* AWP, *tr. by* Terrot Reaveley Glover

Be like God. (LL) God's other eye is good and gold. So bright. Jack Spicer. NeAP; PmAP

Be like the bird, who. Victor Hugo, *French.* CTV; Spl

Be mean with an onion. Recipe: Pastime for the Unemployed. Tom Pickard. NBrP

Be merciful to me, a fool! (LL) The Fool's Prayer. Edward Rowland Sill. APN-2; FaBoBe; PoLF

Be Merry. *Unknown.* RB

Be Mine the Doom. Emily Dickinson. CPO

Be near me when my light is low. 50. Tennyson. CABP; EBVV; EBVVPR; EnVR; HAP; HeIP-4; NOCV; OAEL-2; PFE; PeECV; PoEL-5; SCGP; SCV *Fr.* In Memoriam A. H. H.

Be Never Discouraged. Daniel C. Colesworthy. PWR

Be nobody's darling. Outcast. Alice Walker. NAAAL

Be not afeard: the isle is full of noises. To Dream Again. Shakespeare. OxAEP-1; RB *Fr.* The Tempest. OAEL-1

Be not amazed beloved, if sometimes my song grows dark. Léopold Sédar Senghor. PBMAP

Be Not Silent. David ben Meshullam, *Hebrew.* TrJP

Be not thou so foolish nice. Invitation to Dalliance. *Unknown.* FaBoEE

Be not too wise, nor too foolish. Instructions of King Cormac. Cormac, King of Cashel. PoToHe

Be of good cheer, spirit of Myrrha! To a Courtesan a Thousand Years Dead. Paul Eldridge. PoA

Be Off! Stevie Smith. OxBC

Be one, and one another's all. (LL) Lovers' Infiniteness[e]. Donne. ESCV; MeLP; NOSC; OAEL-1; PoEL-2; SeCP

Be Patient. "George Klingle." PoToHe

Be patient, Morning Star, with Love; though close. Macedonius, *Greek.* GrAn, *tr. by* Adrian Wright

Be patient, solemn nose. Precious Five. W. H. Auden. PeECV

Be plain in dress and sober in your diet. Lady Mary Wortley Montagu. FaBoEE

Be pleasing with thee, Lord, my Rock / Who my redeemer art, *fr.* Bay Psalm Book. Bible, *O.T. See* Psalm 19.

Be praise and glory evermore. (LL) Old Hundredth. William Kethe. FaPoR; NOCV; PeECV

Be prepared. How to Hug Your Three-Year-Old Daughter. Paul B. Janeczko. IFJA

Be proud as Spaniards! Leap for pride, ye fleas! On Donne's First Poem. Coleridge. Ro

Be punctual then to know. *Unknown.* NOEC *Fr.* The Art of Wenching.

Be Quiet! Max Fatchen. FuFo

Be Quiet, Go Away. Wanda Coleman. NAAAL

Be Ready. Carl Sandburg. NOxBChV

Be reasonable, my pain, and think with more detachment. Inward Conversation. Charles Baudelaire, *French.* InPK-6, *tr. by* Robert Bly

Be reckoned [*or* reckon'd] but with herbs and flowers! (LL) The Garden. Andrew Marvell. AWP; ClHu; ESCV; GTBS-P; GeHe; HAP; ImPo; InPS-3; MeLP; NAEL-1; NIP-4; NOBE; NOSC; OAEL-1; OBEV; PoE; PoEL-2; PoLF; PoRA; Poetr; SCGP; SeCP; TFi; TOF; TRP

Be reckoned but with herbs and flowers? Andrew Marvell. *See* The Mower to the Glow-Worms [*or* Glowworms *or* Glo-Worms].

Be rude to strangers. / *moral:* Behave. (LL) Rules and Regulations. "Lewis Carroll." NOBVV; PeVV

Be sad, be cool, be kind. The Long Shadow of Lincoln: A Litany. Carl Sandburg. CBCWP

Be Sad, My Heart. Francis Quarles. NIP-4

Be seated, pray. "A grave appeal?" A Virtuoso. Austin Dobson. PeVV

Be Seeing You. Vasco [*or* Vasko] Popa, *Serbian.* PoSu, *tr. by* Anne Pennington *Fr.* Raw Flesh.

("After the third evening round.") HP, *tr. by* Anne Pennington

Be silent, you still music of the spheres. On a Gentlewoman that Sung and Played upon a Lute. William Strode. NOSC

Be slowly lifted up, thou long black arm. On Seeing a Piece of Our Artillery Brought into Action. Wilfred Owen. GSo

Be so—ashamed of thee. (LL) What Soft—Cherubic Creatures. Emily Dickinson. APN-2; AmPP; HAP; MeMAP; MoAmPo; NALW; WPE

Be steady, on your pranks will rouse the ram. (LL) The Death of Daphnis. Theocritus, *Greek.* AWP, *tr. by* Charles Stuart Calverley

Be still: be still: nor dare. A Holy Hill. "Æ." AWP

Be still, my soul, be still; the arms you bear are brittle. A. E. Housman. MoBrPo; NOBVV; OAEL-2; OBNC; SCGP

Be still O green cliffs of the Dryads. Inscription for a Statue of Pan. *Unknown, Greek.* GrAn, *tr. by* Dudley Fitts

Be still, refrain thyself, and wait. (LL) Put forth thy leaf, thou lofty plane. Arthur Hugh Clough. EBEV; EnVR

Be still, sweet babe, no harm shall reach thee. To an Unborn Infant. Isabella Kelly. ECWP

Be still. The Hanging Gardens were a dream. Trumbull Stickney. APN-2

Be still / Wait. (LL) The Flight. Theodore Roethke. NAAL-2; NoP-4; RB; TRP

Be still, while the music rises about us: the deep enchantment. At a Concert of Music. Conrad Potter Aiken. MoAmPo

Be still with me, as all bells are still! Psalm. Ingeborg Bachmann, *German.* VCWP, *tr. by* Mark Anderson

Be Strong! Maltbie Davenport Babcock. AH; BLPA; FaBoBe; PWR; SoSe-8

("Faint not—fight on! Tomorrow / comes the song.") (LL) CTV

Be sure you paint. Alluding to the One-armed Bandit. David Chapman Berry. BXAP

Be sure your sin will find you out. *Unknown.* CTV *Fr.* The Bible, Numbers 32:23.

Be Swift O Sun. Ronald Allison Kells Mason. PeNZ

Be the Best of Whatever You Are. Douglas Malloch. BLPA

Be the earth unyielding and hard. Poem. Aco Šopov, *Macedonian.* CEEP, *tr. by* Vasa D. Mihailovich

Be the mistress[e] of my choice. What Kind of Mistress[e] He Would Have. Robert Herrick. CaPo; CavPo

Be this was said a grondyn dart leit he glide. Aeolus looses the winds. Virgil, *Latin.* OBCVT, *tr. by* Gawin Douglas

Be thou at peace this night. Nocturne. Edward Davison. CH

Be thou my vision, O Lord of my heart. Prayer. *Unknown, Irish.* TIRV, *tr. by* Eleanor Hull

Be thou then my beauty named. Thomas Campion. AAS

Be thou to others kind and true. Isaac Watts. *See* Our Saviour's Golden Rule.

Be True [*or* Be True Thyself]. Horatius Bonar. FaBoBe; PWR

(Be True.) CTV

Be wise as thou art cruel; do not press. Sonnet 140. Shakespeare. NoSic *Fr.* Sonnets.

Be with me, Beauty, for the fire is dying. On Growing Old. John Masefield. CMoP; ImPo; LiTM; MoBrPo; PoLF; PoRA; SAGP

Be With Me, Lord. George Macdonald. *Fr.* Diary of an Old Soul. TrCP

Be with me, Luis de San Angel, now. Ave Maria. Hart Crane. NOBA; NoAM *Fr.* The Bridge. NAAL-2

Be ye kind one to another. *Unknown.* CTV *Fr.* The Bible, Ephesians 4:32.

Be You. Norman Jordan. NBV

Be[e] you all pleased [*or* pleas'd]? your pleasures grieve not[t] me[e]. Sonnet 9. Mary Sidney, Countess of Montgomery Wroth. BWW; NOSC *Fr.* Pamphilia to Amphilanthus.

Be you to others kind and true. Our Saviour's Golden Rule. Isaac Watts. OxBChV

Be your words made (good sir) of Indian ware. Sonnet 92. Sir Philip Sidney. NoSic *Fr.* Astrophil and Stella. AAS; SiPS

Beach. Sophia De Mello Breyner, *Portuguese.* VCWP, *tr. by* Ruth Fainlight

Beach, The. Robert Graves. OxBSP

Beach Burial. Kenneth Slessor. CBAP

("Sand joins them together, / Enlisted on the other front, The.") (LL) BMAP

Beach Glass. Amy Clampitt. FaBoWP; NoAM; NoP-4; VCAP

Beach in August, The. Weldon Kees. VGW

Beach Party Given by T. Shaughnessy for the Sisters. Josephine Miles. LiLi

Beach Talk. Norman MacCaig. PoA

Beachcomber. George Mackay Brown. FaBoTC; NTP; OxBC

Beaches, The. "Robin Hyde."

("Close under here, I watched two lovers once." FaBoWP; PeNZ

"Cool and certain, their oars will be lifted in dusk." PeNZ

Beaches are full of dirty nails after rain. Coming Back. Ellsworth McGranahan Keane. PBCV

Beachy Head. Charlotte Smith.

From Beachy Head. NoP-4

("I once was happy, when while yet a child." PEW; WPE

Beacon of Hope. Linton Kwesi Johnson. HCP

Beacons from the abode where the Eternal are. (LL) Adonais; An Elegy on the Death of John Keats. Percy Bysshe Shelley. CABP; EBEV; EPCY; FHYEP; ImPo; NOBE; NOBRP; NoP-4; OAEL-2; OBNC; OxAEP-2; PoEL-4; Ro; TFi

Beadle's Testimony, The. Jerome Rothenberg. NNaP

Beads around / my neck / Mt. Kenya away. African Images, Glimpses from a Tiger's Back. Alice Walker. InPS-3

Beads of spring rain. Helen C. Acton. HA

Beagles. William Robert Rodgers. FaBoTw

Beaks of Eagles, The. Robinson Jeffers. NOBA

Beale Street Blues. William Christopher Handy. CrDW

("For to make me go.") (LL) NAAAL

Beam 4. Ronald Johnson. APSN *Fr.* Ark.

Beam 7. Ronald Johnson. APSN *Fr.* Ark.

("May move, in time, the stones themselves to sing.") (LL) PT

("Sound is sea: pattern lapping pattern.") PT

Beam 25, A Bicentennial Hymn. Ronald Johnson. APSN *Fr.* Ark.

Beam 30, The Garden. Ronald Johnson. FTOS

Beam of Wood, A: I am fire-fretted and I flirt with Wind. *Unknown.* EEP, *tr. by* Michael Alexander *Fr.* Riddles (Exeter Book).

Beams. Audre Lorde. NoAM

Beams of April, ere it goes, The. The Silkworm. Vincent Bourne, *Latin.* APo, *tr. by* William Cowper

Bean Eaters, The. Gwendolyn Brooks. BlSi; HAP; HeIP-4; LCAP-2; NALW; PoBA; PoE; Poetr; TAP; TRP; TTY; WeW-3

("And receipts and dolls and clothes, tobacco crumbs, vases and / fringes.") (LL) NoP-4

("Of beads and receipts and dolls and clothes, tobacco crumbs, / vases and fringes.") (LL) PoPoPo

Bean Spasms. Ted Berrigan. PmAP

("And go to the moon.") (LL) SPE

Bean-Stalk, The. Edna St. Vincent Millay. NOxBChV

Beanfield, The. John Clare. BoTP

Beans in blossom with their spots of jet, The. Field Path. John Clare. OxBSP

Beanstalk, Meditated Later, The. Judith Wright. NoAM

Beanstalks, in any breeze, are a slack church parade. The Broad Bean Sermon. Les A. Murray. BMAP

Bear, The. Ted Hughes. APo; FaBoMo

Bear, The. Galway Kinnell. CoAP; InPS-3; NNaP; TAP; TRP; VCAP; VGW

("By which I lived?") (LL) ColAP

Bear, The. Vladimir Aleksandrovich Lugovskoy, *Russian*. TCRP, *tr. by* Gordon McVay

Bear, The. N. Scott Momaday. CDW; HATNAP

Bear: A Totem Dance As Seen by Raven. Peter Blue Cloud. HATNAP

Bear and the Last Person to Remember, The. Robert Penn Warren. *Fr.* Fall Comes in Back-Country Vermont. NYBP; VGW

Bear and the Squirrels, The. Christopher Pearse Cranch. OBCA

Bear cub, chained and tethered to a stake, A. Squaring the Circle. Louis O. Coxe. NYBP

Bear Fat. Linda Hogan. PaTW

Bear in mind. Drum. Langston Hughes. MoAmPo

Bear it, O match unequally, you must. To One Unequally Matched. Walter Savage Landor. CBLP

Bear me to Dictaeus. Acon. Hilda Doolittle. VGW

Bear mother. Ursa Major. Federico García Lorca. PFTM

Bear on the Delhi Road, The. Earle Birney. HeIP-4; MoCV; NOBC; NYBP; NoAM; NoP-4

Bear puts both arms around the tree above her, The. Robert Frost. MoAmPo; NoAM

Bear sleeps in a cellarhole; pine needles, A. New Hampshire. Donald Hall. LCAP-2

Bear [or Bare] that breath[e]s [or breaks] the northern blast the. Upon a Wasp Chilled [or Child] with Cold. Edward Taylor. NAAL-1; NAAL-3; NOBA; NOCV; PoEL-3

Bear Track Plantation: Shortly after Shiloh. Robert Penn Warren. *Fr.* Two Studies in Idealism: Short Survey of American and Human History. CBCWP

Bear us on to the ultimate night. (LL) Exile. Ernest Christopher Dowson. ADE; BoLoP

Bear who eats with a silver spoon, A. Animal Acts. Charles Simic. LCAP-2

Beard-wagging stick-waving beggarman Cynic, A. Lucianus, *Greek*. GrAn, *tr. by* Edwin Morgan

Bearded lady, The. Alan Pizzarelli. HA

Bearded Oaks. Robert Penn Warren. ColAP; FuPo; LiTM; MoAmPo; MoP; NAAL-2; NOBA; NoAM; NoP-4; PoA; PoE; TAP; TwCP

Bearded Woman, by Ribera, The. Paul Muldoon. BiHa

Bearer of evil tidings, The. Robert Frost. MoP; NoAM; SAmP

Bearer of finches and clouds, pale atmosphere. Oxygen. Joan Swift. NYBP

Bearer's Song. Miu Hsi, *Chinese*. ChiP, *tr. by* Arthur Waley

Bearing a torch ablaze at the prow. (LL) The Torch. Walt Whitman. SAmP

Bearing so little ammunition. (LL) The School Children. Louise Glück. AmPA; ColAP; HCAP; PoPoPo; Poetr; WeW-3

Bearing the golden bough of Argicida. So that. (LL) Canto 1. Ezra Pound. AmPP; CMoP; ColAP; MeMAP; MoAmPo; MoP; NoAM; NoP-4; OBVE; PFTM; PoE; VGW

Bearings III: Amber Wall. Wole Soyinka. PBMAP *Fr.* The Shuttle in the Crypt.

Bears. Arthur Guiterman. PoRA

Bears. Adrienne Rich. NYBP

Bears are kept by hundreds within fences, are fed cracked, The. Elizabeth's War with the Christmas Bear. Norman Dubie. LCAP-2; NoAM

Bears became cucumbers. Yury Pavlovich Odarchenko, *Russian*. TCRP, *tr. by* Nina Kossman

Bear's Blood. Ileana Malancioui, *Rumanian*. BoWoP, *tr. by* Stavros Deligiorgis

Bear's Song, The. *Unknown, Haida*. AWP, *tr. by* Constance Lindsay Skinner *Fr.* Three Songs from the Haida.

Beast and bird must bow aside. Epilogue for a Masque of Purcell. Adrienne Rich. NYBP

Beast Flower. Yelena Shwarts, *Russian*. TCRP, *tr. by* Nina Kossman

Beast in Man, The. George Clutesi. HATNAP

Beast in the Space, The. W. S. Graham. FaBoTw; OxAEP-2; PoA

Beast Section, The. Welton Smith. PoBA

Beast stands at my eye, A. The Naked Land. Kenneth Patchen. SPE

Beast with Two Backs, The. Andrew Taylor. NOBAu

Beastly face. Tanka. Ishikawa Takuboku, *Japanese*. MJT, *tr. by* Ueda, Makoto

Beasts and Birds. Adelaide O'Keeffe. CTAV; OxBChV

Beasts in the schoolroom, whose transparent faces, The. Blues for Warren. Thomas McGrath. AF

Beasts in their major freedom / Slumber in peace tonight. Richard Wilbur. AmPP; LCAP-2; TwCP

("Unbridled waters.") (LL) APo

Beasts onely capable of sense, enjoy. John Ford. PoEL-2 *Fr.* The Broken Heart.

Beat at the air till the light blows out. (LL) I Only Am Escaped Alone to Tell Thee. Howard Nemerov. CoAP; HeIP-4; NoAM

Beat! beat! drums!—blow! bugles! blow! Walt Whitman. CBCWP; HeIP-4; InPK-6; InPS-3; NAAL-1; NAAL-3; NCAP; OBWP; PoLF

("So strong you thump O terrible drums—so loud you bugles blow.") (LL) NoP-4

Beat hell out of it. Episode 17. William Carlos Williams. OxBA *Fr.* Paterson.

Beat It Night Dog. Aimé Césaire, *French*. NegPo, *tr. by* Clayton Eshleman *and* Denis Kelly

Beat it with a shoe. Rhapsody. Cynthia Huntington. NAmP90

Beat on, proud billow[e]s! Boreas blow! Mr L'Estrange's Verses in the Prison at Lynn. Sir Roger L'Estrange. NOSC

Beat Poem by an Academic Poet. Vassar Miller. WPE

Beat the drums of skins. War Comes. Zalman Schneour, *Yiddish*. TrJP, *tr. by* Joseph Leftwich

Beat the knife on the plate and the fork on the can. Going In to Dinner. Edward Richard Burton Shanks. OBMV; OxBTC

Beata l'Alma. Sir Herbert Read. FaBoMo

Beaten like an old hound. Mad Day in March. Philip Levine. NYBP

Beaten Track, The. Steve Benson. FTOS

Beaten up. Justice is Done. Oumar Ba. PBMAP

Beating, The. T. R. Hummer. MT

Beating, The. Richard Katrovas. NAmP90

Beating, The. Ann Stanford. SoSe-8; WPE

Beating and beating at an intractable metal. (LL) Blackberrying. Sylvia Plath. HAP; HCAP; NAAL-2; NOBA; NYBP; NoAM; PoPoPo

Beating the drum. The Tattoo. Ania Walwicz. BMAP

Beating their little Bibles till he died. (LL) Grandfather in the Old Men's Home. W. S. Merwin. SAGP

Beatitude. Claire Bateman. CrSp

Beatitudes, The. Bible, *N.T.* *Fr.* St. Matthew.

Beatitudes. Bruce Dawe. GI

Beatrice. Joseph Sheridan Le Fanu.

  Hymn: "Hush! oh ye billows." TIRV

Beats back to his hand and melts once more to wood. (LL) Boomerang. William Hart-Smith. NOBAu; NTP

Beats the golden bird no more. (LL) Elegy: "Let them bury your big eyes." Edna St. Vincent Millay. CMoP; MoAmPo; OxBA; PoRA

Beau Ideal, The. Vũ Hoàng Chu'o'ng, *Vietnamese*. AVP, *tr. by* Huỳnh Sanh Thông

Beaucourt Revisited. Audrey Herbert. PoFWW

Beaufort, fair Beaufort, thou art a favored spot. General Robert Smalls. Josephine D. Henderson Heard. CBWP-4

Beauing, belling, dancing, drinking. The Rakes of Mallow. *Unknown*. OBCoV

Beaulieu. Clarence Major. FTOS

Beau's Reply. William Cowper. FaBoCh

Beauté, La. Charles Baudelaire, *French*. AWP, *tr. by* Lord Alfred Douglas

Beauteous Ethel's father has a, The. A Piazza Tragedy. Eugene Field. NBLV

Beauteous thou art, the spirit knows not how. Elsewhere. "Michael Field." VWP

Beauteous, yea beauteous more than these. Christopher Smart. *Fr.* A Song to David. ImPo; NAEL-1; NOBE; OAEL-1; OBWVE; PoE; PoEL-3

Beautie, I know, is good, and bloud is more. Epistle: To Elizabeth, Countess of Rutland. Horace, *Latin*. OBCVT, *tr. by* Ben Jonson

Beauties in White. Kiên Giang, *Vietnamese*. AVP, *tr. by* Huỳnh Sanh Thông

Beauties of Santa Cruz, The. Philip Freneau.

"Sick of thy northern glooms, come, shepherd, seek." AmPP

Beautiful, The. W. H. Davies. NTP

Beautiful, also, are the souls of my people. (LL) My People. Langston Hughes. MBE; NOxBChV

Beautiful American Word, Sure, The. Delmore Schwartz. VGW

Beautiful and blond they come, the Californians. The Californians. Theodore Spencer. NYBP

Beautiful are the fingers of the loved one. When She Plays upon the Harp or Lute. Moses ibn Ezra, *Hebrew*. TrJP, *tr. by* Solomon Solis-Cohen

Beautiful as the flying legend of some leopard. Judith of Bethulia. John Crowe Ransom. FYAP; FaBoMo; LiTM; MeMAP; NOBA; NoAM

Beautiful as the pomegranate is the white face of Ophrah. The Hot Flame of My Grief. Moses ibn Ezra, *Hebrew*. TrJP, *tr. by* Solomon Solis-Cohen

Beautiful Beeshareen Boy, The. Mathilde Blind. VWP

Beautiful, black-eyed boy. The Beautiful Beeshareen Boy. Mathilde Blind. VWP

Beautiful Black Men. Nikki Giovanni. BPo; NAAAL

Beautiful Black Women. Imamu Amiri Baraka. BPo; PoM

Beautiful cashier's white face has risen once more, The. Before the [*or a*] Cashier's Window in a Department Store. James Wright. CoAP; NYBP

Beautiful Changes, The. Richard Wilbur. CMoP; CoAP; HCAP; InPS-3; PoE

Beautiful Chinese at the computer terminal has notes in, The. In the Red Grove. Andrew Duncan. NBrP

Beautiful city, infected, like a sore, A. Nameless. Natan Zach, *Hebrew*. IP, *tr. by* Warren Bargad *and* Stanley F. Chyet

Beautiful Creatures Brief as These. Douglas G. Jones. MoCV

Beautiful, delicate bright gazelle, The. Love-song. Walter James Turner. OBMV

Beautiful dream was on when I woke up, A. Prison Dreams. Trần Minh Tu'ó'c, *Vietnamese*. AVP, *tr. by* Huỳnh Sanh Thông

Beautiful eyes of the dead, The. Carried Away. Anne Elder. CBAP

Beautiful faces are they that wear. *Unknown*. CTV

Beautiful faces are those that wear. Beautiful Things. Ellen Palmer Allerton. BLPA; PWR

Beautiful girl is very young, The. In the Looking Glass. "Anna Akhmatova," *Russian*. TCRP, *tr. by* Daniel Weissbort

Beautiful girl said something in your praise, A. To a Friend on His Marriage. Frank Templeton Prince. LiTM

Beautiful heights, joy of the world, city of a great king. Jerusalem. Judah Halevi, *Hebrew*. TOF, *tr. by* David Goldstein

Beautiful in the foregone drawing-room and the dance. Jane Austen. Patricia Beer. CABP

Beautiful IRELAND! Who will preach to thee? Who Will Show Us Any Good? Lady Jane Francesca Wilde. VWP

Beautiful is fair, the just is fair, The. Fair and Unfair. Robert Francis. VGW

Beautiful is she, this woman. Love Song. *Unknown, Haida*. AWP, *tr. by* Constance Lindsay Skinner *Fr.* Three Songs from the Haida.

Beautiful Is the Loved One. Moses ibn Ezra, *Hebrew*. TrJP, *tr. by* Solomon Solis-Cohen

Beautiful Ladies. Mcavoy Layne. CDa

Beautiful ladies through the orchard pass. Les Demoiselles de Sauve. John Gray. NOBVV; PeVV

Beautiful Land of Nod, The. Ella Wheeler Wilcox. PWR

Beautiful little children. Kyoto Born in Spring Song. Gary Snyder. MoLi

Beautiful Lunacy! that shapest flight. Thomas Tod Stoddart. NOBRP *Fr.* Death-Wake, The; or, Lunacy.

Beautiful maid of Delgo, I liked your face so black. Shu' Shu' of Delgo. Albert Brodrick. PeSAV

Beautiful Maid of the Mill, The. Wilhelm Müller, *German*. Whither? AWP, *tr. by* Longfellow

Beautiful man and his wife, The. Window Dressing. William Peskett. PNI

Beautiful man is sleeping under a pine tree, A. Monk's Dream. Dave Etter. SeSe

Beautiful Meals. Thomas Sturge Moore. BoTP

Beautiful Melite, in the throes of middle age. Agathias, *Greek*. InMo, *tr. by* Sam Hamill

Beautiful Mistress, A. Thomas Carew. CavPo

Beautiful must be the mountains whence ye come. Nightingales. Robert Bridges. CMoP; ImPo; LiTM; MoBrPo; NOBE; OAEL-2; OBEV; OBMV; OBNC; SCGP; TFi; UnPo

Beautiful, my delight. To Be Sung on the Water. Louise Bogan. VGW

Beautiful natural blossoms. To a Beautiful Pear Tree. James Wright. HAP

Beautiful person awakes, A. Sacrificial Victim. Rie Yoshiyuki, *Japanese*. WPJ, *tr. by* Kenneth Rexroth *and* Ikuko Atsumi

BEAUTIFUL place is the town of Lo-yang, A. Lo-yang. Wen-Ti Chien, *Chinese*. AWP; ChiP, *tr. by* Arthur Waley

Beautiful Railway Bridge of the Silv'ry Tay! William McGonagall. UV *Fr.* The Tay Bridge Disaster.

Beautiful rain falls, the unheeded angel, The. In Time. Kathleen Jessie Raine. WPE

Beautiful River. Robert Lowry. APN-2

Beautiful Ruined Orchard, The. Daniel Berrigan. FYAP

Beautiful Sea, The. Mary E. Tucker. CBWP-1

Beautiful Slave, The. Giovanni Battista Marino, *Italian*. ItIP

Beautiful Snow, The. John Whittaker Watson. BLPA

Beautiful solution, The. When Torrid Rhymes with Forehead. Ray DiPalma. FTOS

Beautiful Soup, so rich and green. The Song of the Mock Turtle. "Lewis Carroll." UV *Fr.* Alice's Adventures in Wonderland.

Beautiful star in heav'n so bright. Star of the Evening. James M. Sayles. UV

Beautiful Strangers, The, *(after sighting an Unidentified Flying Object)*. James Kirkup. SpW

Beautiful summer night, A. Summer Night. Antonio Machado Ruiz, *Spanish*. BLT, *tr. by* Willis Barnstone

Beautiful Swimmer, The. Walt Whitman. EP

Beautiful, tender, wasting away for sorrow. Luscious and Sorrowful. Christina Rossetti. PoEL-5

Beautiful, The! what is not perfect here below. Mary E. Tucker. CBWP-1

Beautiful thing/ I saw you. William Carlos Williams. CMoP *Fr.* Paterson.

Beautiful Things. Ellen Palmer Allerton. BLPA; PWR

Beautiful Toilet, The. Ezra Pound, *tr. fr. Mei Sheng, 140 B.C.* OBVE

Beautiful Train, The. William Empson. OxAEP-2

Beautiful trees make paths beneath themselves. Singing of Thoughts. Juan Chi. CoBCP, *tr. by* Watson, Burton (b. 1925) *Fr.* Singing of Thoughts. CoBCP, *tr. by* Burton Watson

Beautiful Urinals of Paris, The. Charles David Wright. MT

Beautiful was the appearance of Cormac in that assembly. Cormac Mac Airt Presiding at Tara. *Unknown, Irish*. BIrV, *tr. by* Douglas Hyde

Beautiful woman, a cup of wine, and a garden, A. Joy of Life. Moses ibn Ezra. TrJP, *tr. by* Solomon Solis-Cohen *Fr.* The Book of Tarshish.

Beautiful woman, you crown the hours. Dale Zieroth. NOBC

Beautiful women—mdash;we've vowed to be lovers! Liu E. *Fr.* On the Twenty-fourth: Improvisations. CoBLCP, *tr. by* Jonathan Chaves

Beautiful you rise upon the horizon of heaven. The Hymn to the Sun. Akhenaton, *Egyptian*. TTY, *tr. by* J. E. Manchip White

Beautiful Young Nymph Going to Bed, A. Jonathan Swift. ECEV; NOEC

Beautifully Janet slept. Janet Waking. John Crowe Ransom. CMoP; ColAP; FuPo; InPK-6; MeMAP; MoAmPo; MoP; NAAL-2; NoAM; PBMP; PoE; Poetr; RB; TAP

Beauty. Anacreon, *Greek*. OBCVT, *tr. by* Thomas Stanley

Beauty. Laurence Binyon. MoBrPo

Beauty. Madison Cawein. APN-2

Beauty. Sir Richard Fanshawe. *See* Of Beauty.

Beauty. Peter Hille, *German*. AWP, *tr. by* Jethro Bithell

Beauty. Isaac Rosenberg. TrJP

Beauty. Thomas Stanley, *after the Greek of* Anacreon. AWP; OBVE

Beauty. Walt Whitman. WeW-3

Beauty. Elinor Wylie. NAAL-2; OxBA

Beauty—a beam, nay, flame. Fading Beauty. Giovanni Battista Marino, *Italian*. AWP, *tr. by* Samuel Daniel

Beauty about us in the breathe of names. Name Poem. A. J. Seymour. HCP

Beauty Accurst. Richard Le Gallienne. ADE; RACG

Beauty alone will not account for her. Ode 147. Hafiz, *Persian*. EP, *tr. by* Richard Le Gallienne

Beauty and Denial. William Cartwright. BeJo

Beauty and Her Visitors. Winthrop Mackworth Praed. NOBRP

Beauty and Love. Andrew Young. GBL

Beauty and Sadness. Cathy Song. NoAM

Beauty and Terror. Lesbia Harford. CBAP

Beauty and the Beast. Rita Dove. NoAM

Beauty and the Beast. Sylvia Lynd. WPN

Beauty [*or* Beautie], and the life, The. Madrigal. William Drummond, of Hawthornden. OBEV; PoEL-2

Beauty and the Poet. Nam Trân, *Vietnamese*. AVP, *tr. by* Huỳnh Sanh Thông

Beauty as a Shield. Elsie Robinson. BLPA; PoToHe

Beauty Bathing. Anthony Munday. NOBE; OBEV *Fr.* Primaleon of Greece.

(Colin.) GTBS-P

Beauty be not caused—It Is. Emily Dickinson. TAP

Beauty clear and fair. John Fletcher. NOSC; OBEV *Fr.* The Elder Brother.

Beauty does not walk through lovely days. Beauty and Terror. Lesbia Harford. CBAP

Beauty his transient eyes descried. (LL) The Image-Maker. Oliver St. John Gogarty. OBEV; OBMV; PoRA

Beauty I love, yet more than this I love. Faint Love. Arthur Symons. CABP

Beauty in trouble flees to the good angel. Robert Graves. NYBP; OBCoV

Beauty in woman; the high will's decree. Sonnet: He Compares All Things with His Lady, and Finds Them Wanting. Guido Cavalcanti, *Italian*. AWP, *tr. by* D. G. Rossetti

Beauty in your silent towers. Beauty and the Beast. Sylvia Lynd. WPN

Beauty is the straw I clutch at, but to say straw. Amy Witting. NOBAu

Beauty kissed your mouth, and gave the petals. Macedonius, *Greek*. GrAn, *tr. by* Adrian Wright

Beauty lies in the *discovery*, The. (LL) Sonnet: "Sure Lord, there is enough in thee to dry." George Herbert. FSCP; GeHe

Beauty no more the subject be. The Song. Thomas Nabbes. NOSC

Beauty, no other thing is, than a beam[e]. The Definition of Beauty. Robert Herrick. BeJo; CaPo

Beauty of Israel is slain[e] upon thy high places, The. David's Lament. Bible, *O.T.* AWP; OBVE; OBWP; TrJP *Fr.* Second Samuel.

Beauty of Job's Daughters, The. Jay Macpherson. ChIV-1; MoCV; NOBC

Beauty of manhole covers—what of that? The. Manhole Covers. Karl Shapiro. NoAM

Beauty of songs your absence I should not show. Sonnet. Bernadette Mayer. PmAP

Beauty of the Friend it was that taught me, The. Makhfi, *Farsi*. WPOW, *tr. by* Paul Whalley

Beauty of the Stars, The. Moses ibn Ezra, *Hebrew*. TrJP, *tr. by* Solomon Solis-Cohen

Beauty of the unused, The. Unspeakable. Margaret Avison. NOBC

Beauty of Things, The. Robinson Jeffers. PoA

Beauty of wood-boys and wood-men their clear untrimmed faces, The. Song of the Broad-Axe. Walt Whitman. CA

Beauty Rohtraut. Eduard Friedrich Mörike, *German*. AWP; NNPT; OBVE, *tr. by* George Meredith

Beauty sat bathing by a spring. Beauty Bathing. Anthony Munday. EBEvV; GTBS-P; NOBE; OBEV *Fr.* Primaleon of Greece.

Beauty screws her new. Rewrite. E. A. Markham. PBCV

Beauty since. Momcilo Nastasijevic. HSix, *sect.* 6, *tr. by* Charles Simic *Fr.* Deaf Things.

Beauty, since you so much desire. Thomas Campion. OAEL-1

Beauty so sudden for that time of year. (LL) November Cotton Flower. Jean Toomer. ColAP; MoP; NoAM; UnPo

Beauty, sweet love, is like the morning dew. Sonnet: "Beauty, sweet love, is like the morning dew." Samuel Daniel. NOBE; NoSic; OBEV *Fr.* To Delia.

Beauty That All Night Long, A. Jelaluddin Rumi, *Persian*. AWP, *tr. by* Edward Fitzgerald

Beauty the Lover's Gift? Winifred Holtby. WPN

Beauty! thou art a wanderer on the earth. Behold, O Aspasia! I Send You Verses. Walter Savage Landor. OBNC; SCGP *Fr.* Pericles and Aspasia.

Beauty, thou wild fantastic ape. Abraham Cowley. ImPo; PoEL-2

Beauty, Time and Love. Samuel Daniel. OBEV *Fr.* To Delia.
    (Sonnet: "Fair is my love, and cruel as she's fair.") HoPM

Beauty Too of Twisted Trees, A. Philip Sherlock. PBCV

Beauty's Anadems. John Barlas. ADE

Beauty's Transitoriness. Christian Hofmann von Hofmannswaldau, *German*. GePo, *tr. by* George C. Schoolfield

Beaver Pond. Anne Marriott. NOBC

Beaver's Story, The. Vernon Watkins. NYBP

Because. James Philip McAuley. BMAP; CBAP; NOBAu

Because. Tanka. Kondō Yoshimi, *Japanese*. MJT, *tr. by* Makoto Ueda

Because. Emperor Tenji, *Japanese*. OHMPJ, *tr. by* Kenneth Rexroth

Because. B. W. Vilakazi, *Zulu*. PeSA

Because a thermal motif heard. If It's Only Rhythm. Dennis Phillips. FTOS *Fr.* Etudes.

Because all this food is grown in the store. Picketing Supermarkets. Tom Wayman. NIP-4

Because an owl goes home. (LL) Dawn. Gordon Bottomley. BoTP; MoBrPo

Because as they cut it was that special green, they decided. Two Brothers in a Field of Absence. Cynthia MacDonald. NIP-4

Because beer tingles. Beer Drops. Melba Joyce Boyd. BlSi

Because, dear Lord, thy way is rough and steep. Prayer for Shut-Ins. Ruth Winant Wheeler. PoToHe

Because Duke's voice. Twilight Seduction. Yusef Komunyakaa. SeSe

Because he can't work any faster. (LL) See-saw, Margery Daw. *Unknown*. ACTP; LB

Because he dies; he only wishes they would hear him sing. (LL) The Airy Christ. Stevie Smith. ChIV-2; NOCV

Because he got me once and he let me go, O yes, Lord! (LL) Nobody Knows the Trouble I've Had. *Unknown*. APAD; APN-2

Because he had spoken harshly to his mother. Revelation. Robert Penn Warren. NoAM

Because he has bright white teech, Eg- / natius whips out a. Catullus. *See Carmina*, XXXIX.

Because he is young. Yamanoé no Okura. AWP, *tr. by* Arthur Waley *Fr.* Manyo Shu, Part 1 of 4.

Because he puts the compromising chart. Zola. Edwin Arlington Robinson. OxBA

Because he sent a head of cattle on. The Island and the Cattle. Nicholas Moore. SPE

Because he was a butcher and thereby. Reuben Bright. Edwin Arlington Robinson. APN-2; GSo; MeMAP; MoAmPo; NCAP; NOBA; NoP-4; SAGP; Son; TAP

Because her cheek[e]s are near [*or* neere]. (LL) To Lucasta: The Rose. Richard Lovelace. BeJo

Because he's lost the way. A Case in Point. August Kleinzahler. PmAP

Because His Sister Saw Shakespeare in the Moon. Kenneth Patchen. CBNP

Because his nose and face were one festering sore. Orf. Ted Hughes. NoAM

Because his soup was cold, he needs must sulk. House-Mates. Leon Gellert. CBAP; NOBAu

Because I am broke again. Luck's Shining Child. George Garrett. MT

Because I am idolatrous and have besought. Epigram. Ernest Christopher Dowson. OxBSP

"Because I am mad about women." The Wild Old Wicked Man. W. B. Yeats. CMoP; RaBo

Because I breathe not love to ev'ry one. Sir Philip Sidney. *See* Sonnet 54: "Because I breathe not love to every one." ImGa; InPS-3; NoSic *Fr.* Astrophil and Stella. AAS; SiPS

Because I Could Not Dump. Andrea Paterson. BXAP

Because I could not stop for Death. Emily Dickinson. APAD; APN-2; AWP; AmPP; BoWoP; CMoP; ClHu; ColAP; EBEvV; HAP; HeIP-4; ImPo; InPK-6; LiTM; MeMAP; MoAmPo; MoP; NAAL-1; NAAL-3; NALW; NAWM-2; NIP-4; NoAM; NoP-4; OxBA; PAR; PBMP; PBWP; PFE; PoE; PoEL-5; PoPoPo; Poetr; SAGP; SAmP; SCV; SoSe-8; TAP; TFi; TRP; UnPo; WPE; WeW-3

Because I could sing to High Heaven. Caedmon. Aidan Carl Mathews. PBCIP

Because I don't have spit. Anne Waldman. CLPP

Because I don't want you to shear my fleece. (LL) An Answer to the Parson. William Blake. FaBoEE; NBLV; OxBoLi

Because I feel that, in the Heavens above. To My Mother. Edgar Allan Poe. OxBA

Because I had loved so deeply. Compensation. Paul Laurence Dunbar. APN-2; BPo

Because I have a luncheon date. (LL) In Westminster Abbey. John Betjeman. CMoP; InPK-6; NBLV; NIP-4; NOBL; NoAM; OAEL-2; OBSV; OxAEP-2; TOF

Because I have turned my head for years. The Bittern. Sandra McPherson. LCAP-2

Because I know deep in my own heart. Song. Pauli Murray. BlSi

Because I lay my / head on pillows. Why Is God Love, Jack? Allen Ginsberg. FTOS

Because I liked you better. A. E. Housman. CBLP; GBL; NOBVV; OxBTC; PeVV; SAGP

Because I oft, in dark abstracted guise. Sonnet 27. Sir Philip Sidney. CABP; NoSic *Fr.* Astrophil and Stella. AAS; SiPS

Because I once beat you up. For a Far-out Friend. Gary Snyder. BB; NeAP; PoM

Because I paced my thought by the natural world. John Hewitt. CIP-2; PNI

Because I set no snare. Michael's Song. Wilfrid Wilson Gibson. BoTP; NTP

Because I think not ever to return. Ballata: In Exile at Sarzana. Guido Cavalcanti, *Italian*. AWP, *tr. by* D. G. Rossetti

Because I thought that womanhood was all about. Before Throwing a Chicken into an Iowa Valley. Jane Varley. EC3

Because I used to shun. The Spark. Joseph Mary Plunkett. AWP

Because I was content with these poor fields. Musketaquid. Ralph Waldo Emerson. APN-1; PAR

Because I was whipped as a child. Eye of Heart. Olga Broumas. NMM-2

Because I would not dull you with my song. (LL) Sonnet 102. Shakespeare. AWP; OBEV

Because i'm tall my legs are long my left leg's lame. Paper Memorial Stone. Sang Yi, *Korean*. PFTM, *tr. by* Walter Lew

Because I'm writing about the snow not the sentence. Fifth Prose. Michael Palmer. FTOS; NoP-4; PmAP

Because, in the road, I met her foster-nurse. (LL) Remembering Golden Bells. Po Chü-i, *Chinese.* ChiP, *tr. by* Arthur Waley

Because in Vietnam the vision of a Burning Babe. Advent 1966. Denise Levertov. APSN; NNaP

Because it erst was nought, it turns to nought. William Drummond, of Hawthornden. *See* Madrigal: "This life, which seems so fair."

Because it has a very important moral, which is, Don't be a discoverer, be / a promoter. (LL) Columbus. Ogden Nash. FaBoA

Because it is a gray day but not snowy, because traffic grinds by outside. Long, Disconsolate Lines. Jane Cooper. PuP-16

Because it is the day of Palms. Palm Sunday: Naples. Arthur Symons. PeVV

Because it was a pilgrimage. Vespers. C. Dale Young. BAP-96

Because It's Good to Keep Things Straight. Kenneth Patchen. CBNP

Because it's summer a trellis of Gulf air curves over the day. Earth to Tell of the Beasts. David Rivard. NAmP90

Because Kate stood, face pushed to the screen. As If Ending. James Richardson. MoLi

Because mine eyes can never have their fill. Ballata: He Will Gaze upon Beatrice. Dante, *Italian.* AWP, *tr. by* D. G. Rossetti

Because my grief seems quiet and apart. Sonnet. Robert Nathan. TrJP

Because my Lord was born to suffer. Sister Juana Inés de la Cruz. WPoS, *tr. by* Jane Hirshfield *Fr.* The Fifth Villancico, in Alternating Voices, Written for the Feast of the Nativity in Puebla, 1689.

Because my room. Tanka. Maekawa Samio, *Japanese.* MJT, *tr. by* Makoto Ueda

Because my shelter must not be known. Cricket. No Ch'ŏn-myŭng, *Korean.* PBWP, *tr. by* Ko Won

Because my song was bold. Summary for Alastor. Laura Riding Jackson. FuPo

Because of Anger's freeing power. (LL) Anger's Freeing Power. Stevie Smith. NTP; OxBC

Because of body's hunger are we born. Sehnsucht. Anna Wickham. MoBrPo

Because of his long pilgrimage. The Funeral of Ally Flett. George Mackay Brown. FaBoTC

Because of India, before and after. Suniti Namjoshi *and* Gillian Hanscombe. CPO

Because of its erotic and cool underparts and the sunset emblazoned on its. Grid Erectile. Christopher Dewdney. FTOS

Because of My Father's Job. Jim Mitsui. OpBo; UnSA

Because of the change of key midway in "Come Back to Sorrento." Song of Reasons. Robert Pinsky. HCAP

Because of these men's courage, no smoke rose. Simonides, *Greek.* GrAn, *tr. by* Peter Jay

Because of you I have lived. Elegy. Yangshik Kim, *Korean.* CKP, *tr. by* Jaihiun Kim

Because of your long neck. Deer. No Ch'ŏn-myŭng, *Korean.* PBWP, *tr. by* Ko Won

Because of your nose, like a leaf blade. The Wheel. Molly Peacock. RA

Because our being grows in mind. For the Opening of the William Dinsmore Briggs Room. Yvor Winters. CRP

Because peacocks moved like you. What He Said. Peyanar. PLW *Fr.* Nine on Happy Reunion. PLW, *tr. by* A. K. Ramanujan

Because river-fog. River-Fog. Kiyowara Fukuyabu, *Japanese.* AWP, *tr. by* Arthur Waley

Because river-fog. River-Fog. Kiyowara Fukuyabu. AWP *Fr.* Shui Shu. AWP, *tr. by* Arthur Waley

Because she breathed too wildly in the sun. The Sixth Hell. Jerome Rothenberg. *Fr.* The Seven Hells of Jigoku Zoshi. NNaP

Because she had been told, time and / again. Salt. Linda Gregerson. PUP-19

Because she wants to touch him. Parable of the Four-Poster. Erica Jong. LW

Because She Would Ask Me Why I Loved Her. Christopher John Brennan. CBAP

Because the are shame, and cannot flee from it. Wild Turkeys; The Dignity of the Damned. Brigit Pegeen Kelly. NAmP90

Because the Byrds were on his car. Mandolin. Jordan Smith. WeT

Because the Dawn Breaks. Merle Collins. HCP

Because the Dead Sea released its hostages—the taste for salt, a rudder and a sail. Christopher Merrill. PuP-15

Because the folks. Tanka. Tsukamoto Kunio, *Japanese.* MJT, *tr. by* Makoto Ueda

Because the languages are enclosed and heated. Cliff Notes. Bob Perelman. PmAP

Because the mind's eye lit the sun. (LL) The Blue Swallows. Howard Nemerov. NoP-4; Poetr

Because the Moon Comes. Richard Shelton. PaTW

Because the night you asked me. Linda Pastan. CMAP

Because the pleasure-bird whistles after the hot wires. January 1939. Dylan Thomas. SPE

Because the shells were screechinng overhead. (LL) Breakfast. Wilfrid Wilson Gibson. OBMV; OxBTC

Because the warm honey. Sanctuary. Bruce Boyd. NeAP

Because the Wind Remembers. Frank Mkalawile Chipasula. HBAPE

Because their fathers had been drilled. The Last Republicans. Austin Clarke. CIP-2

Because there are avenues. After Tonight. Gary Soto. NoAM

Because there is safety in derision. The Apparitions. W. B. Yeats. CMoP; LiTM; OxBSn; TRP

Because there was a man somewhere in a candystripe silk shirt. Homage to the Empress of the Blues. Robert Earl Hayden. HCAP; LCAP-2; NAAAL; PoBA

Because there was disquiet in the wind. This Poor Man. W. J. Gruffydd, *Welsh.* OBWVE, *tr. by* Gwyn Jones

Because there was no other place. Flee on Your Donkey. Anne Sexton. NYBP; Poetr

Because they are not. The Deceptrices. William Carlos Williams. NYBP

Because they were prisoners. The Pilots. Denise Levertov. InPS-3

Because they were so brave and young. Fingal's Weeping. Neil Munro. NSI

Because they're living; so I leave 'em. (LL) Free Thoughts on Several Eminent Composers. Charles Lamb. OxBoLi; PeLV

Because this evening Miss Hoang Yen. Her Life Runs Like a Red Silk Flag. Bruce Weigl. AF

Because this graveyard is a hill. Visions and Interpetations. Li-Young Lee. NIP-4

Because, this month, when napkins, pretty spoons. Roman Presents. Martial, *Latin.* OBCP, *tr. by* James Michie

Because thou canst not see. The Philosopher to His Mistress. Robert Bridges. LiTM; PoEL-5

Because Thou Did'st Give. Harry Morris. CRP

Because time kept. Pre Domina. Jean Lipkin. PeSA

Because time subdues sharp angles and closes wounds. Burial. Paulin Joachim, *French.* TTY, *tr. by* Oliver Bernard

Because we live in the browning season. Kopis'taya. Paula Gunn Allen. HATNAP; OxWW

Because we see not where the threads have crossed? (LL) Crossed Threads. Helen Hunt Jackson. APN-2; PAR; SDW

Because we suspected / the pillow would say "I know." Lady Ise, *Japanese.* BoWoP, *tr. by* Etsuko Terasaki *and* Irma Brandeis

Because we were baffled. The White Bird. Wilfred Watson. MoCV

Because when they die. On the Suicide of Young Writers. Wilma Stockenström, *Afrikaans.* PeSAV, *tr. by* Stephen Gray

Because women are expected to keep silent about. On Stripping Bark from Myself. Alice Walker. NAAAL

Because you are. Against Silence. Marilyn Hacker. PuP-14

Because you are beautiful I will have to tell you a number / of my secrets. Open Secrets. Gwendolyn MacEwen. LW

Because you are going. Emily Dickinson. MoAmPo

Because you are old and departing I have wetted my handkerchief. Seeing Hsia Chan off by River. Po Chü-i, *Chinese.* TAL, *tr. by* Robert Payne

Because you aren't here to be what I can't think of I need most. Kathleen Fraser. DeD

Because You Asked about the Line between Prose and Poetry. Howard Nemerov. VCAP; WeW-3

Because you care, each task will be much lighter. Frank Crane. PoToHe

Because you have increased my hurt. The Storm. Robert David Cohen. NYBP

Because you have thrown of[f] your Prelate Lord. On the New Forcers of Conscience Under the Long Parliament. Milton. FaBoPV; NAEL-1; NOSC; PBRV; Son

Because you once beat me up. Melon-Slaughterer; or, A Sick Man's Praise for a Well Woman. Robert Peters. BXAP

Because you will not hear it. Macedonius, *Greek.* InMo, *tr. by* Sam Hamill

Because you will suffer soon and die, your choices. Ghetto. Michael Longley. NoP-4; PNI

Because your eyes are slant and slow. Prophetic Soul. Dorothy Parker. LW

Bechuanas—Matclapees. Speech. Chief Mothibi. PeSAV

Becket. Tennyson.

　Duet. APAD; GBL

　("Up with the sun from the sea.") (LL) APAD

Prologue: "Over! the sweet summer closes." GBL

Beckett Kit, The. Linda Gregg. AmPA

Beckie, my luve!—What is't, ye twa-faced tod? Sonnet. George Campbell Hay. OxBS

Become a single being, sure and true. (LL) World Without Peculiarity. Wallace Stevens. FiLi; HCAP

Become essential, man, for if the world should flee. Chance And Essence. "Angelus Silesius." GePo, tr. by George C. Schoolfield Fr. The Cherubical Wanderer.

Becomes at last no meaning and no place. (LL) The Stoic: for Laura von Courten. Edgar Bowers. CoAP; MT

Becoming a Dad. E. A. Guest. PoLF

Becoming an Eskimo isn't hard once you must. Bum's Rush. Michael Dransfield. CBAP

Becoming an osprey frozen skyhigh / to challenge me. (LL) Clear—the senses bright—sitting in the black chair—Rocker. Michael McClure. BB

Becoming dusk,—. Robert Spiess. HA

Becoming Milton. Coleman Barks. RaBo

Bed, The. Ray DiPalma. FTOS

Bed, The. Thom Gunn. EP

Bed, The. Alec Derwent Hope. NoAM; OxBC; OxBSP

Bed, The. Karl Shapiro. NYBP

Bed Book, The. Sylvia Plath.
   "Most Beds are Beds." ChAP

Bed calls. i sit in the dark in the living room. Bedtime Story. Wanda Coleman. NAAAL

Bed in Summer. Robert Louis Stevenson. ACTP; NBLV; OTCP; OxBChV

Bed of Forget-Me-Nots, A. Christina Rossetti. VWP

Bed-Time. Laurence Alma-Tadema. BoTP, CTAV

Bed Time. Peter Davison. UnPo

Bed-time. Thomas Hood. BoTP

Bede's Death Song. The Venerable Bede, Anglo-Saxon. ASW, tr. by Kevin Crossley-Holland.

Bedlam; a Poem on His Majesty's Happy Escape from His German Dominions. Unknown.
   "What mean these loud aerial cracks I hear?" NOEC

Bedlamite, The. Thomas Mozeen. NOEC

Bedouin Song. Bayard Taylor. APN-2; FaBoBe

Bedrock. Gary Snyder. PoE

Beds, The. Elizabeth Spires. NAmP90

Bedtime. Eleanor Farjeon. OTCP

Bedtime. Denise Levertov. TwCP

Bedtime. Unknown. ReMoGo

Bedtime Story. Wanda Coleman. NAAAL

Bedtime Story. Gustav Hasford. CDa

Bedtime Story. Lou Lipsitz. VGW

Bedtime Story. George MacBeth. MoP; SoSe-8

Bedtime Story. Lilian Moore. NTCP

Bedtime Story. Paula Rankin. CMAP

Bedtime Story. Nayo-Barbara Watkins. NBV

Bedtime tears / and evening sorrow. Small Rains. N. M. Bodecker. Spl

Bee, The. Emily Dickinson. MoAmPo

Bee. X. J. Kennedy. OBCA; Spl

Bee, The. Paul Valéry, French. APo, tr. by David Paul

Bee his burnished Carriage, A. Emily Dickinson. NOBA

Bee! I'm expecting you! Letter to Bee. Emily Dickinson. SAmP; TLR; TTTS

Bee is not afraid of me, The. Emily Dickinson. APN-2

Bee-keeper kissed me, The. Unknown, Spanish. BoWoP, tr. by W. S. Merwin

Bee Meeting, The. Sylvia Plath. HCAP; InPS-3; NALW; Poetr; WPE

Bee Mother. Meredith Stricker. LoHo

Bee, the Ant, and the Sparrow, The. Nathaniel Cotton. OxBChV

Bee upon a briar-rose hung, A. The Flesh-Fly and the Bee. Coventry Patmore. FaBoEE

Beech amid the forest lives, The. (LL) Trees. Sara Coleridge. ACTP; BoTP; FPC; OxBChV

Beech boles whiten in the swollen stream, The. Autumn, 1939. Alun Lewis. PoWW

Beech leaves caught in a moment gust, The. Departure. Edmund Blunden. OxBSP

Beechwoods at Knole. Vita Sackville-West. NTP

Beehive. Jean Toomer. GT; PoBA; TTY

Beehive Cell. Richard Murphy. CIP-2

Beehould a cluster to itt selfe a vine. William Alabaster. ESCV Fr. Divine Meditations. Son

Beeman Cliton hews / From the flower fed hive. Apollonides, Greek. GrAn, tr. by Peter Whigham

Been in the Pen So Long. Unknown. AS

Been in the Storm So Long. Unknown. NAAAL

Been on the hummer since ninety-four. A. R. U. Unknown. AS

Beeny Cliff. Thomas Hardy. CABP; OBNC; OxAEP-2; RB

Beer. George Arnold. OBAL

Beer. Charles Stuart Calverley. BXAP
   "But hark! a sound is stealing on my ear."

Beer. Emperor Julian, Greek. GrAn, tr. by Peter Jay

Beer Drops. Melba Joyce Boyd. BlSi

Bees and a honeycomb in the dried head of a horse in a pasture corner—. In Tall Grass. Carl Sandburg. PoA

Bees and lilies there were. Bring the Day! Theodore Roethke. CRP

Bees are Black, with Gilt Surcingles—. Emily Dickinson. APo; NAAL-1; NAAL-3

Bees are flying, The. They taste the spring. (LL) Wintering. Sylvia Plath. NALW

Bees build around red liver. A Poor Christian Looks at the Ghetto. Czeslaw Milosz, Polish. PoSu, tr. by the author; VCWP, tr. by Czeslaw Milosz

Bees build in the crevices, The. The Stare's Nest by My Window. W. B. Yeats. BIrV; GTBS-P; InPS-3; NOBE Fr. Meditations in Time of Civil War.

Bee's Burial, A. Martial, Latin. OBCVT, tr. by Peter Whigham

Bees in the crevices, The. W. B. Yeats. See The Stare's Nest by My Window.

Bee's Last Journey to the Rose, The. Brian Patten. OTCP

Bees rode the scalloped air of the garden. In the Middle of Things, Begin. Beckian Fritz Goldberg. NAmP90

Bees, six tiny legs and wings all lovely. What She Said. Orampokiyar, Tamil. PLW, tr. by A. K. Ramanujan Fr Five on the Riverside Cane. PLW, tr. by A. K. Ramanujan

Bees that have been hiving above the church pond, The. James Keir Baxter. PeNZ Fr. Jerusalem Sonnets.

Beeth hevy again, or elles moot I die. (LL) The Complaint of Chaucer to His [Empty] Purse. Chaucer. ImPo; MiEL; NAEL-1; OAEL-1; SCGP

Beethoven. Bob Cobbing. NBrP Fr. Beethoven Today.

Beethoven. Henrietta Cordelia Ray. CBWP-3

Beethoven. John Hall Wheelock. PoA

Beethoven, Opus 111. Amy Clampitt. NIP-4
   ("Aspire, in its last act, / to walk on air.") (LL) NoP-4
   (Beethoven, Opus III.) NoP-4

Beethoven Today. Bob Cobbing.
   "Beethoven." NBrP

Beethoven's Death Mask. Stephen Spender. OxBTC

Beethoven's Sixth Symphony. Steve Benson. FTOS

Beetle, The. Nikolai Makarovich Oleynikov, Russian. TCRP, tr. by Anatoly Liberman

Beetle on the Shasta Daylight. Shirley Kaufman. NYBP; WPE

Before. William Ernest Henley. MoBrPo Fr. In Hospital.

Before. May Probyn. VWP

Before a Fall. Geoffrey Grigson. SPE

Before a going and coming that goes on forever. . . (LL) Elegy for Alto. Christopher Okigbo. HBAPE; VCWP

Before a grotto of blue-tinted rock. At the Frick. Anthony Hecht. GS

Before a mirror at midnight I compose myself. Self-Portrait as Van Gogh. Peter Cooley. NAmP90

Before a Pack of deep-mouth'd Lusts I flee. Francis Quarles. ESCV Fr. Emblems.

Before a Painting. James Weldon Johnson. GT

Before a Saint's Picture. Walter Savage Landor. OxBChV

Before a Statue of Achilles. George Santayana. APN-2

Before Action. Leon Gellert. CBAP

Before Action. William Noel Hodgson. PoFWW

Before Agincourt. Shakespeare. EBEV Fr. King Henry V.
   "From camp to camp, through the fool womb of time."

Before ah leggo de hand on yu. / Well, yes. (LL) Wukhand. Paul Keens-Douglas. HCP; PBCV

Before an audible sound, an almost recognizable. Prelude to Memorial Song: 100 Years Later. Phillip William George. VoR

Before and After Marriage. Anne Campbell. PoToHe

Before Bannockburn. John Barbour. OxBS Fr. The Bruce.

Before, before he was aware. Comrades: an Episode. Robert Malise Bowyer Nichols. NSI

Before, behind, above. (LL) Interruption. Robert Graves. ImPo; LiTM

Before Breakup on the Chena outside Fairbanks. David McElroy. Poetsp

Before Breughel the Elder. Aleksander Wat, Polish. AF, tr. by Czeslaw Milosz and Leonard Nathan (b. 1924)

Before bulging eyes. The Celebration. Felix Mnthali. PBMAP

Before Chilembwe Tree. Jack A. Mapanje. PBMAP

Before Christmas. John Corben. AYFP

Before Dawn. Horace Hamilton. NYBP

Before Dawn. Alfonsas Nyka-Niliunas, *Lithuanian.* CEEP, *tr.* by Jonas Zdanys

Before dawn i rose thirsty. Other. Lance Henson. VoR

Before daybreak, before dew breaks. Youth. Barend Toerien, *Afrikaans.* PeSA, *tr.* by the author

Before Disaster. Yvor Winters. HoPM; PFE

Before dusk on the lake, the moon just full. Chang Chih-ho. SuSp, *tr.* by Hellmut Wilhelm *Fr.* Fisherman's Songs.

Before Gardens: The Golden Age. Ovid. *See* The Golden Age.

Before Gereint, foe's affliction. Gereint ab Erbin. *Unknown, Welsh.* OBWVE, *tr.* by Joseph P. Clancy

Before God's footstool to confess. Thy Best. Henry Cole. PWR; PoToHe

Before God's last *Put out the Light* was spoken. (LL) Once by the Pacific. Robert Frost. CMoP; GSo; HAP; HeIP-4; LiTM; MeMAP; MoAmPo; NAAL-2; NOBA; PFE; Son; TRP; VGW; WeW-3

Before he collapsed. (LL) Passion of Ravensbrück. János Pilinszky, *Hungarian.* GI, *tr.* by Janos Csokits *and* Ted Hughes; HP, *tr.* by Ted Hughes; AF, *tr.* by Ted Hughes *and* Janos Csokits

Before he died. Equena, *Tlinglit Indian.* STP, *tr.* by James Koller

Before he leaves on his fated journey. Bede's Death Song. The Venerable Bede, *Anglo-Saxon.* ASW, *tr.* by Kevin Crossley-Holland

Before he went to feed with owls and bats. Nebuchadnezzar's Dream. Keats. ChIV-1; KSG

Before her mirror Rebecca combs out her dark hair. Rebecca. Vadim Leonidovich Andreyev, *Russian.* TCRP, *tr.* by Olga Carlisle

Before her wandering feet. (LL) The Rose of the World. W. B. Yeats. ADE; CMoP; MoBrPo; NAEL-2

Before his immense window high as a cathedral window, the great unre-. The Great Unrestrained Sadist. Hans Arp, *German.* PFTM, *tr.* by Joachim Neugroschel

Before Hui-le Peak, sands like snow. At Night atop Shou-hsiang Citadel, Hearing Tartar Flutes. Li Yi, *Chinese.* SuSp, *tr.* by Paul Kroll

Before I can even look. Thinking of My Father on a Bus to Baltimore. Daniel S. Simko. CEEP

Before I could call myself Ángel González. Angel González, *Spanish.* VCWP, *tr.* by Steven Ford Brown *and* Revuelta Gutierrez

Before I die I must just find this rhyme. Leaving for the Front. Alfred Lichtenstein, *German.* PeFWW, *tr.* by Patrick Bridgwater

Before I drove Davy to nursery school. To the Woodville Depot. David Chapman Berry. MT

Before I got my eye put out. Emily Dickinson. APN-2; LiTM; MeMAP; PAR; PoE

Before I have begun to live! (LL) Lines Written in Kensington Gardens. Matthew Arnold. GaP; OBGa

Before I knocked and flesh let enter. Dylan Thomas. FaBoTw; RB

Before I know it, winter and spring depart. Lamenting the Dead. P'an Yüeh, *Chinese.* CoBCP, *tr.* by Burton Watson

Before I laughed with him. What She Said. Maturai Eruttalan Centamputan, *Tamil.* BoLoP, *tr.* by A. K. Ramanujan

Before / I opened my mouth. On Reading Poems to a Senior Class at South High. David Chapman Berry. SoSe-8

Before I regained them. (LL) The Legs. Robert Graves. ImPo; LiTM; PeLV; RB

Before I saw the tall man. Masked Woman's Song. Louise Bogan. NMM-2

Before I see another day. The Complaint of a Forsaken Indian Woman. Wordsworth. Ro

Before I set sail, I will not fail. Skin the Goat's Curse on Carey. *Unknown.* BIrV

Before I sigh my last gasp, let me breathe. The Will. Donne. EBEV; ImPo; NoSic

Before I slept, I saw the nebula. Katherine Doak. MDDM

Before I trust my Fate to thee. A Woman's Question. Adelaide Anne Procter. VWP

Before I Was Born. Solomon ibn Gabirol, *Hebrew.* TOF, *tr.* by David Goldstein

Before I woke I knew her gone. Robert Malise Bowyer Nichols. OBMV *Fr.* The Flower of Flame.

Before in the old time. (LL) Song: "Oh roses for the flush of youth." Christina Rossetti. GTBS-P; NOBVV

Before it came inside. What's That. Anne Sexton. LCAP-2

Before It Is Too Late. Frank Herbert Sweet. PoToHe

Before it was quite unsheathed from reality. (LL) Hurt Hawks. Robinson Jeffers. AmPP; CMoP; ChAP; ColAP; FYAP; LiTM; MoAmPo; MoP; NAAL-2; NOBA; NoAM; NoP-4; OxBA; RB; SAGP; TAP; TFi; TRP; UnPo

Before jade pavilions the new moon dims. *Unknown.* SuSp, *tr.* by Michael E. Workman *Fr.* Spring. *Fr.* Tzu-yeh Songs of the Four Seasons.

Before journeying to the vast sea, I already knew his name. On a Crab. P'i Jih-hsiu, *Chinese.* SuSp, *tr.* by William H. Nienhauser

Before lowering the perfumed curtain to express her love. Tune: "Chrysanthemums Fresh." Liu Yung, *Chinese.* SuSp, *tr.* by James J. Y. Liu

Before man came to blow it right. The Aim Was Song. Robert Frost. SoSe-8

Before me in my endless way. (LL) Stepping Westward. Wordsworth. CH; PoEL-4; Ro; SCGP

Before me / taut pallets of smoke. Clinton. Sterling Plumpp. BkSV *Fr.* Clinton.

Before me / when I look into the mirror. *Unknown, Japanese.* WPJ, *tr.* by Kenneth Rexroth *and* Ikuko Atsumi

Before mine eye to feed my greedy will. George Gascoigne. Son *Fr.* Gascoigne's Memories. AAS

Before morning you shall be here. Alba. Samuel Beckett. BIrV

Before my back was bent I was eloquent. *Unknown.* OBWVE, *tr.* by Gwyn Jones *Fr.* Hateful Old Age.

Before my drift-wood fire I sit. Burning Drift-Wood. John Greenleaf Whittier. APN-1

Before my eyes they come and go. Trumbull Stickney. *Fr.* Pandora's Songs. APN-2 *Fr.* Prometheus Pyrphoros.

Before my face the picture hangs. Robert Southwell. NoSic *Fr.* Upon the Image of Death. CH; NOBE

Before my fourth birthday my father. The Hula Skirt, 1959. Kimiko Hahn. UnSA

Before my lady's window gay. *Unknown.* *Fr.* Medieval Norman Song. AWP, *tr.* by John Addington Symonds

Before myne eye to feede my greedy will. (LL) No Hast But Good. George Gascoigne. AAS; NoSic; Son

Before night comes I think of you and for you before I fall. Léopold Sédar Senghor, *French.* VCWP, *tr.* by Melvin Dixon

Before Olympus. John Gould Fletcher. MoAmPo

Before Parting. Swinburne. CBLP; EP; NOBVV

Before Passover. Seymour Mayne. NOBC

Before People, The. Wesley McNair. CMAP

Before Play. Vasco [*or* Vasko] Popa. *Fr.* Games. RB, *tr.* by Anne Pennington

Before Sedan. Austin Dobson. PeVV

Before she has her floor swept. Portrait by a Neighbour. Edna St. Vincent Millay. OBCA

Before she walked into the river. Last Testaments. Lorna Crozier. LW *Fr.* Last Testaments.

Before Sleep. Fleur Adcock. PeNZ *Fr.* Night-Piece.

Before sleep Baba arranges extra. Moshe Dor, *Hebrew.* IFJA, *tr.* by Barbara Goldberg

Before Sleeping. *Unknown.* CH
  (Prayer: "Matthew, Mark, Luke, and John.") OxBoLi

Before Spring. P. A. Ropes. BoTP

Before Starting. Walker Gibson. *See* Advice to Travelers.

Before sunrise the stork was there. Lake Morning in Autumn. Douglas Livingstone. NoP-4

Before Sunset. Swinburne. CBLP

Before the Actual Cold. Ray A. Young Bear. VoR

Before the Attack. Semyon Petrovich Gudzenko, *Russian.* TCRP, *tr.* by Gordon McVayl

Before the barn-door crowing. Song. John Gay. CTAV; OxBSP; PoEL-3 *Fr.* The Beggar's Opera. OAEL-1

Before the beginning of years. Chorus: "Before the beginning of years." Swinburne. EBVV; EBVVPR; ImPo; NAEL-2; NTP; OBEV *Fr.* Atalanta in Calydon.

Before the Birth of One of Her Children. Anne Bradstreet. BoWoP; ColAP; KTR; NAAL-1; NAAL-3; NOBA; NoP-4; OxBM; PEW; PeECV; WPE; WPOW
  ("Who with salt tears this last farewell did take.") (LL) ColAP; NoP-4; PEW

Before the blond horsemen rode into our village. An Event. Edward Field. CoAP

Before the bright sun rises over the hill. The Gleaner. Jane Taylor. OxBChV

Before the [*or* a] Cashier's Window in a Department Store. James Wright. CoAP; NYBP

Before the cathedral in grandeur rose. How the Great Guest Came. Edwin Markham. BLPA

Before the Court. Aleksandr Blok, *Russian.* TCRP, *tr.* by Geoffrey Thurley

Before the day is everywhere. Martha Blake. Austin Clarke. TIRV

Before the descent. William J. Higginson. HA

Before the dream is gone. For Emma. Luigi Fontanella, *Italian.* NeIt, *tr.* by Michael Palma

Before the eyes of ladies and of kings. Tennyson. *See* And answer made King Arthur, breathing hard.

Before the Fall. Milton. *Fr.* Book IV. OAEL-1 *Fr.* Paradise Lost.

Before the falling summer sun. Musings. William Barnes. HAP; NOBE; OBNC

Before the Feast of Shushan. Anne Spencer. BlSi; NAAAL

Before the gate of Little Su. Bamboo Branch Song of West Lake. Yang Wei-chen, *Chinese.* CoBLCP, *tr. by* Jonathan Chaves

Before the glare o' dawn I rise. The Shearer's Wife. Louis Esson. NOBAu

Before the grass is out the people are out. Paterson. William Carlos Williams. PFTM

Before the Great Void, we burn the fragrant incense. To Purity and Truth. *Unknown, Chinese.* TrJP, *tr. by* William C. White

Before the holidaymakers comes the spring. The Chinese Restaurant in Portrush. Derek Mahon. TRP

Before the indifferent beak could let her drop? (LL) Leda and the Swan. W. B. Yeats. CABP; CMoP; ClHu; EBEV; FaBoSe; GSo; GTBS-P; HAP; HeIP-4; ImPo; InPK-6; LiTM; MoBrPo; MoP; NAEL-2; NAWM-2; NIP-4; NOBE; NoAM; NoP-4; OAEL-2; OxAEP-2; OxBoV; PFE; PoE; PoPoPo; Poetr; SAGP; SCV; SoSe-8; Son; TFi; TRP; WeW-3

Before the Last Battle. *Unknown. Fr.* The Táin. NOIV, *tr. by* Thomas Kinsella

Before the Law stands a doorkeeper. Franz Kafka, *German.* PFTM, *tr. by* Willa Muir *and* Edwin Muir

Before the life leaves me. (LL) As I Came in by Fiddich-Side. *Unknown.* ESPB; RB

Before the light of evening can go out. Charles Brasch. *Fr.* Home Ground. PeNZ

before the Lord, new-born?. (LL) Words from an Old Spanish Carol. *Unknown, Spanish.* PChr, *tr. by* Ruth Sawyer

Before the Map of Russia. "Teffi," *Russian.* TCRP, *tr. by* Albert C. Todd

Before the Mirror. Swinburne. GS *Fr.* Before the Mirror. ("White rose in red rose-garden.") GS

Before the mists descended on your body. Epitaph for a Poet. Homero Aridjis, *Spanish.* STV, *tr. by* John Frederick Nims

Before the Moone should circlewise close both hir hornes in one. Medea's invocation. Ovid, *Latin.* OBCVT, *tr. by* Arthur Golding

Before the Mountain. Elizabeth Libbey. AmPA

Before the mountains were brought forth, before. Christina Rossetti. Son *Fr.* Later Life: A Double Sonnet of Sonnets.

Before the Pacific. Blanca Varela, *Spanish.* BoWoP, *tr. by* Willis Barnstone

Before the paling of the stars. Christina Rossetti. AYFP; TrCP

Before the Peak of Returning Joy the sand was like snow. A Song of War. Li Po, *Chinese.* TAL, *tr. by* Robert Payne

Before the plums fell asleep. On the Way to Mind. Milo De Angelis, *Italian.* NeIt, *tr. by* Lawrence Venuti

Before the Poetry Reading. Louis Simpson. OxBC

Before the prayer begun. (LL) Lady Maisry. *Unknown.* ESPB; OxBB

Before the Press scarce one co'd see. To His Book. Robert Herrick. OxBSP

Before the Rape. Shakespeare. NoSic *Fr.* The Rape of Lucrece.

Before the Roman came to Rye or Caesar conquered Gaul. The Rolling English Wall. Roger Woddis. UV

Before the Roman came to Rye or out to Severn strode. The Rolling English Road. G. K. Chesterton. FaBoCh; NOBE; NOBL; OBEV; OBMV; OxAEP-2; OxBTC; UV

Before the Scales, Tomorrow. Otto René Castillo, *Spanish.* AF, *tr. by* Barbara Paschke *and* David Volpendesta

Before the seas again divide. Valediction. Walter Adolphe Roberts. PBCV

Before the Shrine of the Filial Marquis. Inscribed on a Painting. Ni Tsan, *Chinese.* CoBLCP, *tr. by* Jonathan Chaves

Before the six[t]h day of the next new year. On the Card[e]s, and Dice. Sir Walter Ralegh. ChIV-2; RB; SiPS

Before the solemn bronze Saint Gaudens made. An Ode in Time of Hesitation. William Vaughn Moody. APN-2; CBCWP; OxBA

Before the starry threshold of *Jove['] s* court. Comus; a Masque Presented at Ludlow Castle. Milton. FHYEP; OAEL-1

Before the Statue of Apollo. Saul Tchernichowsky, *Hebrew.* TrJP, *tr. by* L. V. Snowman

Before the Storm. Richard Dehmel, *German.* AWP, *tr. by* Ludwig Lewisohn

Before the Storm. Kenneth O. Hanson. CoAP

Before the Stuff Comes Down. Gary Snyder. HeIP-4

Before the sun goes down. Astrid Hjertenaes Andersen, *Norwegian.* BoWoP, *tr. by* Nadia Christensen

Before the sunlight / splits the dry rock. Aux Leon. . . Women. Honor Ford-Smith. HCP

Before the thing begins we have. Poetry Reading. Vernon Scannell. NOBL

"Before the War." From Our Album. Lawson Fusao Inada. AmPA; PaTW

Before the War. Marilyn Hacker. AmPA

Before the world, I hold that none of these. Albery Allson Whitman. AAP *Fr.* The Octoroon.

Before the world of power you'll fold your arms. Nguyễn Bỉnh Khiêm, *Vietnamese.* AVP, *tr. by* Huỳnh Sanh Thông

Before the world was made. (LL) Before the World Was Made. W. B. Yeats. CBLP; GTBS-P

Before the World Was Made, *fr.* A Woman Young and Old. W. B. Yeats. CBLP; GTBS-P

Before there was a trace of this world of men. Bibi Hayati, *Persian.* EnlH; WPoS, *tr. by* Jane Hirshfield

Before they christened me. Eyes of a Wolf. Vasco [*or* Vasko] Popa, *Serbian.* CEEP, *tr. by* Charles Simic

Before They Made Things Be Alive They Spoke. Lucario Cuevish, *Luiseño Indian.* STP, *tr. by* Jerome Rothenberg

Before they saw through it and found me. (LL) The Diggers. W. S. Merwin. CBNP; SPE

Before this fever of the almost cold. Mirror. Peter De Vries. PoA

Before this grief, mountains must bend down. Dedication. "Anna Andreyevna Akhmatova." PFTM

Before this longing. Her Longing. Theodore Roethke. NAAL-2

Before this, when I was stationed at Hsün-yang. On being Removed from Hsün-yang and Sent to Chung-chou. Po Chü-i, *Chinese.* ChiP, *tr. by* Arthur Waley

Before Throwing a Chicken into an Iowa Valley. Jane Varley. EC3

Before thy door too long of late. 3.10: Extremum Tanain. Horace. AWP, *tr. by* Austin Dobson *Fr.* Odes.

Before Thy Love. Tujin Park, *Korean.* CKP, *tr. by* Jaihiun Kim

Before Waterloo. Thomas Hardy. *See* The Eve of Waterloo.

Before we go to Paradise by way of Kensal Green. (LL) The Rolling English Road. G. K. Chesterton. FaBoCh; NOBE; NOBL; OBEV; OBMV; OxAEP-2; OxBTC; UV

Before we met and you what I had passed. (LL) Meeting and Passing. Robert Frost. GLoP; OxBA

Before we shall again behold. Endimion Porter and Olivia. Sir William Davenant. MeLP; NOBE; NOSC

Before when you left you would always forget. Patrizia Cavalli, *Italian.* NeIt, *tr. by* Judith Baumel

Before which we may not speak or sing or ever stop. (LL) Rain Forest. Dave Jeddie Smith. HCAP; MT

Before you arrive, forget. Africa Says. Carl Phillips. PoPoPo

Before you can learn the trees, you have to learn. Learning the Trees. Howard Nemerov. VCAP

Before You Leave. Ai. GT

Before you left for the Lucky Strike. The Waitress's Kid. Peggy Shumaker. PBCAP

Before you, mother Idoto. Overture. Christopher Okigbo. PBMAP *Fr.* Heavensgate (1961).

Before you praise Spring's advent note. Quatrain. Tu Fu, *Chinese.* TAL, *tr. by* Robert Payne

Before you run out into the street and they shoot. (LL) At first I was given centuries. Margaret Atwood. HAP; WPOW

Before you step out. I Hope I Don't Have You Next Semester, But. Edwin S. Godsey. HoPM

Before you thought of Spring. Emily Dickinson. SAmP

Before your cry. Budded with Child. Meridel Le Sueur. FiLi

Before your face in the moonlight my face. Soyŏng Problems. Sang Yi, *Korean.* PFTM, *tr. by* Walter Lew

Before your hair was ever cut. *Unknown, Greek.* GrAn, *tr. by* Alistair Elliot

Before Your Waking. Anna Gréki, *French.* WPOW, *tr. by* Anita Barrows

Before your wonders I stand, my world. Shimon Halkin, *Hebrew.* MHP, *tr. by* Ruth Finer Mintz

Beg a ten cent mista. Version. Dennis Scott. PBCV

Beg-Innish. John Millington Synge. MoBrPo

Began to tell his tale, as you shall hear. Chaucer. *See* The General Prologue.

Begetting. Dorothea Spears. PeSA

Beggar, The. Margaret E. Bruner. PoToHe

Beggar, The. Thomas Moss. NOEC

Beggar at the Gate, The. Ian Wedde. PeNZ

Beggar Boy, The. Cecil Frances Alexander. OxBChV

"Beggar," he says. Little John a Begging. *Unknown.* ESPB

Beggar in patched robe stands in my doorway, A. From "Ten Poems Recording Things that Happened at the Year's End." Liu K'o-chuang. CoBCP, *tr. by* Burton Watson; CoBCP, *tr. by* Watson, Burton (b. 1925) *Fr.* Ten Poems Recording Things that Happened at the Ye.

Beggar-Laddie, The. *Unknown.* ESPB

Beggar Maid, The. Tennyson. BoTP

Beggar Man, The. Lucy Aikin. OxBChV

Beggar prove thy equal there!, The. (LL) The Birth-Day. Mary Robinson. ECWP; WoRP

Beggar shouts his martial wares, The. Adrian Mitchell. FaBoTw

Beggar to Beggar Cried. W. B. Yeats. CMoP; NoAM; OxAEP-2

Beggar to Burgher. Arthur Rex Dugard Fairburn. PeNZ

Beggar to Mab, the Fairy [or Fairie] Queen, The. Robert Herrick. CaPo

Beggar to the graveyard hied, A. Poverty. *Unknown. Fr.* The Panchatantra. AWP, *tr. by* Arthur Ryder

Beggar Woman, The. William King. ECEV; NOEC

Beggars. Francis Davidson. CH

Beggars have changed places, but the lash goes on, The. (LL) The Great Day. W. B. Yeats. APAD; BlrV; CMoP; OxBSP

Beggar's Holiday, The. John Fletcher. NOSC *Fr.* Beggar's Bush.

Beggar's Opera, The. John Gay. OAEL-1

  Air: "Fox may steal your hens, sir, A." NOEC

  (Act I, Scene ix, Air XI—"A Soldier and a Sailor.") NoP-4

  Air: "Since laws were made for ev'ry degree." NOEC

  Employments of Life, The. PeLV

  ("Thinks his trade as honest as mine.") (LL) OxBoV

  Highwaymen, The.

  "Modes of the court, The."

  "O Polly, you might have toy'd and kist." EnLoPo

  Packington's Pound.

  Song: "Before the barn-door crowing." OxBSP; PoEL-3

  Song: "Can love be controlled by advice?" OxBSP

  Song: "If any wench Venus's girdle wear." PeLV; PoEL-3

  Song: "Thus when the swallow, seeking prey." PoEL-3

  Song: "Were I laid on Greenland's coast." EBEvV, *sect.* I, *pt.* i; CBLP; EnLoPo; NAEL-1; OxBoLi; PeLV; PoEL-3

  (Macheath and Polly.) NOEC

  "Thus I stand like the Turk, with his doxies around." PeLV

  "'Tis woman that seduces all mankind!" OxBoV; PeLV

  What Shall I Do to Show How Much I Love Her?

  Would You Have a Young Virgin?

  Youth and Love. NOBE

  (Youth's the Season.)

Beggar's Serenade. John Heath-Stubbs. BoLoP

Begging. Henry Vaughan. ESCV

Begging Another, on Colour of Mending the Former. Ben Jonson. CBLP; PoEL-2 *Fr.* A Celebration of Charis in Ten Lyric[k] Pieces [*or* Peeces]. BeJo; OxAEP-1; SeCP

Begging at the door of a Master. (LL) A Plea for Mercy. Kwesi Brew. PBMAP

Begging for Food. T'ao Ch'ien, *Chinese.* SuSp, *tr. by* Wu-Chi Liu

Begging strength for his limbs and his trees. (LL) Yellow-coated pomegranate, figs like lizards' necks, A. Philip of Thessalonica, *Greek.* GrAn; OBCVT, *tr. by* Edwin Morgan

begin and end inhaling exhaling. Too Short. Meir Wieseltier, *Hebrew.* IP, *tr. by* Warren Bargad *and* Stanley F. Chyet

Begin before birth with swept-back fins. The Matin Pandemoniums. Richard Eberhart. NYBP

Begin Summer. Ingrid Jonker, *Afrikaans.* PeSA, *tr. by* Jack Cope *and* Uys Krige

Begin to charm, and as thou strok'st mine ears. To Music. Robert Herrick. CaPo

Begin to gleam across the mournful plain? (LL) The Raven Days. Sidney Lanier. APN-2; OxBA

Begin to talk / of HYenaaaAAS. (LL) Hospital/Poem. Sonia Sanchez. BPo; PoBA

Begin unto my God with timbrels. With Timbrels. Bible, Apocrypha. TrJP *Fr.* Judith.

Begin with a kiss[e]. Up Tail[e]s All. Robert Herrick. BeJo

Beginner, The. Rudyard Kipling. FaBoTw *Fr.* Epitaphs of the War [1914–1918]. OBWP

Beginner, / Perpetual beginner. What Can I Tell My Bones? Theodore Roethke. AmPP; NOBA *Fr.* Meditations of an Old Woman.

Beginners. Denise Levertov. CrSp

Beginner's Mind. Margaret Gibson. AFr

Beginning. Alden Nowlan. NOBC

Beginning, The. Vladimir Nikolaevich Sokolov, *Russian.* TCRP, *tr. by* Simon Franklin

Beginning, The. Wallace Stevens. VGW

Beginning. James Wright. ColAP; SAGP; VCAP

Beginning by Example. Christopher Gilbert. Blue. FYAP

Beginning by Value. Christopher Gilbert. GT

Beginning from you, Phoebus, I shall tell the glory. The Argonautica. Apollonius Rhodius, *Greek.* HePo, *tr. by* Barbara Hughes Fowler

Beginning in half darkness. The Morning Track. Edward Parone. NYBP

Beginning in the light as heard, wheel on stone. Stephen Ratcliffe. PT

Beginning my studies the first step pleas'd me so much. Walt Whitman. NAAL-1; NAAL-3; OxBA

Beginning of a Beautiful Day (A Symphony), The. Daniil Kharms, *Russian.* AF, *tr. by* George Gibian

Beginning of a Long Poem on Why I Burned the City, The. Lawrence Benford. TTY

Beginning of Autumn: A Poem to Send to Tzu-yu. Su Tung-p'o, *Chinese.* CoBCP, *tr. by* Burton Watson

Beginning of Spring—A Stroll with My Wife. Hsü Chün-ch'ien, *Chinese.* CoBCP, *tr. by* Burton Watson

Beginning of Summer, The. Po Chü-i, *Chinese.* ChiP, *tr. by* Arthur Waley

Beginning of the Book, The. Edmond Jabès, *French.* AF, *tr. by* Rosemarie Waldrop

Beginning of the End, The. Jon Stallworthy. OxBC

Beginning, The: Some landscape & words about nature. Kirk Lonegren's Home Movie Taking Place Just North of Prince George, with Sound. Sharon Thesen. NOBC

Beginning the Year at Rosebud, S. D. Roberta Hill Whiteman. CDW

Beginning to dangle beneath. In the Marble Quarry. James Dickey. NoP-4

Beginning when I was six I became my father's accomplice. 1. Robert Malise Bowyer Nichols. CLPP *Fr.* Get-Away.

Beginning with a stain, as universe did perhaps. Alice Notley. PmAP

Beginnings. Michael Burns. IFJA

Beginnings. Peter Sirr. PBCIP

Beginnings. *Unknown. Fr.* The Popol Vuh. STP, *tr. by* Munro Edmonson

Beginnings. Michael S. Weaver. PBCAP

Begins the crying. Guitar. Federico García Lorca, *Spanish.* InPK-6, *tr. by* Keith Waldrop

Begone, calm. A Spell of Weather. Eve Merriam. CA

Begonias. Su Tung-p'o, *Chinese.* OHPC, *tr. by* Kenneth Rexroth

Begonia's soil is rich and wet, The. Collusion. Medbh McGuckian. BiHa

Begotten by the meeting of rock with rock. Sea Holly. Conrad Potter Aiken. LiTM

Begotten of the Spleen. Charles Simic. AF; LCAP-2

  ("In the guard towers.") (LL) AF

Beguines who hear these words. *Unknown.* WPoS, *tr. by* Jane Hirshfield *and* Mariko Aratani *Fr.* The Soul Speaks.

Begun before Easter. . . / Sign of the Fish. Thomas McGrath. *Fr.* Letter to an Imaginary Friend, Part Two. NNaP

Behaving Like a Jew. Gerald Stern. LoL; UnSA

  ("His black whiskers and his little dancing feet.") (LL) UnSA

Behaviour of Fish in an Egyptian Tea Garden. Keith Douglas. FaBoMo; RB

Behind a duck, how many ducks? Five? No. Three. This is not the end. (LL) Army. Ciaran Carson. BiHa; PBCIP

Behind a vermilion gate, on the eve of the Skills Festival. Autumn. Fan Ch'eng-ta. SuSp, *tr. by* Irving Y. Lo *Fr.* Seasonal Poems on Fields and Gardens.

Behind a Wall. Amy Lowell. SDW

Behind a web of bottles, bales. The Gombeen. Joseph Campbell. BlrV

Behind Bars, Sel. Fadwa Tuqan, *Arabic.* AF, *tr. by* Hatem Hussaini

Behind Calyx Hall's towers the sun has just set. On a Painting of the Radiant Emperor's Night Revels by Candlelight. Kao Ch'i, *Chinese.* SuSp, *tr. by* Irving Y. Lo

Behind glass, my room is neat. Out of Chaos Out of Order Out. Michele Roberts. BrRo

Behind Grandma's House. Gary Soto. UnSA

Behind her big fan. Tête-à-Tête. May Probyn. VWP

Behind him lay the gray Azores. Columbus. Joaquin Miller. APN-2; CTV; EBEvV; FaBoBe

Behind him the plate glass of the store only cracked. (LL) The Hongo Store 29 Miles Volcano Hilo, Hawaii. Garrett Kaoru Hongo. PoPoPo; WeT

Behind his dinner jacket. He's Doing Natural Life. Conyus. PoBA

Behind King's Chapel what the earth has kept. At the Indian Killer's Grave. Robert Lowell. NOBA; VGW

Behind me, and will not go away. (LL) Follower. Seamus Heaney. CABP; IIP; PNI

Behind Me—dips Eternity. Emily Dickinson. APN-2; PBWP

Behind me I do not see the ancient men. Song on Climbing Yu-chou Gate Tower. Ch'en Tzu-ang, *Chinese.* CoBCP, *tr. by* Burton Watson

Behind: me, wag. (LL) Life, friends, is boring. We must not say so. John Berryman. ColAP; HAP; HCAP; HeIP-4; LiTM; MoP; NAAL-2; NOBA; NoAM; NoP-4; TAP; TRP; TwCP; VCAP

Behind Prison Bars. No Ch'&obreve;n-my&obreve;ng, *Korean.* CKP, *tr. by* Jaihiun Kim

Behind secluded screens the hush of daytime scenes. Summertime. Su Shun-ch'in, *Chinese*. SuSp, tr. by Michael E. Workman

Behind shut doors, in shadowy quarantine. The First Time. Karl Shapiro. VGW

Behind, sun, before, shadow! Silhouette. Annette M'Baye, *French*. PBWP, tr. by Kathleen Weaver

Behind sunglasses. Anita Virgil. HA

Behind the calm famous faces knowledge of what crimes? Collapsible. Tom Raworth. SPE

Behind the gates of sunset. (LL) Eden. Emily Grosholz. FFC; RA

Behind the house the upland falls. After the Pleasure Party. Herman Melville. APN-2; NAAL-1; NAAL-3; PAR; PoEL-5

Behind the Log. Edwin John Pratt.
   "There is a language in a naval log." MoCV

Behind the moth-eaten curtain, 'stead of press. Mary Davys. ECWP *Fr.* The Modern Poet.

Behind the small, fixed windows of the album. Life of a Salesman. Emily Grosholz. RA

Behind the smooth texture. Like an Animal. Jimmy Santiago Baca. AF

Behind the tiller the sea runs thick. High Seas on the Caspian. Boris Petrovich Kornilov, *Russian*. TCRP, tr. by Bernard Meares

Behind the Veil. Andrew Lansdown. NOBAu

Behind the veil, behind the veil. (LL) "So careful of the type?" but no. Tennyson. EBVV; EBVVPR; EnVR; FHYEP; HAP; OAEL-2; OBNC; TOF

Behind the wall of St. John's in the city. The Garden at St. John's. May Swenson. GaP

Behind you / a riot of pallid orphans. Small Country. Claribel Alegría, *Spanish*. BoWoP, tr. by Aliki *and* Willis Barnstone

Behind you, now. Schwerner, Chaney, Goodman. Raymond R. Patterson. NBV

Behold! a proof of Irish sense! Jonathan Swift, *authorship disputed*. CBNP

Behold a Shaking. Christina Rossetti.
   "Blessed that flock safe penned in Paradise." WPoS

Beho[u]ld, a silly [*or* sely *or* little] tender babe. New Prince, New Pomp[e]. Robert Southwell. ESCV; NOBE; NOCV; NoSic; TrCP

Behold, a virgin shall conceive. The Messiah. Bible, *O.T.* AWP *Fr.* Isaiah.

Behold alone / The Woman, opportune to all attempts. Milton. OxBoV *Fr.* Paradise Lost.

Behold, bless ye the Lord, all ye servants of the Lord. Bible, *O.T. See* Psalm 134.

Behold, four Kings in majesty rever'd. The Playing Cards. Alexander Pope. *Fr.* The Rape of the Lock[, an Heroi-Comical Poem]. FHYEP; HAP; ImPo; OAEL-1; OBNV; PeLV; PoEL-3

Behold from sluggish winter's arm. Primo Vere. Giosuè Carducci, *Italian.* AWP, tr. by John Bailey

Behold, God is great, and we know him not. Bible, *O.T. Fr.* Job. NAWM-1

Behold, God of Abraham, God of mercy. Elie Wiesel. HP *Fr.* Ani Maamin, A Song Lost and Found Again.

Behold her, single in the field. The Solitary Reaper. Wordsworth. APAD; AWP; CABP; CH; ClHu; EBEvV; FHYEP; FaBoCh; FaPoR; GTBS-P; HAP; HeIP-4; ImPo; InPS-3; NAEL-2; NOBE; NOBRP; NoP-4; OAEL-2; OBEV; OBNC; OxAEP-2; PoEL-4; PoPoPo; PoRA; Poetr; Ro; SCGP; SCV; SoSe-8; TFi; UnPo; WeW-3

Behold him now his genuine colours wear. Sonnet 32. Anna Seward. CPO

Behold, how eager this our little boy. Of the Boy and Butterfly. John Bunyan. OxBChV

Behold how every man, drawn with delight. Samuel Daniel. NoSic *Fr.* Musophilus; or, Defence of All Learning.

Behold, how good and how pleasant it is. Psalm 133. Bible, *O.T.* AWP; TrJP *Fr.* Psalms.

Behold I see the haven nigh at hand. Edmund Spenser. FHYEP *Fr.* Wood Of Error. AEP

Behold, I send thee to the heights of song. To W. S. M. Arthur W. Monroe. APN-2

Behold, I shew you a mystery: We shall not all sleep, but. The Last Day. Bible, *N.T.* LBC *Fr.* 1 Corinthians, 15. 51.

Behold! in various throngs the scribbling crew. Byron. OAEL-2 *Fr.* English Bards and Scotch Reviewers.

Behold, love, thy power how she despiseth! Sir Thomas Wyatt. GBL

Behold me waiting—waiting for the knife. Before. William Ernest Henley. MoBrPo *Fr.* In Hospital.

Behold, my dearest, how the fragrant rose. To Her Love. Edward May. FaBoEE

Behold my mother! Abu Dulama, *Arabic*. ArPe, tr. by Omar S. Pound

Behold, my servant shall deal prudently. The Song of The Suffering Servant. Bible, *O.T.* NAWM-1 *Fr.* Isaiah.

Behold, O Aspasia! I Send You Verses. Walter Savage Landor. OBNC; SCGP *Fr.* Pericles and Aspasia.

Behold, O Man, *sels.* Edmund Spenser. *Fr.* Wood Of Error. AEP

Behold Pelides with his yellow hair. Before a Statue of Achilles. George Santayana. APN-2

Behold that tree, in Autumn's dim decay. Anna Seward. WoRP *Fr.* Sonnets.

Behold the brand of beauty tossed! The Dancer. Edmund Waller. CBLP

Behold the brave fellow who sits in his Yellow. The All-night Taxi Stand. Kenneth Slessor. BMAP

Behold the child among his new-born blisses. Wordsworth. *Fr.* Ode: Intimations of Immortality [from Recollections of Early Childhood]. AWP; FHYEP; HAP; HeIP-4; NOBE; NOBRP; OAEL-2; OBEV; OBNC; PBMP; PoE; PoEL-4

Behold the child, by Nature's kindly law. Alexander Pope. ECEV *Fr.* An Essay on Man.

Behold the critic, pitched like the *castrati*. Pipling. Theodore Roethke. OBCoV *Fr.* Three Epigrams. NBLV

Behold the Deeds! Henry Cuyler Bunner. NBLV

Behold the dread Mt. Shasta, where it stands. Mount Shasta. John Rollin Ridge. APN-2; PAR

Behold the duck. / It does not cluck. The Duck. Ogden Nash. RB

Behold the ever-tim'rous hare. April. Samuel Thompson. BIrV

Behold the fatal day arrive! Jonathan Swift. PeLV; SCV *Fr.* Verses on the Death of Dr. Swift, D.S.P.D.

Behold the flag! Is it not a flag? "Orpheus C. Kerr." *Fr.* The Rejected "National Hymns." OBAL

Behold, the grave of a wicked man. Why? Stephen Crane. APN-2; MeMAP; NoP-4; TAP *Fr.* The Black Riders [and Other Lines].

Behold, the King of glory now is come. Laurence Clarkson. PBRV *Fr.* A Single Eye All Light, no Darkness.

Behold the manly mesomorph. W. H. Auden. OxBSP *Fr.* Shorts [1948–1957].

Behold, the Meads. Guillaume de Poitiers, *French*. AWP, tr. by Harriet Waters Preston

Behold, the old earth is young again! The Sibyl. Agnes Mary Frances Robinson. VWP

Behold the rocky wall. The Two Streams. Oliver Wendell Holmes. APN-1

Behold, the Shade of Night Is Now Receding. Saint Gregory the Great, *Latin.* AH, tr. by Ray Palmer

Behold this green. Andrea Zanzotto, *Italian*. VCWP, tr. by Ruth Feldman *and* Brian Swann (b. 1940)

Behold the tormented and the fallen angel. Beethoven. John Hall Wheelock. PoA

Behold the works of William Morris. Rondel. *Unknown.* BXAP

Behold this brief hexagonal. Text. Audrey Wurdemann. FYAP

Behold this fleeting world, how all things fade. An Epitaph of the Death of Nicholas Grimald. Barnabe Googe. SCGP

Behold this little volume here enrolled. On the Bible. *Unknown.* NOSC

Behold this needle; when the *Arctick* stone. Francis Quarles. PBRV

Behold this ruin! 'Twas a skull. To a Skeleton. Anna Jane Vardhill. BLPA

Behold this swarthy face, these gray eyes. Walt Whitman. APN-1

Behold those wingèd images. A Legend of the Hive. Robert Stephen Hawker. EBVV

Behold, thou art fair. Bible, *O.T.* OxBM; TrJP *Fr.* The Song of Songs. AWP

Behold three Kings come from the East. For Twelfth Day. Luke Wadding. TIRV

Behold through the veil of distance a pleasing image. Jonathan. "Rachel," *Hebrew*. TrJP, tr. by L. V. Snowman

Behold thy darling, which thy lustfull care. Francis Quarles. ESCV *Fr.* Emblems.

Behold what hap *Pigmalion* had to frame. Samuel Daniel. PBRV *Fr.* Delia.

Behold, whatever wind prevail. The Mid-Day Moon. John Banister Tabb. APN-2

Behold, where Dryden's less presumptuous car. Thomas Gray. EPCY *Fr.* The Progress of Poesy. AWP; GTBS-P; NOEC; OBEV

Behold with Joy. Elhanan Winchester. AH

Behold! wood into bird and bird to wood again. Boomerang. William Hart-Smith. NOBAu; NTP

Behold yon hill, how it is swell'd with pride. Describes the Place Where Cynthia Is Sporting Herself. Philip Ayres. EnLoPo

Behold young Raphael coming back. Raphael. Priscilla Jane Thompson. CBWP-2

Beholde, how good and joyfull a thinge it is, brethren to dwell to gether in unitye. Bible, *O.T. See* Psalm 133.

Beholden or enlarged. Mortar. Elizabeth Robinson. PT

Beholding element, in whose pure eye. The Aspen and the Stream. Richard Wilbur. NYBP

Beija-Flor. Diane Ackerman. NIP-4

Being, The. Hayden Carruth. PoA *Fr.* Contra Mortem.

Being a boy from the hills, brought up. The Welshman in Exile Speaks. T. Harri Jones. OBWVE

Being a colored poet. Jacket Notes. Ishmael Reed. UnSA

Being a friend means, / After all. (LL) Love. Roy Croft. BLPA; FaBoBe; PoToHe

Being a woman, I am. The Wife Speaks. Mary Stanley. PeNZ

Being always / Poor. (LL) Ennui. Langston Hughes. OBAL; OBCA

Being, always to arrange. Martin Carter. HCP

Being Aware. Dennis Cooper. GLP; PmAP

Being black in America. Lonely Eagles. Marilyn Nelson Waniek. NAmP90

Being Called For. Rosemary Dobson. BMAP; CBAP

Being double dead: going, and bidding go[e]. (LL) The Expiration. Donne. CBLP; MeLP; OxBSP

Being drunk upstairs and listening. Green Revolutions. Barbara Guest. FaBoWP

Being half foxt he praiseth Bacchus. Horace, *Latin.* OBCVT, *tr. by* Thomas Flatman

Being her friend, I do not care, not I. John Masefield. FP

Being his resting place. A Dog Sleeping on My Feet. James Dickey. NAAL-2

Being Human. Ruth Stone. IMW

Being in thought of love, I chanced to see. Ballata: He Reveals, in a Dialogue, His Increasing Love for Mandetta. Guido Cavalcanti, *Italian.* AWP, *tr. by* D. G. Rossetti

Being Jewish in a Small Town. Lyn Lifshin. UnSA

Being mighty a master, being a father and fond. (LL) In the Valley of the Elwy. Gerard Manley Hopkins. EnVR; ImPo; NOBVV; NOCV; OxAEP-2; TOF

Being my self captived here in care. Sonnet 73: 'Being my self captived here'. Edmund Spenser. AEP

Being neither white nor black? (LL) Cross. Langston Hughes. ColAP; GT; LiTM; NoP-4; PoBA; PoLF; SAmP; SoSe-8; TAP

Being of sound mind, and in love with the child. Walls. Jay Meek. CMAP

Being on Duty all Night in the Palace and Dreaming of the Hsien-yu Temple. Po Chü-i, *Chinese.* ChiP, *tr. by* Arthur Waley

Being one day at my window all alone. Petrarch. *Fr.* Visions. AWP

Being one day at my window all alone. The Visions. Petrarch. AWP *Fr.* Sonnets to Laura.

Being Pharaoh. Beckian Fritz Goldberg. BAP-95

Being polite to your official guests. (LL) Easter Hymn. Alec Derwent Hope. ChIV-2; GI

Being set in order, to conduct a life. Permanent Wave. Andrew Crozier. NBrP

Being set on the idea. Atlantis. W. H. Auden. OxAEP-2

Being Somebody. Edwin Honig. TAP

Being through weakness to the house confin'd. The Preface to *Divine Songs and Meditacions.* Anne Collins. KTR

Being to timelessness as it's to time. E. E. Cummings. HAP

Being very religious, she devoted most of her time to fear. Episode of Decay. Witter Bynner. OxBM

Being Visited by a Friend During Illness. Po Chü-i, *Chinese.* ChiP, *tr. by* Arthur Waley

Being with you / here, in this room. Margaret Atwood. *Fr.* The Circle Game. MoCV

Being witless it said no prayer. The Death of an Angel. Russell Edson. LCAP-2

Being you, you cut your poetry from wood. The Egg Boiler. Gwendolyn Brooks. PoBA

Being your slave, what should I do[e] but tend. Sonnet 57. Shakespeare. GTBS-P; HAP; NoSic; OBEV; PoEL-2 *Fr.* Sonnets.

Beings' lives gel in my womb. (LL) Pregnancy. Sandra McPherson. LoL; NMM-2

Beinn Naomh. Kathleen Jessie Raine.

    Summit, The. OxBS

Beirut-Hell Express, The. Etel Adnan.

    "Human race is going to the cemetery, The." WPOW

Bel m'es quan lo vens m'alena. Arnaut Daniel, *French.* AWP, *tr. by* Harriet Waters Preston

Belex his flint adjusts and rights. By the Jordan. Herman Melville. NCAP

Belfast. Louis MacNeice. PeECV

Belfast Confetti. Ciaran Carson. BiHa; CIP-2; PNI

Belfast Lough. *Unknown, Irish.* BIrV, *tr. by* John Montague

Belfast Tune. Joseph Brodsky. VCWP

Belfry, The. Laurence Binyon. CH

Belgian, with cumbrous tread and iron boots. Malines. James Kenneth Stephen. OBCoV

Belief. Philip Levine. ColAP

Belief. Josephine Miles. ColAP; FaBoWP; MoP; NoAM; TAP ("Noblesse oblige.") (LL) ColAP

Belief. Ella Wheeler Wilcox. PWR

Belief, and the love, and the truth, The. (LL) Mein Kind, wir waren Kinder. Heinrich Heine, *German.* OBVE, *tr. by* Elizabeth Barrett Browning

Belief and Unbelief. Robert Browning. *Fr.* Bishop Blougram's Apology. EBVVPR; OBNC; PoEL-5

Belief / As unbelief before, Shakes us by fits. Belief and Unbelief. Robert Browning. *Fr.* Bishop Blougram's Apology. EBVVPR; OBNC; PoEL-5

Belief, great mustard seed, sends mountains to the sea. "Angelus Silesius." GePo, *tr. by* George C. Schoolfield *Fr.* The Cherubical Wanderer.

Believe me, if all those endearing young charms. Thomas Moore. BLPA; FaBoBe; ImPo; NAEL-2; OBNC; PoEL-4; Ro ("Same look which she turned when he rose!, The.") (LL) Ro

Believe me, I knew you, though faintly, and I loved, I loved you / All. (LL) The Mother. Gwendolyn Brooks. CrDW; CrSp; MDDM; NAAAL; NALW; NMM-2; PoPoPo

Believe me, knot of gristle, I bleed like a tree. Give Way, Ye Gates. Theodore Roethke. CMoP

Believe me, love, it is not good. To a Girl. Asclepiades, *Greek.* OBCVT, *tr. by* Andrew Lang

Believe me, Love, this vagrant life. To Cordelia. Joseph Stansbury. NOBC

Believe me, sir, I'd like to spend whole days. Martial, *Latin.* OBVE, *tr. by* J. V. Cunningham

Believe not that the world is for naught, made. Isaac Leibush Peretz, *Yiddish.* TrJP, *tr. by* Solomon Liptzin

Believers' Best Buy. Roger Woddis. UV

Believe't, I will. (LL) Madrigal: "How should I love my best?" Edward Herbert, 1st Baron Herbert of Cherbury. PoEL-2; SeCP

Believing in the Absurd. Harold Norse. CLPP

Believing in those inexorable laws. Muriel Rukeyser. Son

Believing the heart was the center of knowledge. No Friends of the Heart. Nancy Eimers. WeT

Belinda lived in a little white house. The Tale of Custard the Dragon. Ogden Nash. OBCA; OTCP; PoRA

Belinda still her downy Pillow prest. Alexander Pope. OxBSn *Fr.* The Rape of the Lock.

Belisarius. Henry Wadsworth Longfellow. APN-1; PoEL-5

Belize Suite. Velma Pollard. HCP

    Road from Xunantunich. HCP

    Sea Wall. HCP

    Xunantunich. HCP

Bell, The. Richard Jones. NAmP90

Bell, The. Kenneth Rexroth. PFTM *Fr.* A Prolegomenon to a Theodicy. "Bell / Too softly and too slowly tolled, The." "Imperceptible light / Scintilla animae." "They were in an unstable condition."

Bell and drum on the south river bank. Following the Rhumes of Chiang Hui-shu. Su Tung-p'o, *Chinese.* CoBCP, *tr. by* Burton Watson

Bell-Birds. Henry Clarence Kendall. NOBAu

Bell horses, bell horses, what time of day? Mother Goose. BoTP; OxNR; ReMoGo

Bell is full of wind, The. Roberto Juarroz. VCWP, *tr. by* W. S. Merwin *Fr.* Sixth Vertical Poetry.

Bell-Man, The. Robert Herrick. BeJo

Bell-rope that gathers God at dawn, The. The Broken Tower. Hart Crane. AmPP; CMoP; ColAP; LiTM; MeMAP; MoAmPo; NOBA; NoAM; NoP-4; OxBA; PoPoPo; Poetr

Bell Speech. Richard Wilbur. MoAmPo

Bell strikes *one*: we take no note of time. Edward Young. ECEV *Fr.* Night Thoughts.

Bell / Too softly and too slowly tolled, The. Kenneth Rexroth. *Fr.* The Bell. PFTM *Fr.* A Prolegomenon to a Theodicy.

Bell Tower. Léonie Adams. MoAmPo

Bell wakes me at 6 in the pale spring dawn, The. Letter from Pretoria Central Prison. Arthur Nortje. HBAPE

Bell was not a jar, when, The. The Suicide Rates. Lewis Warsh. FTOS

Belle Isle, 1949. Philip Levine. ColAP; SAGP; VCAP

Belle Layotte, *tr. of Creole slave song.* George Washington Cable. APN-2

Belle of the Ball-Room, The. Winthrop Mackworth Praed. NOBRP *Fr.* Every-Day Characters.

Bellerophon. Euripides, *Greek.*

    There Are No Gods.

("Doth some one say that there be gods above?")

Bellflower spilling a candlesnuffer's dark hints. Of. Debora Greger. EOEF

Bellies bitter with drinking the/ Weak tears. Final Chorus. Archibald MacLeish. *Fr.* Panic. MoAmPo

Bellman, The. Robert Herrick. CH; CaPo

Bellman himself they all praised to the skies—, The. Fit the Second: The Bellman's Speech. "Lewis Carroll." OBCoV *Fr.* The Hunting of the Snark. CBNP; OBNC; OBNV; PoEL-5

Bellman looked uffish, and wrinkled his brow. Fit the Fourth: The Hunting. "Lewis Carroll." *Fr.* The Hunting of the Snark. CBNP; OBNC; OBNV; PoEL-5

Bellman's Song, The. *Unknown.* EBEV; SCGP

Bellona the fierce, who held man in disdain. On a Lady, Preached into the Colic, by One of Her Lovers. Aaron Hill. ECEV

Bellow of good Master Bull, The. Ballade un Peu Banale. Arthur James Marshall Smith. MoCV

Bellower with the antlers. Suibne Geilt. NOIV

Bellows Maker of Oxford, The. John Hoskyns. FaBoEE

Bellows: O wise man, weigh your words. Cynewulf. ASW, *tr. by* Kevin Crossley-Holland. *Fr.* Riddles (Exeter Book).

Bellrope. Robert Morgan. BLT

Bells. Mateja Matevski, *Macedonian.* CEEP, *tr. by* Dragan Milivojevic

Bells, The. Edgar Allan Poe. APN-1; ChAP; MeMAP; OBAL; OBCA; PoLF; TAP; TFi

Bells, The. Saul Tchernichowsky, *Hebrew.* MHP, *tr. by* Ruth Finer Mintz

Bells, The. *Unknown.* ReMoGo

Bells are booming down the bohreens. Ireland with Emily. John Betjeman. GTBS-P, OxBTC

Bells for John Whiteside's Daughter. John Crowe Ransom. CMoP; ColAP; FuPo; HAP; HeIP-4; HoPM; IMW; InPK-6; InPS-3; LiTM; MeMAP; MoAmPo; MoLi; MoP; NAAL-2; NIP-4; NOBA; NoAM; NoP-4; OxBA; PFE; PoE; Poetr; RB; SAGP; TAP; TFi; UnPo; VGW; WeW 3

Bells from the steeple resound, The. Limerick. John Stanley. PeLi

Bells have wide mouths and tongues, but are too weak. Upon a Ring of Bells. John Bunyan. CH

Bells of Grey Crystal. Dame Edith Sitwell. OxBSP

Bells of Heaven, The. Ralph Hodgson. BoTP; LiTM; MoBrPo; NOBE; OBEV; OxBSP

Bells of hell go ting-a-ling-a-ling, The. *Unknown.* OBCoV *Fr.* Soldiers' Songs of the First World War.

Bells of London, The, *see also* London Bells: "Two sticks and an Apple." *Unknown.* BoTP; LB; OxNR; PoRA

("Here comes a chopper to chop off your head.") (LL) LB; OxNR

("Say the bells at St. Paul's.") (LL) PoRA

Bells of San Blas, The. Henry Wadsworth Longfellow. APN-1; MeMAP; OxBA; PAR

Bells of Shandon, The. Francis Sylvester Mahony. CH; IIP; OBEV

(Shandon Bells, The.) OxAEP-2

Bells of St. Michael. Mary Weston Fordham. CBWP-2

Bells of waiting Advent ring, The. Christmas. John Betjeman. OBCP; OxBTC

Bells of Youth, The. "Fiona Macleod." BoTP

Bells ov Alderburnham, The. William Barnes. EBVV

Belly Dancer. Diane Wakoski. NALW; NoAM

Belly Song. Etheridge Knight. BkSV

Belly waves roll upon waves. Koker. Rooplall Monar. HCP

Belly Woman's Lament. Lillian Allen. PBCV

Belmans Song, A. Thomas Ravenscroft. PBRV

Belongings. Catherine Davis. FFC

Beloved, The. David Roberts, *Welsh.* OBWVE, *tr. by* H. Idris Bell

Beloved, again! (LL) If grief for grief can touch thee. Emily Jane Brontë. GLoP; VWP

Beloved! amid the earnest woes. To F——. Edgar Allan Poe. APN-1

Beloved friends! More glorious times than ours. To My Friends. Johann Christoph Friedrich von Schiller, *German.* AWP, *tr. by* James Clarence Mangan

Beloved, gaze in thine own heart. The Two Trees. W. B. Yeats. OAEL-2

Beloved, I only love thee! let it pass. (LL) Sonnet: "Can it be right to give what I can give?" Elizabeth Barrett Browning. CTC; Son

Beloved, it is good. Dream Song. *Unknown, Pawnee.* OBVE, *tr. by* Francis Densmore

Beloved, let us once more praise the rain. Prelude VII. Conrad Potter Aiken. UnPo *Fr.* Preludes for Memnon; or, Preludes to Attitude.

Beloved, may your sleep be sound. Lullaby. W. B. Yeats. BoLoP; FaBoTw; LoP; OBMV

Belovéd, my Belovéd, when I think. Sonnet. Elizabeth Barrett Browning. Son; WPE *Fr.* Sonnets from the Portuguese.

Beloved, my glory in thee is not ceased. "Michael Field." CPO; VWP

("My spririt grieves.") (LL) VWP

Beloved on the earth. (LL) Late Fragment. Raymond Carver. APAD; LBC

Beloved person must I think, The. Akimine, *Japanese.* AWP; TAL, *tr. by* Arthur Waley *Fr.* Kokin Shu.

Belovèd, thou hast brought me many flowers. Sonnet. Elizabeth Barrett Browning. EBVV; EnVR; LW; OBNC; WPE *Fr.* Sonnets from the Portuguese.

Beloved, what do you want of me? Marguerite Porete, *German.* WPoS, *tr. by* Peter Dronke

Beloved,/ What does it take to put a house in order? Don Mager. GLP *Fr.* Letters from a Married Man.

Beloved, you are like thread in the loom. Ancient Feeling. Wu Wei-yeh, *Chinese.* CoBLCP, *tr. by* Jonathan Chaves

Below. Federico García Lorca. PFTM

Below fair Peebles, on the river's side. Alexander Pennecuik. NOEC *Fr.* A Marriage betwixt Scrape, Monarch of the Maunders, and Blobberlips, Queen of the Gypsies.

Below Freezing. Tomas Tranströmer, *Swedish.* VCWP, *tr. by* Robert Bly

Below Hekla. Selima Hill. FaBoWP

Below Incense Burner Peak I built a new mountain dwelling. A New Thatched Hall. Po Chü-i, *Chinese.* CoBCP, *tr. by* Burton Watson

Below lies one whose name was traced in sand. My Epitaph. David Gray. EBVV

Below Loughrigg. Fleur Adcock. PeNZ

Below me the city was in flames. The Improved Binoculars. Irving Layton. NOBC

Below the dam. John Wills. HA

Below the dancing larches freckled. Joseph Gordon MacLeod. *Fr.* Men of the Rocks. OxBS

Below the gardens and the darkening pines. At Carmel Highlands. Janet Lewis. PoA

Below the Great Wall—the watering hole. The Horse-Watering Hole. Yang Wei-chen, *Chinese.* CoBLCP, *tr. by* Jonathan Chaves

Below the Hall what meets my eyes? The Pine-trees in the Courtyard. Po Chü-i, *Chinese.* ChiP, *tr. by* Arthur Waley

Below the Surface-Stream. Matthew Arnold. NOBVV; OxBSP

Below the thunders of the upper deep;. The Kraken. Tennyson. APo; EnVR; NAEL-2; NoP-4; OAEL-2; OBNC; OxBSn; PeECV; PoEL-5; TOF

Below thir stanes lie Jamie's banes. On a Noisy Polemic. Robert Burns. FaBoEE

Belshazzar! from the banquet turn. To Belshazzar. Byron. ChIV-1

Belshazzar had a Letter. Emily Dickinson. ChIV-1

Belshazzer's Feast. Eloise Bibb. CBWP-4

Belt, The. Eric Chock. IFJA

Be'mi'ster. William Barnes. EBVV

Ben Barley was a barman stout. Gerard Benson. UV

Ben Battle was a soldier bold. Faithless Nelly Gray. Thomas Hood. BXAP; NOBL; NOBRP; UV

Ben Bolt. Thomas Dunn English. APN-1; FaBoBe

Ben Bolt of the salt-sea gale. (LL) Ben Bolt. Thomas Dunn English. APN-1; FaBoBe

Ben, do not leave the stage. An Answer to Mr. Ben Jonson's Ode, to Persuade Him Not to Leave the Stage. Thomas Randolph. BeJo

Ben Jonson. Swinburne. EPCY *Fr.* Sonnets of English Dramatic Poets. Son

Ben Jonson Entertains a Man from Stratford. Edwin Arlington Robinson. AmPP; MoAmPo

Ben Webster: "Did You Call Her Today?" Ron Welburn. SeSe

Bench of Boors, The. Herman Melville. APN-2; NAAL-1; NAAL-3; NoP-4; OBAL; SoSe-8

Benches are broken, the grassplots brown and bare, The. South End. Conrad Potter Aiken. CMoP; HoPM; OxBA

Bend after bend, the long embankment. Tao-chi, *Chinese.* CoBLCP, *tr. by* Jonathan Chaves

Bend as the Bow Bends. Conrad Potter Aiken. CMoP *Fr.* And in the Human Heart. Son

Bend down and touch lightly with my lips the white face in the coffin. (LL) Reconciliation. Walt Whitman. APN-1; HAP; MeMAP; MoAmPo; NAAL-1; NAAL-3; NoP-4; OBWP; OxBA; OxBSP; WeW-3

Bend down my strange face to yours and forgive you. (LL) All My Pretty Ones. Anne Sexton. MoLi; NAAL-3; NoAM

Bend in the River. Simon J. Ortiz. HATNAP; PoPoPo

BEND of the river brings into view two triumphal arches;, A. Arriving at Hsün-yang. Po Chü-i, *Chinese.* ChiP, *tr. by* Arthur Waley

Bend thy bow, Dian! shoot thy silver shaft. The New Moon. William Gilmore Simms. APN-1

Bending above the spicy woods which blaze. October. Helen Hunt Jackson. APN-2

Bending back. Alan Pizzarelli. HA

Bending, I bow my head. Combing. Gladys Cardiff. CDW

Bending the Bow. Robert Duncan. FTOS

Bendix. John Updike. NYBP

Bends all his powers, even unto Stella's grace. (LL) Sonnet 27: "Because I oft, in dark abstracted guise." Sir Philip Sidney. CABP; NoSic

Beneath a gas-mantle that the moths bombard. The West. Michael Longley. BiHa; PBCIP

Beneath a holm repaired two jolly swains. Corydon and Thyrsis. Virgil. AWP, tr. by Dryden Fr. Eclogues.

Beneath a myrtle shade. Song of the Zambra Dance. Dryden. PoEL-3 Fr. The Conquest of Granada.

Beneath a shaggy fir tree. The Devil's Swing. Fyodor Kuz'mich Sologub, Russian. TCRP, tr. by April FitzLyon

Beneath a sky blurred with mist and wind. For Anna Mae Aquash Whose Spirit Is Present Here and in the Dappled Stars. Joy Harjo. PuP-15

Beneath a thundery glaze. Walter James Turner. Fr. The Seven Days of the Sun. OBMV

Beneath a willow entwined with ivy. Boris Pasternak. See Hops.

Beneath all the statistics. New York. Federico García Lorca, Spanish. RaBo, tr. by Robert Bly

Beneath both the feet of Boötes you may see. Aratus, Greek. HePo, tr. by Barbara Hughes Fowler Fr. Phaenomena.

Beneath him with new wonder now he views. Eden. Milton. OBGa Fr. Book IV. OAEL-1 Fr. Paradise Lost.

Beneath its canopy of poisoned air. (LL) On a Line from Valéry. Carolyn Kizer. BAP-95; FFC

Beneath / leaf mold. Marlene Mountain. HA

Beneath me this dark garden plunges, buoyant. Villa D'Este. Edwin Denby. OBGa

Beneath my feet when Flora cast. The Rose. Elizabeth Tollet. ECWP

Beneath my palm-trees, by the riverside. Song of the Indian Maid, The ("Beneath my palm-trees, by the riverside"). Keats. NOBE Fr. Endymion: Poetic Romance.

Beneath my vine's cool shelter. Horace. See Simplicity.

Beneath our eaves the moonbeams play. Moon and Candle-light. William Renton. NOBVV

Beneath our feet, the shuddering bogs. On Yes Tor. Sir Edmund William Gosse. CH

Beneath the blaze of a tropical sun the mountain peaks are the Thrones of Frost. The Blossoming of the Solitary Date-Tree. Coleridge. CBLP

Beneath the branch of the green myrtle. Unknown. Fr. Medieval Norman Song. AWP, tr. by John Addington Symonds

Beneath the brushed wing of the mallard. Lint. Rita Dove. TRP

Beneath the cloud-topp'd mountain. Song of the Desert. Eliza R. Snow. PaTW

Beneath the drear November trees. (LL) Autumnal. Ernest Christopher Dowson. EBVV; OBNC

Beneath the Good how far—but far above the Great. (LL) The Progress of Poesy. Thomas Gray. AWP; GTBS-P; NOEC; OBEV

Beneath the Hollin Tree. (LL) The Bonny Hind. Unknown. ESPB; OxBB

Beneath the lamp the lady bowed. Coleridge. OxBSn Fr. 'Tis the middle of night by the castle clock. Fr. Christabel. FHYEP; NAEL-2; NOBRP; OAEL-2; Ro

Beneath the Malebolge lies Hastings street. Christ Walks in This Infernal District Too. Malcolm Lowry. MoCV; NOBC

Beneath the myrtle's secret shade. The Progress of Love. Robert Dodsley. ECEV

Beneath the Radar—for the RAF and All Low Flying Aircraft. Geraldine Monk. NBrP

Beneath the sagging roof. Ezra Pound. MoAmPo Fr. Hugh Selwyn Mauberley. (Life and Contacts). AmPP; CMoP; InPS-3; LiTM; NOBA; NoAM; TAP

Beneath the shadow of dawn's aerial cope. Hope and Fear. Swinburne. FaBoBe

Beneath the Shadow of the Freeway. Lorna Dee Cervantes. NMM-2; PBCAP

Beneath the shadow of Tongariro mountain. A Song of Yearning. Kohine Whakarua Ponika, Maori. PeNZ, tr. by the author

Beneath the Shrine of the Three Loyal Ones. Wen Cheng-ming. CoBLCP, tr. by Jonathan Chaves Fr. Improvised on Horseback to Say Good-bye to Those Who Are Seeing Me Off.

Beneath the silent eaves, a tinkling as of jade. The Studio for Listening to the Snow. Yang Chi, Chinese. CoBLCP, tr. by Jonathan Chaves

Beneath the sky, the cone-shaped drum is rumbling. Sacrifice. Léon Laleau. NegPo, tr. by Ellen Conroy Kennedy Fr. Black Music.

Beneath the small peach branches. Tune: "Telling of Innermost Feelings"—Wandering in Spring. Ch'en Tzu-lung, Chinese. SuSp, tr. by Bruce Carpenter

Beneath the suffocating night. (LL) Others, I am not the first. A. E. Housman. CMoP; MoBrPo; NOBVV; OxBTC; PoE

Beneath the trees. Memoriae Positum R. G. Shaw. James Russell Lowell. CBCWP

Beneath the umbrageous shadow of a shade. A Pastoral; in the Modern Style. "Worcester." NOEC

Beneath the visiting moon. (LL) Noblest of men, woo't die? Shakespeare. IMW, act V, scene 1; OxAEP-1, sect. IV, xiii

Beneath the willow wound round with ivy. Hops. Boris Pasternak, Russian. BoLoP; TTTS, tr. by Jon Stallworthy and Peter France

Beneath their flames, cities of candelabra. The Chestnut Avenue: at Alton House. Charles Tomlinson. FaBoTw

Beneath these alien stars. Pioneer Woman. Vesta Pierce Crawford. AiP

Beneath these fruit-tree boughs that shed. The Green Linnet. Wordsworth. GTBS-P

Beneath these poppies buried deep. Epitaph on Robert Southey. Thomas Moore. FaBoEE

Beneath these shades, beside yon winding steam. On Visiting the Graves of Hawthorne and Thoreau. Jones Very. TAP

Beneath this fragrant myrtle shade. Anacreon, Greek. OBCVT, tr. by Christopher Smart

Beneath this smooth stone by the bone of his bone. Unknown. FaBoEE

Beneath this sod lie the remains. Epitaph on a Young Poet Who Died before Having Achieved Success. Amy Lowell. OBAL

Beneath this stone a Poet Laureate lies. Epitaph on William Whitehead. Unknown. FaBoEE

Beneath this stone does William Hazlitt lie. W. H. Eheu!. Coleridge. FaBoEE

Beneath this stone in hopes of Zion. At Upton-on-Severn. Unknown. FaBoEE

Beneath this stone lies the body of Hengist. Hengest Cyning. Jorge Luis Borges, Spanish. NYBP, tr. by Norman Thomas Di Giovanni

Beneath this stone lies William Burke. Epitaph. R. P. Weston and Bert Lee (1880–1945). OBCoV

Beneath this tent, clutching this glass of beer. Blues for an Old Blue. Walker Gibson. NYBP

Beneath this world of stars and flowers. The Idea. Agnes Mary Frances Robinson. VWP

Beneath those parts, where stretching to its bound. The Process of Conception. Claude Quillet. ECEV Fr. Callipaedia, or, The Art of Getting Beautiful Children.

Beneath Thy Wing. Hayyim Nahman Bialik, Hebrew. TrJP, tr. by Helena Frank

Beneath Time's roaring cannon. When the Mississippi Flowed in Indiana. Vachel Lindsay. CMoP Fr. Three Poems About Mark Twain.

Beneath yon larkspur's azure bells. The Blue-Bird. Herman Melville. NOBA

Beneath yon ruin'd abbey's moss-grown piles. Thomas, the Younger Warton. NOEC; OxAEP-1 Fr. The Pleasures of Melancholy.

Beneath your cooling coverlet you lie. Radiation Victim. Colin Thiele. NOBAu

Benedicite, What Dreamed I This Night? Unknown. HAP; PoEL-1

Benedictio Domini. Ernest Christopher Dowson. ADE

Benediction. James Berry. OPOU

Benediction. Bible, O.T. OBVE, tr. by William Tyndale Fr. Numbers. (Blessing of the Priests.) TrJP ("Lorde blesse the and kepe the, The.") OBVE, tr. by William Tyndale

Benediction. Stanley Kunitz. VGW

Benediction. Mark Turbyfill. PoA

Benediction of the air, The. (LL) Snow-Bound [or Snow-Bound; a Winter Idyl]. John Greenleaf Whittier. APN-1; AmPP; ColAP; NAAL-3; NOBA; OxBA; PAR; TAP; TFi

Benedictus sis, Oscare! In Honorem Doriani Creatorisque Eius. Lionel Pigot Johnson, Latin. ADE, tr. by Ian Fletcher

Benefactors of the Little Box, The. Vasco [or Vasko] Popa, Serbo-Croatian. HSix, tr. by Charles Simic

Beneficent but blind, my blood. The Prayer of the Arab Physician. Monk Gibbon. TIRV

Benefits and Abuse of Alcohol, The. Eubulus, Greek. NBLV, tr. by Richard Cumberland

Benefits of Sorrow. Lizelia Augusta Jenkins Moorer. CBWP-3

Benicasim. Sylvia Townsend Warner. OBWP

Benign Neglect / Mississippi, 1970. Primus St. John. PoBA

Benjamin, limerick. Ogden Nash. PeLi

Benjamin Banneker Sends His Almanac to Thomas Jefferson. Jay Wright. VCAP

Benjamin Jones Goes Swimming. Aileen Fisher. CTV

Benjamin Jones in confident tones. Benjamin Jones Goes Swimming. Aileen Fisher. CTV

Bent. Martin Carter. HCP; PBCV

Bent, all sleepin, you laugh off. West West. Bruce Andrews. FTOS

Bent double, like old beggars under sacks. Dulce Et Decorum Est. Wilfred Owen. AF; CABP; CMoP; FaBoPV; FaBoTw; HeIP-4; HoPM; InPK-6; LiTM; MoBrPo; NAEL-2; NIP-4; NoAM; NoP-4; OAEL-2; OBWP; PFE; PeFWW; PoE; PoFWW; PoPoPo; PoWW; Poetr; RaBo; SAGP; TFi; TRP; UnPo

Bent like a laboring oar, that toils in the surf of the ocean. Henry Wadsworth Longfellow. *Fr.* Part the First. *Fr.* Evangeline, a Tale of Acadie.

Bent old men and women and dirty children scavenging. Environment. Lionel Kearns. NOBC

Bent over, staggering in panic or despair. Tableau. Judith Wright. CBAP

Bent Sae Brown, The. *Unknown.* ESPB

Bents and Broom, The. *Unknown.* OxBB

Beoleopard; or, The Witan's Whail. *Unknown.* CBNP; OBCoV

Beowulf. Kingsley Amis. OxBC

Beowulf. *Unknown, Anglo-Saxon.* ASW, *tr. by* Kevin Crossley-Holland; OAEL-1, *tr. by* Charles W. Kennedy

   Beowulf and Wiglaf Slay the Dragon. AnOE, *tr. by* Charles W. Kennedy

   Beowulf's Death. AnOE, *tr. by* Charles W. Kennedy

   Beowulf's Funeral. EEP, *tr. by* Michael Alexander

   Coming of Grendel, The. OPOU, *tr. by* Gerald Benson

   Fire-Dragon and the Treasure, The. AnOE, *tr. by* Charles W. Kennedy

   Funeral of Scyld Shefing, The. EEP, *tr. by* Alexander, Michael

   Funeral Pyre, The. AnOE, *tr. by* Charles W. Kennedy

   Grendel.

   "How that glory remains in remembrance." NoP-4, *tr. by* Edward Morgan

   "Hwæt, wē gār dena in gēardagum." CABP

   Last Survivor's Speech, The. NAEL-1, *tr. by* Alfred David

   Lay of Finn, The. AnOE, *tr. by* Charles W. Kennedy

   Lay of the Last Survivor, The. EEP, *tr. by* Michael Alexander

   Mere, The. EEP, *tr. by* Michael Alexander

   "Oft in the hall I have heard my people." HeIP-4, *tr. by* Charles W. Kennedy

   "So Hrothgar's men lived happy in his hall." PoE, *tr. by* Burton Raffel

   Tale of Sigemund, The. AnOE, *tr. by* Charles W. Kennedy

Beowulf and Wiglaf Slay the Dragon. *Unknown.* AnOE, *tr. by* Charles W. Kennedy *Fr.* Beowulf. OAEL-1, *tr. by* Charles W. Kennedy; ASW, *tr. by* Kevin Crossley-Holland

Beowulf's Death. *Unknown.* AnOE, *tr. by* Charles W. Kennedy *Fr.* Beowulf. OAEL-1, *tr. by* Charles W. Kennedy; ASW, *tr. by* Kevin Crossley-Holland

Beowulf's Fight with Grendel's Mother. *Unknown. Fr.* Beowulf. OAEL-1, *tr. by* Charles W. Kennedy; ASW, *tr. by* Kevin Crossley-Holland

Beowulf's Funeral. *Unknown.* EEP, *tr. by* Michael Alexander *Fr.* Beowulf.

Beppo; a Venetian Story. Byron. NOBL; OBNV; OBSV

   "England! with all thy faults I love thee still." UnPo

   Italy versus England. NOBE

   (Italy.)

Bequest of His Heart, A. Alexander Scott. OBEV

Bereaved Swan, The. Stevie Smith. FaBoTw

Bereavement. Elizabeth Barrett Browning. WPE

Bereft. Robert Frost. LiTM; MoAmPo; OxBA; SAGP; SoSe-8

Bereft. Thomas Hardy. BoLoP; NoAM

Bereft. Josephine D. Henderson Heard. CBWP-4

Berg, The. Herman Melville. APN-2; AmPP; ColAP; NCAP; NOBA; NoP-4; PFE; PoEL-5; PoPoPo; TAP

   ("Along thy dense stolidity of walls.") (LL) APN-2

Berkeley. Mairtin O Direain. BiHa

Berlin, a bust. Mbizo. Art Lange. MoNo

Berlin Metro. Desmond O'Grady. BiHa

Berlin Wall Tune, The. Joseph Brodsky, *Russian.* AF, *tr. by* Joseph Brodsky

Bermudas. Andrew Marvell. APAD; AWP; CH; ESCV; FHYEP; FMP; FaBoCh; GeHe; NAEL-1; NOBE; NOCV; NOSC; NoP-4; OBEV; PBRV, PFE, PeECV, PoE, RB; SCGP; SeCP; TFi

   (Song of the Emigrants in Bermuda.) GTBS-P

Bermudas wall'd with Rocks, who does not know. The Garden of Bermuda. Edmund Waller. GaP

Bernadette Murphy, 1943-1955. Thomas Rabbitt. NAmP90

Bernice Got Next to Isis. Leslie Simon. FFC

Berries. Walter De la Mare. MoBrPo

Berry Picking. Irving Layton. HeIP-4; MoCV; NIP-4; NoP-4

Bertha let me run barefoot those weeks. Where We Are. Julia Kasdorf. LoHo

Berthe Morisot. Anne Waldman. PmAP

Bes ware with me! to dede I wende. (LL) I Wende to Dede. *Unknown.* HAP; MiEL

Beseech you, think not I am silent thus. Aeschylus. OBCVT, *tr. by* Elizabeth Barrett Browning *Fr.* Prometheus Bound.

Beshrew me but I love her heartily;. Shakespeare. CTV *Fr.* (Merchant of Venice, The).

Beshrew that heart that makes my heart to groan. Sonnet 133. Shakespeare. OxAEP-1 *Fr.* Sonnets.

Beside a chapel I'd a room looked down. Dread. John Millington Synge. BoLoP; MoBrPo; OxBSP; PFE

Beside a Chrysanthemum. So Chong-Ju, *Korean.* VCWP, *tr. by* David R. McCann

Beside a Deathbed. Vassar Miller. MT

Beside a green meadow a stream used to flow. The Cow and the Ass. Ann Taylor. BoTP; CTAV

Beside a runnel build my shed. After Reading in a Letter Proposals for Building a Cottage. John Clare. OxAEP-2

Beside a spreading elm, from whose high boughs. A Reverie. Joanna Baillie. ECWP; WoRP

Beside green water. Enjoying Retirement ("Beside green water"). Ma Chih-yüan. *Fr.* Three Poems to the Tune "Ssu-k'uai yü." CoBLCP, *tr. by* Jonathan Chaves

Beside her desk, three squat adding machines. White Lanterns. David Wojahn. NAmP90

Beside him in the old Ford pickup. Driving Lesson. Michael Pettit. NAmP90

Beside his heavy-shouldered team. Bullocky. Judith Wright. CBAP

Beside me,—in the car,—she sat. Natura Naturans. Arthur Hugh Clough. CBLP; EnVR; HAP; NOBVV

Beside me in this garden. Korean Mums. James Schuyler. PmAP; VCAP

Beside me she sat, hand hooked and hovering. An Egyptian Passage. Theodore Weiss. TAP

Beside the Bed. Charlotte Mew. BWW; MoBrPo; OxBSP; WPE

Beside the bed where parting life was laid. The Village Preacher. Oliver Goldsmith. *Fr.* The Deserted Village. NOEC; OAEL-1; PoEL-3

Beside the boisterous brook of Green-head Ghyll [*or* Gill]. (LL) Michael [A Pastoral Poem]. Wordsworth. FHYEP; NAEL-2; NOBRP; OAEL-2; OxAEP-2

Beside the Brokenstraw or Licking Creek. John Chapman. Richard Wilbur. OxBC

Beside the Chrysanthemum. So Chong-Ju, *Korean.* CKP, *tr. by* Jaihiun Kim

Beside the gravel pile, the lizard. Of His Life. Wayne Dodd. BLT

Beside the green water. Tune: "Four Pieces of Jade"—Retirement. Ma Chih-yüan, *Chinese.* SuSp, *tr. by* Sherwin S. S. Fu

Beside the haystack in the floods. (LL) The Haystack in the Floods. William Morris. CABP; EBEV; EBNV; EBVV; EnVR; HAP; NAEL-2; NoP-4; OAEL-2; OBNC; OBNV; OxAEP-2; PeVV; PoEL-5; PoRA

Beside the highway. Eve. Dorothy Livesay. NALW

Beside the idle summer sea. Rondel. William Ernest Henley. OBNC

Beside the pond, a rail roosts on a bush. The Rail and the Bullfrog. T(tilde;a)n Đà, *Vietnamese.* AVP, *tr. by* Huỳnh Sanh Thông

Beside the pounding cataracts. The City of the End of Things. Archibald Lampman. NOBC

Beside the river Eden. Kathleen Jessie Raine. *Fr.* By the River Eden. NYBP

Beside the river—mdash;waterbirds, in the river—mdash;fish. Li K'ai-hsien. *Fr.* Impromptu Poems. CoBLCP, *tr. by* Jonathan Chaves

Beside the road. Basho, *Japanese.* TTTS, *tr. by* Kenneth Koch *and* Harold Henderson

Beside the Seaside. John Betjeman.

   "Green shutters, shut your shutters! Windyridge." OxBTC

Beside the sewing-table chained and bent. A Leaf from the Devil's Jest-Book. Edwin Markham. APN-2

Beside the ungathered rice he lay. The Slave's Dream. Henry Wadsworth Longfellow. FaPoR; NAAL-1; NAAL-3

Beside the white / Chickens. (LL) The Red Wheelbarrow. William Carlos Williams. CMoP; ColAP; HeIP-4; HoPM; InPK-6; LiTM; MoAmPo; MoP; NAAL-2; NIP-4; NOBA; NoAM; PoE; Poetr; SAmP; SoSe-8; TAP; TFi; TRP; TTTS; UnPo; WeW-3

Beside the wine. Claustrophobia. Sean O Riordain, *Irish.* NOIV, *tr. by* Thomas Kinsella

Beside, up to my marriage, thirteen years. Robert Browning. EBVVPR *Fr.* The Ring and the Book.

Beside yon straggling fence that skirts the way. The Village Schoolmaster. Oliver Goldsmith. EBEvV *Fr.* The Deserted Village. NOEC; OAEL-1; PoEL-3

Besides the autumn poets sing. Emily Dickinson. OxBA

Besides the grave. (LL) The Hill Wife. Robert Frost. CMoP; HAP; InPS-3; LiTM; NoP-4; RACG

Besides, what else could this be, this toothpick with the long eyelash. The Nipplewhip. Michael Benedikt. WeT

Besieged. Zalman Schneour, *Yiddish.* TrJP, *tr. by* Joseph Leftwich

Besieged Serenity. Vasco [or Vasko] Popa, *Serbo-Croatian*.
   Echo. PoSu
   Journey. PoSu
Bess. William Stafford. NNaP
Bessie. Alvin Aubert. SeSe
Bessie Altmann is home again. April Rape. Marilyn Nelson Waniek. IFJA
Bessie Smith's Funeral. Alvin Aubert. SeSe
Bessy Bell and Mary Gray. Mother Goose. OxNR; ReMoGo
Bessy [or Bessie] Bell and Mary Gray. *Unknown*. ESPB; OxBB
Best, The. Elizabeth Barrett Browning. *See* The Best Thing in the World.
Best? Siv Widerberg, *Swedish*. NTCP, *tr. by* Verne Moberg
Best and brightest, come away! The Invitation. Shelley. CH; GTBS-P; NAEL-2; OBEV
Best-Beloved, The. Francis Quarles. OxBM
Best clock. Best carpet. Best three chairs. Study. Tony Harrison. CABP
Best Cowboy Movie, The. Elizabeth Smither. PeNZ
Best days are the first / To flee., The. (LL) Mantova. James Wright. NNaP; TRP
Best Friend, The. W. H. Davies. OBMV
Best friend? Dog. Judith Nicholls. PeP
Best-loved Night!, The. (LL) Hymn to the Night. Henry Wadsworth Longfellow. APN-1; MeMAP; NOBA; OxBA; PWR; TAP
Best Loved of Africa. Margaret Danner. PoBA
Best Man in the Vield, The. William Barnes.
   Sam and Bob. PeVV, *tr. by* Hualing Nieh, (*Eclogue*)
Best of All, The. Margaret G. Rhodes. BoTP
Best of All. J. M. Westrup. BoTP
Best of all is to be idle. Against Whatever It Is That's Encroaching. Charles Simic. ColAP
Best of all things—is never to be born. Our Course. Theognis, *Greek*. OBCVT, *tr. by* Willis Barnstone
Best of both worlds being got, The. Poets' Corner. Robert Graves. FaBoEE
Best of thy sex! if sacred friendship can. To Phylocles, Inviting Him to Friendship. "Ephelia." KTR; NOSC; WPE
Best Old Fellow in the World, The. *Unknown*. AmFP
Best portion of a good man's life, The. Wordsworth. CTV
Best Religion, The. Heinrich Heine. TrJP, *tr. by* Emma Lazarus *Fr.* Tannhäuser.
Best slave, The. Alcestis on the Poetry Circuit. Erica Jong. AmPA; NALW
Best Slow Dancer, The. David Wagoner. NoAM; VCAP
Best Society. Philip Larkin. FP
Best Thing in the World, The. Elizabeth Barrett Browning. EBVV; NOBVV; SDW; VWP
   (Best, The.) OxBSP
Best thing to give, The. Lord Balfour. CTV
Best thing you have in this, The. Today. Frank Crane. CTV
Best Wishes for the New Year. Trần Tế Xu'o'ng, *Vietnamese*. AVP, *tr. by* Huỳnh Sanh Thông
Best work is made, The. Art. Denise Levertov. CAPP-1
Bestiary, A. Kenneth Rexroth. OBAL
   Aardvark.
   Cat.
   "Deer are gentle and graceful." HoPM
   "Fox is very clever, The." NNaP
   Goat.
   "Herring is prolific, The." HoPM
   Horse. NNaP
   I.
   "Lion is called the king, The." HoPM
   Man.
   Racoon.
   Uncle Sam.
   "Unicorn is supposed, The."
   Vulture. NNaP
   Wolf. NNaP
   You. HoPM
Bestiary, The. *Unknown, Middle English*.
   "Whale is the greatest beast in all the ocean waste." CRP, *tr. by* Richard Wilbur
Bestiary for the Fingers of My Right Hand. Charles Simic. AmPA; LCAP-2
Bestow this day on us the grace. The Festival of the Nativity. Richard De Ledrede, *Latin*. TIRV, *tr. by* Robert Wyse Jackson
Bête Humaine. Francis Brett Young. CH

Beth Gêlert; or, The Grave of the Greyhound. William Robert Spencer. BLPA; EBNV; OBNV
Bethlehem. William Canton. BoTP
Bethlehem. Marina Tsvetayeva, *Russian*. GI, *tr. by* Nina Kossman
Bethsabe Bathing. George Peele. *See* Bethsabe's Song.
Bethsabe's Song. George Peele. ChIV-1; GBL; NOBE; NoSic; OxBSP; OxBoLi; PoEL-2; RB *Fr.* Love of King David and Fair Bethsabe. ChIV-1
   (Bathsheba's Song.) ImPo
   (Bethsabe Bathing.)
   ("Hot sun, cool fire, tempered with sweet air.") KSG; NoP-4
Betjeman, 1984. Charles Causley. NOBL; OxBTC; PeLV; UV
Betrayal. Léon Laleau. NegPo, *tr. by* Ellen Conroy Kennedy *Fr.* Black Music.
Betrayal, The. "Nirala," *Hindi*. OMIP, *tr. by* Arvind Krishna Mehrotra
Betrayal. *Unknown, Greek*. GrIP, *tr. by* Philip Sherrard
Betrayal. Adam Zagajewski, *Polish*. VCWP, *tr. by* Gorczynski, Renata
Betrayed by a maid in her teens. (LL) The Man on the Flying Trapeze. *Unknown*. BLPA; OxBoLi
Betrayed by friend dragged from the garden hailed. Ecce Homunculus. Ronald Allison Kells Mason. PeNZ
Betrothal, A. Edith Jay Scovell. GBL
Betrothed. Louise Bogan. CrSp; NMM-2
Betrothed, The. Aleksandr Andreievich Prokofiev, *Russian*. TCRP, *tr. by* Lubov Yakovleva
Betsy Baker. *Unknown*. OxNR
Betsy, if pencil erasers could sing. 110 Year Old House. Ed Ochester. Poetsp
Better a day in Oxbridge. Stanley J. Sharpless. BXAP
Better a sin which purposed wrong to none. Ellen S. Hooper. PAR
Better Answer to Cloe [or Chloe] Jealous, A. Matthew Prior. AWP; NAEL-1; NOEC; PoEL-3
   (Answer to Cloe [or Chloe] Jealous.) NOBE
Better Be Kind to Them Now. D. J. Enright. PeP
Better born than married, misled. The Grandmother. Wendell Berry. MT
Better Come Drink Wine with Me. Po Chü-i, *Chinese*. CoBCP, *tr. by* Burton Watson
Better disguised than the leaf-insect. The Lake. Ted Hughes. FaBoTw; NYBP
Better for the widow, that she should not live in fear of surprise, The. James Fenton. *Fr.* A German Requiem. NAEL-2; NoAM
Better get drunk and cry. Otomo no Tabito, *Japanese*. OHMPJ, *tr. by* Kenneth Rexroth
Better it were had you borne black earth, o mother, rather than me. Mother of Man. Vesna Parun, *Croatian*. PBWP, *tr. by* Mary Coote
Better, my lover, dead. (LL) The Farmer's Wife. Anne Sexton. HoPM; LiTM
Better never to have met you. Yakamochi, *Japanese*. OHMPJ, *tr. by* Kenneth Rexroth
Better never trouble Trouble. Trouble. David Keppel. PoLF
Better not go to these deep woods. The Great Fountains. Anne Hébert, *French*. BoWoP, *tr. by* Willis Barnstone
Better not to be born; to die is to suffer. Distrust. Chech'on Park, *Korean*. CKP, *tr. by* Jaihiun Kim
Better not to go back to the village. The Malefic Return. Ramón López Velarde, *Spanish*. OBVE, *tr. by* Samuel Beckett
Better one thin frail line of friendship in a letter. The Letter. John Blight. CBAP
Better Resurrection, A. Christina Rossetti. NOBVV; VWP
Better than a closet martinet. What Happened? John Wieners. FTOS; PoM
Better Than Counting Sheep. Robert Penn Warren. AFr
Better than Gold ("Better than grandeur, better than gold"). Abram Joseph Ryan. PoToHe
Better—than Music! For I—who heard it. Emily Dickinson. APN-2
Better the book against the rock. Three Poems about Children. Austin Clarke. CIP-2
Better Things. George Macdonald. PWR
Better to close the book and say good-night. The Double Autumn. James Reeves. OxBSP
Better to live as a rogue and a bum. Mahsati, *Farsi*. WPOW, *tr. by* Deirdre Lashgari
Better to see your cheek grown hollow. Madman's Song. Elinor Wylie. MoAmPo; PoRA
Better to smell the violet cool than sip. Better Things. George Macdonald. PWR
Better trust all and be deceived. Faith. Frances Anne Kemble. FaBoBe
Betty. *Unknown*. FuFo
Betty at the Party. *Unknown*. BoTP

Betty Blue. Mother Goose. OxNR; ReMoGo

Betty Botta bought some butter. The Butter Betty Bought. *Unknown.* FPC

Betty Botter bought some butter. *Unknown.* OTCP; OxNR

Betty by the Sea. Ronald McCuaig. NOBAu

Betty Fuller cried and said, Hit me. A Local Man Remembers Betty Fuller. James Whitehead. MT

Betty Pringle's Pig. Mother Goose. OxNR

(Dirge, A.) CBNP

Betuix twell houris and ellevin. The Amendis to the Telyouris and Sowtaris for the Turnament Maid on Thame. William Dunbar. OBSV

Between. Agnes Nemes Nagy, *Hungarian.* VCWP, *tr. by* Hugh Maxton

Between a Contractor and His Wife. *Unknown.* NOEC

Between a sleep and a sleep. (LL) Chorus: "Before the beginning of years." Swinburne. EBVV; EBVVPR; ImPo; NAEL-2; NTP; OBEV

Between a sunny bank and the sun. Two Houses. Edward Thomas. FaBoCh

Between a Tyrant and a King. The Difference Between a King and a Tyrant. Timothy Kendall. NoSic

Between a wicked rhinoceros trail. Minor Mythology. David Avidan, *Hebrew. tr. by* Warren Bargad *and* Stanley F. Chyet

Between a winter's day and night. The Blue Hour. Margarita Iosifovna Aliger, *Russian.* TCRP, *tr. by* Albert C. Todd

Between an Unemployed Artist and His Wife. *Unknown.* NOEC

Between Awajishima and Suma. *Unknown, Japanese.* WPJ, *tr. by* Kenneth Rexroth *and* Ikuko Atsumi

Between Botallack and the light. A Ballad of a Mine. Robin Skelton. MoBS

Between each layer of tattered, broken flesh. Burial Detail. Andrew Hudgins. CBCWP; MT

Between Equals. Robert Wallace. PFE

Between extremities. Vacillation. W. B. Yeats. NoAM

Between five and fifty. Praise. Jane Cooper. TAP

Between great coloured vanes the butterflies. Wings. Judith Wright. CBAP; NOBAu

Between her breasts is my home, between her breasts. Song of a Man Who Is Loved. D. H. Lawrence. OxBM

Between Here and Illinois. Ralph Pomeroy. Poetsp

Between hunger and love? (LL) Mundus et Infans. W. H. Auden. LiTM; MeMAP; MoBrPo; NoAM

Between leaps to its burrow. (LL) The Jerboa. Marianne Moore. FYAP; NALW

Between living and dreaming. Antonio Machado Ruiz, *Spanish.* EnlH, *tr. by* Robert Bly

Between Love and Death. Frank Stanford. MT

Between me and the rising sun. Cobwebs. E. L. M. King. BoTP

Between me and the sunset, like a dome. The Man against the Sky. Edwin Arlington Robinson. AmPP; CMoP; OxBA

Between me and the wood. Ark Artefact. Jay Macpherson. NOBC *Fr.* The Ark.

Between mountains coils a city. Wind. Abba Kovner, *Hebrew.* IP, *tr. by* Warren Bargad *and* Stanley F. Chyet

Between my finger and my thumb. Digging. Seamus Heaney. BIrV; CIP-2; IIP; InPS-3; NAEL-2; NoP-4; SAGP; TwCP

Between my thighs like a valentine before. (LL) You (I). Tom Clark. PmAP

Between myself and thee! (LL) My Playmate. John Greenleaf Whittier. APN-1; NOBA

Between Ourselves. Audre Lorde. ISC; WPOW

Between Ourselves and the Dead! (LL) Under the Light, yet under. Emily Dickinson. FaBoVe; NCAP

Between periods, / boys at the urinals. Game. Philip Booth. AFr

Between pond and sheepbarn, by maples and watery birches. A Sister on the Tracks. Donald Hall. GM

Between rebellion as a private study and the public. Charles Donnelly. BIrV; CIP-2; IIP

Between Rivers and Seas. Lance Henson. VoR

Between sandbanks marsh reflecting twilight clouds. Birthday Party. Kusano Shimpei, *Japanese.* PFTM, *tr. by* Cid Corman

Between Seasons. Li-Young Lee. TRP

Between Seasons. Anne Welsh. PeSA

Between some god and Buddha, here am I! A Scholar-Laureate in Retirement. Nguyễn Khuyến, *Vietnamese.* AVP, *tr. by* Huỳnh Sanh Thông

Between such animal and human heat. The Partner. Theodore Roethke. EP

Between the avenues of cypresses. Service of All the Dead. D. H. Lawrence. NSI

Between the clod and the midnight. The Interim. Robert Penn Warren. *Fr.* Tale of Time. LCAP-2

Between the conscious and the unconscious, the mind has put up a swing. Kabir, *Hindi.* EnlH, *tr. by* Robert Bly

Between the dark and the daylight. The Children's Hour. Henry Wadsworth Longfellow. APN-1; CTV; ChAP; FPC; FaBoBe; ImGa; OBAL; OBCA; PoEL-5; PoLF; WHSW

Between the dark and the daylight. If. Franklin Pierce Adams. OBAL

Between the dark silent trees. Dionysius. Sophia de Mello Breyner Andresen, *Portuguese.* PBWP, *tr. by* Allan Francovich

Between the form of Life and Life. Emily Dickinson. APN-2; PAR

Between the GARDENING and the COOKERY. A Bookshop Idyll. Kingsley Amis. OxBTC; PeLV

Between the idea and the word. Vladimir Holan, *Czech.* PoSu, *tr. by* Ian *and* Jarmila Milner

Between the Lines. Michael Hamburger. HP

Between the midnight and the morn. The Secret Muse. Roy Campbell. PeSA

Between the oils and canvas. Stroke the white. The Priming Is a Negligee. Alice Fulton. BAP-94

Between the perfect. Somewhere the Equation Breaks Down. Daniel Berrigan. NYBP

Between the Porch and the Altar. Robert Lowell. At the Altar. InPK-6

Between the railway and the mine. The Blackberry. Norman Nicholson. MoBrPo

Between the reeds I saw their bodies gleam. Stéphane Mallarmé. EP, *tr. by* Aldous Leonard Huxley *Fr.* L'Après-Midi d'un Faune.

Between the Traveller and the Setting Sun. Henry David Thoreau. PoEL-4

Between the walls, the brim. Terce. James McMichael. PoA

Between the Wars. Robert Hass. VCAP

Between the wet trees and the sorry steeple. W. H. Louise Imogen Guiney. APN-2

Between the World and Me. Richard Wright. ISC; LiTM; MoP; PoBA

("Now I am dry bones and my face a stony skull staring in yellow surprise / at the sun.") (LL) AF

("Yellow surprise at the sun. . . .") (LL) SSLK

Between their jaws. (LL) Listening to Grownups Quarreling. Ruth Whitman. KaS

Between them is the land of broken colors. The Black Horse Rider. Pierre Loving. SPE

Between thirty and forty one is distracted by the Five Lusts. On Being Sixty. Po Chü-i, *Chinese.* AWP; ChiP, *tr. by* Arthur Waley

Between this and that other country / is neither barricade nor sentry. Journey. Constance Carrier. AFr

Between town and the. The Quarry Pool. Denise Levertov. VGW

Between two fires. (LL) The Conflict. C. Day Lewis. LiTM; MoBrPo; NoP-4

Between two golden tufts of summer grass. Lying in the Grass. Sir Edmund William Gosse. EBVV

Between two rivers. Island. Langston Hughes. HCAP

Between two rivers, / North of the park. Island. Langston Hughes. HCAP *Fr.* Lenox Avenue Mural. HoPM

Between two sister moorland rills. A Fragment. Wordsworth. NOBRP

Between Two Worlds. Rosemary Thomas. NYBP

Between Us. James Merrill. PoE

Between Vicksburg and Rolling Fork. Road. David Chapman Berry. MT

Between Walls. William Carlos Williams. HoPM; TAP; VGW

Between your sheets you soundly sleep. Lady Mary Wortley Montagu. LW; PEW

Betweene the Spyder and the gentle Bee. (LL) Sonnet 71: "I joy to see how in your drawen work." Edmund Spenser. NoP-4; PBRV

Betweens. Norman McCaig. SPE

Betwixt *Atrides* Great, and *Thetis* God-like Son. (LL) The Invocation: "The Wrath of *Peleus* Son, O Muse, resound." Homer, *Greek.* OBVE, *tr. by* Dryden; OBCVT, *tr. by* John Dryden

Betwixt two ridges of plowed[*or* ploughed] land sat [*lay*] Wat. The Hunting of the Hare. Margaret Lucas Cavendish, Duchess of Newcastle. BWW; FaBoVe; KTR; NOSC

BE2c is my 'bus; therefore I shall want, The. The Pilot's Psalm. *Unknown.* NSI; PoWW

Beulah Railway, The. *Unknown.* GM

Beverly Hills, Chicago. Gwendolyn Brooks. Poetr; VGW *Fr.* The Womanhood.

Bewail not much, my parents! Me, the prey. On an Infant. Lucian, *Greek.* OBCVT, *tr. by* William Cowper

Bewailing in my chamber thus allone. He Sees His Beloved. James I, King of Scotland. PoEL-1 *Fr.* The Kingis Quair.

Beware: Do Not Read This Poem. Ishmael Reed. BPo; GT; NIP-4; PoBA

("Space in the lives of their friends, A.") (LL)

Beware of Dogmas. Ebenezer Elliot. FaBoEE

Beware of Ruins. Alec Derwent Hope. NoAM

Beware of the man who denounces ambition. Seventeen Warnings in Search of a Feminist Poem. Erica Jong. AmPA

Beware of thinking nothing's there. Virtual Particles. Frank Wilczek. NBLV

Beware the cuckoo, though she bring. Ernest G. Moll. NOBAu

Beware! The Israelite of old, who tore. The Warning. Henry Wadsworth Longfellow. APN-1; ChIV-1; NCAP; PAR

Beware the Kleptomaniac. The Kleptomaniac. Roger McGough. NOxBChV

Beware. There are fawns. Kydios, *Greek.* InMo, *tr. by* Sam Hamill

Beware: this swellfoot. On Boetian Roads. Nikos Engonopoulos, *Greek.* GrIP, *tr. by* Kimon Friar

Bewick and Graham. *Unknown.* ESPB

Bewick and the Graeme, The. *Unknown.* OxBB

Bewick Finzer. Edwin Arlington Robinson. CMoP; MeMAP; MoAmPo; NAAL-2

Bewildered with the broken tongue. Words in Time. Archibald MacLeish. PoRA

Bewilderment at the Entrance of the Fat Boy into Eden, A. Daryl Hine. NOBC

Bewley's Oriental Café, Westmoreland Street. Paul Durcan. CIP-2

Bewteis of the Fute-Ball, The. *Unknown.* OxBS

Bewty of hir amorus ene, The. Off Womanheid Ane Flour Delice. *Unknown.* OxBS

Bewwitching the blossoms of the spring grove. *Unknown.* SuSp, *tr. by* Ronald C. Miao *Fr.* Spring. SuSp *Fr.* Tzu-yeh Songs of the Four Seasons.

Beyond. *Unknown.* PWR

Beyond all this, the wish to be alone. Wants. Philip Larkin. GTBS-P

Beyond, beneath, within, wherever blood. A Quintina of Crosses. Chad Walsh. TrCP

Beyond, beyond the mountain line. Dreams. Cecil Frances Alexander. NOxBChV

Beyond doubt. Tanka. Sasaki Yukitsuna, *Japanese.* MJT, *tr. by* Makoto Ueda

Beyond empty pews. Nicholas Virgilio. HA

Beyond Fear. Odia Ofeimun. HBAPE

Beyond Gethsemane! (LL) Gethsemane [1914–18]. Rudyard Kipling. APAD; GI; PoFWW

Beyond Imagination. David Rokeah, *Hebrew.* MHP, *tr. by* Ruth Finer Mintz

Beyond is agony. (LL) A Prayer for Indifference. Fanny [or Frances] Macartney Greville. LW; OBEV

Beyond Kerguelen. Henry Clarence Kendall. NOBAu

Beyond Knowledge. Alice Thompson Meynell. ChIV-1

Beyond Melody. Nathan Alterman, *Hebrew.* MHP, *tr. by* Ruth Finer Mintz

Beyond my window in the night. A Town Window. John Drinkwater. BoTP

Beyond Nagel's Funeral Parlor. The Elizabethans Called It Dying. James Schuyler. NeAP; PoM

Beyond Phigalia. Alec Derwent Hope. BMAP

Beyond Religion. Lucretius, *Latin.* AWP, *tr. by* William Ellery Leonard

Beyond stars. L. A. Davidson. HA

Beyond the Alps. Robert Lowell. LCAP-2; NOBA

Beyond the Atlas roams a glutton. The Glutton. Robert Graves. CMoP

Beyond the bamboo fence, cooking fire and smoke. Liu Tsung-yüan. SuSp, *tr. by* Jan W. Walls *Fr.* Farmers.

Beyond the Beaten Way. George Sands Johnson. PWR

Beyond the blind, the rain rattles down, Tune: "Ripples Sifting Sand: A Song." Li Yü, *Chinese.* CoBCP, *tr. by* Burton Watson

Beyond the body itself, we are making / love. Sharon Olds. *See* The Knowing.

Beyond the breakers. Joyce Mansour, *French.* MFP, *tr. by* Martin Sorrell

Beyond the Chagres. James Stanley Gilbert. PoLF

Beyond the dark souks of the old city. The Dig. Lynn Emanuel. PUP-18

Beyond the east gate. *Unknown, Chinese.* TAL, *tr. by* Robert Payne

Beyond the edge of the sepia. Lament for a Cricket Eleven. Kenneth Allott. OxBTC

Beyond the End. Denise Levertov. NeAP; VGW

Beyond the foot of the bed: a seascape whose ocean. On Motel Walls. David Wagoner. DiPo

Beyond the gate the cormorant had gone and not returned. Quatrain. Tu Fu, *Chinese.* SuSp, *tr. by* Jerome P. Seaton

Beyond the glass door. Tanka. Masaoka Shiki, *Japanese.* MJT, *tr. by* Ueda, Makoto

Beyond the grass and shadows at her feet. (LL) Garden Abstract. Hart Crane. GaP; MeMAP; OBGa

Beyond the Grave. Margaret E. Bruner. PoToHe

Beyond the great valley an odd instinctive rising. Ascent to the Sierras. Robinson Jeffers. OxBA

Beyond the hour we counted rain that fell. Old Countryside. Louise Bogan. HAP; WPE

Beyond the Hunting Woods. Donald Justice. CoAmPo; NYBP

Beyond the inmost barriers of the brain. The Owl. Edward Davison. PoA

Beyond the last gate, where I made my first halt. On Scafell Pike. Ted Walker. NYBP

Beyond the last house, where home was. American Portrait: Old Style. Robert Penn Warren. FYAP; Poetr

Beyond the Last Lamp. Thomas Hardy. NOBE; OBNC

Beyond the laughing billboard girl. Leroy Gorman. HA

Beyond the low marsh-meadows and the beach. The Pines and the Sea. Christopher Pearse Cranch. ColAP; PAR

Beyond the mountain passes. Crossing Han River. Li P'in, *Chinese.* OHMPC, *tr. by* Kenneth Rexroth

Beyond the Nigger. Sterling Plumpp. PoBA

Beyond the outstretched hands. Beyond the Nigger. Sterling Plumpp. PoBA

Beyond the people. The Escape Artist. Kevin Young. GT

Beyond the porch. John Wills. HA

Beyond the Profit of Today. *Unknown.* PoToHe

Beyond the sphere which spreads to widest space. Dante. AWP; CTC *Fr.* La Vita Nuova.

Beyond the stone wall. Jug Brook. Ellen Bryant Voigt. MT

Beyond the stream at Seta stretches an endless view. Liu Ya-tzu. SuSp, *tr. by* Wu-chi Liu *Fr.* Miscellaneous Poems on Lake Biwa.

Beyond the temple, a hidden cliff. Yang Shih-ch'i. CoBLCP, *tr. by* Jonathan Chaves *Fr.* A Group of Officials.

Beyond the town a sterile quarter grew. The Poets. Aleksandr Blok, *Russian.* TCRP, *tr. by* Geoffrey Thurley

Beyond time and space. Declaration. Nikolai Ivanovich Glazkov, *Russian.* TCRP, *tr. by* Daniel Weissbort

Beyond treetops I see the slant of a bridge. (LL) Following the Rhumes of Chiang Hui-shu. Su Tung-p'o, *Chinese.* CoBCP, *tr. by* Burton Watson

Beyond Vermont's green hills, against the skies. Richard Henry Wilde. APN-1 *Fr.* Hesperia.

Beyond Words. Robert Frost. Spl; WeW-3

("You wait!") (LL) KaS

Bhagavad-Gita, The. *Unknown, Sanskrit.*

"Hear father yet thou Long-Armed Lord! these latest words I say." TAL, *tr. by* Sir Edward Arnold

"Learn from me, Son of Kunti! also this." TOF, *tr. by* Sir Edwin Arnold

"Learn now, dear Prince! how, if thy soul be set." TAL, *tr. by* Sir Edward Arnold

"Nay, but of such an one." TOF, *tr. by* Sir Edwin Arnold

"Now will I open unto thee—whose heart." TAL, *tr. by* Sir Edward Arnold

"Sovereign soul, The/ Of him who lives self-governed and at peace." TOF, *tr. by* Sir Edwin Arnold

"Steadfast a lamp burns sheltered from the wind." TOF, *tr. by* Sir Edwin Arnold

"Therefore, who doeth work rightful to do." TAL, *tr. by* Sir Edward Arnold

"This, for my soul's peace, have I heard from Thee." TAL, *tr. by* Sir Edward Arnold

"'Those who realize true wisdom'." EnlH

"Who is that BRAHMA? What that Soul of Souls." TAL, *tr. by* Sir Edward Arnold

"Yet hard/ The travail is for such as bend their minds." TOF, *tr. by* Sir Edwin Arnold

Bi-Focal. William Stafford. RB

Bi-lingual. Maria Jastrzebska. NBrP

Biafra. L. V. Mack. PoBA

Bianca. Arthur Symons. PeVV

Bianca Among the Nightingales. Elizabeth Barrett Browning. BrRo; GTBS-P

(Bibbily Boo and Wollypotump). Laura Elizabeth Richards. CTV

Bibbily Boo, the king so free. (Bibbily Boo and Wollypotump). Laura Elizabeth Richards. CTV

Bible, The. David Levi, *Italian.*

"Thou, Zion, old and suffering." TrJP, *tr. by* Mary A. Craig

Bible, The. Lizelia Augusta Jenkins Moorer. CBWP-3

Bible, The. Thomas Traherne. PeECV

Bible Defence of Slavery. Frances Ellen Watkins Harper. APAD; APN-2; PAR

Bible, Ecclesiastes. *See also* Ecclesiastes.

Bible, Ecclesiastes 10:12, The. Bible, *O.T.*

"Words of a wise man's mouth are, The." CTV

Bible, Ephesians 4:32, The. *Unknown.*
  "Be ye kind one to another." CTV
Bible, Exodus. *See also* Exodus.
Bible, Exodus 20:12, The. Bible, *O.T.*
  "Honour thy father and thy mother." CTV
"Bible is a book of race, The." White. Gerald William Barrax. *Fr.* The
  Old Gory. NBV
Bible is an antique Volume, The. Emily Dickinson. APN-2; ChIV-1;
  NAAL-1; NAAL-3; NoP-4; PAR
Bible, Isaiah. *See also* Isaiah.
Bible, Isaiah 6:3.
  "Holy, holy, holy." CTV
Bible, Isaiah 40:31, The. Bible, *O.T.* CTV
Bible, John. *See also* John *and* St. John.
Bible, John 5:24, The. Bible, *N.T.*
  "He that heareth my word." CTV
Bible, Luke. *See also* Luke *and* St. Luke.
Bible, Luke 2:8–20, Phillips, The. Bible, *O.T.*
  "There were some shepherds living in the same part of the country." CTV
Bible, Matthew. *See also* Matthew *and* St. Matthew.
Bible, Matthew 5:3–10.
  From the Sermon on the Mount. CTV
Bible, Matthew 5:3–12, The. CTV
Bible, Matthew 6:9–13, The.
  Lord's Prayer, The. CTV
Bible, Matthew 6:19–21, The.
  "Lay not up for yourselves treasures." CTV
Bible, Numbers. *See also* Numbers.
Bible, Numbers 32:23, The.
  "Be sure your sin will find you out." CTV
Bible or Prayer-Book: I am the scalp of myself, skinned by my foeman.
  Unknown, EEP, *tr. by* Michael Alexander *Fr.* Riddles (Exeter Book).
Bible, Philippians. *See also* Philippians.
Bible, Philippians 4:8, The.
  "Whatsoever things are true." CTV
Bible, Proverbs. *See also* Proverbs.
Bible, Proverbs 3:1–4, The.
  "My son, forget not my law; but let thine heart keep my commandments."
  CTV
Bible, Proverbs 6:6–8, The.
  "Go to the ant, thou sluggard;." CTV
Bible, Proverbs 11:13, The. CTV
Bible, Proverbs 15:1, The. CTV *Fr.* Proverbs.
Bible, Proverbs 16:32, The. CTV *Fr.* Proverbs.
Bible, Proverbs 20:11, The.
  "Even a child is known by his doings." CTV
Bible, Proverbs 22:1, The. CTV *Fr.* The Bible, Proverbs 22:1.
Bible, Psalms. *See also* Psalms.
Bible, Psalm 1:1–3, The. CTV *Fr.* Psalms.
  ("Blessed is every one that feareth the Lord.")
  (Psalm 128.)
Bible, Psalm 92:1, The.
  "It is a good thing to give thanks." CTV
Bible, Psalm 103:1–5, The.
  "Bless the Lord, O my soul." CTV
Bible, Psalm 107:23–31.
  "They that go down to the sea in." CTV
Bible, Psalm 147:1,5,8,9,16–18,7,20, The.
  Psalm 147: "Praise ye the Lord." CTV
Bible, Romans 12:10,11, The.
  "Be kindly affectioned one to." CTV
Bible says Sennacherib's campaign was spoiled, The. Sonnet. C. S. Lewis.
  TrCP
Bible Story. Charles Causley. TOF
Bible Study. Gloria C. Oden. GT
Bibliographer. Josephine Miles. FaBoWP
Bibliolaters. James Russell Lowell.
  "God is not dumb, that he should speak no more." ChIV 1
Bibliotheca Bodleiana. Geoffrey Grigson. GBL
Bibo. Matthew Prior. *See* Epigram: "When Bibo thought fit from the world
  to retreat."
Bibulous eagle behind me at the ball game, The. One to Nothing. Carolyn
  Kizer. OBAL
"Biby's" Epitaph. *Unknown. See* Dahn the Plug'ole.
Bic lighter, A. Tee. Reuben Jackson. UnSA
Bicause I have the still kept fro lyes and blame. Petrarch, *Italian.* OBVE,
  tr. by Sir Thomas Wyatt
Bicentennial Anti-Poem for Italian-American Women. Daniela Gioseffi.
  UnSA
Bickering of vowels on the buses, The. An Irish Childhood in England:
  1951. Eavan Boland. CIP-2

Bicycle, for Derek Peat. David Malouf. BMAP
Bicycle Rider, The. Thomas William Shapcott. CBAP
Bicycles go by in twos and threes, The. Inniskeen Road: July Evening.
  Patrick Kavanagh. CIP-2; MoP; NoAM; Poetr
Bicycles! Tricycles! John Banister Tabb. OBAL
Bid a strong ghost stand at the head. A Prayer for My Son. W. B. Yeats.
  EBEV; OxAEP-2; RaBo; TIRV
Bid me from servitude ascend, / Forever! (LL) The Slave's Complaint.
  George Moses Horton. AAP; CrDW
Bid me no more good-night; because. Good-night. James Shirley. BeJo;
  NOSC
Bid me not go where neither suns nor showers [show'rs]. Valediction.
  William Cartwright. BeJo
Bid me strike a match and blow. (LL) In Memory of Eva Gore-Booth and
  Con Markievicz. W. B. Yeats. FaBoPV; NoAM; OAEL-2; OBMV;
  OxBTC
Bid me to live, and I will live. To Anthea, Who May Command Him
  Anything. Robert Herrick. CaPo; GTBS-P; NOBE; NOSC; OAEL-1;
  OBEV; SeCP
Bid the fond mother spill her infant's blood. To One Who Said I Must Not
  Love. Sarah Fyge Egerton. ECWP
Bid your Papa Goodnight. Sweet exhibition! Mrs. Hopley, on Seeing Her
  Children Say Goodnight to Their Father. Gerard Manley Hopkins.
  FaBoEE
Biding Our Time. Hậu Điền, *Vietnamese.* AVP, *tr. by* Huỳnh Sanh Thông
Bids spheres and atoms in just order move. (LL) Hand and Foot, The [*or*
  Hand and the Foot, The]. Jones Very. APN-1; OxBA; PAR; PoEL-4;
  TAP
Big animals: despondent / at table: unsated, The. Poem. Paul Klee,
  German. PFTM, *tr. by* Anselm Hollo
Big Baboon, The. Hilaire Belloc. MoBrPo
Big Bar. Kenward Elmslie. PmAP
Big Ben is cracked, we needs must own. To Disraeli. Shirley Brooks.
  NOBL
Big Bessie Throws Her Son into the Street. Gwendolyn Brooks. VGW *Fr.*
  A Catch of Shy Fish.
Big Billie Potts was big and stout. The Ballad of Billie Potts. Robert Penn
  Warren. FuPo; NOBA; OxBA
Big Bluejay Composition. Ron Padgett. PmAP
Big box, / Little box. *Unknown.* OxNR
Big Boy came. Catch. Langston Hughes. NoAM
Big Cars. Jane Flanders. PBCAP
Big Chariot, The. *Unknown.* ChiP, *tr. by* Arthur Waley *Fr.* The Book of
  Songs.
Big Chill Variations. Reuben Jackson. UnSA
Big cities are reeking with grief. Limerick. *Unknown.* PeLi
Big doors of the country barn stand open and ready, The. Walt Whitman.
  ColAP *Fr.* Song of Myself.
Big Engines, The. 146th Chorus. Jack Kerouac. NeAP *Fr.* Mexico City
  Blues.
Big enough for an ox, the cauldron. Anyte, *Greek.* GrAn, *tr. by* John
  Heath-Stubbs *and* Carol A. Whiteside
Big farm girl with the dumb prophetic body, The. Bitter Harvest. Alistair
  Campbell. PeNZ
Big, Fat Summer—and the Lean and Hard. Frederick Bock. NYBP
Big feet, / Black feet. Feet. Irene Thompson. BoTP
Big Fire at the Architectural College, The. Andrey Andreievich
  Voznesensky, *Russian.* CLPP, *tr. by* Anselm Hollo
Big Friend of the Stones. Steve Orlen. Poetsp
Big grey elephant, A. Just Jumbo. Eileen Mathias. BoTP
Big Gumbo. William Jay Smith. FuFo
Big guns again. / No speakee well. Imperator Victus. Hart Crane. OxBA
Big heart. Anne Sexton. CrSp
Big House, The. Paul Muldoon. NoAM
Big house, / Little house. *Unknown.* OxNR
Big impression left on me, The. My Answer. Ralph Adamo. MT
Big Island whispered to little island. In the Sea. Brendan Kennelly. BiHa
Big Momma. Don L. Lee. BPo
Big Muddy daddy my daddys gris-gris to the world, A. Mud Water
  Shango. Tom Weatherly. GT; NBV; SeSe
Big Nasturtiums, The. Robert Beverly Hale. NYBP
Big-nose looks best in mountain-coarse clothes. My Man Pa Replies. Li
  Ho, *Chinese.* CoBCP, *tr. by* Burton Watson
Big Plymouth shuddered with all the speed, The. Championship Fight.
  Dave Jeddie Smith. NAmP90
Big 'possum clime little tree. Plantation Proverbs. Joel Chandler Harris.
  CrDW *Fr.* Uncle Remus: His Songs and His Sayings.
Big Rabbit goes to see his baby. *Unknown, Navajo Indian.* STP, *tr. by*
  Jerome Rothenberg
Big Ralph from Rolfe had a black Corvette. The True Ballad of the Great
  Race to Gilmore City. Phil Hey. Poetsp
Big rat, big rat. *Unknown, Chinese.* ChiPo, *tr. by* Arthur Waley; CoBCP,
  tr. by Burton Watson

("Who will moan there for long?") (LL) CoBCP, *tr.* by Burton Watson

Big Rock-Candy Mountain, The. Louis Edward Sissman. GM

Big Rock Candy Mountains, The. *Unknown.* FaBoA; NOBA

Big Rock Candy Mountains, The. *Unknown.* AmFP; OBAL; TTTS

Big rocks into pebbles. Rocks. Florence Parry Heide. NTCP

Big ship sails on the alley alley oh, The. *Unknown.* FaBoVe

Big sound on the ground. (LL) It's over a(see just). E. E. Cummings. OxBA; VGW

Big steel tourist shield says maybe, The. On a Field Trip at Fredericksburg. Dave Jeddie Smith. HCAP; PoPoPo

Big stones of the cistern behind the barn, The. Twilights. James Wright. LCAP-2

Big sweet muscles of an athlete's dream, The. Massacre of the Innocents. Alec Derwent Hope. GI

Big Tease. Ania Walwicz. BMAP

Big tom was a black nigga man. River Town Packin House Blues. Quincy Troupe. LoL

Big trees exposed to the west wind are losing their leaves, The. Reading in the Autumn. Shen Chou, *Chinese.* ImGa

Big-uddered piebald cattle low. Christmas Holiday. Alun Lewis. PoWW

Big Wind. Theodore Roethke. AmPP; CMoP; ColAP; TRP; VGW

Big with great purposes and proud, they sat. Homer. OBVE, *tr.* by William Cowper *Fr.* The Iliad.

Big young bareheaded woman, A. Proletarian Portrait. William Carlos Williams. BLT; OBAL; SAmP; TAP

Big Zeb Johnson. Everett Hoagland. GT

Bigamy. Roy McFadden. PNI *Fr.* Memories of Chinatown.

Bigerlow. *Unknown.* AS

Bigger fish have country cousins here, The. Soldier Bathing. Frank Ormsby. PNI *Fr.* A Northern Spring.

Bigger than earth, certainly. What She Said. Tevakulattar, *Tamil.* PLW, *tr.* by A. K. Ramanujan

Biggest Killing, The. Edward Dorn. VGW

Bight, The. Elizabeth Bishop. FaBoWP; HCAP; NAAL-2; NYBP; RB; VCAP

Biglow Papers, The. James Russell Lowell.

Courtin', The. AmPP; NOBA; OBAL

Letter, A ("This kind o' sogerin' ain't a mite like our October trainin' "). OxBA

Letter, A ("Thrash away, you'll hev to rattle"). AmPP; OxBA

(Mr. Hosea Biglow Speaks.)

Letter Six—The Pious Editors' Creed. APN-1

Rev. Homer Wilbur's "Festina Lente." OBAL

What Mr. Robinson Thinks. AmPP; OBCoV

("Gineral B. is a sensible man.") OBCoV

Bigness of cannon, The. E. E. Cummings. MoAmPo

Bignonia blossoms on both shores, a streamful of water. In a Boat on the Cha River. Chang Yü, *Chinese.* CoBLCP, *tr.* by Jonathan Chaves

Bilberries. Gerda Mayer. Spl

Bile Them Cabbage Down. *Unknown.* AmFP

Bilingual Sestina. Julia Alvarez. FFC

Bill. Peter Kocan. CBAP

Bill 'Awkins. Rudyard Kipling. CBLP

Bill Bailey, Won't You Please Come Home. Hughie Cannon. OBAL

Bill Bubble in a bowler hat. All the Way Back. Laura Riding Jackson. *Fr.* Forgotten Girlhood. RB

Bill Jones had been the shining star upon his college team. Alumnus Football. Grantland Rice. PoLF

Bill the Bachelor lived by himself. Bachelors' Buttons. Maud Morin. BoTP

Bill / Was ill. Careless Talk. Mark Hollis. NBLV

Billboard girl. Leroy Gorman. HA

Billboard Song, The. *Unknown.* CBNP

Billboards. Eric Amann. HA

Billie Holiday's burned voice. Canary. Rita Dove. LoL; SeSe; VCAP

Billie in Silk. Angela Jackson. SeSe

Bill's Story. Mark Doty. PuP-14

Billy. Linda McCarriston. LoL

Billy Batter. Dennis Lee. TLR

Billy, Billy, come and play. *Unknown.* ReMoGo

Billy Boy. Dorothy King. BoTP

Billy Boy. *Unknown.* AmFP; BLPA; HoPM; OxNR

("Where have ye [*or* you] been all the day, / Billy Boy?") OxNR

Billy Budd, Foretopman. Herman Melville.

Billy in the Darbies. APN-2; HAP; NAAL-1; NAWM-2; NCAP; NOBA; OxBoLi; PoEL-5

Billy club, a face, the windshield breaks, A. (LL) Matins: James Brown and His Famous Flames Tour the South, 1958. David Wojahn. NAmP90; PBCAP

Billy Goat. *Unknown.* CTAV

Billy Goat Gruff. The Troll to her Children. Jane Yolen. OTCP

Billy Grimes. *Unknown.* AmFP

Billy in one of his nice new sashes. Tender-Heartedness. Harry Graham. CBNP; NBLV; NOxBChV; PeLV *Fr.* Some Ruthless Rhymes.

Billy in the Darbies. Herman Melville. APN-2; HAP; NAAL-1; NAWM-2; NCAP; NOBA; OxBoLi; PoEL-5 *Fr.* Billy Budd, Foretopman.

Billy the Kid. *Unknown.* FaBoBe

Binary. Chris Wallace-Crabbe. OBCoV

Binary mathematician, A. Limerick. *Unknown.* PeLi

Bind, The. Wayne Brown. PBCV

Bind your straight hair. Thessalian. Winifred Bryher. PoA

Binds us together with you. Chorus of the Rescued. Nelly Sachs, *German.* WPOW, *tr.* by Ruth Mead *and* Matthew Mead; PoSu

Bing Crosby was singing "White Christmas." When I First Saw Snow. Gregory Djanikian. CMAP; UnSA

Bingen on the Rhine. Caroline Elizabeth Norton. BLPA

Bingo. *Unknown.* CH; TTTS

Binnorie; or, The Two Sisters. *Unknown.* OBEV; PoE

(Twa Sisters of Binnorie.) CH; EnSB

Binsey Poplars (Felled 1879). Gerard Manley Hopkins. EBVV; EnVR; InPS-3; NAEL-2; NoAM; RB

(Binsey Poplars.) APAD

Biodrama. Miroslav Holub, *Czech.* CBNP, *tr.* by Ewald Osers

Biographia Literaria. Joan Retallack. FTOS

Biography. Imamu Amiri Baraka. TAP

Biography. Abraham Moses Klein. TrJP

Biography. John Masefield.

"Other bright days of action have seemed great." OxBTC

Biography. Michael Ondaatje. NoAM

Biography. Maura Stanton. CMAP

Biography of an Agnostic. Louis Ginsberg. TrJP

Biography of Southern Rain. Kenneth Patchen. VGW

Biological / and dynastic phenomenon, The. The Art of Picasso. Salvador Dali, *Spanish.* SPE, *tr.* by David Gascoyne

Biology Teacher. Zbigniew Herbert, *Polish.* PoSu, *tr.* by John Carpenter *and* Bogdana Carpenter

Bion. A Pastoral, in Imitation of the Greek of Moschus, bewailing the Death of the Earl of Rochester. Moschus, *Greek.*

"With thee, sweet *Bion*, all the grace of Song." OBCVT, *tr.* by John Oldham

Biped is quite a strange creature, The. Dan Pagis, *Hebrew.* IP, *tr.* by Warren Bargad *and* Stanley F. Chyet

Biplane, The. Steve Orlen. WeT

Biplane shuttles through the telegraph wires, The. Sunday. Philippe Soupault, *French.* PFTM, *tr.* by Anselm Hollo

Birch begins to crack its outer sheath, The. A Young Birch. Robert Frost. SAmP

Birch Canoe. Carter Revard. NoP-4

Birch-Tree at Loschwitz, The. Amy Levy. TrJP

Birches. Robert Frost. AFr; AmPP; CMoP; FaBoVe; HeIP-4; ImGa; LiTM; MeMAP; MoAmPo; MoP; NAAL-2; NoAM; NoP-4; OxBA; PoLF; PoPoPo; PoRA; Poetr; RB; SAmP; SoSe-8; TAP; TFi; TRP

Birches falling down the hillside. (LL) For My Grandmother, Bridget Halpin. Michael Hartnett. BIrV; IIP; PBCIP

Birches stand in their beggar's row, the. February; the Boy Breughel. Norman Dubie. LCAP-2

Bird. Hanmo Chong, *Korean.* CKP, *tr.* by Jaihiun Kim

Bird. Joy Harjo. SeSe

Bird. Chi-ha Kim, *Korean.* CKP, *tr.* by Jaihiun Kim

Bird, A. Chongsam Kim, *Korean.* CKP, *tr.* by Jaihiun Kim

Bird, The. Max Michelson. TrJP

Bird. Agnes Nemes Nagy, *Hungarian.* BoWoP; PoSu, *tr.* by Bruce Berlind

Bird, The. Rabindranath Tagore. SAGP

Bird, The. Henry Vaughan. ESCV; GeHe; OBEV; PoE; PoEL-2

Bird and beast. What She Said. Nannakaiyar, *Tamil.* PLW, *tr.* by A. K. Ramanujan

Bird and the Bell, The. Christopher Pearse Cranch. APN-1

Bird and the Muse. Marya Alexandrovna Zaturenska. PoA

Bird and Waterfall Music. Wang Wei. OHMPC

Bird Appeal. Asa Benveniste. NBrP

Bird at Dawn, The. Harold Monro. BoTP; MoBrPo

Bird Bath, The. Florence Hoatson. BoTP

Bird, bird don't edge me in. The Reply. Theodore Roethke. NYBP

Bird calls me, A. Charles Simic. AmPA

Bird came down the Walk, A. Emily Dickinson. APN-2; AmPP; CMoP; ChAP; ColAP; HeIP-4; LiTM; MeMAP; MoAmPo; NAAL-1; NAAL-3; NCAP; NOBA; NTCP; NoAM; NoP-4; OBAL; OBCA; OxBA; PAR; PoLF; PoRA; SAmP; TFi

("Leap, splashless, as they swim.") (LL) ChAP

Bird Catcher, The. *Unknown, Egyptian.* TTY, *tr.* by Ulli Beier

Bird chirped at my window this morning, A. April. Amy Lowell. CPO

Bird comes / delicately as a little girl, A. Akiko Yosano, *Japanese.* WPJ; WPOW, *tr.* by Kenneth Rexroth *and* Ikuko Atsumi

Bird cried only once, The. Aerin I. Chi-ha Kim, *Korean.* CKP, *tr.* by Jaihiun Kim

Bird does not live / charles christopher parker is dead. The Assassination of Charlie Parker. Arthur Brown. SeSe

Bird flew tangent-wise to the open window, A. Robert Greacen. PNI

Bird flies and I gum it to a concept, A. Letter to Anne Ridler. George Sutherland Fraser. OxBS

Bird flying past my head said previous previous, The. Conrad Potter Aiken. *Fr.* Time in the Rock [or, Preludes to Definition]. VGW

Bird Frau, The. Rita Dove. CMAP

Bird I cannot name crows, A. (LL) A New Poem. Robert Duncan. FTOS

Bird in a Cage, The. *Unknown, Vietnamese.* AVP, *tr.* by Huỳnh Sanh Thông

Bird in a Cage. *Unknown.* AS

Bird in flight parts from the old wood, The. Yüan Mei. *Fr.* Five Poems on Returning to Hangchou. CoBLCP, *tr.* by Jonathan Chaves

Bird in the cage, The. Issa. PeP

Bird in the Hand, A. Vassar Miller. CRP

Bird is calling from the willow, A. *Unknown.* *Fr.* Four Glosses. NOIV

Bird is lost, The. Yardbird's Skull. Owen Dodson. PoBA; VGW

Bird is my neighbor, a whimsical fellow and dim, The. The Crane Is My Neighbor. John Shaw Neilson. CBAP

Bird Language. Christopher Pearse Cranch. APN-1; PAR

Bird-like, my heart was glad to soar and vault. Le Voyage À Cythère. John Gray. ADE

"Bird Lives": Charles Parker [in St. Louis]. Michael S. Harper. AmPA

Bird of Dawning, The. Shakespeare. *Fr.* Hamlet. NAWM-1

(Gracious Time, The.)

Bird of Endless Time, The. James Laughlin. WeW-3

Bird of Night, The. Randall Jarrell. KaS

Bird of Paradise, The. W. H. Davies. NSI

Bird of Power. Jim Tollerud. VoR

Bird of the bitter bright grey golden morn. A Ballad of François Villon. Swinburne. PoEL-5; PoRA

Bird of the moths! that radiant wing. The Butterfly. Robert Stephen Hawker. EBVV

Bird of the woodland, sing me a song. To the Mock-Bird. Mary Weston Fordham. CBWP-2

Bird rests in the air, the stone rests on the land, The. Each In His Own. "Angelus Silesius." GePo, *tr.* by George C. Schoolfield *Fr.* The Cherubical Wanderer.

Bird saw the young Burara girls, twisting their strings, making string figures, The. *Unknown.* NOBAu, *tr.* by Ronald M. Berndt *Fr.* Goulburn Island Song Cycle.

Bird Scarer, The. *Unknown.* ReMoGo

Bird-shaped island, with secretive bird-voices. New Guinea. James Philip McAuley. NOCV

Bird sings the selfsame song, A. The Selfsame Song. Thomas Hardy. CMoP

Bird / sips water / drips music. Keith Bosley. Spl

Bird Song, The. Mrs. Henry Linden. CBWP-4

Bird Song. William Carlos Williams. SAmP

Bird Starver's Cry. *Unknown.* FaBoVe

Bird swerved dapple-white in the blue sky, The. Winged in Gold. Euros Bowen, *Welsh.* OBWVE, *tr.* by the author

Bird that I don't know, A. A Country Life. Randall Jarrell. MoAmPo

Bird, that's fetcht from Phasis flood, The. Out of Petronius. Petronius Arbiter, *Latin.* OBCVT, *tr.* by Richard Crashaw

Bird Was Singing, A. Dietmar von Aist [or Eist], *German.* AWP, *tr.* by Jethro Bithell

Bird watchers top my honors list. Up from the Egg; the Confessions of a Nuthatch Avoider. Ogden Nash. PoRA

Bird-Watching. Dennis Schmitz. LCAP-2

Bird-witted. Marianne Moore. CMoP; NAAL-2

Bird-Woman. Rachel McAlpine. PeNZ

Birdcatcher, The. Ralph Hodgson. MoBrPo

Birdfoot's Grampa. Joseph Bruchac. UnSA

Birdie McReynolds. Samuel Hoffenstein. BXAP; NBLV

Birdie with a yellow bill, A. Time to Rise. Robert Louis Stevenson. ACTP; CTV; OxBChV

Birdies' Breakfast, The. *Unknown.* BoTP

Birdland. Allen Fisher. NBrP

Birdless heaven, seadusk, one lone star, A. Tutto è Sciolto. James Joyce. OBMV

Birds, The. Aristophanes, *Greek.*

  Chorus of Birds. AWP

  (Grand Chorus of Birds.) PoEL-5

  "CHORUS. Ye Children of Man! whose life is a span." OBCVT, *tr.* by John Hookham Frere

Birds, The. William Blake. CH

Birds, The. Coleridge. *See* Answer to a Child's Question.

Birds. Ralph Hawkins. NBrP

Birds. Robinson Jeffers. InPS-3; VGW

Birds, The. Richard Jones. NAmP90

Birds. Ruth Miller. PeSA

Birds. Namsu Park, *Korean.* CKP, *tr.* by Jaihiun Kim

Birds, The. David Posner. NYBP

Birds, The. *Unknown.* PChr

Birds. *Unknown.* AWP *Fr.* The Thousand and One Nights.

Birds. Judith Wright. NoP-4

Birds against the April wind, The. What the Birds Said. John Greenleaf Whittier. APN-1; NOBA; PAR

Birds and Babies close their eyes. (LL) Bed-Time. Laurence Alma-Tadema. CTAV

Birds and bees and butterflies. Out of Doors. E. North. BoTP

Birds and bees, flowers and trees. God's Gifts to Me. Thelma Walton. CTV

Birds and Fishes. Robinson Jeffers. NAAL-2; NoP-4

  ("That is their quality: not mercy, not mind, not goodness, but the beauty / of God.") (LL) NoP-4

Birds and leaves disconnect in Fall. Zimmer in Fall. Paul Zimmer. CA

Birds and periodic blood. 5:30 A.M. Adrienne Rich. NOBA

Birds and sunlight. Yellow. De Leon Harrison. PoBA

Birds and their chatter overwhelm me with feeling, The. *Unknown, Chinese.* CoBCP, *tr.* by Burton Watson

Birds are gone to bed the cows are still, The. Hares at Play. John Clare. NTP; RB

Birds are in the bushes and the wolf is at the door, The. (LL) Everything in Its Place. Arthur Guiterman. NBLV; OBAL; OBCoV

Birds at dawn fly around in confusion now you are gone, The. Lament for Te Heuheu Herea. Te Heuheu Tukino, *Maori.* PeNZ, *tr.* by Margaret Orbell

Birds at Winter Nightfall. Thomas Hardy. MoBrPo

Birds' Ball, The. Charles William Bardeen. BLPA

Birds become frightened when the mountain moon sets. Majestic Valley. Chu Yi-tsun, *Chinese.* SuSp, *tr.* by Chang Yin-nan *and* Lewis C. Walmsley

Birds, birds, birds. Beat Poem by an Academic Poet. Vassar Miller. WPE

Birds come like fishes out of the air, The. Prey to Prey. David Rowbotham. CBAP

Birds / confused by the angle, The. December Eclipse. Margo Lockwood. Poetsp

Birds drip from the trees. Daybreak. Bert Meyers. SPE

Birds feed on birds, beasts on each other prey. Wretched Man. John Wilmot, 2d Earl of Rochester. *Fr.* A Satire [*or* Satyre] against [Reason and] Mankind. NOSC; OAEL-1; OBSV; PoEL-3; SCV

Bird's fire-fangled feathers dangle down, The. (LL) Of Mere Being. Wallace Stevens. NoP-4

Birds / Fly into the depths of our existence. The Seed. Tomasz Jastrun, *Polish.* AF, *tr.* by Michael March *and* Jaroslaw Anders

Birds follow the sun / rain coming on / we drive South. Lady's Days. Larry Neal. NBV

Birds from the Mountains, The. Chang Chi, *Chinese.* OHMPC, *tr.* by Kenneth Rexroth

Birds go fluttering in the air, The. The Silent Snake. *Unknown.* BoTP; CTAV

Birds go to sleep by the sweet, wild twist of her song, The. (LL) The Outlaw of Loch Lene. *Unknown, Modern Irish.* BIrV; CH; GBL; NTP; OBEV, *tr.* by Jeremiah Joseph Callanan

Birds have all left, The. Father's Winter. Justinas Marcinkevičius, *Lithuanian.* CEEP, *tr.* by Jonas Zdanys

Birds have vanished into the sky, The. Li Po, *Chinese.* BLT; EnlH, *tr.* by Sam Hamill

Birds hush. The evening twilight dare not stir. The War Elephant. Chế Lan Viên, *Vietnamese.* AVP, *tr.* by Huỳnh Sanh Thông

Birds in Snow. Hilda Doolittle. PoA

Birds in the first light twitter and whistle, The. A Little Morning Music. Delmore Schwartz. NYBP

Birds in the high Hall-garden. Tennyson. EBVVPR; NAEL-2; PeVV *Fr.* Maud [A Monodrama]. EnVR

Birds' Lament. John Clare. PoEL-4

Bird's Nest, The. *Unknown.* ACTP

Birds Nest in My Arms, The. Gloria Fuertes, *Spanish.* RaBo, *tr. by* Philip Levine

Birds' Nests. John Clare. OAEL-2; OxBSP

Birds' Nests. Millicent Seager. BoTP

Birds' Nests. *Unknown.* BoTP

Birds of a feather flock together. *Unknown.* ACTP; ReMoGo

Birds of Detroit. Greg Pape. PBCAP

Birds of Killingworth, The (The Poet's Tale). Henry Wadsworth Longfellow. MeMAP; OxBA *Fr.* Tales of a Wayside Inn.

(Poet's Tale: The Birds of Killingworth, The.)

"Do you ne'er think what wondrous beings these?"

Birds of Passage, The. Jones Very. NCAP

Birds of Steel, The. W. H. Davies. NSI

Birds of Tin, The. Charles Madge. SPE

Birds on a Powerline. Herbert Asquith. NAAAL

Birds on the School Windowsill, The. Evelyn Dainty. BoTP

Birds, postilions, when. Almost a Spring Poem. Reiner Kunze, *German.* CEEP, *tr. by* Ewald Osers

Birds sang in the wet trees, The. Wet Evening in April. Patrick Kavanagh. OPOU

Birds sang sweet as ony bell, The. Sir Aldingar. *Unknown.* ESPB

Birds saw the people walking along, The. *Aborigine Oral Tradition. Fr.* Moon-Bone Song [*or* Cycle]. CBAP, *tr. by* R. M. Berndt

Birds singing. Jack Kerouac. HA

Bird's Song, A. Dame Edith Sitwell. NALW

Birds the more white, against green stream. Quatrain. Tu Fu, *Chinese.* SuSp, *tr. by* Jerome P. Seaton

Birds, trees and flow'rs they bring to me. Sir John Collings Squire. BXAP *Fr.* The Swallow.

Bird's voice chinks and tinkles, A. July Evening. Norman MacCaig. FaBoTC

Birds Waking. W. S. Merwin. NOBA

Birdshooting season the men. Olive Senior. HCP

Birdsong. Burns Singer. FaBoTw

Birdsong Brook. Wang Wei, *Chinese.* SuSp, *tr. by* Irving Y. Lo

Birdsongs are aging, The. Andrew Joron, *German.* PT, *tr. by* Yvan Goll

Birdsville Track, The. Douglas Stewart.

"Oh the corrugated-iron town." CBAP

Birdwatchers of America. Anthony Hecht. HoPM; NOBA; NoAM

Birdwatching at Fan Lake. Anita Endrezze-Danielson. HATNAP

Birkett's Eagle. Dorothy S. Howard. MoBS

Birks of Aberfeldy, The [Composed on the Spot]. Robert Burns. CTC

Birmingham. Julia Fields. *Fr.* Poems: Birmingham 1962–1964. PoBA

Birmingham. Louis MacNeice. CMoP; MoBrPo; OxAEP-2

Birmingham. Margaret Abigail Walker. PoBA

Birmingham, 1962. Diann Blakely Shoaf. PUP-19

Birmingham and Wolverhampton. James Woodhouse. *Fr.* The Life and Lucubrations of Crispinus Scriblerus. NOEC

Birmingham 1963. Raymond R. Patterson. PoBA

Birth. Edith Bruck, *Italian.* BoWoP, *tr. by* Ruth Feldman *and* Brian Swann (b. 1940)

Birth, A. James Dickey. FiLi; NOBA

Birth. Louise Erdrich. NoP-4; PiM

Birth. Amir Gilbo'a, *Hebrew.* MHP, *tr. by* Ruth Finer Mintz

Birth. George Ella Lyon. CrSp

Birth. Gabriela Melinescu, *Rumanian.* BoWoP, *tr. by* Willis Barnstone *and* Matei Calinescu

Birth. Harold Monro. PoA *Fr.* Strange Meetings.

Birth. Takahashi Shinkichi, *Japanese.* OxBM, *tr. by* Geoffrey Bownas *and* Anthony Thwaite

Birth and the grave, that are not as they were. (LL) Alastor; or, The Spirit of Solitude. Shelley. OAEL-2; Ro

Birth-Bond, The. D. G. Rossetti. Son *Fr.* The House of Life.

Birth-Day, The. Mary Robinson. ECWP; WoRP

Birth-Dues. Robinson Jeffers. MoAmPo

Birth in a Narrow Room, The. Gwendolyn Brooks. BlSi; NoP-4

Birth Is. John Figueroa. PBCV

Birth is Death, Death is Birth. Friedrich von Logau, *German.* GePo, *tr. by* George C. Schoolfield

Birth of a Coachman. Paul Durcan. PBCIP

Birth of a Great Man. Robert Graves. NYBP

Birth of a Shark, The. David Wevill. TwCP

Birth of a Son. Sam Hunt. PeNZ

Birth of Flattery, The. George Crabbe.

"Muse of my Spenser, who so well could sing." EPCY

Birth of Jesus, The. Josephine D. Henderson Heard. CBWP-4

Birth of John Henry, The. Melvin Beaunearus Tolson. BPo; NAAAL; TTY *Fr.* Harlem Gallery.

Birth of Love. Robert Penn Warren. GEA; UnPo; VCAP

Birth of Moshesh, The. David Granmer T. Bereng, *Sotho.* PeSA; TTY, *tr. by* Dan Kunene *and* Jack Cope

Birth of Potchikoo, The. Louise Erdrich. *Fr.* Old Man Potchikoo. HATNAP

Birth of Robin Hood, The. *Unknown.* OAEL-1; OxBB

(Willie and Earl Richard's Daughter.) ESPB

Birth of Shaka, The. Mbuyiseni Oswald Mtshali. PBMAP

Birth of Sohrab, The. Firdausi. TAL, *tr. by* James Atkinson *Fr.* The Shahnamah.

Birth of the Cool. Charles David Wright. MT

Birth of the Foal. Ferenc Juhász, *Hungarian.* RB, *tr. by* David Wevill

Birth of the Squire; an Eclogue, The. John Gay. NAEL-1; NOEC; PoEL-3

Birth of Time, The. Josephine D. Henderson Heard. CBWP-4

Birth of Tragedy, The. Irving Layton. MoCV; NoAM; NoP-4

Birth of Venus, The. Muriel Rukeyser. NALW

Birth of Venus. Constance Urdang. PoA

Birth, old age. Ly Ngoc Kieu, *Vietnamese.* WPoS, *tr. by* Thich Nhat Hanh *and* Jane Hirshfield

Birth Stone. Lorna Goodison. VCWP

Birth Wail, The. Henrietta Tindal. VWP

Birthcry! Raymond Roseliep. HA

Birthday, The. Philip Dacey. AmPA

Birthday. Stanley Plumly. NAmP90

Birthday, A. Christina Rossetti. AWP; CABP; CH; EBEvV; GLoP; ImPo; LW; NAEL-2; NALW; NOBE; NOBVV; OAEL-2; OBEV; PEW; PFE; PeVV; PoE; SDW; TFi; TTTS; UV; VWP; WPE

Birthday Candle, A. Donald Justice. NYBP

Birthday greetings / From a friend. Birthday Wishes to a Physician. Lizelia Augusta Jenkins Moorer. CBWP-3

Birthday Ode to Mr. Alfred Austin, A. Sir Owen Seaman. NOBL

Birthday Party. Kusano Shimpei, *Japanese.* PFTM, *tr. by* Cid Corman

Birthday Poem, A. James Simmons. OxBSP; PNI

Birthday Poem for Thomas Hardy. C. Day Lewis. EBEvV; EPCY

Birthday Poem from Venice. Patricia Beer. OxBC

Birthday Sonnet. Elinor Wylie. MoAmPo

Birthday Sonnet for Grace. Bernadette Mayer. PmAP

Birthday Verses Written in a Child's Album. James Russell Lowell. OxBChV

Birthday Wish, A. Dorothy Nell McDonald. PoToHe

Birthday Wishes to a Husband. Lizelia Augusta Jenkins Moorer. CBWP-3

Birthday Wishes to a Minister of the Gospel. Lizelia Augusta Jenkins Moorer. CBWP-3

Birthday Wishes to a Physician. Lizelia Augusta Jenkins Moorer. CBWP-3

Birthdays. Hilde Domin, *German.* BoWoP, *tr. by* Tudor Morris

Birthdays. C. J. Driver. PeSA

Birthdays. Mother Goose. BLPA; BoTP; FaBoBe; FaBoCh; LB; NBLV; OTCP; OxNR

(Week of Birthdays, A.) ReMoGo

Birthdays from the ocean one desert april noon. That "Craning of the Neck." Isabella Gardner. WPE

Birthdays? yes, in a general way. Sincere Flattery of R. B. James Kenneth Stephen. NOBL

Birthmarks. Rajani Parulekar, *Marathi.* OMIP, *tr. by* Vinay Dharwadker

Birthplace. Tahereh Saffarzadeh, *Farsi.* WPOW, *tr. by* Deirdre Lashgari

Birthplace Revisited. Gregory Corso. NeAP; PoM; VGW

Birthright. John Drinkwater. CH; OxBTC

Biscuit, a basket. Hattie went to Market, A. Hattie Went to Market. Leslie Simon. FFC

Biseth you in this ilke lif. William Herebert. MiEL

Bishop Blomfield's First Charge to His Clergy. Sydney Goodsir Smith. FaBoEE

Bishop Blougram's Apology. Robert Browning. EBVVPR; OBNC; PoEL-5

Bishop Doane on His Dog. George Washington Doane. BLPA; FaBoBe

Bishop Hatto. Robert Southey. OBNV; OBSP

(God's Judgment on a Wicked Bishop.) OBNV

Bishop / High priest of Grenada. Lament for Maurice Bishop. Howard Fergus. PBCV

Bishop James A. Shorter. Josephine D. Henderson Heard. CBWP-4

Bishop of Canterbury, The. *Unknown.* AmFP

Bishop of Chester, The. On Dr. Keene, Bishop of Chester. Thomas Gray. FaBoEE

Bishop Orders His Tomb at Saint Praxed's Church, The. Robert Browning. CABP; EBVV; EBVVPR; EnVR; FHYEP; HAP; HeIP-4; NAEL-2; NAWM-2; NOBVV; NoP-4; OAEL-2; OBAL; PoE; Poetr; SCGP; TFi

Bishop Orders His Tomb in St. Praxed's. Morris Gilbert Bishop. OBAL

Bishop tells us: "When the boys come back," The. "They." Siegfried Sassoon. CMoP; NAEL-2; NoP-4; OBSV; OBWP

Bishop's hand on a widow's breast, A. Russell Lucas. BXAP

Bismark. John Jay Chapman. See Lines on the Death of Bismarck.

Bison, The. Hilaire Belloc. NoAM

Bison Crossing Near Mt. Rushmore. May Swenson. PaTW

Bison in the bath, the image noted, A. Of Bison Men. James Fenton. PeLV Fr. Wild Life Studies.

Bistro Styx, The. Rita Dove. NoP-4

Bit an apple on its red. Green Red Brown and White. May Swenson. VGW

Bit by bit, grain by grain, the self is taken away. Night Sweats. Gwen Head. PuP-16

Bit o' Sly Coorten, A. William Barnes. PeLV

Bit of Colour, A. Horace Smith. BoTP

Bit of jungle in the street, A. Alley Cat. Esther Valck Georges. OTCP; Spl

Bit of Marble, A. Clinton Scollard. APN-2

Bit of security and some silent love, A. (LL) Is all this sorrow? I don't know. Yehuda Amichai, Hebrew. IP, tr. by Warren Bargard and Stanley Chyet

Bit of talcum, A. Reflection on Babies. Ogden Nash. NBLV

Bit of the Book in the morning, A. Margaret Elizabeth Sangster. CTV

Bitch. Carolyn Kizer. NMM-2

Bitch, The. Sergey Aleksandrovich Yesenin, Russian. TCRP, tr. by Daniel Weissbort

Bitch-Kitty, The. Jonathan Williams. PoM

Bite, The. Gerald Stern. APAD

Bite, and the taste of tongues. The Empty Pain-Killer Bottles. Tom Raworth. SPE

Bite back passion. Spring now sets. Li Shang-yin, Chinese. PLT, tr. by A. C. Graham

Bite. The tug of fate, The. (LL) The Pier: Under Pisces. James Merrill. LCAP-2; NoAM

Biting air. Winter Days. Gareth Owen. OBCP

Biting Back. Patricia Smith. GT

Bits and Pieces, The. Chris Wallace-Crabbe.
    Opener. BMAP

Bits of Reminiscence. "Shu Ting," Chinese. VCWP, tr. by Carolyn Kizer

Bits of Silk. Ion Caraion, Romanian. CEEP, tr. by Marguerite Dorian and Elliott B. Urdang

Bits of Wisdom. Benjamin Franklin. CTV

Bitten by a rabid dog, a man sees. Paulus Silentiarius, Greek. InMo, tr. by Sam Hamill

Bitten to dust are the savage feathers of fire. To a Seaman Dead on Land. Kay Boyle. PoA

Bitter aftertaste of spring sky, The. Ballad of Fate. Vadim Nikolaevich Delone, Russian. TCRP, tr. by Nina Kossman

Bitter air, The. L'Aura Amara. Arnaut Daniel, Provençal. CTC, tr. by Ezra Pound

Bitter Angel. Amy Gerstler. PmAP

Bitter batter boop! The Last Cry of the Damp Fly. Dennis Lee. NTCP

Bitter, bitter jewel. Hilda Doolittle. NALW Fr. Tribute to the Angels.

Bitter bullshit rotten white parts / alone., The. (LL) Leroy. Imamu Amiri Baraka. BPo; PmAP; PoBA

Bitter cold, but don't complain when Heaven sends down snow. It Has Snowed Repeatedly and We Can Count On a Good Crop of Wheat and Barley. Lu Yu, Chinese. SuSp, tr. by Burton Watson

Bitter Cold, Living in the Village. Po Chü-i, Chinese. SuSp, tr. by Irving Lo; ChiPo, tr. by Irving Yucheng Lo
    ("In the twelfth month of the Eighth Year.") ChiPo, tr. by Irving Yucheng Lo

Bitter cold. No one is abroad. Unknown, Chinese. OHMPC, tr. by Kenneth Rexroth

Bitter end, A. Persius, Latin. OBCVT, tr. by Thomas Brewster

Bitter for remembrance of the healing which has passed. (LL) Lincoln. John Gould Fletcher. CBCWP; MoAmPo

Bitter for Sweet. Christina Rossetti. GBL

Bitter Fruit of the Tree. Sterling Brown. NoP-4

Bitter Harvest. Alistair Campbell. PeNZ

Bitter Herbs. "Alta." NMM-2

Bitter morning, A. J. W. Hackett. HA

Bitter pinecone may be eaten, The. The Empty Purse. Tu Fu, Chinese. TAL, tr. by Robert Payne

Bitter rain in my courtyard. Wu Tsao, Chinese. BoWoP, tr. by Kenneth Rexroth and Ling Chung

Bitter Sanctuary. Harold Monro. FaBoMo; OBMV

Bitter-Sweet. George Herbert. FHYEP; FMP; GeHe; NOBE; NoP-4; OxBSP

Bitter tea. Penny Harter. HA

Bitter the wind tonight. The Vikings. Unknown, Irish. BIrV, tr. by John Montague

Bitter Withy, The. Unknown. NOCV; NoP-4

Bitter Wood. Martin Carter. HCP

Bitter year it was. What woman ever, A. The Wreath. Robert Graves. BoLoP

Bitterberry daybreak. Ingrid Jonker, Afrikaans. PeSAV, tr. by Cherry Clayton

Bitterer, too, are ye? (LL) The Tuft of Kelp. Herman Melville. APN-2; FaBoEE

Bittern, The. Sandra McPherson. LCAP-2

Bittern booms, A. John Wills. HA

Bittern, I'm sorry to see you stretched. The Yellow Bittern. Cathal Buidhe Mac Giolla Ghunna, Irish. NOIV, tr. by Thomas Kinsella

Bitterness. Anita Virgil. HA

Bitterness of death is on me now, The. The Cup. Jones Very. APN-1

Bittersweet. Joyce Carol Thomas.
    "She / somersaulted." MDDM

Bittersweet growing up the red wall. Robert Kelly. PmAP

Bitto and Nannion do not. Asclepiades, Greek. GrAn, tr. by Alan Marshfield

Bitto gives to Athena. Antipater of Sidon, Greek. GrAn; PGA, tr. by Kenneth Rexroth

Bivouac of the Dead, The. Theodore O'Hara. BLPA

Bivouac on a Mountain Side. Walt Whitman. AiP; CBCWP; OxBA; PoLF

Bix to Buxtehude to Boulez. The Victor Dog. James Merrill. NoAM; NoP-4

Bizerta. George Campbell Hay. FaBoTC

Black. Maxine Chernoff. PmAP Fr. Japan. PmAP

Black A, white E, red I, green U, blue O—vowels. Vowels. Rimbaud, French. TTTS, tr. by Kenneth Koch

Black absence hides upon the past. Stanzas. John Clare. EnLoPo; NOBVV

Black All Day. Raymond R. Patterson. PoBA

Black and blue! (LL) In May. John Millington Synge. SAGP

Black and Blue. Charles Wright. PuP-17

Black and glossy as a bee and curled was my hair. Ambapali, Pali. WPOW, tr. by A. L. Basham

Black and Gold. Nancy Byrd Turner. CTV

Black and White. Shirley Lim. UnSA

Black and White. Michael Smith. HCP; NOxBChV
    ("Lawwwwwd have mercy.") (LL) NOxBChV

Black and White Galaxie, The. Michael S. Weaver. UnSA

Black Angel, The. Henri Coulette. CoAP; NYBP

Black Army, The. S. E. K. Mqhayi, Xhosa. PeSA, tr. by C. M. Mcanyangwa and Jack Cope

Black Art. Imamu Amiri Baraka. BPo; CAPP-1; NAAAL

Black Art, The. Anne Sexton. PoA

Black Artist's role in America is to aid in the destruction / of America as he knows it, The. State/meant. Imamu Amiri Baraka. BB

Black as a chimney is his face. "Sooeep!" Walter De la Mare. BoTP

Black as my fate, or cold as my despair. (LL) On Passing Over a Dreary Tract of Country, and Near the Ruins of a Deserted Chapel, During a Tempest. Charlotte Smith. BoWoP; WPE

Black as my night, anonymous here. An American Memory of Africa. Kofi Awoonor. HBAPE; PBMAP

Black as[—] the centre of an eye, the centre, a blackness. Marina Ivanovna Tsvetayeva. PBWP Fr. Insomnia.

Black Baby. Anita Scott Coleman. FiLi

Black Bagatelles. Rodney Hall. CBAP
    My Coffin Is a Deckchair.
    "October: and the fires go out along the coast."
    They're Dying Just the Same in Station Homesteads.
    World Is a Musician's Cliff House, The.

Black bear does a strange and shuffling dance, The. Bear: A Totem Dance As Seen by Raven. Peter Blue Cloud. HATNAP

Black Bear sang, drumming on a log. Moon of Huckleberries. Phillip William George. VoR

Black bear sits alone, A. Galway Kinnell. RaBo Fr. Lastness.

Black beauty, which above that common light. Sonnet of Black Beauty. Edward Herbert, 1st Baron Herbert of Cherbury. NOSC

Black bird, black voice. In the Orchard. Anne Stevenson. ColAP

Black birds, the wind, cover their heart. (LL) Man of My Time. Salvatore Quasimodo, *Italian*. ItIP

Black Blues. Bloke Modisane. PBA

Black boat, perfect Greek. Sorley MacLean. FaBoTC

Black Book, The. John Berryman.

"Grandfather, sleepless in a room upstairs." VGW

Black Book of Carmarthen, The. *Unknown, Welsh*.

Song of the Graves, The. OBMV, *tr. by* Ernest Rhys

Black Bourgeoisie. Imamu Amiri Baraka. BPo

Black Box, The. Gavin Ewart. OBCoV

Black boy / let me get up from the white man's table of fifty sounds. Melvin Beaunearus Tolson. PoBA

Black boy, the night hides you. Norman Rosten. TrJP

Black bread. (LL) Naturally. Audre Lorde. ISC

Black Bread. Tom Paulin. CIP-2

Black bread and a faithful wife. "Eduard Georgievich Bagritzky," *Russian*. TCRP, *tr. by* Vera Dunham

Black brother, think you life so sweet. Time to Die. Ray Garfield Dandridge. PoBA

Black Bud. Michael Smith. PBCV

Black Buoy. Robert H. Davis. HATNAP

Black Cat. Rilke, *German*. APo; PC, *tr. by* Stephen Mitchell

Black cat among roses, A. The Garden by Moonlight. Amy Lowell. CPO; NMM-2

Black cat, sweet brother. For James Baldwin. Kay Boyle. NMM-2

Black cat yawns, The. Cat. Mary Britton Miller. TLR; WHSW

Black Cloud, The. W. H. Davies. RB

Black clouds spread over the sky. Looking from the Pavilion Over the Lake. Su Tung-p'o, *Chinese*. OHPC, *tr. by* Kenneth Rexroth

Black Cock, The. Ishmael Reed. ISC

Black cock crowed, The. Two o'Clock. Katharine Pyle. *Fr.* The Wonder Clock. OBCA

Black Cottage, The. Robert Frost. CBCWP; VGW

Black Crispus Attucks taught. Dark Symphony. Melvin Beaunearus Tolson. ColAP; NAAAL; SSLK

Black Dada Nihilismus. Imamu Amiri Baraka. PoM

Black Dog. Ray A. Young Bear. CDW

Black Dog, Red Dog. Stephen Dobyns. CMAP

Black doves with white breasts walk the church in circles. In a Naples Bar. Andrejs Eglitis, *Latvian*. CEEP, *tr. by* Inara Cedrins

Black Draftee from Dixie, The. Carrie Williams Clifford. BlSi

Black earth. Farm Picture. Galway Kinnell. AFr

Black Earth. Marianne Moore. FaBoMo

Black English. Richard Katrovas. LTA

Black-Eyed Susan. John Gay. *See* Sweet William's Farewell to Black-Eyed [*or* Black-Ey'd] Susan.

Black-eyed Susie. *Unknown*. AmFP

Black-faced [*or* fac'd] house will love, A. (LL) On the Baptized Ethiopian. Richard Crashaw. ChIV-2; FaBoEE; NoP-4

Black Finger, The. Angelina Weld Grimké. NAAAL; PoBA

Black flies kept nagging in the heat, The. Tao and Unfitness at Inistiogue on the River Nore. Thomas Kinsella. PBCIP

Black fool, why winter here? These frozen skies. Advice to a Raven in Russia [December, 1812]. Joel Barlow. APN-1; AmPP; ColAP; NAAL-1; NAAL-3; NOBA; OBWP; OxBA

Black fox loped out of the hills, The. Dream of a Black Fox. Brendan Kennelly. PBCIP

Black girl black girl. Blackberry Sweet. Dudley Randall. HAP; ISC; InPS-3; KaS; PoBA; SAGP; SoSe-8; WeW-3

Black Girl Goes By, A. Emile Roumer, *French*. TTY, *tr. by* Edna Worthley Underwood

Black glassmaker, The. Jean-Joseph Rabéarivelo. PBMAP *Fr.* Traduits de la Nuit.

Black Gold, blackgold. . . aint no oil. Blackgoldbluseswoman. Kirk Hall. NBV

Black, green and gold at sunset: pageantry. At a Funeral. Dennis Brutus. PBMAP

Black greyed into white a nightmare of bicycling. That Which We Call a Rose. Michael Dransfield. BMAP; CBAP; NOBAu

Black grows the sudden sky, betokening rain. Sudden Shower. John Clare. OxAEP-2

Black Hair. Gary Soto. UnSA

Black hair and red cheeks: for how long? Cui Shaoxuan, *Chinese*. WPoS, *tr. by* Jane Hirshfield

Black Hairs, The. Heinz Pasman, *German*. RaBo, *tr. by* Robert Bly

Black Hat, The. Clayton Eshleman. VGW

Black heart is pulsing to its ant-egg dole. (LL) A Mad Negro Soldier Confined at Munich. Robert Lowell. FaBoMo; OxBC

Black Hen, The. Mother Goose. ReMoGo ("Hickety, pickety, / My black hen.") (LL) BoTP

Black hen, The. Raymond Roseliep. HA

Black Henry. Tejumola Ologboni. NBV

Black history. The Living Truth. Sterling Plumpp. PoBA

Black Hole. Adrian Rumble. SpW

Black Holes, Black Stockings. Olga Broumas, Jane Miller (b. 1925). "Rough Sunday. Wooded plains underwater, seaweed, urchin, sea-horse." WeT

"There's a song of privacy that begins Go away Go away, and stills the." WeT

Black Horse Rider, The. Pierre Loving. SPE

Black Horseman. Branko Miljkovic, *Serbo-Croatian*. HSix, *tr. by* Charles Simic

Black Hose, The. Bruce Weigl. NAmP90

Black I am and much admired. Mother Goose. OxNR

Black in a tentlike cloak, at rest. Incident in Transylvania. Roger McDonald. BMAP

Black in blazonry means. The Buffalo. Marianne Moore. PoA

Black iron fence closes the graves in, A. Visiting Emily Dickinson's Grave with Robert Francis. Robert Bly. LCAP-2

Black Is a Soul. Joseph Blanco White. PoBA

Black is beautiful. Ron Welburn. NBV

Black Is Best. Larry Thompson. MBE; PoBA

Black is not. A Poem Looking for a Reader. Haki R. Madhubuti. ISC

Black is; slavery was; I am. This Child Is the Mother. Gloria C. Oden. BlSi

Black is the color of. What Color Is Black? Barbara Mahone. MBE

Black is the first nail I ever stepped on. Negritude. James A. Emanuel. BPo

Black is the night. What Is Black? Mary O'Neill. NTCP

Black is what the prisons are. The African Affair. Bruce McM. Wright. PoBA

Black Island. Charles Pressoir, *French*. NegPo, *tr. by* Ellen Conroy Kennedy

Black Jackets. Thom Gunn. HeIP-4; NAEL-2; NoP-4; TwCP

Black Jam for Dr. Negro. Mari E. Evans. BPo; PoBA

Black Java Pepper. Arthur Sze. OpBo

Black Jess. Peter Kane Dufault. NYBP

Black Jewel, The. W. S. Merwin. LCAP-2

Black jewel like, The. Akahito, *Japanese*. OHMPJ, *tr. by* Kenneth Rexroth

Black king dance out front of the crowd. Four Poems. Velemir Khlebnikov, *Russian*. PFTM, *tr. by* Paul Schmidt

Black knight. To Josh Gibson (Legendary Slugger of the Old Negro Baseball League). George Mosby Jr. ISC

Black Lace Fan My Mother Gave Me, The. Eavan Boland. BiHa

Black lake, black boat, two black, cut-paper people. Crossing the Water. Sylvia Plath. HCAP; RB

Black leaf owre a white leaf twirls, A. "Hugh MacDiarmid." FaBoTC *Fr.* A Drunk Man Looks at the Thistle.

Black like me. (LL) Dream Variation[s]. Langston Hughes. ISC; MBE; NAAAL; NoP-4; SAGP; SSLK

Black, long-tailed, The. The Yellow Season. William Carlos Williams. MoAmPo

Black Love Black Hope. Doughtry Long. SeSe

Black Magic. Dudley Randall. *See* Blackberry Sweet.

Black Magic. Sonia Sanchez. BPo

Black Magicians / Come home: the pink meat image. The Change: *Kyoto-Tokyo Express*. Allen Ginsberg. APSN

Black Maid to the Fair Boy, The. Henry Reynolds. NOSC

Black Mail. Alice Walker. AmPA

Black Majesty. Countee Cullen. PoBA; VGW

Black Man, A. Sam Cornish. PoBA

Black Man, The. Sergey Aleksandrovich Yesenin, *Russian*. TCRP, *tr. by* Geoffrey Thurley

Black Man, 13th Floor. James A. Emanuel. NBV

Black Man Go Back To The Old Country. High Modes: Vision as Ritual: Confirmation. Michael S. Harper. NBV

Black Man Talks of Reaping, A. Arna Bontemps. BPo; ColAP; NAAAL; PoBA; SSLK

Black Man's Feast. Sarah Webster Fabio. PoBA

Black Man's Lament, The. Léon Damas, *French*. NegPo, *tr. by* Ellen Conroy Kennedy

Black Man's Son, The. Oswald Durand, *French*. TTY, *tr. by* Edna Worthley Underwood; NegPo, *tr. by* Ellen Conroy Kennedy

("At twenty, I loved Lise. She was frail and white.") NegPo, *tr. by* Ellen Conroy Kennedy

Black Man's Sonata, A. Michael S. Weaver. UnSA

Black Maps. Mark Strand. PoA

Black Marigolds. Bilhana, *formerly at. to* Chauras, *Sanskrit.* AWP, *tr. by* E. Powys Mathers

Black Meat. Jean Follain, *French.* BLT, *tr. by* W. S. Merwin

Black men? (LL) Black Woman. Naomi Long Madgett. GT; ISC

Black men with outasight afros. (LL) Beautiful Black Men. Nikki Giovanni. BPo; NAAAL

Black Mesa, The. James Merrill. PoA

Black milk of dawn [*or* daybreak *or* morning] we drink it [*or* you] at dusk [*or* dusktime *or* evening *or* nightfall *or* sundown]. A Death Fugue. Paul Celan, *German.* OBVE, *tr. by* Christopher Middleton; TrJP, *tr. by* Clement Greenberg; CLPP, *tr. by* Jerome Rothenberg; AF, *tr. by* John Felstiner; PoSu, *tr. by* John Felstiner; HP; VCWP, *tr. by* Michael Hamburger

Black Mood. Rosalía de Castro, *Galician.* STV, *tr. by* John Frederick Nims; WeW-3, *tr. by* Dudley Fitts

Black Mother Praying. Owen Dodson. ISC

Black Mother Woman. Audre Lorde. CrSp; MDDM; Poetr

Black Mountain Blues. Bessie Smith. PFTM

Black mountains pricked with pointed pine. The Watershed. Alice Thompson Meynell. VWP

Black Music. Léon Laleau, *French.*

Betrayal. NegPo, *tr. by* Ellen Conroy Kennedy

Cannibal. NegPo, *tr. by* Ellen Conroy Kennedy

Legacies. NegPo, *tr. by* Ellen Conroy Kennedy

Sacrifice. NegPo, *tr. by* Ellen Conroy Kennedy

Voodoo. NegPo, *tr. by* Ellen Conroy Kennedy

Black Music. Yevgeny Borisovich Rein, *Russian.* TCRP, *tr. by* Lubov Yakovleva

Black Muzzle, south sea dog. Su Tung-p'o, *Chinese.* CoBCP, *tr. by* Burton Watson

Black Narcissus. Gerald William Barrax. PoBA

Black Night. / White snow. Aleksandr Blok. AWP, *tr. by* Babette Deutsch *and* Avrahm Yarmolinsky *Fr.* The Twelve. TCRP, *tr. by* Jon Stallworthy *and* Peter France

Black-nosed kitten will slumber all, A. Choosing a Kitten. *Unknown.* CTV

Black November Turkey, A. Richard Wilbur. LCAP-2; NAAL-2

Black, numb fingernails, The. (LL) On a Field Trip at Fredericksburg. Dave Jeddie Smith. HCAP; PoPoPo

Black of brow, with cheeks aglow. A Glance. *Unknown, Irish.* NOIV, *tr. by* Thomas Kinsella

Black one, last as usual, swings her head, The. Fetching Cows. Norman MacCaig. NoP-4; OxBC

Black Orchid. David Jauss. SeSe

Black Ore. René Depestre, *French.* NegPo, *tr. by* Ellen Conroy Kennedy

Black-out. Robinson Jeffers. LiTM

Black Panther, The. John Hall Wheelock. LiTM; PFE

Black panther is sleeping on the crags, The. Sarveshwar Dayal Saxena, *Hindi.* OMIP, *tr. by* Vinay Dharwadker

Black Patch on Lucasta's Face, A. Richard Lovelace. BeJo; CaPo; SeCP

Black Patent Leather Shoes. Karen L. Mitchell. IFJA

Black peak at Xuan Loc, The. It Is Monsoon at Last. Basil T. Paquet. CDa

Black Pebble, The. James Reeves. OTCP

Black People! Imamu Amiri Baraka. BPo

Black People. Ted Joans. MBE

Black people are born singers. On Judgement Day. Sipho Sepamla. PBMAP

BLACK PEOPLE THINK. Awareness. Don L. Lee. MBE; PoBA

Black People: This Is Our Destiny. Imamu Amiri Baraka. CAPP-1

Black Plateau, The. W. S. Merwin. NNaP

Black Poet, White Critic. Dudley Randall. BPo; CoAmP; LTA

("White unicorn?, A .") (LL) LTA

Black Poets should live—not leap. For Black Poets Who Think of Suicide. Etheridge Knight. HeIP-6; InPK-6; LTA; NAAAL; PoBA; SAGP

Black poets / young, The. Charles Bukowski. LTA

Black Power. Raymond R. Patterson. NBV

Black Power. Alvin Saxon. PoBA

Black Power Poem. Ishmael Reed. BPo

Black Pride. Margaret Goss Burroughs. BlSi

Black raven in the snowy dusk. Aleksandr Blok. TCRP, *tr. by* Geoffrey Thurley *Fr.* Three Messages.

Black ravens squawking in the nest. Folk Song. *Unknown, Chinese.* ChiPo, *tr. by* Cecelia Liang

Black reapers with the sound of steel on stones. Reapers. Jean Toomer. BPo; ColAP; GT; HAP; MoP; NoAM; NoP-4; PoBA; Poetr; SoSe-8; TRP; WeW-3

Black Riders [and Other Lines], The. Stephen Crane.

Blades of Grass, The. MoAmPo

Book of Wisdom, The. HoPM; MoAmPo

From The Black Riders and Other Lines. NoP-4

God in Wrath, A. MeMAP; OxBSP; TAP

"God lay dead in Heaven." APN-2; AmPP

Heart, The. APAD; HoPM; MoAmPo

"I SAW A MAN PURSUING THE HORIZON;." APN-2; AmPP; ChAP; GEA; HoPM; MoAmPo; MoMo; NOBA; NoP-4; PBMP

"I stood upon a high place." APN-2; MeMAP

"I walked in a desert." MeMAP; NAAL-2

"If I should cast off this tattered coat." APN-2; PBMP

"It Was Wrong to Do This" Said the Angel. MeMAP

Learned Man [Came to Me Once], A. MeMAP; MoAmPo

"MAN FEARED THAT HE MIGHT FIND AN ASSASSIN, A." APN-2; MeMAP; NAAL-2; NoP-4

Man Saw a Ball of Gold [in the Sky], A. MeMAP

"Many red devils ran from my heart." MeMAP; TAP

"Many workmen / Built a hugh ball of masonry." PFE

Scaped.

"Should the wide world roll away." APN-2; AmPP

"There was set before me a mighty hill." APN-2; MeMAP

"'Think as I think,' said a man." PFE

Why? MeMAP

Youth, A. MoAmPo

(Content.)

Black Riders, The. César Vallejo, *Spanish.* AF; RaBo, *tr. by* Robert Bly

("There are blows in life so violent—I can't answer!") AF, *tr. by* Robert Bly

BLACK RIDERS CAME FROM THE SEA. From The Black Riders and Other Lines. Stephen Crane. APN-2; NAAL-2; NoP-4; TAP *Fr.* The Black Riders [and Other Lines].

Black Riviera, The. Mark Jarman. NAmP90; WeT

Black Rock of Kiltearn. Andrew Young. FaBoTw; RB

Black Rocks. Charles Hubert Sisson. DiPo

Black Rook in Rainy Weather. Sylvia Plath. LiTM; NAAL-2; NoP-4; Poetr

Black Sampson, The. Josephine D. Henderson Heard. CBWP-4

Black Samson of Brandywine. Paul Laurence Dunbar. NAAAL

Black shadow stalks behind the window; last year it stalked right across / the ceiling, A. Children of the Wind. Betti Alver, *Estonian.* CEEP, *tr. by* Ivar Ivask

Black Shawl, The. Lotte Moos. NBrP

Black Sheep, The. Gojko Djogo, *Serbo-Croatian.* AF, *tr. by* Michael March *and* Dušan Puvaić

Black Silk. Tess Gallagher. FaBoWP

Black Sister. Kattie M. Cumbo. BlSi

Black skin against bright green. Black Sister. Kattie M. Cumbo. BlSi

Black Soap. Sandra McPherson. VCAP

Black Soldier Remembers, A. Horace Coleman. CDa

Black Soldier's Civil War Chant. *Unknown. See* Negro Soldier's Civil War Chant.

Black spaces, The. Anita Virgil. HA

Black Spiders. Kathleen Jamie. FaBoTC

Black Spring. Innokenty Fiodorovich Annensky, *Russian.* NNPT, *tr. by* Robert Lowell

Black Star Line. Henry Dumas. PoBA

Black Stone on Top of a White Stone. César Vallejo, *Spanish.* NNPT, *tr. by* Thomas Merton

Black summer, black Vermont. The Mountain. Hayden Carruth. AFr

Black swallows swooping or gliding. The Skaters. John Gould Fletcher. KaS; MoAmPo

Black Swan, The. Randall Jarrell. CMoP; PoE

Black swans with wings over their eyes. For Martin Luther King. Charles Fort. LTA

Black Tambourine. Hart Crane. InPK-6; InPS-3; MeMAP; NoAM; OxBA; OxBSP; TAP

Black Tower, The. W. B. Yeats. CMoP

Black Train, The. Thomas McGrath. GM

Black Trumpeter. Henry Dumas. PoBA

Black velvet flecked with silver points. Dog-watch. Neil Harries. SpW

Black Venus of the Dead, what Sun of Night. Elegy for Dylan Thomas. Dame Edith Sitwell. PoA

Black village of gravestones. Heptonstall. Ted Hughes. OxAEP-2

Black Warrior. Norman Jordan. PoBA

Black was the without eye. Two Legends. Ted Hughes. *Fr.* Crow. PoE

Black water. White waves. Furrows snowcapped. Seamus Heaney. NoAM *Fr.* Station Island.

Black Winter. Frank Stewart. CDa

Black within, and red without. A Chimney. Mother Goose. OxNR; ReMoGo

Black Woman. Naomi Long Madgett. BlSi; GT; ISC; PoBA

Black Woman. Léopold Sédar Senghor, *French*. TTY, *tr. by* Anne Atik

Black Woman Throws a Tantrum. Nayo-Barbara Watkins. NBV

Black—yes, but you are beautiful, O Nature's. The Beautiful Slave. Giovanni Battista Marino, *Italian*. ItIP

Blackberries. Yusef Komunyakaa. NAmP90

Blackberry, The. Norman Nicholson. MoBrPo

Blackberry Blossoms. Lizette Woodworth Reese. SDW

Blackberry Eating. Galway Kinnell. InPK-6; NIP-4; PiM; SoSe-8

Blackberry-Picking. Seamus Heaney. ChAP

Blackberry Sweet. Dudley Randall. HAP; ISC; InPS-3; KaS; SAGP; SoSe-8; WeW-3
   (Black Magic.) PoBA

Blackberry Winter ("If the lady hath any loveliness, let it die"), *see also* Blackberry Winter ("If there be a power of sweetness, let it lie"). John Crowe Ransom. OxBA; PoRA

Blackberrying. Sylvia Plath. HAP; HCAP; NAAL-2; NOBA; NYBP; NoAM; PoPoPo

Blackbird, The. Dinah Maria Mulock Craik. BoTP

Blackbird, The. Phyllis Drayson. BoTP

Blackbird, The. William Ernest Henley. MoBrPo *Fr.* Echoes. (To A. D.) HoPM

Blackbird, The. *Unknown.* NOIV

Blackbird, The. Humbert Wolfe. BoTP; NOxBChV

Blackbird by Belfast Lough, The. *Unknown, Early Irish.* IIP, *tr. by* Frank O'Connor

Blackbird calls in grief, The. *Unknown.* NOIV

Blackbird: Elegy for William Gordon Calvert. Barry MacSweeney. NBrP

Blackbird feeds his fire. Outside, a quick 30 below. (LL) Christmas Comes to Moccasin Flat. James Welch. PaTW

Blackbird of Derrycairn, The. *Unknown, Irish.* BIrV, *tr. by* Austin Clarke

Blackbird sat / In the cedar-limbs, The. (LL) Thirteen Ways of Looking at a Blackbird. Wallace Stevens. CMoP; HCAP; HeIP-4; InPK-6; InPS-3; LiTM; MoP; NAAL-2; NOBA; NoAM; PoE; Poetr; RB; SAmP; TAP; TFi

Blackbird Singing, A. Ronald Stuart Thomas. OBWVE

Blackbird, singing on the highest branch / Of the oak. Argentarius, *Greek.* GrAn, *tr. by* Fleur Adcock

Blackbird whistling / Or just after, The. Wallace Stevens. *See* Thirteen Ways of Looking at a Blackbird.

Blackbird's Field, The. Vasco [or Vasko] Popa, *Serbo-Croatian.* Battle on the Blackbird's Field, The. PoSu, *tr. by* Anne Pennington

Blackboard is erased in the attic, The. Rain Moving In. John Ashbery. NoP-4

Blackboard's white turned dark, The; I. The Relief of Myopia. U. A. Fanthorpe. Spl

Blackbottom. Toi Derricotte. GT; LTA; NAmP90; PBCAP; UnSA ("Whose very existence / tore us down to the human.") (LL) UnSA

Blackcock, The [or The Black Cock]. Joanna Baillie. WoRP

Blacken thy heavens, Jove. Prometheus. Goethe, *German.* AWP, *tr. by* John S. Dwight

Blackened and bleeding, helpless, panting, prone. Chicago. Bret Harte. APN-2; AiP

Blackfriars. Eleanor Farjeon. OxBChV

Blackgoldblueswoman. Kirk Hall. NBV

Blackie, The Electric Rembrandt. Thom Gunn. PFE

Blackie Thinks of His Brothers. Stanley Crouch. GT; PoBA

Black'm saut'm rough'm glower'm saw. Riddle. *Unknown.* FaBoVe

Blackman came walking I. Dreadwalk. Dennis Scott. HCP

Blackness. Primer for Blacks. Gwendolyn Brooks. ISC

Blackness of one quarter lights up the mauve of three, The. The Northland in Cold. Li Ho, *Chinese.* CoBCP, *tr. by* Burton Watson

Blacks in frame houses. Song: I Want a Witness. Michael S. Harper. LTA; UnSA

Blackshawled women of New Mexico, The. Old Women beside a Church. Keith Wilson. Poetsp

Blacksmith. B. K. Pyke. BoTP

Blacksmith Pain. Otto Julius Bierbaum, *German.* AWP, *tr. by* Jethro Bithell

Blacksmiths, The. *Unknown.* FaBoVe; MiEL; RB ("Swart swarthy smiths besmattered with smoke.") RB

Blacksmiths, The. *Unknown. See* Smoke-Blackened Smiths.

Blacksmith's boy went out with a rifle, The. Legend. Judith Wright. NOBAu; NTP; RB

Blacksmith's quite a logical man, The. Palladas, *Greek.* GrAn, *tr. by* Tony Harrison

Blackstone Rangers, The. Gwendolyn Brooks. NoAM; PoBA

Blackthorn. Euros Bowen, *Welsh.* OBWVE, *tr. by the author*

Blackwoman Poems. Don L. Lee. "Soft: the way her eyes view her children." MBE

Blackwood's Edinburgh Magazine, 13 275. Caroline Anne Bowles. "There is a tongue in every leaf." Ro

Bladder Song. Leonard Nathan. BLT

"Blade better, A." Waldere 2. *Unknown, Anglo-Saxon.* ASW, *tr. by* Kevin Crossley-Holland

Blade days—, The. Invisible Autumn. Joseph Ceravolo. FTOS

Blade licks out and acts, A. Thomas Kinsella. BiHa *Fr.* A Technical Supplement.

Blade of Grass Sings to the River, The. Leah Goldberg. TrJP, *tr. by* Robert Friend; MHP, *tr. by* Ruth Finer Mintz *Fr.* Songs of the Stream.

Blade touches the fish heart, over, The. Gutting the Salmon. Robert Adamson. BMAP

Blades of Grass, The. Stephen Crane. MoAmPo *Fr.* The Black Riders [and Other Lines].

Blades of light slide under my eyelids. Awakening to Snow. Sylvia Kantaris. AYFP

Bladyn's Song of Cloten. Charles Montague Doughty. PoEL-5 *Fr.* The Dawn in Britain.

Blah, Blah, Blah. Ira Gershwin. OBAL

Blair Peach died with a broken head. Paul Evans. NBrP *Fr.* The Sofa Book.

Blake Leads a Walk on the Milky Way. Nancy Willard. OBCA

Blake shuts his eyes. Life Mask. Charles Brasch. PeNZ

Blam! Blam! Blam! Pow! Blam! Pow! For a Black Poet. Gerald William Barrax. NBV

Blame me not, Sweet, if here and there. Alibi. Arthur Guiterman. BXAP

Blame Not My Cheekes. Thomas Campion. AAS; SCGP; UnPo

Blame not my lute, for he must sound [or sssnd or Sownde]. Sir Thomas Wyatt. AAS; EBEV; NAEL-1; OAEL-1; PoE; SCGP; SiPS

Blaming Sons. Ch'ien T'ao, *Chinese.* ChiP, *tr. by* Arthur Waley; ChiPo, *tr. by* Burton Watson

Blaming Sons. T'ao Ch'ien, *Chinese.* CoBCP, *tr. by* Burton Watson

Blanche swears her husband's lovely, when a scald. Upon Blanche. Robert Herrick. PFE

Blancheflour and Jellyflorice. *Unknown.* ESPB

Blank Verse by Charles Lloyd and Charles Lamb. Charles Lamb. London. Ro

Blank Verse Written on the Sea Shore. Hannah Cowley. ECWP

Blanket Hog. Paul B. Janeczko. TLR

Blanket, its weight, while we were growing, The. In the Lungs. Milo De Angelis, *Italian.* NeIt, *tr. by* Lawrence Venuti

Blarney castle. Francis Sylvester Mahony. IIP

Blason, A. Alec Derwent Hope. NOBAu

Blasphemers lewd, and swearers shrewd. Michael Wigglesworth. ColAP *Fr.* The Day of Doom.

Blasphemous wretch! How canst thou think or say. Sarah Fyge Egerton. PEW *Fr.* The Female Advocate Or, An Answer to a Late Satyr.

Blasphemy, A. Rodney Jones. WeW-3

Blasphemy. Sachiko Yoshihara, *Japanese.* WPJ, *tr. by* Kenneth Rexroth and Ikuko Atsumi

Blast of War, The. Shakespeare. *See* Henry V at the Siege of Harfleur.

Blast of wind, a momentary breath, A. The Life of Man. Barnabe Barnes. EBEV *Fr.* A Divine Century of Spiritual Sonnets.

Blasted with sighs, and surrounded with tears. Twicknam [or Twickenham] Garden. Donne. EBEV; ESCV; EnLoPo; FMP; GaP; MeLP; OBGa; PoE; PoEL-2; SCGP; SeCP

Blasting from Heaven. Philip Levine. CoAP; WeT

Blasts of Autumn as they scatter round, The. Written in October. Charlotte Smith. NoP-4

Blasts rip Newspaper Gray [or grey] Mannahatta's mid day Air Spires. Friday the Thirteenth. Allen Ginsberg. NNaP

Blatant as factory buildings. Marina Ivanovna Tsvetayeva. PBWP *Fr.* Poem of the End.

Blaze two red eyes as hot as cooking-coals. (LL) Dog. John Crowe Ransom. InPS-3; OBAL

Blazing fire and Christmas treat. (LL) The Garden Year. Sara Coleridge. ACTP; CTV; ChAP; FaBoBe; OTCP; OxBChV

Blazing in darkness, all they wish to see. (LL) The Magi. Louise Glück. PoA

Blazing in Gold and quenching in Purple. Emily Dickinson. NTP

Blazing noon, fierce, unrelenting noon!, The. William Hosack. *Fr.* The Isle of Streams; or, the Jamaica Hermit. PBCV

Blazing stanchions and the corporate lights—, The. Euclid Avenue. Harry Clifton. PBCIP

Blazing sun gets cooled, The. Tavern at Sunset. Jonggil Kim, *Korean.* CKP, *tr. by* Jaihiun Kim

Blazoned in brightness, the Little Dipper gleams. (LL) For the Examination at Ho-nan-fu: Songs of the Twelve Months. Li Ho, *Chinese*. CoBCP, *tr. by* Watson, Burton (b. 1925)

Bleach in the foot-bathtub. Sunday Morning, 1950. Irene McKinney. PBCAP

Bleached wood massed in bone piles. Kalaloch. Carolyn Forché. AmPA; NoAM

Bleak the February light. Kingdom of Heaven. Léonie Adams. MoAmPo

Bleat. Barbara Guest. FTOS

Bled / holding on / to details. Monogram 23. Martina Werner, *German*. BoWoP, *tr. by* Rosemarie Waldrop

Bleeberrying. Jonathan Denwood. MoBS

Bleecker Street. Jean Garrigue. TAP

Bleeding. May Swenson. NALW

Bleeding hearts talk of happy days. Today Is Not Like They Said. Kirk Hall. NBV

Bleeding Nun, The. *Unknown*. NOBRP

Bleeding to death. The counter-attack had failed. (LL) Counter-Attack. Siegfried Sassoon. MoBrPo; OxAEP-2; PeFWW; PoFWW; PoWW

Bleeds drop by drop, and pants his life away. (LL) To Mr. Gay, Who Wrote Him a Congratulatory Letter on the Finishing His House. Alexander Pope. NOEC; OBGa

Bleeds with its death-wound, its wound of love for thee! (LL) Serenade of a Loyal Martyr. George Darley. NOBE; OBEV; OBNC; OxAEP-2

Blend of joy and of hopeless surrender, A. (LL) Last Love. Fyodor Ivanovich Tyutchev, *Russian*. LoP, *tr. by* Vladimir Nabokov

Blenheim. John Philips.
War Poetry. NOEC

Bless earth with Thine Advent, O Saviour Christ! *Unknown*. *Fr.* Christ 1. AnOE, *tr. by* Charles W. Kennedy

Bless Him ("Bless Him, O constant companions"). *Unknown, Hebrew*. TrJP, *tr. by* Israel Abrahams

Bless my desert and give back / song for salt. Diane Di Prima. *See* For H.D.

Bless the Lord, all his works in all places of his dominion: bless the Lord, O my soul. (LL) Psalm 103. Bible, *O.T.* AWP; CTV Psalm 103:1–5.

Bless the Lord, O my soul. O Lord my God. Psalm 104. Bible, *O.T.* NAWM-1; TrJP *Fr.* Psalms.

Bless you, bless you. The Price of Giving Too Much. Vanparanar, *Tamil*. PLW, *tr. by* A. K. Ramanujan

Bless you, bless you, burnie-bee [*or* bonnie-bee]. Mother Goose. BoTP; OxNR

Bless you, earth. Earth's Bounty. Auvaiyar, *Tamil*. PLW, *tr. by* A. K. Ramanujan

Bless you, friend. Listen. What She Said to Her Girl Friend When She Returned from the Hills. Kapilar, *Tamil*. PLW, *tr. by* A. K. Ramanujan

Bless you. Listen to me. What She Said to Her Girl Friend, Her Foster-Mother within Earshot. Kapilar, *Tamil*. PLW, *tr. by* A. K. Ramanujan

Bless you, Mother. On the Appeal from the Race of Sheba: II. Léopold Sédar Senghor, *French*. TTY, *tr. by* John Reed *and* Clive Wake

Bless you, Mother, but listen. What Her Friend Said to the Foster-Mother. Kapilar, *Tamil*. PLW, *tr. by* A. K. Ramanujan

Bless you, Mother, listen. What Her Friend Said to the foster-mother (who is guarding her carefully). Kapilar, *Tamil*. PLW, *tr. by* A. K. Ramanujan

Bless your little cotton socks! (LL) The Ram. Selima Hill. EP; NBrP

Bless'd art Thou, O Lord of all. Prayer before Sleep. Alice Lucas. TrJP

Blesse me! what damps are here? how stiffe an aire? The Charnel-house. Henry Vaughan. FSCP

Blesse yee Jehovah: o my Soul, / Jehovah blesse alone, *fr.* Bay Psalm Book. Bible, *O.T. See* Psalm 103.

Blessed above women/ shall Jael the wife of Heber the Kenite be. Bible, *O.T.* WPOW *Fr.* The Song of Deborah. AWP; BoWoP; PBWP *Fr.* Judges.

Blessed angell not a word replies, The. Ludovico Ariosto. OBVE, *tr. by* Sir John Harington *Fr.* Orlando Furioso.

Blessed are all they that put their trust in him. (LL) Psalm 2. Bible, *O.T.* NAAL-1

Blessed are the files marked action in the inward tray. Beatitudes. Bruce Dawe. GI

Blessed are the flabby people at Walgreen's. Beatitude. Claire Bateman. CrSp

Blessed are the man and the woman, *par. by* Stephen Mitchell. Bible, *O.T. See* Psalm 1.

Blessed are the poor in spirit. From the Sermon on the Mount. Bible, *O.T.* CTV *Fr.* Bible O.T., Matthew 5:3–10.

Blessed are the poor[e] in spirit for theirs is the kingdom[e] of heaven. The Beatitudes. Bible, *N.T.* OBVE *Fr.* St. Matthew.

Blessed are the undefiled in the way. Bible, *O.T. See* Psalm 119.37.

Blessed are they. Euripides. ITG, *tr. by* Merwin, W. S. and George E. Dimock Jr. *Fr.* Iphigeneia at Aulis.

Blessed are they who are pleasant to live with—. Wilhelmina Stitch. PoToHe

Blessed are they who sow but do not reap. Soné, *Hebrew*. TrJP, *tr. by* David Kuselewitz

Blessed [*or* Blesst] are your north parts, for all this long time. To Mr I. L. Donne. SeCP

Blessed Art Thou, O Lord. *Unknown*. TrJP, *tr. by* Theodor H. Gaster *Fr.* The Dead Sea Scrolls.

Blessed Assurance. Fanny Crosby. AH

Blessed be my brain. Robin Morgan. CrSp *Fr.* The Network of the Imaginary Mother.

Blessed Be the Holy Will of God. *Unknown, Irish*. TIRV, *tr. by* Douglas Hyde

Blessed be the Paps which Thou hast Sucked. Bible, *N.T.* BXAP; ChIV-2; NOSC, *tr. by* Richard Crashaw *Fr.* St. Luke.
  (Luke 11; Blessed Be the Paps Which Thou Hast Sucked.)

Blessed be thou, levedy. *Unknown*. MiEL

Blessed be you, Oscar! Who deem me worthy of this book. In Honour of Dorian and his Creator. Lionel Pigot Johnson, *Latin*. ADE, *tr. by* Ian Fletcher

Blessed by the day which bids my grief subside. To Mr. William Long, On His Recovery from a Dangerous Illness, 1785. William Hayley. Son

Blessed Comforter Divine. Lydia Huntley Sigourney. AH

Blessed conversion, and a strange, A. The Conversion of S. Paul. George Wither. ChIV-2

Blessed damozel leaned out, The. D. G. Rossetti. AWP; CABP; EBEvV; EBVV; EnVR; ImPo; NAEL-2; NOBE; NOBVV; NoP-4; OAEL-2; OBEV; OBNC; OxAEP-2; PoE; PoEL-5; TFi

Blessed is every one that feareth the Lord. Bible, *O.T. See* The Bible, Psalm 1:1–3.

Blessed Is Everyone. *Unknown*. AH

Blessed Is God. Bible, Apocrypha. TrJP, *tr. by* D. C. Simpson *Fr.* Tobit.

Blessed is he whose life has not tasted of evil. The Chorus sing of the doom of Thebes' royal family. Sophocles, *Greek*. OBCVT, *tr. by* E. R. Dodds

Blessed is the man. The Bible, Psalm 1:1–3. Bible, *O.T.* CTV *Fr.* Psalms.

Blessed Is the Man. Marianne Moore. ChIV-1

Blessed is the man that walketh not in the counsel of the ungodly [*or* wicked]. Psalm 1. Bible, *O.T., Hebrew*. AWP; TrJP *Fr.* Psalms.

Blesséd Lord, What It Is to Be Young. David McCord. KaS; NTCP

Blessed Mary. *Unknown*. OxBSP

Blessed Match, The. Hannah Senesh, *Yiddish*. TrJP

Blessed offender [*or* offendour], who thyself hast [*or* haist] tried [*or* try'd]. To Saint Mary Magdalen. Henry Constable. NoSic; PoEL-2

Blessed poster girl leaned out, The. The Poster Girl. Carolyn Wells. BXAP

Blessed shall he be, that taketh thy chyldren, and throweth them agaynst the stones. Bible, *O.T. See* Psalm 137.

Blessed sister, holy mother, spirit of the fountain. T. S. Eliot. *Fr.* Ash Wednesday [*or* Ash-Wednesday]. MoAmPo; OxBA; VGW

Blessed that flock safe penned in Paradise. Christina Rossetti. WPoS *Fr.* Behold a Shaking.

Blessed the match that was burned. The Blessed Match. Hannah Senesh, *Yiddish*. TrJP

Blessed Trinity have pity! Childless. Giolla Brighde MacNamee, *Irish*. BIrV, *tr. by* Frank O'Connor

Blessed Virgin Compared to the Air We Breathe, The. Gerard Manley Hopkins. NOBVV; PeVV

Blessed with a joy that only she. The Gift of God. Edwin Arlington Robinson. MoAmPo; OxBA

Blessing, The. Carolyn Kizer. MDDM; NMM-2; Poetr

Blessing, A. James Wright. ChAP; CoAmPo; ITG; InPK-6; InPS-3; NAAL-2; NOBA; NoAM; NoP-4; PoE; PoPoPo; Poetr; RaBo; TRP; TwCP; VCAP; WeT
  ("Into blossom.") (LL) ChAP; CoAmPo; NoP-4; PoPoPo

Blessing a Bride and Groom; a Wedding Night Poem. Robert Peters. BXAP

Blessing for the Blessed, A. Laurence Alma-Tadema.
  "When the sun has left the hill-top." BoTP

Blessing his handiwork, his drawbridge closed. Artificer. X. J. Kennedy. TwCP

Blessing in Disguise, A. John Ashbery. ColAP; PoM

Blessing of the Priests. Bible, *O.T. See* Benediction.

Blessing without Company. *Unknown*. BPo

Blessings as rich and fragrant crown your heads. To the Best, and Most Accomplished Couple. Henry Vaughan. PeECV

Blessings in abundance come. The Good-Night, or Blessing. Robert Herrick. CaPo

Blessings [*or* Blessing] on the hand of women! The Hand That Rocks the Cradle Is the Hand That Rules the World. William Ross Wallace. PoLF

Blessings on thee, little man. The Barefoot Boy. John Greenleaf Whittier. APN-1; CTV; FaBoBe; OBAL; OBCA; PoLF

Blessings on thee, little man. John Greenleaf Whittier. *Fr.* The Barefoot Boy. APN-1; FaBoBe; OBAL; OBCA; PoLF

Blesst all that in Him trust. Bible, *O.T.* *See* Psalm 2.

Blest be the day, and blest the month and year. Petrarch. NAWM-1, *tr. by* Joseph Auslander *Fr.* Sonnets to Laura.

("Father in heaven, after each lost day.") NAWM-1, *tr. by* Bernard Bergonzi

Blest be the God of love. Evensong [*or* Even-Song]. George Herbert. ESCV

Blest be the man, who first the method found. To My Brother at St. John's College in Cambridge. Elizabeth Tollet. ECWP

Blest be the thing that brought the shadow hither. (LL) I Heard a Noise and Wishèd for a Sight. Thomas Bateson. EBEV; HAP; OAEL-1

Blest Be the Wondrous Grace. George Barrell Cheever. AH

Blest, Blest and Happy He. Unknown. GBL

Blest he! whose soul exploring Nature's laws. The Honest life. Virgil, *Latin.* OBCVT, *tr. by* Robert Andrews

Blest is the man who hath not walk'd astray, *par. by* Milton. Bible, *O.T.* See Psalm 1.

Blest Is the Man Whose Tender Breast. Abijah Davis. AH

Blest is the tarn which towering cliffs o'ershade. Sara Coleridge. VWP

Blest leaf! whose aromatic gales dispense. Isaac Hawkins Browne. BXAP; UV *Fr.* A Pipe of Tobacco.

Blest Order, which in power dost so excel[l]. The Priesthood. George Herbert. ESCV

Blest pair of Sirens, pledges of Heaven's joy. Milton. *Fr.* At a Solemn Music[k]. EPCY; GTBS-P; HeIP-4; NOBE; OBEV; PoEL-3; SCGP

Blest pair of *Sirens,* pledges of Heav'ns [*or* Heaven's] joy. At a Solemn Music[k]. Milton. EPCY; GTBS-P; HeIP-4; NOBE; OBEV; PoEL-3; SCGP

Blest Poesy! Oh sent to calm. Helen Maria Williams. NOBRP *Fr.* An Address to Poetry.

Blest privacy! Happy retreat, wherein. My Country Audit. Mildmay Fane, 2d Earl of Westmorland. BeJo; NOSC

Blest the infant Babe. Wordsworth. TOF *Fr.* School-Time. FHYEP *Fr.* The Prelude; Growth of a Poet's Mind [1850 vers.]

Blew It. Michael Castro. SeSe

Blight. Arna Bontemps. ColAP

Blight. Ralph Waldo Emerson. APN-1; NCAP; NOBA

Blight of Love, The. Mary E. Tucker. CBWP-1

Blight rests in your face, The. To a Publisher. . . Cut-out. Imamu Amiri Baraka. NeAP

Blighted apples will not shine. Apple Blight. Paul Zimmer. VGW

Blighter that is at the end of the sea, The. Fernando Pessoa, *Portuguese.* PeSAV, *tr. by* Charles Eglington

Blighters. Siegfried Sassoon. CMoP; FaBoTw; MoP; NoAM; OxBSP; PoFWW; PoWW

("To mock the riddled corpses round Bapaume.") (LL) PoFWW

Blind. John Kendrick Bangs. PoToHe

Blind. Norman V. Pearce. PoToHe

Blind Adolphus. Angela McCabe. AmPA

Blind among enemies, O worse than chains. Milton. KSG *Fr.* Samson Agonistes.

Blind Bartimaeus at the gates. Henry Wadsworth Longfellow. ChIV-2

Blind Beggar, The. Unknown. AmFP

Blind Boy, The. Colley Cibber. GTBS-P; NOEC; OxBChV

Blind Boy's Pranks, The. William Thom. OBEV

Blind but Happy. Fanny Crosby. CTV

Blind child / Guided by his mother, A. Takarai Kikaku, *Japanese.* OHPJ, *tr. by* Kenneth Rexroth

Blind clouds, poisonous vapors hang over this mountain city. Overjoyed at Soviet Russia's Entry into the War. Liu Ya-tzu, *Chinese.* SuSp, *tr. by* Wu-chi Liu

Blind fortune, if thou wants a guide. Fortune's Legacy. Unknown. NOSC

Blind landscape gropes its way, The. On Opening an Old House. Tymoteusz Karpowicz, *Polish.* CEEP, *tr. by* Zak, Ewa

Blind Love. Shakespeare. GTBS-P *Fr.* Sonnets.

(Sonnet 148.)

Blind Man, The, *a fragment.* Anne Batten Cristall. ECWP

Blind Man, The. Ksenya Nekrasova, *Russian.* TCRP, *tr. by* Vera Rich

Blind Man, The. Margaret Elizabeth Sangster. PoToHe

Blind Man, The. Konstantin Mikhailovich Simonov, *Russian.* TCRP, *tr. by* Lubov Yakovleva

Blind Man, The. Yaroslav Vasilevich Smelyakov, *Russian.* TCRP, *tr. by* Simon Franklin

Blind Man, The. Judith Wright. Country Dance. BMAP; CBAP

Blind Man at the Fair, The. Joseph Campbell. AWP

Blind man, blind man. Mother Goose. OxNR

Blind Man Lay beside the Way. Unknown. AS

Blind man selling brushes, A. The Blind Man Who Sells Brushes. David James. CMAP

Blind Man Who Sells Brushes, The. David James. CMAP

Blind man's, The. Raymond Roseliep. HA

Blind Men and the Elephant, The. John Godfrey Saxe. BLPA; BoTP; CTV; FaBoBe; OBCA; OTCP; PoToHe

("Not one of them has seen!") (LL) CTV

Blind Musicians, the blind musicians, The. Unknown, Chinese. TAL, *tr. by* Robert Payne

Blind Old Woman. Clarence Major. PoBA

Blind poet, fiddler, Raftery. For Raftery. Alan Alexander. NOBAu

Blind Poet Looks at the World Outside, A. Nguyễn Đình Chi(cfstilde;e)u, *Vietnamese.* AVP, *tr. by* Huỳnh Sanh Thông

Blind Samson. William Plomer. PeSA

Blind Sheep, The. Randall Jarrell. NYBP; OBAL

Blind Solo, after A Love Supreme. Michael S. Weaver. UnSA

Blind Steersmen. Francis Ernest Kobina Parkes. PBA

Blind Thamyris, and blind Maeonides. Ode to the Human Heart. Edward Laman Blanchard. NOBL

Blind Tramp, The. Lilian Bowes-Lyon. WPN

Blind with love, my daughter. Pain for a Daughter. Anne Sexton. Poetr

Blinded Bird, The. Thomas Hardy. CMoP; LiTM

Blindest buzzard that I know, The. A Sketch. Christina Rossetti. GTBS-P; VWP

Blindfold I should to Myra run. Chloe and Myra. Lady Sophia Burrell. LW *Fr.* Chloe and Myra.

Blindman placed, The. May Swenson. PFE

Blindman's Buff. Peter Viereck. LiTM; MoAmPo

Blindness. Delmira Agustini, *Spanish.* PBWP, *tr. by* D. M. Pettinella

Blindness of Samson, The. Milton. ImPo *Fr.* Samson Agonistes. FHYEP; OAEL-1; PoEL-3

"I, dark in light, exposed."

Blindness we may forgive, but baseness we will smite. (LL) An Ode in Time of Hesitation. William Vaughn Moody. APN-2; CBCWP; OxBA

Blink, a twinkling—I'll be forty soon!, A. Forty. Hoàng Trinh, *Vietnamese.* AVP, *tr. by* Huỳnh Sanh Thông

Blinkered Mind, The. Amy Witting. NOBAu

Blisful lyf, a paisible and a swete, A. Chawcer upon this fyfte meter of the second book. Boethius, *Latin.* OBCVT, *tr. by* Geoffrey Chaucer

Bliss. George Johnston. NOBC

Bliss, The. Tanka. Yosano Tekkan, *Japanese.* MJT, *tr. by* Makoto Ueda

Bliss of man, The (could pride that blessing find). Alexander Pope. NOEC *Fr.* An Essay on Man.

Bliss on high in the heavenly home. (LL) Lo! I have learned of the loveliest of lands. Unknown. AnOE; OAEL-1, *tr. by* Charles W. Kennedy

Blisses about my pilgrimage as pain. (LL) Hap. Thomas Hardy. AWP; CABP; CMoP; EBVV; EnVR; GSo; ImPo; MoBrPo; NAEL-2; NoAM; NoP-4; OAEL-2; PBMP; PFE; Poetr; Son

Blistered and dry was the desert I trod. The Palm. Roy Campbell. MoBrPo

Blithe Fancy lightly builds with airy hands. After Reading Shakspere. Edwin Markham. APN-2

Blizzard. Bella Akhatovna Akhmadulina, *Russian.* TCRP, *tr. by* Albert C. Todd

Blizzard, The. Roger McDonald. NOBAu

Blizzard of Sixty-Six, The. William Daniel Ehrhart. CDa

Blizzard sweeps the streets, A. Aleksandr Blok, *Russian.* TCRP, *tr. by* Geoffrey Thurley

Blizzard wrapped the earth in gloom, The. Winter Night. Boris Pasternak, *Russian.* TCRP, *tr. by* Yakov Hornstein

Blizzards blow and blow, The. To Make Birds Sing. Vladimir Alekseievich Soloukhin, *Russian.* TCRP, *tr. by* Daniel Weissbort

Blizzards of paper. Unlearning to Not Speak. Marge Piercy. CrSp

Blkfern-jungal. Aileen Corpus. BMAP

Bloated / on rotten eggs. The Skunk. Philip Dow. BXAP

Block City. Robert Louis Stevenson. CTV; NTCP

("Coming and going with presents and things!") (LL) NOxBChV

Blockhouse. Olga Kirsch, *Afrikaans.* PeSA, *tr. by* Jack Cope

Blocking the Pass. Charles Madge. FaBoMo

Blocks. Frank O'Hara. HCAP; LCAP-2; SPE

Blocks, The/ which are the buildings and walls. Comforted by Limestone. Edward Dorn. NOBA *Fr.* Oxford.

Blodwen, / Her name like the hours. Her Name like the Hours. Gloria Evans Davies. OBWVE

Bloke I know came rolling home as shickered as he could be, A. Shickered As He Could Be. *Unknown.* NOBAu

Blond. Joseph De Roche. HeIP-4

Blond Bombshell. Lynn Emanuel. NAmP90

Blond-haired, green-eyed, Italian girl. Amazone. Mary Jo Bona. UnSA

Blond light blew away grayness, shadows, mists. Facing Bonnard. Aleksander Wat, *Polish.* BLT, *tr. by* Czeslaw Milosz *and* Leonard Nathan

Blond stones all round-sided. Morning at Point Dume. May Swenson. DiPo

Blonde hair at the edge of the pavement. Mitching. Michael Smith. CIP-2

Blonde neighbor lady tells my wife, The. The Opposite of Green. Alvin Aubert. ISC

Blonde perfume of the painted girl! Opoponax. Theodore Wratislaw. ADE

Blonde White Women. Patricia Smith. GT; UnSA

Blood. Ray Bremser. NeAP

Blood, The. Nina Cassian, *Romanian.* CEEP, *tr. by* Marguerite Dorian *and* Elliott B. Urdang; WPOW, *tr. by* Laura Schiff

Blood. Naomi Shihab Nye. EC3; NMM-2; UnSA
("True Arab knows how to catch a fly in his hands, A.") EC3

Blood. Renate Wood. CMAP

Blood. Franz Wright. LCAP-2

Blood and the Storm. Jure Kastelan, *Croatian.* CEEP, *tr. by* Peter Kastmiler

Blood, blood! The lines of every printed sheet. George Henry Boker. APN-2

Blood falling in drops to the earth. Where Are the Men Seized in This Wind of Madness? Alda do Espírito Santo, *Portuguese.* PBMAP; TTY; WPOW, *tr. by* Alan Ryder

Blood flowed on Vietnam's soil as we rose up. A Deathless Autumn. Ái Lan, *Vietnamese.* AVP, *tr. by* Huỳnh Sanh Thông

Blood flows from my brow, the. "Wintry Dawn." Meir Wieseltier, *Hebrew.* IP, *tr. by* Bargad, Warren and Stanley Chyet; IP, *tr. by* Warren Bargad *and* Stanley F. Chyet *Fr.* Wintry Dawn.

Blood flows in me, but what does it have to do. Living by the Red River. James Wright. NNaP

Blood gushes out of the throat. Slaughterhouse. Masako Takiguchi, *Japanese.* WPJ, *tr. by* Kenneth Rexroth *and* Ikuko Atsumi

Blood in our pockets. (LL) The Subway Witnesses. Lorenzo Thomas. GT

Blood in the Desert's Eyes, The. Syl Cheney-Coker.
Philosopher, The. PBMAP

Blood only blood is able to beat to strike the right note. Whispered. Jiri Orten, *Czech.* AF, *tr. by* Lyn Coffin

Blood or Color. Marjorie Welish. FTOS

Blood-red flower of revolution, The. (LL) Roses and Revolutions. Dudley Randall. BPo; CoAmPo; PoBA; TAP

Blood-red the aloes flank. Farm Gate. Uys Krige, *Afrikaans.* PeSA, *tr. by* Uys Krige *and* Jack Cope

Blood searching in his head without metaphor, The. (LL) Letters and Other Worlds. Michael Ondaatje. NoP-4

Blood-shotten through the bleak gigantic trees. A Winter Twilight. John Banister Tabb. APN-2

Blood-Sister. Adrienne Rich. NAAL-2

Blood-stained, continue cutting weeds and shade. (LL) Reapers. Jean Toomer. BPo; ColAP; GT; HAP; MoP; NoAM; NoP-4; PoBA; Poetr; SoSe-8; TRP; WeW-3

Blood stains how to remove from cotton. Robert Francis. AFr

Blood-strained Banders, The. *Unknown.* AmFP

Blood thudded in my ears. I scuffed. First Confession. X. J. Kennedy. CoAmPo

Bloodhounds look like sad old judges, The. Nice Day for a Lynching. Kenneth Patchen. APAD

Bloods and bucks of this lewd town, The. Horace. *See* 1.25: Ribald Romeos Less and Less Berattle ("Parcius iunctas quatiunt fenestras").

Bloodshot. Tanka. Miyazawa Kenji, *Japanese.* MJT, *tr. by* Makoto Ueda

Bloody and a sudden end, A. John Kinsella's Lament for Mrs. Mary Moore. W. B. Yeats. CMoP; LiTM; OAEL-2; RB

Bloody battle of Bothwell Hill, The. (LL) The Battle of Bothwell Bridge. *Unknown.* OxBB

Bloody Brother, The. John Fletcher *and others.*
Song. PoEL-2

Bloody Fable. Desanka Maksimovic, *Serbo-Croatian.* HSix, *tr. by* Charles Simic

Bloody Hand. Ciaran Carson. PBCIP

Bloody men are like bloody buses. Wendy Cope. APAD; NoP-4

Bloody Pause. "Astra." BrRo

Bloody Sire, The. Robinson Jeffers. CMoP; ImPo; LiTM; PoA

Bloody trunk [*or* Bloudy trunck] of him who did possess[e], The. The Fall. Sir Richard Fanshawe. NOSC; OBVE *Fr.* Il Pastor Fido.

Bloom finished, The. Tanka. Sasaki Yukitsuna, *Japanese.* MJT, *tr. by* Makoto Ueda

Bloom—is Result—to meet a Flower. Emily Dickinson. PoEL-5

Bloom, O my rose! The Gardener. Walter Savage Landor. GaP

Bloom on the fruit is perfect, The. At Les Deux Magots. Maura Dooley. LW

Bloom Street. Angela McCabe. AmPA

Bloomingdale Papers, The. Hayden Carruth.
Words for My Daughter from the Asylum. MoLi

Bloomingdale's. Marilyn Hacker. DeD *Fr.* Love, Death and the Changing of the Seasons.
(Bloomingdale's I.) CPO

Blooms such as wither at finger-touch. Brian Coffey. BIrV *Fr.* Muse, June, Related.

Bloomsbury Snapshot. Connie Bensley. OBCoV

Blossom, The. William Blake. CTAV; FHYEP; Ro *Fr.* Songs of Innocence.

Blossom [*or* Blossome], The. Donne. AWP; ESCV; ImPo; MeLP; NAEL-1; SCGP; SeCP; UnPo

Blossom. Mary Oliver. CrSp

Blossom. May Probyn. VWP

Blossom, The. Shakespeare. OBEV *Fr.* Love's Labour's Lost.
(Love's Perjuries.) OBEV

Blossom into a rose as you are bidden. Valentine Ackland. WPN

Blossom. Is that thing alive? I hear a famisht howl. (LL) Winters close, Springs open, no child stirs, The. John Berryman. NoP-4

Blossoming. Laurie Duesing. DeD

Blossoming of the Solitary Date-Tree, The. Coleridge. CDLP

Blossoms. Frank Dempster Sherman. OBCA

Blossoms bright, the moon dark, shadowed in thin mist. Tune: Deva-like Barbarian. Li Yü, *Chinese.* CoBCP, *tr. by* Burton Watson

Blossoms crowd the branches: too beautiful to endure. Spring-gazing Song. Hsüeh T'ao, *Chinese.* BoWoP, *tr. by* Carolyn Kizer

Blossoms have fallen, The. Princess Shikishi, *Japanese.* BoWoP, *tr. by* Donald Keene

Blossoms of the wood have scattered their spring crimson, Tune: "Crows Crying at Night." Li Yü, *Chinese.* CoBCP, *tr. by* Burton Watson

Blossoms on the pear. Buson, *Japanese.* TAL, *tr. by* Harold G. Henderson

Blot in the 'Scutcheon, A. Robert Browning.
Earl Mertoun's Song. OBEV

Blotto Motto. Homer. *Fr.* Odyssey. NAWM-1, *tr. by* Robert Fitzgerald

Blow, blow, blow. (LL) Blow, Northern Wind. *Unknown.* GBL; OBEV

Blow! blow! The winds are so hoarse they cannot blow! The Winter Storms. Sir William Davenant. NOSC

Blow, blow, thou winter wind. Song. Shakespeare. AWP; CH; CTC; EBEvV; GBL; GTBS-P; ImPo; InPS-3; NAEL-1; NOBE; NoSic; OAEL-1; OBEV; OxAEP-1; PoEL-2; SCGP *Fr.* As You Like It.

Blow, blow, ye spicy breezes. Prospect. Ambrose Bierce. APN-2; OBAL *Fr.* The Devil's Dictionary.

Blow, Boys, Blow [*or* Blow, Bullies, Blow]. *Unknown.* FaBoVe

Blow, Bugle, Blow. Tennyson. ImPo; NOBE; OBEV; UnPo *Fr.* The Princess.
("And murmuring of innumerable bees.") (LL) GTBS-P
(Bugle Song, The.) CTV
("Dying, dying, dying.") (LL) CTV
(Songs from The Princess.) NoP-4
("Splendour falls on castle walls, The.") ChAP

Blow, Northern Wind. *Unknown.* GBL; OBEV

Blow, northerne wind. *Unknown.* MiEL

Blow out the candles of your cake. For K. R. on Her Sixtieth Birthday. Richard Wilbur. APAD

Blow out the jiving smoke the plastik mix the huddling straw of the dying mind. Mission Street Manifesto. Juan Felipe Herrera. PaTW

"Blow out the light," they said, they said. Temper. Rose Fyleman. OxBChV

Blow softly down the valley. The King of Ireland's Cairn. "Ethna Carbery." WPE

Blow the Candle Out ("Come all ye jolly boatsman boys"). *Unknown.* AmFP

Blow the fire, blacksmith. Mother Goose. OxNR

Blow the Man Down. *Unknown.* AS

Blow the Man Down ("I'll put on my boots and I'll blow the man down"). *Unknown.* AmFP

Blow the Winds, I-Ho. *Unknown.* OxBoLi

Blow, thou wind of God! (LL) Ode to the Northeast Wind. Charles Kingsley. FaPoR; OxAEP-2

Blow, West Wind. Robert Penn Warren. ColAP

Blow, wind, blow! and go, mill, go! Mother Goose. OxNR

Blow, winds, and crack your cheek! rage! blow! Lear's Speech to the Storm. Shakespeare. OxAEP-1 *Fr.* King Lear.

Blow, winds, and crack your cheeks! Rage. Shakespeare. SAGP *Fr.* King Lear.

Blow Ye Winds in the Morning. *Unknown.* AmFP

Blow Your Trumpet, Gabriel. *Unknown.* APN-2

Blow Your Trumpets. Donne. *Fr.* Holy Sonnets. ESCV *Fr.* Holy Sonnets.

Blowflies Buzz, The. *Unknown, Aborigine.* NOBAu, *tr. by* Catherine H. Berndt

 (Djalbarmiwi's Song.) CBAP

Blowin' in the Wind. "Bob Dylan." KaS

Blowing hard at the bus stop. Transit. Margaret Avison. FaBoWP

Blown apart by loss, she let herself go. Rita Dove. FFC

Blown from night and the North. (LL) Chorus: "What man is he that yearneth." Sophocles, *Greek.* OBCVT, *tr. by* A. E. Housman

Blown from Sleep's trumpet. (LL) Louse Hunting. Isaac Rosenberg. EBEV; NAEL-2; NSI; NoAM; NoP-4; OxAEP-2; OxBTC; PeFWW

Blown[e] in the morning, thou shalt fade ere noon. A Rose. Sir Richard Fanshawe. AWP; OBEV; PoEL-2 *Fr.* Il Pastor Fido.

Blown in the wind / the silver river. Inscribed on a Snowscape. Yün Shou-p'ing, *Chinese.* CoBLCP, *tr. by* Jonathan Chaves

Blown sand heaps on me, that none may learn, The. Pelicans in the Wilderness (A Grave near Halfa). Rudyard Kipling. PeFWW *Fr.* Epitaphs of the War [1914–1918]. OBWP

Blows birthday candles for the world. (LL) The Birth of Tragedy. Irving Layton. MoCV; NoAM; NoP-4

Blows the Wind Today. To S. R. Crockett. Robert Louis Stevenson. CH; EBVV; NOBE; OBNC

Blows the wind today, and the sun and the rain are flying. To S. R. Crockett. Robert Louis Stevenson. SCGP

Blue. Michael C. Blumenthal. CMAP

Blue. Sally Croft. DeD

Blue. Christopher Gilbert. FYAP *Fr.* Beginning by Example.

Blue: aconite, deadly; / Iris, a grape. The Blue Garden. Barbara Howes. WeT

Blue and the Gray, The. Francis Miles Finch. APN-2; BLPA; CBCWP; FaBoBe

Blue and White. Mary Elizabeth Coleridge. OBEV

Blue and white. Poems at the Porthole. Lorine Niedecker. FTOS

Blue and white tie arrived at the man's neck through, The. Tell Us, Josephine. Ron Padgett. FTOS

Blue Angel, The. Allen Ginsberg. BB

Blue Animals, The. Jon Anderson. AmPA

Blue Arm. Bernard Spencer. NoAM

Blue as the blowpipe's petal of flame. Blue Flag. Dorothy Donnelly. NYBP

Blue-Beard's Closet. Rose Terry Cooke. APN-2

Blue Bell Boy. *Unknown.* ReMoGo

Blue Bird. Ha'un Han, *Korean.* CKP, *tr. by* Jaihiun Kim

Blue-Bird, The. Herman Melville. NOBA

Blue Black. Bloke Modisane. PBA

Blue Blood. James Stephens. MoBrPo; OBCoV; OBMV

Blue, blue is the grass about the river. The Beautiful Toilet. Ezra Pound, *tr. fr. Mei Sheng, 140 B.C.* OBVE

Blue Blue Your Collar. *Unknown, Chinese.* CoBCP, *tr. by* Burton Watson

Blue Bog Children. Roger Weingarten. AmPA

Blue Bonnets over the Border. Sir Walter Scott. OxBS *Fr.* The Monastery.

 (Border Ballad.)

Blue Booby lives, The. James Tate. AmPA; NoAM; SPE

Blue Book 18 Pages 1–4. Steve Benson. FTOS

Blue boughs, green fruit. The Furnished Room. James Merrill. NOBA

Blue Bowl, The. Blanche Bane Kuder. BLPA; FaBoBe

Blue City, The. Alfred Wellington Purdy. NoP-4

Blue Clay. Ellease Southerland. GT

Blue Coat, A. Gertrude Stein. PBWP *Fr.* Tender Buttons.

Blue crane fishing in Cooloola[h]'s twilight, The. At Cooloolah. Judith Wright. BMAP; MoBrPo

Blue Crêpe. Asa Benveniste. NBrP

Blue Cuckoo. *Unknown.* *Fr.* Hunter Poems of the Yoruba. RB, *tr. by* Ulli Beier

blue day, A. March. Elizabeth Jane Coatsworth. AYFP

Blue day / a blue jay, A. March. Elizabeth Jane Coatsworth. Spl

Blue Day Journey, The. Gwyn Jones. OBWVE

Blue duiker, left hindleg, The. A Piece of Earth. Douglas Livingstone. PeSAV

Blue eagle and the demon of the steppes, The. The Staircase with a Hundred Steps. Benjamin Péret, *French.* SPE, *tr. by* David Gascoyne

Blue Elliptic. Joy Harjo. NAmP90

Blue expanse of hyacinthine bloom, The. Memories of a Dorset Childhood in the 1730's. Thomas Cole. *Fr.* The Life of Hubert. NOEC

Blue-eyed Girl. *Unknown.* AmFP

Blue-eyed Mary. Mary Eleanor Wilkins Freeman. OBCA

Blue Flag. Dorothy Donnelly. NYBP

Blue-Fly, The. Robert Graves. APo; CMoP; NAEL-2; NYBP; NoAM; PFE

Blue Fly. Joaquim Maria Machado de Assis, *Portuguese.* TTY, *tr. by* Frances Ellen Buckland

Blue Frog Kisses My Sweetheart. Ljiljana Djurdjic, *Serbo-Croatian.* HSix, *tr. by* Charles Simic

Blue Funk. Joel Oppenheimer. NeAP

Blue Garden, The. Barbara Howes. WeT

Blue-geese, white-geese, you may say. Hilda Doolittle. NOBA *Fr.* The Flowering of the Rod.

Blue Gene. Lawson Fusao Inada. MoNo

Blue Girls. John Crowe Ransom. CMoP; ColAP; GBL; MeMAP; MoAmPo; NoAM; NoP-4; RB; TAP; VGW; WeW-3

 (Vanity of the Blue Girls, The.) FuPo

Blue Glass. Fleur Adcock. FaBoWP

Blue go up & blue go down. American Lights, Seen from Off Abroad. John Berryman. LCAP-2; OBAL; OBCoV

Blue-green bamboo, white sand, village on the river. A Trip to the Village of the River of White Sand. Tao-chi, *Chinese.* CoBLCP, *tr. by* Jonathan Chaves

Blue Guide. Stephen Yenser. BAP-95

Blue Gulf all around us. The Burial of the Dane. Henry Howard Brownell. PAR

Blue heavens have supplanted grass and trees. Talking With the Pyramid. Huy Cận, *Vietnamese.* AVP, *tr. by* Huỳnh Sanh Thông

Blue Heron, The. Theodore Goodridge Roberts. NOBC

Blue hill is my desire, The. Hwang Chin-i, *Korean.* PBWP, *tr. by* Ko Won

Blue hills over the north wall;. Li Po. *See* Taking Leave of a Friend.

Blue Horse. Masako Takiguchi, *Japanese.* WPJ, *tr. by* Kenneth Rexroth *and* Ikuko Atsumi

Blue Horses, The. James McAuley. BMAP

Blue Horses. Ed Roberson. GT; PoBA

Blue Hour, The. Margarita Iosifovna Aliger, *Russian.* TCRP, *tr. by* Albert C. Todd

Blue house at Mills Cross, The. Radio Sky. Norman Dubie. NAmP90

Blue ice curdling on the stream, The. (LL) How still, how happy! These [*or* Those] are words. Emily Jane Brontë. BWW; NOBVV; OBNC; SCGP

Blue in the west the mountain stands. Vickery's Mountain. Edwin Arlington Robinson. MoAmPo

Blue is Our Lady's colour. Blue and White. Mary Elizabeth Coleridge. OBEV

Blue is this night of stars. Inquietude. Pauli Murray. BlSi

Blue Island Intersection. Carl Sandburg. MoAmPo

Blue Jay [*or* Bluejay]. Robert Francis. LCAP-2; WeT

Blue Jay. Paul Lake. RA

Blue jay scuffling in the bushes follows, The. On the Move. Thom Gunn. CMoP; HAP; LiTM; NoP-4; OAEL-2; OxAEP-2; OxBTC; PoE; TRP; TwCP

Blue jays in the pines. Robert Spiess. HA

Blue Jeaned Rock Queen in Search of Happiness on a Blind Thursday at 1/3 Speed and Crying, A. A. K. Redwing. VoR

Blue Juniata. Malcolm Cowley.

 Streets of Air, The. PoA

Blue kingfisher dives on you in fire, The. (LL) Colloquy in Black Rock. Robert Lowell. MoAmPo; NAAL-2

Blue laguna rocks and quivers, The. Port of Holy Peter. John Masefield. OBMV

Blue leather harness slips off glistening shoulders. Radiant Silhouette I. John Yau. OpBo

Blue light is the night harbor-slip. Louis Zukofsky. PoE *Fr.* 29 Poems.

Blue light, morning. This Decoration. Hayden Carruth. NNaP

Blue Lights. Thomas Rabbitt. NAmP90

Blue like Death. James Welch. CDW

Blue, limpid water smoothly flows, like oil. The Bạch-đằng River. *Unknown, Vietnamese.* AVP, *tr. by* Huỳnh Sanh Thông

Blue Meridian, The. Jean Toomer.

 Brown River, Smile. PoBA

Blue mist rises from fragrant herbs in the bronze plate. Yang Yi, *Chinese.* SuSp, *tr.* by Jonathan Chaves

Blue mists surround the mountains now. Lines Written on a Farewell View of the Franconia Mountains at Twilight. Henrietta Cordelia Ray. CBWP-3

Blue Monday. Langston Hughes. SAmP

Blue Monday. *Unknown.* AmFP

Blue Monday. Diane Wakoski. NALW; PmAP

Blue Morning Glory. Anne Pitkin. CrSp

Blue Mountain. Roberta Hill Whiteman. VoR

Blue mountains to the north of the walls. Taking Leave of a Friend. Li Po, *Chinese.* RB, *tr.* by Ezra Pound

Blue mouth of the shark, The. Coming. Robert Kelly. PmAP

Blue Mud Shoal. Yang Shih-ch'i. *Fr.* Ten Scenes at the Hsiao Family Stone Ridge. CoBLCP, *tr.* by Jonathan Chaves

Blue of the heaps of beads poured into her breasts. Blue Monday. Diane Wakoski. NALW; PmAP

Blue Paisley Shirt, The. Thomas William Shapcott. BMAP

Blue peaks are swords and lances thrust at clouds. The Bach-đằng River. Tran Minh-tong (King), *Chinese.* AVP, *tr.* by Huynh Sanh Thông

Blue Rapids. Lu Yu, *Chinese.* CoBCP; SuSp, *tr.* by Burton Watson

Blue Ridge. Ellen Bryant Voigt. NoAM

Blue robe on their shoulder[s], A. The Seven Fiddlers. Sebastian Evans. EBVV

Blue Room, The. Richard Edwards. Spl

Blue Room, The. Lorenz Hart. OBAL

Blue Ruth: America. Michael S. Harper. PoBA

Blue saw in the voice and, suddenly controllable beneath the weight. Space in the light said to be where one / comes from. Stephen Ratcliffe. PT *Fr.* Space in the light said to be where one / comes from.

Blue Shade. Aaron Shurin. FTOS

Blue sky blue water. Home. Calvin Forbes. GT

Blue sky spreads over the fleecy, The. Bird. Chi-ha Kim, *Korean.* CKP, *tr.* by Jaihiun Kim

Blue Sleep. Winifred Bryher. PoA

Blue, so blue that eye of sky. Lament. Jacques Rabémanganjara, *French.* NegPo, *tr.* by Ellen Conroy Kennedy

Blue spaces do not see themselves, The. Stepan Petrovich Shchipachov, *Russian.* TCRP, *tr.* by Daniel Weissbort

Blue Sparks in Dark Closets. Richard Snyder. Poetsp

Blue-Stemmed Grass. Thomas Hornsby Ferril. PaTW

Blue Suburban. Howard Nemerov. ColAP

Blue Swallows, The. Howard Nemerov. NoP-4; Poetr

Blue Tanganyika. Lebert Bethune. PoBA

Blue Tango. Michael Van Walleghen. NAmP90

Blue. The green. The river-bed, The. The Scene. Agnes Nemes Nagy, *Hungarian.* PoSu, *tr.* by Bruce Berlind

Blue Tit on a String of Peanuts. Norman MacCaig. CABP; FaBoTC

("Grain of sawdust being sawn / by the minutest of saws.") (LL) FaBoTC

Blue toads are dying all over Minnesota. Walking through a Cornfield in the Middle of Winter I Stumble over a Cow Pie and Think of the Sixties Press. Barbara Harr. BXAP

Blue unsold tongue, if you could talk. The Overturned Lake. Charles Henri Ford. SPE

Blue vein, bright on her temple, pitifully beating, The. (LL) Boy with His Hair Cut Short. Muriel Rukeyser. LiTM; NALW; NoAM; TwCP; VGW; WPE

Blue water; upon it two possible movements. The Landfall. James Dickey. PoA

Blue West, The. Dahlia Ravikovitch, *Hebrew.* PBWP, *tr.* by Chana Bloch

Blue Wing, The. Donald Hall. CoAmPo

Blue Winter. Robert Francis. LCAP-2

Bluebells. Olive Enoch. BoTP

Bluebells. Juliana Horatia Ewing. BoTP

Bluebells. P. A. Ropes. BoTP

Blueberry Man. David Bergman. GLP

Bluebird. Joyce Peseroff. CMAP

Bluebird alights, The. Michael McClintock. HA

Bluebird & / honeymoon over. Spring. Reed Bye. TTTS

Bluegill rises, A. John Wills. HA

Bluejay sails, A. John Wills. HA

Bluejay screeches from a pine. (LL) What Happened Here Before. Gary Snyder. APSN; NNaP; PoM

Blueness of Stars, The. Elizabeth Kirschner. CMAP

Blues. Edward Kamau Brathwaite. GT

Blues. Léon Damas, *French.* NegPo, *tr.* by Ellen Conroy Kennedy

Blues. John Fuller. NOBL

Blues, The. Langston Hughes. TLR

Blues. Sonia Sanchez. GT

Blues. Léopold Sédar Senghor, *French.* PBMAP

Blues. Derek Walcott. GT; SeSe

Blues 1. Barry Wallenstein. SeSe

Blues 2. Barry Wallenstein. SeSe

Blues Ain' Nothin', De. *Unknown.* AS

Blues ain't culture. Liberation / Poem. Sonia Sanchez. NBV

Blues and Bitterness. Lerone Bennett Jr. PoBA

Blues and blues. Remembered. Sterling Plumpp. GT

Blues are the big thing. Raymond Roseliep. HA

Blues at Dawn. Langston Hughes. SAmP

Blues at Lord's, The. Siegfried Sassoon. PeLV

Blues Don't Change, The. Al Young. GT

Blues for an Old Blue. Walker Gibson. NYBP

Blues for Dan Morin. Lawson Fusao Inada. MoNo

Blues for Franks Wooten. Tom Weatherly. NBV

(Blues for Franks Wooten / House of the Lifting of the Head.) GT

Blues for the Lonely. Jeremy Robson. SeSe

Blues for the Nightowl. Elton Glaser. PBCAP

Blues for Warren. Thomas McGrath. AF

Blues in "C." Ron Overton. SeSe

Blues (in Two Parts), The. Val Ferdinand. NBV

Blues is the black o' the face, The. Black Blues. Bloke Modisane. PBA

Blues lady / with the beaded face. Grinding Vibrato. Jayne Cortez. BlSi

Blues meant Swiss-Up, The. Riding Across John Lee's Finger. Stanley Crouch. GT; PoBA

Blues / Never climb a hill. Get Up, Blues. James A Emanuel. PoBA; SeSe

Blues Note. Bob Kaufman. BB; PoBA

("Ray Charles is a dangerous man ('way cross town), / And I love him.") (LL) BB

Blues Today, The. Mae Jackson. PoBA

Blues walk weeps ragtime. In the Tradition / (Not a White Shadow but Black People Will Be Victorious). Imamu Amiri Baraka. MoNo

Bluesman in pungent mood, The. Tobacco Warehouse Blues. Houston A. Baker Jr. SeSe

Bluesman's Blues, A. Lenard D. Moore. ISC

Bluish, pale, The. Moontan. Mark Strand. NYBP

Bluish twilight sinks with dripping dews, The. The Toad. Gertrud Kolmar, *German.* APo, *tr.* by Henry A. Smith

Blurb for *Anna Livia Plurabelle.* James Joyce. OBCoV

Blurb for *Haveth Childers Everywhere,* A. James Joyce. *See* An Advertisement for Finnegans Wake.

Blush and blow, blush and blow. Sad Spring-Song. Sarah Morgan Bryan Piatt. NCAP

Blush is on the flower, and the bloom is on the tree, The. My Own Cáilin Donn. George Sigerson. FaBoBe

Blustery wind is terrible with song, The. October. Vladimir Ivanovich Narbut, *Russian.* TCRP, *tr.* by Lubov Yakovleva

Bo-be-o-bee sang the mouth. Velemir Khlebnikov, *Russian.* TCRP, *tr.* by Gary Kern

Bo-peep / Little Bo-peep. *Unknown.* OxNR

Bo peeper. *Unknown.* OxNR

Boadicea: An Ode. William Cowper. FaPoR

Boadicea often would goad. Limerick. Douglas Catley. PeLi

Board of War has quelled the mutiny, The. To the Minister Liu. Yü Hsüan-chi, *Chinese.* BoWoP, *tr.* by Geoffrey Waters

Boarded the tain there's no getting off. (LL) Metaphors. Sylvia Plath. HeIP-4; InPK-6; Poetr; SoSe-8

Boarder, The. Louis Simpson. InPK-6

Boarders look so good and new, The. Legend of the Crossing-Sweeper. May Kendall. VWP

Boast not proud English, of thy birth and blood. Roger Williams. SCAP

Boast of heraldry, the pomp of pow'r, The. Thomas Gray. *Fr.* Elegy Written in a Country Churchyard. APAD; AWP; CABP; ClHu; EBEV; EBEvV; FHYEP; FaBoBe; FaRoPV; FaPoR; GTBS-P; HAP; HeIP-4; ImPo; InPK-6; InPS-3; NOBE; NOEC; NoP-4; OAEL-1; OBEV; OxAEP-1; PBMP; PoEL-3; PoLF; PoPoPo; Poetr; SCGP; SCV; TFi; UV; UnPo; WeW-3

Boast of Masopha. Z. D. Mangoaela, *Sotho.* PeSA

Boastful young fellow of Neath, A. Limerick. Frank Richards. PeLi

Boat, A. Richard Brautigan. KaS

Boat, The. Caroline Gilman. OBCA

Boat, The. Robert Pack. CoAP

Boat Builder, The. Mark McWatt. HCP

Boat disappear on the black waters of Lethe?[, The]. Allen Ginsberg. *See* A Supermarket in California.

Boat gathers you in, A. One Reason I Went to Prison. James Moore. CDa

Boat has gone, The. (LL) On the Balcony. D. H. Lawrence. GBL; PoA

Boat is chafing at our long delay, The. Song. John Davidson. OBEV

Boat-load of emigrant Huns, A. The Wreck of the Deutschland. David Annett. BXAP; PeLi

Boat moored, lunch in a lonely village, The. The Dappled Horse. Mei Yao Ch'en, *Chinese*. ChiPo, *tr. by* Burton Watson; CoBCP, *tr. by* Burton Watson

Boat of Cypress Wood, The. *Unknown, Chinese.* ChiPo, *tr. by* Yang Xianyi, Gladys Yang, *and* Hu Shiguang

Boat of sandalwood and oars of magnolia, A. Boating Song. Li Po, *Chinese.* TAL, *tr. by* Robert Payne

Boat People. Yusef Komunyakaa. AF; CDa; PoPoPo

Boat Poem. Bernard Spencer. FaBoTw; OxBTC

Boat-pullers, The. Mei Yao Ch'en, *Chinese.* SuSp, *tr. by* Jonathan Chaves

Boat Song, A. Saint Columbanus, *Latin.* NOIV

Boat Song. Henrietta Cordelia Ray. CBWP-3

Boat Song. Sir Walter Scott. OxAEP-2 *Fr.* The Lady of the Lake.

Boat tilts on your image on the waves, The. The Romantic Movement. Philip Lamantia. CLPP

Boating in Autumn. Lu Yu, *Chinese.* ChiP, *tr. by* Arthur Waley

Boating Song. Li Po, *Chinese.* TAL, *tr. by* Robert Payne

Boatman, The. Jay Macpherson. MoCV

Boatman, have they crossed? "Not all." Doom Ferry. Sir Arthur Thomas Quiller-Couch. EBVV

Boatman he can dance and sing, The. Dance the Boatman. *Unknown.* AiP

Boatman of Ts'ang-lang is quite old, The. Fisherman. Ts'en Shen, *Chinese.* SuSp, *tr. by* C. H. Wang

Boatman's Dance ("Ober de mountains, slick as an eel"). Daniel Decatur Emmett. APN-1

Boatman's Song, A. Wang Chien, *Chinese.* SuSp, *tr. by* William H. Nienhauser

Boatmen / how late you've come! Song of the Transport Workers—Seeing Off Fang Wen-yü on His Way to His Post as Inspector of Transportation. Pien Kung, *Chinese.* CoBLCP, *tr. by* Jonathan Chaves

Boatpond, broken off, looks back at the sky, The. "X." Jean Valentine. NMM-2

Boats. Bernadette Mayer. FTOS

Boats Are Afloat, The. Chu Hsi, *Chinese.* OHPC

Boats at Night. Edward Richard Burton Shanks. CH

Boats in a Fog. Robinson Jeffers. NAAL-2; NoP-4; OxBA

   (Boats in Fog.) BLT

Boats in the Bay. Winifred Holtby. WPN

Boats of orchid-wood float on the river. Gathering Lotus with Singing Girls. Mo Shih-lung, *Chinese.* CoBLCP, *tr. by* Jonathan Chaves

Boats sail on the rivers, / And ships sail on the seas. The Rainbow. Christina Rossetti. OxBChV

Boats sail upstream and downstream alike, The. Poem to the Sun. *Ancient Egyptian Oral Tradition.* TTTS, *tr. by* Christopher Wertz

Boatsong of the Sungari, The. Tonghwan Kim, *Korean.* CKP, *tr. by* Jaihiun Kim

Boatswain! The Tempest. Shakespeare. OAEL-1

Bob and I. Quarrel. Grace Paley. IFJA

Bob Hosey Is Dead. Lloyd Davis. EC2

Bob Robin. Mother Goose. OxNR

Bob Southey! You're a poet—poet-laureate. Dedication. Byron. CTC; OAEL-2; OBSV *Fr.* Don Juan.

Bob Southey! You're a poet—Poet-Laureate. Don Juan. Byron. Ro *Fr.* Dedication: "Bob Southey! You're a poet—poet-laureate." CTC; OAEL-2; OBSV *Fr.* Don Juan.

Bobbing behind the phoenix trees, A. Beauty and the Poet. Nam Trân, *Vietnamese.* AVP, *tr. by* Huỳnh Sanh Thông

Bobbing in the waters of the womb. The Buddha in the Womb. Erica Jong. ColAP

Bobbing with the crowds. The Urban Experience: Part One. Lew Blockcolski. VoR

Bobby Shaftoe's [*or* Shafto's] gone to sea. Mother Goose. CBLP; OxNR; ReMoGo

Bobby Snooks. *Unknown.* ReMoGo

Bobby-soxers exchange clandestine feels. At the Record Hop. Wanda Coleman. NAAAL

Bob's Lane. Edward Thomas. PoE

Bocas: A Daughter's Geography. Ntozake Shange. NAAAL

Boddhisattva Doctrine: Enter / Nirvana only when all beings, sentient. John Cage. APSN *Fr.* Diary: How to Improve the World (You Will Only Make Matters Worse).

Boddynge flourettes bloshes atte the lyghte. Thomas Chatterton. *See* There Lackethe Somethynge Stylle.

Bodega, Goodbye. Edwin Honig. NoAM

Bodies. Vern Rutsala. WeT

Bodies broken on, The. Lucille Clifton. NAAAL

Bodies good to eat a thousand years. Allen Ginsberg. *See* Howl.

Bodies of men and women engirth me, and I engirth them, The. Walt Whitman. *See* Leaves of Grass (1855).

Body, The. William Bronk. VGW

Body. Robert Creeley. FTOS

Body, The. Huy Cận, *Vietnamese.* AVP, *tr. by* Huỳnh Sanh Thông

Body. James Merrill. BAP-96

Body. Sasha Moorsom. APAD

Body, The. Yona Wallach, *Hebrew.* IP, *tr. by* Warren Bargad *and* Stanley F. Chyet

Body and mind, we used to think, were two. Conrad Hilberry. GM

Body and Soul: Poem for Two Readers. John Taggart. FTOS

Body and Spirit I surrendered whole. The Wonder. Rudyard Kipling. *Fr.* Epitaphs of the War [1914–1918]. OBWP

Body Bags. R. S. Gwynn. RA

Body Beside the Ties, The. Kenneth Patchen. CLPP

Body Count. Leonard Nathan. PBCAP

Body, divide-up, why. Saturn. Norma Cole. PT

Body Inside the Soul, The. Bell Hooks. ISC

Body into a finger-ring, for a keepsake forever, A. (LL) Counting Small-Boned Bodies. Robert Bly. CDa; SPE

Body is immobile, left behind, The. Octet Before Winter. Claire Malroux, *French.* VCWP, *tr. by* Marilyn Hacker

Body is like a November birch facing the full moon, The. Solitude Late at Night in the Woods. Robert Bly. VGW

Body is the Soul's [*or* Soules] poor[e] house, or home, The. Robert Herrick. CaPo

Body Is the Victory and the Defeat of Dreams, The. Katerina Anghelaki-Rooke, *Greek.* WPOW, *tr. by* Philip Ram

Body Language. Sylvia Kantaris. LW

Body leaning slightly back, the arms held firm and straight, The. Sonata. John Fuller. DiPo

Body left to merge with the round of the hill? (LL) Poem in the Form of a Coffin-Puller's Song ("A Plain of wild grasses, broad and tangled"). T'ao Ch'ien, *Chinese.* CoBCP, *tr. by* Burton Watson

Body lies under the ground. Dirge. Gavin Bantock. OxBTC

Body, long oppressed, The. This Corruptible. Elinor Wylie. MoAmPo

Body my house / my horse my hound. Question. May Swenson. BLT; LiTM; PFE; SAGP; VGW

Body of a fourteen year old caught playing politics, The. No Man's Land. Gloria Escoffery. PBCV

Body of a Rook. David Wevill. MoCV

Body of a woman, white hills, white thighs. Pablo Neruda, *Spanish.* RaBo, *tr. by* Robert Bly

Body of God, The. D. H. Lawrence. ChIV-2

Body of John. Ronald Allison Kells Mason. PeNZ

Body of man is evolved to a brain, The. For Maulana Karenga & Pharoah Sanders. Imamu Amiri Baraka. APSN

Body of my love is a familiar country, The. Sestina. Mary Stanley. PeNZ

Body of the Great Cat, The. Felicity Bast. PC

Body of the saint, The. Scroll. Geoffrey O'Brien. PT

Body, remember not only how much you were loved. Constantine P. Cavafy, *Greek.* LoP, *tr. by* Rae Dalven

Body Rites. Arnold H. Itwaru. HCP

Body-Snatcher. Ambrose Bierce. APN-2 *Fr.* The Devil's Dictionary.

Body, Soul, And Godhead. "Angelus Silesius." GePo, *tr. by* George C. Schoolfield *Fr.* The Cherubical Wanderer.

Body was given to me—what to do with it, A. Osip Emilevich Mandelstam, *Russian.* TCRP, *tr. by* Albert C. Todd

Body: What bodies else but Man's did Nature make. A Dialogue betwixt the Body and the Mind. Margaret Lucas Cavendish, Duchess of Newcastle. PEW

Body's Beauty. D. G. Rossetti. OAEL-2; Son *Fr.* The House of Life. (Lilith.) PoEL-5

Body's products become, The. Two Sonnets. John Ashbery. VGW; WeT

Body's sad, and I've read everything, The. Breeze from the Sea. Stéphane Mallarmé, *French.* FLP, *tr. by* Alistair Elliot

Boers have poked another, The. Steve Biko is Dead. Jack A. Mapanje. PeSAV

Boethius at Cavalzero. John Macoubrie. CRP

Boetius. Libr. 3. Metr. 6. Boethius, *Latin.* OBCVT, *tr. by* Phineas Fletcher

Bofors A. A. Gun, The. Gavin Ewart. PoWW

Bog and Candle. Robert David Fitzgerald. CBAP

Bog-Face. Stevie Smith. RB

Bog Queen. Seamus Heaney. NoAM; RACG

Boggy wood as full of springs as trees, A. The Idea of Entropy at Maenporth Beach. Peter Redgrove. FaBoMo

Bogland. Seamus Heaney. HeIP-4; NOIV; NoAM; PBCIP; PNI; PoPoPo

Bogs, purgatory, wolves and ease, by fame. Barten Holyday. FaBoEE

Bohemia. Dorothy Parker. NBLV

Bohemians, The. Ivor Gurney. PeFWW

Boiling an Egg. Stanley Cook. OTCP

Boiling Falls. Liu E, *Chinese*. CoBLCP, *tr. by* Jonathan Chaves

Boiling her iron tea-kettle and baking shortcake. Walt Whitman. *See* I believe a leaf of grass is no less than the journey-work of the stars.

Boiling up over the years. Georgy Vladimirovich Ivanov, *Russian*. TCRP, *tr. by* Daniel Weissbort

Bolakins was a very fine mason. Lamkin. *Unknown*. AmFP

Bold Benbow rubs his jovial eyes. Chancery Morals. Winthrop Mackworth Praed. NOBRP

Bold erectness of the girls. The Wheat. Blaze Koneski, *Macedonian*. CEEP, *tr. by* Vasa D. Mihailovich

Bold Jack Donahue. *Unknown*. AmFP

Bold outlines are drawn to encompass. Charcoal. Wilson Harris. PBCV

Bold Pedlar and Robin Hood, The. *Unknown*. AmFP; ESPB

Bold Robin has robed him in ghostly attire. Robin Hood and the Grey Friars. Thomas Love Peacock. OxAEP-2 *Fr.* Maid Marian.

Bold Troubleshooters. Peter Veale. NOBL

Bolding Vedas! Shanks New Nisa! Place-Names of China. Alan Bennett. NOBL; UV

Boldness[e] in Love. Thomas Carew. CaPo

(Boldness in Love.) CavPo

Boll Weevil Song. *Unknown*. AS

Boll-weevil's coming, and the winter's cold. November Cotton Flower. Jean Toomer. ColAP; MoP; NoAM; UnPo

Bollam's Replover, The: Farewell to Jabberwocky. Hugh Haughton. CBNP

Bolsum Brown. *Unknown*. AS

Bolt and bar the shutter. Mad as the Mist and Snow. W. B. Yeats. RaBo

Bolt of lightning struck out of midair, A. Mourning Nguyễn Thái Học and Nguyễn Thị Giang. Phan Bội Châu, *Vietnamese*. AVP, *tr. by* Huỳnh Sanh Thông

Bolt upright, reading her Bible for hours. Great-great-grandmother. Guy Butler. PeSAV

Bolted space. Martin Shea. HA

Bomb City, Bomb City, Bomb City drummed into us. Night and Day. The Other Side. Natalie Hardwick. IIP

Bomb Disposal, The. Ciaran Carson. CIP-2; IIP

Bomb-disposal / combed the area. Peace-Time. Mervyn Morris. PBCV

Bomb Is Made, The. Keith Sinclair. PeNZ

Bomb, it explodes, The. (LL) The Terrorist, He Watches. Wislawa Szymborska, *Polish*. PoSu, *tr. by* Adam Czerniawski

Bomb then, bomb now—doing the breathing arsenic job, we want. Bruce Andrews. PmAP

Bomb Victim in the Cathedral Speaks to a Child, A. Gunars Salis, *Latvian*. CEEP, *tr. by* Baiba Kaugara

Bomb will explode in the bar at twenty past one, The. The Terrorist, He Watches. Wislawa Szymborska, *Polish*. PoSu, *tr. by* Adam Czerniawski

Bombax Tree, The. Fily-Dabo Sissoko, *French*. NegPo, *tr. by* Ellen Conroy Kennedy

Bombed in London. Rudyard Kipling. *Fr.* Epitaphs of the War [1914–1918]. OBWP

Bomber, The. "Brian Vrepont." NOBAu

Bombers. C. Day Lewis. CMoP

Bombers spread out, temperature steady, The. War and Silence. Robert Bly. CAPP-1

Bombing at about ninety miles an hour with the exhaust skittering. Cocktails. Ciaran Carson. BiHa; PBCIP

Bon jour, bon jour a vous! *Unknown*. MiEL

Bona dies, Bona dies. Sir David Lindsay. SeCP *Fr.* Ane Satire [*or* Satyre] of the Three [*or* Thrie] Estaitis.

Bona nox; you're an ox. Kanonentext. Wolfgang Amadeus Mozart, *German*. CBNP, *tr. by* Hugh Haughton

Bond, The. Nuala Ní Dhomhnaill, *Irish*. PBCIP, *tr. by* Medbh McGuckian

Bondmen, and helots, and serfs were we. The Cry of the Oppressed. Henrietta Tindall. VWP

Bondmen of Mizraim/ Were our fathers. Flowering Without End. Stefan Zweig. *Fr.* Jeremiah. TrJP, *tr. by* Eden *and* Cedar Paul

Bonds of Friendship, The. Simon Dach, *German*. GePo, *tr. by* Ingrid Wal[do]e-Engel

Bondsman's gloomy night has passed, The. James Madison Bell. AAP *Fr.* An Anniversary Poem Entitled the Progress of Liberty.

Bone-aged is my white horse. Talysarn. Brenda Chamberlain. OBWVE

Bone and Skin, two millers thin. On Two Monopolists. John Byrom. FaBoEE

Bone China. Richard Percival Lister. NYBP

Bone-Flower Elegy. Robert Earl Hayden. NoAM

Bone-idle, I lie listening to the rain. Dejection. Derek Mahon. PBCIP

Bone that has no Marrow, The. Emily Dickinson. TAP

Bone Thoughts on a Dry Day: Chicago. George Starbuck. NYBP; TwCP

Bone Yard. Jim Barnes. CDW

Boneless tongue, so small and weak, The. The Tongue. Phillips Burrows Strong. PoToHe

Bones, The. W. S. Merwin. CoAmPo

Bones, The. W. S. Merwin. LiTM

Bones and Drums. Ron Welburn. SeSe

Bones of a fish. Tanka. Fumi Saito, *Japanese*. MJT, *tr. by* Ueda, Makoto

Bones of Chuang Tzu, The. Chang Heng, *Chinese*. AWP, *tr. by* Arthur Waley

Bones of Incontention, The. Robert David Cohen. NYBP

Bones of the lonely-wretched spend no quiet nights. Meng Chiao. SuSp, *tr. by* Irving Y. Lo *Fr.* Autumn Meditations.

Bones that cannot bear the light, The. (LL) Genesis. Geoffrey Hill. ChIV-1; HAP; OAEL-2; OxBC; PeECV; TOF

Bones tuned, the body sings. He Hola. Keri Hulme. PeNZ

Boney. *Unknown*. FaBoVe

Bong, Mr., bong, Mr., bong, Mr., bong. (LL) Dirge: "1-2-3 was the number he played but today the number came 3-2-1." Kenneth Fearing. HoPM; NIP-4; PoRA; RB; TrJP

Bonguemba. Antoine-Roger Bolamba, *French*. NegPo, *tr. by* Ellen Conroy Kennedy

Bonhoeffer in his skylit cell. Christmas Trees. Geoffrey Hill. NOCV

Bonie Doon. Robert Burns. NoP-4

Bonnard; a Novel. Richard Howard. CoAP; NYBP

Bonnie Annie. *Unknown*. ESPB

Bonnie Annie Livieston. *Unknown*. OxBB

Bonnie Bower, The. *Unknown*. *See* The Lament of the Border Widow.

Bonnie Broukit Bairn, The. "Hugh MacDiarmid." FaBoCh; FaBoTC; FaBoVe; HAP; InPS-3

Bonnie [*or* Bonny] George [*or* James] Campbell. *Unknown*. AmFP; CH; ESPB; OxBB; OxBoLi; SCGP

("O it's up in the Highlands.") ESPB

Bonnie House o' Airlie, The. *Unknown*. ESPB; OBEV; OxBB; OxBS

Bonnie [*or* Bonny] Kilmeny gaed up the glen. Kilmeny. James Hogg. OBEV; OxAEP-2 *Fr.* The Queen's Wake.

Bonnie Laddie's Lang a-Growin', The. *Unknown*. OxBS

Bonnie lassie, will ye go, will ye go, will ye go. Birks of Aberfeldy, The [Composed on the Spot]. Robert Burns. CTC

Bonnie Lesley. Robert Burns. CTC; GTBS-P; NOBE; OBEV; OxBS

(Saw Ye Bonny Lesley.) OxBS

Bonny Baby Livingston. *Unknown*. ESPB

Bonny Barbara Allan ("In Scarlet Town where I was born"). *Unknown*. AWP; BoLoP; CH; ESPB; HeIP-4; InPK-6; NAEL-1; OxBB

Bonny Bee Hom. *Unknown*. ESPB

Bonny Birdy, The. *Unknown*. ESPB

Bonny Bobby Shaftoe [*or* Shafto]. (LL) Bobby Shaftoe's [*or* Shafto's] gone to sea. Mother Goose. CBLP; OxNR; ReMoGo

Bonny Brown Girl, The. *Unknown*. *See* The Brown Girl.

Bonny Bunch of Roses O, The. *Unknown*. OxBoLi

Bonny Cravet, The. Mother Goose. OxNR

Bonny [*or* Bonnie] Dundee. Sir Walter Scott. FaBoCh; OxBS; OxBoLi; UV *Fr.* The Doom of Devorgoil.

Bonny Earl of Livingston, The. *Unknown*. *See* Fair Mary of Wallington.

Bonny Earl of Murray, The. *Unknown*. ESPB; NOSC; OBEV; OxBB; OxBS; SCGP

Bonny fine maid of a noble degree, A. Robin Hood and Maid Marian. *Unknown*. ESPB

"Bonny heir, and the well-faird heir, The." The Heir of Linne. *Unknown*. ESPB

Bonny Hind, The. *Unknown*. ESPB

(Bonny Heyn, The.) OxBB

Bonny holms of Yarrow!, The. (LL) Yarrow Unvisited [1803]. Wordsworth. GTBS-P; PoRA

Bonny John Seton. *Unknown*. ESPB

Bonny Kilmeny Gaed Up the Glen. James Hogg. *See* Kilmeny.

Bonny Lass of Anglesey, The. *Unknown*. ESPB

Bonny lass, pretty lass, wilt thou be mine? A Proposal. *Unknown*. ACTP

Bonny Lassie O! John Clare. CH

Bonny Lizie Baillie. *Unknown*. ESPB

Bonsai tree / in the attractive pot, The. A Work of Artifice. Marge Piercy. Poetsp

Bonum Est Mihi Quod Humiliasti Me, *abr*. Henry Howard, Earl of Surrey. SiPS

Bonus. A. R. Ammons. HCAP

Bony. Simon J. Ortiz. CDW

Bonze Got Stung By a Bee, The. Ho Xuan Huong, *Vietnamese.* AVP, *tr. by* Huỳnh Sanh Thông

BOO! (LL) Brooklyn Bridge, Brooklyn Bridge. William Jay Smith. KaS

Booby had a little sack, The. Cao Tần, *Vietnamese.* AVP, *tr. by* Huỳnh Sanh Thông

Bood is beabig brighdly, love, The. To Bary Jade. Charles Follen Adams. OBAL

Boogie: 1 A.M. Langston Hughes. APSN

Book, The. William Drummond, of Hawthornden. CH; ChIV-1
   Lessons of Nature, The. GTBS-P
   "Of this fair volume which we 'world' do name." KSG

Book, The. Edmond Jabès, *French.* AF, *tr. by* Rosemarie Waldrop

Book, The. Henry Vaughan. GeHe; PBRV

Book 3, Metrum 11. Boethius, *Latin.* OBCVT, *tr. by* Sir Richard Fanshawe

Book 3, metrum 4. Boethius, *Latin.* OBCVT, *tr. by* Alfred, King of England

Book, a friend, a song, a glass, A. The Happy Life. William Thompson. ECEV

Book and a jug and a dame, A. Limerick. *Unknown.* PeLi

Book-burning Pit, The. Lo Yin, *Chinese.* SuSp, *tr. by* Edward H. Schafer

Book does not begin, he replied, The. The Beginning of the Book. Edmond Jabès, *French.* AF, *tr. by* Rosemarie Waldrop

Book Ends. Tony Harrison. DiPo; NAEL-2 *Fr.* The School of Eloquence. NAEL-2; NoAM

Book: Enemey ended my life, deprived me, An. Cynewulf. ASW, *tr. by* Kevin Crossley-Holland *Fr.* Riddles (Exeter Book).

Book for us to write, like this:, A. Mapping. Robert Kelly. BAP-93

Book Full of Pictures, A. Charles Simic. NoP-4

Book I Held Grew Cold, The. Ernst Toller, *German.* TrJP, *tr. by* Ashley Dukes

Book Moth: "Moth ate a word. To me it seemed, A." Cynewulf. AnOE, *tr. by* Charles W. Kennedy; (*See also* Old English Riddle.) *Fr.* Riddles (Exeter Book).
   ("Bookmoth: A moth devoured words. When I heard.") ASW, *tr. by* Kevin Crossley-Holland

Book of Books, The. Sir Walter Scott. ChIV-1 *Fr.* The Monastery. (Sir Walter Scott's Tribute.)

Book of Cordelia. Susan Howe. *Fr.* White Foolscap/Book of Cordelia. PmAP

Book of During, IV, The. Clark Coolidge. PT

Book of Ephraim, The. James Merrill. *Fr.* The Changing Light at Sandover. NAAL-2
   "Backdrop: The dining room at Stonington." NoAM
   "Correct but cautious, that first night, we asked." NoP-4
   "Life like the periodical not yet." HCAP
   Lost in Translation. FYAP; HCAP; LCAP-2; NAAL-2; NoAM; NoP-4; VCAP
   "Zero hour. Waiting yet again." HCAP

Book of Galahad, The. Jack Spicer. FTOS

Book of Gawain, The. Jack Spicer. PoM *Fr.* The Holy Grail.

Book of Glass, A. David Shapiro. PT; PmAP

Book of hours, The. The Hours. Paul Ramsey. CRP

Book of How, The. Merrill Moore. FuPo; MoAmPo

Book of Hunting. Julians Barnes. WPE

Book of Job and a Draft of a Poem to Praise the Paths of the Living, The. George Oppen. NNaP

Book of Kells, The. Padraic Colum. BIrV; IIP

Book of Music, A. Jack Spicer. APSN; PoM

Book of my enemy has been remaindered, The. Clive James. OBCoV

Book of Myths, The. Joy Harjo. NMM-2

Book of Persephone, The. Robert Kelly. PoM

Book of Praise for Children, The. *Unknown.*
   Child's Offering, A. CTV

Book of Questions, The. Edmond Jabès, *French.*
   "To be in the book. To figure in the book of questions, to be part of it." PFTM, *tr. by* Rosemarie Waldrop

Book of Routh. Carolyn Beard Whitlow. FFC

Book of Ruth and Naomi, The. Marge Piercy. NMM-2

Book of Songs, The. *Unknown, Chinese.*
   Big Chariot, The. ChiP, *tr. by* Arthur Waley
   Oaths of Friendship. FP, *tr. by* Arthur Waley

Book of summer is the butterfly, A. The Butterfly. John Fuller. Spl

Book of Tarshish, The. Moses ibn Ezra, *Hebrew.*
   Joy of Life. TrJP, *tr. by* Solomon Solis-Cohen

Book of the Dead, *sels. Unknown, Egyptian.*

Adoration of the Disk by King Akhnaten and Princess Nefer Neferiu Aten. AWP
   "Cattle roam again across the field, The."
Dead Man Ariseth and Singeth a Hymn to the Sun, The. AWP
He Approacheth the Hall of Judgment. AWP
He Asketh Absolution of God. AWP
He Biddeth Osiris to Arise from the Dead. AWP
He Cometh Forth into the Day. AWP
He Commandeth a Fair Wind. AWP
He Defendeth His Heart against the Destroyer. AWP
He Embarketh in the Boat of Ra. AWP
He Entereth the House of the Goddess Hathor. AWP
He Establisheth His Triumph. AWP
He Holdeth Fast to the Memory of His Identity. AWP
He Is Declared True of Word. AWP
He Is like the Lotus. AWP
   (Death as a Lotus Flower.) TTY, *tr. by* Ulli Beier
He Is like the Serpent Saka. AWP
He Kindleth a Fire. AWP
He Knoweth the Souls of the East. AWP
He Knoweth the Souls of the West. AWP
He Maketh Himself One with Osiris. AWP
He Maketh Himself One with the God Ra. AWP, *tr. by* Robert Hillyer
He Maketh Himself One with the Only God, Whose Limbs Are the Many Gods. AWP
He Overcometh the Serpent of Evil in the Name of Ra. AWP
He Prayeth for Ink and Palette That He May Write. AWP
He Singeth a Hymn to Osiris, the Lord of Eternity. AWP
He Singeth in the Underworld. AWP
He Walketh by Day. AWP
Other World, The. OxBSn, *tr. by* Robert Silliman Hillyer; AWP

Book of the Two Married Women and the Widow, The. William Dunbar.
   Widow Speaks, The. PoEL-1

Book of Thel, The. William Blake. Ro *Fr.* The Book of Thel. NAEL-2; OAEL-2; OBNC; PoE; PoEL-4
   Secrets of the Earth, The. NOBE

Book of Urizen [*or* First Book of Urizen], The. William Blake. NOBRP; Ro
   ("And the salt ocean rolled englobed.") (LL) Ro
   ("Of the primeval priest's assumed power.") Ro

Book of Verses underneath the Bough, A. 12. Edward Fitzgerald. CABP *Fr.* The Rubáiyát of Omar Khayyám of Naishápur.

Book of verses underneath the bough, A. Quatrains. Omar Khayyám. HoPM; NOBE; OBEV; TRP *Fr.* The Rubáiyát of Omar Khayyám [of Naishápúr]. AWP; EBVV; FaBoBe; FaPoR; HAP; NAEL-2; PoEL-5

Book of Wisdom, The. Stephen Crane. HoPM; MoAmPo *Fr.* The Black Riders [and Other Lines].

Book of Wisdom, The. Robert Lowell. ChIV-1

Book of Yolek, The. Anthony Hecht. HP; NoP-4; WeW-3

Book Our Mothers Read, The. John Greenleaf Whittier. *See* Knowledge.

Book Review. Russell Davies. FaBoEE

Book was writ[t] of late called [*or* call'd] *Tetrachordon*, A. On the Detraction Which Followed upon My Writing Certain Treatises. Milton. PoE; Son

Book-Worms, The. Robert Burns. FaBoEE

Book X. Milton. FHYEP *Fr.* Paradise Lost.
   Adam Speaks.
   "Be it so, for I submit; his doom is fair." NAWM-1
   Eve Penitent.
   "Other way Satan went down, Th'." NAEL-1
   "Such was thir song." PeECV
   "Then both ourselves and seed at once to free."
   "Thus Adam himself lamented loud." OAEL-1
   "Thus began / Outrage from lifeless things; but Discord first." NAEL-1

Booke of *Common Pray'r* excels the rest, The. Francis Quarles. PBRV *Fr.* Divine Fancies.

Booker T. and W. E. B. Dudley Randall. MoP; NoAM

Booker Washington Trilogy, The. Vachel Lindsay.
   John Brown. MoAmPo
   Simon Legree—A Negro Sermon. MeMAP; TAP
   (Negro Sermon—Simon Legree, A.) MoAmPo

Bookful Blockhead, The. Alexander Pope. OBSV *Fr.* An Essay on Criticism. NAEL-1; PoEL-3; TFi

Bookmark, A. Thomas M. Disch. RA

Bookmark. Saint Theresa of Avila, *Spanish.* CTC; PoEL-5; WPOW
   (Lines Written in Her Breviary.) AWP, *tr. by* Longfellow

Bookmoth: A moth devoured words. When I heard. Cynewulf. *See* Book Moth: "A Moth ate a word. To me it seemed."

Books. George Mackay Brown. FaBoTC *Fr.* Runes from a Holy Island.

Books, The. (LL)　He Was Lucky. Anna Swirszczynska, *Polish.* HP; PoSu, *tr. by* Magnus J. Krynski *and* Robert A. Maguire

Books and the Man I sing, the first who brings. Alexander Pope. *See* To Dr. Jonathan Swift.

Books are a load of crap. (LL)　A Study of Reading Habits. Philip Larkin. InPK-6; NOBL; OBCoV

Books, books, books! Elizabeth Barrett Browning. WPOW *Fr.* Aurora Leigh. VWP

Books; china; a life / Reprehensibly perfect. (LL)　Poetry of Departures. Philip Larkin. CMoP; HeIP-4; OxBC; PoE; TwCP

Book's Creed, The.　Joseph Seamon Cotter, Sr.　AAP

Books Fall Open. David McCord. OBCA

Books of Ovid's changed shapes, The.　In the Praise of Music. Humphrey Gifford. NoSic

Books of the Old Testament, The.　Thomas Russell. *See* The Names and Order of the Books of the Old Testament.

Bookshop Idyll, A. Kingsley Amis. OxBTC; PeLV

Bookworm: I heard of a wonder, of words moth-eaten;. *Unknown.* EEP, *tr. by* Michael Alexander *Fr.* Riddles (Exeter Book).

Boom! Howard Nemerov. LiTM; NBLV; NIP-4

Boom above my knees lifts, and the boat, The.　Sailing to an Island. Richard Murphy. PBCIP

Boom / The shrill whistle of the wolf. Bird of Power. Jim Tollerud. VoR

Boomerang. William Hart-Smith. NOBAu; NTP

Boomerang, The　Carrie May Nichols. PoToHe

Boomerang. John Perreault. SPE

Boomerang: A Blatantly Political Poem. Quincy Troupe. AF; LTA ("Will have been undone.") (LL)　LTA

Boon nature scattered, free and wild. Flowers and Trees. Sir Walter Scott. OxAEP-2 *Fr.* The Lady of the Lake.

Boon Nature to the woman bows. The Tribute. Coventry Patmore. EBEV; OBNC *Fr.* The Angel in the House.

Booooooooo. spooky ripplings of icy waves. this. American Sonnet (35). Wanda Coleman. BAP-96

Boor's Wooing, The. Anna Wickham. WPN

Boot Hill. Sharlot Mabridth Hall. PaTW

Boot, wet sand and more white along the borders defining a trail of lush / chemicals we adhere to. Kathleen Fraser. PT

Booth Killed Lincoln. *Unknown.* AmFP

Booth led boldly with his big bass drum. General William Booth Enters into Heaven. Vachel Lindsay. AmPP; CMoP; ChIV-2; ImPo; LiTM; MeMAP; MoAmPo; NOBA; OxBA; PoA; PoE; TAP

Booths knew nothing either. They built themselves in. The Old Sipsey Valley Road. Thomas Rabbitt. MT

Boots. Rudyard Kipling. BLPA; FaPoR; MoBrPo

Boots and Shoes. Lilian McCrea. BoTP

Boots are being polished. Where Will You Be? Patricia Parker. GLP

Boots of Spanish Leather. "Bob Dylan." NoP-4

Boots, / Shoes. *Unknown.* OxNR

Booty from the German War. Friedrich von Logau, *German.* GePo, *tr. by* George C. Schoolfield

Booze and the blowens cop the lot. (LL)　Villon's Straight Tip to All Cross Coves. William Ernest Henley, *after* Villon. AWP; CBNP; OxAEP-2; OxBoV

Bop Lyrics. Allen Ginsberg. OBAL

Boppin' is Safer than Grindin'. Thulani Davis. GT

Bora Ring. Judith Wright. NoAM

Border. Taslima Nasrin, *Bengali.* VCWP, *tr. by* Carolyne Wright *and* Farida Sarkar

Border Ballad, A. Thomas Love Peacock. BXAP

Border Ballad. Sir Walter Scott. *See* Blue Bonnets over the Border.

Border clashes flare northeast of the Empire. Song of Yen. Kao Shih, *Chinese.* SuSp, *tr. by* Joseph J. Lee

Border collie has been bred to keep, A　Our Dog Chasing Swifts. U. A. Fanthorpe. Spl

Border Mountain Moon. Lu Yu, *Chinese.* CoBCP, *tr. by* Burton Watson

Bordering Manuscript. James Applewhite. PoA

Borders. Michael S. Weaver. GT

Boreas. Samuel Rowlands. NoSic

Bored. Margaret Atwood. BAP-95

Bored by Ascham and Zeno. The Glad Eye. Paul Muldoon. NoAM

Bored, confused actually. have started several letters. Four Lines of a Black Love Letter Between Teachers. Ed Roberson. NBV

Boredom, and the horror, and the glory, The. (LL)　In Memory of the Unknown Poet, Robert Boardman Vaughn. Donald Justice. DiPo; NoAM

Borgia, thou once wert [*or* were] almost too august.　On Seeing a Hair of Lucretia Borgia. Walter Savage Landor. HAP; SCGP; WeW-3

Boring and boring for food. (LL)　A Legend of the Northland. Phoebe Cary. OBCA; OBSP

Boring executors approach their locks, The.　Poem against Catholics. James Fenton *and* John Fuller. OBSV; PeLV

Boris Pasternak. "Anna Akhmatova," *Russian.* TCRP, *tr. by* Stanley Kunitz *with* Max Hayward

Boris Vilde. Aleksis Rannit, *Estonian.* CEEP, *tr. by* Henry Lymann

Born Again. Forugh Farrokhzad, *Persian.* PBWP, *tr. by* Jascha Kessler *and* Amin Banani

Born, born, we know how it goes. (LL)　Holy Family. Muriel Rukeyser. ChIV-2; MoAmPo

Born crying, and after crying, die. Palladas, *Greek.* GrAn, *tr. by* Tony Harrison

Born I was to be old. Anacreontic. Robert Herrick. CaPo; OxBoLi

Born in a trance, we wake, observe, inquire.　Another and the Same. Samuel Rogers. OBNC *Fr.* Human Life.

Born in another country, under a different flag.　An Irish Requiem. Michael O'Loughlin. PBCIP

Born in the garret, in the kitchen bred.　A Sketch from Private Life. Byron. OBNC

Born in the quarter-night, brash.　Delta Traveller. Charles Wright. AmPA; LCAP-2

Born in wealth and wealthily nursed.　Thomas Hood. EBVV *Fr.* Miss Kilmansegg and Her Precious Leg.

Born in Winter. Francis Quarles. NOSC

Born into those foul times of dusk and dust.　More Thoughts on Nguyễn. Chế Lan Viên, *Vietnamese.* AVP, *tr. by* Huỳnh Sanh Thông

Born like the pines to sing. James Ephriam McGirt. AAP

Born naked. Buried naked. So why fuss? Palladas, *Greek.* GrAn, *tr. by* Tony Harrison

Born, nurtured, wedded, prized, within the pale　Lafayette. Dolley Madison. AiP

Born of good parents, you're a filial son.　A Ricksha Man's Impromptu. Phan Trọng Quảng, *Vietnamese.* AVP, *tr. by* Huỳnh Sanh Thông

Born of rejection, of the boundless snow. (LL)　From the Highest Camp. Thom Gunn. Son; TwCP

Born of the sorrowful of heart. For Paul Laurence Dunbar. Countee Cullen. SSLK *Fr.* Four Epitaphs. PoBA

Born of Woman. Wislawa Szymborska, *Polish.* GI, *tr. by* Magnus J. Krynski *and* Robert A. Maguire

Born on a tabletop in Joe's cafeé. Davy Crockett. *Unknown.* FaBoVe

Born poor and known to few.　Space Captain. John Kitching. SpW

Born salesman, A.　And One for My Dame. Anne Sexton. NoP-4

Born there and scattered out to all four winds.　A Hundred Tongues. Viên Linh, *Vietnamese.* AVP, *tr. by* Huỳnh Sanh Thông

Born to the suburbs.　An Answer of Sorts. Leonard Nathan. WeT

Born to these gentle stones and grass.　Urn Burial. Ted Hughes. EBEV

Born Too Soon. John Fuller *and* James Fentonr. OBCoV

Born two thousand years ago. (LL)　Kid Stuff. Frank Horne. NOxBChV; PChr; PoBA

Born Tying Knots. Samuel Makidemewabe, *Cree Indian.* STP, *tr. by* Howard Norman

Born with all arms, he sought a separate peace.　The Deserter. John Streeter Manifold. CBAP

Born without a Chance. Edmund Vance Cooke. BLPA

Borough, The.　George Crabbe.

　Letter I. CABP

　Peter Grimes. EBNV; ECEV; FHYEP; OBNV; PoEL-4

　("'Again they come!' and muttered as he died.") (LL)　Ro

　("Oppressed the soul with misery, grief, and fear.") (LL)

　(Poor of the Borough, The; Peter Grimes.)

　"He built a mud-wall'd hovel, where he kept."

　Peter Grimes at Aldeburgh.

　"Priest attending, found he spoke at times, The." PoE

　"Thus by himself compelled to live each day." NOBE; OBNC

　Sailing upon the River. OBNC

　Schools. CTC

　Slum Dwelling, A. OBNC

　Vicar, The. OBSV

　"But let applause be dealt in all we may." OBNC

　Winter Views Serene. OBNC

Borrow to your heart's content. *Unknown, Greek.* GrAn, *tr. by* Peter Jay

Borrowed breath. (LL)　When Black People Are. Alfred B. Spellman. ISC

Borrowed wings on his ankles. Perseus. Louis MacNeice. LiTM

Borrowing Rice from Ju-hui. Mei Yao Ch'en, *Chinese.* SuSp, *tr. by* Jonathan Chaves

Boschlog: Being a Cartulary from The Ship of Fools. B. Catling. NBrP

Bosnia. November. And the mountain roads. Sarajevo. Lawrence Durrell. GTBS-P

Bosom of / green buds, A. Mare Nostrum. Joel Oppenheimer. NeAP

Bosom of his Father and his God, The. (LL) Elegy Written in a Country Churchyard. Thomas Gray. APAD; AWP; ClHu; EBEV; EBEvV; ECEV; FHYEP; FaBoBe; FaBoPV; FaPoR; GTBS-P; HAP; HeIP-4; ImPo; InPK-6; InPS-3; NOBE; NOEC; NoP-4; OAEL-1; OBEV; OxAEP-1; PBMP; PFE; PoEL-3; PoLF; PoPoPo; Poetr; SCGP; SCV; TFi; UV; UnPo; WeW-3

Bosom of Thy love, The. (LL) Day Is Past and Gone, The. John Leland. AH; AmFP

Boss, The. James Russell Lowell. NCAP; OBAL

Boss, The. Boris Abramovich Slutsky, *Russian*. TCRP, *tr. by* J. R. Rowland

Boss Communication. Mari E. Evans. SeSe

Boss he had a yaller gal. Git Along Down to Town. *Unknown*. AmFP

Boss i went. Archy Interviews a Pharoah. Don Marquis. OBCoV *Fr.* Archy and Mehitabel.

Boss knows what shape I'm in, The. He tells me. Drunk Last Night with Friends, I Go to Work Anyway. Philip Dow. InPK-6

Boss's Wife, The. *Unknown*. CBAP

Boston. John Collins Bossidy, *also at. to* Samuel C. Bushnell. FaBoEE; NBLV; OBAL; OBCoV; OxBoLi; PeLV

Boston. Edwin Arlington Robinson. APN-2

Boston Ballad [1854], A. Walt Whitman. OBAL
 ("Clear the way there Jonathan!") APN-1
 (Leaves of Grass (1855).) APN-1

Boston Burglar, The. *Unknown*. AmFP

Boston Common. John Berryman. CBCWP

Boston Evening Transcript, The. T. S. Eliot. InPK-6
 ("Readers of the *Boston Evening Transcript*, The.") PFE

Boston has a festival. In the Public Garden. Marianne Moore. NOBA

Boston Hymn. Ralph Waldo Emerson. CBCWP

Boston in Distress. *Unknown*. NOEC

Boston. Lord God, the ocean never to windward. Aspects of Spring in Greater Boston. George Starbuck. NYBP *Fr.* Poems from a First Year in Boston.

Boston Toast, A. John Collins Bossidy. BLPA

Boston Year. Elizabeth Alexander. GT

Bot now the haisty, egir, and wild Dido. Dido's Suicide. Virgil. OBVE, *tr. by* Gawin Douglas *Fr.* The Aeneid [*or* Eneados, *Aeneis*].

Bot of ane bowrd in to bed I sall yow breif yit. William Dunbar. EBEV *Fr.* The Tretis of the Tua Mariit Wemen and the Wedo. OxBS

Bot then kerpe the king, said, "Kithe what ye hatten". *Unknown*. EnVB *Fr.* Winner and Waster.

Botanic Garden, The. Erasmus Darwin.
 ("Descend, ye hovering sylphs! aerial choirs." ECEV
 Kew. OBGa

Botanical Fanaticism. Thylias Moss. TRP

Botanical Trope, A. William Meredith. Poetr

Botany Bay. John Freeth. NOEC

Both bud and fade, both blow and wither. (LL) To A. L.; Persuasions [*or* Perswasions] to Love. Thomas Carew. CaPo; SeCP

Both down together at a blow. (LL) The Presbyterian Knight. Samuel Butler. CABP

Both favor and disgrace you have full known. Nguyễn Trãi, *Vietnamese*. AVP, *tr. by* Huỳnh Sanh Thông

Both gentlemen, or yoemen bould. A True Tale of Robin Hood. *Unknown*. ESPB

Both her mourner and her tomb. (LL) On the Countess Dowager of Pembroke. William Browne. AWP; FaBoEE; HAP; NOBE; NOSC; NoP-4; OAEL-1; OBEV; PoEL-2; PoRA; SCGP; TFi

Both in heart in heart & hand in hand. The Fields from Islington to Marybone. William Blake. FaBoPV; OBNC; OBNV

Both Keats and Boccaccio tell a. Limerick. Joyce Johnson. PeLi

Both Less and More. Richard Watson Dixon. SCGP

Both My Grandmothers ("Both my grandmas came from far away"). Edward Field. CA

Both Plutarch and Pausanius tell a story. Kleomedes. David Wright. MoP

Both robbed of air, we both lie in one ground. Hero and Leander. Donne. FMP; NoSic; SoSe-8

Both Schubert on the waters and Mozart in the din of birds. Osip Emilevich Mandelstam. TCRP, *tr. by* Bernard Meares *Fr.* Ottave.

Both skyed. Japanese Print. Austin Clarke. NOIV

Both the year's [*or* yeares], and the day's [*or* dayes] deep midnight is. (LL) A Nocturnal[l] upon Saint Lucy's [*or* S. Lucies] Day, Being the Shortest Day. Donne. EBEV; ESCV; FHYEP; GBL; MeLP; NAEL-1; NOBE; NOSC; OAEL-1; OxAEP-1; PoE; PoEL-2; SCGP; SeCP; TFi

Both turned, and under open sky adored. Milton. *See* Adam and Eve in the Garden.

Both Ways. William Stafford. CMAP

Both were so shy. Two. Robert Canzoneri. HoPM

Both whom one fire had burnt, one water drowned. (LL) Hero and Leander. Donne. FMP; NoSic; SoSe-8

Both Your Mothers, *for Bieta*. Jerzy Ficowski, *Polish*. HP, *tr. by* Keith Bosley; PoSu

Bothie of Tober-na-Vuolich, The [A Long-Vacation Pastoral]. Arthur Hugh Clough.
 "Ah, you have much to learn, we can't know all things at twenty." FaBoPV
 "As at return of tide the total weight of ocean." FaBoPV
 "But in the interval here the boiling, pent-up water." EnVR
 "But on the morrow Elspie kept out of the way of Philip." EnVR
 Highland Glen near Loch Ericht, A.
 "I have been kissed before, she added, blushing slightly." FaBoVe
 "Nodding and beckoning across, observed of Attaché and Guardsman." FaBoPV
 "Somewhat more splendid in dress, in a waistcoat work of a lady." FaBoVe
 "Then was the dinner served, and the Minister prayed for a blessing." PeLV
 "This is the letter of Hobbes the kilted and corpulent hero." FaBoPV

Bothwell Bridge. *Unknown*. *See* The Battle of Bothwell Bridge.

Botticelli. Three candles. Soft lips suggesting a smile. Judita Vaiiunaite, *Lithuanian*. CEEP, *tr. by* M. G. Slavenas

Botticellian Trees, The. William Carlos Williams. AmPP

Bottle, The. Ralph Knevet. ChIV-2

Bottle contained a little amber and a little, The. Some Glow on the Sill. Clark Coolidge. FTOS

Bottle Creek Blues. Sam Hunt. PeNZ

Bottle-neck. Tribute to Nervous. Kit Robinson. FTOS

Bottle of perfume that Willie sent, The [*or* A]. Limerick. *Unknown*. PeLi

Bottle of Suze, A. Pablo Picasso, *French*. PFTM, *tr. by* Patricia Leighten

Bottled. Jill Breckenridge. LoHo

Bottled [New York]. Helene Johnson. BlSi; PoBA

Bottles. Jane Kenyon. *Fr.* Having It Out With Melancholy. BAP-93

Bottles are empty, the breakfast was good, The. The Morning After. Heinrich Heine, *German*. EP, *tr. by* Louis Untermeyer

Bottles are for sleeping in. Bottles in the Zoological Museum. William Peskett. PNI

Bottles in the Zoological Museum. William Peskett. PNI

Bottom of the sea is cruel, The. (LL) Above the fresh ruffles of the surf. Hart Crane. AmPP; ColAP; MoP; NAAL-2; OxBA; PoE; VGW

Bottom of things is neither life nor death, The. Roberto Juarroz. VCWP, *tr. by* W. S. Merwin *Fr.* Vertical Poetry.

Bottom with your ballast fill was laded, The. (LL) Of an Heroical Answer of a Great Roman Lady to Her Husband. Sir John Harington. BoLoP; OxBM

Bottomed by tugging combs of water. The Swan. William Robert Rodgers. PNI

Bottomless pits. There's one in Castleton. National Trust. Tony Harrison. NAEL-2 *Fr.* The School of Eloquence. NAEL-2; NoAM

Bottom's Dream. Shakespeare. CBNP *Fr.* A Midsummer Night's Dream.

Bottom's Song. Shakespeare. CTC *Fr.* A Midsummer Night's Dream.

Boudoir Feelings. Li Shang-yin, *Chinese*. SuSp, *tr. by* Eugene Eoyang *and* Irving Y. Lo

Boudoir Lament. Yü Hsüan-chi. BoWoP, *tr. by* Geoffrey Waters

Boudoir Thoughts. Hsü Kan, *Chinese*.
 "Deepening shadows bring on sorrow, The." SuSp, *tr. by* Ronald C. Miao
 "Drifting clouds, distant and vast, The." SuSp, *tr. by* Ronald C. Miao
 "Sadly, sadly the season draws to an end." SuSp, *tr. by* Ronald C. Miao
 "Steep, steep the lofty mountain peak." SuSp, *tr. by* Ronald C. Miao

Bouge of Court, The. John Skelton.
 "Sail is up, Fortune ruleth our helm, The." NoSic

Bough, cradle and all. (LL) Hush-a-bye, baby[, on the tree-top]. Mother Goose. LB; OxNR; ReMoGo

Boughs do shake and the bells do ring, The. Harvest Song. *Unknown*. BoTP; OxNR

Boughs, the boughs are bare enough, The. Winter with the Gulf Stream. Gerard Manley Hopkins. CMoP; NoAM

Boughs with apples laden around me whisper. A Cool Retreat. Sappho, *Greek*. OBCVT, *tr. by* Percy Osborn

Bought at the drug store, very cheap; and later pawned. Green Light. Kenneth Fearing. PoE; VGW

Bought / from the flower-peddler's tray. Tune: Magnolia Blossom. Li Ch'ing-chao. PBWP, *tr. by* C. H. Kwock *and* Vincent McHugh

Bought Locks. Martial, *Latin*. AWP, *tr.* by Sir John Harington

Boulders. John Wills. HA

Boulogne to Amiens and Paris. D. G. Rossetti. PeVV *Fr.* A Trip to Paris and Belgium.

Boult to Marina. "Ern Malley." BMAP

Bounce ball! Bounce ball! Song for a Ball-Game. Wilfrid Thorley. BoTP

Bounce, buckram, velvet's dear. *Unknown.* OxNR

Bounce to Pope. Alec Derwent Hope. FP

Bound. Theodore Roethke. PoA

Bound and free. Eudaimon. Kathleen Jessie Raine. PBWP

Bound in a moonlight circle. The 49 Stomp. Lew Blockcolski. VoR

Bound in the women who chain by. For Grizzel McNaught (1709–1792). Annie Finch. FFC

Bound on a voyage of awful length. Henry Highland Garnet. CrDW

Bound to my heart as Ixion to the wheel. Dirge for the New Sunrise. Dame Edith Sitwell. CMoP; MoBrPo *Fr.* Three Poems of the Atomic Bomb.

Bound up it always. Mikata Shami, *Japanese*. OHMPJ, *tr.* by Kenneth Rexroth

Bound with the entrails of thy foe. (LL) A Fly Caught in a Cobweb. Richard Lovelace. BeJo; CaPo; SeCP

Boundaries. José Emilio Pacheco, *Spanish*. STV, *tr.* by John Frederick Nims

Boundary. A. L. Hendriks. PBCV

Bounding Billow, cease thy motion. Stanzas Written between Dover and Calais, in July, 1792. Martha Robinson. ECWP

Boundless, bitter is her sorrow. Tune: "Dreaming of the South." Wen T'ing-yün, *Chinese*. SuSp, *tr.* by William R. Schultz

Boundless Moment, A. Robert Frost. NAAL-2

Boundless the leaves roused by spring. Willow. Li Shang-yin, *Chinese*. PLT, *tr.* by A. C. Graham

Bounds of this court's jurisdiction, The. (LL) Nose. Ambrose Bierce. APN-2; OBAL

Bounty. Josephine Miles. NoAM

Bounty, II, The. Myung Mi Kim. PT

Bounty of Jehovah Praise, The. George Sandys. AH

Bounty of Our Age, The. Henry Farley. FaBoCh; FaBoEE; NOSC

Bouquet of Belle Scavoir. Wallace Stevens. MoAmPo

Bouquet of Objects, A. Elaine Equi. PmAP

Bouquet of zephyr-flowers hitched to a hitching, A. You at the Pump. Frank O'Hara. FTOS

Bouquets. Robert Francis. ChAP

Bourbons. Walter Savage Landor. OBSV

Bourgeoisie. Maksimilian Aleksandrovich Voloshin, *Russian*. TCRP, *tr.* by Albert C. Todd

Bourne, The. Christina Rossetti. OBNC

'Bout th' husband oak [*or* oke], the vine. To Castara, upon an Embrace. William Habington. BeJo *Fr.* Castara.

Bout with Burning. Vassar Miller. LiTM; MT; MoAmPo

Bow, daughter of Babylon, bow thee to dust! Babylon. Tennyson. ChIV-1; KSG

Bow down, mountain, to hear the gladness issuing. Norma Farber. AH

Bow down my soul in worship very low. St. Isaac's Church, Petrograd. Claude McKay. NAAAL; PoBA

Bow down. (Prostrates himself. In Memoriam F.M. Dostoevsky. János Pilinszky. CEEP, *tr.* by Jascha Kessler *Fr.* Three Poems.

Bow hither out of heaven and see and save. (LL) Easter Hymn. A. E. Housman. EBEV; GI

Bow to Allah. Brian G. Gilmore. ISC

Bow-wow, says the dog. Mother Goose. OxNR

Bow, wow, wow, / Whose dog art thou? Caesar's Song. Mother Goose. OxNR; ReMoGo

Bow'd and blessed the Augury. Catullus. *See* Carmen 45 ("Phyllis Corydon clutched to him").

Bowed by the weight of centuries he leans. The Man with the Hoe. Edwin Markham. APN-2; BLPA; GS; MoAmPo; PaTW; TFi

Bowed down / to worship / this perfection. William Carlos Williams. *See* The Gift.

Bower of Bliss, The. Edmund Spenser. PoEL-1 *Fr.* Wood Of Error. AEP
   "And in the midst of all, a fountaine stood." CH
   ("Thence passing forth, they shortly do arrive.") OBGa
   "Eftsoones they heard a most melodious sound." EBEvV; NOBE; PBRV; SCV

Bowge of Courte, The. John Skelton. AAS
   Dreamer Meets Riot, The.

Bowing "New Sabbath" or "Mount Ephraim." (LL) A Church Romance. Thomas Hardy. FaBoTw; NOBE; OxAEP-2; OxBTC; PeECV

Bowl, The. John Wilmot, 2d Earl of Rochester. *See* Upon Drinking in a Bowl.

Bowl he starts with, The. The Man. His Bowl. His Raspberries. Claudia Rankine. GT

Bowl of Roses, A. William Ernest Henley. MoBrPo

Bowlegged, pinchered sand-digger. Statilius Flaccus, *Greek*. GrAn, *tr.* by Barriss Mills

Bowling-Green, The. William Somervile.
   "Where fair Sabrina's wand'ring currents flow." NOEC

Box cars run by a mile long. Work Gangs. Carl Sandburg. GM

Box is only temporary, The. (LL) The Arrival of the Bee Box. Sylvia Plath. FaBoMo; FaBoWP; HCAP; NALW

Box of nails, A. John Wills. HA

Boxcar Poem, The ("Boxcars drift by / clanking, The"). David Young. AmPA; GM

Boxers, The. Paul Whitehead. ECEV *Fr.* Gymnasiad, The, or Boxing Match.

Boxes break / At the corners, The. Christmas Ornaments. Valerie Worth. PChr

Boxes of sleeping pills. Tanka. Nakajō Fumiko, *Japanese*. MJT, *tr.* by Makoto Ueda

Boxing Day. Yusef Komunyakaa. ISC

Boxing the Female. Natasha Le Bel. BAP-96

Boxing the Fox. Pearse Hutchinson. CIP-2

Boy, A. John Ashbery. NeAP

Boy. Mary Kinzie. FFC

Boy, about eleven or twelve, The. Testimony: The United States (1901–1910) Recitative/The South. Charles Reznikoff. FTOS

Boy accepted them, The. Daedalus: The Dirge. George Oppen. FTOS

Boy Actor, The. Noël Coward. OxBTC

Boy, age about eleven, A. On the Photograph "Yarn Mill," by Lewis W. Hine. David Ray. WeT

Boy and Girl. Mother Goose. ReMoGo

Boy and the Deer, The. Andrew Peynetsa. STP, *tr.* by Dennis Tedlock

Boy and the Flute, The. Bjørnstjerne Bjørnson, *Norwegian*. AWP, *tr.* by Sir Edmund Gosse

Boy and the Mantle, The. *Unknown.* ESPB; OxBB

Boy and the Parrot, The. John Hookham Frere. CTAV; OxBChV

Boy and the Snake, The. Charles Lamb *and* Mary Lamb. OxBChV

Boy and the Sparrow. Mother Goose. ReMoGo

Boy at Target Practice; a Contemplation. William Robert Moses. NYBP

Boy at the Paterson Falls. Toi Derricotte. PBCAP

Boy at the Window. Richard Wilbur. RaBo

Boy Breaking Glass. Gwendolyn Brooks. AiP; MoP; NAAL-2; NoAM; NoP-4

Boy! bring an ounce of Freeman's best. Isaac Hawkins Browne. BXAP *Fr.* A Pipe of Tobacco.

Boy, bring me candles on a silver salver. Candles. Hélène Swarth, *Dutch*. WPOW, *tr.* by Jonathan Crewe

Boy Died in My Alley, The. Gwendolyn Brooks. NoAM

Boy Fishing, The. Edith Jay Scovell. FaBoWP

Boy from his bedroom-window, The. At Ballyshannon, Co. Donegal. William Allingham. NOBVV

Boy had run all the way home, The. Mending Crab Pots. Dave Jeddie Smith. MT

Boy has two jobs, A. Herbert Hoover. CTV

Boy He Had an Auger, A. *Unknown.* AS

Boy hid under the house, The. Fear. David Lehman. NAmP90

Boy, hold my wreath for me. The Serenader. *Unknown, Greek.* GrAn, *tr.* by Dudley Fitts

Boy holds a blown glass sparrow in his hand, A. Explanations. Judson Mitcham. PuP-14

Boy! I detest all Persian fopperies. Horace. *See* Simplicity.

Boy, I detest the Persian pomp. Horace. *See* Simplicity.

Boy, I hate their empty shows. Horace, *Latin*. OBCVT, *tr.* by William Cowper

Boy, I hate their empty shows. Simplicity. Horace, *Latin*. AWP; InPK-6; NBLV, *tr.* by William Cowper

Boy in Ice. Laurie Lee. NYBP

Boy in the Barn, The. *Unknown.* ReMoGo

Boy is as old as the stars, A. To My God in His Sickness. Philip Levine. NNaP

Boy just like you took me out to see them, A. What the End Is For. Jorie Graham. NAmP90; NoP-4; PoPoPo

Boy leaves a small house, A. Island School. George Mackay Brown. FaBoTC

Boy Liu in Leafy Mound, visitor of the autumn wind. A Bronze Immortal Takes Leave of Han. Li Ho, *Chinese*. PLT, *tr.* by A. C. Graham

Boy looked out of eyes like Euclid's eyes, The. Form Was the World. Maurice English. NYBP

Boy-mad no longer. Leaving the Boys Behind. Rufinus, *Greek*. GrAn, *tr. by Alan Marshfield*

Boy-Man. Karl Shapiro. NYBP

Boy of Egremond, The. Samuel Rogers. NOBRP

Boy of twelve, shaping a fuselage, The. Models. Howard Nemerov. AF

Boy; or, Son of Rip-off, The. Malcolm Glass. BXAP

Boy, presuming on his intellect, A. At Woodward's Gardens. Robert Frost. PoA

Boy Reading. John Holmes. ImGa

Boy Reciter, The. David Everett. BLPA

Boy Remembers in the Field. Raymond Knister. NOBC

Boy Riding Forward Backward. Robert Francis. LCAP-2

Boy Serving at Table, The. John Lydgate. OxBChV

Boy Shepherds' Simile, The. David Bottoms. MT

Boy sits in the classroom, The. Learning Experience. Marge Piercy. NoAM; WeT

Boy Sleeping. Anne Lauterbach. PmAP

Boy stood on the burning deck, The. Casabianca. Felicia Dorothea Hemans. BLPA; EBEvV; FaBoBe; NOBRP; VWP

Boy stoops, picking greens with his mother, A. Greens. David Ray. VGW

Boy that is good, The [*or* A]. The Description of a Good Boy. Henry Dixon. OxBChV; OxNR

Boy waits on the top step, his hand on the door, The. Black Dog, Red Dog. Stephen Dobyns. CMAP

Boy walking home in twilight, A. Twilight with Xs. Dean Young. WeT

Boy was lying upside-down from me, The. Too Dark. Mark McCloskey. PoA

Boy was shot in Irkutsk, The. Komsomol Song. Iosif Pavlovich Utkin, *Russian*. TCRP, *tr. by Lubov Yakovleva*

Boy who Dreamed the Country Night, The. Christopher Koch. NOBAu

Boy who played and talked and read with me, A. Exile. Donald Hall. NoP-4

Boy who throws the ball, The. The Beadle's Testimony. Jerome Rothenberg. NNaP

Boy with Book of Knowledge. Howard Nemerov. NoP-4

Boy with His Hair Cut Short. Muriel Rukeyser. LiTM; NALW; NoAM; TwCP; VGW; WPE

Boy with Kite. Phoebe Hesketh. AYFP

Boy with yellow hair, his clothes in place, A. War Memento (Somewhere in France 1915). Roger Hecht. CRP

Boyarina Morozova, The. Nikolai Ivanovich Glazkov, *Russian*. TCRP, *tr. by Daniel Weissbort*

Boyhood of Christ, The. Saint Columbanus. NOIV

Boyhood Winter. George Eklund. IFJA

Boyish sleep. Hamlin Garland. APN-2

Boyne Water, The. *Unknown*. FaPoR; IIP; NOIV

BOYO: When I came to this country, I could. Scene 6 The Boat Passage. Gabriel Gbadamosi. NBrP *Fr.* No Blacks, No Irish.

Boys. Winifred M. Letts. TIRV

Boys and girls come out to play. Mother Goose. OxNR

Boys and girls crying with hunger, all over the village. A Painting of Peach Blossom Spring. Shen Chou, *Chinese*. CoBLCP, *tr. by Jonathan Chaves*

Boys and girls, we pledge allegiance. Catullus. *See* Hymn to Diana.

Boys came back. Bands played and flags were flying, The. Fight to a Finish. Siegfried Sassoon. PoFWW

Boy's cocks, Diodore. Epigram. Strato, *Greek*. GrAn, *tr. by Thomas Meyer*

Boys flying kites haul in their white-winged birds. Words. *Unknown*. PoLF

Boys forget about women. The Excuse. Carl H. Greene. NBV

Boys have to slash their fingers to become brothers. Girls trade. An Anointing. Thylias Moss. GT

Boy's Head, A. Miroslav Holub, *Czech*. CBNP, *tr. by Ian Milner and George Theiner*

Boys / I don't promise you nothing. Admonitions. Lucille Clifton. BPo; NALW; NMM-2

Boys in sporadic but tenacious droves. The Horse Chestnut Tree. Richard Eberhart. CMoP; LiTM; MoAmPo; PFE

Boys kicking a ball on a vast square beneath an obelisk. Above Us. Julia Hartwig, *Polish*. BLT, *tr. by Stanislaw Baranczak and Clare Cavanagh*

Boys Make Men. *Unknown*. PWR

Boys of Ch'ien-t'ang practice riding the bore, The. Song of Surfing on the Bore. Cheng Hsieh, *Chinese*. CoBLCP, *tr. by Jonathan Chaves*

Boys of Mullabaun [*or* Mullaghbawn], The. *Unknown*. BIrV

Boys of Sanpete County, The. *Unknown*. AmFP

Boys of these men. Boys of These Men Full Speed. Muriel Rukeyser. NNaP

Boys of These Men Full Speed. Muriel Rukeyser. NNaP

Boy's Poem, A. Alexander Smith.
    "Steamer left the black and oozy wharves, The." PeVV

Boy's Song, A. James Hogg. BoTP; CH; CTV; FaPoR; NOxBChV; OBEV; OTCP; OxAEP-2; OxBChV

Boy's Summer, A. Paul Laurence Dunbar. CA

Boysick (by gadzooks thunderstruck), The. The Honey Lamb. Jonathan Williams. PoM

Bozzy and Piozzi. "Peter Pindar."
    Introduction and Anecdotes. PoEL-3
    Town Eclogue, A. OBCoV

Br-r-r-am-m-m, rackety-am-m, OM, *Am*. What the Motorcycle Said. Mona Van Duyn. NIP-4

Braced in the sinewy vigour of thy breed. The Horse and His Rider. Joanna Baillie. ECWP; NOEC

Bracelet, The. Donne. NoSic

Bracelet. Robert Herrick. OBEV
    ("If I could, I would not so.") (LL) APAD

Bracelet, The. Thomas Stanley. BeJo

Bracelet of Grass, The. William Vaughn Moody. APN-2

Bracelets. William Strode. NOSC

Bracketed by a diesel switcher and five. Note on the L and N. Richmond Lattimore. GM

Brackish reach of shoal off Madaket[—A], A. The Quaker Graveyard in Nantucket. Robert Lowell. CMoP; ColAP; HAP; LiTM; MoP; NAAL-2; NOBA; NoAM; NoP-4; OxBA; OxBoS; PeECV; Poetr; TAP; UnPo; VCAP

Brady. *Unknown*. AS

Braemar. Galway Kinnell. PoA

Braes o' Yarrow, The. *Unknown*. *See* The Dowie Houms o' Yarrow.

Braes of Yarrow, The. John Logan. GTBS-P; SCGP

Braes of Yarrow, The. *Unknown*. ESPB; OxBB

Brag, sweet tenor bull. Basil Bunting. NoAM; NoP-4; PoE *Fr.* Briggflatts [An Autobiography].

Brahma. Ralph Waldo Emerson. APAD; APN-1; AWP; AmPP; ColAP; HAP; ImPo; MeMAP; NOBA; NoP-4; OBEV; OxBA; PAR; PoE; PoRA; TAP; TFi; UV; UnPo

Brahma. Andrew Lang. BXAP; NOBL; PeLV; UV

Brahmin, The. James Montgomery.
    "Once on the mountain's balmy lap reclined." NOBRP

Braid Claith. Robert Fergusson. NOEC; OxBS

Braid of creation / Trembles. Stanley Kunitz. *See* The Snakes of September.

Brain Cells, The. Donald Hall. TAP

Brain Drain. "The Mighty Chalkdust." PBCV

Brain forgets, but the blood will remember, The. The Dark Chamber. Louis Untermeyer. MoAmPo

Brain—is wider than the Sky, The. Emily Dickinson. APN-2; EnlH; MoAmPo; MoP; NAAL-1; NAAL-3; NAWM-2; NCAP; NTP; OxBA; PAR; PoPoPo; Poetr

Brain itself in its skull, The. Harsh Climate. Charles Simic. LCAP-2

Brain on Ice, The El Train Poem. Michael Warr. UnSA

Brain, within its Groove, The. Emily Dickinson. NCAP; NOBA; NoAM; SAmP

Brainless creatures simply fuck. Vive La Différence. Strato, *Greek*. GrAn, *tr. by Teddy Hogge*

Brainsick race that wanton youth ensues, The. *Unknown*. NoSic

Brainstorm. Howard Nemerov. HAP; TRP

Braly Street. Gary Soto. UnSA

Bramble Jam. Irene F. Pawsey. BoTP

Bran, a chaff, a very barley [y]awn, A. Edward Taylor. ChIV-2; NOSC *Fr.* Preparatory Meditations Before My Approach to the Lord's Supper.

Branch, A. Cor Van den Heuvel. HA

Branches of grape-vine thick as ankles. An Elm Tree in Paddington. Robert Adamson. BMAP

Branches' snow is like the cotton fluff, The. The Element Mother. Lorine Niedecker. FTOS

Branchy leafy oak tree, The, Sweeney Praises the Trees. Seamus Heaney. RB

Brandy Glass, The. Louis MacNeice. GEA

Branwell's Sestina. James Reaney. MoCV *Fr.* A Suit of Nettles.

Branwen's Starling. R. Williams Parry, *Welsh*. OBWVE, *tr. by Gwyn Jones*

Brass band plays in a brass oven, A. Moscow: Summer '86. Yevgeny Bunimovich, *Russian*. TCRP, *tr. by Bradley Jordan and Albert C. Todd*

Brass Horse, The. Drummond Allison. FaBoTw

Brass Knuckles. Stuart Dybek. PBCAP

Brass Spittoons. Langston Hughes. MoAmPo; NoAM; Poetr

Brass Tacks. Denise Levertov. InPS-3

Brassica (oleracea) is a cabbage. Cabbage. Rosemary Norman. BrRo

Brats. X. J. Kennedy. NBLV

Brattle Street. Lilacs on Brattle Street. Gail Mazur. PUP-19

Bratzlav Rabbi to His Scribe, The. Jacob Glatstein, *Yiddish.* TrJP, *tr. by* Jacob Sloan

Brave as a postage stamp[, he went his way]. Sporting Goods. Philippe Soupault, *French.* TTTS, *tr. by* Rosemarie Waldrop; PFTM

Brave comrade, answer! When you joined the war. George Henry Boker. APN-2

Brave flowers, that I could gallant it like you. A Contemplation upon Flowers. Henry, Bishop of Chichester King. MeLP; OBEV; SCGP; SeCP

Brave Grant, thou hero of the war. General Grant—the Hero of the War. George Moses Horton. AAP; CBCWP

Brave infant of Saguntum, clear. Ben Jonson. *See* To the Immortal[l] Memory [*or* Memorie] and Friendship of That Noble Pair[e], Sir Lucius Cary and Sir H. [*or* Henry] Morison.

Brave infant of Saguntum, clear[e]. To the Immortal[l] Memory [*or* Memorie] and Friendship of That Noble Pair[e], Sir Lucius Cary and Sir H. [*or* Henry] Morison. Ben Jonson. BeJo; NAEL-1; NOBE; NOSC; OAEL-1; PoEL-2; SeCP

Brave lads in olden musical centuries. Alcaics; to H. F. B. Robert Louis Stevenson. OBEV

Brave Man, The. Wallace Stevens. PBMP; SAmP

Brave Man and Brave Woman. Mrs. Henry Linden. CBWP-4

Brave man has ambitions wide as the four seas, The. Poem without a Category. T'ao Ch'ien, *Chinese.* CoBCP, *tr. by* Burton Watson

Brave man with a sword!, The. (LL) The Ballad of Reading Gaol. Oscar Wilde. ADE; EBVV; NoAM; TIRV

Brave man with a sword!, The. (LL) The Condemned Man. Oscar Wilde. EBEvV; EBNV; MoBrPo; NOBE; NOBVV; NoAM; OBMV; OBNC; TFi; UV

Brave New World. Archibald MacLeish. NOBA; OxBA

Brave New World. Shakespeare. *Fr.* The Tempest. OAEL-1

Brave news is come to town. *Unknown.* OxNR

Brave Old Duke of York, The. *Unknown.* OxNR

Brave Old Oak, The. Henry Fothergill Chorley. FaBoBe

Brave Old Ship, the *Orient*, The. Robert Traill Spence Lowell. FaBoBe

Brave Rover. Max Beerbohm. NBLV

Brave Teuton, though thy awful name. Schemmelfennig. Bret Harte. OBAL

Brave weathercock, I see thou'lt set thy nose. Upon the Weathercock. John Bunyan. OxBChV

Brave, wise, and Venus' son. (LL) In a Bye-Canal. Herman Melville. APN-2; NCAP

Brave youth, to whom Fate in one hour. For a Picture Where a Queen Laments over the Tomb of a Slain Knight. Thomas Carew. CaPo

Bravely from Fairyland he rode, on furlough. The Broken Girth. Robert Graves. BIrV

Bravery runs in my family. Coward. A. R. Ammons. OBAL

Braving the Wilds All Unexplored. Robert Freeman. AH

Braw, snortin', roarin', fearsome beastie. To a Bull Moose. Eugene O'Neill. UV

Brawling of a sparrow in the eaves, The. The Sorrow of Love. W. B. Yeats. NAEL-2; OAEL-2; PeVV

Brazen hypnotics glitter here. Hart Crane. *See* For the Marriage of Faustus and Helen.

Brazen hypnotics glitter here;. For the Marriage of Faustus and Helen. Hart Crane. SeSe *Fr.* For the Marriage of Faustus and Helen. InPS-3; NOBA; NoAM

Brazen Image. Anne Hartigan. CIP-2

Brazen Tongue. William Rose Benét. MoAmPo

Brazil, January 1, 1502. Elizabeth Bishop. BLT; FaBoWP; NoAM; PoPoPo; VCAP

Brazilian Fazenda. Patricia K. Page. FaBoWP

Breach of clear heaven opens, A. Enlightment. Ch'en Yü-yi, *Chinese.* OHMPC, *tr. by* Kenneth Rexroth

Bread. Stanley Burnshaw. TrJP

Bread. James Dickey. LCAP-2

Bread. Huỳnh Phú S(cfstilde;o), *Vietnamese.* AVP, *tr. by* Huỳnh Sanh Thông

Bread. Brendan Kennelly. PBCIP

Bread. W. S. Merwin. SPE; VCAP

Bread. Gabriela Mistral, *Spanish.* WPOW, *tr. by* Allan Francovich *and* Kathleen Weaver

Bread. H. E. Wilkinson. BoTP

Bread and a Pension. Louis Johnson. PeNZ

Bread and milk for breakfast. Christina Rossetti. NTP

Bread and Music. Conrad Potter Aiken. MoAmPo *Fr.* Discordants.

Bread and Wine. Friedrich Hölderlin, *German.*
    "Oh friend, we arrived too late." RaBo

Bread goes up so bread goes up again. Inflation. Nicanor Parra, *Spanish.* AF, *tr. by* Miller Williams

Bread Hot from the Oven, The. John Thompson. NOBC

Bread: I'm told a certain object grows. Cynewulf. ASW, *tr. by* Kevin Crossley-Holland *Fr.* Riddles (Exeter Book).

Bread is a lovely thing to eat. Lovely Things. H. M. Sarson. BoTP

Bread Is Born. Anne Hébert, *French.* BoWoP, *tr. by* Maxine W. Kumin

Bread is poisoned and the air's drunk dry, The. Osip Mandelstam, *Russian.* TCRP, *tr. by* Bernard Meares

Bread Man, The. Lucinda Roy. GT

Bread of Heaven, on Thee We Feed. Josiah Conder. TrCP

Bread of this World; Praises III, The. Thomas McGrath. RaBo

Bread-oh, bread-oh, ten-cent bread. . . . The Bread Man. Lucinda Roy. GT

Bread-Word Giver. John Wheelwright. ChIV-2

Breaded Fish. A. K. Ramanujan. NoP-4

Breaded Meat, Breaded Hands. Michael S. Harper. ISC

Breadth. Circle. Desert. Monarch. Month. Wisdom. John Hollander. PoA

Break, The. Elizabeth Nancy Sargent. NYBP

Break, agonized and clear. Emily Dickinson. *See* Success is counted sweetest.

Break and trail home. The Girl I Left behind Me. *Unknown.* AmFP

"Break, Break, Break." Sir John Collings Squire. BXAP

Break, break, break. Tennyson. AWP; CBLP; CH; CTV; ClHu; EBEvV; EnVR; FHYEP; FaBoBe; FaPoR; GTBS-P; HAP; HeIP-4; ImPo; NAEL-2; NIP-4; NOBE; NOBVV; NoP-4; OBNC; PWR; PoEL-5; PoRA; Poetr; RB; SAGP; SoSe-8; TFi; WeW-3

Break, Fant'sy, from thy cave of cloud. Ben Jonson. *Fr.* The Vision of Delight. PoEL-2

Break from the Bush, A. Yusef Komunyakaa. CDa

Break not my loneliness, O Wanderer! The Dove's Loneliness. George Darley. OBNC

Break not the slumbers of the bride. An Hymeneal Song on the Nuptials of the Lady Anne Wentworth and the Lord Lovelace. Thomas Carew. CaPo

Break[e] of Day. Donne. NAEL-1; SoSe-8

Break of Day in the Trenches. Isaac Rosenberg. CABP; FaBoMo; GTBS-P; MoBrPo; NAEL-2; NOBE; NSI; NoAM; NoP-4; OAEL-2; OBWP; OxAEP-2; PeFWW; PoA; PoFWW; PoWW; TFi

Break off / fallen Catullus. Carmen 8. Catullus, *Latin.* OBVE, *tr. by* Louis Zukofsky *and* Celia Zukofsky; AAS, *tr. by* Thomas Campion

Break off. The phrase disintegrates and dies. Villanelle. Tomas Venclova, *Lithuanian.* CEEP, *tr. by* David McDuff

Break Thou the Bread of Life. Mary Artemisia Lathbury. AH

Break through and stare. (LL) Madrigal: "Your love is dead, lady, your love is dead." Ronald Stuart Thomas. BoLoP; EnLoPo

Break-up, The. Abraham Moses Klein. NOBC

Breakable; heavy; clumsy; the end of a side. 78's. Lloyd Schwartz. WeT

Breake now my heart and dye! Oh no, she may relent. Thomas Campion. AAS

Breakfast. Wilfrid Wilson Gibson. OBMV; OxBTC; PoFWW

Breakfast. Harry Graham. EBNV

Breakfast. Thom Gunn. OxBC

Breakfast. Everette Maddox. MT

Breakfast. Ljubomir Simovic, *Serbo-Croatian.* HSix, *tr. by* Charles Simic

Breakfast. William Carlos Williams. SAmP

Breakfast alone. Alexis Rotella. HA

Breakfast for Barbarians, A. Gwendolyn MacEwen. NOBC

Breakfast in Bed (Influenza in War-time). Donald McDonald. PBCV

Breakfast is drunk down. . . Damp earth. Our Daily Bread. César Vallejo, *Spanish.* GI, *tr. by* James Wright

Breakfast on the Patio. James Harms. CMAP

Breakfast over, islanded by noise. Woman in Kitchen. Eavan Boland. BiHa

Breakfast Song in Time of Diet. Stoddard King. OBAL

Breakfast with Gerard Manley Hopkins. Anthony Brode. BXAP; NOBL

Breakfast with Jerome. Elaine Equi. WWSi

Breaking. Cynthia Huntington. NAmP90

Breaking and Entering. Ralph Angel. NAmP90

Breaking Camp. David Wagoner. PaTW

Breaking from under that thy cloudy veil. Edward Herbert. OxAEP-1

Breaking Green. Michael Ondaatje. NOBC

Breaking Ground. Thom Gunn. OBGa *Fr.* Breaking Ground.

Breaking into a baby's breath. Rapture. Ilsong Kwon, *Korean*. CKP, *tr. by* Jaihiun Kim

Breaking Open. Muriel Rukeyser. AF

Breaking Rocks on Poulo Condore. Phan chu Trinh, *Vietnamese*. AVP, *tr. by* Huỳnh Sanh Thông

Breaking the Chain. Tony Harrison. UV

Breaking the morning ice on the well's bucket was no great hardship. On the Pilgrim's Way in Kent, as It Leads to the Coldrum Stones. "Asphodel." BrRo

Breaking the Surface. George Looney. EC3

Breaking through the first door, he found. Seven Dreams. John Clifford Bayliss. SPE

Breaking Tradition. Janice Mirikitani. NMM-2

Breaking up the clouds. (LL) Pushing. Christopher Gilbert. LTA; SoSe-8

Breaking waves dashed high, The. The Landing of the Pilgrim Fathers [in New England]. Felicia Dorothea Hemans. BLPA; BoTP; FaBoBe; NoP-4; WPE

Breaking with honey buds, shall ever equal. (LL) The Express. Stephen Spender. CMoP; HeIP-4; LiTM; MoBrPo; MoP; NoAM; TwCP

Breaks, and in accents mellifluous, follows the thoughts of the author. (LL) The Metre Colombian. *Unknown*. BXAP; UV

Breaks like the Atlantic Ocean on my head. (LL) Man And Wife. Robert Lowell. AmPP; BoLoP; CoAmPo; ColAP; LoP; NAAL-2; SAGP; VCAP

Breaks up in obelisks on the river. Ice. Ai. FYAP

Breakthrough. Carolyn M. Rodgers. BPo

Breakwaters. Ted Walker. NYBP

Breast/ below ground. The Dance. Robert Kelly. *Fr.* The Book of Persephone. PoM

Breast Examination. Wanda Coleman. GT

Breastes round, and long small armes twain, The. (LL) The Smiling Mouth and Laughing Eyen Grey. Charles, Duc d'Orléans. HAP; MiEL

Breasts. Bhartrihari, *Sanskrit*. EP, *tr. by* John Brough

Breasts. Maxine Chernoff. PmAP

Breasts. Tess Gallagher. AmPA

Breasts. Donald Hall. OBAL

Breasts. Charles Simic. NNaP; RaBo

Breasts of a barmaid of Crale, The. Limerick. *Unknown*. NOBL

Breath, The. Robert Bly. *See* NOTL.

Breath. Mark Strand. HCAP

Breath leaves the sentences and does not come back, A. Losing a Language. W. S. Merwin. NoP-4

Breath of Air, A. James Wright. NOBA

Breath of my life, The—no less. Epigram. Meleager, *Greek*. GrAn, *tr. by* Peter Whigham

Breath of the sun, crowned. Bearings III: Amber Wall. Wole Soyinka. PBMAP *Fr.* The Shuttle in the Crypt.

Breath'd in their distant homes by wife or child! (LL) The Buoy-Bell. Charles Tennyson Turner. GSo

Breathe Dust. Fred Wah. NOBC

Breathe in experience, breathe out poetry—. Poem Out of Childhood. Muriel Rukeyser. NMM-2

Breathe not, hid heart: cease silently. To an Unborn Pauper Child. Thomas Hardy. GTBS-P

Breathed [*or* Breath'd] back again! (LL) Echoes. Thomas Moore. GTBS-P; NOBRP; OxAEP-2

Breathers, The. James Reiss. AmPA

Breathes there the [*or* a] Man [with Soul So Dead]. Caledonia. Sir Walter Scott. BLPA; EBEvV; OxBS; SoSe-8; TFi *Fr.* The Lay of the Last Minstrel.

Breathes there the man, with soul so dead. Sir Walter Scott. *See* Caledonia.

Breathing. James Tate. LCAP-2

Breathing. Rod Willmot. HA

Breathing do I draw that air to me. Song of Breath. Peire Vidal, *French*. AWP, *tr. by* Ezra Pound

Breathing Exercises. Leonard Nathan. PBCAP

Breathing his last music, Mozart is supposed. Lost Letter to James Wright, with Thanks for a Map of Fano. Gibbons Ruark. MT

Breathing something German at the end. The Gift to Be Simple. Howard Moss. Poetsp; TwCP

Breathing Space July. Tomas Transtromer, *Swedish*. RB, *tr. by* Robert Bly

Breathless she stood, her graceful head bent low. Listening Nydia. Henrietta Cordelia Ray. CBWP-3

Breathless swimmer in that cold green element, A. (LL) The Cold Green Element. Irving Layton. NoP-4

Breathless, we flung us on the windy hill. The Hill. Rupert Brooke. MoBrPo; OxBTC; SAGP; Son

Breaths. Birago Diop, *French*. TTY, *tr. by* Anne Atik

Breath's slow, The. Changing Room. John A. Scott. BMAP

Brébeuf and His Brethren. Edwin John Pratt.
　Martyrdom of Brébeuf and Lalemant, 16 March 1649, The. NOBC

Brébeuf and His Brethren. Francis Reginald Scott. NOBC

Bred up at home, full early I begun. Alexander Pope. *Fr.* The Second Epistle of the Second Book of Horace Imitated. TOF

Bredon Hill. A. E. Housman. EBVV; MoBrPo; NAEL-2; OxAEP-2; SoSe-8; UV

Breech, The. Michael McClure. NeAP

Breed in a lively animal. (LL) Two Songs. Adrienne Rich. NIP-4; NOBA; TAP

Breed's described, The: Now, Satire, if you can. Daniel Defoe. OBSV *Fr.* The True-born Englishman.

Breeze from the Sea. Stéphane Mallarmé, *French*. FLP, *tr. by* Alistair Elliot

Breeze in Translation. Belle Waring. NAmP90; PBCAP

Breeze is chasing the zephyr, The. Nobody's Chasing Me. Cole Porter. CBLP

Breeze is on the bluebells, The. Bluebells. Juliana Horatia Ewing. BoTP

Breezes taste, The. September. John Updike. KaS

Breezeways in the tropics winnow the air. A Letter from the Caribbean. Barbara Howes. CoAP; IMW; UnPo

Breezing Dawn of the New Day, The. Mongane Wally Serote. PeSAV

Breitmann in Paris. Charles Godfrey Leland. APN-2

Breitmann in Politics. Charles Godfrey Leland.
　"Dere's a liddle fact in hishdory vitch few hafe onnershtand." OBAL

Brennan on the Moor. *Unknown*. AmFP

Brennbaum. Ezra Pound. MoAmPo *Fr.* Hugh Selwyn Mauberley. (Life and Contacts). AmPP; CMoP; InPS-3; LiTM; NOBA; NoAM; TAP

Brent; a Poem to Thomas Palmer Esq. William Diaper.
　"Had mournful Ovid been to Brent condemned!" OBSV
　"Happy are you, whom Quantock overlooks." NOEC; OBSV

Br'er Sterling and the Rocker. Michael S. Harper. NAAAL

Brereton Omen, The. Felicia Dorothea Hemans.
　"Yes! I have seen the ancient oak." CTC

Bresson's Movies. Robert Creeley. NoP-4; PmAP

Brethren, The. Seamus Deane. PNI

Breton Afternoon. Ernest Christopher Dowson. OBNC

Breughel's Winter. Rutger Kopland, *Dutch*. VCWP, *tr. by* James Brockway

Brevities. Siegfried Sassoon. PoLF

Brewer's Man, The. Leonard Alfred George Strong. OBCoV; PeLV

Brewing of Soma, The. John Greenleaf Whittier. PoEL-4
　"Dear Lord and Father of Mankind." AH; NOCV

Brewing Tea at Moon Pond. Chang Yü. *Fr.* Seven Poems on Living in the Mountains: Seeing Off. CoBLCP, *tr. by* Jonathan Chaves

Breyten Prays for Himself. Breyten Breytenbach, *Afrikaans*. VCWP, *tr. by* Denis Hirson

Brian O'Linn. *Unknown*. CBNP; NBLV; RB
　("Brian O Linn had no breeches to wear.") OBCoV

Brick, The. Paul Roche. NYBP

Brick distinguishes this country. Amsterdam Letter. Jean Garrigue. NYBP; VCAP

Brickie who had a fine tool, A. Limerick. E. O. Parrott. PeLi

Bricklayer tells the busdriver, The. The Continuity. Paul Blackburn. NeAP

Bricklayer's Labours, The. Robert Tatersal. NOEC

Bricklay'r throws his trowel by, The. Religion and the Lower Classes. Evan Lloyd. NOEC *Fr.* The Methodist.

Brid one brere, brid, brid one brere. *Unknown*. MiEL

Bridal Birth. D. G. Rossetti. Son *Fr.* The House of Life.

Bridal Song. Francis Beaumont *and* John Fletcher. *See* Song: "Hold back thy hours, dark night, till we have done."

Bridal Song. Thomas Lovell Beddoes. *See* Bridal Song to Amala.

Bridal Song: "Cynthia, to thy power." Francis Beaumont *and* John Fletcher. OBEV *Fr.* The Maid's Tragedy.

Bridal Song: "Now sleep, bind fast the flood of air." George Chapman. OxBSP *Fr.* The Masque of the Middle Temple and Lincoln's Inn.

Bridal Song: "O come, soft rest of cares, come Night." George Chapman. NOBE; OBEV *Fr.* Hero and Leander. AAS

Bridal Song, A: "Roses, their sharp spines being gone." John Fletcher *and* Shakespeare. NOBE; NOSC; NoSic *Fr.* The Two Noble Kinsmen.

Bridal Song to Amala. Thomas Lovell Beddoes. GBL *Fr.* Death's Jest Book.
　(Song: "We have bathed, where none have seen us.") NOBVV; OBNC

Bridal Songs: "Happy bridegroom! / Now your wedding has come true." Sappho, *Greek*. GrIP, *tr. by* Suzy Q. Groden

Bridal weath. White rhododendron. Dogwood. May, Home after a Year Away. Gail Mazur. NAmP90

Bride, The. Bella Akhatovna Akhmadulina, *Russian*. BoWoP; LiLi, *tr. by* Stephen Stepanchev

Bride, The. Butterfly Wine. *Japanese Oral Tradition, Japanese.* ITG, *tr. by R. H. Blyth*

Bride, A. Harry Fainlight. BoLoP

Bride, The. D. H. Lawrence. NoAM; OxBTC

Bride, The. Sir John Suckling. *Fr.* A Ballad[e] [upon a Wedding]. BeJo; CaPo; EBEV; EBNV; OxBM; SeCP

Bride, The. Tongju Yi, *Korean.* CKP, *tr. by Jaihiun Kim*

Bride cam' out o' the byre, The. Wooed and Married and A'. Alexander Ross. OxBS

Bride loved old words, and found her pleasure marred. James Vincent Cunningham. OBAL *Fr.* Five Epigrams.

Bride-Night Fire, The. Thomas Hardy. EnVR

  "O Tim, my own Tim I must call 'ee—I will!" FaBoVe

Bride of Frankenstein, The. Edward Field. CoAP; HeIP-4

Bride of Lammermoor, The. Sir Walter Scott.

  Lucy Ashton's Song. NOBE; OBEV; OxAEP-2; OxBS; Ro

Bride of Quietness, The. Kelly Cherry. FFC

Bride of the Iconoclasts, The. Benjamin Paul Blood.

  "Stop!—Gaze thro' this hushed gallery! The air." APN-2

Bride she is winsome and bonny, The. Song: Woo'd and married and a'. Joanna Baillie. NoP-4

Bride sits / on a low polished stool, The. The Village Wedding. Angelos Sikelianos, *Greek.* GrIP, *tr. by Edmund Keeley and Philip Sherrard*

Bride Song. Christina Rossetti. OBEV; WPE *Fr.* The Prince's Progress.

Bridegroom, The. Rudyard Kipling. FaBoEE *Fr.* Epitaphs of the War [1914–1918]. OBWP

Bridegroom, beloved of my heart. *Unknown.* WPoS

Bridegroom comes, she sits on the stove, The. Donne. ITG

Bridegroom Dick. Herman Melville.

  "Where's Commander All-a-Tanto?" PoEL-5

Bridegroom of Cana, The. Marjorie Lowry Christie Pickthall. TrCP

Bridegroom of forty-one, / who tomorrow goes off to war, The. Siberian Wooing. Yevtushenko, *Russian.* VCWP, *tr. by Albert C. Todd and James Ragan*

Brides, The. Alec Derwent Hope. HAP

Brides Come to Yuba City, The. Chitra Divakaruni. OpBo; UnSA

Bride's Day. Susan Howe. FTOS *Fr.* Defenestration of Prague.

Bride's Hours, A. Jean Valentine. FaBoWP

Bridge. A. R. Ammons. CoAP; NAAL-2

Bridge, The. Hart Crane. NAAL-2

  Atlantis. LiTM

  Ave Maria. NOBA; NoAM

  Cape Hatteras. InPS-3; MoAmPo

    Power. MoAmPo

  Cutty Sark. FaBoMo

  Powhatan's Daughter.

    Dance, The. LiTM; MoAmPo; OxBA

    Harbor Dawn, The. AmPP; CMoP; LiTM; MoAmPo; NOBA; NoAM; OxBA

    Indiana.

    River, The. AmPP; CMoP; GM; MoAmPo; NOBA; OxBA

    Van Winkle. AmPP; MoAmPo

  Quaker Hill. LiTM

  Three Songs. NAAL-2

    National Winter Garden. EP; InPS-3; LiTM; OxBA

    Southern Cross.

    Virginia.

  To Brooklyn Bridge. AiP; AmPP; ChIV-1; ClHu; ColAP; FaBoA; ImPo; InPS-3; KSG; LiTM; MeMAP; MoAmPo; NOBA; OxBA; PoE; PoPoPo; TFi; TRP

    (Poem: To Brooklyn Bridge.) AmFP; AmPP; CMoP; HAP; HeIP-4; NoAM; TAP; WeW-3

  Tunnel, The. CMoP; MoAmPo; OxBA

Bridge, The. Henry Wadsworth Longfellow. APN-1

Bridge, The. O. V. de L. Milosz, *French.* BLT, *tr. by Czeslaw Milosz and Robert Hass*

Bridge. Christopher Okigbo. PBMAP *Fr.* Heavensgate (1961).

Bridge, The. John Banister Tabb. APN-2

Bridge, The. Charlotte Zolotow. CA

Bridge, and a hot concrete road, A. The Desert of Love. János Pilinszky, *Hungarian.* OBVE, *tr. by Ted Hughes and Janos Csokits*

Bridge-Builder, The. Will Allen Dromgoole. *See* Building the Bridge.

Bridge-Guard in the Karroo. Rudyard Kipling. OBWP

Bridge instead of a Wall, A. *Unknown.* PoToHe

Bridge is certainly the simplest answer, The. Manly Ferry. John Philip. NOBAu

Bridge of Death, The. *Unknown, French.* AWP, *tr. by Andrew Lang*

Bridge of Heraclitus, The. George Reavey. BIrV

Bridge of Sighs, The. Thomas Hood. EBEV; FaPoR; GTBS-P; OBEV; OxAEP-2

Bridge of volumes, The. A World in Yellow. Marcel Duchamp, *French.* PFTM, *tr. by Arturo Schwarz*

Bridge on the Sangarios, A. Agathias, *Greek.* GrAn, *tr. by Guy Davenport*

Bridge over the low-flowing river, A. The River. Paul Zweig. MoLi

Bridge Poem, The. Kate Rushin. GLP

Bridge toll-booth—, The. David E. Lecount. HA

Bridge's iron mesh chases pockets of shadow, The. Love Song During Riot with Many Voices. Lynda Hull. NAmP90

Bridget. Lisa Lewis. BAP-95

Brief Autumnal. *Unknown, Greek.* GrAn; WeW-3, *tr. by Dudley Fitts*

Brief Curriculum. Reiner Kunze, *German.* PoSu, *tr. by Michael Hamburger*

Brief day ending. Frank K. Robinson. HA

Brief Elegie on My Dear Son John, A. John Saffin. SCAP

Brief Essay on Man. Arthur Guiterman. OBAL

Brief Farewell. Anthony Delius. PeSA

Brief History. Richard Hugo. PaTW

Brief is our life, now in the midst of the years. To Adelhard, Archbishop of Canterbury. Alcuin, *Latin.* MLL, *tr. by Helen Waddell*

Brief Journey West, The. Howard Nemerov. NoAM

Brief Letter to Donald Walsh (in memoriam). Angel Cuadra, *Spanish.* AF, *tr. by Katherine Rodriguez Nieto*

Brief Novel (3). Eric Mottram. NBrP

Brief, on a flying night. Chimes. Alice Thompson Meynell. BoTP; CH; MoBrPo; WPE

Brief procession, The. Bessie Smith's Funeral. Alvin Aubert. SeSe

Brief Reflection on Cats Growing in Trees. Miroslav Holub. CBNP, *tr. by Ewald Osers*

Brief Reflection on Charlemagne. Miroslav Holub, *German.* CEEP, *tr. by Stuart Friebert and Dana Habová*

Brief Thoughts on cats Growing on Trees. Miroslav Holub, *Czech.* PoSu, *tr. by Ian Milner and Jarmila Milner*

Brief Thoughts on Cracks. Miroslav Holub, *Czech.* PoSu, *tr. by Ian and Jarmila Milner*

Brief Thoughts on Floods. Miroslav Holub, *Czech.* PoSu, *tr. by Ian and Jarmila Milner*

Brief was the reign of pure poetic truth. Donne. Hartley Coleridge. EPCY

Brief Wyoming Meditation. Diane Di Prima. BB

Briefcase, The. Paul Muldoon. CABP

Briefly It Enters, and Briefly Speaks. Jane Kenyon. CrSp

Brigadier. Arthur James Marshall Smith. MoCV

Briggflatts [An Autobiography]. Basil Bunting.

  "Brag, sweet tenor bull." NoAM; NoP-4; PoE

  "Grass caught in willow tells the flood's height that has subsided." FaBoMo

  "As the player's breath warms the fipple the tone clears."

  "Strong song tows, A." OAEL-2

Bright. (LL) The End of a War. Sir Herbert Read. OBMV; PeFWW

Bright. No Thanks, No. 70. E. E. Cummings. PFTM

Bright. Water Maid. Christopher Okigbo. PBMAP

Bright after Dark. Pearse Hutchinson. PBCIP

Bright and beautiful art thou. October. Mary Weston Fordham. CBWP-2

Bright and early we went down to the fishmarket. Words from Confinement. Cesare Pavese, *Italian.* AF, *tr. by William Arrowsmith*

Bright are the days which the Fates hold in store for us. To William (Whom We Have Missed). P. G. Wodehouse. NOBL

Bright as the day, and like the morning fair. Cloe. George, Granville. FaBoEE; NIP-4

Bright as the light that burns at night. Venetia. Adah Isaacs Menken. CBWP-1

Bright awning is cranked, A. Alan Pizzarelli. HA

Bright Babe! whose awfull beautyes [*or* beauties] make. In the Glorious Epiphanie of Our [*or* Ovr] Lord God[, A Hymn. Svng as by the Three Kings]. Richard Crashaw. ESCV; FSCP; PoEL-2

Bright be the place of thy soul! Byron. HoPM

Bright blossoms seldom last long. T'ao Ch'ien, *Chinese.* SuSp, *tr. by Eugene Eoyang*

Bright burnished day, they are laying fresh roof down. Men Roofing. Eamon Grennan. PBCIP

Bright cards above the fire bring no friends near. Christmas 1944. Denise Levertov. AF

Bright-coloured, mirror-plated, strung with lights. Merry-go-round. James Philip McAuley. CBAP

Bright, consuming Spirit. No power on earth so great as Thee. The Song of Hungarrda. Ngunaitponi. NOBAu

Bright Day, A. W. H. Davies. OBWVE

Bright Day, A. John Montague. CIP-2

Bright drips the morning from its trophied nets. Sonnet of Fishes. George Barker. FaBoMo; Son

Bright enamoured youth above, The. Love's Mystery. Joseph Beaumont. NOSC

Bright flowers and dim moon, enmeshed in thin drifting mist. Tune: "Deva-like Barbarian." Li Yü, *Chinese.* SuSp, *tr. by* Daniel Bryant

Bright-footed Thetis did the sphere aspire. Homer. NoSic, *tr. by* George Chapman. *Fr.* The Iliad.

Bright, glowing Sappho! child of love and song. Ode to Sappho. Elizabeth Oakes Smith. ColAP

Bright green young grass comes up in the garden. Life Is Long. *Unknown, Chinese.* OHMPC, *tr. by* Kenneth Rexroth

Bright-haired am I, my face and body white. First Song. T. Carmi. MHP, *tr. by* Ruth Finer Mintz *Fr.* René's Songs.

Bright-haired Spirit! Golden Brow! Onward to Far Ida. George Darley. OBNC *Fr.* Nepenthe.

Bright hard day over harbour sea, A. Winter Lanscape—Halifax. Douglas Lochhead. NIP-4

Bright-harnessed angels sit in order serviceable. (LL) Hymn on the Morning of Christ's Nativity [*or* On the Morning of Christ's Nativity]. Milton. NAEL-1; NOBE; OBEV

Bright-harnest [*or* harness'd] Angels sit in order serviceable. (LL) On the Morning of Christ's Nativity. Milton. GTBS-P; ImPo; MeLP; NOCV; PoEL-3; SCGP

Bright House. Sumako Fukao, *Japanese.* WPJ, *tr. by* Kenneth Rexroth *and* Ikuko Atsumi

Bright is the ring of words. Robert Louis Stevenson. OBNC

Bright leaps a living brook! (LL) From the Flats. Sidney Lanier. APN-2; NOBA; NoP-4; OxBA

Bright light, swift-winged winds, springs of the rivers, numberless. Aeschylus. GrIP, *tr. by* David Grene *Fr.* Prometheus Bound.

Bright lure seized, the old hook bitten, The. (LL) The Next Poem. Dana Gioia. NoP-4

Bright mirror I braved: the devil in it, The. Cleopatra to the Asp. Ted Hughes. EBEV; RACG

Bright moon appears from the east ridge, The. Moonlit Night at Fragrant Mountain Temple. Wang Shih-chieng, *Chinese.* SuSp, *tr. by* Richard John Lynn

Bright moon born of the sea. Watching the Moon with Thoughts of Far Away. Chang Chiu-ling, *Chinese.* CoBCP, *tr. by* Burton Watson

BRIGHT moon illumines the night-prospect. *Unknown, Chinese.* ChiP, *tr. by* Arthur Waley; BoWoP, *tr. by* Arthur Waley

Bright moon, oh how white it shines, The. *Unknown.* ChiP, *tr. by* Arthur Waley *Fr.* Seventeen Old Poems.

Bright moon rising above T'ien Shan, A. Moon over Mountain Pass. Li Po, *Chinese.* SuSp, *tr. by* Joseph J. Lee

Bright moon shines upon the pavilion, A. Seven Poems of Lament. Ts'ao Chih, *Chinese.* SuSp, *tr. by* Ronald C. Miao

Bright moon slowly, slowly rises, The. The "Slowly, Slowly" Poem. Yüan Hung-tao, *Chinese.* CoBLCP, *tr. by* Jonathan Chaves

Bright moon soars over the Mountain of Heaven, The. The Moon over the Mountain Pass. Li Po, *Chinese.* TAL, *tr. by* Robert Payne

Bright moon, when did you appear?, Tune: "Prelude to Water Music." Su Tung-p'o, *Chinese.* CoBCP, *tr. by* Burton Watson

Bright moon, when will she appear?, The. Tune: "Prelude to Water Music." Su Shih, *Chinese.* SuSp, *tr. by* Eugene Eoyang

Bright moon white and silver, The. *Unknown, Chinese.* SuSp, *tr. by* Charles Hartman

Bright over Europe fell her golden hair. (LL) Letty's Globe. Charles Tennyson Turner. NOBVV; OBEV; PeVV

Bright Queen of Heaven, God's Virgin Spouse. The Knot. Henry Vaughan. MiEL

Bright ran thy line, O Galloway. Lord Galloway. Robert Burns. OxBoLi

Bright ran thy line, O Galloway. Lord Galloway. Robert Burns. OxBoLi *Fr.* Epigrams on Lord Galloway.

Bright shadows of true Rest! some shoots of bliss[e]. Son-Days [dayes]. Henry Vaughan. GeHe; NOSC; SeCP

Bright she is, no daisy whiter. (LL) Madrigal: "My mistress is as fair as fine." Thomas Ravenscroft. CH; OxBoLi

Bright silver penny, A. (LL) The Silver Penny. Walter De la Mare. NOxBChV

Bright spark, shot from a brighter place. The Star[re]. George Herbert. ESCV; PeECV

Bright star[, would I were stedfast as thou art—]. Keats. CABP; CBLP; EnLoPo; GBL; GLoP; GSo; GTBS-P; HAP; ImPo; InPK-6; InPS-3; NAEL-2; NAWM-2; NIP-4; NoP-4; OAEL-2; PFE; PoE; Ro; SCV; Son; TFi

Bright sun lights out over the western bank. T'ao Ch'ien, *Chinese.* SuSp, *tr. by* Eugene Eoyang

Bright, thin, new moon appears, The. New Moon. Tu Fu, *Chinese.* OHPC, *tr. by* Kenneth Rexroth

Bright torment of inspiration of the bare sea. (LL) The Seagull. Siôn Phylip, *Welsh.* PBRV

Bright town, tossed by waves of time to a hill. Ode to Swansea. Vernon Watkins. OBWVE

Bright Tulips, we do know. To a Bed of Tulips. Robert Herrick. CaPo; GaP

Bright vocabularies are transient as rainbows. Precious Moments. Carl Sandburg. MoAmPo

Bright wanderer, fair coquette of heaven, *sl. longer vers.* Shelley. *See* Lines Written in the Bay of Lerici.

Bright watchers are still there, The. (LL) Country Stars. William Meredith. AFr

Brighter sunshine of their own, A. (LL) To the Memory of the Brave Americans. Philip Freneau. AiP; AmPP; PoLF

Brightest of the Bright, The. Egan O'Rahilly, *Irish.* BIrV, *tr. by* James Clarence Mangan

Brightest threads on life's pathway, The. Home and Mother. Hettye Rayburn Ramsey. PWR

Brightly shone the sun in my hut. Those Who Lost Everything. David Diop, *French.* PBA, *tr. by* Langston Hughes

Brightly the sun of summer shone. Memory. Anne Brontë. EBVV

Brightness. Denis Glover. PeNZ

Brightness most bright I beheld on the way, forlorn. Egan O'Rahilly, *Irish.* NOIV, *tr. by* Thomas Kinsella

Brightness of brightness lonely met me where I wandered. Egan O'Rahilly, *Irish.* IIP, *tr. by* Frank O'Connor

Brightness round the rising sun, The. The Spheres. Jones Very. PAR

"Brigid is a caution, sure!"—What's that ye say? Her Sister. "Moira O'Neill." OxBTC

Brill. Clark Coolidge. PmAP

Brilliant-bellied newt flashes, The. Summer Matures. Helene Johnson. BlSi

Brilliant, bright—the flowers of the cold season! The Pavilion for Listening to Fragrance. Chang Yü, *Chinese.* CoBLCP, *tr. by* Jonathan Chaves

Brilliant Day, A. Charles Tennyson Turner. NOBVV

Brilliant fierce eagles. The Lancet. Denis Devlin. NOIV

Brilliant kernel of the night, The. Robert Louis Stevenson. EBVV *Fr.* The Light-Keeper.

Brilliant stills of food, the cozy, The. The Ladies' Home Journal. Sandra M. Gilbert. NIP-4

Brim-shadow, The. Alan Pizzarelli. HA

Brimming Water. Tu Fu, *Chinese.* OHPC, *tr. by* Kenneth Rexroth

Bring a leaf to me. Invitation Standing. Paul Blackburn. VGW

Bring back the life. Give me the Red on the Black of the Bullet (for Claude Reece Jr.) Jayne Cortez. LTA

Bring Daddy home. *Unknown.* OxNR

Bring dreams of Christ to dusky cane-lipped throngs. (LL) Georgia Dusk. Jean Toomer. BPo; NAAL-2; NoAM; NoP-4; PoBA; Poetr

Bring flowers to crown the cup and lute. Stanzas on the Death of Mrs Hemans. Letitia Elizabeth Landon. Ro; VWP *Fr.* New Monthly Magazine, 44 286–8.

Bring forth May flowers. (LL) March winds and April showers. *Unknown.* ACTP; FaBoBe; LB; OxNR; ReMoGo

Bring forth May flowers. (LL) Rain before [*or* Raan afoor] seven. *Unknown.* FaBoBe; FaBoVe; OxNR

Bring in the Wine. Li Ho, *Chinese.* PLT, *tr. by* A. C. Graham

Bring Kateen-beug and Maurya Jude. Beg-Innish. John Millington Synge. MoBrPo

"Bring little children unto me." Sunday Schools. Anna Sawyer. ECWP

Bring me a letter, postman! The Postman. Alice Todd. BoTP

Bring me Men. (LL) Bring me men to match my mountains. Sam Walter Foss. BLPA; FaBoBe

Bring me men to match my mountains. Sam Walter Foss. BLPA; FaBoBe *Fr.* The Coming American.

Bring me my garland, bring me a wreath. The Maniac's Song. Ann Taylor. NOBRP

Bring me my rose-buds, drawer, come. A Frolic[k]. Robert Herrick. FaBoEE

Bring me some figgie hobbin!. (LL) Figgie Hobbin. Charles Causley. NOxBChV; NTP

Bring Me the Cup. Moses ibn Ezra. *Fr.* Wine-Songs. TrJP, *tr. by* Solomon Solis-Cohen

Bring me the sunset in a cup. Emily Dickinson. APN-2; MoAmPo; NOCV

Bring me to the blasted oak. Crazy Jane and the Bishop. W. B. Yeats. CMoP; LiTM

Bring me wine, but wine which never grew. Bacchus. Ralph Waldo Emerson. APN-1; AWP; AmPP; NOBA; OBEV; OxBA; PAR; PoEL-4

Bring now the last flower in to warm this room. At My Mother's Bedside. Marcia Lee Masters. WPE

Bring on the clowns! Jack Prelutsky. OTCP

Bring out the tall tales now that we told. Ghost Story. Dylan Thomas. OBCP

Bring snow-white lilies, pallid heart-flushed roses. The Pantheist's Song of Immortality. Constance Naden. VWP

Bring the biggest bath you've seen. The Song of the Bath. Margaret E. Gibbs. BoTP

Bring the clean water, give out the fresh seed. Elizabeth Barrett Browning. *See* First Book: Young Aurora's Fostermother.

Bring the comb and play upon it! Marching Song. Robert Louis Stevenson. BoTP

Bring the Day! Theodore Roethke. CRP

Bring the good old bugle, boys, we'll sing another song. Marching through Georgia. Henry Clay Work. APN-2; CBCWP; FaPoR

Bring the holy crust of Bread. Charmes. Robert Herrick. BeJo

Bring the North. William Stafford. LCAP-2

Bring the Wine! Li Po, *Chinese*. CoBCP, *tr. by* Burton Watson

Bring them to me. Bring them to me. Bring them to me. Song of the Elk. *Unknown*. APN-2 *Fr.* Minnetare Songs.

Bring us in good ale, and bring us in good ale. *Unknown*. CH; EBEV; MiEL; OAEL-1; OBCoV

Bring visions when you ring my bell. To a Guest. Vladislav Felitsianovich Khodasevich, *Russian*. TCRP, *tr. by* Michael Frayn

Bringers of Beethoven, The. Reiner Kunze, *German*. PoSu, *tr. by* Gordon Brotherston *and* Gisela Brotherston

Bringing a Dead Man Back into Life. Russell Edson. TRP

Bringing Flowers. Roberta Spear. AmPA

Bringing its belly home, slung from a pole. (LL) Fetching Cows. Norman MacCaig. NoP-4; OxBC

Bringing the summer and bringing the sun. (LL) Fly away, fly away over the sea. Christina Rossetti. ACTP; AYFP; CTAV; Spl

Brings him with gold to the shrine, brings him in arms to the gate? (LL) Spirit from Perfecter Ages. Arthur Hugh Clough. EBEV; OBNC; OxAEP-2

Brings my mild father. (LL) Blue Jay [*or* Bluejay]. Robert Francis. LCAP-2; WeT

Briseis, fair as golden Venus, saw. Briseis mourns Patroclus. Homer. OBCVT, *tr. by* Edward, Earl of Derby *Fr.* The Iliad.

Briseis mourns Patroclus. Homer. OBCVT, *tr. by* Edward, Earl of Derby *Fr.* The Iliad.

Brisk Chaunticleer his matins had begun. A Morning-Piece; or, An Hymn for the Hay-Makers. Christopher Smart. NOEC

Brisk methinks I am, and fine. Anacreontic[k] Verse. Robert Herrick. PeLV

Brisk Wind, A. William Barnes. SCGP

Brissit brawnis and broken banis. The Bewteis of the Fute-Ball. *Unknown*. OxBS

Bristled with cities, us the sea received. (LL) A Dream. Matthew Arnold. EnVR; GBL; GTBS-P

Bristol and Clifton. John Betjeman. CMoP

Bristol Channel, The. Thomas Edward Brown. NOBVV

Bristowe Tragedie: or, The Dethe of Syr Charles Bawdin. Thomas Chatterton. OxBB

Britain. Oliver Goldsmith. NOEC *Fr.* The Travel[l]er; or, A Prospect of Society.

Britain's Remembrancer Canto 4. George Wither.
"If by mischance the people in the street." PBRV

Britannia rules the waves. On a Parisian Boulevard. James Kenneth Stephen. NOBL *Fr.* England and America.

Britannia's daughters, much more fair than nice. On Women ("Britannia's daughters"). Edward Young. ECEV *Fr.* Satires. ECEV

Britannia's daughters, much more fair than nice. Edward Young. *Fr.* Love of Fame, the Universal Passion. OBSV

Britannia's isles proclaim. To the First of August. Ann Plato. BlSi

Britannia's Pastorals. William Browne.
"As that Arabian bird (whom all admire)." OAEL-1
Frolic Mariners of Devon, The.
Golden Age, The. NOSC
Memory. OBEV
Morning. NOSC
"Shall I tell you whom I love?" NOSC

Britannia's Pastorals Book 2. William Browne.
"Happyer those times were, when the Flaxen clew." PBRV
"O! should all Potentates whose higher birth." PBRV

Brither-men wha eftir us live on. Ballat o the Hingit. François Villon, *French*. OBVE, *tr. by* Tom Scott

British Army now carries two rifles, The. Identification in Belfast (I.R.A. Bombing). Robert Lowell. OxBC

British Church, The. George Herbert. ESCV; PeECV

British [*or* Brittish] Church, The. Henry Vaughan. ESCV; PeECV

British Connection, The. Padraic Fiacc. PNI

British Garden, A. Wes Magee. OBGa

British Grenadiers, The. *Unknown*. OxBoLi

British Leftish Poetry, 1930-40. "Hugh MacDiarmid." CMoP; FaBoTw; NoAM

British Museum Reading Room, The. Louis MacNeice. LiTM; MoBrPo; NOBE

British Prison Ship, The. Philip Freneau.
Hospital Prison Ship, The. AmPP

Britomart at Isis' Church. Edmund Spenser. PoE *Fr.* Wood Of Error. AEP

Britomart in the House of Busirane. Edmund Spenser. *Fr.* The Legend of Britomartis, or of Chastitie. NAEL-1 *Fr.* Wood Of Error. AEP

Britons never shall [*or* will] be slaves! (LL) Rule, Britannia! James Thomson *and* David Mallet. EBEvV; FaPoR; GTBS-P; NAEL-1; NOEC; OBWP

Brittle beauty [*or* beautie], that nature made so frail[e]. The Frailty and Hurtfulness of Beauty. Henry Howard, Earl of Surrey. AAS; EnLoPo; HoPM; SiPS

Brittle streets, with midnight walking flung, The. Sonnet on a Still Night. James Vincent Cunningham. PoA

Bro Duncannon. C. S. Giscombe. GT *Fr.* (from the "In" Sequence).

Broad-acred Ascra bore me. Mnasalcas, *Greek*. GrAn, *tr. by* Edward Lucie-Smith

Broad and ample he warms himself. Epigram. *Unknown*, *Irish*. NOIV, *tr. by* Thomas Kinsella

Broad and far-reaching, the level plain. Rhyme-Prose on the Desolate City. Pao Chao, *Chinese*. CoBCP, *tr. by* Burton Watson

Broad August burns in milky skies. Day-Dreams. William Canton. NOBVV; NTP

Broad-Ax, The. Walt Whitman. MoAmPo *Fr.* Song of the Broad-Axe. CA

Broad-backed hippopotamus, The. The Hippopotamus. T. S. Eliot. AWP; CBNP; HoPM; ImPo; NAEL-2; OBMV; VGW

Broad-based, broad-fronted, bounteous, multiform. Ben Jonson. Swinburne. EPCY *Fr.* Sonnets of English Dramatic Poets. Son

Broad beach / Sea wind and the sea's irregular rhythm, The. Afternoon: Amagansett Beach. John Hall Wheelock. PoRA

Broad Bean Sermon, The. Les A. Murray. BMAP

Broad Is the Road. Isaac Watts. AH; AmFP

Broad sun, The. The Far-Farers. Robert Louis Stevenson. BoTP

Broad sun-stoned beaches. Midsummer, Tobago. Derek Walcott. OPOU; VCWP

Broadcast. Ivan V. Lalic, *Serbo-Croatian*. HSix, *tr. by* Charles Simic

Broadcast. Philip Larkin. CBLP

Broads. David R. Slavitt. BXAP

Broadway. Mark Doty. WWSi

Broadway. Carl Sandburg. AiP

Broadway. Walt Whitman. NAAL-1; NAAL-3

Broagh. Seamus Heaney. FaBoVe

Brobdingnag. Adrien Stoutenburg. NYBP

Brocade curtains have just rolled back, The. Peonies. Li Shang-yin, *Chinese*. PLT, *tr. by* A. C. Graham

Brock. Paul Muldoon. NoAM; NoP-4

Brocks snuffle from their holt within. The Badgers. Eden Phillpotts. BoTP

Broke drunk &. Uncool. Victoria Rathbun. EC2

Broken, The. W. S. Merwin. LCAP-2

Broken ALTAR, Lord, thy servant rear[e]s, A. The Altar. George Herbert. CABP; ChIV-1; ESCV; GeHe; HoPM; InPS-3; NAEL-1; NOSC; NoP-4; OAEL-1; Poetr; SeCP; TrCP

Broken Appointment, A. Thomas Hardy. GBL; NAEL-2; NOBVV; NoAM ("And marching Time drew on, and wore me numb.") GLoP; NoP-4

Broken, bewildered by the long retreat. Retreat. Wilfrid Wilson Gibson. NSI

Broken bowl. Penny Harter. HA

Broken Bowl, The. James Merrill. PoA

Broken bundle of mirrors. . .!, A. (LL) Near Perigord. Ezra Pound. FaBoMo; LiTM

Broken Chain, The. Dora Greenwell. VWP

Broken Dark, The. Robert Earl Hayden. GT

Broken Doll, The. Nuala Ni Dhomhnaill, *Irish*. BiHa, *tr. by* John Montague

Broken-down hotel on an inhospitable sea, A. Far from Home. Nicholas Christopher. NoP-4

Broken Dreams. Hugo Williams. CBLP

Broken-Face Gargoyles. Carl Sandburg. AmPP; MoAmPo; OxBA

Broken Friendship. Mary Elizabeth Coleridge. VWP

Broken Friendship, The. Stevie Smith. FP

Broken from the bursting bough. The Apple. Ray Smith. TrCP

Broken Girth, The. Robert Graves. BIrV

Broken glass of river, The. Fire Music. Drew Gardner. PT

Broken Heart, The. Donne. EBEV; FSCP

Broken Heart, The. John Ford.
    "Beasts onely capable of sense, enjoy." PoEL-2
    Can You Paint a Thought? PoEL-2
    Love's Martyrs. NOBE
        (Song: "Oh no more, no more, too late.") OxBSP

Broken Heart. Henrietta Cordelia Ray. CBWP-3

Broken Heart, Broken Machine. Richard E. Grant. PoBA

Broken Home, The. James Merrill. ColAP; HAP; HCAP; MoP; NAAL-2; NOBA; NYBP; NoAM; NoP-4; PoPoPo

Broken Home. William Stafford. NNaP

Broken in pieces all asunder. Affliction (4). George Herbert. CABP; ESCV; GeHe; NOSC

Broken, Incan roads. The stones laid perfect. Resurrections. Benjamin Alire Sáenz. PaTW

Broken kite, sprawled. Elizabeth Searle Lamb. HA

Broken Lampstand, The. Wu Wei-yeh, *Chinese*. CoBLCP, *tr. by* Jonathan Chaves

Broken Mirror, The. Bob Perelman. FTOS

Broken Off by the Music. John Yau. EOEF

Broken or sold. Or given away. Or used and forgotten. Or lost. (LL) Green Light. Kenneth Fearing. PoE; VGW

Broken pillar of the wing jags from the clotted shoulder, The. Hurt Hawks. Robinson Jeffers. AmPP; CMoP; ChAP; ColAP; FYAP; LiTM; MoAmPo; MoP; NAAL-2; NOBA; NoAM; NoP-4; OxBA; RB; SAGP; TAP; TFi; TRP; UnPo

Broken sods, a whipped flag, The. A Burial. Seamus Deane. CIP-2; PNI

Broken String, The. *Unknown, Bushman*. PeSA, *tr. by* W. H. I. Bleek; PeSAV
    ("People were those who.") PeSAV

Broken Sword, The. Edward Rowland Sill. *See* Opportunity.

Broken Tower, The. Hart Crane. AmPP; CMoP; ColAP; LiTM; MeMAP; MoAmPo; NOBA; NoAM; NoP-4; OxBA; PoPoPo; Poetr

Broken wagon wheel that rots away beside the river, A. Pioneers. Charles Badger Clark Jr. FaBoBe

Broken window, A. Michael McClintock. HA

Brokendown Countdown. John Rice. SpW

Brome, brome on hill. The Broomfield Hill. *Unknown*. CH

Broncho Dan halts midway of the stream. A Health at the Ford. Robert Cameron Rogers. FaBoBe

Broncho That Would Not Be Broken, The. Vachel Lindsay. MeMAP

Bronx. Joseph Rodman Drake. APN-1

Bronze Age, The. Hesiod, *Greek*. OBCVT, *tr. by* George Chapman

Bronze by gold heard the hoofirons, steelyringing. James Joyce. PFTM *Fr.* Ulysses.

Bronze god running, The. At Guaracara Park. Eric Roach. PBCV

Bronze Immortal Takes Leave of Han, A. Li Ho, *Chinese*. PLT, *tr. by* A. C. Graham

Bronze soldier hitches a bronze cape, The. In Memoriam Francis Ledwidge. Seamus Heaney. CIP-2; NoAM

Bronze warship-beaks, old voyage-avid weapons. Philip of Thessalonica, *Greek*. GrAn, *tr. by* Edwin Morgan

Bronzeville Man with a Belt in the Back. Gwendolyn Brooks. PoBA

Bronzeville Mother Loiters in Mississippi. / Meanwhile, a Mississippi Mother Burns Bacon. Gwendolyn Brooks. SSLK

Bronzeville Woman in a Red Hat. Gwendolyn Brooks. NALW
    (Bronzeville Woman in a Red Hat / Hires Out to Mrs. Miles.) GT

Bronzeville Woman in a Red Hat / Hires Out to Mrs. Miles. Gwendolyn Brooks. *See* Bronzeville Woman in a Red Hat.

Brood her high lonely mysteries. (LL) He Remembers Forgotten Beauty. W. B. Yeats. CTC

Brood of fledging swallows, A. The Lord's Day. Kwangnim Kim, *Korean*. CKP, *tr. by* Jaihiun Kim

Brooding. David Ignatow. PBMP

Brooding Grief. D. H. Lawrence. CMoP; IMW; PoE

Brooding on the eightieth letter of *Fors Clavigera*. Geoffrey Hill. HAP; PoE *Fr.* Mercian Hymns.

Brooding upon its unexerted power. Gas and Hot Air. Morris Gilbert Bishop. OBAL

Brook, The. Tennyson. BoTP; ChAP; EBEvV; FHYEP *Fr.* The Brook; An Idyl. OxAEP-2

Brook, The. Edward Thomas. OAEL-2

Brook; An Idyl, The. Tennyson. OxAEP-2
    Brook, The. BoTP; ChAP; EBEvV; FHYEP
        (Brook's Song, The.) FaBoBe
        ("But I go on for ever.") (LL) ChAP

Brook glides on to the river, The. Reverie. Henrietta Cordelia Ray. CBWP-3

Brook in the City, A. Robert Frost. OxBA

Brook no obscurity, merely plunging deeper. The Rare Birds. Imamu Amiri Baraka. MoNo

Brook speaks with an eloquent tongue, The. Sent to Chief Abbot of Tung-lin Monastery. Su Shih, *Chinese*. SuSp, *tr. by* Chiang Yee

Brooklyn Bound. Barbara Elovic. WWSi

Brooklyn Bridge, Brooklyn Bridge. William Jay Smith. CA; KaS

Brooklyn Heights. John Wain. LiTM; OxBTC

Brooklyn Narcissus. Paul Blackburn. PmAP

Brooklyn Theater Fire, The. *Unknown*. AmFP

Brook's Song, The. Tennyson. *See* The Brook.

Broom, Green Broom. *Unknown*. OxBoLi; PoRA
    (Green Broom.) CH

Broom of Cowdenknows, The. *Unknown*. ESPB

Broom out the floor now, lay the fender by. June. Francis Ledwidge. BIrV; NOIV

Broom Squire's Song, The. *Unknown*. OxNR

Broomfield Hill, The. *Unknown*. AmFP; CH; ESPB; OxBB

Brooms. Charles Simic. AmPA; NNaP

Broon hens keckle and bouk, The. "Hugh MacDiarmid." *See* Farmer's Death.

Brothel echoes with the chime of bells, The. The Old Whore Becomes a Nun. Huỳnh Mẫn Đạt, *Vietnamese*. AVP, *tr. by* Huỳnh Sanh Thông

Brother, The. Peter Everwine. FYAP; NNaP

Brother, The. Semion Yakovlevich Nadson, *Russian*. TrJP, *tr. by* H. Badanes

Brother. Patricia Parker. *See* My Brother.

Brother and Sister. "Lewis Carroll." NOxBChV

Brother and Sister. "George Eliot." NALW
    "But sudden came the barge's pitch-black prow." NOBVV
    I Cannot Choose but Think upon the Time. Son
    "Long years have left their writing on my brow." SDW
    "Our brown canal was endless to my thought." NOBVV
    "Our mother bade us keep the trodden ways."
    School Parted Us. Son
    "Those long days measured by my little feet." NOBVV
    "We had the selfsame world enlarged for each."

Brother and Sisters. Judith Wright. BMAP; FaBoWP

Brother Baptis' on Woman Suffrage. Rosalie Jonas. BlSi

Brother, come! And What Shall You Say? Joseph Cotter, Sr.. PoBA

Brother Fire. Louis MacNeice. AF; MoP; NOBE; NoAM

Brother Green. *Unknown*. AmFP

Brother, Hast Thou Wandered Far. James Freeman Clarke. AH

Brother-in-Law, The. Larry Rubin. MT

Brother Jonathan, Brother Kafka. Vincent O'Sullivan.
    "Figure who stands on the beach, A." PeNZ
    "Last things/ the turning leaves slip in the wind." PeNZ
    "To be in a place for spring and not have lived its winter." PeNZ

Brother, my brother, whither do you pass? To a Face in a Crowd. Robert Penn Warren. FuPo

Brother Number Three comes strolling along. Tune: "Song of the Lunar Palace." Lu Chih, *Chinese*. SuSp, *tr. by* Hellmut Wilhelm

Brother of the Mount of Olives. Paul Monette. NAmP90

Brother of the Streets. Sam Cornish. TRP

Brother soldiers—With them in battle I reached the waters of the Sava. By the Waters of the Sava. Uri Zvi Greenberg, *Hebrew*. MHP, *tr. by* Ruth Finer Mintz

Brother Symmes conversed with her on the ship. Ann Stanford. CRP *Fr.* The Covenant of Grace.

Brother, Though from Yonder Sky. James Henry Bancroft. AH

Brother to the firefly. Morning Light. Mary Effie Lee Newsome. PoBA

Brother where dost thou dwell? Henry David Thoreau. NCAP

Brotherhood. Octavio Paz, *Spanish*. LoL, *tr. by* Eliot Weinberger

Brotherhood. Reginald Shepherd. BAP-95

Brotherhood is not by the blood certainly, The. Speech to Those Who Say Comrade. Archibald MacLeish. OxBA

Brotherhood of Men. Richard Eberhart. PoWW
    "Came lassitude and despair of the mind."
    "Caught there, then, on the Rock. At Corregidor."
    "My mind was heavy and my luck was dark."
    "Rumors of liberation. We could not believe it."

Brotherless Sisters. *Unknown, Serbo-Croatian.* HSix, *tr. by* Charles Simic

Brothers. Robert Currie. Poetsp

Brothers. James Weldon Johnson. NAAAL

Brothers, The. Edwin Muir. GTBS-P; HeIP-4; NTP

Brothers. Marcia Southwick. NAmP90

Brothers. Giuseppe Ungaretti, *Italian.* PeFWW, *tr. by* Jonathan Griffin

Brothers (Adelphi), The. Terence, *Latin.*
   "Elder boy is by adoption mine, The." OBCVT, *tr. by* George Colman

Brothers and men that shall after us be. Ballad of the Gibbet. François Villon, *French.* AWP, *tr. by* Andrew Lang

Brothers and Sisters. Michael Foley. PNI

Brothers at the Bar. Naomi Long Madgett. NBV

Brothers / brothers / everywhere. Utopia. Jewel C. Latimore. BPo

Brothers Grimm grew weaker and flickered, blue light, The. A California Girlhood. Alice Notley. PmAP

Brothers I think we are. Song the Second. *Unknown. Fr.* Two Cherokee Songs of Friendship. APN-2, *tr. by* Samuel L. Mitchill

Brothers Loving Brothers. Vega. ISC

Brothers, my teeth hurt. Strictly for Posterity. Charles Simic. NNaP

Brothers, / this big woman / carries much sweetness / in the folds of her flesh. Song at Midnight. Lucille Clifton. unSA

Brothers: Two Saltimbanques, The. John Logan. LiLi

Brought back from the tedium of dying. Return of a Popular Statesman. Vincent Buckley. CBAP

Brought gifts / home for me. My Daddy, Whenever He Went Some Place. David Huddle. PBCAP

Brought here in slave ships and pitched overboard. Love Your Enemy. Imam Yusef. BPo; GI; TTY

Brought to bed by sickness, cut off from men. Replying to a Poem from My Cousin Hui-lien. Hsieh Ling-yün, *Chinese.* CoBCP, *tr. by* Burton Watson

Brought to burning eyelids sleep. (LL) La Nuit Blanche. Rudyard Kipling. MoBrPo; UV

Brought up as I was to ask of the weather. Point Grey. Daryl Hine. NOBC

Brought up never getting punched. He/She. Stephen Dunn. NAmP90

Broughty Wa's. *Unknown.* ESPB

Brow, brow, brenty. *Unknown.* OxNR

Brown Adam. *Unknown.* ESPB; OxBB

Brown and furry. The Caterpillar. Christina Rossetti. AYFP; BoTP; CTAV; CTV; ChAP; FaBoVe; OxBChV *Fr.* Sing-Song.

Brown and furry / Caterpillar in a hurry. The Caterpillar. Christina Rossetti. BoTP; FaBoVe; OxBChV

Brown arms of the mothering plateau, The. The Lowveld. Charles Eglington. PeSA

Brown Autumn came, and at her solemn close. In the House of the Aylors. Albery Allson Whitman. AAP *Fr.* Not a Man and Yet a Man.

Brown Baby Blues. Una Marson. PBCV

Brown birds brown leaves. Drinking Vodka. Sarah Kirsch, *German.* CEEP, *tr. by* Wayne Kvam

Brown Boy to Brown Girl. Countee Cullen. PoBA

Brown, brittle, wait-a-bit weeds. The Indian Cave Jerry Ramsey Found. William Stafford. NoAM

Brown bunny sits inside his burrow. The Rabbit. Edith King. BoTP

Brown Circle. Louise Glück. NAmP90
   ("To spare my son.") (LL) NMM-2

Brown-coloured Trotter! The Praises of the Canna. *Unknown, Sotho, from French tr. by* Thomas Arbonsset. PeSAV, *v. by* John Croumbie Brown

Brown-dappled fawn, The. The Fawn in the Snow. William Rose Benét. MoAmPo

Brown earth, blue. Astronauts. John Travers Moore. SpW

Brown enormous odor he lived by / was too close, The. The Prodigal. Elizabeth Bishop. ChIV-2; CoAP; GI; LCAP-2; LiTM; NYBP; TwCP

Brown-faced nurse has murmured something unintelligible, The. Microcosmos. Susan Miles OxBTC

Brown Family, The. Colleen Thibaudeau. NOBC

Brown Frog, The. Mary K. Robinson. BoTP

Brown gingham, pink, and skirts of Alice blue. (LL) In an Iridescent Time. Ruth Stone. NMM-2; OxWW

Brown Girl. Angelina Weld Grimké. CPO

Brown Girl, The. *Unknown.* ESPB
   (Bonny Brown Girl, The.)

Brown Girl, Blonde Okie. Gary Soto. NOxBChV

Brown Girl Dead, A. Countee Cullen. GT; TAP

Brown in the snow, a car with a heater. Strangers. William Stafford. NNaP

Brown Is My Love. *Unknown.* CTC; GBL

Brown lilac, roses filled with rain;. World on Sunday. James McAuley. BMAP

Brown lived at such a lofty farm. Brown's Descent; or, The Willy-Nilly. Robert Frost. MoAmPo; PoRA

Brown Lullaby. Adam Small. PeSAV

Brown men shock the brown pools with nets. The Dragonfish. John Balaban. CDa

Brown o' San Juan. "Home, Sweet Home," with Variations ("Brown o' San Juan"). Henry Cuyler Bunner. OBAL *Fr.* Home.

Brown of her—her eyes, her hair, her hair[!], The. (LL) The Farmer's Bride. Charlotte Mew. BWW; BoLoP; CBLP; EBNV; FaBoWP; MoBrPo; NALW; OxBM; OxBTC; WPE

Brown of her—her eyes, her hair, her hair!, The. Charlotte Mew. *See* The Farmer's Bride.

Brown of Ossawatomie. John Greenleaf Whittier. NCAP

Brown owl sits in the ivy bush, The. The Great Brown Owl. Jane Euphemia Browne. OxBChV

Brown Owls come here in the blue evening. Healing Songs. Tohono O'odham, *Papago.* PaTW, *tr. by* Frances Densmore

Brown paper worn next to the skin. B. L. Howarth. BXAP

Brown Penny. W. B. Yeats. BoLoP; CBLP; CMoP; FaBoCh; GLoP; IIP; LiLi

Brown River, Smile. Jean Toomer. PoBA *Fr.* The Blue Meridian.

Brown Robin. *Unknown.* ESPB; OxBB

Brown Robyn's [*or* Robin's] Confession. *Unknown.* CH; ESPB

Brown semicolons move doggedly. The Ant Trap. Joe Rosenblatt. NOBC

Brown Skin Girl. Tommy McClennan. FaBoVe

Brown-skinned boy asleep beneath a clump, A. Mind Pictures. Beatrice Hastings. PeSAV

Brown Thrush, The. Lucy Larcom. BoTP; OBCA
   ("There's a merry brown thrush sitting up in the tree.") NOxBChV
   ("Unless we are as good as can be!") (LL) NOxBChV

Brownies' Celebration, The. Palmer Cox. ODCA

Browning makes the verses. Robert Louis Stevenson. NOBVV

Brown's Descent; or, the Willy-Nilly. Robert Frost. MoAmPo; PoRA

Browny Bee. Irene F. Pawsey. BoTP

Browny Hen, The. Irene F. Pawsey. BoTP

Bruadar and Smith and Glinn. A Curse. *Unknown, Irish.* BIrV, *tr. by* Douglas Hyde

Bruce, The. John Barbour.
   Before Bannockburn. OxBS
   Freedom [*or* Fredome]. FaBoCh; OBEV; OxBS
   "Storys to rede ar delitabill." OxBS

Bruce Ismay's Soliloquy. Derek Mahon. PNI

Brueghel in Naples. Dannie Abse. NIP-4

Brueghel's Winter. Walter De la Mare. GS

Bruised Reed Shall He Not Break, A. Christina Rossetti. OxAEP-2

Bruised Titans, The. Keats. OBNC *Fr.* Hyperion. OAEL-2; Ro

Bruisingly cradled in a Harvard chair. Louis Edward Sissman. NoP-4 *Fr.* Dying: An Introduction.

Brummell at Calais. John Glassco. MoCV

Brunanburg, *see also* Battle of Brunanburh. *Unknown, Anglo-Saxon.* PoE, *tr. by* Kemp Malone

Bruno, our father, joyous, gentle, old. Epitaph for Bruno of Angers. Marbod of Rennes, *Latin.* MLL, *tr. by* Helen Waddell

Brush Fire. Fily-Dabo Sissoko, *French.* NegPo, *tr. by* Ellen Conroy Kennedy

Brush-Fire. U Tam'si Tchicaya, *French.* NegPo, *tr. by* Sangodare Akanji
   ("Fire the river that's to say, The.") PBMAP

Brush in rocks, draw a stream. Yün Shou-p'ing. CoBLCP, *tr. by* Jonathan Chaves *Fr.* Landscape.

Brush Up Your Shakespeare. Cole Porter. OBAL; OBCoV

Brushing away the dust, I opened the broken box. In a Book-Box I Found the Lost Manuscript of a Poem Sent to Me by the Late Kao [Ch'i]. Chang Yü, *Chinese.* CoBLCP, *tr. by* Jonathan Chaves

Brushing back the curls from your famous brow. The Copulating Gods. Carolyn Kizer. Poetr

Brushing my clothes, I followed the sandy dikes. Passing White Banks Pavilion. Hsieh Ling-yün, *Chinese.* SuSp, *tr. by* Francis Westbrook

Brushing my sins. Raymond Roseliep. HA

Brushing out my daughter's dark. 35/10. Sharon Olds. CrSp; MDDM; SAGP

Brussels and Oxford. William Hurrell Mallock. EBVV

Brussels in Winter. W. H. Auden. OxBTC

Brut, The. Layamon.
   Passing of Arthur, The. PoE

Brutal shuddering machines, yellow, bite into given earth. The Landscape Gardeners. Geoffrey Grigson. OBGa

Brute Image. John Ashbery. NoP-4

Brute Strength. Wanda Coleman. PmAP

Bruton Town. *Unknown.* EnSB

Bryan and Pereene. James Grainger. ECEV

Bryan, Bryan, Bryan, Bryan. Vachel Lindsay. CMoP; MeMAP; OxBA; OxBoLi

"Election night at midnight."

"In a nation of one hundred fine, mob-hearted, lynching, relenting, repenting millions."

"July, August, suspense. / Wall Street lost to sense."

"Then we stood where we could see."

"When Bryan came to Springfield, and Altgeld gave him greeting."

"Where it was McKinley, that respectable McKinley."

Bryan O'Lynn was a Dutchman born. Brian O'Linn. *Unknown.* CBNP; FaBoVe; NBLV; RB

Bryan's Last Battle. *Unknown.* AmFP

Bryant. James Russell Lowell. NOBA; TAP *Fr.* A Fable for Critics. NAAL-1; NAAL-3

Brynbwrla. Kingsley Amis. NOBL *Fr.* The Evans Country.

Bryng us all to his blisse! (LL) Robin Hood and the Monk. *Unknown.* EBNV; ESPB; OBNV

Bubble, The. Richard Crashaw. PBRV *Fr.* Bulla.

Bubble; a Song, The. Robert Herrick. CaPo

Bubbled baby gave an abrupt burp, The. Nursery Vignette. Edmund Wilson. OBCoV *Fr.* Easy Exercises in the Use of Difficult Words.

Bubbled with brimming kisses at my mouth. (LL) Willowwood ("I sat with Love upon a woodside well"). D. G. Rossetti. NAEL-2; OAEL-2; PoEL-5

Bubbles. George Garrett. MT

Bubbles. L. Nicholson. BoTP

Bubbles on the Water. Yang Wan-li, *Chinese.* SuSp, *tr. by* Jonathan Chaves

Bubbles soar and die in the sterile bottle, The. Notes for the Chart in 306. Ogden Nash. NYBP

Bubbling brook doth leap when I come by, The. Nature. Jones Very. ColAP

Bubbling Wine. Abu Zakariya, *Arabic.* TTY, *tr. by* A. J. Arberry

Buchenwald. Bin Ramke. WeT

Buck in the Snow, The. Edna St. Vincent Millay. ColAP; NALW; NoP-4

Buckdancer's Choice. James Dickey. HeIP-4; NOBA; NYBP; NoAM; NoP-4; WeT

Buckee Bene. *Unknown.* CH

Bucket, The. Rose Romano. UnSA

Bucket, The. Samuel Woodworth. APN-1

Bucking Bronco. *Unknown.* AmFP

Buckingham Palace. A. A. Milne. OxBChV

Buckles glitter, billies lean, The. American Twilights, 1957. James Wright. CoAP

Bucolic. Aimé Césaire, *French.* VCWP, *tr. by* Clayton Eshleman *and* Annette Smith

Bucolic Eclogues. Ethel Louisa Mason Anderson.

Waking, Child, While You Slept. WPE

Bucolics. W. H. Auden.

Mountains. FaBoPV

Bud fantasies, dreams of an ear of corn. Paean to Eve's Apple. James Liddy. CIP-2

Bud / stands for all things, The. Saint Francis and the Sow. Galway Kinnell. AFr; ChAP; FYAP; InPK-6; RB

Budd, The. Edmund Waller. PBRV

Budded with Child. Meridel Le Sueur. FiLi

Buddha. Arno Holz, *German.* AWP, *tr. by* William Ellery Leonard

Buddha. Jack Kerouac. BB

Buddha, The. Daya Pawar, *Marathi.* OMIP, *tr. by* Eleanor Zelliot *and* Jayant Karve

Buddha and Brahma. Henry Adams. APN-2

Buddha in Glory. Rilke, *German.* EnlH, *tr. by* Stephen Mitchell

Buddha in the Womb, The. Erica Jong. ColAP

Buddha is not more strange. In a Warm Bath. Carl Rakosi. TAP

Buddha, known to men by many names, The. Buddha and Brahma. Henry Adams. APN-2

Buddha taught the Perfect Thusness Way, The. On Reading the Buddha's Scriptures. Nguyễn Bỉnh Khiêm, *Vietnamese.* AVP, *tr. by* Huỳnh Sanh Thông

Buddha took some Autumn leaves. Kenneth Rexroth. BLT *Fr.* The City of the Moon.

Buddhist monastery across a stone bridge, A. I Went to Gold Mountain to Visit a Ch'an Master But He Was Not at Home. Mo Shih-lung, *Chinese.* CoBLCP, *tr. by* Jonathan Chaves

Buddhist Monk Cut and Burned His Own Flesh to Make The Rains Stop—A Man From His Native Place Asked Me to Write a Poem to Send to Him, A. Hsü Wei, *Chinese.* CoBLCP, *tr. by* Jonathan Chaves

Buddhist Priest, A. Ho Xuan Huong, *Vietnamese.* PBWP, *tr. by* Nguyen Ngoc Bich *and* Burton Raffel

Budding floweret blushes at the light, The. There Lackethe Somethynge Stylle. Thomas Chatterton. OxAEP-1 *Fr.* Aella; a Tragycal Enterlude.

Budding young playwright named Coward, A. Limerick. Doris Pulsford. PeLi

Buddy Bolden Cylinder, The. William Matthews. SeSe

Buddy Holly Watching *Rebel Without a Cause*, Lubbock, Texas, 1956. David Wojahn. PBCAP *Fr.* Mystery Train: A Sequence.

Budgie Finds His Voice. Wendy Cope. UV

Budging the sluggard ripples of the Somme. Hospital Barge at Cérisy. Wilfred Owen. RB

Budmouth Dears. Thomas Hardy. CH *Fr.* The Dynasts.

Buds from winter's frost-work lift, The. The Coming of Spring. Henrietta Cordelia Ray. CBWP-3

Buffalo. Henry Dumas. PoBA

Buffalo. Charles Eglington. PeSA

Buffalo, The. Marianne Moore. PoA

Buffalo. Molly Peacock. MoLi; WWSi

Buffalo. *Unknown, Yoruea.* Fr. Hunter Poems of the Yoruba. RB, *tr. by* Ulli Beier

Buffalo Bill opens a pawn shop on the reservation. Evolution. Sherman Alexie. PoPoPo

Buffalo Bill's / defunct / who used to. Portrait. E. E. Cummings. AmPP; CMoP; HeIP-4; InPK-6; NAAL-2; NIP-4; NOBA; OxBSP; PoE; RB; TAP; VGW

Buffalo Blood. Lance Henson. STP

Buffalo Boy. Huang T'ing-chien, *Chinese.* SuSp, *tr. by* Michael E. Workman

Buffalo Boy. *Unknown.* AmFP

Buffalo Boy On a Field of Corpses, The. Phỗ Ðú'c, *Vietnamese.* AVP, *tr. by* Huỳnh Sanh Thông

Buffalo breathed quietly inside, The. The Crow-Children Walk My Circles in the Snow. Ray A. Young Bear. CDW

Buffalo, buffalo, buffalo, buffalo. Death Chant. Peter Blue Cloud. VoR

Buffalo Dusk. Carl Sandburg. ChAP; OBCA

Buffalo Gals, *see also* Lubly Fan *by* Cool White. *Unknown, sometimes at. to* Cool White. APN-2

Buffalo—Isle of Wight Power Cable. Anselm Hollo. PoM

Buffalo / Like Yellowstone National Park, The. Philip Whalen. *See* Further Notice.

Buffalo Skinners, The. *Unknown.* AS; AmFP; RB

Buffaloes are gone, The. Buffalo Dusk. Carl Sandburg. ChAP; OBCA

Buffel's Kop. Roy Campbell. PeSA

Bufo. Alexander Pope. OBSV *Fr.* Epistle to Dr. Arbuthnot. FHYEP; InPS-3; NoP-4; OAEL-1; OxAEP-1; PoE; PoEL-3; TFi

Bug, flower, bird on slipware fired and fluted. Syrinx. James Merrill. HCAP

Bugle Song, The. Tennyson. *See* Blow, Bugle, Blow.

Bugler boy from barrack (it is over the hill), A. The Bugler's First Communion. Gerard Manley Hopkins. NoAM

Bugler's First Communion, The. Gerard Manley Hopkins. NoAM

Bugle's for him, The. Burial. Momcilo Nastasijevic, *Serbo-Croatian.* HSix, *tr. by* Charles Simic

Bugs. Mary Ann Hoberman. OBCA

Cockroach.

Combinations. OBSP

Bugville team was surely up against a rocky game, The. Casey—Twenty Years Later. S. P. McDonald. BLPA

Buick. Marianne Boruch. WeT

Buick. Karl Shapiro. CMoP; HoPM; Poetr

Buik of Alexander, The. John Barbour.

Prologue to the Avowis of Alexander. OxBS

Build for yourself a strong-box. Then Laugh. Bertha Adams Backus. BLPA; PWR; PoToHe

"Build me a nation," said the Lord. Then and Now. Frances Ellen Watkins Harper. PWR

"Build me straight, O worthy Master!" The Building of the Ship. Henry Wadsworth Longfellow. CBCWP

Build then the ship of death, for you must take. D. H. Lawrence. APAD *Fr.* The Ship of Death.

Builder builded a temple, A. Two Temples. Hattie Vose Hall. BLPA

Builder demolishes houses, The. Dialectics. Edvard Kocbek, *Slovenian.* CEEP; PoSu, *tr. by* Michael Scammell *and* Veno Taufer

Builder of Continents, The. "Ping Hsin." *Fr.* The Stars. WPOW, *tr. by* Kai-yu Hsu

Builders. Dmitry Borisovich Kedrin, *Russian*. TCRP, *tr.* by Albert C. Todd

Builders, The. Henry Wadsworth Longfellow. PWR

Builder's Lesson, A. John Boyle O'Reilly. PWR; PoLF; PoToHe

Building, The. As You Come In. Anne Marriott. NOBC

Building. I. E. Dickenga. PWR

Building. Gary Snyder. BB

Building an Outhouse. Ronald Wallace. PBCAP

Building for Eternity. N. B. Sargent. BLPA

Building in Stone. Sylvia Townsend Warner. MoBrPo

Building of Carthage, The. *tr.* by Gavin Douglas. Virgil. OBVE, *tr.* by John Dryden *Fr.* The Aeneid [*or* Eneados, *Aeneis*].

Building of the Ship, The. Henry Wadsworth Longfellow. CBCWP

Ship of State, The. FaBoBe

"Then the Master." NAAL-1; NAAL-3

Building Society Blues. Roger Roughton. SPE

Building the Bridge. Will Allen Dromgoole. WeW-3

(Bridge-Builder, The.) PoToHe

Building the cart again. (LL) Ox Cart Man. Donald Hall. FYAP; InPS-3; LCAP-2; LoL

Building the dollhouse. Rosamond Haas. HA

Built by Hank Wurlitzer, 7 ft. 8 inches, to house the first petrocommunications system. Big Bar. Kenward Elmslie. PmAP

Buke of the Howlat, The. Sir Richard Holland.

Douglas and the Bruce's Heart.

Bulahdelah—Taree Holiday Song Cycle, The. Les A. Murray.

"People are eating dinner in that country north of Legge's Lake, The." BMAP

Bulbs strung along. Christmas Lights. Valerie Worth. PChr

Bulge, The. George Johnston. MoCV

Bulge was Algy, The. (LL) Algy met a bear. *Unknown*. CTV; KaS

Bulging rampart streaked with pink and jade, The. The Watchers. Charles Spear. PeNZ

Bulimia. Denise Duhamel. BAP-94

Bulkhead sweating, and under naked bulbs, The. Mess Deck. Alan Ross. PoWW

Bulky oil lamp, A. Tanka. Shaku Chōkū, *Japanese*. MJT, *tr.* by Makoto Ueda

Bull, The. Ralph Hodgson. LiTM; MoBrPo; NSI; OBMV; OxBTC

Bull, The. Vita Sackville-West. WPE

Bull, The. William Carlos Williams. LiTM; TwCP

Bull Calf, The. Irving Layton. InPK-6

Bull Called Remorse, A. Iain Sinclair. NBrP

Bull Moose, The. Alden Nowlan. NTP

Bull Moses, The. Ted Hughes. Poetr

Bull-roarer, The. Gerald Stern. NAmP90

Bull, the Fleece are crammed [*or* cramm'd], and not a room, The. Audley Court. Tennyson. NOBVV; PeVV

Bull with the fierce eyes that none dares look at. Praises of King George VI. A. Z. Ngani, *Xhosa*. PeSA, *tr.* by Jack Cope

Bulla. Richard Crashaw.

Bubble, The. PBRV

Bulldoze the bed where we made love. Earthmoving Malediction. Heather McHugh. NAmP90

Bulldozer, The. Songbu Yi, *Korean*. CKP, *tr.* by Jaihiun Kim

Bulldozers come, they rip, The. The Development. Marge Piercy. NBLV *Fr.* Sand Roads.

Bullet, A. Sandor Csoori, *Hungarian*. CEEP, *tr.* by Nicholas Kolumban

Bullet passed, The. In a Plantation. Basil T. Paquet. CDa

Bullfight. Miroslav Holub, *Czech*. RB, *tr.* by Ian *and* Jarmila Milner

Bullfinch in Town, The. Henrietta, Lady Luxborough Knight. ECWP

Bullfrog. Ted Hughes. NYBP

Bullfrogs. David Allan Evans. Poetsp

Bullion. Amy Lowell. CPO

Bullock, The. Prelude. Federico García Lorca. PFTM

Bullock: I watched a beast of the weaponed sex. *Unknown*. EEP, *tr.* by Michael Alexander *Fr.* Riddles (Exeter Book).

Bullocky. Judith Wright. CBAP

Bull's eyes and targets. *Unknown*. OxNR

Bully, Boston, Massachusetts, 1987. Martín Espada. LTA; UnSA

("Across the Victorian mustache / and monocle.") (LL) UnSA

Bully night / I do not like. Roger McGough. OTCP

Bulosan Listens to a Recording of Robert Johnson. Alfred Encarnacion. LTA; UnSA

(Bulosan Listens to a Recording of Robert Johnson.) OpBo

("Robert Johnson / Carlos Bulosan— / our names so different, / our song the same.") (LL) UnSA

Bum. W. Dayton Wedgefarth. BLPA

Bumi. Imamu Amiri Baraka. PoBA

Bumpety, bumpety, bump. Fan, the Filly. Wilfrid Thorley. BoTP

Bumpety, bumpety, bump! *Unknown*. *See* The Mischievous Raven.

Bums, on waking. James Dickey. NYBP

Bum's Rush. Michael Dransfield. CBAP

Buna. Primo Levi, *Italian*. AF, *tr.* by Ruth Feldman *and* Brian Swann

Bunch of Blue Ribbons, The. *Unknown*. ReMoGo

Bunch of drifter sons hollered, A. Gottfried Benn, *German*. PFTM, *tr.* by Pierre Joris

Bunch of golden keys is mine, A. Golden Keys. Robert Louis Stevenson. CTV

Bunch of Grapes, The. George Herbert. ChIV-1; ESCV; GeHe; NAEL-1; NOSC; TOF

Bunch of Larks, The. Robert Leighton. EBVV

Bunch of orange buds by mail from Florida, A. (LL) Orange Buds by Mail from Florida. Walt Whitman. NAAL-1; NAAL-3

Bunch of the boys were whooping it up [in the Malamute / saloon;], A. The Shooting of Dan McGrew. Robert W. Service. EBEvV; EBNV; FaBoBe; PoLF; PoRA; RB; SAGP; UV

Bunches of carnations in a tin pitcher. A Joke. Aleksander Wat, *Polish*. BLT, *tr.* by Czeslaw Milosz *and* Leonard Nathan

Bunches of Grapes. Walter De la Mare. NTP; OxBChV

Bundaberg Rum. W. N. Scott. NOBAu

Bundled by Tuc's tight jagged. Notes on a Visit to Le Tuc d'Audoubert. Clayton Eshleman. PmAP

Bundles. Carl Sandburg. MoAmPo

Bundles for Them. Gertrude Stein. PFTM

Bungaloid Growth. Colin Ellis. FaBoEE

Bungalows, The. John Ashbery. CoAP

Bungler, The. Amy Lowell. LW

Bunk Johnson Blowing. Muriel Rukeyser. SeSe

Bunker Hill. George Henry Calvert. FaBoBe

Bunker the ambassador. Does Bunker have a bunker? The Ambassador. Bruce Weigl. CDa

Bunkers, The. Michael O'Loughlin. PBCIP *Fr.* The Shards.

Bunker's Hill, or the Soldier's Lamentation. John Freeth. NOEC

Bunnies are a feeble folk, The. A Bunny Romance. Oliver Herford. OBCA

Bunny and the Baby and the Prophylactic Pup, The. (LL) Strictly Germ-proof. Arthur Guiterman. BLPA; TrJP

Bunny creeps out and caresses his nose. Bunny Rabbit. *Unknown*. BoTP

Bunny Rabbit. *Unknown*. BoTP

Bunny Romance, A. Oliver Herford. OBCA

Bunthorne's Song. Sir William Schwenck Gilbert. CABP; EBVV; OAEL-2 *Fr.* Patience.

(Aesthete, The.) EBVV

Buonaparte. Tennyson. Son

Buoy-Bell, The. Charles Tennyson Turner. GSo; PeVV; Son

Buoys begin clanging like churches. The River That Is East. Galway Kinnell. Poetr

Burd Ellen and Young Tamlane. *Unknown*. ESPB

Burd Helen was her mother's dear. Broughty Wa's. *Unknown*. ESPB

Burd Isabel and Earl Patrick. *Unknown*. ESPB

Burden. Peter Kane Dufault. NoP-4

Burden, The. Francesca Yetunde Pereira. PBA

Burden of Decision, The. Peter Everwine. NNaP

Burdened Ass, The. John Oxenham. NSI

Burdened with family feeling, I went. Burnt. Boris Abramovich Slutsky, *Russian*. HP, *tr.* by Daniel Weissbort

Burdens. Edward Dowden. NOBVV

Burdens of All, The. Frances Ellen Watkins Harper. PWR

Burdock leaves beside the ledge, The. A Brisk Wind. William Barnes. SCGP

Bureau 2. Josephine Miles. NALW

Bureau of Labor Statistics, The. Bureaucratic Limerick. William Harmon. OBAL

Burgeoning trees are thick with leaves, The. East Wind. Ou-yang Hsiu, *Chinese*. OHPC, *tr.* by Kenneth Rexroth

Burgess faces the light the pain. (LL) The Hospital—Retrospections. Kenneth Mackenzie. BMAP

Burgess was drunk when he was admitted. The Hospital—Retrospections. Kenneth Mackenzie. BMAP; CBAP

Burghers, The. Thomas Hardy. EBNV

Burglar Bill. *Unknown*. FuFo

Burglar of Babylon, The. Elizabeth Bishop. InPS-3; NYBP; RB

Burial, A. Seamus Deane. CIP-2; PNI

Burial. Paulin Joachim, *French*. TTY, *tr.* by Oliver Bernard

Burial. Momcilo Nastasijevic, *Serbo-Croatian*. HSix, *tr.* by Charles Simic

Burial, A. Sydney Tremayne. FaBoTC

Burial. Mark Van Doren. MoBS

Burial. Henry Vaughan. GeHe

Burial. Alice Walker. AmPA; LoHo

Burial, The. John Webster. *See* Vanitas Vanitatum.

Burial Detail. Andrew Hudgins. CBCWP; MT

Burial Flags. Ralph Nixon Currey. PoWW

Burial in the East. Pablo Neruda, *Spanish.* TRP, *tr. by* Ben Belitt

Burial of a Fairy Queen. Mary E. Tucker. CBWP-1

Burial of a Fisherman in Hydra. Grace Schulman. BoWoP

Burial of An Irish President. Austin Clarke. BIrV

Burial of King Cormac, The. Sir Samuel Ferguson. NOIV; TIRV

Burial of Latané, The. John Reuben Thompson. CBCWP

Burial of Moses, The. Cecil Frances Alexander. BLPA

Burial of Sir John Moore [after [*or* at] Corunna], The. Charles Wolfe. EBEvV; FaPoR; GTBS-P; NOBE; NOBRP; NTP; OBEV; OBWP; OxAEP-2; PWR; PoRA; TFi; UV

Burial of the Dane, The. Henry Howard Brownell. PAR

Burial of the Dead, The. T. S. Eliot. *See* The Waste Land.

Burial of the Dog. Susan Musgrave. NoAM

Burial of the Linnet, The. Juliana Horatia Ewing. OxBChV

Burial of the Spirit of a Young Poet. Richard Hughes. MoBrPo

Burial Songs. *Unknown, Chinese.* ChiP, *tr. by* Arthur Waley

Burialle of the Dede. Martin Fagg. BXAP

Burials. George Crabbe. OAEL-1 *Fr.* The Parish Register.
  Ancient Virgin, An. OBNC
  Lady of the Manor, The. NOBE; OBNC

Burials. Geoffrey Grigson. PoA

Buried. Christina Rossetti. CBLP

Buried above ground. (LL) Lines Written During a Period of Insanity. William Cowper. ChIV-1; EBEvV; HAP; NOEC; NoP-4; OAEL-1

Buried at Springs. James Schuyler. CoAP; PoM

Buried Graves, The. Brad Leithauser. NoP-4

Buried in a morning Cloud. (LL) EPITAPH. On her Son H. P. at St. Syth's Church where her body also lies Interred. Katherine Philips. CABP; NoP-4; PBRV; PEW

Buried in dust, once dead by fate. Francis Beaumont. *See* Lines on the Tombs in Westminster.

Buried in noontime traffic. The Glade. Robert Kelly. *Fr.* The Book of Persephone. PoM

Buried in this low grave his pale limbs lie. Epitaph for One Killed at Roncesvalles. *Unknown, Latin.* MLL, *tr. by* Helen Waddell

Buried Life, The. Matthew Arnold. CBLP; EnVR; FHYEP; NAEL-2; OAEL-2

Buried Stream, The. James Keir Baxter. OxBC

Buried within the blue vault of the air? (LL) A Dead Mole. Andrew Young. GTBS-P; OxBSP

Burlesque Ode, on the Author's Clearing a New House of Some Workmen, A. George Keate.
  "Midst the fair range of buildings which, new-reared." NOEC

Burlesque upon the Great Frost. Charles Cotton.
  "But, to leave fooling, I assure ye." OBCoV

Burlington Bertie from Bow. William Hargreaves. OBCoV

Burly, dozing, humble-bee. The Humble-Bee. Ralph Waldo Emerson. APN-1; APo; MeMAP; NCAP; NOBA; OxBA

Burma-Shave Roadside Signs. *Unknown.* OBCoV *Fr.* Advertising Rhymes.

Burn, The. Galway Kinnell. Poetr

Burn drowns steadily in its own downpour, The. Waterfall. Seamus Heaney. HeIP-4; Poetr

Burn not too oft who flutters at thy flame. Meleager, *Greek.* GrAn, *tr. by* Peter Whigham

Burn Out Burn Quick. Abraham Reisen, *Yiddish.* TrJP, *tr. by* Joseph Leftwich

Burn Ovid with the rest. Lovers will find. Penal Law. Austin Clarke. BoLoP; GTBS-P; NOIV

Burn this Sari. A. Jayaprabha, *Telugu.* OMIP, *tr. by* V. Narayana Rao *and* A. K. Ramanujan

Burncombe Hollow. William Barnes. OBNC

Burned and dusty garden said, The. An Athenian Garden. Trumbull Stickney. APN-2; GaP; NoP-4

Burned Bridge, The. Ruth Stone. WPE

Burned in this element. Letter II. W. S. Graham. FaBoTC

Burnie bee, burnie bee. *Unknown.* ReMoGo

Burning. Galway Kinnell. CoAP

Burning, The. N. Scott Momaday. HATNAP

Burning. Gary Snyder. NeAP; PoM *Fr.* Myths and Texts.
  Amitabha's Vow.

"Face in the crook of her neck."

John Muir on Mt. Ritter. NOBA

Maitreya the Future Buddha.

Maudgalyâyana Saw Hell.

"Night here, a covert."

Second Shaman Song. NOBA; NeAP; PoM

"Spikes of new smell driven up nostrils."

"Stone-flake and salmon."

Text, The. NAAL-2

"Wash me on home, mama."

Burning Babe, The. Robert Southwell. CH; ESCV; FaBoCh; HAP; HeIP-4; InPS-3; NAEL-1; NOBE; NOCV; NoSic; OAEL-1; OBCP; OBEV; OxAEP-1; PoEL-2; RB; SCGP; TFi; TOF; TRP; TrCP
  ("And straight I callèd unto mind that it was Christmas day.") (LL) AEP; FMP; GEA; NoP-4; OxBSn; PBRV; PoPoPo

Burning Bush. Martin Feinstein. TrJP

Burning Child, The. Amy Clampitt. NMM-2

Burning dinner is not incompetence but war. (LL) What's That Smell in the Kitchen? Marge Piercy. NBLV; NIP-4

Burning Drift-Wood. John Greenleaf Whittier. APN-1

Burning Hills. Michael Ondaatje. NOBC; NoAM

Burning Island. Gary Snyder. APSN; VCAP

Burning Leaves. Ojars Vacietis, *Latvian.* CEEP, *tr. by* Inara Cedrins

Burning Love Letters. Howard Moss. HoPM

Burning Mountain. W. S. Merwin. NYBP

Burning my hart who had him kindly warmd. (LL) Sonnet 2: "Late in the Forest I did Cupid See." Mary Sidney, Countess of Montgomery Wroth. KTR; PBRV

Burning my heart who had him kindly warmed. Mary Sidney, Countess of Montgomery Wroth. *See* Sonnet 2: "Late in the Forest I did Cupid See."

Burning of Auchindown. *Unknown.* *See* Willie Macintosh.

Burning of Paper instead of Children, The. Adrienne Rich. LCAP-2; NAAL-2; VCAP

Burning of the Books, The. Bertolt Brecht, *German.* PoSu, *tr. by* John Willeh

Burning of the Law, The. Meïr of Rothenburg, *Hebrew.* TrJP, *tr. by* Nina Davis Salaman

Burning of the Leaves, The. Laurence Binyon.
  "Now is the time for the burning of the leaves." GTBS-P; NOBE; OxBTC

Burning of the Temple, The. Isaac Rosenberg. FaBoMo; PeFWW; TrJP

Burning Off. Geoffrey Dutton. NOBAu

Burning Shewolf. Vasco [*or* Vasko] Popa, *Serbo-Croatian.* HSix; VCWP, *tr. by* Charles Simic

Burning Shit at An Khe. Bruce Weigl. AF; CDa

Burning the Cat. W. S. Merwin. NIP-4

Burning the Christmas Greens. William Carlos Williams. LiTM; MeMAP; MoP; NAAL-2; NOBA; NoAM

Burning the Dolls. Richard Peabody. IFJA

Burning the Dreams. Muriel Rukeyser. AF

Burning the Letters. Gwendolyn Grew. HoPM

Burning the Letters. Randall Jarrell. MoAmPo

Burning the small dead. Gary Snyder. CAPP-1; NNaP

Burning the Tomato Worms. Carolyn Forché. NMM-2 *Fr.* Burning the Tomato Worms. AmPA
  ("Now pines lift.") NMM-2

Burning under the bleached scalp; behind dry lips / a loaded gun. (LL) Face to Face. Adrienne Rich. LiTM; NAAL-2; NoAM

Burning upon some hidden shore. The Lighthouse. Marjorie Wilson. BoTP

Burning Wheel, The. Aldous Leonard Huxley. ChIV-1

Burnished, burned-out, still burning as the year. The Public Garden. Robert Lowell. OBGa; PoRA; TAP

Burnished silver mask hangs in white air, The. On a Celtic Mask by Henry Moore. Horace Gregory. PoA

Burns up the building: Lord forbid the same. (LL) An Address to the Soul Occasioned by a Rain. Edward Taylor. ColAP; MeMAP; NAAL-1; NAAL-3; NOBA; OxBA; PoEL-3

Burnt. Boris Abramovich Slutsky, *Russian.* HP, *tr. by* Daniel Weissbort

Burnt Bush, The. Jack R. Clemo. FaBoTw

Burnt Child, The. W. S. Merwin. NoAM

Burnt Lands. G. D. Roberts. GSo

Burnt Norton. T. S. Eliot. CMoP; LiTM; MoAmPo; NAAL-2; PoE *Fr.* Four Quartets.

Burnt out year, The. New Year Letter. Edward Kamau Brathwaite. GT

Burnt Ship, A. Donne. EBEV; InPK-6; OBWP

Burnt Sienna. Norman Henry, II Pritchard. GT

Burnt tongue, The. The Last Hiding Places of Snow. Galway Kinnell. FiLi; IMW

Burragorang. Nan McDonald. NOBAu

Burro once, sent by express, A. Advice to Travelers. Walker Gibson. KaS; NBLV

Burrowing deep into earth until the grave is complete. Wolf. Peter Blue Cloud. HATNAP; VoR

Burst agonized and clear! (LL) Success is counted sweetest. Emily Dickinson. APN-2; AWP; CMoP; EBEvV; HeIP-4; ImPo; InPS-3; LiTM; MeMAP; MoAmPo; NAAL-1; NAAL-3; NOBA; NoP-4; OxBA; PAR; PFE; PoPoPo; PoRA; SAmP; TAP; TFi; WPE

Burst into flame. Tadeusz Rózewicz. See Memory of a Dream From the Year 1963.

Burst of iris so that, A. Iris. William Carlos Williams. InPS-3; LCAP-2; WeW-3

Burst, to illumine our tempestuous day. (LL) England in 1819. Shelley. FaBoPV; GSo; NAEL-2; NAWM-2; NOBE; NoP-4; OAEL-2; OxAEP-2; PBMP; PoPoPo; Poetr; Ro; SAGP; Son; TFi; UnPo

Bursting with their own wisdom, the pods were opening. By the Light of the Branches Outside. Ion Caraion, Romanian. CEEP, tr. by Marguerite Dorian and Elliott B. Urdang

Bury Her at Even. "Michael Field." OBMV

Bury it deep, the smile on your red lips. Graves. Chế Lan Viên, Vietnamese. AVP, tr. by Huỳnh Sanh Thông

Bury Me in a Free Land. Frances Ellen Watkins Harper. AAP; BPo; ColAP; CrDW; ISC; NAAAL; PAR

Bury Me Not on the Lone Prairie. Unknown. AS

(Dying Cowboy, The.) FaBoBe

Bury my heart at Wounded Knee. (LL) American Names. Stephen Vincent Benét. FaBoA; OBAL; OxBA

Bury the Great Duke. Ode on the Death of the Duke of Wellington. Tennyson.

Bury the Great Duke. Tennyson. EBVVPR; UV Fr. Ode on the Death of the Duke of Wellington.

("Our loyal passion for our temperate kings.") (LL) UV

Bury the Great Horse. Douglas Garman. UV Fr. Ode on the Death of Haig's Horse.

Bury your heart in some deep green hollow. Saturday Market. Charlotte Mew. WPE

Bury'd in a morning Cloud. Katherine Philips. See EPITAPH. On her Son H. P. at St. Syth's Church where her body also lies Interred.

Burying Ground by the Ties. Archibald MacLeish. GM

Burying Uncle Salomon. David Avidan, Hebrew. IP, tr. by Warren Bargad and Stanley F. Chyet

Bus, The. Leonard Cohen. HeIP-4

Bus, The. "Peter." BoTP

Bus driver. We Thank You! L. E. Cox. BoTP

Bus halts its long brawl, The. At Kfar Kana. Charles Causley. TOF

Bus is waiting at the southern gate, The. James Fenton. Fr. A German Requiem. NAEL-2; NoAM

Bus Ride. Kate Daniels. PBCAP

Bus Stop. Donald Justice. FYAP; LCAP-2; WeT

Bus-Stop on the Somme, The. David Rowbotham. NOBAu

Bus Trip, The. Joel Oppenheimer. NeAP

Bus was taking me, The. To S.V. György Petri, Hungarian. VCWP, tr. by Wilmer, Clive and George Gömöri

Buses came late, each driver sullen. Christmas Bells, Saigon. Walter McDonald. AF

Bush. Josephine Jacobsen. NoP-4

Bush, The. Bernard O'Dowd.

"To other eyes and ears you are a great." CBAP

Bush, The. Victor D. Questel. HCP

Bush, a gathering smoke, The. Blackthorn. Euros Bowen, Welsh. OBWVE, tr. by the author

Bush Justice. Charles Harpur. CBAP

Bush land scrub land. The Country North of Belleville. Alfred Wellington Purdy. NOBC

Bush Navigator: The Last Morning of Hands. Peggy Shumaker. PBCAP

Bush Section, A. Blanche Edith Baughan.

"Logs, at the door, by the fence; broadcast over the paddock." PeNZ

Bush Speaks, The. Ernest G. Moll. NOBAu

Bush that has most briers and bitter fruit, The. The Barberry-Bush. Jones Very. PAR

Bush, The. Yes. It burned like they say it did. Deuteronomy. Robert Bringhurst. NOBC

Bush was on that dump, A. The Burnt Bush. Jack R. Clemo. FaBoTw

Bushed. Earle Birney. MoCV; NOBC; NoAM; NoP-4

Bushed. Charles Lillard. NOBC

Bushed. Barry McKinnon. NOBC

Bushranger, A. Kenneth Slessor. CBAP; NOBAu

Bushwoman lies, The. In a South African Museum. Evangeline Paterson. NBrP

Business. Miryana Basheva, Bulgarian. CEEP, tr. by Brenda Walker

Business Girls. John Betjeman. UV

Business Life, The. David Ignatow. NNaP

Business-like harlot named Draper, A. Limerick. Unknown. PeLi

Business men boast of their skill and cunning. Ch'en Tzu-ang, Chinese. ChiP, tr. by Arthur Waley

Business of Fancydancing, The. Sherman Alexie. PaTW

Business of Love is Cruelty, The. Dean Young. BAP-93

Business of poetry, The. Harold Norse. CLPP

Business Reverses. Edgar Lee Masters. ChIV-2

Busk, Pierce. Maggie O'Sullivan. NBrP

Bussy d'Ambois. George Chapman.

"Ile sooth his plots: and strow my hate with smiles." PoEL-2

"Now all the peacefull regents of the night." PoEL-2

"Now shall we see, that nature hath no end." PoEL-2

Bustan, The. Sadi. See The Gulistan.

Bustle in a House, The. Emily Dickinson. HAP; HeIP-4; NAAL-1; NAAL-3; NoP-4; OxBA; PoEL-5; PoLF; SAmP

Bustopher Jones is not skin and bones. Bustopher Jones: The Cat About Town. T. S. Eliot. OBCoV

Busts of the great composers glimmered in niches. Mrs. Snow. Donald Justice. NoP-4

Busy. Yüan Mei, Chinese. CoBLCP, tr. by Jonathan Chaves

Busy, curious, thirsty fly! On a Fly Drinking out of [or from] His Cup. William Oldys. APAD; ImPo; OBEV; OxAEP-1; SCGP

Busy Heart, The. Rupert Brooke. MoBrPo

Busy in study be thou, child. Demeanour. Unknown. OxBChV

Busy is the life of the weaving woman! Song of the Weaving Woman. Yüan Chen, Chinese. SuSp, tr. by Wu-chi Liu

Busy Man Speaks, A. Robert Bly. CoAmPo

Busy Old Fool. Ian Kelso. BXAP

Busy [or Busie] old fool[e], unruly sun[ne]. The Sun[ne] Rising. Donne. APAD; BoLoP; CABP; CBLP; ClHu; EBEvV; ESCV; FHYEP; FMP; FSCP; GBL; GLoP; HAP; HeIP-4; InPS-3; LoP; MeLP; NAEL-1; NIP-4; NOBE; NOSC; NoP-4; OAEL-1; PBRV; PoE; PoEL-2; PoPoPo; Poetr; SCV; SeCP; TFi; WeW-3

Busy, with an idea for a code, I write. An Obsessive Combination of Ontological Inscape, Trickery and Love. Anne Sexton. PiM

Busy with love, the bumble bee. Meleager, Greek. BoLoP; GrAn, tr. by Peter Whigham

Busy with Many Jobs. Tadeusz Rózewicz, Polish. PoSu, tr. by Adam Czerniawski

Busy with very urgent jobs. Busy with Many Jobs. Tadeusz Rózewicz, Polish. PoSu, tr. by Adam Czerniawski

Busy yellow bee, after his mighty quest, A. Unknown. NOIV

But. Vladimir Holan, Czech. PoSu, tr. by Ian and Jarmila Milner

But a cat too is an extension of God. (LL) Thoughts on Capital Punishment. Rod McKuen. PFE

But a dream within a dream? (LL) A Dream within A Dream. Edgar Allan Poe. AmPP; GBL; MeMAP; NCAP; NOBA; OxBA; TAP

But a flint holds fire. (LL) Flint. Christina Rossetti. ChAP; OxBChV

But a kiss frae aff his rosy lips gi'es strength anew to me. William Miller. See Willie Winkie.

But a large quantity of brandy. A Small Faculty Stag for the Visiting Poet. Earle Birney. OxBC; PeLV

But a little while ago. Winter and Spring. Unknown. BoTP

But a red headed woman make a boy slap his papa down. William Christopher Handy. See St. Louis Blues.

But accept it for friendship's sake. (LL) The Cave of Making. W. H. Auden. FaBoVe; OxAEP-2

But 'accessibility to experience'. Marianne Moore. See New York.

But ae braithless note. Sydney Goodsir Smith. OBVE Fr. The Gangrel Rymour and the Pairdon of Sanct Anne.

But after one such love, can love no more. (LL) The Broken Heart. Donne. EBEV; FSCP

"But ah," Desire still cries, "give me some food." (LL) Sonnet 71: "Who will in fairest book of Nature know." Sir Philip Sidney. InPS-3; NAEL-1; NoP-4; NoSic; OAEL-1; PoE; Poetr

But ah! he left the thorn wi' me. (LL) The Banks O' Doon. Robert Burns. NOBE; NOEC

But Ah! More wondrous still the Charming Fair. (LL) A Compliment to the Ladies. William Blake. BXAP; OBCoV

But ah! what glories yon blue vault emblaze? A Hymn to Indra. Sir William Jones. NOBRP

But, ah! ye maids, beware the gipsy's lures! A Warning against the Gypsies. John Langhorne. ECEV Fr. The Country Justice.

But, alas, who less[e] could do[e] that found so good occasion? (LL) Think'st thou to seduce me then with words that have no meaning? Thomas Campion. NAEL-1; OxAEP-1; OxBSP

But all is new unhallowed ground. (LL) Time draws near the birth of Christ, The. Tennyson. EBVV; OAEL-2

But all too late, grief's out of date. Michael Wigglesworth. NAAL-3 *Fr.* The Day of Doom. NAAL-1; SCAP

But always one, your own both firm and stable. (LL) Sonnet: 'Each man me telleth'. Sir Thomas Wyatt. AEP; SiPS

But always, without fail THE NECK. (LL) Travel[l]er's Curse after Misdirection[, The]. Robert Graves. CMoP; HoPM; LiTM; MoBrPo; NBLV; OBCoV; PFE

But always, your Catullus will be as firm as rock is. Catullus. *See* Carmen 8 ("Break off / fallen Catullus").

But anxious cares the pensive nymph oppressed. Alexander Pope. EBNV; OxAEP-1 *Fr.* The Rape of the Lock[, an Heroi-Comical Poem]. FHYEP; HAP; ImPo; OAEL-1; OBNV; PeLV; PoEL-3

But are not critics to their judgment too? Alexander Pope. *See* 'Tis hard to say, if greater want of skill.

But are not of? (LL) Midnight on the Great Western. Thomas Hardy. CH; NOBE; OxAEP-2

But are these landscapes to be imagined. Ronald Johnson. *Fr.* Letters to Walt Whitman. VGW

But as long-liv'd as present love. (LL) Of English Verse. Edmund Waller. BeJo; CABP; NAEL-1; NOSC; OAEL-1; PoE; SeCP

But, as rewarded, death for to be my meed. (LL) Resound my voice [*or* voyse], ye woods [*or* wodes] that hear [*or* here] me plain. Sir Thomas Wyatt. AEP

But as soon as the pressure of work or people eases off. My Days Go On. Frances Partridge. LBC

But ask now the beasts. Bible, *O.T. Fr.* Job. NAWM-1

But ask whatever else, and we will dare! (LL) Ode Recited at the Harvard Commemoration (July 21, 1865). James Russell Lowell. APN-1; CBCWP; NOBA; OBWP

But at a distance, in another tree. (LL) No Possum, No Sop, No Taters. Wallace Stevens. HCAP; MeMAP; OxBA; TAP; VGW

But at last there came the day, the hour of shovels and buckets. The Angels of the Ruins. Rafael Alberti, *Spanish.* AF, tr. by Geoffrey Connell

But at the common table. (LL) Te Deum. Charles Reznikoff. ChIV-1; TrJP

But at the immolation of a race who cries? (LL) Death of a Whale. John Blight. BMAP; CBAP

But, baby, where are you? (LL) Ballad of Birmingham. Dudley Randall. BPo; HeIP-4; ISC; InPK-6; MoP; NIP-4; NoAM; NoP-4; Poetr; SoSe-8

But Bacchus was not so content: he quyght forsooke their land. King Midas. Ovid. CTC, tr. by Arthur Golding *Fr.* Metamorphoses.

But bargains: those he will not strike. (LL) Age. Walter Savage Landor. FaBoEE; NOBVV; PoEL-4

But be. Archibald MacLeish. *See* Ars Poetica.

But be contended when that fell arest. William Shakespeare. *See* Sonnet 74.

But Bird. Paul Zimmer. PuP-17; SeSe

But break, my heart, for I must hold my tongue! (LL) Frailty, Thy Name is Woman. Shakespeare. IMW; OxAEP-1; SCV

But brims the poisoned well. (LL) Fragments of a Lost Gnostic Poem of the Twelfth [*or* 12th] Century. Herman Melville. APN-2; NOBA; NoP-4; OxBSP; PAR; PoEL-5; PoPoPo

But can see better there, and laughing there. "Pygmies Are Pygmies Still, Though Percht on Alps." Gwendolyn Brooks. ColAP *Fr.* Notes from the Childhood and the Girlhood. LCAP-2

But cannot see our sack behind. (LL) To Varus. Catullus. AWP, tr. by Walter Savage Landor

But caught the mice in his father's barn. Mother Goose. *See* Ding, dong, bell, / Pussy's in the well.

But change the bloody gauze. (LL) The Ballad of Rudolph Reed. Gwendolyn Brooks. PFE; RB

But clasp'd to his bosom, the infant was dead. (LL) The Erl-King. Goethe, *German.* STV, tr. by John Frederick Nims; AWP; OBVE; OxBSn, tr. by Sir Walter Scott

But colorless. Colorless. (LL) Poppies in July. Sylvia Plath. FaBoWP; LCAP-2; RB

But come, come in till then! Come in till then! (LL) Cinderella. Randall Jarrell. LCAP-2; NAAL-2; VCAP

But come. Grief must have its term? Guilt too, then. James Fenton. *Fr.* A German Requiem. NAEL-2; NoAM

But come here, fear / I am alive and you are so afraid / of dying. Joy Harjo. *See* I Give You Back.

But Conrad has not answered a word. (LL) Conrad in Twilight. John Crowe Ransom. MeMAP; OxBA

But copying is, what in her Nature writes. (LL) Sonnet 3: "Let dainty wits cry on the sisters nine." Sir Philip Sidney. NoSic; OAEL-1; Son

But could it come up into a limestone to correct, teeth. Manlius to Coeymans. Clark Coolidge. FTOS

But could not both live and utter it. (LL) My life has been the poem I would have writ. Henry David Thoreau. PAR

But Could You? Vladimir Mayakovsky, *Russian.* TCRP, tr. by Bernard Meares

But Custard keeps crying for a nice safe cage. (LL) The Tale of Custard the Dragon. Ogden Nash. OBCA; OTCP; PoRA

But Cytherea, studious to invent. Cupid at work. Virgil, *Latin.* OBCVT, tr. by William Wordsworth

But day by day I spin my shroud. (LL) Arachne. Rose Terry Cooke. APN-2; APo

But declared she would never leave Portugal. (LL) Limericks, II (iv). Edward Lear. OBCoV; OxBoLi; PeLV; PeLi

But defines, for the fortunate, that joy in which all joys / should rejoice. (LL) Colder Fire. Robert Penn Warren. LiTM

But did not paradise itself contain. Age of Innocence. Graham Hough. PoRA

But do not let us quarrel any more. Andrea del Sarto. Robert Browning. CTC; EnVR; NAEL-2; NOBVV; NoP-4; OAEL-2; PoE; PoEL-5

But does every man feel like this at forty. The Second Life. Edwin Morgan. FaBoTC; OxBS

But doesn't heaven. England, Autumn. Wayne Brown. PBCV

But Don John of Austria rides home from the Crusade. (LL) Lepanto. G. K. Chesterton. EBEvV; EBNV; FaPoR; MoBrPo; OBMV; OBNV; RB

But don't call Mother Damnable names. Around the Corner. Laura Riding Jackson. *Fr.* Forgotten Girlhood. RB

But don't tell the neighbours, you bastard. (LL) Limerick. *Unknown.* OBCoV; PeLi

But drives a blue car through the / stars. (LL) Two Years Later. John Wieners. PmAP; PoM; RaBo

But dropped like Adamant. (LL) 'Twas warm—at first—like Us. Emily Dickinson. APN-2; CMoP; NAWM-2; NCAP; SoSe-8

But Dwell in Darkness. George Chapman. Son *Fr.* A Coronet for His Mistress Philosophy.

But dwell in darkness; for your God is blind. (LL) Love and Philosophy. George Chapman. SCGP; Son

But—'e'll never be the man 'is Father woz. (LL) Chorus of a Song That Might Have Been Written by Albert Chevalier. Max Beerbohm. OBCoV; UV

But equally a want of books and men! (LL) England, 1802, III. Wordsworth. FaBoPV; OBEV; PoEL-4; Son

But ere I could fly thence, it pierced my heart. (LL) Sonnet 20: "Fly, fly, my friends." Sir Philip Sidney. NoSic; OAEL-1

But ere sterne conflict mixt both strengths, faire Paris stept before. Homer. OBVE, tr. by George Chapman *Fr.* The Iliad.

But, fair Iëmpsar (wife of Potiphar). Joshua Sylvester. ChIV-1 *Fr.* The Maidens Blush.

But Fate and gloomy Night encompass thee around. (LL) To the Memory of Mr Oldham. Dryden. AWP; EBEV; EPCY; FP; HAP; InPK-6; InPS-3; NIP-4; NOBE; NOSC; NoP-4; OAEL-1; OxAEP-1; PoE; PoEL-3; PoPoPo; Poetr; SCGP; TFi; TRP

But fear, thirst, hunger, and this huddled chill. (LL) Montana Pastoral. James Vincent Cunningham. MoAmPo; VGW

But Fear Thou Not, O Jacob. Bible, *O.T.* TrJP *Fr.* Jeremiah.

But find while here we dwell our heavenly home. Jones Very. *See* The Origin of Man, I.

But finding nothing, sullenly withdrew. (LL) Range-finding. Robert Frost. MoP; NIP-4; NoAM; OBWP; Poetr; RB

But first one must free oneself. Patrizia Cavalli, *Italian.* VCWP, tr. by Cavalli, Patrizia and Robert McCracken; NeIt, tr. by Robert McCracken and Patrizia Cavalli

But, fool, seek'st not to get into her heart. (LL) Sonnet 11: "In truth, O Love, with what a boyish kind." Sir Philip Sidney. CBLP; PoE

But for a brief / Moment, a poised minute. A Grasshopper. Richard Wilbur. HAP; HoPM

But for an hour's sleep in a filthy bed. Recall. Reed Whittemore. NYBP

But for His bride. (LL) World, The, (1). Henry Vaughan. AWP; ChIV-2; EBEV; ESCV; FMP; FSCP; HAP; ImPo; NAEL-1; NOBE; NOCV; NOSC; OAEL-1; OBEV; OxAEP-1; PBRV; PeECV; PoEL-2; SCGP; SeCP; TFi; TrCP

But for Lust. Ruth Pitter. FaBoTw; OxBTC

But, for such as our earth is now, it lasted long. (LL) The Season of Phantasmal Peace. Derek Walcott. AFr; HCP; PoPoPo; VCWP

But for the broken firing pin. Spider Reeves. Henry Carlile. Poetsp

But for the dew. Tanka. Mori Ōgai, *Japanese.* MJT, tr. by Makoto Ueda

But for The Thing. (LL) The Runes on Weland's Sword. Rudyard Kipling. NoAM; PoEL-5

But for the wits of either Charles's days. Alexander Pope. EPCY *Fr.* The First Epistle of the Second Book of Horace Imitated.

But for their powers, accept my piety. (LL) To William Camden. Ben Jonson. AWP; BeJo; NAEL-1; NOSC

But for them the bombers answer everything. (LL) Second Air Force. Randall Jarrell. CMoP; LiTM; NAAL-2

But for to make it spring againe. (LL) The Hock-Cart, or Harvest Home. Robert Herrick. BeJo; CaPo; EBEV; FaBoPV; NAEL-1; NOSC; OxAEP-1; SeCP

But for women. Tanka. Akiko Yosano, *Japanese.* MJT, tr. by Ueda, Makoto

But for your terror. To Death. Oliver St. John Gogarty. FaBoEE; OBMV

But frankley, gayly shall we get the gods. (LL) Meditation at Kew. Anna Wickham. FaBoTw; MoBrPo; NALW

But from it fly. (LL) A Bridal Song: "Roses, their sharp spines being gone." John Fletcher *and* Shakespeare. NOBE; NOSC; NoSic

But Gawd! it went through my 'eart. (LL) Matey. Patrick MacGill. NSI; PoWW

But get some color and music out of life? (LL) The Investment. Robert Frost. CMoP; OxBA

But gi'e her my breast-knot, white an' blue? (LL) White an' Blue. William Barnes. GBL; GTBS-P

But give me for my soul, those beauteous maids. Those Beauteous Maids. Moses ibn Ezra, *Hebrew.* TrJP, tr. by Solomon Solis-Cohen

But give them me, the mouth, the eyes, the brow! Eurydice to Orpheus. Robert Browning. CBLP; CTC

But grant I may relapse, for want of grace. Alexander Pope. *Fr.* The Second Epistle of the Second Book of Horace Imitated. TOF

But grant, the virtues of a temp'rate prime. Life's Last Scene. Samuel Johnson. *Fr.* The Vanity of Human Wishes [The Tenth Satire of Juvenal Imitated]. EBEV; ECEV; NOEC; OAEL-1; OxAEP-1; PoEL-3; TFi

But gravity lies beneath the dust of his feet. (LL) The Limbo Dancer. Josephine Jacobsen. FFC; PuP-16

But Greece and her foundations are. Shelley. GrIP *Fr.* Hellas.

But gripped, gripped and is now a cenotaph. (LL) Relic. Ted Hughes. NAEL-2; NoP-4

But hark! a sound is stealing on my ear. Charles Stuart Calverley. *Fr.* Beer. BXAP

But hark! the cry is Astur. Horatius. Thomas Babington Macaulay, 1st Baron Macaulay. OBWP *Fr.* Lays of Ancient Rome.

But hark! The sharp beat of the Afric drum. William Hosack. *Fr.* The Isle of Streams; or, the Jamaica Hermit. PBCV

But haven't we always known? "Scientists find universe awash in tiny diamonds." Pat Mayne Ellis. CrSp

But he did for them both by his plan of attack. (LL) The General. Siegfried Sassoon. CMoP; LiTM; NAEL-2; NoAM; NoP-4; OBWP; OxBSP; OxBTC; OxBoLi; PoE; PoFWW

But he didn't catch me. (LL) The Little Turtle. Vachel Lindsay. CTV; NOxBChV; NTCP; OBAL; OBCA; OBSP

But he found it a puz-puz-puzzle. (LL) There was a little dog, and he had a little tail. *Unknown.* CTAV

But he his wonted pride. Satan and His Host. Milton. *Fr.* Book I. FHYEP; NAEL-1; OAEL-1; OxAEP-1 *Fr.* Paradise Lost.

But He Was Cool; or, He Even Stopped for Green Lights. Don L. Lee. BPo; MoP; PoBA

But hear. If you stay, and the child be born. In the Restaurant. Thomas Hardy. MoBrPo *Fr.* Satires of Circumstance in Fifteen Glimpses.

But helpless Pieces of the Game He plays. 69. Edward Fitzgerald. CABP

But her arm—damp, small. Mary Kinzie. FFC

But her sweet odour did them all excel. (LL) Sonnet 64. Edmund Spenser. EBEV; NAEL-1; OAEL-1; Son

But here's the piece, made up to sell. The Landscape. George Daniel. NOSC

But his actual candle blazed with artifice. (LL) A Quiet Normal Life. Wallace Stevens. NAAL-2; NoAM

But his shoes were far too tight. (LL) Incidents in the Life of My Uncle Arly. Edward Lear. CBNP; NOxBChV; OAEL-2; OBCoV; OxBoLi

But hit's mighty ha'd to giggle w'en dey's nuffin' in de pot. (LL) Philosophy. Paul Laurence Dunbar. BPo; NAAAL

"But hold y. . . hold y. . . " says Robin. The Jolly Pinder of Wakefield. *Unknown.* ESPB

But *Horace,* Sir, was delicate, was nice. Persius. OBCVT, tr. by Alexander Pope *Fr.* One Thousand Seven Hundred and Thirty Eight. A Dialogue Something like Horace.

But how can I tell their story / if I was not there? Vocabulary. Ariel Dorfman, *Spanish.* AF, tr. by Ariel Dorfman *and* Edith Grossman

But How It Came from Earth. Conrad Potter Aiken. MoAmPo

But how many merry monthes be in the yeere? Robin Hood and the Curtal Friar. *Unknown.* ESPB

But how much more unfortunate are those. Hilaire Belloc. UV

But how shall we this union well expresse? The Soul and the Body. Sir John Davies. CTC; NOBE; PoEL-2 *Fr.* Nosce Teipsum. NoSic; SiPS

But how thoroughly departmental. (LL) Departmental. Robert Frost. HeIP-4; HoPM; MoAmPo; NAAL-2; NOBA; NOBL; OBAL; PeLV; SAGP; SoSe-8

But howling wind and solitary birds. W. B. Yeats. *See* "Calvary."

But I am completely nourished. (LL) Decade, [A]. Amy Lowell. CPO; MoAmPo; NALW; OxWW

But I Am Growing Old and Indolent. Robinson Jeffers. ColAP; NOBA; TAP

But I Do Not Need Kindness. Gregory Corso. NeAP

But I don't care where the water goes if it doesn't get into the wine. (LL) Wine and Water. G. K. Chesterton. ChIV-1; MoBrPo

But I go on for ever. Tennyson. *See* The Brook.

But I go on forever. (LL) The Brook. Tennyson. BoTP; CTV; EBEvV; FHYEP; FaBoBe

But I remember his hands. (LL) Fifth Grade Autobiography. Rita Dove. ISC; NIP-4

But I remember when the fight was done. Staff Officer. Shakespeare. *Fr.* King Henry IV, Pt. I. NAEL-1

But I shall be gone. (LL) The Sound of Trees. Robert Frost. NoAM; OxBA

But I shall stay at home. (LL) A Country Boy in Winter. Sarah Orne Jewett. APN-2; ColAP; OBCA

But I think mice / Are nice. (LL) (Mice). Rose Fyleman. BoTP; NTCP

But I waked—and all was done. (LL) A Report Song [in a Dream]. Nicholas Breton. GBL; NOBE; NoSic

But I was *born* to other things. (LL) I trust I have not wasted breath. Tennyson. EnVR; FHYEP; OAEL-2

But I was dead, an hour or more. Escape. Robert Graves. MoBrPo

But I was young and foolish, and now am full of tears. (LL) Down by the salley gardens my love and I did meet. W. B. Yeats. CRIP; CMoP; CTC; EBEvV; EBVV; EnLoPo; GLoP; MoBrPo; NAEL-2; NoAM; OBEV; PoEL-5; PoPoPo; SAGP; SoSe-8

But I will make the book of glass. (LL) A Book of Glass. David Shapiro. PT; PmAP

But I will not say so. (LL) Women. ------ Heath. CTC; NoSic

But I would rather be horizontal. I Am Vertical. Sylvia Plath. PiM

But I'd drop dead again. (LL) If I Should Die Tonight. Ben King. NBLV; OBAL; PoLF

But I'd go today. Ultimatum. Philip Larkin. *Fr.* Poetry of Departures. CMoP; HeIP-4; OxBC; PoE; TwCP

But, "if a man die, shall he live again?" Albery Allson Whitman. AAP *Fr.* The Octoroon.

But if I look the ice is gone from the lake. Spring of the Thief. John Logan. NNaP

But if I should ask the king? Answering A Child. Sarah Morgan Bryan Piatt. NCAP

But if I tell you how my heart swings wide. Sunflower Sonnet Number One. June Jordan. Son

But if in endless Drinking you delight. A Poem Dedicated to Mrs. Blennerhasset, the Only Female Member of the Limerick Hell Fire Club. Daniel Hayes. IIP

But if one of those children came near that we have set / on fire. Robert Bly. CDa *Fr.* The Teeth Mother Naked at Last.

But if there be a power too just and strong. Dryden. NOCV *Fr.* Religio Laici.

But if through genuine tenderness of heart. The Art of Preserving Health. John Armstrong. OBGa *Fr.* The Art of Preserving Health.

But if we could see and hear, this Vision—were it not He? (LL) The Higher Pantheism. Tennyson. CABP

But if you break the bloody glass you won't hold up the weather. (LL) Bagpipe Music. Louis MacNeice. CABP; CMoP; EBEvV; GTBS-P; ImPo; LiTM; MoP; NAEL-2; NBLV; NOBE; NOBL; NoAM; NoP-4; OAEL-2; OBSV; OxBTC; PeLV; RB; TFi; UV

But if you don't, I'll lay it on, by G—d! Byron. *See* Poetical Commandments.

But if you [*or* yow] list, my tale shul ye he[e]re. (LL) The Franklin's Prologue. Chaucer. NAEL-1; OAEL-1

'But I'm nothing unusual,' he said. The Undistinguished Visitor. Leo Aylen. SpW

But I'm talking about / Harlem to you! Langston Hughes. *See* Same in Blues.

But I'm the one from whom they stole a button from his trouser leg. Song. Milorad Pavic. HSix *Fr.* Holy Mass For Relja Krilatica.

But I'm the one to whom others spit in the hand when he works. Song. Milorad Pavic. HSix *Fr.* Holy Mass For Relja Krilatica.

But I'm the one who carries a garlic clove in the ear. Song. Milorad Pavic. HSix *Fr.* Holy Mass For Relja Krilatica.

But in her heart a cold December. (LL) All Seasons in One. *Unknown*. GBL; HeIP-4

'But in that Sleep of Death what Dreams may Come?'. Mary Elizabeth Coleridge. VWP

But in the crowding darkness not a word did they say. The Old-Marrieds. Gwendolyn Brooks. PoBA

But in the end one tires of the high-flown. About the Phoenix. James Merrill. NoAM

But in the interval here the boiling, pent-up water. Arthur Hugh Clough. EnVR *Fr*. Bothie of Tober-na-Vuolich, The [A Long-Vacation Pastoral].

But in the shade I will believe what in the sun I loved. (LL) On the Sun Coming Out in the Afternoon. Henry David Thoreau. OxBSP; PoEL-4

But in this country / there is war. Lorna Dee Cervantes. *See* Poem for the Young White Man Who Asked Me How I, An Intelligent, Well-Read Person Could Believe in the War Between Races.

But in Wormie's Wood she shall aye wone'. (LL) Kemp Owyne. Alice Cary. ESPB; EnSB

But is for others undiminished somewhere. (LL) Sad Steps. Philip Larkin. NoAM; NoP-4

But Islands of the Blessed, bless you, son. An Answer. Robert Frost. OBCoV

But it ate a whole in my heart. Argument. Daniel Halpern. BAP-93

But it could be worse. (LL) Sonnet for Minimalists. Mona Van Duyn. FFC; WeW-3

But it is given in friendship. (LL) Visitors. Tu Fu, *Chinese*. BLT; OHPC, *tr. by* Kenneth Rexroth

But it took him a long time / finally to make his mind up to go home. Elizabeth Bishop. *See* The Prodigal.

But it was right that she. His Wife. Shirley Kaufman. LCAP-2

But, John, have you seen the world, said he. Angle of Vision. Robert Rendall. OxBTC

But *Jove* at length with just Resentment fir'd. *Unknown*. OBCVT, *tr. by* William Congreve *Fr*. Hymn to Aphrodite.

But keep that earlier, wilder image bright. (LL) To Cole, the Painter, Departing for Europe. William Cullen Bryant. APN-1; AiP; AmPP; ColAP; GEA; NAAL-1; NAAL-3; PAR; TAP

But kiss and unkiss till we die. Catullus. *See* Carmen 5 ("My sweetest Lesbia, let us live and love").

But kiss him & give him both drink and apparel. (LL) The Little Vagabond. William Blake. FHYEP; NBLV; OBSV; Ro

But know not how, for still I think of you. (LL) Sonnet 30: "Whether the Turkish new moon minded be". Sir Philip Sidney. NoSic; PoE

But know not what's *resisted*. (LL) Address to the Unco Guid, or the Rigidly Righteous. Robert Burns. ChIV-1; NOBE; NOCV; OxBS

But, knowing now that they would have her speak. The Defense of Guenevere. William Morris. NAEL-2

But known of what he died. (LL) The Workbox. Thomas Hardy. InPK-6; NAEL-2; UnPo

But leave, because I cannot as I should! (LL) To John Donne ("Donne, the delight of Phoebus, and each Muse"). Ben Jonson. BeJo; EPCY; NAEL-1

But left the thorn wi' me. (LL) Bonie Doon. Robert Burns. CH; GTBS-P; NoP-4

But ler her go, man, let her go. Catullus. *See* Carmen 8 ("Break off / fallen Catullus").

But let applause be dealt in all we may. George Crabbe. OBNC *Fr*. The Vicar. OBSV *Fr*. The Borough.

But let me now my lovely charge remind. Soame Jenyns. ECEV *Fr*. The Art of Dancing.

But let us hence depart, whilest wether serves and wind. (LL) Eftsoones they heard a most melodious sound. Edmund Spenser. PBRV

But lets the poet see how heav'n can shine. (LL) Coleridge. Theodore Watts-Dunton. GSo

But listen. Go on, tell me the season is over. Alan Wearne. BMAP

But Little John Nobody, that dare not once speak. (LL) Little John Nobody. *Unknown*. CBNP; OxBoLi

But Littleman he can't dance alone. (LL) Dance, Thumbkin, dance. Mother Goose. LB; OxNR; ReMoGo

But lo! at length the day is lingered out. Francis Thompson. OBMV *Fr*. Sister Songs.

But, lo! from forth a copse that neighbours by. The Courser and the Jennet. Shakespeare. NOBE *Fr*. Venus and Adonis.

But lo, Polites, one of Priam's sons. Virgil. *Fr*. The Second Book of Virgil's *Aeneid*. SiPS, *tr. by* Henry Howard, Earl of Surrey *Fr*. The Aeneid [*or* Eneados, *Aeneis*].

But lo! the reaking surface of the vale. John Singleton. *Fr*. A General Description of the West Indian Islands. PBCV

But look a trial down from some far height. Full Vision. Henrietta Cordelia Ray. CBWP-3

But look / but look. Nelly Sachs, *German*. AF, *tr. by* Matthew Mead *and* Ruth Mead

But look in your mirror for the other one. Antonio Machado Ruiz. RaBo, *tr. by* Robert Bly *Fr*. Moral Proverbs and Folk Songs.

But look / look at him out there. What Her Friend Said. Kapilar, *Tamil*. PLW, *tr. by* A. K. Ramanujan

But love curdles to milk in this climate. Harbour. Edward Kamau Brathwaite. PBCV

But love is complicated. (LL) To a Poet. Agnes Nemes Nagy, *Hungarian*. CEEP; PoSu, *tr. by* Bruce Berlind

But love whilst that thou mayst be loved again. Samuel Daniel. NoP-4; NoSic *Fr*. To Delia.

But love whilst that thou mayst be loved again. (LL) The Half-blown Rose. Samuel Daniel. NoP-4; NoSic; SCGP

But lovers are like umbrellas arnt they? Accoutrement. "Marnia." LW

But mark you well the words I say. Horatio Nelson Huggins. *Fr*. Hiroona. PBCV

But Mary stood weeping outside the tomb. John 20:11–18. Rilke. GI *Fr*. St. John.

But may be ravenously unripped in hell? (LL) Sonnet for a Picture. Swinburne. BXAP; OAEL-2; UV

But may I raise up spirits when I please? Marlowe. OxBoV *Fr*. Doctor Faustus.

But Men loved Darkness[e] Rather Than [*or* Then] Light. Richard Crashaw. ChIV-2

But Milton next, with high and haughty stalks. Joseph Addison. EPCY *Fr*. An Account of the Greatest English Poets.

But Money gives me pleasure all the time. (LL) Fatigue. Hilaire Belloc. NBLV; NOBL; OxBTC; UV

But most beautiful of all is the Un-found Island. The Most Beautiful. Guido Gozzano, *Italian*. TTTS, *tr. by* Victoria Pesce

But most by numbers judge a poet's song. Poetical Numbers. Alexander Pope. NIP-4, *ll*. 337–383; ECEV; EPCY; FHYEP; HAP; Poetr *Fr*. An Essay on Criticism. NAEL-1; PoEL-3; TFi

But most of all my knowing I would write to her. Repressed Theme. Barbara Cully. BAP-93

But most of that that most I fear. / What means this? (LL) What means [*or* meaneth *or* menethe] this when I lie [*or* lye] alone. Sir Thomas Wyatt. GBL; SiPS

But Murderous. Stevie Smith. PFE

But My Blood. Rose Romano. UnSA

But my good little man, you have made a mistake. To a Boy-Poet of the Decadence. Sir Owen Seaman. PeLV

But *Nancy* still with me. (LL) In a Letter to A.R.C. on Her Wishing to Be Called Anna. Matilda Barbara Betham-Edwards. ECWP; WoRP

But nane but thee for me. (LL) The False Lover Won Back. *Unknown*. ESPB; OxBB

But nearer than Guardian Angel. Hilda Doolittle. NALW *Fr*. Tribute to the Angels.

But neither stops her song. (LL) I Ask My Mother to Sing. Li-Young Lee. LoL; OpBo; UnSA

But Night determines here, Away. (LL) The Apparition of His Mistress[e] Calling Him to Elizium [*or* Elysium]. Robert Herrick. CaPo; SeCP

But night, the reserved, the reticent, gives more than it takes. (LL) As One Put Drunk into the Packet-Boat. John Ashbery. HAP; HCAP; VCAP

But no one liked to poke up Willie. (LL) Tender-Heartedness. Harry Graham. FPC

But no, the familiar symbol, as that the. Conrad Potter Aiken. *Fr*. Time in the Rock [*or*, Preludes to Definition]. VGW

But nobody seems to know whose. (LL) Limerick. Edward Gorey. OBCoV; PeLi

But none shall thus lament for me! (LL) The Lament of the Captive. Richard Henry Wilde. APN-1; ColAP

But not from her protecting care. (LL) Lullaby: "Beloved, may your sleep be sound." W. B. Yeats. BoLoP; FaBoTw; LoP; OBMV

But not here. (LL) Where Knock Is Open Wide. Theodore Roethke. HAP; VGW

But not in our alley! (LL) Sally in Our Alley. Henry Carey. AWP; BoLoP; FaBoBe; GLoP; GTBS-P; NOBE; NOEC; OBEV; OxAEP-1

But not on a shell, she starts. The Paltry Nude Starts on a Spring Voyage. Wallace Stevens. HCAP

But not pear Jonet! (LL) I have a newe gardin. *Unknown*. OBGa

But Not That One. John Ashbery. LCAP-2

But nothing happens. (LL) Exposure. Wilfred Owen. FaBoMo; InPS-3; NoAM; OBWP; PeFWW; PoFWW; PoWW; RB

But nothing promised is not performed. (LL) To Juan at the Winter Solstice. Robert Graves. CMoP; EBEV; FaBoMo; ImPo; LiTM; MoBrPo; MoP; NAEL-2; NoAM; NoP-4; OAEL-2; PoE; RaBo; TwCP

But now at thirty years my hair is grey. Growing Old. Byron. NOBE; SCV *Fr*. Canto the First. NAEL-2; OAEL-2; PoE *Fr*. Don Juan.

But now came the men of right visiting claims;. Leigh Hunt. EPCY *Fr.* The Feast of the Poets.

But now, encountering the armor forged. Turnus without sword. Virgil, *Latin.* OBCVT, *tr. by* Robert Fitzgerald

But now farewell. I am going a long way. Tennyson. *Fr.* The Passing of Arthur. FHYEP; NAEL-2; OBNC *Fr.* Idylls of the King.

But now had Hesper from the Hero's sight. Joel Barlow. APN-1 *Fr.* The Columbiad.

But now I am home again there is nobody I know. (LL) Fairy Story. Stevie Smith. NOxBChV; OBSP

But now I call him dirty louse. (LL) The Immortals. Isaac Rosenberg. FaBoTw; NSI; TrJP

But now I only know I am,—that's all. (LL) I Feel I Am[, I only know I am]. John Clare. FHYEP; NOBVV; OAEL-2

But now more serious let me grow. Matthew Green. PoEL-3 *Fr.* The Spleen.

But now Mr. Ferritt. And Mr. Ferritt. Judith Wright. MoBrPo

But now my oat proceeds. Milton. OxBoS *Fr.* Lycidas. AWP; CABP; ClHu; EBEV; EBEvV; FHYEP; GTBS-P; HAP; ImPo; InPS-3; NOBE; NOSC; NoP-4; OAEL-1; OBEV; OxAEP-1; PBRV; PFE; PoEL-3; PoPoPo; Poetr; SCGP; TFi; UnPO

But now, no longer deaf to honour's call. Homer. OBVE, *tr. by* Alexander Pope *Fr.* The Iliad.

But now the gentle dew-fall sends abroad. Looking Down on Nether Stowey. Coleridge. *Fr.* Fears in Solitude. FHYEP; OBWP

But now the salmon-fishers moist. Carrying Their Coracles. Andrew Marvell. *Fr.* Upon Appleton House [To My Lord Fairfax]. FaBoPV; GeHe; SeCP

But now this man of hell toward me turned. Philip Freneau. NAAL-1; NAAL-3 *Fr.* The House of Night.

But now you come at noon. (LL) Ten O'Clock Scholar, [The]. Mother Goose. LB; OxNR; ReMoGo

But O! delighting me. (LL) Reason Has Moons. Ralph Hodgson. FaBoCh; MoBrPo; OxBSP

But, o great offspring of the Ocean King. Euripides. OBCVT, *tr. by* Shelley *Fr.* Cyclops.

But, O immortals! What had I to plead. Christopher Smart. NOEC *Fr.* Hymn to the Supreme Being. ChIV-1

But O my Muse, what numbers wilt thou find. A Poem to His Grace the Duke of Marlborough. Joseph Addison. OBWP *Fr.* The Campaign.

But O! the freedom, pleasure and the ease. On Giving Up Smoking. Lawrence Spooner. NOEC *Fr.* A Looking-Glass for Smokers.

But oblivion, not thy forgiveness, FRANCE. Ezra Pound. *See* Canto 80.

But of all the plagues, the greatest is untold. Juvenal. OBSV, *tr. by* Dryden *Fr.* Satires.

But of course you can never be quite sure of these things. (LL) Fearful Symmetry. Basil Bunting. OxBoS; PoA

But oh! how different is each sight and sound. Forest Thoughts. Sir Roger Casement. TIRV

But oh, no man could hold it, for 'twas thine. (LL) The Legacy [or Legacie]. Donne. FMP; SeCP

But oh, that we could sleep up there. (LL) Sleeping on the Ceiling. Elizabeth Bishop. OBGa; TTTS

But ole Mosser hain't cotch me, an' he never will! (LL) Wild Negro Bill. *Unknown.* NAAAL

But on the morrow Elspie kept out of the way of Philip. Arthur Hugh Clough. EnVR *Fr.* Bothie of Tober-na-Vuolich, The [A Long-Vacation Pastoral].

But on the third day Christ arose. Easter. Herman Melville. APN-2 *Fr.* Clarel: A Poem and Pilgrimage in the Holy Land.

But once upon a time. Cranach. Sir Herbert Read. FaBoMo

But one apocalyptic lion's whelp (in flesh). There Is No Opera like "Lohengrin." John Wheelwright. NYBP

But one felt it was doing them good. (LL) Limerick. *Unknown.* OBCoV; PeLi

But one half glaunce, most gladly dye [or die]. (LL) Vanity of Spirit. Henry Vaughan. ESCV; GeHe; NOSC; TOF

But one night went betwixt. (LL) Kind are her answers. Thomas Campion. BoLoP; CBLP; PoEL-2

But only God can make a tree. (LL) Trees. Joyce Kilmer. BLPA; ChAP; EBEvV; FPC; FaBoBe; PFE; UV

But only how did you die. (LL) How Did You Die? Edmund Vance Cooke. BLPA; CTV; PWR

But only not to think about the journey. Irina Ratushinskaya, *Russian.* AF, *tr. by* David McDuff

But only of a voice that sings. (LL) At Home from Church. Sarah Orne Jewett. APAD; APN-2

But only one mother the wide / world over. (LL) Only One Mother. George Cooper. BoTP; CTV; FPC

But only to build memories of spiritual gates. (LL) Emblems of Conduct. Hart Crane. ImPo; LiTM; MeMAP

But Oothoon is not so; a virgin filled with virgin fancies. Desire and Jealousy. William Blake. ECEV *Fr.* Visions of the Daughters of Albion. CABP; OAEL-2; Ro

But peaceful was the night. Milton. FaBoCh *Fr.* Hymn on the Morning of Christ's Nativity [*or* On the Morning of Christ's Nativity]. NAEL-1; NOBE; NOBV; OBEV *Fr.* On the Morning of Christ's Nativity. MeLP; NOCV; NoP-4; PBRV; PoEL-3; SCGP

But perfectly random and coastal. From Arena. Dennis Phillips. FTOS *Fr.* Exile.

But Perhaps [God needs the longing, wherever else should it dwell]. Nelly Sachs, *German.* BoWoP; WPoS, *tr. by* Ruth Mead *and* Matthew Mead

But pinned to the heart of darkness a tattered fire-flag flies. (LL) The Stand-To. C. Day Lewis. NoP-4

But piteous things we are—when I am gone. Robert Malise Bowyer Nichols. *Fr.* Sonnets to Aurelia. OBMV

But pity for the grief they cannot feel. (LL) The Prisoners. Stephen Spender. FaBoMo; MoBrPo

"But plett a wand o bonnie birk." Sweet William's Ghost. *Unknown.* ESPB

But pluck up strength and eat my fill. *Unknown. See* Going on always on and on.

But pray to God that he forgive us all. (LL) The Epitaph in Form of a Ballad. François Villon, *French.* CTC; OxBoV, *tr. by* Algernon Charles Swinburne

But pretty though as / roses is. Three Sayings from Highlands, North Carolina. Jonathan Williams. OBAL

But proves at night a bed of down [or Downe]. (LL) Upon the Sudden Restraint of the Earl[e] of Somerset, Then Falling from Favor [or Favour]. Sir Henry Wotton. NOBC; NOSC; PBRV; SeCP

But Pussy and I / Very gently will play. Jane Taylor. *See* I Like Little Pussy

But reaching is his rule. Gwendolyn Brooks. *See* The Children of the Poor.

But Robin he walkes in the greene fforest. Robin Hood and the Butcher. *Unknown.* ESPB

But Romeo's name speaks heavenly eloquence. (LL) Gallop apace, you fiery-footed steeds [or fierie footed steades]. Shakespeare. CBLP; EBEvV; GBL

But Rosemary will with thee go. (LL) The Dying Man in His Garden. George Sewell. GTBS-P; OBGa

But, ruby my dear. Wanda Coleman. MoNo

But rumors hung about the country-side. At Some Lone Alehouse. Matthew Arnold. *Fr.* The Scholar-Gipsy. EBEV; EBVV; EBVVPR; EnVR; FHYEP; HAP; ImPo; NAEL-2; NOBVV; OAEL-2; OBEV; OBNC; OxAEP-1; PoE; PoEL-5; SCGP; TFi

But sang, "O sea-starved hungry sea." (LL) A Crazed Girl. W. B. Yeats. InPS-3; Son

But say you, if each private Family. Juvenal. OBCVT, *tr. by* Henry Fielding *Fr.* Part of Juvenal's Sixth Satire, Modernized in Burlesque Verse.

But saying, 'Fathers! Fathers!'. (LL) Hunting Civil War Relics at Nimblewill Creek. James Dickey. CoAmPo; WeT

But scarce observ'd, the knowing and the bold. On Gold. Samuel Johnson. *Fr.* The Vanity of Human Wishes [The Tenth Satire of Juvenal Imitated]. EBEV; ECEV; NOEC; OAEL-1; OxAEP-1; PoEL-3; TFi

But see here comes thy reverend Sire. Milton. EBEV *Fr.* Samson Agonistes. FHYEP; OAEL-1; PoEL-3

But see not our own Load behind. Catullus. *See* To Varus.

But see! the well-plumed hearse comes nodding on. Robert Blair. ECEV *Fr.* The Grave.

But seen from the angle of her death. (LL) Burial. Alice Walker. AmPA; LoHo

But shall not question much. (LL) Twice. Christina Rossetti. GBL; NOBE; OBEV; OBNC; TOF; TrCP; VGW

But she is not kind. (LL) In Mind. Denise Levertov. NALW; NMM-2

But she thought she should go back to Sweden. (LL) Limerick: "There was a young lady of Sweden." Edward Lear. CBNP; EBEV; PeVV

But she turned her eyes away. (LL) To Adhiambo. Gabriel Okara. PBMAP

But she who Love long since had swallowed down. Virgil. OBCVT, *tr. by* Sir Richard Fanshawe *Fr.* The Loves of Dido and Aeneas.

But she's divine! (LL) The Water Lady. Thomas Hood. Ro

But shoots its cause, and is a source of joy. (LL) A Choice of Weapons. Stanley Kunitz. LiTM; VGW

But should some snarling critic chance to view. Jane Brereton. ECWP *Fr.* Epistle to Mrs Anne Griffiths.

But Sin on his knees is. Upon a Renaissance Carving. Agnes Gergely, *Hungarian.* CEEP, *tr. by* Timea K. Szell

But, sires, o word forgat I in my tale. Chaucer. EBEV *Fr.* The Pardoner's Tale. FHYEP; NAEL-1; NAWM-1; OAEL-1; PoE *Fr.* The Canterbury Tales.

But So As by Fire. George Oppen. NNaP *Fr.* Some San Francisco Poems.

But something went wrong with the plan: I am still on the train. (LL) Observation Car. Alec Derwent Hope. MoP; NoAM

But soon th'endearments of a husband cloy. Soame Jenyns. ECEV *Fr.* The Modern Fine Lady. NOEC

But still, carrying my illness to the hospital. In the Waiting Room. Patricia Goedicke. NMM-2

"But Still in Israel's Paths They Shine." Carter Revard. VoR

But still the child squealed [*or* squeal'd] on. (LL) Ballad: "The Tender infant, meek and mild." Samuel Johnson. CBNP; OxAEP-1

But still the thunder of Los peals loud and thus the thunder's cry. William Blake. OAEL-2 *Fr.* Jerusalem; The Emanation of the Giant Albion.

But stories somehow lengthen when begun. (LL) Beppo; a Venetian Story. Byron. NOBL; OBNV; OBSV

But sudden came the barge's pitch-black prow. "George Eliot." NOBVV *Fr.* Brother and Sister. NALW

But suh, you've made a mistake. Oh, yes suh! I can't be. Sidney, Looking for her Mother. Dolores Kendrick. ISC

But sun me in the Capitol. (LL) Mithridates. Ralph Waldo Emerson. APN-1; NCAP

But surely the dead must walk again. Trace Elements. Chris Wallace-Crabbe. OxBSn

But sweet sister death has gone debauched today and stalks. David Jones. OBWP; OxAEP-2; PeFWW *Fr.* In Parenthesis.

But take our greatness with our bitterness? (LL) Ancestral Houses. W. B. Yeats. OAEL-2; OBGa

But tell me, child, your choice; what shall I buy You? The Handsome Heart. Gerard Manley Hopkins. FaBoVe

But that from slow dissolving pomps of dawn. Darkness. Arthur Hugh Clough. OxBSP

But That Is Another Story. Donald Justice. CoAP; NoP-4

But that, O me! I both must write and love. (LL) I know that all beneath the moon decays. William Drummond, of Hawthornden. GSo; LoP

But that was nothing to what things came out. Welsh Incident. Robert Graves. CBNP; CMoP; EBEvV; NOBE; OBSP; OxBSn; OxBTC

But that which most I wonder at, which most. Innocence. Thomas Traherne. CABP; ChIV-2; ESCV; MiEL; NOSC

But the beauty of / God. (LL) Birds and Fishes. Robinson Jeffers. NAAL-2

But the best is Radio City Music Hall, one respectful. A One-Way Conversation About Radio City Music Hall. Miroslav Holub, *German.* CEEP, *tr. by* Simko, Daniel

But the breeze has dropped, and silence is the last word. (LL) Fear of Death. John Ashbery. FaBoMo; TAP

But the brief pleasures of life! but the. The Lyf So Short. Palladas, *Greek.* GrAn, *tr. by* Dudley Fitts

But the chief. The Poet the Chief of Artists. Mark Akenside. EPCY *Fr.* The Pleasures of Imagination.

But the child keeps on playing, so I play. (LL) The Lost Children. Randall Jarrell. CoAP; PBMP; TAP

But the choir-boy is happy and gay. (LL) Low Church. Stanley J. Sharpless. NBLV; OBCoV; PeLV

But the clover is honey and sun and the smell of sleep. (LL) Nebuchadnezzar. Elinor Wylie. ChIV-1; KSG; MoAmPo

But the Copperbelt night is a snake. The Leader. Dorothy Livesay. MoCV

But the darkness has passed, and it's daylight at last, and the night has been long—ditto ditto my song—and thank goodness they're both of them over! (LL) Nightmare, [A *or* The]. Sir William Schwenck Gilbert. CBNP; NOBL; NTP; OBCoV; OxBoLi; PBMP; PeLV; PoRA

But the eagle will never fly. (LL) America. Henry Dumas. ChAP

But the future is different. The Future. Angel González, *Spanish.* VCWP, *tr. by* Steven Ford Brown *and* Gutierrez Revuelta

But the harvest time of Love is there. (LL) Love Indestructible. Robert Southey. LBC; OBNC

But the last black horse of all. The Last Ones. "Robin Hyde." PeNZ

But the majestic river floated on. Matthew Arnold. *Fr.* Sohrab and Rustum. EBNV; OBNV

"But the multitude saw why she wore the bandage." (LL) Carl Hamblin. Edgar Lee Masters. CMoP; LiTM; OBSV

But the old men know when an old man dies. (LL) Old Men. Ogden Nash. InPS-3; RB

But the sheet was Belfast linen. (LL) The Ballad of William Bloat. *Unknown.* NOBL; PeLV

But the show was over. (LL) The Artist. William Carlos Williams. InPS-3; LCAP-2; NYBP; RB; SAGP; SAmP

But the sweet little Bees large Monument. (LL) A Black Patch on Lucasta's Face. Richard Lovelace. BeJo; CaPo; SeCP

But the winds. . . But the spaces. . . . Rilke. *See* The Sonnets to Orpheus.

But the Wine-press of Los is eastward of Golgonooza, before the Seat. William Blake. NOBRP *Fr.* Milton.

But the world. (LL) A Kind of Loss. Ingeborg Bachmann, *German.* VCWP, *tr. by* Mark Anderson

But the world shall end when I forget. (LL) Itylus. Swinburne. EBVVPR; UV

But Then and There the Sun Bore Down. N. Scott Momaday. CDW

But then, how it was sweet! (LL) Confessions. Robert Browning. CBLP; GTBS-P; NOBE; NOBVV; PFE

But there ain't no eagle / On a dime. (LL) Fact. Langston Hughes. APSN; PFTM

But there is no joy in Mudville—mighty Casey has struck out. (LL) Casey at the Bat. Ernest Lawrence Thayer. APN-2; AiP; BLPA; CHAP; FaBoA; FaBoBe; OBAL; OBCA; OBCoV; PoRA

But there is no road through the woods. (LL) The Way Through The Woods. Rudyard Kipling. CH; ChAP; EBEvV; FaBoCh; GEA; NOBE; NOxBChV; NTP; NoAM; OBEV; OBNC; OxAEP-2; OxBChV; OxBTC; SAGP; SCGP; WHSW

But there—something rests on your hand and even. Sapphics for Patience. Annie Finch. FFC

But there was / once / a time. Eléni Vakaló, *Greek.* WPOW, *tr. by* John Stathatos

"But they come by tens." (LL) Old Lem. Sterling Brown. BPo; PoBA; TTY

But they did not speak; it was not worth while. (LL) The Toys Talk of the World. Katharine Pyle. NOxBChV

But they knew they were on duty, replacing. Pope's Carnations Knew Him. Thom Gunn. OBGa

But they that wait upon the Lord. The Bible, Isaiah 40:31. Bible, *O.T.* CTV *Fr.* The Bible, Isaiah 40:31.

But thine arithmetic is quite correct. (LL) Fragment of a Greek Tragedy. A. E. Housman. NOBL; PeLV

But this by sure Experiment we know. Ovid. *Fr.* Of the Pythagorean Philosophy. OBVE, *tr. by* Dryden *Fr.* Metamorphoses.

But this fruit-dish (I suppose it is for fruit). A Good Thing. Ray Mathew. CBAP

But this security in Jove the great sea-rector spied. Neptune Goes to the Greeks. Homer. NOSC, *tr. by* George Chapman *Fr.* The Iliad.

But this, so feminine? Donald Davie. OxBTC *Fr.* The Forests of Lithuania.

But this the worke of harts astonishment. (LL) Sonnet 81: "Fair [*or* Fayre] is my love, when her fair [*or* fayre] golden heares." Edmund Spenser. NoP-4

But this view in the museum. Lost in the Galleries. Virginia Hooper. PT

But thou, false infidel! shall writhe. Byron. *Fr.* The Giaour. NOBRP

But thou, Israel, My servant. Israel, My Servant. Bible, *O.T.* TrJP *Fr.* Isaiah.

But thou my deere sweet-sounding lute be still. Richard Lynche. AAS *Fr.* Diella.

But thou, O God, shalt bring them down into the pit of destruction: bloody and deceitful men shall not live out half their days; but I will trust in thee. (LL) Psalm 55. Bible, *O.T.* AWP

But though it scar'd, it did not bite. (LL) The Silken Snake. Robert Herrick. OxBSP; PBRV

But thought the deepening blue thought of the fly. (LL) Truth. Howard Nemerov. HoPM; LiTM

But till that day, plase God, I'll stick to wearin' o' the Green. (LL) The Wearing of [*or* Wearin' o'] the Green. *Unknown.* AWP; FaPoR; IIP; OxBoLi

But 'tis to love, as I love you. (LL) Friendship Between Ephelia and Ardelia. Anne Finch, Countess of Winchilsea. BWW; ECWP; NALW; NoP-4

But to die their creature and be thankful. (LL) The Last of the Fire Kings. Derek Mahon. FaBoPV; PNI

But, to leave fooling, I assure ye. Charles Cotton. OBCoV *Fr.* Burlesque upon the Great Frost.

But to live in the tragic world forever. (LL) A Story About Chicken Soup. Louis Simpson. NNaP; PoE; PoWW; TAP; UnSA

But to the bad children, Christmas does not come. (LL) A Curse on Herod. Amy Witting. ChIV-2; NOBAu

But to the heavens, lo, it fled, for to receive his doom. (LL) In winter's just return, when Boreas gan his reign. Henry Howard, Earl of Surrey. AAS; SiPS

But Troy, alas, me thought above them all. Troy. Thomas, 1st Earl of Dorset Sackville. *Fr.* Induction to "A Mirror for Magistrates." AAS

But true expression, like th' unchanging sun. Alexander Pope. FHYEP *Fr.* An Essay on Criticism. NAEL-1; PoEL-3; TFi

But true Love is a durable fire. Love Indestructible. Sir Walter Ralegh. LBC

But truly keeps its first, last, everlasting day. Donne. *See* The Anniversary [*or* Anniversarie].

But turning toward Ololon in terrible majesty Milton. William Blake. OxAEP-2 *Fr.* Milton.

But 'twas a famous victory. (LL) The Battle of Blenheim. Robert Southey. CABP; FaBoPV; FaPoR; GTBS-P; OBNC; OBWP; OxAEP-2; PBMP; PoLF; Ro; TFi; UV

But twelve short years you lived, my son. His Son. Callimachus, *Greek.* AWP, *tr. by* G. B. Grundy

But Venus first. Sister Juana Inés de la Cruz. BoWoP *Fr.* First Dream.

"But waft the angel on her flight with a Pæan of old days!" (LL) Lenore. Edgar Allan Poe. APN-1; AmPP; PAR

But wanton now, and lolling at our Ease. The Corruption of manners. Juvenal, *Latin.* OBCVT, *tr. by* John Dryden

But war his overturning trumpet blew. Frederick Goddard Tuckerman. APN-2 *Fr.* Sonnets.

But was I the first martyr, who. Stephen to Lazarus. C. S. Lewis. ChIV-2

But was there ever dog that praised his fleas? (LL) To a Poet, Who Would Have Me Praise Certain Bad Poets, Imitators of His and Mine. W. B. Yeats. CTC; FaBoEE

But we are exiles from our fathers' land. (LL) Canadian Boat Song. John Galt *and* "Christopher North." BLPA; FaBoCh; FaPoR; OBEV; OBNC

But we are set to strive to make our mark. Frederick Goddard Tuckerman. TrCP *Fr.* Sonnets.

But we have none! but we have none! (LL) The Mermaidens' Vesper-Hymn. George Darley. BIrV; GBL; NAEL-2; OBNC; PoEL-4

But we have only begun. Beginners. Denise Levertov. CrSp

But we have to see behind all them, there is something. They Receive Instructions Against Chile. Pablo Neruda, *Spanish.* AF, *tr. by* Robert Bly *and* James Wright (1927–80)

But we left him alone with his glory. (LL) The Burial of Sir John Moore [after [*or* at] Corunna]. Charles Wolfe. EBEvV; FaPoR; GTBS-P; NOBE; NOBRP; NTP; OBEV; OBWP; OxAEP-2; PWR; PoRA; TFi; UV

But We Shall Bloom. Haim Guri, *Hebrew.* TrJP, *tr. by* David Kuselewitz

But we, whose sands run low. Helen Waddell. MLL

But we will keep our appointment by the far-off Cloudy / River. (LL) Drinking Alone in the Moonlight. Li Po, *Chinese.* ChiPo, *tr. by* Florence Ayscough *and* Amy Lowell

But weep to have that which it fears to lose. (LL) Sonnet 64. Shakespeare. AEP; AWP; EnLoPo; GTBS-P; HAP; HeIP-4; ImPo; NOBE; NoSic; OAEL-1; OxAEP-1; PoE; PoRA; SCGP; Son

But weighed down by earth and stones. (LL) My love forever! *Unknown.* BIrV; PBWP, *tr. by* Eilis Dillon

But were always a rose. (LL) The Rose Family. Robert Frost. OBAL; OBCA

But what a bruised and broken motley lot we were! Dennis Brutus. *See* Robben Island Sequence.

But what are you, Sir Statue, doing there? To a Statue. Nguyễn Khuyến, *Vietnamese.* AVP, *tr. by* Huỳnh Sanh Thông

But What I'm Trying to Say Mother Is. Ai. MDDM

But what is *He,* who perch'd above the rest. The Mocking Bird. Richard Lewis. APo *Fr.* A Journey from Patapsko to Annapolis.

But what is more thought than a dark over the sun? What is Thought but Won't Hold Still. Clark Coolidge. FTOS

But what is strength without a double share. Milton. ChIV-1 *Fr.* Samson Agonistes. FHYEP; OAEL-1; PoEL-3

But What Is the Reader to Make of This? John Ashbery. InPS-3

But, what of that? (LL) I reason, Earth is short. Emily Dickinson. APN-2; NCAP; TAP

But what the waur am I? (LL) Rigid Body Sings. James Clerk Maxwell. BXAP; UV

But what underneath him lies. (LL) Sonnet ("All my senses, like beacon's flame"). Greville Fulke, 1st Baron Brooke. NOSC; NoSic; PoEL-1

But what you are I do not know. (LL) Carnal Knowledge. Gwen Harwood. BMAP

But whaur's the Minister? (LL) Last Lauch. Douglas Young. NBLV; OxBS

But when a man's in trouble, it's a long freight-train and ride. (LL) The Railroad Blues. *Unknown.* GM

But when Demophilus begins to sing, / The raven dies. (LL) The Raven. Nicarchus of Alexandria. AWP; FaBoEE; OBAL

But when I waked, I saw that I saw not. A Storm at Sea. Donne. NOBE *Fr.* The Storm[e]. NoSic; OxBoS

But when so many had died, so many and at such speed. James Fenton. *Fr.* A German Requiem. NAEL-2; NoAM

But when that comely he covered his wits. The Temptation of Sir Gawain. *Unknown. Fr.* Sir Gawain and the Green Knight. OAEL-1, *tr. by* Brian Stone

But when the Gods and Heroes heard, they brought. Matthew Arnold. PeVV *Fr.* Balder Dead.

But when the Golden-thron'd *Aurora* made. Aurora and Tithonus. *Unknown, Greek.* OBCVT; OBVE, *tr. by* William Congreve *Fr.* The Hymn to Venus

But when the harvest with ripe ears of corn. Autumnal Work. Lucius Junius Moderatus Columella, *Latin.* GaP, *tr. by Unknown*

But when the sun within the eastern house. Catullus. OBCVT, *tr. by* Robert Clayton Casto *Fr.* Attis, after Catullus 63.

But when the water roars around us. The Ocean. Louis Dudek. *Fr.* Provincetown. MoCV

But when the winged Thunder takes his way. The Promised rain. Virgil, *Latin.* OBCVT, *tr. by* John Dryden

But when to mischief mortals bend their will. Alexander Pope. OxAEP-1 *Fr.* The Rape of the Lock[, an Heroi-Comical Poem]. FHYEP; HAP; ImPo; OAEL-1; OBNV; PeLV; PoEL-3

But when you are sad, think, Heaven could give no more. (LL) At Parting. Anne Ridler. APAD; LW

But where are the snows of yester-year? (LL) Ballad[e] of Dead Ladies. François Villon, *French.* AWP; CTC; NNPT; OBVE; PoRA, *tr. by* D. G. Rossetti

But where began the change; and what's my crime? George Meredith. PoEL-5 *Fr.* Modern Love.

But where is County Guy? (LL) A Serenade: "Ah! County Guy, the hour is nigh." Sir Walter Scott. CH; GTBS-P

But where is she? At the seaside? On some hill? Her Story. Diên Nghi, *Vietnamese.* AVP, *tr. by* Huỳnh Sanh Thông

But wherefore did he take away the crown? Shakespeare. OxAEP-1 *Fr.* King Henry IV, Pt. II.

But where's the bloody horse? (LL) On Some South African Novelists. Roy Campbell. FaBoEE; GTBS-P; InPK-6; MoBrPo; NOBL; OBCoV; OxAEP-2; OxBTC; PeLV

But where's the man who counsel can bestow. Alexander Pope. OxAEP-1, *ll.* 631–744 *Fr.* An Essay on Criticism. NAEL-1; PoEL-3; TFi

But which it only needs that we fulfil. (LL) A Prayer in Spring. Robert Frost. AH; TrCP

"But who are [*or* art] thou, with curious beauty graced." Opportunity. Niccolò Machiavelli, *Italian.* AWP, *tr. by* James Elroy Flecker

But who are you? A lover like myself? Speaking to My Photo. Tản Đà, *Vietnamese.* AVP, *tr. by* Huỳnh Sanh Thông

But who can number up his labours? who. Lucretius. OBCVT, *tr. by* James Thomson *Fr.* A Poem Sacred to the Memory of Sir Isaac Newton.

But who is she that walks from yonder hill. A Portrait of the Artist. Mary Leapor. ECWP *Fr.* Mira's Picture, a Pastoral.

But who is this, what thing of sea or land? Delilah. Milton. *Fr.* Samson Agonistes. FHYEP; OAEL-1; PoEL-3

But who killed Johannes, mama. . . ? Lullaby. Jeremy Cronin. PeSAV

But who killed the Jews? (LL) Riddle: "From Belsen a crate of gold teeth." William Heyen. HP

But who shall parcel out. Wordsworth. TOF *Fr.* School-Time. FHYEP *Fr.* The Prelude; Growth of a Poet's Mind [1850 vers.]

But who would loose a gun to-night? Out with a Gun. Vita Sackville-West. WPN

But whoso may, thrice happy man him hold. Edmund Spenser. *Fr.* An Hymn[e] of Heavenly Beauty [*or* Beautie]. PeECV *Fr.* Fowre Hymnes

"But why did he do it, Grandpa?" I said. A Confederate Veteran Tries to Explain the Event. Robert Penn Warren. CBCWP

"But why do you go?" said the lady, while both sat[e] under the yew. Lord Walter's Wife. Elizabeth Barrett Browning. HAP; VWP

But why is Father Larkin talking to the dead? David Jones. PoE *Fr.* In Parenthesis.

But will disclose it in the end. (LL) The Lord of Lorn and the False [*or* Fals] Steward. *Unknown.* ESPB; OxBB

But winter and rough weather. Shakespeare. *See* Song: "Under the greenwood tree."

But with a sure sense of its intrinsic nature. (LL) A Garage in Co. Cork. Derek Mahon. DiPo; PBCIP

But with long use her tears are dry. (LL) Again at Christmas did we weave. Tennyson. EBVV; IMW; OAEL-2; PeECV

But within my gauze curtains, a pair of smiles. (LL) Cool breezes—I sleep by the open window. *Unknown.* CoBCP, *tr. by* Watson, Burton (b 1925)

But wood, with a gift for burning. (LL) Song: "You're wondering if I'm lonely." Adrienne Rich. InPK-6; PBWP

But word is come to Warrington. Sir John Butler. *Unknown.* ESPB

But would not bend to shame. (LL) Vashti. Frances Ellen Watkins Harper. AAP; BlSi; NALW

But Wyatt said true, the scar doth aye endure. (LL) Exhortation to Learn of Others' Trouble. Henry Howard, Earl of Surrey. AAS; FaBoEE; SiPS

But yesterday and he was one of us. To the New Ordained. John D. Sheridan. TIRV

But yesterday the earth drank like a child. A Letter to His Friend Isaac. Judah Halevi, *Hebrew.* TrJP, *tr. by* Emma Lazarus

But yet, alas, the scar shall still remain. (LL) Sighs are my food, drink are my tears. Sir Thomas Wyatt. NoSic; OxBSP; SiPS

But yet in all this interchange of all. Samuel Daniel. EPCY *Fr.* Musophilus; or, Defence of All Learning.

But you can carry the winds. . . and the open spaces. (LL) The Sonnets to Orpheus. Rilke, *German.* RaBo, *tr. by* Robert Bly; APAD

But you, Catullus, your destiny's *obdurate.* Catullus. *See* Carmen 8 ("Break off / fallen Catullus").

But you like none, none you, for constant heart. (LL) Sonnet 53. Shakespeare. CTC; EBEV; ImPo; NoSic; OAEL-1; OBEV; OxAEP-1; SCGP

But You, My Darling, Should Have Married the Prince. Kathleen Spivack. AmPA

But you, Thomas Jefferson. Brave New World. Archibald MacLeish. NOBA; OxBA

But you will die to-day. (LL) Her strong enchantments failing. A. E. Housman. FaBoTw; NOBE; NOBVV; NTP; OAEL-2; PeVV

But your face I coud never see. *Unknown.* *See* The Knight and Shepherd's Daughter.

But your heart—what will it be? (LL) When ice on the pond is three feet thick. *Unknown.* CoBCP, *tr. by* Watson, Burton (b. 1925)

Butch once remarked to me how sinister it was. That Pull from the Left. Louise Erdrich. NoAM

Butcher, A. Thomas Hood. PeLV

Butcher Boy, The. *Unknown.* AmFP

Butcher carves veal for two, The. Hugo Williams. OxBTC

Butcher had prepared the leg of the lamb, The. The Feast. Robert Duncan. APSN *Fr.* Passages.

Butcher Shop. Charles Simic. AF; AmPA; InPK-6; LCAP-2; NNaP

Butchers, The. Homer. OBCVT, *tr. by* Michael Longley *Fr.* The Odyssey.

Butchers and Tombs. Ivor Gurney. PeFWW

Butcher's Apron, The. Diane Wakoski. BAP-96

Butcher's Son, The. Thom Gunn. BAP-93

Butcher's Wife, The. Louise Erdrich. HATNAP; NoP-4

Butter Betty Bought, The. *Unknown.* FPC

Butter Charm. *Unknown.* FaBoVe

Butterbur. My room. Masaoka Shiki, *Japanese.* MJT, *tr. by* Ueda, Makoto

Buttercup, A. *Unknown.* BoTP

Buttercup nodded and said [good-by]. August. Celia Laighton Thaxter. CTV; FPC; ImGa

Buttercups and Daisies. Mary Howitt. BoTP; OxBChV

Buttercups golden and gay. *Unknown.* BoTP

Butterflies. Chang Yü. *Fr.* Twelve Miscellaneous Poems on the Fang Garden. CoBLCP, *tr. by* Jonathan Chaves

Butterflies, butterflies. Corn-grinding Song. *Unknown, Laguna Indian.* AWP, *tr. by* Natalie Curtis

Butterflies in love with evening flowers will not leave until the very end. A Walk in the Country. T'ang Yen-ch'ien, *Chinese.* SuSp, *tr. by* Edward H. Schafer

Butterflies of northern England, The. York: In Memoriam W. H. Auden. Joseph Brodsky. FP

Butterflies paired in ecstatic flight. On a Painting of Ants and Butterflies. Huang T'ing-chien, *Chinese.* SuSp, *tr. by* Michael E. Workman

Butterflies, white butterflies, in the sunshine. Angelina Weld Grimké. GT

Butterfly, The. Pavel Friedmann, *Czech.* HP

Butterfly, The. John Fuller. Spl

Butterfly, The. Robert Stephen Hawker. EBVV

Butterfly, The. Jejuri Arun Kolatkar. AYFP

Butterfly, The. Ron Padgett. *Fr.* Three Animals. TTTS

Butterfly, The. Margaret Rose. BoTP

Butterfly, a [or the] cabbage-white, The. Flying Crooked. Robert Graves. FaBoMo; LiTM; PeLV; RB; TwCP

Butterfly attending the embroidered flowers, A. (LL) The Linen Industry. Michael Longley. CBLP; CIP-2; NoP-4; PBCIP; PNI

Butterfly Bones; or, Sonnet against Sonnets. Margaret Avison. LiTM

Butterfly, butterfly, butterfly, butterfly. Butterfly Song. *Unknown, Acoman Indian.* OBVE; TLR, *tr. by* Frances Densmore

Butterfly Garden, The. Alfred Noyes. OBGa

Butterfly lands on Park Place, A. Alexis Rotella. HA

Butterfly on Rock. Irving Layton. NOBC; NoAM

Butterfly Song. *Unknown, Acoman Indian.* OBVE; TLR, *tr. by* Frances Densmore

Butterfly the ancient Grecians made, The. Psyche. Coleridge. PBMP

Butterfly, the wind blows sea-ward[, strong beyond the garden wall!]. D. H. Lawrence. APo; BLT; NoAM; TTTS
("I saw you vanish into air.") (LL) APo

Butterfly / trapped in a mould. Trapped. Merle Collins. HCP

Butterfly upon the Sky, The. Emily Dickinson. NOxBChV

Butterfly Wine, *song.* *Japanese Oral Tradition.* ITG, *tr. by* R. H. Blyth

Butterfly's Ball [and the Grasshopper's Feast], The. William Roscoe. NOBRP; OxBChV
("For no watchman is waiting for you and for me.") (LL) OxBChV

Butterfly's Ball and the Grasshopper's Feasts, The. Peacock "At Home," The. Catherine Ann Dorset. OxBChV

Button, A. The Sensation Type and His Friends. Michael Davidson. FTOS

Button-grass flats, pale through the drizzle: my eyes. High Country. Tim Thorne. BMAP

Button to chin. *Unknown.* OxNR

Buttoning his fly. Raymond Roseliep. HA

Buttons. Walter De la Mare. PeLi

Buttons. Carl Sandburg. SAGP

Buttons, a farthing a pair. Mother Goose. OxNR; ReMoGo

Buxton, Fyrish, Cove-an-John, Bush Lot, Mahaica. Guyana not Ghana. Marc Matthews. PBCV

Buy a book in brown paper. A Blurb for *Anna Livia Plurabelle.* James Joyce. OBCoV

Buy a love potion, a gin, a double. (LL) Gone Are the Days. Norman MacCaig. CABP

Buy me an ounce and i'll sell you a pound. E. E. Cummings. OxBA

Buy One Now. D. J. Enright. NOBL

Buy our little magazine. Do It Yourself. Joan Aiken. KaS; NOxBChV

Buy the paper, take it home. Coming and Going. Mitchell Goodman. VGW

Buy Us a Little Grain. Christine Lavant, *German.* WPOW, *tr. by* Michael Hamburger

Buy with gold the old associations! (LL) The Golden Mile-Stone. Henry Wadsworth Longfellow. NCAP; PoEL-5

Buying. Jean Follain, *Spanish.* BLT, *tr. by* Heather McHugh

Buying a Dress for My Love. Đông Hồ, *Vietnamese.* AVP, *tr. by* Huỳnh Sanh Thông

Buying a Record. Robert Peters. BXAP

Buying and Selling. Philip Levine. WWSi

Buying Flowers. Po Chü-i, *Chinese.* TAL, *tr. by* Robert Payne

Buying new shoes / takes so long. New Shoes. John Agard. OTCP

Buz, Quoth the Blue Fly. Ben Jonson. *See* A Catch.

Buzz. Jim Tollerud. VoR

Buzz and Hum. Ben Jonson. *See* A Catch.

Buzz Buzz, the Blue Flies. *Unknown, Chinese.* CoBCP, *tr. by* Burton Watson

Buzz frantic. Buzz in the Window. Ted Hughes. NoAM *Fr.* Orts.

Buzz [or buz], quoth the blue fly [or flie]. A Catch. Ben Jonson. CBNP; OxNR *Fr.* Oberon, the Fairy Prince.

Buzz-saw snarled and rattled in the yard, The. "Out, Out—." Robert Frost. ColAP; HAP; HeIP-4; NAAL-2; OxBA; PFE; Poetr; RB; SoSe-8; TRP; UnPo; VGW

Buzz subsides. I have come on stage, The. Boris Pasternak. *See* Hamlet.

Buzz you into unisex twilight. Amazon Club. Kenward Elmslie. PmAP

Buzzard. George Garrett. MT

Buzzard has nothing to fault himself with, The. In Praise of Self-Deprecation. Wislawa Szymborska, *Polish.* BLT, *tr. by* Magnus J. Krynski *and* Robert A. Maguire

Buzzards over Pondy Woods, The. Pondy Woods. Robert Penn Warren. MoAmPo

Buzzing darkly almost like thunder. Mosquitoes. P'i Jih-hsiu, *Chinese.* SuSp, *tr. by* William H. Nienhauser

BuzzZ. Alan Pizzarelli. HA

Bwagamoyo. Lebert Bethune. PoBA

By a bank as I lay. *Unknown.* NoSic

By a broken bridge outside the courier station. Tune: "Song of Divination"—On the Plum Tree. Lu Yu, *Chinese.* SuSp, *tr. by* James J. Y. Liu

By a clear well, within a little field. Of Three Girls and of Their Talk. Giovanni Boccaccio. AWP *Fr.* Sonnets.

By a departing light. Emily Dickinson. APN-2

By a flat rock on the shore of the sea. The Rock. *Unknown, Welsh.* GBL, *tr. by* Geoffrey Grigson

By a forest as I gan fare. *Unknown.* MiEL

By a great, swift water. Aleksander Wat. AF, *tr. by* Milosz, Czeslaw *and* Leonard Nathan *Fr.* Persian Parables.

By a lake below the mountain. The Lady of Trees. Mary Elizabeth Coleridge. VWP

By a peninsula the wanderer sat and sketched. Emblems of Conduct. Hart Crane. ImPo; LiTM; MeMAP

By a quiet little stream on an old mossy log. The Frog and the Bird. Vera Hessey. BoTP

By a route obscure and lonely. Dream-Land [*or* Dreamland]. Edgar Allan Poe. APN-1; AmPP; MeMAP; NAAL-1; NAAL-3; NCAP; NOBA; OxBA; PAR; TAP

By a Stream on Mount T'ien-t'ung. Wang An-shih, *Chinese.* SuSp, *tr. by* Jan W. Walls

By absence, and unkind neglect. The Visit. *Unknown.* ECWP

By Achmelvich Bridge. Norman MacCaig. OxBS

By admonitions taught. (LL) The Answer. Anne Finch, Countess of Winchilsea. NALW; NoP-4

By all means / bless the cloth. John Agard. HCP

By all means sing of love, but if you do. Truest Poetry Is the Most Feigning, The [or, Ars Poetica for Hard Times]. W. H. Auden. NYBP

By all that was lavished upon her / and all that was taken away! Marilyn Chin. *See* How I Got That Name.

By all the glories of the day. Before Action. William Noel Hodgson. PoFWW

By all the published facts in the case. About Children. Phyllis McGinley. OBAL

By an ancient road, abundant thistle plants. Liu Tsung-yüan. SuSp, *tr. by* Jan W. Walls *Fr.* Farmers.

By an Unknown Poet from Eastern Europe, 1955. György Petri, *Hungarian.* VCWP, *tr. by* Wilmer, Clive and George Gömöri

By and by. Epitaph on a Waiter. David McCord. NBLV; NIP-4; OBAL; OBCoV

By and by, the seasons come and go. T'ao Ch'ien. SuSp, *tr. by* Eugene Eoyang *Fr.* The Seasons Come and Go.

By art a poet is not made;. For a Poet. George Wither. ChIV-2

By Arthur's Dale as late I went. Donny Bee Hom. *Unknown.* ESPB

By Babel's Streams. Philip Freneau. AH

By becoming a Cabinet Minister. (LL) On the Birth of His Son. Su Tung-p'o, *Chinese.* AWP; OBVE, *tr. by* Arthur Waley

By being never green. (LL) Telephone Poles. John Updike. FYAP; Poetsp

By Birth I'm a Slave, yet can give you a Crown. Enigma. Matthew Prior. PeLV

By blue Ontario's shore. Walt Whitman. APN-1

   "Are you he who would assume a place to teach or be a poet here in the States?" FaBoPV

   Poet, The. MoAmPo

By broken fence is proved a common field. (LL) Sonnet: "Caelica, I overnight was finely used." Greville Fulke. AAS; Son

By Canoe through the Fir Forest. James Dickey. NYBP *Fr.* On the Coosawattee.

By channels of coolness the echoes are calling. Bell-Birds. Henry Clarence Kendall. NOBAu

By chapel bare, with walls sea-beat. The Haglets. Herman Melville. APN-2

By Cool Siloam's Shady Rill. Reginald Heber. NOCV

By Cypris, Cupid! Meleager, *Greek.* GrAn, *tr. by* Peter Whigham

By dark severance the apparition head. Painted Head. John Crowe Ransom. FuPo; LiTM; MeMAP; MoAmPo; NOBA; NoAM; OxBA

By day and also by night and you are. Ian Wedde. PeNZ *Fr.* Earthly: Sonnets for Carlos.

By day, and were a trouble to my dreams. (LL) Fair seed time had my soul, and I grew up. Wordsworth. PoE

By day his world extends, far, knotted, hot. Boy. Mary Kinzie. FFC

By day she woos me, soft, exceeding fair. The World. Christina Rossetti. BoWoP; NALW; PEW

By day the bat is cousin to the mouse. The Bat. Theodore Roethke. ChAP; OBCA

By day the skyscraper looms in the smoke and sun and has a soul. Skyscraper. Carl Sandburg. ImGa

By day these men ask nothing, and obey. Infantry. Alun Lewis. PoWW

By daybreak a north wind has shaken. After the Chinese. Tess Gallagher. NAmP90

By denying me the seas, the right to run and fly. Osip Emilevich Mandelstam, *Russian.* TCRP, *tr. by* Bernard Meares

By Derwent's rapid stream as oft I strayed. Sonnet VII. Anna Seward Ro *Fr.* Sonnets.

By Derwent's side my father's cottage stood. The Female Vagrant. Wordsworth. Ro

By dint of color. A Dab of Color. Theodore Weiss. VGW

By divination came the Dorians. In Arcadia. Lawrence Durrell. MoBrPo

By drawling out "ye are that head of Gold." (LL) Nebuchadnezzar's Dream. Keats. ChIV-1; KSG

By dream[e]s, each one into a several [or sev'rall] world. (LL) Dream[e]s. Robert Herrick. BeJo; CaPo; HAP; KaS; NAEL-1; OPOU; OxBSP; Spl

By duty bound, and not by custom led. To the Memory of My Dear and Ever Honored Father Thomas Dudley Esq. Who Deceased July 31, 1653, and of His Age 77. Anne Bradstreet. NAAL-1; NAAL-3

By ear, she sd. I, Maximus of Gloucester, to You ("By ear, she sd"). Charles Olson. NeAP *Fr.* The Maximus Poems.

By easy slope to west as if it had. Cheyenne Mountain. Helen Hunt Jackson. APN-2

By eating Miss Foggerty's cake. (LL) Miss Foggerty's Cake. *Unknown.* BLPA; NBLV

By entering the grand lottery. Ryszard Krynicki, *Polish.* CEEP, *tr. by* Magnus J. Krynski *and* Robert A. Maguire

By famine when he died. (LL) Wallet, a rawhide goatskin, a cane, A. Leonidas, *Greek.* GrAn; PGA, *tr. by* Kenneth Rexroth

By fate, not option, frugal Nature gave. Xenophanes. Ralph Waldo Emerson. APN-1; NOBA

By favorable breezes fanned. Cythère. Paul Verlaine, *French.* AWP, *tr. by* Arthur Symons

By feathers green, across Casbeen. The Phoenix. Arthur Christopher Benson. OBEV

By Fiat of Adoration. Oscar Williams. LiTM

By flash in sunshine "to reduce contrast." Snapshot of Adam. James Merrill. EOEF

By Flower-and-Moon Pavilion, I stay my carriage. Liu Ya-tzu. SuSp, *tr. by* Wu-chi Liu *Fr.* Miscellaneous Poems on Lake Biwa.

By Frazier Creek Falls. Gary Snyder. InPS-3

By Godde and Seynt Johne I sweare ye. The Eternale Footeman's Tale. George Moor. BXAP

By God's own light illumined and foreshadowed. (LL) In unplowed Maine he sought the lumberers' gang. Ralph Waldo Emerson. MeMAP; TAP

By-gone September, The. A Flying Visit. Thomas Hood. CBNP

By Goose Lake Mountain, rice and millet grown fat. Shrine Festival. Wang Chia, *Chinese.* CoBCP, *tr. by* Burton Watson

By green waters the footpaths gather. Heraclitus by the Lake. Lucian Blaga, *Romanian.* CEEP, *tr. by* Peter Jay *and* Virgil Nemoianu

By Hallucination Visited. Robert Horan. SPE

By hand, all by her graceful brown hand. (LL) When a Beautiful Woman Gets on the Jutiapa Bus. Belle Waring. NAmP90; PBCAP

By hand-drawn cart, an excursion at evening. Lotus Lake. Ts'ao P'i, *Chinese.* CoBCP; GaP, *tr. by* Burton Watson

By Hatred out of Envy by Despair. (LL) Epigram: "I had gone broke, and got set to come back." James Vincent Cunningham. MoAmPo; OxBSP; VCAP

By he comes *back* at the *gallop* again. (LL) Windy Nights. Robert Louis Stevenson. ACTP; BoTP; FPC; KaS; NTP; OTCP; OxBChV; PoRA

By Heaven! *Unknown, Chinese.* CoBCP, *tr. by* Burton Watson

By Heaven 'tis false, I am not vain. The Defiance. Aphra Behn. EnLoPo

By her arriving immigrant bees. (LL) Blue Horses. Ed Roberson. GT

By Her Aunt's Grave. Thomas Hardy. MoBrPo; PFE *Fr.* Satires of Circumstance in Fifteen Glimpses.

By Her That Is Most Assured to Her Self. Edmund Spenser. *See* Sonnet 58: "Weak is the assurance that weak flesh reposeth."

By her the heaven is in his course contained. Scudamor in the Temple of Venus. Edmund Spenser. PoE *Fr.* Wood Of Error. AEP

By Heraclides. Heraclitus of Halicarnassus, *Greek.* OBCVT; OBVE, *tr. by* William Cowper

By his commandment hee maketh the snow to fall apace. Bible, Apocrypha. OBVE *Fr.* Ecclesiasticus.

By holding my mirror out of the window I see. Motho Ke Motho Ka Batho Babang (A Person Is a Person Because of Other People). Jeremy Cronin. AF

By holding tails. (LL) Holding Hands. Lenore M. Link. FPC; NTCP

By illness pent in lime-tree bower. Lines Written near Linton, on Exmoor. Daniel Gerard Hoffman. BXAP

By its shape, like thrushes in clear evenings. (LL) The Bride. D. H. Lawrence. NoAM; OxBTC

By itself and from a distance. The Brick. Paul Roche. NYBP

By Keats's soul, the man who never stepped. Elizabeth Barrett Browning. EPCY *Fr.* Aurora Leigh. VWP

By keeping you asunder. (LL) Song for a Dance. Francis Beaumont. FaBoCh; NTP

By knocking at my breast. (LL) Though regions far [or farr] divided. Aurelian Townshend. NOSC; PoEL-2

By knowing the sum of our delight. Catullus. *See* Carmen 5 ("My sweetest Lesbia, let us live and love").

By landscape reminded once of his mother's figure. Adolescence. W. H. Auden. MoP; NoAM

By Loch Ness they can toss, like confetti. Limerick. Bill Greenwell. PeLi

By Logan's streams that rin sae deep. Logan Braes. John Mayne. OxBS

By loss; the moment known to Kierkegaard. (LL) Discoveries. Vernon Watkins. ImPo; LiTM

By Man who thirsts to be deceived. (LL) Maia. Ralph Waldo Emerson. APN-1; PAR

By miracles exceeding power of man. Crucifying. Donne. *Fr.* La Corona. ChIV-2; ESCV; Son *Fr.* Holy Sonnets.

By mirrors, horoscopes, / and blood. (LL)　Family Jewels.　Essex Hemphill. GT

By mist.　O. Mabson Southard.　HA

By mourning beauty crowned! (LL)　Ode: "Sleep sweetly in your humble graves."　Henry Timrod.　ColAP; PAR

By moving a single board. (LL)　After weeks of watching the roof leak. Gary Snyder.　KaS

By my cold, clean, whispering spring. (LL)　I, Hermes, have been set up. Anyte, *Greek.*　GrAn; OBVE; PGA, *tr. by* Kenneth Rexroth

By my further dying. (LL)　The Wind Suffers of Blowing.　Laura Riding Jackson.　NoP-4

By myself walking.　Hypochondriacus.　Charles Lamb.　BXAP

By natural instinct they change their Lord. (LL)　Some by their friends, more by themselves thought wise.　Dryden.　ChIV-1; OBSV

By nature I love to dress my hair.　Hsü Pen.　*Fr.* Five Things Sought For— In the Manner of Han Wo.　CoBLCP, *tr. by* Jonathan Chaves

By naughty boys. (LL)　Pigtail.　Tadeusz Różewicz, *Polish.*　HP; PoSu, *tr. by* Adam Czerniawski

By Nebo's lonely mountain.　The Burial of Moses.　Cecil Frances Alexander.　BLPA

By Night.　Robert Francis.　VGW

By night around my temple grove.　Buddha.　Arno Holz, *German.*　AWP, *tr. by* William Ellery Leonard

By night I saw the *Hunter's moon.*　The Indian Gone!　Josiah D. Canning. APN-1

By night on my bed I sought him whom my soul loveth.　On My Bed I Sought Him.　Bible, *O.T.*　TrJP　*Fr.* The Song of Songs.　AWP

By night the rising Star. (LL)　The Other World.　*Unknown, Egyptian.* OxBSn, *tr. by* Robert Silliman Hillyer

By night they haunted a thicket of April mist.　Spectral Lovers.　John Crowe Ransom.　GBL; HeIP-4

By night, Tingribirdi, the hills burned.　Babur.　Dom Moraes.　OMIP

By night we lingered [*or* linger'd] on the lawn.　Tennyson.　EBVV; EnVR; FHYEP; HAP; OAEL-2; OBNC; PeECV; PoEL-5; TOF　*Fr.* In Memoriam A. H. H.

　"Till now the doubtful dusk reveal'd."　GTBS-P

By night within my bed, I roamed here and there.　Michael Drayton. ChIV-1　*Fr.* The Most Excellent Song Which Was Solomon's.

By none but me can the tale be told.　The White Ship.　D. G. Rossetti. OBNV

By noon, as I recall, the sky was clear.　Rural Colloquy with a Painter. Timothy Steele.　CRP

By noon, the bestial roar of surplus-driven labor.　Silence, 2.　Stefan Brecht.　CLPP

By noon the heat became unbearable.　Tea.　Ch'u Ch'uang I, *Chinese.* OHMPC, *tr. by* Kenneth Rexroth

By noon we'll be deep into it—.　Conjugal Visits.　Al Young.　NAAAL

By now after all these years.　Namelessness.　David Wevill.　IFJA

By now I should be entering on the supreme stage.　Pilgrim's Problem.　C. S. Lewis.　TrCP

By now you will have met.　Voice.　W. S. Merwin.　NNaP

By numbers here from shame or censure free.　Poverty in London.　Samuel Johnson.　NOEC; OBSV; OxAEP-1　*Fr.* London: A Poem in Imitation of the Third Satire of Juvenal.　PoEL-3

By only those two stars in Stella's face. (LL)　Sonnet 26: "Though dusty wits dare scorn astrology."　Sir Philip Sidney.　OAEL-1; Son

By our first strange and fatal [*or* fatall] interview.　*See* On His Mistress [*or* Mistris].　John Donne.　BoLoP; CBLP; EBEV; ESCV; GBL; MeLP; NAEL-1; NOBE; NoSic; OxAEP-1; PoEL-2; SCGP; SeCP　*Fr.* Elegies.

By pain of stone and wearing down of bronze.　Upon This Rock.　Ruthven Todd.　PoA

By proxy his bomb exploded, his valour shone. (LL)　From the Irish.　James Simmons.　PBCIP; PNI

By Rail through the Earthly Paradise, Perhaps Bedfordshire.　Denise Levertov.　NNaP

By rights one should experience holy dread.　Eros.　Timothy Steele.　RA

By river and lakes at odds with life I journeyed, wine my freight.　Easing My Heart.　Tu Mu, *Chinese.*　NNPT; PLT, *tr. by* A. C. Graham

By road, a matter of several miles. (LL)　Brown's Descent; or, The Willy-Nilly.　Robert Frost.　MoAmPo; PoRA

By Saint [*or* Saynt] Mary, my lady.　To Mistress [*or* Maystres] Isabell Pennell.　John Skelton.　AAS; CH; InPS-3; NOBE; NoSic; OBEV; OxBoLi; PoEL-1; SCGP; TTTS　*Fr.* The Garland [*or* Garlande *or* Garlands] of Laurel[l].

By scribbled names on walls, by telephone number.　Village Spa.　Phyllis McGinley.　OBCoV

By sheer accident having met him.　Lucky.　Patricia Goedicke.　NMM-2

By silver reeds in a silver stream. (LL)　Silver.　Walter De la Mare.　BoTP; CTV; MoBrPo; PoRA; SAGP; TTTS

By six he's started. I wake to a wince and arrh.　Demolisher.　Alan Gould. BMAP

By sloth on sorrow fathered.　Lollocks.　Robert Graves.　RB

By some derision of wild circumstance.　Reunion.　Edwin Arlington Robinson.　NOBA

By some sad means, when reason holds no sway.　Philip Freneau.　PoEL-4 *Fr.* The House of Night.

By sparrows drawn, there's now no chance.　The Disaster.　Mary Savage. ECWP

By spring banks waterplants are green.　Painting "Solitary Fisherman by a Spring River" The.　Ni Tsan, *Chinese.*　CoBLCP, *tr. by* Jonathan Chaves

By St. Thomas Water.　Charles Causley.　OBSP

By strangers' coasts and waters, many days at sea.　Catullus, CI.　Catullus, *Latin.*　OBCVT, *tr. by* Robert Fitzgerald

By-street was bathed in sun, The.　Andrey Bely.　PFTM, *tr. by* Roger Keys *and* Angela Keys　*Fr.* The Dramatic Symphony.

By Stubborn Stars.　Kenneth Leslie.

　Sonnet: "Silver herring throbbed thick in my seine, The."　NOBC

By such an all-embalming summer day.　Near Helikon.　Trumbull Stickney. *Fr.* Sonnets from Greece.　APN-1

By suddenly coming near. (LL)　The Bat.　Jane Kenyon.　CrSp; LoL

By sundown we came to a hidden village.　Conquerors.　Henry Treece. OBWVE

By Talland Church as I did go.　The Planted Heel.　Sir Arthur Thomas Quiller-Couch.　EBVV

By that long scan of waves, myself call'd back, resumed upon myself.　Walt Whitman.　NAAL-1; NAAL-3　*Fr.* Fancies at Navesink.

By that precious pearl without a / stain. (LL)　Perle, plesaunte to prynces paye.　*Unknown.*　NoP-4

By that summer snapshot on someone else's porch.　I Swear.　Bella Akhatovna Akhmadulina, *Russian.*　TCRP, *tr. by* Albert C. Todd

By that the Maniple hadde his tale ended.　The Introduction to the Parson's Tale.　Chaucer.　NAEL-1　*Fr.* The Canterbury Tales.

By the 5th Generation Louisiana, After Slavery.　Ahmos, II Zu-Bolton. BkSV

By the Arno.　Oscar Wilde.　EBVV

By the ascension [*or* Assention] of thy Lawn, see All. (LL)　To Dianeme ("Show [*or* Shew] me thy feet; show [*or* shew] me thy legs, thy thighs").　Robert Herrick.　CaPo; NOSC

By the Babylonish waters.　By the Waters of Babylon.　Heinrich Heine. TrJP, *tr. by* Charles Godfrey Leland　*Fr.* Hebrew Melodies.

By the bivouac's fitful flame.　Walt Whitman.　BLT; NoAM; NoP-4; OxBA; PoE

By the blue taper's trembling light.　Night Piece on Death.　Thomas Parnell.　NOEC

By the blue wooden sea.　Switchback.　Dame Edith Sitwell.　PBWP

By the Boat House, Oxford.　Anne Stevenson.　FaBoWP

By the bonnie milldams o' Binnorie. (LL)　Binnorie; or, The Two Sisters. *Unknown.*　CH; EnSB; OBEV; PoE

By the Bridge.　Ted Walker.　NYBP

By the Campfire.　Konstantin Mikhailovich Simonov, *Russian.*　TCRP, *tr. by* Lubov Yakovleva

By the child dying at his mother's side.　The Five Sorrowful Mysteries. Francis Jammes, *French.*　GI, *tr. by* Jeffrey Fiskin

By the City Gate.　Ts'ui Hao, *Chinese.*　OHMPC, *tr. by* Kenneth Rexroth

By the crueltie o' his ain maistress. (LL)　Slugabed.　Sydney Goodsir Smith.　FaBoTC

By the crumbling fire we talked.　Witness.　John Montague.　CIP-2

By the Deep Sea.　Byron.　*See* The Ocean.

By the dry road the fathers cough and spit.　The Brief Journey West. Howard Nemerov.　NoAM

By the end of the longest day of the year he could not.　Summer Solstice, New York City.　Sharon Olds.　NAmP90

By the Exeter River.　Donald Hall.　MoBS

By the fierce flames of love I'm in a sad taking.　Love Song.　Royall Tyler.　TAP

By the Fire.　Mother Goose.　OxNR

　(Pussy-cat by [*or* beside] the fire.)　ReMoGo

By the Fire-Side.　Robert Browning.　EBVV; OAEL-2

By the first hour we knew the day's luck.　Rituals along the Arkansas. William Mills.　MT

By the first of August.　I Remember.　Anne Sexton.　AFr; LW

By the flat cup and the splash of new vantage.　1.31.　Horace.　CTC, *tr. by* Ezra Pound　*Fr.* Odes.

By the flow of the inland river.　The Blue and the Gray.　Francis Miles Finch.　APN-2; BLPA; CBCWP; FaBoBe

By the Ford.　Edward Thomas.　OxBSP

By the gas-fire, kneeling.　Olga Poems.　Denise Levertov.　LCAP-2; NNaP

By the gate with star and moon. Medallion. Sylvia Plath. HeIP-4

By the Gold River, in mid-autumn, the bows of our enemy are drawn. Early Geese. Tu Mu, *Chinese*. SuSp

By the hearth a holier Lar! (LL) Celia's Home-Coming. Agnes Mary Frances Robinson. VWP

By the images of things. Epoch. Vladimir Holan, *Czech*. PoSu, *tr. by Ian and Jarmila Milner*

By the injustice of the skies for punishment? (LL) The Cold Heaven. W. B. Yeats. AWP; CTC; GTBS-P; HAP; NoAM; OAEL-2; OxBSP; RB

By the Isar, in the twilight. River Roses. D. H. Lawrence. CMoP; GBL; OAEL-2

By the Jordan. Herman Melville. NCAP

By the lake at Armenonville in the Bois de Boulogne. Armenonville. Edna St. Vincent Millay. NoP-4

By the lamplit stall I loitered, feasting my eyes. Sight. Wilfrid Wilson Gibson. MoBrPo

By the light of a female impersonator. National Assessment. Connie Deanovich. WWSi

By the Light of the Branches Outside. Ion Caraion, *Romanian*. CEEP, *tr. by Marguerite Dorian and Elliott B. Urdang*

By the light of the harvest moon. Moons. Peter Fallon. BiHa

By the light of the moon. (LL) So we'll go no more a-roving. Byron. AWP; BoLoP; CBLP; CH; ClHu; EBEvV; FHYEP; FaPoR; HAP; HeIP-4; ImPo; NAEL-2; NOBE; OAEL-2; OBEV; OPOU; OxBS; OxBSP; PoE; PoEL-4; PoLF; PoRA; Poetr; SCGP; TFi; TTTS

By the Looking-Glass. Augusta Davies Webster. VWP

By the lyre I rose, fell with the flute. Thebes. Honestus, *Greek*. GrAn, *tr. by Peter Jay*

By the Margin of the Great Deep. "Æ." OBEV

By the margin of the ocean, one morning [*or* one pleasant evening] in the month of June. The Bonny Bunch of Roses O. *Unknown*. OxBoLi

By the minutest of saws. (LL) Blue Tit on a String of Peanuts. Norman MacCaig. CABP

By the Moon ("By the moon we sport and play"). John Lyly *and* Thomas Ravenscroft. CH *Fr. The Mayde's Metamorphosis.*

(Urchin's Dance, The.) BoTP

By the new Boot's, a tool-chest with flagpoles. Aberdarcy: The Main Square. Kingsley Amis. NOBL; NoAM; OxBTC *Fr. The Evans Country.*

By the North Gate, the wind blows full of sand. Lament of the Frontier Guard. Li Po, *Chinese*. OBVE; OBWP; VGW, *tr. by Ezra Pound*

By the North Sea. Aleksandr Blok, *Russian*. TCRP, *tr. by Geoffrey Thurley*

By the North Sea. Swinburne.

"Land that is lonelier than ruin, A." PoEL-5

By the old Moulmein Pagoda, lookin' lazy at [*or* eastward to] the sea. Mandalay. Rudyard Kipling. EBEvV; MoBrPo; NOBE; OxAEP-2; PBMP

By the Pasture Bars. George Sands Johnson. PWR

By the Pool at the Third Rosses. Arthur Symons. ADE; OBNC *Fr. In Ireland.*

By the Potomac. Thomas Bailey Aldrich. Son

By the River. Anna McMullen. LBC

By the River. Wang An-shih, *Chinese*. CoBCP, *tr. by Burton Watson*

By the River Ashley. Mary Ursula Bethell.

"Hour is dark. The river comes to its end, The." PeNZ

"Sauntering home from church we lingered." PeNZ

"That bridge from the city, that was Waimakariri." PeNZ

By the River Eden. Kathleen Jessie Raine. NYBP

"Beside the river Eden."

"Lapwing's wavering flight, The."

"Never twice that river."

By the riverbank idly I pick white-budded reeds. Thoughts South of the Yangtze. Yü Hu, *Chinese*. CoBCP, *tr. by Burton Watson*

By the rivers of Babel we sate. Bible, *O.T. See* Psalm 137.

"By the Rivers of Babylon." Mary Weston Fordham. CBWP-2

By the rivers of Babylon, there we sat down, yea, we wept, when [*or* then] we remembered Zion. Psalm 137. Bible, *O.T.* AWP; NAWM-1; OAEL-1; OBSP; TrJP *Fr. Psalms.*

By the Rivers of Babylon We Sat Down and Wept. Byron. ChIV-1

By the Road. Geoffrey Grigson. OxBTC

By the road. Tanka. Saitō Mokichi, *Japanese*. MJT, *tr. by Makoto Ueda*

By the road in spring, rain has added flowers. Tune: "Happy Events Approaching." Ch'in Kuan, *Chinese*. SuSp, *tr. by James J. Y. Liu*

By the Road to the Air-Base. Yvor Winters. PFE

By the road to the contagious hospital. Spring and All. William Carlos Williams. CMoP; ChAP; ColAP; HAP; InPK-6; InPS-3; LiTM; MeMAP; MoAmPo; MoP; NAAL-2; NOBA; NoAM; OxBA; PoE; PoPoPo; TAP; TFi; TRP; UnPo

By the roots of my hair some god got hold of me. The Hanging Man. Sylvia Plath. HCAP; VCAP

By the rude bridge that arched the flood. Concord Hymn. Ralph Waldo Emerson. APN-1; AWP; AiP; AmPP; BLPA; CTV; ClHu; ColAP; EBEvV; FaBoA; FaBoBe; FaPoR; HAP; HeIP-4; MeMAP; NAAL-1; NAAL-3; NOBA; NoP-4; OBWP; OxBA; PAR; PeECV; PoPoPo; TAP; TFi

By the rushy-fringed bank. Sabrina's Song. Milton. NOSC *Fr.* Comus; a Masque Presented at Ludlow Castle. FHYEP; OAEL-1

By the sad waters of separation. Exile. Ernest Christopher Dowson. ADE; BoLoP

By the Saltings. Ted Walker. NYBP

By the same laws which first herself ordain'd. Alexander Pope. *See* First follow Nature, and your judgment frame.

By the Sea. Richard Watson Dixon. OBNC

By the Sea. Christina Rossetti. NOBVV

By the Sea. Iain Crichton Smith.

Dunoon and the Holy Loch. FaBoTC

In the Cafe. FaBoTC

In the Park. FaBoTC

"Sitting here by the foreshore day after day." FaBoTC

By the Sea. Wordsworth. GTBS-P

(Evening on Calais Beach.) OBEV

By the sewage puddles of Sabra and Shatila. You Can't Kill a Baby Twice. Dahlia Ravikovitch, *Hebrew*. VCWP, *tr. by Chana Bloch and Ariel Bloch*

By the spring pond, deep and wide. Duckweed Pond. Wang Wei, *Chinese*. CoBCP, *tr. by Burton Watson*

By the Statue of King Charles [*or* I] at Charing Cross. Lionel Pigot Johnson. MoBrPo; NOBE; OBEV; OBMV; OBNC; PeVV; PoEL-5

By the summer's flare and winter's flaw. John Crowe Ransom. *See* Conrad in Twilight.

By the Swannanoa. William Gilmore Simms. APN-1

By the third day, the rain. Thanksgiving. Steve Hassett. CDa

By the time I get myself out of bed, my wife has left. Tuesday, June 4th, 1991. Billy Collins. BAP-93

By the time the priest started into his sermon. The Divorce Referendum, Ireland, 1986. Paul Durcan. BiHa; PBCIP

By the time you read this. Drive-By Shooting. Elizabeth Cohen. WWSi

By the time you read this. Letter. W. S. Merwin. HAP

By the time you swear you're his. Unfortunate Coincidence. Dorothy Parker. BXAP; LW; NoP-4; PiM

By the Waterfall. Friedrich Adler, *German*. TrJP, *tr. by Jethro Bithell*

By the Waters of Babylon. Heinrich Heine. TrJP, *tr. by Charles Godfrey Leland* *Fr. Hebrew Melodies.*

By the Waters of Babylon. Emma Lazarus. WPE

Currents. PAR

Exodus (August 3, 1492), The.

By the waters of Babylon we sat down and wept. Psalm 137. *Unknown*. NNPT, *tr. by Miles Coverdale*

By the waters of Babylon we sat down and wept. Super Flumina Babylonis. Swinburne. PoEL-5

By the Waters of the Sava. Uri Zvi Greenberg, *Hebrew*. MHP, *tr. by Ruth Finer Mintz*

By the way we met. Shakespeare. OBCoV *Fr. The Comedy of Errors.*

By the Well of Living and Seeing. Charles Reznikoff.

"Highway I was walking on, The." FTOS

By the West Pavilion, on a thousand feet of cliff. Midnight. Tu Fu, *Chinese*. PLT, *tr. by A. C. Graham*

By the Winding River I. Tu Fu, *Chinese*. OHPC, *tr. by Kenneth Rexroth*

By the Winding River II. Tu Fu, *Chinese*. OHPC, *tr. by Kenneth Rexroth*

By the wireless I can hear. Wireless. Rodney Bennett. BoTP

By the women of Marblehead! (LL) Skipper Ireson's Ride. John Greenleaf Whittier. APN-1; NCAP; NOBA; OBAL; OBCA; OxBA; PoLF

By the yellow Nile a temple of black marble. The Memphian Temple. John Barlas. ADE

By thee, thee, only thee. (LL) Thee, Thee, Only Thee. Thomas Moore. GBL; OBNC

By their blight, from strand to strand? (LL) Lines: "At the Portals of the Future." Frances Ellen Watkins Harper. APN-2; PAR

By their nephews and their nieces. (LL) Good and Bad Children. Robert Louis Stevenson. ACTP; ChAP; EBVV; FaBoCh; OBCoV; OxBChV

By them is past in sweetest taste / Hony or Comb of hony, *sel. of par. by* Sir Philip Sidney. Bible, *O.T. See* Psalm 19.

By Themis & wine that made me tipsy. Phanias, *Greek*. GrAn, *tr. by Thomas Meyer*

By themselves in the twilight. Leonidas of Tarentum, *Greek*. PGA, *tr. by Kenneth Rexroth*

By then, by the time my brother. Not Knowing. Gary Soto. NoP-4

By these, by these same chains, O Rome. Alcuin, *Latin*. MLL, *tr. by* Helen Waddell

By thine own named town made famous in thy fall. Michael Drayton. NOSC　*Fr.* Polyolbion.

By this cold shuddering fit of fear. The Glen of Silence. "Hugh MacDiarmid." CMoP

By this exchange of eyes, this encirclement. Robert Graves. ITG

By this [*or* thys] fire [*or* fyre] I warm[e] my handes [*or* handys]. *Unknown.* MiEL

By this good wicked spirit, sweet angel devil. (LL) Evil [*or* Evill] spirit, your beauty, haunts me still, An. Michael Drayton. AAS; GBL; NOBE; NoSic

By this he knew she wept with waking eyes. Modern Love. George Meredith. CABP; EnLoPo; EnVR; GLoP; GSo; HoPM; NAEL-2; NOBVV; NoP-4; OAEL-2; OxBM; PBMP; PoE; PoEL-5; Son　*Fr.* Modern Love.

By this Leander being near the land. Marlowe. EBEV; FaBoSe　*Fr.* Hero and Leander. AAS

("That pulls or shakes it from the golden tree.") (LL) FaBoSe

By this the Northerne wagoner had set. Edmund Spenser. FHYEP; NoSic　*Fr.* Wood Of Error. AEP

By this the sun had sucked up the vast deep. Michael Drayton. NOSC　*Fr.* Noah's Flood.

By this, though deep the evening fell. Battle, The ("By this, though deep the evening fell"). Sir Walter Scott. PoEL-4　*Fr.* Marmion.

By this time had they reached the Stygian pool. Ben Jonson. NOSC　*Fr.* On the Famous Voyage. BeJo

By this time long-gowned Lumen walked abroad. William Rankins. OBSV　*Fr.* Satyrus Peregrinans.

By those soft Tods of wool[l]. A Conjuration, to Electra. Robert Herrick. GBL; PoEL-3

By those true tears y'are weeping. (LL) To a Gentlewoman Objecting to Him His Grey Hairs. Robert Herrick. BeJo; CaPo

By thunders of white silence, overthrown. (LL) Hiram Powers' "Greek Slave." Elizabeth Barrett Browning. GS; NALW

By Timo's locks. Meleager, *Greek*. GrAn, *tr. by* Peter Whigham

By T'ing Yang Waterfall. Hsieh Ling-yün, *Chinese*. OHMPC, *tr. by* Kenneth Rexroth

By tucking her chin in toward her chest, she can look up darkly through. Love: Shyness. Charles Kenneth Williams. CBLP

By unnumbered ways of dream to death. (LL) Immortality. "Æ." AWP; OBMV; TIRV

By viewing Nature, Natures hand-maid, Art. Dryden. OxBoS　*Fr.* Annus Mirabilis.

By Vows of Love Together Bound. Eleazar Thompson Fitch. AH

By Wauchopeside. "Hugh MacDiarmid." EBEV; OxAEP-2

By way of pretext. Yakamochi. AWP, *tr. by* Arthur Waley　*Fr.* Manyo Shu, Part 1 of 4.

By ways remote and distant waters sped. On the Burial of His Brother. Catullus, *Latin*. AWP; IMW; OBCVT, *tr. by* Aubrey Beardsley　*Fr.* Carmina.

By west, under a wilde wode-side. *Unknown.* MiEL

By what appalling dim upheaval. Simon Gerty. Elinor Wylie. OBAL

By what eternal streams. (LL) To One in Paradise. Edgar Allan Poe. AmPP; BoLoP; GLoP; NCAP; OBEV; OxBA; PoLF; TAP

By what right do they call Zeus a lover? Palladas, *Greek*. InMo, *tr. by* Sam Hamill

By what sends. Children's Rhymes. Langston Hughes. BPo; NOxBChV

By which at least I am befriended. (LL) Idiom of the Hero. Wallace Stevens. AFr; OxBA

By which I lived? Galway Kinnell. *See* The Bear.

By who knew enough to save for something. The Black Hose. Bruce Weigl. NAmP90

By woods and water, whose houses are these. The Grand Houses at Lo-yang. Po Chü-i, *Chinese*. ChiP, *tr. by* Arthur Waley

By Yangtse and Han, a stranger who thinks of home. Yangtse and Han. Tu Fu, *Chinese*. PLT, *tr. by* A. C. Graham

By Yangtse and Han the mountains pile their barriers. At the Corner of the World. Tu Fu, *Chinese*. PLT, *tr. by* A. C. Graham

By your breasts. Conversation between the Chevalier de Chamilly and Mariana Alcoforado in the Manner of a Song of Regret. *Unknown*, *Portuguese*. BoWoP, *tr. by* Helen R. Lane

By your unnumbered charities. Hospital for Defectives. Thomas Blackburn. GTBS-P; OxBTC

Bye, bye, baby bunting / Daddy's gone a-hunting. *Unknown.* OxNR; ReMoGo

("Bye, baby bunting.") LB

By'm By. *Unknown.* AS

B'york! but it's lovely under the leaf. Spring Song. Donald Finkel. NYBP

Bypassing rue Descartes. Czeslaw Milosz, *Polish*. VCWP, *tr. by* Gorczynski, Renata and Robert Hass

Byre. Norman MacCaig. FaBoTC

Byrnies, The. Thom Gunn. MoP; NoAM; OxBTC

Byron. J. Gordon Coogler. OBAL

Byron. Joaquin Miller.
In Men Whom Men Condemn as Ill. PoLF

Byron and Shelley and Keats. The Lives and Times of John Keats, Shelley, and George Gordon Noel, Lord Byron. Dorothy Parker. NALW　*Fr.* A Pig's-Eye View of Literature.

Byron, how sweetly sad thy melody! To Lord Byron. Keats. EPCY

Byron on Southey. Byron. OxBoV　*Fr.* The Vision of Judgment.

Byron Recollected at Bologna. Samuel Rogers. *Fr.* Italy. OBNC

Byron's Oak at Newstead Abbey. Timothy Thomas Fortune. AAP

By's beard the Goat, by his bush-tail the Fox. Of Kate's Baldness. John, of Hereford Davies. FaBoEE

Bystander, The. Rosemary Dobson. CBAP

Bytuene [*or* Bytwene *or* Betwene *or* Bitwene *or* Bitweene] Mersh [*or* March *or* Mershe] and [*or* ant] Averil [*or* April]. Alison. *Unknown.* CBLP; MiEL; NAEL-1; NoP-4; OAEL-1; OBEV; PeLV

Byzantium. W. B. Yeats. APAD; CMoP; EBEV; FaBoMo; HAP; InPS-3; LiTM; MoBrPo; MoP; NAEL-2; NAWM-2; NIP-4; NOBE; NoAM; NoP-4; OAEL-2; OxBTC; PoE; Poetr

BZZZZZZZ. Amy Gerstler. PmAP

C

C. C. Rider. Lucille Clifton. GT

C. C. Rider. *Unknown.* AS

C——e, whom providence hath placed. To the Hon. Mrs. C——e. Jane West. ECWP

C.G. Hanzlicek. C. G. Hanzlicek. CMAP

C. L. M. John Masefield. LiTM; MoBrPo; OxBTC

C Major of this life: so, now I will try to sleep, The. (LL) Abt Vogler. Robert Browning. FHYEP; NAEL-2; OAEL-2; TOF

C o y O t e. Marlene Mountain. HA

C / olumbus from his after-. Colombe. Edward Kamau Brathwaite. VCWP

C Stands for Civilization. Kenneth Fearing. TrJP

C. T. at the Five Spot. Thulani Davis. SeSe

C.T.'s variation. Thulani Davis. MoNo; SeSe; WeT
("Some springs the mississipi rose up so high.") WeT

Ca' the ewes [*or* yowes] to the knowes. Robert Burns. OBEV; OxAEP-1

Ca' the yowes to the knowes. *Unknown.* OxBS

Cabal at Nickey Nackey's, The. Aphra Behn. NOSC

Cabaret. Sterling Brown. NAAAL

Cabaret star Viola D'Amore (Violet Dam), who has never heard of. Star, Sun, Moon. Henrikas Radauskas, *Lithuanian*. CEEP, *tr. by* Jonas Zdanys

Cabbage. Rosemary Norman. BrRo

Cabbage in Polish is kapusta—ka*poos*ta. Gary Gildner. CMAP

Cabbages. Renate Wood. CMAP

Cabin-Boy, The. George, 2nd Duke of Buckingham Villiers. NOSC

Cabin Creek Flood, The. *Unknown.* AmFP

Cabin in Minnesota, A. Marvin Bell. HoPM

Cabin North of It All, The. James McMichael. AmPA

Cabin sits alone far up a hill, The. The Wind. Gwendolen Haste. PaTW

Cabin Tale, A. Paul Laurence Dunbar. NAAAL

Cabinet-maker was I for many a long year, A. Chanson du Décervelage, La. Alfred Jarry, *French*. CBNP, *tr. by* Cyril Connolly *and* Simon Taylor　*Fr.* Ubu Cocu.

Cabinet of Seeds Displayed, A. Howard Nemerov. CRP

Cabins. Frank Bird Linderman. PaTW

Cable Ship, The. Harry Edmund Martinson, *Swedish*. RB, *tr. by* Robert Bly

Caboose Thoughts. Carl Sandburg. CMoP

Cachalot, The. Edwin John Pratt.
("Thousand years now had his breed, A." MoCV
"Where Cape Delgado strikes the sea." MoCV

Cackle, cackle, Mother Goose. *Unknown.* CTAV; OxNR

Cackling, smelling of camphor, crumbs of pink icing. Muse. David Wagoner. PoA

Cacoëthes Scribendi. Oliver Wendell Holmes. NBLV; OBCoV

Cactus. Jean-Joseph Rabéarivelo, *French*. NegPo, *tr. by* Ellen Conroy Kennedy; PBMAP
("And replaced them with golden flowers.") (LL) PBMAP
("That multitude of moulded hands.") PBMAP

Cadaver Politic. Tom Paulin. PNI

Cadenza. Ted Hughes. CMoP; NYBP

Cadmus sows teeth. Ovid, *Latin*. OBCVT, *tr.* by John Oldham

Caduceus flies past, with serpents wrought, The. Ambulance. Karl Kirchwey. WWSi

Caedmon. Denise Levertov. NoAM; NoP-4

Caedmon. Aidan Carl Mathews. PBCIP

Caedmon. Norman Nicholson. FaBoTw

Cædmon's Hymn. Caedmon, *Anglo-Saxon*. ASW, *tr.* by Kevin Crossley-Holland; EBEV, *tr.* by Sally Purcell; OAEL-1, *tr.* by Walter Kendrick

Caelia. William Browne. Son

   Lo, I the Man.

   So Sat the Muses.

Caelica. Fanny [*or* Frances] Macartney Greville.

   87. CABP

   99. CABP

Caelica. Fulke Greville.

   Absence and Presence.

      ("*Absence is paine*.") (LL) PBRV

   "Caelica, when I did see you every day." AAS

   Change.

   "*Cupid*, in *Myra's* faire bewitching eyes." PBRV

   "Cupid, thou naughty boy, when thou wert loathed." Son

   Despair.

   Farewell to Cupid.

   From Caelica.

   "Golden age was when the world was young, The." OAEL-1

   "In night, when colors [*or* colours] all to black[e] are cast." AAS; OAEL-1; Son

   "In those years when our sense, desire and wit." NOCV

   "Love, the delight of all well-thinking minds." GBL

   Love's Glory.

   "Manicheans did no idols make, The." NOCV

   Myra. NOBE; OBEV

      ("I with whose colors *Myra* drest her head.") PBRV

      ("*No man can print a kisse, lines may deceive*.") (LL) PBRV

   "Sion lies [*or* Syon lyes] waste, and thy Jerusalem." PeECV, *sect.* CX; ChIV-1; NoSic; PoEL-1

   Sonnet 78: "Little Hearts, where light-wing'd Passion raignes, The." PBRV

   Sonnet ("All my senses, like beacon's flame"). NOSC

   Sonnet: "Caelica, I overnight was finely used."

   Sonnet: "Down[e] in the depth of mine iniquity." NOSC

      ("Downe in the depth of mine iniquity.") PBRV

      ("Thus hath his death rais'd up this soule of mine.") (LL) PBRV

   Sonnet: "Earth with thunder torn, with fire blasted, The."

   Sonnet: "Eternall Truth, almighty, infinite."

   Sonnet: "Love is the peace, whereto all thoughts do strive."

   Sonnet: "Man, dream[e] no more of curious mysteries." NOSC

   Sonnet: "Nurse-life wheat within his green husk growing, The."

      ("Nurse-life wheat within his green husk growing, The.") NoP-4

      ("Turnes all the spirits of Man into desire.") (LL) PBRV

   Sonnet: "O false and treacherous Probability."

   Sonnet: "Three things there be in mans opinion dear[e]." NOSC

   Sonnet: "Whenas [*or* When as] man's life, the light of human lust." NOSC

   "When all this All doth pass from age to age." EBEV; NoSic

   "Wrapt [*or* Wrapped] up, O Lord, in man's degeneration." NoSic

Caelica, I overnight was finely used. Sonnet: "Caelica, I overnight was finely used." Greville Fulke. AAS; Son *Fr.* Caelica.

Caelica, when I did see you every day. Greville Fulke. AAS *Fr.* Caelica.

Caelius, that one, that only Lesbia. Catullus. *See* Carmen 58

   ("My Lesbia, Caelius, that same Lesbia").

Caernarfon, 2 July 1969. T. Glynne Davies, *Welsh*. OBWVE, *tr.* by Joseph P. Clancy

Caesar. W. S. Merwin. LCAP-2

Caesar! renowned in silence as in war. On the Prospect from Westminster Bridge. Elizabeth Tollet. ECWP

Caesar's Song. Mother Goose. ReMoGo

Cæsura. John Ashbery. ChIV-1; KSG

   ("Weather of the soul, vandalized, out-at-elbow. A blight. Spared, though, The.") (LL) KSG

Caesura. Patricia Cumming. MDDM

Caesura. Kenneth Mackenzie. CBAP; NOBAu

Cafe. Czeslaw Milosz, *Polish*. PoSu, *tr.* by Jan Darowski

Café in Warsaw. Allen Ginsberg. HAP

Café of Situations, The. Martin Johnston. BMAP *Fr.* In Transit: A Sonnet Square.

Café: 3 A.M. Langston Hughes. GLP; HCAP

Café Trieste: San Francisco. Joseph Brodsky. EP

Cafe with the hotwire, The. Back to Catfish. Belle Waring. NAmP90

Caffer Commando, The. Thomas Pringle. PeSAV

Cage, The. John Berryman. PoA

Cage, The. David Gascoyne. SPE

Cage, The. John Montague. CIP-2; PNI

Cage, The. James Stephens. OxBTC

Cage, The. Rosamund Marriott Watson. VWP

Cage Bird and Sky Bird. Leslie Norris. OTCP

Cage Walker, The. Yusef Komunyakaa. WWSi

Caged Bird. Maya Angelou. WeW-3

Caged Bird, A. Sarah Orne Jewett. APN-2; ColAP

Caged Bird in Springtime, The. James Kirkup. PeP

Caged in his stone-ribbed side. (LL) Sunk Lyonesse. Walter De la Mare. FaBoCh; LiTM

Caged in old woods, whose reverend echoes wake. Captivity. Samuel Rogers. OBNC

Caged Rats. Ebenezer Elliot. EBEV

Caged Skylark, The. Gerard Manley Hopkins. CMoP; LiTM; MoBrPo; OBMV; SoSe-8; Son

Cages. Marvin Solomon. NYBP

Cain. Irving Layton. MoCV

Cain: a Mystery. Byron.

   "Ah! didst *thou* tempt my mother?" OxBSn

   "And now I will convey thee to thy world." NOBRP

   "Hear, Jehovah! / May the eternal serpent's curse be on him!" NOBRP

   "Oh! thou dead / And everlasting witness! whose unsinking " ChIV-1

Caint call your name. The Hermit Cackleberry Brown, on Human Vanity. Jonathan Williams. OBAL; PoM

Cain't nobody tell me any different. Song No. 3. Sonia Sanchez. FFC; NOxBChV

Caird prevail'd—th' unblushing fair, The. Robert Burns. *Fr.* Love and Libery—A Cantata. NOBRP; NOEC

Cairo Jag. Keith Douglas. PoWW

Cake in the oven, clothes out on the line. Rockin' A Man, Stone Blind. Carolyn Beard Whitlow. FFC

Cake-That-Drifts-in-Water, The. Ho Xuan Huong, *Vietnamese*. AVP, *tr.* by Huỳnh Sanh Thông

Cala-Achí! Ha! Aha! Yeha! Ahau! Wow! Achí! *Unknown*. STP, *tr.* by Nathaniel Tarn *Fr.* Rabinal-Achí.

Calais Sands. Matthew Arnold. EBVVPR

Calamiterror. George Barker.

   Section VI. SPE

Calamity of seals begins with jaws, The. Seals at High Island. Richard Murphy. BiHa; CIP-2; PBCIP

Calcined stones come back, The. Homecoming of Love Amongst Illustrious Ruins. Rafael Alberti, *Spanish*. CLPP, *tr.* by Kenneth Rexroth

Calculating Clara. Harry Graham. PeLV *Fr.* Some Ruthless Rhymes.

Calculation, The. David Wagoner. NYBP

Calculus fit to compute on, A. Limerick. Gina Berkeley. PeLi

Calcutta and I. Sunil Gangopadhyay, *Bengali*. OMIP, *tr.* by Sujit Mukherjee *and* Meenakshi Mukherjee

Caledonia. Colleen J. McElroy. BlSi; NAAAL

Caledonia. Anthony Powell. NOBL

Caledonia. Sir Walter Scott. FaPoR; NOBE; OBEV; OBNC; OxAEP-2; PBMP; Ro *Fr.* The Lay of the Last Minstrel.

   ("Bard may draw his parting groan, The.") (LL) Ro

   ("Breathes there the man, with soul so dead.") Ro

   (Patriot, The.) FaPoR; OBNC

   (Patriotism.) CTV; NOBE; OxAEP-2

   ("Unwept, unhonoured, and unsung.") (LL) CTV

   O Caledonia!

Calendar. Cecil Bødker, *Danish*. BoWoP, *tr.* by Nadia Christensen *and* Alexander Taylor

Calendar of Oengus, The. *Unknown*.

   "This sad world we inhabit." NOIV

Calendar of the Air. Yevgeny Borisovich Rein, *Russian*. TCRP, *tr.* by Lubov Yakovleva

Calendar Rhyme. Flora Willis Watson. BoTP

Calenture. Alastair Reid. NYBP

Calenture, The. Randolph Stow. BMAP

Calf, The. Thomas Hardy. APo

Calf, by Nature and by Genius made, The. School for Calves. Virgil, *Latin*. OBCVT, *tr.* by John Dryden

Calf-Path, The. Sam Walter Foss. PoLF

Caliban. Shakespeare. *See* To Dream Again.

Caliban in Blue. Walter McDonald. CDa

Caliban in the Coal Mines. Louis Untermeyer. MoAmPo; TrJP

Caliban upon Setebos; or, Natural Theology in the Island. Robert Browning. AWP; EBEV; EnVR; FHYEP; NAEL-2; NOBVV; OAEL-2; OxAEP-2; PeVV

Caliban's Journal. Suniti Namjoshi. RACG

Calico-pale paddocks through the window, The. Song for Past Midnight. Geoffrey Lehmann. CBAP

Calico Pie. Edward Lear. FaBoCh; NOxBChV; NTP

California. John Rollin Ridge.
    "And shall we view these miracles and more." APN-2

California. Leon Stokesbury. PFE

California. *Unknown.* AS

California, 1852. Sharyn Jeanne Skeeter. ISC

California Girlhood, A. Alice Notley. PmAP

California Hills in August. Dana Gioia. DiPo; InPK-6

California Madrigal. Bret Harte. APN-2

California Peninsula: El Camino Real. Al Young. GT

California Phrasebook, The. Dennis Schmitz. AmPA

California rolls into. Delia Rexroth. Kenneth Rexroth. FiLi

California song, A. Song of the Redwood-Tree. Walt Whitman. AmPP

California Spring. Charles Wright. ColAP

California Trail. *Unknown.* PaTW

California Winter. Karl Shapiro. AiP

California Winter. Edward Rowland Sill. APN-2

Californian, The. *Unknown.* AmFP

Californians, The. Theodore Spencer. NYBP

Calimachus. Lucian, *Greek.* OBCVT, *tr. by* Timothy Kendall

Caliph shot a gazelle, The. Humorous Verse. Abu Dulama, *Arabic.* TTY, *tr. by* Raoul Abdul

Calisto. John Crowne.
    Song: "Kind lovers, love on." OxBSP

Call, A. Thomas Holley Chivers. Poetr

Call, The. John Hall. MeLP; NOSC

Call, The. Robert Harris. BMAP

Call, The. Dennis Haskell. NOBAu

Call, The. Charlotte Mew. APAD

Call, The. Thomas Osbert Mordaunt. *See* Sound, Sound the Clarion.

Call, The. *Unknown.* OBEV

Call alligator long-mouth. Don't Call Alligator Long-Mouth Till You Cross River. John Agard. NOxBChV

Call and assemble together Aotearoa. Call Together. Kohine Whakarua Ponika, *Maori.* PeNZ, *tr. by* Sam Karetu

Call Awe, then, what you will, long long ago. Freight. John Frederick Nims. GM

Call back your odours, lonely flowers. Night-Blooming Flowers. Felicia Dorothea Hemans. NOBRP

Call Boy. Sterling Brown. GM

Call—and bruise the air. Expression. Isaac Rosenberg. MoBrPo

Call down the hawk from the air. The Hawk. W. B. Yeats. PoA

Call for more pens, more paper, and more ink. (LL) Cacoëthes Scribendi. Oliver Wendell Holmes. NBLV; OBCoV

Call for the robin-redbreast and the wren. A Dirge. John Webster. CH; EBEV; FaBoCh; GTBS-P; HAP; NOBE; NOSC; OBEV; OxAEP-1; PFE; PoEL-2; PoRA; RB; SCGP; TFi   *Fr.* The White Devil.

Call her, call her for me, that girl. Lovers' Song. Kofi Awoonor. PBMAP   *Fr.* Three poems from Rediscovery (1964).

Call in the Midst of the Crowd, A. Alfred Corn.
    Fire: The People. NAAL-2; VCAP

Call in the midst of the crowd, A. Walt Whitman. *See* The Torch.

Call is for belief, The. The Fundament Is Shifted. Abbie Huston Evans. NYBP

Call it a good marriage—. Robert Graves. BoLoP; OxBM; PFE

Call it a louse—I'm. Cid Corman. VGW

Call it neither love nor going madness. Without Name. Pauli Murray. PoBA

Call it not vain; they do not err. The Minstrel Responds to Flattery. Sir Walter Scott. OBNC; OxAEP-2   *Fr.* The Lay of the Last Minstrel.

Call me bad when me start walk de streets. Eighties, De. Frederick Williams. PBCV

Call me no more, O gentle stream. To a River in the South. Sir Henry John Newbolt. CH

Call Me Not Back from the Echoless Shore. *Unknown.* BLPA

Call me not false, beloved. The Bridegroom. Rudyard Kipling. FaBoEE   *Fr.* Epitaphs of the War [1914–1918]. OBWP

Call me Polyxena, the wife of Archelaus. Dioscorides. HePo, *tr. by* Barbara Hughes Fowler   *Fr.* Epigrams.

Call me to the one among your moments. Rilke. EnlH, *tr. by* Stephen Mitchell   *Fr.* Sonnets to Orpheus.

Call not thy wanderer home as yet. Germinal. "Æ." BIrV; MoBrPo; OBEV; OBMV

Call of Aristippus, The. John Gilbert Cooper.
    Elves and Fairies. ECEV

Call of Nature, The. Tony Harrison. NoAM

Call of the Air, The. Jeffery Day. NSI

Call of the Christian, The. John Greenleaf Whittier. NOCV

Call of the Lake, The. Andrey Andreievich Voznesensky, *Russian.* TCRP; VCWP, *tr. by* Stanley Kunitz

Call of the River Nun, The. Gabriel Okara. PBA

Call of Two Birds, The. Basho *and* Shita Yaba, *Japanese.* APo, *tr. by* Geoffrey Bownas *and* Anthony Thwaite

Call out. Call loud: 'I'm ready! Come and find me!'. Hide and Seek. Vernon Scannell. NOxBChV

Call out the colored girls. For the Record. Audre Lorde. LiLi; LoHo

Call the roller of big cigars. The Emperor of Ice-Cream. Wallace Stevens. AmPP; CBNP; CMoP; FaBoMo; HAP; HCAP; HeIP-4; InPK-6; MeMAP; MoP; NAAL-2; NAWM-2; NIP-4; NOBA; NoAM; NoP-4; OxBA; PoE; PoPoPo; Poetr; SAGP; TAP; TFi; TRP; WeW-3

Call the seller of used cars. Sunday Service. Michael Heffernan. BXAP

Call to Action, A. Ch'iu Chin, *Chinese.* PBWP, *tr. by* Kenneth Rexroth *and* Ling Chung

Call to Action, A. Charles Hamilton Sorley. NSI

Call to Arms. "Lu Hsün," *Chinese.* SuSp, *tr. by* William R. Schultz

Call to Arms. Tso Yen-nien, *Chinese.* CoBCP, *tr. by* Burton Watson

Call to mind. Tanka. Maekawa Samio, *Japanese.* MJT, *tr. by* Makoto Ueda

Call Together. Kohine Whakarua Ponika, *Maori.* PeNZ, *tr. by* Sam Karetu

Call yourself alive? Look, I promise you. Temptation. Nina Cassian, *Romanian.* AF; CEEP, *tr. by* Brenda Walker *and* Andrea Deletant

Callaloo. Merle Collins. NBrP

Call'd out by the clap of the Thunder. Robert Herrick. *See* The Hag ("The Hag is astride").

Called Back. Emily Dickinson. MoAmPo

Called dog men. Royals. James Schuyler. FTOS

Called me. I had no winds or clouds. (LL) Song of the Fallen Deer. *Unknown, Pima.* OBVE, *tr. by* Frank Russell

Called [or Cal'd] out by the clap of the thunder. (LL) The Hag ("The Hag is astride"). Robert Herrick. BeJo; CaPo; FaBoCh

Called out on Christmas Eve for a working-party. Devil on Ice. Donald Davie. NoAM

Called Proud. Walter Savage Landor. GBL; GLoP

Caller Herrin'. Carolina Oliphant, Baroness Nairne. OxBS; WoRP

Caller rain frae abune. Frae the Aiolic o Psappho. Sappho, *Greek.* OBCVT, *tr. by* Douglas Young

Caller rain frae abune. Douglas Young. OBVE

Callicles' Song. Matthew Arnold. *See* The Song of Callicles ("Through the black, rushing smoke-bursts").

Calligram, 15 May 1915. Guillaume Apollinaire, *French.* OBWP, *tr. by* O. Bernard

Calligraphy Practice. Ou-yang Hsiu, *Chinese.* CoBCP, *tr. by* Burton Watson

Callin Buddy / Bolden. Callin Buddy. SeSe

Calling all black people, come in, black people, come / on in. (LL) SOS. Imamu Amiri Baraka. BPo; NAAAL; PoBA

Calling all butterflies of every race. Pod of the Milkweed. Robert Frost. LiTM

Calling All Souls. Nguyễn Du, *Vietnamese.* AVP, *tr. by* Huỳnh Sanh Thông

Calling, and Correcting. Robert Herrick. BeJo

Calling black people. SOS. Imamu Amiri Baraka. BPo; MBE; NAAAL; PoBA

Calling on a Taoist Priest in Tai-t'ien Mountain but Failing to See Him. Li Po, *Chinese.* SuSp, *tr. by* Joseph J. Lee

Calling on Peadar O'Donnell at Dungloe. John Hewitt. CIP-2

Calling-One's-Own, song. Ojibway Oral Tradition, Ojibway. ITG, *tr. by* Charles Fenno Thompson *and* Robert Hass

Calling the Child. Karl Shapiro. MoLi

Calling the Doctor (1000 A.D.) Nizami Arudi, *Persian.* ArPe, *tr. by* Omar S. Pound

Calling the Roll. Nathaniel Graham Shepherd. OBCA

Calling to mind[e], mine eie long went about [*or* my eyes went long about]. The Excuse. Sir Walter Ralegh. AAS; SiPS

Calling to [my] mind[e] since first my love begun. Michael Drayton. NOBE; PoEL-2; SCGP   *Fr.* Idea.

Calling Trains. *Unknown.* AmFP

Calliope. *Unknown.* AS

Calliope in the Labour Ward. Elaine Feinstein. BrRo

Callipaedia; or, The Art of Getting Beautiful Children. Claude Quillet, *Latin.*

Process of Conception, The.

Calloused grass lies hard, The. By the Road to the Air-Base. Yvor Winters. PFE

Calls through the valleys of Hall. (LL) Song of the Chattahoochee. Sidney Lanier. APN-2; ColAP; FaBoBe

Calm[e], The. Donne. NoSic; OxBoS

(Calme, The.) PBRV

("I should not then thus feele this miserie.") (LL) PBRV

("Our storme is past, and that storms tyrannous rage.") PBRV

Calm, The. Suicide's Note. Langston Hughes. PoPoPo; SAmP

Calm after the Storm, The. Giacomo Leopardi. ItIP

Calm and alone, in his private derelict sandlorry / named *Albion.* (LL) Gasholders, russet among fields. Mildams, marpools. Geoffrey Hill. HAP; NoAM

Calm and lovely paradise, A. Nathaniel Parker Willis. APN-1 *Fr. Melanie.*

Calm as that second summer which precedes. Charleston. Henry Timrod. APN-2; AmPP; CBCWP; ColAP; NOBA; OxBA; TAP

Calm down, my sorrow, we must move with care. Meditation. Charles Baudelaire, *French.* InPK-6; NAWM-2, *tr. by* Robert Lowell

Calm garden. French Garden. Léopold Sédar Senghor, *French.* NegPo, *tr. by* Ellen Conroy Kennedy

Calm hair, meandering in pellucid gold. (LL) On Seeing a Hair of Lucretia Borgia. Walter Savage Landor. HAP; SCGP; WeW-3

Calm is the landscape when the storm has passed. Peace in the Welsh Hills. Vernon Watkins. GTBS-P; OxBTC

Calm is the morn without a sound. Lincolnshire Wolds and Lincolnshire Sea. Tennyson. EBEV; EBVV; EnVR; FHYEP; HeIP-4; NOBE; OBNC; PeECV; PoEL-5 *Fr.* In Memoriam A H. H.

Calm on the bosom of thy God. Dirge. Felicia Dorothea Hemans. OBEV; WoRP *Fr.* The Siege of Valencia.

Calm, on the Listening Ear of Night. Edmund Hamilton Sears. AH

Calm, sad, secure; behind high convent walls. Nuns of the Perpetual Adoration. Ernest Christopher Dowson. ADE

Calm Soul of All Things! [Make It Mine]. Matthew Arnold. *See* Lines Written in Kensington Gardens.

Calm thou mayst smile, when all around thee weep. (LL) Epigram. "On parent knees, a naked new-born child." Sir William Jones, *after the Sanskrit of* Kalidasa. FaBoEE; OBEV; OxBSP

Calm[e] was the day, and through the trembling air [*or* ayre]. Prothalamion. Edmund Spenser. AAS; AWP; EBEV; GTBS-P; HAP; NoSic; OBEV; TFi

Calm was the day, and through the trembling air. Edmund Spenser. EBEvV; ImPo; SCGP *Fr.* Prothalamion. AAS; AWP; EBEV; GTBS-P; HAP; NoP-4; NoSic; OBEV; TFi

("Calme was the day, and through the trembling ayre.") OxAEP-1

Calm Winter Sleep. Hilary Corke. NYBP

Calme, The. Donne. *See* The Calm[e].

Calmly he smoked till he'd finished his pipe. The Ballad of the Nails. Nikolai Semionovich Tikhonov, *Russian.* TCRP, *tr. by* Michael Frayn

Calmly We Walk Through This April's Day. Delmore Schwartz. *See* For Rhoda.

Calphurnia here, my wife, stays me at home. Shakespeare. OxBSn *Fr.* Julius Caesar.

Caltrop leaves tug on the waves, the lotus quivers in the wind. Lotus-gatherer's Song. Po Chü-i, *Chinese.* SuSp, *tr. by* Irving Y. Lo

Calum thonder, long's the night to your thinking. To a Loch Fyne Fisherman. George Campbell Hay. FaBoTC

Calvary. Padraig De Brun, *Irish.* TIRV, *tr. by* Máire Mhac an tSaoi

Calvary. Sorley MacLean. FaBoTC

Calvary. Edwin Arlington Robinson. GI; MoAmPo; Son

Calvary. *Unknown.* AH

"Calvary." W. B. Yeats. GI; PeECV

("But howling wind and solitary birds.") (LL) GI

"I am Judas." GI

Calverly's. Edwin Arlington Robinson. NoAM

Calvinist Sang. Alexander Scott. OxBS

Calv'ry's tragedy is ended. The Empty Tomb. Clara Ann Thompson. CBWP-2

Calvus to a Fly. Charles Tennyson Turner. NOBVV

Calypso. W. H. Auden. CBLP; PeLV

Calypso / Is a bit of a dipso. Forever Ambrosia. Christopher Darlington Morley. OBAL

Calypsomania. Anthony Brode. PeLV

Calypso's Song to Ulysses. Adrian Mitchell. GBL

Calyx of the Oboe Breaks, The. Conrad Potter Aiken. NYBP

Cam' Ye By [the Salmon Fishers]. *Unknown.* CH

Cambodia. James Fenton. AF

Cambrian. Eeva-Liisa Manner, *Finnish.*

"If they wanted freedom." PBWP

"To move over shifting borders." PBWP

"Turn the page of stone and there." PBWP

Cambrian Night. James Solheim. PuP-15

Cambrian Swain, The. Edward Davies. *Fr. Chepstow: A Poem.* OBWVE

Cambridge. John James. NBrP

Cambridge Elegy. Sharon Olds. IMW

Cambridge ladies who live in furnished souls, The. E. E. Cummings. AmPP; HeIP-4; MoP; NAAL-2; NOBA; NoAM; NoP-4; OBAL; OxBA; Poetr; SAGP; TAP

Cambridge Songs. *Unknown, Latin.*

"Wind is thin." BoWoP, *tr. by* Willis Barnstone

Camden, most reverend head, to whom I owe. To William Camden. Ben Jonson. AWP; BeJo; NAEL-1; NOSC

Came a stranger late among us. In Memory of James M. Rathel. Josephine D. Henderson Heard. CBWP-4

Came back untouched. This man hath travelled well. (LL) To William Roe. ("Roe (and my joy to name) th'art now, to go"). Ben Jonson. BeJo; OAEL-1

Came fresh transfigurings of freshest blue. (LL) Sea Surface Full of Clouds. Wallace Stevens. AmPP; CMoP; MoAmPo; VGW

Came from the savage carpet. (LL) When the Five Prominent Poets. Josephine Jacobsen. NMM-2

Came in my full youth to the midnight cave. Ajanta. Muriel Rukeyser. LiTM; MoAmPo; NNaP

Came lassitude and despair of the mind. Richard Eberhart. *Fr. Brotherhood of Men.* PoWW

Came Neptunus / his mind leaping / like dolphins. Canto 116. Ezra Pound. APSN *Fr. Cantos.*

Came to lakes; came to dead water. A Field of Light. Theodore Roethke. LiTM; TwCP

Came to me— / Who? Basil Bunting, *after the Persian of* Rudaki. BoLoP; OBVE

Came to me— / Who? Rudaki, *Persian.* LoP, *tr. by* Basil Bunting

Came to my side, and put down his head in love. (LL) The Dream. Louise Bogan. InPK-6; LiTM; MoAmPo; NALW; NoAM

Camel. Boris Alekseievich Chichibabin, *Russian.* TCRP, *tr. by* Albert C. Todd

Camel. Laila Akhyaliyya, *Arabic.* BoWoP, *tr. by* Willis Barnstone

Camel and plow. The sharp blade. Tiller of the Soil. Avraham Shlonsky, *Hebrew.* MHP, *tr. by* Ruth Finer Mintz

Camel at the close of day, The. The Kneeling Camel. Anna Temple Whitney. BLPA

Camel-Rider, The. *Unknown, Arabic.* AWP, *tr. by* Wilfrid Scawen Blunt

Camelia. Igor Moiseievich Irtenev, *Russian.* TCRP, *tr. by* Bradley Jordan

Camellias. Linda Pastan. IFJA

Camellias. Tanka. Akiko Yosano, *Japanese.* MJT, *tr. by* Makoto Ueda

Camel's Complaint, The. Charles Edward Carryl. NOxBChV; OBCA; OxBChV *Fr. The Admiral's Caravan.*

(Song of the Camel, The.) OTCP

Camels, the Kings' Camel, The. Leslie Norris. OBCP; PChr

Cameo, The. Edna St. Vincent Millay. FYAP; MeMAP; MoAmPo; UnPo; WPE

Cameo in Sudden Light. Lorenzo Thomas. FTOS

Cameo No. II. June Jordan. BPo

Cameos. Rita Dove. NAmP90

Camera. Ted Kooser. Poetsp

Camera angles. Drear lighting. Mediatrix. David Haynes. NBrP

Camera at the crossing sees the city. Gauley Bridge. Muriel Rukeyser. NNaP

Camera Obscura, The. John Addington Symonds. NOBVV

camera pans a gorgeous snow-filled landscape: rolling hills, large black trees, a frozen river. The snow falls and falls. The camera stops to find Tennyson, in an armchair, in the middle of a snowy field, The. Cinema Vérité: The Death of Alfred, Lord Tennyson. Tom Andrews. BAP-94

Camerados. Bayard Taylor. UnPo

Camilla goes to war. Virgil, *Latin.* OBCVT, *tr. by* John Dryden

Camoëns. Herman Melville. NCAP

Camões, alone, of all the lyric race. Luis de Camões. Roy Campbell. FaBoTw; OxAEP-2; PeSA

Camoes and the Debt. Sophia de Mello Breyner Andresen, *Portuguese.* BoWoP, *tr. by* Willis Barnstone *and* Nelson Cerqueira

Camouflaged, they detach lengths of sea and sky. Destroyers in the Arctic. Alan Ross. PoWW

Camouflaged Troop-Ship. Amy Lowell. AiP

Camouflaging the Chimera. Yusef Komunyakaa. WeT

Camp, The. Mary Robinson. NOBRP

Camp in the Prussian Forest, A. Randall Jarrell. CMoP; HP; MoAmPo; OBWP; OxBC; PoWW

Camp Notes. Mitsuye Yamada. WPOW

In the Outhouse.

On the Bus.

Camp of Souls, The. Isabella Valancy Crawford. NOBC

Camp Site. Denis Glover. PeNZ *Fr.* Arawata Bill.

Campaign, The. Joseph Addison.

Poem to His Grace the Duke of Marlborough, A. OBWP

Campaign. Ciaran Carson. BiHa; CIP-2; PNI

Campaign, The. Josephine Miles. WPE

Campaign. Muriel Rukeyser. GM

Campèa. Andrea Zanzotto, *Italian*. VCWP, *tr. by* Ruth Feldman *and* Brian Swann (b. 1940)

Campesino looked at the air, A. Problems With Hurricanes. Victor Hernandez Cruz. LoL; PmAP

Campfire Extinguished. Raymond Roseliep. HA; InPK-6

Campfireburners. Anatoly Zhigulin, *Russian*. TCRP, *tr. by* Vladimir Lunis *and* Albert C. Todd

Camphor Laurel. Judith Wright. BMAP

Campi Flegrei. Barend Toerien, *Afrikaans*. PeSA, *tr. by the author*

Campidoglio. Robert Garioch, *after* Guiseppe Belli. OBVE

Camping Out. William Empson. CMoP; FaBoMo; OxBTC

Camping Out on Rainy Mountain. Jim Barnes. CDW

Camping Provencal. Notices: (1). Peter Reading. PeLV *Fr.* Travelogue.

Campion white, The. The Lamp Flower. Margaret Cecilia Furse. BoTP

Campo dei Fiori. Czeslaw Milosz. HP

Camptown Races, The. Gwine to Run All Night; or, De Camptown Races. Stephen Collins Foster. OBAL

Campus, The. David Posner. NYBP

Campus on the Hill, The. W. D. Snodgrass. AiP; LiTM; NoAM; TAP; TwCP

Can a sad song take the place of crying? Sad Song. *Unknown, Chinese*. CoBCP, *tr. by* Burton Watson

Can America be reckoned as the country of the free? The Negro Ballot. Lizelia Augusta Jenkins Moorer. CBWP-3

Can anything surprise me more. Fruit Tree. Song-yong Park, *Korean*. CKP, *tr. by* Jaihiun Kim

Can be heavenly. (LL) The Frog Prince. Stevie Smith. HAP; NTP

Can blot the star that shines on Paris now. (LL) Verlaine. Edwin Arlington Robinson. APN-2; NAAL-2; NCAP

Can Bourbon or Nassau claim [*orxit; go*] higher? (LL) On Himself. Matthew Prior. FaBoEE; OBCoV

Can-Can. John Fuller. PeLV *Fr.* Fox-Trot.

Can centre both the worlds of Heaven and Hell. (LL) Stanzas: "Often rebuked, yet always back returning." Emily Jane Brontë. GEA; NALW; NOBVV; OAEL-2; OBEV; OBNC; PBWP; PEW; SCGP; VWP

Can come as often as he wants. (LL) Doesn't he realize / that I am not / like the swaying kelp. Ono no Komachi, *Japanese*. BoWoP; WPJ; WPOW, *tr. by* Kenneth Rexroth *and* Ikuko Atsumi

Can e'er define. Anne Collins. *See* Another Song.

Can ever withstand these woes. Ben King. *See* The Pessimist.

Can get across it if I try. (LL) I May, I Might, I Must. Marianne Moore. ChAP; FaBoWP; OBAL; OxBSP; PFE

Can God delight in such a sight. Michael Wigglesworth. NAAL-3 *Fr.* The Day of Doom. NAAL-1; SCAP

Can he be fair that withers at a blast. Francis Quarles. PeECV *Fr.* Pentelogia.

Can. Hist. Earle Birney. OxBC

Can I explain this to you? Your eyes. The Knife. Keith Douglas. NoAM

Can I forget thee? No, while mem'ry lasts. On Parting with a Friend. Mary Weston Fordham. CBWP-2

Can I go on loving anyone at fifty. The Book of Wisdom. Robert Lowell. ChIV-1

Can I not sin, but thou wilt be. To His Conscience. Robert Herrick. BeJo; ChIV-1; NAEL-1; NoP-4; PoEL-3

Can I not sing but "hoy." The Jolly Shepherd. *Unknown*. NOBE

Can—I—poet. For Some Poets. Mae Jackson. PoBA

Can I Say. Dolly Bird. WPOW

Can I see another's woe. On Another's Sorrow. William Blake. AWP; FHYEP; OxAEP-2; PoEL-4; Ro *Fr.* Songs of Innocence.

"Can I Tempt You to a Pond Walk?" James Schuyler. PoA

Can I, who have for others oft compil'd. Of My Dear Son [*or Deare Sonne*]. Gervase Beaumont. Sir John Beaumont. IMW; NOBE

Can it be. Living Alone with Jesus—. Maxine W. Kumin. UnSA

Can it be growing colder when I begin. Adrienne Rich. NAAL-2 *Fr.* Twenty-one Love Poems. GLP

Can it be right to give what I can give? Sonnet. Elizabeth Barrett Browning. CTC; Son *Fr.* Sonnets from the Portuguese.

Can it be true, that we can meet. Slumbering Passion. Josephine D. Henderson Heard. CBWP-4

Can keep my own away from me. (LL) Waiting. John Burroughs. BLPA; FaBoBe

Can lid smashed into a likeness of the mad English king, George / the Third. (LL) You were wearing your Edgar Allan Poe printed cotton blouse. Kenneth Koch. SPE

Can Life be a blessing. Song from Troilus and Cressida. Dryden. NoP-4 *Fr.* Troilus and Cressida.

Can life's best consciousness of joy. Questioning. Henrietta Cordelia Ray. CBWP-3

Can. Lit. Earle Birney. NOBC

Can love be controlled by advice? Song. John Gay. OxBSP *Fr.* The Beggar's Opera. OAEL-1

"Can make a right Rose Tree." (LL) The Rose Tree. W. B. Yeats. CMoP; FaBoPV; OBMV

Can man forget this story? (LL) A Hymn[e] on the Nativity [*or Nativitie*] of My Saviour. Ben Jonson. BeJo; ChIV-2; TrCP

Can never fail cuckolding two or three spouses. (LL) Two or Three; a Recipe [*or Receipt*] to Make a Cuckold. Alexander Pope. BoLoP; FaBoEE

Can nothing great, and at the height. Chorus. Petronius Arbiter. OBCVT, *tr. by* Ben Jonson *Fr.* Catiline his Conspiracy.

Can nothing settle my uncertain breast. Galatians 6.14. Francis Quarles. ChIV-2

Can one make works which are not works of "art"? Speculations. Marcel Duchamp. PFTM

Can one take captives by writing. Lyn Hejinian. FTOS *Fr.* The Guard.

Can ratt-rime and ragments o' quenry. A Drunk Man Looks at the Thistle. "Hugh MacDiarmid."

Can redwhite & blue I enter. Self World. Clarence Major. NBV

Can someone make my simple wish come true? Lonely Hearts. Wendy Cope. OBCoV

Can steal from us the far-famed name of Homer. (LL) Sky will extinguish its stars, and the sun, The. Philip of Thessalonica, *Greek*. GrAn; OBCVT, *tr. by* Edwin Morgan

Can still propose the old labors. (LL) Heroes. Robert Creeley. NOBA; NoP-4

Can the German language crack and snore and rumble, thunder. The German Language. Friedrich von Logau, *German*. GePo, *tr. by* George C. Schoolfield

Can the lover share his soul. Epithalamium. Walter James Turner. OBMV

Can the Mole Take. C. Day Lewis. OBMV

Can the river alone run? A Flock of Birds. Chung-hee Moon, *Korean*. CKP, *tr. by* Jaihiun Kim

Can the single cup of wine. To his Brother Hsing-chien. Po Chü-i, *Chinese*. ChiP, *tr. by* Arthur Waley

Can there be a collision between picture and application? Steve McCaffery. FTOS *Fr.* Evoba.

Can there be a moon in heaven to-night. Isabelle. James Hogg. BXAP

Can there be anything more mean. On Sir Joshua Reynolds. William Blake. OxBoV

Can these movements which move themselves. Belly Dancer. Diane Wakoski. NALW; NoAM

Can think of all this with nostalgia. (LL) Christmas Family Reunion. Peter De Vries. NBLV; NOBL

Can this decay, but is beginning ever. (LL) A Fragment of Petronius. Petronius Arbiter, *Latin*. EP; LoP; NNPT; OBCVT, *tr. by* Ben Jonson

Can Tho, *favela* of crowing cocks. Herbert Krohn. CDa

Can u walk away from ugly. Positives for Sterling Plumpp. Don L. Lee. PoBA

Can Vei La Lauzeta Mover. Bernard de Ventadour, *Provençal*. APSN, *tr. by* Paul Blackburn

Can we imagine our rewards. (LL) The Picture of Little J. A. in a Prospect of Flowers. John Ashbery. CoAmPo; PmAP

Can we not force from widdowed Poetry. Thomas Carew. *See* An Elegie upon the Death of the Deane of Pauls, Dr. Donne.

Can we not force from widowed poetry. An Elegie upon the Death of the Deane of Pauls, Dr. Donne. Thomas Carew. BeJo; CABP; CaPo; CavPo; EPCY; MeLP; NoP-4; OAEL-1; SeCP

Can Ye Sew Cushions? *Unknown*. FaBoCh

Can You Change a Shilling? Toni Del Renzio. SPE

Can you dig the recognition performance. Garden. Cecil Taylor. MoNo

Can you feel the swell—. Early Triangles. Ron Padgett. FTOS

Can You Imagine. Artur Miedzyrzecki, *Polish*. PoSu, *tr. by* Stanislaw Baranczak *and* Clare Cavanagh

Can you imagine joy. Relining Shelves. Nellie Wong. NMM-2

Can you keep a secret? *Unknown*. LB

Can you make me a cambric [*or cambriek*] shirt. *Unknown*. CBLP; CBNP; OxNR

Can You Paint a Thought? John Ford. PoEL-2 *Fr.* The Broken Heart.

Can your foreigner's nose smell mullets. Who Among You Knows the Essence of Garlic? Garrett Kaoru Hongo. InPS-3; WeT

Cana. Thomas Merton. ChIV-2; GI; TrCP
("Once when our eyes were clean as noon.") GI

Cana. Peter Steele. GI

Cana Revisited. Seamus Heaney. FaBoMo; GI

Canaan. Muriel Spark. NYBP

Canaan, oh Canaan! Benyamin Galai, *Hebrew*. MHP, *tr. by* Ruth Finer Mintz

Canada: Case History: 1973. Earle Birney. PeLV

Canada-I-O ("Come all ye jolly lumbermen and listen to my song"). Ephraim Braley. AmFP

Canada-I-O ("There was a gallant lady all in her tender youth"). *Unknown*. AmFP

Canadian Authors Meet, The. Francis Reginald Scott. NOBC

Canadian Boat Song. John Galt *and* "Christopher North." BLPA; FaBoCh; FaPoR; OBEV; OBNC; OxBS

Canadian Prairies View of Literature, The. David Donnell. NOBC

Canadian Song. *Unknown*. NSI

Canadians. Ivor Gurney. FaBoTw

Canal Bank Walk. Patrick Kavanagh. CIP-2; CMoP; FaBoTw; MoBrPo; NoAM; NoP-4

Canal Street. John Wheelwright. PoA

Canaries in Uncle Arthur's Basement, The. Ed Ochester. CMAP

Canaries were his hobby. The Glass Blower. James Scully. NYBP; TwCP

Canary. Rita Dove. LoL; SeSe; VCAP

Canary, The. Ogden Nash. PeLV

Canary, The. Elizabeth Turner. OxBChV; PeP

Canary-bird, who painted you? The Canary in a Cage. T(stilde;a)n Đà, *Vietnamese*. AVP, *tr. by* Huỳnh Sanh Thông

Canary-birds feed on sugar and seed. The Camel's Complaint. Charles Edward Carryl. CTAV; NOxBChV; OBCA; OTCP; OxBChV *Fr.* The Admiral's Caravan.

Canary in a Cage, The. T(stilde;a)n Đà, *Vietnamese*. AVP, *tr. by* Huỳnh Sanh Thông

Canberra in April. J. R. Rowland. NOBAu

Cancelled Passages of the Poem. Shelley. *Fr.* Adonais; An Elegy on the Death of Keats. EBEV; FHYEP; HoPM; ImPo; NOBRP; OAEL-2; OxAEP-2; PoEL-4; TFi

Cancelled Stanza of the Mask of Anarchy. Shelley. *Fr.* The Mask [*or* Masque] of Anarchy. FHYEP; OBSV; OxAEP-2; RB; SCV

Cancer Cells, The. Richard Eberhart. HAP; LiTM

Cancer garden, protected by buildings, one unfinished. Still, The. Thomas Avena. BAP-96

Cancer Winter. Marilyn Hacker. RA

Cancer's a Funny Thing. John Haldane. OxBTC

Cancion: "O love, I never, never thought." Juan II, of Castile, *Spanish*. AWP, *tr. by* George Ticknor

Cancion: "When I am the sky." Denise Levertov. NALW; PoM

Candaules, King of Lydia. The Queen of Lydia. Charles Hubert Sisson. OxBC

Candelaria and the Sea Turtle. Gladys Cardiff. HATNAP

Candid and generous and just. Friendship. William Cowper. FP *Fr.* Friendship.

Candid Man, The. Stephen Crane. MoAmPo *Fr.* War Is Kind.

Candid Professor confesses, A. Limerick. Thomas Thorneley. PeLi

Candidate, The. Horace, *Latin*.
"I grant it true, that others better tell." OBCVT, *tr. by* George Crabbe

Candidi lectores, callide callete; vestrum fovet Psittacum, etc. (LL) Parrot's Soliloquy. John Skelton. NoSic; OxBoLi; PoEL-1

Candle, A. Mother Goose. ReMoGo

Candle. Jacob Isaac Segal, *Yiddish*. CEEP, *tr. by* Seymour Mayne

Candle. Sachiko Yoshihara, *Japanese*. WPJ, *tr. by* Kenneth Rexroth *and* Ikuko Atsumi

Candle a Saint, The. Wallace Stevens. PoRA

Candle casts dark shadows, The. Li Shang-yin, *Chinese*. OHMPC, *tr. by* Kenneth Rexroth

Candle Indoors, The. Gerard Manley Hopkins. ChIV-2; ImPo; LiTM; OxAEP-2; PoEL-5

Candle-Light. Olive Custance. ADE

Candle lit in darkness of black waters, A. On the Lake. Vita Sackville-West. OBMV

Candle takes the first desperate, The. Homage to Chagall. Duane Niatum. CDW

Candlelight. Kumch'an Hwang, *Korean*. CKP, *tr. by* Jaihiun Kim

Candlemas Day. Sister Mary Madeleva. CRP

Candles. Sylvia Plath. NMM-2

Candles. Hélène Swarth, *Dutch*. WPOW, *tr. by* Jonathan Crewe

Candles Draw Well after All, The. Laura Jensen. LCAP-2

Candles. Red tulips, ninety cents the bunch. Evening Musicale. Phyllis McGinley. OBAL; OBCoV; Son

Candlestick, The. Jaroslav Seifert, *Czech*. AF, *tr. by* Ewald Osers

Candour of the gods is in thy gaze, The. Sonnet XLIII: "Candour of the gods is in thy gaze, The." George Santayana. APN-2 *Fr.* Sonnets.

Candour spurned, and art rewarded. (LL) January, 1795. Mary Robinson. ECWP; WoRP

Candy / Is dandy. Reflections on Ice-breaking. Ogden Nash. AiP; ImPo; LiTM; NBLV; NoP-4; OBAL; PeLV

Candy Lady, The. Laura Boss. UnSA

Candy man was guid tae me, The. *Unknown*. FaBoVe

Cane of Ch'iung Bamboo, The. Hsü Chung-hsing, *Chinese*. CoBLCP, *tr. by* Jonathan Chaves

Canicula. Mary Kinzie. FFC

Canis Major. Robert Frost. KaS; MoAmPo

Canna turn Arthur O'Bower. (LL) The Wind. *Unknown*. FaBoCh; OxNR

Canner, Exceedingly Canny, A. Limerick. Carolyn Wells. PeLi

Cannery Town in August. Lorna Dee Cervantes. NoAM

Cannibal. Thom Gunn. NOxBChV *Fr.* Three for Children.

Cannibal. Léon Laleau. NegPo, *tr. by* Ellen Conroy Kennedy *Fr.* Black Music.

Cannibal Hymn, The. *Unknown, Egyptian*. TTY, *tr. by* Samuel A. B. Mercer

Cannibalism. Diana Chang. WPOW

Canning. Marge Piercy. *Fr.* Six Underrated Pleasures. EC2

Canning Season. Wendy Barkar. IFJA

Cannot for less be told. (LL) The Elixir [*or* Elixer]. George Herbert. BoTP; ESCV; EnlH; FMP; FaBoCh; GeHe; NOSC; NoP-4

Cannot pull it up. (LL) The Well. Mother Goose. OxNR; ReMoGo

"Cannot quite expect that. You ain't ruined," said she. (LL) The Ruined Maid. Thomas Hardy. DoLoP; CMoP; FaBoSe; FaBoVe; HeIP-4; NAEL-2; NBLV; NOBL; NoP-4; OxBTC; PeLV; PeVV; PoPoPo; SCV; TFi; TRP

Cannot, the tempest tells me, disappoint. (LL) Rain, midnight rain, nothing but the wild rain. Edward Thomas. NoP-4

Canny bord ower there. Rape. Tom Pickard. FaBoTw

Canny moment, lucky fit. The Nativity Chant. Sir Walter Scott. FaBoCh *Fr.* Guy Mannering.

Canoer, The. Diane Wakoski. HeIP-4

Canogait [*or* Cano&[;n&];gait] kirkyaird in the failing year. At Robert Fergusson's Grave[, October 1962]. Robert Garioch. FaBoTC; OxBS

Canon Assistant's Tale, The. Chaucer. OxBoV *Fr.* The Canterbury Tale.

Canonical Hours. William Dickey. CoAP

Canonization, The. Donne. CABP; CBLP; ESCV; EnLoPo; FHYEP; FMP; FSCP; FaBoVe; GLoP; HAP; NAEL-1; NAWM-1; NIP-4; NOBE; NOSC; NoP-4; OAEL-1; PBRV; PoE; PoEL-2; PoPoPo; SCGP; SeCP; SoSe-8; TFi; TRP; UnPo

Canopic old Egyptian jugs. Instructions for Your New Osiris. Lorenzo Thomas. PmAP

Canopus. Bert Leston Taylor. NOBL

Canopy of nerve ends. Epiderm. Michael Dransfield. BMAP; CBAP

Canst think the cargoe wherewith ship is fraught. Upon the Decease of Mrs. Anne Griffin. John Fiske. SCAP

Canst thou by searching find out God? Job's Comforters. Bible, *O.T. Fr.* Job. NAWM-1

Canst Thou Draw Out Leviathan with an Hook. Allen Curnow. PeNZ

Canst thou draw out Leviathan with an hook[e]? Leviathan. Bible, *O.T.* OBVE *Fr.* Job. NAWM-1

Canst thou hale up the huge leviathan. Leviathan. Joshua Sylvester. KSG *Fr.* Job Triumphant.

Canst thou imagine where those spirits live. Shelley. *Fr.* Prometheus Unbound. NOBRP; OAEL-2

Canst thou indeed be he that still would sing. Dante. AWP *Fr.* La Vita Nuova.

Cant. Imamu Amiri Baraka. NAAL-2

Can't be a model, there'd be times I. Terri. Alan Wearne. BMAP *Fr.* The Nightmarkets.

Can't find what you can't see / can you? (LL) American History. Michael S. Harper. BPo; HCAP; NoAM; PoPoPo

Cant. 5.6 & c. Elizabeth Singer. ChIV-1; KTR

Can't make excuses for you, Cinque. Cinque. Janet Campbell Hale. VoR

"Can't see out of my left eye." Spinning. Alfred Wellington Purdy. NOBC; NoAM

Can't seem to wake you, kid, guess it. The Body Beside the Ties. Kenneth Patchen. CLPP

Can't Stand It. Vladimir Mayakovsky, *Russian*. TCRP, *tr. by* Bernard Meares

Can't swim; uses credit cards and pills to combat. The Difference Between Pepsi and Coke. David Lehman. PmAP

Can't Tell. Nellie Wong. LTA; OpBo; UnSA

("We wore black arm bands, / put up a sign / in bold letters.") (LL) UnSA

Can't we find some way / to meet again. To Ibn Zaidun. Wallāda, *Arabic*. WPOW, *tr. by* James Monroe *and* Deirdre Lashgari

Can't wring blood from. Lepidoptery. James Sherry. FTOS

Can't You Line It? *Unknown.* NAAAL

Cantares Mexicanos. *Unknown, Aztec.*

Chalcan Female Song. PFTM, *tr. by* John Bierhorst

Cantata. Jack Spicer. APSN

Cantata, A. Jonathan Swift. CBNP

Canter has two stride patterns, one on the right lead and one on the left, The. The Flying Change. Henry Taylor. Poetr

Canterbury Tales, The, *Line numbers in diff. anthologies may refer to diff. manuscript sources, sels.* Chaucer.

Canterbury Tales, The. Geoffrey Chaucer, *Middle English.*

Canon Assistant's Tale, The. OxBoV, *tr. by* David Wright

Cook's Tale, The. BXAP

Franklin's Prologue, The. NAEL-1; OAEL-1

Franklin's Tale, The. NAEL-1; OAEL-1

Friar's Prologue, The. PoE

Friar's Tale, The. PoE

General Prologue, The. FHYEP; NAEL-1; OAEL-1; PoE

("As soon as April pierces to the root.") NAWM-1

("Began to tell his tale, as you shall hear.") (LL) NAWM-1

("His tale anoon, and saide as ye may heere.") (LL) NAEL-1

General Prologue, The. CABP; NoP-4

("His tale anoon, and saide as ye may heere.") (LL) NoP-4

("Whan that Aprill with his shoures soote.") CABP; SAGP, *tr, by* Christopher Burns

("When the sweet showers of April fall and shoot.") SCV, *ll.* 1–42, *mod. vers. by* Nevill Coghill

Madame Eglantine. NOBE

"Marchant was ther with a forked berd, A." CTC

"Sergeant of the Lawe, war and wys, A." CTC

"Somonour was ther with us in that place, A." OBCoV

"This Pardoner had hair as yellow as wax." SCV

Introduction to the Franklin's Prologue and Tale. NAEL-1

Introduction to the Pardoner's Prologue and Tale. FHYEP; NAEL-1; PoE

Introduction to the Parson's Tale, The. NAEL-1

Miller's Prologue, The. NAEL-1; OAEL-1

("There's no sense making earnest out of game.") (LL) NAWM-1

("When the knight had finished, no one, young or old.") NAWM-1

Miller's [*or* Milleres] Tale, The. NAEL-1; OAEL-1; OxBoLi; PeLV

("God save this troop! That's all I have to tell.") (LL) NAWM-1

("*Miller* was a chap of sixteen stone, The.")

("There used to be a rich old oaf.") NAWM-1

"Fair was this yonge wyf, and therwithal." EBEV

Nun's Priest's Prologue, The. FHYEP

(Prologue of the Nun's Priest's Tale, The.) OAEL-1

("This precious priest, this goodly man, Sir John.") (LL) NAWM-1

Nun's Priest's Tale, The. FHYEP; OAEL-1

("And bring us to your holy bliss! Amen.") (LL) NAWM-1

("Poore widwe [*or* widow], somdeel [*or* somedeal] stape in age, A.") NAEL-1

"There liv'd, as Authors tell, in Days of Yore." OBVE

Pardoner's Prologue, The. FHYEP; NAEL-1; OAEL-1; PoE

("'In churches,' said the Pardoner, "when I preach.'"") NAWM-1

("While preaching. Now be still, and I'll begin.") (LL) NAWM-1

Pardoner's Tale, The. FHYEP; NAEL-1; OAEL-1; PoE

("And so they kissed, and rode along their way.") (LL) NAWM-1

("There was a company of young folk living.") NAWM-1

"But, sires, o word forgat I in my tale." EBEV

Death and the Three Revellers. OBNV

"It's of three rioters I have to tell." SCV

Three Rioters, The. EBNV

Prologue to Sir Thopas. NAEL-1

Tale of Sir Thopas, The. BXAP, *ll.* 1–248; NAEL-1, *ll.* 1–252

Wife of Bath's Prologue, The. FHYEP; NAEL-1; OAEL-1, *ll.* 1–862

("Now wol I seye my tale, if ye wol heere.") (LL) PoEL-1

"Experience, though noon auctoritee." OxBoLi; PeLV; RACG

("Al this sentence me liketh every deel.") (LL) RACG

"If there were no authority on earth." OxBM

"Tell me to what conclusion or in aid." OxBM

Wife of Bath's Tale, The. FHYEP; NAEL-1; OAEL-1

("In th'olde dayes of the Kyng Arthour.") OxBSn

("Ther is noon oother incubus but he.") (LL) OxBSn

Cantica: Our Lord Christ: Of Order. Saint Francis of Assisi, *also at. to* Jacopone da Todi, *Italian,* . AWP; OBVE, *tr. by* D. G. Rossetti

Canticle. Michael McClure. NeAP; PoM

Canticle. David Shapiro. TTTS

Canticle for Abba Jacob, A. Marilyn Nelson Waniek. FFC

Canticle for Good Friday. Geoffrey Hill. ChIV-2

Canticle of Darkness. Wilfred Watson. MoCV

Canticle of Living Creatures. Saint Francis of Assisi. ItIP

Canticle of the Sun. Saint Francis of Assisi, *Italian.* EnlH, *tr. by* Stephen Mitchell

Canticle to Apollo, A. Robert Herrick. CaPo

Canticle to the Waterbirds, A. William Everson. APSN; NeAP; PoM

Cantico del Sole. Saint Francis of Assisi, *Italian.* CTC; OBAL, *tr. by* Ezra Pound

Cantinas, The, *see also* The Lighthouse Invites the Storm. Malcolm Lowry.

Delirium in Vera Cruz. FaBoTw; NoP-4; OxBTC

Canto Amor. John Berryman. CoAP; MoAmPo; VGW

Canto I. Samuel Butler. *See* The Presbyterian Knight.

Canto I (excerpt). Vincente Huidobro. PFTM, *tr. by* Eliot Weinberger *Fr.* Altazor.

Canto I: The Trystyng. "Lewis Carroll." *See* Phantasmagoria.

Canto Llano. Anita Endrezze-Danielson. CDW

Canto 7: First Thesis. Tom Weatherly. PoBA

Canto VII. Louis MacNeice. *See* A Fanfare for the Makers.

Canto XXIII. Ludovico Ariosto.

Orlando's Madness. ItIP

Cantor was reading [*or* would chant] Psalms, The. Requiem after Seventeen Years. Dahlia Ravikovitch, *Hebrew.* IP, *tr. by* Warren Bargad *and* Stanley F. Chyet

Cantos. Ezra Pound.

Canto 1. AmPP; CMoP; MeMAP; MoAmPo; MoP; NoAM; NoP-4; OBVE; PFTM; PoE; VGW

Canto 2. AmPP; HAP; MeMAP; MoAmPo; NOBA; NoAM; OxBA; PoA

Canto 3. MeMAP; TAP

Canto 7. NOBA; NoAM

Canto 13. CMoP; FaBoMo; PoE

Canto 17. InPS-3; MeMAP; NAAL-2; OBMV

Canto 36. OBVE

(Canzone: Donna Mi Priegha.) CTC

("Quan ben m'albir e mon ric pensamen.") (LL) OBVE

Canto 45. CMoP; ColAP; LiTM; MeMAP; NAAL-2; NOBA; PoE

Canto 46. "Semi-private inducement." OxBoV

Canto 47. CMoP; PoE; VGW

Canto 80. PoA

("But oblivion, not thy forgiveness, FRANCE.") (LL) FaBoTw

Canto 81. CMoP; FaBoMo; FaBoTw; HAP; MoP; NAAL-2; NOBA; NOBE; NoAM; OxBA; PoE; RaBo; VGW

Canto 90. APSN; VGW

Canto 113. NYBP

From 115. APSN; FaBoMo

Canto 116. APSN

Cantos. Tom Weatherly. PoBA

Coon Fire.

First Thesis.

Gullfish.

Canute at Ely. *Unknown.*

Cnut's Song. PoE

Canyon de Chelly. Simon J. Ortiz. PaTW

Canzone: "Consider the three functions of the tongue." Marilyn Hacker. NoAM

Canzone: "Love, which is least sure and most dared, the pure, keen." Peyton Houston. *Fr.* Sonnet Variations. Son

Canzone: "No better lost than any other woman." Marilyn Hacker. NoAM

Canzone: Donna Mi Priegha. Ezra Pound. *See* Canto 36.

Canzone: He Beseeches Death for the Life of Beatrice. Dante, *Italian.* AWP, *tr. by* D. G. Rossetti

Canzone: He Speaks of His Condition through Love. Folcachiero de' Folcachieri, *Italian.* AWP, *tr. by* D. G. Rossetti

Canzone: His Lament for Selvaggia. Cino da Pistoia, *Italian.* AWP, *tr. by* D. G. Rossetti

Canzone: His Portrait of His Lady, Angiola of Verona. Fazio degli Uberti, *Italian.* AWP, *tr. by* D. G. Rossetti

Canzone: Of His Dead Lady. Giacomino Pugliesi, *Italian*. AWP, tr. by D. G. Rossetti

Canzone: Of His Love, with the Figure of a Sudden Storm. Prinzivalle Doria, *Italian*. AWP, tr. by D. G. Rossetti

Canzone: To Love and to His Lady. Guido Delle Colonne, *Italian*. AWP, tr. by D. G. Rossetti

Canzonet. Mary Robinson. NOBRP

Canzonetta: A Bitter Song to His Lady. Pier Moronelli da Fiorenza, *Italian*. AWP; OBVE, tr. by D. G. Rossetti

Canzonetta: He Will Neither Boast nor Lament to His Lady. Jacopo da Lentino, *Italian*. AWP, tr. by D. G. Rossetti

Canzonetta: Of His Lady, and of His Making Her Likeness. Jacopo da Lentino, *Italian*. AWP, tr. by D. G. Rossetti

Canzonetta: Of His Lady in Absence. Giacomino Pugliesi, *Italian*. AWP, tr. by D. G. Rossetti

Cap, a sword, flowers, A. Yury Pavlovich Odarchenko, *Russian*. TCRP, tr. by Nina Kossman

Cap and Bells, The. W. B. Yeats. MoBrPo; NoAM; RB

Cap tipped back, propped by a window, still can't settle down. Sitting Outdoors. Lu Yu, *Chinese*. CoBCP, tr. by Burton Watson

Cape Ann. T. S. Eliot. NAEL-2; NoAM *Fr.* Landscapes. RB

Cape Ann; a View. John Malcolm Brinnin. NYBP

Cape Breton. Elizabeth Bishop. InPS-3

Cape Coast Castle Revisited. Jo Ann Hall-Evans. BlSi

Cape Cod. George Santayana. APN-2

Cape Coloured Batman. Guy Butler. PeSA

Cape Hatteras. Hart Crane. InPS-3; MoAmPo *Fr.* The Bridge. NAAL-2 Power. MoAmPo

Cape Mootch. Boris Pasternak, *Russian*. LoP, tr. by J. M. Cowen

Cape of Storms, The. John Wheatley. PeSAV

Cape show a glimpse of her bare butt. (LL) Although she's a girl, Dorkion. Asclepiades, *Greek*. GrAn; PGA, tr. by Kenneth Rexroth

Capework of the wind. (LL) Sleepless at Crown Point. Richard Wilbur. InPK-6; WeW-3

Capital is fast asleep at dawn, The. Menshikov. Yaroslav Vasilevich Smelyakov, *Russian*. TCRP, tr. by Lubov Yakovleva

Capital Punishment. Sherman Alexie. BAP-96

Capital Punishment. Nina Cassian, *Romanian*. PoSu, tr. by Nine Cassian

Capital ship for an ocean trip, A. The *Walloping Window-Blind*. Charles Edward Carryl. APN-2; NBLV; OBAL; OBCA *Fr.* Davy and the Goblin.

Capitalism. Mark Levine. PUP-19

Capitals Are Rocked, The. Nikolai Alekseyevich Nekrasov, *Russian*. AWP, tr. by Babette Deutsch *and* Avrahm Yarmolinsky

Cap'n, I Believe. *Unknown*. AS

Capped arbiter of beauty in this street. Hart Crane. FaBoMo; ImPo; LiTM *Fr.* For the Marriage of Faustus and Helen. InPS-3; NOBA; NoAM

Capriccio 9. Lyubomir Levchev, *Bulgarian*. CEEP, tr. by Jascha Kessler *and* Aleksandar Shurbanov

Capriccio of Roman Ruins and Sculpture with Figures, A. J. D. McClatchy. GS

Caprichosa. Angelina Weld Grimké. NMM-2

Capricious, avaricious kind—, A. The Russian Mind. Vyacheslav Ivanovich Ivanov, *Russian*. TCRP, tr. by Albert C. Todd

Capricorn Rising. Nathaniel Mackey. MoNo

Captain, The. Francis Beaumont *and* John Fletcher.

  Away, Delights. NOBE; OBEV

  (Sad Song, The.) GBL

Captain, The. Blanca Varela, *Spanish*. WPOW, tr. by Lynne Alvarez

Captain bold in [*or* from] Halifax, that [*or* who] dwelt in country quarters, A. Miss Bailey's Ghost. George, the Younger Colman. OxBoLi

Captain Bunker. *Unknown*. AmFP

Captain calls his crew to the deck, The. The Landing of Rochambeau. Michael Davidson. FTOS

Captain Car. *Unknown*. See Edom o' Gordon.

Captain Carpenter rose up in his prime. John Crowe Ransom. CBNP; FaBoMo; FuPo; HoPM; ImPo; LiTM; MeMAP; MoAmPo; MoP; NOBA; NoAM; OxBA; TRP; TwCP

Captain Cook. *Aborigine Oral Tradition*. NOBAu, tr. by Percy Mumbulla

Captain Craig. Edwin Arlington Robinson.

  "I doubt if ten men in all Tilbury Town." PoEL-5

Captain Fox sits reading metaphysics. Robert Greacen. PNI

Captain Gungho, my men. The Dead at Quang Tri. Yusef Komunyakaa. CDa

Captain James Leson, U. S. M. C. Bryan Alec Floyd. CDa

Captain Jinks. *Unknown*. BLPA

Captain Kidd ("You captains brave and bold, hear our cries, hear our cries"). *Unknown*. AmFP

Captain Molly. William Collins. ImGa

Captain Noah. Frederick Robert Higgins. KSG

Captain of a Seventy-three, The. (LL) Little Billee. William Makepeace Thackeray. FaBoCh; NOBL; OxAEP-2; OxBB

Captain or Colonel, or Knight in Arms. When the Assault Was Intended to the City. Milton. GTBS-P; OAEL-1; OxAEP-1; SCGP; Son

Captain Quiros and Mr William Lane. Terra Australis. Douglas Stewart. NOBAu

Captain Reece. Sir William Schwenck Gilbert. OBCoV

Captain said, Quack! Quack!, The. (LL) I saw a ship a-sailing. Mother Goose. FaBoBe; LB; NTCP; OxNR; ReMoGo

Captain Spud and His First Mate, Spade. John Ciardi. OBCA

Capt. Smith and Pocahontas. Eloise Bibb. CBWP-4

Captain Stratton's Fancy. John Masefield. MoBrPo; OBEV

Captain Ward and the *Rainbow*. *Unknown*. ESPB

Captain Wattle and Miss Roe. Charles Dibdin. OxBoLi

Captain! we often heretofore. To Our House-Dog Captain. Walter Savage Landor. PoEL-4

Captain Wedderburn's Courtship. *Unknown*. AmFP; ESPB

Captains. Nikolai Stepanovich Gumilyov, *Russian*.

  "On polar and on southern seas." TCRP, tr. by Simon Franklin

Captains among the ghosts, heroes among the Dead! (LL) Hymn to the Fallen. *Unknown, Chinese*. ChiP, tr. by Arthur Waley

Captains Courageous. Frank O'Hara. FTOS

Caption for a Miniature. Joanne Kyger. BB

Captive. Peretz Hirshbein, *Yiddish*. TrJP, tr. by Joseph Leftwich

Captive Dove, The. Anne Brontë. EBVV; VWP

Captive Escaped in the Wilds of America. Addressed to the Hon. Mrs. O'Neill, The. Charlotte Smith. Son

Captive mahogany of a private Roman, The. Roman Elegies. Joseph Brodsky, *Russian*. VCWP, tr. by Joseph Brodsky

Captive of the White City. Ina Coolbrith. PaTW

Captive or king, it's all a matter of chance. The Temple of Hsiang Yü. Li Shan-fu, *Chinese*. SuSp, tr. by Irving Y. Lo

Captive Stone, The. Jim Barnes. CDW

Captived Bee; or, The Little Filcher, The. Robert Herrick. CaPo

Captives, bound in iron bands. The Broken Chain. Dora Greenwell. VWP

Captive's Song. *Unknown, Omaha Native American*. APN-2, tr. by Fannie Reed Giffen

Captivity. Louise Erdrich. HATNAP; NoAM

Captivity, The. Oliver Goldsmith.

  O Memory, Thou Fond Deceiver'. OxBSP

  (Memory.) OBEV

Captivity. Samuel Rogers. OBNC

Captivity: The Minks. Toi Derricotte. *See* The Minks.

Capture of Edwin Alonzo Boyd, The. Peter Miller. MoCV

Captured septemberlight. Late Flowers. Helga Marie Heinze, *German*. CEEP, tr. by Katherine Bradley

Caput apri refero. *Unknown*. MiEL

Caput Tuum Ut Carmelus. "Michael Field." CPO

Car Cemetery, The. Ciaran Carson. CIP-2

Car / I give you over to. Car Wash. Myra Cohn Livingston. NTCP

Car is also / a high-speed hermitage, A. Portrait of the Autist as a New World Driver. Les A. Murray. CBAP

Car is heavy with children, The. The Road Back. Anne Sexton. NYBP

Car je suis La Belle France. (LL) The Deodand. Anthony Hecht. DiPo; NoAM

Car shuddered and stopped, The. Last Love. Nikolai Alekseievich Zabolotsky, *Russian*. TCRP, tr. by Daniel Weissbort

Car Wash. Myra Cohn Livingston. NTCP

Caraguin, The. Robert Dunbar.

  "Angelica has gain'd the dell." PBCV

Caravan. Michael Longley. CIP-2; PNI

Caravan, The. Gwendolyn MacEwen. MoCV

Caravan, The. Madeleine Nightingale. BoTP

Caravans. Irene Thompson. BoTP

Carbon Paper. Martin Sorescu, *Romanian*. CEEP, tr. by Irina Livezeanu

Carcassonne. Gustave Nadaud, *French*. BLPA; FaBoBe, tr. by John R. Thompson

Card comes to tell you, A. Non Piangere, Liù. Peter Porter. CBLP; LBC; OxBC

Card-Players, The. Philip Larkin. BLT; OxBC

Card-Players, The. David Ray. VGW

Card table in the library stands ready, A. Lost in Translation. James Merrill. FYAP; HCAP; LCAP-2; NAAL-2; NoAM; NoP-4; VCAP *Fr.* The Book of Ephraim.

Cardboard box of sugared orange—, A. From Superstition. Boris Pasternak, *Russian*. TCRP, tr. by Yakov Hornstein

Cardigan Bay. John Masefield. OxBoS

Cardinal Bembo's Epitaph on Raphael. Thomas Hardy, *after* Pietro Bembo. FaBoEE

Cardinal Detoxes: A Play in One Act, The. Thomas M. Disch. BAP-94

Cardinal Ideograms. May Swenson. NoP-4; OBCA

Cardinal Newman. Christina Rossetti. NAEL-2

Cardinal's Dog, The. John Glassco. MoCV

Cardplayers, The. Jack Spicer. APSN

Cardplayer's glaze is on Gulliver's eyes, The. Gulliver Plays Cards. Nikolai Semionovich Tikhonov, *Russian*. TCRP, *tr. by* Michael Frayn

Cards and Kisses. John Lyly. HoPM; NOBE; OBEV; PBMP *Fr.* Alexander and Campaspe.

   (Cupid and Campaspe.) GTBS-P; OxAEP-1; SCGP

   ("Cupid and my Campaspe play'd.") GLoP

Care. Josephine Miles. NYBP

Care away, away, away, / Care away for evermore! Care Away. *Unknown*. MiEL; OxBoLi

Care away, away, away, / Murninge away! *Unknown*. MiEL

Care-charmer Sleep[e], son[ne] of the sable night. Sonnet. Samuel Daniel. AAS; CABP; GTBS-P; ImPo; InPS-3; NAEL-1; NIP-4; NOBE; NoP-4; NoSic; OAEL-1; OxAEP-1; PoEL-2; SCGP; Son; TFi *Fr.* To Delia.

Care-charmer sleepe, sweet ease in restles miserie. Sleep. Bartholomew Griffin. AAS; NoSic; SCGP *Fr.* Fidessa, More Chaste than Kind[e].

Care-charming sleep, thou easer of all woes. Sleep Song. John Fletcher. NOSC; OxBSP; OxBoLi; PoEL-2; PoRA; SCGP *Fr.* The Tragedy of Valentinian.

Care thy father once bestowed on me, The. To My Nephew, J. B. Clement Barksdale. OxBSP

Careers. Imamu Amiri Baraka. TRP

Careful man I ought to be, A. The Little Chap Who Follows Me. *Unknown*. PoToHe

Careful: my knife drills your soul. The Killer. A'yunini, *Cherokee Indian*. STP, *tr. by* Jerome Rothenberg

Careful[l] observers may foretell the hour. A Description of a City Shower. Jonathan Swift. HeIP-4; NAEL-1; NOEC; NoP-4; OAEL-1; OBSV; PoE; SCGP; UnPo

Carefully dissected her knee. (LL) Miss Gee. W. H. Auden. EBNV; OxBTC; UV

Careless Content. John Byrom. NOEC; OBCoV

Careless explorer named Blake, A. Limerick. Ogden Nash. PeLi

Careless Gallant, The. Thomas Jordan. HAP; OxBoLi

   (Epicure, The, Sung by One in the Habit of a Town Gallant.) NOBE; PeLV

Careless how it struck those nearest to him. The Stranger. Rilke, *German*. FP, *tr. by* J. B. Leishman

Careless hunter, breaking camp, A. Forest Fire. Vadim Sergeievich Shefner, *Russian*. TCRP, *tr. by* Daniel Weissbort

Careless Love. *Unknown*. AS; UnPo

Careless old cook of Salt Ash, A. Limerick. *Unknown*. PeLi

Careless Talk. Mark Hollis. NBLV

Carentan O Carentan. Louis Simpson. CoAP; MoBS; NOBA; OBWP; PoE; RB; WeT

Cares o' love are sweeter far, The. Robert Burns. PBMP

Cargoes. John Masefield. CABP; CMoP; EBEvV; FaPoR; InPK-6; LiTM; MoBrPo; NOBE; OBEV; OBMV; PoRA; TFi

Cargoes of the Radanites. Harry Alan Potamkin. TrJP

Caria and Philistia considered. Cry Faugh! Robert Graves. MoBrPo

Caribbean Exorcism Poem, A. Kendel Hippolyte. HCP

Caribbean Woman Prayer. Grace Nichols. NBrP

Cariboo Horses, The. Alfred Wellington Purdy. HeIP-4; NOBC

Caribou. Robert Penn Warren. APo

Carious Exposure. Gladys Cardiff. CDW

Carissima Joannissima, ave. Letter from the Alpes-Maritimes. Marilyn Hacker. EOEF

C[h]aritas Nimia; or, The Dear[e] Bargain. Richard Crashaw. ESCV; NOCV; NOSC

Carl Hamblin. Edgar Lee Masters. CMoP; LiTM; OBSV *Fr.* Spoon River Anthology.

Carle He Came o'er the Croft, The. Allan Ramsay. OxBS

Carlton Fisk is My Ideal. Bernadette Mayer. DeD

Carlyle combined the lit'ry life. Thomas Carlyle. Dorothy Parker. NALW *Fr.* A Pig's-Eye View of Literature.

Carlyle on Burns. William Jeffrey. OxBS *Fr.* On Glaister's Hill.

Carm. II. Catullus, *Latin*. OBCVT, *tr. by* Thomas Moore

Carmel Point. Robinson Jeffers. BLT; NAAL-2; NoAM; NoP-4

Carmelite. Raymond Murray, *Irish*. TIRV, *tr. by the author*

Carmen. Victor Hernandez Cruz. PoBA

Carmen Elegiacum. Thomas Morton. SCAP

Carmen, or the Made-Up Girl. Lyubomir Levchev, *Bulgarian*. CEEP, *tr. by* Jascha Kessler *and* Aleksandar Shurbanov

Carmen Possum. *Unknown*. BLPA; NBLV

Carmen Saeculare. Charles Hubert Sisson, *after the Latin of* Horace. OBVE

Carmencita loves Patrick. Little Song. Langston Hughes. TLR

Carmina. Catullus, *Latin*

   Carmen 3. (Death of Lesbia's Bird, The.)   AWP, *tr. by* Samuel Taylor Coleridge

   Carmen 4.   AWP; OBVE

      (Yacht, The.) OBVE

      ("Castor & Pollux / the Dioscuri.") (LL) AWP,

      ("My bean-pod boat you see here.") AWP, *tr. by* John Hookham Frere

      ("To thee, bright Castor, and thy Brother Star!") (LL) OBVE

   Carmen 5.   STV, *tr. by* John Frederick Nims; AAS; AWP; EBEV; GBL; HAP; HeIP-4; InPS-3; NAEL-1; OAEL-1; PoE; PoRA; SCGP; TFi; WeW-3, *tr. by* Thomas Campion; OBVE, *tr. by* William Wordsworth

      ("All the sweets of life in love.") (LL) OBVE, *tr. by* Walter Savage Landor

      ("As shall mocke the envious eye.") (LL) OBVE, *tr. by* Richard Crashaw

      (Carmina, V: To Celia.) EP, *tr. by* Ben Jonson

      ("Come and let us live my Deare.") OBVE, *tr. by* Richard Crashaw

      ("Dear *Lesbia* let us love and play.") OBCVT, *tr. by* Chatwin, John

      ("Glitter green, over such a spell of kisses.") (LL) STV, *tr. by* John Frederick Nims

      ("Lesbia / live with me.") AAS; AWP; EBEV; GBL; HAP; HeIP-4; InPS-3; NAEL-1; OAEL-1; OBVE; PoE; PoRA; SCGP; TFi; WeW-3, *tr. by* Thomas Campion

      ("My *Lesbia* and I did kiss.") (LL) OBCVT, *tr. by* John Chatwin

      ("So let's live—really live!—for love and loving.") STV, *tr. by* John Frederick Nims

      ("That never can again be mine.") (LL) OBVE, *tr. by* William Wordsworth

      ("Then must we sleepe one ever-during night.") (LL) OBCVT, *tr. by* Thomas Campion

      ("These have crimes accounted beene.") (LL) EP; OBVE, *tr. by* Ben Jonson

      ("'Tis with us perpetuall night.") (LL) OBCVT, *tr. by* Johnson, Ben

      (Vivamos, Mea Lesbia, atque Amemus.) EBEV, *tr. by* Thomas Campion

      ("With their evil eyes.") (LL) PFE

      ("You of me & / I of you, / darling, have had.") (LL) AAS; AWP; EBEV; GBL; HAP; HeIP-4; InPS-3; NAEL-1; OAEL-1; PoE; PoRA; SCGP; TFi; WeW-3, *tr. by* Thomas Campion; OBVE, *tr. by* William Wordsworth

   See also Song. To Celia by Ben Jonson.

   Carmen 8.   AAS, *tr. by* Thomas Campion; OBCVT, *tr. by* Douglas Young; STV, *tr. by* John Frederick Nims;

      ("But you, Catullus, your destiny's *obdurate*.") (LL) OBVE, *tr. by* Louis Zukofsky *and* Celia Zukofsky

      OBVE, *tr. by* Louis Zukofsky *and* Celia Zukofsky; OBVE, *tr. by* Thomas Campion

      ("Catullus. / Against the past.") (LL) AAS, *tr. by* Thomas Campion

      ("Catullus, still remember to be strong.") (LL) AWP, *tr. by* William Ellery Leonard

      ("Harden now thy tyred hart, with more than flinty rage.") AAS; OBVE, *tr. by* Thomas Campion

      ("Harden now thy tyred hart with more then flinty rage.") OBCVT, *tr. by* Thomas Campion

      ("O poor Catullus, stupid long enough!") STV, *tr. by* John Frederick Nims

      ("Stupid Catullus! Stubborn soul, endure.") (LL) STV, *tr. by* John Frederick Nims

   Carmen 10. AWP, *tr. by* John Hookham Frere.

      ("Alfenus Varus / buttonholes me.") AWP, *tr. by* John Hookham Frere

      (Fib Detected, A.) AWP, *tr. by* John Hookham Frere

      ("It's common as / well as comic.") (LL) AWP, *tr. by* John Hookham Frere

   Carmen 13. OBVE, *tr. by* Richard Lovelace.

   Carmen 22.

      (To Varus.) AWP, *tr. by* Walter Savage Landor

      ("But see not our own Load behind.") (LL) OBVE, *tr. by* Matthew Prior

      ("Suffenus whom you know, the Witty.") OBVE, *tr. by* Matthew Prior

   Carmen 31. STV, *tr. by* John Frederick Nims; OBVE, *tr. by* Thomas Hardy

      ("And art, mine own unrivalled Fair!") (LL) OBVE, *tr. by* Thomas Hardy

      ("And ring out, all ye laughter-peals of home.") (LL) AWP, *tr. by* Charles Stuart Calverley

      ("Even if one wears oneself out paying for them.") (LL)

      ("If the old home can laugh, let's hear it now.") (LL) STV, *tr. by* John Frederick Nims

("Jewel of the almost islands and the isles.") STV, *tr. by* John Frederick Nims

Carmen 34.

(Hymn to Diana.) AWP, *tr. by* Richard Claverhouse Jebb

Carmen 39. OBVE, *tr. by* Walter Savage Landor

Carmen 40. OBVE, *tr. by* Louis Zukofsky *and* Celia Zukovsky

Carmen 45. OBVE, *tr. by* Abraham Cowley; BoLoP

(Acme and Septimius.) AWP; OBVE, *tr. by* Abraham Cowley

("Than here she grants in Love's requite?") (LL) OBVE, *tr. by* Abraham Cowley; BoLoP

("Whilst on Septimius' panting Breast.") AWP; OBVE, *tr. by* Abraham Cowley

Carmen 51. OBCVI, *tr. by* W. E. Gladstone

(Sappho.) AWP, *tr. by* William Ellery Leonard

("And feels a temporary death.") (LL) OBCVT, *tr. by* Byron

("Equal to Jove that youth must be.") OBCVT, *tr. by* Byron

(Translation from Catullus: Ad Lesbiam.) OBCVT, *tr. by* Byron

Carmen 55. *tr. by* Nahum Tate

Carmen 58. OBVE, *tr. by* Nicholas Amhurst; OBCVT, TR. BY Humphrey Clucas *Fr.* Carmina.

Carmen 61. OxBM, *tr. by* Frederic Raphael *and* Kenneth McLeish

Carmen 63. STV, *tr. by* John Frederick Nims (Attis.) OBVE, *tr. by* Peter Whigham

("Over oceans sped he, Attis, in the speediest of ships.") STV, *tr. by* John Frederick Nims

("Spur the others to fey elation; no mad dogs in the house for me.") STV, *tr. by* John Frederick Nims

Carmen 64. APSN, *tr. by* Louis Zukofsky *and* Celia Zukovsky

Carmen 65 ("Grief reached across the world to get me"). Catullus. *Fr.* Carmina.

("Although entangled in prolonged grief.")

Carmen 69. OBVE, *tr. by* Richard Lovelace *Fr.* Carmina.

(To Rufus.) OBCVT, *tr. by* Richard Lovelace

Carmen 70. OBCVT, *tr. by* Philip Sidney; OBVE, *tr. by* Richard Lovelace; OBVE, *tr. by* Philip Sidney; STV, *tr. by* John Frederick Nims

("In wind or water streame do require to be writ.") (LL) OBCVT; OBVE, *tr. by* Richard Lovelace

("Lovers, we write in rapids streams and wind.") (LL) OBVE, *tr. by* Richard Lovelace

("My Mistresse sayes she'll marry none but me.") OBVE, *tr. by* Richard Lovelace

("Unto no body my woman saith she had rather a wife be.") OBCVT; OBVE, *tr. by* Philip Sidney

("Write on the giddy wind. Write on the stream as it flows.") (LL) STV, *tr. by* John Frederick Nims

Carmen 72. OBVE, *tr. by* Richard Lovelace; OBVE, *tr. by* William Walsh; OxBSP, *tr. by* William Walsh

("I love thee more, but I esteem thee less.") (LL) OBVE; OxBSP, *tr. by* William Walsh

("Me to love more, yet wish thee well much lesse.") (LL) OBVE, *tr. by* Richard Lovelace

("That me alone thou lov'd, you once did say.") OBVE, *tr. by* Richard Lovelace

("Thou saidst that I alone thy heart could move.") OBVE; OxBSP, *tr. by* William Walsh

Carmen 75. AWP, *tr. by* Walter Savage Landor; OBVE, *tr. by* Walter Savage Landor; STV, *tr. by* John Frederick Nims

("How cast down is the mind that took to my Lesbia, culprit.")

("Lesbia! I must love you still.") (LL) AWP; OBVE, *tr. by* Walter Savage Landor

("None could ever say that she.") AWP; OBVE, *tr. by* Walter Savage Landor

("Yet couldn't fall out of love, not for the worst you could do.") (LL) STV, *tr. by* John Frederick Nims

Carmen 85. OBVE, *tr. by* Ezra Pound; OBVE, *tr. by* Richard Lovelace; OBVE, *tr. by* Walter Savage Landor; STV, *tr. by* John Frederick Nims

(De Amore suo.) OBCVT, *tr. by* Richard Lovelace

("Her that I love, I hate! 'How's that, do you know?' they wonder.") STV, *tr. by* John Frederick Nims

("I do not know: I only feel it, and I'm torn in two.") (LL) OBVE, *tr. by* Ezra Pound

("I hate and love. / And if you ask me why.")

("I hate and love, wouldst thou the reason know?") OBCVT; OBVE, *tr. by* Richard Lovelace

("I know not, but I burn and feel it so.") (LL) OBCVT; OBVE, *tr. by* Richard Lovelace

("I love and hate. Ah! never ask why so!") OBCVT, *tr. by* Walter Savage Landor

("I see 'tis folly, but I feel 'tis woe.") (LL) OBCVT; OBVE, *tr. by* Walter Savage Landor

("Know! What's 'know'? I *feel*. Ask any crucified man.") (LL) STV, *tr. by* John Frederick Nims

Carmen 86.

(De Quintia et Lesbia.) OBCVT, *tr. by* RIchard Lovelace

Carmen 92. AWP; OBVE, *tr. by* Jonathan Swift; OBVE, *tr. by* Tom Brown; OBVE, *tr. by* William Walsh; OxBSP, *tr. by* William Walsh

("Each Moment of the long-liv'd Day.") OBVE, *tr. by* Tom Brown

("I love thee more, but I esteem thee less.") (LL) OBCVT; OBVE; OxBSP

("If I don't strangely love her.") (LL) OBVE, *tr. by* Tom Brown

("Lesbia forever on me rails.") AWP; OBVE, *tr. by* Jonathan Swift

(Lesbia from Catullus—Jul. 18th 1736.) OBCVT

(Lesbia Railing.) AWP, *tr. by* Jonathan Swift

("Yet, hang me, but I love her dearly.") (LL) AWP; OBVE, *tr. by* Jonathan Swift

Carmen 96.

(Love and Death.) AWP, *tr. by* H. W. Garrod

Carmen 101. OBCVI, *tr. by* Robert Fitzgerald

"Grief reached across the world to get me." RaBo, *tr. by* Jacob Rabinowitz

(On the Burial of His Brother.) AWP; IMW, *tr. by* Aubrey Beardsley

("Echoing for ever, brother, through a brother's tears. / —'Hail & Farewell'.") (LL) IMW

(Hail and Farewell.) LBC

("Journeying over many seas and through many countries.") IMW

Carmina Burana. *Unknown, Latin.*

"Come, come, my companion." GePo, *tr. by* Sylvia Stevens

"Crown of all travailing." MLL, *tr. by* Helen Waddell

"I am constantly wounded." PGA

"I loved / secretly." BoWoP

"O Fortune." MLL, *tr. by* Helen Waddell

"O happy hour." MLL, *tr. by* Helen Waddell

"She stood in her scarlet gown." MLL, *tr. by* Helen Waddell

"They have crucified their Lord afresh." MLL, *tr. by* Helen Waddell

"What profit to Darius of his reign?" MLL, *tr. by* Helen Waddell

Carnal and the Crane, The. *Unknown.* ESPB

Carnal Knowledge. Thom Gunn. BoLoP; EP

Carnal Knowledge. Gwen Harwood. BMAP; CBAP

Carnal Knowledge I. Gwen Harwood. *See* Carnal Knowledge.

Carnation Milk *Unknown.* InPK-6

(Virtues of Carnation Milk, The.) OBAL

Carnations. Theodore Roethke. BLT

Carnations and Butterflies. Alexander Pope. NOEC *Fr.* Yet, yet a moment, one dim ray of light. NAEL-1; OAEL-1; PoEL-3 *Fr.* The Dunciad.

Carnies. Debra Allbery. PBCAP

Carnival. Primus St. John. CMAP; GT

Carnival. Martin Sorescu, *Romanian.* CEEP, *tr. by* Dan Duescu

Carnival at the River. Robert Greacen. PNI

Carnival Figure of Guatemalan Clay, A. Jeannine Savard. CMAP

Carnival Songs. Lorenzo de' Medici, *Italian.*

Triumph of Bacchus and Ariadne. CTC, *tr. by* Richard Aldington

Caro mio, Pulcinello, kindly hear my wail of woe. A Nocturne at Danieli's. Sir Owen Seaman. UV

Caro ragazzo, yes, sure, let's meet. Part of a Letter to the Codignola Boy. Pier Paolo Pasolini, *Italian.* VCWP, *tr. by* David Stivender *and* J. D. McClatchy (b. 1945)

Carol: "Deep in the fading leaves of night." William Robert Rodgers. OBCP

Carol: "Garden and gardener He made." Thomas Kinsella. TIRV

Carol: "Mary laid her Child among." Norman Nicholson. OBCP

Carol: "Now is the world withdrawn all." Howard Nemerov. TrCP

Carol: "There was a boy bedded in bracken." John Short. FaBoCh; FaBoTw

Carol: "Villagers all, this frosty tide." Kenneth Grahame. *Fr.* The Wind in the Willows.

(Christmas Carol: "Villagers all, this frosty tide.")

Carol: "While shepherds watched their flocks by night." "Saki." NSI; UV

Carol, every violet has. Epilogue. Alfred Noyes. MoBrPo *Fr.* The Flower of Old Japan.

Carol for Advent. John Heath-Stubbs. OxBC

Carol, for Candlemas Day. *Unknown.* NOSC

Carol for the Last Christmas Eve. Norman Nicholson. NOxBChV; OBCP

Carol, in the Park, Chewing on Straws. Judy Grahn. WPOW *Fr.* The Common Woman.

Carol of Agincourt, A. *Unknown.* *See* The Agincourt Carol.

Carol of Death, The. Walt Whitman. *Fr.* Spring. LBC *Fr.* Memories of President Lincoln.

Carol of Patience. Robert Graves. OBCP

Carol of the Brown King. Langston Hughes. PChr

Carol of the Numbers. *Unknown.* AmFP
  (Green Grow the Rushes O.) OxBoLi

Carol of the Poor Children, The. Richard Middleton. OBCP

Carol of the Three Kings. W. S. Merwin. PChr

Carol Singers, The. Margaret G. Rhodes. BoTP

Carola couldn't stop watching. Ups and Downs. Amy Gerstler. DeD

Carolina. Henry Timrod. APN-2; CBCWP

Carolina, in which he was killed. (LL) Robert G. Shaw. Henrietta Cordelia Ray. AAP; BlSi; CBWP-3; Son

Carolina mourns to-day. For he, the gifted. Tribute to Capt. F. W. Dawson. Mary Weston Fordham. CBWP-2

Caroline and Her Young Sailor Bold. *Unknown.* AmFP

Caroline of Edinboro' Town. *Unknown.* AmFP

Caroling softly souls of slavery. (LL) Song of the Son. Jean Toomer. CrDW; ISC; NIP-4; PoBA

Carousel, The. Gloria C. Oden. GT; PoBA

Carp, The. Michael Stevens. CDa

Carp are secrets, The. Lifting Illegal Nets by Flashlight. James Wright. NNaP

Carpe Diem. Thomas Lodge. *See* Pluck the Fruit and Taste the Pleasure.

Carpe Diem. Shakespeare. *See* Sweet-and-Twenty.

Carpenter. George Mackay Brown. OxBC

Carpenter, The. Mary Brent Whiteside. TrCP

Carpenter is intent on the pressure of his hand, The. El Greco: Espolio. Earle Birney. MoCV

Carpenter living in Crewe, A. Limerick. E. O. Parrott. PeLi

Carpenter's Complaint, The. Edward Baugh. HCP; OBCoV; PBCV

Carpenter's Daughter. Cathy Young Czapla. IFJA

Carpenter's made a hole, The. A Hole in the Floor. Richard Wilbur. NOBA

Carpenter's Son, The. John Berryman. ChIV-2

Carpenter's Son, The. A. E. Housman. ChIV-2; MoBrPo; OxAEP-2; PBMP; SAGP; UV

Carpenter's son, carpenter's son. Craftsman. Luci Shaw. TrCP

Carpenter's Wife, The ("O whare hae ye been, my dearest dear"). *Unknown.* OAEL-1; OxBB

Carpenter's Wife, The. *Unknown. See* The Demon Lover.

Carpets cover many floors where I come from. To Vietnam. Charlie Cobb. PoBA

Carrefour. Amy Lowell. BoWoP; LW

Carriage brushes through the bright, The. Solo for Ear-Trumpet. Dame Edith Sitwell. MoBrPo

Carriage from Sweden, A. Marianne Moore. HAP; LiTM; TwCP

Carriage tops flapping in spring wind by the waters of the Ju. Following the Rhymes of Fellow Graduate P'ei Chung-mou. Huang T'ing-chien, *Chinese.* SuSp, *tr. by* Michael E. Workman

Carriages and horses stir up Ch'ang-an's thick dust. Apricot Garden. Yüan Chen, *Chinese.* SuSp, *tr. by* Angela Jung Palandri

Carrickfergus. Louis MacNeice. NAEL-2; NOIV; NoAM; PNI

Carried Away. Anne Elder. CBAP

Carried her unprotesting out the door. The Rites for Cousin Vit. Gwendolyn Brooks. BPo; HAP; NAAAL; NoP-4; WPE; WeW-3 *Fr.* The Womanhood.

Carrier Indians. Ken Belford. NOBC

Carrier Letter. Hart Crane. BoLoP; GLoP
  ("Set in the tryst-ring has but worn more bright.") (LL) GLoP

Carrier of incandescent dreams this, A. Four and More; for Miles Davis. Quincy Troupe. MoNo

Carriers of the Dream Wheel. N. Scott Momaday. CDW; ColAP

Carrion, A. Charles Baudelaire, *French.* AWP, *tr. by* Allen Tate

Carrion. Harold Monro. NSI; PeFWW *Fr.* Youth in Arms.

Carrion Comfort. Gerard Manley Hopkins. CABP; CMoP; EnVR; GSo; HeIP-4; NAEL-2; NoAM; OAEL-2; PoE; PoEL-5; Son; TFi; TOF
  ("Of now done darkness I wretch lay wrestling with (my God!) my God.") (LL) CABP; NoP-4
  (Sonnet.) OBNC

Carrion Crow, The. Thomas Lovell Beddoes. APo *Fr.* Death's Jest Book.
  ("Through a murderer's bones, to and fro, / In the ghosts' moonshine.") (LL) APo

Carrion crow sat upon [*or* on] an oak, The [*or* A]. Mother Goose. LB; OxNR; ReMoGo

Carrion-eater's nobility calls back from God, The. A Dreamed Realization. Gregory Corso. NeAP; PoM; VGW

Carrousel Tune. Tennessee Williams. NBLV; OBAL

Carrowmore. Lucie Brock-Broido. PoPoPo

Carry her over the water. W. H. Auden. FaBoTw; RB *Fr.* Ten Songs.

Carry me. Flavien Ranaivo, *French.* NegPo, *tr. by* Ellen Conroy Kennedy

Carry me ackee go a Linstead market. Linstead Market. *Unknown.* FaBoVe; PBCV

Carry me back to old Virginny. James A. Bland. APN-2; FaBoBe

Carry me back to old Virginny. Notes for a Southern Road Map. Phyllis McGinley. NBLV

Carrying a bunch of marigolds. A Negro Woman. William Carlos Williams. SAmP

Carrying a Cangue Around the Neck. Nguyễn Hữu Huân, *Vietnamese.* AVP, *tr. by* Huỳnh Sanh Thông

Carrying from the courtyard. Song of the Cricket. Lo Fu, *Chinese.* ChiPo, *tr. by* Dominic Cheng

Carrying generations of lust on his tiny feet. Agent of Love. A. K. Redwing. VoR

Carrying her full cargo of roses. (LL) Big Wind. Theodore Roethke. AmPP; CMoP; ColAP; TRP; VGW

Carrying my world. Father. Myra Cohn Livingston. NTCP

Carrying Their Coracles. Andrew Marvell. *Fr.* Upon Appleton House [To My Lord Fairfax]. FaBoPV; GeHe; SeCP

Carrying their packages of groceries in particular. Old Men and Old Women Going Home on the Street Car. Merrill Moore. MoAmPo

Cars in the mirror come swiftly forward, The. Rear Vision. William Jay Smith. NYBP

Cars on the highway filled with speech. George Oppen. APSN *Fr.* Route.

Cars once steel and green, now old. Louis Zukofsky. VGW *Fr.* 29 Poems.

Cars run in a void of utensils, The. George Oppen. APSN *Fr.* Route.

Carse, The. Lewis Spence. FaBoTC

Carson, turn your coat collar up, throw the cigarette from your hand. The Invitation in It, from American Citizen. Kay Boyle. NMM-2

Cartagena. Gary Snyder. BB

Cartagena de Indias. Earle Birney. MoCV

Carthusians. Ernest Christopher Dowson. NAEL-2

Cartload of Shoes, A. Abraham Sutskever, *Yiddish.* CEEP; HP, *tr. by* David G. Roskies

Cartography. Louise Bogan. PiM; TRP

Cartography of the Subtle Heart. Jeni Couzyn. NBrP

Cartoon of slashes on the tide-traced crater. Dylan Thomas. *Fr.* A Sequence of Sonnets.

Caruso: a voice. Sleeping with Women. Kenneth Koch. PoM

Carve delinquency away. Sterilization. Stevie Smith. WPN

Carved in cheap marble, milky & veined. The Lamb. Keith Wilson. Poetsp

Carved on an Areca Nut. Ho Xuan Huong, *Vietnamese.* PBWP, *tr. by* Nguyen Ngoc Bich *and* Burton Raffel

Carving on the jamb of an embrasure, A. The Priory of St Saviour, Glendalough. Donald Davie. OxBC

Caryatid. Léonie Adams. LiTM

Caryatids, The. Andreas Embiricos, *Greek.* GrIP, *tr. by* Kimon Friar

Caryophyllaceae / like a scroungy, The. Spring Coming. A. R. Ammons. HeIP-4; InPK-6

Casa de Pollos. Kathleen Fraser. AmPA

Casa Guidi Windows. Elizabeth Barrett Browning. VWP
  Part I. PEW

Casabianca. Elizabeth Bishop. APAD; FaBoWP; OxBSP; PiM

Casabianca. Felicia Dorothea Hemans. BLPA; EBEvV; FaBoBe; NOBRP; VWP

Casanova on His Deathbed. Philip Casey. BiHa

Casanova was turned by an ankle. Casanova's Ankle. Elizabeth Smither. PeNZ

Casanova's Ankle Elizabeth Smither. PeNZ

CASBAH. Langston Hughes. *See* Neon Signs.

Cascade, The. Edgell Rickword. FaBoTw

Cascadilla Falls. A. R. Ammons. NOBA

Cascando. Samuel Beckett. NOIV

Case, The. Hoffman Reynolds Hays. SPE

Case, The. Karen Volman. BAP-96

Case at Sessions, A. Walter Savage Landor. OBSV

Case in Point. June Jordan. NMM-2

Case in Point, A. August Kleinzahler. PmAP

"Case of Assault," A. Lydia Stephanou, *Modern Greek.* BoWoP, *tr. by* Kimon Friar

Case Study. Gayle Kaune. LoHo

Case to the Civilians, A. *Unknown.* FaBoEE

Cased in your bone and plaster. The Succubus. Harriet Rose. BrRo

Casement's Funeral. Richard Murphy. NOIV; PBCIP *Fr.* The Battle of Aughrim.

Caserta Garden. Richard Wilbur. GaP; OBGa

Casey at the Bat. Ernest Lawrence Thayer. APN-2; AiP; BLPA; ChAP; FaBoA; FaBoBe; OBAL; OBCA; OBCoV; PoRA

Casey Jones. T. Lawrence Seibert. GM

Casey Jones. *Unknown.* AS; AmFP; CTV; OxBoLi; PeLV
("'Why, the Southern Pacific and the / Santa Fe'.") (LL) CTV

Casey Jones has left today. Edward Vincent Swart. PeSA

Casey—Twenty Years Later. S. P. McDonald. BLPA

Casey's Revenge. James Wilson. BLPA

Cash Positive. Peter McDonald. PNI

Cashel of Munster. William English, *Irish.* BIrV; GBL; OBEV, *tr. by* Sir Samuel Ferguson

Cashier, The. Andrey Andreievich Voznesensky, *Russian.* TCRP, *tr. by* W. H. Auden

Casida of Sobbing. Federico García Lorca, *Spanish.* AF, *tr. by* Robert Bly

Casino. Richard Tipping. BMAP

Casket on display, A. Tanka. Tsukamoto Kunio, *Japanese.* MJT, *tr. by* Makoto Ueda

Casket Song, A. Shakespeare. *See* Song: "Tell me where is fancy [or Fancie] bred."

Cassandra. Louise Bogan. HAP; MoAmPo; NALW; PBWP; VGW

Cassandra. Robinson Jeffers. HeIP-4; LiTM

Cassandra. Edwin Arlington Robinson. CMoP; ImPo; LiTM; MeMAP; NoAM; OxBA

Cassandra and Friend. Norman Henry, II Pritchard. GT

Cassandra declining to follow. Limerick. Basil Ransome-Davies. PeLi

Cassandra's Answer. John Montague. BiHa

Cassia hall has collapsed, The. The Deserted Estate at South Garden. Hsü Pen, *Chinese.* CoBLCP, *tr. by* Jonathan Chaves

Cassinus and Peter. Jonathan Swift. OAEL-1

Cassius Hueffer. Edgar Lee Masters. OxBA *Fr.* Spoon River Anthology.

Cast. After the Funeral of Assam Hamady. Sam Hamod. UnSA

Cast a cold eye. W. B. Yeats. FaBoEE *Fr.* Under Ben Bulben. CMoP; HAP; IIP; LiTM; MoP; NAEL-2; NoAM; NoP-4; OxBTC

"Cast down your bucket where you are." Atlanta Exposition Ode. Mary Weston Fordham. AAP; CBWP-2

Cast Off, The. Marge Piercy. NoAM

Cast off all shame. Jana Bai, *Marathi.* WPoS, *tr. by* Vilas Sarang

Cast on 120 stitches, / Rep. to the end of the row. On a Grey-haired Old Lady Knitting at an Orchestral Concert. Suzanne Gardinier. CBAP

Cast on the field from their full height. Second Shadow. Theodore Roethke. PoA

Cast our caps and cares away. The Beggar's Holiday. John Fletcher. NOSC *Fr.* Beggar's Bush.

Cast Shadows. Marcel Duchamp, *French.* PFTM, *tr. by* Arturo Schwarz

Cast the bantling on the rocks. Self-Reliance. Ralph Waldo Emerson. APN-1 *Fr.* Quatrains.

Cast thy bread upon the waters. Bible, *O.T.* AWP, *stanzas* 1–6; OBVE *Fr.* Ecclesiastes.

Cast Thy Bread upon the Waters. Phoebe A. Hanaford. AH

Cast up / with my. To Whom It May Concern. Jon Stallworthy. CBLP

Cast your eyes and look over to the ocean and see ships. Desert Conflict. Calvin Makabo, *Southern Sotho.* PeSAV, *tr. by* Alexander Qoboshane

Castalian Scots, nou may ye cry, Allace! A Fair Cop. Robert Garioch. OBCoV

Castanets. Bernard Spencer. WeW-3

Castara. William Habington.
  Against Them Who Lay Unchastity to the Sex of Women. BeJo; SeCP
  Dialogue between Araphil and Castara, A. BeJo
  "In vain, fair sorceress, thy eyes speak charms." BeJo
  "Nox Nocti Indicat Scientiam." BeJo; MeLP; NOBE; OBEV; SCGP
  Reward of Innocent Love, The. FMP
    ("We saw and woo'd each other's eyes.")
  To a Friend, Inviting Him to a Meeting upon Promise. BeJo
  To Castara ("Do[e] not Their profane orgies hear[e].") BeJo
  To Castara ("Give me a heart where no impure"). BeJo
  To Castara, upon an Embrace. BeJo
  To Castara, upon Beautie. BeJo; SeCP
  To Roses in the Bosom[e] of Castara. BeJo; EnLoPo; MeLP; NOSC; OBEV; SCGP; SeCP
  To the World: the Perfection of Love. BeJo
  Upon Castara's Absence. BeJo

Castara, see that dust, the sportive wind. To Castara, upon Beautie. William Habington. BeJo; SeCP *Fr.* Castara.

Castaway, The. William Cowper. NAEL-1; NOBE; NOBRP; NOEC; OAEL-1; OxBoS; PoE; PoEL-3; PoPoPo; TRP
  ("And whelmed in deeper gulfs than he.") (LL) NoP-4; PoPoPo
  ("Obscurest night involved the sky.") NoP-4; PoPoPo

Castaway. John Nerber. PoA

Castaway, A. Augusta Davies Webster.
  "Well, well, I know the wise ones talk and talk." BrRo

Castellated, tall. The Bat. Dame Edith Sitwell. FaBoMo

Castiglione has many a frontier. The Road to Bologna. Roy Macnab. PeSA

Castilian. Elinor Wylie. ColAP

Casting. Howard Nemerov. OxBSP

Casting. Kevin Young. GT

Casting and Gathering. Seamus Heaney. NoP-4

Casting Fragrance to the Winds. Xuân Diệu, *Vietnamese.* AVP, *tr. by* Huỳnh Sanh Thông

Casting Sequences. Marjorie Welish. FTOS

Casting shadows. Tanka. Kondō Yoshimi, *Japanese.* MJT, *tr. by* Makoto Ueda

Castle. Milton. OxBSN *Fr.* Comus: a Masque Presented at Ludlow.

Castle, The. Edwin Muir. FaBoTC

Castle by the Sea, The. Ludwig Uhland, *German.* AWP, *tr. by* Longfellow

Castle Howard, the Seat of the Rt. Hon. Charles, Earl of Carlisle. Anne, Viscountess Irwin Ingram.

Castle Howard, the Seat of the Rt. Hon. Charles, Earl of Carlisle. Anne, Viscountess Irwin Ingram. OBGa *Fr.* Castle Howard, the Seat of the Rt. Hon. Charles, Earl of Carlisle.

Castle Howard, the Seat of the Rt. Hon. Charles, Earl of Carlisle. OBGa

Castle in Lynn, A. Linda McCarriston. LoL; NMM-2

Castle in the Fire, The. Mary Jane Carr. ChAP

Castle of Indolence, The. James Thomson.
  Land of Indolence, The.
  "Sometimes the pencil, in cool airy halls." PoEL-3

Castle to castle. Caernarfon, 2 July 1969. T. Glynne Davies, *Welsh.* OBWVE, *tr. by* Joseph P. Clancy

Castles. A. Leyeles, *Yiddish.* TiJP, *tr. by* Joseph Leftwich

Castles in the Sand. Dorothy Baker. BoTP

Castles of crystal. Trams. Dame Edith Sitwell. NOxBChV

Castles of iurlionis—rise again, The. Silence. Violeta Palinskaite, *Lithuanian.* CEEP, *tr. by* Irene Pogoželskyte Suboczewski

Castles with lofty. Soldier's Song. Goethe. AWP, *tr. by* Bayard Taylor *Fr.* Faust.

Castleside Song. Wang Ch'ang-ling, *Chinese.* CoBCP, *tr. by* Burton Watson

Castoff Skin. Ruth Whitman. InPK-6

Castor & Pollux / the Dioscuri. Catullus. *See* The Yacht.

Castration of the Pen. Erica Jong. NALW

Castrato. Kenneth Rosen. PuP-15

Casts light for a shadow. (LL) Song: "You are as gold." Hilda Doolittle. LiTM; MoAmPo

Casts up his nets, and there we panting die. (LL) Madrigal: "This world a hunting is." William Drummond, of Hawthornden. SAGP

Casual Meeting. Margaret E. Bruner. PoToHe

Casual Wear. James Merrill. NIP-4 *Fr.* Topics.

Casualties (1970). J. P. Clark Bekederêmo.
  Season of Omens. PBMAP

Casualties are not only those who are dead. J. P. Clark Bekedereme. HBAPE

Casualty. Seamus Heaney. FaBoPV; NAEL-2; PBCIP; PoE

Cat. Sutardji Calzoum Bachri, *Malay.* PC, *tr. by* Harry Aveling

Cat, The. Charles Baudelaire, *French.* PC, *tr. by* William H. Crosby

Cat, The. W. H. Davies. NOBE

Cat. Emily Dickinson. APo

Cat, The. Rose Fyleman. NOxBChV

Cat, The. Issa, *Japanese.* PC, *tr. by* Guest, Harry

Cat, The. Kusatao, *Japanese.* PC, *tr. by* Tze-si Huang

Cat, The. William Matthews. AmPA

Cat. Mary Britton Miller. TLR; WHSW

Cat, The. Ogden Nash. WHSW

Cat. Judith Nicholls. PeP

Cat. Kenneth Rexroth. *Fr.* A Bestiary. OBAL

Cat, The. Raymond Roseliep. HA

Cat. Joe Rosenblatt. NOBC

Cat. Vernon Scannell. PeP

Cat, The. Dame Edith Sitwell. NTP

Cat, The. Lytton Strachey. PC

Cat, A. Edward Thomas. PC

Cat, The. Nguyen Trai, *Vietnamese.* PC, *tr. by* Jess Williamson

Cat and Mouse. Ted Hughes. OxBSP

Cat and the Lute, The. Thomas Master. PC

Cat and the Moon, The. W. B. Yeats. APo; CMoP; CTAV; FaBoCh; PC; TTTS; WHSW

("His changing eye.") (LL) PC

Cat and the Pig, The. Gerard Benson. NOxBChV

Cat and the Weather. May Swenson. HAP; WeW-3

Cat as Cat. Denise Levertov. NOBA; PC

Cat at his dish licks rays of moonlight, The. Moonlight. Rajasekhara, *Sanskrit*. PC, *tr. by* Henry Heifetz

Cat at Night. Adrien Stoutenburg. PC

Cat-call the cat-gut "fiddles"? Fiddlesticks! (LL) Variations on an Air: After Robert Browning. G. K. Chesterton. BXAP; NOBL

Cat came fiddling out of a barn, A. *Unknown*. BoTP; CTAV

Cat, Cat. To Winky. Amy Lowell. PC

Cat, cat, cat. The Song of the Cat. Tristan Klingsor, *French*. PC, *tr. by* Felicity Bast

Cat Changed to a Woman, The. Jean de La Fontaine, *French*. PC, *tr. by* Marianne Moore

Cat Goddesses. Robert Graves. NYBP; OxBSP; PC

Cat has bitten it quite in two, The. (LL) Sing, sing, / What shall I sing? Mother Goose. LB; ReMoGo

Cat has his sport, The. The Innocent. Denise Levertov. KaS

Cat, if you go outdoors you must walk in the snow. On a Night of Snow. Elizabeth Jane Coatsworth. AYFP; MoAmPo; OBCA

Cat in moonlight, The. Cat at Night. Adrien Stoutenburg. PC

Cat in the Dovecote. Avner Trainin, *Hebrew*. MHP, *tr. by* Ruth Finer Mintz

Cat in the Snow. Aileen Fisher. NTCP

Cat-Lady, The. John Barlas. ADE

Cat lies on her back, The. Nativité. André Spire, *French*. PC, *tr. by* Stanley Burnshaw

Cat May Look at a King, A. *Unknown*. OxBoLi

Cat Morgan Introduces Himself. T. S. Eliot. NOBL; PeLV

Cat-naps take in pipe-bowl light. (LL) The Bench of Boors. Herman Melville. APN-2; NAAL-1; NAAL-3; NoP-4; OBAL; SoSe-8

Cat of Cats, The. William Brighty Rands. CTAV; FPC; NOxBChV; OxBChV; PC

Cat on gold-glowing black coals, A. Dream. Raphael Rudnik. PC

Cat on my bosom, The. The Cat as Cat. Denise Levertov. NOBA; PC

Cat on the Mat. J. R. R. Tolkien. PC

Cat runs races with her tail, The. John Clare. OAEL-2 *Fr.* Signs of Winter.

Cat said / on the corner, A. Vietnam #4. Clarence Major. NBV; PoBA

Cat sat asleep by the side of the fire, The. *Unknown*. OxNR

Cat sits on the pavement by the house, A. The Lonely Man. Randall Jarrell. FP; OxBC

Cat takes a look at the weather. Cat and the Weather. May Swenson. HAP; WeW-3

Cat to His Dinner, The. Nancy Willard. PC

Cat Washing. Linda Molony. NOBAu

Cat went here and there, The. The Cat and the Moon. W. B. Yeats. APo; CMoP; CTAV; FaBoCh; PC; TTTS; WHSW

Cat! who hast passed [*or* pass'd] thy grand climacteric. To a Cat. Keats. FaBoCh

Cataclysmic if it were so. "What You See Is Me." Barbara Gibbs. NYBP

Catacomb Suburb. Alastair Fowler. FaBoTC

Catacombs. István Vas, *Hungarian*. CEEP, *tr. by* Emery E. George

Catacombs in San Callisto, The. Rolf Jacobsen, *Norwegian*. BLT, *tr. by* Roger Greenwald

Catalog. Rosalie Moore. NTCP

Catalpa Tree. Miriam Waddington. MoCV

Catalpa Tree on West Twelfth Street, A. Amy Clampitt. BAP-94

Catapulting a Stone. Sokch'o Shin, *Korean*. CKP, *tr. by* Jaihiun Kim

Cataract. Margoret Smith. NYBP

Cataract Isle, The. Christopher Pearse Cranch. APN-1

Cataract of Death far thundering from the heights, The. (LL) Mezzo Cammin. Henry Wadsworth Longfellow. APN-1; ColAP; GSo; NAAL-1; NAAL-3; NCAP; PAR; PoE; TAP

Cataract of Lodore, The. Robert Southey. NOxBChV; NTP; OxBChV

Cataracts flying down a thousand fathoms roll up a raging billow. Liu Ya-tzu. SuSp, *tr. by* Wu-chi Liu *Fr.* Miscellaneous Poems on Lake Biwa.

Catch, A. Henry Aldrich. NOSC; OxBSP

Catch. Robert Francis. InPK-7; RaBo

Catch, The. Brewster Ghiselin. HAP

Catch. Langston Hughes. NoAM

Catch, A. Ben Jonson. CBNP *Fr.* Oberon, the Fairy Prince. (Buzz and Hum.) OxNR

Catch, The. Stanley Kunitz. MoLi

Catch. Mother Goose. OxNR

("Pussy-cat said: 'Mew, mew, mew,' and Robin flew away.") (LL) ReMoGo

Catch, The. Richard Wilbur. DiPo; WeW-3

Catch a Little Rhyme. Eve Merriam. OBCA

Catch a moth in the Amazon; pin it under glass. Every Where and Every When. Arthur Sze. OpBo

Catch her and hold her if you can. Defiance. Walter Savage Landor. CBLP

Catch him coming off the thing after a state of the union. Strategies. Welton Smith. PoBA

Catch him, crow! Carry him, kite! *Unknown*. OxNR

Catch it if you can. (LL) Mix a Pancake. Christina Rossetti. BoTP; NTCP

Catch, my Uncle Jack said. Elizabeth. Michael Ondaatje. NoAM

Catch not my breath, O clamorous heart. Tennyson. NAEL-2 *Fr.* This lump of earth has left his estate. *Fr.* Maud [A Monodrama]. EnVR

Catch of Shy Fish, A. Gwendolyn Brooks.
  Big Bessie Throws Her Son into the Street. VGW
  Garbageman: the Man with the Orderly Mind. CAPP-1

Catch: On a Wet Day. Franco Sacchetti, *Italian*. AWP, *tr. by* D. G. Rossetti
  ("As I was walking pensively through a little wood.") ItIP

Catch What You Can. Jean Garrigue. VGW

Catches tigers / In red weather. (LL) Disillusionment of Ten O'Clock. Wallace Stevens. CBNP; CMoP; InPS-3; NAAL-2; NoAM; OxBA; RB; SAmP; SoSe-8; TRP; TTTS

Catching. Ann Carrel. CMAP

Catching Crabs. David Dabydeen. HCP

Catching One Clear Thought Alive. Paula Gunn Allen. WPOW

Catching the brilliant echoes! (LL) Carmen 31 ("Apple of islands, Sirmio, & bright peninsulas, set"). Catullus. OBVE, *tr. by* Thomas Hardy

Catching Webs. Judith Beveridge. NOBAu

Catechism. Betsy Sholl. CrSp

Catechism, 1958. W. M. Ransom. CDW

Catechism of d Neoamerican Hoodoo Church. Ishmael Reed. NBV

Caterpillar. Emily Dickinson. APo

Caterpillar, The. Christina Rossetti. AYFP; CTAV; CTV; ChAP *Fr.* Sing-Song.
  ("To live again as butterfly.") (LL) BoTP; FaBoVe; OxBChV

Caterpillar, The. Miller Williams. MT

Caterpillar. "I'm learning / To crawl." (LL) The Tickle Rhyme. Ian Serraillier. NTCP; Spl

Caterpillars. Aileen Fisher. TLR

Caterpillar's Lullaby. Jane Yolen. Spl

Catfish and Toad. *Unknown, Vietnamese*. AVP, *tr. by* Huỳnh Sanh Thông

Catharine of Arragon. Eloise Bibb. CBWP-4

Cathedral bell, The. Nicholas Virgilio. HA

Cathedral Builders. John Ormond. NoP-4; PeECV

Cathedral Close, The. Coventry Patmore. *Fr.* The Angel in the House. (Salisbury; the Cathedral Close.) EBVV

Cathedral Is, The. John Ashbery. InPK-6

Cathedral Stones. Ion Gheorghe, *Romanian*. CEEP, *tr. by* Donald Eulert *and* Stefan Avadanei

Cathedrals sway in the blue face of the steel. Citizen. Julia Fields. GT

Cathemerinon 2. Prudentius, *Latin*.
  "Yee night, and darknes, cloudie aire." OBCVT, *tr. by* Alexander Huish

Catherine, describing a perfect circle. Virgin Martyrs. John Heath-Stubbs. OxBC

Catherine said "I think I'll bake." Karla Kuskin. NTCP

Cathexis. Frederick Bryant Jr. NBV; PoBA

Cathleen. *Unknown, Irish*. BIrV, *tr. by* Thomas MacIntyre

Cathleen Sweeping. George Johnston. NOBC

Catholic Bells, The. William Carlos Williams. CMoP; NOBA; OxBA; SAmP

Catiline his Conspiracy. Ovid, *Latin*.
  Mistress keeps her lover on his toes, A. OBCVT, *tr. by* Ben Jonson

Catiline his Conspiracy. Petronius Arbiter, *Latin*.
  Chorus: "Can nothing great, and at the height." OBCVT, *tr. by* Ben Jonson

Catkin. *Unknown*. ACTP; CTV

Catkins flying: floating white snow. Ma Chih-yüan. *Fr.* Two Poems to the Tune "Chin-tzu ching" The Sutra in Gold Characters. CoBLCP, *tr. by* Jonathan Chaves

Catkins, like caterpillars slung arow. Lost Lane. Dorothy, Duchess of Wellington Wellesley. WPE

Catnip from the other side. (LL) The King of Cats Sends a Postcard to His Wife. Nancy Willard. PC

Cato. Charles Hubert Sisson. NOCV

Cato at his wedding. Lucan, *Latin*. OBCVT, *tr. by* P. F. Widdows

Cato in the desert. Lucan, *Latin.* OBCVT, *tr.* by Thomas May

Catoes Morall Distichs: Translated and Paraphras'd, with variations of Expressing, in English verse. Cato Uticensis, *Latin.*

"Interpone tuis, interdum gaudia curis." OBCVT, *tr.* by Sir Richard Baker

Cato's Moral Distichs Englished in Couplets. Cato Uticensis, *Latin.*

"What Men in private whisper, never mind." OBCVT, *tr.* by James Logan

Cats, *see also* Lovers that burn and learnèd scholars cold. Charles Baudelaire, *French.* APo, *tr.* by Richard Howard

Cats. Fazil Hüsnü Daglarca, *Turkish.* PC, *tr.* by Murat Nemet-Nejat

Cats. Francis Scarfe. PeP

("DOG The single creature leads a partial life.") PC

Cats and Dogs. N. M. Bodecker. TLR

Cats and Dogs. Howard Moss. OBAL

Cats are not at all like people. William Jay Smith. PC

Cat's asleep; I whisper *kitten,* The. The Happy Cat. Randall Jarrell. PC

Cat's Conscience, A. *Unknown.* PoLF

Cat's Dream. Pablo Neruda, *Spanish.* PC

Cat's Eye, The. Yorie. PC

Cats making love in the temple. Kawai Chigetsu-Ni, *Japanese.* WPJ, *tr.* by Kenneth Rexroth *and* Ikuko Atsumi

Cats making love in the temple. Propriety. Chigetsu, *Japanese.* PC, *tr.* by Kenneth Rexroth *and* Ikuko Atsumi

Cat's Meat. Harold Monro. OBMV

Cats of Kilkenny, The. *Unknown.* ChAP; PeLi; ReMoGo

Cats of St. Nicholas, The. George Seferis, *Greek.* PC, *tr.* by Edmund Keeley *and* Philip Sherrard

Cat's purr, A. At the Loom. Robert Duncan. VGW *Fr.* Passages.

Cat's run away / With the pudding too!, The. Mother Goose. *See* Sing, sing, / What shall I sing?

Cat's Second Song, The. Nancy Willard. FFC

Cats sleep / Anywhere. Eleanor Farjeon. OTCP; WHSW

Cats sleep fat and walk thin. Catalog. Rosalie Moore. NTCP *Fr.* Catalogue.

Cat's whiskers, The. Penny Harter. HA

Cattail fluff / blows in. Porous. William Carlos Williams. NYBP

Cattle. Ralph Hawkins. NBrP

Cattle. Peter Skrzynecki. CBAP

Cattle in the common field, The. On the Heights. Walter Savage Landor. FaBoEE

Cattle Loading. Gordon Mackay-Warna, *Aborigine.* NOBAu, *tr.* by Georg von Brandenstein

Cattle out of their byres are dungy still, lambs. Gorse Fires. Michael Longley. NoP-4

Cattle roam again across the field, The. *Unknown. Fr.* Adoration of the Disk by King Akhnaten and Princess Nefer Neferiu Aten. AWP *Fr.* Book of the Dead.

Cattle Show. "Hugh MacDiarmid." FaBoMo; HAP; MoBrPo; OBMV; OxBTC

Cattle then are sick, The. (LL) Summer Time on Bredon. Hugh Kingsmill. NOBL; UV

Cattle Thief, The. Emily Pauline Johnson. WPOW

Cattle-trains edge along the river, bringing morning on a white vibration. Ceiling Unlimited. Muriel Rukeyser. MoAmPo

Catullus. / Against the past. Catullus. *See* Carmen 8 ("Break off / fallen Catullus").

Catullus, CI. Catullus, *Latin.* OBCVT, *tr.* by Robert Fitzgerald

Catullus Imitated. Ep. 58. Catullus, *Latin.* OBCVT, *tr.* by Nicholas Amhurst

Catullus man, ye maunna gang sae gyte. Frae Catullus, VIII. Catullus, *Latin.* OBCVT, *tr.* by Douglas Young

Catullus, still remember to be strong. Catullus. *See* Carmen 8 ("Break off / fallen Catullus").

Catullus Talks to Himself. Catullus. *See* Carmen 8 ("Break off / fallen Catullus").

Catullus to Lesbia. Catullus. OBCVT, *tr.* by W. E. Gladstone

Catullus to Lesbia. Catullus. *See* Carmen 5 ("My sweetest Lesbia, let us live and love").

Caught. Rodney Jones. FiLi; NAmP90

Caught and composed, motionless blue, behind. The Desire of Water. Mark Jarman. PoA

Caught at hanger's ends the limp. Goodwill, Inc. Dennis Schmitz. AmPA

Caught between two streams of traffic, in the gloom. T. S. Eliot. Robert Lowell. NOBA; NoAM

Caught in a storm outside Cloud Gate Abbey. Tu Mu. PLT, *tr.* by A. C. Graham *Fr.* Recalling Former Travels.

Caught in my mittens' mohair barbs. The Microscope in Winter. Sandra McPherson. LCAP-2; VCAP

Caught in my private limbo, my. Lusca. John Robert Lee. HCP

Caught in the centre [*or* center] of a soundless field. Myxomatosis. Philip Larkin. CMoP; MoP; NoAM; PFE

Caught me sittin. All is One for Monk. Imamu Amiri Baraka. ISC

Caught shoplifting. Martin Shea. HA

Caught still as Absalom. Chagrin. Isaac Rosenberg. MoBrPo

Caught there, then, on the Rock. At Corregidor. Richard Eberhart. *Fr.* Brotherhood of Men. PoWW

Cauld blaws the wind frae east to west. Up in the Morning Early. Robert Burns. OPOU

Cauld blaws the wind frae north to south. Cold Blows the Wind. John Hamilton. CH

Cauld, grey waater heaves on the neap tide. Itherness. Ellie McDonald. CABP

Cauld Lad of Hilton, The *or* The Wandering Spectre. *Unknown.* OxBoLi (Ghost's Song, The.) FaBoCh

Cauldron. Marilyn Chin. BAP-96

Cause and Effect. Matthew Prior. *See* A Reasonable Affliction.

Cause nobody deals with Aretha—a mother with four children. Poem for Aretha. Nikki Giovanni. BPo; PoBA

Cause of this stab in my side. The Tryst. *Unknown, Welsh.* OBWVE, *tr.* by Joseph P. Clancy

Cause of War, The. *Unknown, Greek.* OBCVT, *tr.* by Thomas Parnell *Fr.* Batrachomyomachia (The Battle of the Frogs and Mice).

Cause thou didst pen *Tetrasticks* clean and sweet. Ad Sabellum. Martial, *Latin.* OBCVT, *tr.* by R. Fletcher

Cause you don't love me. Bad Luck Card. Langston Hughes. NoP-4; SAmP; TRP

Causes are in Time; only their issue, The. The Allegory of the Wolf Boy. Thom Gunn. OxBC

Causes first I purpose to unfould, The. All great things crush themselves. Lucan, *Latin.* OBCVT, *tr.* by Marlowe

Causes of Old Age. John Armstrong. ECEV *Fr.* The Art of Preserving Health.

Caution, The. Catherine Cockburn. LW

Caution Prevents Accidents. Meir Wieseltier, *Hebrew.* IP, *tr.* by Warren Bargad *and* Stanley F. Chyet

Cautionary Limerick. *Unknown.* NBLV

Cautionary Verses to Youth of Both Sexes. Theodore Hook. OxBChV

Cautious Gunslinger, The. An Idle Visitation. Edward Dorn. NOBA; PmAP *Fr.* Gunslinger.

Cautious Gunslinger, The. An Idle Visitation. Edward Dorn. NOBA *Fr.* Gunslinger.

Cautiously the sun rose over the wet sand [*or* shone on the damp sand]. Caution Prevents Accidents. Meir Wieseltier, *Hebrew.* IP, *tr.* by Warren Bargad *and* Stanley F. Chyet

Cavafy in Redondo. Mark Jarman. CMAP

Cavalier Lyric. James Simmons. UV

Cavalier's Escape, The. George Walter Thornbury. FaBoBe

Cavalry Crossing a Ford. Walt Whitman. AiP; AmPP; CBCWP; HeIP-4; InPK-6; InPS-3; MoP; NAAL-1; NAAL-3; NoAM; OxBA; SAmP; TAP; TFi; TRP; UnPo

("Guidon flags flutter gayly in the wind, The.") (LL) BLT; FaBoA; NCAP; NoP-4; PAR

Cave, The. Michael Collier. PuP-15

Cave, The. Arthur Rex Dugard Fairbairn. PeNZ

Cave. John Montague. IIP *Fr.* The Cave of Night.

Cave of Despair, The. Edmund Spenser. OBNV *Fr.* Wood Of Error. AEP

"Ere long they come, where that same wicked wight." NOBE; OAEL-1

Cave of Gold Essence—in Ning-tu, The. T'ang Hsien-tsu, *Chinese.* CoBLCP, *tr.* by Jonathan Chaves

Cave of Making, The. W. H. Auden. FaBoVe; OxAEP-2

Cave of Mammon, The. Edmund Spenser. PoEL-1 *Fr.* Wood Of Error. AEP

Cave of Night, The. John Montague.

Cave. IIP

Cave of Words, The. Vladimir Holan, *Czech.* CEEP, *tr.* by Bronislava Volek *and* Andrew Durkin

Cave we found, but vacant all within, The. Homer. OBVE, *tr.* by Pope *Fr.* Odyssey. NAWM-1, *tr.* by Robert Fitzgerald

Cavendish McKellar. Peter Wesley-Smith. FuFo

Cavern, The. Charles Tomlinson. CMoP

Caverns. Madison Cawein. APN-2

Caverns of the Grave Ive seen, The. William Blake. SCGP

Cavour. Menella Bute Smedley. VWP

Caw caw caw crows shriek in the white sun over grave stones. Allen Ginsberg. BB

Caw Caw Caw / on a far shingle long ago. The Sea and Ourselves at Cape Ann. Lawrence Ferlinghetti. PoM

Caw Caw the Crows Caw Caw. *Unknown, Seneca Indian.* STP, *tr. by* Jerome Rothenberg *and* Richard Johnny John

"Caw," said the rook. Birds' Nests. Millicent Seager. BoTP

Caxtons are mechanical birds with many wings. A Martian Sends a Postcard Home. Craig Raine. NAEL-2; NoAM; NoP-4

CCC campers near West Cummington. The CCC. Thomas Whitbread. NYBP

Ce Dur Appel de l'Espoir (1960). Joseph Miezan Bognini.
  "My days overgrown with coffee blossoms." PBMAP

Ce! la! ho! ho! hu! (LL) Art Thou Gone in Haste? John Webster *and* William Rowley. CH; GBL; OxBoLi

Cean Dubh Deelish. *Unknown. See* Dear Black Head.

Cease murdering the dead. No More Crying Out. Giuseppe Ungaretti, *Italian.* PeFWW, *tr. by* Jon Silkin

Cease rude Boreas blust'ring railers. The Tempest. *Unknown.* AmFP

Cease then, my song, cease the unequal lay. (LL) On Imagination. Phillis Wheatley. AmPP; BlSi; CrDW; NAAAL; OxWW

Cease, Wilberforce, to urge thy generous aim. Epistle to William Wilberforce, Esq., on the Rejection of the Bill for Abolishing the Slave Trade. Anna Laetitia Barbauld. Ro *Fr.* Poems.

Ceaseless snow. Mitsune, *Japanese.* OHMPJ, *tr. by* Kenneth Rexroth

Ceaselessly the weaver, Time. The Weaver. William Henry Burleigh. BLPA

Cecil B. De Mille. Nicolas Bentley. OBCoV

Cecil County. Ron Welburn. PoBA

Cedar and jagged fir. The Lonely Land. Arthur James Marshall Smith. NOBC

Cedar-limbs. Wallace Stevens. *See* Thirteen Ways of Looking at a Blackbird.

Cedar Waxwing on Scarlet Firethorn. Stanley Plumly. NAmP90

Cedars of Lebanon, The. Alphonse Marie Louis de Lamartine, *French.* AWP, *tr. by* Toru Dutt

Céilí. Ciaran Carson. PBCIP
  (It Used to Be.) CIP-2

Ceiling, The. Theodore Roethke. KaS

Ceiling Unlimited. Muriel Rukeyser. MoAmPo

Ceiling wihtout a star. (LL) Child. Sylvia Plath. HCAP; MDDM; PBWP

Celan. "Asya," *Yiddish.* CEEP, *tr. by* Gabriel Preil *and* Howard Schwartz

Celandine. Edward Thomas. OxBTC

Celebrants chanted, The. Four Ways of Dying. Steve Chimombo. HBAPE

Celebrants, The, came chanting, "God is dead!" The Death of God. Howard Nemerov. OxBC; OxBSP

Celebrating the Freak. Cynthia MacDonald. Poetsp

Celebration. Joseph Ceravolo. FTOS

Celebration, The. Felix Mnthali. PBMAP

Celebration. Ray A. Young Bear. CDW

Celebration: Birth of a Colt. Linda Hogan. HATNAP

Celebration for My Mother. Wendy Rose. CDW

Celebration of Charis in Ten Lyric[k] Pieces [*or* Peeces], A. Ben Jonson. BeJo; OxAEP-1; SeCP
  Begging Another, on Colour of Mending the Former. CBLP; PoEL-2
  Her Triumph. CBLP; CTC; EBEV; NOSC; NoP-4; PoEL-2
    (Triumph of Charis, The.) NOBE; TFi
  His Excuse for Loving. NOSC; PoEL-2

Celebration of Nadir. János Pilinszky, *Hungarian.* CEEP, *tr. by* Emery E. George

Celebration of the Body. Daisy Zamora, *Spanish.* LoL, *tr. by* Dinah Livingston

Celestial. Keats. *See* Hyperion.

Celestial Alphabet Event. Jacques Gaffarel. PFTM

Celestial choir. To His Excellency General Washington. Phillis Wheatley. NAAAL; NAAL-1; NAAL-3; WPE

Celestial City, The. Giles, the Younger Fletcher. *Fr.* Christ's Victory and Triumph.

Celestial Evening, October 1967. Charles Olson. PoM *Fr.* The Maximus Poems.

Celestial Fire, The. Yannai, *Hebrew.* NNPT, *tr. by* T. Carmi

Celestial Love. Michelangelo Buonarroti, *Italian.* AWP, *tr. by* John Addington Symonds

Celestial Music. Louise Glück. PuP-14

Celestial Surgeon, The. Robert Louis Stevenson. EBVV; MoBrPo; PoToHe
  ("And stab my spirit broad awake.") (LL) ACTP

Celestial Wisdom. Juvenal. AWP, *tr. by* Samuel Johnson. *Fr.* Satires.

Celia Bleeding, to the Surgeon. Thomas Carew. CavPo; SeCP

Celia Celia. Adrian Mitchell. FaBoEE; OPOU

Celia Singing. Thomas Stanley. BeJo; NOSC

Celia's Home-Coming. Agnes Mary Frances Robinson. OBEV; VWP

Cell, The. Lyn Hejinian.

"In the dark sky there." FTOS

Cell, The, *sonnet.* John Thelwall. NOEC

Cell by cell the baby made herself, the cells. Sara in Her Father's Arms. George Oppen. NNaP

Cell of Himself, The. Arthur Freeman. TwCP

Cell Song. Etheridge Knight. NNaP; PoBA
  ("And are strong.") (LL) GT
  ("Night.") GT

Cellar Door. Sue Standing. EC2
  "Room to go to, A." MDDM

Cells Breathe in the Emptiness. Galway Kinnell. PFE; VGW

Cells hold mock convention in the brain, The. Lobotomy. Kenneth Pitchford. PoA

Celluloid of a photograph holds them well, The. Six Young Men. Ted Hughes. NSI; OBWP; PoWW

Celtic Cross. Norman MacCaig. FaBoTC; OxBS

Celtic Cross, The. Thomas D'Arcy Magee. TIRV

Celtic Lyric, The. Sir John Collings Squire. BXAP

Celtic tribes speak an anapestic lilt. Forked Tongue. Helen Ruggieri. LoHo

Celts, The. Thomas D'Arcy Magee. TIRV

Celts, The. Stevie Smith. NoP-4

Cement-grey floors and walls. On the Island. Dennis Brutus. AF

Cemeteries forever, The. (LL) Little Infinite Poem. Federico García Lorca, *Spanish.* RaBo, *tr. by* Robert Bly

Cemetery, A. Emily Dickinson. MoAmPo

Cemetery at Academy, California, The. Philip Levine. NYBP; WeT

Cemetery in Punta Arenas. Enrique Lihn, *Spanish.* VCWP, *tr. by* David Unger

Cenotaph, The. Charlotte Mew. OxAEP-2; WPE

Cenotaph. John Yau. PmAP

Cenotaph at the Isthmus. Simonides, *Greek.* GrAn, *tr. by* Peter Jay

Cenotaph stands in the Park, The. Greenwood's. Michael Sharkey. NOBAu

Censorship. John Ciardi. NBLV

Censorship. Arthur Waley. OxBTC

Census man, The. Madam and the Census Man. Langston Hughes. SAmP

Centaur, The. May Swenson. FaBoWP; NMM-2; NTP; TwCP
  ("Summer that I was ten, The.") NOxBChV

Centaur does not need a Horse, The. Theodore Roethke. *Fr.* Three Epigrams. NBLV

Centaur Overheard, The. Edgar Bowers. CoAmPo

Centaur, siren [*or* syren], I forgo[e], The. Another. Richard Lovelace. CaPo; PoEL-3

Centaur Song. Hilda Doolittle. VGW

Centaurs, The. Paul Muldoon. BiHa

Centenarian's Story, The. Walt Whitman. CTC

Centenary's Day. Marcus Garvey. PBCV

Centennial of Melville's birth this morning. Japanese City. Kenward Elmslie. PmAP

Center of all centers, core of cores. Buddha in Glory. Rilke, *German.* EnlH, *tr. by* Stephen Mitchell

Center of Attention, The. Daniel Gerard Hoffman. FYAP; UnPo

Center of lake of light. (LL) 127th Chorus. Jack Kerouac. NeAP; PmAP

Centered. P. Inman. FTOS

Centipede adown the street, The. Archy at the Zoo. Don Marquis. NBLV; OBAL *Fr.* Archy and Mehitabel.

Centipede along the threshold crept, The. Thomas Hood. *Fr.* The Haunted House. EBEV

Centipede was happy quite, A. *Unknown.* CTV; OBSP

Central. Ted Kooser. Poetsp

Central Park. Martha Hollander. GaP

Central Park. Robert Lowell. LiTM

Central Park. Julian Symons. PeLV

Central Park Some People (3 P.M.) Nancy Morejón, *Spanish.* PBWP, *tr. by* Sylvia Carranza

Centre of equal daughters, equal sons. America. Walt Whitman. FaBoA

Centuries. Ronald Stuart Thomas. CABP

Century has gone by. And again, A. Variation on Nekrasov. "Naum Korzhavin," *Russian.* TCRP, *tr. by* Vladimir Lunis *and* Albert C. Todd

Century of Hands. Michael Davidson. FTOS

Century Piece for Poor Heine, A. John Logan. NNaP

Century Prayer, The. James Ephriam McGirt. AAP

Century's blind man!, The. (LL) Melting Pot. Michael Echeruo. PBMAP

Century's no longer new, The. A Toast to 2,000. Richard Percival Lister. OBCoV

Ceremon(y)(ies) of Mutability, The. William Harmon. WeT *Fr.* Legion: Civic Choruses.

Ceremonies for Candlemas[se] Eve. Robert Herrick. BeJo; CaPo

Ceremonies for Christmas[se]. Robert Herrick. BeJo; OBCP
    "Wassail the trees, that they may bear." PChr

Ceremony. Kattie M. Cumbo. BlSi

Ceremony. Jewel C. Latimore. BlSi

Ceremony. Richard M. Mishler. CDa

Ceremony, A. Robin Morgan.
    "We will grow old, and older." CrSp

Ceremony. William Stafford. LCAP-2

Ceremony. Richard Wilbur. CoAP; MoP; NAAL-2; NoAM

Ceremony after a Fire Raid. Dylan Thomas. AF; CMoP

Ceremony must be found, The. Speaking of Poetry. John Peale Bishop. OxBA

Ceremony of Sending. *Unknown, Osage Indian.*
    Hidden People and the Star People, The. STP, *tr.* by Barbara Tedlock

Ceremony upon Candlemas Eve. Robert Herrick. OBCP

Cernunnos. Hugh Maxton. CIP-2

Certain Americans refuse to return. Change. Phyllis Janowitz. EOEF

Certain branches cut. October. Denise Levertov. TRP

Certain Choices. Richard Shelton. Poetsp

Certain dark underground eyes. Picture of Loot. Alan Sillitoe. OxBTC

Certain day became a presence to me, A. Variation on a Theme by Rilke. Denise Levertov. CrSp

Certain Dinner For Thirty, A. Martial, *Latin.* OBCVT, *tr.* by Philip Murray

Certain dreams presage true events. Lust. Roo Borson. DeD

Certain Evening, A. G. K. Chesterton. OxAEP-2

Certain Lady, A. Dorothy Parker. NIP-4

Certain Maxims of Archy. Don Marquis. OBAL
    "I once heard the survivors." NBLV

Certain Mercies. Robert Graves. GTBS-P

Certain moments will never change, nor stop being. Thinking about the Past. Donald Justice. MT

Certain painter, leaving in the morning, A. The Saddled Ass. Jean de La Fontaine, *French.* NBLV, *tr.* by Deems Taylor

Certain People. Richard Jones. NAmP90

Certain people would not clean their buttons. The Bohemians. Ivor Gurney. PeFWW

Certain presuppositions are altered. Upland. A. R. Ammons. NOBA

Certain scholar named Mr. Wang, A. *Unknown, Chinese.* CoBCP, *tr.* by Burton Watson

Certain Slant of Sunlight, A. Ted Berrigan. PT

Certain Tall Buildings. Franz Wright. NAmP90

Certain things here are quietly American. Derek Walcott. NAEL-2; NoP-4 *Fr.* Midsummer.

Certain True Woords Spoken Concerning One Benet Corbett after Her Death. Richard Corbet. SeCP

Certain Type of Scientist Speaks, A. Alexander Pope. ECEV *Fr.* Yet, yet a moment, one dim ray of light. NAEL-1; OAEL-1; PoEL-3 *Fr.* The Dunciad.

Certain words disappear from a language. Louisiana Perch. Ron Padgett. FTOS

Certain Year, A. Kunbae Yi, *Korean.* CKP, *tr.* by Jaihiun Kim

Certain Years. Otto Orban, *Hungarian.* CEEP, *tr.* by Jascha Kessler

Certain young chap named Bill Beebee, A. Limerick. *Unknown.* PeLi

Certain young gourmet of Crediton, A. Limerick. Charles Cuthbert Inge. PeLi

Certain Young Lady, A. Washington Irving. FaBoBe

Certain young man of Hilgay, A. Limerick. Ida Thurtle. PeLi

Certain young pate who was addle, A. Limerick. Arthur Shaw. PeLi

Certain young sheik I'm not namin', A. Limerick. *Unknown.* PeLi

Certain youthful lady in Thoulouse, A. Sonnet: Of the Eyes of a Certain Mandetta. Guido Cavalcanti, *Italian.* AWP, *tr.* by D. G. Rossetti

Certainly Metaphysics. Asa Benveniste. NBrP

Certainly the mountain in front. The Ascent. Stefan Aug. Doinas, *Romanian.* CEEP, *tr.* by Peter Jay *and* Virgil Nemoianu

Certainly there was something to their stories. Childe Roland, etc. Elder Olson. OBAL

Certainly they are the same weathered trees. From the Field. Lenard D. Moore. GT

Certainty Before Lunch. John Berryman. LCAP-2; OxBC

Certificate of Live Birth. Kimberly M. Blaeser. UnSA

Cerveteri road. Elena Clementelli. *Fr.* Etruscan Notebook. PBWP, *tr.* by Ruth Feldman *and* Brian Swann (b. 1940)

'Cession's stahted on de gospel way, De. A Spiritual. Paul Laurence Dunbar. BPo

C'est l'arbre de Jesse. The Green Chateau. Wendy Mulford. NBrP

C'est Plus Qu'en Crime, C'est une Faute. David Trinidad. WWSi

Cetewayo, chief of the Zulus. Footnote. Anthony Delius. PeSA

Ceyx and Alcyone. Ovid, *Latin.* NoSic, *tr.* by Arthur Golding *Fr.* Metamorphoses.

Cézanne. Gertrude Stein. TAP

Cha Till Maccruimein (Departure of the 4th Camerons). Ewart Alan Mackintosh. NSI

Chaadayev on Basmannaya. Oleg Grigorevich Chukhonstev, *Russian.* TCRP, *tr.* by Simon Franklin

Chace: "Of the Litter of Whelps," The. Marcus Aurelius Olympis Nemesianus, *Latin.*
    "When now the third revolving Moon appears." OBCVT, *tr.* by William Somervile

Chaeronean Plutarch, to thy deathless praise. Plutarch. Agathias, *Greek.* AWP, *tr.* by Dryden

Chaffinch flies fast, The. Cherry Tree. Ivy O. Eastwick. BoTP

Chagall's Cornflowers. Andrey Andreievich Voznesensky, *Russian.* TCRP, *tr.* by Vera Dunham *and* H. W. Tjalsma

Chagrin. Isaac Rosenberg. MoBrPo

Chahcoal Man. *Unknown.* AS

Chain, The. Maxine W. Kumin. NMM-2

Chain. Audre Lorde. BlSi

Chain of memory is resurrection I am a vain man, The. Charles Olson. APSN

Chain of Pearl, A. Lady Diana Primrose.
    First Pearle, The: Religion. KTR
    Fourth Pearl, The: Temperance. WPE
    ("Golden Bridle of *Bellerophon*, The.") KTR
    Sixth Pearle, The: Justice. KTR

Chain saw stops, The. Robert Spiess. HA

Chained in the market-place he stood. The African Chief. William Cullen Bryant. BLPA; ColAP

Chains are loosed, and at a smack, The. Flight of Leeona. Albery Allson Whitman. AAP *Fr.* Not a Man and Yet a Man.

Chains of Fire. Elsa Gidlow.
    "I know myself linked by chains of fire." CrSp

Chains of hell that hold his friend, The. (LL) 4.7. Horace, *Latin.* NAEL-1; OBVE, *tr.* by Samuel Johnson

Chains that bind my thinking, The. The Searching. Alice S. Cobb. BlSi

Chair. Hagiwara Sakutaro, *Japanese.* PFTM, *tr.* by Hiroaki Sato

Chair, Dog, and Clock. Hilary Corke. NYBP

Chair she sat in, like a burnished throne, The. A Game of Chess. T. S. Eliot. SCV *Fr.* The Waste Land. AmPP; CMoP; FaBoMo; HAP; LiTM; MoAmPo; MoP; NAAL-2; NAEL-2; NAWM-2; NOBA; NOBE; NoAM; NoP-4; OAEL-2; OxAEP-2; OxBA; OxBTC; PoE; TAP; TFi; UnPo

Chair That Is Filled, The. Carrie Biggs. PWR

Chairs. Valerie Worth. NTCP

Chairs in Snow. Elwyn Brooks White. ChAP

Chairs to Mend. *Unknown.* OxNR
    ("I never would cry, Old chairs to mend.") (LL) OxNR
    ("I never would cry old clothes to sell.") (LL) ReMoGo
    (Old Chairs to Mend.) ReMoGo

Chalcan Female Song. *Unknown.* PFTM, *tr.* by John Bierhorst *Fr.* Cantares Mexicanos.

Chalice: I heard a radiant ring, with no tongue. Cynewulf. ASW, *tr.* by Kevin Crossley-Holland *Fr.* Riddles (Exeter Book).

Chalk and Soot. Wassily Kandinsky, *Russian.* PFTM, *tr.* by Elizabeth R. Napier

Chalk mark sex of the nation, on walls we drummers know. Three Modes of History and Culture. Imamu Amiri Baraka. PmAP

Challenge. David Diop, *French.* NegPo, *tr.* by Ellen Conroy Kennedy

Challenge: A Court Ballad, The. Alexander Pope. PoEL-3

Chamber, The. Stuart Dischell. PUP-19

Chambered Nautilus, The. Oliver Wendell Holmes. APN-1; APo; AmPP; ColAP; FaBoBe; HoPM; ImPo; NAAL-3; NCAP; NOBA; NoP-4; PAR; PoEL-5; PoLF; TFi *Fr.* The Autocrat of the Breakfast Table.

Chameleon, The. Matthew Prior. OBSV

Chameleon was wrong, The. A Death Song. Steve Chimombo. HBAPE

Chameleons saw an arc of color, The. The Lord's Chameleons. Peter Klappert. AmPA

Chamois Hunter's Love, The. Felicia Dorothea Hemans. VWP

Chamouny; the Hour Before Sunrise. A Hymn. Coleridge. Ro

Champagne goes straight to my head. Thinking of You, Hiroshima. Betsy Sholl. PBCAP

Champagne Rosee. John Kenyon. OBEV

Championship Fight. Dave Jeddie Smith. NAmP90

Champs d'Honneur. Ernest Hemingway. AiP; PoA

"Champs Elysées of Broadway" says the awning. Elysian Fields. Marilyn Hacker. RA

Chance and chance and thereby starlit. Animula. George Oppen. FTOS

Chance And Essence. "Angelus Silesius." GePo, tr. by George C. Schoolfield Fr. The Cherubical Wanderer.

Chancellor's Nightmare, The. Sir William Schwenck Gilbert. See Nightmare, [A or The].

Chancery Morals. Winthrop Mackworth Praed. NOBRP

Chances, The. John Fletcher.
   "Merciless love, whom nature hath denied." GBL

Chances, The. Wilfred Owen. OxBTC

Chances of rhyme, The. Charles Tomlinson. FaBoMo; PoA

Chances "R." Allen Ginsberg. HCAP

Chandeliers hemorrhage, Tritons, The. Figures in a Ruined Ballroom. George Hitchcock. VGW

Chanel No. 5. Chase Twichell. NAmP90

Ch'ang-an. Ho Ching-ming. CoBLCP, tr. by Jonathan Chaves

Ch'ang-an after snow resembles spring returning. Replying to "On the Occasion of Morning Audience after Snow" Poem by Assistant Secretary Wang of the Board of Sacrifices. Ts'en Shen, Chinese. SuSp, tr. by Daniel Bryant

Ch'ang-an—one slip of moon. Tzu-yeh Song. Li Po, Chinese. CoBCP, tr. by Burton Watson

Ch'ang-ku. Li Ho, Chinese. SuSp, tr. by Maureen Robertson

Chang Liang's face was like a young woman's. Impromptu. Wu Wei-yeh, Chinese. CoBLCP, tr. by Jonathan Chaves

Chang Tuan's Cats. Felicity Bast. PC

Change, The. Abraham Cowley. CBLP; MeLP; SeCP Fr. The Mistress.

Change. Donne. CBLP; EBEV Fr. Elegies.

Change. Robert Graves. OxBTC

Change. Greville Fulke. Fr. Caelica.

Change. Phyllis Janowitz. EOEF

Change, The. Henry, Bishop of Chichester King. NOSC

Change, The. Ellis Ayitey Komey. PBMAP

Change, The. Matabaruka. PBCV

Change, The. David O'Bruadair, Irish. BIrV, tr. by Austin Clarke

Change. Charlotte Zolotow. AYFP

Change blots out change,—their very memory dies. Richard Henry Wilde. APN-1 Fr. Hesperia.

Change in Style, A. Eochadh O'Hussey. NOIV

Change in the Year, A. Wordsworth. AYFP; BoTP
   ("And grass in the green field.") (LL) AYFP
   (To My Sister.) OAEL-2

Change Is Not Always Progress. Don L. Lee. TAP

Change is the law. The new must oust the old. Last of His Tribe. Oodgeroo of the tribe Noonuccal. BMAP

Change: Kyoto-Tokyo Express; the. Allen Ginsberg. APSN

Change. / life if u were a match i wd light u. A Poem to Complement Other Poems. Don L. Lee. BPo; NBV

Change. / life if u were a match i wd light u into something beautiful. change. A Poem to Complement Other Poems. Haki R. Madhubuti. NAAAL

Change me, some God, into that breathing rose! Wordsworth. Son Fr. The River Duddon [A Series of Sonnets].

Change, move, dead clock, that this fresh day. Small Prayer. Weldon Kees. IMW; PoA; VGW

Change My Evil Ways. David Rivard. PUP-18

Change of Address. Kathleen Fraser. NYBP

Change / Polis / is this. (LL) Maximus, to Gloucester, Letter 27. Charles Olson. NOBA; PoE

Change Should Breed Change. William Drummond, of Hawthornden. OBEV

Change thy minde since she doth change. Robert Devereux, 2d Earl of Essex. PBRV

Change, to include a new horse. (LL) A Birth. James Dickey. FiLi; NOBA

Change-up. Don L. Lee. PoBA

Changed. Charles Stuart Calverley. NOBVV

Changed and not changed. Three million years. Fossil, 1975. Janet Lewis. CRP

Changed Mind (or the Day I Woke Up). Tejumola Ologboni. NBV

Changed, Yet Constant. Thomas Stanley. BeJo

Changeful Beauty. Unknown, Greek. EnLoPo, tr. by Andrew Lang

Changeling, The. Charlotte Mew. CH; NOxBChV
   ("I shall never came back again!") (LL) NOxBChV

Changeling, The. Thomas Middleton. FaBoSe; PoEL-2

Changeling VIII. Kristjana Gunnars. NOBC

Changes. "Owen Meredith." PoLF

Changes. May Probyn. VWP

Changing. Tanka. Sasaki Yukitsuna, Japanese. MJT, tr. by Makoto Ueda

Changing Address Books. Michael S. Glaser. UnSA

Changing Diapers. Gary Snyder. RaBo

Changing guests, each in a different mood, The. Inclusiveness. D. G. Rossetti. NAEL-2 Fr. The House of Life.

Changing Light at Sandover, The. James Merrill. NAAL-2

Changing Room. John A. Scott. BMAP

Changing the Wheel. Bertolt Brecht, German. PoSu, tr. by Michael Hamburger

Changing water. Adding aspirin. Nitrogen, potash or. Flowers. Kathleen Fraser. CrSp

Changtzu 33. Chech'on Park, Korean. CKP, tr. by Jaihiun Kim

Channel Crossing. George Barker. GTBS-P

Channel Firing. Thomas Hardy. CABP; CMoP; EBEV; HAP; HeIP-4; ImPo; MoP; NAEL-2; NIP-4; NoAM; NoP-4; OAEL-2; OxAEP-2; OxBTC; PeECV; PeFWW; PoE; PoEL-5; PoPoPo; PoRA; PoWW; Poetr; RB; SoSe-8; TFi; UnPo

Channel moon went down, as ignorance, The. The Outlanders. Andrew Glaze. NYBP

Chanson. Pernette De Guillet, French. PBWP, tr. by Joan Keefe and Richard Terdiman

Chanson. René Vivien. CPO

Chanson Dada. Tristan Tzara, French. PFTM, tr. by Rothenberg, Matthew

Chanson d'Outre Tombe. Philip Whalen. BB

Chanson du Décervelage, La. Alfred Jarry, French. CBNP, tr. by Cyril Connolly and Simon Taylor Fr. Ubu Cocu.

Chansons d'Automne. Paul Verlaine, French. AWP, tr. by Arthur Symons

Chant for Reapers. Wilfrid Thorley. OBEV

Chant for Young/Brothas and Sistuhs, A. Sonia Sanchez. BPo

Chant from the Iroquois Book of Rites. Unknown, Onondaga Native American. APN-2, tr. by Horatio Hale

Chant-Pagan. Rudyard Kipling. FaBoPV

Chant to the Fire-Fly. Unknown, Ojibwa Native American. APN-2, tr. by Henry Rowe Schoolcraft

Chantars No Pot Gaire Valer. Bernard de Ventadour, Provençal. APSN, tr. by Paul Blackburn

Chanted Calendar, A. Sydney Thompson Dobell. BoTP; OBEV Fr. Balder.

Chanticleer. John Chipman Farrar. CTV

Chanticleer. Celia Laighton Thaxter. NOxBChV

Chanting Cherubs, The [A Group by Greenough]. Richard Henry Dana. APN-1

CHANTING IN TIBET HAS NOT CEASED— / IT IS AS IMMORTAL AS MEAT, THE. Moiré. Michael McClure. SPE

Chanting of banishment, / exhaling flame. Elegy for the Time at Hand. "Adunis," Arabic. AF, tr. by Samuel Hazo

Chanting Poems. Wang Chiu-ssu, Chinese. CoBLCP, tr. by Jonathan Chaves

Chanting sun, as ever, rivals, The. Goethe. NAWM-2, tr. by Louis MacNeice Fr. Faust.

Chanting the square deific, out of the One advancing, out of the sides. Walt Whitman. APN-1; NAAL-1; NAAL-3

Chanting These Verses on My Way to Yodoe. Su Man-shu, Chinese. SuSp, tr. by Wu-chi Liu

Chants, The. María Sabina, Mazatec Indian.
   "Ah, Jesu Kri." STP, tr. by Henry Munn

Chants Communal. Horace Logo Traubel.
   What Can I Do? TrJP

Chants to the Deity. Unknown, Ojibwa Native American. APN-2, tr. by Henry Rowe Schoolcraft

Chaos. Still Life: The Table. Theo Van Doesburg, Dutch. PFTM, tr. by Jerome Rothenberg

Chap was so pose that was adi, A. Limerick. Arthur Shaw. PeLi

Chapel at the crossways bore no scar, The. The Guard's Mistake. Edmund Blunden. NSI

Chapel— / like a kneeling mother, A. Landscape With Apparition. Justinas Marcinkevius, Lithuanian. CEEP, tr. by Irene Pogoželskyte Suboczewski

Chapel's cowbell, The. Crusoe's Island. Derek Walcott. VCWP

Chaplet, The. Moses Mendes. TrJP

Chaplinesque. Hart Crane. CMoP; HeIP-4; LiTM; MoP; NAAL-2; NOBA; NoAM; OxBA; VGW

Chapman the Translator. Michael Drayton. EPCY Fr. To Henry Reynolds, of Poets and Poesy.

Chapmen. Unknown. FaBoVe

Chapped loaves of bread whisper through cracked lips. Inevitability. Imants Ziedonis, Latvian. CEEP, tr. by Inara Cedrins

Chapter Heading. Ernest Hemingway. PoA

Chapter One. Stephanie Brown. BAP-93

Chapter II. Elizabeth Singer Rowe. PEW *Fr.* A Paraphrase on the Canticles.

Chapter IV. Elizabeth Singer Rowe. PEW

Chapter V. Elizabeth Singer Rowe. PEW

Character. Detonation. Francesco Cangiullo. PFTM

Character. Ralph Waldo Emerson. OxBSP

Character. Taslima Nasrin, *Bengali*. VCWP, *tr. by* Carolyne Wright *and* Farida Sarkar

Character. Phan Bội Châu, *Vietnamese*. AVP, *tr. by* Huỳnh Sanh Thông

Character, A. Clara Reeve. ECWP

Character, A. Tennyson. EBVVPR

Character and beauty. (LL) The Minks. Toi Derricotte. NAmP90; PuP-15

Character, indistinct, entered, A. Thomas Kinsella. NoAM *Fr.* Songs of the Psyche.

Character of a Critic. Charles Churchill. NOEC *Fr.* The Rosciad.

Character of a Good Parson, The. Dryden. NOCV

Character of a Happy Life, The. Sir Henry Wotton. EBEvV; GTBS-P; NOBE; NOSC; NTP; OBEV

Character of a landscape stands always in a mysterious relation, The. Landscape I. Charles Madge. SPE

Character of a Roundhead, The. *Unknown.* FaBoPV; NOSC

Character of Holland, The. Andrew Marvell. NOBL; PeLV
"Holland, that scarce deserves the name of land." OBSV

Character of Love Seen as a Search for the Lost, The. Kenneth Patchen. CLPP; VGW

Character of Sir Robert Walpole, The. Jonathan Swift. FaBoEE; PoE

Character of the Happy Warrior. Wordsworth. FaBoBe

Characteristics of a Child Three Years Old. Wordsworth. LaPo

Charade. *Unknown.* OxNR

Charcoal. Wilson Harris. PDCV

Chard Whitlow. Henry Reed. BXAP; LiTM; MoBrPo; NBLV; NOBL; NoP-4; OBCoV; OxBTC; PeLV; UV; UnPo

Charge, A. Herbert Trench. OBEV

Charge of the Light Brigade, The. Tennyson. APAD; BLPA; CABP; CTV; ChAP; EBEvV; EnVR; FHYEP; FaBoBe; FaPoR; HoPM; NAEL-2; NOBVV; NoP-4; OBWP; OxAEP-2; PBMP; PeVV; TFi; UV
("Honour the Light Brigade, / Noble six hundred!") (LL) CTV
"Stormed at with shot and shell." Poetr

Charge the the Bread Brigade, The. Ezra Pound *and* Noel Stock. UV *Fr.* The Poems of Alfred Venison, the Poet of Titchfield Street.

Charge to the Poets, A. William Whitehead.
"If nature prompts you, or if friends persuade." OBSV
"Life of writing, unless wondrous short, A." ECEV

Chariot. Stanley Kunitz. BAP-93

Chariot Wheel, A. Auvaiyar, *Tamil*. PLW, *tr. by* A. K. Ramanujan

Charioteer of Delphi, The. James Merrill. GS; GrIP

Charis, guess[e], and do[e] not miss[e]. Claiming [*or* Clayming] a Second Kiss[e] by Desert. Ben Jonson. *Fr.* A Celebration of Charis in Ten Lyric[k] Pieces [*or* Peeces]. BeJo; OxAEP-1; SeCP

Charis one day in discourse. Urging Her of a Promise. Ben Jonson. *Fr.* A Celebration of Charis in Ten Lyric[k] Pieces [*or* Peeces]. BeJo; OxAEP-1; SeCP

Charité Espérance et Foi. Earle Birney. OxBC

Charity. Connie Bensley. FaBoWP

Charity. Henrietta Cordelia Ray. CBWP-3

Charity. *Unknown.* BLPA

Charity lotteries for dream houses, The. Judith Wright. *Fr.* Habitat. CBAP

Charity Overcoming Envy. Marianne Moore. GS; NYBP

Charles and Bruce, Geoff and Ron and Nancy. All Friends Together. Ronald Albert Simpson. NOBAu

Charles Augustus Fortescue. Hilaire Belloc. NoAM

Charles Augustus Milverton. Gavin Ewart. OxBoV

Charles Carville's Eyes. Edwin Arlington Robinson. CMoP; MeMAP; OxBA; TAP

Charles Donnelly. Donagh MacDonagh.
"Of what a quality is courage made." CIP-2

Charles Guiteau. *Unknown.* AmFP

Charles Harpur in his journals long ago. Extinct Birds. Judith Wright. PBWP

Charles II. Andrew Marvell. *Fr.* The Last Instructions to a Painter.

Charles II. *Unknown.* FaBoEE

Charles on Fire. James Merrill. HeIP-4

Charles reaps here like a sickle, The. Professor Kelleher and the Charles River. Desmond O'Grady. CIP-2; PBCIV

Charles Sumner. Charlotte L. Forten Grimke. AAP

Charles Sumner. Henrietta Cordelia Ray. CBWP-3

Charles the First. Shelley.
Song, A: "Widow bird sate mourning for her love, A." NOBE; OBNC; OxBSP; PoEL-4

Charles the King, our Emperor, the Great. The Song of Roland. *Unknown, Old French*. NAWM-1, *tr. by* Frederick Goldin, *abr.*

Charles used to watch Naomi, taking heart. Laboratory Poem. James Merrill. InPK-6; TwCP

Charles XII of Sweden. Samuel Johnson. NOBE *Fr.* The Vanity of Human Wishes [The Tenth Satire of Juvenal Imitated]. EBEV; ECEV; NOEC; OAEL-1; OxAEP-1; PoEL-3; TFi

Charleston. Henry Timrod. APN-2; AmPP; CBCWP; ColAP; NOBA; OxBA; TAP

Charleston Garden, A. Henry Bellamann. PoLF

Charleston in the Eighteen-Sixties. Adrienne Rich. CoAP; NAAL-2

Charley Barley, butter and eggs. *Unknown.* OxNR

Charley, Charley. *Unknown.* OxNR

Charley du Bignon. Mary E. Tucker. CBWP-1

Charley Parker Looked like Buddha. 239th Chorus. Jack Kerouac. BB *Fr.* Mexico City Blues.

Charley Warlie had a cow. *Unknown.* OxNR

Charlie Chaplin. The Charlie Chaplin Poem. Osip Mandelstam, *Russian*. PFTM, *tr. by* Barbara Einzig *and* Jerome Rothenberg

Charlie Chaplin Poem, The. Osip Mandelstam, *Russian*. PFTM, *tr. by* Barbara Einzig *and* Jerome Rothenberg

Charlie Green was a member of Fletcher Henderson's. The Depression. Doug Lang. MoNo

Charlie He's My Darling. Robert Burns. CH; FaBoPV

Charlie MacPherson. *Unknown.* ESPB

Charlie Parker looked like Buddha. Jack Kerouac. *See* 239th Chorus: "Charley Parker Looked like Buddha."

Charlie Parker's on the off ramp. Valentine's Day. Kenneth May. SeSe

Charlie Piccen. L. Murray *and* F. Leigh. OxBoLi

Charlie Wolf used to whittle skinning knives. Halcyon Days. Jim Barnes. CDW; VCAP

Charlie's Sad Date. Rafael Alberti, *Spanish*. CBNP, *tr. by* Mark Strand

Charlot, who my controller is chief. Epistle from Fern Hill. Mary Jones. ECWP

Charlotte Brontë. "Susan Coolidge." OBCA

Charlotte Brontë. Paul Hamilton Hayne. APN-2

Charlotte Brontë said, "Wow, sister! *What* a man!" Limerick. Victor Gray. NOBL; PeLi

Charlotte Corday. Charles Tomlinson. OxBC

Charlotte, Her Book. Elizabeth Bartlett. FaBoWP

Charlottie liv'd on a mountain top in a bleak and lonely spot. The Frozen Girl. *Unknown.* AS

Charm, A. *Unknown, Anglo-Saxon.* RB, *tr. by* Richard Hammer

Charm a single charm is doubtful, A. Nothing Elegant. Gertrude Stein. PBWP *Fr.* Tender Buttons.

Charm against the Toothache, A. John Heath-Stubbs. TwCP

Charm for Lighting the Fire, A. *Unknown, Irish*. NOIV, *tr. by* Thomas Kinsella

Charm for Love and Lasting Affection, A. *Unknown, Irish*. NOIV, *tr. by* Thomas Kinsella

Charm is the measure of attraction's power. What Is Charm? Louisa Carroll Thomas. BLPA

Charm Mary put on the butter, The. A Charm for Love and Lasting Affection. *Unknown, Irish*. NOIV, *tr. by* Thomas Kinsella

Charm me asleep, and melt me so. Robert Herrick. *Fr.* To Music, to Becalm His Fever. BeJo; CaPo; OBEV

Charm me asleep, and melt me so. To Music, to Becalm His Fever. Robert Herrick. BeJo; CaPo; OBEV

Charm of rouge on fragile cheeks, The. Maquillage. Arthur Symons. ADE; OxBSP

Charm Rhyme, A. *Unknown.* FaBoVe

Charme, or an Allay for Love, A. Robert Herrick. FaBoCh

Charmer Turned Ascetic, A. Marippittiyar, *Tamil*. PLW, *tr. by* A. K. Ramanujan

Charmes. Robert Herrick. BeJo

Charming Beauty Bright. *Unknown.* AmFP

Charming girl, full of dejected love, A. For My Wife. Liu Hsiao-Wei, *Chinese*. EP, *tr. by* Anne Birrell

Charming Woman, The. Helen Selina Blackwood. VWP; WPE

Charmion's Lament. Eloise Bibb. CBWP-4

Charms and Knots. George Herbert. KSG

Charms for a Sudden Stitch. *Unknown, Anglo-Saxon.* AnOE, *tr. by* Charles W. Kennedy

Charms for Unfruitful Land. *Unknown, Anglo-Saxon.* AnOE, *tr. by* Charles W. Kennedy

Charms of Nature, The. Joseph Warton. *Fr.* Enthusiast, The; or, The Lover of Nature. PoEL-3

Charms, that call down the moon from out her sphere. To Music, to Becalm a Sweet-sick Youth. Robert Herrick. CaPo

Charnel Ground, The. Allen Ginsberg. BB

Charnel-house, The. Henry Vaughan. FSCP

Charnel thickens into a shadow. . . The boys, meanwhile, The. Vladimir Holan, *Czech.* CEEP, *tr. by* Miroslav Hanak

Charon. Louis MacNeice. FaBoTw; PNI

Charon, *see also* Charon *tr. by* Gavin Douglas. Virgil. OBVE, *tr. by* John Dryden *Fr.* The Aeneid [*or* Eneados, Aeneis].

Charon, *see also* Charon *tr. by* Dryden. Virgil. OBVE, *tr. by* Gawin Douglas *Fr.* The Aeneid [*or* Eneados, Aeneis].

Charon! Thou slave! Thou fool! Thou Cavalier [*or* Cavaleer]! A Mock Charon. Richard Lovelace. CaPo

Charon's Cosmology. Charles Simic. HCAP; PoPoPo

Chartist's Complaint, The. Ralph Waldo Emerson. NCAP

Chartivel. Marie de France, *French.*
    Song from "Chartivel." AWP

Chartres. Edith Wharton. APN-2

Chase, The. William Somervile.
    Hare-hunting. NOEC
    "See! there she goes." ECEV

Chase, The. John Webster *and* William Rowley. *See* Art Thou Gone in Haste?

Chased from my calling to this hackneyed trade. James Kennedy. NOEC *Fr.* The Exile's Reveries.

Chasing the Bird. Robert Creeley. MoNo

Chasm. A. R. Ammons. OBAL

Chaste Florimel. Matthew Prior. BoLoP

Chaste Stranger, The. James Tate. NoAM

Chaste trees, dark-clustered, The. A Leaf in Love and War. Veṛipātiya Kāmakkaṇṇiyār, *Tamil.* PLW, *tr. by* A. K. Ramanujan

Chastity. Milton. *Fr.* Comus; a Masque Presented at Ludlow Castle. FHYEP; OAEL-1

Chastity ("I Mean That Too, But Yet a Hidden Strength"). Milton. NOSC *Fr.* Comus; a Masque Presented at Ludlow Castle. FHYEP; OAEL-1

Château, The. Henry Reed. NoP-4

Chateaux en Espagne. Henrietta Cordelia Ray. CBWP-3

Chatsworth. Charles Cotton. OBGa *Fr.* The Wonders of the Peak.

Chattanooga. Ishmael Reed. NAAAL

Chatte-Show Host came with us, yclept Wogan, A. Chaucer: The Wogan's Tale. Stanley J. Sharpless. UV

Chatter of birds two by two raises a night song joining a litany of running water. Prairie Waters by Night. Carl Sandburg. NAAL-2

Chattering finch and water-fly. The Skeleton. G. K. Chesterton. FaBoTw

Chattering swallow! what shall we. The Swallow. Thomas Stanley. AWP

Chatting on deck was Dryden too. Walter Savage Landor. EPCY *Fr.* To Wordsworth.

Chaucer. Hartley Coleridge.
    "No doubt he well invented, nobly felt." EPCY

Chaucer. Henry Wadsworth Longfellow. APN-1; AWP; HeIP-4; MeMAP; NOBA; OBEV; OxBA; PoE; PoRA; Son; TAP; TFi

Chaucer, Langland, Douglas, Dunbar, with all your. Ode to the Medieval Poets. W. H. Auden. PoA

Chaucer: The Wogan's Tale. Stanley J. Sharpless. UV

Chaucer's Wishes for his 'Troilus'. Chaucer. *See* Go, Little Book.

Chaunt of the Brazen Head, The. Winthrop Mackworth Praed.
    "I think the thing you call Renown." OBSV

Chaunts of Life. Mathilde Blind. VWP *Fr.* The Ascent of Man.

Chaunts of the Brazen Head, The. Winthrop Mackworth Praed. NOBRP

Chawcer upon this fyfte meter of the second book. Boethius, *Latin.* OBCVT, *tr. by* Geoffrey Chaucer

Che is with-out longing. (LL) I Have a Young Sister. *Unknown.* CH; EBEV; EnVB; FaBoVe; InPS-3; MiEL; NAEL-1; OAEL-1; PeLV; PoEL-1

Cheap Replicas of the Eiffel Tower. Elton Glaser. PBCAP

Cheat, The. Joseph Beaumont. NOSC

Cheat of Cupid; or, The Ungentle Guest, The. Robert Herrick. AWP; OBVE

Chee, chee, chee. (LL) Robert of Lincoln. William Cullen Bryant. FaBoBe; OBCA

Cheekbone footprint husk if only they could write. Centered. P. Inman. FTOS

Cheer, The. William Meredith. AFr

Cheer and salute for the Admiral, and here's to the Captain bold, A. The Men behind the Guns. John Jerome Rooney. BLPA; FaBoBe

Cheer for the Consumer. Nixon Waterman. OBAL

Cheer up, cheer up! my own Jeannette, tho' far away I go. Jeannot's Answer. Charles Jefferys. BLPA

Cheer up, my mates, the wind does fairly blow. Abraham Cowley. OxAEP-1

Cheerfu' supper done, wi' serious face, The. Robert Burns. *Fr.* The Cotter's Saturday Night transcribed to Robert Aiken [*or* R. A****], Esq. FaBoBe; NOBRP; PoLF

Cheerful arn he blaws in the marn, The. The Cheerful Horn. *Unknown.* CH

Cheerful Chilterns, The. Frank Sidgwick. BXAP

Cheerful Girls at Smiller's Bar, The. Jack A. Mapanje. HBAPE; PeSAV (Cheerful Girls at Smiller's Bar, 1971, The.) PBMAP ("Preservation of our traditional / et cetera. . . , The.") (LL) PBMAP

Cheerful Horn, The. *Unknown.* CH

Cheerful old bear at the zoo, A. *Unknown.* CTV

Cheerleaders, The. Jack Matthews. CMAP

Cheers, Cheers for Old Cha Cha Ass ("Cheers, cheers for old Patchogue High"). Walta Borawski. GLP

Cheeses, pâté. Rod Willmot. HA

Cheetie-Poussie-Cattie, O. *Unknown.* FaBoCh

Chef Yeats, that master of the use of herbs. Michael Hartnett. NOIV *Fr.* A Farewell to English.

Chekhov, my country is Ward 6. Ward 6. Tanure Ojaide. HBAPE

Chelmsfords Fate. Benjamin Tompson. SCAP

Chemicals ripen the citrus. In California. Donald Davie. NoAM

Chemin Des Dames. Crosbie Garstin. NSI

Chemistry of Character, The. Elizabeth Dorney. BLPA

Ch'en-hsi County. Ho Ching-ming, *Chinese.* CoBLCP, *tr. by* Jonathan Chaves

Cheng-tao Temple. Tai Piao-yüan, *Chinese.* CoBLCP, *tr. by* Jonathan Chaves

Chengtu. Tu Fu, *Chinese.* TAL, *tr. by* Robert Payne

Chepstow: A Poem. Edward Davies. OBWVE

Chercheuses de Poux, Les. Rimbaud. AWP, *tr. by* T. Sturge Moore *Fr.* Illuminations.

Chernobyl. Mary Jo Salter. FFC

Cherokee, The. Mary Weston Fordham. CBWP-2

Cherokee Love Song, A. John Rollin Ridge. APN-2; PaTW

Cherries. Joe Lamb. RaBo

Cherries. Zalman Schneour, *Yiddish.* TrJP, *tr. by* Joseph Leftwich

Cherries; a Parable. Thomas Moore. OBSV

Cherry. Stuart Dybek. PBCAP

Cherry, A. *Unknown.* ReMoGo

Cherry and pear are white. The Crowns. John Freeman. CH

Cherry-Blossom Wand, The. Anna Wickham. MoBrPo

Cherry blossoms, The. Spring. Princess Shikishi, *Japanese.* PBWP, *tr. by* Hiroaki Sato

Cherry blossoms. Tanka. Kanoko Okamoto, *Japanese.* MJT, *tr. by* Makoto Ueda

Cherry blossoms. Tanka. Tawara Machi, *Japanese.* MJT, *tr. by* Makoto Ueda

Cherry Bombs. Alice Fulton. NAmP90

Cherry Fair, The. *Unknown.*
    "This lyfe, I see, is but a cheyre feyre."

Cherry-lipped Adonis. Richard Barnfield. Son *Fr.* Cynthia.

Cherry petals. Tanka. Kanoko Okamoto, *Japanese.* MJT, *tr. by* Makoto Ueda

Cherry-ripe. Robert Herrick. BeJo; CH; CaPo; EBEvV; OBEV; PeLV

Cherry Robbers. D. H. Lawrence. MoBrPo

Cherry Tree. Ivy O. Eastwick. BoTP

Cherry Tree, The. Thom Gunn. GLP; Poetsp

Cherry-Tree Carol, The. *Unknown.* AmFP; EBEV; ESPB; EnSB; HeIP-4; OAEL-1; OBCP; OxBB; OxBoLi; PeECV; SCGP; TFi

Cherry tree is down, and dead, that was so high, The. Small Dark Song. Philip Dacey. CMAP

Cherry Trees, The. Edward Thomas. NAEL-2; OBWP; PeFWW; Spl

Cherry year, A. *Unknown.* OxNR

Cherrylog Road. James Dickey. CoAP; ColAP; HAP; HCAP; InPS-3; MT; NAAL-2; NIP-4; NYBP; Poetr; TwCP; WeW-3

Cherubical Wanderer, The. "Angelus Silesius," *German.*
    Abomination Of Evil, The. GePo, *tr. by* George C. Schoolfield
    "Belief, great mustard seed, sends mountains to the sea." GePo, *tr. by* George C. Schoolfield
    Body, Soul, And Godhead. GePo, *tr. by* George C. Schoolfield
    Chance And Essence. GePo, *tr. by* George C. Schoolfield
    Each In His Own. GePo, *tr. by* George C. Schoolfield
    God Is Nothing Physical. GePo, *tr. by* George C. Schoolfield

God Is To Me What I Desire. GePo, *tr. by* George C. Schoolfield

I Am As God And God As I. GePo, *tr. by* George C. Schoolfield

Light Exists In The Fire, The. GePo, *tr. by* George C. Schoolfield

"Love is a twin to death; it makes my senses dead." GePo, *tr. by* George C. Schoolfield

Man Is The Highest Thing. GePo, *tr. by* George C. Schoolfield

More Abandoned, The More Divine, The. GePo, *tr. by* George C. Schoolfield

One Knows Not What One Is. GePo, *tr. by* George C. Schoolfield

Only His Son Is With God. GePo, *tr. by* George C. Schoolfield

"Rose, regarded here by your external eyes, The." GePo, *tr. by* George C. Schoolfield

Secret Virginity, The. GePo, *tr. by* George C. Schoolfield

Sin. GePo, *tr. by* George C. Schoolfield

Spiritual Alchemy, The. GePo, *tr. by* George C. Schoolfield

Spiritual Ark And The Manna-Vessel, The. GePo, *tr. by* George C. Schoolfield

Spiritual Impregnation, The. GePo, *tr. by* George C. Schoolfield

Take Therefore That You May Have. GePo, *tr. by* George C. Schoolfield

To St. Augustine. GePo, *tr. by* George C. Schoolfield

Treasure Lies In the Cornerstone, The. GePo, *tr. by* George C. Schoolfield

Virtue's Goal Is God. GePo, *tr. by* George C. Schoolfield

Whoever Has Become All Divine. GePo, *tr. by* George C. Schoolfield

Chesapeake. Gerta Kennedy. NYBP

Chess. Martin Sorescu, *Romanian*. CEEP, *tr. by* Donald Eulert *and* Stefan Avadanei

Chess Piece Cornered. John Kinsella. BMAP

Chess Play, The. Nicholas Breton. NoSic

"Chessie," the Chesapeake and Ohio's. Our Flag Was Still There. Richard Tillinghast. WeT

Chest starts up again., The. (LL) The Assassination of John Lennon as Depicted by Madame Tussaud Wax Museum, Niagara Falls, Ontario, 1987. David Wojahn. NAmP90; PBCAP

Chestnut Avenue: at Alton House, The. Charles Tomlinson. FaBoTw

Chestnut Buds. Evelyn M. Williams. BoTP

Chestnut tree stands in the line of sight, A. St. Asaph's. Kingsley Amis. OxBTC

Chestnut's a fine tree, The. A Christmas-Tree Song. Rodney Bennett. BoTP

Chestnuts for Verdi. Roberta Spear. WeT

Chevy Chase. *Unknown.* EnSB; OxBB

(Hunting of the Cheviot, The.) EnVB

Chewing Chawing Gum. *Unknown.* AmFP

Chewing cud. Cow. Joan Fern Shaw. IFJA

Chewing [of] the Cud, The. Robert Herrick. ChIV-1

Cheyenne Mountain. Helen Hunt Jackson. APN-2

Chez Jane. Frank O'Hara. CoAP; ColAP; NOBA; NeAP; NoAM; PoA; PoE

Ch'i-yü-ko. *Unknown, Chinese.* CoBCP, *tr. by* Burton Watson

Chiang Lin-chi Treats Me to Mudfish. Mei Yao Ch'en, *Chinese.* SuSp, *tr. by* Jonathan Chaves

Chiang-nan¹ is a glorious and beautiful land. Song of the Men of Chin-ling. Hsieh T'iao, *Chinese.* ChiP, *tr. by* Arthur Waley

Ch'iang Village. Tu Fu, *Chinese.*

"Flocks of chicken clucking from every corner." SuSp, *tr. by* Irving Y. Lo

"From the jagged edges of purple clouds to the west." SuSp, *tr. by* Irving Y. Lo

Chiapas. Gary Soto. NoAM

Chic Freedom's Reflection. Alice Walker. InPS-3

Chicago. Margaret Walker Alexander. GT

Chicago. Bret Harte. APN-2; AiP

Chicago. Lola Ridge. PoA

Chicago. Carl Sandburg. AiP; AmPP; CMoP; ColAP; LiTM; MoAmPo; MoP; NAAL-2; NOBA; NoAM; OxBA; PoA; Poetr; TAP; TFi; TRP; UnPo; VGW

("Player with Railroads and Freight Handler to the Nation.") (LL) FaBoA; NoP-4; SAGP

Chicago *Defender* Sends a Man to Little Rock, The. Gwendolyn Brooks. CrDW; NAAAL; PoBA; Poetr

Chicago Exposition Ode. Mary Weston Fordham. CBWP-2

Chicago: "Manual of Style" is really neat, The. John Tranter. NoAM *Fr.* Crying in Early Infancy.

Chicago: Near West-Side Renewal. Dennis Schmitz. AmPA

Chicago Picasso, The. Gwendolyn Brooks. BPo; LiTM *Fr.* Two Dedications.

(Two Dedications.) NAAAL

Chicago Poem. Lew Welch. BB; NeAP; PoM

Chicago ran a fever of a hundred and one that groggy Sunday. The Shooting of John Dillinger outside the Biograph Theater July 22, 1934. David Wagoner. CoAP; FYAP; RB

Chicago, Summer Past. Richard Snyder. Poetsp

Chick! my naggie. *Unknown.* OxNR

Chickadee. Brendan Galvin. CMAP

Chickadees should never. Natural Selection. Jess Williamson. PC

Chicken, The. Vladimir Holan, *Czech.* PoSu, *tr. by* Ian *and* Jarmila Milner

Chicken. *Unknown. Fr.* Hunter Poems of the Yoruba. RB, *tr. by* Ulli Beier

Chicken blessed and caressed. *Unknown.* NOEC *Fr.* A Collection of Hymns. . . of the Moravian Brethren.

Chicken, she chided early, should not wait. Sunday Chicken. Gwendolyn Brooks. ColAP *Fr.* Notes from the Childhood and the Girlhood. LCAP-2

Chicken thaws, blood, A. Eden. Claudia Rankine. GT

Chickens. William Carlos Williams. *See* The Red Wheelbarrow.

Chickens a-crowin' on Sourwood Mountain. Sourwood Mountain. *Unknown.* AS

Chickory. Zerubavel Gal'ed, *Hebrew.* TrJP

Chide, chide no more away. Expectation. Thomas Stanley. BeJo

Chief Defect of Henry King, The. Henry King, Who Chewed Bits of String, and Was Early Cut Off in Dreadful Agonies. Hilaire Belloc. FuFo; NBLV; OBCoV; OxAEP-2; PeLV

Chief Leschi of the Nisqually. Duane Niatum. CDW

Chief of all. Samson's Complaint. Milton. NOSC *Fr.* Samson Agonistes. FHYEP; OAEL-1; PoEL-3

Chief of the civil administration / of the occupying power reflects, The. Pilate. Donald Davie. GI

Chief of the West, Darkling, The. David Knight. MoCV

Chief Petty Officer. Charles Causley. OxBTC

Chief Stewardess on a Boeing, The. Limerick. Paul Alexander. PeLi

Chiefly to Mind Appears. C. Day Lewis. MoBrPo

Chieftain Iffucan of Azcan in caftan. Bantams in Pine-Woods. Wallace Stevens. CMoP; InPS-3; MeMAP; NOBA; NoAM; OxBA; PFE; SAmP; UnPo

Chieftain to the Highlands bound, A. Lord Ullin's Daughter. Thomas Campbell. BoTP; FaPoR; GTBS-P; NOBRP

Child. Sylvia Plath. HCAP; MDDM; PBWP

Child. Raymond Roseliep. KaS

Child, The. Judith Wright. BMAP

Child (a boy) bouncing, A. To. William Carlos Williams. OBAL

Child, and all children. To a Christmas Two-Year-Old. Luci Shaw. TrCP

Child and Maiden. Sir Charles Sedley. GTBS-P *Fr.* The Mulberry Garden. (To Chloris.) OBEV

Child and Sea. Blaga Dimitrova, *Bulgarian.* CEEP, *tr. by* Jascha Kessler *and* Aleksandar Shurbanov

Child and the Mariner, The. W. H. Davies. CH

Child Asleep, A. J. P. Clark Bekederemo. PBMAP *Fr.* A Reed in the Tide.

Child at Brighton has been left to drown, A. Ballade of Genuine Concern. Hilaire Belloc. EBEvV

Child awaits the angel, The. The Angel. Alfred Hayes. TrJP

Child Bearers, The. Anne Sexton. BoWoP

Child Beater. Ai. BoWoP

Child, big black woman, pretty kitchen towels. (LL) Bronzeville Woman in a Red Hat. Gwendolyn Brooks. GT; NALW

Child brought blue clay from the creek, The. The Image. Robert Hass. BLT

Child climbs to the island's highest point, The. Edouard Glissant. NegPo, *tr. by* Ellen Conroy Kennedy *Fr.* The Indies.

Child Compassion, The. Margot Ruddock. OBMV

Child / Curious and innocent, A. To Robert Louis Stevenson. William Ernest Henley. MoBrPo

Child, Do Not Throw This Book About. Hilaire Belloc. EBEV; NoAM

Child draws another inscrutable house, The. Elizabeth Bishop. *See* Sestina: "September rain falls on the house."

Child Dying, The. Edwin Muir. FaBoTw; GTBS-P; PoWW; RB

Child Frightened by a Thunderstorm. Ted Kooser. KaS

Child Harold. John Clare.

Stanzas from "Child Harold." OBNC

Child I left your class to have, The. For Elizabeth Bishop. Sandra McPherson. NMM-2

Child, I warn thee in all wise. Symon's Lesson of Wisdom for All Manner of Children. *Unknown.* OxBChV

Child in my arms. Tanka. Sasaki Yukitsuna, *Japanese.* MJT, *tr. by* Makoto Ueda

Child in Prison, A. Gofraidh Fionn O'Dalaigh. NOIV

Child, Invisible Fire. Marcia Southwick. NAmP90

Child is born in blood, O child of blood, The. (LL) New Year's Day. Robert Lowell. CoAmPo

Child is father to the man, The. Triolet. Gerard Manley Hopkins. NOBL; NOBVV; NTP *Fr.* A Trio of Triolets.

Child is like a sailor cast up by the sea, The. Lucretius. *See* Like a shipwreck'd Sailor tost.

Child is not dead, The. The Child Who Was Shot Dead by Soldiers at Nyanga. Ingrid Jonker, *Afrikaans.* PeSA, *tr. by* Jack Cope *and* Uys Krige; PeSAV, *tr. by* Jack Cope *and* William Plomer

Child is Revenant to the Man, The. Vincent Buckley. BMAP

Child, is thy father dead? Ebenezer Elliot. NOBRP

Child-King, The. Morris Wintchevsky, *Yiddish.* TrJP, *tr. by* Alter Brody

Child Life. Mary E. Tucker. CBWP-1

Child listen / I am singing. White-arm, *Crow Indian.* STP, *tr. by* W. S. Merwin *after* Robert Lowie

Child Maurice. *Unknown.* ESPB

Child[e] My Choice [*or* Choyse], A. Robert Southwell. PeECV

Child Myro made this tomb, The. Anyte, *Greek.* GrAn, *tr. by* Sally Purcell

Child need not be very clever, A. Grandpa Is Ashamed. Ogden Nash. OBCoV

Child next door is defective because the mother, The. Robert Penn Warren. FuPo *Fr.* To a Little Girl, One Year Old, in a Ruined Fortress.

Child Noryce is a clever young man. Child Maurice. *Unknown.* ESPB

Child not yet is lulled to rest, The. Cradle-Song at Twilight. Alice Thompson Meynell. NOBVV; VWP

Child of Delight! with sunbright hair. R.C. Emily Jane Brontë. *Fr.* The Two Children. PoEL-5

Child of distress, who meet'st the bitter scorn. To the Poor. Anna Laetitia Barbauld. ECWP; NoP-4

Child of Europe. Czeslaw Milosz, *Polish.* AF, *tr. by* Jan Darowski

Child of maize! Red Monkey. *Unknown. Fr.* Hunter Poems of the Yoruba. RB, *tr. by* Ulli Beier

Child of my love! though thou be bright as day. Shadow. Mary Elizabeth Coleridge. VWP

Child of my winter, born. Heart's Needle. W. D. Snodgrass. CAPP-1

Child of My Winter Born. W. D. Snodgrass. MoAmPo *Fr.* Heart's Needle. CAPP-1

Child of Nature is the *better* man, The. (LL) On the Civilization of the Western Aboriginal Country. Philip Freneau. APN-1; PaTW

Child of Our Time. Eavan Boland. CIP-2

Child of patient industry. Invitation to the Bee. Charlotte Smith. OxBChV

Child of silence and shadow. Yvonne Caroutch, *French.* BoWoP, *tr. by* David Cloutier

Child of that hour when rock and ocean meet. (LL) Hatteras Calling. Conrad Potter Aiken. ColAP

Child of the potent spell and nimble eye. Henry Headly. ECEV *Fr.* An Invocation to Melancholy.

Child of the Romans. Carl Sandburg. NAAL-2

Child of the season of adventure, child of the heart. Elizabeth Nancy Sargent. NYBP

Child of the sun, in whom his rays appear. La Gialletta Gallante, or the Sunburned Exotic Beauty. Edward Herbert. NOSC

Child on the Judgment Seat, The. Elizabeth Rundle Charles. BLPA

Child on the Shore, The. Ursula K. Le Guin. KaS

Child on Top of a Greenhouse. Theodore Roethke. KaS; LCAP-2; NOxBChV; NoP-4; VGW

Child Owlet. *Unknown.* ESPB

Child Poems. Hilda Doolittle. Socratic. HoPM

Child Reads an Almanac, The. Francis Jammes, *French.* AWP, *tr. by* Ludwig Lewisohn

Child reads on; her basket of eggs stands by, The. The Child Reads an Almanac. Francis Jammes, *French.* AWP, *tr. by* Ludwig Lewisohn

Child running wild in woods of Lissadell. Remembering Con Markievicz. C. Day Lewis. IIP

Child said *What is the grass?*, A. Walt Whitman. *See* Grass.

Child said *What is the grass?* fetching it to me with full hands, A. Grass. Walt Whitman. ColAP; NoP-4; PAR *Fr.* Song of Myself. AmPP; MoAmPo; NAAL-3; NOBA; OxBA

Child saw the bombers skate like stones across the fields, The. Come to the Stone. Randall Jarrell. VGW

Child screams in his room, Rage, The. Unjustly Punished Child. Sharon Olds. PBCAP

Child Screening a Dove from a Hawk, A. Letitia Elizabeth Landon. NOBRP

Child Shall Lead, A. Audre Lorde. FiLi

Child should always say what's [true], A. Whole Duty of Children. Robert Louis Stevenson. CTV; NBLV; OxBChV

Child stood in the shed, The. The child went mad. The Carpenter's Son. John Berryman. ChIV-2

Child, take your basket down. First Gathering. Eleanor Farjeon. AYFP

Child Taken from the Mother, The. Minnie Bruce Pratt. GLP

Child tears itself free of my hands, The. Child and Sea. Blaga Dimitrova, *Bulgarian.* CEEP, *tr. by* Jascha Kessler *and* Aleksandar Shurbanov

Child, the current of your breath is six days long. Unknown Girl in the Maternity Ward. Anne Sexton. MoP; NoAM

Child to His Sick Grandfather, A. Joanna Baillie. CABP; ECWP; NOEC; RACG; WoRP

Child Waters. *Unknown.* ESPB; OxBB

Child! we must quit these visionary scenes. Epilogue. Hannah More. ECWP *Fr.* The Search after Happiness.

Child went out one day, A. I Eat Kids Yum Yum! Dennis Lee. TLR

Child Who Was Shot Dead by Soldiers at Nyanga, The. Ingrid Jonker, *Afrikaans.* PeSA, *tr. by* Jack Cope *and* Uys Krige; PeSAV, *tr. by* Jack Cope *and* William Plomer

Child, who went gathering the flowers of death. Haroun Al-Rachid for Heart's-Life. *Unknown.* AWP *Fr.* The Thousand and One Nights.

Child with a Cockatoo. Rosemary Dobson. CBAP

Child / With ancient face. One Acre. Jean Goulbourne. HCP

Child, with many a childish wile. To Cupid. Joanna Baillie. LW

Child with Six Fingers. Carol Muske. AmPA

Child, you were conceived in my upstairs room. To a Child Born in Time of Small War. Helen Sorrells. WPE

Childcity, Aprilcity. Paris. Gregory Corso. VGW

Childe Harold's Pilgrimage. Byron.
  Canto 3. Ro
    "In my youth's summer I did sing of One." NOBRP
    "Lake Leman woos me with its crystal face." NOBRP
    "Sky is changed!—and such a change! Oh night, The." NOBRP
    "There is a very life in our despair." NOBRP
  Canto 4. GS
    "Come, blue-eyed maid of heaven!—but thou, alas!" NOBRP
    Dedication: To Ianthe. OBNC
    Dying Gladiator, The. NOBE
    Eve of Waterloo, The. EBEvV; FaBoBe; FaBoCh; NOBE; OBNC
    Fatal Spell, The. OBNC
    "He, who, grown aged in this world of woe." EPCY
    "Is thy face like thy mother's, my fair child!" OAEL-2
    "Lake Leman woos me with its crystal face." InPS-3; PoEL-4
    Ocean, The. PoEL-4
      (By the Deep Sea.) OBNC
      "And I have loved thee, Ocean! and my joy." OxBoS
      Sea, The. FaBoBe; ImPo
      (Ocean, The.) TFi
      "Thou glorious mirror, where the Almighty's form." OxBoS
      To the Ocean.
    "Oh, thou! in Hellas deemed of heavenly birth." NAEL-2
    "Once more upon the waters! yet once more!" FHYEP
    "Stop! for thy tread is on an empire's dust!" InPS-3
    "Where'er we tread 'tis haunted, holy ground." GrIP

Childe Maurice hunted the Silver Wood. *Unknown. See* Gill Morice stood in stable-door.

Childe Roland, etc. Elder Olson. OBAL

Childe Roland to the Dark Tower Came. Robert Browning. EnVR; NAEL-2; NOBVV; NoP-4; OAEL-2; OBNV; PeVV; PoE; PoPoPo

Childe Rolandine. Stevie Smith. BrRo

Childe Watters in his stable stoode. Child Waters. *Unknown.* ESPB; OxBB

Childheart, time alone is not enough. A Late Spring. James Scully. NYBP

Childhood. Jens Baggesen, *Danish.* AWP, *tr. by* Longfellow

Childhood. William Barnes. NOBVV

Childhood. Anne Bradstreet. KTR *Fr.* The Four Ages of Man.

Childhood. Edith Bruck, *Italian.* AF, *tr. by* Ruth Feldman

Childhood. Frances Darwin Cornford. FaBoWP; KaS; OxBSP; OxBTC

Childhood. Chitra Divakaruni. OpBo

Childhood. Donald Justice. LCAP-2

Childhood. Edwin Muir. CMoP; FaBoTC; HeIP-4; NoP-4

Childhood. Sherod Santos. FiLi

Childhood. Maura Stanton. CMAP

Childhood. Sharan Strange. GT

Childhood. Henry Vaughan. NOSC

Childhood. Margaret Abigail Walker. NoP-4; PBWP; PoBA; Son; WPOW

Childhood and prime womanhood were spent in the / nailer's darg. (LL) Brooding on the eightieth letter of *Fors Clavigera.* Geoffrey Hill. HAP; PoE

Childhood, boyhood, young manhood. Preface to the Suite. Robert Duncan. FTOS *Fr.* Poems from the Margins of Thom Gunn's Moly.

Childhood in Jacksonville, Florida. Jane Cooper. TAP

Childhood is health. (LL) Holy Baptism (2). George Herbert. ChIV-2; PoEL-2

Childhood is not from birth to a certain age and at a certain age. Childhood Is the Kingdom Where Nobody Dies. Edna St. Vincent Millay. FaBoWP; NALW

Childhood is the village of Rosycheekly. Metamorphoses. Yevtushenko, *Russian.* TCRP, *tr. by* Arthur Boyars *and* Simon Franklin

Childhood of a Spy. Dick Davis. DiPo

Childhood of a Stranger. Claire Bateman. CrSp

Childhood of a Voice. Martin Carter. HCP

Childhood of an Equestrian, The. Russell Edson. AmPA

Childhood Painting Lesson. Henry Rago. WHSW

Childhood remembrances [or memories] are always a drag. Nikki-Rosa. Nikki Giovanni. BlSi; CrSp; FaBoA; GT; HeIP-4; ISC; MoP; NAAAL; PBMP; PoBA; SSLK; TAP; UnSA

Childhood Scenes in Four Seasons. Helen G. Quigless. BkSV

Childhood's Retreat. Robert Duncan. NoAM

Childish Game, A. Reinmar von Hagenau, *German.* AWP, *tr. by* Jethro Bithell

Childish Prank, A. Ted Hughes. CABP; OAEL-2; OxBC

Childless. Giolla Brighde MacNamee, *Irish.* BIrV, *tr. by* Frank O'Connor

Childless couple, The. Restoration. Jeffrey Skinner. PBCAP

Childless Father, The. Wordsworth. CH

Childlessness. James Merrill. CoAmPo; ColAP

Childlike, with childish things not put away. (LL) R.A.F. (Aged Eighteen). Rudyard Kipling. LiLi; PoWW

Children. Russell Edson. AmPA

Children. Bill Manhire. PoNZ

Children. Sandra McPherson. FaBoWP

Children. Pāṇṭiyaṉ Ariyutai Nampi, *Tamil.* PLW, *tr. by* A. K. Ramanujan

Children. Po Chü-i, *Chinese.* ChiP, *tr. by* Arthur Waley

Children. Charles Reznikoff. FTOS

Children, The. Iain Crichton Smith. SpW

Children. Teaching the Children. Myra Sklarew. CRP

Children, The. Constance Urdang. CoAP

Children, The. William Carlos Williams. SAmP

Children are at the door. At the Door. Lillie Fuller Merriam. PoToHe

Children are dumb to say how hot the day is. The Cool Web. Robert Graves. AWP; GTBS-P; MoP; NAEL-2; NoAM; OxBTC; PoA; Poetr; SCV

Children are hiding among the raspberry canes, The. Mark Jarman. WeT

Children aren't happy with nothing to ignore. The Parent. Ogden Nash. LiLi; Spl

Children at Christmas in 1945. Vladimir Holan, *Czech.* AF, *tr. by* C. G. Hanzlicek *and* Dana Habova

Children Band, The. Sir Aubrey De Vere. OBEV

Children believe in clover, magic numbers. The Sacred Children. Hoffman Reynolds Hays. SPE

Children, billy goat, have put crimson reins, The. Anyte. HePo, *tr. by* Barbara Hughes Fowler *Fr.* Epigrams.

Children born of fairy stock. I'd Love to Be a Fairy's Child. Robert Graves. BoTP; ChAP

Children, brown as earth, continue to laugh away. Main Temple Street, Puri. Jayanta Mahapatra. VCWP

Children cried "Mummy!," The. Massacre of the Boys. Tadeusz Rózewicz, *Polish.* GI; HP, *tr. by* Adam Czerniawski; AF, *tr. by* Robert A. Maguire *and* Magnus Jan Krynski

Children dear, was it yesterday. Matthew Arnold. BoTP *Fr.* The Forsaken Merman. EBEV; EBVVPR; FHYEP; FaBoCh; FaPoR; NAEL-2; NTP; OBNV; OBSP

Children do not ask the proper questions. Leaping into the Gulf. Patricia Beer. OxBC

Children do not grow up. Biting Back. Patricia Smith. GT

Children don't know what worry means! Su Tung-p'o, *Chinese.* CoBCP, *tr. by* Burton Watson

Children enter, The. Sundown at Darlington 1878. Lance Henson. VoR

Children go, The. Kenneth Mackenzie. BMAP

Children go forward with their little satchels, The. The School Children. Louise Glück. AmPA; ColAP; HCAP; PoPoPo; Poetr; WeW-3

Children have a society of their own, The. John Cage. APSN *Fr.* Diary: How to Improve the World (You Will Only Make Matters Worse).

Children have put purple, The. Anyte, *Greek.* PGA, *tr. by* Kenneth Rexroth

Children have tied you, billy-goat, with bright, The. Anyte, *Greek.* GrAn, *tr. by* Sally Purcell

Children have vanished. (LL) Grand Abacus. John Ashbery. SPE

Children, if you dare to think. Warning to Children. Robert Graves. CBNP; FaBoCh; NOxBChV; NTP; NoP-4; OAEL-2

Children in daylight, The. (LL) Lucy's Letter. James Berry. FaBoVe; HCP

Children in the Wood, The. *Unknown. See* The Babes in the Wood ("Now ponder well, you parents dear").

Children like the block, The. Margaret Atwood. *Fr.* The Circle Game. MoCV

Children March, The. Elizabeth Riddell. CBAP

Children of dreams are in terror, The. A Text for These Distracted Times. Rodney Hall. CBAP

Children of Greenock, The. W. S. Graham. FaBoTC; FaBoTw

Children of Light. Robert Lowell. CMoP; NAAL-2; OxBA

Children of Lir. Susan Howe. *Fr.* White Foolscap/Book of Cordelia. PmAP

Children of Love. Harold Monro. MoBrPo

Children of my happier prime. Immolated. Herman Melville. NCAP

Children of Saigon, The. Walter McDonald. AF

Children of the Epoch. Wislawa Szymborska, *Polish.* AF, *tr. by* Grazyna Drabik *and* Austin Flint

Children of the future Age. A Little Girl Lost. William Blake. FHYEP; Ro *Fr.* Songs of Experience.

Children of the Mist. Rosamund Marriott Watson. VWP

Children of the Night, The. Edwin Arlington Robinson. APN-2; OxBA

Children of the Poor, The. Gwendolyn Brooks. WPE, *sect.* I, *pt.* 1-2; PoA, *sect.* I, *pt.* 1-3; NAAAL *Fr.* The Womanhood.
("But reaching is his rule.") (LL) NAAAL
"First fight. Then fiddle. Ply the slipping string." InPK-6; NIP-4; PFE; Poetr
"What shall I give my children? who are poor." BPo; PoA; WPE

Children of the Wind. Betti Alver, *Estonian.* CEEP, *tr. by* Ivar Ivask

Children of the Working Class. John Weiners. BB

Children of the world are on the march, The. The Children March. Elizabeth Riddell. CBAP

Children of wealth in your warm nursery. Elizabeth Daryush. WPN

Children of yesterday. Song of Hope. Mary Artemisia Lathbury. BLPA

Children on the lawn / joined hand to hand, The. Margaret Atwood. *Fr.* The Circle Game. MoCV

Children on the lawn / joined hand to hand, The. The Circle Game. Margaret Atwood. MoCV

Children—or. Or a Play. Leslie Scalapino. FTOS

Children picking up our bones. A Postcard from the Volcano. Wallace Stevens. GEA; HAP; HCAP; MeMAP; NoAM; SAmP; WeW-3

Children Playing Checkers at the Edge of the Forest. Adrienne Rich. LCAP-2; WeW-3

Children run shouting, The. Glimpses. Philippe Jaccottet, *French.* VCWP, *tr. by* Derek Mahon

Children sleep at night. Laura Riding Jackson. *Fr.* Forgotten Girlhood. RB

Children, the Sandbar, That Summer. Muriel Rukeyser. LCAP-2

Children they move stand, The. Clear. Angelo Lewis. PoBA

Children / this is the blood. Brother of the Streets. Sam Cornish. TRP

Children Waking: Indian Hill Station. Ralph Nixon Currey. PeSA

Children Walking Home from School through Good Neighborhood. Donald Justice. DiPo; NIP-4

Children wandered up and down, The. The Cruise of the *Mystery*. Celia Laighton Thaxter. OBCA

Children were around my feet like dogs, The. Seventh Birthday of the First Child. Sharon Olds. PBCAP

Children were frightened by crescendoes, The. A Fete. Larry Eigner. NeAP

Children were shouting together, The. Frolic. "Æ." BoTP; MoBrPo

Children, when was. Napoleon. Miroslav Holub, *Czech.* PoSu; ChAP, *tr. by* Polakova, Kaca

Children who love more than they hate. Families. Thomas Blackburn. OxBSP

Children, why do you fear, why turn away? For Miriam. Marjorie Oludhe Macgoye. WPOW

Children, you are very little. Good and Bad Children. Robert Louis Stevenson. ACTP; ChAP; EBVV; FaBoCh; OBCoV; OxBChV

Children's Ball-Bouncing Song. *Unknown.* NOBAu

Children's Bells, The. Eleanor Farjeon. BoTP; CH

Children's Carol, The. Eleanor Farjeon. PChr

Children's Crusade 1939. Bertolt Brecht, *German.* MoBS, *tr. by* Michael Hamburger

Children's Hospital. Olive Senior. HCP

Children's Hour, The. Henry Wadsworth Longfellow. APN-1; CTV; ChAP; FPC; FaBoBe; ImGa; OBAL; OBCA; PoEL-5; PoLF; WHSW

Children's Letters, The. Dorothy Livesay. NALW; NOBC

Children's Rhymes. Langston Hughes. BPo; InPS-3; NOxBChV

Children's Rhymes and Parodies. *Unknown.* NOBAu

Children's Song, The. Rudyard Kipling. *Fr.* Puck of Pook's Hill.

Children's Song. *Unknown, Nepalese.* PC, tr. by Kumar Prakesh

Children's toys? (LL) Nursery Rhyme of Innocence and Experience. Charles Causley. NOxBChV

Children's Train, The. Dorianne Laux. GM

Children's voices in the orchard. New Hampshire. T. S. Eliot. FaBoCh; GTBS-P; NoAM; WeW-3 *Fr.* Landscapes. RB

Child's a plaything for an hour, A. Parental Recollections. Mary Lamb. OBEV; OxBSP

Child's Calendar, A. John Updike.
    August. AYFP; OBCA
    May. AYFP; NOxBChV; OBCA
    ("Look at some baseball / On TV.") (LL) NOxBChV

Child's castle crumbles; hot air shimmers, The. Mercury Bay Eclogue. M. K. Joseph. PeNZ

Child's Christmas Carol, A. Christine Chaundler. BoTP

Child's Christmas Day, A. *Unknown.* OBCP

Child's Christmas in Wales, A. Dylan Thomas.
    When I was a boy. SAGP

Child's Creed, A. *Unknown.* CTV

Child's Dream, A. Frances Darwin Cornford. NOxBChV

Child's Evening Prayer, A. Coleridge. OxBChV

Child's eyes to see. The Vision Clear. J. M. Westrup. BoTP

Child's First Grief, The. Felicia Dorothea Hemans. BLPA
    (First Grief, The.) CH

Child's foot is not yet aware it's a foot, The. To the Foot from Its Child. Pablo Neruda, *Spanish.* RB, tr. by Alastair Reid

Child's gaze. August Stramm. *See* Battlefield.

Child's Grace, A, *see also* Grace at Kirkudbright. *Unknown. Fr.* Two Graces.

Child's Grave, Hale County, Alabama. Jim Simmerman. WeW-3

Child's Guide to Welfare, A. D. J. Enright. CBNP

Child's Laughter, A. Swinburne. NTP; PoLF

Child's Morning Prayer, A. Jeannie Kirby. BoTP

Child's Offering, A. *Unknown.* CTV *Fr.* The Book of Praise for Children.

Child's Parliment. Chenjerai Hove. HBAPE

Child's Pet, A. W. H. Davies. CH; RB

Child's Prayer, A. William Canton. BoTP

Child's Prayer, A. Siegfried Sassoon. BoTP

Child's Prayer, A. *Unknown.* BoTP

Child's Present, A. Robert Herrick. *See* To His Saviour, a Child; a Present, by a Child.

Child's Return, The. Phyllis Shand Allfrey. PBCV

Child's Sight, The. Hy Sobiloff. VGW

Child's Song. Gerald Louis Gould. BoTP

Child's Song. Robert Lowell. RB

Child's Song. Sir Thomas More. ChAP

Child's Song in Spring. Edith Nesbit. BoTP; NOxBChV; OxBChV

Child's Song of Christmas, A. Marjorie Lowry Christie Pickthall. BoTP

Child's Thought, A. Robert Louis Stevenson. BoTP

Child's Visit to the Biology Lab, A. Kathleen Spivack. AmPA

Child's Winter Evening, A. Gwen John. CH

Child's wisdom is in saying, The. The Child's Sight. Hy Sobiloff. VGW

Chilean Elegies: 5, The. The Interior. Tom Wayman. NOBC

Chile's flag has three colors. The Flag of Chile. Teresa de Jesús, *Spanish.* AF, tr. by Maria Proser, Arlene Scully *and* James Scully

Chill, A. Christina Rossetti. BoTP

Chill and harsh the year draws to its close;. Ch'ien T'ao, *Chinese.* ChiP, tr. by Arthur Waley

Chill leaves soughing / scatter sounds of rain. Autumn Sentiments. Yüan Hao-wen, *Chinese.* SuSp, tr. by Irving Y. Lo

Chill of dawn grows on the tips of yellow chrysanthemum twigs, The. Tune: "Partridge Sky." Huang T'ing-chien, *Chinese.* SuSp, tr. by James J. Y. Liu

Chill-rushing, / Hush-hushing, / Hush—hushing. (LL) The Main-Deep. James Stephens. MoBrPo; OBMV; UnPo

Chill wind and dew repeat the autumn scene. Hibiscus Flowers. Li Shang-yin, *Chinese.* SuSp, tr. by Eugene Eoyang *and* Irving Y. Lo

Chill wind stirs at horizon's end. At Horizon's End, Thinking of Li Po. Tu Fu, *Chinese.* SuSp, tr. by Eugene Eoyang

Chill'd by unkind Honora's alter'd eye. Sonnet 12. Anna Seward. CPO

Chilled by excess of passion. We Drink Farewell. Tu Mu, *Chinese.* OHMPC, tr. by Kenneth Rexroth

Chilled by the Blasts of Adverse Fate. Jacob Duché. AH

Chilled in this Irish pub I wish my loves. John Berryman. FaBoMo; LCAP-2 *Fr.* Dream Songs.

Chilled with salt dew, tossed on dark waters deep. A Mermaiden. Thomas Hennell. FaBoTw

Chillen Get Shoes. Sterling Brown. NoP-4

Chilling breath of midwinter arrives, The. *Unknown, Chinese.* SuSp, tr. by Dell R. Hales

Chillingham. Mary Elizabeth Coleridge. BoTP

Chilly Night, A. Christina Rossetti. VWP

Chilterns, The. Rupert Brooke. MoBrPo

Chimaeras, The. W. H. Auden. MeMAP

Chimayo. Gloria Vando. LoHo

Chimera. Barbara Howes. TwCP

Chimes. Alice Thompson Meynell. BoTP; CH; MoBrPo; WPE

Chimes. D. G. Rossetti. OBNC

Chimes. Michael Smith. PBCIP

Chimney, A. Mother Goose. OxNR; ReMoGo

Chimney, breathing a little smoke, A. February. James Schuyler. NeAP

Chimney of my neighbour's house. Soliloquy to Absent Friends. Douglas G. Jones. MoCV

Chimney Sweeper, The ("Little black thing among the snow, A"). William Blake. EBEvV; FHYEP; NAEL-2; NAWM-2; NOEC; OAEL-2; RB; Ro *Fr.* Songs of Experience.

Chimney Sweeper, The. *Unknown.* AmFP

Chimney Sweeper, The ("When my mother died I was very young"). William Blake. CH; FHYEP; FaBoPV; HeIP-4; InPK-6; NAEL-2; NAWM-2; NOEC; OAEL-2; OxAEP-2; OxBChV; PoE; Poetr; Ro; SCGP; SoSe-8; TFi *Fr.* Songs of Innocence.

Chimney-Sweeper's Complaint, The ("Chimney sweeper's boy am I, A"). Mary Alcock. ECWP; NOEC

Chimney-Tops. *Unknown.* BoTP

Chimneys: colder. Reindeer Report. U. A. Fanthorpe. OBCP

Chimneys, rank on rank, The. Evening. Richard Aldington. MoBrPo

Ch'in Chia's Wife's Reply. Ch'in Chia, *Chinese.* BoWoP; ChiP, tr. by Arthur Waley

Ch'in emperor guarded the land against Tartar foes, The. The Great Wall. Chu Ch'ing-yü, *Chinese.* SuSp, tr. by Irving Y. Lo

Chin-ling. Liu Yu Hsi, *Chinese.* SuSp, tr. by Paul Kroll

China. Dorianne Laux. DeD; LW

China. Bob Perelman. FTOS

China has many people and many heroes. *Unknown.* ChiPo

China island dream. Empire Smoke, Forgeries, Salient and The Ritz. Ray DiPalma. FTOS

China Maniacs. May Probyn. VWP

China Observed Through Greek Rain in Turkish Coffee. Henrik Nordbrandt, *Danish.* VCWP, tr. by Nordbrandt, Henrik and Alexander Taylor

Chinashop at seaborde. Civility a Bogey. Margaret Avison. NOBC

Chinchopper, chin. (LL) Forehead, Eyes, Cheeks, Nose, Mouth, and Chin. Mother Goose. FaBoVe; LB; OxNR; ReMoGo

Chinese Banquet, A. Kitty Tsui. CPO; GLP

Chinese Camp, Kamloops (circa 1883). Andrew Suknaski. NOBC

Chinese Checker Players, The. Richard Brautigan. PFE

Chinese Drawings. Witter Bynner.
    "What though they conquer us?" NoP-4

Chinese Fireworks Banned in Hawaii. Eric Chock. PuP-16

Chinese Food in the Fifties. Alberto Rios. PUP-20

Chinese Garden, The. Horace Gregory. OBGa

Chinese Hot Pot. Wing Tek Lum. UnSA

Chinese Laundry. Yury Kazarnovsky, *Russian.* TCRP, tr. by Bradley Jordan

Chinese Nightingale, The. Vachel Lindsay. MoAmPo

Chinese Poem. Iain Crichton Smith. FaBoTC

Chinese Poems: Arthur Waley. "C. A. Fair." PeSA

Chinese Restaurant in Portrush, The. Derek Mahon. TRP

Chinese Sandmen. *Unknown.* FuFo

Chinese Temple. Sándor Weöres, *Hungarian.* CEEP, tr. by Emery E. George

Chinese Ulysses, A. Kazuko Shiraishi, *Japanese.* WPJ, tr. by Kenneth Rexroth *and* Ikuko Atsumi

Chinese Villanelle. John Yau. PmAP

Chinese Winter. Frederick Robert Higgins. BIrV

Ching a Ring. James Robinson Planché. NOBL

Ch'ing-yang Ford. *Unknown, Chinese.* CoBCP, tr. by Burton Watson

Chingwe's Hole, you devoured the Chief's prisoners. Glory Be to Chingwe's Hole. Jack A. Mapanje. HBAPE

Chinoiserie. Charles Wright. AmPA

Chinoiseries. Amy Lowell. PoRA

Chinook Songs. *Unknown, Chinook Native American.* APN-2, tr. by Franz Boas

Chios. Ioanna Tsatsos, *Greek.* GrIP, tr. by Jean Demos

Chip. George Starbuck. OBAL

Chip chip cherry. Riddle. *Unknown.* FaBoVe

Chip on His Shoulder, A. *Unknown.* BLPA

Chipmunk, The. Herman Melville. NCAP

Chipmunk can't drag it along. Alonzo Gonzales, *Navajo Indian.* STP, *tr. by* Jerome Rothenberg

Chipmunk chewing the Chippendale. Exit, Pursued by a Bear. Ogden Nash. NYBP

Chipmunk was standing. Alonzo Gonzales, *Navajo Indian.* STP, *tr. by* Jerome Rothenberg

Chipmunk's Day, The. Randall Jarrell. OBCA

Chipmunks jump, and / Greensnakes slither. Valentine. Donald Hall. NTCP

Chippewa Love Song. *Unknown, Chippewa Indian.* BoWoP, *tr. by* Frances Densmore, *ad. by* Willis Barnstone

Chirp Chirp the Katydids. *Unknown, Chinese.* CoBCP, *tr. by* Burton Watson

Chisel in hand stood a sculptor boy. Life Sculpture. George Washington Doane. BLPA

Chiswick. Thomas Maurice. OBGa *Fr. Richmond Hill.*

Chitterabob Mob's cat. (LL) There was a man, and his name was Dob. *Unknown.* CTAV

Ch'iu-p-u teems with white gibbons. Li Po. SuSp, *tr. by* Irving Lo *Fr. Songs of Ch'iu-p'u.*

Chivvy. Michael Rosen. OTCP

"Chkk! chkk!" hopper-grass. Confucius. *Fr. Shao and the South.* CTC, *tr. by* Ezra Pound

Chloe. Sir Edward De Stein. NSI

Chloe and Myra. Lady Sophia Burrell. LW *Fr. Chloe and Myra.*

Chloe Divine. Thomas D'Urfey. OBEV

Chloe, why wish you that your years. To Chloe, Who Wished Herself Young Enough for Me. William Cartwright. BeJo; NOSC; OBEV; OxAEP-1

Chloe's a nymph in flowery groves. Chloe Divine. Thomas D'Urfey. OBEV

Chloe's father is a professor of linguistics. Elegy for Chloe Nguyen. Marilyn Chin. UnSA

Chloris [*or the Complaint of the Passionate Despised Shepheard*]. William Smith.
  "Feed, silly sheep, although your keeper pineth." Son
  "Some in their harts their mistris colours bears." AAS

To the Most Excellent and Learned Shepherd, Colin Clout. AAS; Son

Chloris, forbear a while. Song. Henry Bold. GBL; NOSC

Chloris in the Snow. William Strode. NOBE; OBEV
  (On a Gentlewoman Walking in the Snow.) NOSC; OxBSP

Chloris, it is not thy disdain. Sidney Godolphin. BeJo

Chloris, since first our calm of peace. To Chloris, upon a Favour Received. Edmund Waller. OxBSP

Chockablock Once a man was traveling through the woods, and. Charles Olson. FTOS *Fr. The Maximus Poems.*
  ("I live underneath / the light of day.")

Chocolate-coloured paint and the July sun. The Dying Synagogue at South Terrace. Thomas McCarthy. BiHa

Chocolate Milk. Ron Padgett. TTTS

Chocolate treat, A. (LL) Harlem Sweeties. Langston Hughes. LiTM; TTY

Chocolates. Louis Simpson. InPS-3; OBCoV; OxBC

Choice. David Bromige. FTOS

Choice, The. Hilary Corke. NYBP

Choice. James Vincent Cunningham. VGW

Choice, The. Soame Jenyns. ECEV

Choice, The. John Masefield. MoBrPo *Fr. Lollingdon Downs.*

Choice. Angela Morgan. PoLF

Choice, The. Robert Morgan. SpW

Choice, The. John Pomfret. FP; NOEC *Fr. The Choice.*

Choice. Flavien Ranaivo, *French.* NegPo, *tr. by* Ellen Conroy Kennedy

Choice, The. D. G. Rossetti. ChIV-2; GTBS-P; OBEV *Fr. The House of Life.*

Choice, The. Nahum Tate. OxBSP

Choice, The. George Wither. OBEV

Choice, The. W. B. Yeats. CMoP; NoAM; OxBSP; OxBTC

Choice of the Cross, The. Dorothy Leigh Sayers. TrCP *Fr. The Devil to Pay.*

Choice of Weapons, A. Stanley Kunitz. LiTM; VGW

Choice of Weapons, A. Phyllis McGinley. PFE

Choice soul, in whom, as in a glass, we see. The Doom of Beauty. Michelangelo Buonarroti, *Italian.* AWP, *tr. by* John Addington Symonds

Choicer than all / flush of youth. Paulus Silentiarius, *Greek.* GrAn, *tr. by* Andrew Miller

Choicer than the Mermaid Tavern? (LL) Lines on the Mermaid Tavern. Keats. FHYEP; FaBoBe; GTBS-P; PoRA; SCGP

Choir Invisible, The. "George Eliot." EBVV; OBNC

Choir of angels glorified the great hour, The. Crucifixion. "Anna Andreyevna Akhmatova." IMW *Fr. Requiem 1935-1940.* BoWoP, *tr. by* Richard McKane

Choir of angels glorified the hour, A. "Anna Andreyevna Akhmatova." *See* Crucifixion.

Choir of Day, The. William Blake. *See* The Lark's Song.

Choirmaster's Burial, The. Thomas Hardy. PeECV

Choise of Valentines, The. Thomas Nashe. PBRV

Choke all week in the fumes and air stinking. Plainsong. Vladislav Felitsianovich Khodasevich, *Russian.* TCRP, *tr. by* Michael Frayn

Choked sunset glow. Roads. Peter Huchel, *German.* HP; PoSu, *tr. by* Michael Hamburger

Choker's Lane. Kenneth Slessor. BMAP

Choking through the whole attack. (LL) Champs d'Honneur. Ernest Hemingway. AiP; PoA

Chomei at Toyama. Basil Bunting. OxBTC

Chongno Street. Un Ko, *Korean.* CKP, *tr. by* Jaihiun Kim

Chook, chook, chook, chook, chook. *Unknown.* OxNR

Choose. Carl Sandburg. Spl

Choose judiciously thy friends; for to discard them / is undesirable. Of Friendship. Charles Stuart Calverley. FP

Choose now among this fairest number. Song. William Browne. GBL

Choose Something like a Star. Robert Frost. MoAmPo

Choosing a Kitten. *Unknown.* CTV

Choosing a Mast. Roy Campbell. FaBoTw; NoP-4; PeSA

Choosing a Name. Charles Lamb *and* Mary Lamb. OxBChV

Choosing a Name. Anne Ridler. NOBE

Choosing a Stone. John Haines. WeT

Choosing Coffins. Raymond Souster. MoCV

Choosing Shoes. Frida Wolfe. ChAP

Choosing the Blues. Angela Jackson. ISC

Choosing Their Names. Thomas Hood. ACTP; NOxBChV; PeP

Chop-Cherry. Robert Herrick. CavPo; EnLoPo; GLoP
  ("Another snapp'd [*or* snappt] the cherry.") (LL) EnLoPo

Chopin. Marilyn Nelson. RA

Chops Are Flyin, *Chops are flyin everywhere / and there's nothin says Louis / but old Duke left in there. / Get away, Duke, get away!.* Stanley Crouch. GT

Chord, The. Abdur-Rahman Slade Hopkinson. HCP

Chord. Langston Hughes. APSN

Chords knotted together like insane nouns. Tom Clark. *See* You (IV).

Chords Passages 14. Robert Duncan. FTOS

Choric Song. Tennyson. *See* Song of the Lotus-Eaters.

Choric Song of the Lotus-Eaters. Tennyson. *See* Song of the Lotus-Eaters.

Chorus: "All ye that handle harp and viol." Moses Hayyim, of Padua Luzzatto, *Hebrew.* TrJP, *tr. by* Nina Davis Salaman *Fr. Unto the Upright Praise.*

Chorus. W. H. Auden. *See* The Wanderer.

Chorus: "Babylon, I did not come to you for the sake of coming." Matsemela Manaka. PeSAV *Fr. Pula.*

Chorus: "Can nothing great, and at the height." Petronius Arbiter. OBCVT, *tr. by* Ben Jonson *Fr. Catiline his Conspiracy.*

Chorus: "Fair Salamis, the billow's roar." Sophocles, *Greek.* AWP, *tr. by* Winthrop Mackworth Praed *Fr. Ajax.*

Chorus: "Great Fortune is an hungry thing." Aeschylus. AWP, *tr. by* Gilbert Murray *Fr. Agamemnon.* NAWM-1, *tr. by* Robert Fagles

Chorus: "If I drink water while this doth last." Thomas Love Peacock. NBLV *Fr. Crotchet Castle.*

Chorus: "In the name of the people." Matsemela Manaka. PeSAV *Fr. Pula.*

Chorus: "Let the Priests of the Raven of dawn, no longer in deadly black." William Blake. *Fr. The Marriage of Heaven and Hell.* NAEL-2; NOBRP; OAEL-2

Chorus: "Oh, may my constant feet not fail." Sophocles, *Greek. Fr. Oedipus the King [or Oedipus Rex].* NAWM-1, *tr. by* Robert Fagles

Chorus. Sophocles, *Greek.* PiM, *tr. by* Robert Fagles *Fr. Antigone.* NAWM-1, *tr. by* Robert Fagles

Chorus: "Summer holds, The: upon its glittering lake." W. H. Auden. *Fr. The Dog beneath the Skin.* OxBTC

Chorus: "Sweet are the ways of death to weary feet." Euripides, *Greek.* OBEV, *tr. by* John Byrne Leicester Warren, Lord de Tabley *Fr. Medea.*

Chorus. Swinburne. *See* The Hounds of Spring.

Chorus: "Those mindes that wholy dote upon delight." Lady Elizabeth Carey. KTR *Fr. Mariam.* WPE

Chorus: "We do not wish anything to happen." T. S. Eliot. OxBTC *Fr. Murder in the Cathedral.*

Chorus: "We have not been happy, my Lord, we have not been too happy."

Chorus: "What man is he that yearneth." Sophocles, *Greek.* AWP *Fr.* Oedipus at Colonus.

(Chorus reflect on Oedipus' fate, The.) OBCVT, *tr.* by Alfred Edward Housman

Chorus: "You are the town and we are the clock." W. H. Auden. *Fr.* The Dog beneath the Skin. OxBTC

Chorus assisted, bringing cups of tea, The. (LL) Epilogue to a Human Drama. Stephen Spender. AF; CMoP

Chorus: "Before the beginning of years." Swinburne. EBVV; EBVVPR; OBEV *Fr.* Atalanta in Calydon.

(Man.)

Chorus for Survival. Horace Gregory.

"Ask no return for love that's given." MoAmPo; VGW

Chorus from "Hellas." Shelley. *See* Chorus: "World's great age begins anew, The."

Chorus-leading, splashing out the wine. (LL) A Postcard from North Antrim. Seamus Heaney. PBCIP; PNI

Chorus of a Song That Might Have Been Written by Albert Chevalier. Max Beerbohm. OBCoV; UV

Chorus of Angels. John Henry, Cardinal Newman. NOCV; PoEL-5 *Fr.* The Dream of Gerontius.

(Fifth Choir of Angelicals.) NOBVV

Chorus of Birds. Aristophanes. AWP *Fr.* The Birds.

(Grand Chorus of Birds.) PoEL-5

Chorus of Nymphs, A. Andrey Voznesensky, *Russian.* VCWP, *tr.* by Vera Dunham *and* H. W. Tjalsma

Chorus of Priests. 1st Baron Brooke Fulke Greville. *See* Chorus Sacerdotum.

Chorus of Satyrs, Driving Their Goats. Euripides, *Greek.* AWP *Fr.* The Cyclops.

Chorus of the Dead. Nelly Sachs, *German.* PFTM, *tr.* by Ruth Mead *and* Matthew Mead

Chorus of the Rescued. Nelly Sachs, *German.* WPOW, *tr.* by Ruth Mead *and* Matthew Mead; PoSu

Chorus of the Stars. Nelly Sachs, *German.* PFTM, *tr.* by Michael Roloff

Chorus of the Unborn. Nelly Sachs, *German.* NYBP, *tr.* by Ruth Mead *and* Matthew Mead

Chorus of the Years. Thomas Hardy. *See* The Field of Waterloo.

Chorus Primus of Bashaws or Cadis. Greville Fulke. NOSC *Fr.* Mustapha.

Chorus recall Helen's flight, The. Aeschylus, *Greek.* OBCVT, *tr.* by Edward Fitzgerald

Chorus reflect on Oedipus' fate, The. Sophocles. *See* Chorus: "What man is he that yearneth."

Chorus Sacerdotum. Greville Fulke. HAP; NAEL-1; NOBE; OAEL-1; PoEL-5 *Fr.* Mustapha.

(Chorus of Priests.) NoSic; OxAEP-1

("O wearisome condition of humanity!") NoP-4

Chorus sing of escape, The. Euripides, *Greek.* OBCVT, *tr.* by Hilda Doolittle *Fr.* Hippolytus.

Chorus sing of the doom of Thebes' royal family, The. Sophocles, *Greek.* OBCVT, *tr.* by E. R. Dodds

Chorus sing of the laws of the gods, The. Sophocles, *Greek.* OBCVT, *tr.* by Robert Fagles

Chorus sing the doom of Helen, The. Aeschylus, *Greek.* OBCVT, *tr.* by Louis MacNeice

Chorus to the Gods. John Dryden. OxBSP *Fr.* The Secular Masque. NAEL-1; OxAEP-1; PoE; PoEL-3; SCGP

(Chorus to the Gods.) OxBSP

Chorus: "To throw away the key and walk away." W. H. Auden. *See* The Walking Tour.

Chorus: "World's great age begins anew, The." Shelley. EBEV; HAP; NOBE; OAEL-2; PoEL-4 *Fr.* Hellas.

(Chorus from "Hellas.") AWP

(Final Chorus, The.)

Chorus: "Worlds on worlds are rolling ever." Shelley. NAEL-2 *Fr.* Hellas.

Ye Children of Man! whose life is a span. Aristophanes. OBCVT, *tr.* by John Hookham Frere *Fr.* The Birds.

Choruses from "The Rock." T. S. Eliot.

"Eagle soars in the summit of heaven, The." OBMV

"I journeyed to the suburbs, and there I was told." UV

Chose to have it out at last / on your own premises. (LL) I Am in Danger—Sir—. Adrienne Rich. HCAP; NALW; NOBA

Chosen. Marilyn Nelson Waniek. FFC; NAmP90

Chosen, fr. A Woman Young and Old. W. B. Yeats. BoLoP; CMoP

Chosen of God. Stefan Zweig. *Fr.* Jeremiah. TrJP, *tr.* by Eden *and* Cedar Paul

Chosen Ruby, and the Reprobate, The. (LL) In the Dark None Dainty. Robert Herrick. CaPo; CavPo

Chosen Three, on Mountain Height, The. David H. Ela. AH

Chou and the South. Confucius, *Chinese.*

"In the South be drooping trees." CTC, *tr.* by Ezra Pound

Chou and the South. *Unknown.* CTC, *tr.* by Ezra Pound *Fr.* Shi King.

Chough. Rex Warner. PoRA

Chough and crow to roost are gone, The. The Outlaw's Song. Joanna Baillie. OBEV

Pese anger not thyself so I thee pray. Publius Terentius Afer. OBCVT, *tr.* by Unknown *Fr.* The Girl from Andros (Andria).

Chriseaster. Molly Peacock. FFC

Christ. *Unknown, Greek.* GrAn, *tr.* by Guy Davenport

Christ and Satan. *Unknown, Anglo-Saxon.*

Lamentations of the Fallen Angels. AnOE, *tr.* by Charles W. Kennedy

Christ and the Little Ones. Julia Gill. BLPA

Christ and the Pagan. John Banister Tabb. TrCP

Christ and the Soldier. Siegfried Sassoon. NoP-4

Christ Child, The. Mary Weston Fordham. CBWP-2

Christ child lay on Mary's lap, The. Christmas Carol. G. K. Chesterton. BoTP; OBCP

Christ Church Meadows, [Oxford]. Donald Hall. NYBP

Christ Climbed Down / from His bare Tree. Lawrence Ferlinghetti. GI; VGW

Christ Crucified. Richard Crashaw. OBEV

Christ for the World! We Sing. Samuel Wolcott. AH

"Christ has risen." Whoever believes that / Should not behave as we do. Czeslaw Milosz. GI, *tr.* by Czeslaw Milosz *and* Leonard Nathan (b. 1924) *Fr.* "Six Lectures in Verse."

Christ hath a garden walled around. Isaac Watts. FaBoCh

Christ home, Christ and his mother and all his hallows. (LL) The Starlight Night. Gerard Manley Hopkins. APAD; EnVR; GTBS-P; InPS-3; LiTM; MoBrPo; NAEL-2; PoE

Christ, I have read, did to His chaplains say. Salutation. Robert Herrick. CavPo; ChIV-2

Christ I Wudint Know Normal if I Saw It When. Bill Bissett. NOBC

Christ in Alabama. Langston Hughes. PoBA

Christ in Flanders. Lucy Whitmell. NSI

Christ in the Clay-Pit. Jack R. Clemo. GTBS-P

Christ in the Universe. Alice Thompson Meynell. MoBrPo; NOBE; OxAEP-2; VWP

Christ Inviting Sinners to His Grace. Henry Alline.

Amazing Sight! The Saviour Stands. AH

Christ is a nigger. Christ in Alabama. Langston Hughes. PoBA

Christ Is Arisen. Goethe. TrCP *Fr.* Faust.

(Easter Chorus.)

Christ is now risen again. Of the Resurrection. Miles Coverdale. ChIV-2

Christ keep the Hollow Land. Song: "Christ keep the Hollow Land." William Morris. PoEL-5 *Fr.* The Hollow Land.

Christ made [or maketh] to man a fair present. Divine Love. *Unknown.* OAEL-1

Christ, My Beloved. William Baldwin. NOCV; OxBSP

Christ, my Life, my Only Treasure. During His Courtship. Charles Wesley. NOCV

Christ of His gentleness. In the Wilderness. Robert Graves. CH; ChIV-2; MoBrPo

Christ 1. *Unknown, Anglo-Saxon.* AnOE, *tr.* by Charles W. Kennedy

Advent Lyrics. ASW

"'O my Joseph, Jacob's son,'" ASW, *tr.* by Kevin Crossley-Holland

"You govern the locks, You open life." ASW, *tr.* by Kevin Crossley-Holland

"Bless earth with Thine Advent, O Saviour Christ!"

"Hail, O most worthy in all the world!"

"O holy Jerusalem, Vision of peace."

"To the King. / Thou art the wall-stone rejected."

Christ risen was rarely recognized by sight. For They Shall See God. Luci Shaw. TrCP

Christ! These are her angels! The Unicorn and the Lady. Jean Garrigue. NYBP

Christ 3. *Unknown, Anglo-Saxon.*

Last Judgment, The. AnOE, *tr.* by Charles W. Kennedy

Christ to His Spouse [or The Beloved to the Spouse]. William Baldwin. NOCV

Christ to seek the lost was sent. Sympathy. Lizelia Augusta Jenkins Moorer. CBWP-3

Christ 2. Cynewulf, *Anglo-Saxon.*

Voyage of Life, The. AnOE

Christ Walks in This Infernal District Too. Malcolm Lowry. MoCV; NOBC

Christ was not sad, i' th' garden, for His own. Christ's Sadness. Robert Herrick. CavPo

CHRIST was the Word that spake it. *Unknown.* NoSic

Christ washed the feet of Judas!   The Feet of Judas.   George Marion McClellan.   AAP

Christ! What are patterns for? (LL)   Patterns.   Amy Lowell.   AWP; BoWoP; MoAmPo; NoP-4; OxBA; PBMP; WHSW

Christ, whose glory fills the skies.   Morning Hymn.   Charles Wesley.   TOF

Christ, you walked on the sea.   In the Twentieth Century.   James Philip McAuley.   ChIV-2

Christabel.   Coleridge.   FHYEP; NAEL-2; NOBRP; OAEL-2; Ro

("'Tis the middle of night by the castle clock.")   Ro

Christabel and Geraldine.

"In the touch of this bosom there worketh a spell."   RB

Scars Remaining, The.   OBNC

"'Tis the middle of night by the castle clock."

"Beneath the lamp the lady bowed."   OxBSn

"'Tis the middle of night by the castle clock."   CH; FaBoVe

Christabel and Geraldine.   Coleridge.   *Fr.* Christabel.   FHYEP; NAEL-2; NOBRP; OAEL-2; Ro

"In the touch of this bosom there worketh a spell."   RB

Christchurch, N. Z.   Earle Birney.   OxBC

Christendom.   Thomas Traherne.   PoEL-2

Christening, A.   Donald Davie.   OxBC

Christian, Be Up.   Robert Nathan.   AH

Christian constellations run, The.   The Circle.   Lizelia Augusta Jenkins Moorer.   CBWP-3

Christian Ethics.   Thomas Traherne.

"All music, sauces, feasts, delights and pleasures."   OxBSP

"Contentment is a sleepy thing."   NOCV

("For man to act as if his soul did see.")   NOCV

Christian Forbearance.   William Blake.   *See* A Poison Tree.

Christian has trousers on.   *Unknown.*   CBNP

Christian psalm for thee, A. (LL)   Ruth [or, The Influences of Nature]   Wordsworth.   GTBS-P; PoEL-4

Christian Rome.   Hildebert, *Latin.*   MLL, *tr. by* Helen Waddell

Christiana.   Peter Redgrove.   OxBC

Christianite.   William Stafford.   NoAM

Christians awake, salute the happy morn.   A Hymn for Christmas Day.   John Byrom.   ECEV; NOCV; PoEL-3

Christian's "Good-Night," The.   Sarah Doudney.   BLPA

Christian's Prayer, The.   *Unknown.*   CTV

Christian's Reply to the Philosopher, The.   Sir William Davenant.   MeLP   Life and Death.

Christina.   Dora Greenwell.   VWP

Christina.   Yona Wallach, *Hebrew.*   IP, *tr. by* Warren Bargad *and* Stanley F. Chyet

Christine to Her Son.   Christine de Pisan, *French.*   BoWoP, *tr. by* Barbara Howes

Christlike is my behaviour.   Aldous Leonard Huxley.   OBCoV   *Fr.* Antic Hay.

Christmas.   John Betjeman.   OBCP; OxBTC

Christmas, The.   Doll.   Myra Cohn Livingston.   TLR

Christmas.   Steve Hassett.   CDa

Christmas.   George Herbert.   GeHe; NOSC; PeECV; TOF; TrCP

Christmas.   Leigh Hunt.   OBCP

Christmas.   Jonggil Kim, *Korean.*   CKP, *tr. by* Jaihiun Kim

Christmas.   Peter McDonald.   PNI

Christmas.   Mary I. Osborn.   BoTP

Christmas.   Henry Timrod.   APN-2

Christmas.   Giuseppe Ungaretti, *Italian.*   NNPT, *tr. by* Michael Hamburger

Christmas 1956.   György Petri, *Hungarian.*   VCWP, *tr. by* Wilmer, Clive and George Gömöri

Christmas 1971.   Iain Crichton Smith.   FaBoTC

Christmas and Common Birth.   Anne Ridler.   FaBoTw

Christmas and Death.   Janet Frame.   PeNZ

Christmas at Freelands.   James Stephens.   TIRV; TrCP

Christmas at Sea.   Robert Louis Stevenson.   CH; EBVV; FaBoBe; PeVV

Christmas Ballad.   Saint John of the Cross, *Spanish.*   STV, *tr. by* John Frederick Nims

Christmas Bells.   Henry Wadsworth Longfellow.   AH; OBCP; PChr

("Of peace on earth, good-will to men.") (LL)   CTV

Christmas bells, awake and ring.   Christmas Morning.   Harry Behn.   PChr

Christmas Bells, Saigon.   Walter McDonald.   AF

Christmas Bills.   Joseph Hatton.   OBCP

Christmas, Boston Nineteen Eighty Nine.   Patricia Jones.   WWSi

Christmas Card.   Ted Hughes.   OBCP

Christmas Carol: "Angel told Mary, An."   Harry Behn.   PChr

Christmas Carol: "Christ child lay on Mary's lap, The."   G. K. Chesterton.   BoTP; OBCP

Christmas Carol: "Close to a quarter of a century since then."   T. H. Parry-Williams, *Welsh.*   OBWVE, *tr. by* Joseph P. Clancy

Christmas Carol: "God bless the master of this house."   *Unknown.*   BoTP; CTV

("And a Happy New Year.") (LL)   CTV

Christmas Carol, A: "God rest you merry gentlemen."   G. K. Chesterton.   UV

Christmas Carol, A: "In the bleak mid-winter."   Christina Rossetti.   ACTP; InPS-3; NOBVV; VWP

My Gift.   PChr

("Give Him my heart.") (LL)   CTV

Christmas Carol, A: "Thank God, thank God, we do believe."   Christina Rossetti.   PChr

Christmas Carol: "Three outas from the [High] bleak Karoo."   D. J. Opperman, *Afrikaans.*   PeSA; PeSAV, *tr. by* Anthony Delius

Christmas Carol: "Villagers all, this frosty tide."   Kenneth Grahame.   *See* Carol: "Villagers all, this frosty tide."

Christmas Caroll Sung to the King in the Presence at White-Hall, A.   Robert Herrick.   PChr

"Darling of the world is come, The."   PChr

Christmas Carols.   Patricia Beer.   OxBC

Christmas Carols.   Henry Wadsworth Longfellow.   BoTP

Christmas Childhood, A.   Patrick Kavanagh.   IIP

"My father played the melodion."   PChr; RB

Christmas come tomorrow.   Christmas with the Holy Family.   Susan Cavin.   GLP

Christmas comes but once a year.   Mother Goose.   OxNR; ReMoGo

Christmas comes like this: Wise men.   Christmas Comes to Moccasin Flat.   James Welch.   CDW; NoAM; PaTW

Christmas Creek.   Henry Clarence Kendall.   CBAP

Christmas Day.   Roy Fuller.   OBCP

Christmas Day.   Christopher Smart.   OBCP   *Fr.* The Nativity of Our Lord.   EBEV; HAP; NOBE; PoEL-3; SCGP *Fr.* Hymns and Spiritual Songs for the Fasts and Festivals of the Church of England.

Christmas Day.   Andrew Young.   OBCP

Christmas Day in the Workhouse.   George R. Sims.   BLPA; EBNV

(In the Workhouse.)   OBCP

Christmas day is come; let all prepare for mirth.   Luke Wadding.   NOSC; TIRV

Christmas Day. 1696.   Nicholas Hasluck.   NOBAu   *Fr.* Rottnest Island.

Christmas Day; the Family Sitting.   John Meade Falkner.   ChIV-2; NOCV; OxBTC

Christmas declares the glory of the flesh.   Christmas and Common Birth.   Anne Ridler.   FaBoTw

Christmas Dinner.   Michael Rosen.   OBCP

Christmas dinner was at two, The.   A Summer Christmas in Australia.   Douglas Brook Wheelton Sladen.   OBCP

Christmas Eve.   Patricia Beer.   OBCP

Christmas-Eve.   Robert Browning.

Earth Breaks Up.   TrCP

Christmas Eve.   Charlotte Druitt Cole.   BoTP

Christmas Eve.   John Davidson.   *See* A Ballad of Hell.

Christmas Eve.   Sascha Feinstein.   SeSe

Christmas Eve.   Lizelia Augusta Jenkins Moorer.   CBWP-3

Christmas Eve.   Karl Shapiro.   NYBP

Christmas Eve.   George Swede.   HA

Christmas Eve.   Edna Kingsley Walla.   BoTP

Christmas Eve, and twelve of the clock.   The Oxen.   Thomas Hardy.   APo; BoTP; CABP; CMoP; ChAP; EBEV; HAP; InPK-6; LiTM; MoBrPo; MoP; NOBE; NTP; NoAM; OAEL-2; OBCP; OxAEP-2; OxBTC; PChr; PeECV; Poetr; RB; SoSe-8; TFi; TOF; TRP; WeW-3

Christmas Eve in Whitneyville, 1955.   Donald Hall.   UnPo

Christmas Eve: My Mother Dressing.   Toi Derricotte.   NAmP90

Christmas Eve Service at Midnight at St. Michael's.   Robert Bly.   NNaP

Christmas Eve, South, 1865.   Mary E. Tucker.   CBWP-1

Christmas Eve under Hooker's Statue.   Robert Lowell.   CoAmPo; OxBA

Christmas Everywhere.   Phillips Brooks.   PWR

("Christmas to-night!") (LL)   CTV

Christmas Exchange, The.   Arthur Guiterman.   CTV

Christmas Family Reunion.   Peter De Vries.   NBLV; NOBL

Christmas Folk-Song, A.   Lizette Woodworth Reese.   OBCA; TrCP

Christmas Ghost, A.   Priscilla Jane Thompson.   CBWP-2

Christmas Ghost-Story, A.   Thomas Hardy.   OBWP

Christmas hath made an end.   Carol, for Candlemas Day.   *Unknown.*   NOSC

Christmas Holiday.   Alun Lewis.   PoWW

Christmas Hymn.   *Unknown, Irish.*   TIRV, *tr. by* Douglas Hyde

Christmas Hymn, A.   Richard Wilbur.   ChIV-2; OBCP; PChr; TrCP

Christmas in the Midwest.   Maureen Seaton.   LoHo

Christmas in the Wood. Frances Mary Frost. TrCP

Christmas is coming [*or* a-coming], / And the geese are getting fat. *Unknown.* NTCP; OxNR; PChr; ReMoGo

Christmas is my name, far have I gone, have I gone, have I gone. A Song Bewailing the Time of Christmas, So Much Decayed in England. *Unknown.* NoP-4; PBRV

Christmas Is Really for the Children. Steve Turner. OBCP

Christmas Landscape. Laurie Lee. OBCP

Christmas Letter Home. George Sutherland Fraser. OxBTC

Christmas Letter, 1970. May Sarton.
    "'Yes,' you say, "of course at Christmas." CrSp

Christmas Lights. Valerie Worth. PChr

Christmas Lullaby for a New-Born Child. Yvonne Gregory. NOxBChV

Christmas Mass for a Little Atheist Jesus. Claude Maillard, *French.* BoWoP, *tr.* by Maxine W. Kumin *and* Judith Kumin

Christmas Message, A. Gavin Ewart. FaBoMo

Christmas Morn. *Unknown. See* Words from an Old Spanish Carol.

Christmas Morning. Harry Behn. PChr

Christmas Morning. Elizabeth Madox Roberts. MoAmPo; NOxBChV; PChr

Christmas Morning I. Carol Freeman. KaS; PChr; PoBA; TTY
    ("Ragdoll.") (LL) KaS

Christmas Mourning. Vassar Miller. ChIV-2; MoAmPo

Christmas Night. B. E. Milner. BoTP

Christmas Night. Lawrence Sail. OBCP

Christmas Night in the Quarters. Irwin Russell.
    Fust Banjo, De. BLPA

Christmas night: the solstice storm. The Narrows of Birth. William Everson. PoM

Christmas 1959 et Cetera. Gerald William Barrax. PChr

Christmas 1944. Denise Levertov. AF

Christmas 1970. Spike Milligan. OBCP

Christmas 1962. Paul Mariah. GLP

Christmas: 1924. Thomas Hardy. FaBoEE; OBCP

Christmas Ornaments. Valerie Worth. PChr

Christmas Package, A. David McCord.
    "My stocking's where." PChr
    "That broken star." PChr

Christmas Party. Kate Daniels. NAmP90

Christmas Party, The. Adeline White. BoTP

Christmas Prayer, A. George Macdonald. PChr

Christmas Prayer, A. Robert Louis Stevenson. TrCP

Christmas Revel, A. Dafydd Bach ap Madog Wladaidd, *Welsh.* OBWVE

Christmas Rhyme, A. George Sands Johnson. PWR

Christmas Rhyme: North Tyrone. *Unknown.* FaBoVe

Christmas Rose, The. C. Day Lewis. TIRV

Christmas Rush, The. Clara Ann Thompson. CBWP-2

Christmas, season of streamers, coloured lights. Christmas Story (1980). Pat Arrowsmith. BrRo

Christmas Sermon, A. Robert Louis Stevenson.
    To Be Honest, to Be Kind. PoLF

Christmas Shopping. Louis MacNeice. OBCP

Christmas Song ("Trees are all bare not a leaf to be seen, The"). *Unknown.* NTP

Christmas Song, A. *Unknown. See* Long, Long Ago.

Christmas Song: "Why do the bells for Christmas ring?" Eugene Field. BoTP
    (Song.) CTV
    ("Therefore little children sing.") (LL) CTV

Christmas, South, 1866. Mary E. Tucker. CBWP-1

Christmas Spider, The. Michael Richards. Spl

Christmas Star. Boris Pasternak, *Russian.* GI, *tr.* by Nina Kossman; TCRP, *tr.* by Yakov Hornstein
    ("Christmas star was looking at the Maiden, The.") (LL) GI, *tr.* by Nina Kossman
    ("It was winter.") GI, *tr.* by Nina Kossman

Christmas Story (1980). Pat Arrowsmith. BrRo

Christmas Thank You's. Mick Gowar. OBCP

Christmas, the Year One, A.D. Sara Henderson Hay. PoRA

Christmas Thoughts, by a Modern Thinker. William Hurrell Mallock. NOBVV

Christmas Times. Maggie Pogue Johnson. CBWP-4

Christmas to-night! Phillips Brooks. *See* Christmas Everywhere.

Christmas Tree, The. Patricia Beer. OBCP

Christmas Tree, A. William Burford. SoSe-8

Christmas Tree. Stanley Cook. OBCP

Christmas Tree, The. Peter Cornelius. PChr

Christmas Tree, The. Isabel De Savitzky. BoTP

Christmas Tree, The. Lizelia Augusta Jenkins Moorer. CBWP-3

Christmas Tree. Laurence Smith. OBCP

Christmas Tree, The. John Walsh. AYFP

Christmas-Tree Song, A. Rodney Bennett. BoTP

Christmas Trees. Geoffrey Hill. NOCV

Christmas twigs crispen and needles rattle, The. New Year's Poem. Margaret Avison. LiTM; NOBC

Christmas Verse, A. "Kay." BoTP

Christmas was in the air and all was well. Karma. Edwin Arlington Robinson. AmPP; CMoP; FP; HeIP-4; MoAmPo; TrCP

Christmas Wish, A. Rose Fyleman. BoTP

Christmas with the Holy Family. Susan Cavin. GLP

Christopher. Diane Glancy. PUP-18

Marlowe. Swinburne. EPCY   *Fr.* Sonnets of English Dramatic Poets. Son

Christopher Robin Changes Guard with Dylan Thomas. Bill Greenwell. UV

Christopher Robin goes / Hoppity, hoppity. Hoppity. A. A. Milne. NTCP

Christopher Smart. Stanley Shaw. UV

Christopher White. *Unknown.* ESPB

Christo's. Paul Muldoon. CIP-2

Christ's Bounty. *Unknown, Irish.* TIRV, *tr.* by Brendan Kennelly

Christ[e]'s Childhood[e]. Robert Southwell. ChIV-2

Christ's Kirk on the Grene. James V, King of Scotland. OxBS
    "Than Robene Roy begouth to revell."

Christ's Life Our Code. Benjamin Copeland. AH

Christ's Nativity. Henry Vaughan. ESCV

Christ's Passion. Abraham Cowley. ChIV-2

Christ's Promise. Bible, *N.T.* LBC   *Fr.* John, 8. 21.

Christ's Reply. Edward Taylor. NAAL-1; NAAL-3; PoEL-3   *Fr.* God's Determinations [touching his Elect].

Christ's Resurrection and Ascension. Philip Doddridge. NOCV

Christ's Sadness. Robert Herrick. CavPo

Christ's sake, look / out where yr going. (LL) I Know a Man. Robert Creeley. InPS-3; NIP-4; NOBA; OxBSP; PoM; VCAP

Christs Sleeping Friends. Robert Southwell. ESCV

Christ's teeth ascended with him into heaven. The Linen Workers. Michael Longley. BiHa; CIP-2   *Fr.* Wreaths.

Christs Victorie, and Triumph in Heaven, and Earth, over, and after death. Giles, the Younger Fletcher.
    "As when the cheerfull Sunne, elamping wide." PBRV

Christ's Victory and Triumph. Giles, the Younger Fletcher.
    Celestial City, The.

Christus Natus Est. Countee Cullen. ChIV-2

Chrome Babies Eating Chocolate Snowmen in the Moonlight. A. K. Redwing. VoR

Chronic Meanings. Bob Perelman. PmAP

Chronica. Else Lasker-Schüler, *German.* PFTM, *tr.* by Durchslag, Audri and Jeanette Litman-Demeestère

Chronicle. Mei-Mei Berssenbrugge. OpBo

Chronicle, A. *Unknown.* CBNP
    (Life Story.) OBSP

Chronicle; a Ballad, The. Abraham Cowley. OxAEP-1

Chronicler, The. Alexander Bergman. TrJP

Chronology. Turner Cassity. PoA

Chronos, Chronos, mend thy pace. Dryden. *See* The Secular Masque.

Chronos, Chronos, mend thy ways. The Secular Masque. Dryden. NAEL-1; PoE; PoEL-3; SCGP

Chrysalides. Thomas Kinsella. BIrV

Chrysanthemums. Irene McKinney. PBCAP

Chrysanthemums in the Eastern Garden, The. Po Chü-i, *Chinese.* ChiP, *tr.* by Arthur Waley

Chrysanthemums last too long for these ravenous ladies. Starved Lovers. Archibald MacLeish. MeMAP

Chrysoberyl: The Eye of the Cat. Felicity Bast. PC

Chu Ch'ên Village. Po Chü-i, *Chinese.* ChiP, *tr.* by Arthur Waley

Chuang Tzu and Hui Tzu were hundreds of years old. Dick Barnes. GI

Chuang Tzu, The Monist. Po Chü-i, *Chinese.* ChiP, *tr.* by Arthur Waley

Chuck it, Smith ! (LL) Antichrist, or the Reunion of Christendom; an Ode. G. K. Chesterton. NOBE; NOBL; OBSV; OxAEP-2

Chuck Will's Widow Song. *Unknown.* BPo

Chüeh-chü. Tu Fu, *Chinese.* CoBCP, *tr.* by Burton Watson

Chums, The. Theodore Roethke. FP

Chung-i Temple, The. Wen Cheng-ming, *Chinese.*
    "Around the temple, pines and cedars." CoBLCP, *tr.* by Jonathan Chaves
    "At the lacquered table—my recent calligraphy." CoBLCP, *tr.* by Jonathan Chaves
    "Day drags on, as long as a year!, The." CoBLCP, *tr.* by Jonathan Chaves

"Fine breeze blows through the temple halls, A." CoBLCP, *tr. by* Jonathan Chaves

"Floating threads of spider webs hang." CoBLCP, *tr. by* Jonathan Chaves

"In the sixth month, outside the gate." CoBLCP, *tr. by* Jonathan Chaves

"Tea bowls, incense burning—a good feeling here!" CoBLCP, *tr. by* Jonathan Chaves

"These long verandahs seem to be washed clean." CoBLCP, *tr. by* Jonathan Chaves

"This little courtyard—mdash;the wind is pure." CoBLCP, *tr. by* Jonathan Chaves

Chunks of night. Shadows. Patricia Hubbell. Spl

Church and State. W. B. Yeats. CMoP

Church and the World walked far apart, The. The Church Walking with the World. Matilda Caroline Edwards. BLPA

Church Bells, The. Mrs. Henry Linden. CBWP-4

Church Bells. Clara Ann Thompson. CBWP-2

Church bells howitzers aloft to oust who suspect they've come as idea of beauty must. The Impatient Heart. Bruce Andrews. FTOS

Church bells ring—it is the Sabbath day, The. The Lifting of the Cloud. Thomas Macdonagh. TIRV

Church Burning: Mississippi. James A. Emanuel. PoBA

Church, / Chapel. *Unknown.* OxNR

Church Festivals. Christopher Harvey. NOSC

Church-Floor[e], The. George Herbert. EBEV; ESCV; MeLP; NOSC; OAEL-1; PeECV

Church Going. Philip Larkin. CABP; CMoP; GTBS-P; HeIP-4; LiTM; MoBrPo; MoP; NAEL-2; NIP-4; NoAM; NoP-4; OAEL-2; Poetr; SCV; SoSe-8; TFi; TwCP; UnPo

Church in the heart, The. Morris Abel Beer. PoToHe

Church is a business, and the rich, The. After Lorca. Robert Creeley. CoAmPo; InPS-3; LCAP-2; PmAP

Church is an iceberg, The. Winter Night. Charles Simic. HCAP

Church Ladies. Nancy Travis. ISC

Church Lock-and-Key. George Herbert. GeHe

Church-Lock and Key. George Herbert. ESCV; GeHe; OxBSP

Church Militant, The. George Herbert.
    "Religion stands on tip-toe in our land." PBRV

Church Monuments. George Herbert. ESCV; GeHe; HAP; NAEL-1; NOCV; NOSC; OAEL-1; PoE; TRP

Church Mouse commends: tapeworms and slugs grow wings. Critics and Poets. Geoffrey Grigson. FaBoEE

Church-Music[k]. George Herbert. ESCV; GeHe; OxBSP

Church of a Dream, The. Lionel Pigot Johnson. ADE; CABP; OAEL-2; OBMV

Church of Heaven's triumphal Car, The. Live, Evil Veil. John Wheelwright. ChIV-1

Church of San Antonio de la Florida, The. Paul Petrie. NYBP

Church-Porch, The. George Herbert. FP *Fr.* The Church-Porch. ESCV
    "Drink not the third glass, which thou canst not tame."

Church Romance, A. Thomas Hardy. FaBoTw; NOBE; OxAEP-2; OxBTC; PeECV

Church steeple fingers the sky, The. Asleep in the City. Michael Smith. PBCIP

Church the Garden of Christ, The. Isaac Watts. NOCV; PeECV

Church tower crowned the town, A. The Glass Town. Alastair Reid. NYBP

Church Walking with the World, The. Matilda Caroline Edwards. BLPA

Churches are best for prayer, that have least light. Dark Churches. Donne. *Fr.* A Hymn[e] to Christ, at the Author's Last Going into Germany. EBEV; MeLP

CHURCHES built to please the Priest. (LL) Love and Liberty—A Cantata. Robert Burns. NOBRP; NOEC; PoE; PoEL-4

Churches, Chapels, Stores, and Houses. A General Description of Men and Things in Cape Town. Frederic Brooks. PeSAV

Churches of Rome and of England, The, *much abr.* Dryden. *Fr.* The Hind and the Panther.

Church's One Foundation, The. Samuel John Stone. UV

Church's publication, The. Believers' Best Buy. Roger Woddis. UV

Churchyard leans to the sea with its dead, The. The Old Churchyard of Bonchurch. Philip Bourke Marston. EBVV; OBNC

Churchyard on the Sands, The. John Byrne Leicester Warren, 3d Baron De Tabley. CH; GBL; OBNC

Churl that wants another's fare, The. The Dog in the River. Phaedrus, *Latin. tr. by* Christopher Smart.

Churlyshe Cat, The. John Skelton. *See* O Cat of Carlishkind.

Churning (or lovemaking): Young man made for the corner, A. Cynewulf. *See* Three Riddles from *The Exeter Book.*

Churning the compost, dazed. To Earth. James Applewhite. PoA

Chyrsanthemums. Yün Shou-p'ing, *Chinese.*

"As we say farewell to autumn." CoBLCP, *tr. by* Jonathan Chaves

Cibber! write all thy verses upon glasses. Alexander Pope. FaBoEE

Cicada. Li Shang-yin, *Chinese.* SuSp, *tr. by* Eugene Eoyang *and* Irving Y. Lo

Cicada, The. Ou-yang Hsiu, *Chinese.* AWP; ChiP, *tr. by* Arthur Waley

Cicada. Adrien Stoutenburg. NYBP

Cicada cries out, The. *Unknown, Japanese.* OHMPJ, *tr. by* Kenneth Rexroth

Cicada sings, The. *Unknown, Japanese.* OHPJ, *tr. by* Kenneth Rexroth

Cicadas. Richard Wilbur. NOBA

Cicadas. Xue Tao, *Chinese.* APo, *tr. by* Jeanne Larsen

Cicadas in brambled foliage, The. The House-Builders. Kamala Das. PBWP

Cicadas sing, The. Ono no Komachi, *Japanese.* APo, *tr. by* Jane Hirshfield *and* Mariko Aratani

Cicadas were loud and what looked like a child's, The. The White Pilgrim: Old Christian Cemetary. Brigit Pegeen Kelly. BAP-93

Cicala stoned with dew. Meleager, *Greek.* GrAn, *tr. by* Peter Whigham

Cider and Vesalius. John Peck. AmPA

Cigar bands and glinting, dimestore lockets. (LL) Who I Think You Are. Elizabeth Alexander. FFC; RA

Cigar Smoke, Sunday, after Dinner. Louise Townsend Nicholl. FYAP

Cigarette smoke drifted, The. The Bandit. Vladimir Aleksandrovich Lugovskoy, *Russian.* TCRP, *tr. by* Gordon McVay

Cigarette smoke floated. Milne's Bar. Norman MacCaig. FaBoTw

Cigarettes in my mouth. The End of an Ethnic Dream. Jay Wright. MoNo; SeSe

Cigarettes will spoil yer life. *Unknown.* AS

Cigars. Olafs Stumbrs. CEEP

Cill Chais. *Unknown, Irish.* NOIV, *tr. by* Thomas Kinsella

Climabuella. Bayard Taylor. BXAP

Cincinnati. Mitsuye Yamada. UnSA

Cinderella. Olga Broumas. InPK-6

Cinderella. Randall Jarrell. LCAP-2; NAAL-2; VCAP

Cinderella. Ruby C. Saunders. BlSi

Cinderella. Anne Sexton. HeIP-4; InPS-3; NAAL-2; SAGP
    ("That story.") (LL) SAGP

Cinders of the desert, The. (LL) But Bird. Paul Zimmer. PuP-17; SeSe

Cinema—an asian girl with an african name. Rifacimento. Paul Violi. PmAP

Cinema is cruel, The. An Image of Leda. Frank O'Hara. HCAP; LCAP-2

Cinema Point. Philip Mead. BMAP

Cinema Vérité: The Death of Alfred, Lord Tennyson. Tom Andrews. BAP-94

Cinnabar Well—I don't know where it is. Searching for Herb Brazier and Cinnabar Well, I Also Saw the Waterfall of Singing Strings. Alongside Was the Cliff of the Lord of the Mountain. Tao-chi, *Chinese.* CoBLCP, *tr. by* Jonathan Chaves

Cinnamon Peeler, The. Michael Ondaatje. NOBC

Cino. Ezra Pound. VGW

Cinq Ans Après. Frank Gelett Burgess. OBAL; OBCoV; TFi
    (Confession.) NBLV

Cinquain: A Warning. Adelaide Crapsey. *See* The Warning.

Cinque. Janet Campbell Hale. VoR

Cinquevalli is falling, falling. Edwin Morgan. FaBoTC

Cinyras and Myrrha, Out of the Tenth Book of Ovid's Metamorphoses. Ovid, *Latin.*
    "'Twas now the mid of Night, when Slumbers close." OBCVT, *tr. by* John Dryden

Circe. John Byrne Leicester Warren, 3d Baron De Tabley. NOBVV

Circe. Hilda Doolittle. PoRA

Circe. William Gibson. PoA

Circe. Homer. OBCVT, *tr. by* Alexander Pope *Fr.* The Odyssey.

Circe. Louis MacNeice. OBMV

Circe. Augusta Davies Webster. VWP

Circe a lute she on—you say. Enchanter's Nightshade. Richard Caddel. NBrP

Circe / Mud Poems. Margaret Atwood.
    "I made no choice / I decided nothing." NALW
    "It's the story that counts." NALW
    "Men with the heads of eagles." NoAM
    "People come from all over to consult me, bringing their limbs." NALW
    "This story was told to me by another traveller." NALW

Circle, The. Lizelia Augusta Jenkins Moorer. CBWP-3

Circle, A. Theodore Spencer. NYBP

Circle, a Square, a Triangle and a Ripple of Water, A. Jane Cooper. TAP

Circle Game, The. Margaret Atwood. MoCV

"And you play the safe game / the orphan game."

"Being with you / here, in this room."

"Children like the block, The."

"Children on the lawn / joined hand to hand, The."

"However, / in all their games."

"Returning to the room: / I notice how."

"Summer again; / in the mirrors of this room."

Circle Jerk. Andrei Codrescu. PmAP

Circle of Struggle. William Pitt Root. NYBP

Circle of Totems, The. Peggy Shumaker. PBCAP

Circle of Weeping, The. Amir Gilbo'a, *Hebrew*. MHP, *tr. by* Ruth Finer Mintz

Circle to the left, Old Brass Wagon. Old Brass Wagon. *Unknown*. AS

Circle with a Hole in the Middle, The. Peter Kostakis. MoNo

Circles. Harry Behn. CA
   ("Things to draw with compasses, The.") CTV

Circles. Ralph Waldo Emerson. APN-1

Circles. Celia Gilbert. MDDM

Circles never fully round, but change, The. Perspective of Co-ordination. Arthur Davison Ficke. PoA

Circling by the fire. Stories. J. Patrick Lewis. NOxBChV

Circling shadow on the measured dial, The. Chronology. Turner Cassity. PoA

Circling the Daughter. Etheridge Knight. MoLi

Circling the Sun, at a respectful distance. Problems Of Gender. Robert Graves. LoP

Circuit closes, The. House and heart. Winter Night. Louis O. Coxe. NYBP

Circuit Judge, The. Edgar Lee Masters. FaBoEE *Fr.* Spoon River Anthology.

Circuit of Apollo, The. Anne Finch, Countess of Winchilsea. NALW
   ("To loose three parts in four from amongst womankind.") (LL) CABP

Circulation, The. Thomas Washbourne. NOCV

Circumambulating Arunachala. Gary Snyder. BB

Circumambulation of Mt. Tamalpais. Andrew Hoyem. PoA

Circumstance, The. Hart Crane. PFTM

Circumstance. Tennyson. CBLP

Circumstance. John Townsend Trowbridge. APN-2

Circumstances. Richard Jackson. PuP-17

Circus, The. Kenneth Koch. PmAP

Circus Animals' Desertion, The. W. B. Yeats. CMoP; EPCY; FaBoMo; FaBoTw; MoP; NAEL-2; NAWM-2; NIP-4; NOBE; NOIV; NoAM; NoP-4; OAEL-2; OxBTC; TFi

Circus at the Barber's Shop. Kendrick Smithyman. PeNZ

(Circus Elephant). Kathryn Worth. CTV

Circus Garland, A. Rachel Lyman Field.
   Epilogue: "Nothing now to mark the spot." OBCA
   Equestrienne. OBCA
   Gunga. OBCA
   Parade. OBCA
   Performing Seal, The. OBCA

Circus lions roared. In Tsvetnoy Boulevard, The. The Pipe. German Borisovich Plisetsky, *Russian*. TCRP, *tr. by* Keith Boseley

Circus Parade, The. Katharine Pyle. OBCA

Circus-Postered Barn, The. Elizabeth Jane Coatsworth. MoAmPo

Circus-Rider to Ringmaster. Thomas Hardy. RACG

Circus runaway, tattooed from head to toe in yellow. Finding the Tattooed Lady in the Garden. Pattiann Rogers. MT

Circus shines, like a shield, The. Nikolai Alekseievich Zabolotsky, *Russian*. TCRP, *tr. by* Daniel Weissbort

Circus tent, The. Eric Amann. HA

Cirque d'Hiver. Elizabeth Bishop. InPS-3
   ("Well, we have come this far.") (LL) ChAP

Cirrhosis. A. L. Hendriks. HCP

Cirrus bow of surf is blown, The. A Fantasy of Little Waters. James Scully. NYBP

Citadel. Edward Kamau Brathwaite. VCWP

Citation and Examination of William Shakespeare, The. Walter Savage Landor.
   Maid's Lament, The. OBEV; OBNC; RACG
   ("And, oh! pray too for me!") (LL) RACG

Cities, The. "Æ." OBMV

Cities. Grigory Mikhailovich Pozhenyan, *Russian*. TCRP, *tr. by* Lubov Yakovleva

Cities and towns, ye haunts of wretchedness! Industrial Evils. Joseph Cottle. NOEC *Fr.* Malvern Hills.

Cities are walled. It is a cruel land. Memory. Babette Deutsch. PoA

Cities Drowned. Sir Henry John Newbolt. CH

Cities Have Fallen, The. Fragano Ledgister. PBCV

Cities of dream wander under the bark of a December forest, The. A December Forest. Vesna Krmpotic, *Croatian*. WPOW, *tr. by* Vasa D. Mihailovich

Cities of the Plain, The. John Greenleaf Whittier. ChIV-1; NCAP

Citizen. Julia Fields. GT

Citizen. Chris Wallace-Crabbe. CBAP

Citizen, myself, or personal friend. Allen Tate. *See* Gay citizen, myself, and thoughtful friend.

Citizen of—the World, A. Donald McDonald. PBCV

Citizens and Sky. Phillis Levin. FFC

Citizen's Way, The. Vladimir Burich, *Russian*. TCRP, *tr. by* Albert C. Todd

Citizenship; Form 8889512, Sub-Section Q. G. K. Chesterton. OxBoLi

Cit's Country Box, The. Robert Lloyd. NOEC
   ("Some three or four mile out of town.") OBGa

City. Joseph Bruchac. CDW

City, The. Constantine P. Cavafy, *Greek*.
   ("You said, 'I will go to another land, I will go to another sea'.") NNPT, *tr. by* Rae Dalven
   ("You've destroyed it everywhere in the world.") (LL) AF, *tr. by* Edmund Keeley

City, The. Robert Creeley. LCAP-2

City. Angel González, *Spanish*. VCWP, *tr. by* Steven Ford Brown *and* Revuelta Gutierrez

City. Langston Hughes. SSCS

City, The. Ogden Nash. CBNP

City. Michael Smith. PBCIP

City, The. James Thomson. *See* Proem: "Lo, thus, as prostrate, 'In the dust I write'."

City Afternoon. John Ashbery. HeIP-4; InPK-6; NIP-4

City asleep / City asleep. The City Dump. Felice Holman. SSCS

City Baseball. Liz Rosenberg. CA

City Blues. Christine Craig. HCP

City branching blindly through the clouds, The. Citizens and Sky. Phillis Levin. FFC

City bred. Moon. Frances Horovitz. BrRo

City built in darkness and cold air, A. Peter Levi. CRP *Fr.* Pancakes for the Queen of Babylon.

City by the Sea, The. Josephine D. Henderson Heard. CBWP-4

City cactus. Discovery. Zhao Zhenkai, *Chinese*. VCWP, *tr. by* McDougall, Bonnie S. and Chen Maiping

City Called Heaven. *Unknown*. NAAAL

City Child, The. Tennyson. ACTP; BoTP; NOxBChV; OxBChV

City Christmas. Phyllis McGinley. OBCoV

City Clerk, The. Thomas Ashe. EBVV

City defenseless by day one sees desolation, A. Amir Gilbo'a, *Hebrew*. IP, *tr. by* Warren Bargad *and* Stanley F. Chyet

City Dump, The. Felice Holman. SSCS

City dwellers all complain, The. August. Michael Lewis. AYFP

City Eclogue, A. "W. J." NOEC

City Eclogue. "W. J." NOEC

City, etched in the black metal of sunset, is called Resurrection, / city of my birth, The. Winter Landscape. Alfonsas Nyka-Niliunas, *Lithuanian*. CEEP, *tr. by* Jonas Zdanys

City, Evening, and an Old Man: Me, The. "Dhoomil," *Hindi*. OMIP, *tr. by* Vinay Dharwadker

City falls, The. (LL) Battle Report. Bob Kaufman. ISC; MoNo; TTY

City Garden, A. W. S. Braithwaite. GT

City Gent. Craig Raine. NoAM

City Girl in the Country. Elizabeth Smither. PeNZ

City Girls. Aina Kraujiete, *Latvian*. CEEP, *tr. by* Inara Cedrins

City growing fast with a new lot number assigned, The. The Dove in Songbukdong. Kwangsop Kim, *Korean*. CKP, *tr. by* Jaihiun Kim

City Hall. Belle Randall. CRP

City Hall of Maritzburg, one silver-misted dawn, The. The Comrades Marathon. Chris Mann. PeSAV

City has spread quietly, suddenly. Everywhere, The. New Delhi, 1974. Vinay Dharwadker. OMIP

City in death with the streets caved in and the traffic lights / still, A. The Catacombs in San Callisto. Rolf Jacobsen, *Norwegian*. BLT, *tr. by* Roger Greenwald

City in the Full Moon, The. Hrubín František, *Czech*.
   "When the great wind blew the streetlights out." CEEP, *tr. by* Don Mager

City in the Sea, The. Edgar Allan Poe. APN-1; AmPP; ColAP; KSG; MeMAP; NAAL-1; NAAL-3; NCAP; NOBA; NoP-4; OxBA; PAR; PoE; PoEL-4; SCV; TAP; TFi; TRP

("Hell, rising from a thousand thrones, / Shall do it reverence.") (LL) ColAP

City in Which I Love You, The. Li-Young Lee. ChIV-1

City in your smile, A. Detente. Tom Pickard. NBrP

City is a crowded lift, The. Paul Evans. NBrP *Fr.* The Sofa Book.

City is beseiged, none may enter or leave, The. A Convert Comes to the City. Nathan Alterman. MHP, *tr. by* Ruth Finer Mintz. *Fr.* The Joy of the Poor.

City is covered with places you, The. Eddy Van Vliet, *Flemish.* VCWP, *tr. by* John Van Tiel

City is crossed by the river, The. Landscape of the Capibaribe River. João Cabral de Melo Neto, *Portuguese.* VCWP, *tr. by* Richard Zenith

City is of Night, The; perchance of Death. James Thomson. EBVV; PoEL-5 *Fr.* The City of Dreadful Night. OBNC

City is silent, The. Dawn Over the Mountains. Tu Fu, *Chinese.* OHPC, *tr. by* Kenneth Rexroth

City Limits, The. A. R. Ammons. HCAP; MoP; NAAL-2; NOBA; NoAM; NoP-4; PoPoPo; Poetr; VCAP

City Limits. Ted Kooser. GM

City looks flimsy as a movie set, The. (LL) Shoe Shop. Barton Sutter. EC3; SoSe-8

City, Lord, Where Thy Dear Life, The. William E. Dudley. AH

City Lyrics. Nathaniel Parker Willis. APN-1

City Morning, The. Sir William Davenant. NOSC *Fr.* Gondibert.

City Mouse and the Garden Mouse, The. Christina Rossetti. BoTP; FaBoBe; NTCP *Fr.* Sing-Song.

City of Dreadful Night, The. James Thomson. OBNC

"Although lamps burn along the silent streets." EBVV

"Anear the centre of that northern crest." GS

"As I came through the desert thus it was."

"City is of Night, The; perchance of Death." EBVV; PoEL-5

City's Queen, The. NOBE

"He stood alone within the spacious square." NOBVV

"I wandered in a suburb of the north." NOBVV

"Large glooms were gathered in the mighty fane." EBEV; OAEL-2

"Mighty river flowing dark and deep, The." EBVV; EnVR

Proem: "Lo, thus, as prostrate, 'In the dust I write'." OxBS

(City, The.) NOBE

"What men are they who haunt these fatal glooms." EBVV

City of Esteli, The. June 10. Magdalena de Rodriguez, *Spanish.* WPOW, *tr. by* Nina Serrano

City of Home is reached only in dreams, The. Thomas William Shapcott. BMAP

City of Men. Aaron Shurin. FTOS

City of orgies, walks and joys. Walt Whitman. APN-1

City of Slaughter, The. Hayyim Nahman Bialik, *Hebrew.* TrJP, *tr. by* A. M. Klein

City of Sleep, The. Rudyard Kipling. NTP

City of the End of Things, The. Archibald Lampman. NOBC

City of the Moon, The. Kenneth Rexroth.

"Buddha took some Autumn leaves." BLT

City of the Silent, The. William Gilmore Simms.

"With ruder pomp, in more barbaric taste." APN-1

City of White Emperor, The. Tu Fu, *Chinese.* SuSp, *tr. by* Wu-Chi Liu

City of Yes and the City of No, The. Yevtushenko, *Russian.* TCRP, *tr. by* Tina Tupkina-Glaessner *and* Geoffrey Dutton *and* Igor Mezhakoff-Koriakin

City opens its streets, the. The Transparent Life. Luigi Fontanella, *Italian.* NeIt, *tr. by* W. S. Di Piero

City Park. Christine Crow. SSCS

City Pigeons. Helen Chasin. WeW-3

City planners. To the New Annex to the Detroit County Jail. Richard W. Thomas. PoBA

City Rain. Kit Wright. AYFP

City rises, The. A Poem for Democrats. Imamu Amiri Baraka. CAPP-1

City Shower, A. Jonathan Swift. *See* A Description of a City Shower

City shuffles through the snow, the whirling snow, and I, indifferent, The. Dead of Winter. Anthony Towne. NYBP

City Songs. Mark Van Doren. NYBP

City Sparrow. Jane Mayhall. TAP

City-Storm. Harold Monro. MoBrPo

City Visions. Emma Lazarus. APN-2

City Walk-up, Winter 1969. Carolyn Forché. Poetr

City was full of blue devils, The. What the City Was Like. James Tate. WWSi

City where I was born, Radautz in Bukovina, cast me out when I was / ten, The. The Souvenir. Dan Pagis, *Hebrew.* IP, *tr. by* Warren Bargad *and* Stanley F. Chyet

City, whose streets are wavering reflections. Canal Street. John Wheelwright. PoA

City With Towers. Vitězslav Nezval, *Czech.* PFTM, *tr. by* Jerome Rothenberg *and* Frantiseak Deak

City without Walls. W. H. Auden. NYBP

City Worker, The. Edith Jay Scovell. WPN

City's pale-blooded, The. City Girls. Aina Kraujiete, *Latvian.* CEEP, *tr. by* Inara Cedrins

City's Queen, The. James Thomson. NOBE *Fr.* The City of Dreadful Night. OBNC

Civil Blood. Jill Breckenridge.

General John Cabell Breckinridge. CBCWP

Civil Defense. Kenneth Burke. OBAL

Civil Elegies. Dennis Lee.

"Often I sit in the sun and brooding over the city, always." NOBC

Civil Rights. Ira Sadoff. LTA

Civil Riot. George Douglas Howard Cole.

"And you'll say a nation totters." OxBTC

Civil Servant, The. Michael Longley. BiHa *Fr.* Wreaths.

Civil Service, The, *mod. by* Donald Attwater. William Langland. NOCV *Fr.* The Vision of Piers Plowman.

Civil Song. Pier Paolo Pasolini, *Italian.* VCWP, *tr. by* Norman MacAfee *and* Luciano Martinengo

Civil War. Austin Clarke.

"They are the spit of virtue now." NOIV

Civil War, The. Suzanne Rhodenbaugh. CBCWP

Civil War. Maksimilian Aleksandrovich Voloshin, *Russian.* TCRP, *tr. by* Albert C. Todd

Civil war of that household, The. (LL) A Small Farm. Michael Hartnett. CIP-2; PBCIP

Civil Wars, The. Samuel Daniel.

"It was upon the twilight of that day." OBWP

"Place there is, where proudly raised there stands, A." NoSic

Civile Wares betweene the Howses of Lancaster and Yorke, The. Lucan, *Latin.*

"I sing the civill Warres, tumultuous Broyles." OBCVT, *tr. by* Samuel Daniel

Civilian. Josephine Miles. WPE

Civilian and Soldier. Wole Soyinka. AF; PBMAP

Civilisation is hooped together, brought. Meru. W. B. Yeats. GSo; NoAM; OAEL-2; PoA; PoPoPo

Civilities of Lamplight. Charles Tomlinson. OxBC

Civility a Bogey. Margaret Avison. NOBC

Civilization. Yüan Chieh, *Chinese.* ChiP, *tr. by* Arthur Waley

Civilization Aha. Sipho Sepamla. PBMAP

Civilization and Its Discontents. John Ashbery. CAPP-1; LCAP-2; TwCP

Civilizations are viscous. History shipwrecks, Gold slips from God no. Disdained Apparitions. René Char, *French.* AF, *tr. by* Paul Mann

Civill Warres of Rome, Discours'd to his Royall Highness, Prince Charles, The. Virgil, *Latin.*

"Others may breathing Mettals softer grave." OBCVT, *tr. by* Sir Richard Fanshawe

Clach Eanchainn. Geoffrey Fraser Dutton. FaBoTC

Clack your beaks you cormorants and kittiwakes. A Canticle to the Waterbirds. William Everson. APSN; NeAP; PoM

Clacking and gouging when huddled. Snapshot of a Crab-Picker among Barrels Spilling Over, Apparently at the End of Her Shift. Dave Jeddie Smith. NoAM

Clad in a vestment wrought with passion-flowers. To a Passionist. Lionel Pigot Johnson. ADE

Clad in the wealthy robes his genius wrought. On Shakespeare and Voltaire. Thomas Holcroft. NOEC

Claflin's Alumni. Lizelia Augusta Jenkins Moorer. CBWP-3

Claim, The. Edith Nesbit. NOBVV

Claim naught but th' honour of the victory. (LL) Masque of the Virtues against Love. Mary Monck. ECWP; NOEC

Claim to Love. Giovanni Battista Guarini, *Italian.* AWP, *tr. by* Thomas Stanley

Claiming. Anita Virgil. HA

Claiming [*or* Clayming] a Second Kiss[e] by Desert. Ben Jonson. *Fr.* A Celebration of Charis in Ten Lyric[k] Pieces [*or* Peeces]. BeJo; OxAEP-1; SeCP

Claiming Kin. Ellen Bryant Voigt. WeT

Claims no particular status in space, or being of its own. (LL) Jealousy. Mei-Mei Bersssenbrugge. OpBo; PmAP

Clair de Lune. Gwen Harwood. BMAP

Clair de Lune. Anthony Hecht. NYBP

Clair de Lune. Paul Verlaine, *French.* AWP, *tr. by* Arthur Symons

Clairvoyant Journal. Hannah Weiner.
    "How can I describe anything when all these interruptions keep *arriving* and then." PmAP

Clambering up the Cold Mountain path. Han-shan, *Chinese.* EnlH, *tr. by* Gary Snyder

Clamming. Reed Whittemore. NYBP; TAP

Clammy cement, The. Dennis Brutus. PeSAV
    ("Cold / the clammy cement.") AF
    ("We begin to move / awkwardly.") (LL) AF

Clamor. Anne Lauterbach. PmAP

Clamour of the wind making music. Saint Columcille, *Irish.* BIrV, *tr. by* John Montague

Clams. Rin Ishigaki, *Japanese.* PBWP, *tr. by* Hiroaki Sato

Clan MacLean, The. Sorley MacLean. FaBoTC

Clan Meeting: Births and Nations: A Blood Song. Michael S. Harper. NoAM

Clan of stony desert women, A. Velemir Khlebnikov. TCRP, *tr. by* Gary Kern *Fr.* A Night in the Trench.

Clang! Clang! Clang! The Firemen. James Keir Baxter. NOxBChV

Clanking past the crest of a dune. Bad Run at King's Rest. Douglas Livingstone. PeSAV

Clap, clap handies. Clap Handies. *Unknown.* ReMoGo

Clap, clap the double nightcap on! William Gifford. Walter Savage Landor. FaBoEE; GTBS-P

Clap Handies. *Unknown.* ReMoGo

Clap hands, clap hands / Hie, Tommy Randy. *Unknown.* OxNR

Clap hands, clap hands / Till father comes home. *Unknown.* OxNR

Clap hands, Daddy comes / With his pocket full of plums. *Unknown.* OxNR

Clap hands, Daddy's coming / Up the waggon way. *Unknown.* OxNR

Clap Your Hands for Herod. Josef Hanzlik, *Czech.* OBCP, *tr. by* Ian Milner

Clapping Chant, A. *Unknown.* FaBoVe

Clara strolled in the garden with the children. Souvenir of the Ancient World. Carlos Drummond de Andrade, *Portuguese.* ChAP; VCWP, *tr. by* Mark Strand

Clare de Kitchen. *Unknown.* BLPA

Clarel: A Poem and Pilgrimage in the Holy Land. Herman Melville.
    Afterward.
        ("Saturnian Age, the Golden!") (LL) NCAP
        ("Seedsmen of old Saturn's land.") NCAP
    Concerning Hebrews. APN-2
    Dirge: "Stay, Death. Not mine the Christus-wand." APN-1; NCAP
    Easter. APN-2
    Epilogue: "If Luther's day expand to Darwin's year." APN-2; NCAP
    Hostel, The. APN-2
    Inscription, The: "While yet Rolfe's foot in stirrup stood." APN-2
    Medallion, The. APN-2
    Of Mortmain. APN-2
    Of Rome. OxBA
    On Mammon. OxBA
    Pillow, The. APN-2
    Prelusive. AmPP
    Recluse, The. APN-2
    Sodom. AmPP
    Symphonies. APN-2
    Ungar and Rolfe. OxBA
        ("Such earnestness! such wear and tear.")
    Via Crucis. APN-2; NCAP

Clarence Lee from Tennessee. Shel Silverstein. OBCA

Clarence Mangan. Thomas Kinsella. CIP-2

Clarence Short Bull died. Sitting Bull's Will versus the Sioux Treaty of 1868 and Monty Hall. A. K. Redwing. VoR

Claret laird, A. Hierarchy. George Mackay Brown. FaBoTC *Fr.* Runes from a Holy Island.

Clari, the Maid of Milan. John Howard Payne.
    Home, Sweet Home! APN-1; BLPA; EBEvV; FaBoBe

Clarimonde. Théophile Gautier. AWP *Fr.* Taches Jaunes, Les.

Clarissa Harlowe Poem, The. Gavin Ewart. OxBoV

Claritas. Denise Levertov. VGW

Clarity. A. R. Ammons. HCAP; TAP

Clark Colven and his gay ladie. Clerk Colvill. *Unknown.* ESPB; EnSB; OxBB

Clash in Arms of the Achaians and Trojans. Homer, *Greek.* OBCVT, *tr. by* George Meredith *Fr.* The Iliad.

Clash of salutation. As keels thrust into shingle. Geoffrey Hill. NoAM *Fr.* Mercian Hymns.

("Wine, urine and ashes.") (LL) NoP-4

Clasp you the God within yourself. The Last Round. Anna Wickham. MoBrPo

Claspe, The. Margaret Lucas Cavendish, Duchess of Newcastle. BWW; PBRV

Clasped around warm weeks in tents. Actually Swallowed. Douglas Messerli. FTOS

Clasping of Hands. George Herbert. PoEL-2

Class Incident from Graves. Alan Brownjohn. OxBTC

Class Song of '91. Eloise Bibb. CBWP-4

Classic. A. R. Ammons. NOBA

Classic Ballroom Dances. Charles Simic. LCAP-2; WeW-3

Classic Case, A. Gilbert Sorrentino. NeAP

Classic Encounter. "Christopher Caudwell." OxBTC

Classic landscapes of dreams are not, The. The Snowfall. Donald Justice. CRP; Poetr; VGW

Classic Scene. William Carlos Williams. NAAL-2; OxBA

Classic Verses. Rade Drainac, *Serbo-Croatian.* HSix, *tr. by* Charles Simic

Classic Waits for Me, A. Elwyn Brooks White. BXAP; NYBP

Classical Head, The. John Forbes. *See* Four Heads & How to Do Them.

Classical Quatrain, A. Paul Goodman. VGW

Classics Society. Tony Harrison. NoP-4 *Fr.* The School of Eloquence. NAEL-2; NoAM

Classroom at the Mall, The. R. S. Gwynn. RA

Claud Cockburn. Thomas McCarthy. PBCIP

Claude Allen. *Unknown.* AmFP

"Claude Monet sur son lit do mort." Michael White. BAP-94

Claude to Eustace: "Ah, let me look, let me watch, let me wait, unhurried, unprompted!" Arthur Hugh Clough. EnVR *Fr.* Amours de Voyage. NOBVV

Claude to Eustace. Arthur Hugh Clough. *See* Juxtaposition.

Claude to Eustace: "I am in love, meantime, you think; no doubt you would think so." Arthur Hugh Clough. EnVR; FaBoVe *Fr.* Amours de Voyage. NOBVV

Claude to Eustace: "Juxtaposition is great,—but, you tell me, affinity greater." Arthur Hugh Clough. CBLP *Fr.* Amours de Voyage. NOBVV

Claude to Eustace: "No, the Christian faith, as at any rate I understood it." Arthur Hugh Clough. EnVR *Fr.* Amours de Voyage. NOBVV

Claude to Eustace: "Shall we come out of it all, some day, as one does from a tunnel?" Arthur Hugh Clough. EBVVPR *Fr.* Amours de Voyage. NOBVV

Claude to Eustace: "There are two different kinds, I believe, of human attraction." Arthur Hugh Clough. *Fr.* Amours de Voyage.

Claude to Eustace: "These are the facts. The uncle, the elder brother, the squire." Arthur Hugh Clough. FaBoVe *Fr.* Amours de Voyage. NOBVV

Claude to Eustace: "Tibur is beautiful, too, and the orchard slopes, and the Anio." Arthur Hugh Clough. *Fr.* Amours de Voyage. NOBVV

Claude to Eustace: "Yes, we are fighting at last, it appears. This morning, as usual." Arthur Hugh Clough. EBVV; OxAEP-2; PeVV *Fr.* Amours de Voyage. NOBVV

Claudian's Old Man of Verona. Claudian. *See* The Old Man of Verona.

Claudian's Rufinus: or, The Court Favourite's Overthrow. Claudian, *Latin.*
    "He pass'd his Journey, to the Court arriv'd." OBCVT, *tr. by* Aaron Hill

Claudio's Lament: "Done to death by slanderous tongues." Shakespeare. *See* Epitaph: "Done to death by slanderous tongues."

Claudio's Lament: "Pardon, goddess of the night." Shakespeare. *See* Song: "Pardon, goddess of the night."

Claudius Gilbert. John Wilson. SCAP

Claudy. James Simmons. BiHa; CIP-2; PBCIP

Claus von Stauffenberg. Thom Gunn. OBWP

Claustrophobia. Sean O Riordain, *Irish.* NOIV, *tr. by* Thomas Kinsella

Clavering. Edwin Arlington Robinson. VoR

Clavicles for a Great Poetic Game. René Daumal, *French.* PFTM, *tr. by* Pierre Joris *Fr.* Clavicles for a Great Poetic Game.

Clawed green-eyed. Song. Lenrie Peters. PBMAP

Clay is the word and clay is the flesh. Patrick Kavanagh. NoAM; NoP-4; OxBTC *Fr.* The Great Hunger.

Clay of their departed lover, The. (LL) Woodnotes I ("For this present, hard"). Ralph Waldo Emerson. AmPP; NOBA

Clay, sand, and rock, seem of a diff'rent birth. Barten Holyday. FaBoEE

Clay when the wire slackens, sheds its velvet light. John Wilkinson. NBrP

Clean. Ann Turner. SSCS

Clean as a lady. Tulip. Humbert Wolfe. MoBrPo

Clean bones crying in the flesh, The. (LL) Full Moon. Elinor Wylie. NoP-4

Clean, green, windy billows notching out the sky. Cardigan Bay. John Masefield. OxBoS

Clean in the light, with nothing to remember. Aspects. Norman MacCaig. OxBS

Clean is the autumn wind. Verses. Li Po, *Chinese*. TAL, *tr. by* Robert Payne

Clean otter, I have not seen other, The. Into the Ark. John Blight. BMAP

Clean slate, with your own face on, A. (LL) You're. Sylvia Plath. FaBoTw; FaBoWP; RB

Clean the spittoons, boy. Brass Spittoons. Langston Hughes. MoAmPo; NoAM; Poetr

Clean vowel / is my morning, A. Vowel. Nina Cassian, *Romanian*. AF, *tr. by* Brenda Walker *and* Andrea Deletant

Cleaning a Fish. Dave Jeddie Smith. NoAM

Cleaning the Well. Fred Chappell. MT

Cleaning woman opened the rusty door, A. The Church of San Antonio de la Florida. Paul Petrie. NYBP

Cleanliness. Charles Lamb *and* Mary Lamb. OxBChV

Cleanly rush of the mountain air, The. The Dead Knight. John Masefield. CH; GTBS-P

Cleanly, sir, you went to the core of the matter. A Correct Compassion. James Kirkup. FaBoTw; OxBTC

Cleanness. *Unknown, Middle English.*
"He who would acclaim Cleanness in becoming style." NOCV, *tr. by* Brian Stone

Clear. Angelo Lewis. PoBA

Clear After Rain. Tu Fu, *Chinese*. BLT; OHPC, *tr. by* Kenneth Rexroth

Clear and bright is the splendor. The Day of Cold Food. Li Ch'ing-chao, *Chinese*. OHPC, *tr. by* Kenneth Rexroth

Clear and Colder. Robert Frost. OBCoV

Clear and cool, clear and cool. The River's Song. Charles Kingsley. ACTP   *Fr. The Water Babies.*

Clear Ankor, on whose silver sanded shore. Another to the River Ankor. Michael Drayton. NOSC   *Fr.* Idea.

Clear [*or* Cleere] are her eyes. Upon Her Eyes. Robert Herrick. BeJo

Clear as my ash tree through the glass. Housing. Denise Riley. NBrP

Clear Autumn. I gaze out into. Overlooking the Desert. Tu Fu, *Chinese*. OHPC, *tr. by* Kenneth Rexroth

Clear Bright. Huang T'ing-chien, *Chinese*. OHMPC, *tr. by* Kenneth Rexroth

Clear Bright. Li Ch'ing-chao, *Chinese*. BoWoP, *tr. by* Kenneth Rexroth

Clear, bright and full of mid-month days. (LL) A Song Of Chang Ching-Yüan Picking Lotus Flowers. Wen T'ing-yün, *Chinese*. LoP; SuSp, *tr. by* William R. Schultz

Clear bright morning, with its scented air, The. The Fair Morning. Jones Very. GSo; NOBA

Clear brown eyes, kindly and alert, with 12-20 vision, The. Portrait. Kenneth Fearing. MoAmPo

Clear cedar air and. A Fine Line. Art Lange. MoNo

Clear Channel. Lorenzo Thomas. FTOS

Clear cool note of the cuckoo which has ousted the legitimate nest-holder, The. Sincere Flattery of W. W. (Americanus). James Kenneth Stephen. NOBL

Clear dawn adorns the day of the Cold Food Festival, A. Tune: "Sand of Silk-washing Stream." Wei Chuang, *Chinese*. SuSp, *tr. by* Lois Fusek

Clear Evening after Rain. Tu Fu, *Chinese*. OHPC, *tr. by* Kenneth Rexroth

Clear fall afternoon beckons, A. Grigory Mikhailovich Pozhenyan, *Russian*. TCRP, *tr. by* John Glad

Clear full moon. *Unknown, Japanese.* OHMPJ, *tr. by* Kenneth Rexroth

Clear [*or* Cleere] had the day been [*or* bin] from the dawn[e]. The Sixt Nimphall. Michael Drayton. BoTP   *Fr.* Muses' Elysium [*or* Elizium].

Clear Midnight, A. Walt Whitman. HAP; NTP; OxBSP; PAR; SAmP; Spl

Clear moon arcs, The. Red Rock Ceremonies. Anita Endredze-Danielson. VoR

Clear moon brightly shining in the night. Mei Sheng *and* Fu I. *Fr.* Nineteen Old Poems of the Han. CoBCP, *tr. by* Burton Watson

Clear moon brightly shining in the night. *Unknown, Chinese.* CoBCP, *tr. by* Burton Watson

Clear Night[, thumb-top of a moon, a back-lit sky]. Charles Wright. MT; SAGP; VCAP

Clear night in harvest time, A. I Pass the Night at General Headquarters. Tu Fu, *Chinese*. OHPC, *tr. by* Kenneth Rexroth

Clear, noon sky at midsummer is God's eye, A. Cosmic Eye. A. K. Redwing. VoR

Clear ocean seems, The. The Double Vision of Manannan. *Unknown, Irish.* BIrV, *tr. by* John Montague

Clear pond, The. Then and Now. Kapilar, *Tamil*. PLW, *tr. by* A. K. Ramanujan

Clear Shell, A. Frances Bellerby. FaBoWP

Clear spring, A. Tanka. Akiko Yosano, *Japanese*. MJT, *tr. by* Makoto Ueda

Clear stream girdles the long copse, The. On Returning to Sung Mountain. Wang Wei, *Chinese*. SuSp, *tr. by* Paul W. Kroll

Clear the brown path, to meet his coulter's gleam! The Ploughman. Oliver Wendell Holmes. CA

Clear the land, thatch the rush for roof. Meditation Hall. Liu Tsung-yüan, *Chinese*. SuSp, *tr. by* Jan W. Walls

Clear—the senses bright—sitting in the black chair—Rocker. Michael McClure. BB; NeAP   *Fr.* Peyote Poem. PoM

Clear the way and build the road! The Road. Zalman Schneour, *Yiddish*. TrJP, *tr. by* Joseph Leftwich

Clear the way there Jonathan! Walt Whitman. *See* A Boston Ballad [1854].

Clear transparent sea with light, The. Introduction. Horatio Nelson Huggins. *Fr.* Hiroona. PBCV

Clear vowels rise like balloons, The. (LL) Morning Song. Sylvia Plath. BoWoP; ColAP; HCAP; HeIP-4; InPK-6; InPS-3; LCAP-2; NAAL-2; NIP-4; NOBA; NTP; NoP-4; PoPoPo; SAGP; VCAP

Clear water in a brilliant bowl. The Poems of Our Climate. Wallace Stevens. MeMAP; NoP-4; OxBA; SoSe-8; TwCP

Clear water of the imperial pond, The. Ise Tayu, *Japanese*. BoWoP; WPJ, *tr. by* Kenneth Rexroth *and* Ikuko Atsumi

Clear weather of juniper, The. Sloe Gin. Seamus Heaney. PNI

Clear wind—what is it?, The. Lotus Viewing. Su Tung-p'o, *Chinese*. CoBCP, *tr. by* Burton Watson

Clearances. Seamus Heaney. CIP-2; PBCIP; PNI
"Cool that came off sheets just off the line, The."
"Fear of affectation made her affect."
"I thought of walking round and round a space."
"In the last minutes he said more to her."   PNI
"When all the others were away at Mass."   BLT; PNI

Clearances, The. Iain Crichton Smith. FaBoTC

Cleare moving cristall, pure as the Sunne beames. Sonnet. Sir William Alexander, Earl of Stirling. OxBS   *Fr.* Aurora.

Clearing, The. Peter Everwine, *after the Nahuatl Indian*. NNaP

Clearing, The. Robert Graves. NYBP

Clearing at Dawn. Li Po, *Chinese*. AWP, *tr. by* Arthur Waley

Clearing Away. Andrew Taylor. BMAP

Clearing brush away. Taking to the Woods. Henry Taylor. MT

Clearing for the Plough. Ernest G. Moll. NOBAu

Clearing Station. Wilhelm Klemm, *German*. PeFWW, *tr. by* David McDuff

Clearing the Air. Nancy Willard. CrSp

Clearista. Meleager, *Greek*. OBCVT, *tr. by* Andrew Lang

Clearly and without emotion / about the need for action, about killing people, / I wanted him. (LL) Action Would Kill It / A Gamble. Robert Adamson. BMAP

Clearly we'd found the rim of something. Tremendous Mood Swings. Burlin Barr. BAP-94

Clearly your day has passed. The Boyarina Morozova. Nikolai Ivanovich Glazkov, *Russian*. TCRP, *tr. by* Daniel Weissbort

Clearness for me, frailty for her. (LL) In a Glass-Window for Inconstancy. Edward Herbert, 1st Baron Herbert of Cherbury. OxBSP; SeCP

Clears the morning of doves. The Wind in the Trees. Cathy Song. OpBo

Clearsightedness. Andrew Salkey. PBCV

Cleator Moor. Norman Nicholson. FaBoTw

Cleavage. A. R. Ammons. OBAL

Cleave and *Cleave*. Brenda Hillman. WeT

Cleaving, The. Li-Young Lee. NAmP90; OpBo; PuP-16

Cleitagoras. Leonidas of Tarentum, *Greek*. AWP, *tr. by* William M. Hardinge

Clementine. Percy Montross. *See* Oh, My Darling Clementine.

Clementine. *Unknown.* CTV

Clementine. *Unknown.* KaS

Clenched ignorant against the sky! (LL) The Armadillo. Elizabeth Bishop. ColAP; HCAP; MoP; NAAL-2; NOBA; NYBP; NoAM; NoP-4; Poetr; TAP; VCAP; VGW

Cleombrotus the bruiser. Lucilius, *Greek*. GrAn, *tr. by* Peter Porter

Cleomenes. Dryden.
One Happy Moment. OBEV
(Song.)

Cleon the poet (from the sprinkled isles). Robert Browning. OAEL-2 Greece.

Cleon the poet, (from the sprinkled isles). Greece. Robert Browning. *Fr.* Cleon the poet (from the sprinkled isles). OAEL-2

Cleonicos. Edward Cracroft Lefroy. AWP   *Fr.* Echoes from Theocritus.

Cleopatra. Samuel Daniel.
"O fearfull, frowning nemesis." PoEL-2

Cleopatra. Shakespeare. *Fr.* Antony and Cleopatra.
(Cleopatra's Barge.)

Cleopatra. William Wetmore Story. APN-1

Cleopatra Dying. Thomas Stephens Collier. BLPA; FaBoBe

Cleopatra to the Asp. Ted Hughes. EBEV; RACG

Cleopatra's Barge. Shakespeare. *See* Cleopatra.

Cleopatra's Death. Shakespeare. *See* Anthony and Cleopatra.

Cleopatra's Lament. Shakespeare. UnPo *Fr.* Antony and Cleopatra.

Cleric once heard with dismay, A. Limerick. Joan Dare. PeLi

Clerical Oppressors. John Greenleaf Whittier. NAAL-1

Clerihew: "Savonarola." Edmund Clerihew Bentley. CBNP *Fr.* Clerihews.

Clerihew: "Spinoza / Collected curiosa." *Unknown.* NOBL

Clerihews. Edmund Clerihew Bentley.

     "After dinner Erasmus." OBCoV

     "Art of Biography, The." NOBL; NTP; PeLV

     Clerihew: "Savonarola." CBNP

     "'Dinner-time?' said Gilbert White." OBCoV

     George III. PeLV

     "How vigilant was Spenser." OBCoV

     "I am not Mahomet." NOBL

     "Intrepid Ricardo, The." OBCoV

     J. S. Mill. OxBoLi; PeLV

     Lord Clive. PeLV

     "'No,' said Charles Peace." NOBL

     "'No, sir,' said General Sherman." NOBL; OBCoV

     "Sir Christopher Wren." NBLV; PeLV

     "'Susaddah!' exclaimed Ibsen." OBCoV

     "There exists no proof as." NOBL

     "When their lordships asked Bacon." OBCoV

     "Wynkyn de Worde." OBCoV

Clerimont's Song. Ben Jonson. NOSC; OAEL-1; PoE; SeCP *Fr* Epicoene; or, The Silent Woman.

     (Clerimont's Song.) NOSC; OAEL-1; PoE; SeCP

     ("Still to be neat, still to be dressed.") NoP-4; PoPoPo

Clerk Colvill. *Unknown.* ESPB; EnSB; OxBB

Clerk Saunders[and May Margaret]. *Unknown.* ESPB; OBEV; OxBS

     ("Clinking bell gaed thro' the toun, The.") EBNV

     "Is there ony room at your head, Saunders?"

Clerk Ther Was of Caunterbrigge Also, A. Walter William Skeat. BXAP

Clerk ther was of Oxenford also, A. Chaucer. *See* The Canterbury Tales.

Clerke ther was, a puissant wight was hee, A. Ye Clerke of Ye Wethere. *Unknown.* BXAP

Clerks, The. Edwin Arlington Robinson. APN-2; MoAmPo; NAAL-2; PoEL-5

Clerks. Boris Abramovich Slutsky, *Russian.* TCRP, *tr.* by J. R. Rowland

Clerk's Twa Sons o Owsenford, The. *Unknown.* ESPB

Cleveland Lyke Wake Dirge, The. *Unknown. See* Lyke-Wake Dirge, The [*or* A].

Clever Hen, The. *Unknown.* ReMoGo

Clever man builds a city, A. Woman. *Unknown.* AWP, *tr.* by H. A. Giles *Fr.* Shi King.

Clever Peter and the Ogress. Katharine Pyle. OBCA

Clever showpiece nature here displays!, A. The Man-and-Wife Mountain. Ho Xuan Huong, *Vietnamese.* AVP, *tr.* by Huỳnh Sanh Thông

Clever Skipper, The. *Unknown.* AmFP

Clever Tom Clinch Going to Be Hanged. Jonathan Swift. NOIV

Clever Woman, A. Mary Elizabeth Coleridge. BrRo; VWP

Cliché can be true: You hate to open the paper. Insomnia: The Distances. Sydney Lea. RA

Clichés for an Unfaithful Husband. Jane King. HCP

Cliches with worn wit combined. On a Lover of Books. Geoffrey Grigson. FaBoEE

Click Go the Shears. *Unknown.* NOBAu

Clickety-clack. Song of the Train. David McCord. NTCP

Client, the patron, the age, The. Juvenal, *Latin.* OBCVT, *tr.* by John Dryden

Cliff, The. David Rowbotham. NOBAu

Cliff dweller ruins. Foster Jewell. HA

Cliff Klingenhagen had me in to dine. Edwin Arlington Robinson. APN-2; AmPP; MeMAP; MoAmPo; NCAP; Son

Cliff Notes. Bob Perelman. PmAP

Cliff of the Ancient Tomb, The. Chang Yü. *Fr.* Seven Poems on Living in the Mountains: Seeing Off. CoBLCP, *tr.* by Jonathan Chaves

Cliff-Top, The. Robert Bridges. BoTP

Cliffs are tinged red. The Summit. Chiyong Chong, *Korean.* CKP, *tr.* by Jaihiun Kim

Cliffs at Manzanilla, The. Jan Carew. PBCV

Cliffs of scarlet cloud gleam in the west. The Return. Tu Fu, *Chinese.* TAL, *tr.* by Robert Payne

Cliffs that rise a thousand feet. Sailing Homeward. Chan Fang-sheng, *Chinese.* AWP; ChiP; FaBoCh, *tr.* by Arthur Waley

Clifton. Joan Larkin. GLP

Clifton Chapel. Sir Henry John Newbolt. OBEV

Clifton Grove. Henry Kirke White.

     "Lo! in the West, fast fades the ling'ring light." OBNC

Climate of Paradise, The. Louis Simpson. NOBA

Climate succumbing continuously as water gathered. Nebraska. Barbara Guest. FTOS

"Climate's very healthy once you're used to being dead," The. (LL) On Learning to Adjust to Things: John Ciardi. KaS

Climax of passion, the dancers are trembling, The. Rumba. José Zacarías Tallet, *Spanish.* TTY, *tr.* by Sangodare Akanji

Climb. Rapunzel. Olga Broumas. CPO

Climb at *Court* for me that will. Seneca. *See* Senec. Traged. ex Thyeste Chor. 2.

Climb Mount Fuji. Avedik Issahakian. ChAP

Climbed high, to gaze upon the sea. Ancient Air. Li Po, *Chinese.* BLT, *tr.* by J. P. Seaton

Climbers, The. W. H. Auden. MeMAP

Climbin up de mountain. Trouble Oh. *Unknown.* PBCV

Climbing. Lucille Clifton. GT; LoL

Climbing. Gloria Fuertes, *Spanish.* PBWP, *tr.* by Philip Levine

Climbing. Jennifer Maiden. BMAP; CBAP

Climbing a Solitary Islet in the River. Hsieh Ling-yün, *Chinese.* SuSp, *tr.* by Francis Westbrook

Climbing, climbing, the path of stones. Temple of the Ocean of Awakening. Shen Chou, *Chinese.* CoBLCP, *tr.* by Jonathan Chaves

Climbing from the Lethal dead. Orpheus. Yvor Winters. NOBA; VGW

Climbing Gannett. Roberta Hill Whiteman. HATNAP

Climbing high, sadly I gaze at the Mountain of Eight Immortals. Passing by Huai-yin I Have Feelings. Wu Wei-yeh, *Chinese.* CoBLCP, *tr.* by Jonathan Chaves

Climbing K'uai Pavilion. Huang T'ing-chien, *Chinese.* SuSp, *tr.* by Michael E. Workman

Climbing Mount Yang. Yüan Hung-tao, *Chinese.* CoBLCP, *tr.* by Jonathan Chaves

Climbing northward. The Herds. W. S. Merwin. NYBP

Climbing Phoenix Terrace at Chin-ling. Li Po, *Chinese.* SuSp, *tr.* by Joseph J. Lee

Climbing P'iao-miao Peak. Wu Wei-yeh, *Chinese.* CoBLCP, *tr.* by Jonathan Chaves

Climbing rung after rung the scrambling-. Davy by Starlight. Raymond Wilson. SpW

Climbing Stone Drum Mountain Above the Shores of Shang-shu. Hsieh Ling-yün, *Chinese.* SuSp, *tr.* by Francis Westbrook

Climbing the Chagrin River. Mary Oliver. Poetr

Climbing the Heights. Tu Fu, *Chinese.* SuSp, *tr.* by Wu-Chi Liu

Climbing the Ling-Ying Terrace and Looking North. Po Chü-i, *Chinese.* BLT, *tr.* by Arthur Waley

Climbing the Ling-ying Terrace and Looking North. Po Chü-i, *Chinese.* ChiP, *tr.* by Arthur Waley

Climbing the peak of Tamalpais the loose. The Impossible Poem. George Oppen. NNaP *Fr.* Some San Francisco Poems.

Climbing the rutted path, the lights of the town. The Phases of Darkness. Paul Petrie. TAP

Climbing the stairway grey with urban midnight. Effort at Speech. William Meredith. AFr

Climbing the Terrace of Kuan-yin and Looking at the City of Ch'ang-an. Po Chü-i, *Chinese.* ChiP, *tr.* by Arthur Waley

Climbing the Tower by the Pond. Hsieh Ling-yün, *Chinese.* SuSp, *tr.* by Francis Westbrook

Climbing through the January snow, into the Lobo canyon. Mountain Lion. D. H. Lawrence. FaBoVe; OxBTC; RB

Climbing to a Mountain Monastery. Tu Hsün-ho, *Chinese.* SuSp, *tr.* by Edward H. Schafer

Climbing to Lo-yu Plateau, before Leaving for Wu-hsing. Tu Mu, *Chinese.* PLT, *tr.* by A. C. Graham

Climbing to the Top of the City Walls at Kan-yü. Wang T'ing-hsiang, *Chinese.* CoBLCP, *tr.* by Jonathan Chaves

Climbing Up to the Lo-yu Plain. Tu Mu, *Chinese.* SuSp, *tr.* by Irving Y. Lo

Climbing You. Erica Jong. PoA

Climbs back up to claim herself again. (LL) The Woman Hanging from the Thirteenth Floor Window. Joy Harjo. GLP; HATNAP

Climbs to a soul in grass and / flowers. James Russell Lowell. *See* What [*or* And what] Is So Rare as a Day in June?

Clinging / to lost / horizons / i. (LL) Upon Leaving the Parole Board Hearing. Conyus. GT

Clinging to my breast, no stronger. Spinster's Lullaby. Vassar Miller. BoWoP; NMM-2

Clinic Day. Jo Barnes. BrRo

Clink, clink, clinkety-clink. The Milkman. Clive Sansom. BoTP

Clinking bell gaed thro' the toun, The. *Unknown*. *See* Clerk Saunders[and May Margaret].

Clio. Martha Sansom.
   NoTL. LW

Cliona. Catherine Twomey. IIP

Clio's. Mick Imlah. CBLP

Clio's Picture. *Unknown*.
   "Here let the Muse perform the painter's art." ECWP

Clio's Protest. Richard Brinsley Sheridan. FaBoEE

Clip-clop go water-drops and bridles ring. Nude in a Fountain. Norman MacCaig. OxBS

Clipped / separated / piled up. Mulch. Adam David Miller. NBV

Clippety cloppety, / Cesare Borgia. Chip. George Starbuck. OBAL

Clipping the same sad alnage of the years. (LL) The Clerks. Edwin Arlington Robinson. APN-2; MoAmPo; NAAL-2; PoEL-5

Cloak, The. James McAuley. BMAP

Cloak, The. Norman Henry, II Pritchard. GT

Cloak of Laughter. Abigail Cresson. PoToHe

Clock. Edward Kamau Brathwaite. MoNo

Clock, The. Mother Goose. ReMoGo

Clock. Valerie Worth. TLR

Clock-A-Clay [The Lady Bug]. John Clare. APo; EBEV; EBVV; EnVR; NAEL-2; NOxBChV; OAEL-2; OBNC; PoEL-4

Clock gleams, The. 1941. Everette Maddox. MT

Clock in the Old Jewish Ghetto, The. Vitězslau Nezval, *Czech*. NNPT, *tr. by* Ewald Osers

Clock in the Square, A. Adrienne Rich. HeIP-4

Clock just now has nothing more to say, The. (LL) The Campus on the Hill. W. D. Snodgrass. AiP; LiTM; NoAM; TAP; TwCP

Clock of my days winds down, The. The Alligator Bride. Donald Hall. CoAmPo; SPE

Clock on Hancock Street. June Jordan. FaBoWP

Clock says, The, "When will it be morning?" After Lorca. Ted Hughes. PoA

Clock shows nearly five, The. To a Salesgirl, Weary of Artificial Holiday Trees. James Wright. NYBP

Clock stopped, A. Emily Dickinson. APN-2; AmPP; NAAL-1; NAAL-3; PAR; PoEL-5
   ("And Him.") (LL) NoP-4

Clock stops ticking, The. Stroke. Mike Lowery. Poetsp

Clock strikes five—the watchman goes, The. Lady Sophia Burrell. ECWP *Fr.* Verses to a Lady, on Her Saying She Preferred Commonalty to an Irish Peerage.

Clock strikes one that just struck two, The. Emily Dickinson. APN-2

Clock without Hands. John Frederick Nims. PoA

Clockface. Rhyll McMaster. BMAP

Clockface. Judith Thurman. Spl

Clocks. Louis Ginsberg. TrJP

Clocks are sorry, the clocks are very sad, The. Psalm and Lament. Donald Justice. DiPo

Clocks begin, civicly simultaneous, The. At Delft. Charles Tomlinson. NYBP

Clocks blue seconds fold over me. Paregoric Babies. Jim Carroll. PmAP

Clock's so huge you can watch the minute hand, The. Grand Central Station, 20 December 1987. Bruce Bawer. RA

Clocks strike in the distance. On My Child's Death. Joseph, Freiherr von Eichendorff, *German*. IMW, *tr. by* W. D. Snodgrass

Clock's untiring fingers wind the wool of darkness, The. Cradle Song. Louis MacNeice. MoBrPo

Clocks were running as usual so they waited only. The Fathers of a Star. Zbigniew Herbert, *Polish*. CEEP, *tr. by* Czesw Miosz

Clockwise and counter-clockwise turning. (LL) A Poem Beginning with a Line by Pindar. Robert Duncan. CoAmPo; NNaP; NeAP; PmAP; PoM; VCAP

Clockwork beings, winding out their lives. Insects. Isidor Schneider. TrJP

Clockwork skating Wordsworth on the ice, A. Xmas for the Boys. Gavin Ewart. OBSV

Clod or the Pebble, The. William Blake. EnLoPo; FHYEP; InPS-3; NAEL-2; NOBE; OBNC; OxAEP-2; OxBSP; PoE; RB; SCGP; SCV; TFi *Fr.* Songs of Experience.
   (Clod and the Pebble, The.) APAD; GLoP; NoP-4; Ro

Clodian Songbook. Christian Karlson Stead.
   "Air New Zealand." PeNZ
   "Fucking, I feel at one with the world." PeNZ

Clods, as if Inform'd with some new Soul, The. Cadmus sows teeth. Ovid, *Latin*. OBCVT, *tr. by* John Oldham

Clods' friability lulls iron to sleep. August Stramm. *See* Battlefield.

Cloe ("Bright as the day, and like the morning fair"). George, Baron Lansdowne Granville. FaBoEE; NIP-4

C[h]loe. Alexander Pope. AWP; NOBE; OBSV *Fr.* Epistle [II,] to a Lady[: Of the Characters of Women]. NAEL-1; NOEC

Cloe, blooming sweet as May. To Cloe. Hildebrand Jacob. NOEC

Cloe, by your command, in verse I write. A Letter from Artemisa in the Town, to Chloe [*or* Cloe], in the Country. John Wilmot, 2d Earl of Rochester. PoE

Cloe, dear JACK, that once victorious name. Catullus Imitated. Ep. 58. Catullus, *Latin*. OBCVT, *tr. by* Nicholas Amhurst

Cloe to Artimesa. *Unknown*. ECWP

Cloe's the wonder of her sex. To Cloe. George, Baron Lansdowne Granville. FaBoEE; NBLV; OxBSP

Clogged and soft and sloppy eyes. The Parents: People Like Our Marriage Maxie and Andrew. Gwendolyn Brooks. ColAP *Fr.* Notes from the Childhood and the Girlhood. LCAP-2

Cloister. Conrad Potter Aiken. MoAmPo *Fr.* Preludes for Memnon; or, Preludes to Attitude.

Clonakilty. *Unknown*. FaBoEE

Clonfeacle. Paul Muldoon. CIP-2

Clonmacnoise. Angus O'Gillan. *See* The Dead at Clonmacnois [*or* Clonmacnoise].

Clonmel Jail. *Unknown, Irish*. BIrV, *tr. by* Valentin Iremonger

Cloodburst an' soarin' mune. Cloudburst and Soaring Moon. "Hugh MacDiarmid." NoAM

Cloosmit the herring, hosts in the night. Ko-Ishin-Mit Goes Fishing. George Clutesi. HATNAP

Clora come view my Soul, and tell. The Gallery. Andrew Marvell. ESCV; MeLP; NoP-4; PBRV; PoE

Clorinda and Damon. Andrew Marvell. ESCV; FMP; SeCP
   ("For all the world is our Pan's choir.") (LL) FMP

Cloris, I cannot say your eyes. To Cloris. Sir Charles Sedley. BoLoP

Cloris, it is not thy disdaine. Song: "Chloris, it is not thy disdaine." Sidney Godolphin. MeLP

Cloris misfortunes that can be exprest. Song. Elizabeth Wilmot, Countess of Rochester. KTR

Close. Robert Duncan. PmAP

Close by the basement door-step. A Toad. Elizabeth Akers Allen. OBCA

Close by the creepered wall. Snake. J. D. McClatchy. APo

Close by the host. Tanka. Mori Ōgai, *Japanese*. MJT, *tr. by* Makoto Ueda

Close by those meads, for ever crowned with flow'rs. Hampton Court. Alexander Pope. EBEvV; EBNV; OBSV; OxBoLi *Fr.* The Rape of the Lock[, an Heroi-Comical Poem]. FHYEP; HAP; ImPo; OAEL-1; OBNV; PeLV; PoEL-3

Close by, to the north, there were two oranges. Jean-Joseph Rabéarivelo, *French*. NegPo, *tr. by* Ellen Conroy Kennedy

Close cleaving unto Silence, into sound. Whisper. John Banister Tabb. APN-2

Close Encounter, A. Adrian Rumble. SpW

Close is lust's expectation. On a Bath-House in which Both Men and Women Bathe. Paulus Silentiarius, *Greek*. GrAn, *tr. by* Andrew Miller

Close now the door; shut down the light. The Supremer Sacrifice. Suzanne Gardinier. CBAP

Close Quarters. John Banister Tabb. OBAL

Close the dim eyes, for expression hath left them. Lines on a Dead Girl. Priscilla Jane Thompson. CBWP-2

Close the forest behind you, the door. Return from the Convention. Reiner Kunze, *German*. CEEP, *tr. by* Lori Fisher

Close thine eyes, and sleep secure. On a Quiet Conscience. Charles I, King of England. CH

Close to a house on a piece of ground. The Garden. Bernadette Mayer. FTOS

Close to a quarter of a century since then. Christmas Carol. T. H. Parry-Williams, *Welsh*. OBWVE, *tr. by* Joseph P. Clancy

Close to Aminta, on the Loss of Her Lover. Sarah Dixon. ECWP

Close to nature my brother, your thoughts ring softly. To an Indian Poet. Patty L. Harjo. VoR

Close to the fireside confined. The Invitation from a Country Cottage. Martha Sansom. ECWP

Close to the gates a spacious garden lies, *see also* "Without the hall, and close upon the gates" *and* "To left and right, outside, he saw an orchard." The Gardens of Alcinous. Homer, *Greek*. GaP; OAEL-1; OBVE, *tr. by* Alexander Pope *Fr.* Odyssey. NAWM-1, *tr. by* Robert Fitzgerald

Close to the gates a spacious garden lies. The Gardens of Alcinous. Alexander Pope. OBGa, *tr. by* Alexander Pope *Fr.* Odyssey.

Close to the sod. The Snowdrop. Anna Bunston DeBary. BoTP

Close under here, I watched two lovers once. "Robin Hyde." FaBoWP; PeNZ *Fr.* The Beaches.

Close-up. A. R. Ammons. PoA

Close-up. Heather McPherson. PeNZ

Close up the casement, draw the blind. Shut Out That Moon. Thomas Hardy. CMoP; NOBE; NoAM

Close up they're seen in fine detail. A Painting of One Hundred Wild Geese. Tai Piao-yüan, *Chinese.* CoBLCP, *tr. by* Jonathan Chaves

Close up wolf about my mouth. Animal. Bill Griffiths. NBrP

Close-ups of Summer. Norman MacCaig. OxBC

"Close Your Eyes!" Arna Bontemps. GT; PoBA
    ("Woodman on the hill must have his rest, A.") (LL) GT

Closed Door, The. Theodosia Pickering Garrison. BLPA; PoToHe

Closed Doors. Marie Thorson. PWR

Closed is that curious ear by Death's cold hand. Thomas Gray's View of Nature. William Mason. EPCY; NOEC *Fr.* The English Garden.

Closed like confessionals, they thread. Ambulances. Philip Larkin. FaBoTw; NAEL-2; NoP-4; OxBC

Closed Mill. Maggie Anderson. PBCAP

Closed over wounds. (LL) Roads. Peter Huchel, *German.* HP; PoSu, *tr. by* Michael Hamburger

Closed their wounds. Peter Huchel. *See* Roads.

Closed window looks down, A. Ka 'Ba. Imamu Amiri Baraka. BPo; CAPP-1; CrDW; ISC; NBV; PmAP; TAP; UnSA

Closed World, The. Denise Levertov. NoP-4

Closer in. Bro Duncanson. C. S. Giscombe. GT *Fr.* (from the "In" Sequence).

Closer to escaping into day / trams. Lorenzo Thomas. *See* Electricity of Blossoms.

Closer to us than most of our close friends. Frederick Kuh, Manx Cat. Robert Lowell. FP

Closing, A. May Miller. ISC

Closing Album, The. Louis MacNeice.
    Dublin. CIP-2; IIP; OxBTC

Closing cycle rich in good, The. (LL) Tonight ungathered let us leave. Tennyson. EBVV; FHYEP; OAEL-2

Closing of the Rodeo, The. William Jay Smith. AiP; TwCP

Closing the House. Jim Wayne Miller. MT

Closing Time. David Wagoner. NYBP

Closure. Douglas Messerli. FTOS

Clote (Water-Lily), The. William Barnes. FaBoVe; PoEL-4

Cloth of Gold. Francis Reginald. MoCV

Cloth-plant grew till it covered the thorn bush, The. *Unknown. See* Widow's Lament.

Cloth-plant grew till it covered the thorn bush, The. Widow's Lament. *Unknown, Chinese.* BoWoP *Fr.* Shih Ching.

Cloth socks, straw sandals, robe of coarse cloth. Walking to the Temple of Precious Light. Wen Cheng-ming, *Chinese.* CoBLCP, *tr. by* Jonathan Chaves

Clothed in buckskin, clothed in homespun. Pioneers. Aileen Fisher *and* Olive Rabe. CA

Clothed in yellow, red and green. *Unknown.* OxNR

Clothes. Wislawa Szymborska, *Polish.* PoSu, *tr. by* Grazyna Drabik *and* Sharon Olds

Clothes Do But Cheat and Cozen [*or* Cousen] Us. Robert Herrick. CaPo

Clothes-Line, The. Charlotte Druitt Cole. BoTP

Clothes make no sound when I tread ground. The Swan. Cynewulf. RB, *tr. by* Geoffrey Grigson *Fr.* Riddles (Exeter Book).

Clothes Make the Man. Jack Conway. NBLV

Clothes Maketh the Man. Theodore Weiss. NoAM

Clothes on the Washing Line. Frank Flynn. OTCP

Clothes Pit, The. Douglas Dunn. OxBTC

Clothespin, The. Rhonda Bower. IFJA

Clothing us in a robe of more than glory. (LL) The Coliseum. Edgar Allan Poe. APN-1; AmPP; NOBA

Clotho. Hilaire Kirkland. *Fr.* Clotho, Lachesis, Atropos. PeNZ

Clotho, Lachesis, Atropos. Hilaire Kirkland. PeNZ
    Atropos.
    Clotho.
    Lachesis.
    "When them old hooters had plenty eating material."

Cloud, The. Shelley. CABP; FHYEP; LaPo; NAEL-2; NoP-4; PWR; PoEL-4
    ("As still as a brooding dove.") (LL) LaPo

Cloud, The. Derek Walcott. ChIV-1

Cloud and water, lonely, desolate. Mooring at Night at the River Mouth, I Heard a Flute—Sent to My Elder Brother Hsi-ch'iao. Wang Shih-chieng, *Chinese.* CoBLCP, *tr. by* Jonathan Chaves

Cloud-backed heron will not move, The. The Heron. Vernon Watkins. GTBS-P; TwCP; UnPo

Cloud capped peaks fill the eyes. On a Visit to Ch'ung Chen Taoist Temple. Y'ü Hs'üan-Chi, *Chinese.* ChiPo; PBWP, *tr. by* Kenneth Rexroth *and* Ling Chung

Cloud—cloud—cloud— hurls. It. Gary Snyder. LCAP-2

Cloud doth gather, the green wood roar, The. Thekla's Song. Johann Christoph Friedrich von Schiller. AWP *Fr.* The Piccolomini.

Cloud Factory, The. John Haines. SPE

Cloud Fantasy. Henrietta Cordelia Ray. CBWP-3

Cloud fields change into furniture. An Emphasis Falls on Reality. Barbara Guest. FTOS; PmAP

Cloud in Trousers, The. Vladimir Mayakovsky, *Russian.*
    "Maria! Maria! Maria!" TCRP, *tr. by* Bernard Meares
    Prologue: "I'll mock those thoughts of yours." TCRP, *tr. by* Bernard Meares
    "You think this is some malarial dream?" TCRP, *tr. by* Bernard Meares

Cloud is the post office between continents, The. To Modigliani to Prove to Him That I Am a Poet. Max Jacob, *French.* TrJP, *tr. by* Wallace Fowlie

Cloud-maidens that float on for ever. Aristophanes. *See* Song of the Clouds.

Cloud-maidens that float on forever. Song of the Clouds. Aristophanes. AWP, *tr. by* Oscar Wilde *Fr.* The Clouds.

Cloud moved close, A. The bulk of the wind shifted. The Visitant. Theodore Roethke. CMoP; PoE; RB; TRP; UnPo

Cloud no bigger than a button, A. Old Champagne Glass. Eddy Van Vliet, *Dutch.* VCWP, *tr. by* John Van Tiel

Cloud of dust on the long white road, A. The Teams. Henry Lawson. CBAP

Cloud of witnesses. To whom? To what?, A. A Fanfare for the Makers. Louis MacNeice. NOBE *Fr.* Autumn Sequel.

Cloud Parade, The. Laura Jensen. LCAP-2

Cloud possessed the hollow field, A. The High Tide at Gettysburg. Will Henry Thompson. BLPA; CBCWP; FaBoBe

Cloud-puffball, torn tufts, tossed pillows [] flaunt forth, then [chevy on / an air-]. That Nature Is a Heraclitean Fire and of the Comfort of the Resurrection. Gerard Manley Hopkins. EnVR; EnlH; FaBoMo; FaBoVe; GTBS-P; NoP-4; OAEL-2; PFTM; PoE; PoEL-5

Cloud reflections float on flooded paddles. On the Way to Huang-ch'ang River. Wang Shih-chieng, *Chinese.* SuSP, *tr. by* Richard John Lynn

Cloud River. Charles Wright. MT

Cloud Song. Henrietta Cordelia Ray. CBWP-3

Cloud Unfolding, The. Ernesto Trejo. LTA

Cloudburst and Soaring Moon. "Hugh MacDiarmid." NoAM

Clouded Evening, Late September. Sydney Lea. RA

Clouded Morning, The. Jones Very. GSo; NOBA

Clouded Sky. Miklós Radnóti, *Hungarian.* HP, *tr. by* Polgar, Steven, S. Berg, and S. J. Marks

Clouded with snow / The cold winds blow. Winter. Walter De la Mare. OAEL-2; OBMV

Clouds, The. Aristophanes, *Greek.*
    "Rise up and come, immortal Clouds." GrIP, *ll.* 275–290, *tr. by* Kenneth Mcleish
    Song of the Clouds. AWP, *tr. by* Oscar Wilde
    ("Cloud-maidens that float on for ever.") OBCVT, *tr. by* Oscar Wilde

Clouds. Rupert Brooke. OBEV; OBMV; OxBTC

Clouds. The Complete Sound-Poems of Hugo Ball. Hugo Ball. PFTM

Clouds, The. Thomas M. Disch. RA

Clouds. Penny Harter. HA

Clouds. Philip Levine. LCAP-2

Clouds, The. Mirabai, *tr. from Medieval Hindi; English version by* Robert Bly. EnlH

Clouds. Francis Webb. BMAP

Clouds, The. William Carlos Williams. Poetr; VGW

Clouds and the stars didn't wage this war, The. For the Record. Adrienne Rich. NIP-4; VCAP

"Clouds and water block the way home." The Ailing Japanese Monk. Hsiang Ssu, *Chinese.* CoBCP, *tr. by* Burton Watson

Clouds are swept into the sunset—mdash;a sky beyond the sky. Chu Yün-ming. CoBLCP, *tr. by* Jonathan Chaves *Fr.* Poem Inscribed on a Landscape Painting.

Clouds as I see them, rising, The. Denise Levertov. VCAP

Clouds darken the plain. Hand. Edouard Roditi. SPE

Clouds fill the sky. The Morning after. . . Love. Kattie M. Cumbo. BlSi

Clouds float through dreams, are nowhere to be seen. Nguyễn Bỉnh Khiêm, *Vietnamese.* AVP, *tr. by* Huỳnh Sanh Thông

Clouds Gathering. Charles Simic. ColAP

Clouds go, nevertheless / In their direction, The. (LL)   The Death of a Soldier.   Wallace Stevens.   OBWP; OxBSP; SAmP; SoSe-8

Clouds had made a crimson crown, The.   A Moment.   Mary Elizabeth Coleridge.   LW; PEW

Clouds have come up from the south, the Nile's.   Yehuda Amichai.   IP, *tr. by* Bargad, Warren *and* Stanley Chyet   *Fr.* Achziv.   IP, *tr. by* Warren Bargad *and* Stanley F. Chyet

Clouds Have Left the Sky, The.   Robert Bridges.   CH

Clouds hover over the river's waves, the evening's in a haze.   On a Painting by Hsia Kuei Entitled "Returning in Wind and Snow to a Village Home."   Kao Ch'i, *Chinese*.   SuSp, *tr. by* Irving Y. Lo

Clouds of dust arise, rolling up from earth.   Song of the Promise of the Buffalo.   *Unknown*.   APN-2, *tr. by* Alice C. Fletcher   *Fr.* The Hako.

Clouds of Evening.   Robinson Jeffers.   MoAmPo

Clouds of incense mounting in the air, The.   Palm Sunday.   Theodore Wratislaw.   ADE

Clouds of the heavens.   Ephesos.   Duris, *Greek*.   GrAn, *tr. by* Peter Jay

Clouds on the Sea.   Ruth Dallas.   PeNZ   *Fr.* Letter to a Chinese Poet.

Clouds over Islands.   James Seay.   MT

Clouds pass over, endless.   Passover: the Injections.   William Heyen.   HP

Clouds scattered across the sky all so far away.   The Words.   Lee Harwood.   SPE

Clouds scud in patches on the dawning sky.   The Boatsong of the Sungari.   Tonghwan Kim, *Korean*.   CKP, *tr. by* Jaihiun Kim

Clouds shouldered a path up the mountains, The.   The Drought.   Gary Soto.   NoAM

Clouds spout upon her.   Rain on a Grave.   Thomas Hardy.   OxAEP-2

Clouds That Are So Light, The.   Edward Thomas.   FaBoTw

Clouds that drift so far and free.   The Wife's Thoughts.   Hsü Kan, *Chinese*.   CoBCP, *tr. by* Burton Watson

Clouds, the source of rain, one stormy night, The.   Lost in Heaven.   Robert Frost.   MoAmPo

Clouds were fishbone, The.   Walden in July.   Donald Junkins.   NYBP

Clouds were mountains, that day, behind the real mountains, The.   The View from Skates in Berkeley.   Quincy Troupe.   UnSA

Clouds, which rise with thunder, slake, The.   All's Well.   John Greenleaf Whittier.   OxBSP

Cloudy Bay.   Eileen Duggan.   PeNZ

Cloudy Day.   Jimmy Santiago Baca.   InPS-3; LoL

Cloudy morning.   *Unknown, Japanese*.   OHMPJ, *tr. by* Kenneth Rexroth

Cloudy quiver over Pairc-na-lee, A. (LL)   In the Seven Woods.   W. B. Yeats.   CMoP; NoAM

Clove, salmon knocking.   For Lerida.   David St. John.   AmPA

Clover.   Sidney Lanier.   APN-2; ColAP

Clover's simple Flame, The.   Emily Dickinson.   APN-2

Clown, The.   Margaret E. Bruner.   PoToHe

Clown, The.   Janet Frame.   PeNZ

Clown, The.   Donald Hall.   NYBP

Clownlike, happiest on your hands.   You're.   Sylvia Plath.   FaBoTw; FaBoWP; RB

Clown's Song, The.   Shakespeare.   CTC   *Fr.* Twelfth Night.
   (Come Away, Death.)   PoRA
   (Dirge.)   OBEV
   (Feste's Song.)

Club, The.   Mitsuye Yamada.   LoHo
   ("That is how we left him / forever.") (LL)   NMM-2

Club cloakroom as soothing franchise, hats.   To The Great Hard-Bop Pianists.   Joel Lewis.   MoNo

Clucking Hen, The.   *Unknown*.   BoTP

Clues are everywhere, The.   For My Father Looking for My Uncle.   Jorie Graham.   MoLi

Clues to what they remembered had been pasted into an album, The.   Cenotaph.   John Yau.   PmAP

Clumped murmuring above a sump of loam.   The Woodlot.   Amy Clampitt.   HCAP

Clumsy clot of shadow in the fold, A   A Moth.   Henry Bellyse Baildon.   NOBVV

Clumsy cross burns, A.   Pillar of Flame.   Barbara Unger.   LoHo

Clumsy Guys.   Tomaz Salamun.   PUP-18

Cluster, A.   Tanka.   Fumi Saito, *Japanese*.   MJT, *tr. by* Makoto Ueda

Clustered beside the road are a van.   Serenade for Winds.   T. Alan Broughton.   CMAP

Clustered trees filled with the sounds of autumn.   Yüan Hao-wen.   SuSp, *tr. by* Stephen West   *Fr.* Random Verses on Mountain Life.

Clusters in Thy vineyard turn to gold, O God, Then.   Grape-gathering.   Avraham Shlonsky, *Hebrew*.   TrJP, *tr. by* I. M. Lask

Clusters of cold-weather blossoms.   Ch'ien Ch'ien-i.   *Fr.* In Lamplight, Watching My Wife Preparing a Flower Arrangement—Playfully Inscribing Four Poems.   CoBLCP, *tr. by* Jonathan Chaves

Clutching a fist of hair.   Alexis Rotella.   HA

Clyde's Water. A.   *Unknown*.   ESPB

Clyde's Waters.   *Unknown*.   OxBB

Clymène, A.   Paul Verlaine.   AWP, *tr. by* Arthur Symons

Clytemnestra triumphant over the bodies of Agamemnon and Cassandra.   Aeschylus, *Greek*.   OBCVT, *tr. by* Robert Fagles

Cnut's Song.   *Unknown*.   PoE   *Fr.* Canute at Ely.

Co-operation.   J. Mason Knox.   BLPA

Coach, / Carriage.   *Unknown*.   OxNR

Coachman, The.   Mother Goose.   ReMoGo

Coachman sits like a king, The.   Movement.   Nikolai Alekseievich Zabolotsky, *Russian*.   TCRP, *tr. by* Daniel Weissbort

Coal.   Audre Lorde.   BlSi; NALW; NBV; NoAM; PoBA; VCAP
   ("Love is a word, another kind of open.")   PiM
   ("Now take my word for jewel in the open light.") (LL)   NoP-4; PiM
   ("Take my word for jewel in your open light.") (LL)   NAAAL

Coal-black raven, coal-black devil.   The Raven.   Nikolai Ivanovich Glazkov, *Russian*.   TCRP, *tr. by* Daniel Weissbort

Coal Diggin' Blues.   *Unknown*.   AmFP

Coal Fire in Winter, A.   Thomas McGrath.   RaBo

Coal Loadin' Blues.   *Unknown*.   AmFP

Coal Miner's Goodbye, A.   *Unknown*.   AmFP

Coal Train.   Jay Parini.   GM

Coal train, The.   Anita Virgil.   HA

Coal-white bird appears this spring, A.   Almanac Verse.   Samuel Danforth.   SCAP

Coals go out, The.   Galway Kinnell.   RaBo   *Fr.* Middle of the Way.

Coast hills at Sovranes Creek, The.   The Place for No Story.   Robinson Jeffers.   AiP

Coast-Road, The.   Robinson Jeffers.   PaTW

Coast, The: Norfolk.   Frances Darwin Cornford.   OxBTC

Coast View, A.   Charles Harpur.
   "Dead city walls may pen us in, but still."   CBAP

Coastline.   Elaine Feinstein.   BrRo

Coastline never alters for the fisherman, The.   Eddy Van Vliet, *Flemish*.   VCWP, *tr. by* Matthew Blake

Coat.   Vicki Feaver.   LW

Coat, The.   Dennis Lee.   TLR

Coat, A.   W. B. Yeats.   CMoP; EPCY; IIP; LiTM; NAEL-2; NoAM; OxAEP-2; OxBSP; PoEL-5

Coat-of-Mail: Dank earth, wondrously cold, The.   Cynewulf.   ASW, *tr. by* Kevin Crossley-Holland   *Fr.* Riddles (Exeter Book).

Coat of Mail: The womb of the wold, wet and cold.   *Unknown*.   EEP, *tr. by* Michael Alexander   *Fr.* Riddles (Exeter Book).

Coats.   Jane Kenyon.   IFJA

Coax me to-morrow, by forswearing all.   Ovid.   *See* Elegies.

Coaxing My Illness.   Mai Th(tilde;a)o, *Vietnamese*.   AVP, *tr. by* Huỳnh Sanh Thông

Cob, thou nor soldier, thief, nor fencer art.   To Pertinax Cob.   Ben Jonson.   BeJo

Cobalt.   Rolf Jacobsen, *Norwegian*.   BLT, *tr. by* Roger Greenwald

Cobb Would Have Caught It.   Robert Fitzgerald.   HAP; TwCP

Cobble thrown a hundred years ago, A.   Clearances.   Seamus Heaney.   CIP-2; PBCIP; PNI

Cobbler, The.   *Unknown*.   BoTP

Cobbler, cobbler, mend my shoe.   Mother Goose.   LB; OxNR
   ("Get it done by half-past eight.") (LL)   LB

Cobbler, cobbler, mend my shoe.   *Unknown*.   ACTP

Coble o Cargill, The.   *Unknown*.   ESPB

Cobra is the night image of a chinese water-print.   North Express.   Joyce Mansour, *French*.   WPOW, *tr. by the author*

Cobweb, The.   Raymond Carver.   BLT

Cobwebs.   E. L. M. King.   BoTP

Cobwebs.   Christina Rossetti.   CABP; NAEL-2; NALW; VWP

Coca Cola and Coco Frio.   Martín Espada.   UnSA

Cocaine Lil [and Morphine Sue].   *Unknown*.   AS; CBNP; OxBoLi; RB

Cochineals and fig colours ripple.   Dining Out.   Judith Beveridge.   BMAP

Cock, A.   Anyte, *Greek*.   GrAn, *tr. by* Sally Purcell

Cock-A-Doodle-Do.   *Unknown*.   ReMoGo

Cock a doodle doo!   *Unknown*.   ACTP

Cock-a-doodle-doo! I want my leftover rice!   Children's Song.   *Unknown, Nepalese*.   PC, *tr. by* Kumar Prakesh

Cock-a-doodle-doo! / My dame has lost her shoe.   Mother Goose.   BoTP; LB; OxNR; ReMoGo

Cock-a-doodle-doo the brass-lined rooster goes [*or* says].   Dog.   John Crowe Ransom.   InPS-3; OBAL

Cock-a-Hoop.   Isabella Gardner.   WPE

Cock and Bull Story, A. *Unknown.* ReMoGo

Cock and Hen: I saw two wonderful and weird creatures. *Unknown.* EEP, *tr. by* Michael Alexander *Fr.* Riddles (Exeter Book).

Cock and Hen: I watched a couple of curious creatures. Cynewulf. ASW, *tr. by* Kevin Crossley-Holland *Fr.* Riddles (Exeter Book).

Cock and the Bull, The. Charles Stuart Calverley. BXAP

Cock and the Fox, The. Jean de La Fontaine, *French.* AWP, *tr. by* Elizur Wright

Cock and the Hen, The. Geoffrey Chaucer. *See* The Nun's Priest's Tale.

Cock and the Hen, The. *Unknown.* ReMoGo

Cock and the Pearl, The. Max Jacob, *French.*
"I thought he was bankrupt." PFTM, *tr. by* Bill Zavatsky

Cock at Sea. Constantine A. Trypanis. PFE

Cock before Dawn. Norman MacCaig. OxBC

Cock, cock, cock, cock. The Cock and the Hen. *Unknown.* OxNR; ReMoGo

Cock-Crow. Ralph Nixon Currey. PeSA

Cock-Crow. Edward Thomas. GTBS-P; MoBrPo; NTP; OxBSP; RB

Cock-Crow. *Unknown.* ReMoGo

Cock-crow and early-rise! Dawn. Joseph Kumbirai, *Shona.* PeSAV, *tr. by* Douglas Livingstone

Cock-crow Song. *Unknown, Chinese.* ChiP, *tr. by* Arthur Waley

Cock-crowing. Henry Vaughan. ESCV; GeHe; OAEL-1; PBRV

Cock crows / But no queen rises, The. Depression before Spring. Wallace Stevens. OBAL

Cock doth crow / To let you know, The. Mother Goose. OxNR

Cock-fight, The. Ts'ao Chih, *Chinese.* ChiP, *tr. by* Arthur Waley

Cock has crow's an hour ago, The. The Morning Quatrains. Charles Cotton. NOSC; PeECV

Cock is crowing, The. Written in March [While Resting on the Bridge at the Foot of Brother's Water]. Wordsworth. ACTP; BoTP; CTV; ChAP; NAEL-2; NTCP; PBMP; SCGP; UnPo

Cock of Glory is the *coq français,* The. The French, 1870-1871. *Unknown.* FaBoEE

Cock Robin got up early. *Unknown.* ACTP; BoTP; OxNR

Cock that crowed this dawn up, heard, The. Copernicus. Robert David Fitzgerald. NOBAu

Cock, warm roosting 'mid his feathers mates, The. A Winter's Day. Joanna Baillie. WoRP

Cock, warm roosting midst his feathered dames, The. Morning. Joanna Baillie. ECWP *Fr.* A Winter Day.

Cockaigne: A Dream. Louis Edward Sissman. DiPo

Cockatoo hears gamelan, The. Allegory. Jenny Mueller. BAP-94

Cocked up a squint eye and said, "I bloody did that." (LL) Cathedral Builders. John Ormond. NoP-4; PeECV

Cocker of Snooks, A. Phyllis Gotlieb. NOBC

Cocklorel would needs have the devil his guest. Dinner for the Devil. Ben Jonson. NOSC *Fr.* The Gypsies Metamorphosed.

Cocklorrel woulds needs have the devil his guest. Ben Jonson. CBNP

Cockney of the North, The. Harry Graham. UV

Cockney's Garden, The. Edgar Bateman. OBGa

Cockroach. Mary Ann Hoberman. *Fr.* Bugs. OBCA

Cocks and Mares. Ruth Stone. RaBo

Cocks crow in the morn. Cock-Crow. *Unknown.* ReMoGo

Cock's crow means profit, The. Tseng Jui. SuSp, *tr. by* Wayne Schlepp *Fr.* Tune: "Sheep on Mountain Slope"—Lamenting the Times.

Cock's on the housetop blowing his horn, The. A Cock and Bull Story. *Unknown.* ReMoGo

Cock's on the wood pile, The. *Unknown.* OxNR

Cockscomb, A. Tanka. Kanoko Okamoto, *Japanese.* MJT, *tr. by* Makoto Ueda

Cocktail is a pleasant drink, The. R-E-M-O-R-S-E. George Ade. NBLV; OBAL; OBCoV; PeLV

Cocktail Party, The. T. S. Eliot.
"Then no doubt it's all for the best." OxBM
"Yes a very important discovery." OxBM

Cocktails. Ciaran Carson. BiHa; PBCIP

Cocoa coursing through their veins. (LL) In Praise of Cocoa, Cupid's Nightcap. Stanley J. Sharpless. NBLV; PeLV

Cocoa Morning. Bob Kaufman. NBV

Coconut for Katerina, A. Sandra McPherson. LCAP-2

Cocoon. Rin Ishigaki, *Japanese.* WPOW, *tr. by* Ayusawa Takako

Cocoon, The. Larry Levis. CMAP

Cocoon. David McCord. OBCA

Cocumscussoc is my village. History as Apple Tree. Michael S. Harper. AFr

Cod inert as an old boot. Mid-Channel. Gwen Harwood. BMAP

Coda. "Ern Malley." BMAP

Coda. Marilyn Hacker.
Conclusion: "Did you love well what very soon you left?" NoAM

Coda. Louis MacNeice. CBLP

Coda. Ezra Pound. NOBA; SAGP

Coda. James Tate. AmPA; NYBP

Coda. William Carlos Williams. NOBA

Coda, Overture. Eleanor Wilner. NMM-2

Coda: The Higher Keys. James Merrill.
"Empty perfection, as I take you in." NoAM

Code, The. Robert Frost. OBNV; PoA; UnPo

Code Book Lost. Robert Penn Warren. Poetr

Code Poem for the French Resistance. Leo Marks. APAD

Codex. Stephen Rodefer. PmAP

Codex Minor. Rachel Hadas. EOEF

Codicil. Ruth Stone. BoWoP

Codicil. Derek Walcott. MoP; NoAM

Coelia. William Percy.
"Judged by my goddess' doom to endless pain." Son
"Relent, my dear yet unkind Coelia." AAS; Son

Coffee. Wanda Coleman. ISC

Coffee. James Vincent Cunningham. MoAmPo; VGW

Coffee. Gary Hotham. HA

Coffee and cigarettes in a clean café. Small Comfort. Katha Pollitt. CrSp

Coffee and jasmine on a tray. Convalescence. James Philip McAuley. CBAP

Coffee and Tea. *Unknown.* ReMoGo

Coffee cups cool on the Vicar's harmonium. A Game of Consequences. Paul Dehn. NOBL

Coffin, The. Heinrich Heine, *German.* AWP, *tr. by* Louis Untermeyer

Coffin, as I crossed the common lane, The. Hannah, A Plaintive Tale. Robert Southey. Ro *Fr.* Monthly Magazine, 4 287.

Coffin bearing the face of a boy, A. A Mirror for the Twentieth Century. "Adunis," *Arabic.* AF, *tr. by* Abdullah Al-Udhari

Coffin was lowered, The. Lowering the Coffin. Mogwol Park, *Korean.* CKP, *tr. by* Jaihiun Kim

Coffin-Worm, The. Ruth Pitter. MoBrPo

Cog the ah marring maggots, say by now 'we love,' mean us? Catullus. *See* Carmina, LXXII.

Cogitabo Pro Peccato Meo. William Habington. ChIV-1

Cogito Ergo. Jerzy Ficowski, *Polish.* PoSu, *tr. by* Frank J. Corliss, Jr., *and* Grazyna Sandel

Coil there and squat, and pay your fee? (LL) Interview with Doctor Drink. James Vincent Cunningham. OxBSP; VGW

Coiled asp, The. My Grandfather. Joanne Hotchkiss. CrSp

Coiled like a lyncher's rope. Portrait in Georgia. Jean Toomer. NAAL-2

Coilyear, gudlie in feir, tuke him be the hand, The. *Unknown.* OxBS *Fr.* Rauf Coilyear.

Coin, The. Edwin Morgan. FaBoTC *Fr.* Sonnets from Scotland.

Coin of the Realm. Patricia Goedicke. CMAP

Coins for the ferry, The. (LL) Being Called For. Rosemary Dobson. BMAP; CBAP

Coins handsome as Nero's; of good substance and. Geoffrey Hill. FaBoMo; HAP; NoAM *Fr.* Mercian Hymns.

Coins in the hand. On Her Decision to Stop Wearing Clothes. Mahadevi, *Kannada.* WPoS, *tr. by* Jane Hirshfield

Cokboy. Jerome Rothenberg. PmAP
"Comes a brown."
"Saddlesore I came."

Cokkils. Sydney Goodsir Smith. OxBS; PoA

Cold. Brian Coffey. CIP-2

Cold, The. Lance Henson. CDW

Cold. Poems About Prison. Dennis Brutus. PBMAP

Cold. Dorothy Roberts. NOBC

Cold, The. Charles Simic. HCAP

Cold air drains down from the peaks. In the Mountains as Autumn Begins. Wen T'ing-yün, *Chinese.* OHMPC, *tr. by* Kenneth Rexroth

Cold airs from the river creep, The. Children of the Mist. Rosamund Marriott Watson. VWP

Cold and clear-cut face, why come you so cruelly meek. Tennyson. EBVVPR *Fr.* Maud [A Monodrama]. EnVR

Cold and Quiet. Jean Ingelow. SDW

Cold and raw the north wind doth blow. Winter. Mother Goose. ReMoGo

Cold and the colors of cold: mineral, shell. Robert Francis. LCAP-2; PoA

Cold and the cranes. Migratory Noon. Joseph Ceravolo. FTOS

Cold Are the Crabs. Edward Lear. CBNP; NAEL-2

Cold as no love, and wild with all negation. Quand on n'a pas ce que l'on aime, il faut aimer ce que l'on a—. Stevie Smith. FaBoEE

Cold as No Plea. The Death Sentence. Stevie Smith. NoP-4

Cold as the breath of winds that blow. Lucasta's World. Richard Lovelace. BeJo; CaPo; SeCP

Cold blood or warm, crawling or fluttering. Pet Shop. Louis MacNeice. PeP

Cold-blooded Creatures. Elinor Wylie. OxBSP

Cold-blooded in warm waters, my Nurse. Among Sharks. Alfred M. Lee. AmPA

Cold blows the blast--the night's obscure. George, the Younger Colman. NOEC *Fr.* Maid of the Moor, The; or, The Water-Fiends.

Cold Blows the Wind. John Hamilton. CH

Cold blows the winter wind: 'tis Love. Love at the Door. Meleager, *Greek.* AWP, *tr. by* John Addington Symonds

Cold bugle calls, and the city moves on, A. (LL) Armistice Day. Charles Causley. NAEL-2; NoP-4; OBWP

Cold Cash. Stephen Berg. BAP-93

Cold Ceremony. Hannah More. ECWP *Fr.* Bas Bleu, The; or, Conversation.

Cold chain of life presseth heavily on me tonight, The. Fragment. Adah Isaacs Menken. CBWP-1

Cold, cold! / Cold tonight is broad Moylurg. A Song of Winter. *Unknown, Middle Irish.* CH, *tr. by* Kuno Meyer

Cold, cold the year draws to its end. Old Poem. *Unknown, Chinese.* AWP; BoWoP, *tr. by* Arthur Waley

Cold! cold! 'tis a chilly clime. Robert Southey. NOBRP *Fr.* Thalaba the Destroyer.

Cold! Cold! / Wide Lurg Plain is cold tonight. *Unknown.* NOIV

Cold Colloquy. Patrick Anderson. NOBC *Fr.* Poem on Canada.

Cold comes about, The. North Dakota, North Light. N. Scott Momaday. HATNAP

Cold coming we had of it, A. Journey of the Magi. T. S. Eliot. EBEvV; FaBoCh; FaBoMo; GI; HAP; HeIP-6; ImPo; InPK-6; LiTM; MoAmPo, NAEL-2; NIP-4; NOCV; NoP-4; OBCP; OBMV; OxBTC; PBMP; PChr; PoE; Poetr; TAP; TFi; TRP; TwCP

Cold days sit where it's warm. Written on the Wall of Pan-shan Temple. Wang An-shih, *Chinese.* CoBCP, *tr. by* Burton Watson

Cold / December nights I'd go. Touched. Olga Broumas. NMM-2

Cold drool on his chin, warm drool in his lap, a sigh. A Dimpled Cloud. Frederick Seidel. FYAP

Cold Fear. Elizabeth Madox Roberts. WPE

Cold February. Hal Summers. AYFP

Cold felt cold until our blood, The. Phantasia for Elvira Shatayev. Adrienne Rich. NALW

Cold Fire. George Starbuck. NYBP

Cold floors. Endurance. Dennis Brutus. VCWP

Cold Fly. Yang Wan-li, *Chinese.* CoBCP, *tr. by* Burton Watson

Cold Fly, The. Yang Wan-li, *Chinese.* SuSp, *tr. by* Jonathan Chaves

Cold, gray dawn of the morning after, The. (LL) R-E-M-O-R-S-E. George Ade. NBLV; OBAL; OBCoV; PeLV

Cold Green Element, The. Irving Layton. NOBC; NoP-4

Cold grey walls. San Francisco County Jail Cell B-6. Conyus. PoBA

Cold has put blue horses where lambs were, The. Blue Horses. Ed Roberson. GT; PoBA

Cold Heaven, The. W. B. Yeats. AWP; CTC; GTBS-P; HAP; NoAM; OAEL-2; OxBSP; RB

Cold holds its own, inside and out. Si Monumentum Requiris. Daryl Hine. EOEF

Cold hue newly clears, a belt of haze, The. Autumn Spring. Hsüeh T'ao, *Chinese.* SuSp, *tr. by* Eric W. Johnson

Cold in the earth—and the deep snow piled above thee! Remembrance. Emily Jane Brontë. BoLoP; BoWoP; BrRo; CABP; CBLP; CH; EBEV; EBVV; EnLoPo; EnVR; GLoP; HAP; IMW; LBC; NAEL-2; NALW; NOBE; NOBVV; NoP-4; OBNC; OxAEP-2; PBWP; PEW; PoE; PoEL-5; PoPoPo; Poetr; TFi; VWP; WPE; WeW-3

Cold Irish Earth, The. Knute Skinner. InPK-6

Cold Is the North Wind. *Unknown, Chinese.* CoBCP, *tr. by* Burton Watson

Cold is the winter. The wind is risen. *Unknown.* NOIV

Cold, Isn't It. Tom Leonard. FaBoTC

Cold Kiss, The. Thomas Stanley. CBLP

Cold Lantern, The. Yang Wan-li, *Chinese.* SuSp, *tr. by* Jonathan Chaves

Cold limbs of the air, The. A Mountain Wind. "Æ." AWP

Cold Lost Marbles. William S. Burroughs. BB

Cold Lunch. William Corbett. PmAP

Cold Meteorite, The. William Reed Huntington. APN-2

Cold mist, sparse. Evening Bell from Misty Temple. Ma Chih-yüan. *Fr.* Three Poems to the tune "Lo-mei Feng." CoBLCP, *tr. by* Jonathan Chaves

Cold morning early. Two Mornings. Lawrence McGaugh. PoBA

Cold mornings, he would warm his hands. Coroner. Elton Glaser. PBCAP

Cold Mountain is full of weird sights. *Unknown, Chinese.* CoBCP, *tr. by* Burton Watson

Cold Mountain Poem No. 158. Han-shan, *Chinese.* PC, *tr. by* Brooks, E. Bruce

Cold Mountain Poems. Han-shan, *Chinese.* ChiPo, *tr. by* Gary Snyder

Cold mountain turns dark green. Wang Wei, *Chinese.* TAL, *tr. by* Robert Payne

Cold, my dear,—cold and quiet. Cold and Quiet. Jean Ingelow. SDW

Cold Night. Ch'en Shih-tao, *Chinese.* CoBCP, *tr. by* Burton Watson

Cold night, the sidewalk we walk on icy, A. Christmas Eve Service at Midnight at St. Michael's. Robert Bly. NNaP

Cold nights outside the taverns in Wyoming. Accountability. William Stafford. LCAP-2

Cold of autumn's frost penetrates the curtain, The. Tune: "Immortal's Auspicious Crane, An"—On Plum Blossoms. Hsin Ch'i-chi, *Chinese.* SuSp, *tr. by* Irving Y. Lo

Cold Oxford unfamiliar now, around. Above the High. Geoffrey Grigson. EnLoPo

Cold Pastoral. Diotimus, *Greek.* GrAn, *tr. by* Dudley Fitts

Cold penetrates to the river's shore. To the Tune "Flowers in the Rain." Yang Shen, *Chinese.* CoBLCP, *tr. by* Jonathan Chaves

Cold remote islands, The. Night. Louise Bogan. NoP-4; Poetr; UnPo

Cold Rendering, A. *Unknown.* BXAP

Cold season—birds all head for warmer climes. Viên Linh, *Vietnamese.* AVP, *tr. by* Huỳnh Sanh Thông

Cold, Sharp Lamentation. Douglas Hyde, *Irish.* OBMV, *tr. by* Lady Augusta Gregory

Cold snap. Five o'clock. Aubade. Richard Kenney. NoP-4

Cold spot on the heart repeats, A. Deep. Timothy Holmes. PeSAV

Cold spring, A. Elizabeth Bishop. ColAP; TwCP

Cold Spring. Kao Ch'i, *Chinese.* SuSp, *tr. by* Irving Y. Lo

Cold stars and the whores. (LL) Street Corner College. Kenneth Patchen. CLPP; MoAmPo

Cold steel may penetrate the flesh. Heart Wounds. Claire Richcreek Thomas. PoToHe

Cold Term. Imamu Amiri Baraka. BPo

Cold / the clammy cement. Dennis Brutus. *See* The Clammy cement.

Cold / the clammy cement. Dennis Brutus. *See* The Clammy cement.

Cold transparent ham is on my fork—, The. Sonnet to Vauxhall. Thomas Hood. OBCoV; PoEL-4

Cold was the night wind, drifting fast the snow[s] fell. The Widow. Robert Southey. NOBRP; NOEC; UV

Cold water falling out of the split rock. Leonidas of Tarentum, *Greek.* GrAn, *tr. by* Peter Levi

Cold, we sit in the warmth. Written on the Wall of Halfway Mountain Temple. Wang An-shih, *Chinese.* SuSp, *tr. by* Jan W. Walls

Cold-Weather Love. Ronald G. Everson. MoCV

Cold white snowy [*or* snowie] nunnery, The. The Virgins. Donne. *Fr.* The Litanie. PoEL-2

Cold wind at evening, A. Ballad of Yi River. Ho Ching-ming, *Chinese.* CoBLCP, *tr. by* Jonathan Chaves

Cold wind blows from the far sky, A. To Li Po at the Sky's End. Tu Fu, *Chinese.* ChiPo, *tr. by* Witter Bynner

Cold wind stirs the blackthorn, A. Endure Hardness. Christina Rossetti. NOBVV

Cold winter morning. Jim Handlin. HA

Cold winter's in the wood. In the Wood. Eileen Mathias. BoTP

Cold world awakens, The. (LL) If the Owl Calls Again. John Haines. CoAP; CoAmPo; HeIP-4

Colder. Erica Jong. LW

Colder Fire. Robert Penn Warren. FuPo; LiTM; MoLi *Fr.* To a Little Girl, One Year Old, in a Ruined Fortress.

("Past paths where on their appointed occasions men climb, / and pass.") (LL) MoLi

("Should rejoice.") (LL) FuPo

Coldly, sadly descends. Rugby Chapel. Matthew Arnold. EBVVPR; EnVR; PeECV; PoEL-5

Cole Porter's Son. Gerrit Henry. EOEF

Cole, that unwearied prince of Colchester. Variations on an Air Composed on Having to Appear in a Pageant as Old King Cole. G. K. Chesterton. NOBL

Cole Younger. *Unknown.* AmFP

Colebrook Dale. Anna Seward.
"Scene of superfluous grace, and wasted bloom." PEW
"While neighbouring cities waste the fleeting hours." NOEC

Coleman Valley Road. Gerald Stern. BAP-93; PUP-18

Colenso Rhymes for Orthodox Children. Bret Harte. OBAL

Coleridge. Washington Allston. APN-1

Coleridge. Medbh McGuckian. CIP-2

Coleridge. Ronald Stuart Thomas. TOF

Coleridge. Theodore Watts-Dunton. GSo; Son

Coleridge caused his wife unrest. Theme and Variation. Peter De Vries. NYBP

Coleridge received the Person from Porlock. Thoughts about the Person from Porlock. Stevie Smith. NAEL-2; NoAM; NoP-4

Cole's Island. Charles Olson. PoM *Fr.* The Maximus Poems.

Colin. Anthony Munday. *See* Beauty Bathing.

Colin Clout. John Skelton.
  "And if ye stand in doubt." NAEL-1; OAEL-1
  "Doctors that learned be." OBSV
  "For though my rhyme be ragged." OBCoV

Colin Clout's Come Home Again. Edmund Spenser.
  "Of loves perfection perfectly to speake." OAEL-1

Colin, my dear and most entire beloved. To the Most Excellent and Learned Shepherd, Colin Clout. William Smith. AAS; Son *Fr.* Chloris [*or the* Complaint of the Passionate Despised Shepheard].

Colin, my deare, when shall it please thee sing. November. Edmund Spenser. PoEL-1 *Fr.* The Shepheardes [*or* Shepeards *or* Shepherd's] Calender.

Colin, well fits thy sad cheer this sad stound. A Pastoral Eclogue upon the Death of Sir Philip Sidney Knight. Lodowick Bryskett. NoSic

Colin, you can tell my words are crippled now. James Keir Baxter. PeNZ *Fr.* Jerusalem Sonnets.

Coliseum, The. Edgar Allan Poe. APN-1; AmPP; NOBA

Colkelbie Sow. *Unknown.*
  "Penny lost in the lak, The." OxBS

Collaboration: Letter to Charlie Chaplin. Peter Orlovsky. CLPP

Collage for Richard Davis—Two Short Forms, A. De Leon Harrison. PoBA

Collapsible. Tom Raworth. SPE

Collapsible lover, the spider in iniquitousness, The. Anthology of Nouns. Parker Tyler. PoA

Collar, The. George Herbert. AWP; CABP; ClHu; EBEV; FMP; FSCP; FaBoVe; GeHe; HAP; HeIP-4; ImPo; InPS-3; MeLP; NAEL-2; NIP-4; NOBE; NOCV; NOSC; NoP-4; OAEL-1; OBWVE; PBRV; PoE; PoEL-2; PoPoPo; PoRA; SCGP; SCV; SeCP; TFi; TOF; WeW-3
  ("And I reply'd, *My Lord.*") (LL) FSCP; PBRV

Collarbone [*or* Collar-Bone] of a Hare, The. W. B. Yeats. CBNP; NTP; OxAEP-2; OxBTC; RB

Collect Call. Mcavoy Layne. CDa

Collecting Antiques. Cheng Hsieh, *Chinese.* CoBLCP, *tr. by* Jonathan Chaves

Collection, The. Zhao Zhenkai, *Chinese.* VCWP, *tr. by* McDougall, Bonnie S. and Chen Maiping

Collection of Emblemes, Ancient and Moderne, A. George Wither.
  Husbandman, The. NOSC
  Marigold, The. NOSC
  Planting. NOSC
  Spade and the Wreath, The. NOSC
  "Spade, for labour stands. The ball with wings, The." NOSC

Collection of Hymns. . . of the Moravian Brethren, A. *Unknown.*
  "Chicken blessed and caressed." NOEC
  "What does a bird in Cross's air." NOEC

Collective Invention, The. Chris Wallace-Crabbe. BMAP

Collective Portrait, The. Robert Finch. MoCV

Collector, The. Desiré Flynn. BrRo

Collector's Marginalia, The. Peter Sirr. PBCIP

Collects her motions into shape. (LL) Nude Descending a Staircase. X. J. Kennedy. APAD; CoAmPo; HoPM; NIP-4; OxBSP; PoA; SAGP

Colleen Rue. *Unknown.* BIrV

College Colonel, The. Herman Melville. CBCWP; LiLi; NCAP; OBWP

Colley's Run-I-O. *Unknown.* AmFP

Collier, The. Vernon Watkins. FaBoTw; OBWVE

Collier Lass, The. Frankie Armstrong. BrRo

Collier's Wedding, The. Edward Chicken.
  "At last the beef appears in sight." NOEC

Collier's Wife, The. D. H. Lawrence. FaBoVe; OxBTC

Collins. Lionel Pigot Johnson. OxAEP-2

Colloam. P. Inman. FTOS

Colloquy. Weldon Kees. NYBP

Colloquy in Black Rock. Robert Lowell. MoAmPo; NAAL-2

Colloquy with John Keats, 'And the Lord destroyeth the imagination of all them that had not the truth with them' Odes of Solomon 24.8. "Ern Malley." BMAP

Collusion. Medbh McGuckian. BiHa

Collyn Clout. John Skelton.
  "Over this the foresayd lay." PBRV

Colney Hatch forever. (LL) The Pilot's Psalm. *Unknown.* NSI; PoWW

Colobus Monkey. *Unknown.* Fr. Hunter Poems of the Yoruba. RB, *tr. by* Ulli Beier

Cologne. Coleridge. FaBoEE; NBLV; PBMP

Colombe. Edward Kamau Brathwaite. VCWP

Colon Bay. *Unknown.* FaBoVe

Colonel, The. Carolyn Forché. InPS-3; LoL; OBWP; SoSe-8
  ("Some of the ears on the floor were / pressed to the ground.") (LL) LoL

Colonel. Kate Llewellyn. NOBAu

Colonel Chartres. John Arbuthnot. *See* Epitaph on Colonel Francis Chartres.

Colonel Cold strode up the Line. Winter Warfare. Edgell Rickword. OBWP; OxBTC; PeFWW; PoFWW; PoWW

Colonel Fantock. Dame Edith Sitwell. MoBrPo; OBMV

Colonel Fazackerley [Butterworth-Toast]. Charles Causley. NOxBChV; OTCP

Colonel from Cheltenham stopped everyone, A. W. H. Auden. *Fr.* A Happy New Year. OBSV

Colonel in a casual voice, The. Gallantry. Keith Douglas. NAEL-2; NoAM; NoP-4; OBWP

Colonels here in solemn manner meet, The. Thomas Brown. FaBoEE

Colonel's Soliloquy, The. Thomas Hardy. OBWP

Colonial Nomenclature. John Dunmore Lang. NOBAu

Colonists / unearth their wealth. Shaman Breaks. Gerald Vizenor. HATNAP

Colonization in Reverse. Louise Bennett. OBCoV; PBCV

Colonizin in reverse. (LL) Colonization in Reverse. Louise Bennett. OBCoV; PBCV

Colonus' Praise. Sophocles. OBVE; OBCVT, *tr. by* W. B. Yeats *Fr.* Oedipus at Colonus.

Colophon. Oliver St. John Gogarty. OBMV

Colophon for Lan-t'ing Hsiu-hsi. John Peck. AmPA

Colophon to a Roll of Erinna's Poems. Asclepiades, *Greek.* GrAn, *tr. by* Lee T. Pearcy

Color, The. Tanka. Ishikawa Takuboku, *Japanese.* MJT, *tr. by* Makoto Ueda

Color ain't no faucet. Within the Veil. Michelle Cliff. NAAAL

Color, Caste, Denomination. Emily Dickinson. PBMP; TAP

Color, even whiteness, reaches / the body as a name. Claire Needell. PT *Fr.* Reaches the Body.

Color of coral and of your lips, The. From the French. Charles North. FTOS

Color of ice and fire and solitude, The. (LL) Farewell to an idea. . . A cabin stands. Wallace Stevens. CMoP; HCAP; PoE *Fr. The* Auroras of Autumn

Color of silence is the oyster's color, The. Earliness at the Cape. Babette Deutsch. FYAP; NYBP

Color of the flowers / has faded, The. Ono no Komachi, *Japanese.* BoWoP, *tr. by* Kenneth Rexroth

Color of the Grave is Green, The. Emily Dickinson. PoE

Color Sergeant, The, (On an Incident at the Battle of San Juan Hill). James Weldon Johnson. GT

Colorado Blvd. Lorna Dee Cervantes. NAmP90; PaTW

Colorado Trail, The. *Unknown.* AS

Colored cowboy named Nat Love. Deadwood Dick. Elizabeth Alexander. RA

Colored Hats. Gertrude Stein. TTTS *Fr.* Tender Buttons.

Colored Heroes, Hark the Bugle. Robert Charles O'Hara Benjamin. AAP

Colored leaves, The. Hitomaro, *Japanese.* OHPJ, *tr. by* Kenneth Rexroth

Colored pictures/ of all things to eat: dirty. Charles Olson. NeAP; NoAM *Fr.* Songs of Maximus. TAP

Colored Soldiers, The. Paul Laurence Dunbar. AAP; APN-2; CBCWP; NAAAL

Colorful frames are erected beside the Yellow River, The. Li K'ai-hsien. CoBLCP, *tr. by* Jonathan Chaves *Fr.* Watching the Swinging.

Coloring Book. Robert Farnsworth. IFJA

Coloring high means that the strange reason is in front. An Umbrella. Gertrude Stein. TTTS *Fr.* Tender Buttons.

Colorizing: Turner Broadcasting Enterprises, Computer Graphics Division, Burbank, California, 1987. David Wojahn. PBCAP *Fr.* Mystery Train: A Sequence.

Colors. Fortunato Depero, *Italian.* PFTM, *tr. by* Victoria Nes Kirby

Colors are words' little sisters. They can't become soldiers. Cobalt. Rolf Jacobsen, *Norwegian.* BLT, *tr. by* Roger Greenwald

Colors for Mama. Barbara Mahone. PoBA

Colors of Desire, The. David Mura. LoL; NAmP90

Colors of Night, The. N. Scott Momaday. PaTW

Colors of spring have returned to West Lake, A. Song of Spring at West Lake, A, Sent to Circuit Officer Hsieh. Ou-yang Hsiu, *Chinese.* SuSp, *tr. by* Irving Y. Lo

Colors of the country, powerful river. At the River Tower Parting from My Younger Brother, Fu-ling. Wu Wei-yeh, *Chinese*. CoBLCP, *tr. by* Jonathan Chaves

Colors of the Dark One have penetrated Mira's body; all the [other colors washed out], The. Why Mira Can't Go Back to Her Old House. Mirabai, *Rajasthani*. EnlH; WPoS, *tr. by* Robert Bly

Colors of the flowers fade, The. Ono no Komachi, *Japanese*. WPJ, *tr. by* Kenneth Rexroth *and* Ikuko Atsumi

Colors of tulips and roses are not the same, The. Asadullah Khan Ghalib, *Urdu*, *tr. by* Jane Hirshfield

Colors on the elephant's body, The. What She Said to Her Friend. Kapilar, *Tamil*, PLW, *tr. by* A. K. Ramanujan

"Colors," she said, "are never so fine." The Green and the Black. Anthony Bailey. NYBP

Colors shifting. Time of Fish Dying. Gabriela Melinescu, *Rumanian*. BoWoP, *tr. by* Stavros Deligiorgis

Colors we depend on are, The. The Love Bit. Joel Oppenheimer. PoM

Colossal: / Like towers and pavilions from the flat plain. Hsü Wei, *Chinese*. SuSp, *tr. by* Irving Y. Lo

Colosseum. Harold Norse. TrJP

Colossians 3:3. George Herbert. *See* Our Life Is Hid with Christ in God.

Colossus, The. Sylvia Plath. AFr; FaBoWP; HCAP; LiTM; NALW; NOBA; NoAM; NoP-4; Poetr; TAP; VCAP

Colour. Adeline White. BoTP

Colour it cherry-red and call it Death-Wish Valley—that's the message. Loveliest of Counties, Shropshire Now. Ian Sainsbury. BXAP

Colour meant nothing. Anyone. To an Expatriate Friend. Mervyn Morris. PBCV

Colour of the olives who shall say?, The. Tuscan Olives. Agnes Mary Frances Robinson. VWP

Colour-Scheme. Edward Baugh. PBCV

Coloured lanterns lit the trees, the grass, The. Episode of a Night of May. Arthur Symons. PeVV *Fr.* Scènes de la Vie de Bohème.

Coloured long-shore fishermen unfurl, The. The Gamblers. Anthony Delius. PeSA

Colours of water and bamboo wash each other. Stopping on a Journey at the East Water Pavilion at Lo-ch'eng. Meng Chiao, *Chinese*. PLT, *tr. by* A. C. Graham

Coltish horseplay of the locker room, The. The Feast of Stephen. Anthony Hecht. HAP; NoAM; VCAP

Coltrane and My Father. Ralph Sneeden. SeSe

Coltrane Memorial, A. David Henderson. MoNo

Coltrane must understand how. Soul. D. L. Graham. PoBA

Columbia. *Unknown*. AmFP

Columbia, all hail! Chicago Exposition Ode. Mary Weston Fordham. CBWP-2

Columbia, the Gem of the Ocean. Thomas à Becket. CTV

Columbia, the Gem of the Ocean. *Unknown*. FaBoBe

Columbia, Trust the Lord. *Unknown*. AH

Columbiad, The. Joel Barlow. NCAP *Fr.* The Columbiad.

"But now had Hesper from the Hero's sight." APN-1

"Eager he look'd. Another train of years." AmPP

"From Mohawk's mouth, far westing with the sun." APN-1

"From sultry Mobile's gulf-indented shore." APN-1

"He spoke; and silent tow'rd the northern sky." APN-1

("My friends, I love your fame; I joy to raise.") NCAP

"Now graceful truce suspends the burning war." APN-1

Columbian poet, whom we've all respected. Letter to an American Visitor. Alex Comfort. OxBTC

Columbia's Agony. "Orpheus C. Kerr." OBAL

Columbine, The. Jones Very. ColAP; GSo; NOBA; PAR

Columbus. Joaquin Miller. APN-2; CTV; EBEvV; FaBoBe

Columbus. Ogden Nash. FaBoA

("Discoverer, be a promoter.") (LL) NoP-4

Columbus. Muriel Rukeyser. AF

Columbus Day. Jimmie Durham. HATNAP; LTA

Columbus discovered America. A Concise History of the World. Ira Sadoff. AmPA

Columbus may have worked the wind. America Is Hard to See. Robert Frost. AiP; FaBoA

Columbus Reaches Juana, 1492. Ralph Gustafson. NOBC

Columbus to Ferdinand. Philip Freneau. OBCA

Column of lemon sky lit one hill, A. The Civil War. Suzanne Rhodenbaugh. CBCWP

Columns. Meir Wieseltier, *Hebrew*. IP, *tr. by* Warren Bargad *and* Stanley F. Chyet

Columns and Caryatids. Carolyn Kizer. WPE

Columns constructed from delirious dust. Lovely Stuff. Diane Ward. PmAP

Columns of the Temple of Olympian Zeus. Nicolas Calas, *Greek*. GrIP, *tr. by* Kimon Friar

Colville 1964. Kendrick Smithyman. PeNZ

Com, Shuppere, Holy Gost, ofsech oure thoughtes. William Herebert. MiEL

Comanche Ghost Dance: An Impression. Lance Henson. VoR

Comarnad it is a very bonny place. Richie Story. *Unknown*. ESPB

Comb and the Mirror, The. Elizabeth Spires. FFC

Combat, The. Edwin Muir. CMoP; FaBoTC; MoBrPo; NOBE

Combat, The. Thomas Stanley. AWP

Combat raged not long, but ours the day, The. The Burial of Latané. John Reuben Thompson. CBCWP

Combat Zone/War Stories. Lynda Hull. PUP-19

Combe was ever dark, ancient and dark, The. Edward Thomas. GTBS-P; RB

Combed thru the piers the wind. The Translucent Mechanics. George Oppen. NNaP *Fr.* Some San Francisco Poems.

Combinations. Mary Ann Hoberman. OBSP *Fr.* Bugs. OBCA

Combine grinds into the hearts, The. Harvest. David James. CMAP

Combines crossed the wheat field, The. Wheat. Diane Glancy. CRP

Combing. Gladys Cardiff. CDW

Combing the attic for anything extra. Brother of the Mount of Olives. Paul Monette. NAmP90

Combing. The poem of the act of the mind. (LL) Of Modern Poetry. Wallace Stevens. ColAP; MoP; NAAL-2; NoAM; OxBA; Poetr; TAP

Come! William Barnes. CH

Come a *brimmer* (my bullies) drink whole ones or nothing. Alexander Brome. PBRV *Fr.* The Prisoners.

Come again to the place. After the Visit. Thomas Hardy. NOBE; OBNC

Come againe ho, hey (LL) Hey ho, what shall I say? Thomas Ravenscroft. PBRV

Come all gallant [*or* you gallant] seamen that unite a meeting. The Death of Nelson. *Unknown*. OxBoLi

Come all good people, I'd have you draw near. Poor Naomi. *Unknown*. APN-2

Come, all my good people, and listen to my song. Tittery-Irie-Aye. *Unknown*. AmFP

Come all my jolly seamen, likewise the landsmen, too. *Cumberland* and the *Merrimac*. . . *Unknown*. AmFP

Come all ye bold undaunted ones who brave the winter's frost. Fifteen Ships on Georges Banks. *Unknown*. AmFP

Come all ye Colonizationists. Old Liberia Is Not the Place for Me. Joshua McCarter Simpson. AAP

Come All Ye Fair and Tender Ladies. *Unknown*. AmFP

Come all ye foreign strolling gentry. John Byrom. *Fr.* Four Epigrams on the Naturalization Bill. NOBL

Come all ye gentle Christians [*or* Christian people], wherever you may be. Charles Guiteau. *Unknown*. AmFP

Come, all ye good people, my story to hear. Poor Ellen Smith. *Unknown*. AmFP

Come all ye jolly boatsman boys. Blow the Candle Out. *Unknown*. AmFP

"Come all ye jolly fellows, who delight in a gun." Polly Vaughn. *Unknown*. AmFP

Come all ye jolly lumbermen and listen to my song. Canada-I-O. Ephraim Braley. AmFP

Come, all ye jolly sailors bold. *Arethusa*, The. Prince Hoare. FaPoR

Come all ye jolly shepherds. When the Kye Comes Hame. James Hogg. OxBS

Come all ye knights, ye knights of Molites. The Sons of Levi. *Unknown*. AmFP

Come all ye Lewiston fac'try girls. The Factory Girl's Come-All-Ye. *Unknown*. AmFP; OBAL

Come, all ye men of England, and listen unto me. Verses. William Henry. PeSAV

Come All Ye Mourning Pilgrims. John A. Granade. AH

Come, All Ye People. George R. Seltzer. AH

Come all ye rounders, for I want you to hear. Casey Jones. T. Lawrence Seibert. GM

Come, all ye seamen [*or* you sailors] bold. Admiral Benbow. *Unknown*. EnSB

Come all ye [*or* you] true born shanty-boys, wherever you may be [*or* whoever that ye be]. The Jam on Gerry's Rock. *Unknown*. AS; AmFP

Come all ye wits, that with immortal rhymes. Invites Poets and Historians to Write in Cynthia's Praise. Philip Ayres. Son

Come all ye [*or* you] young fellows that [*or* who] follow the sea. Blow the Man Down. *Unknown*. AS; AmFP

Come all ye young people and all my relations. Mr. Davis's Experience. *Unknown.* AmFP

Come all you bold sailors that follow the lakes. Red Iron Ore. *Unknown.* AS

Come, all you brave gallants, and listen a while. Robin Hood and the Butcher. *Unknown.* ESPB

Come all you brave young shanty-boys. James Whaland. *Unknown.* AS

Come all you fair gallants, fair gallants attend. Pretty Polly of Topsham. *Unknown.* AmFP

Come all you fine young fellows with hearts so warm and true. Flat River Girl. *Unknown.* AS

Come all you gallant heroes, I'd have you lend an ear. Major André. *Unknown.* AmFP

Come all you gallant poachers, that ramble free from [*or* void of] care. Van Dieman's Land. *Unknown.* NOBAu; PeVV

Come all you girls and all you boys. Kitty Morey. *Unknown.* AmFP

Come all you good people / From all over the World. Lula Vires. *Unknown.* AmFP

Come all you heroes, where'er you be. The Dying Sergeant. *Unknown.* AmFP

Come all you jolly cowboys and listen to my song. The Buffalo Skinners. *Unknown.* RB

Come all you jolly fellows, come listen to my song. The Shanty Boys and the Pine. *Unknown.* AmFP

Come all you jolly freighters that ever hit the road. Freighting from Wilcox to Globe. *Unknown.* AmFP

Come all you jolly-hearted sailors. False Nancy. *Unknown.* AmFP

Come all you jolly highwaymen and outlaws of the land. Bold Jack Donahue. *Unknown.* AmFP

Come all you jolly lumbermen, and listen to my song. Colley's Run-I-O. *Unknown.* AmFP

Come all you jolly lumbermen, I'd have you for to know. The Banks of the Gaspereaux. *Unknown.* AmFP

Come all you jolly railroad men, and I'll sing you if I can. Way Out in Idaho. *Unknown.* AmFP

Come all you jolly seamen who plough that restless deep. Jimmy Judge. *Unknown.* AmFP

Come all you jolly shanty boys that work the shanty and go. Turner's Camp on the Chippewa. *Unknown.* AmFP

Come all you Lachlan men, and a sorrowful tale I'll tell. The Streets of Forbes. Jack McGuire. CBAP; NOBAu

Come all you loyal Unionists, wherever you may be. Virginia's Bloody Soil. *Unknown.* AmFP

Come all you men and maidens. Rufus Mitchell's Confession. *Unknown.* AmFP

Come, all you painters, all you who are the best. Anacreon, *Greek.* InMo, *tr. by* Sam Hamill

Come all you people from every land. Ellen Flannery. *Unknown.* AmFP

Come all you pretty fair maids. Green Willow, Green Willow. *Unknown.* AmFP

Come all you pretty fair maids, I pray you attend. My New Garden Field. *Unknown.* AmFP

Come all you rounders [*or* muckers] if you want [*or* for I want you *or* that want] to hear. Casey Jones. *Unknown.* AS; AmFP; CTV; OxBoLi; PeLV

Come all you sons of Erin, attention now I crave. Morrissey and the Russian Sailor. *Unknown.* AS

Come all you sons of freedom and listen to my theme. Once More a-Lumbering Go. *Unknown.* AmFP

Come all you sporty fellows. Stackalee. *Unknown.* APN-2

Come all you thoughtless young men, a warning take by me. The Murder of Maria Marten by W. Corder. *Unknown.* OxBoV

Come All You Tonguers. *Unknown.* PeNZ

Come all you very merry London girls that are disposed to travel. The Maidens of London's Brave Adventures, Or, a Boon Voyage Intended for the Sea. Laurence Price. NOSC

Come all you young and handsome ladies. Little Sparrow. *Unknown.* AmFP

Come all you young ladies and make no delay. *Unknown.* OxNR

Come all you young people, a story I will tell. Naomi (Omie) Wise. *Unknown.* AmFP

Come all you young people / That live far and near. The Murder of Goins. *Unknown.* AmFP

Come all you young people who handle the gun. Shooting of His Dear. *Unknown.* OxBoLi

Come all young girls, both far and near, and listen unto me. The Female Transport. *Unknown.* NOBAu

Come, all young girls, pay attention to my noise. Kansas Boys. *Unknown.* AS

Come all young men and ladies, come fathers and mothers, too. The Rowan County Crew. James William Day. AmFP

Come all young men and maidens, come listen to my rhyme. Caroline of Edinbilo' Town. *Unknown.* AmFP

Come, all young men, taking warning by me. Married and Single Life. *Unknown.* AmFP

Come along boys, and listen to my tale. The Old Chisholm Trail. *Unknown.* FaBoBe

Come along in then, little girl! From a Very Little Sphinx. Edna St. Vincent Millay. NOxBChV

Come along, 'tis the time, ten or more minutes past. Le Diner. Arthur Hugh Clough. OBCoV; OBSV *Fr.* Spectator ab Extra. OBCoV; OxBoLi; PeLV; PeVV

Come, And Be My Baby. Maya Angelou. OPOU

Come and let us live my Deare. Catullus. *See* Carmen 5 ("My sweetest Lesbia, let us live and love").

Come and listen to the chiming. Bells of St. Michael. Mary Weston Fordham. CBWP-2

"Come and see! Come and see!" What the Thrush Says. Queenie Scott-Hopper. BoTP

Come and see my shining palace built upon the sand! (LL) Second Fig. Edna St. Vincent Millay. NALW; NoP-4; PoA

Come and see our French goods—you can try 'em. Limerick. *Unknown.* PeLi

Come and take my milk. (LL) Song: "Sweet beast, I have gone prowling." W. D. Snodgrass. MoAmPo; NYBP

Come ant daunce wyt me, / in irlaunde. *Unknown. See* I Am from Ireland.

Come at dawn, good friend. *Unknown, Spanish.* BoWoP, *tr. by* Willis Barnstone

Come at last to this point. Akiko Yosano, *Japanese.* OHMPJ, *tr. by* Kenneth Rexroth

Come away! Come away! The Song of the Beasts (Sung, on one night, in the cities, in the darkness). Rupert Brooke. APo

Come away, come away, death. The Clown's Song. Shakespeare. CTC; GBL; GTBS-P; NOBE; NoP-4; NoSic; OBEV; PoEL-2; PoRA; TFi *Fr.* Twelfth Night.

Come away, come, sweet love. John Dowland. GBL; NAEL-1; NoSic; PoEL-2

Come away! come, sweet love! To His Love. *Unknown.* NoP-4

Come Away, Death. Shakespeare. *See* The Clown's Song.

Come away, / Make no delay. Doomsday. George Herbert. GeHe; SeCP

Come away to the skies. For His Wife, on Her Birthday. Charles Wesley. NOCV

Come away with me, Tom. The Invitation. Charles Kingsley. NOBVV

Come Back, Alexander. Sati Kumar, *Punjabi.* OMIP, *tr. by* Manohar Bandopadhyay

Come Back Blues. Michael S. Harper. PoBA

Come back early or never come. (LL) Autobiography. Louis MacNeice. NOIV; PNI; RB

Come back in love, come back in pain. (LL) Poem for My Father. Toi Derricotte. MoLi; NMM-2

Come back Paul. (LL) Two little dicky birds. *Unknown.* LB; OxNR

Come back to me! my life is young. Karazah to Karl. Adah Isaacs Menken. CBWP-1

Come back to me, O ye, my children. Mother's Recall. Mary Weston Fordham. CBWP-2

Come back to me, who wait and watch for you. Christina Rossetti. *Fr.* Monna Innominata. BWW

Come, balm of night, oh nightingale. Hans Jakob Christoffel von Grimmelshausen, *German.* GePo, *tr. by* George C. Schoolfield

Come balmy sleep! tired Nature's soft resort! To Sleep. Charlotte Smith. Son; WPE

Come, be my camera. Documentary. Claribel Alegría, *Spanish.* LoL; VCWP, *tr. by* D. J. Flakoll

Come, blessed ones, and sit on thrones. Michael Wigglesworth. NAAL-3 *Fr.* The Day of Doom. NAAL-1; SCAP

Come, blue-eyed maid of heaven!—but thou, alas! Byron. NOBRP *Fr.* Childe Harold's Pilgrimage.

Come, break with time. Louise Bogan. MoAmPo

Come, bring the children. Let them. Summer Solstice. Peter Blue Cloud. *Fr.* Within the Seasons. HATNAP

Come, bring with a noise. Ceremonies for Christmas[se]. Robert Herrick. BeJo; OBCP

Come, brother, come. Let's lift it. Cotton Song. Jean Toomer. BPo

Come build in the empty house of the stare. (LL) The Stare's Nest by My Window. W. B. Yeats. BIrV; FaBoPV; GTBS-P; InPS-3; NOBE

Come butter come! Butter Charm. *Unknown.* FaBoVe; OxBSn

Come, butter, come. Mother Goose. OxNR

Come Buy! Come Buy! Shakespeare. *See* Autolycus as Peddler.

Come buy, come buy. (LL) Worrying Fruit. Christina Rossetti. BoTP; EBEvV

Come carders an spinners an wayvers as weel. Factory Workers' Song. *Unknown.* FaBoVe

Come, chearfull day, part of my life, to mee. Come, Cheerful Day! Thomas Campion. AAS

Come cheer up my lads. Heart of Oak. David Garrick. NOEC; OxBoLi

Come, Cheerful Day! Thomas Campion. AAS

Come child, and with your sunbeam gaze assign. The Green Eye. James Merrill. PoA

Come Christmas. David McCord. PChr

Come close to me, dear friends; still closer; thus! Paracelsus. Robert Browning.

Come closer, kind, white, long-familiar friend. Age and Death. Emma Lazarus. SDW

Come closer to me. Leaves of Grass (1855). Walt Whitman. APN-1

Come closer yet, my honeysuckle, my sweetheart Jinny. The Land of Whipperginny. Robert Graves. NTP

Come Come. Marc Matthews. HCP

Come, come dear Night! Love's mart of kisses. Epithalamion Teratos. George Chapman. NoSic *Fr.* Hero and Leander. AAS

Come, come, Flipote; it's time I left this place. Tartuffe. Molière, *French.* NAWM-2, *tr. by* Richard Wilbur

Come, come, my companion. *Unknown, German.* GePo, *tr. by* Sylvia Stevens *Fr.* Carmina Burana.

Come, come, my love, the bush is growing. With Garments Flowing. John Clare. GBL

Come, come, no time for lamentation now. No Time for Lamentation Now. Milton. *Fr.* Samson Agonistes. FHYEP; OAEL-1; PoEL-3

Come, come, what doe I here? Henry Vaughan. ESCV

Come, cousin Cuba, me yerry some news. Quaco Sam. *Unknown.* PBCV

Come, cuddle your head on my shoulder, dear. The Beautiful Land of Nod. Ella Wheeler Wilcox. PWR

Come, cut thy throte, and have thy throte-ball out! Lovers' Debouchment. William Zaranka. BXAP

Come dance a jig. Mother Goose. OxNR

Come Dance with Kitty Stobling. Patrick Kavanagh. MoP; NoAM; Poetr

Come, dark-eyed Sleep, thou child of Night. And on My Eyes Dark Sleep by Night. "Michael Field." LW; OBMV

Come darkest night, be[e]coming sorrow best. Sonnet 19. Mary Sidney, Countess of Montgomery Wroth. NOSC *Fr.* Pamphilia to Amphilanthus.

Come, day, glad day, day running out of the night. Glad Day. Louis Untermeyer. TrJP

Come, dear children, let us away. The Forsaken Merman. Matthew Arnold. EBEV; EBVVPR; FHYEP; FaBoCh; FaPoR; NAEL-2; NTP; OBNV; OBSP

Come, Death, I'd have a word with thee. Motley. Walter De la Mare. HoPM; PoWW

Come Dora, my darling, my angel, and help me to ask him to dine. (LL) Lord Walter's Wife. Elizabeth Barrett Browning. HAP; VWP

Come down at dawn from windless hills. Sunrise on Rydal Water. John Drinkwater. LiTM

Come down from heaven to meet me when my breath. Invocation. Siegfried Sassoon. MoBrPo

Come down from the Cross, my soul, and save thyself. Descent from the Cross. "Michael Field." PoWW

Come down, O Christ, and help me! reach thy hand. E Tenebris. Oscar Wilde. ChIV-2; GSo; MoBrPo; NAEL-2; OxAEP-2; Son; TIRV

Come down to Kew in lilac-time (it isn't far from London!). (LL) The Barrel-Organ. Alfred Noyes. MoBrPo; PoRA

Come down to you. (LL) To the Muse. James Wright. NAAL-2; NNaP

Come, drunks and drug-takers; come, perverts unnerved! Several Voices Out of a Cloud. Louise Bogan. NALW

Come, Every Soul. John H. Stockton. AH

Come feed with me and be my love. The Passionate Profiteer to His Love. "Sagittarius." OBCoV

Come! fill a fresh bumper, for why should we go. Ode for a Social Meeting. Oliver Wendell Holmes. OBAL

Come, fill the cup, and in the fire of spring. Omar Khayyám. TRP; UV *Fr.* The Rubáiyát of Omar Khayyám [of Naishápúr]. AWP; EBVV; FaBoBe; FaPoR; HAP; NAEL-2; PoEL-5

Come, follow, follow me. The Fairies. *Unknown.* BoTP

Come, follow me by the smell. Onyons. Jonathan Swift. BIrV *Fr.* Verses Made for the Women Who Cry Apples, etc.

Come forth from thy oozy couch. Imitation of Julia A. Moore. "Mark Twain." OBAL

Come forth, old lion, from thy den. On Himself. Walter Savage Landor. FaBoEE

Come forth, you workers! Réveille. Lola Ridge. WPE

Come forthe, sire sergeaunt, with your stately mace. The Dance. *Unknown.* PoEL-1, *tr. by* John Lydgate *Fr.* The Dance of Death.

Come fresh-from-the-oven flakes direct from the heart of the corn. (LL) Breakfast with Gerard Manley Hopkins. Anthony Brode. BXAP; NOBL

Come, friendly bombs, and fall on Slough. Slough. John Betjeman. APAD; MoBrPo; NoAM; OxAEP-2

Come, Friends and Neighbors, Come. Lewis Hartsough. AH

Come, friends, if you will listen, a story I will tell. The Sherman Cyclone. *Unknown.* AmFP

Come from a distant country. At Birth. Anthony Thwaite. PFE

Come from the confines of the sunset world. Prudentius, *Latin.* MLL, *tr. by* Helen Waddell

Come from Thy Palace. Thomas Randolph. OxBSP *Fr.* The Conceited Pedlar.

Come, gaze with me upon this dome. E. E. Cummings. NoAM; OxBA

Come, gentle sleep, death's image though thou art. Thomas, the Younger Warton, *Latin.* OBVE, *tr. by* William Wordsworth

Come, gentlemen all, and listen a while. Robin Hood and the Bishop. *Unknown.* ESPB

Come gie's a sang, Montgomery cry'd. Tullochgorum. John Skinner. OxBS

"Come girlies and fellas, as quick as you can." Mutton Bird Man. Rhyll McMaster. NOBAu

Come, give me kisses, Rhodope. Paulus Silentiarius, *Greek.* InMo, *tr. by* Sam Hamill

Come go with me out to the Field. Lee Ann Brown. PT

Come, Gobrys, there are other gods besides the Muses. Argentarius, *Greek.* GrAn, *tr. by* Fleur Adcock

Come, Gorgo, put the rug in place. "Michael Field." VWP *Fr.* Variations on Sappho.

Come, Happy Children. *Unknown.* AH

Come Harken unto Me. *Unknown.* AH

"Come here, come here, you freely feed." Kemp Owyne. *Unknown.* ESPB; EnSB; OxBB

Come here, I want to show you something. Sightseeing. Rita Dove. GT

Come Here, Little Robin. *Unknown.* BoTP

Come here, said my hostess, her face making room. A Literary Dinner. Vladimir Nabokov. OBAL; PeLV

Come here, thou proud pretender unto arts. There's Life in a Mussel; a Meditation. George Farewell. NOEC

Come hither, Child! and rest. Villanelle of Sunset. Ernest Christopher Dowson. ADE

Come hither to the hedge, and see. To the Muse. Jean Adams. ECWP

Come hither, womankind and all their worth. Kissing. Edward Herbert, 1st Baron Herbert of Cherbury. EnLoPo; NOSC

Come, hoist the sail, the fast let go! Pleasure Boat, The [*or* Pleasure-Boat, The]. Richard Henry Dana. APN-1

Come Holy Spirit, Dove Divine. Adoniram Judson. AH

Come, holy tortoise shell. Sappho, *Greek.* BoWoP, *tr. by* Willis Barnstone

Come / Home. The Shortest and Sweetest of Songs. George Macdonald. NOBVV

Come Home. *Unknown, Zulu.* PeSA, *tr. by* Jack Cope

Come home, come home! and where an home hath he. Arthur Hugh Clough. HAP

Come Home, Father[!]. Henry Clay Work. APN-2

Come home with white gulls waving across gray. Winter Landscape. Stephen Spender. MoBrPo

Come, Hooker, come forth of thy native soile. Yee Shall Not Misse of a Few Lines in Remembrance of Thomas Hooker. Edward Johnson. SCAP

Come hugging your breasts. Light Behind the Rain. Michael Longley. CBLP

Come, human dogs, interfertilitate. The Eugenist. Robert Graves. FaBoEE

Come, I will make the continent indissoluble. For You O Democracy. Walt Whitman. APN-1; UV

Come In. Robert Frost. AmPP; LiTM; MoAmPo; NOBA; NoP-4; PFE; RaBo; TRP

Come in at the low-silled window. Being Called For. Rosemary Dobson. BMAP; CBAP

Come in, Aunt Jemima. Wintah Styles, De. Maggie Pogue Johnson. CBWP-4

Come in, Gentlemen—he said. No inconvenience. Look through. Search. Yannis Ritsos, *Greek.* NNPT, *tr. by* Nikos Stangos

Come in. I've just been dying for you. Song of Songs. Yelena Kryukova, *Russian.* TCRP, *tr. by* Albert C. Todd

Come in the garden. The Snowman. E. M. Adams. BoTP

Come in, Tom longtail, come short hose and round. *Unknown.* EBEV

Come inside the weather. By Hallucination Visited. Robert Horan. SPE

Come into animal presence. Denise Levertov. HeIP-4

Come into dinner squalls the dame. Snaps for Dinner, Snaps for Breakfast, and Snaps for Supper. OBAL

Come into the Army, Maud. "Sagittarius." UV

Come into the garden, Maud. Song. Tennyson. AWP; EBEvV; EBVV; EBVVPR; EnVR; FHYEP; GaP; NOBE; NOBVV; OAEL-2; OBGa; OxAEP-2; PoE; UV *Fr.* Maud [A Monodrama]. EnVR

Come Into the Night Grove. Elizabeth Libbey. CMAP

Come into the orchard, Anne. Swinburne. UV

Come into the Whenceness Which. Whenceness of the Which. *Unknown.* UV

Come is the ending day, Troy's hour is come. Virgil. MLL, *tr.* by Helen Waddell *Fr.* The Aeneid [*or* Eneados, *Aeneis*].

Come July in my native village. The Grapes. Yuksa Yi, *Korean.* CKP, *tr.* by Jaihiun Kim

Come, Landlord, Fill the Flowing Bowl. *Unknown.* OxBoLi

Come lasses and lads, take leave of your dads. The Rural Dance about the Maypole. *Unknown.* OxBoLi

Come learn with me the fatal song. The Mighty Heart. Ralph Waldo Emerson. *Fr.* Woodnotes II ("As sunbeams stream through liberal space"). NOBA

Come leave the loathèd stage. Ode to Himself. Ben Jonson. BeJo; EPCY; NAEL-1; OAEL-1; SeCP

Come, let me sound thy depths, unquiet sea. To My Own Heart. Maria Jane Jewsbury. VWP

Come, let me take thee to my breast. Robert Burns. CBLP

Come, let me write. 'And to what end?' To ease. Sonnet 34. Sir Philip Sidney. *Fr.* Astrophil and Stella. AAS; SiPS

Come let us be going my brothers. Come Home. *Unknown, Zulu.* PeSA, *tr.* by Jack Cope

Come, let us build a temple to oblivion. Tabernacle. D. H. Lawrence. ChIV-1; KSG

Come let us burne our severall horrid peeces. Antemasque, The: Witches the Nomber Beinge Five. Lady Jane Cavendish. KTR *Fr.* A Pastorall.

Come, let us down. Ode: Hastening His Friend into the Country. Eldred Revett. NOSC

Come, let us go a-roaming! Travellers. Arthur St. John Adcock. BoTP

Come, let us join this festal lay. Rally Song. Mary Weston Fordham. CBWP-2

Come, let us now resolve at last. The Reconcilement. John, Duke of Buckingham and Normandy Sheffield. OBEV

Come let us now to each discover. The Lover. "Eliza." KTR

Come, let us sigh a requiem over love. Robert Malise Bowyer Nichols. *Fr.* Sonnets to Aurelia. OBMV

Come, let us tell the weeds in ditches. Last Hill in a Vista. Louise Bogan. FaBoWP

Come, Let Us Tune Our Loftiest Song. Robert A. West. AH

Come, let us walk. Spring in Virginia. Ramona Wilson. VoR

Come let's begin to revel't out. Madrigal. *Unknown.* BoTP

Come, let's go climb on that jasmine-mantled rock. What Her Girlfriends Said to Her. Okkur Macatti, *Tamil.* BoWoP, *tr.* by A. K. Ramanujan

Come, let's to bed. Mother Goose. LB; OxBoLi; OxNR; ReMoGo

Come lie down next to me and rest. And Later by Myself. Ory Bernstein, *Hebrew.* IP, *tr.* by Warren Bargad *and* Stanley F. Chyet

Come light and listen, you gentlemen all. Robin Hood and the Beggar, I. *Unknown.* ESPB

Come listen a while and give ear to my song. Hard Times. *Unknown.* AmFP

Come listen a while, you gentlemen all. Robin Hood Newly Revived. *Unknown.* ESPB

Come listen to me, you gallants so free. Robin Hood and Allen [*or* Allin]-a-Dale. *Unknown.* ESPB; FaBoBe; OxAEP-1

Come, listen to my story, ye landsmen, one and all. Raging Canawl. *Unknown.* AS

Come, listen to my tragedy, good people, young and old. Mary Wyatt and Henry Green. *Unknown.* AmFP

Come, little babe. Cradle Song. Nicholas Breton. NOBE; OBEV; RACG

Come, little infant, love me now. Young Love. Andrew Marvell. OxAEP-1

Come, Little Leaves. The Wind and the Leaves. George Cooper. BoTP

Come Live with Me. Naomi Marks. BXAP

"Come live with me and be my love." Bacchanal. Peter De Vries. BXAP; NBLV; NOBL; OBAL

Come live with me[e], and be[e] my love. The Bait[e]. Donne. CBLP; HoPM; InPK-6; InPS-3; NAEL-1; NOSC; OAEL-1; PFE; PoRA; RB

Come, live with me and be my love. Samuel Hoffenstein. NBLV *Fr.* Invocation.

Come live with me and be my love. Love Under the Republicans (Or Democrats). Ogden Nash. PBMP

Come live with me[e] and be my Love. The Passionate Shepherd [*or* Sheepheard] To His Love. Marlowe. AAS; AEP; APAD; AWP; BoLoP; CABP; CBLP; CTC; ClHu; EBEvV; FaBoBe; GEA; GLoP; GTBS-P; HAP; HeIP-4; HoPM; ImPo; InPK-6; InPS-3; NAEL-1; NBLV; NIP-4; NOBE; NoP-4; NoSic; OAEL-1; OBEV; OxAEP-1; PBMP; PFE; PoE; PoLF; PoPoPo; PoRA; Poetr; RB; SAGP; SCV; SiPS; TFi; TRP; TTTS; UV; WeW-3

Come, live with me and be my love. Song. C. Day Lewis. BoLoP; NIP-4; OBMV; Poetr *Fr.* Two Songs. HAP; NoAM

Come live with me and be my wife. The Passionate Shepherd to His Love. Delmore Schwartz. PFE; SCGP

Come, love, for now the night and day. Song for Autumn. Andrew Young. GBL

Come lovely and soothing Death. The Carol of Death. Walt Whitman. APAD; SCV *Fr.* Spring. LBC *Fr.* Memories of President Lincoln.

Come, lovely Muse, desert for me. Invocation. Samuel Hoffenstein. BXAP

Come, Madam, come, all rest my powers defy [*or* defie]. To His Mistress Going To Bed. Donne. BoLoP; CBLP; NoSic; OAEL-1; OxAEP-1; OxBM; PoE; SeCP *Fr.* Elegies.

Come! Marget, come!—the team is at the gate! The Country Lovers; or, Isaac and Marget Going to Town, on a Summer's Morning. George Smith. NOEC

Come, master of the rosy art. Anacreon's Portrait of His Mistress. Anacreon, *Greek.* OBCVT, *tr.* by Leigh Hunt

Come, memory, let us seek them there in the shadows. (LL) On the Death of Friends in Childhood. Donald Justice. CoAmPo; CoIAP; InPK-6; LCAP-1

Come, Muse, migrate from Greece and Ionia. The Muse in the New World. Walt Whitman. MoAmPo *Fr.* Song of the Exposition.

Come, my beloved. From the Garden. Anne Sexton. LW

Come, my beloved. Song. Bible, O.T. WPoS, *tr.* by Chana Bloch *and* Ariel Bloch *Fr.* The Song of Solomon.

Come, my beloved, let us go up the shining mountain, and sit together. *Abanaki Oral Tradition, Abanaki.* ITG, *tr.* by John Reade *and* Robert Hass

Come, my brothers. The Only Tourist in Havana Turns His Thoughts Homeward. Leonard Cohen. MoCV; MoP

Come my Celia, let us prove, *after* Catullus, Carmen 5. Song. To Celia. Ben Jonson. AEP; BeJo; CBLP; FMP; NoP-4; OAEL-1; OBVE; OxAEP-1; PFE; PoPoPo; SeCP; TFi *Fr.* Volpone. NAEL-1

Come, my Corinna, come[, let's go *or* goe a-Maying]. (LL) Corinna's Going A-Maying. Robert Herrick. AEP; BeJo; CABP; CaPo; HAP; InPS-3; NAEL-1; NIP-4; NOBE; NOSC; NoP-4; OAEL-1; OBEV; PBRV; PoE; PoEL-3; PoPoPo; SCGP; SeCP; TFi

Come (my dear) whilst young conspires. Time Recover'd. Thomas Stanley, *after the Italian of* Girolamo Casone. OBVE

Come, my little Robert, near. Cleanliness. Charles Lamb *and* Mary Lamb OxBChV

Come, my *Lucasia*, since we see. Friendship's Mystery, To My Dearest Lucasia. Katherine Philips. CPO; KTR; PBRV; PEW

Come, my songs, let me express our baser passions. Further Instructions. Ezra Pound. PoA; TwCP *Fr.* Lustra.

Come my tan-faced children. Pioneers! O Pioneers! Walt Whitman. FaBoBe; PaTW

Come my true Consort in my Joyes and Care! Paulinus of Nola. OBCVT, *tr.* by Henry Vaughan *Fr.* St. Paulinus to his Wife Therasia.

Come, mysterious night. A Hymn to Night. Max Michelson. TrJP

Come, neighbour, take a walk with me. Hannah More. ECWP *Fr.* Gin-Shop, The; A Peep into Prison.

"Come, neighbours, no longer be patient and quiet." The Riot; or, Half a Loaf Is Better than No Bread. Hannah More. NOEC; PEW

Come not in here, Nuncle, here's a spirit. Lear's Madness. Shakespeare. CBNP *Fr.* King Lear.

Come Not Near My Songs. *Unknown, Shoshone Indian.* AWP; WPE, *tr.* by Mary Austin

Come not the earliest petal here, but only. Quiet. Marjorie Lowry Christie Pickthall. NOBC

Come Not the Seasons Here. Edwin John Pratt. NoP-4

Come not, when I am dead. Go By. Tennyson. GBL; GLoP; OBNC; PeVV

Come now, and let us wake them: time. Serenade. *Unknown, German.* AWP, *tr.* by Jethro Bithell

Come now behold. The Glory of and Grace in the Church Set Out. Edward Taylor. AmPP *Fr.* God's Determinations [touching his Elect].

Come now, my friend, you must not say. "Ivan Venediktovich Elagin," *Russian.* TCRP, *tr.* by Helen Matveyeff

"Come now, my love, the moon is on the lake;." Albery Allson Whitman. AAP *Fr.* Twasinta's Seminoles; Or Rape of Florida.

"Come now," said Bell, "this is choice." Limerick. Frank Richards. PeLi

Come now ye rural deities and show. The Country Seat. Sir John, of Penicuik Clerk. OBGa *Fr.* The Country Seat.

Come, O Friend, to Greet the Bride. Solomon Halevi Alkabez, *Hebrew into German.* TrJP, *tr. by* Heine; *English vers. by* Louis Untermeyer

Come, O Sabbath Day. Gustav Gottheil. AH

Come, O thou traveller unknown. Wrestling Jacob. Charles Wesley. NOBE; NOCV; NOEC; OBEV; OxAEP-1; PeECV; PoEL-3; TOF

Come o'er the hills, and pass unto the wold. A Winter Hymn—to the Snow. Ebenezer Jones. OBNC

Come o'er the stream, Charlie. McLean's Welcome. James Hogg. OxBS

Come on, come on! And where you go. Ben Jonson. *Fr.* Pleasure Reconciled to Virtue. NAEL-1; OAEL-1

Come on! Come on! This hillock hides the spire. Sunday Afternoon Service in St. Enodoc Church, Cornwall. John Betjeman. NOCV

Come on, good fellow, make an end. A Dialogue between Death and Youth. *Unknown.* NoSic

Come on in. Imamu Amiri Baraka. *See* SOS.

Come On In, the Senility Is Fine. Ogden Nash. AiP

Come on, make haste—please, won't you hurry up? Xuân Diệu, *Vietnamese.* AVP, *tr. by* Huỳnh Sanh Thông

Come on, Mama, we'll slake the lime. Gennady Krasnikov, *Russian.* TCRP, *tr. by* Vladimir Lunis *and* Albert C. Todd

Come on, my fellow pilgrims, come. Sarah Lancaster. AmFP

Come On, My Lucky Lads. Edmund Blunden. PeFWW

Come on, my partners in distress. Charles Wesley. NoP-4

Come on out of there with your hands up, Charlie. Patriotic Ode on the Fourteenth Anniversary of the Persecution of Charlie Chaplin. Bob Kaufman. PoBA

Come on out, we are burning a fairy! (LL) Limerick: "Some Harvard men, stalwart and hairy." Edward Gorey. OBAL; OBCoV

Come on Percy, my pillion-proud, be. Cyril Connolly. OBCoV *Fr.* Where Engels Fears to Tread.

Come on, sir; here's the place. Stand still. Dover, the Samphire Cliff. Shakespeare. OxAEP-1 *Fr.* King Lear.

Come on, sir. Now, you set your foot on shore. Ben Jonson. PoEL-2 *Fr.* The Alchemist. FaBoSe

Come on then, ye dwellers by nature in darkness. Chorus of Birds. Aristophanes. AWP; PoEL-5 *Fr.* The Birds.

Come on, ye critics! Find one fault who dare. On Mr. Edward Howard, upon His British Princes. Charles, 6th Earl of Dorset Sackville. OBSV

Come on, you. . . Do you want to live forever? (LL) Losers. Carl Sandburg. CMoP; MoAmPo; NoAM

Come once again and love me. (LL) Lady Greensleeves. *Unknown.* EBEvV; GBL; NoSic; OxAEP-1; PoEL-2

Come, Ophrah, fill my cup—but not with wine. The Splendor of Thine Eyes. Moses ibn Ezra, *Hebrew.* TrJP, *tr. by* Solomon Solis-Cohen

Come. Or if not remain where. Ex Voto. Virgil Teodorescu, *Romanian.* CEEP, *tr. by* Donald Eulert *and* Stefan Avadanei

Come out come out come out. Moon Eclipse Exorcism. *Unknown, Alsea Indian.* STP, *tr. by* Armand Schwerner

Come out, come out, this sunny day. Hay-Time. C. M. Lowe. BoTP

Come out from the bath. (LL) The Bath. Gary Snyder. NNaP; PmAP; TAP; VCAP

Come Out into the Sun. Robert Francis. NYBP

Come out, love—the night is enchanting! City Lyrics. Nathaniel Parker Willis. APN-1

Come out of Crete / and find me here. Sappho, *Greek.* OBVE, *tr. by* Guy Davenport

Come out of your body among us & we're all one. How to Get Grizzly Spirit. *Unknown, Tlingit Indian.* STP, *tr. by* James Koller

Come over here. Dance to the Amulets. U Tam'si Tchicaya. PBMAP

Come, passer-by, sit in this plane-tree's shade. Inscription on a Statue. Hermocreon, *Greek.* GrAn, *tr. by* Alistair Elliot

Come Peace, on snowy pinions. Ode to Peace. Mary Weston Fordham. CBWP-2

Come people; Aaron's dressed [*or* dresst *or* drest]. (LL) Aaron. George Herbert. ChIV-1; FSCP; GeHe; MeLP; NOSC; OAEL-1; PeECV

Come, Phoenix, come, if such a bird there be. On the Phoenix. Jean Adams. ECWP

Come pity [*or* pitie] us, all ye, who see. The Widow's Tears [*or* Widdowes Teares]: or, Dirge of Dorcas. Robert Herrick. ChIV-2

Come play with me;. To a Squirrel at Kyle-Na-No. W. B. Yeats. APo; CTAV; ChAP

Come play with me said the sun. Play. Frank Asch. NTCP

Come praise Colonus' horses and come praise. Colonus' Praise. Sophocles. OBVE, *tr. by* W. B. Yeats; OBCVT, *tr. by* W. B. Yeats *Fr.* Oedipus at Colonus.

Come, Precious Soul. *Unknown.* AH

Come quick, come quick, come quick, come quick! (LL) The Watch. Frances Darwin Cornford. InPK-6; MoBrPo; OxBTC; PFE; SAGP

Come quickly—as soon as. Lady Izumi, *Japanese.* LoP, *tr. by* Mariko Aratani

Come right in this house, Will Johnson! Mrs. Johnson Objects. Clara Ann Thompson. BlSi; CBWP-2

Come! rouse ye brothers, rouse! a peal now breaks. Spirit Voice, The; or Liberty Call to the Disfranchised (State of New York). Charles Lewis Reason. AAP

"Come saddle me my fastest steed." Geordie. *Unknown.* AmFP; ESPB; OxBB

Come, said my soul. Walt Whitman. NOBA

"Come!" said Old Shellover. Old Shellover. Walter De la Mare. BoTP; OxBChV

Come, saints and sinners, hear me tell. A Parody. Frederick Douglass. NAAL-1; NAAL-3; NAWM-2 *Fr.* Narrative of the Life of Frederick Douglass, an American Slave.

Come sapless blossom, creep not stil on earth. The Sap. Henry Vaughan. ESCV

Come See the Place Where the Lord Lay. Richard Crashaw. ChIV-2

Come show thy Durham Breast. Emily Dickinson. NCAP

Come sing, come sing, come sing come sing sing / And sing. (LL) Yardbird's Skull. Owen Dodson. PoBA; VGW

Come sing with me in chorus: it's nothing, all we know. Antonio Machado Ruiz, *Spanish.* STV, *tr. by* John Frederick Nims

Come, Sire, come. The Unicorn. Ion Gheorghe, *Romanian.* CEEP, *tr. by* Loring R. Taylor

Come sit beneath my pine. On a Statue of Pan. *Unknown, Greek.* GrAn, *tr. by* W. G. Shepherd

Come sleep, Oh sleep, the certain knot of peace. Sonnet 39. Sir Philip Sidney. GSo; NAEL-1; NODE; NoSic; OBEV; OxAEP-1; PoF; PoRA; SCGP; SCV; Son; TFi *Fr.* Astrophil and Stella. AAS; SiPS

Come slowly—Eden! Emily Dickinson. CMoP; FaBoVe; NALW; NCAP

Come smoke a coca-cola. The Billboard Song. *Unknown.* CBNP

Come, sons of summer, by whose toil[e]. The Hock-Cart, or Harvest Home. Robert Herrick. BeJo; CaPo; EBEV; FaBoPV; NAEL-1; NOSC; OxAEP-1; SeCP

Come soon, soon! (LL) To Night. Shelley. AWP; CH; FHYEP; GTBS-P; NAEL-2; OAEL-2; OBEV; OBNC; PoLF; PoRA; TFi

Come, sorrow, come! bring all thy cries. Fletcher's Lament for his friend. John Fletcher. FP

Come, sound up your trumpets and beat up your drums. The Young Earl of Essex's Victory over the Emperor of Germany. *Unknown.* ESPB

Come sounding thro' the town. (LL) The Bonny Earl of Murray. *Unknown.* ESPB; NOSC; OBEV; OxBB; OxBS; SCGP

Come, spread foam rubber on the floor. I Can't Have a Martini, Dear, but You Take One, or, Are You Going to Sit THere Guzzling All Night? Ogden Nash. PoRA

Come spur [*or* spurre] away. An Ode to Mr. [*or* Master] Anthony Stafford to Hasten Him into the Country. Thomas Randolph. BeJo; NOBE; NOSC; OBEV

Come, stack arms, men! Pile on the rails. Stonewall Jackson's Way. John Williamson Palmer. CBCWP

Come, stir the fire. Safe. James Walker. AYFP; OBCP

Come suddenly, O Lord, or slowly come. Take Ye Heed, Watch and Pray. Jones Very. ChIV-2

Come! supper is ready. The Good Moolly Cow. Eliza Lee Cabot Follen. OBCA

Come take up your hats, and away let us haste. The Butterfly's Ball [and the Grasshopper's Feast]. William Roscoe. NOBRP; OxBChV

Come tawny bees. Diodorus Zonas, *Greek.* GrAn, *tr. by* Alistair Elliot

Come the oak before the ash. *Unknown.* ACTP

Come the quick trumpet of the Judgement Day? (LL) Lament for a Leg. John Ormond. NoP-4

Come, the wind may never again. D.G.C. to J.A. Emily Jane Brontë. BrRo; EnLoPo

Come then, and like two doves with silvery [*or* silv'rie] wings. The Apparition of His Mistress[e] Calling Him to Elizium [*or* Elysium]. Robert Herrick. CaPo; SeCP

Come then, as ever, like the wind at morning! Invocation to Youth. Laurence Binyon. OBEV

Come then, my soule, approach this royall Burse. Francis Quarles. ESCV *Fr.* Emblems.

Come then sick youth unto my sacred skill. Ovid. OBCVT, *tr. by* F. L. Lucas *Fr.* The Remedies for Love.

Come, thou monarch of the vine. A Drinking Song. Shakespeare. NoSic *Fr.* Antony and Cleopatra.

Come thou, who art the wine and wit. His Winding-Sheet. Robert Herrick. CaPo; OBEV

Come Thunder. Christopher Okigbo. PBMAP

("Last lighted torch of the century. . . , The.") (LL) VCWP

("Now THAT the triumphant march has entered the last street.") HBAPE

Come tip a few with me. Alcaeus, *Greek.* InMo, *tr. by* Sam Hamill

Come to a sign. 4-Way Stop. Myra Cohn Livingston. KaS

Come to guard us, come to bless us. The Triple Benison. Henrietta Cordelia Ray. CBWP-3

Come to me, as you come. Kenneth Rexroth. APSN *Fr.* The Love Poems of Marichiko.

Come to me broken dreams and all. The Still Voice of Harlem. Conrad Kent Rivers. PoBA

Come to me, Eros, if you needs must come. To the God of Love. Edmund George Valpy Knox. NOBL

Come to me from Crete to this holy temple. Sappho, *Greek.* WPOW, *tr. by* Richmond Lattimore

Come to me God; but do not come. To God. Robert Herrick. CavPo

Come to me, grief, for ever. A Funerall Song. *Unknown.* CH

Come to me in my dreams, and then. Longing. Matthew Arnold. GLoP; PoLF; SoSe-8

Come to me in the night—we shall sleep closely together [*or* Let us sleep entwined]. Love Song. Else Lasker-Schüler, *German.* BoWoP; TrJP, *tr. by* Michael Gillespie

Come to me in the silence of the night. Echo. Christina Rossetti. BoLoP; CH; EBEvV; EBVV; GBL; GLoP; LBC; LW; NOBE; NoP-4; OAEL-2; OBNC; PEW; PoE; PoEL-5; SDW; VWP

Come to me pig, you who dress yourself as a courtier. Flirting with a Pig. Aleksandar Ristović, *Serbo-Croatian.* HSix, *tr. by* Charles Simic

Come to me when the swelling wind assails the wood with a sealike roar. Late Light. Edmund Blunden. EnLoPo

Come to my longing Arms, my lovely care. Virgil. OBCVT, *tr. by* John Dryden *Fr.* The Second Pastoral. Or, Alexis.

Come to my window in the evening twilight. Sunset. Hayyim Nahman Bialik, *Hebrew.* TrJP, *tr. by* Helena Frank

Come to Noah's for wine and strong waters. Limerick. *Unknown.* PeLi

Come to shameful common sense or reason. (LL) Mayakovsky's Suicide Note. Vladimir Mayakovsky, *Russian.* TCRP, *tr. by* Bernard Meares

Come to Sunny Prestatyn. Sunny Prestatyn. Philip Larkin. NoAM; OBCoV

Come to term the started child shocks. Multipara: Gravida 5. Marie Ponsot. CLPP; VGW

Come to the festal board tonight. The Festal Board. *Unknown.* BLPA

Come to the judgment, golden threads. The Judgment of the May. Richard Watson Dixon. OBNC

Come to the Stone. Randall Jarrell. VGW

Come to the window! You're the painter used. Requiescam. Trumbull Stickney. ColAP

Come to these lonely woods to die alone? The Dying Raven. Richard Henry Dana. APN-1

Come to this shrine. String Bean. Luis J. Rodriguez. EC3

Come to weep out the night. (LL) To the Willow-Tree. Robert Herrick. CaPo; OBEV; SCGP

Come to your heaven, you [*or* yowe] heavenly choirs [*or* quires]. New Heaven, New War[re]. Robert Southwell. ChIV-2; ESCV; NOBE; NoP-4

Come towering, armed in adamant and gold. (LL) Beneath yon ruin'd abbey's moss-grown piles. Thomas, the Younger Warton. NOEC; OxAEP-1

Come, try this exercise. In the Dark. James Merrill. LCAP-2

"Come, try your skill, kind gentlemen." The Gipsy Girl. Ralph Hodgson. MoBrPo; SAGP

Come unto Me, When Shadows Darkly Gather. Catharine H. Watterman. AH

Come unto these yellow sands. Ariel's Song: "Come unto these yellow sands." Shakespeare. BoTP; CH; CTC; EBEvV; FaBoCh; NOBE; NOSC; NoSic; OBEV; PoEL-2; SCGP; SoSe-8; TFi; TTTS *Fr.* The Tempest. OAEL-1

Come up from the fields father, here's a letter from our Pete. Walt Whitman. APN-1; CBCWP; MoAmPo; OBWP; OxBA; SAmP; UnPo

Come Up, Methuselah. C. Day Lewis. OBMV

Come up, my horse, to Budleigh Fair. *Unknown.* OxNR

Come up to me at early dawn. Invitation. Solomon ibn Gabirol, *Hebrew.* TrJP, *tr. by* Israel Zangwill

Come, virgin tapers of pure wax. Epithalamium. Richard Crashaw. NOCV

Come visit my pancake collection. The Pancake Collector. Jack Prelutsky. OBCA

Come, walk with me. Emily Jane Brontë. NOBVV

Come, warm your hands. Driftwood. Witter Bynner. FYAP

Come Wary One. Ruth Manning-Sanders. CH

Come we shepheards whose blest Sight. In the Holy Nativity of Our Lord God. Richard Crashaw. ESCV; FSCP; GeHe; HAP; MeLP; PoEL-2

Come, wed me, Lady Singleton. Lady "Rogue" Singleton. Stevie Smith. FaBoWP; OPOU; OxBSP

Come wee Shepheards who have seene. A Hymne of the Nativity, Sung by the Shepheards. Richard Crashaw. PBRV

Come wench, are we almost at the well. Fair Maiden. George Peele. PoEL-2 *Fr.* The Old Wives' [*or* Wife's] Tale.

Come, when no graver cares employ. To the Rev. F. D. Maurice. Tennyson. GTBS-P; NOBVV; PeECV

Come when you're called. Good Advice. Mother Goose. OxNR; ReMoGo

"Come, wife," said good old Farmer Gray. The Little Dog under the Wagon. *Unknown.* PoLF

Come, "Will," let's be good friends again. Sunshine after Cloud. Josephine D. Henderson Heard. CBWP-4

Come with clean hands. *Unknown, Greek.* GrAn, *tr. by* Edward Lucie-Smith

Come with me. Parker's Mood. Clarence Beeks. NAAAL

Come with me and you may see. A Christmas Rhyme. George Sands Johnson. PWR

Come with me into those things that have felt this despair for so long. Robert Bly. CAPP-1; NOBA; NoAM

Come with me to the mushroom. Tale of Mushrooms. Lynda Hiott. CTV

Come with our voices, let us war. The Musical Strife; in a Pastoral Dialogue. Ben Jonson. BeJo

Come with rain, O loud Southwester! To the Thawing Wind. Robert Frost. OxBA

Come worthy Greek, Ulysses [*or* Vlisses], come. Ulysses and the Siren [*or* Syren]. Samuel Daniel. HAP; NAEL-1; NOBE; NoP-4; OBEV; OxAEP-1; PoE; PoEL-2

Come ye hither all, whose taste. The Invitation. George Herbert. ChIV-1; ESCV

Come, ye thankful people, come. Henry Alford. CTV

Come ye, whose hearts the tyrant sorrows wound. Stanzas Written under Aeolus' Harp. Amelia Alderson Opie. Ro *Fr.* Poems.

Come yee my servants of my father Blessed. (LL) Upon the First Sight of New England, June 29, 1638. Thomas Tillam. AH; SCAP

Come, yellow broom. A Glimpse. Robert Duncan. FTOS

Come you, ascend the ladder; all come in; all sit down. Invocation to the U' wannami. *Unknown, Zuni.* APN-2; PaTW, *tr. by* Matilda Coxe Stevenson

Come you, cartoonists. Halsted Street Car. Carl Sandburg. NAAL-2

Come you gallants all, to you I do call. Robin Hood's Chase. *Unknown.* ESPB

Comeahead then comeahead. Love Song of Tommo Frogley. Roger Crawford. UV

Comedian as the Letter C, The. Wallace Stevens. OxBA

Comedian Gets a Curtain Lecture, The. Nguyễn Khuyến, *Vietnamese.* AVP, *tr. by* Huỳnh Sanh Thông

Comedy of Errors, The. Shakespeare.
"By the way we met." OBCoV

Comedy of the World, The. Huỳnh Thúc Kháng, *Vietnamese.* AVP, *tr. by* Huỳnh Sanh Thông

Comely and capable one of our race. On the Portrait of a Woman About to Be Hanged. Thomas Hardy. CMoP

Comely young widow named Ransom, A. Limerick. *Unknown.* PeLi

Comes a brown. Corkby, Part Two. Jerome Rothenberg. NNaP *Fr.* Cokboy. PmAP

Comes a time. The Poet in Old Age Fishing at Evening. Desmond O'Grady. CIP-2

Comes back with the reply, 'Yes, you're another's'. (LL) I despise neo-epic verse sagas. Callimachus, *Greek.* GrAn; OBCVT, *tr. by* Peter Jay

Comes Death, and takes the table clean away. (LL) A Comparison of the Life of Man. Richard Barnfield. NoSic; OxBSP

Comes home dull with coal-dust deliberately. Her Husband. Ted Hughes. OxBC

Comes like an idiot, babbling and strewing flowers. (LL) Spring. Edna St. Vincent Millay. BoWoP; MeMAP; MoAmPo; NoP-4; SAGP

Comes not the springtime here. Come Not the Seasons Here. Edwin John Pratt. NoP-4

Comes of his own accord to me. He That None Can Capture. May Swenson. LW

Comes once to set, it makes eternal night. (LL) Pastoral[1], A: "Oh [*or* O] happy golden age." Torquato Tasso. AWP; OBVE, *tr. by* Leigh Hunt; OAEL-1; PoEL-2, *tr. by* Samuel Daniel

Comes out like a ribbon lies flat on the brush. (LL) Poem, or Beauty Hurts Mr. Vinal. E. E. Cummings. FaBoA; InPS-3; MoAmPo; NAAL-2; OBAL; OxBA; PFTM; PeLV; TRP

Comes the day, when he must die. Muspilli. *Unknown, German.* GePo, *tr. by* Carroll Hightower

Comes the deer to my singing. Hunting-Song. *Unknown, Navajo.* AWP, *tr. by* Natalie Curtis

Comes the smiling / mortician. (LL) 25. Lawrence Ferlinghetti. CAPP-1; CLPP

Comes the time when it's later. A Wicker Basket. Robert Creeley. HAP; MoP; NoAM; Poetr

Comes walking barefoot. Sojourner Truth. Robert Earl Hayden. *Fr.* Stars. LCAP-2

Comet. Federico García Lorca. PFTM

Comet, The. Maria Luisa Spaziani, *Italian*. NeIt, *tr.* by Beverly Allen

Comet at Yell'ham, The. Thomas Hardy. CMoP; GBL

Comets and Princes. Samuel Johnson. FaBoEE

Comfort. Maura Stanton. SoSe-8

Comfort for a wedded pair! (LL) The Ballad of Hiram Hover. Bayard Taylor. BXAP; OBAL

Comfort in Puirtith. Helen B. Cruickshank. OxBS

Comfort-Maker. Jerry W. Ward Jr. ISC

Comfort myself when that my hap is nought. (LL) Love's Fidelity. Petrarch. AAS; HAP; NoSic; SiPS, *tr.* by Henry Howard, Earl of Surrey

Comfort that does not comprehend. (LL) The Return. Edna St. Vincent Millay. MeMAP; MoAmPo; MoP; NoAM; OxBA; Poetr

Comfort thee, oh thou mourner, yet awhile! To the Sister of Charles Lamb. Walter Savage Landor. Ro

Comfort thyself, my wo[e]ful heart. Sir Thomas Wyatt. SiPS

Comfort to a Youth That Had Lost His Love. Robert Herrick. NOBE; OBEV

Comfort ye, comfort ye my people. Bible, *O.T.* OBVE, *stanzas* 1–8; TrJP *Fr.* Isaiah.

Comfortable Words. Gillian Allnutt. NBrP

Comfortably fixed for clothing and food, children married off. Half in the Family, Half Out. Po Chü-i, *Chinese*. CoBCP, *tr.* by Burton Watson

Comforted by Limestone. Edward Dorn. NOBA *Fr.* Oxford.

Comforters, The. Dora Sigerson Shorter. CH

Comic Adventures of Old Mother Hubbard and Her Dog, The. Sarah Catherine Martin. CBNP; OxBChV

("Dog said, Bow wow, The.") (LL) LB

Comical Revenge, The. Sir George Etherege.
Song: "Ladies, though to your conquering eyes." OxBSP

Comin' thro' the Rye. Robert Burns. UV

Comin[g] thro' [*or* through] the rye, poor body. Robert Burns. CBLP; FaBoVe; OxAEP-2; OxBS

Coming. Robert Kelly. PmAP

Coming. Philip Larkin. MoBrPo; OxBTC

Coming Across. Mehri, *Farsi*. WPOW, *tr.* by Deirdre Lashgari

Coming Again to Heng-yang, I Mourn for Liu Tsung-yüan. Liu Yu Hsi, *Chinese*. SuSp, *tr.* by Daniel Bryant

Coming American, The. Sam Walter Foss.
"Bring me men to match my mountains." BLPA; FaBoBe

Coming and Going. Robert Francis. TLR

Coming and Going. Mitchell Goodman. VGW

Coming and going these several seasons. Abiku. J. P. Clark Bekedereme. HBAPE

Coming and going these several seasons. Abiku. J. P. Clark Bekedermo. PBMAP *Fr.* A Reed in the Tide.

Coming and going with presents and things! Robert Louis Stevenson. *See* Block City.

Coming around the corner of a dream. Cockaigne: A Dream. Louis Edward Sissman. DiPo

Coming around the corner of the dark trail . . . what was wrong with the. The Inquisitors. Robinson Jeffers. MoAmPo

Coming around the Horn. John A. Stone. AmFP

Coming at an end, the lovers. A Book of Music. Jack Spicer. APSN; PoM

Coming at Night to a Fisherman's Hut. Chang Chi, *Chinese*. BLT, *tr.* by J. P. Seaton

Coming Back. Joseph Bruchac. CDW

Coming Back. Ellsworth McGranahan Keane. PBCV

Coming Back Home. Ray A. Young Bear. CDW

Coming back one evening through deserted fields. Through All Your Abstract Reasoning. Brian Patten. FaBoTw

Coming back over the col between. Strength through Joy. Kenneth Rexroth. FYAP; VGW

Coming Back to America. James Dickey. NYBP; WeT

Coming back to this generous island. Returning to Store Bay. Barbara Howes. Poetsp

Coming by evening through the wintry city. At a Bach Concert. Adrienne Rich. NIP-4

Coming down into an air brown as whiskey, the plane. Autobiography, Chapter XLII: Three Days in Louisville. Jim Barnes. HATNAP

Coming down the mountain in the twilight. Where the Hayfields Were. Archibald MacLeish. AFr

Coming Down to It. Malcolm Glass. BXAP

Coming from Evening Church. Charles Causley. NTP

Coming from Kansas. Myra Cohn Livingston. NOxBChV

Coming from Montreal. Upstate. Simon J. Ortiz. LTA

Coming from the south. Six Ten Sixty-Nine. Conyus. GT; PoBA

Coming from the woods. Richard Wright. KaS

Coming, going, the waterbirds. On Non-dependence of Mind. Dogen. EnlH

Coming Home. D. F. Brown. CDa

Coming Home. Daniel S. Simko. CEEP

Coming Home, *Detroit*, 1968. Philip Levine. WWSi

Coming home, I find you still in bed. Abortion. Ai. BoWoP

Coming Home in March. Harold Littlebird. VoR

Coming Home Late at Night. Tu Fu, *Chinese*. BLT, *tr.* by J. P. Seaton

Coming home late through the smoky. Brian Turner. PeNZ

Coming home with the last load I ride standing. Emergency Haying. Hayden Carruth. NNaP

Coming Homeward out of Spain. Barnabe Googe. NoSic

Coming in again, you know the town by boards it makes eyes touch. Autobiography: Last Chapter. Jim Barnes. CDW

Coming in off the dock after writing. Station. Sharon Olds. PBCAP

Coming into the store at first angry. The Man Who Finds That His Son Has Become a Thief. Raymond Souster. NOBC

"Coming" is an empty word, "going" leaves no trace. Li Shang-yin, *Chinese*. SuSp, *tr.* by James J. Y. Liu

Coming of Age. Michael Palma. UnSA

Coming of Age in the County Jail. Carter Revard. VoR

Coming of Dusk upon a Village in Haiti, The. Henry Rago. HoPM

Coming of Good Luck, The. Robert Herrick. FaBoEE; OxBSP; Spl

Coming of Grendel, The. *Unknown*. OPOU, *tr.* by Gerald Benson *Fr.* Beowulf. OAEL-1, *tr.* by Charles W. Kennedy; ASW, *tr.* by Kevin Crossley-Holland

Coming of His Feet, The. Lyman Whitney Allen. BLPA

Coming of John, The. Amus Mor. MoNo, SoSe

Coming of Kali, The. Lucille Clifton. NMM-2

Coming of Light, The. Mark Strand. HCAP

Coming of Raka, The. N. P. van Wyk Louw, *Afrikaans*. PeSAV, *tr.* by Guy Butler *Fr.* Raka.

Coming of Spring, The. Nora Perry. PWR

Coming of Spring, The. Henrietta Cordelia Ray. CBWP-3

Coming of Teddy Bears, The. Dennis Lee. TLR

Coming of that limpid star is twice, The. Sonnet 6. Louise Labé, *French*. BoWoP, *tr.* by Willis Barnstone

Coming of the Cold, The. Theodore Roethke. OBCP

Coming of the Plague, The. Weldon Kees. ChIV-1; VGW

Coming of the White Man, The. Patrick Anderson. MoCV *Fr.* Poem on Canada.
"Wide was the land."

Coming of War, The; Actaeon. Ezra Pound. CMoP; PoA; PoE

Coming of Wisdom with Time, The. W. B. Yeats. FaBoEE; SoSe-8

Coming out of the house on a fresh March morning. March 1st. Kathleen Spivack. NYBP

Coming out of the house to die. Robert Duncan. SPE

Coming out of the mountains of a summer evening. St. Gervais. Michael Roberts. FaBoCh

Coming Right Up. A. R. Ammons. OBCoV

Coming Storm, The. Herman Melville. APN-2

Coming Suddenly to the Sea. Louis Dudek. NOBC

Coming through the Craigs o' Kyle. O'er the Muir Amang the Heather. Jean Glover. RACG

Coming through the rye. The Rose Farmer. Herman Melville. APN-2

Coming to cottonwoods, an. Prospecting. A. R. Ammons. CoAmPo

Coming [*or* Comming] to kiss[e] her lips [*or* lyps], (such grace I found). Sonnet 64. Edmund Spenser. EBEV; NAEL-1; OAEL-1; Son *Fr.* Amoretti. AAS

Coming to the farm that winter afternoon. Burragorang. Nan McDonald. NOBAu

Coming to This. Mark Strand. HCAP; SAGP; VCAP

Coming up England by a different line. I Remember, I Remember. Philip Larkin. NOBL; NTP

Coming up the green lane from the sea. Tryst. John Hewitt. BiHa

Coming was an empty promise, you have gone, and left no footprint. Li Shang-yin, *Chinese*. PLT, *tr.* by A. C. Graham

Coming winter and a summoning / odour of balsam. (LL) Himalayan Balsam. Anne Stevenson. EP

Coming Woman, The. Mary Weston Fordham. CBWP-2

Comings, goings, hard to settle down. Seeing Off Wang Yüan-chao—Reprise. Wu Wei-yeh, *Chinese*. CoBLCP, *tr.* by Jonathan Chaves

Command, The. Avraham Huss, *Hebrew*. MHP, *tr.* by Ruth Finer Mintz

Commandeered. Lucy Gertrude Moberley. NSI

Commandeering the Wind. Su Shun-ch'in, *Chinese*. SuSp, *tr. by* Irving Y. Lo

Commander Lowell. Robert Lowell. VGW

Commanding asker, if it be. The Fair Beggar. Richard Lovelace. BeJo

Commandments. D. H. Lawrence. GI

Commemoration. Sir Henry John Newbolt. FaBoTw

Commemoration Ode. Harriet Monroe.
　Washington. FaBoBe

Commemorative of a Naval Victory. Herman Melville. HAP; UnPo

Commencement. Constance Carrier. WPE

Commendations of Mistress Jane Scrope, The. John Skelton. *Fr.* Phyllyp Sparowe [*or* Philip Sparrow]. AAS; PoEL-1

Commendatory Sonnets. Edmund Spenser.
　To the Right Worshipfull, My Singular Good Frend, Master Gabriell Harvey, Doctor of the Lawes. NoSic

Commendatory Verses to Edmund Spenser's Fairy Queen. Sir Walter Ralegh.
　Another of the Same. SiPS
　Vision upon This Concei[p]t of the Faerie [*or* Faery] Queen[e], A. NAEL-1; NoSic; SCGP; Son
　("And cursed the access of that celestial thief!") (LL) NoP-4
　(Of Spenser's Faery Queen.) SiPS

Comment. Dorothy Parker. LW; NBLV; NIP-4; OBAL; OBCoV *Fr.* Some Beautiful Letters.
　("And I am Marie of Rumania.") (LL) LW

Comment on Curb. Langston Hughes. APSN *Fr.* Lenox Avenue Mural. HoPM

Commentary Applied to Spiritual Things. Saint John of the Cross, *Spanish*. TOF, *tr. by* K. Kavanaugh *and* O. Rodrigues

Commentary Text Commentary Text Commentary Text. David Shapiro. PmAP

Commerce or contemplation. (LL) Large Bad Picture. Elizabeth Bishop. NYBP; OxBC

Commination, A. Alec Derwent Hope. ChIV-2

Comming to kisse her lyps, (such grace I found). Edmund Spenser. *See* Sonnet 64: "Coming [*or* Comming] to kiss[e] her lips [*or* lyps], (such grace I found)."

Commingling sky, A. Freely Espousing. James Schuyler. FTOS; NeAP; NoP-4

Commiserating with the Poor. Li K'ai-hsien, *Chinese*. CoBLCP, *tr. by* Jonathan Chaves

Commission. Ezra Pound. BoLoP; TwCP

Commissioner bet me a pony, The—I won, The. Robert, Viscount Sherbrooke Lowe. NOBAu *Fr.* Songs of the Squatters.

Commissioner bet me a pony, The—I won. Songs of the Squatters. Robert, Viscount Sherbrooke Lowe. NOBAu

Commit—flirtation with the muse of Moore. (LL) Poetical Commandments. Byron. OxBoLi; PeLV, *canto* 1, *stanzas* 204–206

Committee, The. C. Day Lewis. CMoP

Committee, The—now a permanent body. Dream. Marianne Moore. NYBP

Committee's fat, The. Un-American Investigators. Langston Hughes. BPo

Common a-Took In, The. William Barnes. EnVR

Common Bill. *Unknown*. AS

Common Bill. *Unknown*. AS; AmFP

Common Cormorant [*or* Shag], The. Christopher Isherwood. FaBoCh; NBLV; NOxBChV

Common Dawn. Guy Butler. PeSA

Common Dust. Georgia Douglas Johnson. PoBA; TTY

Common Fate of Books, The. Margaret Lucas Cavendish, Duchess of Newcastle. PBRV

Common Form. Rudyard Kipling. FaBoEE; FaBoTw; PeFWW *Fr.* Epitaphs of the War [1914–1918]. OBWP

Common garden snail can't watch, The. Good Heavens. Pattiann Rogers. PuP-17

Common Grave, The. James Dickey. CoAP

Common Ground, A. Denise Levertov. PoM

Common Lover's Song, The. Flavien Ranaivo. *See* Love Song: "Do not love me, my friend."

Common Man, The. Arthur James Marshall Smith. NOBC

Common man I might have been, The. In Brief. Angel Cuadra, *Spanish*. AF, *tr. by* Katherine Rodriguez Nieto

Common miracle. Miracle Mart. Wislawa Szymborska, *Polish*. PoSu, *tr. by* Adam Czerniawski

Common Occurrence, A. Priscilla Jane Thompson. CBWP-2

Common Prayer. Lynn Ungar. CrSp

Common Road, The. Silas H. Perkins. BLPA; FaBoBe

Common Sacrifice to Honour fall, A. (LL) Sarpedon's Speech to Glaucus. Homer, *Greek*. OBCVT; OBVE, *tr. by* Sir John Denham

Common Sense. Alan Brownjohn. NOxBChV *Fr.* Pitman's Common Sense Arithmetic, 1917.

Common Sense: A Poem. *Unknown*.
　"We still have bards who, with aspiring head." EPCY

Common speech is, spend and God will send, The. Magnum Vectigal Parsimonia. George Gascoigne. NoSic

Common tasks are beautiful if we. Grace Noll Crowell. PoToHe

Common Things. Paul Laurence Dunbar. GT

Common Woman, The. Judy Grahn.
　Carol, in the Park, Chewing on Straws. WPOW
　Ella, in a Square Apron, Along Highway 80. NALW; NMM-2
　("As a rattlesnake.") (LL) NMM-2
　"She holds things together, collects bail." NALW

Common woman is as common / as a rattlesnake, The. (LL) Ella, in a Square Apron, Along Highway 80. Judy Grahn. NALW

Commonplace Day, A. Thomas Hardy. NOBVV

Commonplace I sing, The. Walt Whitman. MoAmPo

Communal Krakovyak. Vladimir Druk, *Russian*. TCRP, *tr. by* Albert C. Todd

Commune above her in a drift of wings. (LL) Assumption. Padraic Fallon. BIrV; NOIV

Commune for Me, The. Viktor Fiodorovich Bokov, *Russian*. TCRP, *tr. by* Bernard Meares

Communication in Whi-te. Don L. Lee. BPo

Communication of His Thirtieth Birthday. Marvin Bell. CoAP

Communication to Nancy Cunard, A. Kay Boyle. NMM-2

Communication to the City Fathers of Boston. George Starbuck. NYBP

Communion. P. M. Snider. PoToHe

Communion Hymn. George Seaver. TIRV

Communion II. U Tam'si Tchicaya, *French*. NegPo, *tr. by* Ellen Conroy Kennedy

Communion of Saints: The Poor Bastard under the Bridge. Marie Ponsot. VGW

Communist Poem, 1935. Valentine Ackland. WPN

Commuted Sentence, The. Stevie Smith. OxAEP-2

Commuter. Lisel Mueller. GM

Commuter. Elwyn Brooks White. NBLV

Commuters. Betsy Hearne. SSCS

Como lo Siento. Lorna Dee Cervantes. NoAM

Companion, The. Edwin Arlington Robinson. NoAM

Companion—North-East Dug-Out. Ivor Gurney. FP

Companions. Charles Stuart Calverley. NOBL
　(Companions, a Tale of a Grandfather.) PeLV

Companions, The. Howard Nemerov. NYBP

Companions, a Tale of a Grandfather. Charles Stuart Calverley. *See* Companions.

Companions of my favourite hours. Sappho Burns Her Books and Cultivates the Culinary Arts. Elizabeth Moody. ECWP

Companions of the Spring. (LL) To the Cuckoo. Michael Bruce, *rev. by* John Logan. NOEC; OBEV

Companion's Progress, A. Paul Laurence Dunbar. GT

Company, The. Robert Creeley. FTOS

Company. Michael Longley. IIP

Company in Loneliness. *Unknown*. NOIV

Company of the Birds, The. Sasha Moorsom. APAD

Company of vessels on the sea, A. Battle Problem. William Meredith. NYBP

Comparatives. *Unknown*. ACTP

Compared with loss of thee will not seem so. (LL) Sonnet 90. Shakespeare. AWP; EBEV; NOBE; NoSic; OBEV; OxAEP-1; PoEL-2

Comparison, The. Thomas Carew. BeJo

Comparison, A. William Cowper. OxBSP

Comparison, The. Donne. PeLV *Fr.* Elegies.

Comparison, A. John Chipman Farrar. WHSW

Comparison, The. *Unknown*.
　"Let dirty streets be paved with flow'ry green." NOEC

Comparison betwixt a Whore and a Booke, A. John Taylor.
　"Me thinks I heare some Cavillers object." PBRV

Comparison of Hands One Day Late Summer El Sobrante. Wendy Rose. HATNAP

Comparison of the Life of Man, A. Richard Barnfield. NoSic; OxBSP

Comparisons. Christina Rossetti. OxBChV

Comparisons will be made. To the Writers' Worship in Zomba. Felix Mnthali. PeSAV

Compass Poem. Bill Griffiths. NBrP

Compassion for the Farmers. Li K'ai-hsien, *Chinese*. CoBLCP, *tr. by* Jonathan Chaves

Compassionate Fool, The. Norman Cameron. GTBS-P; OxBSP; OxBTC; RB

Compelling a recognition. (LL) Paring the Apple. Charles Tomlinson. CMoP; OxBTC; PoE; TRP

Compensation. E. M. Brainard. PoToHe

Compensation. Paul Laurence Dunbar. APN-2; BPo

Compensation. Harry Graham. CBNP; PeLV   *Fr. Some Ruthless Rhymes.*

Compensation. Robinson Jeffers. MoAmPo

Compensation. Henrietta Cordelia Ray. CBWP-3

Compensation ("Why should I keep holiday"). Ralph Waldo Emerson. APN-1; MeMAP; TAP

Compensation ("Wings of Time are black and white, The"). Ralph Waldo Emerson. APN-1; AmPP; NOBA; PAR

Competitive product you said you'd send, The. (LL) A Consumer's Report. Peter Porter. NoP-4

Complacencies of the peignoir, and late. Sunday Morning. Wallace Stevens. AmPP; CMoP; ColAP; HAP; HCAP; HeIP-4; ImPo; InPS-3; LiTM; MeMAP; MoAmPo; MoP; NAAL-2; NAWM-2; NIP-4; NOBA; NoAM; NoP-4; OxBA; PoA; PoE; PoPoPo; Poetr; SAmP; SoSe-8; TAP; TFi; TRP

Complacent Cliff-Dweller, The. Margaret Fishback. PoLF

Complacent old Don of Divinity, A. Limerick. *Unknown.* PeLi

Complacent they tell us, hard hearts and derisive. Woman's Future. May Kendall. VWP

Complacent Tortoise, The. Brian Patten. OBSP

Complaining. George Herbert. ChIV-1

Complaint, The. Mark Akenside. OBEV

Complaint. Alistair Paterson. *Fr. Incantations for Warriors.* PeNZ

Complaint   William Carlos Williams. SAmP

Complaint, A. Wordsworth. NOBE; PoEL-4; Ro

Complaint. James Wright. NOBA; SAGP; TAP; VGW

  ("And now lies down, who was my moon or more.") (LL) SAGP

Complaint about Exile, A. Mairi MacLeod, *Gaelic*. PBWP, *tr. by* Joan Keefe

Complaint Against the Arsonist. Stanley Plumly. PUP-18

Complaint by Night of the Lover Not Beloved, A. Henry Howard, Earl of Surrey, *after* Petrarch. AAS; AWP; EBEV; NAEL-1; OAEL-1; OBVE; SiPS; Son

  (Complaint by Night, A.) SCGP

Complaint of a Forsaken Indian Woman, The. Wordsworth. Ro

Complaint of a Lover Rebuked. Henry Howard, Earl of Surry, *after* Petrarch. *Fr. Sonnets to Laura.*

  ("Love that liveth and reigneth in my thought.") PFE; SiPS

Complaint of a Neglected Wife. Meng Chiao, *Chinese*. PLT, *tr. by* A. C. Graham

Complaint of Ariadna, The. Catullus, *Latin*.

  "There on th'extreamest Beach, and farthest Sand." OBCVT, *tr. by* William Bowles

Complaint of Chaucer to His [Empty] Purse, The. Chaucer. ImPo; MiEL; NAEL-1; OAEL-1; SCGP

  (Complaint to His Purse.) NoP-4

  ("Have minde upon my supplicacioun.") (LL) NoP-4

Complaint of Henry Duke of Buckingham, The. Thomas, 1st Earl of Dorset Sackville. *See* Induction to "A Mirror for Magistrates."

Complaint of Love. Sir Philip Sidney. PoEL-1; SiPS   *Fr. Arcadia.*

Complaint of Rosamond, The. Samuel Daniel.

  Lonely Beauty. CTC

Complaint of the Absence of Her Lover Being upon the Sea. Henry Howard, Earl of Surrey. AAS; EBEV; GBL; NOBE; OBEV

  (Seafarer, The.) SiPS

Complaint of the Black Knight, The. John Lydgate. *Fr. The Complaint of the Black Knight.*

Complaint of the Fair Armoress [*or* Armouress], The. François Villon, *French*. AWP; CTC; OBVE, *tr. by* Algernon Charles Swinburne

Complaint of the Morpethshire Farmer, The. Basil Bunting. CTC

Complaint of Troilus, The. Chaucer. NOBE; OBEV   *Fr. Troilus and Criseyde [or Criseide].* EnVB

Complaint That His Ladie After She Knew of His Love Kept Her Face Alway Hidden from Him, *sl. diff vers.* Henry Howard, Earl of Surrey. PoEL-1

Complaint to a Court Poet. Rashidi Samarqandi, *Persian*. ArPe, *tr. by* Omar S. Pound

Complaint to His Purse. Chaucer. *See* The Complaint of Chaucer to His [Empty] Purse.

Complaint: To the Muse. Philip Whalen. BB

Complaint unto Pity, The. Chaucer. MiEL

Complaints of Poverty, The. Nicholas James.

  "May poverty, without offence, approach." NOEC

Complaisant Swain, The. Ovid. AWP, *tr. by* F. A. Wright   *Fr. Amores.*

Complaynt. Anne Waldman. FiLi

Complaynt of the Comoun weill of Scotland, The. Sir David Lindsay. *See* The Compleynt of the Comoun Weill of Scotland.

Complement, The. Thomas Carew. CBLP

Complements. Like figures in statuary. Sun and Moon. Mary Kinzie. FFC

Complete Birth if the Cool, The. C. D. Wright. LCAP-2

Complete Cynic, The. Keith Preston. NBLV

Complete Destruction. William Carlos Williams. SAmP

Complete in Thee, No Work of Mine. Aaron R. Wolfe. AH

Complete Sound-Poems of Hugo Ball, The. Hugo Ball. PFTM

Complete the picture. (LL) The Hunters in the Snow. William Carlos Williams. GS

Complete with photomatic *stimmung*. Our Lady. John Godfrey. PmAP

Compleynt of feire Anelida and fals Arcite, The. Publius Papinius Statius, *Latin*.

  "When Thesus with werres longe and grete." OBCVT, *tr. by* Geoffrey Chaucer

Compleynt of the Comoun Weill of Scotland, The. Sir David Lindsay. OxBS   *Fr. The Dreme.*

  ("And thus as we wer talking to and fro.") PBRV

  (Complaynt of the Comoun weill of Scotland, The.) PBRV

Compliment to the Ladies, A. William Blake. BXAP

  (Imitation of Pope   A Compliment to the Ladies.) OBCoV

Compline. Donald Davie. *Fr. Horae Canonicae.* CRP

Components. Roger McDonald. CBAP

Compose compose beds. Sacred. Gertrude Stein. OBAL

Composed as I am, like others. Elements of Composition. A. K. Ramanujan. VCWP

Composed at Neidpath Castle, the Property of Lord Queensberry,1803. Wordsworth. GTBS-P

Composed at Rydal on May Morning, 1838. Wordsworth. LaPo   *Fr. Memorials of a Tour in Italy, 1837.*

Composed at Sunset at the Dunes of Ho-yen. Ts'en Shen, *Chinese*. SuSp, *tr. by* Ronald C. Miao

Composed at the Request of a Lady, and Descriptive of Her Feelings. Maria Gowen Brooks. APN-1; PAR

Composed at thirty, my funeral oration: Here lies. A Funeral Oration. David Wright. PeSAV

Composed by the Sea-Side, near Calais, August, 1802. Wordsworth. Son

Composed, generally defined. The Map. Mark Strand. NYBP

Composed in One of the Valleys of Westmoreland, on Easter Sunday. Wordsworth. ChIV-2

Composed in the Composing Room. Franklin Pierce Adams. NIP-4; OBAL

Composed in the Tower before his execution. 'More Light! More Light!'. Anthony Hecht. AF; CoAP; CoAmPo; HAP; HP; NOBA; NoAM; NoP-4; OBWP; Poetr; RB; TwCP; UnPo; VCAP; VGW

Composed Near Calais on the Road Leading to Ardres, August 7, 1802. Wordsworth. FaBoPV

Composed Near the Bay Bridge (after a wild party). Marilyn Chin. WWSi

Composed on a Journey Homeward; the Author Having Received Intelligence of the Birth of a Son. Coleridge. Son

Composed on a Spring Day on the Farm. Wang Wei, *Chinese*. ChiPo, *tr. by* Chang Yin-nan *and* Lewis C. Walmsley

Composed on Horseback, Returning from Lakeview Pavilion at Hangchow, Presented to Yü-ju and Lo-tao. Wang An-shih, *Chinese*. SuSp, *tr. by* Jan W. Walls

Composed on the Theme "Willows by the Riverside." Yü Hsüan-chi, *Chinese*. SuSp; WPOW, *tr. by* Jan W. Walls

Composed upon an Evening of Extraordinary Splendour and Beauty. Wordsworth. OAEL-2

Composed upon Westminster Bridge[, September 3, 1802]. Wordsworth. APAD; AWP; CABP; CH; ChAP; ClHu; FaBoCh; GSo; GTBS-P; HAP; HeIP-4; ImPo; InPK-6; InPS-3; NAEL-2; NAWM-2; NOBRP; NoP-4; OAEL-2; OBNC; OPOU; PBMP; PFE; PoE; PoEL-4; PoLF; PoPoPo; Ro; SCGP; Son; TFi; UnPo

Composed While under Arrest. Mikhail Yuryevich Lermontov, *Russian*. AWP, *tr. by* Max Eastman

Composer, The. W. H. Auden. MeMAP

Composing mortals with immortal fire. (LL) Song for St. Cecilia's Day. W. H. Auden. FaBoTw; TwCP

Composition. Peter Blue Cloud. VoR

Composition, The. Jean Kenward. PeP

Composition of the Chalcans, A. Chalcan Female Song. *Unknown*. PFTM, *tr. by* John Bierhorst   *Fr. Cantares Mexicanos.*

Compositions in harmony. Big Bluejay Composition. Ron Padgett. PmAP

Compost. James Grainger. NOEC   *Fr. The Sugar Cane.*

Compost Heap, The. Vernon Watkins. NYBP

Compromise. Akhtar-ul-Iman, *Urdu*. OMIP, *tr.* by C. M. Naim *and* Vinay Dharwadker

Compromise, The. Ibn al-Rumi, *Arabic*. ArPe, *tr.* by Omar S. Pound

Compromised by sorrow. Elegy for Chief Sealth. Duane Niatum. CDW

Compulsion as the Critical Element in a Defined Perversion. Bin Ramke. WeT

Compulsive Qualifications. Richard Howard. PoA
   "Richard, may I ask a question? What is an episteme?"
   "Richard, what will it be like when you ask the questions?"

Computation, The. Donne. CBNP; FMP; NoSic; OxBSP; SoSe-8

Computer's First Christmas Card, The. Edwin Morgan. PChr

Computer's First Christmas Card, The. Edwin Morgan. NOxBChV

Computer's First Proverbs, The. Peter Finch. NBrP

Comrade. Philippe Soupault, *French*. PFTM, *tr.* by Pat Nolan

Comrade and Confidant to me. (LL) Autumn day its course has run—The Autumn evening falls, The. Charlotte Brontë. NOBVV; SDW

Comrade, comrade, come away. The Midsummer Apple Tree. Naomi Mitchison. WPN

Comrade Stalin, you are a great scholar. Yuz Aleshkovsky, *Russian*. TCRP, *tr.* by Sarah W. Bliumis

Comrades: an Episode. Robert Malise Bowyer Nichols. NSI

Comrades and friends! with whom, where'er. Carm. II. Catullus, *Latin*. OBCVT, *tr.* by Thomas Moore

Comrades, leave me here a little, while as yet 't is early morn. Granny's House. Phoebe Cary. APN-2

Comrades, leave me here a little, while as yet 'tis early morn. Locksley Hall. Tennyson. EBEV; EBVVPR; EnVR; FaBoBe; ImPo; NAEL-2; OAEL-2

Comrades Marathon, The. Chris Mann. PeSAV

Comrades, the morning breaks, the sun is up. Hafiz. AWP, *tr.* by Richard Le Gallienne *Fr.* Odes.

Comus; a Masque Presented at Ludlow Castle. Milton. FHYEP; OAEL-1; OxBSn
   (Mask, A.)
   "Bacchus, that first from out the purple grape."
   Chastity ("I Mean That Too, But Yet a Hidden Strength"). NOSC
   Comus' Summons. NOSC
      (Comus Speaks.) NOBE
   Comus's Praise of Nature. PoEL-3
   Echo. OBEV
      (Lady Sings, The.) NOBE
   Mask, A. OxAEP-1
      "Nay, lady, sit; if I but wave this wand." OxAEP-1
   Resources.
   Sabrina.
      Sabrina. CH; NOBE; OBEV
      Sabrina's Song. NOSC
   Spirit's Epilogue, The. NOSC
      (Spirit Epiloguizes, The.) NOBE
   Temperance and Virginity.

Comus' Summons. Milton. NOSC *Fr.* Comus; a Masque Presented at Ludlow Castle. FHYEP; OAEL-1

Comus's Song. Ben Jonson. *See* Hymn to Comus.

Concealed in the style of a late manner. Drawing Room Drama. Virginia Hooper. PT

Conceit. Mervyn Laurence Peake. Spl

Concei[p]t begotten by the eyes. Sir Walter Ralegh. NoSic; SiPS

Conceit upon the Feet. William Zaranka. BXAP

Conceited Pedlar, The. Thomas Randolph.
   Come from Thy Palace. OxBSP

Conceived on a mattress of human hair. Innocence. Wislawa Szymborska, *Polish*. PoSu, *tr.* by Jan Darowski

Concentration Camp Blues. Henry Dumas. SeSe

Concentration Constellation. Lawson Fusao Inada. PaTW

Concentric. Richard Kostelanetz. TAP

Concept like "I," which I am told by many, A. I Brood about Some Concepts, for Example. Alicia Ostriker. PBCAP

Conception. Joseph Ceravolo. FTOS

Conception. Josephine Miles. APAD; ColAP; FaBoWP

Conception, an Archbishop said, The. Limerick. "L. E. J." PeLi

Conception is interesting, to: to see, as though reflected. Wet Casements. John Ashbery. NAAL-2; PoM

Concepts and Their Bodies (The Boy in the Field Alone). Pattiann Rogers. MT

Concerning a Girl. Tanikawa Shuntaro, *Japanese*. VCWP, *tr.* by Harold Wright

Concerning Death. Sister Mary Madeleva.
   I Ask My Teachers. CRP

Concerning Dragons. H. D. C. Pepler. NOxBChV

Concerning Hebrews. Herman Melville. APN-2 *Fr.* Clarel: A Poem and Pilgrimage in the Holy Land.

Concerning Himself. Paul Fleming, *German*. GePo, *tr.* by George C. Schoolfield

Concerning My Neighbors, the Hittites. Charles Simic. VCAP

Concerning One Responsible Negro with Too Much Power. Nikki Giovanni. BPo

Concerning that exploit of yours. (LL) That Exploit of Yours. Ford Madox Ford. PeFWW; PoWW

Concerning the Afterlife, the Indians of Central California Had Only the Dimmest Notions. Robert Hass. LoL

Concerning the Awakening of My Soul. Henriëtte Roland-Holst, *Dutch*. WPOW, *tr.* by Jonathan Crewe

Concerning the bees and the flowers. Limerick. *Unknown*. PeLi

Concerning the Dead Women: The Munitions Plant Explosion: June, 1918. Elizabeth Libbey. AmPA

Concerning the Fruit-bringing Autumn Season. Catharina Regina von Greiffenberg, *German*. GePo, *tr.* by George C. Schoolfield

Concerning the King of Sweden. Georg Rudolph Weckherlin, *German*. GePo, *tr.* by George C. Schoolfield

Concerning the Wolffsbrunnen near Heidelberg. Martin Opitz, *German*. GePo, *tr.* by George C. Schoolfield

Concerning your letter in which you ask. With Mercy for the Greedy. Anne Sexton. HCAP; TOF; VCAP

Concert. Josephine Miles. NALW

Concert. Robert Sward. VGW

Concert conductor in Rio, A. Limerick. *Unknown*. PeLi

Concert-hall was crowded the night of the Crash, The. Paper Anniversary. Muriel Rukeyser. NoAM

Concert Party. Siegfried Sassoon. NSI

Concert Party: Busseboom. Edmund Blunden. NSI; PoFWW

Concert's what the English like, A. *Unknown*. PeSAV, *tr.* by Stephen Gray

Conch. Elwyn Brooks White. LiLi

Conchobor, what are you thinking, you. *Unknown*. *Fr.* Exile of the Sons of Uisliu. NOIV, *tr.* by Thomas Kinsella

Concierge at the front gate where relatives, The. Aeterna Poetae Memoria. Archibald MacLeish. Son

Concise History of the Vietnam War: 1965–1968, A. Ron Weber. CDa

Concise History of the World, A. Ira Sadoff. AmPA

Conclusion: "Did you love well what very soon you left?" Marilyn Hacker. NoAM *Fr.* Coda.

Conclusion: "If what began (look far and wide) will end." John Frederick Nims. PoA

Conclusion: "Image dance of change, An." Siegfried Sassoon. MoBrPo

Conclusion: "In one of those excursions (may they ne'er)." Wordsworth. OAEL-2; OBNC *Fr.* The Prelude; Growth of a Poet's Mind [1850 vers.]
   "In one of those excursions (may they ne'er)." EBEV, book 14, *ll.* 1–119
   "It was a close, warm, breezeless summer night." PoEL-4

Conclusion. Ovid, *Latin*. OBCVT, *tr.* by Arthur Golding; CTC *Fr.* Metamorphoses.
   ("Now have I brought a woork too end which neither *Joves* fierce wrath.") OBCVT, *tr.* by Arthur Golding

Conclusion. After the Manner of Horace, ad librum suum, The. Horace, *Latin*. OBCVT, *tr.* by Allan Ramsay

Conclusion I reach at the Tate, The. Limerick. "Tallis." PeLi

Conclusion of a Letter to the Rev. Mr. C——, The. Mary Barber. CABP; ECWP

Conclusion of the Matter, The. Christopher Smart. ChIV-1; KSG *Fr.* Hymns for the Amusement of Children.

Concord Cats. Richard Eberhart. PC

Concord Hymn. Ralph Waldo Emerson. AWP; AiP; AmPP; BLPA; CTV; ClHu; ColAP; FaBoA; FaBoBe; FaPoR; HAP; HeIP-4; MeMAP; NOBA; NoP-4; OBWP; OxBA; PeECV; PoPoPo; TAP; TFi
   (Hymn[:] Sung at the Completion of the Concord Monument, April 19, 1836.) APN-1; EBEvV; NAAL-1; NAAL-3

Concordat Proviso Ascendant. Christopher Dewdney.
   "She is liquid darkness occult with desire." FTOS

Concrete Cat. Dorthi Charles. InPK-6; KaS

Concubine next door, The. Girlfriend. Taeko Tomioka, *Japanese*. WPJ, *tr.* by Kenneth Rexroth *and* Ikuko Atsumi

Condemne me not for making such a coyle. Excuse for So Much Writ upon My Verses. Margaret Lucas Cavendish, Duchess of Newcastle. KTR

Condemned. Philippe Soupault, *French*. AF, *tr.* by Schmidt, Paulette

Condemned Man, The. Oscar Wilde. EBNV *Fr.* The Ballad of Reading Gaol. CABP; OBNV; OxAEP-2

Condemned [*or* Condemn'd] to hope's delusive mine. On the Death of Dr [*or* Mr] Robert Levet [a Practiser in Physic]. Samuel Johnson. ChIV-2; EBEV; InPS-3; NAEL-1; NOBE; NOEC; NoP-4; OAEL-1; OBEV; OxAEP-1; PFE; PeECV; PoE; PoEL-3; SCGP; SCV; TFi

Condemning the Moongod Nanna. Enheduanna, *ad. by* Aliki *and* Willis Barnstone, *Sumerian.* BoWoP

Condition Blue/ Dress. Ron Welburn. NBV

Condition of Desire. Harry Mathews. EOEF

Conditions. Essex Hemphill.
    XXII. NAAAL
    XXIV. NAAAL

CONDOLENCES. . . from our swollen lips laden with condolences. Elegy for Slit-Drum. Christopher Okigbo. HBAPE

Condom Tree, The. Chase Twichell. NAmP90

Condoms. Ronald Wallace. MoLi

Conduct of Kings, The. (King) Lê Thánh–tông, *Chinese.* AVP, *tr. by* Huỳnh Sanh Thông

Conduct your blooming in the noise and whip of the whirlwind. (LL) The Second Sermon on the Warpland. Gwendolyn Brooks. BPo; NOBA; PoBA

Conductor's hands were black with money, The. Charon. Louis MacNeice. FaBoTw; PNI

Confab. Kenneth Rosen. AmPA

Confederacy. Elise Paschen. FFC

Confederate Flags, The. Ambrose Bierce. CBCWP

Confederate Memorial Day. *Unknown.* CBCWP

Confederate Veteran Tries to Explain the Event, A. Robert Penn Warren. CBCWP

Conference among ourselves we called, A. George Gascoigne. OBWP *Fr.* The Fruits of War.

Conference is on Glass, in, The. Deceptively Like a Solid. Roald Hoffmann. BAP-94

Conference of the Birds, The. Farid-uddin Attar, *Persian.* TOF, *tr. by* Afkham Darbandi *and* Dick Davis
    "Dervish wept to feel the violence of, A."
    "Hallaj's corpse was burnt and when the flame."
    "In India lives a bird that is unique."

Conferences, adjournments, ultimatums. Louis MacNeice. FaBoPV; OxBTC *Fr.* Autumn Journal.

Confess We All, before the Lord. John Wilson. AH

Confessio Amantis. John Gower.
    "Among these othre of Slouthes kinde." EnVB, *sect.* IV
    Parting of Venus and Old Age, The. PoEL-1

Confessio Fidei. Dryden. NOBE *Fr.* The Hind and the Panther. (Private Judgement Condemned.)

Confession. Frank Gelett Burgess. *See* Cinq Ans Après.

Confession. Pearl Cleage. ISC

Confession, The. Peter Cooley. AmPA

Confession. George Herbert. ESCV

Confession. Ho Xuan Huong, *Vietnamese.* AVP, *tr. by* Huỳnh Sanh Thông

Confession, A. Robert Mezey. AmPA; PFE

Confession and Salute to the Fire. Lyubomir Levchev, *Bulgarian.* CEEP, *tr. by* Ewald Osers

Confession of Cleopas, The. Eric Pankey. GI

Confession of Faith. Elinor Wylie. MoAmPo

Confession Overheard in a Subway. Kenneth Fearing. LiTM

Confession Stone, The. Owen Dodson. TTY

Confession to J. Edgar Hoover. James Wright. CAPP-1; CoAmPo

Confession to Malcolm. Conyus. NBV

Confessional. Frank Bidart. GLP

Confessional, The. Nathaniel Parker Willis. APN-1

Confessional Poem. Louis Jenkins. RaBo

Confessional Poetry. Tony Harrison. DiPo

Confessions. Robert Browning. CBLP; GTBS-P; NOBE; NOBVV; PFE

Confessions of the Life Artist. Thom Gunn. CMoP

Confessors, The. Donne. *Fr.* The Litanie. PoEL-2

Confide In a Friend. *Unknown.* PoToHe

Confiding always on His excellent greatness. (LL) Johannes Milton, Senex. Robert Bridges. CMoP; PeECV; PoEL-5

Configurations. Grace Nichols. LW

Confinement. Tanka. Saitō Mokichi, *Japanese.* MJT, *tr. by* Ueda, Makoto

Confirmation, A. William Daniel Ehrhart. CDa

Confirmation, The. Edwin Muir. OxBM; OxBS

Confirmers, The. A. R. Ammons. TAP

Confiscating Salt. Wang An-shih, *Chinese.* CoBCP, *tr. by* Burton Watson

Conflict, The. C. Day Lewis. LiTM; MoBrPo; NoP-4

Conflict. Kwangnim Kim, *Korean.* CKP, *tr. by* Jaihiun Kim

Conflict of Convictions, The. Herman Melville. APN-2; CBCWP; NOBA

Confluences at San Francisco. Elton Glaser. PBCAP

Confounded Nonsense. Thomas Hood Jr. CBNP

Confounding deities, not men. (LL) Nebuchadnezzar's Kingdom-Come. David Rowbotham. ChIV-1; NOBAu

Confront the darkness in another place. (LL) The Woods. Derek Mahon. NOIV; PBCIP

Confrontation with an Artist. Elisabeth Eybers. PeSAV

Confrontations with the Devil in the Form of Love. Judy Grahn. "My name is Judith meaning." NMM-2

Confronting a longing. Poem to My Death. Julia De Burgos, *Spanish.* BoWoP, *tr. by* Grace Schulman

Confronting each other the pictures stare. The Royal Portraits. William Dean Howells. APN-2

Confronting the solitude. Song to Be Written on a Wave. José Emilio Pacheco, *Spanish.* STV, *tr. by* John Frederick Nims

Confronting the wind, late autumn trees. Drunk, Facing Crimson Leaves. Po Chü-i, *Chinese.* CoBCP, *tr. by* Burton Watson

Confucian scholars love strange antiquity. Drinking Wine. Lin Hung, *Chinese.* SuSp, *tr. by* Irving Y. Lo

Confused with my life, that is commonplace and solitary. (LL) Next Day. Randall Jarrell. HAP; HCAP; MoP; NAAL-2; NYBP; NoAM; NoP-4; Poetr; VCAP; WeW-3

Confusion. Christopher Hervey. BXAP; UV

Confusion. Nino Nikolov, *Bulgarian.* CEEP, *tr. by* Ewald Osers

Confusion of Planes We Must Wander in Sleep, The. Bruce Weigl. NAmP90

Confusion of song. On the radio. Clouded Evening, Late September. Sydney Lea. RA

Confusion's plenty lies in every way. The Farmyard. John Clare. EnVR

Congealed vapors surge in vast space. Seeing Off Editor Wang Chou-tz'u and Secretary Lin Shih-lai on Their Mission as Envoys to the Ryūkyū Islands. Wang Shih-chieng, *Chinese.* CoBLCP, *tr. by* Jonathan Chaves

Congo, The. Vachel Lindsay. CMoP; MeMAP; MoAmPo; NOBA; OxBA; PoRA; TAP

'Congo is myself' (Lumumba), The. U Tam'si Tchicaya. PBMAP *Fr.* Le Ventre (1964).

Congratulating a Friend On His New Dentures. Tô Giang T(stilde;u)', *Vietnamese.* AVP, *tr. by* Huỳnh Sanh Thông

Congregation was scandalised, The. Robert Sat. Tom Matthews. PNI

Congressman Visits the Grade School, The. James B. Hathaway. IFJA

Congressmen came out to see Bull Run, The. Stephen Vincent Benét. CBCWP *Fr.* John Brown's Body.

Congruence of the complement is vain, if it exists, The. (LL) To a Steam Roller. Marianne Moore. BoWoP; CMoP; FaBoMo; MeMAP; MoAmPo; OxBA; PoPoPo; VGW

Coniagui women, The. Audre Lorde. NAAL-2; NALW

Conies had their hiding-place, The. He "Had Not Where to Lay His Head." Frances Ellen Watkins Harper. PWR

Conjergal rights! conjergal rights! Thomas Edward Brown. PeVV *Fr.* In the Coach.

Conjugal. Russell Edson. PmAP

Conjugal Visits. Al Young. NAAAL

Conjugation of the Paramecium, The. Muriel Rukeyser. NMM-2

Conjunction. Robert Graves. LoP

Conjunction. Semyon Izrailevich Lipkin, *Russian.* TCRP, *tr. by* Albert C. Todd

Conjunction of Jupiter and Venus, The. William Cullen Bryant. APN-1

Conjunctions. Eamon Grennan. PBCIP

Conjuration, to Electra, A. Robert Herrick. GBL; PoEL-3

Conjured. Sterling Brown. NoP-4

Conjuring Against Alien Spirits. Quincy Troupe. ISC

Conjuring Roethke. James Tate. OBAL

Conkers. Barrie Wade. AYFP

Connais-Tu le Pays? Richard Shelton. NYBP

Connecticut. Fitz-Greene Halleck.
    "They burnt their last witch in CONNECTICUT." APN-1

Connie Deanovich. Connie Deanovich. WWSi

Connivingly my dreaming-book. Edgar Allan Poe. *See* Introduction: "Romance, who loves to nod and sing."

Connoisseur of Chaos. Wallace Stevens. LiTM; PFTM

Connoisseur of pearl, A. African China. Melvin Beaunearus Tolson. ColAP; PoBA

Connoisseurs of coition aver. Limerick. *Unknown.* PeLi

Connoisseuse of Slugs, The. Sharon Olds. APAD; DeD; LW

"Conquer the gloomy night of thy sorrow." Defiance. Solomon ibn Gabirol, *Hebrew.* TrJP, *tr. by* Emma Lazarus

Conquered the flower-maidens, and the wide embrace. Parsifal Imitated from the French of Paul Verlaine. John Gray. ADE

Conqueror of a Forbidden Landscape. Amryl Johnson. NBrP

Conqueror Worm, The. Edgar Allan Poe. APN-1; AWP; ImPo; MeMAP; NCAP; NOBA

Conquerors, The. Phyllis McGinley. PBMP

Conquerors. Henry Treece. OBWVE

Conquest [or His Lady's Might]. Philippe Desportes. AWP

Conquest, The. Oliver St. John Gogarty. OBMV

Conquest. Pauli Murray. GT

Conquest of Granada, The. Dryden.
    Song of the Zambra Dance. PoEL-3

Conquistador. Archibald MacLeish.
    Prologue: "And the way goes on in the worn earth." NoAM

Conrad, Conrad, aren't you old. Conrad in Twilight. John Crowe Ransom. FuPo; MeMAP; OxBA *Fr.* Sixteen Poems in Eight Pairings.

Conrad in Twilight. John Crowe Ransom. FuPo; MeMAP; OxBA *Fr.* Sixteen Poems in Eight Pairings.
    ("By the summer's flare and winter's flaw.") (LL) FuPo

Consanguinity of sound, The. (LL) First know, my friend, I do not mean. Matthew Green. ECEV; NOEC

Conscience. George Herbert. ESCV

Conscience. Charles William Stubbs. BLPA

Conscientious Objector. Edward Davison. NSI

Conscientious Objector. Edna St. Vincent Millay. WPOW

Conscientious Objector, The. Karl Shapiro. OxBA

Conscious. Wilfred Owen. NSI; PoWW

Conscript, The. Wilfrid Wilson Gibson. PoFWW

Consecration, A. John Masefield. MoBrPo

Consejos y Documentos al Rey Dom Pedro. Santob de Carrion, *Spanish.* Jewish Poet Counsels a King, A. TrJP

Consents to his inexorable will. (LL) Playboy. Richard Wilbur. MoP; NOBA; NoAM; SAGP

Consequences. William Meredith.
    My Acts. VCAP
    Of Choice. VCAP
    Of Love. VCAP

Consequences of Waking, The. Vickie Karp. WWSi

Consequently the tongue is a chair. (LL) The Domestic Stones (fragment). Hans Arp, *French.* CBNP; SPE, *tr. by* David Gascoyne

Conservation. Horace, *Latin.* GaP, *tr. by* James Michie

Conservatrix of Milesien. Ezra Pound. *Fr.* Hugh Selwyn Mauberley. (Life and Contacts). AmPP; CMoP; InPS-3; LiTM; NOBA; NoAM; TAP

Conserves. David Mus. PoA *Fr.* The Joy of Cooking.

Conserving the Magnitude of Uselessness. A. R. Ammons. NoAM

Consider a coral or guano atoll. Manichean Geography I. Tom Paulin. PNI

Consider a new habit—classical. Arras. Patricia K. Page. MoCV

Consider Famous Men, Dai Bach. Idris Davies. OBWVE

Consider for a moment how the body of a dancer. Female Dancer. James Camp. Son

Consider Icarus, pasting those sticky wings on. To a Friend Whose Work Has Come to Triumph. Anne Sexton. InPK-6; PFE

Consider, O my soul, what morn is this! A Meditation for Christmas. Selwyn Image. OBEV

Consider, praise, remember all of these. All of These. Denis Glover. PeNZ

Consider the case of the many-minded men. Friday Evening. Sean Lucy. CIP-2

Consider the egg. It's a miracle. Eggomania. Felicia Lamport. NBLV

Consider the Emperor Nero. Limerick. *Unknown.* PeLi

Consider the lowering Lynx. Limerick. Langford Reed. PeLi

Consider the mysterious salt. In Time Like Air. May Sarton. NYBP

Consider the sea's insatiate lust. The Island. Brendan Kennelly. PBCIP

Consider the sea's listless chime. The Sea-Limits. D. G. Rossetti. EnVR; NAEL-2; OAEL-2 *Fr.* The House of Life.

Consider the significance. Wire. Rod Moran. NOBAu

Consider the three functions of the tongue. Canzone. Marilyn Hacker. NoAM

Consider them both in paradise. W. H. Auden & Mantan Moreland. Al Young. LTA

Consider These, for We Have Condemned Them. C. Day Lewis. ImPo; LiTM

Consider this and in our time. W. H. Auden. FaBoMo; OxAEP-2

Consider this small dust, here in the glass. The Hour Glass. Ben Jonson. GLoP; ImPo

Considerable Speck, A. Robert Frost. MoAmPo; OBAL; PBMP; SAmP

Considerate Crocodile, The. Amos Russell Wells. OBCA

Consideration for Others. Christopher Smart. *See* Mutual Subjection.

Considerations. David Helwig. NOBC

Consideratus Considerandus. John Saffin. SCAP

Considered Reply to a Child, A. Jonathan Price. BoLoP

Considering How Exaggerated Music Is. Leslie Scalapino. FTOS

Considering how to run. (LL) Centipede was happy quite, A. *Unknown.* CTV; OBSP

Considering the Snail. Thom Gunn. LiTM; NAEL-2; TwCP

Consign to thee and come to dust. Shakespeare. *See* Song: "Fear no more the heat o' the Sun."

Consistent disciples of Marx. Limerick. A. Cinna. PeLi

Consolation. Arthur Guiterman. BXAP

Consolation. Milton. LBC *Fr.* Samson Agonistes. FHYEP; OAEL-1; PoEL-3

Consolation. Henry Howard, Earl of Surrey. AAS; EBEV; EnLoPo; NOBE; SiPS

Consolation. Dimitris Tsaloumas. BMAP

Consolation. W. B. Yeats. OxBSP

Consolation, The. Edward Young. NOEC *Fr.* Night Thoughts.

Consolation Aria. Johann Christian Günther, *German.* GePo, *tr. by* George C. Schoolfield

Consolation in War. Lewis Mumford. NYBP

Consolation of Philosophy, The. Boethius, *Latin.*
    "None from thy laws are free." OBCVT, *tr. by* J. T. [Michael Walpole]

Consolation of Philosophy, The ("De Consolacione Philosophie"). Boethius, *Latin to* Middle English.
    "Alas, the ignorance of unhappy men." MLL, *tr. by* Helen Waddell
    "All human kind on earth." NoSic, *tr. by* Queen Elizabeth I
    Book III. Metre 6. OBCVT, *tr. by* Johnson, Samuel and Hester Thrale [later Piozzi]
    "Happy he whose eyes have view'd." OBVE, *tr. by* Samuel Johnson
    "Happy, too happy was the world." MLL, *tr. by* Helen Waddell
    Happy Too Much. CTC, *tr. by* Queen of England Elizabeth I
    "He that hath set his headlong heart." MLL, *tr. by* Helen Waddell
    "He who has made his reckoning with life." MLL, *tr. by* Helen Waddell
    "Heu Quam Praecipih Mersa Profundo." MLL, *tr. by* Helen Waddell
    Heu Quam Precipiti. OBMV, *tr. by* John Walton
    "Hither, O captives, hither let you come." MLL, *tr. by* Helen Waddell
    Huc omnes pariter. OBMV, *tr. by* John Walton
    Lib. 2. Metrum 5. OBCVT, *tr. by* Henry Vaughan
    New Year's Eve. MLL, *tr. by* Helen Waddell
    "O Father, give the spirit power to climb." MLL, *tr. by* Helen Waddell
    "O Maker of the starry world." MLL, *tr. by* Helen Waddell
    "O thou whose pow'r o'er moving worlds presides." OBVE, *tr. by* Samuel Johnson
    "O Thou whose reason guides the universe." MLL, *tr. by* Helen Waddell
    "Songs I wrote when I was young and ardent, The." MLL, *tr. by* Helen Waddell
    "Stars hidden by dark clouds." MLL, *tr. by* Helen Waddell
    "Then night was shaken from me." MLL, *tr. by* Helen Waddell
    "There is no race of men." MLL, *tr. by* Helen Waddell
    "This bird was happy once in the high trees." MLL, *tr. by* Helen Waddell
    "This concord tempers then the elements." MLL, *tr. by* Helen Waddell
    "Though countless as the Grains of Sand." OBVE, *tr. by* Samuel Johnson
    "What pleasure in such vehement commotion." MLL, *tr. by* Helen Waddell
    "Who thought in high midsummer." MLL, *tr. by* Helen Waddell

Consolation to Empty Pitchers. K. S. Narasimhaswami, *Kannada.* OMIP, *tr. by* A. K. Ramanujan

Consolations. Paul Ramsey. *Fr.* Three Epigrams. CRP

Consolations After an Affair. James Tate. WeT

Consolations of Art. Roy Fuller. OxBC

Consolations of Philosophy. Derek Mahon. BIrV; CIP-2

Consolatory Poem Dedicated unto Mr. Cotton Mather, A. Nicholas Noyes. SCAP

Consoling the Yü Farmers. Fan Ch'eng-ta, *Chinese.* SuSp, *tr. by* Wu-chi Liu

Consoling Wu Te-cheng on the Death of His Son. Shen Chou, *Chinese.* CoBLCP, *tr. by* Jonathan Chaves

Consorting with Angels. Anne Sexton. NALW; NMM-2

Conspiracy. Claire Bateman. CrSp

Conspiracy. Jack Spicer. APSN

Conspiracy's to make us thin, The. Size three's. Used. Rita Dove. NAmP90

Conspirators, The. Frederic Prokosch. LiTM

Constable Calls, A. Seamus Heaney. FaBoPV; NOIV *Fr.* Singing School.

Constancy. "Michael Field." CPO; VWP

Constancy[e]. Sidney Godolphin. BeJo; NOSC

Constancy. John Wilmot, 2d Earl of Rochester. OBEV

Constancy Rewarded. Coventry Patmore. OxBSP *Fr.* The Angel in the House.

Constancy to an Ideal Object. Coleridge. NAEL-2; NOBRP

Constant, The. A. R. Ammons. HAP; WeW-3

Constant Bridegrooms, The. Kenneth Patchen. LiTM

Constant Cannibal Maiden, The. Wallace Irwin. OBAL

Constant keeping past of shaken trees, A. London to Folkestone. D. G. Rossetti. EnVR

Constant keeping-past of shaken trees. D. G. Rossetti. PeVV, *pt. I Fr.* A Trip to Paris and Belgium.

("Constant keeping past of shaken trees.") EnVR

Constant Labor, A. James W. Thompson. BPo

Constant Lover, The. Louis Simpson. NYBP

Constant Lover, A [*or* The]. Sir John Suckling. CBLP; ImPo; NOSC; OxAEP-1; PBMP *Fr.* A Poem with the Answer.

(Constant Lover, The.) GLoP; SAGP

("Out upon it.") GLoP; NoP-4; SAGP

(Sir S.J.)

Constant Mouse, The. *Unknown, Vietnamese.* AVP, tr. by Huỳnh Sanh Thông

Constant North, The. J. F. Hendry. OxBS

Constant Penelope sends to thee, careless Ulysses. Ovid, *Latin.* EnLoPo; GBL; NAEL-1; NoSic; OAEL-1

Constant starburst showers us, A. Ivar Grunthal, *Estonian.* CEEP, tr. by Ivar Ivask

Constant to none, but ever false to me. An Elegye. Thomas Campion. AAS *Fr.* Observations in the Art of English Poesie.

Constantine's Vision of the Cross. Cynewulf. *Fr.* Elene. AnOE, tr. by Charles W. Kennedy

Constantinople (New Rome). *Unknown, Greek.* GrAn, tr. by Peter Jay

Constantly near you, I never in my entire. The Horse Show. William Carlos Williams. CMoP; FiLi; NOBA; TAP; VGW

Constantly present and lovely. (LL) Before there was a trace of this world of men. Bibi Hayati, *Persian.* EnlH; WPoS, tr. by Jane Hirshfield

Constantly risking absurdity. Lawrence Ferlinghetti. LiTM; NeAP; PmAP; PoM; Poetr; SAGP; TAP

Constellation like day; the horizon behind it by lights, A. Nocturnal Landscape. Anton Schnack, *German.* PeFWW, tr. by Christopher Middleton

Constellation of Dead Brothers. Victor Serge, *Russian.* AF, tr. by James Brook

Constellation Quilt, The. Mei-Mei Berssenbrugge. OpBo

Constellations, The. William Cullen Bryant. APN-1

Constitution and the *Guerriére*, The. *Unknown.* AmFP

Constructed Space, The. W. S. Graham. PoA

Consulting summer's clock. Emily Dickinson. SAmP

Consumer's Report, A. Peter Porter. NOBL; NTP; NoP-4

Consummation. Musaeus, *Greek.* OBCVT, tr. by Unknown

Consumptive, The. Priscilla Jane Thompson. CBWP-2

Contact. John F. Deane. TIRV

Contagion. James Tate. CMAP

Container, The. Cid Corman. VGW

"Containing Communism." Charlie Cobb. PoBA

Contemplate all this work of Time. Tennyson. EBVV; EnVR; OAEL-2 *Fr.* In Memoriam A. H. H.

Contemplation. John Frederick Nims. InPK-6

Contemplation. Francis Thompson.

"From stones and poets you may know." APAD

"Nature one hour appears a thing unsexed." OBNC

Contemplation, a furtive act, A. The Third Kind of Interior Word. Albert Mobilio. PT

Contemplation of Our State in Our Deathbed. Donne. *Fr.* The Second Anniversary [*or* Anniversarie]. ESCV; SeCP *Fr.* Of the Progres[se] of the Soule, the Second Anniversarie.

Contemplation of the Heavens. Bill Manhire. PeNZ

Contemplation upon Flowers, A. Henry, Bishop of Chichester King. MeLP; OBEV; SCGP; SeCP

Contemplations. Anne Bradstreet. ColAP *Fr.* Contemplations. AmPP; NAAL-3; PoEL-3; SCAP; WPE

("Some time now past in the autumnal tide.") ColAP

Contemplations. ColAP

("Some time now past in the autumnal tide.") ColAP

"I wist not what to wish, yet sure thought I." PBWP

"Mariner that on smooth waves doth glide, The." WPOW

"Shall I then praise the heavens, the trees, the earth." NOSC; PBWP

"Silent alone, where none or saw, or heard." PBWP

"So he that saileth in this world of pleasure." WPOW

"When I behold the heavens as in their prime." PBWP

Contemplations of Mary. Roy McFadden. PNI

Contemporania. Ezra Pound.

Tenzone. MeMAP; PoA

Contemporaries all surpassed, see one. William Cowper. EPCY *Fr.* Table Talk.

Contemporary. Hortense King Flexner. PoA

Contemporary Criticism, A. William Wetmore Story.

"He thanked me for my kindness, disagreed." APN-1

Contemporary Culture and the Letter "K." Alfred Corn. NoP-4

Contemporary Muse, The. Edgell Rickword. OBSV

Contempt. Rodney Jones. BAP-94

Contempt of Poetry, The. Edmund Spenser. *See* October.

Contemptuous of his home beyond. A Frog's Fate. Christina Rossetti. NOBVV

Contend in a sea which the land partly encloses. The Yachts. William Carlos Williams. AmPP; CMoP; HeIP-4; ImPo; LiTM; MeMAP; MoAmPo; MoP; NOBA; NoAM; NoP-4; OxBA; PoE; SAmP; TFi

Content. Barnabe Barnes. *Fr.* Parthenophil and Parthenophe.

Content. Stephen Crane. *Fr.* The Black Riders [and Other Lines].

Content and Resolute. William Drummond of Hawthornden. PBRV

Content and Ri[t]ch[e]. Robert Southwell. ChIV-2; NoSic

"I wrastle not with rage."

Content, content! within a quiet room. Dora Greenwell. PoToHe

Content thee, greedy heart. The Size. George Herbert. GeHe

Content though blind, had I no better guide. (LL) To Mr. Cyriack Skinner upon His Blindness. Milton. NOSC; OxAEP-1; PeECV; Son

Content to bid the War aloof in Peace? Homer. *See* The Goddess intervenes between Achilles and Agamemnon.

Contendeder—to die. (LL) My Portion is Defeat—today. Emily Dickinson. APN-2; OBWP

Contention between Four Maids Concerning That Which Addeth Most Perfection to That Sex. Sir John Davies. SiPS

Contention betwixt a Wife, a Widow, and a Maid, A. Sir John Davies. SiPS

Contention of Ajax and Ulysses, The. James Shirley.

Death the Leveller. FaPoR; GTBS-P; ImPo; NOBE; OBEV; PBMP; UnPo

(Dirge.) AWP; GEA; NoP-4; OAEL-1; PoEL-2

Contentment. Charles Stuart Calverley. NOBVV

Contentment. Nathaniel Cotton. OxBChV

Contentment. William Cowper. ChIV-2 *Fr.* Olney Hymns.

Contentment. Oliver Wendell Holmes. APN-1; AmPP; OxBA; PWR *Fr.* The Autocrat of the Breakfast Table.

Contentment. Sir Philip Sidney. *See* Get Hence Foule Griefe.

Contentment is a sleepy thing. Thomas Traherne. NOCV *Fr.* Christian Ethics.

("For man to act as if his soul did see.") NOCV

Contents of an Ink-bottle, The. Mary Elizabeth Coleridge. VWP

Contest Snake, The. Cheng Hsieh, *Chinese.* CoBLCP, tr. by Jonathan Chaves

Continental Divide, The. Maria Flook. WeT

Continent's End. Robinson Jeffers. AWP

Continual Conversation with a Silent Man. Wallace Stevens. LiTM

Continually they cackle thus. Sir Osbert Sitwell. PoWW *Fr.* How Shall We Rise to Greet the Dawn?

Continuation of a Long Poem of These States. Allen Ginsberg.

S.F. Southward. NAAL-2

Continuation of Life. Boris Petrovich Kornilov, *Russian.* TCRP, tr. by Bernard Meares

Continuation of *The Cook's Tale*, The. William Zaranka. BXAP

Continued. Matthew Arnold. Son

Continuity. "Æ." MoBrPo

Continuity, The. Paul Blackburn. NeAP

Continuity. Stella Gibbons. WPN

Continuous Thunder. Aaron Shurin. PT

Continuous Time. Milo De Angelis, *Italian.* NeIt, tr. by Lawrence Venuti

Contours. Noël Coward. UV

Contra Mortem. Hayden Carruth. PoA

Being, The. PoA

Contraband. Denise Levertov. BLT

Contraception,—that's the bizarre, proper slang. The Crystal Palace. John Davidson. PeVV

Contract. (For The Destruction and Rebuilding of Paterson), A. Imamu Amiri Baraka. FTOS

Contradictions: Tracking Poems. Adrienne Rich.

"My mouth hovers across your breasts." LW

Contrary Theses (I). Wallace Stevens. OxBA; SAmP

Contrary to popular belief, the lowest circle of hell is not. Pan Cogito's Thoughts on Hell. Zbigniew Herbert, *Polish.* FaBoPV, *tr.* by Adam Czerniawski

Contrary to / tales you told us. Anti-Father. Rita Dove. IFJA

Contrast, A. James Russell Lowell. NCAP

Contrast, A. Menella Bute Smedley. VWP

Contrast, The. Royall Tyler.
"Father and I went to camp." NAAL-3
"Marblehead's a rocky place." NAAL-3
Prologue: "Exult each patriot heart!—this night is shewn." NAAL-3
Song: "Sun sets in night, and the stars shun the day, The." NAAL-3

Contrasts. Đặng Thái Thuyên, *Vietnamese.* AVP, *tr.* by Huỳnh Sanh Thông

Contre Jour. Elizabeth Bartlett. FaBoWP

Contretemps, The. Thomas Hardy. CMoP; LiTM

Contribution on Pornography, A. Wislawa Szymborska, *Polish.* PoSu, *tr.* by Adam Czerniawski

Contrite Heart, The. William Cowper. *Fr.* Olney Hymns.

Contrition. Ralph Knevet. ChIV-2

Contrition. Henry More. NOSC *Fr.* Psychozoia, or, the Life of the Soul.

Controlled woolgathering is my work too. (LL) Sheepdog Trials in Hyde Park. C. Day Lewis. MoP; NoAM; OxBTC

Conundrum of the Workshops, The. Rudyard Kipling. MoBrPo

Convalescence. Noël Coward. TTTS

Convalescence. James Philip McAuley. CBAP

Convalescence. Lynne McMahon. NAmP90

Convalescing in London. Thomas M. Disch. RA

Convent in '45, The. Maria Luisa Spaziani, *Italian.* Nelt, *tr.* by Beverly Allen

Convent of Pleasure, The. Margaret Lucas Cavendish, Duchess of Newcastle.
Song: "My cabinets are oyster-shells." WPE
(Sea-Goddess, The.) OxBoS

Convent Threshold, The. Christina Rossetti. NALW; NoP-4; VWP
"I tell you what I dreamed last night." PeVV

Conventionalist, The. Stevie Smith. LiLi

Convergence of the Twain, The. Thomas Hardy. CABP; FaBoTw; HeIP-4; InPK-6; InPS-3; LiTM; MoBrPo; MoP; NAEL-2; NIP-4; NoAM; NoP-4; OAEL-2; OxBTC; PBMP; PFE; PeVV; PoPoPo; Poetr; SCGP; TFi

Conversation. John Berryman. LiTM

Conversation. Buson, *Japanese.* NTCP

Conversation. Rose Fyleman. BoTP

Conversation. Dan Pagis, *Hebrew.* VCWP, *tr.* by Stephen Mitchell

Conversation, A. Gisèle Prassinos, *French.* PFTM, *tr.* by Pierre Joris

Conversation at Midnight. "Adelina Efimovna Adalis," *Russian.* TCRP, *tr.* by Bernard Meares

Conversation between the Chevalier de Chamilly and Mariana Alcoforado in the Manner of a Song of Regret. *Unknown, Portuguese.* BoWoP, *tr.* by Helen R. Lane

Conversation brings us so close! Opening. Looking into a Face. Robert Bly. NOBA

Conversation goodnightthankyou. (LL) A Word in Edgeways. Charles Tomlinson. CABP; NOBL

Conversation in Front of a Helicopter. Rosario Murillo, *Spanish.* CLPP, *tr.* by Alejandro Murguía

Conversation in Gibraltar 1943. Charles Causley. PoWW

Conversation in the Bush. Arthur Rex Dugard Fairburn. PeNZ *Fr.* Album Leaves.

Conversation in the Drawingroom, The. Weldon Kees. SPE

Conversation of a Private and the Virgin. Nikolai Ivanovich Glazkov, *Russian.* TCRP, *tr.* by Daniel Weissbort

Conversation of Prayer, The. Dylan Thomas. EBEV; GTBS-P; OxAEP-2

Conversation of prayers about to be said, The. Dylan Thomas. NoP-4

Conversation Overheard. Quincy Troupe. NAAAL

Conversation Through the Door, A. Anna Swirszczynska, *Polish.* AF, *tr.* by Czeslaw Milosz

Conversation with a Fireman from Brooklyn. Tess Gallagher. CrSp
("Love you.") (LL) IFJA

Conversation with a Neighbor. Olga Fiodorovna Berggolts, *Russian.* TCRP, *tr.* by Daniel Weissbort

Conversation with cancer, The. Death Who. Philip Hodgins. BMAP

Conversations are simple: about food, The. Under the Window: Ouro Prêto. Elizabeth Bishop. NYBP; VCAP

Conversations in Courtship. *Unknown, Egyptian.*
"Darling, you only, there is no duplicate." CTC, *tr.* by Ezra Pound

Conversations in Crisis. Audre Lorde. Poetr

Conversations in Mayan. Alonzo Gonzales Mó, *Mayan.* STP, *tr.* by Allan F. Burns

Conversations in the Mountains. Li Po, *Chinese.* RaBo; TAL, *tr.* by Robert Payne

Conversations on the Plurality of Worlds. Molly Bendall. PUP-20

Conversations with Strangers. George Buchanan. PNI

Conversion. Frances Angermayer. PoLF

Conversion. Thomas Ernest Hulme. FaBoMo; OxBSP

Conversion of S. Paul, The. George Wither. ChIV-2

Conversion of stones into bread would be a supernatural miracle, The. From "The Prolific and the Devourer." W. H. Auden. GI *Fr.* "Prolific and the Devourer," The.

Convert, The. G. K. Chesterton. ChIV-2

Convert, The. Margaret Danner. BPo

Convert Comes to the City, A. Nathan Alterman. MHP, *tr.* by Ruth Finer Mintz *Fr.* The Joy of the Poor.

Convert's but a fly, that turns about, A. Samuel Butler. FaBoEE

Convict. Edward Vincent Swart. PeSAV

Convict, The. Wordsworth. Ro

Convict Song, The. Alfred Cruickshank. PBCV

Conviction fills the body. Radio. Barrett Watten. PmAP

Conviction IV. Stevie Smith. LW

Convicts' Rum Song. *Unknown.* FaBoVe; NOBAu

Convict's Tour to Hell, A. Francis MacNamara. NOBAu

Convoy Escort. Rudyard Kipling. *Fr.* Epitaphs of the War [1914–1918]. OBWP

Convulsed at a checked impulse of the heart. (LL) Message from her set his brain aflame, A. George Meredith. EnVR; NOBVV

Convulsed, foaming immortal blood: farewell. (LL) A Professor's Song. John Berryman. HeIP-4; MoP; NAAL-2; NOBA; NoAM; OxBC

Convulsions came; and, where the field. The Apparition. Herman Melville. APN-2; NCAP

Coo-Coo. *Unknown.* AS

Cooing pigeons, nursling swallows, all quiet without a sound. Spring Day. Su Shih, *Chinese.* SuSp, *tr.* by Irving Y. Lo

Cook, The. Ray A. Young Bear. CDW

Cook admired the native courage, made. Rex Ingamells. NOBAu *Fr.* The Great South Land.

Cook became the compote's bride, The. Procurers. Novella Nikolaevna Matveyeva, *Russian.* TCRP, *tr.* by Deming Brown

Cook called McMurray, A. Ogden Nash. PeLi

Cook crows—cock-a-doodle-doo!—the east grows bright, The. On the Hall of Precious Virtue. Yang Shih-ch'i, *Chinese.* CoBLCP, *tr.* by Jonathan Chaves

Cookers, The: A Song of the Transport. Sir Alan Patrick Herbert. NSI

Cookie was hard the way only women can be hard/not street or. Tantrum Girl Responds to Death. Michelle T. Clinton. BAP-94

Cook's Tale, The. Chaucer. BXAP *Fr.* The Canterbury Tales.

Cooks who'd roast a sucking-pig. Roasted Sucking Pig. *Unknown.* BXAP

Cooky-Nut Trees, The. Albert Bigelow Paine. OBCA

Cool and certain, their oars will be lifted in dusk. "Robin Hyde." PeNZ *Fr.* The Beaches.

Cool as from underground springs and pure enough to drink. (LL) The Man-Moth. Elizabeth Bishop. CBNP; LiTM; MoAmPo; MoP; NALW; NOBA; NoAM; Poetr

Cool black night thru the redwoods. First Party at Ken Kesey's with Hell's Angels. Allen Ginsberg. PmAP; TRP

Cool breezes—I sleep by the open window. *Unknown.* CoBCP, *tr.* by Burton Watson; CoBCP, *tr.* by Burton Watson *Fr.* Tzu Yeh Songs.

Cool earth, calm heaven—smoothly waters flow. War. Đông Hồ, *Vietnamese.* AVP, *tr.* by Huỳnh Sanh Thông

Cool in its dream, I kissed the stone. The Stream Sings to the Stone. Leah Goldberg. MHP, *tr.* by Ruth Finer Mintz *Fr.* Songs of the Stream.

Cool it is, and still. Basho, *Japanese.* TAL, *tr.* by Harold G. Henderson

Cool it Mag. Margaret Are You Drug. George Starbuck. InPK-6

Cool of bamboo invades my room, The. Restless Night. Tu Fu, *Chinese.* ChiPo; CoBCP, *tr.* by Burton Watson

Cool perfume of bamboo pervades my room. Summer Night. Tu Fu, *Chinese.* TAL, *tr.* by Robert Payne

Cool red rose and a pink cut pink, A. Red Roses. Gertrude Stein. TTTS *Fr.* Tender Buttons.

Cool reek of the field. Reek of companions. (LL) Cobb Would Have Caught It. Robert Fitzgerald. HAP; TwCP

Cool Retreat, A. Sappho, *Greek.* OBCVT, *tr.* by Percy Osborn

Cool shadows blanked dead cities, falling. Falling. Bob Kaufman. PoBA

Cool small evening shrunk to a dog bark and the clank of a bucket, A. Full Moon and Little Frieda. Ted Hughes. NTP; OPOU; OxBC; OxBSP

Cool that came off sheets just off the line, The. Seamus Heaney. *Fr.* Clearances. CIP-2; PBCIP; PNI

Cool Tombs. Carl Sandburg. AmPP; CBCWP; CMoP; ColAP; HAP; HeIP-4; MoAmPo; MoP; NAAL-2; NOBA; NoAM; OxBSP; PoLF; TAP; TFi

("In the dust. . . in the cool / tombs.") (LL) CBCWP; ColAP

Cool Web, The. Robert Graves. AWP; GTBS-P; MoP; NAEL-2; NoAM; OxBTC; PoA; Poetr; SCV

Coole Park and Ballylee, 1931. W. B. Yeats. CMoP; GTBS-P; NOIV; NoAM; OBGa; OBMV

Coole Park, 1929. W. B. Yeats. CABP; IIP; OAEL-2; OBMV

Coolie Chinee, The. Septimus Winner. OBAL

Coolie Mother. David Dabydeen. HCP; NBrP

Coolie Odyssey. David Dabydeen. NBrP

Coolie Son. David Dabydeen. HCP

Coolness. John Wills. HA

Coon Can (Poor Boy). *Unknown.* AS

Coon Fire. Tom Weatherly. *Fr.* Cantos. PoBA

Coon Hunt. Thomas Rabbitt. MT

Coon Song. A. R. Ammons. MoP; NOBA

Coons, The. James Bertolino. CMAP

Cooper. James Russell Lowell. NOBA; OxBA; TAP *Fr.* A Fable for Critics. NAAL-1; NAAL-3

Cooper, whose name is with his country's woven. Red Jacket. Fitz-Greene Halleck. APN-1

Cooper's Hill. Sir John Denham. BeJo; CABP; PBRV; SeCP

Cooper's Hill. Sir John Denham. CABP

"Here have I seen the king, when great affairs." PoE

"O could I flow like thee, and make thy stream." EPCY

Thames, The. NOSC

Thames from Cooper's Hill, The.

"There Faunus and Sylvanus keep their courts."

Coora Flower, The. Gwendolyn Brooks. NoP-4

Coordinating cities gulls still gull, and, arms binged with wine, as wine. Ted Greenwald. FTOS *Fr.* Licorice Chronicles.

Cootchie, Miss Lula's servant, lies in marl Elizabeth Bishop. FaBoWP

Cop holds me up like a fish, The. Fish. Larry Levis. AmPA

Copa: The Barmaid. Virgil, *Latin.* NNPT, *tr. by* Jack Lindsay

Cope sent a letter frae Dunbar. Johnnie Cope. Adam Skirving. OxBS

Copernicus. Robert David Fitzgerald. NOBAu

Cophetua. "Hugh MacDiarmid." OxBS

Copie out onely that, and save expense. George Herbert. *See* Jordan (2)(II): "When first my lines [*or* verse] of heavenly [*or* heav'nly] joy[e]s made mention."

Coplas. Antonio Machado Ruiz, *Spanish.* AF, *tr. by* Robert Bly

Coplas about the Soul Which Suffers with Impatience to See God. Saint John of the Cross, *Spanish.*

"I live without inhabiting/ Myself." OBVE, *tr. by* Roy Campbell

Copper cobra comes out of his slit, The. The Banded Cobra. C. Louis Leipoldt, *Afrikaans.* PeSA, *tr. by* Uys Krige, Jack Cope, *and* Ruth Miller

Copperhead, The. Linda Gregg. AFr

Copter lays flat the rice stalks, The. Ceremony. Richard M. Mishler. CDa

Coptic Socks. Roy Fuller. OBCoV

Copulate in the foam. (LL) News for the Delphic Oracle. W. B. Yeats. CMoP; FaBoMo; LiTM; NoAM

Copulating Gods, The. Carolyn Kizer. Poetr

Copy of an Intercepted Despatch from His Excellency Don Strepitoso Diabolo. Thomas Moore. OBSV

Copy of Verses, A. John Wilson. SCAP

Copy [*or* copie] out only that, and save expense. (LL) Jordan. "When first my lines [*or* verse] of heavenly [*or* heav'nly] joy[e]s made mention." George Herbert. ESCV; GeHe; NAEL-1; NOSC; OAEL-1; OBWVE; SeCP

Copy-writer's Dream, The. Bruce Dawe. BMAP

Copycat, copycat / Shadow's a copycat! Robert Heidbreder. OTCP

Coquettes with doctors; hoards her breath. The Old Beauty. Phyllis McGinley. FaBoEE

Coracle Fishers, The. Robert Bloomfield. *Fr.* The Banks of Wye. OBNC

Coral and emerald shade. Almora Spring. Sumitranandan Pant, *Hindi.* OMIP, *tr. by* David Rubin

Coral and shells are heaped until it seems. The Clouds. Thomas M. Disch. RA

Coral Grove, The. James Gates Percival. APN-1; ColAP

Coral Reef, The. John Blight. NOBAu

Coral Reef, The. Laurence Lieberman. CoAP

Coralie. Frederick Goddard Tuckerman. NCAP

Corals and Shells. William Bronk. APSN

Cordate head meanders through himself, The. Pit Viper. N. Scott Momaday. CDW; HATNAP

Cordelia's / In stony / Lonesome / Ground! (LL) Stony Lonesome. Langston Hughes. NOBA; SAmP

'Cordin to de present perdicament. Subtlety. Bruce St. John. PBCV

Cordon Negro. Essex Hemphill. GLP

Cordova. Ibn Zaydun, *Arabic.* AWP, *tr. by* H. A. R. Gibb

Core of masculinity does not derive from being male, The. Jelaluddin Rumi, *Persian.* RaBo, *tr. by* Coleman Barks

Corfu appears, and then the distant blue. On the Ferry, Toward Patras. Emily Grosholz. RA

Coridon and Phillis. Robert Greene. *See* Phillis and Coridon.

Coridon's Song. John Chalkhill. NOSC

Corinna Bathes. George Chapman. *Fr.* Ovid's Banquet of Sense.

Corinna, from Athens, to Tanagra. Walter Savage Landor. OBEV *Fr.* Pericles and Aspasia.

(Corinna to Tanagra.) OBNC

Corinna In Vendome. Pierre de Ronsard, *French.* LoP, *tr. by* Alistair Elliot; BoLoP, *tr. by* Robert Mezey

Corinna, pride of Drury Lane. A Beautiful Young Nymph Going to Bed. Jonathan Swift. ECEV; NOEC

Corinna's Going A-Maying. Robert Herrick. AEP; BeJo; CABP; CaPo; HAP; InPS-3; NAEL-1; NIP-4; NOBE; NOSC; NoP-4; OAEL-1; OBEV; PBRV; PoE; PoEL-3; PoPoPo; SCGP; SeCP; TFi

Corinne at the Capitol. Felicia Dorothea Hemans. BrRo; VWP

Corinne's Last Love-Song. Lady Jane Francesca Wilde. VWP

Coriolan. T. S. Eliot. OBWP

Triumphal March.

Coriolanus. Shakespeare.

"All tongues speak of him, and the bleared sights." FaBoPV

"He that will give good words to thee, will flatter." FaBoPV

"Madam, the Lady Valeria come to visit you." OxAEP-1

"Read it not, noble lords." OxAEP-1

"Why dost not speak?" OxAEP-1

Corkby, Part Two. Jerome Rothenberg. NNaP

Cormac Mac Airt Presiding at Tara. *Unknown, Irish.* BIrV, *tr. by* Douglas Hyde

Cormorant has, The. Tails and Heads. Suzanne Knowles. RB

Cormorant in His Element, The. Amy Clampitt. InPK-6

(Cormorant in Its Element, The.) NoP-4

Cormorant still screams, The. Late. Louise Bogan. PBWP; VGW

Cormorants. John Blight. CBAP

Corn, The. Daniel David Moses. HATNAP

Corn comes up, the rain descends, The. Atsá'lei Song. *Unknown. Fr.* The Night Chant. APN-2, *tr. by* Washington Matthews

Corn-grinding Song. *Unknown, Laguna Indian.* AWP, *tr. by* Natalie Curtis

Corn has stood ripe on the stalks for months, The. The Frost in the Corn. Robert McAlmon. AiP

Corn King beckoning to his Spring Queen, The. (LL) A Girl in a Library. Randall Jarrell. NAAL-2; NOBA; NoAM

Corn-Pone-y, The. Carolyn Wells. *Fr.* A Baker's Dozen of Wild Beasts. OBCA

Corn Rigs Are Bonnie. Robert Burns. *See* Song: "It was upon a Lammas night."

Corn Song. *Unknown, Ojibwa Native American.* APN-2, *tr. by* Henry Rowe Schoolcraft

Corn-Stalk Fiddle, THe. Paul Laurence Dunbar. AAP

Corneille's Pompey. Katherine Philips.

Cornelia's Defiance. NOSC

Corner bank has lost a great window, The. High Wind at the Battery. Ralph Pomeroy. NYBP

Corner Knot, The. Robert Graves. NYBP

Corner of Thistle Street, two slack shillings jangled. Politico. Carol Ann Duffy. FaBoTC

Cornered and trapped, The. For Mack C. Parker. Pauli Murray. PoBA

Cornfields in Accra. Christine Ama Ata Aidoo. WPOW

Cornhusk bag. Talking Designs. Liz Sohappy Bahe. CDW

Cornish Emigrant's Song, The. Robert Stephen Hawker. EBVV

Cornkind. Frank O'Hara. CLPP

Cornucopia. Christopher Pearse Cranch. APN-1

Corona. Paul Celan. PoSu, *tr. by* Michael Hamburger

Coronach. Alexander Scott. FaBoTC; OxBS

Coronary Thrombosis. William Price Turner. OxBS

Coronation ceremony was in Belize this time, The. Mosquito Kingdom. Ernesto Cardenal, *Spanish.* VCWP, *tr. by* Donald D. Walsh

Coroner. Elton Glaser. PBCAP

Coroner's Jury. Leonard Alfred George Strong. OxBTC

Coronet, The. Andrew Marvell. ESCV; FHYEP; FMP; FSCP; GeHe; MeLP; NAEL-1; NOCV; NOSC; NoP-4; PBRV; PoE; SCGP; TOF

Coronet for His Mistress Philosophy, A. George Chapman.

But Dwell in Darkness. Son

Love and Philosophy.

Love Flows Not from My Liver. Son

Corporal. Ambrose Bierce. APN-2; OBAL   *Fr.* The Devil's Dictionary.

Corporal Charles Chungtu, U. S. M. C. Bryan Alec Floyd. CDa

"Corporal Green!" the orderly cried. Calling the Roll. Nathaniel Graham Shepherd. OBCA

Corporal Kevin Spina, U. S. M. C. Bryan Alec Floyd. CDa

Corporal Pym. Walter De la Mare. FaBoEE

Corporal Who Killed Archimedes, The. Miroslav Holub, *Czech.* PoSu, *tr. by* Ian *and* Jarmila Milner

Corporate Entity. Archibald MacLeish. OBAL

Corposant. Peter Redgrove. OxBTC

Corps d'Esprit. Heather McHugh. AmPA

Corpse, The. Jagannath Prasad Das, *Oriya.* OMIP, *tr. by* Jayanta Mahapatra

Corpse-bearing. Thomas Ashe. EBVV; NOBVV

Corpse in the House. Jure Kastelan, *Croatian.* CEEP, *tr. by* Peter Kastmiler

Corpse-Keeper, The. *Unknown, Catalan.* BoWoP, *tr. by* W. S. Merwin

Corpse lies smilin' underfit, The. (LL) The Dead Liebknecht. "Hugh MacDiarmid." FaBoPV; OBVE

Corpse / was wrapped like *panettone* in Italian tinfoil, The. Robert Lowell. *See* Sailing Home from Rapallo.

Corpses in the Wood. Ernst Toller, *German.* TrJP, *tr. by* E. Ellis Roberts

Corpus Christi Carol, The. *Unknown.* CH; EBEV; EnVB; HAP; MiEL; NAEL-1; NOBE; NoP-4; OAEL-1; SCV; TFi

   (Knight of the Grail, The.) OBEV

   ("Lully, lullay, lully, lullay.") (LL) NoP-4

   ("Lully, lulley, lully, lulley.") TFi

Corpus Christi Carol, The. *Unknown.* HAP

Correct but cautious, that first night, we asked. James Merrill. NoP-4   *Fr.* The Book of Ephraim.

Correct Compassion, A. James Kirkup. FaBoTw; OxBTC

Correction of proofs + desires in speed. Filippo Tommaso Marinetti. PFTM, *tr. by* Richard J. Pioli   *Fr.* Zang Tumb Tuuum.

Correggio's Cupolas at Parma. Aubrey Thomas De Vere. Son

Correlated Greatness. Francis Thompson. *See* All's Vast.

Correspondence. Henri Coulette. DiPo

Correspondence. Peter Reading. PeLV

Correspondence between Mr. Harrison in Newcastle and Mr. Sholto Peach Harrison in Hull. Stevie Smith. NBLV; OxBC

Correspondence School Instructor Says Goodbye to His Poetry Students, The. Galway Kinnell. NOBA; NoAM; NoP-4; TAP

Correspondence: / when I have sad thoughts. Lady Ise, *Japanese.* BoWoP, *tr. by* Etsuko Terasaki *and* Irma Brandeis

Correspondences. Charles Baudelaire, *French.* AWP, *tr. by* Allen Tate

Correspondences. Christopher Pearse Cranch. APN-1; PAR

Correspondences. Robert Duncan. PoM

Correspondences. Anne Stevenson.

   Love Letter, A: Ruth Arbeiter to Major Paul Maxwell. OxBM

Corridor. Federico García Lorca, *Spanish.* CBNP

Corrugated iron shack. One room, A. The Cradle. Roland Robinson. NOBAu

Corrupt Man in the French Pub, The. Brian Higgins. OxBTC

Corruption. Henry Vaughan. ESCV; GEA; GeHe; NAEL-1; NOCV; NOSC; OAEL-1; SeCP

Corruption of manners, The. Juvenal, *Latin.* OBCVT, *tr. by* John Dryden

Corrymeela. "Moira O'Neill." AWP

Corsair, The. Byron.

   Sunset over the Aegean. OBNC

Corsica. Anna Laetitia Barbauld.

   On General Paoli and the Corsican Struggle for Liberty. ECWP

Corsons Inlet. A. R. Ammons. CoAP; ColAP; MoP; NAAL-2; NOBA; NoAM; NoP-4; PoE; VCAP

Cortège. Paul Verlaine, *French.* AWP; OBVE, *tr. by* Arthur Symons

Cortège for Colette. Jean Garrigue. NYBP

Cortez's Horse. Pat Mora. UnSA

Corydon and Thyrsis. Virgil. AWP, *tr. by* Dryden   *Fr.* Eclogues.

Corydon's Farewell, on Sailing in the Late Expedition Fleet. *Unknown.* NOEC

Cosmetics do no good. Steve Kowit. BLT

Cosmic disaster! (LL) *Paradise Lost* as a Haiku. Stanley J. Sharpless. BXAP; OBCoV

Cosmic Eye. A. K. Redwing. VoR

Cosmic Leviathan, that monstrous fish. Cosmogony. Edgell Rickword. FaBoTw

Cosmogony. David Chapman Berry. BXAP

Cosmogony. Edgell Rickword. FaBoTw

Cosmos in London. Arthur Nortje. HBAPE; PeSAV

Cosmus hath more discoursing in his head. Sir John Davies. NoSic; PBRV   *Fr.* Epigrams.

Cost, The. Anthony Hecht. OxBC

Cost of Seriousness, The. Peter Porter. NoAM

Costa Geriatrica. Stanley J. Sharpless. PeLV

Costumes are a kind of late-colonial, The. Totalled. Peter McDonald. PNI

Cot, The. Grover Amen. NYBP

Côte d'Azur. Katherine Hoskins. NYBP

Côte de Liesse. Daryl Hine. NoP-4

Cotillion, Act II, Scene iv, Air IV. John Gay. NoP-4

Cottage, The. Jones Very. APN-1; OxBA

Cottage Behind the Railway, The. Josef Hanzlik, *German.* CEEP, *tr. by* Ewald Osers

Cottage in Grasmere Vale, A. Dorothy Wordsworth. Ro

   ("And the tall pine-trees tower above.") (LL) Ro

Cottage in the Wood, A. Russell Edson. LCAP-2

Cottage Pictures. Samuel Jackson Pratt. OBGa   *Fr.* Cottage Pictures.

Cottage Song. John Drinkwater. UV

Cottage Street, 1953. Richard Wilbur. FaBoMo; HCAP; PoPoPo

Cottager to Her Infant, (By My Sister), The. Dorothy Wordsworth, *Third and fourth stanzas by* Wordsworth. CH; NTP; OxBChV; TTTS

   (To My Niece Dorothy, a Sleepless Baby.) CABP

Cottager's Complaint, on the Intended Bill for Enclosing Sutton-Coldfield, The. John Freeth. NOEC

Cotter's Saturday Night transcribed to Robert Aiken [*or* R. A****], Esq., The. Robert Burns. FaBoBe; NOBRP; PoLF

Cotton. Harry Edmund Martinson, *Swedish.* RB, *tr. by* Robert Bly

Cotton blankets left in the cold. Liu E.   *Fr.* On the Fifteenth Day of the Eighth Month: Watching a Rainstorm from a Tower in Seoul. CoBLCP, *tr. by* Jonathan Chaves

Cotton Boll, The. Henry Timrod. APN-2; AmPP

Cotton Song. Jean Toomer. BPo

Cottonmouth Country. Louise Glück. CoAP

Cottonwood, willow, and briar. Leaves like Fish. Gladys Cardiff. CDW

Couch Fantasy. Adrian C. Louis. NAmP90

Cough, a creaking stair, A. (LL) Still Life. Reed Whittemore. CoAP; CoAmPo

Coughed up those shirts and flagged the train. (LL) The Goat. *Unknown.* CTAV; PoLF

Could be anything. A is unknown, A. Thomas M. Disch. *See* Zewhyexary.

Could Beatrice have written like Dante. Epigram. "Anna Akhmatova," *Russian.* TCRP, *tr. by* Stanley Kunitz *with* Max Hayward

Could build so strong in a weak heart. (LL) The Church-Floor[e]. George Herbert. EBEV; ESCV; MeLP; NOSC; OAEL-1; PeECV

Could but compose man's image and his cry. (LL) The Sorrow of Love ("The Brawling of a sparrow in the eaves"). W. B. Yeats. NAEL-2; OAEL-2; PeVV

Could die out there. You / could live forever. (LL) Instructions to the Double. Tess Gallagher. FaBoWP; NMM-2

Could fathom to this pond's black bed. (LL) The Midnight Skaters. Edmund Blunden. FaBoTw; GTBS-P; MoBrPo; NOBE; PeFWW

Could I but become a crimson rose. *Unknown, Greek.* GrAn, *tr. by* W. G. Shepherd

Could I but live again. Pisgah-Sights. II. Robert Browning. ChIV-1

Could I not ride indefinite. Emily Dickinson. SAmP

Could I Say I Touched You. Harold Littlebird. VoR

Could I take me to some cavern for mine hiding. O for the Wings of a Dove. Euripides. AWP, *tr. by* Gilbert Murray   *Fr.* Hippolytus.

Could it be, Bud. For Bud. Michael S. Harper. MoNo; PoE

Could it be Madness—this? (LL) First Day's Night had come, The. Emily Dickinson. ImPo; LiTM; NCAP; OxBA; PoE; TRP; WPOW

Could man be drunk for ever. A. E. Housman. LiTM; NAEL-2; OBMV

Could mortal lip divine. Emily Dickinson. RB

Could not once blinding me, cruel[l], suffice? Samson to His De [*or* a] lilah. Richard Crashaw. ChIV-1

Could not say no—I am in trouble now! An Unwed Mother. Ho Xuan Huong, *Vietnamese.* AVP, *tr. by* Huỳnh Sanh Thông

Could our first father, at his toilsome plough. Adam Posed. Anne Finch, Countess of Winchilsea. ChIV-1; ECWP

Could we be so now! (LL) Even So. D. G. Rossetti. NOBE; NOBVV; OBNC

Could ye come back to me, Douglas, Douglas. Douglas, Douglas, Tender and True. Dinah Maria Mulock Craik. BLPA

Could you bid an acorn. Lover's Reply to Good Advice. Richard Hughes. MoBrPo

Could you come back to me, Douglas, Douglas. Dinah Maria Mulock Craik. *See* Douglas, Douglas, Tender and True.

Could you register birds. Holocaust. Myra Sklarew. CRP

Could you, so arrantly of earth, so cool. Animal. Max Eastman. FYAP

Couldn't put Humpty Dumpty together again. (LL) Humpty Dumpty sat on a wall. Mother Goose. FaBoBe; LB; OxBoLi; OxNR; ReMoGo

Could'st thou (O Earth) live thus obscure, and now. George Alsop. SCAP

Councell Given to Master Bartholmew Withipoll. George Gascoigne. AAS

Council of Satan, The. Milton. PoEL-3 *Fr.* Book I. FHYEP; NAEL-1; OAEL-1; OxAEP-1 *Fr.* Paradise Lost.

COUNCIL ON THE POWDER, THE. John Gneisenau Neihardt. PaTW *Fr.* The Song of the Indian Wars.

Council Pool's chockablock, The. Debbie and Co. John Tranter. BMAP

Councils. Marge Piercy. CrSp

Counsel. Roy Campbell. LBC

Counsel of Moderation, A. Francis Thompson. MoBrPo

Counsel to Girls. Robert Herrick. *See* To [the] Virgins, to Make Much of Time.

Counsel to Unreason. Léonie Adams. PoA

Counsels of Sigrdrifa. *Unknown.* AWP *Fr.* The Elder Edda.
(Part of the Lay of Sigrdrifa.) OBVE

Count Carrots. Gerda Mayer. OBSP

Count each affliction, whether light or grave. Sorrow. Aubrey Thomas De Vere. BLPA

Count, if you can, every leaf on every tree. Anacreon, *Greek.* InMo, *tr. by* Sam Hamill

Count of Senlis at His Toilet, The. John Byrne Leicester Warren, 3d Baron De Tabley. PeVV

Count on dead fingers of time the years that pass. Poem for Garcia Lorca. George Woodcock. NOBC

Count Ten. Bonaro W. Overstreet. PoToHe

Count the mirrors, count the walled-in windows. Roll Call of Mirrors. Ivan V. Lalic, *Serbo-Croatian.* HSix, *tr. by* Charles Simic

Count the number of times boards crack. Insomnia. Wyatt Prunty. RA

Count the transmutations of solar years. Solar Years. David Rokeah, *Hebrew.* MHP, *tr. by* Ruth Finer Mintz

Count them. The Onus of Mercy. Yehuda Amichai, *Hebrew.* IP, *tr. by* Warren Bargad *and* Stanley F. Chyet

Count up those books whose pages you have read. Indolence. Vernon Watkins. FaBoTw

Count wandered all night through the woods, The. Orlando's Madness. Ludovico Ariosto. ItIP *Fr.* Canto XXIII.

Count Your Blessings. Mrs. Henry Linden. CBWP-4

Countdown   takeoff. To the Moon and Back. William Plomer. OBCoV

Counter-Attack. Siegfried Sassoon. MoBrPo; OxAEP-2; PeFWW; PoFWW; PoWW
("Bleeding to death. The counterattack had failed.") (LL) SAGP
(Counterattack.) SAGP

Counter-Example, The. David Shapiro. PmAP

Counter Play. Ion Barbu, *Romanian.* CEEP, *tr. by* Thomas Amherst Perry *and* George Preda

Counter-Revolution. W. H. Oliver. PeNZ

Counterattack. Siegfried Sassoon. *See* Counter-Attack.

Counterblast against Garlic, A. Horace. NBLV, *tr. by* Roswell Martin Field *Fr.* Epodes.

Counterfable of Orpheus. Marie-Claire Bancquart, *French.* MFP, *tr. by* Martin Sorrell

Counterfeiter, The. Michael Davitt, *Irish.* PBCIP, *tr. by* Philip Casey

Counterfeiter, The. Greg Williamson. RA

Counterlove, A. *Unknown.* NoSic

Counterpart, The. Elizabeth Jennings. LiTM; TOF

Counterparts. Stephen Dobyns. PoA

Counterparts. Octavio Paz, *Spanish.* EP, *tr. by* Eliot Weinberger

Counterpoint, A. Robert Creeley. NeAP

Countershadow, The. Philip Booth. NYBP

Countess of Anglesey lead Captive by the Rebels, at the Disforresting of Pewsam, The. Sir William Davenant. PBRV

Countess of Dufferin, The. Helen Selina Blackwood, Countess of Dufferin. OxAEP-2

Countesse of Douglas out of her boure she came, The. The Knight of Liddesdale. *Unknown.* ESPB

Countesse of Pembrokes Arcadia, The. Sir Philip Sidney.
"Such maner time there was (what time I n'ot)." PBRV
"Then do I thinke in deed, that better it is to be private." PBRV

Counting. Peter Everwine. IMW

Counting-out Rhyme. Eve Merriam. KaS

Counting-out Rhyme. Edna St. Vincent Millay. InPK-6; NOxBChV; Poetr; SoSe-8; TTTS

Counting-out Rhyme, A. *Unknown.* ReMoGo

Counting-out Rhymes. *Unknown.*

"Eenie, meenie, minie, mo / Catch a thief by the toe." ImGa; OxNR

"Hinty, minty, cuty, corn." ImGa

"One-ery, Ore-ery, Ickery, Ann." ImGa

"One potato, two potato." ImGa

"Out goes the rat." ImGa

Counting Sheep. Russell Edson. LCAP-2

Counting Small-Boned Bodies. Robert Bly. CDa; SPE

Counting the Beats. Robert Graves. GBL; GTBS-P; HAP; OxAEP-2; OxBTC; WeW-3

Counting the Children. Dana Gioia. RA

Counting the eyes that see. (LL) The Message on Cape Cod. Michael S. Weaver. GT; PBCAP

Counting the Mad. Donald Justice. CoAmPo; NIP-4; NoP-4; TRP; UnPo

Counting the singles carefully. (LL) After Midnight. Louis Simpson. BLT; NoAM

Counting the Stars. Tongju Yun, *Korean.* CKP, *tr. by* Jaihiun Kim

Countless forests we pass hour after hour, The. Travelling Alone. Robin Fulton. FaBoTC

Countless great lords and statesmen of past regimes, The. Thoughts on T'ien-chin Bridge. Shao Yung, *Chinese.* CoBCP, *tr. by* Burton Watson

Countless things escape easily out of me. Afternoon 3. Saburoh Kuroda. SPE

Countries tears, be ye my spring, The; my hill. To the Memory of the Learned and Reverend, Mr. Jonathan Mitchell. Francis Drake. SCAP

Country and Town. Charles Morris. NOEC

Country Bedroom, The. Frances Darwin Cornford. MoBrPo

Country beneath / the earth has a green sun, The. Procedures for Underground. Margaret Atwood. NALW

Country Boy in Winter, A. Sarah Orne Jewett. APN-2; ColAP; OBCA

Country Burial. Janet Lewis. CRP

Country Burying (1919). Robert Penn Warren. LiTM

Country Child, The. Irene Thompson. BoTP

Country Clergy, The. Ronald Stuart Thomas. GTBS-P; OxBTC; PeLCV

Country Clergyman's Trip to Cambridge, The. Thomas Babington Macaulay, 1st Baron Macaulay. OBSV; OxBoLi; PeLV

Country Club Romance, A. Derek Walcott. OxBC

Country Cottage. Tu Fu, *Chinese.* OHPC, *tr. by* Kenneth Rexroth

Country Curate, The. Henry Taylor. NOEC

Country Dance. Edward Baugh. PBCV

Country Dance. Dame Edith Sitwell. MoP; NoAM

Country Dance, A. Charles Tennyson Turner. NOBVV

Country Dance. Judith Wright. BMAP; CBAP *Fr.* The Blind Man.

Country Doctor, The. Will M. Carleton. BLPA

Country Faith, The. Norman Gale. BoTP; OBEV

Country God, A. Edmund Blunden. MoBrPo

Country Gods. Cometas, *Greek.* FaBoCh, *tr. by* T. F. Higham

Country Graveyard. Charles Pressoir, *French.* NegPo, *tr. by* Edna Worthley Underwood

Country Greeting. Frank Steele. Poetsp

Country Gulliver, A. The Reports Come In. J. D. Reed. NYBP

Country? have lost our pride / as nationals no man can die for billboards / as have for freedom. Spring 61. Lenore Kandel. BB

Country House. Ch'u Ch'uang I, *Chinese.* OHMPC, *tr. by* Kenneth Rexroth

Country House, The. Louis Simpson. NOBA

Country is not named, The. Dürer's Vision. John Haines. WeT

Country Justice, The. John Langhorne.
Gypsies. NOEC
Poor, The. NOEC
Warning against the Gypsies, A. ECEV

Country kid in Mississippi I drew water, A. A Little More Traveling Music. Al Young. NBV

Country Letter. John Clare. EnVR

Country Life. Horace. AWP, *tr. by* Dryden *Fr.* Epodes.

Country Life. Chenjerai Hove. HBAPE

Country Life, A. Randall Jarrell. MoAmPo

Country Life: To His Brother, M. Tho. Herrick. Robert Herrick. CaPo; SeCP

Country Life, to the Honored Mr. Endymion Porter[, Groome of the Bed-Chamber to His Maj.], The. Robert Herrick. BeJo

Country Lovers; or, Isaac and Marget Going to Town, on a Summer's Morning, The. George Smith. NOEC

Country Man, The. George Farewell.
"Crunking crane heard high amongst the clouds, The." NOEC

Country Midwife: A Day, The. Ai. GT

Country-Mouse, The. Abraham Cowley, *after the Latin of* Horace. OBVE; SeCP

Country Mouse and the City Mouse, The. Richard Scrafton Sharpe *and* Mrs. Pearson. OxBChV

Country North of Belleville, The. Alfred Wellington Purdy. NOBC

Country Nun. Geoff Page. CBAP

Country of a Thousand Years of Peace, The. James Merrill. NoP-4

Country of Dust, The. Vahan Tekeyan, *Armenian.* AF, *tr. by* Hovanessian, Diana Der and Marzbed Margossian

Country of early October had no fruit, The. The Words of Evening. Yves Bonnefoy, *French.* VCWP, *tr. by* Richard Pevear

Country of hunchbacks!—where the strong, straight spine. Sonnet to Gath. Edna St. Vincent Millay. BoWoP; CMoP; MoAmPo

Country of No Lack. Jean Starr Untermeyer. MoAmPo

Country of the dead, The. Jared Angira. PBMAP

Country of Water. Bernice Ames. WPE

Country Parson turn'd in Years, The. Horace. OBCVT, *tr. by* William Diaper *Fr.* An Imitation of the Seventeenth Epistle of the First Book of Horace. Address'd to Dr. S[wi]ft.

Country Pathway, A. James Whitcomb Riley. CA

Country Pleasures. Martial, *Latin.* AWP, *tr. by* F. A. Wright

Country Press. Rosemary Dobson. FaBoWP; NOBAu

Country rings around with loud alarms, The. The Militia. Dryden. OBSV *Fr.* Cymon and Iphigenia. EPCY; OBNV

Country Road, The. Tế Hanh, *Vietnamese.* AVP, *tr. by* Huỳnh Sanh Thông

Country roads are yellow and brown. Street Lanterns. Mary Elizabeth Coleridge. BoTP; PoRA

Country Scene. Wu Wei-yeh, *Chinese.* CoBLCP, *tr. by* Jonathan Chaves

Country School. Ted Kooser. KaS

Country Seat, The. Sir John, of Penicuik Clerk. OBGa

Country she inhabits, where pale people, The. The Other Side. Meredith Stricker. LoHo

Country Song, A. Sir Philip Sidney. SiPS *Fr.* Arcadia.

Country Song, A. Douglas Stewart. NOBAu

Country Stars. William Meredith. AFr; VCAP

Country Store, The. *Unknown.* BLPA

Country Summer. Léonie Adams. LiTM; MoAmPo

Country Thought. Sylvia Townsend Warner. MoBrPo

Country Town, A. Philip James Bailey.
    "We live in deeds, not years; in thoughts, not breaths." PoToHe

Country Towns. Kenneth Slessor. CBAP

Country Villa. Jean Garrigue. TAP

Country Walk, The. John Dyer.
    "I am resolved, this charming day." ECEV

Country Walk, A. Thomas Kinsella. CIP-2; CMoP

Country / was back in the hands of the patriots, The. Poem. Fred Levinson. AmPA

Country Wedding, The. Thomas Hardy. UnPo

Country Wife, The. Dana Gioia. RA

Country Wisdoms. Maggie Anderson. PBCAP

Country without a Mythology, A. Douglas Le Pan. MoCV; NOBC

Country Woman Elegy. Margaret Gibson. CrSp; MT

Country Wooing. Sir John Collings Squire.
    "So lay the youth with Mary in his arms." BXAP

Countryman's Return, The. Dylan Thomas. OxBTC

Country's Crisis, The. Brian Merriman. BIrV, *tr. by* David Marcus *Fr.* The Midnight Court. NOIV, *tr. by* Thomas Kinsella

Countryside. Jane Miller. PUP-19

Counts itself lucky. Meleager, *Greek.* GrAn, *tr. by* Peter Whigham

County Ball, The. Coventry Patmore. EBVV *Fr.* The Angel in the House.

County Ball, The. Winthrop Mackworth Praed.
    County Member, The. OBNC

County of Mayo, The. Thomas Flavell, *Irish.* BIrV; IIP; OBEV, *tr. by* George Fox

Coup-clock Clicks, The. Brian Meeks. PBCV

Couple, The. Ana Blandiana, *Rumanian.* WPOW, *tr. by the author and* William M. Murray

Couple, The. Sandra Hochman. NYBP

Couple. Walter Stone. NYBP

Couple from old Aberystwyth, A. Limerick. Stuart Woods. PeLi

Couple of angels get in, A. Hotel North. Yongt'ae Kim, *Korean.* CKP, *tr. by* Jaihiun Kim

Couple of Swells, A. Irving Berlin. OBCoV

Couple Overheard, The. William Meredith. HoPM

Couple there was in Blefuscu, A. Limerick. W. F. N. Watson. PeLi

Couple Waiting, A. Matthew Sweeney. BiHa

Coupled to life. (LL) Vigil. Giuseppe Ungaretti, *Italian.* PeFWW, *tr. by* Jonathan Griffin

Couples. Kate Jennings. BMAP

Couplet: February 24, 1847. Henry Wadsworth Longfellow. APN-1

Couplets, XX. Robert Mezey. FYAP

Couplings buckled, cracked, collapsed. The Wreck of the Circus Train. Hayden Carruth. GM

Courage. "Anna Akhmatova," *Russian.* TCRP, *tr. by* Stanley Kunitz *with* Max Hayward

Courage. Matthew Arnold. OAEL-2

Courage. George Herbert. CTV

Courage. Sadi. AWP, *tr. by* Sir Edwin Arnold *Fr.* The Gulistan.

Courage, a Tale. Thom Gunn. GLP

"Courage!" he said, and pointed toward the land. The Lotus-Eaters. Tennyson. EBEvV; EBVVPR; EnVR; FHYEP; NAEL-2; NoP-4; OAEL-2; PoEL-5; SCGP

Courage my Soul, now learn to wield. A Dialogue Between The Resolved Soul and Created Pleasure. Andrew Marvell. ESCV; FSCP; GeHe; MeLP; OAEL-1; SeCP

Courage, my Soul! now to the silent wood. Peace. Bhartrihari, *Sanskrit.* AWP, *tr. by* Paul Elmer More

Courage, poor heart of stone! Tennyson. *Fr.* Maud [A Monodrama]. EnVR

Courage that my mother had, The. Edna St. Vincent Millay. NALW

Courage to Live. Grace Noll Crowell. PoToHe

Courage to wait, The. Greater Courage. Natan Zach, *Hebrew.* PoSu, *tr. by* Peter Everwine *and* Shulamit Yasny-Starkman

Courage: your tongue has left. Stutterer. Alan Dugan. CAPP-1; NYBP

Coureurs de Bois. Douglas Le Pan. MoCV; NOBC

Couriers, The. Sylvia Plath. LCAP-2

Course, The. Robert Huff. CoAP

Course bread and water's most their fare. Roger Williams. SCAP

Course of a Particular, The. Wallace Stevens. HCAP

Course of a Year, The. George Sands Johnson. PWR

Courser and the Jennet, The. Shakespeare. NOBE *Fr.* Venus and Adonis.

Coursing in emptiness. Lal Ded, *Kashmiri.* WPoS, *tr. by* Jane Hirshfield

Court considered the country's crisis, The. The Country's Crisis. Brian Merriman. BIrV, *tr. by* David Marcus *Fr.* The Midnight Court. NOIV, *tr. by* Thomas Kinsella

Court Historian, The. George Walter Thornbury. PeVV

Court holds open contests for good men, The. Exhortation to Learning. *Unknown, Vietnamese.* AVP, *tr. by* Huỳnh Sanh Thông

Court is kept att leeue London, The. Hugh Spencer's Feats in France. *Unknown.* ESPB

Court lady Addresses Her Lover, A. Edward, 17th Earl of Oxford De Vere. NoSic

Court of Love, The. *Unknown.*
    "On May-day, when the lark began to rise." NoSic

Court of Sapience. John Lydgate.
    Lament: "Farewell Mercy, farewell thy piteous grace." PoEL-1

Court the vain blessing from a woman's pen. (LL) Maidenhead. "Ephelia." PEW

Courteous Indian, The. Roger Williams. NOSC

Courteous Knight, The. *Unknown. See* The Baffled Knight.

Courteous pagan shall condemn[e], The. The Courteous Indian. Roger Williams. NOSC; SCAP

Courteously self-assured, although alone. Charlotte Corday. Charles Tomlinson. OxBC

Courtesan. Angela Shaw. BAP-94

Courtesan with Fan. Elizabeth Spires. WeT

Courtesies of good-morning and good-evening. On Dwelling. Robert Graves. CMoP; FaBoMo; OxBSP

Courtesy, A Trenchant Grace, A. Cyrus Cassells. GT

Courtesy is a quality of soul / refinement impossible to purchase. F. E. Elwell. CTV

Courtesy Tips. *Unknown.* CTV

Courtier's a Riddle, A. Ralph Schomberg. *Fr.* The Judgment of Paris. TrJP

Courtier's Life, The. Sir Thomas Wyatt. FaBoEE

Courtin', The. James Russell Lowell. AmPP; NOBA; OBAL *Fr.* The Biglow Papers.

Courting the Faerie Queen. Margaret Lucas Cavendish, Duchess of Newcastle. NOSC

Courting the Famous Figures at the Grotto of Improbable Thought. Brigit Pegeen Kelly. BAP-94

Courtling, I rather thou shouldst utterly. To Censorious Courtling. Ben Jonson. NOSC

Courtship, The. Ann Beresford. LW

Courtship. Rita Dove. LCAP-2

Courtship. Musaeus, *Greek.* OBCVT, *tr. by Unknown*

Courtship. Mark Strand. HCAP; PoPoPo

Courtship of Inanna and Dumuzi, The. *Ancient Sumerian Oral Tradition, Sumerian.*

"Inanna sang." ITG, *tr. by* Diane Wolkstein *and* Samuel Noah Kramer

Courtship of the Yonghy-Bonghy-Bo, The. Edward Lear. EnLoPo; OAEL-2; OxBM

Courtyard, The. Eddy Van Vliet, *Flemish.* VCWP, *tr. by* John Van Tiel

Courtyard, quiet, The. Rainy Night. Ho Ching-ming, *Chinese.* CoBLCP, *tr. by* Jonathan Chaves

Courtyards in Delft. Derek Mahon. CIP-2; PBCIP; PNI

Cousin. David Huddle. CDa

Cousin, it's of you I always dream. El Sueño de la Razón. Jane Cooper. FaBoWP *Fr.* March.

Cousin Jack Song. Charley Tregonning. AmFP

Cousin Kate. Christina Rossetti. VWP

Cousin Mary. Wanda Coleman. GT; MoNo

Cousin Nancy. T. S. Eliot. OBAL; OxBSP

Cousin Nell. Roger McGough. FuFo

Cousin Reggie. Roger McGough. FuFo

Cousins if i be betrayed. Crazy Horse Instructs the Young Men But In Their Grief They Forget. Lucille Clifton. PaTW

Couturier from Haverford West, A. Limerick. E. O. Parrott. PeLi

Covenant of Grace, The. Ann Stanford.
   "Brother Symmes conversed with her on the ship." CRP

Coventry Carol. *Unknown.* PChr

Cover Her Face. Thomas Kinsella. CIP-2

Cover my eyes with your palm. Ruth Miller. *Fr.* Cycle. PeSA

Cover nine kingdoms as thou lie'st asleep. (LL) Lines on the Death of Bismarck. John Jay Chapman. APN-2; PoEL-5

Cover us with your pools of fir. (LL) Oread. Hilda Doolittle. AWP; CMoP; ColAP; HeIP-4; InPS-3; MoAmPo; MoP; NAAL-2; NALW; NOBA; NoAM; OxBA; PoPoPo; Poetr; TAP

Cover your teeth. (LL) Kalaloch. Carolyn Forché. AmPA; NoAM

Covered Bridge. Robert Penn Warren. AiP

Covered with a glory that had lost its luster. Georgy Vladimirovich Ivanov, *Russian.* TCRP, *tr. by* Daniel Weissbort

Covered with rags and cardboard and nothing. The Women's Room in Pennsylvania Station. Kate Daniels. GM

Covered with snow, the herd, with none to guide. Without the Herdsman. Diotimus, *Greek.* AWP, *tr. by* John William Burgon

Covered with yellow leaves. Memory Gardens. Allen Ginsberg. NNaP

Covering / a given distance, a countryside. Eccentricity of the Middle Ground. Mary Margaret Sloan. PT

Covering the Subject. Richard Armour. CTV

Covers it, like a stone covered in grass. (LL) Of the Lady Pietra degli Scrovigni. Dante, *Italian.* AWP; OAEL-2; OBVE, *tr. by* D. G. Rossetti

Covetous Nebraskaites, The. Elymas Payson Rogers. AAP *Fr.* The Repeal of the Missouri Compromise Considered.

Covetousness. Peter Idley. OxBChV

Covets nothing that it has let go. This then you may know / as the hero. (LL) The Hero. Marianne Moore. CMoP; NOBA; OxBA; PoA

Cow, The. Theodore Roethke. OBAL; OBCA

Cow. Joan Fern Shaw. IFJA

Cow, The. Robert Louis Stevenson. CTAV; CTV; FPC; NTCP; OxBChV; PWR; TLR; WHSW

Cow, The. Ann Taylor. CTAV; OxBChV

Cow and a calf, A. *Unknown.* OxNR

Cow and the Ass, The. Ann Taylor. BoTP; CTAV

Cow Boy. Vincente Huidobro, *Spanish.* PFTM, *tr. by* David Guss

Cow Boy's Lament. *Unknown.* PaTW

Cow-Boy's Song, The. Anna Maria Wells. OBCA

Cow eats green grass, The. Response to Rimbaud's Later Manner. Thomas Sturge Moore. CABP; OBMV

Cow in Apple Time, The. Robert Frost. APo; MoAmPo; OxBSP; PoLF

Cow is of the bovine ilk, The. Ogden Nash. NBLV; NoP-4; RB

Cow of morning spurted, The. The Last Vision of Eoghan Rua Ó Súilleabháin. Michael Hartnett. PBCIP

Cow of Our Time, A. Thomas M. Disch. EOEF

Cow Perseverance, The. Frederick D'Aguiar. HCP

Cow walks away from him, The. Thomas in the Fields. Lois Moyles. NYBP

Cow Worship. Gerald Stern. IFJA; LoL

Coward. A. R. Ammons. OBAL

Coward, The. Rudyard Kipling. FaBoEE; FaBoTw; PeFWW *Fr.* Epitaphs of the War [1914–1918]. OBWP

Coward, The. Eve Merriam. TrJP

Cowards fear to die, but Courage stout. On the Snuff of a Candle. Sir Walter Ralegh. FaBoEE; SiPS

Cowboy, The. John Antrobus. FaBoBe

Cowboy Film. Tom Matthews. PNI

Cowboy Sayings. *Unknown.* CA

Cowboy Song. Charles Causley. PoRA

Cowboy stands beneath, The. Vaquero. Edward Dorn. NeAP; PoM

Cowboys, come and hear a story of Roy Bean in all his glory. Roy Bean. *Unknown.* OBAL

Cowboy's Lament, The, *see also* St. James Infirmary *and* The Bad Girl's Lament. *Unknown.* APN-2; ChAP
   (Streets of Laredo, The.) AmFP; RB

Cowboy's Lament, The. Smoky Mountains. *Unknown.* AmFP

Cowboy's Life, The. James Barton Adams. CTV

Cowboy's Life Is a Very Dreary Life, The. *Unknown.* AmFP

Cowherd, The; a Song. Ch'u Kuang-hsi, *Chinese.* SuSp, *tr. by* Joseph J. Lee

Cowhorn-crowned, shockheaded, cornshuck-bearded. The Knight, Death, and the Devil. Randall Jarrell. ColAP; GS; WeW-3

Cowlady cowlady. Ladybird. *Unknown.* FaBoVe

Cowley's Style. Walter Savage Landor. EPCY

Cowper, the poet of the fields. John Clare. EPCY

Cowper's Grave. Elizabeth Barrett Browning. OxAEP-2

Cowper's Tame Hare. Norman Nicholson. PoBA

Cows. James Reeves. NOxBChV; NTCP; NTP

Cows bring in the last light, The. The Black Plateau. W. S. Merwin. NNaP

Cows graze across the hill. Peter Kocan. NOBAu

Cows they had, many, like heavy clouds drifting in the meadow. The Wheelbarrow. Russell Edson. LCAP-2

Cowslips for her covering. (LL) An Epitaph upon a Virgin. Robert Herrick. CaPo; FaBoEE; OxBoLi; PoEL-3

Coxcomb, The. Joseph Hall. OxAEP-1

Coxcomb bird, so talkative and grave, The. Alexander Pope. ImPo *Fr.* Epistle I, to Sir Richard Temple, Lord Cobham.

Coy Nature (which remain'd, though aged grown). Abraham Cowley. *Fr.* Ode upon Doctor Harvey. PoEL-2

Coyne's. John Ennis. PBCIP

Coyote, The. Carter Revard. VoR

Coyote and the Locust, The. *Unknown.* AWP

Coyote Fragments. Lance Henson. HATNAP

Coyote / running. Sweat Song. Peter Blue Cloud. VoR

Coyotes are howling, The. George John Whyte-Melville. NOxBChV

Coyote's song, A. New Realism. Joseph Ceravolo. PmAP

Crab has got the sun in its claws, The. July. John Heath-Stubbs. AYFP

Crab is in again, his monthly house, The. Anne Ridler. WPN

Crabbed age and youth cannot live together. A Madrigal. Shakespeare. EBEvV; GBL; GTBS-P; InPS-3; NoSic; OBEV *Fr.* The Passionate Pilgrim.

Crabs. Marge Piercy. NBLV

Crack, The. Clark Coolidge. PmAP

Crack, The. Michael Goldman. NYBP

Crack. Yusef Komunyakaa. WWSi

Crack, The. Denise Levertov. NALW

Crack! crack! As the Flower of the Grass. May Probyn. VWP

Crack in the Wall Holds Flowers. Adam David Miller. PoBA

Crack ran through our hearthstone long ago, A. The Refugees. Edwin Muir. NoAM

Crack—recall it vividly as first fabric. Light. Richard Kenney. Son

Crack soldiers get no sleep, The. Li K'ai-hsien. *Fr.* Songs of the Frontier. CoBLCP, *tr. by* Jonathan Chaves

Cracked Looking Glass. Jean Garrigue. VCAP

Cracked Portraits. Agha Shahid Ali. OpBo

Cracking a Few Hundred Million Years. A. R. Ammons. EC3

Cracking whips, off to the wine shop. The Streets of Ch'ang-an. Ch'u Kuang-hsi, *Chinese.* CoBCP, *tr. by* Burton Watson

Cracks, The. Robert Creeley. CoAmPo

Cracks in eight log buildings, counting sheds. Montana Ranch Abandoned. Richard Hugo. PaTW

Cracks on the walls, The. Star Blanket. Ray A. Young Bear. CDW

Crackup, last day of Carnival, first of Lint. Drinking Sappho Brand Ouzo. Martin Johnston. BMAP *Fr.* In Transit: A Sonnet Square.

Cradle, The. Roland Robinson. NOBAu

Cradle, at a distance, of a kind, A. Half-Built Boat in a Hayfield. Norman MacCaig. FaBoTC

Cradle Hymn. Martin Luther. BoTP
   ("Till morning is nigh.") (LL) CTV

Cradle Hymn, A. Isaac Watts. OBEV; OxBChV; PoEL-3; SCGP

Cradle Logic of Autumn, The. En mi país otoño nace de una flor seca, de algunos pájaros . . . o del vaho penetrante de ciertos ríos de la llanura. Jay Wright. BAP-95

Cradle Song: "Angels are bending, The." W. B. Yeats. NOBVV

Cradle Song, A: "Angels are stooping, The." W. B. Yeats. NOxBChV

Cradle Song: "Clock's untiring fingers wind the wool of darkness, The." Louis MacNeice. MoBrPo

Cradle Song: "Come, little babe." Nicholas Breton. NOBE; OBEV (Sweet Lullaby, A.) RACG

Cradle Song, A: "Sleep baby sleep! / Thy father watches the sheep." *Unknown.* BoTP

Cradle Song: "Sleep, my child, my little daughter." *Unknown, Yiddish.* TrJP, *tr. by* Joseph Leftwich

Cradle Song, A: "Sleep, sleep, beauty bright." William Blake. OBEV; PoLF

Cradle Song, A: "Sweet dreams form a shade." William Blake. FHYEP; OBCP; Ro *Fr.* Songs of Innocence.
("Heaven and earth to peace beguiles.") (LL) Ro

Cradle Song: "What does little birdie say?" Tennyson. BoTP; OxBChV *Fr.* Sea Dreams.

Cradle Song, A: "O men from the fields!" Padraic Colum. TIRV

Cradle Song, A: "Golden slumbers kiss your eyes." Thomas Dekker *and others.* OxBChV; SCGP *Fr.* The Pleasant Comedy of Patient Grissell [*or* Grissel *or* Grissill].
(Lullaby: "Golden slumbers kiss your eyes.")

Cradle Song at Bethlehem. E. J. Falconer. BoTP

Cradle-Song at Twilight. Alice Thompson Meynell. NOBVV; VWP

Cradle Will Rock, The. Marc Blitzstein.
Art for Art's Sake. TrJP

Cradled and warm, fur-warm, in the she-wolf's lair. Wolf-Boy. David Malouf. CBAP

Cradlesong, A. Tố Hữu, *Vietnamese.* AVP, *tr. by* Huỳnh Sanh Thông

Craft I left in was called Esau, The. Sheenagh Pugh. SpW

Craft with which I don't know how to deal. (LL) The Mind, Intractable Thing. Marianne Moore. LiTM; NYBP

Craftsman. Luci Shaw. TrCP

Craftsmanship. Nikolai Nikolaevich Ushakov, *Russian.* TCRP, *tr. by* John Glad

Craftsmen. Vita Sackville-West. OxBTC

Craftsmen of the Little Box, The. Vasco [*or* Vasko] Popa, *Serbo-Croatian.* CEEP; HSix, *tr. by* Charles Simic

Crafty Butcher, The. Susan Hampton. BMAP; NOBAu

Crafty Farmer, The. *Unknown.* AmFP; ESPB

Crafty Farmer, The. *Unknown.* ESPB

Crafty Miss of London; or, The Fryar Well Fitted, The. *Unknown.* OxBB

Craggy rocks, crouching like elephants. Climbing Mount Yang. Yüan Hung-tao, *Chinese.* CoBLCP, *tr. by* Jonathan Chaves

Cramped, and the bright sun shining on its tusks. (LL) Gratitude. Louise Glück. FaBoWP; TRP

Cramped like sardines on the Queens, and sedated. Tourists. Howard Moss. NYBP; NoP-4; OBCoV; PeLV

Cranach. Sir Herbert Read. FaBoMo

Cranberry nose and a tin-can hat, A. Mister Snow Man. Bertha Wilcox Smith. CTV

Cranberry Song, The. Barney Reynolds. AmFP

Crane. Joseph Langland. NYBP

Crane, The. Charles Tomlinson. MoBrPo

Crane, The. Tu Mu, *Chinese.* SuSp, *tr. by* John M. Ortinau

Crane from the shore standing at the top of the steps, The. Going Alone to Spend a Night at the Hsien-Yu Temple. Po Chü-i, *Chinese.* ChiP, *tr. by* Arthur Waley

Crane Is My Neighbor, The. John Shaw Neilson. CBAP

Cranes, The. Po Chü-i, *Chinese.* ChiP; OBVE, *tr. by* Arthur Waley

Cranes of Ibycus, The. Emma Lazarus. APN-2

Crankadox leaned o'er the edge of the moon, The. Craqueodoom. James Whitcomb Riley. OBAL

Cranmer was person of this parish. Charles Hubert Sisson. FaBoTw

Crapshooters. Carl Sandburg. VGW

Craqueodoom. James Whitcomb Riley. OBAL

Crash / and the door flew. Revolution. Pentti Saarikoski, *Finnish.* EC2, *tr. by* Anselm Hollo

Crash / Take Valium Sleep / Dream and, / forget it. Things To Do in Providence. Ted Berrigan. PT

Crashes into the orchestra, which explodes. (LL) Cadenza. Ted Hughes. CMoP; NYBP

Crass Times Redeemed by Dignity of Souls. Peter Viereck.
"Tenderness of dignity of souls, The." HoPM

Craswall. Roland Mathias. OBWVE

Crateas the doctor and Damon the sexton. *Unknown, Greek.* GrAn, *tr. by* Peter Porter

Craving of Samuel Rouse for clearance to create, The. The Slave and the Iron Lace. Margaret Danner. BPo

Crawled near my mind's poor birds. (LL) Dramatic Fragment. Trumbull Stickney. InPK-6; OxBA; OxBSP

Crawled near my mind's poor birds. (LL) Sir, say no more. Trumbull Stickney. APN-2; InPK-6; OxBA; OxBSP

Crawlin' aboot like a snail in the mud. The Image o' God. Joe Corrie. ChIV-1; OxBS

Crawling glaciers pierce me with the spears. Shelley. FHYEP *Fr.* Prometheus Unbound. NOBRP; OAEL-2

Crawls from the dry grass. (LL) Exeunt. Richard Wilbur. HeIP-4; PoLF; Poetsp

Crayfish, The. Guillaume Apollinaire, *French.* APo, *tr. by* Roger Shattuck

Crazed. Walter De la Mare. OxBSP

Crazed. Mary E. Tucker. CBWP-1; RACG

Crazed Girl, A. W. B. Yeats. InPS-3; Son

Crazed life, The. At the Van Gogh exibition. Toki Zenmaro, *Japanese.* MJT, *tr. by* Makoto Ueda

Crazed Man in Concentration Camp. Agnes Gergely, *Hungarian.* BoWoP, *tr. by* Edwin Morgan

Crazy as hell and typical of us. Making Contact. John Streeter Manifold. CBAP

Crazy as white shines in summer. City Baseball. Liz Rosenberg. CA

Crazy Bill to the Bishop. Robert Peters. BXAP

Crazy Courage. Alma Villanueva. BAP-96

Crazy Dog Events. Jerome Rothenberg. RaBo

Crazy Horse Instructs the Young Men But In Their Grief They Forget. Lucille Clifton. PaTW

Crazy Horse Monument. Peter Blue Cloud. HATNAP; UnSA

Crazy Horse Names His Daughter. Lucille Clifton. PaTW

Crazy Horse Speaks. Sherman Alexie. UnSA

Crazy Horse: The Last Morning. Lance Henson. VoR

Crazy Jane and Jack the Journeyman, *fr.* Words for Music Perhaps. W. B. Yeats. CMoP

Crazy Jane and the Bishop, *fr.* Words for Music Perhaps. W. B. Yeats. CMoP; LiTM

Crazy Jane Grown Old Looks at the Dancers, *fr.* Words for Music Perhaps. W. B. Yeats. CMoP; EBEV

Crazy Jane on God, *fr.* Words for Music Perhaps. W. B. Yeats. CMoP; EBEV; OxBTC; RACG

Crazy Jane on the Day of Judgment, *fr.* Words for Music Perhaps. W. B. Yeats. CMoP

Crazy Jane on the Mountain. W. B. Yeats. CMoP

Crazy Jane Reproved, *fr.* Words for Music Perhaps. W. B. Yeats. CMoP

Crazy Jane Talks with the Bishop, *fr.* Words for Music Perhaps. W. B. Yeats. BoLoP; CABP; CMoP; EBEV; InPK-6; MoP; NAEL-2; NoAM; NoP-4; OAEL-2; OxAEP-2; PFE; PoE; PoPoPo; TOF; TRP

Crazy pigeon strutting outside my cell. Etheridge Knight. NBV

Crazy Quilt. Jane Wilson Joyce. CrSp

Crazy Song to the Air of "Dixie." "Andy Lee." AS

Crazy Weather. John Ashbery. ColAP; PoE

Crazy Woman, The. Gwendolyn Brooks. NALW

Creak, creak, loom and shuttle, hidden beyond the trees. Hearing Loom and Shuttle. Yü Chi, *Chinese.* CoBLCP, *tr. by* Jonathan Chaves

Cream-Puffin, The. Carolyn Wells. *Fr.* A Baker's Dozen of Wild Beasts. OBCA

Cream Song, The. Apirana Ngata, *Maori.* PeNZ, *tr. by* Margaret Orbell

Creamcheese babies square and downy as bolsters. The Peaceable Kingdom. Marge Piercy. TwCP

Created, The. Jones Very. APN-1; NOCV
("There is nought for thee by thy haste to gain.") PAR

Created Clay. Maimee Lee Brown. PWR

Created purely from glass the saint stands. In Piam Memoriam. Geoffrey Hill. OxBC

Creation. Sir Richard Blackmore.
Digestive System, The. ECEV

Creation. Mary Weston Fordham. CBWP-2

Creation. Robin Gurr. NOBAu

Creation, The. James Weldon Johnson. ChIV-1; MoAmPo; NAAAL; PBMP; PoBA; PoRA; TrCP
("Amen. Amen.") (LL) ISC; KSG; SAGP; SSLK
(Creation: A Negro Sermon, The.) KSG

Creation. Simon J. Ortiz. CDW; ColAP; HATNAP

Creation: Enduring the Creator, He who now guides. Cynewulf. ASW, *tr. by* Kevin Crossley-Holland *Fr.* Riddles (Exeter Book).

Creation fires my tongue. Praise of Creation. George Moses Horton. AAP

Creation Myth Haiku. Gavin Ewart. APAD

Creation Myth on a Moebius Band. Howard Nemerov. OBCoV

Creation of Light, The. Sister Maura. CRP

Creation of My Lady, The. Francesco Redi, *Italian.* AWP, *tr.* by Sir Edmund Gosse

Creation's and Creator's crowning good. To the Body. Coventry Patmore. CABP; EnVR; OAEL-2; PoEL-5 *Fr.* The Unknown Eros.

Creation's Lord, We Give Thee Thanks. William deWitt Hyde. AH

Creations mildest charms are there combined. Britain. Oliver Goldsmith. NOEC *Fr.* The Travell[l]er; or, A Prospect of Society.

Creative Process, The. Mark Akenside. NOEC *Fr.* The Pleasures of Imagination.

Creative Process, The. Amrita Pritam, *Punjabi.* OMIP, *tr.* by Amrita Pritam and Arlene Zide

Creator of Infinities. Chadwick Hansen. AH

Creator Spirit, by whose aid. Veni Creator Spiritus. Charlemagne *and* Hrabanus Maurus (*fl.* 9th cent.), *par.* by Dryden. AWP; FaPoR

Creatrix. Anna Wickham. MoBrPo

Creature of charm is the gerbil, A. Limerick. *Unknown.* PeLi

Creature to pet and spoil, A. Kob Antelope. *Unknown, Yoruba. Fr.* Hunter Poems of the Yoruba. RB, *tr.* by Ulli Beier

Creatures all eyes and brows, and tresses streaming. Correggio's Cupolas at Parma. Aubrey Thomas De Vere. Son

Creatures Rest, The. Alkman, *Greek.* APo, *tr.* by John Hollander

Creatures that live in a wave, glass-housed. Garfish. John Blight. BMAP

Creatures that rustle in the shadows, all the crooked. Green Light. Rolf Jacobsen. EC3

Creatures that we met this morning, The. Discovery of the New World. Carter Revard. SoSe-8; VoR

Credences of Summer. Wallace Stevens. MeMAP

Creditor to His Proud Debtor, The. George Moses Horton. AAP; NAAAL

Credo. Brewster Ghiselin. PoA

Credo. Robinson Jeffers. MoAmPo

Credo. Georgia Douglas Johnson. PoBA

Credo. Jane Kenyon. BAP-93 *Fr.* Having It Out With Melancholy. BAP-93

Credo. Maxine W. Kumin. NMM-2

Credo. Edwin Arlington Robinson. AmPP; CMoP; LiTM; MeMAP; MoAmPo; NAAL-2; OxBA; PFE; TAP; TrCP

Creed, A. Edwin Markham. BLPA; FaBoBe

Creed. Anne Spencer. NMM-2

Creed. Mary Ashley Townsend. BLPA; FaBoBe

Creed of Mr. Nicholas Culpeper. Patricia Beer. OxBC

Creeds of the Bells. George W. Bungay. PWR

Creek, The. Roland Robinson. NOBAu

Creek of the Four Graves, The. Charles Harpur.
    "I verse a settler's tale of olden times." CBAP

Creek, shining, The. W. W. Eustace Ross. MoCV

Creep into thy narrow bed. The Last Word. Matthew Arnold. APAD; NOBE; OAEL-2; OBNC; PBMP; PFE; PoEL-5; SCGP

Creeper grows over thorn. Alba. Confucius. CTC, *tr.* by Ezra Pound *Fr.* Songs of T'ang.

Creeping and healing. (LL) The Minimal. Theodore Roethke. HCAP; MoP; NOBA; NoAM; RB

Creeping serrate line of dusty red, A. Fighting Fire. Hamlin Garland. APN-2

Creeps in half wanton, half asleep. Wagner. Rupert Brooke. FaBoTw; NOBL; PeLV

Creepy little creepers are insinuatingly. A. R. Ammons. BAP-93 *Fr.* Garbage. BAP-93

Creide's Lament for Cael. *Unknown.* NOIV

Créide's Lament for Dínertech. *Unknown.* NOIV

Cremation. Robinson Jeffers. BLT

Cremation of Sam McGee, The. Robert W. Service. NOBC; OBCoV; OBNV; PoLF; SAGP
    ("*Was that night on the marge of Lake Lebarge / cremated Sam McGee.*") (LL) ChAP

Crematorium. John Betjeman. PoA

Crepe de Chine. Tennessee Williams. NYBP

Crept like a frightened girl. (LL) The Harlot's House. Oscar Wilde. ADE; EBVV; MoBrPo; NAEL-2; NoAM; PFE

Crepuscular. Richard Howard. TwCP

Crepuscule. Angela Shaw. BAP-96

Crepuscule with Nellie. Charles Simic. SeSe

Crescendoes are indigo scarves. Gonsalves. Ron Welburn. SeSe

Crescent Moon. William Renton. NOBVV

Crescent moon hangs on the tip of the willows, A. Ch'ien Ch'ien-i. SuSp, *tr.* by Irving Y. Lo *Fr.* Willow Branch Songs.

Crescent moon shines, The. Mei Yao Ch'en, *Chinese.* OHPC, *tr.* by Kenneth Rexroth

Crescent moon with silver sheen aglow, The. Sunset Thought. Henrietta Cordelia Ray. *Fr.* A Group of Musings. CBWP-3

Crescent, tiny as the curtain hook, The. The Moon. Hsüeh T'ao, *Chinese.* SuSp, *tr.* by Eric W. Johnson

Cresseid's Complaint against Fortune. Robert Henryson. *Fr.* The Testament of Cresseid. OxBS

Cressida. James Keir Baxter.
    Bar Room Conversation. PeLV
    In the Lecture Room. PeLV

Cressida's Leprosy. Robert Henryson. *Fr.* The Testament of Cresseid. OxBS

Crest Jewel, The. James Stephens. MoBrPo

Crethis. Callimachus, *Greek.* AWP, *tr.* by Richard Garnett

Creusa. Virgil. NoSic *Fr.* The Aeneid [*or* Eneados, *Aeneis*].

Crew Practice on Lake Bled, in Jugoslavia. James Scully. NYBP

Crib, The. Robert Finch. OBCP

Cricket, The. Vincent Bourne, *Latin.* PoLF, *tr.* by William Cowper

Cricket. No Ch'ŏn-myŭng, *Korean.* PBWP, *tr.* by Ko Won

Cricket, The. Konstantin Mikhailovich Simonov, *Russian.* TCRP, *tr.* by Lubov Yakovleva

Cricket, The. Frederick Goddard Tuckerman. APN-2; NCAP; NOBA; PAR

Cricket; an Heroic Poem. James Dance.
    "When the returning sun begins to smile." NOEC

Cricket and the greshope wenten hem to fight, The. Nonsense. *Unknown.* EBEV

Cricket at Oxford. Alan Ross. PeLV

Cricket cries, The. Fujiwara no Go-Kyōgoku, *Japanese.* OHPJ, *tr.* by Kenneth Rexroth

Cricket Heard. Lady Izumi, *Japanese.* APo, *tr.* by Jane Hirshfield

Cricket Kept the House, The. Edith Matilda Thomas. OBCA

Cricket, lovely cricket. Victory Calypso, Lord's 1950. Egbert Moore. ("Lord Beginner"). OBCoV; PeLV

Cricket on a rubbish-tip, A. Winter Cricket. John Heath-Stubbs. OBCP

Cricket ripples sorrow, A. Song of Cricket. Hyonggi Yi, *Korean.* CKP, *tr.* by Jaihiun Kim

Cricket, you'll sing no more. Aristodicus of Rhodes, *Greek.* GrAn, *tr.* by Barriss Mills

Cricketer. R. C. Scriven. AYFP

Cricketers of Flanders, The. *Unknown.* NSI

Crickets. David McCord. NTCP

Crickets. Larry Wiggin. HA

Crickets and gardenias attempted to fill my senses, The. Summer. Helen G. Quigless. BkSV *Fr.* Childhood Scenes in Four Seasons.

Crickets and locusts, cicadas. Rosalía de Castro, *Galician.* PBWP, *tr.* by Benjamin M. Woodbridge, Jr.

Crickets' chirps become increasingly urgent. Upon Passing the Homestead. Huang T'ing-chien, *Chinese.* SuSp, *tr.* by Michael E. Workman

Crickety Creek. Arkady Kutilov, *Russian.* TCRP, *tr.* by Bradley Jordan

Cried a man on the Salisbury Plain. Myra Cohn Livingston. KaS

Cried a scientist watching this creature dart by. Hummingbird. X. J. Kennedy. NOxBChV

Cried, *ah!* and can *Death enter Paradise?*. (LL) Madrigal: "The Beauty [*or* Beautie], and the life." William Drummond, of Hawthornden. OBEV; PoEL-2

Cried Innocence, "Mother, my thumbs, my thumbs!" The Tortured. May Sarton. FFC

Cried out the hollows of the sea. (LL) On a Political Prisoner. W. B. Yeats. FaBoPV; IIP; OAEL-2; OBMV

Cried the Fox. Tennessee Williams. PFE

Cried the maid: "You must marry me, Hume!" Limerick. P. W. R. Foot. PeLi

Crier, The. Michael Drayton. *See* The Cryer.

Crier, The. Philip Kahclamet, *Wishram Chinook Indian.* STP, *tr.* by Dell Hymes

Cries From Chiapas. Muriel Rukeyser. CPO

Cries of London, The. *Unknown.* OPOU

Cries still linger on the battlefield. Kingdom of Silence. Amir Gilbo'a, *Hebrew.* IP, *tr.* by Warren Bargad and Stanley F. Chyet

Crime. Robert Penn Warren. FuPo

Crime and Punishment. Kahlil Gibran. PoToHe *Fr.* The Prophet.

Crime and Punishment. Paul Lake. RA

Crime at Its Best. Stoddard King. NBLV

Crime of the Ages, The. Augusta Cooper Bristol. APN-2

Crimes of Lugalanne. Enheduanna, *Sumerian.* BoWoP, *ad.* by Aliki and Willis Barnstone

Crimes of Passion: The Phone Caller. Terry Stokes. AmPA

Crimes of Passion: The Slasher. Terry Stokes. AmPA

Crimp and whorl of conch, The. A Mantelpiece of Shells. Ruthven Todd. NYBP

Crimson-budded rose. A View of my garden. Masaoka Shiki, *Japanese*. MJT, *tr. by* Ueda, Makoto

Crimson dragonfly, A. Kenneth Yasuda. HA

Crimson nor yellow roses, nor. Eros D'Aute. Theodore Wratislaw. GBL

Crimson roses burn and glow, The. Vigil. Richard Dehmel, *German*. AWP, *tr. by* Ludwig Lewisohn

Crimson Tent. John Dos Passos. PoA

Crines in a windin' sheet. (LL) Farmer's Death. "Hugh MacDiarmid." FaBoVe

Criole Candjo, *tr. of Creole slave song*. George Washington Cable. APN-2

Cripple Creek. *Unknown*. APN-2; AmFP

Cripple Dick upon a stick. *Unknown*. OxNR

Cripple for Life; or, The Poor Volunteer, The. *Unknown*. AmFP

Crisp / pale green, The. Salad La Raza. Janet Campbell Hale. VoR

Crispus Attucks McCoy. Sterling Brown. BPo

Crist, buyere of alle icoren. William Herebert. MiEL

Critic, A. Walter Savage Landor. FaBoEE

Critic advises, A. Black Poet, White Critic. Dudley Randall. BPo; CoAmPo; LTA

Critic leaves at curtain fall, The. Elwyn Brooks White. NBLV *Fr*. Definitions.

Critical Condition. Sang Yi, *Korean*. Precipice. PFTM, *tr. by* Walter Lew

Critical Observations. Archibald MacLeish. OBAL

Criticisms. Li Ho, *Chinese*. "Southern hills, how mournful!, The." PLT, *tr. by* A. C. Graham

Criticks, ye are grown so much unkind of late. Prologue. Delariviere Manley. KTR *Fr*. The Royal Mischeif.

Critics. Martial, *Latin*. AWP, *tr. by* Sir John Harington

Critics, The. Theodore Spencer. NYBP

Critics. Jonathan Swift. *Fr*. On Poetry: a Rhapsody. OBSV

Critics and Connoisseurs. Marianne Moore. AmPP; CMoP; FaBoWP; MeMAP; NOBA; NoAM; OxBA; Poetr

Critics and Poets. Geoffrey Grigson. FaBoEE

Critics cry unfair, The. In Defense of Black Poets. Conrad Kent Rivers. BPo

Critics: in your sight. Sister Juana Inés de la Cruz. *Fr*. A Satirical Romance. PBWP, *tr. by* Judith Thurman

Critics say that epics have died out, The. From Book 5. Elizabeth Barrett Browning. NALW; NoP-4; PBWP; PeVV *Fr*. Aurora Leigh. VWP

Critter. W. M. Ransom. CDW

Cro-Kill. Anthony Lawrence. NOBAu

Cro-Magnons carried stones for books. Lawrence Ferlinghetti. BB

Croak of a raven hoar, The! Mammon Marriage. George Macdonald. BoLoP; EBVV

"Croak!" said the Toad, "I'm hungry, I think." *Unknown*. CTAV

Croaked the Eagle: "Nevermore." "Sagittarius." UV

Croaker Papers, The. Fitz-Greene Halleck *and* Joseph Rodman Drake. National Painting [*or* Paintings], The. APN-1

Croaking frog in a well sees the sky from end to end, A. Yüan Hao-wen. SuSp, *tr. by* Irving Y. Lo *Fr*. On Poetry.

Crocheting. Miroslav Holub, *German*. CEEP, *tr. by* Stuart Friebert *and* Dana Hábová

Crocodile, A. Thomas Lovell Beddoes. APo; NOBVV; RB *Fr*. The Last Man.

Crocodile, The. "Lewis Carroll." CTAV; ChAP; HoPM *Fr*. Alice's Adventures in Wonderland.

Crocodile once dropped a line, A. Oliver Herford. OBCA

Crocodile wept bitter tears, The. William Jay Smith. OBCA

Crocus armies from the dead, The. Veni Coronaberis. Geoffrey Hill. DiPo; NoP-4

Crocus Night. James Schuyler. PoM

Crocus Turn and Gods, The. Joseph Ceravolo. PT *Fr*. Book III of Fits of Dawn.

Crocus, while the days are dark, The. Round the Year. Coventry Patmore. BoTP; EBVV

Crocuses, The. Frances Ellen Watkins Harper. BlSi

Crocuses. Anna M. Platt. BoTP

Crofters few but crafty. Shore Tullye. Robert Rendall. OxBS

Crofter's Kitchen, Evening. Norman MacCaig. FaBoTC

"Crom Cruach and his sub-gods twelve." The Burial of King Cormac. Sir Samuel Ferguson. NOIV; TIRV

Cromwell, our chief [*or* cheif] of men, who through a cloud. To the Lord General[l] Cromwell[, on the Proposals of Certain Ministers at the Committee for the Propagation of the Gospel *or* May 1652]. Milton.

FaBoPV; GSo; IIP; NAEL-1; NOSC; NoP-4; PBRV; PoPoPo; SCGP; Son

Crooked bank still winds to something new, The. Sneyd Davies. NOEC *Fr*. A Voyage to Tintern Abbey.

Crooked / beneath a denim. Dreams. Charles Cooper. PoBA

Crooked ear, crooked ear, / Walker at night. Corn Song. *Unknown, Ojibwa Native American*. APN-2, *tr. by* Henry Rowe Schoolcraft

Crooked fireworks. Tanka. Fumi Saito, *Japanese*. MJT, *tr. by* Ueda, Makoto

Crooked, like bough the march wind bends wallward across the sleet. The Lavender Woman. Lizette Woodworth Reese. APN-2

Crooked paths go every way, The. The Goat Paths. James Stephens. AWP; CH; SCGP; UnPo

Crooked River. Li Shang-yin, *Chinese*. PLT, *tr. by* A. C. Graham

Croon. Langston Hughes. PFTM

Croon on Hennacliff, A. Robert Stephen Hawker. NOBVV

Cropdusting, The. William Zaranka. BXAP

Croppy Boy, The. William B. McBurney. TIRV

Croppy Boy, The. *Unknown*. AmFP; NOIV; OxBoLi

Crops are all gathered, The. Harvest Sacrifice. Su Tung-p'o, *Chinese*. OHPC, *tr. by* Kenneth Rexroth

Crops like hedgehogs, high-crown'd hats. Modern Male Fashions. Mary Robinson. NOBRP

Cross[e], The. George Herbert. ESCV

Cross. Langston Hughes. ColAP; GT; LiTM; NoP-4; PoBA; PoLF; SAmP; SoSe-8; TAP

Cross, The. Allen Tate. AWP; ChIV-2; MoAmPo; OxBA

Cross, The. Jones Very. NCAP

Cross, The. Tongju Yun, *Korean*. CKP, *tr. by* Jaihiun Kim

Cross at the morning. Once and Upon. Madeline Gleason. NeAP

Cross between a bakehouse and a bell tower, A. Elegy. Oleg Grigorevich Chukhontsev, *Russian*. TCRP, *tr. by* Simon Franklin

Cross Country. Rod Moran. NOBAu

Cross Cut. Peter Davison. ColAP

Cross Divide. Tom Raworth. NBrP

Cross-framed square of kitchen light, A. Back Steps Lookout. Rhyll McMaster. BMAP

Cross leaves marks the tree we fancy, A. An Owl Is an Only Bird of Poetry. Robert Duncan. NeAP; PoM

Cross of boy with man within is an, The. On a Prize Crucifix by a Student Sculptor. Robert Logan. CAPP-1

Cross of Snow, The. Henry Wadsworth Longfellow. APN-1; ColAP; GSo; HeIP-4; MeMAP; NOBA; NoP-4; OxBA; TAP

Cross Over the River. Sam Cornish. MBE

Cross-Patch. *Unknown*. LB

Cross Patch / Draw the latch. Mother Goose. OxNR; ReMoGo

Cross-Road Epitaph, A. Amy Levy. VWP

Cross staggered him. At the cliff-top, The. Canticle for Good Friday. Geoffrey Hill. ChIV-2

Cross Talk. Cyril Cusack. TIRV

Cross, the Cross, The. Tortoise-Shell. D. H. Lawrence. CMoP; FaBoVe; NAEL-2; OAEL-2; OxAEP-2

'Cross the ford o' Kabul river in the dark! (LL) Ford o' Kabul River. Rudyard Kipling. FaBoTw; PeVV

Cross, the icon, The. The Paradox. Francesca Yetunde Pereira. PBA

Cross Ties. X. J. Kennedy. HoPM

Cross-tree, The. Robert Herrick. CavPo

Cross Was His Own, The. *Unknown*. BLPA

Crosscauseway, Bristo Street, and Potterrow. Green Breeks. Douglas Dunn. FaBoPV

Crossed Apple, The. Louise Bogan. HeIP-4; NALW; RACG

Crossed out *delete* and wrote his patient *stet*. (LL) The Proof. Richard Wilbur. CRP; OxBSP

Crossed Threads. Helen Hunt Jackson. PAR; SDW ("Silken threads by viewless spinner spun, The.") APN-2

Crosses. Robert Herrick. CaPo

Crossing, The. Paul Blackburn. NYBP

Crossing. Philip Booth. GM

Crossing, The. Aleksandr Trifonovich Tvardovsky. TCRP, *tr. by* April FitzLyon *Fr*. Vasily Tyorkin.

Crossing. Diane Ward. FTOS

Crossing alone the nighted ferry. A. E. Housman. GTBS-P; NOBE; NoP-4; OxBSP

Crossing Brooklyn Ferry. Walt Whitman. APN-1; AmPP; ColAP; FaBoA; InPS-3; MoP; NAAL-1; NAAL-3; NCAP; NOBA; NoAM; NoP-4; PAR; TAP ("Me, and more in my meditations, than you might suppose.") (LL) PiM

Crossing Disappearing behind Them. Marjorie Welish. PmAP

Crossing Han River. Li P'in, *Chinese*. OHMPC, *tr.* by Kenneth Rexroth

Crossing Kansas by Train. Donald Justice. AiP; NYBP

Crossing Lake Pontchartrain, vertiginous, hands gripping the wheel, / the bridge beneath me. Solo, New Orleans. Diann Blakely Shoaf. PUP-20

Crossing Nation. Allen Ginsberg. AiP

Crossing Over. William Meredith. NoAM

Crossing South of Li-chou, A. Wen T'ing-yün, *Chinese*. SuSp, *tr.* by William R. Schultz

Crossing the Atlantic. Anne Sexton. NoAM

Crossing the Bar. Tennyson. APAD; ChIV-2; ClHu; EBVV; EBVVPR; FaPoR; HeIP-4; ImPo; NAEL-2; NOBE; NOBVV; NoP-4; OAEL-2; OBEV; OBNC; OxBoS; PBMP; PWR; PeECV; PoLF; PoRA; SoSe-8; TFi; TrCP

   ("When I have crossed the bar.") (LL) PFE; SAGP

Crossing the Desert in a Pram. Selima Hill. NBrP

Crossing the Frontier. Li Meng-yang, *Chinese*. CoBLCP, *tr.* by Jonathan Chaves

Crossing the Hsiang River at Night. Meng Hao Jan, *Chinese*. SuSp, *tr.* by Daniel Bryant

Crossing the Lang-yeh Mountain with a Friend. Wei Ying-wu, *Chinese*. SuSp, *tr.* by Wu-Chi Liu

Crossing the Park. Howard Moss. ImGa; NYBP

Crossing the ridge, the woodcutter loses his way. Li K'ai-hsien. CoBLCP, *tr.* by Jonathan Chaves *Fr.* Describing My Feelings upon Encountering Snow.

Crossing the River. Yang Shih-ch'i, *Chinese*. CoBLCP, *tr.* by Jonathan Chaves

Crossing the river I pluck the lotus flowers;. *Unknown*. ChiP, *tr.* by Arthur Waley *Fr.* Seventeen Old Poems.

Crossing the shallow holdings high above sea. The Hungry Grass. Donagh MacDonagh. BIrV; IIP

Crossing the street. The Broken Home. James Merrill. ColAP; HAP; HCAP; MoP; NAAL-2; NOBA; NYBP; NoAM; NoP-4; PoPoPo

Crossing the Water. Sylvia Plath. HCAP; RB

Crossing the Yangtze in a Strong Wind. Wang Shih-chieng, *Chinese*. CoBLCP, *tr.* by Jonathan Chaves

Crossing the Yellow River: June 12. Yüan Hao-wen, *Chinese*. SuSp, *tr.* by Stephen West

Crossing there under the trees with leaden pace. False Enchantment. Jean Starr Untermeyer. MoAmPo

Crossing this lake at night in a shell canoe. Maine Lake at Night. Harry Morris. CRP

Crossing Ts'en River. Yang Wan-li, *Chinese*. SuSp, *tr.* by Jonathan Chaves

Crotchet Castle. Thomas Love Peacock.

   Chorus: "If I drink water while this doth last." NBLV

   Priest and the Mulberry-Tree, The. BoTP; OxAEP-2

Crouched beneath a snowbound sky. The Grey Ones. Louis MacNeice. CMoP

Crouched in a sandbagged bunker. War Games. Walter McDonald. CDa

Crouched in its giant green the Indian hid. Vacant Lot. Dudley Randall. NoAM

Crouched on one knee one. Autumn Warrior. Barney Bush. HATNAP

Crouched [*or* Crouch'd] on the pavement close by Belgrave Square. West London. Matthew Arnold. FP; GSo; SCGP; Son

Crouched on their women woven saddle rugs. The Great Horse Fair. Desmond O'Grady. PBCIP

Crouching to the whizzing storms. (LL) February. John Clare. NOBE; OBNC

Crow, The. Cecil Frances Alexander. BoTP; CTAV

Crow, The. Rita Boumi-Pappas, *Modern Greek*. PBWP, *tr.* by Kimon Friar

Crow. Robert Grenier. PmAP

Crow. Ted Hughes. PoE

   That Moment. UV

   Two Legends.

Crow after crow darts into the woods; the passers-by are few. Late Spring. Fan Ch'eng-ta. SuSp, *tr.* by Irving Y. Lo *Fr.* Seasonal Poems on Fields and Gardens.

Crow and Pie. *Unknown*. ESPB

Crow and the Fox, The. Jean de La Fontaine, *French*. AWP, *tr.* by Edward Marsh

Crow caws in the moonlight, A. *Unknown, Japanese*. OHMPJ, *tr.* by Kenneth Rexroth

Crow-Children Walk My Circles in the Snow, The. Ray A. Young Bear. CDW

Crow Cries at Night, The. Po Chü-i, *Chinese*. SuSp, *tr.* by Irving Y. Lo

Crow flew guiltily off. (LL) Crow's First Lesson. Ted Hughes. MoP; NoAM

Crow flies off, The. Larry Gates. HA

Crow, in pulpit lone and tall. In the Pauper's Turnip-Field. Herman Melville. OxBSP; PoEL-5

Crow in the snowy pine, A. Nicholas Virgilio. HA

Crow is only an anvil, The. Chickadee. Brendan Galvin. CMAP

Crow Jane. Imamu Amiri Baraka. BB; PoM

Crow / on either shoulder, A. (LL) The Boxcar Poem ("The Boxcars drift by / clanking"). David Young. GM

Crow or crowd with its detached features of twig bark and plunder walks to, The. Allegory. Carla Harryman. FTOS

Crow realized God loved him. Crow's Theology. Ted Hughes. GI

Crow Resting. "Edward Pygge." BXAP

Crow sat perched upon an oak, A. The Crow and the Fox. Jean de La Fontaine, *French*. AWP, *tr.* by Edward Marsh

Crow went on laughing. (LL) A Childish Prank. Ted Hughes. CABP; OAEL-2; OxBC

Crowd, The. John Masefield. OxBTC

Crowd and Not Evening Or Light. Leslie Scalapino.

   Series—3, The. PmAP

Crowd at the ball game, The. At the Ball Game. William Carlos Williams. CMoP; MoP; NOBA; NoAM; OxBA; PoE

Crowd fear: blown paper and uprooted ferns. The Spring Festival on the River. John Peck. AmPA

Crowd was gathering beneath the tent, A. The Clown. Margaret E. Bruner. PoToHe

Crowded Street, The. William Cullen Bryant. NCAP

Crowded Ways of Life. Walter S. Gresham. BLPA

Crowdieknowe. "Hugh MacDiarmid." InPS-3; OxBS

Crowds amassed with sudden bursts of. The. Victoria Station. Luigi Fontanella, *Italian*. NeIt, *tr.* by Michael Palma

Crowds of shuffling feet pass over the bridge. The Goddess Chiao. *Unknown, Chinese*. CoBCP, *tr.* by Burton Watson

Crowds pour from the train. My, what a crew—like people possessed! The Mother. Nikolai Ivanovich Dementyev, *Russian*. TCRP, *tr.* by Lubov Yakovleva *and* Max Hayward

Crowfield. Adrian Henri. AYFP

Crown, The. Donne. *See* La Corona.

Crown me with roses whilst I live. Abraham Cowley. OBVE *Fr.* Epicure ("Underneath this myrtle shade, The"). AWP

Crown of all travailing. *Unknown, Latin*. MLL, *tr.* by Helen Waddell *Fr.* Carmina Burana.

Crown of Days. *Unknown, Hebrew*. TrJP, *tr.* by Herbert Loewe

Crown of Happiness. Anne Hébert, *French*. BoWoP, *tr.* by Willis Barnstone

Crown of ivy! I submit my head, A. On Receiving a Crown of Ivy from the Same. Leigh Hunt. Son

Crown of Sonnets Dedicated to Love, A. Mary Sidney, Countess of Montgomery Wroth.

   In This Strange Labyrinth How Shall I Turn? NAEL-1

Crown of Windflowers, A. Christina Rossetti. OxBChV

Crown Prince of Dullness, The. Dryden. NOBE *Fr.* MacFlecknoe; or, A Satire [*or* Satyr] upon the True-Blue [*or* -Blew] Protestant Poet T. S. CBNP; FHYEP; HAP; OAEL-1; OBSV; OxBoLi; PeLV; Poetr; TFi

   ("Thou last great prophet of tautology.") (LL) NOSC

Crown your Bacchus with lettuce leaves, not ivy. Lucilius, *Greek*. GrAn, *tr.* by Peter Porter

Crowned, girdled, garbed and shod with light and fire. Marlowe. Swinburne. EPCY *Fr.* Sonnets of English Dramatic Poets. Son

Crowned with flowers, I saw fair Amarillis. *Unknown*. EnLoPo

Crowning a bluff where gleams the lake below. Pontoosuce. Herman Melville. APN-2; NOBA; NCAP

Crowns, The. John Freeman. CH

Crowns all thy mean affairs. (LL) Waldeinsamkeit. Ralph Waldo Emerson. APN-1; NOBA; PAR

Crows, The. Louise Bogan. FaBoWP; NALW; NMM-2

Crows, The. David McCord. MoAmPo

Crows, The. Maria Valli. CRAP

Crows. Valerie Worth. ImGa

Crows are cawing, The. Coming and Going. Robert Francis. TLR

Crows are come again to pick my eyes, The. Soliloquy on Death. F. K. Fiawoo. PBA

Crows came in, The. Caw Caw the Crows Caw Caw. *Unknown, Seneca Indian*. STP, *tr.* by Jerome Rothenberg *and* Richard Johnny John

Crows crowd croaking overhead. Summer Evening. John Clare. BoTP

Crow's-Eye View. Sang Yi.

   Poem No. II. PFTM

Crow's First Lesson. Ted Hughes. MoP; NoAM

Crows mark, The. African Day. Gloria de Sant'Ana, *Portuguese*. PBWP, *tr.* by Allan Francovich *and* Kathleen Weaver

Crow's Theology. Ted Hughes. GI

Crow's Way. Duane Niatum. CDW

Crucified. Francis Quarles. NOSC

Crucified Jesus on a yellow cross. Crucifixion. Ljubomir Simovic, *Serbo-Croatian.* HSix, *tr. by* Charles Simic

Crucified Lord, you swim upon your cross. Lachrimae Verae. Geoffrey Hill. NAEL-2; NoAM *Fr.* Lachrimae; or Seven Tears Figured in Seven Passionate Pavans.

Crucifix, The. Daniel Berrigan. CRP

Crucifix, A. John Gray. ADE

Crucifix Corner. Ivor Gurney. NSI

Crucifix in a Deathhand. Charles Bukowski. PmAP

Crucifixa. Marie-Madeleine, *German.* CPO, *tr. by* Lillian Faderman, Brigitte Eriksson *and* Frankie Hucklenbroich

Crucifixion. "Anna Andreyevna Akhmatova." GI, *tr. by* Stanley Kunitz and Max Hayward; IMW *Fr.* Requiem 1935-1940. BoWoP, *tr. by* Richard McKane

("Choir of angels glorified the hour, A.") GI, *tr. by* Stanley Kunitz and Max Hayward

("Into her secret eyes. Nobody dared.") (LL) GI, *tr. by* Stanley Kunitz and Max Hayward

Crucifixion, The. Mary Weston Fordham. CBWP-2

Crucifixion. Ljubomir Simovic, *Serbo-Croatian.* HSix, *tr. by* Charles Simic

Crucifixion, The. *Unknown, Irish.* TIRV, *tr. by* Kuno Meyer

Crucifixion. *Unknown.* BPo; TAP

Crucifixion of Our Blessed Lord. Christopher Smart. ChIV-2 *Fr.* Hymns and Spiritual Songs for the Fasts and Festivals of the Church of England.

Crucifixion to the World by the Cross of Christ. Isaac Watts. ECEV; NOCV; NOEC; PeECV

(Hymn.) AmFP; FaPoR

Cruciform. Winifred Welles. NYBP

Crucifying. Donne. *Fr.* La Corona. ChIV-2; ESCV; Son *Fr.* Holy Sonnets.

Crude Foyer. Wallace Stevens. LiTM; MeMAP

Cruel arrows gone, The. Fleche. Larry Eigner. VGW

Cruel Brother, The, *vers.* B. *Unknown.* ESPB

Cruel Brother, The. *Unknown.* AmFP; ESPB; OxBB

Cruel, Clever Cat. Geoffrey Taylor. FaBoEE

Cruel girls we loved, The. Mothers and Daughters. David Campbell. BMAP

Cruel Mistress, A. Thomas Carew. CavPo

Cruel Mother, The. *Unknown.* AmFP; ESPB; InPK-6; OxBB

Cruel Sister, The. *Unknown. See* The Two Sisters.

CRUEL, you pull away too soon your lips whenas you kiss me. *Unknown.* NoSic

Cruell Maid, The. Robert Herrick. CaPo

Crueller than owl or eagle. Ted Hughes. HAP *Fr.* Skylarks.

Cruelties. Robert Herrick. CavPo

Cruelty has a Human heart. A Divine Image. William Blake. ChIV-1; NAEL-2; NoP-4; OBNC; RB; Ro *Fr.* Songs of Experience.

Cruise, The. Robert Dunbar.

"Summit gain'd how glorious the reward, The." PBCV

Cruise of the *Mystery*, The. Celia Laighton Thaxter. OBCA

Cruising. Gig Ryan. BMAP

Crum Appointment, The. Lizelia Augusta Jenkins Moorer. CBWP-3

Crumble Hall. Mary Leapor.

In the Kitchen. ECWP

Crumbled rock of London is dripping under, The. Sonnet. Roy Fuller. PoA

Crumbling Infrastructure, The. Thomas M. Disch. EC3

Crumbling is not an instant's Act. Emily Dickinson. AmPP; NCAP; NOBA

("Slippingis Crash's law.") (LL) NCAP

Crumbs or the Loaf. Robinson Jeffers. CMoP

Crumpled handkerchief. Third-Class Car on a Night Train (three poems). Ōkuma Nobuyuki, *Japanese.* MJT, *tr. by* Makoto Ueda

Crumpled like an embroidered pillowcase. Kinged. Shalin Hai-Jew. UnSA

Crunch, The. Gerda Mayer. OBSP

Crunking crane heard high amongst the clouds, The. George Farewell. NOEC *Fr.* The Country Man.

Crusaders knew the Holy Places, The. Jenny Mastoraki, *Modern Greek.* BoWoP; PBWP, *tr. by* Nikos Germanakos

Crusader's wife slipped from the garrison, A. Limerick. Ogden Nash. PeLi

Cruse, The. Louise Townsend Nicholl. NYBP

Crush the manroot, swallow what you desire. Learning the Spells; a Diptych. Anita Endrezze-Danielson. CDW

Crushed by the waves upon the crag was I. Sea Dirge. Archias of Byzantium, *Greek.* AWP, *tr. by* Andrew Lang

Crushed Flower, The. Mary E. Tucker. CBWP-1

Crushing out life than waving me farewell! (LL) Kashmiri Song. "Laurence Hope." BLPA; FaBoBe

Crusoe had provided all the necessaries and was more or less at leisure in. Paul Valéry, *French.* PFTM, *tr. by* Corke, H.

Crusoe in England. Elizabeth Bishop. FaBoVe; HCAP; PoPoPo; RACG

Crusoe's Island. Derek Walcott. VCWP

Crustaceans. Roy Fuller. NoAM

Crutches. Robert Herrick. CaPo

Cry, 'All flesh is grass'. (LL) On a Clergyman's Horse Biting Him. *Unknown.* ChIV-1; FaBoEE; NBLV; OxBoLi

Cry, baby, cry, / Put your finger in your eye. *Unknown.* ReMoGo

Cry, Cock-a-diddle-dow! (LL) Ariel's Song: "Come unto these yellow sands." Shakespeare. BoTP; CH; CTC; EBEvV; FaBoCh; NOBE; NOSC; NoSic; OBEV; PoEL-2; SCGP; SoSe-8; TFi; TTTS

Cry, crow. Sonnet. Hayden Carruth. NNaP; Son

Cry Faugh! Robert Graves. MoBrPo

Cry from the Canadian Hills, A. Lilian Leveridge. BLPA

Cry from the Ghetto, A. Morris Jacob Rosenfeld, *Yiddish.* TrJP, *tr. by* Charles Weber Linn

Cry "God for Harry, England, and Saint George!" (LL) Henry V at the Siege of Harfleur. Shakespeare. EBEvV; OxAEP-1

Cry "Infidel!" Alfred Gibbs Campbell. AAP

Cry of a Stone, The. Anna Trapnell.

"O he is a rest that requires." PBRV

"Therefore John read how that thou wouldst." ChIV-2; KTR

Cry of battle, The. Labor Day (four poems). Ōkuma Nobuyuki, *Japanese.* MJT, *tr. by* Makoto Ueda

Cry of Birth. J. P. Clark Bekedermo. PBMAP *Fr.* A Reed in the Tide.

Cry of Blood, and of a Broken Covenant, The. Sir William Mure.

"O Heavens! O Earth! heer I must pause a space." PBRV

Cry of Europe, The. Sorley MacLean. FaBoTC

Cry of South Africa, The. Olive Schreiner. PeSAV

Cry of the Animals, The. Mary Howitt. VWP

Cry of the Child, The. William Zaranka. BXAP

Cry of the Children, The. Elizabeth Barrett Browning. EBVV; OxAEP-2; VWP

"They look up with their pale and sunken faces."

Cry of the Daughter of My People, The. Bible, *O.T.* TrJP *Fr.* Jeremiah.

Cry of the Dreamer, The. John Boyle O'Reilly. BLPA

Cry of the Oppressed, The. Henrietta Tindall. VWP

Cry of the Peoples, The. Alter Brody. TrJP

Cry of the stag, The. Yakamochi, *Japanese.* OHPJ, *tr. by* Kenneth Rexroth

Cry of those being eaten by America, The. Those Being Eaten by America. Robert Bly. CoAP

Cry out for Sakhr when a dove with necklaces. Elegy for Her Brother Sakhr. Al-Khansa, *Arabic.* BoWoP, *tr. by* Willis Barnstone

Cry, The, is: "Back to God!" Without respite. The Homeward Journey. Leonard Aaronson. TrJP

Cry went through me like a stab of a knife, A. W. H. Auden. *Fr.* A Happy New Year. OBSV

Cryer, The. Michael Drayton. PoEL-2; SCGP

(Crier, The.) NOSC

Crying. Scott Montgomery. HA

Crying Asia! that famous place. The Marriage of Hector and Andromache. Sappho, *Greek.* OBVE, *tr. by* Guy Davenport

Crying in Early Infancy. John Tranter.

"Chicago 'Manuel of Style' is really neat, The." NoAM

"Giving up women is worse than animal laxatives." NoAM

"It's bad luck with a coughing baby." CBAP

"Spy bears his bald intent like a maniac, The." CBAP

"Sweat is a style of the body." NoAM

"They burn the radio and listen to the blues." NoAM

Crying only a little bit. Galway Kinnell. ChAP; KaS; NTCP

Crying out for the help of me. (LL) The Holy Well ("As it fell out one May morning"). *Unknown.* FaBoCh; NOCV

Crying plovers, The. Fujiwara No Sueyoshi, *Japanese.* OHMPJ, *tr. by* Kenneth Rexroth

Crying unseen, birds awaken me from my sleep. Impressions. Lu Yu, *Chinese.* SuSp, *tr. by* Irving Y. Lo

Crying white candle, A. The Haunted. Brad Leithauser. RA

Cryptic philosopher, Kant, The. Limerick. "E. F. C." PeLi

Crystal, The. George Barker. LiTM; OBMV

Crystal Cabinet, The. William Blake. CH; FaBoCh; OAEL-2; OBNC; PoEL-4; Ro

("I filled with woes the passing wind.") (LL) Ro

Crystal, flawless beauty on the brows, A. A Portrait. "Michael Field." VWP

Crystal Gazer, The. Sara Teasdale. MoAmPo

Crystal Lithium, The. James Schuyler. PmAP; PoM; VCAP

Crystal Palace, The. John Davidson. PeVV

Crystal parting the meads. The River in the Meadows. Léonie Adams. MoAmPo

Crystal Text, The. Clark Coolidge. PT

Crystallization of color, A. Aurora Borealis. Edouard Roditi. SPE

Crystals kissed / in cabinets of amethyst and frost. Geoffrey Hill. *See* The Laurel Axe.

Crystals like Blood. "Hugh MacDiarmid." HAP; RB

Crystals of fog have frozen on the thorns. Wanting News. Sydney Tremayne. FaBoTC

Cú Chuimne in his youth. Epitaph for Cú Chuimne. *Unknown, Irish.* NOIV, *tr. by* Thomas Kinsella

Cu Chuimne in youth. *Unknown, Irish.* BIrV, *tr. by* John V. Kelleher

Cuba. Thomas MacDermot. PBCV

Cuba. Paul Muldoon. CIP-2; PNI

Cuba, disheveled, naked to the waist. On a Monument to Martí. Walter Adolphe Roberts. PBCV; TTY

Cuba Libre. Imamu Amiri Baraka. BB

Cuba Night. Dave Jeddie Smith. NAmP90

Cuba, 1962. Ai. AmPA

Cubana bird touched down, The. Waiting for Fidel. John Agard. PBCV

Cubic inch of some stars, A. Blue Tit on a String of Peanuts. Norman MacCaig. CABP; FaBoTC

Cubical Domes, The. David Gascoyne. SPE

Cubicled women / pecking at computers. The Secret of the Legal Secretary's Cigarette Smoke. Martín Espada. FiLi

Cubist Portrait. Marjorie Allen Seiffert. PoA

Cuchulain Comforted. W. B. Yeats. CMoP; LiTM; OAEL-2; TOF

Cuchulainn. Michael O'Loughlin. BiHa; PBCIP

Cuckolded husbands have no certain sign. Palladas, *Greek.* GrAn, *tr. by* Tony Harrison

Cuckoo. Robert Desnos, *French.* PFTM, *tr. by* Armand Schwerner

Cuckoo, The. Gerard Manley Hopkins. MoBrPo; OxBSP; RB; TTTS

Cuckoo, The. *Unknown.* BoTP; FaBoVe; RB

Cuckoo!/ Cuckoo! Chiyojo, *Japanese.* WPJ, *tr. by* Kenneth Rexroth *and* Ikuko Atsumi

Cuckoo: Abandoned unborn by my begetters. *Unknown.* EEP, *tr. by* Michael Alexander *Fr.* Riddles (Exeter Book).

Cuckoo and the gowk, the. Riddle. *Unknown.* FaBoVe

Cuckoo, are you calling me. The Cuckoo Wood. Edmund Beale Sargant. NSI

Cuckoo calls from the bamboo grove, The. *Unknown, Chinese.* OHMPC, *tr. by* Kenneth Rexroth

Cuckoo calls its flock—it's when the rice, The. Tố Hũ'u, *Vietnamese.* AVP, *tr. by* Huỳnh Sanh Thông

Cuckoo calls. / When I look there is only, A. Sanesada, *Japanese.* OHPJ, *tr. by* Kenneth Rexroth

Cuckoo, cherry tree. *Unknown.* FaBoVe

Cuckoo comes in April, The. *Unknown.* OxNR

Cuckoo cries / Go home, go home, The. Tune: "Song of Great Virtue"—Spring. Kuan Han-ch'ing, *Chinese.* SuSp, *tr. by* Jerome P. Seaton

Cuckoo, cuckoo, cherry tree. *Unknown.* OxNR

Cuckoo, cuckoo / What do you do? *Unknown.* CTAV; LB; OxNR ("Go I must.") (LL) OxNR

Cuckoo, glad cuckoo, Oh! where wilt thou rest to-night? Cuckoo Song. Henrietta Cordelia Ray. CBWP-3

Cuckoo: In former days my father and mother [*or* mother and father]. Riddle: Cuckoo. Cynewulf. AnOE, *tr. by* Charles W. Kennedy; ASW, *tr. by* Kevin Crossley-Holland *Fr.* Riddles (Exeter Book).

Cuckoo is a bonny [*or* fine *or* merry] bird, The. *Unknown.* AmFP; NTP; OxNR

Cuckoo, noisy among the Shenbaka flowers. Andal, *Tamil.* BoWoP, *tr. by* Willis Barnstone

Cuckoo on Mt. Chiri, The. Sugwon Song, *Korean.* CKP, *tr. by* Jaihiun Kim

Cuckoo Song. Rudyard Kipling. NTP

Cuckoo Song. Henrietta Cordelia Ray. CBWP-3

Cuckoo-throb, the heartbeat of the Spring, The. Ardour and Memory. D. G. Rossetti. OAEL-2 *Fr.* The House of Life.

Cuckoo—to welcome in the spring! (LL) Trico's Song. John Lyly. CH; NOBE; NoSic; OBEV; SCGP

Cuckoo Waltz. *Unknown.* AS

Cuckoo Wood, The. Edmund Beale Sargant. NSI

Cuckoo's double note, The. Wiltshire Downs. Andrew Young. GTBS-P; NTP; OxBTC

Cucumber, The. Nazim Hikmet, *Turkish.* VCWP, *tr. by* Randy Blasing *and* Mutlu Konuk

Cuddie [*or* Cuddy], for shame hold up thy heavy[e] head. October. Edmund Spenser. NAEL-1; OAEL-1 *Fr.* The Shepheardes [*or* Shepeards *or* Shepherd's] Calender.

Cuddled in the dark. 4½ Months: Halfway Song. George Barlow. ISC

Cudgeled Husband, The. Jonathan Swift. *See* Three Epigrams.

Cuernavaca. Ory Bernstein. *Fr.* Poems from Mexico. IP, *tr. by* Warren Bargad *and* Stanley F. Chyet

Cui Bono? Horace Smith *and* James Smith (1775–1839). NOBRP

Cuillins tower, The. Iain Crichton Smith. FaBoTC *Fr.* The White Air of March.

Cuisine Bourgeoise. Wallace Stevens. MeMAP

Culbin Sands. Andrew Young. GTBS-P; OxBS; OxBTC

Culloden and After. Iain Crichton Smith. OxBS

Culprit Fay, The. Joseph Rodman Drake. APN-1

Elfin Knight, An. BoTP

Cult of the Celtic, The. Anthony C. Deane. BXAP; NOBL; PeLV

Cultivated Signals types. Footnote to Enright's "Apocalypse." Martin Bell. FaBoMo

Cultivation. Mrs. Henry Linden. CBWP-4

Cultural Exchange. Langston Hughes. BPo; PoBA

Cultural Notes. Kenneth Fearing. CMoP; PoE

Cultural Trip, A. Opal Palmer Adisa. GT

Culture and Anarchy. Adrienne Rich. NALW

Culture as Exhibit. "Ern Malley." BMAP

Cultured gentleman, mature, congenial, refined. Personal. Samuel Yellen. NYBP

Cultured Girl Again, The. Ben King. OBAL

Cultures. Gloria Anzaldúa. UnSA

Cum here, Mandy, what's you chewin'. When Daddy Cums from Wuk. Maggie Pogue Johnson. CBWP-4

Cumae. Merrill Moore. FuPo

Cumberland, The. Henry Wadsworth Longfellow. CBCWP

Cumberland and the *Merrimac.* . . The. *Unknown.* AmFP

Cumberland Gap. *Unknown.* APN-2

Cumberland Rocks. Barbara Hoole. Ro *Fr.* Poems.

Cumberland Station. Dave Jeddie Smith. HCAP

Cumberland's Crew, The. *Unknown.* AmFP

Cumnor Hall. William Julius Mickle. OxBB

Cuncta Semper. Rodolfo Di Biasio, *Italian.* NeIt, *tr. by* Stephen Sartarelli

Cunjah Man, De. James Edwin Campbell. AAP

Cunning and art he did not lack. The Allansford Pursuit. Robert Graves. RB

Cunning Clerk, The. *Unknown.* OxBB

Cunning Painter, that with curious care, The. Joshua Sylvester. PBRV *Fr.* Saluste du Bartas' Devine Weekes.

Cup, The. Anacreon, *Greek.* GrIP, *tr. by* Thomas Stanley

Cup, The. John Oldham. AWP

Cup, The. Jones Very. APN-1

Cup, The. Judith Wright. FaBoWP

Cup clinks out, my friend, The. Apollonides, *Greek.* GrAn, *tr. by* Peter Whigham

Cup takes its sweet joy and tells how it touches, The. Meleager. HePo, *tr. by* Barbara Hughes Fowler *Fr.* I'll Twine White Violets. NIP-4, *tr. by* Goldwin Smith

Cupbearer, O victorious Falcon, come! Qorratu'l-Ayn. WPOW, *tr. by* Deirdre Lashgari *Fr.* He the Beloved.

Cupboard, The. Walter De la Mare. NTCP

Cupid. Bernard O'Dowd. NOBAu

Cupid. Sir Philip Sidney. SiPS *Fr.* Arcadia.

Cupid a Plowman. Moschus. *See* Cupid Turned Plowman.

CUPID abroad was lated in the night. A Night Visitor. Robert Greene. NoSic

Cupid and Campaspe. John Lyly. *See* Cards and Kisses.

Cupid and Death. James Shirley.

Song: "Victorious men of earth, no more." BeJo

(Last Conqueror, The.) GTBS-P

Cupid and my Campaspe played [*or* playd]. Cards and Kisses. John Lyly. CBLP; GBL; GTBS-P; HoPM; NOBE; NoSic; OBEV; OxAEP-1; PBMP; PoRA; SCGP *Fr.* Alexander and Campaspe.

Cupid as he lay among. The Wounded Cupid. Song. Anacreon, *Greek.* AWP; LoP; OBCVT; OBVE, *tr. by* Robert Herrick

Cupid at Venus' breast. Meleager, *Greek.* GrAn, *tr. by* Peter Whigham

Cupid at work. Virgil, *Latin.* OBCVT, *tr. by* William Wordsworth

Cupid, because thou shin'st in Stella's eyes. Sonnet 12. Sir Philip Sidney. *Fr.* Astrophil and Stella. AAS; SiPS

Cupid, begon! who wou'd on thee rely. To his false Mistress. Ovid, *Latin.* OBCVT, *tr. by* Sir Charles Sedley

Cupid Far Gone. Richard Lovelace. CaPo

Cupid, I hate thee, which I'd have thee know. Michael Drayton. SCGP

Cupid, in *Myra's* faire bewitching eyes. Fulke Greville. PBRV *Fr.* Cælica.

Cupid Lost. Mary Sidney, Countess of Montgomery Wroth. *See* Sonnet 2: "Late in the Forest I did Cupid See."

Cupid, thou naughty boy, when thou wert loathed. Fulke Greville. Son *Fr.* Caelica.

Cupid Turned Plowman. Moschus, *Greek.* AWP, *tr. by* Matthew Prior (Cupid a Plowman.) OBVE

Cupid's Call. James Shirley. BeJo; NOSC

Cupid's Wrongs Vindicated. Martin Parker. "Thou knowst I lov'd thee well." PBRV

Cupio Dissolvi. William Habington. ChIV-2

Cupping her chin and lying there, the Bren. Defensive Position. John Streeter Manifold. MoBrPo

Cur foretells the knell of parting day, The. Elegy. Ambrose Bierce. APN-2; OBAL *Fr.* The Devil's Dictionary.

Curate Thinks You Have No Soul, The. St. John Lucas. BLPA

Curative Powers of Silence, The. Al Young. GT

Cure, The. Alfred Noyes. FuFo

Cure at Porlock, A. Amy Clampitt. NoAM

Cure for Fault Finding, A. Strickland W. Gillilan. *See* Watch Yourself Go By.

Cure for Poetry, A. Annabella Blount. ECWP

Cure for Poetry, A. *Unknown, after the Latin of* George Buchanan. FaBoEE

Cured, I am frizzled, stale and small. (LL) Home after Three Months Away. Robert Lowell. HCAP; MoLi; PBMP

Curfew. Teresa de Jesús, *Spanish.* AF, *tr. by* Maria Proser, Arlene Scully *and* James Scully

Curfew. Paul Éluard, *French.* BoLoP, *tr. by* Quentin Stevenson

Curfew. Henry Wadsworth Longfellow. APN-1; MeMAP; OxBA

Curfew Must Not Ring Tonight [*or* To-Night]. Rose Hartwick Thorpe. APN-2; BLPA; FaBoBe

Curfew tolls the hour of locking up, The. Elegy in Newgate. William Cobbett. UV

Curfew tolls the knell of parting day, The. Diversions of the Re-Echo Club. Carolyn Wells. OBAL

Curfew tolls the knell of parting day, The. Thomas Gray. PBMP; UV *Fr.* Elegy Written in a Country Churchyard. APAD; AWP; CABP; ClHu; EBEV; EBEvV; FHYEP; FaBoBe; FaBoPV; FaPoR; GTBS-P; HAP; HeIP-4; ImPo; InPK-6; InPS-3; NOBE; NOEC; NoP-4; OAEL-1; OBEV; OxAEP-1; PBMP; PoEL-3; PoLF; PoPoPo; Poetr; SCGP; SCV; TFi; UV; UnPo; WeW-3

("And Melancholy marked him for her own.") (LL)   PBMP

Curfew tolls the knell of parting day, The. If Gray Had Had to Write His Elegy in the Cemetery of Spoon River Instead of in That of Stoke Poges. Sir John Collings Squire. BXAP

Curing Homosexuality. Jim Everhard. GLP

Curio's rich sideboard seldom sees the light. On a Stingy Beau. John Winstanley. FaBoEE

Curiosity. Alastair Reid. PC; SoSe-8

Curiosity-Shop, The. Peter Redgrove. OxBC

Curious is this stonework! The Fates destroyed it. The Ruin. *Unknown, Anglo-Saxon.* EBEV, *tr. by* Gavin Bone

Curious knot God made in paradise, A. Upon Wedlock and Death of Children. Edward Taylor. AmPP; ColAP; NAAL-1; NAAL-3; NoP-4

Curious music that I hear, The. (LL) The Land of Nod. Robert Louis Stevenson. ACTP; FPC; PWR

Curious tale that threaded through the town, A. Le loupgarou. Derek Walcott. OxBSn

Curious, the assembly that forms before a door, a large door always. Jews in Hell. Tom Mandel. PmAP

Curious wits, seeing dull pensiveness, The. Sonnet 223. Sir Philip Sidney. *Fr.* Astrophil and Stella. AAS; SiPS

Curl Up and Diet. Ogden Nash. OBCoV

Curliest Thing, The. *Unknown.* BoTP

Curling them around. Cutting Greens. Lucille Clifton. CrSp; GT

Curly Locks [!] Curly Locks [!] wilt thou be mine? Mother Goose. LB; OxNR; ReMoGo

Curr dhoo, curr dhoo. Mother Goose. OxNR

Currency Lads may fill their glasses, The. The Lass in the Female Factory. *Unknown.* NOBAu

Current, The. James Merrill. NYBP

Currents. Emma Lazarus. PAR *Fr.* By the Waters of Babylon. WPE

Curricle and hansom, The. The Great Garret, or 100 Wheels. James McMichael. AmPA

Curriculum Vitae. Ingeborg Bachmann, *German.* BoWoP, *tr. by* Jerome Rothenberg

Curriculum vitae. Marie-Claire Bancquart, *French.* MFP, *tr. by* Martin Sorrell

Curriculum Vitae. Robert Gray. NOBAu

Curriculum Vitae. Lawrence Joseph. PBCAP

Curse, The. John Hollander. UnPo

Curse. Kalju Lepik, *Estonian.* CEEP, *tr. by* Ivar Ivask

Curse, The. John Millington Synge. FaBoEE; NOIV; OBCoV

Curse, A. *Unknown, Irish.* BIrV, *tr. by* Douglas Hyde

Curse. A Song, The. Robert Herrick. CaPo

Curse for a Nation, A. Elizabeth Barrett Browning. NALW; WPE; WPOW ("I send it over the Western Sea.") (LL) VWP

Curse of Cromwell, The. W. B. Yeats. BIrV; IIP

Curse of Kehama, The. Robert Southey.
Kehama's Curse.
("For ever and ever.") (LL) OBNC
Love Indestructible. OBNC

Curse of the Cat Woman. Edward Field. WeW-3

Curse on Herod, A. Amy Witting. ChIV-2; NOBAu

Curse on the star, dear Harry, that betrayed. An Epistle from a Half-Pay Officer in the Country to His Friend in London. Richardson Pack. NOEC

Curse on Uruk, A. Enheduanna, *Sumerian.* BoWoP, *tr. by* Aliki *and* Willis Barnstone

Curse the tongue in my head. Good Night! Good Night! John Holmes. PoToHe

Curse upon Edward, The. Thomas Gray. OBEV

Curse upon that faithless maid, A. Song. Aphra Behn. WPE *Fr.* Emperor of the Moon.

Cursed Be the Day. Bible, *O.T.* TrJP *Fr.* Jeremiah.

Curses. Ljubomir Simovic, *Serbo-Croatian.* HSix, *tr. by* Charles Simic

Cursive crawl, the squared-off characters, The. Writing. Howard Nemerov. NYBP; VCAP

Curtain. Lance Henson. VoR

Curtain of daybreak is hanging, The. First Daylight Song. *Unknown.* APN-2, *tr. by* Washington Matthews *Fr.* The Mountain Chant.

Curtain of the Wedding Bed, The. Liu Hsün's Wife, *Chinese.* ChiP, *tr. by* Arthur Waley

Curtain rung down on his wise old age, The. *Unknown, Greek.* GrAn, *tr. by* W. G. Shepherd

Curtains. Ruth Stone. NAmP90

Curtains drawn back, the door ajar. Robinson at Home. Weldon Kees. CoAP; NYBP

Curtains in the House of the Metaphysician, The. Wallace Stevens. PoA

Curtains now are drawn, The. Thomas Hardy. CMoP

Curtains of rock. Orpheus in the Underworld. David Gascoyne. FaBoTw

Curtains were half drawn, the floor was swept, The. After Death. Christina Rossetti. GBL; GSo; LoP; NAEL-2; NALW

Curtis Fuller. Rick Madigan. SeSe

Curvd lines toe-drawn, round cornerd squares, The. Hop, Skip, and Jump. Gary Snyder. LCAP-2

Curve of the path was to the left, The. The Nose, the Grand Canyon, and the Sixties. Arthur Vogelsang. BAP-95

Curve of the Water. Hilda Morley. PmAP

Curved clouds are sailing, like yachts with spinnakers. Flotilla. Clive Sansom. AYFP

Curving. Tropical Fish. Christopher Vernon Hassall. PeP

Curving, leaping line of light, A. Prairie Fires. Hamlin Garland. OBCA

Curzon! thou shouldst be living at this hour. Sonnet to the "Most Distinguished Chancellor" that Oxford Has Had. Max Beerbohm *and* William Rothenstein. UV

Cushie Butterfield. George Ridley. FaBoVe; NTP

Cushy cow bonny, let down thy milk. Mother Goose. CTAV; OxNR; ReMoGo

Custard, The. Robert Herrick. PFE

Custer Lives in Humbolt County. Janet Campbell Hale. VoR

Custer's Last Charge. Frederick Whittaker. PoLF

Custom, in this small article I find. On Snuff-Taking. Elizabeth Teft. ECWP

Custom Job: Hank Williams, Jr., and the Death Car, 1958. David Wojahn. PBCAP *Fr.* Mystery Train: A Sequence.

Custom of the World, The. Louis Simpson. BoLoP

Customize the Grass. Peter Finch. NBrP

Customs Change. *Unknown.* OxBChV

Cut. Sylvia Plath. TAP

Cut brambles long enough. Sun Bu-er, *Chinese.* WPoS, *tr. by* Jane Hirshfield

Cut branches back for a day. Trail Crew Camp at Bear Valley. 9000 Feet. Gary Snyder. HCAP

Cut down, and up again as blithe as ever. (LL) Ianthe's Troubles. Walter Savage Landor. GBL; NOBE; OBEV; OBNC

Cut Flower, A. Karl Shapiro. HAP; WeW-3

Cut grass lies frail. Philip Larkin. NTP; NoAM; OxBC; RB

Cut loose, without devotion, a man becomes a comic. Without Devotion. Marie Howe. NAmP90

Cut the Grass. A. R. Ammons. HAP; Poetr; TAP; WeW-3

Cut the pear or I cut the pear. On Entries Emptiness. Dennis Phillips. FTOS

Cut them on Monday, you cut them for health. *Unknown.* OxNR

Cut thistles in May. *Unknown.* OxNR

Cut yer name across me backbone. Convicts' Rum Song. *Unknown.* FaBoVe; NOBAu

Cute secretary, none cuter, A. Limerick. Ogden Nash. PeLi

Cutstone Pond. Chao Meng-fu. *Fr.* Twenty-Eight Poems Inscribed on T'ien-kuan Mountain. CoBLCP, *tr. by* Jonathan Chaves

Cutter risen from the mollusks, it is a god, A. The Memoirs. Carl Rakosi. PoA

Cutting back / wherever the weather. The Pruning. Adam David Miller. NBV

Cutting Edge, The. Philip Levine. NYBP

Cutting Greens. Lucille Clifton. CrSp; GT

Cutting Prow, The. Edward Sanders. PmAP

Cutting that jungle road from Lugardville. Surveyor. Guy Butler. PeSA

Cutting up an Ox. Chuang Tzu, *Chinese.* EnlH, *tr. by* Thomas Merton

Cuttings ("Sticks-in-a-drowse droop over sugary loam"). Theodore Roethke. ColAP; HCAP; LCAP-2; MoP; NAAL-2; NOBA; NoAM; OBGa; TAP; UnPo

Cuttings ("This urge, wrestle, resurrection of dry sticks"). Theodore Roethke. ColAP; HCAP; LCAP-2; MoP; NAAL-2; NOBA; NoAM; OBGa; TAP; TRP; UnPo; VCAP

Cutty Sark. Hart Crane. FaBoMo *Fr.* The Bridge. NAAL-2

Cutty Wren, The. *Unknown.* OxBoLi; UV

Cuz he's black and poor. About Atlanta. Ntozake Shange. ISC

C'wa nou, what wey suld I chap o this door? Aristophanes. OBCVT, *tr. by* Douglas Young *Fr.* The Frogs.

Cwmrhydyceirw Elegiacs. Vernon Watkins. PoA

Cyanide jar seals life, as sonnets move, The. Butterfly Bones; or, Sonnet against Sonnets. Margaret Avison. LiTM

Cyclamens. "Michael Field." NOBVV; VWP

Cycle. Gottfried Benn, *German.* PFTM, *tr. by* Francis C. Golffing

Cycle. Ruth Miller. PeSA

"Cover my eyes with your palm."

"Dropped leaf, The."

"To eat pain like bread is a condition."

Cycle. Bobbi Sykes. BMAP

Cycle Akhmatova, The. Marina Tsvetayeva, *Russian.*

". . . In my melodious city cupolas burn." AF, *tr. by* Mary Maddock

Cycle for Mother Cabrini, A. John Logan.

"Saint, who overlaps." CRP

Cycle of life is a worrisome thing, The. On Covering the Bones of Chang Chin, the Hired Man. Liu Tsung-yüan, *Chinese.* SuSp, *tr. by* Jan W. Walls

Cycle sings, A. Nature. Walter Stone. NYBP

Cyclist, The. Marge Piercy. NoAM

Cyclists, The. Amy Lowell. WPE

Cyclop! if any ask thee who imposed. Ulysses Insults over the Cyclops. Homer. NOSC, *tr. by* George Chapman *Fr.* Odyssey. NAWM-1, *tr. by* Robert Fitzgerald

Cyclops. Euripides, *Greek.*

"But, o great offspring of the Ocean King." OBCVT, *tr. by* Shelley

Chorus of Satyrs, Driving Their Goats. AWP

Love Song: "One with eyes the fairest." AWP

Cyclops. Ovid. CTC, *tr. by* Arthur Golding *Fr.* Metamorphoses.

Cyclops, The. Theocritus, *Greek.*

"Thus sweetly sad of old, the *Cyclops* strove." OBCVT, *tr. by* Richard Duke

Cyclops and No-Man. Homer. OBCVT, *tr. by* George Chapman *Fr.* The Odyssey.

Cyclops, The ("And so an easier life"). Theocritus. AWP *Fr.* Idylls.

("For love there is no other drug, Nicias.") HePo, *tr. by* Barbara Hughes Fowler

Cyder. John Philips.

Apple-Culture. OxAEP-1

Cymbals crash, The. A Victory Dance. Alfred Noyes. NSI; PoLF

Cymbeline. Shakespeare.

Aubade: "Hark! hark! tahe lark at heaven's gate sings." OBEV

"How found you him?" OxAEP-1

Song: "Fear no more the heat o' the Sun." CTC; EBEvV; NOSC; PoE; PoEL-2

("Consign to thee and come to dust.") (LL) GTBS-P; PFE

(Dirge.) OAEL-1

(Fidele.) GTBS-P; OBEV

"With fairest flowers./ Whilst summer lasts." EBEV; RB

Song: "Hark! hark! the lark at heaven's gate sings." EBEvV; NOSC

Cymochles and Phaedria. Edmund Spenser. *Fr.* Wood Of Error. AEP

Cymon and Iphigenia. Dryden. EPCY; OBNV

Militia, The. OBSV

Power of Love, The.

Cymru. David Gwenallt Jones, *Welsh.* OBWVE, *tr. by* Gwyn Jones

Cynderaxa kind and good. Trim's Song: The Fair Kitchen-Maid. Sir Richard Steele. OxBSP *Fr.* The Funeral.

Cynic, The. St. George Tucker. OBAL

"Once at a merry wedding feast." NBLV

Cynic Satire, A. John Marston. NoSic *Fr.* Satires.

Cynic says: Now that we know, A. Limerick. Thomas Thorneley. PeLi

Cynical Portraits. Louis Paul. NBLV

Cynical sage with a kink, A. Limerick. Hassall Pitman. PeLi

Cynthia. Richard Barnfield.

Cherry-lipped Adonis. Son

Sighing, and Sadly Sitting by My Love. Son

Cynthia in the Snow. Gwendolyn Brooks. TLR

Cynthia Matz, with my finger in your cunt. Each Day. David Ignatow. NNaP

Cynthia on Horseback. Philip Ayres. EnLoPo

Cynthia, to thy power. Bridal Song. Francis Beaumont *and* John Fletcher. OBEV *Fr.* The Maid's Tragedy.

Cynthia's Revels. Ben Jonson.

Glove, The. GBL

Hymn to Diana. AWP; CH; GTBS-P; HAP; NOBE; OBEV; PoRA; SeCP; TFi

(Hesperus' Hymne[e] to Cynthia.)

(Hymn to Cynthia.) NOSC; PoE; SCGP

Song: "Slow, slow fresh fount, keep time with my salt tears." OxBSP; PoEL-2; SeCP

(Echo's Lament for Narcissus.) CH; OxAEP-1

Cypassis, that a thousand ways trim'st hair. 2.8. Ovid. EBEV, *tr. by* Marlowe *Fr.* Elegies.

Cypress stood up like a church, The. Bianca Among the Nightingales. Elizabeth Barrett Browning. BrRo; GTBS-P

Cypresses. Robert Francis. LCAP-2

Cypresses. D. H. Lawrence. NAEL-2

Cypris who puts the sea to rest. Philodemus, *Greek.* GrAn, *tr. by* William Moebius

Cyriack, this three years['] day these eyes, though clear. To Mr. Cyriack Skinner upon His Blindness. Milton. NOSC; OxAEP-1; PeECV; Son

Cyriack, whose Grandsire on the Royal Bench. To Cyriack Skinner. Milton. GTBS-P; NOSC; NoP-4; OBEV; OxAEP-1; Son

Cyril and Methodius. Aleksandar Vuco, *Serbo-Croatian.* HSix, *tr. by* Charles Simic

Cyril Connolly. Enemies of Promise. Edmund Wilson. OBCoV

Cythera. David Ferry. DiPo; GS

Cythère. Paul Verlaine, *French.* AWP, *tr. by* Arthur Symons

Cywdd to Morvydd, The. Dafydd ap Gwilym, *Welsh.* NOEC

Czar's Last Christmas Letter: A Barn in the Urals, The. Norman Dubie. NoAM

Czestochowa, Jasna Gora, Auschwitz, Nova Huta. Lolek. John Jordan. TIRV

D

D Blues. Calvin C. Hernton. PoBA

D. C. Karl Shapiro. NYBP

D   dronken. *Unknown.* MiEL

D.G.C. to J.A. Emily Jane Brontë. BrRo; EnLoPo

D. G. Rossetti. Dorothy Parker. NALW *Fr.* A Pig's-Eye View of Literature.

D. H. Lawrence and James Joyce. Humbert Wolfe. FaBoEE

D is for Dog. W. H. Davies. OxBSP

D.O.A. Tim Dlugos. EC3

D-Y Bar. James Welch. CDW

D-Zug. Julian Croft. NOBAu

Da Silva Gives the Cue. Walter Hart Blumenthal. TrJP

Dab of Color, A. Theodore Weiss. VGW

Dabbling in the Dew. *Unknown.* CH

Dacca Gauzes, The. Agha Shahid Ali. NoP-4

Daccus is all bedaub'd with golden lace. Against Gaudy-Bragging-Undoughty Daccus. John, of Hereford Davies. FaBoEE

Dachshund leads a quiet life, The. Dachshunds. William Jay Smith. OBAL

Dachshunds ("Dachshund leads a quiet life, The"). William Jay Smith. OBAL

Dad a da da. Aborigine Sound Poem. *Unknown.* PFTM

Dad and the Cat and the Tree. Kit Wright. OTCP

Dad pushed my mother down the cellar stairs. Those Paperweights with Snow Inside. Molly Peacock. RA

Dad waited while Mum bought the ham. Limerick. Coral E. Copping. PeLi

Dada, having only a few years or months or days to live, looks for a law-. Artichokes. Georges Ribemont-Dessaignes, *French.* PFTM, *tr. by* Pierre Joris

Dada Manifesto on Feeble and Bitter Love. Tristan Tzara, *French.* PFTM, *tr. by* Barbara Wright *Fr.* Dada Manifesto on Feeble and Bitter Love.

Dada would have liked a day like this. Lawrence Ferlinghetti. NeAP *Fr.* Pictures of a Gone World.

Daddy. Sylvia Plath. BoWoP; CMoP; CoAP; ColAP; HCAP; HP; HeIP-4; InPK-6; InPS-3; LiTM; MoLi; MoP; NAAL-2; NALW; NIP-4; NMM-2; NOBA; NoAM; NoP-4; PoE; PoPoPo; Poetr; TFi; TwCP; UnPo; VCAP

Daddy. Warning. Langston Hughes. PFTM

Daddy and Mummy. Life Story. Taeko Tomioka, *Japanese.* WPOW, *tr. by* Harry Guest, Lynn Guest, *and* Kajima Shozo

Daddy at the stove or sink. Large. June Jordan. MoLi *Fr.* War and Memory.

Daddy, daddy, you bastard, I'm through. (LL) Daddy. Sylvia Plath. BoWoP; CMoP; CoAP; ColAP; HCAP; HP; HeIP-4; InPK-6; InPS-3; LiTM; MoLi; MoP; NAAL-2; NALW; NIP-4; NMM-2; NOBA; NoAM; NoP-4; PoE; PoPoPo; Poetr; TFi; TwCP; UnPo; VCAP

Daddy eat dog shark, malingay. Dog Shark. *Unknown.* PBCV

Daddy Fell into the Pond. Alfred Noyes. ChAP; NOxBChV

Daddy Long-legs and the Fly, The. Edward Lear. CBNP

Daddy Poem, A. William J. Harris. ISC

("My father is a hand-/ some guy.") NBV

("'You're good looking / for a colored man'.") (LL) UnSA

Daddy sits / in his brown. Sunflowers and Saturdays. Melba Joyce Boyd. BISi

Daddy would drop purple-veined vines. Banking Potatoes. Yusef Komunyakaa. NAAAL; NoP-4

Daddy's Friends. Esther Iverem. GT

Dae what ye wull ye canna parry. "Hugh MacDiarmid." EBEV; OxAEP-2 *Fr.* A Drunk Man Looks at the Thistle.

Daedal of my death, A. Madrigal. William Drummond, of Hawthornden. NOSC

Daedalus. Leonid Nikolaevich Martynov, *Russian.* TCRP, *tr. by* J. R. Rowland

Daedalus. Ovid. CTC; OBVE, *tr. by* Arthur Golding *Fr.* Metamorphoses.

Daedalus. Alastair Reid. NYBP

Daedalus: The Dirge. George Oppen. FTOS

Daemon, The. Louise Bogan. NYBP

Daemon, The. Mikhail Yuryevich Lermontov, *Russian.*

"On the sightless seas of ether." AWP, *tr. by* Babette Deutsch *and* Avrahm Yarmolinsky

Dæmonic and the Celestial Love, The. Ralph Waldo Emerson. APN-1 *Fr.* Initial, Dæmonic, and Celestial Love.

Daffadowndilly. Mother Goose. CTV

Daffodil. Waldo Williams, *Welsh.* OBWVE, *tr. by* Gwyn Jones

Daffodil Song, The. Michael Drayton. AEP *Fr.* The Shepherd's Garland. (Shepheard's Daffodil, The.)

Daffodils. P. A. Ropes. BoTP

Daffodils. Wordsworth. CTV; ChAP; ImPo; Ro

Daffodils shiver. Early Spring. Adrian Henri. AYFP

Daffy-down-dilly is new come to town [*or* Daffadowndilly has come up to town]. Daffadowndilly. Mother Goose. CTV; NTCP; OxNR

Dafney parades her resentment of this city. Dafney's Lamentation. W. C. Morton. EC2

Dafney's Lamentation. W. C. Morton. EC2

Daft Days, The. Robert Fergusson. CABP; NOEC; OxAEP-1

Dafydd ap Gwilym Resents the Winter. Rolfe Humphries. NYBP

Dagger, The ("Dagger rests in a drawer, A"). Jorge Luis Borges, *Spanish.* NYBP, *tr. by* Norman Thomas Di Giovanni

Dagger. Mikhail Yuryevich Lermontov, *Russian.* AWP, *tr. by* Max Eastman

Dagger-hilt crusted with flaming gems, A. Beauty's Anadems. John Barlas. ADE

Dagger rests in a drawer, A. The Dagger. Jorge Luis Borges, *Spanish.* NYBP, *tr. by* Norman Thomas Di Giovanni

Dago shovelman sits by the railroad track, The. Child of the Romans. Carl Sandburg. NAAL-2

Daguerreotype Taken in Old Age. Margaret Atwood. BoWoP; NoAM

Dahlias are black. Tanka. Saitō Mokichi, *Japanese.* MJT, *tr. by* Makoto Ueda

Dahn the Plug'ole. *Unknown.* RB, *tr. by* Robert Bly ("Biby's" Epitaph.) NOxBChV

Dahomey. Audre Lorde. NAAL-2

Dai horse neighs against the bleak wind of Etsu, The. South-Folk in Cold Country. Ezra Pound, *after the Chinese.* OBVE

Daily Daily, The. Nicolás Guillén, *Spanish.* National Police Headquarters. PFTM, *tr. by* Vera M. Kutzinski

Daily going out, The. Waterpot. Grace Nichols. PBCV

Daily Habits. Herberto Padilla, *Spanish.* VCWP, *tr. by* Alastair Reid *and* Alexander Coleman

Daily Living. Rosemary Dobson. Folding the Sheets. NOBAu

Daily News. Tom Clark. SPE

Daily Space. João Cabral de Melo Neto, *Portuguese.* VCWP, *tr. by* W. S. Merwin

Daily the Drum. Anne Wilkinson. NOBC

Daily the neighbour's dog is withdrawn to the park. Hilaire Kirkland. *Fr.* Observations. PeNZ

Daily the Ocean between Us. Patricia Goedicke. TAP

Daily the wind-flowers age, and so do I. Weaving Love-Knots. Hsüeh T'ao. BoWoP, *tr. by* Carolyn Kizer

Daily, though no ears attended. The Obedient. Rudyard Kipling. *Fr.* Epitaphs of the War [1914–1918]. OBWP

Daily to turn in Paul's, and help the trade. (LL) On English Monsieur. Ben Jonson. AEP; NBLV; NoP-4

Daily Trials. Oliver Wendell Holmes. PoEL-5

Daily Wages. Amrita Pritam, *Punjabi.* PBWP, *tr. by the author and* Charles Brasch

Daily walked the fair and lovely. The Azra. Heinrich Heine, *German.* AWP, *tr. by* John Hay

Daily warmth we, The. John Cage. APSN *Fr.* Diary: How to Improve the World (You Will Only Make Matters Worse).

Dainty Baby Austin! The King of Oo-Rinktum-Jing. James Whitcomb Riley. NOxBChV

Dainty little maiden, whither would you wander? The City Child. Tennyson. ACTP; BoTP; NOxBChV; OxBChV

Dainty Miss Apathy. Pooh! Walter De la Mare. HAP; OBCoV; PeLV

Dainty white lilies, and sad flowers well prized. (LL) Brown Is My Love. *Unknown.* CTC; GBL

Daisies. Louise Glück. AFr

Daisies. Frank Dempster Sherman. CTV

Daisies, The. James Stephens. AWP

Daisies and Grasses. *Unknown.* BoTP

"Daisies and kingcups and honeysuckle-flowers'". (LL) The City Child. Tennyson. ACTP; BoTP; NOxBChV; OxBChV

Daisies of Florence. Kathleen Jessie Raine. NYBP

Daisies so bright. Daisies and Grasses. *Unknown.* BoTP

Daisy, The. James Montgomery. Field Flower, A. BoTP

Daisy, The. Tennyson. EnLoPo; NOBVV; OBNC; PoEL-5

Daisy. Francis Thompson. AWP; MoBrPo; OBEV; OBNC

Daisy. William Carlos Williams. MoAmPo

Daisy, The. Marya Alexandrovna Zaturenska. MoAmPo

Daisy and Lily. Waltz. Dame Edith Sitwell. BWW

Daisy, dead and dry. (LL) For the Candle Light. Angelina Weld Grimké. BISi; NAAAL

Daisy Fraser. Edgar Lee Masters. CMoP; HAP; PoE *Fr.* Spoon River Anthology.

Dakota: Five Times Six. Joseph Hansen. NYBP

Dakota Land. *Unknown.* AS

Dakota: October, 1822, Hunkpapa Warrior. Rod Taylor. WeW-3

Dakota Wheat-Field, A. Hamlin Garland. OBCA

Dalliance of the Eagles, The. Walt Whitman. APo; AmPP; HAP; HeIP-4; NAAL-1; NAAL-3; NoP-4; SAGP; SAmP; TAP; TRP

Dalyaunce. *Unknown.* CH

Dam, The. Muriel Rukeyser. PFTM

Dam Neck, Virginia. Richard Eberhart. PoWW

Damages, Two Hundred Pounds. William Makepeace Thackeray. OBSV

Damastes (Also Known As Procrustes) Speaks. Zbigniew Herbert, *Polish.* PoSu, *tr. by* John Carpenter *and* Bogdana Carpenter

Dame, get up and bake your pies. *Unknown.* BoTP; OxNR

Dame Music. Stephen Hawes. PoEL-1 *Fr.* The Pastime of Pleasure. OBGa

Dame Nature. Edmund Spenser. PoEL-1 *Fr.* Wood Of Error. AEP

Dame Nature, the goddess, one very bright day. On the Late Improvements at Nuneham, the Seat of the Earl of Harcourt. William Whitehead. OBGa

Dame, said the Panther, times are mended well. Dryden. PoEL-3 *Fr.* The Hind and the Panther.

Dame Trot and her cat. Mother Goose. BoTP; CTAV; OxNR; ReMoGo

Dame Wiggins of Lee. *Unknown.* FaBoBe; OxBChV *Fr.* Dame Wiggins of Lee [and Her Seven Wonderful Cats].

Dames of France are fond and free, The. The Girl I Left behind Me. Thomas Osborne Davis. FaBoBe

Damit blackman. Domestics. Kattie M. Cumbo. BlSi

Damn it all! all this our South stinks peace. Sestina: Altaforte. Ezra Pound. CMoP; ColAP; FaBoTw; ImPo; MoAmPo; NOBA

Damn it, honey, neither one of us. In the Twenty-Fifth Year of Marriage, It Goes On. Alicia Ostriker. PBCAP

Damn that celibate farm, that cracker-box house. Censorship. John Ciardi. NBLV

Damn the snow. Elegy for Thelonious. Yusef Komunyakaa. WeT

Damn you, lady, get out of my blood for good. Robin Morgan. NMM-2

Damnation follows death in other men. On Poets. Alexander Pope. FaBoEE

Damn'd for thy false Apostasy. (LL) To My Inconstant Mistress [*or* Mistris]. Thomas Carew. BeJo; CaPo; CavPo; EnLoPo; GBL; GLoP; MeLP; NOBE; NoP-4; OBEV; SAGP; SeCP; TFi

Damned bird, why have you ruined my sleep. Argentarius, *Greek.* GrAn, *tr. by* Fleur Adcock

Damned Minoan crevices, that I clog them up! Paranoia in Crete. Gregory Corso. NeAP

Damned Women. Charles Baudelaire, *French.* BoLoP, *tr by* Roy Campbell

Damocles. Robert Graves. NYBP

Damoetas and Daphnis. Theocritus, *Greek.* HePo, *tr. by* Barbara Hughes Fowler *Fr.* Idylls.

Damon and Cupid. John Gay. EnLoPo

DAMON and Phyllis squared. *Unknown.* NoSic

Damon & Pythias. Robert Creeley. LCAP-2

Damon, come drive thy flocks this way. Clorinda and Damon. Andrew Marvell. ESCV; FMP; SeCP

Damon the Mower. Andrew Marvell. ESCV; GeHe; NAEL-1; NOSC; OAEL-1

Damp[e], The. Donne. NOSC; SeCP

Damsel, The. Omar ben Abi Rabi'a, *Arabic.* AWP, *tr. by* W. G. Palgrave

Damsel came in midnight rain, A. Over, Over. Thomas Love Peacock. OxAEP-2 *Fr.* Maid Marian.

Damsel of Peru, The. William Cullen Bryant. APN-1

Damside. Margaret Atwood. LCAP-2

Dan Ellis's Boys. *Unknown.* AmFP

Danaans wept for you, Achilles, gathering round, The. The Heroes meet again in the underworld. Homer. OBCVT, *tr. by* David Constantine *Fr.* The Iliad.

Danaë. Barbara Howes. WPE

Dance, The. Wendell Berry. ITG

Dance, The. Thomas Campion. FaBoCh *Fr.* The Ayres that Were Sung and Played, at *Brougham Castle* in *Westmerland*, in the Kings Entertainment.

Dance, The. Hart Crane. LiTM; MoAmPo; OxBA *Fr.* Powhatan's Daughter. *Fr.* The Bridge. NAAL-2

Dance, The. Gareth Alban Davies, *Welsh.* OBWVE, *tr. by* Gwyn Jones

Dance, The. Robert Duncan. NeAP

Dance, The. Cornelius Eady. GT

Dance. Haim Guri, *Hebrew.* IP, *tr. by* Warren Bargad *and* Stanley F. Chyet

Dance, The. Daniel Halpern. ChAP

Dance, The. Robert Kelly. *Fr.* The Book of Persephone. PoM

Dance, The. Irene McKinney. PBCAP

Dance, The. Theodore Roethke. *Fr.* Four for Sir John Davies. MoAmPo; NOBA; NoAM

Dance, The. Siamanto, *Armenian.* AF, *tr. by* Peter Balakian *and* Nevart Yaghlian

Dance, The. Edmund Spenser. *See* The Dance of the Graces.

Dance, The. Mark Strand. LCAP-2

Dance, The. *Unknown.* PoEL-1, *tr. by* John Lydgate *Fr.* The Dance of Death.

Dance, The. William Carlos Williams. AmPP; CMoP; HAP; HeIP-4; InPK-6; LiTM; MeMAP; MoP; NAAL-2; NIP-4; NOBA; NoAM; NoP-4; OxBA; PoE; PoPoPo; Poetr; SAmP; SoSe-8; TAP; TFi

("In Breughel's great picture, The Kermess.") NoP-4; PoPoPo

Dance a baby diddy. Mother Goose. OxNR

Dance begins: to end about a form, The. The Desert Music. William Carlos Williams. APSN

Dance begins with the sun descending, The. Marrakech. Richard Eberhart. LiTM

Dance Bodies #1. Eugene B. Redmond. ISC

Dance, dance in this museum case. Love Song to Eohippus. Peter Viereck. MoAmPo

Dance Figure. Ezra Pound. HeIP-4; MoAmPo

Dance Floor on the Mountain, The. Pentti Saarikoski, *Finnish.* "Winter solstice." VCWP, *tr. by* Herbert Lomas

Dance For Ma Rainey, A. Al Young. ISC; NAAAL; NBV; UnSA ("To prove how proud we are.") (LL) ISC ("To prove we're still here.") (LL) NBV

Dance for Militant Dilettantes, A. Al Young. NBV; PoBA

Dance Half Done, The. Mary Ann Larkin. IIP

Dance in the Rain. Ana Blandiana, *Romanian.* CEEP, *tr. by* Irina Livezeanu

Dance in the township hall is nearly over, The. Country Dance. Judith Wright. BMAP; CBAP *Fr.* The Blind Man.

Dance is on the Bridge of Death, The. The Bridge of Death. *Unknown, French.* AWP, *tr. by* Andrew Lang

Dance, little baby, dance up high. The Baby's Dance. Mother Goose, *at. to* Mother Goose. OxBChV; OxNR; ReMoGo

Dance of birds, The. (LL) Kopis'taya. Paula Gunn Allen. HATNAP

Dance of blue-bells in the shady places, A. Sweet Surprises. Sarah Doudney. BoTP

Dance of Death, A. "Michael Field." ADE

Dance of Death, The. *Unknown, French.*

  Dance, The. PoEL-1, *tr. by* John Lydgate

Dance of Despair, The. Hayyim Nahman Bialik, *Hebrew.* TrJP, *tr. by* A. M. Klein

Dance of Dust, The. Louis Untermeyer. BXAP

Dance of feathers, the dance of birds, The. Paula Gunn Allen. *See* Kopis'taya.

Dance of Love, The. Sir John Davies. *Fr.* Orchestra; or, A Poem[e] of Da[u]ncing. NoSic; SiPS

Dance of Saul with the Prophets, The. Saul Tchernichowsky, *Hebrew.* TrJP, *tr. by* I. M. Lask

Dance of the Elephants, The. Michael S. Harper. LCAP-2

Dance of the Graces, The. Edmund Spenser. *Fr.* Wood Of Error. AEP

  (Dance, The.)

Dance of the Greased Women, The. Tristan Tzara. PFTM, *tr. by* Pierre Joris *Fr.* Poemes Negres.

Dance of the Infidels. Al Young. MoNo; NBV; PoBA; SeSe

Dance of the Letters. Vince Gotera. OpBo

Dance of the Macabre Mice. Wallace Stevens. CMoP; NOBA; OxBA; PFTM

Dance of the Rain, The. Eugène Marais, *Afrikaans.* PeSA, *tr. by* Jack Cope *and* Uys Krige

Dance of the Rain Gods. *Unknown, Cora Indian.* STP, *tr. by* Anselm Hollo

Dance of the Sevin Deidly Synnis, The. William Dunbar. OxBS; PoE

Dance of the Soul. Vladimir Shchirovsky, *Russian.* TCRP, *tr. by* Bradley Jordan

Dance Poem. Michele Murray.

  "I am giving you the dark birds of night." MDDM

Dance She Does, The. Harryette Mullen. ISC

Dance Song. *Unknown, Chinese.* ChiP; FaBoCh, *tr. by* Arthur Waley

Dance-Song of the Lightning. *Unknown, Hottentot.* PeSA

Dance the Boatman. *Unknown.* AiP

Dance there upon the shore. To a Child Dancing in the Wind. W. B. Yeats. IIP; PFE

Dance, Thumbkin, dance. Mother Goose. LB; OxNR; ReMoGo

Dance to the Amulets. U Tam'si Tchicaya. PBMAP

Dance to thee daddy, my little lamb. (LL) Dance to your [*or* thee] daddy. Mother Goose. FaBoVe; OxNR; ReMoGo

Dance to your [*or* thee] daddy. Mother Goose. FaBoVe; LB; OxNR; ReMoGo

  ("When the boat / comes in.") (LL) LB

Dance with Banderillas. Richard Duerden. NeAP

Dance with me. . . dance with me. . . we are the song. . . we. Three/ Quarters Time. Nikki Giovanni. CA

Dance with you, my sweet brown Harlem girl. (LL) Juke Box Love Song. Langston Hughes. NAAAL; PoBA; SAmP; TTTS

Danced round the dreadful thing in fiendish glee. (LL) The Lynching. Claude McKay. ColAP; CrDW; GT; PoBA

Dancer, The. Joseph Campbell. OBMV

Dancer, The. Sadi. AWP, *tr. by* Sir Edward Arnold *Fr.* The Gulistan.

Dancer, The. Walter James Turner. NOBAu; OBMV

Dancer, The. Edmund Waller. CBLP

Dancer, The. Al Young. PoBA

Dancer! / A one-headed drum. A Poet to a Dancer. Auvaiyar, *Tamil.* PLW, *tr. by* A. K. Ramanujan

Dancer, or the dance, The. (LL) On a Female Rope-Dancer. *Unknown.* LiLi

Dancers at the Moy. Paul Muldoon. BIrV

Dancers Exercising. Amy Clampitt. NoAM

Dancer's Life, A. Donald Justice. LCAP-2

Dancers of Colbek, The. Robert Mannyng. PoE *Fr.* Handling Sin.

Dancers of Huai-nan, The. Chang Heng, *Chinese.* ChiP, *tr. by* Arthur Waley

Dancers with cane whistles. Memory. Elizabeth Cook-Lynn. *Fr.* Journey. HATNAP

Dancer's world, A. The Twist. Alfred B. Spellman. ISC

Dances and Songs of the Winter Ceremonial. *Unknown, Kwakiutl.* APN-2, *tr. by* Franz Boas

  Hā′ mats'a Song Composed about Fifty Years Ago.

  Hā′ mats'a Song, La′ Lasiqoala.

  Hā′ mats'a Song of the Koskimo.

  Hā′ mats'a Song of the Lau′ itsîs.

  Kî′ nqalaLala Song.

  Ku′ nXulaL, Thunder Bird Dance.

  Song for Pacifiying the Excited Nū′ LmaL.

  Song of a Bear Dancer Named Walas Nā′ nē (Great Bear).

  Song of a Salmon Dancer.

  Song of Nū′ LmaL, La′ Lasiqoala.

  Song of the Ghost Dancer.

  Song of the Ghost Dancer of the La′ Lasiqoala, A.

  Song of the Ia′ kîm.

  Song of the Ts'ē′ k'ois, A.

Dances like Italy, imagining red. (LL) Walt Whitman at Bear Mountain. Louis Simpson. CoAmPo; LiTM; TRP

Dances of Death. Aleksandr Blok, *Russian.*

  "Night, street, a lamp, a chemist's window." OBVE, *tr. by* Jon Stallworthy *and* Peter France

  "Night, the street, the lamp, the drugstore, The." TCRP, *tr. by* Yakov Hornstein

Dancing, The. Gerald Stern. LCAP-2; LoL; UnSA

Dancing Bear, The. Rachel Lyman Field. KaS; NTCP

Dancing Bear, The. Albert Bigelow Paine. OBCA

Dancing Cabman, The. John Bingham Morton. NOBL

Dancing Concerning a Form of Women, A. Robert Duncan. FTOS

Dancing Girl, The. John Barlas. ADE

Dancing-Girl's Song. Kshetrayya, *Telugu.* BoWoP, *tr. by* Tambimuttu *and* R. Appalaswamy

Dancing on the Shore. M. M. Hutchinson. BoTP

Dancing, phosphorescent drops. Yaroslav Vasilevich Smelyakov, *Russian.* TCRP, *tr. by* Simon Franklin

Dancing Pleiads and eternal men, The. (LL) Bacchus. Ralph Waldo Emerson. APN-1; AWP; AmPP; NOBA; OBEV; OxBA; PAR; PoEL-4

Dancing School. Jonathan Holden. Poetsp

Dancing Sea, The. Sir John Davies. *Fr.* Orchestra; or, A Poem[e] of Da[u]ncing. NoSic; SiPS

Dancing Songs. *Unknown.* PBCV

  "Hipsaw! my deaa! you no do like a-me!"

  "Tajo, tajo, tajo! tajo, my mackey massa!"

Dancing the Shout to the True Gospel; or, The Song Movement Sisters Don't Want Me to Sing. Rita Mae Brown. CrSp

Dancing with God. Stephen Dunn. NIP-4

Dancing with Poets. Ellen Bryant Voigt. CrSp

Dandelion Greens. Jane Flanders. CrSp

Dandelion Puff, The. Mary K. Robinson. BoTP

Dandelions. Louis MacNeice. *See* Nature Notes: Dandelions.

Dandelions. Gerda Mayer. Spl

Dandelions. Craig Raine. NoAM

Dandelions. Will D. Stanton. SoSe-8

Dandelions, The. *Unknown.* BoTP

Dandelions for Chains ("Dandelions meet me wherever I am"). Sarah Kirsch, *German.* WPOW, *tr. by* Michael Hamburger

Dandelions purr in their sleep. Of Dandelions & Tourists. Joe Rosenblatt. NOBC

Dandelions, wrecked on their stems, The. Late Dandelions. Ben Belitt. NYBP

Dándole la mano a Mongo. Martín Espada. SeSe

Dane-Geld. Rudyard Kipling. OxBTC

Danger! September 1, 1923. Toki Zenmaro, *Japanese.* MJT, *tr. by* Makoto Ueda

Dangers of the Journey to the Happy Land. Joseph Ceravolo. PT

Daniel and Abigail. Epitaph. Miguel de Barrios, *Spanish.* TrJP

Daniel at Breakfast. Phyllis McGinley. OBSV; OxBM

Daniel Boone. Stephen Vincent Benét. KaS

Daniel in the lion's den. Nebuchadnezzar's Kingdom-Come. David Rowbotham. ChIV-1; NOBAu

Daniel Webster's Horses. Elizabeth Jane Coatsworth. MoAmPo; OBCA

Danish Cradle Song, A. *Unknown.* BoTP

Danish Wit. John Hollander. NBLV

Dank fens of cedar; hemlock-branches gray. Frederick Goddard Tuckerman. *See* Dark fens of cedar; hemlock-branches gray.

Dannie Abse, Douglas Dunn. On Consulting "Contemporary Poets of the English Language." Anthony Thwaite. PeLV

Danny. Malcolm Cowley. PoA

Danny. John Millington Synge. PeVV

Danny dead of heart attack. Landed Fish. Marge Piercy. WeT

Danny Deever. Rudyard Kipling. EBEvV; EBVV; FaPoR; GTBS-P; InPS-3; MoBrPo; NAEL-2; NOBE; NOBVV; NoAM; OxBTC; OxBoLi; PBMP; PeVV; PoLF; SCGP; SCV; TFi; UnPo

Danny Murphy. James Stephens. BoTP

Dans ce miroir. On imagine les anges. Guillaume Apollinaire, *French.* PiM, *tr. by* Kenneth Koch

Dans l'Allée. Paul Verlaine. *See* L'Allée.

Danse Africaine. Langston Hughes. NAAAL

Danse Russe. William Carlos Williams. CMoP; InPS-3; NOBA; NoP-4; PoE; Poetr; RaBo; SAGP; SAmP; TAP

Dante. William Cullen Bryant. APN-1

Dante. Robert Duncan.

  Little Language, A. FTOS

  ("I know a little language of my cat, though Dante says.") FTOS

Dante. Henry Wadsworth Longfellow. NCAP

Dante. Michelangelo Buonarroti, *Italian.* AWP, *tr. by* Longfellow

Dante. Henrietta Cordelia Ray. CBWP-3

Dante, a sigh that rose from the heart's core. To Dante: He Reports, in a Feigned Vision, the Successful Issue of Lapo Gianni's Love. Guido Cavalcanti, *Italian.* AWP, *tr. by* D. G. Rossetti

Dante, a dark oracle. Inscription for a Portrait of Dante. Giovanni Boccaccio. AWP *Fr.* Sonnets.

Dante, Cecco, your good friend. Sonnet: To Dante on the Last Sonnet of the Vita Nuova. Cecco Angiolieri, da Siena, *Italian.* AWP, *tr. by* D. G. Rossetti

Dante, if I jest and lie. Sonnet: To Dante (He Writes to Dante, Then in Exile at Verona, Defying Him as No Better Than Himself). Cecco Angiolieri, da Siena, *Italian.* AWP, *tr. by* D. G. Rossetti

Dante in Becchina's praise. Sonnet: He Rails against Dante, Who Had Censured His Homage to Becchina. Cecco Angiolieri, da Siena, *Italian.* AWP, *tr. by* D. G. Rossetti

Dante, if thou within the sphere of Love. To Dante in Paradise, after Fiammetta's Death. Giovanni Boccaccio. AWP *Fr.* Sonnets.

Dante, whenever this thing happeneth. To Dante: He Conceives of Some Compensation in Death. Cino da Pistoia, *Italian.* AWP, *tr. by* D. G. Rossetti

Dante's Inferno, Canto XXXIV (The Final Canto). Robert Pinsky. PUP-20

Danton is waiting to die. Dead Leaves. Aleksandar Ristovic, *Serbo-Croatian.* HSix, *tr. by* Charles Simic

Danube to the Severn gave, The. The Hushing of the Wye. Tennyson. EBVV; EBVVPR; EnVR; GTBS-P *Fr.* In Memoriam A. H. H.

Daphnaïda. Edmund Spenser.

  Elegy, An: "She fell away in her first ages spring." OBEV

Daphne. John Lyly. *Fr.* Midas.

  (Song of Daphne to the Lute, A.)

Daphne and Apollo. Ovid. NOEC, *tr. by* Matthew Prior *Fr.* Metamorphoses.

Daphne knows, with equal ease. Jonathan Swift. NOBL

Daphne Stillorgan. Denis Devlin. CIP-2

Daphne with her thighs in bark. Ezra Pound. *Fr.* Hugh Selwyn Mauberley. (Life and Contacts). AmPP; CMoP; InPS-3; LiTM; NOBA; NoAM; TAP

Daphnis dearest, wherefore weave me. Appeal. Edith Nesbit. LW

Daphnis the fair-skinned, who plays country songs. Theocritus, *Greek.* GrAn, *tr. by* Anthony Holden

Daphnis to Ganymede. Richard Barnfield. *See* The Affectionate Shepherd.

Dapple-gray. Mother Goose. ReMoGo

Dappled Horse, The. Mei Yao Ch'en, *Chinese.* ChiPo, *tr. by* Burton Watson; CoBCP, *tr. by* Burton Watson

Dappled sky, a world of meadows, A. Jean Ingelow. OBNC; PEW *Fr.* Divided.

Dar es-Salaam: Harbour of Peace. Breyten Breytenbach, *Afrikaans.* AF, *tr. by Denis Hirson*

Dar es-Salaam: it's when night is darkest. Dar es-Salaam: Harbour of Peace. Breyten Breytenbach, *Afrikaans.* AF, *tr. by Denis Hirson*

Darby and Joan were dressed in black. *Unknown.* OxNR

Dardanelles 1916. Padraic Fallon. CIP-2

Dare a mighty *row* in Zion an' de *debbil's gittin' high,.* Linin' ub De Hymns, De. Daniel Webster Davis. AAP

Dare frame thy fearful symmetry? (LL) The Tyger. William Blake. APAD; AWP; BoTP; CH; CTAV; ChAP; ClHu; FPC; FaBoBe; FaBoCh; FaBoPV; FaPoR; HAP; HeIP-4; HoPM; ImPo; InPK-6; InPS-3; NAWM-2; NIP-4; NOBE; NOBRP; NOEC; NOxBChV; NoP-4; OAEL-2; OBEV; OBNC; OPOU; PBMP; PFE; PeECV; PoE; PoEL-4; PoLF; PoPoPo; PoRA; RB; Ro; SAGP; SCGP; SCV; SoSe-8; TFi; TTTS; UnPo; WHSW

Dare I in such momentous points advise. Soame Jenyns. ECEV *Fr.* The Art of Dancing.

Dare to be true. Courage. George Herbert. CTV

Dare to Do Right. George Lansing Taylor. PWR

Dare you see a Soul *at the White Heat?.* Emily Dickinson. APN-2; NALW; WPoS

Daredevil. Ania Walwicz. BMAP

Daring young lady of Guam, A. Limerick. *Unknown.* PeLi

Darius Green and His Flying-Machine. John Townsend Trowbridge. FaBoBe; OBAL; OBCA; OxBChV; PoLF

Dark, The. Myra Cohn Livingston. TLR

Dark, The. Anita Virgil. HA

Dark accurate plunger down the successive knell. The Subway. Allen Tate. NOBA

Dark against the sky yonder distant line. Song to the Trees and Streams. *Unknown.* APN-2, *tr. by Alice C. Fletcher Fr.* The Hako.

Dark Age Glosses. Louis MacNeice.
  "After long trouble in a tacdious way." KTP

Dark an' stormy may come de wedder. Slave Marriage Ceremony Supplement. *Unknown.* BPo; CrDW; TAP

Dark and Dark. William Robert Moses. WeT

Dark and dim, the Bamboo Grove Monastery. Saying Goodby to the Monk Ling-ch'e. Liu Ch'ang-ch'ing, *Chinese.* SuSp, *tr. by Dell R. Hales*

Dark and Falling Summer, The. Delmore Schwartz. ImGa; NYBP

Dark angel who art clear and straight. Serenade: Any Man to Any Woman. Dame Edith Sitwell. NALW

Dark Angel, with thine aching lust. Lionel Pigot Johnson. ADE; GTBS-P; MoBrPo; NOBE; NOBVV; OAEL-2; OBMV; OxAEP-2
  ("Divine, to the Divinity.") (LL) ADE

Dark Area. Russell Atkins. GT

Dark as the grave wherein my friend is laid. . . (LL) It was a dismal and a fearful night. Abraham Cowley. BeJo; NOBE; OxAEP-1

Dark as the spring river, the earth. Farm Wife. Ellen Bryant Voigt. MT

Dark as wells, his eyes. Long Person. Gladys Cardiff. CDW

Dark Blood. Margaret Abigail Walker. NALW

Dark-blue clouds of night, in dusky lines, The. A Summer's Day. Joanna Baillie. WoRP

Dark Blue Hussars. Nikolai Nikolaievich Aseyev, *Russian.* TCRP, *tr. by Lubov Yakovleva with Daniel Weissbort*

Dark branches. Alaskan Mountain Poem #1. Leslie Marmon Silko. VoR

Dark breast feathers of a future storm. (LL) Crazy Horse Monument. Peter Blue Cloud. UnSA

Dark bricks hold the fire alight, The. Overnight. Valentine Ackland. WPN

Dark brother touches me, The. Will Inman. GLP *Fr.* 108 Tales of a Po 'Buckra.

Dark Brown. Michael McClure.
  (Fuck Ode). BB

Dark brown is the river. Where Go the Boats? Robert Louis Stevenson. CTV; FaBoBe; FaBoCh; NOxBChV; NTCP; NTP; OxBChV; TLR; WHSW

Dark cave, that ever dost cool shades retain. Medoro's Inscription Book XXIII. Ludovico Ariosto, *Italian.* NOBRP, *tr. by William Parsons Fr.* Orlando Furioso.

Dark Chamber, The. Louis Untermeyer. MoAmPo

Dark chocolate fungus, A. Walking, when the Lake of the Air is Blue with Spring. J. S. Harry. BMAP

Dark Churches. Donne. *Fr.* A Hymn[e] to Christ, at the Author's Last Going into Germany. EBEV; MeLP

Dark circle around my body and my daughter. (LL) May 1968. Sharon Olds. NAmP90; NIP-4

Dark Conclusions. Ruth Stone. BoWoP

Dark Country, A. Derek Mahon. BIrV

Dark cul de sac, A. The Mother Tongue. Carolina Hospital. LoHo

Dark, dark, far mists rise. Things Seen. Wang Shih-chieng, *Chinese.* CoBLCP, *tr. by Jonathan Chaves*

Dark, dark lay the drifters, against the red west. *Kilmeny.* Alfred Noyes. NSI

Dark, deep, and cold the current flows. Plaint. Ebenezer Elliot. OBEV

Dark, deeply. A red. Inside the River. James Dickey. PoA

Dark Dialogues, The. W. S. Graham. OxBS
  "Almost I, yes, I hear."
  "Now in the third voice."

Dark drum the vanishing horses' hooves. (LL) The Closing of the Rodeo. William Jay Smith. AiP; TwCP

Dark earth drinks the sky, The. Anacreon, *Greek.* InMo, *tr. by Sam Hamill*

Dark earth, furry as a bear, / Grumbled too!, The. (LL) Dark Song. Dame Edith Sitwell. CMoP; FaBoTw; PBWP

Dark Edge of Europe, The. Desmond O'Grady.
  "Twist of cloth on the flat stones, A." PBCIP

Dark Eleanor and Henry sat at meat. The Rose of the World. John Masefield. PoRA

Dark eleventh hour, The. Ulster. Rudyard Kipling. FaBoPV; IIP

Dark-Eyed Gentleman, The. Thomas Hardy. MoBrPo; NBLV; UnPo

Dark eyed, / O woman of my dreams. Dance Figure. Ezra Pound. HeIP-4; MoAmPo

Dark Farmhouses. Charles Simic. LCAP-2

Dark fens of cedar; hemlock-branches gray. Frederick Goddard Tuckerman. APN-2 *Fr.* Sonnets.
  ("Dank fens of cedar; hemlock-branches gray.") PAR

Dark filthy blood was drying on my ear. (LL) Postcard (Found on His body after He Was Killed by the Nazis). Miklós Radnóti, *Hungarian.* HP, *tr. by Polgar, Steven, S. Berg, and S. J. Marks, S. J.; RaBo, tr. by Steven Polgar, Stephen Berg, and S. J. Marks*

Dark foreboding haunts me lest I die, A. Thomas MacDermot. PBCV *Fr.* San Gloria.

Dark Forest, The. Edward Thomas. SAGP

Dark fragrance, sparse shadows. Night of the Fifteenth, Second Month. Yüan Mei, *Chinese.* CoBLCP, *tr. by Jonathan Chaves*

Dark-haired girl, who holds my thoughts entirely, The. Peggy Browne. Turlough Carolan, *Irish.* BIrV, *tr. by Austin Clarke*

Dark hall. Great green liquid windows, A. Thomas Kinsella. BiHa *Fr.* A Technical Supplement.

Dark Harbor. Mark Strand.
  "I recall that I stood before the breaking waves." BAP-93
  "Is it you standing among the olive trees." BAP-93; NoP-4
  "It is true, as someone has said, that in." NoP-4
  "Out here, dwarfed by mountains and a sky of fires." BAP-93

Dark head sits brooding its, A. Song of the Andoumboulou: 7. Nathaniel Mackey. FTOS

Dark hills at evening in the west. Edwin Arlington Robinson. APAD; AiP; HAP; ImPo; LiTM; MoAmPo; NoAM

Dark hills distant in the setting sun. Encountering a Snowstorm, I Stay with the Recluse of Mount Hibiscus. Liu Ch'ang-ch'ing, *Chinese.* SuSp, *tr. by Dell R. Hales*

Dark Horse. Phillis Levin. FFC

Dark House, The. *Unknown.* NTCP

Dark house, by which once more I stand. Tennyson. EBEV; EBVV; EBVVPR; EnVR; FHYEP; GTBS-P; HAP; HeIP-4; ImPo; NOBE; OAEL-2; OBNC; PoEL-5; SCGP; SCV; SoSe-8; UnPo *Fr.* In Memoriam A. H. H.

Dark in the cubicle boxed from snow-darkness of night. History during Nocturnal Snowfall. Robert Penn Warren. DiPo

Dark is kind and cozy, The. God's Dark. John Martin. PoLF

Dark is soft, like fur. Rhyme for Night. Joan Aiken. TLR

Dark is the forest and deep, and overhead. The Dark Forest. Edward Thomas. SAGP

Dark is the stair, and humid the old walls. The Belfry. Laurence Binyon. CH

Dark lintels, the blue and foreign stones, The. Adrienne Rich. NALW; NoAM *Fr.* Twenty-one Love Poems. GLP

Dark look, and overhanging thorn. (LL) Poem: "I cannot tell, not I, why she." Walter Savage Landor. GBL; OAEL-2

Dark Lord of Savaiki, The. Alistair Campbell. PeNZ

Dark Mirror. Calvin Forbes. GT

Dark Morning, The. Thomas Merton. PoA

Dark Mountains. Milton Lockyer, *Yindjibarndi.* CBAP, *tr. by Frank Wordick*

Dark Night, The. Saint John of the Cross, *Spanish.* STV; WeW-3, *tr. by John Frederick Nims*
  (Obscure Night of the Soul, The.) AWP; OBMV, *tr. by Arthur Symons*

Dark Night. Tản Đà, *Vietnamese.* AVP, *tr. by Huỳnh Sanh Thông*

Dark o'clock. The Bed. Ray DiPalma. FTOS

Dark one are you restless. The Armies Enter Cuailnge. *Unknown. Fr.* The Táin. NOIV, *tr. by Thomas Kinsella*

Dark Phrases. Ntozake Shange. BlSi *Fr.* For Colored Girls Who Have Considered Suicide When the Rainbow Is Enuf.

Dark Pines under Water. Gwendolyn MacEwen. NOBC

Dark Planet, The. John Heath-Stubbs. OAEL-2

Dark plume fetch me from yon blasted yew, A. Return. Wordsworth. HAP *Fr.* The River Duddon [A Series of Sonnets].

Dark Portrait, A. Lawrence Ferlinghetti. PmAP

Dark Prophecy: I Sing of Shine. Etheridge Knight. BPo; LTA; PBCAP

Dark purple light rises in the north, The. Song of Creation. *Hopi Oral Tradition, Hopi.* PaTW, *tr. by* Frank Waters

Dark Romance. Lucha Corpi, *Spanish.* WPOW, *tr. by* Catherine Rodriguez-Nieto

Dark Room, The. Enrique Lihn, *Spanish.* VCWP, *tr. by* David Unger

Dark Rosaleen. Owen Roe MacWard *and* Hugh O'Donnell, *Irish.* AWP; BIrV; CH; IIP; NOIV; OBEV; OxAEP-2, *tr. by* James Clarence Mangan

Dark rose the walls, a church and prison joined. Albery Allson Whitman. AAP *Fr.* Twasinta's Seminoles; Or Rape of Florida.

Dark seaweeds. Tanka. Miyazawa Kenji, *Japanese.* MJT, *tr. by* Makoto Ueda

Dark smokes ascend, dark smokes ascend. Opium. Thế Lữ', *Vietnamese.* AVP, *tr. by* Huỳnh Sanh Thông

Dark Song. Dame Edith Sitwell. CMoP; FaBoTw; PBWP

Dark Song. Martha Zweig. IFJA

Dark Stag, The. Isabella Valancy Crawford. NOBC

Dark streets are deserted, The. After Midnight. Louis Simpson. BLT; NoAM

Dark swimmers, The. Larry Eigner. PoM

Dark Symphony. Melvin B. Tolson. ColAP; NAAAL; SSLK

Dark Testament. Pauli Murray. BlSi

Dark theme keeps me here, A. In Evening Air. Theodore Roethke. NYBP; TAP

Dark Thing Inside the Day, A. Linda Gregg. BLT

Dark, thinned, beside the wall of stone. In Time of Grief. Lizette Woodworth Reese. APN-2

Dark thoughts are my companions. I have wined. Epigram. James Vincent Cunningham. VGW

Dark-time. The little ones like bees. Little Lullaby. Irving Feldman. NYBP

Dark to me is the earth. Dark to me are the heavens. The Desolate City. *Unknown, Arabic.* AWP; OBEV, *tr. by* Wilfrid Scawen Blunt

Dark was the day for Childe Rolandine the artist. Childe Rolandine. Stevie Smith. BrRo

Dark Was the Night. *Unknown.* AmFP

Dark waters into crystalline brilliance break. Troopship: Mid-Atlantic. Wilfrid Wilson Gibson. NSI

Dark Welcome, The. James Keir Baxter. PeNZ *Fr.* Five Sestinas.

Dark whispers. Night Gives Old Woman the Word. Gail Tremblay. HATNAP

Dark wind blows in the forest, crows and magpies mourn. Ballad of a Ferocious Tiger. Kao Ch'i, *Chinese.* SuSp, *tr. by* Irving Y. Lo

Dark Wings. James Stephens. PoA

Dark woman, head bent, listening for something, A. Adrienne Rich. PaTW

Dark Wood, The. Dante, *Italian.* BiHa, *tr. by* Seamus Heaney *Fr.* Inferno. NAWM-1, *tr. by* John Ciardi *Fr.* Divina Commedia.

(Inferno, Canto I, The.) PiM, *tr. by* Seamus Heaney

("Where the straight road had been lost sight of.") (LL) PiM, *tr. by* Seamus Heaney

Dark wrath of people, The. Georg Trakl. *See* In the East.

Dark young pine, at the center of the earth originating. *Unknown, Navajo.* WPoS, *tr. by* Gladys A. Reichard

Darkened bedroom, the double bed, The. Driving Wheel. Sherley Anne Williams. BlSi

Darkened copies of all trees, The. (LL) An Emphasis Falls on Reality. Barbara Guest. FTOS; PmAP

Darkened farmhouse is asleep, The. Saving the Harvest. Geoffrey Lehmann. CBAP

Darkened Mind, The. James Russell Lowell. NCAP

Darkened Windows. Ronald Bottrall. PoA

Darkening. Anita Virgil. HA

Darkening Garden, The. *Unknown.* BoTP

Darkening Hotel Room. Alfred Corn. VCAP

Darkening was like riches in the room, The. Rilke. *See* From a Childhood.

Darker by far than any coalpit stone. (LL) The Preface: "Infinity, when all things it beheld." Edward Taylor. AmPP; HAP; MeMAP; NAAL-1; NAAL-3; NOBA; OxBA; SCAP

Darkling Chicken, The. Robert Peters. BXAP

Darkling eye and golden hair. Lee. Rose Cecil O'Neill. CPO

Darkling I listen; and for many a time. Keats. *Fr.* Ode to a Nightingale. AWP; CABP; ClHu; EBEV; FaBoBe; GEA; GTBS-P; HAP; HeIP-4; ImPo; InPS-3; NAEL-2; NAWM-2; NOBE; NOBRP; NoP-4; OAEL-2;

OBEV; OBNC; PFE; PoE; PoEL-4; PoPoPo; PoRA; RB; Ro; SCGP; SoSe-8; TFi; TOF; UnPo

Darkling Thrush, The. Thomas Hardy. APo; CABP; CMoP; ClHu; EBVV; HAP; ImPo; InPS-3; LiTM; MoBrPo; MoP; NAEL-2; NIP-4; NOBE; NOBVV; NoAM; NoP-4; OAEL-2; OBEV; OBNC; PFE; PoE; PoPoPo; Poetr; RB; SoSe-8; TFi; TOF; UnPo

Darkmotherscream is a Siberian dance. Andrey Andreievich Voznesensky, *Russian.* RaBo; TCRP, *tr. by* Robert Bly *and* Vera Dunham

Darkness. Byron. CABP; GEA; NAEL-2; OAEL-2; PoE; PoEL-4; Ro

Darkness. Joseph Campbell. BIrV

Darkness. Arthur Hugh Clough. OxBSP

Darkness. Paavo Haavikko, *Finnish.*

"Days become years. Years." VCWP, *tr. by* Herbert Lomas

Darkness and rain and the wind. Loneliness. Ivan Alekseievich Bunin, *Russian.* TCRP, *tr. by* Yakov Hornstein

Darkness and stars i' the mid-day! they invite. A Rhapsody. Henry Vaughan. BeJo; NAEL-1

Darkness—and white. The Twelve. Aleksandr Blok, *Russian.* TCRP, *tr. by* Jon Stallworthy *and* Peter France

Darkness at the break of noon. It's Alright, Ma (I'm Only Bleeding). "Bob Dylan." FiLi

Darkness begins a. After Christmas. John Corben. AYFP

Darkness begins a / retreat. After Christmas. Michael Richards. OBCP

Darkness came early, though not yet cold. The Apple-raid. Vernon Scannell. NOxBChV

Darkness comes out of the earth. Twilight. D. H. Lawrence. OBMV

Darkness crumbles away, The. Break of Day in the Trenches. Isaac Rosenberg. CABP; FaBoMo; GTBS-P; MoBrPo; NAEL-2; NOBE; NSI; NoAM; NoP-4; OAEL-2; OBWP; OxAEP-2; PeFWW; PoA; PoFWW; PoWW; TFi

Darkness falls like a wet sponge. The Picture of Little J. A. in a Prospect of Flowers. John Ashbery. CoAmPo; PmAP

Darkness has called to darkness, and disgrace. As a Plane Tree by the Water. Robert Lowell. CMoP; CoAP; LiTM; MoAmPo; NOBA; OxBA

Darkness has feathered all night. Dawn Feeding. Leslie Ullman. NAmP90

Darkness is closing around us, The. In Orbit. Henry Taylor. BXAP

Darkness is not dark, nor sunlight the light of the sun. Foal. Vernon Watkins. OxBTC

Darkness lifts, imagine, in your lifetime, The. The Undertaking. Louise Glück. FaBoWP

Darkness marks the distance where river meets ocean. Autumn River. T'ang Hsien-tsu, *Chinese.* CoBLCP, *tr. by* Jonathan Chaves

Darkness Music. Muriel Rukeyser. BoWoP

Darkness of her eyes!, The. (LL) The Gipsy Girl. Ralph Hodgson. SAGP

Darkness of trees, The. But So As by Fire. George Oppen. NNaP *Fr.* Some San Francisco Poems.

Darkness reigned. Sacrifice. Nana Issaia, *Modern Greek.* BoWoP, *tr. by* Helle Tzalopoulou Barnstone

Darkness stares from everywhere and no one's here. The Last Poem. Jiri Orten, *Czech.* AF, *tr. by* Lyn Coffin

Darkness still shadows the mountain road. I Spend the Night in a Room by the River. Tu Fu, *Chinese.* SuSp, *tr. by* Mark Perlberg

Darkness that man must dread at last. (LL) Tenebrae. Austin Clarke. BIrV; CIP-2; NOIV

Darkness: the rain sluiced down; the mire was deep. The Redeemer. Siegfried Sassoon. PoFWW

Darkness was a richness in the room, The. From a Childhood. Rilke, *German.* TrJP, *tr. by* C. F. MacIntyre

Darkness was born in the forest. I found it there. Desanka Maksimovic, *Serbo-Croatian.* HSix, *tr. by* Charles Simic

Darkness wears off, and, dawning into light. The Figures on the Frieze. Alastair Reid. NYBP

Darky Sunday School. *Unknown.* OxBoLi

Darlene's Hospital. John Ashbery. ColAP

Darling! because my blood can sing. E. E. Cummings. OxBA

Darling Cory. *Unknown.* AmFP

Darling, each morning a blooded rose. Corinna In Vendome. Pierre de Ronsard, *French.* LoP, *tr. by* Alistair Elliot; BoLoP, *tr. by* Robert Mezey

"Darling," he said, "I never meant." Forgetfulness! Josephine D. Henderson Heard. CBWP-4

Darling, he said, I never meant. Two Truths. Helen Hunt Jackson. LW

Darling Henriette, if fate were symmetrical. Casanova on His Deathbed. Philip Casey. BiHa

Darling, how long before this breath will cease? Evanishings. Mary E. Tucker. CBWP-1

Darling, I won't be your hot love. Sulpicia, *Latin.* BoWoP, *tr. by* Aliki *and* Willis Barnstone

Darling, it's frightening! When a poet loves. Boris Pasternak, *Russian*. LoP, *tr. by* J. M. Cowen

Darling little Tom and Harry. The Octopus. Stevie Smith. WPN

Darling of the world is come, The. Robert Herrick. PChr *Fr.* A Christmas Caroll Sung to the King in the Presence at White-Hall.

Darling, on the moving stairs. And No Regrets. Lex Banning. NOBAu

Darling Shell, where hast thou bene. Walter Savage Landor. CBLP

Darling, the plates have been cleared away. Beauty and the Beast. Rita Dove. NoAM

Darling, you only, there is no duplicate. *Unknown*. CTC, *tr. by* Ezra Pound *Fr.* Conversations in Courtship.

Darned Mounseer, The. Sir William Schwenck Gilbert. NOBL *Fr.* Ruddigore.

Dar's a skool in West Virginny. To Professor Byrd Prillerman. Maggie Pogue Johnson. CBWP-4

Dar's plenty t'ings to write erbout. Dat Mule ob Brudder Wright's. Maggie Pogue Johnson. CBWP-4

Dart, The. "Eliza." KTR

Dart of Izdabel prevails! 'twas dipt, The. The Dying Indian. Joseph Warton. NOEC; OxAEP-1

Dartmoor: Sunset at Chagford. Thomas Edward Brown. NOBVV

Dartmouth Women's Prison, 1992. Lynda Hull. PUP-19

Darwin. Lorine Niedecker. APSN

Darwin Descending. Russell Edson. LCAP-2

Darwin in 1881. Gjertrud Schnackenberg. NoAM; NoP-4

Darwinism. Agnes Mary Frances Robinson. VWP

Darwinism in the Kitchen. *Unknown*. NBLV

Darya Vlasyevna, my neigbor. Conversation with a Neighbor. Olga Fiodorovna Berggolts, *Russian*. TCRP, *tr. by* Daniel Weissbort

Das Kapital. Imamu Amiri Baraka. PoM

Dash down yon cup of Samian wine! (LL) Isles of Greece, the isles of Greece!, The. Byron. AWP; FaPoR; NOBE; OBEV; OxAEP-2

Dash him to dust, and let the world repose. (LL) Advice to a Raven in Russia [December, 1812]. Joel Barlow. APN-1; AmPP; ColAP; NAAL-1; NAAL-3; NOBA; OBWP; OxBA

Dasius, chucker-out / at the Turkish Baths. Martial, *Latin*. OBVE, *tr. by* Peter Porter

Dass Cap'm Cayetano. The Song of Cayetano's Circus. George Washington Cable. APN-2

Dat Mule ob Brudder Wright's. Maggie Pogue Johnson. CBWP-4

Dat Sunshine Special comin' around de bend. C. C. Rider. *Unknown*. AS

Data. Joseph Ceravolo. PT

Data, data, data. Transfigured Night. Ralph Gustafson. MoCV

Data in the glass jar: some ten scorpions, The. In the Laboratory. Dan Pagis, *Hebrew*. PoSu, *tr. by* Robert Friend

Date. Sarah Kirsch, *German*. CEEP, *tr. by* Wayne Kvam

Date With Robbe-Grillet, A. Elaine Equi. PeVV; PmAP

Dates. *Unknown*. AWP *Fr.* The Thousand and One Nights.

Dates on bridges, The. History and Abstraction. Thomas Lux. AmPA

Datur Hora Quieti. Sir Walter Scott. GTBS-P

Datura Hunting Song. *Pima Oral Tradition, Pima*. PaTW, *tr. by* Frank Russell

Dauber. John Masefield.
"All through the windless night the clipper rolled." CMoP
Rounding the Horn. MoBrPo

Daufuskie. Mari E. Evans. BlSi

Daughter, A. Lee Upton. CMAP

Daughter. Ellen Bryant Voigt. MT

"Daughter, how the door is creaking." Evening Prayer. Arthur Fitger, *German*. AWP, *tr. by* Jethro Bithell

Daughter, I must commend thy noble heart. Euripides. OBCVT, *tr. by* George Gascoigne *Fr.* The Phoenician Women.

Daughter, lying on a snow-white bed. To My Daughter. N. Balamani Amma, *Malayalam*. OMIP, *tr. by* N. Balamani Amma

Daughter-my-mother / you have observed my worst. The Blessing. Carolyn Kizer. MDDM; NMM-2; Poetr

Daughter of Admetus, A. Thomas Sturge Moore. FaBoTw

Daughter of earth and child of the wave be appeased. William Everson. NoAM *Fr.* Tendril in the Mesh.

Daughter of Jairus, The. Marina Tsvetaeva, *Russian*. BoWoP, *tr. by* Paul Schmidt

Daughter of Jove, relentless Power. Hymn to Adversity. Thomas Gray. GTBS-P

Daughter of Liberty! whose knife. Hymn to the Guillotine. "Peter Pindar." NOBRP

Daughter of Night, chaotic Queen! Ode to the German Drama. *Unknown*. NOEC

Daughter of the farrier, The. *Unknown*. ACTP

Daughter of th'Italian heaven! Corinne at the Capitol. Felicia Dorothea Hemans. BrRo; VWP

Daughter, take this amulet. Mwana Kupona Msham. WPOW, *ad. by* Deirdre Lashgari *Fr.* Poem to Her Daughter.

Daughter to that good Earl[e], once President. To the Lady Margaret Ley. Milton. GTBS-P; OBEV

Daughters. "Astra." BrRo

Daughters, 1900. Marilyn Nelson Waniek. FFC

Daughter's Brooch, The. Jeannine Savard. CMAP

Daughter's Difficulties as a Wife, A: Mrs. Reuben Chandler to Her Mother in New Orleans. Anne Stevenson. OxBM

Daughters, in the wind's boisterous roughing. Vernal Equinox. Ruth Stone. MoAmPo

Daughter's job: without a murmur, The. Household Fires. Indira Sant, *Marathi*. OMIP, *tr. by* Vinay Dharwadker

Daughters of Albion hear her woes, & eccho back her sighs, The. (LL) Visions of the Daughters of Albion. William Blake. CABP; OAEL-2

Daughters of Beulah! Muses who inspire the Poets Song. William Blake. PeECV *Fr.* Milton.

Daughters of Blum, The. Charles Wright. CoAP

Daughters of Jerusalem. Chapter V. Elizabeth Singer Rowe. PEW

Daughters of Jove, whose voice is melody. Hymn to Selene. *Unknown*. AWP *Fr.* Homeric Hymns.

Daughters of Mne [*or* The] Seraphim led round their sunny flocks, The. William Blake. *See* The Book of Thel.

Daughters of Mne Seraphim led round their sunny flocks, The. The Book of Thel. William Blake. Ro *Fr.* The Book of Thel. NAEL-2; OAEL-2; OBNC; PoE; PoEL-4

Daughters of Pandarus, The. Homer. *Fr.* Odyssey. NAWM-1, *tr. by* Robert Fitzgerald

Daughters of Time, the hypocritic Days. Days. Ralph Waldo Emerson. APN-1; AmPP; ColAP; HAP; HeIP-4; MeMAP; NAAL-1; NAAL-3; NCAP; NOBA; NoP-4; OxBA; OxBSP; PAR; PfE; PoE; PoEL-4, TAP, TFi

Daughters of War. Isaac Rosenberg. PeFWW

Dauncing (bright Lady) then began to bee. The Praise of Dancing. Sir John Davies. NOBE; PoEL-2 *Fr.* Orchestra; or, A Poem[e] of Da[u]ncing. NoSic; SiPS

Dauntless master, as he starts the human tale, The. (LL) Puella Parvula. Wallace Stevens. HCAP; LCAP-2

Dave Dirt's dog is a horrible hound. Heads or Tails? Kit Wright. OTCP

Daventry Wonder, The. "Agricola." NOEC

David. Linda Pastan. CRP

David. Charles Reznikoff. ChIV-1

David and Bathsheba in the Public Garden. Robert Lowell. ChIV-1

David and [Fair] Bethsabe. George Peele. *See* Love of King David and Fair Bethsabe.

David and Goliath. Nathaniel Crouch. OxBChV

David and Goliath. Michael Drayton.
"Our sacred Muse, of Israel's Singer sings." ChIV-1

David and Goliath. Priscilla Jane Thompson. CBWP-2

David and Goliath. P. Hately Waddell. ChIV-1

David and his three captains bold. David in the Cave of Adullam. Charles Lamb. ChIV-1

David and I that summer cut trails on the Survey. Earle Birney. NOBC

David Drummond's destinie. The Coble o Cargill. *Unknown*. ESPB

David Garrick. Oliver Goldsmith. NOEC *Fr.* Retaliation. OxBoLi

David in the Cave of Adullam. Charles Lamb. ChIV-1

David Lowston. *Unknown*. PeNZ

David ross called up from syracuse and wanted to know if. David Antin. PmAP

David sang to his hooknosed harp. King David. Stephen Vincent Benét. ChIV-1

David Talamántez on the Last Day of Second Grade. Rosemary Catacalos. BAP-96

David the king was grieved and moved. David's Lamentation. William Billings. AmFP

David Walker (1785–1830). Rita Dove. NAAAL

Davideis. Abraham Cowley.
Gabriel's Appearance. NOSC
"Michal her modest flames sought to conceal." ChIV-1
Music and Poetry. EPCY
Number, Weight, and Measure. NOSC
"So covetous Ballaam with fond intent." ChIV-1
Supplication, A. GTBS-P
(Music.) OxAEP-1

David's Epitaph on Jonathan. Francis Quarles. ChIV-1

David's Lament. Bible, *O.T.* TrJP *Fr.* Second Samuel.

(David's Lament for Saul and Jonathan.) AWP

David's Lament for Jonathan. Peter Abelard, *Latin.* NAWM-1, *tr. by* Helen Waddell

David's Lament for Saul and Jonathan. Bible, *O.T. See* David's Lament.

David's Lamentation. William Billings. AmFP

David's Peccavi. Robert Southwell. ChIV-1

David's Song to Saul. Christopher Smart. KSG *Fr.* "Song to David, A."

Davis Matlock. Edgar Lee Masters. LiTM *Fr.* Spoon River Anthology.

Davy and the Goblin. Charles Edward Carryl.
    Robinson Crusoe's Story. PoRA
    Walloping Window-Blind, The. NBLV; OBAL; OBCA
    (Nautical Ballad, A.) APN-2; OBAL

Davy by Starlight. Raymond Wilson. SpW

Davy Crockett. *Unknown.* FaBoVe

Davy Davy Dumpling. *Unknown.* OxNR

Dawlish Fair. Keats. NTP; PeLV

Dawn. Nirmalprabha Bardoloi, *Assamese.* OMIP, *tr. by* D. N. Bezbarua

Dawn. Gordon Bottomley. BoTP; MoBrPo

Dawn. Jeni Couzyn. NBrP

Dawn. Jeffery Day. NSI

Dawn. Paul Laurence Dunbar. PoLF

Dawn. John Ford. OBEV *Fr.* The Lover's Melancholy.

Dawn. Philippe Jaccottet, *French.* VCWP, *tr. by* W. S. Merwin

Dawn. Joseph Kumbirai, *Shona.* PeSAV, *tr. by* Douglas Livingstone

Dawn. "Rachel," *Hebrew.* TrJP, *tr. by* A. M. Klein

Dawn. Rimbaud. TTTS, *tr. by* Enid Rhodes Peschal *Fr.* Illuminations.

Dawn. Betsy Sholl. LTA

Dawn. George Swede. HA

Dawn, The. Tennyson. NAEL-2

Dawn, The. *Unknown.* PoToHe

Dawn. Ella Wheeler Wilcox. PWR

Dawn. William Carlos Williams. MoAmPo

Dawn after dawn after dawn / then suddenly the Dark One. Ammianus, *Greek.* GrAn, *tr. by* Tony Harrison

Dawn after dawn comes on the wine. Ammianus, *Greek.* PGA, *tr. by* Kenneth Rexroth

Dawn after mortal dawn, with vulgar joy / Acclaim the sun. (LL) A Black November Turkey. Richard Wilbur. LCAP-2; NAAL-2

Dawn: and foot on the cold stair treading [or]. Aubade for Hope. Robert Penn Warren. FuPo; MoAmPo

Dawn and night of fighting, lovers like actual wars. Sonnet: Kamikaze. Bernadette Mayer. FTOS

Dawn; and the jew's-harp's sawing seesaw song. Pilots, Man Your Planes. Randall Jarrell. MoAmPo

Dawn at Chiao Mountain, Seeing Off K'un-lun on His Way Back to Ching-k'ou. Wang Shih-chieng, *Chinese.* SuSp, *tr. by* Richard John Lynn

Dawn. Birds sing in the courtyard. Spring Morning. Ch'en Yü-yi, *Chinese.* OHMPC, *tr. by* Kenneth Rexroth

Dawn breaks, snow patches lie on the slopes. After Snow—Impromptu. Yü Chi, *Chinese.* CoBLCP, *tr. by* Jonathan Chaves

Dawn Chorus. Mary Holtby. UV

Dawn: Clear Skies. Yang Shih-ch'i, *Chinese.* CoBLCP, *tr. by* Jonathan Chaves

Dawn crack of sounds known, The. This Earth, My Brother. Kofi Awoonor. VCWP

Dawn departs, the morning is begun, The. My Mother. Claude McKay. NAAAL

Dawn Dissolves the Monsters. Paul Éluard, *French.* AF, *tr. by* Lloyd Alexander

Dawn drizzle [*or* Dawndrizzle] ended dampness steams from. Anglo Saxon Street. Earle Birney. HeIP-4; NOBC

Dawn edges its way through the crowd of huddled trees. An October Morning. Jayanta Mahapatra. OMIP

Dawn enters; here Love wakens; here is day. (LL) Nuptial Song. John Byrne Leicester Warren, 3d Baron De Tabley. GTBS-P; PeVV

Dawn enters; my Love wakes; here is day. John Byrne Leicester Warren, 3d Baron De Tabley. *See* Nuptial Song.

Dawn Feeding. Leslie Ullman. NAmP90

Dawn. First light tearing. Clouds. Philip Levine. LCAP-2

Dawn Has Yet to Ripple In. Melville Cane. MoAmPo

Dawn Hippo. Sydney Clouts. PeSA

Dawn Horse, The. William Harmon. FYAP

Dawn: I half-open the gate. Spring. Chang Yü. *Fr.* The Four Seasons in the Mountains. CoBLCP, *tr. by* Jonathan Chaves

Dawn in a tree of birds, A. Kenneth Rexroth. InPK-6

Dawn in Britain, The. Charles Montague Doughty.

Bladyn's Song of Cloten. PoEL-5

Gauls Sacrifice, The. FaBoTw

Hymn to the Sun. FaBoTw

Roman Officer Writes, A. FaBoTw

Dawn in January. Lance Henson. CDW

Dawn in Stone City. Li Ho, *Chinese.* PLT, *tr. by* A. C. Graham

Dawn in the Heart of Africa. Patrice Emery Lumumba. PBA; TTY

Dawn in the Valley. Fily-Dabo Sissoko, *French.* NegPo, *tr. by* Ellen Conroy Kennedy

Dawn is, in essence, sinister as fire. Dew. Jennifer Maiden. CBAP

Dawn is smiling on the dew that covers, The. The Genesis of Butterflies. Victor Hugo, *French.* AWP, *tr. by* Andrew Lang

Dawn. Leni Riefenstahl. Pol Pot. Frederick Seidel. BAP-94

Dawn lightly laid her rosy hand. (LL) A Ballad of a Nun. John Davidson. MoBrPo; UV

Dawn, / like petals of drenched roses. Fish. Bhanuji Rao, *Oriya.* OMIP, *tr. by* Jayanta Mahapatra

Dawn moon struggles to shine its light, The. On Failing the Examination. Meng Chiao, *Chinese.* CoBCP, *tr. by* Burton Watson

Dawn of a New Humankind, The. Du Tử Lê, *Vietnamese.* AVP, *tr. by* Huỳnh Sanh Thông

Dawn of a pleasant morning in May. Lee to the Rear. John Randolph Thompson. CBCWP

Dawn of Love, The. Henrietta Cordelia Ray. BlSi; CBWP-3

Dawn of the Space Age. John Ciardi. OBAL

Dawn on the drab North Sea! North Sea. Jeffery Day. NSI; PoWW

Dawn on the East Coast. Alun Lewis. OBWP

Dawn Over the Mountains. Tu Fu, *Chinese.* OHPC, *tr. by* Kenneth Rexroth

Dawn overtook Scheherazade and she fell silent. The Telling. Andrew Hudgins. RA

Dawn Patrol, The. Paul Bewsher. NSI

Dawn Raid on an Orchard. Tom Pickard. NBrP

Dawn / rose like a hand at the edge of dark. Crazy Horse: The Last Morning. Lance Henson. VoR

Dawn shakes the candle, shoots a flame. May It Be. Boris Pasternak, *Russian.* TrJP, *tr. by* C. M. Bowra

Dawn, streaks of rose-brown, dry. Living Together. Jean Valentine. LCAP-2

Dawn that cares for nobody. February. W. S. Merwin. NNaP

Dawn Wail for the Dead. Oodgeroo of the tribe Noonuccal. BMAP

Dawn Wail for the Dead. Kath Walker. CBAP

Dawn was apple-green, The. Green. D. H. Lawrence. GBL; LoP; MoBrPo; PoA

Dawn with a young, restive hand erased. Morning Joy. Marie Under, *Estonian.* CEEP, *tr. by* Ivar Ivask

Dawning. Richard Watson Dixon. NOBVV

Dawning, The. George Herbert. ESCV; NOSC

Dawning, The. Henry Vaughan. GeHe; NOCV

Dawning Fair, Morning Wonderful. *Unknown.* AH

Dawning of morn, the daylight's sinking, The. Thee, Thee, Only Thee. Thomas Moore. GBL; OBNC

Dawn's Carol. Henrietta Cordelia Ray. CBWP-3

Dawn's orb orange-raw shining over Palisades. We Rise on Sun Beams and Fall in the Night. Allen Ginsberg. CLPP

Dawn's precise pronouncement waits, The. The Edge of Day. Laurie Lee. NYBP

Dawn's Rose. Ted Hughes. *Fr.* Crow. PoE

Day, The. Roy Fuller. OxBTC

Day. Cecil Arthur Spring-Rice. BoTP

Day, A. William Leroy Stidger. PoToHe; SoSe-8

Day 20. Bruce Beaver. BMAP *Fr.* Odes and Days.

Day after Chasing Porcupines. James Welch. NoAM

Day after Conference, The. Josephine D. Henderson Heard. CBWP-4

Day after day as the day sets. Tirzah. Jacob Cohen, *Hebrew.* MHP, *tr. by* Ruth Finer Mintz

Day after day I sit and write. Advice to Young Ladies. Ann Plato. AAP

Day after day it goes on. How Much Longer? Robert Mezey. OBWP

Day after day I've longed for my husband. Yosami, the wife of Hitomaro, *Japanese.* WPJ, *tr. by* Kenneth Rexroth *and* Ikuko Atsumi

Day after day my silk dresses grow more loose. The New Wife. Ng Shao, *Chinese.* OHMPC, *tr. by* Kenneth Rexroth

Day after day, O lord of my life, shall I stand before thee face to face? Rabindranath Tagore. OBMV *Fr.* Gitanjali.

Day after day spring's glory vies with the glorious sun. Li Shang-yin, *Chinese.* PLT, *tr. by* A. C. Graham

Day after decapitation, The. The Head. Padraic Fallon. CIP-2

Day after Sunday, The. Phyllis McGinley. MoAmPo; OBSV; UnPo

Day agone, as I rode sullenly, A. Dante. AWP *Fr.* La Vita Nuova.

Day and Night. Eugenio Montale, *Italian.* AF, *tr.* by William Arrowsmith

Day and Night. James Stephens. BoTP

Day and night are never weary. Greek Epigram. Ezra Pound. MoAmPo

Day and Night Handball. Stephen Dunn. AmPA

Day at a Time, *For the artist of environment, time too must be flexible.* Michael Dransfield. BMAP

Day at the Farm, A. "L. J." BoTP

Day Aviva Came to Paris, The. Irving Layton. MoCV

Day befo' Thanksgibin', De. Maggie Pogue Johnson. CBWP-4

Day before April, The. Mary Carolyn Davies. BoTP

Day before Christmas. Marchette Chute. NTCP

Day Before They Bombed Nagasaki, The. Rebecca Baggett. CrSp

Day began with dismal dougt, The. *Unknown.* PoToHe

Day Begins at Governor's Square Mall. Leon Stokesbury. MT

Day begins to droop, The. Winter Nightfall. Robert Bridges. MoBrPo; OBEV; SCGP

Day-break and a candle end. (LL) The Wild Old Wicked Man. W. B. Yeats. CMoP; RaBo

Day-Breakers [or Daybreakers], The. Arna Bontemps. PoBA

Day breaks, the. Morning Inscription. Miodrag Pavlovic, *Serbo-Croatian.* HSix, *tr.* by Charles Simic

Day breaks—the first rays of the riising Sun, stretching her arms, The. Sunrise Sequence. *Unknown, Aborigine.* NOBAu, *tr.* by Ronald M. Berndt *Fr.* The Dulngulg Song Cycle.

Day by day more brutal and more savage. In the Bottomless Pit. Maksimilian Aleksandrovich Voloshin, *Russian.* TCRP, *tr.* by Yakov Hornstein

Day by Day the Manna Fell. Josiah Conder. TrCP

Day by day the Organ-Builder in his lonely chamber wrought. The Legend of the Organ-Builder. Julia Caroline Ripley Dorr. BLPA; FaBoBe

Day changed, The. A Page from the New Diary. Nida Fazli, *Urdu.* OMIP, *tr.* by Baidar Bakht *and* Leslie Lavigne

Day concludes burning, The. Desmond O'Grady. CIP-2 *Fr.* The Dying Gaul.

Day creeps down. The moon is creeping up. The Man on the Dump. Wallace Stevens. HAP; NAWM-2; NoAM

Day darkens. Bob Boldman. HA

Day dawns with scent of must and rain, The. Mirror in February. Thomas Kinsella. CIP-2; GTBS-P; NoAM

Day drags on, as long as a year!, The. Wen Cheng-ming. CoBLCP, *tr.* by Jonathan Chaves *Fr.* The Chung-i Temple.

Day draws to a close, The. Rotation (1). Un-gyo Kang, *Korean.* CKP, *tr.* by Jaihiun Kim

Day Dream, A. Emily Jane Brontë. NALW

Day-dream, A. Mary Elizabeth Coleridge. VWP

Day-Dream, The ("If thou wert here, these tears were tears of light!"). Coleridge. Ro

Day-Dreamer. *Unknown, German.* CTV, *tr.* by Louis Untermeyer

Day-Dreams. William Canton. NOBVV; NTP

Day Dreams. Tso Ssu, *Chinese.* ChiP, *tr.* by Arthur Waley

Day Dreams, or Ten Years Old. Margaret Johnson. BLPA

Day ends that way, with brilliant colors, so lovely, without, The. Not Even Mythology. Yannis Ritsos, *Greek.* AF, *tr.* by Edmund Keeley

Day! / Faster and more fast. Pippa Passes. Robert Browning.

Day felled / the roaming troop. On the Way. Peter Huchel, *German.* CEEP, *tr.* by Michael Hamburger

Day Flight. Jack Davis. CBAP

Day goes down red darkling, The. Desolate. Gerald Massey. EBVV

Day ground down; but sheer walls, The. Difficulties of Falling Asleep. Zsuzsa Rakovszky, *Hungarian.* CEEP, *tr.* by Barbar Howes *and* Margot Archer

Day grows old, the low-pitched lamp hath made, The. Yet a Little While Is the Light With You. Francis Quarles. ChIV-2

Day had been a day of wind and storm, The. After a Tempest. William Cullen Bryant. APN-1

Day has her star, as well as Night. The Two Stars. W. H. Davies. MoBrPo

Day has pleasures of its own, The. I Love the Night. Matilda Caroline Edwards. PWR

Day! hast thou two faces. The Chartist's Complaint. Ralph Waldo Emerson. NCAP

Day He Died, The. Ted Hughes. OxAEP-2

Day he first spoke to me of love, The. When He Spoke to Me of Love. M. A. Mokhomo, *Sotho.* PeSA, *tr.* by Dan Kunene *and* Jack Cope

Day he was to leave, The. The Hand. Phạm Hồ, *Vietnamese.* AVP, *tr.* by Huỳnh Sanh Thông

Day I had in mind, The. Tanka. Masaoka Shiki, *Japanese.* MJT, *tr.* by Makoto Ueda

Day I put him off the sun outside, The. Long Tour: The Country Music Star Explains Why He Put off the Bus and Fired a Good Lead Guitar in West Texas. James Whitehead. MT

Day I was born, The. Tanka. Maekawa Samio, *Japanese.* MJT, *tr.* by Makoto Ueda

Day in an' day oot on his auld farrant loom. A Song for February. Thomas Given. FaBoVe

Day in August, A. Frank Ormsby. IIP; PBCIP; PNI

Day in June, A ("And what is so fair as a day in June?"). James Russell Lowell. *See* What [*or* And what] Is So Rare as a Day in June?

Day in May you left me, a day in May I lose you, A. Yannis Ritsos. GrIP, *tr.* by Kimon Friar *Fr.* Epitaphios.

Day in the City, A. Louis Edward Sissman. NYBP

Day in the Life, A. Stef Pixner. BrRo

Day in the Life of . . . , A. Conyus. GT

Day in the Life of a Poet, A. Quincy Troupe. NBV

Day invited me to walk, The. To Mrs.———, on the Death of Her Husband. Hannah Wallis. ECWP

Day is again begun. Richard Watson Dixon. OBNC

Day is chilly, birds each lean upon another, The. Returning from Kuang-ling. Ch'in Kuan, *Chinese.* SuSp, *tr.* by Stephen West

Day is cold, and dark, and dreary, The. The Rainy Day. Henry Wadsworth Longfellow. AWP; PoLF

Day is colorless like Swiss characters in a novel, The. For Guillaume Apollinaire. William Meredith. CoAP

Day is curled [*or* curl'd] about again [*or* agen], The. An Anniversary on the Hymeneals of My Noble Kinsman, Thomas Stanley, Esquire. Richard Lovelace. CaPo

Day is dark and dreary, The. If. Franklin Pierce Adams. OBAL

Day is done, and darkness, The. Phoebe Cary. NoAM; BXAP; OBAL

Day is done, and the darkness, The. Henry Wadsworth Longfellow. APN-1; BLPA; ChAP; FaBoBe; MeMAP; NCAP; NOBA; OxBA; PWR; PoRA

Day is drawing to its fall, A. First Sight of Her and After. Thomas Hardy. FaBoVe; PoEL-5

Day Is Dying in the West. Mary Artemisia Lathbury. AH

Day is ending, The. Afternoon in February. Henry Wadsworth Longfellow. APN-1; ColAP

Day is great and strong—, The. World Without Peculiarity. Wallace Stevens. FiLi; HCAP

Day is long; the worn noon dreams, The. Noon's Dream-Song. Eugene Lee-Hamilton. NOBVV

Day is o'er and twilight's shade, The. Gerarda. Eloise Bibb. AAP; CBWP-4

Day Is Past and Gone, The. John Leland. AH; AmFP

Day is past, the sun is set, The. Evening. Thomas Miller. ACTP; NOxBChV; OxBChV

Day / is ready to close, The. Saturday Night in the Village. Giacomo Leopardi, *Italian.* OBVE, *tr.* by Robert Lowell

Day is the children's friend. The Prejudice against the Past. Wallace Stevens. LiTM

Day is turning ghost, The. A Commonplace Day. Thomas Hardy. NOBVV

Day Lady Died, The. Frank O'Hara. HCAP; LCAP-2; MoNo; MoP; NAAL-2; NOBA; NeAP; NoAM; NoP-4; PmAP; PoE; PoM; Poetr; RaBo; TRP; VCAP

Day lay in the glass and the blood was gone., The. (LL) The Last Supper. Oscar Williams. ImPo; LiTM

Day, like our souls, is fiercely dark. Battle Song. Ebenezer Elliot. OxAEP-2

Day-long bluster of the storm was o'er, The. The Drowned Spaniel. Charles Tennyson Turner. PeVV

Day-long cold hard rain drove, The. Surviving. James Welch. CDW; HATNAP

Day my father calls to say he'll buy, The. Asparagus. Jody Gladding. BAP-95

Day my father died, The. Mervyn Morris. HCP

Day my girl is lost for an hour, The. The Quest. Sharon Olds. NAmP90

Day of anger after the holy night, The. News from a Pacified Area. James Keir Baxter. OxBC

Day of Atonement. Charles Reznikoff. ChIV-1; KSG

Day of Cold Food, The. Li Ch'ing-chao, *Chinese.* OHPC, *tr.* by Kenneth Rexroth

Day of Denial, The. Jones Very. NOBA

Day of Doom, The. Michael Wigglesworth. NAAL-1; SCAP

   "Adulterers and whoremongers / were there, with all unchaste." ColAP

   "All filthy facts, and secret acts." NAAL-3

   "All silence keep, both goats and sheep." NAAL-3

   "Apostates and run-aways." ColAP

   "Blasphemers lewd, and swearers shrewd." ColAP

   "But all too late, grief's out of date." NAAL-3

"Can God delight in such a sight." NAAL-3

"Come, blessed ones, and sit on thrones." NAAL-3

"Had your intent been to repent." NAAL-3

"Others argue, and not a few." NAAL-3

"Still was the night, serene and bright." ColAP; NAAL-3
  ("This was their song, their cups among, / the evening before.") (LL) ColAP

"Then to the bar, all they drew near." OBCA

"There also stand a num'rous band." ColAP

"These words appall and daunt them all." NAAL-3

"They wring their hands, their caitiff-hands." NAAL-3

"Thus all men's pleas the Judge with ease." NAAL-3

"Thus everyone before the throne." NAAL-3
  ("Moreover, there with them appear.") ColAP
  ("Who not at all thereon did call, / or took in vain the same.") (LL) ColAP

"Thus he doth find of all mankind." NAAL-3

"Thus shall they lie, and wail, and cry." NAAL-3

"Unto the saints with sad complaints." NAAL-3

"Wallowing in all kind of sin." ColAP

"With cords of love God often strove." NAAL-3

"Wond'rous crowd then 'gan aloud, A." NAAL-3

Day of glory! Welcome day! The Fourth of July. John Pierpont. CTV

Day of God! Thou Blessed Day. Hannah Flagg Gould. AH

Day of heat. The woods burning. Time, A. Monkey. Vladislav Felitsianovich Khodasevich, *Russian.* TCRP, *tr. by* Michael Frayn

Day of her wedding, she crouches in the kitchen, The. The Feast of St. Tortoise. Nancy Willard. LCAP-2

Day of hunting done. Twilight in California. Philip Dow. AmPA

Day of Judgement, The. Jonathan Swift. BIrV; ChIV-1; NOBE; NOEC; OAEL-1; OBSV; SCGP

Day of Judgement. Henry Vaughan. ChIV-2

Day of Judgement [*or* Judgment]; an Ode, The. Isaac Watts. ECEV; HAP; NOBE; NOEC; OBEV
  (Day of Judgement, The.) ChIV-2; SCGP
  ("Shout the Redeemer.") (LL) NoP-4

Day of Judgment, The. Thomas of Celano, *Latin.* TIRV, *tr. by* Wentworth Dillon

Day of Judgment is here, The. So Bring the Order for My Execution. Faiz Ahmad Faiz, *Urdu.* VCWP, *tr. by* Agha Shahid Ali

Day of Mourning at Yên-Báy, The. Đằng Phu'o'ng, *Vietnamese.* AVP, *tr. by* Huỳnh Sanh Thông

Day of My Death, The. Pier Paolo Pasolini, *Italian.* VCWP, *tr. by* Lawrence Ferlinghetti *and* Francesca Valente; GI, *tr. by* Max Hayward *and* Lawrence R. Smith
  ("And he has remained alone.") (LL) GI, *tr. by* Max Hayward *and* Lawrence R. Smith

Day of my double birth, if such the year. John Thelwall. NOEC *Fr.* Lines Written at Bridgewater, 27 July 1797.

Day of Resurrection, The. Saint John of Damascus, *Greek.* TrCP, *tr. by* John Mason Neale

Day of sea in the sky, made. Sophia De Mello Breyner, *Portuguese.* VCWP, *tr. by* Ruth Fainlight

Day of sunny face and temper, A. Big Bessie Throws Her Son into the Street. Gwendolyn Brooks. VGW *Fr.* A Catch of Shy Fish.

Day of the Dead. Patricia Jones. WWSi

Day of the fête, The—and what a day for it. School Cadets. Anne Elder. CBAP

Day of the Two Bodies. Jim Daniels. PUP-19

DAY OF THE VERNAL WINDS/1967. David Henderson. *See* Do Nothing Till You Hear from Me.

Day of Wrath, that dreadful day, The. The Day of Judgment. Thomas of Celano, *Latin.* TIRV, *tr. by* Wentworth Dillon

Day on Kind Continent. Robert David Cohen. NYBP

Day on the Planet, A. Brian Morse. NOxBChV

Day on which you, The. Enumeration. Ilse Aichinger, *German.* AF, *tr. by* Chappel, Allen H.

Day seemed suddenly to give to black-&-white, The. Meridian. David St. John. NAmP90

Day she visited the dissecting room, The. Two Views of a Cadaver Room. Sylvia Plath. CMoP

Day Song. Lance Henson. HATNAP

Day That I Have Loved. Rupert Brooke. PoLF

Day that I was christened, The. Godmother. Dorothy Parker. PoRA

Day that my dear came to us, The. Early Mornings. *Unknown.* AS, *tr. by* Louis Untermeyer

Day that they stole her tiger's-eye ring, The. On Becoming a Tiger. Lorna Goodison. GT

Day the bombs hit Hellabrunn, The. In the Menagerie. Oleg Grigorevich Chukhonstev, *Russian.* TCRP, *tr. by* Simon Franklin

Day the fat woman, The. The Beach in August. Weldon Kees. VGW

Day the Perfect Speakers Left, The. Leonard Nathan. WeT

Day the Tide, The. Philip Booth. CoAP

Day the wind was hardly, A. Letter VI. W. S. Graham. FaBoMo; FaBoTC

Day the Winds, The. Josephine Miles. FaBoWP

Day They Came for Our House, The. Don Mattera. PeSAV

Day They Cleaned Up the Border El Salvador, February, 1981, The. Wendy Rose. HATNAP

Day they laid your grandfather away, The. Second Wind. Fred Chappell. MT

Day they strung the cable from America to Europe, The. Cotton. Harry Edmund Martinson, *Swedish.* RB, *tr. by* Robert Bly

Day Thou Gavest, Lord, Is Ended, The. John Ellerton. EBVV; FaPoR

Day time failed began as usual, The. Burial of a Fisherman in Hydra. Grace Schulman. BoWoP

Day took such a time to pass, The. Note. Dimitris Tsaloumas. BMAP

Day transports fallen snows, muddied, mildewed, ruined, The. Spring over the City. Anne Hébert, *French.* PBWP, *tr. by* Kathleen Weaver

Day Trip. Carole Satyamurti. OPOU

Day Twenty-three. Victor Coleman. NOBC

Day wanes. The evening-glow sinks into the lonely river, The. Fireworks. Yohan Chu, *Korean.* CKP, *tr. by* Jaihiun Kim

Day was a year at first, The. Theodore Spencer. PFE

Day was clear as fire, The. The Killer. Judith Wright. BMAP

Day was close, overcast like a grey belly, The. Winter. Philip Salom. NOBAu

Day was cloudy. No one could come to a decision, The. The Last Day. George Seferis, *Greek.* AF, *tr. by* Edmund Keeley *and* Philip Sherrard

Day was here when it was his to know, The. The New Tenants. Edwin Arlington Robinson. NoAM

Day was one of weariness, The. The Beggar. Margaret E. Bruner. PoToHe

Day We Buried Our Bully, The. Mbuyiseni Oswald Mtshali. PeSAV

Day we die, The. *Southern Bushmen Oral Tradition.* BLT

Day wears on, The. John Wills. HA

Day when Charmus ran with five, The. A Mighty Runner. Edwin Arlington Robinson. MeMAP; OBAL

Day when Charmus ran with five, The. A Mighty Runner. Nicarchus of Alexandria. MeMAP; OBAL *Fr.* Variations of Greek Themes.

Day when I rose at dawn from the bed of perfect health, refresh'd, The. Walt Whitman. ITG *Fr.* When I Heard at the Close of Day.

Day when it will not matter, The. John Glassco. MoCV

Day Which Endures Not, A. A. G. Prys-Jones, *Welsh.* OBWVE, *tr. by* Anthony Conran

Day will come when I will, The. A Farewell to a Southern Melody. Huang O, *Chinese.* BoWoP, *tr. by* Kenneth Rexroth *and* Ling Chung

Day will come, when't shall be said, The. Jonathan Swift. NOIV *Fr.* The Life and Character of Dean Swift.

Day will dawn, when one of us shall harken, The. One of Us Two. Ella Wheeler Wilcox. PoToHe

Day will rise and the sun from eastward. Song. George Campbell Hay. OxBS

Day will soon be gone, The. Michinobu. *Fr.* Hyaku-Nin-Isshu. AWP, *tr. by* Curtis Hidden Page

Day with the Foreign Legion, A. Reed Whittemore. CoAP; CoAmPo; LiTM

Day you appeared I began to speak, The. To Your Question. Duane Niatum. CDW

Day You Are Reading This, The. William Stafford. PoA

Day you came, The. Breasts. Tess Gallagher. AmPA

Day you came naked to Paris, The. The Day Aviva Came to Paris. Irving Layton. MoCV

Day you died, The. A Poem for my Brother. Sonia Sanchez. NMM-2

Day you died a cold New England wind, The. Post-Larkin Triste. Mary Karr. PuP-15

Day Zimmer Lost Religion, The. Paul Zimmer. InPK-6; PBCAP

Daybreak. Richard Henry Dana. APN-1

Daybreak. Linda Hogan. NMM-2

Daybreak. Galway Kinnell. BLT; ChAP

Daybreak. Henry Wadsworth Longfellow. BoTP; PWR; PoLF

Daybreak. George Marion McClellan. AAP

Daybreak. W. S. Merwin. NAAL-2

Daybreak. Bert Meyers. SPE

Daybreak. Stephen Spender. BoLoP

Daybreak. *Unknown, at. to* John Donne. *See* Aubade.

Daybreak, and she left her poppy-seed roll. For That Day Only. Grace Schulman. WWSi

Daybreak / Have you already seen the dawn. Three Dawns. Jean-Joseph Rabéarivelo, *French*. NegPo, tr. by Ellen Conroy Kennedy

Daybreak in a Garden. Siegfried Sassoon. BoTP

Daybreak in Alabama. Langston Hughes. FaBoA

Daybreak / mingles blood. Philippe Jaccottet, *French*. MFP, tr. by Martin Sorrell

Daybreak: the household slept. Father and Child. Gwen Harwood. CBAP; WPE

Daydreaming on the Trail. Miyazawa Kenji, *Japanese*. PFTM, tr. by Gary Snyder

Daylight announces. Sunrise Comes to Second Avenue. Thylias Moss. TRP

Daylight cranked the start of work. Father. Rajandaye Ramkissoon-Chen. HCP

Daylight. For everyone but me. *Nap*. Dreams by No One's Daughter. Leslie Ullman. PBCAP

Daylight, full of small dancing particles. Jelaluddin Rumi, *Persian*. LoL, tr. by Coleman Barks

Daylights. Rosanna Warren. NoAM

Daylong this tomcat lies stretched flat. Esther's Tomcat. Ted Hughes. OxBC

Days. Ralph Waldo Emerson. APN-1; AmPP; ColAP; HAP; HeIP-4; MeMAP; NAAL-1; NAAL-3; NCAP; NOBA; NoP-4; OxBA; OxBSP; PAR; PFE; PoE; PoEL-4; TAP; TFi

Days. Philip Larkin. EBEV; FaBoMo; NTP; OxAEP-2; OxBC; OxBSP; PeECV; PiM; RB; TOF

Days and Nights. Kenneth Koch.
Stones of Time, The. NoAM

Days are cold. The Cottager to Her Infant, (By My Sister). Dorothy Wordsworth, *Third and fourth stanzas by* Wordsworth. CABP; CH; NTP; OxBChV; TTTS

Days are sad, it is the holy tide, The. The Holy Tide. Frederick Tennyson. OBEV

Days are short, The. January. John Updike. NOxBChV

Day's at end and there's nowhere to go. Allen Tate. *Fr.* More Sonnets at Christmas. LiTM

Days become years. Years. Paavo Haavikko. VCWP, tr. by Herbert Lomas *Fr.* Darkness.

Days can be sunny. I Got Rhythm. Ira Gershwin. CBLP

Days damp has shuffled bent of back into the. Paul Brown. NBrP *Fr.* De Rebus.

Days dawn on us that make amends for many. The Interpreters. Swinburne. PoEL-5

Days Drawing In. Edith Jay Scovell. FaBoWP *Fr.* The First Year.

Day's exhaustion brings me to the valley of sleep, The. I and I. Khalil-ur-Rahman Azmi, *Urdu*. OMIP, tr. by C. M. Naim *and* Norman H. Zide

Days fail: night broods over afternoon, The. Days Drawing In. Edith Jay Scovell. FaBoWP *Fr.* The First Year.

Days go I remain, The. (LL) The Mirabeau Bridge. Guillaume Apollinaire, *French*. BoLoP, tr. by Quentin Stevenson; OBVE, tr. by W. S. Merwin

Days Gone By, The. James Whitcomb Riley. APN-2; OBCA

Days grow and the stars cross over, The. Darkness Music. Muriel Rukeyser. BoWoP

Days grow long, the mountains, The. South Wind. Tu Fu, *Chinese*. BLT; OHPC, tr. by Kenneth Rexroth

Days grow shorter, the nights grow longer, The. Ella Wheeler Wilcox. BLPA

Day's grown old, the fainting sun, The. Evening Quatrains. Charles Cotton. NOSC; PoEL-3; SCGP

Day's in dread of losing her bright features, The. Ausiàs March, *Catalan*. STV, tr. by John Frederick Nims

Days in White. Ingeborg Bachmann, *German*. BoWoP, tr. by Daniel Huws

Days into weeks. Up and Down. Rachel Hadas. FiLi

Days like this, off Jake's, the August fog. Jake's Wharf. Philip Booth. NYBP

Day's noise was draining away in my mind, The. Man in the middle of the street. Petronius Arbiter, *Latin*. OBCVT, tr. by Tim Reynolds

Days of 1901. Constantine P. Cavafy, *Greek*. EP, tr. by Rae Dalven

Days of 1908. Constantine P. Cavafy, *Greek*. PFTM, tr. by Edmund Keeley and Phillip Sherrard

Days of Adam were 930 years, The. D. J. Enright. OBCoV *Fr.* Paradise Illustrated.

Days of fiesta, The. Tío-Vivo, or the Merry-go-round. Federico García Lorca, *Spanish*. CBNP

Days of 'Forty-Nine [*or* '49], The. *Unknown, att. to* Charley Rhodes. APN-2

Days of my youth left me long ago, The. The Chrysanthemums in the Eastern Garden. Po Chü-i, *Chinese*. ChiP, tr. by Arthur Waley

Days of 1992, *"Pray for the souls of the antisemites."* Marilyn Hacker. BAP-95

Days of 1956. Robin Magowan. SPE

Days of 1941 and '44. James Merrill. GLP

Days of 1964. James Merrill. CoAP; HCAP; NAAL-2; PoE; VCAP

Days of old, The. Grass Flower. Yangshik Kim, *Korean*. CKP, tr. by Jaihiun Kim

Days of Our Youth, The. *Unknown, Arabic*. AWP, tr. by Wilfrid Scawen Blunt

Days of Rain; the Rivers Have Overflowed. Su Tung-p'o, *Chinese*. CoBCP, tr. by Burton Watson

Days of spring are here, The! the eglantine. Hafiz. AWP, tr. by Gertrude Lowthian Bell *Fr.* Odes.

Days of the Unicorns. The. Phyllis Webb. NOBC

Days pass easy over these ancient hills. We Are a People. Lance Henson. VoR

Day's Ration, The. Ralph Waldo Emerson. APN-1

Days sparkling with ever new joys. (LL) Your Presence. David Diop, *French*. PBMAP

Day's sweetest moments are at dawn. Dawn. Ella Wheeler Wilcox. PWR

Days themselves, The. Position. Léon Damas, *French*. NegPo, tr. by Ellen Conroy Kennedy

Days Too Short. W. H. Davies. MoBrPo

Days went by, The. I took up the old days. Tuscan Life. Elizabeth Barrett Browning. *Fr.* Aurora Leigh. VWP

Dayseye hugging the earth, The. The Daisy. William Carlos Williams. MoAmPo

Daystar. Rita Dove. LCAP-2; NAAAL; NIP-4; OxWW

Daytime. Outside. Closeup. Not Allowed to Make a Movie in This Country. David Avidan. *Fr.* Traveling in the City. IP, tr. by Warren Bargad *and* Stanley F. Chyet

Daytrip to Paradox. Dara Wier. CMAP

Dazzle. Dorothy Roberts. NOBC

Dazzle on the sea, my darling, The. Leaving Barra. Louis MacNeice. EBEV

Dazzled blood, The. Faustus Triumphant. Thom Gunn. FaBoMo

Dazzled [*or* Dazel'd] thus with height of place. Upon the Sudden Restraint of the Earl[e] of Somerset, Then Falling from Favor [*or* Favour]. Sir Henry Wotton. NOBE; NOSC; PBRV; SeCP

Dazzling and tremendous how quick the sun-rise would kill me. Walt Whitman. ColAP *Fr.* Song of Myself.

DDD. Bruce Andrews. FTOS

De. Robert Alan Jamieson. FaBoVe

De Aegypto. Ezra Pound. VGW

De Ambiente. Tatiana De la Tierra. GLP

De Amore. Ernest Christopher Dowson. OBNC

De Amore suo. Catullus. *See Carmina*, LXXXV.

De Civitate Hominum. Thomas MacGreevy. CIP-2

De Cœnatione Micae. Martial, *Latin*. FaBoCh, tr. by Robert Louis Stevenson

De Gellia. Martial, *Latin*. OBCVT, tr. by R. Fletcher

De Gustibus. Robert Browning. FHYEP; InPS-3; SCGP

De histrice. Ex Claudiano. Claudian, *Latin*.
"Her longer head like a swines snowt doth show." OBCVT, tr. by Thomas Randolph

De Hortis Julii Martialis. Martial, *Latin*. GaP, tr. by Robert Louis Stevenson

De Imagine Mundi. John Ashbery. FaBoMo

De Libro suo. Martial, *Latin*. OBCVT, tr. by R. Fletcher

De M. Antonio. Martial, *Latin*. OBCVT, tr. by Robert Louis Stevenson

De Morte. Sir Henry Wotton. NOSC; OxBSP

De Naevo in Facie Faustinae. Thomas Bastard. FaBoEE

De Natura Rerum. Yves Bonnefoy, *French*. VCWP, tr. by Lisa Sapinkopf

De nex' day de hide drap off'n yō' back. (LL) Jack and Dinah Want Freedom. *Unknown*. NAAAL

De Ponto. Ovid, *Latin*. OBVE, tr. by Henry Vaughan

De Principe Bono et Malo. Sir Thomas More. PBRV

De Profundis. George Gascoigne.
"From depth of dole wherein my soul doth dwell." ChIV-1
"Skies gan scowl, o'ercast with misty clouds, The." ChIV-1

De Profundis. David Gascoyne. PoWW

De Profundis. Dorothy Parker. NAAL-2

De Profundis. Georg Trakl, *German*. PFTM, tr. by James Wright

De Profundis ("From depth of grief"). Bible, *O.T. See* Psalm 130.

De Puero Balbutiente. Thomas Bastard. NoSic; OxBSP

De Quincey in Glasgow. Edwin Morgan. FaBoTC *Fr.* Sonnets from Scotland.

De Quintia et Lesbia. Catullus, *Latin*. OBCVT, tr. by Richard Lovelace *Fr.* Carmina.

De railroad bridge's. Homesick Blues. Langston Hughes. GM; NAAAL

De Rebus. Paul Brown.
"Almost believed in." NBrP
"Days damp has shuffled bent of back into the." NBrP
"Don't talk to me." NBrP
"Saltpetre sucked up the cigarette with." NBrP
"This morning trampled." NBrP
"Unbowel the meaning." NBrP
De Regimine Principium. Thomas Hoccleve.
Lament for Chaucer. OBEV
"O maister deere and fader reverent!" EBEV
Prologue: "Musing upon the restless bisinesse." PoEL-1
De Rerum Natura (On the Nature of Things). Lucretius, *Latin*.
Address to Venus. AWP, *tr. by Spenser*
("Great *Venus*, Queene of beautie and of grace.") OBCVT, *tr. by Edmund Spenser*
("And quiet to the weary World restore.") (LL) EP, *tr. by John Dryden*
Against the Fear of Death. AWP; OAEL-1; OBVE, *tr. by Dryden*
Argument of the Fourth Booke, The. KTR, *tr. by Lucy Hutchinson*
"Like a shipwreck'd Sailor tost." OBCVT, *tr. by William Wordsworth*
No Single Thing Abides. AWP, *tr. by W. H. Mallock*
"Nor will ingenious women, free from pride." KTR, *tr. by Lucy Hutchinson*
"Now since the members of the world we view." OBVE, *tr. by Thomas Creech*
Suave Mari Magno. AWP, *tr. by W. H. Mallock*
What Has This Bugbear Death. CTC, *tr. by Dryden*
"Why only in the spring are roses borne?" KTR, *tr. by Lucy Hutchingson*
De Sade. John Fuller. NBLV; PeLV
De Se. John Weever. FaBoEE
De Souza Prabhu. Eunice De Souza. FaBoVe
De talles' tree in Paradise. Blow Your Trumpet, Gabriel. *Unknown*. APN-2
Dea ex Machina. John Updike. UV
Deacon Brown's Conclusion. George Sands Johnson. PWR
Deacon Jones' Grievance. Paul Laurence Dunbar. AAP
Deacon Morgan. Naomi Long Madgett. BlSi
Deacon's Masterpiece; or, The Wonderful "One-Hoss Shay," The. Oliver Wendell Holmes. APN-1; AmPP; NAAL-3; NOBA; OBAL; OBCA; OxBA; PoLF; PoRA; TAP; TFi *Fr.* The Autocrat of the Breakfast Table.
(Wonderful "One-Hoss Shay," The.) FaBoBe
Deacon's wife was a bit desirish, The. Pride of Ancestry. Robert Frost. OBAL
Dead. René Arcos, *French*. PeFWW, *tr. by Christopher Middleton*
Dead. Ambrose Bierce.
"Done with the work of breathing; done." LiLi
Dead, The. C. Day Lewis. TwCP
Dead, The. Louis Dudek. NOBC
Dead, The. Charles Heavysege. NOBC
Dead. Lionel Pigot Johnson. OBNC; PoEL-5
Dead, The. Susan Mitchell. WeT
Dead, The. Mark Strand. HeIP-4
Dead, The. Jones Very. APN-1; HAP; NOBA; NoP-4; OxBA; PAR; TAP
Dead abide with us! Though stark and cold, The. Mathilde Blind. GSo
Dead and divine and brother of all, and here again he lies. (LL) A sight in camp in the daybreak gray and dim. Walt Whitman. AmPP; BLT; CBCWP; MoP; NAAL-1; NoAM; OxBA; PoE; PoEL-5; SAmP; TAP
Dead are a cadmium blue, The. Charles Wright. HCAP *Fr.* Homage to Paul Cézanne. VCAP
Dead are always looking down on us, they say, The. Billy Collins. EC3
Dead are always searched, The. The Enemy Dead. Bernard Gutteridge. PoWW
Dead are gone and with them we cannot converse;, The. *Unknown*. ChiP, *tr. by Arthur Waley* *Fr.* Seventeen Old Poems.
Dead are selfish, The. Diatribe Against the Dead. Angel González, *Spanish*. VCWP, *tr. by Steven Ford Brown and Gutierrez Revuelta*
Dead are together as pure souls, The. (LL) In Broad Daylight I Dream of My Dead Wife. Mei Yao Ch'en, *Chinese*. OHPC, *tr. by Kenneth Rexroth; OxBM*
Dead are waiting for us in our rooms, The. Charles Wright. *Fr.* Homage to Paul Cézanne. VCAP
Dead are with us to stay, The. Charles Wright. *Fr.* Homage to Paul Cézanne. VCAP
Dead at Clonmacnois [*or* Clonmacnoise], The. Angus O'Gillan, *Irish*. APAD; OBEV; OBMV, *tr. by Thomas William Rolleston*
(Clonmacnoise.) IIP
Dead at foot of castle wall. (LL) Fast rode the knight. Stephen Crane. MeMAP; NAAL-2

Dead at Quang Tri, The. Yusef Komunyakaa. CDa
Dead at Villers-Bretonneux, The. Inscription at Villers-Bretonneux. Geoff Page. NOBAu
Dead Baby, The. William Carlos Williams. NAAL-2
Dead-Beat, The. Wilfred Owen. PeFWW
Dead beetle lies on a country road, A. Seen From Above. Wislawa Szymborska, *Polish*. PoSu, *tr. by Grazyna Drabik and Sharon Olds*
Dead before Death. Christina Rossetti. NAEL-2; NALW
Dead Beggar, an Elegy Addressed to a Lady, The. Charlotte Smith. BWW
Dead bents and thistles start to grow. (LL) Sudden Thaw. Andrew Young. FaBoTC; NTP
Dead Bird. David R. Slavitt. BXAP
Dead birds fell, but no one had seen them fly, The. Some Dreams They Forgot. Elizabeth Bishop. NoAM
Dead bodies adrift. River in Hell (two poems). Miyazawa Kenji, *Japanese*. MJT, *tr. by Makoto Ueda*
Dead Body Itself, The. Sharon Olds. PuP-16
Dead Boy. John Crowe Ransom. CMoP; FaBoMo; FuPo; MeMAP; NoAM; NoP-4; OxBA; PoE; TwCP
Dead boy living among men as a man, A. A Head. James Schuyler. PoM
Dead Brother, The. *Unknown*. EnSB
Dead Butterfly, The. Denise Levertov. NoP-4
Dead by the side of the road, The. (LL) The Dead by the Side of the Road. Gary Snyder. HAP; InPS-3
DEAD CAN SING, THE. For the Dead Lecturer. Diane Di Prima. BB
Dead can sleep, The. I Am Dead But I Know the Dead Are Not Like This. Charles Bukowski. PmAP
Dead cat. Michael McClintock. HA
Dead cats, and turnip-tops, come tumbling down the flood. (LL) A Description of a City Shower. Jonathan Swift. HeIP-4; NAEL-1; NOEC; OAEL-1; OBSV; PoE; SCGP; UnPo
Dead Center. Chester Kallman. PoA
Dead Center. Ruth Whitman. NYBP
Dead center in the rain over Stephansplatz. Vienna in the Rain. Jay Meek. CMAP
Dead Child Speaks, A. Nelly Sachs, *German*. HP; PoSu, *tr. by Ruth Mead and Matthew Mead*
Dead Christ. Andrew Hudgins. RA
Dead Cities. Madison Cawein. APN-2
Dead city walls may pen us in, but still. Charles Harpur. CBAP *Fr.* A Coast View.
Dead Cleopatra lies in a crystal casket. Conrad Potter Aiken. PoA *Fr.* Discordants.
Dead Color. Charles Wright. HCAP; LCAP-2
Dead cones upon the altar [*or* alder] shook. (LL) In Memory of Jane Fraser [*or* Frazer]. Geoffrey Hill. MoP; NAEL-2; NoAM; OxBTC
Dead Cow Farm. Robert Graves. PoWW
Dead Crab, The. Andrew Young. FaBoTw; RB
Dead dandelions, bald as drumsticks. Dandelions. Craig Raine. NoAM
Dead! dead! the Child I lov'd so well! On the Death of His Son. Charles Wesley. NOCV
Dead Dog. Vernon Scannell. OxBC
Dead don't get around / Much anymore, The. (LL) Nostalgia and Complaint of the Grandparents. Donald Justice. LCAP-2; NoAM
Dead drunk, he mutters. (LL) Rhyming with Tzu-yu's "Treading the Green." Su Tung-p'o, *Chinese*. CoBCP, *tr. by Burton Watson*
Dead Embryos. Judit Tóth, *Hungarian*. WPOW, *tr. by Laura Schiff*
Dead fall around us like rain, The. Charles Wright. *Fr.* Homage to Paul Cézanne. VCAP
Dead Father, The. Bernd Jentzsch, *German*. CEEP, *tr. by Ewald Osers*
Dead Feast of the Kol-Folk, The. John Greenleaf Whittier. PoEL-4
Dead Fiddle, The. Humbert Wolfe. TrJP
Dead Fly. Eiléan Ní Chuilleanáin. CIP-2
Dead for Two Years, Erhart Arranges to Meet Me in a Dream. John Balaban. CDa
Dead Foxhunter, The. Robert Graves. PoFWW
Dead Friend, The. Agnes Mary Frances Robinson. VWP
Dead Hand. W. S. Merwin. InPK-6
Dead hangs the fruit on that tall tree. Burial of the Spirit of a Young Poet. Richard Hughes. MoBrPo
Dead have no doubt, The. At the Mass Graveyard. Eve Shelnutt. CMAP
Dead have remembered, The. Posthumous Rehabilitation. Tadeusz Rózewicz, *Polish*. FaBoPV; HP, *tr. by Adam Czerniawski*
Dead. He died in Detroit, his beard. Etheridge Knight. *Fr.* Two Poems for Black Relocation Centers. NNaP
Dead Heroes, The. Isaac Rosenberg. MoBrPo; NSI
Dead Horse, The. Cecília Meireles, *Portuguese*. PBWP, *tr. by James Merrill*

Dead Horse, The. *Unknown.* AS

Dead Horse Bay. Robert Adamson. NOBAu

Dead Host's Welcome, The. John Fletcher. OxAEP-1 *Fr.* The Lover's Progress.

Dead in Europe, The. Robert Lowell. LiTM; OxBA; OxBC

Dead in Frock Coats, The. Carlos Drummond de Andrade, *Portuguese.* PFTM

Dead in his meagreness. (LL) In the Prison Pen. Herman Melville. PoEL-5; TAP

Dead in other lands are settled, The. The Order of the Dead. J. P. Clark Bekederemo. HBAPE

Dead in Queens lean westward from their stones, The. A Day in the City. Louis Edward Sissman. NYBP

Dead in the cold, a song-singing thrush. Last Rites. Christina Rossetti. FaBoVe; OxBChV

Dead in the rice paddies, dead on the nameless hills. (LL) Ode for the American Dead in Asia. Thomas McGrath. AiP; RaBo; VGW

Dead in There. Langston Hughes. APSN

Dead in via, The. La Préface. Charles Olson. PoM

Dead is Columba: the world's arch. Saint Columba. Lionel Pigot Johnson. TIRV

Dead! Is it possible? He, the bold rider. Custer's Last Charge. Frederick Whittaker. PoLF

Dead is now that blackguard and buried in earth. Translation by Mark Willhardt. William Dunbar. RACG

Dead is the root[e] whence all these fancies [or fancyes] grew[e]. (LL) A Farewell to False Love. Sir Walter Ralegh. BoLoP; NAEL-1; NoSic; SiPS

Dead Knight, The. John Masefield. CH; GTBS-P

Dead Lady Canonized, The. Imamu Amiri Baraka. CAPP-1

Dead Leaf, A. Howard Moss. NYBP

Dead Leaves. Aleksandar Ristovic, *Serbo-Croatian.* HSix, *tr. by* Charles Simic

Dead leaves are falling in the dormant air. The Bridge. O. V. de L. Milosz, *French.* BLT, *tr. by* Czeslaw Milosz *and* Robert Hass

Dead leaves, one-time fair, The. A Word to the West End. Thomas Ashe. EBVV

Dead lemon like a cowled old woman crouching in the cold, A. For *Under the Volcano.* Malcolm Lowry. NOBC

Dead Letters. Frank Manley. Poetr

Dead lie on Givenchy field, The. Givenchy Field. "H. d'A. B." NSI

Dead Liebknecht, The. "Hugh MacDiarmid." FaBoPV; OBVE

Dead, long dead. Tennyson. EBVVPR *Fr.* Maud [A Monodrama]. EnVR

("As the churches have killed their Christ.") (LL) OAEL-2

Dead Love. Elizabeth Siddal. LW; NOBVV

Dead man, A/ who never caused others to die. W. H. Auden. OAEL-2 *Fr.* Marginalia.

Dead Man Ariseth and Singeth a Hymn to the Sun, The. *Unknown.* AWP *Fr.* Book of the Dead.

Dead Man Dragged from the Sea, The. Carl Gardner. PoBA

Dead man is introduced back into life. They take him to a country fair, to a, The. Bringing a Dead Man Back into Life. Russell Edson. TRP

Dead man lay quietly, The. Waking the Dead. Alasdair Maclean. FaBoTC

Dead man touched me with his hand, A. Mariya Avakkumova, *Russian.* TCRP, *tr. by* Albert C. Todd

Dead Man's Dump. Isaac Rosenberg. FaBoMo; GTBS-P; LiTM; NAEL-2; NSI; NoAM; NoP-4; OBWP; PeFWW; PoWW; TrJP

("And the startled blood may stop.") (LL) PoFWW

("Or a piper coming from far away?") (LL) NoP-4

Dead March, A. Mary C. Gillington. PeVV

Dead Men, The. Sophia de Mello Breyner Andresen, *Portuguese.* PBWP, *tr. by* Allan Francovich

Dead Mole, A. Andrew Young. GTBS-P; OxBSP

Dead Monkey, The. William Olsen. NAmP90

Dead-Mule Tree: A Song of Wisdom. Sir Alan Patrick Herbert. NSI

Dead of the Wilderness, The. Hayyim Nahman Bialik, *Hebrew.* AWP, *tr. by* Maurice Samuel

Dead of Winter. Anthony Towne. NYBP

Dead! One of them shot by the sea in the east. Mother and Poet. Elizabeth Barrett Browning. NAEL-2; NALW; VWP

Dead or living. The Seed is in Me. José Craveirinha. PBMAP

Dead Ox, The. Virgil, *Latin.* OBCVT, *tr. by* Charles Stuart Calverley

Dead person, I wander, a. Exile. Ingeborg Bachmann, *German.* PoSu, *tr. by* Daniel Huws

Dead piled up, thick, fragrant, on the fire escape, The. Autumn Leaves. Marilyn Chin. PiM

Dead Poet, The. Lord Alfred Bruce Douglas. ADE; GSo

Dead Poet, The. Alfred Wellington Purdy. NOBC

Dead poets stalk the air. Rainy Night at the Writers' Colony. Josephine Jacobsen. TAP

Dead Ponies. Brenda Chamberlain. OBWVE; WPE

Dead rising from the boiling seas, The. (LL) Fears of the Eighth Grade. Toi Derricotte. GT

Dead scents I couldn't bear bore. Year of the Bird. Brian Swann. AmPA

Dead Sea Scrolls, The. *Unknown, Hebrew.*

Blessed Art Thou, O Lord. TrJP, *tr. by* Theodor H. Gaster

Lo, I Am Stricken Dumb. TrJP, *tr. by* Theodor H. Gaster

My Soul in the Bundle of Life. TrJP, *tr. by* E. Margaret Rowley

Though Mine Eye Sleep Not. TrJP, *tr. by* Theodor H. Gaster

Dead Seal [near McClure's Beach], The. Robert Bly. NNaP

Dead Seal. Alfred Wellington Purdy. MoCV; MoP

Dead Shall Be Raised Incorruptible, The. Galway Kinnell. NOBA; PoE

Dead shall rise again, The. The Raising of Lazarus. Lucille Clifton. CrSp

Dead shalt thou lie; and nought. Sapphic Fragment. Sappho, *Greek.* OBCVT, *tr. by* Thomas Hardy

Dead sheep / beside the highway. Preparations. Leslie Marmon Silko. VoR

Dead Sister, The. Caroline Gilman. OBCA

Dead Soldier. Nicolás Guillén, *Spanish.* TTY, *tr. by* Langston Hughes

Dead Soldiers. James Fenton. AF; NoAM; NoP-4; OBWP

Dead Soldiers, The. Max Plowman. PoWW

Dead soul's epitaph in every face!, A. (LL) The Street. James Russell Lowell. GSo; Son

Dead Sparrow, The. William Cartwright. CH

Dead stare out of empty sockets, The. Arthur James Marshall Smith. NOBC

Dead Statesman, A. Rudyard Kipling. FaBoEE; NBLV; OPOU; PoFWW; PoWW *Fr.* Epitaphs of the War [1914–1918]. OBWP

Dead Still. Andrey Andreievich Voznesensky, *Russian.* BoLoP; LoP, *tr. by* Richard Wilbur

Dead! the glorious Dead!—And shall they rise?, The. The Magic Glass. Felicia Dorothea Hemans. NOBRP

Dead, The ("These hearts were woven"). Rupert Brooke. CH; PeFWW; PoA; SoSe-8 *Fr.* 1914.

Dead, they do not come from cemeteries, The. Corpse in the House. Jure Kastelan, *Croatian.* CEEP, *tr. by* Peter Kastmiler

Dead, they'll burn you up with electricity. Argentarius, *Greek.* PGA, *tr. by* Kenneth Rexroth

Dead to the Living, The. Edith Nesbit. VWP

Dead to the world in love my parents lie. My Parents En Route. David Ferry. WeT

'Dead,' was all he answered. (LL) The Death of the Hired Man. Robert Frost. AmPP; CMoP; HeIP-4; HoPM; MoAmPo; NAAL-2; NoP-4; OxBA; SAGP; SAmP

Dead Water. Wen Yi-tuo, *Chinese.* PFTM, *tr. by* Arthur Sze

Dead Weasel, A. David Helwig. NOBC

Dead Will Not Praise You, The. David Shapiro. KSG

Dead will not rehabilitate us, The. (LL) Posthumous Rehabilitation. Tadeusz Rózewicz, *Polish.* HP, *tr. by* Adam Czerniawski

Dead Wingman, The. Randall Jarrell. PoWW

Dead Words, The. Vernon Watkins. LiTM

Dead, you will lie under a yard of earth. Argentarius, *Greek.* GrAn, *tr. by* Fleur Adcock

Deader they die here, or at least. One Voter out of Sixteen. Robert Penn Warren. *Fr.* Fall Comes in Back-Country Vermont. NYBP; VGW

Deadly Dance, The. *Unknown, Aztec Indian.* STP, *tr. by* Edward Kissam

Deadly Kisses. Pierre de Ronsard, *French.* AWP, *tr. by* Andrew Lang

Deadly Seven, The. Sydney Bernard Smith. PeLi

Deadly Weapon. Beatrix Gates. GLP

Deadman's Dirge. George Darley. *See* The Sea-Ritual.

Dead's right grain, The. The Future and the Ancestor. André Chedid, *French.* WPOW, *tr. by* Samuel Hazo *and* Mirène Ghossein

Deadsong. Don Domanski. NOBC

Deadwood Dick. Elizabeth Alexander. RA

Deaf-and-Dumb School. Anthony Delius. PeSA

Deaf, giddy, helpless, left alone. On His Own Deafness. Jonathan Swift. BIrV; FaBoEE

Deaf, giddy, odious to my friends. Jonathan Swift. *See* On His Own Deafness.

Deaf Girl Playing. James Tate. CMAP; LCAP-2

Deaf is like. Barry O. Higgs. PeSA

Deaf-Mute in the Pear Tree. Patricia K. Page. NoAM; NoP-4; PoE

Deaf-Mutes. Nikolai Ivanovich Glazkov, *Russian.* TCRP, *tr. by* Daniel Weissbort

Deaf Poem. Tess Gallagher. PUP-18

Deaf Things. Momcilo Nastasijevic, *Serbo Croatian.*

"Beauty since." HSix, *sect.* 6, *tr. by* Charles Simic

"I know by the arrow of darkness." HSix, *sect.* 3, *tr. by* Charles Simic

"It has hardened." HSix, *sect.* 2, *tr. by* Charles Simic

"Not one whisper." HSix, *sect.* 1, *tr. by* Charles Simic

"Pain / so it turned black." HSix, *sect.* 10, *tr. by* Charles Simic

Deaf to God, who calls and walks. Doomsday Morning. Genevieve Taggard. MoAmPo

Deafness. Richard Ryan. BIrV; PBCIP

Dealer, bewitched by gain-promising dreams, A. Bush Justice. Charles Harpur. CBAP

Dealer in shirt-sleeves told his assistant Jenny, The. Newcombe at the Croydon Gallery. Arthur Nortje. HBAPE

Dealing Scraps. Ruth Garnett. ISC

Dean, adult education may seem silly. Lucretius versus the Lake Poets. Robert Frost. OBCoV

Dean-Bourn, farewell; I never look to see. To Dean-bourn, a Rude River in Devon, by Which Sometimes He Lived. Robert Herrick. BeJo; CaPo; CavPo; PBRV

Dean Inge. Humbert Wolfe. FaBoEE

Dean of Paul's did search for his wife, The. Fragment of a Song on the Beautiful Wife of Dr. John Overall. *Unknown.* BoLoP

Dean of the University said, The. May 1968. Sharon Olds. NAmP90; NIP-4

Dear Albert, of Saxe-Coburg-Gotha. Limerick. W. F. N. Watson. PeLi

Dear Alice! you'll laugh when you know it. The Talented Man. Winthrop Mackworth Praed. CABP; NOBL; OBCoV; PeLV

Dear and great Angel, wouldst thou only leave. The Guardian-Angel. Robert Browning. PeECV

Dear, and very dear relation. To Ann Lear. Edward Lear. CBNP

Dear Ann, wherever you are. For Ann Scott-Moncrieff. Edwin Muir. GTBS-P

Dear Antigone, / after going over all the arguments. Letter. Leonard Nathan. PBCAP

Dear architect of fine *Chateaux en l'air.* To William Hayley, Esq.: In Reply to His Solicitation to Write with Him in a Literary Work. William Cowper. Son

Dear Auntie / Oh, what a nice jumper. Christmas Thank You's. Mick Gowar. OBCP

Dear, back my wounded heart restore. The Divorce. Thomas Stanley. FMP; MeLP

Dear Bill, I dawdled answering your letter. February 25. Marilyn Hacker. CPO

Dear Bill, / When I search the past for you. A Letter to William Carlos Williams. Kenneth Rexroth. NNaP

Dear Black Head. *Unknown, Gaelic.* BIrV, *tr. by* Sir Samuel Ferguson (Cean Dubh Deelish.) GBL

Dear Boy, What a superlative day for a funeral. Micheál Mac Liammóir. Paul Durcan. PBCIP

Dear boy, you will not hear me speak. Pangloss's Song: A Comic-Opera Lyric. Richard Wilbur. MoP; NBLV; NoAM

Dear Brethren, Are Your Harps in Tune? Eunice Smith. AH

Dear brother Robin, this comes from us all. Country Letter. John Clare. EnVR

Dear brother, would you know the life. Ralph Waldo Emerson. APN-1; OxBA

Dear brothers and sisters, we love one another. The Ark. Noah Calwell Cannon. AAP

Dear child, first-born, what I could give outright. Hand-Shadows. Jarold Ramsey. NIP-4

Dear child, these words which briefly I declare. The Maiden's Best Adorning. *Unknown.* OxBChV

"Dear children," they asked in every town. The Wise Men Ask the Children the Way. Heinrich Heine, *German.* OBCP, *tr. by* Geoffrey Grigson

DEAR CHRIS / It is 3:17 a.m. in New York city, yes, it is. Ted Berrigan. *See* Sonnet LXXVII: "It is 3:17 a.m. in New York city, yes, it is."

Dear Cleo, I can't complain about your absence. To the Muse. Philip Whalen. PoM

Dear Cloe [*or* Chloe], how blubbered is that pretty face! A Better Answer to Cloe [*or* Chloe] Jealous. Matthew Prior. AWP; NAEL-1; NOBE; NOEC; OxAEP-1; PoEL-3

Dear Col'nel, COBHAM's and your country's Friend! The Second Epistle of the Second Book of Horace Imitated. Alexander Pope. TOF

Dear Colonel, name the day. From a Young Woman to an Old Officer Who Courted Her. Elizabeth Frances Amherst. ECWP

Dear common flower, that grow'st beside the way. To the Dandelion. James Russell Lowell. ColAP; NAAL-1 *Fr.* To the Dandelion. NAAL-3

Dear common flower, that grow'st beside the way. To the Dandelion. James Russell Lowell. NAAL-3

Dear Craoibhin Aoibhin, look into our case. At The Abbey Theatre. W. B. Yeats. Son

Dear creature by the fire a-purr. The Cat. Lytton Strachey. PC

Dear critic, who my lightness so deplores. To a Captious Critic. Paul Laurence Dunbar. BPo

Dear, damn'd, distracting Town, farewell! A Farewell to London in the Year 1715. Alexander Pope. Son

Dear Dave: Rain five days and I love it[. A relief]. Letter to Wagoner from Port Townsend. Richard Hugo. NNaP

Dear, dear, dear. The Thrush's Song. *Unknown, Gaelic.* CH, *tr. by* William MacGillivray

Dear, dear! what can the matter be? Oh, Dear! *Unknown.* ReMoGo

Dear Denise: Long way from, long time since Boulder[. I hope]. Letter to Levertov from Butte. Richard Hugo. NNaP

Dear Dennice: I'm this close but the pass is tough this year. Letter to Scanlon from Whitehall. Richard Hugo. NNaP

Dear / Diana. Andy-Diana DNA Letter. Andrew Weiman. HAP

Dear Doctor, I have read your play. Epistle from Mr Murray to Dr Polidori. Byron. OBCoV

Dear Doctor of St Mary's. Song upon Miss Harriet Hanbury, Addressed to the Revd Mr Birt. Sir Charles Hanbury Williams. OBCoV

Dear Doll, while the tails of our horses are plaiting. Letter 1. Thomas Moore. NOBRP *Fr.* The Fudge Family in Paris.

Dear Dolly, stay thy scampering joints one minute. Ode to a Country Hoyden. "Peter Pindar." NOEC

Dear, doting Dick, for O! she saved my life. (LL) Privy-Love for My Landlady. George Farewell. NOEC; OBCoV

Dear Dove, that bear'st to my sole-laboring ark. Ad Amicam. Francis Thompson. Son

Dear dreamer, help me to take off. Another Fan. Stéphane Mallarmé, *French.* FLP; LoP, *tr. by* Alistair Elliot

Dear Earth my Nurse, who bar'st and dost relieve me. A Prayer. Oppian, *Greek.* OBCVT, *tr. by* Thomas Stanley

Dear earth, take old Amyntichus to your heart. *Unknown, Greek.* GrAn, *tr. by* Alistair Elliot

Dear Echo, do me a favour; it's somewhat. . . *Some what?*. Gauradas, *Greek.* GrAn, *tr. by* Peter Jay

Dear Ellen, when you read these lines, O, throw them not aside! Lines to Ellen, the Factory Girl. Ellen Johnston. VWP

Dear Emily, my tears would burn your page. To Emily Dickinson. Yvor Winters. Son

Dear Eustatio, I write that you may write me an answer. Arthur Hugh Clough. EBVV; EBVVPR; FaBoVe; OxAEP-2 *Fr.* Amours de Voyage. NOBVV

Dear, farewell, a little while. Anacreontic, on Parting with a Little Child. Samuel Wesley. NOEC

Dear father and dear mother: Let me crave. Erotion. Martial, *Latin.* AWP, *tr. by* Kirby Flower Smith

Dear Father, Look Up. "Orpheus C. Kerr." OBAL

Dear father, mother, sister, come listen while I tell. The Ashland Tragedy. Elijah Adams. AmFP

Dear fellow-artist, why so free. To a Young Beauty. W. B. Yeats. CMoP

Dear fellow castaway, the cruise ships. Weathering the Depths. Alfred M. Lee. AmPA

Dear Female Heart, I am sorry for you. Stevie Smith. FaBoEE; NALW

Dear Fergusson—They've Ramsay's statue clean. Letter to Robert Fergusson. Alexander Scott. OxBS

Dear Folks. Patrick Kavanagh. FaBoTw

Dear Frank, Here is a poem. Josephine Miles. NALW

Dear Frank, with fancy, fire and style. Upon an Ingenious Friend, Over-Vain. Thomas Fitzgerald. OxBSP

Dear Frère Jacques. Letter to a Benedictine Monk. Marilyn Nelson Waniek. GT

Dear friend, be silent and with patience see. To My Noble Friend Master William Browne: Of the Evil Time. Michael Drayton. CABP

Dear friend! Believe me, Love's not always blind. Love Has Eyes. William Forster. CBAP

Dear friend, far off, my lost desire. Tennyson. EBVVPR; FHYEP; OAEL-2 *Fr.* In Memoriam A. H. H.

Dear friend, I fear my heart will break. Out of French. Sir Charles Sedley. FaBoEE

Dear friend, I pray thee, if thou wouldst be proving. Friendship. Ella Wheeler Wilcox. PoToHe

Dear Friend, since you have chosen to associate. Tennyson's Poems. Josephine D. Henderson Heard. CBWP-4

Dear friend, the here-there emphasis is made. Letter. Janet Frame. PeNZ

Dear friend! whose holy, ever-living lines. The Match. Henry Vaughan. ESCV

Dear Friend, Whose Presence in the House. James Freeman Clarke. AH

Dear friends, and here I say friends. To my Friends. Primo Levi, *Hebrew*. FP, *tr. by* Ruth Feldman *and* Brian Swann (b. 1940)

Dear friends, left darkling in the long eclipse. Prelude to a Volume Printed in Raised Letters for the Blind. Oliver Wendell Holmes. APN-1

Dear friends, there is no cause for so much sympathy. Illness. Po Chü-i, *Chinese*. ChiP, *tr. by* Arthur Waley

Dear friends, we are gathered together. A Tribute to the Bride and Groom. Priscilla Jane Thompson. CBWP-2

Dear Fronto, famed alike in peace and war. Country Pleasures. Martial, *Latin*. AWP, *tr. by* F. A. Wright

Dear galway / it is flooding here, in missouri. A Poem to Galway Kinnell. Etheridge Knight. NNaP

Dear gentle hands have stroked my hair. Mother's Hands. W. Dayton Wedgefarth. PoToHe

Dear gentle soul, who went so soon away. Do This Favour For Me. Luis de Camões, *Portuguese*. BoLoP; LBC, *tr. by* Roy Campbell

Dear George, were Sarum palace mine. 18th Ode 1st Book, translated or rather Imitated. Horace, *Latin*. OBCVT, *tr. by* Thomas Burnet

Dear ghosts, dear presences, O my dear parents. Sadness, An Improvisation. Donald Justice. PUP-20

Dear girl, you're growing very thin. To a Sick Friend. Hannah Wallis. ECWP

Dear God. Garry Cleveland Myers. CTV

Dear God, I didn't know that Cytherea was bathing. Rufinus Domesticus. HePo, *tr. by* Barbara Hughes Fowler *Fr.* Epigrams.

Dear God, I have a little dog. Hoping for a Dog. Sophie Way. PeP

Dear God, I keep praying. A Prayer for the Young and Lovely. Helen Steiner Rice. CTV

Dear gods, set me free from all the pain. Agamemnon. Aeschylus, *Greek*. NAWM-1, *tr. by* Robert Fagles

Dear, had the world in its caprice. Respectability. Robert Browning. CBLP, EnLoPo

Dear Happy Souls. Eunice Smith. AH

Dear Harp of My Country. Thomas Moore. NOIV

Dear hearts, whose love has been so sweet to know. Last Words. Helen Hunt Jackson. SDW

Dear heavenly Father. Christian Holt. CTV

Dear hope! Earth's dowry and heaven's debt! Answer for Hope. Richard Crashaw. MeLP; NOBE; NOSC

Dear Husband. Yambo Ouologuem, *French*. NegPo, *tr. by* Ellen Conroy Kennedy

Dear, I must be gone. Parting. W. B. Yeats. FaBoTw

Dear, if unsocial privacies obsess me. Epigram. James Vincent Cunningham. VGW

Dear, if you change, I'll never choose again. John Dowland. EnLoPo; PoEL-2

Dear———, I'll gie ye some advice. To an Artist. Robert Burns. PBMP

Dear, in the terrible hour. More than They that Watch for the Morning. May Probyn. VWP

Dear J.D.: One should think of Chief Joseph here[, coming soft]. Letter to Reed from Lolo. Richard Hugo. NNaP

Dear Jack, this white mug that with Guinness I fill. William Makepeace Thackeray. OBCoV

Dear Jim: This is as far as I ever chased a girl. Letter to Welch from Browning. Richard Hugo. NNaP

Dear John, Dear Coltrane. Michael S. Harper. AmPA; ISC; LoL; NAAAL; NIP-4; VCAP

("*Love supreme, a love supreme*— A.") (LL) LoL; NAAAL

Dear John: This is a Dear John letter from booze. Letter to Logan from Milltown. Richard Hugo. NNaP

Dear John Wayne. Louise Erdrich. UnSA

Dear John, whoever now takes pen to write. James Philip McAuley. CBAP *Fr.* A Letter to Dryden.

Dear Kenward, / What a pearl. A Stone Knife. James Schuyler. FTOS

Dear kindly Sergeant Krupke. Gee, Officer Krupke. Stephen Sondheim. OBAL

Dear Knight, how great a drudge is he. Hudibras and Milton Reconciled. William Somervile. NOEC

Dear Lamp, she swore by you. Asclepiades, *Greek*. GrAn, *tr. by* Edward Lucie-Smith

Dear Land of Hope, thy hope is crowned. Land of Hope and Glory. Arthur Christopher Benson. FaPoR

Dear Lela is my joy and crown. Lela's Charms. Lizelia Augusta Jenkins Moorer. CBWP-3

Dear *Lesbia* let us love and play. Catullus. *See* Carmen 5 ("My sweetest Lesbia, let us live and love").

Dear letters, fond letters. Love Letters. Josephine D. Henderson Heard. CBWP-4

Dear little bird, the Graces' favourite. Tymnes, *Greek*. GrAn, *tr. by* Peter Jay

Dear little Bog-Face. Bog-Face. Stevie Smith. RB

Dear Liza, I is bin down town. Nigger's Got to Go, De. Daniel Webster Davis. AAP

Dear Lizbie Browne. To Lizbie Browne. Thomas Hardy. FaBoVe; NOBVV; OxAEP-2

Dear lord, accept a sinful heart. Self-Acquaintance. William Cowper. NOCV *Fr.* Olney Hymns.

Dear Lord and Father of Mankind. John Greenleaf Whittier. AH; NOCV *Fr.* The Brewing of Soma. PoEL-4

Dear Lord, Behold Thy Servants. Hosea, I Ballou. AH

Dear Lord, receive my son, whose winning love. Of His Dear Son, Gervase. Sir John Beaumont. OBEV *Fr.* Of My Dear Son, Gervase Beaumont. NOBE

Dear Lord, we give Thee thanks for. Thanks. *Unknown*. CTV

Dear lords of life, stump-toothed, with ragged breath. Geoffrey Hill. DiPo *Fr.* The Mystery of the Charity of Charles Péguy.

"Dear love, dost thou sleep fairly?" Parting at Morning. Dietmar von Aist [*or* Eist], *German*. AWP, *tr. by* Frank C. Nicholson

Dear [*or* Deare] love, for nothing less[e] than thee. The Dream[e]. Donne. CBLP; ESCV; FMP; MeLP; OAEL-1; OBEV; SeCP; TOF

Dear love, I am resolved with thee to live. A Posy. Sir Robert Ayton. NOSC

Dear love / 'tis less than I have vowed. Love. Al-Abbas ibn al-Ahnaf, *Arabic*. ArPe, *tr. by* Omar S. Pound

"Dear love, why should you weep." A Lost World. Robert Graves. NYBP

Dear Love you'd better know. Amymone. Rufinus, *Greek*. GrAn, *tr. by* Alan Marshfield

Dear Lucy, you know what my wish is. Ad Ministram. Horace, *Latin*. OBCVT, *tr. by* William Makepeace Thackeray

Dear Maiden. Heinrich Heine, *German*. AWP, *tr. by* John Todhunter

Dear Mama. Letter. Langston Hughes. PoE

Dear Mama (2). Wanda Coleman. NMM 2

Dear Mama, / Time I pay rent and get my food. Letter. Langston Hughes. PoE *Fr.* Lenox Avenue Mural. HoPM

Dear Mamma, if you just could be. A Lesson for Mamma. Sydney Dayre. OBCA; OxBChV

Dear man from the city. What Her Girl Friend Said when He Sent a Flattering Minstrel on His Behalf. Orampokiyar, *Tamil*. PLW, *tr. by* A. K. Ramanujan

Dear March, Come in. Emily Dickinson. NTP

Dear Margie, hello. It is 5:15 a.m. Ted Berrigan. PmAP *Fr.* The Sonnets.

Dear Martin, / Bumped into Arthur tonight. Correspondence. Peter Reading. PeLV

Dear Martin Folkes, dear scholar, brother, friend. John Byrom. NOBL *Fr.* A Full and True Account of a Horrid and Barbarous Robbery.

Dear Marvin: Months since I left broke down and sobbing. Letter to Bell from Missoula. Richard Hugo. NNaP

Dear Mary, thou didst see thy first-born Son. Prayer to Mother Mary. Padraic Pearse. TIRV

Dear matted squirrel tongue. Radiant Silhouette V. John Yau. OpBo

Dear me! what signifies a pin. The Pin. Ann Taylor. OxBChV

Dear Men and Women. John Hall Wheelock. IMW; NYBP

Dear Michiko, / Do songs sound different in prison? Letters from Poston Relocation Camp (1942–45). David Mura. LTA

Dear Mickey. Dahlia Ravikovitch, *Hebrew*. IP, *tr. by* Warren Bargad *and* Stanley F. Chyet

Dear Miss. Herman Gladwin. PeNZ

Dear Miss Miller. Letter to a Substitute Teacher. Gary Gildner. Poetsp

Dear Miss Roper, It seems, George Vernon, before we left Rome, said. Mary Trevellyn to Miss Roper. Arthur Hugh Clough. FaBoVe *Fr.* Amours de Voyage. NOBVV

Dear Mr Fisher I am writing. Paraphrases. Roy Fisher. PeLV

Dear Mistress, do not grieve for me. Leo to His Mistress. Henry Dwight Sedgwick. BLPA

Dear Moly, why so oft in tears? 3.7. Horace. OBVE, *tr. by* George Stepney *Fr.* Odes.

Dear Mother. Ebba M. Leaf. PWR

Dear mother cease complaints, and wipe your eyes. New England. Anne Bradstreet. KTR *Fr.* A Dialogue between Old England and New.

Dear Mother, dear Mother, the Church is cold. The Little Vagabond. William Blake. FHYEP; NBLV; OBSV; Ro *Fr.* Songs of Experience.

Dear Mother, Thank you for the egg cosy. Sister Agnes Writes to Her Beloved Mother. Paul Durcan. OBCoV

Dear Mr. Editor: I wish to say. A Grievance. James Kenneth Stephen. BXAP

Dear Mr. Noman, does it ever strike you. On Noman, a Guest. Hilaire Belloc. FaBoEE

Dear native Brook. Sonnet to the River Otter. Coleridge. OAEL-2; Ro; Son

Dear native brook! Like Peace, so placidly. Written in Early Youth, the Time an Autumnal Evening. Coleridge. LaPo *Fr.* Effusions.

Dear native brooks, your ways I have pursued. Wordsworth. Ro

Dear, near and true—no truer Time himself. A Dedication. Tennyson. OxBSP

Dear Night! this world's defeat. Diversely Holy Darkness. Henry Vaughan. *Fr.* The Night. ChIV-2; EBEV; ESCV; FSCP; GeHe; MeLP; NAEL-1; NOBE; NOCV; NoP-4; OAEL-1; OBEV; OBWVE; OxAEP-1; PoEL-2; SCGP; TFi; TOF

Dear object of defeated care! Lines Written beneath a Picture. Byron. OxBSP; Ro

Dear object of my love, whose pow'rful charms. Sarah Hazard's Love Letter. John Ellis. NOEC

Dear Obour / Our crossing was without. A Letter from Phillis Wheatley. Robert Earl Hayden. NAAAL; NoAM

Dear! of all happy in the hour, most blest. Safety. Rupert Brooke. EnLoPo *Fr.* 1914.

Dear old equivocal and closest friend. The Author to His Body on Their Fifteenth Birthday, 29.2.80. Howard Nemerov. NoAM

Dear one, forgive my appearing before you like this. A Victorian Hangman Tells His Love. Bruce Dawe. NoAM

Dear Paulus it's a busy trade of late. Lines Descriptive of Thomson's Island. Benjamin Lynde. SCAP

Dear Peggy, since the single state. Advice to a Young Lady Lately Married. Esther Lewis. ECWP

Dear Phoebus, hear my only vow. The Poetess's Bouts-Rimés. *Unknown.* NOEC

Dear Pound, I am leaving England. (LL) Villanelle: The Psychological Hour. Ezra Pound. CTC; NAAL-2

Dear Queenie, though it breaks my heart. The Handmaid of Religion. Edgell Rickword. OBSV

Dear Reader. Peter Meinke. Poetsp

Dear Reader. James Tate. SPE

Dear Reliques of a dislodg'd Soul, whose lack. Death's Lecture. Richard Crashaw. SeCP

Dear Reynolds, as last night I lay in bed. Epistle to John Hamilton Reynolds. Keats. OBNC *Fr.* To J. H. Reynolds, Esq.

Dear Reynolds! as last night I lay in bed. To J. H. Reynolds, Esq. Keats.

Dear Saint Brigid of The Kine. Invocation to Saint Bride. John Irvine. TIRV

Dear Samson, / I put your hair. Love Letter. Carole C. Gregory Clemmons. BlSi

Dear San: Everybody doesn't write poetry. Feeling and Form. Marilyn Hacker. NoAM

Dear Saviour, If These Lambs Should Stray. Abby Bradley Hyde. AH

Dear school of my childhood. Lines to an Old School-House. Priscilla Jane Thompson. CBWP-2

Dear Serious Novel. Exchange of Letters. Wendy Cope. OBCoV

Dear singer. A Guide to Patrons. Alattur Killar, *Tamil.* PLW, *tr. by* A. K. Ramanujan

Dear Sir. Walter De la Mare. OBCoV

Dear Sir, your astonishment's odd. A Reply. *Unknown.* NBLV; NOBL; PeLi

Dear Sir, You're quite wrong about me. Limerick. M. Trench. PeLi

Dear Sirs. In Response to Executive Order 9066: All Americans of Japanese Descent Must Report to Relocation Centers. Dwight Okita. UnSA

Dear Sirs: Is it not time we formed a Boston. Communication to the City Fathers of Boston. George Starbuck. NYBP

Dear Sister, my resentment had not been. Virgil. OBVE, *tr. by* Sir John Denham *Fr.* The Aeneid [*or* Eneados, *Aeneis*].

Dear Smith [*or* S****], the sleest, paukie thief. To James Smith. Robert Burns. HoPM

Dear Son, Leave Thy Weeping. *Unknown.* CTC

Dear Stella, midst the pious sorrow. Verses Inviting Stella to Tea on the Public Fast-Day. Anna Seward. ECWP

Dear steps may die away. Room. Robert Finch. MoCV

Dear these three who have come to see me. In Praise of Three Young Men. Lochlann Og O Dalaigh. NOIV

Dear, they said that woman resembled you. In My Fashion. Dannie Abse. OxBM

Dear things! we would not have you learn too much. Womankind. Gerald Massey. NOBVV

Dear Thomas, didst thou never pop. A Simile. Matthew Prior. NOEC

Dear, Though the Night Is Gone. W. H. Auden. BoLoP; CBLP

Dear[e], though to part it be a hell. To Dianeme. Robert Herrick. CaPo

Dear to my soul! then leave me not forsaken! Henry Constable. AAS; CBLP *Fr.* Diana.

Dear Uncle Stranger. Conrad Potter Aiken. ColAP; NOBA; NoAM

Dear uplands, Chester's favorable fields. Clover. Sidney Lanier. APN-2; ColAP

Dear urge no more that killing cause. To Celia Pleading Want of Merit. Thomas Stanley. MeLP; NOSC

Dear vent'rous Book, e'en take thy Will. The Conclusion. After the Manner of Horace, ad librum suum. Horace, *Latin.* OBCVT, *tr. by* Allan Ramsay

Dear, when I did from you remove. Another [Madrigal]. Edward Herbert, 1st Baron Herbert of Cherbury. NOSC

Dear, when we sit in that high, placid room. Touché. Jessie Redmond Fauset. BlSi

Dear Whoever-You-Are-That-You-Are. A Letter from the Pygmies. Theodore Weiss. VGW

Dear, why do you say you love. Song, A: On His Mistress. Sir Robert Ayton. NOSC

Dear, why make you more of a dog than me? Sonnet 59. Sir Philip Sidney. GBL *Fr.* Astrophil and Stella. AAS; SiPS

Dear, why should you command me to my rest. Michael Drayton. *See* Night and Day.

Dear World. Paula Gunn Allen. HATNAP

Dear youth, too early lost, who now art laid. On the Death of a Young and Favorite Slave. Martial, *Latin.* AWP, *tr. by* Goldwin Smith

Deare cherish this, and with it[t] my soules will. Sonnet 26. Mary Sidney, Countess of Montgomery Wroth. BWW *Fr.* Pamphilia to Amphilanthus.

Deare eyes farewell, my Sunne once, now my end. Lindamira's Complaint. Mary Sidney, Countess of Montgomery Wroth. *Fr.* Urania.

Deare friend sit down, and bear awhile this shade. The Palm-tree. Henry Vaughan. ESCV

Deare [*or* Dear], why should you command [*or* commaund] me to my rest. Night and Day. Michael Drayton. AAS; NOBE; PoEL-2; Son *Fr.* Idea.

Dearest Barry. An Answer to Thomas Barry. Pierce Fitzgerald, *Irish.* TIRV, *tr. by* Joan Keefe

Dearest Evelyn, I often think of you. The Jungle Husband. Stevie Smith. FaBoWP; NBLV; NIP-4; RB

Dearest Friend, Thou Art in Love. Heinrich Heine. TrJP, *tr. by* Emma Lazarus *Fr.* Homeward Bound.

Dearest, I am getting seedy. To My Wife. Clarence Day. OxBM

Dearest, I did not think four years ago. To Helen. Winthrop Mackworth Praed. NOBVV

Dearest, if I almost cease to weep for you. Love's Guerdons. Edith Nesbit. NOBVV

Dearest! if you those fair Eyes (wondring) stick. To his Wife at Rome, when he was sick. Ovid, *Latin.* OBCVT, *tr. by* Henry Vaughan

Dearest Louisa, Enquire if you please about Mr. Claude. Georgina Trevellyn to Luisa. Arthur Hugh Clough. FaBoVe *Fr.* Amours de Voyage. NOBVV

Dearest love, do you remember. When This Cruel War Is Over. Charles Carroll Sawyer. AmFP

Dearest Reader. Michael Palmer. FTOS

Dearest Spot on Earth, The. W. T. Wrighton. FaBoBe

Dearest, thy tresses are not threads of gold. The Comparison. Thomas Carew. BeJo

Dearest, we are like two flowers. Frimaire. Amy Lowell. CPO

Dearest, / You must know that I think of you continually. Love Letter, A: Ruth Arbeiter to Major Paul Maxwell. Anne Stevenson. OxBM *Fr.* Correspondences.

Dearly beloved Cousin, these. The Epistle of Deborah Dough. Mary Leapor. ECWP; NoP-4

Dearly beloved gentle knight. Walther von der Vogelweide, *German.* GePo, *tr. by* Frederick Goldin

Dearly loved children. Potato Peel. *Unknown.* CTAV

Death. Maxwell Bodenheim. TrJP

Death, The. Hayden Carruth. FiLi *Fr.* Mother.

Death. John Clare. GTBS-P

Death. Roy Fuller. NoAM

Death. Patty L. Harjo. VoR

Death. Thomas Hood. *See* Sonnet: "It is not death, that sometime in a sigh."

Death. Bill Knott. PBCAP; SPE

Death. Rilke, *German.* PFTM, *tr. by* Pierre Joris

Death. Sherod Santos. WeT

Death. William Bell Scott. NOBVV

Death. John A. Stone. MT

Death. *Unknown, Welsh.* OBWVE; RB, *tr. by* Aneirin Talfan Davies

Death. *Unknown.* BLPA

Death. *Unknown.* RaBo

Death. Henry Vaughan. ChIV-1

Death. William Carlos Williams. NAAL-2; OxBA; VGW

Death. W. B. Yeats. OxAEP-2; OxBSP

Death Again. T. Hope. BXAP

Death, always cruel, Pity's foe in chief. Dante. AWP *Fr.* La Vita Nuova.

Death, an Ode. John Forbes. BMAP

Death and Co. Sylvia Plath. CMoP; CoAmPo; LCAP-2

Death and darkness, get you packing. Easter Hymn. Henry Vaughan. ChIV-2; ESCV

Death and Doctor Hornbook [A True Story]. Robert Burns. OxBS

Death and Empedocles 444 B.C. Horace Gregory. PoA

Death, and it is broken. The Instrument. Kathleen Jessie Raine. PoA

Death and Love. Ben Jonson. NOBE *Fr.* The Sad Shepherd. (Song.) SeCP

Death and Passion of Our Lord Jesus Christ, The. Elizabeth Middleton. "Unhappy merchant, Thus t'expose thy Lord." KTR

Death and Rebirth. Jean-Baptiste Tati-Loutard. PBMAP

Death and Resurrection. Priscilla Jane Thompson. CBWP-2

Death and the Bridge. Robert Lowell. HCAP

Death and the Dancer. Muriel Rukeyser. AF

Death and the Lady. Léonie Adams. MoAmPo

Death and the Plowman. Sidney Keyes. OxBTC

Death and the Sun. Derek Mahon. BiHa

Death and the Three Revellers. Chaucer. OBNV *Fr.* The Pardoner's Tale. FHYEP; NAEL-1; NAWM-1; OAEL-1; PoE *Fr.* The Canterbury Tales.

Death-angel smote Alexander McGlue, The. Out of the Hurly-Burly. "Max Adeler." OBAL

Death as a Lotus Flower. *Unknown. See* He Is like the Lotus.

Death as History. Jay Wright. PoBA

Death at Pocono Lake Preserve. Robert Bagg. WeT

Death at Suppertime. Phyllis McGinley. PBMP

Death at Winson Green, A. Francis Webb. BMAP

Death[,] be not proud, though some have called thee. Holy Sonnet. Donne. EBEvV; FHYEP; HAP; HeIP-4; ImPo; InPK-6; InPS-3; MeLP; NAEL-1; NAWM-1; NIP-4; NOBE; NOSC; OAEL-1; OPOU; OxAEP-1; PBMP; PoE; PoEL-2; PoRA; Poetr; SCGP; SCV; SeCP; SoSe-8; TRP; TrCP; WeW-3 *Fr.* Holy Sonnets. ESCV *Fr.* Holy Sonnets.

Death be not proud, thy hand gave not this blow. Elegy. Lucy Harington, Countess of Bedford. PeECV; WPE

Death, become a shewolf. Crown of Happiness. Anne Hébert, *French.* BoWoP, *tr. by* Willis Barnstone

Death Bed, The. Waring Cuney. PFE

Death-Bed, The. Thomas Hood. GTBS-P; NOBE; OBEV; OBNC

Death Bed. Thomas Kinsella. CIP-2; PBCIP

Death-Bed, A. Rudyard Kipling. PoWW

Death-Bed, The. Siegfried Sassoon. AF; LiTM; NSI; PeFWW; PoFWW

Death-Bed Song. *Unknown.* AmFP

Death before forty's no bar. Lo! Obit on Parnassus. F. Scott Fitzgerald. NBLV; NYBP

Death by Drowning. Elizabeth Brewster. NOBC

Death by Water. T. S. Eliot. OBVE *Fr.* The Waste Land. AmPP; CMoP; FaBoMo; HAP; LiTM; MoAmPo; MoP; NAAL-2; NAEL-2; NAWM-2; NOBA; NOBE; NoAM; NoP-4; OAEL-2; OxAEP-2; OxBA; OxBTC; PoE; TAP; TFi; UnPo

Death came before Marriage, Philaenion. Perses, *Greek.* GrAn, *tr. by* Peter Whigham

Death Came for Michael Rockinghorse early one morning. Natan Zach, *Hebrew.* IP, *tr. by* Warren Bargad *and* Stanley F. Chyet

Death Camp. Irena Klepfisz. GLP

Death can be so lazy at times. Death of a Lady. J. P. Clark Bekedereme. HBAPE

Death, can you too be enamored? To Death. Johann Wilhelm Ludwig Gleim, *German.* GePo, *tr. by* George C. Schoolfield

Death Certificate. Rui Knopfli, *Portuguese.* PeSAV, *tr. by the author*

Death Chant. Peter Blue Cloud. VoR

Death Circus, The. John Tranter. CBAP

Death claimed the last pure dusky seaside sparrow. Noted in The New York Times. Maxine W. Kumin. AFr

Death comes in quantity from solved. The Tolerance of Crows. Charles Donnelly. CIP-2

Death Crown. Robert Morgan. MT

Death culture swarms, The. Los Angeles, 1980. Paula Gunn Allen. NMM-2

Death Described by His True Effects. George Chapman. NOSC *Fr.* Eugenia.

Death designs swirl high above faces that are of disbelief. War Walking Near. Ray A. Young Bear. CDW

Death devours all lovely things. Passer Mortuus Est. Edna St. Vincent Millay. CMoP; FaBoWP; MoAmPo; OxBA

Death did not come to my mother. Conception. Josephine Miles. APAD; ColAP; FaBoWP

Death does away with sickness; Hell cures chance. Consolations. Paul Ramsey. *Fr.* Three Epigrams. CRP

Death, Don't Be Boring. Roy Kelly. BXAP

Death favoured me from the first, well knowing I could not endure. The Favour. Rudyard Kipling. *Fr.* Epitaphs of the War [1914–1918]. OBWP

Death feeds us up, keeps an eye on our weight. Palladas, *Greek.* GrAn, *tr. by* Tony Harrison

Death for the Dark Stranger. Thomas McGrath. VGW

Death fought; before giving in. (LL) The Sacrifice. Frank Bidart. GLP; VCAP

Death from Cancer. Robert Lowell. TwCP *Fr.* In Memory of Arthur Winslow.

Death from Cancer. Edith Jay Scovell. WPN

Death Fugue, A. Paul Celan, *German.* TrJP, *tr. by* Clement Greenberg; CLPP, *tr. by* Jerome Rothenberg; AF; PoSu, *tr. by* John Felstiner; HP; VCWP, *tr. by* Michael Hamburger

("Dein aschenes Haar Shulamith.") (LL) AF, *tr. by* John Felstiner

(Fugue of Death.) OBVE, *tr. by* Christopher Middleton

Death gallops up the bridge of red railtie girders. Death and the Bridge. Robert Lowell. HCAP

Death gapes to its hinges. (LL) Harbach 1944. János Pilinszky, *Hungarian.* PoSu, *tr. by* Janos Csokits *and* Ted Hughes; HP, *tr. by* Ted Hughes; AF, *tr. by* Ted Hughes *and* Janos Csokits

Death Grapple, The. Robert Graves. EP

Death has no features of his own. Gwen Harwood. NOBAu

Death has torn ten years from us. Philodemus, *Greek.* PGA, *tr. by* Kenneth Rexroth

Death hath deprived me of my dearest friend. A Remembrance of My Friend Mr. Thomas Morley. John Davies, of Hereford. OxBSP; PFE

Death himself. L M F B R. Gary Snyder. PoM

Death, I repent. Invocation of Death. Kathleen Jessie Raine. OxBTC *Fr.* Two Invocations of Death.

Death, if thou wilt, fain would I plead with thee. A Dialogue. Swinburne. PoEL-5

Death in Leamington. John Betjeman. NoP-4; OxAEP-2; RB

Death in Life. Thomas Vaux, 2d Baron Vaux of Harrowden. NoSic

Death in Spring, A. Amir Gilbo'a, *Hebrew.* IP, *tr. by* Warren Bargad *and* Stanley F. Chyet

Death in the Dawn. Wole Soyinka. PBMAP *Fr.* Idanre and Other Poems (1967).

Death in the Desert, A. Charles Tomlinson. CABP

Death in the Evening. Miroslav Holub, *Czech.* PoSu, *tr. by* George Theiner

Death in Yorkville. Langston Hughes. PoBA

Death Invited. May Swenson. WPE

Death Invoked, *song.* Philip Massinger. *See* Song.

Death is a Dialogue between. Emily Dickinson. WPoS

Death Is a Door. Nancy Byrd Turner. BLPA

Death is a matter of mathematics. Barry Amiel. PoWW

Death is all metaphors, shape in one history. Dylan Thomas. CMoP; Son *Fr.* A Sequence of Sonnets.

Death is another milestone on their way. The Funeral. Stephen Spender. CMoP; MoBrPo; NoAM

Death is before me today. Egyptian Poem. *Unknown.* APAD

Death is in the air—. Anniversary. Dorothy Hewett. BMAP

Death is in your house, but I'm out here. The Heartless Art. Tony Harrison. NoP-4

Death is more than. One X. E. E. Cummings. FaBoMo

Death is not death, for death is but the borning day. Birth is Death, Death is Birth. Friedrich von Logau, *German.* GePo, *tr. by* George C. Schoolfield

Death Is Not Evil, Evil Is Mechanical. D. H. Lawrence. PBMP

Death is not harsh: Death is our lot: but harsh. Epitaph from a Tomb in Asia Minor. *Unknown, Greek.* GrAn, *tr. by* Peter Whigham

Death/ Is nothing to us, has no relevance. Lucretius. *See* Against the Fear of Death.

Death is only a technical correction of the market. Answer Yes or No. Robert Penn Warren. *Fr.* Tale of Time. LCAP-2

Death is only an old door. Death Is a Door. Nancy Byrd Turner. BLPA

Death is stronger than all the governments. Death Snips Proud Men. Carl Sandburg. CMoP

Death is the *Cook* of *Nature*; and we find. Nature's Cook. Margaret Lucas Cavendish, Duchess of Newcastle. BWW; PBWP; PEW

Death is the strongest of all living things. Warning to One. Merrill Moore. MoAmPo

Death is the supple Suitor. Emily Dickinson. NALW; NCAP

Death knocks all night at my door. Journey to the Place of Ghosts. Jay Wright. GT; VCAP

Death lay in ambush. Christopher Okigbo. PBMAP; TTY *Fr.* Distances.

Death lies dead. (LL) A Forsaken Garden. Swinburne. EBEV; EBEvV; GTBS-P; GaP; NOBE; NOBVV; NoP-4; OAEL-2; OBNC; OxAEP-2; SCGP

Death loved him the best. (LL) Envy. Adelaide Anne Procter. VWP

Death loves rich people. Funny Poem. Bill Knott. PBCAP

Death March. Charles Fishman. CDa

Death Mask of John Clare, The. Edmund Blunden. EPCY

Death May Be Very Gentle. Oliver St. John Gogarty. PoRA

Death, my companion, who shall quit me soon. Alec Brock Stevenson. FuPo

Death, my lifes Mistress, and the soveraign Queen. To His Mistress for Her True Picture. Edward Herbert, 1st Baron Herbert of Cherbury. SeCP

Death neither wish, nor fear to see. (LL) A Happy Life. Martial, *Latin.* FMP, *tr. by* Sir Richard Fanshawe

Death never troubled Damocles. Damocles. Robert Graves. NYBP

Death News. Allen Ginsberg. BB; MoP

Death of a Cat, The. Louis MacNeice. PC *Fr.* The Death of a Cat.

Death of a Chief. Khadambi Asalache. PBMAP

Death of a Distant In-law. Patricia Traxler. BAP-94

Death of a Fly. Goethe, *German.* STV, *tr. by* John Frederick Nims

Death of a Friend. Witter Bynner. IMW

Death of a Friend. Pauli Murray. PoBA

Death of a Gardener. Phoebe Hesketh. OBGa

Death of a Girl in Budapest, The. Ch'unsu Kim, *Korean.* CKP, *tr. by* Jaihiun Kim

Death of a Grandparent. Mrs. Jennette Bonneau. Mary Weston Fordham. CBWP-2

Death of a Lady. J. P. Clark Bekederêmo. HBAPE

Death of a Naturalist. Seamus Heaney. HAP; NoAM; OxBC; WeW-3

Death of a Negro Poet, The. Conrad Kent Rivers. BPo

Death of a Oaxaquenian. Malcolm Lowry. CLPP

Death of a Poet. Charles Causley. OxBTC

Death of a Ram. Sedulius Scottus, *Latin.* NOIV

Death of a Soldier, The. Wallace Stevens. OBWP; OxBSP; SAmP; SoSe-8

Death of a Son. Jon Silkin. GTBS-P; MoP; OxBTC

Death of a Starling, The. Catullus. *See* The Death of Lesbia's Bird.

Death of a Toad, The. Richard Wilbur. CMoP; LiTM; MoP; NAAL-2; NoAM; PFE; PoA; Poetr

Death of a Vermont Farm Woman. Barbara Howes. MoAmPo

Death of a Warrior, The. Jenny Mastoraki, *Modern Greek.* BoWoP, *tr. by* Kimon Friar

Death of a Whale. John Blight. BMAP; CBAP

Death of a Young Son by Drowning. Margaret Atwood. BoWoP; NOBC

Death of Adonis, The. Philip Ayres, *after the Greek of* Theocritus. OBVE

Death of Adonis, The. Shakespeare. NoSic *Fr.* Venus and Adonis.

Death of Adonis, The. Theocritus, *Greek.* NNPT, *tr. by* Philip Ayres

Death of Alexander, The. *Unknown.* OxBS

(When Alysandyr Our King Was Dede.) FaBoCh

Death of Allegory, The. Billy Collins. WeW-3

Death of an Aircraft. Charles Causley. MoBS

Death of an Angel, The. Russell Edson. LCAP-2

Death of an Irishwoman. Michael Hartnett. CIP-2; IIP; PBCIP

Death of an Old Woman. Alasdair Maclean. FaBoTC

Death of Artemidora, The. Walter Savage Landor. OBNC *Fr.* Pericles and Aspasia.

Death of Camilla. Virgil, *Latin.* OBCVT, *tr. by* Nicholas Brady

Death of Chet Baker, The. Miller Williams. SeSe

Death of Cleopatra. Shakespeare. *See* Antony and Cleopatra.

Death of Daphnis, The. Theocritus. HePo, *tr. by* Barbara Hughes Fowler; AWP, *tr. by* Charles Stuart Calverley *Fr.* Idylls.

("Sweet is the whispering of that pine tree, goatherd.") HePo, *tr. by* Barbara Hughes Fowler

Death of David, The. Hayyim Nahman Bialik, *Hebrew.* TrJP, *tr. by* Herbert Danby, *ad. by* Sholom J. Kahn

Death of Digenis, The. *Unknown, Greek.* GrIP, *tr. by* Richard Stoneman

Death of Don Pedro, The. *Unknown, Spanish.* AWP, *tr. by* John Gibson Lockhart

Death of Dr. King. Sam Cornish. PoBA

(Death of Dr. King #1.) MBE

Death of Europe, The. Charles Olson. NeAP

Death of faithful Dobbin I deplore, The. An Elegy on the Death of Dobbin, the Butterwoman's Horse. Francis Fawkes. NOEC

Death of General Uncebunke, The; a Biography in Little. Lawrence Durrell. "My uncle sleeps in the image of death." FaBoMo

Death of God, The. Howard Nemerov. OxBC; OxBSP

Death of Grant, The. Ambrose Bierce. CBCWP

Death of Hamlet. Shakespeare. *Fr.* Hamlet. NAWM-1

Death of Hektor, The. Brian Coffey. "Homer where born swhee buried of whom the son." BiHa

Death of Hoel, The. Thomas Gray. NOEC

Death of Irish, The. Aidan Carl Mathews. PBCIP

Death of Ivan, The. "David Samuilovich Samoylov," *Russian.* TCRP, *tr. by* Lubov Yakovleva

Death of Justice, The. Walter Everette Hawkins. PoBA

Death of King Edward VII, The. *Unknown.* OxBoLi

Death of King George V. John Betjeman. *See* "New King Arrives in His Capital by Air. . . ."—Daily Newspaper.

Death of Kings, The. Shakespeare. TRP *Fr.* Let's Talk of Graves. FaBoBe *Fr.* King Richard II.

Death of Lesbia's Bird, The. Catullus. AWP, *tr. by* Samuel Taylor Coleridge *Fr.* Carmina.

Death of Lincoln, The. William Cullen Bryant. NAAL-1; TAP (Abraham Lincoln.) NAAL-3

("Oh, slow to smite and swift to spare.") NCAP

Death of Little Boys. Allen Tate. FuPo

Death of Lord Warriston, The. *Unknown.* OxBB

Death of Marilyn Monroe, The. Sharon Olds. HeIP-4

Death of Moses, The. "George Eliot." ChIV-1

Death of Moses, The. Frances Ellen Watkins Harper. AAP *Fr.* Moses: A Story of the Nile.

Death of Moses, The. *Unknown, Hebrew.* TrJP, *tr. by* Alice Lucas

Death of My Aunt. *Unknown.* OxBoLi

Death of Myth-making, The. Sylvia Plath. PoA

Death of Nelson, The. *Unknown.* OxBoLi

Death of Othello. Shakespeare. *Fr.* Othello.

Death of Parcy Reed, The. *Unknown.* ESPB

("God send the land deliverance.") IBB

Death of Potchikoo, The. Louise Erdrich. *Fr.* Old Man Potchikoo. HATNAP

Death of Priam, The. Virgil. OBVE, *tr. by* Sir John Denham *Fr.* The Aeneid [*or* Eneados, Aeneis].

Death of Queen Jane, The. *Unknown.* AmFP

("Queen Jeanie, Queen Jeanie, travel'd six weeks and more.") ESPB

Death of Robert, Earl of Huntingdon. Anthony Munday.

Dirge: "Weep, weep, ye woodmen, wail." CTC

Death of Robin Hood, The. *Unknown.* EnSB

Death of Samson, The. Milton. *See* No Time for Lamentation Now.

Death of Samuel Adams, The. *Unknown.* AmFP

Death of Saul, The. Philip Levine. ChIV-1

Death of Sir Nihil, book the *n*th. Tywater. Richard Wilbur. CMoP; CoAmP; LiTM; TRP

Death of Slavery, The. William Cullen Bryant. CBCWP

Death of Sohrab, The. Matthew Arnold. *Fr.* Sohrab and Rustum. EBNV; OBNV

Death of Sohrab, The. Firdausi. TAL, *tr. by* James Atkinson *Fr.* The Shahnamah.

Death of Southwell, The. John Logan. "Topcliffe's horses shake." CRP

Death of Tammuz, The. Saul Tchernichowsky, *Hebrew.* TrJP, *tr. by* L. V. Snowman

Death of the Ball Turret Gunner, The. Randall Jarrell. CMoP; ClHu; ColAP; HAP; HeIP-4; HoPM; InPK-6; LCAP-2; LiTM; MT; MoAmPo; NAAL-2; NIP-4; NOBA; NoAM; NoP-4; OBWP; OxBA; PoE; PoPoPo; PoWW; Poetr; RB; SAGP; SoSe-8; TAP; TFi; UnPo; VCAP; VGW

Death of the Bird, The. Alec Derwent Hope. BMAP

Death of the Bosun's Mate. Louis Johnson. PeNZ

Death of the Day. Walter Savage Landor. NoP-4

Death of the Fathers, The. Anne Sexton.
Santa. AFr

Death of the Flowers, The. William Cullen Bryant. OBCA; PoLF

Death of the Gods; an Ode Written in Imitation of Pindar, The. L. Ker. NOEC

Death of the Hired Man, The. Robert Frost. AmPP; CMoP; HeIP-4; HoPM; MoAmPo; NAAL-2; NoP-4; OxBA; SAGP; SAmP

Death of the Kapowsin Tavern. Richard Hugo. NAAL-2

Death of the King's Canary, The. William Empson. "Not your winged lust but his must now change suit." UV

Death of the Miners or, The Widows of the Earth. Raymond Mazisi Kunene, *Zulu.* PeSAV, *tr. by the author*

Death of the Moon, The. David Wagoner. PoA

Death of the Novel, The. David Young. AmPA

Death of the Pilot Whales, The. Peter Meinke. PBCAP

Death of the Polar Explorers. Gabriel Gbadamosi. HBAPE

Death of the Sheriff, The. Robert Lowell. MoAmPo

Death of the small commune, The. Marge Piercy. WeT

Death, of thee do I make my moan. To Death, of His Lady. François Villon, *French.* AWP, *tr. by* D. G. Rossetti

Death of Thomas Merton. Harry Clifton. PBCIP

Death of Venus, The. Robert Creeley. NOBA

Death of Vitellozzo Vitelli, The. Irving Feldman. TwCP

Death of Will, The. Charles Tomlinson. OxBC

Death of Wyatt, The. Henry Howard, Earl of Surrey. SiPS ("Dyvers thy death doo dyverslye bemone.") AAS

Death on a Live Wire. Michael Baldwin. MoBS

Death ("Once he will miss, twice he will miss"). *Unknown.* AWP *Fr.* The Thousand and One Nights.

Death Poems in September. Diane Di Prima. BB

Death Rites II. *Unknown.* TTY, *tr. by* C. M. Bowra

Death roodly knocked him off his perch. On a Government Surveyor. Albert Brodrick. PeSAV

Death Room, The. Robert Graves. NYBP

Death Scene, A. Emily Jane Brontë. OxAEP-2

Death Seed. Ricarda Huch, *German.* PBWP, *tr. by* Susan C. Strong

Death Sentence, The. Stevie Smith. NoP-4

Death shall be death forever unto thee. Forever Dead. Sappho, *Greek.* AWP, *tr. by* William Ellery Leonard

Death, since I find not one with whom to grieve. Canzone: He Beseeches Death for the Life of Beatrice. Dante, *Italian.* AWP, *tr. by* D. G. Rossetti

Death Snips Proud Men. Carl Sandburg. CMoP

Death Song, A. Steve Chimombo. HBAPE

Death Song[, A]. Paul Laurence Dunbar. PoLF

Death Song. Robert Stephen Hawker. OBNC

Death Song ("I'll keep your shirt white"). *Unknown, Turkish.* BoWoP, *tr. by* Reza Baraheni *and* Zahra-Soltan Shokoohtaezeh

Death Song ("Leave the window open"). *Unknown.* BoWoP, *tr. by* Reza Baraheni *and* Zahra-Soltan Shokoohtaezeh

Death Song, A. William Morris. NAEL-2

Death Song. *Unknown, Ojibwa Native American.* APN-2, *tr. by* Henry Rowe Schoolcraft

Death Song for Owain ab Urien. Taliesin, *Welsh.* OBWVE, *tr. by* Anthony Conran

Death Song of White Antelope, The. *Cheyenne Oral Tradition, Cheyenne.* PaTW, *tr. by* George Bird Grinnell

Death Songs ("I'm the snow on mountains"). *Unknown, Turkish.* BoWoP, *tr. by* Reza Baraheni *and* Zahra-Soltan Shokoohtaezeh

Death Songs. L. V. Mack. PoBA

Death Sonnet I. Gabriela Mistral, *Spanish.* BoWoP, *tr. by* David Garrison

Death Stands above Me[, whispering low]. Walter Savage Landor. NOBE; NoP-4; OAEL-2; OBNC; OxBSP; PFE; PoEL-4

Death stepped out of the television. The Gods Ash Their Cigarettes. S. K. Kelen. BMAP

Death Sunyata Chant: A Rite for Passing Over. Diane Di Prima. BB

Death surrounds itself with the living. Mississippi. E. Ethelbert Miller. GT

Death Survey. Mongane Wally Serote. PeSAV

Death Sweet. Thomas Lovell Beddoes. NOBVV

Death takes our loved ones—. Selfishness. Margaret E. Bruner. PoToHe

Death, that is small respecter of distinction. Trainwrecked Soldiers. John Frederick Nims. GM

Death, that struck when I was most confiding. Emily Jane Brontë. EBVV; OBNC

Death the Consequence of the Fall. Dryden. *Fr.* The State of Innocence. NOCV

Death the dancer poked his skull. We Show You That Death as a Dancer. Hamish Henderson. PoWW

Death. / The death of a million. Pastoral. Ron Loewinsohn. NeAP

Death, the friend behind phenomenon. A Game of Chance. Howard Moss. PoA

Death, the Last Visit. Marie Howe. NAmP90

Death the Leveller. James Shirley. FaPoR; GTBS-P; ImPo; NOBE; OBEV; PBMP; UnPo *Fr.* The Contention of Ajax and Ulysses. (Dirge.) AWP; GEA; NoP-4; OAEL-1; PoEL-2

Death the Painter. Anthony Hecht. NoP-4

Death, Thou Hast Seized Me. Isaac Luzzatto, *Hebrew.* TrJP, *tr. by* Nina Davis Salaman

Death, thou wast once an uncouth hideous thing. George Herbert. ESCV; FSCP; GeHe; NAEL-1; NoP-4; SeCP

Death, though [*or* tho] I see him not, is near. Age. Walter Savage Landor. FaBoEE; NOBVV; PoEL-4

Death, thou'rt a cordial old and rare. The Stirrup-Cup. Sidney Lanier. AmPP

Death to him 's a Strange surprise. Seneca. *See* Senec. Traged. ex Thyeste Chor. 2.

Death to the Lady said. Death and the Lady. Léonie Adams. MoAmPo

Death to Van Gogh's Ear! Allen Ginsberg. VGW

Death took my father. Manos Karastefanís. James Merrill. TAP

Death took these early, to our land's great honour. On the Athenians Who Died at the Hellespont, 440–39 B.C. *Unknown, Greek.* GrAn, *tr. by* Peter Jay

Death Valley. Sorley MacLean. FaBoTC

Death-Wake, The; or, Lunacy. Thomas Tod Stoddart. "Beautiful Lunacy! that shapest flight." NOBRP "He sate like winter o'er the wasted year." NOBRP Mirthful Lunacy. OBNC Song: "'Tis light to love thee living, girl, when hope is full and fair." NOBRP

Death was at hand. Sean O Riordain, *Irish.* NOIV, *tr. by* Thomas Kinsella

Death was lovely. Raid on a Cheyenne Village. Diane Glancy. LoHo

Death was there, sitting by the roadside. Climbing. Gloria Fuertes, *Spanish.* PBWP, *tr. by* Philip Levine

Death, when you come to me, tread with a footstep. So Might It Be. John Galsworthy. PoLF

Death Who. Philip Hodgins. BMAP

Death, why hast thou made life so hard to bear. Canzone: Of His Dead Lady. Giacomino Pugliesi, *Italian.* AWP, *tr. by* D. G. Rossetti

Death, why so cruel [*or* soe crewill]? What! no other way. Bacon's Epitaph, Made by His Man. John Cotton. SCAP

Death will not correct. Proofs. Tadeusz Rózewicz, *Polish.* PoSu, *tr. by* Adam Czerniawski

Death you are a dreadful fellow. Death, Don't Be Boring. Roy Kelly. BXAP

Death, you're more successful than America. Death, an Ode. John Forbes. BMAP

Deathbed, A. John Hawthorn. NOEC *Fr.* The Journey and Observations of a Countryman.

Deathless Aphrodite, throned in flowers. Ode to Aphrodite. Sappho, *Greek.* AWP, *tr. by* William Ellery Leonard

Deathless Autumn, A. Ái Lan, *Vietnamese.* AVP, *tr. by* Huỳnh Sanh Thông

Deathplace, A. Louis Edward Sissman. NoP-4

Death's Guerdon. Lizette Woodworth Reese. APN-2

Death's Head. Phyllis Gotlieb. NOBC

Death's head on your head you neede not weare, A. Thomas Dudley, Ah! Old Must Dye. *Unknown.* SCAP

Death's Jest Book. Thomas Lovell Beddoes. Bridal Song to Amala. GBL (Song: "We have bathed, where none have seen us.") NOBVV; OBNC Carrion Crow, The. APo ("Through a murderer's bones, to and fro, / In the ghosts' moonshine.") (LL) APo Dirge: "Swallow leaves her nest, The." OBNC; PoEL-4 (Song from the Waters.) NOBE Dirge: "We do lie beneath the grass." NOBVV; OBNC (Sibilla's Dirge.) NOBE Envoi, L': "Who findeth comfort in the stars and flowers." OBNC "Fair and bright assembly, A: never strode." CTC Sailors' Song. OxAEP-2 Song by Isbrand. NOBVV; OBNC ("New dodo is finished—oh come to my nest!, The.") (LL) Ro ("Squats on a toadstool under a tree.") Ro Song on the Water. FaBoCh Wolfram's Dirge. NOBE; OBEV; OxAEP-2 (Dirge: "If Thou wilt ease Thine heart.") OBNC; PoEL-4

Death's Lecture. Richard Crashaw. SeCP

Death's memories are graves. John Clare. FHYFP

Deaths of Orpheus and Hercules, The. Seneca. OBVE *Fr.* Medea.

Death's pale cold orb has turned to an eclipse. Avalon. Thomas Holley Chivers. APN-1

Death's the Classic Look. John Ciardi. PoA

Death's Transfiguration. Israel Zangwill. TrJP

Death's Valley. Walt Whitman. GS

Death's Vision. John Reynolds. Mysteries Revealed after Death. NOEC

Deathward. John Lyle Donaghy. BIrV

Deathwatch. Michael S. Harper. AmPA; NAAAL; PoBA

Debasement is the password of the base. The Answer. Bei Dao, *Chinese.* AF, *tr. by* Bonnie S. McDougall

Debate: Question, Quarry, Dream. Robert Penn Warren. VGW

Debbie and Co. John Tranter. BMAP

Debits and Credits. Rudyard Kipling.
  We and They. NoAM

Deborah Dough. Mary Leapor. *See* The Epistle of Deborah Dough.

Debout. U Tam'si Tchicaya, *French.*
  "Here is the stream again under the rainbow." PBA, *tr. by* E. S. Yntema

Debridement. Michael S. Harper. NoAM

Debris of Life and Mind. Wallace Stevens. SAmP

Debt, The. Paul Laurence Dunbar. ColAP

Debt, The. Lee Upton. CMAP

Debt is paid, The. The Past. Ralph Waldo Emerson. FaBoCh; MeMAP; PoEL-4; TAP

Decade, [A]. Amy Lowell. MoAmPo; NALW
  (Decade, A.) CPO; OxWW

Décadent to His Soul, The. Richard Le Gallienne. ADE

Décadent was speaking to his soul, The. The Décadent to His Soul. Richard Le Gallienne. ADE

Decadent's Lyric, A. Lionel Pigot Johnson. ADE

Decades behind me. A Right-of-Way: 1865. William Plomer. PeLV

Decampment. Ernst Stadler, *German.* PeFWW, *tr. by* David McDuff

Decay. John Clare. EnVR

Decay. George Herbert. ESCV; SCGP; SeCP

Decay, and life's end is death. Robinson Jeffers. *See* The Purse-Seine.

Decay of Piety. Wordsworth. TrCP

Decease, Release. Robert Southwell. *See* At Fotheringay.

Deceased. Cid Corman. VGW

Deceased, The. Keith Douglas. FaBoTw

Deceav'd and undeceav'd to be. The Self-Deceaver. Thomas Stanley. OBVE

Deceit goes well with a Fall afternoon. Deep Dusk. Gyula Illyés, *Hungarian.* CEEP, *tr. by* Nicholas Kolumban

Deceit in the Park. Patrick Hare. OBGa

Deceiv'd Deceiver, and Imposter cheated! Prologue. Mary Pix. KTR *Fr.* The Deceiver Deceived.

Deceiver Deceived, The. Mary Pix.
  Prologue: "Deceiv'd Deceiver, and Imposter cheated!" KTR

Deceiving world, that with alluring toys. A Palinode. Robert Greene. NoSic *Fr.* Greene's Groatsworth of Wit.

December. John Clare. OBCP

December. Lucille Clifton. NOxBChV

December. Christopher Pearse Cranch. APN-1

December. Robert Francis. LCAP-2

December. Josephine D. Henderson Heard. CBWP-4

December. Maurice Kenny. HATNAP

December. Ron Padgett. SPE

December. Henrietta Cordelia Ray. CBWP-3

December. Folgore da San Geminiano. *Fr.* Sonnets of the Months. AWP, *tr. by* D. G. Rossetti

December. Gary Snyder. InPS-3 *Fr.* Six Years.

December 14, 1979: A Poetry Reading. Stanislaw Baranczak, *Polish.* AF, *tr. by* Magnus J. Krynski

December 7 always brings christmas early. Amy Uyematsu. LTA

December 9th. Eileen Myles. PmAP

December, a weekday. Waiting for Lesser Duckweed: On a Proposal of Issa's. Sandra McPherson. BAP-93

December. An arctic wind, new. Wall Calendar. Dan Pagis, *Hebrew.* VCWP, *tr. by* Tsipi Keller

December, and the closing of the year. Christmas Eve in Whitneyville, 1955. Donald Hall. UnPo

December at Yase. Gary Snyder. *Fr.* Four Poems for Robin. MoP; NNaP; NOBA; NoAM

December Day, Hoy Sound. George Mackay Brown. OxBS

December Eclipse. Margo Lockwood. Poetsp

December 15, 1811. Poem for My Family: Hazel Griffin and Victor Hernandez Cruz. June Jordan. BPo

December finds him. James Bottle's Year. Alastair Reid. FaBoTC

December Forest, A. Vesna Krmpotic, *Croatian.* WPOW, *tr. by* Vasa D. Mihailovich

December Fragments. Richmond Lattimore. PChr

December Morning, *sonnet.* Anna Seward. ECWP

December narrows our day to a thread of light. Song in the Cold Season. Samuel French Morse. PoA

December nights are frosts and stars. Helen Waddell. MLL

December 1974: a Lament. Abdur-Rahman Slade Hopkinson. PBCV

December of My Springs, The. Nikki Giovanni. GT

December: Prayer to St. Nicholas. John Heath-Stubbs. OBCP

December Stillness. Siegfried Sassoon. CMoP

December sun sits low over hedgegrows, glitter. What Shines in Winter Burns. T. R. Hummer. MT

December: the trees chafing. Mile Hill. Dennis Schmitz. LCAP-2

December 30th. Ivor Gurney. NAEL-2

December 21st. Jean Valentine. LCAP-2

December 24 and George McBride Is Dead. Richard Hugo. HoPM

December 27, 1966. Louis Edward Sissman. DiPo

December's Husbandry. Thomas Tusser. NoSic *Fr.* Five Hundred Points of Good Husbandry.

Decent docent doesn't doze, The. History of Education. David McCord. OBAL

Deception. Alfred Corn. PoA

Deception. Josephine D. Henderson Heard. CBWP-4

Deceptions. Philip Larkin. CMoP; GTBS-P; OxAEP-2
  ("To burst into fulfilment's desolate attic.") (LL) FaBoSe

Deceptive Grin of the Gravel Porters, The. Gavin Ewart. FaBoMo

Deceptively Like a Solid. Roald Hoffmann. BAP-94

Deceptrices, The. William Carlos Williams. NYBP

Decision. M. P. Flynn. CTV

Decision, The. Theodore Roethke. CRP; VGW

Decision, A. Edith Södergran, *Swedish.* PBWP, *tr. by* Jaakko A. Ahokas

Decision. *Unknown.* PoToHe

Deck thyself, maiden. Esthonian Bridal Song. Johann Gottfried von Herder, *German.* AWP, *tr. by* W. Taylor

Decked, stacked, pillaged from. The Middle Passage and After. Larry Neal. NBV

Decks awash, / Mast-top dipping. Archilochus, *Latin.* OBVE, *tr. by* Guy Davenport

Declaimer, The. Henry Baker. NOEC

Declair, ye bankis of Helicon. *Unknown.* OxBS *Fr.* The Bankis of Helicon.

Declaration. Nikolai Ivanovich Glazkov, *Russian.* TCRP, *tr. by* Daniel Weissbort

Declaration, The. Nathaniel Parker Willis. OBAL

Declaration of the Death of John Lewes, A. Thomas Gilbart. NoSic

Declaration of the Word as Such. Aleksei Eliseievich Kruchyonykh, *Russian.* PFTM, *tr. by* Anna Lawton *and* Herbert Eagle

Declare, my pretty maid. The Philanderer. Moses Mendes. *Fr.* The Chaplet. TrJP

Declare, O mind, from fond desires excluded. A Counterlove. *Unknown.* NoSic

Declension. Stephen Sandy. PoA

Decline of an Empire. Dan Pagis, *Hebrew.* IP, *tr. by* Warren Bargad *and* Stanley F. Chyet

Deconstruction of Emily Dickinson, The. Galway Kinnell. PUP-20

Decoration. Mary Ursula Bethell. PeNZ

Decoration. Louise Bogan. MoAmPo

Decoration Day. Josephine D. Henderson Heard. CBWP-4

Decorations climbing up the loft on a wobbly ladder. My Christmas; Mum's Christmas. Sarah Forsyth. OBCP

Decorator is mixing his plaster, The. Moon over Prague. Vitězslav Nezval, *Czech.* AF, *tr. by* Ewald Osers

Decoy. John Ashbery. PoM

Decoy Partridge, A. Simmias [*or* Simias] of Rhodes, *Greek.* GrAn, *tr. by* Peter Jay

Decoys, The. W. H. Auden. CMoP; PoE

Decrees of God, The. Chao Ying-tou, *Chinese.* TrJP, *tr. by* William C. White

Decrepit Old Gasman, A. Limerick: "Decrepit old gas man named Peter, A." *Unknown.* SoSe-8

Dedicated, The. Philip Larkin. OxBC

Dedicated Dancing Bull and the Water Maid, The. Stevie Smith.
  "Hop hop, thump thump." WPE

Dedicated to a Young Lady Representing the Indian Race at Howard University. Alfred Islay Walden. AAP

Dedicated to Dr. W. H. Sheppard. Maggie Pogue Johnson. CBWP-4

Dedicated to the Right Rev'd D. A. Payne. Mary Weston Fordham. CBWP-2

Dedication. "Anna Andreyevna Akhmatova." PFTM

Dedication. Māris aklais, *Latvian.* CEEP, *tr. by* Inara Cedrins

Dedication, A: "Anchored now to Neptune's temple floor, this." Macedonius, *Greek.* GrAn, *tr. by* Adrian Wright

Dedication: "Bob Southey! You're a poet—poet-laureate." Byron. CTC; OAEL-2; OBSV *Fr.* Don Juan.
  Don Juan. Ro
  "If, fallen in evil days on evil tongue." EPCY
  "You gentlemen, by dint of long seclusion." EPCY

Dedication, A. Karin Boye, *Swedish.*
  "I feel your steps in the hall." PBWP, *tr.* by Nadia Christensen

Dedication. "Lewis Carroll." *Fr.* The Hunting of the Snark. CBNP; OBNC; OBNV; PoEL-5

Dedication, A: "Dear, near and true—no truer Time himself." Tennyson. OxBSP

Dedication: "Had there been peace there never had been riven." Drummond Allison. FaBoTw

Dedication: "Health to great Gloucester—from a man unknown." Charles Churchill. OBSV

Dedication: "I would the gift I offer here." John Greenleaf Whittier. APN-1; OxBA

Dedication. Irena Klepfisz. *See* Bashert.

Dedication: "Let us honour if we can." W. H. Auden. PeLV *Fr.* Shorts [1927–1932].

Dedication. N. P. van Wyk Louw, *Afrikaans.* PeSAV, *tr.* by Hugh Finn

Dedication, The: "My God, thou that didst dye for me." Henry Vaughan. ESCV

Dedication, A: "My new-cut ashlar takes the light." Rudyard Kipling. PoEL-5 *Fr.* Life's Handicap.

Dedication: "Private faces in public places." W. H. Auden. PeLV *Fr.* Shorts [1927–1932].

Dedication: "Tall unpopular men." Oliver St. John Gogarty. OBMV

Dedication, A: "They are rhymes rudely strung with intent less." Adam Lindsay Gordon. CBAP

Dedication: "Unto the blithe and lordly fellowship." Folgore da San Geminiano. *Fr.* Sonnets of the Months. AWP, *tr.* by D. G. Rossetti

Dedication: "You whom I could not save / Listen to me." Czeslaw Milosz, *Polish.* AF, *tr.* by Czeslaw Milosz

Dedication: A Spear. Anyte, *Greek.* GrAn, *tr.* by John Heath-Stubbs *and* Carol A. Whiteside

Dedication Day. Maggie Pogue Johnson. CBWP-4

Dedication Day Poem. Lizelia Augusta Jenkins Moorer. CBWP-3

Dedication I: "To that clear majesty which in the north." Sir John Davies. *See* To Queen Elizabeth.

Dedication II: "Strongest and the noblest argument, The." Sir John Davies. SiPS *Fr.* Nosce Teipsum. NoSic; SiPS

Dedication of a Torch. Crinagoras, *Greek.* GrAn, *tr.* by Alistair Elliot

Dedication of My First Son, A. Mildmay Fane, 2d Earl of Westmorland. BeJo

Dedication of the Cook. Anna Wickham. MoBrPo; NALW

Dedication to Aphrodite, A. Hedylos, *Greek.* GrAn, *tr.* by William Moebius

Dedication to G**** H******* Esq, A. Robert Burns.
  "Morality, thou deadly bane." OBSV

Dedication to Hunger. Louise Glück.
  From the Suburbs. FaBoWP; NALW

Dedication: To Ianthe. Byron. OBNC *Fr.* Childe Harold's Pilgrimage.

Dedication: To Leigh Hunt, Esq. Keats. *See* To Leigh Hunt, Esq.

Dedication to My Wife, A. T. S. Eliot. BoLoP; OxBM

Dedication to St. Michael. Alcuin, *Latin.* MLL, *tr.* by Helen Waddell

Dedication to the Final Confrontation. Lloyd M. Corbin Jr. PoBA

Dedication to the Poet Laureate. Byron. *See* Dedication: "Bob Southey! You're a poet—poet-laureate."

Dedications, I: To His Very Friend, Master Richard Martin. Sir John Davies. SiPS *Fr.* Orchestra; or, A Poem[e] of Da[u]ncing. NoSic; SiPS

Dedications, II: To the Prince. Sir John Davies. SiPS *Fr.* Orchestra; or, A Poem[e] of Da[u]ncing. NoSic; SiPS

Dedicatory Epistle, with a Book of 1949. Roy Fuller. PeLV

Dedicatory Ode. Hilaire Belloc.
  They Say That in the Unchanging Place. PoLF

Dedicatory Sonnet to S. T. Coleridge. Hartley Coleridge. OAEL-2; Son

Dee dee dee dee dee wee weee eeeeee wee we. Communication in Whi-te. Don L. Lee. BPo

Deean Tractorman, Clear, The. Edith Anne Robertson. OxBS

Deean Tractorman, Deleerit, The. Edith Anne Robertson. OxBS

Deed / that was done in the Beginning, The. Clerks. Boris Abramovich Slutsky, *Russian.* TCRP, *tr.* by J. R. Rowland

Deeds Done and Suffered by Light. Clayton Eshleman. APSN

Deeds of Kindess. *Unknown.* CTV

Deem as ye list. Upon good cause. Sir Thomas Wyatt. SiPS

Deem not, devoid of elegance, the sage. Written in a Blank Leaf of Dugdale's "Monasticon." Thomas, the Younger Warton. Son

Deem unplausible. (LL) Color, Caste, Denomination. Emily Dickinson. PBMP; TAP

Deep. Timothy Holmes. PeSAV

Deep and boundless, the long autumn night. Ts'ao P'i, *Chinese.* SuSp, *tr.* by Ronald C. Miao

Deep, and silent, and wide. With the Tide: A Cry of Weakness. Louisa Sarah Bevington. PEW *Fr.* Two songs.

Deep and vast is parting sorrow as the sun slants. Miscellanies of the Year Chi-hai. Kung Tzu-chen, *Chinese.* SuSp, *tr.* by Irving Y. Lo

Deep as this hour, ready again to sleep. (LL) Night Feeding. Muriel Rukeyser. MDDM; NMM-2; NoP-4; WPE

Deep breath Inhale the drums Feet begin. For Sharol Graves. "Chrystos." CPO

Deep calleth unto deep. Dial Call. Christopher Darlington Morley. NBLV

Deep Dusk. Gyula Illyés, *Hungarian.* CEEP, *tr.* by Nicholas Kolumban

Deep in a distant bay, and deeply hidden. The Lonely Isle. Claudian, *Latin.* AWP, *tr.* by Howard Mumford Jones

Deep in a kingfisher hall, someone is heavy with wine. Inscribed on the Fan of a Wealthy Old Man. Shen Chou, *Chinese.* SuSp, *tr.* by Irving Y. Lo

Deep in a vale, a stranger now to arms. The American Soldier. Philip Freneau. TAP

Deep in a vale where rocks on every side. Sonnet. Gustav Rosenhane, *Swedish.* AWP, *tr.* by Sir Edmund Gosse

Deep in her seventh month, my sister dozes. Sonnet 2. Debra Bruce. FFC *Fr.* ("Light They Make, The").

Deep in my heart I hear them, the gaunt hounds pacing. The Hounds of the Soul. Louis Ginsberg. TrJP

Deep in my notebook a lily pad floats away. Matsuo Allard. HA

Deep in rank grass. Nicholas Virgilio. HA

Deep in the air the past appears. The Greeks. Tom Clark. PoA

Deep in the brain, far back. (LL) Night Crow. Theodore Roethke. HoPM; InPK-6; OxBSP; VGW

Deep in the brown bosom. Bangkok. Francis Reginald Scott. MoCV

Deep in the fading leaves of night. Carol. William Robert Rodgers. OBCP

Deep in the forest there is a pond. After the Anonymous Swedish. James Harrison. VGW

Deep in the grass there lies a dead gazelle. Maytime. *Unknown.* AWP, *tr.* by L. Cranmer-Byng *Fr.* Shi King.

Deep in the leafy fierceness of the wood. Apollo and Daphne. Yvor Winters. Son

Deep in the mountain. Sarumaru, *Japanese.* OHPJ, *tr.* by Kenneth Rexroth

Deep in the mountain wilderness. Wang Wei, *Chinese.* OHMPC, *tr.* by Kenneth Rexroth

Deep in the night. Ransetsu, *Japanese.* OHMPJ, *tr.* by Kenneth Rexroth

Deep in the night and unable to sleep. Juan Chi. SuSp, *tr.* by Charles Hartman *Fr.* Poems Expressing My Feelings.

Deep in the nightmare of narrative, narrating. Brotherhood. Reginald Shepherd. BAP-95

Deep in the rippling spring. May Ushida. KaS

Deep in the roaring tide he plunged to endless night. (LL) Bard, The [A Pindaric Ode]. Thomas Gray. GTBS-P; NOBE; NOEC; OAEL-1; OxAEP-1

Deep in the shady sadness of a vale. Hyperion. Keats. OAEL-2; Ro

Deep in the shady sadness of a vale. Saturn. Keats. OxAEP-2, *book* I–III; FHYEP; NOBRP; OBNC; PoEL-4 *Fr.* Hyperion.

Deep in the Siberian mine. Message to Siberia. Aleksandr Sergeyevich Pushkin, *Russian.* AWP; TTY, *tr.* by Max Eastman

Deep in the wave is a coral grove. The Coral Grove. James Gates Percival. APN-1; ColAP

Deep in the winter plain, two armies. Two Armies. Stephen Spender. OBWP; OxBTC

Deep in the wood I made a house. August. Katharine Pyle. OBCA

Deep in the wood's recesses cool. The Watcher in the Wood. Dora Sigerson Shorter. SDW

Deep in this grave her bones remain. Reflections, Written on Visiting the Grave of a Venerated Friend. Ann Plato. BlSi

Deep in Winter. Tu Fu, *Chinese.* PLT, *tr.* by A. C. Graham

Deep in your cheeks. Origins. Keorapetse Kgositsile. PoBA

Deep intelligence living at peace would have, The. (LL) Life at War. Denise Levertov. NMM-2; VGW

Deep into autumn the acorns ripen. Lament of a Woman Acorn-gatherer. P'i Jih-hsiu, *Chinese.* SuSp, *tr.* by William H. Nienhauser

Deep into the midst of a great, dark, wood. The Snail's Lesson. Priscilla Jane Thompson. CBWP-2

Deep lane, poor families; I have few friends. At the End of Spring. Yü Hsüan-chi, *Chinese.* BoWoP, *tr.* by Geoffrey Waters

Deep Mining. Irene McKinney. PBCAP

Deep night. I cannot sleep. Yuan Chi, *Chinese.* OHMPC, *tr.* by Kenneth Rexroth

Deep on the convent-roof the snows. St. Agnes' Eve. Tennyson. OBEV

Deep peace, pure white of the moon to you. "Fiona Macleod." BoTP *Fr.* Invocation of Peace.

Deep prolonged entry with the strong pink cock. She Loves. Olga Broumas. GLP

Deep red bogs divided. Richard Murphy. CIP-2 *Fr.* The Battle of Aughrim.

Deep River. Eugène Marais, *Afrikaans.* PeSAV, *tr. by* Hugh Finn

Deep river, my home is over Jordan. *Unknown.* BPo; BkSV; CrDW; TAP ("There's nobody there for to turn me out.") (LL) APN-2

Deep scar engraved in the bark's dark silver, A. Vadim Leonidovich Andreyev, *Russian.* TCRP, *tr. by* Belinda Brindle

Deep Season. Virginia Hooper. PT

Deep snow. Betty Drevniok. HA

Deep Spring. *Unknown.* AmFP

Deep sunk in floods of grief. Bible, *O.T. See* Psalm 130.

Deep-sworn Vow, A. W. B. Yeats. CMoP; OAEL-2; PoE; UnPo

Deep under the willows' shade the horse treads proudly. Passing by Kamata. Su Man-shu, *Chinese.* SuSp, *tr. by* Wu-chi Liu

Deep waters silent roul, so Grief like mine. Elegy on the Earl of Rochester. Anne Wharton. KTR; NOSC

Deep Well. Roland Robinson.
"I am at Deep Well where the spirit-trees." CBAP; NOBAu

Deep well knows it certainly, The. World-Secret. Hugo von Hofmannsthal, *German.* TrJP, *tr. by* Charles Wharton Stork

Deep within the stream. J. W. Hackett. HA

Deep wooden note, A. Overheard. Denise Levertov. PoM

Deepening-Green Pavilion. Chu Yi-tsun, *Chinese.* SuSp, *tr. by* Chang Yin-nan *and* Lewis C. Walmsley

Deepening shadows bring on sorrow, The. Hsü Kan. SuSp, *tr. by* Ronald C. Miao *Fr.* Boudoir Thoughts.

Deeper, ever so little deeper. (LL) Dead, long dead. Tennyson. EBVVPR

Deeper than sleep but not so deep as death. Night Feeding. Muriel Rukeyser. MDDM; NMM-2; NoP-4; WPE

Deeply repentant of my sinful ways. Gaspara Stampa, *Italian.* WPOW, *tr. by* Lorna De' Lucchi

Deer, The. "Asya," *Yiddish.* CEEP, *tr. by* Gabriel Preil *and* Howard Schwartz

Deer. John Drinkwater. CH

Deer. No Ch'&obreve;n-my&obreve;ng, *Korean.* CKP, *tr. by* Jaihiun Kim

Deer. No Ch'ŏn-myŏng, *Korean.* PBWP, *tr. by* Ko Won

Deer and the Snake, The. Kenneth Patchen. MoAmPo

Deer are gentle and graceful. Kenneth Rexroth. HoPM *Fr.* A Bestiary. OBAL

Deer are just thankful it's over, The. Thanksgiving. Liz Rosenberg. PBCAP

Deer carcass hangs from a rafter, The. Gathering the Bones Together. Gregory Orr. AmPA; Poetsp; WeT

Deer Cloud. Susan Clements. UnSA

Deer feed on. Upon Leaving the Parole Board Hearing. Conyus. GT; PoBA

Deer Fence. Wang Wei. *Fr.* Twenty Views of Wang-ch'uan. CoBCP, *tr. by* Burton Watson

Deer gather in flocks by nature. Living in the Mountains. Tai Shu-lun, *Chinese.* SuSp, *tr. by* William H. Nienhauser

Deer is humble, lovely as God made her, The. The Deer and the Snake. Kenneth Patchen. MoAmPo

Deer Isle. Philip Booth. VGW

Deer Lay Down Their Bones, The. Robinson Jeffers. NoAM

Deer-of-the-Waters: he laboured hard on his grammar. Red Indian Corpse. Peter Redgrove. OxBC

Deer on pine mountain, The. Onakatomi Yoshinobu, *Japanese.* OHPJ, *tr. by* Kenneth Rexroth

Deer Park. John Montague. PBCIP

Deer Sing. Confucius, *Chinese.*
Fraternitas. CTC; OBVE

Deer Song. Leslie Marmon Silko. VoR

Deer walking quietly on the soft red earth. (LL) New Apartment. Linda Hogan. UnSA

Deer were bounding like blown leaves, The. Fire on the Hills. Robinson Jeffers. CMoP; RaBo

Deer which lives, The. Onakatomi Yoshinobu. *Fr.* Shui Shu. AWP, *tr. by* Arthur Waley

Deevil's Waltz, The. Sydney Goodsir Smith. FaBoTw

Defeat, A. Denise Levertov. PBWP

Defeat may serve as well as victory. Victory in Defeat. Edwin Markham. PoLF

Defeat of the Norsemen, The. Sedulius Scottus, *Latin.*
"Heavens, ocean, and all earth, rejoice!" NOIV

Defeat of Turnus, The. Virgil. OBVE, *tr. by* Gawin Douglas *Fr.* The Aeneid [*or* Eneados, *Aeneis*].

Defence of Poetry, A. Giolla Brighde Mac Con Midhe. NOIV

Defend the bad against the worse. (LL) Where Are the War Poets? C. Day Lewis. FaBoMo; NoP-4; OBWP; OxBSP; OxBTC

Defend Us, Lord, from Every Ill. John Hay. AH

Defender— / a partner doesn't dance with prison bars. Poem for the Wife of an Imprisoned Leader *especially for* Winnie Mandela. James Berry. NBrP

Defending you, my country, hurts. The Battle Hymn of the Republic. Rafael Campo. BAP-95

Defenestration of Prague. Susan Howe.
Bride's Day. FTOS

Defense of Fort McHenry. Francis Scott Key. *See* The Star-Spangled Banner.

Defense of Guenevere, The. William Morris. NAEL-2

Defense of the Alamo, The. Joaquin Miller. FaBoBe

Defense Rests. Vassar Miller. MoAmPo

Defensive measures. Ovid, *Latin.* OBCVT, *tr. by* Overbury, Sir Thomas

Defensive Position. John Streeter Manifold. MoBrPo

Defensive Rapture. Barbara Guest. FTOS

Deferment. Marcel Duchamp. PFTM

Deferred. Langston Hughes. APSN

Defiance, The. Aphra Behn. EnLoPo

Defiance. Walter Savage Landor. CBLP

Defiance. Solomon ibn Gabirol, *Hebrew.* TrJP, *tr. by* Emma Lazarus

Defied,—no past is mine, no future: look at me! (LL) Eurydice to Orpheus. Robert Browning. CBLP; CTC

Defiled Is My Name Full Sore. Anne Boleyn. WPE

Definition. Grace Noll Crowell. PoToHe

Definition. Lauren Shakely. FYAP

Definition for Blk/Children. Sonia Sanchez. PoBA

Definition of Beauty, The. Robert Herrick. BeJo; CaPo

Definition of Blue. John Ashbery. NAAL-2

Definition Of Love, The. Andrew Marvell. BoLoP; CBLP; EBEV; ESCV; FHYEP; FMP; FSCP; GBL; GLoP; GeHe; HoPM; ImPo; InPS-3; LoP; MeLP; NAEL-1; NOBE; NOSC; NoP-4; OAEL-1; OBEV; PBRV; PoEL-2; SCGP; SeCP; TFi; UnPo

Definition of Nature. Eugene B. Redmond. NBV; PoBA

Definition of the Soul. Boris Pasternak, *Russian.* TrJP, *tr. by* Babette Deutsch

Definitionless in this strict atmosphere. (LL) A Lovely Love. Gwendolyn Brooks. BPo; NAAAL

Definitions. Joseph Joel Keith. PoToHe

Definitions. Elwyn Brooks White.
"Critic leaves at curtain fall, The." NBLV

Definitions for Mendy. David Antin. APSN

Deflowering. Mahmood Jamal. NBrP

Deformed Mistress, The. Sir John Suckling. BXAP

Deft, practised, eager. Usquebaugh. Wendy Cope. UV

Deftly, admiral, cast your fly. Song. W. H. Auden. GTBS-P *Fr.* Five Songs.

Degas. Paul Monette. AmPA

Degenerate Age, A. Solomon ibn Gabirol, *Hebrew.* TrJP, *tr. by* Emma Lazarus

Degenerate Douglas! O [*or* oh,] the unworthy lord! Composed at Neidpath Castle, the Property of Lord Queensberry,1803. Wordsworth. GTBS-P

Degli Sposi. Rika Lesser. FYAP

Degrees of Gray in Philipsburg. Richard Hugo. CoAP; NAAL-2; NoAM; TRP; VCAP

Deh 'Pon Um Again. Michael McTurk. PBCV

Deid is now that divour and dollin in erd. The Widow Speaks. William Dunbar. PoEL-1 *Fr.* The Book of the Two Married Women and the Widow.

Deid is now that dyvour and dollin in erd. The Widow Has Buried Her Second Husband. William Dunbar. RACG *Fr.* The Tua Mariit Wemen and the Wedo.

Deid sall ye ligg, and ne'er a memorie. Douglas Young, *after the Greek of* Sappho. OBVE

Deign[e] at my hands this crown[e] of prayer and praise. La Corona. Donne. ChIV-2; ESCV; Son *Fr.* La Corona. ChIV-2; ESCV; Son *Fr.* Holy Sonnets.

Deign, Laura—now again the rainy season's here. Girl with Mind Wandering. Paul Valéry, *French.* STV, *tr. by* John Frederick Nims

Deil [*or* De'il] cam fiddling through the town, The. The De'il's [*or* Deil's] Awa wi' th' Exciseman. Robert Burns. OBCoV

De'il's [*or* Deil's] Awa wi' th' [*or* the] Exciseman, The. Robert Burns. OBCoV

Dein aschenes Haar Shulamith. Paul Celan. *See* A Death Fugue.

Deirdre. James Stephens. AWP; CMoP; OBMV; PoRA

Deirdre's [or Deidre's] Lament for the Sons of Usnach. *Unknown, Irish.* IIP; NOIV, *tr.* by Sir Samuel Ferguson

Deity of Love Incorporate, A. Edward Taylor. TAP *Fr.* Preparatory Meditations Before My Approach to the Lord's Supper.

Déjà Vu. Shirley Kaufman. NMM-2

Dejection. Coleridge. FHYEP; HeIP-4; NAEL-2; NAWM-2; NOBE; NOBRP; OAEL-2; OBNC; OxAEP-2; PoE; PoEL-4; TFi; TOF
(Dejection: An Ode, written 4 April 1802.) Ro
("Thus mayest thou ever, evermore rejoice.") (LL) NoP-4; PoPoPo
"Grief without a pang, void, dark, and drear, A." IMW

Dejection. Derek Mahon. PBCIP

Dejection. Georg Trakl, *German.* PeFWW, *tr.* by Michael Hamburger

Déjeuner Sur l'Herbe. Bruce Beaver. BMAP

Dejeuner Sur L'Herbe. Tu Fu, *Chinese.* BLT, *tr.* by Carolyn Kizer

Delacroix pentit Chopin's heid. Ye Mongers Aye Need Masks for Cheatrie. Sydney Goodsir Smith. OxBS

Delay. Elizabeth Jennings. NIP-4; OPOU; OxBTC

Delay Has Danger. George Crabbe. NOBRP

Delay, whose parents Phlegm and Slumber are. William Hammond. CBLP

Delayed Action. Christian Morgenstern, *German.* RB, *tr.* by W. D. Snodgrass and Lore Segal

Delectable little seeds. Sesame. Jack Marshall. PuP-16

Delia. Samuel Daniel.
"Behold what hap *Pigmalion* had to frame." PBRV
Sonnet 5: "Whilst Youth and Error". AEP
Sonnet 34. CABP

Delia, Delia, why didn't you run? Delia Holmes. "Whistling Bill" Ruff. AmFP

Delia Rexroth. Kenneth Rexroth. FiLi

Delia Very Angry. *Unknown.* NOEC

Deliberate as scrimshaw. Cat Washing. Linda Molony NOBAu

Deliberately, long ago / the carcasses. From an Old House in America. Adrienne Rich. NNaP; TRP

Delicate eyes that blinked blue Rockies all ash. On Neal's Ashes. Allen Ginsberg. BB; PmAP; PoM

Delicate, firm, whole flesh of the still unburned, The. (LL) Advent 1966. Denise Levertov. APSN; NNaP

Delicate girl was eager to air, The. Princess Elizabeth of Bohemia, as Perdita. Frank O'Hara. PoA

Delicate grasses, faint wind on the bank. A Traveler at Night Writes His Thoughts. Tu Fu, *Chinese.* ChiPo; CoBCP, *tr.* by Burton Watson

Delicate old injuries, the spines of names and leaves. (LL) Indian Boarding School: The Runaways. Louise Erdrich. HATNAP; NoAM; UnSA

Delicate, Plummeting Bodies, The. Stephen Dobyns. FYAP

Delicate sound of a moth; a page turning. The Moths. Sean O Riordain, *Irish.* NOIV, *tr.* by Thomas Kinsella

Delicate young Negro stands, A. Anonymous Drawing. Donald Justice. CoAP; HeIP-4

Delicately bordered by poplars. (LL) In the Dordogne. John Peale Bishop. OBWP; PeFWW; PoWW; VGW

Delicious, *fine* Sugar Hill. Langston Hughes. *See* Harlem Sweeties.

Delicious morning! how thy gentle beams. Blank Verse Written on the Sea Shore. Hannah Cowley. ECWP

Délie. Maurice Scève, *French.* FLP, *tr.* by Alistair Elliot

Delight in books from evening. Francis Daniel Pastorius. NOSC; SCAP

Delight in Disorder. Robert Herrick. APAD; BeJo; CABP; CaPo; CavPo; ClHu; EBEV; EBEvV; EP; EnLoPo; FaBoSe; HAP; HeIP-4; InPK-6; InPS-3; NAEL-1; NIP-4; NOBE; NOSC; NoP-4; OAEL-1; OBEV; OxAEP-1; PBMP; PBRV; PeLV; PoE; PoRA; Poetr; SAGP; SCGP; SeCP; TFi; TRP; WeW-3
("Sweet disorder in the dress, A.") APAD; CABP; CavPo; EP; FaBoSe; NoP-4; SAGP

Delight is as the flight. Emily Dickinson. NCAP

Delight of Humane kind, and Gods above. Address to Venus. Lucretius, *Latin.* OBVE, *tr.* by Dryden; EP, *tr.* by John Dryden *Fr.* De Rerum Natura (On the Nature of Things).

Delight of Solitariness, The. Sir Philip Sidney. *See* Solitariness.

Delight Song of Tsoai-Talee, The. N. Scott Momaday. CDW; InPK-6; PaTW

Delighted, incredulous bride, A. Maud Fitzgerald. *Unknown.* PeLi

Delightful. Audre Lorde. *See* On a Night of the Full Moon.

Delightful, book, your trip. Aoibhinn, A Leabhráin, Do Thriall. *Unknown, Irish.* BIrV, *tr.* by Flann O'Brien

Delightful change from the town's abode. Barnyard Melodies. Fred Emerson Brooks. OBAL

Delightful mansion! blest retreat! A Thought in a Garden. John Hughes. ECEV

Delights of the Door, The. Francis Ponge, *French.* RaBo, *tr.* by Robert Bly

Delilah. Milton. *Fr.* Samson Agonistes. FHYEP; OAEL-1; PoEL-3

Delilah. Ellen Bryant Voigt. CrSp

Delineaments of the Giants, The. William Carlos Williams. NoAM *Fr.* Paterson.

Delirious the drought raved birds stretched on the fence. Remember. Ion Caraion, *Romanian.* AF, *tr.* by Marguerite Dorian and Elliott B. Urdang

Delirium in Vera Cruz, *also appears independently of* Cantinas *in* CP-Lowry. Malcolm Lowry. FaBoTw; NoP-4; OxBTC *Fr.* The Cantinas.

Deliver me from mine enemies, O my God. Bible, *O.T. See* Psalm 59.

Deliver us for thy descent. Donne. *Fr.* The Litanie. PoEL-2

Deliverance. Frances Ellen Watkins Harper. WPOW

Deliverance. "Ping Hsin," *Chinese.* ChiPo, *tr.* by Kai-yu Hsu

Deliverance from a Fit of Fainting. Anne Bradstreet. TAP

Delivered at the Knighting of Lord Durgling by Great Bruce-Jean. Jean Toomer. GT

Delivered / palpable / ours. (LL) Snapshots of a Daughter-in-Law. Adrienne Rich. FaBoWP; HCAP; NAAL-2; NALW; NIP-4; NoAM; NoP-4; Poetr; VCAP

Deliverer, The. Milton. *Fr.* Samson Agonistes. FHYEP; OAEL-1; PoEL-3

Delivering the Times, 1952-1944. David Huddle. PBCAP

DeLiza drive the car to fetch, Alexis. DeLiza Spend the Day in the City. June Jordan. NoAM

DeLiza Spend the Day in the City. June Jordan. NoAM

Dell, The. Gavin Ewart. OxBC

Dell's hounds leap like the damned around the trunk. Coon Hunt. Thomas Rabbitt. MT

Delos. Lawrence Durrell. GrIP; OxAEP-2

Delos. Bernard Spencer. NoAM

Delphic Dawn. Euripides, *Greek.* GrIP, *tr.* by Ronald Frederick Willetts *Fr.* Ion.

Delta, The. Michael Dennis Browne. NYBP

Delta. Adrienne Rich. LoL; NIP-4; PiM

Delta Traveller. Charles Wright. AmPA; LCAP-2

Delug'd with tears, by what you heard before. To My Honoured Patron Humphery Davie. Benjamin Tompson. SCAP

Deluge 1939, The. Saunders Lewis, *Welsh.* OBWVE, *tr.* by Gwyn Morgan

Dem Belly Full. Legon Cogil and Carlton Barrett. PBCV

Dem say him born. For Don Drummond. Lorna Goodison. PBCV

Dem say / who say? Black Bud. Michael Smith. PBCV

Demagogue, The. Phyllis McGinley. FaBoEE

Demand for truth, The. (LL) "Wintry Dawn." Meir Wieseltier, *Hebrew.* IP, *tr.* by Bargad, Warren and Stanley Chyet

Demanding that I explain / my treachery. (LL) Blonde White Women. Patricia Smith. GT; UnSA

Demands more Praise than Tongues can give. (LL) The Church the Garden of Christ. Isaac Watts. PeECV

Demands my soul, my life, my all. (LL) Crucifixion to the World by the Cross of Christ. Isaac Watts. AmFP; ECEV; FaPoR; NOCV; NOEC; OxAEP-1; PeECV

Demands of the Muse. Vernon Watkins. PoA

Deme as Ye List Uppon Goode Cause. Sir Thomas Wyatt. PoEL-1

Demeanour. *Unknown.* OxBChV

Dementia Praecox. Morris Gilbert Bishop. PoA

Demeter. Genevieve Taggard. NMM-2

Demeter and Cora. Dora Greenwell. VWP

Demeter Grieving. Michele Roberts. NBrP

Demeter has torn off. Demeter Grieving. Michele Roberts. NBrP

Demeter Mourning. Rita Dove. NAAAL *Fr.* Mother Love.

Demeter's Prayer to Hades. Rita Dove. NAAAL *Fr.* Mother Love.

Demiurge. D. H. Lawrence. GI

Demiurge's Laugh, The. Robert Frost. OxBA

Democracy works (*entre nous*). Limerick. W. Stewart. PeLi

Democratic Barber; or, Country Gentleman's Surprise, The. John Parrish. NOEC

Democritus and Heraclitus. Matthew Prior. OxBSP

Democritus, dear droll, revisit Earth. Democritus and Heraclitus. Matthew Prior. OxBSP

Demodocus sings the fall of Troy. Homer. OBCVT, *tr.* by George Chapman *Fr.* The Odyssey.

Demodocus sings the fall of Troy. Homer. OBCVT, *tr.* by Robert Fitzgerald *Fr.* The Odyssey.

Demographics. Catherine Bowman. BAP-94

Demolisher. Alan Gould. BMAP

Demolition, The. Anne Stevenson. OxBSP

Demon in Paradise. Minuchihri, *Persian.* ArPe, *tr.* by Omar S. Pound

Demon Lover, The. *Unknown.* EnSB; HAP; PBMP; SCGP; TFi; UnPo; WeW-3
(Carpenter's Wife, The.) OAEL-1; OxBB

(James Harris.) ESPB

(House Carpenter, The.) AmFP

Demonstrators who filled the streets of Seoul, The. It's Not the Same. Tomoko Fukunaka, *Japanese*. WPJ, *tr. by* Kenneth Rexroth *and* Ikuko Atsumi

Demoted I Arrive at Lan-t'ien Pass and Show This Poem to My Brother's Grandson Han Hsiang. Han Yü, *Chinese*. SuSp, *tr. by* Charles Hartman

Demure you are over your left shoulder. Lines on a Boer War Pin-up Girl Seen in the Falcon Hotel, Bude. Christopher Hope. PeSAV

Den of the bear. John Wills. HA

Denial, A. Elizabeth Barrett Browning. GBL; OBNC

Denial[l]. George Herbert. ESCV; GeHe; NAEL-1; NOBE; OAEL-1; PoEL-2; TOF

("And mend my ryme.") (LL) FSCP; PBRV

(Denial.) FMP; NoP-4

Denied, / Like Bessie. Of Walter White's Father in the Rain. Houston A. Baker Jr. SeSe

Denim and silk pooled at our feet upstairs. Gramercy Park. Marilyn Hacker. DeD *Fr.* Love, Death and the Changing of the Seasons.

Dennis's Sky Leopard. Thylias Moss. IFJA

Denouement. Ruth Stone. BoWoP

Dense as a horse mane is. Marina Ivanovna Tsvetayeva. PFTM *Fr.* Poem of the End.

Dense on the stream the vapours lay. The Mowers: An Anticipation of the Cholera, 1848. Charles MacKay. EBVV

Dense ravine, no inch, A. Portola Valley. Amy Clampitt. EOEF

Dense white clouds embrace Thunder Peak. Written during My Stay at White Clouds Monastery on West Lake. Su Man-shu, *Chinese*. SuSp, *tr. by* Wu-chi Liu

Dented spider like a snowdrop white, A. In White. Robert Frost. TRP

Dentist, A. *Unknown*. FaBoEE

(Epitaph on a Dentist.) OxBoLi

Dentists continue to water their lawns even in the rain. The Great Society. Robert Bly. NoAM

Dentist's Window, A. James Keir Baxter. OxBC

Denunciation; or, Unfrock'd Again. Philip Whalen. NeAP

Denying they have been. (LL) The Snow. Emily Dickinson. ACTP; SoSe-8; WHSW

"Deo Gracias!" (LL) Adam Lay Bound. *Unknown*. CH; CTC; ChIV-2; EnVB; HAP; InPS-3; MiEL; NAEL-1; NOBE; NOCV; OAEL-1; OxBoLi; PeLV; PoE; PoEL-1; TFi; TOF; TRP; WeW-3

Deo Gracias, Anglia. *Unknown*. *See* The Agincourt Carol.

Deo gracias [*or* gracias], Anglia, / Redde pro victoria. The Agincourt Carol. *Unknown*. EBEV; NoP-4; OAEL-1

Deodand, The. Anthony Hecht. DiPo; NoAM

Deor. *Unknown, Anglo-Saxon*. EBEV, *tr. by* John Wain; ASW, *tr. by* Kevin Crossley-Holland; EEP, *tr. by* Michael Alexander

("Wayland knew the wanderer's fate.") EEP, *tr. by* Michael Alexander

Deor. *Unknown, Anglo-Saxon*. EBEV, *tr. by* John Wain

Deornamentation. Ion Caraion, *Romanian*. CEEP, *tr. by* Marguerite Dorian *and* Elliott B. Urdang

Deor's Lament. *Unknown, Anglo-Saxon*. AnOE; OAEL-1, *tr. by* Charles W. Kennedy

Depairt, depairt, depairt [*or* Departe, departe, departe]. Lament of the Master of Erskine. Alexander Scott. CH; GBL

Depart,— be off,— excede,— evade,— erump! (LL) Aestivation [an Unpublished Poem, by My Late Latin Tutor]. Oliver Wendell Holmes. NOBL; OBAL

Departed Youth. Hannah Cowley. CABP; ECWP

Departing at dawn, carriage bells ajingle. An Early Walk on Shang Mountain. Wen T'ing-yün, *Chinese*. SuSp, *tr. by* William R. Schultz

Departing Boat, The. Yongch'ol Park, *Korean*. CKP, *tr. by* Jaihiun Kim

Department of Plants and Structures— obsolete, the old name. George Oppen. APSN *Fr.* Route.

Departmental. Robert Frost. HeIP-4; HoPM; MoAmPo; NAAL-2; NOBA; NOBL; OBAL; PeLV; SAGP; SoSe-8

Departure. Edmund Blunden. OxBSP

Departure. Van K. Brock. MT

Departure. Louise Glück. GM

Departure. Thomas Hardy. Son

Departure. Edna St. Vincent Millay. MoAmPo

Departure, The. William Vaughn Moody. APN-2

Departure. Coventry Patmore. NOBE; OBEV; OBNC *Fr.* The Unknown Eros.

Departure, The. Trumbull Stickney. ColAP

Departure. Wang Wei, *Chinese*. TAL, *tr. by* Robert Payne

Departure. Mildred Weston. FFC

Departure, The. Reed Whittemore. TAP

Departure; an Elegy, The. Henry, Bishop of Chichester King. SeCP

Departure Aria. Johann Christian Günther, *German*. GePo, *tr. by* George C. Schoolfield

Departure in Middle Age. Roland Mathias. CRP; OBWVE

Departure in the Dark. C. Day Lewis. TwCP

Departure of the Prodigal Son*, The. Rilke, *German*. GI, *tr. by* David Curzon, Lori Seibel *and* Will Alexander Washburn

Departure's Girl-friend. W. S. Merwin. CoAmPo

Dependencies, The. Howard Nemerov. VCAP

Depending on the Light. Andrea Potos. IFJA

Depiction of Childhood. Franz Wright. BLT *Fr.* After Picasso.

Deportation. "M. B.," *Polish*. TrJP, *tr. by* A. Glanz-Leyeles

Depose your finger of that Ring. Sonnet. Richard Lovelace. CavPo

Deposition. Kurt Bartsch, *German*. CEEP, *tr. by* Wayne Kvam

Deposition, The. Thomas Stanley. CBLP

Deposition from Love, A. Thomas Carew. BeJo; CaPo; CavPo; MeLP

Depot Blues. *Unknown*. AmFP

Depot in Rapid City. Roberta Hill Whiteman. BoWoP

Depreciating Her Beauty. Wilfrid Scawen Blunt. OBMV *Fr.* The Love Sonnets of Proteus.

Depressed by a Book of Bad Poetry, I Walk toward an Unused Pasture and Invite the Insects to Join Me. James Wright. CoAmPo

Depressed by the Death of the Horse That He Bought from Robert Bly. Henry Taylor. BXAP

Depression. Wendy Cope. FaBoWP

Depression, The. Doug Lang. MoNo

Depression before Spring. Wallace Stevens. OBAL

Depression Days. Pat Mora. UnSA

Depression in Winter. Jane Kenyon. LoL

Deprived of his enemy, shrugged to a standstill. John Berryman. CAPP-1; LCAP-2 *Fr.* Dream Songs.

Deprived of the green of that exclusive golf course, the scotch. Epistle to the Gentiles. Alfred Hayes. TrJP

Depth or the duration of his woe. (LL) On Being Cautioned against Walking on an Headland Overlooking the Sea, because It Was Frequented by a Lunatic. Charlotte Smith. ECWP; WoRP

Der lived a king inta da aste. King Orfeo. *Unknown*. ESPB; OxBB; OxBoLi

Der noble Ritter Hugo. Ballad. Charles Godfrey Leland. APN-2

Der teufel's los in Bal Mabille. Breitmann in Paris. Charles Godfrey Leland. APN-2

Derailment: A Delirium. Steve Chimombo. HBAPE

Derby Ram, The. *Unknown*. AmFP; CBNP; NTP; OxNR; ReMoGo

("As I was going to Derby.") OxNR

(Wonderful Derby Ram, The.) BoTP

Derelict. Young Ewing Allison. BLPA; FaBoBe

Derelict, The. Rudyard Kipling. NoAM

Dere's a beeg jam up de reever, w'ere rapide is runnin' fas'. The Log Jam. William Henry Drummond. NOBC

Dere's a liddle fact in hishdory vitch few hafe onnershtand. Charles Godfrey Leland. OBAL *Fr.* Breitmann in Politics.

Dere's no hidin' place down dere. *Unknown*. APN-2; BPo

Dermis. Anthony McNeill. PBCV

Dern frae aa men. (LL) For a Wife in Jizzen. Douglas Young. FaBoTC

Derry. Seamus Deane. CIP-2; IIP

Derry Morning. Derek Mahon. IIP; NOIV

Dervish wept to feel the violence of, A. Farid-uddin Attar. *Fr.* The Conference of the Birds. TOF, *tr. by* Afkham Darbandi *and* Dick Davis

Dervorgilla's supremely lovely daughter. Portrait with Background. Oliver St. John Gogarty. OBMV

Derwent; an Ode. Sir John Carr. Memories of Childhood. NOEC

Derzhavin. Georgy Arkadevich Shengeli, *Russian*. TCRP, *tr. by* Daniel Weissbort

Désamère. Alice Notley. PT

Descartes and the Stove. Charles Tomlinson. FaBoMo

Descartes at Daybreak. Aidan Carl Mathews. CIP-2

Descend, fair Truth, celestial maid, descend. Ode to Truth. Mary Whateley. ECWP

DESCEND from heaven O muse Melpomene. An Epitaph of Our Late Queen Mary. George Cavendish. NoSic

Descend, while three birds watch and the fourth flies. (LL) Winter Landscape. John Berryman. GS; LiTM; MoAmPo; TwCP

Descend, ye hovering sylphs! aerial choirs. Erasmus Darwin. ECEV *Fr.* The Botanic Garden.

Descendant I am of Emperor Kao-yang, A. Yüan, Ch'ü. Ch'u Yüan, *Chinese*. SuSp, *tr. by* Wu-chi Liu *Fr.* Li Sao.

Descendant of the ancestor Kao-yang. Encountering Sorrow. *Unknown, Chinese.* CoBCP, *tr. by* Burton Watson; CoBCP, *tr. by* Burton Watson, *at. to* Ch'u Yüan

Descended of an ancient line. To Maecenas. Horace. FaPoR; OBVE *Fr.* Odes.

Descending. Ioan Alexandru, *Romanian.* CEEP, *tr. by* Donald Eulert *and* Stefan Avadanei

Descending. Valentin Iremonger. EnLoPo

Descending by the mountain-side. Guide and Guard. Herman Melville. NCAP

Descending Chestnut Ridge. Donald Davidson. FuPo *Fr.* Hermitage.

Descending Figure. Louise Glück. FaBoWP

Descending the Ridge of Flying Clouds. T'ang Hsien-tsu, *Chinese.* CoBLCP, *tr. by* Jonathan Chaves

Descending to the cave where the Archangel / made his announcement. Nazareth. Rosario Castellanos, *Spanish.* GI, *tr. by* Magda Bogin

Descends the snow. Henry Wadsworth Longfellow. *See* Snow-Flakes.

Descent beckons, the. William Carlos Williams. HAP; SAmP; WeW-3

Descent from the Cross. "Michael Field." WPE

Descent into Hell, The. William Langland. PoEL-1 *Fr.* The Vision of Piers Plowman.

Descent of Fire, The. Jeannine Savard. CMAP

Descent of Odin, The. Thomas Gray. OxAEP-1

Descent of the Child, The. Susan Langstaff Mitchell. TIRV

Descent of the Vulture, The. Marya Alexandrovna Zaturenska. WPE

Descent of Winter, The. William Carlos Williams.
"To freight cars in the air." InPK-6

"Describe the Borough."—Though our idle tribe. Letter I. George Crabbe. CABP *Fr.* The Borough.

Describe: The Rain on Dasaswamedh Ghat. Allen Ginsberg. FTOS
("Kali Ma tottering up steps to shelter tin roof, feeling her way.") BB

Describes the Place Where Cynthia Is Sporting Herself. Philip Ayres. EnLoPo

Describing circle after circle. The Vulture. Aleksandr Blok, *French.* NNPT, *tr. by* Jon Stallworthy *and* Peter France

Describing My Feelings upon Encountering Snow. Li K'ai-hsien, *Chinese.*
"Crossing the ridge, the woodcutter loses his way." CoBLCP, *tr. by* Jonathan Chaves

Describing My Feelings While Living in Retirement by the Riverside: Seven Poems to the Tune "Ch'ing-p'ing-yüeh," *with music.* Yang Chi, *Chinese.* CoBLCP, *tr. by* Jonathan Chaves

Describing My Feelings While Living in the Spring Quarters at Chiang-ning: Four Poems to the Tune "Ching-p'ing-yëh." Yang Chi, *Chinese.* CoBLCP, *tr. by* Jonathan Chaves

Description, A. Edward Herbert, 1st Baron Herbert of Cherbury. SeCP

Description of a City Shower, A. Jonathan Swift. HeIP-4; NAEL-1; NOEC; OAEL-1; OBSV; PoE; UnPo
(City Shower, A.) SCGP

Description of a City Shower, A. Jonathan Swift. NoP-4

Description of a Good Boy, The. Henry Dixon. OxBChV; OxNR

Description of a New England Spring. John Josselyn. SCAP

Description of an Author's Bedchamber, A. Oliver Goldsmith. BIrV

Description of an Irish Feast, The. Hugh MacGowran, *Irish.* NOIV; OBCoV, *tr. by* Jonathan Swift

Description of Cookham, The. Aemilia Bassano Lanyer. CABP; KTR; NoP-4; OBGa; PBRV

Description of Elizium, The. Michael Drayton. OAEL-1 *Fr.* Muses' Elysium [*or* Elizium].

Description of Hagia Sophia. Paulus Silentiarius, *Greek.* GrIP, *tr. by* Richard Stoneman

Description of London, A. John Bancks. NOEC; OBCoV

Description of Love, A. Sir John Beaumont. NOSC

Description of Maidenhead, A. John Wilmot, 2d Earl of Rochester. NOBL

Description of Perfect Beauty. Christian Hofmann von Hofmannswaldau, *German.* GePo, *tr. by* George C. Schoolfield

Description of Sir Geoffrey Chaucer, The. Robert Greene. CTC; NoSic; SCGP *Fr.* Greene's Vision.
(Sir Chaucer.) FaBoCh

Description of Some Confederate Soldiers, A. Randall Jarrell. CBCWP

Description of Spring in London, A. *Unknown.* NOEC

Description of Spring, Wherein Each Thing Renews Save Only the Lover. Henry Howard, Earl of Surrey, *after* Petrarch. OBEV
("Eche care decayes, and yet my sorow springes.") (LL) PBRV
("Soot season, that bud and bloom forth brings, The.") AEP

Description of the Contrarious Passions in a Lover. Petrarch. Son *Fr.* Sonnets to Laura.

Description of the Morning, A. Jonathan Swift. EBEV; ECEV; HAP; HeIP-4; InPS-3; NOBE; NOEC; NoP-4; OAEL-1; OxAEP-1; PoPoPo; Poetr; SoSe-8; TFi

("And School-Boys lag with Satchels in their Hands.") (LL) PFE

Description of the Shepherd and His Wife, The. Robert Greene. NoSic

Description of Tyme, A. Alexander Montgomerie. OxBS

Description of Virtue. Nicholas Grimald. *See* Virtue.

Description of Wallace, A. Henry the Minstrel. *See* Schir William Wallace.

Descriptive Poem, Addressed to Two Ladies at Their Return from Viewing the Mines, near Whitehaven, A. John Dalton.
Agape the sooty collier stands. NOEC

Dese Bones Gwine to Rise Again. *Unknown.* AS; OxBoLi

Desecration of the Han Tombs, The. Chang Tsai, *Chinese.* ChiP, *tr. by* Arthur Waley

Desert. Birago Diop, *French.* NegPo, *tr. by* Ellen Conroy Kennedy

Desert, The. Edmond Jabès, *French.* AF, *tr. by* Rosemarie Waldrop

Desert. Del Marie Rogers. MDDM

Desert caller, The. Eyeful Glances. Niyi Osundare. HBAPE

Desert Conflict. Calvin Makabo, *Southern Sotho.* PeSAV, *tr. by* Alexander Qoboshane

Desert Flowers. Keith Douglas. FaBoTw

Desert Has Many Teachings, The. Mechthild von Magdeburg, *German.* WPoS, *tr. by* Jane Hirshfield

Desert, II, The. Edmond Jabès, *French.* AF, *tr. by* Rosemarie Waldrop

Desert in the Sea. Brian Swann. AmPA

Desert Landscape. Agha Shahid Ali. OMIP

Desert Lark, The. Eugène Marias, *Afrikaans.* PeSA, *tr. by* Uys Krige *and* Jack Cope

Desert moves out on half the horizon, The. The Supper after the Last. Galway Kinnell. NOBA

Desert Music, The. William Carlos Williams. APSN

Desert of Love, The. János Pilinszky, *Hungarian.* OBVE, *tr. by* Ted Hughes *and* Janos Csokits

Desert Places. Robert Frost. AFr; AmPP; CMoP, InPK-6, MoAmPo; MoP; NAAL-2; NOBA; NoAM; OxBA; PFE; PoE; RB; SoSe-8; TAP; TRP; UnPo

Desert Warfare. Michael Longley. CIP-2

Deserted city, residence of Ch'en emperors. The Residence of the Emperors of Ch'en. Yang Wei-chen, *Chinese.* CoBLCP, *tr. by* Jonathan Chaves

Deserted Estate at South Garden, The. Hsü Pen, *Chinese.* CoBLCP, *tr. by* Jonathan Chaves

Deserted Garden, The. Elizabeth Barrett Browning. GaP

Deserted Home, A. Sidney Royce Lysaght. CH

Deserted Homestead, The. Loren C. Eiseley. PoA

Deserted House, The. Johannes Bobrowski, *German.* CEEP, *tr. by* Ruth Mead *and* Matthew Mead

Deserted House, The. Mary Elizabeth Coleridge. BoTP; CH

Deserted House. Dorothy, Duchess of Wellington Wellesley.
Epilogue: "He is not dead nor liveth." OBMV

Deserted islands, broken sherds of land. Antipater of Thessalonica, *Greek.* GrAn, *tr. by* Alistair Elliot

Deserted Mountain, The. *Unknown, Irish.* BIrV, *tr. by* John Montague

Deserted mountain, streams and stones, A. Searching for the Ruins of the Pavilion of the Drunken Old Man. Yang Shih-ch'i, *Chinese.* CoBLCP, *tr. by* Jonathan Chaves

Deserted street, shadows of trees and houses, locked doors—. Vista. Faiz Ahmad Faiz, *Urdu.* VCWP, *tr. by* Agha Shahid Ali

Deserted Village, The. Oliver Goldsmith. NOEC; OAEL-1; PoEL-3
Deserted Village, The. ECEV; FHYEP; ImPo; NOBE; NoP-4; OxAEP-1; TFi
"Even now the devastation is begun." EBEV
"Ill fares the land, to hastening ills a prey." OBSV; UV
"O luxury! Thou curst by Heaven's decree." BIrV
"Sweet Auburn! parent of the blissful hour." EBEV
"Sweet smiling village, loveliest of the lawn." NOIV
Village, The ("Sweet was the sound, when oft at evening's close"). IIP
"Yes! let the rich deride, the proud disdain." OBSV

Deserted Village, The. "Robin Hyde." PeNZ; WPE

Deserted wharf. Chuck Brickley. HA

Deserter, The. John Philpot Curran. OxAEP-1

Deserter, The. Gilbert Frankau. PoFWW

Deserter, The. A. E. Housman. OBMV

Deserter, The. John Streeter Manifold. CBAP

Deserter, A. Charles Reznikoff. TRP

Deserter, The. Stevie Smith. FaBoWP

Desertion of Beauty and Strength, The. *Unknown. Fr.* Everyman. NAEL-1; NAWM-1; OAEL-1; PoEL-1

Desertion of the Women and Seals, The. George Mackay Brown. OxBC

Desertmartin. Tom Paulin. CIP-2; PBCIP; PNI

Design. Robert Frost. CMoP; ColAP; HeIP-4; InPK-6; InPS-3; MoP; NAAL-2; NOBA; NoAM; NoP-4; PBMP; PoPoPo; Poetr; RaBo; SAmP; SoSe-8; Son; TAP; TFi; TRP

Design, The. Clarence Major. PoBA

Design in Living Colors. Adrienne Rich. GaP

Design, or chance, makes others wive. Of the Marriage of the Dwarfs. Edmund Waller. CBLP

Designer sits, head in hand, The. Peter Redgrove. OxBC

Désillusion. Lady Jane Francesca Wilde. VWP

Desire. "Æ." OBMV; TIRV

Desire. Claribel Alegría, *Spanish*. LoL, *tr. by* D. J. Flakoll

Desire. Stephen Dobyns. NAmP90

Desire. Lynn Emanuel. WWSi

Desire. Alison Fell. FaBoTC

Desire. Paul Hoover. PmAP

Desire. D. H. Lawrence. CBLP

Desire. Molly Peacock. RA

Desire. Kurt Schwitters, *German*. PFTM, *tr. by* Jerome Rothenberg

Desire. Leslie Ullman. NAmP90

Desire 1. Thulani Davis. ISC

Desire and Jealousy. William Blake. ECEV *Fr.* Visions of the Daughters of Albion. CABP; OAEL-2; Ro

Desire, get your bow ready / and go quietly after / another mark. Archias, *Greek*. GrAn, *tr. by* Alan Marshfield

Desire has failed, desire has failed. Grasshopper Is a Burden. D. H. Lawrence. FaBoVe

Desire is a witch. C. Day Lewis. CMoP

Desire Is Dead. D. H. Lawrence. FaBoEE

Desire may be dead. Desire Is Dead. D. H. Lawrence. FaBoEE

Desire of Dominion. Timothy Kendall. NoSic

Desire of Water, The. Mark Jarman. PoA

Desire of wine and all delicious drink. Milton. *Fr.* Samson Agonistes. FHYEP; OAEL-1; PoEL-3

Desire of your hands white. Ancient Winter. Salvatore Quasimodo. ItIP

Desire, though thou my old companion art. Sonnet 72. Sir Philip Sidney. AEP; NAEL-1; PBRV *Fr.* Astrophil and Stella. AAS; SiPS

Desire to be in Two Places at Once, The. Charles Henri Ford. PC

Desired, the snow falls upward. Letter 5. Michael Palmer. FTOS *Fr.* Letters to Zanzotto.

Desires. Connie Bensley. FaBoWP

Desire's green / and gold corona / in the wavering branch. Joseph Donahue. PT

Desires of Men and Women. John Berryman. LiTM

Desiring his imprisoned Muse to enlarge. On the Doctors' Telling Him that till He Left off Making Verses He Was Not Fit to be Discharged. James Carkesse. NOSC

Desiring nought but how to kill desire. (LL) Thou blind man's mark, thou fool's self-chosen snare, *Wr. considered Sonnet CIX of* Astrophil and Stella. Sir Philip Sidney. HeIP-4; ImPo; NAEL-1; NOBE; SCGP; SiPS; Son

Desk, The. David Bottoms. MT; WeW-3

Desk, The. Cid Corman. VGW

Desk. Marina Tsvetayeva, *Russian*. FP, *tr. by* Elaine Feinstein

Desks. Dave Jeddie Smith. HCAP

Desmet, Idaho, March 1969. Janet Campbell Hale. VoR

Desolate. Sydney Thompson Dobell. OBNC

Desolate. Gerald Massey. EBVV

Desolate and lone. Lost. Carl Sandburg. AmPP; CMoP

Desolate City, The. *Unknown, Arabic*. AWP; OBEV, *tr. by* Wilfrid Scawen Blunt

Desolate poems of chaotic times—could I bear. Ch'ien Ch'ien-i. *Fr.* Miscellaneous Feelings at West Lake. CoBLCP, *tr. by* Jonathan Chaves

Desolate rhythm of dying recurs, The. Fall. Michael Smith. CIP-2

Desolate that cry as though world were unworthy. Chough. Rex Warner. PoRA

Desolate, this rainy autumn evening. What Strikes My Eye. Wang Shih-chieng, *Chinese*. SuSp, *tr. by* Richard John Lynn

Desolation. Jack Davis. BMAP

Desolation. Amy Lowell. PoA

Desolation. *Unknown, Welsh*. OBWVE, *tr. by* Aneirin Talfan Davies

Desolation in Zion. Bible, *O.T.* TrJP *Fr.* Lamentations.

"Desolation Is a Delicate Thing." Elinor Wylie. MoAmPo

Despair. Andrey Bely, *Russian*. TCRP, *tr. by* Bernard Meares

Despair. Emily Dickinson. *See* I cannot live with You.

Despair. Greville Fulke. *Fr.* Caelica.

Despair. Maxine W. Kumin. FFC

Despair. Denise Levertov. NNaP

Despair. Aleksandar Ristovic, *Serbo-Croatian*. HSix, *tr. by* Charles Simic

Despair. Edmund Spenser. *Fr.* Wood Of Error. AEP

Despair. Tom Wayman. CDa

Despair and Hope. Israel Zangwill. TrJP

Despair, anger, grief. Black Java Pepper. Arthur Sze. OpBo

Despair before us, vanity behind. (LL) Sonnet XXV: "As in the midst of battle there is room." George Santayana. APN-2; AWP

Despair is big with friends I love. Of Choice. William Meredith. VCAP *Fr.* Consequences.

Despair of all, and hope for none! Despair and Hope. Israel Zangwill. TrJP

Despairing Lover, The. William Walsh. FaBoCh; NBLV; NOBL; OxBoLi; PeLV

Despair's advantage is achieved. Emily Dickinson. PAR

Desperate spinster of Clare, A. Limerick. *Unknown*. PeLi

Despisals. Muriel Rukeyser. CPO; NMM-2

Despise not any man that lives. Sam Walter Foss. PoToHe *Fr.* Work for Small Men.

Despised and Rejected. Katharine Lee Bates. TrCP

Despised and Rejected. Christina Rossetti.
"Then I cried out upon him: Cease." PeVV

Despite my lifelong wish to live. The Gong Dance. Sokch'o Shin, *Korean*. CKP, *tr. by* Jaihiun Kim

Despite the reigning darkness. The Great Masturbator. Salvador Dali, *French*. PFTM, *tr. by* Marcel Jean

Despite the weatherman, who in hibiscus. Breakfast on the Patio. James Harms. CMAP

Desponding Phyllis was endued. Phyllis [*or* Phillis] [*or* Progress of Love, The]. Jonathan Swift. EBNV; OAEL-1; OBCoV; OBSV; PoE; PoEL-3

Desportes. Sir Arthur Gorges.
"Tell me, my heart, how wilt thou do." NoSic

Despot treads thy sacred sands, The. Carolina. Henry Timrod. APN-2; CBCWP

Despot's heel is on thy shore, The. My Maryland. James Ryder Randall. APN-2; CBCWP; FaBoBe

Destination or an origin?, A. Infinity Effect at the Hôtel Soubise. Alfred Corn. EOEF

Destination: Tule Lake Relocation Center, May 20, 1942. Jim Mitsui. OpBo

Destinations. Josephine Jacobsen. WPE

Destined for greatness, he lies on his stomach, a pacifier. Pages of an Album. Dan Pagis, *Hebrew*. IP, *tr. by* Warren Bargad *and* Stanley F. Chyet

Destined to sway supreme. For Asopichus of Orchomenus: Winner in the Stade Run. Pindar, *Greek*. OBCVT, *tr. by* Robert Fagles

Destined while living to sustain. An Epitaph on Herself. Mehetabel Wright. ECWP

Destinie. Abraham Cowley. MeLP
"Me from the womb the midwife Muse did take." EPCY

Destiny. Sir Edwin Arnold. NOBVV; OxBSP; PoLF

Destiny. Eloise Bibb. CBWP-4

Destiny. Maria Luisa Spaziani, *Italian*. NeIt, *tr. by* Beverly Allen

Destiny guide me always. The Chorus sing of the laws of the gods. Sophocles, *Greek*. OBCVT, *tr. by* Robert Fagles

Destroy the heavy yoke beneath which you are bound! To Germany. Georg Rudolph Weckherlin, *German*. GePo, *tr. by* George C. Schoolfield

Destroyer and Preserver; hear, O hear! Shelley. *See* Ode to the West Wind.

Destroyer of a Soul, The. Lionel Pigot Johnson. ADE

Destroyers. Sir Henry Head. NSI

Destroyers. "Klaxon." NSI

Destroyers, The. Albert Rowe. SpW

Destroyers in Collision. Rudyard Kipling. *Fr.* Epitaphs of the War [1914–1918]. OBWP

Destroyers in the Arctic. Alan Ross. PoWW

Destroyers Off Jutland. Reginald McIntosh Cleveland. NSI

Destroying Angel. Hilary Corke. NYBP

Destroying life alone, not peace! (LL) Lines Written in the Bay of Lerici. Shelley. NAEL-2; OAEL-2

Destruction. Joanne Kyger. BLT

Destruction of Jerusalem, The. Thomas Deloney.
"Our Savior Christ tracing the bordering hills." ChIV-2

Destruction of Jerusalem by the Babylonian Hordes, The. Isaac Rosenberg. PeFWW

Destruction of Letters. Babette Deutsch. WPE

Destruction of Sennacherib, The. Byron. APAD; BLPA; CABP; CTV; ChAP; ChIV-1; EBEvV; FHYEP; FaBoBe; FaBoCh; FaPoR; HAP; HeIP-4; InPS-3; NoP-4; OBWP; OxAEP-2; PBMP; PoLF; RB; SCGP; TFi; TrCP; WeW-3

Destruction of Sodom, The. Daryl Hine. ChIV-1

Destruction of the Grecian Fort, The. Homer. OBVE, *tr. by* Alexander Pope *Fr.* The Iliad.

Destruction that brings an eagle from heaven is better than mercy, The. (LL) Fire on the Hills. Robinson Jeffers. CMoP; RaBo

Desultory Thoughts in London. Charles Lloyd.
  "Where have I wander'd, London, from thy haunts?" NOBRP

Desunt nonnulla. (LL) On Hellespont, guilty of true love's blood. Marlowe. NoSic; OAEL-1; PoE; PoEL-2

Detach, Invading. Ron Padgett. FTOS

Detail. Mary Ursula Bethell. PeNZ

Detected little things: a peach pit basket watch chain charm, an ivory cross wound. Father or Son. James Schuyler. FTOS

Detectives from the vice squad. Café: 3 A.M. Langston Hughes. GLP; HCAP

Detente. Tom Pickard. NBrP

Detergent's mixed with pinches of my love. Washing My Wife's Clothes. Luân Hoán, *Vietnamese.* AVP, *tr. by* Huỳnh Sanh Thông

Determination. John Henrik Clarke. PoBA

Determined, Dared, and Done. (LL) A Song to David. Christopher Smart. ImPo; NAEL-1; NOBE; OAEL-1; OBWVE; PoE; PoEL-3

Determined gait, A. The Announcer. Vladimir Nikolaevich Kornilov, *Russian.* TCRP, *tr. by* Daniel Weissbort

Determined to try. Tanka. Saitō Mokichi, *Japanese.* MJT, *tr. by* Ueda, Makoto

Determinism. Maurice Evan Hare. OBCoV

Detestable race, continue to expunge yourself, die out. Apostrophe to Man. Edna St. Vincent Millay. NALW; PBMP

Detonation. Francesco Cangiullo. PFTM

Detour. Michael Longley. CIP-2

Detroit Conference of Unity and Art. Nikki Giovanni. HoPM

Detroit River. Constance Fenimore Woolson. APN-2

Deuce: 12:23 a.m. Barbara Anderson. NAmP90

Deus "Sex" Machina. Harriet Mandelbaum. PeLi

Deuteronomy. Bible, *O.T.*
  "For the Lordes parte is his folke." OBVE, *tr. by* William Tyndale
  Give Ear, Ye Heavens. TrJP

Deuteronomy. Robert Bringhurst. NOBC

Deuteronomy 30.19. Francis Quarles. ChIV-1

Deutschland. Hugh Maxton. PBCIP

Developing a Wife. Andrew Taylor. BMAP; CBAP

Development. D. J. Enright. OxBSP

Development, The. Marge Piercy. NBLV *Fr.* Sand Roads.

Development of Idiotcy, A. Ebenezer Jones. OBNC; PeVV

Devil, A. Zbigniew Herbert, *Polish.* RB, *tr. by* Czeslaw Milosz

Devil, The. Robert Southey. NOxBChV

Devil and the Governor, The. William Forster.
  "In New South Wales, as I plainly see." CBAP

Devil and the Princess. *Unknown.* FaBoVe

Devil and the Shepherd, The. Fazil Abdulovich Iskander, *Russian.* TCRP, *tr. by* Daniel Weissbort

Devil below was ringing his knell, The. (LL) The Inchcape Rock. Robert Southey. EBEvV; EBNV; FaBoBe; OBNV; OBSP; OxAEP-2

Devil damn thee black, thou cream-faced loon—, The. Paul Dehn. OBCoV *Fr.* Potted Swan.

Devil-Dancers, The. William Plomer. PeSA; PeSAV

Devil, having nothing else to do, The. On Lady Poltagrue, A Public Peril. Hilaire Belloc. MoBrPo; OBCoV; OxBoV

Devil, I safely can aver, The. Shelley. OxBoV *Fr.* Peter Bell the Third.

Devil! I tell thee without nubbs or jubbs. After Reading the Life of Mrs. Catherine Stubbs in Isaac Ambrose's "War with the Devils." Isaac Hann. NOCV

Devil in Texas, The. *Unknown.* NBLV; RB

Devil is a gentleman, and asks you down to stay, The. The Aristocrat. G. K. Chesterton. OBCoV

Devil Is an Ass, The. Ben Jonson. OxBSn

Devil is dead, good people all, The. The Devil's Funeral. Mary Elizabeth Coleridge. NALW

Devil now knew his proper cue, The. Shelley. OBSV *Fr.* Peter Bell the Third.

Devil on Ice. Donald Davie. NoAM

Devil take the human race!, The. Ill Humor. Goethe, *German.* STV, *tr. by* John Frederick Nims

Devil to Pay, The. Dorothy Leigh Sayers.
  Choice of the Cross, The. TrCP

Devil was more generous than Adam, The. Samuel Butler. FaBoEE

Devil, we're told, in hell was chained, The. Hell in Texas. *Unknown.* BLPA

Devil, who plays a deep part, The. Limerick. "Little Billee." PeLi

Devilish and the dark, the dying and diseas'd, The. The Rounded Catalogue Divine Complete. Walt Whitman. NAAL-1; NAAL-3

Devilish little wheels. (LL) Nobody. Novica Tadic, *Serbo-Croatian.* HSix; VCWP, *tr. by* Charles Simic

Devilish Mary. *Unknown.* AmFP

Devils. Norman Mailer. OBAL

Devil's Advice to Story-Tellers, The. Robert Graves. LiTM; MoP; NAEL-2; NoAM

Devils Clowns and Women. Rochelle Owens. DeD

Devil's Dictionary, The. Ambrose Bierce.
  Alone. APN-2
  Body-Snatcher. APN-2
  Corporal. APN-2; OBAL
  Egotist. APAD; APN-2; OBAL
  Elegy: "Cur foretells the knell of parting day, The." APN-2; OBAL
  "Freedom, as every schoolboy knows." APN-2
  Gorgon. APN-2
  Hypochondriasis. APN-2
  Lead. APN-2; OBAL
  Nose. APN-2; OBAL
  Orthography. APN-2; OBAL; PeLi
  Prospect. APN-2; OBAL
  "Rimer quenches his unheeded fires, The." APN-2
  Safety-Clutch. APN-2; OBAL

Devil's Funeral, The. Mary Elizabeth Coleridge. NALW

Devil's Law Case, The. John Webster.
  Vanitas Vanitatum. NOBE; OBEV
  (Burial, The.) CH

Devil's Nine Questions, The. *Unknown.* AmFP

Devil's no longer a myth, The. Limerick. "Little Billee." PeLi

Devil's on his bike, lead shoes, The. A Carnival Figure of Guatemalan Clay. Jeannine Savard. CMAP

Devil's Swing, The. Fyodor Kuz'mich Sologub, *Russian.* TCRP, *tr. by* April FitzLyon

Devils there may be, and Gods but one. (LL) Sonnet: "Three things there be in mans opinion dear[e]." Fulke, 1st Baron Brooke Greville. NOCV; NOSC; NoSic; PoEL-1

Devil's Thoughts, The. Coleridge. CBNP; OBSV; OxBoLi; PeLV

Devoide of reason, thrale to foolish ire. Thomas Lodge. AAS *Fr.* Phyllis.

Devolution. Molly Peacock. FFC

Devolution of the Nude. Lynne McMahon. NAmP90

Devonshire Song, A. William Strode. PoEL-2

Devotion. Paul Fleming, *German.* GePo, *tr. by* F. Warnke

Devotion is a heavy cross. Boris Pasternak, *Russian.* LoP, *tr. by* J. M. Cowen

Devotional Sonnet, A. Timothy Steele. CRP

Devouring Time, blunt thou the lion's paws. Sonnet 19. Shakespeare. AWP; EBEV; HeIP-4; ImPo; NAEL-1; NoSic; OAEL-1; OxAEP-1; PoE; PoEL-2; SCGP *Fr.* Sonnets.

Devouring time blunt thou the Lyons pawes. Shakespeare. See Sonnet 19.

Devout Fits. Donne. ESCV *Fr.* Holy Sonnets.
  ("Oh, to vex me, two contraries meet in one.") ChIV-2

Devout Lover, A. Thomas Randolph. HoPM; OBEV

Dew. Jennifer Maiden. CBAP

Dew clear and bright. Tune: "Phoenix Hairpin"—Crab Apple. Ku T'ai-ch'ing, *Chinese.* SuSp, *tr. by* Irving Y. Lo

Dew drops in the morning. Today Will Pass. Lemn Sissay. NBrP

Dew is on the grasses, dear, The. Youth. Georgia Douglas Johnson. NAAAL

Dew it trembles on the thorn, The. Silent Love. John Clare. Ro

Dew of the rouge-flower, The. Haiku. Chiyojo, *Japanese.* PBWP, *tr. by* R. H. Blyth

Dew on a Dusty Heart. Jean Starr Untermeyer. MoAmPo

Dew on roses. Ma Chih-yüan. *Fr.* Three Poems to the tune "Lo-mei Feng." CoBLCP, *tr. by* Jonathan Chaves

Dew on the garlic, The. Dew on the Young Garlic Leaves. T'ien Hung, *Chinese.* OHMPC, *tr. by* Kenneth Rexroth

Dew on the leek. *Unknown, Chinese.* CoBCP, *tr. by* Burton Watson

Dew on the secret orchid. The Grave of Little Su. Li Ho, *Chinese.* PLT, *tr. by* A. C. Graham

Dew on the Young Garlic Leaves. T'ien Hung, *Chinese.* OHMPC, *tr. by* Kenneth Rexroth

Dew-rinsed. Cicadas. Xue Tao, *Chinese.* APo, *tr. by* Jeanne Larsen

Dew sate on *Julia's* haire. Upon Julia's Haire Fill'd with Dew. Robert Herrick. PBRV

Dew, the rain and moonlight, The. A Net to Snare the Moonlight. Vachel Lindsay. PoLf

Dew was falling fast, the stars began to blink, The. Pet Lamb, The; A Pastoral. Wordsworth. OxBChV

Dewdrops sob in the roof-gutters, The. The Last Day. Wen I-to, *Chinese.* ChiPo, *tr. by* Kai-yu Hsu

Dews of summer night[e] did fall[e], The. Cumnor Hall. William Julius Mickle. OxBB

Dewy the earth with tears. Epitaph for His Niece, Sophia. Paul the Deacon, *Latin*. MLL, *tr. by* Helen Waddell

Dexter Gordon's tenor sax. February in Sydney. Yusef Komunyakaa. NAAAL

Dey is times in life when Nature. When de Co'n Pone's Hot. Paul Laurence Dunbar. AAP

Dey tell me Joe Turner he done come. Joe Turner Blues. *Unknown*. AS

Dey want me to help score d ambush. (LL) Badman of the Guest Professor. Ishmael Reed. SSLK

Dey was hard times jes 'fo' Christmas round our neighborhood one year. An Indignation Dinner. James David Corrothers. NAAAL

Dey was talkin' in de cabin, dey was talkin' in de hall. When Dey 'Listed Colored Soldiers. Paul Laurence Dunbar. BPo; CBCWP

Dey's a so't o' threatenin' feelin' in de blowin' of de breeze. Soliloquy of a Turkey. Paul Laurence Dunbar. BPo

Dharma is like an Avocado!, The. Avocado. Gary Snyder. PmAP

Diagnosis of our hist'ry proves, A. "Orpheus C. Kerr." *Fr.* The Rejected "National Hymns." OBAL

Diakka, The. Gerald Massey. NOBVV

Dial, The. Thomas Cole. APN-1

Dial Call. Christopher Darlington Morley. NBLV

Dial is dark, 'tis but half-past one, The. A Rhyme of the Sun-Dial. William Bell Scott. NOBVV

Dial life— / And Him, The. (LL) Clock stopped, A. Emily Dickinson. APN-2; AmPP; NAAL-1; NAAL-3; PAR; PoEL-5

Dial Tone, The. Howard Nemerov. NYBP

Dialectic. Victor Serge, *Russian*. AF, *tr. by* James Brook

Dialectical Poem #1. Campbell McGrath. WeT

Dialectics. Edvard Kocbek, *Slovenian*. PoSu, *tr. by* Michael Scammell *and* Veno Taufer; CEEP, *tr. by* Veno Taufer *and* Michael Scammell

Dialogue, The. Vladimir Burich, *Russian*. TCRP, *tr. by* Katya Olmstead

Dialogue, A. Elizabeth Carter. CABP; ECWP

("I shall snap off my chains and fly freely away.") (LL) CABP

Dialogue. Leah Goldberg, *Hebrew*. MHP, *tr. by* Ruth Finer Mintz

Dialogue, A. George Herbert. FSCP; GeHe; NOSC; OBEV

Dialogue. Norkiko Ibaragi, *Japanese*. WPJ, *tr. by* Kenneth Rexroth *and* Ikuko Atsumi

Dialogue, A. David Ignatow. NNaP

Dialogue. Richard Lovelace. CavPo

Dialogue. James McAuley. BMAP

Dialogue, A. Lizelia Augusta Jenkins Moorer. CBWP-3

Dialogue. Howard Nemerov. NYBP

Dialogue. Adrienne Rich. TAP

Dialogue, A. Swinburne. PoEL-5

Dialogue—2 Dollmakers. Gregory Corso. NeAP

Dialogue after Enjoyment. Abraham Cowley. BoLoP

Dialogue between a Squeamish Cotting Mechanic and His Sluttish Wife, in the Kitchen. Edward Ward. NOEC *Fr.* Nuptial Dialogues.

Dialogue between Araphil and Castara, A. William Habington. BeJo *Fr.* Castara.

Dialogue, between Crab and Gillian. Thomas D'Urfey. NOEC *Fr.* The Bath; or, The Western Lass.

Dialogue between Death and Youth, A. *Unknown*. NoSic

Dialogue between Father and Daughter. Robert Browning. OBCoV

Dialogue between Melancholy and Mirth, A. Margaret Lucas Cavendish, Duchess of Newcastle. BWW

Thoughts Several Be.

Dialogue between Old England and New, A. Anne Bradstreet.

New England. KTR

Old England. KTR

Dialogue between the Head and Heart, A. Gavin Ewart. CBLP

Dialogue Between The Resolved Soul and Created Pleasure, A. Andrew Marvell. ESCV; FSCP; GeHe; MeLP; OAEL-1; SeCP

Dialogue between the Soul and [the] Body, A. Andrew Marvell. ESCV; GeHe; HAP; InPS-3; MeLP; NAEL-1; OAEL-1; OxAEP-1; PoEL-2; SeCP; SoSe-8; TFi

(Dialogue Between the Soul and Body, A.) FMP; FSCP; NoP-4

("O who shall from this Dungeon raise.") FMP; FSCP

Dialogue between Thyrsis and Dorinda, A. Andrew Marvell. SeCP

Dialogue betwixt God and the Soul, A. Sir Henry Wotton. MeLP; PeECV

Dialogue betwixt Man, and Nature, A. Margaret Lucas Cavendish, Duchess of Newcastle. PBRV

Dialogue betwixt the Body and the Mind, A. Margaret Lucas Cavendish, Duchess of Newcastle. PEW

Dialogue betwixt Time and a Pilgrim[e], A. Aurelian Townshend. NOBE; OAEL-1; PoEL-2; SeCP

Dialogue in Imitation of that between Horace and Lydia, A. Horace, *Latin*. OBCVT, *tr. by Unknown*

Dialogue in Winter. Tomas Venclova, *Lithuanian*. CEEP, *tr. by* David McDuff

Dialogue: Lover and Lady. Ciullo d'Alcamo, *Italian*. AWP, *tr. by* D. G. Rossetti

Dialogue of Self and Soul, A. W. B. Yeats. CMoP; FaBoMo; LiTM; MoBrPo; NAEL-2; NoAM; PoE

"Living man is blind and drinks his drop, A." RaBo

Dialogue on Finding Someplace to Live. Lori Storie-Pahlitzsch. LoHo

Diameter of the bomb was thirty centimeters, The. Yehuda Amichai, *Hebrew*. PoSu, *tr. by* Bernhard Frank

Diamond Cut Diamond. Ewart Milne. FaBoCh; PC

Diamond of Character, The. Kabita Sinha, *Bengali*. OMIP, *tr. by* Swapna Mitra *and* Carolyne Wright

Diamonds are forever so I gave you quartz. The Hardness Scale. Joyce Peseroff. TRP

Diamonds are mined. . . oil is discovered. A Poem (for Langston Hughes). Nikki Giovanni. SSLK

Dian, Isis, Artemis, whate'er thy name. Walter James Turner. *Fr.* The Seven Days of the Sun. OBMV

Dian, that fain would cheer her friend the Night. Sonnet 97. Sir Philip Sidney. *Fr.* Astrophil and Stella. AAS; SiPS

Diana. Henry Constable.

"Dear to my soul! then leave me not forsaken!" AAS; CBLP

"Hope, like the hyaena [*or* hyena], coming to be old." EnLoPo; SCGP; Son

"Miracle of the world, I never will deny." SCGP

Of his Mistress, upon Occasion of her Walking in a Garden. OBGa

Resolved to Love. Son

"Whilst Ec[c]ho cries [*or* cryes], 'What shall become of me[e]?'." AAS

Diana guardeth our estate. Hymn to Diana. Catullus. AWP, *tr. by* Richard Claverhouse Jebb *Fr.* Carmina.

Diana was a white girl. What abou' de Law? Adam Small, *Afrikaans*. PeSAV, *tr. by* Carrol Lasker

Diana's Hunting-Song. Dryden. NOBE *Fr.* The Secular Masque. NAEL-1; OxAEP-1; PoE; PoEL-3; SCGP

Diaphenia like the daffadowndilly. Henry Constable. CH; GLoP; GTBS-P; NOBE; PoEL-2

Diary, The. Goethe, *German*. STV, *tr. by* John Frederick Nims

Diary. David Wagoner. CoAP

Diary. Mary Wilson. Spl

Diary: How to Improve the World (You Will Only Make Matters Worse). John Cage.

Abundance. APSN

"Boddhisattva Doctrine: Enter / Nirvana only when all beings, sentient." APSN

"Daily warmth we, The." APSN

"Get it, / she said, so it's unknown which parent." APSN

"Hearing of past actions." APSN

"Lazy dog (a bomb containing ten), The." APSN

"LET'S CALL IT THE / COLLECTIVE CONSCIOUSNESS (WE'VE GOT." APSN

"Mother wrote to say: 'Stay / in Europe. Soak up as much beauty as you'." APSN

"Since the / Spirit's omnipresent, there's a difference." APSN

"The / children have a society of their own." APSN

"They dance the world as." APSN

"To / know whether or not art is contemporary." APSN

"We've / poisoned our food, polluted our air." APSN

Diary of a Church Mouse. John Betjeman. OxBTC

Diary of an Old Soul. George Macdonald. TrCP

Diary of Francis Kilvert, The. *Unknown*.

"Little health, A." FP

Diary of the Waning Moon, The. Abutsu the Nun [*or* Abutsu-Ni], *Japanese*.

"Shore wind is cold on my travel clothes, The." PBWP, *tr. by* Edwin O. Reischauer

Diary Page 69. Reiner Kunze, *German*. CEEP, *tr. by* Lori Fisher

Diary without Dates, A. Chio Nakamura, *Japanese*. WPJ, *tr. by* Kenneth Rexroth *and* Ikuko Atsumi

Diatribe Against the Dead. Angel González, *Spanish*. VCWP, *tr. by* Steven Ford Brown *and* Revuelta Gutierrez

Diatribe of the Kite, The. Norman Dubie. NAmP90

Dic Siôn Dafydd. Thomas Jacob Thomas, *Welsh*. OBWVE, *tr. by* H. Idris Bell

Dick, a Maggot. Jonathan Swift. NBLV

Dick and Colin at the Salmon Nets. Naomi Mitchison. WPN

Dick and Jane. Judith Kroll. AmPA

Dick Briggs a wealthy farmer's son. Dick Briggs from Australia. Charles Robert Thatcher. NOBAu

Dick Hairbrain Learns the Social Graces. John Trumbull. *Fr.* The Progress of Dulness. AmPP

Dick is the one with the weenie. Dick and Jane. Judith Kroll. AmPA

Dick o' the Cow. *Unknown.* ESPB; IBB; OxBB

Dick Tracy chases Eighty-Eight Keys. Clinton. Sterling Plumpp. BkSV *Fr.* Clinton.

Dick Tracy's yellow Hat and Blacksuit. Peter Orlovsky. BB

Dick Turpin and Black Bess. *Unknown.* AmFP

Dickensian borough of Coketown, The. Limerick. Martin Fagg. PeLi

Dickery Dean. Dennis Lee. TLR

Dickery, dickery, dare. (LL) Dickery [or dickory], dickery [or dickory], dare. Mother Goose. OxNR; ReMoGo

Dickinson. Annie Finch. FFC

Dicky-Birds. Natalie Joan. BoTP

"Dictates of nature prove school-knowledge weak, The." Repentance. George Alexander Stevens. NOEC

Dictators, The. Pablo Neruda, *Spanish.* AF, *tr. by* Robert Bly

Dictionary definition of change, The. The Age of Plastic. John Forbes. BMAP

Did a wind come just as you got up or were. Dysraphism. Charles Bernstein. FTOS

Did all the lets and bars appear. The March into Virginia. Herman Melville. CBCWP; ColAP; HAP; ImPo; NAAL-1; NAAL-3; NCAP; NoP-4; PoE; PoPoPo; TAP

Did any seer of ancient time forbode. The Steam Threshing-Machine. Charles Tennyson Turner. OBNC

Did but the law appoint us one. A Popular Functionary. Charles Dibdin. NOEC

Did he meet Lud at the Fleet Gate? did count the top David Jones. EBEV *Fr.* The Anathemata.

Did he strike soundings off Vecta Insula? Angle-Land. David Jones. NoAM *Fr.* The Anathemata.

Did I boast of liberty? Sonnet 45. Mary Sidney, Countess of Montgomery Wroth. LW; PEW *Fr.* Urania.

Did I create that sky? Yes, for, if it was. Jack Kerouac. CLPP *Fr.* The Scripture of the Golden Eternity.

Did I evah tell you, Sonny. Uncle Jimmie's Yarn. Priscilla Jane Thompson. CBWP-2

Did I ever tell you that Mrs. McCave. Too Many Daves. "Dr. Seuss." OBCA

Did I ever think. Ono no Takamura. AWP, *tr. by* Arthur Waley *Fr.* Kokin Shu.

Did I follow Truth wherever she led. Herman Altman. Edgar Lee Masters. OxBA *Fr.* Spoon River Anthology.

Did I hear it half in a doze. Tennyson. *Fr.* Maud [A Monodrama]. EnVR

Did I, my lines intend for public[k] view. The Introduction. Anne Finch, Countess of Winchilsea. BWW; NAEL-1; NALW; NoP-4; WPOW

Did I not say we grow old. Rufinus, *Greek.* GrAn, *tr. by* Alan Marshfield

Did I not tell you, my soul, "By Cypris, you will be caught." Meleager. HePo, *tr. by* Barbara Hughes Fowler *Fr.* I'll Twine White Violets. NIP-4, *tr. by* Goldwin Smith

Did I step on your train? Before. May Probyn. VWP

Did it go wrong just about a hundred. Counter-Revolution. W. H. Oliver. PeNZ

Did it not tremble with the strings! Edgar Allan Poe. *See* Introduction: "Romance, who loves to nod and sing."

Did ivver ye see the like o' that? Pride. Violet Jacob. OxBS

Did John's Music Kill Him? Alfred B. Spellman. NAAAL; SeSe

Did love him faithfully. (LL) Uncle Ananias. Edwin Arlington Robinson. MoAmPo; NIP-4

Did my father curse his father for his lust I wonder. The Young Man Thinks of Sons. Ronald Allison Kells Mason. PeNZ

Did my hand ever touch your hair? Birth. Takahashi Shinkichi, *Japanese.* OxBM, *tr. by* Geoffrey Bownas *and* Anthony Thwaite

Did Not. Thomas Moore. BoLoP; GLoP; PeLV

(Quantum Est Quod Desit.) APAD; EnLoPo

Did not the heavenly rhetoric of thine eye. The Heavenly Rhetoric. Shakespeare. ImPo; Son *Fr.* Love's Labour's Lost.

Did not true love disdain to own. On the Infrequency of Celia's Letters. William Hammond. CBLP

Did Ophelia ask Hamlet to bed? Limerick. A. Cinna. PeLi

Did Our Best Moment last. Emily Dickinson. NOBA

Did Shriner die or make it to New York? A Disappearance in West Cedar Street. Louis Edward Sissman. TwCP

Did / Somebody / Die? (LL) World War II. Langston Hughes. HCAP; PoPoPo

Did somebody give you a pat on the back? Pass. Edmund Vance Cooke. PWR

Did Someone Say "Babies"? Ogden Nash. OxBM

Did someone say that there would be an end. All Souls. May Sarton. CrSp; IMW

Did soon draw in again [or agen]. (LL) Upon Her Feet. Robert Herrick. BeJo; CBLP; CaPo; OxBSP; PoE

Did summon us in his delightful round. Wordsworth. *See* Fair seed time had my soul, and I grew up.

Did the Harebell loose her girdle. Emily Dickinson. FaBoVe; NCAP

Did the people of Nara[1]. In Nara (two poems). Mori Ōgai, *Japanese.* MJT, *tr. by* Makoto Ueda

Did the people of Viet Nam [use lanterns of stone?]. What Were They Like? Denise Levertov. HeIP-4; NIP-4; OBWP; SAGP; VGW; WPE

Did their Catullus walk that way? (LL) The Scholars. W. B. Yeats. APAD; CMoP; NoP-4; OAEL-2; PoA

"Did they dare, did they dare, to slay Owen Roe O'Neil?" Lament for the Death of Eoghan Ruadh O'Neill. Thomas Osborne Davis. NOIV

Did This Happen to Your Mother? Did Your Sister Throw Up a Lot? Alice Walker. ISC

Did those twelve fairies curse the gal at birth? The Girl Without a Sex. Ho Xuan Huong, *Vietnamese.* AVP, *tr. by* Huỳnh Sanh Thông

Did we not underwrite them when we were born? (LL) Elegy for Minor Poets. Louis MacNeice. CABP; PNI

Did ye ever hear o guid Earl o Bran. Earl Brand. *Unknown.* ESPB

Did ye ever sleep at the foot o' the bed. Sleepin' at the Foot o' the Bed. Luther Patrick. BLPA

Did Ye See Me? Robert Garioch. OBCoV

Did you ask dulcet rhymes from me? To a Certain Civilian. Walt Whitman. CBCWP

"Did You Call Me, Father?" Mary E. Tucker. CBWP-1

Did you eever iver ever. Hand-clapping Rhyme. *Unknown.* NTCP

Did you eever, iver, over. *Unknown.* KaS

Did You Ever, Ever, Ever. *Unknown.* AS

Did you ever have a chipmunk for a friend? Jessie Orton Jones. CTV *Fr.* (XII from Secrets).

Did you ever hear about Cocaine Lil? Cocaine Lil [and Morphine Sue]. *Unknown.* AS; CBNP; OxBoLi; RB

Did You Ever Hear an English Sparrow Sing? Bertha Johnston. BLPA

Did you ever hear of Captain Wattle? Captain Wattle and Miss Roe. Charles Dibdin. OxBoLi

Did you ever hear of Editor Whedon. Daisy Fraser. Edgar Lee Masters. CMoP; HAP; PoE *Fr.* Spoon River Anthology.

Did you ever hear the story 'bout Willy the Weeper? Willy the Weeper. *Unknown.* AS

Did you ever make some small success. You Too. Edmund Vance Cooke. PWR

Did you ever see an alligator. Arlo Will. Edgar Lee Masters. PBMP *Fr.* Spoon River Anthology.

Did you ever see such a thing in your life, / As three blind mice? [or Three blind mice]. (LL) Three blind mice, see how they run! Mother Goose. LB; OxNR; ReMoGo

Did you ever see the day. On the Prince's Death, to the King. Sir Robert Ayton. NOSC

Did you ever sit and ponder, sit and wonder, sit and think. Life's a Funny Proposition after All. George M. Cohan. PoLF

Did you ever think as the hearse rolls by. The Hearse Song. *Unknown.* AS

Did you go at all to Chicago? The Stockyard. Sir John Collings Squire. OxBTC

Did you hear of the curate who mounted his mare. The Priest and the Mulberry-Tree. Thomas Love Peacock. BoTP; OxAEP-2 *Fr.* Crotchet Castle.

Did you know. Realization. Günter Kunert, *German.* CEEP, *tr. by* Michael Hamburger

Did you love well what very soon you left? Conclusion. Marilyn Hacker. NoAM; RA *Fr.* The Cook.

Did you read in the seabooks of the oldfashioned frigate-fight? Walt Whitman. PAR *Fr.* Song of Myself.

Did you see him go by here tonight? The Stranger. Aldo Palazzeschi, *Italian.* PFTM, *tr. by* Jerome Rothenberg

Did you see in the shadowy woods. An Event Which Makes No News. Kazue Shinkawa, *Japanese.* WPJ, *tr. by* Kenneth Rexroth *and* Ikuko Atsumi

Did you see me walking by the Buick Repairs? Song. Frank O'Hara. TTTS

Did you see my wife, did you see, did you see. *Unknown.* OxNR

Did you tackle that trouble that came [your way]. How Did You Die? Edmund Vance Cooke. BLPA; CTV; PWR

Did you take me because you loved me? Kenneth Rexroth. APSN *Fr.* The Love Poems of Marichiko.

Did you think all that stuff you gave me. Materialism. R. P. Dickey. Poetr

Did you waste his time. Brief Novel (3). Eric Mottram. NBrP

Didactic Piece. Louise Bogan. NoAM

Didactic Sonnet. Melvin Walker La Follette. PoA

Diddie Wa Diddie. "Blind" Blake. CBNP

Diddle, diddle, dumpling, my son John. (LL) Diddle, diddle, dumpling, my son John. Mother Goose. BoTP; LB; OxNR; ReMoGo

Diddle, diddle, dumpling, my son John. Mother Goose. BoTP; LB; OxNR; ReMoGo

Diddlety, diddlety, dumpty. (LL) Diddlety, diddlety, dumpty. Mother Goose. LB; OxNR

Didn't a certain woman. Tanka. Nakajō Fumiko, *Japanese.* MJT, tr. by Makoto Ueda

Didn't acknowledge receipt. The Suicide. Joyce Carol Oates. Poetsp

Didn't Chet Baker know. Speed Ball. Yusef Komunyakaa. SeSe

Didn't He Ramble. James Simmons. PNI

Didn't I say last night it will snow? Breakfast. Ljubomir Simovic, *Serbo-Croatian.* HSix, tr. by Charles Simic

Didn't like jazz, he once claimed. William Carlos Williams. Cornelius Eady. GT

Didn't my Lord Deliver Daniel. *Unknown.* AH; APN-2; NAAAL ("An' why not every man?") (LL) NAAAL

Didn't Sappho say her guts clutched up like this? Sources. Marilyn Hacker. DeD *Fr.* Love, Death and the Changing of the Seasons.

Didn't you say we should trace. Before Chilembwe Tree. Jack A. Mapanje. PBMAP

Dido among the Shades. Virgil. *See* Dido in the Elysian Fields.

Dido by Night. Virgil. OBVE, tr. by Henry Howard, Earl of Surrey *Fr.* The Aeneid [or Eneados, Aeneis].

Dido in the Elysian Fields. Virgil, *Latin.* OBCVT, tr. by John Dryden *Fr.* The Aeneid [or Eneados, Aeneis].
(Dido among the Shades.)

Dido My Dear, Alas, Is Dead. Edmund Spenser. *Fr.* November. PoEL-1 *Fr.* The Shepheardes [or Shepeards or Shepherd's] Calender.

Dido: Swarming. Kathleen Spivack. PoA

Dido to Her Sister Anna. Virgil. OBVE, tr. by Henry Howard, Earl of Surrey *Fr.* The Aeneid [or Eneados, Aeneis].

Dido's death. Virgil, *Latin.* OBCVT, tr. by Sir Richard Fanshawe

Dido's farewell. Ovid. OBCVT, tr. by George Turberville *Fr.* The Heroides.

Dido's last night. Virgil, *Latin.* OBCVT, tr. by John Dryden

Dido's reproaches. Virgil, *Latin.*
"Whyles in this sorte he dyd hys tale pronounce." OBCVT, tr. by Henry Howard, Earl of Surrey

Dido's Suicide. Virgil. OBVE, tr. by Gawin Douglas *Fr.* The Aeneid [or Eneados, Aeneis].

Didst thou not find the place inspired [or inspir'd]. Upon My Lady Carlisle's [or Carlile's] Walking in Hampton Court Garden. Sir John Suckling. BeJo; CABP; CaPo; CavPo; NoP-4

Didyme waved an olive branch at me. Asclepiades, *Greek.* InMo, tr. by Sam Hamill

Didyme waved her wand at me. Asclepiades, *Greek.* GrAn; PGA, tr. by Kenneth Rexroth

Die. Novica Tadic, *Serbo-Croatian.* HSix, tr. by Charles Simic

Die blauen Veilchen der Äugelein. Heinrich Heine, *German.* AWP, tr. by James Thomson

Die, die my shriek, you will not be heard. Die My Shriek. Aaron Kushniroff, *Yiddish.* TrJP, tr. by Joseph Leftwich

Die, dying clasped [or clasp'd] in his embrace. (LL) Fatima. Tennyson. GBL; UnPo

Die is cast, and we must part, The. The Parting. Josephine D. Henderson Heard. CBWP-4

Die is cast, come weal, come woe, The. Marriage. Mary Weston Fordham. CBWP-2

Die Lotusblume ängstigt. Heinrich Heine, *German.* AWP, tr. by James Thomson

Die Musik, An. David Malouf. CBAP

Die My Shriek. Aaron Kushniroff, *Yiddish.* TrJP, tr. by Joseph Leftwich

DiE not before thy day, poor man condemned. *Unknown.* NoSic

Die oftener—Not so vitally. (LL) Nature—sometimes sears a Sapling. Emily Dickinson. NAAL-1; NAAL-3

Die, pussy, die. *Unknown.* OxNR

Die single, and thine image dies with thee. (LL) Sonnet 3. Shakespeare. ImPo; NAEL-1; NoP-4; SCGP

Die soon. (LL) We real cool. We. Gwendolyn Brooks. KaS; LiLi; NoP-4

Die while you're alive. Bunan, *Japanese.* EnlH, tr. by Stephen Mitchell

Die, wild country, like the eaglehawk. Australia 1970. Judith Wright. CBAP; NoAM

Died. . . . Elizabeth Barrett Browning. NOBVV

Died from fatigue, three laundresses together all. *Unknown.* FaBoEE

Died, Sir Charles Wetherell's laundress, honest Sue. *Unknown.* FaBoEE

Diehard. Judith Moffett. PoA

Diehards, The. Ruth Pitter. OBGa

Diella. Richard Lynche.
"But thou my deere sweet-sounding lute be still." AAS
Soon as the Azure-colored Gates. Son
What Sugared Terms. Son

Dieppe, *author's tr. of his* Dieppe ("Encore le dernier reflux"). Samuel Beckett. NOIV

Dies. (LL) Asleep, My Love? Shakespeare. CTC; EBEvV

Dies Irae. Thomas Babington Macaulay, 1st Baron Macaulay. ChIV-2

Dies Irae. Thomas of Celano, *Latin.* AWP; TIRV, tr. by Richard Crashaw (Day of Judgment, The.) OBVE

Diesel fumes rise. Dinner on the Miami River. Greg Pape. PBCAP

Diesel translator / Prose poem combine. Auction; Saturday 2:00. Donald D. Olsen. EC2

Diesel trucks past the Scrovegni chapel. Ian Wedde. PeNZ *Fr.* Earthly: Sonnets for Carlos.

Diet, The. Maureen Burge. BrRo

Dieter bit his sealskin mitts, and pulled. Bush Navigator: The Last Morning of Hands. Peggy Shumaker. PBCAP

Dieu Qu'il la Fait. Charles, Duc d' Orléans, *French.* AWP, tr. by Ezra Pound

Difference. Mark Doty. BAP-94

Difference, The. Rowland Howard. CTV

Difference. T. Harri Jones. OBWVE

Difference, The. Stoddard King. OBAL

Difference, The. Tadhg Dall O'Huiginn, *Irish.* BIrV, tr. by Robin Flower

Difference Between a King and a Tyrant, The. Timothy Kendall. NoSic

Difference between Despair, The. Emily Dickinson. NAAL-1; NAAL-3

Difference Between Pepsi and Coke, The. David Lehman. PmAP

Difference between poetry and rhetoric, The. Power. Audre Lorde. GLP; NoAM

Difference between those / coming, The. The Lives of Thomas—Episodes and Prayers. John High. PT

Difference between you and me, The. Half-Breed. Cherríe Moraga. UnSA

Difference of Opinion with Lygdamus. Ezra Pound. MeMAP *Fr.* Homage to Sextus Propertius.

Difference of Zoos, A. Gregory Corso. VGW

Difference to him!, The. (LL) He Lived amidst th' Untrodden Ways. Hartley Coleridge. NOBL; PFE; PeLV; UV

Difference to me!, The. (LL) Jacob. Phoebe Cary. APAD; APN-2; OBAL; PAR

Difference to me. (LL) Song: "She dwelt among the untrodden ways." Wordsworth. AWP; BLPA; BoLoP; EBEvV; EnLoPo; GTBS-P; HAP; HeIP-4; IMW; ImPo; NIP-4; NOBRP; OxAEP-2; OxBSP; PBMP; PWR; Poetr; Ro; UV; UnPo; WeW-3

Differences between rich and poor, king and queen. Rank. Lincoln Kirstein. FaBoA; OBWP

Different. Clere Parsons. APAD; FaBoTw

Different Cereal, A. John Yau. PT

Different Dimensions. Ikuko Atsumi, *Japanese.* WPJ, tr. by Kenneth Rexroth *and* Ikuko Atsumi

Different Horizon. Aimé Césaire, *French.* VCWP, tr. by Clayton Eshleman *and* Annette Smith

Different Image, A. Dudley Randall. BPo; TAP

Different Love Poem / We Need a Change, A. Ntozake Shange. UnSA *Fr.* Okra to Greens /.

Different Poem, A. Onésima Silveira. PBMAP

Different task remains, A; the secret paths. Poetic Genius. Mark Akenside. NOEC *Fr.* The Pleasures of Imagination.

Difficult Adjustment, A. Lauris Edmond. FaBoWP

Difficult Land, The. Edwin Muir. FaBoTC

Difficult Rhyme, A. Mother Goose. ReMoGo

Difficulties of Falling Asleep. Zsuzsa Rakovszky, *Hungarian.* CEEP, tr. by Barbar Howes *and* Margot Archer

Difficulties, the impossibilities. The. Robert Lowell. HCAP *Fr.* Mexico.

Difficulty to think at the end of day, The. A Rabbit Is King of the Ghosts. Wallace Stevens. NoAM; PBMP; TTTS

Difficulty was, it was, The. In the Beginning Was a Word. Robert Graves. PoA

Diffugere nives, redeunt iam gramina campis. Horace, *Latin.* OBCVT, tr. by Jim McCulloch

Dig, The. Lynn Emanuel. PUP-18

Dig and Be Dug In Return. Langston Hughes. *See* Motto.

Dig in. Wicker throne. Scratch that. Keep moving. Dressd to kill. Burgundy jumpsuit. Ron Silliman. *See* Not this. / What then?

Dig My Grave. *Unknown.* AmFP

Digdog. Ruth Pitter. WPN

Digenis is wrestling for his soul, earth trembles at his struggle. The Death of Digenis. *Unknown, Greek.* GrIP, *tr. by* Richard Stoneman

Digestive System, The. Sir Richard Blackmore. ECEV *Fr.* Creation.

Diggers, The. W. S. Merwin. CBNP; SPE

Digger's Song, The. Barcroft Henry Boake. NOBAu

Diggers' Song, The. *Unknown.* PBRV

Digger's Song, The. Gerrard Winstanley. FaBoPV; NOSC

Digging. Seamus Heaney. BIrV; CIP-2; IIP; InPS-3; NAEL-2; NoP-4; SAGP; TwCP

Digging. Edward Thomas. GaP; MoBrPo; OxBTC

Digging and building tire men out. Poem of the Western Fields. Wu Wei-yeh, *Chinese.* CoBLCP, *tr. by* Jonathan Chaves

Digging deep in the garden. Planting Roses. Phillis Levin. FFC

Digging earth for puddles, she would wake stranded. Steps. Roberta Hill Whiteman. VoR

Digging for China. Richard Wilbur. ImGa; TwCP

Digging for Indians. Gary Gildner. AmPA; PBCAP

Digging in the Streets of Gold. Barry Seiler. UnSA

Digging Sing, A. *Unknown.* FaBoVe

Digging / toward a Lenten extreme. Year. Milo De Angelis, *Italian.* NeIt, *tr. by* Lawrence Venuti

Digging was always my worst work. Grandfather in the Garden. Robert Minhinnick. OBGa

Diggins-Oh, The. *Unknown.* NOBAu

Dignity of Labor, The. Robert Bersohn. NBLV

Dignity of room, the value of rareness, The. (LL) November Surf. Robinson Jeffers. NAAL-2; OxBA

Digression, A. Richard Wilbur. BAP-94

Dilemma. Patricia Beer. OxBC

Dilemma. David Ignatow. VGW

Dilemma, The. Sir John Collings Squire. OBCoV; PoFWW

Dilemma, The. Anna Wickham. WPN

Dilemma of the Elm. Genevieve Taggard. MoAmPo

Diligent in the burnt fields above the sea. Find. Josephine Miles. WPE

Dillar, a dollar, A. Ten O'Clock Scholar, [The]. Mother Goose. ACTP; LB; OxNR; ReMoGo

Dilly Dilly. *Unknown.* OxNR

Dilly Dilly Piccalilli. Clyde Watson. NTCP

Dim afternoon December afternoon. December. Robert Francis. LCAP-2

Dim apparition thou!—and bitter in my tear. (LL) Eyam. Anna Seward. ECWP

Dim, as the borrow'd beams of moon and stars. Reason and Religion. Dryden. NOSC; OAEL-1 *Fr.* Religio Laici.

Dim, as the borrowed beams of moon and stars. Religio Laici. Dryden.

Dim boy claps because the others clap, The. The Freaks at Spurgin Road Field. Richard Hugo. LCAP-2; NoAM; SoSe-8

Dim boy claps because the others clap, The. (LL) The Freaks at Spurgin Road Field. Richard Hugo. LCAP-2; NoAM; SoSe-8

Dim, gradual thinning of the shapeless gloom. The Troops. Siegfried Sassoon. CMoP; PeFWW

Dim grey wastes of the silent hills. Helen Waddell. MLL

Dim light of daybreak now. Dawn Wail for the Dead. Kath Walker. BMAP; CBAP

Dim the light in your faces: be passionless in the room. The Image. Richard Hughes. OBMV

Dim vales—and shadowy floods. Fairyland [*or* Fairy-Land]. Edgar Allan Poe. APN-1; NAAL-1; NAAL-3

Dim wind pillared the hills: stiller than mist it seemed. Sunrise Trumpets. Joseph Auslander. TrJP

Dime for Jesus who had died for men, A. (LL) Karma. Edwin Arlington Robinson. AmPP; CMoP; FP; HeIP-4; MoAmPo; TrCP

Dime Found in the Snow, A. James Tate. WeT

Dime store. The goldfish swam in the murky. Kite. Laura Jensen. LCAP-2

Dimensions. Laura Riding Jackson. FuPo

Dimly remembering how your life made. Remembering Aunt Helen. Vassar Miller. WeT

Dimly seen but off-center. Wood irons in the box. Rhymes with Monk. Clark Coolidge. MoNo

Dimme eyes, deaf ears, cold stomach shew. Verses Found in Thomas Dudley's Pocket after His Death. Thomas Dudley. SCAP

Dimmed Observation. Abba Kovner, *Hebrew.* IP, *tr. by* Warren Bargad *and* Stanley F. Chyet

Dimpled Cloud, A. Frederick Seidel. FYAP

Dimpling its tranquil surface. (LL) From Beachy Head. Charlotte Smith. NOBRP; NoP-4

Dimply damsel, sweetly smiling. Ode: To Miss Margaret Pulteney. Ambrose Philips. OxAEP-1; Poetr; UV

Din of work is subdued, The. Lullaby. W. H. Auden. FaBoMo; GLP; NoAM

Din quiets. I step onto the boards, The. Hamlet. Boris Pasternak, *Russian.* GI, *tr. by* Nina Kossman

Dinah Kneading Dough. Paul Laurence Dunbar. NAAAL

Dinah Shore sings of America. Racial Memories. Elizabeth Mische John. LoHo

Dined with Auden. He'd been at Milwaukee. Auden at Milwaukee. Stephen Spender. AiP

Diners in the Kitchen, The. James Whitcomb Riley. CTAV; OBAL

Ding dang, bell rang. *Unknown.* OxNR

Ding ding ding! Esanzo. Antoine-Roger Bolamba, *French.* NegPo, *tr. by* Ellen Conroy Kennedy

Ding Dong. Arthur Clement Hilton. BXAP

Ding-Dong! *Unknown.* BoTP

Ding, dong, bell. (LL) Ariel's Song: "Full fathom [*or* fadom] five thy father lies." Shakespeare. CH; CTC; EBEvV; GTBS-P; NAEL-1; NoSic; OAEL-1; OBEV; PoEL-2; SCGP; TFi

Ding, dong, bell, / Pussy's in the well. Mother Goose. OxNR; ReMoGo ("But caught the mice in his father's barn.") (LL) LB

Ding dong bell! Pussy's in the well! *Unknown.* ACTP

Ding-Donging. Laura Riding Jackson. NoP-4

Dingle dingle doosey. *Unknown.* OxNR

Dingty diddlety. Mother Goose. FaBoVe; OxNR

Dingy donkey, formal and unchanged, A. A Fable. John Hookham Frere. UV

Dining Out. Judith Beveridge. BMAP

Dining-Room Tea. Rupert Brooke. MoBrPo

Dinkey-Bird, The. Eugene Field. FPC

Dink's Song. *Unknown.* OxBoLi

Dinky. Theodore Roethke. OBAL; OBCA

Dinky Di. *Unknown.* NOBAu

Dinner at Le Caprice. Rachel Wetzsteon. RA

Dinner at the Mongoloid's. Larry Rubin. MT

Dinner for the Devil. Ben Jonson. NOSC *Fr.* The Gypsies Metamorphosed.

Dinner for thirty, A. A Certain Dinner For Thirty. Martial, *Latin.* OBCVT, *tr. by* Philip Murray

Dinner Guest: Me. Langston Hughes. BPo; LTA; SSLK

Dinner on the Miami River. Greg Pape. PBCAP

Dinner Party 1940. Philip Sherlock. PBCV

"Dinner-time?" said Gilbert White. Edmund Clerihew Bentley. OBCoV *Fr.* Clerihews.

Dinner was over, the tablecloth gone, The. A Poem on the Supposition of the Book Having Been Published and Read. Elizabeth Hands. ECWP; WoRP

Dino. Michael Lassell. GLP *Fr.* Times Square Poems.

Dinogad's speckled petticoat. Dinogad's Petticoat. *Unknown, Welsh.* OBWVE; RB, *tr. by* Gwyn Williams

Dinosaur died, and small, The. The Naked Ape. John Updike. EOEF

Dinosaurs. Carolyn Stoloff. NYBP

Dinosaurs. Valerie Worth. NTCP

Dinosaurs and Larger Issues. Irena Klepfisz. CPO

Dinosaurs are not all dead, The. Steam Shovel. Charles Malam. NTCP

Dinosaurs wept angry tears. Abba Kovner, *Hebrew.* IP, *tr. by* Warren Bargad *and* Stanley F. Chyet

Diodorus the hunchback / Went to Socles the quack. Nicarchus of Alexandria, *Greek.* GrAn, *tr. by* Peter Porter

Diogenes. Morris Gilbert Bishop. NBLV

Diogenes. Arthur Rex Dugard Fairburn. PeNZ

Diogenes, that wise old bird. The Complete Cynic. Keith Preston. NBLV

Diomede Mourns His Fate and That of His Friends to the Latian Ambassador Who Seeks His Alliance against Aeneas. Virgil. OBVE, *tr. by* John Dryden *Fr.* The Aeneid [*or* Eneados, *Aeneis*].

Dion. Plato, *Greek.* GrAn, *tr. by* Peter Jay

Dion of Tarsus. *Unknown, Greek.* AWP, *tr. by* Alma Strettell

Dionysiaca. Nonnus, *Greek.* OBCVT, *tr. by* Elizabeth Barrett Browning *Fr.* Dionysiaca.

Dionysius. Sophia de Mello Breyner Andresen, *Portuguese.* PBWP, *tr. by* Allan Francovich

Dionysus as Psychiatrist. Robert Pinsky. HCAP *Fr.* Essay on Psychiatrists.

Diophon, seeing / another man. Lucilius, *Greek.* GrAn, *tr. by* Peter Porter

Dioptric. Ion Barbu, *Romanian.* CEEP, *tr. by* Thomas Amherst Perry

Dioramacist does not know, The. The Museum of the Second Creation. Sandra McPherson. LCAP-2

Dip down upon the northern shore. Tennyson. EBVV *Fr.* In Memoriam A. H. H.

Dipped. Tanka. Masaoka Shiki, *Japanese.* MJT, *tr. by* Makoto Ueda

Dipping into Death like a soup. (LL) A Dreamed Realization. Gregory Corso. NeAP; PoM; VGW

Dipsychus [and the Spirit]. Arthur Hugh Clough.

Dipsychus. Arthur Hugh Clough. CABP *Fr.* Dipsychus [and the Spirit].
(From Dipsychus.) NoP-4

Dipsychus. CABP
(From Dipsychus.) NoP-4
How Pleasant It Is to Have Money. NOBE
I Dreamt a Dream. NAEL-2
"I'm not a judge, I own; in short." EnVR
Public Garden, The. PeLV
"Scene is different, and the place, The." PeVV, *scene* I
Temptation. PeLV
"'There is no God,' the wicked saith.'" NoP-4V
"Yet I could think, indeed, the perfect call." OBNC

Dipt by itself, and we were glad at heart. (LL) Audley Court. Tennyson. NOBVV; PeVV

Diptych. Birago Diop, *French.* NegPo, *tr. by* Ellen Conroy Kennedy; PBMAP
("And for those who return.") (LL) PBMAP
("Sun hung by a thread, The.") PBMAP

Dirce. Walter Savage Landor. AWP; CTC; EBEV; FaBoEE; GBL; HAP; NOBE; NoP-4; OAEL-2; OBEV; OBNC; OxAEP-2; OxBSP; PoEL-4; PoRA; SCGP; TFi; WeW-3 *Fr.* Pericles and Aspasia.

Direction. Barbara Guest. WPE

Direction. Roberta Hill Whiteman. CDW

Directions, The. Christopher Gilbert. GT

Directions. William Matthews. AmPA

Directions for Dreamfishing. Martin Johnston. CBAP

Directions in Our Blood. Barney Bush. HATNAP

Directions that you took. Old Haven. Jean Garrigue. WPE

Directions to a Rebel. William Robert Rodgers. LiTM

Directions to the lunatic asylum were confusing, The. Like a Scarf. James Tate. BAP-94

Directions to the Nomad. James Welch. CDW

Directive. Robert Frost. AFr; AmPP; CMoP; ColAP; HAP; ImPo; InPS-3; LiTM; MeMAP; MoAmPo; NAAL-2; NOBA; NoAM; NoP-4; PoE; SAGP; SAmP; TFi

Director, The. Edmund George Valpy Knox. OBCoV

Dirge: "Body lies under the ground." Gavin Bantock. OxBTC

Dirge, A: "Call for the robin-redbreast and the wren." John Webster. NOBE; OBEV *Fr.* The White Devil.
("For with his nails he'll dig them up again.") (LL) PFE
(Land Dirge, A.) CH; GTBS-P

Dirge: "Calm on the bosom of thy God." Felicia Dorothea Hemans. OBEV; WoRP *Fr.* The Siege of Valencia.

Dirge: "Her house is become like a man dishonored." Bible, Apocrypha. TrJP *Fr.* First Maccabees.

Dirge: "I make this dirge for you Miss Mary Binning I miss you." *Unknown, Hawaiian.* BoWoP, *tr. by* Armand Schwerner

Dirge: "If Thou wilt ease Thine heart." Thomas Lovell Beddoes. *See* Wolfram's Dirge.

Dirge: "It is the endless dance of the dead." Quincy Troupe. PoBA

Dirge: "Naiad, hid beneath the bank." William Johnson Cory. OBNC

Dirge: "1-2-3 was the number he played but today the number came 3-2-1." Kenneth Fearing. HoPM; NIP-4; PoRA; RB; TrJP

Dirge: "Ring out your bells [*or* belles], let mourning shows [*or* shewes] be spread." Sir Philip Sidney. NoSic; OxAEP-1; SiPS
(Litany, A: "Ring out your bells.") GBL; UnPo
("Ring out your bells, let mourning shows be spread.") NoP-4

Dirge, A: "Rough wind, that moanest loud." Shelley. NAEL-2; NOBE; PFE; PoRA; SAGP; SCGP

Dirge: "Stay, Death. Not mine the Christus-wand." Herman Melville. APN-1; NCAP *Fr.* Clarel: A Poem and Pilgrimage in the Holy Land.

Dirge: "Swallow leaves her nest, The." Thomas Lovell Beddoes. OBNC; PoEL-4 *Fr.* Death's Jest Book.
(Song from the Waters.) NOBE
("Swallow leaves her nest, The.") PoEL-4

Dirge: "We do lie beneath the grass." Thomas Lovell Beddoes. NOBVV; OBNC *Fr.* Death's Jest Book.
(Sibilla's Dirge.) NOBE

Dirge: "Weep, weep, ye woodmen, wail." Anthony Munday. CTC *Fr.* Death of Robert, Earl of Huntingdon.

Dirge, A: "Who died? Why does the music speak such grief?" Huy Cận, *Vietnamese.* AVP, *tr. by* Huỳnh Sanh Thông

Dirge, A: "Why were you born when the snow was falling?" Christina Rossetti. EBVV; NOBVV; SCGP

Dirge. Shakespeare. *See* The Clown's Song.

Dirge. James Shirley. *See* Death the Leveller.

Dirge for McPherson, A. Herman Melville. CBCWP; PoEL-5

Dirge for the New Sunrise. Dame Edith Sitwell. CMoP; MoBrPo *Fr.* Three Poems of the Atomic Bomb.

Dirge for the Ninth of Ab. *Unknown, Hebrew.* TrJP, *tr. by* Nina Davis Salaman

Dirge for Three Trumpets, *chain poem. Unknown.* SPE

Dirge for Two Veterans. Walt Whitman. APN-1; BLT; CBCWP; MoAmPo; PoEL-5

Dirge in "Cymbeline." William Collins. NOBE; SCGP
(Fidele, A.) NOEC
(Song from Shakespeare's Cymbeline, A.) CABP

Dirge in Jazz Time. Vassar Miller. FFC

Dirge in Woods. George Meredith. NAEL-2; OBEV; OBNC; PFE

Dirge of Jephthah's Daughter, The. Robert Herrick. ChIV-1

Dirge of St. Malo, The, *tr. of Creole slave song.* George Washington Cable. APAD; APN-2

Dirge of the Three Queens. John Fletcher *and* Shakespeare. OBEV *Fr.* The Two Noble Kinsmen.

Dirge Without Music. Edna St. Vincent Millay. CMoP; IMW; MeMAP

Dirigible, The. Chris Wallace-Crabbe. CBAP

Diringer's *The Alphabet: A Key to the History of Mankind.* Stephanie Strickland. LoHo

Dirt and / clean them clean them clean them. The Streetcleaner's Lament. Patricia Hubbell. SSCS

Dirt of my flesh, defeated, underground. (LL) At the Executed Murderer's Grave. James Wright. HCAP; VCAP

Dirt road, A. Robert Spiess. HA

Dirtiest Man in the World, The. Shel Silverstein. OBCA

Dirty Earth that hides her, The. (LL) Loving Mad Tom. *Unknown.* CBNP; NOSC

Dirty grey of the day at a Flanders dawn. Repetition. Anthony Rhodes. NSI

Dirty Hand, The. Carlos Drummond de Andrade, *Portuguese.* PFTM, *tr. by* Mark Strand

Dirty Little Accuser, The. Norman Cameron. OxBS

Dirty money and the sleazy hearts, The. The Matadors. Josephine Jacobsen. TAP

Dirty Niggers. Jacques Roumain, *French.* NegPo, *tr. by* Ellen Conroy Kennedy

Dirty Panes. Judith Barrington. IFJA

Dirty river by religious explorers, The. Mystic River. John Ciardi. NYBP

Dirty tears are falling. (LL) Walking [*or* Walkin'] Around. Pablo Neruda, *Spanish.* SPE, *tr. by* Robert Bly

Dirty word hops in the cage of the mind like the Pondicherry vulture, The. Karl Shapiro. CoAP; InPK-6; PoA

Dis[h], a dis[h], a green grass, A. Green Grass. *Unknown.* BoTP; CH; OxBoLi; OxNR

Dîs Aliter Visum; or, Le Byron de Nos Jours. Robert Browning. CBLP; NAEL-2

Dis is gospel weathah sho'. Song of Summer. Paul Laurence Dunbar. APN-2

Dis is Ned dat am er-speakin'. Ned's Psalm of Life for the Negro. Joseph Cotter, Sr.. AAP

Dis Long Time, Gal. *Unknown.* PBCV

Dis Mornin', Dis Evenin', So Soon. *Unknown.* AS

Dis sun are hot. This Sun Is Hot. *Unknown.* BPo

Dis Time No Stan' Like befo' Time. James Martinez. PBCV

Dis-ya dutty, a we create it. Michael Smith. HCP

Disabled. Wilfred Owen. CMoP; InPS-3; LiTM; MoP; NAEL-2; NSI; NoAM; OBWVE; OxBTC; PeFWW; PoFWW; PoPoPo; SCGP

Disabled Debauchee, The. John Wilmot, 2d Earl of Rochester. BoLoP; HAP; NAEL-1; NOBL; OBSV
(Maim[e]'d Debauchee, The.) PoEL-3; SCGP

Disabled Debauchee, The. Grace Buchanan Sherwood. NoP-4

Disabled garment worker, The. In the Age of Postcapitalism. Lawrence Joseph. PBCAP

Disappear. Let a race of men now rise and take control. Margaret Abigail Walker. *See* For my people [everywhere singing their slave songs repeatedly: their].

Disappearance. Willis Barnstone. IMW

Disappearance in West Cedar Street, A. Louis Edward Sissman. TwCP

Disappeared Woman I. Marjorie Agosin, *Spanish.* LoHo, *tr. by* Cola Franzen

Disappearing. David Clewell. IFJA

Disappearing Act. Laurel Blossom. MoLi

Disappointed Shrimper, The. P. A. Ropes. BoTP

Disappointed Wife, The. Mehetabel Wright. *See* Address to Her Husband.

Disappointment, A. Joanna Baillie. NOEC; WoRP

Disappointment, The. Aphra Behn. CABP; LW; NALW; NOSC; NoP-4; PEW
  ("Finding beneath the verdant Leaves a Snake.") (LL) LW
  ("Had damn'd him to the hell of impotence.") (LL) CABP; NoP-4

Disappointment. Mary E. Tucker. CBWP-1

Disarmed with so genteel an air. The Answer. Anne Finch, Countess of Winchilsea. NALW; NoP-4

Disarticulated / arm torn out. Last Affair: Bessie's Blues Song. Michael S. Harper. HCAP; LCAP-2

Disaster. Charles Stuart Calverley. NBLV

Disaster, The. Mary Savage. ECWP

Disaster has struck the people. Tune: "Decorous and Pretty"—Respectfully Offered to Circuit Inspector Kao. Liu Chih, *Chinese*. SuSp, *tr. by* Richard John Lynn

Disasters numb within us, The. Life at War. Denise Levertov. NMM-2; VGW

Disbelief in Yourself Is Indispensable. Yevtushenko, *Russian*. TCRP, *tr. by* Albert C. Todd

Discant, descant. (LL) We chant and enchant. Velemir Khlebnikov, *Russian*. NNPT, *tr. by* Paul Schmidt

Discarded papers trembled in the sudden flurry. Deep Season. Virginia Hooper. PT

Discharge me? No! He knew I did just right. (LL) The Code. Robert Frost. OBNV; PoA; UnPo

Disciple, The. Oscar Wilde. OAEL-2

Disciples Asleep at Gethsemane. Paul Kane. GI

Discipline. George Herbert. FHYEP; FSCP; GeHe; MeLP; NAEL-1; NOBE; NOCV; NoP-4; OBEV; OxAEP-1; PoLF

Disciplined in the school of hard campaigning. 3.2. Horace. OBWP, *tr. by* James Michie *Fr. Odes.*

Disconsolate I / from the thinning line. Witness to Death. Richmond Lattimore. VGW

Discontented Student, The. St. George Tucker. OBAL

Discontents in Devon. Robert Herrick. BeJo; CaPo; OxBSP

Discordants. Conrad Potter Aiken.
  Bread and Music. MoAmPo
  "Dead Cleopatra lies in a crystal casket." PoA

Discords. Fabio Doplicher, *Italian*. NeIt, *tr. by* Dana Gioia

Discourse of Beasts, A. Margaret Lucas Cavendish, Duchess of Newcastle. PEW

Discourse of Melancholy, A. Margaret Lucas Cavendish, Duchess of Newcastle. GEA; NOSC

Discourse of the Good Thief, The. Nicanor Parra, *Spanish*. GI, *tr. by* Miller Williams

Discourse on Colonialism. Aime Cesaire *and* Rene Depestre, *French*.
  "How did you come to develop the concept of Negritude?" PFTM, *tr. by* Joan Pinkham

Discourse on Method, The. Herberto Padilla, *Spanish*. VCWP, *tr. by* Alastair Reid *and* Alexander Coleman

Discourse on Peace, The. Jacques Prévert, *French*. CLPP, *tr. by* Lawrence Ferlinghetti

Discover Me. Opal Palmer Adisa. GT

Discoverer. James Michie. DiPo

Discoverer, be a promoter. Ogden Nash. *See* Columbus.

Discoveries. Vernon Watkins. ImPo; LiTM

Discovering Lasseter. Conal Fitzpatrick. NOBAu

Discovering the Photograph of Lloyd, Earl, and Priscilla. Lynn Emanuel. WWSi

Discovering Your Subject. Pattiann Rogers. MT

Discovery. Hilaire Belloc. OxBSP

Discovery. Gu Cheng, *Chinese*. VCWP, *tr. by* Eva Hung

Discovery. Benjamin Keech. PoToHe

Discovery, The. Gwendolyn MacEwen. NOBC

Discovery. Hilda Schiff. HP

Discovery. Zhao Zhenkai, *Chinese*. VCWP, *tr. by* McDougall, Bonnie S. *and* Chen Maiping

Discovery of America, The. James Logie Robertson. NOBVV

Discovery of LSD a True Story, The. Anselm Hollo. PoM

Discovery of the New World. Carter Revard. SoSe-8; VoR

Discovery of the Pacific, The. Thom Gunn. HeIP-4

Discredited for some time to come. (LL) War Has Been Given a Bad Name. Bertolt Brecht, *German*. NNPT; PoSu, *tr. by* John Willett; HP, *tr. by* Willet, John

Discreet. Maria Flook. EOEF

Discreet householder exclaims on the grandsire, A. Old Man Playing with Children. John Crowe Ransom. MeMAP

Discreet, not cryptic. I write to you from the garden. A Message. Fleur Adcock. DiPo

Discrete Series 1929–1933. George Oppen. PFTM

Discriminator, The. Vernon Scannell. OxBC

Discussing divorce. Alexis Rotella. HA

Discussions in the trenches often coupled pleasant wenches. Trench Fever. Robert Swan. NSI

Disdain me not without desert. Sir Thomas Wyatt. SiPS

Disdain Me Still. William Herbert, Earl of Pembroke. CBLP

Disdain Punished. Dryden. EBNV; NOSC *Fr.* Theodore and Honoria, From [Fables Ancient and Modern from] Boccace.

Disdain Returned. Thomas Carew. CavPo; PFE *Fr.* Disdain Returned. BeJo
  ("Lovely cheeks, or lips or eyes.") (LL) GTBS-P
  (True Beauty, The.) GTBS-P

Disdained Apparitions. René Char, *French*. AF, *tr. by* Paul Mann

Disdaining butterflies. The Woman Who Loved Worms. Colette Inez. CMAP; NMM-2

Disdains to crop a weed, and will not come. (LL) Madrigal: "My thoughts hold mortal[l] strife." William Drummond, of Hawthornden. GTBS-P; NOBE; NOSC; OBEV; OxBSP

Disdain'st we see thee stained with other's light. (LL) Madrigal. Sir Philip Sidney. NoSic; SiPS

Diseases of Bath; a Satire, The. *Unknown.*
  "If to the Pump Room in the morn we go." NOEC

Disembarking at Quebec. Margaret Atwood. PoE

Disentangling our lives. The X-Ray. Andrew Elliott. PNI

Disfigure me, Lord. Take pity on me. Antipsalm. Novica Tadic, *Serbo-Croatian*. HSix; VCWP, *tr. by* Charles Simic

Disgrace. David Hall. CDa

Disguised in my mouth as a swampland. In the Morning. Jayne Cortez. BlSi

Disgusted with crimes that are piffling and messy. Crime at Its Best. Stoddard King. NBLV

Dish for a Poet, A. *Unknown.* OBCP

Dishonest Miller, The. *Unknown.* AmFP

Disillusion. Maureen Burge. BrRo

Disillusion. Bessie B. Decker. PoToHe

Disillusionment. Virginia Graham. NBLV

Disillusionment of Ten O'Clock. Wallace Stevens. CBNP; CMoP; ChAP; InPS-3; NAAL-2; NoAM; OxBA; RB; SAmP; SoSe-8; TRP; TTTS
  ("In red weather.") (LL) ChAP

Disinherited. Donne. FMP

Disinherited, The. Charles Spear. PeNZ

Disintegrating at low speeds. To Live at the Speed of Biography. Yona Wallach, *Hebrew*. IP, *tr. by* Warren Bargad *and* Stanley F. Chyet

Disintegration. Richard Kostelanetz. InPK-6

Disk falling from negative charges. Lightning. Will Alexander. PT *Fr.* Lightning.

Disloyal Lines to an Alumnus. Edmund Wilson. OBCoV

Dismantled Ship, The. Walt Whitman. AmPP; OxBA

Dismiss the instruments that for your pleasure. Music in Venice. Louis Simpson. NYBP

Dismissing Progress and Its Progenitors. George Reavey. SPE

Dismissing reports and men, he put pressure on the. Geoffrey Hill. HAP *Fr.* Mercian Hymns.

Dismounting, I offer you wine. Seeing Someone Off. Wang Wei, *Chinese*. SuSp, *tr. by* Irving Y. Lo

Disobedience. A. A. Milne. NOxBChV; NTCP; OTCP; TLR; UV

Disorder, The. Marilyn Chin. LoL

Disorder and Frailty. Henry Vaughan. ChIV-1

Disown. Rae Armantrout. FTOS

Dispatch this note to our hero at once. (LL) After the Broken Arm. Ron Padgett. CoAmPo; SPE

Dispensary, The. Sir Samuel Garth. OBSV
  "As bold Mirmillo the grey dawn descries." ECEV

Dispenser of wide-wasting woe. Cowley's Style. Walter Savage Landor. EPCY

Display thy breasts, my Julia. Upon Julia's Breasts. Robert Herrick. CaPo; NoP-4

Dispossessed, The. John Berryman. VGW

Dispossessed, The. Thomas Kinsella. NOCV

Dispossessed. Evangeline Paterson. NBrP

Dispossessions. Jane Cooper. FaBoWP

Dispraise of Absalom, The. *Unknown, Irish*. BIrV, *tr. by* Robin Flower

Dispute between Women, A. *Unknown, Eskimo*. STP, *tr. by* Tom Lowenstein

Dispute of the Heart and Body of François Villon, The. François Villon, *French.* AWP; OBVE, *tr. by* Swinburne

Dispute over Suicide, A. *Unknown, Egyptian.* TTY, *tr. by* T. Eric Peet

Disquieting Muses, The. Sylvia Plath. NALW; NMM-2

Disregard. Ai. NoAM

Dissatisfaction with Metaphysics. William Empson. CMoP

Disseminating their / Circumference. (LL) Poets light but Lamps, The. Emily Dickinson. APN-2; HeIP-4

Dissent of trees over the space of roots, The. This Spring. Regina DeCormier-Shekejian. LoHo

Dissert, A. Margaret Lucas Cavendish, Duchess of Newcastle. PEW

Dissolution of the world proovd from the mortality of every part, The. Lucretius, *Latin.* OBCVT, *tr. by* Lucy Hutchinson

Dissolve us in pleasure, and soft repose. (LL) Would You Have a Young Virgin? John Gay. EnLoPo; NAEL-1

Disswasion hearing her assigne my helpe. Rachel Speght. PBRV *Fr.* The Dreame.

Distaff, The. Erinna, *Greek.* WPOW, *tr. by* Marylin Arthur

Distaff Side, The. Harry Clifton. PBCIP

Distance. Anthony Delius. PeSA

Distance. Evacuation. Pol N Ndu. PBMAP

Distance. Peter Everwine. NNaP

Distance. Eugene B. Redmond. SeSe

Distance. Xuân Diệu, *Vietnamese.* AVP, *tr. by* Huỳnh Sanh Thông

Distance. Andrea Zanzotto, *Italian.* VCWP, *tr. by* Ruth Feldman *and* Brian Swann (b. 1940)

Distance between us becomes lightning, The. Moment of Parting. Stefan Aug. Doinas, *Romanian.* CEEP, *tr. by* Peter Jay *and* Petru Popescu

Distance doesn't matter, Francisco. Extracts: From the Journal of Elisa Lynch. Maura Stanton. AmPA

Distance from Loved Ones. James Tate. FiLi

Distance / is one trick of the mind. Walking in the Midst of Others. Michael Tarachow. EC2

Distance of a City. James Berry. PBCV

DISTANCE, OVERTURE. "Theatre." Anne-Marie Albiach, *French.* MFP, *tr. by* Martin Sorrell

Distance Spills Itself, The. Yocheved Bat-Miriam, *Hebrew.* MHP, *tr. by* Ruth Finer Mintz

Distance that the dead have gone, The. Emily Dickinson. MeMAP

Distances. Claire Bateman. WeT

Distances, The. Jim Carroll. PoA

Distances. Otto René Castillo, *Spanish.* AF, *tr. by* Margaret Randall

Distances. Philippe Jaccottet, *French.* VCWP, *tr. by* Derek Mahon

Distances. Jeremy Kingston. NYBP

Distances, The. W. S. Merwin. NOBA

Distances. Christopher Okigbo.
   "Death lay in ambush." PBMAP; TTY

Distances, The. Charles Olson. NAAL-2; NeAP

Distances (1964). Christopher Okigbo.
   "From flesh into phantom." PBMAP

Distances to the Friend, The. Jonathan Williams. NeAP

Distant, The. Yannis Ritsos, *Greek.* VCWP, *tr. by* Edmund Keeley

Distant and faint the Herd-Boy Star. *Unknown, Chinese.* SuSp, *tr. by* Dell R. Hales

Distant balloon, A. Nicholas Virgilio. HA

Distant Drum, The. Calvin C. Hernton. GT; TTY

Distant Footsteps, The. César Vallejo, *Spanish.* RaBo, *tr. by* James Wright *and* John Knoepfle

Distant Fury of Battle, The. Geoffrey Hill. NoP-4

Distant Mountains. Ou-yang Hsiu, *Chinese.* CoBCP, *tr. by* Burton Watson

Distant Orgasm, The. James Tate. AmPA

Distant roads in the aftermath of war. Wu Wei-yeh, *Chinese.* CoBLCP, *tr. by* Jonathan Chaves

Distant Runners, The. Mark Van Doren. LiTM; MoAmPo

Distant Seychelles are not so remote, The. Eireann. Osbert Lancaster. NOBL; PeLV *Fr.* Afternoons with Baedeker.

Distant soughing of pine forests caresses my ear, The. Yitzhak Lamdan. MHP, *tr. by* Ruth Finer Mintz *Fr.* In the Khamsin.

Distant thunder. Gary Hotham. HA

Distant View. Uys Krige, *Afrikaans.* PeSA, *tr. by* Uys Krige *and* Jack Cope

Distant Winter, The. Philip Levine. VGW

Distaste. Ammianus, *Greek.* GrAn, *tr. by* Peter Jay

Distich. Shuraikh, *Arabic.* TrJP

Distil not poison in mine ears. Song. John Hall. OxBSP

Distilled Water. M. K. Joseph. PeNZ

Distinct Call of the Alligator, The. Betsy Sholl. PBCAP

Distinctions. Charles Tomlinson. CMoP

Distinguish carefully between these two. The Justice of the Peace. Hilaire Belloc. NOBVV; OBSV

Distinguished, and familiar, and aloof. (LL) Epigram: "And what is love? Misunderstanding, pain." James Vincent Cunningham. CRP; HAP; HoPM; PoA

Distinguished the belt feed lever from the belt holding pawl. (LL) The Fury of Aerial Bombardment. Richard Eberhart. CMoP; FYAP; FaBoMo; HeIP-4; HoPM; InPK-6; LiTM; MoP; NIP-4; NoAM; NoP-4; OBWP; PoWW; RB; TAP; TwCP; UnPo; VGW

Distracted Puritan, The. Richard Corbet. BeJo; OBCoV; OxBoLi

Distracted with care. The Despairing Lover. William Walsh. FaBoCh; NBLV; NOBL; OxBoLi; PeLV

Distraction. Henry Vaughan. GeHe; SeCP

Distractions and the Human Crowd. Stevie Smith. OxBC

Distress. Flavien Ranaivo, *French.* NegPo, *tr. by* Ellen Conroy Kennedy

Distribution of Honours for Literature. Walter Savage Landor. FaBoEE

Distribution of Poetry. Jorge de Lima, *Portuguese.* PFTM, *tr. by* John Nist

District's been demolished, sown with salt, The. Combat Zone/War Stories. Lynda Hull. PUP-19

Distrust. Chech'on Park, *Korean.* CKP, *tr. by* Jaihiun Kim

Distrust ("To safeguard man from wrongs, there nothing must"). Robert Herrick. CaPo

Distrust the pomp of Caesar. Valentin Petrovich Katayev, *Russian.* TCRP, *tr. by* Bernard Meares

Disturbed by consciousness. Satori. Gayl Jones. BlSi

Disturbed, the kudu are running. On Clouds. Douglas Livingstone. PeSAV

Disturbing some brush. Foster Jewell. HA

Disturbing the Sallies Forth. Clark Coolidge. FTOS

Disturbing to have a person. Poem. Barbara Guest. FaBoWP

Disused Shed in Co. Wexford, A. Derek Mahon. BiHa; CABP; CIP-2; FaBoPV; NOIV; NoP-4; OxBC; PBCIP; PNI

Disused Temple, The. Norman Cameron. OxBS; OxBTC

Ditchdigger, The. Igor Moiseievich Irtenev, *Russian.* TCRP, *tr. by* John High

Ditty: "I went into my garden to gather some herbs." Sister Bertken, *Dutch.* WPOW, *tr. by* Jonathan Crewe

Ditty: "If you refuse me once, and think again." Edward Herbert, 1st Baron Herbert of Cherbury. NOSC

Ditty: "Why dost thou hate return instead of love." Edward Herbert, 1st Baron Herbert of Cherbury. NOSC

Ditty, A: In Praise of Eliza, Queen of the Shepherds. Edmund Spenser. OBEV *Fr.* April. NAEL-1; OBEV; PoEL-1 *Fr.* The Shepheardes [*or* Shepeards *or* Shepherd's] Calender.

(Ditty, A: "See where she sits upon the grassy green.") FaBoCh

Ditty, A. Sir Philip Sidney. *See* The Bargain.

Divan, The. Hafiz. *See* Odes.

Dīvāni Shamsi Tabrīz. Jelaluddin Rumi, *Persian.*
   "Man of God is drunken without wine, The." TAL, *sect.* I–IX, *tr. by* Reynold A. Nicholson

Dive could come who was its fledgling first, The. Nijinsky. Parker Tyler. PoA

Diver, The. Robert Earl Hayden. AmPP; BPo; NAAAL
   ("Measured rise.") (LL) NAAAL

Diver, The. Edward Leslie Mayo. CoAP

Diver, The. W. W. Eustace Ross. NOBC

Diver. Ronald Albert Simpson. CBAP

Diverne stands in the kitchen as they dance. Diverne's Waltz. Marilyn Nelson Waniek. FFC

Diverne wanted to die, that August night. Chosen. Marilyn Nelson Waniek. FFC; NAmP90

Diverne's Waltz. Marilyn Nelson Waniek. FFC

Divers, The. Peter Quennell. MoBrPo

Divers[e] [*or* Dyvers] doth[e] use, as I have heard and kno[w]. Sir Thomas Wyatt. AAS; NAEL-1; SiPS; Son

Divers [*or* Diverse] thy death do diversely bemoan. The Death of Wyatt. Henry Howard, Earl of Surrey. SiPS

Diverse strangers flower and diverge. Crossing Disappearing behind Them. Marjorie Welish. PmAP

Diversely Holy Darkness. Henry Vaughan. *Fr.* The Night. ChIV-2; EBEV; ESCV; FSCP; GeHe; MeLP; NAEL-1; NOBE; NOCV; NoP-4; OAEL-1; OBEV; OBWVE; OxAEP-1; PoEL-2; SCGP; TFi; TOF

Diversions of the Re-Echo Club. Carolyn Wells. OBAL

Diverting History of John Gilpin, The. William Cowper. EBNV; FaBoBe; OBNV

Dives and Lazarus ("As it fell out upon a day [*or* one day]"). *Unknown.* ESPB; OxBB

Dives and Lazarus ("There was a man in olden times"). *Unknown.* AmFP

Dives and Laz'us. *Unknown.* TTY

Dives, when you and I go down to Hell. To Dives. Hilaire Belloc. ChIV-2; OBSV

Divided. Walter De la Mare. CBLP

Divided. Jean Ingelow. VWP

"Dappled sky, a world of meadows, A." OBNC; PEW

Divided Touch, Divided Color. Kathleen Peirce. BAP-94

Divina Commedia. Dante, *Italian*.

Inferno. NAWM-1, *tr. by* John Ciardi

"And now we walked along the solid mire." OBVE, *tr. by* Robert Lowell

Dark Wood, The. BiHa, *tr. by* Seamus Heaney

"Earnest I look'd." OxBSn, *tr. by* Henry Cary

(Inferno, Canto I, The.) PiM, *tr. by* Seamus Heaney

("Where the straight road had been lost sight of.") (LL) PiM, *tr. by* Seamus Heaney

"Middle of life's journey; I, The." STV, *tr. by* John Frederick Nims

Pier delle Vigne. HoPM, *tr. by* John Ciardi

Ugolino. FaBoPV, *tr. by* Seamus Heaney

Divina Commedia, *Introductory poem to Longfellow's tr. of* The Divine Comedy. Henry Wadsworth Longfellow. APN-1; OxBA; TAP

"Oft have I seen at some cathedral door." HAP

Divination by a Daffadill [*or* Daffodil]. Robert Herrick. CaPo

Divine approval is thy sweetest praise. (LL) To My Father. Henrietta Cordelia Ray. AAP; BlSi; CBWP-3; Son

Divine by the name of McWhinners, A. Limerick. *Unknown*. PeLi

Divine Century of Spiritual Sonnets, A. Barnabe Barnes.

God's Virtue. NOCV

No More Lewd Lays. Son

Divine destroyer, pit[t]y me no more. A La Bourbon. Richard Lovelace. CaPo; CavPo

Divine Fancies. Francis Quarles.

"Booke of *Common Pray'r* excels the rest, The." PBRV

"I saw him dead; I saw his Body fall." PBRV

"I wish a greater knowledge, then t'attaine." PBRV

On Death. PeECV

On God's Favour. PeECV

On Our Saviour's Passion. PeECV

On the Life of Man. PeECV

Divine Image, A ("Cruelty has a Human heart"). William Blake. ChIV-1; NAEL-2; NoP-4; OBNC; RB; Ro *Fr.* Songs of Experience.

Divine Image, The ("To Mercy, Pity, Peace and Love"). William Blake. APAD; BoTP; ChAP; FHYEP; NAEL-2; NOBE; NOBRP; NOEC; NoP-4; OAEL-2; OBNC; PeECV; PoE; PoEL-4; Ro *Fr.* Songs of Innocence.

Divine Insect, The. John Hall Wheelock. NYBP

Divine Love. Michael Benedikt. AmPA; CoAP; CoAmPo

Divine Love. *Unknown*. OAEL-1

Divine Meditations. William Alabaster. Son

"Beehould a cluster to itt selfe a vine." ESCV

"Haile gracefull morning of eternall Daye." ESCV

"Jesu, thie love within mee is soe maine." ESCV

"My soule a world is by Contraccion." ESCV

"Night, the starless[e] night of passion, The." ESCV

"Now I have found thee, I will ever more." ESCV

"Now that the midd day heate doth scorch my shame." ESCV

"O starry Temple of unvalted space." ESCV

"Sunne begins uppon my heart to shine, The." ESCV

"Three sortes of teares doe from myne eies distraine." ESCV

"Way feare with thy projectes, noe false fyre, A." ESCV

"What meaneth this, that Christ an hymne did singe." ESCV

"When without tears I looke on Christ, I see." ESCV

Divine Meditations. Donne. *See* Holy Sonnets.

Divine Mission, The. Alfred Gibbs Campbell. AAP

Divine Mistress, A. Thomas Carew. BeJo; CavPo

Divine Office of the Kitchen, The. Cecily Hallack. PoLF

Divine one, my Lysi. My Divine Lysi. Sister Juana Inés de la Cruz. CPO

Divine Rapture, A. Francis Quarles. *See* My Beloved Is Mine, and I Am His; He Feedeth among the Lillies.

Divine Revenge, *epigram*. Friedrich von Logau, *German*. GePo, *tr. by* George C. Schoolfield

Divine Sonnet, A. William Alabaster. NoSic

Divine, to the Divinity. (LL) Dark Angel, with thine aching lust. Lionel Pigot Johnson. ADE

Divine Weeks and Works of Guillaume de Saluste Sieur Du Bartas, The. Joshua Sylvester.

Tower of Babel, The. NoSic

Divine Wooer, The. Phineas Fletcher.

"Me Lord? can'st Thou mispend." TOF

Divinely Superfluous Beauty. Robinson Jeffers. HeIP-4; MoAmPo

Diviners, The. Mary Oliver. WPE

Diving. Charlotte Brontë. PEW

Diving into the Wreck. Adrienne Rich. ColAP; HCAP; HeIP-4; InPK-6; InPS-3; MoP; NAAL-2; NALW; NIP-4; NOBA; NoAM; NoP-4; OxWW; PoPoPo; Poetr

Divinities. W. S. Merwin. PoA

Divinity. George Herbert. NOSC

Division. John Ratti. NYBP

Division of an Estate. George Moses Horton. NAAAL

Division of O'Dowd, The. Alan Wearne. BMAP *Fr.* The Nightmarkets.

Divorce, The. Hans Magnus Enzensberger, *German*. EP, *tr. by* Michael Hamburger; OxBM

("At first it was only an imperceptible quivering of.") EP, *tr. by* Michael Hamburger

("This is the bunch of keys. This is the scar.") (LL) EP, *tr. by* Michael Hamburger

Divorce. Adam Koehn. AiP

Divorce, The. Thomas Stanley. FMP; MeLP

Divorce. Anna Wickham. MoBrPo; NALW; SAGP

Divorce of a Lover, The ("Divorce me nowe good death"). George Gascoigne. AAS

Divorce Referendum, Ireland, 1986, The. Paul Durcan. BiHa; PBCIP

Divorce Song. *Unknown, Tsimshian Indian*. STP, *tr. by* Carl Cary

Divorced, but friends again at last. The Onion, Memory. Craig Raine. NAEL-2; NoAM; NoP-4

Divorcee. C. Webster Wheelock. SoSe-8

Divorcing. Denise Levertov. NALW

Dixie [*or* Dixie's Land]. Daniel Decatur Emmett. APN-1; CBCWP; FaBoA

Dizzy, lost, yet unbewailing! (LL) Hymn to the Spirit of Nature. Shelley. CH; GTBS-P; NOBE; PoE; PoEL-4

Djalbarmiwi's Song. *Unknown*. *See* The Blowflies Buzz.

Djanbun's the platypus. He was a man one time. The Platypus. *Aborigine Oral Tradition*. NOBAu

Do. Melvin Beaunearus Tolson. *See* On the Founding of Liberia.

Do' a-stan'in' on a jar, fiah a-shinin' thoo. Howdy, Honey, Howdy! Paul Laurence Dunbar. PoLF

Do all condole my woe. (LL) The Good Shepherd's Sorrow for the Death of His Beloved Son. Anne, Duchess of Arundel Howard. NOSC; WPE

Do all the good you can. John Wesley's Rule. *Unknown*. CTV

Do As You Would Be Done By. Matilda Caroline Edwards. PWR

Do be my enemy—for friendship's sake. William Blake. *See* On Hayley.

Do[e] but consider this small dust. The Hour-Glass [*or* Houre-Glasse]. Ben Jonson. BeJo; EnLoPo; NIP-4; OAEL-1; SeCP

Do chóireoinn leaba duit. Leaba Shíoda. Nuala Ni Dhomhnaill. CABP

Do diddle di do. Jim Jay. Walter De la Mare. CBNP

Do gorillas have birthdays? Questions My Son Asked Me, Answers I Never Gave Him. Nancy Willard. LCAP-2

Do I believe in Angels? Yes. The Angel's Visit. Eugene Field. PWR

Do I give off in the wee. The Sickness of Friends. Henri Coulette. NYBP

Do I? / It might be so. (LL) A Slice of Wedding Cake. Robert Graves. BoLoP; NAEL-2; NOBE; OxBTC

Do I not know that groping for light in darkness. To a Friend. Boris Pasternak, *Russian*. TCRP, *tr. by* Yakov Hornstein

"Do I see a hat in the road?" I said. The Old Sussex Road. Ian Serraillier. NTCP

Do I sleep? do I dream? Further Language from Truthful James. Bret Harte. NOBL

Do It Now! *Unknown*. BLPA

Do it well or not at all. (LL) Always Finish. *Unknown*. BLPA; CTV; FaBoBe

Do It Yourself. Joan Aiken. KaS; NOxBChV

Do It Yrself. Larry Eigner. NeAP; PoM

Do leân down low in Linden Lea. (LL) My Orcha'd in Linden Lea. William Barnes. EBVV; FaBoVe; NOBVV

Do London's Mayor; or Germans, the Pope's pride. (LL) Jealosie. Donne. CBLP; ESCV

"Do look at those pigs as they lie in the straw." The Pigs. Jane Taylor. CTAV

Do, Lord, Remember Me. *Unknown*. AmFP

Do make thee blush at any time / Blame not my lute. (LL) Blame not my lute, for he must sound [*or* sssnd *or* Sownde]. Sir Thomas Wyatt. AAS; EBEV; NAEL-1; OAEL-1; PoE; SCGP; SiPS

Do men suppose, when God's free-giving hand. The Spade and the Wreath. George Wither. NOSC *Fr.* A Collection of Emblemes, Ancient and Moderne.

Do nettles mar the month of May. Nettles in May. Euros Bowen, *Welsh*. OBWVE, *tr. by the author*

Do not account that for thine own. Isabella Whitney. *Fr.* Sweet Nosegay, A, or Pleasant Posy. WPE

Do not allow the sun to dim. Sunbeams. Avner Trainin, *Hebrew*. MHP, *tr. by* Ruth Finer Mintz

Do Not Ask. Christine Lavant, *German*. WPOW, *tr. by* Michael Hamburger

Do not ask: where? We Go. Karl Wolfskehl, *German*. TrJP, *tr. by* Carol North Valhope *and* Ernst Morwitz

Do not assume I came out on Christopher Street. Assumption about the Harlem Brown Baby. Salih Michael Fisher. GLP

Do not bathe her in blood. An Abortion. Frank O'Hara. TAP

Do not be afraid of no. Gwendolyn Brooks. ColAP *Fr.* Notes from the Childhood and the Girlhood. LCAP-2

Do not be angry if I tell you. The Sofa. Medbh McGuckian. PBCIP; PNI

Do not be offended because. An Excuse for Not Returning the Visit of a Friend. Mei Yao Ch'en, *Chinese*. OHPC, *tr. by* Kenneth Rexroth

Do not beguile my heart. Complaining. George Herbert. ChIV-1

Do not complain of three-score, 'the time of obedient ears'. (LL) On Being Sixty. Po Chü-i, *Chinese*. ChiP, *tr. by* Arthur Waley

Do not conceal[e] thy radiant eyes. To Cynthia, on Concealment of Her Beauty. Sir Francis Kynaston. MeLP; NOBE

Do not conceive that I shall here recount. A Virgin Declares Her Beauties. Francesco da Barberini, *Italian*. AWP, *tr. by* D. G. Rossetti

Do not despair. For Johnny. John Pudney. OBWP

Do not disdain, O straight upraised pine, *speech of Pamela*. Graven Thoughts. Sir Philip Sidney. SiPS *Fr.* Arcadia.

Do not enforce the tired wolf. Prelude to an Evening. John Crowe Ransom. MoAmPo; OxBA *Fr.* Sixteen Poems in Eight Pairings.

Do not enforce the tired wolf. Prelude to an Evening. John Crowe Ransom. SPE *Fr.* Sixteen Poems in Eight Pairings.

Do Not Expect Again a Phoenix Hour. C. Day Lewis. CMoP; FaBoMo; LiTM; MoBrPo; NoAM; OxBTC; PoRA

Do not expect, bewildered by your tears. No Easy Answer. John Lehmann. LBC

Do not fear to put thy feet. The River[-]God's Song. John Fletcher. ITG; NOSC; SCGP *Fr.* The Faithful Shepherdess.

Do not fill postcards with memories. Face Lost in the Wilderness. Fadwa Tuqan, *Arabic*. AF, *tr. by* Naomi Shihab Nye

"Do not force me with present favor." Lady Hsi. Lady Wang Wei, *Chinese*. CoBCP, *tr. by* Burton Watson

Do not forget, my dear, that once we loved. Valediction. Vita Sackville-West. WPN

Do Not Go Gentle ("Do not go gentle into Death's esteemed vale"). Tim Hopkins. BXAP

Do not go gentle into that good night. Dylan Thomas. APAD; CABP; ChAP; ClHu; EBEvV; HAP; HeIP-4; HoPM; InPK-6; InPS-3; LiTM; MoBrPo; MoP; NAEL-2; NIP-4; NOBE; NoAM; NoP-4; OAEL-2; OxAEP-2; OxBTC; PBMP; PFE; PeECV; PiM; PoE; PoPoPo; Poetr; RB; SAGP; SCV; SoSe-8; TFi; TOF; TRP; TwCP; UV; UnPo; WeW-3

Do not go sober into that dim light. Roger Woddis. UV

Do not imagine that the exploration. The Discovery. Gwendolyn MacEwen. NOBC

Do not let any woman read this verse! Deirdre. James Stephens. AWP; CMoP; OBMV; PoRA

Do not look for him. Elegy. Leonard Cohen. HeIP-4

Do not look for the stones. Eastern River. Peter Huchel, *German*. CEEP, *tr. by* Michael Hamburger

Do not lose sight. You Who Occupy Our Land. Manuela Margarido, *Portuguese*. WPOW, *tr. by* Allan Francovich

Do not love me, cousin. Flavien Ranaivo. *See* Love Song: "Do not love me, my friend."

Do not love me, my friend. Love Song. Flavien Ranaivo, *French*. PBA

Do not make things too easy. Martha Baird. LW

Do not ridicule the small. On a Small Bath. *Unknown, Greek.* GrAn, *tr. by* Robin Skelton

Do not say "Godspeed" to me, wicked heart. Callimachus. HePo *Fr.* Epigrams.

Do not say that time once gone can never be returned! Yüan Mei. *Fr.* Moments of Fullfillment—mdash;Writing Down Miscellaneous. CoBLCP, *tr. by* Jonathan Chaves

Do not seek too much fame. Old Song. *Unknown.* RaBo

Do not smile to yourself. Lady Otomo no Sakanoé, *Japanese*. OHPJ, *tr. by* Kenneth Rexroth

Do not speak to us of dreams, speak to us of autumn in. The Gardens of Ravished Psyche. George Barker. OBGa

Do not suddenly break the branch, or. Usk. T. S. Eliot. FaBoCh; NOCV; PeECV *Fr.* Landscapes. RB

"Do not take a bath in Jordan." Scotch Rhapsody. Dame Edith Sitwell. TwCP

Do not tell me, my brother, to reach. Mirrors, Without Song. Keorapetse Kgositsile. PBMAP *Fr.* The Present is a Dangerous Place to Live.

Do[e] not their profane orgies hear[e]. To Castara ("Do[e] not Their profane orgies hear[e].") William Habington. BeJo *Fr.* Castara.

Do Not Think. Carol Freeman. MBE

Do not think I am not grateful for your small. Gratitude. Louise Glück. FaBoWP; TRP

Do not torment me, lady. *Unknown.* NOIV

Do Not Turn Away. Kumeroa Ngoingoi Pewhairangi, *Maori*. PeNZ, *tr. by* Sam Karetu

Do not weep maiden, for war is kind. War Is Kind. Stephen Crane. APN-2; AmPP; LiTM; MeMAP; NAAL-2; NOBA; NoP-4; OBWP; PoLF; RaBo; TAP *Fr.* War Is Kind.

Do not wonder when the wench declines. Catullus. *See* Carmen 69 ("That no fair woman will, wonder not why").

Do not you mark how *passionate*, how *wild*. Sophocles. OBCVT, *tr. by* Christopher Wase *Fr.* Electra.

Do Nothing Till You Hear from Me. David Henderson. GT; PoBA ("Day of the vernal winds/1967.") (LL) GT

Do parks get lonely. Snowy Benches. Aileen Fisher. KaS

Do People moulder equally. Emily Dickinson. ChIV-2

Do sit down, Metro. Get up and set. Friends in Private. Herodas, *Greek*. HePo, *tr. by* Barbara Hughes Fowler

Do Skyscrapers ever grow tired. Skyscrapers. Rachel Lyman Field. ChAP; NOxBChV; SSCS

Do So. Denise Riley. NBrP

Do something, brother. M. Gopalakrishna Adiga, *Kannada*. OMIP, *tr. by* A. K. Ramanujan

Do Stella love. Fools, who doth it deny? (LL) Sonnet 104: "Envious wits, what hath been mine offence." Sir Philip Sidney. PoE; Son

Do tell me, Hermes, what was it like when the soul. Lucianus, *Greek*. GrAn, *tr. by* Edwin Morgan

Do the Baby Cake-Walk. Clyde Watson. NTCP

Do the Dead Know What Time It Is? Kenneth Patchen. HoPM; MoAmPo

Do the Others Speak of Me Mockingly, Maliciously? Delmore Schwartz. ChIV-1

Do the vain world no form or beauty see. (LL) Cant. 5.6. Elizabeth Singer. ChIV-1; KTR

Do the wife and baby travelling to see. The Sick Nought. Randall Jarrell. OxBA

Do they call virtue there ungratefullness? Sir Philip Sidney. *See* Sonnet 31: "With how sad steps, O Moon, thou climb'st the skies!"

Do they call 'Virtue' there—ungratefulness? (LL) Sonnet 31: "With how sad steps, O Moon, thou climb'st the skies!" Sir Philip Sidney. AEP; AWP; BoLoP; CABP; CH; EnLoPo; GBL; GLoP; GSo; HAP; HeIP-4; InPS-3; LoP; NAEL-1; NOBE; NoSic; OBEV; OxAEP-1; PBMP; PoE; PoEL-1; PoRA; SCGP; Son; TFi; TRP

Do They Return? Samuel Johnson. LBC

Do they think of me now. Making the Children Behave. William Daniel Ehrhart. CDa

Do they whisper behind my back? [Do they speak]. Do the Others Speak of Me Mockingly, Maliciously? Delmore Schwartz. ChIV-1

Do things then happen. Melting Milk. Bill Berkson. PmAP

Do This Favour For Me. Luis de Camões, *Portuguese*. LBC, *tr. by* Roy Campbell

Do we indeed desire the dead. Tennyson. EBVVPR; EnVR; OAEL-2 *Fr.* In Memoriam A. H. H.

Do what you are going to do, and I will tell about it. Sharon Olds. *See* I Go Back to May 1937.

Do what you are going to do, and I will tell you about it. (LL) I Go Back to May 1937. Sharon Olds. BLT

Do What You Can. Lawrence Joseph. PBCAP; WWSi

Do with me, God! as Thou didst deal with John. To God. Robert Herrick. ChIV-2

Do ye hear the children weeping, O my brothers. The Cry of the Children. Elizabeth Barrett Browning. EBVV; OxAEP-2; VWP

Do ye indeed speak righteousness, O congregation? Bible, *O.T. See* Psalm 58.

Do ye ken hoo to fush for the salmon? Master and Man. Sir Henry John Newbolt. OxBTC

Do ye, o congregation. Psalm 58. *Unknown.* NoP-4

Do you ask what the birds say? / The sparrow, the dove. Answer to a Child's Question. Coleridge. BoTP; CTAV; FaBoBe; NOxBChV; NTP; OxBChV

Do you believe in evolution, oh, thing of easy answers? Darwin Descending. Russell Edson. LCAP-2

Do you blame me that I loved him? A Double Standard. Frances Ellen Watkins Harper. AAP; BlSi; CrDW; NAAAL; PWR

Do you carrot all for me? *Unknown.* CBNP; ChAP

Do you come to me to bend me to your will. A Woman to Her Lover. Christina Walsh. BrRo

Do you envy, my comrades-in-arms. Viktor Aleksandrovich Sosnora, *Russian*. TCRP, *tr. by* Daniel Weissbort

Do you ever think of me, Kitty Kline? Kitty Kline. *Unknown*. AmFP

Do you give yourself to me utterly. Sleep. Kenneth Slessor. BMAP

Do you grieve no costly offering. A Love Token. Adelaide Anne Procter. SDW

Do you have a sweet thought, Cerinthus. Sulpicia, *Latin*. BoWoP, *tr. by* Aliki *and* Willis Barnstone

Do you have the poems of Han-shan in your house? *Unknown*, *Chinese*. CoBCP, *tr. by* Burton Watson

Do you know. The Tree. Cinda Thompson. CrSp

Do you know me now? From the Ballad of Evil. N. P. van Wyk Louw, *Afrikaans*. PeSA, *tr. by* Anthony Delius

Do you know me now? Skinny, cadaverous bitch. Goethe. OxBSn, *tr. by* David Luke *Fr.* Faust.

Do you know that once. Overnight Guest. Ramona Wilson. VoR

Do you know that your soul is of my soul such part. To My Son. Margaret Johnston Grafflin. BLPA; PoToHe

Do you know the neighbor who lives in your block. Your Neighbor. H. Howard Biggar. PoToHe

Do you know the old man who. The Wild Flower Man. Lu Yu, *Chinese*. OHPC, *tr. by* Kenneth Rexroth

Do you know the story of Hamelin Town? Rat Trap. Mick Gowar. NOxBChV

Do you know what. Fancy. Robert Creeley. NOBA

Do you know what happened in August here? Roslyn Malamud the Coup. Anna Deavere Smith. OxWW *Fr.* Fires in the Mirror.

Do you know what is bad? Bad and Good. Alexander Resnikoff. NTCP

Do you know why the old woman sings? Why the Old Woman Limps. Lupenga Mphande. HBAPE

Do you know you have asked for the costliest thing. A Woman's Question. Lena Lathrop, *wrongly at. to* Elizabeth Barrett Browning. BLPA, PoToHe

Do you lazily nurse your knee and muse? What Are You Doing? Edmund Vance Cooke. PWR

Do you like marigolds? Marigolds. Louise Driscoll. BoTP

Do you look for a rainbow, Love, in this wet weather. Wet Weather. Patricia Low. VGW

Do you love her? Inquisition. Gloria Wade-Gayles. ISC

Do you make me notice you! (LL) The Reminder. Thomas Hardy. CMoP; ChAP; OBCP

"Do you mind the news while we eat?" Dinner Party 1940. Philip Sherlock. PBCV

Do you ne'er think what wondrous beings these? Henry Wadsworth Longfellow. *Fr.* Birds of Killingworth, The (The Poet's Tale). MeMAP; OxBA *Fr.* Tales of a Wayside Inn.

"Do you not find something very strange about him?" The Assassination. Robert Silliman Hillyer. MoAmPo

Do you not hear the Aziola cry? The Aziola. Shelley. EBEV

Do you not know that I need to touch you. Frances Horovitz. LW

Do you not see the Running Horse River flowing along the Sea of Snow. Song of the Running Horse River, A: Presented on Seeing General Feng Off on a Campaign to the West. Ts'en Shen, *Chinese*. SuSp, *tr. by* Daniel Bryant

"Do you not wish to renounce the Devil?" Epigram. Armand Lanusse, *French*. TTY, *tr. by* Langston Hughes

Do you, now, as the news becomes known. Pay-off. Kenneth Fearing. CMoP

Do you recall the Vardar River. In Memoriam. A. B. L. Hodgson. NSI

Do you remember. Friend. Hone Tuwhare, *Maori*. PeNZ, *tr. by* Kumeroa Ngoingoi Pewhairangi

Do you remember an Inn. New Tarantella. Paul Griffin. UV

Do you remember an Inn. Tarantella. Hilaire Belloc. APAD; CH; EBEvV; FaBoCh; MoBrPo; OBMV; RB; UV

Do you remember an inn, Miranda? It lost its licence of course. Footnote to Belloc's "Tarantella." John Heath-Stubbs. OBCoV

Do you remember how I beat on the door. A Door. W. S. Merwin. LCAP-2

Do you remember how we went. To Another Housewife. Judith Wright. NALW

Do you remember/ How you won. To James. Frank Horne. BPo *Fr.* Letters [*or* Notes] Found near a Suicide. PoBA

Do you remember me? or are you proud? Ianthe's Question. Walter Savage Landor. OBNC *Fr.* Ianthe.

Do you remember Mr. Goodbeare, the carpenter. Elegy for Mr. Goodbeare. Sir Osbert Sitwell. MoBrPo

Do You Remember 1926? Idris Davies. OBWVE

Do you remember that night? *Unknown*, *Irish*. BIrV, *tr. by* Eugene O'Curry

Do you remember the lizard? The Lizard. Rona Murray. NOBC

Do you remember? We were in a room. The Raiment We Put On. Kelly Cherry. FFC

Do you remember, when you were first a child. Message from Home. Kathleen Jessie Raine. WPE

Do you see? Evening falls. Seventh Eclogue. Miklós Radnóti, *Hungarian*. PFTM, *tr. by* Clayton Eshleman *and* Gyula Kodolanyi

Do you see me! 'One with this world'. *Unknown*, *Yokuts*. FaBoA, *tr. by* A. L. Kroeber

Do you see this grain of sand. A Grain of Sand. Frances Ellen Watkins Harper. PWR

Do you see this square old yellow Book, I toss. Robert Browning. FaBoVe *Fr.* The Ring and the Book.

Do you smell smoke? Phobiphilia. Robin Morgan. EC2

Do you still have a demon in your heart? When I Was Saved. Andrew Hudgins. PuP-17

Do you still remember? On the faces. Afterword. János Pilinszky, *Hungarian*. CEEP, *tr. by* Emery E. George

Do You Think? Josephine D. Henderson Heard. CBWP-4

Do you think I know what I'm doing? Jelaluddin Rumi, *Persian*. LoL, *tr. by* Coleman Barks

Do you think of me as I think of you. L.E.L.'s Last Question. Elizabeth Barrett Browning. Ro; VWP

Do you think of me as I think of you? (LL) L.E.L.'s Last Question. Elizabeth Barrett Browning. Ro; VWP

'Do you think we'll ever get to see Earth, sir?'. Sheenagh Pugh. SpW

"Do you think you will hug the shore, Captain, to-day?" Hugging the Shore. Mary E. Tucker. CBWP-1

Do you want to know his name? The Porch. Ronald Stuart Thomas. NOCV

—Do you want to return. The River Silence. Leonid Nikolaevich Martynov, *Russian*. TCRP, *tr. by* J. R. Rowland

Do your balls hang low? Song *Unknown*. NSI

Do Your Best. Mrs. Henry Linden. CBWP-4

Doan't You Be What You Ain't. Edwin Milton Royle. BLPA

Dobbin. George Bowering. NOBC

Docker. Seamus Heaney. HeIP-4; IIP; MoP; NOIV; Poetr

Doctor, The. Roger Woddis. UV

Doctor asked her what she wanted done, The. Edna St. Vincent Millay. *Fr.* Sonnets from an Ungrafted Tree. NALW

Doctor asked him if he dreamed at night, The. The Patient. Nicholas Moore. SPE

Doctor Bell fell down the well. *Unknown*. FuFo

Dr. Berman, my old lady listens to you. Deuce: 12:23 a.m. Barbara Anderson. NAmP90

Dr. Booker T. Washington to the National Negro Business League. Joseph Cotter, Sr.. AAP

Doctor Bottom was preparing to leave. Medical Aid. Walter Hard. BXAP

Doctor, doctor, it fits real fine. Vet's Rehabilitation. Ray Durem. PoBA

Doctor Faustus. Marlowe. NAEL-1; OAEL-1

  "Ah, Doctor Faustus, that I might prevail." FaBoSe

  "But may I raise up spirits when I please?" OxBoV

  End of Doctor Faustus, The. PoEL-2

  "First will I question with thee about hell." OxBSn

  Helen. ImPo

  "Now, Faustus, what wouldst thou have me do?" OxBSn

Doctor Faustus was a good man. Mother Goose. LB

Doctor Fell. Thomas Brown, *after the Latin of* Martial. FaBoEE; NBLV; OBCoV; OBVE; OxNR

  (Non Amo Te.) AWP

Doctor Foster is a good man. Dr. Foster. *Unknown*. ACTP; OxNR

Doctor Foster went to Gloucester [*or* Glo'ster]. Mother Goose. ACTP; LB; OxBoLi; OxNR; ReMoGo

Dr. Foster. *Unknown*. ACTP

Doctor Frolic. Robert Pinsky. NoAM

Doctor Gliedschirm, skin specialist, surgeries 14–16 hours or by appointment. James Fenton. *Fr.* A German Requiem. NAEL-2; NoAM

"Dr. Halley never eat any thing." Edmond Halley. Roy Fuller. OxBC

Doctor Johnson. Soame Jenyns. FaBoEE; OBSV

Dr. Johnson, when sober or pissed. Limerick. A. Cinna. PeLi

Dr. Johnson's Ghost. Elizabeth Moody. ECWP; OxBSn

Dr. King's photograph. Report from the Skull's Diorama. Yusef Komunyakaa. LTA

Doctor loves the patient, The. The Bed. Alec Derwent Hope. NoAM; OxBC; OxBSP

Dr. Newman with the crooked pince-nez. Robert Graves. PeLV *Fr.* Grotesques. CMoP

Doctor, of great skill and fame, A. Fair and Softly goes far or, The Wary Physician. Laetitia Pilkington. PEW

Dr. Potatohead Talks to Mothers. Judith Johnson Sherwin. MoP

Doctor punched my vein, The. Scyros. Karl Shapiro. HoPM; ImPo; LiTM

Dr. Stupid says. The Exciting New Concept of Art Therapy. Marlys West. IFJA

Dr Szasz, professor, sir. A Footnote Extended. Dannie Abse. HP

Doctor Who Sits at the Bedside of a Rat, The. Josephine Miles. VGW

Doctor, you say there are no haloes. Monet Refuses the Operation. Lisel Mueller. FYAP

Doctors, The. Donne. *Fr.* The Litanie. PoEL-2

Doctors attended behind each chair. W. H. Auden. *Fr.* A Happy New Year. OBSV

Doctor's fortunate indeed, A. The Physicians' Fortune. Friedrich von Logau, *German.* GePo, *tr.* by George C. Schoolfield

Doctor's Journal Entry for August 6, 1945, A. Vikram Seth. OMIP

Doctors' Row. Conrad Potter Aiken. HAP

Doctor's Story, The. Will M. Carleton. BLPA

Doctors tender of their fame, The. Jonathan Swift. NOBL *Fr.* Verses on the Death of Dr. Swift, D.S.P.D.

Doctors that learned be. John Skelton. OBSV *Fr.* Colin Clout.

Documentary. Claribel Alegría, *Spanish.* LoL; VCWP, *tr.* by D. J. Flakoll

Documentary Film. "Ern Malley." BMAP

Dodder twines around the *huang-po* tree, The. The Woman Née Wu. Wu Chia-chi, *Chinese.* CoBLCP, *tr.* by Jonathan Chaves

Dodder vine trails with the long wind, The. Old *Chüeh-chü. Unknown, Chinese.* CoBCP, *tr.* by Burton Watson

Doddledy, doodledy, doodledy, dan. *Unknown.* OxNR

Dodger, The. *Unknown.* AmFP

Dodo. Henry Carlile. Poetsp

Doe at Evening, A. D. H. Lawrence. APo

Doe of the mountains east. Mother / Deer / Lady. Harold Littlebird. VoR

Doeg, though without knowing how or why. John Dryden *and* Nahum Tate. FHYEP; PoEL-3 *Fr.* Absalom and Achitophel, Pt. II.

Does a man ever give up hope, I wonder. Truth at Last. Edward Rowland Sill. APN-2

Does Charidas lie beneath you? If you mean. Callimachus, *Greek.* GrAn, *tr.* by Peter Jay

Does everyone have to die? Yes, everyone. Fable. Merrill Moore. LiLi

Does he know the road to Flanders, does he know the criss-cross tracks. The Flight to Flanders. Lessel Hutcheon. NSI

Does he think of me in the merry throng. The Question. Josephine D. Henderson Heard. CBWP-4

Does it become a girl so wise. Walter Savage Landor. CBLP

Does It Matter?[—losing your legs?]. Siegfried Sassoon. MoBrPo; PeFWW; PoFWW; PoWW

Does it wear a yarmulka. What Is a Jewish Poem? Myra Sklarew. CRP

Doe's leap, A. Peggy Lyles. HA

Does man love Art? Man visits Art, but squirms. The Chicago Picasso. Gwendolyn Brooks. BPo; LiTM; NAAAL *Fr.* Two Dedications.

Does mother get praised as often as she should. The Woman Back in the Kitchen. Nicholas Lloyd Ingraham. PWR

Does my voice reach you? You are. Light Years and the Love Lost in the Oleanders. Alane Rollings. WeW-3

Does my voice sound strange? I am sitting. Talking to You Afterwards. Peter Porter. BMAP

Does now like one of them appear. (LL) Upon Appleton House [To My Lord Fairfax]. Andrew Marvell. FaBoPV; GeHe; SeCP

Does our own soil produce the bread they sell? Bread. Huỳnh Phú Sổ, *Vietnamese.* AVP, *tr.* by Huỳnh Sanh Thông

Does Spring Come to These Forfeited Fields? Sanghwa Yi, *Korean.* CKP, *tr.* by Jaihiun Kim

Does That Answer Your Question, Mr Shakespeare? Stanley J. Sharpless. PeLV

Does that bird. Princess Nukada, *Japanese.* WPJ, *tr.* by Kenneth Rexroth *and* Ikuko Atsumi

Does the day break. Dawn. Nirmalprabha Bardoloi, *Assamese.* OMIP, *tr.* by D. N. Bezbarua

Does the Eagle know what is in the pit? Thel's Motto. William Blake. *Fr.* The Book of Thel. NAEL-2; OAEL-2; OBNC; PoE; PoEL-4

Does the Elephant remember. (Circus Elephant). Kathryn Worth. CTV

Does the lily flower open? Star Song of the Bushman Women. *Unknown, Bushman.* PeSA, *tr.* by W. H. I. Bleek

Does the mouth refuse? Russians Breathing. Philip Hammial. NOBAu

Does the policeman sleep with his boots on. Song. Gerda Mayer. PeLV

Does the road wind up-hill all the way? Uphill [*or* Up-Hill]. Christina Rossetti. APAD; BLPA; CABP; CH; EBEvV; EBVV; FaBoBe; HAP; InPK-6; LBC; NAEL-2; NALW; NOBE; NTP; NoP-4; OAEL-2; OBEV;

OBNC; PEW; PFE; PoE; PoPoPo; PoRA; Poetr; SDW; TFi; TrCP; WPE; WeW-3

Does the Spearmint Lose Its Flavor on the Bedpost Overnight? Billy Rose. OBAL

Does the trick worth forty wenches. (LL) Song: "Love a woman? You're [*or* Y'are] an ass." John Wilmot, 2d Earl of Rochester. GBL; NBLV; NOBL; NOSC; PeLV

Does this water. At the Well. Leonard Nathan. PBCAP

Does thy life destroy. (LL) The Sick Rose. William Blake. APAD; AWP; BoLoP; CABP; ClHu; EBEvV; EP; EnLoPo; FHYEP; FaBoSe; GEA; HAP; HeIP-4; InPK-6; InPS-3; NAEL-2; NAWM-2; NIP-4; NOBE; NOBRP; NOEC; NoP-4; OAEL-2; OBNC; OPOU; OxAEP-2; OxBSP; PFE; PoE; PoEL-4; PoPoPo; Poetr; RB; Ro; SCGP; SoSe-8; TFi; TRP; WeW-3

Doesn't he realize / that I am not / like the swaying kelp. Ono no Komachi, *Japanese.* BoWoP; WPJ; WPOW, *tr.* by Kenneth Rexroth *and* Ikuko Atsumi

Doesn't make any sense. (LL) Out beyond ideas of wrongdoing and rightdoing. Jelaluddin Rumi, *Persian.* BLT, *tr.* by Barks, Coleman and John Moyne; EnlH, *tr.* by Coleman Barks *and* John Moyne

"Doesn't that feel great?" Self-Storage. Alice Fulton. NAmP90

Dog. David Chapman Berry. BXAP

Dog, The. Valentin Iremonger. BIrV

Dog. Ingrid Jonker, *Afrikaans.* PBWP, *tr.* by Jack Cope *and* William Plomer

Dog. Harold Monro. MoBrPo

Dog, The. Ogden Nash. Spl

Dog. Judith Nicholls. PeP

Dog. John Crowe Ransom. InPS-3; OBAL

Dog, A. Gertrude Stein. TTTS *Fr.* Tender Buttons.
 ("Little monkey goes like a donkey that means to say that means to say, A.") PFTM

Dog, The. Gerald Stern. WeW-3

Dog, alive, Lucy, my light, sleeps, The. Poem to Begin the Second Decade of AIDS. Boyer Rickel. WeT

Dog ambles across the empty, dusty road, A. Chimayo. Gloria Vando. LoHo

Dog and a Boy, A. Richard Katrovas. NAmP90

Dog barked itself, The. The Dog Which Barked Itself Out. Tymoteusz Karpowicz, *Polish.* PoSu, *tr.* by Andrzej Busza *and* Bogdan Czaykowski

Dog-barking. Night in the Village. Christoph Eisenhuth, *German.* CEEP, *tr.* by Allen H. Chappel

Dog barks amid the sound of water, A. Calling on a Taoist Priest in Tai-t'ien Mountain but Failing to See Him. Li Po, *Chinese.* SuSp, *tr.* by Joseph J. Lee

Dog barks and is for the moment a dog heard, The. David Ignatow. WeT

Dog barks from a cloud, The. Adolescence. Gregory Orr. Poetsp

Dog beneath the Skin, The. W. H. Auden. OxBTC
 "We are girls of different ages."

Dog body and cat mind, The. Jenny Joseph. BrRo

Dog called Sesamë slewed out. Stray Dog, near Ecully. Margaret Avison. PoA

Dog came in the kitchen, A. Vladimir's Song. Samuel Beckett. CBNP *Fr.* Waiting for Godot.

Dog Creek Mainline. Charles Wright. AmPA; LCAP-2; WeT

Dog Day Lesson. John Hughes. PNI

Dog-Day Night. Robert Francis. WeT

Dog Day Vespers. Charles Wright. LCAP-2

Dog Days. Derek Mahon. OPOU

Dog Days 1978. Jim Barnes. EC2

Dog, Dog in My Manger. George Barker. ImPo; LiTM

Dog downstairs is howling back, The. Krakow and the Girl of Twelve. Marianne Boruch. WeT

Dog Fight. Eric Rolls. NOBAu

Dog Fox Field, The test for feeblemindedness was, they had to make up a sentence using the words dog, fox and field. Les A. Murray. BMAP

Dog from Malta, The. Tymnes. *See* A Maltese Dog.

Dog Hospital. Peter Wild. AmPA

Dog in the Lifeboat, A. Joyce Peseroff. CMAP

Dog in the River, The. Phaedrus, *Latin.* AWP, *tr.* by Christopher Smart

Dog it was that died, The. (LL) An Elegy on the Death of a Mad Dog. Oliver Goldsmith. BLPA; FaBoBe; FaBoCh; NBLV; NOEC; NOIV; NTP; OBNV; OxAEP-1; TFi

Dog loved its churlish life, The. Lupercalia. Ted Hughes. CMoP

Dog must see your corpse, The. The last thing that you feel. Dog Prospectus. Peter Redgrove. OxBC

Dog Named Ego, the Snowflakes as Kisses, A. Delmore Schwartz. LiTM

Dog of Art, The. Denise Levertov. MoP; NoAM

Dog Prospectus. Peter Redgrove. OxBC

Dog Sacrifice at Lake Ronkonkoma. William Heyen. AmPA

Dog said, Bow wow, The. Sarah Catherine Martin. *See* The Comic Adventures of Old Mother Hubbard and Her Dog.

Dog scatters her body in sleep, The. Biography. Michael Ondaatje. NoAM

Dog searches until he finds me, The. In and Out. Jane Kenyon. BAP-93; LoL *Fr.* Having It Out With Melancholy. BAP-93

Dog Shark. *Unknown.* PBCV

Dog Show. Laurie Anderson. OxWW

Dog Sleeping on My Feet, A. James Dickey. NAAL-2

Dog stops barking after Robinson has gone, The. Robinson. Weldon Kees. MoP; NYBP

DOG The single creature leads a partial life. W. H. Auden. *See* Cats and Dog.

Dog-tired, suisired, will now my body down. The Poet's Final Instructions. John Berryman. Son; VGW

Dog trots freely in the street, The. Lawrence Ferlinghetti. HoPM

Dog was there, outside her door, The. W. H. Davies. MoBrPo

Dog-watch. Neil Harries. SpW

Dog Which Barked Itself Out, The. Tymoteusz Karpowicz, *Polish.* PoSu, *tr. by* Andrzej Busza *and* Bogdan Czaykowski

Dog who knew the winter felt no spleen, The. The Watcher. Ruth Stone. NYBP

Dog will come when he is called, The. Beasts and Birds. Adelaide O'Keeffe. CTAV; OxBChV

Dog will often steal a bone, A. A Cat's Conscience. *Unknown.* PoLF

Dog with daisies for eyes, The. The Dog of Art. Denise Levertov. MoP; NoAM

Dogalypse. Andrey Andreievich Voznesensky, *Russian.* CLPP, *tr. by* M. S., C. L., V. R., *and* L. Ferlinghetti

Doggerel by a Senior Citizen. W. H. Auden. NBLV; NOBL

Dogget Gap. *Unknown.* AmFP

Doggies went to the mill, The. *Unknown.* BoTP; OxNR

Dogknotting in Quezaltenango. Vincent O'Sullivan. PeNZ

Dogmatic Egg, The. Ion Barbu, *Romanian.* CEEP, *tr. by* Donald Eulert *and* Stefan Avadanei

Dogs. Laurie Duggan.
     South Coast Haiku. BMAP

Dogs, The. Michael S. Weaver. PBCAP

Dogs Are Shakespearean, Children Are Strangers. Delmore Schwartz. NoAM; Poetr

Dogs bark ably: in Accra, The. Many Worlds Are Walked Once. Kojo Laing. HBAPE

Dog's / body zipped, A. At the Crossroads. Thomas Kinsella. NoAM

Dog's Death. John Updike. Poetr; Poetsp

Dogs Gambol. Novica Tadic, *Serbian.* VCWP, *tr. by* Charles Simic

Dogs in the Loft. Phan chu Trinh, *Vietnamese.* AVP, *tr. by* Huỳnh Sanh Thông

Dogs in the Morning Light. Bruce Dawe. NoAM

Dogs ran in the woods today, The. The Hunt Goes By. Howard Nemerov. *Fr.* Epigrams. OBAL

Dog's Song. Robert Wallace. TLR

Dog's Vigil, A. Margaret E. Bruner. PoToHe

Dogwood blossoms, lovely and full—. Betsy Sholl. CrSp *Fr.* Spring Fragments.

Dogwood flakes / what is green. Variations Done for Gerald Van De Wiele. Charles Olson. NOBA; NeAP; NoAM; NoP-4

Doing, a filthy pleasure is, and short. A Fragment of Petronius. Petronius Arbiter, *Latin.* EP; LoP; NNPT; OBCVT, *tr. by* Ben Jonson

Doing a filthy pleasure is, and short. Ben Jonson. PFE

Doing all right so far! (LL) Optimist fell ten stories, The. *Unknown.* FuFo

Doing Justice. Bruce Cutler. EC2

Doing the routine things / around the house. Stephen Dunn. *See* The Routine Things Around the House.

Doing Time in Baltimore. Judith Baumel. WWSi

Dol and Roger. Laetitia Pilkington. PEW

Dole of the King's Daughter, The. *Unknown, French.* AWP, *tr. by* Oscar Wilde

Doll, The. Peyton Houston. *Fr.* Sonnet Variations. Son

Doll. Myra Cohn Livingston. TLR

Doll. Josephine Miles. NALW

Doll, The. Gregory Orr. AmPA

Doll. John Wieners. FTOS

Doll in the doll-maker's house, A. The Dolls. W. B. Yeats. CMoP; NoAM; PoE

Dolls. David St. John. LCAP-2

Dolls, The. W. B. Yeats. CMoP; NoAM; PoE

Doll's hair concealing, A. Partial Resemblance. Denise Levertov. CoAP

Dolls Museum in Dublin, The. Eavan Boland. NoP-4

Dolls' Wash, The. Juliana Horatia Ewing. OxBChV

Dolor. Josephine Miles. FaBoWP

Dolor. Theodore Roethke. AmPP; CMoP; HCAP; HeIP-4; HoPM; LiTM; MoP; NoAM; OPOU; OxBSP; PBMP; PoA; TRP

("Glazing the pale hair, the duplicate gray standard faces.") (LL) SAGP

Dolores. Swinburne.
     "O lips full of lust and of laughter." UV

Dolorous, here he made his stand. He Who Loved Beauty. Alec Brock Stevenson. FuPo

Dolphin. Robert Lowell. NOBA; NoAM; VCAP

Dolphin plunge, fountain play. Invocation. Louis MacNeice. NTP

Dolphins, The. Carol Ann Duffy. NBrP

Dolphins play, The. The Aquarium. Thom Gunn. NOxBChV *Fr.* Three for Children.

Dolphins were Men, (Tradition hands the Tale). Oppian. APo, *tr. by* William Diaper *Fr.* Halieutica.

Dom Pedro, The. *Unknown.* AmFP

Domaine Public. Geoffrey Hill. OxBC *Fr.* Four Poems Regarding the Endurance of Poets.

Dome of Sunday, The [*or* A]. Karl Shapiro. CMoP; CoAP; LiTM; MoAmPo; NoAM; OxBA

Dome Poem. Dave Jeddie Smith. PoA

Domestic Asides; or, Truth in Parentheses. Thomas Hood. PeLV

Domestic Mysticism. Lucie Brock-Broido. PoPoPo

Domestic Philosopher, The. *Unknown.* ECWP

Domestic Poem. Eileen Moeller. CrSp

Domestic Poems. Thomas Hood.
     Serenade, A. NBLV

Domestic Scene. Michael Hartnett. BIrV

Domestic Stones (fragment), The. Hans Arp, *French.* CBNP; SPE, *tr. by* David Gascoyne

Domestic Storm, A. Priscilla Jane Thompson. CBWP-2

Domestic Tranquility. Gerald William Barrax. GT

Domesticity of Giraffes, The. Judith Beveridge. BMAP

Domestics. Kattie M. Cumbo. BlSi

Domicilium. Thomas Hardy. GaP; OBGa

Domination of Black ("At night, by the fire"). Wallace Stevens. AmPP; MoAmPo; OxBA

Domineering Eagle and the Inventive Bratling, The. Guy Wetmore Carryl. OBAL

Domingo Limón. Alberto A. Ríos. BAP-96

Dominic Francis Xavier Brotherton-Chancery. Pastoral. Gavin Ewart. OxBC

Dominica Pentecostes. Aubrey Thomas De Vere. TIRV

Dominus Illuminatio Mea. Richard Doddridge Blackmore. OBEV

Domus Caedet Arborem. Charlotte Mew. NTP; PBWP

Don. Anthony McNeill. PBCV

Don and Dave and Di—. The Ballad of Don and Dave and Di. John Heath-Stubbs. EBNV

Don Baty, the Draft Resister. Muriel Rukeyser. NNaP

Don Giovanni. Lorenzo Da Ponte, *Italian.*
     "Giovinette, Che Fate All'Amore." TrJP, *tr. by* Natalie MacFarren
     "Little lady, you are not going to like this." OxBoV, *tr. by* Amanda Holden *and* Anthony Holden

Don Juan. Byron. Ro *Fr.* Dedication: "Bob Southey! You're a poet—poet-laureate." CTC; OAEL-2; OBSV *Fr.* Don Juan.
     "All this she told with some confusion and." OxBSn
     "And thus they wandered forth, and hand in hand." EP
     Canto the Eleventh. NOBRP
         "In the great world—which, being interpreted." OxBoLi; PeLV
     Juan in England. FaBoVe, *canto* 11, *stanza* 8–20
         "Juan knew several languages—as well." OAEL-2
         "Over the stones still rattling, up Pall Mall." NOBL
         "To our theme. The man who has stood on the Acropolis." InPS-3; OBSV
         "'Where is the world!' cries Young at eighty." FaBoPV
     Canto the First. NAEL-2; OAEL-2; PoE
         Canto I. CABP
         Donna Julia. PoEL-4
         Growing Old. NOBE; SCV
         My Days of Love Are Over. OBNC
         Poetical Commandments. OxBoLi; PeLV, *canto* 1, *stanzas* 204–206
         "Poor Julia's heart was in an awkward state." NOBRP
         "Sagest of women, even of widows, she." NOBL; PeLV
         "They tell me 'tis decided you depart." CBLP
         "They tell me 'tis decided; you depart." NOBRP
         "What is the end of fame? 'Tis but to fill." OBCoV
         "Young Juan wandered by the glassy brooks." EPCY; OBCoV

("Like Coleridge into a metaphysician.") (LL) EPCY
Canto the Third.
  "Hail, Muse! et caetera.--We left Juan sleeping." OAEL-2
  Hesperus the Bringer. AWP
  (Evening.)
  "I know that what our neighbours call *longueurs*." OBSV
  "Isles of Greece, the isles of Greece!, The." AWP; FaPoR; NOBE;
    OBEV; OxAEP-2
  "Milton's the prince of poets—so we say." NOBL
  "We learn from Horace, Homer sometimes sleep." EPCY
  Dedication: "Bob Southey! You're a poet—poet-laureate." CTC; OAEL-2;
    OBSV
  Don Juan. Ro
  "If, fallen in evil days on evil tongue." EPCY
  "You gentlemen, by dint of long seclusion." EPCY
  Fragment: "I would to heaven that I were so much clay." CTC; NAEL-2;
    NOBL; OAEL-2; OxBSP
  "Grim reader, did you ever see a ghost?" OxBSn
  Lady Adeline Amundeville. PoEL-4
Don Juan. D. H. Lawrence. PoA
Don Juan. Sappho, *Greek.*
  "Oh Hesperus! thou bringest all good things." OBCVT, *tr. by* Byron
Don Juan had got out on Shooter's Hill. Juan in England. Byron. FaBoVe,
  canto 11, *stanza* 8–20 *Fr.* Canto the Eleventh. NOBRP *Fr.* Don Juan.
Don Juan in Hell. Charles Baudelaire, *French.* AWP, *tr. by* James Elroy
  Flecker
Don Juan is coming in the morning. Sarah Kirsch, *German.* CEEP, *tr. by*
  Tanaquil Taubes
Don Juan's Address to the Sunset. Robert Malise Bowyer Nichols. OBMV
Don' Let Yo' Watch Run Down. *Unknown.* AS
Don Quixote in England. Henry Fielding.
  Hunting Song. OxBoLi; PeLV
Don Surly, to aspire the glorious name. On Don Surly. Ben Jonson.
  FaBoEE; NAEL-1
Donagh MacDonagh. James Liddy. BiHa
Donahue's Sister. Thom Gunn. NoAM
Donal Og. *Unknown, Irish.* RB, *tr. by* Lady Augusta Gregory
Donal[l] Oge [*or* Og]: Grief of a Girl's Heart. *Unknown, Modern Irish.*
  GBL; PBWP; RB, *tr. by* Lady Augusta Gregory
Donald, he's come to this town. Dugall Quin. *Unknown.* ESPB
Donald of the Isles. *Unknown. See* Lizie Lindsay.
Done is a battell on the dragon blak. On the Resurrection of Christ.
  William Dunbar. ChIV-2; EnVB; NOCV; OxBS; PoEL-1
Done playing the lute, but still full of feeling. Pien Kung. *Fr.* Paintings.
  CoBLCP, *tr. by* Jonathan Chaves
Done to death by slanderous tongues. Epitaph. Shakespeare. CTC *Fr.*
  Much Ado about Nothing.
Done with the work of breathing; done. Ambrose Bierce. LiLi *Fr.* Dead.
Done with trying—no one's awake—it's dark. Morning. Edward Foster.
  PT
Donegal Hush Song, A. Cathal O'Byrne. TIRV
Dong, sounds the brass in the east. Henry David Thoreau. APAD; APN-1
Dong with a luminous Nose. (LL) The Dong with a Luminous Nose.
  Edward Lear. CBNP; EBNV; EBVV; NOBVV; NOxBChV; OxAEP-2;
  PoEL-5
Dong with a Luminous Nose, The. Edward Lear. CBNP; EBNV; EBVV;
  NOBVV; NOxBChV; OxAEP-2; PoEL-5
Donkey, The. G. K. Chesterton. ACTP; APo; CTAV; ChIV-2; EBEvV;
  FaPoR; GI; InPK-6; MoBrPo; OBEV; PFE; PoLF; RB
Donkey, The. Rose Fyleman. BoTP
Donkey, The. Theodore Roethke. OBCA
Donkey, The. *Unknown.* PeP
Donkey and the Lapdog, The. Jean de La Fontaine, *French.* OBVE, *tr. by*
  Marianne Moore
Donkey doctor came covered with rain, The. Big Friend of the Stones.
  Steve Orlen. Poetsp
Donkey, donkey, do not bray. *Unknown.* OxNR
Donkey, donkey, old and gray. *Unknown.* ACTP; ReMoGo
Donkey Riding. *Unknown.* ACTP
Donkey's tail is very nice, A. The Monotony Song. Theodore Roethke.
  ChAP
Donna Julia. Byron. PoEL-4 *Fr.* Canto the First. NAEL-2; OAEL-2; PoE
  Fr. Don Juan.
Donne. Hartley Coleridge. EPCY
Donne, the delight of Phoebus, and each Muse. To Donne. Ben Jonson.
  BeJo; EPCY; NAEL-1
Donner Party, The. George Keithley.
  From Land Logic. PaTW

Donnybrook. James Stephens. TIRV
Donought would have everything. Song. Ebenezer Elliot. NOBVV
Don's Holiday. George Rostrevor Hamilton. OBCoV
Don't ape what must be born in one. The Donkey and the Lapdog. Jean de
  La Fontaine, *French.* OBVE, *tr. by* Marianne Moore
Don't ask about the Six Dynasties of the Sui Palace. Wang T'ing-hsiang.
  CoBLCP, *tr. by* Jonathan Chaves *Fr.* Song of Wu-ch'eng.
Don't Ask Me for That Love Again. Faiz Ahmad Faiz, *Urdu.* VCWP, *tr.*
  by Agha Shahid Ali
Don't ask me what to wear. Sappho, *Greek.* PBWP, *tr. by* Mary Barnard
Don't Ask Me Who I Am. James A. Randall Jr. BPo
Don't ask whose face it is when you see me. Humiliation in Its Disguises.
  Andrew Crozier. NBrP
Don't Be Afraid, I Am With You. Peter Porter. LBC
Don't be afraid of dying. The glass of water. Couplets, XX. Robert
  Mezey. FYAP
Don't be dismayed, woman, by my fierce form. Annunciation. Primo Levi,
  Hebrew. AF, *tr. by* Ruth Feldman; GI, *tr. by* Ruth Feldman *and* Brian
  Swann (b. 1940)
Don't Be Fourteen (In Mississippi). Jerry W. Ward Jr. BkSV
Don't be like. On the birth of my son. Toki Zenmaro, *Japanese.* MJT, *tr.*
  by Makoto Ueda
Don't be literary, darling, don't be literary. Sasha Moorsom. APAD
Don't be oversure of your cherry-tree. Vizma Belševica, *Latvian.* CEEP, *tr.*
  by Inara Cedrins
Don't be polite. How to Eat a Poem. Eve Merriam. ChAP
Don't be scared of the dark. Dark Song. Martha Zweig. IFJA
Don't be startled, Supernatural One. Healing Prayer to the Salmon-Berry
  Vines. *Kwakiutl Oral Tradition, Kwakiutl.* PaTW, *tr. by* Franz Boas
Don't believe the hype. Public Enemy. NAAAL
Don't bite your nails. Amanda! Amanda! Robin Klein. OTCP
Don't blame me, ladies, if I've loved. No sneers. Sonnet 24. Louise Labé,
  French. BoWoP, *tr. by* Willis Barnstone
Don't bother telling me about the programs. TV. John Forbes. BMAP;
  CBAP
Don't bow down before [to] the little box. The Enemies of the Little Box.
  Vasco [*or* Vasko] Popa, *Serbo-Croatian.* HSix, *tr. by* Charles Simic
Don't Call Alligator Long-Mouth Till You Cross River. John Agard.
  NOxBChV
Don't care didn't care. *Unknown.* NTP; OTCP
Don't-Care—he didn't care. *Unknown.* ACTP
Don't-Care Negro, The. Joseph Cotter, Sr. AAP
Don't care where you come from. African. Peter Tosh. PBCV
Don't Count. Ory Bernstein, *Hebrew.* IP, *tr. by* Warren Bargad *and* Stanley
  F. Chyet
Don't. Crow and butcher bird. Sick Woman. John Kinsella. BMAP
Don't cry / over the happy dead. *Unknown, Greek.* GrAn, *tr. by* Peter
  Porter
Don't Cry, Scream. Haki R. Madhubuti. SeSe
Don't cut it to make a flute. The Bamboo by Li Ch'e Yun's Window. Po
  Chü-i, *Chinese.* OHMPC, *tr. by* Kenneth Rexroth
Don't deceive us. (LL) Song of the Bald Eagle. *Unknown.* STP
Don't doubt it, they remember. Maps. Susan Mitchell. MoLi
Don't dress for it. Chiyojo, *Japanese.* BoWoP, *tr. by* David Ray
Don't drive me out of my mind. Second Honeymoon. *Unknown, Irish.*
  BIrV, *tr. by* Augustus Young
Don't fash yourself, man! Don't complain. Palladas, *Greek.* GrAn, *tr. by*
  Tony Harrison
Don't fear me! there's the gray beginning. Zooks! Robert Browning. *See*
  Fra Lippo Lippi.
Don't fear me! There's the grey beginning. Zooks! (LL) Fra Lippo Lippi.
  Robert Browning. CTC; EBVV; EBVVPR; EnVR; FHYEP; OAEL-2;
  OxAEP-2
Don't fight, honey. Mama's Report. Michael S. Harper. FiLi
Don't Forget. Stephen Berg. PoA
Don't forget the crablike / hands. The Hands. Denise Levertov. NeAP;
  PoM
Don't forget when the sticks are ready for picking. Alice Sadongei.
  HATNAP
Don't give everything. David Foster. NOBAu *Fr.* The Fleeing Atalanta.
Don't Give Up. C. C. Cameron. PoToHe *Fr.* Success.
Don't Give Up. Phoebe Cary. CTV
"Don't give yo / right name no / No NO." (LL) Blackie Thinks of His
  Brothers. Stanley Crouch. GT
Don't go. Larry Eigner. PoM
Don't go climbing up to the blue clouds. Po Chü-i. *Fr.* Better Come Drink
  Wine with Me. CoBCP, *tr. by* Burton Watson

Don't go hide in the deep mountains. Better Come Drink Wine with Me. Po Chü-i. CoBCP, *tr.* by Watson, Burton (b. 1925) *Fr.* Better Come Drink Wine with Me. CoBCP, *tr.* by Burton Watson

Don't go into the realm of red dust. Po Chü-i. *Fr.* Better Come Drink Wine with Me. CoBCP, *tr.* by Burton Watson

Don't go off and be a farmer. Po Chü-i. *Fr.* Better Come Drink Wine with Me. CoBCP, *tr.* by Burton Watson

Don't Go Out of the Door. Li Ho, *Chinese.* PLT, *tr.* by A. C. Graham

Don't grieve. Anything you lose comes round. Jelaluddin Rumi, *Persian.* EnlH, *tr.* by Coleman Barks and A. J. Arberry

Don't Grow Old. Allen Ginsberg.
V. Father Death Blues. CLPP

Don't halt your voyage, sailor, nor drop sail. Johannes Barbucollas, *Greek.* GrAn, *tr.* by Peter Jay

Don't hand me over with a word, Toihau. Reply to a Marriage Proposal. Irihapeti Rangi Te Apakura, *Maori.* PBWP, *tr.* by Roger Oppenheim *and* Allen Curnow

Don't help-on the big chariot;. The Big Chariot. *Unknown.* ChiP, *tr.* by Arthur Waley *Fr.* The Book of Songs.

Don't hide the madness. (LL) On Burroughs' Work. Allen Ginsberg. NAAL-2; NOBA

Don't Hope to Gain by What Has Preceded. Joanne Kyger. PoM

Don't judge men by their gravestones. Antipater of Thessalonica, *Greek.* GrAn, *tr.* by Alistair Elliot

Don't kill that fly! Avedik Issahakian. ChAP

Don't kiss the mouth of Alphaeus. *Unknown, Greek.* InMo, *tr.* by Sam Hamill

Don't Knock the Rawleigh's Man. Vincent O'Sullivan. PeNZ

Don't know. But that' where we're going. (LL) The Scattered Congregation. Tomas Tranströmer, *Swedish.* RaBo, *tr.* by Robert Bly

Don't know / Nice, though. (LL) Ode on a Grecian Urn Summarized. Desmond Skirrow. NIP-4; NOBL

Don't Know No English. Nicolás Guillén, *Spanish.* PFTM, *tr.* by Langston Hughes

Don't know why I. Angola Question Mark. Langston Hughes. BPo; TTY

Don't laugh because it's muddy—year-end wine brewed in country homes. A Trip to Mountain West Village. Lu Yu, *Chinese.* CoBCP, *tr.* by Burton Watson

Don't leave me. Ion of Chios, *Greek.* InMo, *tr.* by Sam Hamill

Don't let freezing hands play with these pearls. Meng Chiao. SuSp, *tr.* by Stephen Owen *Fr.* Apricots Die Young.

Don't let her get out of your sight. (LL) The Craftsmen of the Little Box. Vasco [or Vasko] Popa, *Serbo-Croatian.* CEEP; HSix, *tr.* by Charles Simic

Don't let it matter much, Philaenis. Tymnes, *Greek.* GrAn, *tr.* by Alistair Elliot

Don't let me fall. Prayers: I. Kadya Molodovsky, *Yiddish.* WPoS, *tr.* by Kathryn Hellerstein

Don't let me lose you. How Tuesday Began. Kathleen Fraser. NYBP

Don't let that horse / eat that violin. Lawrence Ferlinghetti. APAD; CBNP; RB

Don't let them bother you, she said. Typographical Errors. Geof Hewitt. IFJA

Don't let them die out. Now Poem. For Us. Sonia Sanchez. PoBA

Don't lie down again. Lying Down. *Unknown, Bella Bella Indian.* STP, *tr.* by Franz Boas

Don't lock me in wedlock, I want. About Marriage. Denise Levertov. NALW

Don't look for the flaws as you go. Christina Rossetti. CTV

Don't love me, my sweet [or dear]. Song of a Common Lover. Flavien Ranaivo, *French.* TTY, *tr.* by Alan Ryder; PBMAP

Don't lower your eyes. Lady Freedom Among Us. Rita Dove. LoL

Don't make me go out eat goose. Ebenezer Californicus. August Kleinzahler. PmAP

Don't Move Away. Nino Nikolov, *Bulgarian.* CEEP, *tr.* by Ewald Osers

Don't offend. Song of the Breed. Carroll Arnett. LTA

Don't open the little box. The Craftsmen of the Little Box. Vasco [or Vasko] Popa, *Serbo-Croatian.* CEEP; HSix, *tr.* by Charles Simic

Don't pay any attention. Martial, *Greek.* PGA, *tr.* by Kenneth Rexroth

Don't Quit. *Unknown.* BLPA
(You Mustn't Quit.) PoToHe

Don't read odes, boy, timetables. For a Senior College Textbook. Hans Magnus Enzensberger. PoSu

Don't read this one out loud. Deaf Poem. Tess Gallagher. PUP-18

Don't remove the glasses and plates. Instructions for a Waitress. Yehuda Amichai, *Hebrew.* PoSu, *tr.* by Harold Schimmel

Don't resemble me. Tanka. Fumi Saito, *Japanese.* MJT, *tr.* by Makoto Ueda

Don't run anymore. Quiet. How softly it rains. After Paradise. Czeslaw Milosz, *Polish.* ITG, *tr.* by Czeslaw Milosz *and* Robert Hass (b. 1941); EP

Don't say, don't say there is no water. The Fountain. Denise Levertov. CrSp

Don't say goodbye to the Porkpie Hat that rolled. Larry Neal. GT; MoNo ("Again, this time from the chorus.") (LL) ISC; SeSe
("Don't say goodbye to the pork-pie hat that rolled along on.") SeSe

Don't say: How can Phoenix Hill. Tune: "Happy Events Approaching." Kuan Yün-shih. SuSp, *tr.* by Richard John Lynn *Fr.* Medley of Southern and Northern Tunes—Scenic Tour of West Lake.

Don't say there are only hills and slopes at West Lake. Abandoning the Plans of Visiting West Lake. Hsü Wei, *Chinese.* SuSp, *tr.* by Irving Y. Lo

Don't say to me. On Wishes. Mahmoud Darwish, *Arabic.* VCWP, *tr.* by Denys Johnson-Davies

"Don't scold me, ladies, if I have loved." Louise Labé. *See* Sonnet 24: "Don't blame me, ladies, if I've loved. No sneers."

Don't seek me where the myrtles bloom! My Camping Ground. Morris Jacob Rosenfeld, *Yiddish.* TrJP, *tr.* by Aaron Kramer

Don't send me a dove. To The Beloved. "Anna Akhmatova," *Russian.* LoP, *tr.* by Judith Hemschemeyer

Don't set sail! Love-Poem. Fêng Mêng-lung, *Chinese.* ChiP, *tr.* by Arthur Waley

Don't shirk. Good Advice. Hilaire Belloc, *German.* CTV, *tr.* by Louis Untermeyer

Don't shoo the morning flies away. Han Yü, *Chinese.* SuSp, *tr.* by Kenneth Hanson

Don't sing: a song. Drops of Gall. Gabriela Mistral, *Spanish.* BoWoP, *tr.* by David Garrison

Don't sing "The Song of Everlasting Sorrow." Ma-wei. Yüan Mei, *Chinese.* CoBLCP, *tr.* by Jonathan Chaves

Don't sleep! for your paddle fell into the water and your spear. Song of Parents Who Want to Wake Up Their Son. *Unknown, Kwakiutl Indian.* TTTS

Don't sleep, look! Ingrid Jonker, *Afrikaans.* WPOW, *tr.* by Elizabeth Jones

Don't steal. Thou'lt never thus compete. Ambrose Bierce. NBLV

Don't step. The Cracks. Robert Creeley. CoAmPo

Don't stop after beating the swords. An Appendix to the Vision of Peace. Yehuda Amichai, *Hebrew.* PoSu, *tr.* by Glenda Abramson *and* Tudor Parfitt

Don't suppose that the weightless phantom. The Titans. Betti Alver, *Estonian.* BoWoP, *tr.* by Willis Barnstone and Felix Oinas

Don't sweep away this green after the rain. Moss below the Stairs. Kao Ch'i, *Chinese.* CoBLCP, *tr.* by Jonathan Chaves

Don't take the cups and dishes. Instructions for the Waitress. Yehuda Amichai, *Hebrew.* IP, *tr.* by Warren Bargad and Stanley F. Chyet

Don't talk to me. Paul Brown. NBrP *Fr.* De Rebus.

Don't Talk to Me about Bread. E. A. Markham. HCP; PBCV

Don't talk to me about trees having branches and roots. On Trees. Alan Dugan. NoAM

Don't talk to me of love. I've had an earful. In Paris with You. James Fenton. NoP-4

Don't tell lies with your tears. Poseidippus, *Greek.* InMo, *tr.* by Sam Hamill

Dont' tell me I'm getting gray. Paulus Silentiarius, *Greek.* PGA, *tr.* by Kenneth Rexroth

Don't tell me objects don't have feelings. Living with the Boss. Ken Smith. NBrP

Don't the moon look lonesome shining through the trees? Sent for You Yesterday. Jimmy Rushing. NAAAL

Don't thee think, Zurrr, I be zo amazin'. Limerick. Elizabeth H. Lister. PeLi

Don't think governments end the world. The blast. Molly Peacock. NAmP90

Don't think I haven't noticed you. The Muses. Marilyn Hacker. NMM-2

Don't think it will fall to your lot. Limerick. Leslie Johnson. PeLi

Don't think / that I don't know. Sous-Entendu. Anne Stevenson. LW; OxBSP

Don't throw your arms around me in that way. Footnote to John II: 4. Ronald Allison Kells Mason. PeNZ

Don't touch me. The Hermaphrodite's Song. Lorna Mitchell. BrRo

Don't touch my corpse. Standing Coffin. Tamura Ryuichi, *Japanese.* AF, *tr.* by Christopher Drake

Don't touch that. And stop your whining too. What I Heard at the Discount Department Store. David Budbill. RaBo; TRP

Don't touch that fruit, Eve. *Paradise Lost* as a Haiku. Stanley J. Sharpless. BXAP; OBCoV

Don't trace out your profile. Antonio Machado Ruiz. RaBo, *tr.* by Robert Bly *Fr.* Moral Proverbs and Folk Songs.

Don't travel beyond. Immigrant. Arthur Nortje. PeSAV

Don't wait for the lamplighter. Alcaeus, *Greek.* InMo, *tr. by* Sam Hamill

Don't wait for the wind to blow you through the door. Moving In. Paul Engle. PoA

Don't Walk beside the Big Carriage. *Unknown, Chinese.* CoBCP, *tr. by* Burton Watson

Don't walk like a drunken sailor,. Fracture Santa Monica. Gail Mazur. BAP-95

Don't waste yourself, dragging out the life of a vagrant. Leonidas of Tarentum, *Greek.* GrAn, *tr. by* Peter Jay

Don't we talk of then are unsealed they efflorescing. Giant Philosophical Otters. Jackson Mac Low. FTOS

Don't weep for me—I'll live on. Incantation. Bella Akhatovna Akhmadulina, *Russian.* TCRP, *tr. by* Albert C. Todd

Don't worry about growing old. Prayerwheel: 2. David Meltzer. NeAP

Don't worry baby. Broken Heart, Broken Machine. Richard E. Grant. PoBA

Don't worry, nobody has the. The Secret. Charles Bukowski. RaBo

Don't worry / One night we'll find that deserted kinema. If Life's a Lousy Picture, Why Not Leave before the End. Roger McGough. OxBTC

Don't worry, spiders. Issa. ChAP; PiM

Don't worry, you'll get there! You're close. Philippe Jaccottet, *French.* MFP, *tr. by* Martin Sorrell

Don't worry. You're in darkness. Instructions to a Seed. David Curzon. GI

Dont Worry Yr Hair. Bill Bissett. NOBC

Don't write poems about what's happening. Looking for Poetry. Carlos Drummond de Andrade, *Portuguese.* ChAP, *tr. by* Mark Strand

Don't ya tell Henry. "Bob Dylan." CBNP

Don't You Be like the Foolish Virgin. *Unknown.* AH

Don't you care for my love? she said bitterly. Intimates. D. H. Lawrence. BoLoP; CBLP; NBLV; OxBSP; RaBo

Don't you feel sorry. Moles. Aileen Fisher. CTV

Don't You Hear that Whistle Blowin'. Denise Levertov. GM

Don't you know. The Ox-Soldier. Oumar Ba. PBMAP

Don't you love my baby, mam. Infant Song. Charles Causley. NOxBChV; OxBC

Don't you remember sweet Alice, Ben Bolt. Ben Bolt. Thomas Dunn English. APN-1; FaBoBe

Don't you see, north of Ch'ang-an, by the bridge over Wei River. The Weary Road. Lu Chao-lin, *Chinese.* SuSP, *tr. by* Robin D. S. Yates

Don'ts. D. H. Lawrence. LiTM; OxBoLi; PeLV

Doodle doodle doo, / The Princess lost her shoe. The Lost Shoe. *Unknown.* ReMoGo

Dooley Is a Traitor. James Michie. OxBTC

Doom Ferry. Sir Arthur Thomas Quiller-Couch. EBVV

Doom is dark and deeper than any sea-dingle. The Wanderer. W. H. Auden. CMoP; GTBS-P; MeMAP; MoP; NoAM; RB; WeW-3

Doom of Beauty, The. Michelangelo Buonarroti, *Italian.* AWP, *tr. by* John Addington Symonds

Doom of Devorgoil, The. Sir Walter Scott.
   Bonny [*or* Bonnie] Dundee. FaBoCh; OxBS; OxBoLi; UV

Doomed Garden, A. Octavio Paz, *Spanish.* GaP, *tr. by* Eliot Weinberger

Doomed in the depths to dwell. Thanksgiving. David Abenatar Melo, *Spanish.* TrJP, *tr. by* Henry Hart Milman

Doomed Spaceman, The. Ted Walker. SpW

Doomsayers, The. Pattiann Rogers. LoHo

Doomsday. George Herbert. GeHe; SeCP

Doomsday. Elinor Wylie. NoP-4

Doomsday Morning. Genevieve Taggard. MoAmPo

Doon Deeside cam Inverey. The Baron of Braikley. *Unknown.* OxBB

Door, The. W. H. Auden. Son *Fr.* The Quest.

Door, The. Robert Creeley. NeAP; NoAM; PoM; VGW

Door, A. W. S. Merwin. LCAP-2; SPE

Door, The. Leonard Alfred George Strong. MoBrPo

Door, The. Charles Tomlinson. PoA

Door. Valerie Worth. CA

Door and Window Bolted Fast. Mani Leib, *Yiddish.* TrJP, *tr. by* Joseph Leftwich

Door behind me was you, The. You (I). Tom Clark. PmAP; SPE *Fr.* You.

Door-Bell, The. Charlotte Becker. PoToHe

Door closes on pain and confusion, The. The Room. Galway Kinnell. AFr

Door Creaked Three Times, The. Sandor Csoori, *Hungarian.* CEEP, *tr. by* Nicholas Kolumban

Door does not turn; in my window, no face, The. Purity. Avigdor Hame'iri, *Hebrew.* MHP, *tr. by* Ruth Finer Mintz

Door is before you again and the shrieking, The. Mark Strand. NoAM

Door is closing, The. Prayer to my Muse. Vassar Miller. NMM-2

"Door is shut fast, The." Who's In. Elizabeth Fleming. BoTP

Door isn't locked. You walk, The. In the Gloaming. Jennifer Maiden. BMAP

Door of Hope, The. Lizelia Augusta Jenkins Moorer. CBWP-3

Door slam, The. After the First Frost. Lew Blockcolski. VoR

Door still swinging to, and girls revive, The. A Dream of Fair Women. Kingsley Amis. NoAM; OAEL-2

Door sunk in a hillside, with a bolt, A. The Icehouse in Summer. Howard Nemerov. MoP; NoAM

Door swung open, The. Kenneth Mackenzie. BMAP

Door that someone opened wide, The. The Message. Jacques Prévert, *French.* WeW-3, *tr. by* John Frederick Nims

Door to mine, The. (LL) I Remember. Anne Sexton. LW

Door was shut, as doors should be, The. Jack Frost. "Gabriel Setoun." BoTP

Door was shut. I looked between, The. Shut Out. Christina Rossetti. NALW

Doorbell buzzed, The. It was past three o'clock. The Australian Dream. David Campbell. CBAP

Doors. Tom Clark. CoAmPo

Doors. Thérèse Plantier, *French.* BoWoP, *tr. by* Willis Barnstone *and* Elene Kolb

Doors flapped open in Ulysses' house, The. The Return. Edwin Muir. CMoP

Doors open by themselves, The. The Chicken. Vladimir Holan, *Czech.* PoSu, *tr. by* Ian *and* Jarmila Milner

Doors open on the sands, doors open on exile. "St.-John Perse." AF, *tr. by* Denis Devlin *Fr.* Exile.

Doors, the little doors, swing wide, The. (LL) Jim Desterland. Hyam Plutzik. RB; VGW; WeT

Doors, where my heart was used to beat. Tennyson. EnVR; FHYEP; OBNC; PoEL-5; SCV *Fr.* In Memoriam A. H. H.

Dope. Imamu Amiri Baraka. APSN

Doper's Dream. Don Receveur. CDa

Dora versus Rose. Austin Dobson. NOBL

Dora Williams. Edgar Lee Masters. HAP *Fr.* Spoon River Anthology.

Dorcas, be off! & tell her this. Meleager, *Greek.* GrAn, *tr. by* Peter Whigham

Doré knew this overhang. View from the Gorge. Ben Belitt. NYBP

Doreen had a round face. Janice Mirikitani. UnSA

Doretha wore the short blue lace last night. The Reception. June Jordan. FaBoWP

Doria. Ezra Pound. MoAmPo

Doricha. Poseidippus, *Greek.* AWP; FaBoEE; OBVE; OBCVT, *tr. by* E. A. Robinson *Fr.* Variations of Greek Themes.

Doricha, your soft bones are. Poseidippus, *Greek.* GrAn, *tr. by* Edward Lucie-Smith

Dorinda's sparkling wit, and eyes. On Dorinda. Charles, 6th Earl of Dorset Sackville. NOSC; OBEV; OxBSP

Doris. William Congreve. NOEC

Doris and Philemon. Sir John Collings Squire.
   "Now the declining fulgent orb of day." BXAP

Doris, I that could repell. The Snow-Ball. Thomas Stanley. CBLP

Dormouse, The. Charlotte Druitt Cole. BoTP

Doron's Description of Samela. Robert Greene. *See* Samela.

Doron's Jigge. Robert Greene. PoEL-2 *Fr.* Menaphon.

Dorothy Q. Oliver Wendell Holmes. NOBA

Dorothy Rose had a turned-up nose. The Rhyme of Dorothy Rose. Pauline Frances Camp. FPC

Dorothy Wordsworth, dying, did not want to read. My Sisters, O My Sisters. May Sarton. NALW

Dorothy's Dower. Phoebe Cary. PAR

Dos Geshray (The Scream). Jerome Rothenberg. FTOS

Dose of a mere, The. The Discovery of LSD a True Story. Anselm Hollo. PoM

Dosn't thou 'ear my 'erse's legs, as he canters awaäy? Northern Farmer: New Style. Tennyson. EnVR; NAEL-2; OBCoV; OxAEP-2; PeVV

Dossier of the Torturer. Michael Benedikt. WeT

Dost see how unregarded now. Sonnet. Sir John Suckling. BeJo; CaPo; CavPo; NOSC

Dost tha hear my horse's feet, as he canters away? Lord Tennyson and Lord Melchett. D. H. Lawrence. FaBoEE

Dost therefore swell and pout with pride. A Tyrant in Sleep, Naught Differeth from a Common Man. Timothy Kendall. NoSic

Dost thou forget. Shakespeare. OxAEP-1 *Fr.* The Tempest. OAEL-1

Dost thou remember ever, for my sake. Mathilde Blind. OBNC *Fr.* Love in Exile.

Dot a dot dot dot a dot dot. Weather. Eve Merriam. NOxBChV; TLR

Dotes less on Nature, then on Art. (LL) Art above Nature, to Julia. Robert Herrick. BeJo; CABP; NOSC

Doth dye unknowen, dazed with dreadfull face. (LL) Senec. Traged. ex Thyeste Chor. 2. Seneca, *Latin.* AAS; NoSic; OBCVT; OBVE; PoEL-1; SiPS, *tr. by* Sir Thomas Wyatt

Doth make my heart give to my tongue the lie! (LL) Sonnet 47: "What, have I thus betrayed my liberty?" Sir Philip Sidney. GBL; NAEL-1; NoP-4; PoEL-1

Doth not a Tenarif[e], or higher hill. Donne. *Fr.* The First Anniversary [*or* Anniversarie]. NAEL-1 *Fr.* Anatomy [*or* Anatomie] of the World, An[: The First Anniversary].

Doth not thou, Castara, read. A Dialogue between Araphil and Castara. William Habington. BeJo *Fr.* Castara.

Do[e]th rise [*or* ryse] again and greater wood [*or* wode] do[e]th bind [*or* bynd]. (LL) He is not de[a]d that sometime [*or* somtyme] hath a fall. Sir Thomas Wyatt. AAS; OBVE

Doth some one say that there be gods above? Euripides. *See* There Are No Gods.

Doth someone say that there be gods above? There Are No Gods. Euripides. OBCVT, *tr. by* John Addington Symonds *Fr.* Bellerophon.

Doth then the world go thus, doth all thus move? William Drummond, of Hawthornden. GTBS-P

Doth warm our hands, and make them write of love. (LL) Love (1). George Herbert. GeHe; HoPM; Son

Dotito is our brother. Charles Mungoshi. PeSAV

D'Où Venons Nous? Que Sommes Nous? Où Allons Nous. A. L. Hendriks. PBCV

Double, The. Irving Feldman. NYBP

Double Autumn, The. James Reeves. OxBSP

Double Ballad of Good Counsel, A. François Villon, *French.* AWP, *tr. by* Swinburne

Double Bass. Sue May. NBrP

Double Bed. Carol Rumens. LW

Double boiler fixed on fiery wheels, A. On Shakespeare Critics. Alec Derwent Hope. OxBC *Fr.* Dunciad Minor.

Double curtains hang deep in the room of Never Grieve. Li Shang-yin, *Chinese.* PLT, *tr. by* A. C. Graham

Double Dactyl. Chris Wallace-Crabbe. OBCoV

Double Dactyls. Eric Salzman. OBCoV

Double Dactyls. E. William Seaman. OBCoV

Double Date. Lincoln Kirstein. PeLV

Double, double toil and trouble. Song of the Witches. Shakespeare. *Fr.* Thrice the Brinded Cat Hath Mewed. RB *Fr.* Macbeth.

Double Elegy. Michael S. Harper. NoAM

Double Feature. Robert Earl Hayden. NoAM

"Double flesh / Double way." Freud: Dying London, He Recalls the Smoke of His Cigar Beginning to Sing. James Schevill. TAP

Double-Goer, The. Daryl Hine. MoCV

Double-headed Snake, The. John Newlove. MoCV

Double-horned, nocturnal Moon. Philodemus, *Greek.* GrAn, *tr. by* William Moebius

Double-lived in regions new! (LL) Ode: "Bards of passion and of mirth." Keats. FHYEP; GTBS-P; OBEV; OxAEP-2

Double Looking Glass, The. Alec Derwent Hope. CBAP

Double-Play, The. Robert Wallace. CMAP; PFE

Double Rock, The, *sonnet.* Henry, Bishop of Chichester King. CBLP; NOSC; SeCP

Double Sestine [*or* Sestina]. Sir Philip Sidney. ImPo; PoEL-1 *Fr.* Arcadia.
("Our morning hymne this is, and song at evening.") (LL) PBRV
("*Strephon.* Ye Goat-herd gods, that love the grassy.") GEA
("Ye goatherd gods, that love the grassy mountains.") NoP-4

Double Shame, The. Stephen Spender. LiTM

Double Sonnet. Anthony Hecht. Son

Double Standard, The. Franklin Pierce Adams. OBAL

Double Standard, A. Frances Ellen Watkins Harper. AAP; BlSi; CrDW; NAAAL; PWR

Double Take at Relais de L'Espadon. Thadious M. Davis. BlSi

Double Transformation, The. Oliver Goldsmith. OBCoV; OBNV

Double Trouble. David Trinidad. PmAP

Double Vision of Manannan, The. *Unknown, Irish.* BIrV, *tr. by* John Montague

Doubled at their feet. (LL) King Harald's Trance. George Meredith. EBNV; PeVV

Doubly unfortunate are those who dwell in Hell—. Lucilius, *Greek.* GrAn, *tr. by* Peter Porter

Doubt. Mary Elizabeth Coleridge. NALW

Doubt, A. Sarah Morgan Bryan Piatt. NCAP

Doubt. Tennyson. *Fr.* In Memoriam A. H. H.

Doubt crept into a heart one day, A. Clara Ann Thompson. CBWP-2

Doubt no longer miracles. Miracles. Arna Bontemps. NAAAL

Doubt of future foes exiles my present joy, The. Elizabeth I, Queen of England. CTC; NAEL-1; NALW; NoP-4; NoSic; PBWP; WPE
("To poll their tops that seek such change or gape for future joy.") (LL) NoP-4; PEW

Doubt of Martyrdom, A. Sir John Suckling. *See* Sonnet: "O[h]! for some honest lover's ghost."

Doubt there hath been, when with his golden chain. Sonnet 58. Sir Philip Sidney. *Fr.* Astrophil and Stella. AAS; SiPS

Doubt which ye misdeem, fair love, is vain, The. Edmund Spenser. *See* Sonnet 65.": "The Doubt which ye misdeeme, fayre love, is vaine."

Doubt which ye misdeeme, fayre love, is vaine, The. Sonnet 65." Edmund Spenser. NAEL-1 *Fr.* Amoretti. AAS

Doubt you to whom my Muse these notes intendeth [*or* entendeth]. First Song. Sir Philip Sidney. OxAEP-1 *Fr.* Astrophil and Stella. AAS; SiPS

Doubtful divines, lawyers that wrangle most. Saturn's Three Sons. Robert Hayman. NOSC *Fr.* Owen's Epigrams.

Doubting. Louis Simpson. NNaP

Doubts. Rupert Brooke. CH

Douglas and the Bruce's Heart. Sir Richard Holland. *Fr.* The Buke of the Howlat.

Douglas, Douglas, Tender and True. Dinah Maria Mulock Craik. BLPA; LW
("Could you come back to me, Douglas, Douglas.") LW

Douglas, Douglas, tender and true. (LL) Douglas, Douglas, Tender and True. Dinah Maria Mulock Craik. LW

Douglas Tragedy, The. *Unknown. See* Earl Brand (The Douglas Tragedy).

Douglass. Paul Laurence Dunbar. AAP; CBCWP; GSo; NAAAL; Son

Douglass was someone who. Frederick Douglass: 1817-1895. Langston Hughes. BPo; CDCWP

Doun by the baundstaund, by the ice-cream barrie. In Princes Street Gairdens. Robert Garioch. FaBoTC

Doun throu the sea. Cokkils. Sydney Goodsir Smith. OxBS; PoA

Dour thing in olive trees, The. Olive Trees. Bernard Spencer. NoAM

Dousing clean a thousand old cares. A Night with a Friend. Li Po, *Chinese.* CoBCP, *tr. by* Burton Watson

Dove, The. Victor James Daley. NOBAu

Dove. Norma Farber. PChr

Dove, A. Ted Hughes. OxBC

Dove and the Wren, The. Mother Goose. ReMoGo

Dove Apologies to His God for Being Caught by a Cat, The. Anthony Eaton. PeSA

Dove has brought an olive branch to eat, The. (LL) Where the Rainbow Ends. Robert Lowell. HCAP; NoAM

Dove, I think, is more suited, The. Raven's Monologue. Ivan V. Lalic, *Serbo-Croatian.* HSix, *tr. by* Charles Simic

Dove in Songbukdong, The. Kwangsop Kim, *Korean.* CKP, *tr. by* Jaihiun Kim

"Dove-Love." Judith Wright. NIP-4; NoAM

Dove of liberty sat on an egg, The. The American Eagle. D. H. Lawrence. OAEL-2

Dove of New Snow, The. Vachel Lindsay. MoAmPo

Dove of rarest worth, A. Judah Halevi, *Hebrew.* TrJP, *tr. by* Amy Levy

Dove purrs—over and over the dove, The. "Dove-Love." Judith Wright. NIP-4; NoAM

Dove says, Coo[, coo], The. The Dove and the Wren. Mother Goose. BoTP; CTAV; OxNR; ReMoGo

Dove stays in the garden, The. *Ambo Oral Tradition. Fr.* Five Ghost Songs. TTTS

Dove that ventured outside, flying far from the dovecote. Rilke, *German.* EnlH, *tr. by* Stephen Mitchell

Dove walks with sticky feet, The. Pastoral. Kenneth Patchen. CLPP

Dover Beach. Matthew Arnold. APAD; AWP; BLPA; CABP; ClHu; EBVV; EBVVPR; FaBoBe; GTBS-P; HAP; HeIP-4; HoPM; ImPo; InPK-6; InPS-3; NAEL-2; NIP-4; NOBE; NOBVV; NoP-4; OAEL-2; OBNC; OxBoS; PBMP; PFE; PeVV; PoE; PoEL-5; PoPoPo; PoRA; SAGP; SCGP; SCV; TFi; TOF

Dover Bitch, The. Anthony Hecht. BXAP; NBLV; NIP-4; NOBA; NOBL; OBAL; PFE; PeLV; UnPo; VGW
("And sometimes I bring her a bottle of *Nuit d' Amour.*") (LL) PFE
(Dover Bitch: A Criticism of Life, The.) Poetr; TRP

Dover Cliffs. William Lisle Bowles. OxAEP-2

Dover, the Samphire Cliff. Shakespeare. *Fr.* King Lear.

Dover to Munich. Charles Stuart Calverley. NOBL

Doves. E. J. Falconer. BoTP

Doves, The. Katharine Tynan. AWP

Doves come down for bread on the sun-warmed stone, The. (LL) Pro Patria. Constance Carrier. AFr

Dove's Loneliness, The. George Darley. OBNC

Doves the speckled doves, The. In Aix. Grace Paley. NMM-2

Dowager. John Montague. IIP

Dowager Duchess of Spout, The. Limerick. Edward Gorey. PeLV; PeLi

Dowie Dens of Yarrow, The. *Unknown.* IBB

Dowie Houms o' Yarrow, The. *Unknown.* OBEV; OxBS
(Braes o' Yarrow, The.) ESPB

Down a blackened alley. La Llorona. Greg Pape. AmPA

Down a broad river of the western wilds. The Indian Woman's Death-Song. Felicia Dorothea Hemans. NoP-4; PEW; Ro

Down all the lanterned Bagdad of our youth. On Reading the Life of Haroun Er Reshid. Madison Cawein. APN-2

Down among the roots like a half-. Nuchal, a Fragment. Thomas Kinsella. PBCIP

Down among the smelly dungeons. The Prisoner. Eduard Friedrich Mörike, *German.* CBNP, *tr. by* Christopher Middleton

Down and Out. Clarence Leonard Hay. BLPA

Down and out. Langston Hughes. PoE

Down-and-Out Fighter and the Spring Nymph, A. Trần Huy Liệu, *Vietnamese.* AVP, *tr. by* Huỳnh Sanh Thông

Down at the docks. Kenneth Koch. VGW

Down below / I run from street to street. I Run With a Pair of Compasses Stuck in the Back of My Head. Novica Tadic, *Serbo-Croatian.* HSix, *tr. by* Charles Simic

Down by the brook which glides through yonder vale. Robin; a Pastoral Elegy. John Dobson. NOEC

Down by the church-way walk, and where the brook. An Ancient Virgin. George Crabbe. OBNC *Fr.* Burials. OAEL-1 *Fr.* The Parish Register.

Down by the gate of the orchard. Spring Whistles. Lucy Larcom. OBCA

Down by the greenhouse. Dirty Panes. Judith Barrington. IFJA

Down by the meadows, chasing butterflies. *Unknown.* BoTP

Down by the ocean side where ships were sailing. The Nightingales of Spring. *Unknown.* AmFP

Down by the river. *Unknown.* OxNR

Down by the salley gardens my love and I did meet;. W. B. Yeats. CBLP; CMoP; CTC; EBEvV; EBVV; EnLoPo; GLoP; MoBrPo; NAEL-2; NoAM; OBEV; PoEL-5; PoPoPo; SAGP; SoSe-8

Down by the Station, Early in the Morning. John Ashbery. HCAP

Down by the weeping willow. Florella; or, The Jealous Lover. *Unknown.* AmFP

Down by the Wild Mustard River. The Wild Mustard River. *Unknown.* AmFP

Down by yon garden green. The Laird of Wariston. *Unknown.* ESPB

Down! Down! Eleanor Farjeon. NTCP

Down, Down Derry Down. *Unknown.* AS

Down, down, in millions, blending. The Snow-Flakes. Priscilla Jane Thompson. CBWP-2

Down / Down into the fathomless depths. Black Is a Soul. Joseph Blanco White. PoBA

Down, down into the great world's flowering. (LL) The Gardener to His God. Mona Van Duyn. GaP; RACG; TrCP; UnPo; WPE

Down, down with the Devil. (LL) Simon Legree—A Negro Sermon. Vachel Lindsay. MeMAP; MoAmPo; TAP

Down drop of the blackbird, The. Three Spring Notations on Bipeds. Carl Sandburg. AWP

Down flew the shaft of the god. A Love Affair. Arnold Bennett. OxBTC

Down from the bridge rail. Clement Hoyt. HA

Down from the Country. John Blight. BMAP; CBAP

Down from the north on the north wind flying. And Stands There Sighing. Elizabeth Jane Coatsworth. KaS

Down from the purple mist of trees on the mountain. The Bull Moose. Alden Nowlan. NTP

Down from the tower, back at sea-level. The Reel World. Jim Hall. CMAP

Down-Hearted Blues. Albert Hunter *and* Louie Austin. NAAAL

Down here now / summer's burnt skeins. In Blanco County. Russell T. Fowler. NOBC

Down hills floating by heart on the bulldozed land. (LL) For Robert Frost. Galway Kinnell. NOBA; VGW

Down home / he sets on a stoop. Neighbor. Langston Hughes. APSN; PFTM

Down I came to wash my soul. Tuskegee, Tuskegee! Lance Jeffers. BkSV

Down in a Coal Mine. J. B. Geoghegan. AmFP

Down in a green and shady bed. The Violet. Jane Taylor. WoRP

Down in Atlanta. Slim in Atlanta. Sterling Brown. NoP-4

Down in Carlisle there lived a lady. The Lady of Carlisle. *Unknown.* AmFP

Down in Dallas, down in Dallas. X. J. Kennedy. PFE

Down in Dumbarton there wonnd a rich merchant. Bonnie Annie. *Unknown.* ESPB

Down in front of Casey's old brown wooden stoop. The Sidewalks of New York. James W. Blake. BLPA; FaBoBe

Down in history we find it and in grandest works of art. Negro Heroines. Lizelia Augusta Jenkins Moorer. CBWP-3

Down in some lone valley, in some lonesome place. Pretty Saro. *Unknown.* AmFP

Down in some lonesome piney grove. Lonesome Dove. *Unknown.* AmFP

Down in St. Louis at 12th and Carr. Brady. *Unknown.* AS

Down in the bass / That steady beat. Easy Boogie. Langston Hughes. APSN

Down in the bleak December bay. The Mayflower. Erastus Wolcott Ellsworth. FaBoBe

Down in the bottom built for comfort. (LL) Impressions / of Chicago; For Howlin' Wolf. Quincy Troupe. NAAAL; NBV

Down in the cabin all things were gay. Thwarted. Priscilla Jane Thompson. CBWP-2

Down in the deep, dumb worlds are waiting, silent;. Letter to My Wife. Miklós Radnóti, *Hungarian.* AF, *tr. by* Emery E. George

Down in the dell. Sunrise. Henrietta Cordelia Ray. BlSi *Fr.* Idyl. CBWP-3

Down in the depth of mine iniquity. 99. Fanny [*or* Frances] Macartney Greville. CABP *Fr.* Caelica.

Down in the depth of mine iniquity. Sonnet: "Down[e] in the depth of mine iniquity." Greville Fulke. NOSC; NoSic *Fr.* Caelica.

Down in the field. M. P. Flynn. CTV

Down in the flood of remembrance, I weep like a child for the past. (LL) Piano. D. H. Lawrence. APAD; CABP; CMoP; GTBS-P; HAP; HeIP-4; InPK-6; MoBrPo; MoP; NAEL-2; NOBE; NoAM; NoP-4; OAEL-2; OPOU; OxBSP; PoE; Poetr; RB; SCGP; TFi; TRP; UnPo; WeW-3

Down in the Frantic Mountains. A Survey. William Stafford. RB

Down in the grassy hollow. Merry Little Men. Kathleen M. Chaplin. BoTP

Down in the hole we go, boys. Lament while Descending a Shaft. *Unknown.* AmFP

Down in the Lonesome Garden. *Unknown.* BPo

Down in the meadow. *Unknown.* CBNP

Down in the mine, in the dark, dismal drift. Only a Miner. *Unknown.* AmFP

Down in the orchard. Geoffrey Hill. HAP *Fr.* The Pentecost Castle.

Down in the south, by the waste without sail on it. Beyond Kerguelen. Henry Clarence Kendall. NOBAu

Down in the Valley. *Unknown.* CrDW

Down in the valley, valley so low. *Unknown.* AS
("And back it in care of the Birmingham Jail.") (LL) APN-2

Down in yon garden sweet and gay. Willy Drowned in Yarrow. *Unknown.* GTBS-P

Down in Yonder Meadow [where the green grass]. *Unknown.* ACTP; CH

Down [*or* Downe] lay the shepherd swain. Hye Nonny Nonny Noe. *Unknown.* NOBL; PeLV

Down let the shrine of Moloch sink. Henry Highland Garnet. CrDW

Down mountain roads like scars across a fist. At Tripolis. Constance Carrier. WPE

Down near the end of a wandering lane. A Rhyme of the Dream-Maker Man. William Allen White. PoLF

Down near The river. Spring of Work Storm. Joseph Ceravolo. FTOS

Down on My Luck. Arthur Rex Dugard Fairburn. PeNZ

Down poured the rain; the closed window streamed. The Storm. Margaret Stanley-Wrench. LW

Down rippling, The. Frank K. Robinson. HA

Down she comes from her vermilion tower, her face freshly adorned. A Song of Spring Replying to a Poem by Po Chü-yi. Liu Yu Hsi, *Chinese.* SuSp, *tr. by* Daniel Bryant *and* Ronald C. Miao

Down streams of centuries grown old. Women of My Land. Frankie Armstrong. BrRo

Down stucco sidestreets. Dublinesque. Philip Larkin. NoAM; OxBC

Down the assembly line they roll and pass. The Brides. Alec Derwent Hope. HAP

Down the billboard girl's bare belly. Leroy Gorman. HA

Down the blue night the unending columns press. Clouds. Rupert Brooke. OBEV; OBMV; OxBTC

Down the Canongate. Old Edinburgh. Norman MacCaig. FaBoTC

Down the centuries, eternal. From a Venetian Sequence. Adèle Naudé. PeSA

Down the close, darkening lanes they sang their way. The Send-Off. Wilfred Owen. MoBrPo; NSI; OBWP; OBWVE; OxBTC; PeFWW; PoWW; RB; SAGP

Down the cloud ladder, but the problem has not been solved. (LL) Our Youth. John Ashbery. CoAmPo; VGW; WeT

Down the coast south of here. Earth. Jim Tollerud. VoR

Down the dawn-brown. The Current. James Merrill. NYBP

Down the dead streets of sun-stoned Frederiksted. The Virgins. Derek Walcott. OxBC; SoSe-8

Down the dim aisle of standing pullman coaches. Departure. Mildred Weston. FFC

Down the dripping pathway dancing through the rain. Rainy Song. Max Eastman. FaBoBe

Down the Glimmering Staircase. Siegfried Sassoon. PoLF *Fr.* Vigils. CMoP

Down the green hill-side fro' the castle window. Lady Jane. Sir Arthur Thomas Quiller-Couch. PeLV

Down the imperturbable street. (LL) An Aspect of Love, Alive in the Ice and Fire. Gwendolyn Brooks. BPo; CAPP-1; TAP

Down the irrationally humped. Origins. Vincent Buckley. BMAP

Down the long avenues the north wind. 5°. Nicholas Christopher. WWSi

Down the long hall she glistens like a star. Venus of the Louvre. Emma Lazarus. APN-2; GS; PAR

Down the long path beneath the garden wall. A Dream. Vita Sackville-West. WPN

Down the M4. Dannie Abse. OxBC

Down the narrow Calle where the moonlight cannot enter. Venetian Nocturne. Agnes Mary Frances Robinson. VWP

Down the Nile. Robert Lowell. HCAP

Down the North Channel Paul Jones did steer just at break of day. (LL) The Yankee Man-of-War. *Unknown.* AmFP; FaBoBe

Down the red stock route. Song for the Cattle. David Campbell. NOBAu

Down the road someone is practising scales. Sunday Morning. Louis MacNeice. FaBoMo; MoBrPo; NAEL-2; NIP-4; OxAEP-2; Son

Down the rock chute into the tombs of the kings they grope these battling sandalled. This Is the Life. Louis MacNeice. NoAM

Down the slimy rope into the impossible! The Poem Films Itself. J. S. Harry. BMAP

Down the street the ground is feeling so. The Directions. Christopher Gilbert. GT

Down the valley gan he track. The Palmer. Robert Greene. NoSic

Down the waves of the Yang-tse-Kiang. Ballade of the Chinese Lover. Stuart Merrill. APN-2

Down the white steps, into the night, she came. Victory. Lionel Pigot Johnson. NOBVV

Down the winding lanes of Moscow, down its hopeless. Elegies on the Cardinal Points. Yelena Shwarts, *Russian.* VCWP, *tr. by* Michael Molnar

Down the Wolf river. Feasts of Death, Feasts of Love. Stuart Z. Perkoff. NeAP

Down their carved [*or* chiselled] names the rain-drop ploughs. (LL) During Wind and Rain. Thomas Hardy. CMoP; GTBS-P; HAP; NAEL-2; OAEL-2; OxBTC; PeVV; PoE; TFi; TOF; TRP

Down, down then, thou rogue thou, red three-cornered / varlet. The Clarissa Harlowe Poem. Gavin Ewart. OxBoV

Down there a poor woman. The Potter. *Unknown, Geez.* TTY, *tr. by* Halim El-Dabh

Down there where I was. The Story of My Life. Carroll Arnett. VoR

Down through the earth as a last gift. Meleager, *Greek.* PGA, *tr. by* Kenneth Rexroth

Down to dark leaf-mold. O. Mabson Southard. HA

Down to me quickly, down! I am such dust. The Mummy Invokes his Soul. "Michael Field." VWP

Down to the Mire. *Unknown.* WPoS

Down to the Puritan marrow of my bones. Puritan Sonnet, IV. Elinor Wylie. BoWoP; BoWoP; SAGP *Fr.* Wild Peaches. ColAP; FaBoWP; LiTM; LoP; NAAL-3; NALW; OxBA; WPE

Down to the river! into the street! (LL) II. Allen Ginsberg. CLPP

Down to the Sacred Wave. Samuel Francis Smith. AH

Down under green. RMS Lusitania. Richmond Lattimore. PFE

Down under the bridge you. Shakti. Rae Desmond Jones. BMAP

Down, up—a single dot of red. Pitch-Ball. Yang Chi. CoBLCP, *tr. by* Jonathan Chaves *Fr.* Ten Poems on the Tuan-yang Festival.

Down valley a smoke haze. Mid-August at Sourdough Mountain Lookout. Gary Snyder. ColAP; HAP; InPK-6; LoL; NoP-4; PaTW; TAP; VCAP

Down, Wanton, Down! Robert Graves. BoLoP; CBLP; CMoP; EP; FaBoTw; HeIP-4; InPK-6; LiTM; MoP; NAEL-2; NoAM; OAEL-2; PoE; Poetr

Down where New York's a-glare at night. Exiles. Patrick O'Connor. TIRV

Down where the Dream Woman dwells. (LL) The Paradox. Paul Laurence Dunbar. AAP; PoBA

Down with the lambs. *Unknown.* OxNR

Down with the Rosemary and Bay[e]s. Ceremonies for Candlemas[se] Eve. Robert Herrick. BeJo; CaPo

Down with the rosemary, and so. Ceremony upon Candlemas Eve. Robert Herrick. OBCP

Down you go alone, so late, into the surge-black fissure. (LL) You Will Know When You Get There. Allen Curnow. NoP-4; PeNZ

Down, you mongrel, Death! The Poet and His Book. Edna St. Vincent Millay. MoAmPo

Downe in the depth of mine iniquity. Fulke Greville. *See* Sonnet: "Down[e] in the depth of mine iniquity."

Downe to the king's most bright-kept baths they went. Homer. CTC, *tr. by* George Chapman *Fr.* Odyssey. NAWM-1, *tr. by* Robert Fitzgerald

Downed Black Pilot Learns How to Fly, A. Horace Coleman. CDa

Downfall. Georg Trakl, *German.* AF, *tr. by* Simko, Daniel

Downfall of Heathendom, The. *Unknown, Irish.* IIP, *tr. by* Frank O'Connor

Downfall of the Gael, The. Fearflatha O'Gnive, *Late Middle Irish.* AWP, *tr. by* Sir Samuel Ferguson

Downhill [*or* Down hill] I came, hungry, and yet not starved. The Owl. Edward Thomas. AF; APo; ChAP; EBEV; FaBoTw; GTBS-P; MoP; NAEL-2; NIP-4; NOBE; NoAM; NoP-4; OAEL-2; OBWVE; OxAEP-2; PeFWW; PoE; Poetr; RB; SCGP; TFi; TRP; UnPo

Downland Crisis, A. Wyndham Lewis. "Ale they drink in Giggleswick, The." UV

Downpour. Daisy Zamora, *Spanish.* CLPP, *tr. by* Barbara Paschke

Downstairs I laugh, I sport and jest with all. L.E.L E. L. Christina Rossetti. VWP

Downstream. Thomas Kinsella. PBCIP

Downtown Los Angeles: / In the baroque lobby. Bagpipes at the Biltmore. Robert Conquest. OBCoV

Downtown, on the precinct wall. Field Trip. Carol Muske. WWSi

Downward to darkness, on extended wings. (LL) Sunday Morning. Wallace Stevens. AmPP; CMoP; ColAP; HAP; HCAP; HeIP-4; InPS-3; LiTM; MeMAP; MoAmPo; MoP; NAAL-2; NAWM-2; NIP-4; NOBA; NoAM; NoP-4; OxBA; PoA; PoE; PoPoPo; Poetr; SAmP; SoSe-8; TAP; TFi; TRP

Dow's Flat. Bret Harte. FaBoBe

Dowsed coals fume and hiss after your meal, The. The Book of Yolek. Anthony Hecht. HP; NoP-4; WeW-3

Dowser, The. Edwin Morgan. FaBoTC; NoP-4

Doxology. Josephine D. Henderson Heard. CBWP-4

Doxology. Bert Leston Taylor. OBAL

Doxy, oh! thy glaziers shine. The Maunder's Praise of His Strowling Mort. *Unknown.* CBNP; OxBoLi; PeLV

Doyen of walls. Apologia (Nkomati). Wole Soyinka. HBAPE

Doze, The. James Reeves. CTV

Dozen dozen in her place, A. (LL) Constant Lover, A [*or* The]. Sir John Suckling. BeJo; CBLP; CavPo; EBEvV; GLoP; ImPo; NBLV; NOSC; NoP-4; OxAEP-1; PBMP; PBRV; PeLV; PoE; SAGP

Dozen false starts, A. Riding a Nervous Horse. Vicki Hearne. APo

Dozen sparrows scuttled on the frost, A. France. Douglas Dunn. LBC; OxBM

Dozens of girls would storm up. Embraceable You. Ira Gershwin. CBLP

Dozens of wrangling sparrows have built their. Power Transformer. Ian Wedde. PeNZ *Fr.* Earthly: Sonnets for Carlos.

Dozing on the Porch with an Oriental Lap-Rug. Richard Tillinghast. WeT

Draft for a Contemporary Love Poem. Tadeusz Rózewicz, *Polish.* EP, *tr. by* Adam Czerniawski

Draft for an Ancestor. George MacBeth. FaBoTC

Draft Horse, The. Robert Frost. CMoP; HeIP-4; HoPM; PFE; PoE; SAmP; TRP

Draft of a Modern Love Poem. Tadeusz Rózewicz, *Polish.* PoSu, *tr. by* Magnus J. Krynski; VCWP, *tr. by* Magnus J. Krynski *and* Robert A. Maguire

("In a modern love poem.") (LL) BLT, *tr. by* Czeslaw Milosz

(Sketch for a Modern Love Poem, A.) BLT, *tr. by* Czeslaw Milosz

Draft of a Reparations Agreement Dan Pagis, *Hebrew.* AF; HP; PoSu, *tr. by* Stephen Mitchell

("And will emigrate / to the sky.") (LL) AF, *tr. by* Stephen Mitchell

Drafted. Su Wu, *Chinese.* OHMPC, *tr. by* Kenneth Rexroth

Drafts for a Quatrain. Edmund Wilson. OBAL

Drafty winds and fine rain. Spring Joy. Chu Shu-chen, *Chinese.* ChiPo, *tr. by* Kenneth Rexroth *and* Ling Chung

Dragging his hunger through the sky. The Vulture. Samuel Beckett. *Fr.* Echo's Bones. NoAM

Dragging in Winter. David McElroy. AmPA

Dragon, The. Mary Mullineaux. BoTP

Dragon, The. Edmund Spenser. *Fr.* Wood Of Error. AEP

Dragon-Fly, The. Walter Savage Landor. OBEV

(Lines to a Dragon-Fly.) OBNC

Dragon-fly strives patiently, The. Haiku. José Juan Tablada, *Spanish.* PBMP, *tr. by* Samuel Beckett

Dragon has come, A. Olive Dove. OTCP

Dragon Mouth Cliff. Chao Meng-fu. *Fr.* Twenty-Eight Poems Inscribed on T'ien-kuan Mountain. CoBLCP, *tr. by* Jonathan Chaves

Dragon never rears its head before sending down torrential rain. Filled with Emotions on the Moon-ferrying Bridge at Arashiyama. Liu Ya-tzu, *Chinese.* SuSp, *tr. by* Wu-chi Liu

Dragon Night. Jane Yolen. OTCP

Dragon Skate. Gladys Cardiff. CDW

Dragon that our seas did raise his crest, The. Of the Great and Famous. . . Sir Francis Drake, and of My Little-Little Selfe. Robert Hayman. CH; FaBoCh

Dragon-Tiger Terrace. Yang Shih-ch'i, *Chinese.* CoBLCP, *tr. by* Jonathan Chaves

Dragonfish, The. John Balaban. CDa

Dragonflies were here before us, friend, The. Woodniche. Aidan Carl Mathews. APAD

Dragonfly, The. Louise Bogan. HeIP-4; Poetr

Dragonfly. J. D. McClatchy. APo

Dragonfly, The. Howard Nemerov. PoA

Dragonfly blue as the June Atlantic, A. Between Equals. Robert Wallace. PFE

Dragonfly / Dead on the snow. Gary Snyder. BLT

Dragonfly-Mother, The. Denise Levertov. InPS-3

Dragons and snakes tangle in my dream; they can hardly recoil. Liu Ya-tzu, *Chinese.* SuSp, *tr. by* Wu-chi Liu

Drags his tail on the ground, damn thief. Thief. Novica Tadic, *Serbo-Croatian.* CEEP; HSix, *tr. by* Charles Simic

Drained Cup, The. D. H. Lawrence. CBLP; FaBoVe

Drained spittle from his pipe, then scrammed. (LL) To William Carlos Williams. Galway Kinnell. NoAM; Poetr

Drake he's in his hammock an' a thousand mile away. Drake's Drum. Sir Henry John Newbolt. EBEvV; FaBoCh; FaPoR; OBMV; PoRA; UV

Drake, who the world hast conquered like a scroll. To the Noble Sir Francis Drake. Thomas Beedome. OxBSP

Drake's Drum. Sir Henry John Newbolt. EBEvV; FaBoCh; FaPoR; OBMV; PoRA; UV

Drama of our time is the coming of all men into one fate, The. Rites of Participation. Robert Duncan. PFTM *Fr.* Rites of Participation.

Drama's Vitallest Expression is the Common Day. Emily Dickinson. NOBA

Dramatic Fragments. Trumbull Stickney.
    "I heard a river thro' the valley wander." APN-2
    ("I hear a river thro' the valley wander.") NoP-4
    "Sir, say no more." APN-2; InPK-6; OxBA; OxBSP

Dramatic Scenes and Other Poems. "Barry Cornwall."
    Dream, A. Ro

Dramatic Symphony, The. Andrey Bely, *Russian.*
    "By-street was bathed in sun, The." PFTM, *tr. by* Roger Keys *and* Angela Keys

Drances in debate. Virgil, *Latin.* OBCVT, *tr. by* Sir Richard Maitland

Drank lonesome water. Lonesome Water. Roy Helton. MoAMPo

Drank tonight at Eastern Slope, sobered up, drank again, Tune: "Immnortal at the River." Tune: Immortal at the River. Su Tung-p'o, *Chinese.* CoBCP, *tr. by* Burton Watson

Dransfield, who wrote. Eight xx. Laurie Duggan. BMAP

Draped in khaki, Jurgis. Jurgis Petrakas, the Workers' Angel, Organizes the First Miners' Strike in Exeter, Pennsylvania. Anthony Petrosky. FYAP

Drat my hateful birthday. Sulpicia, *Latin.* PBWP, *tr. by* John Dillon

Draw a bucket of water. *Unknown.* FaBoVe

Draw a deep breath. Hold it. Let it go. Healing the World from Battery Park. Tim Dlugos. BAP-93

Draw a little closer, comrades! The Fisherman's Story. Henrietta Cordelia Ray. CBWP-3

Draw a pail of water. *Unknown.* BoTP; FaBoVe; LB; OxNR

Draw in your head and sleep the long way home. (LL) Meticulous, past midnight in clear rime. Hart Crane. ColAP; NAAL-2; PoE

Draw me nere [*or* near], draw me nere [*or* near]. *Unknown.* EBEV

"Draw me," the cypress said. Childhood Painting Lesson. Henry Rago. WHSW

Draw near [*or* neer], / You lovers that complain. The Exequies. Thomas Stanley. BeJo; MeLP

Draw near, / And list what with our council we have done. Shakespeare. OxAEP-1 *Fr.* King Richard II.

Draw near, young men, and learn of me. McAfee's Confession. *Unknown.* AmFP

Drawer. Zbigniew Herbert, *Polish.* VCWP, *tr. by* Czeslaw Milosz and Peter Dale Scott

Drawer of My Writing Desk, The. Boris Petrovich Kornilov, *Russian.* TCRP, *tr. by* Bernard Meares

Drawing near unto the merry month of May. (LL) Old May Song. *Unknown.* BoTP; CH

Drawing on the Traditions. Cris Cheek.
    "Succulence by implication pinks the eye with condensation, A." NBrP

Drawing Room Drama. Virginia Hooper. PT

Drawing you, heavy with sleep to lie closer. Sylvia Townsend Warner. WPN

Drawings of the Song Animals. Duane Niatum. HATNAP

Drawn by old Homer's hand, the rose. Helen like the Rose. Evan Lloyd. OBWVE *Fr.* The Powers of the Pen.

Drawn by Stones, by Earth, by Things That Have Been in the Fire. Marvin Bell. VCAP

Drawn on the blackboard. School and Nature. Jean Follain, *French.* BLT, *tr. by* W. S. Merwin

Drawn on the burden of light. Bleat. Barbara Guest. FTOS

Draws rein and sings to the swing of the tide. (LL) The Phantom Horsewoman. Thomas Hardy. CMoP; NOBE; PoEL-5

Draws tears, or blood [*or* bloud]. (LL) The Dawning. George Herbert. ESCV; NOSC

Drayman, The. Walt Whitman. *Fr.* Song of Myself. AmPP; MoAMPo; NAAL-3; NOBA; OxBA

Dread. John Millington Synge. BoLoP; MoBrPo; OxBSP; PFE

Dread are the death-pale Kings. Still-Heart. Frank Pearce Sturm. OBMV

Dreaded Task, The. Margaret E. Bruner. PoToHe

Dreadful case of murder, A. Execution of Alice Holt. *Unknown.* OxBoLi; OxBoV

Dreadful Dinotherium he, The. Hilaire Belloc. NOBL *Fr.* A Moral Alphabet.

Dreadful Fate of Naughty Nate, The. John Kendrick Bangs. OBCA

"Dreadful Has Already Happened, The." Mark Strand. HCAP; NoAM; VCAP

Dreadnought, The. *Unknown.* AmFP

Dreadwalk. Dennis Scott. HCP

Dream, A. Bella Akhatovna Akhmadulina, *Russian.* BoWoP, *tr. by* Jean Valentine *and* Olga Carlisle

Dream, A. Matthew Arnold. EnVR; GBL; GTBS-P *Fr.* Switzerland.

Dream, The. Aphra Behn. PBWP; RACG *Fr.* A Voyage to the Isle of Love.

Dream, The. "Brian Bendo." NOEC

Dream, The. John Peale Bishop. LiTM

Dream, A. William Blake. CH; FHYEP; NOBRP; Ro *Fr.* Songs of Innocence.

Dream, The. Louise Bogan. InPK-6; LiTM; MoAMPo; NALW; NoAM

Dream. Elizabeth Cook-Lynn. *Fr.* Journey. HATNAP

Dream, A. "Barry Cornwall." Ro *Fr.* Dramatic Scenes and Other Poems.

Dream, A. W. H. Davies. CBLP

Dream. Richard Watson Dixon. EBEV; NOBVV; PeVV; SCGP

Dream[e], The. Donne. CBLP; ESCV; FMP; MeLP; OAEL-1; OBEV; SeCP; TOF

Dream, The. Irving Feldman. VCAP

Dream, The. Robert Earl Hayden. NBV

Dream, The ("I dreamed that, buried in my fellow clay"). *Unknown.* NOEC

Dream, The. David Ignatow. CoAP; NNaP

Dream. Nana Issaia, *Modern Greek.* BoWoP, *tr. by* Helle Tzalopoulou Barnstone

Dream, A. Maggie Pogue Johnson. CBWP-4

Dream, A. Evan Jones. NOBAu

Dream[e], The. Ben Jonson. BeJo; CBLP; NOBE; NOSC; PoEL-2

Dream, A. Keats. OBNC *Fr.* The Fall of Hyperion. OAEL-2
    Garden-Dream, A. GaP

Dream, The ("Last night I supped on lobster; it nearly drove me mad"). *Unknown.* OxBoLi

Dream, The. William Matthews. PuP-16

Dream. Novella Nikolaevna Matveyeva, *Russian.* TCRP, *tr. by* Deming Brown

Dream. Josephine Miles. PoA

Dream, A. Milton. *See* On His Deceased Wife.

Dream. Marianne Moore. NYBP

Dream, The. Paul Petrie. TAP

Dream, The. Felix Pollak. RaBo

Dream, The. Lola Ridge. NMM-2

Dream, The. Theodore Roethke. EP; NYBP; UnPo

Dream. Raphael Rudnik. PC

Dream, A. Vita Sackville-West. WPN

Dream, The. Sir Edward Sherburne. OxBSP

Dream, A. Rachel Speght. WPE

    "My grief, quoth I, is called Ignorance." KTR

Dream, A. Sir John Suckling. ChIV-2

Dream, A. May Swenson. NMM-2

Dream, The. May Swenson. DeD   *Fr.* Poet to Tiger. GLP

Dream, A. Tanka. Kondō Yoshimi, *Japanese.* MJT, *tr. by* Makoto Ueda

Dream. Vahan Tekeyan, *Armenian.* AF, *tr. by* Hovanessian, Diana Der and Marzbed Margossian

Dream, A. Charles Tomlinson. OxBC

Dream. *Unknown, Eskimo.* STP, *tr. by* Armand Schwerner

Dream, A. Charles Williams. OBEV

Dream, A [*or* The]. William Allingham. BIrV; NOBVV

Dream about a Piano, A. Yury Davydovich Levitansky, *Russian.* TCRP, *tr. by* Sophie Lund

Dream about Our Master, William Shakespeare, The. Hyam Plutzik. RB

Dream after dream I see the wrecks that lie. Posted. John Masefield. Son

Dream, after Reading Dante's Episode of Paolo and Francesca, A. Keats. NOBRP

Dream at Night, A. Mei Yao Ch'en, *Chinese.* BLT; OHPC, *tr. by* Kenneth Rexroth

Dream Barker. Jean Valentine. VGW

Dream behind the. Here. Bob Orr. PeNZ

Dream Below the Sun, The. Antonio Machado Ruiz. Roads. IMW, *tr. by* Willis Barnstone

Dream Boogie. Langston Hughes. APSN; AmPP; HCAP; NAAAL; PFTM; SSLK

    ("Y-e-a-h!.") (LL) NAAAL; PFTM; SSLK

Dream Boogie: Variation. Langston Hughes. APSN

    ("For the Freedom Train.") (LL) SSLK

    ("Tinkling treble.") SSLK

Dream Broke, A. William Cartwright. NOSC

Dream Called Life, The. Pedro Calderón de la Barca, *Spanish.* AWP, *tr. by* Edward Fitzgerald

Dream Come True. Molly Peacock. RA

Dream Data. Robert Duncan. NeAP

Dream Deferred. Langston Hughes. *See* Harlem.

Dream Dream, The. Michael Davidson. FTOS

Dream, Dump-Heap, and Civilization. Robert Penn Warren. AFr

Dream Fairy, The. Thomas Hood. BoTP

Dream Feast (Three Poems), The. Anita Endrezze-Danielson. VoR

Dream fluently, still brothers, who when young. To the Etruscan Poets. Richard Wilbur. OxBC

Dream House. Catherine Parmenter-Newell. PoToHe

Dream in a dream the heavy soul somewhere. Canto Amor. John Berryman. CoAP; MoAmPo; VGW

Dream is an old and forgotten truth, A. Everyone Will Write Poetry. Branko Miljkovic, *Serbo-Croatian.* HSix, *tr. by* Charles Simic

Dream it was in which I found myself, A. The Dream Called Life. Pedro Calderón de la Barca, *Spanish.* AWP, *tr. by* Edward Fitzgerald

Dream Kitchen, The. Sandra M. Gilbert. IFJA

Dream-Land [*or* Dreamland]. Edgar Allan Poe. APN-1; AmPP; MeMAP; NAAL-1; NAAL-3; NOBA; OxBA; PAR; TAP

Dream Land. Christina Rossetti. BrRo

Dream-Language of Fergus, The. Medbh McGuckian. CIP-2

Dream Lesbian Lover. "Chrystos." CPO

Dream-Love. Christina Rossetti. CH; HAP; PoEL-5

Dream Maiden, A. Harriet Hamilton King. VWP

Dream May 18, 1958. Peter Orlovsky. BB

Dream not, O Soul, that easy is the task. Help. John Greenleaf Whittier. Son

Dream of a Baseball Star. Gregory Corso. BB; PmAP; VGW

Dream of a Black Fox. Brendan Kennelly. PBCIP

Dream of a Boy Who Lived at Nine Elms, The. William Brighty Rands. OxBChV

Dream of a summer day: a hearse. A Summer Day. Robert Greacen. PNI

Dream of Comparison, A. Stevie Smith. BWW

Dream of Completion, The. Shirley Kaufman. LCAP-2

Dream of Death, A. W. B. Yeats. GBL

Dream of Dying, A. Leslie Monsour. FFC

Dream of Elfland, A. Henrietta Cordelia Ray. CBWP-3

Dream of Fair Women, A. Kingsley Amis. NoAM; OAEL-2

Dream of Gerontius, The. John Henry, Cardinal Newman.

    Chorus of Angels. NOCV; PoEL-5

    (Fifth Choir of Angelicals.) NOBVV

Dream of Glass Bangles, A. Agha Shahid Ali. OpBo; WeT

Dream of Governors, A. Louis Simpson. NYBP

Dream of Heaven, A. Li Ho, *Chinese.* PLT, *tr. by* A. C. Graham

Dream of Husbands, A. Alberto A. Ríos. NoAM

Dream of Instant Total Representation, The. Anselm Hollo. PmAP

Dream of Jealousy, A. Seamus Heaney. NoP-4

Dream of Judgement, A. Douglas Dunn. OxBC

Dream of Mind: The Gap, A. Charles Kenneth Williams. BAP-93

Dream of Mountaineering, A. Po Chü-i, *Chinese.* BLT; ChiP, *tr. by* Arthur Waley

Dream of Pairing. Ntozake Shange. GT

Dream of Rebirth. Roberta Hill Whiteman. CDW

Dream of Retarded Children, A. Robert Bly. LoL

Dream of Sappho, A. Rose Cecil O'Neill. CPO

Dream of the Artfairy. Carl Morse. GLP

Dream of the Cabbage Caterpillars, The. Libby Houston. AYFP

Dream of the Cross, The. *Unknown, Anglo-Saxon.* EBEV, *tr. by* Sally Purcell

Dream of the Forgotten Lover. Lucia Fox, *Spanish.* BoWoP, *tr. by* R. Maghan

Dream of the Quartz Pebble, The. Vasco [*or* Vasko] Popa. PoSu, *tr. by* Anne Pennington   *Fr.* The Quartz Pebble.

    (Dream of the Pebble.) CEEP, *tr. by* Charles Simic

    ("Hand springs out of the earth, A.") CEEP, *tr. by* Charles Simic

Dream of the Rood, A. Cynewulf, *Old English.* AnOE; OAEL-1, *tr. by* Charles W. Kennedy

Dream of the Rood, The ("Listen! I will describe the best of dreams"). *Unknown, Anglo-Saxon.* ASW, *tr. by* Kevin Crossley-Holland

Dream of the Rood, The. *Unknown, Anglo-Saxon.* EEP; NOCV, *tr. by* Michael Alexander

Dream of the Unknown, The. Shelley. *See* The Question ("I dream'd that, as I wander'd by the way").

Dream of Trains, A. Mark Van Doren. GM

Dream of Venus, A. Bion, *Greek.* AWP, *tr. by* Leigh Hunt

Dream of Winter. George Mackay Brown. FaBoTw

Dream, or the Type of the Rising Sun, A. Jean Adams. ECWP; NOEC

Dream Orpheum Balcony. Tom Dent. BkSV

Dream-Pedlary. Thomas Lovell Beddoes. BoTP; CH; FaBoBe; HAP; NOBE; OBEV; OBNC; OxAEP-2; PoEL-4; Ro

    ("Ever to last!") (LL) Ro

Dream, ploughman, of what agriculture brings. Elegy for the Lost Parish. Douglas Dunn. DiPo

Dream Poem. Mary Jo Bona. UnSA

Dream Question, A. Thomas Hardy. ChIV-1

Dream Record: June 8 1955. Allen Ginsberg. CoAmPo; NOBA

Dream Sequence, Part 9. Naomi Long Madgett. BPo

Dream Ship, The. W. K. Holmes. BoTP

Dream Song. Lewis Alexander. PoBA; WHSW

Dream Song. *Unknown, Pawnee.* OBVE, *tr. by* Francis Densmore

Dream Songs. John Berryman.

    324. An Elegy for W.C.W., The Lovely Man. NoP-4

    April Fool's Day, or St. Mary Egypt. ChIV-2

    "At Henry's bier let some thing fall out well." NoP-4

    "Chilled in this Irish pub I wish my loves." FaBoMo; LCAP-2

    "Deprived of his enemy, shrugged to a standstill." CAPP-1; LCAP-2

    Dream Song 4. PoPoPo

    Dream Song 45. PoPoPo

    Dream Song 384. PoPoPo

    Dream Song 55. ChIV-2

    "Full moon. Our Narragansett gales subside." CoAP

    "Glories of the world struck me, made me aria, once, The." HCAP

    "God bless Henry. He lived like a rat." CAPP-1

    "He lay in the middle of the world, and twitcht." HCAP; PoE

    "He yelled at me in Greek." FYAP

    "Henry sats in de bar and was odd." ColAP; HCAP; PoPoPo; VCAP

    ("Of a newborn child.") (LL) ColAP

    Henry's Confession. LCAP-2; MoP; NAAL-2; NoAM; PoE; TwCP; VCAP

    "Henry's mind grew blacker the more he thought." FaBoMo; NOBA

    "Henry's pelt was put on sundry walls." MoP; NoAM; Poetr; TRP

    "How this woman came by the courage, how she got." TAP

    "Huffy Henry hid the day." CBNP; ColAP; HCAP; NAAL-2; NoP-4; PoE; VCAP

    "I am, outside. Incredible panic rules." VCAP

    "I can't get him out of my mind, out of my mind." NoP-4

    "I have moved to Dublin to have it out with you." MoP; NoAM; TRP

    "Ill lay he long, upon this last return." TAP

    "I'm cross with god who has wrecked this generation." FaBoMo

"Irish have the thickest ankles in the world, The." TAP

Lay of Ike, The. LCAP-2

"Life, friends, is boring. We must not say so." ColAP; HAP; HCAP; HeIP-4; LiTM; MoP; NAAL-2; NOBA; NoAM; NoP-4; TAP; TRP; TwCP; VCAP

"Love her he doesn't but the thought he puts." FaBoMo

Sabbath. LCAP-2

"Seedy Henry rose up shy in de world." HCAP; VCAP

So Long? Stevens. HAP; HCAP; NOBA

"Some good people, daring and subtle voices." HCAP

Song 385. MoLi

"Supreme my holdings, greater yet my need." CRP

"That dark brown rabbit, lightness in his ears." TwCP

"That's enough of that, Mr Bones. *Some* lady you make." NAAL-2; VCAP

"There are voices, voices. Light's dying. Birds have quit." CAPP-1

"There sat down, once, a thing on Henry's heart." CAPP-1; HAP; HCAP; NoP-4; PoE; VCAP

"Thin as a sheet his mother came to him." FiLi

"This world is gradually becoming a place." MoP; NOBA; NoAM; SAGP

"Three 'coons came at his garbage. He be cross." LCAP-2

"Three limbs, three seasons smashed; well, one to go." HCAP

"Thunder & the flaw of their great quarrel, The." VCAP

"Turning it over, considering, like a madman." MoP; NoAM

"Welcome, grinned Henry, welcome fifty-one!" TAP

"You couldn't bear to grow old, but we grow old." TAP

"Your face broods from my table, Suicide." CAPP-1; TAP

Dream that stole o'er us in the time. Charlotte Brontë. PEW *Fr.* Retrospection.

Dream, The; An Epistle to Mr. Dryden. Elizabeth Thomas. KTR

Dream Thief. Nathaniel Mackey. GT

Dream Time. Anthony Thwaite. DiPo

Dream 2: Brian the Still-Hunter. Margaret Atwood. BoWoP; CrSp

Dream Variation[s]. Langston Hughes. HAP; NAAAL; NAAL-2; NOBA; NoP-4; PoBA; SAGP; SSLK; SAmP

("Night coming tenderly / Black like me.") (LL) HAP; NAAL-2; NOBA; PoBA; SAmP

Dream where land, The. The Island of Mirrors. Ricardo Pau-Llosa. CMAP

Dream within A Dream, A. Edgar Allan Poe. AmPP; GBL; MeMAP; NCAP; NOBA; OxBA; TAP

Dream within a Song, A. Henrietta Cordelia Ray. CBWP-3

Dream you remember yet. (LL) Ave atque Vale. Rosamund Marriott Watson. NOBE; OAEL-2; OBEV; OBNC

Dreame, The. Rachel Speght.

"*Disswasion* hearing her assigne my helpe." PBRV

Dreamed Realization, A. Gregory Corso. NeAP; PoM; VGW

Dreamer. Jean Binta Breeze. HCP

Dreamer Meets Riot, The. John Skelton. *Fr.* The Bowge of Courte. AAS

Dreamer of Dreams. William Herbert Carruth. PoLF

Dreamer, visionary, green-eyed sluggard! Mikhail Valentinovich Kulchitsky, *Russian.* TCRP, *tr. by* Daniel Weissbort

Dreamers. Siegfried Sassoon. GSo; MoBrPo; NoAM; Son

("Soldiers are citizens of death's gray land.") GSo

'Dreamers?' Ah, no! else he was a dreamer. Louisa Sarah Bevington. VWP

Dreaming. Larry Wiggin. HA

Dreaming Child, The. Felicia Dorothea Hemans. NOBRP

Dreaming Frankenstein. Liz Lochhead. FaBoTC

Dreaming I sat by the fire last night. The Saturday Tub. Mary Gilmore. NOBAu

Dreaming of a Dead Lady. Shên Yo, *Chinese.* ChiP, *tr. by* Arthur Waley

Dreaming of Li Po. Tu Fu, *Chinese.* CoBCP, *tr. by* Burton Watson

"Drifting clouds pass by all day long." SuSp, *tr. by* Eugene Eoyang

"Parted by death, we swallow remorse." SuSp, *tr. by* Eugene Eoyang

Dreaming of Master Chung-lu. K'ang Hai, *Chinese.* CoBLCP, *tr. by* Jonathan Chaves

Dreaming of Yüan Chên. Po Chü-i, *Chinese.* ChiP, *tr. by* Arthur Waley

Dreaming that I went with Li and Yü to Visit Yüan Chên. Po Chü-i, *Chinese.* ChiP; FP, *tr. by* Arthur Waley

Dreaming the flower I have never seen. (LL) Moly. Thom Gunn. CABP; HAP; MoP; NoAM; Poetr

Dreaming Up Mother. Robert Adamson. BMAP

Dreamlike leap, A. For the Record. Roy Blount, Jr. OBAL

Dreams. Cecil Frances Alexander. NOxBChV

Dreams. Charles Cooper. PoBA

Dreams. Nikki Giovanni. PoBA

Dream[e]s. Robert Herrick. BeJo; CaPo; HAP; KaS; NAEL-1; OPOU; OxBSP; Spl

Dreams. Helen Hunt Jackson. APN-2

Dreams. Caroline Elizabeth Norton. Ro

Dreams. Edgar Allan Poe. NCAP

"Oh! that my young life were a lasting dream!" AmPP; MeMAP; OxBA; Poetr; TAP, *ll.* 1–12

Dreams. Arthur Symons. PoA

Dreams. Henry Timrod. APN-2; PAR

Dreams. Thomas Traherne. FMP

Dreams. *Unknown.* ReMoGo

Dreams. Israel Zangwill. TrJP

Dreams Ahead, The. Edwin Carlile Litsey. PoToHe

Dreams Are Also Wounds. Breyten Breytenbach, *Afrikaans.* VCWP, *tr. by* André Brink

"Dreams Are the Royal Road to the Unconscious." Paul Goodman. PoA

Dreams by No One's Daughter. Leslie Ullman. PBCAP

Dreams fled away, this country bedroom, raw. Another September. Thomas Kinsella. BIrV; CABP; CIP-2; NoP-4

Dreams in German. "David Martin." NOBAu

("I dream / of embroidering / new skin.") (LL) UnSA

Dreams in Harrison Railroad Park. Nellie Wong. OpBo; UnSA

Dreams in War Time. Amy Lowell.

"I dug a grave under an oak-tree." BoWoP

Dreams of Beauty. Adah Isaacs Menken. CBWP-1

Dreams of Johnson Grass. Colleen J. McElroy. WeT

Dreams of Life. Timothy Thomas Fortune.

"O, Life of Dreams! O, Dreams of Life!" AAP

"Upon the future life we build." AAP

Dreams of Water. Donald Justice. LCAP-2; NYBP

Dreams that delude with flying shade men's minds. We Are Such Stuff as Dreams. Petronius Arbiter, *Latin.* AWP, *tr. by* Howard Mumford Jones

Dreams, Whimsies, and no more. Seneca. *See* Seneca's Troas, Act 2. Chorus.

Dreams worn out like small coins taken out of circulation. Rade Drainac. HSix, *tr. by* Charles Simic *Fr.* Opus III.

Dreamscape in Kümmel. Harold Witt. NYBP

Dreamt I today [*or* to-day] the dream of yesternight. Sonnet V. George Santayana. APN-2 *Fr.* Sonnets.

Dreamtime Lives Again, The. Jan Carew. HCP

Dreamtime, / The first ones lived, those of long ago. Lalai (Dreamtime). Sam Woolagoodjah. NOBAu

Dreamwork, the mnemonic flicker. The Burning Child. Amy Clampitt. NMM-2

Dreamy cars graze on the dewy boulevard. James Tate. LCAP-2

Dreamy in a darkling bar. Ode to a Nightingale. Roy Kelly. BXAP

Drearie trumpet blew a dreadfull blast, The. Edward Fairfax. PBRV *Fr.* Tasso's Godfrey of Bulloigne Book 4.

Dreary Black Hills, The. *Unknown.* AmFP; AS

Dreary Change, The. Sir Walter Scott. NAEL-2; OAEL-2; OBNC

Dreary lay the long road, dreary lay the town. The Toy Band. Sir Henry John Newbolt. BoTP

Dredge of that gravity, being without experience, The. (LL) In the Yukon. Ralph Gustafson. NoP-4

Dregs. Ernest Christopher Dowson. OBMV; SAGP

Dreme, The. Sir David Lindsay.

Compleynt of the Comoun Weill of Scotland, The. OxBS

("And thus as we wer talking to and fro.") PBRV

(Complaynt of the Comoun weill of Scotland, The.) PBRV

Of the Realme of Scotland. OxBS

Drenching night drags on: no sleep or snore, The. Egan O'Rahilly, *Irish.* NOIV, *tr. by* Thomas Kinsella

Drenching rain hisses down, cooling the evening. Days of Rain; the Rivers Have Overflowed. Su Tung-p'o, *Chinese.* CoBCP, *tr. by* Burton Watson

Drenching rain hisses down, cooling the evening. Days of Rain; the Rivers Have Overflowed. Su Tung-p'o. CoBCP, *tr. by* Burton Watson; CoBCP *Fr.* Days of Rain; the Rivers Have Overflowed: Two Poems.

Dresden. Ciaran Carson. CIP-2; PBCIP; PNI

Dresdener. Remembering Dresden. Van K. Brock. HP

Dress me in green. *Unknown, Spanish.* BoWoP, *tr. by* Willis Barnstone

Dress of Fire, A. Dahlia Ravikovitch, *Hebrew.* VCWP, *tr. by* Chana Bloch *and* Ariel Bloch

Dress of Hà-Đông silk, The. Sa Nguyên, *Vietnamese.* AVP, *tr. by* Huỳnh Sanh Thông

Dress that my brother has put on is thin, The. Lady Otomo no Sakanoé. AWP, *tr. by* Arthur Waley *Fr.* Manyo Shu, Part 1 of 4.

Dressed as a drag queen. Tiger Lady. Yusef Komunyakaa. CDa

Dressed in his clumsy, stiff, aquatic clothes. The Diver. Edward Leslie Mayo. CoAP

Dressed in the colours of a country day. From the Painting "Back from Market" by Chardin. Eavan Boland. PBCIP

Dressed man and a naked man, A. George Orwell. EBEV

Dressed Up. E. Ethelbert Miller. IFJA

Dresses. Kathleen Fraser. LiLi

Dressing. Henry Vaughan. ESCV

Dressing My Daughter. George Eklund. IFJA

Dressing Stations, The. Norman Dubie. AmPA

Dressing Up. Jackie Kay. CPO

Drew one angel—borne, see, on my bosom! (LL) One Word More. Robert Browning. EnVR; PoEL-5

Drew shatters into rivulets on crunched cellophane. A. R. Ammons. BAP-93 *Fr.* Garbage. BAP-93

Dried Apple Pies. *Unknown.* BLPA

Dried Fruit. Philip Dow. BXAP

Dried leaves as I bow and pass smiling. (LL) The Young Housewife. William Carlos Williams. ColAP; HeIP-4; NAAL-2; TAP

Dried up old cactus. June. Elaine Feinstein. BrRo

Drift. Alberta Turner. LCAP-2

Drift descends like rattling dust, The. Avalanche. Adrien Stoutenburg. NYBP

Drift on through slumber to a dream, and through a dream / to death. (LL) Music. George Du Maurier, *after the French of* Sully-Prudhomme. SAGP

Drift-Wood. Clara Ann Thompson. CBWP-2

Drifter. Norman MacCaig. FaBoTC

Drifter off Tarentum, A. Rudyard Kipling. FaBoEE; NSI; PeFWW; PoWW *Fr.* Epitaphs of the War [1914–1918]. OBWP

Drifters. Bruce Dawe. BMAP; CBAP; NoAM

Drifting and innocent and like snow. Christmas Letter Home. George Sutherland Fraser. OxBTC

Drifting clouds disgorge a bright moon, The. Song of "Night After Night," A. Ou-yang Hsiu, *Chinese.* SuSp, *tr. by* Irving Y. Lo

Drifting clouds, distant and vast, The. Hsü Kan, *Chinese.* SuSp, *tr. by* Ronald C. Miao *Fr.* Boudoir Thoughts.

Drifting clouds pass by all day long. Tu Fu, *Chinese.* SuSp, *tr. by* Eugene Eoyang *Fr.* Dreaming of Li Po.

Drifting in casually, one by one. (LL) Icarus. Valentin Iremonger. BIrV; CIP-2

Drifting night in the Georgia pines. O Daedalus, Fly Away Home. Robert Earl Hayden. HAP; NAAAL; PoBA

Drifting off the wheel of a past. First Spring. Duane Niatum. HATNAP

Drifting Sands and a Caravan. Yolande Langworthy. BLPA

Drifts That Bar My Door. Adah Isaacs Menken. CBWP-1

Driftwood. Witter Bynner. FYAP

Drill Man Blues. George Sizemore. AmFP

Drill, Ye Tarriers, Drill. Thomas F. Casey. GM

Drilling in Russell Square. Edward Richard Burton Shanks. OBMV

Drink. Anacreon, *Greek.* OBCVT, *tr. by* Charles Goodall

Drink. John L. Stanizzi. EC3

Drink. William Carlos Williams. OxBA

Drink and be merry, merry, merry boys. The Song. Thomas Morton. NAAL-3

Drink and be whole again beyond confusion. (LL) Directive. Robert Frost. AFr; AmPP; CMoP; ColAP; HAP; ImPo; InPS-3; LiTM; MeMAP; MoAmPo; NAAL-2; NOBA; NoAM; NoP-4; PoE; SAGP; SAmP; TFi

Drink and dance and laugh and lie. The Flaw in Paganism. Dorothy Parker. NBLV

Drink and Drown Your Cares. Cao Bá Quát, *Vietnamese.* AVP, *tr. by* Huỳnh Sanh Thông

Drink, Asklepiades. Asclepiades, *Greek.* GrAn, *tr. by* Alistair Elliot

Drink deep, my heart, of brightest noon. Afternoon Light. Jacob Fichman, *Hebrew.* MHP, *tr. by* Ruth Finer Mintz

Drink, Friends. Moses ibn Ezra. *Fr.* Wine-Songs. TrJP, *tr. by* Solomon Solis-Cohen

Drink, gossips mine! *Unknown. Fr.* Medieval Norman Song. AWP, *tr. by* John Addington Symonds

Drink, my bull, from the river; I am here to guard you / with my spear. (LL) The Magnificent Bull. *Dinka Oral Tradition.* PeP

Drink no more. Echo. Simon Pettet. PT

Drink not the third glass, which thou canst not tame. George Herbert. *Fr.* The Church-Porch. ESCV

Drink of Milk, A. John Montague. PNI

Drink of Spring, A. John Ennis. CIP-2; PBCIP

Drink of Water, A. Seamus Heaney. OxBC; TRP

Drink On. Mary E. Tucker. CBWP-1

Drink on, tho' Night be spent and Sun do shine. Alcaeus. OBCVT, *tr. by* Philip Ayres *Fr.* A Drinking Ode of Alcæus.

Drink to drown my sorrows and restart, A. Palladas, *Greek.* GrAn, *tr. by* Tony Harrison

Drink[e] to me, only, [*or* onely] with thine eyes, *adapted from the Greek of* Philostratus. To Celia. Ben Jonson. APAD; AWP; BeJo; BoLoP; CBLP; ClHu; EBEvV; EnLoPo; FaBoBe; GBL; GLoP; GTBS-P; ImPo; InPK-6; NAEL-1; NOBE; NOSC; NoP-4; OAEL-1; OBEV; OBVE; OxAEP-1; PoE; PoEL-2; PoLF; SAGP; SCGP; SeCP; SoSe-8; TFi; UV

'Drink was the end of you, Anacreon'. Julianus of Egypt, *Greek.* GrAn, *tr. by* W. S. Merwin

Drink wonder, my heart, drink in the wonder. Shin Shalom, *Hebrew.* MHP, *tr. by* Ruth Finer Mintz

Drinke and be merry, merry, merry boyes. Song. Thomas Morton. SCAP

Drinker, glutton supreme. Simonides, *Greek.* GrAn, *tr. by* Peter Jay

Drinking. Anacreon, *Greek.* BeJo; NNPT; NOBE; OBCVT; OBEV; OBVE; OxAEP-1; SeCP, *tr. by* Abraham Cowley

Drinking. Chu Yün-ming, *Chinese.* CoBLCP, *tr. by* Jonathan Chaves

Drinking. Abraham Cowley. PFE

Drinking against men, Kallistion. A Dedication to Aphrodite. Hedylos, *Greek.* GrAn, *tr. by* William Moebius

Drinking Alone beneath the Moon. Li Po, *Chinese.*
   "If Heaven weren't fond of wine." SuSp, *tr. by* Irving Lo
   "Pot of wine among the flowers, A." SuSp, *tr. by* Irving Lo

Drinking Alone in Moonlight. Li Po, *Chinese.* TAL, *tr. by* Robert Payne

Drinking Alone in the Moonlight. Li Po, *Chinese.* AWP; ChiPo, *tr. by* Florence Ayscough *and* Amy Lowell

Drinking Alone under Moonlight. Li Po, *Chinese.* TAL, *tr. by* Robert Payne

Drinking alone without knowing the coming of dusk. To Amuse Myself. Li Po, *Chinese.* SuSp, *tr. by* Joseph J. Lee

Drinking at Night in the Western Pavilion of the Fa-hua Temple. Liu Tsung-yüan, *Chinese.* SuSp, *tr. by* Jan W. Walls

Drinking at Night with Yen Kung-mou. Shen Chou, *Chinese.* CoBLCP, *tr. by* Jonathan Chaves

Drinking at the Cave Mouth. Tsung Ch'en, *Chinese.* CoBLCP, *tr. by* Jonathan Chaves

Drinking at the Lake, First It's Sunny, Then It Rains. Su Shih, *Chinese.* SuSp, *tr. by* Irving Y. Lo

Drinking Back. Franz Wright. LCAP-2

Drinking Bout Beneath the Open Sky. Slavko Mihalic. *See* Drinking Spree Beneath the Open Sky.

Drinking Cold Water. Peter Everwine. NNaP

Drinking Fountain, The. Robert Duncan. CLPP

Drinking is done, the lamps extinguished, The. New Year's Eve. Wen Cheng-ming, *Chinese.* CoBLCP, *tr. by* Jonathan Chaves

Drinking Ode of Alcæus, A. Alcaeus, *Greek.*
   "Drink on, tho' Night be spent and Sun do shine." OBCVT, *tr. by* Philip Ayres

Drinking on East Slope at night. Listening to the River. Su Tung-p'o, *Chinese.* TAL, *tr. by* Robert Payne

Drinking Sappho Brand Ouzo. Martin Johnston. BMAP *Fr.* In Transit: A Sonnet Square.

Drinking Song. Robert Burns. *Fr.* Love and Libery—A Cantata. NOBRP; NOEC
   ("Who have character to lose.") (LL) NBLV

Drinking-Song, A. Henry Carey. OBEV

Drinking Song. Robert Fergusson. OxAEP-1

Drinking Song, A. Shakespeare. NoSic *Fr.* Antony and Cleopatra.

Drinking Song. Richard Brinsley Sheridan. *See* Song: "Here's to the maiden [*or* maid] of bashful fifteen."

Drinking Song. James Kenneth Stephen. NOBL; PeLV

Drinking Song, A. Trần Dạ Từ', *Vietnamese.* AVP, *tr. by* Huỳnh Sanh Thông

Drinking Song. *Unknown.* NOBL

Drinking Song, A. W. B. Yeats. BoLoP; GLoP; LoP; OAEL-2

Drinking Spree Beneath the Open Sky. Slavko Mihalic, *Croatian.* PoSu, *tr. by* Peter Kastmiler
   (Drinking Bout Beneath the Open Sky.) CEEP, *tr. by* Peter Kastmiler
   ("With my large eyes which needed nothing.") (LL) CEEP, *tr. by* Peter Kastmiler

Drinking the Wind. "Tan Ying," *Chinese.* WPOW, *tr. by* Kenneth Rexroth *and* Ling Chung

Drinking together in the evening we are human. Antimedon, *Greek.* GrAn, *tr. by* Peter Jay

Drinking until drunk, the day is nearly gone. Sobering Up. Yüan Chen, *Chinese.* SuSp, *tr. by* Dell R. Hales

Drinking Vodka. Sarah Kirsch, *German.* CEEP, *tr. by* Wayne Kvam

Drinking Wine. Ch'ien Ch'ien-i, *Chinese.* SuSp, *tr. by* Irving Y. Lo

Drinking Wine. Lin Hung, *Chinese.* SuSp, *tr. by* Irving Y. Lo

Drinking Wine. Mo Shih-lung, *Chinese.* CoBLCP, *tr. by* Jonathan Chaves

Drinking Wine. T'ao Ch'ien, *Chinese.* CoBCP, tr. by Burton Watson

"Autumn chrysanthemums have beautiful color." SuSp, tr. by Wu-chi Liu

"Green pine grows in eastern garden, A." SuSp, tr. by Wu-chi Liu

"I built my hut in a place where people live." CoBCP, tr. by Burton Watson

"Old friends know what I like." SuSp, tr. by Wu-chi Liu

"Prosperity and decline have no fixed dwelling." CoBCP, tr. by Burton Watson

"Unsettled, a bird lost from the flock." SuSp, tr. by Wu-chi Liu

"Way's been lost for a thousand years, The." CoBCP, tr. by Burton Watson

Drinking with Friends amongst the Blooming Peonies. Liu Yu Hsi, *Chinese.* OHMPC, tr. by Kenneth Rexroth

Drip Drip or Not Bloody Likely. Gerda Mayer. PeLV

Drip drip, the rain on paulownia leaves. Pouring Out My Feelings after Parting from Yüan Chen. Po Chü-i, *Chinese.* CoBCP, tr. by Burton Watson

Drip in darkness like a leaking pipe in the cellar. (LL) Evening Hawk. Robert Penn Warren. APo; ColAP; NAAL-2; NoP-4; VCAP

Dripping with sweat he bends down. The One-Armed Man in the Undergrowth. Bertolt Brecht, *German.* PoSu, tr. by Derek Bowman

Drips surprise. They talk too, The. Fag-End. Philip O'Connor. SPE

Drive a Tractor. *Unknown.* NBLV

Drive-By Shooting. Elizabeth Cohen. WWSi

Drive-In, The. R. S. Gwynn. RA

Drive In, The. Michael S. Harper. AFr

Drive-ins are out, to start with. Movie-Going. John Hollander. CoAP

Drive nails into my tongue. (LL) Mothers, Daughters. Shirley Kaufman. BoWoP; CrSp; NMM-2

Drive off that golden oriole. Spring Sorrow. Chin Ch'ang-hsü, *Chinese.* OHMPC, tr. by Kenneth Rexroth

Drive on, sharp wings, and cry above. The Redshanks. Julian Bell. OBMV

Drive to Lone Ranger, A. Ray A. Young Bear. AF

Driven by hunger I leave my home. Begging for Food. T'ao Ch'ien, *Chinese.* SuSp, tr. by Wu-chi Liu

Driven out, and compel'd to be chaste. (LL) I laid me down upon a bank. William Blake. EnLoPo; GBL

Driver, The. James Dickey. VGW

Dríver, drive fáster and máke a good rún. Calypso. W. H. Auden. CBLP; PeLV

Driver rubbed at his nettly chin, The. To the Four Courts, Please. James Stephens. BIrV; MoBrPo; UnPo

"Driver, what stream is it?" I asked, well knowing. The Lordly Hudson. Paul Goodman. CoAP; VGW

Drivers dread suicides. Rhythm. Yevgeny Mikhailovich Vinokurov, *Russian.* TCRP, tr. by Daniel Weissbort

Drivers, therefore, didn't do, The. (LL) Limerick: "A Man hired by John Smith and Co." "Mark Twain." InPK-6; PeLi

Drivin' Steel. *Unknown.* AS

Drivin' steel, drivin' steel. Hammer Man. *Unknown.* AS

Driving. Alan Pizzarelli. HA

Driving around, I will waste more time. (LL) Driving to Town Late to Mail a Letter. Robert Bly. HeIP-4; InPK-6; VGW

Driving By. Robert Wallace. CMAP

Driving Cattle to Casas Buenas. Roy Campbell. PeSA

Driving Cross-Country. X. J. Kennedy. TwCP

Driving down the concrete artery. The White Man Pressed the Locks. James C. Kilgore. InPK-6

Driving Home. Peter Kane Dufault. PFE

Driving Home the Cows. Kate Putnam Osgood. CBCWP

Driving, I come for a while. Late at Night. William Stafford. NNaP

Driving in Oklahoma. Carter Revard. HATNAP; VoR

Driving in the Park. *Unknown.* OxBoLi; PeLV

Driving into Enid. Michael Van Walleghen. FYAP

Driving keel, cut from the forest—look—travels the current, The. A Boat Song. Saint Columbanus, *Latin.* NOIV

Driving late at night I pass. Sleep. Dana Naone. CDW

Driving Lesson. Michael Pettit. NAmP90

Driving My Parents Home at Christmas. Robert Bly. IFJA

Driving / ruffian / fluff. Battle of India and Europe. Aleksei Eliseievich Kruchyonykh, *Russian.* CBNP, tr. by Vladimir Markov

Driving Saw-Logs on the Plover. *Unknown.* AS

Driving south and travelling. Maintrunk Country Roadsong. Sam Hunt. PeNZ

Driving the Big Chrysler across the Country of My Birth. Michael S. Harper. MoNo

Driving the perfect length of Ireland. To a Cuckoo at Coolanlough. Medbh McGuckian. PBCIP

Driving through Essex I smell the wild privet and. Thinking of War. Naomi Mitchison. WPN

Driving through Minnesota during the Hanoi Bombings. Robert Bly. Poetr

Driving through thick bush. Geoffrey Lehmann. *Fr. Ross's Poems.* CBAP

Driving to Town Late to Mail a Letter. Robert Bly. HeIP-4; InPK-6; VGW

Driving toward the Lac Qui Parle River. Robert Bly. CoAMPo; LCAP-2; WeT

Driving Wheel. Sherley Anne Williams. BlSi

Drizzle, The. China Observed Through Greek Rain in Turkish Coffee. Henrik Nordbrandt, *Danish.* VCWP, tr. by Henrik Nordbrandt and Alexander Taylor

Drizzle, drizzle, drop, drop, the rain at Winding Pond. Tune: "Deva-like Barbarian." *Unknown, Chinese.* SuSp, tr. by Hellmut Wilhelm

Drizzling Easter Morning, A. Thomas Hardy. CMoP

Drizzling rain, A. Michael McClintock. HA

Drizzling rain set in, A. (LL) The Rosy Bosom'd Hours. Coventry Patmore. EnLoPo; NOBVV

Dromedary has one hump, The. How to Tell a Camel. J. Patrick Lewis. TLR

Drone of airplane neared, and dimmed away, The. Immanent. Walter De la Mare. PoA

Drone v. Worker. Ebenezer Elliot. FaBoPV; OBSV

Droning a drowsy syncopated tune. The Weary Blues. Langston Hughes. ColAP; FaBoA; ISC; MoP; NAAAL; NOBA; NoAM; NoP-4; PoPoPo; SAmP

Droop under doves' wings silent, breathing shapes. The Night Nurse Goes Her Round. John Gray. OBNC

Drop a Pebble in the Water. James William Foley. BLPA; PoToHe

Drop a Stone. *Unknown.* PWR

Drop down, drop down, white snowflakes! Winter's Song. *Unknown, Bohemian.* BoTP

Drop, drop, slow tears. Hymn. Phineas Fletcher. OxBSP; PeECV

Drop from above. (LL) Grace. George Herbert. ChIV-1; GeHe

Drop of Dew, A. Shmuel Halkin, *Yiddish.* TrJP, tr. by Jacob Sonntag

Drop of dew on an autumn lotus leaf, A. On Dewdrop. Wei Ying-wu, *Chinese.* SuSp, tr. by Irving Y. Lo

Drop of ocean. Alan Pizzarelli. HA

Drop of sepia in the fragrant vase, The. Dusk. Abraham Z. Lopez-Penha, *Spanish.* TrJP, tr. by Thomas Walsh

Drop the Wires. Hugh Seidman. AmPA

Dropped by memory. (LL) After a hundred years. Emily Dickinson. APN-2; AWP; OxBA

Dropped into the Ether Acre. Emily Dickinson. NCAP

Dropped leaf, The. Ruth Miller. *Fr. Cycle.* PeSA

Dropped petals of a broken lotus-moon. No Less than Prisoners. Frederick Thomas Bennett Macartney. CBAP

Dropping By the Guava Graveyard in So'n-La. Trần Huy Liệu, *Vietnamese.* AVP, tr. by Huỳnh Sanh Thông

Dropping the reins, we dismount from the ornate carriage. Hand in Hand; a Song. Shen Yüeh, *Chinese.* SuSp, tr. by Richard B. Mather

Dropping Your Aitches. Joseph Warren Beach. NYBP

Drops of Gall. Gabriela Mistral, *Spanish.* BoWoP, tr. by David Garrison

Drops out and all our day is done. (LL) Winter with the Gulf Stream. Gerard Manley Hopkins. CMoP; NoAM

Drought. Oumar Ba, *French.* PBWP, tr. by Kathleen Weaver

Drought. David Holbrook. OxBTC

Drought, The. Gary Soto. NoAM

Drought. Trần Tế Xu'o'ng, *Vietnamese.* AVP, tr. by Huỳnh Sanh Thông

Drought. Sitanshu Yashashchandra, *Gujarati.* OMIP, tr. by Saleem Peeradina, Jayant Parek, Rasik Shah, *and* Ghulam Mohammed Sheikh

Drought Year. Judith Wright. NoAM

Drove-Road, The. Wilfrid Wilson Gibson. OxBTC

Drover, A. Padraic Colum. AWP; MoBrPo; OBMV; RB

Drover's Boy, The. Ted Egan. NOBAu

Drowned, The. David Bottoms. MT

Drowned, The. Norman MacCaig. OxBC

Drowned Children, The. Louise Glück. HCAP; VCAP

Drowned in the perilous sea of music. Music. Namjo Kim, *Korean.* CKP, tr. by Jaihiun Kim

Drowned Spaniel, The. Charles Tennyson Turner. PeVV

Drowned truck-driver was propped on the slab, A. Little Aster. Gottfried Benn, *German.* PFTM, tr. by Babette Deutsch

Drowning is not so pitiful. Emily Dickinson. CMoP; NCAP; OxBSP

Drowsy sun went slowly to his rest, The. Evening. James Stephens. MoBrPo

Drug of the incomprehensible. The Bad Habit. Charles Henri Ford. SPE

Drug Store. Karl Shapiro. CMoP; OxBA; TwCP

Drugs. Dennis Cooper. PmAP

Drugs. Jacquie Jones. ISC

Drugs are a tuition. Going to School in France or America. Tom Clark. CoAmPo

Drugs made Pauline vague. Stevie Smith. FaBoWP

Drugs of War, The. Les A. Murray. BMAP

Druk. / Druker. / Druksome. Drukascripts. Vladimir Druk, *Russian*. TCRP, *tr. by* John High *and* Katya Olmsted

Drukascripts. Vladimir Druk, *Russian*. TCRP, *tr. by* John High *and* Katya Olmsted

Drum. Langston Hughes. MoAmPo

Drum-footed black elephant's calf, The. What Her Friend Said Criticizing Him to Give Her Strength. Kuriyiraiyar, *Tamil*. PLW, *tr. by* A. K. Ramanujan

Drum on your drums, batter on your banjos [*or* banjoes]. Jazz Fantasia. Carl Sandburg. AiP; MoAmPo; Poetr; SAGP

Drum sounds from the high city wall as the lampwick burns, The. Tune: "Song of Picking Mulberry." Wang Kuo-wei, *Chinese*. SuSp, *tr. by* Ching-i Tu

Drum; the Narrative of the Demon of Tedworth, The. Dame Edith Sitwell. FaBoTw

Drum thumps, faraway, A. The House-Slave. Mervyn Morris. PBCV

Drumbeat is constant as surf, The. At Bon Odori. Jim Mitsui. OpBo

Drumdrumdrum, A. The Wall. Gwendolyn Brooks. PoBA *Fr.* Two Dedications.

Drumlin Prayer. Tom MacIntyre. CIP-2

Drumlin Woodchuck, A. Robert Frost. NOBA; NoAM

Drummer, The. Bruce Beaver. BMAP

Drummer Boy of Shiloh, The. *Unknown*. AmFP

Drummer Hodge. Thomas Hardy. AWP; EBEV; GTBS-P; HAP; InPS-3; MoP; NAEL-2; NOBVV; NoAM; NoP-4; OBWP; OxAEP-2; PeFWW; Poetr; WeW-3

Drummer, or the Haunted House, The. Joseph Addison. "In this grave age, when comedies are few." OxBSn

Drums mutter for war, and soon we must begin, The. Advice for a Journey. Sidney Keyes. PoWW

Drums / Then again drums. A. J. Seymour. PBCV

Drunk. Carroll Arnett. VoR

Drunk as drunk on turpentine. Pablo Neruda, *Spanish*. BoLoP, *tr. by* Christopher Logue; LoP, *tr. by* W. S. Merwin

Drunk came in out of the cold, A. What Did They Have In Mind? Nikolai Ivanovich Glazkov, *Russian*. TCRP, *tr. by* Daniel Weissbort

Drunk, Climbing to the Peak of Iron Tomb on Wei Mountain. Li K'ai-hsien, *Chinese*. CoBLCP, *tr. by* Jonathan Chaves

Drunk, Facing Crimson Leaves. Po Chü-i, *Chinese*. CoBCP, *tr. by* Burton Watson

Drunk, he leans back in his boat. Wu Chen. *Fr.* Paintings of Fishermen. CoBLCP, *tr. by* Jonathan Chaves

Drunk I have been. And drunk I was that night. To Laura Phelan: 1880-1906. Leon Stokesbury. MT

Drunk, I left the western pavilion. Tune: "Butterflies Lingering over Flowers." Yen Chi-tao, *Chinese*. SuSp, *tr. by* An-yan Tang

Drunk I observe the golden dance of stars. Argentarius, *Greek*. GrAn, *tr. by* Alistair Elliot

Drunk in the Furnace, The. W. S. Merwin. LiTM; MoP; NAAL-2; NoAM; NoP-4; PoE; Poetr; TwCP

Drunk in the kitchen, I ring God. Telephoning God. Gary Soto. PBCAP

Drunk Last Night with Friends, I Go to Work Anyway. Philip Dow. InPK-6

Drunk Man, The. *Unknown, Aborigine*. NOBAu

Drunk Man Looks at the Thistle, A. "Hugh MacDiarmid."

Drunk Man Looks at the Thistle, A. "Hugh MacDiarmid."
  "Black leaf owre a white leaf twirls, A." FaBoTC
  "Dae what ye wull ye canna parry." EBEV; OxAEP-2
  Farewell to Dostoevski. FaBoTC; NAEL-2
  "Jean! Jean! Gin she's no' here it's no' oor bed." FaBoTC
  Man and the Infinite. FaBoTC
  Problem Child, The. FaBoTC
  Repetition Complex. FaBoTC
  Stick-nest in Ygdrasil, A. FaBoTC
  Thistle's Characteristics, The. FaBoTC
  Yet Ha'e I Silence Left. NAEL-2

Drunk Too Soon. Yüan Chen, *Chinese*. SuSp, *tr. by* Dell R. Hales

Drunk water cold and clear from an inexhaustible hidden fountain. (LL) The Wilderness. Kathleen Jessie Raine. BoWoP; WPE

Drunk with the unmixed wine. (LL) A Thought from Propertius. W. B. Yeats. OAEL-2; OxBSP

Drunk with wine, I slap my spring robe. Yen Chi-tao, *Chinese*. SuSp, *tr. by* An-yan Tang

Drunkard, The. Bible, *O.T.* TrJP *Fr.* Proverbs.

Drunkard, The. William Carlos Williams. PFE

Drunkard and the Pig, The. *Unknown*. OBAL

Drunkard cannot meet a Cork, A. Emily Dickinson. InPS-3

Drunkards, The. Malcolm Lowry. NYBP

Drunkards are rolling slowly, The. Jelaluddin Rumi, *Persian*. EnIH, *tr. by* Robert Bly

Drunkard's Doom, The. *Unknown*. AS

Drunkard's Nocturnes, A. "Sasha Chorny," *Russian*. TCRP, *tr. by* Bernard Meares

Drunkard's Wife, The. Mary E. Tucker. CBWP-1

Drunken Americans. John Ashbery. HCAP

Drunken Fisherman, The. Robert Lowell. AmPP; CMoP; ChIV-2; ImPo; LiTM; NOBA; OxBA; VGW

Drunken night in my house with a, A. Dream Record: June 8 1955. Allen Ginsberg. CoAmPo; NOBA

Drunken Poem. David Helwig. NOBC

Drunken Rose, The. Amarou, *Sanskrit*. AWP, *tr. by* E. Powys Mathers

Drunken sun / totters among the clouds, The. Orgy (That Is, Vegetable Market, at Sarno). Gina Labriola, *Italian*. WPOW, *tr. by* Edgar Pauk

Drunkenness, *epigram*. Friedrich von Logau, *German*. GePo, *tr. by* George C. Schoolfield

Dry. Samuel Hoffenstein. BXAP

Dry brown coughing beneath their feet, The. Beverly Hills, Chicago. Gwendolyn Brooks. Poetr; VGW *Fr.* The Womanhood.

Dry earth near this salt sea, The. Laocoön. Wilson Harris. PBCV

Dry heat of the Tassajara canyon. Letter to Jeanne (at Tassajara). Diane Di Prima. BB

Dry Leaves, Dry Leaves. *Unknown, Chinese*. CoBCP, *tr. by* Burton Watson

Dry Loaf. Wallace Stevens. MeMAP; NOBA; OxBA; PoRA; RaBo

Dry River. *Unknown*. FaBoVe

Dry River Bed. Andrew Salkey. PBCV

Dry Root in a Wash. Simon J. Ortiz. HATNAP

Dry-rot at ease till the Judgment-day! (LL) Sibrandus Schafnaburgensis. Robert Browning. CTC; EBVV; OBGa

Dry Salvages, The. T. S. Eliot. AiP; NoP-4; OxBA *Fr.* Four Quartets. "River is within us, the sea is all about us, The." OxBoS

Dry, summer day. Robert Spiess. HA

Dry tree with an empty honeycomb, A. The Tomb of Heracles. James McAuley. BMAP *Fr.* The Hero and the Hydra.

Dry Your Tears, Africa! Bernard Dadié, *French*. TTY, *tr. by* Donatus Ibe Nwoga

Drying Clothes. Yang Wan-li, *Chinese*. SuSp, *tr. by* Jonathan Chaves

Dryness is upon the house, A. In Honor of David Anderson Brooks, My Father. Gwendolyn Brooks. MoLi

Du bist wie eine Blume. Heinrich Heine. TrJP, *tr. by* Emma Lazarus; AWP, *tr. by* Kate Freiligrath Kroeker *Fr.* Homeward Bound.
  ("Thou Seemest Like a flower.") TrJP, *tr. by* Emma Lazarus

Dual, The. Richard Lovelace. CaPo

Dual Site, The. Michael Hamburger. TwCP

Dualism. Ishmael Reed. NAAAL

Dualisms. Tennyson. EnVR

Dub Eleven. Jeff Nuttall. NBrP

Dubbement dere of down and dales, The. *Unknown*. EnVB *Fr.* Pearl.

Dubious Foreigner. Cyril Dabydeen. HCP

Dublin. Louis MacNeice. CIP-2; IIP; OxBTC *Fr.* The Closing Album.

Dublin Girl, Mountjoy, 1984. Dermot Bolger. BiHa

Dublin Made Me. Donagh MacDonagh. OxBTC

Dublinesque. Philip Larkin. NoAM; OxBC

Duchess of Malfi, The. John Webster. NAEL-1
  "O that it were possible we might." IMW
  Shrouding of the Duchess of Malfi, The. NOBE; OBEV
  (Hearke, Now Every Thing Is Still.)
  "What hideous noyse was that?" PoEL-2
  "Yond's the Cardinall's window: This fortification." PoEL-2
  "I am Duchess of Malfy still." OxBoV

Duchesses. David Campbell. NOBAu

Duchess's Lullaby, The. "Lewis Carroll." CBNP *Fr.* Alice's Adventures in Wonderland.
  (Lullaby, A.) NOxBChV

Duck. John Lyle Donaghy. BIrV

Duck, The. Edith King. BoTP

Duck, The. Ogden Nash. RB

Duck. Valerie Worth. NTCP

Duck and a drake, A. Ducks and Drakes. Mother Goose. OxNR; ReMoGo

Duck and the Kangaroo, The. Edward Lear. OxBChV

Duck-chasing. Galway Kinnell. TwCP; VGW

Duck fats rot in the roasting pan, The. Throwing Out the Flowers. Gwendolyn Brooks. ColAP *Fr.* Notes from the Childhood and the Girlhood. LCAP-2

Duck feathers. David Lloyd. HA

Duck patrol is waddling down the odd-number side of Raglan, The. Army. Ciaran Carson. BiHa; PBCIP

Duck Pond at Mini's Pasture, a Dozen Years Later, The. Philip Dow. AmPA

Duck who had got such a habit of stuffing, A. The Notorious Glutton. Ann Taylor. OxBChV

Ducks. Norman Ault. BoTP

Ducks. Frederick William Harvey.
  "Yes, ducks are valiant things." BoTP

Ducks and Drakes. Mother Goose. ReMoGo

Ducks, at first, except they didn't. Seals in the Inner Harbor. Brendan Galvin. CMAP

Duck''s Ditty. Kenneth Grahame. BoTP; CTAV; FPC; NOxBChV; NTCP; OTCP; OxBChV; WHSW *Fr.* The Wind in the Willows.

Ducks flew up from the Morton Pond, The. The Run to Mourne End Wood. John Masefield. EBNV *Fr.* Reynard the Fox.

Ducks have turned to stone, the lovers untwined, The. The Garden. Debora Greger. GaP

Ducks in pairs drowse on the warm sand. (LL) South Wind. Tu Fu, *Chinese.* BLT; OHPC, *tr. by* Kenneth Rexroth

Ducks land, The. William J. Higginson. HA

Duckweed. Leopold Staff, *Polish.* PoSu, *tr. by* Adam Czerniawski

Duckweed Pond. Wang Wei, *Chinese.* CoBCP, *tr. by* Burton Watson

Due of the Dead, The. William Makepeace Thackeray. OBWP

Duel, The. Eugene Field. APN-2; CTV; FPC; FaBoBe; NOxBChV; OBAL; OBCA; PoLF; PoRA; TFi

Duel with Verses over a Great Man. *Unknown, Hebrew.* TrJP
  Epigram I: "Thou Guide to doubt, be silent evermore."
  Epigram II: "Thou fool profane, be silent!"
  Epigram III: "Forgive us, son of Amram, be not wroth."
  Epigram IV: "What thought ye to burn, when ye kindled the pyre."
  Epigram V: "Against the guide of Truth."
  Epitaph I: "Here lies a man, and still no man."

Duellist, The. Charles Churchill.
  "First (entitled to the place), The." OBSV

Duende. Nina Zivancevic, *Serbo-Croatian.* HSix, *tr. by* Charles Simic

Duenna, The. Richard Brinsley Sheridan.
  Air: "I ne'er could any lustre see." NOEC
  "Oh, the days when I was young." OxAEP-1
  Song: "Give Isaac the nymph who no beauty can boast." NOIV

Duet, A. Thomas Sturge Moore. OBEV

Duet. Theodore Roethke. OBCoV

Duet. Tennyson. GBL *Fr.* Becket.
  ("Up with the sun from the sea.") (LL) APAD

Duet for a Chair and a Table. Jack Spicer. APSN

Duet for One Voice. Linda Pastan. NMM-2

Dug-Out, The. Siegfried Sassoon. CH; MoBrPo; NSI; PoFWW

Dugall Quin, *vers. A and B. Unknown.* ESPB

Duh, duh, duh, DUM! (LL) Double Dactyls. E. William Seaman. OBCoV; WeW-3

Duino Elegies. Rilke, *German.*
  First Duino Elegy, The. PFTM, *tr. by* J. B. Leishman and Stephen Spender
    ("Emptiness first / felt the vibration that now charms us and comforts and helps?") PFTM, *tr. by* J. B. Leishman and Stephen Spender
    ("Who, if I cried, would hear me among the angelic orders?") PFTM, *tr. by* J. B. Leishman and Stephen Spender
    "Not wooing, no longer shall wooing, voice that has outgrown it." EnlH, *tr. by* Stephen Mitchell
    "Why, if this interval of being can be spent serenely." EnlH; NAWM-2

Duke Ellington Dream, The. Paul Zimmer. PBCAP

Duke is the lad to frighten a lass, The. Thomas Moore. OBCoV

Duke o' Athole's Nurse, The. *Unknown.* OxBB; ESPB

Duke Of Buccleuch, The. J. A. Phelp. NOBAu

Duke of Buckingham, The. Alexander Pope. NOBE *Fr.* Epistle III, to Allen Lord Bathurst.

Duke of Gordon has three daughters, The. The Duke of Gordon's Daughter. *Unknown.* ESPB

Duke of Gordon's Daughter, The ("Duke of Gordon has three daughters, The"). *Unknown.* ESPB

Duke of York's Statue, The. Walter Savage Landor. FaBoEE

Duke was in his hammock and a thousand miles away, The. The Great Poll-Tax Victory of '88. Noel Petty. UV

Duke's Song, The. Mary Sidney, Countess of Montgomery Wroth. WPE *Fr.* Urania.
  ("And friendship by her are dissolved, / suffered unspoken.") (LL) RACG
  ("If a clear fountain still keeping a sad course.") RACG

Dulce Et Decorum Est. Wilfred Owen. CABP; CMoP; FaBoPV; FaBoTw; HeIP-4; HoPM; InPK-6; LiTM; MoBrPo; NAEL-2; NIP-4; NoAM; NoP-4; OAEL-2; OBWP; PFE; PeFWW; PoE; PoFWW; PoPoPo; PoWW; Poetr; RaBo; SAGP; TFi; TRP; UnPo
  ("Old Lie: Dulce et decorum est / Pro patria mori, The.") (LL) AF

Dulce it is, and *decorum,* no doubt, for the country to fall, to. Arthur Hugh Clough. EBVV; EnVR; FaBoPV; OxAEP-2 *Fr.* Amours de Voyage. NOBVV

Dull as I was, to think that a Court Fly. A Black Patch on Lucasta's Face. Richard Lovelace. BeJo; CaPo; SeCP

Dull. Dull indeed! What shall it e'er be thus? Edward Taylor. ChIV-1 *Fr.* Preparatory Meditations Before My Approach to the Lord's Supper.

Dull evening in a run-down village, A. Earth Poem. Mahmoud Darwish, *Arabic.* AF, *tr. by* Abdullah Al-Udhari

Dull Is My Verse. Walter Savage Landor. PoEL-4

Dull people, A. From Colony to Nation. Irving Layton. NOBC

Dull sleep instructs, nor sport vain dreams in vain. (LL) Night Thoughts. Edward Young. NOEC; OxAEP-1

Dull, Sullen Prisoners. Alexander Pope. ECEV; NOBE; NOEC; OAEL-1; OBEV; SCGP

Dull to myself and almost dead to these. The Bad Season Makes the Poet Sad. Robert Herrick. BeJo; CaPo; CavPo; NAEL-1; SCGP

Dull unwashed windows of eyes. A Poem Some People Will Have to Understand. Imamu Amiri Baraka. BPo; GT; NOBA; RaBo; SAGP

Dull water spirit—and Protean god. Fog. Henry David Thoreau. APN-1

Dulled by the slow glare of the yellow bulb. A Wartime Dawn. David Gascoyne. LiTM

Dulness[e]. George Herbert. ESCV

Dulness is ever apt to magnify. (LL) Some to Conceit alone their taste confine. Alexander Pope. OxAEP-1, *ll.* 289–393 *Fr.* An Essay on Criticism

Dulngulg Song Cycle, The. *Unknown.*
  Sunrise Sequence. NOBAu, *tr. by* Ronald M. Berndt

Dumb are the trumpets, cymbals. Solomon. Heinrich Heine, *German.* TrJP, *tr. by* Emma Lazarus

Dumb, / Bloodied, the severed. A Grafted Tongue. John Montague. BIrV; CIP-2; PBCIP

Dumb Friend, A. Christina Rossetti. FP

Dumb genius blows. From Another Room. Gregory Corso. NeAP

Dumb herd scowled, The. The Cashier. Andrey Andreievich Voznesensky, *Russian.* TCRP, *tr. by* W. H. Auden

Dumb Insolence. Adrian Mitchell. NOxBChV

Dumb Oxen. Sister Mary Madeleva. CRP *Fr.* Of Mary.

Dumb Soldier, The. Robert Louis Stevenson. OxBChV

Dumb thing near a drunken man., A. (LL) The Dumb World. W. H. Davies. OBWVE; OxBTC

Dumb World, The. W. H. Davies. OBWVE; OxBTC

Dumbfounding, The. Margaret Avison. NOBC

Dummer the shepherd sacrific'd. Epitaph. Cotton Mather. SCAP

Dump, The. Greg Kuzma. PoA

Dumping (left over from the autumn). Enemy Encounter. Padraic Fiacc. IIP; PNI

Dumpy Ducky. Lucy Larcom. OBCA

Dun-Colour [*or* Dun-Color]. Ruth Pitter. PoRA

Dun shades quiver down the lone long fallow. A Poem for Max Nordau. Edwin Arlington Robinson. APN-2

Dunbar. Anne Spencer. NAAAL

Duncan and his brother was playing pool. Brady. *Unknown.* AS

Duncan Gray cam here to woo. Robert Burns. GTBS-P

Duncan Spoke of a Process. Imamu Amiri Baraka. CAPP-1

Dunce, The. Jacques Prévert, *French.* MFP, *tr. by* Martin Sorrell

Dunce, The. *Unknown.* OxNR

Dunciad, The. Alexander Pope.
  To Dr. Jonathan Swift. OxAEP-1, *book* I, *ll.* 1–330; CBNP, *book* I, *ll.* 1–84, *first edition vers.;* OBSV; PoE
    ("And the hoarse nation croaked, 'God save King Log!'.") (LL) OxAEP-1, *book* I, *ll.* 1–330
    ("Books and the Man I sing, the first who brings.") CBNP, *book* I, *ll.* 1–84, *first edition vers.*
    ("In clouded Majesty here Dullness shone.") (LL) PoE
    "Here she beholds the chaos dark and deep." FHYEP
    "Yet, yet a moment, one dim ray of light." NAEL-1; OAEL-1; PoEL-3

Carnations and Butterflies. NOEC

Certain Type of Scientist Speaks, A. ECEV

Idle Pursuits. ECEV, book IV, ll. 565–604

"More had she spoke, but yawn'd—All nature nods." FHYEP

Reign of Chaos, The. EBEV; FaBoPV; SCV

(Triumph of Dullness [or Dulness], The.) NOBE; NOEC

"She comes! she comes! the sable throne behold." ECEV

Young Traveller Is Presented to the Goddess Dulness, A. NOEC

Dunciad Minor. Alec Derwent Hope.

"Now Muse assist me, aptly to describe." BXAP

On Shakespeare Critics. OxBC

Dunes are graying that were blackest. Aubade: The Desert. Frederick Bock. PoA

Dunes stir sleepily, The. Cities. Grigory Mikhailovich Pozhenyan, *Russian.* TCRP, *tr. by* Lubov Yakovleva

Dungeon, The. Coleridge. Ro

Dungeon horrible, on all sides round, A. Milton. *Fr.* Book I. FHYEP; NAEL-1; OAEL-1; OxAEP-1 *Fr.* Paradise Lost.

Dunna thee tell me it's his'n, mother. Whether or Not. D. H. Lawrence. MoBrPo

Dunoon and the Holy Loch. Iain Crichton Smith. FaBoTC *Fr.* By the Sea.

Duns Scotus, say, with Scotus Eriugena. (LL) Sushi. Paul Muldoon. CABP; CIP-2

Duns Scotus's Oxford. Gerard Manley Hopkins. CABP; EBEV; GTBS-P; NAEL-2; NoAM; OBMV; OxAEP-2; PeECV; PoEL-5

Dunt Dunt Dunt Pittie Pattie. *Unknown.* FaBoVe

Duo-Tang. Kenward Elmslie. FTOS

Duomo, The. Maria Luisa Spaziani, *Italian.* NeIt, *tr. by* Beverly Allen

Durand of Blonden. Ludwig Uhland, *German.* AWP, *tr. by* James Clarence Mangan

Durban, Birmingham. Question and Answer. Langston Hughes. RPo

Dürer: Innsbruck, 1495. "Ern Malley." BMAP; CBAP

Dürer would have seen a reason for living. The Steeple-Jack. Marianne Moore. BoWoP; CMoP; ColAP; FaBoMo; FaBoWP; HAP; InPS-3; NOBA; NoAM; NoP-4; OxBA; PBWP; PoPoPo; Poetr; WPE *Fr.* Part of a Novel, Part of a Poem, Part of a Play.

Dürer's Vision. John Haines. WeT

Durham. Tony Harrison. NoAM

Durham. *Unknown, Anglo-Saxon.* ASW, *tr. by* Kevin Crossley-Holland

"Durham," "Devonia," "Allendale,"—their houses, those. A Summer Cloud. Waldo Williams, *Welsh.* OBWVE, *tr. by* Joseph P. Clancy

Durham Field. *Unknown.* ESPB

Duriesdyke. Swinburne. OxBB

During a Bombardmant by V-Weapons. Roy Fuller. OxBSP

During a break. Tanka. Mori Ōgai, *Japanese.* MJT, *tr. by* Makoto Ueda

During a cozy hour of rain, I wondered. St. Bartholomew's Night. Bella Akhatovna Akhmadulina, *Russian.* TCRP, *tr. by* Albert C. Todd

During a fit. Tanka. Kitahara Hakushū, *Japanese.* MJT, *tr. by* Makoto Ueda

During a trip. Masaoka Shiki, *Japanese.* MJT, *tr. by* Makoto Ueda

During a trip. Tanka. Sasaki Yukitsuna, *Japanese.* MJT, *tr. by* Makoto Ueda

During an illness. Masaoka Shiki, *Japanese.* MJT, *tr. by* Makoto Ueda

During December's Death. Delmore Schwartz. NYBP

During His Courtship. Charles Wesley. NOCV

During his great speech the prosecutor. The Trial. Zbigniew Herbert, *Polish.* AF, *tr. by* John Carpenter *and* Bogdana Carpenter

During long walks. Janet Sutherland. NBrP

During March while hoeing long rows. Hoeing. Gary Soto. PBCAP

During Music. Arthur Symons. NOBVV

During one period I remember. Eveningsong 2. Ramona Wilson. VoR

During our argument. Alexis Rotella. HA

During the Depression my grandmother. One Foot in the Door. Anne Elder. CBAP

During the early winter. Poem for Shane on Her Brother's Birthday. Donald T. Sanders. TTTS

During the Eichmann Trial. Denise Levertov. HP

During the final minutes of the raid. Mushroom Clouds. John Engman. NAmP90

During the holidays. Holidays. Eva Mylonas, *Modern Greek.* BoWoP, *tr. by* Kimon Friar

During the Pageant at Medicine Lodge. Charles G. Ballard. VoR

During the plague I came into my own. Tarantula or the Dance of Death. Anthony Hecht. CoAP

During the rainy season. Miya Shūji, *Japanese.* MJT, *tr. by* Makoto Ueda

During the Reign of the Queen of Persia. Joan Chase.

"One early spring evening when Celia was fourteen." DeD

During the season of cut organs we. Initiation. Jayne Cortez. PoBA

During the winter she began. Division. John Ratti. NYBP

During Wind and Rain. Thomas Hardy. CMoP; GTBS-P; HAP; NAEL-2; NoP-4; OAEL-2; OxBTC; PFE; PeVV; PoE; TFi; TOF; TRP

("Down their carved names the rain-drop ploughs.") (LL) NoP-4; PFE

Durst ye not stoop to play the fools for him? (LL) On Those That Deserve It. Francis Quarles. NOCV; NOSC

Dusk. Frank Mkalawile Chipasula. HBAPE *Fr.* Nightsong.

Dusk, The. Robert Gray. BMAP

Dusk. Abraham Z. Lopez-Penha, *Spanish.* TrJP, *tr. by* Thomas Walsh

Dusk. Gabriela Mistral, *Spanish.* BoWoP, *tr. by* David Garrison

Dusk. Helen Welshimer. PoToHe

Dusk. / Above the / water hang the. Swan and Shadow. John Hollander. InPK-6; NoP-4; PoA; VCAP

Dusk comes early in the shaft. Twilight. Paul Engle. PFE

Dusk, first lights coming on. Window-Dreaming with SAS. Haim Guri, *Hebrew.* IP, *tr. by* Warren Bargad *and* Stanley F. Chyet

Dusk from rock to rock a waterthrush. John Wills. HA

Dusk-haired and gold-robed o'er the golden wine. For "The Wine of Circe" by Edward Burne-Jones. D. G. Rossetti. UV

Dusk in Creason's Park comes on slow. Late Afternoon, Late in the Twentieth Century. Jeffrey Skinner. PBCAP

Dusk in My Backyard. Keith Wilson. BLT

Dusk in the Country. Harry Edmund Martinson, *Swedish.* RB, *tr. by* Robert Bly

Dusk in Winter. W. S. Merwin. BLT

Dusk: July. Marilyn Hacker. FFC

Dusk must become your light. Sitting with Lester Young. Paul Zimmer. SeSe

Dusk / no dawns, and silver linings. No Dawns. Julianne Perry. PoBA

Dusk of Horses, The. James Dickey. ColAP; LiTM; NYBP; WeT

Dusk or dawn, maybe a bridge. Kafka Poem. Lisa Zeidner. CMAP

Dusk over the lake. Virgil Hutton. InPK-6

Dusk settles in. Road from Xunantunich. Velma Pollard. HCP *Fr.* Belize Suite. HCP

Dusk, the ivy thick with sparrows. Temple Near Quang Tri, Not on the Map. Bruce Weigl. CDa

Dusky night rides down the sky, The. Hunting Song. Henry Fielding. OxBoLi; PeLV *Fr.* Don Quixote in England.

Dust. Rupert Brooke. MoBrPo; OxBTC

Dust. Allen Grossman. PuP-15

Dust. P. A. Ropes. BoTP

Dust. Kathleen Spivack. BoWoP

Dust. Randolph Stow. CBAP

Dust and clay. Ascension Hymn. Henry Vaughan. ESCV; GeHe; NOSC; TrCP

Dust and dirt blow into my trailing face. (LL) Gabriel's Blues. Calvin Forbes. PoA; WeT

Dust, as they say, settled, The. Gwendolyn Brooks. *See* The Third Sermon on the Warpland.

Dust as we are, the immortal spirit grows. Wordsworth. SCV *Fr.* Introduction—Childhood and School-Time. FHYEP *Fr.* The Prelude; Growth of a Poet's Mind [1850 vers.]

Dust Bowl. Langston Hughes. PoA

Dust Bowl. P. Inman.

"Field dodd." FTOS

Dust cools easily. South Texas Summer Rain. Rebecca Gonzales. AiP

Dust had covered us both, and the dust was white, The. (LL) George Robinson: Blues. Muriel Rukeyser. NNaP; RACG

Dust of all the saints of the ages, The. Cymru. David Gwenallt Jones, *Welsh.* OBWVE, *tr. by* Gwyn Jones

Dust of Snow. Robert Frost. CMoP; ChAP; OxBA; OxBSP; PFE; SAmP; SoSe-8; TAP; UnPo; WeW-3

Dust of Timas, The. Sappho, *Greek.* AWP, *tr. by* E. A. Robinson *Fr.* Variations of Greek Themes.

Dust storms whipped. Putting an End to the War Stories. Larry Moffi. CDa

Dust thou art, but dust carefully. Ralph Hodgson. *Fr.* Flying Scrolls. FaBoTw

Dust to Dust. Thomas Hood. NBLV

Dust to the dust; Death takes the clay. (LL) The Forest of the Dead. James Griffyth Fairfax. NSI; PoWW

Dust was too thick every summer. Every winter. Brief History. Richard Hugo. PaTW

Dust World. Adrian C. Louis. UnSA

Duster, dust away, my friend. André Spire, *French.* TrJP, *tr. by* Jethro Bithell

Dusting. Rita Dove. HCAP; HeIP-4; LCAP-2; NoP-4; PoPoPo; Poetr

("Maurice.") (LL) NoP-4; PoPoPo

Dusting off the board, I sit down happily to play. Wei-ch'i Chess. Li K'ai-hsien, *Chinese.* CoBLCP, *tr. by* Jonathan Chaves

Dustman, The. Clive Sansom. BoTP

Dustman, The. *Unknown.* BoTP

Dusty Answer, A. George Meredith. *Fr.* Modern Love.

Dusty Miller, The. *Unknown.* ReMoGo

Dusty pickup, The. Richard Crist. HA

Dusty road is mine to tread, A. Pedlar Jim. Florence Hoare. BoTP

Dusty, with some skeleton of. The Yahrtzeit Light. Lyn Lifshin. UnSA

Dutch, The. George Canning. PeLV
(Epigram: Dutch, The.) OxBoLi

Dutch Lover, The. Aphra Behn.
Song: "Ah false Amyntas, can that hour." WPE
Willing Mistriss, The. FaBoSe; LW
("Oh! who can guess the rest?") (LL) NALW
(Willing Mistress, The.) NALW

Dutch Proverb, A. Matthew Prior. FaBoEE; NOEC; OBCoV

Dutty Tough. Louise Bennett. PBCV

Duty. Bible, *O.T.* LBC *Fr.* 2 Samuel, 19.

Duty. Ralph Waldo Emerson. *See* I Can.

Duty. Ellen S. Hooper. BLPA

Duty, or Truth at Work. Lizelia Augusta Jenkins Moorer. CBWP-3

Duty—that's to say, complying. Arthur Hugh Clough. EBVV; EnVR

Duw gwyddiad mai da y gweddai. Dafydd ap Gwilym. CABP, *tr. by* Arthur James Johnes *Fr.* Mis Mai.

Dvonya. Louis Simpson. NNaP; NOBA

Dwarf, The. Wallace Stevens. MeMAP

Dwarf barefooted, chanting, The. The Peasants. Alun Lewis. LiTM; PoWW

Dwarf of Disintegration. Oscar Williams. ImPo; LiTM

Dwell, awful Silence, on the shady hills. Pan Piping. Plato, *Greek.* FaBoEE, *tr. by* Thomas Stanley

Dweller and a joy, A. (LL) To the Snipe. John Clare. FaBoPV; OBNC

Dweller in hollow places, hills and rocks. Echo. Madison Cawein. APN-2

Dweller on Helicon, son. Roman Epithalamion. Catullus, *Latin.* ITG, *tr. by* Martin, Charles and Robert Hass

Dwelling-Place, The. Henry Vaughan. GeHe; MeLP; NOSC; PeECV

Dwindled and harsh, dead-white and cloudy-clear. (LL) Wild Peaches. Elinor Wylie. LoP

D'ye ken John Peel with his coat so gay [*or* gray]? John Peel. John Woodcock Graves. CH; OxBoLi

Dyer, The. *Unknown.* OxNR

Dying. Adah Isaacs Menken. CBWP-1

Dying. Robert Pinsky. HCAP; VCAP

Dying. John Stigall. CRP

Dying Airman, The. *Unknown.* AS; OxBoLi; PeLV; RB

Dying: An Introduction. Louis Edward Sissman. NYBP
"Bruisingly cradled in a Harvard chair." NoP-4

Dying Away. William Meredith. NoAM

Dying Californian, The. *Unknown.* AmFP

Dying Child, The. Mary Howitt. VWP

Dying Child, The. Letitia Elizabeth Landon. VWP

Dying Child's Request, The. Hannah Flagg Gould. OBCA

Dying Christian to His Soul, The. Alexander Pope, *par. fr. the Latin of* Emperor Hadrian. AWP; OBEV
(Ode: The Dying Christian to His Soul.) ChIV-2

Dying Cowboy, The. *Unknown. See* Bury Me Not on the Lone Prairie.

Dying day pinches the tot. Daily News. Tom Clark. SPE

Dying, dying, dying. Tennyson. *See* Blow, Bugle, Blow.

Dying firelight slides along the quirt, A. The End of the Weekend. Anthony Hecht. CoAmPo; FaBoMo; HAP; LiTM; WeW-3

Dying Garden, The. Howard Nemerov. Poetsp

Dying Gaul, The. Desmond O'Grady. BIrV; PBCIP
"Day concludes burning, the." CIP-2

Dying Girl, The. Mary Weston Fordham. CBWP-2

Dying Gladiator, The. Byron. NOBE *Fr.* Childe Harold's Pilgrimage.

Dying Hobo, The. *Unknown.* AmFP

Dying Hogger, The. *Unknown.* AS

Dying in Massachusetts. Donald W. Baker. PuP-15

Dying Indian, The. Joseph Warton. NOEC; OxAEP-1

Dying Man in His Garden, The. George Sewell. GTBS-P
(Soliloquy.) OBGa

Dying Mine Brakeman, The. Orville Jenks. AmFP

Dying Prostitute, The; an Elegy. Thomas Holcroft. NOEC

Dying Raven, The. Richard Henry Dana. APN-1

Dying Sergeant, The. *Unknown.* AmFP

Dying Song. Anton Ulrich, *German.* GePo, *tr. by* George C. Schoolfield

Dying Speech of an Old Philosopher. Walter Savage Landor. *See* On His Seventy-Fifth Birthday.

Dying sun, shine warm a little longer! Lament for Pasiphaë. Robert Graves. FaBoTw

Dying Swan, The. Thomas Sturge Moore. OBMV

Dying Swan, The. Tennyson. APo

Dying Synagogue at South Terrace, The. Thomas McCarthy. BiHa

Dying Tiger—moaned for Drink, A. Emily Dickinson. InPK-6

Dying Viper, A. "Michael Field." ADE; CABP

Dying Wife to Her Husband, A. Moses ibn Ezra, *Hebrew.* TrJP

Dying with Amish Uncles. Julia Kasdorf. PBCAP

Dying with the Wrong Name, Three parts of an unfinished poem. Sam Hamod. UnSA

Dying Words of Stonewall Jackson, The. Sidney Lanier. APN-2; CBCWP

Dying Year, The. Clara Ann Thompson. CBWP-2

Dykes, The. Rudyard Kipling. OBWP

Dylan, Two Days, *for Dylan Corbett.* Patricia Smith. GT

Dylan, Who Is Dead. Samuel Allen. PoBA

Dynamite Song. *Unknown.* AmFP

Dynastic Hymn. *Unknown, Chinese.* ChiP, *tr. by* Arthur Waley

Dynasts, The. Thomas Hardy.
Budmouth Dears. CH
Eve of Waterloo, The. OAEL-2; OBWP
Field of Talavera, The. CMoP
Field of Waterloo, The. FaBoCh
(Chorus of the Years.) CMoP
Men Who March Away. CH
Night of Trafalgar, The. FaBoCh; MoBrPo; OBMV
(Trafalgar.) CH

"Dynasty of apples," A. (LL) Another Sarah. Anne Porter. KSG

Dysraphism. Charles Bernstein. FTOS

Dyvers thy death doo dyverslye bemone. Henry Howard, Earl of Surrey. *See* The Death of Wyatt.

Dzhansukh, the shepherd, met a devil. The Devil and the Shepherd. Fazil Abdulovich Iskander, *Russian.* TCRP, *tr. by* Daniel Weissbort

Dzogbese Lisa has treated me thus. Songs of Sorrow. Kofi Awoonor. HBAPE; PBMAP

E

E-E-K! Mice. David Marsh. CTV

E hó hì ura bhì. Waulking Song: Two. Minnie Bruce Pratt. GLP

E. Jarvis-Thribb (17) and Keith's Mum. On the Tercentenary of Milton's Death. Gavin Ewart. OxBC

E. P. Ode Pour l'Election de Son Sepulchre. Ezra Pound. HAP; MoAmPo; MoP; NAAL-2; NoAM; VGW *Fr.* Hugh Selwyn Mauberley. (Life and Contacts). AmPP; CMoP; InPS-3; LiTM; NOBA; NoAM; TAP
("All things save Beauty alone.") (LL) NoP-4
(Hugh Selwyn Mauberley.) MeMAP; NoP-4

E Questo il Nido in Che la Mia Fenice? Alec Derwent Hope. OxBC

E-ri-e, The. *Unknown.* AS

E. S. L. Charles Martin. RA

E stands for egg. Hilaire Belloc. NoAM *Fr.* A Moral Alphabet.

E. T. Jean Kenward. SpW

E Tenebris. Oscar Wilde. ChIV-2; MoBrPo; NAEL-2; OxAEP-2; Son; TIRV
(E Tenebris[2].) GSo

E-th-io-piaaaaa! (LL) Number Four. Doughtry Long. MBE

È, the Feasting Florentines. Daniel Gerard Hoffman. VGW

E u w / i a o. Heights. Aleksei Eliseievich Kruchyonykh. CBNP

E Uni Que A The Hi A Tho, Father. Roberta Hill Whiteman. VoR

'E was sittin' on a door-step. The Road to Vagabondia. Dana Burnet. PoLF

'E was warned agin 'er. The Sergeant's Weddin'. Rudyard Kipling. OBCoV; OxBTC

Each a glimpse and gone for ever! (LL) From a Railway Carriage. Robert Louis Stevenson. BoTP; OxBChV

Each alighted. Tanka. Kitahara Hakushū, *Japanese.* MJT, *tr. by* Makoto Ueda

Each and All. Ralph Waldo Emerson. APN-1; AWP; AmPP; ColAP; MeMAP; NAAL-1; NAAL-3; NCAP; NOBA; OxBA; PAR; TAP

Each beast can choose his fere according to his mind. Of a Lady That Refused to Dance with Him. Henry Howard, Earl of Surrey. SiPS

Each Bird Walking. Tess Gallagher. CrSp; FaBoWP; FiLi; NAmP90

Each blest drop, on each blest limb [*or* limme]. On the Water of Our Lord's Baptism[e]. Richard Crashaw. GeHe

Each body has its art, its precious prescribed. Still Do I Keep My Look, My Identity. . . . Gwendolyn Brooks. PoA

Each burning deed and thought! (LL) The Village Blacksmith. Henry Wadsworth Longfellow. APN-1; AiP; CTV; EBEvV; FaBoBe; FaPoR; OBAL; OBCA; PAR; PWR; UV

Each care-worn face is but a book. The Strangers. Jones Very. APN-1; OxBA

Each colour sits beside. Thomas A. Clark. NBrP Fr. Sixteen Sonnets.

Each cord of wood that warms this house. Physics One. Marie Harris. EC3

Each Day. David Ignatow. NNaP

Each Day. Sister Maura. CRP

Each day I grow poorer by the day. Written at Random. Lu Yu, Chinese. SuSp, tr. by Irving Y. Lo

Each day I live, each day the sea of light. Poem against the Rich. Robert Bly. CAPP-1; NOBA

Each day I long so much to see. The One Who Is at Home. Franciso Albanez, Spanish. RaBo, tr. by Robert Bly

Each day I sink in sleep, as into death. Of the Resurrection of the Body. Marbod of Rennes, Latin. MLL, tr. by Helen Waddell

Each day, I take the lift from the sublet down. The Beds. Elizabeth Spires. NAmP90

Each day into the upper air. Election Reflection. M. Keel Jones. NBLV

Each day the tide withdraws; chills us; pastes. Wreaths. Geoffrey Hill. PoA

Each day with so much ceremony / begins. Anaphora. Elizabeth Bishop. AFr

Each element to water yields. Pindar. OBCVT, tr. by Ambrose Philips Fr. The First Olympionique of Pindar. To Hiero of Syracuse, victorious in the Horse-race.

Each face in the street is a slice of bread. Dread. W. S. Merwin. SPF; VCAP

Each face its own phantom. Cartagena de Indias. Earle Birney. MoCV

Each find in each a just, unshaken friend. (LL) An Elegy on a Maiden Name. Jane Cave. CABP; ECWP

Each for himself is still the rule. In the Great Metropolis. Arthur Hugh Clough. EnVR

Each form of beauty's but the new disguise. The Unimaginative. Madison Cawein. APN-2

Each Found Himself at the End Of. . . . Ebbe Borregaard. NeAP

Each grain of sand has an architecture, but. Proposition II. Keith Waldrop. InPK-6

Each holiday celebrated with real extravagance. Morning. Charles D'Ambrosio. PUP-19

Each hour has some glory all its own. The Hour's Glory. Henrietta Cordelia Ray. CBWP-3

Each house had its ghost. Sigmund Freud. Howard Nemerov. PoA

Each In His Own. "Angelus Silesius." GePo, tr. by George C. Schoolfield Fr. The Cherubical Wanderer.

Each in His Own Tongue. William Herbert Carruth. BLPA

Each instant comes with a price, the blue-edged bill. The Cradle Logic of Autumn. Jay Wright. BAP-95

Each is beautiful. Tell Our Daughters. Besmilr Brigham. CrSp

Each known mile comes late. The Train Runs Late to Harlem. Conrad Kent Rivers. PoBA

Each Lon was a notable man. Limerick. L. G. Udall. PeLi

Each lonely and earthly, wanting to be celestial. (LL) His Body. Sandra McPherson. LoL

Each lover's longing leads him naturally. To Dante: He Interprets Dante's Dream. Cino da Pistoia, Italian. AWP, tr. by D. G. Rossetti

Each man is limited by inborn traits. Love Is Kind. Benjamin Keech. PoToHe

Each man me telleth I change most my device [or devise]. Sonnet: 'Each man me telleth'. Sir Thomas Wyatt. AEP; SiPS

Each man on this slow train. Farewell to You. Elizabeth Alexander. GT

Each man to his forced march; this is mine. Hitchhiker. Jack Marshall. NYBP

Each minute the last minute. (LL) Living. Denise Levertov. BLT; OPOU; VGW; WPE

Each moment is surrounded. Ray DiPalma. PmAP

Each Moment of the long-liv'd Day. Catullus. See Carmen 92 ("Lesbia loads me night & day with her curses").

Each More Melodious Note I Hear. Henry David Thoreau. OxBSP; PFE

Each Morning. Imamu Amiri Baraka. PoBA Fr. Hymn for Lanie Poo. BB

Each morning and each noon. Moving. Jeanne Foster. CrSp

Each morning I awake. Tanka. Sasaki Yukitsuna, Japanese. MJT, tr. by Makoto Ueda

Each morning, it's a custom now with me. Mother, I Am Still Here With You. Bàng Bá Lân, Vietnamese. AVP, tr. by Huỳnh Sanh Thông

Each morning she is wheeled into the picture. Living in the La Brea Tar Pits. Nancy Vieira Couto. PBCAP

Each morning the birds awake me. Morning Vigil. Phillip William George. VoR

Each morning they bring me the condemned man's brekker. Analogy. Brian Higgins. FaBoTw

Each morning they pass over. The Starling Migration. Jeffrey Skinner. PBCAP

Each Mortal has his Pleasure: None deny. Horace. OBCVT, tr. by Alexander Pope Fr. The First Satire of the Second Book of Horace, Imitated: To Mr. Fortescue.

Each naked branch, the yellow leaf or brown. The Robe. Jones Very. NCAP

Each new daybreak we are born again. Palladas, Greek. GrAn, tr. by Tony Harrison

Each night a star to guide thy feet to Heaven. (LL) Opportunity. Walter Malone. BLPA; FaBoBe; PWR

Each night father fills me with dread. Limerick. Edward Gorey. PeLi

Each night I float into levels of cislunar. Dreams of Johnson Grass. Colleen J. McElroy. WeT

Each night I read you stories—. 1001 Nights. Ronald Wallace. EC2

Each night / the dead man. Twilight of Vanity. Vyacheslav Kupriyanov, Russian. TCRP, tr. by Albert C. Todd

Each night with moist leaves. Bamboo Elegy: Two. Edmond Yi-teh Chang. OpBo

Each object by a few short years how changed! A Visit to the Author's Paternal Seat. Richard Polwhele. NOEC Fr. The Influence of Local Attachment.

Each of them must have terrified. In Memory of the Utah Stars. William Matthews. Poetsp

Each of these microscopic points and lines is in itself a complete world. Universe of the Rose. Chimako Tada, Japanese. VCWP, tr. by Kirsten Vidaeus

Each of us holds a locked razor. (LL) Waking in the Blue. Robert Lowell. CoAP; HCAP; MoAmPo; UnPo

Each of us like you. Adonis. Hilda Doolittle. AWP

Each of us pursues his trade. The Scholar and the Cat. Unknown, Irish. PC, tr. by Frank O'Connor

Each one making possible the next. (LL) From a Survivor. Adrienne Rich. LoL; NALW

Each other satire humbler arts has known. Mock-Epic Satire. Walter Harte. EPCY

Each page a day. Rondeaux. Laura Moriarty. PT

Each photographed face. Valerio Magrelli, Italian. NeIt, tr. by Dana Gioia

Each picture was a painted memory. An Hour in a Studio. Richard Watson Gilder. APN-2

Each poet with a different talent writes. Wentworth Dillon, 4th Earl of Roscommon. EPCY Fr. An Essay on Translated Verse.

Each prayer is answered. Unknown. CTV

Each shaped. Tanka. Akiko Yosano, Japanese. MJT, tr. by Makoto Ueda

Each small gleam was a voice. Stephen Crane. APN-2 Fr. War Is Kind.

Each sockeye of adulterous claim. Little Hans. Steve McCaffery. FTOS

Each star a rung. A Prison Evening. Faiz Ahmad Faiz, Urdu. VCWP, tr. by Agha Shahid Ali

Each storm-soaked flower has a beautiful eye. Rain. Vachel Lindsay. CMoP; RaBo

Each subtlety hard for the pedant to solve. Coming Across. Mehri, Farsi. WPOW, tr. by Deirdre Lashgari

Each summer day the sun loosens. The Women of Maine. Rush Rankin. CMAP

Each Sunday evening the nuns took us / for a walk. The Walk. Chitra Divakaruni. PUP-19

Each Sunday I climb the mountain to picnic. Picnic. Nellie Wong. OpBo

Each time breath draws through me. This Body. Michael Cuddihy. CMAP

Each time, greenbones, you pressed the neat trigger. Boy at Target Practice; a Contemplation. William Robert Moses. NYBP

Each time I order her to go. Forgiveness. Alice Walker. MDDM

Each time it's a surprise, finding a shell. Mussels. David Keller. CMAP

Each time my body threatens and acts up. Coaxing My Illness. Mai Tho, Vietnamese. AVP, tr. by Huỳnh Sanh Thông

Each to itself. What clew, what clew? (LL) Afterward. Herman Melville. APN-2

Each traveller prays, "Let me be far from any." Journey to Iceland. W. H. Auden. PoA

Each Tuesday above a roadway. Daniil Kharms, Russian. TCRP, tr. by Bradley Jordan

Each way the turn. The Turn. Robert Creeley. FTOS; LCAP-2

Each wishing for the sword that severs all. (LL) Modern Love. George Meredith. CABP; EnLoPo; EnVR; GLoP; GSo; HoPM; NAEL-2; NOBVV; NoP-4; OAEL-2; OxBM; PBMP; PoE; PoEL-5; Son

Each with each has borne in patience. To Edom. Heinrich Heine, *German.* TrJP

Each year. Tanka. Nakajō Fumiko, *Japanese.* MJT, *tr. by* Makoto Ueda

Each year for a short season. Folk Wisdom. Thomas Kinsella. TwCP

Each year I have a birthday. A Giant's Cake. Evelina San Garde. BoTP

Each year, the court expands. The Old Pro's Lament. Paul Petrie. TAP

Each year the dead grow less dead, and nudge. Charles Wright. *Fr.* Homage to Paul Cézanne. VCAP

Each year when peach trees blossomed forth. The Old Calligrapher. Vũ Đình Liên, *Vietnamese.* AVP, *tr. by* Huỳnh Sanh Thông

Eadwacer. *Unknown, Anglo-Saxon.* PBWP, *tr. by* Kemp Malone; WPE (Wulf and Eadwacer.) CIP-2, *ad. by* Richard Ryan; BoWoP, *tr. by* Willis Barnstone *and* Elene Kolb

Eager he look'd. Another train of years. Joel Barlow. AmPP *Fr.* The Columbiad.

Eager note on my door said "Call me," The. Poem. Frank O'Hara. NOBA; NoAM; PmAP; Poetr; SPE

Eager Spring. Gordon Bottomley. MoBrPo

Eager Street. Kendra Kopelke. AiP

Eagerly / Like a woman hurrying to her lover. Four Glimpses of Night. Frank Marshall Davis. PoBA

Eagerness of objects to, The. Interior (With Jane). Frank O'Hara. LCAP-2

Eagle. Robin Skelton. NOBC

Eagle, The. Tennyson. APAD; APo; BoTP; CH; CTAV; CTV; ChAP; ClHu; FHYEP; FPC; FaBoCh; GTBS-P; HeIP-4; InPK-6; NAEL-2; NOBVV; NTCP; NTP; NoP-4; OAEL-2; OxBSP; PFE; Poetr; SAGP; SCGP; TFi; TRP; UnPo

Eagle, The. "Aleksandr Iakovlevich Yashin," *Russian.* TCRP, *tr. by* Daniel Weissbort

Eagle above Us, The. Santiago Altamirano, *Cora Indian.* STP, *tr. by* Anselm Hollo

Eagle and the Beetle, The. Jean de La Fontaine, *French.* OBVE, *tr. by* Elizur Wright

Eagle and the Mole, The. Elinor Wylie. AWP; BoWoP; LiTM; MoAmPo; NALW; UnPo

Eagle-Feather Fan, The. N. Scott Momaday. CDW; NoP-4

Eagle for an Emperor. Falconry. Anne Wilkinson. MoCV

Eagle has Landed, The. Adrian Rumble. SpW

Eagle in New Mexico. D. H. Lawrence.
"Towards the sun, towards the south-west." RB

Eagle in the Land of Oz. Don Receveur. CDa

Eagle is my power, The. The Eagle-Feather Fan. N. Scott Momaday. CDW; NoP-4

Eagle looked at this changing world, The. Mount Eagle. John Montague. BiHa; IIP

Eagle of Pengwern. *Unknown, Welsh.* PBWP, *tr. by* Gwyn Williams

Eagle of the north-west, thou hast heard the voice of the Reim-kennar. (LL) The Song of the Reim-Kennar. Sir Walter Scott. OAEL-2; OBNC

Eagle of the tomb, whose tomb is this? Why. *Unknown, Greek.* GrAn, *tr. by* Peter Whigham

Eagle Poem. Joy Harjo. CrSp; HATNAP; WeT; WeW-3

Eagle so caught in some bursting cloud, An. Shelley. *Fr.* Prometheus Unbound. NOBRP; OAEL-2

Eagle soars in the summit of heaven, The. T. S. Eliot. OBMV *Fr.* Choruses from "The Rock."

Eagle Song. Gordon Bottomley. MoBrPo *Fr.* Suilven and the Eagle.

Eagle That Is Forgotten, The. Vachel Lindsay. AWP; CMoP; MeMAP; MoAmPo; NOBA; OxBA

Eagle Valor, Chicken Mind. Robinson Jeffers. OxBA; OxBSP

Eagle! why soarest thou above that tomb? Spirit of Plato. *Unknown, Greek.* AWP; OBCVT; OBVE, *tr. by* Shelley.

Eagles and butterflies (and some other things). Nina Berberova, *Russian.* TCRP, *tr. by* Albert C. Todd

Eagles gather on the place of death, The. Jones Very. TAP

Eagle's nest on the head of an old redwood on one of the, An. The Beaks of Eagles. Robinson Jeffers. NOBA

Eagles, that wheel above our crests. The Cedars of Lebanon. Alphonse Marie Louis de Lamartine, *French.* AWP, *tr. by* Toru Dutt

Eaper Weaper, chimney sweeper. *Unknown.* OxBoLi

Ear, The. Louis MacNeice. OxBSP

Ear Ear [stripestripestripestripe]. Concrete Cat. Dorthi Charles. InPK-6; KaS

Ear-string, An. William Strode. NOSC

Earl Bothwell. *Unknown.* ESPB

Earl Brand. *Unknown.* AmFP

Earl Brand. *Unknown.* ESPB; OxBB

Earl Brand (The Douglas Tragedy). *Unknown.* NTP
(Douglas Tragedy, The.) NoP-4

Earl Crawford. *Unknown.* ESPB

Earl March look'd on his dying child. The Maid of Neidpath. Thomas Campbell. GTBS-P

Earl Mertoun's Song. Robert Browning. OBEV *Fr.* A Blot in the 'Scutcheon.

Earl of Aboyne, The. *Unknown.* ESPB

Earl of Cassillis' ladie, The. (LL) The Gypsy Laddie. *Unknown.* ESPB; EnSB

Earl of Errol, The. *Unknown.* ESPB

Earl of Mar's Daughter, The. *Unknown.* CH; ESPB

Earl of Westmoreland, The. *Unknown.* ESPB

Earl of Wigton had three daughters, The. Richie Story. *Unknown.* ESPB

Earl Percie of Northumberland. Chevy Chase. *Unknown.* EnSB

Earl Rothes. *Unknown.* ESPB

Earle of Somerset. Sir Henry Wotton. *See* Upon the Sudden Restraint of the Earl[e] of Somerset, Then Falling from Favor [*or* Favour].

Earlier in the evening the moon. The Moon. Robert Creeley. VGW

Earliest Spring. William Dean Howells. *See* In Earliest Spring.

Earliest Spring. Denise Levertov. LCAP-2

Earliness at the Cape. Babette Deutsch. FYAP; NYBP

Earlobe. Leonid Andreievich Zavalnyuk, *Russian.* TCRP, *tr. by* Albert C. Todd

Early Affection. George Moses Horton. AAP

Early Arrival: Sydney. Vivian Smith. NOBAu

Early autumn enters my rickety house. Thoughts in Early Autumn: Thirty Rhymes Sent to Lu-wang. P'i Jih-hsiu, *Chinese.* SuSp, *tr. by* Irving Y. Lo

Early Autumn in the Mountains. Wen T'ing-yün, *Chinese.* SuSp, *tr. by* William R. Schultz

Early autumn, white rabbits. Wang Chien. SuSp, *tr. by* William H. Nienhauser *Fr.* Palace Poems.

Early bird got up and whet his beak, The. A Birthday Ode to Mr. Alfred Austin. Sir Owen Seaman. NOBL

Early bird may catch the worm, The. Samuel Hoffenstein. NBLV *Fr.* As the Crow Flies, Let Him Fly.

Early blossoms—could a single. Permanence in Change. Goethe. HoPM; STV, *tr. by* John Frederick Nims

Early Chaplin, The. Wiktor Woroszylski, *Polish.* CEEP, *tr. by* Magnus J. Krynski *and* Robert A. Maguire

Early Copper. Carl Sandburg. HeIP-4

Early Death. Hartley Coleridge. OBEV

Early Death, An. Daniel Halpern. FiLi

Early dew woos the half-opened flowers, An. Haroun's Favorite Song. *Unknown.* AWP *Fr.* The Thousand and One Nights.

Early Discoveries. David Malouf. CBAP

Early, each morning, Martha Blake. Martha Blake at Fifty-one. Austin Clarke. CIP-2; NOIV

Early Electric! With what radiant hope. The Metropolitan Railway. John Betjeman. EBEV; OxAEP-2; OxBTC

Early Evening Quarrel. Langston Hughes. SAmP; UnPo

Early Geese. Tu Mu, *Chinese.* SuSp

Early Graves, The. Friedrich Gottlieb Klopstock, *German.* GePo, *tr. by* J. W. Thomas

Early I rose. Love Song. *Unknown, Papago Indian.* AWP, *tr. by* Mary Austin

Early in the Morning. Li-Young Lee. LoL

Early in the Morning. Louis Simpson. CoAmPo; TRP

Early in the morning. Jules Supervielle, *French.* MFP, *tr. by* Martin Sorrell

Early in the morning. A Watering Rhyme. P. A. Ropes. BoTP

Early in the morning I hear monkeys call from the mouth of the gorge. West Cliff. Chu Yi-tsun, *Chinese.* SuSp, *tr. by* Chang Yin-nan *and* Lewis C. Walmsley

Early in the spring when the snow is all gone. A Trip to the Grand Banks. Amos Hanson. AmFP

Early January. W. S. Merwin. VGW

Early Levée, An. Po Chü-i. *Chinese.* ChiP, *tr. by* Arthur Waley

Early light of the rising sun shines on the beams of my house, The. Getting Up Early on a Spring Morning. Po Chü-i, *Chinese.* ChiP, *tr. by* Arthur Waley

Early Losses: a Requiem. Alice Walker. BlSi

Early Lynching. Carl Sandburg. ChIV-2; MoAmPo

Early may fly the Babylonian wo[e]. (LL) On the Late Massacre [*or* Massacher] in Piedmont [*or* Piemont]. Milton. AWP; GTBS-P; HAP; HeIP-4; NAEL-1; NOBE; NOCV; OAEL-1; OBWP; PoEL-3; Poetr; SCGP; Son; TFi; TRP; UnPo; WeW-3

Early Morn. W. H. Davies. CH

Early Morning, The. Hilaire Belloc. BoTP; OxBSP; Spl; TLR

Early Morning Meadow Song. Charles Dalmon. CH

Early morning over Rouen, hopeful. Rouen. May Wedderburn Cannan. NAEL-2; OBWP; OxBTC

Early morning, the day before yesterday. Green Snake. B. R. Lakshman Rao, *Kannada.* OMIP, *tr. by* A. K. Ramanujan

Early morning woman. Joy Harjo. CrSp

Early Mornings. *Unknown.* AS, *tr. by* Louis Untermeyer

Early, my God, without delay. Isaac Watts. AmFP

Early Noon. Ingeborg Bachmann, *German.* AF, *tr. by* Mark Anderson

Early on a Monday morning. Kevin Barry. *Unknown.* AS

Early on a pleasant day. The Mocking-Bird. Joseph Rodman Drake. APN-1

Early on the morning of Monday. Omens. *Unknown, Gaelic.* RB, *tr. by* Alexander Carmichael

Early Pregnancy. Penelope Shuttle. BrRo

Early Rebels, The. Mervyn Morris. PBCV

Early Rising. John Godfrey Saxe. PoLF

Early, sober, and alone. (LL) Epitaph on a Party Girl. Richard Usborne. FaBoEE; OBCoV

Early Spring. Adrian Henri. AYFP

Early Spring. Sidney Keyes. MoBrPo

Early Spring, An. Stephen Sartarelli. PT

Early spring's sweet blush, The. Eloise Bibb. CBWP-4

Early Summer: At the Riverside, Seeing Off Li Chiu-ho as He Returns to Yeh with the Books I Lent Him. Li K'ai-hsien, *Chinese.* "Not a day goes by without someone borrowing books from me." CoBLCP, *tr. by* Jonathan Chaves

Early Summer in the Year Jen-tzu (1672)—Playfully Painted in the Manner of Ts'ao Yün-hsi. Yün Shou-p'ing, *Chinese.* CoBLCP, *tr. by* Jonathan Chaves

Early Summer Sea-Tryst. Frederick Thomas Bennett Macartney. CBAP

Early Summer Waking from a Nap. Yang Wan-li, *Chinese.* SuSp, *tr. by* Sherwin S. S. Fu

Early sun on Beaulieu water. Youth and Age on Beaulieu River, Hants. John Betjeman. FaBoTw; TwCP

Early Sunday Morning. John A. Stone. MT

Early Supper. Barbara Howes. WeT

Early that afternoon, as we keep. The "Portland" Going Out. W. S. Merwin. NYBP

Early thou goest forth, to put to rout. To a "Tenting" Boy. Charles Tennyson Turner. OBNC

Early Thoughts of Marriage. Nathaniel Cotton. OxBChV

Early to bed and early to rise. *Unknown.* FaBoBe; LB

 ("Early to bed, early to rise.") CTV

 ("'Tis time to rise.") (LL) LB

Early Triangles. Ron Padgett. FTOS

Early Waking. Léonie Adams. LiTM

Early Walk on Shang Mountain, An. Wen T'ing-yün, *Chinese.* SuSp, *tr. by* William R. Schultz

Early we set out from Ch'en-hsi ferry. Ch'en-hsi County. Ho Ching-ming, *Chinese.* CoBLCP, *tr. by* Jonathan Chaves

Earlye, Earlye, in the Spring. *Unknown.* AmFP

Earnest, earthless, equal, attuneable, vaulty, voluminous,. . . stupendous. Spelt from Sibyl's Leaves. Gerard Manley Hopkins. CMoP; EnVR; FaBoMo; LiTM; NOBVV; OAEL-2; TOF

Earnest elements of nature. (LL) Boats in a Fog. Robinson Jeffers. BLT; NAAL-2; NoP-4; OxBA

Earnest I look'd. Dante. OxBSn, *tr. by* Henry Cary *Fr.* Divina Comedia.

Earnest Liberal's Lament, The. Ernest Hemingway. OBAL; OBSV

Earnest young leftie named Tariq. Limerick. Bernard Levin. PeLi

Earning a Dinner. Matthew Prior. NBLV

Earrings Dangling and Miles of Desert. Gary Snyder. APSN *Fr.* Mountains and Rivers without End: The Market.

Ears. Sonja Åkesson, *Swedish.* WPOW, *tr. by* Joanna Bankier

Ear's Delight, The. George Chapman. NoSic *Fr.* Ovid's Banquet of Sense.

Ears in the turrets hear. Dylan Thomas. FaBoTw

Ears on the floor were pressed to the ground. (LL) The Colonel. Carolyn Forché. InPS-3; OBWP; SoSe-8

Earth. Margaret Atwood. PoE

Earth ("Grasshopper, your fairy [*or* tiny] song"). John Hall Wheelock. MoAmPo

Earth, The. David Gwenallt Jones, *Welsh.* OBWVE, *tr. by* Dyfnallt Morgan

Earth. Czeslaw Milosz. ITG, *tr. by* Czeslaw Milosz *and* Robert Hass (b. 1941) *Fr.* The Garden of Earthly Delights.

Earth ("'Planet doesn't explode of itself, A,' said drily"). John Hall Wheelock. LiTM; SAGP; SoSe-8

 ("'Planet doesn't explode of itself,' said drily, A.") SAGP

Earth, The. Anne Sexton. SAGP

Earth. Yaroslav Vasilevich Smelyakov, *Russian.* TCRP, *tr. by* Albert C. Todd

Earth. Jules Supervielle, *French.* MFP, *tr. by* Martin Sorrell

Earth. Ann Taylor. NOxBChV

Earth. Jim Tollerud. VoR

Earth, The. Jones Very. APN-1; OxBA

Earth a flower. For Nothing. Gary Snyder. NNaP

Earth / a part of Ocean / again, The. Nathaniel Mackey. *See* The Phantom Light of All Our Day.

Earth and Fire. Vernon Watkins. NYBP

Earth and Goddess of Birth. Macedonius, *Greek.* GrAn, *tr. by* Alistair Elliot

Earth and I Gave You Turquoise. N. Scott Momaday. CDW; HATNAP; UnPo

Earth and sky are infinities / Where our cries cannot venture. Joseph Miezan Bognini. PBMAP

Earth and sky black. Camp Site. Denis Glover. PeNZ *Fr.* Arawata Bill.

Earth and water, air and stars. Immortality. "Nicolai Maksimovich Minsky," *Russian.* TrJP, *tr. by* Babette Deutsch

Earth Angel. Jeffrey Skinner. PBCAP

Earth Asks and Receives Rain, The. Phyllis Haring. PeSA

Earth bleeds / as a breast bleeds, The. Kassak. Birago Diop, *French.* NegPo, *tr. by* Ellen Conroy Kennedy

Earth Breaks Up. Robert Browning. TrCP *Fr.* Christmas-Eve.

Earth Buried. Kenneth Mackenzie. CBAP

Earth did tremble, and heaven's closed eye, The. On Our Saviour's Passion. Francis Quarles. PeECV *Fr.* Divine Fancies.

Earth does not ever grow fat, The. Ngoni Burial Song. *Unknown, Zulu.* PeSA

Earth does not understand her child. The Return. Edna St. Vincent Millay. MeMAP; MoAmPo; MoP; NoAM; OxBA; Poetr

Earth exhales, The. (LL) Slough. John Betjeman. APAD; MoBrPo; NoAM; OxAEP-2

Earth Felicities, Heavens Allowances. Richard Steere. SCAP

Earth fills her lap with pleasures of her own. Wordsworth. *Fr.* Ode: Intimations of Immortality [from Recollections of Early Childhood]. AWP; FHYEP; HAP; HeIP-4; NOBE; NOBRP; OAEL-2; OBEV; OBNC; PBMP; PoE; PoEL-4

Earth for the sun her lover. Spring Song. John Milton, *Latin.* MLL, *tr. by* Helen Waddell

Earth from a distance, The. Optics. Alan Sillitoe. SpW

Earth goes on the earth glittering in gold, The. Inscribed in Melrose Abbey. *Unknown.* FaBoEE

Earth grown old, yet still so green. Advent. Christina Rossetti. TrCP

Earth had wanted us all to itself, The. Mighty Forms. Brenda Hillman. PuP-16; WeT

Earth has borne a little son. The Aconite. A. M. Graham. BoTP

Earth has many keys, The. Emily Dickinson. APN-2

Earth has [*or* hath] not anything to show [*or* shew] more fair. Composed upon Westminster Bridge[, September 3, 1802]. Wordsworth. APAD; AWP; CABP; CH; ChAP; ClHu; FaBoCh; GSo; GTBS-P; HAP; HeIP-4; ImPo; InPK-6; InPS-3; NAEL-2; NAWM-2; NOBRP; NoP-4; OAEL-2; OBNC; OPOU; PBMP; PFE; PoE; PoEL-4; PoLF; PoPoPo; Ro; SCGP; Son; TFi; UnPO

Earth Has Shrunk in the Wash. William Empson. CMoP

Earth his bones, the heavens possess his ghost, The. Henry Howard, Earl of Surrey. *See* Tribute to Wyatt.

Earth holds the sunlit. For Spring. Douglas G. Jones. NOBC

Earth in beauty dressed. Her Anxiety. W. B. Yeats. OPOU

Earth in her mercy permits us to repeat. Wedding Song. Patricia Storace. FFC

Earth in Spring, The. Judah Halevi, *Hebrew.* TrJP, *tr. by* Edward G. King

Earth is a beautiful place, The. The Third Sermon on the Warpland. Gwendolyn Brooks. BPo; NAAAL; SeSe

Earth is a place on which England is found, The. Geography. G. K. Chesterton. OBSV *Fr.* Songs of Education.

Earth is a prison to man all his life, The. The Prison. Samuel Hanagid, *Hebrew.* NNPT, *tr. by* T. Carmi

Earth is a woman who imagines us. She sings. Robert Kelly. *Fr.* The Book of Persephone. PoM

Earth / is a wonderful, The. Poem for Friends. Quincy Troupe. PoBA

Earth is God's, with all she bears, The. Bible, *O.T. See* Psalm 24.

Earth is sweet with roses, The. Easter Eve. Prudentius, *Latin.* MLL, *tr. by* Helen Waddell

Earth is taken: this is not your home, The. (LL) Travelogue for Exiles. Karl Shapiro. MoAmPo; TrJP

Earth is the Lord's and the fulness thereof, The. Psalm 24. Bible, *O.T.* AWP; TrJP *Fr.* Psalms.

Earth is weary of our foolish wars, The. Let Us Have Peace. Nancy Byrd Turner. PoToHe

Earth keeps some vibration going, The. Edgar Lee Masters. CMoP; NoAM; OxBA; TAP *Fr.* Spoon River Anthology.

Earth-ling, The, *Countless years ago the people of Alzorus used the planet Earth as a lunatic asylum. They called the people they dumped there 'Earth-lings'.* Brian Patten. SpW

Earth looks, The. Tanka. Akiko Yosano, *Japanese.* MJT, *tr. by* Makoto Ueda

Earth, my likeness. Walt Whitman. APN-1; MeMAP; OxBA

Earth, ocean, air, belovèd brotherhood! Alastor; or, The Spirit of Solitude. Shelley. OAEL-2; Ro

Earth, ocean, air, belovèd brotherhood! Invocation. Shelley. NAEL-2 *Fr.* Alastor; or, The Spirit of Solitude. OAEL-2; Ro

Earth outside, The. Muzahim al-Ugaili, *Arabic.* ArPe, *tr. by* Omar S. Pound

Earth Poem. Mahmoud Darwish, *Arabic.* AF, *tr. by* Abdullah Al-Udhari

Earth puts her colours by. Envoi. P. H. B. Lyon. BoTP

Earth rais'd up her head. Earth's Answer. William Blake. ChIV-1; FHYEP; InPS-3; NAEL-2; NAWM-2; NOBRP; NOEC; OAEL-2; PoE *Fr.* Songs of Experience.

Earth rebelled, The. / The good and patient earth. And the Earth Rebelled. Yuri Suhl, *Yiddish.* TrJP, *tr. by* Max Rosenfeld

Earth, receive an honoured guest. W. H. Auden. FaBoTw *Fr.* In Memory of W. B. Yeats. CMoP; EPCY; GEA; HAP; HeIP-4; HoPM; IIP; ImPo; LiTM; MeMAP; MoBrPo; NOBE; NoAM; NoP-4; OAEL-2; OxAEP-2; OxBTC; PFE; Poetr; TFi; TRP; UnPo; WeW-3

Earth rises blue above the ragged grey. Earthrise. Judith Nicholls. SpW

Earth said to Death. Helen Waddell. MLL

Earth Screaming. Esther Iverem. GT

Earth sees in thee. To Sultan Murad II. James Clarence Mangan, *Turkish.* NOIV

Earth shook, stumbled, shuddered, The. Last Men on Mars. Alan Bold. SpW

Earth shows her face to the moon, The. Eclipse II. Linda Hogan. HATNAP

Earth, Sky. Sydney Clouts. PeSA

Earth Song. Thomas Love Peacock. VoR

Earth spins to my finger-tips and, The. The Globe in North Carolina. Derek Mahon. BiHa; PBCIP

Earth stopped. The Holy City hit a mountin. Joshua. X. J. Kennedy. ChIV-1

Earth that lightly covers her, The. (LL) Upon a Child That Died [*or* Dyed]. Robert Herrick. BeJo; CH; CaPo; InPK-6; NoP-4; OBEV; PFE; Poetr

Earth to Tell of the Beasts. David Rivard. NAmP90

Earth Took of Earth. *Unknown.* HAP

Earth Trembles Waiting. Blanche Shoemaker Wagstaff. PoLF

Earth Tremor in Lugano. James Kirkup. NYBP

Earth turns / like a rainbow, The. When You Read This Poem. Pinkie Gordon Lane. BlSi

Earth was green, the sky was blue, The. A Green Cornfield. Christina Rossetti. ACTP; BoTP

Earth was young, the world was fair, The. The Saxon Legend of Language. Mary Weston Fordham. AAP; CBWP-2

Earth will be going on a long time, The. Lute Music. Kenneth Rexroth. TAP

Earth with swallowing drunken showers, The. Paraphras'd from Anacreon. Anacreon, *Greek.* MoBrPo, *tr. by* Charles Cotton

Earth with thunder torn[e], with fire blasted, The. Sonnet: "Earth with thunder torn, with fire blasted, The." Fulke Greville. AAS; NoSic *Fr.* Caelica.

Earth Worm, The. Denise Levertov. NOBA

Earth wraps your body, Kallisto, in its lap. Epitaph from Piraeus. *Unknown, Greek.* GrAn, *tr. by* Peter Jay

Eartha my mother's name, now earth. Crinagoras, *Greek.* GrAn, *tr. by* Alistair Elliot

Earthly bare, / How it blows you! dumb. Ode I. Erich Arendt, *German.* CEEP, *tr. by* David Scrase

Earthly Paradise, The. William Morris. *See* An Apology.

Apology, An. AWP; EBVV; EnVR; NAEL-2; OAEL-2; OBNC

(Earthly Paradise, The.) NoP-4

November. EnVR

October. EnVR; OBNC

Outlanders, The. EBVV

Prologue: The Wanderers. EBVV

(Introduction.) EnVR

Road of Life, The. OBNC

"Under a bent when the night was deep." PChr

Earthly roses at God's call have made, The. On the Death of a Pious Lady. Olof Wexionius, *Swedish.* AWP, *tr. by* Sir Edmund Gosse

Earthly: Sonnets for Carlos. Ian Wedde.

"By day and also by night and you are." PeNZ

"Diesel trucks past the Scrovegni chapel." PeNZ

"'If thy wife is small bend down to her and'." PeNZ

Power Transformer. PeNZ

Earthmoving Malediction. Heather McHugh. NAmP90

Earthquake. Robert Arthur Douglas Ford. NOBC

Earthquake. Li K'ai-hsien, *Chinese.*

"Earthquake covered Shansi and Shensi, The." CoBLCP, *tr. by* Jonathan Chaves

Earthquake of 1886, The. Josephine D. Henderson Heard. CBWP-4

Earthquake terrified us all. The house trembled, the, An. Four Days: Earthquake. Gary Young. PuP-17

Earthquaked, my house collapsed. Antiphilus, *Greek.* GrAn, *tr. by* Lee T. Pearcy

Earthrise. Judith Nicholls. SpW

Earth's Answer. William Blake. ChIV-1; FHYEP; InPS-3; NAEL-2; NAWM-2; NOBRP; NOEC; OAEL-2; PoE *Fr.* Songs of Experience.

("Earth raised up her head.") Ro

Earth's Bounty. Auvaiyar, *Tamil.* PLW, *tr. by* A. K. Ramanujan

Earth's first Adam, he lay in the grass. Adam and Eve. Itsik Manger, *Yiddish.* TrJP, *tr. by* Jacob Sonntag

Earth's Holocaust. James Schuyler. FTOS

Earth's Immortalities. Robert Browning.

Love. EnLoPo; GLoP

Earth's increase, foison plenty. Shakespeare. *Fr.* The Tempest. OAEL-1

Earth's Lyric. Bliss Carman *and* Richard Hovey (1864–1900). APN-2

Earthset. Judith Nicholls. SpW

Earthworker's God is Healed, The. Bernadette Mayer. FTOS

Earthworm, The. Harry Edmund Martinson, *Swedish.* RB; RaBo, *tr. by* Robert Bly

Earthworms. Parody. Martha Paley Francescato, *Spanish.* BoWoP, *tr. by* Willis Barnstone

Earthy Anecdote. Wallace Stevens. CMoP; RB; SAmP

Early [*or* Earthly] nourris [*or* nouris *or* nourrice] sits and sings, An. The Great Silkie of Sule Skerry. *Unknown.* ESPB; FaBoCh; OxBB

Ease. William Cowper. *Fr.* The Sofa. *Fr.* The Task.

Ease. Po Chü-i, *Chinese.* ChiP; Spl, *tr. by* Arthur Waley

("I wonder if the courtiers at the Western Capital know of these things, or not?") (LL) ChiP, *tr. by* Arthur Waley

Ease came with song, he could not buy with gold. (LL) Cyclops, The ("And so an easier life"). Theocritus. HePo, *tr. by* Barbara Hughes Fowler; OBVE, *tr. by* Elizabeth Barrett Browning

Ease is the pray'r of him who, in a whaleboat. Sapphics: At the Mohawk-Castle, Canada. Thomas Morris. NOEC

Ease, is the weary Merchant's Pray'r. Translation of the 16th Ode of the 2d. Book of Horace. Horace, *Latin.* OBCVT, *tr. by* William Cowper

Ease your weary limbs, stranger, under this elm—. Anyte, *Greek.* GrAn, *tr. by* John Heath-Stubbs *and* Carol A. Whiteside

Easie earth that covers her, Th'. (LL) Upon a Child. Robert Herrick. OBEV

Easier to encapsulate your lives. Granddaughter. Adrienne Rich. *Fr.* Grandmothers. HCAP; NAAL-2; NoAM

Easiest Room in Hell, The. Peter Porter. BMAP

Easing a savior's birth. (LL) Tempt Me No More. C. Day Lewis. MoBrPo; OBMV; PoA

Easing My Heart. Tu Mu, *Chinese.* NNPT; PLT, *tr. by* A. C. Graham

East and West. Ernest Francisco Fenollosa.

Separated East, The. APN-2

East Anglian Bathe. John Betjeman. NoP-4

East Bronx. David Ignatow. CoAmPo

East Coast Journey. James Keir Baxter. NoP-4; PeNZ

East Coker. T. S. Eliot. HAP; VGW *Fr.* Four Quartets.

East Gate Willows. *Unknown, Chinese.* ChiPo, *tr. by* Rewi Alley

East is a clear violet mass, The. A Street Scene. Lizette Woodworth Reese. OBCA

East London. Matthew Arnold. SCGP

East looking down from the Chieh-shih. Viewing the Ocean. Ts'ao Ts'ao, *Chinese.* CoBCP, *tr. by* Burton Watson

East of the eastern ocean. Song of a Dream Journey over the Vast Sea. Yang Wei-chen, *Chinese.* CoBLCP, *tr. by* Jonathan Chaves

East of the Library, Across from the Odd Fellows Building. August Kleinzahler. WWSi

East of the river there's a foul bird. A Parable. Ch'en Tzu-lung, *Chinese.* SuSp, *tr. by* Irving Y. Lo

East of the salt village, low and narrow. Wu Chia-chi, *Chinese.* CoBLCP, *tr. by* Jonathan Chaves

East of the sun's slant, in the vineyard that never failed. Harvest. Gary Soto. PBCAP

East St. Louis Blues. *Unknown.* AmFP

East the ocean, west the Himalaya. A Eulogy of the Sagely Virtue of His Imperial Majesty Emperor Shih-tsu. Chao Meng-fu, *Chinese*. CoBLCP, *tr. by* Jonathan Chaves

East Wind. Ou-yang Hsiu, *Chinese*. OHPC, *tr. by* Kenneth Rexroth

East Wind asperges Boston with Lynn's sulphurous brine, An. Father. John Wheelwright. UnPo

East wind blows gently, The. Begonias. Su Tung-p'o, *Chinese*. OHPC, *tr. by* Kenneth Rexroth

East wind blows in the street to-day, The. A March Day in London. Amy Levy. VWP

East wind, knowing I plan to walk through the hills, The. On the Road to Hsin-ch'eng. Su Tung-p'o, *Chinese*. CoBCP, *tr. by* Burton Watson

East wind sighs, the fine rains come, The. Li Shang-yin, *Chinese*. PLT, *tr. by* A. C. Graham

East wind stirs fine dust on the roads. Rhyming with Tzu-yu's "Treading the Green." Su Tung-p'o, *Chinese*. CoBCP, *tr. by* Burton Watson

East wind whirling, light clouds in strands, The. Tune: "Beautiful Lady Yü, The"—Spring Sorrow. Ch'en Liang, *Chinese*. SuSp, *tr. by* Hellmut Wilhelm

East wind's whistlin' cauld an' shrill, The. A Schule Laddie's Lament on the Lateness o' the Season. James Logie Robertson. NOBVV

Easter ("I got me flowers to straw [*or* strew *or* strow] Thy [*or* the] way"). George Herbert. BoTP; CH; FHYEP; FaBoCh; NAEL-1; NOBE; OBEV

Easter. Herman Melville. APN-2 *Fr.* Clarel: A Poem and Pilgrimage in the Holy Land.

Easter. Howard Nemerov. NoP-4

Easter. Frank O'Hara. SPE

Easter ("Rise heart; thy Lord is risen. Sing his praise"). George Herbert. ESCV; FMP; GeHe; NAEL-1; PoWW; PeECV; TrCP

Easter. Charles Hubert Sisson. OxBSP

Easter. Edmund Spenser. *See* Sonnet 68: "Most glorious Lord of Life that on this day."

Easter '68. Basil T. Paquet. CDa

Easter again, and a small rain falls. The Other Side of the River. Charles Wright. MT; VCAP

Easter at Christmas. Alun Lewis. PoWW

Easter Bonnet, The. Clara Ann Thompson. CBWP-2

Easter Bunny Blues or All I Want for Xmas Is the Loop, The. Ebon Dooley. PoBA

Easter Carol. Henrietta Cordelia Ray. CBWP-3

Easter Chick, An. Thirza Wakley. BoTP

Easter Chorus. Goethe. *See* Christ Is Arisen.

Easter Dawn. Kofi Awoonor. PBMAP

Easter dawn! Morning, Noon, And. Hawley Truax. NYBP

Easter Day. Richard Crashaw. FMP

Easter-Day. Henry Vaughan. ESCV; PeECV

Easter Day. Oscar Wilde. OxAEP-2

Easter Day. Naples, 1849. Arthur Hugh Clough. EBVVPR

Easter Eve. Prudentius, *Latin*. MLL, *tr. by* Helen Waddell

Easter Eve. Muriel Rukeyser. VGW

Easter Garland, An. Carol Rumens. FaBoWP

Easter has come around. W. D. Snodgrass. VCAP *Fr.* Heart's Needle. CAPP-1

Easter Hymn. Alec Derwent Hope. ChIV-2; GI

Easter Hymn. A. E. Housman. EBEV; GI

Easter Hymn. Henry Vaughan. ChIV-2; ESCV

Easter Light, The. Clara Ann Thompson. CBWP-2

Easter lilies! Can you hear. On Easter Day. Celia Laighton Thaxter. CTV

Easter Monday. Christina Rossetti. NOCV

Easter Morn. Josephine D. Henderson Heard. CBWP-4

Easter Morning. A. R. Ammons. HCAP; NAAL-2; NoAM; PoPoPo

("Flood of burn breaking across us now / from the sun.") (LL) PoPoPo

Easter Morning. Amy Clampitt. ChIV-2

Easter Morning. Edmund Spenser. *See* Sonnet 68: "Most glorious Lord of Life that on this day."

Easter Night. Alice Thompson Meynell. BrRo; ChIV-2

Easter 1984. Les A. Murray. ChIV-2

Easter 1916. W. B. Yeats. CMoP; FaBoMo; FaBoPV; FaPoR; GEA; HAP; HeIP-4; IIP; InPS-3; LiTM; MoP; NAEL-2; NAWM-2; NIP-4; NOBE; NOIV; NoAM; NoP-4; OAEL-2; OBWP; OxAEP-2; OxBTC; PoE; PoPoPo; TFi

Easter, 1968. May Sarton. CrSp

Easter; or, Spring-Time. Lizelia Augusta Jenkins Moorer. CBWP-3

Easter Praise. Rodney Bennett. BoTP

Easter Roses. Robert Grenier. FTOS *Fr.* Phantom Anthems.

Easter Song, An. *Unknown*. MiEL

Easter Sunday. Allen Ginsberg. FTOS

Easter Sunday, 1985. Charles Martin. RA

Easter: Wahiawa, 1959. Cathy Song. OpBo

Easter-Wings. George Herbert. CABP; ChIV-1; ESCV; FHYEP; FMP; FSCP; GeHe; HAP; HeIP-4; InPK-6; InPS-3; MeLP; NAEL-1; NIP-4; NOSC; NoP-4; OAEL-1; PBRV; PFE; PoE; PoEL-2; PoPoPo; Poetr; SeCP; TFi; TOF; TRP; TrCP; WeW-3

Eastern Gate, The. *Unknown, Chinese*. ChiP, *tr. by* Arthur Waley

Eastern guard tower. Haiku. Etheridge Knight. BPo; MoP; TAP

Eastern mountains/ and western mountains. Yüan Hung-tao. CoBLCP, *tr. by* Jonathan Chaves *Fr.* Passing by the Hot Springs at Hua-ch'ing Palace.

Eastern neighbor, western neighbor. Yang Chi. CoBLCP, *tr. by* Jonathan Chaves *Fr.* Scenes.

Eastern River. Peter Huchel, *German*. CEEP, *tr. by* Michael Hamburger

Eastern Slope. Su Tung-p'o, *Chinese*.

"Abandoned earthworks nobody tends." CoBCP, *tr. by* Burton Watson

"I planted rice before Spring Festival." CoBCP, *tr. by* Burton Watson CoBCP

"Little stream used to cross my land, A." CoBCP, *tr. by* Burton Watson CoBCP

Eastern spices I bring with me. Venio ex Oriente. Nuala Ni Dhomhnaill. BiHa

Eastern Tempest. Edmund Blunden. MoBrPo

Eastern Wall stands high and long;, The. *Unknown*. ChiP, *tr. by* Arthur Waley *Fr.* Seventeen Old Poems.

Eastern War Time. Adrienne Rich.

"Memory lifts her smoky mirror: 1943." NoP-4

Eastmuir king, and Wastmuir king. Fause Foodrage. *Unknown*. ESPB

Eastward, etched in purple by a sun. Appalachian Convalescence. Robert Conquest. OxBC

Eastward Ho! A Succession. David Bromige. FTOS

Eastward spurs tip backward from the sun, The. Nigger's Leap, New England. Judith Wright. NOBAu

Eastward, the faint glimmer of the early dawn. Starting Early from Yü-p'u Deep. Meng Hao Jan, *Chinese*. SuSp, *tr. by* Daniel Bryant

Eastward the sea and sky, and a lengthening evening. Evening View at River Pavilion, Inviting Guest. Po Chü-i, *Chinese*. SuSp, *tr. by* Irving Y. Lo

Easy as cove-water rustles its pebbles and shells. Part of a Letter. Richard Wilbur. CMoP

Easy Boogie. Langston Hughes. APSN

Easy Decision, An. Kenneth Patchen. PFE

Easy Exercises in the Use of Difficult Words. Edmund Wilson.

Lakeside. OBCoV

Nursery Vignette. OBCoV

Scène de Boudoir. OBCoV

Easy in the presence of her lover. (LL) Laboratory Poem. James Merrill. InPK-6; TwCP

Easy is the triolet. William Ernest Henley. PFE

Easy Life. Pamela Mordecai. HCP

Easy Morning's Ride, An. (LL) A Hummingbird. Emily Dickinson. APN-2; HeIP-4; NAAL-1; NAAL-3; NoP-4; PoEL-5; SoSe-8

Easy Rider Blues. Blind Lemon Jefferson. GM

Easy rider, see what you done done, Lawd, Lawd. *Unknown*. CrDW

Easy way out. Nayo-Barbara Watkins. NBV

Eat / 300 feet. The Anthropophagites See a Sign on NC Highway 177 That Looks like Heaven. Jonathan Williams. OBAL

Eat and drink. Sun-Watchers. Abba Kovner, *Hebrew*. IP, *tr. by* Warren Bargad *and* Stanley F. Chyet

Eat and Walk. James Norman Hall. BLPA

Eat as I go. Denise Levertov. *See* Stepping Westward.

Eat, Eat me, Soul, and thou shalt never die. (LL) Meditation 8 (First Series). Edward Taylor. AmPP; ChIV-2; ColAP; MeMAP; NAAL-1; NAAL-3; NOBA; NoP-4; OxBA; PoEL-3; SCAP; TAP

Eat, eat, while there is bread. Tewa Song of War. *Unknown, Mayan*. PBMP, *tr. by* Daniel G. Brinton

Eat! Gyrate! Quick! Rose Garland Sonnet. Simon Pettet. PT

Eat me to the root. Vine v. Goat. Euenus, *Greek*. GrAn, *tr. by* Alistair Elliot

"Eat my cake, eat," cried the young. To the Last Wedding Guest. Horace Gregory. NYBP

Eat thou and drink; tomorrow thou shalt die. The Choice. D. G. Rossetti. ChIV-2

Eat what you wish; I'll teach ye all to die. Death Described by His True Effects. George Chapman. NOSC *Fr.* Eugenia.

Eat your banana, Annie dear. Sales Talk for Annie. Morris Gilbert Bishop. NBLV

Eat Your Heart Out, Edward Lear! Roger Woddis. UV

Eaten away by light. (LL) Daguerreotype Taken in Old Age. Margaret Atwood. BoWoP; NoAM

Eaters saddened every heart in Tenejapa, The. A Story of the Eaters.
  Santiago Mendes Zapata, *Tzeltal Indian*. STP, *tr. by* W. S. Merwin
'Eathen in 'is blindness bows down to wood an' stone, The. Rudyard
  Kipling. OxBTC
Eating Alone. Li-Young Lee. TRP; WeW-3
Eating Babies. Chana Bloch. FiLi
Eating Bamboo-Shoots. Po Chü-i, *Chinese*. ChiP; OBVE, *tr. by* Arthur
  Waley
Eating cherries off a plate. (LL) One, two, three, four, / Mary at the cottage
  door. Mother Goose. LB; OxNR
Eating Poetry. Mark Strand. MoP; NoAM; PFE; TAP
Eating Shepherd's-purse. Mei Yao Ch'en, *Chinese*. SuSp, *tr. by* Jonathan
  Chaves
Eating the Elephant Whole. Jonathan Small. HCP
Eating the Forest. D. F. Brown. CDa
Eating the living germs of grasses. Song of the Taste. Gary Snyder.
  LCAP-2
Eau-Forte. Francis Stewart [*or* "Frank"] Flint. OxBTC
Eaves. Ellis Jones, *Welsh*. OBWVE, *tr. by* Anthony Conran
Eavesdropper. Breyten Breytenbach, *Afrikaans*. PeSAV, *tr. by* Ernst van
  Heerden
Ebb and Flow, The. Edward Taylor. AmPP; SCAP
Ebb on, tide, moving swiftly outwards! Invalid's Song. Harata Tangikuku,
  Maori. PeNZ, *tr. by* Margaret Orbell
Ebb slips from the rock, the sunken, The. Night. Robinson Jeffers. AWP;
  ColAP; MoAmPo; NOBA; OxBA
Ebb Tide, The. Robert Southey. OBNC
Ebb-tide to me as to the sea; old age brings me reproach [*or* Ebb tide has
  come for me: / My life drifts downward]. The Hag of Beare.
  Unknown, Irish. BIrV; PBWP, *tr. by* John Montague; OBVE, *tr. by*
  Lady August Gregory; NOIV, *tr. by* Thomas Kinsella
Ebb / with the flow. Daufuskie. Mari E. Evans. BlSi
Ebba Dawson: Mardel Rest Home, Haskell, New Jersey. Maria Gillan.
  CrSp
Ebba sits at the window. Ebba Dawson: Mardel Rest Home, Haskell, New
  Jersey. Maria Gillan. CrSp
Ebbtide at Sundown. "Michael Field." VWP
Ebenezer Californicus. August Kleinzahler. PmAP
Ebony Wood. Jacques Roumain, *French*.
  "Negro peddler of revolt." NegPo, *tr. by* Ellen Conroy Kennedy
Ecce Homo. David Gascoyne. ChIV-2; LiTM; NoP-4; OBWP; PeECV *Fr.*
  Miserere.
Ecce Homo. Sándor Weöres, *Hungarian*. CEEP, *tr. by* Emery E. George
Ecce Homunculus. Ronald Allison Kells Mason. PeNZ
Ecce Puer. James Joyce. BIrV; ChIV-2; EBEV; IMW; MoP; NoAM; TrCP
Eccentric propositions of its fate, The. (LL) Men Made Out of Words.
  Wallace Stevens. MeMAP; NOBA; OxBSP; TAP; VGW
Eccentricity of the Middle Ground. Mary Margaret Sloan. PT
Eccles Street, Bloomsday, 1982. Harry Clifton. PBCIP
Ecclesiastes. Bible, *O.T. See also* Bible, Ecclesiastes.
  "Cast thy bread upon the waters." AWP, *stanzas* 1–6; OBVE
  It Is Better. TrJP
  Remember Now Thy Creator. AWP; OBVE
  (Remember Then Thy Creator.) TrJP
  Time for Everything, A.
    ("And a time to hate; a time of war, and a time / of peace.") (LL)
    (Ecclesiastes 3, 1–8.)
    ("For everything there is a season.")
  "Vanity of vanities, saith the Preacher, vanity of vanities; all is vanity."
    TrJP, *sect.* I, *ll.* 2–9; FaBoPV; NAWM-1; PBMP
    ("There is no remembrance of former things.) PBMP
Ecclesiastes. G. K. Chesterton. ChIV-1; MoBrPo; OxBSP
Ecclesiastes. Derek Mahon. BIrV; CIP-2; ChIV-1; PNI
Ecclesiastes 3, 1–8. Bible, *O.T. See* A Time for Everything.
Ecclesiastical Chronicle, An. John Heath-Stubbs.
  "Year of Our Lord two thousand one hundred and seven, The." NOBL
Ecclesiastical Sonnets. Wordsworth.
  Edward VI. EPCY
  Inside of King's College Chapel, Cambridge. OBNC
    (Within King's College Chapel, Cambridge.) GTBS-P
  Mutability. EBEV; HeIP-4; InPK-6; LaPo; NOBE; NoP-4; OAEL-2;
    OBEV; PoEL-4
  Pilgrim Fathers, The. AiP
  Trepidation of the Druids. Son
Ecclesiasticus. Bible, Apocrypha.
  "All flesh waxeth old as a garment." OBVE
  "By his commandment hee maketh the snow to fall apace." OBVE

Music. TrJP
O Death. TrJP
Our Fathers. TrJP
Test of Men, The. TrJP
Ecclesiazusae, The. Aristophanes, *Greek*.
  "O glorious Eie, thou miracle of Sight." OBCVT, *tr. by* Oldisworth,
    Nicholas
Eche care decayes, and yet my sorow springes. (LL) Description of Spring,
  Wherein Each Thing Renews Save Only the Lover. Henry Howard, Earl
  of Surrey, *after* Petrarch. PBRV
Eche man me telleth I chaunge moost my devise. Sir Thomas Wyatt. AAS
Echo, The. William Barnes. SCGP
Echo. Madison Cawein. APN-2
Echo. Walter De la Mare. OBMV
Echo. Pamela Grey, Viscountess Grey of Fallodon. CH
Echo. Milton. OBEV *Fr.* Comus; a Masque Presented at Ludlow Castle.
  FHYEP; OAEL-1
  (Lady Sings, The.) NOBE
Echo. Thomas Moore. LBC *See* Echoes.
  ("Faintly answering still the notes once that were so dear.") (LL) LBC
Echo. Ovid, *Latin*. OBCVT, *tr. by* Arthur Golding
Echo. Simon Pettet. PT
Echo. Vasco [*or* Vasko] Popa. PoSu *Fr.* Besieged Serenity.
Echo. Christina Rossetti. BoLoP; CH; EBEvV; EBVV; GBL; GLoP; LW;
  NOBE; NoP-4; OAEL-2; OBNC; PEW; PoE; PoEL-5; SDW; VWP
Echo. George Santayana. APN-2
Echo. Sir Philip Sidney. SiPS *Fr.* Arcadia.
  (Echo Song.)
Echo, An. Sir William Alexander, Earl of Stirling. NOSC
Echo. John Banister Tabb. APN-2
Echo:/ mimic, / last sip. Euodos, *Greek*. GrAn, *tr. by* Robin Skelton
Echo always mocks the sound, The. Rabindranath Tagore. PoA *Fr.*
  Epigrams.
Echo and Narcissus. Gerda Mayer. PeLV
Echo and the Ferry. Jean Ingelow. EBVV
Echo Canyon. *Unknown*. AmFP
Echo Club, The. Bayard Taylor.
  Night the Second: All or Nothing. APN-2
  Night the Sixth: Hadramaut. APN-2
  Night the Eighth: Camerados. APN-2
Echo-Elf Answers, The. Thomas Hardy. CBLP
Echo from Willow-Wood, An. Christina Rossetti. CABP
Echo, I ween, will in the wood reply. A Gentle Echo on Woman. Jonathan
  Swift. NBLV
Echo of childhood stalks before me, An. Cry of Birth. J. P. Clark
  Bekedermo. PBMAP *Fr.* A Reed in the Tide.
Echo of fireplace on the dividing wall, An. Louise Herlin, *French*. MFP, *tr.
  by* Martin Sorrell
Echo of insects where the lamplight thins. At Ch'ang-ku, Reading: To Show
  to My Man Pa. Li Ho, *Chinese*. CoBCP, *tr. by* Burton Watson
Echo of the clocktower, footstep. Prayer. Dana Gioia. NoP-4
Echo Reverie. Henrietta Cordelia Ray. CBWP-3
Echo Song. Sir Philip Sidney. *See* Echo.
Echo, the beating of the tide. Prophecy on Lethe. Stanley Kunitz. PoA
Echo to a Rock. Edward Herbert, 1st Baron Herbert of Cherbury. PoEL-2
Echo, tongueless, sings her sweet. Satyrus, *Greek*. GrAn, *tr. by* Robin
  Skelton
Echo your thought in ours? 'Destroy! Destroy!'. (LL) Brother Fire. Louis
  MacNeice. AF; MoP; NOBE; NoAM
Echoes. William Ernest Henley.
  Blackbird, The. MoBrPo
    (To A. D.) HoPM
  "I am the reaper." OBNC
  Invictus. APAD; BLPA; CABP; EBEvV; FaBoBe; FaPoR; HoPM; ImPo;
    MoBrPo; NOBE; OBEV; OBMV; OBNC; SAGP
  Margaritæ Sorori [I. M.]. MoBrPo; NOBE; OBEV; OBNC
    (I. M. Margaritae Sorori.) CABP
  On the Way to Kew. MoBrPo
  "We'll go no more a-roving by the light of the moon." MoBrPo
Echoes, The. Raymond Mazisi Kunene. PBMAP
Echoes. Emma Lazarus. APN-2; GSo; PAR
Echoes. Audre Lorde. NoP-4
Echoes. Naomi Long Madgett. SeSe
Echoes. Thomas Moore. GTBS-P; OxAEP-2
  (Echo.) NOBRP
Echoes. John Banister Tabb. APN-2
Echoes. Ronald Stuart Thomas. OxAEP-2

Echoes from Theocritus. Edward Cracroft Lefroy, *after the Greek of* Theocritus.

  Cleonicos. AWP

  Epitaph of Eusthenes, The. AWP

  Flute of Daphnis, The. AWP

  Grave of Hipponax, The. AWP

  Monument of Cleita, The. AWP

  Sacred Grove, A. AWP

  Sylvan Revel, A. AWP

  Thyrsis. AWP

Echoes of the hymns return. Grandfather's Sermon and Michael Smith. E. A. Markham. PBCV

Echoes of wheels and singing lashes. "Furnley Maurice." NOBAu

Echoing for ever, brother, through a brother's tears. / —'Hail & Farewell'. Catullus. *See* On the Burial of His Brother.

Echoing [or Ecchoing] Green, The. William Blake. BoTP; CH; FHYEP; NAEL-2; NTP; OxAEP-2; PoE; UnPo *Fr.* Songs of Innocence.

  ("Sun does arise, The.") Ro

Echoing Old Man Mu's Poem, "Inscribed on Shen Lang-ch'ien's Little Landscape, Autumn Willows at Stone Cliff." Wang Shih-chieng, *Chinese.* CoBLCP, *tr. by* Jonathan Chaves

Echoless, ignorant,— / What then? (LL) If I should cast off this tattered coat. Stephen Crane. APN-2; PBMP

Echo's Bones. Samuel Beckett. NoAM

Echo's Complaint. Henrietta Cordelia Ray. CBWP-3

Echo's Lament for Narcissus. Ben Jonson. *See* Song: "Slow, slow fresh fount, keep time with my salt tears."

Eclipse. Anita Endrezze-Danielson. CDW

Eclipse. Ed Roberson. GT

Eclipse, The. Henry Vaughan. OxBSP

Eclipse and glory of her kind?, The. (LL) On His Mistress [or Mistris], the Queen of Bohemia. Sir Henry Wotton. BoLoP; CBLP; EnLoPo; FaBoCh; GBL; GTBS-P; HAP; MeLP; NOBE; NOSC; OBEV; SCGP; SeCP; TFi

Eclipse II. Linda Hogan. HATNAP

Eclipse of the Moon, The. Lu T'ung, *Chinese.* PLT, *tr. by* A. C. Graham

Eclipses. Nancy Sullivan. TAP

Eclogue: "Men talking, The." George Oppen. FTOS

Eclogue for Christmas, An. Louis MacNeice. FaBoMo; NoAM; OBMV

Eclogue IV: The Poet. Charles Jenner. AWP

  Soliloquy in the Suburbs, A. NOEC

Eclogue IV: Winter. Joseph Brodsky, *Russian.* TCRP, *tr. by* Joseph Brodsky

Eclogues. Alexander Barclay.

  "Winter snowes, all covered is the grounde, The." PBRV

Eclogues. Virgil, *Latin.*

  Corydon and Thyrsis. AWP, *tr. by* Dryden

  Lycidas and Moeris. AWP, *tr. by* Dryden

  "MelibŒus. O fortunate old man!" OBCVT, *tr. by* Samuel Palmer

  Messiah, The. AWP, *tr. by* Dryden; OBVE, *tr. by* Sir John Beaumont

    ("Sicilian Muses, sing we greater things.") OBVE, *tr. by* Sir John Beaumont

  Shepherd's Gratitude, The. AWP, *tr. by* Charles Stuart Calverley

Economics. Alvin Aubert. MT

Ecstacy, An. Richard Crashaw. OxAEP-1

Ecstasy, The. Donne. BoLoP; CABP; FHYEP; FMP; FSCP; GLoP; HAP; ImPo; InPS-3; LoP; NAEL-1; NOBE; NoP-4; OAEL-1; OBEV; PoE; TFi; TOF

  (Extasie, The.) CBLP; ESCV; EnLoPo; MeLP; PoEL-2; SeCP

  ('Small change, when we are to bodies gone.') CABP; FSCP; FMP; GLoP; LoP; NoP-4

Ecstasy. Hélène Swarth, *Dutch.* WPOW, *tr. by* Jonathan Crewe

Ecstasy. Walter James Turner. CH

Ecstasy, 1 *st., at. to* John Leland. *Unknown.* AmFP

Ecstasy of the moon. (LL) Mandoline. Paul Verlaine, *French.* AWP; OBMV, *tr. by* Arthur Symons

Ecstatic bird songs pound. Dawn. William Carlos Williams. MoAmPo

Ecstatic fleece that ripples to your nape. The Head of Hair. Charles Baudelaire, *French.* EP, *tr. by* Richard Howard

Ecstatic Longing. Goethe, *German.* STV, *tr. by* John Frederick Nims

Ecstatic thought's the thing. Poetry. Mary Elizabeth Fullerton. GI; NOBAu

Eddi, priest of St. Wilfrid. Eddi's Service. Rudyard Kipling. OBCP

Eddie and the Birthday. Michael Rosen. NOxBChV

Eddie Priest's Barbershop and Notary. Kevin Young. ISC

Eddie the spaghetti nut. The Spaghetti Nut. Jack Prelutsky. ChAP

Eddi's Service. Rudyard Kipling. OBCP

Eden. Emily Grosholz. FFC; RA

Eden. Milton. GaP *Fr.* Book IV. OAEL-1 *Fr.* Paradise Lost. (Paradise Lost.) OBGa

  ("Southward through Eden went a river large.") GaP

Eden. Claudia Rankine. GT

Eden. James Simmons. PNI

Eden. Thomas Traherne. ChIV-1; ESCV; GeHe; PoEL-2

Eden. David Woo. OpBo

Eden After Dark. Richard Shelton. CDa

Eden Is a Zoo. Margaret Atwood. WPE

Eden is that old-fashioned House. Emily Dickinson. ChIV-1; KSG; NALW

Eden of that dim lake, An. (LL) The Lake: To———. Edgar Allan Poe. APN-1; MeMAP; NAAL-1; NAAL-3

Eden Rock. Charles Causley. NTP; NoP-4

Eden Says No. Robert Johnstone. PNI

Edenhall. "Susan Coolidge." OBCA

Edgar A. Guest Considers "The Old Woman Who Lived in a Shoe" and the Good Old Verities at the Same Time. Louis Untermeyer. OBAL *Fr.* Mother Goose Up-to-Date.

  (Edgar A. Guest Syndicates the Old Woman Who Lived in a Shoe.) MoAmPo

Edgar Allan Poe. Timothy Thomas Fortune. AAP

Edge, The. Robert Creeley. FTOS

Edge, The. Rosemary Dobson. NOBAu

Edge. Robert David Fitzgerald. CBAP

Edge. Sylvia Plath. FaBoWP; HCAP; NAAL-2; NALW; PFE; PoE; PoPoPo; TAP; VCAP

Edge, The. Sandra Price. LoHo

Edge Effect. Sandra McPherson. BAP-96

Edge-Hill; or, The Rural Prospect Delineated and Moralised. Richard Jago. Instructions on landscaping. OBGa

  Iron Industry in Birmingham, The. NOEC

  Sage Philosophy. ECEV

Edge of Autumn, The. Michael Anania. NoAM

Edge of Day, The. Laurie Lee. NYBP

Edge of our bed was a wide grid, The. Sisters in Arms. Audre Lorde. NMM-2

Edge of the cancer, The. Front Lines. Gary Snyder. PoE

Edge of the light. (LL) How Poetry Comes to Me. Gary Snyder. LoL; PoPoPo; SAGP

Edge of the sky, The. Songs and Chants. *Unknown, Southern Paiute Native American.* APN-2, *tr. by* John Wesley Powell

Edge of the War (1939–), The. William Montgomerie. FaBoTC

Edges of the gorges hack up sun and moon, The. Meng Chiao. SuSp, *tr. by* Stephen Owen *Fr.* Laments of the Gorges.

Edging each other towards consummation. In the Borghese Gardens. Charles Tomlinson. OBGa

Edible World, The. David Bromige. FTOS

Edificio Sayonara. John Yau. PT

Edinburgh after Flodden. William Edmonstoune Aytoun.

  "Then the Provost he uprose." OBWP

Edith B——and her mother on a Sunday afternoon. Liz Rosenberg. UnSA *Fr.* Prose Poems.

'Edith is fair,' the painter said. The Two Artists. Constance Naden. VWP

Editor Whedon. Edgar Lee Masters. CMoP; FaBoEE; NOBA; OBSV; OxBA; PoE *Fr.* Spoon River Anthology.

Editor's Wooing, The. "Orpheus C. Kerr." OBAL

Edmond Halley. Roy Fuller. OxBC

Edmonton, thy cemetery. Stevie Smith. OxBTC

Edmund Burke. Oliver Goldsmith. NOEC *Fr.* Retaliation. OxBoLi

Edmund Davie 1682; Annagram. Benjamin Tompson. SCAP

Edna St. Vincent Millay Exhorts Little Boy Blue. Louis Untermeyer. MoAmPo *Fr.* Mother Goose Up-to-Date.

Edna's Alphabet. Barry Humphries. OBCoV

Edna's Hymn. Barry Humphries. NOBAu

Edom. Isaac Watts. AmFP

Edom o' Gordon. *Unknown.* OxBB

  (Captain Car.) ESPB

Educated Feller. *Unknown.* PaTW

Education by stone: through lessons, An. João Cabral de Melo Neto, *Portuguese.* VCWP, *tr. by* James Wright

Education of Nature, The. Wordsworth. GTBS-P *Fr.* Lucy. FHYEP; NOBE; OAEL-2; OBEV; OBNC; SCGP; TFi

Education's Martyr. May Kendall. VWP

Edvard Munch. Charles Wright. HCAP

Edward [or Edward, Edward]. *Unknown.* AmFP; CH; ClHu; EBEV; EBEvV; ESPB; FaPoR; HAP; HoPM; InPK-6; InPS-3; NAEL-1; NOBE; NoP-4; OBEV; OxBB; OxBS; PoEL-1; PoRA; SCGP; SoSe-8; TFi; TRP

("Sic counsels ye gave to me, O.") (LL) NoP-4

"Edward back from the Indian Sea." Neglectful Edward. Robert Graves. MoBrPo

Edward Lear. W. H. Auden. OxAEP-2

Edward Lear in February. Christopher Middleton. TwCP

Edward/ Paterson has grown older. William Carlos Williams. NoAM *Fr.* Paterson.

Edward the Dyke and Other Poems. Judy Grahn.
   "In the place where." NALW

Edward the Third had seven sons. The Ballad of Banners (1944). John Lehmann. MoBS

Edward VI. Wordsworth. EPCY *Fr.* Ecclesiastical Sonnets.

Edwardus Comes Clarendoniae. Bibliotheca Bodleiana. Geoffrey Grigson. GBL

Edwin in the Lowlands Low. *Unknown.* AmFP

Edwin, The Minstrel. James Beattie. OxAEP-1

Edwin, your father has never ceased to be. Veterans of the Wars. Edgar Lee Masters. CBCWP

Ee calazi. Hammer-Song. *Unknown.* FaBoVe

Eeeveryyee time. Trips. Nikki Giovanni. CA

Eek! / Her legs are caught in something. The Orlando Commercial. George MacBeth. NOBL; PeLV

Eel, The. Eugenio Montale, *Italian.* STV; WeW-3, tr. by John Frederick Nims
   ("Eel, the siren, The.") PFTM, tr. by Cid Corman
   ("Immersed in your mud, can you / not believe her a sister?") (LL) PFTM, tr. by Cid Corman

Eel, The. Ogden Nash. NOxBChV; NTCP
   ("And the way they feels.") (LL) NOxBChV

Eel, the North Sea siren, The. Eugenio Montale. LoP, tr. by Robert Lowell

Eels and Tortoises. William Diaper. *See* The Sex-life of Fish.

Eemis-Stane, The. "Hugh MacDiarmid." FaBoTC; NAEL-2

E'en as a lovely flower. Du bist wie eine Blume. Heinrich Heine. AWP, tr. by Kate Freiligrath Kroeker *Fr.* Homeward Bound.

E'en as the sculptor chisels patiently. The Tireles Sculptor. Henrietta Cordelia Ray. CBWP-3

E'en like two little bank-dividing brooks. The Best-Beloved. Francis Quarles. OxBM

Eenie, meenie, mackeracka. *Unknown.* OxNR

Eenie, meenie, minie, mo. (LL) Eenie, meenie, minie, mo / Catch a thief by the toe. *Unknown.* ImGa; OxNR

Eenie, meenie, minie, mo / Catch a thief by the toe. *Unknown.* ImGa; OxNR *Fr.* Counting-out Rhymes.

Eenity, feenity, fickety, feg. *Unknown.* OxNR

Eeny meeny figgety fig. Tig. *Unknown.* FaBoVe

Eeny, weeny, winey, wo. *Unknown.* OxNR

Ef ah could, ah sholy would. Railroad Section Leader's Song. *Unknown.* GM

Ef I had wings like Noah's dove. Dink's Song. *Unknown.* OxBoLi

Ef there's thousands o' my mind. (LL) Letter, A ("Thrash away, you'll hev to rattle"). James Russell Lowell. AmPP; OxBA

Effendi. Michael S. Harper. PoBA

Effervescence and Evanescence. Keith Preston. OBAL

Effet de Neige. John Hollander. GS

Efficiency Apartment. Gerald William Barrax. PoBA

Efficient Wife's Complaint, The. Confucius. CTC, tr. by Ezra Pound *Fr.* Airs of Pei.

Effigies, The. Felicia Dorothea Hemans. NOBRP

Effingham, Grenville, Raleigh, Drake. Admirals All. Sir Henry John Newbolt. FaPoR

Effort at Speech. William Meredith. AFr

Effort at Speech between Two People. Muriel Rukeyser. FYAP; MoAmPo; Poetr; TrJP; TwCP

Effortlessly, / Love flows from God into man. Mechthild von Magdeburg, *German.* EnlH, tr. by Jane Hirshfield
   ("Effortlessly.") WPoS, tr. by Jane Hirshfield
   ("Must sound.") (LL) WPoS, tr. by Jane Hirshfield

Effusions. Coleridge.

Eolian Harp, The. FHYEP; NAEL-2; NOBRP; OAEL-2; Ro
   (Aeolian Harp, The.) NoP-4
   ("My pensive Sara.") NoP-4; Ro
   ("Peace, and this Cot, and thee, heart-honored ("... and this Cot [or cot], and thee...") Maid!") NoP-4; Ro

On a Discovery Made Too Late. GSo; Son

To a Young Ass. OxAEP-2

To the Rev. [or Reverend] W. L. Bowles. Son

Eftsoones they heard a most melodious sound. Edmund Spenser. EBEvV; NOBE; PBRV; SCV *Fr.* The Bower of Bliss. PoEL-1 *Fr.* Wood Of Error. AEP

Eftsoons they saw an hideous host array'd. Sea Monsters. Edmund Spenser. *Fr.* Wood Of Error. AEP

Egalitarian and full of plastics. Epigoni Go French Line. Turner Cassity. WeT

Egan O Rahilly. *Unknown, Irish.* EBEV; OBMV, tr. by James Stephens

Egg, The. Clarence Day. NBLV

Egg and the Machine, The. Robert Frost. MoAmPo

Egg Boiler, The. Gwendolyn Brooks. PoBA

Egg for Easter, An. Irene F. Pawsey. BoTP

Egg I have chosen is sandy brown, The. Boiling an Egg. Stanley Cook. OTCP

Egg is a grand thing for a journey, An. How the Hen Sold Her Eggs to the Stingy Priest. Nancy Willard. LCAP-2

Egg of fire. the egg of water. the egg of wind in the silk bag. the egg of air, The. The Man. The Woman. Hans Arp, *German.* PFTM, tr. by Joachim Neugroschel

Egg of pure gold, An. Mother Goose. *See* Old Mother Goose.

Egg so round on the outside, An. To Beat or Not to Beat. Nina Iskrenko, *Russian.* TCRP, tr. by John High *and* Katya Olmsted

Egg Thoughts. Russell Hoban. NTCP; OTCP

Eggleston was a taxi-driver. Cynical Portraits. Louis Paul. NBLV

Eggomania. Felicia Lamport. NBLV

Eggplants Have Pins and Needles, The. Novella Nikolaevna Matveyeva, *Russian.* WPOW, tr. by Daniel Weissbort

Eggs. Sharon Olds. CrSp

Eggs. Susan Wood. SoSe-8

Eggs for Breakfast. Irene F. Pawsey. BoTP

Egles byrde hath spred his wings, The. John Heywood. PBRV *Fr.* A Ballad on the Marriage of Philip and Mary.

Egnatius has fine teeth, and those. Carmina, XXXIX. Catullus. OBVE, tr. by Walter Savage Landor *Fr.* Carmina.

Ego. Philip Booth. TwCP

Ego. Norman MacCaig. GTBS-P

Ego. Robert Siegel. PoA

Ego Dominus Tuus. W. B. Yeats. CMoP; EPCY

Ego-perverted love. (LL) The Mess of Love. D. H. Lawrence. CBLP; OAEL-2

Ego Tripping [(There May Be a Reason Why)]. Nikki Giovanni. CrSp; MoP; Poetsp; RaBo
   (Ego Tripping.) ISC
   ("I mean. . . . I . . . can fly / like a bird in the sky. . . .") (LL) GT

'Egoisme à Deux'. Louisa Sarah Bevington. VWP

Egoisme à Deux. Louisa S. Guggenberger. NOBVV

Egoist is not / good for himself. (LL) The Immoral Proposition. Robert Creeley. LiTM; NeAP; PoM

Egotist. Ambrose Bierce. APAD; APN-2; OBAL *Fr.* The Devil's Dictionary.

Egrets. Tu Mu, *Chinese.* SuSp, tr. by Irving Y. Lo; APo, tr. by Irving Yucheng Lo; PLT, tr. by A. C. Graham

Egypt. Wendy Mulford. NBrP

Egyptian Cat, The. D. J. Enright. PC

Egyptian Dancer at Shubra. Bernard Spencer. NoAM

Egyptian Passage, An. Theodore Weiss. TAP

Egyptian Poem. *Unknown.* APAD

Egyptian Pulled Glass Bottle in the Shape of a Fish, An. Marianne Moore. NALW; PBWP

Egyptian Register. "Ern Malley." BMAP

Egypt's Favorite. Sir Francis Hubert.
   Joseph in Carcere. ChIV-1
   Joseph in Carcere: or, the Innocent Prisoner. KSG

Egypt's might is tumbled down. Mary Elizabeth Coleridge. CH

Egypt's might is tumbled down. Coleridge. APAD

Egypts Pyramids inclose their Kings. Mary Sidney, Countess of Montgomery Wroth. *Fr.* Urania.

Eh-Ros-ka, the Warrior's Dance. *Unknown.* APN-2 *Fr.* War Dance. APN-2, tr. by George Catlin

Eheu Fugaces. "Thomas Ingoldsby." FaBoEE; OxBoLi

Eia, with handbells, jews' harps, risible. Geoffrey Hill. DiPo *Fr.* Hymns to Our Lady of Chartres.

Eidolons. Walt Whitman. APN-1

Eight Aspects of Melissa. Lawrence Durrell.
   Visitations. MoBrPo

Eight Cows. Carol J. Pierman. CMAP

Eight Days in April. Marilyn Hacker. FFC

Eight Early Poems. Kenneth Patchen.

At the New Year. LiTM

Eight hands across, form a ring. Mississippi Sawyer. *Unknown.* AmFP

Eight months ago, on Christmas Day. Family Holiday. Raymond Wilson. PeP

Eight O'Clock. A. E. Housman. CMoP; InPK-6; MoBrPo; MoP; NoAM; OxBSP; PFE; PoE; Poetr; SoSe-8

Eight o'clock. The Postman. Christina Rossetti. CTV

Eight Sandbars on the Takano River. Gary Snyder. NOBA; VGW

Eight Six Foxtrot—Eight Six Foxtrot. Gliding Baskets. Frank A. Cross, Jr. CDa

Eight xx. Laurie Duggan. BMAP

Eight year old and the heifer, An. Apprehension. Phillip McCaffrey. EC2

Eight years ago this May. A Spring Night in Shokoku-ji. Gary Snyder. VGW *Fr.* Four Poems for Robin. MoP; NNaP; NOBA; NoAM

Eighteen. Maria Banus, *Rumanian.* BoWoP; LiLi, *tr. by* Willis Barnstone *and* Matei Calinescu

1887. A. E. Housman. FaPoR; NIP-4; NOBVV; SCGP; UnPo

1845. Jackson MacLow. APSN *Fr.* The Presidents of the United States of America.

1841 (I). Jackson MacLow. APSN *Fr.* The Presidents of the United States of America.

1841 (II). Jackson MacLow. APSN *Fr.* The Presidents of the United States of America.

Eighteen Hundred and Eleven. Anna Laetitia Barbauld. NOBRP

1892-1941. Louis Zukofsky. PoA

1808 Wordsworth dies from fall while hiking in Scotland. Other Lives of the Romantics. Jane Flanders. PBCAP

1805. Robert Graves. FaBoCh; OBCoV; OBSV; PeLV

1809. Jackson MacLow. APSN *Fr.* The Presidents of the United States of America.

1801. Jackson MacLow. APSN *Fr.* The Presidents of the United States of America.

1801. Wordsworth. Son

1817. Jackson MacLow. APSN *Fr.* The Presidents of the United States of America.

Eighteen-Seventy. Rimbaud, *French.*

  Evil. OBWP, *tr. by* Robert Lowell

  ("Whilst the red spittle of the grape-shot sings.")

  Napoleon after Sedan. FaBoPV; OBWP, *tr. by* Robert Lowell

  Poster of Our Dazzling Victory at Saarbrucken, A. FaBoPV; OBWP, *tr. by* Robert Lowell

  Sleeper in the Valley, The. AWP, *tr. by* Ludwig Lewisohn; OBWP, *tr. by* Robert Lowell

  ("There's a green hollow where a river sings.") AWP, *tr. by* Ludwig Lewisohn

  To the French of the Second Empire. FaBoPV; OBWP, *tr. by* Robert Lowell

18:VI:82. David Meltzer. MoNo

1837. Jackson MacLow. APSN *Fr.* The Presidents of the United States of America.

1825. Jackson MacLow. APSN *Fr.* The Presidents of the United States of America.

1829. Jackson MacLow. APSN *Fr.* The Presidents of the United States of America.

Eighteen Verses Sung to a Tatar Reed Whistle. Ts'ai Yen, *Chinese.*
  "I have no desire to live, but I am afraid of death." WPOW
  "I never believed that in my broken life." BoWoP; WPOW
  "I was born in a time of peace." BoWoP; PBWP; WPOW
  "Seventeenth stanza, The. My heart aches, my tears fall." WPOW
  "Sun sets, The. The wind moans." BoWoP; WPOW
  "Tatar chief forced me to become his wife, A." WPOW

Eighteenth century, The. As I Sat in the Armchair of the Tsar. Bulat Shalvovich Okudzhava, *Russian.* TCRP, *tr. by* Deming Brown

Eighteenth-Century Medical Illustration: The Infant in its Little Room. Ann Townsend. PUP-20

18th Ode 1st Book, translated or rather Imitated. Horace, *Latin.* OBCVT, *tr. by* Thomas Burnet

Eighteenth of October, The. The Fire of Frendraught. *Unknown.* ESPB; OxBB

Eighth Air Force. Randall Jarrell. MoP; NOBA; NoAM; NoP-4; OBWP; PoWW; TRP; VCAP

Eighth and the Thirteenth, The. Alicia Ostriker. BAP-96

Eighth child of an eighth child, your wilful advent. Birth of a Great Man. Robert Graves. NYBP

Eighth Elegy. Children's Elegy. Muriel Rukeyser.
  "That is what they say, who were broken off from love." LCAP-2

Eighth of Shostakovich, The. The Eighth and the Thirteenth. Alicia Ostriker. BAP-96

Eighth Sky. Michael Palmer. FTOS

Eighth Song. Sir Philip Sidney. NoSic *Fr.* Astrophil and Stella. AAS; SiPS

Eighties, De. Frederick Williams. PBCV

'Eighty-nine was bad. Graves at Elkhorn. Richard Hugo. UnPo; VCAP

80 papers / was all there was. Delivering the Times, 1952-1944. David Huddle. PBCAP

Eileen Aroon. Gerald Griffin.
  "When like the rising day." OBEV

Eileithyia, brought safe. Leonidas of Tarentum, *Greek.* PGA, *tr. by* Kenneth Rexroth

Eileithyia, once more. Callimachus, *Greek.* GrAn, *tr. by* Peter Jay

Ein Complaint. Virginia Graham. OBCoV

Ein feste Burg ist unser Gott. Martin Luther. CTC, *tr. by* M. Woolsey Stryker

Ein Fichtenbaum steht einsam. Heinrich Heine, *German.* AWP, *tr. by* James Thomson

Eine Kleine Snailmusik. May Sarton. NBLV

Einstein's Bathrobe. Howard Moss. VCAP

Eire. David O'Bruadair, *Irish.* BIrV, *tr. by* Austin Clarke

Eireann. Osbert Lancaster. NOBL; PeLV *Fr.* Afternoons with Baedeker.

Eisenhower Years, The. Paul Zimmer. PBCAP

Eisenhower's Visit to Franco, 1959. James Wright. CAPP-1

Either at my friend's daughter's. Without Looking. Patricia Goedicke. NMM-2

Either get out of the [my] house or conform to my tastes, woman. Martial, *Latin.* FaBoEE; NNPT; OBCVT, *tr. by* James Michie

Either heard or taught. Song for a Thin Sister. Audre Lorde. OxWW

Either I mistake your shape and making quite. Shakespeare. OxBSn *Fr.* A Midsummer Night's Dream.

Either I'm swimming toward a floating discotheque its dancers. Treason's Choice. Phillp Hammial. BMAP

Either nude & pulled behind as well as. A Bull Called Remorse. Iain Sinclair. NBrP

Either she was foul, or her attire was bad. 3.6. Ovid, *Latin.* CABP; EP; OBVE, *tr. by* Marlowe *Fr.* Elegies.

Either the lunches or the dead soldiers. (LL) Dead Soldiers. James Fenton. AF; NoAM; NoP-4; OBWP

Either you will / go through this door. Prospective Immigrants Please Note. Adrienne Rich. AiP; PoPoPo; VGW

8th Ode of Book I. of Horace imitated in the Cumberland Manner and Dialect, The. Horace, *Latin.* OBCVT, *tr. by* Josiah Relph

Ejaculating into their vaginas—young girls of the western tribes. *Unknown.* NOBAu, *tr. by* Ronald M. Berndt *Fr.* Goulburn Island Song Cycle.

Ejected Wife, The. *Unknown, Chinese.* OBVE, *tr. by* Arthur Waley

El-a-noy. *Unknown.* AS

El Abandonado. *Unknown, Spanish.* AS, *tr. by* Frank J. Dobie

El Aghir. Norman Cameron. *See* Green, Green Is El Aghir.

El Alamein. Steve Crow. HATNAP

El Alamein. Sydney Goodsir Smith. FaBoTC *Fr.* Armageddon in Albyn.

El Alamein Revisited. Roy Macnab. PeSA

El Camino Verde. Paul Blackburn. PmAP

El Corrido de Gregorio Cortez. *Unknown, Spanish.* PaTW, *tr. by* Paredes, Américo

El Día de los Muertos. Rafael Campo. RA

El Dorado. Edgar Allan Poe. *See* Eldorado.

El Dorado. Richard Ryan. BIrV

El Greco. Edward Leslie Mayo. HoPM

El Greco: Espolio. Earle Birney. MoCV

El-Hajj Malik El-Shabazz. Robert Earl Hayden. PoBA
  (El-Hajj Malik El-Shabazz (Malcolm X).) NAAAL

El Heroe. Sylvia Townsend Warner. WPN

El Hombre. William Carlos Williams. CMoP; SAmP

El;in the top of his head:to tell / him. (LL) Plato told / him:he couldn't. E. E. Cummings. AmPP; CTC; MoP; NOBA; NoAM; OxBA; PoE

El Ropero. Antonio Di Montorio. TrJP

El Sueño de la Razón. Jane Cooper. FaBoWP *Fr.* March.

Elaine, pretending it was salt. E. Aitken. UV

Elaine sleeps most of the day. She's the prettiest invalid I've ever seen. The True Bride. Amy Gerstler. PmAP

Elate of heart and confidence of fame, *fr.* 1790 *vers.* Coleridge. EPCY *Fr.* Monody on the Death of Chatterton.

Elavil, Ludiomil, Doxepin. Bottles. Jane Kenyon. BAP-93 *Fr.* Having It Out With Melancholy. BAP-93

Elbows cut wind. Near the front. Dip in ground. The Ballad of the Blue Envelope. Nikolai Semionovich Tikhonov, *Russian.* TCRP, *tr. by* Michael Frayn

Elder boy is by adoption mine, The. Terence. OBCVT, *tr. by* George Colman *Fr.* The Brothers (Adelphi).

Elder Brother, The. John Fletcher.
  "Beauty clear and fair." NOSC; OBEV
Elder Edda, The, *sels. Unknown, Old Norse.*
  Counsels of Sigrdrifa. AWP
    (Part of the Lay of Sigrdrifa.) OBVE
  First Lay of Gudrun, The. AWP, *tr. by* William Morris *and* Eirikr
    Magnusson
    Gudrun Laments over Sigurd. OBVE
  Lay [*or* Short Lay] of Sigurd, The. AWP, *tr. by* William Morris *and*
    Eirikr Magnusson
    "And now one prayer." OBVE
  Voluspo. AWP, *tr. by* Henry Adams Bellows
Elder Sister, The. Sharon Olds. NIP-4
Elder Stonegate treats the body like a dream. Written in Jest on Elder
    Stonegate's Eastern Balcony. Liu Tsung-yüan, *Chinese.* SuSp, *tr. by*
    Jan W. Walls
Elderblossom. Johannes Bobrowski, *German.* AF, *tr. by* Matthew Mead
Elderly bride of Port Jervis, An. Limerick. Ogden Nash. PeLi
Elderly Lady Crossing on Green. Wyatt Prunty. RA
Elders and officers line the returning road. Good-bye to the People of
    Hangchow. Po Chü-i, *Chinese.* ChiP, *tr. by* Arthur Waley
Elder's Reproof to his Wife, An. 'Abdillaahi Muuse, *Somali.* TTY, *tr. by*
    B. W. Andrzejewski *and* I. M. Lewis
Eldorado. Edgar Allan Poe. APN-1; AWP; AmPP; CTV; ChAP; ColAP;
    FPC; FaBoBe; FaBoCh; LiLi; MeMAP; NCAP; NOBA; NOxBChV;
    NTP; NoP-4; OxBA; TAP
    (El Dorado.) APAD
    ("If you seek for El Dorado!") (LL) APAD
Eleanor (she spoiled in a British climate). Canto 7. Ezra Pound. NOBA;
    NoAM *Fr.* Cantos.
Eleanora Duse. Amy Lowell.
    "Seeing you stand once more before my eyes." SAGP
Eleazar Wheelock. Richard Hovey. OBAL
Elect. Mary Ursula Bethell. PeNZ
Elect, The. Peter Cooley. CMAP
Elected Knight, The. *Unknown, Danish.* AWP, *tr. by* Longfellow
Elected Silence. Siegfried Sassoon. MoBrPo
Elected Silence, sing to me. The Habit of Perfection. Gerard Manley
    Hopkins. ChIV-2; ImPo; MoBrPo; MoP; NoAM; OBEV; OBMV;
    OxAEP-2; PoRA; Poetr; RB; TFi
Elected virgins, The. Wedding in Hanover. Lorna Goodison. GT
Election, The. Sitakant Mahapatra, *Oriya.* OMIP, *tr. by* Sitakant Mahapatra
Election, The. Leonard Nathan. PBCAP
Election Eve, with Cat. Alex Skovron. BMAP
Election night at midnight. Vachel Lindsay. *Fr.* Bryan, Bryan, Bryan,
    Bryan. CMoP; MeMAP; OxBA; OxBoLi
Election Reflection. M. Keel Jones. NBLV
Election Speech for the Presidency of the United States of Chinamerica.
    David Avidan, *Hebrew.* IP, *tr. by* Warren Bargad *and* Stanley F. Chyet
Election Time. Lamont B. Steptoe. UnSA
Election Time. *Unknown.* UV
Electra. György Petri, *Hungarian.* VCWP, *tr. by* Wilmer, Clive and George
    Gömöri
Electra. Sophocles, *Greek.*
    "Do not you mark how *passionate,* how *wild.*" OBCVT, *tr. by* Christopher
    Wase
Electric Cop, The. Victor Hernandez Cruz. PoBA
Electric Eel, The. Ron Padgett. *Fr.* Three Animals. TTTS
Electric Elegy. Adam Zagajewski, *Polish.* VCWP, *tr. by* Renata
    Gorczynski, Benjamin Ivry, *and* C. K. Williams
Electricity Breadthwise. Marcel Duchamp. PFTM
Electricity of Blossoms, *for Janet.* Lorenzo Thomas. FTOS; GT
    ("Closer to escaping into day / trams.") (LL) GT
Electrocution. Lola Ridge. WPE
Electrodes attached to a flautist's cheeks. First Night. Michael Hofmann.
    CBLP
Elegance. Christopher Smart. NOCV *Fr.* Hymns for the Amusement of
    Children.
Elegance in the extreme. Ntozake Shange. SeSe
Elegant use of foliage and grace, An. More. Gertrude Stein. PBWP *Fr.*
    Tender Buttons.
Elegant Women, The. Tu Fu, *Chinese.* SuSp, *tr. by* Mark Perlberg
Elegiac Ballad, An. Hannah Cowley. ECWP
Elegiac Stanzas Suggested by a Picture of Peele Castle, in a Storm [Painted
    by Sir George Beaumont]. Wordsworth. GTBS-P; NAEL-2; NOBRP;
    NoP-4; OAEL-2; OBNC; PoE; Ro
    (Suggested by a Picture of Peele Castle, in a Storm, Painted by Sir George
    Beaumont.) GS

Elegiac Verse. Henry Wadsworth Longfellow.
    "Peradventure of old, some bard in Ionian Islands." APN-1
Elegiack Verse on Mr. Elijah Corlet, An. Nehemiah Walter. SCAP
Elegie: His Parting from Her. Donne. *See* His Parting from Her.
Elegie Made by Mr. Aurelian Townshend in Remembrance of the Ladie
    Venetia Digby, An. Aurelian Townshend. SeCP
Elegie: "Nature's lay ideot, I taught thee to love." Donne. OxAEP-1;
    SeCP *Fr.* Elegies.
    (Elegy VII.) NoP-4
    ("Nature's lay idiot, I taught thee to love.") FMP; NoP-4
Elegie on the Deploreable Departure of the Honored and Truely Religious
    Chieftain John Hull, An. John Saffin. SCAP
Elegie upon the Death of the Deane of Pauls, Dr. John Donne, An. Thomas
    Carew. MeLP; PBRV; SeCP
    ("Can we not force from widdowed Poetry.") PBRV
    (Elegy upon the Death of Doctor [*or* Dr.] Donne, Dean of Paul's, An.)
    BeJo; EPCY; OAEL-1
    (Elegy upon the Death of the Dean of [St.] Paul's, Dr. John Donne, An.)
    CaPo
  On the Death of Donne. NOBE
Elegie upon The Death of the Reverend. . . Mr. Thomas Shepard, An.
    Urian Oakes. SCAP
    "Away loose-reined careers of poetry!" NOCV
Elegie V: His Picture. Donne. *See* His Picture.
Elegies. André Marie de Chénier, *French.* AWP, *tr. by* Arthur Symons
    "Every Man has his sorrows; yet each still."
    "Well, I would have it so. I should have known."
    "White nymph wandering in the woods by night, A."
Elegies. Donne.
  Autumnal[l], The. FSCP; InPS-3; NOSC; PoEL-2
  Change. CBLP; EBEV
  Comparison, The. PeLV
  Elegie: "Nature's lay ideot, I taught thee to love." OxAEP-1; SeCP
    (Elegy VII.) NoP-4
    ("Nature's lay idiot, I taught thee to love.") FMP; NoP-4
  His Parting from Her. EBEV
    (Elegie: His Parting from Her.)
  His Picture. FSCP; PBRV
    (Elegie V: His Picture.) MeLP; OxAEP-1
    ("To feed on that, which to disus'd tasts seemes tough.") (LL) PBRV
    ("To feed on that, which to disused tastes seemes tough.") (LL) FSCP
  "In such white robes heav'n's angels used to be." OxBSn
  Jealosie. CBLP; ESCV
  Love's Progress. OAEL-1
  On His Mistress [*or* Mistris]. BoLoP; CBLP; EBEV; ESCV; NAEL-1;
    NoSic; PoEL-2
    ("By our first strange and fatal interview.") CABP; FSCP
    (Elegy on His Mistress.) GBL; MeLP; SCGP
    (On His Mistress.) CABP; FSCP
  Perfume, The. ESCV; FSCP; NoSic; SeCP
  Sapho To Philaenis. RACG
    (Sappho to Philaenis.)
  To His Mistress Going To Bed. BoLoP; FSCP; LoP; NoSic; OAEL-1;
    PBRV; PoE
    ("Come, Madam, come, all rest my powers defy.") FSCP; GLoP; LoP;
    NoP-4
    (Elegy XIX. To His Mistress Going to Bed.) NoP-4
    (Going to Bed.) FaBoSe
    (To His Mistris Going to Bed.) CBLP; OxAEP-1; SeCP
    ("What needst thou have more covering then a man.") (LL) FaBoSe;
    PBRV
Elegies. Douglas Dunn.
    "She sat up on her pillows, receiving guests." NoP-4
Elegies. Marlowe. LoP
Elegies. Hugh Maxton. PBCIP
Elegies. Ovid, *Latin.*
  1.2. AWP, *tr. by* Marlowe, *sl. diff. vers.*
  1.3. EBEV, *tr. by* Marlowe
  1.4. NoSic, *tr. by* Marlowe; BoLoP, *tr. by* Dryden
    ("Coax me to-morrow, by forswearing all.") (LL) BoLoP, *tr. by* Dryden
    (Elegies 1.4.) CABP, *tr. by* Marlowe
    ("Your husband will be with us at the treat.") BoLoP, *tr. by* Dryden
  1.5. BoLoP; EBEV; GBL; NoSic; OBVE; OxAEP-1, *tr. by* Marlowe
    (Elegy 5.) EP; NNPT, *tr. by* Marlowe
    ("In summers heate and mid-time of the day.") OBCVT, *tr. by* Marlowe
    ("*Jove* send me more such after-noones as this.") (LL) OBCVT, *tr. by*
    Marlowe

1.14. AWP, *tr. by* Kirby Flower Smith

1.15. NoSic, *tr. by* Marlowe

(Elegies 1.15.) CABP, *tr. by* Marlowe

("Envy, why carpest thou my time is spent so ill.") CABP, *tr. by* Marlowe

2.1. EP, *tr. by* Peter Green; OBVE, *tr. by* Marlowe

2.8. EBEV, *tr. by* Marlowe

2.10. EBEV, *tr. by* Marlowe

Elegies 3.1: "Old wood stands uncut, of long years' space, An." CABP, *tr. by* Marlowe

3.6. OBVE, *tr. by* Marlowe

(Elegies 3.6.) CABP, *tr. by* Marlowe

3.13. OBVE, *tr. by* Marlowe

Elegy 9b: "If I heard a voice from heaven say 'Live without'." Ovid, *Latin.* EP, *tr. by* Peter Green

Elegies. Propertius, *Latin.* AWP

"Ah woe is me, of passion naught I knew." AWP, *tr. by* F. A. Wright

Hylas. AWP, *tr. by* F. A. Wright

Revenge to Come. AWP, *tr. by* Kirby Flower Smith

"Stab me with sword, or poison strong."

Elegies 1.iv: "Far from the tender Tribe of Boys remove." Tibullus, *Latin.* EP, *tr. by* John Dart *Fr.* Odes.

("He'll struggle, but at length comply with ease.") (LL) OBCVT, *tr. by* John Dart

Elegies, I.iv: "Yield prompt compliance to the maid's desires." Tibullus, *Latin.* EP, *tr. by* James Grainger

"Elegies By the Senses." Meir Wieseltier, *Hebrew.* IP, *tr. by* Bargad, Warren and Stanley Chyet *Fr.* Elegies by the Senses.

Elegies for the Hot Season. Sandra McPherson. AmPA

Elegies on the Cardinal Points. Yelena Shwarts, *Russian.* VCWP, *tr. by* Michael Molnar

Elegist, The. Geoff Page. BMAP

Elegy. Frank Bidart. HCAP

Elegy. Joseph Brodsky, *Russian.* AF, *tr. by* Joseph Brodsky

Elegy, An. Yüan Chên, *Chinese.* NNPT, *tr. by* Witter Bynner

Elegy. Arthur L. Clements. UnSA

Elegy. Raymond Mazisi Kunene. PBMAP

Elegy. Linda Pastan. IFJA

Elegy. Anna Seward. CPO

Elegy. Chidiock Tichborne. *See* Tichborne's Elegy.

Elegy: "April again, and it is a year again." Sidney Keyes. NoP-4

Elegy: "Because of you I have lived." Yangshik Kim, *Korean.* CKP, *tr. by* Jaihiun Kim

Elegy: "Cross between a bakehouse and a bell tower, A." Oleg Grigorevich Chukhonstev, *Russian.* TCRP, *tr. by* Simon Franklin

Elegy: "Cur foretells the knell of parting day, The." Ambrose Bierce. APN-2; OBAL *Fr.* The Devil's Dictionary.

Elegy: "Death be not proud, thy hand gave not this blow." Lucy, Countess of Bedford Harington. PeECV; WPE

Elegy: "Do not look for him." Leonard Cohen. HeIP-4

Elegy: "Fled is the swiftness of all the white-footed ones." Joseph Auslander. TrJP

Elegy: "Floods of tears well from my deepest heart, The." Immanuel di Roma, *Italian.* TrJP, *tr. by* J. Chotzner

Elegy. Carolyn Forché. LoL

Elegy: "Friend, whose unnatural early death." David Gascoyne. FaBoTw; TwCP

Elegy: "From the old settlements only the writings." Slavko Mihalic. PoSu, *tr. by* Charles Simic

Elegy: "Gnu up at the zoo, The." John Hall Wheelock. NYBP

Elegy: "He has held." Perevin Muruvalar, *Tamil.* PLW, *tr. by* A. K. Ramanujan

Elegy: "I die for Your holy word without regret." Antonio Enriquez Gomez, *Spanish.* TrJP

Elegy: "I expected him to look dead in the casket." Richard Hugo. GM

Elegy: "I know but will not tell." Alan Dugan. NIP-4

Elegy: "I lay down in my grave." Maya Angelou. CrSp

Elegy: "I must wait for a stranger to knock on my door." David Ignatow. NNaP

Elegy: "If he found a little liquor." Auvaiyar, *Tamil.* PLW, *tr. by* A. K. Ramanujan

Elegy: "In pain she bore the son who her embrace." Moses ibn Ezra, *Hebrew.* TrJP, *tr. by* Solomon Solis-Cohen

Elegy, An: "Last, best-loved daughter of old Hsieh, you who foolishly ran off." Yüan Chen, *Chinese.* OxBM

Elegy: "Let day, let night, come no more." Auvaiyar, *Tamil.* PLW, *tr. by* A. K. Ramanujan

Elegy [*or* Elegie], An: "Let me be what I am, as Virgil cold." Ben Jonson. PoEL-2; SeCP

Elegy: "Let them bury your big eyes." Edna St. Vincent Millay. CMoP; MoAmPo; OxBA; PoRA *Fr.* Memorial to D. C.

Elegy, An: "Love, give me leave to serve thee, and be wise." Thomas Randolph. NOSC

Elegy: "My thoughts impelled me to the resting-place." Moses ibn Ezra, *Hebrew.* TrJP, *tr. by* Emma Lazarus

Elegy. *Nahuatl Oral Tradition, Spanish.* PaTW, *tr. by* Miguel Léon-Portilla and Grace Lobanov

Elegy: "No more, no more Jewish townships in Poland," *in honour of the Warsaw Ghetto uprising, April 19, 1943.* Antoni Slonimski, *Polish.* HP, *tr. by* Komen, Isaac

Elegy: "Noon is beautiful, The: the perfect wheel." Yvor Winters. VGW

Elegy: "Nor Hammond's love nor Shenstone's was sincere." John, Lord Dreghorn Maclaurin. NOEC

Elegy: "Not only doesn't the Ohio." Gregory Orr. WeT

Elegy: "O [*or* Oh] snatch'd away in beauty's bloom!" Byron. GTBS-P

Elegy, An: "O youngest, best-loved daughter of Hsieh." Yüan Chen, *Chinese.* IMW, *tr. by* Witter Bynner

Elegy: "Pages of history open, The." Sandra M. Gilbert. PoA

Elegy, An: "She fell away in her first ages spring." Edmund Spenser. OBEV *Fr.* Daphnaïda.

Elegy: "They are lang deid, folk that I used to ken." Robert Garioch. FaBoTC; OxBS

Elegy: "This bright burning pyre." Auvaiyar, *Tamil.* PLW, *tr. by* A. K. Ramanujan

Elegy: "Those reckless hosts rush to the wells." Baruch of Worms, *Hebrew.* TrJP

Elegy, An: "Though beauty be the mark of praise." Ben Jonson. BeJo; NoP-4, OBEV

Elegy: "Tonight the moon is high, to summon all." William Bell. FaBoTw

Elegy: "What's to be hoped from seeing her again?" Goethe. *Fr.* Trilogy of Passion. STV, *tr. by* John Frederick Nims

Elegy: "Who would I show it to." W. S. Merwin. HCAP

Elegy: "Wind won't come to draw smiles in dream sand, The." Yehuda Amichai, *Hebrew.* IP, *tr. by* Warren Bargad *and* Stanley K. Chyet

Elegy: "Wood is bare, The: a river-mist is steeping, The." Robert Bridges. EBVV; IMW

Elegy: "Young will not wear it, The." Kutavayir Kirattanar, *Tamil.* PLW, *tr. by* A. K. Ramanujan

Elegy V: [Separation of Man from God]. George Barker. FaBoTw

Elegy VII. Donne. *See* Elegie: "Nature's lay ideot, I taught thee to love."

Elegy VII. Ezra Pound. VGW *Fr.* Homage to Sextus Propertius.

Elegy 11: "Ah me, my friend! it will not, will not last!" William Shenstone. NOEC

Elegy 19 (A Kiss): "Without a soul, a mind, a breath, or pulse." Pierre de Ronsard, *French.* EP, *tr. by* Alistair Elliot

(Elegy xix /(A Kiss).) FLP, *tr. by* Alistair Elliot

Elegy XIX. To His Mistress Going to Bed. Donne. *See* To His Mistress Going To Bed.

Elegy and Flame. Horace Gregory. FYAP

Elegy before Death. Edna St. Vincent Millay. CMoP; LiTM; MeMAP

Elegy: Breece D'J Pancake. Franz Wright. NAmP90

Elegy, An: December, 1970. Edgar Bowers. MT

Elegy does not raise its wistful tone in downpour of southern shine, An. To Tarshish. Shimon Halkin, *Hebrew.* MHP, *tr. by* Ruth Finer Mintz

Elegy: E. W. Louis Edward Sissman. NYBP

Elegy for 6 So Far. Greg Ryan. BMAP

Elegy for a Dead Soldier. Karl Shapiro. HAP; LiTM; OBWP; OxBA

Elegy for a Diver. Peter Meinke. Poetsp

Elegy for a Forest Clear-Cut by the Weyerhaeuser Company. David Wagoner. NoAM

Elegy for a Nature Poet. Howard Nemerov. HoPM

Elegy for a School-Friend. Augustus Young. BIrV

Elegy for a Schoolmate. Vincent O'Sullivan. PeNZ

Elegy for a White Cock. Mei Yao Ch'en, *Chinese.* SuSp, *tr. by* Jonathan Chaves

Elegy for Alto. Christopher Okigbo. HBAPE; VCWP

Elegy for Chief Sealth. Duane Niatum. CDW

Elegy for Chloe Nguyen, (1955–1988). Marilyn Chin. UnSA

Elegy for Dr. Donne. Edward Herbert.

"Having delivered now what praises are." EPCY

Elegy for Drowned Children. Bruce Dawe. BMAP; NOBAu

Elegy for Dylan Thomas. Dame Edith Sitwell. PoA

Elegy for Ernest Hemingway, An. Thomas Merton. BLT

Elegy for Five, An. Richard Palmer Blackmur. PFE

Elegy for Her Brother Sakhr. Al-Khansa, *Arabic*. WPOW, *tr. by* Bridget Connelly; BoWoP, *tr. by* Willis Barnstone

Elegy (for Himself). Moses Rimos of Majorca, *Hebrew*. TrJP, *tr. by* Israel Abrahams

Elegy for His Daughter Ellen. Goronwy Owen, *Welsh*. OBWVE, *tr. by* George Borrow

Elegy for Integral Domains, The. Norman Dubie. NAmP90

Elegy for Jack Bowman. Joseph Bruchac. CDW

Elegy for Jack Moffat. Charlotte Painter. IMW

Elegy for Jane. Theodore Roethke. AmPP; CoAP; ColAP; HAP; HCAP; IMW; InPK-6; InPS-3; LiLi; LiTM; MoAmPo; MoLi; NoP-4; PoE; PoPoPo; Poetr; SAGP; TAP; TFi; TRP; TwCP; WeW-3

Elegy for Lyn James. Leslie Norris. OBWVE

Elegy for Mangochi Fishermen, An. Jack A. Mapanje. PBMAP

Elegy for Minor Poets. Louis MacNeice. CABP; PNI

Elegy for Mr. Goodbeare. Sir Osbert Sitwell. MoBrPo

Elegy for My Father. Howard Moss. CoAP; LiTM

Elegy for My Father. Mark Strand. HCAP; LCAP-2

    Empty Body, The. UnPo

    New Year, The. UnPo

Elegy for My Father, Who Is Not Dead. Andrew Hudgins. RA

Elegy for My Mother. Andrey Andreievich Voznesensky, *Russian*. TCRP, *tr. by* William Jay Smith *and* F. D. Reeve

Elegy for My Sister. Howard Moss. VCAP

Elegy for Neal Cassady. Allen Ginsberg. CLPP

Elegy for Slit-Drum. Christopher Okigbo. HBAPE

Elegy for the Dead of Soweto. Thembinkosi Ndlovu, *Zulu*. PeSAV, *tr. by* Chris Mann

Elegy for the Duke. Robert Dana. SeSe

Elegy for the Giant Tortoises. Margaret Atwood. BoWoP

Elegy for the Lost Parish. Douglas Dunn. DiPo

Elegy for the Monastery Barn. Thomas Merton. VGW

Elegy for the Nightbound. Anthony Cronin. PBCIP

Elegy for the Other. Cleopatra Mathis. MT

Elegy for the Prefect of Vĩnh-tu'ò'ng. Ho Xuan Huong, *Vietnamese*. AVP, *tr. by* Huỳnh Sanh Thông

Elegy for the Time at Hand. "Adunis," *Arabic*. AF, *tr. by* Samuel Hazo

Elegy for the Unknown Soldier. Michael O'Loughlin. PBCIP

Elegy for the Wife of a Friend. Yü Hsüan-chi, *Chinese*. BoWoP, *tr. by* Geoffrey Waters

Elegy for Thelonious. Yusef Komunyakaa. WeT

Elegy for Tru'o'ng Định. Nguyễn Đình Chiểu, *Vietnamese*. AVP, *tr. by* Huỳnh Sanh Thông

Elegy for Two Banjos. Karl Shapiro. TrJP

Elegy for W. C. W., the Lovely Man, An. John Berryman. *See* 324. An Elegy for W.C.W., The Lovely Man.

Elegy for William Soutar. William Montgomerie. OxBS

Elegy for Wright & Hugo. Norman Dubie. NoAM

Elegy for Yards, Pounds, and Gallons. David Wagoner. PoA

Elegy in a Country Churchyard. G. K. Chesterton. FaPoR; MoBrPo; NSI; OBWP; OxBSP; PoFWW

Elegy in a Kensington Churchyard. Muriel Spark. FaBoTC

Elegy in a Presbyterian Burying-Ground. Robert Noble Denison Wilson. BIrV

Elegy in a Spider's Web. Laura Riding Jackson. PFTM

Elegy in a Theatrical Warehouse. Kenneth Fearing. NYBP

Elegy in an Abandoned Boatyard. Dave Jeddie Smith. VCAP

Elegy in Memory of the Worshipful Major Thomas Leonard Esq, An. Samuel Danforth Jr. SCAP

Elegy in Newgate. William Cobbett. UV

Elegy Is Preparing Itself, An. Donald Justice. CRP; HoPM

Elegy: Ise Lamenting the Death of Empress Onshi. Lady Ise, *Japanese*. BoWoP; IMW, *tr. by* Etsuko Terasaki *and* Irma Brandeis

Elegy Just in Case. John Ciardi. TwCP

Elegy: "My Prime of Youth Is But a Frost of Cares." Chidiock Tichborne. *See* Tichborne's Elegy.

Elegy: "O spare a tear for poor Tom Hood." Martin Fagg. *See* Elegy on Thomas Hood.

Elegy of Fortinbras. Zbigniew Herbert, *Polish*. CEEP; FaBoPV; PoSu, *tr. by* Czeslaw Milosz; BLT; VCWP, *tr. by* Czeslaw Milosz and Peter Dale Scott

    ("And that water these words what can they do what can they / do prince.") (LL) CEEP, *tr. by* Czeslaw Milosz; BLT, *tr. by* Czeslaw Milosz and Peter Dale Scott

Elegy of the Wind. Christopher Okigbo. VCWP

Elegy on a Favorite Cat, An. Anne Francis.

    "When cats like him submit to fate." ECWP

Elegy on a Lady, Whom Grief for the Death of Her Betrothed Killed. Robert Bridges. OBEV

Elegy on a Maiden Name, An. Jane Cave. CABP; ECWP

Elegy on a Young Thrush Which Escaped from the Writer's Hand. Helen Maria Williams. ECWP

Elegy on an X-ray Photo of My Skull. Yelena Shwarts, *Russian*. VCWP, *tr. by* Michael Molnar

Elegy on Any Lady by George Moore. Max Beerbohm. FaBoEE

Elegy on Ben Jonson, An. John Cleveland. MeLP

Elegy on Cynddylan, The. *Unknown, Welsh*.

    "Stand out, maids, and look on the land of Cynddylan." OBWVE, *tr. by* Kenneth Hurlstone Jackson

Elegy on D. D. Sidney Godolphin. BeJo

Elegy on His Mistress. Donne. *See* On His Mistress [*or* Mistris].

Elegy on Donne. Sidney Godolphin.

    "Passion's excess for thee we need no fear." EPCY

Elegy on the Death of a Mad Dog, An. Oliver Goldsmith. BLPA; FaBoBe; FaBoCh; NBLV; NOEC; NOIV; OBNV; OxAEP-1; TFi *Fr.* The Vicar of Wakefield.

    (On the Death of a Mad Dog.) NTP

Elegy on the Death of Bingo Our Trench Dog. Sir Edward De Stein. NSI

Elegy on the Death of Dobbin, the Butterwoman's Horse, An. Francis Fawkes. NOEC

Elegy on the Death of Her Husband. Anne, Duchess of Arundel Howard. *See* The Good Shepherd's Sorrow for the Death of His Beloved Son.

Elegy on the Death of John Keats, An. Shelley. OBNC *Fr.* Adonais; An Elegy on the Death of Keats. EBEV; FHYEP; HoPM; ImPo; NOBRP; OAEL-2; OxAEP-2; PoEL-4; TFi

    ("I weep for Adonais—he is dead!") CABP

    (Mourn Not for Adonais.) NOBE

Elegy on the Death of Mr Sterne. Miles Peter Andrews. NOBRP

Elegy on the Dust. Thom Gunn. NoAM

Elegy on the Earl of Rochester. Anne Wharton. KTR; NOSC

Elegy [*or* Elegie] on the Lady Jane Pawlet [*or* Paulet], [Marchioness of Winton], An. Ben Jonson. SeCP

    "How did she leave the world? with what contempt?"

Elegy on Thomas Hood. Martin Fagg. NOBL; UV

    (Elegy: "O spare a tear for poor Tom Hood.") BXAP

Elegy over a Tomb. Edward Herbert. MeLP; NOBE; OBEV; OBWVE; PoEL-2

Elegy, to an Old Beauty, An. Thomas Parnell. ECEV; NOEC

Elegy: To Spring. Michael Bruce.

    "Farewell, ye blooming fields! ye cheerful plains!" NOEC

Elegy to the Memory of an Unfortunate Lady. Alexander Pope. ECEV; NOBE; NOEC; OAEL-1; OBEV; SCGP

Elegy upon His Tomb in Herndon-Hill Church, Erected by His Wife, Who Speaks, An. James Howell. OBWVE

Elegy upon Old Freeman, An. Matthew Stevenson.

    "Here in this homely cabinet." NOSC

Elegy upon S[ir] W[alter] R[aleigh], An. Henry, Bishop of Chichester King. NOSC

Elegy upon the Death of Doctor [*or* Dr.] Donne, Dean of Paul's, An. Thomas Carew. *See* An Elegie upon the Death of the Deane of Pauls, Dr. Donne.

Elegy Upon the Death of His Own Father, An. Richard Corbet. BeJo; NOSC

Elegy upon the Death of Mrs. A. Behn, the Incomparable Astrea, An. *Unknown*. KTR

Elegy upon the Death of That Holy Man of God Mr. John Allen, An. Edward Taylor. PoEL-3

Elegy upon the Death of the Dean of [St.] Paul's, Dr. John Donne, An. Thomas Carew. *See* An Elegie upon the Death of the Deane of Pauls, Dr. Donne.

Elegy: "When in the mirror of a permanent tear." Gene Derwood. ImPo; LiTM

Elegy Written in a Country Churchyard. Thomas Gray. APAD; AWP; ClHu; EBEV; EBEvV; FaBoBe; FaPoR; GTBS-P; HAP; HeIP-4; ImPo; InPK-6; InPS-3; NOBE; NOEC; NoP-4; OAEL-1; OBEV; OxAEP-1; PoEL-3; PoLF; PoPoPo; Poetr; SCV; TFi; UnPo; WeW-3

    ("Bosom of his Father and his God, The.") (LL) CABP

    (Elegy Wrote in a Country Church Yard, An.) ECEV

    "Curfew tolls the knell of parting day, The." UV

    ("And Melancholy marked him for her own.") (LL) PBMP

    Epitaph: "Here rests his head upon the lap of earth." FHYEP; FaBoPV; SCGP

Elegy Written in a Country Coal-Bin. Christopher Darlington Morley. OBAL

Elegy Wrote in a Country Church Yard, An. Thomas Gray. *See* Elegy Written in a Country Churchyard.

Elegye, An: "Constant to none, but ever false to me." Thomas Campion. AAS *Fr.* Observations in the Art of English Poesie.

Elektra's Keening. Sophocles, *Greek.* OBCVT, *tr. by* Pound, Ezra (1885-1972) and Rudd Fleming

Element. Patricia K. Page. MoCV

Element Mother, The. Lorine Niedecker. FTOS

Element of mischief contributed, An. Summer Breezes. Frank O'Hara. FTOS

Element that utters doves, angels and cleft flames. Air. Kathleen Jessie Raine. MoBrPo

Elemental. D. H. Lawrence. NoP-4

Elementary. Jim Tollerud. VoR

Elementary Cosmogony. Charles Simic. NNaP

Elementary Scene, The. Randall Jarrell. CMoP; PoE

Elementary School Classroom in a Slum, An. Stephen Spender. FaBoMo; MoBrPo; TwCP; UnPo

Elements, The. W. H. Davies. MoBrPo

Elements, The. Tom Lehrer. UV

Elements have merged into solicitude, The. The Racer's Widow. Louise Glück. AmPA; NYBP

Elements of Composition. A. K. Ramanujan. VCWP

Elements of San Joaquin, The. Gary Soto. PBCAP; PaTW; UnSA

("For any of us.") (LL) UnSA

   Rain. NoAM

   Wind. NoAM

Elena. Pat Mora. UnSA

Elena's Song. Sir Henry Taylor. OBEV; RACG *Fr.* Philip van Artevelde.

Elene. Cynewulf, *Anglo-Saxon.* AnOE, *tr. by* Charles W. Kennedy

Elephant, The. Herbert Asquith. BoTP; CTAV

Elephant, The. Hilaire Belloc. BoTP

Elephant [II], The ("Elephant hunter, take your bow!"). *Unknown, Gabon Pigmy.* TTY, *tr. by* C. M. Bowra

Elephant [I], The ("Elephant who brings death"). *Unknown, Yoruba.* TTTS; TTY, *tr. by* Gbadamosi *and* Ulli Beier

Elephant. Pablo Neruda, *Spanish.*

   "Gross innocent." TTTS

Elephant ("Tall-topped acacia, you, full of branches"). *Unknown.* PeSA

Elephant. *Unknown. Fr.* Hunter Poems of the Yoruba. RB, *tr. by* Ulli Beier

Elephant always carries his trunk, The. The Elephant's Trunk. Alice Wilkins. ImGa

Elephant beaten with candy and little pops and chews. A Sound. Gertrude Stein. TTTS *Fr.* Tender Buttons.

Elephant hunter, take your bow! The Elephant [II]. *Unknown, Gabon Pigmy.* TTY, *tr. by* C. M. Bowra

Elephant is like a wall, The. E. J. Falconer. BoTP

Elephant Is Slow to Mate, The. D. H. Lawrence. LiTM

Elephant of long service to a circus, An. The Retirement of the Elephant. Russell Edson. AmPA

Elephant of Moissel, hear my pious prayer. Léopold Sédar Senghor, *French.* NegPo, *tr. by* Ellen Conroy Kennedy *Fr.* Return of the Prodigal Son.

Elephant on a ball presents a Shakespearean spectacle, An. The Modern circus. Pierre McOrlan, *French.* MFP, *tr. by* Martin Sorrell

Elephant, or the Force of Habit, The. A. E. Housman. NOBL

Elephant Rock. Primus St. John. PoBA

Elephant, the huge old beast, The. The Elephant Is Slow to Mate. D. H. Lawrence. LiTM

Elephant who brings death. The Elephant [I]. *Unknown, Yoruba.* TTTS; TTY, *tr. by* Gbadamosi *and* Ulli Beier

Elephants. Tô Hũ'u, *Vietnamese.* AVP, *tr. by* Huỳnh Sanh Thông

Elephants Are Different to Different People. Carl Sandburg. MoAmPo

Elephants Are in the Yard, The. Indran Amirthanayagam. OpBo

Elephants Dying, The. Michael C. Blumenthal. NoAM

"Elephants in bed," my daughter says. Vision. Louis Johnson. PeNZ

Elephant's Trunk, The. Alice Wilkins. ImGa

Elephants walking. Holding Hands. Lenore M. Link. FPC; NTCP

Eletelephony. Laura Elizabeth Richards. CTV; ImGa; NBLV; NOxBChV; NTCP; OBCA; OxBChV

Eleusis. Trumbull Stickney. *Fr.* Sonnets from Greece. APN-1

Élévation. Charles Baudelaire, *French.* AWP, *tr. by* Arthur Symons

Elevator. Naomi Shihab Nye. IFJA

Elevator Man Adheres to Form, The. Margaret Danner. PoBA

Elevator Man, 1949. Rita Dove. LoL; NAmP90

("*Slender breath of the piper, The.*") (LL) LoL

Elevator operator. Mr. 'Gator. N. M. Bodecker. NTCP

Eleven. Archibald MacLeish. HAP; MeMAP; WeW-3

Eleven A.M. on My Day Off, My Sister Phones Desperate for a Babysitter. Sharon Hashimoto. OpBo

Eleven Addresses to the Lord. John Berryman. OxBC

   "After a Stoic, a Peripatetic, a Pythagorean."

   "Fearful I peer upon the mountain path."

   "Germanicus leapt upon the wild lion in Smyrna."

   "Holy, & holy. The damned are said to say."

   "Holy, as I suppose I dare to call you."

   "If I say Thy name, art Thou there ? It may be so."

   "Master of beauty, craftsman of the snowflake." UnPo

   Prayer for the Self, A.

   "Sole watchman of the flying stars, guard me." UnPo

   "Surprise me on some ordinary day."

   "Under new management, Your Majesty."

Eleven he courts, twelve he marries. (LL) One I love, two I love. *Unknown.* LB; OxNR

1100 Exposition. Newletter from My Mother. Michael S. Harper. PoBA

Eleven o'clock and the bar is empty. The Hat Factory. Paul Durcan. BiHa

Eleven o'clock, and the curtain falls. End of the Comedy. Louis Untermeyer. PoA

Eleven Rock Poems. Gustaf Sobin. PmAP

Eleven struck. Check the little clock. The Mighty Ocean. Ilya L'vovich Selvinsky, *Russian.* TCRP, *tr. by* Daniel Weissbort

11/10 Again. Lucille Clifton. GT

Eleven-thirty and hot. The Cyclist. Marge Piercy. NoAM

Elevens. Marilyn Hacker. RA

11th: and Last Booke of the Ocean to Scinthia, The. Sir Walter Ralegh *See* The Ocean's Love to Cynthia.

Eleventh-Century Sanskrit, The. Vidyakara, *Sanskrit.*

   Four Poems. SAGP, *tr. by* Daniel H. H. Ingalls

Eleventh Song. Sir Philip Sidney. NoSiC; OxAEP-1 *Fr.* Astrophil and Stella. AAS; SiPS

   ("And from lowts to run away.") (LL) PBRV

   (Voices at the Window.) NOBE; OBEV

   ("Who is it that this darke night.") PBRV

Eleventh Vertical Poetry. Roberto Juarroz, *Spanish.*

   "Every word is a doubt." VCWP, *tr. by* Mary Crow

Elf. Sándor Weöres, *Hungarian.* CEEP, *tr. by* Emery E. George

Elf and the Dormouse, The. Oliver Herford. FPC; FaBoBe

Elfer Hill. *Unknown, Danish.* AWP, *tr. by* Robert Jamieson

Elfin Knight, An. Joseph Rodman Drake. BoTP *Fr.* The Culprit Fay.

   (Fairy in Armor, A.)

Elfin Knight, The. *Unknown.* AmFP

Elfin Knight, The. *Unknown.* ESPB

Elfin Pedlar, The. George Darley. BoTP

Elfin People Fill the Tubes, The. Winifred M. Letts. BoTP

Eli, Eli. Miriam Kessler. CrSp

Eli, Eli. Judith Wright. BMAP; CBAP; GI

Elia, thy reveries and visioned themes. To Elia (unsigned). John Clare. Ro *Fr.* London Magazine, 6 151.

Elijah Speaking. Doug Fetherling. NOBC

Elijah this / The Children of Israel that. The Nile. Albert Goldbarth. NAmP90

Elijah's Wagon knew no thill. Emily Dickinson. ChIV-1

Elinda's [*or* Ellinda's] Glove. Richard Lovelace. CBLP; CaPo; NOSC

   (Elinda's Glove.) CavPo

   ("Thou snowy farm with thy five tenements!") CavPo

Elinor Frost's Marble-Topped Kneading Table. Pattiann Rogers. LoHo

Elinor Glyn. *Unknown.* OBCoV

Elinor Wylie fell in love with Shelley. A Thought in Time. Robert Silliman Hillyer. NYBP

Elinour Rumming. John Skelton.

   "Instead of coin and money." NoSiC

Elisa ("Ye dainty nymphs, that in this blessed brook"). Edmund Spenser. *See* The Lay to Eliza.

Elise. Alan Wearne. BMAP *Fr.* The Nightmarkets.

Elixir [*or* Elixer], The. George Herbert. BoTP; FMP; ESCV; EnlH; FaBoCh; GeHe; NoP-4; NOSC

Elixir, The. Emma Lazarus. SDW

Elixir. Richard Murphy. BiHa

Eliza Harris. Frances Ellen Watkins Harper. AAP; NAAAL

Eliza in Uncle Tom's Cabin. Eloise Bibb. CBWP-4

Elizabeth. Michael Ondaatje. NoAM

Elizabeth, Elspeth, Betsy, and Bess. Mother Goose. OxNR; ReMoGo

Elizabeth, frigidly stretched. This Houre Her Vigill. Valentin Iremonger. CIP-2; NOIV; OxBTC

Elizabeth in Italy. Richard Weber. BoLoP

Elizabeth, Listening. Sabina Grogan. PUP-20

Elizabeth of Bohemia. Sir Henry Wotton. *See* On His Mistress [*or* Mistris], the Queen of Bohemia.

"Elizabeth the Beloved." Sylvia Townsend Warner. MoBrPo

Elizabeth Walters is my name. Elizabeth Walters. FaBoVe

Elizabethan & Nova Scotian Music. Charles North. PmAP

Elizabethans Called It Dying, The. James Schuyler. NeAP; PoM

Elizabeth's War with the Christmas Bear. Norman Dubie. LCAP-2; NoAM

Elk on Mutability, The. John Bensko. MT

Elk, The Whelk, The. Robert Williams Wood. NBLV

Elk Uncovers the Heavens, The. John Bensko. MT

Ella, fell a / Maple tree. Picnic. Hugh Lofting. NOxBChV; OTCP

Ella, in a Square Apron, Along Highway 80. Judy Grahn. NALW *Fr.* The Common Woman.
    ("As a rattlesnake.") (LL) NMM-2

Ella Mi Fu Rapita! Gavin Ewart. NoAM

Ella Speed. *Unknown.* AmFP

Ellas and the Statues. Gülten Akin, *Turkish.* PBWP, *tr. by* Nermin Menemencioglu

Ellen Fitzarthur: A Metrical Tale. Caroline Anne Bowles.
    Stanzas. Ro

Ellen Flannery. *Unknown.* AmFP

Ellen Learning to Walk. Frances Sargent Osgood. ColAP

Ellen West. Frank Bidart. NAAL-2; RACG
    ("Your *Ellen.*") (LL) PoPoPo

Ellenore. William Taylor. NOBRP

Ellie Mae Leaves in a Hurry. Peter Klappert. PFE

Ellington is dead. Elegy for the Duke. Robert Dana. SeSe

Elliott Hawkins. Edgar Lee Masters. OxBA *Fr.* Spoon River Anthology.

Elm. Sylvia Plath. NOBA; NoAM; NoP-4; Poetr
    (Elm Speaks, The.) NYBP

Elm is turned to crystal, The. Weather. William Meredith. NYBP; Poetr

Elm, laburnum, hawthorn, oak. Trees. Fleur Adcock. OBGa

Elm Speaks, The. Sylvia Plath. *See* Elm.

Elm Street. Alberta Turner. CMAP

Elm Tree in Paddington, An. Robert Adamson. BMAP

Elms. Louise Glück. NoAM

Elms are bad, sinister trees. Breakwaters. Ted Walker. NYBP

Elms have to fight, The. Home Movies. Carter Revard. VoR

Eloi, Eloi, Lama Sabachthani? D. H. Lawrence. GI

Eloisa. Alexander Pope. *Fr.* Eloisa to Abelard. NAEL-1; PoEL-3; RACG

Eloisa to Abelard. Alexander Pope. NAEL-1; PoEL-3; RACG
    Life of a Nun. ECEV

Elopement and civil wedding. . . the sham squire. The Distaff Side. Harry Clifton. PBCIP

Eloquent between the formal hedges. Affair of Honour. George Whalley. MoCV

Elphin knight sits on yon hill, The. The Elfin Knight. *Unknown.* ESPB

Elsa Wertman. Edgar Lee Masters. MoP; NoAM; OxBA *Fr.* Spoon River Anthology.

Else a great Prince in prison lies. Denise Levertov. VGW

Else tears heap all within one clay-cold hill. (LL) To Emily Dickinson. Hart Crane. CMoP; ColAP; NIP-4; NOBA; NoAM; NoP-4; Son; TAP

Elsewhere. "Michael Field." VWP

Elsewhere. Derek Walcott. HCP

Elsie Marley is grown so fine. *Unknown.* OxNR

Elusive Maid, The. Abraham ibn Chasdai, *Hebrew.* TrJP, *tr. by* J. Chotzner

Elustrious Dame whose vertues rare doe shine. An Acrostick on Mrs. Elizabeth Hull. John Saffin. SCAP

Elves and Fairies. John Gilbert Cooper. ECEV *Fr.* The Call of Aristippus.

Elves' Dance, The. John Lyly *and* Thomas Ravenscroft. CH *Fr.* The Mayde's Metamorphosis.

Elvin Jones Gretsch Freak. David Henderson. SeSe

Elvin's Blues. Michael S. Harper. BPo; LoL

Elwha River, The. Gary Snyder. NoAM

Elysee. Larry Eigner. VGW

Elysian Fields. Marilyn Hacker. RA

Elysium is as far as to. Suspense. Emily Dickinson. AWP; MoAmPo; OxBA; WPE

Em pom pee para me. A Clapping Chant. *Unknown.* FaBoVe

Emancipation. Priscilla Jane Thompson. CBWP-2

Emancipation. *Unknown.* BLPA

Emancipation Day. Lizelia Augusta Jenkins Moorer. CBWP-3

Emancipators, The. Randall Jarrell. PoA

Emariculdfe. "E. C." Son

Embalmer. Rossana Ombres, *Italian.* NeIt, *tr. by* Ruth Feldman

Embalmment. "Michael Field." VWP

Embankment (The Fantasia of a Fallen Gentleman on a Cold, Bitter Night), The. Thomas Ernest Hulme. EBEV; FaBoMo; GTBS-P; OPOU; OxBSP; OxBTC
    (Embankment, The.) APAD
    ("Once, in finesse of fiddles found I ecstasy.") APAD

Embarcation. Thomas Hardy. OBWP

Embarkation, The, *sels.* Henry Wadsworth Longfellow. *Fr.* Part the First. *Fr.* Evangeline, a Tale of Acadie.

Embarkation for Cythera, The. David Ferry. GS

Embarkation, 1942. John Jarmain. PoWW

Embarrassed the moon with his curses & songs. (LL) Because of My Father's Job. Jim Mitsui. OpBo; UnSA

Embarrassing Episode of Little Miss Muffet, The. Guy Wetmore Carryl. OBCA

Embassy. W. H. Auden. LiLi *Fr.* Sonnets from China.

Ember Week, Reseda. Stephen Yenser. EOEF

Emblem. Roy Fisher. NBrP

Emblem of England's ancient faith. To an Oak Tree. Sir Walter Scott. OBNC *Fr.* Waverley.

Emblem of Two Foxes, An. Barry Spacks. HoPM

Emblems. Douglas Dunn. FaBoMo

Emblems. Francis Quarles.
    "At length, by flight, I over-went the Pack." ESCV
    "Before a Pack of deep-mouth'd Lusts I flee." ESCV
    "Behold thy darling, which thy lustfull care." ESCV
    "Come then, my soule, approach this royall Burse." ESCV
    Epigram: "My soul, thy love is dear: 'twas thought a good." OAEL-1
    "How shall my tongue expresse that hallow'd fire." ESCV
    I Am My Beloved's, and His Desire Is towards Me. OxAEP-1
    "If lust should chase my soule, made swift by fright." ESCV
    "Let Grace conduct thee to the paths of peace." ESCV
    My Beloved Is Mine, and I Am His; He Feedeth among the Lillies. MeLP; NOBE; OBEV
    (Divine Rapture, A.) GLoP; OBEV
    ("E'en like two little bank-dividing brooks.") GLoP
    ("World's but theirs; but my Beloved's mine, The.") (LL) GLoP
    "My Soule is like a Bird; my Flesh, the Cage." ESCV
    "Not as the thirsty soyle desires soft showres." ESCV
    Stay My Steps in Thy Paths, That My Feet Do Not Slide. NOSC
    "This furnish't Ark presents the greedy view." ESCV
    Wherefore Hidest Thou Thy Face, and Holdest Me for Thine Enemy [*or* Enemie]? MeLP; NOSC; OxAEP-1
    "Worldly wisdome of the foolish man, The." ESCV
    "World's a Floore, whose swelling heapes retaine, The." ESCV

Emblems. Allen Tate. AWP; VGW

Emblems of Conduct. Hart Crane. ImPo; LiTM; MeMAP

Emblems of Love. Lascelles Abercrombie.
    Epilogue: "What shall we do for Love these days?" MoBrPo
    Small Fountains. CH
    Hymn to Love. OBEV
    Woman's Beauty. MoBrPo

Embodied close, the lab'ring Grecian train. Homer. OBVE, *tr. by* Alexander Pope *Fr.* The Iliad.

Embodiment of what, The. Lyric. Arthur Gregor. TAP

Embrace at first and then a loving kiss, An. Four Poems. Vidyakara. SAGP, *tr. by* Daniel H. H. Ingalls *Fr.* The Eleventh-Century Sanskrit.

Embrace the Blade. Joyce Mansour, *French.* PBWP, *tr. by* Carol Cosman

Embraceable You. Ira Gershwin. CBLP

Embracing low-falutin. The Countryman's Return. Dylan Thomas. OxBTC

Embracing the young mother from behind. Peyanar. PLW *Fr.* Seven Said by the Foster-Mother. PLW, *tr. by* A. K. Ramanujan

Embracing this woman. Peyanar. PLW *Fr.* Seven Said by the Foster-Mother. PLW, *tr. by* A. K. Ramanujan

Embro to the Ploy. Robert Garioch. FaBoTC; OxBS

Embroidered in a tapestry of green. Design in Living Colors. Adrienne Rich. GaP

Embroidery. Catherine Nomura Crystal. AiP

Embroidery (I), An. Denise Levertov. NMM-2

Emerald, The. James Merrill. FiLi *Fr.* Up and Down.

Emerald is as green as grass, An. Flint. Christina Rossetti. ChAP; OxBChV *Fr.* Sing-Song.

Emerald is as green as grass, An. Flint. Christina Rossetti. OxBChV

Emeralds are singing on the grasses, The. How Many Heavens. Dame Edith Sitwell. TrCP

Emeralds big as half the county. (LL) Ireland never was contented. Walter Savage Landor. FaBoEE; GTBS-P; OBCoV; OxBSP; OxBoLi; PeLV

Emerge, and shine upon the Aral Sea. (LL) Sohrab and Rustum. Matthew Arnold. EBNV; OBNV

Emerge, and shine upon the Aral Sea. (LL) Sohrab Dead. Matthew Arnold. EBEvV; GTBS-P; NOBE; PeVV

Emergency Haying. Hayden Carruth. NNaP

Emerges daintily, the skunk. The Wood Weasel. Marianne Moore. CMoP

Emerging. Tanka. Miyazawa Kenji, *Japanese.* MJT, *tr. by* Makoto Ueda

Emerging from the unlit room at dusk. (LL) Father and Daughter. Cathy Song. MoLi; OpBo

Emerging hot and rosy. Anita Virgil. HA

Emerging through the automatic doors. The Library. Timothy Steele. RA

Emerson. James Russell Lowell. NOBA *Fr.* A Fable for Critics. NAAL-1; NAAL-3

(Fable for Critics, A.) NCAP

("While a cloud that floats o'er is reflected within it.") (LL) AmPP; OxBA; TAP

("Will be some very great person over again.") (LL) NCAP

Emerson. Henrietta Cordelia Ray. CBWP-3

Emigrant, The. Alexander McLachlan.

Arrival, The. NOBC

Song: "Old England is eaten by Knaves." NOBC

Emigrant, The. Standish O'Grady.

Winter in Lower Canada. NOBC

Emigrant/Immigrant ("From the people"). Rina Ferrarelli. LoHo

Emigrant/Immigrant ("Slight accent, A"). Rina Ferrarelli. LoHo

Emigrant Ship, The. Henry Dalton. PBCV

Emigrant Song. "S. Ansky," *Yiddish.* TrJP, *tr. by* Joseph Leftwich

Emigrant's Cabin, The. Thomas Pringle. PeSAV

Emigration. Eleanor Wilner. NMM-2

Emigration Trains, The. Thomas McCarthy. PBCIP

Emily Brontë. C. Day Lewis. GTBS-P

Emily Brontëë: Du hast Diamanten. Robert Bridges. EPCY

Emily Carr. Wilfred Watson. MoCV; NOBC

Emily, delirium's your province. Dartmouth Women's Prison, 1992. Lynda Hull. PUP-19

Emily Dickinson. Lucha Corpi. NMM-2

Emily Dickinson. Michael Longley. CIP-2

Emily Dickinson, Bismarck and the Roadrunner's Inquiry. Ray A. Young Bear. HATNAP

Emily Dickinson in Southern California. X. J. Kennedy. NBLV; OBCoV

Emily Dickinson's To-Do List. Andrea Carlisle. IFJA

Emily Geiger. *Unknown.* PoLF

Emily Hardcastle, Spinster. John Crowe Ransom. CMoP; MeMAP; OxBSP

Emily Wants to Play. Mary Jo Salter. NMM-2

Emily Writes Such a Good Letter. Stevie Smith. OBCoV

Emily's Haunted Housman. David Cummings. BXAP

Emily's Words. Leslie Monsour. FFC

Eminent scholar "took the bull by the horns," The. Arrow. Rita Dove. NMM-2

Emmeline Grangerford's "Ode to Stephen Dowling Bots, Dec'd." "Mark Twain." NBLV; OBAL *Fr.* The Adventures of Huckleberry Finn.

(Ode to Stephen Dowling Bots, Dec'd.) APN-2; Poetr

Emmet is an ant (archaic), The. Ogden Nash. OBCoV

Emmett Till. Wanda Coleman. NAAAL

Emmett Till. James A. Emanuel. NIP-4; PoBA

Emmonsail's Heath in Winter. John Clare. PoEL-4

Emmy's exquisite youth and her virginal air. Emmy. Arthur Symons. ADE; OBNC

Emotional the / fox at an am. Brill. Clark Coolidge. PmAP

Empedocles came coughing through the smoke. To the Thoughtful Reader. William Meredith. NoAM

Empedocles on Etna. Matthew Arnold.

"And lie thou there." EnVR

Hymn of Empedocles. OBEV

Song of Callicles, The ("Through the black, rushing smoke-bursts"). NOBE; OAEL-2; OBEV

Empedocles on Etna. Herbert B. Mallalieu. PoA

Emperor, The. Tu Fu, *Chinese.* AWP, *tr. by* E. Powys Mathers

Emperor Butterfly. Anna Kiss, *Magyar.* EC2, *tr. by* Nicholas Columban

Emperor Marcus Aurelius, The. Limerick. "Yorick." PeLi

Emperor of China Speaks, The. Hugo von Hofmannsthal, *German.* GaP, *tr. by* Michael Hamburger

Emperor of Ice-Cream, The. Wallace Stevens. AmPP; CBNP; CMoP; FaBoMo; HAP; HCAP; HeIP-4; InPK-6; MeMAP; MoP; NAAL-2; NAWM-2; NIP-4; NOBA; NoAM; NoP-4; OxBA; PoE; PoPoPo; Poetr; SAGP; TAP; TFi; TRP; WeW-3

Emperor of the East, The. Philip Massinger.

Song. OxAEP-1

Emperor of the Moon. Aphra Behn.

Song: "All joy to mortals, joy and mirth." WPE

Song: "Curse upon that faithless maid, A." WPE

Emperor's city, a place of fame and profit, The. A Quiet House in Ch'ang-lo Ward. Po Chü-i, *Chinese.* CoBCP, *tr. by* Burton Watson

Emphasis Falls on Reality, An. Barbara Guest. FTOS; PmAP

Empire Builders. Archibald MacLeish. OxBA

(Museum Attendant, The.) GM

("There is nothing to see of America but land.") (LL) GM

Empire Day. G. K. Chesterton. *See* Geography.

Empire Is No More. William Blake. *Fr.* America; a Prophecy. OAEL-2

Empire of Dreams. Charles Simic. BLT; LCAP-2; VCAP

Empire Smoke, Forgeries, Salient and The Ritz. Ray DiPalma. FTOS

Empire Sofa, The. Thomas Hornsby Ferril. PaTW

Employment: "He that is weary, let him sit." George Herbert. FaBoVe; SeCP

(Employment (1).) GeHe

(Employment (2).) GeHe

Employments of Life, The. John Gay. PeLV *Fr.* The Beggar's Opera. OAEL-1

("Thinks his trade as honest as mine.") (LL) OxBoV

Emplumada. Lorna Dee Cervantes. NoAM; PBCAP

Empress Brand Trim; Ruby Reminisces, The. Sherley Anne Williams. BlSi

Empress herself served tea to Su Tung-po, The. Lew Welch. BB

Empress Receives the Head of a Taiping Rebel, The. Sarah Gorham. FFC

Empress's Cat, The. Felicity Bast. PC

Empryce of prys, imperatrice. William Dunbar. EBEV *Fr.* Ane Ballat of Our Lady. OxBS

Emptied with weeping. At the Badr Trench. Safiya bint Musafir, *Arabic.* WPOW, *tr. by* Bridget Connelly *and* Deirdre Lashgari

Empties Coming Back. Angelo de Ponciano. BLPA

Emptiness first / felt the vibration that now charms us and comforts and helps? Rilke. *See* The First Duino Elegy.

Emptiness of man is not like, The. João Cabral de Melo Neto, *Portuguese.* VCWP, *tr. by* Galway Kinnell

Emptiness of the day, The. Roberto Juarroz. VCWP, *tr. by* W. S. Merwin *Fr.* Fifth Vertical Poetry.

Empty as Death. Pyong-hwa Cho, *Korean.* CKP, *tr. by* Jaihiun Kim

Empty Bed Blues. Bessie Smith. OBAL; UnPo

Empty bell, The. Secret. Pierre Reverdy, *French.* PFTM, *tr. by* Kenneth Rexroth

Empty boat, floating, adrift, An. (LL) Written on the Wall at Chang's Hermitage. Tu Fu, *Chinese.* OHPC, *tr. by* Kenneth Rexroth

Empty Body, The. Mark Strand. UnPo *Fr.* Elegy for My Father. HCAP; LCAP-2

Empty carousel in a deserted park, An. The Carousel. Gloria C. Oden. GT; PoBA

Empty corse to waver with the wind, The. (LL) Execution of the faithless maids. Homer, *Greek.* OBCVT, *tr. by* Alexander Pope

Empty Dwelling Places. Kenneth Patchen. PoA

Empty elevator, An. Jack Cain. HA

Empty / flowerpot, The. (LL) Poem. "As the cat / climbed over." William Carlos Williams. InPS-3; PFE; SoSe-8; TTTS

Empty Glen, The. R. Crombie Saunders. OxBS

Empty Heart, An. Samuel Johnson. LBC

Empty highway, The. Nicholas Virgilio. HA

Empty hills, no one in sight. Deer Fence. Wang Wei. *Fr.* Twenty Views of Wang-ch'uan. CoBCP, *tr. by* Burton Watson

Empty House, The. William Dean Howells. APN-2

Empty House. Stephen Spender. NYBP; PCP

Empty House, The. Max Williams. CBAP

Empty, I echo to the least footfall. Barren Woman. Sylvia Plath. OxBSP

Empty, illusory life. The Enchanted Region; or, Mistaken Pleasures. Walter Harte. EBEV

Empty Kettle. Louis Oliver. HATNAP

Empty mailbox. Marlene Mountain. HA

Empty out your pockets nighttime, Daddy. Who I Think You Are. Elizabeth Alexander. FFC; RA

Empty Pain-Killer Bottles, The. Tom Raworth. SPE

Empty perfection, as I take you in. James Merrill. NoAM *Fr.* Coda: The Higher Keys.

Empty Purse, The. Tu Fu, *Chinese.* TAL, *tr. by* Robert Payne

Empty room. Jack Cain. HA

Empty room begins to growl, The. Echo. Vasco [*or* Vasko] Popa. PoSu *Fr.* Besieged Serenity.

Empty rumour, that second world beyond the seas, An. Ma-wei. Li Shang-yin, *Chinese.* PLT, *tr. by* A. C. Graham

Empty sky, a world of heather, An. Divided. Jean Ingelow. VWP

EMPTY TAG. (LL) What [*or* And what] Is So Rare as a Day in June? James Russell Lowell. FaBoBe; ImGa

Empty Tomb, The. Clara Ann Thompson. CBWP-2

Empty Vessel. "Hugh MacDiarmid." FaBoTC; FaBoTw; OxBS

Empty Warriors. Don L. Lee. RaBo

Empty your mind of all thoughts. Lao Tzu. EnlH *Fr.* Tao Te Ching.

Emu makes, though prone to fret, The. Leon Gellert. PeP

Emu Shot. Tjinapirrgarri, *Aborigine.* NOBAu, *tr. by* Georg von Brandenstein

Emulation, The. Sarah Fyge Egerton. CABP; ECWP; NOEC; PEW

Emulation, The: A Pindarick Ode. *Unknown.* KTR

En Bateau. Paul Verlaine, *French.* AWP, *tr. by* Arthur Symons

En-Dor. Rudyard Kipling. OxBSn

En Famille. Dame Edith Sitwell. NALW

En las Internas Entrañas. Saint, of Avila Theresa, *Spanish.* WPOW, *tr. by* Father Benedict Zimmerman

En Route. Duncan Campbell Scott. NOBC

En route to the picnic they drive through their history. Picnic: the Liberated. M. Carl Holman. PoBA

Enacting someone's notion of themselves. Aunt Jemima of the Ocean Waves. Robert Earl Hayden. LCAP-2; PoBA

Enamel Girl, The. Genevieve Taggard. MoAmPo

Enamoured of the miniscule / of the careful and compact. Michael Hartnett. BIrV

Encantadas, The. Richard Kenney.

"One might as well conceive this story in the cirrose." EOEF

Encased and shining in a bead of amber. A Bee's Burial. Martial, *Latin.* OBCVT, *tr. by* Peter Whigham

Encased in talent like a uniform. The Novelist. W. H. Auden. MeMAP

Encelado and the Facts. Agnes Gergely, *Hungarian.* CEEP, *tr. by* Emery E. George

Encelado Sulfato XVII, King of the Cobalts. Encelado and the Facts. Agnes Gergely, *Hungarian.* CEEP, *tr. by* Emery E. George

Encelado: you and I. Gnosis. Agnes Gergely, *Hungarian.* CEEP, *tr. by* Emery E. George

Enchanted frame assures the image of a loved one, An. Veil. Marjorie Welish. PmAP

Enchanted Island, The. Letitia Elizabeth Landon. CABP; NOBRP

Enchanted Region; or, Mistaken Pleasures, The. Walter Harte. EBEV

Enchanted Shell, The. Henrietta Cordelia Ray. CBWP-3

Enchanted Shirt, The. John Milton Hay. BLPA

Enchanted thing: how can two chosen words. The Gazelle. Rilke, *German.* APo, *tr. by* Stephen Mitchell

Enchanter's Nightshade. Richard Caddel. NBrP

Enchantment. Lewis Alexander. PoBA

Enchantment, The. Thomas Otway. OBEV

Enchantment, The. Theocritus. CTC; OBVE, *tr. by* Thomas Creech *Fr.* Idylls.

("Where is my bay? Bring it, Thestylis. Where are my charms?") HePo, *tr. by* Barbara Hughes Fowler

Encinctured with a twine of leaves. The Fruit Plucker. Coleridge. CH; FaBoCh; OBNC

Enclosed with a Letter to My Family—For Shu. Yang Shih-ch'i, *Chinese.* CoBLCP, *tr. by* Jonathan Chaves

Encompass me, my lover. The Constant North. J. F. Hendry. OxBS

Encounter, The. Paul Blackburn. NeAP

Encounter. Denis Devlin. BIrV

Encounter. Uys Krige, *Afrikaans.* PeSA, *tr. by the author*

Encounter. Czeslaw Milosz, *Polish.* PiM, *tr. by* Czeslaw Milosz *and* Lillian Vallee; ChAP

Encounter, The. Edgell Rickword. OxBTC

Encounter. August Stramm, *German.* PFTM, *tr. by* Jerome Rothenberg

Encounter. Marion Strobel. LW

Encounter at St. Martin's. Ken Smith. OPOU

Encounter in the Cage Country. James Dickey. CAPP-1

Encountering a Snowstorm, I Stay with the Recluse of Mount Hibiscus. Liu Ch'ang-ch'ing, *Chinese.* SuSp, *tr. by* Dell R. Hales

Encountering Sorrow, *or* Li Sao. *Unknown, Chinese.* CoBCP, *tr. by* Burton Watson, *at. to* Ch'u Yüan

Encouragement. Mrs. Henry Linden. CBWP-4

Encouragement to Exile. Petronius Arbiter, *Latin.* AWP, *tr. by* Howard Mumford Jones

Encouragements to a Lover. Sir John Suckling. *See* Song: "Why so pale and wan, fond lover?"

End, The. Allen Ginsberg. CoAmPo

End, The. Walter Savage Landor. *See* On His Seventy-Fifth Birthday.

End, The. Wilfred Owen. CH; ChIV-1

End, An. Christina Rossetti. CBLP; GBL; SDW

End, The. Mark Strand. TRP

End. Virgil, *Latin.* OBCVT, *tr. by* John Dryden

End and the Beginning, The. Wislawa Szymborska, *Polish.* VCWP, *tr. by* Stanislaw Baranczak *and* Clare Cavanagh

End / as it ends. (LL) The Poem of the End. Marina Tsvetayeva, *Russian.* BrRo

End came as I drove it down the road, The. Last of the Poet's Car. Tony Connor. OxBTC

End came easy for most of us, The. The Man from Washington. James Welch. CDW; HATNAP; NoAM; PoPoPo; RaBo

End Circulates in the Wide Space of Summer, The. Paul Zweig. WeT

End / conscience. Stéphane Mallarmé. PFTM, *tr. by* Pierre Joris *Fr.* Le Livre.

End Is Near the Beginning, The. David Gascoyne. SPE

End, Middle, Beginning. Anne Sexton. PoE

End of a Campaign. Hamish Henderson. PoWW

End of a Course. Ivor Armstrong Richards. CRP

End of a Dynasty, The. Zbigniew Herbert, *Polish.* FaBoPV, *tr. by* Czeslaw Milosz

End of a long stillness. Dawn in January. Lance Henson. CDW

End of a thing, The. December. Lucille Clifton. NOxBChV

End of a War, The. Sir Herbert Read. OBMV; PeFWW

End of a Year. Robert Lowell. HCAP

End of an Ethnic Dream, The. Jay Wright. MoNo; SeSe

End of Another Home Holiday. D. H. Lawrence. EBEV; FaBoMo; OxAEP-2

End of ARt, The. Reiner Kunze, *German.* PoSu, *tr. by* Michael Hamburger

End of Clonmacnois, The. *Unknown, Irish.* CIP-2, *tr. by* Frank O'Connor

End of Doctor Faustus, The. Marlowe. PoEL-2 *Fr.* Doctor Faustus. NAEL-1; OAEL-1

End of Dodona II, The. Yannis Ritsos, *Greek.* VCWP, *tr. by* Edmund Keeley

End of Ends. . . in God's Beginning's lost, The. (LL) Clover. Sidney Lanier. APN-2; ColAP

End of everything approaches, The. Doomsday. Elinor Wylie. NoP-4

End of Faustus, The. Marlowe. *See* The End of Doctor Faustus.

End of His Work, The. Robert Herrick. CaPo

End of Human Reign on Bashan Hill, The. Bernadette Mayer. FTOS

End of It, The. Francis Thompson. NOBVV; OxBSP

End of Love, The. George Meredith. *See* Modern Love.

End of Man Is Death, The. Moses ibn Ezra, *Hebrew.* TrJP, *tr. by* Solomon Solis-Cohen

End of May, The. William Morris. NOBVV

End of Play. Robert Graves. EBEV

End of Sorrow, The. Edmond Fleg. *Fr.* The Wall of Weeping. TrJP, *tr. by* Humbert Wolfe

End of Summer. Stanley Kunitz. LoL; MoAmPo; Poetsp; SAGP; VGW

(End) of Summer (1966). Bill Knott. *See* Two Vietnam Poems: (1966).

End of summer suggested the way, The. Autumn Leaves. James Cushing. SeSe

End of summer: the spruces put out a few green shoots. Amazons. Louise Glück. NAmP90

End of the Affair. Geoffrey Grigson. GBL

End of the Affair, The. James Simmons. PBCIP

End of the Boo[c]k[e]s, of the Ocean's Love to Cynthia [*or* Scinthia], and the Beginning[e] of the 12 [*or* 22] Boo[c]k, Entreating of Sorrow, The. Sir Walter Ralegh. *See* A Poem Entreating of Sorrow.

End of the cold spell. Marlene Mountain. HA

End of the Comedy. Louis Untermeyer. PoA

End of the Flower World (A.D. 2300). Stanley Burnshaw. TrJP

End of the Game. Artur Miedzyrzecki, *Polish.* PoSu, *tr. by* Artur Miedzyrzecki *and* John Batki

End of the Journey, The. May Probyn. VWP

End of the Line, The. Thomas McGrath. GM

End of the Parade, The. William Carlos Williams. NYBP

End of the Picnic. Francis Webb. BMAP; NOBAu

End of the Questionnaire. Dan Pagis, *Hebrew.* NNPT, *tr. by* Stephen Mitchell; PoSu, *tr. by* Robert Friend

End of the Suitors, The. Homer. *Fr.* Odyssey. NAWM-1, *tr.* by Robert Fitzgerald

End of the Trip. David Avidan, *Hebrew   Fr.* Traveling in the City. IP, *tr. by* Warren Bargad *and* Stanley F. Chyet

End of the Weekend, The. Anthony Hecht. CoAmPo; FaBoMo; HAP; LiTM; WeW-3

End of the Whole Matter, The. Albery Allson Whitman. AAP *Fr.* Not a Man and Yet a Man.

End of the World, The. Gordon Bottomley. CH; MoBrPo

End of the World. Else Lasker-Schüler, *German.* BoWoP, *tr. by* Willis Barnstone *and* Michael Gillespie

End of the World, The. Archibald MacLeish. CMoP; GSo; HoPM; ImPo; InPK-6; LiTM; MeMAP; MoAmPo; NOBA; NoAM; OBAL; OxBA; PBMP; PFE; SAGP; Son; TAP; TFi; VGW

End of the World, The. João Cabral de Melo Neto, *Portuguese.* VCWP, *tr. by* James Wright

End of the world: it was given to me to see it, The. Thomas McGrath. AF

End of the Year, The. Su Tung-p'o, *Chinese.* OHPC, *tr. by* Kenneth Rexroth

End of their journey, I descended too, The. (LL) The Traveller. John Berryman. GM; PoA; VGW

End or a Beginning, An. Bei Dao, *Chinese.* AF, *tr. by* Bonnie S. McDougall

End To It, An. Asa Benveniste. NBrP

End to Myth, An. Charles Buckmaster. BMAP

End To Tears, An. Bible, *N.T.* LBC *Fr.* The Revelation of St John The Divine.

End was more of a melting, The. The Death of Will. Charles Tomlinson. OxBC

End was quick and bitter, The. Quick And Bitter. Yehuda Amichai, *Hebrew.* BoLoP; LoP; VCWP, *tr. by* Assia Gutmann; IP, *tr. by* Warren Bargad *and* Stanley F. Chyet

End your groan, and come away. (LL) The Shrouding of the Duchess of Malfi. John Webster. CH; HAP; NOBE; OBEV; SCGP

Ended, ere it begun. Emily Dickinson. APN-2

Endimion. John Lyly.

"Pinch him, pinch him black and blue." NoSic

"Stand! Who goes there?" NoSic; OBCoV

Endimion Porter and Olivia. Sir William Davenant. MeLP

(Song: "Endimion Porter and Olivia.") MeLP; NOSC

Ending, The. Paul Engle. NYBP

Ending. Gavin Ewart. NBLV; OxBSP; SoSe-8

Ending up tending shop up in Fiesole. (LL) Tourists. Howard Moss. NYBP; NoP-4; OBCoV; PeLV

Endless. Muriel Rukeyser. NYBP

Endless blue mountains disperse, The. On the Tower of Gathering Remoteness. Su Tung-p'o, *Chinese.* TAL, *tr. by* Robert Payne

Endless downpour: misty wood. Ivan Alekseievich Bunin, *Russian.* TCRP, *tr. by* Simon Franklin

Endless lanes sunken in the clay. The Trenches. Frederic Manning. NOBAu; NSI; PoWW

Endless repetitions of his own murmurous blood, The. (LL) A Letter. Anthony Hecht. NYBP; OxBC

Endless Song, The. Ruth McEnery Stuart. OBAL

Endlessly gaze at Mount Wu. Mount Wu Is High. Lu Chao-lin, *Chinese.* SuSp, *tr. by* Robin D. S. Yates

Endlessly over the water. The Sweetness of Nature. *Unknown, Irish.* IIP; TIRV, *tr. by* Frank O'Connor

Endowed with Ch———l's strength and Low———r's face. (LL) Epistle from Mrs. Yonge to Her Husband. Lady Mary Wortley Montagu. NAEL-1; NALW; NoP-4

Ends. Robert Frost. TRP

Ends. (LL) My Brother. Patricia Parker. CPO

Ends of Things were heard no more, The. Amir Gilbo'a, *Hebrew.* IP, *tr. by* Warren Bargad *and* Stanley F. Chyet

Endsight, *for Union Carbide, A.D. Hope and Sir P. Hasluck, Askin, Clutha etc.* Michael Dransfield. BMAP

Endurance. Elizabeth Akers Allen. PoToHe

Endurance. Dennis Brutus. VCWP

Endure Hardness. Christina Rossetti. NOBVV

Endure what life God gives and ask no longer span. Sophocles. OBMV, *tr. by* W. B. Yeats *Fr.* Oedipus at Colonus.

Enduring is the bust of bronze. The Duke of York's Statue. Walter Savage Landor. FaBoEE

Endymion. Keats.

Endymion. Keats. LaPo *Fr.* Endymion: Poetic Romance.

("From our dark spirits.") (LL) OPOU

("Full of sweet dreams, and health, and quiet breathing.") (LL) PFE

("Pouring unto us from the heaven's brink.") (LL) Ro

("Pouring unto us from the heaven's /brink brink.") (LL) APAD; CTV; LaPo

("Thing of beauty is a joy for ever, A.") APAD; CTV; LaPo; PFE; Ro

"Seasons four, The." LaPo

Endymion. Thomas Kinsella. PBCIP

Endymion: Poetic Romance. Keats.

Endymion. LaPo

("From our dark spirits.") (LL) OPOU

("Full of sweet dreams, and health, and quiet breathing.") (LL) PFE

("Pouring unto us from the heaven's brink.") (LL) APAD; CTV; LaPo; Ro

("Thing of beauty is a joy for ever, A.") APAD; CTV; LaPo; PFE; Ro

Hymn to Pan. PoEL-4

("Oh thou, whose mighty palace roof doth hang.") Ro

"O sovereign power of love! O grief! O balm!" OBNC

Song of the Indian Maid. NOBE; OBEV

Song of the Indian Maid, The ("Beneath my palm-trees, by the riverside"). NOBE

Eneas wonderit the greitnes of Cartiage. The Building of Carthage. Virgil. OBVE, *tr. by* Gawin Douglas *Fr.* The Aeneid [*or* Eneados, *Aeneis*].

Enemies of Promise. Edmund Wilson. OBCoV

Enemies of the Little Box, The. Vasco [*or* Vasko] Popa, *Serbo-Croatian.* HSix, *tr. by* Charles Simic

Enemies, / take care. A Chariot Wheel. Auvaiyar, *Tamil.* PLW, *tr. by* A. K. Ramanujan

Enemy, The. Randolph Stow. NOBAu

Enemy, The. Alice Walker. GT

Enemy, The. Dorothy, Duchess of Wellington Wellesley. WPN

Enemy Dead, The. Bernard Gutteridge. PoWW

Enemy Encounter. Padraic Fiacc. IIP; PNI

Enemy had burned his cottage home, The. Mikhail Vasilevich Isakovsky, *Russian.* TCRP, *tr. by* Lubov Yakovleva

Enemy in the Fortress, The. Marbod of Rennes, *Latin.* MLL, *tr. by* Helen Waddell

Enemy [*or* en'my] of life, decayer of all kind, The [*or* Th']. Sir Thomas Wyatt. OxBSP; SiPS

Enemy roamed the desert and everyone itched, The. (LL) A Day with the Foreign Legion. Reed Whittemore. CoAP; CoAmPo; LiTM

Enemy's Eyes, The. Emma Lee Warrior. HATNAP

Energetic Women. D. H. Lawrence. InPS-3

Energy. Victor Hernandez Cruz. PoBA

Energy in Sweden. Kenneth Koch. NoP-4

Enfant perdu. Heinrich Heine, *German.* AWP, *tr. by* Lord Houghton

Enfidaville. Keith Douglas. PoWW

Enfolding sunny spots of greenery. Coleridge. *See* Kubla Khan; or, A Vision in a Dream.

Enforc'd to seek some covert nigh at hand. Wood Of Error. Edmund Spenser. AEP

Enfranchising cable, silvered by the sea. Granite and Steel. Marianne Moore. NYBP

Engaged. Octavio Paz, *Spanish.* PBMP, *tr. by* Muriel Rukeyser

Engagement. Nichita Stanescu, *Romanian.* CEEP, *tr. by* Mariana Carpinisan *and* Mark Irwin

Engine, The. Ella Wheeler Wilcox. APN-2

Engine and tender, old loaf-shaped Pullman. The Old Trip by Dream Train. Brendan Galvin. GM

Engine Driver, The. "G. S. O." BoTP

Engineers' Corner. Wendy Cope. OBCoV

Engines of Gloom and Affection. John Yau. PmAP

England. Marianne Moore. MeMAP; MoAmPo

England. Mary Jo Salter. DiPo

England. *Unknown.* FaBoEE; OxBSP

England, a happy land we know. The Ghost. Charles Churchill. OxBSn *Fr.* The Ghost.

England and America. James Kenneth Stephen.

On a Parisian Boulevard. NOBL

On a Rhine Steamer. FaBoA; NOBL; NOBVV; OBCoV; PeLV

England and America, 1863. Richard Monckton, 1st Baron Houghton Milnes. EBVV

England and Switzerland 1802. Wordsworth. *See* Thought[s] of a Briton on the Subjugation of Switzerland.

England, Autumn. Wayne Brown. PBCV

England! awake! awake! awake! William Blake. FHYEP; NoP-4; OBNC *Fr.* Jerusalem; The Emanation of the Giant Albion.

England be your sepulchre. (LL) Song to the Men of England. Shelley. CABP; InPS-3; NAEL-2; PBMP

England, 1802, V. Wordsworth. OBEV

England, 1802, I. Wordsworth. *See* Written in London, September, 1802.

England, 1802, II. Wordsworth. *See* London 1802.

England, 1802, III. Wordsworth. OBEV

England, 1802 ("It is not to be thought of"). Wordsworth. NOBE; OBEV (We Must Be Free or Die.) FaPoR

England Expects. Ogden Nash. PeLV

England Expects? Sir Owen Seaman. NOBL

England in 1819. Shelley. FaBoPV; NAEL-2; NAWM-2; NOBE; NoP-4; OAEL-2; OxAEP-2; PBMP; PoPoPo; Poetr; Ro; SAGP; Son; TFi; UnPo (Sonnet: England in 1819.) GSo

England, My England. William Ernest Henley. MoBrPo; OBEV; PoLF

England, my England—you have been my tutrix. W. H. Auden. OBSV *Fr.* Letter to Lord Byron.

England that was the glory of the earth. On the Death of Henry the Lion. Hildebert, *Latin.* MLL, tr. by Helen Waddell

England! the time is come when thou shouldst wean. Sonnet. Wordsworth. Son

England to Her Sons. William Noel Hodgson. PoFWW

England, unlike junior nations. Remember Suez? Adrian Mitchell. OxBTC

England! with all thy faults I love thee still. Byron. UnPo *Fr.* Beppo; a Venetian Story. NOBL; OBNV; OBSV

England's Alfred Abroad. Sir Owen Seaman. UV

England's Dead. Felicia Dorothea Hemans. NoP-4

England's Heroical Epistles. Michael Drayton.

    Owen Tudor to Queen Katherine. NoSic

    Queen Katherine to Owen Tudor. NoSic

England's ingratitude still blots. What Jenner Said on Hearing in Elysium That Complaints Had Been Made of His Having a Statue [in Trafalgar Square]. Shirley Brooks. FaBoEE

England's lads are miniature men. Boy-Man. Karl Shapiro. NYBP

England's Sovereigns in Verse. *Unknown.* BLPA

England's Standard. Thomas Macaulay. *Fr.* The Armada. FaBoCh; FaPoR

England's sun was slowly setting o'er the hill-tops far away. Curfew Must Not Ring Tonight [*or* To-Night]. Rose Hartwick Thorpe. APN-2; BLPA; FaBoBe

English. Osbert Lancaster. NOBL; PeLV *Fr.* Afternoons with Baedeker.

English Alphabet, An. *Unknown.* CBNP

English Are Frosty, The. Alice Duer Miller. PoLF *Fr.* The White Cliffs.

English as nice, The. D. H. Lawrence. NoP-4; PoPoPo; RaBo

English Ballad, on the Taking of Namur by the King of Great Britain, 1695, An. Matthew Prior. PoEL-3

English Bards and Scotch Reviewers. Byron.

    "As Sisyphus against the infernal steep." OBSV

    "Behold! in various throngs the scribbling crew." OAEL-2

    "Illustrious Holland! hard would be his lot." OBSV

    "Next comes the dull disciple of thy school." EPCY

    "Shall gentle Coleridge pass unnoticed here." EPCY

    "There be who say, in these enlightened days." EPCY

    "Thus Lays of Minstrels—may they be the last! -." EPCY

    "Time has been, when yet the muse was young, The." FHYEP

    "Time was, ere yet in these degenerate days." EPCY; FHYEP

    "When Vice triumphant holds her sov'reign sway." FHYEP

William Lisle Bowles. OBNC

English Beach Memory: Mr. Thuddock. Sir Osbert Sitwell. NYBP

English Cocker: Old and Blind. Robert Penn Warren. APo

English Cousin Comes to Scotland. Jackie Kay. NOxBChV

English Garden, The. William Mason.

    Alcander's Flower Garden. OBGa

    "Nor, Shenstone, thou / Shalt pass withou thy meed, thou son of peace!" EPCY

    Some Early gardenists. OBGa

    Thomas Gray's View of Nature. EPCY; NOEC

English Girl. *Unknown, Chinese.* OBMV, tr. by E. Powys Mathers

English Girl Eats Her First Mango. John Agard. HCP

English Graves, The. G. K. Chesterton. NSI

English Lessons. Boris Pasternak, *Russian.* NNPT, tr. by Mark Rudman *and* Bohdan Boychuk

English Liberal. Geoffrey Taylor. FaBoEE

English muskets went bim! bim!, The, *tr. of Creole slave song.* George Washington Cable. APN-2

English professor named Brooks, An. Limerick. D. H. Cudmore. PeLi

English Queen, The. Henry Lawson. NOBAu

English Songs. "Barry Cornwall."

    Poet's Thought, A. Ro

English-Speaking Persons Will Find Translations. Michael S. Glaser. UnSA

English Succession, The. *Unknown.* OxBChV

English Teeth, English Teeth! Teeth. Spike Milligan. OPOU

English Thornton. Edgar Lee Masters. OxBA *Fr.* Spoon River Anthology.

English Traveller, The. Plautus Titus Maccius, *Latin.* From Mostellaria. OBCVT, tr. by Thomas Heywood

English Was Only a Second Language. Walta Borawski. GLP

Englishman, The. Sir William Schwenck Gilbert. NOBL *Fr.* H. M. S. Pinafore.

Englishman at the Table, The. James Cawthorn. ECEV *Fr.* Of Taste; an Essay.

Englishman from Holland, An. *Unknown, French.* CBNP

Englishman in Italy, The. Robert Browning. PoEL-5

Englishman in the old days, An. Carl Sandburg. FYAP *Fr.* The People, Yes.

Englishman's Home, The. Harry Graham. CBNP; PeLV *Fr.* Some Ruthless Rhymes.

Engraved on the case. Gold Watch. Patrick Kavanagh. InPS-3

Engraved on the Collar of a Dog, Which I Gave to His Royal Highness. Alexander Pope. *See* Epigram Engraved on the Collar of a Dog Given [*or* Which I Gave] to His Royal Highness.

Enhancement of life. Blood's to defeat its preordination or. Quasi Quasi. . . as If Repeated. Glenda George. NBrP

Enhances Nature now. (LL) Further in Summer than the Birds. Emily Dickinson. APN-2; AmPP; NOBA; NoP-4; PoE; PoEL-5

Enigma. Catherine Maria Fanshawe. OBCoV

Enigma, An. Edgar Allan Poe. Son

Enigma. Matthew Prior. PeLV

Enigma No. 6. Augusta Davies Webster. VWP

Enigma rules, and the heart has no certainty. (LL) Flux. Richard Eberhart. Poetsp; VGW

Enigma Variations. David Lehman. NAmP90

Enigma Variations. The. Paul Petrie. NYBP

Enigma was plagued with vertigo, The. Romance. Richard Stull. EOEF

Enigmatical, tremulous. The Barrel-Organ. Arthur Symons. NOBVV

Enion Replies from the Caverns of the Grave. William Blake. OBNC *Fr.* Vala; or The Four Zoas.

Enion's Lamentation. William Blake. *See* Night II (Enion's Lament).

Enitharmon Revives with Los. William Blake. OBNC *Fr.* Vala; or The Four Zoas.

Enjoy it a', ye've nae mair for't. (LL) Ode to Mr. F— [*or* Mr. Forbes]. Allan Ramsay, *after* Horace. NOEC; OBVE

Enjoy such liberty. Richard Lovelace. *See* To Althea, from Prison.

Enjoy your fortune as if you were about to die. Lucianus, *Greek.* GrAn, tr. by Edwin Morgan

Enjoy your time, my soul! another race. Enjoyment. Theognis, *Greek.* AWP, tr. by John Hookham Frere

Enjoyed them precisely with a sharp pencil. (LL) The Cancer Cells. Richard Eberhart. HAP; LiTM

Enjoying Coolness. Wang Wei, *Chinese.* SuSp, tr. by Hugh M. Stimson

Enjoying [*or* Injoying] of myself I lie [*or* lye]. (LL) Love Made in the First Age[: To Chloris]. Richard Lovelace. BeJo; CaPo; NAEL-1; OAEL-1; SeCP

Enjoying Retirement ("Beside green water"). Ma Chih-yüan. *Fr.* Three Poems to the Tune "Ssu-k'uai yü." CoBLCP, tr. by Jonathan Chaves

Enjoying Retirement (ldquo;The wine just purchased"). Ma Chih-yüan. *Fr.* Three Poems to the Tune "Ssu-k'uai yü." CoBLCP, tr. by Jonathan Chaves

Enjoyment. Theognis, *Greek.* AWP, tr. by John Hookham Frere

Enjoyment of sex, although great, The. Limerick. *Unknown.* PeLi

Enkindled Spring, The. D. H. Lawrence. NoAM

Enlarge your fortifications, Zeus. Philip of Macedon. Alcaeus, *Greek.* GrAn, tr. by Alistair Elliot

Enlightenment. Ch'en Yü-yi, *Chinese.* OHMPC, tr. by Kenneth Rexroth

Enlisted on the other front. (LL) Beach Burial. Kenneth Slessor. CBAP

Enlisted Today. *Unknown.* CBCWP

Enmeshed in steel stands a stone. The Captive Stone. Jim Barnes. CDW

Enmeshment. Lewis Warsh. FTOS

Enmeshment is an enter. Closure. Douglas Messerli. FTOS

Ennui. Langston Hughes. OBAL; OBCA

Ennui. Peter Viereck. NYBP

Enobarbus, Antony. Shakespeare. OxAEP-1 *Fr.* Antony and Cleopatra.

Enoch. Bible, Pseudepigrapha.

    Seven Metal Mountains. TrJP

Enoch. Jones Very. ChIV-1; HAP

ENORMOUS BLISS of American death, The. Reading Frank O'Hara in a Mexican Rainstorm. Michael McClure. BB

Enormous cloud-mountains that form over Point Lobos and into the sunset. Clouds of Evening. Robinson Jeffers. MoAmPo

Enormous Hand, The. Jorge de Lima, *Portuguese*. PFTM, *tr. by* June Jordan

Enormous tragedy of the dream in the peasant's bent / shoulders, The. Ezra Pound. AF *Fr.* Pisan Canto 124.

Enosis. Christopher Pearse Cranch. *See* Gnosis.

Enough! John Bunyan. *See* The Shepherd Boy Sings [in the Valley of Humiliation].

Enough. Digby Mackworth Dolben. EBVV

Enough. Tom Masson. OBAL

Enough. Marianne Moore. NOBA

Enough: and leave the rest to fame. An Epitaph upon —. Andrew Marvell. OBEV

Enough, Catullus, of this silly whining. Catullus, *Latin*. LoP, *tr. by* James Michie

Enough complaining. An Arab Chieftain to His Young Wife. Abid ibn al-Abras, *Arabic*. ArPe, *tr. by* Omar S. Pound

Enough for you. (LL) For Bud. Michael S. Harper. MoNo

Enough is never enough—That voice comes back—Suave. Stan Rice. MoLi *Fr.* Incanto.

Enough kind Heaven! to purpose I have liv'd. To Mrs. W. on Her Excellent Verses. Aphra Behn. KTR

Enough! Let this season end. Arthur Gregor. TAP

Enough, my Muse, of earthly things. Christ's Passion. Abraham Cowley. ChIV-2

Enough of snivelling! Shove our papers in the desk. Osip Emilevich Mandelstam, *Russian*. TCRP, *tr. by* Bernard Meares

Enough of those who study the oblique. A Good Resolution. Roy Campbell. OBSV

Enough of Thought, Philosopher. The Philosopher. Emily Jane Brontë. BWW

"Enough," she said. But the dust still rained around [or about] her. Dust. Randolph Stow. CBAP

Enough snow over last night's ice. Mercy. Bruce Weigl. CDa

Enough to make him homesick, what home was / really like. (LL) I've Got a Home in That Rock. Raymond R. Patterson. MBE

Enough! we're tired, my heart and I. My Heart and I. Elizabeth Barrett Browning. VWP

Enough when it's not just a game? (LL) Step on His Head. James Laughlin. IFJA

Enough! Why should a man bemoan. Per Iter Tenebricosum. Oliver St. John Gogarty. OBMV

Enough women over thirty are at Redbones. Raising a Humid Flag. Thylias Moss. GT

Enough's enough: don't wait, don't hope. Despair. Andrey Bely, *Russian*. TCRP, *tr. by* Bernard Meares

Enquiry after Peace. A Fragment. Anne Finch, Countess of Winchilsea. ECWP; PoE

Enraptured by earth, rain and sunrise. Ten Girls. Luchezar Elenkov, *Bulgarian*. CEEP, *tr. by* Ewald Osers

Enrica, 1865. Christina Rossetti. NALW

Enrich my resignation as I usurp those far. Hart Crane. PoA

Ensamples of Our Savior. Robert Southwell. PoEL-2

Enslaved. Claude McKay. BPo; NAAAL

Enslaved by passions, swelled with pride. The Execration. Elizabeth Thomas. ECWP

Ensnaring Flower of Psalms. Rossana Ombres, *Italian*. NeIt, *tr. by* Ruth Feldman

Ensuing Copy the Late Printer Hath Been Pleased to Honour, by Mistaking It Among Those of the Most Ingenious and Too Early Lost Sir John Suckling, The. Sir John Suckling *and* Owen Feltham (c.1602–1668). *See* Song: "When, dearest, I but think on [or of] thee."

Entailed Farm, The. John Glassco. MoCV; NOBC

Entangled. Mathilde Blind. VWP

Entanglement. Francis Sparshott. MoCV

Enter and learn the story of the rulers. Inscriptions on the City of Brass. *Unknown*. AWP *Fr.* The Thousand and One Nights.

Enter and see this tomb, sirs, do not fear. Epitaph on Some Bottles of Sack and Claret Laid in Sand. Robert Wild. NOSC

Enter Harlem. Walk with de Mayor of Harlem. David Henderson. PoBA

Enter in the circle. Edouard J. Maunick. NegPo, *tr. by* Ellen Conroy Kennedy *Fr.* As Far as Yoruba Land.

Enter the dream-house, brothers and sisters, leaving. Newsreel. C. Day Lewis. MoBrPo

Enter the story here: their battle lost. The Story. Kevin Hart. BMAP

Enter without knocking, hard–working ant. This Morning. Charles Simic. BAP-93

Entered [or Enter'd or Entred] for both, far[re] above their desert! (LL) Obedience. George Herbert. ESCV; GeHe

Entered in the Minutes. Louis MacNeice.

Night Club. OxBSP

Entered that brilliant intimate. Only Alice. Josephine Jacobsen. FFC

Entered to race, Barabbas was scratched. The Passion of Jesus Considered as an Uphill Race. Alfred Jarry, *French*. PFTM, *tr. by* Gary Fletcher

Entering—takes away, The. (LL) I had been hungry, all the Years. Emily Dickinson. ImPo; LiTM; MeMAP; MoAmPo; NALW; SAmP; WPoS

Entering the hall, she meets the new wife. The Ejected Wife. *Unknown, Chinese*. OBVE, *tr. by* Arthur Waley

Entering the Mouth of P'eng-li Lake. Hsieh Ling-yün, *Chinese*. SuSp, *tr. by* Francis Westbrook

Entering the publisher's warehouse, a foreign young lady. Anecdote from William IV Street. D. J. Enright. OxBC

Enters—and is lost in Balms. (LL) Come slowly—Eden! Emily Dickinson. CMoP; FaBoVe; NALW; NCAP

Entertained by song and dance here in this wine pavilion. Pleasures of Shinbashi. Liu E, *Chinese*. CoBLCP, *tr. by* Jonathan Chaves

Entertainer, The. Bruce Beaver. NOBAu

Entertainment Industry, The, *mod. by* Donald Attwater. William Langland. NOCV *Fr.* The Vision of Piers Plowman.

Entertainment of War, The. Roy Fisher. FaBoMo

Entertainment, or Porch-Verse, at the Marriage of Mr. Henry Northleigh [or Hen. Northly] and the Most Witty Mrs. Lettice Yard, The. Robert Herrick. CaPo

Enthrone thy Rosy-selfe within mine Eyes. (LL) The Reflexion. Edward Taylor. ChIV-1, *sect.* IV, (*Division* I); AmPP; MeMAP; OxBA

Enthusiast, The. Herman Melville. ChIV-1; NAAL-1; NAAL-3

Enthusiast, The; or, The Lover of Nature. Joseph Warton. PoEL-3

"Ye green-robed Dryads, oft at dusky eve." ECEV, *ll.* 1–15; NOEC

Enthusiastically hurting a clouded yellow bud and. A New Cup and Saucer. Gertrude Stein. TTTS *Fr.* Tender Buttons.

Enticed to the release of the sky. (LL) Seals, Terns, Time. Richard Eberhart. LiTM, MoAmPo

Entire country is overrun with private property, The. Gypsy. Josephine Miles. MoP; NoAM

Entire, more than entire have we been devastated! Tears of the Fatherland, Anno Domini 1636. Andreas Gryphius, *German*. GePo, *tr. by* George C. Schoolfield

Entire night, An. Giuseppe Ungaretti. *See* Vigil.

Entirely. Louis MacNeice. CMoP

Entirely beautiful, The. (LL) Lullaby: "Lay your sleeping head, my love." W. H. Auden. PiM

Entrain airport: New York, Chicago, west. Valediction to My Contemporaries. Horace Gregory. MoAmPo

Entrance and exit wounds are silvered clean. Recalling War. Robert Graves. AF; CMoP; LiTM; NoAM; OAEL-2; OBWP; PeFWW; PoWW

Entreaty. Robert Fitzgerald. OxBSP

Entrepreneur chicken shed his tail feathers, surplus, The. Josephine Miles. MoP; NoAM

Entropic Villanelle. Thomas M. Disch. RA

Entry in an Unknown Hand. Franz Wright. CMAP; NAmP90

Entwined on the bed in the dark. Two Shapes. Arthur Gregor. TAP

Enueg I. Samuel Beckett. CIP-2

Enueg II. Samuel Beckett. NoAM

Enumeration. Ilse Aichinger, *German*. AF, *tr. by* Chappel, Allen H.

Envelope, The. Maxine W. Kumin. CrSp; NALW

Envelope looks so peculiar, The. Aleksandr Semionovich Kushner, *Russian*. TCRP, *tr. by* Paul Graves *and* Carol Ueland

Enveloping Echo, The. Ion Caraion, *Romanian*. AF; CEEP, *tr. by* Marguerite Dorian *and* Elliott B. Urdang

Enviable Isles, The. Herman Melville. NCAP

Envies, The. George Bowering. NOBC

Envious and foul disease, could there not be. An Epigram. To the Small-Pox. Ben Jonson. NOSC

Envious wits, what hath been mine offence. Sonnet 104. Sir Philip Sidney. PoE; Son *Fr.* Astrophil and Stella. AAS; SiPS

Environment. Lionel Kearns. NOBC

Environs. Larry Eigner. FTOS; NeAP

Environs of Vanholt I. Charles Spear. PeNZ

Envisioning faces where the streets have parted. (LL) The Rebirth of Venus. Mary Jo Salter. FFC; WWSi

Envoi: "Earth puts her colours by." P. H. B. Lyon. BoTP

Envoi: "Go little book, par avion." Richard Tillinghast. MT

Envoi: "God, thou great symmetry." Anna Wickham. MoBrPo

Envoi. "Hear me, whom I betrayed." James Vincent Cunningham. VGW

Envoi. James McAuley. BMAP

Envoi: "My country is not a country." Eli W. Mandel. NOBC

Envoi: "Princess, you trapped a guileless Mayor." G. K. Chesterton. OxBoV

Envoi: "Sun in the mouth of the day." Robley Wilson Jr. PBCAP

Envoi: "Take of me what is not my own." Kathleen Jessie Raine. NOBE

Envoi: "There's a whisper down the field where the year has shot her yield." Rudyard Kipling. OBEV

Envoi: "What has want to give." Kathleen Jessie Raine. WPE

Envoi: "Go, dumb-born book." Ezra Pound. *See* Envoi (1919).

Envoi, L': "Who findeth comfort in the stars and flowers." Thomas Lovell Beddoes. OBNC *Fr.* Death's Jest Book.

Envoi (1919). Ezra Pound. HAP; MoP; UnPO; VGW *Fr.* Hugh Selwyn Mauberley. (Life and Contacts). AmPP; CMoP; InPS-3; LiTM; NOBA; NoAM; TAP

   (Envoi: "Go, dumb-born book.") MoAmPo; OxBA

Envoi: Washington Square Park. Myra Cohn Livingston. SSCS

Envoy: "Go, songs, for ended is our brief, sweet play." Francis Thompson. MoBrPo

Envoy: "Good Night, at last." Robert Duncan. VGW *Fr.* Passages.

Envoy: "Legend of Felix is ended, the toiling of Felix is done, The." Henry Van Dyke. BLPA *Fr.* The Toiling of Felix.

Envoy: "They are not long, the weeping and the laughter." Ernest Christopher Dowson. *See* Vitae Summa Brevis Spem Nos Vetat Incohare Longam.

Envoy to Scogan. Chaucer. EnVB

Envy. "Naum Korzhavin," *Russian*. TCRP, *tr.* by Vladimir Lunis and Albert C. Todd

Envy. Charles Lamb *and* Mary Lamb (1764–1847). OxBChV; WoRP

Envy. Adelaide Anne Procter. NOBVV; VWP

Envy. Edmund Spenser. *Fr.* Wood Of Error. AEP

Envy of Poor Lovers, The. Austin Clarke. CIP-2; CMoP

Envy the mad killer who lies in the ditch and grieves. Crime. Robert Penn Warren. FuPo

Envy, why carpest thou my time is spent so ill. Ovid. *See* Elegies 1.15.

Envy with heavy heart asked for shrift. William Langland. NAEL-1 *Fr.* The Vision of Piers Plowman.

Envying the Pelican. Richard Weber. CIP-2

Enzensberger at 'Exiles'. John Tranter. BMAP

Eolian Harp, The. Coleridge. FHYEP; NAEL-2; NOBRP; OAEL-2 *Fr.* Effusions.

   (Aeolian Harp, The.) NoP-4

   ("My pensive Sara.") NoP-4; Ro

   ("Peace, and this Cot, and thee, heart-honored Maid!") (LL) NoP-4; Ro

Ephemeral Past, The. Antonio Machado Ruiz, *Spanish*. NNPT, *tr.* by Charles Tomlinson *and* Henry Gifford

Ephesos. Duris, *Greek*. GrAn, *tr.* by Peter Jay

Ephraim Repenting. William Cowper. ChIV-1 *Fr.* Olney Hymns.

Epi-Strauss-ium. Arthur Hugh Clough. EnVR; NAEL-2

Epic. Patrick Kavanagh. BIrV; CABP; CIP-2; NOIV; NoP-4

Epic, The [Morte d'Arthur], *conclusion to* Morte d'Arthur. Tennyson. NAEL-2 *Fr.* Morte d'Arthur. EnVR

Epic, The [Morte d'Arthur], *introduction to* Morte d'Arthur. Tennyson. NAEL-2 *Fr.* Morte d'Arthur. EnVR

Epicoene; or, The Silent Woman. Ben Jonson.

   Clerimont's Song. NOSC; OAEL-1; PoE; SeCP

   ("Still to be neat, still to be dressed.") NoP-4; PoPoPo

Epicure, The. Abraham Cowley. OxAEP-1

Epicure, The ("Fill the bowl with rosie [*or* rosy] wine"). Abraham Cowley. BeJo; SeCP

Epicure, Dining at Crewe, An. Limerick. *Unknown*. NBLV; NTCP; PeLi; PeLV

Epicure, The, Sung by One in the Habit of a Town Gallant. Thomas Jordan. *See* The Careless Gallant.

Epicure ("Underneath this myrtle shade, The"). Abraham Cowley, *after the Greek of* Anacreon. AWP; OBEV

   (Another.) SeCP

   "Crown me with roses whilest I live." OBVE

Epicurean. William James Linton. EBVV

Epicurean Ode, An. John Hall. CBLP; MeLP; NOSC

Epicurean Reminiscences of a Sentimentalist. Thomas Hood. CBNP; PeLV

Epicurus praised. Lucretius, *Latin*. OBCVT, *tr.* by Thomas Creech

Epidaurus: / you loved it. Hilda Morley. EC2

Epidemic / of freedom, An. Vyacheslav Kupriyanov, *Russian*. TCRP, *tr.* by Albert C. Todd

Epiderm. Michael Dransfield. BMAP; CBAP

Epigoni Go French Line. Turner Cassity. WeT

Epigram. Ebenezer Elliot. *See* On Communists.

Epigram. Samuel Johnson. *See* The Turnip Vendor.

Epigram. Su Tung-p'o. OHPC

Epigram: "After some years Bohemian came to this." James Vincent Cunningham. VGW

Epigram: "And now I, Meleager, am among them." Meleager, *Greek*. GrAn, *tr.* by Peter Whigham

Epigram: "And now you're ready who while she was here." James Vincent Cunningham. *Fr.* Five Epigrams.

Epigram: "And what is love? Misunderstanding, pain." James Vincent Cunningham. CRP; HAP; HoPM; PoA

Epigram: "As honey in wine / wine, honey." Meleager, *Greek*. GrAn, *tr.* by Peter Whigham

Epigram: "As the body denies the means to look." Pernette De Guillet, *French*. PBWP, *tr.* by Joan Keefe *and* Richard Terdiman

Epigram: "At ten a clock, when I the fire rake." Francis Daniel Pastorius. SCAP

Epigram: "At 12 o'clock in the afternoon." Meleager, *Greek*. GrAn, *tr.* by Peter Whigham

   (At 12 O'clock.) EP, *tr.* by Peter Whigham

Epigram: "Because I am idolatrous and have besought." Ernest Christopher Dowson. OxBSP

Epigram: "Boy's cocks, Diodore." Strato, *Greek*. GrAn, *tr.* by Thomas Meyer

Epigram: "Breath of my life, The—no less." Meleager, *Greek*. GrAn, *tr.* by Peter Whigham

Epigram: "Broad and ample he warms himself." *Unknown*, *Irish*. NOIV, *tr.* by Thomas Kinsella

Epigram: "Could Beatrice have written like Dante." "Anna Akhmatova," *Russian*. TCRP, *tr.* by Stanley Kunitz *with* Max Hayward

Epigram: "Dark thoughts are my companions. I have wined." James Vincent Cunningham. VGW

Epigram: "Dear, if unsocial privacies obsess me." James Vincent Cunningham. VGW

Epigram: "'Do you not wish to renounce the Devil?'." Armand Lanusse, *French*. TTY, *tr.* by Langston Hughes

Epigram: "Fair Beatrice tucks her coat up somewhat high." John Taylor. NOSC

Epigram: "Gold priests, wooden chalices." *Unknown*, *Irish*. NOIV, *tr.* by Thomas Kinsella

Epigram: "Golden casket I designed, A." John Swanwick Drennan. BIrV

Epigram: "Golden one is gone from the banquets, The." Hilda Doolittle. PoA

Epigram: "Good Fortune, when I hailed her recently." James Vincent Cunningham. VCAP

Epigram: "Great woe, fire & war come on me." Skythinos, *Greek*. GrAn, *tr.* by Thomas Meyer

Epigram: "Heat goes deep as cold." *Unknown*, *Irish*. NOIV, *tr.* by Thomas Kinsella

Epigram: "Here lies my wife. Eternal peace." James Vincent Cunningham. NIP-4; OBAL

Epigram: "Here lies New Critic who would fox us." James Vincent Cunningham. MoAmPo; OBAL

Epigram: "Hetero-sex is best for the man of a serious turn of mind." Argentarius, *Greek*. GrAn, *tr.* by Fleur Adcock

Epigram: "Homer was poor. His scholars live at ease." James Vincent Cunningham. VGW

Epigram: "How we desire desire! Joy of surcease." James Vincent Cunningham. VGW

Epigram: "I am provoked." Strato, *Greek*. GrAn, *tr.* by W. G. Shepherd

Epigram: "I delight in the prime of a boy of twelve." Strato, *Greek*. GrAn, *tr.* by Thomas Meyer

Epigram: "I had gone broke, and got set to come back." James Vincent Cunningham. MoAmPo; OxBSP; VCAP

Epigram: "I loved thee beautiful and kind." Robert, Earl Nugent Nugent. NOEC

Epigram: "I was thirsty." Meleager, *Greek*. GrAn, *tr.* by Peter Whigham

Epigram: "I who by day am function of the light." James Vincent Cunningham. VGW

Epigram: "If men be judged wise." Joseph Solomon Del Medigo, *Hebrew*. TrJP

Epigram: "In whose will is our peace? Thou happiness." James Vincent Cunningham. VGW

Epigram: "It is true that I held Thero fair." Meleager, *Greek*. GrAn, *tr.* by Peter Whigham

Epigram: "King, observing with judicious eyes, The." Joseph Trapp. FaBoEE

Epigram: "King to Oxford sent a troop of horse, The." Sir William Browne. FaBoEE

Epigram: "Kissing Hippomenes, I crave." Paulus Silentiarius, *Greek*. GrAn, *tr.* by Andrew Miller

Epigram: "Lasses, like nuts at bottom brown." Allan Ramsay. FaBoEE

Epigram: "Life flows to death as rivers to the sea." James Vincent Cunningham. VGW

Epigram: "Long hair, endless curls trained by the devoted." Strato, *Greek.* GrAn, *tr. by* Teddy Hogge

Epigram: "Look how yon lecher's legs are worn away." John Taylor. NOSC

Epigram: "Loss of our learning brought darkness, weakness and woe." *Unknown, Greek.* NOIV, *tr. by* Thomas Kinsella

Epigram: "Love signed the contract blithe and leal." John Swanwick Drennan. BIrV

Epigram: "Lusty wench as nimble as an eel, A." John Taylor. NOSC

Epigram: "Member of the modern great, A." John Cunningham. FaBoEE

Epigram: "Midas, they say, possessed the art of old." "Peter Pindar." NIP-4

Epigram: "Milo's from home; and, Milo being gone." Martial, *Latin.* OBVE, *tr. by* Elijah Fenton

Epigram: "My heart still hovering round about you." Robert, Earl Nugent Nugent. NOEC

Epigram: "My soul, sit thou a patient looker-on." Francis Quarles. NOBE; PoToHe

(Epigram: Respice Finem.) OBEV

Epigram: "My soul, thy love is dear: 'twas thought a good." Francis Quarles. OAEL-1 *Fr.* Emblems.

Epigram: "Naked I came, naked I leave the scene." James Vincent Cunningham. *See* Epitaph for Someone or Other.

Epigram: "Need from excess—excess from folly growing." Samuel Bishop. NOEC

Epigram: "Nicander, ooh, your leg's got hairs!" Alcaeus, *Greek.* GrAn, *tr. by* Tony Harrison

Epigram: "On parent knees, a naked new-born child." Sir William Jones, *after the Sanskrit of* Kalidasa. FaBoEE; OBEV

(Moral Tetrastich, A.) OxBSP

Epigram: "Poverty? wealth? seek neither." Kassia, *Greek.* WPOW, *tr. by* Patrick Diehl

Epigram: "'Prepare to meet the King of Terrors,' cried." Ebenezer Elliot. NOBVV

Epigram: "Says a Reverend Priest to a less Rev'rend friend." *Unknown.* NOBRP

Epigram: "Since first you knew my am'rous smart." Robert, Earl Nugent Nugent. NOEC

Epigram: "There chanced to meet together in an inn." John Taylor. NOSC

Epigram: "There was this gym-teacher." Strato, *Greek.* GrAn, *tr. by* Teddy Hogge

Epigram: "This is my curse, Pompous, I pray." James Vincent Cunningham. HAP

Epigram: "Those snooty boys in all their purple drag!" Strato, *Greek.* GrAn, *tr. by* Tony Harrison

Epigram: "Thy nags (the leanest things alive)." Matthew Prior. FaBoEE

Epigram: "Time heals not: it extends a sorrow's scope." James Vincent Cunningham. IMW; VGW

Epigram: "Time was when once upon a time, such toys." Glaukos, *Greek.* GrAn, *tr. by* Peter Jay

Epigram: "This *Humanist* Whom No Beliefs Constrained." James Vincent Cunningham. RB; VGW

Epigram: "To John I ow'd great obligation." Matthew Prior. FaBoEE; OBVE

(Quits.) AWP

Epigram: "Tom's sickness did his morals mend." Matthew Prior. FaBoEE

Epigram: "'Twas not so in my time,' surly Grumio exclaims." Samuel Bishop. NOEC

Epigram: "Wealth covers sin—the poor." Kassia, *Greek.* WPOW, *tr. by* Patrick Diehl

Epigram: "Were I a king, I could command content." Edward De Vere. *See* Poem: "Were I a king, I could command content."

Epigram: "When Bibo thought fit from the world to retreat." Matthew Prior. FaBoEE

Epigram: "When other Ladies to the Shades go down." Alexander Pope. OxBSP; PoEL-3

(Bibo.) CBNP

Epigram: "While Adam slept, from him his Eve arose." *Unknown.* FaBoEE

Epigram: "Whilst maudlin Whigs deplore their Cato's fate." Nicholas Rowe. ECEV

Epigram: "Why all the racket, you chattering birds?" *Unknown, Greek.* GrAn, *tr. by* Thomas Meyer

Epigram: "Wife, there are some points on which we differ from each other." Martial, *Latin.* OxBM

Epigram: "Within this mindless vault." James Vincent Cunningham. RB; VGW

Epigram: "Woman working hard and wisely, A." Kassia, *Greek.* WPOW, *tr. by* Patrick Diehl

Epigram: "Women, as some men say, unconstant be." George Wither. NOSC

Epigram: "World laid low, and the wind blew like a dust, The." *Unknown, Irish.* NOIV, *tr. by* Thomas Kinsella

Epigram: "Yes, every poet is a fool." Matthew Prior. FaBoEE

Epigram: "You ask me how Contempt who claims to sleep." James Vincent Cunningham. VCAP

Epigram: "You were a pretty boy once, Archestratus, and." Philip of Thessalonica, *Greek.* GrAn, *tr. by* Edith Morgan

Epigram I: "Thou Guide to doubt, be silent evermore." *Unknown. Fr.* Duel with Verses over a Great Man. TrJP

Epigram II: "Thou fool profane, be silent!" *Unknown. Fr.* Duel with Verses over a Great Man. TrJP

Epigram III: "Forgive us, son of Amram, be not wroth." *Unknown. Fr.* Duel with Verses over a Great Man. TrJP

Epigram IV: "What thought ye to burn, when ye kindled the pyre." *Unknown. Fr.* Duel with Verses over a Great Man. TrJP

Epigram IV.v: Of Treason. Sir John Harington. *See* Of Treason.

Epigram V: "Against the guide of Truth." *Unknown. Fr.* Duel with Verses over a Great Man. TrJP

Epigram VII: Winifred. Hugh Crompton. NOSC

Epigram LXVII: Time, the Interpreter. Hugh Crompton. NOSC

Epigram 29: "Gentlewoman of the dealing trade, A." Samuel Rowlands. NOSC

Epigram 34: "Lesbia, why are your amours." Martial, *Latin.* EP, *tr. by* James Michie

Epigram, A Supposed Construction. John Taylor. NOSC

Epigram: Dutch, The. George Canning. *See* The Dutch.

Epigram Engraved on the Collar of a Dog Given [*or* Which I Gave] to His Royal Highness. Alexander Pope. FaBoEE; InPK-6; NOEC; NTCP; OxBSP

(Engraved on the Collar of a Dog, Which I Gave to His Royal Highness.) ImPo; OxBoLi; SoSe-8; TTTS

Epigram from the French: "Sir, I admit your general [*or* gen'ral] Rule." Alexander Pope, *also at. to* Matthew Prior *and to* Coleridge. FaBoEE

(Fool and the Poet, The.) NBLV

Epigram in a Maid of Honour's Prayer-Book. Alexander Pope. FaBoEE

Epigram on a Lawyer's Desiring One of the Tribe to Look with Respect to a Gibbet. Robert Fergusson. OxBS

Epigram on an Academic Visit to the Continent. Richard Porson. OxBoLi; PeLV

(Porson's Visit to the Continent.) FaBoEE

Epigram on Fasting. Jonathan Swift. OBVE

Epigram on Florio. John Winstanley. FaBoEE

Epigram: On Inclosures. *Unknown.* OxBoLi

(On Enclosures.) FaBoEE

Epigram on Milton. Dryden. *See* Lines Printed under the Engraved Portrait of Milton [In Tonson's Folio of the "Paradise Lost"].

Epigram on One Who Made Long Epitaphs. Alexander Pope. FaBoEE

Epigram on Scolding, An. Jonathan Swift. FaBoEE; FaBoVe

Epigram: On Sir Roger Phillimore. *Unknown.* NBLV

Epigram on the Feuds between Handel and Bononcini. John Byrom. FaBoEE; NOBL; NOEC

Epigram on the First of April. John Winstanley. NOEC

Epigram on Woman, An. Philip Ayres. FaBoEE

Epigram out of Plato To Madam Amara, An. *Unknown, Greek.* OBCVT, *tr. by* Charles Goodall

Epigram: Political Reflexion. Howard Nemerov. *See* The Sparrow in the Zoo.

Epigram: Respice Finem. Francis Quarles. *See* Epigram: "My soul, sit thou a patient looker-on."

Epigram. To the Household. 1630, An. Ben Jonson. BeJo; Son

Epigram. To the Small-Pox, An. Ben Jonson. NOSC

Epigrams. Antipater of Sidon, *Greek.*

"Artemeias, surely when you from the nether world's bark." HePo, *tr. by* Barbara Hughes Fowler

"Here beside the threshing floor, O hardworking ant." HePo, *tr. by* Barbara Hughes Fowler

"I, who used to ward off the starlings and that snatcher." HePo, *tr. by* Barbara Hughes Fowler

"Let the four-clustered ivy flourish about you, Anacreon." HePo, *tr. by* Barbara Hughes Fowler

"Myriad times, Ptolemy, your father, myriad times." HePo, *tr. by* Barbara Hughes Fowler

"Tell me, woman, your parents, your name, your land. B. Calliteles." HePo, *tr. by* Barbara Hughes Fowler

"This is the barrow of grizzled Maronis, on which you see." HePo, *tr. by* Barbara Hughes Fowler

"To Pallas, three girls, all of an age, skilled as the spider." HePo, *tr. by* Barbara Hughes Fowler

"To Pan three brothers hung up these tools of the trade." HePo, *tr. by* Barbara Hughes Fowler

Epigrams. Anyte, *Greek.*

"Children, billy goat, have put crimson reins, The." HePo, *tr. by* Barbara Hughes Fowler

"For her locust, nightingale of the fields, and her cricket that slept." HePo, *tr. by* Barbara Hughes Fowler

"No longer, as before, will you wake at dawn and flap." HePo, *tr. by* Barbara Hughes Fowler

"No longer shall I exult in the floating seas and arch." HePo, *tr. by* Barbara Hughes Fowler

"Often on this her daughter's tomb did Cleina grieve." HePo, *tr. by* Barbara Hughes Fowler

"This tomb Damis built for his courageous horse." HePo, *tr. by* Barbara Hughes Fowler

Epigrams. Asclepiades, *Greek.*

"I am not yet twenty-two and I am tired of living." HePo, *tr. by* Barbara Hughes Fowler

"Lysidice dedicated to you, Cypris." HePo, *tr. by* Barbara Hughes Fowler

"This is the sweet work of Erinna, not much, of course." HePo, *tr. by* Barbara Hughes Fowler

Epigrams. Bassus, *Greek.*

"I'm not planning to turn into gold. Somebody else." HePo, *tr. by* Barbara Hughes Fowler

Epigrams. Callimachus, *Greek.*

"At dawn we buried Melanippus. At sunset." HePo, *tr. by* Barbara Hughes Fowler

"Do not say 'Godspeed' to me, wicked heart." HePo, *tr. by* Barbara Hughes Fowler

"'Goodbye, O sun,' said Cleombrotus of Ambracia." HePo, *tr. by* Barbara Hughes Fowler

"Here Philip the father buried." HePo, *tr. by* Barbara Hughes Fowler

"Hesiod's is the theme and his the style." HePo, *tr. by* Barbara Hughes Fowler

"I hate the cyclic poem, nor do I rejoice." HePo, *tr. by* Barbara Hughes Fowler

"On the mountain, Epicydes the hunter seeks." HePo, *tr. by* Barbara Hughes Fowler

"Someone told me, Heracleitus." HePo, *tr. by* Barbara Hughes Fowler

("For Death, he taketh all away, but them he cannot take.") (LL) OBCVT, *tr. by* William Johnson Cory

("They told me, Heraclitus, they told me you were dead.") OBCVT, *tr. by* William Johnson Cory

"These gifts to Aphrodite." HePo, *tr. by* Barbara Hughes Fowler

"Timon, for you exist no more." HePo, *tr. by* Barbara Hughes Fowler

"Whoever passes by my tomb, know." HePo, *tr. by* Barbara Hughes Fowler

"Would that there had never been swift ships!" HePo, *tr. by* Barbara Hughes Fowler

"You pass the tomb of Battus' son, well skilled." HePo, *tr. by* Barbara Hughes Fowler

Epigrams. Crinagoras, *Greek.*

"You toss now to the left; you toss now to the right." HePo,, *tr. by* Barbara Hughes Fowler

Epigrams. Sir John Davies.

"Amongst the poets Dacus numbered is." NoSic

"Cosmus hath more discoursing in his head." NoSic; PBRV

("As none at all can perfect passage finde.") (LL) PBRV

"Fine youth Ciprius is more terse and neat, The." NoSic

"Philo the gentleman, the fortune teller." NoSic

"Titus the brave and valorous gallant." NoSic

Epigrams. Dioscorides, *Greek.*

"Call me Polyxena, the wife of Archelaus." HePo, *tr. by* Barbara Hughes Fowler

"Eros, that bane of men, molded soft as marrow." HePo, *tr. by* Barbara Hughes Fowler

"Lamisca, who breathed her last in lamentable pangs of labor." HePo, *tr. by* Barbara Hughes Fowler

"They drive me mad, those rosy lips, forever prattling." HePo, *tr. by* Barbara Hughes Fowler

Epigrams. Diotimus, *Greek.*

"Polyaenus' daughter, Scyllis, came to the wide gates." HePo, *tr. by* Barbara Hughes Fowler

"What use to suffer in labor, give birth to children, if she." HePo, *tr. by* Barbara Hughes Fowler

Epigrams. Erinna, *Greek.*

"I am the grave of Baucis the bride. Passing by." HePo, *tr. by* Barbara Hughes Fowler

"Stele and my Sirens and mournful pitcher that hold." HePo, *tr. by* Barbara Hughes Fowler

Epigrams. Leonidas of Tarentum, *Greek.*

Fisherman, The. AWP, *tr. by* Andrew Lang

"Forever brigands and pirates, the Cretans are never just." HePo, *tr. by* Barbara Hughes Fowler

"Get out of my hut, you stealthy vermin! Leonidas'." HePo, *tr. by* Barbara Hughes Fowler

"Gloomy minister of Hades who sail this stream." HePo, *tr. by* Barbara Hughes Fowler

"His ball, beautiful leaved, and his noisy boxwood rattle." HePo, *tr. by* Barbara Hughes Fowler

"If the tombstone placed over me is small to see and close." HePo, *tr. by* Barbara Hughes Fowler

"Old Platthis often thrust away her morning's sleep." HePo, *tr. by* Barbara Hughes Fowler

Spinning Woman, The. AWP, *tr. by* Andrew Lang

"Theris, thrice-old, who got his living from." HePo, *tr. by* Barbara Hughes Fowler

"Thundering sea, why in savage storm did you plunge." HePo, *tr. by* Barbara Hughes Fowler

"To Gluttony and Guzzling, that fastidious gourmet." HePo, *tr. by* Barbara Hughes Fowler

"To Pallas, Theris, cunning of hand, dedicated." HePo, *tr. by* Barbara Hughes Fowler

"Wallet, the hide of a goat, tough and untanned, a stick, A." HePo, *tr. by* Barbara Hughes Fowler

"Whoever then are you? Whose wretched bones are these." HePo, *tr. by* Barbara Hughes Fowler

Epigrams. Meleager. *See* I'll Twine White Violets.

Epigrams. Mnasalcas, *Greek.*

"Say, stranger, that this is the tomb of the mare Aethyia." HePo, *tr. by* Barbara Hughes Fowler

Epigrams. Howard Nemerov.

Absent-Minded Professor. OBAL

April. OBAL

Hunt Goes By, The. OBAL

Invocation: "Wasp, climbing the window pane." OBAL

"Lucilius the poet has informed me." OBAL

Mythological Beast. OBAL

Old Story, An. OBAL

Sparrow in the Zoo, The. MoP; OBAL

(Epigram: Political Reflexion.) NIP-4

Spiral Shell, A. OBAL

Epigrams. Philodemus, *Greek.*

"I fell in love with Demo of Paphos. No big surprise." HePo, *tr. by* Barbara Hughes Fowler

"In the middle of the night I slipped away from my husband." HePo, *tr. by* Barbara Hughes Fowler

"I've been in love. Who hasn't? I went out and got drunk." HePo, *tr. by* Barbara Hughes Fowler

"O foot, O leg, O thighs for which I rightly died." HePo, *tr. by* Barbara Hughes Fowler

"O two-horned moon, you love the parties that last all night." HePo, *tr. by* Barbara Hughes Fowler

"Philaenion is small and swart, but her hair curls more." HePo, *tr. by* Barbara Hughes Fowler

"Xanthippe's strumming, her chatter, her speaking eye, her song." HePo, *tr. by* Barbara Hughes Fowler

Epigrams. Rufinus Domesticus, *Greek.*

"Dear God, I didn't know that Cytherea was bathing." HePo, *tr. by* Barbara Hughes Fowler

"Lamplighter, if you can't set two equally." HePo, *tr. by* Barbara Hughes Fowler

"Melissias denies her love, but her body screams." HePo, *tr. by* Barbara Hughes Fowler

"Rhodoclea, I send you this wreath which I wove with my own hands." HePo

"Silver-footed girl was bathing, letting the water, The." HePo, *tr. by* Barbara Hughes Fowler

"Time has not quenched your beauty. Much of your bygone prime." HePo, *tr. by* Barbara Hughes Fowler

"When Pallas and golden-sandaled Hera saw Maeonis." HePo, *tr. by* Barbara Hughes Fowler

Epigrams. Rabindranath Tagore.

"Echo always mocks the sound, The." PoA

Epigrams. Tymnes, *Greek.*

Maltese Dog, A. FaBoCh; FaBoEE; Spl, *tr. by* Edmund Blunden

(Dog from Malta, The.) OBCVT, *tr. by* Edmund Blunden; GrAn

"Stone says that it covers here the white dog, The." HePo

Epigrams and Epitaphs. C. S. Lewis.

"Save yourself. Run and leave me. I must go back." EBEV

Epigrams must be curt, nor seem. Walter Savage Landor. FaBoEE

Epigrams of Martial, The. Laurie Duggan.
One xxxvii. BMAP

Epigrams on Lord Galloway. Robert Burns.
Lord Galloway. OxBoLi
On Lord Galloway. FaBoEE
(On the Same Nobleman.)

Epigrams to Ernesto Cardenal in Defense of Claudia. Dionne Brand.
"Give up the bitterness." PBCV

Epigraph. William Blake. OBNC *Fr.* Jerusalem; The Emanation of the Giant Albion.
"I give you the end of a golden string." NTP

Epigraph: "In the sea of life." Gu Cheng, *Chinese.* ChiPo, *tr.* by Helen F. Siu *and* Zelda Stern

Epilogue: "After our Epilogue this crowd dismisses." William Congreve. *Fr.* The Way of the World. NAEL-1

Epilogue: "At the midnight in the silence of the sleep-time." Robert Browning. EnVR; NAEL-1; NOBE; OBNC

Epilogue: "Away, for we are ready to a man!" James Elroy Flecker. NOBE *Fr.* The Golden Journey to Samarkand.

Epilogue: "Carol, every violet has." Alfred Noyes. MoBrPo *Fr.* The Flower of Old Japan.

Epilogue: "Child! we must quit these visionary scenes." Hannah More. ECWP *Fr.* The Search after Happiness.

Epilogue: "He is not dead nor liveth." Dorothy, Duchess of Wellington Wellesley. OBMV *Fr.* Deserted House.

Epilogue: "Heaven, which man's generations draws." Francis Thompson. MoBrPo *Fr.* A Judgment in Heaven.

Epilogue: "I have crossed an ocean." Grace Nichols. HCP

Epilogue: "I have seen flowers come in stony places." John Masefield. FaBoEE; OxBTC

Epilogue: "I, the genius Severyanin." "Igor Severyanin," *Russian.* TCRP, *tr.* by Bernard Meares

Epilogue: "If Luther's day expand to Darwin's year." Herman Melville. APN-2; NCAP *Fr.* Clarel: A Poem and Pilgrimage in the Holy Land.

Epilogue: "Like the stalks of wheat in the fields." Heinrich Heine. TrJP, *tr.* by Emma Lazarus *Fr.* The North Sea.
(Epilogue: "Like the ears of wheat in a wheat-field growing.") AWP, *tr.* by Louis Untermeyer

Epilogue: "Nothing now to mark the spot." Rachel Lyman Field. OBCA *Fr.* A Circus Garland.

Epilogue: "Now my charms are all o'erthrown." Shakespeare. CTC *Fr.* The Tempest. OAEL-1

Epilogue: "O chansons foregoing." Ezra Pound. OxBA

Epilogue: "On the first of the Feast of Feasts." Robert Browning. ChIV-2

Epilogue: "Our Poet tells me I am very pretty." Mary de la Rivière Manley. KTR *Fr.* The Royal Mischeif.

Epilogue: "Phoenix on the hot sirocco's breath." Herbert B. Mallalieu. PoA

Epilogue. Shakespeare. UV *Fr.* The Tempest. OAEL-1

Epilogue: "Soldier, there is a war between the mind." Wallace Stevens. ColAP *Fr.* Notes toward a Supreme Fiction.

Epilogue: "That death might not be casual." Burns Singer. FaBoTw

Epilogue: "There I learned how faces fall apart." "Anna Andreyevna Akhmatova." *Fr.* Requiem 1935-1940. BoWoP, *tr.* by Richard McKane

Epilogue: "Those blessèd structures, plot and rhyme." Robert Lowell. HCAP; NAAL-2; NoAM; NoP-4; PoPoPo; SAGP; VCAP

Epilogue: "Thus far, with rough and all-unable pen." Shakespeare. CTC *Fr.* King Henry V.

Epilogue: "Time is a thing." Stephen Spender. MoBrPo

Epilogue: "Truly my Satan thou art but a dunce." William Blake. HAP; ImPo; OAEL-2; OBNC; PeECV; PoE; WeW-3 *Fr.* The Gates of Paradise. PoEL-4
(To the Accuser Who Is the God of This World.) FHYEP; OxBSP; SCGP

Epilogue: "Well, when all is said and done." "Æ." MoBrPo

Epilogue: "What Epilogues are made, for who can tell." Catherine Trotter. KTR *Fr.* Queen Catharine; or, The Ruines of Love.

Epilogue: "What shall we do for Love these days?" Lascelles Abercrombie. MoBrPo *Fr.* Emblems of Love.
Small Fountains. CH

Epilogue: "With heart at rest I climbed the citadel's." Charles Baudelaire, *French.* AWP, *tr.* by Arthur Symons

Epilogue for a Masque of Purcell. Adrienne Rich. NYBP

Epilogue: "Now the hungry lion roars." Shakespeare. *See* The Fairy Blessing.

Epilogue: " 'O where are you going?' said reader to rider." W. H. Auden. FaBoCh; LiTM *Fr.* Five Songs.
(Song: " 'O where are you going?' said reader to rider.") OAEL-2

Epilogue to a Human Drama. Stephen Spender. AF; CMoP

Epilogue to a Poetry Reading. M. K. Joseph. PeNZ

Epilogue to Alun Mabon. John Ceiriog Hughes, *Welsh.* OBWVE, *tr.* by H. Idris Bell

Epilogue to Casualties. J. P. Clark Bekederemo. HBAPE

Epilogue to Robinson Crusoe. Dan Pagis, *Hebrew.* IP, *tr.* by Warren Bargad *and* Stanley F. Chyet

Epilogue to "The Parson's Wedding." Thomas Killigrew. NOSC

Epilogue to the Satires, in Two Dialogues. Alexander Pope. OAEL-1
Art of Satire, The. ECEV
(Power of Ridicule, The.) NOBE
"Spare then the person, and expose the vice." OBSV
Triumph of Vice, The. NOBE; OBSV

Epilogue to "The Sister." Oliver Goldsmith.
"Lud! what a group the motley scene discloses!" OBSV

Epilogue to *Tyrannic[k] Love.* Dryden. OBCoV *Fr.* Tyrannic Love.

Epimanes. Flavius Vopiscus, *Latin.*
"Thousand, a thousand, a thousand, A." OBCVT, *tr.* by Edgar Allan Poe

Epiphanies of the Voodoo Gods. René Depestre, *French.*
Attibon Legba. NegPo, *tr.* by Ellen Conroy Kennedy
Prelude. NegPo, *tr.* by Ellen Conroy Kennedy

Epiphany. Pem Kremer. CrSp

Epiphany. Nancy Paddock. LoHo

Epiphany. Christopher Smart. NOCV *Fr.* Hymns and Spiritual Songs for the Fasts and Festivals of the Church of England.

Epiphany. Andrea Zanzotto, *Italian.* VCWP, *tr.* by Ruth Feldman *and* Brian Swann

Epipsychidion, *see also* Fragments Connected with Epipsychdion. Shelley.
"Let us become the overhanging day." OAEL-2
Longest Journey, The. OxBM
"One stood on my path who seemed." LaPo
"She met me, Stranger, upon life's rough way." EP
"Spouse! Sister! Angel! Pilot of the Fate." CBLP
"Thy wisdom speaks in me, and bids me dare." OAEL-2
"True Love in this differs from gold and clay." FHYEP; OBNC

Episode of a Night of May. Arthur Symons. PeVV *Fr.* Scènes de la Vie de Bohème.

Episode of Decay. Witter Bynner. OxBM

Episode 17. William Carlos Williams. OxBA *Fr.* Paterson.

Epistemology. Richard Wilbur. CRP; NOBA; NoAM; OxBSP

Epistle: "How happy you who varied joys pursue." Lady Mary Wortley Montagu. ECWP

Epistle, An: "Is Friends fled, or Love grown cold?" Mary Mollineux. KTR

Epistle, An, Addressed to Sir Thomas Hanmer, on His Edition of Shakespeares Works. William Collins.
"O might some verse with happiest skill persuade." EPCY

Epistle Answering to One That Asked to Be Sealed of the Tribe of Ben, An. Ben Jonson. BeJo; FP

Epistle Containing the Strange Medical Experience of Karshish, the Arab Physician, An. Robert Browning. ChIV-2; NAEL-2

Epistle from a Half-Pay Officer in the Country to His Friend in London, An. Richardson Pack. NOEC

Epistle from Fern Hill. Mary Jones. ECWP

Epistle from Mr Murray to Dr Polidori. Byron. OBCoV

Epistle from Mr. Pope to Dr. Arbuthnot, An. Alexander Pope. *See* Epistle to Dr. Arbuthnot.

Epistle from Mrs. Yonge to Her Husband. Lady Mary Wortley Montagu. NAEL-1; NALW; NoP-4

Epistle I, to Sir Richard Temple, Lord Cobham. Alexander Pope.
"Coxcomb bird, so talkative and grave, The." ImPo

Epistle II: To a Socialist in London. Robert Bridges. *See* The Power of Ridicule.

Epistle II: To Mr. Pope, From Oxford. Edward Young.
"If satire charms, strike faults, but spare the man." EPCY

Epistle III, to Allen Lord Bathurst. Alexander Pope.
Duke of Buckingham, The. NOBE

Epistle in Form of a Ballad to His Friends. François Villon, *French.* AWP, *tr.* by Swinburne

Epistle IV, to Richard Boyle, Earl of Burlington. Alexander Pope. OAEL-1
(Epistle IV: Of the Use of Riches.) PoEL-3
Timon's Villa.
("And Splendour borrows all her rays from Sense.") PoE; *ll.* 99–180
("And swear no day was ever passed so ill.") (LL) OBSV
("Who never mentions Hell to ears polite.") (LL) ECEV

Epistle of Deborah Dough, The. Mary Leapor. ECWP; NoP-4
("Deborah Dough.") (LL) NoP-4

Epistle of Othea to Hector (A Lytil Bibell of Knyghthod), The. Christine de Pisan, *French*.

"Phoebus, the goddess variant and changeable." PBWP, *tr.* by Joan Keefe

Epistle to a Lady, An. Mary Leapor. BWW; CABP; ECWP; NOEC

Epistle [II,] to a Lady[: Of the Characters of Women]. Alexander Pope. NAEL-1; NOEC

(To a Lady.) OAEL-1; OxBoLi

C[h]loe. AWP; NOBE; OBSV

Ghosts of Beauty, The. OBSV

Epistle to a Young Friend. Robert Burns. EBEV

Epistle to Artemisia. Mary Leapor.

Patrons of My Early Song, The. ECWP

Epistle to Augusta. Byron. FHYEP

Epistle to Baron Delvig. Oleg Grigorevich Chukhonstev, *Russian*. TCRP, *tr. by* Simon Franklin

Epistle to Be Left in the Earth. Archibald MacLeish. CMoP; MoAmPo; NOBA; SAGP

Epistle to Clemena, Occasioned by an Argument She Had Maintained Against the Author. Elizabeth Thomas. ECWP

Epistle to Dr. Arbuthnot, *in imitation of* Horace (*Satires*, Prologue). Alexander Pope. FHYEP; InPS-3; OAEL-1; OxAEP-1; PoE; PoEL-3; TFi

(Epistle from Mr. Pope to Dr. Arbuthnot, An.) NOEC

("Shut, shut the door, good John! (fatigued, I said).") NoP-4

("Thus far was right—the rest belongs to Heaven.") (LL) NoP-4

Apologia pro Vita Sua. NOBE

Atticus ("Peace to all such! but were there one whose fires"). AWP; InPK-6; NOBE; TRP

"Bard whom pilf'red pastorals reknown, The." OBSV

Bufo. OBSV

Epistle to Dr Arbuthnot, An: "There are, who to my person pay their court." FP

"Shut, shut the door, good *John*! fatigu'd I said." OBCoV

Sporus. AWP; NOBE; OBSV

("Let Sporus tremble—A. What? that thing of silk.") OxBoV

"Why did [*or* do] I write? what sin to me unknown." EBEV; EPCY; TOF

"Yet let me flap this bug with gilded wings." ECEV

Epistle: To Elizabeth, Countess of Rutland. Horace, *Latin*. OBCVT, *tr.* by Ben Jonson

Epistle to Elizabeth, Countess of Rutland. Ben Jonson. BeJo

Epistle to George Keats. Keats.

"Ah, my dear friend and brother." FHYEP

Epistle to Her Friends at Gartmore. Susanna Blamire. ECWP

Epistle to J. Lapraik, an Old Scotch Bard. Robert Burns. Ro

Epistle to John Guthrie. Sydney Goodsir Smith. OxBS

Epistle to John Hamilton Reynolds. Keats. OBNC *Fr.* To J. H. Reynolds, Esq.

Epistle to John Walker, Esq., An. "Eliza." ECWP *Fr.* A Tour to the Glaciers of Savoy.

Epistle. To Katharine, Lady Aubigny. Ben Jonson. BeJo

Epistle to Lady Bowyer, An. Mary Jones. ECWP

("How much of paper's spoiled! what floods of ink!") PEW

("Patriots! who sell their country for a place!") (LL) PEW

Epistle to Lord Burlington. Alexander Pope. OBGa *Fr.* Epistle to Lord Burlington.

Epistle to Master John Selden, An. Ben Jonson. BeJo

("Pernicious enemy.") (LL) FP

Epistle to Miss [*or* Miss Teresa] Blount, on Her Leaving the Town after the Coronation. Alexander Pope. BoLoP; EBEV; FHYEP; LoP; NAEL-1; NOBE; NOEC; PoEL-3

Epistle to Mr. Alexander Pope. Andrew Lang.

"From mortal gratitude, decide, my Pope." EPCY

Epistle to Mr. Pope Occasioned by His Characters of Women, An. Anne, Viscountess Irwin Ingram.

"Female mind like a rude fallow lies, A." ECWP

Epistle to Mrs Anne Griffiths. Jane Brereton.

"But should some snarling critic chance to view." ECWP

Epistle to My Friend J. B, An. Robert Dodsley. NOEC .

Epistle to My Gardener. Nicolas Boileau-Despéaux, *French* OBGa, *tr.* by John Ozell *Fr.* Epistle to My Gardener.

Epistle. To Prince Henrie. Samuel Daniel.

"Theare be great Prince, such as will tell us howe." PBRV

Epistle to Robert Nugent, Esq. with a Picture of Doctor Swift in Old Age, An. William Dunkin.

"Hibernia's Helicon is dry." NOEC

Epistle to Sir Richard Temple. Alexander Pope.

Wharton ("Wharton! the scorn and wonder of our days"). AWP

Epistle to the Gentiles. Alfred Hayes. TrJP

Epistle to the King of Sweden, An. Susanna Centlivre.

"To thee—rude warrior, who, we once admired." ECWP

Epistle to the President of the Scottish Society of Antiquaries: On Being Chosen a Correspondent Member. Alexander Geddes. OxBS

Epistle to the Rappalloan. Archibald MacLeish. PoA

Epistle to the Right Hon. Charles James Fox, An. Thomas Maurice.

"How cursed that country, how severe its doom." NOEC

Epistle to the Right Honourable William Pulteney, Esq. John Gay.

French Fops. ECEV

Epistle to William Wilberforce, Esq., on the Rejection of the Bill for Abolishing the Slave Trade. Anna Laetitia Barbauld. Ro *Fr.* Poems.

Epistle Written in the Country to the Right Honourable the Lord Lovelace, An. Soame Jenyns.

"In days, my Lord, when mother Time." OBSV

"Nor can I for my soul delight." ECEV

Epistles. Horace, *Latin*.

1.1. AWP, *tr.* by Abraham Cowley

Part of the Seventh Epistle of the First Book of Horace Imitated: And Address'd to a Noble Peer. OBCVT, *tr.* by Jonathan Swift

Epistles to Mr. Pope. Edward Young.

"These labouring wits, like paviours, mend our ways." OBSV

Epitaph. Marie-Claire Bancquart, *French*. MFP, *tr.* by Martin Sorrell

Epitaph. Katherine Philips. *See* EPITAPH. On her Son H. P. at St. Syth's Church where her body also lies Interred.

Epitaph. *Unknown*. OBCoV

Epitaph. U Tam'si Tchicaya. PBMAP *Fr.* L'Arc Musical (1970).

Epitaph, An. Sir William Watson. FP

Epitaph: "Again, traveller, you have come a long way led by that star." Thomas McGrath. RaBo

Epitaph: "Angler rose, he took his rod, The." Robert Louis Stevenson. OBCoV

Epitaph: "Athenagoras begot Eubulus—." Chairemon, *Greek*. GrAn, *tr. by* Richard Evans

Epitaph: "Beneath this stone lies William Burke." R. P. Weston *and* Bert Lee (1880–1945). OBCoV

Epitaph: "Daniel and Abigail." Miguel de Barrios, *Spanish*. TrJP

Epitaph: "Done to death by slanderous tongues." Shakespeare. CTC *Fr.* Much Ado about Nothing.

Epitaph: "Dummer the shepherd sacrific'd." Cotton Mather. SCAP

Epitaph, An: "Erected by her sorrowing brothers." C. S. Lewis. OBCoV

Epitaph: "Fate to beauty still must give." Claudian, *Latin*. AWP, *tr. by* Howard Mumford Jones

Epitaph: "For this she starred her eyes with salt." Elinor Wylie. MoAmPo

Epitaph: "From out the stormy sea unto the shore." Azariah di Rossi, *Hebrew*. TrJP, *tr.* by A. B. Rhine

Epitaph: "Glassblower lies here at rest, A." John Bingham Morton. FaBoEE

Epitaph, An: "He worshipped at the altar of Romance." Colin Ellis. OxBTC

Epitaph: "Her grieving parents cradled here." Sylvia Townsend Warner. MoBrPo

Epitaph: "Here I— / What does." Paulus Silentiarius, *Greek*. GrAn, *tr. by* Andrew Miller

Epitaph, An: "Here lie I, once a witty fair." Samuel Wesley. NOEC

Epitaph: "Here lie John Hughes and Sarah Drew." Lady Mary Wortley Montagu. CABP; ECWP; FaBoEE

Epitaph I: "Here lies a man, and still no man." *Unknown*. *Fr.* Duel with Verses over a Great Man. TrJP

Epitaph, An: "Here lies a most beautiful lady." Walter De la Mare. ImPo; LiTM; MoBrPo; OBEV; RB

Epitaph: "Here lies a simple Jew." "Sholom Aleichem," *Yiddish*. TrJP, *tr.* by Joseph Leftwich

Epitaph, An: "Here lies Nachshon, a man of great renown." Isaac Benjacob, *Hebrew*. TrJP, *tr.* by Joseph Chotzner

Epitaph: "Here lies Sir Tact, a diplomatic fellow." Timothy Steele. InPK-6; NBLV

Epitaph, An: "Here lies Stephen Pwanya." Julius Chingono. PeSAV

Epitaph: "Here lies the body of Richard Hind." Francis, Lord Jeffrey. FaBoEE; OxBoLi

Epitaph, An: "Here lieth under this marble ston." *Unknown*. MiEL

Epitaph: "Here rests his head upon the lap of earth," *see also* Shelley's "Hic sinu fessum caput hospitali." Thomas Gray. FHYEP; FaBoPV; SCGP *Fr.* Elegy Written in a Country Churchyard. APAD; AWP; CABP; ClHu; EBEV; EBEvV; FHYEP; FaBoBe; FaBoPV; FaPoR; GTBS-P; HAP; HeIP-4; ImPo; InPK-6; InPS-3; NOBE; NOEC; NoP-4; OAEL-1; OBEV; OxAEP-1; PBMP; PoEL-3; PoLF; PoPoPo; Poetr; SCGP; SCV; TFi; UV; UnPo; WeW-3

Epitaph, An: "His friends he loved. His direst earthly foes." Sir William Watson. NOBVV

Epitaph: "I am old." Christopher Logue. OxBTC

Epitaph: "I, an unwedded wandering dame." Sylvia Townsend Warner. MoBrPo

Epitaph: "I lived in those times. For a thousand years." Robert Desnos, *French.* PFTM, *tr. by* Kenneth Rexroth

Epitaph: "I never cared for Life: Life cared for me." Thomas Hardy. FaBoEE; LiLi

Epitaph: "I, Richard Kent, beneath these stones." Sylvia Townsend Warner. MoBrPo

Epitaph, An: "I was buried near this dyke [*or* Dike]." William Blake. FaBoEE; OBCoV

Epitaph, An: "I was, I am not; smiled, that since did weep." Thomas Heywood. OxBSP

Epitaph: "Implacable angel / Has shot his dart, The." Leone da Modena, *Hebrew.* TrJP

Epitaph, An: "Interred [*or* Interr'd] beneath this marble stone." Matthew Prior. OBCoV

Epitaph: "It was for you that the mountains shook at Sinai." *Unknown.* TrJP

Epitaph: "John Bird, a laborer, lies here." Sylvia Townsend Warner. MoBrPo

Epitaph: "Last year the child died." Olive Senior. PBCV

Epitaph: "Like silver dew are the tears of love." Alfred Edgar Coppard. OBMV

Epitaph, An: "Like thee I once have stemm'd the sea of life." James Beattie. OBEV

Epitaph: "Malcolm Lowry." Malcolm Lowry. OBCoV

Epitaph: "Man who in his life trusts in this world, A." *Unknown.* TrJP

Epitaph: "Meek Francis lies here, friend, without stop or stay." Matthew Prior. FaBoEE

Epitaph: "Mr. Heath-Stubbs as you must understand." John Heath-Stubbs. OxBTC

Epitaph: "My brother is skull and skeleton now." William Montgomerie. OxBS

Epitaph: "My friend, judge not me." *Unknown.* NOSC

Epitaph, An: "My name—my country—what are they to thee." Paulus Silentiarius, *Greek.* FaBoEE; OBVE

(No Matter.) AWP, *tr. by* William Cowper

Epitaph: "Nor practising virtue nor committing crime." Geoffrey Taylor. FaBoEE

Epitaph: "O King, give Angilbert thy rest." Angilbert, *Latin.* MLL, *tr. by* Helen Waddell

Epitaph: "Of many things adulterate." Tristan Corbière, *French.* AWP, *tr. by* Joseph T. Shipley

Epitaph: "Old man is gone, The." John Figueroa. HCP

Epitaph: "One whom I knew, a student and a poet." Alex Comfort. MoBrPo

Epitaph: "Or many things adulterate." Tristan Corbière, *French.* AWP, *tr. by* Joseph T. Shipley

Epitaph: "Roots of mankind are tangled in my hair, The." Wendy Rose. CDW

Epitaph: "See here, nice Death, to please his palate." Alexander Pope. FaBoEE

Epitaph: "Serene descent, as a red leaf's descending." Sara Teasdale. PoA

Epitaph: "Sir, you should notice me: I am the Man." Lascelles Abercrombie. MoBrPo

Epitaph: "Stone cries from the wall, The." *Unknown.* TrJP

Epitaph: "Stop, Christian passer-by!—Stop, child of God." Coleridge. NAEL-2; NOCV; OAEL-2; PeECV

Epitaph: "They hanged him on a clement morning, swung." Dennis Scott. HCP; PBCV

Epitaph: "This is the end of him, here he lies." Amy Levy. NOBVV; PEW; TrJP

(Epitaph (On a Commonplace Person who Died in Bed).) CABP; VWP

Epitaph: "This stone, with not unpardonable pride." John Sparrow. OBCoV

Epitaph: "Time and the World, whose magnitude and weight." Robert Southey. OBNC

Epitaph: "Time that brings [*or* bringes] all things to light." Thomas Morton. NOSC; SCAP

Epitaph: "To the chimney a bull's horns." Ljubomir Simovic, *Serbo-Croatian.* HSix, *tr. by* Charles Simic

Epitaph: "Tread softly; bid a solemn music sound." John Bingham Morton. FaBoEE

Epitaph: "Underneath this marble stone." Abraham Cowley. *See* Epitaph of Pyramus and Thisbe.

Epitaph: "Underneath this wooden cross there lies." Karl Shapiro. *Fr.* Elegy for a Dead Soldier. HAP; LiTM; OBWP; OxBA

Epitaph, An: "When I am gone." Josephine D. Henderson Heard. AAP; CBWP-4

Epitaph: "When I shall be without regret." James Vincent Cunningham. InPK-6

Epitaph: "Young then, / we were bored already." Eleanor Wilner. ChIV-1

Epitaph after Reading Ronsard's Lines from Rabelais. John Millington Synge. FaBoEE

Epitaph, An: On a Man for Doing Nothing. John Hoskyns. NOSC

Epitaph: Atticus. Paulus Silentiarius, *Greek.* GrAn, *tr. by* Andrew Miller

Epitaph. Caecil. Boulstr. Edward Herbert. SeCP

Epitaph: Chryseomallus the Mime. Paulus Silentiarius, *Greek.* GrAn, *tr. by* Andrew Miller

Epitaph Ending in And, The. William Stafford. LCAP-2

Epitaph for a Beatnik Poet. Guy Owen. CRP

Epitaph for a Cat. Margaret E. Bruner. PoLF

Epitaph for a Concord Boy. Stanley Young. ChAP

Epitaph for a Godly Man's Tomb, An. Robert Wild. FaBoEE

Epitaph for a Good Mouser. Anne Stevenson. Spl

Epitaph for a Judge. Benedict Jeitteles, *Hebrew.* TrJP, *tr. by* Joseph Chotzner

Epitaph for a Meat-Packer. Guy Owen. CRP

Epitaph for a Poet. Homero Aridjis, *Spanish.* STV, *tr. by* John Frederick Nims

Epitaph for a Postal Clerk. X. J. Kennedy. NIP-4

Epitaph for a Scientist. Lex Banning. NOBAu

Epitaph For Belaud. Joachim Du Bellay, *French.*
  "There are cats (not he)." PC, *tr. by* Felicity Bast

Epitaph for Bruno of Angers. Marbod of Rennes, *Latin.* MLL, *tr. by* Helen Waddell

Epitaph for Castlereagh, An. Byron. FaBoEE

Epitaph for Cleonicus. Alexander of Pleuron, *Greek.* GrAn, *tr. by* W. S. Merwin

Epitaph for Cú Chuimne. *Unknown, Irish.* NOIV, *tr. by* Thomas Kinsella

Epitaph for Erotion. Martial, *Latin.* FaBoEE, *tr. by* James Michie

Epitaph for G. B. Shaw. Max Beerbohm. FaBoEE

Epitaph for George Moore. Thomas Hardy. FaBoEE

Epitaph for His Niece, Sophia. Paul the Deacon, *Latin.* MLL, *tr. by* Helen Waddell

Epitaph for James Smith. Robert Burns. EBEV

Epitaph for Mael Mhuru. *Unknown.* NOIV

Epitaph for Maria Wentworth. Thomas Carew. *See* Maria Wentworth.

Epitaph for Mr. Moses Levy. *Unknown.* TrJP

Epitaph for My Cat. Jean Garrigue. TAP

Epitaph for My Dog. Phan Bội Châu, *Vietnamese.* AVP, *tr. by* Huỳnh Sanh Thông

Epitaph for One Killed at Roncesvalles. *Unknown, Latin.* MLL, *tr. by* Helen Waddell

Epitaph for One Who Would Not Be Buried in Westminster Abbey ("Heroes, and Kings! your distance keep") Alexander Pope. FaBoEE

Epitaph for Paulinus of Aquileia and Arno of Salzburg. Alcuin, *Latin.* MLL, *tr. by* Helen Waddell

Epitaph for Peter Stuyvesant. Henricus Selyns. SCAP

Epitaph for Sir Henry Lee. *Unknown.* FaBoEE

Epitaph for Sir Lawrence Tanfield. Lady Elizabeth Tanfield. NOSC

Epitaph for Someone or Other. James Vincent Cunningham. OBAL; PFE; TRP *Fr.* Five Epigrams.

(Epigram: "Naked I came, naked I leave the scene.") VGW

Epitaph for St. Amand, Bishop of Utrecht. Alcuin, *Latin.* MLL, *tr. by* Helen Waddell

Epitaph for the Poet. George Barker. OxBSP

Epitaph for the Race of Man. Edna St. Vincent Millay.
  "Here lies, and none to mourn him but the sea." HeIP-4
  "O Earth, unhappy planet born to die." HeIP-4
  "See where Capella with her golden kids." CMoP; MoAmPo

Epitaph for the Western Intelligentsia. Richard Allen. NOBAu

Epitaph for [*or* on] Thomas Clere. Henry Howard, Earl of Surrey. *See* Epitaph on Thomas Clere.

Epitaph for Vysotsky. Andrey Andreievich Voznesensky, *Russian.* TCRP, *tr. by* William Jay Smith

Epitaph for William Pitt. Byron. FaBoEE

Epitaph from a Tomb in Asia Minor. *Unknown, Greek.* GrAn, *tr. by* Peter Whigham

Epitaph from Athens. *Unknown, Greek.* GrAn, *tr. by* Peter Jay

Epitaph from Athens. *Unknown, Greek.* GrAn, *tr. by* Richmond Lattimore

Epitaph from Piraeus. *Unknown, Greek.* GrAn, *tr. by* Peter Jay

Epitaph from *The Great Gatsby.* F. Scott Fitzgerald. OxBM *Fr.* The Great Gatsby.

Epitaph in Christ Church, Bristol, on Thomas Turner, Twice Master of the Company of Bakers. Francis, Lord Jeffrey. *See* In Christ Church, Bristol, on Thomas Turner, Twice Master of the Company of Bakers.

Epitaph in Dialogue on the Sceptic Philosopher Pyrrho. Julianus of Egypt, *Greek*. GrAn, *tr. by* Lee T. Pearcy

Epitaph in Form of a Ballad, The. François Villon, *French*. CTC; OxBoV, *tr. by* Algernon Charles Swinburne

[Epitaph] In Obitum M.S., X Maij [*or* Maii], 1614. William Browne. FaBoEE; NOBE; OBEV

Epitaph in Sirmio. David Morton. PoLF

Epitaph in St. Olave's, Southwark, on Mr. Munday. *Unknown.* OxBoLi

Epitaph in the Bermuda Tongue, Which Must Be Pronounced With the Accent of the Grunting of a Hog. John Taylor. CBNP

Epitaph in the Borghese Gardens. *Unknown, Greek.* GrAn, *tr. by* Peter Whigham

Epitaph in the Utopian Tongue. John Taylor. CBNP

Epitaph Intended for Sir Isaac Newton. Alexander Pope. *See* Intended for Sir Isaac Newton.

Epitaph: Iohannis Sande. Thomas Bastard. FaBoEE

Epitaph of a Dog. *Unknown, Greek.* FP; GrAn, *tr. by* Dudley Fitts

Epitaph of a Girl. *Unknown, Greek.* GrAn, *tr. by* Dudley Fitts

Epitaph of a Nicene Actor. *Unknown, Greek.* GrAn, *tr. by* Dudley Fitts

Epitaph of a Sailor. Antiphilus, *Greek.* GrAn, *tr. by* Dudley Fitts

Epitaph of a Sailor. Damagetus, *Greek.* GrAn, *tr. by* Dudley Fitts

Epitaph of Cleonicus. Theocritus, *Greek.* FaBoEE, *tr. by* Charles Stuart Calverley

Epitaph of Dionysia. *Unknown.* OBEV

Epitaph of Erotion, The. Leigh Hunt. OBCVT

Epitaph of Eusthenes, The. Edward Cracroft Lefroy. AWP *Fr.* Echoes from Theocritus.

Epitaph of Felis, The. John Jortin, *Latin.* PC, *tr. by* Samuel Courtauld

Epitaph of Graunde [*or* La Graunde] Amoure, The. Stephen Hawes. EBEV; FaBoEE; NoSic; OBEV *Fr.* The Pastime of Pleasure. OBGa

Epitaph of Hipponax. Theocritus, *Greek.* FaBoEE, *tr. by* Charles Stuart Calverley

Epitaph of Maister Win Drowned in the Sea, An. George Turberville. FaBoEE

Epitaph of Nearchos. Ammianus, *Greek.* WeW-3, *tr. by* Dudley Fitts

Epitaph of Our Late Queen Mary, An. George Cavendish. NoSic

Epitaph of Pyramus and Thisbe. Abraham Cowley. FaBoEE

(Epitaph: "Underneath this marble stone.") EnLoPo

Epitaph of Sardanapalos, The. *Unknown, Greek.* PGA, *tr. by* Kenneth Rexroth

Epitaph of Sir Thomas Gravener, [Knight], An. Sir Thomas Wyatt. SiPS

Epitaph of the Death of Nicholas Grimald, An. Barnabe Googe. SCGP

Epitaph on a Betrothed Girl. Erinna, *Greek.* GrAn, *tr. by* Lenore Mayhew

Epitaph on a Child Killed by Procured Abortion. *Unknown.* NOEC

Epitaph (On a Commonplace Person who Died in Bed). Amy Levy. *See* Epitaph: "This is the end of him, here he lies."

Epitaph on a Dentist. *Unknown.* *See* A Dentist.

Epitaph on a Diamond Digger. Albert Brodrick. PeSAV

Epitaph on a Dormouse. *Unknown.* OxBChV

Epitaph on a Fir-Tree. Richard Murphy. FaBoTw

Epitaph on a Great Sleeper. Sir Aston Cokayne. FaBoEE

Epitaph on a Hare. William Cowper. HAP; NOEC; NoP-4; PeP; PoEL-3; PoPoPo

Epitaph on a Jacobite. Thomas Babington Macaulay. *See* A Jacobite's Epitaph.

Epitaph on a Party Girl. Richard Usborne. FaBoEE; OBCoV

Epitaph on a Pessimist. Thomas Hardy. FaBoEE; PFE; TRP

Epitaph on a Robin Redbreast, An. Samuel Rogers. FaBoEE

Epitaph on a Schoolmaster. Robert Burns. FaBoEE

Epitaph on a Tomb near Rome. *Unknown, Greek.* GrAn, *tr. by* Frank Kuenstler

Epitaph on a Tyrant. W. H. Auden. AF; HeIP-4; MeMAP; NoAM; OxBSP; OxBoV; RB

Epitaph on a Waiter. David McCord. NBLV; NIP-4; OBAL; OBCoV

Epitaph on a Willing Girl. Thomas Rowlandson. FaBoEE

Epitaph on a Young Child. Ivor Gurney. FaBoEE

Epitaph on a Young Poet Who Died before Having Achieved Success. Amy Lowell. OBAL

Epitaph on Achilles. *Unknown, Greek.* AWP, *tr. by* William M. Hardinge

Epitaph on an Army of Mercenaries. A. E. Housman. EBEvV; NSI; NoP-4; SCGP; SoSe-8

Epitaph on an Infant. Crinagoras, *Greek.* AWP, *tr. by* John William Burgon

Epitaph on an Irish Priest. *Unknown.* FaBoEE

Epitaph on an Unfortunate Artist. Robert Graves. FaBoEE; NOBL; OBCoV

Epitaph on Charles I. James Graham, Marquess of Montrose. *See* His Metrical Vow.

Epitaph on Charles II. John Wilmot, 2d Earl of Rochester. SCGP

Epitaph on Claudy Phillips, a Musician, An. Samuel Johnson. *See* An Epitaph upon the Celebrated Claudy Phillips, Musician, Who Died Very Poor.

Epitaph on Colonel Francis Chartres. John Arbuthnot. FaBoEE

(Colonel Chartres.) OBSV

Epitaph on Dr. Donne, Dean of Paul's, An. Richard Corbet. BeJo; EPCY

Epitaph on Dr. Johnson. William Cowper. EPCY

Epitaph on Dr. Keene. Thomas Gray. FaBoEE

Epitaph on Dr. Keene's Wife. Thomas Gray. FaBoEE

Epitaph on Dr Samuel Johnson. Soame Jenyns. ECEV

Epitaph on Elizabeth, L. H. Ben Jonson. BeJo; FaBoEE; HAP; NAEL-1; NIP-4; NOSC; NoP-4; OBEV; PoE; Poetr; SCGP; SeCP

EPITAPH. On her Son H. P. at St. Syth's Church where her body also lies Interred. Katherine Philips. NOSC; PBRV; PEW

("Bury'd in a morning Cloud.") (LL) KTR; NOSC

(Epitaph.) NoP-4

(Epitaph on her Son *H. P.* at St. Syth's Church.) KTR

Epitaph on Herself, An. Mehetabel Wright. ECWP

Epitaph on Himself. Coleridge. FaBoEE

Epitaph on Himself. Alexander Pope. FaBoEE

Epitaph on Himself. Matthew Prior. *See* On Himself.

Epitaph on Himself. Shakespeare. PFE

Epitaph on Hogarth. Samuel Johnson. *See* An Epitaph on William Hogarth.

Epitaph on James Moore Smythe. Alexander Pope. FaBoEE

Epitaph on John Knott. *Unknown.* FaBoEE

Epitaph on Lady Ossory's Bullfinch. Horace, 4th Earl of Orford Walpole. *Fr.* Epitaphs [*or* Epitaph] on Two Piping-Bullfinches of Lady Ossory's, Buried under a Rose-Bush in Her Garden. FaBoEE; NOEC

Epitaph on Laurence Sterne. David Garrick. FaBoEE

Epitaph on M. H, An. Charles Cotton. EBEV; FaBoEE

Epitaph on Maria Wentworth. Thomas Carew. PoEL-3

Epitaph on Master Philip Gray, An. Ben Jonson. FaBoEE

Epitaph on Master Vincent Corbet[t], An. Ben Jonson. BeJo

Epitaph on Peter Robinson. Francis, Lord Jeffrey. *See* On Peter Robinson.

Epitaph on Prince Frederick. *Unknown.* *See* On Prince Frederick.

Epitaph on Prince Henry. Hugh Holland. FaBoEE

Epitaph On Robert Southey. Thomas Moore. FaBoEE

Epitaph on Solomon Pavy, [Salomon *or* Salathiel Pavy], a Child of Q[ueen] El[izabeth's] Chapel. Ben Jonson. BeJo; GEA; HoPM; NAEL-1; NOBE; NOSC; OAEL-1; OBEV; PoEL-2; SCGP; SeCP; TFi; UnPo

Epitaph on Sir Philip Sidney. Fulke Greville. SCGP

Epitaph on Sir Philip Sidney, An. James I, King of England. Son

Epitaph on Sir Philip Sidney. Sir Walter Ralegh. SiPS

Epitaph on Sir Thomas Wyatt. Henry Howard, Earl of Surrey. *See* Tribute to Wyatt.

Epitaph on Sir Walter Pye. John Hoskyns. FaBoEE

Epitaph on Some Bottles of Sack and Claret Laid in Sand. Robert Wild. NOSC

Epitaph on the Admirable Dramatic Poet, W. Shakespeare, An. Milton. *See* On Shakespear[e].

Epitaph on the Countess[e] Dowager of Pembroke. William Browne. *See* On the Countess Dowager of Pembroke.

Epitaph on the Duke of Buckingham. *Unknown.* PBRV

Epitaph on the Duke of Grafton. Sir Fleetwood Shepherd. FaBoEE

Epitaph on the Earl of Leicester [*or* Leceister]. Sir Walter Ralegh. RB; SiPS

Epitaph on the Earl of Strafford. John Cleveland. FaBoEE; FaBoPV; NOBE; NOSC; PeECV

("Speechlesse still, and never crie.") (LL) PBRV

Epitaph on the Fart in the Parliament House. John Hoskyns. FaBoEE

Epitaph on the Favourite Dog of a Politician. Hilaire Belloc. OBSV

Epitaph on the Lady Mary Vill[i]ers. Thomas Carew. BeJo; CaPo; CavPo; FaBoEE; NOBE; OBEV

("Lady *Mary* Villers lyes, The.") PBRV

Epitaph on the Lady Mary Villiers, An. Thomas Carew. *See* Another [Epitaph on Lady Mary Villiers] ("This little vault, this narrow room").

Epitaph on the Monument of Sir William Dyer at Colmworth, 1641. Lady Catherine Dyer. BoLoP; EnLoPo; OxBM *Fr.* Sir William Dyer, Knight.

Epitaph on the Monument of Sir William Strode. William Strode. NOSC

Epitaph on the Politician Himself. Hilaire Belloc. FaBoEE; MoBrPo; NBLV; OBSV

Epitaph on the Stanton-Harcourt Lovers. Alexander Pope. FaBoEE *Fr.* Three Epitaphs on John Hewet and Sarah Drew. NIP-4

Epitaph on the Tombstone of a Child, the Last of Seven That Died Before. Aphra Behn. CABP; KTR; NOSC

Epitaph on Thomas Clere. Henry Howard, Earl of Surrey. AAS; OBWP; SiPS

(Epitaph for [or on] Thomas Clere.) NoSic

Epitaph on Tuft-Hunter. Thomas Moore. FaBoEE

Epitaph on William Hogarth, An. Samuel Johnson. EBEV

(Epitaph on Hogarth.) OxAEP-1

Epitaph on William Jones. *Unknown.* FaBoEE

Epitaph on William Whitehead. *Unknown.* FaBoEE

Epitaph Placed on His Daughter's Tomb. "Mark Twain." PoLF, *ad. by* Robert Richardson

Epitaph: "Posterity will ne'er survey." An Epitaph for Castlereagh. Byron. FaBoEE

Epitaph: Sappho. Pinytos, *Greek.* GrAn, *tr. by* Lee T. Pearcy

Epitaph: Snake River. Lance Henson. VoR

Epitaph to a Dog. Byron. BLPA

Epitaph to Let, An. Paulus Silentarius, *Greek.* OBCVT, *tr. by* Leigh Hunt

Epitaph to Mrs Freland, in Edwelton churchyard, Nottinghamshire, 1741. *Unknown.*

"She drank good ale, strong punch and wine." LiLi

Epitaph upon —, An. Andrew Marvell. OBEV

Epitaph upon a Child, An. Robert Herrick. FaBoEE

Epitaph upon a Sober Matron, An. Robert Herrick. CaPo

Epitaph upon a Virgin, An. Robert Herrick. CaPo; FaBoEE; OxBoLi; PoEL-3

Epitaph upon a Young Married Couple, An. Richard Crashaw. *See* An Epitaph Upon Husband and Wife Who Died and Were Buried Together.

Epitaph Upon Husband and Wife Who Died and Were Buried Together, An. Richard Crashaw. EBEV; NOBE; OBEV; OxAEP-1; OxBM

(Epitaph upon a Young Married Couple, An.) FaBoEE; SeCP

Epitaph upon That Profound and Learned Casuist, the Late Ordinary of Newgate, An. Thomas Brown. OBSV

Epitaph upon the Celebrated Claudy Phillips, Musician, Who Died Very Poor, An. Samuel Johnson. NOEC

(Epitaph on Claudy Phillips, a Musician, An.) OxAEP-1

Epitaph Upon the Lady Elizabeth, Second Daughter to his Late Majesty, An. Henry Vaughan. BeJo

Epitaph Upon the Right Honorable Sir Philip Sidney. *Unknown.*

"He was (woe worth that word!) to each well thinking mind." EPCY

Epitaph upon Thomas, Lord Fairfax, An. George, 2d Duke of Buckingham Villiers. NOSC

Epitaphios. Yannis Ritsos, *Greek.*

"Day in May you left me, a day in May I lose you, A." GrIP, *tr. by* Kimon Friar

Epitaphium Cithariastriae. Victor Gustave Plarr. EnLoPo; NBLV

Epitaphium Meum. William Bradford. SCAP

Epitaphs. Robert Francis.

"Everyman/ Preacher or lecher, saint or sot." CRP

Epitaphs for some Space Beasts. Wes Magee. SpW

Epitaphs from Karansko Cemetery. Ljubomir Simovic, *Serbo-Croatian.* HSix, *tr. by* Charles Simic

Epitaphs of the War [1914–1918]. Rudyard Kipling. OBWP

Actors.

Batteries Out of Ammunition.

Beginner, The. FaBoTw

Bombed in London.

Bridegroom, The. FaBoEE

Common Form. FaBoEE; FaBoTw; PeFWW

Convoy Escort.

Coward, The. FaBoEE; FaBoTw; PeFWW

Dead Statesman, A. FaBoEE; NBLV; OPOU; PoFWW; PoWW

Destroyers in Collision.

Drifter off Tarentum, A. FaBoEE; NSI; PeFWW; PoWW

Equality of Sacrifice. FaBoTw

Ex-Clerk.

Favour, The.

Grave Near Cairo, A.

Hindu Sepoy in France.

Journalists.

Native Water-Carrier (M.E.F.)

Obedient, The.

Only Son, An.

Pelicans in the Wilderness (A Grave near Halfa). PeFWW

R.A.F. (Aged Eighteen). PoWW

(R.A.F. [Aged Eighteen].) LiLi

Raped and Revenged.

Rebel, The.

Refined Man, The. FaBoEE; FaBoTw; PeFWW

Salonikan Grave.

Servant, A. PeFWW

Shock.

Sleepy Sentinel, The.

Son, A. FaBoEE; PeFWW

Two Canadian Memorials.

Unknown Female Corpse. PoWW

V.A.D. (Mediterranean).

Wonder, The.

Epitaphs [*or* Epitaph] on Two Piping-Bullfinches of Lady Ossory's, Buried under a Rose-Bush in Her Garden. Horace, 4th Earl of Orford Walpole. FaBoEE; NOEC

Epitaphy of la Graunde Amoure. Stephen Hawes. *See* The Epitaph of Graunde [*or* La Graunde] Amoure.

Epithalamion. Richard Crashaw. ITG, *tr. by* Robert Hass

Epithalamion. Edmund Spenser, *English.*

Epithalamion I–IV. James Liddy.

"I know nothing but this scene." BiHa

Epithalamion: "Singing, today I married my white girl." Dannie Abse. OBWVE

"Now is this love already forth to come." ITG, *tr. by* Robert Hass

Epithalamion: "These are the small hours when." Michael Longley. CIP-2

Epithalamion: "Ye learned sisters which have oftentimes." Edmund Spenser. AAS; BoLoP; FHYEP; InPS-3; NOBE; NoSic; OAEL-1; OBEV; OxAEP-1; PoEL-3

("And for short time an endlesse moniment.") (LL) CABP; NoP-4; PBRV; PoPoPo

"Wake, now my love, awake; for it is time." GBL

Epithalamion for Lawyers, An. John Donne, *English.* ITG, *tr. by* Robert Hass

Epithalamion Made at Lincoln's Inn [*or* Lincolnes Inne]. Donne. SeCP

Epithalamion: or, a Song. Ben Jonson. BeJo

Epithalamion Teratos. George Chapman. NoSic *Fr.* Hero and Leander. AAS

Epithalamion/Wedding Dawn. Michael Dennis Browne. CMAP

Epithalamium. Sappho, *Greek.*

Epithalamium: "Can the lover share his soul." Walter James Turner. OBMV

Epithalamium: "Come, virgin tapers of pure wax." Richard Crashaw. NOCV

Epithalamium: "Hymen, god of marriage bed." Joseph Rutter. NOSC

Epithalamium: "Hymen hath together tied." R. Hatton. NOSC

Epithalamium: "Lo! Hymen passes through th' admiring crowds." *Unknown.* ECWP

"Happy bridegroom, Hesper brings." OBCVT, *tr. by* Alfred Edward Housman

Epithalamium: "So you are married, girl. It makes me sad." Roy McFadden. PNI

Epithalamium: "This girl all in white is my crystal of light." Francis Warner. OxBM

Epithalamium: "Voice that breathed o'er Eden, The." John Keble. NOCV

Epithalamium: "Let mother Earth." Sir Philip Sidney. *See* Long Their Coupled Joys Maintain.

Epithalamium: To Mistress M. A. Martin Lluellyn [*or* Lluelyn]. NOSC

Epithalamy. Alexander Brome. NOSC

Epithalamy to Sir Thomas Southwell and His Lady, An. Robert Herrick. CaPo

Epitomé (1962). U Tam'si Tchicaya.

"I was naked for the first kiss of my mother." PBMAP

Scorner, The. PBMAP

"What do I want with a thousand stars in broad daylight." PBMAP

Epitrepontes (The Arbitration), The. Menander, *Greek.*

"What do you say to this? The thought has just." OBCVT, *tr. by* Murray, Gilbert

Epoch. Vladimir Holan, *Czech.* PoSu, *tr. by* Ian *and* Jarmila Milner

Epoch ends, the world is still, The. Matthew Arnold. OAEL-2 *Fr.* Bacchanalia; or, The New Age.

Epode: "Not to know vice at all, and keep[e] true state." Ben Jonson. BeJo; SeCP

Epode 2. Horace, *Latin.*

"With such delights he can forget." OBCVT, *tr. by* Charles Hubert Sisson

Epodes. Horace, *Latin*.

Counterblast against Garlic, A. NBLV, *tr. by* Roswell Martin Field

Country Life. AWP, *tr. by* Dryden

Praises of a Country Life, The. OBVE; SeCP. *tr. by* Ben Jonson

("At th'Calends, puts all out againe.") (LL) OBCVT, *tr. by* Ben Jonson

("*Happie* is he, that from all Businesse cleere.") OBCVT, *tr. by* Ben Jonson

(Praises of a Countrie life, The.) OBCVT, *tr. by* Ben Jonson

Epos. Harold Rosenberg. PoA

Eppie Morrie. *Unknown*. ESPB; OxBB

Epygrams. John Heywood.

"Wilt thou use turners craft still? ye by my trouth." PBRV

Equal, An. *Unknown*. ReMoGo

Equal to Jove that youth must be. Catullus. *See* Sappho.

Equality. Nina Cassian, *Romanian*. IFJA, *tr. by* Brenda Walker

Equality, father! Your dream has come true. Edith Bruck, *Italian*. AF, *tr. by* Ruth Feldman; EC2, *tr. by* Ruth Feldman

Equality of Sacrifice. Rudyard Kipling. FaBoTw *Fr.* Epitaphs of the War [1914–1918]. OBWP

Equanimity. Les A. Murray. BMAP; NOBAu

("Where nothing is diminished by perspective.") (LL) BMAP

Equestrian fell from his horse, An. The Childhood of an Equestrian. Russell Edson. AmPA

Equestrienne. Rachel Lyman Field. OBCA *Fr.* A Circus Garland.

Equilibrists, The. John Crowe Ransom. CMoP; FuPo; HAP; LiTM; MeMAP; MoP; NAAL-2; NOBA; NoAM; OxBA; TAP

Equinox, The. DuBose Heyward. PoA

Equinox 1980. Peter Davison. NoP-4

Equipment. E. A. Guest. PoToHe

Equity in death. Homer. OBCVT, *tr. by* Alexander Pope *Fr.* The Iliad.

Er-Heb beyond the Hills of Ao-Safai. The Sacrifice of Er-Heb. Rudyard Kipling. PeVV

Era of the Vari-Vue, The. Gary Fincke. PUP-20

Erasers are the nicest things! *Unknown*. PoToHe

Erce, Erce, Erce, mother of earth. Charms for Unfruitful Land. *Unknown*, *Anglo-Saxon*. AnOE, *tr. by* Charles W. Kennedy

Erd sould trymbill, the firmament sould schaik, The. Quod Dunbar to Kennedy. William Dunbar. OxBoLi

Ere famous Winthrops bones are laid to rest. Chelmsfords Fate. Benjamin Tompson. SCAP

Ere God had built the mountains. Wisdom. William Cowper. ChIV-1 *Fr.* Olney Hymns.

E're I forget the zenith of your love. To My Cosen Mrs. Ellinor Evins. George Alsop. SCAP

Ere I freeze, to sing bravely. Poem of the Frost and Snow. Lewis Morris, *Welsh*. OBWVE, *tr. by* Anthony Conran

Ere I had known the world and understood. Sonnet. John Clare. Ro

Ere I had told / Ten birthdays when among the mountain-slopes. Wordsworth. TOF *Fr.* Introduction—Childhood and School-Time. FHYEP *Fr.* The Prelude; Growth of a Poet's Mind [1850 vers.]

Ere I know it—next moment I dance at the King's! (LL) Laboratory, The [Ancien Régime]. Robert Browning. EnVR; NAEL-2; OBEV

Ere I prove false to faith, or strange to you. (LL) Dear, if you change, I'll never choose again. John Dowland. EnLoPo; PoEL-2

Ere, in the northern gale. Autumn Woods. William Cullen Bryant. APN-1

Ere it passes, barefoot boy! (LL) The Barefoot Boy. John Greenleaf Whittier. APN-1; CTV; FaBoBe; OBAL; OBCA; PoLF

Ere lang the waves war foamin'. (LL) The Mermaid. *Unknown*. CH; ESPB

Ere long they come, where that same wicked wight. Edmund Spenser. NOBE; OAEL-1 *Fr.* The Cave of Despair. OBNV *Fr.* Wood Of Error. AEP

Ere my heart beats too coldly and faintly. The Truants. Walter De la Mare. MoBrPo

Ere on my bed my limbs I lay. A Child's Evening Prayer. Coleridge. OxBChV

Ere on my bed my limbs I lay, / It hath not been my use to pray. The Pains of Sleep. Coleridge. FHYEP; NAEL-2; OBNC; Ro

E're since hath in her Sun-shine liv'd. (LL) Lucasta's World. Richard Lovelace. BeJo; CaPo; SeCP

Ere sleep comes down to soothe the weary eyes. Paul Laurence Dunbar. APN-2; ColAP; NAAAL

Ere space exists, or earth, or sky. The Lord Is King. *Unknown*, *Hebrew*. TrJP, *tr. by* Solomon Solis-Cohen

Ere [*or* Or] that I wist[!] / Farewell, unkissed[!]. (LL) What should I say. Sir Thomas Wyatt. NoSic; SCGP

Ere the beard of thistle sails. The Seasons. Thomas Holcroft. NOEC

Ere their story die. (LL) In Time of "The Breaking of Nations." Thomas Hardy. BoLoP; CMoP; ChIV-1; EBEV; EBEvV; HAP; LiTM; MoBrPo;

MoP; NAEL-2; NOBE; NoAM; NoP-4; OAEL-2; OBEV; OBWP; OPOU; OxAEP-2; PoWW; Poetr; RB; TFi; WeW-3

Ere yet they win that verge and line. The Recluse. Herman Melville. APN-2 *Fr.* Clarel: A Poem and Pilgrimage in the Holy Land.

Ere yet your footsteps quit the place. Verses Addressed to a Friend, Just Leaving a Favourite Retirement. Samuel Henley. NOEC

Erected by her sorrowing brothers. An Epitaph. C. S. Lewis. OBCoV

Erica. Mary Ursula Bethell. PeNZ

Ericstane Brooch, The. Valerie Gillies. FaBoTC

Eride. Trumbull Stickney.

Eride, V. APN-2

Erie Canal, The. William S. Allen. AS

("I've got an old mule and her name is Sal.") APN-2

(Low Bridge, Everybody Down.) APN-2

Erige Cor Tuum ad Me in Caelum. Hilda Doolittle. CMoP

Erinna. Antipater of Sidon, *Greek*. AWP, *tr. by* A. J. Butler

Erinna's *Distaff*. Antipater of Sidon, *Greek*. GrAn, *tr. by* Peter Jay

Erl-King, The. Goethe, *German*. AWP; OBVE; OxBSn, *tr. by* Sir Walter Scott

("Life throbb'd in the sweet baby's bosom no more.") (LL) NOBRP, *tr. by* Matthew Gregory Lewis

("Who spurs on the road when day is done.") STV, *tr. by* John Frederick Nims

Erlinton. *Unknown*. ESPB

Erminia's steed this while his mistress bore. Torquato Tasso. NoSic, *tr. by* Edward Fairfax *Fr.* Godfrey of Bulloigne; or, The Recoverie of Jerusalem.

Erolog. Michael Palmer. FTOS

Eros. Robert Bridges. CABP; CMoP; NOBE; PoEL-5

Eros. Ralph Waldo Emerson. APN-1; FaBoBe

Eros. "Michael Field." VWP

Eros. Timothy Steele. RA

Eros at Temple Stream. Denise Levertov. NALW

Eros cast in wax, molded into a candle, An. Anacreon, *Greek*. InMo, *tr. by* Sam Hamill

Eros D'Aute. Theodore Wratislaw. GBL

Eros has changed his quiver. Paulus Silentiarius, *Greek*. PGA, *tr. by* Kenneth Rexroth

Eros Out of the Sea. Dilys Bennett Laing. PoA

Eros, playing among the roses. Anacreon, *Greek*. InMo, *tr. by* Sam Hamill

Eros seizes and shakes my very soul. Sappho, *Greek*. InMo, *tr. by* Sam Hamill

Eros taught Pratalidas his adolescent beauty. Leonidas of Tarentum, *Greek*. GrAn, *tr. by* Peter Levi

Eros, that bane of men, molded soft as marrow. Dioscorides. HePo, *tr. by* Barbara Hughes Fowler *Fr.* Epigrams.

Eros, thou yet behold'st me? Shakespeare. EBEV; OxAEP-1 *Fr.* Antony and Cleopatra.

Eros Turannos. Edwin Arlington Robinson. CMoP; GBL; GLoP; HAP; HeIP-4; LiTM; MeMAP; MoAmPo; MoP; NAAL-2; NOBA; NoAM; NoP-4; OxBA; PoA; PoE; PoPoPo; Poetr; TAP; TFi; TRP

Eros, why should one or two small notes. The Goad. "Michael Field." VWP

Erosion. Linda Pastan. NIP-4

Erotion. Martial, *Latin*. AWP, *tr. by* Kirby Flower Smith

Erotion. Swinburne. PoEL-5

Erotion rests here, in the. Martial, *Greek*. PGA, *tr. by* Kenneth Rexroth

Erotocritos. Vizentzos Cornaros, *Greek*.

"Observe how Eros works his magic spells." GrIP, *tr. by* Theodore P. Stephanides

Err shall they not, who resolute explore. Translations from the *Medea* of Euripedes. Euripides. *Fr.* Medea. NAWM-1; OxBM

Errant storm does not ask many questions, The. Stellar Hour. Betti Alver, *Estonian*. CEEP, *tr. by* Ivask, Astrid

Errantry. Robert Fitzgerald. NYBP

Errata. Charles Simic. NNaP

Erratum. E. J. Thribb. PeLV

Errore. Pier Giorgio Di Cicco. NOBC

Erskineville. The sun came round a corner. Pioneer Lane. Michael Dransfield. NOBAu

Erthe Toc of Erthe. *Unknown*. HAP

Erthe tok of erthe erthe with woh. *Unknown*. MiEL

Erudite demon, a fiend in topology, An. Möbius Strip-Tease. Alec Derwent Hope. OBCoV

Erudite, solemn / The pious bird. Rev Owl. Abraham Moses Klein. TrJP

Eruption: Pu'u Ō'ō. Garrett Kaoru Hongo. LoL

'E's crowdin' us out!—'er majesty's poet—soldier an' sailor too! (LL)
  Ballad: "As I was walkin' the jungle round, a-killin' of tigers an' time."
  Guy Wetmore Carryl. BXAP; NBLV
Es fällt ein Stern herunter. Heinrich Heine, German. AWP, tr. by Richard
  Garnett
E's Finch. Paul Verlaine, French. FLP, tr. by Alistair Elliot
Es Stehen Unbeweglich. Heinrich Heine, German. AWP; TrJP, tr. by James
  Thomson
Es war einmal. . . No, it's too heavy. Märchenbilder. John Ashbery.
  LCAP-2; NOBA
Esanzo. Antoine-Roger Bolamba, French. NegPo, tr. by Ellen Conroy
  Kennedy
Escape. Edmund Blunden. NSI
Escape. Robert Graves. MoBrPo
Escape, The. Ivor Gurney. OxBSP
Escape. Georgia Douglas Johnson. PoBA
Escape, The. William Stafford. NNaP
Escape, The. Mark Van Doren. MoAmPo
Escape. Elinor Wylie. ChAP; MoAmPo
  ("Silver wasp-nests hang like fruit, The.") (LL) ChAP
Escape Artist, The. Kevin Young. GT
Escape at Bedtime. Robert Louis Stevenson. CTV; OTCP
Escape from the weekday tune. Which deadens and endures. (LL) Sunday
  Morning. Louis MacNeice. FaBoMo; MoBrPo; NAEL-2; NIP-4;
  OxAEP-2; Son
Escape me? / Never. Life in a Love. Robert Browning. FHYEP; OBNC
Escape to Love. Patrick MacDonogh.
  "Alone and Godless, stopped by the sudden edge." BIrV
Escaped from Germany—. History and Reality. Stephen Spender. HP
Escorting Candidates to the Examination Hall. Po Chü-i, Chinese. ChiP, tr.
  by Arthur Waley
Eshu. Adesanya Alakoye. ISC
Eskimo Baby, An. Lucy Diamond. BoTP
Eskimo Girl, The. David Ray. LTA
Eskimo Occasion. Judith Rodriguez. CBAP; FaBoWP; NOBAu
Eskimos in Manitoba. Recital. John Updike. OBAL
Esmeralda! Now we rest. Lines Written in Oregon. Vladimir Nabokov.
  NYBP
ESP. Carter Revard. VoR
España, Aparta de me Este Caliz. César Vallejo, Spanish.
  Masses. RB, tr. by Robert Bly
Especially he loves. God Poem. Stanley Moss. VGW
Especially in weeping. Valerio Magrelli, Italian. NeIt, tr. by Dana Gioia
Especially on hot summer Sundays. Hot Summer Sunday. A. L. Hendriks.
  PBCV
Especially when the October wind. Dylan Thomas. MoBrPo; OBWVE;
  OxAEP-2; OxBSP
Esposito, Fiorani, Fogagnolo. To the Fifteen of Piazzale Loreto. Salvatore
  Quasimodo, Italian. AF, tr. by Jack Bevan
Espresso. Carol Lee Saffoti. UnSA
Essay on Concrete, An. Douglas Messerli. FTOS
Essay on Criticism. Alexander Pope. Fr. An Essay on Criticism. NAEL-1;
  NoP-4; PoEL-3; TFi
  ("Flies o'er th' unbending corn, and skims along the main.") (LL) PFE
  ("Flies o'er the unbending corn, and skims along the main.") (LL) HAP
  ("Reader's threaten'd (not in vain) with 'sleep,' The.") (LL) PFE
  Alps on Alps.
  ("Whole at once is bold, and regular, The.") (LL) ImPo
  Art of Poetry, The. ECEV
  "Avoid extremes; and shun the fault of such." FHYEP
  Bookful Blockhead, The. OBSV
  "But true expression, like th' unchanging sun." FHYEP
  "But where's the man who counsel can bestow." OxAEP-1, ll. 631–744
  "First follow Nature, and your judgment frame." EPCY; FHYEP
  ("Are Nature still, but Nature methodized.") (LL) HAP
  "In wit, as nature, what affects our hearts." HAP
  "Little learning is a dangerous [or dang'rous] thing, A." EBEvV; HAP;
  HoPM; NOBE; PoLF, ll 215–251
  (Whole at once is bold, and regular, The.) ImPo, ll 215–252
  "Of all the causes which conspire to blind." OxAEP-1
  Plain Fools. OBSV
  Poetical Numbers.
  ("Flies o'er the unbending corn, and skims along the main.") (LL)
  EPCY; FHYEP; Poetr
  ("That, like a wounded snake, drags its slow length along.") (LL)
  ECEV; HAP
  "Pride, Malice, Folly, against Dryden rose." EPCY

Servile Herd, The. OBSV
"Some beauties yet no precepts can declare." HAP
"Some to Conceit alone their taste confine." OxAEP-1, ll. 289–393; EPCY
  ("As bodies perish through excess of blood.") (LL) EPCY
"Still green with bays each ancient altar stands." EPCY
"Thus critics, of less judgment than caprice." OAEL-1
"'Tis hard to say, if greater want of skill." OAEL-1, ll. 1–266; HAP
  ("But are not critics to their judgment too?") (LL) HAP
"True wit is Nature to advantage dressed." HAP
"Unhappy wit, like most mistaken things." EPCY
Essay on Epic Poetry, An. William Hayley.
  "Apart, and on the sacred hill retired." EPCY
Essay on Friendship. Mary Leapor.
  "To Artemisia.—'Tis to her we sing." PEW
Essay on Language. Wanda Coleman. PmAP
Essay on Lunch. Walker Gibson. NYBP
Essay on Man, An. Alexander Pope.
  "All are but parts of one stupendous whole." FHYEP
  "All Nature is but art, unknown to thee." ECEV
  "Awake, my St. John! leave all meaner things." NAEL-1; PoEL-3
  "Behold the child, by Nature's kindly law." ECEV
  "Bliss of man, The (could pride that blessing find)." NOEC
  "Far as creation's ample range extends." ECEV
  "For forms of government let fools contest." ECEV
  "Hope humbly then; with trembling pinions soar." EBEvV
  Know Thyself. NOBE, ll. 1–18
  (Paragon of Animals, The.)
  (Riddle of the World.)
  "Look round our world; behold the chain of love." FHYEP
  "Nor think, in nature's state they blindly trod." OAEL-1
  "Placed on this isthmus of a middle state." WeW-3
  "What if the foot, ordain'd the dust to tread." FaBoPV
  "What would this Man? Now upward will he soar." HeIP-4
  "What's fame? A fancied life in others' breath." FHYEP
Essay on Man. Unknown. PoToHe
Essay on Marriage. Anne Finch.
  "O, love, in your sweet name enough." FaBoTw
Essay on Memory. Robert David Fitzgerald.
  "Rain in my ears: impatiently there raps." CBAP
Essay on Psychiatrists. Robert Pinsky.
  Dionysus as Psychiatrist. HCAP
  Invocation: "It's crazy to think one could describe them." NoAM
  (Lakeside Identification, A.) NoP-4
  ("Yes, crazy to suppose one could describe them.") NoP-4
  Mad, The. NoAM
  Peroration, Concerning Genius. NoAM
  Proposition. HCAP; NoAM
  Some Terms. HCAP
  Their Patients. NoAM
  Their Philistinism Considered. NoAM
  Their Seriousness, with Further Comparisons. NoAM
  Their Speech, Compared with Wisdom and Poetry. NoAM; PoA
Essay on Satire, Particularly on The Dunciad, An. Walter Harte.
  "Above all flattery, all thirst of gain." EPCY
  "In Albion then, with equal lustre bright." EPCY
Essay on the Different Styles of Poetry, The. Thomas Parnell.
  "Here all the passions, for their greater sway." EPCY
Essay on Translated Verse, An. Wentworth Dillon.
  "Each poet with a different talent writes." EPCY
  "Have we forgot how Raphael's numerous prose." EPCY
Essay on William Carlos Williams, An. Victor Hernandez Cruz. PmAP
Essay on Woman, An. Mary Leapor. BWW; ECWP; NOEC
Esse. Czeslaw Milosz. TOF
Essence Is Not in the Living, The. Mairtin O Direain. BiHa, tr. by Douglas
  Sealy and Tomás MacSiomóin
Essence of Existence, The. 182nd Chorus. Jack Kerouac. NeAP Fr.
  Mexico City Blues.
Essence of ink, The. Yün Shou-p'ing. CoBLCP, tr. by Jonathan Chaves
  Fr. In My Boat, Painting a Picture of Going Home by Boat.
Essence of orchids in her tumbled hair, a goddess of spring. A Song Of
  Chang Ching-Yüan Picking Lotus Flowers. Wen T'ing-yün, Chinese.
  LoP; SuSp, tr. by William R. Schultz
Essential oils—are wrung. Emily Dickinson. APN-2; AmPP; PBMM
Essential poem at the centre [or center] of things, The. A Primitive like an
  Orb. Wallace Stevens. NOBA

Essentially description, night. (1978, Remembering 1962). C. S. Giscombe. GT

Essie Parrish in New York. Elsie Parrish, *Kashia Pomo Indian.* STP, *tr. by* George Quasha

Est tamen invidia mors tibi continua. (LL) Philip Sparrow. John Skelton. AAS; NOBE; OAEL-1; OxBoLi; PeLV; PoEL-1

Esta. Linda Gregg. AFr

Está Muy Caliente. George Bowering. MoCV

Establish thy serenity o'er the fields. (LL) Haze. Henry David Thoreau. NCAP; TAP

"Established" is a good word, much used in garden books. Time. Mary Ursula Bethell. APAD; FaBoWP; OBGa

Establishment has taken to the hills. First Letter to an Irish Novelist. Roy McFadden. PNI

Estate, The. Charles Brasch.
"What have you seen on the summits, the peaks that plunge their." PeNZ

Estate and an earldom at seventy-four, An! Horace, 4th Earl of Orford Walpole. FaBoEE

Estelí / this mountain town means something. Resurrection. Joy Harjo. HATNAP

Estelle irons khaki and navy. City Blues. Christine Craig. HCP

Esteville fire begins to burn. On Summer. George Moses Horton. AAP

Esther [a Young Man's Tragedy]. Wilfrid Scawen Blunt.
I Will Not Tell the Secrets. Son
"When I hear laughter from a tavern door." OBMV
With Esther. OBEV

Esther K. Comes to America: 1931. Jerome Rothenberg. NNaP

Esther's Tomcat. Ted Hughes. OxBC

Esthete in Harlem. Langston Hughes. BPo; ColAP

Esthétique du Mal. Wallace Stevens. LiTM
"He was at Naples writing letters home." CMoP; MeMAP; NOBA
"Life is a bitter aspic. We are not." CMoP
"Sun, in clownish yellow, but not a clown, The." NOBA

Esthonian Bridal Song. Johann Gottfried von Herder, *German.* AWP, *tr. by* W. Taylor

Estonia. A private dacha. Irina Znamenskaya, *Russian.* TCRP, *tr. by* Vera Dunham

Estranged in site. The Parthenon. Herman Melville. NCAP

Estrangements. William Pitt Root. IFJA

Estray, The. Forceythe Willson. APN-2

E[a]strich, thou feather[e]d fool[e] and easy [*or* easie] prey. Lucasta's Fan[ne], with a Looking-Glass[e] in It. Richard Lovelace. CaPo; CavPo

Estuarial Republic, The. Douglas Dunn. FaBoMo

Estuary. Ted Walker. NYBP

Esyllt. Glyn Jones. OBWVE

Et cetera. (LL) The Cheerful Girls at Smiller's Bar. Jack A. Mapanje. HBAPE; PeSAV

Et Cetera. Léon Damas, *French.* NegPo, *tr. by* Ellen Conroy Kennedy

Et cætera, et cætera, et cætera. (LL) Austrian Army, An. Alaric Alexander Watts. BLPA; NOBL; PeLV

Et in Arcadia Ego. W. H. Auden. CMoP

Et in Leucadia Ego. Michael Davidson. PmAP

Et Incarnatus Est. William Langland. NOBE *Fr.* The Vision of Piers Plowman.

Et Quid Amabo Nisi Quod Aenigma Est. Stephen Sandy. NYBP

Et the pie-dough. (LL) The Diners in the Kitchen. James Whitcomb Riley. CTAV

État. Anne-Marie Albiach, *French.*
"Of the unended in the speed of." PBWP, *tr. by* Paul Auster

Etch in the memory of your bones. For Mark James Robert Essex d. 1973. Alvin Aubert. BkSV

Etched Away From. Paul Celan, *German.* OBVE, *tr. by* Michael Hamburger

Eternal Aphrodite. Sappho, *Greek.* OBCVT, *tr. by* Groden, Suzy Q.

Eternal City, The. A. R. Ammons. HCAP

Eternal Father, Strong to Save. William Whiting. FaPoR; NOCV

Eternal Female groand! [*or* groan'd!] it was heard all over the Earth, The. A Song of Liberty. William Blake. *Fr.* The Marriage of Heaven and Hell. NAEL-2; NOBRP; OAEL-2

Eternal gates' terrific porter lifted the northern bar, The. The Secrets of the Earth. William Blake. NOBE *Fr.* The Book of Thel. NAEL-2; OAEL-2; OBNC; PoE; PoEL-4

Eternal God[,] (for whom who ever [*or* whoever] dare). Upon the Translation of the Psalms by Sir Philip Sidney, and the Countess of Pembroke His Sister. Donne. EPCY

Eternal God, How They're Increased. Cotton Mather. AH

Eternal God! maker of all. The Book. Henry Vaughan. GeHe; PBRV

Eternal God, our life is but. A Prayer. "Yehoash," *Yiddish.* TrJP, *tr. by* Isidore Goldstick

Eternal God, whose power upholds. Henry Hallam Tweedy. AH

Eternal Goodness, The. John Greenleaf Whittier.
"I know not what the future hath." NOCV

Eternal Image, The. Ruth Pitter. MoBrPo; OxBTC

Eternal Jew, The. Jacob Cohen, *Hebrew.* TrJP, *tr. by* I. M. Lask

Eternal King, grant me true quietness. Angilbert's Prayer. Angilbert, *Latin.* MLL, *tr. by* Helen Waddell

Eternal Landscape, The. Lenard D. Moore. GT

Eternal Light! Thomas Binney. NOCV

Eternal lightning of Lenin's bones, The. (LL) The Skeleton of the Future. "Hugh MacDiarmid." MoBrPo; OBMV

Eternal Love, maintain thy life in me. (LL) Splendidis longum valedico nugis. Sir Philip Sidney. AEP; GSo; PFE

Eternal Masculine. William Rose Benét. AWP; MoAmPo

Eternal nature! When thy giant hand. On Slavery. Thomas Campbell. Ro *Fr.* The Pleasures of Hope.

Eternal pain! (LL) Philomela. Matthew Arnold. EBVVPR; FHYEP; OAEL-2; OBEV; UnPo

Eternal Paraclete, to thee. (LL) Veni Creator Spiritus. Charlemagne *and* Hrabanus Maurus (*fl.* 9th cent.), *par. by* Dryden. AWP; FaPoR

Eternal reciprocity of tears. (LL) Insensibility. Wilfred Owen. CMoP; FaBoTw; InPS-3; LiTM; NoP-4; OBWP; OxAEP-2; OxBTC; PeFWW; PoWW

Eternal Return, The. Robert Silliman Hillyer. AiP; NYBP

Eternal Road, The. Franz Werfel, *German.*
Ye Sorrowers. TrJP, *tr. by* Ludwig Lewisohn

Eternal Sabbath. Isaac Leibush Peretz, *Yiddish.* TrJP, *tr. by* Joseph Leftwich

Eternal son of God for sin did die, The. The Authors of Confession. Elizabeth Major. KTR *Fr.* Honey on the Rod.

Eternal Spirit of the chainless Mind! The Prisoner of Chillon. Byron. PoLF

Eternal Spirit of the chainless Mind! Sonnet on Chillon. Byron. GSo; GTBS-P; PBMP *Fr.* The Prisoner of Chillon. PoLF

Eternal Spirit, Source of Light. Samuel Davies. AH

ETERNAL sprite, which art in heaven the love. To God the Holy Ghost. Henry Constable. NoSic

Eternal, Thou. Saint Ambrose, *Latin.* MLL, *tr. by* Helen Waddell

Eternal Values. Grace Noll Crowell. PoToHe

Eternal Years, The. Frederick William Faber. PWR

Eternale Footeman's Tale, The. George Moor. BXAP

Eternall and all-working God, which wast. Michael Drayton. PoEL-2 *Fr.* Noah's Flood.

Eternall Truth, almighty, infinite. Sonnet: "Eternall Truth, almighty, infinite." Greville Fulke. NoSic *Fr.* Caelica.

Eternally distant, luminous in the air. (LL) The Book of How. Merrill Moore. FuPo

Eternally in summer air. Kenneth Rexroth. *See* The Signature of All Things.

Eternities. Norman Mailer. NYBP

Eternities before the first-born day. Mother Night. James Weldon Johnson. Son

Eternity. Bozhidar Bozhilov, *Bulgarian.* CEEP, *tr. by* Jascha Kessler *and* Aleksandar Shurbanov

Eternity ("He who binds to himself a joy"). William Blake. APAD; AWP; EBEV; EnlH; FaBoEE; ImPo; NOBE; NTP; NoP-4; OBNC; OxBSP; Poetr; RB; SCGP; SoSe-8; Spl *Fr.* Several Questions Answered.

Eternity. Josephine D. Henderson Heard. CBWP-4

Eternity. Robert Herrick. CavPo

Eternity. James Whitcomb Riley. GSo

Eternity is passion, girl or boy. Whence Had They Come? W. B. Yeats. BoLoP

Eternity of Love Protested. Thomas Carew. BeJo; MeLP
(Song: Eternity of Love Protested.) NOSC

Eternity of Nature, The. John Clare. EBEV

Eternity, thou thunderous word. Johann Rist. GePo, *stanzas* 1–3, *tr. by* Z. Philip Ambrose *Fr.* Eternity, Thou Thunderous Word.

Ethan Boldt. Roger Weingarten. AmPA

Ethel in her crimson row boat. Chateaux en Espagne. Henrietta Cordelia Ray. CBWP-3

Ethelstan. George Darley.
O'er the Wild Gannet's Bath. PoEL-4

Ether Insatiable. May Kendall. CABP

Ethereal minstrel! pilgrim of the sky! To the Skylark. Wordsworth. GTBS-P

Ethical schizophrenia you called it. Goin' to the Territory. Michael S. Harper. NAAAL

Ethick. Robert Bridges. OxBTC *Fr.* The Testament of Beauty.

Ethics. Linda Pastan. InPK-6

Ethics for Everyman. Roger Woddis. NOBL

Ethiopia. Kate Daniels. PBCAP

Ethiopia. Frances Ellen Watkins Harper. NAAAL

Ethiopia for Tifa, *for Tifa.* Audre Lorde. LiLi

Ethnic Life, The. Daniel Halpern. AmPA

Ethnocide. Howard Fergus. PBCV

Ethnogenesis. Henry Timrod. APN-2; AmPP; NOBA; OxBA

Ethnologists up with the Sioux. Limerick. *Unknown.* PeLi

Etiquette. Sir William Schwenck Gilbert. FaBoCh

Etlekhe Verter Oyf Mame-Loshn / A Few Words in the Mother Taunge. Irena Klepfisz. *See* A Few Words in the Mother Tongue.

Etrick Forest is a fair forest[e]. The Outlaw Murray. *Unknown.* ESPB; OxBB

Etruscan Notebook. Elena Clementelli, *Italian.* PBWP, *tr. by* Ruth Feldman *and* Brian Swann

Etruscan Tombs. Agnes Mary Frances Robinson. PeVV

Ettrick. Lady John Scott. LW; SoSe-8; WPE

Ettricke Foreste is a feir forestle. The Sang of the Outlaw Murray. *Unknown.* IBB

Etude in Glass. Janina Degutyte, *Lithuanian.* CEEP, *tr. by* M. G. Slavenas

Étude Réaliste. Swinburne.

"Baby's feet, like sea-shells pink, A." WeW-3

Etudes. Dennis Phillips.

If It's Only Rhythm. FTOS

Euch, are you having your period? "Alta." NMM-2

Euclid alone has looked on Beauty bare. Edna St. Vincent Millay. CMoP; GSo; HeIP-4; MeMAP; MoAmPo; NAAL-2; NoP-4; Son; TAP

Euclid Avenue. Harry Clifton. PBCIP

Eudaimon. Kathleen Jessie Raine. PBWP

Eugenia. George Chapman.

Death Described by His True Effects. NOSC

Eugenio. Hugh Henry Brackenridge *and* Philip Freneau. *Fr.* The Rising Glory of America. AiP

Eugenist, The. Robert Graves. FaBoEE

Eulogy, The. Carol Muske. PBCAP

Eulogy for a Hermit Crab. Pattiann Rogers. WeT

Eulogy for Hasdai ibn Shaprut. *Unknown, Hebrew.* TrJP, *tr. by* Israel Abrahams

Eulogy for Populations. Ron Welburn. PoBA

Eulogy of the Sagely Virtue of His Imperial Majesty Emperor Shih-tsu, A. Chao Meng-fu, *Chinese.* CoBLCP, *tr. by* Jonathan Chaves

Eulogy on My Own Portrait, A. Yang Shih-ch'i, *Chinese.* CoBLCP, *tr. by* Jonathan Chaves

Eumares. Asclepiades, *Greek.* AWP, *tr. by* Richard Garnett

Eumelos had a Maltese dog. Tymnes, *Greek.* PGA, *tr. by* Kenneth Rexroth

Eumenides, The. Aeschylus, *Greek.* NAWM-1, *tr. by* Robert Fagles

"She-kin, show our force. Join hands!" OBCVT, *tr. by* Tony Harrison

Eumenides at Home, The. James Agate. BXAP

Eunica scorned [*or* skornde] me, when her I would have sweetly kissed [*or* kist]. Neteheard. Theocritus, *Greek.* NoSic; OBVE *Fr.* Idylls.

Eunica skorned me, when her I would have sweetly kist. Theocritus. *See* Neteheard.

Eunice is tired of pain, everyone else's. Some Gangster Pain. Gillian Conoley. CMAP

Eunuch Unique. Francis Picabia, *French.* PFTM, *tr. by* Tom Mandel *Fr.* Eunuch Unique.

Euphene. Ben Jonson.

Picture of the Body, The. NOSC

Euphemisms of the love-blind. Lucretius, *Latin.* OBCVT, *tr. by* John Dryden

Euridice. "Alta." NMM-2

Euripides. Thucydides, *Greek.* GrAn, *tr. by* Peter Jay

Europa. Moschus, *Greek.* HePo, *tr. by* Barbara Hughes Fowler

"Into the Mead he comes, nor (seen) doth fright." OBCVT, *tr. by* Thomas Stanley

Europa. William Plomer. MoBS

Europa. Anatol Stern, *Polish.* PFTM, *tr. by* Stefan Themerson *and* Michael Horowitz

Europa (in Athens) does business / at truly reasonable rates. Antipater of Thessalonica, *Greek.* GrAn, *tr. by* Andrew Miller

Europa kisses sweetly. Rufinus Domesticus, *Greek.* InMo, *tr. by* Sam Hamill

Europa's kiss / even if. Rufinus, *Greek.* GrAn, *tr. by* Alan Marshfield

Europe and America. David Ignatow. NNaP; PBMP; UnPo

Europe / Is endowed with the first move. Calvin Forbes. NBV

Europe, Late. Dan Pagis, *Hebrew.* HP, *tr. by* Stephen Mitchell

Europe lies in ruins: a black headline story. 1945. Sheila Cussons, *Afrikaans.* PeSA, *tr. by* Jack Cope *and* Uys Krige

European Crimes. Charles Churchill. *Fr.* Gotham. NOEC

European Shoe is constructed of grass and reed, [bound,] The. Michael Benedikt. AmPA; CoAmPo; TwCP

Europe's Prisoners. Sidney Keyes. PoWW

Eurotas said to the goddess of love. Leonidas of Tarentum, *Greek.* GrAn, *tr. by* Peter Levi

Euryalus and Nisus Meet Their Deaths. Virgil. NoSic, *tr. by* Thomas Phaer *Fr.* The Aeneid [*or* Eneados, *Aeneis*].

Eurydice. Hilda Doolittle.

"At least I have the flowers of myself." NMM-2

"So for your arrogance." NMM-2

"So you have swept me back." NALW; NMM-2; VGW

("I had forgot you / and the past.") (LL) NMM-2

Eurydice. Rachel Blau DuPlessis.

"Back arched like a bow." DeD

"She will lie naked." DeD

"Since the narcissus bud." DeD

"Where is the bird?" DeD

Eurydice to Orpheus. Robert Browning. CBLP

(Orpheus and Eurydice.) CTC

Eutawville Lynching, The. Lizelia Augusta Jenkins Moorer. CBWP-3

Euthymiae Raptus; or, The Teares of Peace. George Chapman.

"And, now gives Time, her states description." PoEL-2

Justice. NOSC

Learning ("So Learned Men in Controversies Spend"). NOSC

Peace Discovers the Poet. NOSC

Peace of Death, The. NOSC

Eutopia. Francis Turner Palgrave. EBVV; OBGa

Eutychides. Edwin Arlington Robinson, *after the Greek of* Lucilius. OBAL

Eutychides the thief was in a rare. Lucilius, *Greek.* GrAn, *tr. by* Peter Porter

Eutychides, who wrote the songs. Lucilius. OBAL *Fr.* Variations of Greek Themes.

Eutychos was prolific as a painter. Lucilius, *Greek.* InMo, *tr. by* Sam Hamill

Eutychus. Rosemary Dobson. ChIV-2

Eutychus the painter / Fathered twenty sons. Lucilius, *Greek.* GrAn, *tr. by* Alistair Elliot

Evacuation. Pol N Ndu. PBMAP

Evadne. Hilda Doolittle. BoWoP; LW

Evahmo'. . . . Sterling Brown. *See* Southern Road.

Evan just had the white birch lined up. Fear and Anger in the Mindless Universe. Hayden Carruth. NNaP

Evanescent. Tanka. Akiko Yosano, *Japanese.* MJT, *tr. by* Ueda, Makoto

Evanescent hue whose pearly gleam, An. An Ideal. Henrietta Cordelia Ray. CBWP-3

Evangelical vicar in want. Limerick. Ronald Arbuthnott Knox. PeLi

Evangeline. Henry Wadsworth Longfellow.

"Talk not of wasted affection." CTV

Tale of Acadie, A. MeMAP

From Evangeline. NoP-4

Evangeline made her. Straight Talk from Plain Women. Sherley Anne Williams. GT

Evangelle. Anne Waldman. PT

Evanishings. Mary E. Tucker. CBWP-1

Evans Country, The. Kingsley Amis.

Aberdarcy: The Chaucer Road. NOBL

Aberdarcy: The Main Square. NOBL; NoAM; OxBTC

Aldport (Mystery Tour). NOBL

Brynbwrla. NOBL

Fforestfawr. NOBL

Langwell. NOBL; OxBC

Pendydd. NOBL

Evarra and His Gods. Rudyard Kipling. MoBrPo

Evasion, An. Douglas Livingstone. PeSA

Evasive souls, of whom the wise lose track. The Imaginative Life. Geoffrey Hill. NoAM

Eve. Arthur J. Bull. UnPo

Eve. David Gascoyne. GTBS-P

Eve. Oliver Herford. OBAL

Eve. Dorothy Livesay. NALW

Eve. Milton. *See* Adam and Eve in the Garden.

Eve. Howard Nemerov. CRP

Eve. Christina Rossetti. CH; ChIV-1; GTBS-P; NALW; NIP-4; PoEL-5; Poetr

Eve. *Unknown, Irish.* BIrV, *tr. by* Thomas Macdonagh

Eve am I, great Adam's wife. *Unknown.* NOIV

Eve & her envy roving slammed me down. Gislebertus' Eve. John Berryman. LCAP-2

Eve is madly in love with Hugh. Office Friendships. Gavin Ewart. FP; PeLV

Eve Names the Animals. Susan Donnelly. Poetr

Eve of Christmas had arrived, The. A Christmas Ghost. Priscilla Jane Thompson. CBWP-2

Eve of St Agnes, The. Keats. CABP; EBNV; EP; FHYEP; HAP; HoPM; ImPo; NAEL-2; NOBRP; NoP-4; OAEL-2; OBNC; OBNV; OxAEP-2; PoE; PoEL-4; PoLF; Poetr; Ro; TFi; TRP
  "Then by the bed-side, where the faded moon." PFE

Eve of Saint John, The. Sir Walter Scott. PoEL-4

Eve of St. Mark, The. Keats. CH

Eve of Waterloo, The. Byron. EBEvV; FaBoBe; FaBoCh; NOBE; OBNC *Fr.* Childe Harold's Pilgrimage.

Eve of Waterloo, The. Thomas Hardy. OAEL-2; OBWP *Fr.* The Dynasts.

Eve Oh Eve. Taslima Nasrin, *Bengali.* VCWP, *tr. by* Carolyne Wright *and* Mohammad Nurul Huda

Eve Penitent. Milton. *Fr.* Book X. FHYEP *Fr.* Paradise Lost.

Eve (Rachel). Michael S. Harper. MoLi

Eve-Song. Mary Gilmore. CBAP; LW

Eve tempts Adam. Milton. FaBoSe *Fr.* Paradise Lost.

Eve the fox swung. Paula Gunn Allen. NMM-2

Eve to Adam. Milton. *Fr.* Book IV. OAEL-1 *Fr.* Paradise Lost.

Eve to Her Daughters. Judith Wright. NALW; NoP-4

Eve to Lilith. Michelene Wandor. NBrP

Eve, with her basket, was. Ralph Hodgson. CH; ChIV-1; LiTM; MoBrPo; TrCP; UnPo

Evelyn. Priscilla Jane Thompson. CBWP-2

Even. Anne Morrow Lindbergh. AiP

Even a child is known by his doings. Bible, *O.T.* CTV *Fr.* The Bible, Proverbs 20:11.

Even a feather in flight can sketch. Day and Night. Eugenio Montale, *Italian.* AF, *tr. by* William Arrowsmith

Even a flaming fire can be snatched. Empress Jito, *Japanese.* WPJ, *tr. by* Kenneth Rexroth *and* Ikuko Atsumi *Fr.* Manyo Shu, Part 1 of 4.

Éven a priést or a pólitician. (LL) Calypso. W. H. Auden. CBLP; PeLV

Even a Pyrrhonist. A Lot of Night Music. Anthony Hecht. OxBC; Poetr

Even a rock. How I Come to You. Molly Peacock. RA

Even after Confession. On a Catholic Childhood. Janet Campbell Hale. VoR

Even as a child, of sorrow that we give. Pride of Youth. D. G. Rossetti. OBNC *Fr.* The House of Life.

Even as a holy martyr sheds her blood. (LL) Stanzas on Mutability. Hugo von Hofmannsthal, *German.* TrJP, *tr. by* Jethro Bithell

Even as a young man. Once More Fields and Gardens. T'ao Ch'ien, *Chinese.* AWP, *tr. by* Amy Lowell *and* Florence Ayscough

Even as children they were late sleepers. The Undead. Richard Wilbur. CAPP-1; CoAP; CoAmPo; OxBC

Even as I hold you. Alice Walker. MT; WeW-3

Even as the cattle in the winter woods. For France. Claudian, *Latin.* MLL; OBCVT, *tr. by* Helen Waddell

Even as the day when it is yet at dawning. Canzone: Of His Love, with the Figure of a Sudden Storm. Prinzivalle Doria, *Italian.* AWP, *tr. by* D. G. Rossetti

Even as the others mock, thou mockest me. Dante. AWP *Fr.* La Vita Nuova.

Even as the sun with purple-colour'd face. Shakespeare. FaBoSe
  ("Even as the sunne with purple-coulord face.") PBRV
  ("So he were like him, and by Venus side.") (LL) PBRV

Even as the wandering traveler doth stray. John Hall. ChIV-1

Even as we kill. On the Birth of My Son, Malcolm Coltrane. Julius Lester. PoBA

Even ashes of lovers find no rest. (LL) The Hour-Glass [*or* Houre-Glasse]. Ben Jonson. BeJo; EnLoPo; GLoP; ImPo; NIP-4; OAEL-1; SeCP

Even at prayer, our eyes look inward. Asadullah Khan Ghalib, *Urdu.* EnlH, *tr. by* Jane Hirshfield

Even before I speak, she serves. (LL) Nani. Alberto A. Ríos. UnSA

Even Buddha is lost in this land. Tassajara, 1969. Diane Di Prima. BB

Even by force I make the night surrender. Fingerprints. Jaroslav Seifert, *German.* CEEP, *tr. by* Ewald Osers

Even clothed in wrinkles, dear Philinna. Paulus Silentiarius, *Greek.* InMo, *tr. by* Sam Hamill

Even dead the old man grows. Hipponax. Alcaeus, *Greek.* GrAn, *tr. by* Alistair Elliot

Even during war, moments of delicate peace. Muriel Rukeyser. TrJP *Fr.* Letter to the Front.

Even fine steel thinly made. For a Broken Needle. Hazel Hall. NMM-2; PaTW

Even flaming fire. Empress Jito. *See* Even a flaming fire can be snatched.

Even for the wind there was no room. The Way the Bird Sat. Ray A. Young Bear. CDW; VoR

Even from earthly love thy face avert not. Nuru'ddin Abdu 'R-Rahman Jami, *Persian.* TOF, *tr. by* E. G. Browne

Even from the beach I could sense it. Attack of the Crab Monsters. Lawrence Raab. AmPA

Even gods resent my paradise. Hors de Combat. "Anvari," *Persian.* ArPe, *tr. by* Omar S. Pound

Even here I taste, having eaten it / all these years. (LL) Red Dust. Philip Levine. NNaP; NoAM

Even if God did not exist, religion would still be holy and divine. Fuses I and II. Charles Baudelaire, *French.* PFTM, *tr. by* Norman Cameron

Even if I am only more dust. Pompeius, *Greek.* GrAn, *tr. by* Dennis Schmitz

Even if one wears oneself out paying for them. Catullus. *See* Carmen 31 ("Apple of islands, Sirmio, & bright peninsulas, set").

Even if the geraniums are artificial. The Geraniums. Genevieve Taggard. VGW

Even if you are killed, you die. The Bus-Stop on the Somme. David Rowbotham. NOBAu

Even if you can't shape your life the way you want. As Much As You Can. Constantine P. Cavafy, *Greek.* GrIP; RB, *tr. by* Edmund Keeley *and* Philip Sherrard

Even in bed I pose: desire may grow. Carnal Knowledge. Thom Gunn. BoLoP; EP

Even in death they prosper; even in the death. Necropolis. Karl Shapiro. PoA

Even in dreams. Lady Ise, *Japanese.* WPJ, *tr. by* Kenneth Rexroth *and* Ikuko Atsumi

Even in my dreams / I must no longer meet you. Lady Ise, *Japanese.* BoWoP, *tr. by* Etsuko Terasaki *and* Irma Brandeis

Even in my dreams you have denied yourself to me. To Kalon. Ezra Pound. PoA

Even in repentance there is pleasure. Elizaveta Kuzmina-Karavayeva, *Russian.* TCRP, *tr. by* Thomas E. Bird

Even in September noon, the groundhog. Upon Hearing of My Friend's Marriage Breaking Up. Dean Young. BAP-94

Even in sleep my eyes are on the elements. An Astronomer's Journal. Jane Shore. PoA

Even in the age. Narihira, *Japanese.* OHPJ, *tr. by* Kenneth Rexroth

Even in the bluest noonday of July. To Mrs. Will H. Low. Robert Louis Stevenson. NOBVV

Even in the moment of our earliest kiss. Edna St. Vincent Millay. HeIP-4; VGW

Even in youth. (LL) An Ode: "High-spirited friend, / I send not balms, nor corsives to your wound." Ben Jonson. BeJo; OBEV

Even invisible things. Even Invisible Things (two poems). Ōkuma Nobuyuki, *Japanese.* MJT, *tr. by* Makoto Ueda

Even Invisible Things (two poems). Ōkuma Nobuyuki, *Japanese.* MJT, *tr. by* Makoto Ueda

Even is come; and from the dark Park, hark. A Nocturnal Sketch. Thomas Hood. PeLV

Even Memphis smells pretty. Last Night in Elvisville. Lydia Tomkiw. WWSi

Even my loves are measured by wars. Yehuda Amichai. PoSu, *tr. by* Yehuda Amichai *and* Ted Hughes *Fr.* Patriotic Songs.

Even now I wish that you had been there. Swans Mating. Michael Longley. IIP; PNI

Even now my breast bone's aching. Part of a Bird. Nina Cassian, *Romanian.* PoSu, *tr. by* Andrea Deletant *and* Brenda Walker

Even now / My thought is all of this gold-tinted king's daughter. Black Marigolds. Bilhana, *formerly at. to* Chauras, *Sanskrit.* AWP, *tr. by* E. Powys Mathers

Even now that care which on thy crown attends. To the Thrice-Sacred Queen Elizabeth. Mary Sidney Herbert, Countess of Pembroke. NALW; NoP-4

Even now that Care which on thy Crowne attends. Mary Sidney Herbert, Countess of Pembroke. *See* To the Thrice-Sacred Queen Elizabeth.

Even now the devastation is begun. Oliver Goldsmith. EBEV *Fr.* The Deserted Village. NOEC; OAEL-1; PoEL-3

Even now the fragrant darkness of her hair. Terre Promise. Ernest Christopher Dowson. NOBVV

Even now there are places where a thought might grow. A Disused Shed in Co. Wexford. Derek Mahon. BiHa; CABP; CIP-2; FaBoPV; NOIV; NoP-4; OxBC; PBCIP; PNI

Even now this landscape is assembling. All Hallows. Louise Glück. AmPA; HCAP; PoPoPo

Even of [or for] the children of Israel, a people near unto him. Praise ye the Lord [or him. Hallelujah]. (LL) Psalm 148. Bible, *O.T. Hebrew.* TrJP

Even on clear nights, lead the most supple children. The Great Bear. John Hollander. ColAP; LiTM; NYBP; NoAM; TwCP

Even on Sunday. Robin Blaser. FTOS

Even on the quietest days the distant. Ford Manor. Derek Mahon. PBCIP

Even or odd, of all days in the year. Shakespeare. SCV *Fr.* Romeo and Juliet.

Even ordinarily, parting is difficult. Yang Shih-ch'i. CoBLCP, *tr. by* Jonathan Chaves *Fr.* Inscribed on a Painting of Bamboo Presented to Lecturer Ch'en Upon His Departure to Resume His Duties at Nanking.

Even So. D. G. Rossetti. NOBE; NOBVV; OBNC

Even so deep in the jungle they were not safe. The Garden of Ships. Douglas Stewart. CBAP

Even so distant, I can taste the grief. Deceptions. Philip Larkin. CMoP; FaBoSe; GTBS-P; OxAEP-2

'Even so!' said the Queen. (LL) Jealousy. Mary Elizabeth Coleridge. CH; EnLoPo; LW; OBNC; WPE

Even such is time, that [or which] takes in trust. Verses Made the Night before He Died [or Dyed]. Sir Walter Ralegh. AAS; FaBoEE; HAP; ImPo; NAEL-1; NOBE; NTP; NoSic; OBEV; OxBSP; PeECV; PoRA; RB; SCGP; SiPS; TFi; TRP

Even such is Time, which takes in trust. Verses Made the Night before His Beheading. Sir Walter Ralegh. CABP

Even than all lovely lights, and roses, are? (LL) Dark fens of cedar; hemlock-branches gray. Frederick Goddard Tuckerman. APN-2; PAR

Even that desperate gaiety is gone. There Is No Riot. Martin Carter. PBCV

Even the air could kill us. (LL) Angels in Winter. Nancy Willard. ColAP

Even the bad news came slowly and was afraid. Washington Heights, 1959. Michael C. Blumenthal. HCAP

Even the barnacle has certain rights. This Octopus Exploits Women. James Fenton. CBNP; NoAM

Even the black gloves. Tanka. Fumi Saito, *Japanese.* MJT, *tr. by* Ueda, Makoto

Even the dark end of Belmont Avenue. Walking by the Cliffside Dyeworks. Robert Carnevale. UnSA

Even the dirt kept breathing a small breath. (LL) Root Cellar. Theodore Roethke. AmPP; ColAP; HeIP-4; InPK-6; NoP-4; PFE; SAGP; VCAP

Even the dissident ones speak. America. John Newlove. NOBC

Even the dumb beasts. How They Communicate. Lucretius, *Latin.* APo, *tr. by* Rolfe Humphries

Even the Eagles Must Gather. Alma Villanueva. FFC

Even the fat slug. Everything in the Garden is Lovely. Alasdair Aston. OBGa

Even the graves are not tended in Russia. Georgy Vladimirovich Ivanov, *Russian.* TCRP, *tr. by* Daniel Weissbort

Even the liveliest of us had. Another and Another and. Theodore Weiss. DiPo

Even the long-dead are willing to move. Gentle Communion. Pat Mora. NIP-4

Even the most die-hard liberals. A Lonely Affair. Reuben Jackson. GT

Even the night will blossom as the rose. (LL) On Growing Old. John Masefield. CMoP; ImPo; LiTM; MoBrPo; PoLF; PoRA; SAGP

Even the rainbow has a body. The Rainbow. D. H. Lawrence. NTP

Even the sky here in Connecticut has it. A Winter without Snow. J. D. McClatchy. FYAP

Even the spring water. The Cutting Edge. Philip Levine. NYBP

Even the sun-clouds this morning cannot manage such skirts. Poppies in October. Sylvia Plath. FaBoWP; HCAP; LCAP-2; NoAM

Even the sun, still warm. August/Fresno 1973. Roberta Spear. AmPA

Even the walls are flowing, even the ceiling. Variation on Heraclitus. Louis MacNeice. MoP; NoAM

Even the whales now. Tom Matthews. PNI

Even then I said. Antiphilus, *Greek.* GrAn, *tr. by* Alan Marshfield

Even this late it happens. The Coming of Light. Mark Strand. HCAP

Even this love's heat must be its curb and rein. (LL) Cantica: Our Lord Christ: Of Order. Saint Francis of Assisi, *also at. to* Jacopone da Todi, *Italian.* AWP; OBVE, *tr. by* D. G. Rossetti

Even This Shall Pass Away. Theodore Tilton. BLPA

Even this suburb has overcome Death. Easter. Howard Nemerov. NoP-4

Even though he lies underground. Erucius of Cyzicus, *Greek.* GrAn, *tr. by* Peter Levi

Even though my hands / are rough from much rice-pounding. *Unknown, Japanese.* BoWoP, *tr. by* Kenneth Yasuda

Even time, An. What I Do. Denise Riley. NBrP

Even to each other. Merely to be mere, ly to be. (LL) Song Form. Imamu Amiri Baraka. ChAP; TTTS

Even to the children/ on the disenchanted shore. The Blade of Grass Sings to the River. Leah Goldberg. TrJP, *tr. by* Robert Friend *Fr.* Songs of the Stream.

Even to thy pure and most most loving breast. (LL) Sonnet 110. Shakespeare. AEP; EBEV; NoSic; OxAEP-1

Even tonight and I need to take a walk and clear. Poem About My Rights. June Jordan. GLP; ISC; NAAAL; NMM-2; NoAM

Even under a petroglyphic coastal overcast. Edge Effect. Sandra McPherson. BAP-96

Even uprooted, still their flowers. Always, In March. Ion Caraion, *Romanian.* CEEP, *tr. by* Marguerite Dorian *and* Elliott B. Urdang

Even we, / Even so. (LL) Dirge in Woods. George Meredith. NAEL-2; OBEV; OBNC; PFE

Even when a man has earned much. Children. Pāṇṭiyaṉ Ariyutai Nampi, *Tamil.* PLW, *tr. by* A. K. Ramanujan

Even when black Saturn. Pāri's Green Land, Remembered. Kapilar, *Tamil.* PLW, *tr. by* A. K. Ramanujan

Even when I cross those places. Six on the Desert Ways. Otalantaiyar, *Tamil.* PLW, *tr. by* A. K. Ramanujan

Even when I fall asleep early. Insomnia. Lu Yu, *Chinese.* OHMPC, *tr. by* Kenneth Rexroth

Even while. Tanka. Tsukamoto Kunio, *Japanese.* MJT, *tr. by* Makoto Ueda

Even while he sung Sir Proteus rose. Thomas Love Peacock. CBNP *Fr.* Sir Proteus, a Satirical Ballad.

Even with insects—. Avedik Issahakian. ChAP

Even with its own ax to grind, sometimes. The Mind, Intractable Thing. Marianne Moore. LiTM; NYBP

Even with the good knight Charlemain. (LL) Ballad of the Lords of Old Time. François Villon, *French.* AWP; PeVV, *tr. by* Swinburne

Evenen in the Village. William Barnes. EBVV

Evenfall, so slow on hills, hath shot, The. The Lights of London. Louise Imogen Guiney. APN-2

Evening. Richard Aldington. MoBrPo

Evening, An. William Allingham. EnLoPo; NOBVV

Evening. Joanna Baillie. ECWP *Fr.* A Summer Day.

Evening. Byron. *See* Hesperus the Bringer.

Evening. John Clare. NOBVV

Evening. Charles Cotton. *See* Evening Quatrains.

Evening. Emily Dickinson. BoTP

Evening. Hilda Doolittle. CMoP; FaBoMo; VGW; WPE

Evening. Andreas Gryphius, *German.* GePo, *tr. by* George C. Schoolfield

Evening. Beatrice Hawley. MoLi

Evening. King D. Kuka. VoR

Evening. Emma Lazarus. APN-2 *Fr.* Phantasies.

Evening. W. S. Merwin. NAAL-2

Evening. Thomas Miller. ACTP; NOxBChV; OxBChV

Evening. Helen G. Quigless. BkSV

Evening. Dame Edith Sitwell. MoBS

Evening. James Stephens. MoBrPo

Evening, The. Georg Trakl, *German.* PFTM, *tr. by* Robert Firmage

Evening. *Unknown.* BoTP

Evening. Victor Van Vriesland, *Dutch.* TrJP, *tr. by* Adriaan J. Barnouw

Evening. James Wright. NOBA; NYBP

Evening! A flight of pigeons in clear sky! The Flute; a Pastoral. José-Maria de Heredia, *French.* AWP, *tr. by* H. J. C. Grierson

Evening; an Elegy. Horace Smith. BXAP

Evening, and Maidens. William Barnes. OBEV

Evening and morning old Platthis kept. Leonidas of Tarentum, *Greek.* PGA, *tr. by* Kenneth Rexroth

Evening and the flat land. Prairie Spring. Willa Silbert Cather. PaTW

Evening—another evening—and the lights flare. Thomas McGrath. *Fr.* Letter to an Imaginary Friend, Part Two. NNaP

Evening, as slow thy placid shades descend. Sonnet 5. William Lisle Bowles. NOBRP; NOEC

Evening before Rain. Leonard Alfred George Strong. OxBTC

Evening Bell from a Misty Temple. Wen Cheng-ming, *Chinese.* CoBLCP, *tr. by* Jonathan Chaves

Evening Bell from Misty Temple. Ma Chih-yüan. *Fr.* Three Poems to the tune "Lo-mei Feng." CoBLCP, *tr. by* Jonathan Chaves

Evening calm envelops the cold city. Listening to the Washblock in the Moonlight. Liu Ch'ang-ch'ing, *Chinese.* SuSp, *tr. by* Dell R. Hales

Evening came, a child was missing. Little Bell. Mary E. Tucker. CBWP-1

Evening clouds dispersed. Tune: "Joy All Under Heaven"—Sunset on the Western Hill. Hsü Tsai-ssu, *Chinese.* SuSp, *tr. by* Sherwin S. S. Fu

Evening comes and sorrow crowds my mind. Kasa no Iratsume, *Japanese.* WPJ, *tr. by* Kenneth Rexroth *and* Ikuko Atsumi

Evening comes. My mind is troubled. Li Shang-yin, *Chinese.* OHMPC, *tr. by* Kenneth Rexroth

Evening comes with an onslaught of wind and rain, Tune: "Song of Picking Mulberry." Li Ch'ing-chao, *Chinese.* CoBCP, *tr. by* Burton Watson

Evening Contemplation. George Washington Doane. AH; BLPA; FaBoBe

Evening Dance of the Grey Flies. Patricia K. Page. NOBC

Evening darkens over, the. Robert Bridges. CMoP; HAP; NOBVV; PoEL-5; SCGP

Evening darkens until. *Unknown, Japanese.* OHMPJ, *tr. by* Kenneth Rexroth

Evening Ebb. Robinson Jeffers. NoAM
  ("Ocean has not been so quiet for a long while; five night- / herons, The.") BLT

Evening falls on the smoky walls. Ballad of the Londoner. James Elroy Flecker. EnLoPo

Evening: for Chang Chi and Chou K'uang. Han Yü, *Chinese.* PLT, *tr. by* A. C. Graham

Evening, Gertrude. Anne Batten Cristall. ECWP

Evening has brought its. Witnesses. W. S. Merwin. LCAP-2

Evening Hawk. Robert Penn Warren. APo; ColAP; NAAL-2; NoP-4; VCAP

Evening Hour. Robert Penn Warren. MT

Evening Hymn. William Henry Furness. FaBoBe

Evening Hymn, An. Thomas Ken. OxBChV

Evening Hymn in the Hovels. Francis Lauderdale Adams. OxBS

Evening in Paradise. Milton. NOBE, *ll.* 598–656 *Fr.* Book IV. OAEL-1 *Fr.* Paradise Lost.

Evening in the Garden Clear after Rain. Ch'u Ch'uang I, *Chinese.* OHMPC

Evening in the Sanitarium. Louise Bogan. FYAP; FaBoWP; NALW; TwCP

Evening in the Village. Lu Yu, *Chinese.* OHPC, *tr. by* Kenneth Rexroth

Evening in the yard. Peyanar. PLW *Fr.* Seven Said by the Foster-Mother. PLW, *tr. by* A. K. Ramanujan

Evening is clogged with gnats as the light fails. Alceste in the Wilderness. Anthony Hecht. CoAmPo; PoA

Evening is coming, The. Bed-time. Thomas Hood. BoTP

Evening is part of the jig-saw truth of her. Ode in Honour. Francis Scarfe. SPE

Evening is tawny on the old. Gold. Martin Donisthorpe Armstrong. BoTP

Evening Land, The. D. H. Lawrence. FaBoA

Evening lecture. Scott Montgomery. HA

Evening lies along the horizon and gives blood. Yehuda Amichai, *Hebrew.* IP, *tr. by* Warren Bargad *and* Stanley F. Chyet

Evening Lights on the River. Chiang Shih-ch'üan, *Chinese.* OHMPC, *tr. by* Kenneth Rexroth

Evening Lull, An. Walt Whitman. NAAL-1; NAAL-3

Evening Meal in the Twentieth Century. John Holmes. AiP

Evening Musicale. Phyllis McGinley. OBAL; OBCoV; Son

Evening News, The. Audre Lorde. NAAL

Evening Nixon called his last troops off, The. April 30, 1975. John Balaban. CDa

Evening of Home Movies, An. Constance Urdang. PFE

Evening of My Birthday, The. Yang Shih-ch'i, *Chinese.* CoBLCP, *tr. by* Jonathan Chaves

Evening of Russian Poetry, An. Vladimir Nabokov. NYBP

Evening of the Mind, The. Donald Justice. VCAP

Evening of the Whirlwind. Amir Gilbo'a, *Hebrew.* MHP, *tr. by* Ruth Finer Mintz

Evening on Calais Beach. Wordsworth. *See* By the Sea.

Evening on the Moselle. Ausonius, *Latin.* OBCVT, *tr. by* Helen Waddell

Evening on the Potomac. Richard Hovey. APN-2

Evening Out, The. Ogden Nash. MoAmPo

Evening outdoors is only a larger lobby. One-Night Expensive Hotel. Ronald G. Everson. NOBC

Evening passes fast away, The. Self-Interrogation. Emily Jane Brontë. BWW

Evening Prayer. Arthur Fitger, *German.* AWP, *tr. by* Jethro Bithell

Evening Prayer, ad. fr. Psalm 140, 141. Thomas Merton. ChIV-1

Evening Prayer. Henrietta Cordelia Ray. CBWP-3

Evening Prayer, An. *Unknown.* CTV

Evening Prayer. *Unknown, Hebrew.* TrJP, *tr. by* Solomon Solis-Cohen

Evening Prayer, at a Girls' School. Felicia Dorothea Hemans. VWP

Evening Primrose. John Clare. CH

Evening Primrose, The. Christopher Pearse Cranch. APN-1

Evening Quatrains. Charles Cotton. NOSC; SCGP
  (Evening.) PoEL-3

Evening Quiet. Jovan Hristic, *Serbo-Croatian.* HSix, *tr. by* Charles Simic

Evening red and morning gray. *Unknown.* FaBoBe; FaBoVe; OxNR

evening river is level and motionless—, The. Flowers and Moonlight on the Spring River. Yang-Ti, Emperor of Sui Dynasty, *Chinese.* ChiP, *tr. by* Arthur Waley

Evening Scene, An. Coventry Patmore. ACTP

Evening Scene, An. Zhao Zhenkai, *Chinese.* VCWP, *tr. by* McDougall, Bonnie S. and Chen Maiping

Evening Scene at Twin Forests. Chin Nung, *Chinese.* CoBLCP, *tr. by* Jonathan Chaves

Evening sitdown vision. Allen Ginsberg. *See* Sunflower Sutra.

Evening Song, An. Alcaeus, *Greek.* GrIP, *tr. by* James S. Easby-Smith

Evening Song. Sherwood Anderson. GM

Evening Song. Kenneth Fearing. SPE

Evening Song. John Fletcher. *See* Folding the Flocks.

Evening Song. Edith King. BoTP

Evening Song. Sidney Lanier. UnPo

Evening Song. Jean Toomer. BPo; GT

Evening Song. Philipp von Zesen, *German.* GePo, *tr. by* George C. Schoolfield

Evening Star, The. *Aborigine Oral Tradition. Fr.* Moon-Bone Song [*or* Cycle]. CBAP, *tr. by* R. M. Berndt

Evening star, The. Nick Avis. HA

Evening star. William J. Higginson. HA

Evening Star, The. Henry Wadsworth Longfellow. APN-1

Evening star. Hal Roth. HA

Evening star that in the vaulted skies, The. Verse Written in the Album of Mademoiselle. Pierre Dalcour, *French.* TTY, *tr. by* Langston Hughes

Evening Star who gathers everything. Sappho. WPoS

Evening sun, The. John Wills. HA

Evening sun sets beyond the western ranges, The. Spending the Night at the Hillside Lodge of Master Yeh and Waiting for My Friend Ting. Meng Hao Jan, *Chinese.* SuSp, *tr. by* Daniel Bryant

Evening sun sinks. Returning Sails at a Distant Shore. Ma Chih-yüan. *Fr.* Three Poems to the tune "Lo-mei Feng." CoBLCP, *tr. by* Jonathan Chaves

Evening sun was sinking down, The. Emily Jane Brontë. CH

Evening swallows keep twittering by my curtain. Late Spring. Yüan Chen, *Chinese.* SuSp, *tr. by* Dell R. Hales

Evening, the heather, The. Invasion Summer. Laurie Lee. OxBSP

Evening Thought, An [: Salvation by Christ with Penitential Cries]. Jupiter Hammon. CrDW

Evening traffic homeward burns. Before Disaster. Yvor Winters. HoPM; PFE

Evening Twilight. Heinrich Heine. AWP, *tr. by* John Todhunter *Fr.* The North Sea.

Evening View as the Snow Clears. Chia Tao, *Chinese.* SuSp, *tr. by* Stephen Owen

Evening View at River Pavilion, Inviting Guest. Po Chü-i, *Chinese.* SuSp, *tr. by* Irving Y. Lo

Evening View from the Bell Tower at P'ing-ch'ang. T'ang Hsien-tsu, *Chinese.* CoBLCP, *tr. by* Jonathan Chaves

Evening Walk. Sonja Åkesson, *Swedish.* WPOW, *tr. by* Joanna Bankier

Evening Walk, The. Nazim Hikmet, *Turkish.* AF, *tr. by* Randy Blasing *and* Mutlu Konuk

Evening was in the wood, louring with storm. Haunted. Siegfried Sassoon. CMoP

Evening-Watch, The. Henry Vaughan. ESCV; FMP

Evening Waterfall. Carl Sandburg. ImPo

Evening without Angels. Wallace Stevens. VGW

Evenings ever more wailing lapse into my world's evening. Denis Devlin. NOIV *Fr.* Memoirs of a Turcoman Diplomat.

Evenings I hear. A Plague of Starlings. Robert Earl Hayden. NoAM

Evenings in the Sea. Eleanor Lerman. WeT

Evening's Love, An. Dryden.
  After the Pangs of a Desperate Lover. PeLV

Evenings, / the stream now sounds. The Wanderer. Johannes Bobrowski, *German.* CEEP, *tr. by* Juliette Victor-Rood

Eveningsong. Ramona Wilson. VoR

Eveningsong 2. Ramona Wilson. VoR

Evenlode, The. Hilaire Belloc. OxAEP-2

Evensong. Paul Gerhardt, *German.* GePo, *tr. by* Ingrid Walde-Engel

Evensong [*or* Even-Song]. George Herbert. ESCV

Evensong. C. S. Lewis. TIRV; TrCP

Event, The. Rita Dove. CMAP; NoAM
  ("Gently shirred.") (LL) NAAAL

Event, An. Edward Field. CoAP

Event, The. Thomas Sturge Moore. OBMV

Event. Sylvia Plath. NOBA

Event, An. Richard Wilbur. AFr

Event on the Street, An. Daniil Kharms. AF

Event Which Makes No News, An. Kazue Shinkawa, *Japanese*. WPJ, *tr. by* Kenneth Rexroth *and* Ikuko Atsumi

Event's already happened, The. Muertes. Robert Mazzocco. WWSi

Events by Moonlight. Michael Benedikt. WeT

Eventual Proteus. Margaret Atwood. MoCV

Eventually you will find. Where It's At. A. L. Hendriks. HCP

Ever a toiling *child* doth make us sad. A Voice from the Factories. Caroline Elizabeth Norton. VWP *Fr.* A Voice from the Factories.

Ever at night have I looked up for thee. The Planet Jupiter. Epes Sargent. APN-1

Ever been kidnapped. Kidnap Poem. Nikki Giovanni. BPo; Poetr; TAP

Ever charming, ever new. John Dyer. *See* Prospects.

Ever deeper. Tanka. Fumi Saito, *Japanese*. MJT, *tr. by* Ueda, Makoto

Ever, ever come? (LL) Beyond the Hunting Woods. Donald Justice. CoAmPo; NYBP

Ever-Fixed Mark, An. Kingsley Amis. MoP; NoAM

Ever gratefully, Your little friend. . . . (LL) Matinees. James Merrill. HCAP; NOBA

Ever let the Fancy roam. Fancy. Keats. GTBS-P; OBEV

Ever mine [*or* myn] hap[pe] is slack and slo[w] in coming [*or* commyng]. Petrarch, *Italian*. OBVE, *tr. by* Sir Thomas Wyatt

Ever moulded by the lips of man. (LL) To Virgil [*or* Vergil]. Tennyson. AWP; EBVVPR; GTBS-P; OAEL-2; PoEL-5

Ever perfect, ever in them- / selves eternal [*or* eternall]. (LL) Laura. Thomas Campion. AAS; EnLoPo; InPK-6; InPS-3; NAEL-1; NOBE; NOSC; OAEL-1; OBEV; PoE; PoEL-2; TFi; TRP

Ever perfect, ever in them- / Selves eternal. Thomas Campion. *See* Laura.

Ever Present. Philip Ayres. OxBSP

Ever seem them close, (LL) An Autumn Morning in Shokoku-ji. Gary Snyder. HAP; VGW; WeW-3

Ever since boyhood it has been my joy. The Everlasting Mercy. Sir John Collings Squire. BXAP

Ever since I realized there was someone callt. No More Love Poems #1. Ntozake Shange. BlSi *Fr.* For Colored Girls Who Have Considered Suicide When the Rainbow Is Enuf.

Ever since i was knee high to a grasshopper they said i had cute cheeks. Marble surfaces. Joanne Burns. BMAP

Ever since Miss Susan Johnson lost her jockey, Lee. Yellow Dog Blues. William Christopher Handy. NAAAL

Ever since my daughters started to walk. The Green Tree. James Reiss. AmPA

Ever since the great planes were murdered at the end of the gardens. Domus Caedet Arborem. Charlotte Mew. NTP; PBWP

Ever since the time when I was a lusty boy. Realizing the Futility of Life. Po Chü-i, *Chinese*. ChiP, *tr. by* Arthur Waley

Ever since they've left the Tennessee ridge. The Event. Rita Dove. CMAP; NAAAL; NoAM

Ever since T'ien-pao, this silence and desolation. The Man with No Family to Take Leave of. Tu Fu, *Chinese*. CoBCP, *tr. by* Burton Watson

Ever Since Uncle John Henry Been Dead. *Unknown*. AS

Ever singing "Die, oh die." (LL) The Phantom-Wooer. Thomas Lovell Beddoes. NAEL-2; OxBSn; Ro

Ever so close. Tanka. Saitō Mokichi, *Japanese*. MJT, *tr. by* Ueda, Makoto

Ever to last! Thomas Lovell Beddoes. *See* Dream-Pedlary.

Ever upward like a kite. If We Try. George Sands Johnson. PWR

Ever Watchful. Ta' Abbata Sharra, *Arabic*. AWP, *tr. by* W. G. Palgrave

Evergreen Cemetery. Alfred Wellington Purdy. MoCV

Evergreen shadow and the pale magnolia, The. Souls Lake. Robert Fitzgerald. TwCP

Everlasting Arms, The, *Moulton*, Modern Reader's Bible. Bible, *O.T. See* Psalm 91.

Everlasting cat!, The. (LL) The Cat of Cats. William Brighty Rands. CTAV; FPC; NOxBChV; OxBChV; PC

Everlasting Forests, The. Dahlia Ravikovitch, *Hebrew*. BoWoP, *tr. by* Chana Bloch

Everlasting Gospel, The. William Blake.

   "Vision of Christ that thou dost see, The." ChIV-2

   "Was Jesus Chaste? or did he." ChIV-2

   "Was Jesus Humble? or did he." ChIV-2

Everlasting green, The. (LL) The Holly and the Ivy. *Unknown*. CH; PChr

Everlasting Mercy, The. Sir John Collings Squire. BXAP

Everlasting night, An. (LL) A Hymne to Christ, at the Author's Last Going into Germany. Donne. EBEV; ESCV; MeLP; NAEL-1; NOSC; OxAEP-1; PeECV

Everlasting omen of what is. (LL) Often I Am Permitted to Return to a Meadow. Robert Duncan. CMoP; ColAP; NOBA; PmAP

Everlasting Sorrow, The. Po Chü-i, *Chinese*. ChiPo, *tr. by* Witter Bynner

Everlasting universe of things, The. Mont Blanc. Shelley. InPS-3; NAEL-2; NIP-4; NOBRP; NoP-4; OAEL-2; Ro

Everlasting Voices, The. W. B. Yeats. AWP

Everness. Jorge Luis Borges, *Spanish*. APAD, *tr. by* Richard Wilbur

Every being in the universe. Lao Tzu. EnlH *Fr.* Tao Te Ching.

Every boy knows what it's like. What Every Boy Knows. "Antler." GLP

Every branch big with it. Snow in the Suburbs. Thomas Hardy. CMoP; EBEvV; MoBrPo; OAEL-2; OBMV; OxBTC

Every Bush New Springing. *Unknown*. PoEL-2

Every Cache. Robert Johnstone.

   "He's a high clear forehead." PNI

   "Various instants I'm not with you." PNI

Every child may joy to hear. (LL) Introduction: "Piping down the valleys wild." William Blake. AWP; ChAP; ClHu; FaBoBe; FaBoCh; HeIP-4; ImPo; InPS-3; NAEL-2; NAWM-2; NOBE; NOBRP; NOEC; NOxBChV; NoP-4; OAEL-2; OBEV; OBNC; OxBChV; PoE; PoEL-4; Ro; SoSe-8; TFi

Every child who has gardening tools. Garden Lore. Juliana Horatia Ewing. OxBChV

Every choice is always the wrong choice. Whole Love. Robert Graves. ITG

Every Christian Born of God. *Unknown, German*. AH

Every city in America is approached. Kissing Stieglitz Goodbye. Gerald Stern. LCAP-2

Every Day. Ingeborg Bachmann, *German*. BoWoP, *tr. by* Christopher Middleton; PBWP, *tr. by* Michael Hamburger

   ("War is no longer declared.") PBWP, *tr. by* Michael Hamburger

Every Day. Günter Kunert, *German*. CEEP, *tr. by* Michael Hamburger

Every Day. Felix Mendelssohn. CTV

Every Day. Mary I. Osborn. BoTP

Every day. Outside the Furnace. Aziz Qaisi, *Urdu*. OMIP, *tr. by* Baidar Bakht *and* Leslie Lavigne

Every day a wilderness—now. Dusting. Rita Dove. HCAP; HeIP-4; LCAP-2; NoP-4; PuPuPo; Poetr

Every day almost at the same hour. A Bird. Chongsam Kim, *Korean*. CKP, *tr. by* Jaihiun Kim

Every day brings a ship. Letters. Ralph Waldo Emerson. OxBSP

Every-Day Characters. Winthrop Mackworth Praed.

   Belle of the Ball-Room, The. NOBRP

   Portrait of a Lady in the Exhibition of the Royal Academy. NOBL; PeLV; PoEL-4

   Vicar, The. OBEV; OBNC; OxAEP-2; PoEL-4

Every day I burn a stick of incense. Joanne Kyger. BB

Every day I meet the horses. Horses at Valley Store. Leslie Marmon Silko. VoR

Every day I peruse the box scores for hours. Baseball and Classicism. Tom Clark. PmAP

Every day I receive the Imperial favor. Enclosed with a Letter to My Family—For Shu. Yang Shih-ch'i, *Chinese*. CoBLCP, *tr. by* Jonathan Chaves

Every day I see from my window. Wild Oats. Norman MacCaig. OxBTC

Every day is a fresh beginning. New Every Morning. "Susan Coolidge." APAD

Every day is a long pause without seams. The Silence. Vern Rutsala. CDa

Every day is as old. As New and as Old. Martin Carter. PBCV

Every day on the way home from. By the Winding River I. Tu Fu, *Chinese*. OHPC, *tr. by* Kenneth Rexroth

Every day our bodies separate. Villanelle. Marilyn Hacker. AmPA

Every day that their sky droops down. Moles. William Stafford. NYBP

Every eleven years they appear. Sun Spots. Christopher Buckley. PuP-16

Every evening, bent over the bright. Valerio Magrelli, *Italian*. NeIt, *tr. by* Dana Gioia

Every evening, down into the hardweed. Hardweed Path Going. A. R. Ammons. HCAP; UnPo; VGW

Every few years, down at the Florida Keys. The Death of the Pilot Whales. Peter Meinke. PBCAP

Every Friday morning my grandfather. Ancestors. Edward Kamau Brathwaite. NoP-4

Every game that Harvey plays. Harvey Always Wins. Jack Prelutsky. NTCP

Every heavenly orbit is furrowed into a rose-garden. Changtzu 33. Chech'on Park, *Korean*. CKP, *tr. by* Jaihiun Kim

Every hour and every minute. A Vow for New Year's. Mary Carolyn Davies. PoToHe

Every hour, every moment. Hilda Doolittle. NALW; NoAM *Fr.* Tribute to the Angels.

Every inch of you, a terrible vision, not bear, but virgin! (LL) Elizabeth's War with the Christmas Bear. Norman Dubie. LCAP-2; NoAM

Every lady in this land. Mother Goose. OxNR; ReMoGo

Every little while I crash a Camel. *Unknown.* NSI

Every Man has his sorrows; yet each still. André Marie de Chénier. *Fr.* Elegies. AWP, *tr. by* Arthur Symons

Every Man in His Humour. Ben Jonson. In Defence of Poetry. EPCY

Every man wants to be a stud. Cocks and Mares. Ruth Stone. RaBo

Every metaphor sounds the same. John Wilkinson. NBrP

Every moment we were together. First Meetings. Arseny Aleksandrovich Tarkovsky, *Russian.* TCRP, *tr. by* Albert C. Todd

Every morn I lift my head. Ralph Waldo Emerson. APN-1 *Fr.* Monadnoc.

Every morning. Daily Habits. Herberto Padilla, *Spanish.* VCWP, *tr. by* Alastair Reid *and* Alexander Coleman

Every morning. Marichiko, *Japanese.* OHMPJ, *tr. by* Kenneth Rexroth

Every morning. Stafford in Kansas. James Baker Hall. BXAP

Every morning. Work We Hate and Dreams We Love. Jimmy Santiago Baca. LoL

Every Morning After Killing Thousands of Angels. Ryuichi Tamura, *Japanese.* VCWP, *tr. by* Christopher Drake

Every morning at break of day. The Trains. "Seumas O'Sullivan." BoTP

Every morning he is astounded again. Terminally Ill. Anna Swirszczynska, *Polish.* PoSu, *tr. by* Czeslaw Milosz *and* Leonard Nathan (b. 1924)

Every morning I break trail. Changeling VIII. Kristjana Gunnars. NOBC

Every morning I forget how it is. Poem. Charles Simic. NNaP

Every morning I get up. To the Tune "A Floating Cloud Crosses Enchanted Mountain." Huang O, *Chinese.* BoWoP, *tr. by* Kenneth Rexroth *and* Ling Chung

Every morning, I / Wake alone, dreaming my. Kenneth Rexroth. APSN *Fr.* The Love Poems of Marichiko.

Every morning I went to her charity and learned. To a Red-headed Do-good Waitress. Alan Dugan. Son

Every morning, in the dust. A Sparrow in the Dust. Ruth Domino, *Italian.* BoWoP, *tr. by* Daniel Hoffman *and* Jerre Mangione

Every morning she'd smear something brown. Man Arrested in Hacking Death Tells Police He Mistook Mother-in-Law for Raccoon. Susan Bartels Ludvigson. MT

Every morning the curtain rises. Claire Malroux, *French.* VCWP, *tr. by* Marilyn Hacker

Every morning the Pope kisses Africa. Kinshasa. Walid Bitar. WeT

Every morning the prisoner hears. The Prisoner. William Plomer. PeSA

Every morning the sun comes, the sun. (LL) The Arc Inside and Out. A. R. Ammons. NoP-4

Every morning there is war again. Clearing Station. Wilhelm Klemm, *German.* PeFWW, *tr. by* David McDuff

Every morning they hold hands. Suburban Lovers. Bruce Dawe. NOBAu

Every morning you return from a long. The Morning Roar of the City. Slavko Mihalic. PoSu, *tr. by* Charles Simic

Every night. Gary Hotham. HA

Every night, as my grandfather sat. The Guild. Sharon Olds. RaBo

Every night I dream we're fighting, armies raise. General John Cabell Breckinridge. Jill Breckinridge. CBCWP

Every night I dream we're fighting, armies raised. General John Cabell Breckinridge. Jill Breckinridge. CBCWP *Fr.* Civil Blood.

Every night my prayers I say. System. Robert Louis Stevenson. PWR

Every night / the ex-mental patient. The Music of Astronomy. Martín Espada. AFr

Every night the fireflies were our eyes. Fireflies. Faustin Charles. PBCV

Every night when I went to bed. The Lament of the Unmarried Girl. Brian Merriman. OBVE, *tr. by* Frank O'Connor *Fr.* The Midnight Court. NOIV, *tr. by* Thomas Kinsella

Every October millions of little fish come along the shore. Birds and Fishes. Robinson Jeffers. NAAL-2; NoP-4

Every old man I see. Memory of my Father. Patrick Kavanagh. InPS-3; RB

Every one of these, stood, separate, upright, above ground. David Jones. PeECV *Fr.* In Parenthesis.

Every one of us saw it. Silence. Alvin Aubert. MT

Every path a green lady. Four Songs from the Book of Samuel. Eli W. Mandel. MoCV

Every peak is a crater. This is the law of volcanoes. Adrienne Rich. NAAL-2; NALW; NoAM *Fr.* Twenty-one Love Poems. GLP

Every planet is a small plane. The Plane: Earth. Sun-Ra. PoBA

Every poor fellow reminds me of my father. The Lullaby. Laura Riding Jackson. MoLi

Every Second Thought. Theodore Weiss. "Grey and dankish thing, A." DiPo

Every Shuiler Is Christ. Joseph Campbell. TIRV

Every silver. 9.1.59: VI. Pablo Picasso, *French.* CLPP, *tr. by* Paul Blackburn

Every stance seemed crooked. He had. Saint Ras. Anthony McNeill. PBCV

Every store keeps a book for complaints. Yevgeny Mikhailovich Vinokurov, *Russian.* TCRP, *tr. by* Albert C. Todd

Every summer. Braly Street. Gary Soto. UnSA

Every summer. Lemonade Stand. Myra Cohn Livingston. TLR

Every Sunday she prepared the brown oak table. The Poet of the Mountains. Thomas McCarthy. CIP-2

Every Thing. Harold Monro. MoBrPo

Every thread of summer is at last unwoven. Puella Parvula. Wallace Stevens. HCAP; LCAP-2

Every Thursday morning. The Dustman. Clive Sansom. BoTP

Every time I climb a tree. Five Chants. David McCord. NOxBChV; NTCP

Every [or Ev'ry] Time I Feel the [or de] Spirit. *Unknown.* APN-2

Every time I hear that march from Lohengrin. Makin' Whoopee. Gustave Kahn. OBCoV

Every time I smell Lava soap it is 1948. The Story of Lava. David Allan Evans. Poetsp

Every time I write a letter. Writing Letters. Rodney Bennett. BoTP

Every time Lady Lowbodice swoons. Lady Lowbodice. *Unknown.* PeLV; PeLi

Every time the bucks went clattering. Earthy Anecdote. Wallace Stevens. CMoP; RB; SAmP

Every time we go on the pier. Oh Erica, Not Again! Max Fatchen. FuFo

Every Time We Say Goodbye. James Cushing. SeSe

Every time you hear me sing this song. The Railroad Blues. *Unknown.* AmFP; GM

Every Town a Home Town. Kaniyan Punkunran, *Tamil.* PLW, *tr. by* A. K. Ramanujan

Every town with black Catholics has a St. Peter Claver's. St. Peter Claver. Toi Derricotte. LTA; PBCAP

Every Where and Every When. Arthur Sze. OpBo

Every whipped ideal save for / the one just mentioned. The Lyric Can Snare. Lee Ann Brown. PT

Every wild she-bird has nest and mate in the warm April weather. The Virgin Martyr. Ada Cambridge. NOBAu

Every word is a doubt. Roberto Juarroz. VCWP, *tr. by* Mary Crow *Fr.* Eleventh Vertical Poetry.

Every year in June—up here, that's the month for lilacs. What the Light Was Like. Amy Clampitt. FaBoWP

Every year men harvest grapes, not seeing. Macedonius, *Greek.* GrAn, *tr. by* Adrian Wright

Every year they try to rob us. Berlin Metro. Desmond O'Grady. BiHa

Every year without knowing it I have passed the day. For the Anniversary of My Death. W. S. Merwin. BLT; CAPP-1; CoAP; ColAP; HCAP; InPK-6; LiLi; NAAL-2; NOBA; PoPoPo; Poetr; VCAP

Everybody but Me. Margaret Goss Burroughs. BlSi

Everybody dug a hole and lived in it. Theory. David Huddle. CDa

Everybody else, then, going. Exeunt Omnes. Thomas Hardy. FaBoVe; UV

Everybody gets the blues. Surplus Blues. Raymond R. Patterson. IFJA

Everybody knew Clifton Cockerell was not half bright. The Beating. T. R. Hummer. MT

Everybody knows her, for they see her every day. Pay Your Debts. Mrs. Henry Linden. CBWP-4

Everybody knows that. Expandable Language. Thulani Davis. MoNo

Everybody loved Chick Lorimer in our town. Gone. Carl Sandburg. NOBA

Everybody wants an intelligent son. At the Washing of My Son. Su Tung-p'o, *Chinese.* OHPC, *tr. by* Kenneth Rexroth

Everybody wants to know. Poem for Two Daughters. Ishmael Reed. MoLi

Everybody who has a baby thinks everybody who hasn't a baby. Did Someone Say "Babies"? Ogden Nash. OxBM

Everybody who's anybody longs to be a tree. Horse and Tree. Rita Dove. TRP

"Everybody's Reading Li Po" Silkscreened on a Purple T-Shirt. Yusef Komunyakaa. WWSi

Everyday. Indian Girl. Lenard D. Moore. GT

Everyday History. Sandor Csoori, *Hungarian.* VCWP, *tr. by* Len Roberts

Everyday / I think about dying. Survivor. Roger McGough. OBCoV

Everyday Things. Jean Ayer. BoTP

Everymaid. John Oxenham. TrCP

Everyman. Siegfried Sassoon. MoBrPo

Everyman, *Old English Morality Play.* *Unknown.* NAEL-1; NAWM-1; OAEL-1; PoEL-1

Everyman/ Preacher or lecher, saint or sot. Robert Francis. CRP *Fr.* Epitaphs.

Everyone at Lake Kearney had a nickname. Sway. Louis Simpson. NoAM

Everyone drinks Havdolah wine. Havdolah Wine. Miriam Ulinover, *Yiddish.* CEEP, tr. by Seth L. Wolitz.

Everyone grows younger; my thinning hair. Figures of Authority. Edward Watkins. NYBP

Everyone grumbled. The sky was gray [*or* grey]. Daddy Fell into the Pond. Alfred Noyes. ChAP; NOxBChV

Everyone had turned off their televisions. Petroglyph. Joy Harjo. NAmP90

Everyone has only one leg. Great Infirmities. Charles Simic. ChAP

Everyone in me is a bird. In Celebration of My Uterus. Anne Sexton. CrSp; NALW

Everyone is asleep. Enomoto Seifu-Jo, *Japanese.* WPJ, tr. by Kenneth Rexroth *and* Ikuko Atsumi

Everyone is gone. Everyone. Blue. Christopher Gilbert. FYAP *Fr.* Beginning by Example.

Everyone is young, young, young. David Davidovich Burlyuk, *Russian.* TCRP, tr. by Albert C. Todd

Everyone Knows the World Is Ending. Alice Fulton. EOEF

Everyone notices they are inseparable. The Sisters. Josephine Jacobsen. NMM-2

Everyone passes under the moon. Meir Wieseltier, *Hebrew.* IP, tr. by Warren Bargad *and* Stanley F. Chyet

Everyone possesses something sad. Tanikawa Shuntaro, *Japanese.* IFJA, tr. by Harold Wright

Everyone Sang. Siegfried Sassoon. APAD; EBEvV; GTBS-P; MoBrPo; NAEL-2; NOBE; NSI; NoAM; NoP-4; OBEV; OBWP; OPOU; OxBSP; OxBTC; TrJP

Everyone says / what they do. Life Is a Killer. John Giorno. PmAP

Everyone silent, moving. . . .Take my hand. Speak to me. (LL) Effort at Speech between Two People. Muriel Rukeyser. FYAP; MoAmPo; Poetr; TrJP; TwCP

Everyone speaks of the sad autumn with a heavy heart. Sounds of Autumn. Lu Yu, *Chinese.* SuSp, tr. by Irving Y. Lo

Everyone suddenly burst out singing. Everyone Sang. Siegfried Sassoon. APAD; EBEvV; GTBS-P; MoBrPo; NAEL-2; NOBE; NSI; NoAM; NoP-4; OBEV; OBWP; OPOU; OxBSP; OxBTC; TrJP

Everyone talking at once. Alexis Rotella. HA

Everyone thinks I am poisonous. I am not. The Tarantula. Reed Whittemore. CoAP

Everyone thinks me a cannibal. When Negro Teeth Speak. Ouologuem Yambo. PBMAP

Everyone wants to meet *him.* (LL) Lines to Ralph Hodgson Esqre. T. S. Eliot. NBLV; OBAL; PeLV

Everyone will have his turn. The Jaguar is Getting Ready. Anna Hajnal, *Hungarian.* CEEP, tr. by Juliette Victor-Rood

Everyone Will Write Poetry. Branko Miljkovic, *Serbo-Croatian.* HSix, tr. by Charles Simic

Everyone's going to ride tomorrow. Gabriel's Blues. Calvin Forbes. PoA; WeT

Everyone's on about Walter's willy. Underneath the Archers *or* What's All This about Walter's Willy? Kit Wright. OBCoV

"Everyone's sick! The soldiers poison the air." (LL) From Trollope's Journal. Elizabeth Bishop. CBCWP; FaBoPV

Everything as in a good old-fashioned novel. Vladimir Nikolaevich Sokolov, *Russian.* TCRP, tr. by Simon Franklin

Everything began here. Snowfall in Boston. Otto Orban, *Hungarian.* CEEP, tr. by Timea K. Szell

Everything but mere being just like this. (LL) The Two Parents. "Hugh MacDiarmid." FaBoTw; OxBTC

Everything / can be retouched. The Need for Censorship. Reiner Kunze, *German.* PoSu, tr. by Michael Hamburger

Everything changes. Ode to a Country Childhood. Olafs Stumbrs, *Latvian.* CEEP, tr. by Olafs Stumbrs

Everything changes. We plant. Cicely Herbert. OPOU

Everything! Counter and scales. Business Reverses. Edgar Lee Masters. ChIV-2

Everything: Eloy, Arizona, 1956. Ai. AmPA

Everything ended with the Honeymoon. Loyal Housewife. Daisy Zamora, *Spanish.* LoL, tr. by Margaret Randall

Everything, / everything. Wislawa Szymborska. *See* In Praise of My Sister.

Everything fades away beyond oneself. Looking in a Mirror the Day before the Advent of Autumn. Li Yi, *Chinese.* SuSp, tr. by William H. Nienhauser

Everything flows. Denise Levertov. NAAL-2 *Fr.* Olga Poems.

Everything has been arranged too carefully. The Room. Lawrence Raab. CMAP

Everything has been checked. My inventory is ready. Elizaveta Kuzmina-Karavayeva, *Russian.* TCRP, tr. by Albert C. Todd

Everything has its limit, including sorrow. To Urania. Joseph Brodsky, *Russian.* AF, tr. by Joseph Brodsky

Everything has lasted till today. The Unknown Soldier. Alun Lewis. MoBrPo

Everything here is curtained in darkness. Bulat Shalvovich Okudzhava, *Russian.* TCRP, tr. by Deming Brown

Everything I do is against meaning. Against Meaning. Andrei Codrescu. PmAP

Everything I do is stitched with its color. (LL) Separation. W. S. Merwin. HAP; NoP-4; SAGP

Everything I say / is a garment. (LL) Sous-Entendu. Anne Stevenson. LW

Everything in Its Place. Arthur Guiterman. NBLV; OBAL; OBCoV

Everything in the Garden is Lovely. Alasdair Aston. OBGa

Everything is black and gold. Black and Gold. Nancy Byrd Turner. CTV

Everything Is Going to Be All Right. Derek Mahon. PBCIP

Everything is laughing, singing. It Is a Pleasant Day. *Unknown.* BoTP

Everything is, once was not. Life after Death. Richard W. Thomas. PoBA

Everything Is Plundered[, betrayed, sold]. "Anna Akhmatova," *Russian.* WPoS, tr. by Stanley Kunitz and Max Hayward; WPOW, tr. by Stanley Kunitz

Everything Is Round. Gabriela Mistral, *Spanish.* PBWP, tr. by D. M. Pettinella

Everything lives and nothing is dead. The Fugs. Edward Sanders. PoM

Everything passes and vanishes. William Allingham. NOBVV

Everything revolved at first, then settled. Words. Wayne Brown. HCP

Everything sounds funny in a funny magazine. Paper on Humor. Andrei Codrescu. PmAP

Everything That Acts Is Actual. Denise Levertov. NoAM

Everything that happens to me these days. Sonnet 1. Julia Alvarez. FFC *Fr.* ("33").

Everything that has been said for several centuries. Atlantis. John Engman. NAmP90

Everything that lives has its own proper pride. Proper Pride. D. H. Lawrence. FaBoEE

Everything that touches us, me and you. Rilke. ITG, tr. by Stephen Mitchell *Fr.* Love Song.

Everything they do will succeed. Bible, *O.T. See* Psalm 1.

Everything was happening for the first time. As we travelled through. There. Philip Mead. BMAP

Everything was put to use. The Seven Words. Jerzy Ficowski, *Polish.* PoSu, tr. by Keith Bosley *and* Krystyna Wandycz

Everything was simple, yet triumphant. For the Unveiling of a Memorial. Daniil Leonidovich Andreyev, *Russian.* TCRP, tr. by Bradley Jordan

Everything was yellow. The Painters. Judith Hemschemeyer. Poetsp

Everything we look upon is blest. (LL) A Dialogue of Self and Soul. W. B. Yeats. CMoP; FaBoMo; LiTM; MoBrPo; NAEL-2; NoAM; PoE

Everything we stand up in. Spectrum. Aidan Carl Mathews. PBCIP

Everything will be forsaken then. Apocrypha. János Pilinszky, *Hungarian.* PoSu, tr. by Ted Hughes

Everything you have heard about me. The Witch's Story. Lawrence Raab. CMAP

Everything's a metaphor, some wise. History. Rita Dove. FFC

Everything's a metaphor, some wise. History. Rita Dove. NAAAL *Fr.* Mother Love.

Everything's laughter / everything dust. Glycon, *Greek.* GrAn, tr. by Peter Jay

Everything's / so far away. The Sadness of Leaving. Eileen Myles. PmAP

Everything's still on down the rows of cells of beds with men / asleep. The Great Escape. Ralph Adamo. MT

"Everything's the same old way," she said tenderly. The Same Old Way. "Igor Severyanin," *Russian.* TCRP, tr. by Bernard Meares

Everythng's just as it was: fine hard snow. The Guest. "Anna Akhmatova," *Russian.* RaBo, tr. by Jane Kenyon *and* Vera Dunham

Everytime a thunderstorm comes. My Mother is a God Fearing Woman. Cornelius Eady. ISC

Everytime I read Pessoa I think. Salutations to Fernando Pessoa. Allen Ginsberg. BAP-95

Everywhere. Plantings. Catalina Cariaga. LoHo

Everywhere about is landscape as far as foot can feel. Homage to Paul Delvaux. Ramon Guthrie. PoE

Everywhere else we wrapped our bodies. The Locker Room. Nora Mitchell. IFJA

Everywhere, everywhere, Christmas [tonight!]. Christmas Everywhere. Phillips Brooks. CTV; PWR

Everywhere, everywhere, following me. Camerados. Bayard Taylor. UnPo

Everywhere, everywhere, following me. Night the Eighth: Camerados. Bayard Taylor. APN-2 *Fr.* The Echo Club.

Everywhere fish wheeled and fled. Noah. Wayne Brown. PBCV

Everywhere I look in the garden. Déjeuner Sur l'Herbe. Bruce Beaver. BMAP

Everywhere petals are flying. By the Winding River II. Tu Fu, *Chinese*. OHPC, *tr.* by Kenneth Rexroth

Everywhere the windows give up nothing. The Letter. Lynda Hull. PUP-19

Everywoman Her Own Theology. Alicia Ostriker. CrSp

Eves Apologie. Emilia Lanier. BoWoP *Fr.* Salve Deus Rex Judaeorum.

Eve's Commentary. Michelene Wandor. NBrP

Eve's tinted shadows slowly fill the fane. Sir Walter Scott at the Tomb of the Stuarts in St. Peter's. Richard Monckton, 1st Baron Houghton Milnes. EBVV

Eviction, The. William Allingham. BIrV; NOIV *Fr.* Laurence Bloomfield in Ireland.

Eviction. Lucille Clifton. NTCP
  (The First.) InPS-3

Eviction. Michelle T. Clinton. ISC

Evidence. Toki Zenmaro, *Japanese*. MJT, *tr.* by Makoto Ueda

Evidence at the Witch Trials. James Keir Baxter. OxBC

Evidence Read at the Trial of the Knave of Hearts. "Lewis Carroll." GTBS-P; NOBVV; OxBoLi; PBMP; PeLV *Fr.* Alice's Adventures in Wonderland.
  (Verses from the Trials of the Knave of Hearts.) CBNP

Evidently Chicken Town. John Cooper Clarke. FaBoPV

Evil. Rimbaud. OBWP, *tr.* by Robert Lowell *Fr.* Eighteen-Seventy.

Evil Days, The. D. J. Enright. OBCoV

Evil Days, The. Boris Pasternak, *Russian*. GI, *tr.* by Nina Kossman

Evil Eye, The. John Ciardi. MoBS

Evil, if rightly understood. On the Origin of Evil. John Byrom. NOEC

Evil Is No Black Thing. Sarah Webster Fabio. PoBA

Evil Man, An! Richard Beer-Hofmann. TrJP, *tr.* by Ludwig Lewisohn *Fr.* Graf von Charolais, Der.

Evil Nigger Waits for Lightnin'. Imamu Amiri Baraka. NOBA

Evil [*or* Evill] spirit, your beauty, haunts me still, An. Michael Drayton. AAS; GBL; NOBE; NoSic *Fr.* Idea.

Evil That Men Do, The. Queen Latifah. NAAAL

Evil word it is, / This Love, An. (LL) In Memory of Radio. Imamu Amiri Baraka. BB; NAAAL; NAAL-2; NeAP; PoM; Poetr

Ev'n for your sake. (LL) Address to the Deil. Robert Burns. NOEC; OAEL-1; OxBS; PoEL-4

Ev'n from my heart the strings do break. Thomas Campion. *See* When to Her Lute Corinna [*or* Corrina] Sings.

Ev'n from my heart the strings do break. (LL) When to Her Lute Corinna [*or* Corrina] Sings. Thomas Campion. NoP-4

Ev'n God himself, being pressed for my sake. (LL) The Bunch of Grapes. George Herbert. ChIV-1; ESCV; GeHe; NAEL-1; NOSC; TOF

Ev'n [*or* E'en *or* Even] like two little bank-dividing brooks [*or* brookes]. My Beloved Is Mine, and I Am His; He Feedeth among the Lillies. Francis Quarles. MeLP; NOBE; OBEV *Fr.* Emblems.

Ev'n on board the Lisbon Packet? (LL) Lines to Mr Hodgson. Byron. NBLV; OBCoV; OxBoS

Ev'n sated with variety [*or* Varietie]. (LL) The Scrutiny [*or* Scrutinie]. Richard Lovelace. BeJo; BoLoP; CaPo; EnLoPo; GBL; MeLP; NOSC; SeCP

Evoba. Steve McCaffery.
  "Can there be a collision between picture and application?" FTOS

Evocation. Nichita Stanescu, *Romanian*. CEEP, *tr.* by Irina Livezeanu

Evolution. Sherman Alexie. PoPoPo

Evolution. John Blight. CBAP

Evolution. Langdon Smith. BLPA; FaBoBe

Evolution. John Banister Tabb. APAD; APN-2
  ("Life again.") (LL) APAD

Evolution. Israel Zangwill. TrJP

Evolution: A Science Fiction. Melinda Mueller. PUP-20

Evolution from the Fish. Robert Bly. MoP; NOBA; NoAM

Evolutionary Hymn. C. S. Lewis. NOBL

Ev'rybody's building the big ships and the boats. Quinn the Eskimo. "Bob Dylan." RaBo

Ewes and lambs, loving the far hillplaces, The. Ad Limina. Joseph Campbell. BIrV

Ex-Basketball Player. John Updike. InPK-6; NYBP; TRP

Ex-Clerk. Rudyard Kipling. *Fr.* Epitaphs of the War [1914–1918]. OBWP

Ex-Deputy Sheriff Remembers the Eastern Oklahoma Murderers, An. Jim Barnes.
  Summerfield. HATNAP, *sect.* i

Ex-Judge at the Bar, An. Melvin Beaunearus Tolson. NAAAL

Ex Nihilo. David Gascoyne. GTBS-P *Fr.* Miserere.

Ex Ore Infantium. Francis Thompson. BoTP; OxBChV

Ex-Queen Among the Astronomers, The. Fleur Adcock. FaBoWP; NALW; NoP-4

Ex Vermibus. "Hugh MacDiarmid." CABP

Ex Voto. Virgil Teodorescu, *Romanian*. CEEP, *tr.* by Donald Eulert *and* Stefan Avadanei

Ex-Voto for a Shipwreck. Aimé Césaire, *French*. PFTM, *tr.* by Clayton Eshleman *and* Annette Smith

Exactly the contents of one, and exactly the contents of two, and which is / ahead? Walt Whitman. *See* I have heard what the talkers were talking, the talk of the beginning and the end.

Exactly the value of one and exactly the value of two, and which is ahead? (LL) I have heard what the talkers were talking, the talk of the beginning and the end. Walt Whitman. ColAP *Fr.* Song of Myself

Exaltatio Humanae Naturae. William Alabaster. NoSic

Exaltation. Franz Werfel, *German*. TrJP, *tr.* by Edith Abercrombie Snow

Examination, The. W. D. Snodgrass. CAPP-1; CoAmPo; SAGP
  ("They nod, whispering, 'One of ours; one of ours. Yes. / Yes'.") (LL) CoAmPo

Examination, The. Priscilla Jane Thompson. CBWP-2

Examination at the Womb-Door. Ted Hughes. NAEL-2; NoP-4; OxBC

Examination Question. *Unknown*. OBCoV

Examiner, no. 385 316, The. Leigh Hunt.
  To Hampstead. Ro

Example, The. W. H. Davies. MoBrPo

Example of Kant's sterling wit, An. Limerick. Victor Gray. PeLi

Example, pattern: lead them to thy light. (LL) St. Simeon Stylites. Tennyson. NOBVV; OAEL-2

Exasperated, worn, you conjure a mansion. Desires of Men and Women. John Berryman. LiTM

Exceeding sorrow / Consumeth my sad heart! O Mors! Quam Amara Est Memoria Tua Homini Pacem Habenti In Substantiis Suis. Ernest Christopher Dowson. ADE; OBMV

Excelente Balade of Charitie, An. Thomas Chatterton. EBEV; NOEC; OxAEP-1

Excelsior! (LL) Excelsior. Henry Wadsworth Longfellow. EBEvV; FaPoR; NAAL-1; NAAL-3; OBCA; OBSP; UV

Excelsior, *see* The Shades of Night *by* Housman *for par.* Henry Wadsworth Longfellow. EBEvV; FaPoR; NAAL-1; NAAL-3; OBCA; OBSP; UV
  ("Like a falling star / Excelsior!") (LL) PFE

Excelsior. *Unknown*. BXAP

Excelsior. Walt Whitman. SAmP

Except. Wendell Berry. EC2

Except a certain awful look / of terrible depression. (LL) In Golden Gate Park that day. Lawrence Ferlinghetti. PmAP; RB

Except as meals. (LL) The Eel. Ogden Nash. NTCP

Except for the fat. Return. John Robert Lee. PBCV

Except ourselves, we have no other prayer. Without Ceremony. Vassar Miller. MoAmPo

Except the Heaven had come so near. Emily Dickinson. SAmP

Except the Lord build the house. Psalm 127. Bible, *O.T.* TrJP *Fr.* Psalms.

Except the Lord, That He for Us Had Been. Henry Ainsworth. AH

Except the rare time. Tanka. Yosano Tekkan, *Japanese*. MJT, *tr.* by Makoto Ueda

Except thy beauty, virtues, and thy friend. (LL) Time. Giles Fletcher, the Elder. AAS; EBEV

Except you'l think of her you left behind. "Ephelia." *See* First Farewell to J.G G.

Excepting the diner. Poem to Be Read at 3 A.M. Donald Justice. HoPM

Excerpt from a Report to the Galactic Council. Robert Conquest. OxBC

Excess of lemon, whether on the phone. The Lair. Rachel Hadas. FFC

Exchange. George Rostrevor Hamilton, *after the Greek of* Plato. FaBoEE

Exchange, The. Alicia Ostriker. NMM-2

Exchange. Dabney Stuart. HoPM

Exchange in greed the ungraceful signs. Thrust. The Violent Space. Etheridge Knight. BPo

Exchange Of Feelings, An. Paul Verlaine, *French*. FLP; LoP, *tr.* by Alistair Elliot

Exchange of Fire. Susan Musgrave. BAP-95

Exchange of Letters. Wendy Cope. OBCoV

Exchange of Poems by Tung-yang Stream, An. Hsieh Ling-yün, *Chinese*. CoBCP, *tr.* by Burton Watson

Exchanges. Ernest Christopher Dowson. OBMV

Excise the er from exercise. Or from. And What Do You Get. Heather McHugh. BAP-95

Excitation. Lorenzo Thomas. FTOS

Excited as a sophisticated boy at his first. Matins and Lauds. Marie Ponsot. CLPP

Excited woodwinds, staccato strings in noisy clamor. Tune: "Squabbling Quails." Kuan Yün-shih. SuSP, *tr.* by Richard John Lynn *Fr.* Medley of Southern and Northern Tunes—Scenic Tour of West Lake.

Excitement. Louise Bennett. PBCV

Excitement of too much, An. German Bite. Iain Sinclair. NBrP

Exciting New Concept of Art Therapy, The. Marlys West. IFJA

Exclamation. Octavio Paz, *Spanish*. ChAP, *tr. by* Eliot Weinberger

Exclusive Blue. Robert Francis. CRP

Excrement Poem, The. Maxine W. Kumin. AFr; FaBoWP

Excursion. Niyi Osundare. HBAPE

Excursion, The. Tu Fu, *Chinese*. AWP, *tr. by* Amy Lowell *and* Florence Ayscough

Excursion, The. Wordsworth. OBGa; LaPo

    identical to lines 754–860 of The Recluse; Home at Grasmere. FHYEP; PoE

Excursion of the Speech and Hearing Class, The. David Wagoner. VCAP

Excursion to Ravenna of A Young Girl with Her Parents. Rossana Ombres, *Italian*.

    Afternoon Hours. PeFWW

    Morning Hours. NeIt

Excursion to the Dragon Pool Temple on Chung-nan, An. Meng Chiao, *Chinese*. PLT, *tr. by* A. C. Graham

Excursion to the Suburbs, An. Tsung Ch'en, *Chinese*.

    "Side by side, we ride out of the city." CoBLCP, *tr. by* Jonathan Chaves

Excuse, The. Carl H. Greene. NBV

Excuse, The. Sir Walter Ralegh. AAS; SiPS

Excuse for Not Returning the Visit of a Friend, An. Mei Yao Ch'en, *Chinese*. OHPC, *tr. by* Kenneth Rexroth

Excuse for So Much Writ upon My Verses. Margaret Lucas Cavendish, Duchess of Newcastle. KTR; PEW

    ("Condemn me not for making such a coil.") PEW

Excuse me. Half-caste. John Agard. NBrP

Excuse me I thought for a moment you were someone I know. I Thought It Was Harry. William Bronk. APSN

Excuse me, isn't that you I see concealed underneath there. Thoughts. Michael Benedikt. CoAmPo; SAGP

Excuse, my lord, the liberty I take. Letter to Lord Byron. W. H. Auden.

Excuse of Absence, An. Thomas Carew. CaPo; SeCP

Exeat. Stevie Smith. NAEL-2; NoAM

Execration, The. Elizabeth Thomas. ECWP

Execration upon Vulcan, An. Ben Jonson. BeJo; SeCP

Execution, The. Vladimir Nabokov, *Russian*. TCRP, *tr. by* Vladimir Nabokov

Execution. James A. Randall Jr. BPo

Execution of Alice Holt. *Unknown*. OxBoLi; OxBoV

Execution of King Charles, The. Andrew Marvell. PoRA

Execution of Madame du Barry, The. J. J. Bray. NOBAu

Execution of Memory, The. Jerzy Ficowski, *Polish*. HP, *tr. by* Keith Bosley

Execution of the faithless maids. Homer, *Greek*. OBCVT, *tr. by* Alexander Pope *Fr.* Odyssey. NAWM-1, *tr. by* Robert Fitzgerald

Executioner arrives on the scene, The. Revenge. Slave Gorgo Dimoski, *Yugoslav*. CEEP, *tr. by* Ewald Osers

Executioner yawned. From his axe the blood was still dripping, The. Imagerie d'Epinal. Aleksander Wat, *Polish*. AF, *tr. by* Czeslaw Milosz *and* Leonard Nathan

Executive. John Betjeman. NOBL

Executive's Death, The. Robert Bly. CoAP

Exempla. James Fenton.

    "For the context of the basidiocarp Singer states." PeLV

    Pitt-Rivers Museum, Oxford, The. FaBoMo

    South Parks Road. PeLV

Exeo in a spasm. Enueg I. Samuel Beckett. CIP-2

Exequies, The. Thomas Stanley. BeJo; MeLP

Exequy, The. Henry, Bishop of Chichester King. GBL; GLoP; HAP; LoP; MeLP; OxBM; PoEL-2; SCGP; SeCP

    (Exequy on [*or upon*] His Wife.) BoLoP; NOBE; OBEV; PeECV; TFi

    (Exequy: To his Matchless Never to be Forgottn Friend, An.) NOSC

    ("Till wee shall Meet, and Never part.") (LL) PBRV

    Stay For Me There. LBC

    ("I shall at last sit down with thee.") (LL) LBC

Exequy, An. Peter Porter. NoAM; NoP-4; OxBC

Exercise. W. S. Merwin. NOBA

Exercise No. 2. William Carlos Williams. SAmP

Exercise of Affection, The. Sir Robert Ayton. NOSC

Exercises in Scriptural Writing. Carl Rakosi.

    "Sandlewood comes to my mind." ChIV-1; KSG

Exert thy voice, sweet harbinger of Spring! To the Nightingale. Anne Finch, Countess of Winchilsea. ECWP; NALW; WPE

Exerted by this grey and shuttered town. (LL) French. Osbert Lancaster. NOBL; PeLV

Exeter Riddle, An. Gavin Ewart. OxBC

Exeunt. Richard Wilbur. HeIP-4; PoLF; Poetsp

Exeunt Omnes. Thomas Hardy. FaBoVe; UV

Exhausted from depression. Ilya Krichevsky, *Russian*. TCRP, *tr. by* Albert C. Todd

Exhausted now her sighs, and dry her tears. Walter Savage Landor. CBLP; FaBoEE

Exhibition: a hundred years of Edinburgh life, An. Museums and Journeys. Robin Fulton. FaBoTC

Exhortation of a Father to His Children, The. Robert Smith. OxBChV

Exhortation to Learn of Others' Trouble. Henry Howard, Earl of Surrey. FaBoEE

    (Lines to Ratclif.) SiPS

Exhortation to Learning. *Unknown, Vietnamese*. AVP, *tr. by* Huỳnh Sanh Thông

Exhortation to Prayer. William Cowper. NOCV *Fr.* Olney Hymns.

Exhorting Myself. Ssu-k'ung Shu, *Chinese*. SuSp, *tr. by* Hellmut Wilhelm

Exhumation. Elizabeth Spires. WeT

Exile. Ingeborg Bachmann, *German*. PoSu, *tr. by* Daniel Huws

Exile. Mbella Sonne Dipoko. PBMAP

Exile. Ernest Christopher Dowson. ADE; BoLoP

Exile. Marta Fenyves. LoHo

Exile. Erich Fried, *German*. AF, *tr. by* Georg Rapp

Exile. Donald Hall. NoP-4

Exile. George Rostrevor Hamilton, *after the Greek of* Isidoros of Aigai. FaBoEE

Exile. Li Shang-yin, *Chinese*. PLT, *tr. by* A. C. Graham

Exile. "St.-John Perse," *French*.

    "Doors open on the sands, doors open on exile." AF, *tr. by* Denis Devlin

Exile. Dennis Phillips.

    From Arena. FTOS

Exile. Karl Shapiro. CRP *Fr.* Adam and Eve.

Exile. Theognis, *Greek*. OBCVT, *tr. by* Andrew Miller

Exile in Japan. Su Man-shu, *Chinese*. BLT, *tr. by* Kenneth Rexroth

Exile in Nigeria. Ezekiel Mphahlele. PBA

Exile lingering here, An. (LL) Infelix. Adah Isaacs Menken. AAP; CBWP-1; PAR

Exile of Erin, The. *Unknown*. NOBAu

Exile of the Sons of Uisliu. *Unknown, Irish*. NOIV, *tr. by* Thomas Kinsella

Exile, Representative. Breyten Breytenbach, *Afrikaans*. AF, *tr. by* Denis Hirson

Exiled. Edna St. Vincent Millay. PoRA

Exiled Heart, The. Maurice Lindsay. OxBS

Exiled under silver birch and conifers. Lure of the Cascadura. John C. M. Lyons. NBrP

Exiles. "Æ." BIrV; MoBrPo

Exiles, The. W. H. Auden. OxBTC

Exiles. Judy F. Ham. LoHo

Exiles. Patrick O'Connor. TIRV

Exiles, The. Paul Ramsey. *Fr.* Three Epigrams. CRP

Exiles: Ends. Leonard Schwartz. PT

Exiles have departed, The. Iain Crichton Smith. FaBoTC *Fr.* The White Air of March.

Exile's Letter. Li Po, *Chinese*. CTC; FaBoMo; OxBA, *tr. by* Ezra Pound

Exile's Letter: After the Failed Revolution. Marilyn Chin. LoHo

Exile's Letter (Or: An Essay on Assimilation). Marilyn Chin. OpBo

Exile's Return, The. Robert Lowell. AmPP; OxBA

Exile's Return, The. Slavko Mihalic. PoSu, *tr. by* Peter Kastmiler *and* Charles Simic

Exile's Reverie, The. Mary Weston Fordham. CBWP-2

Exile's Reveries, The. James Kennedy.

    "Chased from my calling to this hackneyed trade." NOEC

Existing always, always to be blest. (LL) At distance far approaching to the tomb. Philip Freneau. NAAL-1; NAAL-3

Exit. Edwin Arlington Robinson. MoAmPo; OxBSP

Exit Line. John Ciardi. WeW-3

Exit on Feedback. Gavin Selerie. NBrP

Exit, Pursued by a Bear. Ogden Nash. NYBP

Exits and Entrances. Naomi Long Madgett. BlSi

Exmatriate. Jacqueline Lapidus. LoHo

Exodus. Bible, *O.T. See also* Bible, Exodus.

    "Let us synge unto the Lorde, for he is become glorious." OBVE, *tr. by* William Tyndale

    "Then sang Moses and the children of Israel this song." OBWP

Exodus. Horst Bienek, *German*. AF, *tr. by* Matthew Mead

Exodus. Anita Endrezze-Danielson. CDW

Exodus. George Oppen. ChIV-1; KSG; MoLi

Exodus. Charles Reznikoff. ChIV-1

Exodus. *Unknown, Anglo-Saxon.*
  Parting of the Red Sea, The. AnOE, *tr. by* Charles W. Kennedy
Exodus (August 3, 1492), The. Emma Lazarus. *Fr.* By the Waters of Babylon. WPE
Exodus from Egypt, The. Ezechiel of Alexandria, *Greek.* TrJP, *tr. by* E. H. Gifford
Exodus to Connacht. Fear Dorcha O'Meallain, *Irish.* FaBoPV; TIRV, *tr. by* Thomas Kinsella
Exorcism of the Straight/Man/Demon. Aaron Shurin. GLP
Exotic Scent. Charles Baudelaire, *French.* EP; FLP, *tr. by* Alistair Elliot
Expandable Language. Thulani Davis. MoNo
Expanded waters gather on the plain, The. The Flood. Ovid. *Fr.* The Floods, by nature enemies to land. OBVE, *tr. by* Dryden *Fr.* Metamorphoses.
Expanding in the chill. Cold-Weather Love. Ronald G. Everson. MoCV
Expansive puppets percolate self-unction. The Canadian Authors Meet. Francis Reginald Scott. NOBC
Expatriates. David Woo. OpBo
Expect na, Sir, in this narration. A Dedication to G**** H******* Esq. Robert Burns.
Expect No Turbulence. Barbara Ferland. PBCV
Expect nothing. Live frugally. Alice Walker. AmPA
Expectans Expectavi. Charles Hamilton Sorley. FaBoCh
Expectant faces brimmed the waiting square. Rome Sunday[,] June 1960. John Hewitt. TIRV
Expectant Mother. Penelope Shuttle. BrRo
Expectation. Thomas Stanley. BeJo
Expected Guest, The. Sidney Keyes. PoWW
Expense of spirit in a waste of shame, The. Shakespeare. *See* Sonnet 129.
Expense of spirit in a waste of shame, The [*or* Th']. Sonnet 129. Shakespeare. AWP; EBEV; GBL; HAP; HeIP-4; ImPo; InPS-3; NAEL-1; NIP-4; NOBE; NoSic; OAEL-1; OBEV; OxAEP-1; PoE; PoEL-2; Poetr; SCGP; SCV; Son; TFi; UnPO *Fr.* Sonnets.
Expensive Wife, The. Judah ibn Sabbatai. TrJP *Fr.* The Gift of Judah the Woman-Hater.
Experience, The. Bruce Bennett. PeECV
Experience. Mei-Mei Berssenbrugge. PT
Experience. Ralph Waldo Emerson. APN-1; MeMAP; PoEL-4; TAP
Experience. Lesbia Harford. CBAP
Experience. Dorothy Parker. NAAL-2
Experience. James Simmons. BIrV
Experience, The. Edward Taylor. AmPP *Fr.* Preparatory Meditations Before My Approach to the Lord's Supper.
Experience. Edith Wharton. APN-2
Experience of writing you these love leters, The. The Ticket. John Ashbery. WeT
Experience, though noon auctoritee. Chaucer. OxBoLi; PeLV; RACG *Fr.* The Wife of Bath's Prologue. FHYEP; NAEL-1; OAEL-1, *ll.* 1–862 complete *Fr.* The Canterbury Tales.
  ("Al this sentence me liketh every deel.") (LL) RACG
Experience, though noon auctoritee. The Wife of Bath's Prologue. Chaucer. FHYEP; NAEL-1; OAEL-1, *ll.* 1–862 complete *Fr.* The Canterbury Tales.
Experienced men, inured to city ways. John Gay. OAEL-1 *Fr.* Trivia; or, The Art of Walking the Streets of London.
Experienced wife, An. A Midwife's Story; Two. Anne Szumigalski. NOBC
Experiment. Wislawa Szymborska, *Polish.* PoSu, *tr. by* Magnus F. Krynski
Experiment Degustatory. Ogden Nash. ChAP
Experiment escorts us last. Emily Dickinson. APN-2
Experimental Animals. Miroslav Holub, *German.* CEEP, *tr. by* Simko, Daniel
Experiments with God. Karen Gershon. HP
Experts, The. Jack Myers. NAmP90
Expiration, The. Donne. CBLP; MeLP; OxBSP
  (Being double dead, going, and bidding, go[e].) EP; LoP
  ("So, so, break off this last lamenting kiss.") LoP
Explaining the Evening News to Corbyn. James Harms. CMAP
Explanation of America, An. Horace, *Latin.*
  "You of course live in the way that is truly right." OBCVT, *tr. by* Robert Pinsky
Explanation of America, An. Robert Pinsky. Serpent Knowledge. ColAP; NAAL-2
Explanation of the Exhibit, An. Rodney Jones. MoLi
Explanations. Judson Mitcham. PuP-14
Explanatory Note. Yevgeny Bunimovich, *Russian.* TCRP, *tr. by* Albert C. Todd
Explicit Snow. Norman MacCaig. FaBoTC

Exploding before my very eyes. Peyote Vision. Lew Blockcolski. VoR
Exploiter of the shadows. Fox. Clifford Dyment. OxBSP
Exploration. Daniel Hoffman. CoAP
Explore the beauty of our land. The Odyssey. Sipho Sepamla. AF
Explorer. Alan Brownjohn. AYFP
Explorers as Seen by the Natives. Doug Fetherling. NOBC
Explorers will come, The. Margaret Atwood. MoCV
Explosion, The. Philip Larkin. EBEV; FaBoMo; HAP; NAEL-2; NoAM; NoP-4; OxAEP-2; OxBC; PeECV; RB; SCV; WeW-3
Explosive Decibel Journeys. Will Alexander. PT
Exposed to lose his life as well as breeches. (LL) To our theme. The man who has stood on the Acropolis. Byron. InPS-3; OBSV
Exposing his plate to the air. Limerick. Joyce Johnson. PeLi
Expostulation, An. Isaac Bickerstaffe. OBCoV
Expostulation, The. Elizabeth Singer Rowe. PEW
Expostulation and Reply. Wordsworth. FHYEP; NAEL-2; NOBRP; OAEL-2
  ("Why, William, on that old grey stone.") Ro
Exposure. Seamus Heaney. PBCIP; PNI
Exposure. Wilfred Owen. FaBoMo; InPS-3; NoAM; OBWP; PeFWW; PoFWW; PoWW; RB
  ("Pause over half-known faces. All their eyes are ice, / But nothing happens.") (LL) AF
Express. William Allingham. NOBVV
Express. Vincente Huidobro, *Spanish.* PFTM, *tr. by* David Guss
Express, The. Stephen Spender. CMoP; HeIP-4; LiTM; MoBrPo; MoP; NoAM; TwCP
Express Train. Karl Kraus, *German.* TrJP, *tr. by* Albert Bloch
Express train 1256 races alongside hidden, remote villages. House. Rolf Jacobsen, *Norwegian.* BLT, *tr. by* Roger Greenwald
Expressing My Feelings. Meng Chiao, *Chinese.* SuSp, *tr. by* Stephen Owen
Expressing My Feelings. Shen Chou. *See* To the Tune "Nan-hsiang-tzu."
Expression. Thom Gunn. OxBC
Expression. Isaac Rosenberg. MoBrPo
Expulsion, The. Gerald Stern. LCAP-2
Expulsion of Hagar, The. Eloise Bibb. CBWP-4
Exquisite bartender at Sweeney's, The. Limerick. *Unknown.* PeLi
Exquisite / Blue frog, An. Blue Frog Kisses My Sweetheart. Ljiljana Djurdjic, *Serbo-Croatian.* HSix, *tr. by* Charles Simic
Exquisite stillness! What serenities. Don Juan's Address to the Sunset. Robert Malise Bowyer Nichols. OBMV
Exquisite torment, dainty Mrs. Hargreaves. Sapphics. Wyndham Lewis. NOBL; PeLV
Extasie, The. Abraham Cowley. SeCP
Extasie, The. Donne. *See* The Ecstasy.
Extempore Effusion upon the Death of James Hogg. Wordsworth. EBEV; NOBE; OAEL-2; SCV
  ("And Ettrick mourns with her their Shepherd dead!") (LL) Ro
  (Extempore Effusion, Upon Reading, in the Newcastle Journal, the Notice of the Death of the Poet, James Hogg.) Ro
Extempore [Verses] Intended to Allay the Violence of Party-Spirit. John Byrom. NOBL; PeLV
  (Jacobite Toast.) FaBoEE
Extempore—On Being Shown a Beautiful Country Seat Belonging to Maxwell of Cardoness. Robert Burns. OBGa
Extend, there where you venture and come back. Walk on the Moon. N. Scott Momaday. CRP
Extended Sonnet on the Death of Isaac Danziger, *love poem.* Meir Wieseltier, *Hebrew.* IP, *tr. by* Warren Bargad *and* Stanley F. Chyet
  (Extended Sonnet on the Death of Isaac Danzinger.) IP, *tr. by* Warren Bargad *and* Stanley F. Chyet
Exterior—to Time. (LL) This was a Poet—It is That. Emily Dickinson. APN-2; AmPP; NAAL-1; NAAL-3; NCAP; NOBA; PAR
Extinct Birds. Judith Wright. PBWP
Extinct volcanoes are silent. Volcanoes. Bella Akhatovna Akhmadulina, *Russian.* PBWP, *tr. by* W. H. Auden
Extinguish, one by one. Vicki Raymond. NOBAu
Extinguish that delight. (LL) A Last Confession. W. B. Yeats. BoLoP; CBLP; CMoP; HAP; NIP-4; OAEL-2
Extinguishes all hope! (LL) The Mad Gardener's Song. "Lewis Carroll." CBNP; OxBChV; PBMP
Extra Joyful Chorus for Those Who Have Read This Far, An. Robert Bly. SPE
'Extra Terrestrial' they called you, spilling. E. T. Jean Kenward. SpW
Extract. Paul Bowles. PoA
Extract from a Diary. János Pilinszky, *Hungarian.* PoSu, *tr. by* Peter Jay
Extract from Addresses to the Academy of Fine Ideas, An. Wallace Stevens. LiTM
Extract from Memoirs. Howard Nemerov. OxBC
Extract from Romance. Dame Edith Sitwell. WPN

Extract from Solitude. Vita Sackville-West.

Extract the juice which is itself a Light. Paracelsus. Diane Di Prima. PT

Extract the quint-essence. Francis Daniel Pastorius. SCAP

Extracts: From the Journal of Elisa Lynch. Maura Stanton. AmPA

Extraordinary patience of things!, The. Carmel Point. Robinson Jeffers. BLT; NAAL-2; NoAM; NoP-4

Extravagant Drunkard's Wish, The. Edward Ward. CBNP; NOEC

Extreme scab take thee and thine, for me, The. (LL) To the Sour[e] Reader. Robert Herrick. NBLV; NoP-4; SeCP

Extreme Unction. Ernest Christopher Dowson. ADE; MoBrPo; OAEL-2; OBMV; PeECV; PeVV

Extremes. James Whitcomb Riley. FPC

Exuberant, restless. West Lake. Kenneth O. Hanson. CoAP

Exult each patriot heart!—this night is shewn. Prologue. Royall Tyler. NAAL-3 *Fr.* The Contrast.

Exultation. Hywel ab Owain Gwynedd, *Welsh.* OBWVE, *tr. by* Gwyn Williams

Exultation is the going. Emily Dickinson. APN-2; OxBoS

Exulting in his Strength, he seems to dare. Turnus and the Wanton Courser. Virgil. OBVE, *tr. by* John Dryden *Fr.* The Aeneid [*or* Eneados, *Aeneis*].

Eyam. Anna Seward.

Eyam. Anna Seward. CABP; ECWP

("Dim Apparition thou—and bitter is my tear!") (LL) CABP

"In scenes paternal, not beheld through years." NOEC

Eye, The. Michael Benedikt. CoAmPo

Eye, The. Robert Herrick. CaPo

Eye, The. Robinson Jeffers. ImPo; LiTM; NOBA; NoAM; OxBA

Eye and Ear, The. Jones Very. APN-1

Eye and Tooth. Robert Lowell. NAAL-2

Eye Blade. George Evans. AF

Eye can hardly pick them out, The. At Grass. Philip Larkin. HAP; OxBTC; RB; WeW-3

Eye closes, An. Inn. Pierre Reverdy, *French.* PFTM, *tr. by* Patricia Terry

Eye for an Eye, An. Christine M. Donald. GLP

Eye for an Eye, An. Homer. *Fr.* Odyssey. NAWM-1, *tr. by* Robert Fitzgerald

Eye in the Rock, The. John Haines. PaTW

Eye is meant to see things, An. Someone Digging in the Ground. Jelaluddin Rumi, *Persian.* RaBo, *tr. by* Coleman Barks

Eye Mask. Denise Levertov. BLT

Eye of God. Jim Tollerud. VoR

Eye of Heart. Olga Broumas. NMM-2

Eye of looking back were well, An. Ben Jonson. *Fr.* Pleasure Reconciled to Virtue. NAEL-1; OAEL-1

Eye of the earth; and what it watches is not our wars. (LL) The Eye. Robinson Jeffers. ImPo; LiTM; NOBA; NoAM; OxBA

Eye of this storm is not quiet, The. To a Gone Era. Irma McClaurin. BlSi

Eye-Opener. Malcolm Lowry. NoP-4

Eye opening is a mouth seeing, The. Eyesight II. Robert Duncan. SPE

Eye sees more than the heart knows, The. William Blake. *See* Visions of the Daughters of Albion.

Eye sit here, now, inside my fast thickening breath. Reflections on Growing Older. Quincy Troupe. GT

Eye: solitude. Ecce Homo. Sándor Weöres, *Hungarian.* CEEP, *tr. by* Emery E. George

Eye standing up eye lying down eye sitting. Making Feet and Hands. Benjamin Péret, *French.* SPE, *tr. by* David Gascoyne

Eye, the cauldron of morning. (LL) Ariel. Sylvia Plath. CMoP; HCAP; HeIP-4; LCAP-2; MoP; NAAL-2; NALW; NOBA; NoAM; NoP-4; PBWP; PoE; Poetr; VCAP

Eye unacquitted by whatever it holds in allegiance, The. Didactic Piece. Louise Bogan. NoAM

Eye use to write poems about burning. Boomerang: A Blatantly Political Poem. Quincy Troupe. AF; LTA

Eye winker. *Unknown.* OxNR

Eyeful Glances. Niyi Osundare. HBAPE

Eyeglasses. Tom Clark. CoAmPo

Eyeing the Eyes of One's Mistress. Ebenezer Jones. NOBVV

Eyeless labourer in the night, The. Woman to Man. Judith Wright. BMAP; CBAP; NoP-4; WPE

Eyelid is twitching. On the open mouth, An. Sextet. Joseph Brodsky, *Russian.* TCRP, *tr. by* Joseph Brodsky

Eyelids glowing, some chill morning, The. Monet: 'Les Nymphéas'. W. D. Snodgrass. CoAP; CoAmPo

Eyelids meet. He'll catch a little nap, The. In the Smoking-Car. Richard Wilbur. CoAmPo; GM; LiTM; MoAmPo

Eyelids of eve fall together at last, The. The Eve of Waterloo. Thomas Hardy. OAEL-2; OBWP *Fr.* The Dynasts.

Eyes, The. Tanka. Nakajō Fumiko, *Japanese.* MJT, *tr. by* Makoto Ueda

Eyes. Vladimir Dmitrievich Tsybin, *Russian.* TCRP, *tr. by* Lubov Yakovleva

EYES always open eyes. Eyewash. Niall Montgomery. SPE

Eyes and Tears. Andrew Marvell. FSCP; GeHe

Eyes, Calm beside Thee (Lady, Could'st Thou Know!). Robert Browning. Son

Eyes caught by beauty, fancy by eyes caught. The Husband of To-Day. Edith Nesbit. VWP

Eyes Fastened with Pins. Charles Simic. VCAP

Eyes filled with speaking fire. Irenaeus Referendarius, *Greek.* GrAn, *tr. by* Andrew Miller

Eyes fixed. Tanka. Yosano Tekkan, *Japanese.* MJT, *tr. by* Makoto Ueda

Eyes / flatterers of Soul. Meleager, *Greek.* GrAn, *tr. by* Peter Whigham

Eyes in the Air. Gilbert Frankau. NSI

Eyes knees and of your Etcetera. (LL) My sweet old etcetera. E. E. Cummings. AmPP; CMoP; HeIP-4; InPS-3; OBAL; OBWP; OxBA; PeFWW

Eyes like the morning star. The Colorado Trail. *Unknown.* AS

Eyes look front in humans, The. Teleology. May Swenson. VCAP

Eyes:. . . . . . . Medium. All There Is to Know about Adolph Eichmann. Leonard Cohen. InPK-6

Eyes of a Wolf. Vasco [*or* Vasko] Popa, *Serbian.* CEEP, *tr. by* Charles Simic

Eyes of body, being blindfold by night, The. Valentine Ackland. WPN

Eyes of grey—a sodden quay. The Lovers' Litany. Rudyard Kipling. CBLP

Eyes of heavenly essence, O breasts of the purity of breasts. Poem for a Lost Lover. Syl Cheney-Coker. PBMAP

Eyes of men running, falling, screaming. *Unknown.* OBWP

Eyes of Night-Time. Muriel Rukeyser. BoWoP

Eyes of slain stag. In Some Seer's Cloud Car. Christopher Middleton. TwCP

Eyes of twenty centuries, The. Judas Iscariot. Stephen Spender. MoBrPo; NIP-4

Eyes open on the beach. Eyes Watch the Stars. Christopher Okigbo. PBMAP *Fr.* Heavensgate (1961).

Eyes open to a cry of pulleys, The. Love Calls Us to the Things of This World. Richard Wilbur. AmPP; CMoP; ColAP; HAP; HeIP-4; InPS-3; MoAmPo; NIP-4; NoAM; NoP-4; PoE; PoRA; Poetr; SAGP; TAP; TFi; UnPo; VCAP; VGW

Eyes red, the lips blue, The. The Three Seamstresses. Isaac Leibush Peretz, *Yiddish.* TrJP, *tr. by* Joseph Leftwich

Eye's roundness between the bars. Language Mesh. Paul Celan, *German.* VCWP, *tr. by* Michael Hamburger

Eyes shut tight. Madness. Sachiko Yoshihara, *Japanese.* BoWoP, *tr. by* James Kirkup *and* Shozo Tokunaga

Eyes So Tristful. Diego de Saldaña, *Spanish.* AWP, *tr. by* Longfellow

Eyes socketing instrumentation. Folkway. Gábor Görgey, *Hungarian.* CEEP, *tr. by* Jascha Kessler

Eyes that drew from me such fervent praise, The. Petrarch. NAWM-1, *tr. by* Edwin Morgan. *Fr.* Sonnets to Laura.

Eyes that glass fear, though fear on furtive foot. A Hare. Walter De la Mare. EBEV

Eyes that last I saw in tears. T. S. Eliot. NOBE

Eyes that weep for pity of the heart, The. Dante. AWP *Fr.* La Vita Nuova.

Eyes, the Blood, The. David Meltzer. PoM

Eyes turn topaz, The. (LL) Hugh Selwyn Mauberley. (Life and Contacts). Ezra Pound. AmPP; CMoP; InPS-3; LiTM; NOBA; NoAM; TAP

Eyes Watch the Stars. Christopher Okigbo. PBMAP *Fr.* Heavensgate (1961).

Eyesight II. Robert Duncan. SPE

Eyewash. Niall Montgomery. SPE

Ez Malindy sings. (LL) When Malindy Sings. Paul Laurence Dunbar. AAP; APN-2; ISC; NAAAL; PoBA

Ezek'el saw de wheel. Ezekiel, You and Me. *Unknown.* AS *See* Ezekiel Saw the Wheel.

Ezekiel. Bible, *O.T.*

Lamentation. TrJP

Thy Mother Was like a Vine. TrJP

Ezekiel. John Greenleaf Whittier. ChIV-1

Ezekiel Saw the Wheel. *Unknown.* APN-2; NoP-4

("Ezek'el saw de wheel.") AS

(Ezekiel Saw the Wheel.) NoP-4

("'Way up in the middle o' the air.") (LL) NoP-4

Ezekiel, You and Me. *Unknown.* AS

Ezra Pound. Robert Lowell. MoP; NAAL-2; NOBA; NoAM

Ezra Pound and Robert Bridges. Robert Bagg. WeT

Ezra Pound's Eye. Anne Hussey. WeT

Ezra, whom not with eye nor with ear have I ever. Epistle to the Rapalloan. Archibald MacLeish. PoA

Ezry. Archibald MacLeish. NOBA

F

F. de Samara to A. G. A. Emily Jane Brontë. NALW

Fa La La. John Hilton. *See* Madrigal: "My mistress frowns when she should play."

Fa, Mi, Fa, Re, La, Mi. *Unknown.* InPK-6

Fab Four Tour Deutschland: Hamburg, 1961. David Wojahn. PBCAP *Fr.* Mystery Train: A Sequence.

Fable. Eugenio de Andrade, *Portuguese.* VCWP, *tr. by* Alexis Levitin

Fable. James Facos. NBLV

Fable, A. John Hookham Frere. UV

Fable, A: "In Æsop's tales an honest wretch we find." Matthew Prior. NoP-4

Fable. Merrill Moore. LiLi

Fable: "Mountain and the squirrel, The." Ralph Waldo Emerson. APN-1; AmPP; BoTP; FaBoBe; ImPo; MeMAP; NBLV; OBAL; OBCA; TFi

Fable: "Once upon a time / there was a lonely wolf." János Pilinszky, *Hungarian.* OBVE; PoSu; RB, *tr. by* Ted Hughes *and* Janos Csokits

Fable: "There is an inevitability." Norman Harris. NYBP

Fable: "Under a dung-cake." D. J. Opperman, *Afrikaans.* PeSA; PeSAV, *tr. by* Jack Cope

Fable at the beginning of the monsoon, The. A Monsoon Day Fable. Jayanta Mahapatra. VCWP

Fable for Critics, A. James Russell Lowell. NAAL-1; NAAL-3; NCAP
See Emerson.
  Bryant. NOBA; TAP
  Cooper. NOBA; OxBA; TAP
  Emerson. AmPP; NOBA; OxBA; TAP
    ("While a cloud that floats o'er is reflected within it.") (LL) AmPP; OxBA; TAP
    ("Will be some very great person over again.") (LL) NCAP
  Hawthorne. AmPP; NOBA; OxBA; TAP
    ("For making him fully and perfectly man.") (LL) OxBA
  Holmes. NOBA
  Irving. TAP
  Lowell. AmPP; NOBA; OxBA; TAP
  Poe and Longfellow. AmPP; OxBA; PAR
    (Poe.) TAP
    ("There comes Poe with his raven, like Barnaby Rudge.") PAR; OBCoV
  "There are truths you Americans need to be told." OBSV
  Whittier. AmPP; NOBA; OxBA

Fable of the Piece of Glass and the Piece of Ice, The. John Hookham Frere. OxBChV

Fable of the Speckled Cow. D. J. Opperman, *Afrikaans.* PeSA, *tr. by* Jack Cope, Uys Krige, *and* Ruth Miller

Fable of the War, A. Howard Nemerov. OBWP

Fable of the Young Man and His Cat, The. Christopher Pitt. ECEV

Fable XXI: The Rat-catcher and Cats. John Gay. OxAEP-1

Fabled queen of love, The. (LL) Sonnet: "When Phoebe formed a wanton smile." William Collins. EnLoPo; OxBSP

Fables. John Gay.
  Mother, the Nurse, and the Fairy, The. PeLV
  Poet and the Rose, The. PeLV
  Wild Boar and the Ram, The. NOEC

Fabrication of Ancestors. Alan Dugan. CBCWP; NoAM

Fabulary Satire IV. Daryl Hine. NOBC

Fabullus I will treat you handsomely. *Carmina,* XIII. Catullus. OBVE, *tr. by* Richard Lovelace *Fr.* Carmina.

Fabulous Wizard of Oz, The. Limerick. *Unknown.* PeLi

Façade. Dame Edith Sitwell.

Façade. Dame Edith Sitwell.
  Hornpipe. FaBoMo; GTBS-P; OAEL-2
  "I Do Like To Be Beside the Seaside." PFTM
  Sir Beelzebub. BoWoP; FaBoMo; FaBoWP; HoPM; MoBrPo; NALW; OBCoV; OxBTC
  Trio for Two Cats and a Trombone. NAEL-2; PBWP

Face, A. Robert Browning. CTC

Face, The. Anthony Euwer. OBAL; PeLi *Fr.* The Limeratomy.
  (My Face.) PoLF

Face, The. Susan Mitchell. NAmP90

Face, A. Marianne Moore. OxBSP

Face, The. Edwin Muir. GTBS-P

Face. Sounds. Wassily Kandinsky, *Russian.* PFTM, *tr. by* Elizabeth R. Napier

Face. Jean Toomer. NoP-4

Face, A? There. Between Us. James Merrill. PoE

Face-down; odor. Terror. Denise Levertov. PoE

Face down on the sled. The Pilot. Renate Wood. CMAP

Face flashing free child-arms. This. Adrienne Rich. FiLi

Face framed in a pink lace baby's hood was youth and age, A. The Dead Monkey. William Olsen. NAmP90

Face from the Past, A. Menella Bute Smedley. VWP

Face (Guillemont), The. Frederic Manning. NSI

Face in the crook of her neck. Gary Snyder. *Fr.* Burning. NeAP; PoM *Fr.* Myths and Texts.

Face in the Mirror, The. Robert Graves. CABP

Face Lost in the Wilderness. Fadwa Tuqan, *Arabic.* AF, *tr. by* Naomi Shihab Nye

Face of all the world is changed, I think, The. Sonnet. Elizabeth Barrett Browning. CTC *Fr.* Sonnets from the Portuguese.

Face of Helen, The. Marlowe. *See* Helen.

Face of his hours reflected?, The. (LL) Hours continuing long, sore and heavy-hearted. Walt Whitman. PoPoPo

Face of Love, The. Ingrid Jonker, *Afrikaans.* PeSA, *tr. by* Jack Cope

Face of the autumn moon freezes, The. Meng Chiao. PLT, *tr. by* A. C. Graham *Fr.* Autumn Thoughts.

Face of the Horse, The. Nikolai Alekseievich Zabolotsky, *Russian.* RB; TCRP, *tr. by* Daniel Weissbort

Face of the landscape is a mask, The. Mask. Stephen Spender. MoBrPo

Face of the precipice is black with lovers, The. Salvador Dali. David Gascoyne. FaBoMo; OxBTC; SPE

Face of the Waters, The. Robert David Fitzgerald. CBAP

Face sings, alone, The. A Poem for Willie Best. Imamu Amiri Baraka. CAPP-1

Face that should content me wonders [*or* wondrous] well, A. Sir Thomas Wyatt. CTC; EnLoPo

Face the Animal. Jean Follain, *French.* BLT, *tr. by* Heather McHugh

Face to Face. Adrienne Rich. LiTM; NAAL-2; NoAM

Face to Face. K. V. Tirumalesh, *Kannada.* OMIP, *tr. by* A. K. Ramanujan

Face to face with the sunflower. The Secret Joy. Mary Webb. BoTP

Face upon [*or* on] the Floor, The. Hugh Antoine D'Arcy. BLPA; FaBoBe

Face which, duly as the sun, The. Elizabeth Barrett Browning. LBC

Face wrapping a champagne glass. Bob Boldman. HA

Face yellowed, The. The Betrayal. "Nirala," *Hindi.* OMIP, *tr. by* Arvind Krishna Mehrotra

Faces. David Chapman Berry. BXAP

Faces. John Ciardi. WeW-3

Faces, The. Robert Creeley. NoAM

Faces. Walt Whitman. PoEL-5
  (Leaves of Grass (1855).) APN-1
  ("Sauntering the pavement or riding the country byroad here then are faces.") APN-1

Faces and Skulls. Jan Carew. PBCV

Faces are lifted up in the jumpy light, The. White Noise. Laurie Sheck. WWSi

Faces at the First Farmworkers Constitutional Convention. José Montoya. "Just the other day." PaTW

Faces greying faster than loam-crumbs on a harrow. Judge Not. Theodore Roethke. ChIV-2; GI

Faces hover on the windows. Masks. Judit Tóth, *Hungarian.* CEEP, *tr. by* Emery E. George

Faces I Love, The. Gerald Stern. LoL

Faces in a door a row of faces. On Parade. Fragano Ledgister. PBCV

Faces in the Street. Henry Lawson. CBAP

Faces may alter, names can't change. Nathaniel Lee to Sir Roger L'Estrange. Nathaniel Lee. FaBoEE

Faces of the children, The. Without Song. Grace Nichols. PBCV

Faces surround me that have no smell or color no time. Chain. Audre Lorde. BISi

Facile as can be the boat you see, my guests, says. Catullus. *See* The Yacht.

Facing a streetlight under batty moths. The Calculation. David Wagoner. NYBP

Facing Bonnard. Aleksander Wat, *Polish.* BLT, *tr. by* Czeslaw Milosz *and* Leonard Nathan

Facing Change. Dr. Tony Lake. LBC

Facing It. Yusef Komunyakaa. MT; NAAAL; PoPoPo; TRP

Facing me, the blustering evening rain besprinkles the sky over the river. Tune: "Eight Beats of a Kan-chou Song." Liu Yung, *Chinese.* SuSp, *tr. by* James J. Y. Liu

Facing the Chair. "Hugh MacDiarmid." FaBoMo

Facing the palm of fire. Meditation for this Day. Antonio Machado Ruiz, *Spanish.* CLPP, *tr. by* Kenneth Rexroth

Facing west from California's shores. Walt Whitman. MoAmPo; NAAL-1; NAAL-3; PaTW; TAP

Facing Wine with Memories of Lord Ho. Li Po, *Chinese.* CoBCP, *tr. by* Burton Watson

Facing you, on the wall, across your bed. Yün Shou-p'ing. CoBLCP, *tr. by* Jonathan Chaves *Fr.* Mourning for Lü Hui-chiu.

Fact. Langston Hughes. APSN; PFTM

Fact. Kenneth Rexroth. OBAL

Fact is / that i don't hate any body any more, The. Some Me of Beauty. Carolyn M. Rodgers. NMM-2

Fact of the matter is, Jack, The. Limerick. John Stanley. PeLi

Fact that we survive it compels us, The. Beyond Fear. Odia Ofeimun. HBAPE

Factory. "Antler."

  "Machines waited for me, The." CLPP

  "Ungag our souls!! Unstrangle our souls!! Unsmother our souls!!" CLPP

Factory, The. Aleksandr Blok, *Russian*. TCRP, tr. by Yakov Hornstein

Factory. Andre Breton *and* Philippe Soupault. PFTM, tr. by David Gascoyne *Fr.* The Magnetic Fields.

Factory Girl's Come-All-Ye, The. *Unknown*. AmFP; OBAL

Factory windows are always broken. Vachel Lindsay. ImPo; MeMAP; OBCA; OxBSP

Factory Workers' Song. *Unknown*. FaBoVe

Facts of Life, The. Ronald Wallace. PBCAP

Facts of Life, Ballymoney. Eamon Grennan. PBCIP

Fade in the sound of summer music. Notes for a Movie Script. M. Carl Holman. PoBA

Fade the kingfisher blue, trim the red, blend the colors. Yüan Hao-wen. SuSp, tr. by Irving Y. Lo *Fr.* On Poetry.

Faded. Augusta Davies Webster. VWP

Faded, and the hill slept. (LL) He Fell among Thieves. Sir Henry John Newbolt. EBVV; FaPoR; OBEV; OBWP; OxBTC

Faded back last night. Talking. Robert Creeley. FTOS

Faded Boy—in sallow Clothes, A. Emily Dickinson. PoEL-5

Faded flowers of the bed sheets autumn night. Marlene Mountain. HA

Fading Beauty. Giovanni Battista Marino, *Italian*. AWP, tr. by Samuel Daniel

Fading Beauty. *Unknown*. FaBoEE

Fading chimes, The. The Old Temple. Zhao Zhenkai, *Chinese*. ChiPo, tr. by Bonnie S. McDougall

Fading dream lingers by the hills on the screen. Tune: "Song of Divination." Chu Yi-tsun, *Chinese*. SuSp, tr. by Irving Y. Lo

Fading in the most important place we have yet devised. Linda Gregg. *See* The Shopping-Bag Lady.

Fading-Leaf and Fallen-Leaf. Richard Garnett. EBVV

Fading, sick, again I hear of war. Wu Wei-yeh. *Fr.* Country Scene. CoBLCP, tr. by Jonathan Chaves

Fading Skiff, The. Henrietta Cordelia Ray. CBWP-3

Fado Singer. Wole Soyinka. HBAPE

Faerie Fair, The. Florence Harrison. BoTP

Faerie Queene, The. Edmund Spenser.

  Address to Venus. AWP

  Arthur's Fight with Orgoglio and Duessa. EBNV

  "As when a ship, that flyes faire under saile." FHYEP

  "Ay me, how many perils doe unfold [*or* enfold]." FHYEP; OAEL-1

  Balme. CH

  "Behold I see the haven nigh at hand." FHYEP

  Bower of Bliss, The. PoEL-1

    "And in the midst of all, a fountaine stood." CH

    Bower of Bliss, The. OBGa

    "Eftsoones they heard a most melodious sound." EBEvV; NOBE; PBRV; SCV

  Britomart at Isis' Church. PoE

  "By this the Northerne wagoner had set." FHYEP; NoSic

  Cave of Despair, The. OBNV

  "Ere long they come, where that same wicked wight." NOBE; OAEL-1

  Cave of Mammon, The. PoEL-1

  Dame Nature. PoEL-1

    ("And Nature's self did vanish, whither no man wist.") (LL) AEP

    (Nature.) AEP

    ("Then forth issued (great goddess) great Dame Nature.") AFP

  "Faire knight (quoth he) Hierusalem that is." FaBoPV

  Fight of the Red Cross Knight and the Heathen Sansjoy, The. FHYEP; NoSic

  "For round about, the walls yclothed were." PBRV

  Garden of Adonis, The. NOBE; OBGa; PoEL-1

    ("Possesseth him, and of his sweetnesse takes her fill.") (LL) OBGa

    ("She brought her to her ioyous Paradize.") OBGa

    "In that same gardin all the goodly flowres." NOBE

  "Gentle knight was pricking on the plaine, A." EBEV; FHYEP; NAEL-1; OAEL-1; Poetr

  Guyon's Voyage to the Bower of Bliss. NoSic

    "Two dayes now in that sea he sayled has." OxBoS

"Hard is the doubt, and difficult to deeme." OAEL-1

"He making speedy way through spersed ayre." NoSic

"He was to weet a man of full ripe years." UV, *sect.* 4, *canto* 3

"High time now gan it wex for Una faire." FHYEP

Hill of the Graces, The. NOBE

House of Busyrane, The. NoSic

House of Richesse, The. CH

"In such luxurious plentie of all pleasure." OAEL-1

In the Bower of Bliss. GaP

  ("O horrible enchantment, that him so did blend.") (LL) FaBoSe

"It fortuned (as faire it then befell)." OAEL-1

Legend of Britomartis, or of Chastitie, The. NAEL-1

Legend of the Knight of the Red Crosse, or of Holinesse, The. EPCY; FHYEP; NAEL-1; OAEL-1

  ("It was a chosen plot of fertile land.") AEP

  (Phaedria's Island: The Faerie Queene II.vi. 12–17.) AEP

  ("Refuse such fruitless toil, and present pleasures choose.") (LL) AEP

"Like as the tide that comes from th' Ocean main." HoPM

Mask of Cupid, The.

  "First was Fancy, like a lovely boy, The." NOBE

  "Noble Mayde, still standing, all this vewd, The." PoEL-1

Mutability. AEP; PoEL-1

  ("And death instead of life have sucked from our Nurse.") (LL) AEP

  ("What man that sees the ever-whirling wheel.") AEP

Mutability Claims to Rule the World. NoSic

Nature's Reply to Mutability. NOBE

Nought is on earth more sacred or divine. OAEL-1

"Nought is there under heav'ns wide hollownesse." FHYEP

"Nought vnder heauen so strongly doth allure." NoSic

"Now, at the time that was before agreed." OAEL-1

"O goodly golden chaine, wherewith yfere." FHYEP

Pageant of the Seasons and the Months, The. OxAEP-1

"Right well I w[r]ote most mighty Soueraine [*or* soueraine]." NoSic; OAEL-1

Scudamor in the Temple of Venus. PoE

"So as they travelled, the drouping night." OAEL-1

"So forth she comes, and to her coche does clyme." NAEL-1; OAEL-1

"So oft as I with state of present time." OAEL-1

"Then said that royall Pere in sober wise." OAEL-1

"Thence forward by that painfull way they pas." OAEL-1

"Therein was writ, how often thundering Jove." OxBSn

"They sate to meat, and Satyrane his chaunce." OAEL-1

"Tho when as chearelesse night ycovered had." OAEL-1

"Tho when they came to the sea coast, they found." PBRV

"Thus being entered, they behold around." OAEL-1

Vision of the Graces, The. NoSic

"Well may I weene, faire ladies, all this while." OAEL-1

What If Some Little Paine the Passage Have. CH

"What man is he, that boasts of fleshly might." FHYEP

"What man so wise, what earthly wit so ware." FHYEP

"When I bethinke me on that speech whyleare." NoSic; OAEL-1

"Whilom, as antique stories tellen us." EPCY

"Who now does follow the foule Blatant Beast." FHYEP

"Who travels [*or* trauels] by the wearie wandring way." OxAEP-1

Wood of Error. AEP

"Young knight, what ever that dost armes professe." FHYEP

Faery Beam upon You, The. Ben Jonson. BeJo *Fr.* The Gypsies Metamorphosed.

(Song.) OxBSP

Faery Song. Keats. CH

Faesulan Idyll. Walter Savage Landor. Ro

Fafnir. Alec Derwent Hope. BMAP

Fag-End. Philip O'Connor. SPE

Faggots and their friends now live in Ramrod, The. Larry Mitchell. GLP

Faggots created a rite of cleansing, The. The faggots sit in a circle. Sons and Fathers. Larry Mitchell. GLP

Faggots of ash, elm, oak. A Heap of Faggots. Andrew Young. FaBoTC

Fagots blazed, the caldron's smoke, The. The Brewing of Soma. John Greenleaf Whittier. PoEL 4

Faht's in there? What's in There? *Unknown*. CH

Failing the Examination. Meng Chiao, *Chinese*. SuSp, tr. by Stephen Owen

Failings, The. Paul Zimmer. CMAP

Failure, A. C. Day Lewis. NOBE

Failure. Kate Tucker Goode. PWR

Failure. Henrietta Cordelia Ray. CBWP-3

Failure and Success. Richard Watson Gilder. PWR

Failure of an Invention. Safiya Henderson-Holmes. UnSA

Failure, the longed-for valley, takes him in. (LL) In the Smoking-Car. Richard Wilbur. CoAmPo; GM; LiTM; MoAmPo

Failure to write is a personal failure, The. Instrumentum Vocale. Kevin Magee. PT

Failures. May Kendall. VWP

Fain would I be sleeping, dreaming. The Plaint of the Wife. *Unknown, Russian.* AWP, *tr. by* W. R. S. Ralston

Fain would I change that note. No Other Choice. Tobias Hume. EBEV; GBL; NOBE; PoEL-2

Fain would I have a pretty thing. A Proper Song, Entitled: Fain Would I Have a Pretty Thing to Give unto My Lady. *Unknown.* NoSic

Fain would I kiss my Julia's dainty leg. Her Legs. Robert Herrick. NOSC; PFE

Fain would I rival thee. To the Eagle. Mary Weston Fordham. CBWP-2

Fain would I wed a fair young man that night and day could please me. Thomas Campion. NAEL-1

Fain would my Muse the flow'ry Treasures sing. The Garden. Alexander Pope. GaP; OBGa

Faint and more faint amid the world of dreams. A Poet's Love. Letitia Elizabeth Landon. Ro *Fr.* Life and Literary Remains of L.E.L.

Faint Falls the Gentle Voice. Henry Timrod. AH

Faint flush spread all over her cheeks, still sleepy-eyed, A. Tune: "Sand of Silk-washing Stream." Wu Wei-yeh, *Chinese.* SuSp, *tr. by* Irving Y. Lo

Faint-flushed buds awake within the cup, The. The Awakening. Henrietta Cordelia Ray. CBWP-3

Faint Love. Arthur Symons. CABP

Faint Music. Walter De la Mare. FaBoCh

Faint now in the evening pallor. Silver Jubilee. Llewelyn Wyn Griffith. OBWVE

Faint shines the far moon. The Road. Nikolay Platonovich Ogarev, *Russian.* AWP, *tr. by* P. E. Matheson

Faintheart in a Railway Train. Thomas Hardy. CBLP; CTC; EnLoPo

Faintly answering still the notes that once were so dear. (LL) Echo. Thomas Moore. GLoP; GTBS-P; NOBE; OBEV; OBNC; PoEL-4

Faintly white. Tanka. Yosano Tekkan, *Japanese.* MJT, *tr. by* Makoto Ueda

Fair am I, mortals, as a stone-carved dream. Beauté, La. Charles Baudelaire, *French.* AWP, *tr. by* Lord Alfred Douglas

Fair Amazon of Heaven who tookst in hand. To Saint Margaret. Henry Constable. NoSic

Fair Amoret is gone astray. A Hue and Cry after Fair Amoret. William Congreve. NOEC; OBEV

Fair and bright assembly, A: never strode. Thomas Lovell Beddoes. CTC *Fr.* Death's Jest Book.

Fair and Fair. George Peele. OBEV *Fr.* The Arraignment of Paris. (Oenone and Paris.) NOBE

Fair and free soul of poesy, O Keats! Keats. Walter Savage Landor. EPCY

Fair and scornful, do thy worst. *Unknown.* OBCoV

Fair and Softly goes far or, The Wary Physician. Laetitia Pilkington. PEW

Fair and Unfair. Robert Francis. VGW

Fair Annie. *Unknown.* CH; ESPB; OxBB

Fair Annie an Sweet Willie. Lord Thomas and Fair Annet. *Unknown.* ESPB

Fair Annie had a costly bower. The Holy Nunnery. *Unknown.* ESPB

Fair Annie of Lochryan. *Unknown.* AS

Fair are the bells of this bright-flowering weed. Poet and Botanist. Constance Naden. VWP

Fair[e] as unshaded light; or as the day. To the Queen[e], Entertain[e]d at Night by the Countess[e] of Anglesey. Sir William Davenant. MeLP; NOSC

Fair at Windgap, The. Austin Clarke. OxBTC

Fair Beatrice tucks her coat up somewhat high. Epigram. John Taylor. NOSC

Fair Beauty Bride, The. *Unknown.* AmFP

Fair Beggar, The. Richard Lovelace. BeJo

Fair bosom! fraught with virtue's richest treasure. Sonnet 76. Edmund Spenser. NIP-4 *Fr.* Amoretti. AAS

Fair boy, alas, why fliest thou me. The Black Maid to the Fair Boy. Henry Reynolds. NOSC

Fair boy, how gay the morning must have seemed. Hyacinthus. Olive Custance. ADE

Fair Cassidy. *Unknown, Irish.* BIrV, *tr. by* Donagh MacDonagh

Fair cheek under a merry blue eye, two brows, A. The Beloved. David Roberts, *Welsh.* OBWVE, *tr. by* H. Idris Bell

Fair Cloris in a pig-stye lay. Song: "Fair Chloris in a pigsty lay." John Wilmot, 2d Earl of Rochester. NOSC

Fair Cop, A. Robert Garioch. OBCoV

Fair copy of my Celia's face. To T. H., a Lady Resembling My Mistress. Thomas Carew. CaPo

Fair Cynthia, all the Homage that I may. Thoughts on the Sight of the Moon. Sarah Kemble Knight. SCAP

Fair Cynthia mounted on her sprightly pad. Cynthia on Horseback. Philip Ayres. EnLoPo

Fair[e] daffodils [*or* daffadills], we weep to see. To Daffodils [*or* Daffadills]. Robert Herrick. APAD; AWP; AYFP; BeJo; CaPo;

EBEvV; FaBoCh; GTBS-P; InPS-3; NOBE; NOSC; NTP; NoP-4; OBEV; OxAEP-1; PoEL-3; PoRA; SCGP; SeCP; TFi; TTTS; UnPo

Fair Damsel from London, The. *Unknown.* AmFP

Fair Danubie is praised for being wide. Rivers. Thomas Storer. FaBoCh

Fair[e] Days; or, Dawn[e]s Deceitful[l]. Robert Herrick. CaPo

Fair displays a hundred goods and wares, The. At an Exposition. Nguyễn Khuyến, *Vietnamese.* AVP, *tr. by* Huỳnh Sanh Thông

Fair Excellence! such strange Commands you lay. To the Honoured *Eugenia,* Commanding Me to Write to Her. "Ephelia." KTR

Fair Exchange. Aileen Fisher. NOxBChV

Fair eyes, sweet lips, dear heart, that foolish I. Sonnet 43. Sir Philip Sidney. *Fr.* Astrophil and Stella. AAS; SiPS

Fair fa' your honest, sonsie face. To a Haggis. Robert Burns. FaBoVe

Fair famous flood, which sometimes did divide. Sonnet: On the River Tweed. Sir Robert Ayton. NOSC

Fair flower of fifteen springs, that still. To His Young Mistress. Pierre de Ronsard, *French.* AWP, *tr. by* Andrew Lang

Fair Flower of Northumberland, The. *Unknown.* ESPB; OxBB

Fair flower, that dost so comely grow. The Wild Honey Suckle. Philip Freneau. AmPP; ColAP; NAAL-1; NAAL-3; NOBA; OxBA; PoEL-4; PoLF; TAP

Fair, fragile Una, golden-haired. The Enchanted Shell. Henrietta Cordelia Ray. CBWP-3

Fair friend, 'tis true, your beauties move. Ben Jonson. NOSC

Fair girl tripping out to meet her love, A. The Power of Interval. John Byrne Leicester Warren, 3d Baron De Tabley. NOBVV; OxBSP

Fair Golden Age! When milk was th' on[e]ly food. The Golden Age. Sir Richard Fanshawe. NOSC; OAEL-1; OBVE *Fr.* Il Pastor Fido.

Fair, great, and good, since seeing you, we see. To the Countess of Salisbury. Donne. PeECV

Fair gull on the water's bank. The Seagull. Siôn Phylip, *Welsh.* OBWVE, *tr. by* Joseph P. Clancy

Fair Helen. *Unknown.* *See* Helen of Kirconnell.

Fair Hills of Ireland, The. *Unknown, Modern Irish.* OBEV, *tr. by* Sir Samuel Ferguson

Fair Hope with lucent light in her glad eyes. The Quest of the Ideal. Henrietta Cordelia Ray. CBWP-3

Fair Ines. Thomas Hood. OBEV

Fair insect! that, with threadlike legs spread out. To a Mosquito. William Cullen Bryant. NCAP

Fair Iris I love, and hourly I die. Mercury's Song [to Phaedra]. Dryden. AWP; NOSC; OxBSP; PBMP; PoEL-3 *Fr.* Amphitryon.

"Fair is Alexis," I no sooner said. On Alexis. Plato, *Greek.* AWP, *tr. by* Thomas Stanley

Fair is her body, bright her eye. *Unknown. Fr.* Medieval Norman Song. AWP, *tr. by* John Addington Symonds

Fair is my dove, my loved one. Marriage Song. Judah Halevi, *Hebrew.* TrJP, *tr. by* Alice Lucas

Fair is my Love and cruel as she's fair. Beauty, Time and Love. Samuel Daniel. AAS; GSo; HoPM; NOBE; OBEV *Fr.* To Delia.

Fair[e] is my love that feeds among the lilies. Faire Is My Love. Bartholomew Griffin. GBL; PoEL-2 *Fr.* Fidessa, More Chaste than Kind[e].

Fair [*or* Fayre] is my love, when her fair [*or* fayre] golden heares. Sonnet 81. Edmund Spenser. Son *Fr.* Amoretti. AAS

Fair is not my face. A Woman Grows Soon Old. Larin Paraske, *Finnish.* PBWP, *tr. by* Jaakko A. Ahokas

Fair is Our Lord's Own City. *Unknown, Irish.* TIRV, *tr. by* Coslett Quin

Fair Is Too Foul an Epithet. Marlowe. *Fr.* Tamburlaine the Great.

Fair Isabel sat in her bower door. Hind Etin. *Unknown.* OxBB

Fair Isabell of Rochroyall. *Unknown.* OxBB

Fair Isle at Sea—thy lovely name. Robert Louis Stevenson. NOBVV

Fair Janet. *Unknown.* ESPB; OxBB

Fair lady Isabel sits in her bower sewing. Lady Isabel and the Elf-Knight. *Unknown.* ESPB

Fair lady, what's your face to me? Love for Enjoying. James Shirley. BeJo

Fair lady, will you travel. The Wooing of Etain. *Unknown, Irish.* BIrV, *tr. by* John Montague

Fair Lass of Islington, The. *Unknown.* OxBB

Fair little girl sat under a tree, A. Good Night and Good Morning. Richard Monckton, 1st Baron Houghton Milnes. BoTP; OxBChV

Fair lovely Maid, or if that Title be. To the Fair Clarinda, Who Made Love to Me, Imagin'd More Than Woman. Aphra Behn. CABP; CPO; EP; NALW; NoP-4; PEW

Fair Lucy was sitting in her own cabin door. *Unknown.* AmFP ("Lizie Wan sits at her father's bower door.") FaBoVe

Fair Lunacy! I see thee, with a crown. Mirthful Lunacy. Thomas Tod Stoddart. OBNC *Fr.* The Death-Wake; or, Lunacy.

Fair Maid by the Shore, The. *Unknown.* AmFP

Fair maid, had I not heard thy baby cries. To a Lofty Beauty, from Her Poor Kinsman. Hartley Coleridge. OxAEP-2

Fair Maid of Amsterdam, The. *Unknown.* OxBoLi; PeLV; RB

Fair maid sat in her bower-door, A. The False Lover Won Back. *Unknown.* ESPB

Fair maid who, the first of May. The First of May. *Unknown.* ReMoGo

Fair Maiden. George Peele. PoEL-2 *Fr.* The Old Wives' [*or* Wife's] Tale.

Fair maiden, fair maiden. Invocation to the Muse. Richard Hughes. MoBrPo

Fair maiden, white and red. A Voice [Speaks] from the Well. George Peele. CBNP; FaBoCh; NOBE; OxBoLi *Fr.* The Old Wives' [*or* Wife's] Tale.

Fair Margaret and Sweet William ("As it fell out in a long summer's day"). *Unknown.* ESPB; OxBB

Fair Margaret and Sweet William ("Little Marg'et sitting in her high hall door"). *Unknown.* AmFP

Fair Margret was a young ladye. Proud Margret. *Unknown.* ESPB; OxBB

Fair Marjorie sat i her bower-door. Young Benjie. *Unknown.* ESPB

Fair Mary of Wallington. *Unknown.* ESPB
(Bonny Earl of Livingston, The.) OxBB

Fair Mary sat at her father's castle gate. Willie of Winsbury. *Unknown.* AmFP

Fair Melody: To Be Sung by Good Christians, A. Hans Sachs, *German.* GePo, *tr.* by Catherine Winkworth

Fair Mildred wide her lattice threw. Mildred's Doves. Henrietta Cordelia Ray. CBWP-3

Fair morn unbars her gates of gold. Dawn's Carol. Henrietta Cordelia Ray. CBWP-3

Fair Morning, The. Jones Very. GSo; NOBA

Fair mouth's broken tooth, A. (LL) August 1914. Isaac Rosenberg. EBEV; NOBE; OBWP; OxBTC; PeFWW

Fair Musidora starry-eyed. Musidora's Vision. Henrietta Cordelia Ray. CBWP-3

Fair nights beneath the mellow moon. The Maid of Ehrenthal. Henrietta Cordelia Ray. CBWP-3

Fair now is the springtide, now earth lies beholding. The Message of the March Wind. William Morris. OBNC

Fair one! if thus kind you be. To the Tune—"Once I Lov'd a Maiden Fair." Patrick Carey. CBLP

Fair one, to you this monitor I send. Mira to Octavia. Mary Leapor. ECWP

Fair Phoebe and Her Dark-eyed Sailor. *Unknown.* AmFP

Fair Phyllis I saw sitting all alone. *Unknown.* GBL

Fair[e] pledges of a fruitful tree. To Blossoms. Robert Herrick. BeJo; CaPo; GTBS-P; NAEL-1; NOSC; OBEV; SCGP; SeCP

Fair princess[e] of the spacious air. The Falcon. Richard Lovelace. CaPo

Fair Protarchus doesn't want to. Alcaeus, *Greek.* GrAn, *tr.* by Thomas Meyer

Fair proud, now tell me, why should fair be proud. Sonnet 27. Edmund Spenser. Son *Fr.* Amoretti. AAS

Fair rebel to thyself and time. The Revenge. Pierre de Ronsard, *French.* AWP, *tr.* by Thomas Stanley

Fair, Rich, and Young. Sir John Harington, *after the Latin of* Martial. FaBoEE; NIP-4

Fair rocks, goodly rivers, sweet woods, when shall I see peace? Echo. Sir Philip Sidney. SiPS *Fr.* Arcadia.

Fair Rosa was a lovely child. *Unknown.* FaBoVe

Fair Salamis, the billow's roar. Chorus. Sophocles. AWP, *tr.* by Winthrop Mackworth Praed *Fr.* Ajax.

Fair seagull on the water's edge, bright-feathered breast, rich your state. Siôn Phylip. *See* The Seagull.

Fair seed time had my soul, and I grew up. Wordsworth. HAP; PoE *Fr.* Introduction—Childhood and School-Time. FHYEP *Fr.* The Prelude; Growth of a Poet's Mind [1850 vers.]
("Did summon us in his delightful round.") (LL) PoEL-4
("Work like a sea?") (LL) HAP

Fair shadow, faithless as my sun! The Dream. Sir Edward Sherburne. OxBSP

Fair ship, that from the Italian shore. Tennyson. EBVV; EBVVPR; EnVR; OAEL-2 *Fr.* In Memoriam A. H. H.

Fair Singer, The. Andrew Marvell. EnLoPo; FSCP; MeLP; NOBE; NoP-4; PoEL-2; SCGP

Fair sinks the summer evening now. Emily Jane Brontë. BWW

Fair Star of evening, Splendo[u]r of the west. Composed by the Sea-Side, near Calais, August, 1802. Wordsworth. Soe

Fair [*or* Faire] stood the wind for France. Agincourt. Michael Drayton. EBEvV; EBNV; FaBoBe; FaBoCh; NTP; OBEV; OxAEP-1

Fair summer droops, droop men and beasts therefore. Baning Summer. Thomas Nashe. NoSic; OxBSP; SCGP *Fr.* Summer's Last Will and Testament.

Fair, the young acacia, thick with leaves. The Young Acacia. Hayyim Nahman Bialik, *Hebrew.* TrJP, *tr.* by Helena Frank

Fair these broad meads—these hoary woods are grand. Canadian Boat Song. John Galt and "Christopher North." BLPA; FaBoCh; FaPoR; OBEV; OBNC; OxBS

Fair Thou Art. Mordecai ben Isaac, *Hebrew.* TrJP, *tr.* by Herbert Loewe

Fair-tinted cheeks, clear eyelids drawn. Cimabuella. Bayard Taylor. BXAP

Fair Trade. Gary Soto. BAP-96

Fair Ursly, in a merry mood. Annibal Cruceius, *Latin.* FaBoEE

Fair Virtue, the Mistress of Philarete. George Wither.
Author's Resolution, The. AWP; OBEV
Sonnet: "I wandered out a while agone." NOSC

Fair[e] was the dawn[e], and but e'ne now the skies. Fair[e] Days; or, Dawn[e]s Deceitful[l]. Robert Herrick. CaPo

Fair was this yonge wyf, and therwithal. Chaucer. EBEV *Fr.* The Miller's [*or* Milleres] Tale. NAEL-1; NAWM-1; OAEL-1; OxBoLi; PeLV *Fr.* The Canterbury Tales.

Fair witch crept to a young man's side, A. The Witch-Bride. William Allingham. NOBVV; OxBSn

Fair ye be sure, but cruel and unkind. Sonnet 56. Edmund Spenser. Son *Fr.* Amoretti. AAS

Faire Is My Love. Bartholomew Griffin. GBL; PoEL-2 *Fr.* Fidessa, More Chaste than Kind[e].

Faire knight (quoth he) Hierusalem that is. Edmund Spenser. FaBoPV *Fr.* Wood Of Error. AEP

"Faire sir," quoth she, "be not displeasd at all." Edmund Spenser. *Fr.* Wood Of Error. AEP

Faire [*or* fayre] soule, how long shall veyles thy graces shroud? At Home in Heaven. Robert Southwell. ESCV; EnVR

Fairest action of our human life, The. Lady Elizabeth Carey. *Fr.* Mariam. WPE

Fairest blossom of the garden dies, The. (LL) Vision V. William Browne. CH; NOSC; OBEV; PFE

Fairest day that ever yet has shone, The. The Lost. Jones Very. APAD; APN-1; NOBA; NoP-4; PAR

Fairest flower, all flowers excelling. To a Child [of] Five Years Old. Nathaniel Cotton. ECV; OxBChV

Fairest isle, all isles excelling. Song of Venus. Dryden. OxBoLi; PoEL-3 *Fr.* King Arthur.

Fairest Lord Jesus. *Unknown, German.* CTV

Fairest Nymph that ever bless'd our Shore. A Song. Mary Pix. KTR *Fr.* The Spanish Wives.

Fairest of stars, that with your persant light. Balade Simple. John Lydgate. GBL

Fairest of trees under heaven and on earth. Hymn to the Orange. *Unknown, Chinese.* SuSp, *tr.* by Wu-Chi Liu

Fairest things are those which live, The. Song. Mary Russell Mitford. NOBRP

Fairest things have fleetest end, The. Too Soon. Francis Thompson. LBC

Fairfax, whose name in armes through Europe rings. On the Lord Gen[eral] Fairfax at the Siege of Colchester. Milton. NOSC

Fairground. W. H. Auden. NYBP

Fairies, The. William Allingham. CH; FPC; FaBoCh; NOBE; NOBVV; NOxBChV; OBEV; OTCP; OxBChV; TFi

Fairies. Rose Fyleman. OxBChV

Fairies, The. *Unknown.* BoTP

Fairies Are Dancing All Over the World, The. Michael Rumaker. GLP

Fairies are taken into the world, The. Scenes of Childhood. Carl Morse. GLP

Fairies break their dances, The. A. E. Housman. OxBSP; PeVV

Fairies' Farewell, The. Richard Corbet. BeJo; NOSC; OxAEP-1 *Fr.* Her Boreale.

Fairies Feast, The. Charles Montague Doughty. CH

Fairies hold a fair, they say, The. The Faerie Fair. Florence Harrison. BoTP

Fairies' Lullaby, The. Shakespeare. *See* Fairy Land, 2.

Fairies' Song, The. Jane Taylor. NOBRP

Fairweill. *Unknown.* OxBS

Fairy [*or* Faery *or* Faiery] beam[e] upon you, The. The Faery Beam upon You. Ben Jonson. BeJo; EBEV; FaBoCh; OxBSP *Fr.* The Gypsies Metamorphosed.

Fairy Blessing, The. Shakespeare. OxBoLi *Fr.* A Midsummer Night's Dream.
(Epilogue: "Now the hungry lion roars.")
(Lion of Winter, The.)

Fairy Cobbler, The. A. Neil Lyons. BoTP

Fairy Dream, A. Dorothy Graddon. BoTP

Fairy Feet. Phyllis L. Garlick. BoTP

Fairy Flute, The. Rose Fyleman. BoTP

Fairy in Armor, A. Joseph Rodman Drake. *See* An Elfin Knight.

Fairy Land, 1. Shakespeare. OBEV *Fr.* A Midsummer Night's Dream.
(Fairy Song ("Over hill, over dale").) NOBE

Fairy Land, 2. Shakespeare. OBEV *Fr.* A Midsummer Night's Dream.

Fairy Maimounè, The. John Moultrie. NOBRP

Fairy Music. Enid Blyton. BoTP

Fairy Ring, The. *Unknown.* BoTP

Fairy Ring, The. Andrew Young. Spl

Fairy Shoemaker, The. Phyllis L. Garlick. BoTP

Fairy Sleep and Little Bo-Peep, The. *Unknown.* BoTP

Fairy Song. W. B. Yeats. *See* The Wind Blows out of the Gates of the Day.

Fairy Story. Stevie Smith. NOxBChV; OBSP

Fairy Story. Robert Penn Warren. NYBP

Fairy Straighttalk. Carl Morse. GLP
Fairy Tale. Miroslav Holub, *Czech*. RB, *tr. by* George Theiner
Fairy Tale about Rain, A. Bella Akhatovna Akhmadulina, *Russian*. TCRP, *tr. by* Albert C. Todd
Fairy Tales. "Shu Ting," *Chinese*. VCWP, *tr. by* Donald Finkel
Fairy Temple; or, Oberon's Chapel, The. Robert Herrick. CaPo
Fairy Thorn, The. Sir Samuel Ferguson. CH
Fairy Went a-Marketing, A. Rose Fyleman. BoTP; OxBChV
Fairyland [*or* Fairy-Land]. Edgar Allan Poe. APN-1; NAAL-1; NAAL-3
Fairy's Reply to Saturn, The. Thomas Hood. *Fr.* The Plea of the Midsummer Fairies. OBNC
Faith. Frances Anne Kemble. FaBoBe
Faith, *epigram*. Friedrich von Logau, *German*. GePo, *tr. by* George C. Schoolfield
Faith. Czeslaw Milosz, *Polish*. RaBo, *tr. by* Robert Hass, Robert Pinsky *and* Renata Gorcynski
Faith. George Santayana. *See* Sonnet III: "O world, thou choosest not the better part!"
Faith. Christopher Smart. ChIV-1 *Fr.* Hymns for the Amusement of Children.
Faith. *Unknown*. PoToHe
Faith. Ella Wheeler Wilcox. PoToHe
Faith and Works. Muriel Spark. OxBSP
"Faith" bleats—to understand! (LL) I should have been too glad, I see. Emily Dickinson. APN-2; MeMAP; NOCV; PAR
Faith for Tomorrow. Thomas Curtis Clark. PoToHe
Faith hasn't got no eyes, but she long-legged. Zora Neale Hurston. NAAAL
Faith Healing. Philip Larkin. ChIV-2; GI; NoAM
Faith, Hope, and Charity Are the Prospects of Manhood. Leigh Hunt. ChIV-2
"Faith" is a fine invention. Emily Dickinson. APN-2; AmPP; MeMAP; NAAL-1; NAAL-3; NCAP; NOBA; NoP-4; OxBA; PAR; TAP
Faith—is the Pierless Bridge. Emily Dickinson. AmPP; NCAP
"Faith, master, whither you will." Captain Car; or, Edom o Gordon. *Unknown*. ESPB
Faith (wench) I cannot court thy sprightly eyes. Sir John Davies. PBRV
Faithful as enemy, or friend. (LL) Roosters. Elizabeth Bishop. ChIV-2; LiTM; NALW
Faithful Frances Ellen Harper! Mrs. Francis Ellen Harper. George Clinton Rowe. AAP
Faithful friend from flattering foe. (LL) Philomel. Richard Barnfield. AWP; CH; GBL; GTBS-P; NOBE; OBEV
Faithful mother tongue. My Faithful Mother Tongue. Czeslaw Milosz, *Polish*. VCWP, *tr. by* Czeslaw Milosz *and* Robert Hass (b. 1941)
Faithful Shepherdess, The. John Fletcher.
    Folding the Flocks. CH
    God of Sheep, The. FaBoCh
    Hymn to Pan. NOBE; OBEV
    River[-]God's Song, The. NOSC
        (Song: "Do not fear to put thy feet.") SCGP
    Satyr's Song.
    Satyr's Song, The ("Softly Gliding as I Go"). NOSC
Faithful watcher sits alone, A. The Watcher. Clara Ann Thompson. CBWP-2
Faithful Wife, The. Patricia Beer. LW
Faithful Wife, A. Chang Chi, *Chinese*. OHMPC, *tr. by* Kenneth Rexroth
Faithfull lovers keepe from hence. Mary Sidney. *Fr.* Urania.
Faithfully tinying at twilight voice. E. E. Cummings. NYBP
Faithless Nelly Gray. Thomas Hood. BXAP; NOBL; NOBRP; UV
Faithless Sally Brown. Thomas Hood. NOBL; OBNV
Faithless Shepherdess, The. *Unknown*. *See* The Unfaithful Shepherdess.
Faithless the watch that I kept: now I have none to keep. The Sleepy Sentinel. Rudyard Kipling. *Fr.* Epitaphs of the War [1914–1918]. OBWP
Faithless Wife, The. Federico García Lorca, *Spanish*. BoLoP, *tr. by* A. L. Lloyd
Faking Boy, The. *Unknown*. RB
Fakir (a religious well known in the East), A. Richard Owen Cambridge. ECEV
Falcon, The. Richard Lovelace. CaPo
Falcon and the Dove, The. Sir Herbert Read. FaBoMo
Falcon Drinking. Dimitris Tsaloumas. BMAP
Falcon soars, The. Angelica the Doorkeeper. *Unknown*, *Serbian*. RB, *tr. by* Anne Pennington
Falcon to the Falconer, The. Jonathan Steffen. APAD
Falconry. Anne Wilkinson. MoCV
Falero, lero, loo. (LL) I loved a lass, a fair one. George Wither. CH; GBL; GLoP; NOBE; NOSC; OBEV
Falkland at Newbury, 1643. Hugh Conway. EBVV
Fall, The. William Barnes. PoEL-4
Fall. Laure-Anne Bosselaar. APAD
Fall, The. Russell Edson. LCAP-2
Fall, The. Sir Richard Fanshawe. NOSC *Fr.* Il Pastor Fido.
    (Great Favorit Beheaded, A.) OBVE

Fall. Robert Francis. VGW
Fall. Robert Hass. AmPA
Fall. George Cabot Lodge. APN-2
Fall, The. Sarah Maguire. LW
Fall, The. Milton. PoEL-3 *Fr.* Book IX. FHYEP; NAEL-1; NAWM-1; OAEL-1 *Fr.* Paradise Lost.
Fall, The. John Wilmot, 2d Earl of Rochester. ChIV-1; EnLoPo
Fall, The. Jeannine Savard. CMAP
Fall. Michael Smith. CIP-2
Fall, The. Edmund Waller. NOSC
Fall Again, The. Howard Nemerov. CoAmPo
Fall and the bees. Where do these evenings take me. In a Park, in Siena, at Twilight. Ory Bernstein, *Hebrew*. IP, *tr. by* Warren Bargad *and* Stanley F. Chyet
Fall back, all worlds, into the abyss. Feast of the Most Holy Trinity. Aubrey Thomas De Vere. TIRV
Fall chrysanthemums have beautiful colors. T'ao Ch'ien. *Fr.* Drinking Wine. CoBCP, *tr. by* Burton Watson
Fall Comes in Back-Country Vermont. Robert Penn Warren. NYBP; VGW
Fall days are not entirely free of heat. Sitting at Night on the Moonlit Terrace. Yang Wan-li, *Chinese*. CoBCP, *tr. by* Burton Watson
Fall Down, (in Memory of Eric Dolphy). Calvin C. Hernton. GT; PoBA
    ("You died.") (LL) GT
Fall, gáll themsélves, and gásh góld-vermílion. (LL) The Windhover. Gerard Manley Hopkins. APAD; CABP; CMoP; ClHu; EBEvV; EBVV; EnVR; GEA; GTBS-P; HAP; InPK-6; InPS-3; LiTM; MoBrPo; MoP; NAEL-2; NOBE; NOBVV; NoAM; NoP-4; OAEL-2; OBNC; OxAEP-2; PFE; PeECV; PoE; PoEL-5; PoPoPo; PoRA; Poetr; RB; SCGP; SCV; TFi; TOF; TRP; UnPo
Fall golden on the patience of the dead. (LL) Many Are Called. Edwin Arlington Robinson. GI; MeMAP; OxBA
Fall In. Harold Begbie. NSI
Fall In. Lincoln Kirstein. MoP
Fall in Long Island. Lake Success. Robert Conquest. OxBC
Fall Is Here, The. Mrs. Henry Linden. CBWP-4
Fall, leaves, fall; die, flowers, away;. Song. Emily Jane Brontë. AYFP; CH; FaBoCh; OxBSP; PoEL-5
Fall 1961. Robert Lowell. OBWP; VGW
    ("Oriole's swinging nest!") (LL) GEA
Fall of Da Nang, The. Gerald McCarthy. CDa
Fall of Hyperion, The. Keats. OAEL-2
    (Fall of Hyperion: A Dream, The.) Ro
    Dream, A. OBNC
    Garden-Dream, A. GaP
    "Fanatics have their dreams, wherewith they weave." TOF
    "Towards the altar sober-paced I went." TOF
Fall of Icarus: Brueghel. Joseph Langland. PFE
Fall of J. W. Beane, The. Oliver Herford. OBAL
Fall of Leaves. Derek S. Savage. PoA
Fall of Light, The. Elizabeth Kirschner. CMAP
Fall of night. Basho, *Japanese*. TAL, *tr. by* Harold G. Henderson
Fall of Rock, A. William Plomer. PeSAV
Fall of Rome, The. W. H. Auden. InPS-3; OAEL-2; OxBTC; PFE; UnPo
Fall of the Angels, The. Milton. *See* Satan as Rebel-Liberator.
Fall of the City, The. Archibald MacLeish.
    Voice of the Studio Announcer. HoPM
Fall of / velvet plum points and umber aureolae, The. Mastectomy. Wanda Coleman. NAAAL
Fall. Peppercorns / rouge into salmon roe. From the Bus to E. L. at Atascadero State Hospital. Lorna Dee Cervantes. NAmP90
Fall River. David Rivard. PBCAP
Fall wind in pinyons. Foster Jewell. HA
Fall winds wail in mulberry branches. Castleside Song. Wang Ch'ang-ling, *Chinese*. CoBCP, *tr. by* Burton Watson
Fallen / angels. Homework Assignment on the Subject of Angels. Tadeusz Rózewicz, *Polish*. VCWP, *tr. by* Magnus J. Krynski *and* Robert A. Maguire
Fallen Angels, The. Milton. *See* Satan Defiant.
Fallen birch leaf. Virginia Brady Young. HA
Fallen Blossoms. Yang Wan-li, *Chinese*. SuSp, *tr. by* Sherwin S. S. Fu
Fallen Elm, The. John Clare. FHYEP; FaBoPV
Fallen flower I see. A Flying Flower. Arakida Moritaké, *Japanese*. APo, *tr. by* Geoffrey Bownas *and* Anthony Thwaite
Fallen Flowers. Li Shang-yin, *Chinese*. SuSp, *tr. by* James J. Y. Liu
Fallen flowers rise. Haiku. Arakida Moritaké, *Japanese*. SoSe-8, *tr. by* Harold G. Henderson
Fallen flowers should still be mourned. In Heaven. Ssu-k'ung Shu, *Chinese*. SuSp, *tr. by* Irving Y. Lo
Fallen from heaven, lies across. River. Ted Hughes. NAEL-2; NoP-4
Fallen Fruit, A. Bùi Công Trù'ng, *Vietnamese*. AVP, *tr. by* Huỳnh Sanh Thông
Fallen horse. Geraldine Clinton Little. HA
Fallen leaves are scattered by evening rain. Regretful Thoughts. Yü Hsüan-chi, *Chinese*. BoWoP, *tr. by* Geoffrey Waters

Fallen leaves are the banknotes of the Polish government-in-exile. Lyricism of an Autumn Day. Kwanggun Kim, *Korean*. CKP, *tr. by* Jaihiun Kim
Fallen Majesty. W. B. Yeats. PoA
Fallen Petals. Hyonggi Yi, *Korean*. CKP, *tr. by* Jaihiun Kim
Fallen pile! I ask not what has been thy fate. Netley Abbey. William Lisle Bowles. Son
Fallen Star, The. George Darley. OBEV
Fallen Tower of Siloam, The. Robert Graves. ChIV-2
Fallen Yew, A. Francis Thompson. MoBrPo
Fallen Zulu Commander, The. C. M. Van den Heever, *Afrikaans*. PeSA, *tr. by* Uys Krige *and* Jack Cope
Falling. James Dickey. LCAP-2; MT; NYBP; NoAM
Falling. Bob Kaufman. PoBA
Falling Asleep. Siegfried Sassoon. MoBrPo; OxBTC
Falling Asleep over the Aeneid. Robert Lowell. MoAmPo; OxBA
Falling flower, The. Haiku. Arakida Moritaké, *Japanese*. SoSe-8, *tr. by* Babette Deutsch
Falling forever. Oche Iron. Peter Blue Cloud. HATNAP
Falling from a sleeve. Wild Sleeve. Marjorie Welish. FTOS
Falling from Stardom. Jonathan Holden. CMAP
Falling from the ridge. Emperor Yozei, *Japanese*. OHPJ, *tr. by* Kenneth Rexroth
Falling, I caught the curtain. On the Other Side. Czeslaw Milosz, *Polish*. PoSu, *tr. by* Jan Darowski
Falling in Love at Sixty-Five. Mona Van Duyn. NoP-4
Falling Leaf, A. Trần Gia Thoại, *Vietnamese*. AVP, *tr. by* Huỳnh Sanh Thông
Falling leaves leave the trees. Poem on Falling Leaves. Liu E, *Chinese*. CoBLCP, *tr. by* Jonathan Chaves
Falling Moon. Roberta Hill Whiteman. CDW
Falling night / in a brief symphony of candied light, The. Garrett Kaoru Hongo. *See* Winnings.
Falling Petals. Chi-hun Cho, *Korean*. CKP, *tr. by* Jaihiun Kim
Falling separate into the dark. Late at Night. William Stafford. NNaP
Falling Snow. Amy Lowell. ColAP
Falling Snow. *Unknown*. CTV
Falling Star, The. "Ping Hsin." PBWP *Fr.* Spring Waters.
Falling Star, The. Sara Teasdale. ChAP; OBCA
Falling Water. John Koethe. BAP-95
Fallow Deer. Thomas Hardy. *See* The Fallow Deer at the Lonely House.
Fallow Deer at the Lonely House, The. Thomas Hardy. AWP; CH; CMoP; OxBSP; RB; TTTS
  (Fallow Deer.) CTAV
  ("Fourfooted, tiptoe.") (LL) APo; CTAV
  ("One without looks in tonight.") APo; CTAV
Fallow fields, dark pewter sky. Winter Drive. James Philip McAuley. BMAP; PoA
Falls, The. F. D. Reeve. NYBP
Falls Funeral. John Montague. CIP-2
Falls of Glomach, The. Andrew Young. OxBS
Falltime. Carl Sandburg. PoA
Falmouth. William Ernest Henley. *See* Home.
Fals fox came unto our croft, The. *Unknown*. MiEL
False Achitophel, The. Dryden. *See* Achitophel: The Earl of Shaftsbury.
False and faithless as thou art. Charlotte Bury. Ro *Fr.* Poems on Several Occasions.
False Arrest. Cornelius Eady. LTA
False beauty who, although in semblance fair. Ballade to His Mistress. François Villon, *French*. WeW-3, *tr. by* Norman Cameron
False Country of the Zoo. Jean Garrigue. LiTM
False dreams, all false. Iliad. Humbert Wolfe. MoBrPo
False Enchantment. Jean Starr Untermeyer. MoAmPo
False, ere I come, to two or three. (LL) Song. "Go and catch a falling star." Donne. AWP; CBNP; ClHu; EBEV; EBEvV; ESCV; FHYEP; FSCP; HAP; HeIP; HoPM; ImPo; InPK-6; InPS-3; MeLP; NAEL-1; NAWM-1; NBLV; NIP-4; NOBE; NOSC; NoP-4; NoSic; OBEV; OxAEP-1; PBMP; PFE; PoE; PoEL-2; SeCP; SoSe-8; TFi
False Friends-like. William Barnes. NOBVV
False Heart, The. Hilaire Belloc. FaBoCh; FaBoEE; OxBSP
  (For False Heart.) MoBrPo
False [*or* Faulce] hope which feeds but[t] to destroy, and spill. Sonnet 35. Mary Sidney, Countess of Montgomery Wroth. KTR; NAEL-1 *Fr.* Pamphilia to Amphilanthus.
False Knight upon [*or* on] the Road, The. *Unknown*. AmFP; CH; ESPB; EnSB
  (False Knight and the Wee Boy, The.) FaBoCh; OxBS; OxBoLi
False life! a foil and no more. Quickness. Henry Vaughan. FMP
False life! a foil and no more. Quickness. Thomas Stanley. GeHe; MeLP; NOBE; NOCV; NOSC; SeCP
False Love. John Lilliat. EBEV
False Love. Sir Walter Ralegh. *See* A Farewell to False Love.
False Lover Won Back, The. *Unknown*. ESPB; OxBB
False Nancy. *Unknown*. AmFP
False One, The. Lucan, *Latin*.
  "Sit: sit all." OBCVT, *tr. by* John Fletcher

False Poets and True. Thomas Hood. EPCY
False Security. John Betjeman. CMoP; NoAM; NoP-4
False Sir John a wooing came. May Colven [*or* May Colvin]. *Unknown*. OxBB; PBMP
False Though She Be [to me and love]. William Congreve. BoLoP; EnLoPo; GLoP; NOBE; OBEV; OxBSP
False words of the Buddhists and Taoists, The. Yang Shih-ch'i. *Fr.* Rhymed Words Sent to My Eldest Son. CoBLCP, *tr. by* Jonathan Chaves
False world, good night: since thou hast brought. To the World [A Farewell for a Gentlewoman, Virtuous and Noble]. Ben Jonson. BeJo; SeCP
False Youth: Autumn: Clothes of the Age. James Dickey. MT
Falsehood. William Cartwright. OBEV
Falso Brilhante. Nathaniel Mackey. NAAL
Fame. Josephine D. Henderson Heard. CBWP-4
Fame. Robert Herrick. FaBoEE
Fame. Charlotte Mew. BrRo; InPK-6; PBWP; VWP
Fame. Vladimir Nabokov, *Russian*. TCRP, *tr. by* Vladimir Nabokov
Fame. Virgil, *Latin*. OBVE, *tr. by* John Dryden. *Fr.* The Aeneid [*or* Eneados, *Aeneis*].
  "Queen whom sense of Honor cou'd not move, The." OBCVT, *tr. by* John Dryden
Fame and Friendship. Austin Dobson. OBEV
Fame is a bee. Emily Dickinson. NoP-4
Fame is a fickle food. Emily Dickinson. SAmP; TAP
Fame is a food that dead men eat. Fame and Friendship. Austin Dobson. OBEV
Fame let thy trumpet sound. A Song. Joel Barlow. AmPP
Fame Makes Us Forward. Robert Herrick. CaPo
Fame, wisdom, love, and power were mine. 'All Is Vanity, Saith the Preacher.' Byron. ChIV-1; KSG; TrCP
Famed big-hitter in cricket, A. Limerick. Douglas Catley. PeLi
Famed ship *California*, a ship of high renown, The. The Girls around Cape Horn. *Unknown*. AmFP
Fame's pillar here at last we set. The Pillar of Fame. Robert Herrick. BeJo; CaPo; CavPo; NIP-4; NoP-4; SeCP
Familial. Jacques Prévert, *French*. CLPP, *tr. by* Lawrence Ferlinghetti
Familiar Epistle, A. Ann Murry. WPE
Familiar Epistle to J. B. Esq, A. Robert Lloyd.
  "Mark yon round parson, fat and sleek." ECEV, *ll.* 1–60; OBSV Public Schools. NOEC
Familiar Faces, Long Departed. Robert Silliman Hillyer. NYBP
Familiar Friends. James Sterling Tippett. BoTP
Familiar Oxen. Oumar Ba. PBMAP
Familiar Poem from Nisa to Fulvia of the Vale. Ann Yearsley. ECWP
Familiar pull of the slow train, The. Homecoming. Desmond O'Grady. IIP
Familiar Spirits. Lyall Tao Tschung Yu. OxBSn
Familiar Story. Alan Shapiro. DiPo; NIP-4
Families. Thomas Blackburn. OxBSP
Families Album, The. Michael S. Harper. AFr
Families, when a child is born. On the Birth of His Son. Su Tung-p'o, *Chinese*. AWP; OBVE, *tr. by* Arthur Waley
Family. Nissim Ezekiel. OBCoV *Fr.* Songs for Nandu Bhende.
Family, The. William Freedman. IFJA
Family [*or* Familie], The. George Herbert. ESCV
Family, The. Donna R. Lydston. PoToHe
Family. Josephine Miles. FYAP; FaBoWP
Family. Eve Shelnutt. CMAP
Family Cat, The. Roy Fuller. OxBC
Family Court. Ogden Nash. PeLV
Family Evening. Daniel Huws. NYBP
Family Fool, The. Sir William Schwenck Gilbert. NBLV *Fr.* Yeoman of the Guard.
Family Fortunes. Charles Hubert Sisson. OxBC
Family Goldschmitt, The. Henri Coulette. CoAP
Family Grove. Albert Goldbarth. HCAP
Family History. Irving Feldman. VCAP
Family Holiday. Raymond Wilson. PeP
Family Is All There Is, The. Pattiann Rogers. NIP-4; PuP-14
Family Jewels, *for Washington, D.C.* Essex Hemphill. GLP; GT
Family Man, The. Bruce Dawe. BMAP
Family Man, A. Maxine W. Kumin. TAP
Family Matter, A. Allen Curnow. *Fr.* Trees, Effigies, Moving Objects. PeNZ
Family Name, The. Charles Lamb. Son
Family of Love, The. James Philip McAuley.
  Song of Shem. ChIV-1
Family Outing—a Celebration. Nicki Jackowska. BrRo
Family Photograph. Gerald Vizenor. VoR
Family Photograph 1939, A. James Keir Baxter. OxBC
Family Pictures. Mervyn Morris. PBCV
Family Plot, October. Gail Mazur. NAmP90
Family Portrait. Carlos Drummond de Andrade, *Portuguese*. VCWP, *tr. by* Elizabeth Bishop

Family Portrait. Tanikawa Shuntaro, *Japanese*. VCWP, *tr. by* Harold Wright

Family portrait not too stale to record, A. Father and Son: 1939. William Plomer. PeSA

Family Portraits. Mary E. Tucker. CBWP-1

Family Pride. T. S. Venugopalan, *Tamil*. OMIP, *tr. by* Rajagopal Parthasarathy

Family Prime. Mark Van Doren. VGW

Family Procession, A. J. P. Clark Bekederemo. HBAPE

Family Reunion. Louise Erdrich. HATNAP; NoAM

Family Reunion. Anne S. Perlman. CMAP

Family story tells, and it was told true, The. Funnel. Anne Sexton. MoAmPo

Family tombs, The. Inscribed on Sun An-chih's "Painting of Pines and Catalpas." Chao Meng-fu, *Chinese*. CoBLCP, *tr. by* Jonathan Chaves

Family Week at Oracle Ranch. James Merrill. BAP-94

Family were gathered, The. Kisimiso. Musaemura Bonus Zimunya. HBAPE

Famine Road, The. Eavan Boland. FaBoWP

Famine Year, The. Lady Jane Francesca Wilde. IIP; TIRV

Famish me, nor over-fill. (LL) What Kind of Mistress[e] He Would Have. Robert Herrick. CaPo; CavPo

Famished end to my tale this night, A. Maghnas O Domhnaill. NOIV

Famished plain, The. Come Back, Alexander. Sati Kumar, *Punjabi*. OMIP, *tr. by* Manohar Bandopadhyay

Famous. Naomi Shihab Nye. LoL

Famous Flower of Serving-Men; or, The Lady Turn'd Serving-Man, The. *Unknown*. ESPB; OxBB

Famous kingdom of the birds, The. Somewhere Is Such a Kingdom. John Crowe Ransom. CMoP

Famous philosopher, Kant, The. Limerick. C. S. Cook. PeLi

Famous Poet. Ted Hughes. LiTM

Famous poet Everette, The. The Great Man's Death: An Anecdote. Everette Maddox. MT

Famous Tay Whale, The. William McGonagall. PeVV

Famous theatrical actress, A. Limerick. *Unknown*. PeLi

Famously she descended, her red hair. A Recollection. John Peale Bishop. Son

Fan, The. Eugenio Montale, *Italian*. AF, *tr. by* William Arrowsmith

Fan from Korea, A. Chu Yün-ming, *Chinese*. CoBLCP, *tr. by* Jonathan Chaves

Fan, the Filly. Wilfrid Thorley. BoTP

Fanaticism? No. Writing is exciting. Baseball and Writing. Marianne Moore. BoWoP; FaBoA

Fanatics have their dreams, wherewith they weave. The Fall of Hyperion. Keats. OAEL-2; Ro

Fanatics have their dreams, wherewith they weave. Keats. TOF *Fr.* The Fall of Hyperion. OAEL-2

Fanatics have their dreams, wherewith they weave. Prest her cold finger closer to her lips. Keats. *Fr.* The Fall of Hyperion. OAEL-2

Fancies at Navesink. Walt Whitman.
  "By that long scan of waves, myself call'd back, resumed upon myself." NAAL-1; NAAL-3
  "Had I the choice to tally greatest bards." Poetr; SoSe-8

Fancy, A. Thomas Carew. BeJo; NOSC; PBRV
  ("Marke how this polisht Easterne sheet.") PBRV
  ("To fold up silkes, may wrap up wit.") (LL) PBRV

Fancy. Robert Creeley. NOBA

Fancy. Keats. OBEV
  (Realm of Fancy, The.) GTBS-P

Fancy, A. Gérard de Nerval, *French*. FLP, *tr. by* Alistair Elliot

Fancy. Jonathan Smedley. OxBSP

Fancy, and I, last Evening walkt. To Amoret Gone from Him. Henry Vaughan. BeJo; MeLP; SeCP

Fancy and Imagination. Henrietta Cordelia Ray. CBWP-3

Fancy Another Day Gone. Lorine Niedecker. FTOS *Fr.* This Condensery: The Complete Writing of Lorine Niedecker, 1985.

Fancy Dress. Dorothea MacKellar. NOBAu

Fancy (quoth he) farewell, whose badge I long did bear. The Green Knight's Farewell to Fancy. George Gascoigne. NoSic

Fancy the Copt. Coptic Socks. Roy Fuller. OBCoV

Fancy the Sunrise—left the door ajar! (LL) I know some lonely Houses off the Road. Emily Dickinson. APN-2; MoAmPo; OxBA; PoRA

Fancy, which that I have served long, The. The Restless Heart. Henry Howard, Earl of Surrey. SiPS

Fancy's Knell. A. E. Housman. FaBoCh; PoRA

Fane Wald I Luve. Sir John, of Penicuik Clerk. OxBS

Fanfare for the Makers, A. Louis MacNeice. NOBE *Fr.* Autumn Sequel. (Canto VII.)

FANFARE of drums, wooden bells: iron chapter. Thunder Can Break. Christopher Okigbo. HBAPE

Fannie has the sweetest foot. Thomas Bailey Aldrich. OBAL

Fannie / lou / hamer / never / heard / of. Sam Cornish. LTA

Fanning away the heat. A Friend Comes to Visit on a Summer Night. Mo Shih-lung, *Chinese*. CoBLCP, *tr. by* Jonathan Chaves

Fanny. Fitz-Greene Halleck.
  "Fanny was younger once than she is now." CTC
  "We owe the ancients something. You have read." OBAL

Fanny Brawne's Letter Put Unopened In Keats's Coffin. Valentine Ackland. WPN

Fanny Foo-Foo was a Japanese girl. The Japanese Lovers. *Unknown*. BLPA

Fanny! If in your arms my soul could slip. Keats to Fanny Brawne. Edgar Lee Masters. PoA

Fanny was younger once than she is now. Fitz-Greene Halleck. CTC *Fr.* Fanny.

Fanny's Removal in 1714. John Winstanley. NOEC

Fantasia. Dorothy Livesay. MoCV

Fantasies of old age. Merced. Adrienne Rich. NOBA

Fantastic Rock, The. Wu Chen, *Chinese*. CoBLCP, *tr. by* Jonathan Chaves

Fantastic Simile, A. Thomas Lovell Beddoes. Son

Fantasy. Gwendolyn B. Bennett. BlSi

Fantasy, A. Mathilde Blind. VWP

Fantasy of an African Boy. James Berry. HCP; NTP; PBCV

Fantasy of Little Waters, A. James Scully. NYBP

Fantasy spaceman, The. Star Trek III. Richard Harteis. GLP

Fantasy under the Moon. Emmanuel Boundzeki-Dongala, *French*. TTY, *tr. by* Gerald Moore *and* Ulli Beier

Fantasy under the Moon. Emmanuel Dongala. PBMAP

Fantoches. Paul Verlaine. AWP; OBMV, *tr. by* Arthur Symons

Far across the waves, the wing of a gull. The Voices. Jean-Baptiste Tati-Loutard. PBMAP

Far and near. Tanka. Mori Ōgai, *Japanese*. MJT, *tr. by* Makoto Ueda

Far and near, and now, from never. Beauty. Isaac Rosenberg. TrJP

Far / and / wee. E. E. Cummings. *See* In Just- / spring when the world is mud-.

Far and wide / outside St. Vincent. Soufrière. Andrew Salkey. PBCV

Far as creation's ample range extends. Alexander Pope. ECEV *Fr.* An Essay on Man.

Far as man can see. Song of the Rain Chant. *Unknown, Navajo*. AWP, *tr. by* Natalie Curtis Burlin

Far Away. Jane Miller. BAP-96

Far Away. Vũ Hoàng Chu'o'ng, *Vietnamese*. AVP, *tr. by* Huỳnh Sanh Thông

Far Away and Long Ago. "Rubén Dario," *Spanish*. PFTM, *tr. by* Denise Levertov

'Far away is where I've come from,' said the wind. What the Wind Said. Russell Hoban. AYFP

Far away on a state farm called Victory. Griboyedov's Waltz. Aleksandr Bashlachov, *Russian*. TCRP, *tr. by* Sarah W. Bliumis

Far away the spring comes down among clustered peaks. Cold Spring. Kao Ch'i, *Chinese*. SuSp, *tr. by* Irving Y. Lo

Far back under a ledge. Elizabeth Searle Lamb. HA

Far back up country does enormous things. (LL) The Scales. William Empson. CBLP; CMoP; FaBoMo; LiTM

Far back when I went zig-zagging. Orion. Adrienne Rich. MoP; NAAL-2; NIP-4; NoAM; NoP-4; Poetr; WPE

Far be remov'd each painted scene! Invocation. To Horror. Hannah Cowley. NOBRP

Far beyond all the girls of Pirelli. Limerick. I. D. M. Morley. PeLi

—Far brighter than this gaudy melon-flower! (LL) Home-Thoughts, From Abroad. Robert Browning. APAD; AWP; BoTP; CABP; ClHu; EBEvV; EBVV; FHYEP; FaBoBe; FaPoR; HeIP-4; ImPo; NAEL-2; NOBE; NOBVV; NoP-4; OBEV; OBNC; PBMP; PoLF; PoRA; TFi; UV

Far court opens for us all July, The. Prothalamion. Maxine W. Kumin. NYBP

Far Cry after a Close Call, A. Richard Howard. NYBP; UnPo

Far Cry from Africa, A. Derek Walcott. HeIP-4; MoP; NAEL-2; NoAM; NoP-4; PBCV; PFE; TTY; UnPo

Far down, down through the city's great gaunt gut. Subway Wind. Claude McKay. PBCV

Far down the purple wood. The Constant Bridegrooms. Kenneth Patchen. LiTM

"Far enough down is China," somebody said. Digging for China. Richard Wilbur. ImGa; TwCP

Far, far. Far, Far a City Lies. Abba Kovner. HP, *tr. by* Shirley Kaufman *Fr.* 'My Little Sister'.

Far far away, the Herdboy Star. Mei Sheng *and* Fu I. *Fr.* Nineteen Old Poems of the Han. CoBCP, *tr. by* Burton Watson

Far, far, far are my silver waters drawn. Song of the Oktahutchee. Alexander L. Posey. APN-2

Far far from gusty waves these children's faces. An Elementary School Classroom in a Slum. Stephen Spender. FaBoMo; MoBrPo; TwCP; UnPo

Far far from here. The Song of Callicles. Matthew Arnold. GTBS-P *Fr.* Empedocles on Etna.

Far, far from home they rode on their excursions. Two Englishmen. Douglas Stewart. CBAP

Far, far out lie the white sails all at rest. An Ocean Musing. Henrietta Cordelia Ray. CBWP-3

Far, far sea (its waters blue and cool), The. Robinson Crusoe. Soubhagya Kumar Mishra, *Oriya.* OMIP, *tr.* by Jayanta Mahapatra

Far, far southward, the forest is white, not merely. Caribou. Robert Penn Warren. APo

Far far the least of all, in want. The Prisoners. Stephen Spender. FaBoMo; MoBrPo

Far, faraway, steep mountain paths. Shih Te, *Chinese.* SuSp, *tr.* by James M. Hargett

Far-Farers, The. Robert Louis Stevenson. BoTP

Far-fetched with tales of other worlds and ways. Home From Abroad. Laurie Lee. APAD

Far Field, The. Theodore Roethke. ColAP; NAAL-2; NoAM *Fr.* North American Sequence.

Far from a cultural centre he was used. W. H. Auden. CMoP; NoAM *Fr.* Sonnets from China.

Far from Africa: Four Poems. Margaret Danner. PoBA
  Garnishing the Aviary. BPo

Far from Home. Nicholas Christopher. NoP-4

Far from Italy, far from my native Tarentum. Leonidas of Tarentum, *Greek.* GrAn, *tr.* by Fleur Adcock

Far from kingdoms. Patrizia Cavalli, *Italian.* NeIt; VCWP, *tr.* by Judith Baumel

Far from Love the Heavenly Father. Emily Dickinson. APN-2

Far from Our Friends. Jeremy Belknap. AH

Far from our garden at the edge of a gulf. The Gulf. Denise Levertov. NNaP

Far from the deep roar of the Aegean main. Farewell. Plato, *Greek.* AWP, *tr.* by Charles Whibley

Far from the Madding Crowd. Nixon Waterman. BLPA; FaBoBe

Far from the parlour have your kitchen placed. William King. ECEV *Fr.* The Art of Cookery.

Far from the Rappahannock, the silent. Into the Duck Charged Air. John Ashbery. APSN

Far from the sun and summer gale. Thomas Gray. EPCY *Fr.* The Progress of Poesy. AWP; GTBS-P; NOEC; OBEV

Far from the tender Tribe of Boys remove. Elegies I.iv. Tibullus, *Latin.* EP; OBCVT, *tr.* by John Dart *Fr.* Odes.

Far from the thronged luxurious town. On Honour. Bernard Mandeville. NOEC

Far from the Vistula, along the northern plain. Auschwitz. Salvatore Quasimodo, *Italian.* AF, *tr.* by Jack Bevan

Far from the vulgar haunts of men. On the Same. Roy Campbell. OBCoV; OxBTC

Far from their homes they lie, the men who fell. On a War-worker, 1916. Arundell James Kennedy Esdaile. NSI

Far from this atmosphere that music sounds. Music. Henry David Thoreau. APN-1; PAR

Far from thy dearest self, the scope. To His Mistress in Absence. Torquato Tasso, *Italian.* AWP, *tr.* by Thomas Stanley

Far from your crumpled mountains, plains that vultures ponder. Jamaica. Louis Simpson. PBCV

Far greater numbers have been lost by hopes. Samuel Butler. FaBoEE

Far hence amid an isle of wondrous beauty. Old Ireland. Walt Whitman. IIP

Far in a western brookland. A. E. Housman. AWP; PoEL-5

Far in the east, far below. House Song to the East. *Unknown, Navajo Indian.* TTTS

Far in the land of sunny South. A Southern Scene. Priscilla Jane Thompson. CBWP-2

Far in the purple valleys of illusion. The Purple Valleys. Madison Cawein. APN-2

Far in the West there lies a desert land, where the mountains. Henry Wadsworth Longfellow. *Fr.* Part the Second. *Fr.* Evangeline, a Tale of Acadie.

Far in the woods my stealthy flute. The Magic Flute. W. D. Snodgrass. NYBP

Far inland / go my sad thoughts. *Unknown, Eskimo.* BoWoP, *tr.* by Knud Rasmussen, *ad.* by Willis Barnstone

Far moon maketh lovers wise, The. Moonlight. Walter De la Mare. EnLoPo

Far off a lonely hound. The Hounds. John Freeman. OBMV; OxBSP

Far-off a young State rises, full of might. Farther. John James Piatt. APN-2

Far off, above the plain the summer dries. Second Air Force. Randall Jarrell. CMoP; LiTM; NAAL-2

Far-off / at the core of space. Swan. D. H. Lawrence. CMoP; PoE

Far off brough, A. *Unknown.* FaBoVe

Far off I see the River at Meng Ford. Song of the Breaking of the Willow. *Unknown, Chinese.* CoBCP, *tr.* by Burton Watson

Far-off, most secret, and inviolate Rose. The Secret Rose. W. B. Yeats. ADE; NAEL-2

Far-off mountains hide you from me, The. Absent Lover. *Unknown, Xhosa.* PBA, *tr.* by A. C. Jordan

Far Off-Shore. Herman Melville. OxBoS

Far off the sea is grey and still as the sky. Week-End by the Sea. Edgar Lee Masters. MoAmPo

Far, oh, far is the Mango island. The Constant Cannibal Maiden. Wallace Irwin. OBAL

Far out at sea. White Horses. Irene F. Pawsey. BoTP

Far out beyond the city's lights, away from din and roar. The Country Store. *Unknown.* BLPA

Far out of sight forever stands the sea. The Slow Pacific Swell. Yvor Winters. ColAP; NOBA

Far shore, The. Elizabeth Searle Lamb. HA

Far Side of Introspection, The. Alfred M. Lee. CoAP

Far spread the moory ground, a level scene. The Moors. John Clare. EnVR

Far Sweeter than Honey. Abraham ibn Ezra, *Hebrew.* TrJP, *tr.* by Israel Abrahams

Far up the cold mountain the stony path slopes. Travelling in the Mountains. Tu Mu, *Chinese.* PLT, *tr.* by A. C. Graham

Far up the dim twilight fluttered. The Unknown God. "Æ." MoBrPo

Far Up the River. Tu Fu, *Chinese.* OHPC, *tr.* by Kenneth Rexroth

Far up the River—hark! 'tis the loud shock. A Flight of Wild Ducks. Charles Harpur. NOBAu

Far Within Us. Vasco Popa, *Serbo-Croatian.*
  "Look that is that uninvited." PoSu, *tr.* by Anne Pennington
  "Streets of your glances, The." PoSu, *tr.* by Anne Pennington
  "These are your lips." PoSu, *tr.* by Anne Pennington

Fara Diddle Dyno. Thomas Weelkes. CBNP; FaBoCh
  (Madrigal.) OxBoLi; PeLV

Faraway hands are folded and folded. The Starry Night. George Starbuck. NYBP

Faraway Places. Walter McDonald. CDa

Fare Thee Well. *Unknown, Chippewa.* PBMP, *tr.* by Frances Densmore

Fare thee well! and if for ever. Byron. BLPA; CBLP; NOBRP; OBNC; PoEL-4

Fare Well. Walter De la Mare. EBEvV; GTBS-P; NOBE; NoP-4; OBEV

Fare well fare well, kind poetry my friend. She Begining to Study Phisick, Takes Her Leave of Poetry. Jane Barker. KTR

Fare you well, my blue-eyed girl. Blue-eyed Girl. *Unknown.* AmFP

Fare You Well, My Darling. *Unknown.* AmFP

Fareweel to a' our Scotish fame. Such a Parcel of Rogues in a Nation. Robert Burns. OxBS

Farewel, dear daughter Sara; now Thou'rt gone. In Saram. John Cotton. SCAP

Farewel to Love, A. Elizabeth Singer. KTR

Farewel to Worldly Joyes, A ("Farewel to unsubstantial joyes"). Anne Killigrew. BoWoP
  (Farewell to Worldly Joys, A.) CABP
  ("Farewell ye unsubstantial joys.") CABP

Farewel ye guilded follies, pleasing troubles. *Unknown.* MeLP

Farewele Advent; Cristemas [*or* Christemas] is cum [*or* come]. James Ryman. MiEL

Farewell. Ivor Gurney. FP

Farewell. Sir Walter Scott. *See* Farewell Thou Minstrel Harp.

Farewell, A. Coventry Patmore. GLoP; GTBS-P *Fr.* The Unknown Eros.

Farewell, A. Sir Philip Sidney. NOBE; SiPS

Farewell: "Autumn already!—But why regret an eternal sun if we are embarked on." Rimbaud, *French.* PFTM, *tr.* by Louise Varese

Farewell: "Far from the deep roar of the Aegean main." Plato, *Greek.* AWP, *tr.* by Charles Whibley

Farewell, A. George Gascoigne. NOBE; SCGP *Fr.* The Adventures of Master F. I.

Farewell, The: "Gone, gone,—sold and gone." John Greenleaf Whittier. AWP; NCAP

Farewell: "Good-bye!—no [*or* nay] do not grieve that it is over." Harriet Monroe. PoA

Farewell: "I search / for the straight path." Florence Dacey. LoHo

Farewell, A [*or* The]: "It was a' for our rightfu' king." Robert Burns. CH; IIP; OBEV

Farewell! Letitia Elizabeth Landon. VWP

Farewell: "Linden blossomed, the nightingale sang, The." Heinrich Heine, *German.* AWP, *tr.* by John Todhunter

Farewell: "My boat goes west, yours east." Ch'ao Li-houa, *Chinese.* BoWoP, *tr.* by J. P. Seaton

Farewell, A: "My fairest child, I have no song to give you." Charles Kingsley. BLPA; EBVV; OxBChV

Farewell, A: "My horse's feet beside the lake." Matthew Arnold. EnVR *Fr.* Switzerland.

Farewell: "Not soon shall I forget—a sheet." Katharine Tynan. CH

Farewell: "Shores of my native land." Isaac Toussaint L'Ouverture, *French.* TTY, *tr.* by Edna Worthley Underwood

Farewell: "Smell of death was in the air, The." John Press. PoRA

Farewell, A: "Venus, take my votive glass." Matthew Prior. *See* The Lady Who Offers Her Looking-Glass to Venus.

Farewell: "Well, you have gone now, comrades." Ewart Alan Mackintosh. NSI

Farewell, A: "What is there left to be said?" Arthur Rex Dugard Fairburn. PeNZ

Farewell: "You sang round-dance songs." Liz Sohappy Bahe. CDW

Farewell, adieu, that courtly life. Haltersick's Song. John Pickering. NoSic *Fr.* Horestes.

Farewell, all my welfare. Sir Thomas Wyatt. GBL; SiPS

Farewell and adieu to you noble hearties. Tom Deadlight. Herman Melville. APN-2; NCAP

Farewell and adieu to you, Spanish ladies. Spanish Ladies. *Unknown.* FaBoCh

Farewell!—and never think of me. Song. Letitia Elizabeth Landon. VWP

Farewell at the Moment of Parting. Agostinho Neto, *Portuguese.* PBMAP

Farewell awhile, beautiful Italy! Farewell to Italy. Frances Anne Kemble. VWP

Farewell!—but whenever you welcome the hour. Long, Long Be My Heart with Such Memories Filled. Thomas Moore. FaBoBe

Farewell, Captain. In bygone days. Vladimir L'vovich Korvin-Piotrovsky, *Russian.* TCRP, *tr.* by Bradley Jordan

Farewell dear babe, my heart's too much content! In Memory of My Dear Grandchild Elizabeth Bradstreet Who Deceased August, 1665, Being a Year and Half Old. Anne Bradstreet. ColAP; NAAL-1; NAAL-3; NOCV; SCAP; WPE

Farewell, dear love! Since thou wilt needs be gone. *Unknown.* NoSic

Farewell, dear scenes, for ever closed to me. Lines Written upon a Window-Shutter at Weston. William Cowper. NOEC

Farewell, false Friend!—our scenes of kindness close! Sonnet 19. Anna Seward. CPO

Farewell, false love, the oracle of lies. A Farewell to False Love. Sir Walter Ralegh. BoLoP; NAEL-1; NoSic; SiPS

Farewell, farewell! Before our prow. Dover to Munich. Charles Stuart Calverley. NOBL

Farewell, farewell! but this I tell. Coleridge. *Fr.* The Rime of the Ancient Mariner. CABP; CH; EBEV; EBNV; FHYEP; FaBoBe; FaBoCh; HAP; HeIP-4; HoPM; ImPo; InPS-3; NOBE; NoP-4; OAEL-2; OBEV; OBNC; OBNV; OxAEP-2; OxBoS; PeECV; PoE; PoEL-4; PoPoPo; SCGP; TFi; TOF

"Farewell, farewell, my pretty maid." The True Lover's Farewell. *Unknown.* AS

Farewell--farewell to thee, Araby's daughter! The Peri's Lament for Hinda. Thomas Moore. OBNC *Fr.* Lalla Rookh.

Farewell, farewell, Your Royal Highness. (LL) A Luncheon. Max Beerbohm. NOBL; OBSV; OxBTC; PeLV; UV

Farewell Folk Song. *Unknown, Greek.* GrIP, *tr.* by Loring N. Danforth

Farewell, for evermore! John Skelton. *See* Philip Sparrow.

Farewell Frost; or, Welcome the Spring. Robert Herrick. CaPo

Farewell, German radio with your green eye. Electric Elegy. Adam Zagajewski, *Polish.* VCWP, *tr.* by Renata Gorcyznski, Benjamin Ivry, and C. K. Williams

Farewell has long been said; I have forgone thee. After a Parting. Alice Thompson Meynell. NOBVV

Farewell! I go to sleep; but when. The Evening-Watch. Henry Vaughan. ESCV; FMP

Farewell, I say, farewell to the incomplete. Leonid Lavrov. TCRP, *tr.* by Lubov Yakovleva *Fr.* Notes on the Impossible.

Farewell in a Dream. Stephen Spender. MoBrPo

Farewell, incomparable element. Hymn to Earth. Elinor Wylie. LiTM; MoAmPo

Farewell, love, and all thy law[e]s forever. A Renouncing of Love. Sir Thomas Wyatt. AAS; AEP; CBLP; GBL; GSo; NAEL-1; NoSic; OAEL-1; SCGP; SiPS; Son

Farewell Mercy, farewell my piteous grace. Lament. John Lydgate. PoEL-1 *Fr.* Court of Sapience.

Farewell my Betty, and farewell my Annie. A Song. Christian Carstairs. ECWP

Farewell my dearer half, joy of my heart. First Farewell to J.G G. "Ephelia." LW; NOSC

Farewell, my lute!—and would that I. Sappho's Song. Letitia Elizabeth Landon. VWP *Fr.* The Improvisatrice and Other Poems.

Farewell, my younger brother! Last Words of the Prophet. *Unknown.* APN-2, *tr.* by Washington Matthews *Fr.* The Mountain Chant.

Farewell, my Youth! for now we needs must part. Ave atque Vale. Rosamund Marriott Watson. NOBE; OAEL-2; OBEV; OBNC

Farewell now, poesy's secret cell, thy ordered grace. Farewell to Hendre Fechan. William Phylip, *Welsh.* OBWVE, *tr.* by H. Idris Bell

Farewell, O Prince, farewell, O sorely tried! Theodor Herzl. Israel Zangwill. TrJP

Farewell of an Old Man. Tu Fu, *Chinese.* SuSp, *tr.* by Michael E. Workman

Farewell, old friend, we part at last. My Old Straw Hat. Eliza Cook. BrRo

Farewell old year. The New Year. Bible, *O.T.* CTV

Farewell once more,—and yet again farewell! George Henry Boker. APN-2 *Fr.* Sonnets: A Sequence on Profane Love.

Farewell Once More to My Friend Yen at Feng Chi Station. Tu Fu, *Chinese.* OHPC, *tr.* by Kenneth Rexroth

Farewell Poem. Tu Mu, *Chinese.*
"Passion too deep seems like none." PLT, *tr.* by A. C. Graham

Farewell, politics, utterly! What can I do? I can not. Arthur Hugh Clough. FaBoPV *Fr.* Amours de Voyage. NOBVV

Farewell Rewards and *Faeries.* A Proper New Ballad Intituled The Faer Yes Farewell: Or God-A-Mercy Will. Richard Corbett. PBRV

Farewell, rewards and fairies. The Fairies' Farewell. Richard Corbet. BeJo; NOSC; OxAEP-1 *Fr.* Her Boreale.

Farewell rewards and Fairies. A Proper New Ballad, Intitled The Fairies' Farewell. Richard Corbet. PeLV; SCGP

"Farewell, Romance!" the Cave-men said. The King. Rudyard Kipling. CABP

Farewell Song, A. Huỳnh Thúc Kháng, *Vietnamese.* AVP, *tr.* by Huỳnh Sanh Thông

Farewell Song. Nikolai Mikhailovich Rubtsov, *Russian.* TCRP, *tr.* by Bradley Jordan and Katya Zubritskaya

Farewell, sweet boy; complain not of my truth. Farewell to Cupid. Fulke Greville. GBL; Son *Fr.* Caelica.

Farewell (sweet Cooke-ham) where I first obtain'd. The Description of Cooke-ham. Emilia Lanier. KTR; PBRV; NoP-4; CABP

"Farewell, sweet Jane, for I must go across the flowing sea." Sweet Jane. *Unknown.* AmFP

Farewell, Sweet Mary. *Unknown.* AmFP

Farewell, the bell upon a ram's neck hung. Corydon's Farewell, on Sailing in the Late Expedition Fleet. *Unknown.* NOEC

Farewell, the reign of cruelty! Sir Thomas Wyatt. SiPS

Farewell, this world! I take my leve for ever. The Cherry Fair. *Unknown.* EnVB; MiEL

Farewell! Thou art too dear[e] for my possessing. Sonnet 87. Shakespeare. CBLP; EBEV; EBEvV; GTBS-P; ImPo; InPS-3; NAEL-1; NOBE; NoSic; OAEL-1; OBEV; OxAEP-1; PoEL-2; Son; TFi *Fr.* Sonnets.

Farewell, thou child of my right hand and joy;. On My First Son [*or* Sonne]. Ben Jonson. AWP; BeJo; CABP; ClHu; EBEV; FaBoEE; HAP; HoPM; IMW; InPK-6; InPS-3; NAEL-1; NIP-4; NOBE; NOSC; NoP-4; OAEL-1; OBSP; PBMP; PBRV; PFE; PoE; PoEL-2; PoPoPo; Poetr; RB; RaBo; SCGP; SeCP; TFi; TRP; WeW-3

Farewell thou fertyll soyle. Goyng towardes Spayne. Barnabe Googe. PBRV

Farewell thou little Nook of mountain-ground. Wordsworth. OBGa

Farewell Thou Minstrel Harp. Sir Walter Scott. OBNC *Fr.* The Lady of the Lake.

Farewell, thou Thing, time-past so known[e], so dear. His Farewell [*or* Farewell] to Sack. Robert Herrick. BeJo; CaPo; CavPo; NAEL-1; SeCP

Farewell to a Friend. Hsüeh T'ao, *Chinese.* SuSp, *tr.* by Eric Johnson

Farewell to a Jovial Friend. Gloria Escoffery. PBCV

Farewell to a Southern Melody, A. Huang O, *Chinese.* BoWoP, *tr.* by Kenneth Rexroth and Ling Chung

Farewell to Allen University. Josephine D. Henderson Heard. CBWP-4

Farewell to America. To Mrs. S. W, A. Phillis Wheatley. NoP-4

Farewell to an idea. . . A cabin stands. Wallace Stevens. CMoP; HCAP; PoE *Fr.* The Auroras of Autumn.

Farewell to an idea. . . The mother's face. Wallace Stevens. HCAP; PoE *Fr.* The Auroras of Autumn.

Farewell to Anactoria. Sappho, *Greek.* AWP, *tr.* by Allen Tate

Farewell to Arms, A. Aleksandr Petrovich Mezhirov, *Russian.* TCRP, *tr.* by Deming Browm

Farewell to Arms, A. George Peele. NOBE; OBEV; OBWP; OxAEP-1; PoRA *Fr.* Polyhymnia.
("His golden locks time hath to silver turned.") NoP-4
(Old Knight, The.)
(Sonnet, A: "His golden locks time hath to silver turned.") InPS-3; PoEL-2

Farewell to Autumn. Oleg Grigorevich Chukhonstev, *Russian.* TCRP, *tr.* by Simon Franklin

Farewell to barn and stack and tree. A. E. Housman. CMoP; MoBrPo; UnPo

Farewell to Bath. Lady Mary Wortley Montagu. WPE

Farewell, To C. E. G. A. Charles Kingsley. BoTP

Farewell to Cupid. Fulke Greville. *Fr.* Caelica.

Farewell to Dostoevski. "Hugh MacDiarmid." FaBoTC; NAEL-2 *Fr.* A Drunk Man Looks at the Thistle.

Farewell to English, A. Michael Hartnett.
"Chef Yeats, that master of the use of herbs." NOIV
"Gaelic is the conscience of our leaders." CIP-2
"Half afraid to break a promise." NOIV

Farewell to False Love, A. Sir Walter Ralegh. BoLoP; NAEL-1; NoSic (False Love.) SiPS

Farewell to Fan Yun at An Ch'eng. Shen Yüeh, *Chinese.* OHMPC, *tr. by* Kenneth Rexroth

Farewell to Florida. Wallace Stevens. NoAM

Farewell to Folly. Robert Greene.
Maesia's Song. CTC; UnPo
(Song: "Sweet are the thoughts that savour of content.") PoEL-2

Farewell to Hendre Fechan. William Phylip, *Welsh.* OBWVE, *tr. by* H. Idris Bell

Farewell to Hiruharama. Haere Ra. James Keir Baxter. PeNZ

Farewell to Ireland. Saint Columcille. AWP, *tr. by* Douglas Hyde

Farewell to Italy. Frances Anne Kemble. VWP

Farewell to Kingsbridge. *Unknown.* ECEV

Farewell to Kurdistan. Rosemary Tonks. OxBTC

Farewell to London in the Year 1715, A. Alexander Pope. OBCoV

Farewell to Love. Donne. OAEL-1

Farewell to Love. Sir John Suckling. CaPo; CavPo

Farewell to Maria. Tadeusz Borowski, *Polish.* HP, *tr. by* Tadeuszt Pióro

Farewell to My Mother. "Placido," *Spanish.* TTY, *tr. by* James Weldon Johnson

Farewell to My Scooter. Mbuyiseni Oswald Mtshali. PeSAV

Farewell to Narcissus. Robert Horan. NYBP

Farewell to New Zealand. Wynford Vaughan-Thomas. NOBL

Farewell to one now silenced quite. Parted. Alice Thompson Meynell. PeVV

Farewell to Pāri's Hill. Kapilar, *Tamil.* PLW, *tr. by* A. K. Ramanujan

Farewell to Shen Yueh. Fan Yun, *Chinese.* OHMPC, *tr. by* Kenneth Rexroth

Farewell to the bushy clump close to the river. John Clare. NoP-4

Farewell to the Court. Sir Walter Ralegh. NoSic; SiPS
(Like Truthless Dreams.) Son

Farewell to the Highlands, farewell to the North. My heart's in the Highlands, my heart is not here. Robert Burns. AWP; ChAP; ImPo

Farewell to the Muse, A. Maria Jane Jewsbury. VWP

Farewell to Tobacco, A. Charles Lamb. OxBoLi

Farewell to two envoys from the Yüan court. Tran Minh-tong (King), *Chinese.* AVP, *tr. by* Huỳnh Sanh Thông

Farewell to Van Gogh. Charles Tomlinson. CMoP; GTBS-P; NoP-4; PoE

Farewell to Worldly Joys, A. Anne Killigrew. *See* A Farewel to Worldly Joyes ("Farewel to unsubstantial joyes").

Farewell to You. Elizabeth Alexander. GT

Farewell, too little and too lately known. To the Memory of Mr Oldham. Dryden. AWP; EBEV; EPCY; FP; HAP; InPK-6; InPS-3; NIP-4; NOBE; NOSC; NoP-4; OAEL-1; OxAEP-1; PoE; PoEL-3; PoPoPo; Poetr; SCGP; TFi; TRP

Farewell, twin sons of Neokles. On Epicurus and Themistokles. Menander, *Greek.* GrAn, *tr. by* Alan Marshfield

Farewell ungrateful[l] traitor [*or* traytor], / Farewell my perjured swain. Love's Despair. Dryden. BoLoP; EnLoPo; HAP; NOBE *Fr.* The Spanish Friar [*or* Fryar].

Farewell, Unkind! Farewell! to me, no more a father! *Unknown.* EnLoPo

Farewell Voyaging World! Conrad Potter Aiken. NYBP

Farewell: "What should I say." Sir Thomas Wyatt. GBL; NOBE (Revocation, A.) OBEV

Farewell with a Mischeife. George Gascoigne. AAS

Farewell, ye blooming fields! ye cheerful plains! Michael Bruce. NOEC *Fr.* Elegy: To Spring.

Farewell ye unsubstantial joys. Anne Killigrew. *See* A Farewel to Worldly Joyes.

Farewell you everlasting hills! I'm cast. Mans Fall, and Recovery. Henry Vaughan. ESCV

Farewells from Paradise. Elizabeth Barrett Browning. OBEV

Farm, The. Donald Hall. LiTM

Farm, The. Archibald MacLeish. AFr

Farm boys wild to couple. The Sheep Child. James Dickey. HCAP; MT; MoP; NOBA; NoAM; TAP; VCAP

Farm by the Lake, The. Chu Hsi, *Chinese.* OHPC, *tr. by* Kenneth Rexroth

Farm Families. Lu Yu, *Chinese.* CoBCP, *tr. by* Burton Watson

Farm Families. Lu Yu. ChiPo, *tr. by* Burton Watson

"Snug—the robe sewn from coarse cotton." CoBCP, *tr. by* Watson, Burton (b. 1925)

Farm families have few leisure months. Watching the Wheat-Reapers. Po Chü-i, *Chinese.* SuSp, *tr. by* Irving Lo

Farm Gate. Uys Krige, *Afrikaans.* PeSA, *tr. by* Uys Krige *and* Jack Cope

Farm-hands, passing at the end of the day, The. The Lonely Woman. Valentine Ackland. WPN

Farm Implements and Rutabagas in a Landscape. John Ashbery. CBNP; CoAP; PmAP

Farm on the Great Plains, The. William Stafford. HAP; VGW

Farm Picture. Galway Kinnell. AFr

Farm Picture, A. Walt Whitman. BLT; InPS-3; TRP

Farm Routine. Ch'u Kuang-hsi, *Chinese.* SuSp, *tr. by* Joseph J. Lee

Farm Wife. Ellen Bryant Voigt. MT

Farmer, The. Mary Elizabeth Fullerton. CBAP

Farmer, The. *Unknown.* AS

Farmer, The. Ellen Bryant Voigt. MT; WeW-3

Farmer and the Farmer's Wife, The. Paul Gerhardt Hiebert. NBLV

Farmer and the Raven, The. *Unknown. See* The Mischievous Raven.

Farmer and the Shanty Boy, The. *Unknown.* AmFP

Farmer drives by, A. Arizona Zipper. HA

Farmer Goes Beserk. Anne Elder. CBAP

Farmer had a daughter whose beauty ne'er was told, A. The Banks of Sweet Dundee. *Unknown.* AmFP

Farmer has a receipt, but the yamen still presses for tax payment. Pressing for Tax Payment. Fan Ch'eng-ta. SuSp, *tr. by* Wu-chi Liu *Fr.* Four Songs in Imitation of Wang Chien.

Farmer is busy, so busy, to-day, The. Haymaking. E. M. Adams. BoTP

"Farmer, is the harvest ready?" Bread. H. E. Wilkinson. BoTP

Farmer John. John Townsend Trowbridge. PWR

Farmer Kalligenes sowed his wheat. The Astrologer. Agathias, *Greek.* GrAn, *tr. by* Guy Davenport

Farmer Nguyen. William Daniel Ehrhart. CDa

Farmer of Tilsbury Vale, The. Wordsworth. EBEV

Farmer once planted some little brown seeds, A. A Growing Rhyme. J. M. Westrup. BoTP

Farmer ploughs into the ground, The. Seed. Herman Charles Bosman. PeSA

Farmer Remembers the Somme, The. Vance Palmer. NOBAu

Farmer say to de weevil, De. Ballet [*or* Ballit] of de Boll Weevil, De. *Unknown.* AS; NOBA

Farmer sleeps under a printed stone, The. The Apple-Tree Man. Charles Causley. OBSP

Farmer went trotting on [*or* upon] his grey mare. The Mischievous Raven. *Unknown.* BoTP; LB; OxNR; ReMoGo

Farmers. Liu Tsung-yüan, *Chinese.*
"Beyond the bamboo fence, cooking fire and smoke." SuSp, *tr. by* Jan W. Walls
"By an ancient road, abundant thistle plants." SuSp, *tr. by* Jan W. Walls

Farmers. Thomas Lux. LCAP-2

Farmers. Kathleen Peirce. PBCAP

Farmer's Boy, The. Robert Bloomfield.
Moonlight. . . Scattered Clouds. OBNC
Spring. Ro

Farmer's Boy, A. *Unknown.* CTAV; PeP

Farmer's Bride, The. Charlotte Mew. BWW; BoLoP; CBLP; EBNV; FaBoWP; MoBrPo; NALW; OxBM; OxBTC; WPE
("Brown of her—her eyes, her hair, her hair!, The.") (LL) CABP; LW; NoP-4; RACG; SAGP; VWP

Farmer's clothes are soaked through and never dried, The. Ise Tayu, *Japanese.* WPJ; WPOW, *tr. by* Kenneth Rexroth *and* Ikuko Atsumi

Farmer's Curst Wife, The. *Unknown.* AmFP; ESPB

Farmer's Death. "Hugh MacDiarmid." FaBoVe
("Broon hens keckle and bouk, The.") FaBoVe

Farmer's eyes are dark; the; he speaks in song. On the Welsh Marches. Walter Stone. NYBP

Farmer's goose, who in the stubble, The. The Progress of Poetry. Jonathan Swift. NOIV

Farmers on the Gorge lead a hard life. Consoling the Yü Farmers. Fan Ch'eng-ta, *Chinese.* SuSp, *tr. by* Wu-chi Liu

Farmer's Soliloquy, The. Robert Charles O'Hara Benjamin. AAP

Farmer's son is good and mad, The. Recitative: "Farmer's son is good and mad," The. Ronald McCuaig. NOBAu

Farmer's Song at Can Tho. Herbert Krohn. CDa

Farmer's Thoughts, A. Ch'u Kuang-hsi, *Chinese.* CoBCP, *tr. by* Burton Watson

Farmer's Wife, The. Anne Sexton. HoPM; LiTM

Farmer's wife looked out of the dairy, The. The Rival. Sylvia Townsend Warner. MoBrPo

Farmhand lay all hidden, A. Steinmar, *German*. GePo, *tr. by* James J. Wilhelm

Farmhouse lingers, though averse to square, The. A Brook in the City. Robert Frost. OxBA

Farmhouse seems centuries ago, The. On Craigie Hill. Stewart Conn. FaBoTC

Farming Family Invites the Guest to Stay Overnight, A. Fan Ch'eng-ta. SuSp, *tr. by* Wu-chi Liu *Fr.* Four Songs in Imitation of Wang Chien.

Farms at Wei River, The. Wang Wei, *Chinese*. SuSp, *tr. by* Paul W. Kroll

Farmwife. Betsy Sholl. CrSp

Farmyard, The. A. A. Attwood. BoTP

Farmyard, The. John Clare. EnVR

Farr off from these a slow and silent stream. The Place of the Damned. Milton. *Fr.* Book II. FHYEP; NAEL-1; OxAEP-1 *Fr.* Paradise Lost.

Farragut, Farragut / Old Heart of Oak. William Tuckey Meredith. CBCWP; FaBoBe

Farrar! to thee these early lays I owe. Studley Park. John Langhorne. OBGa

Farrell O'Reilly. Oliver St. John Gogarty. OxBTC

Farther. John James Piatt. APN-2

Farther and farther. Lenard D. Moore. HA

Farther Away. Veronica Porumbacu, *Romanian*. CEEP, *tr. by* Dorian, Marguerite and Elliott Urdang

Farther east it wouldn't be on the map. Midwest Town. Ruth Delong Peterson. CA

Farther in the summer than the birds. Emily Dickinson. *See* Further in Summer than the Birds.

Farther than I have been. The Summit. Kathleen Jessie Raine. OxBS *Fr.* Beinn Naomh.

Farthest from any war, unique in time. Hollywood. Karl Shapiro. LiTM; OxBA

Farthest Thunder that I heard, The. Emily Dickinson. NAAL-1; NAAL-3

Farthing, A. *Unknown*. OxNR

Fascicle 34 Poem 9. Emily Dickinson. *See* My Life Had Stood—A Loaded Gun.

Fascinating Poet's Dream, A. *Unknown*. PFE

Fascination of What's Difficult, The. W. B. Yeats. APAD; BIrV; NAEL-2; OxAEP-2; PoEL-5

Fascist, erect and irate, A. Limerick. Thomas Thorneley. PeLi

Fa'se Footrage. *Unknown*. *See* Fause Foodrage.

Fashion. Ada Cambridge. NOBAu

Fashion. Horace Twiss. BXAP

Fashion changes! Maidens do not wear, The. Andrew Lang. EPCY *Fr.* To Lord Byron.

Fashionable blood. Drip Drip or Not Bloody Likely. Gerda Mayer. PeLV

Fashioned After the Manner of Master Geoffrey Chaucer in His Assembly of Fowls. Thomas, the Elder Warton. ChIV-1

("Of feathered fowls, that fan the buxom air.") KSG

(Paraphrase on Leviticus Chapter XI, After the Manner of Master Geoffrey Chaucer in His Assembly of Fowls, A.) KSG

Fast-anchor'd eternal O love! O woman I love! Walt Whitman. APN-1

Fast asleep on the wooden bench. Warru. Jack Davis. BMAP

Fast Ball. Jonathan Williams. NeAP

Fast Break. Edward Hirsch. DiPo; EOEF; VCAP

Fast breaks. Lay ups. With Mercury's. Slam, Dunk, and Hook. Yusef Komunyakaa. ISC

Fast falls the snow, O lady mine. To F. C. Mortimer Collins. NOBVV

Fast-locked the land for weeks. Of ice we dream. Silver Lake. Brigit Pegeen Kelly. NAmP90

Fast rode the knight. Stephen Crane. MeMAP; NAAL-2 *Fr.* War Is Kind.

Fasten the chamber! Blue-Beard's Closet. Rose Terry Cooke. APN-2

Faster, Faster/ O Circe, Godess. The Strayed Reveller. Matthew Arnold. EBVVPR; OAEL-2

Faster than fairies, faster than witches. From a Railway Carriage. Robert Louis Stevenson. BoTP; OxBChV

Fasti (Roman Feast-Days). Ovid, *Latin*.

Story of Lucretia out of Ovid de Fastis. / Book II, The. OBCVT, *tr. by* Thomas Creech

Fat black bucks in a wine-barrel room. The Congo. Vachel Lindsay. CMoP; MeMAP; MoAmPo; NOBA; OxBA; PoRA; TAP

Fat black woman want, The. Tropical Death. Grace Nichols. HCP

Fat Budgie, The. John Lennon. NBLV

Fat cat came into my drawing room, A. Face to Face. K. V. Tirumalesh, *Kannada*. OMIP, *tr. by* A. K. Ramanujan

Fat cat on the mat, The. Cat on the Mat. J. R. R. Tolkien. PC

Fat friar stroking golf balls, The. Walking along the Hudson. Donald Petersen. CoAP

Fat girls have more fun in the woods. Bernadette Murphy, 1943-1955. Thomas Rabbitt. NAmP90

Fat / is the soul of this flesh. Eating Babies. Chana Bloch. FiLi

Fat-kneed god! Feeder of mangy leopards! You Also, Gaius Valerius Catullus. Archibald MacLeish. NoAM; TAP

Fat lady, The. Alan Pizzarelli. HA

Fat Man in the Mirror, The, *after* Werfel. Robert Lowell. PoA

Fat Men, The. Cyril Dabydeen. PBCV

Fat men go about the streets, The. Ballade of the Poetic Life. Sir John Collings Squire. OBMV

Fat-tailed Dwarf Lemur, in bed, A. Limerick. Gerry Hamill. PeLi

Fat torpedoes in bursting jackets. Fourth of July. Rachel Lyman Field. CTV

Fat White Woman Speaks, The. G. K. Chesterton. OBCoV; UV

Fatal Dream; or, The Unhappy Favourite, The. Emanuel Collins. NOEC

Fatal Hour arrives so rashly sought, The. The Moment of battle. Publius Papinius Statius, *Latin*. OBCVT, *tr. by* William S. Lewis

Fatal Interview. Edna St. Vincent Millay.

Love Is Not All. Son

Fatal Love. Matthew Prior. NBLV

Fatal Spell, The. Byron. OBNC *Fr.* Childe Harold's Pilgrimage.

Fatal volume, The. Marina Tsvetayeva, *Russian*. GI, *tr. by* Nina Kossman

Fatales Poetae. Henry Parrot. FaBoEE

Fatality. D. H. Lawrence. PeECV

Fate. Ralph Waldo Emerson. APN-1; NoP-4 *Fr.* Quatrains.

Fate. Susan Marr Spalding. BLPA; PoToHe

Fate and the Younger Generation. D. H. Lawrence. OxBoLi

Fate brought three men to birth. Petronius Arbiter. MLL, *tr. by* Helen Waddell *Fr.* Satyricon.

Fate didn't hustle Gessius to his death. Palladas, *Greek*. GrAn, *tr. by* Tony Harrison

Fate gave the word, the arrow sped. A Mother's Lament for the Death of Her Son. Robert Burns. HoPM

Fate in Incognito. Michael Benedikt. OBAL

Fate is like a race. Archaic Hippocamp. Ion Caraion, *Romanian*. CEEP, *tr. by* Marguerite Dorian *and* Elliott B. Urdang

Fate is the master of everything it is vain to fight against fate. Seneca. OBCVT, *tr. by* Ted Hughes *Fr.* Oedipus.

Fate on the left hand, and Death on the right. And Again. Humphrey Evans. BXAP

Fate succumbs. Marginalia. W. H. Auden.

Fate to beauty still must give. Epitaph. Claudian, *Latin*. AWP, *tr. by* Howard Mumford Jones

Fateful slumber floats and flows, The. For the Briar Rose. William Morris. NOBVV

Fates of Men (Exeter Book). *Unknown, Old English*. AnOE, *tr. by* Charles W. Kennedy

Fates of the Apostles. Cynewulf, *Anglo-Saxon*.

"Now I pray the man who may love this lay." AnOE, *tr. by* Charles W. Kennedy

Father. Paul Carroll. NeAP

Father. Sharon Doubiago. NMM-2

Father. Margit Kaffka, *Hungarian*. PBWP, *tr. by* Laura Schiff

Father. Jean Lipkin. PeSA

Father. Myra Cohn Livingston. NTCP

Father. Rajandaye Ramkissoon-Chen. HCP

Father, The. Jean Valentine. MoLi *Fr.* The Messenger. LCAP-2

Father. John Wheelwright. UnPo

Father, and bard revered! to whom I owe. Dedicatory Sonnet to S. T. Colerige. Hartley Coleridge. OAEL-2; Son

Father and Child. Gwen Harwood. CBAP; WPE

Father and Child, *fr.* A Woman Young and Old. W. B. Yeats. PFE

Father and Daughter. Sonia Sanchez. FFC; GT

Father and Daughter. Cathy Song. MoLi; OpBo

Father and His Children, The. *Unknown*. OxBChV

Father and I drove to the sand-quarry across the ruined marshlands. Sand-Quarry with Moving Figures. Muriel Rukeyser. MoLi; NoP-4

Father and I in the Woods. David McCord. NOxBChV

Father and I went to camp. Royall Tyler. NAAL-3 *Fr.* The Contrast.

Father and mother joined to breed a snail. Snail. Ho Xuan Huong, *Vietnamese*. AVP, *tr. by* Huỳnh Sanh Thông

Father and Son. Robert Greacen. PNI

Father and Son. Frederick Robert Higgins. BIrV; OBMV

(Memory of His Father, A.) LBC

("Yes, one in a graven silence no bird speaks.") (LL) LBC

Father and Son. Stanley Kunitz. AF, *tr. by* Jack Bevan; MoP; Poetr; TwCP

Father and Son: 1939. William Plomer. PeSA

Father Animus and Zimmer. Paul Zimmer. CMAP

Father calls me William, sister calls me Will. Jest 'fore Christmas. Eugene Field. PoLF

Father dead and mother dead. The Female Principle. Alec Derwent Hope. OxBC

Father dead, loved one dead. Motionless Faces. Carlos Drummond de Andrade, *Portuguese*. PFTM; VCWP, *tr. by* Mark Strand

Father, dear father, come home with me now! Come Home, Father[!]. Henry Clay Work. APN-2

Father Father Son and Son. Jon Swan. NYBP

Father, father, where are you going? The Little Boy Lost. William Blake. FHYEP; NoP-4; Ro *Fr.* Songs of Innocence.

Father from Asia. Shirley Lim. UnSA

Father grew up here. Red Hills of Home. Chenjerai Hove. HBAPE

Father Grumble. *Unknown.* AmFP

Father, he cried, after the critics' chewing. A Sacrificed Author. Howard Nemerov. GI *Fr.* Gnomes.

Father, Hear the Prayer We Offer. Love Maria Willis. AH

Father heard his children scream. The Stern parent. Harry Graham. CBNP; PeLV *Fr.* Some Ruthless Rhymes.

Father Hunger and Son. Roger Weingarten. NAmP90

Father! I bless thy name that I do live. In Him We Live [& Move & Have Our Being]. Jones Very. APN-1; OxBA

Father, I expect your eyes. Before the Mountain. Elizabeth Libbey. AmPA

Father, I have launched my bark. The Pilgrim. Emma Catherine Embury. OBCA

Father, I know that all my life. My Times Are in Thy Hand. Anna L. Waring. PWR

Father! I Own Thy Voice. Samuel Wolcott. AH

Father! I wait thy word—the sun doth stand. The Son. Jones Very. NCAP

Father, I will not ask for wealth or fame. The Higher Good. Theodore Parker. FaBoBe

Father in heaven, after each lost day. Petrarch. *See* Blest be the day, and blest the month and year.

Father in the Railway Buffet. U. A. Fanthorpe. FaBoWP

Father, in Thy Mysterious Presence Kneeling. Samuel Johnson. AH

Father, in Thy starry tent. Rest in Peace. Wilfred John Funk. PoLF

Father is the number one small town fry cook. The Old Dream Oven. Jacinto Jesús Cardona. IFJA

Father, it was an honor to be here, in the dugout. Poem for My Father. Quincy Troupe. LTA

Father, it was honor to be there, in the dugout. Quincy Troupe. *See* Poem for My Father.

Father John's bread was made of rye. Rye Bread. W. S. Braithwaite. GT

Father Malloy. Edgar Lee Masters. OxBA *Fr.* Spoon River Anthology.

Father Mat. Patrick Kavanagh. CMoP

  "In a meadow/ Beside the chapel three boys were playing football." CIP-2; PoE

Father Missouri takes his own. Foreclosure. Sterling Brown. GT; PoBA

Father, Mother, and me. We and They. Rudyard Kipling. NoAM *Fr.* Debits and Credits.

Father! no amaranths e'er shall wreathe my brow. Sara Coleridge. VWP

Father of All! In every [*or* ev'ry] Age. The Universal Prayer [Deo Opt. Max.] Alexander Pope. BLPA; FaBoBe; NoP-4

Father of Famine. Richard Ryan. PBCIP

Father of heaven, and him, by whom. Donne. NOCV *Fr.* The Litanie. PoEL-2

Father of lights! what sunny [*or* sunnie] seed. Cock-crowing. Henry Vaughan. ESCV; GeHe; OAEL-1; PBRV

Father of love! Evening Prayer. Henrietta Cordelia Ray. CBWP-3

Father of My Country, The. Diane Wakoski. NoAM; TAP

  "If George Washington / had not." MoLi

Father of My Father. Lawson Fusao Inada. UnSA

Father of Rivers! standing by thy side. Richard Henry Wilde. APN-1 *Fr.* Hesperia.

Father of the Faithful said, The. Faith. Christopher Smart. ChIV-1 *Fr.* Hymns for the Amusement of Children.

Father of Women, A. Alice Thompson Meynell. *See* Father of Women, A [Ad Sororem E. B.]

Father of Women, A [Ad Sororem E. B.] Alice Thompson Meynell. BrRo; NALW; WPE; VWP

Father, on the first day on the Hunting Moon. The First Day of the Hunting Moon. Patricia Low. VGW

Father, / one day longer on this earth than you. My Father, My Son. John Malcolm Brinnin. NYBP

Father or Son. James Schuyler. FTOS

Father our, he-who is at-the-height, name Thy let-it-be. Bible, *N.T.* *See* Prayer of-Lord.

Father, part of his double interest. Donne. *Fr.* Holy Sonnets. ESCV *Fr.* Holy Sonnets.

Father Poem. Joel Oppenheimer. PoM

Father Riley's Horse. Andrew Barton Paterson. NOBAu

Father-Sequence. Luigi Fontanella, *Italian*. NeIt, *tr. by* Michael Palma

Father Short came down the lane. *Unknown.* OxNR

Father Son and Holy Ghost. Audre Lorde. MoLi; NAAAL; NoAM; PoBA

Father studied theology through the mail. A Book Full of Pictures. Charles Simic. NoP-4

Father, / the Santa Claus suit. Anne Sexton. *See* Santa.

Father, / the Santa Claus suit / you bought. Santa. Anne Sexton. AFr *Fr.* The Death of the Fathers.

Father, the Year Is Fallen. Audre Lorde. PoBA

Father, this year's jinx rides us apart. All My Pretty Ones. Anne Sexton. MoLi; NAAL-2; NoAM

Father, thy hand/ Hath reared. William Cullen Bryant. *Fr.* A Forest Hymn. APN-1; TAP

Father! Thy wonders do not singly stand. The Spirit Land. Jones Very. HAP

Father was to her, and to me. Fever. Judith Ortiz Cofer. MoLi

Father, we thank Thee for the night. A Child's Prayer. *Unknown.* BoTP

Father, when I am in my grave, kind Father. Christina. Dora Greenwell. VWP

Father, who designs his babe a priest, The. William Cowper. OBSV *Fr.* Tirocinium; or, A Review of Schools.

Father, Who Mak'st Thy Suff'ring Sons. Arthur Cleveland Coxe. AH

Father, whom I knew well for forty years. The Gardener. John Hall Wheelock. NYBP

Father, whom I murdered every night but one. Elegy for My Father. Howard Moss. CoAP; LiTM

Father! whose hard and cruel law. The Death of Grant. Ambrose Bierce. CBCWP

Father will descend, The. Songs of the Kiowa. *Unknown, Kiowa*. APN-2, *tr. by* James Mooney *Fr.* Ghost-Dance Songs.

Father William. "Lewis Carroll." BXAP; CBNP; ChAP; HoPM; NOBL; NOBVV; OBCoV; OxBChV; PeLV; PoLF; PoRA; TFi; UV; UnPo *Fr.* Alice's Adventures in Wonderland.

  "'You are old,' said the youth, "and your jaws are too weak.'" OxBM

Father wore an overcoat with a narrow velvet collar, The. Poem: Alte Zachen. Abba Kovner, *Hebrew*. AF, *tr. by* Shirley Kaufman; IP, *tr. by* Warren Bargad *and* Stanley F. Chyet

Father, You Learn to Die. Jim Handlin. EC3

Father, you must have been. Offering. Thomas McGrath. RaBo

Father, you turn your hands toward me. Father from Asia. Shirley Lim. UnSA

Fatherland Song. BjØrnstjerne BjØrnson, *Norwegian*. AWP, *tr. by* William Ellery Leonard

Fatherless boy, thirteen, walks and weeps, The. Ballad of the Fatherless Boy. Wang Chiu-ssu, *Chinese*. CoBLCP, *tr. by* Jonathan Chaves

Fathers. Robert Creeley. FTOS

Fathers, The. Edwin Muir. OxBS

Fathers, The. Siegfried Sassoon. MoP

Fathers, The. Ann Stanford. IMW

Fathers and Sons. Tom Leonard. CABP; FaBoTC

Father's Day. Ruth Stone. NMM-2

Father's Death, A. John Hewitt. PNI

Father's gone a-flailing. *Unknown.* OxNR

Father's Love, The. Mary E. Tucker. CBWP-1

Fathers: naked, you stand for their big faces. This Is a Poem for the Dead. Michael Ryan. AmPA

Father's Notes of Woe, A. Sir Walter Scott. OBNC *Fr.* The Lay of the Last Minstrel.

Fathers of a Star, The. Zbigniew Herbert, *Polish*. CEEP, *tr. by* Czesw Miosz

Father's Story. Elizabeth Madox Roberts. ImGa

Father's Testament, A. Judah ibn Tibbon, *Hebrew*. TrJP, *tr. by* Israel Abrahams

Fathers will hear you, The. (LL) The Children's Bells. Eleanor Farjeon. BoTP; CH

Father's Winter. Justinas Marcinkevius, *Lithuanian*. CEEP, *tr. by* Jonas Zdanys

Fatigue. Hilaire Belloc. NBLV; NOBL; OxBTC; UV

Fatima. Tennyson. GBL; UnPo

Fatness. Alan Ansen. CoAP

Fatted / on herbs, swollen on crabapples. The Porcupine. Galway Kinnell. NOBA

Fattened sky, The. The Fifth Hell. Jerome Rothenberg. *Fr.* The Seven Hells of Jigoku Zoshi. NNaP

Faucon hath born my mak away, The. (LL) The Corpus Christi Carol. *Unknown.* CH; EBEV; EnVB; HAP; ImPo; MiEL; NAEL-1; NOBE; OAEL-1; OBEV; SCV; TFi

Fault of the Age, The. Ella Wheeler Wilcox. PWR

Fault was mine, the fault was mine, The. Tennyson. *Fr.* Maud [A Monodrama]. EnVR

Faun, The. Ezra Pound. FaBoCh; FaBoTw

Faun Sees Snow for the First Time, The. Richard Aldington. MoBrPo

Fause Foodrage, *vers. B and C. Unknown.* ESPB

Fause Foodrage. *Unknown.* ESPB

(Fa'se Footrage.) OxBB

Faust. John Ashbery. TwCP

Faust. Goethe, *German.*
   "Chanting sun, as ever, rivals, The." NAWM-2, *tr. by* Louis MacNeice
   Christ Is Arisen. TrCP
   "Do you know me now? Skinny, cadaverous bitch." OxBSn, *tr. by* David Luke
   Lose This Day Loitering. PoLF, *tr. by* John Anster
   Soldier's Song. AWP, *tr. by* Bayard Taylor
   Spirit of Evil, The. OxBoV, *tr. by* Bayard Taylor

Faustina hath a spot upon her face. De Naevo in Facie Faustinae. Thomas Bastard. FaBoEE

Faustina, or Rock Roses. Elizabeth Bishop. FaBoMo

Faustine. Swinburne. EBVVPR

Faust's Servant. Roy Fuller. OxBTC

Faustus. Alec Derwent Hope. NOBAu

Faustus Triumphant. Thom Gunn. FaBoMo

Favorite Flower, The. Celia Laighton Thaxter. AiP

Favorite Grandson Braid. Phillip William George. VoR

Favorite has no friend!, A. Thomas Gray. *See* Ode on the Death of a Favourite [*or* Favorite] Cat, Drowned in a Tub [*or* Bowl] of Gold Fishes.

Favorite Iraqi Soldier. Stephen Dobyns. BAP-93

Favorite Little Shrine, A. Enrique Lihn. VCWP

Favorite Slave's Story, The. Priscilla Jane Thompson. AAP; CBWP-2; RACG

Favour. Robert David Fitzgerald. CBAP

Favour, The. Rudyard Kipling. *Fr.* Epitaphs of the War [1914–1918]. OBWP

Favourite Swain, The. Elizabeth Hands. WoRP

Favourite Village, The. James Hurdis.
   Peasants at Work. ECEV

Favourite's fall, The. Juvenal, *Latin.* OBCVT, *tr. by* Thomas Morris

Fawn in the Snow, The. William Rose Benét. MoAmPo

Fawnia. Robert Greene. OBEV; PoEL-2 *Fr.* Pandosto.
   (In Praise of His Loving and Best-beloved Fawnia.) PoEL-2

Fawn's Foster-Mother. Robinson Jeffers. MoP; NOBA; NoAM

Fear, The. Lascelles Abercrombie. OBMV

Fear. Devdas Chhotray, *Oriya.* OMIP, *tr. by* Jayanta Mahapatra

Fear. Anna Hajnal, *Hungarian.* BoWoP, *tr. by* Daniel Hoffman

Fear, A. Francis Ledwidge. NOIV

Fear. David Lehman. NAmP90

Fear. Thomas Love Peacock. VoR

Fear. Vittoria Aganoor Pompili, *Italian.* PBWP, *tr. by* Brenda Webster

Fear and Anger in the Mindless Universe. Hayden Carruth. NNaP

Fear, as I see the spring go. Kuan Han-ch'ing. SuSp, *tr. by* Jerome P. Seaton *Fr.* Tune: "Green Jade Flute."

Fear death?—to feel the fog in my throat. Prospice. Robert Browning. APAD; FHYEP; ImPo; NAEL-2; PFE; PoLF; PoRA; SAGP; TrCP

Fear God—obey his just decree. The Conclusion of the Matter. Christopher Smart. ChIV-1; KSG *Fr.* Hymns for the Amusement of Children.

Fear it has faded and the night. Schoolgirls Hastening. John Shaw Neilson. NOBAu

Fear, jealousy and murder are the same. Gamecock. James Dickey. HoPM; UnPo

Fear me, virgin whosoever. Herman Melville. *See* After the Pleasure Party.

Fear no longer for the lone grey birds. End of the Flower World (A.D. 2300). Stanley Burnshaw. TrJP

Fear no more the heat o' the Sun. Song. Shakespeare. APAD; AWP; CH; CTC; ClHu; EBEV; EBEvV; FaBoCh; GBL; GTBS-P; HAP; ImPo; InPS-3; NAEL-1; NOBE; NOSC; NoP-4; NoSic; OAEL-1; OBEV; OxAEP-1; PBMP; PFE; PoE; PoEL-2; PoPoPo; PoRA; RB; SCGP; SCV; SoSe-8; TFi *Fr.* Cymbeline.

Fear not, dear love, that I'll reveal. Secrecy [*or* Secresie] Protested. Thomas Carew. CaPo; PFE; SeCP

Fear Not: For They That Be With Us. Jones Very. ChIV-1

Fear Not, Poor Weary One. Thomas Cogswell Upham. AH

Fear not, shepherds, for I bring. Angel's Song. Charles Causley. OBCP

Fear of affectation made her affect. Seamus Heaney. *Fr.* Clearances. CIP-2; PBCIP; PNI

Fear of Death. John Ashbery. FaBoMo; TAP

Fear of death disturbs me constantly, The. Prayer. Gabrielle de Coignard, *French.* WPOW, *tr. by* Raymond Oliver

Fear of loneliness, the wish, The. The Price. Anne Stevenson. DiPo

Fear of Love, The. Wendell Berry. EC2

Fear of poetry is the, The. Reading Time : 1 Minute 26 Seconds. Muriel Rukeyser. PBWP

Fear of Shoplifting. Maureen Seaton. FFC

Fear of Subways. Maureen Seaton. FFC

Fear of the Earth. Alex Comfort. MoBrPo

Fear of the Lord, The. Bible, *O.T.* TrJP *Fr.* Proverbs.

Fear passes from man to man. Charles Simic. HCAP; WeW-3

Fear Test: Integrity of Heroes. James Simmons. CIP-2

Fear the one who has sharp weapons. Song of the Lioness for Her Cub. *Unknown, Hottentot.* BoWoP, *tr. by* Thomas Hahn

Feare not, litle flocke, for it is your fathers good pleasure to give you the kingdome. Bible, *N.T.* OBVE *Fr.* St. Luke.

Fearful I peer upon the mountain path. John Berryman. *Fr.* Eleven Addresses to the Lord. OxBC

Fearful night sinks, The. Hymn to the Sun. *Unknown.* TTTS

Fearful of beauty, I always went. The Enamel Girl. Genevieve Taggard. MoAmPo

Fearful Symmetry. Basil Bunting. PoA

Fearful the chamber's quiet; the veiled windows. A Development of Idiotcy. Ebenezer Jones. OBNC; PeVV

Fearing. Tanka. Ishikawa Takuboku, *Japanese.* MJT, *tr. by* Makoto Ueda

Fearing that Albion should turn his back against the Divine Vision. William Blake. OAEL-2 *Fr.* Jerusalem; The Emanation of the Giant Albion.

Fearless, The. Mortimer J. Adler. PoA

Fearless One. Genrik Veniaminovich Sapgir, *Russian.* TCRP, *tr. by* Albert C. Todd

Fears and Tears. *Unknown.* ReMoGo

Fears any one his bride lest she a virgin be not. Reasons for and against Marrying Widows. Henricus Selyns. SCAP

Fears in Solitude. Coleridge. FHYEP; OBWP
   (Fears in Solitude. Written April 1798, during the Alarms of an Invasion.) Ro
   ("Love, and the thoughts that yearn for humankind.") (LL) Ro
   "On the green sheep-track, up the heathy hill." OBNC

Fears in Solitude. Written April 1798, during the Alarms of an Invasion. Coleridge. *See* Fears in Solitude.

Fears of the Eighth Grade. Toi Derricotte. GT; InPS-3

Feast, The. Robert Duncan. APSN *Fr.* Passages.

Feast and noon grew high, and Sacrifice, The. Milton. EBEV *Fr.* Samson Agonistes. FHYEP; OAEL-1; PoEL-3

Feast Day. Ellen Bryant Voigt.
   "O mild Christ." CrSp

Feast o' Saint [*or* St.] Stephen, The. Ruth Sawyer. OBCP

Feast of Blood, The. Joseph Fawcett. NOEC *Fr.* The Art of War.

Feast of St. Tortoise, The. Nancy Willard. LCAP-2

Feast of Stephen, The. Anthony Hecht. HAP; NoAM; VCAP

Feast of Stephen, The. Kevin Nichols. OBCP

Feast of the Assumption of the Virgin, The. Ellen Bryant Voigt. CrSp

Feast of the Monkeys, The. John Philip Sousa. OBAL

Feast of the Most Holy Trinity. Aubrey Thomas De Vere. TIRV

Feast of the Poets, The. Leigh Hunt.
   "But now came the men of right visiting claims;." EPCY
   "'Twas in eighteen eleven those bards came to dine;." EPCY

Feast of the Ram's Horn. Harvey Shapiro. VGW

Feasts, The. Boris Pasternak, *Russian.* TCRP, *tr. by* Yakov Hornstein

Feast's begun / And the wine is done, The. Water Song. Solomon ibn Gabirol, *Hebrew.* TrJP, *tr. by* Israel Abrahams

Feasts of Death, Feasts of Love. Stuart Z. Perkoff. NeAP

Feat of Gardening, The. John Gardner. OBGa *Fr.* The Feat of Gardening.
   Feat of Gardening, The. OBGa

Feather, The. Lilian Bowes-Lyon. LW

Feather, The. Vernon Watkins. FaBoTw

Feather Bag, Stick Bag. Kim R. Stafford. CMAP

Feather, feather, if it was a feather. Poem about a Ball in the Nineteenth Century. William Empson. CBNP

Feather for My Cap, A. Ivy O. Eastwick. BoTP

Feather Plucked from the Tail of the Fiery Hen, A. Novica Tadic, *Serbo-Croatian.* HSix, *tr. by* Charles Simic

Feather that all, The. Abukbo. Jim Barnes. *Fr.* Four Things Choctaw. HATNAP

"Feathered fowl's in your orchard, father, A." Brown Robin. *Unknown.* ESPB

Feather'd millions form'd for speed. Bible, *O.T. See* Psalm 148.

Feathered songster chaunticleer, The. Bristowe Tragedie: or, The Dethe of Syr Charles Bawdin. Thomas Chatterton. OxBB

Feathered Dances. Kenward Elmslie. PmAP

Feathered Friends. Robert Peters. BXAP

Feathers blacken against the sun. Manifest Destiny. Anita Endrezze-Danielson. CDW

Feathers in a fan, The. Man. Humbert Wolfe. MoBrPo

Feathers of the willow, The. Song. Richard Watson Dixon. CH; FaBoCh; GTBS-P; NOBE; OBEV; OBNC; PFE

Feathers or Lead? James Richard Broughton. NeAP

Feathers up fast, and steeples; then in clods. The Fountain. Donald Davie. GTBS-P; NoP-4; OxBTC

Featherstone's Doom. Robert Stephen Hawker. OBNC

Feathery forests are blown back, frost rends, The. Winter. John Lyle Donaghy. BIrV

February. John Clare. NOBE; OBNC *Fr.* The Shepherd's [*or* Shepheards] Calendar.

February. John Heath-Stubbs. AYFP; OBCP

February. W. S. Merwin. NNaP

February. Lolly Quinones. IMW

February. Dorothy Una Ratcliffe. BoTP

February. Henrietta Cordelia Ray. CBWP-3

February. Folgore da San Geminiano. *Fr.* Sonnets of the Months. AWP, *tr. by* D. G. Rossetti

February. James Schuyler. NeAP

February 23. Marilyn Hacker. CPO

February 8, 1980: And No One Has Warned Me. Stanislaw Baranczak, *Polish.* AF, *tr. by* Magnus J. Krynski

February: A Thaw. John Clare. *See* February.

February Afternoon. Edward Thomas. NoAM; PeFWW; PoWW

February, and the wind has begun. What a Boy Can Do. Alberto A. Ríos. IFJA

February 11, 1977. Frederick Morgan. DiPo

February Evening in New York. Denise Levertov. NoAM

February. Germination's moment. Judit Tóth, *Hungarian.* CEEP, *tr. by* Emery E. George

February. Get your ink and weep. Boris Pasternak, *Russian.* TCRP, *tr. by* Yakov Hornstein

February in Sydney. Yusef Komunyakaa. NAAAL

February is the love and wrath of weather. Blizzard. Bella Akhatovna Akhmadulina, *Russian.* TCRP, *tr. by* Albert C. Todd

February Morning. King D. Kuka. VoR

February Park. Gerald Vizenor. VoR

February road to the river is mud / and dirty snow, The. To Be Here. Linda Gregg. AFr

February; the Boy Breughel. Norman Dubie. LCAP-2

February: Thinking of Flowers. Jane Kenyon. LoL

February 13, 1980. Lucille Clifton. "Twenty-one years of my life you have been." CrSp; MDDM

February Twilight. Sara Teasdale. AYFP; OBCA

February's Forgotten Mitts. Raymond Knister. NOBC

Feckless Dinner-Party, The. Walter De la Mare. FP; FaBoTw

Fed up with the circle. Vasco Popa. *See* The Adventure of the Quartz Pebble.

Fedele and Fortunio. Anthony Munday. Fedele's Song.

Fedele's Song. Anthony Munday. *Fr.* Fedele and Fortunio.

Federation. W. T. Goodge. NOBAu

Fee, fi, fo, fum. *Unknown.* OxNR

Feed Ma Lamz. Tom Leonard. FaBoTC

Feed, silly sheep, although your keeper pineth. William Smith. Son *Fr.* Chloris [*or* the Complaint of the Passionate Despised Shepheard].

Feed still thy self, thou fondling, with belief. *Unknown.* NoSic

Feed the Mexican Back into Her. Cherríe Moraga. GLP

Feeding, The. Toi Derricotte. NMM-2

Feeding, The. Lou Lipsitz. CDa

Feeding, The. Joel Oppenheimer. NeAP

Feeding a Child. Nuala Ni Dhomhnaill, *Irish.* CIP-2, *tr. by* Michael Hartnett

Feeding Ducks. Norman MacCaig. FaBoTC; OxBS

Feeding Ground. Thomas McCarthy. CIP-2

Feeding the Dog. Russell Edson. RaBo

Feeding the Dove. Velemir Khlebnikov, *Russian.* TCRP, *tr. by* Gary Kern

Feeding the ducks at the Howard Johnson Motel. Susan Mitchell. NAmP90

Feeding the Lions. Norman Jordan. PoBA

Feeding the Sun. Bill Knott. PBCAP

Feel for your bad fall how could I fail. A Sympathy, A Welcome. John Berryman. NYBP; NoP-4

Feel Free. Natasha Tarpley. ISC

Feel free. To Bobby Seale. Lucille Clifton. MBE; PoBA

"Feel me to do right," our father said on his deathbed. May Swenson. MoLi; NMM-2

Feel my eye breaking. (LL) The Window. Robert Creeley. FTOS; NOBA; NoAM; PmAP; TAP; VGW

Feel of Hands, The. Thom Gunn. EP

Feel of it was hairy and coarse, The. Pulling a Pig's Tail. Dave Jeddie Smith. NAmP90

Feel the sharpness. The Meeting. Ramona Wilson. VoR

Feeling, The. William Bronk. VGW

Feeling a pain in his breast, when he speaks. Ellas and the Statues. Gülten Akin, *Turkish.* PBWP, *tr. by* Nermin Menemencioglu

Feeling and Form. Marilyn Hacker. NoAM

Feeling constricted by the dusty city. In the Second Month of Summer, Taking My Family to the Villages East of the City. Li K'ai-hsien, *Chinese.* CoBLCP, *tr. by* Jonathan Chaves

Feeling Fucked/Up Up. Etheridge Knight. GT; NNaP; PBCAP; RaBo

Feeling it with me. Walking on Water. James Dickey. ChIV-2

Feeling my face has the terrible shine of fish. Element. Patricia K. Page. MoCV

Feeling Old Age. Liu Tsung-yüan, *Chinese.* SuSp, *tr. by* Jan W. Walls

Feeling Sorry for Myself. Lu Yu, *Chinese.* CoBCP, *tr. by* Burton Watson

Feeling the urge my mother. Birth. Edith Bruck, *Italian.* BoWoP, *tr. by* Ruth Feldman *and* Brian Swann (b. 1940)

Feeling Through. Alvin Aubert. BkSV

Feeling Type and His Friends, The. Michael Davidson. FTOS

Feelings and Emotions. Xuân Diệu, *Vietnamese.* AVP, *tr. by* Huỳnh Sanh Thông

Feelings Come As I Pass through Wu-chiang. Wu Wei-yeh, *Chinese.* CoBLCP, *tr. by* Jonathan Chaves

Feelings go up into the air, The. Some Feelings. Michael Benedikt. CoAmPo

Feelings I don't have I don't have, The. To Women, as Far as I'm Concerned. D. H. Lawrence. InPS-3; OxBSP; RaBo

Feelings in Nature ("Bamboo fishing coat, purple official gown"). Ma Chih-yüan. *Fr.* Four Poems to the Tune "Ch'ing-chiang yin." CoBLCP, *tr. by* Jonathan Chaves

Feelings in Nature ("Forest and brook—mdash;who has gone"). Ma Chih-yüan. *Fr.* Four Poems to the Tune "Ch'ing-chiang yin." CoBLCP, *tr. by* Jonathan Chaves

Feelings in Nature ("In the western village the day grows long"). Ma Chih-yüan. *Fr.* Four Poems to the Tune "Ch'ing-chiang yin." CoBLCP, *tr. by* Jonathan Chaves

Feelings in Nature ("Woodcutter wakes as mountain moon hangs low, The"). Ma Chih-yüan. *Fr.* Four Poems to the Tune "Ch'ing-chiang yin." CoBLCP, *tr. by* Jonathan Chaves

Feelings of a Republican on the Fall of Bonaparte. Shelley. Son

Feelings Wakened by a Mirror. Po Chü-i, *Chinese.* CoBCP, *tr. by* Burton Watson

Fees, The! The fees! The mighty fees! God or Mammon. Alfred Cruickshank. PBCV

Feet. Irene Thompson. BoTP

Feet at their loveliest are like two hands. Conceit upon the Feet. William Zaranka. BXAP

Feet covered with mud, the smell of meat on their breath. Making Fun of the Well at the Inn below the Mountain. Chu Yün-ming, *Chinese.* CoBLCP, *tr. by* Jonathan Chaves

Feet folded under her. Sweet Oranges. Mary Logue. EC3

Feet O' Jesus. Langston Hughes. ISC

Feet of Judas, The. George Marion McClellan. AAP

Feet of morning the feet of noon and the feet of evening, The. The Domestic Stones (fragment). Hans Arp, *French.* CBNP; SPE, *tr. by* David Gascoyne

Feigned Courage. Yitzhak Lamdan. OxBChV

Feld, groes or goers, hus, doeg, dung. Returning to Roots of First Feeling. Robert Duncan. PoA

Felicia Hemans. Elizabeth Barrett Browning. VWP
(Stanzas Addressed to Miss Landon, and suggested by her 'Stanzas on the Death of Mrs Hemans'.) Ro
("Thou bay-crowned living one, who o'er.") Ro
("Were softer than her singing.") (LL) Ro

Felicitie of a mind imbracing vertue, that beholdeth the wretched desyres of the worlde, The. Lucretius, *Latin.* OBCVT, *tr. by Unknown*

Felicitous Life, A. Czeslaw Milosz, *Polish.* PoSu, *tr. by Czeslaw Milosz and Lillian Vallee*

Felicitous phenomenon! (LL) O To Be A Dragon. Marianne Moore. CTC; ChIV-1; KSG; NALW; NMM-2

Felicity the healer isn't young. Doctor Frolic. Robert Pinsky. NoAM

Feliks Skrzynecki. Peter Skrzynecki. CBAP

Felix Antonius. Sir Henry John Newbolt. FP

Felix Holt: The Radical. "George Eliot." LW *Fr.* Felix Holt, the Radical.

Felix, qui patriis. . . and Imitated from Claudian. Claudian, *Latin.* OBCVT, *tr. by Stephen Duck*

Felix Randal the farrier, O is he dead then? my duty / all ended. Gerard Manley Hopkins. EBEV; EBVV; EnVR; FaBoMo; FaBoVe; GTBS-P; HAP; ImPo; InPS-3; LiTM; MoBrPo; MoP; NAEL-2; NOBE; NoAM; NoP-4; OBEV; OBNC; OxAEP-2; PeECV; PoE; PoPoPo; PoRA; Poetr; SAGP; SCGP; Son; TFi; WeW-3

("Felix Randal the farrier, O he is dead then? [my duty all ended].") CABP; FP

Felix rapina. The flap. The Feast of the Assumption of the Virgin. Ellen Bryant Voigt. CrSp

Felixstowe, or, The Last of Her Order. John Betjeman. OxBTC

Fell the edge of the knife. Shoriken. Charles Brasch. PeNZ

Felled Plane Tree, The. Anna Hajnal, *Hungarian.* BoWoP, *tr. by William Jay Smith*

Feller isn't thinkin' mean, A. Out Fishin'. E. A. Guest. PoLF

Felling a Tree. Ivor Gurney. FaBoVe

Fellow compositors. The Printer's Error. Aaron Fogel. BAP-95

Fellow countrymen. He Was a Man of Jokes outside Office. Oswald Basize Dube. PeSAV

Fellow from far Erewhon, A. Limerick. W. F. N. Watson. PeLi

Fellow Mortal, A. John Masefield. OxAEP-2

Fellow Passenger. Valerie Gillies. FaBoTC

Fellow who fucked but as few can, A. Limerick. *Unknown.* PeLi

Fellow who sits in the air-conditioned office, The. At the Back of Progress. . . . Taslima Nasrin, *Bengali.* VCWP, *tr. by* Carolyne Wright *and* Mohammad Nurul Huda

Fellow, you have no flair for art, I fear. The Sitting Bard. Sir Owen Seaman. NOBL

Fellowship. "Michael Field." VWP

Fellowship. *Unknown.* BLPA

Felo de Se. Thomas Blackburn. OxBTC

Felo de Se. Richard Hughes. OBMV

Felo de Se. Amy Levy. VWP

Felt for thee as a lover or a child! (LL) England, 1802, V. Wordsworth. GTBS-P; OBEV

Feltons Epitaph. *Unknown.* PBRV

Felucca and Pinnace. The Waterfront Girls. Rufinus, *Greek.* GrAn, *tr. by* Alan Marshfield

Female Advocate Or, An Answer to a Late Satyr, The. Sarah Fyge Egerton. "Blasphemous wretch! How canst thou think or say." PEW

Female and the Silence of a Man, The. June Jordan. NAAAL; NMM-2

Female Dancer. James Camp. Son

"Female genital, like the blank page anticipating the poem, The." Sentience. Sandra McPherson. PoA

Female giants, fauna of women. The Women of Rubens. Wislawa Szymborska, *Polish.* WPOW, *tr. by* Celina Wieniewska

Female God, The. Isaac Rosenberg. FaBoTw

Female is fertile, and discipline, The. Praise for Sick Women. Gary Snyder. NeAP

Female mind like a rude fallow lies, A. Anne, Viscountess Irwin Ingram. ECWP *Fr.* An Epistle to Mr. Pope Occasioned by His Characters of Women.

Female of the Species, The. Rudyard Kipling. BLPA

Female Philosopher, The. Charlotte Dacre. NOBRP

Female Principle, The. Alec Derwent Hope. OxBC

Female spider / swept her legends into her palms. Roots of Blue Bells. Nia Francisco. HATNAP

Female Transport, The. *Unknown.* NOBAu

Female Vagrant, The. Wordsworth. Ro

Female Wits, The: A Song by a Lady of Quality. *Unknown.* NOSC

Female's Lamentations, The; or, The Village in Mourning. Hannah Wallis. ECWP

Femina. Daphne Marlatt. NOBC

Femina Contra Mundum. G. K. Chesterton. OxAEP-2

Feminine mouth in Utopia, The. Limerick. W. F. N. Watson. PeLi

Feminism. Denise Duhamel. BAP-93; IFJA

Feminism. Carolyn M. Rodgers. NMM-2

Feminism, baby, feminism. Male Rage Poem. Pier Giorgio Di Cicco. NOBC

Femme et Chatte. Paul Verlaine, *French.* AWP; OBVE, *tr. by* Arthur Symons

("They were just playing, lady and cat.") PC, *tr. by* Felicity Bast

Femmes Damnées. Charles Baudelaire. CPO, *tr. by* Carlyle Ferren MacIntyre *Fr.* Les Fleurs du Mal.

Femmes Damnées. John Gray. ADE

Fence beyond fence from breakfast. The Names of the Humble. Les A. Murray. CBAP

Fence or an Ambulance, A. Joseph Malins. BLPA

Fence Wire. James Dickey. NYBP; VGW

Fencing. Anthony Lawrence. NOBAu

Fencing instructor named Fisk, A. Limerick. *Unknown.* PeLi

Fencing School. John Streeter Manifold. CBAP

Feral Pioneers, The. Ishmael Reed. PoBA; UnPo

Ferdinand De Soto lies. The Distant Runners. Mark Van Doren. LiTM; MoAmPo

Ferdinando and Elvira; or, The Gentle Pieman. Sir William Schwenck Gilbert. OBCoV

Fergusson, tho twa-hunder year. To Robert Fergusson. Robert Garioch. FaBoTC

Ferishtah's Fancies. Robert Browning. When I Vexed You. OxBSP

Fern. Ted Hughes. NYBP

Fern and flower, safely keep. The Cat to His Dinner. Nancy Willard. PC

Fern Hill. Dylan Thomas. CABP; CMoP; ChAP; ClHu; GEA; GTBS-P; HAP; HeIP-4; ImPo; InPK-6; InPS-3; LiTM; MoBrPo; MoP; NAEL-2; NIP-4; NOBE; NTP; NoAM; NoP-4; OAEL-2; OBWVE; OxBTC; PoE; PoLF; PoPoPo; PoRA; Poetr; SAGP; SoSe-8; TFi; TRP; TwCP

Fernando ("Fernando has a basketball"). Marci Ridlon. NTCP

Ferniehirst Castle. Richard Hugo. NoAM

Ferries go out with the bodies from the morgue, The. PBS. Robert Mazzocco. WWSi

Ferris Wheel, The. Wyatt Prunty. RA

Ferry Me Across. B. P. Nichol. FTOS

Ferry Me across the Water. Christina Rossetti. NTP; OxBChV; TLR *Fr.* Sing-Song.

(Ferryman, The.) BoTP

Ferry Pirate, The. Douglas Oliver. NBrP

Ferryboat and the Traveler, The. Yong-un Han, *Korean.* CKP, *tr. by* Jaihiun Kim

Ferrying across the river. The Traveler. Mogwol Park, *Korean.* CKP, *tr. by* Jaihiun Kim

Ferryman, The. Christina Rossetti. *See* Ferry Me across the Water.

Ferryman's Song at Binh Minh. Herbert Krohn. CDa

Fertile and rank and rich the coastal rains. Advent. William Everson. NeAP; TrCP

Fertile Muck, The. Irving Layton. NOBC; NoAM

Fervid breath of our flushed Southern May, The. Evening on the Potomac. Richard Hovey. APN-2

Festal Board, The. *Unknown.* BLPA

Feste's Song. Shakespeare. *See* Song: "When that I was and a little tiny boy."

Feste's Song. Shakespeare. *See* The Clown's Song.

Feste's Song ("When that I was and a little tiny boy"). Shakespeare. *See* Song: "When that I was and a little tiny boy."

Festival of the Nativity, The. Richard De Ledrede, *Latin.* TIRV, *tr. by* Robert Wyse Jackson

Festive draperies override the claims of. A Naming Day. Odia Ofeimun. HBAPE; PBMAP

Festus Conrad. Melvin B. Tolson. GT

Fet Walks Melody Home. Gary Hyland. IFJA

Fetch in the holly from the tree. Holly and Mistletoe. Eleanor Farjeon. PChr

Fetch me a red flower from that meadow. Speech Warts. Myra Sklarew. CRP

Fetchin Water. Claude McKay. PBCV

Fetching Cows. Norman MacCaig. NoP-4; OxBC

Fete, A. Larry Eigner. NeAP

Fete confused me, The. Guests played the part of gods. Sigismundo. Linda Gregg. AmPA

Feud, The. Sydney Lea. RA

Feuerzauber. Louis Untermeyer. TrJP

Feuilles d'Automne. Victor Hugo, *French.*
    Heard on the Mountain. AWP, *tr. by* Francis Thompson
    Sunset, A. AWP, *tr. by* Francis Thompson

Fever. Bella Akhatovna Akhmadulina, *Russian.* TCRP, *tr. by* Elaine Feinstein

Fever. Judith Ortiz Cofer. MoLi

Fever, The. Rosemary Dobson. FaBoWP

Fever, A. Donne. OAEL-1

Fever. Thom Gunn. EP

Fever 103°. Sylvia Plath. CMoP; FaBoWP; NOBA; NoAM; VCAP; VGW ("To Paradise.") (LL) ColAP

Fever Toy, The. Charles Wright. AmPA

Feverish Propositions. Rosemarie Waldrop. FTOS *Fr.* The Reproduction of Profiles.

Feverish room and that white bed, The. White Heliotrope. Arthur Symons. BoLoP; EBEV; GLoP; LoP; PeVV

Fevers and plagues, and all their noxious stores. (LL) But now this man of hell toward me turned. Philip Freneau. NAAL-1; NAAL-3

Few are the moonlit nights that I've cared for. Last Stop. George Seferis, *Greek.* AF, *tr. by* Edmund Keeley *and* Philip Sherrard

Few beds are stonier than one shared by a sleeper. Bed Time. Peter Davison. UnPo

Few bones, A. Galway Kinnell. *Fr.* The Dead Shall Be Raised Incorruptible. NOBA; PoE

Few Days in the South in February, A. Eleanor Ross Taylor. CBCWP

Few even o' the criminals, cravens, and fools. First Hymn to Lenin. "Hugh MacDiarmid." FaBoTC

Few ever came to help you speak or sell. Peter Dale. NOCV *Fr.* The Fragments.

Few Facts about Me, A. Charles North. PmAP

Few flakes appear, A. Chuck Brickley. HA

Few hairs, made fewer by the comb. Master Liu Painted a Portrait of Me in My Old Age and Asked Me to Write a Poem About the Picture. Yang Wan-li, *Chinese.* SuSp, *tr by* Jonathan Chaves

Few Happy Matches. Isaac Watts. NOEC

Few hours ago a woman went on a walk, A. The Legend of Hell. C. D. Wright. LCAP-2

Few Lines to Fill up a Vacant Page, A. John Danforth. SCAP

Few men in any age have second sight. To a Reviewer Who Admired My Book. John Ciardi. OBAL

Few minutes ago, I stepped onto the deck, A. The Cobweb. Raymond Carver. BLT

Few minutes late / For the Freedom Train, A. (LL) Dream Boogie: Variation. Langston Hughes. APSN

Few months obliterate, A. (LL) Brag, sweet tenor bull. Basil Bunting. NoAM; NoP-4; PoE

Few nights ago I was half-watching the news on television and half-reading to my daughter, A. The Last Deaths. Charles Kenneth Williams. MoLi

Few of the Bird-Family, A. James Whitcomb Riley. NOxBChV

Few people are talking low in a boat, A. (LL) Driving toward the Lac Qui Parle River. Robert Bly. CoAmPo; LCAP-2; WeT

Few people could hope to compare. Limerick. J. Endersby. PeLi

Few quick drying globs of gold acrylic, A. Tricks of the Trade. Gloria Escoffery. HCP

Few sashay, a few finagle, A. I Knew I'd Sing. Heather McHugh. WeT

Few, save the poor, feel for the poor. The Poor. Letitia Elizabeth Landon. VWP

Few scraps of the wind, A. A Smaller Love Song. Tong-gyu Hwang, *Korean.* CKP, *tr. by* Jaihiun Kim

Few sights were lovelier. Seeing Cousin Phyllis Off. Richard Howard. WeT

Few Sirens, A. Alice Walker. CrSp

Few Things Can More Inflame. C. Day Lewis. OBMV

Few things to desire can so prod us. Limerick. W. F. N. Watson. PeLi

Few thought he was even a starter. Clement Attlee. OBCoV

Few times only, then away, A. Night Song for a Woman. Alfred Wellington Purdy. NOBC

Few, wild handfuls of rock, A. Padraic's Point. Gabriel Gbadamosi. NBrP

Few words are best; I wish you well. To Mr. C., St. James's Place, London, October 22nd. Alexander Pope. OxBSP

Few Words in the Mother Tongue, A. Irena Klepfisz. LoHo

    (Etlekhe Verter Oyf Mame-Loshn / A Few Words in the Mother Tounge.) CPO

Few years back and they told me Black, A. A Poem about Intelligence for My Brothers and Sisters. June Jordan. LTA; UnSA

Fforestfawr. Kingsley Amis. NOBL *Fr.* The Evans Country.

Fhairshon swore a feud. The Massacre of the Macpherson. William Edmonstoune Aytoun. BXAP

Fiascherino. Charles Tomlinson. NoAM

Fiat Lux. Lynda Hull. WWSi

Fib Detected, A. Catullus. *See* Carmen 10 ("Varus, whom I chanced to meet").

Fiction: A Message. Gavin Ewart. OxBC

Fiction and the Reading Public. Philip Larkin. NOBL; OBSV

Fiction-Makers, The. Anne Stevenson. DiPo

Fiction: The House Party. Gavin Ewart. PeLV

Fiddle, The. Neil Munro. BoTP

Fiddle-de-dee! High June. Catherine A. Morin. BoTP

Fiddle-I-Fee. *Unknown.* AmFP

Fiddle, we know, is diddle: and diddle, we take it, is dee. (LL) The Higher Pantheism in a Nutshell. Swinburne. BXAP; CABP; CBNP; EnVR; PeVV

Fiddler and his wife, The. *Unknown.* OxNR

Fiddler Jones. Edgar Lee Masters. LiLi

Fiddler of Dooney, The. W. B. Yeats. EBVV; FaBoCh; NBLV; OxAEP-2

Fiddler settles in, The. Lament for the O'Neills. John Montague. CIP-2

Fidele, A. William Collins. *See* Dirge in "Cymbeline."

Fidele. Shakespeare. *See* Song: "Fear no more the heat o' the Sun."

Fidelia Arguing with Her Self on the Difficulty of Finding the True Religion. Jane Barker. KTR

Fidelis. Adelaide Anne Procter. BLPA; FaBoBe

Fidelity. Thomas Lodge. *See* Phillis 2.

Fidelity and love are two different things, like a flower and a gem. D. H. Lawrence. CBLP

    ("Man and woman are like the earth, that brings forth flowers.") ITG

Fidelity Rewarded. Dora Greenwell. VWP

Fidessa, More Chaste than Kind[e]. Bartholomew Griffin.

    Faire Is My Love. GBL; PoEL-2

    "My ladies haire is threeds [or threads] of beaten gold." AAS

Fie fie fie fie fie! (LL) Madrigal: "Ay me, alas, heigh ho, heigh ho!" Thomas Weelkes. FaBoCh; OxBoLi

Fie [or Fye], foolish Earth, think[e] the heaven wants glory Love's Glory. Fulke Greville. PoEL-1; Son *Fr.* Caelica.

Fie on all courtesy, and unruly winds. The Coxcomb. Joseph Hall. OxAEP-1

Fie on Eastern Luxury. Horace. *See* Simplicity.

Fie on Love. James Shirley. OxBSP

Fie, school of Patience, fie; your lesson is. Sonnet 56. Sir Philip Sidney. NAEL-1 *Fr.* Astrophil and Stella. AAS; SiPS

Fie [or Fy] tedious Hope, why do[e] you still rebel[l]? Sonnet 27. Mary Sidney, Countess of Montgomery Wroth. NOSC *Fr.* Pamphilia to Amphilanthus.

Fie upon hearts that burn with mutual fire[!]. Against Fruition. Sir John Suckling. BeJo; CaPo

Field, A. *Unknown, Greek.* GrAn, *tr. by* Peter Jay

Field, The. Jean Valentine. LCAP-2

Field and Forest. Randall Jarrell. LCAP-2; VGW

Field, bright green, laps sunshine up, The. The Man Who Sleeps Out in the Fields. Bùi Khải Nguyên, *Vietnamese.* AVP, *tr. by* Huỳnh Sanh Thông

Field daisies, wild lichens—each a mint coin. Stanza Written in Jest. Yang Wan-li, *Chinese.* SuSp, *tr. by* Sherwin S. S. Fu

Field Daisy, The. Jane Taylor. BoTP

Field Day. William Robert Rodgers. BIrV; IIP; PNI

Field dodd. P. Inman. FTOS *Fr.* Dust Bowl.

Field Flower, A. James Montgomery. BoTP *Fr.* The Daisy.

Field Flowers. Louise Glück. AFr

Field Full of Folk, The. William Langland. *See* Prologue: "In a summer season, when soft was the sun."

Field-Glasses. Andrew Young. GTBS-P; RB

Field Hospital, A. Randall Jarrell. NoP-4

Field Hospital, The. Paul Muldoon. CIP-2; PNI

Field Manoeuvres. Richard Aldington. PeFWW; PoFWW

Field-Mouse, The. Enid Blyton. BoTP

Field Mouse, The. William Sharp. FPC

Field mouse follows its own shadow, The. Snowfall; a Poem about Spring. James Wright. NoAM

Field of Autumn. Laurie Lee. LiTM

Field of Glory, The. Edwin Arlington Robinson. MoAmPo

Field of golden wheat there grows, A. Harvest Song. Richard Dehmel, *German.* AWP, *tr. by* Ludwig Lewisohn

Field of Light, A. Theodore Roethke. LiTM; TwCP

Field of poetry ends here, The. The Dump. Greg Kuzma. PoA

Field of stones, A. Irthing Valley. Frances Horovitz. NBrP

Field of Talavera, The. Thomas Hardy. CMoP *Fr.* The Dynasts.

Field of the Caribou, The. John Haines. WeT

Field of the Cloth of Gold, The. Patrick Joseph Hartigan. NOBAu

Field of the Grounded Arms, The. Fitz-Greene Halleck. PoEL-4

Field of Waterloo, The. Thomas Hardy. FaBoCh *Fr.* The Dynasts. (Chorus of the Years.) CMoP

Field Path. John Clare. OxBSP

Field Poem. Gary Soto. PBCAP

Field Trip. Carol Muske. WWSi

Field Trip, The. Ellen Bryant Voigt. IFJA

Field Trip. Kevin Young. GT

Field was clouded with a lilac heat, The. In The Wood. Boris Pasternak, *Russian.* LoP, *tr. by* J. M. Cowen

Field Work. Doug Cockrell. Poetsp

Field Work. Seamus Heaney. CBLP

Fieldmouse, The. Cecil Frances Alexander. CTAV; OxBChV

Fields, The. W. S. Merwin. HCAP

Fields and mountains. Naito Joso, *Japanese.* OHMPJ, *tr. by* Kenneth Rexroth

Fields and mountains turn. Ransetsu, *Japanese.* OHMPJ, *tr. by* Kenneth Rexroth

Fields are chill, The; the sparse rain has stopped. Clearing at Dawn. Li Po, *Chinese.* AWP, *tr. by* Arthur Waley

Fields are white, The. Nothing to Do. James Ephriam McGirt. AAP

Fields flame with it, endless, blue, The. Indigo. Chitra Divakaruni. OpBo

Fields from Islington to Marybone, The. William Blake. FaBoPV; OBNV *Fr.* Jerusalem; The Emanation of the Giant Albion. (Prelude: "Fields from Islington to Marybone, The.") OBNC

Fields of golden rape. May. Roger McGough. AYFP

Fields of Learning. Josephine Miles. NoAM ("Going out into the fields of learning.") LiLi (Paths.) LiLi

Fields, Teruko-san, are threshed, The. A good. The Hibakusha's Letter (1955). David Mura. OpBo

Fields Where We Slept. Muriel Rukeyser. NNaP

Fiend / Saw undelighted all delight, all kind, The. Milton. FaBoPV *Fr.* Book IV. OAEL-1 *Fr.* Paradise Lost.

Fierce and brooding holocaust of faith, The. Edgar Bowers. *Fr.* Two Poems on the Catholic Bavarians. CRP

Fierce Dream, The. Jeffrey Wainwright. DiPo

Fierce musical cries of a couple of sparrowhawks hunting on the headland, The. Birds. Robinson Jeffers. InPS-3; VGW

Fierce passions discompose the mind. Contentment. William Cowper. ChIV-2 *Fr.* Olney Hymns.

Fierce they drove on, impatient to destroy. Homer. OBVE, *tr. by* Alexander Pope *Fr.* The Iliad.

Fierce *Turnus* first to nearer distance drew. Turnus kills Pallasy. Virgil, *Latin.* OBCVT, *tr. by* John Dryden

Fierce west wind. Tune: "Remembering the Lady of Ch'in"—Loushan Pass. Mao Tse-tung, *Chinese.* SuSp, *tr. by* Eugene Eoyang

Fierce wind urges me to change into my quilted cotton gown. Strolling in the Countryside. Chao Yi, *Chinese.* SuSp, *tr. by* Chang Yin-nan *and* Lewis C. Walmsley

Fierce wrath of Solomon. The Burning of the Temple. Isaac Rosenberg. FaBoMo; PeFWW; TrJP

Fiercely the battle raged and, sad to tell. Corporal. Ambrose Bierce. APN-2; OBAL *Fr.* The Devil's Dictionary.

Fiery Declarations (two poems). Ōkuma Nobuyuki, *Japanese.* MJT, *tr. by* Makoto Ueda

Fiery palm tree in front of me, The. Today's Meditation. Antonio Machado Ruiz, *Spanish.* AF, *tr. by* Robert Bly

Fiery songs, their five long toes trembling in the soaked earth, The. (LL) Johnson's Cabinet Watched by Ants. Robert Bly. MoP; NOBA

Fiery Sun was mounted now on hight, The. Virgil. OBCVT, *tr. by* Edmund Spenser *Fr.* Virgils Gnat.

Fiery wheel without beginning. Sunflower. Tuvia Rivner, *Hebrew.* MHP, *tr. by* Ruth Finer Mintz

Fiery young fellow called Bryant, A. Barney Blackley. PeLi

Fife and Drum. Dryden. *Fr.* A Song for St Cecilia's Day [1687]. AWP; FHYEP; FaBoTw; GTBS-P; HAP; ImPo; InPS-3; NOSC; OAEL-1; OBEV; OxAEP-1; PoEL-3; SCGP; TFi

Fife Tune. John Streeter Manifold. CBAP; ImPo; InPS-3; LiTM; NBLV; NOBAu

Fifteen. Jan Freeman. OxWW *Fr.* Autumn Sequence.

Fifteen. Paula Rankin. CMAP

Fifteen Acres, The. James Stephens. BoTP

Fifteen Boys, or Perhaps Even More. Bella Akhatovna Akhmadulina, *Russian.* WPOW, *tr. by* Daniel Weissbort

Fifteen churches lie here. At Dunwich. Anthony Thwaite. MoBS

Fifteen Days of Judgment, The. Sebastian Evans. NOBVV

Fifteen foresters in the Braid alow. Johnie Cock. *Unknown.* ESPB

"Fifteen men on the dead man's chest." Derelict. Young Ewing Allison. BLPA; FaBoBe

Fifteen men on the Dead Man's Chest. Pirate Ditty. Robert Louis Stevenson. NOBVV *Fr.* Treasure Island.

Fifteen Million Plastic Bags. Adrian Mitchell. OBSV; OxBTC

Fifteen Ships on Georges Banks. *Unknown.* AmFP

Fifteen to Eighteen. Marilyn Hacker. GLP

Fifteen years ago the edict came: peace with the invader. Border Mountain Moon. Lu Yu, *Chinese.* CoBCP, *tr. by* Burton Watson

Fifteen years in the coal mine. Coal Diggin' Blues. *Unknown.* AmFP

15th Kühl-Psalm, The. Quirinus Kuhlmann, *German.* GePo, *tr. by* George C. Schoolfield

Fifteenth passes with drums and in armour, The. Centuries. Ronald Stuart Thomas. CABP

15th Raga: For Bela Lugosi. David Meltzer. *Fr.* Ragas. NeAP

Fifteenth Volume, The. Po Chü-i, *Chinese.* ChiP, *tr. by* Arthur Waley

Fifth Book. Elizabeth Barrett Browning. PEW

Fifth Choir of Angelicals. John Henry, Cardinal Newman. *See* Chorus of Angels.

Fifth day of the fifth month. Hsü Wei. CoBLCP, *tr. by* Jonathan Chaves *Fr.* Lotus.

Fifth-Floor Window, The. Lola Ridge. WPE

Fifth Grade Autobiography. Rita Dove. ISC; NIP-4

Fifth Hell, The. Jerome Rothenberg. *Fr.* The Seven Hells of Jigoku Zoshi. NNaP

Fifth month, golden plums are ripe. Evening in the Garden Clear after Rain. Ch'u Ch'uang I, *Chinese.* OHMPC

Fifth Movement: Autobiography. Louis Zukofsky. PFTM *Fr.* Poem Beginning "The."

Fifth Ode of Horace, The. Horace. *See* Odes.

Fifth Ode of Horace. Lib. I, The. Milton. PBRV

Fifth Philosopher's Song. Aldous Leonard Huxley. OBCoV

Fifth Prose. Michael Palmer. NoP-4; PmAP ("And the tribe to show you its tongue. It has only one.") (LL) FTOS

Fifth Season, The. Reg Saner. FYAP

Fifth Sense, The. Patricia Beer. MoBS

Fifth Song. Sir Philip Sidney. *Fr.* Astrophil and Stella. AAS; SiPS

Fifth Vertical Poetry. Roberto Juarroz, *Spanish.* "Emptiness of the day, The." VCWP, *tr. by* W. S. Merwin

Fifth Villancico, in Alternating Voices, Written for the Feast of the Nativity in Puebla, 1689, The. Sister Juana Inés de la Cruz, *Spanish.* "Because my Lord was born to suffer." WPoS, *tr. by* Jane Hirshfield

Fifth year of the new Son of Heaven, The. The Eclipse of the Moon. Lu T'ung, *Chinese.* PLT, *tr. by* A. C. Graham

Fifties, The. Ira Sadoff. AmPA

Fifty. Kenneth Rexroth. TAP

Fifty cents apiece. Good Hot Dogs. Sandra Cisneros. NOxBChV

Fifty Faggots. Edward Thomas. MoBrPo; PeFWW; PoWW

50–50. Langston Hughes. NOBA; NoAM; PoE; SAGP

Fifty Gunner, The. Frank A. Cross Jr. CDa

59th Light Poem: for La Monte Young and Marian Zazeela—6 November 1982. Jackson MacLow. PmAP

Fifty, not having expected to arrive here. Journey toward Evening. Phyllis McGinley. NYBP

Fifty Quatrains. "Michael Field." VWP

Fifty-six new sonnets by tomorrow night. (LL) Notes for a Sonnet. Edward Pygge. BXAP; OBCoV

Fifty thousand people uprooted by mfecane. The Mantatee Horde. Mtutuzeli Matshoba. PeSAV

Fifty times the rose has flower'd and faded. On the Jubilee of Queen Victoria. Tennyson. UnPo

Fifty wizards working in the wind. A Poem to Explain Everything about a Certain Day in Vermont. Genevieve Taggard. NYBP

Fifty Years. James Weldon Johnson. NAAAL

Fig flames inward on the bough, and I, The. The Red Mullet. Robert Penn Warren. APo

Fig for the Lower House, A. Patrick Carey. NOSC

Fig for Thee, Oh! Death, A. Edward Taylor. NAAL-1; NAAL-3

Fig for those by law protected!, A. Robert Burns. *See* Drinking Song.

Fig-tree, a falling woolshed, a filled-in well, A. Mullabinda. David Rowbotham. CBAP

Fig-trees, weird fig-trees. Bare Fig-trees. D. H. Lawrence. FaBoVe

Figgie Hobbin. Charles Causley. NOxBChV; NTP

Fight at Finnsburg, The. *Unknown, Anglo-Saxon.* EEP, *tr. by* Michael Alexander

Fight of the Red Cross Knight and the Heathen Sansjoy, The. Edmund Spenser. FHYEP; NoSic *Fr.* Wood Of Error. AEP

Fight of the Year, The. Robert McGough. OBCP

Fight thou with shafts of silver, and o'[e]rcome. Money Gets the Mastery [*or* Masterie]. Robert Herrick. CaPo

Fight to a Finish. Siegfried Sassoon. PoFWW

Fight was at its hottest, The. Rev. Andrew Brown, over the Hill to Rest. Josephine D. Henderson Heard. CBWP-4

Fight was over, and the battle won, The. An Allegory. Barcroft Henry Boake. CBAP

Fight With An Angel. Tadeusz Różewicz, *Polish*. PoSu, *tr. by* Victor Contoski

Fight your little fight, my boy. Don'ts. D. H. Lawrence. LiTM; OxBoLi; PeLV

Fighter, The. Samuel Ellsworth Kiser. BLPA

Fighter's Thoughts of Spring, A. Lê Đức Thọ, *Vietnamese*. AVP, *tr. by* Huỳnh Sanh Thông

Fighting Fire. Hamlin Garland. APN-2

Fighting in mud we turn to Thee. Prayer for Those on the Staff. Julian Grenfell. PoFWW

Fighting nature of the intellect, The. Vast Light. Richard Eberhart. CMoP

Fighting on the South Frontier. Li Po, *Chinese*. TAL, *tr. by* Robert Payne

Fighting Race, The. Joseph I. C. Clarke. BLPA

Fighting South of the Castle. *Unknown, Chinese*. AWP, *tr. by* Arthur Waley

Fighting South of the Ramparts. *Unknown, Chinese*. ChiP, *tr. by* Arthur Waley

Fights, The. Milton Acorn. MoCV; NOBC

Fights God for cursed Amalek? That hand. Meditatio Septima. Francis Quarles. ChIV-1

Figlio Maggiore. Robert Fitzgerald. NoP-4

Figmental mannequin, Turk's-head for the trap. To the Eternal Feminine. Tristan Corbière, *French*. EP, *tr. by* Carlyle Ferren MacIntyre

Figs. D. H. Lawrence. EP; OAEL-2

Figtrees. Agnes Nemes Nagy, *Hungarian*. CEEP, *tr. by* Bruce Berlind

Figure a Poem Makes, The. Jim Hall. CMAP

Figure, A/ perhaps John the Evangelist. Vision at Knock. Gerry Murphy BiHa

Figure is not anatomical, The. Limerick. Thomas Thorneley. PeLi

Figure it out for yourself, my lad. Equipment. E. A. Guest. PoToHe

Figure of Eight. Louis MacNeice. OxBSP

Figure of this world I can compare, The. The World as Garden. George Gascoigne. GaP

Figure or figures unknown. Grocery. Charles Simic. AFr

Figure out what to wear—white dress? Emily Dickinson's To-Do List. Andrea Carlisle. IFJA

Figure stood a crucifix against the door, The. Message from a Cross. Max Harris. NOBAu

Figure the hell with. Horace. *See* Ribald Romeos Less and Less Berattle ("Parcius iunctas quatiunt fenestras").

Figure who stands on the beach, A. Vincent O'Sullivan. PeNZ *Fr.* Brother Jonathan, Brother Kafka.

Figured Wheel, The. Robert Pinsky. NoAM

Figurehead, The. Léonie Adams. WPE

Figurehead, The. Maria Luisa Spaziani, *Italian*. NeIt, *tr. by* Beverly Allen

Figures, The. Robert Creeley. UnPo

Figures in a Ruined Ballroom. George Hitchcock. VGW

Figures in the fields against the sky! Poem. Antonio Machado Ruiz, *Spanish*. AWP, *tr. by* John Dos Passos

Figures of Authority. Edward Watkins. NYBP

Figures of light and dark, these two are walking. Effet de Neige. John Hollander. GS

Figures of the Human. David Ignatow. WeT

Figures on the Frieze, The. Alastair Reid. NYBP

Filaments of light. In the New Sun. Philip Levine. NNaP

File-Hewer's Lamentation, The. Joseph Mather. FaBoPV; NOEC

File into yellow candle light, fair choristers of King's. Sunday Morning, King's Cambridge. John Betjeman. PeECV

Filene's department store. Ladders. Elizabeth Alexander. FFC

Filial Republic, A. Susan Wheeler. BAP-93

Filipino Boogie. Jessica Hagedorn. UnSA

Filipino Hombre, A. *Unknown*. AS

Fill and Illumined. Joseph Ceravolo. ChIV-1

Fill High the Bowl. John Keble. NOCV

Fill me my Wine in Cristall; thus, and thus. How he would drinke his Wine. Martial, *Latin*. OBCVT, *tr. by* Robert Herrick

Fill the bowl with rosie [*or* rosy] wine. The Epicure. Abraham Cowley. BeJo; SeCP

Filled out gourd rots, the, The. Motion's Holdings. A. R. Ammons. NoAM

Filled with Emotions on the Moon-ferrying Bridge at Arashiyama. Liu Ya-tzu, *Chinese*. SuSp, *tr. by* Wu-chi Liu

Filled with the final weariness. Boris Abramovich Slutsky, *Russian*. TCRP, *tr. by* J. R. Rowland

Filled with water. Family Portrait. Tanikawa Shuntaro, *Japanese*. VCWP, *tr. by* Harold Wright

Filling an Order. John Townsend Trowbridge. OBAL

Filling her compact and delicious body. Dream Song 4. John Berryman. BoLoP; CAPP-1; ColAP; HAP; HCAP; NoP-4; OBAL; PoPoPo; VCAP *Fr.* Dream Songs.

Filling Station. Elizabeth Bishop. FaBoMo; HAP; HCAP; InPK-6; NYBP; NoP-4; VCAP; WeW-3

Filling the Gap. Lawson Fusao Inada. MoNo; OpBo

Filling the mind. The Clouds. William Carlos Williams. Poetr; VGW

Filling us with such bowels of. Sext. Donald Davie. *Fr.* Horae Canonicae. CRP

Filling you and / singing. (LL) Waiting. Jane Cooper. CrSp; NMM-2; TAP

Film Noir: Train Trip Out. Lynn Emanuel. BAP-95

(Film Noir: Train Trip Out of Metropolis.) PUP-20

Film Vermouth: Six o'Clock Show. Magda Portal, *Spanish*. PBWP, *tr. by* Allan Francovich *and* Kathleen Weaver

Filming with weak, white blossoms. (LL) Poem: "In the early evening, as now, a man is bending." Louise Glück. HCAP; Poetr

Filthy young fellow called Lawrence, A. Limerick. Bill Greenwell. PeLi

Fin, A. Bob Boldman. HA

Fin de Siècle. Edmund Vance Cooke. BLPA

Final adventure of Skinny Marcus—. Lucilius, *Greek*. GrAn, *tr. by* Peter Porter

Final Chorus. Archibald MacLeish. *Fr.* Panic. MoAmPo

Final Chorus, The. Shelley. *See* Chorus: "World's great age begins anew, The."

Final Curtain. Roger Woddis. UV

Final Curve. Langston Hughes. MBE

Final Exam. Dan Pagis, *Hebrew*. IP, *tr. by* Warren Bargad *and* Stanley F. Chyet

Final Hunger, The. Vassar Miller. LiTM

Final issues of heart and mind, The. (LL) Unbosoming. "Michael Field." CPO; VWP

Final Moments, The. Edwin John Pratt. NOBC *Fr.* The Titanic.

Final Notations. Adrienne Rich. NMM-2

Final Painting, The. Lee Harwood. SPE

Final Prayer. Enheduanna, *Sumerian*. BoWoP, *tr. by* Aliki *and* Willis Barnstone

Final Soliloquy of the Interior Paramour. Wallace Stevens. ColAP; HAP; HCAP; LCAP-2

Final Soliloquy on a Randy Rooster (in a Key of Yellow). Robert Peters. BXAP

Final Sonnet, A. Ted Berrigan. FTOS; PmAP *Fr.* The Sonnets.

Final Thing, A. Li-Young Lee. FiLi

Finale. Sue Lenier. LW

Finality broods upon the things that pass. A Walk by the Charles. Adrienne Rich. NYBP

Finally. Vittoria Aganoor Pompili, *Italian*. PBWP, *tr. by* Brenda Webster

Finally, among the bottles shining. The Lady in the Barbershop. Raphael Rudnik. NYBP

Finally, from your house there is no view. Water Island. Howard Moss. CoAP; NYBP; NoP-4

Finally, one arrives at the place. Golgotha. Andrew Lansdown. ChIV-2

Finally retired pensionless. Big Momma. Don L. Lee. BPo

Finally stays no more away. Consolation Aria. Johann Christian Günther, *German*. GePo, *tr. by* George C. Schoolfield

Finally, to forgo love is to kiss a leaf. Rescue the Dead. David Ignatow. CoAmPo; VGW; WeT

Finally to make his mind up to go home. (LL) The Prodigal. Elizabeth Bishop. ChIV-1; CoAP; LCAP-2; LiTM; NYBP; TwCP

Find. Josephine Miles. WPE

Find me, and turn thy back on heaven. (LL) Brahma. Ralph Waldo Emerson. APAD; APN-1; AWP; AmPP; ColAP; HAP; ImPo; MeMAP; NOBA, NoP-4; OBEV; OxBA; PAR; PoE; PoRA; TAP; TFi; UV; UnPo

Find out cursed policies of man. (LL) The Heart Is Deep. Roger Wolcott ChIV-1; SCAP

"Find rest in Him!" One knows the parsons' tags. Charlotte Mew. ChIV-2 *Fr.* Madeleine in Church.

Find the fair Pierides! (LL) A Garden Song. Austin Dobson. OBGa

Find their sole voice [*or* speech] in that victorious brow. (LL) Shakespeare. Matthew Arnold. EBVVPR; EPCY; FHYEP; HeIP-4; OBEV; OxAEP-2; SCGP; Son

Find they've won themselves only empty names? (LL) Poem without a Category ("The Brave man has ambitions wide as the four seas"). T'ao Ch'ien, *Chinese*. CoBCP, *tr. by* Burton Watson

Find thy body by the wall! (LL) The Last Word. Matthew Arnold. APAD; NOBE; OAEL-2; OBNC; PBMP; PFE; PoEL-5; SCGP

Find Uncle Fred's photograph. Well You Needn't. Dave Etter. SeSe

Finder, The. Robin Blaser. FTOS

Finder Found, The. Edwin Muir. PoA

Finder of a Horseshoe, The. Osip Mandelstam, *Russian*. TCRP, *tr. by* Bernard Meares

Finding, A. Ted Kooser. CMAP

Finding a Chet Baker Album in the Dimestore 2-for-$1 Pile. David Hilton. MoNo

Finding a Long Gray Hair. Jane Kenyon. LoL

Finding a Teacher. W. S. Merwin. NNaP

Finding all of the stops. (LL) San Sepolcro. Jorie Graham. HCAP; VCAP

Finding beneath the verdant Leaves a Snake. Aphra Behn. *See* The Disappointment.

Finding God's taboos totalitarian. Limerick. Basil Ransome-Davies. PeLi

Finding gold *A* left. Exchange. George Rostrevor Hamilton, *after the Greek of* Plato. FaBoEE

Finding is the first Act. Emily Dickinson. NOBA

Finding Serenity. Yüan Mei, *Chinese*. CoBLCP, *tr. by* Jonathan Chaves ("I'll ask, 'Now, really, beyond the sky, / is there another sky?'.") (LL) ChiPo, *tr. by* Jonathan Chaves

Finding the Tattooed Lady in the Garden. Pattiann Rogers. MT

Finding the Way Back. Gerald McCarthy. CDa

Finding Them Lost. Howard Moss. CoAP; NYBP

Finding this cavern. Foster Jewell. HA

Finding those beams (which I must ever love). Absence. Sir Philip Sidney. SiPS

Finds a tree of unrecorded species. Literary Excellence. Robert Harris. BMAP

Finds ways enough to ease thine heaviness. (LL) Of Money. Barnabe Googe. GEA; NBLV; NoSic; SoSe-8

Fine and Mellow. Billie Holiday. NAAAL

Fine as wine! / Life is fine! (LL) Life Is Fine. Langston Hughes. NBLV; SAmP

Fine breeze blows through the temple halls, A. Wen Cheng-ming. CoBLCP, *tr. by* Jonathan Chaves *Fr.* The Chung-i Temple.

Fine Day, A. Michael Drayton. *See* The Sixt Nimphall.

Fine day! A good sign, A. April in Town. Yury Ryashentsev, *Russian*. TCRP, *tr. by* Daniel Weissbort

Fine Day for Straw Hats, A. Louis Simpson. PBCV

Fine delight that fathers thought; the strong, The. To R. B. Gerard Manley Hopkins. CMoP; EPCY; EnVR; GTBS-P; OAEL-2; OxAEP-2

Fine evening may I have. Courtship. Rita Dove. LCAP-2

Fine feelings under blockade! Cargoes just in from Kamschatka! Winter Coming On. Martin Bell, *after the French of* Jules Laforgue. FaBoMo; OBVE; OxBTC

Fine! Fine! Isaac Rosenberg. PeFWW *Fr.* Moses.

Fine fish to net. Ezra Pound, *after the Chinese*. OBVE

Fine game is grab-bag, a fine game to see, A! Grab-Bag. Helen Hunt Jackson. OBCA

Fine, green pajama cotton, The. Size and Sheer Will. Sharon Olds. Poetr

Fine knacks for ladies, cheap, choice, brave and new! Unknown. CH; EBEV; HAP; NoP-4; NoSic; OAEL-1

Fine knacks for ladies, cheape choise brave and new. John Dowland. PBRV

Fine Line, A. Art Lange. MoNo

Fine Madam Would-Be, wherefore° should you fear. To Fine Lady Would-Be. Ben Jonson. FaBoEE; NOSC; NoP-4; OxBSP

Fine merry franions. Going or Gone. Charles Lamb. BXAP

Fine Old English Gentleman, The. *Unknown*. CH

Fine Old English Gentleman; New Version, The. Charles Dickens. NOBVV; OBSV

Fine rain, gentle thunder. Tune: "Full River Red"—A Four-season Song on the Hardships and Joys of Farming Life. Cheng Hsieh, *Chinese*. SuSp, *tr. by* Irving Y. Lo

Fine romance! with no kisses!, A. Dorothy Fields. OBCoV

Fine view, but I'm still getting thinner. Tune: "Pleasure of Returning to the Fields: A Prelude." Huang T'ing-chien, *Chinese*. SuSp, *tr. by* James J. Y. Liu

Fine weather since yesterday. Han Yü. PLT, *tr. by* A. C. Graham *Fr.* The South Mountains.

Fine will be the day. (LL) If bees stay at home. *Unknown*. OxNR

Fine Young Folly. William Habington. *See* Pretty Sport.

Fine youth Ciprius is more terse and neat, The. Sir John Davies. NoSic *Fr.* Epigrams.

Fineness of midnight. Midnight. Gabriela Mistral, *Spanish*. BoWoP, *tr. by* David Garrison

Finesse be first, whose elegance deplores. Six Poets in Search of a Lawyer. Donald Hall. NYBP

Fingal's Weeping. Neil Munro. NSI

Finger Folk. H. M. Tharp. BoTP

Finger-nails. Paolo Buzzi, *Italian*. PFTM, *tr. by* Felix Stefanile

Finger of death touched me, The. He Is Gone. Anna Swirszczynska, *Polish*. PoSu, *tr. by* Czeslaw Milosz *and* Leonard Nathan

Finger Play. *Unknown*. BoTP; CTAV

Finger Play for a Snowy Day, A. *Unknown*. BoTP

Fingernail Sunrise. Vernon Watkins. NYBP

Fingerprints. Jaroslav Seifert, *German*. CEEP, *tr. by* Ewald Osers

Fingers lie in the lap, The. Year's End. Ellen Bryant Voigt. NoAM

Fingers probe. Claire Malroux, *French*. VCWP, *tr. by* Marilyn Hacker

Fingers / slowly opening. (LL) The Needle: For a Friend Who Disappeared. Franz Wright. CMAP; OPOU

Fingers smelling always of onions. (LL) I Am Becoming My Mother. Lorna Goodison. GT; OPOU

Finigan's Wake. *Unknown*. *See* Finnegan's Wake.

Finis. Basho, *Japanese*. EP, *tr. by* Nobuyuki Yuasa

FINIS. (LL) The Day of Doom. Michael Wigglesworth. NAAL-1; SCAP

Finished. Kate Llewellyn. NOBAu

Finished Gentleman, A. Geoffrey Dutton. NOBAu

Finished Man, A. Richard Wilbur. AFr

Finistére. Thomas Kinsella. PBCIP

Finite Intuition. Milo De Angelis, *Italian*. NeIt, *tr. by* Lawrence Venuti

Finnegans Wake. James Joyce.
   Ballad of Persse O'Reilly, The. CBNP; PeLV
   Ondt and the Gracehoper, The. BIrV

Finnegan's Wake. *Unknown*. CBNP; NBLV
   (Finigan's Wake.) BLPA

Finnes and Laplands are acquainted well, The. Thomas Heywood. OxBSn *Fr.* Hierarchie of the Blessed Angells.

Finnesburh Fragment, The. *Unknown, Anglo-Saxon*. ASW; OBWP, *tr. by* Kevin Crossley-Holland

Finnigin to Flannigan. Strickland W. Gillilan. FaBoBe

Finn's Wishes. Desmond O'Grady, *Irish*. CIP-2, *tr. by the author*

Fire. William Carpenter. Poetsp

Fire. Amiya Chakravarty, *Bengali*. OMIP, *tr. by* Sujit Mukherjee

Fire, The. Robert Creeley. NOBA

Fire. Fazil Hüsnü Daglarca. CRP

Fire, The. Robert Duncan. APSN; VGW *Fr.* Passages.

Fire. Langston Hughes. NOBA

Fire. Mark O'Connor. NOBAu

Fire. Luis J. Rodriguez. UnSA

Fire. Ann Taylor. NOxBChV

Fire. Dorothy, Duchess of Wellington Wellesley. OBMV

Fire alight / in the other window as it. Open Air Where. Larry Eigner. PmAP

Fire and Ice. Robert Frost. AmPP; CMoP; EBEvV; FaBoEE; HeIP-4; HoPM; InPK-6; LiTM; MoAmPo; MoP; NAAL-2; NOBA; NoAM; PFE; OxBA; Poetr; RaBo; SoSe-8; TAP; TFi
   ("Is also great / And would suffice.") (LL) ColAP

Fire and sword with ease subdues. (LL) Beauty. Thomas Stanley, *after the Greek of* Anacreon. AWP; OBVE

Fire at Alexandria, The. Theodore Weiss. NoAM; PoA; SAmP; TAP

Fire-Bringer, The. William Vaughn Moody.
   Pandora Speaks.

Fire burns bright on my hearth to-night, The. The Fire Guest. George Alfred Townsend. PWR

Fire Burns Low, The. John Leax. TrCP

Fire darkens, the wood turns black, The. Song for the Sun That Disappeared behind the Rainclouds. *Hottentot Oral Tradition*. ChAP; TTTS; TTY, *tr. by* Ulli Beier

Fire-Dragon and the Treasure, The. *Unknown*. AnOE, *tr. by* Charles W. Kennedy. *Fr.* Beowulf. OAEL-1, *tr. by* Charles W. Kennedy; ASW, *tr. by* Kevin Crossley-Holland

Fire falls, the night, The. Summer Is a Poem by Ovid. Douglas G. Jones. NIP-4

Fire Fetched Down, The. George Bradley. BAP-94

Fire, fire. Song. Henry Bold. GBL

Fire! Fire! said [*or* says] the town crier. *Unknown*. OxNR

Fire-flies come stagg'ring down the dark, The. Paul Laurence Dunbar. *See* A Summer's Night.

Fire-fly, fire-fly, light me to bed. Chant to the Fire-Fly. *Unknown, Ojibwa Native American*. APN-2, *tr. by* Henry Rowe Schoolcraft

Fire Guest, The. George Alfred Townsend. PWR

Fire, Hair, Meat and Bone. Fred Johnson. PoBA

Fire high up in air, The. A Bird's Song. Dame Edith Sitwell. NALW

Fire I praise was once perduring flame, The. Allen Tate. PoA *Fr.* Sonnets of the Blood.

Fire in leaf and grass, The. Living. Denise Levertov. BLT; OPOU; VGW; WPE

Fire in my meditation burned. Henry Ainsworth. AH; ChIV-1

Fire in the heavens, and fire along the hills. Christopher John Brennan. CBAP; NOBAu *Fr.* The Quest of Silence.

Fire in the Hole. Gary Snyder. NAAL-2

Fire in the olive groves throughout the night. Vineta. Charles Spear. PeNZ

Fire in the Snow, The. Vernon Watkins. LiTM

Fire in the Stone, The. Tuvia Rivner, *Hebrew.* MHP, *tr. by* Ruth Finer Mintz

Fire is burning clear and blithely, The. The Darkened Mind. James Russell Lowell. NCAP

Fire is out, and spent the warmth thereof, The. Dregs. Ernest Christopher Dowson. OBMV; SAGP

Fire is out, the house dark, The. (LL) The Nurse's Lament. Mary Elizabeth Coleridge. NOBVV; OxBSP

Fire is passing up through the soles of my feet!, A. (LL) Evolution from the Fish. Robert Bly. MoP; NOBA; NoAM

Fire Island. May Swenson. PoA; TAP

Fire-kindled satellite. Napkin and Stone. Vernon Watkins. NYBP

Fire-mist and a planet, A. Each in His Own Tongue. William Herbert Carruth. BLPA

Fire more priceless than diamonds rare. The Father's Love. Mary E. Tucker. CBWP-1

Fire Music. Drew Gardner. PT

Fire of Drift-Wood, The. Henry Wadsworth Longfellow. APN-1; AmPP; MeMAP; NAAL-1; NAAL-3; NCAP; NOBA; OxBA; TAP

Fire of Frendraught, The. *Unknown.* ESPB; OxBB

Fire of Meditation burns, The. A Præfatory Poem to the Little Book, Entituled, Christianus per Ignem. Nicholas Noyes. SCAP

Fire of our victims, The. The Knell. Muhammad Al-Faituri, *Arabic.* TTY, *tr. by* Samir M. Zoghby

Fire: On earth there's a warrior of curious origin. Cynewulf. ASW, *tr. by* Kevin Crossley-Holland *Fr.* Riddles (Exeter Book).

Fire on the Hills. Robinson Jeffers. CMoP; RaBo

Fire Parcel. Peter Kostakis. MoNo

Fire Poem, The. Theodore Enslin. CRP

Fire-Queen. Ruth Fainlight. PoA

Fire rides calmly in the air. At War. Charles Madge. FaBoMo

Fire Seven Times Tried This, The. Shakespeare. CTC *Fr.* The Merchant of Venice.

Fire shimmied & reached up. Temples of Smoke. Yusef Komunyakaa. NAmP90

Fire Side, The; a Pastoral Soliloquy. Isaac Hawkins Browne. NOEC *Fr.* The Foundling Hospital for Wit.

Fire station's delight, The. Susan Hampton. NOBAu

Fire Support Burk. Steve Denning. CDa

Fire that cancels all that is. Burning Love Letters. Howard Moss. HoPM

Fire the Babysitter. David Avidan, *Hebrew.* IP, *tr. by* Warren Bargad *and* Stanley F. Chyet

Fire the heather. Joseph Gordon MacLeod. *Fr.* Men of the Rocks. OxBS

Fire, the lamp, and I, were alone together, The. Mary Elizabeth Coleridge. VWP

Fire: The People. Alfred Corn. NAAL-2; VCAP *Fr.* A Call in the Midst of the Crowd.

Fire the river that is to say, the. Brush-Fire. U Tam'si Tchicaya, *French.* NegPo, *tr. by* Sangodare Akanji

Fire, the rope, the bullet, and the ax, The. Nikolai Semionovich Tikhonov, *Russian.* TCRP, *tr. by* Michael Frayn

Fire threatens, The. The Hyena Addressing Her Young Ones. *Unknown, Hottentot.* PeSAV, *tr. by* W. H. I. Bleek

Fire to see my wrongs for anger burneth, The. The Wronged Lover. Sir Philip Sidney. SiPS *Fr.* Arcadia.

Fire-Truck, A. Richard Wilbur. AiP

Fire Us with Ice, Burn Us with Snow. Mary Monk. LW

Fire was furry as a bear, The. Dark Song. Dame Edith Sitwell. CMoP; FaBoTw; PBWP

Fire, water, woman, are man's ruin! A Dutch Proverb. Matthew Prior. FaBoEE; NOEC; OBCoV

Fire will not ask me to make its bed, The. Asseverations. Arthur Nortje. HBAPE

Fire, with well-dried logs supplied, The. Sir Walter Scott. OBCP

Fire within fire, desire in deity. (LL) The Kiss. D. G. Rossetti. NOBVV; Son

Firebell for Peace. Joyce Lee. NOBAu

Fireblade / Flame scimitar's cutting edge. Suncoming. Oliver La Grone. NBV

Firebombers, The. Anne Sexton. SAGP

Firebombing, The. James Dickey. CAPP-1; OBWP

Firebowl. Sydney Clouts. PeSAV

Firebrand. Harry Crosby. SPE

Firebreathers at the Café Deux Magots, The. Miller Williams. MT

Firecrackers sounding like shots of handguns rattle. A Late Fourth. John Hollander. AFr

Fired Pot, The. Anna Wickham. FaBoTw; FaBoWP; LW; OxBTC

Fired up over the chess, cards, poems. Having Led a Charmed Life, He Had to be Hanged Twice. Mac Wellman. FTOS

Fireflies. Faustin Charles. PBCV

Fireflies. Paul Fleischman. NOxBChV

Fireflies [*or* Fire-flies] come stagg'ring down the dark, The. (LL) A Summer's Night. Paul Laurence Dunbar. APN-2

Fireflies float noiseless. Canicula. Mary Kinzie. FFC

Fireflies in the Garden. Robert Frost. OxBSP; SAmP

Fireflies' light, The. Chine-Jo, *Japanese.* WPJ, *tr. by* Kenneth Rexroth *and* Ikuko Atsumi

Fireflies throw. May Swenson. APo

Firefly. Elizabeth Madox Roberts. NTCP

Firefly, airplane, satellite, star—. Back Yard, July Night. William Cole. KaS

Firefly light. Summer. Ramona Wilson. VoR

Fire-light. Homer. *See* Night Piece: the Trojans outside Troy.

Firelight. Edwin Arlington Robinson. NoAM

Firelight. John Greenleaf Whittier. *Fr.* Snow-Bound [*or* Snow-Bound; a Winter Idyl]. APN-1; AiP; AmPP; NAAL-3; NOBA; OxBA; TAP; TFi

Firelight in sunlight, silver-pale. The Marriage of Heaven and Earth. Howard Nemerov. NYBP

Fireman Save My Child. *Unknown. See* No More Booze.

Firemen, The. James Keir Baxter. NOxBChV

Firemen, firemen! Help! X. J. Kennedy. CA

Fireplace, The. Michael S. Harper. GT

Fires. Elizabeth Fleming. BoTP

Fires / Burn in my heart. Kenneth Rexroth. APSN *Fr.* The Love Poems of Marichiko.

Fire's here, that won't be forgotten. Log. David Bromige. FTOS

Fires in Illinois. John James Piatt. APN-2

Fires in the fall! (LL) Autumn Fires. Robert Louis Stevenson. NOxBChV; NTP

Fires in the Mirror. Anna Deavere Smith.
    Roslyn Malamud the Coup. OxWW

Firestone. David Rivard. PBCAP

Firewing. Breyten Breytenbach, *Afrikaans.* VCWP, *tr. by* Ernst van Heerden

Firewood, iron-ware, and cheap tin trays. (LL) Cargoes. John Masefield. CABP; CMoP; EBEvV; FaPoR; InPK-6; LiTM; MoBrPo; NOBE; OBEV; OBMV; PoRA; TFi

Fireworks. Yohan Chu, *Korean.* CKP, *tr. by* Jaihiun Kim

Fireworks. Babette Deutsch. NYBP; Poetr

Fireworks. Valerie Worth. NTCP

Fireworks explode like thunderclaps all over Chungking. On Hearing the News of the Japanese Surrender. Liu Ya-tzu, *Chinese.* SuSp, *tr. by* Wu-chi Liu

Firing back at my heavy heart. Aleksandr Rudolfovich Gangnus, *Russian.* TCRP, *tr. by* Bradley Jordan

Firm and well-fixed foundation. Robert Herrick. *See* The Pillar of Fame.

Firm as young bones, fine as blown spume, still. Paradigm. Babette Deutsch. TrJP

Firm Belief. *Unknown.* PoToHe

Firm of Happiness, Limited, The. Norman Cameron. FaBoTw

Firmament breaks up. In black eclipse, The. A Word for the Hour. John Greenleaf Whittier. NCAP

Firmament Displays on High, The. Barend Toerien, *Afrikaans.* PeSA, *tr. by the author*

Firmament Doth Shake, The. Ken Edwards. NBrP

Firmly, sweetly, / refusing. Portrait of a Woman (and a Man). John Figueroa. PBCV

Firmness. Anthony Hecht. OBAL

Firs / born Xmas day. Christopher Reid. FaBoVe *Fr.* Memres of Alfred Stoker.

First, The. Grace Cavalieri. UnSA

First / A far thud. Fireworks. Valerie Worth. NTCP

First a monkey, then a man. Dawn of the Space Age. John Ciardi. OBAL

First a razor then a fact. (LL) Fifth Prose. Michael Palmer. NoP-4; PmAP

First a sea: soft sands, muds, and marls. What Happened Here Before. Gary Snyder. APSN; NNaP; PoM

First a terror of choice, but that was done. I Had a Terror—Since September. Gerald William Barrax. MT

First Actor to Hamlet. Ivan V. Lalic, *Serbo-Croatian*. HSix, *tr. by* Charles Simic

First Adventurer for her fame I stand, The. Prologue. Delariviere Manley. KTR *Fr. The Lost Lover.*

First Aid at 4 A.M. Christopher Bursk. InPK-6

First Americans, The. (LL) When Something Happens. James A. Randall Jr. SSLK

First Anniversary [*or* Anniversarie], The. Donne. NAEL-1 *Fr. Anatomy [or Anatomie] of the World, An[: The First Anniversary].*

"And new philosophy calls all in doubt." NOSC

First Anniversary of the Government under O.C, The. Andrew Marvell.

"'Is this, saith one, the Nation that we read'." PBRV

First, April, she with mellow show[e]rs. The Four Sweet Months. Robert Herrick. AYFP; BoTP

First, are you our sort of a person? The Applicant. Sylvia Plath. NAAL-2; NOBA; PoPoPo; TwCP

First, at a window of the vacant house. The Windows. Chris Wallace-Crabbe. BMAP

First Atlantic Telegraph, The. Jones Very. NCAP

First Attempt in Rhyme, A. Thomas Hood. OBCoV

First Autumn Night. Katie Donovan. BiHa

First beginning was Sellinger's Round, The. *Unknown*. CBNP

First Birth, The. Rodney Jones. MT

First blossom was the best blossom, The. Apple Blossom. Louis MacNeice. NTP; PeECV; RB

First blow caught me sideways, my jaw, The. The Beating. Ann Stanford. SoSe-8; WPE

First Book, The. Rita Dove. LoL

First Book: Young Aurora's Fostermother. Elizabeth Barrett Browning. PEW *Fr. Aurora Leigh.* VWP

("Bring the clean water, give out the fresh seed.") (LL) PEW

First-born, The. Jack Davis. BMAP

First born of Chaos, who so fair didst come. Hymn: To Light. Abraham Cowley. MeLP; OxAEP-1

First Boyfriend. Sharon Olds. DeD

First calls of the migrant geese, no more cicadas. Li Shang-yin. PLT, *tr. by* A. C. Graham *Fr. The Lady in the Moon.*

First came the primrose. A Chanted Calendar. Sydney Thompson Dobell. BoTP; OBEV *Fr. Balder.*

First Canzone of the Convito, The. Dante, *Italian*. OBVE, *tr. by* Shelley

First Carolina Said-Song. A. R. Ammons. OBAL

First cat that was ever killed by Care, The. (LL) New England. Edwin Arlington Robinson. HeIP-4; MeMAP; MoAmPo; NAAL-2; NOBA; OxBA; PoPoPo; TAP

First Chance Twice. Fanny Howe. FTOS

First chap to fuck little Sophie, The. Limerick. Victor Gray. PeLi

First Child, Born Out of Breach in Mid-May. Sherod Santos. *Fr. The Sheltering Ground.* Son

First—Chill—then Stupor—then the letting go—. (LL) After great pain a formal feeling comes—. Emily Dickinson. APN-2; AmPP; BoWoP; HAP; HeIP-4; IMW; InPS-3; MoAmPo; NAAL-1; NAAL-3; NALW; NAWM-2; NIP-4; NOBA; NoAM; NoP-4; OxWW; PAR; PFE; PoE; PoPoPo; Poetr; SAGP; SAmP; TAP; TFi; TRP; UnPo

First Circle, The. Kofi Awoonor. HBAPE; PBMAP; VCWP

First Circle, The. S. K. Kelen. BMAP

First Claims Poem. Victor Hernandez Cruz. NBV

First clan of autumn, thistleball on a stem. Thistledown. James Merrill. UnPo

First cold rain. Basho, *Japanese*. TTTS, *tr. by* Kenneth Koch *and* Harold Henderson

First colour? Just like a captive, The. Three-Coloured Banner. János Pilinszky, *Hungarian*. PoSu, *tr. by* Peter Jay

First come I. My name is Jowett. Henry Charles Beeching. FaBoEE; NOBL; PeLV *Fr. Balliol Rhymes.*

First comes the logic of substitution. The Secret Life of Gilbert Bond. Joan Retallack. FTOS

First Confession. X. J. Kennedy. CoAmPo

First Corinthians. Bible, *N.T.*

Greatest of These, The.

First Corinthians at the Crossroads. Bruce Dawe. NoAM

First country to die was normal in the evening, The. The Last War. Kingsley Amis. OBSV; OxBC; SAGP

First cries were, The. Mother Poem. Joel Oppenheimer. PoM

First Cycle of Love Poems. George Barker.

My Joy, My Jockey, My Gabriel. MoBrPo

1st Dance—Making Things New—6 February 1964. Jackson MacLow. FTOS; PmAP

First Date, The. David Avidan. *Fr. Samson, Our Hero.* IP, *tr. by* Warren Bargad *and* Stanley F. Chyet

First dawn comes, The. *Unknown, Japanese*. OHMPJ, *tr. by* Kenneth Rexroth

First Day, The. Christina Rossetti. BoLoP; FaBoBe; GBL; GLoP *Fr. Monna Innominata.* BWW

("I wish I could remember that first day.") LBC; LW; LoP

(Sonnet.) LW

First Day, The. Elizabeth Spires. PUP-20

First Day at School. Roger McGough. NOxBChV

First day he had gone, The. A Space in the Air. Jon Silkin. TrJP

First day he was travelling in Asia, The. The Shape-Changer. Chris Wallace-Crabbe. NOBAu

First day I shot dope, The. Summer Words of [*or* for] a Sistuh [*or* Sister] Addict. Sonia Sanchez. BPo; BlSi; NAAL; UnPo

First day of Christmas, The. The Twelve Days of Christmas. *Unknown*. AmFP; OxBoLi; OxNR; PChr

First day of false spring, I hit the street, The. Green Market, New York. Julia Kasdorf. LoHo

First day of kindergarten I slice my four-years' thumb. Susans. Susan Clements. UnSA

First day of May Jack. Poem. Tony Baker. NBrP

First Day of School, The. Tru'o'ng Anh Thụy, *Vietnamese*. AVP, *tr. by* Huỳnh Sanh Thông

First Day of Spring, The. Pien Kung, *Chinese*. CoBLCP, *tr. by* Jonathan Chaves

First Day of the Hunting Moon, The. Patricia Low. VGW

First day of the week he spoke to them, The. Eutychus. Rosemary Dobson. ChIV-2

First day of this month I saw. Snowdrops. George MacBeth. OBCP

First day she passed up and down through the Heavens, The. Petrarch. OBMV *Fr. Sonnets to Laura.*

First day the Germans came into the city, The. Massacres. Charles Reznikoff. APSN

First-Day Thoughts. John Greenleaf Whittier. APN-1; AmPP; TrCP

First daylight on the bittersweet-hung. Meridian. Amy Clampitt. GEA

First Daylight Song. *Unknown*. APN-2, *tr. by* Washington Matthews *Fr. The Mountain Chant.*

First Days, The. James Wright. *See* Mantova.

First Day's Night had come, The. Emily Dickinson. ImPo; LiTM; NCAP; OxBA; PoE; TRP; WPOW

First days of spring—the sky. Ryokan, *Japanese*. EnlH, *tr. by* Stephen Mitchell

First Death. Donald Justice. IMW; MT

First Death in Nova Scotia. Elizabeth Bishop. CoAP; FaBoWP; LCAP-2; NOBA; NYBP

First Did I Fear. Giles, the Elder Fletcher. Son *Fr. Licia.*

First Dimension of Skunk, The. Ray A. Young Bear. HATNAP

First Dream. Sister Juana Inés de la Cruz, *Spanish*.

"But Venus first." BoWoP

First Drift. Ron Padgett. FTOS

First drum roll—and he's a coil of air, limbs in all directions, he, The. Acrobatics. Dan Pagis, *Hebrew*. IP, *tr. by* Warren Bargad *and* Stanley F. Chyet

First Duino Elegy, The. Rilke, *German*. PFTM, *tr. by* J. B. Leishman *and* Stephen Spender *Fr. Duino Elegies.*

("Emptiness first / felt the vibration that now charms us and comforts and helps?") (LL) PFTM, *tr. by* J. B. Leishman *and* Stephen Spender

("Who, if I cried, would hear me among the angelic orders?") PFTM, *tr. by* J. B. Leishman *and* Stephen Spender

First Early Mornings Together. Robert Pinsky. ColAP

First Elegy for the Dead in Cyrenaica. Hamish Henderson. OxBS

First enters wearing the neon armour, The. Ten Types of Hospital Visitor. Charles Causley. OxBC

First (entitled to the place), The. Charles Churchill. OBSV *Fr. The Duellist.*

First Epistle of the First Book of Horace Imitated, The. Horace, *Latin*. Profiteers. ECEV, *tr. by* Alexander Pope.

First Epistle of the Second Book of Horace, Imitated, The. Horace, *Latin*.

"But for the wits of either Charles's days." EPCY, *tr. by* Alexander Pope

"Milton's strong pinion now not heaven can bound." EPCY

"Of little use the man you may suppose." EBEV, *tr. by* Alexander Pope.

"Our rural Ancestors, with little blest." OBCVT, *tr. by* Alexander Pope

"Shakespeare (whom you and every playhouse bill)." EPCY

"We conquered France, but felt our captive's charms." EPCY

"Who now reads Cowley? if he pleases yet." EPCY

First Farewell to J.G.G. "Ephelia." LW; NOSC

("Except you'l think of her you left behind.") (LL) LW

First, feel, then feel, then. Young Soul. Imamu Amiri Baraka. BPo

First few wounds are nearly invisible, The. Shooting a Farmhouse. Ted Kooser. PBCAP

First Fig. Edna St. Vincent Millay. APAD; AiP; ChAP; EBEvV; FaBoWP; NALW; NoAM; NoP-4; PoA; PoLF; TAP

First fight. Then fiddle. Ply the slipping string. Gwendolyn Brooks. InPK-6; NIP-4; PFE; Poetr *Fr.* The Children of the Poor. WPE, *sect.* I, *pt.* 1-2; PoA, *sect.* I, *pt.* 1-3; NAAAL *Fr.* The Womanhood.

First flakes of winter seen through glass. Lyric. T. Alan Broughton. CMAP

First flower grows as high as the sunshine, The. Flowers. Edith Jay Scovell. WPN

First follow Nature, and your judgment frame. Alexander Pope. EPCY; FHYEP; HAP *Fr.* An Essay on Criticism. NAEL-1; PoEL-3; TFi ("Are Nature still, but Nature methodized.") (LL) HAP

First, for effusions due unto the dead. Upon His Sister-in-Law, Mistress Elizabeth Herrick. Robert Herrick. CaPo

First forget what time it is. Exercise. W. S. Merwin. NOBA

First form your artful looks with studious care. The Art of Coquetry. Charlotte Lennox. ECWP; LW *Fr.* The Art of Coquetry.

First Friday bell shatters the morning. Anson Gonzalez. HCP

First fruits from her fruitful bed, The. Dioscorides, *Greek.* GrAn, *tr. by* Peter Whigham

First full moon of overgrown buffalo. America's Wounded Knee. Phillip William George. VoR

First Gathering. Eleanor Farjeon. AYFP

First Grade. Phillip William George. VoR

First Grade. William Stafford. PiM

First Grey Hair, The. Mary E. Tucker. CBWP-1

First Grief, The. Felicia Dorothea Hemans. *See* The Child's First Grief.

First having read the book of myths. Diving into the Wreck. Adrienne Rich. ColAP; HCAP; HelP-4; InPK-6; InPS-3; MoP; NAAL-2, NALW, NIP-4; NOBA; NoAM; NoP-4; OxWW; PoPoPo; Poetr

First he gave me / his heart. It was. Pomegranate. Louise Glück. NMM-2

First hear the story of Kaspar the rosy-cheeked. Fräulein Reads Instructive Rhymes. Maxine W. Kumin. NYBP; Poetsp

First horn lifts its arm over the dew-lit grass, The. The House Slave. Rita Dove. NoAM

First hot night, The. Anita Virgil. HA

First Hymn to Lenin. "Hugh MacDiarmid." FaBoTC

First I looked on, after a long time far from home, The. American Change. Allen Ginsberg. HCAP

First I lowered my head. A Woman's Song, about Men. *Unknown, Eskimo into French.* STP, *tr. by* Paul-Emile Victor; *English vers. by* Armand Schwerner

First I saw the white bear, then I saw the black;. At the Zoo. William Makepeace Thackeray. CTAV; NTCP; OxBChV

First, I want to make you come in my hand. Noces. Marilyn Hacker. DeD *Fr.* Love, Death and the Changing of the Seasons.

First I went down to the street. A Ballad of Going Down to the Store. Miron Bialoszewski, *Polish.* BLT, *tr. by* Czeslaw Milosz

First I would have a face exactly fair. How to Choose a Mistress. Edmond Prestwich. NOSC

First, I would have her be beautiful. Selecting a Reader. Ted Kooser. PBCAP

First idea was man walking through space in a tower, The. For the New World. Edward Hirsch. WWSi

First Impressions. Alfred Grant Walton. PoToHe

First in a carriage. *Unknown.* OxNR

First in his pride the orient sun's display. Hilaire Belloc. FaBoEE

First in the North. The black sea-tangle beaches. The Mythical Journey. Edwin Muir. NoAM; OxBS

First indication was this repeated tic, the latch jigging and clicking, The. Asylum. Ciaran Carson. PNI

First inkling I had of the beast's agony, The. An Abortion. Liz Lochhead. NBrP

First inroads were made in our 19-aughts. Contemporary Culture and the Letter "K." Alfred Corn. PNI

First Invasion of Ireland, The. *Unknown, Irish.* BIrV, *tr. by* John Montague

First is a park, The. A Four-Light Window. Agnes Nemes Nagy, *Hungarian.* VCWP, *tr. by* Hugh Maxton

First it was only an imperceptible quivering of the skin. The Divorce. Hans Magnus Enzensberger, *German.* OxBM

First king was Pharamond, The; after him came. Kings of France. Mary W. Lincoln. BLPA

First know, my friend, I do not mean. Matthew Green. ECEV; NOEC *Fr.* The Spleen.

First lady of the throne room, The. The Restoration of Enheduanna to Her Former Station. Enheduanna, *Sumerian.* BoWoP, *ad. by* Aliki *and* Willis Barnstone

First Lawcase, The. *Unknown, Irish.* BIrV, *tr. by* John Montague

First Lay of Gudrun, The. *Unknown.* AWP, *tr. by* William Morris *and* Eirikr Magnusson. *Fr.* The Elder Edda.
Gudrun Laments over Sigurd. OBVE

First Lesson. Philip Booth. TwCP

First Lessons. Marilyn Chin. LoHo

First let me show you with the pointer. Map. Martin Sorescu, *Romanian.* VCWP, *tr. by* Longley, Michael and Joana Russell-Gebbett

First, let me view what noxious nonsense reigns. Richard Savage. OBSV *Fr.* The Authors of the Town.

First Letter from Tamara A. Reiner Kunze, *German.* PoSu, *tr. by* Ewald Osers

First Letter to an Irish Novelist. Roy McFadden. PNI

First Letter to the Corinthians, The. *Bible, N.T.*
"Though I speak in the tongues of men or of angels: if I have no love, I am." ITG, *tr. by* Stephen Mitchell

First Light. Thomas Kinsella. BIrV; CMoP; PoE

First Limick. Ogden Nash. PeLi

First line of a poem, The. How to Read the First Line. Gabriel Preil, *Yiddish.* CEEP, *tr. by* Laya Firestone

First Lord's Song, The. Sir William Schwenck Gilbert. PeLV *Fr.* H. M. S. Pinafore.

First Love. Thomas Campion. GBL; OxBoLi

First Love. John Clare. BoLoP; EnLoPo; GBL; GLoP; HAP; NOBVV; NoP-4; PoPoPo; Ro

First Love. Mary Dorcey. BrRo

First Love. Judith Hemschemeyer. Poetsp

First Love. Elizabeth Jennings. LW

First Love. Sharon Olds. FYAP

First Love. Jean Valentine. NMM-2

First love is first death. There is no other. The Sequel. Delmore Schwartz. LiTM

First Maccabees. Bible, Apocrypha.
Dirge: "Her house is become like a man dishonored." TrJP
Great Mourning. TrJP
Judas Maccabeus. TrJP

First Madrigal. Anna Swirszczynska, *Polish.* CEEP, *tr. by* Magnus J. Krynski *and* Robert A. Maguire

First, make a letter like a monument. The Book of Kells. Padraic Colum. BIrV; IIP

First man—you are his child, he is your child, The. Song of the Flood. *Unknown, Navajo Indian.* TTTS

First Meditation. Theodore Roethke. LCAP-2; NOBA *Fr.* Meditations of an Old Woman.

First Meetings. Arseny Aleksandrovich Tarkovsky, *Russian.* TCRP, *tr. by* Albert C. Todd

First melt, The. Michael McClintock. HA

First Memory. Louise Glück. PiM

First Men on Mercury, The. Edwin Morgan. CBNP; PeLV; SpW
("You'll remember Mercury.") (LL) FaBoTC

First Merseburg Spell. *Unknown, German.* GePo, *tr. by* Carroll Hightower

First Monday Scottsboro Alabama. Tom Weatherly. PoBA

First Month: at Ch'ung-jang House. Li Shang-yin, *Chinese.* PLT, *tr. by* A. C. Graham

First month dawn. Auspice. Brooks Haxton. CMAP

First month of his absence, The. Song (On Seeing Dead Bodies Floating Off the Cape). Alun Lewis. LiTM; NAEL-2; NoP-4; OBWP

First month of winter: cold air comes. *Unknown, Chinese. Fr.* Nineteen Old Poems of the Han. CoBCP, *tr. by* Burton Watson

First morning after anyone's death, is it important, The. Thomas Hardy. Norman Dubie. LCAP-2

First morning of Three Mile Island: those first disquieting, uncertain, mystifying hours, The. Tar. Charles Kenneth Williams. VCAP

First Movement. Padraic Fiacc. PNI

First Murderer, The. Bible, O.T. OxBoV *Fr.* Genesis.

First-name-only business beggars history, The. Larkin. Gibbons Ruark. DiPo

First Necessity, A. (LL) Faith—is the Pierless Bridge. Emily Dickinson. AmPP; NCAP

First Nemæan Ode of Pindar, The. Pindar, *Greek.*
"How *early* has young *Chromius* begun." OBCVT, *tr. by* Abraham Cowley

First Night, A. Peter Kane Dufault. DiPo; NoP-4

First Night. Michael Hofmann. CBLP

First night. San Juan: 1979. Cheryl Clarke. CPO

First night God created was too weak, The. Reunion with a Ghost. Ai. DeD

First night, the first night, The. Carol for the Last Christmas Eve. Norman Nicholson. NOxBChV; OBCP

First night when I came home, The. Our Goodman. *Unknown.* AmFP; OBAL

First night you were gone. Place, Places. Melvin Dixon. ISC

1st. No other God exists than Mighty Me. Ten New Commandments. Robert Greacen. PeLV

First nobody liked us; they said we smelled. American Dream: First Report. Joseph Papaleo. UnSA

First Nowell the angel did say, The. *Unknown.* PChr

First Ode of the Fourth Book of Horace, The. Horace, *Latin.* OBCVT, *tr. by* Alexander Pope

First of all do you remember the way a bear goes through. Destruction. Joanne Kyger. BLT

First of all it has to be anecdotal; ideas don't exist. The Canadian Prairies View of Literature. David Donnell. NOBC

"First of all, it's all true." Creation. Simon J. Ortiz. CDW; ColAP; HATNAP

First of all, it's being nine years old and. What It's Like to Be a Black Girl (For Those of You Who Aren't). Patricia Smith. UnSA

First of all my dreams was of, The. E. E. Cummings. NYBP; VGW

First of all people was Adam, The. Moira Blyth. PeLi

First of all / the old icon clears its throat. Waking Up. Jerzy Harasymowicz, *Polish.* CEEP, *tr. by* Victor Contoski

First of April, some do say, The. All Fools' Day. *Unknown.* AYFP; BoTP; CTV

First of August. A. J. Seymour. PBCV

First of August in Jamaica, The. Joshua McCarter Simpson. AAP

First of Autumn, The. Meng Hao Jan, *Chinese.* SuSp, *tr. by* Paul W. Kroll

First of God by whom all grace is spread. Sources of Good Counsel. Peter Idley. OxBChV

First of May, The. *Unknown.* ReMoGo

First of May, The. Masaoka Shiki, *Japanese.* MJT, *tr. by* Ueda, Makoto

First of summer, lovely sight. *Unknown.* NOIV

First of that train which cursed the wave. To the First Slave Ship. Lydia Huntley Sigourney. ColAP

First of the first, / Such I pronounce Pompilia, then as snow. Robert Browning. EBVPR *Fr.* The Ring and the Book.

First of the gods I honor in my prayer is Mother Earth. The Eumenides. Aeschylus, *Greek.* NAWM-1, *tr. by* Robert Fagles

First of the Month, The. Adrian C. Louis. NAmP90

First of the undecoded messages read: "Popeye sits in thunder," The. Farm Implements and Rutabagas in a Landscape. John Ashbery. CBNP; CoAP; PmAP

First Offense. David Lehman. PmAP

First Olympionique of Pindar. To Hiero of Syracuse, victorious in the Horse-race, The. Pindar, *Greek.*

"Each element to water yields." OBCVT, *tr. by* Ambrose Philips

First on TV, A. David Ignatow. RaBo

First or Last. Thomas Hardy. CMoP

First paint a cage. Jacques Prévert, *French.* CBNP

First pale shoots, The. On a Picture of Your House. Douglas G. Jones. NOBC

First Party at Ken Kesey's with Hell's Angels. Allen Ginsberg. PmAP; TRP

("Cool black night thru redwoods.") CoAmPo

First Pearle, The: Religion. Lady Diana Primrose. KTR *Fr.* A Chain of Pearl.

First person to set foot on land was Noah's daughter, The. Ballad of Noah's Daughter. Rossana Ombres, *Italian.* NeIt, *tr. by* Ruth Feldman

First Person—1981. D. F. Brown. CDa

First Philosopher's Song. Aldous Leonard Huxley. AWP

First poem in the book, The. Passages. Mark Vinz. IFJA

First Practice. Gary Gildner. AmPA

First Praise. William Carlos Williams. VGW

First Prayer for the Hottentotsgod. Breyten Breytenbach, *Afrikaans.* AF, *tr. by* Denis Hirson

First Pregnancy. "Alta." NMM-2

First Prelude. Francis J. Smith. CRP

First principles of Epicurean physics. Lucretius, *Latin.* OBCVT, *tr. by* John Nott

First Problem. Aimé Césaire, *French.* NegPo, *tr. by* Ellen Conroy Kennedy

First Psalm (Posthumous). Bertolt Brecht, *German.* PFTM, *tr. by* Anselm Hollo

First rape a people. Pan Recipe. John Agard. HCP; PBCV

First Reader, The. Winfield Townley Scott. PoA

First Reader Santee Training School, 1873, The. Diane Glancy. LTA

First retainer / he gave to her, The. A Marriage. Robert Creeley. LiTM; NeAP; PoPoPo; RaBo

First Robin. Jane Yolen. NOxBChV

First Rondeau: After a French Poet of the Fourteenth Century. Johann Nikolaus Götz, *German.* GePo, *tr. by* George C. Schoolfield

First Rule. Maurice Kenny. HATNAP

First Samuel. Bible, *O.T.*

Hannah's Song of Thanksgiving. AWP

(Song of Hannah, The.) TrCP, *ad. by* Michael Drayton

Hannah's Thanksgiving. BoWoP

First Satire of the Second Book of Horace, [Imitated: To Mr. Fortescue], The. Horace, *Latin,* OAEL-1, *tr. by* Alexander Pope.

"Alas, young man! your days can ne'er be long." EPCY, *tr. by* Alexander Pope

"Pope: Each Mortal has his Pleasure: None deny." OBCVT, *tr. by* Alexander Pope

"With all a woman's virtues but the pox." OBSV, *tr. by* Alexander Pope

First Satyr of Aulus Persius Flaccus. In Dialogue betwixt the Poet and His Friend, or Monitor, The. Persius, *Latin.*

"Friend: Your Satyrs, let me tell you, are too fierce." OBCVT, *tr. by* John Dryden

First see those ample melons—brindled o'er. A Basket Of Summer Fruit. Charles Harpur. NOBAu

First sentence: Her cheap perfume. Seduced by Analogy. Bob Perelman. FTOS

First Sex. Sharon Olds. NMM-2

First she heard a sound. The Sound. Robert Kelly. PoM

First shot out of that sling, The. After Goliath. Kingsley Amis. NOBL; OxBTC

First Sight. Philip Larkin. NTCP

First Sight of Her and After. Thomas Hardy. FaBoVe; PoEL-5

First sign was your hair, The. I'm Just a Stranger Here, Heaven Is My Home. Carole C. Gregory Clemmons. PoBA

First Six Seals, The. David Wojahn. PUP-18

First Six Verses of the Ninetieth Psalm, The. Robert Burns. ChIV-1

First Snow in Alsace. Richard Wilbur. NoP-4; OBWP

First snow is never all the snows there were. Explicit Snow. Norman MacCaig. FaBoTC

First Snow on an Airfield. John Ciardi. PoA

First snow was sleet, The. It swished heavily. Sleet. Norman MacCaig. AYFP; OBCP

First snow wet against the windshield. In the Third Month. David Ray. RaBo

First Snowfall, The. James Russell Lowell. BLPA; FaBoBe; TAP

"Snow had begun in the gloaming, The."

First Snowflake. N. M. Bodecker. TLR

First Solitude, The. Luis de Góngora y Argote, *Spanish.* OBVE, *tr. by* Edward Meryon Wilson

First Song. T. Carmi. MHP, *tr. by* Ruth Finer Mintz *Fr.* René's Songs.

First Song. Galway Kinnell. LiLi; LiTM; NoP-4; Poetr; TwCP

First Song. Sir Philip Sidney. OxAEP-1 *Fr.* Astrophil and Stella. AAS; SiPS

First Song of Moses, The. George Wither. ChIV-1

First Song of the Exploding Stick. *Unknown.* APN-2, *tr. by* Washington Matthews *Fr.* The Mountain Chant.

First Song of the Thunder. *Unknown.* APN-2, *tr. by* Washington Matthews *Fr.* The Mountain Chant.

First sorrow of autumn, The. The Seven Sorrows. Ted Hughes. NAEL-2

First Spring. Duane Niatum. HATNAP

First Spring Day, The. Christina Rossetti. FaBoVe

First Spring Morning. Robert Bridges. BoTP

First stands the lofty Washington. Our Presidents. *Unknown.* BLPA

First Steps Up Parnassus. Michael Drayton. NOBE

("And so my deare friend, for this time adue.") (LL) PBRV

("My dearely loved friend how oft have we.") PBRV

(To my most dearely-loved friend Henery Reynolds Esquire, of Poets and Poesie.) PBRV

First Stone of the New Castle, The. *Unknown, Dutch.* PeSAV, *tr. by* H. C. V. Leibbrandt

First strawberry, The. Original Strawberry. Nancy Willard. LCAP-2

First, suicide notes should be. Suicide. Alice Walker. GT

First Sunday I missed Mass on purpose, The. The Day Zimmer Lost Religion. Paul Zimmer. InPK-6; PBCAP

First / tale of Gotham City, the Beggar, The. The Beggar at the Gate. Ian Wedde. PeNZ

First Thanksgiving, The. Jack Prelutsky. NTCP

First Thanksgiving of All. Nancy Byrd Turner. ChAP

First that broke silence was good old Ben, The. Sir John Suckling. EPCY Fr. A Session[s] of the Poets. BeJo

1st, The. Lucille Clifton. *See* Eviction.

First the crow is heard. Then. Nina Cassian, *Romanian.* CEEP, tr. by Schiff, Laura and Virgil Nemoianu

First the melody, clean and hard. How High the Moon. Lance Jeffers. PoBA; SeSe

First the pleasures fire the heart. From Belfast to Suffolk. William Peskett. PNI

First, the scene endlessly diminishes. Travelling Backward. Gene Baro. NYBP

First, the two men stand pondering. Verona. James Wright. NNaP

First there was a dream not wholly mine. Clouds over Islands. James Seay. MT

First there was a god of night and tempest. From Mythology. Zbigniew Herbert, *Polish.* FaBoPV, tr. by Czeslaw Milosz

First there was putting hot-water bottles to it. Inevitable. John Betjeman. MoBrPo

First there was the island. The Sea and Other Stories. Jennifer Rankin. NOBAu

First there was the lamb on knocking knees. Dylan Thomas. CMoP Fr. A Sequence of Sonnets.

First there were two of us, then there were three of us. The Storm. Walter De la Mare. NOxBChV; NTP

First Thesis. Tom Weatherly. Fr. Cantos. PoBA

First they came for the Jews. Pastor Niemoller. APAD; HP

First they slaughtered the angels. Lenore Kandel. BB

First they take it away. My Father's Body. William Matthews. PuP-17

First they were stiff and gaudy. The Magi. George Garrett. MT

First Thing. Kit Robinson. FTOS

First thing I saw in the morning, The. Mantova. James Wright. NNaP; TRP

First Things. Lucienne Desnoues, *French.* WPOW, tr. by Miller Williams

First Things First. W. H. Auden. CBLP; NYBP

First things first. Douglas Florian. NOxBChV

First Time, The. Karl Shapiro. VGW

First Time: 1950. Honor Moore. FFC; GLP

First time he kissed me, he but only kissed. Sonnet. Elizabeth Barrett Browning. BLPA; CTC; FaBoBe; LW Fr. Sonnets from the Portuguese.

First time I entered France, not by storm, The. Avec Amour. Robyn Selman. BAP-95

First time I flew over Florida I was amazed, The. The Distinct Call of the Alligator. Betsy Sholl. PBCAP

First time I lied to my baby, I told him that it was his face, The. How Lies Grow. Maxine Chernoff. PmAP

First time I looked seaward, westward. Lone Kauri Road ("First time I looked seaward, westward"). Allen Curnow. Fr. Trees, Effigies, Moving Objects. PeNZ

First time I saw her between her embroidered curtains, The. Tune: "Joy in Spring's Coming"—Seven Songs. *Unknown, Chinese.* SuSp, tr. by Wayne Schlepp

First time I saw her, light was falling, The. The Queen. Paul Zimmer. CMAP

First time I saw the sea, The. Tiho, the Carib. Jan Carew. HCP

First time I saw you, The. *Unknown, Japanese.* OHMPJ, tr. by Kenneth Rexroth

First time I walked, The. Oranges. Gary Soto. NoAM; WeW-3

First time I was sweet sixteen. Nayo-Barbara Watkins. NBV

First Time In. Ivor Gurney. FaBoVe; NoP-4

("Are sung—but never more beautiful than there under the guns' noise.") (LL) NoP-4

First time my father overheard me listening. Three Oranges. Charles Bukowski. BAP-93

First time out. Lives. Derek Mahon. PBCIP

First time that the sun rose on thine oath, The. Sonnet. Elizabeth Barrett Browning. EnVR; NAEL-2; WPE Fr. Sonnets from the Portuguese.

First to climb the parapet, The. The Cricketers of Flanders. *Unknown.* NSI

First To Go, The. Joyce Grenfell. LBC

First to God and then to you. (LL) My Gostly Fader, I Me Confesse. Charles, Duc d' Orléans. BoLoP; EnLoPo; EnVB; GBL; MiEL; NOBE

First to the Corse the weeping Consort flew. Homer. OBCVT, tr. by Alexander Pope Fr. The Odyssey.

First, to the feet, as they bear what you have grown to live in. Praise. William Matthews. AmPA

First Tooth, The. Charles Lamb *and* Mary Lamb. ACTP; OxBChV; WoRP

First travelers to the coves of the Blue Ridge. The Hollow. Robert Morgan. MT

First Travels of Max. John Crowe Ransom. MoAmPo; NTP

("As hath been, lo, these many generations.") MoAmPo

First turn to me after a shower. Work in Progress. Bernadette Mayer. DeD; PmAP

First two nights, The. Dinosaurs and Larger Issues. Irena Klepfisz. CPO

First Villancico, Written for the Nativity of Our Lord, Puebla, 1689, The. Sister Juana Inés de la Cruz, *Spanish.*

"Since Love is shivering." WPoS, tr. by Alan S. Trueblood

First Voice, The. "Lewis Carroll." Fr. The Three Voices. BXAP

First Walk on the Moon. May Swenson. RACG

First was Fancy, like a lovely boy, The. Edmund Spenser. NOBE Fr. The Mask of Cupid. Fr. Wood Of Error. AEP

First we locked our fingers, wove them. My Blood Brother. Frank Mkalawile Chipasula. HBAPE

First week the soil was clean, The. Digging for Indians. Gary Gildner. AmPA; PBCAP

First were invented. (LL) The Elf and the Dormouse. Oliver Herford. FPC; FaBoBe

First when Maggie [*or* Maggy] was my care. Whistle o'er the Lave o't. Robert Burns. OxBS

First will I question with thee about hell. Marlowe. OxBSn Fr. Doctor Faustus.

First William the Norman. *Unknown.* OxNR

First Winter: Joy. Peggy Shumaker. PBCAP

First Year, The. Edith Jay Scovell.

Days Drawing In. FaBoWP

First you bite your fingernails. American Rhapsody. Kenneth Fearing. MoAmPo

First you must blow a bottle round your sleep. Directions for Dreamfishing. Martin Johnston. CBAP

First you must have. Instructions for Building Straw Huts. Yusef Komunyakaa. GT

First, you think they are dead. Lobsters in the Window. W. D. Snodgrass. NYBP; TAP; TRP

Firstborn Land, The. Ingeborg Bachmann, *German.* BoWoP, tr. by Daniel Huws

Firste stok, fader of gentilesse, The. Gentilesse. Chaucer. AWP; MiEL; NAEL-1; OAEL-1

Fisbo. Robert Malise Bowyer Nichols.

"Talking of Ezra Pound and long-dead pantos." OBSV

Fish, The. Elizabeth Bishop. ChAP; FaBoWP; HAP; HeIP-4; HoPM; InPK-6; LiTM; MoAmPo; MoP; NAAL-2; NALW; NOBA; NTP; NoAM; NoP-4; PoE; PoPoPo; Poetr; RB; TFi; TRP

Fish, The. Rupert Brooke. APo

Fish. Daniel Halpern. AmPA

Fish. Larry Levis. AmPA

Fish, The. Marianne Moore. AmPP; ColAP; FaBoWP; MeMAP; MoAmPo; MoP; NAAL-2; NoAM; NoP-4; OxBA; PBMP; Poetr

Fish. Bhanuji Rao, *Oriya.* OMIP, tr. by Jayanta Mahapatra

Fish. Joe Rosenblatt. NOBC

Fish. Emily Townsend. NYBP

Fish and Bird. Rosemary Brinckman. BoTP

Fish and Chips on the Merry-Go-Round. K. O. Arvidson. PeNZ

Fish and Corn. George Mackay Brown. FaBoTC Fr. Runes from a Holy Island.

Fish Answers, A. Leigh Hunt. NBLV; SCGP Fr. The Fish, the Man, and the Spirit. HAP; NOBL; NTP; OBEV; PoEL-4

(Fish Replies, A.) PeLV

Fish at Mass, The. *Unknown, Latin.* BIrV, tr. by J. F. Webb

Fish bones walked the waves off Hatteras. Cottonmouth Country. Louise Glück. CoAP

Fish cannot drown in water, A. Mechthild von Magdeburg, *German.* EnlH; WPoS, tr. by Jane Hirshfield

Fish Cooking. Huran Kim, *Korean.* CKP, tr. by Jaihiun Kim

Fish Cove. Blaise Cendrars, *French.* BLT, tr. by Monique Chefdor

Fish Crier. Carl Sandburg. OxBA

Fish dripping, A. W. W. Eustace Ross. MoCV; NTP

Fish Fact. Pamela Alexander. IFJA

Fish (fly-replete, in depth of June). Heaven. Rupert Brooke. EBEV; HoPM; LiTM; MoBrPo; NOBE; NSI; PoRA

Fish / fowl. Lorine Niedecker. *See* Paean to Place.

Fish has laid her succulent eggs. Vicissitudes of the Creator. Archibald MacLeish. MeMAP

Fish in a Painting. Ho Ching-ming, *Chinese.* CoBLCP, tr. by Jonathan Chaves

Fish in River: "My house is not quiet, I am not loud." Cynewulf. AnOE, tr. by Charles W. Kennedy Fr. Riddles (Exeter Book).

Fish in the Stone, The. Rita Dove. GT; HCAP; Poetr

("He knows why the scientist / in secret delight / strokes the fern's voluptuous braille.") (LL) GT

Fish in the unruffled lakes. W. H. Auden. BoLoP; CBLP; CMoP; LoP; MoBrPo; MoP. *Fr.* Twelve Songs.

Fish leaping. Where the Lilies Were in Flower. Kumattur Kannanar, *Tamil.* PLW, *tr. by* A. K. Ramanujan

Fish man chats with the passers by, The. Fish Peddler. Mei Yao Ch'en, *Chinese.* OHPC, *tr. by* Kenneth Rexroth

Fish of the sea couldn't come. How They Brought the Good News by Sea. Norma Farber. PChr

Fish Peddler. Mei Yao Ch'en, *Chinese.* OHPC, *tr. by* Kenneth Rexroth

Fish Peddler and Cobbler. Kenneth Rexroth. NNaP

Fish Replies, A. Leigh Hunt. *See* A Fish Answers.

Fish Shop Windows. Geoffrey Dutton. NOBAu

Fish skeleton, A. Tanka. Maekawa Samio, *Japanese.* MJT, *tr. by* Makoto Ueda

Fish Story: How Language Carries Us into the Unknown. Brigitte Frase. LoHo

Fish-teeming sea. Amergin. *Fr.* Amergin's Songs. NOIV

Fish, the Man, and the Spirit, The. Leigh Hunt. HAP; NOBL; NTP; OBEV; PoEL-4

　Fish Answers, A. NBLV; SCGP

　(Fish Replies, A.) PeLV

　To a Fish. NBLV; PeLV; SCGP

Fish took a notion, A. Tip-Toe Tail. Dixie Willson. NTCP

Fish Turns Into a Man, and Then Into a Spirit, and Again Speaks, The. Leigh Hunt. *Fr.* The Fish, the Man, and the Spirit. HAP; NOBL; NTP; OBEV; PoEL-4

Fish wade / through black jade, The. Marianne Moore. AmPP; FaBoWP; MoAmPo; MoP; NoAM; OxBA

Fish weeps in the, The. *Unknown, Chinese.* OHMPC, *tr. by* Kenneth Rexroth

Fisher, The. Roderic Quinn. CBAP

Fisher Street. Thylias Moss. GT

Fisherman, The. Goethe, *German.* STV, *tr. by* John Frederick Nims

Fisherman, The. Leonidas of Tarentum. AWP, *tr. by* Andrew Lang *Fr.* Epigrams.

Fisherman, The. Jay Macpherson. NOBC

Fisherman, The. Janice Mirikitani. OpBo

Fisherman. Ou-yang Hsiu, *Chinese.* BLT; OHPC, *tr. by* Kenneth Rexroth

Fisherman, The. Su Shih, *Chinese.*

　"Fisherman drinks, The." SuSp, *tr. by* Irving Y. Lo

　"Fisherman, laughing, The." SuSp, *tr. by* Irving Y. Lo

　"Fisherman wakes, The." SuSp, *tr. by* Irving Y. Lo

　"Fisherman's drunk, The." SuSp, *tr. by* Irving Y. Lo

Fisherman. Ts'en Shen, *Chinese.* SuSp, *tr. by* C. H. Wang

Fisherman, The. W. B. Yeats. CMoP; HAP; NoAM

Fisherman drinks, The. Su Shih. SuSp, *tr. by* Irving Y. Lo *Fr.* The Fisherman.

Fisherman goes out at dawn, The. Abbie Farwell Brown. FPC

Fisherman in wellingtons, A. Gaelic Stories. Iain Crichton Smith. FaBoTC

Fisherman, laughing, The. Su Shih. SuSp, *tr. by* Irving Y. Lo *Fr.* The Fisherman.

Fisherman on a Southern Stream. Lu Kuei Meng, *Chinese.* SuSp, *tr. by* Robin D. S. Yates

Fisherman Speaks His Mind, A. Nguyễn Đình Chiều, *Vietnamese.* AVP, *tr. by* Huỳnh Sanh Thông

Fisherman wakes, The. Su Shih. SuSp, *tr. by* Irving Y. Lo *Fr.* The Fisherman.

Fisherman's drunk, The. Su Shih. SuSp, *tr. by* Irving Y. Lo *Fr.* The Fisherman.

"Fisherman's Honor," The. Li Ch'ing-chao, *Chinese.* WPoS, *tr. by* Jane Hirshfield

Fisherman's hut, by the mouth of the river. Coming at Night to a Fisherman's Hut. Chang Chi, *Chinese.* BLT, *tr. by* J. P. Seaton

Fisherman's Lyric. Chao Meng-fu, *Chinese.* CoBLCP, *tr. by* Jonathan Chaves

Fisherman's Rhyme. *Unknown.* FaBoVe

Fisherman's Song, The. Thomas D'Urfey. NOSC

Fisherman's Songs. Chang Chih-ho, *Chinese.*

　"Before dusk on the lake, the moon just full." SuSp, *tr. by* Hellmut Wilhelm

　"Near the rim of Hsi-sai Mountain, white egrets fly." SuSp, *tr. by* Irving Y. Lo

　"Oh, about the joy of owning a crab hut at Sung-chiang!" SuSp, *tr. by* Hellmut Wilhelm

Fisherman's Story, The. Henrietta Cordelia Ray. CBWP-3

Fisherman's swapping a yarn for a yarn, The. The Flower-Boat. Robert Frost. PoA

Fisherman's Whore, The. Dave Jeddie Smith. CMAP

Fisherman's Wife, The. Amy Lowell. BoWoP

Fishermen. Basil Bunting. PoA

Fishermen. Song. Primus St. John. GT

Fishermen, The. Theocritus. AWP; OBVE, *tr. by* Charles Stuart Calverley *Fr.* Idylls.

Fishermen among the fireweed, The. By Rail through the Earthly Paradise, Perhaps Bedfordshire. Denise Levertov. NNaP

Fishermen and Cormorants. Phan Thanh Giản, *Chinese.* AVP, *tr. by* Huỳnh Sanh Thông

Fishermen at Ballyshannon. Limbo. Seamus Heaney. CIP-2; NoAM; OxBC

Fishermen, Drowned beyond the West Coast. Vivian Smith. CBAP

Fishermen, like thieves, shake out their silver. Derek Walcott. PBCV *Fr.* Another Life.

Fishermen who go, The. What She Said. Ammuvanar, *Tamil.* PLW, *tr. by* A. K. Ramanujan

Fishermen will relate that in the South. The Lord of the Isle. Stefan George, *German.* AWP, *tr. by* Ludwig Lewisohn

Fishermen's fires glitter and fade. Staying Overnight on the Banks of Embroidered River. Li K'ai-hsien, *Chinese.* CoBLCP, *tr. by* Jonathan Chaves

Fishermen's Song. *Unknown, Maori.* PeNZ, *tr. by* Margaret Orbell

Fisherwoman, The. David Ignatow. LiLi

Fishes are born in water. Man Is Born in Tao. Chuang Tzu, *Chinese.* BLT, *tr. by* Thomas Merton

Fishes swim in water clear. *Unknown.* OxNR

Fishing. Dorothy, Duchess of Wellington Wellesley. OBMV

Fishing. Wordsworth. *Fr.* Introduction—Childhood and School-Time. FHYEP *Fr.* The Prelude; Growth of a Poet's Mind [1850 vers.]

Fishing alone in a frail boat. Walking Out. Betty Adcock. MT

Fishing at dawn, trap them east of town. A Fishing Trapping Song. Wen T'ing-yün, *Chinese.* SuSp, *tr. by* William R. Schultz

Fishing boats have returned, The! "Ping Hsin." PBWP, *tr. by* Julia C. Lin *Fr.* Three Poems.

Fishing Boats in Martigues. Roy Campbell. FaBoEE; OxBSP

Fishing cove and long lines of fishermen's huts, A. Ch'ien Ch'ien-i. SuSp, *tr. by* Irving Y. Lo *Fr.* Poems Written in Prison.

Fishing in the Wei River. Po Chü-i, *Chinese.* ChiP, *tr. by* Arthur Waley

Fishing on a wide river from a boat. Supreme Death. Douglas Dunn. FaBoMo

Fishing, one morning early in July. Lines in Memory of My Father. Basil Payne. IIP

Fishing Pole, The ("Fishing pole's a curious thing, A"). Mary Carolyn Davies. CTV

Fishing Rod, The. Shen Yüeh, *Chinese.* SuSp, *tr. by* Richard B. Mather

Fishing-Tackle, The. Bertolt Brecht, *German.* PoSu, *tr. by* Lee Baxendall

Fishing the White Water. Audre Lorde. GT

Fishing Trapping Song, A. Wen T'ing-yün, *Chinese.* SuSp, *tr. by* William R. Schultz

Fishing Village. Louis Dudek. *Fr.* Provincetown. MoCV

Fishmarket closed, the fishes gone into flesh, The. The Avenue Bearing the Initial of Christ into the New World. Galway Kinnell. CoAmPo *Fr.* The Avenue Bearing the Initial of Christ into the New World.

Fishnet. Robert Lowell. HCAP; VCAP

Fish's Nightsong. Christian Morgenstern. WeW-3

Fist Fight. Doug Cockrell. Poetsp

Fist of red fire, a flower, A. First Love. Elizabeth Jennings. LW

Fistful of News, A. Antoine-Roger Bolamba. PBMAP

Fit against the Country, A. James Wright. WeT

Fit for the soul to wear those clothes again. (LL) Soul and Body. Margaret Lucas Cavendish, Duchess of Newcastle. PEW

Fit of Rhyme [*or* Rime] against Rhyme [*or* Rime], A. Ben Jonson. BeJo; OAEL-1; PoEL-2; SeCP

　(Fit of Rhyme Against Rhyme, A.) NoP-4

　("Rhyme, the rack of finest wits.") NoP-4

　("Was the founder!") (LL) NoP-4; PBRV

Fit of Something against Something, A. Alan Ansen. WeT

Fit Only for Apollo. Francis Beaumont. *See* Song for a Dance.

Fit only for barbarians. (LL) Translation. Roy Fuller. NOBE; OxBTC

Fit place to observe the transit of Venus, A. Tahiti. Louis Johnson. PeNZ

Fit the Fifth: The Beaver's Lesson. "Lewis Carroll." *Fr.* The Hunting of the Snark. CBNP; OBNC; OBNV; PoEL-5

Fit the First: The Landing. "Lewis Carroll." EBEvV *Fr.* The Hunting of the Snark. CBNP; OBNC; OBNV; PoEL-5

Fit the Fourth: The Hunting. "Lewis Carroll." *Fr.* The Hunting of the Snark. CBNP; OBNC; OBNV; PoEL-5

Fit the Second: The Bellman's Speech. "Lewis Carroll." OBCoV *Fr.* The Hunting of the Snark. CBNP; OBNC; OBNV; PoEL-5

Fit the Seventh: The Banker's Fate. "Lewis Carroll." *Fr.* The Hunting of the Snark. CBNP; OBNC; OBNV; PoEL-5

Fit the Sixth: The Barrister's Dream. "Lewis Carroll." EBNV *Fr.* The Hunting of the Snark. CBNP; OBNC; OBNV; PoEL-5

Fitter said: "Madame, vous avez maigri," The. The Fitting. Edna St. Vincent Millay. NALW

Fitting, The. Edna St. Vincent Millay. NALW

Fitting Room. Lois Marie Harrod. IFJA

Fitz Adam's Story. James Russell Lowell. AmPP

Fitz-Eustace's Song. Sir Walter Scott. CH; GTBS-P *Fr.* Marmion. (Song.) NOBRP; PoEL-4

Fitzi in the Yearbook. Lyn Lifshin. DeD

Fitzroy. Andrew Taylor. BMAP

Five. Dennis Phillips. FTOS *Fr.* Twenty Questions.

Five Arabic Verses in Praise of Wine. *Unknown, Arabic.* TrJP, *tr. by* Hartwig Hirschfeld

Five barrels of flour seventy sticks. Making Old Bones. Alberta Turner. LCAP-2

Five Bells. Kenneth Slessor. CBAP; NOBAu; PoRA

("*Five bells.*") (LL) BMAP

Five best doctors anywhere, The. O. S. Hoffman. PoToHe

Five Birds Rise. William Hayward. NYBP

Five bolts of hanging silk. Returning from the Seventy-Two Mountains. Hsü Wei, *Chinese.* CoBLCP, *tr. by* Jonathan Chaves

Five buds were on the parent tree. Family Portraits. Mary E. Tucker. CBWP-1

Five Chants. David McCord. NOxBChV

Five-color robe of embroidered silk, A. Yang Chi, *Chinese.* CoBLCP, *tr. by* Jonathan Chaves

Five crackpots got together, talked big things. Cao Tần, *Vietnamese.* AVP, *tr. by* Huỳnh Sanh Thông

Five daughters, in the slant light on the porch. Daughters, 1900. Marilyn Nelson Waniek. FFC

Five Dawn Skies in November. David Wagoner. VCAP

Five-Day Rain, The. Denise Levertov. NeAP

Five days five nights of rain, rush. Spring And. Elizabeth Libbey. CMAP

5°. Nicholas Christopher. WWSi

Five Domestic Interiors. Vernon Scannell. OxBC

5.8.1942 / In Memory of Janusz Korczak. Jerzy Ficowski, *Polish.* HP, *tr. by* Keith Bosley

Five Epigrams. James Vincent Cunningham.

"Bride loved old words, and found her pleasure marred." OBAL

Epigram: "And now you're ready who while she was here."

Epitaph for Someone or Other. OBAL; PFE; TRP

(Epigram: "Naked I came, naked I leave the scene.") VGW

"Lip was a man who used his head." OBAL

Five Eyes. Walter De la Mare. PC

515 Madison Avenue. Rhapsody. Frank O'Hara. NoAM

Five-Finger Exercises. T. S. Eliot.

Lines for Cuscuscaraway and Mirza Murad Ali Beg. NBLV; NTP; OBAL; OBCoV; PeLV; UV

Lines to Ralph Hodgson Esqre. NBLV; OBAL; PeLV

Five-Fingered Maple, The. Kate Louise Brown. BoTP

Five Flower World Variations. *Unknown, Yaqui Indian.* STP, *tr. by* Jerome Rothenberg

Five for the Grace of Man. Winfield Townley Scott. VGW

5.40. The Bay View. After the office. Aberdarcy: The Chaucer Road. Kingsley Amis. NOBL *Fr.* The Evans Country.

5 4 3. Aldrin Collins and Armstrong. Michael Rosen. SpW

Five geese deploy mysteriously. Bas-Relief. Carl Sandburg. ColAP

Five Ghost Songs. *Ambo Oral Tradition.* TTTS

Five gleaming crows. In Air. Peter Clarke. PBA

Five Groups of Verse. Charles Reznikoff.

After I Had Worked All Day. VGW

Five Hens, The. *Unknown.* OxNR

Five hours, (and who can do it less in?). The Lady's Dressing Room. Jonathan Swift. NoP-4

Five Hundred Points of Good Husbandry. Thomas Tusser.

Advice of Housewives. NoSic

December's Husbandry. NoSic

Five inches from. Desire. Paul Hoover. PmAP

Five Little Brothers. Ella Wheeler Wilcox. BoTP

Five Little Chickens. *Unknown.* CTAV

(Wishes.) BoTP

("'You must come here and scratch'.") (LL) CTAV

Five little monkeys. The Monkeys and the Crocodile. Laura Elizabeth Richards. CTV

Five Little Sisters Walking in a Row. Five Sisters. Kate Greenaway. BoTP

Five Men. Zbigniew Herbert, *Polish.* PoSu, *tr. by* Czeslaw Milosz *and* Peter Dale Scott

Five-Minute Orlando Macbeth, The. George MacBeth. NOBL; PeLV

Five minutes, five minutes more, please! Bedtime. Eleanor Farjeon. OTCP

Five months after your death, I come like the others. Elegy for a Forest Clear-Cut by the Weyerhaeuser Company. David Wagoner. NoAM

Five Nocturnes. Robert Frost.

Were I in Trouble. OxBSP

Five O'Clock Shadow. John Betjeman. PFE

Five on the Crabs. Orampokiyar, *Tamil.*

What Her Girl Friend Said to the foster-mother ("If you think, mother"). PLW, *tr. by* A. K. Ramanujan

What Her Girl friend Said to the Foster-Mother ("In his fields, mother"). PLW, *tr. by* A. K. Ramanujan

What She Said ("In his place, mother / field-crabs cut into the pink"). PLW, *tr. by* A. K. Ramanujan

What She Said ("In his place, mother, / mud-spattered spotted crabs"). PLW, *tr. by* A. K. Ramanujan

Five on the Riverside Cane. Orampokiyar, *Tamil.*

What She Said ("Bees, six tiny legs and wings all lovely"). PLW, *tr. by* A. K. Ramanujan

What She Said ("Green creepers planted inside the house"). PLW, *tr. by* A. K. Ramanujan

What She Said ("Hovering like the heron"). PLW, *tr. by* A. K. Ramanujan

What She Said ("In the full river"). PLW, *tr. by* A. K. Ramanujan

What She Said ("Like the high fanning tufts on swift horses"). PLW, *tr. by* A. K. Ramanujan

Five. One. Laurie Duggan. BMAP *Fr.* The Ash Range.

Five oxen, grazing in a flowery mead. On a Seal. Plato, *Greek.* AWP; FaBoEE, *tr. by* Thomas Stanley

5 Poems. Robert Gray. CBAP

Five Poems about Poetry. George Oppen.

From Virgil. NNaP

Gesture, The. NNaP

Five Poems for Grandmothers. Margaret Atwood.

"How little I know / about you finally." CrSp

Five Poems on Returning to Hangchou. Yüan Mei, *Chinese.* CoBLCP, *tr. by* Jonathan Chaves

Five rivers, like the fingers of a hand. Ebenezer Elliot. NOBRP *Fr.* The Village Patriarch.

Five Sestinas. James Keir Baxter.

Dark Welcome, The. PeNZ

Five Sisters. Kate Greenaway. BoTP

Five soldiers fixed by Mathew Brady's eye. Looking into History. Richard Wilbur. VCAP; VGW

Five Songs. W. H. Auden.

Epilogue: " 'O where are you going?' said reader to rider." FaBoCh

(Song: " 'O where are you going?' said reader to rider.") OAEL-2

Love Song: "For what as easy." PeLV

Proof, The. OAEL-2

Song: "Deftly, admiral, cast your fly." GTBS-P

"Starling and a willow-wren, A." FaBoMo

"That night when joy began." OxBTC; SoSe-8

Five Sorrowful Mysteries, The. Francis Jammes, *French.* GI, *tr. by* Jeffrey Fiskin

Five Souls. W. N. Ewer. NSI

Five Stages of Grief, The. Linda Pastan. IMW

Five-string, The. Po Chü-i, *Chinese.* ChiP, *tr. by* Arthur Waley

Five Students, The. Thomas Hardy. CMoP; GTBS-P; PoEL-5

Five summer days, five summer nights. The Blue-Fly. Robert Graves. APo; CMoP; NAEL-2; NYBP; NoAM; PFE

Five Things Sought For—In the Manner of Han Wo. Hsü Pen, *Chinese.* CoBLCP, *tr. by* Jonathan Chaves

Five Things White. Edward May. FaBoEE

5:30 A.M. Adrienne Rich. NOBA

5:32, The. Phyllis McGinley. NMM-2; OxBM; WPE *Fr.* I Know a Village.

529 1983. Gerda Mayer. Spl

Five Unmistakable Marks, The. David Jones. NAEL-2 *Fr.* In Parenthesis.

"Across upon this undulated board of verdure chequered bright." NoAM

Five Voyages of Arnor, The. George Mackay Brown. FaBoTC

Five Were Foolish. Arthur J. Hodge. AH

Five Words for Joe Dunn on His 22nd Birthday. Jack Spicer. PoM

Five years ago we knew such ecstasies. Interim. Frank Ormsby. CIP-2

Five years have passed [or past]; five summers, with the length. Lines Composed a Few Miles Above Tintern Abbey on Revisiting the Banks of the Wye During a Tour. Wordsworth. EBEvV; FHYEP; HeIP-4; ImPo; InPS-3; NOBRP; OAEL-2; OBNC; OxAEP-2; PoEL-4; Poetr; SCGP; TFi

Five years since you died and I am. Letter to a Dead Father. Richard Shelton. PBCAP

Fivesucked the features of my girl by glory. Nicholas Moore. PoA

Fix. Michael Dransfield. NOBAu

Fixed Ideas. Kenneth Slessor. BMAP

Fixed in the fireplace. The Fireplace. Michael S. Harper. GT

Fixer of Midnight. Reuel Denney. OBAL

Fixture, A. May Swenson. NYBP

Flaccus gave me, the silver lamp. Statilius Flaccus, *Greek*. GrAn, tr. by W. G. Shepherd

Flag. Ch'ihwan Yu, *Korean*. CKP, tr. by Jaihiun Kim

Flag-covered coffin. Nicholas Virgilio. HA

Flag Goes By, The. Henry Holcomb Bennett. FaBoBe; PWR

Flag is passing by!, The. (LL) The Flag Goes By. Henry Holcomb Bennett. FaBoBe; PWR

Flag of Chile, The. Teresa de Jesús, *Spanish*. AF, tr. by Maria Proser, Arlene Scully and James Scully

Flagpole Sitter, The. Donald Finkel. CoAP

Flags of all sorts. Things We Dreamt We Died For. Marvin Bell. CoAP

Flags of war like storm-birds fly, The. The Battle Autumn of 1862. John Greenleaf Whittier. CBCWP

Flake diamond of / the sea. Larry Eigner. PoM

Flakes pour to the black dead. In the Camp There Was One Alive. Randall Jarrell. HP

Flame and wood and blackened stones like these. Haim Guri, *Hebrew*. IP, tr. by Warren Bargad and Stanley F. Chyet

Flame beneath the pot that boils the water, The. (LL) Lobsters. Howard Nemerov. PBMP; PFE

Flame burns in the morning, A. Le Chariot. John Wieners. VGW

Flame-Heart. Claude McKay. GT

Flame out, you glorious skies. The Dead Heroes. Isaac Rosenberg. MoBrPo; NSI

Flame-red moon, the harvest moon, The. The Harvest Moon. Ted Hughes. AYFP

Flame the westward skies adorning. A. E. H. Kingsley Amis. PFE

Flame tongues, A. Thrace. Peter Huchel, *German*. CEEP, tr. by Rich Ives

Flames and Dangling Wire. Robert Gray. BMAP; NOBAu

Flames are shooting. Song of the Fire-Charm. *Unknown, Chippewa Indian*. STP, tr. by Frances Densmore; *English vers.* by Jerome Rothenberg

Flames, the arrows, all lie here, The. (LL) Another [Epitaph on Lady Mary Villiers] ("This little vault, this narrow room"). Thomas Carew. BeJo; CaPo; CavPo; OBEV; SeCP

Flames were already eating. Hannah. Judy Grahn. NMM-2 *Fr.* Helen you Always Were / The Factory.

Flaming Heart, The. Richard Crashaw. NAEL-1; OAEL-1; PoEL-2

(Flaming Heart, The [Upon the Booke and Picture of Teresa. As She Is Usually Expressed with a Seraphim Beside Her].) ESCV

("Unto all life of mine may die.") (LL) CABP

("Vnto all life of mine may dy.") (LL) FSCP

("Well meaning readers! you that come as freinds.") FSCP

"Live in these conquering leaves; live all the same." OxAEP-1

"O Heart! the equal poise of love's both parts." GeHe

Upon the Book and Picture of the Seraphical Saint Teresa. NOBE; OBEV

Flaming Terrapin, The. Roy Campbell.

"Maternal Earth stirs redly from beneath." MoBrPo

Flamingo, what has brought you here? *Unknown, Sanskrit*. APo, tr. by John Brough

Flamingos, The. Rilke, *German*. APo, tr. by Stephen Mitchell

Flammonde. Edwin Arlington Robinson. AmPP; CMoP; LiTM; MeMAP; NoAM

Flaneur, The. Oliver Wendell Holmes. APN-1

Flannan Isle. Wilfrid Wilson Gibson. CH; PoRA

Flannery O'Connor. Dorothy Walters. PoRA

Flap, flap, the captive bird in the cage. The Scholar in the Narrow Street. Tso Ssu, *Chinese*. AWP; ChiP, tr. by Arthur Waley

Flap, flap, the sounds of autumn. Spending the Night in an Inn at Swatow and Writing about My Feelings, Sent to Liang Shih-wu. Huang Tsun-hsien, *Chinese*. SuSp, tr. by An-yan Tang

Flap, flap, you curtain in front of our bed! The Curtain of the Wedding Bed. Liu Hsün's Wife, *Chinese*. ChiP, tr. by Arthur Waley

Flapper, The. Charles Larcom Graves. NSI

Flapping of ducks' wings, The. Autumn. Andrey Andreievich Voznesensky, *Russian*. TCRP, tr. by Stanley Kunitz

Flash. Lee Bennett Hopkins. SSCS

Flash Cards. Rita Dove. LoL; PoPoPo

Flash Colonial Barman, The. William W. Coxon. NOBAu

Flash Crimson. Carl Sandburg. MoAmPo

Flash of blue, A. The Kingfisher. Dyneley Hussey. NSI

Flash of lightning does not satisfy thirst, A. Modern Love Songs. *Unknown, Somali*. TTY, tr. by B. W. Andrzejewski and I. M. Lewis

Flash, sort belts, dresses, shirts, baby clothes. (LL) First Time: 1950. Honor Moore. FFC

Flashed [or flasht] out between the middle and extre[a]me. (LL) The Definition of Beauty. Robert Herrick. BeJo; CaPo

Flashing and glimmering at the edge of the horizon. (LL) East Coast Journey. James Keir Baxter. NoP-4; PeNZ

Flashing light, this ancient mirror. Song of the Ch'in-Dynasty Mirror—Written for Yüan Sung-li. Wang Shih-chieng, *Chinese*. CoBLCP, tr. by Jonathan Chaves

Flashing messengers of light and swiftness. Ian McDonald. HCP *Fr.* The Poison-Maker. HCP

Flashing through falling sunlight. Fall of Icarus: Brueghel. Joseph Langland. PFE

Flat as to an eagle's eye. George Meredith. PeVV *Fr.* The Nuptials of Attila.

Flat as to an eagle's eye. The Nuptials of Attila. George Meredith.

Flat end of sorrow here, The. The First Circle. Kofi Awoonor. HBAPE; PBMAP; VCWP

Flat on the bank I parted. The Trout. John Montague. IIP; NoP-4; PBCIP; PNI; PoE

Flat One, A. W. D. Snodgrass. LiTM

Flat River Girl. *Unknown*. AS

Flatted Fifths. Langston Hughes. MoNo

Flattened your words against your speaking mouth. (LL) Hearing your words, and not a word among them. Edna St. Vincent Millay. CMoP; ColAP; MoP; NoAM; Poetr; VGW

Flaubert in Egypt. Robert Penn Warren. NoAM

Flaubert wanted to write a novel. Style. Howard Nemerov. NoAM

Flaunt of the sunshine I need not your bask. Walt Whitman. *Fr.* Song of Myself. AmPP; MoAmPo; NAAL-3; NOBA; OxBA

Flautist boasts but God's enraged—, The. Elegy on an X-ray Photo of My Skull. Yelena Shwarts, *Russian*. VCWP, tr. by Michael Molnar

Flavia's a name a deal too free. *Unknown*. FaBoEE

Flavor of vanilla drifts, A. Dark Romance. Lucha Corpi, *Spanish*. WPOW, tr. by Catherine Rodriguez-Nieto

Flavor the speaking of this one. Not to Forget Miss Dickinson. Marshall Schacht. LiTM

Flavour in mild times, there are no great men, The. Climbing to Lo-yu Plateau, before Leaving for Wu-hsing. Tu Mu, *Chinese*. PLT, tr. by A. C. Graham

Flaw, A. "Michael Field." VWP

Flaw in Paganism, The. Dorothy Parker. NBLV

"Flawless" is the word, no doubt, for this third of May. Hourglass. Josephine Jacobsen. BAP-93; NoP-4

Flax. Ivan Alekseievich Bunin, *Russian*. AWP, tr. by Babette Deutsch and Avrahm Yarmolinsky

Flaxen-headed cow-boy, as simple as may be, A. Air. John O'Keefe. NOEC

Flaxman. Margaret Fuller. APN-1; PAR

Fle[e] fro[m] the pres[s] [or prees] and dwelle with so[o]th[e][ ]fastnesse. Truth. Chaucer. AWP; EnVB; MiEL; NAEL-1; NoP-4; OAEL-1; SCGP

Flea, The. Donne. APo; BoLoP; EBEV; EP; ESCV; FMP; FSCP; HoPM; ImPo; InPK-6; InPS-3; NAEL-1; NBLV; NIP-4; NoP-4; NoSic; OAEL-1; OxAEP-1; PFE; PoE; Poetr; SCV; SeCP; TFi

Flea. Raymond Roseliep. HA

Flea and a fly in a flue, A. *Unknown*. FPC

("Flue.") (LL) CTV

Flea flew by a bee, A. The bee. Combinations. Mary Ann Hoberman. OBSP *Fr.* Bugs. OBCA

Fleadh Cheoil. Pearse Hutchinson. PBCIP

Fleance. Michael Longley. CIP-2; PNI

Fleche. Larry Eigner. VGW

Fled are the frosts, and now the fields appear[e]. Farewell Frost; or, Welcome the Spring. Robert Herrick. CaPo

Fled are those times, when, in harmonious strains. Truth in Poetry. George Crabbe. EPCY; FHYEP *Fr.* The Village.

Fled gasping from the House. (LL) I Years had been from Home. Emily Dickinson. NOBA; OxBA; PoRA; SAmP

Fled is that music—Do I wake or sleep? (LL) Ode to a Nightingale. Keats. AWP; CABP; ClHu; EBEV; FaBoBe; GEA; GTBS-P; HAP; HeIP-4; ImPo; InPS-3; NAEL-2; NAWM-2; NOBE; NOBRP; NoP-4; OAEL-2; OBEV; OBNC; PFE; PoE; PoEL-4; PoPoPo; PoRA; RB; Ro; SCGP; SoSe-8; TFi; TOF; UnPo

Fled is the swiftness of all the white-footed ones. Elegy. Joseph Auslander. TrJP

Flee always from the snare. (LL) A Rondel of Luve [or Love]. Alexander Scott. BoLoP; OBEV; OxBS

Flee on Your Donkey. Anne Sexton. NYBP; Poetr

Fleece, The. John Dyer.
"Ah gentle shepherd, thine the lot to tend." PoEL-3
Happy Workhouse and the Good Effects of Industry, The. NOEC
Treating Sheep Ailments. ECEV
Urban Progress. ECEV, ll. 1–20

Fleeing across the roofs. (LL) The Roofwalker. Adrienne Rich. CoAP; NAAL-2; SAGP

Fleeing Atalanta, The. David Foster.
"Alchemists say the Stone turns lead to gold." NOBAu
"Don't give everything." NOBAu
"Seeking heat men become cold, and look for meaning." NOBAu

Fleeing From Bandits. Nguyễn Đình Chiều, Vietnamese. AVP, tr. by Huỳnh Sanh Thông

Fleeing from my fellow-countrymen. 1940. Bertolt Brecht, German. HP, tr. by Willet, John

Fleeing from threatened flood, they sailed. The First Invasion of Ireland. Unknown, Irish. BIrV, tr. by John Montague

Fleeing sandpipers, The. J. W. Hackett. HA

Fleeing the short-haired mad executives. The Climbers. W. H. Auden. MeMAP

Fleet Astronomer can bore, The. Vanity [or Vanitie] (1). George Herbert. FMP; FSCP; GeHe; NOSC; NoP-4

Fleet ships encountering on the high seas. Good Ships. John Crowe Ransom. MeMAP; WeW-3

Fleeting birds may soon in ocean swim, The. To Miss Laetitia Van Lewen. Constantia Grierson. ECWP; WPE

Fleeting glory or decay—are wind and lightning. A Monk of Auspicious Fortune Monastery Asking Me to Name a Pavilion. Su Shih, Chinese. SuSp, tr. by Chiang Yee

Fleeting Passion, A. W. H. Davies. NSI

Fleeting Time. Unknown, Vietnamese. AVP, tr. by Huỳnh Sanh Thông

Fleggit Bride, The. "Hugh MacDiarmid." OxBS

Fleming Helphenstine. Edwin Arlington Robinson. MeMAP

Flemington Racecourse. Kevin Hart. NOBAu

Flesh, and cars, tar, dug holes beneath stone. A Contract. (For The Destruction and Rebuilding of Paterson). Imamu Amiri Baraka. FTOS

Flesh and the Spirit, The. Anne Bradstreet. AmPP; ChIV-2; NAAL-1; NAAL-3; NOBA; OxBA; OxWW; SCAP; TAP

Flesh chase night, weather booming and dark. Major Bowes' Diary. Imamu Amiri Baraka. NAAL-2

Flesh-Fly and the Bee, The. Coventry Patmore. FaBoEE

Flesh, I Have Knocked at Many a Dusty Door. John Masefield. LiTM Fr. Sonnets.

Flesh is sad, alas, The! and all the books are read. Sea-Wind. Stéphane Mallarmé, French. AWP, tr. by Arthur Symons

Flesh of the Young Men Is Burning, The. Lance Jeffers. BkSV

Flesh to feed hell's worm upon. (LL) After Death. Swinburne. NOBVV; OxBSn; PeVV

Flesh will heal and pain will fade. Claire Richcreek Thomas. PoToHe

Fleshing his dream of the beautiful, needful thing. (LL) Frederick Douglass. Robert Earl Hayden. CBCWP; HCAP; ISC; NAAAL; NIP-4; PBMP; PFE; PoBA; PoPoPo; Son; TTY; VCAP

Fletcher's Lament for his Friend. John Fletcher. FP

Flew up to the moon. Mother Goose. See Old Mother Goose.

Flicker, The. Lew Blockcolski. VoR

Flicker flies by. Bend in the River. Simon J. Ortiz. HATNAP; PoPoPo

Flicker of a movement—could have been executed differently. (LL) Work. Gyula Illyés, Hungarian. PFTM, tr. by William Jay Smith

Flickering curtain, scintillations, junebugs. Wavering. Denise Levertov. PmAP

Flickering of incessant rain. John Gould Fletcher. Fr. Irradiations. MoAmPo

Flies. Jack Kerouac. CLPP

Flies, flies are on the plane tree, on the streets. (LL) As a Plane Tree by the Water. Robert Lowell. CMoP; CoAP; LiTM; MoAmPo; NOBA; OxBA

Flies o'er th' unbending corn, and skims along the main. Alexander Pope. See An Essay on Criticism.

Flies screaming like a jay. (LL) Deaf-Mute in the Pear Tree. Patricia K. Page. NoP-4

Flight. Charles Stuart Calverley. OBCoV

Flight. Jorge Guillén, Spanish. BLT, tr. by Reginald Gibbons

Flight, The. John Haines. SPE

Flight. Barbara Howes. NYBP

Flight, The. Theodore Roethke. NAAL-2; RB; TRP Fr. The Lost Son. HAP; HCAP; LiTM; VGW
(Lost Son, The.) NoP-4

Flight. Jean Starr. BAP-96

Flight, The. Sara Teasdale. LW

Flight from Bootle, The. John Betjeman. PeLV

Flight from Manhattan, The. Les A. Murray. BMAP Fr. The Sydney Highrise Variations.

Flight in the Desert, The. William Everson. ChIV-2; VGW

Flight into Egypt, The. Peter Quennell. ImPo; LiTM

Flight into Midian. Frances Ellen Watkins Harper. AAP Fr. Moses: A Story of the Nile.

Flight is past: and man forgot, The. (LL) Sic Vita. Henry, Bishop of Chichester King. NOBE; NOSC; OxBSP; SCGP; SeCP

Flight is the bird's value. Aesthetic. Norman Rosten. PoA

Flight of fancy and breath of fresh air, . . . A. I Applied for the Board. Jimmy Santiago Baca. LoL

Flight of Leeona. Albery Allson Whitman. AAP Fr. Not a Man and Yet a Man.

Flight of Love, The. Shelley. See Lines: "When the lamp is shattered [or shatter'd]."

Flight of the Bucket, The. Rudyard Kipling. BXAP

Flight of the Duchess, The. Robert Browning.
"And were I not, as a man may say, cautious." OBCoV

Flight of the Earls, The, 1607. Fearghal Og MacWard, Irish.
"All Ireland's now one vessel's company." BIrV

Flight of the Roller Coaster. Raymond Souster. NOBC

Flight of the Spirit. Felicia Dorothea Hemans. Son

Flight of the White South Africans, The. Christopher Hope. PeSAV

Flight of Wild Ducks, A. Charles Harpur. NOBAu

Flight out of Time. Hugo Ball, German.
Flight out of Time. PFTM, tr. by Pierre Joris and Jerome Rothenberg

Flight to Flanders, The. Lessel Hutcheon. NSI

Flight to Italy. C. Day Lewis.
"Winged bull trundles to the wired perimeter, The." OxBTC

Flights. Roger McDonald. CBAP

Flighty young lady from Loddon, A. Limerick. Ida Thurtle. PeLi

Fling Out the Banner! George Washington Doane. AH

Fling this useless book away. Written in a Lady's Prayer Book. John Wilmot, 2d Earl of Rochester. BoLoP; NOSC

Fling weh de wash pan, drop de cloes! Excitement. Louise Bennett. PBCV

Flinging the frisbee. Alan Pizzarelli. HA

Flint. Christina Rossetti. OxBChV Fr. Sing-Song.
(Precious Stones.) ChAP

Flint Hills, The. Lew Blockcolski. VoR

Flintlike, her feet struck. Night Walk. Sylvia Plath. NYBP

Flip, clack! The windscreen wipers clear. Seven Rainy Months. William Plomer. OxBTC

Flippancies. Richard Wilbur.
Star System, The. NBLV
What's Good for the Soul is Good for Sales. NBLV

Flippantly, / In the cinemas past sleep. Before Dawn. Horace Hamilton. NYBP

Flipping eck, cor blimey, strewth. Taking the Plunge. John Mole. NOxBChV

Flirt, The. W. H. Davies. EnLoPo

Flirting with a Pig. Aleksandar Ristovic, Serbo-Croatian. HSix, tr. by Charles Simic

Flitting, The. John Clare. FaBoPV; OxAEP-2

Flitting, The. Medbh McGuckian. PBCIP; PNI

Flitting, with little leathern sails dispread. (LL) Fashioned After the Manner of Master Geoffrey Chaucer in His Assembly of Fowls. Thomas, the Elder Warton. ChIV-1; KSG

Float over us, Florence, your banners. History as Decoration. Rosanna Warren. DiPo

Float up again. Celan. "Asya," Yiddish. CEEP, tr. by Gabriel Preil and Howard Schwartz

Floating across the lake. Not Thinking of America. Judith Kroll. AmPA

Floating clouds and worldly affairs. Wen Cheng-ming. CoBLCP, tr. by Jonathan Chaves. Fr. Improvised on Horseback to Say Good-bye to Those Who Are Seeing Me Off.

Floating clouds, before my eyes. Inscribed on a Painting of Sailboats on the River—Seeing Off Yen-chi on His Journey to Ch'ang-an. Yün Shou-p'ing, *Chinese.* CoBLCP, *tr. by* Jonathan Chaves

Floating, floating on misty waves. Fisherman's Lyric. Chao Meng-fu, *Chinese.* CoBLCP, *tr. by* Jonathan Chaves

Floating, floating, the river waters. Wang Chiu-ssu. *Fr.* After Reading the Poems of Master Han Shan. CoBLCP, *tr. by* Jonathan Chaves

Floating, floating weightless. Swimming Pool. Myra Cohn Livingston. NOxBChV

Floating, floating, your boat sets sail. Song of the Merchant's Wife. Yang Wei-chen, *Chinese.* CoBLCP, *tr. by* Jonathan Chaves

Floating Island at Hawkshead. Dorothy Wordsworth. PEW; Ro

Floating perfectly through the net. (LL) Fast Break. Edward Hirsch. DiPo; EOEF; VCAP

Floating Petals. Jan Barry. CDa

Floating Poem, Unnumbered, The. Adrienne Rich. NALW; NoAM *Fr.* Twenty-one Love Poems. GLP

(Floating Poem, The.) NMM-2

Floating scent encircles the curved shore. Lotuses on the Crooked Pond. Lu Chao-lin, *Chinese.* SuSp, *tr. by* Paul W. Kroll

Floating Series. Leslie Scalapino.

Floating Series 1. DeD

Floating Series 2. DeD

Third Part. DeD

Floating threads of spider webs hang. Wen Cheng-ming. CoBLCP, *tr. by* Jonathan Chaves *Fr.* The Chung-i Temple.

Floats the white moon. (LL) Winter. Walter De la Mare. OAEL-2; OBMV

Flock. Lance Henson. VoR

Flock of Birds, A. Chung-hee Moon, *Korean.* CKP, *tr. by* Jaihiun Kim

Flock of crows high from the Northland flies, A. Autumn. Detlev, Freiherr von Liliencron, *German.* AWP, *tr. by* Ludwig Lewisohn

Flock of Guinea Hens Seen from a Car, A. Eudora Welty. NYBP

Flock of sheep that leisurely pass by, A. To Sleep. Wordsworth. GTBS-P

Flock of winds came winging [*or* flying] from the North, A. The Roaring Frost. Alice Thompson Meynell. EBVV; WPE

Flocking together. Vultures—in the midst of war. Shaku Chōkū, *Japanese.* MJT, *tr. by* Makoto Ueda

Flocks of birds fly high and vanish. Sitting Alone in Ching-t'ing Mountain. Li Po, *Chinese.* SuSp, *tr. by* Irving Y. Lo

Flocks of chicken clucking from every corner. Tu Fu. SuSp, *tr. by* Irving Y. Lo *Fr.* Ch'iang Village.

Flodden Field. *Unknown.* ESPB

Flood. Ch'ien T'ao, *Chinese.* ChiP, *tr. by* Arthur Waley

Flood, The. John Clare. RB

Flood. James Joyce. MoBrPo

Flood, The. Ovid. *Fr.* The Floods, by nature enemies to land. OBVE, *tr. by* Dryden *Fr.* Metamorphoses.

Flood. *Unknown, Vietnamese.* AVP, *tr. by* Huỳnh Sanh Thông

Flood, The. Dara Wier. NAmP90

Flood of burn breaking across us now / from the sun. A. R. Ammons. *See* Easter Morning.

Flood recedes, The. Ovid, *Latin.* OBCVT, *tr. by* Arthur Golding

Flood-Tide below me! I see you face to face! Crossing Brooklyn Ferry. Walt Whitman. APN-1; AmPP; ColAP; FaBoA; InPS-3; MoP; NAAL-1; NAAL-3; NCAP; NOBA; NoAM; NoP-4; PAR; PiM; TAP

Flood Water. *Unknown, Aborigine.* NOBAu, *tr. by* Mungayana Nundhirribala

Flood Year. Judith Wright. NoAM

Flooded Mind. Norman MacCaig. OxBC

Flooding with a brilliant mist. To the Moon. Goethe, *German.* STV, *tr. by* John Frederick Nims

Floodlights in the guard towers, The. (LL) Begotten of the Spleen. Charles Simic. LCAP-2

Floods all the soul with its melodious seas. . (LL) Milton. Henry Wadsworth Longfellow. AWP; AmPP; GSo; TAP

Floods, by nature enemies to land, The. Ovid. OBVE, *tr. by* Dryden *Fr.* Metamorphoses.

Floods Clap Their Hands, The. Bible, *O.T. See* Psalm 98.

Floods of men. All the Spirit Powers Went to Their Dancing Place. Gary Snyder. UnPo

Floods of tears well from my deepest heart, The. Elegy. Immanuel di Roma, *Italian.* TrJP, *tr. by* J. Chotzner

Floods Swell around Me, Angry, Appalling. Zachary Eddy. AH

Floodtide. Askia Muhammad Touré. PoBA

Flooer o the Gean. George Campbell Hay. OxBS

Floor and the Ceiling, The. William Jay Smith. OBCA

Floor Is Dirty, The. Edward Field. CoAP; NeAP

Floor is something we must fight against. Whilst seemingly, The. Russell Edson. WeT

Floor Plans. Maxine Scates. PBCAP

Floorboards creak, The. New Apartment. Linda Hogan. HATNAP; UnSA

Floral Apron, The. Marilyn Chin. LoL

("How to honor the village, the tribe, / that floral apron.") (LL) UnSA

Florella; or, The Jealous Lover. *Unknown.* AmFP

Florence. Nina Zivancevic, *Serbo-Croatian.* HSix, *tr. by* Charles Simic

Florence Vane. Philip Pendleton Cooke. APN-1

Florida. Dannie Abse. OxBC

Florida. Elizabeth Bishop. TwCP

("Whimpers and speaks in the throat / of the Indian Princess.") (LL) FaBoA

Florida. Carl Rakosi. TAP

Florida Beach, The. Constance Fenimore Woolson. APN-2

Florida Road Workers. Langston Hughes. MoAmPo

Florin to the willing guard, A. The Rosy Bosom'd Hours. Coventry Patmore. EnLoPo; NOBVV

Florio, one ev'ning, brisk, and gay. Epigram on Florio. John Winstanley. FaBoEE

Florist was told, cyclamen or azalea, The. Lines to Accompany Flowers for Eve. Carolyn Kizer. BoWoP

Florrie Abraham Witness. Jack A. Mapanese. "There are times when their faith in gods." HBAPE

Florist's Vade-Mecum, The. Samuel Gilbert. OBGa *Fr.* The Florist's Vade-Mecum.

Florist's Vade-Mecum, The. OBGa

Florus, canst thou define that innate spark. To Mr. ———, an Unlettered Poet, on Genius Unimproved. Ann Yearsley. NOEC

Flos Lunae. Ernest Christopher Dowson. OBMV; PeVV

Flotilla. Clive Sansom. AYFP

Flounders in mud. O Jesus, make it stop! (LL) Attack. Siegfried Sassoon. MoBrPo; NOBE; OxBTC; PoFWW

Flour is exhaustion. Kitchen. Laura Jensen. LCAP-2

Flour of England, fruit of Spain. A Plum Pudding. Mother Goose. OxNR; ReMoGo

Flourish of silver, A. Deer Park. John Montague. PBCIP

Flourish of sunlight in the room where, A. Claud Cockburn. Thomas McCarthy. PBCIP

Flourishing his head around. The Cat. Kusatao, *Japanese.* PC, *tr. by* Tze-si Huang

Flow Chart. John Ashbery.

"Still in the published city but not yet." PmAP

Flow, flow—he's often near water. Inscribed on a Painting of Bamboo. Wu Chen, *Chinese.* CoBLCP, *tr. by* Jonathan Chaves

Flow, flow the waves hated. Illusions. Ralph Waldo Emerson. APN-1; NCAP

Flow gently, sweet Afton, among thy green braes. Robert Burns. AWP; FaBoBe; ImPo; NAEL-2

Flow swiftly into thee, and in thee ever end. (LL) Upon Nothing. John Wilmot, 2d Earl of Rochester. NOSC; OBSV; OxAEP-1; PoEL-3

Flower, The. Robert Creeley. PmAP

Flower, The. George Herbert. AWP; ESCV; FMP; FSCP; GeHe; NAEL-1; NOBE; NOCV; NoP-4; OBGa; PBRV; PoEL-2; SeCP

Flower, A. Po Chü-i, *Chinese.* TAL, *tr. by* Robert Payne

Flower and not a flower; of mist yet not of mist, A. P'u—Hua Fei Hua. Po Chü-i, *Chinese.* IMW, *tr. by* Duncan Mackintosh

Flower and the Leaf, The. The Lady of the Arbour. OBGa *Fr.* The Flower and the Leaf.

"And at the last I cast my mine eye aside." WPE

Flower, and yet not a flower, A. Tune: "Flower unlike Flower." Po Chü-i, *Chinese.* SuSp, *tr. by* Eugene Eoyang

Flower blooms, A. Tanka. Kanoko Okamoto, *Japanese.* MJT, *tr. by* Makoto Ueda

Flower-Boat, The. Robert Frost. PoA

Flower Chorus. Ralph Waldo Emerson. BoTP

Flower Ensnarer of Psalms. Rossana Ombres, *Italian.* BoWoP, *tr. by* I. L. Salomon

Flower-feasting bee, why do you touch upon. Meleager. HePo, *tr. by* Barbara Hughes Fowler *Fr.* I'll Twine White Violets. NIP-4, *tr. by* Goldwin Smith

Flower-fed buffaloes of the spring, The. Vachel Lindsay. CMoP; GM; MoAmPo; NOBA; OBCA; PoE; RB; TRP; VGW

("Flower-fed buffalos of the spring, The.") CA

Flower Given to My Daughter, A. James Joyce. OBMV; RB; RaBo

Flower Herding on Mount Monadnock. Galway Kinnell. HeIP-4; LCAP-2; NOBA; NoAM

(Flower-herding Pictures on Mount Monadnock.) CoAmPo

Flower in the crannied wall. Tennyson. BLPA; CTV; ImPo; InPK-6; NAEL-2; PBMP; TFi

Flower in the leaves, only as heaven pleases. Deep in Winter. Tu Fu, *Chinese*. PLT, *tr. by* A. C. Graham

Flower Is Looking, A. Harold Monro. MoBrPo *Fr*. Strange Meetings.

Flower is not visible, The. Precipice. Sang Yi. PFTM, *tr. by* Walter Lew *Fr*. Critical Condition.

Flower is withered on the stem, The. The Nurse's Lament. Mary Elizabeth Coleridge. NOBVV; OxBSP

Flower Market, The. Po Chü-i, *Chinese*. ChiP, *tr. by* Arthur Waley

Flower Market. Pierre Reverdy, *French*. PFTM, *tr. by* Kenneth Rexroth

Flower Master, The. Medbh McGuckian. PNI

Flower / my heart, The. Poem to Be Recited Every 8 Years While Eating Unleavened Tamales. *Unknown, Aztec Indian*. STP, *tr. by* Anselm Hollo

Flower of Flame, The. Robert Malise Bowyer Nichols.
"Before I woke I knew her gone." OBMV

Flower of Mullein, A. Lizette Woodworth Reese. MoAmPo

Flower of Old Japan, The. Alfred Noyes.
Epilogue: "Carol, every violet has." MoBrPo

FLOWER of roses, angels' joy. Hymn to the Virgin. *Unknown*. NoSic

Flower of the flock. On Sweet Killen Hill. Tom MacIntyre. CIP-2; PBCIP

Flower of the foam of the waves. Captive of the White City. Ina Coolbrith. PaTW

Flower of the pear-tree gathers and turns to fruit, The. At the End of Spring. Po Chü-i, *Chinese*. ChiP, *tr. by* Arthur Waley

Flower of the race, The. Gentlemen. Geoffrey Taylor. FaBoEE

Flower of the vine! Stornelli and Strambotti. Agnes Mary Frances Robinson. VWP

Flower of This Purple Dye. Shakespeare. CTC *Fr*. A Midsummer Night's Dream.

Flower of Virtue is the heart's content, The. Sonnet: Of Virtue. Folgore da San Geminiano, *Italian*. AWP, *tr. by* D. G. Rossetti

Flower of waves, A. Lady Ise, *Japanese*. BoWoP, *tr. by* Etsuko Terasaki *and* Irma Brandeis

Flower-Patterned Snake. So Chong-Ju, *Korean*. VCWP, *tr. by* David R. McCann

Flower Poem. Alec Derwent Hope. BMAP

Flower Pot, The. David Shimoni, *Hebrew*. MHP, *tr. by* Ruth Finer Mintz

Flower pot. William Carlos Williams. *See* Poem: "As the cat / climbed over."

Flower-Rain Terrace, The. Tao-chi, *Chinese*. CoBLCP, *tr. by* Jonathan Chaves

Flower-seller's fat, The. The Flower-Seller. Eleanor Farjeon. BoTP

Flower Shadows. Mo Shih-lung, *Chinese*. CoBLCP, *tr. by* Jonathan Chaves

Flower Songs. Nezahualcoyotl. PaTW

Flower that smiles to-day [*or* today], The. Mutability. Shelley. LaPo; NAEL-2; NoP-4; OBNC

Flower-tinted cheek, the flowery close, A. Hafiz. TAL, *tr. by* Gertrude Lowthian Bell *Fr*. Odes.

Flower-tree. Sang Yi, *Korean*. CKP, *tr. by* Jaihiun Kim

Flower unblown; a book unread; A. The New Year. Horatio Nelson Powers. PoToHe

Flower was offered to me, A. William Blake. *See* My Pretty Rose-Tree.

Flower was offered [*or* offerd] to me, A. My Pretty Rose-Tree. William Blake. BoLoP; FHYEP; NAEL-2; NOBRP *Fr*. Songs of Experience.

Flowering Absence, A. John Montague. BiHa; CIP-2; PBCIP

Flowering azaleas dotting / the roadside. The Land of Flowering Azaleas. Tong-yop Shin, *Korean*. CKP, *tr. by* Jaihiun Kim

Flowering Bars, The. Charles Donnelly. CIP-2

Flowering Cherry, The. Janet Frame. PeNZ

Flowering of the Rod, The. Hilda Doolittle.
"Blue-geese, white-geese, you may say." NOBA
"It is no madness to say." FaBoMo

Flowering Plums. Han Yü, *Chinese*. GaP, *tr. by* Hans H. Frankel

Flowering poppies. Tanka. Miya Shūji, *Japanese*. MJT, *tr. by* Makoto Ueda

Flowering tree does not spare itself, The. Wang T'ing hsiang, *Chinese*. CoBLCP, *tr. by* Jonathan Chaves

Flowering War, The. *Unknown, Aztec Indian*. STP, *tr. by* Jerome Rothenberg

Flowering Without End. Stefan Zweig. *Fr*. Jeremiah. TrJP, *tr. by* Eden *and* Cedar Paul

Flowerpot. William Carlos Williams. *See* Poem: "As the cat / climbed over."

Flowers. Margaret Atwood. NoP-4

Flowers. Roo Borson. NOBC

Flowers. Wendy Cope. NoP-4

Flowers. D. J. Enright. OBGa

Flowers. Kathleen Fraser. CrSp

Flowers. (LL) Impression de Nuit; London. Lord Alfred Bruce Douglas. ADE

Flowers. Edith Jay Scovell. WPN

Flowers achieve their own floweriness and its's a miracle. Flowers and Men. D. H. Lawrence. FaBoEE

Flowers along the palace, The. Waiting for Audience on a Spring Night. Tu Fu, *Chinese*. OHPC, *tr. by* Kenneth Rexroth

Flowers always know what they. Jessie Orton Jones. CTV *Fr*. (VI from Secrets).

Flowers and Men ("Flowers achieve their own floweriness and its's a miracle"). D. H. Lawrence. FaBoEE

Flowers and Moonlight on the Spring River. Yang-Ti, Emperor of Sui Dynasty, *Chinese*. ChiP, *tr. by* Arthur Waley

Flowers, and tall-stalked grasses, and a bee. Ivan Alekseievich Bunin, *Russian*. GI, *tr. by* David Curzon *and* Vladislav I. Guerassev

Flowers and Trees. Sir Walter Scott. OxAEP-2 *Fr*. The Lady of the Lake.

Flowers are dead, The. Scenery. Ted Joans. PoBA

Flowers—at ease and tall. The king is dead. (LL) No Swan So Fine. Marianne Moore. MeMAP; NALW; NoP-4; OxBA; PoA; UnPo

Flowers bloom. Flowers in the Mountains. Sowol Kim, *Korean*. CKP, *tr. by* Jaihiun Kim

Flowers bloom, flowers fall. To Send Away Melancholy. Huang Tsun-hsien, *Chinese*. SuSp, *tr. by* An-yan Tang

Flowers by the Sea. William Carlos Williams. CMoP; MoAmPo; NoAM; RB; TAP

Flowers can be cousins of the stars. There Are Different Gardens. Carl Sandburg. ImGa

Flowers did not seem to unfurl from slow bulbs, The. An Easter Garland. Carol Rumens. FaBoWP

Flowers! Down to the river! into the street! Allen Ginsberg. *See* Howl.

Flowers drift downstream—a dismal thing, this world! Fleeting Time. *Unknown, Vietnamese*. AVP, *tr. by* Huỳnh Sanh Thông

Flowers, flowers, high-nō! *Unknown*. CDNP

Flowers for Luis Bunuel. Stuart Z. Perkoff. NeAP

Flower's fragrance is a woman's virtue, A. The Orchid House. Medbh McGuckian. CABP

Flowers from growing, your flowers. (LL) For James Dean. Frank O'Hara. NNaP; NeAP

Flowers get a darkening brilliance now, The. The Dying Garden. Howard Nemerov. Poetsp

Flowers hast thou in thyself, and foliage. Sonnet: To His Lady Joan, of Florence. Guido Cavalcanti, *Italian*. AWP, *tr. by* D. G. Rossetti

Flowers have fenced-in. The Clearing. Peter Everwine, *after the Nahuatl Indian*. NNaP

Flowers have lost their withered red, The. Spring Scene. Su Tung-p'o, *Chinese*. TAL, *tr. by* Robert Payne

Flowers I called Christ's when I was four, The. (LL) Supernatural Love. Gjertrud Schnackenberg. NoP-4

Flowers in bud on the trees, The. On the Death of a New Born Child. Mei Yao Ch'en, *Chinese*. OHPC, *tr. by* Kenneth Rexroth

Flowers in legions bloomed around in forest, scrub, and marsh. Tasmanian Scenes. Louisa Meredith. NOBAu

Flowers in the Mountains. Sowol Kim, *Korean*. CKP, *tr. by* Jaihiun Kim

Flowers in the Valley. *Unknown*. OxBoLi

Flowers in the Ward. John Shaw Neilson. CBAP

Flowers in Town, The. Stanley Cook. AYFP

Flowers leaves stems / lips hands eyes. Still Life. "Shahryar," *Urdu*. OMIP, *tr. by* Gopi Chand Narang *and* David Paul Douglas

Flowers left thick at nightfall in the wood, The. In Memoriam (Easter, 1915). Edward Thomas. GTBS-P; NOBE; NoP-4; OBWP; OBWVE; OxBTC; PeFWW; Spl

Flower's Name, The. Robert Browning. CTC; GaP *Fr*. Garden Fancies. (Garden Fancies.) OBGa

Flowers need irrigation, The. Busy. Yüan Mei, *Chinese*. CoBLCP, *tr. by* Jonathan Chaves

Flowers nodding gaily, scent in air. A Duet. Thomas Sturge Moore. OBEV

Flowers of Darkness. Frank Marshall Davis. PoBA

Flowers of fire. (LL) To the Tune "Soaring Clouds." Huang O, *Chinese*. BoWoP; PBWP; WPOW, *tr. by* Kenneth Rexroth *and* Ling Chung

Flowers of Love and Persuasion. (LL) Love has found out how to mix. Asclepiades, *Greek*. GrAn; PGA, *tr. by* Kenneth Rexroth

Flowers of Perdita, The. Shakespeare. *Fr*. The Winter's Tale.

Flowers of Politics, I, The. Michael McClure. NeAP

Flowers of Politics, II, The. Michael McClure. NeAP

Flowers of the Forest, The. Alison Rutherford Cockburn. ECWP

Flowers of the Forest, The. Jane Elliot. CH; ECWP; FaBoCh; NoP-4; OxBS; SCGP; WPE
(Lament for Flodden, The.) GTBS-P; OBEV

Flowers of the willow, light, fluffy by the second moon. Willow Catkins. Hsüeh T'ao, *Chinese*. SuSp, *tr. by* Eric W. Johnson

Flowers rare and sweet I sent, whose delicate white. White Lilies. Theodore Wratislaw. ADE

Flowers say goodbye to me, The. Sergey Aleksandrovich Yesenin, *Russian*. TCRP, *tr. by* Geoffrey Thurley

Flowers shall hang upon the palls. Death. John Clare. GTBS-P

Flowers that in thy garden rise, The. Song. Sir Henry John Newbolt. FaBoTw

Flowers through the window. Nantucket. William Carlos Williams. HAP; InPS-3; OxBA; TAP; TRP; WeW-3

Flowers upon the rosemary spray, The. The Rosemary Spray. Luis de Góngora y Argote, *Spanish*. AWP, *tr. by* E. Churton

Flowers whirl away, The. Kintsune, *Japanese*. OHPJ, *tr. by* Kenneth Rexroth

Flowers will do us no good on our tombstones. *Unknown*, *Greek*. PGA, *tr. by* Kenneth Rexroth

Flowing of all men's tears beneath the sky, The. (LL) Before the Mirror. Swinburne. GS; OBEV

Flowrets—wreaths—thy banks along. To a Gentleman, Who Desired Proper Materials for a Monody. *Unknown*. NOEC

Flue. (LL) Flea and a fly in a flue, A. *Unknown*. CTV

Flukum couldn't stand the strain. Flukum. A Poem for Black Relocation Centers. Etheridge Knight. NNaP *Fr.* Two Poems for Black Relocation Centers. NNaP

Flunked out and laid-off. The Eisenhower Years. Paul Zimmer. PBCAP

Flush / a Play. Leslie Scalapino. PmAP

Flush or Faunus. Elizabeth Barrett Browning. VWP

("You see this dog; it was but yesterday.") FP

Flush with the pond the lurid furnace burned. The Steam Threshing-Machine. Charles Tennyson Turner. OBNC

Flute, The. Sophia De Mello Breyner, *Portuguese*. VCWP, *tr. by* Ruth Fainlight

Flute. Sokch'o Shin, *Korean*. CKP, *tr. by* Jaihiun Kim

Flute; a Pastoral, The. José-Maria de Heredia, *French*. AWP, *tr. by* H. J. C. Grierson

Flute Holes. Chaesam Park, *Korean*. CKP, *tr. by* Jaihiun Kim

Flute-music. Rabindranath Tagore, *Bengali*. OMIP, *tr. by* William Radice

Flute Notes from a Reedy Pond. Sylvia Plath. FaBoMo

Flute of Daphnis, The. Edward Cracroft Lefroy. AWP *Fr.* Echoes from Theocritus.

Flute of interior time is played whether we hear it or not, The. Kabir, *Hindi*. ITG, *tr. by* Robert Bly

Fluteplayers from Finmarken. Carl Rakosi. FTOS

Flutes, and the harp on the plain. Home on the Range, February 1962. Edward Dorn. CoAmPo

Fluting filniriri. Oaten Pipe. Ha'un Han, *Korean*. CKP, *tr. by* Jaihiun Kim

Flutter flutter on clothes and cap, jujube flowers fall. Tune: Sand of Silk-washing Stream. Su Tung-p'o, *Chinese*. CoBCP, *tr. by* Burton Watson

Flutter flutter on clothes and cap, jujube flowers fall, Tune: "Sand of Silk-washing Stream." Tune: Sand of Silk-washing Stream ("Flutter, flutter, on clothes and cap, jujube flowers fall"). Su Tung-p'o. CoBCP, *tr. by* Burton Watson; CoBCP *Fr.* Along the Road to Stone Lake.

Fluttering Leaves. Rodney Bennett. BoTP

Flux. Richard Eberhart. Poetsp; VGW

Flux. Simonides, *Greek*. OBCVT, *tr. by* Willis Barnstone

Fly, The. Philip Ayres, *after the Spanish of* Quevedo. OBVE

Fly, The. William Blake. CTAV; FHYEP; NOBRP; NOxBChV; OxAEP-2; PBMP; Ro *Fr.* Songs of Experience.

("If I live / Or if I die.") (LL) CTAV

("Little fly.") Ro

Fly, The. Walter De la Mare. OTCP

Fly, The. Barnabe Googe. CH

Fly, The. Miroslav Holub, *Czech*. PoSu; RB, *tr. by* Milner *and* George Theiner; VCWP, *tr. by* Stuart Friebert *and* Dana Hábová

("She sat on the willow bark.") VCWP, *tr. by* Stuart Friebert *and* Dana Hábová

Fly. W. S. Merwin. ChAP; NNaP

Fly, The. Ogden Nash. OBCoV

Fly, The. William Oldys. *See* On a Fly Drinking out of [*or* from] His Cup.

Fly, The. Karl Shapiro. LiTM; MoP; NoAM; PBMP; PFE; SoSe-8

Fly, A. Tanka. Saitō Mokichi, *Japanese*. MJT, *tr. by* Ueda, Makoto

Fly. Larry Wiggin. HA

Fly about a Glass[e] of Burnt Claret, A. Richard Lovelace. CaPo

Fly away, fly away over the sea. Christina Rossetti. ACTP; AYFP; CTAV; Spl

Fly-Away Horse, The. Eugene Field. CTAV

Fly by night / black galaxy / friendly galaxy. Lee Morgan. David Henderson. SeSe

Fly Caught in a Cobweb, A. Richard Lovelace. BeJo; CaPo; SeCP

Fly down, Death: call me. Madboy's Song. Muriel Rukeyser. MoAmPo; TrJP

Fly envious Time, till thou run out thy race. On Time. Milton. ImPo; OBEV; SCGP

Fly-flicking cattle-tail, quiet byre. Summer Reflection. Cyril Cusack. TIRV

Fly, fly, my friends. Sonnet 20. Sir Philip Sidney. AEP; NoSic; OAEL-1 *Fr.* Astrophil and Stella. AAS; SiPS

Fly [*or* Flie] hand in hand to heav'n! (LL) Sunday. George Herbert. GeHe; PeECV; TrCP

Fly hence O! joy noe longer heere abide. Sonnet 29. Mary Sidney, Countess of Montgomery Wroth. KTR *Fr.* Pamphilia to Amphilanthus.

Fly hence, shadows, that do keep. Dawn. John Ford. OBEV *Fr.* The Lover's Melancholy.

Fly in December. Robert Wallace. NYBP

Fly is brushed off the pale forehead, The. Mistake. Haim Guri, *Hebrew*. IP, *tr. by* Warren Bargad *and* Stanley F. Chyet

Fly is dying hard, The. Mayday. Ed Roberson. PoBA

Fly, Muse, thy wonted themes, nor longer seek. "Break, Break, Break." Sir John Collings Squire. BXAP

Fly not thus my brow of snow. Ode 51. Anacreon, *Greek*. OBCVT, *tr. by* Thomas Moore

Fly on the Water, A. Paul Zweig. WeT

Fly or beetle on their track, The. The Shepherd Boy. John Clare. NOBVV

Fly she sat in Shamble row, The. The Fly's Wedding. *Unknown*. CBNP

Fly That Flew into My Mistress'[s] Eye, A. Thomas Carew. CaPo

Fly[e] to her heart; hover about her heart. Her Heart. Bartholomew Griffin. AAS *Fr.* Fidessa, More Chaste than Kind[e].

Fly to him I love the best. (LL) Bless you, bless you, burnie-bee [*or* bonnie-bee]. Mother Goose. BoTP; OxNR

Fly to the desert, fly with me. Thomas Moore. BIrV *Fr.* Lalla Rookh.

Flyer's Fall. Wallace Stevens. MeMAP; SAmP

Flyfisherman in Wartime. Leonard Bacon. FYAP

Flying. Michael Dransfield. BMAP

Flying. J. M. Westrup. BoTP

Flying at Night. Ted Kooser. InPK-6; PBCAP

Flying Bells. Yüan Mei, *Chinese*. CoBLCP, *tr. by* Jonathan Chaves

Flying catkins, flying floss, where have they gone? Tune: "Immortal at the River"—Winter Willow. Na-lan Hsing-te, *Chinese*. SuSp, *tr. by* Irving Y. Lo

Flying Change, The. Henry Taylor. Poetr

Flying Cloud, The. *Unknown*. AmFP

Flying Crooked. Robert Graves. FaBoMo; LiTM; OxBSP; PeLV; RB; TwCP

Flying Deeper into the Century. Pier Giorgio Di Cicco. NOBC

Flying Dutchman, The. Ian D. Colvin. PeSAV

Flying Fish, The. Jack Cope. PeSA

Flying Fish, The. John Gray. NOBVV

Flying Fish, The. John Gray.

"Of the birds that fly in the farthest sea." OBNC

Flying Flower, A. Arakida Moritaké, *Japanese*. APo, *tr. by* Geoffrey Bownas *and* Anthony Thwaite

Flying,—flying beyond all lower regions. A Poet's Hope. William Ellery Channing. PAR

Flying Fowl, and Creeping Things, Praise Ye the Lord. Isaac Watts. ChIV-1

Flying Fox. Thomas William Shapcott. CBAP

Flying Friendly Skies. Turner Cassity. MT

Flying from the dry pall of the city. The Gray Woods Exploding. Earle Birney. NoAM

Flying Home. Gabriel Gbadamosi. NBrP

Flying Home from Utah. May Swenson. WPE

Flying Horse was in jail. The Urban Experience: Part Two. Lew Blockcolski. VoR

Flying Inn, The. G. K. Chesterton.

Wine and Water. ChIV-1; MoBrPo

Flying low on the level sky of her final enduring. (LL) Penelope's Despair. Yannis Ritsos, *Greek*. GrIP, *tr. by* Edmund Keeley

Flying Noises. Thomas Lux. LCAP-2

Flying out from. Issa, *Japanese*. EnlH, *tr. by* Stephen Mitchell

Flying Petals. Hsiao Kang, *Chinese*. OHMPC, *tr. by* Kenneth Rexroth

Flying sand darkens the air, the moon is a dull yellow. Li K'ai-hsien. *Fr.* Songs of the Frontier. CoBLCP, *tr. by* Jonathan Chaves

Flying saucers, levitation. Moon Rocks, Moon in the Man. David Byrne. CBNP

Flying Scrolls. Ralph Hodgson. FaBoTw

"Movement, she explained, would bring poetry to the rich, The."

Flying Tailor, The. James Hogg. BXAP

Flying Temple. Milorad Pavic, *Serbo-Croatian.* HSix, *tr.* by Charles Simic

Flying up a valley in the Alps where the rock. Lufthansa. John Tranter. BMAP; NOBAu

Flying Visit, A. Thomas Hood. CBNP

Flying word from here and there, A. The Master. Edwin Arlington Robinson. CBCWP; LiTM; MoAmPo

Fly's Wedding, The. *Unknown.* CBNP

Flyting o' Life and Daith, The. Hamish Henderson. OxBS

Fo' a yeah or mo' on this roof I'se layed. The Signal Fire. Aeschylus. CTC, *tr.* by Dallam Simpson *Fr.* Agamemnon. NAWM-1, *tr.* by Robert Fagles

Foal, The. William Renton. NOBVV

Foal. Vernon Watkins. OxBTC

Foam fluttered on the sea like birds' wings. Hills of Salt. Dahlia Ravikovitch, *Hebrew.* WPOW, *tr.* by Chana Bloch

Foaming white wave washes over a grave, A. Exultation. Hywel ab Owain Gwynedd, *Welsh.* OBWVE, *tr.* by Gwyn Williams

Foam's Frail Power. Joseph Mallord William Turner. OxBoS

Fo'c'sle had gone under the creep, The. The Final Moments. Edwin John Pratt. NOBC *Fr.* The Titanic.

Focus. Adrienne Rich. FaBoWP

Fod. *Unknown.* AmFP

Foetus. Phyllis Haring. PeSA

Foetus kicks. Janice Bostok. HA

Fog. Louise Imogen Guiney. APN-2

Fog. Gary Hotham. HA

Fog. Henry David Thoreau. APN-1

Fog at Liang-hsiang. Yüan Mei, *Chinese.* CoBLCP, *tr.* by Jonathan Chaves

Fog comes / on little cat feet, The. Carl Sandburg. AmPP; CTV; ChAP; HeIP-4; InPK-6; MoAmPo; NAAL-2; OBCA; SAGP; Spl; TAP; TFi; TTTS

Fog Dream, The. Sandra M. Gilbert. PoA

Fog hanged over the park, the night cold, and, clean. And, Hinges. Ted Greenwald. FTOS

Fog has settled, The. Claire Pratt. HA

Fog in November, trees have no heads. Leonard Clark. AYFP

Fog lifting above the fields. Mussel Rock/Lowtide—Santa Cruz, California 1959. Jeff Tagami. OpBo

Fog obscures the deserted mountain. A Man in Hangchou Spread Word that I Had Died. Chen-chü Heard of This and Was Upset, So I Have Written This To Send Him. Ni Tsan, *Chinese.* CoBLCP, *tr.* by Jonathan Chaves

Fog of night envelops the flowering trees, The. T'ang Yin. CoBLCP, *tr.* by Jonathan Chaves *Fr.* Spring—River—Flower—Moon—Night.

Fog over the base: the beams ranging. A Front. Randall Jarrell. NoP-4; OBWP; OxBC; PoWW; VGW

Fog smog fog smog. Windshield Wiper. Eve Merriam. KaS

Fog. The road I usually wander down. Georgy Vladimirovich Ivanov, *Russian.* TCRP, *tr.* by Daniel Weissbort

Fog veils the river and the mountains. Taking the Ferry at Ta-kao at Dawn. Yang Wei-chen, *Chinese.* SuSp, *tr.* by Jonathan Chaves

Fogged hill-scene on an enormous continent, A. Hunger. Adrienne Rich. NMM-2

Foggy, Foggy Dew, The. *Unknown.* AS; OxBoLi; PeLV

Foggy moon, bird-calls in the flowers at dawn. Twenty-first Day of the Seventh Month. Henry Vaughan, *Chinese.* CoBLCP, *tr.* by Jonathan Chaves

Fol de riddle, lol de riddle, hi ding do. (LL) Carrion crow sat upon [*or* on] an oak, The [*or* A]. Mother Goose. LB; OxNR; ReMoGo

Fold away all your bright-tinted dresses. Hospital Duties. *Unknown.* CBCWP

Fold home, fast fold thy child. (LL) The Blessed Virgin Compared to the Air We Breathe. Gerard Manley Hopkins. NOBVV; PeVV

Fold it up carefully, lay it aside. The Jacket of Gray. Caroline Augusta Ball. CBCWP

Fold of my flesh. Sleep Close to Me. Gabriela Mistral, *Spanish.* PBWP, *tr.* by D. M. Pettinella

Fold us music-drunken in. (LL) Merlin II. Ralph Waldo Emerson. PAR; PoEL-4

Folded close under deepening snow. (LL) The First Snowfall [*or* Snow-Fall]. James Russell Lowell. BLPA; FaBoBe; TAP

Folded delicately into shape. The Nun's Dance. Chi-hun Cho, *Korean.* CKP, *tr.* by Jaihiun Kim

Folded hands and darkened eyes. The Stone. Walter De la Mare. WeW-3

Folded Skyscraper, A. William Carlos Williams. Hemmed-in Males. PoRA

Folders, papers, proofs, maps. Artists' Letters. Thomas Kinsella. BiHa

Folding clothes / I think of folding you. Sorting Laundry. Elisavietta Ritchie. SoSe-8

Folding sheets. Marge Piercy. *Fr.* Six Underrated Pleasures. EC2

Folding the Flocks. John Fletcher. CH *Fr.* The Faithful Shepherdess. (Evening Song.) (Priest's Chant, The.)

Folding the paper money, tearing the bills. (LL) The Struggle. Toi Derricotte. IFJA; LTA; PBCAP

Folding the Sheets. Rosemary Dobson. NOBAu *Fr.* Daily Living.

Foliage, bees and flowers. . . walking alone under low skies. Poet. Luchezar Elenkov, *Bulgarian.* CEEP, *tr.* by Jascha Kessler *and* Aleksandar Shurbanov

Foliage foliage. Ivar Ivask, *Estonian.* CEEP, *tr.* by Ivar Ivask

Foliage of Vision. James Merrill. VGW

Folk Museum, The. Medbh McGuckian. CIP-2

Folk Singer of the Thirties, A. James Dickey. GM

Folk Song: "O I'm off to Hullaboola where the climate's never cooler." Bruce Beaver. OBCoV

Folk Song. *Unknown, Chinese.* ChiPo, *tr.* by Cecelia Liang

Folk-Songs. Chan Fang-sheng, *Chinese.* ChiP, *tr.* by Arthur Waley

Folk Songs For Today. Nguyễn Tất Nhiên, *Vietnamese.* AVP, *tr.* by Huỳnh Sanh Thông

Folk Tune. Joseph Brodsky. EP

Folk Who Live in Backward Town, The. Mary Ann Hoberman. OBCA

Folk Wisdom. Thomas Kinsella. TwCP

Folks ain't got no right to censuah othah [*or* uthah] folks about dey habits. Accountability. Paul Laurence Dunbar. APN-2; PoLF

Folks and Me. Lucile Crites. PWR

Folks at home half the time are thinkin' about dirt, The. Soap, the Oppressor. Burges Johnson. PoLF

Folks downstairs brought him home, The. Dylan, Two Days. Patricia Smith. GT

Folks, I'm telling you. Advice. Langston Hughes. GEA; NBLV; SAmP

Folks need a lot of loving in the morning. Need of Loving. Strickland W. Gillilan. BLPA; PoToHe

Folks on both sides, see what I'm bearing here? Carrying a Cangue Around the Neck. Nguyễn Hữu Huân, *Vietnamese.* AVP, *tr.* by Huỳnh Sanh Thông

Folkway. Gábor Görgey, *Hungarian.* CEEP, *tr.* by Jascha Kessler

Follies of Adam, The. Theodore Roethke. ChIV-1

Follow a shadow [*or* shaddow], it still flies you. Song. That Women Are But Men's Shadows. Ben Jonson. BeJo; NOBE; OBEV; OxBSP; SeCP

Follow back from the gull's bright arc and the osprey's plunge. Water Ouzel. William H. Matchett. CoAP; NYBP

Follow, follow[e] / Though with mischiefe. Thomas Campion. EnLoPo *Fr.* Observations in the Art of English Poesie.

Follow him. (LL) He Who Knows. ("He who knows not and knows not [that he knows not]"). *Unknown, Arabic.* CTV, *tr.* by *Unknown*

Follow its lazy main street lounging. Hawthorne. Robert Lowell. AFr

Follow my Bangalorey Man. *Unknown.* OxNR

Follow pattern kill Cadogan. Yes, Lord. Bajan Litany. Bruce St. John. PBCV

Follow The Gleam. (LL) Merlin and the Gleam. Tennyson. FHYEP; NTP; OAEL-2

Follow thy fair sun unhappy shadow. Thomas Campion. AAS; CH; EnLoPo; NOBE; NOSC; NoP-4; NoSic; OBEV; PoEL-2; SCGP; UnPo ("Sun still proved, the shadow still disdained, The.") (LL) NoP-4; PBRV

Follow your saint, follow with accents sweet. Thomas Campion. AAS; EBEV; EnLoPo; HAP; NOBE; NOSC; NoSic; OAEL-1; OBEV; OxAEP-1; PoE

Followed the bird in the long forest where it cried. In Her Song She Is Alone. Jon Swan. NYBP

Follower. Seamus Heaney. CABP; IIP; PNI

Following forbidden streets. The Wraith-Friend. George Barker. OBMV

Following Her to Sleep. Jeffrey McDaniel. BAP-94

Following His Rhymes and Answering the Poems of My Friend Next Door on Recent Events. Tai Piao-yüan, *Chinese.* "South of the house, north of the house." CoBLCP, *tr.* by Jonathan Chaves

Following the Army on Campaign. Wang Ch'ang-ling, *Chinese.* "At Jad Gate Pass mountain ridges several thousand-fold." SuSp, *tr.* by Ronald C. Miao "In the citadel of Jade Gate Pass, elm leaves early scatter yellow." SuSp, *tr.* by Ronald C. Miao "P'i-p'a begins the dance, midst changing new sounds, The." SuSp, *tr.* by Ronald C. Miao

Following the Rhumes of Chiang Hui-shu. Su Tung-p'o, *Chinese.* CoBCP, *tr.* by Burton Watson

Following the Rhymes of Autumn Night Song by Meng Tzu-chou, Signatory Official of the Board of Rites. Yü Chi, *Chinese.* CoBLCP, *tr.* by Jonathan Chaves

Following the Rhymes of Bamboo Branch Songs in Response to Yüan Po-chang. Yü Chi, *Chinese.* CoBLCP, *tr. by* Jonathan Chaves

Following the Rhymes of Chang Hsün, in My Study in Late Spring. Huang T'ing-chien, *Chinese.* SuSp, *tr. by* Michael E. Workman

Following the Rhymes of Chiang Hui-shu. Su Tung-p'o. *See* Following the Rhumes of Chiang Hui-shu.

Following the Rhymes of Fellow Graduate P'ei Chung-mou. Huang T'ing-chien, *Chinese.* SuSp, *tr. by* Michael E. Workman

Following the Rhymes of Kao Chi-ti's Poem: "We Had Planned to Travel to Cloud Cliff But Couldn't Because of Rain." Hsü Pen, *Chinese.* CoBLCP, *tr. by* Jonathan Chaves

Following the Rhymes of Magistrate Liu's Poems on Entertaining Two Assistant Premiers at Pine-Snow Temple. Hsü Chung-hsing, *Chinese.*
  "Trees are ancient, thick with patterns of moss, The." CoBLCP, *tr. by* Jonathan Chaves

Following the Rhymes of Shao-pao Huang's Poem on Being Moved While Visiting the Farmers. Yang Shih-ch'i, *Chinese.* CoBLCP, *tr. by* Jonathan Chaves

Following the Rhymes of the Six Poems "Thinking of the Past at Ku-Su and Ch'ien-t'ang." Ni Tsan, *Chinese.* CoBLCP, *tr. by* Jonathan Chaves

Following the Rhymes of Wang An-shih's Poem "Inscribed on the Wall of the Temple of Western Great Unity." Huang T'ing-chien, *Chinese.* SuSp, *tr. by* Michael E. Workman

Following the Rhymes of Yang T'ing-ho's Poem, "On the Road Back, Accompanying the Imperial Retinue on a Visit to the Tombs of Former Emperors." Li Tung-yang, *Chinese.* CoBLCP, *tr. by* Jonathan Chaves

Following the Rhymes of Yü-chai's Poems on Autumn. Ni Tsan, *Chinese.*
  "You ask when I will go back home." CoBLCP, *tr. by* Jonathan Chaves

Following the roads. Ono no Komachi, *Japanese.* OHMPJ, *tr. by* Kenneth Rexroth

Following their road of exit, they stooped over and came out. *Zuni Oral Tradition.* APN-2, *tr. by* Matilda Coxe Stevenson *Fr.* History Myth of the Coming of the A' shiwi as Narrated by 'Kiäklo.

Follows the naked work, profoundly moved by it. (LL) Story of a Hotel Room. Rosemary Tonks. APAD; LW; OxBTC

Follows the others stick in / hand triumphant to disaster. William Carlos Williams. *See* The Parable of the Blind.

Folly Of Being Comforted, The. W. B. Yeats. GBL; HeIP-4; LoP; NAEL-2; PFE

Folly's Song. Thomas Dekker *and others.* NOSC

Fond Affection. *Unknown.* AS

Fond aged man, why doe you on me gaze. Mary Sidney, Countess of Montgomery Wroth. *Fr.* Urania.

Fond greeting, hillock there, A. Laoiseach Mac an Bhaird. NOIV

Fond man *Musophilus,* that thus dost spend. Poet and Critic. Samuel Daniel. NoSiC; PBRV *Fr.* Musophilus; or, Defence of All Learning.

Fond man, that canst believe [*or* beleeve] her blood. Celia Bleeding, to the Surgeon. Thomas Carew. CavPo; SeCP

Fond nymphs, from us true pleasure learn. In Derision of a Country Life. Edward Ravenscroft. NOSC

Fond woman, which wouldst [*or* would'st] have thy husband die. Jealosie. Donne. CBLP; ESCV *Fr.* Elegies.

Fond words have oft been spoken to thee, sleep! To Sleep. Wordsworth. Son

Fondle me. Marrow of My Bone. Mari E. Evans. BPo

"Fondling," she saith, "since I have hemmed thee here." Shakespeare. OAEL-1 *Fr.* Venus and Adonis.

Foo to the Infinite. Clayton Eshleman. MoNo

Food. Josephine Jacobsen. NMM-2

Food and Drink. Louis Untermeyer. MoAmPo

Food-Factory Kitchen. Vladimir Salimon, *Russian.* TCRP, *tr. by* Vera Dunham

Food for Fire, Food for Thought. Robert Duncan. NeAP

Food for Thought. Val Ferdinand. NBV

Food of Love. Carolyn Kizer. Poetr; RaBo

Food of Love, The. Shakespeare. *Fr.* Twelfth Night.

Food of the north tastes too much of the fat of the pig, The. D. H. Lawrence. FaBoEE

Food will be given to me, food will be given to me, because I obtained this magic treasure. Hä' mats'a Song Composed about Fifty Years Ago. *Unknown. Fr.* Dances and Songs of the Winter Ceremonial. APN-2, *tr. by* Franz Boas

Fool, The. Kenneth Mackenzie. BMAP

Fool, The. Padraic Pearse. TIRV

Fool, The. Novica Tadic, *Serbo-Croatian.* HSix, *tr. by* Charles Simic

Fool, a fool, A!—I bet a fool i' the forest. A Cold Rendering. *Unknown.* BXAP

Fool, a fool! I met a fool i' the forest, A. Motley's the Only Wear. Shakespeare. OBCoV *Fr.* As You Like It.

Fool and False. *Unknown. Fr.* The Panchatantra. AWP, *tr. by* Arthur Ryder

Fool and the Poet, The. Alexander Pope. *See* Epigram from the French.
  "Sir, I admit your general [*or* gen'ral] Rule."

Fool hath said in his heart, The, There is no God. Psalm 14. Bible, *O.T.* TrJP *Fr.* Psalms.

Fool In Love, A. Xuân Diệu, *Vietnamese.* AVP, *tr. by* Huỳnh Sanh Thông

Fool much bit by fleas put out the light, A. Richard Lovelace, *after the Greek of* Lucian. FaBoEE

Fool of nature, stood with stupid eyes, The. The Power of Love. Dryden. *Fr.* Cymon and Iphigenia. EPCY; OBNV

"Fool," said my Muse to me, "look in thy heart and /write." (LL) Sonnet 1: "Loving in truth, and fain[e] in verse my love to show." Sir Philip Sidney. AWP; EBEV; EPCY; GBL; GLoP; GSo; HAP; ImPo; InPS-3; LoP; NAEL-1; NoSiC; OAEL-1; OxAEP-1; PoE; Poetr; SCGP; Son; TFi

Fool, take up thy shaft again. Song. Thomas Stanley. EnLoPo

Fool there was and he made his prayer, A. The Vampire. Rudyard Kipling. NOBVV

Fool there was, and she lowered her pride, A. Woman's Answer to "The Vampire," A. Felicia Blake. BLPA

Fool, to put up four crosses at your door. Jonathan Swift. FaBoEE

Fooled me once and you fooled me bad. All Night Long Fooling Me. *Unknown.* AmFP

Foolish Child. *Unknown, Akan.* PBA, *tr. by* J. B. Danquah

Foolish eyes, thy streams give over. Song. Martha Sansom. ECWP

Foolish Flowers. Rupert Sargent Holland. CTV

Foolish impatient apricot trees. Vegetable Destiny. Nina Cassian, *Rumanian.* PBWP, *tr. by* Michael Impey *and* Brian Swann

Foolish little maiden bought a foolish little bonnet, A. What the Choir Sang about the New Bonnet. M. T. Morrison. BLPA

Foolish man rides here, A. In the Heart of the Desert. Al-Tirimmah, *Arabic.* ArPe, *tr. by* Omar S. Pound

Foolish men who accuse. She Proves the Inconsistency of the Desires and Criticism of Men Who Accuse Women of What They Themselves Cause. Sister Juana Inés de la Cruz, *Spanish.* BoWoP, *tr. by* Aliki *and* Willis Barnstone

Foolish prater, what dost thou. The Swallow. Abraham Cowley. EBEV; OBEV; OxAEP-1

Foolish rhythm turns in my idle head, A. A Tune. Arthur Symons. BoLoP; LBC; OBNC

Foolish useless man who had done nothing, A. Brummell at Calais. John Glassco. MoCV

Fools and Wise Men, *epigram.* Friedrich von Logau, *German.* GePo, *tr. by* George C. Schoolfield

Fool's disease, The. (LL) Flee on Your Donkey. Anne Sexton. NYBP; Poetr

Fools have power over wise men: each transactions, each affair. Fools and Wise Men. Friedrich von Logau, *German.* GePo, *tr. by* George C. Schoolfield

Fools in Love's College. John Lyly. *See* O Cupid! Monarch over Kings.

Fool's Prayer, The. Edward Rowland Sill. APN-2; FaBoBe; PoLF
  "'Tis not by guilt the onward sweep."

Fool's Preferment, A. Thomas D'Urfey.
  I'll Sail upon the Dog-Star. FaBoCh; OxBoLi

Fool's prophecy, The. Shakespeare. CBNP *Fr.* King Lear.

Fools! Sit down and wait for them to crumble! (LL) On the Fly-Leaf of Pound's Cantos. Basil Bunting. FaBoTw; NoAM; OxBTC

Fool's Song. Thomas Holcroft. CBNP; NOEC

Fools, they are the only nation. Nano's Song. Ben Jonson. *Fr.* Volpone. NAEL-1

Foot, The. Alice Jones. BAP-94

Foot-fall of her parting soul is softer than her singing, The. (LL) Felicia Hemans. Elizabeth Barrett Browning. VWP

Foot Fire Burn Dance. Natasha Le Bel. BAP-96

Foot Inspection. Siegfried Sassoon. EP

Foot of death has printed on my chest, The. Shudder [, The]. Donald Hall. NYBP

Foot of the tower. An angle where the darkness, The. Thomas Kinsella. PBCIP *Fr.* Nightwalker.

Foot Race Song. *Unknown, Pima.* OBVE, *tr. by* Frank Russell

Foot Soldiers. John Banister Tabb. OBAL

Foot-Washing, The. A. R. Ammons. ChIV-2

Foot-Washing, The. George Ella Lyon. CrSp; OxWW

Football. Louis Jenkins. RaBo

Football. Walt Mason. KaS

Football. "Nikolai Karpovich Otrada," *Russian.* TCRP, *tr. by* Daniel Weissbort

Football, The. Arizona Zipper. HA

Footbinding. Patricia Beer. NoP-4

Footnote. Anthony Delius. PeSA

Footnote at "Figure of Speech." Tina Darragh. FTOS

Footnote Extended, A, for Thomas Szasz's *Karl Kraus and the Soul Doctors*. Dannie Abse. HP

Footnote to Belloc's "Tarantella." John Heath-Stubbs. OBCoV

Footnote to Enright's "Apocalypse." Martin Bell. FaBoMo

Footnote to Howl. Allen Ginsberg. CAPP-1; CLPP

Footnote to John II: 4. Ronald Allison Kells Mason. PeNZ

Footnote to Tennyson. Gerald Bullett. UV

Footnote to the Amnesty Report on Torture. Margaret Atwood. NoAM

Footnote to the Lord's Prayer. Kay Smith.
    "Heaven which art in Heaven Our Father in Heaven." TrCP

Footnotes to "The Autobiography of Bertrand Russell." Mona Van Duyn.
    "This seems, in a world where love must take its chances." HAP

Footpath. Stella Ngatho. WPOW

Footpath would have been enough, A. The Entailed Farm. John Glassco. MoCV; NOBC

Footpaths Cross in the Rice Field. "Lin Ling." *Unknown.* PBWP, *tr. by* Kenneth Rexroth *and* Ling Chung

Footprint on the Air, A. Naomi Lewis. NOxBChV

Footprints. Dan Pagis, *Hebrew.* VCWP, *tr. by* Stephen Mitchell

Footprints made on the sands of. *Unknown.* CTV

Footprints of the Heart-of-the-Daybreak, The! Heart-of-the-Daybreak. Eugène Marais, *Afrikaans.* PeSA, *tr. by* Uys Krige *and* Jack Cope

Footprints on the Glacier. W. S. Merwin. MoP; NoAM

Footsteps, The. Paul Valéry, *French.* FLP; LoP, *tr. by* Alistair Elliot

For a Black Child. David Diop, *French.* NegPo, *tr. by* Ellen Conroy Kennedy

For a Black Poet. Gerald William Barrax. NBV

For a Broken Needle, Hazel Hall. NMM-2; PaTW

For a Brother. Richard Frost. BAP-95

For a Child Expected. Anne Ridler. LiTM

For a chrysanthemum to bloom. Beside the Chrysanthemum. So Chong-Ju, *Korean.* CKP, *tr. by* Jaihiun Kim

For a colored man. (LL) A Daddy Poem. William J. Harris. ISC; NBV

For a Coming Extinction. W. S. Merwin. HCAP; NNaP; PoE; PoPoPo; VCAP

For a creed that will not let you dance? (LL) Magalu. Helene Johnson. BlSi; PoBA

For a Daughter Gone Away. Brendan Galvin. GM

For a dawn moon, hard to hold its light. Failing the Examination. Meng Chiao, *Chinese.* SuSp, *tr. by* Stephen Owen

For a Dead Lady. Edwin Arlington Robinson. CMoP; FYAP; HeIP-4; HoPM; LiTM; MoAmPo; MoP; NOBA; NoAM; OxBA; PoEL-5; PoRA; TFi

For a dream's sake. (LL) Mirage. Christina Rossetti. BoLoP; PoRA

For a Far-out Friend. Gary Snyder. BB; NeAP; PoM

For a Father. Anthony Cronin. FaBoTw

For a few thousand battered books. (LL) E. P. Ode Pour l'Election de Son Sepulchre. Ezra Pound. FaBoMo; HAP; MeMAP; MoAmPo; MoP; NAAL-2; NoAM; OxBA; UnPo; VGW; NOBE; PoE; TRP

For a forehead: Kansas skies. Cosmogony. David Chapman Berry. BXAP

For a former Macon waiter. (LL) Robert Whitmore. Frank Marshall Davis. BPo; PoBA

For a Fountain. "Barry Cornwall." OBEV

For a generation. The Hermit's Curse. Richard Harteis. CMAP

For a good decade. The Drunk in the Furnace. W. S. Merwin. LiTM; MoP; NAAL-2; NoAM; NoP-4; PoE; Poetr; TwCP

For a hundred days grenades have been piercing. The Lieutenant. Konstantin Mikhailovich Simonov, *Russian.* TCRP, *tr. by* Lubov Yakovleva

For a hundred miles the west wind carries the fragrance of millet. Yün Shou-p'ing. CoBLCP, *tr. by* Jonathan Chaves *Fr.* On the Painting "Joys of Village Life."

For a Lady I Know. Countee Cullen HeIP-4; InPK-6; NIP-4; OBAL; SSLK; TAP; TRP *Fr.* Four Epitaphs. PoBA

(Lady I Know, A.) MoAmPo

For a Lady's Summons of Non-Entry. William Drummond, of Hawthornden. NOSC

For a Lamb. Richard Eberhart. CMoP; ColAP; LiTM; OxBSP; RB; SoSe-8

For a little gold, Zeus bought Danae. Parmenion of Macedon, *Greek.* InMo, *tr. by* Sam Hamill

For a little more time. The last of it. Marina Ivanovna Tsvetayeva. *See* The Poem of the End.

For a long day and a night we read the names. Reading the Names of the Vietnam War Dead. Thomas McGrath. CDa

For a long time I haven't seen such a young face. Faina Grimberg, *Russian.* TCRP, *tr. by* John High *and* Ivan Burkin

For a long time I've been searching for words. Voyvodina. Ivan Gadjanski, *Serbo-Croatian.* HSix, *tr. by* Charles Simic

For a long time, not a year, not two. Valentin Petrovich Katayev, *Russian.* TCRP, *tr. by* Albert C. Todd

For a long time we've been apart. While It Was Raining. Wen Cheng-ming, *Chinese.* CoBLCP, *tr. by* Jonathan Chaves

For a long time we've called ourselves grown-ups. The Prospectors' Little Waltz. Aleksandr Arkadevich Galich, *Russian.* TCRP, *tr. by* Gene Sosin

For a maid again I'll never be. (LL) Waly, Waly [Love Be Bonny]. *Unknown.* ESPB; EnLoPo; EnSB; GTBS-P; HAP; NOSC; OBEV; OxBB; OxBS; TFi

For a man that's dedicated. Vote for Lunn. *Unknown.* FaBoVe

For a Man Who Walked Sideways. Martin Carter. PBCV

For a Masseuse and Prostitute. Kenneth Rexroth. NNaP

For a minute, daughter, for an afternoon. The Prevention of Stacy Miller. Peter Miller. MoCV

For a Mocking Voice. Eleanor Farjeon. CH

For a moment. Tanka. Maekawa Samio, *Japanese.* MJT, *tr. by* Makoto Ueda

For a moment all that it touches back to wonder. (LL) The Beautiful Changes. Richard Wilbur. CMoP; CoAP; HCAP; InPS-3; PoE

For a moment I saw a surging river. Impermanence. Lal Ded, *Kashmiri.* BoWoP

For a moment pause. The Mound. Thomas Hardy. OxBTC

For a moment, unaware. *Unknown, Burmese.* PBWP, *tr. by* U Win Pe

For a Mouthy Woman. Countee Cullen. ChIV-1; OBAL; PoBA

For a Neighbor Girl. Yü Hsüan-chi. *See* Advice to a Neighbour Girl.

For a New Home. Rosa Zagnoni Marinoni. PoToHe

For a night—any night—that bends. Poem of the Dawn and the Night. Rodolfo Di Biasio, *Italian.* NeIt, *tr. by* Stephen Sartarelli

For a night when sleep eludes you, I have. Better Than Counting Sheep. Robert Penn Warren. AFr

For a Pastoral Family. Judith Wright.
    I To my Brothers. BMAP

For a Picture Where a Queen Laments over the Tomb of a Slain Knight. Thomas Carew. CaPo

For a Poet. Countee Cullen. TTY

For a Poet. George Wither. ChIV-2

For a Quick Exit. Norma Farber. KaS

For a ráinbow fóoting it nor hé for his bónes rísen. (LL) The Caged Skylark. Gerard Manley Hopkins. CMoP; LiTM; MoBrPo; OBMV; SoSe-8; Son

For a saving grace, we didn't see our dead. The War in the Air. Howard Nemerov. ColAP; DiPo; VCAP

For a season there must be pain. The Widower. Rudyard Kipling. CBLP; LBC; OxBM

For a Senior College Textbook. Hans Magnus Enzensberger. PoSu

For a single beautiful word. (LL) Parsley. Rita Dove. CMAP; HCAP; LoL; NAAAL; NoAM; NoP-4; PoPoPo; VCAP

For a solemn opening. We Survived Them. Anna Swirszczynska, *Polish.* AF, *tr. by* Czeslaw Milosz

For a Statue of Chaucer at Woodstock. Mark Akenside. EPCY

For a Stone Girl at Sanchi. Gary Snyder. BB

For a Suicide, a Little Early Morning Music. Gibbons Ruark. MT

For a Swarm of Bees, *a magical charm. Unknown, Anglo-Saxon.* ASW, *tr. by* Kevin Crossley-Holland

For A' That and A' That. Shirley Brooks. UV

For A' That and A' That ["Is there, for honest poverty"]. Robert Burns. FaBoBe; FaBoPV; FaPoR; NAEL-2; OAEL-1; OxAEP-2; TFi; UV
    (Man's a Man for A' That, A.) ImPo; OxBS
    ("Shall brothers be for a' that—.") (LL) CABP

For A' That and A' That. *Unknown.* BXAP

For a' the gowd in Christentie. (LL) Kinmont Willie. *Unknown.* ESPB; IBB; OxBB

For a thing done, repentance is no good. Sonnet: He Is Past All Help. Cecco Angiolieri, da Siena, *Italian.* AWP, *tr. by* D. G. Rossetti

For a thousand miles along the river, when the ice begins to close. Pien River Blocked by Ice. Tu Mu, *Chinese.* PLT, *tr. by* A. C. Graham

For a thousand miles the oriole sings, crimson against the green. Spring in Chiang-nan. Tu Mu, *Chinese.* PLT, *tr. by* A. C. Graham

For a thousand years, you, African, suffered like a beast. Dawn in the Heart of Africa. Patrice Emery Lumumba. PBA; TTY

For a time self-evident light all tremendously clear. Work. Denise Riley. NBrP

For a trophy on this pine tree. (LL) This beast which preyed on sheep. Leonidas, *Greek.* GrAn; PGA, *tr. by* Kenneth Rexroth

For A Venetian Pastoral By Giorgone (In the Louvre). D. G. Rossetti. GS

For a Violin, Somewhat Nervously. Vladimir Mayakovsky, *Russian.* TCRP, *tr. by* Bernard Meares

For a Virgin Lady. Countee Cullen. MoAmPo

For a War Memorial. G. K. Chesterton. PoWW

For a while a year is a long time. Wholes. Larry Eigner. PmAP

For a while there we had 25-inch Chinese peasant families. The Not-so-good Earth. Bruce Dawe. CBAP

For a Wife in Jizzen. Douglas Young. FaBoTC; OxBS

For a Wine Festival. Vernon Watkins. OxBTC

For a Winnebago Brave. Joseph Bruchac. CDW

For a Woman Murdered While Running at Land's End, October 1979. Patricia Kirkpatrick. LoHo

For a Woodscolt Miscarried. John William Corrington. MT

For a year he'd collect. The Milkman and His Son. Thomas Lux. LCAP-2

For a Young Artist. Robert Earl Hayden. NoAM

For aa da scraimin stars at hing. Gallow Hill. William J. Tait. OxBS

For action, I chant out loud, for quiet, I just think. Wu Chen. *Fr.* Poems Inscribed on Paintings of Bamboo. CoBLCP, *tr. by* Jonathan Chaves

For Adelaide. Bessie Rayner Parkes. VWP

For Adolf Eichmann. Primo Levi, *Italian.* AF, *tr. by* Ruth Feldman *and* Brian Swann (b. 1940)

For Adrian. Derek Walcott. AFr

For Advanced Seminar Students Only. David Avidan. *Fr.* Samson, Our Hero. IP, *tr. by* Warren Bargad *and* Stanley F. Chyet

For age is opportunity no less. Henry Wadsworth Longfellow. PoToHe *Fr.* Morituri Salutamus.

For Alexis Christa von Hartmann: Proved Not Guilty. William Stafford. CMAP

For All Blasphemers. Stephen Vincent Benét. OxBA

For All Mary Magdalenes. Desanka Maksimovic, *Croatian.* WPOW, *tr. by* Vasa D. Mihailovich

For All My Brothers and Sisters. Dick Lourie. CDa

For all of us destiny is undivided. Nikolai Stefanovich, *Russian.* TCRP, *tr. by* Albert C. Todd

For all that [*or* this] lady's hire. (LL) Dapple-gray. Mother Goose. BoTP; LB; OxNR; ReMoGo

For all the scenes that Day's bright eye pervades! (LL) Night. Ann Radcliffe. NOBRP; WPE

For all the vision that took fire this night. Burning Bush. Martin Feinstein. TrJP

For all the world is our Pan's choir [*or* Quire]. (LL) Clorinda and Damon. Andrew Marvell. ESCV; SeCP

For all those beaten, for the broken heads. Litany for Dictatorships. Stephen Vincent Benét. OxBA

For All Unwed Mothers. Robert Fleming. ISC

For all we have and are. Rudyard Kipling. FaPoR; NSI

For all your days prepare. Preparedness. Edwin Markham. MoAmPo

For Allan, Who Wanted to See How I Wrote a Poem. Robert Frost. PChr

For Alva Benson, and for Those Who Have Learned to Speak. Joy Harjo. HATNAP; UnSA

For America is a lady rocking on a porch in an unpainted house on an. Sixth Psalm. Anne Sexton. LCAP-2

For among My People are found wicked men. As Fowlers Lie in Wait. Bible, *O.T.* TrJP *Fr.* Jeremiah.

For Amy Lowell. Countee Cullen. PoA

For an Album. Adrienne Rich. VCAP

For An Amorous Lady. Theodore Roethke. LoP; NBLV

For an Emigrant. Randall Jarrell. OxBA

For an Epitaph at Fiesole. Walter Savage Landor. FaBoEE; OBNC

For an Ex-Far East Prisoner of War. Charles Causley. OxBC

For an officer / in the old Capital, fox fur. Ezra Pound, after the Chinese. OBVE

For Andy Goodman—Michael Schwerner—and James Chaney. Margaret Abigail Walker. BPo

For Angela. Zack Gilbert. PoBA

For Angus MacLeod. Iain Crichton Smith. OxBS

For Ann Scott-Moncrieff. Edwin Muir. GTBS-P

For Anna Mae Aquash Whose Spirit Is Present Here and in the Dappled Stars. Joy Harjo. PuP-15

For Anne Gregory. W. B. Yeats. CMoP; ImPo; LiTM; NAEL-2; OxAEP-2; Poetr

For Annie. Edgar Allan Poe. APN-1; AmPP; ColAP; MeMAP; NOBA; OBEV; OxBA

("With the thought of the light / Of the eyes of my Annie.") (LL) ColAP

For any of us. Gary Soto. *See* The Elements of San Joaquin.

For Art Blakey and the Jazz Messengers. Keorapetse Kgositsile. SeSe

For Artaud. Michael McClure. NeAP

For Asopichus of Orchomenus: Winner in the Stade Run. Pindar, *Greek.* OBCVT, *tr. by* Robert Fagles

For at the window of my house. She of the Impudent Face. Bible, *O.T.* TrJP *Fr.* Proverbs.

For aught that a lie saith, fear. (LL) The Lake of Gaube. Swinburne. CABP; NAEL-2; OAEL-2

For August, be your dwelling thirty towers. August. Folgore da San Geminiano. CTC *Fr.* Sonnets of the Months. AWP, *tr. by* D. G. Rossetti

For auld land syne. Robert Burns. *See* Auld Lang Syne.

For auld Robin Gray he is kind unto me. (LL) Auld Robin Gray. Lady Anne Lindsay. CH; ECWP; GTBS-P; NOEC; OBEV; PeSAV; WPE

For authorities whose hopes. The Paper Nautilus. Marianne Moore. FaBoWP; NALW; VGW

For awhile I too was haunted by. Amnesiac. Mark Osaki. CDa

For aye unsought-for slept among his ashes cold. (LL) The Eve of St Agnes. Keats. CABP; EBNV; EP; FHYEP; HAP; HoPM; ImPo; NAEL-2; NOBRP; NoP-4; OAEL-2; OBNC; OBNV; OxAEP-2; PoE; PoEL-4; PoLF; Poetr; Ro; TFi; TRP

For Baby. *Unknown.* ReMoGo

For Barbara, who said She Couldn't Visualize Two Women Together. Ellen Bass. NMM-2

For bards, like these, who neither sing nor say. On His Own Poetry. Charles Churchill. NOEC *Fr.* The Prophecy of Famine.

For beautie, wit, and matchlesse dignitie / yeeld to *Samela.* Robert Greene. *See* Samela.

For being so black. My Father. James Berry. PBCV

For best of bone and blood. (LL) Fowls [*or* Foweles *or* Fowles] in the frith. *Unknown.* FaBoVe; HAP; MiEL; NAEL-1; NoP-4; OxBSP

For best work. Lorine Niedecker. VGW

For beste of boon and blood. *Unknown. See* Fowls [*or* Foweles *or* Fowles] in the frith.

For Bill Hawkins, a Black Militant. William J. Harris. PoBA

For Black Poets Who Think of Suicide. Etheridge Knight. HeIP-4; InPK-6; LTA; NAAAL; PoBA; SAGP

For brave comportment, wit without offence. To His Honoured and Most Ingenious Friend Mr. Charles Cotton. Robert Herrick. CaPo; CavPo; NOSC

For breakfast—war and coffee. Pilots. Battle News. Samuel Hazo. CDa

For, brother, what are we? Thomas Wolfe. RaBo

For Brothers Everywhere. Tim Seibles. NAmP90

For Bud. Michael S. Harper. MoNo; PoE

For by tomorrow [*or* to morrow], I may think[e] so too. (LL) Woman's Constancy. Donne. ESCV; FMP; FSCP; NBLV; NOSC; NoP-4; SAGP

For C. Philip Whalen. NeAP; VGW

For Carlos Charles Bucillio. Alice Sadongei. HATNAP

For carrion crows to feed upon. (LL) The Dirge of St. Malo. George Washington Cable. APAD; APN-2

For centuries only painters, poets and sculptors. The Aging Actress Sees Herself a Starlet on the Late Show. Miller Williams. MT

For centuries sadhus live and die. Circumambulating Arunachala. Gary Snyder. BB

For certain he hath seen all perfectness. Dante. AWP *Fr.* La Vita Nuova.

For certain, I did not live thus in this world. "Naum Korzhavin," *Russian.* TCRP, *tr. by* Albert C. Todd

For change of solitude. (LL) Happiness Makes Up in Height for What It Lacks in Length. Robert Frost. MoAmPo; SoSe-8

For Charlie and his men. (LL) Charlie He's My Darling. Robert Burns. CH; FaBoPV

For Christmas Day. Luke Wadding. TIRV, *tr. by* Thomas Kinsella

For Christopher Columbus. A. J. Seymour. PBCV

   "And so the day beginning."

   "He dreamed not that the ocean would bear ships."

For City Spring. Stephen Vincent Benét. BXAP; NBLV

For Colored Girls Who Have Considered Suicide When the Rainbow Is Enuf. Ntozake Shange.

   "At 4:30 AM/ she rose." BoWoP

   Dark Phrases. BlSi

   I Sat Up One Night. CrSp

   No More Love Poems #1. BlSi

For Consciousness. Mervyn Morris. PBCV

For Contemporary Artist Pien Wei-Ch'I. Cheng Hsieh, *Chinese.* SuSp, *tr. by* Irving Y. Lo; ChiPo, *tr. by* Irving Yucheng Lo

For conversation when we meet again. (LL) I, being born a woman and distressed. Edna St. Vincent Millay. BoLoP; GLoP; LW; LoP; NALW; NIP-4; NoP-4

For Cool Papa Bell. Tom Dent. ISC

For Cora Lightbody, R.N. John Glassco. PoA

For cover—the tall forest. A Landscape Painted on a Fan—Echoing a Poem by Wen Cheng-ming. Chu Yün-ming, *Chinese.* CoBLCP, *tr. by* Jonathan Chaves

For Craig Who Leapt Off a Cliff in to Hummingbird Light. Diane Wakoski. PmAP

For Crethis' store of tales and pleasant chat. Crethis. Callimachus, *Greek.* AWP, *tr. by* Richard Garnett

For dame and doodle-doo. (LL) Cock-a-doodle-doo! / My dame has lost her shoe. Mother Goose. BoTP; LB; OxNR; ReMoGo

For dateless consummation dateless days. To My Lady. E. S. Miller. Son

For Daughters of Magdalen. Countee Cullen. ChIV-2

For David Shapiro. David Lehman. PoA

For dawn, wind / off the river. Crow Jane. Imamu Amiri Baraka. BB; PoM

For days now, / It's been a real binge. Tune: "Distant Red Window." Chou Pang-yen, *Chinese.* SuSp, *tr. by* Irving Y. Lo

For days now the ham radio operators wait in vain. Yevtushenko. Matija Beckovic, *Serbo-Croatian.* HSix, *tr. by* Charles Simic

For days you find it one long zero hour. Marking Time. Peter Steele. NOBAu

For de Lawd. Lucille Clifton. IMW; PoBA; TAP; TwCP

(For DeLawd.) MBE

("For their sons gone / just pushing.") (LL) MBE

For Death, he taketh all away, but them he cannot take. Callimachus. *See* Someone told me, Heraclitus.

For Death, he taketh all away, but them he cannot take. (LL) Heraclitus. William Johnson Cory, *par. from the Greek of* Callimachus. AWP; EBEvV; EBVV; FP; FaBoEE; FaPoR; InPK-6; NOBE; OBEV; OBNC; OxAEP-2; OxBSP; PoRA; SCGP; UV

For Death, not for Love, hast thou. Clearista. Meleager, *Greek.* OBCVT, *tr. by* Andrew Lang

For Death thou art a Mower too. (LL) Damon the Mower. Andrew Marvell. ESCV; GeHe; NAEL-1; NOSC; OAEL-1

For deep deer-copse beneath Mount Han. Ezra Pound, after the Chinese. OBVE

For DeLawd. Lucille Clifton. *See* For de Lawd.

For Deliverance from a Fever. Anne Bradstreet. NAAL-1; NAAL-3; NALW

For Demeter winnowing, for the Hours who haunt the furrows. Diodorus Zonas, *Greek.* GrAn, *tr. by* Alistair Elliot

For dogs, / was made for / men. (LL) To Bobby Seale. Lucille Clifton. MBE

For Don Drummond. Lorna Goodison. PBCV

For Douglas whom the cloud and eddy rejected. A Funeral Oration. Drummond Allison. PoWW

For Dr. and Mrs. Dresser. Margaret Avison. MoCV

For dred to fall I stond not fast. (LL) It may be good like it who list. Sir Thomas Wyatt. PBRV

For dred to fall I stond not fast. Sir Thomas Wyatt. *See* It may be good like it who list.

For Drum Hadley. Harold Littlebird. VoR

For dwelling in milk. (LL) Two Hundred and Twenty-Eighth Chorus. Jack Kerouac. NeAP; PmAP

For each breath of the south-wind makes a new bamboo! (LL) Eating Bamboo-Shoots. Po Chü-i, *Chinese.* ChiP, *tr. by* Arthur Waley

For each ecstatic instant. Emily Dickinson. NAAL-1; NAAL-3

For each repentant soul. (LL) Rouen, Place de la Pucelle. Maria White Lowell. APAD; APN-2

For ears to hear Your outdoor. Thanks for Hearing. Layne Felsted. CTV

For Edward Hicks. David Helwig. NOBC

For eighty years we lived the fate of beasts. Independence Day. Phan Trọng Quảng, *Vietnamese.* AVP, *tr. by* Huỳnh Sanh Thông

For Elaine de Kooning. Hilda Morley. PmAP

For Eleanor and Bill Monahan. William Carlos Williams. CRP; VGW

For Eli Jacobson. Kenneth Rexroth. RaBo

For Elizabeth Bishop. Sandra McPherson. NMM-2

For Emily (Dickinson). Maureen Owen. PmAP

For Emma. Luigi Fontanella, *Italian.* NeIt, *tr. by* Michael Palma

For Esther. Stanley Plumly. GM; LCAP-2

For Eusi, Ayi Kwei and Gwen Brooks. Keorapetse Kgositsile. PoBA

For ever and ever. Robert Southey. *See* Kehama's Curse.

For ever, Fortune, wilt thou prove. James Thomson. GTBS-P

For ever hard to meet, and as hard to part. Li Shang-yin, *Chinese.* PLT, *tr. by* A. C. Graham

For ever shall I be called virgin. Epitaph of a Girl. Unknown, *Greek.* GrAn, *tr. by* Dudley Fitts

For every bird there is this last migration. The Death of the Bird. Alec Derwent Hope. BMAP

For every evil under the sun. Mother Goose. LB; OxNR; ReMoGo

For every letter drink a glass. Martial, *Latin.* OBCVT, *tr. by* Nash, T. R.

For every parcel I stoop down to seize. The Armful. Robert Frost. CMoP; OxBSP; PiM

For every year, he grew a new tooth. The Man Who Became Old. Alberto A. Ríos. NoAM

For every year of life we light. A Birthday Poem. James Simmons. OxBSP; PNI

For everyone. The Swimmer's Moment. Margaret Avison. NOBC

For everyone's nourishment. Paraphrase. János Pilinszky, *Hungarian.* CEEP, *tr. by* Emery E. George

For everything there is a season. Bible, *O.T. See* A Time for Everything.

For Example (1): Stepping Out. Anne Lauterbach. PT

For Example (5): Song of the Already Sung. Anne Lauterbach. PT

For Exmoor. Jean Ingelow. OBEV

For eyes he waves greentipped. Slug in Woods. Earle Birney. NOBC; NoP-4

For Eyes to Bless You. Pamela Mordecai. PBCV

For False Heart. Hilaire Belloc. *See* The False Heart.

For Farmers. Harley Elliott. EC2

For fear my cradle prove my urn. (LL) Youth and Beauty. Aurelian Townshend. GBL; SeCP

For fear of finding something worse. (LL) Jim Who Ran Away from His Nurse, and Was Eaten by a Lion. Hilaire Belloc. EBNV; NOxBChV; NoAM; OBSP; OxAEP-2; OxBChV; PeLV

For fear that she wyle your fancy frae me. (LL) Whistle, and I'll Come to You, My Lad. Robert Burns. CBLP; OxAEP-2; OxBoLi

For fear they burn a hole through two-foot steel. (LL) Spoils. Robert Graves. HAP; NYBP; Son; WeW-3

FOR few nights' solace in delicious bed. To St Mary Magdalen. Henry Constable. ChIV-2; NoSic

For fifty thousand years man has been dreaming of powers. Unnatural Powers. Robinson Jeffers. PBMP

For 5p at a village fête I bought. On First Looking into Chapman's Hesiod. Peter Porter. NOBAu

For flowers that bloom about our feet. Spring Prayer. Ralph Waldo Emerson. BoTP

For Fog and Fate no charm is found. Destroyers in Collision. Rudyard Kipling. *Fr.* Epitaphs of the War [1914–1918]. OBWP

For forms of government let fools contest. Alexander Pope. ECEV *Fr.* An Essay on Man.

For forty years, for forty-one. This Dim and Ptolemaic Man. John Peale Bishop. LiTM

For forty years I shunned the lust. For a Virgin Lady. Countee Cullen. MoAmPo

For France. Claudian, *Latin.* MLL; OBCVT, *tr. by* Helen Waddell

("To-night there is no watch upon the Rhine.") (LL) OBCVT, *tr. by* Helen Waddell

For Freckle-Faced Gerald. Etheridge Knight. BPo

For Friends Only. W. H. Auden. FP *Fr.* Thanksgiving for a Habitat.

For friendship. Robert Creeley. *See* For friendship / make a chain that holds.

For friendship / make a chain that holds. Robert Creeley. VCAP

("For friendship.") PiM

For gay bard, barren summer. Lament for Lleucu Llwyd. Llywelyn Goch ap Meurig Hen, *Welsh.* OBWVE, *tr. by* Joseph P. Clancy

For George Santayana. Robert Lowell. CMoP; NAAL-2; VGW

For Geraldine. Tony Baker. NBrP

For Glaukos, for the Nereids. Lucianus, *Greek.* PGA, *tr. by* Kenneth Rexroth

For God, our God is a gallant foe. Ballad for Gloom. Ezra Pound. LiTM; MoAmPo

For God shall bring every work into judgment, with every secret thing, whether it be good, or whether it be evil. (LL) Remember Now Thy Creator. Bible, *O.T.* AWP; OBVE; TrJP

For God While Sleeping. Anne Sexton. CAPP-1

For God's forsaken the buffalo range and the damned old buffalo. (LL) The Buffalo Skinners. Unknown. AS; AmFP; RB

For God's sake be careful or someone will hear you! (LL) Sacred and Profane Love, or, There's Nothing New under the Moon Either. Peter De Vries. NBLV; OBCoV

For God's sake [or Godsake] hold your tongue, and let me love. The Canonization. Donne. CABP; CBLP; ESCV; EnLoPo; FHYEP; FMP; FSCP; FaBoVe; HAP; NAEL-1; NAWM-1; NIP-4; NOBE; NOSC; NoP-4; OAEL-1; PoE; PoEL-2; PoPoPo; SCGP; SeCP; SoSe-8; TFi; TRP; UnPo

For God's sake, let us sit upon the ground. Shakespeare. HoPM *Fr.* Let's Talk of Graves. FaBoBe *Fr.* King Richard II.

For God's sake mark that fly. Nulla Fides. Patrick Carey. SCGP

For in much wisdom is much grief: and he that increaseth knowledge increaseth sorrow. (LL) Vanity of vanities, saith the Preacher, vanity of vanities; all is vanity. Bible, *O.T.* TrJP, *sect.* I, *ll.* 2–9; FaBoPV; NAWM-1

For Innocents' Day. Luke Wadding. NOIV; TIRV

For Instance. Robert McAlmon. PoA

For it is only He / That helps the weak and low. Bible, *O.T.* See Psalm 130.

For it makes us tell the story of our whole lives. (LL) Rejoicing at the Arrival of Chi'en Hsiung. Po Chü-i, *Chinese.* ChiP, *tr.* by Arthur Waley

For it will be as when a man going on a journey called his servants and entrusted to them his property. Matthew 25:14–30; "For it will be as when a man." Jorge Luis Borges. GI *Fr.* St. Matthew.

For it's up with the bonnets of Bonny Dundee. (LL) Bonny [*or* Bonnie] Dundee. Sir Walter Scott. FaBoCh; OxBS; OxBoLi; UV

For J. W. Rafael Campo. RA

For James Baldwin. Kay Boyle. NMM-2

For James Dean. Frank O'Hara. NNaP; NeAP

For Jan, in Bar Maria. Carolyn Kizer. VGW

For Jane. Charles Bukowski. HoPM

For Jane Myers. Louise Glück. FaBoWP

For January I give you vests of skin. January. Folgore da San Geminiano. *Fr.* Sonnets of the Months. AWP, *tr.* by D. G. Rossetti

For Jean Vincent d'Abbadie, Baron St.-Castin. Alden Nowlan. NOBC

For Jessica, My Daughter. Mark Strand. MoLi

For John Berryman. Robert Lowell. FP; NOBA

For John Chappell. Gary Snyder. NNaP

For John Clare. John Ashbery. FYAP

For John Keats, Apostle of Beauty. Countee Cullen. *Fr.* Four Epitaphs. PoBA

For Johnny. John Pudney. ODWP

For Josef Herman. Burns Singer. FaBoTC

For joy. (LL) Upon a Spider Catching a Fly. Edward Taylor. AmPP; MeMAP; NOBA; NoP-4; OxBA; PeECV; PoEL-3; SCAP; TAP

For July, in Sierra, by the willow-tree. July. Folgore da San Geminiano. *Fr.* Sonnets of the Months. AWP, *tr.* by D. G. Rossetti

For just a brief while every day. Rendezvous. Mary Scott Fitzgerald. PoToHe

For Just Men Light Is Sown. Michael Wigglesworth. AH

For K. R. on Her Sixtieth Birthday. Richard Wilbur. APAD

For Kai Snyder. Philip Whalen. PoM

For Kay Boyle. Muriel Rukeyser. NMM-2

For Kelly, Missing in Action. Walter McDonald. CDa

For knighthood is not in the feats of war. The True Knight [*or* True Knighthood]. Stephen Hawes. OBEV *Fr.* The Pastime of Pleasure. OBGa

For Ku Yen-hsien, A Poem for Him to Give to His Wife. Lu Yün, *Chinese.* CoBCP, *tr.* by Burton Watson

For Kuo Hsiang. Yü Hsüan-chi, *Chinese.* BoWoP, *tr.* by Geoffrey Waters

For lack of knowledge do my people die! My People Are Destroyed for Lack of Knowledge. Jones Very. ChIV-1

For Langston Hughes. Etheridge Knight. NBV

For Lerida. David St. John. AmPA

For Li Po. Tu Fu, *Chinese.* SuSp, *tr.* by Eugene Eoyang

For life goes not backward nor tarries with yesterday. (LL) On Children. Kahlil Gibran. OxBM; PoToHe

For Life I had never cared greatly. Thomas Hardy. CMoP; LiTM; NoAM

For light doth seize my brain / With frantic pain. (LL) Mad Song. William Blake. NAEL-2; NOEC; OAEL-2; PoE; PoEL-4

For Lil Louis. Tom Dent. BkSV

For listening and instructional purposes. A Drive to Lone Ranger. Ray A. Young Bear. AF

For little dreams to go. (LL) Hold Fast Your Dreams. Louise Driscoll. BLPA; FaBoBe

For Lo! My Jonah How He Slumped. John Wilson. AH

For lo! the board with cups and spoons is crown'd. Alexander Pope. UV *Fr.* The Rape of the Lock[, an Heroi-Comical Poem]. FHYEP; HAP; ImPo; OAEL-1; OBNV; PeLV; PoEL-3

For lo! the sea that fleets about the land. The Dancing Sea. Sir John Davies. *Fr.* Orchestra; or, A Poem[e] of Da[u]ncing. NoSic; SiPS

For, lo, the winter is past. Lo, the Winter Is Past. Bible, *O.T.* CTV *Fr.* The Song of Songs. AWP

For, Lord, the Crowded Cities Be. Rilke, *German.* AWP; TrJP, *tr.* by Ludwig Lewisohn

For lost honour among thieves. (LL) The Thieves. Robert Graves. BoLoP; CMoP; GTBS-P; LiTM; LoP; OAEL-2

For Lotus Flower. Li Shang-yin, *Chinese.* SuSp, *tr.* by Eugene Eoyang *and* Irving Y. Lo

For Louis Armstrong, A Ju-Ju. Sarah Webster Fabio. SeSe

For Love, (For Bobbie). Robert Creeley. CoAmPo; NOBA; PmAP; VCAP

For love Appollo (his Godhead set aside). The Power of love over gods them selves. Seneca, *Latin.* OBCVT, *tr.* by Unknown

For love he offered me his perfect world. Gift to a Jade. Anna Wickham. OxBSP

For love—I would. The Warning. Robert Creeley. NeAP; TAP; VGW

For love no time has she, or inclination. Soame Jenyns. OBSV *Fr.* The Modern Fine Lady. NOEC

For love of mayde and moder thyn benigne! Amen. (LL) Go, Little Book ("Go, litel book, go litel myn tragedy"). Chaucer. EPCY; OAEL-1

For love there is no other drug, Nicias. Theocritus. *See* Cyclops, The ("And so an easier life").

For Love's sake, kiss[e] me once again[e]. Begging Another, on Colour of Mending the Former. Ben Jonson. CBLP; PoEL-2 *Fr.* A Celebration of Charis in Ten Lyric[k] Pieces [*or* Peeces]. BeJo; OxAEP-1; SeCP

For Love's Sake Only. Elizabeth Barrett Browning. *See* Sonnet: "If thou must love me, let it be for nought."

For M.S. Singing *Fruhlingsglaube* in 1945. Frances Darwin Cornford. BrRo

For Mack C. Parker. Pauli Murray. PoBA

For making him fully and perfectly man. (LL) Hawthorne. James Russell Lowell. OxBA

For Malcolm: After Mecca. Gerald William Barrax. PoBA

For Malcolm Who Walks in the Eyes of Our Children. Quincy Troupe. PoBA

For Malcolm X. Nanina Alba. PoBA

For Malcolm X. Margaret Abigail Walker. BPo; NAAAL; PoBA; Son

For Malcolm's eyes, when they broke. A Poem for Black Hearts. Imamu Amiri Baraka. CAPP-1; NAAAL; PoBA; PoM

For Malcolm's eyes, when they broke. A Poem for Black Hearts. LeRoi Jones *and* Imamu Amiri Baraka. SSLK

For man is between the pinchers while his soul is shaping and purifying. Christopher Smart. ChIV-1 *Fr.* Fragment B. *Fr.* Jubilate Agno

For man to act as if his soul did see. Thomas Traherne. *See* Contentment is a sleepy thing.

For many a year I've watched the ships a-sailing to and fro. The Ships. J. J. Bell. BoTP

For many distant travelers. Acoma. William Oandasan. HATNAP

For many, many days together. Riding Together. William Morris. EnVR; NOBE; OAEL-2

For many thousand ages. Es Stehen Unbeweglich. Heinrich Heine, *German.* AWP; TrJP, *tr.* by James Thomson

For many unsuccessful years. Advice to a Lover. Thomas Yalden. ECEV

For Mao Tse-tung; a Meditation on Flies and Kings. Irving Layton. NOBC

For Margaret. Stanley Moss. FiLi; IMW

For Maria Magdalenes. Desanka Maksimovic, *Serbo-Croatian.* HSix, *tr.* by Charles Simic

For Marianne Moore's Birthday. Kay Boyle. NMM-2

For Mark James Robert Essex d. 1973. Alvin Aubert. BkSV

For Martin Luther King. Charles Fort. LTA

For Maulana Karenga & Pharoah Sanders. Imamu Amiri Baraka. APSN

For me a tragedy's most important act is the sixth. Theater Impressions. Wislawa Szymborska, *Polish.* VCWP, *tr.* by Magnus J. Krynski *and* Robert A. Maguire

For me, one there, two horses wait. The Wizard's Funeral. Richard Watson Dixon. NOBVV; PeVV

For me, the naked and the nude. The Naked and the Nude. Robert Graves. EP; NYBP; SoSe-8

For me, the tears that welled. Aeschylus. GrIP, *tr.* by Robert Fagles *Fr.* Agamemnon. NAWM-1, *tr.* by Robert Fagles

For Medgar Evers. David Ignatow. LTA

For men do often learn when they do teach. (LL) To Donne. Sir Henry Wotton. NOSC; NoSic

For mercy, courage, kindness, mirth. A Song. Laurence Binyon. BoTP; MoBrPo

For merit here below, who equals it? The Rice Mill. Phan Văn Tri, *Vietnamese.* AVP, *tr.* by Huỳnh Sanh Thông

For methinks thou stays [*or* stay'st] too long. (LL) A Madrigal: "Crabbed age and youth cannot live together." Shakespeare. EBEvV; GBL; GTBS-P; InPS-3; NoSic; OBEV

For Miklos Radnóti: 1909-1944. Kate Daniels. NAmP90

For Miles. Gregory Corso. MoNo

For mine, I ween, is free.] (LL) Johnie Cock. *Unknown.* ESPB; OxBB

For Miranda. Gregory Corso. MoLi

For Miriam. Marjorie Oludhe Macgoye. WPOW

For Miss Tin in Hue. John Balaban. CDa

For Monk. Michael McClure. SeSe

For months / my books were stacked. February Park. Gerald Vizenor. VoR

For months the letters from his mother came. Sequence. Marilyn Nelson Waniek. PuP-14

For more than sixty years he has been blind. War Blinded. Douglas Dunn. DiPo; OBWP

For morn, my dome of blue. A Child's Prayer. Siegfried Sassoon. BoTP

For mortals, mortal things. And all things leave us. Lucianus, *Greek*. GrAn, *tr. by* Edwin Morgan

For Mother on Father's Day. James Tate. FiLi

For "Mr. Dudley," a Black Spy. James A. Emanuel. BPo; NBV

For Mrs. Cam, Whose Name Means "Printed Silk." John Balaban. CDa

For Musia's Grandchildren. Irving Layton. NOBC

For My Ancestors. Rolfe Humphries. PoRA

For my beautiful, dutiful Lily Adair. (LL) Lily Adair. Thomas Holley Chivers. APN-1; OBAL

For My Contemporaries. James Vincent Cunningham. CoAP; VCAP

For My Daughter. Weldon Kees. CoAP; MoLi

For My Daughter. John Logan. CRP

For My Daughter. Sharon Olds. DeD

For My Daughter in Reply to a Question. David Ignatow. MoLi

For My Daughter's Twenty-First Birthday. Jeanne Murray Walker. MDDM

For my dreams of your image that blossoms a rose in the deeps of my heart. (LL) The Lover Tells of the Rose in His Heart. W. B. Yeats. CMoP; MoBrPo

For My Father. Louise Glück. MoLi *Fr.* Metamorphosis. MoLi

For My Father. Paul Potts. FaBoTw

For My Father. Philip Schultz. IFJA

For My Father Looking for My Uncle. Jorie Graham. MoLi

For My Father's Mother Who Has Alzheimer's. M. Eliza Hamilton. IFJA

For My Funeral. A. E. Housman. CoAP

For My Godmother. Astride Ivaska, *Latvian*. CEEP, *tr. by* Inara Cedrins

For My Grandmother. Countee Cullen. MoAmPo; SSLK; VGW *Fr.* Four Epitaphs. PoBA

For My Grandmother, Bridget Halpin. Michael Hartnett. BIrV; IIP; PBCIP

For My Great-Grandfather: A Message Long Overdue. Maxine W. Kumin. UnSA

For My Lover, Returning to His Wife. Anne Sexton. CBLP; HCAP; NMM-2; Poetr; SAGP; UnPo; WPE

("As for me, I am a watercolor. / I wash off.") (LL) NMM-2

For My Mother. Doris Brett. NOBAu

For My Mother. David Diop, *French*. NegPo, *tr. by* Ellen Conroy Kennedy

For My Mother. Louise Glück. UnPo

For My Mother. June Jordan. BoWoP

For My Mother. Philip Schultz. FiLi; NAmP90

("My hand of peace, this wound which does not heal.") (LL) FiLi

For My Mother. Iain Crichton Smith. OxBS

For My Mother. Ellen Bryant Voigt. NIP-4

For My Mother: Genevieve Jules Creeley. Robert Creeley. PoM; TRP

For My Mother, Who Lives. Lorraine Duggin. LoHo

For My Neverborn. Nancy Shiffrin. EC3

For My Own Monument. Matthew Prior. OBEV

(For His Own Epitaph.) FaBoEE

For my part, I never care. Lips Tongueless[e]. Robert Herrick. CaPo

For my part, I'le not meddle with the cause. Homer. CTC, *tr. by* George Chapman *Fr.* Odyssey. NAWM-1, *tr. by* Robert Fitzgerald

For My People. Wendy Rose. CDW

For my people [everywhere singing their slave songs repeatedly: their]. Margaret Abigail Walker. ISC; NAAAL; PBMP; PoBA; SAGP; SSLK

("Disappear. Let a race of men now rise and take control.") (LL) SSLK

("Let a race of men now rise and take control.") (LL) NAAAL

("Of men now rise and take control!") (LL) SAGP

("Take control!") (LL) ISC

For my poor passage to the stall of Night? (LL) On an Anniversary. John Millington Synge. FaBoEE; NOIV; OBMV

For my sister's sake. Hitomaro. AWP, *tr. by* Arthur Waley *Fr.* Manyo Shu, Part 1 of 4.

For My Son Noah, Ten Years Old. Robert Bly. InPS-3; LoL; RaBo

For My Torturer, Lieutenant D——. Leila Djabali, *French*. WPOW, *tr. by* Anita Barrows

For My Unborn and Wretched Children. Alfred B. Spellman. PoBA

For My Wife. Liu Hsiao-Wei, *Chinese*. EP, *tr. by* Anne Birrell

For Napoleon. (LL) Napoleon. Miroslav Holub, *Czech. tr. by* Káča Poláčková ChAP; PoSu

For nations vague as weed. Nothing to Be Said. Philip Larkin. OxBTC

For nearly a month. Drought. Sitanshu Yashashchandra, *Gujarati*. OMIP, *tr. by* Saleem Peeradina, Jayant Parek, Rasik Shah, *and* Ghulam Mohammed Sheikh

For nearly a week that open-aired autumn. Ground Elder. Leonard Clark. OBGa

For never a begger need now despair, And every rogue has a chance. (LL) The Speculators. William Makepeace Thackeray. OBCoV; OBSV

For New Year, Postumus, ten years ago. A Roman Thank-You Letter. Martial, *Latin*. OBCP, *tr. by* James Michie

For Nicholas, Born in September. Tod Perry. NYBP

For night comes. Gunnar Ekelof, *Swedish*. IFJA, *tr. by* Robert Bly

For No Clear Reason. Robert Creeley. VGW

For No Good Reason. Peter Redgrove. PoE

For no watchman is waiting for you and for me. William Roscoe. *See* The Butterfly's Ball [and the Grasshopper's Feast].

For noble minds, the worst of miseries. Poverty. Theognis, *Greek*. AWP, *tr. by* John Hookham Frere

For none can call againe the passèd time. (LL) Sonnet 70: "Fresh Spring the herald of love's mighty king." Edmund Spenser. NoP-4; PBRV

For none for these waterburners at night may rest. (LL) The Blacksmiths. *Unknown*. FaBoVe; MiEL; RB

For None see God and live. (LL) To pile like Thunder to its close. Emily Dickinson. APN-2; NCAP

For Nothing. Gary Snyder. NNaP

For nothing now can ever come to any good. (LL) Stop All the Clocks, Cut Off the Telephone. W. H. Auden. MoBrPo; RB

For now, and since first break of dawne the Fiend. Satan tempts Eve. Milton. FaBoSe *Fr.* Paradise Lost.

For now it's eight o'clock *or* For it's now eight o'clock. William Miller. *See* Willie Winkie.

For now, love thou, I rede, Christ, as I thee tell. Love is Life. Richard Rolle of Hampole. PoEL-1 *Fr.* A Song of the Love of Jesus. PoEL-1

For O! reflect, poetic daughter, / 'Twas hapless Britain's laurel-water. Anna Seward. *See* Verses Inviting Stella to Tea on the Public Fast-Day.

For oak and elm have pleasant leaves. The Ballad of Reading Gaol. Oscar Wilde. NoAM *Fr.* The Ballad of Reading Gaol. CABP; OBNV; OxAEP-2

For often my mammy has told. Air. Henry Brooke. *Fr.* Jack the Giant Queller; an Antique History. NOEC

For once. Portrait of Jonah with woman. Marie-Claire Bancquart, *French*. MFP, *tr. by* Martin Sorrell

For once, I hardly noticed what I ate. Runaways Café II. Marilyn Hacker. NoAM

For once it doesn't matter that you've gone. Troubadour. Peter Sirr. BiHa

For Once, Then, Something. Robert Frost. GEA; NOBA; NoAM

For one beloved Friend alone. Shelley. *See* With a Guitar, to Jane.

For one brief day, did Queenie stay. Queenie. Mary Weston Fordham. CBWP-2

For one human being to love another human being: that is perhaps the. Rilke. ITG, *tr. by* Stephen Mitchell *Fr.* Letters to a Young Poet.

For One Lately Bereft. Margaret E. Bruner. PoToHe

For one long term, or e'er her trial came. Inscription. George Canning. FaBoEE

For One Moment. David Ignatow. NNaP

For one short week I leave, with anxious heart. Eyam. Anna Seward. CABP; ECWP

For One Who Died Young. Hoffman Reynolds Hays. SPE

For One Who Is Serene. Margaret E. Bruner. PoToHe

For one who says he feels. Petra von Morstein, *German*. BoWoP, *tr. by* Rosemarie Waldrop

For other beds the priests there used none. Britomart at Isis' Church. Edmund Spenser. PoE *Fr.* Wood Of Error. AEP

For other fruits my father was indifferent. My Father and the Figtree. Naomi Shihab Nye. UnSA

For our belovèd Jane alone. (LL) With a Guitar, to Jane. Shelley. FHYEP; GTBS-P; OAEL-2

For our Dragon hath vanquish'd [*or* vanquished] the St. George. (LL) A Mock Song. Richard Lovelace. BeJo; CaPo

For Our Lady. Sonia Sanchez. NAAAL

For "Our Lady of the Rocks." D. G. Rossetti. EBEV

(For Our Lady of the Rocks By Leonardo da Vinci.) GS

For our own private reasons. Reasons. Thomas James. PoA

For our Red Army there was no fear in. The Long March. Mao Tse-tung, *Chinese*. ChiPo, *tr. by* Rewi Alley

For P—Celtic: found text from Machen. Bill Griffiths. NBrP

For P[ope] has wrote upon their tomb. (LL) Epitaph. "Here lies John Hughes and Sarah Drew." Lady Mary Wortley Montagu. CABP

For Paddy Mac. Padraic Fallon. CIP-2; IIP

For Paul Laurence Dunbar. Countee Cullen. SSLK *Fr.* Four Epitaphs. PoBA

For Period exhaled. (LL) Great Streets of silence led away. Emily Dickinson. APN-2; NOCV

For physic and farces his equal there scarce is. On Sir John Hill, M. D., Playwright. David Garrick. FaBoEE; NBLV

For Poets. Al Young. PoBA

For Polla. Uku Masing, *Estonian*. CEEP, tr. by Ivar Ivask

For poor Cock Robin. (LL) Who killed Cock [or poor] Robin? [or Here lies Cock Robin]. Mother Goose. AmFP; CBNP; CTAV; OxBoLi; OxNR; ReMoGo; UV

For prodigal read generous. E. E. Cummings. FaBoEE; PBMP

For Raftery. Alan Alexander. NOBAu

For rage and dignity no words compare. A Classical Quatrain. Paul Goodman. VGW

For reading I can recommend. "Domaine Public." Geoffrey Hill. OxBC *Fr.* Four Poems Regarding the Endurance of Poets.

For Real. Jayne Cortez. PoBA

For repose I have sighed and have struggled; have sigh'd and have struggled in vain. Felo de Se. Amy Levy. VWP

For reputation of the art. The Ghost. Charles Churchill. OxBSn *Fr.* The Ghost.

For Rhoda. Delmore Schwartz. MoAmPo; OxBA *Fr.* The Repetitive Heart.

  (Calmly We Walk Through This April's Day.) LiTM

For Righteousness' Sake. John Greenleaf Whittier. PoEL-4

For rigorous teachers seized my youth. Matthew Arnold. FHYEP *Fr.* Stanzas from the Grande Chartreuse. EBVV; EnVR; NAEL-2; OAEL-2; PoE; PoEL-5

For Robert Desnos. Tristan Tzara, *French*. AF, tr. by Mary Ann Caws

For Robert Frost. Galway Kinnell. NOBA; VGW

For Ronald King Our Brother. Sherley Anne Williams. WeT

For Rosa Yen, Who Lived Here. Greg Pape. AmPA

For round about, the wals yclothed were. Edmund Spenser. PBRV *Fr.* The Faerie Queene.

For Saint John's Day. Luke Wadding. TIRV

For Saint Stephen's Day. Luke Wadding. TIRV

For Sale. Robert Lowell. AFr; CoAmPo

For Sale or Rent. *Unknown*. PoToHe

For Sammy Younge. Charlie Cobb. PoBA

For Saturday. Christopher Smart. FaBoCh; NOEC; OxBChV *Fr.* Hymns for the Amusement of Children.

  (Hymn for Saturday.) OxBChV

  (Hymns for Saturday.) NOxBChV

For Saundra. Nikki Giovanni. BPo; NAAAL; TTY

For Scholars and Pupils. George Wither. OxBChV

For seasons beyond count, age. Species. Philip Booth. AFr

For seeing / brightness within, A. A New Light. William Hawkins. MoCV

For seven long years I had declared my passion. The Cywdd to Morvydd. Dafydd ap Gwilym, *Welsh*. NOEC

For seven years, eyesockets like caves. Rilke. Wayne Brown. HCP

For Several Days I Have Not Visited the Garden Pavilion—A Poem Sent to My Pet Crane. Wang Chiu-ssu, *Chinese*. CoBLCP, tr. by Jonathan Chaves

For several miles I have heard the chill waters. Passing by a Mountain Village: Evening. Chia Tao, *Chinese*. SuSp, tr. by Stephen Owen

For several months. P.C. Plod versus the Dale St. Dog Strangler. Roger McGough. MoP; OBSP

For several weeks I have been reading. Expression. Thom Gunn. OxBC

For Several Years I Have Wanted To Grow a Garden, But Have Never Finished One. This Year It Is Already Halfway Through Summer, and This Has Made Me Despondent. Chu Yün-ming, *Chinese*. CoBLCP, tr. by Jonathan Chaves

For shame, thou everlasting wooer [or Woer]. The Antiplatonic[k]. John Cleveland. CBLP; NOSC; PBRV; SeCP

For Sharol Graves. "Chrystos." CPO

For she came of the better kin. (LL) Little Musgrave and Lady Barnard. *Unknown*. ESPB; OxBB

For Sheridan. Robert Lowell. HCAP

For Sidney Bechet. Philip Larkin. NoP-4

For Signs. Thom Gunn. PoE

For Simon Rodia: The sudden appearance, at once, of. Time Traveler's Potlatch. Philip Lamantia. CLPP

For Singing In Good Mood. Lebert Bethune. GT

For Sistuhs Wearin' Straight Hair. Carolyn M. Rodgers. NAAAL

For Sleep. Larry Eigner. FTOS

For Snow. Eleanor Farjeon. CH

For so long / We looked into mirrors. Us. Julius Lester. PoBA

For so should it be. (LL) A Maid of Kent. *Unknown*. CBLP; OxBoLi

For Soldiers. Humphrey Gifford. CH; NoSic

For Some Poets. Mae Jackson. PoBA

For some semitropical reason. Tarantulas on the Lifebuoy. Thomas Lux. LCAP-2

For some, the sea. Bathing Song. Anne Ridler. NYBP

For some the shuttle leaping in the sun. Rosa Luxembourg. Eileen Duggan. PeNZ

For some we loved, the loveliest and the best. Omar Khayyám. TRP *Fr.* The Rubáiyát of Omar Khayyám [of Naishápúr]. AWP; EBVV; FaBoBe; FaPoR; HAP; NAEL-2; PoEL-5

For some years he still would harden as he. The Fall. Sarah Maguire. LW

For Someone Temporizing. Thomas Erwin, *German*. CEEP, tr. by A. Leslie Willson

For spoiling her nice new clothes. (LL) Little Polly Flinders. Mother Goose. LB; OxNR; ReMoGo

For sport my *Julia* threw a Lace. The Silken Snake. Robert Herrick. OxBSP; PBRV

For Spring. Douglas G. Jones. NOBC

For Spring By Sandro Botticelli. D. G. Rossetti. GS

For Starters. Victoria McCabe. CRP

For Steph. Wendy Rose. CDW

For Stephen Dixon. Zack Gilbert. PoBA

For still 'tis only dawning Day. (LL) The Burial of King Cormac. Sir Samuel Ferguson. NOIV; TIRV

For Stuart Porter, Who Asked for a Poem That Would Not Depress Him Further. Jeffrey Skinner. PBCAP

For such as you, I do believe. Mother. Hermann Hagedorn. PoToHe

For such company decks such solitariness. (LL) Solitariness. Sir Philip Sidney. NoSic; PoEL-1; SCGP; SiPS

For Summer has o'er-brimmed their clammy cells. Keats. *See* To Autumn.

For Sunday's play he never makes excuse. The Lout. John Clare. EnVR

For surely whiteness. Draft for a Contemporary Love Poem. Tadeusz Rózewicz, *Polish*. EP, tr. by Adam Czerniawski

For surfeits sooner kill than fasts. (LL) Against Absence. Sir John Suckling. CaPo; CavPo

For sweet things dying. (LL) A Dirge. "Why were you born when the snow was falling?" Christina Rossetti. EBVV; NOBVV; SCGP

For Talbot's de dog, and James is de ass. (LL) Lilli Burlero [or Lilliburlero]. Thomas Wharton, 1st Marquess of Wharton. NOIV; OxBoLi

For Talking, Saint Didacus, 1968. Denise Nico Leto. UnSA

For ten miles the mountains rise. The Farm by the Lake. Chu Hsi, *Chinese*. OHPC, tr. by Kenneth Rexroth

For ten miles, till day at last breaks. (LL) Starting Early from the Ch'u-ch'êng Inn. Po Chü-i, *Chinese*. BLT; ChiP, tr. by Arthur Waley

For ten years I never left my books;. After Passing the Examination. Po Chü-i, *Chinese*. ChiP, tr. by Arthur Waley

For That Day Only. Grace Schulman. WWSi

For that fair[e] blessed mother-maid. The Virgin Mary. Donne. *Fr.* The Litanie. PoEL-2

For that goatfucker, goatfooted. Leonidas of Tarentum, *Greek*. tr. by Kenneth Rexroth GrAn; PGA; OBCVT,

For That He Looked Not upon Her. George Gascoigne. NoP-4

For that I never knew you, I only learned to dread you. St. Roach. Muriel Rukeyser. GLP

For that rare, random descent. (LL) Black Rook in Rainy Weather. Sylvia Plath. LiTM; NAAL-2; NoP-4; Poetr

For that the sonnet no doubt was my own true. Late Sonnet. Hayden Carruth. Son

For that they housed Him from the cold! (LL) A Christmas Folk-Song. Lizette Woodworth Reese. OBCA; TrCP

For that's the best cure for a little pussy cat. (LL) Who's that ringing at my door bell? *Unknown*. FaBoCh; OxNR

For the Air is purified by prayer which is made aloud and with all our might. Christopher Smart. *Fr.* Fragment B. *Fr.* Jubilate Agno.

For the Anniversary of My Death. W. S. Merwin. BLT; CAPP-1; CoAP; ColAP; HCAP; InPK-6; LiLi; NAAL-2; NOBA; PoPoPo; Poetr; VCAP

  ("And boding not knowing to what.") (LL) BLT

For the Athenian Dead at Plataia. Simonides, *Greek*. GrAn, tr. by Peter Jay

For the Baptist. William Drummond, of Hawthornden. *See* Saint John Baptist.

For the Baptiste. William Drummond of Hawthornden. PBRV

For the Barren Woman. Desanka Maksimovic, *Serbo-Croatian*. GI, tr. by Ivo Soljan

For the black plunge-line nightdress. (LL) The Skunk. Seamus Heaney. NAEL-2; NoP-4; OxBC; PoE

For the Bones of Josef Mengele, Disinterred June 1985. Robert Bringhurst. NIP-4

For the Book of Love. Jules Laforgue, *French*. AWP, tr. by Jethro Bithell; NNPT, tr. by Vernon Watkins

For the Boy Who Was Dodger Point Lookout Fifteen Years Ago. Gary Snyder. BB

For the Briar Rose. William Morris. NOBVV

For the bumps bangs and scratches of. Auto Mobile. A. R. Ammons. OBAL

For the Candle Light. Angelina Weld Grimké. BlSi; NAAAL

For the Cenotaph of a Lost Soldier. Theon, *Greek*. GrAn, *tr. by* Dudley Fitts

For the child of her love is no longer a slave! (LL) Eliza Harris. Frances Ellen Watkins Harper. AAP; NAAAL

   (She's Free!) BiSi; Son

For the Children. Thomas Love Peacock. VoR

For the Children or the Grown-ups? *Unknown*. OBCP

For the clouds above the garden in Papenburg. Homesick. Helmut Heissenbüttel, *German*. CLPP, *tr. by* Jerome Rothenberg

For the Color of my Mother. Cherríe Moraga. NMM-2; UnSA

For the Common Market. Michael Burn. OBCoV

For the Company Underground. Francis MacNamara. NOBAu

For the context of the basidiocarp Singer states. James Fenton. PeLV *Fr.* Exempla.

For the correct / yes. (LL) In Celebration of My Uterus. Anne Sexton. CrSp; NALW

For the country will bring us no peace. (LL) Raleigh Was Right. William Carlos Williams. NIP-4; NoAM; Poetr; RB

For the Courtesan Ch'ing Lin. Wu Tsao, *Chinese*. BoWoP; WPOW, *tr. by* Kenneth Rexroth *and* Ling Chung

For the Dancer of the King of Wu. Li Po, *Chinese*. TAL, *tr. by* Robert Payne

For the Dead. Adrienne Rich. NAAL-2

For the Dead Lecturer. Diane Di Prima. BB

For the dear memory of what, you know, / You never were. (LL) Among His Books. Edith Nesbit. PEW

For the Death of 100 Whales. Michael McClure. BB

For the dim regions whence my father[s] came. Outcast. Claude McKay. NAAAL; PoBA

For the disciple nothing had changed. The mood was still. The Lament Upon the Waters. John Ashbery. FTOS

For the doubling of flowers is the improvement of the gard'ner's talent. Christopher Smart. ChIV-2; NOEC *Fr.* Fragment B. *Fr.* Jubilate Agno.

For the Evening Land. David Shapiro. BAP-96

For the Examination at Ho-nan-fu: Songs of the Twelve Months. Li Ho, *Chinese*. CoBCP, *tr. by* Burton Watson

For the expectant is the glory. Zealots of Yearning. David Rokeah, *Hebrew*. MHP, *tr. by* Ruth Finer Mintz

For the Fallen. Laurence Binyon. EBEvV; NOBE; OBEV; OBWP; OxBTC; PoFWW

For the Family of Cuchonnacht O Dalaigh. David O'Bruadair, *Irish*. NOIV, *tr. by* Thomas Kinsella

For the First Manned Moon Orbit. James Dickey.

   "So long." AiP

For the first time. A Poem for Positive Thinkers. Barbara Mahone. PoBA

For the first time, now for the first time seen. (LL) Green. D. H. Lawrence. GBL; LoP; MoBrPo; PoA

For the first time since anyone remembers. Rhapsody on Main Street. Patrick Williams. PNI

For the first twenty years [*or* yeares], since yesterday. The Computation. Donne. CBNP; FMP; NoSic; OxBSP; SoSe-8

For the floating world? (LL) I, who cut off my sorrows. Akazome Emon, *Japanese*. BoWoP; WPJ; WPOW, *tr. by* Kenneth Rexroth *and* Ikuko Atsumi

For the Fly-Leaf of a School-Book. Norman Cameron. OxBS

For the fount of life undying. Paradise. Peter Damian, *Latin*. MLL, *tr. by* Helen Waddell

For the Freedom Train. Langston Hughes. *See* Dream Boogie: Variation.

For the Ghost of Elinor Wylie. Winifred Holtby. WPN

For the girl, it was a growing up. Moon of the First Communion. Kathleen Norris. CrSp

For the Girls 'cause They Know. Harold Littlebird. VoR

For the God of Peyote. *Unknown, Huichol Indian*. STP, *tr. by* Jerome Rothenberg

For the Good of the Pythian Order. Mrs. Henry Linden. CBWP-4

For the Grave of a Peace-Loving Man. Hans Magnus Enzensberger, *German*. VCWP, *tr. by* Enzensberger, Hans Magnus *and* Michael Hamburger

For the great flint to come singing into his heart. (LL) Bushed. Earle Birney. MoCV; NOBC; NoAM; NoP-4

For the Jellicle Moon and the Jellicle Ball. (LL) The Song of the Jellicles. T. S. Eliot. EBEvV; FaBoCh; ImGa; OxBChV

For the Kindling of the Light on Easter Eve. Prudentius, *Latin*. MLL, *tr. by* Helen Waddell

For the Lady Olivia Porter; a Present upon a New Year's Day. Sir William Davenant. MeLP; NOSC

For the last time Beowulf uttered his boast. Beowulf and Wiglaf Slay the Dragon. *Unknown*. AnOE, *tr. by* Charles W. Kennedy *Fr.* Beowulf. OAEL-1, *tr. by* Charles W. Kennedy; ASW, *tr. by* Kevin Crossley-Holland

For the Last Time, Fire. Dennis Scott. PBCV

For the last time I wash the shirt. I Wash the Shirt. Anna Swirszczynska, *Polish*. BLT, *tr. by* Czeslaw Milosz *and* Leonard Nathan

For the Last Time on My Native Estate, *fragment*. Ilya Iankelevich Gabai, *Russian*. TCRP, *tr. by* Albert C. Todd

For the Lord is good; his mercy is everlasting; and his truth endureth to all generations. (LL) Psalm 100. Bible, *O.T., Hebrew*. NOCV

For the Lord knoweth the way of the righteous: but the way of the ungodly shall perish. (LL) Psalm 1. Bible, *O.T., Hebrew*. AWP; EnlH; SCAP; TrJP

For the Lord knows th' upright way of the just, / And the way of bad men to ruin must, *par. by* Milton. Bible, *O.T.* *See* Psalm 1.

For the Lord of Caves. Allama Prabhu, *Kanaada*. PFTM, *tr. by* A. K. Ramanujan

For the Lorde promised hys blessynge, and lyfe for evermore. Bible, *O.T.* *See* Psalm 133.

For the Lordes parte is his folke. Bible, *O.T.* OBVE, *tr. by* William Tyndale *Fr.* Deuteronomy.

For the Lord's Day Evening. Isaac Watts. OxBChV

For the Magdalene. William Drummond, of Hawthornden. ChIV-2; PoEL-2

For the man was she made by the Eden tree. Ballade of Lovers. May Probyn. VWP

For the Market. Jane Mayhall. TAP

For the Marriage of Faustus and Helen. Hart Crane. SeSe; InPS-3; NOBA; NoAM

   ("Brazen hynotics glitter here.")

   "Capped arbiter of beauty in this street." FaBoMo; ImPo; LiTM

   "Mind has shown itself at times, The."

For the Marsh's Birthday. James Wright. NYBP

For the Master's Use. *Unknown*. BLPA

For the mighty wind arises, roaring seaward, and I go. (LL) Locksley Hall. Tennyson. EBEV; EBVVPR; EnVR; FaBoBe; ImPo; NAEL-2; OAEL-2

For the mind in harmony with the Tao. Seng-ts'an. *See* The Mind of Absolute Trust.

For the Missing in Action. John Balaban. AF; PuP-15

For the Moment. Pierre Reverdy, *French*. TTTS, *tr. by* Ron Padgett

For the Monk San-tsang on His Return to the Western Regions. Li Tung, *Chinese*. CoBCP, *tr. by* Burton Watson

For the New Union Dead in Alabama. Edward Dorn. PoM

For the New World. Edward Hirsch. WWSi

For the nightemare. *Unknown*. MiEL

For the Nightly Ascent of the Hunter Orion over a Forest Clearing. James Dickey. TwCP

For the Obese. Paula Rankin. CMAP

For the old Kentucky home, far away. (LL) My Old Kentucky Home[, Good Night!]. Stephen Collins Foster. APN-2; FaBoBe; PoLF

For the One Who Would Take Man's Life in His Hands. Delmore Schwartz. LiTM; MoAmPo; VGW

For the Opening of the William Dinsmore Briggs Room. Yvor Winters. CRP

For the Palace that lies desolate. We Sit Solitary. *Unknown*. TrJP

For the Passing of Groucho's Pursuer. John Hollander. *See* To the Lady Portrayed by Margaret Dumont.

For the past. D. H. Lawrence. *See* Piano.

For the Poet Who Said Poets Are Struck by Lightning Only Two or Three Times. Peter Klappert. NBLV

For the Poets. Jayne Cortez. PmAP

For the Poor. Ho Hyongman, *Korean*. CKP, *tr. by* Jaihiun Kim

For the Poorman's nosegay is an introduction to a Prince. (LL) For the doubling of flowers is the improvement of the gard'ner's talent. Christopher Smart. ChIV-2; NOEC

For the Rain It Raineth Every Day. Robert Graves. NYBP

For the raindrop, joy is in entering the river. Asadullah Khan Ghalib, *Urdu*. EnlH, *tr. by* Jane Hirshfield

For the Record. Roy Blount, Jr. OBAL

For the Record. George Jonas. MoCV

For the Record. Audre Lorde. LiLi; LoHo

   ("And they weren't even / sisters.") (LL) LiLi

For the Record. Roy McFadden. PNI

For the Record. Adrienne Rich. NIP-4; VCAP

For the resounding valor of milennia to come. Osip Emilevich Mandelstam, *Russian*. TCRP, *tr. by* Bernard Meares

For the Safety of Lovers. John James. NBrP

For the sake of a night. Stewardess of the Empress Kōka, *Japanese*. OHPJ, *tr. by* Kenneth Rexroth

For the sake of a night of a little sleep. The daughter of Minamoto no Toshitaka, *Japanese*. WPJ, *tr. by* Kenneth Rexroth *and* Ikuko Atsumi

For the Sake of Retrieval. Linda Bierds. NAmP90

For the sea is his truest home! (LL) The Sea-Gull. Mary Howitt. BoTP; CTAV; OxBChV

For the second course, last night, a custard came. The Custard. Robert Herrick. PFE

For the self you did not value? (LL) To a Comrade in Arms. Alun Lewis. FaBoTw; MoBrPo

For the seven lakes, and by no man these verses. Canto 49. Ezra Pound. PFTM

For the Sexes the Gates of Paradise. William Blake. *See* The Gates of Paradise.

For the Sin. *Unknown, Hebrew*. TrJP

For the Sisters of the Hôtel Dieu. Abraham Moses Klein. NoP-4

For the site of the Kingdom of Heaven. (LL) Loss of something ever felt I, A. Emily Dickinson. ChIV-2; NALW; NCAP

For the Sleepwalkers. Edward Hirsch. FYAP

For the smell. Leroy Gorman. HA

For the sound we revere. For Art Blakey and the Jazz Messengers. Keorapetse Kgositsile. SeSe

For the Spartan Dead at Plataia. Simonides, *Greek*. GrAn, *tr. by* Peter Jay

For the Spartan Dead at Thermopylai (480 B.C.). Simonides, *Greek*. OBCVT, *tr. by* Peter Jay; GrAn

("Go tell at Sparta, traveler passing by.") WeW-3

(On the Spartan Dead at Thermopylae.) WeW-3

For the spiritual musick is as follows. Christopher Smart. NOEC *Fr.* Fragment B. *Fr.* Jubilate Agno.

For the Student Strikers. Richard Wilbur. OxBC

For the Sun Declined. Yitzhak Lamdan, *Hebrew*.

"Where am I, O awesome friend?" TrJP, *tr. by* Simon Halkin

"For the tenth time, dull Daphnis," said Chloe. Limerick. *Unknown*. PeLi

For the Theft of Cattle, *a magical charm*. *Unknown, Anglo-Saxon*. ASW, *tr. by* Kevin Crossley-Holland

For the Thing we call Moon contains. Chords Passages 14. Robert Duncan. FTOS

For the three dead children. (LL) Lament for Tadhg Cronin's Children. Michael Hartnett. PBCIP; RB

For the Union Dead. Robert Lowell. AmPP; CBCWP; CoAP; ColAP; FYAP; FaBoPV; HAP; HCAP; HeIP-4; InPS-3; LCAP-2; LiTM; MoP; NAAL-2; NOBA; NoAM; NoP-4; OBWP; PoE; Poetr; SCV; TFi; TRP; TwCP; UnPo; VCAP; WeW-3

("Old South Boston Aquarium stands / in a Sahara of snow now, The.") AFr

("Savage servility / slides by on grease, A.") (LL) AFr; FaBoA; PoPoPo

For the Unveiling of a Memorial. Daniil Leonidovich Andreyev, *Russian*. TCRP, *tr. by* Bradley Jordan

For the vanished mother / of a Black girl. Audre Lorde. *See* Story Books on a Kitchen Table.

For the voyage of oblivion awaits you. (LL) The Ship of Death. D. H. Lawrence. CMoP; FaBoTw; GTBS-P; MoBrPo; MoP; NAEL-2; NoAM; NoP-4; OAEL-2; OxAEP-2

For "The Wine of Circe" by Edward Burne-Jones. D. G. Rossetti. UV

For the woman / African in ancestry. A Freedom Song for the Black Woman. Carole C. Gregory Clemmons. BlSi

For the Woman at the Fast-Food Fish Place Who Called Me Pig. Gary Margolis. IFJA

For the Women of Poland: December 1981. Jane Hirshfield. WeT

For the Word Is Flesh. Stanley Kunitz. VGW

For the Yonghy-Bonghy-Bo. (LL) The Courtship of the Yonghy-Bonghy-Bo. Edward Lear. EnLoPo; OAEL-2; OxBM

For the Young Who Want To. Marge Piercy. Poetsp

For thee and for myself no quiet find. (LL) Sonnet 27. Shakespeare. HeIP-4; NoSic; SCGP

For thee I shall not die. O Woman, Shapely as the Swan. *Unknown, Irish*. IIP, *tr. by* Douglas Hyde; BIrV, *tr. by* Padraic Colum

For thee to wear, but this of thine own Blood. (LL) On Our Crucified Lord, Naked and Bloody. Richard Crashaw. HoPM; NOSC; OAEL-1; OxBSP; SeCP; TrCP

For their sons gone / just pushing. Lucille Clifton. *See* For de Lawd.

For them the sun shines at full strength—while we here walk in night. Afterlife in Elysium. Pindar, *Greek*. OBCVT, *tr. by* Willis Barnstone

For there is an African virtue of the tree. Edouard J. Maunick. NegPo, *tr. by* Ellen Conroy Kennedy *Fr.* As Far as Yoruba Land.

For there is hope for a tree. Bible, *O.T. Fr.* Job's Entreaty. AWP *Fr.* Job. NAWM-1

For there is no friend like a sister. Christina Rossetti. *Fr.* Goblin Market. CPO; EBEV; FaBoSe; NAEL-2; NALW; NOBVV; NOxBChV; OBNV; OxAEP-2; VWP

For there is no God found stronger than death; and death is a sleep. (LL) Hymn to Proserpine. Swinburne. EBVV; EnVR; NAEL-2; OAEL-2; OBNC; PoEL-5

For there is one more fair than thou, beloved of Alexis. (LL) Hexametra Alexis in Laudem Rosamundi. Robert Greene. GBL; PoEL-2

For there the Lord commanded the blessing, even life for evermore [*or* for ever]. (LL) Psalm 133. Bible, *O.T.* AWP; TrJP

For these dead Birds sigh a prayer. (LL) The Phoenix and the Turtle. Shakespeare. ImPo; NOBE; NoP-4; NoSic; OAEL-1; OBEV; OxAEP-1; PBRV; PeECV; PoEL-2; SCGP

For they appeal from tyranny to God. (LL) Sonnet on Chillon. Byron. GSo; GTBS-P; PBMP

For they come of a gentle kind. (LL) The Oyster. Sir Walter Scott. FaBoCh; NTP

For they know when their Shepherd is nigh. (LL) The Shepherd. William Blake. BoTP; ChAP; FHYEP; Ro

For they never came back again. (LL) What Became of Them? *Unknown*. BoTP; CTAV; OBCA; OxBChV

For They Shall See God. Luci Shaw. TrCP

For they were sent to do judgement on him! (LL) Bishop Hatto. Robert Southey. OBNV; OBSP; OxAEP-2

For they'd left all their tails behind 'em. Mother Goose. *See* Little Bo-Peep has lost her sheep.

For thine is the kingdom. Lord's Prayer. D. H. Lawrence. PeECV

For thine own Duplicity. (LL) "Heavenly Father"—take to thee. Emily Dickinson. APN-2; PoEL-5

For thinking on my dearie. (LL) Simmer's a pleasant time. Robert Burns. NOEC; PoEL-4

For thirteen days / she had threatened / and forced me dark. Friendly Town #3. Safiya Henderson-Holmes. UnSA

For this. Tanka. Nakajō Fumiko, *Japanese*. MJT, *tr. by* Makoto Ueda

For this agility chance found. The Age Demanded. Ezra Pound. *Fr.* Mauberly (1920). *Fr.* Hugh Selwyn Mauberley. (Life and Contacts). AmPP; CMoP; InPS-3; LiTM; NOBA; NoAM; TAP

For this and for all enclosures like it the archetype. The Cave of Making. W. H. Auden. FaBoVe; OxAEP-2

For this is not the road against which stand enemy lines. Piyyut for Rosh Hashana. Haim Guri, *Hebrew*. MHP, *tr. by* Ruth Finer Mintz

For This Is Wisdom. "Laurence Hope." PoLF *Fr.* The Teak Forest. (Wisdom?)

For this particular silence. (LL) The Memory of Elena. Carolyn Forché. LoL; NoAM

For this present, hard. Woodnotes I ("For this present, hard"). Ralph Waldo Emerson. AmPP; NOBA

"For this same night att [Bucklesfeildberry]." Little Musgrave and Lady Barnard. *Unknown*. ESPB

For this she starred her eyes with salt. Epitaph. Elinor Wylie. MoAmPo

For this the ancient stars were hurled. Evolution. Israel Zangwill. TrJP

For this the monk is to blame. (LL) The Weak Monk. Stevie Smith. BoWoP; FaBoTw

For this your mother sweated in the cold. To Jesus on His Birthday. Edna St. Vincent Millay. ChIV-2; HeIP-4; TrCP

For Thomas Moore. James Simmons. BiHa; PBCIP

For Thomas Stearns Eliot on the Occasion of His One Hundredth Birthday. Thomas Rabbitt. NAmP90

For Those my unbaptized Rhymes [*or* Rhimes]. His Prayer for Absolution. Robert Herrick. BeJo; CavPo

For those of us who live at the shoreline. A Litany for Survival. Audre Lorde. NAAAL

For those that never know the light. The Children of the Night. Edwin Arlington Robinson. APN-2; OxBA

For those vicissitudes by which men die. (LL) La Gioconda. "Michael Field." ADE; CABP; PeVV

For Those Who Always Fear the Worst. *Unknown*. NBLV

For Those Who Fail. Joaquin Miller. PoToHe

For those who place their blooms on new-made graves. Time's Hand Is Kind. Margaret E. Bruner. PoToHe

For Those Who Will Live Forever. Thomas Rabbitt. CMAP

For those who worship Thee there is no death. The Trees of Life. Jones Very. NOBA

For thou art of her clay. (LL) The Lacking Sense. Thomas Hardy. CMoP; PoEL-5

For thou art with me here upon the banks. Wordsworth. *Fr.* Lines Composed a Few Miles Above Tintern Abbey on Revisiting the Banks

of the Wye During a Tour. EBEvV; FHYEP; HeIP-4; InPS-3; NoP-4; OAEL-2; OBNC; OxAEP-2; PoEL-4; Poetr; SCGP; TFi

For though my rhyme be ragged. John Skelton. OBCoV *Fr.* Colin Clout.

For though the eaves were rabbeted. Henry David Thoreau. NCAP; OxBSP; PoEL-4

For though ye be true of your tongue and honestly earn. Good Works. William Langland. NOCV *Fr.* The Vision of Piers Plowman.

For three days the wind blew northeast. March Storm, Poquoson, Virginia, 1963. Dave Jeddie Smith. CMAP

For three years, diabolus in the scale. Ezra Pound. *Fr.* Mauberley (1920). *Fr.* Hugh Selwyn Mauberley. (Life and Contacts). AmPP; CMoP; InPS-3; LiTM; NOBA; NoAM; TAP

For three years I sadly listened. Wen Cheng-ming. CoBLCP, *tr.* by Jonathan Chaves *Fr.* Improvised on Horseback to Say Good-bye to Those Who Are Seeing Me Off.

For three years, out of key with his time. E. P. Ode Pour l'Election de Son Sepulchre. Ezra Pound. FaBoMo; HAP; MeMAP; MoAmPo; MoP; NAAL-2; NoAM; NoP-4; OxBA; UnPo; VGW *Fr.* Hugh Selwyn Mauberley. (Life and Contacts). AmPP; CMoP; InPS-3; LiTM; NOBA; NoAM; TAP

For Thurman Thomas. Reuben Jackson. ISC

For thus I leave the world, the flesh, and devil. (LL) This is my play's [*or* playes] last scene, here heavens appoint. Donne. EBEV; FaBoVe; MeLP; SeCP; Son

For Thus saith The Lord to the men of Judah and Jerusalem. Bible, *O.T.* OBVE *Fr.* Jeremiah.

"For thy soul's health to shed his dearest blood?" (LL) Now Pontius Pilate is to judge the cause. Emilia Lanyer. NALW; NOSC

For to Admire. Rudyard Kipling. MoBrPo

For to-day we have naming of parts. Henry Reed. *See* Naming Of Parts.

For to his light, what other is not blind? (LL) Psalm 147. Bible, *O.T.* NOCV

For to make him she exhausted all her store. (LL) Elegy on the Earl of Rochester. Anne Wharton. KTR; NOSC

For to make me go. William Christopher Handy. *See* Beale Street Blues.

For to please ourselves, truly, is more than we can. (LL) On an Unsociable Family. Elizabeth Hands. ECWP; WoRP

For to sit upon a serpent's knee.' (LL) Dives and Lazarus. ("As it fell out upon a day [*or* one day]"). Unknown. ESPB; OxBB

For today we have naming of parts. (LL) Naming Of Parts. Henry Reed. APAD; EBEvV; HoPM; ImPo; InPS-3; MoBrPo; NOBE; NoP-4; OxBTC; PoPoPo; PoRA; Poetr; RaBo; SAGP; SoSe-8; TFi; UV; UnPo

For Tom Numkena, Hopi/Spokane. Harold Littlebird. VoR

For Travelers Going Sidereal. Limerick. Robert Frost. OBAL; PeLi

For treuthe [*or* trewthe] telleth that love [*or* loue] is triacle to abate sinne [*or* of hevene]. The Incarnation. William Langland. OBEV; PoEL-1 *Fr.* The Vision of Piers Plowman.

For Twelfth Day. Luke Wadding. TIRV

For twenty years and more surviving after. Widows. Edgar Lee Masters. MoAmPo

For 20 years they hid your words. Freedom. Carolina Hospital. LoHo

For Two Children. David Malouf. BMAP

For two months the dust of the capital. On First Returning from Taking the Examinations: Feelings at Cloud-Stop Pavilion. Wen Cheng-ming, *Chinese.* CoBLCP, *tr.* by Jonathan Chaves

For two nights. Fire Support Burk. Steve Denning. CDa

For two who. For Two Who Slipped Away Almost Entirely. Alice Walker. CrSp

For two years I looked forward. Breakfast. Thom Gunn. OxBC

For Uncle Jim's deep-fried, all-fat, real gone / whale steaks. (LL) Naughty Boy. Robert Creeley. HeIP-4; NOBA; NoAM

For *Under the Volcano.* Malcolm Lowry. NOBC

For us, born into a still. C. Day Lewis. CMoP *Fr.* Overtures to Death.

For us, his creatures and his foes, hath died. (LL) Why are we[e] by all creatures waited on? Donne. NOCV; PoE; PoEL-2; TrCP

For us like any other fugitive. Another Time. W. H. Auden. MeMAP; OxBA

For Us No Night Can Be Happier. Nikolaus Ludwig, Graf von Zinzendorf, *German.* AH

For vacant hours of man's destructive leisure. To a Gentleman Who Invited Me to Go A-Fishing. Elizabeth Moody. ECWP

For vanished Hellas and Hebraic pain. (LL) Venus of the Louvre. Emma Lazarus. APN-2; GS; PAR

For Venus' ceston every line you make. (LL) A Sonnet to the Noble Lady, the Lady Mary Wroth. Ben Jonson. BeJo; NoP-4

For vulgar praise, doth it too dearly [*or* dearly] buy. (LL) To My Book. Ben Jonson. BeJo; FaBoVe; NAEL-1

For W.C.W ("Rhyme is after, The"). Robert Creeley. FTOS; LCAP-2

For W C W. Harvey Shapiro. WeT

For Walter Lowenfels. Wendy Rose. CDW

For Walter Washington. Tom Dent. NBV

For Want of a Male a Shoe Was Lost. Colleen J. McElroy. WeT

For want of a nail[, the shoe was lost]. Mother Goose. FaBoBe; LB; OxNR; ReMoGo

("And all for the want of a horseshoe nail.") (LL) LB

For want of a nail, the shoe was lost. Tremendous Trifles. Rowland Howard. CTV

For want of [*or* I] will in woe I plain. Sir Thomas Wyatt. SiPS

For wars his life and half a world away. A Lullaby. Randall Jarrell. HCAP; OxBC

For water-ices, cheap but good. A Grace for Ice-Cream. Allan M. Laing. OBCoV

For We Are Thy People. *Unknown.* TrJP

For we have thought the longer thoughts. Chapter Heading. Ernest Hemingway. PoA

For we know that in Heaven above at this moment *he's* saving *God.* (LL) Addition to Kipling's "The Dead King (Edward VII), 1910." Max Beerbohm. FaBoEE; OBCoV

For wealth as wide as weariness? (LL) Odes, 3.1. Horace. AWP, *tr.* by Abraham Cowley; OBVE, *tr.* by Gerard Manley Hopkins

For weariness of life, not love of Thee. (LL) To Heaven. Ben Jonson. BeJo; ChIV-2; HAP; NAEL-1; NOCV; NOSC; SCGP; SeCP; TRP; UnPo

For weeks and weeks the autumn world stood still. How One Winter Came in the Lake Region. Wilfred Campbell. NOBC

For weeks before it comes I feel excited, yet when it. Afterthought. Elizabeth Jennings. NOxBChV; OBCP

For weeks now. Haciendo Apenas la Recolección. Tino Villanueva. UnSA

For weeks now certain hours of every day. Heirloom. Robin Morgan. NMM-2

For wha ere had a lealer luve. Brown Adam. *Unknown.* ESPB

For what are husbands for, but to praise their wives? (LL) The Divorce Referendum, Ireland, 1986. Paul Durcan. BiHa; PBCIP

For what as easy. Love Song. W. H. Auden. PeLV Fr. Five Songs.

For what seemed to be the whole night. Ostiones Y Cangrejos Moros. Ricardo Pau-Llosa. CMAP

For what the world admires I'll wish no more. The Resolve. Mary Lee, Lady Chudleigh. ECWP; WPE

For what to-morrow shall disclose. Quid Sit Futurum Cras Fuge Quaerere. Matthew Prior. FaBoEE

For what we owe to other days. Exit. Edwin Arlington Robinson. MoAmPo; OxBSP

For whatever did it—the cider. A Cure at Porlock. Amy Clampitt. NoAM

For when it dawn'd—they dropp'd their arms. Coleridge. *See* The Loud wind never reached the ship.

For when the rushing Winds begin to blow. Lava-flow. *Unknown.* OBCVT, *tr.* by Jabez Hughes *Fr.* Aetna.

For when they meet, the tensile air. The Paradigm. Allen Tate. NOBA

For which all long has never yet been built. (LL) Peace in the Welsh Hills. Vernon Watkins. GTBS-P; OxBTC

For which the intricate Alps are a single nest. (LL) Connoisseur of Chaos. Wallace Stevens. LiTM; PFTM

For while through winding Ways I took my Flight. Aeneas sees his wife. Virgil, *Latin.* OBCVT, *tr.* by John Dryden

For Whitsuntide. Hildebert, *Latin.* MLL, *tr.* by Helen Waddell

For Who? Mary Weston Fordham. CBWP-2

For whom are you intended, wine in the corked bottle. Old Motif. Aleksandar Ristovic, *Serbo-Croatian.* HSix, *tr.* by Charles Simic

For whom now will you comb your hair in lover's fashion? Paulus Silentiarius, *Greek.* GrAn, *tr.* by Andrew Miller

For whom the possessed sea littered, on both shores. Requiem for the Plantagenet Kings. Geoffrey Hill. CABP; NAEL-2; NoAM

For whore and rogue; and dog and bitch. (LL) An Epigram on Scolding. Jonathan Swift. FaBoEE; FaBoVe

For whosoever will save his life shall lose it. Matthew 10:25–26. Bible, *N.T.* PBMP

For why[?] the gains [*or* gaines) doth se[e]ldom[e] quit[te] the charge. (LL) All were to[o] little for the merchant's [*or* merchauntes) hand[e]. George Gascoigne. AAS; Son

For Widower—wanted, house-keeper. Limerick. *Unknown.* PeLi

For William Edward Burghardt Du Bois on His Eightieth Birthday. Bette Darcie Latimer. PoBA

For Willyce. Patricia Parker. CPO; NMM-2

For wishing to be King. (LL) Silvio's Complaint: A Song, To a Fine Scotch Tune. Aphra Behn. KTR; RACG

For with his nail[e]s he'll dig them up again [*or* agen]. (LL) A Dirge: "Call for the robin-redbreast and the wren." John Webster. CH; EBEV; FaBoCh; GTBS-P; HAP; NOBE; NOSC; OBEV; OxAEP-1; PoEL-2; PoRA; RB; SCGP; TFi

For with his nails he'll dig them up again. John Webster. *See* A Dirge: "Call for the robin-redbreast and the wren."

For women grieve to think they must be old. (LL) Sonnet: "Beauty, sweet love, is like the morning dew." Samuel Daniel. NOBE; NoSic; OBEV

For Women shall you Taylors have. Isabella Whitney. BWW *Fr.* The Manner of Her Will and What She Left to London and to All Those in It, at Her Departing. NoSic

For X. Louis MacNeice. BoLoP; EnLoPo *Fr.* Trilogy for X.

For years he's gone over her parting words. No, Go On. Maura Dooley. LW

For years I had not seen such a town. Reunion. Judith Herzberg, *Dutch.* BoWoP, *tr. by* Shirley Kaufman

For years I have been a coal miner. A Coal Miner's Goodbye. *Unknown.* AmFP

For years I thought I knew, at the bottom of the dream. The Meeting. Louise Bogan. NYBP; NoAM

For years I waited for this to happen to me. The Chamber. Stuart Dischell. PUP-19

For years I've heard. Poem. Robin Blaser. NeAP

For years I've suffered from extreme poverty. Writing Poetry in the Back Garden. Chao Yi, *Chinese.* SuSp, *tr. by* Chang Yin-nan *and* Lewis C. Walmsley

For years now I have heard the cracking of. Studying Physics with My Daughter. Jeanne Murray Walker. WeW-3

For years we endured his insolence. Mask-Maker. Michael Jackson. PeNZ

For years you wallowed in the scholar's world. Nguyễn Trãi, *Vietnamese.* AVP, *tr. by* Huỳnh Sanh Thông

For You. James Moore. PuP-14

For You. Lawrence Raab. CMAP

For You. Carl Sandburg. MoAmPo

For You. James Harvey Spencer. PWR

For you fleas too. Avedik Issahakian. ChAP

For you, for you I am trilling these songs. (LL) For You O Democracy. Walt Whitman. APN-1; UV

For you I have emptied the meaning. Louis Zukofsky. NoAM

For you I have slept. Michael Ondaatje. NoP-4 *Fr.* Rock Bottom.

For you / I will be a ghetto jew. The Genius. Leonard Cohen. MoCV

For you I would put on embroidered robes. Hymn. Jane King. HCP

For You, Mamá. Cherríe Moraga. GLP

For You, My Son. Horace Gregory. MoAmPo

For You O Democracy. Walt Whitman. APN-1; UV

For you only can say "Wee! wee!" (LL) The Three Little Pigs. Sir Alfred Scott Gatty. ACTP; BoTP; OxBChV

For you Time past could not forget. Hymn to Proust. Gavin Ewart. NYBP

For you, tormentors. (LL) Where Are the Men Seized in This Wind of Madness? Alda do Espírito Santo, *Portuguese.* TTY; WPOW, *tr. by* Alan Ryder

For your offence. (LL) Rosalind's [*or* Rosalynd's] Madrigal[l]. Thomas Lodge. CBLP; NOBE; NoSic; OBEV; PoEL-2; SCGP

For your own mother, you remain Baby. And for His Mother. John Wheelwright. FiLi

For Zbigniew Herbert, Summer, 1971, Los Angeles. Larry Levis. CMAP; FYAP

For Zion's Sake. Bible, *O.T.* TrJP *Fr.* Isaiah.

Forbear bold Youth. An Answer to Another Persuading a Lady to Marriage. Katherine Philips. HAP; LW; OBEV; PBRV; PEW; WeW-3

Forbear this liquid fire, fly. A Fly about a Glass[e] of Burnt Claret. Richard Lovelace. CaPo

Forbear, thou great good husband, little ant. The Ant. Richard Lovelace. CaPo

Forbearance. Coleridge. ChIV-2

Forbearance. Ralph Waldo Emerson. MeMAP; TAP

Forbearance of kinsmen's wrongs. The Tiger. Kuṟamakaḷ Iḷaveyiṉi, *Tamil.* PLW, *tr. by* A. K. Ramanujan

Forbidden, The. Phyllis Haring. PeSA

Forbidden gate, palace trees, a moon's flitting trace. Presented to a Lady within the Palace. Chang Yü, *Chinese.* SuSp, *tr. by* Ronald C. Miao

Forc'd from home, and all its pleasures. The Negro's Complaint. William Cowper. CABP

Force. *Unknown.* OBCoV *Fr.* Advertising Rhymes.

Force. Derek Walcott. OxBC

Force-feeding swans—let me tell. Farmers. Thomas Lux. LCAP-2

Force of Love, The. Samuel Jones. NOEC

Force that through the green fuse drives the flower, The. Dylan Thomas. APAD; CABP; CMoP; EBEV; FaBoMo; InPS-3; LiTM; MoBrPo; MoP; NAEL-2; NOBE; NoAM; NoP-4; OBWVE; OxAEP-2; OxBTC; PBMP; PoE; Poetr; RB; SCV; TFi; UnPo

Forced by circumstance, I'll feign to be his wife. You Eat the Figs, So Sit Beneath the Tree. Phan Bội Châu, *Vietnamese.* AVP, *tr. by* Huỳnh Sanh Thông

Forced by soft violence of prayer. Matthew Green. ECEV *Fr.* The Spleen.

Forced Feelings. Wang Chiu-ssu, *Chinese.*
  "You think I am happy." CoBLCP, *tr. by* Jonathan Chaves

Forced March. Miklós Radnóti, *Hungarian.* AF, *tr. by* Emery E. George

Forced Music, A. Robert Graves. MoBrPo

Ford Madox Ford ("Lobbed ball plops, then dribbles to the cup, The"). Robert Lowell. OxBC; TwCP

Ford Madox Ford ("Taking Ford's dictation on Samuel Butler"). Robert Lowell. OxBC

Ford Manor. Derek Mahon. PBCIP

Ford o' Kabul River. Rudyard Kipling. FaBoTw; PeVV

Fording the River. Seamus Deane. PBCIP; PNI

'Fore I'll return again. (LL) Son David. *Unknown.* OxBB; OxBS

Foreboding, The. Robert Graves. GBL; PoA

Foreboding. John Haines. CoAmPo

Forecast. Howard Fergus. PBCV

Forecast. Josephine Miles. NoAM

Foreclosure. Sterling Brown. GT; PoBA
  ("And the old river rolls on, sleepily to the gulf.") (LL) GT

Forefathers. Edmund Blunden. NOBE; NoP-4; OBEV; OBMV; OxBTC

Forehead, Eyes, Cheeks, Nose, Mouth, and Chin. Mother Goose. ReMoGo

Forehead without scalp, dry shell without yolk of eye. Crinagoras, *Greek.* GrAn, *tr. by* Alistair Elliot

Foreign. Carol Ann Duffy. NBrP

Foreign Affairs. Stanley Kunitz. LiTM; NYBP

Foreign Aid. Lionel Kearns. NOBC

Foreign Children. Robert Louis Stevenson. BoTP; GoJo-1

Foreign Exchange. Marion Winik. IFJA

Foreign Gate, The. Sidney Keyes.
  "Moon is a poor woman, The." NoP-4; OBWP

Foreign Lands. Robert Louis Stevenson. BoTP

Foreign room, slab faces, dusty panes, A, The Rebel General. Chris Wallace-Crabbe. CBAP

Foreign Ruler, A. Walter Savage Landor. OBSV; PFE

Foreign thing desertless in origin, A. (LL) Apologia pro Vita Sua. A. R. Ammons. HCAP; NOBA

Foreign Ways. Diana Chang. UnSA

Foreign Woman. Rosario Castellanos, *Spanish.* WPOW, *tr. by* J. M. Cohen

Foreigners. Meredith Stricker. LoHo

Foreigners at the Fair. Fred Emerson Brooks. OBAL

Forensic Jocularities. Sir George Rose. OxBoLi

Forensic Medicine. Gieve Patel. OMIP

Forerunners. Ralph Waldo Emerson. APN-1; OBEV; OxBA

Forerunners, The. George Herbert. ESCV; GeHe; NAEL-1; NoP-4; TOF
  ("So all within be livelier then before.") (LL) FSCP; PBRV

Foreseen for so many years: these evils, this monstrous violence. May-June, 1940. Robinson Jeffers. LiTM; MoAmPo

Foresight. Lincoln Kirstein. OBWP; PoWW

Forest. Jean Garrigue. LiTM; NOBA

Forest, The. Miroslav Holub, *Czech.* PoSu, *tr. by* George Theiner

Forest. Angus Martin. FaBoTC

Forest, The. Edward Thomas. *See* Lights Out.

Forest. Judit Tóth, *Hungarian.* CEEP, *tr. by* Emery E. George

Forest and brook—mdash;who has gone. Feelings in Nature ("Forest and brook—mdash;who has gone"). Ma Chih-yüan. *Fr.* Four Poems to the Tune "Ch'ing-chiang yin." CoBLCP, *tr. by* Jonathan Chaves

Forest animals walk there. What She Said. Kapilar, *Tamil.* PLW, *tr. by* A. K. Ramanujan

Forest Birds (A Woman Speaks). Chu Yün-ming, *Chinese.* CoBLCP, *tr. by* Jonathan Chaves
  "What can I do, I love you so much!"
  "You and I are like birds in a forest."

Forest bitter, spiky, The. Melpomene. Peter Huchel, *German.* CEEP, *tr. by* Michael Hamburger

Forest drips and glows with green, The. Rainforest. Judith Wright. OPOU

Forest felled, A. Publius Papinius Statius, *Latin.* OBCVT, *tr. by* Walter Harte

Forest Fire. Vadim Sergeievich Shefner, *Russian.* TCRP, *tr. by* Daniel Weissbort

Forest Hymn, A. William Cullen Bryant. APN-1; TAP
  "Father, thy hand/ Hath reared."

Forest Lake. Edith Södergran, *German.* WPoS, *tr. by* Stina Katchadourian

Forest Leaves in Autumn. John Keble.
  November. OBEV; OBNC

Forest nuns, who sheltered us and healed, The. The Krankenhaus of Leutkirch. Richmond Lattimore. NYBP

Forest of Europe. Derek Walcott. PBCV

Forest of the Dead, The. James Griffyth Fairfax. NSI; PoWW

Forest of yellow bamboo trees, The. B. S. Mardhekar, *Marathi*. OMIP, tr. by Vinay Dharwadker.

Forest road, The. Charlotte Mew. VWP

Forest Song. Sir Shane Leslie. TIRV

Forest stands, The. John Wills. HA

Forest Thoughts. Sir Roger Casement. TIRV

Forest was fair and wide, The. Tristrem and the Hunters. Thomas of Erceldoune. OxBS *Fr.* Sir Tristrem.

Forests are branches of a tree lying down. Flying Home from Utah. May Swenson. WPE

Forests grow pink and lacy in the dawn, The. Russian Woman. "Igor Severyanin," *Russian*. TCRP, tr. by Bernard Meares

Forests of Lithuania, The. Donald Davie. "But this, so feminine?" OxBTC

Forests were on fire, The. Two Drops. Zbigniew Herbert, *Polish*. RB, tr. by Czeslaw Milosz

Foresworn now the love-vows! Meleager, *Greek*. GrAn, tr. by Peter Whigham

Forever. (LL) The Club. Mitsuye Yamada. LoHo

Forever Ambrosia. Christopher Darlington Morley. OBAL

Forever brigands and pirates, the Cretans are never just. Leonidas of Tarentum. HePo, tr. by Barbara Hughes Fowler *Fr.* Epigrams.

Forever Dead. Sappho, *Greek*. AWP, tr. by William Ellery Leonard

Forever in My Dream and in My Morning Thought. Henry David Thoreau. PoEL-4

Forever in the back seat of the car. King over Israel. Dahlia Ravikovitch, *Hebrew*. IP, tr. by Warren Bargad and Stanley F. Chyet

Forever intervene! (LL) Our lives are Swiss. Emily Dickinson. APN-2; NOBA; TAP

Forever, it comes from the head. / *Where does it end?*. Venom. James Dickey. PoA

Forever, life-long. (LL) To O.E.A E. A. Claude McKay. GT

Forever over now, forever, forever gone. The Cameo. Edna St. Vincent Millay. FYAP; MeMAP; MoAmPo; UnPo; WPE

Forever Parted: Graveyard. Gu Cheng, *Chinese*. VCWP, tr. by J. P. Seaton and Mu Yi

Forever the little thud of names, falling. Empty Dwelling Places. Kenneth Patchen. PoA

Forever the Snake. Jennifer Rankin. BMAP

Forever; 'tis a single word! Charles Stuart Calverley. NOBL; NOBVV

Forever, yes, forever I'll love you. Xuân Diệu, *Vietnamese*. AVP, tr. by Huỳnh Sanh Thông

Forevermore. Jones Very. NCAP

Foreword to a Book of Poems. Xuân Diệu, *Vietnamese*. AVP, tr. by Huỳnh Sanh Thông

Foreword to New Numbers. Christopher Logue. OxBTC

Forfeit their Paradise by their pride. (LL) The Flower. George Herbert. AWP; ESCV; FMP; FSCP; GeHe; NAEL-1; NOBE; NOCV; NoP-4; OBGa; PBRV; PoEL-2; SeCP

Forfeiture, The. Henry King, Bishop of Chichester. NOSC

Forge me a tool, my Seamus. His Request. Owen Roe O'Sullivan, *Irish*. BIrV, tr. by Joan Keefe

Forget each kindness that you do. A Memory System. *Unknown*. PWR

Forget it. (LL) Blues. Derek Walcott. GT; SeSe

Forget It. *Unknown*. PoLF

Forget Me Not. Austin Clarke. CIP-2

Forget-Me-Not, The. *Unknown*. BoTP

Forget-Me-Nots. Yevgeny Mikhailovich Vinokurov, *Russian*. TCRP, tr. by Daniel Weissbort

Forget not this. Sir Thomas Wyatt. *See* A Supplication.

Forget not yet the tried intent. A Supplication. Sir Thomas Wyatt. AAS; FaBoVe; GTBS-P; HAP; NAEL-1; NOBE; NoP-4; NoSic; OBEV; PoPoPo; SCGP; SiPS

Forget roadside crossings. How to See Deer. Philip Booth. Poetsp

Forget six counties overhung with smoke. Prologue: The Wanderers. William Morris. EBVV; EnVR *Fr.* The Earthly Paradise.

Forget the past and live the present hour. Now. Sarah Knowles Bolton. PWR

Forget Thee? John Moultrie. BLPA; FaBoBe; PoToHe

Forget thine anguish. Meditations. Solomon ibn Gabirol, *Hebrew*. TrJP, tr. by Emma Lazarus

Forget to mail my letter to my friend Death. Overdue Balance Sheet. Thérèse Plantier, *French*. BoWoP, tr. by Maxine W. Kumin and Judith Kumin

Forget What Did. Philip Larkin. NoAM

Forget your life. Say *God is Great*. Get up. Say Yes Quickly. Jelaluddin Rumi, *Persian*. EnlH, tr. by Coleman Barks and A. J. Arberry; RaBo, tr. by Coleman Barks and John Moyne

Forgetful Number. Vasco [*or* Vasko] Popa. HSix, tr. by Charles Simic *Fr.* The Yawn of Yawns.

Forgetfulness! Josephine D. Henderson Heard. CBWP-4

Forgetting. Tanka. Ishikawa Takuboku, *Japanese*. MJT, tr. by Ueda, Makoto

Forgetting daily self, my truest self I find. (LL) Flaxman. Margaret Fuller. APN-1; PAR

Forgetting follies, faults forgiving, *par.* by Countess of Pembroke, Mary Sidney Herbert. Bible, *O.T. See* Psalm 130.

FORGETTING God. Sir Thomas Seymour. NoSic

Forgetting Greek. Rachel Hadas. WeT

Forgetting. Yes, I will forget it all. Vahan Tekeyan, *Armenian*. AF, tr. by Hovanessian, Diana Der and Marzbed Margossian

Forgive and Forget. Frances Sargent Osgood. PAR

Forgive and Forget. "Totius," *Afrikaans*. PeSA, tr. by Anthony Delius

"Forgive—forget! I own the wrong!" Forgive and Forget. Frances Sargent Osgood. PAR

Forgive Me. Shakti Chattopadhyay, *Bengali*. OMIP, tr. by Prithvindra Chakravarty and Ulli Beier

Forgive me Head Master. A Portrait of the Self as Nation, 1990–1991. Marilyn Chin. PUP-19

Forgive me if I speak possessively of him. To a New Daughter-in-Law. *Unknown*. PoToHe

Forgive me, if I wound your ear. In a Letter to A.R.C. on Her Wishing to Be Called Anna. Matilda Barbara Betham-Edwards. ECWP; WoRP

Forgive me, my God, and overlook my sins. His Illness. Solomon ibn Gabirol, *Hebrew*. TOF, tr. by David Goldstein

Forgive me, Sire, for cheating your intent. Norman Cameron. FaBoEE; FaBoTC; GTBS-P; OxBS; OxBSP

Forgive me that I pitch your praise too low. Apology for Understatement. John Wain. OxBTC; PFE

Forgive me, you whom they cast in a name. Prayer. Avraham Shlonsky, *Hebrew*. MHP, tr. by Ruth Finer Mintz

Forgive, O Lord, my little jokes on Thee. Robert Frost. LiTM; Poetr; SAmP

Forgive, O Lord, this worldly one. A Prayer for Forgiveness. Aengus the Culdee, *Irish*. TIRV, tr. by Eoin Neeson

Forgive the hours spent listening to radios. Looking at a Dead Wren in My Hand. Robert Bly. NNaP

"Forgive these nigguhs that know not what they do." Gwendolyn Brooks. *See* The Rites for Cousin Vit.

"Forgive these nigguhs that know not what they do." (LL) Riot. Gwendolyn Brooks. BPo; CAPP-1; NAAAL; NALW; NBV; PoBA; TAP

Forgive us, son of Amram, be not wroth. Epigram III. *Unknown*. *Fr.* Duel with Verses over a Great Man. TrJP

Forgive your son! (LL) Ecce Puer. James Joyce. BIrV; ChIV-2; EBEV; IMW; MoP; NoAM; TrCP

Forgiven. Margaret Elizabeth Munson Sangster. PoToHe

Forgiven Past, The. Laura Riding Jackson. PBWP

Forgiveness. Alice Walker. MDDM

Forgiveness. John Greenleaf Whittier. GSo; TrCP

Forgiveness Dream. Jean Valentine. LCAP-2; NMM-2

Forgo the charming Muses! No, in spite. Elizabeth Singer Rowe. PEW *Fr.* To one that persuades me to leave the Muses.

Forgotten Girlhood. Laura Riding Jackson. RB

Forgotten Man, The. Edwin Markham. PoLF

Forgotten? / What it was about? / What the matter was? ((((((Hollanditis)))))). Simon Vinkenoog, *Dutch*. CLPP, tr. by Charles McGeehan

Fork. Charles Simic. AmPA; ChAP; ColAP; HCAP; LCAP-2; PoPoPo; TRP; WeW-3

Fork of the Road, The. William Renton. NOBVV

Forked Radish, A. Jonathan Price. CBLP

Forked Tongue. Helen Ruggieri. LoHo

Forlorn. William Dean Howells. APN-2

Forlorn and glum the couples go. The Houses. Eden Phillpotts. OxBTC

Forlorn and lonely, my time will never come. Parting from Wang Wei. Meng Hao Jan, *Chinese*. SuSp, tr. by Daniel Bryant

Forlorn and lost, who's standing by the field? To a Scarecrow. Tản Đà, *Vietnamese*. AVP, tr. by Huỳnh Sanh Thông

Forlorn Saphira, with reclining head. Against Homosexuality. Thomas Gilbert. NOEC *Fr.* View of the Town, A. In an Epistle to a Friend.

Form, as any taper, fine, A. Modern Female Fashions. Mary Robinson. NOBRP

Form decreed of tree and flower, The. Dominica Pentecostes. Aubrey Thomas De Vere. TIRV

Form is the woods: the beast. Poem. James Harrison. VGW

Form of Chiasmus; The Chiasmus of Forms, The. Michael Davidson. PmAP

Form of Epitaph, A. Laurence Whistler. GTBS-P

Form of Passion, A. David McFadden. NOBC

Form Rejection Letter. Philip Dacey. AmPA

Form Was the World. Maurice English. NYBP

Formal as a minuet or sonnet. Mystery Story. Howard Nemerov. NBLV

Formal exercise for withered fingers, A. Old Fisherman with Guitar. George Mackay Brown. FaBoTC; OxBC

Formed long ago, yet made today. Mother Goose. OxNR

Former Barn Lot. Mark Van Doren. MoAmPo

Former Beauties. Thomas Hardy. CBLP; NoAM; OBMV; OBNC *Fr.* At Casterbridge Fair.

Formerly a Slave. Herman Melville. APN-2; TAP

Formerly I thought of you twice. Four Notions of Love and Marriage. N. Scott Momaday. HATNAP

Forming Child Poems. Simon J. Ortiz. CDW

Forms. Tadeusz Rózewicz, *Polish.* CEEP, *tr. by* Victor Contoski

Forms of Love, The. George Oppen. NNaP

Forms of the Earth at Abiquiu. N. Scott Momaday. CDW

Forms of the Implicit Love of God. Simone Weil, *French.*
   "When one human being is attached to another by a bond of affection that." ITG, *tr. by* Stephen Mitchell

Fornication is a filthy business. Petronius Arbiter, *Greek.* PGA, *tr. by* Kenneth Rexroth

Forsake me not thus, Adam, witness Heav'n. Eve Penitent. Milton. *Fr.* Book X. FHYEP *Fr.* Paradise Lost.

Forsaken. Zalman Schneour, *Yiddish.* TrJP, *tr. by* Joseph Leftwich

Forsaken, The. Duncan Campbell Scott. NOBC

Forsaken. *Unknown.* AmFP

Forsaken Bride, The. *Unknown. See* Waly, Waly [Love Be Bonny].

Forsaken Garden, A. Swinburne. EBEV; EBEvV; GTBS-P; GaP; NOBE; NOBVV; NoP-4; OAEL-2; OBGa; OBNC; OxAEP-2; SCGP
   ("As a god self-slain on his own strange altar, / Death lies dead.") (LL) OBGa

Forsaken Merman, The. Matthew Arnold. EBEV; EBVVPR; FHYEP; FaBoCh; FaPoR; NAEL-2; NTP; OBNV; OBSP
   "Children dear, was it yesterday." BoTP

Forsaken of all comforts but these two. Upone Tabacco. Sir Robert Ayton. OxBS

Forsaken Wife, The. Elizabeth Thomas. ECWP; LW

Forsaken Wife, The. Ts'ao Chih, *Chinese.* CoBCP, *tr. by* Burton Watson

Forsaken woods, trees with sharp storms opressed. Robert Sidney. NoSic

"Forsaking all"—You mean. The Word. Margaret Avison. MoCV

Forsee or more control than robin or wren. (LL) Fifty Faggots. Edward Thomas. MoBrPo; PeFWW; PoWW

Forsythia. Mary Ellen Solt. BoWoP

Fort by the oak trees there, The. The Fort of Rathangan. Berchan, *Old Irish.* CH; FaBoCh, *tr. by* Kuno Meyer

Fort of Ard Ruide, The. *Unknown.* NOIV

Fort of Rathangan, The. Berchan, *Old Irish.* CH; FaBoCh, *tr. by* Kuno Meyer

Fort or Castle of Hope, The. Margaret Lucas Cavendish, Duchess of Newcastle.
   "Some with sharp swords, to tell O most accursed!" PEW

Fort Wayne. Jack Spicer. CBNP

Forth at the threshold of the desert—profession of his father: dealer in scent-bottles. (LL) Anabasis. "St.-John Perse," *French.* PFTM, *tr. by* Thomas Stearns Eliot

Forth Feasting. William Drummond, of Hawthornden.
   "What blust'ring noise now interrupts my sleep." NOSC

Forth from his den to steal he stole. Burglar Bill. *Unknown.* FuFo

Forth from its scabbard, pure and bright. The Sword of Robert Lee. Abram Joseph Ryan. CBCWP

Forth from the east, up the ascent of Heaven. Matthew Arnold. PeVV *Fr.* Balder Dead.

Forth from the purple battlements he fared. Sir Eggnogg. Bayard Taylor. BXAP

Forth goes the weeding dame; her daily task. Peasants at Work. James Hurdis. ECEV *Fr.* The Favourite Village.

Forth into the warm darkness faring wide. Wings in the Dark. John Gray. NOBVV

Forth, to the alien gravity. The Launch. Alice Thompson Meynell. PeVV; WPE

Forth went the candid man. The Candid Man. Stephen Crane. MoAmPo *Fr.* War Is Kind.

Forties, fateful forties, The. "David Samuilovich Samoylov," *Russian.* TCRP, *tr. by* Lubov Yakovleva

Forties Flick. John Ashbery. FTOS; NoAM

Fortification of New Ross, The. *Unknown, Norman French.*
   "I have a whim to speak in verse." NOIV

Fortitude. Noël Coward. LBC

Fortitude. Christopher Smart. ChIV-2 *Fr.* Hymns for the Amusement of Children.

Fortnight before Christmas Gypsies were everywhere, A. The Gypsy. Edward Thomas. NoAM; NoP-4

Fortress, The. Anne Sexton. LiTM

Fortù, fortù, my beloved one. The Englishman in Italy. Robert Browning. PoEL-5

Fortunate, / Being articulate. Nocturne of the Self-evident Presence. Thomas MacGreevy. BIrV; CIP-2

Fortunate Traveller, The. Derek Walcott. NoAM

Fortune. Charles Madge. FaBoMo

Fortune. *Unknown.* HeIP-4

Fortune. Sir Thomas Wyatt. AAS; SiPS

Fortune a Goddess is to Fools alone. Juvenal, *Latin.* OBCVT, *tr. by* John Dryden, the younger

Fortune always boosts the dumb. The Weighing-In. Ibn al-Rumi, *Arabic.* ArPe, *tr. by* Omar S. Pound

Fortune and Virtue. Thomas Dekker *and others.* NoSic *Fr.* Old Fortunatus.

Fortune beyond my loveliest daydreams fulfilled is my. Roman Elegy Ia. Goethe, *German.* EP, *tr. by* Michael Hamburger

Fortune Cookie Blues. Amy Uyematsu. LTA

Fortune did not mean to give you promotion. On a Worthless Politician. *Unknown, Greek.* GrAn, *tr. by* Peter Jay

Fortune doth frown. Sir Thomas Wyatt. NoSic

Fortune favours the Brave, old Proverbs say. Mr Cromek to Mr Stothard. William Blake. FaBoEE

Fortune has brought me down--her wonted way. His Children. Hittan of Tayyi. AWP *Fr.* Hamasah.

Fortune hath taken away my love. Sir Walter Ralegh. NoSic
   ("Fortune hath taken thee away, my love.") NoP-4
   ("No fortune base shall ever alter me.") (LL) NoP-4
   "Thus now I leave my love in fortunes." PBRV

Fortune hath taken thee away, my love. Sir Walter Ralegh. *See* Fortune hath taken away my love.

Fortune, Nature, Love, long have contended about me, *speech of Dorus.* Sir Philip Sidney. *Fr.* Arcadia.

Fortune smiles, cry holy day! [*or* holiday]. Fortune and Virtue. Thomas Dekker *and others.* NoSic *Fr.* Old Fortunatus.

Fortune-tellers say I won't last long. Antipater of Thessalonica, *Greek.* PGA, *tr. by* Kenneth Rexroth

Fortune's Legacy. *Unknown.* NOSC

Fortunes locked in the Hua-kai stars, why seek anything. Self-mockery. "Lu Hsün," *Chinese.* SuSp, *tr. by* William R. Schultz

Fortunes of Men, The. *Unknown, Anglo-Saxon.* ASW, *tr. by* Kevin Crossley-Holland
   "Another shall hang from the gallows' height."

Fortunes of War. Kit Wright. PeLV

Fortunes of War, I Tell You Plain, The. *Unknown.* InPK-6

Fortune's Treachery. Judah Halevi, *Hebrew.* TrJP, *tr. by* Solomon Solis-Cohen

Forty. Hoàng Trinh, *Vietnamese.* AVP, *tr. by* Huỳnh Sanh Thông

Forty Days. John Wheelwright.
   Second Ascension of Christ, The. NOCV

48 Words for a Woman's Dance Song. Jerome Rothenberg. PoM

Forty-five Years Since the Fall of the Ch'ing Dynasty. Philip Whalen. *See* 10:X:57, 45 Years Since the Fall of the Ch'ing Dynasty.

Forty *li* through Chü-yang Pass. Yang Shih-ch'i. CoBLCP, *tr. by* Jonathan Chaves *Fr.* Ten Miscellaneous Poems Written as a Member of the Imperial Retinue on an Inspection Tour of the Frontier—We Reached Hsüan-fu and Then Returned.

40— Love. Roger McGough. OBCoV; Poetr

'49 dawn set me high on a roaring yellow tractor, The. In Kansas. Carter Revard. HATNAP

49 Stomp, The. Lew Blockcolski. VoR

Forty—that's not so old! Written for the Pavilion of the Drunken Old Man at Ch'u-chou. Ou-yang Hsiu, *Chinese.* CoBCP, *tr. by* Burton Watson

43. Jimmy Santiago Baca. PuP-14

Forty-two years ago (to me if to no one else). Star-Gazer. Louis MacNeice. NAEL-2; NoP-4

Forty years back, when much had place. George Meredith (1828-1909). Thomas Hardy. EPCY

Forward abrupt. Night and a Distant Church. Russell Atkins. PoBA

Forward exults on the run, The. Soccer. Nikolai Alekseievich Zabolotsky, *Russian.* TCRP, *tr. by* Daniel Weissbort

Forward or Back. Aaron Shurin. FTOS

Forward rush by the lamp in the gloom, A. The Contretemps. Thomas Hardy. CMoP; LiTM

Forward, sons of the tribe! Tambourine song for Soldiers Going into Battle. Hind bint Utba, *Arabic*. WPOW, *tr. by* Bridget Connelly *and* Deirdre Lashgari

Forward violet thus did I chide, The. Sonnet 99. Shakespeare. OxAEP-1 *Fr.* Sonnets.

Forward Youth that would appear, The. An Horatian Ode upon Cromwell's Return from Ireland. Andrew Marvell. CABP; EBEV; ESCV; FMP; FSCP; GTBS-P; GeHe; HAP; IIP; InPS-3; NOBE; NOSC; NoP-4; OAEL-1; OBEV; OBWP; OxAEP-1; PBRV; PoEL-2; PoPoPo; SCGP; SeCP; TFi

Fossil. E. D. Blodgett. NOBC

Fossil, A. May Kendall. VWP

Fossil, The. Boynton Merrill Jr. CRP

Fossil, 1975. Janet Lewis. CRP

Fossil Raindrops, The. Harriet Prescott Spofford. OBCA

Fossils, The. Galway Kinnell. NYBP

Foster-Mother's. I never saw the man whom you describe. Foster-Mother's Tale. William Wordsworth. Ro

Foul canker of fair virtuous action. To Detraction I Present My Poesie. John Marston. NoSic *Fr.* The Scourge of Villainy [*or* Villanie].

Foul fa' the breast first treason bred in. Hobie [*or* Hobbie] Noble. *Unknown.* ESPB; IBB; OxBB

Foul hyena's prey, The. (LL) The African Chief. William Cullen Bryant. BLPA; ColAP

Foul Line—1987. Colleen J. McElroy. LTA; NMM-2

Foul sod covers a bad one here. Crinagoras, *Greek*. GrAn, *tr. by* Alistair Elliot

Foules Rondel. Chaucer. *See* Roundel: "Now welcom[e], Somer [*or* Summer] with thy sunne soft."

Found. Goethe, *German*. STV, *tr. by* John Frederick Nims

Found. Carol Muske. AmPA

Found a family, build a state. Fragments of a Lost Gnostic Poem of the Twelfth [*or* 12th] Century. Herman Melville. APN-2; NOBA; NoP-4; OxBSP; PAR; PoEL-5; PoPoPo

Found a hole with a light in it, and saying. The Little Random Creatures. *Unknown, Fox Indian.* STP, *tr. by* Armand Schwerner

Found and Lost. Robert Long. NAmP90

Found dead a rat—no case could sure be harder. *Unknown.* FaBoEE

Found dead he had worsted God! (LL) Little East of Jordan, A. Emily Dickinson. ChIV-1; NoP-4

Found him with crabs upon his face. (LL) The Newcomer's Wife. Thomas Hardy. BoLoP; OxBTC

Found in the garden—dead in his beauty. The Burial of the Linnet. Juliana Horatia Ewing. OxBChV

Found in the Woods. Irene F. Pawsey. BoTP

Found Parable. J. D. McClatchy. BAP-94

Found—Who Lost? Mary E. Tucker. CBWP-1

Foundations, The. Jennifer Maiden. BMAP

Foundations. Leopold Staff, *Polish*. BLT, *tr. by* Czeslaw Milosz; PoSu, *tr. by* Adam Czerniawski

Foundations of American Industry, The. Donald Hall. CA

Founder, The. Gerald Stern. NAmP90

Founder thou; these are thy race!, The. (LL) Experience. Ralph Waldo Emerson. APN-1; MeMAP; PoEL-4; TAP

Founding of New Hampshire, The. Carl Rakosi. FTOS

Foundling Hospital for Wit, The. Isaac Hawkins Browne. Fire Side, The; a Pastoral Soliloquy. NOEC

Fount there is, doth overfling, A. At the Fountain. Marcabrun, *French*. AWP, *tr. by* Harriet Waters Preston

Fountain, The. William Cowper. *See* Praise for the Fountain Opened.

Fountain, The. Donald Davie. GTBS-P; NoP-4; OxBTC

Fountain. Elizabeth Jennings. WPE

Fountain, The. Don Allen Johnson, *Arabic*. AWP, *tr. by* Dulcie L. Smith

Fountain, The. Denise Levertov. CrSp

Fountain, The. James Russell Lowell. BoTP; OBCA

Fountain, The. Wordsworth. GTBS-P; OxAEP-2

Fountain, a Bottle, a Donkey's Ears and Some Books, A. Robert Frost. VGW

Fountain, a house of stone, A. Herberto Padilla, *Spanish*. VCWP, *tr. by* Alastair Reid *and* Alexander Coleman

Fountain at the Tomb, The. Nicias, *Greek*. AWP, *tr. by* Charles Merivale

Fountain, coolest fountain. Ballad of the Cool Fountain. *Unknown, Spanish*. BoWoP, *tr. by* Edwin Honig

Fountain from Wilderness Stone, A, *par. by* David Rosenberg. Bible, *O.T. See* Psalm 114.

Fountain of light, Light, Source of light. Prayer at Night. Alcuin, *Latin*. MLL, *tr. by* Helen Waddell

Fountain of living light. A Hymn to Su'rya. Sir William Jones. NOBRP

Fountain of tears, river of grief. Christine de Pisan, *French*. WPOW, *tr. by* Joanna Bankier

Fountain, that springest on this grassy slope. William Cullen Bryant. APN-1

Fountain to which we, The. Bath. John Godfrey. FTOS

Fountains ("Proud fountains, wave your plumes"). Sir Osbert Sitwell. MoBrPo

Fountains ("This night is pure and clear as thrice refinèd silver"). Sacheverell Sitwell. MoBrPo

Fountains are dry and the roses over, The. The Manor Garden. Sylvia Plath. FaBoWP; LCAP-2

Fountains in the Sea. Martin Sorescu, *Romanian*. VCWP, *tr. by* Seamus Heaney *and* Joana Russell-Gebbett

Fountains mingle with the river, The. Love's Philosophy. Shelley. APAD; BLPA; BoLoP; FHYEP; FaBoBe; GLoP; GTBS-P; HoPM; OxAEP-2; PBMP; PoToHe; SCGP

Fountains of the boiling stars, the flowers on the foreland, the ever-returning roses of dawn, The. (LL) Apology for Bad Dreams. Robinson Jeffers. AmPP; MoAmPo; NOBA; OxBA

Fountains that frisk and sprinkle. Ballade Made in the Hot Weather. William Ernest Henley. MoBrPo

Four a.m. At the reactor an alarm begins. Glow-boys. John Tranter. BMAP

Four adobe walls. Bougainvilleas. Stanzas for an Imaginary Garden. Octavio Paz. OBGa

Four Ages of Man, The. Anne Bradstreet. Childhood. KTR

Four Ages of Man, The. W. B. Yeats. TrCP

4 A.M. and still snowing. Elegy for the Other. Cleopatra Mathis. MT

4 a.m. freight comes pounding and shaking through the fall night, The. Don't You Hear that Whistle Blowin'. Denise Levertov. GM

Four and Eight. Ffrida Wolfe. BoTP

Four and More; for Miles Davis. Quincy Troupe. MoNo

4½ Months: Halfway Song. George Barlow. ISC

Four and twenty bonny boys. Sir Hugh; or, The Jew's Daughter. *Unknown.* CH; ESPB; EnSB; OxBB

Four-and-twenty Highland men. Eppie Morrie. *Unknown.* ESPB; OxBB

Four-and-twenty ladies fair. Bonny Baby Livingston. *Unknown.* ESPB

Four and twenty noblemen they rode thro Banchory fair. Glenlogie; or, Jean o Bethelnie. *Unknown.* ESPB

Four and twenty nobles sits in the king's ha. Glenlogie; or, Jean o Bethelnie. *Unknown.* ESPB

Four and twenty tailors / went to kill a snail. The Snail. Mother Goose. LB; OxNR; ReMoGo

Four-and-twenty tailors went to kill a snail. *Unknown.* ACTP

Four arms, two necks, one wreathing. Song. *Unknown.* CBLP

Four be the things I am wiser to know. Inventory. Dorothy Parker. NBLV

Four Best Things, The. Robert Herrick. *See* Four[e] Things Make Us Happy Here.

Four Bird Songs. Simon J. Ortiz. HATNAP

Four blue stones in this thrush's nest. The Nest. Andrew Young. Spl

Four boards of the coffin lid, The. After Death. Swinburne. NOBVV; OxBSn; PeVV

Four by four, in column of route. Marching. Isaac Rosenberg. NSI

Four centuries of sleep they say. African Sleeping Sickness. Wanda Coleman. PmAP

Four Chinatown Figures. Garrett Kaoru Hongo. NAmP90

Four Christmas Carols. *Unknown, Spanish*. "How cold the snow." PChr, *tr. by* Cheli Durán

4 Daughters. Lucille Clifton. IFJA

Four Days: Earthquake. Gary Young. PuP-17

Four days long the guns had thundered. Salonika Campaign. Owen Rutter. NSI *Fr.* The Song of Tiadatha.

Four days with you, my father three months dead. The Stream. Mona Van Duyn. NMM-2; VCAP

Four dazzling points of phosphor gleamed. (LL) Femme et Chatte. Paul Verlaine, *French*. PC, *tr. by* Felicity Bast

Four decades, I've aroused the southeast with flute and sword. To a Friend, Using the Same Rhymes of a Poem He Sent Me. Liu Ya-tzu, *Chinese*. SuSp, *tr. by* Wu-chi Liu

Four Ducks on a Pond. William Allingham. EBEvV; NOBVV; NOIV; OxAEP-2

Four Epigrams on the Naturalization Bill. John Byrom. NOBL "Come all ye foreign strolling gentry." "Now upon sale, a bankrupt island." "This act reminds me, ge'men, under favour."

Four Epitaphs. Countee Cullen. PoBA For a Lady I Know. HeIP-4; InPK-6; NIP-4; OBAL; SSLK; TAP; TRP

(Lady I Know, A.) MoAmPo

For John Keats, Apostle of Beauty.

For My Grandmother. MoAmPo; SSLK; VGW

For Paul Laurence Dunbar. SSLK

Four feet up, under the bruise-blue. Small Woman on Swallow Street. W. S. Merwin. CoAP; MPo

Four-fifty. The palings of Trinity Church. The Mill-Race. Anne Winters. BAP-96

Four fingers o' his right han'. (LL) Brown Adam. *Unknown.* ESPB; OxBB

Four foot box, a foot for every year, A. (LL) Mid-Term Break. Seamus Heaney. InPS-3; PoPoPo

Four-footed, silent, resilient, feathered. Mythological Beast. Howard Nemerov. *Fr.* Epigrams. OBAL

Four for Sir John Davies. Theodore Roethke. MoAmPo; NOBA; NoAM
Dance, The.

Four gents up and swing Sally Goodin. Sally Goodin. *Unknown.* AmFP

Four Glimpses of Night. Frank Marshall Davis. PoBA

Four Glosses. *Unknown.* NOIV

"Bird is calling from the willow, A."

"How lovely it is today!"

"Little bird, The."

"Wall of woodland overlooks me, A."

Four Heads & How to Do Them. John Forbes. CBAP

(Classical Head, The.) BMAP

Four hooves rang out and now are still. Early Waking. Léonie Adams. LiTM

Four Horses, The. James Reeves. TLR

Four III. E. E. Cummings. FaBoMo

Four in the Morning. Wislawa Szymborska, *Polish.* BLT tr. by Magnus J. Krynski *and* Robert A. Maguire

("If we're to go on living.") (LL) PiM

Four Japanese Paintings. Arthur Davison Ficke.

Wave Symphony, The. PoA

Four-Light Window, A. Agnes Nemes Nagy, *Hungarian.* VCWP, tr. by Hugh Maxton

Four Lines of a Black Love Letter Between Teachers. Ed Roberson. NBV

Four little children. The Lost Angel. Philip Levine. NOBA

Four May Poems. *Unknown.* See Lusty May.

Four May Poems. *Unknown.* See Quhen Flora Had O'erfret the Firth.

Four May Poems: "Be glaid, al ye that luvaris bene." *Unknown.* OxBS

Four May Poems, II. *Unknown.* OxBS

Four men stood by the grave of a man. Alexander the Great. *Unknown.* CH

Four[e] Monarchies, The. Anne Bradstreet.

Semiramis. KTR

Four Most Important Words, The. Important Words. F. E. Elwell. CTV

Four Mountain Wolves. Leslie Marmon Silko. VoR

Four Nights' Drunk, The. *Unknown.* See Our Goodman.

Four Notions of Love and Marriage. N. Scott Momaday. HATNAP

Four o'clock. Letters from Chankiri Prison. Nazim Hikmet, *Turkish.* PFTM, tr. by Randy Blasing and Mutlu Konuk

Four o'Clock Flower Blues. *Unknown.* AmFP

Four of July. Robert Newton Peck. CA

Four on a Sidewalk. *Unknown.* CA

4 Or 5 Tadpoles. Kusano Shimpei, *Japanese.* PFTM, tr. by Cid Corman

4 Part Geometry Lesson, A. Robin Blaser. NeAP

Four Paths. Nikolai Ivanovich Glazkov, *Russian.* TCRP, tr. by Daniel Weissbort

Four-Paws. Helen Parry Eden. BoTP

Four pelicans went over the house. Pelicans. Robinson Jeffers. MoAmPo

Four Poems. Velemir Khlebnikov, *Russian.* PFTM, tr. by Paul Schmidt

Four Poems. Vidyakara. SAGP, tr. by Daniel H. H. Ingalls *Fr.* The Eleventh-Century Sanskrit.

Four Poems for Robin. Gary Snyder. MoP; NNaP; NOBA; NoAM

Autumn Morning in Shokoku-ji, An. HAP; VGW; WeW-3

Four Poems for Robin. BB

Spring Night in Shokoku-ji, A. VGW

Four Poems for The St. Louis Sporting News. Jack Spicer. PoM

Four Poems from the Sequence "Singing of the Moon." Yang Shen, *Chinese.* CoBLCP, tr. by Jonathan Chaves

To the Tune "Chieh san ch'eng" ("I love the autumn moon").

To the Tune "Chieh san ch'eng" ("I love the spring moon").

To the Tune "Yu hu-lu" ("I love the summer moon").

To the Tune "Yu hu-lu" ("I love the winter moon").

Four Poems On the Ch'ung-wu Festival. Chang Yü, *Chinese.* CoBLCP, *tr. by* Jonathan Chaves

Artemisia Tiger, The.

Hundred-Fold Cord, The.

Four Poems Regarding the Endurance of Poets. Geoffrey Hill.

Domaine Public. OxBC

Four Poems to the Tune "Ch'ing-chiang yin." Ma Chih-yüan, *Chinese.* CoBLCP, tr. by Jonathan Chaves

Feelings in Nature ("Bamboo fishing coat, purple official gown").

Feelings in Nature ("Forest and brook—who has gone").

Feelings in Nature ("In the western village the day grows long").

Feelings in Nature ("Woodcutter wakes as mountain moon hangs low, The").

Four Portraits. Judita Vaiiunaite, *Lithuanian.*

Nausicaa. CEEP, tr. by Irene Pogoželskyte Suboczewski

Four Preludes on Playthings of the Wind. Carl Sandburg. CMoP; MoAmPo; NOBA

Four Quartets, sels. T. S. Eliot.

Burnt Norton. CMoP; LiTM; MoAmPo; NAAL-2; PoE

Dry Salvages, The. AiP; NoP-4; OxBA

"River is within us, the sea is all about us, The." OxBoS

East Coker. HAP; VGW

Little Gidding. FaBoMo; FaBoPV; FaBoTw; GTBS-P; MoP; NAEL-2; NAWM-2; NOBA; NOBE; NoAM; OAEL-2; OxAEP-2; OxBTC; PeECV; TAP; TFi

"Ash on an old man's sleeve." FaBoTw

Four Quartz Crystal Clocks. Marianne Moore. AmPP; TwCP

Four Quatrains. Jelaluddin Rumi, *Persian.*

"In the shambles of love, they kill only the best." RaBo, tr. by Coleman Barks *and* John Moyne

"Tonight with wine being poured." RaBo, tr. by Coleman Barks *and* John Moyne

"Two strong impulses: One." RaBo, tr. by Coleman Barks *and* John Moyne

"Where is a foot worthy to walk a garden." RaBo, tr. by Coleman Barks *and* John Moyne

Four Recollections. Shen Yüeh, *Chinese.* SuSp, tr. by Richard B. Mather

Four Resurrections in the Valley of the Ghosts. Yehuda Amichai, *Hebrew.* VCWP, tr. by Benjamin Harshav *and* Barbara Harshav

Four roads lead out of the town. Alice Greene. PeSAV

Four sails of the mill, The. Lubber Breeze. Thomas Sturge Moore. CH

Four Saints in Three Acts. Gertrude Stein.

"Pigeons on the grass alas." TAP

Four Scarlet Berries. Mary Vivian. BoTP

Four-score and seven, so the papers say. The Old Boatman of Death's River. R. Williams Parry, *Welsh.* OBWVE, tr. by Joseph P. Clancy

Four seas, five continents—the world's astir. The Ship An-Nam. Tản Đà, *Vietnamese.* AVP, tr. by Huỳnh Sanh Thông

Four seasons fill the measure of the year. The Human Seasons. Keats. GTBS-P; LaPo; PoPoPo

Four Seasons in the Mountains, The. Chang Yü, *Chinese.* CoBLCP, tr. by Jonathan Chaves

Four Seasons of His Discontent. Roger Weingarten. NAmP90

Four Seasons of the Year, The. Anne Bradstreet. SCAP

Four Sheets to the Wind and a One-Way Ticket to France. Conrad Kent Rivers. BPo; PoBA

Four Songs from the Book of Samuel. Eli W. Mandel. MoCV

Four Songs in Imitation of Wang Chien. Fan Ch'eng-ta, *Chinese.*

Farming Family Invites the Guest to Stay Overnight, A. SuSp, tr. by Wu-chi Liu

Pressing for Tax Payment. SuSp, tr. by Wu-chi Liu

Reeling Silk. SuSp, tr. by Wu-chi Liu

Rejoicing the Spirits. SuSp, tr. by Wu-chi Liu

4 squirrels / are as busy as monks. Maine Vastly Covered with Much Snow. John Tagliabue. InPK-6

Four Stanzas Written in Anxiety. George Jonas. MoCV

Four stiff-standers. *Unknown.* LB; OxNR

Four sweaters are woven upon me. Springer Mountain. James Dickey. CAPP-1

Four Sweet Months, The. Robert Herrick. AYFP; BoTP

Four talked about the pine tree. One defined it by genus, species, and. Conversation. Dan Pagis, *Hebrew.* VCWP, tr. by Stephen Mitchell

Four Tao philosophers as cedar waxwings. Waxwings. Robert Francis. BLT; LCAP-2; RaBo

Four Things [a man must learn to do]. Henry Van Dyke. CTV; PoLF; PoToHe

Four things are white, the fifth exceeds the rest. Five Things White. Edward May. FaBoEE

Four Things Choctaw. Jim Barnes. HATNAP

    Abukbo.

    Baii.

    Isuba.

    Nashoba.

Four things in any land must dwell. Hilaire Belloc. CTV

Four[e] Things Make Us Happy Here. Robert Herrick. CaPo

    (Four Best Things, The.) Spl

Four times the sun had risen and set; and now on the fifth day. The Embarkation. Henry Wadsworth Longfellow. *Fr.* Part the First. *Fr.* Evangeline, a Tale of Acadie.

Four Trees—upon a solitary Acre. Emily Dickinson. APN-2; PoEL-5

Four *Tz'u* from Tun-huang. *Unknown, Chinese.* CoBCP, *tr. by* Burton Watson

    Tune: Eternal Longing.

    Tune: Magpie on the Branch.

4-Way Stop. Myra Cohn Livingston. KaS

Four Ways of Dying. Steve Chimombo. HBAPE

Four wet winters and now the dry. Runoff. William Everson. NoAM

Four white heifers with sprawling hooves. The Orotava Road. Basil Bunting. NoAM

Four Winds. Hal Porter. NOBAu

Four winds and seven seas have called me friend. From Life to Love. Countee Cullen. ChIV-1; KSG

Four winds contend on the sea's face. A Vision of Beasts. John Heath-Stubbs. ChIV-1

Four Winds dry their wooden shoes, The. (LL) Fishing Boats in Martigues. Roy Campbell. FaBoEE; OxBSP

Four-Word Lines. May Swenson. GLP; WPE

Four-year-old girl, A. The Coons. James Bertolino. CMAP

Four years ago I met your death here. Letter from Chicago. May Sarton. NALW

Four years ago I started reading Proust. A Bookmark. Thomas M. Disch. RA

Four years ago, / in this knot of a village north of the university. The Madwoman of Papine. Abdur-Rahman Slade Hopkinson. PBCV

Four years!—and didst thou stay above. Geist's Grave. Matthew Arnold. NOBVV

Four years at school left me taller. Size Is Relative. Chuck Martin. IFJA

Fourfooted, tiptoe. Thomas Hardy. *See* The Fallow Deer at the Lonely House.

Fourscore and seven years ago our. The Gettysburg Address. Abraham Lincoln. CTV

Fourteen, a sonneteer thy praises sings. A Sonnet upon Sonnets. Robert Burns. GSo; Son

Fourteen good measur'd verses make a sonnet. (LL) A Sonnet upon Sonnets. Robert Burns. GSo; Son

14 July 1956. Laurence David Lerner. PeSA

Fourteen Men. Mary Gilmore. CBAP

1492. Emma Lazarus. APN-2; PAR; WPE

Fourteen small broidered berries on the hem. What the Sonnet Is. Eugene Lee-Hamilton. GSo; HoPM; Son

(1422 amsterdam avenue). The Old Buildings. Pedro Juan Pietri. UnSA

Fourteen-year-old boy is out rambling alone, A. Backside to the Wind. Paul Durcan. PBCIP

14-Year-Old Convalescent Cat in the Winter, A. Gavin Ewart. OPOU; OxBSP

Fourteen-year-old, why must you giggle and dote. The Conventionalist. Stevie Smith. LiLi

Fourteen years old, learning the alphabet. The Reading Lesson. Richard Murphy. PBCIP

Fourteenth Ode of the Second Book of Horace, The. Horace, *Latin.* OBCVT, *tr. by* John Potenger

Fourteenth of July, The. *Unknown, Vietnamese.* AVP, *tr. by* Huỳnh Sanh Thông

Fourteenth Olympick Ode, The. Pindar, *Greek.* OBCVT, *tr. by* Gilbert West

14th Street was gutted in 1968. Cheryl Clarke. UnSA

Fourth and fifth months are when the tea is best in mountain groves, The. On Hearing that Holders of the *Chin-shih* Degree Are Dealing in Tea. Mei Yao Ch'en, *Chinese.* SuSp, *tr. by* Jonathan Chaves

Fourth Book of Sibylline Oracles, The. "The Jewish Sibyl," *Greek.*

    There Is a City. TrJP, *tr. by* Bohn

Fourth Dance Poem. Gerald William Barrax. PoBA

Fourth Day of the Flood, The. George Keithley. EC3

Fourth month: summer already, The. *Unknown, Chinese.* SuSp, *tr. by* C. H. Wang

Fourth Ode to Persephone. Robert Kelly. *Fr.* The Book of Persephone. PoM

Fourth of July. Rachel Lyman Field. CTV

Fourth of July, The. John Pierpont. CTV

4th of July. William Carlos Williams. PoA

Fourth of July in Maine. Robert Lowell. CAPP-1

Fourth Pearl, The: Temperance. Lady Diana Primrose. KTR; WPE *Fr.* A Chain of Pearl.

    ("Golden Bridle of *Bellerophon*, The.") KTR

Fourth Poem of a Canto of Accusation. Costa Andrade, *Portuguese.* PBMAP

4th Sheppard Speakes This, The. Lady Jane Cavendish. KTR *Fr.* A Pastorall.

Fourth Song, The. Francis Beaumont. NOSC *Fr.* The Masque of the Inner Temple and Gray's Inne.

4th Song. John Berryman. *See* Dream Song 4.

Fourth Song. Sir Philip Sidney. GBL; HAP; NAEL-1; NoP-4; NoSic *Fr.* Astrophil and Stella. AAS; SiPS

Fourth Song the Night Nurse Sang. Robert Duncan. VGW

Fourth watch, the moon sinks, paper window calm. Inscribed on a Painting of Bamboo. T'ang Yin, *Chinese.* CoBLCP, *tr. by* Jonathan Chaves

Fourth Wish. Alberta Turner. LCAP-2

40 Days and 40 Nights. Henri Cole. PoPoPo

Fowl of the air, and the fish of the sea, and whatsoever passeth through the paths of the sea, The, *sel., vv. 3–8.* Bible, *O.T. See* Psalm 8.

Fowler, The. Wilfrid Wilson Gibson. NTP

Fowls [*or* Foweles *or* Fowles] in the frith. *Unknown.* FaBoVe; HAP; MiEL; NAEL-1; OxBSP

    ("For beste of boon and blood.") (LL) GEA; NoP-4

Fowr Epigrams frae Theognis o Megara. Theognis, *Greek.*

    "I've been a gangrel bodie, I've been to Sicilie." OBCVT, *tr. by* Douglas Young

Fowre Hymnes, *sels.* Edmund Spenser.

    Hymne of Heavenly Beautie, An. PeECV

Fowre muckle angels wi their trumpets, stalkin. Judgment Day. Robert Garioch, *after the Italian of* Giuseppe Belli. OBVE

Fox. David Campbell. CBAP

Fox. Clifford Dyment. OxBSP

Fox, The. Philip Levine. SoSe-8

Fox, The. R. Williams Parry, *Welsh.* OBWVE, *tr. by* Gwyn Williams

Fox and crow, their dirty business finished, The. Fabulary Satire IV. Daryl Hine. NOBC

Fox and the Ape Go to Court, The. Edmund Spenser. NoSic *Fr.* Mother Hubbard's Tale.

Fox and the Crow, The. Jean de La Fontaine, *French.* NAWM-2; OBVE, *tr. by* Marianne Moore

Fox and the Grapes, The. Phaedrus, *Latin.* OBCVT, *tr. by* Christopher Smart

Fox at your neck and snakeskin on your feet, A. Leaving Something Behind. David Wagoner. CoAP

Fox came into my garden, A. Charles Causley. OTCP

Fox Dancing. Suzanne Knowles. RB

Fox don't make a fauz pas! A. Polka. John Fuller. PeLV *Fr.* Fox-Trot.

Fox flees the farm in a red rogue dazzle. For Hani, Aged Five, That She Be Better Able to Distinguish a Villain. Gene Baro. NYBP

Fox Glove Song. Christina Beer. PeNZ

Fox he came lolloping, lolloping, The. Hunting Song. Donald Finkel. CoAP; MoBS

Fox is after dinner, too, The. (LL) The Sycophantic Fox and the Gullible Raven. Guy Wetmore Carryl. BLPA; NBLV; OBCA; PBMP

Fox is very clever, The. Kenneth Rexroth. NNaP *Fr.* A Bestiary. OBAL

Fox jumped up one winter's night, A. A Visit from Mr. Fox. *Unknown.* BLPA; OxNR

Fox knew well, that before they tore him, The. John Masefield. OBNV *Fr.* Reynard the Fox.

Fox may steal your hens, sir, A. Air. John Gay. NOEC; NoP-4 *Fr.* The Beggar's Opera. OAEL-1

Fox set out in hungry plight, The. *Unknown. See* A Visit from Mr. Fox.

Fox-Trot. John Fuller.

    Can-Can. PeLV

    Polka. PeLV

Fox Who Watched for the Midnight Sun, The. Norman Dubie. LCAP-2

Fox, with TOOKE to grace his side. Acme and Septimius; or, The Happy Union Celebrated at the Crown and Anchor Tavern. Catullus. OBCVT, *tr. by* George Ellis

Fox woman / dances, string of blue beads. Second Skins—a Peyote Song. Joseph Bruchac. CDW

Foxes, The. Janet Frame. WPE

Foxglove bells, with lolling tongue, The. Foxgloves. Mary Webb. BoTP

Foxglove by the cottage door, The. Four and Eight. Ffrida Wolfe. BoTP

Fox's Counsel, The. Huw Llwyd, *Welsh.* OBWVE, *tr. by* Joseph P. Clancy

Fox's Song. Barbara Angell. ImGa

Fra banc to banc fra wod to wod I rin. Sonet. Mark Alexander Boyd. EBEV; HAP; InPK-6; OBEV; PBRV; Son

Fra Lippo Lippi. Robert Browning. CTC; EBVV; EBVVPR; EnVR; FHYEP; OAEL-2; OxAEP-2

    ("Don't fear me! there's the gray beginning. Zooks!") (LL) NoP-4

Fracture Santa Monica. Gail Mazur. BAP-95

Frae Catullus, VIII. Catullus, *Latin.* OBCVT, *tr. by* Douglas Young

Frae great Apollo, poet say. The Poet's Wish; an Ode. Allan Ramsay, *after* Horace. OBVE

Frae nirly, nippin', Eas'lan' breeze. Ille Terrarum. Robert Louis Stevenson. OxBS

Frae the Aiolic o Psappho. Sappho, *Greek.* OBCVT, *tr. by* Douglas Young

Fragile. U Tam'si Tchicaya, *French.*

    "I am no longer master of my tears." NegPo, *tr. by* Ellen Conroy Kennedy

Fragile blades of grass. The Builder of Continents. "Ping Hsin." *Fr.* The Stars. WPOW, *tr. by* Kai-yu Hsu

Fragile light of my fading eyes, The. Body Rites. Arnold H. Itwaru. HCP

Fragment. Betti Alver, *Estonian.* CEEP, *tr. by* Ivar Ivask

Fragment: "As for him who." William Carlos Williams. Spl

Fragment, A: "Between two sister moorland rills." Wordsworth. NOBRP

Fragment, A. Anne Brontë. VWP

Fragment: "Cold chain of life presseth heavily on me tonight, The." Adah Isaacs Menken. CBWP-1

Fragment. Ray DiPalma. FTOS

Fragment: "He is an inharmonious note." Sir Roger Casement. TIRV

Fragment: "I am as brisk." Keats. CBNP

Fragment: "I cannot find my way to Nazareth." Yvor Winters. OBSV

Fragment: "I saw his round mouth's crimson deepen as it tell." Wilfred Owen. OAEL-2

Fragment, A: "'I saw the Sibly at Cumæ'." D. G. Rossetti. PeVV

Fragment, A: "I walked [*or* walk'd] along a stream for pureness rare." Gervase Markham. CTC

Fragment: "I would to heaven that I were so much clay." Byron. CTC; NAEL-2; NOBL; OAEL-2; OxBSP *Fr.* Don Juan.

Fragment, A: "In Cloe's chamber, she and I." John Bancks. NOEC

Fragment: "Isn't ligature—or is it ligament?—a lovely word?" Rupert Brooke. NSI

Fragment: "Language has not the power to speak what love indites." John Clare. FaBoEE; OAEL-2; OBNC; OxBSP; PoEL-4

Fragment: "My lips (the inconstancy of man!)." Rupert Brooke. NSI

Fragment: "O grant that like to Peter I." Keats. CBNP

Fragment, A: "Our fancies are but joys all unexprest." Henrietta Cordelia Ray. CBWP-3

Fragment, A: "Thou strainest through the mountain fern." Robert Louis Stevenson. NOBVV

Fragment: "Wake the serpent not—lest he." Shelley. SCGP

Fragment 113: "Not honey, / not the plunder of the bee." Hilda Doolittle. NAAL-2

Fragment 36: "I know not what to do." Hilda Doolittle. CMoP; NALW; OxBA; VGW

    (Fragment Thirty-Six.) CPO

Fragment A. Christopher Smart. *Fr.* Jubilate Agno.

    "Let Anaiah bless with the Dragon-fly, who sails over the pond by the wood-side and feedeth on the cresses." FaBoVe, *ll.* 100–113

    "Rejoice in God, O ye Tongues; give the glory to the Lord, and the Lamb." FaBoVe, *ll.* 1–22

Fragment B. Christopher Smart. *Fr.* Jubilate Agno.

    "For I bless the PRINCE of PEACE and pray that all the guns may be nail'd up, save such as are for the rejoicing days." InPS-3

    "For man is between the pinchers while his soul is shaping and purifying." ChIV-1

    "For the doubling of flowers is the improvement of the gard'ner's talent." ChIV-2; NOEC

    "For the spiritual musick is as follows." NOEC

    "Let Elizur[e] rejoice with the Partridge, who is a prisoner of state and is proud of his keepers." PoEL-3

    "Let Ephah bless with Buprestis, the Lord endue us with temperance and humanity, till every cow have her mate!" NOEC

    "Let Peter rejoice with the Moon Fish who keeps up the life in the waters by night." ChIV-2

    "Let Shobi rejoice with the Kastrel—blessed be the name JESUS in falconry and in the MALL." NOEC

    My Cat Jeoffry. APo; CABP; FaBoCh; PeP; PoE; RB

    ("For he purrs in thankfulness, when God tells him he's / a good Cat.") (LL) PeP

(From Jubilate Agno.) NoP-4; PoPoPo

Fragment: December 18, 1847. Henry Wadsworth Longfellow. APN-1

Fragment Descriptive of the Miseries of War. Charlotte Smith. ECWP

Fragment for the Dark. Elizabeth Jennings. FaBoWP

Fragment from the Golden Age. János Pilinszky, *Hungarian.* CEEP, *tr. by* Emery E. George

Fragment from "The Maladjusted: A Tragedy." Morris Gilbert Bishop. NBLV

Fragment: "Mountain summits sleep, glens, cliffs, and caves, The." Alcman, *Greek.* AWP

Fragment of a Greek Tragedy. A. E. Housman. NOBL; PeLV

Fragment of a Poem on Hunting, A. Thomas Tickell.

    "Such be the dog, I charge, thou mean'st to train." ECEV

Fragment of a Song on the Beautiful Wife of Dr. John Overall. *Unknown.* BoLoP

Fragment of a Sonnet. Pierre de Ronsard, *French.* AWP; OBVE, *tr. by* Keats

Fragment of an English Opera. A. E. Housman. OBCoV

Fragment of an Ode to Maia Written on May Day, 1818. Keats. OAEL-2; OBEV; PoEL-4

Fragment of Death. François Villon. *See* A Fragment on Death.

Fragment of Petronius, A. Petronius Arbiter, *Latin.* BoLoP; OBVE; OxBSP

    (Fragment of Petronius Arbiter, A.) OBCVT, *tr. by* Ben Jonson

Fragment of Petronius, Paraphras'd, A. Petronius Arbiter, *Latin.* OBCVT, *tr. by* John Oldham

Fragment on Death, A. François Villon, *French.* CTC; PeVV, *tr. by* Swinburne

    (Fragment of Death.) AWP

Fragment Thirty-Six. Hilda Doolittle. *See* Fragment 36: "I know not what to do."

Fragmented Address to the FBI. Diane Di Prima. BB

Fragmenti. Ezra Pound. PoA

Fragments, The. Peter Dale.

    "Few ever came to help you speak or sell." NOCV

Fragments. Catherine Maria Fanshawe. BXAP

Fragments. Gerard Manley Hopkins.

    "How looks the night? There does not miss a star." OxBSP

Fragments. Letitia Elizabeth Landon.

    Secrets. VWP

Fragments: "Locke sank into a swoon." W. B. Yeats. NoAM

Fragments join in me with their own music, The. (LL) The Poem as Mask. Muriel Rukeyser. CrSp; NALW; NMM-2; OxWW

Fragments of a Lost Gnostic Poem of the Twelfth [*or* 12th] Century. Herman Melville. APN-2; NOBA; OxBSP; NoP-4; PoEL-5; PoPoPo

Fragments of Ancient Poetry, Collected in the Highlands of Scotland. James Macpherson.

    "I sit by the mossy fountain; on the top of the hill of winds." NOEC

Fragments of Ten Poems. Gábor Görgey, *Hungarian.* CEEP, *tr. by* Jascha Kessler

Fragments of the Green Island. Errol Francis.

    "If only / Under the canopy of stars." NBrP

Fragments, / Refuse of the soul. Gottfried Benn, *German.* AF, *tr. by* Vernon Watkins

Fragrance comes from the scent I wear, The. *Unknown.* CoBCP, *tr. by* Burton Watson *Fr.* Tzu Yeh Songs.

Fragrance of her life, The. (LL) My Mother's Garden. Alice E. Allen. BLPA; FaBoBe

Fragrance of Life, Odor of Death. Denise Levertov. AF

Fragrance of the red lotus fades, The. Poem to the Tune of "Yi chian mei." Li Ch'ing-chao, *Chinese.* WPOW, *tr. by* Marsha Wagner

Fragrance would call me out of the house, A. Catching Webs. Judith Beveridge. NOBAu

Fragrances that like a wind disturb. The Islands Where I Was Born. Gloria Rawlinson. PeNZ

Fragrant grass in front of the courtyard. Spoken to Pines and Bamboos. Wei Chuang, *Chinese.* SuSp, *tr. by* Robin D. S. Yates

Fragrant Hands. Faiz Ahmad Faiz, *Urdu.* VCWP, *tr. by* Agha Shahid Ali

Fragrant perfume that even now fills the road! (LL) Out the southern gate at sundown. *Unknown.* CoBCP, *tr. by* Burton Watson (b. 1925)

Fragrant prayer upon the air, A. A Poem to Be Said on Hearing the Birds Sing. Biddy Crummy, *Irish.* AWP, *tr. by* Douglas Hyde

Fragrant the Prayer. *Unknown, Irish.* TIRV, *tr. by* Alice Furlong

Fragrant Thy Memories. "Judah," *Hebrew.* TrJP, *tr. by* Herbert Loewe

Fragrant Tree, The. Shen Yüeh, *Chinese.* SuSp, *tr. by* Richard B. Mather

Frail and tenuous mist lingers on baffled and intricate branches, A. Leaves. Frederic Manning. NOBAu

Frail[e] as our flesh, crumble to dust. (LL) Maria Wentworth. Thomas Carew. BeJo; CaPo; MeLP; PeECV; SCGP

Frail as the Cord, and brittle as the Urn. (LL) Pass we the ills, which each man feels or dreads. Matthew Prior. NOEC; PoEL-3

Frail as the leaves that quiver on the sprays. Homer. OBVE, *tr. by* Samuel Johnson *Fr.* The Iliad.

Frail branches of the arbor, The. When the Moon is in the River of Heaven. Ou-yang Hsiu, *Chinese.* OHPC, *tr. by* Kenneth Rexroth

Frail duration of a flower, The. (LL) The Wild Honey Suckle. Philip Freneau. AmPP; ColAP; NAAL-1; NAAL-3; NOBA; OxBA; PoEL-4; PoLF; TAP

Frail frail, lone-growing bamboo. Mei Sheng *and* Fu I. *Fr.* Nineteen Old Poems of the Han. CoBCP, *tr. by* Burton Watson

Frail frail, lone-growing bamboo. *Unknown, Chinese.* CoBCP, *tr. by* Burton Watson

Frail golden flowers that perish at a breath. Candle-Light. Olive Custance. ADE

Frail in the blades. For the Poor. Hyongman Ho, *Korean.* CKP, *tr. by* Jaihiun Kim

Frail Life! in which, through mists of human breath. Life and Death. Sir William Davenant. *Fr.* The Christian's Reply to the Philosopher. MeLP

Frail scorched grasses are ripped now, The. Drought. Oumar Ba, *French.* PBWP, *tr. by* Kathleen Weaver

Frail sound of a tunic trailing, A. Poem. Antonio Machado Ruiz, *Spanish.* AWP, *tr. by* John Dos Passos

Frail the white rose and frail are. A Flower Given to My Daughter. James Joyce. OBMV; RB; RaBo

Frailty. George Herbert. NOCV

Frailty and Hurtfulness of Beauty, The. Henry Howard, Earl of Surrey. HoPM

Frailty, Thy Name is Woman. Shakespeare. *Fr.* Hamlet. NAWM-1 ("O, that this too too sullied flesh would melt.") IMW

Frame. Adrienne Rich. NMM-2

Frame for the Angels, A. Paul Smyth. "Spring that I was six I found in the woods, The." CRP

Frame within frame, the evolving conversation. Dancers Exercising. Amy Clampitt. NoAM

Framed. Claire Harris. PBCV

Framed in her phoenix fire-screen, Edna Ward. Cottage Street, 1953. Richard Wilbur. FaBoMo; HCAP; PoPoPo

Framer of the earth and sky. Hymn. Saint Ambrose, *Latin.* TrCP

Framing. Michael Davidson. FTOS

Frammenti Romani. Kathleen Fraser. PT

France. Coleridge. (France: An Ode.) Ro ("Ye clouds, that far above me float and pause.") Ro

France. Douglas Dunn. OxBM (Summer.) LBC

France: An Ode. Coleridge. *See* France.

Francesca of Rimini. Dante. *Fr.* Inferno. NAWM-1, *tr. by* John Ciardi *Fr.* Divina Commedia.

Francie-the-Possessed. Oswald Durand, *French.* NegPo, *tr. by* Ellen Conroy Kennedy

Francine's Room. Louise Erdrich. NoAM

Francis Beaumont's Letter from the Country to Jonson. Francis Beaumont. SeCP

François Villon. Bulat Shalvovich Okudzhava, *Russian.* TCRP, *tr. by* Deming Brown

Francus. Sir John Davies. *See* In Francum.

Frangipani. Theodore Wratislaw. ADE

Frank Albert and Viola Benzena Owens. Ntozake Shange. BlSi

Frank Baker's my name, and a bachelor I am. *Unknown.* *See* Starving to Death on a Government Claim.

Frank Costello eating spaghetti in a cell at San Quentin. Mafioso. Sandra M. Gilbert. UnSA

Frank James, the Roving Gambler. *Unknown.* AmFP

Frank O'Hara. Bruce Beaver. BMAP *Fr.* Letters to Live Poets. CBAP

Frank Plume, a spark about the town. The Inquisitive Bridegroom. William Somervile. ECEV

Frank, will['lt live handsomely? Trust not too far. Advice to My Best Brother, Colonel Francis Lovelace. Richard Lovelace. BeJo

Frankfurt. János Pilinszky, *Hungarian.* PoSu, *tr. by* Janos Csokits *and* Ted Hughes (Frankfurt 1945.) AF, *tr. by* Ted Hughes *and* Janos Csokits ("Then their hearts tasted the full sadness.") (LL) AF, *tr. by* Ted Hughes *and* Janos Csokits

Frankfurt 1945. János Pilinszky. *See* Frankfurt.

Frankie and Albert were sweethearts, ev'ryboy knows. *Unknown.* *See* Frankie was a good woman.

Frankie and Johnny. Josie. *Unknown.* AS; AmFP; EBEvV; EBNV; NIP-4; NOBA; NTP; OxBoLi; RB; UnPo

Frankie and Johnny were lovers. *Unknown.* *See* Josie.

Frankie Blues. *Unknown.* AS

Frankie Silvers. Frances Silvers. AmFP

Frankie was a good woman. *Unknown, sometimes att. to* Hughie Cannon. APN-2 ("Frankie and Albert were sweethearts, ev'ryboy knows.") AS ("He was yo' man, now he's dead an' gone.") (LL) AS

Frankie was a good woman. Frankie Blues. *Unknown.* AS

Franklin Bridge in Philadelphia, The. Miroslav Holub, *German.* CEEP, *tr. by* Daniel Simko

Franklin Hyde. Hilaire Belloc. NBLV

Franklin sailed a key-hung kite. Fable. James Facos. NBLV

Franklin's Prologue, The. Chaucer. NAEL-1; OAEL-1 *Fr.* The Canterbury Tales.

Franklin's Tale, The. Chaucer. NAEL-1; OAEL-1 *Fr.* The Canterbury Tales.

Frantic as a prentice poet. Niyi Osundare. HBAPE, *sect.* V *Fr.* Moonsongs.

Frantic throes of Saul, The. Christopher Smart. *See* O thou, that sit'st upon a throne.

Franz Kafka always wished. Franz Kafka (II). Wiktor Woroszylski, *Polish.* CEEP, *tr. by* Magnus J. Krynski *and* Robert A. Maguire

Franz Kafka (I). Wiktor Woroszylski, *Polish.* CEEP, *tr. by* Magnus J. Krynski *and* Robert A. Maguire

Franz Kafka (II). Wiktor Woroszylski, *Polish.* CEEP, *tr. by* Magnus J. Krynski *and* Robert A. Maguire

Frater Ave Atque Vale. Tennyson. EBVV; GTBS-P; HAP; InPS-3; NAEL-2; NoP-4; OxBSP

Fraternitas. Confucius. CTC: OBVE *Fr.* Deer Sing.

Frau Bauman, Frau Schmidt, and Frau Schwartze. Theodore Roethke. CoAP; MoP; NAAL-2; NOBA; NYBP; NoAM; TAP

Fraudulent Days. Michael Benedikt. PoA

Fraudulent perhaps in that they gave. Swans. Lawrence Durrell. MoBrPo

Fräulein Reads Instructive Rhymes. Maxine W. Kumin. NYBP; Poetsp

Fray of Suport, The. *Unknown.* IBB

Frayed cables bear perilously the antiquated lift. Hospice. Lynda Hull. PuP-15

Freak. Chandrashekhar Patil, *Kannada.* OMIP, *tr. by* A. K. Ramanujan

Freak is the other, The. Celebrating the Freak. Cynthia MacDonald. Poetsp

Freaks at Spurgin Road Field, The. Richard Hugo. LCAP-2; NoAM; SoSe-8

Freckled and frivolous cake there was, A. The Frivolous Cake. Mervyn Laurence Peake. CBNP; PeLV

Freckles numberless as stars on my forehead. My Portrait. Moyshe-Leyb Halpern, *Yiddish.* TrJP, *tr. by* Joseph Leftwich

Fred Pickering never asked why. The Playground. Gregory Harrison. NOxBChV

"Fred, where is north?" West-Running Brook. Robert Frost. MoAmPo; NOBA; NoP-4

Freddie Hubbard's music / is an hour late. The Left Bank Jazz Society. Michael S. Weaver. UnSA

Freddy. Stevie Smith. LW

Fredensborg. Friedrich Gottlieb Klopstock, *German.* GePo, *tr. by* George C. Schoolfield

Frederick Douglass. Sam Cornish. PoBA

Frederick Douglass. Joseph Cotter, Sr.. AAP

Frederick Douglass. Paul Laurence Dunbar. CBCWP; PoBA

Frederick Douglass. Robert Earl Hayden. CBCWP; HCAP; ISC; NAAAL; NIP-4; PBMP; PFE; PoBA; PoPoPo; Son; TTY; VCAP

Frederick Douglass: 1817-1895. Langston Hughes. BPo; CBCWP

Frederick Kuh, Manx Cat. Robert Lowell. FP

Frederiksted, Dusk. Derek Walcott. NoAM

Free at last [*or* las'], at last [*or* las']. I Thank God I'm Free at Las'. *Unknown.* APN-2; BPo; CrDW; PBMP; TAP

Free Beseiged, The. Dionysios Solomos, *Greek.* Temptation. GrIP, *tr. by* Rae Dalvin

Free bird leaps / on the back of the wind, A. Caged Bird. Maya Angelou. WeW-3

Free evening fades, outside the windows fastened with decorative iron grilles, The. Evening in the Sanitarium. Louise Bogan. FYAP; FaBoWP; NALW; TwCP

Free Fantasia on Japanese Themes. Amy Lowell. MoAmPo

Free Fire Zone. Igor Bobrowsky. CDa

Free Grace. Charles Wesley. NOCV

Free hands. Hands. Bernard Dadié, *French.* NegPo, *tr. by* Ellen Conroy Kennedy

Free I have my own self-reliance. I Drift in the Wind. Ingrid Jonker, *Afrikaans.* PeSA; WPOW, *tr. by* Jack Cope

Free Labor. Frances Ellen Watkins Harper. PAR

Free Little Bird. *Unknown.* AmFP

Free One, A. W. H. Auden. CMoP; OxAEP-2

Free Parliament Litany, A. *Unknown.* OxBoLi

Free Puerto Rico. Puerta Rica. Victor Hernandez Cruz. LoL

Free Radicals. James Sherry. FTOS

Free Silver. *Unknown.* AmFP

Free Thoughts on Several Eminent Composers. Charles Lamb. OxBoLi; PeLV

Free till eventide. Piraeus. Haim Guri, *Hebrew.* IP, *tr. by* Warren Bargad *and* Stanley F. Chyet

Free to travel, he still couldn't be shown how lucky. David Walker (1785–1830). Rita Dove. NAAAL

Free Union. André Breton, *French.* PFTM; TTTS, *tr. by* David Antin

(Freedom of Love.) NNPT; SPE, *tr. by* Edouard Roditi

("My wife with eyes of water-level of air earth and fire.") (LL) NNPT; SPE, *tr. by* Edouard Roditi

("My wife with the hair of a wood fire.") NNPT; SPE, *tr. by* Edouard Roditi

Free Up de Lan, White Man. Mutabaruka. PBCV

Free woman, A. At last free! The mother of Sumangala, *Pali.* BoWoP, *tr. by* Willis Barnstone

Freeborn Pindaric never does refuse. A Pindaric on the Grunting of a Hog. Samuel Wesley. NOBL

Freedom. Joan Agnew. BoTP

Freedom [*or* Fredome]. John Barbour. FaBoCh; OBEV; OxBS *Fr.* The Bruce.

Freedom. Wimal Dissanayake. ChAP

Freedom. Ralph Waldo Emerson. APN-1

Freedom. Carolina Hospital. LoHo

Freedom. Abraham ibn Ezra, *Hebrew.* TrJP, *tr. by* Solomon Solis-Cohen

Freedom, *epigram.* Friedrich von Logau, *German.* GePo, *tr. by* George C. Schoolfield

Freedom. Sean O Riordain, *Irish.* TIRV, *tr. by* Coslett Quin

Freedom. Charles Lewis Reason.

"O Freedom! Freedom! O! how oft." AAP

Freedom. "Jan Struther." LW

Freedom a Come Oh! *Unknown.* FaBoVe; PBCV

Freedom; a Poem, Written in Time of Recess from the Rapacious Claws of Bailiffs. Andrew Brice.

Poet's Terror at the Bailiffs of Exeter, The. NOEC

Freedom and Discipline. Hayden Carruth. MoNo

Freedom and Love. Thomas Campbell. GLoP; GTBS-P

Freedom and Truth. Margaret Fuller. PAR

Freedom, as every schoolboy knows. Ambrose Bierce. APN-2 *Fr.* The Devil's Dictionary.

Freedom at last. Cincinnati. Mitsuye Yamada. UnSA

Freedom at McNealy's. Priscilla Jane Thompson. CBWP-2

Freedom fighter, she said, A. Antigone Kefala. BMAP

Freedom for the Mind. William Lloyd Garrison. FaBoBe

Freedom Hair. Raymond Washington. NBV

Freedom in Peril. "Sagittarius." UV

Freedom in the Air. *Unknown.* NAAAL

Freedom is a dream. Dark Testament. Pauli Murray. BlSi

Freedom is more than a word, more than the base coinage. The *Nabara.* C. Day Lewis. EBNV; OBNV

Freedom is Walking toward Us. Tien Ch'ien, *Chinese.* ChiPo, *tr. by* Kai-yu Hsu

Freedom, New Hampshire. Galway Kinnell. LCAP-2

Freedom of Love. André Breton. *See* Free Union.

Freedom of the wholly mad, The. The Phenomenology of Anger. Adrienne Rich. PoE

Freedom Song for the Black Woman, A. Carole C. Gregory Clemmons. BlSi

Freedom to worship God. (LL) The Landing of the Pilgrim Fathers [in New England]. Felicia Dorothea Hemans. BLPA; BoTP; FaBoBe; NoP-4; WPE

Freedom Train. Langston Hughes. GM

Freedom will not come. Langston Hughes. PoBA

Freely Espousing. James Schuyler. FTOS; NeAP; NoP-4

Freely floats the boat of cypress wood. The Boat of Cypress Wood. *Unknown, Chinese.* ChiPo, *tr. by* Yang Xianyi, Gladys Yang, *and* Hu Shiguang

Freely the dead bracken breaks to your stride. Argenteuil County. Peter Dale Scott. MoCV

Freeman, I treat tonight, and treat your friends. The Invitation. Leonard Welsted. NOEC

Freend, foe; past, present, future. "Hugh MacDiarmid." OAEL-2 *Fr.* Second Hymn to Lenin.

Freeway 280. Lorna Dee Cervantes. NoAM; PaTW; WeW-3

Freeze-Frame. Alison Fell. FaBoTC; NBrP

("And the cats / wicked on the wall.") (LL) FaBoTC

Freeze, freeze, thou bitter sky. Shakespeare. *Fr.* Song: "Blow, blow, thou winter wind." CTC; EBEvV; OxAEP-1; PoEL-2 *Fr.* As You Like It.

Freeze-up annexes the sea even, The. Michael Longley. CABP

Freezing my smile. Tanka. Tawara Machi, *Japanese.* MJT, *tr. by* Makoto Ueda

Freezing Night. T'ao Hung Ching, *Chinese.* OHMPC, *tr. by* Kenneth Rexroth

Freight. John Frederick Nims. GM

Freight Cars. Stephen Dobyns. GM

Freight Train, Freight Train. Alvin Greenberg. GM

Freight trains are pulling in. Attila József, *Hungarian.* AF, *tr. by* John Batki

Freighter, gay with rust, The. Jews at Haifa. Randall Jarrell. MoAmPo

Freighting from Wilcox to Globe. *Unknown.* AmFP

Freind! for your epitaphs I'm griev'd. Epigram on One Who Made Long Epitaphs. Alexander Pope. FaBoEE

French. Osbert Lancaster. NOBL; PeLV *Fr.* Afternoons with Baedeker.

French, 1870-1871, The. *Unknown.* FaBoEE

French are a race among races, The. Limerick. *Unknown.* PeLi

French clocks struck two-thirty, and above, The. Under the Arc de Triomphe: October 17. Marilyn Hacker. PoA

French Dress, *epigram.* Friedrich von Logau, *German.* GePo, *tr. by* George C. Schoolfield

French Fops. John Gay. ECEV *Fr.* Epistle to the Right Honourable William Pulteney, Esq.

French Garden. Léopold Sédar Senghor, *French.* NegPo, *tr. by* Ellen Conroy Kennedy

French Historie, The. Anne Dowriche.

"So him at first *De Nance* commanded was to kill." PBRV

French Horn. Robin Behn. PUP-18

French Lisette: A Ballad of Maida Vale. William Plomer. OBCoV; OxBoV

French National Holiday, The. Nguyễn Khuyến, *Vietnamese.* AVP, *tr. by* Huỳnh Sanh Thông

French Peasants. Monk Gibbon. TIRV

French poodle espied in the hall, A. Limerick. *Unknown.* PeLi

French Prisoner, The. János Pilinszky, *Hungarian.* PoSu, *tr. by* Janos Csokits *and* Ted Hughes

Frenzied sea is roaring day and night, The. The Sea and the Sands. H. H. T., *Vietnamese.* AVP, *tr. by* Huỳnh Sanh Thông

Frenzy. George Crabbe. NOBE *Fr.* Sir Eustace Grey.

Frenzy softens the air. Radiant Silhouette IV. John Yau. OpBo

Frequent oil your safety-clutch. (LL) Safety-Clutch. Ambrose Bierce. APN-2; OBAL

Fresco. Martin Sorescu, *Romanian.* CEEP, *tr. by* Irina Livezeanu; VCWP, *tr. by* Enright, D. J. and Joana Russell-Gebbett

Fresco Come to Life. Boris Pasternak, *Russian.* AF, *tr. by* Jon Stallworthy *and* Peter France

Fresco: Departure for an Imperialist War. Thomas McGrath. AF

Fresco of Swans and Bears, A. Robert Wallace. CMAP

Fresco-Sonnets to Christian Sethe. Heinrich Heine, *German.* AWP, *tr. by* John Todhunter

Fresh Air. Kenneth Koch. CAPP-1; NNaP; NeAP

"Supposing that one walks out into the air." OBCoV

Fresh Air, The. Harold Monro. CH

Fresh and fair the morn awaketh. Morn. Josephine D. Henderson Heard. CBWP-4

Fresh breezes waft across march orchid fragrance as. Tune: "Moth Fluttering Against Lamp." Kuan Yün-shih. SuSp, *tr. by* Richard John Lynn *Fr.* Medley of Southern and Northern Tunes—Scenic Tour of West Lake.

Fresh, changeful, constant, upward, like thee! (LL) The Fountain. James Russell Lowell. BoTP; OBCA

Fresh Cheese and Cream. Robert Herrick. CBLP

Fresh clad from heaven in robes of white. Verses for an Album. Charles Lamb. NOBRP

Fresh fields and woods! the Earth's fair face. Retirement. Henry Vaughan. ChIV-1

Fresh Flowers. Wang An-shih, *Chinese.* CoBCP, *tr. by* Burton Watson

Fresh from the dewy hill, the merry year. Song. William Blake. PeECV

Fresh from the Void. Masaoka Shiki, *Japanese.* OHMPJ, *tr. by* Kenneth Rexroth

Fresh Green, The. So Chong-Ju, *Korean.* CKP, *tr. by* Jaihiun Kim

Fresh new leaves. During an illness. Masaoka Shiki, *Japanese*. MJT, *tr. by* Ueda, Makoto

Fresh oil pours through your curls. Saul Re-enthroned. Meir Wieseltier, *Hebrew*. IP, *tr. by* Warren Bargad *and* Stanley F. Chyet

Fresh Paint. Boris Pasternak, *Russian*. TrJP, *tr. by* Babette Deutsch

Fresh savannas of the Sangamon, The. The Painted Cup. William Cullen Bryant. APN-1

Fresh Spring the herald of love's mighty king. Sonnet 70. Edmund Spenser. AWP; HAP; InPS-3; NoP-4; OBEV; PBRV; PoE; Son *Fr.* Amoretti. AAS

Fresh strewings [*or* strowings] allow. The Peter-penny. Robert Herrick. CaPo

Fresh were the breathings of the nightborn gale. Wild Nature. Charles Newton. NOEC *Fr.* Stanzas.

Fresh wind strains. Azov's shallow sea. Watermelon. "Eduard Georgievich Bagritzky," *Russian*. TCRP, *tr. by* Vera Dunham

Fresher and fresher comes the air. The blue. John Neal. APN-1 *Fr.* The Battle of Niagara.

Freshly fallen snow. Nick Avis. HA

Freshly lit cigarette in his mouth. Improvisation for Piano. Michael S. Weaver. UnSA

Freshmen. Barry Spacks. NYBP

Fret not thyself because of. Psalm 37: "Fret not thyself because of evildoers." Bible, *O.T.* CTV *Fr.* Psalms.

Freud: Dying London, He Recalls the Smoke of His Cigar Beginning to Sing. James Schevill. TAP

Friar had said his paternosters duly, The. Necrological. John Crowe Ransom. FuPo; MeMAP

Friar in the Well, *vers.* B. *Unknown.* ESPB

Friar in the Well, The, *vers.* A. *Unknown.* ESPB

Friar Lubin. Clément Marot, *French*. AWP, *tr. by* Longfellow

Friar of Orders Gray, The. *Unknown.* NOEC

Friar's Prologue, The. Chaucer. PoE *Fr.* The Canterbury Tales.

Friar's Tale, The. Chaucer. PoE *Fr.* The Canterbury Tales.

Friday. Sir Walter Scott. BoTP

Friday before Labor Day, The. In the Way Back. Debi Kang Dean. UnSA

Friday Evening. Sean Lucy. CIP-2

Friday evening coos up in the attic. Abraham Sutskever. CEEP, *tr. by* Seymour Mayne *Fr.* Mother.

Friday Night. Robert Graves. LoP

Friday Night. Linda Hogan. NMM-2

Friday night's dream, on Saturday told. Dreams. *Unknown.* ReMoGo

Friday the Thirteenth. Allen Ginsberg. NNaP

Friday. Wet Dusk. Christopher Logue. OxBTC

Friday's all-staff meeting dissolves. Indian College Blues. Adrian C. Louis. NAmP90; PaTW

Fridge clicks, hums; light flows across, The. Joseph. Timothy Steele. RA

Friend, A. Santob De Carrion. TrJP *Fr.* Proverbios Morales.

Friend, A. Paul Klee, *German*. PFTM, *tr. by* Anselm Hollo

Friend, The. Marge Piercy. CrSp; NALW; NMM-2; Poetr

Friend, A. Sir Thomas N. Talfourd. PoToHe

Friend. Hone Tuwhare, *Maori*. PeNZ, *tr. by* Kumeroa Ngoingoi Pewhairangi

Friend, A. *Unknown.* PoToHe

Friend Advises Me to Stop Drinking, A. Mei Yao Ch'en, *Chinese*. HoPM; OHPC, *tr. by* Kenneth Rexroth

Friend, Ah You Have Changed! Frank Mkalawile Chipasula. HBAPE

Friend at a cocktail party tells me, A. Talk to Me, Baby. Michael Dennis Browne. CMAP

Friend Cato. Anna Wickham. MoBrPo

Friend Col and I, both full of whim. David Garrick. FaBoEE

Friend Comes to Visit on a Summer Night, A. Mo Shih-lung, *Chinese*. CoBLCP, *tr. by* Jonathan Chaves

Friend, coming in a friendly wise. If Any Be Pleased to Walk into My Poor Garden. Francis Daniel Pastorius. SCAP

Friend dies one night, A. Drugs. Dennis Cooper. PmAP

Friend, don't be angry. Mirabai, *Hindi*. BoWoP, *tr. by* Willis Barnstone *and* Usha Nilsson

Friend, his seas swell and roar. What She Said. Ammuvanar, *Tamil*. PLW, *tr. by* A. K. Ramanujan

Friend, hope for the Guest while you are alive. To Be a Slave of Intensity. Kabir, *Hindi*. APAD; RaBo, *tr. by* Robert Bly

Friend, how can I meet my lord? Mirabai, *Hindi*. BoWoP, *tr. by* Willis Barnstone *and* Usha Nilsson

Friend, if the mute and shrouded dead. Love and Death. Catullus. AWP, *tr. by* H.W. Garrod *Fr.* Carmina.

Friend in a tipi in the, A. Two Fawns That Didn't See the Light This Spring. Gary Snyder. HCAP

Friend in my mountain-side demesne. To A Gardener. Robert Louis Stevenson. OBGa

Friend in Need Will Be Around in Five Minutes, A. Ogden Nash. FP

Friend in the Garden, A. Juliana Horatia Ewing. BoTP; CTAV; OxBChV; PeP

Friend is a person, A. *Unknown.* CTV

Friend is sometimes desert, A. Eugenio de Andrade. VCWP, *tr. by* Alexis Levitin *Fr.* White on White.

"Friend / like someone who gets drunk secretly." What She Said to Her Girl Friend, and What Her Girl Friend Said in Reply. Uruttiran, *Tamil*. PLW, *tr. by* A. K. Ramanujan

Friend, listen. What She Said. Ammuvanar, *Tamil*. PLW, *tr. by* A. K. Ramanujan

Friend of Humanity and the Knife Grinder, The. George Canning *and* John Hookham Frere. BXAP; OBCoV; UV
  (Sapphics.) NOBRP; NOEC

Friend of mine who raised six daughters and, A. Case in Point. June Jordan. NMM-2

Friend of Ronsard, Nashe and Beaumont. On a Birthday. John Millington Synge. GBL; OBMV

Friend of that poor queen, The. (LL) Deirdre. James Stephens. AWP; CMoP; OBMV; PoRA

Friend of the Family, A. Louis Simpson. NNaP

Friend of the Fourth Decade, The. James Merrill. NYBP

Friend of the wise! and teacher of the good! To Wordsworth. Coleridge. EPCY; FHYEP; NAEL-2; OAEL-2

Friend of the wretched! wherefore should the eye. Ode to Death. Charlotte Smith. NoP-4

Friend of Two, A. Wilbur Dick Nesbit. PoLF

Friend, on This Scaffold Thomas More Lies Dead. James Vincent Cunningham. CRP; InPK-6

Friend, Ortho of Syracuse gives thee this charge. Ortho's Epitaph. Theocritus, *Greek*. FaBoEE, *tr. by* Charles Stuart Calverley

Friend! / Poor, foolish blossom! Beauty. Peter Hille, *German*. AWP, *tr. by* Jethro Bithell

Friend remarks to the Prophet, "Why is it," A. Jelaluddin Rumi, *Persian*. LoL, *tr. by* Coleman Barks

Friend sparrow, do not eat, I pray. Basho, *Japanese*. AWP, *tr. by* Curtis Hidden Page

Friend—the face I wallow toward. What I Like. Alice Fulton. WeW-3

Friend, the Old Man that was last year. Than, Mau. John Balaban. CDa

Friend, there be they on whom mishap. Contentment. Charles Stuart Calverley. NOBVV

Friend thinks he knows best, A. The Late Victorian Girl. Bill Manhire. PeNZ

Friend to Birds. Eric Groch, *Czech and Slovak*. CEEP, *tr. by* Eric Groch

Friend told me, A. Alone. Michael S. Harper. ISC

Friend Who Just Stands By, The. Bertye Young Williams. PoLF; PoToHe

Friend, whose unnatural early death. Elegy. David Gascoyne. FaBoTw; TwCP

Friend, with regard to this same hare. To the Rev. Mr. Powell. Christopher Smart. OBWVE

Friend writes, We're not talking about any port, A. Report from Another Country. Charlene Langfur. LoHo

Friend you resemble, A. Song the First. *Unknown. Fr.* Two Cherokee Songs of Friendship. APN-2, *tr. by* Samuel L. Mitchill

Friend, you seem thoughtful. I not wonder much. A Sea Dialogue. Oliver Wendell Holmes. OBAL

Friend: Your Satyrs, let me tell you, are too fierce. Persius. OBCVT, *tr. by* John Dryden *Fr.* The First Satyr of Aulus Persius Flaccus. In Dialogue betwixt the Poet and His Friend, or Monitor.

Friendless and faint, with martyred steps and slow. Calvary. Edwin Arlington Robinson. GI; MoAmPo; Son

Friendly Address, A. Thomas Hood. PoEL-4

Friendly Beasts, The. *Unknown.* PChr

Friendly Cinnamon Bun, The. Russell Hoban. OTCP

Friendly cow all red and white, The. The Cow. Robert Louis Stevenson. CTAV; CTV; FPC; NTCP; OxBChV; PWR; TLR; WHSW

Friendly Game of Football, A. Edward Dyson. CBAP

Friendly Town #1. Safiya Henderson-Holmes. UnSA

Friendly Town #3. Safiya Henderson-Holmes. UnSA

Friends. John Ashbery. LCAP-2

Friends, The. Bertolt Brecht, *German*. PoSu, *tr. by* Michael Hamburger

Friends. Abbie Farwell Brown. CTV

Friends. Thomas Curtis Clark. PoToHe

Friends. Ray Durem. PoBA

Friends. Mikhail Arkadyevich Svetlov, *Russian*. TCRP, *tr. by* Daniel Weissbort

Friends. *Unknown.* CTV

Friends. W. B. Yeats. FP; IIP; MoP; NoAM

Friends are unhappy; their long night. Winter Work. Peter Fallon. CIP-2; PBCIP

Friends Beyond. Thomas Hardy. EBVV; FaBoVe; GTBS-P; NOBVV; OBEV

Friends Departed. Henry Vaughan. OBEV

Friend's Greeting, A. E. A. Guest. BLPA

Friends, I account the fortune of my wife. Euripides. OBCVT, *tr.* by Robert Browning *Fr.* Alcestis.

Friends in Private. Herodas, *Greek.* HePo, *tr.* by Barbara Hughes Fowler

Friends / our dear sister. Goodbye Party for Miss Pushpa T. S. Nissim Ezekiel. OBCoV

Friends, Outside, Night. David Keller. CMAP

Friends repeat: "All means are good." Olga Fiodorovna Berggolts, *Russian.* TCRP, *tr.* by Albert C. Todd

Friends, Romans, countrymen, lend me your ears. Mark Antony Addresses the Mob. Shakespeare. EBEvV; FaPoR; OxAEP-1 *Fr.* Julius Caesar.

Friends who come to see you, The. Sleep. James Schuyler. GLP

Friends—With a Difference. Mary Elizabeth Coleridge. VWP

Friends, / you are lucky you can talk. Vidya, *Sanskrit.* BoWoP, *tr.* by Willis Barnstone

Friendship. William Cowper. FP

Friendship. Dinah Maria Mulock Craik. BLPA; PoToHe

Friendship, The. Toi Derricotte. IFJA; PBCAP

Friendship. Elizabeth Jennings. FP

Friendship. Octavio Paz, *Spanish.* FP, *tr.* by Charles Tomlinson

Friendship. Katherine Philips. FP

Friendship. Cole Porter. FP

Friendship. Sadi. AWP, *tr.* by L. Cranmer-Byng *Fr.* The Gulistan.

Friendship. Shel Silverstein. NTCP

Friendship. Henry David Thoreau. FP

Friendship. *Unknown, Aztec Indian.* FP

Friendship. Ella Wheeler Wilcox. PoToHe

Friendship After Love. Ella Wheeler Wilcox. APAD; APN-2; LW

Friendship, as some sage poet sings. On the Aphorism "L'Amitié est l'Amour sans Ailes." Charlotte Smith. CABP; PEW

Friendship Between Ephelia and Ardelia. Anne Finch, Countess of Winchilsea. BWW; ECWP; NALW; NoP-4

Friendship in Emblem, or the Seal, to my Dearest Lucasia. Katherine Philips. CABP; PBRV

Friendship in Perfection. Andrew Michael Ramsay. NOEC

Friendship is like a garden of. Growing Friendship. *Unknown.* CTV

Friendship needs no studied phrases. *Unknown.* PoToHe

Friendship's Mystery, To My Dearest Lucasia. Katherine Philips. CPO; PBRV; PEW

  (Friendship's Mysterys, to my dearest Lucasia.) KTR

  ("Grows deathless by the sacrifise.") (LL) KTR

Frigate Jones, the Pussyfooter ("Frigate Jones was very slow and fat"). Kenneth Burke. OBAL

Frightened / by the sound of my own voice. Lawrence Ferlinghetti. TAP

Frightened Flier Goes North, The. Judith Kazantzis. BrRo

Frightened Man, The. Louise Bogan. FaBoWP

Frightened Ploughman, The. John Clare. EnVR; PoEL-4

Frigid and sweet Her parting Face. Emily Dickinson. CPO

Frimaire. Amy Lowell. CPO

Frisco-City. Blaise Cendrars, *French.* BLT, *tr.* by Monique Chefdor

Frisky lamb / And a frisky child, A. Christina Rossetti. BoTP; CTAV; FPC; WHSW

Frithiof's Saga. Esaias Tegnér, *Swedish.* AWP, *tr.* by Longfellow

  Frithiof's Farewell. AWP, *tr.* by Longfellow

  Frithiof's Homestead. AWP, *tr.* by Longfellow

Frivolous Cake, The. Mervyn Laurence Peake. CBNP; PeLV

Fro Niz - nil - imbo. (LL) Metamorphosis. Wallace Stevens. InPK-6; VGW

Frog, The. Hilaire Belloc. CTAV; CTV; ChAP; FaBoBe; NOxBChV; NTCP; OxBChV

Frog, The. Rose Fyleman. BoTP

Frog, A, *epigram.* Friedrich von Logau, *German.* GePo, *tr.* by George C. Schoolfield

Frog. Marlene Mountain. HA

Frog, The. Francis Ponge, *French.* BLT, *tr.* by Beth Archer

Frog. Tanka. Saitō Mokichi, *Japanese.* MJT, *tr.* by Ueda, Makoto

Frog, The. *Unknown.* NBLV; NOxBChV; NTCP; RB

Frog and the Bird, The. Vera Hessey. BoTP

Frog Autumn. Sylvia Plath. OxBSP

  ("Our folk thin / Lamentably.") (LL) PFE

Frog, gem-green, A—like the Jamaican wave. Origami. Abdur-Rahman Slade Hopkinson. HCP

Frog He Would A-Wooing Go, A. Mr. Frog Went a-Courting. Mother Goose. AS; AmFP; OxNR

Frog in the Swimming Pool, The. Debora Greger. BAP-94; NoP-4

Frog Prince, The. Robert Pack. Poetr

Frog Prince, The. Stevie Smith. HAP; NTP

Frog under you, A. The Wife. Denise Levertov. EP

Frog Voices. James Bertolino. EC2

Frog went a-courting, away did ride, huh-huh, A. *Unknown.* BLPA

Froggie Went a-Courting. *Unknown.* AmFP

Frogologist, The. Brian Patten. OTCP

Frogs, The. Aristophanes, *Greek.*

  "C'wa nou, what wey suld I chap o this door?" OBCVT, *tr.* by Douglas Young

Frogs. Buddhadeva Bose, *Bengali.* OMIP, *tr.* by Buddhadeva Bose

Frog's Fate, A. Christina Rossetti. NOBVV

Frogs time out of mind, The. Aesop's Fable of the Frogs. Jean de La Fontaine, *French.* OBVE, *tr.* by John Hookham Frere

Frolic. "Æ." BoTP; MoBrPo

Frolic[k], A. Robert Herrick. FaBoEE

Frolic architecture of the snow, The. (LL) The Snow-Storm. Ralph Waldo Emerson. APN-1; AmPP; FaBoBe; MeMAP; NAAL-1; NAAL-3; NCAP; NOBA; NoP-4; OxBA; PAR; PoE; PoEL-4; PoLF; PoPoPo; TAP; TFi; UnPo

Frolic Mariners of Devon, The. William Browne. *Fr.* Britannia's Pastorals.

Frolicking. Tanka. Mori Ōgai, *Japanese.* MJT, *tr.* by Makoto Ueda

From 66 to 70 A.D. Rome and Palestine tore. Wars of Imperialism. John Foulcher. NOBAu

From a branch / The bird called. The Bird. Max Michelson. TrJP

From a Childhood. Rilke, *German.* TrJP, *tr.* by C. F. MacIntyre; RaBo, *tr.* by Robert Bly

  ("Darkening was like riches in the room, The.") TTTS, *tr.* by M D Herter Norton

From a church across the street. Ave Maria. Barbara Ferland. PBCV

From a Correct Address in a Suburb of a Major City. Helen Sorrells. WPE

From a crumpled wartime diary. Aleksandr Trifonovich Tvardovsky, *Russian.* TCRP, *tr.* by Peter Norman

From a distance, I watch. Practical Concerns. William J. Harris. PoBA

From a donkey, excuse me, one lesson is given. Fanny Howe. FTOS

From a fish store window, on their deathbed of ice. The Consequences of Waking. Vickie Karp. WWSi

From a flour mill. Tanka. Tsukamoto Kunio, *Japanese.* MJT, *tr.* by Makoto Ueda

From a Full Heart. A. A. Milne. NSI

From A Funeral Song, Upon the Decease of Annes His Mother. Nicholas Grimald. NoP-4 *Fr.* A Funeral Song, Upon the Decease of Annes His Mother.

From a German War Primer. Bertolt Brecht, *German.* AF, *tr.* by John Willett, Ralph Manheim and Erich Fried

From a high mountain I see how the banks of a river. The Banks of a River. Abraham Sutskever, *Yiddish.* CEEP, *tr.* by Ruth Whitman

From a Lavatory Wall. *Unknown.* FaBoEE

From a little basket on the kitchen shelf I was about to. Concerning a Girl. Tanikawa Shuntaro, *Japanese.* VCWP, *tr.* by Harold Wright

From a little seed. Little Things. Eileen Mathias. BoTP

From a London Bookshop. *Unknown.* NBLV

From a lonesome old house, near Holbeach Wash-way. From the Country, to Mr. Rowe in Town. Susanna Centlivre. ECWP

From a long way, and Pilgrimage for Love. Mary Sidney, Countess of Montgomery Wroth. *Fr.* Urania.

From a Museum Man's Album. John Hewitt. OxBTC

From a new peony. Sonnet for Minimalists. Mona Van Duyn. FFC; WeW-3

From a passing train at twilight. Renewal Notice. Bruce Dawe. BMAP

From a Photograph. George Oppen. FTOS

From a place I came. Kathleen Jessie Raine. OxBTC *Fr.* Two Invocations of Death.

From a precipitous cliff, a withered pine hangs upside down. Tune: "Intoxication in the East Wind" Autumn Scenery. Lu Chih, *Chinese.* SuSp, *tr.* by Sherwin S. S. Fu

From a Railway Carriage. Robert Louis Stevenson. BoTP; OxBChV

From a Republican Grave: Daniel Henry Deniehy, 1828–1865. Philip Mead. NOBAu

From a rived tree, that stands beside the grave. Sonnet. Anna Seward. ECWP

From a ruler that's a curse. Litany. Charles Cotton. OBSV

From a slip of the foot you may soon. Bits of Wisdom. Benjamin Franklin. CTV

From a Spanish Cloister. G. K. Chesterton. UV

From a Survivor. Adrienne Rich. LoL; NALW

From a Talk. Yevgeny Yevtushenko, *Russian.* CLPP, *tr. by* Anselm Hollo

From a thousand Chinese dinners, one cookie. Robert Mezey. RaBo *Fr.* A Thousand Chinese Dinners.

From a thousand hills, bird flights have vanished. River Snow. Liu Tsung-yüan, *Chinese.* CoBCP, *tr. by* Burton Watson

From a thread in space, endless and unbroken. Without unravelling. Jacques Dupin. VCWP, *tr. by* Paul Auster *Fr.* Songs of Rescue.

From a tower the stone sea. Two Cities. Judit Tóth, *Hungarian.* CEEP, *tr. by* Emery E. George

From a Train Window. Edna St. Vincent Millay. GM

From a Venetian Sequence. Adèle Naudé. PeSA

From a Very Little Sphinx. Edna St. Vincent Millay. NOxBChV; OBAL

From a Village. Ana Blandiana, *Romanian.* CEEP, *tr. by* Irina Livezeanu

From a Walking Song. Charles Williams. BoTP

From a Window in Princes Street. William Ernest Henley. EBVV

From a woman, the gods turned me into stone. Niobe. *Unknown, Greek.* GrAn, *tr. by* Peter Jay

From a Woman to a Greedy Lover. Norman Cameron. FaBoEE *Fr.* Three Love Poems. FaBoTw; GTBS-P

From a woman's dream of being. Written in Water. Amy Clampitt. NMM-2

From a world more full of weeping than he can / Understand. (LL) The Stolen Child. W. B. Yeats. CMoP; NAEL-2; NoP-4

From a Young Woman to an Old Officer Who Courted Her. Elizabeth Frances Amherst. ECWP

From across the stream, on the side of the opposite hill. Not Seeing Is Believing. Paul Petrie. TAP

From Age to Age They Gather. Frederick Lucian Hosmer. AH

From Albert to Bapaume. Alec Waugh. NSI

From all my lame defeats and oh! much more. The Apologist's Evening Prayer. C. S. Lewis. TrCP

From All Peoples. Nathan Alterman, *Hebrew.* "When our children cried in the shadow of the gallows." TrJP, *tr. by* Simon Halkin

From All Sides Laughter Shall Strike Them. Amir Gilbo'a, *Hebrew.* MHP, *tr. by* Ruth Finer Mintz

From all the circle of the hills. (LL) Somersby, Lincolnshire; after Leaving the Refectory. Tennyson. EBVV; FHYEP; GTBS-P; GaP; OBNC; PeECV; PoEL-5; SCV

From America. James M. Whitfield. APN-2; BPo

From America comes the little huming-bird. Vermont Apollinaire. William Corbett. PmAP

From among ten thousand trees autumn wind rises. Sent in Lieu of a Letter to Shih-wu, Lan-ku, and Other Friends. Huang Tsun-hsien, *Chinese.* SuSp, *tr. by* An-yan Tang

From among the miserable soldiers. (LL) And Their Winter and Night in Disguise. George Oppen. APSN; NNaP

From Amphitryon. Plautus Titus Maccius. OBCVT, *tr. by* Nicholas Udall *Fr.* A Newe enterlued for chyldren to playe named Jacke Jugeler.

From an Afternoon Caller. Sister Mary Madeleva. CRP

From an airtight office window. Downpour. Daisy Zamora, *Spanish.* CLPP, *tr. by* Barbara Paschke

From an Apocryphal Gospel. Jorge Luis Borges. GI, *tr. by* Norman Thomas Di Giovanni *Fr.* An Apocryphal Gospel.

From an ass to an analyst and back. Joyce Mansour, *French.* MFP, *tr. by* Martin Sorrell

From an Asylum; Kathy Chattle to Her Mother, Ruth Arbeiter. Anne Stevenson. BrRo

From an island teeming with parrots. Epilogue to Robinson Crusoe. Dan Pagis, *Hebrew.* IP, *tr. by* Warren Bargad *and* Stanley F. Chyet

From an Old House in America. Adrienne Rich. NNaP; TRP

From an old house shaded with macrocarpas. James Keir Baxter. PeNZ *Fr.* Pig Island Letters.

From anger into the pit of sleep. Wife to Husband. Fleur Adcock. PeNZ

From Another Room. Gregory Corso. NeAP

From appetite to innocence. (LL) The Garden. Robert Penn Warren. GaP; PoA

From Arena. Dennis Phillips. FTOS *Fr.* Exile.

From Ariadne's Crown. A Shooting Star. Edith Matilda Thomas. ChAP

From Arranmore the weary miles I've come. Mavrone. Arthur Guiterman. BXAP

From art, from nature, from the schools. Tennyson. OAEL-2 *Fr.* In Memoriam A. H. H.

From Battle Clamour. Samuele Romanelli, *Hebrew.* TrJP, *tr. by* Nina Davis Salaman

From Baudelaire. "Michael Field." ADE

From Beachy Head. Charlotte Smith. NoP-4 *Fr.* Beachy Head.

From before the beginning of the universe. (LL) Say Yes Quickly. Jelaluddin Rumi, *Persian.* EnlH, *tr. by* Coleman Barks *and* A. J. Arberry; RaBo, *tr. by* Coleman Barks *and* John Moyne

From behind a crag, as though round a corner. The Eagle. "Aleksandr Iakovlevich Yashin," *Russian.* TCRP, *tr. by* Daniel Weissbort

From behind he looks like a man. China. Dorianne Laux. DeD; LW

From behind me. Cor Van den Heuvel. HA

From behind the Bars. Fadwa Tuqan, *Arabic.* From the Diary of----. WPOW, *tr. by* Hatem Hossaini

From behind the mirror, a row of mirrors. The Woman in the Mirror. Stefan Aug. Doinas, *Romanian.* CEEP, *tr. by* Donald Eulert *and* Stefan Avadanei

From being anxious, or secure. Donne. *Fr.* The Litanie. PoEL-2

From being driven mad by a scold. (LL) Tell Me, Tell Me. Marianne Moore. LiTM; NYBP

From Belfast to Suffolk. William Peskett. PNI

From below, the waist-thick pine. Yggdrasill. Paul Muldoon. PBCIP

From Belsen a crate of gold teeth. Riddle. William Heyen. HP; SoSe-8

From Beowulf. *Unknown.* NoP-4

From between my own teeth I come out smoking. The Hungry Man's Wheel. César Vallejo, *Spanish.* PFTM, *tr. by* Clayton Eshleman *and* Jose Rubia Barcia

From bill to breast a snake. Swan. Edward Lowbury. GTBS-P

From birth he's worn a home-spun cotton shirt. Ode to the Toad. *Unknown, Vietnamese.* AVP, *tr. by* Huỳnh Sanh Thông

From black against the nothing. Phantasmatikon. Stephen Sartarelli. PT

From black branches. (LL) Love Song: "Sweep the house clean." William Carlos Williams. LoP; MoAmPo; SAmP

From Blenheim's clocktower a cheerful bell bangs out. Distilled Water. M. K. Joseph. PeNZ

From blossoms comes. Li-Young Lee. TRP

From Bosch's Hill. Tymoteusz Karpowicz, *Polish.* CEEP, *tr. by* Zak, Ewa

From Boston south he talks of citrus fruit. My Father's Watch. Thomas Rabbitt. CMAP

From boy to man, from man to boy, would chop and change degree. . . . Henry Howard, Earl of Surrey. *See* Laid in my quiet bed, in study as I were.

From branching chandeliers they bell. Yellow Delicious. Samuel Hazo. IFJA

From breakfast on through all the day. The Land of Nod. Robert Louis Stevenson. ACTP; FPC; PWR

From breezeway or through front porch screen. The Sheets. Timothy Steele. DiPo

From Brooklyn, over the Brooklyn Bridge, on this fine morning. Invitation to Miss Marianne Moore. Elizabeth Bishop. NALW

From Bulgaria thick, wild cannon pounding rolls. Picture Postcards. Miklós Radnóti, *Hungarian.* AF, *tr. by* Emery E. George

From Caelica. Greville Fulke. NoP-4 *Fr.* Caelica.

From Calpe's rock, with loss of leg. The Soldier That Has Seen Service. *Unknown.* NOEC

From camp to camp, through the fool womb of time. Shakespeare. *Fr.* Before Agincourt. EBEV *Fr.* King Henry V.

From Canaan Joseph shall return, whose face. Hafiz. TAL, *tr. by* Gertrude Lowthian Bell *Fr.* Odes.

From cavities of bones. From the Cavities of Bones. Patricia Parker. BlSi

From Chekiang I Went to Hsin-an and Climbed Even-with-the-Clouds Mountain. On the Way Back There Were Many Beautiful Sights at the Inns Where I Stayed and Yet I Could Not Write One Word of Poetry. When I Got Back to the Main Road I Wrote These Four Lines to Make Fun of Myself. Hsü Wei, *Chinese.* CoBLCP, *tr. by* Jonathan Chaves

From childhood's hour I have not been. Alone. Edgar Allan Poe. APAD; APN-1; MeMAP; NAAL-1; NAAL-3; NTP; PAR; PoEL-4

From Clee to heaven the beacon burns. 1887. A. E. Housman. FaPoR; NIP-4; NOBVV; SCGP; UnPo

From Colony to Nation. Irving Layton. NOBC

From Countless Hearts. Gail Brook Burket. AH

From Creature to Ghost. Pauline Hanson. TAP

From darkness / I go onto the road / of darkness. Lady Izumi, *Japanese.* BoWoP, *tr. by* Willis Barnstone ("From darkness / Into the path of darkness.") PBWP, *tr. by* Edwin A. Cranston

From darkness where no stars shine. The Observed Observer. Alan Gould. BMAP

From dawn till now that it is growing dusk. Robert Browning. EBVVPR *Fr.* The Ring and the Book.

From dawn to dark, and back from dark to dawn. Hedylos, *Greek.* GrAn, *tr. by* William Moebius

From Death and dark Oblivion, ne'er the same. The Mind of the Frontispiece to a Book. Ben Jonson. GS

From death to life thou mightst him yet recover. (LL) Since There's No Help. Michael Drayton. AAS; AEP; AWP; BoLoP; CABP; ClHu; EnLoPo; GBL; GEA; GLoP; GSo; GTBS-P; HAP; HeIP-4; ImPo; InPS-3; LoP; NAEL-1; NOBE; NOSC; OAEL-1; OBEV; OPOU; PBMP; PFE; PoEL-2; PoPoPo; SAGP; SCGP; SCV; SoSe-8; Son; TFi

From deep sleep. Nightmare. James A. Emanuel. BPo

From deepest need cry out, oh hungered heart! Quirinus Kuhlmann, *German.* GePo, tr. by George C. Schoolfield

From depth of dole wherein my soul doth dwell. George Gascoigne. ChIV-1 *Fr.* De Profundis.

F[f]rom depth of[f] sin[n] and from a deep [*or* diepe] despair [*or* dispaire]. Bible, *O.T. See* Psalm 130.

From depths of woe I cry to you. Martin Luther, *German.* GePo, tr. by F. Samuel Janow

From distant Annam there came a gift. Too Brilliant. Po Chü-i, *Chinese.* ChiPo, tr. by Rewi Alley

From distant grove I hear the occasional knell of a monastery bell. Inscribed on the Painting of "Garden for Retirement": Pavilion of Sincerity, on Rocky Mountain. Chu Yi-tsun, *Chinese.* SuSp, tr. by Chang Yin-nan and Lewis C. Walmsley

From Drogheda all along the coast, the Irish sea. Back to Dublin. Robert Arthur Douglas Ford. MoCV

From dusk to dawn I sit under the canopy of a pine. In the Country. Ssu-k'ung Shu, *Chinese.* SuSp, tr. by Hellmut Wilhelm

From Eastertide to Eastertide. A Ballad of a Nun. John Davidson. MoBrPo; UV

From ech greene tree whereon the rayes of firie *Phebus* glowde. Ovid. *See* The Golden Age.

From every place you cast your wandering eyes. Castle Howard, the Seat of the Rt. Hon. Charles, Earl of Carlisle. Anne, Viscountess Irwin Ingram. OBGa *Fr.* Castle Howard, the Seat of the Rt. Hon. Charles, Earl of Carlisle

From everything a little remained. Residue. Carlos Drummond de Andrade, *Portuguese.* VCWP, tr. by Mark Strand

From Exile. Dafydd Benfras, *Welsh.* OBWVE, tr. by Anthony Conran

From fair Jamaica's fertile plains. Lines. "Ada." BlSi

From fairest creatures we desire increase. Sonnet 1. Shakespeare. CTC; HeIP-4; ImPo; NoP-4 *Fr.* Sonnets.

From Far Away. Delmira Agustini, *Spanish.* PBWP, tr. by D. M. Pettinella

From far, from eve and morning. A. E. Housman. APAD; CMoP; HAP; MoBrPo; NoP-4; PoEL-5

From far she's come, and very old. Age in Youth. Trumbull Stickney. ColAP

From Father to Son. Emyr Humphreys. OBWVE

From fealty to light. (LL) The Enthusiast. Herman Melville. ChIV-1; NAAL-1; NAAL-3

"From fear to fear, successively betrayed." Reflection from Rochester. William Empson. PoA

From Feathers to Iron. C. Day Lewis.
    Now She Is like the White Tree-Rose. CMoP; FaBoTw; MoBrPo

From first light we fear falling. Hotel Fire: New Orleans. Paul Ruffin. InPK-6

From flesh into phantom. Christopher Okigbo. PBMAP *Fr.* Distances (1964).

From flower that captivates me. The Sea of Lemon. Yojong Kim, *Korean.* CKP, tr. by Jaihiun Kim

From forth th' Elisian Fields. Mad Maudlin is Come. *Unknown.* CBNP

From frozen climes, and endless tracks [*or* tracts] of snow. A Winter-Piece. Ambrose Philips. NOEC

From furthest Spirit—God. (LL) On a Columnar Self. Emily Dickinson. APN-2; NoP-4

From Generation to Generation. Sir Henry John Newbolt. FaBoTw

From ghoulies and ghosties. Things That Go Bump in the Night. *Unknown.* NTCP

From Gloucester Out. Edward Dorn. NOBA; PmAP; PoM

From Gloucester out. (LL) From Gloucester Out. Edward Dorn. NOBA; PmAP; PoM

From God's side even of such a simple thing? (LL) To a Daisy. Alice Thompson Meynell. VWP

From gorge to gorge. Elena Clementelli. *Fr.* Etruscan Notebook. PBWP, tr. by Ruth Feldman and Brian Swann (b. 1940)

From green and blue things and arguments that cannot be proven. (LL) Canal Bank Walk. Patrick Kavanagh. CIP-2; CMoP; FaBoTw; MoBrPo; NoAM; NoP-4

From Green Mountain. William Reed Huntington. APN-2

From green to grey. Alexis Rotella. HA

From Greenland's cisy mountains. From Greenland's Icy Mountains. Reginald Heber. FaPoR

From Greenland's Icy Mountains. Reginald Heber. FaPoR

From groves of spice. Hindu Cradle Song. Sarojini Naidu [*or* Nayadu]. BoTP

From harmony, from heav'nly [*or* heav'nly] harmony. A Song for St Cecilia's Day [1687]. Dryden. AWP; FHYEP; FaBoTw; GTBS-P; HAP; ImPo; InPS-3; NOSC; OAEL-1; OBEV; OxAEP-1; PoEL-3; SCGP; TFi

From Harvest to January. Charles Tennyson Turner. NOBVV

From having done nothing up to now. Reality. Léon Damas, *French.* NegPo, tr. by Ellen Conroy Kennedy

From heaped-up mound of earth and from the heart. The Poem of Jacobus Sadoletus on the Statue of Laocoon. Jacopo Sadoleto, *Italian.* GS, tr. by H. S. Wilkinson

From Hear to Air. Douglas Messerli. FTOS

From heart through mind into image. Words of Tayko-mol. William Oandasan. HATNAP

From Heart to Heart. William Channing Gannett. AH

From heaven above to earth I come. Martin Luther, *German.* GePo

From Heaven High I Come to You. Martin Luther, *German.* PChr

From Heaven's Gate to Hampstead Heath. The Ballad of Hampstead Heath. James Elroy Flecker. MoBrPo

From hence began that Plot, the nation's curse. Dryden. *Fr.* Absalom and Achitophel, Pt. I. EBEvV; FHYEP; FaBoPV; HAP; NOSC; OAEL-1; PoE

From her bed's high and odoriferous roome. Homer. CTC, tr. by George Chapman *Fr.* Odyssey. NAWM-1, tr. by Robert Fitzgerald

From her neon window. Alexis Rotella. HA

From her room in Fu-chou tonight. Moonlight Night. Tu Fu, *Chinese.* CoBCP, tr. by Burton Watson

From Heraclitus. Alan Dugan. PoA

From here do I send. Medicine Songs. *Unknown, Omaha Native American.* APN-2, tr. by Francis La Flesche

From here, the quay, one looks above to mark. The Harbour Bridge. Thomas Hardy. NoAM

From here through tunnelled gloom the track. The Railway Junction. Walter De la Mare. OxBTC

From here to the frontiers of this world. The Panther. *Unknown, Anglo-Saxon.* ASW, tr. by Kevin Crossley-Holland

From here to there / To Washington Square. *Unknown.* OxNR

From high on the spectrum, the prisms ponder. Dioptric. Ion Barbu, *Romanian.* CEEP, tr. by Thomas Amherst Perry

From Him. Andra Davis. IFJA

From his brimstone bed at break of day. The Devil's Thoughts. Coleridge. CBNP; OBSV; OxBoLi; PeLV

From his brimstone bed at the break of day. The Devil. Robert Southey. NOxBChV

From his circuits round the district. Lady Macbeth. Nikolai Nikolaevich Ushakov, *Russian.* TCRP, tr. by Daniel Weissbort

From his garden bed our Lord. The Harvesting of the Roses. Menahem ben Jacob, *Hebrew.* TrJP

From his heavenly Father, our Fortress and Strength. (LL) The Wanderer. *Unknown, Anglo-Saxon.* AnOE; NAWM-1; OAEL-1, tr. by Charles W. Kennedy

From his library in Surrey. Nothing Sacred. Roger Woddis. NOBL

From his mouth he takes out. The Night Game of the Maker of Faces. Novica Tadic, *Serbo-Croatian.* HSix, tr. by Charles Simic

From his nose. Gulliver in Lilliput. Alexander Pope. FuFo

From his own solitude to the world unheeding. Llewelyn Wyn Griffith. OBWVE *Fr.* The Barren Tree.

From his pouch he took his colors. Henry Wadsworth Longfellow. *Fr.* Picture-Writing. APN-1 *Fr.* The Song of Hiawatha.

From his shoulder Hiawatha. Hiawatha's Photographing. "Lewis Carroll." BXAP; NOBL; PeLV

From his small city Columbus. Voyage. Josephine Miles. LiTM

From hollows of a tree. Fable of the Speckled Cow. D. J. Opperman, *Afrikaans.* PeSA, tr. by Jack Cope, Uys Krige, and Ruth Miller

From holy flower to holy flower. The Study of a Spider. John Byrne Leicester Warren, 3d Baron De Tabley. APo; NOBVV

From Holy Sonnets. Donne. NoP-4 *Fr.* Holy Sonnets. ESCV *Fr.* Holy Sonnets.
    ("Thou hast made me, and shall thy work decay?") GSo; NoP-4

From Homegrown: An Asian-American Anthology of Writers. Colleen J. McElroy. LTA

From honey-dew of milking. Feeding a Child. Nuala Ni Dhomhnaill, *Irish.* CIP-2, tr. by Michael Hartnett

From house to house he goes. *Unknown.* BoTP

From inside the bird a dream hums itself out and turns. These Horses Came. Ray A. Young Bear. CDW

From it[t] self[e] never turning [*or* turnynge]. (LL) The Holy Land of Walsingham. *Unknown, sometimes at. to Sir Walter Ralegh.* AAS;

BoLoP; CBLP; EnLoPo; EnSB; FaBoCh; GBL; HAP; InPS-3; NOBE; NTP; NoSic; OBEV; OxAEP-2; PoEL-2; RB; SCGP; TFi

From its dancers circulates among the other / dancers. The Dance. Robert Duncan. NeAP

From its sources which well. Robert Southey. *See* The Cataract of Lodore.

From joy I part, still living in annoy. (LL) A Farewell. Sir Philip Sidney. GBL; NOBE; SiPS

From joy I part still living in annoy. (LL) To Mary: 'It Is the Evening Hour'. John Clare. BoLoP; EnLoPo; GBL

From Jubilate Agno. Christopher Smart. *See* My Cat Jeoffry.

From June to December. Wendy Cope.
  "You know exactly what to do." APAD

From Keith Laurence's gracious patio. Old Talk, or West Indian History. Edward Baugh. HCP

From lake-caves the tortoise-heads protrude. The Fantastic Rock. Wu Chen, *Chinese*. CoBLCP, *tr. by* Jonathan Chaves

From lake Tung-t'ing we travel west. On the Way to Pa-ling. Yüan Mei, *Chinese*. CoBLCP, *tr. by* Jonathan Chaves

From Land Logic. George Keithley. PaTW *Fr.* The Donner Party.

From left to right, she leads the eye. Myth on Mediterranean Beach: Aphrodite as Logos. Robert Penn Warren. HAP

From Life to Love. Countee Cullen. ChIV-1; KSG

From Lines of Swinburne. Charles Bernstein. FTOS

From lofty Roofs the Gods repuls'd before. Ovid. OBCVT, *tr. by* John Dryden *Fr.* Baucis and Philemon, Imitated, From the Eighth Book of Ovid's Metamorphose.

From Lois in London. Angela McCabe. AmPA

From low to high doth dissolution climb. Mutability. Wordsworth. EBEV; HeIP-4; InPK-6; LaPo; NOBE; NoP-4; OAEL-2; OBEV; PoEL-4 *Fr.* Ecclesiastical Sonnets.

From Lucy: Holiday Reflections. James Berry. PBCV

From Manzanilla come! (LL) I taste a liquor never brewed. Emily Dickinson. PFE

From marrying in haste, and repenting at leisure. A New Litany, Occasioned by an Invitation to a Wedding. Elizabeth Thomas. ECWP

From masons laying up brick. Mason's Trick. James Hayford. InPK-6

From Matilda Betham's Notes. Matilda Barbara Betham-Edwards. *See* Power of Women, The.

From Matlock Bath's half-timbered station. Matlock Bath. John Betjeman. NYBP

From me, who whilom sung the town. A Ballad to Mrs. Catherine Fleming in London from Malshanger Farm in Hampshire. Anne Finch, Countess of Winchilsea. ECWP

From mental mists to purge a nation's eyes. George Canning. NOEC *Fr.* New Morality.

From Miss Biddy Fudge to Miss Dorothy———. Thomas Moore. PeLV *Fr.* The Fudge Family in Paris.

From moccasins to shoes. First Grade. Phillip William George. VoR

From Mohawk's mouth, far westing with the sun. Joel Barlow. APN-1 *Fr.* The Columbiad.

From Molepolole and Morogoro. Reflexions on the Seizure of the Suez, and on a Proposal to Line the Banks of That Canal with Billboard Advertisements. Howard Nemerov. NBLV

From momentary work, a wrench, to just fall forward. Jean Day. FTOS

From Monna Innominata. Christina Rossetti. CABP *Fr.* Monna Innominata. BWW

From moonwater, from mirror mist, a slender porcelain. Gift Hour. Maria Banus, *Rumanian*. BoWoP, *tr. by* Willis Barnstone *and* Matei Calinescu

From morn to [*or* till] midnight, all day through. Expectans Expectavi. Charles Hamilton Sorley. FaBoCh

From morning on Rain wouldn't leave my side. A Fairy Tale about Rain. Bella Akhatovna Akhmadulina, *Russian*. TCRP, *tr. by* Albert C. Todd

From mortal gratitude, decide, my Pope. Andrew Lang. EPCY *Fr.* Epistle to Mr. Alexander Pope.

From Mostellaria. Plautus Titus Maccius. OBCVT, *tr. by* Thomas Heywood *Fr.* The English Traveller.

From Mt. Arima / over the bamboo plains of Ina. Daini no Sanmi, *Japanese*. WPJ, *tr. by* Kenneth Rexroth *and* Ikuko Atsumi

From My Arm-Chair. Henry Wadsworth Longfellow. BLPA

From my city bed in the dawn I see a raccoon. Science Fiction. Reed Whittemore. KaS

From My Diary. Yaroslav Vasilevich Smelyakov, *Russian*. TCRP, *tr. by* Simon Franklin

From My Diary, July 1914. Wilfred Owen. FaBoMo; LiTM; MoBrPo

From my disease's danger, and from thee. (LL) To Doctor Empiric[k]. Ben Jonson. FaBoEE; NoP-4; SeCP

From my father and mother I inherited land enough. Han-shan, *Chinese*. ChiP, *tr. by* Arthur Waley

From my favorite place in the Chung-nan Mountains. Oxhead Temple. Ssu-k'ung Shu, *Chinese*. SuSp, *tr. by* Hellmut Wilhelm

From my front wheels the scared rabbits. Iowa, June. Michael Dennis Browne. AmPA

From my high love I look at that poor world there. Kenneth Patchen. MoAmPo

From my high window I can watch. Winter in Minneapolis. Richard Ryan. PBCIP

From My Lai the Thunder Went West. Richard Ryan. CIP-2

From my lyre within the sky. (LL) Israfel. Edgar Allan Poe. APN-1; AWP; AmPP; ImPo; MeMAP; NAAL-1; NAAL-3; NOBA; OxBA; PAR; PoE; PoEL-4; TAP

From my mother, the antique mirror. Heritage. Linda Hogan. UnSA

From My Mother's Home. Leah Goldberg. *Fr.* My Mother's House.

From my mother's sleep I fell into the State. The Death of the Ball Turret Gunner. Randall Jarrell. CMoP; ClHu; ColAP; HAP; HeIP-4; HoPM; InPK-6; LCAP-2; LiTM; MT; MoAmPo; NAAL-2; NIP-4; NOBA; NoAM; NoP-4; OBWP; OxBA; PoE; PoPoPo; PoWW; Poetr; RB; SAGP; SoSe-8; TAP; TFi; UnPo; VCAP; VGW

From my neighbor's ashcan. Richard Wilbur. *See* Junk.

From My Parisian Diary. Mbella Sonne Dipoko. PBMAP

From my personal album. For Malcolm X. Nanina Alba. PoBA

From My Window. Mary Elizabeth Coleridge. OBNC

From My Window. Zaro Weil. AYFP

From my years young in dayes of youth. Epitaphium Meum. William Bradford. SCAP

From my youth up I never liked the city. I Return to the Place I Was Born. T'ao Ch'ien, *Chinese*. OHMPC, *tr. by* Kenneth Rexroth

From Mythology. Zbigniew Herbert, *Polish*. FaBoPV, *tr. by* Czeslaw Milosz

From narrow provinces. The Moose. Elizabeth Bishop. DiPo; FaBoWP; NAAL-2; NALW; NoP-4

From near the sea, like Whitman my great predecessor, I call. Ode: Salute to the French Negro Poets. Frank O'Hara. GLP; NNaP; NeAP; PoM

From needing danger, to be[e] good. Donne. *Fr.* The Litanie. PoEL-2

From noise of scare-fires rest ye free. The Bellman. Robert Herrick. CH; CaPo

From non-being into being: the cloud peaks gather. Sent to a Ch'an Master. Han Wo, *Chinese*. SuSp, *tr. by* Irving Y. Lo

From now on let birds tell you of our life. Letter of the 26th June. Philippe Jaccottet, *French*. MFP, *tr. by* Martin Sorrell

From Number Nine, Penwiper Mews. Limerick. Edward Gorey. OBCoV; PeLi

From Oberon, in fairy land. Robin Goodfellow. *Unknown*. FaBoCh

From Olney Hymns. William Cowper. *See* Light Shining out of Darkness.

From one of the white throats which it hid among? (LL) Vision by Sweetwater. John Crowe Ransom. CMoP; FaBoMo; MeMAP; NOBA; OxBA; RB

From one shaft at Cleator Moor. Cleator Moor. Norman Nicholson. FaBoTw

From one that's base but merely has succeeded. (LL) Words. W. H. Auden. OxBSP; PeLV

From one unus'd in pomp of words to raise. To My Venerable Friend, the President of the Royal Academy. Washington Allston. APN-1

From One Who Stays. Amy Lowell. BoWoP; IMW

From Orford Ness to Shingle Street. Dawn on the East Coast. Alun Lewis. OBWP

From Our Album. Lawson Fusao Inada. AmPA

From our dark spirits. Keats. *See* Endymion.

From our low seat beside the fire. The Call. Charlotte Mew. APAD

From out a book into my lap. A Withered Rose. "Yehoash," *Yiddish*. TrJP, *tr. by* Isidore Goldstick

From out of a wood did a cuckoo fly. The Birds. *Unknown*. PChr

From out of the waters it came with a moan. The Beast in Man. George Clutesi. HATNAP

From out the crowd of vanity and noise. A New Cantata. Clara Reeve. ECWP

From out the stormy sea unto the shore. Epitaph. Azariah di Rossi, *Hebrew*. TrJP, *tr. by* A. B. Rhine

From Pamphilia to Amphilanthus. Mary Sidney, Countess of Montgomery Wroth. NoP-4 *Fr.* Pamphilia to Amphilanthus.

From past to present, year has followed year. Self-Reflection. Nguyễn Bỉnh Khiêm, *Chinese*. AVP, *tr. by* Huỳnh Sanh Thông

From pent-up aching rivers. Walt Whitman. APN-1; BoLoP; GLoP; NAAL-1; NAAL-3; NOBA; OxBM

From Persian looms the silk *he* wove. To Mr. Blanchard, the Celebrated Aeronaut in America. Philip Freneau. APN-1

From pitch and catch. Fungo. Stanley Plumly. AmPA

From plains that reel to southward, dim. Heat. Archibald Lampman. NOBC; NTP

From plane of light to plane, wings dipping through. Evening Hawk. Robert Penn Warren. APo; ColAP; NAAL-2; NoP-4; VCAP

From Plane to Plane. Robert Frost. MoAmPo

From Poetical Sketches. William Blake. *See* To the Muses.

From Poetry and Marriage. Wendell Berry. ITG *Fr.* Poetry and Marriage.

From point A a wind is blowing to point B. After the Broken Arm. Ron Padgett. CoAmPo; SPE

From prehistoric distance, beyond clocks. Street Fight. Harold Monro. FaBoTw

From Prison. Todros ben Judah Abulafia, *Hebrew.* TOF, *tr. by* David Goldstein

From Psyche. Mary Tighe. NoP-4 *Fr.* Psyche, with Other Poems, 3rd edition.

From purple rhetoric of evening skies. (LL) Nearing Again the Legendary Isle. C. Day Lewis. FaBoTw; MoBrPo

From Rich Uneasy America to My Friend Christopher Logue. Adrian Mitchell. SeSe

From Riot Rimes U.S.A. #78. Raymond R. Patterson. MBE

From Riot Rimes U.S.A. #79. Raymond R. Patterson. MBE

From Rite and Ordinance abused they fled. The Pilgrim Fathers. Wordsworth. AiP *Fr.* Ecclesiastical Sonnets.

From Room to Room. Jane Kenyon. LoL

From rude darkness the heroes rose. Passing Chao-ling Again. Tu Fu, *Chinese.* CoBCP, *tr. by* Burton Watson

From Salve Deus Rex Judæorum. Aemilia Bassano Lanyer. NoP-4 *Fr.* Salve Deus Rex Judæorum.

From Sand River to Ts'ai Rock. Yang Chi, *Chinese.*
  "After my illness, so hard to be a traveler." CoBLCP, *tr. by* Jonathan Chaves

From Sappho to myself, consider the fate of women. One. Carolyn Kizer. NMM-2, VCAP *Fr.* Pro Femina.

From say, the sea, a purity of space. (LL) Metonymy as an Approach to a Real World. William Bronk. APSN; VGW

From Scars Where Kestrels Hover. W. H. Auden. FaBoPV; OxBTC

From sea to shining sea! (LL) America the Beautiful. Katharine Lee Bates. APN-2; BLPA; CTV; EBEvV; FaBoA; FaBoBe; TAP

From Several Questions Answered. William Blake. *See* Question Answered, The [*or* A].

From Sex, This Sea. Douglas G. Jones. NOBC

From shadows of rich oaks outpeer. The Pike. Edmund Blunden. LiTM

From shores of Senegal, from Lake Omandaba. O My Swallows! Ernst Toller, *German.* TrJP, *tr. by* Ashley Dukes

From six o'clock I traversed to and fro. Verses to Miss——. J. Wilde. NOEC

From snow that melted only yesterday. (LL) Spring Pools. Robert Frost. AmPP; ColAP; NAAL-2; NOBA; NoAM; OxBA

From "Songs of a Wanderer." Aleksander Wat, *Polish.* BLT, *tr. by* Czeslaw Milosz *and* Leonard Nathan

From Songs of Innocence. William Blake. *See* Introduction: "Piping down the valleys wild."

From Sonnets. Shakespeare. *See* Sonnet 1.

From sopranino to contrabass. (LL) Vow. John Updike. NYBP; PeLV

From Sorrow Sorrow Yet Is Born. Tennyson. OxBSP

From *Spoke / Aug 19.* Hannah Weiner. FTOS

From stainless steel basins of water. The Operation. W. D. Snodgrass. InPK-6; TAP

From Stanzas in Meditation. Gertrude Stein. NoP-4 *Fr.* Stanzas in Meditation.

From Stirling Castle we had seen. Yarrow Unvisited [1803]. Wordsworth. GTBS-P; PoRA

From Stone to Steel. Edwin John Pratt. NoP-4

From stones and poets you may know. Francis Thompson. APAD *Fr.* Contemplation.

From sultry Mobile's gulf-indented shore. Joel Barlow. APN-1 *Fr.* The Columbiad.

From Sunset to Star Rise. Christina Rossetti. VWP

From Superstition. Boris Pasternak, *Russian.* TCRP, *tr. by* Yakov Hornstein

From Susquehanna's farthest springs. The Indian Student; or, Force of Nature. Philip Freneau. OxBA

From tempting Satan to tempt us. Donne. *Fr.* The Litanie. PoEL-2

From "Ten Poems Recording Things that Happened at the Year's End." Liu K'o-chuang. CoBCP, *tr. by* Burton Watson. *Fr.* Ten Poems Recording Things that Happened at the Ye.

From ten to five we whacked the waves. Bath after Sailing. John Updike. OxBoS

From that blest bed the hero came. Andrew Marvell. *Fr.* Upon Appleton House [To My Lord Fairfax]. FaBoPV; GeHe; SeCP

From that dire era, bane to Sarum's pride. On Bishop Burnet's Being Set on Fire in His Closet. Thomas Parnell. ECEV

From that far land to him? (LL) Indian Names. Lydia Huntley Sigourney. APN-1; ColAP; PAR

From that first flash when awful Love took flame. Sonnet 4. Louise Labé, *French.* BoWoP, *tr. by* Willis Barnstone

From that first night. Lady Izumi, *Japanese.* PBWP, *tr. by* Edwin A. Cranston

From that high apple-tree, my love. The Apple Tree. James Keir Baxter. OxBC

From that last acre on oblivion's heap. Edna St. Vincent Millay Exhorts Little Boy Blue. Louis Untermeyer. MoAmPo *Fr.* Mother Goose Up-to-Date.

From that they found most lovely, most abhorred. Beginning. Alden Nowlan. NOBC

From the Antique. Christina Rossetti. EnLoPo: PEW

From the Arabic: An Imitation. Shelley. OBEV

From the ash-colored steel of images. Spring and the Ashura. Miyazawa Kenji, *Japanese.* PFTM, *tr. by* Gary Snyder

From the back it looks like a porch. For Esther. Stanley Plumly. GM; LCAP-2

From the Ballad of Evil. N. P. van Wyk Louw, *Afrikaans.* PeSA, *tr. by* Anthony Delius

From the barbed body, wires. Yearbook. Milo De Angelis, *Italian.* NeIt, *tr. by* Lawrence Venuti

From the bathing machine came a din. Limerick. Edward Gorey. OBAL; OBCoV; PeLi

From the beginning. Teika, *Japanese.* OHMPJ, *tr. by* Kenneth Rexroth

From the besieged Ardea all in post. The Rape of Lucrece. Shakespeare.

From the besieged hills. St Sava's Forge. Vasco [*or* Vasko] Popa. PoSu, *tr. by* Anne Pennington *Fr.* St Sava's Spring.

From the black beach and broad expanse of sea. Thomas Parnell. ChIV-1 *Fr.* Hezekiah.

From The Black Riders and Other Lines. Stephen Crane. NoP-4 *Fr* The Black Riders [and Other Lines].

From the black trunk I shake out. Yuba City School. Chitra Divakaruni. LTA; LoHo; OpBo; UnSA

From "The Blue Notebook" No. 12. Daniil Kharms, *Russian.* TCRP, *tr. by* Bradley Jordan

From the bump / floating down river. Issa, *Japanese.* BLT, *tr. by* Lucien Stryk *and* Takashi Ikemoto

From The Bramble Hedge. Joan Downar. AYFP

From the Bridge. Claribel Alegría, *Spanish.* AF, *tr. by* D. J. Flakoll ("Surrounding me.") (LL) VCWP, *tr. by* D. J. Flakoll

From the Brothers Grimm to Sister Sexton to Mother Goose; One Transmogrification. David Cummings. BXAP

From the bucket's edge. Returning from Abroad. Ōkuma Nobuyuki, *Japanese.* MJT, *tr. by* Makoto Ueda

From the bus I see graffiti. Kevin of the N.E. Crew. Elizabeth Alexander. FFC

From the Bus to E. L. at Atascadero State Hospital. Lorna Dee Cervantes. NAmP90

From the Canton of Expectation. Seamus Heaney. CIP-2

From the Cavities of Bones. Patricia Parker. BlSi

From the Chinese. Michael Smith. CIP-2; PBCIP

From the cities where from caves. Cancelled Stanza of the Mask of Anarchy. Shelley. *Fr.* The Mask [*or* Masque] of Anarchy. FHYEP; OBSV; OxAEP-2; RB; SCV

From the cliff-top it appeared a place of defeat. The Cave. Arthur Rex Dugard Fairburn. PeNZ

From the closed garden. Hymen. Hilda Doolittle.

From the cold hands of guards. Letters Come to Prison. Shahid. GLP

From the colour the nature. Canto 90. Ezra Pound. APSN; VGW *Fr.* Cantos.

From the Country, to Mr. Rowe in Town. Susanna Centlivre. ECWP

From the Cradle to the Graave, or, through Working and Sweating, Suffering and Hardship, even through Prayyer into Damnation. Adolf Wolfli, *German.*
  "And now: And now: here begins Our Voyage, hunters and naturalists of indefatigable enthusiasm." PFTM, *tr. by* Aaron H. Esman

From the crowded platform. Girl. Hugo Williams. CBLP

From the crypt of the church of St. Giles. Limerick. *Unknown.* PeLi

From the dark mood's control. The Recovery. Edmund Blunden. MoBrPo

From the Dark Tower. Countee Cullen. BPo; ColAP; CrDW; LiTM; NAAAL; NAAL-2; PoBA; Son

From the dark woods that breathe of fallen showers. The Zebras. Roy Campbell. MoBrPo

From the dark yard by the sheepbarn the cock crowed. The Henyard Round. Donald Hall. Poetsp

From the day you retired to this home of three paths. The Retreat of Liu Kuo-pao. Chang Yü, *Chinese.* CoBLCP, *tr. by* Jonathan Chaves

From the depth of the dreamy decline of the dawn through a notable nimbus of nebulous moonshine. Nephelidia. Swinburne. BXAP; EnVR; HoPM; PeVV *Fr.* The Heptalogia.

From the desert I come to thee. Bedouin Song. Bayard Taylor. APN-2; FaBoBe

From the Diary of----. Fadwa Tuqan. WPOW, *tr.* by Hatem Hossaini *Fr.* From behind the Bars.

From the dream where we made love. *Unknown, Japanese.* WPJ, *tr.* by Kenneth Rexroth *and* Ikuko Atsumi

From the dress-box's plashing tis–. The Catch. Richard Wilbur. DiPo; WeW-3

From the dull confines of the drooping West. His Return to London. Robert Herrick. BeJo; CaPo; NAEL-1

From the dust of my bosom! (LL) Anne Rutledge. Edgar Lee Masters. CBCWP; CMoP; HAP; ImPo; LiTM; MoAmPo; MoP; NOBA; NoAM; OxBA; TFi

From the elephant paddock one day. Limerick. Frank Richards. PeLi

From the Embassy. Robert Graves. PoA

From the evening darkness. Tanka. Saitō Mokichi, *Japanese.* MJT, *tr.* by Ueda, Makoto

From the eyes endlessly falls. The Diamond of Character. Kabita Sinha, *Bengali.* OMIP, *tr.* by Swapna Mitra *and* Carolyne Wright

From the fair head, for ever, and for ever! (LL) Hampton Court. Alexander Pope. EBEvV; EBNV; OBSV; OxBoLi

From the Field. Lenard D. Moore. GT

From the field's plane tree. Diodorus Zonas, *Greek.* GrAn, *tr.* by Dennis Schmitz

From the fingertips of a lady. The Piano. Pong-gon Chon, *Korean.* CKP, *tr.* by Jaihiun Kim

From the first cave, the first farm, the first sage. Violence. Robert Lowell. NoAM

From the first it had been like a. Bronzeville Mother Loiters in Mississippi. / Meanwhile, a Mississippi Mother Burns Bacon. Gwendolyn Brooks. SSLK

From the first only saying. Teaching Myself to Read. Karen Fiser. IFJA

From the first shock of leaves their alliance. Park Poem. Paul Blackburn. PmAP

From the first tap on the deep stairway. At the Grave of Hazel Hall. Sandra McPherson. NMM-2

From the Flats. Sidney Lanier. APN-2; NOBA; NoP-4; OxBA

From the forests and highlands. Hymn of Pan. Shelley. FaBoCh; OBEV; PoEL-4

From the four corners of the earth. Carl Sandburg. CMoP *Fr.* The People, Yes.

From The Four Quartets. T. S. Eliot. *See* Little Gidding.

From the frantic weather into his creaking tomb. His Necessary Darkness. Nancy Sullivan. TAP

From the freeway you can almost. New York City Mira Mira Blues. Gloria Vando. LoHo

From the French. Charles North. FTOS

From the Front: The Song of the Trench, December, 1914. C. W. Blackall. NSI

From the Frontier of Writing. Seamus Heaney. CABP; PoPoPo

From the Garden. Anne Sexton. LW

From the Garden of the Women Once Fallen. Lorna Goodison. VCWP

From the geyser ventilators. Business Girls. John Betjeman. UV

From the great trees the locusts cry. In August. Hamlin Garland. APN-2

From the Greek. Ptolemy, *Greek.* OBCVT, *tr.* by Bridges, Robert

From the Greek Anthology. Crinagoras, *Greek.* PGA, *tr.* by Kenneth Rexroth

From the Grove Press. Anthony Hecht. OBAL; OBCoV

From the hag [*or* hagg] and hungry [*or* hungrie] goblin. Tom o'Bedlam. *Unknown.* CBNP; CH; EBEV; EnSB; FaBoCh; GEA; HAP; ImPo; NOBE; NTP; NoP-4; OAEL-1; OxBoLi; PoEL-2; PoRA; RB; TFi; WeW-3

From the half / of the sky. The Approach of the Storm. *Unknown, Chippewa.* OBVE; TTTS, *tr.* by Frances Densmore

From the Hazel Bough. Earle Birney. HeIP-4; NIP-4

From the heart of a flower. Leave It to Me Blues. Joel Oppenheimer. VGW

From the hector of France to the cully of Britain. (LL) A Satire on Charles II. John Wilmot, 2d Earl of Rochester. NOSC; PeLV

"From the Hell of the planetary souls?," *sl. longer vers.* Edgar Allan Poe. *See* Ulalume [*or* Ulalume—a Ballad].

From the high Alpine pass. Petronius Arbiter. MLL, *tr.* by Helen Waddell *Fr.* Satyricon.

From the high line spun over us, we hang on to. Confluences at San Francisco. Elton Glaser. PBCAP

From the Highest Camp. Thom Gunn. Son; TwCP

From the hodge porridge. The Farmer's Wife. Anne Sexton. HoPM; LiTM

From the House of Yemanjá. Audre Lorde. NALW; NoAM; NoP-4

From the icy niche where men placed you. Death Sonnet I. Gabriela Mistral, *Spanish.* BoWoP, *tr.* by David Garrison

From the Indians who welcomed the pilgrims. Winter in America. Gil Scott-Heron. ISC

From the Irish. James Simmons. PBCIP; PNI

From the Isle of Awaji. *Unknown, Japanese.* WPJ, *tr.* by Kenneth Rexroth *and* Ikuko Atsumi

From the jagged edges of purple clouds to the west. Tu Fu. SuSp, *tr.* by Irving Y. Lo *Fr.* Ch'iang Village.

From the jaws of the final beast. (LL) God lay dead in Heaven. Stephen Crane. APN-2; AmPP

From the Joke Shop. Roy Fuller. OxBC

From the land of refuge. Week-Seek. Jim Tollerud. VoR

From the local office, orders flying thicker than comb's teeth. Confiscating Salt. Wang An-shih, *Chinese.* CoBCP, *tr.* by Burton Watson

"From the long fronds." What Her Girl Friend Asked and What She Replied Regarding His Return. *Unknown, Tamil.* PLW, *tr.* by A. K. Ramanujan

From the loutishness of learning. (LL) Gnome. Samuel Beckett. BIrV; OxBSP

From the Meadow. Peter Everwine. PuP-17

From the meadows of bliss even the angel goes. Fredensborg. Friedrich Gottlieb Klopstock, *German.* GePo, *tr.* by George C. Schoolfield

From the mind. Chiyojo, *Japanese.* WPoS, *tr.* by Jane Hirshfield *and* Mariko Aratani

From the moment. Tanka. Tawara Machi, *Japanese.* MJT, *tr.* by Makoto Ueda

From the moment of your birth. God's Little Angel. Patrick J. Murray. TIRV

From the Monkey House and Other Cages: Monkey II. Irena Klepfisz. GLP

From the Moorish city. Roads. Antonio Machado Ruiz, *Spanish.* IMW, *tr.* by Willis Barnstone *Fr.* The Dream Below the Sun.

From the Most Distant Time. Emperor Wu of Han, *Chinese.* OHMPC, *tr.* by Kenneth Rexroth

From the mountains we come. Warrior Nation Trilogy. Lance Henson. ImGa; VoR

From the music of two voices and the light of one sweet smile. (LL) Stanzas—April, 1814. Shelley. OBEV; OBNC; SCGP

From the New World. Jorie Graham. NMM-2

From the North Saskatchewan. Eli W. Mandel. NOBC

From the North send a message. Murasaki Shikibu, *Japanese.* WPJ, *tr.* by Kenneth Rexroth *and* Ikuko Atsumi

From the Nursery. Jane Kenyon. BAP-93 *Fr.* Having It Out With Melancholy. BAP-93

(1 From the Nursery.) LoL

From the old settlements only the writings. Elegy. Slavko Mihalic. PoSu, *tr.* by Charles Simic

From the old slave shack I chose my lady. Trellie. Lance Jeffers. NBV

From the oracular archives and the parchment. Dylan Thomas. CMoP *Fr.* A Sequence of Sonnets.

From the other world. (LL) Milkweed. James Wright. ColAP; LCAP-2; NOBA; RaBo

From the Painting "Back from Market" by Chardin. Eavan Boland. PBCIP

From the people. Emigrant/Immigrant. Rina Ferrarelli. LoHo

From the pier, at dusk, the dim. The Buried Graves. Brad Leithauser. NoP-4

From the pole of the flower vendor. Tune: "Magnolia Blossoms, Abbreviated." Li Ch'ing-chao, *Chinese.* SuSp, *tr.* by Eugene Eoyang

From the porch; from the hayrick where her prickled. Mood Indigo. William Matthews. WeW-3

From the porch, if they hold to what there is. When Our Voices Broke Off. James Seay. MT

From the Prison House. Adrienne Rich. NNaP

From the private ease of Mother's womb. Baby Song. Thom Gunn. RB *Fr.* Three Songs.

From the Provençal of William of Poitiers. William of Aquitaine, *Provençal.* MLL, *tr.* by Helen Waddell

From the Rain Forest. Desiré Flynn. BrRo

From the ravine pours silent angry darkness. From the Diary of----. Fadwa Tuqan. WPOW, *tr.* by Hatem Hossaini *Fr.* From behind the Bars.

From the Righteous Man Even the Wild Beasts Run Away. David Bromwich. PoA

From the riverbank / She hails a boat. Tune: "River Messages." Wen T'ing-yün, *Chinese.* SuSp, *tr.* by William R. Schultz

From the rocky-bound Atlantic to the south Pacific shore. The Wabash Cannonball. Delmore Brothers. GM

From the round window, everything is blue. Vision from the Blue Window. Ernesto Cardenal, *Spanish.* VCWP, *tr.* by Marc Zimmerman

From the ruins of that place. (LL) Voice and Address. Michael Palmer. FTOS; PmAP

From the sad eaves the drip-drop of the rain! Desolate. Sydney Thompson Dobell. OBNC

From the scripture. Rotogravure. Errol Francis. NBrP

From the Sermon on the Mount. Bible, *O.T.* CTV *Fr.* Bible O.T., Matthew 5:3–10.

From the Skein of the Straight Line. Tymoteusz Karpowicz, *Polish.* CEEP, *tr. by* Zak, Ewa

From The Slave Trade. Hannah More. NoP-4 *Fr.* The Slave Trade.

From the slopes of the mountain. Clear Bright. Li Ch'ing-chao, *Chinese.* BoWoP, *tr. by* Kenneth Rexroth

From the small life that loves with tooth and nail. Coventry Patmore. FaBoEE

From the sombre clouds fell slow. Snow Song. Henrietta Cordelia Ray. CBWP-3

From the soul of a man who was homeless. Peace at the Goal. Ella Wheeler Wilcox. PWR

From the south they come. War Songs. *Unknown, Ojibwa Native American.* APN-2, *tr. by* Henry Rowe Schoolcraft

From the sphere of our sorrow? (LL) To———: "One word is too often profaned." Shelley. BoLoP; CBLP; EBEvV; GLoP; GTBS-P; ImPo; NOBE; OBEV; OBNC; OxAEP-2; PoLF; TFi

From the Spotted Night. Ray A. Young Bear. AF; HATNAP

From the start, each living thing's. Sergey Aleksandrovich Yesenin, *Russian.* TCRP, *tr. by* Daniel Weissbort

From the stately violence of the State. The Broken Mirror. Bob Perelman. FTOS

From the Suburbs. Louise Glück. FaBoWP; NALW *Fr.* Dedication to Hunger.

From the Sun Itself. Roberta Hill Whiteman. HATNAP

From the sustaining air. Larry Eigner. PoM

From the tall pavilion the guests have all departed. Fallen Flowers. Li Shang-yin, *Chinese.* SuSp, *tr. by* James J. Y. Liu

From the tawny light. Everything That Acts Is Actual. Denise Levertov. NoAM

From the Telephone. Florence Ripley Mastin. LW

From the Temple of Longing. Roger Weingarten. NAmP90

From the thick cover of unknowingness. On the Curve-Edge. Abbie Huston Evans. NYBP

From the thin slats of the Venetian blinds. Underwood. Howard Moss. TwCP

From the third floor I beckon to the child. Calling the Child. Karl Shapiro. MoLi

From the Tibetan. John Hewitt. PNI

From the time we were caught up. Town Pier Parking Lot. Brendan Galvin. CMAP

From the time you came into my house. Sad Remembrance. Mei Yao Ch'en, *Chinese.* CoBCP, *tr. by* Burton Watson

From the top here. X L E B. Jack Hirschman. CLPP

From the top of Dragon Gate. Inscribed on My Ink Landscape Painting. Tao-chi, *Chinese.* CoBLCP, *tr. by* Jonathan Chaves

From the top of high *Caucasus. Unknown.* CBNP

From the tragic-est novels at Mudie's. Dora versus Rose. Austin Dobson. NOBL

From the Train. Marjorie Wilson. BoTP

From the train window at daybreak. At Daybreak. Adam Zagajewski, *Polish.* VCWP, *tr. by* Renata Gorcyznski, Benjamin Ivry, *and* C. K. Williams

From the Travels of Gulliver. Suniti Namjoshi. GLP

From the trucks we see. Graves Registration. Basil T. Paquet. CDa

From the uttermost part of the earth. I Waste Away. Bible, *O.T.* TrJP *Fr.* Isaiah.

From the very first coming down. The Letter. W. H. Auden. FaBoTw; MoP; NoAM

From the Waitress Papers. Sharon Doubiago. NMM-2

From the wan dream that was her waking day. Edna St. Vincent Millay. *Fr.* Sonnets from an Ungrafted Tree. NALW

From the War. Aleksandr Petrovich Mezhirov, *Russian.* TCRP, *tr. by* Deming Brown

From the water's depth. Tanka. Shaku Chōkū, *Japanese.* MJT, *tr. by* Makoto Ueda

From the Wave. Thom Gunn. NAEL-2; NoP-4; OxBoS

From the west. An African Thunderstorm. James David Rubadiri. PBMAP

From the west comes Harold, with a bitter smile. Harold. David Ignatow. LTA

From the west to the fabulous east. Limerick. *Unknown.* PeLi

From the white plain where stands the water. Song of the Stricken Twins. *Unknown. Fr.* The Night Chant. APN-2, *tr. by* Washington Matthews

From the wilderness remote he breaks. The Red-Man. Frank Prewett. HATNAP

From the wind I get / the predicate of plants. Saved. Maria Teresa Horta, *Portuguese.* PBWP, *tr. by* Suzette Macedo

From the window. Alexis Rotella. HA

From the Window Down. Louis O. Coxe. NYBP

From the window of a train. Night Coach. Phillis Levin. RA

From the window of my grandfather's. Late Gothic. Phyllis Gotlieb. NOBC

From the Window of the Beverly Wilshire Hotel. Michael McClure. SPE

From the winter wind. Michael Rosen. Spl

From the years. Things Kept. William Dickey. NYBP

From Thee to Thee. Solomon ibn Gabirol, *Hebrew.* TrJP, *tr. by* Israel Abrahams

From their journeys our dreams return. Pavel Grigoryevich Antokolsky, *Russian.* TCRP, *tr. by* Bernard Meares

From thence into the open fields he fled. A Pastoral. Edmund Spenser. *Fr.* Wood Of Error. AEP

From thence took first their Rise, thither at last must Flow. (LL) Hymn: To Light. Abraham Cowley. MeLP; OxAEP-1

From these bare trees. Chinese Winter. Frederick Robert Higgins. BIrV

From these high walls I look at the town below. After Collecting the Autumn Taxes. Po Chü-i, *Chinese.* BLT, *tr. by* Arthur Waley; ChiP, *tr. by* Arthur Waley

From this depth—I came only to draw water. Song of the Brightness of Water. Karol Wojtyla. CRP

From this high place all things flow. Watershed. Robert Penn Warren. PoA

From this late-flowering lust. (LL) Late-Flowering Lust. John Betjeman. CMoP; EP

From this lone village rises dimly a wisp of smoke. Chanting These Verses on My Way to Yodoe. Su Man-shu, *Chinese.* SuSp, *tr. by* Wu-chi Liu

From this range it all goes out with becoming. Cattle. Ralph Hawkins. NBrP

From this swaying city. Birthday Poem from Venice. Patricia Beer. OxBC

From this father's quality. (LL) Cradle Song: "Come, little babe." Nicholas Breton. NOBE; OBEV; RACG

From this ultimate dim Thule. (LL) Dream-Land [*or* Dreamland]. Edgar Allan Poe. APN-1; AmPP; MeMAP; NAAL-1; NAAL-3; NCAP; NOBA; OxBA; PAR; TAP

From this, unto the last of daies. (LL) Easter Hymn. Henry Vaughan. ChIV-2; ESCV

From this valley they say you are going. Red River Valley. *Unknown.* APN-2; AS; FaBoBe

From thorax of storms the voices of verbs. George Barker. ImPo; LiTM *Fr.* Pacific Sonnets.

From those few famous silkworms smuggled. Angels Grieving over the Dead Christ. Gjertrud Schnackenberg. BAP-93

From [fly] those Windings and that Shade! (LL) Give me, O indulgent fate! Anne Finch, Countess of Winchilsea. ECWP; NOSC

From three dark places Christ came forth this day. Upon Christ's Nativity or Christmas. Rowland Watkyns. OBWVE

From three sources, / vital sources flowing in dull shades of red. Oleg Khlebnikov. TCRP, *tr. by* Bradley Jordan *Fr.* Miracle Workers.

From thy patient, who while here. Accompanying a Gift. Lizelia Augusta Jenkins Moorer. CBWP-3

From today thou shalt have a (certain) time of dying. The Horse Cursed by the Sun. *Unknown, Hottentot.* PeSAV, *tr. by* W. H. I. Bleek

From Tomorrow On. *Unknown, Yiddish.* TrJP, *tr. by* Joseph Leftwich

From tomorrow's mist-fall till Time be sped! (LL) The Eve of Waterloo. Thomas Hardy. OAEL-2; OBWP

From too much love of living. Swinburne. IMW *Fr.* The Garden of Proserpine. AWP; BLPA; FaPoR; HAP; NAEL-2; NOBE; NOBVV; OBNC; PoE; PoEL-5; PoRA; SCV

From Travancore to Tripoli. Ballad of the Oedipus Complex. Lawrence Durrell. OBCoV

From Trollope's Journal. Elizabeth Bishop. CBCWP; FaBoPV

From troubles of the world. Ducks. Frederick William Harvey.

From Tuscan came my lady's worthy race. Henry Howard, Earl of Surrey. AAS; SiPS

From up here in the crow's nest. Jesus Dies. Anne Sexton. CrSp; RACG

From V. C. (a Gentleman of Verona). Gavin Ewart. OxBC

From Venice was that afternoon. Jean Garrigue. NOBA

From Villahermosa, / in Tabasco. Postcard from Mexico, 16.X.1973. Andrew Salkey. PBCV

From Virgil. George Oppen. NNaP *Fr.* Five Poems about Poetry.

From Water-Tower Hill to the brick prison. Point Shirley. Sylvia Plath. NIP-4; Poetr

From what great sleep. Watts. Alvin Saxon. PoBA

From what once was, from the crazy nights. Veronica Porumbacu, *Romanian*. CEEP, *tr. by* Dorian, Marguerite and Elliott Urdang

From what proud star I know not, but I found. The Giant Puffball. Edmund Blunden. FaBoTw

From Whence Doth This Union Arise? Thomas Baldwin. AH

From whence, vile poet, didst thou glean thy wit. To Poet Edmund Waller, Occasioned for His Writing a Panegyric on Oliver Cromwell. Charles Cotton. EPCY

From where. Tanka. Saitō Mokichi, *Japanese*. MJT, *tr. by* Ueda, Makoto

From where dark clouds of curling smoke arise. Susanna Blamire. ECWP; NOEC *Fr.* Stoklewath; or, The Cumbrian Village.

From where have you learned to wipe the tears. To My Mother. Hannah Senesh, *Yiddish*. MDDM, *tr. by* Ruth Finer Mintz

From where I am. Drinking Back. Franz Wright. LCAP-2

From where I live, from windows on four sides. Juniper. Robert Francis. VGW

From where I stand now. 12 October. Myra Cohn Livingston. NTCP

From where I stand, Professor Pagels. Proton Decay. Robert Pack. ColAP

From where I stand the sheep stand still. Sheep. Robert Francis. LCAP-2

From where I stood at the field's immaculate edge. Ice Plant in Bloom. W. S. Di Piero. PaTW

From where you are. Stone Buddha (two poems). Ōkuma Nobuyuki, *Japanese*. MJT, *tr. by* Makoto Ueda

From Whitehall Stairs, whence oft with distant view. Whitehall Stairs. Aaron Hill. NOEC

From Whitsuntide to Whitsuntide. A Ballad of a Bun. Sir Owen Seaman. UV

From whose large mouth for verse all that since live. Manilius Marcus. OBCVT, *tr. by* John Florio *and* Matthew Gwinne *Fr.* The Astronomica.

From Wibbleton to Wobbleton is fifteen miles. *Unknown*. OxNR

From Winchester, twenty miles away! (LL) Sheridan's Ride. Thomas Buchanan Read. APN-2; CBCWP; FaBoBe

From winter, plague, and pestilence, good Lord, deliver us! (LL) Autumn Hath All the Summer's Fruitful Treasure. Thomas Nashe. NoSic; OAEL-1; SCGP

From winter-sleep. Ladybug's Christmas. Norma Farber. PChr

From witty men and mad . The Poet. Thomas Randolph. OxBSP

From woe to weale, from hell to heavenly raigne. (LL) At Fotheringay. Robert Southwell. NoSic; PoEL-2

From Wynyard's Gap the livelong day. A Trampwoman's Tragedy. Thomas Hardy. NAEL-2; OBNC; OBNV

From year to year the contest grew. James M. Whitfield. CBCWP *Fr.* A Poem Written for the Celebration of the Fourth Anniversary of President Lincoln's Emancipation Proclamation.

From yonder wood, make blue-eyed Eve proceed. Progress of Evening. Walter Savage Landor. OBNC

From Yoshino / Mountain the autumn. Fujiwara no Masatsune, *Japanese*. OHPJ, *tr. by* Kenneth Rexroth

From you have I been absent in the spring. Sonnet 98. Shakespeare. AWP; EBEV; GLoP; ImPo; LoP; NAEL-1; NOBE; NoSic; OBEV; OxAEP-1 *Fr.* Sonnets.

From you I want more than I've ever asked. To the Days. Adrienne Rich. BAP-93; LoL *Fr.* Not Somewhere Else, But Here. BAP-93

From you, Ianthe, little troubles pass. Ianthe's Troubles. Walter Savage Landor. GBL; NOBE; OBEV; OBNC *Fr.* Ianthe.

From you, Rose, I do not like. Rondeau for You. Mário de Andrade, *Portuguese*. TTY, *tr. by* John Nist

From your arm. (LL) Inside Out. Diane Wakoski. CoAP; NYBP

From your eyes. Sokchong Shin, *Korean*. CKP, *tr. by* Jaihiun Kim

From your eyes I thought. Silences; a Dream of Governments. Jean Valentine. LCAP-2

From Zeus let us begin, him we mortals never. Proem. Aratus. HePo, *tr. by* Barbara Hughes Fowler *Fr.* Phaenomena.

Fronleichnam. D. H. Lawrence. GBL

Front, A. Randall Jarrell. NoP-4; OBWP; OxBC; PoWW; VGW

Front Lines. Gary Snyder. PoE

Front Page. Abba Kovner, *Hebrew*. IP, *tr. by* Warren Bargad *and* Stanley F. Chyet

Front Street. Howard Moss. NYBP

Front Window, The. Rae Desmond Jones. BMAP

Frontier, The. John Hewitt. BIrV

Frontier of rage that exists, The. Askia M. Toure. ISC

Frontier Songs. Lu Lun, *Chinese*.
   "Moon blackens, geese fly high." SuSp, *tr. by* Ronald C. Miao
   "Select fine arrows and call for falcons." SuSp, *tr. by* Ronald C. Miao
   "Woods darken, grasses startled by wind." SuSp, *tr. by* Ronald C. Miao
Frontier Songs, First Series. Tu Fu, *Chinese*.
   "If you draw a bow, draw the strongest." SuSp, *tr. by* Ronald C. Miao
   "Sad, sad they leave their old village." SuSp, *tr. by* Ronald C. Miao

"Sharpen the sword in the Sobbing Waters." SuSp, *tr. by* Irving Y. Lo

Frontispiece. May Swenson. CoAP; WPE

Frost. Stella Benson. OxBTC

Frost. Vita Sackville-West. GaP

Frost and snow, frost and snow. Ariel. David Campbell. CBAP

Frost at Midnight. Coleridge. CABP; EBEV; FHYEP; HAP; NAEL-2; NOBE; NOBRP; NoP-4; OAEL-2; OBNC; PoE; PoEL-4; Poetr; Ro; TFi; TOF

"Frost performs its secret ministry, The." OPOU
   Silent Icicles, The.

Frost at Midnight. Mary Jo Salter. RA

Frost covers the reeds of the marsh. Kenneth Rexroth. APSN *Fr.* The Love Poems of Marichiko.

Frost Eyebrows was the favorite cat. Felicity Bast. PC

Frost falls only to melt in the valley. Living in Exile at Ch'ien-nan. Huang T'ing-chien, *Chinese*. SuSp, *tr. by* Michael E. Workman

Frost glitters on the chrysanthemums. Tu Fu. *See* Stars and Moon on the Yangtse.

Frost has sealed. Tree in December. Melville Cane. MoAmPo

Frost in the air and music in the air. The Waits. John Freeman. BoTP

Frost in the Corn, The. Robert McAlmon. AiP

Frost is All Over, The. Pearse Hutchinson. PBCIP

Frost lies white, The. Yakamochi, *Japanese*. OHPJ, *tr. by* Kenneth Rexroth

Frost-locked all the winter. Spring. Christina Rossetti. OBNC

Frost looked forth, one still, clear night, The. Hannah Flagg Gould. BLPA

Frost performs its secret ministry, The. Frost at Midnight. Coleridge. CABP; EBEV; FHYEP; HAP; NAEL-2; NOBE; NOBRP; NoP-4; OAEL-2; OBNC; PoE; PoEL-4; Poetr; Ro; TFi; TOF

Frost-sad, clouds of white hair. Miscellaneous Poems Written While in Jail. Ch'ien Ch'ien-i, *Chinese*. CoBLCP, *tr. by* Jonathan Chaves

Frost shall freeze; fire melt wood. Maxims (Exeter Book). *Unknown*, *Anglo-Saxon*. AnOE, *tr. by* Charles W. Kennedy

Frost, 1654, The: To Mr. W.L. Thomas Shipman.
   "Streams are fettered, and with us as rare, The." NOSC

Frosty Christmas Eve, A. Noel; Christmas Eve, 1913. Robert Bridges. NOCV; OBCP; PoEL-5

Frosty Night, A. Robert Graves. CH; MoBS; MoBrPo; OxBTC

Frosty wind harries the *wu-t'ung*, A. Han Yü, *Chinese*. PLT, *tr. by* A. C. Graham *Fr.* Autumn Thoughts. CoBCP, *tr. by* Burton Watson

Froude informs the Scottish youth. A Hymn on Froude and Kingsley. William Stubbs. FaBoEE

Frounyng fates have taken hence, The. Calimachus. Lucian, *Greek*. OBCVT, *tr. by* Timothy Kendall

Frowardness of the Elect in the Work of Conversion, The. Edward Taylor. SCAP *Fr.* God's Determinations [touching his Elect].

Frown[e] death immediately. (LL) A La Bourbon. Richard Lovelace. CaPo; CavPo

Frozen Boy, The. Brian W. Aldiss. OxBM

Frozen breaths, The. George Swede. HA

Frozen clouds in the dark gloomy air. Tune: "Midnight Music." Liu Yung, *Chinese*. SuSp, *tr. by* James J. Y. Liu

Frozen Girl, The. *Unknown*. AS

Frozen Greenhouse, The. Thomas Hardy. OBGa

Frozen ground is broken, The. In February. P. A. Ropes. BoTP

Frozen Hands. Joseph Bruchac. CDW

Frozen Hero, The. Thomas H. Vance. NYBP

Frozen in the ice. Masaoka Shiki, *Japanese*. OHMPJ, *tr. by* Kenneth Rexroth

Frozen Logger, The. *Unknown*. OBAL

Frozen lost dead with hunger. August Bank Holiday. Jacques Prévert, *French*. MFP, *tr. by* Martin Sorrell

Frozen Man, The. Kit Wright. AYFP

Frozen Ocean, The. Viola Meynell. CH

Frozen Rain. Michael Longley. PBCIP

Frozen river is drifted deep with snow, The. In the Evening I Walk by the River. Ou-yang Hsiu, *Chinese*. OHPC, *tr. by* Kenneth Rexroth

Frozen Witness, The. Nick Piombino. FTOS

Frozen Zone; or, Julia Disdainful, The. Robert Herrick. CaPo
   (Julia Disdainful: or, The Frozen Zone.) CavPo

Frugal Repasts. Lynda Hull. NAmP90

Frugal snail, with forecast of repose, The. The Housekeeper. Vincent Bourne, *Latin*. PoLF, *tr. by* Charles Lamb

Fruit. Kenward Elmslie. FTOS

Fruit. Philippe Jaccottet, *French*. MFP, *tr. by* Martin Sorrell

Fruit, The. Denise Levertov. *See* O Taste and See.

Fruit and Flower Painter. Herman Melville. NCAP

Fruit bat swings on its branch, a tongueless bell, The. (LL) The Hotel Normandie Pool. Derek Walcott. HCP; VCWP

Fruit falls off, and that's when it's all ripe, A. A Fallen Fruit. Bùi Công Trừng, *Vietnamese.* AVP, *tr. by* Huỳnh Sanh Thông

Fruit of all the service that I serve, The. Sir Thomas Wyatt. SiPS

Fruit of Knowledge, The. Robert Johnstone. PNI

Fruit of Loneliness. May Sarton. PoA

Fruit, of the Earth. Cyril Dabydeen. PBCV

Fruit of the Flower. Countee Cullen. PoLF

Fruit of the Tree, The. David Wagoner. NYBP

Fruit on the trees is aging fast, The. Words to a Song. Agnes Nemes Nagy, *Hungarian.* BoWoP, *tr. by* Bruce Berlind

Fruit Plucker, The. Coleridge. CH

    (In a Moonlight Wilderness.) FaBoCh

Fruit Tree. Song-yong Park, *Korean.* CKP, *tr. by* Jaihiun Kim

Fruit-tree's branch by very wealth, The. The Penalty of Virtue. *Unknown. Fr.* The Panchatantra. AWP, *tr. by* Arthur Ryder

Fruit white and lustrous as a pearl. The Lychee. Wang I, *Chinese.* FaBoCh, *tr. by* Arthur Waley

Fruited Month, The. Zalman Schneour, *Hebrew.* MHP, *tr. by* Ruth Finer Mintz

Fruitful earth drinks up the rain. All Things Drink. Thomas Stanley, *after the Greek of* Anacreon. AWP

Fruits of War, The. George Gascoigne.

    "Conference among ourselves we called, A." OBWP

Fruits you give me are more savory than others, The. Marguerite Burnat-Provins, *French.* BoWoP, *tr. by* Cassia Berman

Frustrated. May Probyn. VWP

Frutas. Ricardo Pau-Llosa. CMAP

Frutta di Mare. Geoffrey Scott. OBMV

Fry says a word. Rosellen Brown. FFC

Fryar was walking in Exeter-Street, A. The Crafty Miss of London; or, The Fryar Well Fitted. *Unknown.* OxBR

Frying Trout While Drunk. Lynn Emanuel. NAmP90

Fúar liom an adhaighsi dh'Aodh. A Winter Campaign. Eochaidh Ó Heóghusa. CABP

Fuchsia Hedges in Connacht. Padraic Colum. TIRV

Fuck I want to be bound by devotion! Tortured. African Sunday. Maureen Owen. PmAP

Fuck Ode. Michael McClure. BB *Fr.* Dark Brown.

Fucked the Mountain. The Song of Ullikummi. Charles Olson. PFTM

Fucking cops are fucking keen, The. Evidently Chicken Town. John Cooper Clarke. FaBoPV

Fucking, I feel at one with the world. Christian Karlson Stead. PeNZ *Fr.* Clodian Songbook.

Fudge Family in Paris, The. Thomas Moore.

    "After dreaming some hours of the land of Cockaigne." BIrV

    "At length, my Lord, I have the bliss." OBSV

    From Miss Biddy Fudge to Miss Dorothy———. PeLV

    Letter 1. NOBRP

    "Oh Dick! You may talk of your writing and reading." OBCoV

Fuego. Dionisio D. Martinez. WWSi

Fugitive, The. Alice Thompson Meynell. NOCV

Fugitive, The. Priscilla Jane Thompson. CBWP-2

Fugitive Pieces and Reminiscences of Lord Byron with Some Original Poetry, Letters and Recollections of Lady Caroline Lamb, ed. I. Nathan. Lady Caroline Lamb.

    "My heart's fit to break, yet no tear fills my eye." Ro

Fugitive returned on New Year's Eve, The. Festus Conrad. Melvin B. Tolson. GT

Fugitive Slaves, The. Jones Very. TAP

Fugitive Slave's Apostrophe to the North Star, The. John Pierpont. APN-1

Fugs, The. Edward Sanders. PoM

Fugue. Howard Nemerov. TAP

Fugue of Death. Paul Celan. *See* A Death Fugue.

Fuimus Fumus. Joshua Sylvester. FaBoEE

Full and True Account of a Horrid and Barbarous Robbery, A. John Byrom.

    "Dear Martin Folkes, dear scholar, brother, friend." NOBL

Full autumn moon, A. Jim Handlin. HA

Full be the year, abundant be the grain. Ezra Pound, *after the Chinese.* OBVE

Full day—. Today Tutu Is Beating the Same Burru As Me. Lebert Bethune. GT

Full days come striding with measured, The. Concerning the Awakening of My Soul. Henriëtte Roland-Holst, *Dutch.* WPOW, *tr. by* Jonathan Crewe

Full early in the morning. *Unknown.* BoTP

Full Fathom Five. Arthur Rex Dugard Fairburn. PeNZ

Full fathom [*or* fadom] five thy father lies. Ariel's Song. Shakespeare. AWP; ClHu; EBEV; EBEvV; FaBoCh; GTBS-P; HAP; HoPM; ImPo;

InPK-6; InPS-3; NAEL-1; NOBE; NOSC; NTP; NoSic; OBEV; OPOU; OxBSP; PoE; PoEL-2; PoRA; TFi *Fr.* The Tempest. OAEL-1

Full fathom five thy father lies. June Mercer Langfield. SCGP

Full in her glory, she as Tirzah fair. The Prophet Jeremiah and the Personification of Israel. Eleazar ben Kalir, *Hebrew.* TrJP, *tr. by* Nina Davis Salaman

Full in the hand, heavy. September Afternoon at Four O'Clock. Marge Piercy. NIP-4

Full many a glorious morning have I seen[e]. Sonnet 33. Shakespeare. AWP; EBEV; EBEvV; HAP; ImPo; NIP-4; NoSic; OAEL-1; OxAEP-1; PoRA; SCGP; Son; TFi *Fr.* Sonnets.

Full many sing to me and thee. The Barren Shore. Coventry Patmore. GBL

Full Moon. Robert Graves. NOBE

Full Moon. Robert Earl Hayden. BPo; GT

Full Moon. Vita Sackville-West. NTP

Full Moon. Sappho, *Greek.* AWP, *tr. by* William Ellery Leonard

Full Moon. Tu Fu. OHPC

Full Moon. Elinor Wylie. NALW; NoP-4

Full Moon and Little Frieda. Ted Hughes. NTP; OPOU; OxBC; OxBSP

Full Moon at Tierz; before the Storming of Huesca. John Cornford. OBWP

Full moon easterly rising, furious, The. A Love Story. Robert Graves. CMoP; FaBoTw; NAEL-2

Full Moon in Malta. "Asphodel." BrRo

Full moon is partly hidden by cloud, The. A Fable of the War. Howard Nemerov. OBWP

Full moon on the Colosseum, The. Colosseum. Harold Norse. TrJP

Full moon on the night of the seventeenth, A. The Night of the Seventeenth. Li K'ai-hsien, *Chinese.* CoBLCP, *tr. by* Jonathan Chaves

Full moon. Our Narragansett gales subside. John Berryman. CoAP *Fr.* Dream Songs.

Full moon rising on the waters of my heart. Evening Song. Jean Toomer. BPo; GT

Full Moon; Santa Barbara. Sara Teasdale. OBCA

Full moon shines across the lawn, The. Translation from a Lost Source. Richard Caddel. NBrP

Full Moon that Strikes the Earth Cold. Karen McCosker. APAD

Full moonlit night people. The Net of Moon. *Unknown, Pawnee Indian.* STP, *tr. by* Jerome Rothenberg

Full-nelsoned in earth's arms the Crusher sleeps. Last Lines on a Wrestler. X. J. Kennedy. CRP

Full night. The moon has yet to rise. Sodom. Herman Melville. AmPP *Fr.* Clarel: A Poem and Pilgrimage in the Holy Land.

Full of courage and promise like the geese gone away. The Prince Enters the Forest. Henri Cole. DiPo

Full of her long white arms and milky skin. The Equilibrists. John Crowe Ransom. CMoP; FuPo; HAP; LiTM; MeMAP; MoP; NAAL-2; NOBA; NoAM; OxBA; TAP

Full of life now, compact, visible. Walt Whitman. APN-1

Full of rain, the word. Ramola Dharmaraj. BAP-94

Full of sentiment, clever at mechanics, and we love our luxuries. (LL) Ave Caesar. Robinson Jeffers. FaBoPV; MoP; NOBA; NoAM; OxBA; OxBSP

Full of superstition. The New Notebook. Maria Banus, *Rumanian.* PBWP, *tr. by* Laura Schiff *and* Dana Beldiman

Full of sweet dreams, and health, and quiet breathing. Keats. *See* Endymion.

Full of years and seasoned like a salt timber. Islandman. Brenda Chamberlain. OBWVE

Full oft doth Mat. with Topaz dine. Earning a Dinner. Matthew Prior. NBLV

Full oft of old the islands changed their name. Epitaph on an Infant. Crinagoras, *Greek.* AWP, *tr. by* John William Burgon

Full often as I rove by path or stile. Wind on the Corn. Charles Tennyson Turner. EBVV

Full September moon sheds floods of light, The. A September Night. George Marion McClellan. AAP

Full summer and at noon; from a waste bed. Noon. "Michael Field." NOBVV

Full Tide. Paraire Henare Tomoana, *Maori.* PeNZ, *tr. by* Margaret Orbell

Full Vision. Henrietta Cordelia Ray. CBWP-3

Full Well I Know. Hartley Coleridge. Son

Full well I know that she is there. Gertrude Stein. PoA *Fr.* Stanzas in Meditation.

Full well it may be seen. Sir Thomas Wyatt. SiPS

Full well, my gentle sir, I know. To an Artful Theatre Manager. Lorenzo Da Ponte. TrJP, *tr. by* John Mazzinghi *Fr.* Il Capriccio Dramatico.

Full well, Tibaldi, did thy kindred mind. On Seeing the Picture of Æolus by Pelegrino Tibalbi, in the Institute at Bologna. Washington Allston. APN-1

Full year since, I took this eager city, A. An Irishman in Coventry. John Hewitt. BIrV; CIP-2; IIP; PNI

Fuller and Warren. Moses Whitecotton. AmFP

Fullfillment. Eunice Tietjens. PoToHe

Fulling Cloth for Clothes. Hsieh Hui-lien, *Chinese*. CoBCP, *tr. by* Burton Watson

Fullness of the Deity, The. (LL) The Night. Henry Vaughan. ChIV-2; EBEV; ESCV; GeHe; MeLP; NAEL-1; NOBE; NOCV; OAEL-1; OBEV; OBWVE; OxAEP-1; PoEL-2; SCGP; TFi; TOF

Fulvia, our Consul bids me thank thee: why. Familiar Poem from Nisa to Fulvia of the Vale. Ann Yearsley. ECWP

Fum and Hum, the Two Birds of Royalty. Thomas Moore. OBSV

Fumbling for the live nerve. Winter. Rae Armantrout. FTOS

Fumetti. Robert Long. NAmP90

Fun. Leroy F. Jackson. CTV

Fundament Is Shifted, The. Abbie Huston Evans. NYBP

Funeral, The. Walter De la Mare. CMoP

Funeral[l], The. Donne. AWP; BoLoP; EBEV; ESCV; EnLoPo; FSCP; HeIP-4; ImPo; MeLP; NAEL-1; NAWM-1; NoP-4; OAEL-1; OBEV; PoEL-2; PoRA; SCGP; SeCP; TFi

("That, since you would have none of me, I bury some of you.") (LL) GLoP

Funeral, The. Norman Dubie. InPK-6; NoAM

Funeral, The. Donald Hall. Son

Funeral, The. "M. J.," *Polish*. TrJP, *tr. by* A. Glanz-Leyeles

Funeral, The. Stephen Spender. CMoP; MoBrPo; NoAM

Funeral, The. Sir Richard Steele.

Trim's Song: The Fair Kitchen-Maid. OxBSP

Funeral Elegy Upon that Pattern and Patron of Virtue, A. John Norton. SCAP

Funeral Eva. Koroneu. RaBo

Funeral gent led us, The. Choosing Coffins. Raymond Souster. MoCV

Funeral Home, The. Robert Mezey. LiTM

Funeral Hymn upon the Obsequies of a Friend, A. Prudentius, *Latin*.
"Now, earth, take to thy cold embrace." OBCVT, *tr. by* Simon Patrick

Funeral in the East. Pablo Neruda, *Spanish*. TRP, *tr. by* Robert Bly

Funeral Lament (Kommos) from Epiros. *Unknown, Modern Greek*. BoWoP, *tr. by* Elene Margot Kolb

Funeral Music. Geoffrey Hill.
"My little son, when you could command marvels." NoAM
"Not as we are but as we must appear." NoAM

Funeral of Ally Flett, The. George Mackay Brown. FaBoTC

Funeral of Martin Luther King, Jr, The. Nikki Giovanni. BPo

Funeral of Philip Sparrow, The. John Skelton. *Fr.* Phyllyp Sparowe [*or* Philip Sparrow]. AAS; PoEL-1

Funeral of Scyld Shefing, The. *Unknown*. EEP, *tr. by* Alexander, Michael *Fr.* Beowulf. OAEL-1, *tr. by* Charles W. Kennedy; ASW, *tr. by* Kevin Crossley-Holland

Funeral Oration, A. Drummond Allison. PoWW

Funeral Oration, A. David Wright. PeSAV

Funeral Oration for a Mouse. Alan Dugan. HAP; Poetr

Funeral Plainsong from a Younger Woman to an Older Woman, A. Judy Grahn. DeD; GLP

Funeral Pyre, The. *Unknown*. AnOE, *tr. by* Charles W. Kennedy *Fr.* Beowulf. OAEL-1, *tr. by* Charles W. Kennedy; ASW, *tr. by* Kevin Crossley-Holland

Funeral Rites. Seamus Heaney. BiHa; PBCIP

Funeral[l] Rites of the Rose, The. Robert Herrick. CaPo; NOSC; OBEV
("And closed her up as in a tomb.") (LL) PFE
("Rose was sick and, smiling, died, The.") PFE

Funeral Sermon, Soweto. Wole Soyinka. VCWP

Funeral Service. Cecil Gray. HCP

Funeral Song. Hayiaku, *Tlingit Indian*. STP, *tr. by* James Koller

Funeral Song. *Unknown, Sotho*. PeSA, *tr. by* Dan Kunene *and* Jack Cope

Funeral Song, Upon the Decease of Annes His Mother, A. Nicholas Grimald.
From A Funeral Song, Upon the Decease of Annes His Mother. NoP-4
"I, in your frutefull woomb conceyved, born was." PBRV

Funeral[l] stone, A. To Laurels. Robert Herrick. CaPo

Funerall Hymne out of Prudentius, A. Prudentius, *Latin*.
"O God, the soules pure fi'ry Spring." OBCVT, *tr. by* Sir John Beaumont

Funerall Song, A. *Unknown*. CH

Funerary Portraits. Rosanna Warren. NoAM

Funfair, henhouse of pleasure. Peoples House. Nikolai Alekseievich Zabolotsky, *Russian*. TCRP, *tr. by* Daniel Weissbort

Fungo. Stanley Plumly. AmPA

Fungus Fingers, The. Wes Magee. SpW

Funk Lore. Imamu Amiri Baraka. UnSA

Funky Butt Legacy Song (An Epic in Progress), The. Kofi Natambu. MoNo

Funky Football. Ruby C. Saunders. BlSi

Funnel. Anne Sexton. MoAmPo

Funnel-web spider, snake and octopus. Pelicans. Judith Wright. BMAP

Funny Folk. Robert Fisher. FuFo

Funny Grotto, The. Ho Xuan Huong, *Vietnamese*. AVP, *tr. by* Huỳnh Sanh Thông

Funny Man. Charles Bukowski. EC2

Funny Poem. Bill Knott. PBCAP

Funny thing is that he's reading a paper, The. The Sandwich Man. Ron Padgett. CoAmPo

Fur in see bi west Spayngne. The Land of Cokaygne. *Unknown*. NOIV

Furies, The. Liz Lochhead.
"Mad Meg on my mantelpiece." FaBoTC

Furious Gun, The. Sir Thomas Wyatt. PoE

Furious Versions. Li-Young Lee. PuP-14

Furious words and minerals which destroy, The. (LL) Two Armies. Stephen Spender. OBWP; OxBTC

Furnace, The. Thomas Kinsella. BiHa

Furnace Blast, The. John Greenleaf Whittier. CBCWP

Furnace fire lights up earth and sky, The. Li Po. SuSp, *tr. by* Irving Lo *Fr.* Songs of Ch'iu-p'u.

Furnace of Colors, The. Vernon Watkins. NYBP

Furnace tolls the knell of falling steam, The. Elegy Written in a Country Coal-Bin. Christopher Darlington Morley. OBAL

Furnished Room, The. James Merrill. NOBA

Furnished room beyond the stinging of, A. Good-bye for a Long Time. Roy Fuller. CBLP

Furniture. Phyllis Beauvais. NYBP

Furniture: humble, dependent. Judith Wright. *Fr.* Habitat. CBAP

'Furrow' is inexact: / no ship could be. On Water. Charles Tomlinson. OxBoS

Furry coat has the bear to wear, A. The Pig's Tail. Norman Ault. BoTP

Furry Home, The. J. M. Westrup. BoTP

Further, advancing further. (LL) For X. Louis MacNeice. BoLoP; EnLoPo

Further Advantages of Learning. Kenneth Rexroth. TAP

Further adventure of Skinny Marcus—. Lucilius, *Greek*. GrAn, *tr. by* Peter Porter

Further Adventures With You. C. D. Wright. LCAP-2

Further in Summer than the Birds. Emily Dickinson. APN-2; AmPP; NOBA; NoP-4; PoE
("Farther in the summer than the birds.") PoEL-5

Further Instructions. Ezra Pound. TwCP *Fr.* Lustra.

Further Language from Truthful James. Bret Harte. NOBL

Further Notice. Philip Whalen. PoM; VGW
("Buffalo / Like Yellowstone National Park, The.") (LL) BB

Further off is the measured force the word of the sea. Edouard J. Maunick, *French*. PBMAP *Fr.* Les Manèges de la Mer (1964).
("Never say no when I speak to you from afar. . . .") (LL) VCWP, *tr. by* Gerald Moore

Furtive blow, more like, A. There was I. Leda's Version. James Harrison. NIP-4

Fury. Lucille Clifton. LoL

Fury against the Moslems at Uhud. Hind bint Utba, *Arabic*. WPOW, *tr. by* Bridget Connelly *and* Deirdre Lashgari

Fury heard, while on *Cocytus' Brink, The. Tisiphone responds. Publius Papinius Statius, *Latin*. OBCVT, *tr. by* Alexander Pope

Fury of Aerial Bombardment, The. Richard Eberhart. CMoP; FYAP; FaBoMo; HeIP-4; HoPM; InPK-6; LiTM; MoP; NIP-4; NoAM; NoP-4; OBWP; PoWW; RB; TAP; TwCP; UnPo; VGW
("Distinguished the belt feed lever from the belt holding paw.") (LL) ColAP

Fury of Flowers and Worms, The. Anne Sexton. BoWoP

Fury of Overshoes. Anne Sexton. LCAP-2; NIP-4

Fury said to a mouse, That. A Long Tale. "Lewis Carroll." CBNP; NoAM; OBCoV

Fury this Friday broke through my wall, The. In Memory of a Friend. George Barker. OxBTC

Fury's Field. Cecil Bodker, *Danish*. PBWP, *tr. by* Nadia Christensen

Fus time dem kar me go a Bellevue was fi di dactar an de lanlard operate, De. Riddym Ravings (The Mad Woman's Poem). Jean Binta Breeze. NBrP

Fuscara, or the Bee Errant. John Cleveland. CBLP

Fuscus is free, and hath the world at will. In Fuscum. Sir John Davies. FaBoEE

Fuses I and II. Charles Baudelaire, *French*. PFTM, *tr. by* Norman Cameron

Fust Banjo, De. Irwin Russell. BLPA *Fr.* Christmas Night in the Quarters.

Fusty Christopher. (LL) To Christopher North. Tennyson. FaBoEE; PeLV

Futility. Wilfred Owen. APAD; CMoP; FaBoMo; GTBS-P; MoBrPo; NAEL-2; NSI; NoAM; NoP-4; OBWP; PeFWW; RB

Future, The. Angel González, *Spanish.* VCWP, *tr. by* Steven Ford Brown *and* Revuelta Gutierrez

Future, The. James Oppenheim. TrJP

Future. Vicki Viidikas. BMAP

Future ain't what it used to be, The. Pharaoh. Jane Kenyon. LoL

Future and the Ancestor, The. André Chedid, *French.* WPOW, *tr. by* Samuel Hazo *and* Mirène Ghossein

Future Conditional. Marilyn Hacker. CPO; DeD *Fr.* Love, Death and the Changing of the Seasons.

Future is for tomorrow, The. Anna Gréki, *French.* WPOW, *tr. by* Mildred P. Mortimer

Future is timid and wayward, The. Ruth Fainlight. CMAP

Future Peace and Glory of the Church, The. William Cowper. *See* Hymn 10.

Future Verdict, The. Ada Cambridge. NOBAu

Future Work. Fleur Adcock. DiPo

Futurism Wants to Transform the Variety Theater into a Theater of Amazement, Record-setting, and Body-madness. Filippo Tommaso Marinetti. PFTM, *tr. by* R. W. Flint *and* Arthur A. Coppotelli *Fr.* The Variety Theater Manifesto.

Fuzzy fellow, without feet, A. Emily Dickinson. TAP

Fuzzy-Wuzzy. Rudyard Kipling. MoBrPo

Fuzzy wuzzy, creepy crawly. Lillian Schulz Vanada. CTV

Fuzzy Wuzzy was a bear. *Unknown.* NTCP

Fwap! Alan Pizzarelli. HA

Fy Satyre fie, shall each mechanick slave. John Marston. PBRV *Fr.* The Scourge of Villanie.

Fyllr. *Unknown.* NBrP

G

G. B. Shaw wrote to Yeats: "P'raps it's mad of me." Limerick. W. A. Rathkey. PeLi

G / G / G / Gold Goldsmith's. . . . Grasshopper. J. D. McClatchy. APo

G. K. Chesterton. Humbert Wolfe. TrJP

G. K. Chesterton on His Birth. A. E. Housman. NBLV

G. M. B. Donald Davie. OxBC

G stands for goat and also. Goat. Kenneth Rexroth. *Fr.* A Bestiary. OBAL

Gaa-a-Muna, a Mountain Flower. Harold Littlebird. VoR

Gaberlunzie Man, The. *Unknown.* EnSB; OxBB; OxBS

"Gables are not burning, The." The Finnesburh Fragment. *Unknown, Anglo-Saxon.* ASW; OBWP, *tr. by* Kevin Crossley-Holland

Gabriel. Adrienne Rich. VGW

Gabrielle, the terrapin, whose tiny eyes. The Terrapin. Elizabeth Smither. PeNZ

Gabriel's Appearance. Abraham Cowley. NOSC *Fr.* Davideis.

Gabriel's Blues. Calvin Forbes. PoA; WeT

Gadflies swarm on the weary horse. On Mount Ching. Meng Chiao, *Chinese.* PLT, *tr. by* A. C. Graham

Gaelic is the conscience of our leaders. Michael Hartnett. CIP-2 *Fr.* A Farewell to English.

Gaelic Songs. Iain Crichton Smith. FaBoTC

Gaelic Stories. Iain Crichton Smith. FaBoTC

Gaeltacht. Pearse Hutchinson. BIrV; PBCIP

Gaeta from wool and weaving first began. In Gaetam. Thomas Bastard. FaBoEE

Gaffer Gray. Thomas Holcroft. NOEC; OxAEP-1

Gaffer in Love, A. Y Vân Tử', *Vietnamese.* AVP, *tr. by* Huỳnh Sanh Thông

Gaily bedight / A gallant knight. Eldorado. Edgar Allan Poe. APAD; APN-1; AWP; AmPP; CTV; ChAP; ColAP; HPC; FaBoBe; FaBoCh; LiLi; MeMAP; NCAP; NOBA; NOxBChV; NTP; NoP-4; OxBA; TAP

Gaily into Ruislip Gardens. Middlesex. John Betjeman. OxBTC

Gaily they grow, the quiet throng. Heather Flowers. Eliseus Williams, *Welsh.* OBWVE, *tr. by* Kenneth Hurlstone Jackson

Gain without gladness. Liadain. *Unknown.* WPOW, *tr. by* Frank O'Connor

Gal, I'm tellin you, I'm tired to true. The Lament of the Banana Man. Evan Jones. PBCV

Galactic Government Health Warning. Alpha-B375-Earth Visitors' Guide. . . Section. John Cunliffe. SpW

Galang dada / galang gwaan yaw sah. Reggae fi Dada. Linton Kwesi Johnson. NBrP; PBCV

Galataea. Callimachus, *Greek.*

"Or rather the sacred fish with the golden faces." HePo, *tr. by* Barbara Hughes Fowler

Galatians 6.14. Francis Quarles. ChIV-2

Galaxies. Alan Gould. NOBAu

Gale in April. Robinson Jeffers. MoAmPo

Gales. Anne Stevenson. Spl

Galilee Shore. Allen Ginsberg. ChIV-2; FTOS

("With the blue-dark dome old-starred at night, green boat-lights purring over.") FTOS

Gallant Château. Wallace Stevens. MoAmPo

Gallant foeman in the fight, A. Robert E. Lee. Julia Ward Howe. CBCWP

Gallant laird of Lamington, The. Katharine Jaffray. *Unknown.* ESPB

Gallant Ship, The. Sir Walter Scott. BoTP

Gallantry. Keith Douglas. NAEL-2; NoAM; OBWP

("(Air commented in a whisper, The).") (LL) NoP-4

Gallants attend, and hear a friend. The Battle of the Kegs. Francis Hopkinson. OBAL

Gallants, / If, as you say, you Love Varietie. Prologue. "Ephelia." KTR *Fr.* The Pair-Royal of Coxcombs.

Gallery, The. Andrew Marvell. ESCV; MeLP; NoP-4; PoE

("To crown her Head, and Bosome fill.") (LL) PBRV

Gallery of My Heart. King D. Kuka. VoR

Gallery Shepherds. Patricia Beer. OxBC

Galley, The. Petrarch. GBL; PoEL-1 *Fr.* Sonnets to Laura.

(Lover Compareth His State to a Ship in Perilous Storm Tossed on the Sea, The.) GBL; PoEL-1

Galley of Count Arnaldos, The. Henry Wadsworth Longfellow. OBEV

Galley-Slave, The. Rudyard Kipling. PeVV

Galliass, The. Walter De la Mare. FaBoTw

Gallio's Song. Rudyard Kipling. ChIV-2

Gallipoli. Sidney Walter Powell.

Song of Blood, A. NSI

Gallipoli. Mary Morison Webster. NSI

Gallon of gin and a flitch of pork, A. Obsequy for Dylan Thomas. James Keir Baxter. PeLV

Gallop a dreary dun. (LL) Master and Man. Mother Goose. OxNR; ReMoGo

Gallop apace, you fiery-footed steeds [*or* fierie footed steades]. Shakespeare. CBLP; EBEvV; GBL *Fr.* Romeo and Juliet.

Galloping around, north and south. T'ang Yin. CoBLCP, *tr. by* Jonathan Chaves *Fr.* Miscellaneous Feelings.

Galloping Cat, The. Stevie Smith. BrRo

Galloping collection of boards, The. Somewhere. Robert Creeley. NoAM

Gallow Hill. William J. Tait. OxBS

Gallows, The. Edward Thomas. GEA; InPS-3; MoBrPo; MoP; NoAM; SCGP; UnPo

Gallows in my garden, people say, The. A Ballade of Suicide. G. K. Chesterton. NBLV; OBCoV

Galoshes. Rhoda Warner Bacmeister. NTCP

Gal's Cry for a Dying Lover. Langston Hughes. NAAAL

Galveston with a seawall. Wasn't That a Mighty Storm? *Unknown.* AmFP

Galway is a blackguard place. Clonakilty. *Unknown.* FaBoEE

Galway Races. *Unknown.* OxBoLi

Galya, Mother, and My Daughter Anna. Yevgeny Borisovich Rein, *Russian.* TCRP, *tr. by* Bernard Meares

Gamble. Linda Hogan. HATNAP

Gamblers, The. Anthony Delius. PeSA

Gambler's life I do admire, du-da, du-da. *Unknown.* AmFP

Gambling. Vince Gotera. OpBo

Gambling. Royall Tyler. TAP

Gamboling Man, The. *Unknown.* AS

Game. Philip Booth. AFr

Game, The. Edvard Kocbek, *Slovene.* PoSu, *tr. by* Michael Scammell *and* Veno Taufer

Game after Supper. Margaret Atwood. FaBoWP; LCAP-2

Game at Salzburg, A. Randall Jarrell. NoAM

Game called kick the can, which used to last about a month, A. We Used to Play. Don Welch. Poetsp

Game of Chance, A. Howard Moss. PoA

Game of Chess, A. T. S. Eliot. SCV *Fr.* The Waste Land. AmPP; CMoP; FaBoMo; HAP; LiTM; MoAmPo; MoP; NAAL-2; NAEL-2; NAWM-2; NOBA; NOBE; NoAM; NoP-4; OAEL-2; OxAEP-2; OxBA; OxBTC; PoE; TAP; TFi; UnPo

Game of Chess, A. Phan chu Trinh, *Vietnamese.* AVP, *tr. by* Huỳnh Sanh Thông

Game of Consequences, A. Paul Dehn. NOBL

Game of Life, The. John Godfrey Saxe. BLPA

Game on the Fingers, A. *Unknown.* CBNP

Game Resumed. Richmond Lattimore. NYBP

Game was ended, and the noise at last had died, The. Football. Walt Mason. KaS

Gamecock. James Dickey. HoPM; UnPo

Gamekeeper of Lady Chatterley, The. Limerick. Gerry Hamill. PeLi

Games. Ory Bernstein, *Hebrew.* IP, *tr. by* Warren Bargad *and* Stanley F. Chyet

Games. Sandra McPherson. LCAP-2

Games. Vasco [*or* Vasko] Popa, *Serbo-Croatian.* RB, *tr. by* Anne Pennington

  Ashes. HSix, *tr. by* Charles Simic

  He. CBNP; PoSu

  ("Some bite off the others.") NNPT, *tr. by* Anne Pennington

  Hide-and-Seek. HSix, *tr. by* Charles Simic

  Hunter. HSix, *tr. by* Charles Simic

  Nail, The. PoSu

  Rose Thieves, The. HSix

  Seed, The. PoSu

Gammer Gurton's Needle, *sels.* William Stevenson *and* John Still.

  Back and Side Go Bare, Go Bare. HeIP-4; NAEL-1

  (Song of Ale, A.) SCGP

  Jolly Good Ale and Old. OBEV

Gampta, my little grey sister. The Desert Lark. Eugène Marias, *Afrikaans.* PeSA, *tr. by* Uys Krige *and* Jack Cope

Ganaderia. Ricardo Pau-Llosa. CMAP

Gane were but the winter cauld. Gone Were but the Winter Cold. Allan Cunningham. CH

Gang doun wi' a sang, gang doun. (LL) Song: "Whaur yon broken brig hings owre;." William Soutar. FaBoTC; OxBS

Gang-gang-suwole. Tongju Yi, *Korean.* CKP, *tr. by* Jaihiun Kim

Gang of labourers on the piled wet timber, A. Morning Work. D. H. Lawrence. MoBrPo

Gang wanted to give Oedipus Rex a going away present, The. Oedipus. Josephine Miles. SoSe-8; WPE

Ganga. Thomas Blackburn. MoBS

Ganges, The. Norman Dubie. LCAP-2

Gangrel Rymour and the Pairdon of Sanct Anne, The. Sydney Goodsir Smith, *after the French of* Tristan Corbiére.

  "But ae braithless note." OBVE

Gangrene. Philip Levine. VGW

Gangster's Death, The. Ishmael Reed. PoBA

Gap between the Sunday papers and lunch, The. (LL) Against Coupling. Fleur Adcock. CBLP; NALW

Gap in the Cedar, The. Roy Scheele. Poetsp

Gape, gape, gorlin'. Ex Vermibus. "Hugh MacDiarmid." CABP

Garage in Co. Cork, A. Derek Mahon. DiPo; PBCIP

Garage Sale. Karl Shapiro. Poetsp

Garage Sale as a Spiritual Exercise, The. Thomas M. Disch. GI

Garbage. A. R. Ammons. BAP-93

Garbage is bagged, deposited in the dump, and several, The. Little Cape Cod Landscape. Charles North. FTOS

Garbage went over the fantail, boiling into blue. Memories of Mess Duty and the War. Christopher Howell. CDa

Garbageman: the Man with the Orderly Mind. Gwendolyn Brooks. CAPP-1 *Fr.* A Catch of Shy Fish.

García Lorca. Louis Dudek. MoCV; NOBC

García Lorca Murdered in Granada. John Streeter Manifold. CBAP

García Lorca tasted. The Drinking Fountain. Robert Duncan. CLPP

Garden, The. Rae Armantrout. FTOS

Garden. Michael Bullock. OBGa

Garden, The. Abraham Cowley. OBGa

Garden. Hilda Doolittle. NoAM

  Heat. CMoP; HeIP-4; InPK-6; MoAmPo; OxBA; PiM; TAP; TRP; UnPo

Garden, The. Louise Glück. AmPA; HCAP; NAAL-2; NoP-4; VCAP

Garden, The. Debora Greger. GaP

Garden, The. Nicholas Grimald. GaP; OAEL-1

  ("Seed, leaf, flower, fruit, herb, bee, and tree, and more than I may sing.") (LL) OBGa

Garden, The. John Hollander. GaP

Garden. D. H. Lawrence. *See* Trees in the Garden.

Garden, A. Andrew Marvell. OBEV *Fr.* Upon Appleton House [To My Lord Fairfax]. FaBoPV; GeHe; SeCP

Garden, The, *see also* Hortus. Andrew Marvell. AWP; ClHu; ESCV; GeHe; HAP; ImPo; InPS-3; MeLP; NAEL-1; NIP-4; NOBE; NOSC; OAEL-1; PoE; PoEL-2; PoLF; PoRA; Poetr; SCGP; SeCP; TFi; TOF; TRP

  ("Be reckon'd but with herbs and flow'rs!") (LL) FSCP; PBRV

  ("Be reckoned but with herbs and flowers?") (LL) FMP; GaP; OBGa; PoPoPo

  (Thoughts in a Garden.) GTBS-P; OBEV

Garden, The. Bernadette Mayer. FTOS

Garden, The, *in imitation of* Cowley. Alexander Pope. GaP; OBGa

Garden, The. Ezra Pound. AWP; HeIP-4; MoAmPo; NIP-4; OxBSP; TwCP

  ("Will commit that indiscretion.") (LL) NoP-4; PoPoPo

Garden, The. Edwin Arlington Robinson. GaP

Garden, The. Vita Sackville-West. OBGa

Garden, The. James Shirley. BeJo; NOSC

  ("My self to die, and prove my own.") (LL) GaP; OBGa

Garden, The. Mark Strand. ColAP; NoAM

Garden, The. Joshua Sylvester. OBGa

Garden. Cecil Taylor. MoNo

Garden, The. Jones Very. APN-1; OxBA; PAR; TAP

Garden, The. Robert Penn Warren. GaP; PoA

Garden. Rosanna Warren. GaP

Garden, The. John Greenleaf Whittier. OBGa

Garden, The. Oscar Wilde. PoRA *Fr.* Impressions.

Garden Abstract. Hart Crane. GaP; MeMAP; OBGa

Garden and gardener He made. Carol. Thomas Kinsella. TIRV

Garden at St. John's, The. May Swenson. GaP

Garden by Moonlight, The. Amy Lowell. CPO; NMM-2

Garden By The Sea, A. William Morris. CH; EBEvV; NOBE; OAEL-2; OBNC; PoEL-5 *Fr.* The Life and Death of Jason.

  ("Anigh the murmuring of the sea.") (LL) GaP; LBC

  (Nymph's Song to Hylas, The.) OBEV

Garden Calendar. N. M. Bodecker. TLR

Garden called Gethsemane / In Picardy it was, The. Gethsemane [1914–18]. Rudyard Kipling. APAD; FaBoTw; GI; PeFWW; PoFWW

Garden did not bloom, The. Gethsemane A. D. Dolores Kendrick. FFC

Garden-Dream, A. Keats. GaP *Fr.* A Dream. OBNC *Fr.* The Fall of Hyperion. OAEL-2

Garden Fancies. Robert Browning.

  Flower's Name, The. CTC; GaP

  (Garden Fancies.) OBGa

  Sibrandus Schafnaburgensis. CTC; EBVV; OBGa

  ("Plague take all your pendants, say I!") OBGa

Garden flew round with the angel, The. The Pleasures of Merely Circulating. Wallace Stevens. OBAL

Garden God, The. Richard Eberhart. OBGa

Garden Hose, The. Beatrice Janosco. NTCP

Garden in a garden; a green spot, A. On Keats, 18 January, 1948 (Eve of St Agnes). Christina Rossetti. EPCY

Garden in September, The. Robert Bridges. GaP; OBGa

Garden in the middle of a hundred acres is half-covered with moss, The. Tune: "Sand of Silk-washing Stream." Wang An-shih, *Chinese.* SuSp, *tr. by* James J. Y. Liu

Garden inclosed is my sister, my spouse; a spring shut up, a fountain / sealed, A. The Song of Solomon. Bible, *O.T.* OBGa *Fr.* The Song of Solomon.

Garden is a loathsome thing, God wot, A. My Garden. P. R. Hines. UV

Garden is a lovesome thing, God wot!, A. My Garden. Thomas Edward Brown. EBEvV; InPK-6; OBEV; OBGa; PoLF; UV

Garden is a *lovesome* thing? What rot!, A. My Garden. J. A. Lindon. InPK-6

Garden is frightful! It drips, it listens, The. The Weeping Garden. Boris Pasternak, *Russian.* GaP, *tr. by* Eugene M. Kayden

Garden is not a place, A. A Doomed Garden. Octavio Paz, *Spanish.* GaP, *tr. by* Eliot Weinberger

Garden Living. Wu Wei-yeh, *Chinese.* CoBLCP, *tr. by* Jonathan Chaves

Garden Lore. Juliana Horatia Ewing. OxBChV

Garden. Nothing catches fire, The. (LL) The Public Garden. Robert Lowell. OBGa; PoRA; TAP

Garden of Adonis, The. Edmund Spenser. NOBE; PoEL-1 *Fr.* Wood Of Error. AEP

  ("Possesseth him, and of his sweetnesse takes her fill.") (LL) OBGa

  ("She brought her to her ioyous Paradize.") OBGa

  "In that same gardin all the goodly flowres." NOBE

Garden of Amour, The. Guillaume de Lorris *and* Jean de Meun. PoEL-1, *tr. by* Geoffrey Chaucer *Fr.* The Romance [*or* Romaunt] of the Rose.

  ("Garden *or* gardin was, by measuring, The.") OBGa, *tr. by* Chaucer

  ("That casten up full good savour.") (LL) OBGa, *tr. by* Chaucer

Garden of Appleton House, The ("When in the east the morning ray"). Andrew Marvell. NOBE *Fr.* Upon Appleton House [To My Lord Fairfax]. FaBoPV; GeHe; SeCP

Garden of Bermuda, The. Edmund Waller. GaP

Garden of Earthly Delights, The. Czeslaw Milosz, *Polish.*

Earth. ITG. *tr.* by Czeslaw Milosz *and* Robert Hass

Garden of Epicurus, The. George Meredith. GaP

Garden of Gethsemane, The. Boris Pasternak, *Russian*. GI, *tr. by* Nina Kossman

Garden of Joy, The. Isaac Rosenberg. GaP

Garden of Love, The. William Blake. APAD; AWP; EnLoPo; FHYEP; GBL; GLoP; GaP; HAP; NAEL-2; NoP-4; OBGa; OxAEP-2; PoE; PoPoPo; RB; Ro; SCGP; TFi; TOF; TRP *Fr.* Songs of Experience.

Garden of Old People, The. Miroslav Holub, *German*. CEEP, *tr. by* Stuart Friebert *and* Dana Hábová

Garden of Proserpina, The. Edmund Spenser. *Fr.* Wood Of Error. AEP

Garden of Proserpine, The. Swinburne. CABP; GaP; NoP-4; PeVV; TFi *Fr.* The Garden of Proserpine. AWP; BLPA; FaPoR; HAP; NAEL-2; NOBE; NOBVV; OBNC; PoE; PoEL-5; PoRA; SCV

"From too much love of living." IMW

Garden of Shadow, The. Ernest Christopher Dowson. OBNC

Garden of Ships, The. Douglas Stewart. CBAP

Garden of Shushan! Before the Feast of Shushan. Anne Spencer. BlSi; NAAAL

Garden of Situations, A. Jack Anderson. PoA

Garden of Song, The. Moses ibn Ezra, *Hebrew*. TOF, *tr. by* David Goldstein

Garden of the Gods, The. Thom Gunn. GaP

Garden of the Sexes, The. Jay Macpherson. GaP

Garden of Theophrastus, The. Peter Huchel, *German*. AF, *tr. by* Simko, Daniel

Garden of Writing, The. Nicolas Boileau-Despéaux, *French*. GaP, *tr. by* John Hollander

Garden Party. Sir Herbert Read. OBGa

Garden Poem. Ian Hamilton Finlay. OBGa

Garden saw I full of blosmy boughs, A. Love's Garden. Chaucer. GaP

Garden Seat, The. Angelina Weld Grimké. NMM 2

Garden Seat, The. Thomas Hardy. GaP; HAP; RB

Garden shut, a fountain sealed, A. Jay Macpherson. GaP

Garden Song, A. Austin Dobson. OBEV; OBGa; OBNC

Garden Song, A. George R. Sims. NOBVV; OBCoV; OBGa

Garden that recalls the past, A. In Winter. Saigyo. GaP, *tr. by* Watson, Burton *Fr.* Sixty-four Tanka.

Garden, The ("How vainly men themselves amaze"). Andrew Marvell. AWP; HAP; InPS-3; MeLP; NIP-4; NOBE; OAEL-1; PoEL-2; PoLF; PoRA; SeCP

"What wondrous life is this I lead!" CH

Garden was, by mesuring, The. The Garden of Amour. Guillaume de Lorris *and* Jean de Meun (d. 1305). PoEL-1, *tr. by* Geoffrey Chaucer *Fr.* The Romance [*or* Romaunt] of the Rose.

Garden we walked in, The. Green Grass and Yellow Balloons. Etheridge Knight. GT

Garden where he broods is like a riddle, The. The Wartburg, 1521–22. Timothy Steele. RA

Garden, Wilderness. Michael Hamburger. OBGa

Garden Window, The. Aaron Hill. OBGa

Garden Year, The. Sara Coleridge. ChAP; FaBoBe; OTCP

(Around the Year.) CTV

(Months, The.) OxBChV

Gardener, The. Robin Becker. CrSp

Gardener. Ralph Waldo Emerson. OxBA *Fr.* Quatrains.

Gardener, The. Robert Graves. GaP; OBGa

Gardener, The. Sidney Keyes. MoBrPo

Gardener, The. Walter Savage Landor. GaP

Gardener, The. Louis MacNeice. IIP *Fr.* Novelettes.

Gardener. Dom Moraes. OBGa

Gardener, The. Craig Raine. UV

Gardener. A. H. Snow. OBGa

Gardener, The. Rabindranath Tagore. OBMV

Gardener. Mark Van Doren. GaP

Gardener, The. Rowland Watkyns. NOSC

Gardener, The. John Hall Wheelock. NYBP

Gardener came running, The. Incident in a Rose Garden. Donald Justice. CRP

Gardener does not love to talk, The. Robert Louis Stevenson. GaP; OBGa

Gardener Janus Catches a Naiad. Dame Edith Sitwell. MoBrPo; OBGa

Gardener stands in his bower-door, The. *Unknown*. ESPB

Gardener to His God, The. Mona Van Duyn. GaP; RACG; TrCP; UnPo; WPE

Gardener wi' His Paidle; or, The Gardener's March, The. Robert Burns. OBGa

Gardeners. Douglas Dunn. OBGa

Gardeners, The. Christopher Reid. DiPo

Gardener's daughter, The. The Prophetic Child. Geoffrey O'Brien. PT

Gardener's Daughter, The. Tennyson. OBGa

Gardener's Preface, The. Allen Fisher. NBrP

Gardener's rule applies to youth and age, The. Adage. Henry James Byron. NBLV

Gardens. Neil Curry. OBGa

Gardens, The. Abbé Jacques de Lille. OBGa *Fr.* The Gardens.

Gardens, gardens, and we are gardeners. Gardeners. Douglas Dunn. OBGa

Garden's grillwork gate, The. Plainness. Jorge Luis Borges, *Spanish*. NYBP, *tr. by* Norman Thomas Di Giovanni

Gardens No Emblems. Donald Davie. GaP; LiTM; OAEL-2; OBGa

Garden of Alcinous, The, *see also* Alkinoos' Garden. Homer, *Greek*. GaP; OAEL-1; OBVE, *tr. by* Alexander Pope; OBVE, *tr. by* George Chapman *Fr.* Odyssey. NAWM-1, *tr. by* Robert Fitzgerald

Gardens of Proserpine, The. Turner Cassity. PoA

Gardens of Ravished Psyche. George Barker. OBGa

Gardens of the Villa D'Este, The. Anthony Hecht. ColAP; OBGa

Garden's quit with me: as yesterday, The. Joseph Beaumont. NOSC

("Paradise I planted see / On open Calvary, A.") (LL) OBGa

Gardens We Have Left. David Mura. OpBo

Gardin was, by measuring, The. Guillaume de Lorris *and* Jean de Meun (d. 1305). *See* The Garden of Amour.

Gardner of the World, The. (LL) Summer Sun. Robert Louis Stevenson. MoBrPo; PWR

Gare du Midi. W. H. Auden. OxBSP

Garfish. John Blight. BMAP

Gargoyle. Thomas Rabbitt. MT

Gargoyle. Carl Sandburg. MoP; NOBA; NoAM

Gargoyle. Robert B. Shaw. CRP

Garland, The. Vladimir Sokolov, *Russian*. TCRP, *tr. by* Albert C. Todd

Garland. *Unknown*. NBrP

Garland and the Girdle, The. Michelangelo Buonarroti, *Italian*. AWP, *tr. by* John Addington Symonds

Garland briefer than a girl's, The. (LL) To an Athlete Dying Young. A. E. Housman. CMoP; ChAP; HAP; HeIP-4; ImPo; InPK-6; LiTM; MoBrPo; MoP; NAEL-2; NIP-4; NoAM; NoP-4; PBMP; PFE; PoE; PoEL-5; PoRA; Poetr; SAGP; SCGP; SoSe-8; TFi; TRP; UnPo; WeW-3

Garland for a Propagandist. Ted Pauker. NOBL

Garland for Advancing Years, A. William Bell Scott. GSo

Garland for Heliodora, A. Meleager, *Greek*. AWP, *tr. by* "Christopher North"

Garland [*or* Garlande *or* Garlands] of Laurel[l], The. John Skelton.

Lullay, Lullay, Like a Child. SCGP

(Lullay, Lullay.) ImPo

To Maystres Jane Blenner-Haiset. AAS

To Mistress [*or* Maystres] Isabell Pennell. AAS; InPS-3; NOBE; NoSic; OBEV; OxBoLi; PoEL-1; SCGP; TTTS

(In Praise of Isabel Pennell.) CH

To Mistress [*or* Maystres] Margaret Hussey. AAS; EBEV; EnLoPo; HoPM; InPS-3; NAEL-1; NBLV; NOBE; NTP; NoSic; OAEL-1; OBEV; PeLV; PoE; PoEL-1; PoRA; SCGP; SCV; TFi

("Merry Margaret.") NoP-4

(Mistress Margaret Hussey.) FaBoCh

To Mistress Margery Wentworth. EBEV; EnLoPo; NOBE; OAEL-1; OBEV

Garland of Precepts, A. Phyllis McGinley. NBLV

Garland of roses, whether you come. Martial, *Latin*. FaBoEE, *tr. by* James Michie

Garland on the Wrist, A. Jaroslav Seifert, *Czech*. CEEP, *tr. by* Ewald Osers

Garlands fade that Spring so lately wove, The. Sonnet Written at the Close of Spring [*or* Elegiac Sonnet]. Charlotte Smith. ECWP

Garlands of fatted words are strung through the city. Silence. Miroslav Holub, *Czech*. PoSu, *tr. by* Ian *and* Jarmila Milner

Garlic. Jeanne Foster. CrSp

Garments of inattention, oh mere items. Teaching Swift to Young Ladies. William Dickey. PoA

Garnie, I wish I was a sea gull. A Poem by Garnie Braxton. James Wright. LiLi

Garnishing the Aviary. Margaret Danner. BPo *Fr.* Far from Africa: Four Poems. PoBA

Garrisons pent up in a little fort. Sonnet of Brotherhood. Ronald Allison Kells Mason. PeNZ

Gas and Hot Air. Morris Gilbert Bishop. OBAL

Gas fire, The. The Persian. Stevie Smith. FaBoWP

Gas flaring on the yellow platform; voices running up and down;. The Night-Ride. Kenneth Slessor. BMAP

Gas from a Burner. James Joyce.

"Ladies and gents, you are here assembled." IIP

Gas is good, The. Petit Guignol. Philip Hammial. BMAP
Gas-lamps abandoned by the night burn on. Baudelaire in Brussels.
Anthony Cronin. BIrV
Gas ring's hoarse exhaling wheeze, The. Twinings Orange Pekoe. Judith
Moffett. PoA
Gas Station, The. Charles Kenneth Williams. VCAP
Gas was on in the Institute, The. A Shropshire Lad. John Betjeman.
MoBS
Gasa, the aggressive one. The Praises of Field-marshal J. C. Smuts.
Nongejeni Zuma, *Zulu.* PeSAV, *tr. by* Harry C. Lugg
Gasbags. *Unknown.* NOBL
Gasco. Günter Grass, *German.* CLPP, *tr. by* Jerome Rothenberg
Gascoigne's Good-Morrow. George Gascoigne. AAS; NOCV; NoSic
("To see that joyful day.") (LL) CABP
Gascoigne's [*or* Gascoygnes] Good-Night. George Gascoigne. AAS;
NOCV; NoSic
Gascoigne's Lullaby [*or* Lullabie]. George Gascoigne. *See* The Lullaby [*or*
Lullabie] of a Lover.
Gascoigne's Memories. George Gascoigne.
"All were to[o] little for the merchant's [*or* merchauntes] hand[e]." AAS;
Son
"And every year a world my will did deem." Son
"Before mine eye to feed my greedy will." Son
"For why? The gains doth seldom quit the change." Son
No Hast But Good. NoSic
"No haste but good, where wisdome makes the waye." AAS; Son
"To prink me up and make me higher placed." Son
Gascoigne's Woodmanship. George Gascoigne. AAS; NoSic; PoEL-1
(Gascoignes wodmanship.) PBRV
("Tedious tale in rhyme, but little reason, A.") (LL) CABP
("Tedious tale in rime, but little reason. / *Haud ictus sapio.* A.") (LL)
PBRV
Gashed by the slashings of a harsh season. The Vertex. Yuksa Yi,
Korean. CKP, *tr. by* Jaihiun Kim
Gashed, from her long immobility on the sea-bed. The Arrival of the
Titanic. William Dickey. BAP-96
Gasholders, russet among fields. Mildams, marpools. Geoffrey Hill. HAP;
NoAM *Fr.* Mercian Hymns.
("Gasholders, russet among fields. Milldams, marlpools.") NoP-4
("In his private derelict sandlorry / named *Albion.*") (LL) NoP-4
Gaslight. Kwanggun Kim, *Korean.* CKP, *tr. by* Jaihiun Kim
Gasoline. Tanka. Kitahara Hakushū, *Japanese.* MJT, *tr. by* Makoto Ueda
Gasp sounded, The. A Poem. Mongane Wally Serote. PeSAV
Gasparillo Remembered. Anson Gonzalez. HCP
Gassing the woodchucks didn't turn out right. Woodchucks. Maxine W.
Kumin. HoPM; NIP-4; Poetr
Gate, The. Edwin Muir. CMoP; LiTM
Gate at the End of Things, The. *Unknown.* BLPA
Gate Lodge. Richard Murphy. PBCIP
Gate, red lights revolving in the leaves. (LL) First Party at Ken Kesey's
with Hell's Angels. Allen Ginsberg. CoAmPo; PmAP; TRP
Gate Tower of Ch'i-an City, The. Tu Mu, *Chinese.* PLT, *tr. by* A. C.
Graham
Gate was open, The; the fence under the aspens, fallen. Mountain Corral.
Helen Sorrells. WPE
Gatemouth Moore. *See* II. Song of the Reverend Gatemouth Moore. Etheridge
Knight. BkSV *Fr.* Three Songs.
Gateposts. Medbh McGuckian. BiHa; PBCIP
Gates clanged and they walked you into jail, The. The Conscientious
Objector. Karl Shapiro. OxBA
Gates fly open with a pretty sound, The. Under the Hill. Daryl Hine.
MoCV
Gates of Hell, The. Dante. *Fr.* Inferno. NAWM-1, *tr. by* John Ciardi *Fr.*
Divina Commedia.
Gates of Paradise, The. William Blake. PoEL-4
Epilogue: "Truly my Satan thou art but a dunce." HAP; ImPo; OAEL-2;
OBNC; PeECV; PoE; WeW-3
(To the Accuser Who Is the God of This World.) FHYEP; OxBSP;
SCGP
Gate's Open, The. John Blight. CBAP
Gates to England, The. Marjorie Wilson. BoTP
Gateway, The. Alec Derwent Hope. BoLoP
Gather for festival. Hilda Doolittle. MoAmPo *Fr.* Songs from Cyprus.
Gather into the mind. First of August. A. J. Seymour. PBCV
Gather noble death. Cumae. Merrill Moore. FuPo
Gather or take fierce degree. A Short Poem for Armistice Day. Sir Herbert
Read. PeFWW

Gather round while I sing you of Wernher von Braun. Wernher von Braun.
Tom Lehrer. OBCoV
Gather the Rose. Edmund Spenser. *See* Song of Bliss.
Gather the sacred dust. Lines. Abram Joseph Ryan. APN-2
Gather while you may. Rose. Kathleen Jessie Raine. WPE
Gather ye bank-notes while ye may. Election Time. *Unknown.* UV
Gather, ye brave sons of Ukadi Awaka! Moon Song. Chuba Nweke. PBA
Gather Ye Rosebuds. Laurence Fowler. BXAP
Gather ye rosebuds while ye may. On Lady A———. Nicolas Bentley.
OBCoV
Gather ye rosebuds while ye may. To [the] Virgins, to Make Much of
Time. Robert Herrick. AWP; BLPA; BeJo; BoLoP; CaPo; CavPo;
ClHu; EBEvV; EnLoPo; GBL; GLoP; GTBS-P; HAP; HeIP-4; ImPo;
InPK-6; InPS-3; LoP; NAEL-1; NBLV; NIP-4; NOBE; NOSC; NoP-4;
OAEL-1; OBEV; OxAEP-1; PBMP; PFE; PoE; PoEL-3; PoPoPo; Poetr;
SAGP; SCGP; SCV; SeCP; SoSe-8; TFi; UV
Gathered at the River. Denise Levertov. CrSp
Gathered in inter-admiration. When the Five Prominent Poets. Josephine
Jacobsen. NMM-2; TAP
Gathering, The. Edwin John Pratt. MoCV *Fr.* Towards the Last Spike.
Gathering, The. Sir Walter Scott. OBNC *Fr.* The Lady of the Lake.
Gathering fuel in vacant lots. T. S. Eliot. *See* Preludes.
Gathering in the Days. Gareth Owen. NOxBChV
Gathering Leaves. Stanley Cook. AYFP
Gathering Leaves. Robert Frost. RB; VGW
Gathering Lotus. Chu Ch'ing-yü, *Chinese.* SuSp, *tr. by* Irving Y. Lo
Gathering Lotus with Singing Girls. Mo Shih-lung, *Chinese.* CoBLCP, *tr.*
by Jonathan Chaves
Gathering Mushrooms. Paul Muldoon. BiHa; CIP-2; NoP-4; PBCIP; PNI
Gathering of the Grand Army, The. Charlotte L. Forten Grimke. AAP
Gathering Place, The. Alan Alexander. NOBAu
Gathering the Bones Together. Gregory Orr. AmPA; Poetsp; WeT
Gathering tomatoes has no art. Picking Pole Beans. Marge Piercy. *Fr.* Six
Underrated Pleasures. EC2
Gaudy painted hangings, fringed by many a tatter. The Dancing Girl. John
Barlas. ADE
Gauge. Langston Hughes. APSN
Gauguin. Derek Walcott. NoAM *Fr.* Midsummer.
Gauguin's White Horse. Vicki Hearne. GS
Gauley Bridge is a good town for Negroes, they let us stand. George
Robinson: Blues. Muriel Rukeyser. NNaP; RACG
Gauls Sacrifice, The. Charles Montague Doughty. FaBoTw *Fr.* The Dawn
in Britain.
Gaunt in gloom. Nightpiece. James Joyce. PoA
Gaunt man, Abraham Lincoln, woke one morning, The. Stephen Vincent
Benét. *See* John Brown's Prayer.
Gaunt thing, The. Babylon Revisited. Imamu Amiri Baraka. BPo; MoP;
NoAM
Gauze. Rising was as hard as having died. (LL) Lazarus. Agnes Nemes
Nagy, *Hungarian.* PoSu, *tr. by* Frederic Will
Gave back Endymion in a dream-like tale. (LL) Sonnet Written in Keats's
Endymion. Thomas Hood. EPCY; Ro
Gave me things I. Swallow the Lake. Clarence Major. FTOS; GT;
NAAAL; PmAP; PoBA; WeT
Gave proof through the night. Poem to My Sister, Ethel Ennis, Who Sang
"The Star-spangled Banner" at the Second Inauguration of Richard
Milhous Nixon. June Jordan. TAP
Gawain and the Lady of the Castle. *Unknown.* EBEV *Fr.* Sir Gawain and
the Green Knight. OAEL-1, *tr. by* Brian Stone
Gawayn spurred on, and he picked out a path. Sir Gawayn Goes to Receive
His Return Blow from the Green Knight. *Unknown.* *Fr.* Sir Gawain
and the Green Knight. OAEL-1, *tr. by* Brian Stone
Gay, The. "Æ." OBMV
Gay blade on the gentle hedgerow. Daffodil. Waldo Williams, *Welsh.*
OBWVE, *tr. by* Gwyn Jones
Gay citizen, myself, and thoughtful friend. Allen Tate. *Fr.* More Sonnets at
Christmas. LiTM
Gay colors flow. Miyoko Goto, *Japanese.* WPJ, *tr. by* Kenneth Rexroth
and Ikuko Atsumi
Gay full story is authentic verve fabulous jay gull stork. Bernadette Mayer.
PmAP
Gay, Ghastly, Holiday! (LL) 'Tis so appalling—it exhilirates. Emily
Dickinson. NCAP; PoE
Gay go up and gay go down. The Bells of London. *Unknown.* BoTP;
CBNP; LB; OxBoLi; OxNR; PeLV; PoRA
Gay Goshawk [*or* Goss-Hawk], The. Anna Gordon Brown. ESPB; OxBB;
WPE
Gay little Girl-of-the-Diving-Tank. At the Carnival. Anne Spencer. BlSi;
NAAAL

Gay occident of saffron hue, The. Foam's Frail Power. Joseph Mallord William Turner. OxBoS

Gay Old Hag, The. *Unknown.* BIrV

Gay Psalm from Fort Valley, A. Louie Crew. GLP

Gay Robin Is Seen No More. Robert Bridges. BoTP

Gay soccer spectator from Wix, A. Limerick. Cyril Mountjoy. PeLi

Gay summer's bliss, good-bye! Dietmar von Aist [*or* Eist], *German.* GePo, *tr. by* J. W. Thomas

Gaze at the world—a tangled game of chess. Stepping Out of the World. *Unknown, Vietnamese.* AVP, *tr. by* Huỳnh Sanh Thông

Gaze North-east. *Unknown, Irish.* BIrV, *tr. by* John Montague

Gaze not on Swans, in whose soft breast. On His Mistress. Henry Noel *and* William Strode. PoEL-2

Gaze not on thy beauties pride. Song: Good Counsel to a Young Maid. Thomas Carew. CaPo

Gaze not upon my outside, friend. Apple Dumplings. Mary E. Tucker. CBWP-1

Gazelle, The. Rilke, *German.* APo, *tr. by* Stephen Mitchell

Gazelle calf, O my children, The. D. H. Lawrence. OxBTC; RB

Gazelle-girl / gazelle. King Solomon Vistas. Ian Wedde. PeNZ

Gazelle I send you to the wolves not in the wood they're. Amir Gilbo'a, *Hebrew.* IP, *tr. by* Warren Bargad *and* Stanley F. Chyet

Gazelles, The. Thomas Sturge Moore. OBMV

Gazing and gazing in the glass. A Lesson for Beautiful Women. Alastair Reid. FaBoTC

Gazing as I climbed a high peak. Han Yü. PLT, *tr. by* A. C. Graham *Fr.* The South Mountains.

Gazing at Ch'ang-po Mountain. Li K'ai-hsien, *Chinese.* CoBLCP, *tr. by* Jonathan Chaves

Gazing thro' her chamber window. Reflection. Christina Rossetti. VWP

Gazing upon him now, severe and dead. Sonnet 17. Edna St. Vincent Millay. NMM-2 *Fr.* Sonnets from an Ungrafted Tree. NALW

Gazing upwards. Tanka. Tawara Machi, *Japanese.* MJT, *tr. by* Makoto Ueda

Gazing west—the isles of paradise. Waiting for the Ferry at Inchŏn. Liu E, *Chinese.* CoBLCP, *tr. by* Jonathan Chaves

Geat race then reared up for him, The. Beowulf's Funeral. *Unknown.* EEP, *tr. by* Michael Alexander *Fr.* Beowulf.

Geate A-Vallen To, The. William Barnes. EnVR

Gebir. Walter Savage Landor.
  "Now to Aurora, borne by dappled steeds." NOBRP
  Shepherd and the Nymph, The. OBNC
  "Sleepless, with pleasure and expiring fears." NOBRP

Gebit, gebit, gebit, gebit. *Unknown.* CBNP

Gee, but it's hard to love someone, when that someone don't love you. Down-Hearted Blues. Albert Hunter *and* Louie Austin. NAAAL

Gee i like to think of dead it means nearer because deeper firmer. E. E. Cummings. HoPM

Gee, Officer Krupke. Stephen Sondheim. OBAL

Gee up, Neddy, to the fair. *Unknown.* OxNR

Geese. Mark Cox. NAmP90

Geese, The. Jorie Graham. HCAP

Geese Blood. Barbara Guest. FTOS

Geese Gone Beyond. Gary Snyder. NoAM

Geese have gone, The. Cor Van den Heuvel. HA

Geese in the pond are drifting, five. Wandsworth Common. David Bromwich. PoA

Gehazi. Rudyard Kipling. FaBoPV

Geist's Grave. Matthew Arnold. NOBVV

Gellia nere mourns her fathers losse. De Gellia. Martial, *Latin.* OBCVT, *tr. by* R. Fletcher

Gem-like stars, The. Midnight. Henrietta Cordelia Ray. *Fr.* Idyl. CBWP-3

Gem of the crimson-colour'd Even. To the Evening Star. Thomas Campbell. GTBS-P; OBNC

Gemini Castor and his twin-starred Castor. Catullus. *See* The Yacht.

Gems and jewels let them heap. In a Garret. Herman Melville. OBAL

Gems of dew wilt and wound the maple trees in the wood. Autumn Meditation. Tu Fu, *Chinese.* PLT, *tr. by* A. C. Graham

Gemwood. Marvin Bell. CMAP

Genau'r Glyn, Tywyn, each day from these to Rhys's halls. Ode to Rhys ap Maredudd of Tywyn. Dafydd Nanmor, *Welsh.* OBWVE, *tr. by* H. Idris Bell

Gendarme came, The. Turn Your Eyes Away. Ruth Stone. NAmP90

Gene sat on a rock, dangling our map. The Route of the Táin. Thomas Kinsella. PBCIP

Genealogical Reflection. Ogden Nash. OBAL

Genealogy. Joan Larkin. LoHo

Genealogy. Eléni Vakaló, *Modern Greek.* PBWP, *tr. by* Paul Merchant

Geneology. Bob Kaufman. NBV

General, The. G. K. Menzies. NSI

General, The. Siegfried Sassoon. CMoP; LiTM; NAEL-2; NoAM; NoP-4; OBWP; OxBSP; OxBTC; OxBoLi; PoE; PoFWW

General B. F. Butler. Ambrose Bierce. CBCWP

General Communion, A. Alice Thompson Meynell. NOCV; WPE

General conquers Russia, The. Honest with Oneself. "Don Aminado," *Russian.* TCRP, *tr. by* Albert C. Todd

General Description of Men and Things in Cape Town, A. Frederic Brooks. PeSAV

General Description of the West Indian Islands, A. John Singleton. PBCV

General Elliott, The. Robert Graves. PeLV

General Grant—the Hero of the War. George Moses Horton. AAP; CBCWP

General inspecting the trenches, The. Sir Alan Patrick Herbert. NSI; PoWW

General John Cabell Breckinridge. Jill Breckinridge. CBCWP *Fr.* Civil Blood.

General Matthei Drives Home through Santiago. Stephen Dobyns. CMAP

General once lived named de Gaulle, A. Limerick. Paul Bristow. PeLi

General Prologue, The. Chaucer. FHYEP; NAEL-1; NAWM-1; OAEL-1; PoE *Fr.* The Canterbury Tales.
  ("As soon as April pierces to the root.") NAWM-1
  ("Began to tell his tale, as you shall hear.") (LL) NAWM-1
  ("His tale anoon, and saide as ye maye heere.") (LL) NAEL-1
  Canterbury Tales, The. SAGP, *tr. by* Burns, Christopher
    ("Clerk ther was of Oxenford also, A.")
    (Seven Pilgrims: A Clerk.)
  ("His tale anoon, and saide as ye maye heere.") (LL) NoP-4
  ("Whan that Aprill with his shoures soote.") CABP
  ("When the sweet showers of April fall and shoot.") SCV, *ll.* 1–42, *mod. vers. by* Nevill Coghill
  Madame Eglantine. NOBE
  "Marchant was ther with a forked berd, A." CTC
  "Sergeant of the Lawe, war and wys, A." CTC
  "Somonour was ther with us in that place, A." OBCoV
  "This Pardoner had hair as yellow as wax." SCV

General Review of the Sex Situation. Dorothy Parker. NAAL-2

General Robert Smalls. Josephine D. Henderson Heard. CBWP-4

General Secretary's feet whispered over the red carpet, The. Anteroom: Geneva. Denis Devlin. CIP-2

General Store. Rachel Lyman Field. ChAP

General, there's a battle / between your orders and my songs. Song of the Juggler. Herberto Padilla, *Spanish.* AF, *tr. by* Alastair Reid

General Truths. David Avidan, *Hebrew.* IP, *tr. by* Bargad, Warren and Stanley Chyet *Fr.* Samson, Our Hero. IP, *tr. by* Warren Bargad *and* Stanley F. Chyet

General will be shot in the face, The. A Respect for Law and Order. John Hughes. PNI

General William Booth Enters into Heaven. Nicholas Vachel Lindsay. AmPP; CMoP; ChIV-2; ImPo; LiTM; MeMAP; MoAmPo; NOBA; OxBA; PoA; PoE; TAP
  ("(Bass drum beaten loudly).") ColAP

General wonder in our land. *Unknown.* NOIV

Generalities. Robert Conquest. OxBC

Generation. Rae Armantrout. FTOS

Generation, A. Gu Cheng, *Chinese.* VCWP, *tr. by* Sam Hamill

Generation. Audre Lorde. NBV; Poetr

Generation Gap, The. Ruby C. Saunders. BISi

Generation of the Seeds, or the Origin of Corn, The. *Unknown, Zuni.*
  "Lo! ye children of men and the Mother." APN-2, *tr. by* Frank Hamilton Cushing

Generations. Ivor Gurney. NTP

Generations 1. Sam Cornish. GT

Generations 2. Sam Cornish. GT

Generations of the virgin are tattooed on her unblemished belly, The. Poem of any Virgin. Jorge de Lima, *Portuguese.* PFTM, *tr. by* Dudley Poore

Generations unfold from our faces. Bones and Drums. Ron Welburn. SeSe

Generic Elbows. Bernadette Mayer. FTOS

"Generosity of her love provides, The." The Grand Guignols of Love. Michael Benedikt. AmPA

Genes confessing. (LL) The Weakness. Toi Derricotte. GT; LTA

Genesis. Bible, *O.T.* OBGa *Fr.* Genesis.
  "And God saw that the wickedness of man was great." NAWM-1
  "And Joseph was brought down to Egypt." NAWM-1
  "And Noah was six hundred years old when the flood of waters." NAWM-1

And the Lord God planted a garden eastward in Eden. OAEL-1

"And the whole earth was of one language, and of one speech." NAWM-1

And there came two angels to Sodom at even. HoPM

First Murderer, The. OxBoV

"In the beginning God created the heaven and the earth." NAWM-1

"Joseph, being seventeen years old, was feeding the flock with his brethren." NAWM-1

"Now the serpent was more subtil than any beast of the field." OxBoV

"See, the smelle of my sone is as the smell of a feld." OBVE, *tr. by* William Tyndale

Genesis. Caedmon, *Anglo-Saxon.*

  Noah's Flood. AnOE, *tr. by* C. W. Kennedy

  Temptation and Fall of Man, The. AnOE, *tr. by* C. W. Kennedy

Genesis. Anghel Dumbrveanu, *Romanian.* CEEP, *tr. by* Adam J. Sorkin *and* Irina Grigorescu Pan

Genesis. Brian Higgins. FaBoTw

Genesis. Geoffrey Hill. ChIV-1; HAP; OAEL-2; OxBC; PeECV; TOF

Genesis. Evan Jones. PBCV

Genesis. Theodore Roethke. KSG

Genesis. K. Satchidanandan, *Malayalam.* OMIP, *tr. by* K. Satchidanandan

Genesis. Delmore Schwartz.

  You Are a Jew! TrJP

Genesis. Jules Alan Wein. TrJP

Genesis of Butterflies, The. Victor Hugo, *French.* AWP, *tr. by* Andrew Lang

Genesis XXIV. Arthur Hugh Clough. ChIV-1

  ("And Isaac brought her / to his mother's tent.") (LL) KSG

  ("Who is this Man / that walketh in the field.") KSG

Genetics. Richard Harteis. CMAP

Geneva. Alastair Reid. NYBP

Geneva was the wild one. The Ballad of Aunt Geneva. Marilyn Nelson Waniek. FFC; GT; RA

Genial poets, pink-faced. Goodbye to Tolerance. Denise Levertov. NoAM

Genie in the Jar, The. Nikki Giovanni. SeSe

Genie's Prayer Under the Kitchen Sink. Rita Dove. RACG

Genitalia. George Tysh. PT

Genitals of woods, The. Mikajo Yagi, *Japanese.* WPJ, *tr. by* Kenneth Rexroth *and* Ikuko Atsumi

Genius, The. Leonard Cohen. MoCV

Genius, *limerick.* R. J. P. Hewison. PeLi

Genius. Philip Levine. NoAM

Genius, The. Archibald MacLeish. MeMAP

Genius Child. Langston Hughes. PoPoPo

Genius is power. Adah Isaacs Menken. CBWP-1

Genius Loci. Margaret Louisa Woods. OBEV

Genius, or Muse, whate'er thou art! whose thrill. Robert Merry. NOBRP *Fr.* The Laurel of Liberty. A Poem.

Genius, technique—you'd swear the pair unsuited. Nature and Art. Goethe, *German.* STV, *tr. by* John Frederick Nims

Genius, that power which dazzles mortal eyes. Success. C. C. Cameron. PoToHe

Genius was 81, The. The Cutting Prow. Edward Sanders. PmAP

Geniuses of countless nations. Reprise. Ogden Nash. OxBM

Genoa. Dino Campana, *Italian.* PFTM, *tr. by* Charles Wright

Gent, Nugget, Swank, and *Dude.* Thirteen. Ronald Wallace. PBCAP

Genteel in personage, / Conduct and equipage. The Maid's Husband. Henry Carey. ECEV

Gentian weaves her fringes, The. Emily Dickinson. PoRA

Gentile or Hebrew or simply a man. Luke XXIII. Jorge Luis Borges, *Spanish.* GI, *tr. by* David Curzon

Gentilesse. Chaucer. AWP; NAEL-1; OAEL-1

Gentle Anarchist, The. Brunton Stephens. NOBAu

Gentle and smiling as before. The Wheel. Robert Earl Hayden. BPo

Gentle Annie, willow wind, the West, A. Four Winds. Hal Porter. NOBAu

Gentle as a maiden's dream. The Snow Storm. Mary Weston Fordham. CBWP-2

Gentle as Moon on Water. Yona Wallach, *Hebrew.* IP, *tr. by* Warren Bargad *and* Stanley F. Chyet

Gentle at last, and as clean as ever. Grandfather in the Old Men's Home. W. S. Merwin. CoAmPo; LiTM; SAGP

Gentle breeze has died down, The. To the Tune "Spring at Wu Ling." Li Ch'ing-chao, *Chinese.* OHMPC, *tr. by* Kenneth Rexroth

Gentle breeze, morning dew. I Wake Up Alone. Li Shang-yin, *Chinese.* OHMPC, *tr. by* Kenneth Rexroth

Gentle breeze rustles through reeds and rushes, A. In a boat, Getting Up at Night. Su Shih, *Chinese.* ChiPo; SuSp, *tr. by* Irving Y. Lo

Gentle Check, The. Joseph Beaumont. NOSC

Gentle, cheerful ticking of a clock, The. Quiet Days. Mildred T. Mey. PoToHe

Gentle Christ? (LL) Marban, a Hermit Speaks. *Unknown, Irish.* BIrV; CIP-2, *tr. by* Michael Hartnett

Gentle Communion. Pat Mora. NIP-4

Gentle East wind is blowing, A. On the Siu Cheng Road. Su Tung-p'o, *Chinese.* OHPC, *tr. by* Kenneth Rexroth

Gentle Echo on Woman, A. Jonathan Swift. NBLV

Gentle footsteps on the sand. The Crows. Maria Valli. CBAP

Gentle hands that never weary. Lines to Mother. Rose M. Stein. PWR

Gentle Heart, A: Two. Judith Johnson Sherwin. BoWoP

Gentle hunter. Leopard. *Unknown. Fr.* Hunter Poems of the Yoruba. RB, *tr. by* Ulli Beier

Gentle Jesus meek and mild. Mrs. William H. Dietz. CTV

Gentle Jesus Meek and Mild. Charles Wesley. OxBChV

Gentle knight was pricking on the plaine, A. Edmund Spenser. EBEV; FHYEP; NAEL-1; OAEL-1; Poetr *Fr.* Wood Of Error. AEP

Gentle Locke sits down to write his famous treatise. At Work. Artur Miedzyrzecki, *Polish.* PoSu, *tr. by* Artur Miedzyrzecki *and* John Batki

Gentle lords and ladies gay. (LL) Hunting Song. Sir Walter Scott. GTBS-P; SCGP

Gentle Mary, noble maiden, give us help! Prayer to the Virgin. Saint Columcille, *Irish.* TIRV, *tr. by* Kuno Meyer *and* John Strachan

Gentle of hand, the Dean of St. Patrick's guided. A Sermon on Swift. Austin Clarke. BIrV

Gentle River, Gentle River. *Unknown, Spanish.* AWP, *tr. by* Thomas Percy

Gentle rodent in its cage. *Unknown.* PeP

Gentle Shepherd, The. Allan Ramsay.

  Wawking of the Fauld, The. SCGP

  (Peggy.) OBEV

Gentle slopes are green to remind you, The. The Five Unmistakable Marks. David Jones. NAEL-2 *Fr.* In Parenthesis.

Gentle squire would gladly entertain, A. Joseph Hall. NoSic *Fr.* Virgidemiarum.

Gentle thought there is will often start, A. Dante. AWP *Fr.* La Vita Nuova.

Gentle wind that waves, The. Kitty and I. W. H. Davies. CBLP

Gentle Wind [fans the calm night], A. Fu Hsüan, *Chinese.* AWP; ChiP, *tr. by* Arthur Waley

Gentle Word, A. *Unknown.* PoToHe

Gentle youth, forbear. Hero Feels the Shaft of Love. Marlowe. GBL *Fr.* Hero and Leander. AAS

Gentleman, The. Menahem ben Judah Lonzano, *Hebrew.* TrJP, *tr. by* A. B. Rhine

Gentleman Aged Five before the Mirror. John Wain. PFE

Gentleman cam oure the sea, A. The Cruel Brother. *Unknown.* ESPB

Gentleman in hunting rode astray, A. The Beggar Woman. William King. ECEV; NOEC

Gentleman, most wretched in his lot, A. Reformation. Anne Finch, Countess of Winchilsea. ECWP

Gentleman's Study, in Answer to The Lady's Dressing-Room, The. "Miss W——." ECWP

Gentlemen. Geoffrey Taylor. FaBoEE

Gentlemen, as we take our seats. The Rehearsal. Horace Gregory. VGW

"Gentlemen, look on this wonder." The Adhesive Autopsy of Walt Whitman. Jonathan Williams. PoM

Gentlemen-Rankers. Rudyard Kipling. NOBVV

Gentlemen, / the situation is tragic. State of the Union. Aimé Césaire, *French.* NegPo, *tr. by* Denis Kelly

Gentlemen who have got to be classics and are now old, The. Letter to the Academy. Langston Hughes. AF

Gentleness of the slant October light, The. Where It Ends. William Bronk. APSN

Gentlest air, thou breath of lovers. A Sigh. Anne Finch. ECWP

Gentlest fair, mourn, mourn no moe. (LL) Weep No More. John Fletcher. CH; OBEV; OxAEP-1

Gentlest of women, put your weapons by. Lay Your Arms Aside. Pierce Ferriter, *Irish.* BIrV, *tr. by* Eiléan Ní Chuilleanáin

Gentlewoman of the dealing trade, A. Epigram 29. Samuel Rowlands. NOSC

Gently about this tomb wind gently O Ivy. At the Tomb of Sophokles. Simmias [*or* Simias] of Rhodes, *Greek.* GrAn, *tr. by* Dudley Fitts

Gently dip: but not too deepe. The Voice from the Well [of Life Speaks to the Maiden]. George Peele. InPS-3; NOBE; NoSic; PoEL-2; RB *Fr.* The Old Wives' [*or* Wife's] Tale.

Gently, gently prithee, time. *Unknown.* NOSC

Gently gripped by the. Rilke. GaP, *tr. by* Snow, Edward *Fr.* The Parks.

Gently I stir a white feather fan. In the Mountains on a Summer Day. Li Po, *Chinese*. AWP; ChiP, *tr. by* Arthur Waley

Gently I took that which ungently came. Forbearance. Coleridge. ChIV-2

Gently I wave the visible world away. The Absinthe-Drinker. Arthur Symons. FaBoTw; NOBVV

Gently shirred. Rita Dove. *See* The Event.

Gently, so as not to rouse / His skinny girl. Lucilius, *Greek*. GrAn, *tr. by* Alistair Elliot

Gently stroke a wound. Joyce Mansour, *French*. MFP, *tr. by* Martin Sorrell

Gently, the ocean waves. Sappho. Marie-Madeleine, *German*. CPO, *tr. by* Lillian Faderman, Brigitte Eriksson *and* Frankie Hucklenbroich

Gently to hear, kindly to judge, our play. (LL) A Muse of Fire. Shakespeare. OxAEP-1; SCV

Genuine Poem, Found on a Blackboard in a Bowling Alley in Story City, Iowa. Ted Kooser. KaS

Genuine, you are interested in poetry. (LL) Poetry. Marianne Moore. AmPP; BoWoP; CMoP; ColAP; FaBoWP; HAP; HeIP-4; ImGa; ImPo; LiTM; MoAmPo; MoP; NAAL-2; NALW; NIP-4; NOBA; NoAM; NoP-4; OxBA; PoE; PoPoPo; Poetr; TAP; TFi; UnPo

Geocentric. Pattiann Rogers. NAmP90

Geode, the troll's melon. James Merrill. HCAP *Fr.* In Nine Sleep Valley.

Geographers, The. Karl Shapiro. OxBA

Geography. G. K. Chesterton. OBSV *Fr.* Songs of Education.

Geography. Michael Dransfield.

"In the forest, in unexplored." CBAP

"Sky ceases. There is only." CBAP

Geography. Kenneth Koch. NoAM

Geography: a Song. Howard Moss. OBCoV

Geography Lesson. Carol Rumens. FaBoWP

Geography of Lunch, A. Mary Jo Schimelpfenig. IFJA

Geological Hymn. Joseph Ceravolo. PmAP

Geologist and Millions of Years, A. Xuân Diệu, *Vietnamese*. AVP, *tr. by* Huỳnh Sanh Thông

Geometrical Place. Günter Eich, *German*. AF, *tr. by* David Young

Geometry. Rita Dove. CMAP; HCAP; HeIP-4; Poetr

Geometry of sky, The. The Technicians. Jean Kenward. SpW

Geordie [An Old Ballad]. *Unknown*. AmFP; ESPB; OxBB

Georg Trakl. Else Lasker-Schüler, *German*. PFTM, *tr. by* Durchslag, Audri and Jeanette Litman-Demeestère

George. Dudley Randall. BPo; CoAmPo; NoAM

George I--Star of Brunswick. William Makepeace Thackeray. *Fr.* The Georges. FaBoEE

George II. H. J. Daniel. *Fr.* The Georges. FaBoEE

George III. Edmund Clerihew Bentley. PeLV *Fr.* Clerihews. ("Art of Biography, The.")

George III. Byron. *Fr.* The Vision of Judgment. OAEL-2

George III. Robert Lowell. FaBoPV

George III. William Makepeace Thackeray. *Fr.* The Georges. FaBoEE

George III and the Sailor. "Peter Pindar." NOEC *Fr.* The Royal Tour, and Weymouth Amusements. OxBoLi

George III Visits Whitbread's Brewery. "Peter Pindar." NOEC *Fr.* Instructions to a Celebrated Laureat.

George IV. William Makepeace Thackeray. *Fr.* The Georges. FaBoEE

George Allen. *Unknown*. AmFP

George Alow came from the South. *George Aloe* and the *Sweepstake, The*. *Unknown*. ESPB

George and Genevieve. George Hugnet. Gertrude Stein. NoAM

George and me. Letter to a Boy at School. Anna Wickham. NOxBChV

George Burns likes to insist that he always. Of Time and the Line. Charles Bernstein. FTOS; PmAP

George Collins came home last Saturday night. Lady Alice. *Unknown*. AmFP

George Collins come home last Friday night. Lady Alice. *Unknown*. AmFP

George Copway's Dream Song. *Unknown, Ojibwa Native American*. APN-2, *tr. by* George Copway

George Crabbe. Edwin Arlington Robinson. APN-2; CMoP; LiTM; MeMAP; MoAmPo; NAAL-2; NOBA; NoP-4; OxBA; PoEL-5; TAP

George Grosz. Else Lasker-Schüler, *German*. PFTM, *tr. by* Durchslag, Audri and Jeanette Litman-Demeestère

George Hugnet. Gertrude Stein. NoAM

George! I dunno how you do it George. Toronto Board of Trade Goes Abroad. Earle Birney. PeLV

George Marrow's 1011th Dream. Juhan Viiding, *Estonian*. CEEP, *tr. by* Ivar Ivask

George Meredith (1828-1909). Thomas Hardy. EPCY

George Moses Horton, Myself. George Moses Horton. AAP; NAAAL

George Robinson: Blues. Muriel Rukeyser. NNaP; RACG

George Sand. Dorothy Parker. NALW *Fr.* A Pig's-Eye View of Literature.

"George," she said, "come out of the rain!" The Man in the Rain. Van K. Brock. MT

George Stephenson said: "These repairs." Limerick. Frank Richards. PeLi

George the First was always reckoned. The Georges. Walter Savage Landor. FaBoEE; NIP-4; OBCoV; OBSV; PFE

George the Third. Byron. *Fr.* The Vision of Judgment. OAEL-2 (George III.)

George the Third. George III. Edmund Clerihew Bentley. CBNP; NOBL; OxBoLi; PeLV *Fr.* Clerihews.

George the Third's Soliloquy. Philip Freneau. NOBA

George Washington. *Unknown*. CTV

George Washington never owned a camel. 1789. Jackson MacLow. APSN *Fr.* The Presidents of the United States of America.

George Washington said to his dad. Limerick. Frank Richards. PeLi

George Washington, your name is on my lips. Patriotic Poem. Diane Wakoski. VGW

Georges, The. Walter Savage Landor. FaBoEE; NIP-4; OBCoV; OBSV; PFE

Georges, The. William Makepeace Thackeray. FaBoEE

George I--Star of Brunswick.

George II.

George III.

George IV.

Georgia. Bin Ramke. MT

Georgia Dusk. Jean Toomer. BPo; NAAL-2; NoAM; NoP-4; PoBA; Poetr

Georgiad, The. Roy Campbell.

"Hail, mediocrity, beneath whose spell." MoBrPo

"Next him Jack Squire through his own tear-drops sploshes." OxBTC

Georgian Spring. Roy Campbell. OBSV

Georgics. Virgil, *Latin*.

Knowing About Horses. APo, *tr. by* John Dryden

Of Bees. APo, *tr. by* John Dryden

Signs of Rain. APo, *tr. by* John Dryden

"Until Jove let it be, no colonist." OBCVT, *tr. by* Robert Fitzgerald

"What makes a plenteous harvest." AWP, *tr. by* Dryden

Georgics of Hesiod, The. Hesiod.

Winter. NOSC, *tr. by* George Chapman

Georgie Porgie, pudding and pie. Mother Goose. LB; OxNR; ReMoGo

Georgie Wedlock. *Unknown*. AmFP

Georgina Trevellyn to Luisa: "At last, dearest Louisa, I take up my pen to address you." Arthur Hugh Clough. EBVVPR *Fr.* Amours de Voyage. NOBVV

Georgina Trevellyn to Luisa: "Dearest Louisa, Enquire if you please about Mr. Claude." Arthur Hugh Clough. FaBoVe *Fr.* Amours de Voyage. NOBVV

Gerald the Bitter, with your polished smile. The Widow's Curse. *Unknown, Irish*. NOIV, *tr. by* Thomas Kinsella

"Gerald's here!" my mother called. A Voice in the Garden. Selima Hill. FaBoWP

Geranium. Edward Dorn. PmAP

Geranium, The. Theodore Roethke. CoAP; UnPo; WeW-3

Geranium, The. Richard Brinsley Sheridan. BoLoP; EP

Geranium, houseleek, laid in oblong beds. Poem. John Gray. ADE; NOBVV

Geranium in my studio window, The. The Motion. Josephine Jacobsen. NMM-2

Geraniums. Wilfrid Wilson Gibson. NSI

Geraniums, The. Genevieve Taggard. VGW

Geraniums, South London. Ken Edwards. NBrP

Gerarda. Eloise Bibb. AAP; CBWP-4

Gereint ab Erbin. *Unknown, Welsh*. OBWVE, *tr. by* Joseph P. Clancy

Germ, The. Ogden Nash. RB

Germ of new life, whose powers expanding slow. To a Little Invisible Being Who Is Expected Soon to Become Visible. Anna Laetitia Barbauld. ECWP; WoRP

German Bite. Iain Sinclair. NBrP

German Frontier at Basel: 1942 and 1992, The. Hilda Schiff. HP

German Graves, The. Sir Alan Patrick Herbert. NSI

German Language, The, *epigram*. Friedrich von Logau, *German*. GePo, *tr. by* George C. Schoolfield

German Prisoners. Joseph Lee. NSI

German Requiem, A. James Fenton. HP; NAEL-2; NoAM

Germanicus leapt upon the wild lion in Smyrna. John Berryman. *Fr.* Eleven Addresses to the Lord. OxBC

Germans in Greek, The. Porson on German Scholarship. Richard Porson. FaBoEE

Germany of three confessions now shall keep a single one. One Faith and No Faith. Friedrich von Logau, *German*. GePo, *tr. by* George C. Schoolfield

Germinal. "Æ." BIrV; MoBrPo; OBEV; OBMV

Gerneralissimo Yuan Shih Kai. Cauldron. Marilyn Chin. BAP-96

Geron and Histor. Sir Philip Sidney. SiPS *Fr.* Arcadia.

Gerontion. T. S. Eliot. AmPP; CMoP; EBEV; GTBS-P; HAP; ImPo; InPS-3; LiTM; MoP; NAAL-2; NOBA; NoAM; OAEL-2; OxAEP-2; OxBA; TAP; TFi

  "Vacant shuttles / Weave the wind. I have no ghosts." UV

Gertrude and Gulielma, sister-twins. Frederick Goddard Tuckerman. HAP *Fr.* Sonnets.

Gertrude Stein at Snails Bay. Peter Porter. OxBC

Gertrude's Prayer. Rudyard Kipling. APAD

Gest of Robyn Hode. *Unknown*. ESPB; OxBB

  "They toke togyder theyr counsell." PeECV

Gestalt at Sixty. May Sarton.

  "I am not ready to die." CrSp

Gestalt me out! Slang to the point of meat-eating, imperative ornament, dislike. Bruce Andrews. FTOS

Gesture. Donald Finkel. InPK-6

Gesture, The. George Oppen. NNaP *Fr.* Five Poems about Poetry.

Gesture by a Lady with an Assumed Name, A. James Wright. CoAmPo; LiTM

Gesture of an Ionic column returning your face. Noli Me Tangere. Jan Polkowski, *Polish*. AF, *tr. by* Michael March *and* Jaroslaw Anders

Gesture the gesture the gesture the gesture, The. Michael McClure. NeAP; PmAP *Fr.* Hymn to St. Geryon.

Get a Transfer. *Unknown*. BLPA

Get all the gold and silver that you can. W. B. Yeats. APAD *Fr.* Vacillation.

Get Angry, Compass. Michiko Inoue, *Japanese*. WPJ, *tr. by* Kenneth Rexroth *and* Ikuko Atsumi

Get-Away. Robert Malise Bowyer Nichols.

  1. CLPP

"Get away from Eros!" Archias, *Greek*. GrAn, *tr. by* Peter Jay

Get away, they're all gone. Chops Are Flyin. Stanley Crouch. GT

"Get down, get down, lovin' Henry," she cried. Loving Henry. *Unknown*. AmFP

Get drunk, my boy, don't weep, you're. Asclepiades, *Greek*. PGA, *tr. by* Kenneth Rexroth

Get hence foul[e] grief[e], the canker of the mind[e]. Get Hence Foule Griefe. Sir Philip Sidney. PoEL-1; SiPS *Fr.* Arcadia.

Get Hence Foule Griefe. Sir Philip Sidney. PoEL-1 *Fr.* Arcadia.

  (Contentment.) SiPS

Get him that enormous cauldron on the tripod. Alkman's Supper. Alcman, *Greek*. OBCVT, *tr. by* Willis Barnstone

Get him and be gone as one shaped awry; he disturbs the order here. (LL) When the clouds' swoln bosoms echo back the shouts of the many and strong. Thomas Hardy. CMoP; ChIV-1; LiTM; NoAM; OxBTC

Get it done by half-past eight. Mother Goose. *See* Cobbler, cobbler, mend my shoe.

Get it, / she said, so it's unknown which parent. John Cage. APSN *Fr.* Diary: How to Improve the World (You Will Only Make Matters Worse).

Get on Board, Little Children. *Unknown*. PBMP

Get out of my hut, you stealthy vermin! Leonidas'. Leonidas of Tarentum. HePo, *tr. by* Barbara Hughes Fowler *Fr.* Epigrams.

Get out the lunch-box of your dreams. Jim Crow Car. Langston Hughes. GM

Get ready your money and come to me. *Unknown*. OxNR

Get the Gasworks. David Ignatow. InPK-6

Get thee a ship well-rigged and tight. In Praise of Fidelia. Mildmay Fane, 2d Earl of Westmorland. BeJo; NOSC; OxBSP

Get thee behind me. Even as heavy-curled. "Retro Me, Sathana." D. G. Rossetti. ChIV-2

Get There If You Can and See the Land. W. H. Auden. InPS-3

Get to Hell Outa Here. "The Mighty Sparrow." PBCV

Get up and bar the door. (LL) Get Up and Bar the Door. *Unknown*. AmFP; EnSB; ESPB; HeIP-4; NoP-4; OxBS; PBMP

Get up at once, now, Margaret May! Eggs for Breakfast. Irene F. Pawsey. BoTP

Get Up, Blues. James A. Emanuel. PoBA; SeSe

Get up, get up for shame [the blooming morn *or* Morne]. Corinna's Going A-Maying. Robert Herrick. AEP; BeJo; CABP; CaPo; HAP; InPS-3; NAEL-1; NIP-4; NOBE; NOSC; NoP-4; OAEL-1; OBEV; PBRV; PoE; PoEL-3; PoPoPo; SCGP; SeCP; TFi

Get up, get up, you lazy-head. *Unknown*. ACTP; NTCP

"Get up!" "Marlene?" I smell the April rain. Mark Stern Wakes Up. Frederick Feirstein. RA

"Get up, our Anna dear, from the weary spinning wheel." The Fairy Thorn. Sir Samuel Ferguson. CH

"Get up!" the caller calls, "Get up!" Joseph Skipsey. InPK-6; NOBVV

Get ye up from the wrath of God's terrible day! The Cities of the Plain. John Greenleaf Whittier. ChIV-1; NCAP

Get your flag out of my face, it tickles! Last Will and Testament. Hans Magnus Enzensberger. PoSu

Gethsemane [1914–18]. Rudyard Kipling. APAD; GI; PoFWW

  ("I drank it when we met the gas / Beyond Gesthemane!") (LL) FaBoTw; PeFWW

Gethsemane A. D. Dolores Kendrick. FFC

Gettin de Spirit. Una Marson. PBCV

Gettin' Straight. Mcavoy Layne. CDa

Getting Across. Carter Revard. VoR

Getting at the Root of the Matter. Henry Taylor. BXAP

Getting Berries. *Unknown, Bella Bella Indian*. STP, *tr. by* Franz Boas

Getting Dirty. Dorthi Charles. TLR

Getting Down. "Chrystos." CPO

Getting Down to Get Over. June Jordan. TAP

Getting Firewood. *Unknown, Bella Bella Indian*. STP, *tr. by* Franz Boas

Getting Happy. Forrest Hamer. BAP-94

Getting in the Wood. Gary Snyder. NoAM

Getting Inside the Miracle. Luci Shaw. TrCP

Getting old, I retire to this little mountain district. Late in the Year K'uei-yu (1333), Staying at the Temple of the Upper Regions. Yü Chi, *Chinese*. CoBLCP, *tr. by* Jonathan Chaves

Getting on Horseback. Yü Chi, *Chinese*. CoBLCP, *tr. by* Jonathan Chaves

Getting Out. Cleopatra Mathis. SoSe-8

Getting out of bed one day, you broke. Elegy for My Sister. Howard Moss. VCAP

Getting the Mail. Galway Kinnell. UnPo

Getting the Message. Maxine W. Kumin. BAP-95

Getting There. Edward Baugh. HCP

Getting There. Sylvia Plath. GM

Getting Through. James Merrill. NYBP

Getting through with the world. Approach to a City. William Carlos Williams. PoRA

Getting to Rome. *Unknown*. NOIV

Getting Up. Lilian McCrea. BoTP

Getting Up Early on a Spring Morning. Po Chü-i, *Chinese*. ChiP, *tr. by* Arthur Waley

Getting Up in Winter. Emperor Ch'ien Wen-Ti, *Chinese*. BLT, *tr. by* Kenneth Rexroth

Getting Warm. Rae Armantrout. FTOS

Getting Well. Ngân Giang, *Vietnamese*. AVP, *tr. by* Huỳnh Sanh Thông

Gettysburg. Edgar Lee Masters. CBCWP

Gettysburg Address, The. Abraham Lincoln. CTV

Gettysburg, July 1, 1863. Jane Kenyon. CBCWP

Gettysburg Ode. Bayard Taylor. CBCWP

Geyser, The. Agnes Nemes Nagy, *Hungarian*. PoSu, *tr. by* Bruce Berlind

Ghaists; a Kirk-yard Eclogue, The. Robert Fergusson. OxBS

Ghazal. Iftiqar Arif. NBrP

Ghazal on signs of Love and Occupation. Philip Salom. BMAP

Ghede Poem. Nathaniel Mackey. PmAP

Ghetto. Michael Longley. NoP-4; PNI

Ghetto, The. Lola Ridge.

  "I room at Sodos'—in the little green room." NMM-2

Ghetto. Guy Tirolien, *French*. NegPo, *tr. by* Ellen Conroy Kennedy

Ghetto Lovesong—Migration. Carole C. Gregory Clemmons. PoBA

Ghona Widow's Lullaby, The. Thomas Pringle. PeSAV

Ghost. Nina Cassian, *Romanian*. PoSu, *tr. by* Christopher Hewitt

Ghost, The. Charles Churchill. OxBSn

  "Pomposo (insolent and loud)." OBSV

Ghost, The. Hilary Corke. NYBP

Ghost, The. Walter De la Mare. CMoP; EnLoPo; LiTM; LoP; MoBrPo; NOBE; OAEL-2; OxBSn; OxBTC

Ghost. Christian Morgenstern, *German*. OxBSn, *tr. by* W. D. Snodgrass

Ghost, The. Agnes Nemes Nagy, *Hungarian*. PoSu, *tr. by* Bruce Berlind

Ghost, The. Fitz-James O'Brien. NOEC

Ghost, The. Iain Crichton Smith. NOxBChV

Ghost & Shaman. *Unknown, Bella Bella Indian*. STP, *tr. by* Franz Boas

Ghost appears in the dark of winter, The. The Ghost of Soul-making. Michael S. Harper. NAAAL

Ghost at Anlaby, The. Randolph Stow. NOBAu

Ghost Dance Songs. *Arapaho Oral Tradition, Arapaho.* PaTW, *tr.* by James Mooney

Ghost-Dance Songs. *Unknown.*

"I' yehe! my children." STP

Songs of the Arapaho. APN-2, *tr.* by James Mooney

"My children, when at first I liked the whites." STP

Songs of the Kiowa. APN-2, *tr.* by James Mooney

Songs of the Paiute. APN-2

Songs of the Sioux. APN-2

"We shall live again." STP

Ghost-grey the fall of night. A Robin. Walter De la Mare. CMoP

Ghost in the Martini, The. Anthony Hecht. DiPo; NoP-4; OxBC

Ghost is gone in rags, The. *Ambo Oral Tradition. Fr.* Five Ghost Songs. TTTS

Ghost is someone: death has left a hole, A. Robert Lowell. PoA

Ghost of a Ghost, The. Brad Leithauser. RA

Ghost of a little white kitten, The. The Little Cat Angel. Leontine Stanfield. BLPA

Ghost of a mouldy larder is one thing, A: whiskery bread. Corposant. Peter Redgrove. OxBTC

Ghost of Abel, The. William Blake. ChIV-1

Ghost of an Education, The. James Michie. NYBP

Ghost of another comes to visit and we hold, The. The Dance. Mark Strand. LCAP-2

Ghost of Edward. Joanna Baillie. ECWP *Fr.* Night Scenes of Other Times.

Ghost of Fadon, The. Joanna Baillie. NOBRP

Ghost of Ninon would be sorry now, The. Veteran Sirens. Edwin Arlington Robinson. NOBA

Ghost of our blood, I worship You. Adoramus Te, Christe. David Ó Bruadair, *Irish.* NOIV, *tr.* by Thomas Kinsella

Ghost of Soul-making, The. Michael S. Harper. NAAAL

Ghost Sickness. Luis Alberto Urrea. BAP-96

Ghost Song. Jack Spicer. APSN

Ghost Story. Dylan Thomas. OBCP

Ghost Tantras. Michael McClure.

"PLEASURE FEARS ME, FOOT ROSE, FOOT BREATH." BB

Ghost that loved a lady fair, A. The Phantom-Wooer. Thomas Lovell Beddoes. NAEL-2; OxBSn; Ro

Ghost, though invisible, still is like a place, A. Black Cat. Rilke, *German.* APo, *tr.* by Stephen Mitchell

Ghost Voice. Roy Fuller.

"Why do we return? Not in the darkened rooms." LBC

Ghost-Who-Walks, The. Colleen J. McElroy. GT

Ghostie Men. Tom Leonard.

"Baa baa black sheeep." NBrP

"Right inuff / ma language is disgraceful." FaBoTC

"Ulstir fur fucks sake." NBrP

Ghostly Father, The. Peter Redgrove. MoBS

Ghostly Gladness. Richard Rolle of Hampole. HAP

Ghostly Tree. Léonie Adams. MoAmPo

Ghosts. Dorianne Laux. EC3

Ghosts. Mary Oliver. Poetr

Ghosts, The. Thomas Love Peacock. OBCoV

Ghosts. Alastair Reid. NYBP

Ghosts do exist; death does not finish everything. Propertius, *Latin.* OBCVT, *tr.* by Jim Powell

Ghosts II. Lauris Edmond. PeNZ

Ghosts in the Carpet. Robert Morgan. WeT

Ghosts man the phantom ships that ply between. Gallipoli. Mary Morison Webster. NSI

Ghosts of Beauty, The. Alexander Pope. OBSV *Fr.* Epistle [II,] to a Lady[: Of the Characters of Women]. NAEL-1; NOEC

Ghosts of hedgers and ditchers. Ash Keys. Michael Longley. PBCIP

Ghosts of the Buffaloes, The. Vachel Lindsay. MeMAP, MoAmPo

Ghosts, places, stories, questions. Vincent Buckley. NOBAu

Ghost's Song, The. *Unknown. See* Cauld Lad of Hilton, The *or* The Wandering Spectre.

Ghosts there must be with me in this old house. Solitude. Walter De la Mare. CMoP

Ghoul, The. Jack Prelutsky. OBCA

Ghoul Care. Ralph Hodgson. MoBrPo

Giant Decorative Dahlias. Molly Holden. OxBTC

Giant Has Swallowed the Earth, A. Pattiann Rogers. MT

Giant Jojo. Michael Rosen. FuFo

Giant Killer. George Garrett. CRP

Giant Otters. Jackson Mac Low. FTOS

Giant Philosophical Otters. Jackson Mac Low. FTOS

Giant Puffball, The. Edmund Blunden. FaBoTw

Giant Red Woman. Clarence Major. GT

Giant Rocket. Wes Magee. NOxBChV

Giant sparkler, / Lights of the river. "A" 4 ("Giant sparkler, / Lights of the river"). Louis Zukofsky. VGW *Fr.* A.

Giant Steps. John Taggart. MoNo

Giant Thunder[, striding home]. James Reeves. NOxBChV; OTCP

Giant Tortoise. Anthony Hecht. APo

Giant whispering and coughing from. Broadcast. Philip Larkin. CBLP

Giantess, The, *see also tr.* by Roy Campbell, "Of old when Nature, in her verve defiant," *and tr.* by Karl Shapiro, "When Nature once in lustful hot undress." Charles Baudelaire, *French.* EP; FLP, *tr.* by Alistair Elliot

Giantesses, female fauna. The Women of Rubens. Wislawa Szymborska, *Polish.* PoSu, *tr.* by Magnus F. Krynski; VCWP, *tr.* by Magnus J. Krynski *and* Robert A. Maguire

Giant's Cake, A. Evelina San Garde. BoTP

Giaour, The. Byron. NOBRP

"But thou, false infidel! shall writhe."

Gibber, The. Theodore Roethke. NAAL-2 *Fr.* The Lost Son. HAP; HCAP; LiTM; VGW

Gibraltar. Wilfrid Scawen Blunt. OBEV

"Gie corn to my horse, mither." The Mother's Malison; or, Clyde's Water. *Unknown.* ESPB

Gi'e me a lass with a lump of land. Lass with a Lump of Land. Allan Ramsay. NOEC

Gif ye kip the schule. I Winna Let On. James King Annand. NOxBChV

Gife Langour. Henry Stuart, Lord Darnley. OxBS

Gift. Gerald William Barrax. MT

Gift, The. Margaret E. Bruner. PoToHe

Gift, The. John Ciardi. LiTM

Gift, The. Robert Creeley. NOBA

Gift, The. Greg Delanty. BiHa

Gift, The. Hilda Doolittle. CPO

Gift, The. Louise Glück. FaBoWP; FiLi

Gift, The. Mark Jarman. WeT

Gift, The. Li-Young Lee. LoL; OpBo; RaBo; UnSA

Gift, The. N. Scott Momaday. NoP-4

Gift, The. Ed Ochester. Poetsp

Gift, The. William Stafford. PuP-16

Gift, The. Sara Teasdale. LW

Gift, A. *Unknown, Greek.* GrAn, *tr.* by Guy Davenport

Gift, The. William Carlos Williams. ChIV-2

("Bowed down / to worship / this perfection.") (LL) GI

Gift, The. Francis Brett Young. NSI

Gift for my Mother's 90th Birthday. Maude Meehan. NMM-2

Gift for the Queen. *Unknown.* OxNR

Gift for you should not be vulgar, A. Inscribed on a Painting of Windy Bamboo, to Be Presented to Tzu-kan. Hsü Wei, *Chinese.* SuSp, *tr.* by Chiang Yee

Gift from Kenya. May Miller. BlSi

Gift Horse. Yusef Komunyakaa. GT

Gift Hour. Maria Banus, *Rumanian.* BoWoP, *tr.* by Willis Barnstone *and* Matei Calinescu

Gift of God, The. Edwin Arlington Robinson. MoAmPo; OxBA

Gift of Great Value, A. Robert Creeley. LCAP-2

Gift of Judah the Woman-Hater, The. Judah ibn Sabbatai. Expensive Wife, The. TrJP

Gift of Love. Sowol Kim, *Korean.* CKP, *tr.* by Jaihiun Kim

Gift of Sight. Robert Graves. EP

Gift of Song, The. Anthony Hecht. NYBP

Gift of Speech, The. Sadi. AWP, *tr.* by L. Cranmer-Byng *Fr.* The Gulistan.

Gift of Tongues, The. Robert Morgan. MT

Gift Outright, The. Robert Frost. AiP; AmPP; CMoP; ColAP; FaBoA; LiTM; MeMAP; MoAmPo; MoP; NAAL-2; NOBA; NoAM; NoP-4; OxBA; PoPoPo; Poetr; TFi; TRP

Gift Shop in Pecs. Len Roberts. PuP-16

Gift to a Jade. Anna Wickham. OxBSP

Gift to Be Simple, The. Howard Moss. Poetsp; TwCP

Gift was delivered to Laura, A. Edward Gorey. CBNP *Fr.* The Listing Attic.

Gifts. Mary Elizabeth Coleridge. PBWP; VWP

Gifts. Juliana Horatia Ewing. LW

Gifts, The. John Heath-Stubbs. OxBC

Gifts. Amryl Johnson. HCP

Gifts. Emma Lazarus. TrJP

Gifts. Judy Ruiz. IFJA

Gifts. "Shu Ting," *Chinese.* VCWP, *tr. by* Carolyn Kizer

Gifts. Karen Snow. FYAP

Gifts. James Thomson. OBEV *Fr.* Sunday up the River.

Gifts as Tokens of Love. Trần Dạ Tù', *Vietnamese.* AVP, *tr. by* Huỳnh Sanh Thông

Gifts Misused. Letitia Elizabeth Landon. VWP

Gifts of God, The. George Herbert. *See* The Pulley.

Gifts to a Lady. Antiphilus, *Greek.* GrAn, *tr. by* W. S. Merwin

Gigantic beauty of a stallion, fresh and responsive to my caresses, A. Walt Whitman. ImGa *Fr.* Song of Myself. AmPP; MoAmPo; NAAL-3; NOBA; OxBA

Gigantic Grandfather. Karl Heinrich Marx. Hans Magnus Enzensberger, *German.* FaBoPV, *tr. by* Michael Hamburger

Gil Brenton. *Unknown.* ESPB; OxBB

Gil Morrice. *Unknown.* OxBB

Gila Desert in Arizona, The. Miroslav Holub, *German.* CEEP, *tr. by* Simko, Daniel

Gilbert Stuart Portrait of Washington, The. Ted Kooser. CMAP

Gilbertus Glanvil, whose heart was as hard as an anvil. *Unknown, Latin.* FaBoEE, *tr. by* Matthew Prior

Giles Collins he said to his old mother. Lady Alice. *Unknown.* ESPB

Giles Johnson, Ph.D. Frank Marshall Davis. BPo; PoBA

Gilgamesh. Herbert Mason.
    "I asked unanswerable questions a child asks." IMW

Gill Morice stood in stable-door. *Unknown.* ESPB
    ("Childe Maurice hunted the Silver Wood.") OBSP

Gillespie. Sir Henry John Newbolt. PeVV

Gilly Silly Jarter. *Unknown.* OxNR

Gimme $25.00 / and the change. Request. Langston Hughes. PFTM

Gin a body meet a body. Comin' thro' the Rye. Robert Burns. UV

Gin a body meet a body. Rigid Body Sings. James Clerk Maxwell. BXAP; UV

Gin I were on my milkwhite steed. The Bents and Broom. *Unknown.* OxBB

Gin she this sight did see! (LL) Rose the Red and White Lil[l]y. *Unknown.* ESPB; OxBB

Gin-Shop, The; A Peep into Prison. Hannah More.
    "Come, neighbour, take a walk with me." ECWP

Gin the Goodwife Stint. Basil Bunting. CTC; OxBoS

Gin ye hae'd corneich airth an' time. To His Coy Mistress. Gerry Hamill. BXAP

Gineral B. is a sensible man. James Russell Lowell. *See* What Mr. Robinson Thinks.

Ginevra. Samuel Rogers. OxAEP-2; PoLF

Ginger Bread Mama. Doughtry Long. BPo; PoBA

Ginger-flowers. Kenneth Mackenzie. BMAP

Gingerbread Heart. Aleksandar Ristovic, *Serbo-Croatian.* HSix, *tr. by* Charles Simic

Gingerbread Man, The. *Unknown.* ACTP

Gingerbread man gave a gingery shout, The. Rowena Bastin Bennett. ChAP

Gingerly walked the hare. Two Laments. *Unknown, Chinese.* ChiP, *tr. by* Arthur Waley

Gingham dog and the calico cat, The. The Duel. Eugene Field. APN-2; CTV; FPC; FaBoBe; MoNBChV; OBAL; OBCA; PoLF; PoRA; TFi

Gingilee. Moyshe-Leyb Halpern, *Yiddish.* TrJP, *tr. by* Joseph Leftwich

Ginkgo, cottonwood, pin oak, sweet gum, tulip tree. The Shapes of Leaves. Arthur Sze. IFJA

Ginkgoes in Fall. Howard Nemerov. HCAP

Ginny at a table of young men belly dancing. Soup Kitchen. Betsy Sholl. PBCAP

Ginza Samba. Robert Pinsky. PUP-18

Giorno dei Morti. D. H. Lawrence. NOBE

Giotto's Campanile. Guy Butler. PeSA

Giovanni Azania. Don Mattera. PeSAV

Giovanni da Fiesole on the Sublime. Richard Howard. GS

"Giovinette, Che Fate All'Amore." Lorenzo Da Ponte. TrJP, *tr. by* Natalie MacFarren *Fr.* Don Giovanni.

Gipsies: "Snow falls deep; the forest lies alone, The." John Clare. CH; PoEL-4
    (Gypsies.) NoP-4

Gipsies came to Lord Cassilis' gate, The. Johnny Faa, the Lord of Little Egypt. *Unknown.* EnSB

Gipsies lit their fire by the chalk-pit anew, The. The Idlers. Edmund Blunden. BoTP; CH

Gipsies seek wide sheltering woods again, The. John Clare. FHYEP

Gipsies tell me my life-line's a short one, The. Antipater of Thessalonica, *Greek.* GrAn, *tr. by* Tony Harrison

Gipsy Girl, The. Ralph Hodgson. MoBrPo
    (Gypsy Girl, The.) SAGP

Gipsy Jane. William Brighty Rands. BoTP

Gipsy Laddie, The. *Unknown.* FaBoCh; OxBoLi

Gipsy Man. Dorothy King. BoTP

Gipsy-Night. Richard Hughes. OBWVE

Gipsy Queen. John Alexander Chapman. OBEV

Gipsy Trail, The. Rudyard Kipling. PoRA

Giraffe, The. Nikolai Stepanovich Gumilyov, *Russian.* TCRP, *tr. by* Yakov Hornstein
    "Listen: / There roams, far away, by the waters of Clead."

Giraffe, The. Ron Padgett. *Fr.* Three Animals. TTTS

Giraffe. Stanley Plumly. AmPA; ChAP

Giraffe. *Unknown, Hottentot.* PeSAV, *tr. by* W. H. I. Bleek; PeSA, *tr. by* W. H. I. Bleek
    ("Thou who descendest river by river.") PeSAV

Giraffe and Tree. Walter James Turner. CH

Giraffes, yes, even the strongest. Limerick. Frank Davies. PeLi

Girandole. Dorothy Donnelly. NYBP

Girandole. Gustaf Sobin. APSN

Gird up thy loins now like a man. Out of the Whirlwind. Bible, *O.T.* AWP *Fr.* Moreover the Lord answered Job, and said. OBVE *Fr.* Job. NAWM-1

Gird your beard three times with a belt and light a stove. Flying Temple. Milorad Pavic, *Serbo-Croatian.* HSix, *tr. by* Charles Simic

Girdle, A. William Strode. NOSC

Girdle round the Earth, A. Anthony Thwaite. PeLV

Girl, A. "Michael Field." CPO; VWP

Girl, The. Sharon Olds. NMM-2

Girl. Octavio Paz, *Spanish.* STV, *tr. by* John Frederick Nims

Girl, A. Ezra Pound. MoAmPo; NOxBChV

Girl. *Unknown, Serbian.* RB, *tr. by* Anne Pennington

Girl. Hugo Williams. CBLP

Girl and Baby Florist Sidewalk Pram Nineteen Seventy Something. Kenneth Koch. NoP-4

Girl and Her Fawn, The. Andrew Marvell. *See* The Nymph and Her Fawn.

Girl at Her Devotions, A. Letitia Elizabeth Landon. VWP

Girl at the Chu Lai Laundry. Bruce Weigl. CDa

Girl at the Seaside. Richard Murphy. BIrV

Girl at the Window. Pinkie Gordon Lane. GT

Girl attacked me once with a number 2 Eagle pencil, A. A Blasphemy. Rodney Jones. WeW-3

Girl, Boy, Flower, Bicycle. M. K. Joseph. PeNZ

Girl brought me into the house of love, The. A Secret Kept. Judah Al-Harizi, *Hebrew.* NNPT, *tr. by* David Goldstein

Girl by Green River, The. *Unknown, Chinese.* OHMPC, *tr. by* Kenneth Rexroth

Girl by the River. Federico García Lorca, *Spanish.* CBNP

Girl (captured; later, freed), The. For Miss Tin in Hue. John Balaban. CDa

Girl Caught Napping By Day, A. Ho Xuan Huong, *Vietnamese.* AVP, *tr. by* Huỳnh Sanh Thông

Girl Combs Her Hair, A. Li Ho, *Chinese.* PLT, *tr. by* A. C. Graham

Girl comes out of a doorway in the morning, A. Back Street. Arthur Rex Dugard Fairburn. PeNZ *Fr.* Album Leaves.

Girl Cousin, The. Gérard de Nerval, *French.* FLP, *tr. by* Alistair Elliot

Girl fits her body, The. Night Vision. Lucille Clifton. UnSA

Girl Friend Describes the Bull Fight, The. Uruttiran, *Tamil.* PLW, *tr. by* A. K. Ramanujan

Girl from Andros (Andria), The. Publius Terentius Afer, *Latin.*
    "CHREMES. Pese anger not thyself so I thee pray." OBCVT, *tr. by Unknown*

Girl from Ch'ang-kan is just fourteen years old, The. Cheng Hsieh, *Chinese.* CoBLCP, *tr. by* Jonathan Chaves

Girl from Flower Mountain, The. Han Yü, *Chinese.* SuSp, *tr. by* Charles Hartman

Girl gathering lotus upon a brook, A. Upon a Brook. Ku K'uang, *Chinese.* SuSp, *tr. by* Irving Y. Lo

Girl grows up hidden in far-off rooms, A. In a Boat on a Summer Evening. Lu Yu, *Chinese.* CoBCP, *tr. by* Burton Watson

Girl grows up hidden in innermost rooms, A. In a Boat on a Summer Evening, I Heard the Cry of a Water Bird. Lu Yu, *Chinese.* SuSp, *tr. by* Burton Watson

Girl Held without Bail. Margaret Abigail Walker. BPo; PoBA

Girl Help. Janet Lewis. HeIP-4; InPK-6

Girl I Call Alma, The. Linda Gregg. AmPA

Girl I Left behind Me, The. Thomas Osborne Davis. FaBoBe

Girl I Left behind Me, The. *Unknown.* AmFP

Girl in a grey frock. A Grey Frock. Zinaida Hippius, *Russian.* PBWP, *tr. by* Temira Pachmuss

Girl in a house dress, pushing open the window, The. Remembering in Oslo the Old Picture of the Magna Carta. Robert Bly. WeT

Girl in a Library, A. Randall Jarrell. NAAL-2; NOBA; NoAM

Girl in a Nightgown. Wallace Stevens. OxBA

Girl in poor clothes, her skin lustrous as jade, A. A Teahouse at Hoshioka. Liu E, *Chinese.* CoBLCP, *tr. by* Jonathan Chaves

Girl in the Hall, The. John A. Stone. MT

Girl in the Kitchen. "Vaidehi," *Kannada.* OMIP, *tr. by* A. K. Ramanujan

Girl in the lane, The. Mother Goose. OxNR; ReMoGo

Girl in the tea shop, The. The Tea Shop. Ezra Pound. HeIP-4

Girl in trousers wheeling a red baby, The. Metamorphoses. Roy Fuller. OxBTC

Girl lithe and tawny, the sun that forms. Pablo Neruda, *Spanish.* EP, *tr. by* W. S. Merwin

Girl / loosens her bra, The. Alan Pizzarelli. HA

Girl Named Spring, A. Betsy Sholl. PBCAP

Girl Next Door, The. Nguyễn Bính, *Vietnamese.* AVP, *tr. by* Huỳnh Sanh Thông

Girl of All Periods: An Idyll, The. Coventry Patmore. EnVR

Girl of fifteen. James Weldon Johnson. GT

Girl of Mt. Hua, The. Han Yü, *Chinese.* CoBCP. *tr. by* Burton Watson

Girl of Six from the Ghetto Begging in Smolna Street in 1942, A. Jerzy Ficowski, *Polish.* HP, *tr. by* Keith Bosley

Girl of the yellow, heavy-yellow, gold-yellow hair. The Cry of Europe. Sorley MacLean. FaBoTC

Girl of Yueh, The. Li Po, *Chinese.* TAL, *tr. by* Robert Payne

Girl on the Land, The. Alice Thompson Meynell. VWP

Girl on the stairs listens to her father, A. Tours. Charles David Wright. MT

Girl Powdering Her Neck. Cathy Song. NoP-4

Girl, Prince, Lizard. Heather Ross Miller. MT

Girl Sings to the Stream, The. Leah Goldberg. MHP, *tr. by* Ruth Finer Mintz *Fr.* Songs of the Stream.

Girl strapped in the bare mechanical crib, The. Song and Story. Ellen Bryant Voigt. BAP-93

Girl Tearing Up Her Face. Susan Mitchell. BAP-96

Girl threw an apple to a cloud, A. *Unknown, Serbo-Croatian.* HSix, *tr. by* Charles Simic

Girl to Soldier on Leave. Isaac Rosenberg. PeFWW

Girl today, dreaming, A. Auf dem Wasser zu Singen. Stephen Spender. EnLoPo

Girl was singing in the choir with fervor, A. Aleksandr Blok, *Russian.* TCRP, *tr. by* Jon Stallworthy *and* Peter France

Girl, when rejecting me you never guessed. To a Jilt. Martin Donisthorpe Armstrong. FaBoEE

Girl who is bespectacled, A. Lines Written to Console Those Ladies Distressed by the Lines 'Men Never Make Passes, etc'. Ogden Nash. PeLV

Girl Who Loved the Sky, The. Anita Endrezze-Danielson. HATNAP

Girl who sells melons beside the stream, The. Melon Girl. Mei Yao Ch'en, *Chinese.* OHPC, *tr. by* Kenneth Rexroth

Girl who was touring Zambesi, A. Limerick. *Unknown.* PeLi

Girl with all that raising, A. Ballad of the Girl Whose Name Is Mud. Langston Hughes. SAmP

Girl with Doves. Stephen Gray. PeSA

Girl with Long Dark Hair. Stephen Gray. PeSA

Girl with Mind Wandering. Paul Valéry, *French.* STV, *tr. by* John Frederick Nims

Girl with Pitcher. Ruth Dallas. PeNZ

Girl with the beautiful legs, The. The Tides. Paul Blackburn. PoM

Girl with the Green Skirt. Dana Naone. CDW

Girl Without a Sex, The. Ho Xuan Huong, *Vietnamese.* AVP, *tr. by* Huỳnh Sanh Thông

Girl   working the xerox in the stationery store, The. For Emily (Dickinson). Maureen Owen. PmAP

Girl Writing a Letter. William Carpenter. BAP-95

Girl Writing Her English Paper, The. Robert Wallace. Poetsp

Girl wrote that once, A. The Sky Is Full of Blue and Full of the Mind of God. Kathleen Norris. CrSp

Girl, your young loveliness. White Swan. A. Glanz-Leyeles, *Yiddish.* CEEP, *tr. by* Keith Bosley

Girlfriend. Taeko Tomioka, *Japanese.* WPJ, *tr. by* Kenneth Rexroth *and* Ikuko Atsumi

Girls, The. Nights in Nha Trang. Jan Barry. CDa

Girls. Kenneth Rosen. AmPA

Girls, The. Diane Wakoski. NMM-2

Girls and boys come out to play. *Unknown.* ACTP; BoTP; LB; ReMoGo

Girls are simply the prettiest things. My Cat and I. Roger McGough. OxBTC

Girls around Cape Horn, The. *Unknown.* AmFP

Girls Bathing, Galway 1965. Seamus Heaney. InPS-3

Girls, brighter than wine, are clothed and naked, The. Night Club. Francis Reginald Scott. NOBC

Girls Can We Educate We Dads? James Berry. NOxBChV

Girl's desire moves among her bangles, The. Gagan Gill, *Hindi.* OMIP, *tr. by* Mrinal Pande *and* Arlene Zide

Girl's far treble, muted to the heat, The. Milkmaid. Laurie Lee. APAD; BoLoP; FaBoTw

Girl's footsteps, A. Theology of Rain. Alfonsas Nyka-Niliunas, *Lithuanian.* CEEP, *tr. by* Jonas Zdanys

Girl's Garden, A. Robert Frost. GaP

Girl's Hair, A. Dafydd ab Edmwnd, *Welsh.* OBWVE, *tr. by* Gwyn Williams

Girl's Head, A. Katherine Gallagher. NOBAu

Girls in Their Seasons. Derek Mahon. BoLoP

Girl's Lamentation, The. William Allingham. TIRV

Girls Looking for Lice. Rimbaud. FLP, *tr. by* Alistair Elliot *Fr.* Illuminations.

Girls of Llanbadarn, The. Dafydd ap Gwilym, *Welsh.* DiPo, *tr. by* Leslie Norris; OBWVE, *tr. by* Rolfe Humphries

Girls of the riverside, Nereids, did you see. Pan Asks about Daphnis. Diodorus Zonas, *Greek.* GrAn, *tr. by* Alistair Elliot

Girls of Yueh, The. Li Po, *Chinese.* TAL, *tr. by* Robert Payne

Girls on mopeds rode to Fécamp parties. The Musical Orchard. Douglas Dunn. FaBoMo

Girls on the Bridge. Derek Mahon. NoP-4

Girls' School. Alan Moore. BiHa

Girls scream. School's Out. W. H. Davies. OBMV

Girl's Song, A. *Unknown.* APN-2, *tr. by* Franz Boas *Fr.* Songs of the Kwakiutl Indians.

Girls today in society, The. Brush Up Your Shakespeare. Cole Porter. OBAL; OBCoV

Girls wake, stretch, and pad up to the door, The. Apartment Cats. Thom Gunn. PC

Girls Working in Banks. Karl Shapiro. WeW-3

Girt in my guiltless gown, as I sit here and sew. A Woman's Answer. Henry Howard, Earl of Surrey. SiPS

Girt with a boyish grab for boyish task. Dedication. "Lewis Carroll." *Fr.* The Hunting of the Snark. CBNP; OBNC; OBNV; PoEL-5

Gislebertus' Eve. John Berryman. LCAP-2

Git Along Down to Town. *Unknown.* AmFP

Git out o' bed, you rascals. Call Boy. Sterling Brown. GM

Gita Govinda, The. Jayadeva, *Sanskrit.*

    Hymn to Vishnu. AWP, *tr. by* Sir Edwin Arnold

    "Sandal and garment of yellow and lotus garlands upon his body of blue." TAL, *tr. by* George Keyt

Gitanjali. Rabindranath Tagore.

    "Day after day, O lord of my life, shall I stand before thee face to face?" OBMV

    I Have Got My Leave. OBMV

    If It Is Not My Portion. OBMV

    On the Slope of the Desolate River. OBMV

    Thou Art the Sky. OBMV

Giuffre's Nightmusic. Thomas McGrath. *See* Guiffre's Nightmusic.

Giuseppe, da barber, ees greata for "mash." Mia Carlotta. Thomas Augustin Daly. NBLV

Giv but to things their tru esteem. Right Apprehension. Thomas Traherne. PoEL-2

Give a man a horse he can ride. Gifts. James Thomson. OBEV *Fr.* Sunday up the River.

. . . *give a man his.* Wait for Me. Robert Creeley. NOBA

Give all to love;. Ralph Waldo Emerson. APN-1; AWP; AmPP; ColAP; GLoP; MeMAP; NOBA; OBEV; OxBA; PoEL-4; PoLF; TAP

("Gods arrive, The.") (LL) GLoP

Give, and take the cash. Strato, *Greek.* GrAn, *tr. by* W. G. Shepherd

Give back my dead! The Cry of South Africa. Olive Schreiner. PeSAV

Give beauty all her right. Thomas Campion. AAS

Give Crabbe, dear Helen, on your shelf. To Helen, with Crabbe's Poems: a Birthday Present. Winthrop Mackworth Praed. EPCY

Give ear my children to my words. John Rogers' Exhortation to His Children. *Unknown.* OBCA *Fr.* The New England Primer.

Give Ear, O God, to My Loud Cry. Thomas Prince. AH

Give ear, O heavens, to that which I declare. Henry Ainsworth. AH; ChIV-1

Give ear, O my people, to my law. Bible, *O.T. See* Psalm 78.

Give ear to my prayer, O God. Bible, *O.T. See* Psalm 55.

Give Ear, Ye Heavens. Bible, *O.T.* TrJP *Fr.* Deuteronomy.

Give, give me back that Trifle you despise. The Request of Alexis. Sarah Dixon. LW

Give God thy heart. Motto for a Sundial. *Unknown.* FaBoEE

Give greatly of your grunts, O pig. Hymn to Joy. Julia Cunningham. PChr

Give him the darkest inch your shelf allows. George Crabbe. Edwin Arlington Robinson. APN-2; CMoP; LiTM; MeMAP; MoAmPo; NAAL-2; NOBA; NoP-4; OxBA; PoEL-5; TAP

Give Isaac the nymph who no beauty can boast. Song. Richard Brinsley Sheridan. NOIV *Fr.* The Duenna.

Give it all back, even what you were just handed. Lover Man. James Cushing. SeSe

Give Lucinda pearl nor stone. To the New Year [For the Countess of Carlisle]. Thomas Carew. CaPo

Give me a chair. Song of the Poor Man. *Unknown.* TTY, *tr. by* Anselm Hollo

Give me a color. America. Wendy Rose. CDW

Give me a doctor, partridge-plump. W. H. Auden. OBCoV *Fr.* Shorts [1948–1957].

Give me a Girle (if one I needs must meet). Women. Palladas, *Greek.* BeJo; OBCVT, *tr. by* William Cartwright

Give me a good digestion, Lord, / And also something to digest. An Ancient Prayer. Thomas Henry Basil Webb. BLPA; CTV; FaBoBe; PoToHe

Give me a happy heart and suasive tongue. A Happy Heart. Josephine D. Henderson Heard. CBWP-4

Give me a harsh land to wring music from. This Land. Ian Mudie. NOBAu

Give me a heart where no impure. To Castara ("Give me a heart where no impure"). William Habington. BeJo *Fr.* Castara.

Give me a man that is not dull. His Desire. Robert Herrick. OxBSP

Give me a mattress on the ship's poop some day. Antiphilus, *Greek.* GrAn, *tr. by* Peter Jay

Give me a pen. Testament of a Rebel. Breyten Breytenbach, *Afrikaans.* PeSAV, *tr. by* André P. Brink

Give me a royal niche--it is my due. George III. William Makepeace Thackeray. *Fr.* The Georges. FaBoEE

Give me a son. The blessing sent. The Mother, the Nurse, and the Fairy. John Gay. PeLV *Fr.* Fables.

Give me a thrill, says the reader. Fiction and the Reading Public. Philip Larkin. NOBL; OBSV

Give me, give me Buriano. Bacchus's Opinion of Wine, and Other Beverages. Francesco Redi. AWP; OBVE *Fr.* Bacchus in Tuscany.

Give me, great God! said I, a little farm. Verses Written in the Chiosk [of the British Palace], at Pera, Overlooking [the City of] Constantinople. Lady Mary Wortley Montagu. ECEV; ECWP

Give me hunger / O you gods that sit and give. At a Window. Carl Sandburg. FaBoBe; PoToHe

Give Me Jesus. *Unknown.* BPo

Give me leave to rail at you. Song. John Wilmot, 2d Earl of Rochester. NOSC

Give me more love or more disdain. Mediocrity in Love Rejected. Thomas Carew. BeJo; NoP-4

Give me my captive soul, or take. Church Lock-and-Key. George Herbert. GeHe

Give me, my love, that billing kiss. The Kiss. Thomas Moore. EnLoPo

Give me my robe, put on my crown; I have. Death of Cleopatra. Shakespeare. OxAEP-1 *Fr.* Antony and Cleopatra.

Give me my Scallop[-]shell of quiet. The Passionate Man[']s Pilgrimage. Sir Walter Ralegh. AAS; ChIV-2; EBEvV; NOBE; NoSic; OBEV; PeECV; PoE; PoEL-2; PoRA; RB; SCGP; SiPS; TFi

Give me new Phœnix wings to fly at my desire. (LL) On Sitting Down to Read "King Lear" Once Again. Keats. CABP; EBEV; EPCY; GSo; NAEL-2; NoP-4; PoPoPo; Ro

Give me no gift! Less than thyself were nought. Broken Friendship. Mary Elizabeth Coleridge. VWP

Give me, O indulgent fate! Anne Finch, Countess of Winchilsea. ECWP; NOSC *Fr.* The Petition for an Absolute Retreat. PoEL-3; WPE

Give me one kiss. To Dianeme. Robert Herrick. CaPo; FaBoBe

Give me one small smothering of earth. Leonidas of Tarentum, *Greek.* GrAn, *tr. by* Peter Levi

Give Me Peace. Andrey Andreievich Voznesensky, *Russian.* TCRP, *tr. by* Max Hayward

Give me quietness and peace. . . . Give Me Peace. Andrey Andreievich Voznesensky, *Russian.* TCRP, *tr. by* Max Hayward

Give me something to eat. Poor Crow! Mary Mapes Dodge. OBCA

Give me sweet nectar in a kiss. *Unknown.* FaBoEE

Give me that man that dares bestride. His Cavalier. Robert Herrick. CaPo; CavPo

Give me that old-time religion. Old-Time Religion. *Unknown.* APN-2

Give me the Daulian bird and Locrian Arsinoë. From V. C. (a Gentleman of Verona). Gavin Ewart. OxBC

Give me the lowest place: not that I dare. The Lowest Place. Christina Rossetti. NOBVV

Give me the Muse whose generous force. Isaac Watts. EPCY *Fr.* The Adventurous Muse.

Give me the Red on the Black of the Bullet (for Claude Reece Jr.) Jayne Cortez. LTA

Give me the right of way. Irish. Paul Celan, *German.* OBVE, *tr. by* Michael Hamburger

Give me the splendid silent sun with all his beams full-dazzling. Walt Whitman. CBCWP; HAP; MoAmPo; NOBA

Give me the woman here. Sir John Suckling. *See* Sonnet: "O[h]! for some honest lover's ghost."

Give me the wretched refuse of your teams: pitchers with sore elbows. Amurrika! Philip Appleman. BXAP

Give me this day a faith not personal. Allen Tate. *Fr.* More Sonnets at Christmas. LiTM

Give me those flowers there, Dorcas. Reverend sirs. Shakespeare. OxAEP-1 *Fr.* The Winter's Tale.

Give Me Three Grains of Corn, Mother. Amelia Blandford Edwards. AS; BLPA

Give me truths; / For I am weary of the surfaces. Blight. Ralph Waldo Emerson. APN-1; NCAP; NOBA

Give Me What the Tree Has [and what it won't lose]. Natan Zach, *Hebrew.* IP, *tr. by* Warren Bargad *and* Stanley F. Chyet

Give me wide walls to build my house of Life. Wide Walls. *Unknown.* PoToHe

Give me your hand old Revolutionary. The Centenarian's Story. Walt Whitman. CTC

Give me your pardon, sir. I have done you wrong. Shakespeare. *Fr.* Hamlet. NAWM-1

Give me your silver knife, right here. Maris Acklais, *Latvian.* CEEP, *tr. by* Inara Cedrins

Give me yourself one hour; I do not crave. Request. "Laurence Hope." SAGP

Give *Mee* the *Free* and *Noble Stile.* The Claspe. Margaret Lucas Cavendish, Duchess of Newcastle. BWW; PBRV

Give money me, take friendship whoso list. Of Money. Barnabe Googe. GEA; NBLV; NoSic; SoSe-8

Give my heart. (LL) A Christmas Carol: "In the bleak mid-winter." Christina Rossetti. ACTP; InPS-3; NOBVV; VWP

Give Not Our Blankets, Tax-Fed Squire. Ebenezer Elliot. Son *Fr.* The Year of Seeds.

Give over, now, red roses. Warning of Winter. Mary Ursula Bethell. FaBoWP; PeNZ

Give pardon, blessèd soul, to my bold cries. On the Death of Sir Philip Sidney. Henry Constable. NoSic; OBEV

Give patient eare to something I man saye. Admonition to Montgomerie. James I, King of England. GTBS-P; OxBS

Give Peace in These Our Days, O Lord. Edmund Grindal. AH

Give Peace, O God, the Nations Cry. John W. Norris. AH

Give place all ye that doth rejoice. Sir Thomas Wyatt. SiPS

Give place, ye lovers (here before). Henry Howard, Earl of Surrey. AAS; SiPS

Give place, you ladies, and be gone! A Praise of His Lady. John Heywood. OBEV

Give sorrow words; the grief that does. Shakespeare. IMW *Fr.* Macbeth.

Give store of days, good Jove, give length of years. Juvenal. OBSV, *tr. by* Henry Vaughan *Fr.* Satires.

Give T'anks. Mervyn Morris. HCP

Give Thanks. *Unknown.* CTV

Give thanks for this turn for the better. A Change in Style. Eochadh O'Hussey. NOIV

Give thanks unto Him, and bless His name, *sel., v. 4.* Bible, *O.T. See* Psalm 100.

Give the barber a pinch of snuff. (LL) Barber, barber, shave a pig. Mother Goose. LB; OxNR; ReMoGo

Give the king thy judgments, O God. Bible, *O.T. See* Psalm 72.

Give the sounds of the curved mated phonographs. Three Found Poems. George Hitchcock. OBAL

Give them back / to me. Blues. Léon Damas, *French.* NegPo, *tr. by* Ellen Conroy Kennedy

Give them me. Give them. / No. Harold Monro. *See* Overheard on a Saltmarsh.

Give them my regards when you go to the school reunion. More of a Corpse Than a Woman. Muriel Rukeyser. NALW; NMM-2

Give them thy fingers, me thy lips to kiss. (LL) Sonnet 128. Shakespeare. NAEL-1; OxAEP-1; PoE

Give thou my sacred relics burial [*or* Reliques Buriall]. (LL) His Return to London. Robert Herrick. BeJo; CaPo; NAEL-1

Give to barrows, trays, and pans. Art. Ralph Waldo Emerson. APN-1

Give to me the life I love. The Vagabond. Robert Louis Stevenson. OxAEP-2

Give unto the Lord, O ye mighty. Psalm 29. Bible, *O.T.* AWP *Fr.* Psalms.

Give up the bitterness. Dionne Brand. PBCV *Fr.* Epigrams to Ernesto Cardenal in Defense of Claudia.

"Give us your very best table," I swaggered, taking the head waiter aside and. Jet Set Melodrama. Michael Brownstein. FTOS

Give way, and be ye ravished [*or* ravish'd] by the sun. To Marygolds. Robert Herrick. CavPo; NAEL-1

Give way, give way ye Gates, and win. The Wassaile. Robert Herrick. PBRV

Give Way, Ye Gates. Theodore Roethke. CMoP

Giveaway, The. Phyllis McGinley. PBMP; PoRA

Given away in poems, only their solitude kept. (LL) The Correspondence School Instructor Says Goodbye to His Poetry Students. Galway Kinnell. NOBA; NoAM; NoP-4; TAP

"Given faith," sighed the vicar of Deneham. Limerick. *Unknown.* PeLi

Given flesh returns nothing but bread, The. Aileen Kelly. ChIV-2

Given the limitation of trees, what if each. The New Language. Elizabeth Robinson. PT

Given their natural inclinations toward betrayal. Bodies. Vern Rutsala. WeT

Given to a Lady Who Asked Me to Write a Poem. Janet Little. ECWP

Given to love. (LL) Agony, An. As Now. Imamu Amiri Baraka. AmPP; BPo; LiTM; NAAL-2; PoE

Givenchy Field. "H. d'A. B." NSI

Giving. Nora B. Cunningham. LW

Giving. *Unknown.* PoToHe

Giving and Forgiving. Thomas Grant Springer. PoToHe

Giving Back the Flower. Sarah Morgan Bryan Piatt. APN-2

Giving birth in Greek. Judith Hemschemeyer. WeT

Giving her mother's / zealous eye. Paulus Silentiarius, *Greek.* GrAn, *tr. by* Andrew Miller

Giving oneself to the dentist or doctor who is a good one. The Kind of Act Of. Robert Creeley. NeAP

Giving Potatoes. Adrian Mitchell. NBLV; RB

Giving Rabbit to My Cat Bonnie. Anne Stevenson. FaBoWP

Giving Thanks, *sel., v.* 4. Bible, *O.T. See* Psalm 100.

Giving Up Smoking. Wendy Cope. APAD

Giving up women is worse than animal laxatives. John Tranter. NoAM *Fr.* Crying in Early Infancy.

Giving, while the rain lasts, soft noises. Eaves. Ellis Jones, *Welsh.* OBWVE, *tr. by* Anthony Conran

Gizzard and some ruby inner parts, A. Lament. Margaret Avison. HAP

Glad at the Cold (1955). Alan Dugan. NoAM

Glad, but not flush'd with gladness. Before the Mirror. Swinburne. OBEV *Fr.* Before the Mirror.

Glad Christmas comes, and every hearth. December. John Clare. OBCP

Glad Day. Louis Untermeyer. TrJP

Glad Eye, The. Paul Muldoon. NoAM

Glad that I live am I. A Little Song of Life. Lizette Woodworth Reese. OBCA

Glade, The. Robert Kelly. *Fr.* The Book of Persephone. PoM

Gladstone was still respected. Yeux Glauques. Ezra Pound. MoAmPo *Fr.* Hugh Selwyn Mauberley. (Life and Contacts). AmPP; CMoP; InPS-3; LiTM; NOBA; NoAM; TAP

Glamis thou art, and Cawdor; and shalt be. Shakespeare. OxAEP-1 *Fr.* Macbeth.

Glamour of the end attic, the smell of old, The. Perdita. Louis MacNeice. PoA

Glance, The. George Herbert. ESCV

Glance, A. *Unknown, Irish.* NOIV, *tr. by* Thomas Kinsella

Glance back four years (yes, nearly four years now. A Poem for February First 1975. Kay Boyle. NMM-2

Glance in White Space. Clark Coolidge. FTOS

Glanced down at Shannon from the sky-way. Irish-American Dignitary. Austin Clarke. BIrV

Glare from the brass horn makes sun-brown satin fit smoothly the girl by the, The. Fancy Another Day Gone. Lorine Niedecker. FTOS *Fr.* This Condensery: The Complete Writing of Lorine Niedecker, 1985.

Glasgerion, *vers.* B. *Unknown.* ESPB

Glasgow 1956. Gerald Mangan. FaBoTC

Glasgow Peggie. *Unknown.* ESPB

Glasgow Schoolboys, Running Backwards. Douglas Dunn. OxBC

Glasgow Sonnets. Edwin Morgan. FaBoTC

Glasgow Street. William Montgomerie. OxBS

Glasnevin Cemetery. Michael O'Loughlin. PBCIP

Glass. W. S. Merwin. SPE

Glass, The. Sharon Olds. NIP-4

Glass. Takako Uchino Lento, *Japanese.* BoWoP, *tr. by the author*

Glass Blower, The. James Scully. NYBP; TwCP

Glass Enclosure, The. Michael Brownstein. FTOS

Glass Falling. Louis MacNeice. AYFP

Glass falls lower, The. Sad Green. Sylvia Townsend Warner. MoBrPo

Glass goblet, A. Bring in the Wine. Li Ho, *Chinese.* PLT, *tr. by* A. C. Graham

Glass has been falling all the afternoon, The. Storm Warnings. Adrienne Rich. AiP; NAAL-2; NIP-4

Glass House. Diane Ward. PmAP

Glass is going down. The sun, The. Glass Falling. Louis MacNeice. AYFP

Glass I've wanted to live. Through You. Edwin Honig. TAP

Glass King, The. Eavan Boland. CIP-2

Glass of Beer, A. James Stephens. CMoP; InPK-6; MoP; NBLV; OBCoV; OBMV; OxBS; OxBTC; PFE; RB

(Righteous Anger.) MoBrPo

Glass of Water, The. Iain Crichton Smith. FaBoTC

Glass of Water, The. Wallace Stevens. MeMAP; MoAmPo; OxBA; TAP

Glass on the picture from the Bible, The. Darkening Hotel Room. Alfred Corn. VCAP

Glass Town, The. Alastair Reid. NYBP

Glass was the Street—in tinsel Peril. Emily Dickinson. OxBA

Glassblower lies here at rest, A. Epitaph. John Bingham Morton. FaBoEE

Glassed with cold sleep and dazzled by the moon. Train Journey. Judith Wright NoP-4; PBWP

Glassily strand the sea. (LL) The Undead. Richard Wilbur. CAPP-1; CoAP; CoAmPo; OxBC

Glassine envelopes trampoline the pigmeat into a final awakening. The Glass Enclosure. Michael Brownstein. FTOS

Glaucopis. Richard Hughes. OBMV

Glaucus, pilot of the Nessus strait, born. On the Death of the Ferryman, Glaucus. Antiphilus, *Greek.* GrAn, *tr. by* W. S. Merwin

Glaukon and Korydon, mountain herdsmen. Erucius of Cyzicus, *Greek.* GrAn, *tr. by* Peter Levi

Glazed day crumbles to its fall, The. Provincetown, Mass. Harvey Shapiro. PoA

Glazier, The. Stéphane Mallarmé, *French.* OBVE, *tr. by* Keith Bosley

Glazing the pale hair, the duplicate gray [*or* grey] standard faces. (LL) Dolor. Theodore Roethke. AmPP; CMoP; HCAP; HeIP-4; HoPM; LiTM; MoP; NoAM; OPOU; OxBSP; PBMP; PoA; TRP

Glazunoviana. John Ashbery. LCAP-2; VCAP

Gleam of irrecoverable gold, The. (LL) Sunken Gold. Eugene Lee-Hamilton. GSo

Gleamed a resplendent star. At Christmas-Tide. Henrietta Cordelia Ray. CBWP-3

Gleaming sliver. Tanka. Kitahara Hakushū, *Japanese.* MJT, *tr. by* Makoto Ueda

Gleaming—sunken stones. O. Mabson Southard. HA

Gleaner, The. Jane Taylor. OxBChV

Gleaning. David Shimoni, *Hebrew.* MHP, *tr. by* Ruth Finer Mintz

Gleanings. Lorna Goodison. HCP

Glee-fulfiller, fruit-producer, cook who glad the year can feed. Concerning the Fruit-bringing Autumn Season. Catharina Regina von Greiffenberg, *German.* GePo, *tr. by* George C. Schoolfield

Glee—The great storm is over. Emily Dickinson. APN-2

Glen of Silence, The. "Hugh MacDiarmid." CMoP

Glen tells me you've become comatose. San Fransisco Ward. Charles Plymell. EC3

Glenaradale. Walter Chalmers Smith. OBEV; PeVV

Glenarm. John Lyle Donaghy. OBEV; PoEL-4

(Ianthe.) PoEL-4

(To Ianthe.) NOBE

("Verse: 'Past ruin'd [*or* ruined] Ilion Helen lives.'") OBEV

Glenaveril. "Owen Meredith."

Tears. EBVV

Glencoe. Douglas Stewart.

"Sigh, wind in the pine." CBAP

Glengormley. Derek Mahon. CIP-2; IIP

Glenkindie was once a harper gude. Glasgerion. *Unknown.* ESPB

Glenlogie; or, Jean o Bethelnie, *vers.* A. *Unknown.* ESPB

Glenlogie; or, Jean o Bethelnie, *vers.* B. *Unknown.* ESPB

Glenn Miller and I were heroes. 179th Chorus. Jack Kerouac. NeAP *Fr.* Mexico City Blues.

Glens, The. John Hewitt. IIP

Glib little beer-buff from Troon, A. Limerick. Bill Greenwell. PeLi

Glib page / the nearsighted priestess. Pythia. Stefan Aug. Doinas, *Romanian.* CEEP, *tr. by* Stavros Deligiorgis

Glide gently, thus for ever glide. Remembrance of Collins, Composed upon the Thames near Richmond. Wordsworth. EPCY

Gliding / as he sinks two into the chains. Michael S. Harper. *See* Makin' Jump Shots.

Gliding Baskets. Frank A. Cross, Jr. CDa

Gliding through the still air, he made no sound;. The Return of Persephone. Alec Derwent Hope. BMAP

Glimmering morning. Michael McClintock. HA

Glimpse, A. Frances Darwin Cornford. OBMV

Glimpse, A. Robert Duncan. FTOS

Glimpse. William Noel Hodgson. PoFWW

Glimpse. Pearl Cleage Lomax. PoBA

Glimpse, A. John Wieners. FTOS

Glimpse from the Past. Ilse Aichinger, *German.* AF, *tr. by* Allen H. Chappel

Glimpse of a once-loved face, The. What Do They Say. Gary Snyder. NNaP

Glimpse of an Open Dream. David Avidan, *Hebrew.* IP, *tr. by* Warren Bargad *and* Stanley F. Chyet

Glimpse through an interstice caught, A. Walt Whitman. APN-1; AmPP; EP; OxBA; RaBo

("Speaking little, perhaps not a word.") (LL) EP

Glimpsed from the train, which takes shadow for truth. Vladimir Holan, *Czech.* PoSu, *tr. by* Ian *and* Jarmila Milner

Glimpsed through a Lens. Yevgeny Borisovich Rein, *Russian.* TCRP, *tr. by* Bernard Meares

Glimpsed world, halfway through the film, A. The Malice of Innocence. Denise Levertov. NNaP

Glimpses. Christopher Gilbert. GT

Glimpses. Philippe Jaccottet, *French.* VCWP, *tr. by* Derek Mahon

Glimpses of Infancy. Priscilla Jane Thompson. CBWP-2

Glinting like water. Mary Kinzie. FFC

Glion?—Ah, twenty years, it cuts. Obermann Once More. Matthew Arnold. PoEL-5

Glisk of the Great. Robert Garioch. FaBoTC

Glitter green, over such a spell of kisses. Catullus. *See* Carmen 5 ("My sweetest Lesbia, let us live and love").

Glitter of mica at the windy corners. Home Town Elegy. George Sutherland Fraser. FaBoTC

Glittering, adroit, the Sicilian wonder. Death and Empedocles 444 B.C. Horace Gregory. PoA

Glittering bridge. The Bridge. Charlotte Zolotow. CA

Glittering colors of the day are fled, The. To the Moon. Helen Maria Williams. NoP-4

Glittering, glittering, fireflies in the grass. Tsung Ch'en. *Fr.* Miscellaneous Words on the Lake. CoBLCP, *tr. by* Jonathan Chaves

Glittering leaves of the rhododendrons, The. Green Symphony. John Gould Fletcher. MoAmPo

Glittering rises in flocks, The. The Approaches. W. S. Merwin. NOBA

Glittering topaz in your glass, The. At a Danse Macabre. Charles Spear. PeNZ

Gloat, glittering talmudist. Talmudist. Stanley Burnshaw. DiPo

Globe. Elizabeth Spires. WeT

Globe, a paper of the Tories, The. A Suggestion Made by the Posters of the *Globe.* J. E. Thorold Rogers. FaBoEE

Globe and Traveller, no. 6733. Elizabeth Barrett Browning. Stanzas on the Death of Lord Byron. Ro

Globe in North Carolina, The. Derek Mahon. BiHa; PBCIP

Globe of th'earth on which we dwell, The. On the Tack. Thomas Hearne. ECEV

Glog-Hole, The. "Hugh MacDiarmid." NTP

Gloire de Dijon. D. H. Lawrence. CMoP; EnLoPo; GBL; GLoP; NoAM

Gloom of death is on the raven's wing, The. The Raven. Edwin Arlington Robinson, *after* Nicarchus. AWP; FaBoEE; OBAL

Gloom of death is on the raven's wing, The. The Raven. Nicarchus of Alexandria. AWP; FaBoEE; OBAL *Fr.* Variations of Greek Themes.

Gloom of night had overspread the land, The. The Nativity. Mary Weston Fordham. CBWP-2

Glooms of the live-oaks, beautiful-braided and woven. The Marshes of Glynn. Sidney Lanier. AmPP; ImPo; NOBA; NoP-4; OxBA *Fr.* Hymns of the Marshes. APN-2

Gloomy am I, oppressed and sad. The Poet's Arbour in the Birchwood. Edward Williams, *Welsh.* OBWVE, *tr. by* Kenneth Hurlstone Jackson

Gloomy and dark art thou, O chief of the mighty Omahas. To the Driving Cloud. Henry Wadsworth Longfellow. PoEL-5

Gloomy Cathedral, A. Paris. Gertrud Kolmar, *German.* PBWP, *tr. by* David Kipp

Gloomy grammarians in golden gowns. Of the Manner of Addressing Clouds. Wallace Stevens. PoA

Gloomy hulls, in armor [*or* armour] grim, The. The *Temeraire.* Herman Melville. APN-2; GS; NCAP

Gloomy lowering of the sky, The. Written on a Gloomy Day, in Sickness. Susanna Blamire. ECWP

Gloomy minister of Hades who sail this stream. Leonidas of Tarentum. HePo, *tr. by* Barbara Hughes Fowler *Fr.* Epigrams.

Gloomy night embraced the place. The Shepherds' Hymn. Richard Crashaw. NOBE *Fr.* In the Holy Nativity of Our Lord God. GeHe; PoEL-2

Gloomy Night of Sadness, The. *Unknown.* AH

Gloomy rain. Tanka. Kondō Yoshimi, *Japanese.* MJT, *tr. by* Makoto Ueda

Gloomy thought, Ben Bulben, A. The Deserted Mountain. *Unknown, Irish.* BIrV, *tr. by* John Montague

Gloriana Dying. Sylvia Townsend Warner. FaBoWP

Glories of our blood and state, The. Death the Leveller. James Shirley. AWP; BeJo; EBEvV; FaPoR; GEA; GTBS-P; HAP; ImPo; NOBE; NoP-4; OAEL-1; OBEV; PBMP; PBRV; PFE; PeECV; PoEL-2; PoRA; SCGP; UnPo *Fr.* The Contention of Ajax and Ulysses.

Glories of the world struck me, made me aria, once, The. John Berryman. HCAP *Fr.* Dream Songs.

Glorious image of the Maker's beauty, The. Sonnet 61. Edmund Spenser. Son *Fr.* Amoretti. AAS

Glorious Maid, whose soule to Heaven is gone, The. The Arguement. Anna Hume. KTR *Fr.* Triumphs of Death.

Glorious Strike of the Builders, The. *Unknown.* FaBoVe

Glorious the sun in mid career. Christopher Smart. FaBoCh *Fr.* A Song to David. ImPo; NAEL-1; NOBE; OAEL-1; OBWVE; PoE; PoEL-3

Glorious Things of Thee Are Spoken. John Newton. NOCV; NOEC

Glorious Wonders of the DEITY, The. (LL) Eden. Thomas Traherne. ChIV-1; ESCV; GeHe; PoEL-2

Glory. Marianne Moore. NYBP

Glory. Joseph Wise. AH

Glory and Enduring Fame. William Gilmore Simms. Son

Glory and loveliness have passed away. To Leigh Hunt, Esq. Keats. OBNC; Son

Glory Be to Chingwe's Hole. Jack A. Mapanje. HBAPE

Glory be to God for dappled things. Pied Beauty. Gerard Manley Hopkins. APAD; AWP; CABP; CMoP; ChAP; ClHu; EBEvV; EBVV; EnVR; EnlH; FaBoMo; GTBS-P; HAP; HeIP-4; HoPM; ImPo; InPK-6; InPS-3; LiTM; MoBrPo; MoP; NAEL-2; NOBE; NOBVV; NTP; NoAM; NoP-4; OAEL-2; OBEV; OBMV; OBNC; OxAEP-2; OxBSP; PBMP; PoE; PoPoPo; PoRA; Poetr; RB; RaBo; SAGP; SCGP; SCV; SoSe-8; TFi; TTTS; UV; WeW-3

Glory be to God for Hopkins' verse. Pied Beauty. Stanley J. Sharpless. UV

Glory be to God on high. The Incarnation. Charles Wesley. NOCV

Glory be to those. Baker's prayer. Sasaki Yukitsuna, *Japanese.* MJT, *tr. by* Makoto Ueda

Glory Dead. *Unknown.* PBCV

Glory, Glory. . . . Raymond R. Patterson. MBE

Glory, Glory, Glory to the heroes!!! On Trash. Vladimir Mayakovsky, *Russian.* TCRP, *tr. by* Daniel Weissbort

Glory is of the sun, too, and the sun of suns. D. H. Lawrence. OxBSP

Glory of and Grace in the Church Set Out, The. Edward Taylor. AmPP *Fr.* God's Determinations [touching his Elect].

Glory of evening was spread through the west, The. The Convict. Wordsworth. OxBSP

Glory of God, The, *sl. diff. vers.* Bible, *O.T. See* Psalm 19.

Glory of my Work, and Me, The. (LL) His Prayer for Absolution. Robert Herrick. BeJo; CavPo

Glory of Nature, The. Frederick Tennyson. OBNC

Glory of the beauty of the morning, The. Edward Thomas. OxBTC; TOF

Glory of the Day Was in Her Face, The. James Weldon Johnson. PoBA

Glory of the Garden, The. Rudyard Kipling. OBGa

"Oh, Adam was a gardener, and God." CTV

Glory of Women. Siegfried Sassoon. NAEL-2; NoP-4; OBWP; OxAEP-2; PeFWW; PoFWW

Glory to God and to God's Mother chaste. To Dante (He Commends the Work of Dante's Life). Giovanni Quirino, *Italian.* AWP, *tr. by* D. G. Rossetti

Glory to Osiris, the Prince of Everlastingness. He Singeth a Hymn to Osiris, the Lord of Eternity. *Unknown.* AWP *Fr.* Book of the Dead.

Glory to Thee, My God, This Night. Thomas Ken. NOCV

Glory to you, oh pain, sorrow unending! The Grey-eyed King. "Anna Akhmatova," *Russian.* PBWP, *tr. by* Robert Tracy

Glory Trumpeter, The. Derek Walcott. GT; NAEL-2; NoP-4; SeSe

Glose. Michael Malinowitz. EOEF

Gloss. Padraic Fiacc. CIP-2; PNI

Gloss. David McCord. OBAL

Gloss to Matthew V 27–28. Alec Derwent Hope. GI

Gloucester Moors. William Vaughn Moody. APN-2; NOBA; OxBA "This earth is not the steadfast place."

Glove, The. Harold Bond. NYBP

Glove, The. Ben Jonson. GBL *Fr.* Cynthia's Revels.

Glow and beauty of the stars, The. Sappho, *Greek.* BoWoP, *tr. by* Willis Barnstone

Glow-boys. John Tranter. BMAP

Glow, little glow-worm, fly of fire. The Glow-Worm. Johnny Mercer. OBAL

Glow of eyes being handed back their sight, The. (LL) Rogue and Jar: 4/27/77. Thulani Davis. MoNo; SeSe

Glow-Worm, The. Johnny Mercer. OBAL

Glow-Worm, The. Charlotte Smith. BWW

Glow-Worms. P. A. Ropes. BoTP

Glowing, festive, warm, the moon looked down. Thalero. Angelos Sikelianos, *Greek.* GrIP, *tr. by* Edmund Keeley *and* Philip Sherrard

Glowworm. David McCord. NTCP

Glowworm, The. Thomas Stanley. BeJo; NOSC

Glowworm in a garden prayed, A. A Very Minor Poet Speaks. Isabel Valle. BLPA

Gloze Upon This Text, *Dominus iis opus habet*, A. George Gascoigne. ChIV-2

Glue and a small amount of alum. Pictures of the Floating World. Miyazawa Kenji, *Japanese.* PFTM, *tr. by* Hiroaki Sato

Glunk! / I toss my heels up to my head. Oiseaurie. Margaret Widdemer. BXAP

Glutton, The. Robert Graves. CMoP

Glutton [*or* Glutton in the Tavern], The. William Langland. PoE *Fr.* The Vision of Piers Plowman.

Glutton, The. John Oakman. OxBChV

Glycine's Song. Coleridge. CH; OBEV *Fr.* Zapolya. (Song.)

Glykon, glory of Asia / born in Pergamum. Antipater of Thessalonica, *Greek.* GrAn, *tr. by* Alistair Elliot

Glyn Cynon Wood. *Unknown, Welsh.* OBWVE, *tr. by* Gwyn Williams

Gnarly and bent and deaf's a pos'. Zeke. Leonard Alfred George Strong. MoBrPo

Gnat, The. Joseph Beaumont. NOSC

Gnawed by lichens. The Meditation Rock. Mo Shih-lung, *Chinese.* CoBLCP, *tr. by* Jonathan Chaves

Gnawed by a beetle. (LL) My lover capable of terrible lies. Kaccipettu Nannakaiyar, *Tamil.* BoWoP; PBWP; WPOW, *tr. by* A. K. Ramanujan

Gnawing the Breast. Sandra McPherson. LCAP-2

Gnawing the highway's edges, its black mouth. The Swamp. Derek Walcott. GT

Gnomes. Samuel Beckett. BIrV; OxBSP

Gnomes. Howard Nemerov. Sacrificed Author, A. GI

Gnomic Verses. William Blake. "Abstinence sows sand all over." EBEV; FaBoEE; GBL; OxBM; PFE "Angel that presided o'er my birth, The." InPK-6; OxBSP; RB "Great things are done when Men and Mountains meet." OxBSP Sword and the Sickle, The.

Gnomic Verses (Exeter Book). *Unknown. See* Maxims (Exeter Book).

Gnosis. Christopher Pearse Cranch. APN-1; ColAP (Enosis.) PAR

Gnosis. Agnes Gergely, *Hungarian.* CEEP, *tr. by* Emery E. George

Gnostic Prelude. James McAuley. BMAP

Gnostics on Trial. Linda Gregg. EC2

Gnu up at the zoo, The. Elegy. John Hall Wheelock. NYBP

Go. Elizabeth I, Queen of England. *See* When I was fair and young, then [*or* and] favour graced me;.

Go ahead: say what you're thinking. Daisies. Louise Glück. AFr

Go and ask Robin to bring the girls over. Vision by Sweetwater. John Crowe Ransom. CMoP; FaBoMo; MeMAP; NOBA; OxBA; RB

Go and catch a falling star. Song. Donne. AWP; ClHu; EBEV; EBEvV; FHYEP; FSCP; HAP; HeIP-4; ImPo; InPK-6; InPS-3; NAEL-1; NAWM-1; NIP-4; NOBE; NOSC; NoP-4; NoSic; OBEV; OxAEP-1; PBMP; PFE; PoE; SoSe-8; TFi

Go and find *work.* (LL) What the Chairman Told Tom. Basil Bunting. NoP-4; OxBTC

Go Ask the Dead. Thomas McGrath. AF; CDa ("You have climbed to the moon on a ladder of dead / man's bones!") (LL) CDa

Go bet, penny, go bet, go! *Unknown.* MiEL

Go bind thou up young dangling apricots. Richard II. Shakespeare. OBGa *Fr.* King Richard II.

Go Blow Fire, A. Michael Smith. HCP

Go bow thy head in gentle spite. To a Lily. James Matthew Legaré. APN-2

Go boy, and thy good mistress tell. Macbeth. Horace Smith. BXAP

Go Bring Me Back My Blue-eyed Boy. *Unknown.* AS

"Go Bring Me," Said the Dying Fair. William Hunter. AH

Go By. Tennyson. OBNC

Go by! linked fin by fin! most odiously. (LL) A Fish Answers. Leigh Hunt. NBLV; PeLV; SCGP

Go call a careful painter, let him show. Of the French Kings Nativity. Benjamin Harris. SCAP

Go child, who is my sin and nothing more. (LL) Unknown Girl in the Maternity Ward. Anne Sexton. MoP; NoAM

Go, daughters of Zion. The Death of Tammuz. Saul Tchernichowsky, *Hebrew.* TrJP, *tr. by* L. V. Snowman

Go deeper than love, for the soul has greater depths. D. H. Lawrence. ITG

Go Down Death. James Weldon Johnson. BkSV; ISC; PoBA

Go down, Moses. *Unknown.* AH; BPo; BkSV; CrDW; NAAAL; NOBA; NoP-4; PeECV ("When Israel was in Egypt land.") PeECV

Go Down, O Sun, Out from the Motu River. Te Aomuhurangi te Maaka, *Maori.* PeNZ, *tr. by the author*

Go Down, Old Hannah. *Unknown.* AmFP; NAAAL

Go down to Kew in lilac-time, in lilac-time, in lilac-time. The Barrel-Organ. Alfred Noyes. BoTP; MoBrPo; PoRA

Go, draw aside the curtain, and discover. Shakespeare. OxAEP-1 *Fr.* The Merchant of Venice.

Go, dumb-born book. Envoi (1919). Ezra Pound. HAP: MoAmPo; MoP; OxBA; UnPo; VGW *Fr.* Hugh Selwyn Mauberley. (Life and Contacts). AmPP; CMoP; InPS-3; LiTM; NOBA; NoAM; TAP

Go farther! let it serve to trample on. (LL) Sonnet: "What can I give thee back, O liberal." Elizabeth Barrett Browning. BWW; OxAEP-2

Go fetch to me a pint o'wine. The Silver Tassie. Robert Burns. NOBE; OBEV

Go find Avicenna. Calling the Doctor (1000 A.D.) Nizami Arudi, *Persian.* ArPe, *tr. by* Omar S. Pound

Go, flaunting Rose! The Aesthete to the Rose. *Unknown.* BXAP

"Go, Flee?"—A man like me does not flee! Prophet, Go, Flee! Hayyim Nahman Bialik, *Hebrew.* MHP, *tr. by* Ruth Finer Mintz

Go For Broke. André Breton, *French.* PFTM, *tr. by* David Antin

Go, for they call you, Shepherd, from the hill. The Scholar-Gipsy. Matthew Arnold. EBEV; EBVV; EBVVPR; EnVR; FHYEP; HAP; ImPo; NAEL-2; NOBE; NOBVV; NoP-4; OAEL-2; OBEV; OBNC; OxAEP-1; PoE; PoEL-5; SCGP; TFi

Go;—for 'tis Memorial morning. Memorial Day. Clara Ann Thompson. CBWP-2

Go forth my little volume. God Speed. George Clinton Rowe. AAP

Go from me: I am one of those who fall. Mystic and Cavalier. Lionel Pigot Johnson. ADE; MoBrPo

Go from me, summer friends, and tarry not. From Sunset to Star Rise. Christina Rossetti. VWP

Go from me. Yet I feel that I shall stand. Sonnet. Elizabeth Barrett Browning. BWW; CBLP; LW; OBEV; OxAEP-2 *Fr.* Sonnets from the Portuguese.

"Go get me some of your father's gold." Pretty Polly. *Unknown.* AS

Go Get the Axe. *Unknown.* AS

Go! go! go! seek some other where, importune me no more. Elizabeth I, Queen of England. *See* When I was fair and young, then [*or* and] favour graced me;.

Go, go, queint folies, sugred sin. Idle Verse. Henry Vaughan. MiEL

Go, grieving rimes of mine, to that hard stone. Petrarch. NAWM-1 *Fr.* Sonnets to Laura.

Go, Hart. *Unknown.* OxBS

Go, Heart, unto the Lamp of Licht. Go, Hart. *Unknown.* OxBS

Go hert, hurt with adversité. *Unknown.* MiEL

Go hmmmp hmmmmp hmmmmmp. (LL) Tapping. Jayne Cortez. ISC; MoNo

Go home, stupid. Ultimatum: Kid to Kid. Langston Hughes. NOxBChV

Go home, you see, well I wouldn't run a risk like that. (LL) My Hat. Stevie Smith. BrRo; CBNP

Go! hunt the whiter ermine, and present. For the Lady Olivia Porter; a Present upon a New Year's Day. Sir William Davenant. MeLP; NOSC

Go I must. *Unknown. See* Cuckoo, cuckoo / What do you do?

Go, idle Boy! I quit thy pow'r. The Adieu and Recall to Love. Robert Merry. NOBRP

Go Idle Lines. Thomas Watson. Son *Fr.* The Tears of Fancy.

Go, ill-sped book, and whisper to her or. John Berryman. BoLoP

Go in, enter this landscape. It's still dark. Dialogue in Winter. Tomas Venclova, *Lithuanian.* CEEP, *tr.* by David McDuff

Go inside a stone. Stone. Charles Simic. ChAP; InPS-3

Go, let the fatted calf be killed. The Welcome. Abraham Cowley. BoLoP *Fr.* The Mistress.

Go, litel book, go litel myn tragedy. Go, Little Book ("Go, litel book, go litel myn tragedy"). Chaucer. EPCY; OAEL-1 *Fr.* Troilus and Criseyde [*or* Criseide]. EnVB

Go little book, par avion. Envoi. Richard Tillinghast. MT

Go, litull bill, and command me hertely. She Saw Me in Church. *Unknown.* MiEL

Go[e], lovely rose[—ous sweet and fair]. Song. Edmund Waller. AWP; BeJo; BoLoP; CABP; CTC; ClHu; EBEvV; EnLoPo; GBL; GLoP; GTBS-P; HAP; HeIP-4; InPK-6; LoP; NAEL-1; NOBE; NOSC; NoP-4; OAEL-1; OBEV; OxAEP-1; OBEV; PoE; PoEL-3; PoPoPo; PoRA; Poetr; SeCP; SoSe-8; TFi; UnPo; WeW-3

Go, loving woodbine, clip with lovely grace. On a Pair of Garters. Sir John Davies. SiPS

Go measure the distance from Cape Town to Pretoria. Measure for Measure. Sipho Sepamla. AF; PeSAV

Go, my flock, go get you hence. Ninth Song. Sir Philip Sidney. NoSic *Fr.* Astrophil and Stella. AAS; SiPS

Go, my songs, seek your praise from the young and from the intolerant. Ité. Ezra Pound. HAP; MoAmPo

Go, my songs, to the lonely and the unsatisfied. Commission. Ezra Pound. BoLoP; TwCP

Go, my thought, as long as a word clear enough for flight. Ingeborg Bachmann, *Hebrew.* PoSu, *tr.* by Mark Anderson

Go not, happy day. Tennyson. EBVV *Fr.* Maud [A Monodrama]. EnVR

Go not to the hills of Erinn. The Wind on the Hills. Dora Sigerson Shorter. NOBVV

Go not too frequently thy friends to see. Advice to Bores. Abraham ibn Chasdai, *Hebrew.* TrJP, *tr.* by J. Chotzner

Go not too near a House of Rose. Emily Dickinson. MoAmPo; NIP-4

Go on! Go on! A Sermon at Clevedon. Thomas Edward Brown. NOBVV

Go on! go on! and love away! The Perfidious. Walter Savage Landor. CBLP

Go on, high ship, since now, upon the shore. Farewell to Florida. Wallace Stevens. NoAM

Go on; I'll follow thee. (LL) Angels and ministers of grace defend us! Shakespeare. EBEV; OxAEP-1

Go on, tell me the season is over. Alan Wearne. BMAP

Go on the Scout they say. Thorow. Susan Howe. APSN; PT

Go Out. Eileen Mathias. BoTP

Go out and camp somewhere. You're lying down. Mapooram. *Aborigine Oral Tradition.* NOBAu, *tr.* by Fred Biggs

Go out in the midday sun. (LL) Mad Dogs and Englishmen. Noël Coward. NBLV; NOBL; PeLV

Go out in this dear summertide. Paul Gerhardt, *German.* GePo, *tr.* by George C. Schoolfield

Go out with a small flashlight and a star chart. Things to Do around a Ship at Sea. Gary Snyder. CAPP-1

Go peni go. (LL) Penny. *Unknown.* EnVB; FaBoVe; MiEL

Go[e], perjured [*or* perjur'd] man, and if thou e'er [*or* ere] return. The Curse. A Song. Robert Herrick. CaPo

Go, perjured youth, and court what nymph you please. To Philaster. Sarah Fyge Egerton. ECWP

Go pretty [*or* prettie] child and bear[e] this flower. To His Saviour, a Child; a Present, by a Child. Robert Herrick. BeJo; ChIV-2; OxBChV; PeECV; SeCP; TrCP

Go Right along the Seashore. *Unknown.* PeNZ

Go, rose, my Chloe's bosom grace. Love's Emblem. John Clare. NIP-4

Go, Sad Complaint. Charles, Duc d' Orléans. EnVB

Go sad or sweet or riotous with beer. The Old Women. George Mackay Brown. NoP-4; OxBS

Go, said old Lyce, senseless lover, go. Lyce. William Walsh. BoLoP

Go, silly worm, drudge, trudge, and travell. Omnia Somnia. Joshua Sylvester. FaBoEE

Go Slow. Langston Hughes. LiTM

Go slow, my soul, to feed thyself. Emily Dickinson. APN-2

Go slowly, go slowly, oh moon, upon your way. We are sowing by your light. They That Sow at Night. Shin Shalom, *Hebrew.* MHP, *tr.* by Ruth Finer Mintz

Go[e], smiling soul[e]s, your new-built cages break[e]. To the Infant Martyrs. Richard Crashaw. ChIV-2; GeHe; NAEL-1; NoP-4; OxBSP

Go softly now in the presence of circles. Summer Adjustments. Anne S. Perlman. CMAP

Go softly past the graveyard where. Leonidas of Tarentum, *Greek.* GrAn; OBCVT, *tr.* by Fleur Adcock

Go softly, you whose careless feet. Boot Hill. Sharlot Mabridth Hall. PaTW

Go, solitary wood, and henceforth be. On the Death of a Nightingale. Thomas Randolph. BeJo

Go, songs, for ended is our brief, sweet play. Envoy. Francis Thompson. MoBrPo

Go, Soul [*or* Goe soule], the body's [*or* bodies] guest. The Lie. Sir Walter Ralegh. AAS; CTC; EBEV; FaBoPV; GEA; HAP; ImPo; NAEL-1; NOBE; NoP-4; NoSic; PBRV; PoEL-2; PoPoPo; RB; SCGP; SCV; SiPS; TFi

Go soule, go sweetest soule for ever blest. Ludovico Ariosto. OBVE, *tr.* by Sir John Harington *Fr.* Orlando Furioso.

Go stay with someone else now, make a young man happy. (LL) In Illness, Dismissing My Singing Girl. Ssu-k'ung Shu, *Chinese.* CoBCP, *tr.* by Burton Watson

Go, swallow, and tell, now that the summer is dying. Cwmrhydyceirw Elegiacs. Vernon Watkins. PoA

Go Take the World. Jay Macpherson. MoCV

Go talk with those who are rumored to be unlike you. For the Student Strikers. Richard Wilbur. OxBC

Go tell at Sparta, traveler passing by. Simonides. *See* For the Spartan Dead at Thermopylai (480 B.C.).

Go tell Aunt Rhody [*or* Nancy]. The Old Gray Goose. *Unknown.* AmFP

Go tell him to clear me one acre of ground. The Elfin Knight. *Unknown.* AmFP

Go tell the king—the carven hall is felled. *Unknown, Greek.* GrAn, *tr.* by Peter Jay

Go tell the king: the daedal. The Last Utterance of the Delphic Oracle. *Unknown, Greek.* OBVE, *tr.* by Kenneth Rexroth

Go tell the Spartans, thou that passest by. Thermopylae. Simonides, *Greek.* AWP; OBVE; OBWP, *tr.* by William Lisle Bowles

Go, the rich *Chariot* instantly prepare;. The Muse. Abraham Cowley. CABP; EPCY; PBRV

Go, then, and join the murmuring city's throng! To a Friend. William Lisle Bowles. Son

Go then, my dove, but now no longer mine. Cotton Mather. AiP; SCAP

Go thou forth, my book, though late. To His Book. Robert Herrick. CaPo

Go thou gentle whispering wind. A Prayer to the Wind. Thomas Carew. BeJo; CavPo

Go, thou that vainly dost mine eyes invite. Sonnet. Henry King, Bishop of Chichester. OxBSP

Go thou thy way, and I go mine. Mizpah. Julia Aldrich Baker. BLPA; FaBoBe

Go Thou to Rome. Shelley. *Fr.* Adonais; An Elegy on the Death of Keats. EBEV; FHYEP; HoPM; ImPo; NOBRP; OAEL-2; OxAEP-2; PoEL-4; TFi

Go through the gates with closed eyes. "Close Your Eyes!" Arna Bontemps. GT; PoBA

Go Throw Them Out. Moyshe-Leyb Halpern, *Yiddish.* CEEP, *tr.* by Ruth Whitman

Go to bed early wake up with joy. *Unknown.* BoTP

Go to bed first. *Unknown.* OxNR

Go to bed late. *Unknown.* CTV; OxNR

Go to bed, Tom. *Unknown.* OxNR

Go to Old Ireland. *Unknown.* AmFP

Go to sleep, go to sleepy. All the Pretty Little Horses. *Unknown.* AmFP

Go to sleep, my baby goblin. Mother Goblin's Lullaby. Jack Prelutsky. NOxBChV

Go to sleep. Night is a coal pit. Lullaby for a Daughter. James Harrison. MoLi

Go to sleep—though of course you will not. A Goodnight. William Carlos Williams. MoAmPo

Go to Sleepy. *Unknown.* AS

Go to sleepy, little baby. (LL) All the Pretty Little Horses. *Unknown.* AmFP; OxBoLi; TTTS

Go to the Ant [Thou Sluggard]. Bible, *O.T.* TrJP *Fr.* Proverbs. (Reproof, A.)

"Go to the Ant." Stanley J. Sharpless. NOBL

Go to the ant, thou sluggard;. Bible, *O.T.* CTV *Fr.* The Bible, Proverbs 6:6–8.

Go to the ant, you sluggard. Proverbs 6:6. David Curzon. ChIV-1

Go to the moon / white folks going to the moon / going to. Moon Bound. Raymond Washington. NBV

Go to the patch some afternoon. How to Make Rhubarb Wine. Ted Kooser. PBCAP

Go to the western gate, Luke Havergal. Luke Havergal. Edwin Arlington Robinson. APN-2; AWP; AmPP; GBL; LiTM; MeMAP; MoAmPo; NAAL-2; NCAP; NOBA; NoAM; PoEL-5; TFi; UnPo

Go up among the mountains when the storm. Sonnet III. Written at Midnight, on Helm Crag. John Wilson. Ro *Fr.* The Isle of Palms and Other Poems.

Go, Valentine. Robert Southey. Son

Go wailing verse, the infants of my love. Samuel Daniel. NoP-4

Go, wash thyself in Jordan—go, wash thee and be clean! Naaman's Song. Rudyard Kipling. ChIV-1

Go 'way, fiddle! folks is tired o' hearin' you a-squawkin. Fust Banjo, De. Irwin Russell. BLPA *Fr.* Christmas Night in the Quarters.

Go 'Way f'om Mah Window. *Unknown.* AS

Go 'way from dat window, "My Honey, My Love." Song to the Runaway Slave. *Unknown.* BPo

Go where glory waits thee. Thomas Moore. OBNC

Go where my mind will. Tune: "Four Pieces of Jade"—Idle Leisure. Kuan Han-ch'ing, *Chinese.* SuSp, *tr. by* Jerome Seaton

Go where we will, at ev'ry time and place. Against Sodomy. Charles Churchill. ECEV *Fr.* The Times.

Go with a perm or a duck tail. How to Dress Like a Femmy Dyke. Jane Barnes. GLP

Go Work in My Vineyard. Frances Ellen Watkins Harper. PWR

Go ye afar. Go teach all nations. Missionary Hymm. James Burke. TIRV

Go you, O winds that blow from north to south. To Pandora. Alexander Craig. Son

"Go, your lover lives!" said Cromwell; "Curfew shall not ring tonight!" (LL) Curfew Must Not Ring Tonight. Rose Hartwick Thorpe. BLPA; FaBoBe

Goad, The. "Michael Field." VWP

Goanna chases grasshopper. *Unknown, Aborigine.* NOBAu, *tr. by* Mungayana Nundhirribala

Goat. Kenneth Rexroth. *Fr.* A Bestiary. OBAL

Goat, The. *Unknown.* CTAV; PoLF

Goat can climb anything, but, A. Maltese Goat. Nigel Dennis. PFE

Goat-foot choros the. Japanese Presentation I and II. Joan Retallack. FTOS

Goat-foot Pan has quit his flocks. Meleager, *Greek.* GrAn, *tr. by* Peter Whigham

Goat Paths, The. James Stephens. AWP; CH; SCGP; UnPo

Goat was nibbling on a vine, A. The Vine and the Goat. Aesop, *Greek.* AWP, *tr. by* William Ellery Leonard

Goat's-Leaf. Marie de France. PBWP, *tr. by* Aline Allard

Goats on the roof. John Wills. HA

Goats were still, The. Summer, At Home. Mary Clark. IFJA

Goblin, The. Jack Prelutsky. TLR

Goblin lives in our house, in our house, in our house, A. Rose Fyleman. BoTP; NTCP

Goblin Market. Christina Rossetti. CPO; EBEV; FaBoSe; NAEL-2; NALW; NOBVV; NOxBChV; OBNV; OxAEP-2; VWP

  "'Good folk,' said Lizzie." FaBoVe

  "Laughed every goblin." BrRo

God, A. Ted Hughes. GI

God? Cristoir O'Flynn. TIRV

God. Boris Abramovich Slutsky, *Russian.* TCRP, *tr. by* J. R. Rowland

God (3). Marina Tsvetayeva, *Russian.* WPoS, *tr. by* Paul Graves

God a great railway to heaven has planned. The Beulah Railway. *Unknown.* GM

God, a man at Yale, adopted a monkey. Monkey. Josephine Miles. LiTM

God, A Poem. James Fenton. DiPo; NoAM; NoP-4; OBCoV

God aloft in majesty. God Supreme. Abraham ibn Ezra, *Hebrew.* TOF, *tr. by* David Goldstein

God alone is God! Mohammed rassoul *Allah!.* Desert. Birago Diop, *French.* NegPo, *tr. by* Ellen Conroy Kennedy

God and Saint [*or* Sanct] Peter was gangand be the way. How the First Hielandman of God Was Made. *Unknown.* OBSV

God and the devil in these letters. The Postman's Bell Is Answered Everywhere. Horace Gregory. MoAmPo; NYRP

God and the devil still are wrangling. For a Mouthy Woman. Countee Cullen. ChIV-1; OBAL; PoBA

God and Yet a Man, A? *Unknown.* HAP; MiEL

God appears, and God is Light. William Blake. *Fr.* Auguries of Innocence. EBEV; FaBoCh; FaPoR; ImPo; OAEL-1; OBNC; OxAEP-2; OxBoLi; PeECV; PoEL-4; TFi

God, Are You There? Helen Steiner Rice. CTV

God banish from your house. Benediction. Stanley Kunitz. VGW

God be here, God be there. *Unknown.* OxNR

God be in my head. The Knight's Prayer. *Unknown.* BoTP

(God be praised!) the Georges ended. (LL) The Georges. Walter Savage Landor. FaBoEE; NIP-4; OBCoV; OBSV; PFE

God Be with You. *Unknown.* PoToHe

God be with you in the Springtime. Through the Year. Julian S. Cutler. BLPA

God Be with You till We Meet Again. Jeremiah Eames Rankin. AH

God being with thee when we know it not. (LL) By the Sea. Wordsworth. AWP; FHYEP; GSo; GTBS-P; HeIP-4; ImPo; NAEL-2; NIP-4; NOBRP; NoP-4; OAEL-2; OBEV; OxAEP-2; PoEL-4; PoLF; SCGP; Son; TFi

God bless all policemen. Goodbat Nightman. Roger McGough. MoP

God bless America. Irving Berlin. CTV

God Bless America. John Fuller. OBSV; PeLV

God bless Henry. He lived like a rat. John Berryman. CAPP-1 *Fr.* Dream Songs.

God bless our good and gracious King. Impromptu on Charles II. John Wilmot, 2d Earl of Rochester. FaBoEE; NBLV; NOBL; NTP; OBSV; OxAEP-1; PeLV

God bless our meat. *Unknown.* OxNR

God Bless Our Native Land. Frances Ellen Watkins Harper. PWR

God bless the field and bless the furrow. The Robin's Song. C. Lovat Fraser. BoTP

God bless the King!—I mean the Faith's Defender. Extempore [Verses] Intended to Allay the Violence of Party-Spirit. John Byrom. FaBoEE; NOBL; PeLV

"God bless the man who first invented sleep!" Early Rising. John Godfrey Saxe. PoLF

God bless the master of this house. Christmas Carol. *Unknown.* BoTP; CTV

God bless this house from thatch to floor. *Unknown.* OxNR

God bless us all! That's quite another thing. (LL) Extempore [Verses] Intended to Allay the Violence of Party-Spirit. John Byrom. FaBoEE; NOBL; PeLV

God bless you! (LL) Christmas is coming [*or* a-coming], / And the geese are getting fat. *Unknown.* NTCP; OxNR; PChr; ReMoGo

God Bless You. *Unknown.* PoToHe

God bless you. Guilt is magical. (LL) Adultery. James Dickey. MT; TAP

God-born before the Sons of God, she hurled. Music. Madison Cawein. APN-2

God braced me with His firm hand. The Tool of Fate. "Yehoash," *Yiddish.* TrJP, *tr. by* Isidore Goldstick

God breathed. Creation. Robin Gurr. NOBAu

God bring you safe from the death sleep of night. A Donegal Hush Song. Cathal O'Byrne. TIRV

God broke into my house last night. Scapegoat. William Robert Rodgers. CIP-2

God broke upon this upturned field; trees. Body of a Rook. David Wevill. MoCV

God brought perfect man to fruition. Limerick. Douglas Catley. PeLi

God caught his eye. (LL) Epitaph on a Waiter. David McCord. NBLV; NIP-4; OBAL; OBCoV

God certainly wasn't. Blasphemy. Sachiko Yoshihara, *Japanese.* WPJ, *tr. by* Kenneth Rexroth *and* Ikuko Atsumi

God, consider the soul's need. Death Song for Owain ab Urien. Taliesin, *Welsh.* OBWVE, *tr. by* Anthony Conran

God created his image. Fill and Illumined. Joseph Ceravolo. ChIV-1

God decided he was tired. Budgie Finds His Voice. Wendy Cope. UV

God did forbid the Israelites, to bring. The Ass[e]. Robert Herrick. ChIV-1

God does for virtue goal and urge and crown afford. Virtue's Goal Is God. "Angelus Silesius." GePo, *tr. by* George C. Schoolfield *Fr.* The Cherubical Wanderer.

God does not live to explain. (LL) New Hampshire, February. Richard Eberhart. LiTM; TwCP

God don't want no coward soldiers. God's Goin' to Set This World on Fire. *Unknown.* AS

God doth dwell in men, from th' blessed seats, A. In Consort to Wednesday, Jan. 1st. 1701. Richard Henchman. SCAP

God, ever gracious God! Here I myself debase. Night Thoughts Concerning a Dream. Daniel Casper von Lohenstein, *German.* GePo, *tr. by* George C Schoolfield

God Everywhere. Abraham ibn Ezra, *Hebrew.* TrIP, *tr. by* D. E. de L

God exists, though he doesn't exist. Phallus. Kazuko Shiraishi. BoWoP, *tr. by* Ikuko Atsumi

God, / for Mercy's sake. Rabbi Nachman of Bratzlav, *Hebrew.* BLT, *tr. by* Zalman Schachter. *Fr.* The Torah of the Void.

God. For the most part I do without. The Cardinal Detoxes: A Play in One Act. Thomas M. Disch. BAP-94

God from His Throne with Piercing Eye. Joseph Steward. AH

God gave His children memory. Roses in December. Geoffrey Anketell Studdert-Kennedy. BLPA

God gave my son in trust to me. My Son. James D. Hughes. BLPA

God, give me back the simple faith that I so long have clung to. A Prayer for Faith. Margaret Elizabeth Sangster. PoToHe

God Give to Men. Arna Bontemps. BPo; ColAP

God, Give Us Men! Josiah Gilbert Holland. BLPA

God gives them sleep on ground, on straw. Roger Williams. SCAP

God gives us joy that we may give. Giving. *Unknown*. PoToHe

God! / glad I'm black. Blue Black. Bloke Modisane. PBA

God, God, be lenient her first night there. Prayer for a Very New Angel. Violet Alleyn Storey. BLPA

God grant thee thine own wish, and grant thee mine. Donne. OBVE

God guard me from those thoughts men think. A Prayer for Old Age. W. B. Yeats. IIP

God had released her. (LL) The Widow. Robert Southey. NOBRP; NOEC; UV

God has a Right Hand, but is quite bereft. The Right Hand. Robert Herrick. CavPo

God Has Mercy [*or* Pity] on Kindergarten Children. Yehuda Amichai, *Hebrew*. IP, *tr. by* Warren Bargad *and* Stanley F. Chyet

God has not appeared to the birds. (LL) "Calvary." W. B. Yeats. PeECV

God Hasn't Made Room. Mririda n'Ait Attik. PBWP, *tr. by* Daniel Halpern *and* Paula Paley

God heard the embattled nations sing and shout. The Dilemma. Sir John Collings Squire. OBCoV; PoFWW

God help who follows his father's craft! The Passing of the Poets. Fearflatha O'Gnive. NOIV

God help who looks upon Enniskillen. A Visit to Enniskillen. Tadhg Dall O'Huiginn. NOIV

God, how I envy you these great oak roots. A Jew Walks in Westminster Abbey. Aubrey Hodes. TrJP

God! How I Long for You. Kenneth Mackenzie. CBAP

God, how my mouth swam. Sparrow Hills. Wilson Robley, Jr. PBCAP

God! how they plague his life, the three damned sisters. The Little Brother. James Reeves. OxBTC

God, I know nothing, my sense is all nonsense. A Grace. Donald Hall. LoL

God I love thee in Thy robe of roses. Zebaoth. Else Lasker-Schüler, *German*. TrJP, *tr. by* Jethro Bithell

God, I need a job because I need money. Prayer. Alan Dugan. NoAM

God if he exists. The Man Root. Kazuko Shiraishi, *Japanese*. WPJ, *tr. by* Kenneth Rexroth *and* Ikuko Atsumi

God if he isn't is. Phallic Root. Kazuko Shiraishi. WPOW

God, if this were enough. If This Were Faith. Robert Louis Stevenson. OBNC

GOD-IN-HIMSELF / I feel the evil of absence in my eternal heart. Preface *or* The Drama of Absence in an Eternal Heart. Roger Gilbert-Lecomte, *French*. PFTM, *tr. by* Pierre Joris

God in His wisdom made the fly. The Fly. Ogden Nash. OBCoV

God in Wrath, A. Stephen Crane. MeMAP; OxBSP; TAP *Fr.* The Black Riders [and Other Lines].

God Is. Roland Mathias. CRP

God is a distant—stately Lover. Emily Dickinson. APN-2; NCAP

God is a pure no-thing. "Angelus Silesius," *German*. EnlH, *tr. by* Stephen Mitchell

God is above the sphere of our esteem. What God Is. Robert Herrick. BeJo; NOSC

God Is Everywhere. Christina Rossetti. CTV

God is Good. It Is a Beautiful Night. Wallace Stevens. SAmP

God is in Heaven. Yes. (LL) I have nothing to say about the war. Yehuda Amichai, *Hebrew*. PoSu, *tr. by* Yehuda Amichai *and* Ted Hughes

God is indeed a jealous God. Emily Dickinson. NOBA; SAGP

God is it who transcends. (LL) Prologue: "The Poet's age is sad: for why?" Robert Browning. EnVR; OAEL-2

God Is Love. Sir John Bowring. FaBoBe

God is love. Then by inversion. History of Ideas. James Vincent Cunningham. NIP-4; VCAP

God is my staff, my path, my goal, my game, my fire. God Is To Me What I Desire. "Angelus Silesius." GePo, *tr. by* George C. Schoolfield *Fr.* The Cherubical Wanderer.

God is near, and / difficult to grasp, The. Patmos. Friedrich Hölderlin, *German*. GrIP; OBVE, *tr. by* David Gascoyne

God is no botcher, but when God wrought you two. On Botching. John Heywood. FaBoEE

God is not dumb, that he should speak no more. James Russell Lowell. ChIV-1 *Fr.* Bibliolaters.

God is not on[e]ly merciful, to call. Calling, and Correcting. Robert Herrick. BeJo

God Is Nothing Physical. "Angelus Silesius." GePo, *tr. by* George C. Schoolfield *Fr.* The Cherubical Wanderer.

God is older than the sun and moon. Maximus. D. H. Lawrence. BLT; TOF

God is our refuge and strength, a very present help in trouble. Psalm 46. Bible, *O.T.* AWP *Fr.* Psalms.

God is our strength and our refuge: therefore will we not tremble. Hexameters[; Paraphrase of Psalm XLVI]. Coleridge. ChIV-1

God is praise and glory. Psalm of Battle. *Unknown*. AWP *Fr.* The Thousand and One Nights.

God is still glorified. Building in Stone. Sylvia Townsend Warner. MoBrPo

God is the great urge that has not yet found a body. The Body of God. D. H. Lawrence. ChIV-2

God is the Most High. Muhammedan Call to Prayer. Bilal, *Arabic*. TTY, *tr. by* Raoul Abdul

God Is To Me What I Desire. "Angelus Silesius." GePo, *tr. by* George C. Schoolfield *Fr.* The Cherubical Wanderer.

God Is Working His Purpose Out. Arthur Campbell Ainger. FaPoR

God, keep me still unsatisfied. (LL) Prayer: "God, though [*or* although] this life is but a wraith." Louis Untermeyer. MoAmPo; TrJP

God kept / a secret. Mark Jarman. *See* Questions for Ecclesiastes.

God knows it, I am with you. To a Republican Friend, 1848. Matthew Arnold. EBVVPR

God knows, teaching the Renaissance I could use it. Why I Don't Speak Italian. Arthur L. Clements. UnSA

God knows, that's too much terror for your years. The Chord. Abdur-Rahman Slade Hopkinson. HCP

God knows / We have our troubles too. High to Low. Langston Hughes. HCAP; PoPoPo

God knows what beat him down into that deadland. At the Entrance. Douglas Stewart. CBAP

God knows what happened to the candlestick. The Candlestick. Jaroslav Seifert, *Czech*. AF, *tr. by* Ewald Osers

God knows what was done to you. (Frank O'Hara). Bruce Beaver. BMAP *Fr.* Letters to Live Poets. CBAP

God lay dead in Heaven. Stephen Crane. APN-2; AmPP *Fr.* The Black Riders [and Other Lines].

God leaned out of himself one day. A Whole New Scene. John Fuller. NOxBChV

God, let me be a giver, and not one. Let Me Be a Giver. Mary Carolyn Davies. PoToHe

God let me find the lonely ones. Prayer for a Day's Walk. Grace Noll Crowell. PoToHe

God let never soe old a man. Old Robin of Portingale. *Unknown*. ESPB

God loafs around heaven. The Earth. Anne Sexton. SAGP

God love you. A Poem for the Old Man. John Wieners. NeAP

God love you now, if no one else will ever. Ode for the American Dead in Asia. Thomas McGrath. AiP; RaBo; VGW

God loves us all, I'm pleased to say. God's Love. Vikram Seth. TRP

God Lyaeus, Ever Young. John Fletcher. OBEV *Fr.* The Tragedy of Valentinian.

God made a wonderful mother. A Wonderful Mother. Pat O'Reilly. BLPA

God made Him birds in a pleasant humour. The Making of Birds. Katharine Tynan. TIRV

God made Himself an awful rose of dawn. (LL) The Vision of Sin. Tennyson. EBVVPR; OAEL-2

God made my mother on an April day. My Mother. Francis Ledwidge. TIRV

God made the bees. Mother Goose. Spl

God made the bees. *Unknown*. LiLi

God made the sex-shop keeper. Fiona Pitt-Kethley. UV

God made the sugar cane grow where it's hot. Bundaberg Rum. W. N. Scott. NOBAu

God made the wicked grocer. The Song against Grocers. G. K. Chesterton. OBCoV; TAP

God makes all things for good; 'tis man. Man Leavens the Batch. Mildmay Fane, 2d Earl of Westmorland. BeJo

God makes sech nights all white an' still. The Courtin'. James Russell Lowell. AmPP; NOBA; OBAL *Fr.* The Biglow Papers.

God moves in a mysterious way. Light Shining out of Darkness. William Cowper. CABP; EBEV; EBEvV; ECEV; FHYEP; FaBoCh; ImPo; NOBE; NOCV; NoP-4; PWR; PoEL-3; SCGP; TFi; TOF *Fr.* Olney Hymns.

God must have a big eye to see everything. Jack Spicer. NeAP; PmAP *Fr.* Imaginary Elegies.

God, O God, whom I have begged. A Poem in Praise of Colum Cille. Dallán Forgaill. NOIV

God of Abraham, of Isaac, and of Jacob. *Unknown*, *Yiddish*. TrJP, *tr. by* Olga Marx

God of Bethel Heard Her Cries, The. Richard Allen. AH

God of day rolls his car up the slopes, The. Guido's Aurora. Henry David Thoreau. APN-1

God of his goodnes, praysed that he be. *Unknown.* NOIV Fr. The Praise of Waterford.

God of Mercy. Kadya Molodovsky, *Yiddish.* WPOW, tr. by Irving Howe

God of Might, God of Right. *Unknown.* TrJP

God of My Life! Benjamin Colman. AH

God of Nature in the field of Grace, The. (LL) Against Hope. Richard Crashaw. CABP; MeLP; NOBE; NOSC

God of Our Fathers. Melancthon Woolsey Stryker. AH

God of Our Fathers, Bless This Our Land. John Henry Hopkins, Jr. AH

God of our fathers, known of old. Recessional. Rudyard Kipling. AWP; BLPA; CABP; CTV; EBEvV; FaBoPV; MoBrPo; NOBE; NOBVV; NoAM; NoP-4; OBEV; OBNC; OxAEP-2; PWR; SAGP; SCGP; TFi; UV; UnPo

God of Our Fathers, Whose Almighty Hand. Daniel C. Roberts. AH

God of peace! before thee. Hymn of Freedom. Michael J. Barry. TIRV

God of Peace, in Peace Preserve Us. Ernst W. Olson. AH

God of Sheep, The. John Fletcher. FaBoCh Fr. The Faithful Shepherdess. (To Pan.)

God of Smoke listens idly in the heat, The. Backyard. John Tranter. BMAP

God of song and laughter long ago, The. But. Vladimir Holan, *Czech.* PoSu, tr. by Ian *and* Jarmila Milner

God of the Nations. Walter Russell Bowie. AH

God of the Nations, Near and Far. John Haynes Holmes. AH

God of the Prophets! Bless the Prophets' Sons. Denis Wortman. AH

God of the strong, God of the weak. Richard Watson Gilder. AH

God of the World. Israel Najara, *Hebrew.* TrJP, tr. by Israel Abrahams

God of the World, Thy Glories Shine. Sewall Sylvester Cutting. AH

God of War, The. Bertolt Brecht, *German.* AF, tr. by Michael Hamburger; FaBoPV

God of War, Money Changer of Dead Bodies, The. Aeschylus. Fr. Agamemnon. NAWM-1, tr. by Robert Fagles

God of your fathers, known of old. Post-Recessional. G. K. Chesterton. UV

God or Mammon. Alfred Cruickshank. PBCV

God ordered motion, but ordained no rest. (LL) Man. Henry Vaughan. ESCV; FMP; GeHe; MeLP; NOBE; NOCV; OBEV; PoEL-2; SCGP

God ought to bow profoundly for the favour. (LL) Exhausted now her sighs, and dry her tears. Walter Savage Landor. CBLP; FaBoEE

God our fathers formerly knew. Headlined in Heaven. Paul Grano. NOBAu

God, pity broken little families. A Prayer for Broken Little Families. Violet Alleyn Storey. PoToHe

God pity me whom (god distinctly has). E. E. Cummings. SeSe

God pity the wretched prisoners. In Prison. Michael Smith. PWR

God Poem. Stanley Moss. VGW

God prosper long our Gracious King. An Ode for the New Year. John Gay. OxBoLi

God Replies, XXXVIII: 2–41. Bible, *O.T.* Fr. Then the Lord Answered. ("Who is this that darkeneth counsel by words without knowledge?"). AWP Fr. Job. NAWM-1

God rest that Jewy woman. Song for the Clatter-Bones. Frederick Robert Higgins. ChiV-1; ImPo; OBMV

God rest the soul of Ireland. After the Flight of the Earls. Fearflatha O'Gnive. NOIV

God Rest Ye Merry, Gentlemen. Derek Walcott. GT

God rest you merry gentlemen. A Christmas Carol. G. K. Chesterton. UV

God Rest You [*or* ye] Merry, Gentlemen. Dinah Maria Mulock Craik. UV

God rings the bells, earth rings the bells, the sky itself is ringing. The Last Mass in Hagia Sophia. *Unknown, Greek.* GrIP, tr. by Richard Stoneman

God rot the guts and the guts' indulgences. Palladas, *Greek.* GrAn, tr. by Tony Harrison

GOD said, *Let Newton be!* and All was Light. (LL) Intended for Sir Isaac Newton. Alexander Pope. ECEV; FaBoEE; InPK-6; PFE; WeW-3

God said, "Let there be light, and there was light." Mysteries of Life. Mary E. Tucker. CBWP-1

God save great George our King. God Save the King. *Unknown.* EBEvV

God save great Thomas Paine. Joseph Mather. NOEC

God save our gracious King. God Save the King. James Elroy Flecker. NSI

God Save the King. James Elroy Flecker. NSI

God Save the King. *Unknown.* EBEvV

God save the King, that King that sav'd the land. Benjamin Harris. SCAP

God Save the People. Ebenezer Elliot. BLPA

God Save the Plough. Lydia Huntley Sigourney. OBAL

God save this troop! That's all I have to tell. (LL) The Miller's [*or* Milleres] Tale. Geoffrey Chaucer, *Middle English.* NAWM-1

"God scatters beauty as he scatters flowers." Walter Savage Landor. FaBoEE

God Send Easter. Lucille Clifton. CrSp

God send her well to speede! (LL) The Boy and the Mantle. *Unknown.* ESPB; OxBB

God send the Devil is a gentleman. The Knight Fallen on Evil Days. Elinor Wylie. MoAmPo

God send the land deliverance. *Unknown. See* The Death of Parcy Reed.

God send us a little home. A Prayer for a Little Home. Florence Bone. BLPA; FaBoBe

God send vs alle good endyng! (LL) Chevy Chase. *Unknown.* EnSB; EnVB; OxBB

God sende hem so[o]ne [a] verray pestilence [!]. (LL) The Wife of Bath's Tale. Geoffrey Chaucer. FHYEP; NAEL-1; OAEL-1

God sent us here to make mistakes. Mistakes. Ella Wheeler Wilcox. PoToHe

God sent us wit to banish far. Peace in the World. John Galsworthy. PoLF

God Set Us Here. Nicasius de Sillè, *Dutch.* AH

God signs to us. Inventing Sin. George Ella Lyon. CrSp

God sits on the firmament arch. The Creation of Light. Sister Maura. CRP

God Sour the Milk of the Knacking Wench. Alden Nowlan. MoCV

God Speaks to the Soul. Mechthild von Magdeburg, *German.* WPoS, tr. by Oliver Davies

God Speed. George Clinton Rowe. AAP

God Speed the Plough! *Unknown.* EnVB

God spoke once in the dark. The Precision. Yvor Winters. SPE

God stopped and the car. Not Singing. Kate Daniels. PBCAP

God strengthen me to bear myself. Who Shall Deliver Me? Christina Rossetti. TOF

God Supreme. Abraham ibn Ezra, *Hebrew.* TOF, tr. by David Goldstein

God Supreme! To Thee We Pray. Penina Moise *and* Edward N. Calisch. AH

God, that all this mightes may. *Unknown.* MiEL

God That Doest Wondrously. Moses ibn Ezra, *Hebrew.* TrJP, tr. by Solomon Solis-Cohen

God, that mad'st her well regard her. Dieu Qu'il la Fait. Charles, Duc d' Orléans, *French.* AWP, tr. by Ezra Pound

God the Artist. Angela Morgan. BLPA; PoToHe

God the Eater. Stevie Smith. BWW

God, the Eternal! Infinite! All-wise! Cain: A Mystery. Byron.

God, the rabbis tell us, never assigns. Getting the Message. Maxine W. Kumin. BAP-95

God then. Denise Levertov. CrSp Fr. Mass for the Day of St. Thomas Didymus.

God— / they fear you, they hold you so. Testimony. Carolyn M. Rodgers. BPo

God, thou great symmetry. Envoi. Anna Wickham. MoBrPo

God, though [*or* although] this life is but a wraith. Prayer. Louis Untermeyer. MoAmPo; TrJP

God thought about you, and so I am here. George Macdonald. *See* Where did You Come From, Baby Dear?

God thought of you, and so I am here. (LL) Where did You Come From, Baby Dear? George Macdonald. BLPA; OxBChV; WHSW

God to Be First Served. Robert Herrick. OxBChV

God to Man. *Unknown.* Fr. The Talmud. TrJP

God to Thee We Humbly Bow. George Henry Boker. AH

God told Noah about the rainbow sign. Lining Track. *Unknown.* AmFP

God tole Hezykiah. Little Black Train Is A-Comin'. *Unknown.* GM

God tried to teach Crow how to talk. Crow's First Lesson. Ted Hughes. MoP; NoAM

God wants the souls of the faithful. The Marrano. Barry Goldensohn. NAmP90

God wants to be thought of. Julian of Norwich. CrSp

God was sick, / gravely. César Vallejo. *See* Have You Anything to Say in Your Defense?

God, we don't like to complain. Caliban in the Coal Mines. Louis Untermeyer. MoAmPo; TrJP

God, when he walked on earth. Robinson Jeffers. *See* Shine, Perishing Republic.

God, when you thought of a pine tree. God the Artist. Angela Morgan. BLPA; PoToHe

God who also watched over me / was my old granny's friend. (LL) To the Anxious Mother. Valente Goenha Malangatana, *Portuguese.* PBMAP

God who created me. Prayers. Henry Charles Beeching. BoTP; OBEV

God who fled down with a standard yard, The. William Empson. PoA Fr. Bacchus. NoAM

God who mounts the winged winds, The. Homer. OBVE, tr. by Pope Fr. Odyssey. NAWM-1, tr. by Robert Fitzgerald

God, Whom Shall I Compare to Thee? Judah Halevi, *Hebrew*. TrJP, *tr. by* Alice Lucas

God, whose love and joy. "Angelus Silesius," *German*. EnlH, *tr. by* Stephen Mitchell

God will have all or none; serve Him, or fall. Neutrality Loathsome. Robert Herrick. ChIV-1; NoP-4

God with honour hang your head. At the Wedding March. Gerard Manley Hopkins. ITG

God / you aint. I Wonta Thank Ya. Tejumola Ologboni. NBV

God, you could grow to love it, God-fearing, God. Ecclesiastes. Derek Mahon. BIrV; CIP-2; ChIV-1; PNI

God / You do not mind if I an unbaptized. Prayer of a Pagan Woman. Cothrai Gogan. TIRV

Goddess, The. Denise Levertov. LiTM; NALW; NOBA; NeAP; PoM

Goddess. Judith Johnson Sherwin. BoWoP

Goddess adored! who gained my early love. The Housewife's Prayer on the Morning Preceding a Fete. Elizabeth Moody. ECWP

Goddess capricious is Fame, A. Limerick. Langford Reed. PeLi

Goddess Chiao, The. *Unknown, Chinese*. CoBCP, *tr. by* Burton Watson

Goddess excellently bright. (LL) Hymn to Diana. Ben Jonson. AWP; CH; EBEvV; GTBS-P; HAP; InPS-3; NAEL-1; NOBE; NOSC; NoP-4; OAEL-1; OBEV; PoE; PoEL-2; PoRA; SCGP; SeCP; TFi

Goddess Fortune be praised (on her toothed wheel), The. The Unpredicted. John Heath-Stubbs. BoLoP; OxBC

Goddess, how oft you bent the silver bow. Callimachus. OBCVT, *tr. by* William Dodd   *Fr.* Hymn to Diana.

Goddess intervenes between Achilles and Agamemnon, The. Homer, *Greek*. *Fr.* The Iliad.

     ("Content to bid the War aloof in Peace?") (LL) OBCVT, *tr. by* John Dryden

Goddess of threads gladly. *Unknown. Fr.* The Saga of Gisli. OBVE, *tr. by* George Johnston

Goddess rising, asks her guests to stay, The. Spellbound. Homer. *Fr.* Odyssey. NAWM-1, *tr. by* Robert Fitzgerald

Goddess stands in front of the cave, The. On the occasion of becoming an echo. Anselm Hollo. PT

Goddess swore: then seiz'd my hand, and led, The. Circe. Homer. OBCVT, *tr. by* Alexander Pope   *Fr.* The Odyssey.

Goddesse bade the nymphs remove, The. *Unknown*. OBVE, *tr. by* Thomas Stanley   *Fr.* The Vigil of Venus. GBL, *tr. by* Allen Tate; AWP, *tr. by* Thomas Stanley

Godes moder be. (LL) I syng of a mayden that is makeles. *Unknown*. CABP; NoP-4

Godfrey Gordon Gustavus Gore—. William Brighty Rands. FPC

Godfrey of Bulloigne; or, The Recoverie of Jerusalem. Torquato Tasso, *Italian*.

     "Erminia's steed this while his mistress bore." NoSic, *tr. by* Edward Fairfax

     "Joyous birds, hid under greenewood shade, The." OBVE

     "Palace great is builded rich and round." NoSic, *tr. by* Edward Fairfax

     "Sweet Armida tooke this charge on hand, The." OBVE

Godhorse. Kojo Laing. HBAPE

Godiva. David Chapman Berry. BXAP

Godiva. Tennyson. EBVVPR

Godlike. Anselm Hollo. PmAP

Godlings are born racily. Nativities. U. A. Fanthorpe. NoP-4

Godly Dream, A. Elizabeth Melvill, Lady Culross. WPE

Godmother. Dorothy Parker. PoRA

Gododdin, The. Aneirin, *Welsh*.

     "Men went to Catraeth, keen their war-band." OBWVE, *tr. by* Joseph P. Clancy

     "Men went to Gododdin, laughter-loving." OBWP, *tr. by* Joseph P. Clancy

     "To Cattraeth's vale in glitt'ring row." OBVE, *tr. by* Thomas Gray

Gods, The. Dennis Lee. NOBC

God's A-Gonna Trouble the Water. *Unknown*. NAAAL

God's Absence. Mechthild von Magdeburg, *German*. WPoS, *tr. by* Oliver Davies

Gods are happy, The. The Strayed Reveller to Ulysses. Matthew Arnold. OBEV   *Fr.* The Strayed Reveller. EBVVPR; OAEL-2

Gods are Mighty, The. N. P. van Wyk Louw, *Afrikaans*. PeSA, *tr. by* Jack Cope

Gods are not more blest than he, The. Sapho's Ode out of Longinus. Sappho, *Greek*. OBCVT, *tr. by* William Lisle Bowles

God's armies of Heaven, with pinions extended. Pro Patria. Adah Isaacs Menken. CBWP-1

Gods Ash Their Cigarettes, The. S. K. Kelen. BMAP

God's blessings all are uniform. They Are the Same. Priscilla Jane Thompson. CBWP-2

Gods boundles bownties gods promise ever abyding. Mary Sidney Herbert, Countess of Pembroke. PBRV   *Fr.* Psalm 89 Misericordias.

God's boundless mercy is, to sinful man. God's Mercy. Robert Herrick. BeJo

Gods, by right of Nature, must possess, The. Lucretius, *Latin*. OBCVT, *tr. by* John Wilmot, 2d Earl of Rochester

Gods chase / Round vase. Ode on a Grecian Urn Summarized. Desmond Skirrow. NIP-4; NOBL

God's child in Christ adopted—Christ my all. My Baptismal Birthday [*or* Birth-Day]. Coleridge. ChIV-2; NOCV

God's Controversy with New-England. Michael Wigglesworth. SCAP

God's Dark. John Martin. PoLF

God's Determinations [touching his Elect]. Edward Taylor. SCAP

     Christ's Reply. NAAL-1; NAAL-3; PoEL-3

     Forwardness of the Elect in the Work of Conversion, The. SCAP

     Glory of and Grace in the Church Set Out, The. AmPP

     God's Selecting Love in the Decree. PoEL-3

     Joy of Church Fellowship Rightly Attended, The. AmPP; MeMAP; NAAL-1; NAAL-3; OxBA; SCAP

     Preface, The: "Infinity, when all things it beheld." AmPP; HAP; MeMAP; NAAL-1; NAAL-3; NOBA; OxBA; SCAP

     Soul's Groan to Christ for Succo[u]r, The. NAAL-1; NAAL-3; PoEL-3

God's Electric Power. Mrs. Henry Linden. CBWP-4

God's Family. Sigitas Geda, *Lithuanian*. CEEP, *tr. by* Jonas Zdanys

God's favour like the sun, whose beams appear. On God's Favour. Francis Quarles. PeECV   *Fr.* Divine Fancies.

God's Fire upon Children ("God's fire upon cities"). Meir Wieseltier, *Hebrew*. IP, *tr. by* Warren Bargad *and* Stanley F. Chyet

God's fire upon cities. God's Fire upon Children. Meir Wieseltier, *Hebrew*. IP, *tr. by* Warren Bargad *and* Stanley F. Chyet

God's Gifts. Albrecht von Johannsdorf, *German*. GePo, *tr. by* F. C. Nicholson

God's Gifts to Me. Thelma Walton. CTV

God's Glory. Bible, *O.T. See* Psalm 19.

God's Goin' to Set This World on Fire. *Unknown*. AS

God's grace has surely been overabundant. To My Friends. Yuly Markovich Daniel, *Russian*. TCRP, *tr. by* David Burg *and* Arthur Boyars

God's Grandeur. Gerard Manley Hopkins. APAD; AWP; CABP; CMoP; ChAP; ClHu; EBVV; EnlH; GSo; HAP; ImPo; InPK-6; LiTM; MoBrPo; MoP; NAEL-2; NIP-4; NOBE; NOBVV; NoAM; NoP-4; OAEL-2; OBNC; PFE; PeVV; PoE; PoPoPo; RaBo; SCGP; SoSe-8; Son; TFi; TrCP; UnPo; WeW-3

God's Harp. Gustav Falke, *German*. AWP, *tr. by* Ludwig Lewisohn

Gods have heard me, Lyce, The. 4.13: Revenge ("Audivere, Lyce"). Horace. AWP, *tr. by* Louis Untermeyer   *Fr.* Odes.

Gods have taken alien shapes upon them, The. Exiles. "Æ." BIrV; MoBrPo

God's head for a paperweight, A. The Desk. Cid Corman. VGW

Gods *Houses*, almost like *Troyes Ilion*,. John Taylor. PBRV   *Fr.* Here followeth the unfashionable fashion, or the too too homely Worshipping of God.

Gods in Vietnam. Eugene B. Redmond. PoBA

Gods it is I ask to release me from this watch, The. Agamemnon. Aeschylus. NAWM-1, *tr. by* Louis MacNeice

God's Judgment on a Wicked Bishop. Robert Southey. *See* Bishop Hatto.

God's Little Angel. Patrick J. Murray. TIRV

God's Love. Vikram Seth. TRP

God's Mercy. Robert Herrick. BeJo

God's Mercy, *mod. by* Donald Attwater. William Langland. NOCV   *Fr.* The Vision of Piers Plowman.

Gods of Africa regard me, The. Distance. Anthony Delius. PeSA

Gods of heaven are irrational, The. Kasa no Iratsume, *Japanese*. WPJ, *tr. by* Kenneth Rexroth *and* Ikuko Atsumi

Gods of the Copybook Headings, The. Rudyard Kipling. FaPoR; NoAM; OBSV; OxBTC

Gods of the Nile, should this stout fellow here. A Grave Near Cairo. Rudyard Kipling. *Fr.* Epitaphs of the War [1914–1918]. OBWP

Gods of the storm and the giants of the earth, The. The Ascent of Vasco da Gama. Fernando Pessoa, *Portuguese*. PeSAV, *tr. by* F.E.G. Quintanilha

God's other eye is good and gold. So bright. Jack Spicer. NeAP; PmAP   *Fr.* Imaginary Elegies.

God's philosophical and so can wait. Palladas, *Greek*. GrAn, *tr. by* Tony Harrison

God's Plan for Spring. Nancy Byrd Turner. CTV

God's plan made a hopeful beginning. Limerick. *Unknown*. PeLi

God's Praises. *Unknown, Irish*. TIRV, *tr. by* Brendan Kennelly

God's Precepts Perfect, vv. 7–9 of sl. diff. vers. Bible, *O.T. See* Psalm 19.

God's querulous calling. (LL) Theology. Ted Hughes. FaBoMo; NAEL-2; NoAM; NoP-4

God's Remembrance. Francis Ledwidge. TIRV

God's Residence. Emily Dickinson. SAmP

God's Selecting Love in the Decree. Edward Taylor. PoEL-3 *Fr.* God's Determinations [touching his Elect].

Gods the Court deckt of Alcinous, The. (LL) The Gardens of Alcinous. Homer. OAEL-1; OBVE, *tr.* by George Chapman

Gods! The Gods!, The. D. H. Lawrence. CMoP

Gods their god-like fun, The. (LL) Letter to My Sister. Anne Spencer. BlSi; NAAAL; NMM-2; PoBA

Gods themselves with us do dwell, The. (LL) The Mower Against Gardens. Andrew Marvell. CABP; EBEV; ESCV; FaBoPV; GaP; NAEL-1; NOSC; NoP-4; OAEL-1; OBGa; OxAEP-1; PBRV; PoE; PoEL-2

God's Virtue. Barnabe Barnes. NOCV *Fr.* A Divine Century of Spiritual Sonnets.

God's ways are strange; He chastens those. Margaret E. Bruner. PoToHe

God's Ways, Not Our Ways. Henrietta Cordelia Ray. AAP; CBWP-3

Gods will ask, The. Xunantunich. Velma Pollard. HCP *Fr.* Belize Suite. HCP

God's Will for You and Me. *Unknown.* SoSe-8

Gods! with what pride I see the titled slave. Charles Churchill. OBSV *Fr.* The Author.

God's words are golden grains. To Every Believer. Uku Masing, *Estonian.* CEEP, *tr.* by Ivar Ivask

God's World. Edna St. Vincent Millay. CMoP; FaBoBe; MoAmPo; PFE; SAGP; TrCP

Gods Wrote, The. Keorapetse Kgositsile. GT

Godspeed. John Greenleaf Whittier. GSo; Son

Goe and catche a falling starre. Donne. *See* Song: "Go and catch a falling star."

Goe, happy Rose, and, enterwove. To the Rose, a Song. Robert Herrick. SeCP

Goe little book, and once a week shake hands. Ad Librum. Samuel Danforth Jr. SCAP

Goes all the way down. (LL) Lament: "Someone is dead." Anne Sexton. CoAmPo; WPE

Goes flaring down to Baggot Street. (LL) Baggot Street Deserta. Thomas Kinsella. CIP-2; CMoP; NoAM

Goes on, and the moon in the breast of man is cold. (LL) The Moon and the Night and the Men. John Berryman. CoAP; GEA; VCAP; VGW

Goes through the mud. *Unknown.* OxNR

Goes way back to the days / my father a young man. Cousin Mary. Wanda Coleman. MoNo

Goethe and Brentano. Andrew Taylor. BMAP *Fr.* Travelling to Gleis-Binario.

Goethe in Weimar sleeps, and Greece. Memorial Verses. Matthew Arnold. CABP; NAEL-2; OAEL-2

Goethe's Blues. Denise Levertov. FaBoWP

Goff; an Heroi-comical Poem, The. Thomas Mathison.
  Victory on the Last Green. NOEC

Goggled mother with her children / stomp on the tar road. The Families Album. Michael S. Harper. AFr

Goin' Back T'morrer. Hamlin Garland. OBAL

Goin' 'cross the Mountain. *Unknown.* AmFP

Goin' down to Cripple Creek, goin' at a run. Cripple Creek. *Unknown.* AmFP

Goin' down to the delta. Mississippi Blues. *Unknown.* AmFP

Goin' Down to Town. *Unknown.* AS

Goin' to Chicago Blues. *Unknown.* NAAAL

Goin' to the Territory. Michael S. Harper. NAAAL

Goin' up State Street, comin' down Main. Take a Whiff on Me. *Unknown.* NOBA

Going, for my mother-in-law, Gladys. Bruce Dawe. BMAP

Going. Peter Everwine. NNaP

Going, The. Thomas Hardy. CBLP; EBFV; LoP; NOBE; OxAEP-2; SCGP; UnPo

Going. Philip Larkin. CMoP

Going Alone to Spend a Night at the Hsien-Yu Temple. Po Chü-i, *Chinese.* ChiP, *tr.* by Arthur Waley

Going and Staying. Thomas Hardy. CMoP; NoAM

Going Back Patiently. Frank Mkalawile Chipasula. HBAPE

Going Barefoot. Judith Thurman. AYFP

Going Blind. Rilke, *German.* BLT, *tr.* by Walter Arndt

Going by far. Hyon-jong Chong, *Korean.* CKP, *tr.* by Jaihiun Kim

Going Down Hill on a Bicycle. Henry Charles Beeching. NOxBChV; OBEV

Going Down on America. Kelly Cherry. CMAP

Going-elsewhere of ripples incessantly shaping, The. (LL) Swimming Chenango Lake. Charles Tomlinson. FaBoMo; MoP; NoAM

Going for Peaches, Fredericksburg, Texas. Naomi Shihab Nye. MT

Going from us at last. The Escape. Mark Van Doren. MoAmPo

Going, Going. Philip Larkin. NoAM; OxAEP-2

Going / Gone / Don't be going. Candle. Sachiko Yoshihara, *Japanese.* WPJ, *tr.* by Kenneth Rexroth and Ikuko Atsumi

Going Home. Robert Bridges. LBC

Going Home. Richard Caddel. NBrP

Going Home. Wing Tek Lum. UnSA

Going Home. Robert W. Service. NSI

Going Home to Mayo, Winter, 1949. Paul Durcan. CIP-2; PBCIP

Going In to Dinner. Edward Richard Burton Shanks. OBMV; OxBTC

Going into Breeches. Charles Lamb *and* Mary Lamb (1764–1847). OxBChV

Going on always on and on. *Unknown, Chinese.* SuSp, *tr.* by Charles Hartman
  ("But pluck up strength and eat my fill.") (LL) CoBCP, *tr.* by Burton Watson
  ("On and on, going on and on.") CoBCP, *tr.* by Burton Watson

Going on boats but. The Series—3. Leslie Scalapino. PmAP *Fr.* Crowd and Not Evening Or Light.

Going or Gone. Charles Lamb. BXAP

Going out into the fields of learning. Josephine Miles. *See* Fields of Learning.

Going Out Through the North Gate of Chi. Pao Chao, *Chinese.* SuSp, *tr.* by Daniel Bryant

Going Out to the Country on a Boat Trip, Sheltering from Rain Beneath a Tree. Kao Ch'i, *Chinese.* CoBLCP, *tr.* by Jonathan Chaves

Going Rate, The. Michael Lassell. GLP *Fr.* Times Square Poems.

Going the Rounds; a Sort of Love Poem. Anthony Hecht. BoLoP

Going to Bed. Donne. *See* To His Mistress Going To Bed.

Going to Chicago, sorry that I can't take you. Goin' to Chicago Blues. *Unknown.* NAAAL

Going to Church. Coventry Patmore. PeVV *Fr.* The Angel in the House.

Going to Mass after Fifteen Years. Maxine Scates. PBCAP

Going to Mass Last Sunday. Donagh MacDonagh. BIrV

Going to Remake This World. James Welch. CDW

Going to School. Karl Shapiro. TrJP

Going to School in France or America. Tom Clark. CoAmPo

Going to Sea. Douglas Messerli. FTOS

Going to sleep, I cross my hands on my chest. Death. Bill Knott. PBCAP; SPE

Going to the Ministry with Chao Tzu-ch'i. Yü Chi, *Chinese.* CoBLCP, *tr.* by Jonathan Chaves

Going to the Mountains with a Little Dancing Girl, Aged Fifteen. Po Chü-i, *Chinese.* ChiP, *tr.* by Arthur Waley

Going Under of the Evening Land, The. Mekeel McBride. CMAP

Going up for the assault that morning. Walt. Ted Hughes. NoP-4

Going up the river, or down, their tuneless look. Barges on the Hudson. Babette Deutsch. WPE

Going up through the hill called the vineyard. The Vineyard. W. S. Merwin. NNaP

Going up to Sotheby's. Muriel Spark. FaBoTC

Going Uptown to Visit Miriam. Victor Hernandez Cruz. LoL

Going Westwards. Sorley MacLean. FaBoTC

Golagros and Gawane. *Unknown.*
  "Thai passit in thare pilgramage." OxBS

Gold. Martin Donisthorpe Armstrong. BoTP

Gold. Donald Hall. CoAmPo; SAGP

Gold and all this werdis [werldes] win. I Would Be Clad in Christ's Skin. *Unknown.* EnVB; MiEL

Gold-armoured ghost from the Roman road, The. The Youth with Red-gold Hair. Dame Edith Sitwell. FaBoTw

Gold Braid. A. A. Milne. NSI

Gold Coast Customs. Dame Edith Sitwell.
  "One fantee wave." OBMV

Gold-colored [*or* coloured] skin of my Lebanese friends, The A Trip to Four or Five Towns. John Logan. CoAP; NNaP

Gold cross-bow brooch, The. The Ericstane Brooch. Valerie Gillies. FaBoTC

Gold cut the knot of otherwise. Paulus Silentarius, *Greek.* GrAn; OBCVT, *tr.* by Andrew Miller

Gold dung and urinous straw from the horse garages. Midsummer: XXX. Derek Walcott. AFr *Fr.* Midsummer.

Gold-flaked plaster body, The. The Fall. Jeannine Savard. CMAP

Gold Glade. Robert Penn Warren. CRP; Poetr; TRP

Gold in the Mud, The. Gerrit Lansing. PT

Gold Is the Son of Zeus: Neither Moth nor Worm May Gnaw It. "Michael Field." OBMV

Gold I've none, for use or show. Lyric[k] for Legacies. Robert Herrick. BeJo

Gold Leaves. G. K. Chesterton. OxBTC

Gold of a ripe oat straw, gold of a southwest moon. Falltime. Carl Sandburg. PoA

Gold on Mule. Thomas Lux. CMAP

Gold on Oak Leaves. George Oppen. FTOS

Gold or iv'ry's not intended. 2.18. Horace. OBVE, tr. by Christopher Smart Fr. Odes.

Gold priests, wooden chalices. Epigram. Unknown, Irish. NOIV, tr. by Thomas Kinsella

Gold said her golden. Gold on Oak Leaves. George Oppen. FTOS

Gold savours well, though it be got. Isabella Whitney. Fr. Sweet Nosegay, A, or Pleasant Posy. WPE

Gold-Seekers, The. Hamlin Garland. FaBoBe

Gold, / Silver. Unknown. OxNR

Gold survives the fire that's hot enough. Timer. Tony Harrison. Fr. The School of Eloquence. NAEL-2; NoAM

Gold tane from the kings harbengers. Robin Hood and Queen Katherine. Unknown. ESPB

Gold tape gently billowing with her breathing. Mars and Venus. Rachel Hadas. GS

Gold that was my hair has turned, The. Marina Tsvetayeva, Russian. WPoS, tr. by Paul Graves

Gold Tooth Blues. Tennessee Williams. OBAL

Gold Watch. Patrick Kavanagh. InPS-3

Gold will not buy this voyage. Looking for a Country under Its Original Name. Colleen J. McElroy. BlSi

Gold wings across the sea! The Song of Jehane du Castel Beau. William Morris. Fr. Golden Wings. OBNC

Goldbrown upon the sated flood. Flood. James Joyce. MoBrPo

Golden Age, The. William Browne. NOSC Fr. Britannia's Pastorals.

Golden Age, The. Sir Richard Fanshawe. NOSC; OAEL-1 Fr. Il Pastor Fido.

Golden Age. Mac Hammond. EOEF

Golden Age, The. Hesiod, Greek. OBCVT, tr. by Charles Elton

Golden Age, The. Artur Miedzyrzecki, Polish. PoSu, tr. by Stanislaw Baranczak and Clare Cavanagh

Golden Age, The. Ovid, Latin. OAEL-1 Fr. Metamorphoses.
  (Before Gardens: The Golden Age.) GaP, tr. by Arthur Golding
  ("From ech greene tree whereon the rayes of firie Phebus glowde.") (LL) OBCVT, tr. by Arthur Golding
  ("Then sprang up first the golden age, which of itself.") GaP, tr. by Arthur Golding
  ("Whereon the rayes of fiery / Phœbus glowed.") (LL) GaP, tr. by Arthur Golding

Golden Age, The. Torquato Tasso. See Pastoral[l], A: "Oh [or O] happy golden age."

Golden age was when the world was young, The. Fulke Greville. OAEL-1 Fr. Caelica.

Golden apples of the sun, The. (LL) The Song Of Wandering Aengus. W. B. Yeats. ADE; APAD; CH; CMoP; ChAP; FaBoCh; MoBrPo; NTP; OTCP; PBMP; PoEL-5; PoRA; RaBo; SAGP; TFi; TTTS

Golden Bells. Po Chü-i, Chinese, tr. by Arthur Waley BLT; ChiP

Golden Bough. Elinor Wylie. MoAmPo; PBWP

Golden bridle of Bellerephon. Fourth Pearl, The: Temperance. Lady Diana Primrose. WPE Fr. A Chain of Pearl.

Golden Bridle of Bellerophon, The. Lady Diana Primrose. See Fourth Pearl, The: Temperance.

Golden Calf. Norman MacCaig. ChIV-1; OxBS

Golden casket I designed, A. Epigram. John Swanwick Drennan. BIrV

Golden cloud slept for her pleasure, A. The Mountain. Mikhail Yuryevich Lermontov, Russian. AWP, tr. by Max Eastman

Golden cradle under you, and you young, A. He Meditates on the Life of a Rich Man. Douglas Hyde, Irish. OBMV, tr. by Lady Augusta Gregory

Golden eagle swooped out of the sky, The. Salmon Drowns Eagle. Malcolm Lowry. MoCV

Golden Fleece, The. Oscar Williams. PoA

Golden flood the weightless seat, The. Spacepoem 3: Off Course. Edwin Morgan. SpW

Golden Gate, The. Vikram Seth.
  "How ugly babies are! How heedless." OBCoV

Golden gift that nature did thee give, The. Henry Howard, Earl of Surrey. AAS; SiPS

Golden globe incontinent, The. Midsummer Day in France. Alexander Hume. Fr. Of the Day Estivall. NOCV; OxBS

Golden Glove, The. Unknown. AmFP

Golden grove has whispered its last, The. The Rowan Tree Fire. Sergey Aleksandrovich Yesenin, Russian. TCRP, tr. by Geoffrey Thurley

Golden hair that Gulla wears, The. Bought Locks. Martial, Latin. AWP, tr. by Sir John Harington

Golden head by golden head. Laura and Lizzie Asleep. Christina Rossetti. Fr. Goblin Market. CPO; EBEV; FaBoSe; NAEL-2; NALW; NOBVV; NOxBChV; OBNV; OxAEP-2; VWP

Golden Hour, The. Thomas Moore. OBNC Fr. Lalla Rookh.

Golden Island; or, the Darian Song, The. Unknown. KTR

Golden Journey to Samarkand, The. James Elroy Flecker.
  "And how beguile you? Death has no repose." OxBTC
  Epilogue: "Away, for we are ready to a man!" NOBE

Golden Jubilee of Wilberforce. Mrs. Henry Linden. CBWP-4

Golden Keys. Robert Louis Stevenson. CTV

Golden light has presently, The. Evening Song. Philipp von Zesen, German. GePo, tr. by George C. Schoolfield

Golden Mean, The. Henry Howard, Earl of Surrey, after Horace. OBVE; SiPS

Golden Mile-Stone, The. Henry Wadsworth Longfellow. NCAP; PoEL-5

Golden mists o'er Cloudland wreathing. Fancy and Imagination. Henrietta Cordelia Ray. CBWP-3

Golden Moonrise. W. S. Braithwaite. PoBA

Golden one is gone from the banquets, The. Epigram. Hilda Doolittle. PoA

Golden Palace, The. Unknown, Chinese. ChiP, tr. by Arthur Waley

Golden Pheasant. Mating Pair. William Hart-Smith. NOBAu

Golden prince of pictorial war, A. (LL) Uccello. Gregory Corso. NeAP; PoM

Golden Road to Barcelona: 1992, The. Martin Fagg. UV

Golden Season. Kurtis Lamkin. IFJA

Golden Shower, The. Roy Campbell.
  "Here, where relumed by changing seasons, burn." OxBTC

Golden slumbers kiss your eyes. Cradle Song, A: "Golden slumbers kiss your eyes." Thomas Dekker and others. NoSic; OxAEP-1; OxBChV; SCGP Fr. The Pleasant Comedy of Patient Grissell [or Grissel or Grissill].

Golden spider of the sky, The. Solar Myth. Genevieve Taggard. MoAmPo

Golden State. Frank Bidart. NoAM

Golden sun that brings the day, The. In Praise of the Sun. "A. W." CTC

Golden sun upon his fiery wheels, The. Michael Drayton. NoSic Fr. Idea's Mirrour.

Golden [or Goldyn] Targe, The. William Dunbar. OxBS
  Poet's Dream, The. PoEL-1

Golden trees of England, The. The Jungle Trees. Marjorie Wilson. BoTP

Golden Vanitie, The. Unknown. EnSB

Golden Vanity, The. Unknown. CH; FaBoCh; PBMP; OxBoV
  ("He sank beneath the Lowland sea.") (LL) PBMP
  (Sweet Trinity (The Golden Vanity), The.) ESPB

Golden Violet, The. Letitia Elizabeth Landon.
  Song: "My heart is like the failing hearth." NOBRP
  Song: "Where, O! where's the chain to fling." NOBRP

Golden Wedding, The. David Gray. FaBoBe

Golden Wings. William Morris. OBNC

Golden wings of time, The. The Transition—S.M. Alfred Islay Walden. AAP

Golden, within this golden hive. Danaë. Barbara Howes. WPE

Goldenrod [or Golden-rod] is yellow, The. September [Days Are Here]. Helen Hunt Jackson. APN-2; AYFP; OBCA; PoLF

Goldfish. Barrie Wade. OTCP

Goldfish in the Garden Pond. Valerie Worth. NOxBChV

Goldfish on the Writing Desk. Max Brod, German. TrJP, tr. by Babette Deutsch and Avrahm Yarmolinsky

Goldfish Wife, The. Sandra Hochman. NYBP; UnPo

Goldie Sapiens. P. J. Kavanagh. OBCoV

Goldilocks. Mick Imlah. FaBoTC

Golf Links [lie so near The mill], The. Sarah Norcliffe Cleghorn. ImPo; InPK-6; KaS; NIP-4; PoLF

Golfer's Rubaiyat, The. H. W. Boynton. BXAP

Golgotha. X. J. Kennedy. NYBP

Golgotha. Andrew Lansdown. ChIV-2

Golgotha is a mountain, a purple mound. Arna Bontemps. NAAAL

Goliardic Song. Anthony Hecht. OBCoV

Goliath and David. Robert Graves. PoFWW

Goliath and David. Louis Untermeyer. TrJP

Goliath was known for ferocity. Limerick. Frank Richards. PeLi

Goliathus goliathus, the one banana. The Zoo. Gilbert Sorrentino. NeAP

Goll Mac Morna Parts from His Wife. Unknown. NOIV

Gollihar / Burned the winter grass from his fields.   Rahab.   Diane Glancy.   CRP

Golly, How Truth Will Out.   Ogden Nash.   MoAmPo

Golly, it's hard.   Decision.   M. P. Flynn.   CTV

Gombeen, The.   Joseph Campbell.   BIrV

Gondibert.   Sir William Davenant.

   City Morning, The.   NOSC

   Praise and Prayer.   OBEV

      ("*Praise,* is devotion fit for mighty Mindes!")   PBRV

Gondibert Book 2.   Sir William Davenant.

   "There, when they thought they saw in well sought Books."   PBRV

Gondoliers, The.   Sir William Schwenck Gilbert.

   "There lived a King, as I've been told."   OBCoV

Gone.   Mary Elizabeth Coleridge.   OBEV; OBNC; VWP

Gone, A.   Larry Eigner.   NeAP

Gone.   Carl Sandburg.   NOBA

Gone are the coloured princes, gone echo, gone laughter.   The Ruin.   Richard Hughes.   OBMV

Gone Are the Days.   Norman MacCaig.   CABP; OxBC

Gone are the drab monosyllabic days.   Tilth.   Robert Graves.   FaBoEE; OBSV

Gone are the games we played all night.   Mahsati, *Farsi.*   WPOW, *tr. by* Deirdre Lashgari

Gone as his mouth's last sighs. (LL)   The Burning of the Temple.   Isaac Rosenberg.   FaBoMo; PeFWW; TrJP

Gone Away.   Hugo Williams.   IFJA

Gone, gone again.   Edward Thomas.   OxAEP-2; PeFWW; PoWW

Gone   Gone / Another weaver of black dreams has gone.   For Langston Hughes.   Etheridge Knight.   NBV

Gone, gone,—sold and gone   The Farewell.   John Greenleaf Whittier.   AWP; NCAP

Gone, I say and walk from church.   The Truth the Dead Know.   Anne Sexton.   ColAP; IMW; LCAP-2; MoAmPo; NoAM; NoP-4; PBWP; TAP; VCAP

Gone in the Wind.   James Clarence Mangan, *after the German of* Friedrich Rückert.   TIRV

Gone is the city, gone the day.   The Right Kind of People.   Edwin Markham.   BLPA; PoToHe

Gone Is the Sleepgiver.   Penelope Shuttle.   BrRo

Gone Is Youth.   son of Jandal Salamah.   *Fr.* The Mufaddaliyat.   AWP, *tr. by* Sir Charles Lyall

Gone now the baby's nurse.   Home after Three Months Away.   Robert Lowell.   HCAP; MoLi; PBMP

Gone she is a long, long way.   Upon a Maid.   Robert Herrick.   CaPo

Gone the three ancient ladies.   Frau Bauman, Frau Schmidt, and Frau Schwartze.   Theodore Roethke.   CoAP; MoP; NAAL-2; NOBA; NYBP; NoAM; TAP

Gone to seed, ailanthus, the poverty.   Ornithology.   Lynda Hull.   SeSe

Gone to sleep I wake up.   The Wrong Way Round.   Peter Handke, *German.*   CBNP, *tr. by* Michael Hamburger

Gone were but the Winter.   Spring Quiet.   Christina Rossetti.   BoTP; CH; GTBS-P; InPS-3; PoE; PoEL-5; WPE   *Fr.* Spring Fancies.

Gone Were but the Winter Cold.   Allan Cunningham.   CH

Gone, with all her sparkling beauty.   Mary E. Tucker.   CBWP-1

"Goneys an' gullies an' all o' the birds o' the sea."   Sea Change.   John Masefield.   FaBoTw; OBMV; RB

Gong, A.   Odia Ofeimun.   PBMAP

Gong Dance, The.   Sokch'o Shin, *Korean.*   CKP, *tr. by* Jaihiun Kim

Gonna dig my grave both long and narrow.   Dig My Grave.   *Unknown.*   AmFP

Gonna Lay My Head Down on Some Railroad Line.   *Unknown.*   AmFP

Gonna talk about you when I get on my knees. (LL)   I been rebuked and I been scorned.   *Unknown.*   BkSV; NAAAL

Gonsalves.   Ron Welburn.   SeSe

Good Advice.   Hilaire Belloc, *German.*   CTV, *tr. by* Louis Untermeyer

Good Advice.   Mother Goose.   ReMoGo

Good afternoon, General Ball.   Collect Call.   Mcavoy Layne.   CDa

Good aged Bale, that with thy hoary hairs.   To Doctor Bale.   Barnabe Googe.   NoSic

Good and Bad.   Edward Wallis Hoch.   CTV

Good and bad and right and wrong.   James Stephens.   MoBrPo

Good and bad are in my heart.   The Twins.   James Stephens.   RaBo

Good and Bad Children.   Robert Louis Stevenson.   ACTP; ChAP; EBVV; FaBoCh; OBCoV; OxBChV

Good and Bad Luck.   John Milton Hay.   *See* Good Luck and Bad ("Good luck is the gayest of all gay girls").

Good and Clever.   Elizabeth Wordsworth.   OxBTC

Good, and great God, can I not think[e] of thee.   To Heaven.   Ben Jonson.   BeJo; ChIV-2; HAP; NAEL-1; NOCV; NOSC; SCGP; SeCP; TRP; UnPo

Good and great God! How should [*or* sho'd] I fear[e].   No Coming to God without Christ.   Robert Herrick.   OxBSP

Good Appetite.   Mark Van Doren.   OxBSP; Spl

Good bailiff of my farm, that snug domain.   Horace, *Latin.*   OBVE, *tr. by* John Conington

Good, better, best.   Comparatives.   *Unknown.*   ACTP; OxNR

Good Boy, A.   Robert Louis Stevenson.   PWR

Good Boy, The.   *Unknown.*   AS

Good brother *Philip,* I have borne you long.   Sonnet 83.   Sir Philip Sidney.   PBRV   *Fr.* Astrophil and Stella.   AAS; SiPS

Good-By.   Grace Denio Litchfield.   PoToHe

Good-by and Keep Cold.   Robert Frost.   CMoP

Good-by can be a happy word.   Margaret E. Bruner.   PoToHe

Good-by er Howdy-do.   James Whitcomb Riley.   CTC

Good-By Liza Jane.   *Unknown.*   AS

Good-by, my son, good-by.   The Wayward Son.   Mrs. Henry Linden.   CBWP-4

Good-by *or* Goodbye , good-by to summer!   Robin Redbreast.   William Allingham.   FaBoBe; OxBChV

Good-by, sweetheart, our days of bliss.   The Parting Lovers.   Mrs. Henry Linden.   CBWP-4

Good-by, the tears are in my eyes.   Rondel.   François Villon, *French.*   AWP, *tr. by* Andrew Lang

Good-by, you big lummux, I'm glad you backed out!   *Unknown.*   *See* Sweet Betsey from Pike.

Good-bye.   Walter De la Mare.   SAGP

Good-bye—and hail! my Fancy. (LL)   Good-Bye, My Fancy! (" Farewell dear mate, dear love!").   Walt Whitman.   ImPo; MeMAP; NAAL-3; SAmP; TAP

Good-bye for a Long Time.   Roy Fuller.   CBLP

Good-bye, little desk at school, good-bye.   Vacation Time.   Frank Hutt.   BoTP

Good-bye 'Liza Jane.   *Unknown.*   AS

Good-bye, my Fancy!   Walt Whitman.   ImPo; MeMAP; NAAL-3; SAmP; TAP

Good-bye Nellie.   *Unknown.*   NSI

Good-bye!—no [*or* nay] do not grieve that it is over.   Farewell.   Harriet Monroe.   PoA

Good-bye! Off for Kansas.   John Willis Menard.   AAP

Good-bye, proud world! I'm going home.   Ralph Waldo Emerson.   MeMAP; PWR; PoToHe; TAP

"Good-bye," said the river, "I'm going downstream."   Howard Nemerov.   WeW-3

Good-Bye to the Mezzogiorno.   W. H. Auden.   OxBTC

Good-bye to the People of Hangchow.   Po Chü-i, *Chinese.*   ChiP, *tr. by* Arthur Waley

Good-bye ye bloody scenes of long ago!   Good-bye! Off for Kansas.   John Willis Menard.   AAP

"Good-bye," you said, and your voice was an echo.   Tak for Sidst.   Babette Deutsch.   PoA

Good Captain, Maker of the light.   For the Kindling of the Light on Easter Eve.   Prudentius, *Latin.*   MLL, *tr. by* Helen Waddell

Good Catholic girl, she didn't mind the cleaning.   Snow White and the Seven Deadly Sins.   R. S. Gwynn.   SoSe-8

Good Cheer.   John Skoyles.   CMAP

Good children, refuse not these lessons to learn.   A Schoolmaster's Admonition.   *Unknown.*   OxBChV

Good christian Reader judge me not.   God's Controversy with New-England.   Michael Wigglesworth.   SCAP

Good Christians all, both great and small.   The Avondale Mine Disaster.   *Unknown.*   AmFP

Good come out of / prison. (LL)   Cell Song.   Etheridge Knight.   NNaP; PoBA

Good Counsel.   *Unknown, Turkish.*   NOIV, *tr. by* James Clarence Mangan

Good Counsel.   *Unknown, Welsh.*   OBWVE, *tr. by* Glyn Jones

Good Counsel to a Young Maid.   Thomas Carew.   *See* Song: Good Counsel to a Young Maid.

Good creatures, do you love your lives.   I Counsel You Beware.   A. E. Housman.   PFE; PeVV

Good Creed, A.   *Unknown.*   *See* The Little Word.

Good dame looked from her, The.   The Leak in the Dike.   Phoebe Cary.   CTV

Good dame Mercy with dame Charite, The.   The Seven Deadly Sins.   Stephen Hawes.   PoEL-1   *Fr.* The Pastime of Pleasure.   OBGa

Good day's work, two contracts made, A.   Between a Contractor and His Wife.   *Unknown.*   NOEC

Good Dr. ARTHUR SHADWELL, who lends lustre to a name. The Flapper. Charles Larcom Graves. NSI

Good Dream, The. Denise Levertov. NNaP

Good evening, daddy! / I know you've heard. Boogie: 1 A.M. Langston Hughes. APSN

Good faith, Mr. Parson, excuse me from that! (LL) On Marriage. Thomas Flatman. EnLoPo; NOBL; PeLV

Good Filya. Nikolai Mikhailovich Rubtsov, *Russian*. TCRP, tr. by Lubov Yakovleva

Good folk [*or* folke], for gold or hire [*or* hyre]. The Cryer. Michael Drayton. NOSC; PoEL-2; SCGP

Good folk, go gain. God's Gifts. Albrecht von Johannsdorf, *German*. GePo, tr. by F. C. Nicholson

"Good folk," said Lizzie. Christina Rossetti. FaBoVe   *Fr.* Goblin Market. CPO; EBEV; FaBoSe; NAEL-2; NALW; NOBVV; NOxBChV; OBNV; OxAEP-2; VWP

Good folks ever will have their way. The Doctor's Story. Will M. Carleton. BLPA

Good for good is only fair. Good Counsel. *Unknown, Welsh*. OBWVE, tr. by Glyn Jones

Good Fortune, when I hailed her recently. Epigram. James Vincent Cunningham. VCAP

Good Frend. Hilda Doolittle.
  "Time has an end, they say." NOBA; VGW

Good Friday. Christy Brown. TIRV

Good Friday. George Herbert. GeHe

Good Friday. Christina Rossetti. ChIV-2; PoEL-5

Good Friday and the Present Crucifixion. Vincent Buckley. CBAP

Good Friday. Driving Weekend. Elizabeth Spires. WWSi

Good Friday: For Lack of an Orchestra. Jack Spicer. APSN

Good Friday: Rex Tragicus, or, Christ Going to His Cross[e]. Robert Herrick. NOSC

Good Friday [*or* Goodfriday], 1613. Riding Westward. Donne. ChIV-2; ESCV; FSCP; InPS-3; MeLP; NAEL-1; NOCV; NOSC; NoP-4; OAEL-1; PBRV; PeECV; PoE; PoEL-2; SeCP; TFi

Good Friday. Somewhere a death. Good Friday and the Present Crucifixion. Vincent Buckley. CBAP

Good Friday was the day. The Martyr. Herman Melville. CBCWP; ColAP; NCAP; PoEL-5; TAP

Good friend, for Jesus' sake forbear. Epitaph on Himself. Shakespeare. PFE

Good Gad! who's this? What's this, my son? The Democratic Barber; or, Country Gentleman's Surprise. John Parrish. NOEC

Good Girl. Molly Peacock. FFC

Good glory, give a look at Sporting Beasley. Sporting Beasley. Sterling Brown. NAAAL

Good God! and can it be that such a nook. The Milking Shed. John Clare. CH

'Good God!' said God, 'I've got my work cut out'. (LL) The Dilemma. Sir John Collings Squire. OBCoV; PoFWW

Good God, what a night that was. Petronius Arbiter, *Latin*. BoLoP; EP; PGA, tr. by Kenneth Rexroth

Good gray [*or* grey] guardians of art, The. Museum Piece. Richard Wilbur. APAD; CMoP; CoAmPo; FaBoMo; InPK-6; NIP-4; TAP; TRP

Good Grease. Mary TallMountain. UnSA

Good Great Man, The. Coleridge. PWR

Good heaven, I thank thee since it was designed. On Myself. Anne Finch, Countess of Winchilsea. NoP-4; OxBSP

Good Heaven! this mystery of life explain. Ad Coelum. William Pattison. OxBSP

Good Heavens. Pattiann Rogers. PuP-17

Good Hot Dogs. Sandra Cisneros. NOxBChV

Good house, and ground whereon, A. The Salt Garden. Howard Nemerov. OBGa

Good hunting, rabbit-catcher and bird-catcher. Leonidas of Tarentum, *Greek*. GrAn, tr. by Peter Levi

Good in Everything. Shakespeare. PoToHe   *Fr.* As You Like It.

Good in graves as heavenly seed are sown, The. The Christian's Reply to the Philosopher. Sir William Davenant. MeLP

Good is the wine that is in love with us. The Sixth Sense. Nikolai Stepanovich Gumilyov, *Russian*. TCRP, tr. by Yakov Hornstein

Good King Wenceslas went out. Children's Rhymes and Parodies. *Unknown*. NOBAu

Good ladies, ye [*or* you] that have your pleasure in exile. The Lady Again Complains. Henry Howard, Earl of Surrey. SiPS

Good Linemen Live in a Closed World. James Whitehead. MT

Good-looking, I'll never stoop for you. Mahsati, *Farsi*. WPOW, tr. by Deirdre Lashgari

Good Lord. Good Lord in That Heaven. *Unknown*. WPoS

Good Lord, behold this dreadful[l] enemy. The Soul's Groan to Christ for Succo[u]r. Edward Taylor. NAAL-1; NAAL-3; PoEL-3   *Fr.* God's Determinations [touching his Elect].

Good Lord Graeme is to Carlisle gane. Graeme and Bewick. *Unknown*. EnSB

Good Lord in That Heaven. *Unknown*. WPoS

Good Lord Nelson had a swollen gland, The. A Ballad of the Good Lord Nelson. Lawrence Durrell. ImPo; LiTM; PeLV

"Good lord of the land, will you stay thane." Lord Maxwell's Last Goodnight. *Unknown*. ESPB; OxBB

Good Lord Saved Her, The. Anna Swirszczynska, *Polish*. PoSu, tr. by Magnus J. Krynski *and* Robert A. Maguire

Good Luck and Bad ("Good luck is the gayest of all gay girls"). John Milton Hay, *after the German of* Heine. FaBoEE; NBLV
  (Good and Bad Luck.) OBAL

Good luck, bad luck are both the Maker's works. Cao Bá Quát, *Vietnamese*. AVP, tr. by Huỳnh Sanh Thông

Good Luck Gold. Janet S. Wong. NOxBChV

Good luck is the gayest of all gay girls. Good Luck and Bad. John Milton Hay, *after the German of* Heine. FaBoEE; NBLV; OBAL

Good madam, when ladies are willing. To a Lady Making Love. Lady Mary Wortley Montagu. LW

Good Madam with kynd speach and promise fayr. To my Lady Rogers. Martial, *Latin*. OBCVT, tr. by Sir John Harington

Good Man, The. *Unknown, Irish*. TIRV, tr. by Robin Flower

Good Man, The. *Unknown*. *Fr.* The Talmud. TrJP

Good Man Has No Shape, The. Wallace Stevens. MeMAP

Good Man in Hell, The. Edwin Muir. MoBrPo

Good man ther[e] was of religioun [*or* religion], A. The Good Parson. Chaucer. NOCV   *Fr.* The General Prologue. FHYEP; NAEL-1; NAWM-1; OAEL-1; PoE   *Fr.* The Canterbury Tales.

Good manners may in Seven Words be found. Of Courtesy. Arthur Guiterman. Spl

Good mechanics are all of one mind. Limerick. Douglas Catley. PeLi

Good medicin for sor eyen. *Unknown*. MiEL

Good Medicine. *Unknown*. PWR

Good men and true! in this house who dwell. The Croppy Boy. William B. McBurney. TIRV

Good men and women gone too soon to bed. (LL) Dear Uncle Stranger. Conrad Potter Aiken. ColAP; NOBA; NoAM

Good Mistress Dishclout, what's the matter? Written by Desire of a Lady, on an Angry, Petulant Kitchen-Maid. Jane Cave. ECWP

Good Moolly Cow, The. Eliza Lee Cabot Follen. OBCA

Good mornin', blues. Good Morning, Blues. Jimmy Rushing. NAAAL

Good Morning. Rose Fyleman. BoTP

Good morning[, good-morning!" the General said]. The General. Siegfried Sassoon. CMoP; LiTM; NAEL-2; NoAM; NoP-4; OBWP; OxBSP; OxBTC; OxBoLi; PoE; PoFWW

Good Morning. Carl Rakosi. FTOS

Good morning, Algernon: Good morning, Percy. On Mundane Acquaintances. Hilaire Belloc. FaBoEE; OBCoV; OxBTC

Good morning, and How do you do? Ninety-Nine. Elizabeth Godley. NOxBChV

Good Morning, Blues. Jimmy Rushing. NAAAL

Good morning daddy! Dream Boogie. Langston Hughes. APSN; AmPP; HCAP; MBE; NAAAL; PFTM; SSLK   *Fr.* Lenox Avenue Mural. HoPM

Good morning, Father Francis. *Unknown*. OxNR

Good morning, fox of the cave. The Fox's Counsel. Huw Llwyd, *Welsh*. OBWVE, tr. by Joseph P. Clancy

'Good morning! good morning! our work is begun!'. (LL) Good Night and Good Morning. Richard Monckton, 1st Baron Houghton Milnes. BoTP; OxBChV

Good morning, Life—and all. A Greeting. W. H. Davies. MoBrPo

Good Morning—Midnight. Emily Dickinson. NALW

Good morning, Mistress and Master. *Unknown*. OxNR

Good morning, Mrs Roebeck. Christ have mercy! (LL) On Mundane Acquaintances. Hilaire Belloc. FaBoEE; OBCoV; OxBTC

Good morning to You, Almighty God. Kaddish. Levi-Yitzhok of Berditchev, *Yiddish*. TrJP, tr. by Joseph Leftwich

Good-Morrow, The. Donne. APAD; CABP; FMP; FSCP; ITG; LoP; NoP-4
  ("Love so alike that none do slacken, none can die.") (LL) APAD; CABP; NoP-4

Good Morrow. Thomas Heywood. *See* Matin Song.

Good morrow bids the cock, th' owl bids good night. Of a Husbandman. Joshua Sylvester. NOSC

Good morrow to the day so fair. The Mad Maid's Song. Robert Herrick. AWP; CH; CaPo; EnLoPo; GEA; OAEL-1; OBEV; RACG

Good morrow to the morn next to my gold. Aristophanes. OBCVT, *tr.* by Thomas Randolph *Fr.* Plutus.

Good morrow to thy sable beak. Blackcock, The [*or* The Black Cock]. Joanna Baillie. WoRP

Good morrow to you, Valentine. *Unknown.* OxNR

Good Mr. Peeps or Peps or Pips. The Gospel of Mr. Pepys. Christopher Darlington Morley. NBLV

Good name is better than precious oil, A. It Is Better. Bible, *O.T.* TrJP *Fr.* Ecclesiastes.

Good name is rather to be chosen, A. The Bible, Proverbs 22:1. Bible, *O.T.* CTV *Fr.* The Bible, Proverbs 22:1.

Good-nature is thy sterling name. Loveliness. Christopher Smart. NOCV *Fr.* Hymns for the Amusement of Children.

Good News from New England. Edward Johnson. SCAP

Good news, good news. (LL) Letter Written on a Ferry While Crossing Long Island Sound. Anne Sexton. CoAP; NAAL-2; NYBP; TwCP

Good news. It seems he loved them after all. A Song about Major Eatherly. John Wain. OxBTC

Good Night. Ruth Ainsworth. BoTP

Good Night. Eleanor Farjeon. NOxBChV; NTP; OTCP

Good Night. Thomas Hood. OTCP; Spl

Good-night. James Shirley. BeJo
  (Goodnight.) NOSC

Good Night! Gilbert Sorrentino. FTOS

Good-Night. Edward Thomas. FP

Good Night! William Carlos Williams. SAmP

Good Night and Good Morning. Richard Monckton, 1st Baron Houghton Milnes. BoTP; OxBChV

Good Night, at last. Envoy. Robert Duncan. VGW *Fr.* Passages.

Good-night, big world. Back to the Ghetto. Jacob Glatstein, *Yiddish.* TrJP, *tr. by* Joseph Leftwich

Good-night; ensured release. Parta Quies. A. E. Housman. NOBE

Good night for the fireplace to be, A. The Heat in the Room. Weldon Kees. SPE

Good night, God bless you. *Unknown.* OxNR

Good Night! Good Night! John Holmes. PoToHe

"Good night.". . . "Good night." Muriel Stuart. *See* In The Orchard.

Good night! Good night! / Far flies the light. Victor Hugo, *French.* BoTP

Good night Marcus put out the light. To Marcus Aurelius. Zbigniew Herbert, *Polish.* VCWP, *tr. by* Miosz, Czeslaw and Peter Dale Scott

Good night, my two little cloud ladies. For the Girls 'cause They Know. Harold Littlebird. VoR

Good-Night, or Blessing, The. Robert Herrick. CaPo

"Good Night," Says the Owl. Lady Erskine Crum. BoTP

Good night, sweet repose. *Unknown.* OxNR

Good night to the Season! 'Tis over! Goodnight to the Season! Winthrop Mackworth Praed. NOBE; NOBL; OBCoV; OBNC; OxBoLi; PeLV; PoEL-4

Good night to the Year Academic. A Grouchy Good Night to the Academic Year. Ted Pauker. NOBL; PeLV

Good Night, Willie Lee, I'll See You in the Morning. Alice Walker. CrSp; IMW; ISC; NAAAL; WeW-3
  ("At the end.") (LL) ISC

Good of the Chaplain to enter Lone Bay. Billy in the Darbies. Herman Melville. APN-2; HAP; NAAL-1; NAWM-2; NCAP; NOBA; OxBoLi; PoEL-5 *Fr.* Billy Budd, Foretopman.

Good Old Days, The. Barbara Fried. NBLV

Good Old Dog, The. Toi Derricotte. InPS-3

Good old, honest Deacon Brown. Deacon Brown's Conclusion. George Sands Johnson. PWR

Good old Mother Fairie. To Mother Fairie. Alice Cary. OBCA

"Good old times"—all times when old are good, The. The Age of Bronze. Byron.

Good Parson, The, *mod. vers. by* H.C. Leonard. Chaucer. *Fr.* The General Prologue. FHYEP; NAEL-1; NAWM-1; OAEL-1; PoE *Fr.* The Canterbury Tales.

Good people all, of every sort. An Elegy on the Death of a Mad Dog. Oliver Goldsmith. BLPA; FaBoBe; FaBoCh; NBLV; NOEC; NOIV; NTP; OBNV; OxAEP-1; TFi *Fr.* The Vicar of Wakefield.

Good people draw near as you pass along. Alphabetical Song on the Corn Law Bill. *Unknown.* OxBoLi

Good people, give attention, a story you shall hear. Lord Delamere. *Unknown.* ESPB

Good people give attention, and listen for a while. The Queen's Dream. *Unknown.* PeVV

Good people I pray. The Orange. Matthew Prior. PeLV

Good people, what, will you of all be bereft. A Ballad on the Taxes. Edward Ward. OxBoLi

Good Play, A. Robert Louis Stevenson. ACTP; OTCP; PWR

Good prince, what? The dog that keeps, A. Of a Good Prince and an Evil. Timothy Kendall. NoSic

Good rain knows its season, A. Spring Night, A—Rejoicing in Rain. Tu Fu, *Chinese.* SuSp, *tr. by* William H. Nienhauser

Good rain knows its season, A. Spring Rain. Tu Fu, *Chinese.* OHMPC, *tr. by* Kenneth Rexroth

Good reader! if you e'er have seen. Nonsense. Thomas Moore. FaBoEE

Good repute is water carried in a sieve. Lalleswari, *Kashmiri.* WPOW, *tr. by* George Grierson, *ad. by* Deirdre Lashgari

Good Resolution, A. Roy Campbell. OBSV

Good Samaritan et Al, The. Stephen Mitchell. GI

Good schoolmaster, pray give your classes a rest. To a Schoolmaster. Martial, *Latin.* OBCVT, *tr. by* F. A. Wright

Good Shepherd: Atlanta, 1981, The. Ai. RACG; WWSi

Good Shepherd's Sorrow for the Death of His Beloved Son, The. Anne, Duchess of Arundel Howard. NOSC
  (Elegy on the Death of Her Husband.) WPE

Good Ships. John Crowe Ransom. MeMAP; WeW-3

Good sir, whose powers are these? Shakespeare. *Fr.* Hamlet. NAWM-1

Good sportsmanship we hail, we sing. Richard Armour. ChAP; KaS

Good Style. Tom Leonard. FaBoTC

Good sword and a trusty hand, A! The Song of the Western Men. Robert Stephen Hawker. EBEvV; FaPoR; OBNC; OxAEP-2

Good Taste. Christopher Logue. OBSP

Good Thanksgiving, A. "Marian Douglas." PoLF

Good Thing, A. Ray Mathew. CBAP

Good things go by so softly, The. Back to it. Larry Eigner. FTOS

Good thoughts are the threads. Katherine Maurine Haaff. PoToHe

Good time of the year, The. Bernard de Ventadour, *French.* STV, *tr. by* John Frederick Nims

Good time will never come back again, The. Parting from Su Wu. Li Ling, *Chinese.* ChiP, *tr. by* Arthur Waley

Good Times. Lucille Clifton. AmPA; BPo; ISC; InPS-3; MBE; PoBA; SoSe-8; TAP; TRP; TwCP

Good Town, The. Edwin Muir. CMoP

Good traveler has no fixed plans, A. Lao Tzu. EnlH *Fr.* Tao Te Ching.

Good Wife, The. Bible, *O.T. See* The Virtuous Woman.

Good Will to Men—Christmas Greetings in Six Languages. Dorothy Brown Thompson. OBCP

Good Wish. *Unknown, Gaelic.* FaBoCh, *tr. by* Alexander Carmichael

Good wood. Food for Fire, Food for Thought. Robert Duncan. NeAP

Good wood died: hacked, chopped, rent, burnt black, The. Dialectical Poem #1. Campbell McGrath. WeT

Good Works, *mod. by* Donald Attwater. William Langland. NOCV *Fr.* The Vision of Piers Plowman.

Good World. Velemir Khlebnikov, *Russian.*
  "And so the castles of world trade." TCRP, *tr. by* Gary Kern

Good Wyf [*or* Wif] was ther of bisyde [*or* biside] Bathe, A. Seven Pilgrims: A Wyf of Bathe. Chaucer. EBEV *Fr.* The General Prologue. FHYEP; NAEL-1; NAWM-1; OAEL-1; PoE *Fr.* The Canterbury Tales.

Goodbat Nightman. Roger McGough. MoP

Goodby Betty, don't remember me. E. E. Cummings. CMoP; PoE

Goodbye. Bella Akhatovna Akhmadulina, *Russian.* BoWoP, *tr. by* Barbara Einzig

Goodbye. Bill Knott. SPE

Goodbye. Alun Lewis. BoLoP; NAEL-2; NoP-4; OBWP; OxBM; OxBTC; PoWW

Goodbye. Robert Long. IFJA

Goodbye. Adrian Mitchell. OPOU

Goodbye. Virgil Teodorescu, *Romanian.* CEEP, *tr. by* Stavros Deligiorgis

Goodbye, bright creature. In the Cloud of Unknowing. Carol Rumens. DiPo

Goodbye David Tamunoemi West. Margaret Danner. BPo

Goodbye, Goldeneye. May Swenson. NoP-4

Goodbye, goodbye. Here come the cows. James Tate. *See* The Lost Pilot.

Goodbye: I bite the word back. Paulus Silentiarius, *Greek.* GrAn, *tr by* Andrew Miller

Goodbye, lady in Bangor, who sent me. The Correspondence School Instructor Says Goodbye to His Poetry Students. Galway Kinnell. NOBA; NoAM; NoP-4; TAP

Goodbye, Little Bonny Blue Eyes. *Unknown.* AmFP

Goodbye, my friend, goodbye. Sergey Aleksandrovich Yesenin, *Russian.* TCRP, *tr. by* Geoffrey Thurley

Goodbye Nkrumah. Diane Di Prima. PoM

Goodbye Note to Debbie Fuller: Pass It On. David Clewell. IFJA

"Goodbye, O sun," said Cleombrotus of Ambracia. Callimachus. HePo *Fr.* Epigrams.

Goodbye Party for Miss Pushpa T. S. Nissim Ezekiel. OBCoV

Goodbye, Sally. James Simmons. BIrV

"Goodbye Sun!" said the Ambracian. Callimachus, *Greek*. GrAn, *tr. by* Peter Jay

Goodbye to Brigid / An Agnus Dei. Padraic Fiacc. CIP-2

Goodbye to London. Louis MacNeice. PeECV

Goodbye to Regal. Daniel Huws. NYBP

Goodbye to Serpents. James Dickey. NYBP

Goodbye to the Bay of Naples. Wendy Mulford. NBrP

Goodbye to Tolerance. Denise Levertov. NoAM

Goodbye / Until such time as bobolinks do dine. To Janet. Ralph Pomeroy. NYBP

Goodbye, Winter, / The days are getting longer. Prognosis. Louis MacNeice. CMoP; NOBE

Goodhousekeeping #17. Safiya Henderson-Holmes. ISC

Goodliest Pearle in faire *Eliza's* Chaine, The. First Pearle, The: Religion. Lady Diana Primrose. KTR *Fr.* A Chain of Pearl.

Goodly Child, A. *Unknown*. OxBChV

Good[-]Morrow, The. Donne. AWP; BoLoP; CBLP; ClHu; EBEV; ESCV; EnLoPo; FHYEP; FaBoBe; FaBoVe; HoPM; ImPo; InPS-3; MeLP; NAEL-1; NAWM-1; NOSC; OAEL-1; OxAEP-1; PoE; PoEL-2; PoRA; Poetr; SCV; SeCP; SoSe-8; TFi

Goodnight. John Ciardi. OBAL

Goodnight. James Shirley. *See* Good-night.

Goodnight, The. Louis Simpson. PBMP

Goodnight. Stevie Smith. FaBoWP

Goodnight, A. William Carlos Williams. MoAmPo

Goodnight, Achilles. Enrique Lihn, *Spanish*. VCWP, *tr. by* Alastair Reid

Goodnight to the Season! Winthrop Mackworth Praed. NOBE; NOBL; OBCoV; OBNC; OxBoLi; PeLV; PoEL-4

Goodtime Jesus. James Tate. LCAP-2; WeT

Goodwill, Inc. Dennis Schmitz. AmPA

Goody Blake and Harry Gill: A True Story. Wordsworth. Ro

Goodyere, I am [*or* I'm] glad and grateful to report. To Sir Henry Goodyere. Ben Jonson. NOSC

Goops are gluttonous and rude, The. Table Manners II. Frank Gelett Burgess. CTV

Goops they lick their fingers, The. Table Manners. Frank Gelett Burgess. CTV; OBCA

Goose. Richard Emil Braun. NoAM

Goose and the Gander, The. *Unknown*. RB

Goose Fish, The. Howard Nemerov. CMoP; HeIP-4; LiTM; NIP-4; NoAM; NoP-4; PoE; Poetr

Goose-Girl, The. Edith Nesbit. VWP

Goose Pond's imaginable snows. Stanley Kunitz. PoA

Gooseberry Fool ("Gooseberry's no doubt an oddity, The"). Amy Clampitt. NoAM

Gooseberry's no doubt an oddity, The. Gooseberry Fool. Amy Clampitt. NoAM

Goosey, goosey, gander[, where *or* whither shall I wander? shall I wander?]. Mother Goose. CTAV; LB; OxNR; ReMoGo

Goosey, goosey gander, / Who stands yonder? Betsy Baker. *Unknown*. OxNR

Gorbo, as thou cam'st this way. The Daffodil Song. Michael Drayton. AEP *Fr.* The Shepherd's Garland.

Gorby and the Rats. Obeyd-i-Zàkànì, *Persian*. PC, *tr. by* Omar Pound

Gordian knot need not be cut, The. (LL) Charity Overcoming Envy. Marianne Moore. GS; NYBP

Goree. Niyi Osundare. HBAPE

Gorée ten miles offshore beckons. Everett Hoagland. GT

Gorey at the Biennale. Martin Johnston. BMAP

Gorg, a Detective Story. B. P. Nichol. NOBC

Gorgeous grew the common walls about me. Impromptu. Mary Elizabeth Coleridge. VWP

Gorges of Wu are hoary and in the season of mist and rain, The. Liu Yu Hsi. SuSp, *tr. by* Daniel Bryant *Fr.* Bamboo Branch Song.

Gorgo, a Cretan bitch, on a deer's track. Antipater of Thessalonica, *Greek*. GrAn, *tr. by* Alistair Elliot

Gorgo and Praxinoa. Theocritus, *Greek*. HePo, *tr. by* Barbara Hughes Fowler *Fr.* Idylls.

Gorgon. Ambrose Bierce. APN-2 *Fr.* The Devil's Dictionary.

Gorilla Gorilla. Bruce Dawe. NoAM

Gorilla lay on his back, The. Au Jardin des Plantes. John Wain. OxBTC

Gormley's Laments. Gormley, Queen of Ireland, *Irish*.

"I have loved thirty by three." PBWP, *tr. by* Joan Keefe

Gorse Fires. Michael Longley. NoP-4

Gorselight, yellow, the slopes. Matière de Bretagne. Paul Celan, *German*. VCWP, *tr. by* Michael Hamburger

Gosling following its neck to the bug. Marlene Mountain. HA

Gospel. Kevyn Arthur. PBCV

Gospel of Mr. Pepys, The. Christopher Darlington Morley. NBLV

Gospel train is moving, The. *Unknown*. GM

Gosport Tragedy, The. *Unknown*.
(Pretty Polly.) AmFP

Gossip. Mrs. Henry Linden. CBWP-4

Gossip grows like weeds. Hitomaro, *Japanese*. OHPJ, *tr. by* Kenneth Rexroth

Got a Home in That Rock, *see also* Home in That Rock *and* I Got a Home in Dat Rock. *Unknown*. APN-2

Got a peek / at the moon. Last Night. Onuora Oku. PBCV

Got Dem Blues. *Unknown*. AS

Got up and dressed up. 113th Chorus. Jack Kerouac. NeAP; PmAP *Fr.* Mexico City Blues.

Got up this morning. One Thousand Nine Hundred and Sixty-Eight Winters. Jaci Earley. MBE; PFE

Got up, went to school. Diary. Mary Wilson. Spl

Gotham. Charles Churchill. NOEC

Gothic church. At one end of an aisle, A. A Crucifix. John Gray. ADE

Gothic columns of petrified motion. M. G. Mainwaring. TOF

Gothic Dusk, The. Frederic Prokosch. PoA

Gothic Landscape. Irving Layton. TrJP

Gothic looks solemn, The. On Oxford. Keats. OBCoV; OxAEP-2; PeLV; SCGP

Goulburn Island Song Cycle. *Unknown, Aborigine*.

"Bird saw the young Burara girls, twisting their strings, making string figures, The." NOBAu, *tr. by* Ronald M. Berndt

"Ejaculating into their vaginas—young girls of the western tribes." NOBAu, *tr. by* Ronald M. Berndt

"They saw the young girls twisting their strings, Goulburn Island." NOBAu, *tr. by* Ronald M. Berndt

"They seize the young girls of the western tribes, with their swaying." NOBAu, *tr. by* Ronald M. Berndt

Gourd Dancer, The. N. Scott Momaday. CDW

Gourd has still its bitter leaves, The. I Wait My Lord. *Unknown*. AWP, *tr. by* Helen Waddell *Fr.* Shi King.

Gourmand, The. Harry Graham. UV

Gourmet challenged me to eat, A. Experiment Degustatory. Ogden Nash. ChAP

Gourmet's Love-Song, The. P. G. Wodehouse. NOBL

Gout. Lewis Warsh. FTOS

Gout and Wings. Charles Tennyson Turner. NOBVV

Gouzeaucourt: The Deceitful Calm. Edmund Blunden. PeFWW

Govern a life. (LL) Words. Sylvia Plath. APAD; CoAmPo; HCAP; NAAL-2; NALW; PoE; Poetr; VCAP

Governante, The. Dame Edith Sitwell. BWW *Fr.* The Sleeping Beauty.

Government building, not my own home, A. Written when Governor of Soochow. Po Chü-i, *Chinese*. ChiP, *tr. by* Arthur Waley

Government had just been overthrown, The. Mimosas. Louis Aragon, *French*. CBNP

Government wine of Peking is sweeter than honey, The. Hsieh Chin. CoBLCP, *tr. by* Jonathan Chaves *Fr.* Things Experienced upon Withdrawal from Court.

Governor loves to go mapping—round and round, The. Sydney Cove, 1788. Peter Porter. NoAM

Governor of Huai-yang, arm and leg to the ruler, The. In a Provincial Capital Sick in Bed. Hsieh T'iao, *Chinese*. CoBCP, *tr. by* Burton Watson

Governor of the Ollie Street, The. Ahmos, II Zu-Bolton. BkSV

Governor your husband lived so long, The. John Berryman. NOBA *Fr.* Homage to Mistress Bradstreet.

Gowan glitters on the sward, The. The Trysting Bush. Joanna Baillie. WPE

Goyng towardes Spayne. Barnabe Googe. PBRV

Gr-r-r—there go, my heart's abhorrence! Soliloquy of the Spanish Cloister. Robert Browning. FHYEP; FaBoVe; ImPo; InPK-6; NAEL-2; NIP-4; NOBL; NOBVV; NoP-4; OAEL-2; OxBoV; PeVV; TOF; UV

Grab-Bag. Helen Hunt Jackson. OBCA

Grabbing one of. Tanka. Akiko Yosano, *Japanese*. MJT, *tr. by* Makoto Ueda

Grace. Ralph Waldo Emerson. APN-1; AmPP; NCAP

Grace, A. Donald Hall. LoL

Grace. Joy Harjo. NAmP90

Grace. George Herbert. ChIV-1; GeHe

Grace Abounding. A. R. Ammons. HCAP

Grace after Meals. *Unknown, Hebrew*. TrJP, *tr. by* Alice Lucas

Grace and Thanksgiving. Elizabeth Gould. BoTP

Grace at Kirkudbright, *see also* A Child's Grace. Robert Burns. NTP; OxBSP

Grace before Meat. Robert David Fitzgerald. NOBAu

Grace by his priest; *The feast is ended.* (LL) Oberon's Feast. Robert Herrick. BeJo; CaPo; NOSC

Grace for a Child. Robert Herrick. AWP; CTV; InPS-3; NAEL-1; PFE; PoE; TFi

(Another Grace for a Child.) BeJo; NOSC; NTP; OxBChV; SCGP

Grace for Children, A. Robert Herrick. OxBChV

Grace for Ice-Cream, A. Allan M. Laing. OBCoV

Grace for Light. "Moira O'Neill." TIRV

Grace is the focal point. Bar Giamaica, 1959-60. Charles Wright. EOEF

Grace, Majesty, and the calm bliss of life. Two Worlds. Richard Watson Gilder. GS

Grace more then thine [*or* thyne], that [*or* but] God's, the world hath none. (LL) At Home in Heaven. Robert Southwell. ESCV; EnVR

Grace-Note, The. Denise Levertov. CoAmPo

Grace of Animals, The. Richard Harteis. GLP

Grace of God and the Meth-Drinker, The. Sydney Goodsir Smith. FaBoTC

Grace of the Way. Francis Thompson.
 "Now of that vision I, bereaven." MoBrPo

Grace of Tullies eloquence doth excell, The. Classics Society. Tony Harrison. NoP-4 *Fr.* The School of Eloquence. NAEL-2; NoAM

Grace on which we fix our gaze; pillar. Nicole at Thirteen. Gregory Orr. MoLi

Grace, thou source of each perfection. Epiphany. Christopher Smart. NOCV *Fr.* Hymns and Spiritual Songs for the Fasts and Festivals of the Church of England.

Grace to be born and live as variously as possible. Sonnet LV. Ted Berrigan. FTOS *Fr.* The Sonnets.

Grace to be said at the Supermarket. Howard Nemerov. SoSe-8

Graceful Acacia. Walter Savage Landor. PoEL-4

Graceful as acorus or lotus flower. Aliter. Confucius. *Fr.* Songs of Ch'en. CTC, *tr. by* Ezra Pound

Graceful Bastion, The. William Carlos Williams. NYBP

Gracefullest leaper, the dappled fox-cub. Young Reynard. George Meredith. HoPM

Graces da[u]nced and Apollo played, The. (LL) Gratiana Dancing [*or* Dauncing] and [*or* &] Singing. Richard Lovelace. BeJo; CaPo; MeLP; OBEV

Graces, if the beautiful Dionysios. *Unknown, Greek.* GrAn, *tr. by* Peter Jay

Graces of the Holy Ghost, The. *Unknown, Irish.* TIRV, *tr. by* Douglas Hyde

Graciela. Gary Soto. NoAM

Graciela wouldn't fuck me. De Ambiente. Tatiana De la tierra. GLP

Gracing the tide-warmth, this seagull. The Seagull. Dafydd ap Gwilym, *Welsh.* OBWVE, *tr. by* Glyn Jones

Gracious Goodness. Marge Piercy. Poetsp

Gracious Saviour let me make. Thou Lovest Me. Josephine D. Henderson Heard. CBWP-4

Gracious Saviour, We Adore Thee. Sewall Sylvester Cutting. AH

Gracious Time, The. Shakespeare. *See* The Bird of Dawning.

Gracius and gay. *Unknown.* MiEL

Grackle's voice is less than mellow. Ogden Nash. CBNP; NBLV

Gradation. Charles Bernstein. FTOS

Gradual bud and bloom and seedfall speeded up. July 4th. May Swenson. PoA

Gradual self-effacement of the dead, The. (LL) Song (On Seeing Dead Bodies Floating Off the Cape). Alun Lewis. LiTM; NAEL-2; NoP-4; OBWP

Gradually even this disappears. What remains. Of All the Splendor. Ory Bernstein, *Hebrew.* IP, *tr. by* Warren Bargad *and* Stanley F. Chyet

Graecinus (well I wot) thou told'st me once." 2.10. Ovid. EBEV, *tr. by* Marlowe *Fr.* Elegies.

Graeme and Bewick. *Unknown.* EnSB

Graf von Charolais, Der. Richard Beer-Hofmann, *German.*
 "Evil Man, An!" TrJP, *tr. by* Ludwig Lewisohn

Graffiti. Julian Croft. NOBAu

Graffiti. Alice Archer Sewall James. NBLV

Graffiti. Jane Yolen. SSCS

Graft anneal upon perennial trees. (LL) Invitation To Juno. William Empson. CBLP; CMoP; FaBoMo

Grafted Bud, The. Mary Weston Fordham. CBWP-2

Grafted Tongue, A. John Montague. BIrV; CIP-2; PBCIP

Grail, The. Sidney Keyes. FaBoTw

Grain-Barge Wife, The. Wu Chia-chi, *Chinese.* CoBLCP, *tr. by* Jonathan Chaves

Grain for Emperor Huan. *Unknown, Chinese.* ChiPo, *tr. by* Rewi Alley

Grain of Sand, A. Frances Ellen Watkins Harper. PWR

Grain of sand, the beginning of the desert, The. Maria Luisa Spaziani, *Italian.* NeIt, *tr. by* Beverly Allen

Grain of sawdust being sawn / by the minutest of saws. Norman MacCaig. *See* Blue Tit on a String of Peanuts.

Grains of corn were planted, The. Story of the Corn. K. Fisher. BoTP

Grains of Rice. Phan Văn Trị, *Vietnamese.* AVP, *tr. by* Huỳnh Sanh Thông

Grains of snow ride down here as bits. Letter from a Black Soldier. Bill Anderson. VGW

Gra'ma was a little bit of a thing. Colleen J. McElroy. NMM-2

Gramercy, Death, as you've my love to win. Sonnet: He Argues His Case with Death. Cecco Angiolieri, da Siena, *Italian.* AWP, *tr. by* D. G. Rossetti

Gramercy Park. Marilyn Hacker. DeD *Fr.* Love, Death and the Changing of the Seasons.

Grammar, A. Andrei Codrescu. SPE

Grammar commences with a five line curse. Palladas, *Greek.* OBVE, *tr. by* Tony Harrison

Grammar Lesson. Linda Pastan. Poetsp

Grammar of cause, The. Prolegomena To A Theodicy. Kenneth Rexroth. PFTM

Grammar-Rules. Sir Philip Sidney. *See* Sonnet 63: "O Grammer rules, ô now your virtues show."

Grammarian's daughter, The. Palladas, *Greek.* GrAn, *tr. by* Peter Jay

Grammarian's Funeral, A. Robert Browning. NAEL-2; NOBVV; PeECV

Grammer's Shoes. William Barnes. EBVV; EnVR

Grampa. Dennis Scott. NTP; PBCV

Granada (1000 A.D.) Abu Ishaq al-Ilbin, *Arabic.* ArPe, *tr. by* Omar S. Pound

Grand Abacus. John Ashbery. PoA; SPE

Grand ancient, Gothic, mark this ample dome. Lake, The; Or, Modern Improvement in Landscape. Anna Seward. OBGa

Grand Army Plaza. June Jordan. ISC

Grand attempt some Amazonian dames, A. On a Fortification at Boston Begun by Women. Benjamin Tompson. NOSC; SCAP

Grand Ballet. Frances Darwin Cornford. WPN

Grand Canyon, The. James Merrill. TAP

Grand Central Hotel, The. Roy McFadden. PNI

Grand Central Station, 20 December 1987. Bruce Bawer. RA

Grand Chorus of Birds. Aristophanes. *See* Chorus of Birds.

Grand conglomerate hills of Araby, The. Night the Sixth: Hadramaut. Bayard Taylor. APN-2 *Fr.* The Echo Club.

Grand-Dad, they say you're old and frail. A Child to His Sick Grandfather. Joanna Baillie. CABP; ECWP; NOEC; RACG; WoRP

Grand Duo. James Schuyler. FTOS

Grand Entry, The. Gary Snyder. NoAM

Grand Finale. Irving Layton. NOBC

Grand Guignols of Love, The. Michael Benedikt. AmPA

Grand Houses at Lo-yang, The. Po Chü-i, *Chinese.* ChiP, *tr. by* Arthur Waley

Grand Night, A. D. J. Enright. NSI

Grand old Duke of York, The. *Unknown.* BoTP
 ("O, the grand old Duke of York.") LB

Grand-Père. Robert W. Service. NSI

Grand Projection. Rodney Jones. BAP-93

Grand Rapids. Julia A. Moore. OBAL

Grand rough old Martin Luther. The Twins. Robert Browning. FaBoVe

Grand Tradition of Western Culture, The. Julia Stein. LoHo

Granddaddy longlegs did twilight, The. Ohio Valley Swains. James Wright. NNaP

Granddaughter. Adrienne Rich. *Fr.* Grandmothers. HCAP; NAAL-2; NoAM

Grandest ship-of-war which e'er to sea was known, The. She Is the Greatest Wealth. Georg Rudolph Weckherlin, *German.* GePo, *tr. by* George C. Schoolfield

Grandest writer of late ages, The. Distribution of Honours for Literature. Walter Savage Landor. FaBoEE

Grandeur of Ghosts. Siegfried Sassoon. MoBrPo; ODMV

Grandeurs of his Babylonian heart, The. (LL) All's Vast. Francis Thompson. GTBS-P; MoBrPo; OBMV; Son

Grandfa' Grig / Had a pig. *Unknown.* OxNR

Grandfather. George Bowering. NOBC

Grandfather. Michael S. Harper. LCAP-2; NAAAL; TAP; VCAP

Grandfather. Lance Henson, *Cheyenne Indian.* CDW; HATNAP, *tr. by* Lance Henson

Grandfather. Derek Mahon. OxBC

Grandfather / advised me. Lorine Niedecker. NMM-2

Grandfather and Grandmother in Love. David Mura. TRP

Grandfather at the Indian Health Clinic. Elizabeth Cook-Lynn. HATNAP; UnSA

Grandfather-in-law. David Mura. LoL

Grandfather in the Garden. Robert Minhinnick. OBGa

Grandfather in the Old Men's Home. W. S. Merwin. CoAmPo; LiTM; SAGP

Grandfather Poem, A. William J. Harris. MBE; PoBA

Grandfather puts down his tea-glass. A Night in Odessa. Louis Simpson. NNaP

Grandfather, sleepless in a room upstairs. John Berryman. VGW Fr. The Black Book.

Grandfather Was Queer, Too. Bob Kaufman. NAAAL

Grandfather's Clock. Henry Clay Work. BLPA

Grandfather's Rockery. David Woo. OpBo

Grandfather's Sermon and Michael Smith. E. A. Markham. PBCV

Grandma. Ann Johnson. CTV

Grandma, come back, I forgot. The Morning Baking. Carolyn Forché. LoL

Grandma Fire. Charles G. Ballard. VoR

Grandma in the Shower. Dale M. Kushner. UnSA

Grandma lit the stove. History. Gary Soto. PBCAP

Grandma sleeps with / my sick. Medicine. Alice Walker. CrSp

Grandma stuffed her fur coat into the icebox. Ode. Philip Schultz. NAmP90

Grandma's Bureau. Robert Morgan. EOEF; WeW-3

Grandma's Lost Balance. Sydney Dayre. OBCA

Grandma's Man. James Welch. NoAM

Grandmither, Think Not I Forget. Willa Cather. WPE

Grandmother. Paula Gunn Allen. MDDM

Grandmother, The. Wendell Berry. MT

Grandmother. Grace Cavalieri. UnSA

Grandmother. Siv Cedering Fox. PBCAP

Grandmother. Marilyn Krysl. CrSp

Grandmother, The. Gérard de Nerval, French. IMW, tr. by Barbara Howes

Grandmother. Fily-Dabo Sissoko, French. NegPo, tr. by Ellen Conroy Kennedy

Grandmother, a Caribbean Indian, Described by My Father. Yvonne Sapia. UnSA

Grandmother Came Down to Visit Us, The. Joseph Bruchac. CDW

Grandmother Grace. Ronald Wallace. Poetr

Grandmother, I dreamed of you again. The Visit. Phillip William George. IMW; VoR

Grandmother Jackson. David Jackson. OBCP

Grandmother Remembers, A. Janet Lewis. PaTW

Grandmother Sleeps. Liz Sohappy Bahe. CDW

Grandmother Watching at Her Window. W. S. Merwin. VGW

Grandmothers, The. Mary Oliver. WPE

Grandmothers. Adrienne Rich. HCAP; NAAL-2; NoAM

Mary Gravely Jones. MDDM

Grandmothers Land. William Oandasan. HATNAP

Grandmother's love. Love Necessitates. Eugene B. Redmond. ISC

Grandmother's mirror. Penny Harter. HA

Grandmother's mother: her age, I guess. Dorothy Q. Oliver Wendell Holmes. NOBA

Grandmother's Old Armchair. Unknown. BLPA

Grandmothers' Song. Nellie Wong. FFC

Grandmothers who wring the necks. Classic Ballroom Dances. Charles Simic. LCAP-2; WeW-3

Grandpa dropped his glasses once. Leroy F. Jackson. CTV

Grandpa, I saw you die in the Indian hospital at Pawnee. Hartico. Anna Walters. VoR

Grandpa Is Ashamed. Ogden Nash. OBCoV

Grandpapa. Harry Graham. OBCoV

Grandparents. Sheila Bramfit. OxBM

Grandparents. Robert Lowell. ColAP; LiTM

Grandpa's .45. W. M. Ransom. CDW

Grandson, The. James Scully. NYBP

Grandson Is a Hoticeberg, A. Margaret Danner. BlSi

Grandsons still unborn, The. Georg Trakl. See Grodek.

Grange, The. Stevie Smith. OBCoV

Granite and Cypress. Robinson Jeffers. AmPP

Granite and Grass. Donald Hall. AFr; DiPo

("On Ragged Mountain birches twist from rifts in granite.") AFr

Granite and Steel. Marianne Moore. NYBP

Granite is grass in the holy meadow of the soul's repose. (LL) Granite and Grass. Donald Hall. AFr; DiPo

Grannie's Birthday. Eliza Ogilvy. VWP

Granny. Spike Milligan. FuFo

Granny and I with dear Dadu. A Very Odd Fish. D'Arcy Wentworth Thompson. OxBChV

Granny Crack. James Reaney. NOBC

Granny in de Market Place. Amryl Johnson. HCP

Granny's House. Phoebe Cary. APN-2

Gran's Green Parrot. Wes Magee. PeP

Grant Heaven could once have given us liberty. Predestination and Free Will. Dryden. Fr. The State of Innocence. NOCV

Grant me, indulgent Heaven, a rural seat. The Choice. Nahum Tate. OxBSP

Grant me sweet Christ the grace to find. The Hermitage. Unknown, Irish. IIP, tr. by Frank O'Connor

Grant me the great and solemn breath withdrawn. Invocation and Prelude. Stefan George, German. AWP, tr. by Ludwig Lewisohn

Grant that no Hobgoblins fright me. Prayer. John Day. Spl

Grant us, O God! great Ruler of the Skies! Translation of "Pax Bello Potior." Unknown, Latin. NOBRP, tr. by Unknown

Granted that what we summon is absurd. T. R. Donald Hall. PoA

Granted, we die for good. Table Talk. Wallace Stevens. NoP-4

Grape-gathering. Avraham Shlonsky, Hebrew. TrJP, tr. by I. M. Lask

Grape Stakes. Roy Zarucchi. EC3

Grapes. Unknown, Greek. AWP, tr. by Alma Strettell

Grapes, The. Yuksa Yi, Korean. CKP, tr. by Jaihiun Kim

Grapes Making. Léonie Adams. FYAP; UnPo

Graphemics. Jack Spicer. VGW

"Walden Pond/ All those noxious gases rising from it." VGW

Grappa in September. Cesare Pavese, Italian. RaBo, tr. by William Arrowsmith

Grasmere. Amy Clampitt. PiM

Grasping my flying cane, several feet of wood. Drunk, Climbing to the Peak of Iron Tomb on Wei Mountain. Li K'ai-hsien, Chinese. CoBLCP, tr. by Jonathan Chaves

Grasping with opposite hand the side of his pram. Outside the Supermarket. Roy Fuller. OxBC

Grass, The. George Bowering. MoCV

Grass. Carl Sandburg. AWP; ColAP; MoAmPo; MoP; NAAL-2; NOBA; NoAM; NoP-4; OBWP; OxBA; PeFWW; PoLF; PoPoPo; Poetr; SAGP; TFi

("Let me work.") (LL) NoP-4; PoPoPo; SAGP

Grass. Walt Whitman. ImPo Fr. Song of Myself. AmPP; MoAmPo; NAAL-3; NOBA; OxBA

("Child said What is the grass?, A.") ImPo; SAmP

Grass basks greedily in the sun. Alan Bold. FaBoTC

Grass below—above the vaulted sky, The. (LL) I am: yet what I am none cares or knows. John Clare. EBEV; EBVV; EnVR; FHYEP; GTBS-P; HAP; NAEL-2; NOBE; NOBVV; OAEL-2; OBEV; OBNC; OxAEP-2; PeECV; PoEL-4; TFi; TOF; TRP

Grass below; above, the meadow, The. (LL) Written in Northampton County Asylum. John Clare. PBMP; PFE

Grass bends, The: blades crack from a wind. Camping Out on Rainy Mountain. Jim Barnes. CDW

Grass caught in willow tells the flood's height that has subsided. Basil Bunting. FaBoMo Fr. Briggflatts [An Autobiography].

Grass cuts our feet as we wend our way, The. The Young Prince and the Young Princess. John Ashbery. CoAmPo

Grass Flower. Yangshik Kim, Korean. CKP, tr. by Jaihiun Kim

Grass-green and aspen-green. Variables of Green. Robert Graves. FaBoEE

Grass grows over the dead rails. Still Life with Cleaning Lady. Kurt Bartsch, German. CEEP, tr. by Wayne Kvam

Grass has not yellowed on the paths by the river, The. In Imitation of Ancient-style Poetry. Pao Chao, Chinese. SuSp, tr. by Daniel Bryant

Grass hath such a simple faith, The. Mary Morison Webster. PeSA

Grass hovel filled with wind and dust. Wang Fan-chih, Chinese. SuSp, tr. by Eugene Eoyang

Grass is half-covered with snow, The. Snowfall in the Afternoon. Robert Bly. NOBA; SPE

Grass is very green, my friend, The. A Unison. William Carlos Williams. NOBA

Grass Leaves. Un-gyo Kang, Korean. CKP, tr. by Jaihiun Kim

Grass lies flattened. Suyong Kim, Korean. CKP, tr. by Jaihiun Kim

Grass manoeuvres under passing swans. Picnic. Kenward Elmslie. FTOS

Grass on Ancient Plain, a Song of Farewell. Po Chü-i, Chinese. SuSp, tr. by Irving Y. Lo

Grass on the Cliff. Robinson Jeffers. PoA Fr. The Trumpet.

Grass on the Mountain, The. Mary Austin. PaTW

Grass on the Mountain, The. Unknown, Paiute Indian. AWP, tr. by Mary Austin

Grass path lasts. Anita Virgil. KaS

Grass people bow, The. To Turn Back. John Haines. CoAmPo; TRP

Grass purpled by fallen Judas flowers. In the Spring Garden. Geoffrey Grigson. OBGa

Grass resurrects to mask, to strangle. The Distant Fury of Battle. Geoffrey Hill. NoP-4

Grass shakes. / Smoke streaks, no, The. Growing Dark. James Schuyler. GLP

Grass singed and low. Chickory. Zerubavel Gal'ed, *Hebrew.* TrJP

Grass Widows. Robert B. Shaw. CRP

Grasse-Hopper, The. Richard Lovelace. *See* The Grasshopper.

Grasse: The Olive Trees. Richard Wilbur. NAAL-2; NOBA; NYBP; NoAM

Grasshopper, The. Anacreon, *Greek.* OBCVT, *tr. by* Abraham Cowley

Grasshopper, The. Abraham Cowley, *after the Greek of* Anacreon. AWP; BeJo; NOSC; OAEL-1; OBVE; OxAEP-1

Grasshopper, The. Richard Lovelace. BeJo; CaPo; CavPo; EBEV; FaBoPV; NAEL-1; NOBE; NOSC; NoP-4; OAEL-1; OBEV; SCGP; TFi

(Grasse-Hopper, The.) MeLP; PBRV

(Grasshopper: To My Noble Friend, Mr. Charles Cotton, The.) APo

("O thou that swing'st upon the waving hair.") APo; CavPo; NoP-4

("That wants himself is poor indeed.") (LL) APo; CavPo; NoP-4

("That wants himselfe, is poore indeed.") (LL) PBRV

Grasshopper. J. D. McClatchy. APo

Grasshopper, A. Michael McClintock. HA

Grasshopper, A. Richard Wilbur. HAP; HoPM

Grasshopper and Cricket, The. Keats. *See* On the Grasshopper and [the] Cricket.

Grasshopper and the Bird, The. James Reeves. OTCP

Grasshopper and the Cricket, The. Leigh Hunt. *See* To the Grasshopper and the Cricket.

Grasshopper and the Elephant, The. *Unknown.* CTV

Grasshopper and the Glowworm, The. William Wilkie.
   True Knowledge. ECEV

Grasshopper Green. Nancy Dingman Watson. BoTP

Grasshopper Is a Burden. D. H. Lawrence. FaBoVe

Grasshopper said, The. The Grasshopper and the Bird. James Reeves. OTCP

Grasshopper thrice-happy! who. Thomas Stanley, *after the Greek of* Anacreon. NOSC; OBVE

Grasshopper: To My Noble Friend, Mr. Charles Cotton, The. Richard Lovelace. *See* The Grasshopper.

Grasshopper Wings. *Unknown, Chinese.* CoBCP, *tr. by* Burton Watson

Grasshopper, your fairy [*or* tiny] song. Earth. John Hall Wheelock. MoAmPo

Grasshoppers. John Clare. EnVR; TTTS

Grasshopper's among some grassy hills, The. (LL) On the Grasshopper and [the] Cricket. Keats. APo; BoTP; FHYEP; FaBoBe; ImPo; NIP-4; OAEL-2; OxAEP-2; Poetr; Son; TTTS

Grasshoppers beware. The Cropdusting. William Zaranka. BXAP

Grasshoppers / Chirping in the sleeves. Kawai Chigetsu-Ni, *Japanese.* WPJ; WPOW, *tr. by* Kenneth Rexroth *and* Ikuko Atsumi

Grasshoppers four a-fiddling went. Rilloby-Rill. Sir Henry John Newbolt. BXAP

Gratiana Dancing [*or* Dauncing] and [*or* &] Singing. Richard Lovelace. BeJo; CaPo; MeLP; OBEV

("Graces danced, and Apollo play'd, The.") (LL) CavPo

("*Graces* daunced, and *Apollo* play'd, The.") (LL) PBRV

(Gratiana Dancing and Singing.) CavPo

Gratitude. Louise Glück. FaBoWP; TRP

Gratitude. György Petri, *Hungarian.* VCWP, *tr. by* Wilmer, Clive *and* George Gömöri

Gratitude. Christopher Smart. NOEC *Fr.* Hymns for the Amusement of Children.

Gratitude to Mother Earth, sailing through night and day. Prayer for the Great Family. Gary Snyder. HAP; WeW-3

Gratitude to the Unknown Instructors. W. B. Yeats. EnlH

Gratulatory to Mr. Ben Johnson for His Adopting of Him to Be His Son, A. Thomas Randolph. BeJo

Grave, The. Robert Blair.
   All Impelled Onward Alike. OxAEP-1
   "But see! the well-plumed hearse comes nodding on." ECEV
   Grave-yard on a Stormy Night, The. OxAEP-1
   "Oft in the lone church-yard at night I've seen." OxAEP-1
   Peace the End of the Good Man. OxAEP-1
   "Sickly taper / By glimmering through thy low-browed misty vaults, The." ECEV
   "Whilst some affect the sun, and some the shade." NOEC

Grave, The. Rudyard Kipling. NSI

Grave, A. Marianne Moore. CMoP; FaBoWP; GEA; HAP; HeIP-4; MeMAP; MoP; NAAL-2; NOBA; NoAM; NoP-4; OxBoS; PoE; Poetr; TAP; TFi; TRP; UnPo; WPE; WeW-3

("In which if they turn and twist, it is neither with volition / nor consciousness.") (LL) GEA

Grave and the Rose, The. Victor Hugo, *French.* AWP, *tr. by* Andrew Lang

Grave but ends the struggle!—Follows then, The. The Triumph. William Gilmore Simms. Son

Grave charge in Mayfair bathroom case. Headline History. William Plomer. OBCoV

Grave Doubts. Patricia Beer. NoP-4

Grave has the bones and dumb name of Sappho, The. Epitaph: Sappho. Pinytos, *Greek.* GrAn, *tr. by* Lee T. Pearcy

Grave in Hollywood Cemetery, Richmond, A. Margaret Junkin Preston. CBCWP

Grave in the earth, A. A Kind of Hope. Reiner Kunze, *German.* CEEP, *tr. by* Ewald Osers

Grave in Ukraine, A. Saul Tchernichowsky, *Hebrew.* TrJP, *tr. by* L. V. Snowman

Grave moral Spenser after these came on. Michael Drayton. EPCY *Fr.* To Henry Reynolds, of Poets and Poesy.

Grave Near Cairo, A. Rudyard Kipling. *Fr.* Epitaphs of the War [1914–1918]. OBWP

Grave no conquest gets, Death hath no sting, The. (LL) Elegy: "Death be not proud, thy hand gave not this blow." Lucy Harington, Countess of Bedford. PeECV; WPE

Grave number twenty-four. Udude. Pol N Ndu. PBMAP

Grave of a Poetess, The. Felicia Dorothea Hemans. Ro; VWP

Grave of Hipponax, The. Edward Cracroft Lefroy. AWP *Fr.* Echoes from Theocritus.

Grave of Keats, The. Shelley. *See* Go Thou to Rome.

Grave of Little Su, The. Li Ho, *Chinese.* PLT, *tr. by* A. C. Graham

Grave of Love, The. Thomas Love Peacock. CH; OxAEP-2; OxB5P

Grave of Marmousette, The. Antoine Girard *and* Sieur de Saint-Amant, *French.* FLP, *tr. by* Alistair Elliot

Grave said to the Rose, The. The Grave and the Rose. Victor Hugo, *French.* AWP, *tr. by* Andrew Lang

Grave wise man that had a great rich lady, A. Of an Heroical Answer of a Great Roman Lady to Her Husband. Sir John Harington. BoLoP; OxBM

Grave-Yard, The. Jones Very. NOBA

Grave-yard on a Stormy Night, The. Robert Blair. OxAEP-1 *Fr.* The Grave.

Gravelly Run. A. R. Ammons. CoAP; NAAL-2; NoAM; PoA; VCAP

Graven Thoughts. Sir Philip Sidney. SiPS *Fr.* Arcadia.

Graves. Chế Lan Viên, *Vietnamese.* AVP, *tr. by* Huỳnh Sanh Thông

Graves, The. Gregor Strnisa, *Slovenian.* CEEP, *tr. by* Michael Scammell

Graves Are Made to Waltz On. Peter Viereck. PoA

Graves at Elkhorn. Richard Hugo. UnPo; VCAP

Grave's Cherub, The. Sydney Clouts. PeSA

Graves grow deeper, The. The Dead. Mark Strand. HeIP-4

Graves of a Household, The. Felicia Dorothea Hemans. FaPoR; NOBRP; WPE

Graves Registration. Basil T. Paquet. CDa

Graves the rain makes wet and sleek, The. *Unknown.* OBWVE, *tr. by* Gwyn Jones *Fr.* The Stanzas of the Graves.

Graves! Where in dust are laid our dearest hopes! Vigilantius, or a Servant of the Lord Found Ready. Cotton Mather. SCAP

Gravestone at Corinth, A. *Unknown, Greek.* GrAn, *tr. by* Peter Jay

Graveyard, The. Hayyim Nahman Bialik, *Hebrew.* TrJP, *tr. by* Bertha Beinkinstadt

Graveyard at Bald Eagle Ridge. John Balaban. CDa

Graveyard by the Sea, The. Paul Valéry, *French.* STV, *tr. by* John Frederick Nims

Graveyard—who makes his home in that yard?, The. *Unknown, Chinese.* CoBCP, *tr. by* Burton Watson

Gravity's the villain in this piece—. Jack Matthews. CMAP

Gravy Train, The. R. R. Davidson. NOBAu

Gray are the pages of record. Black Samson of Brandywine. Paul Laurence Dunbar. NAAAL

Gray-blue shadows lift. Starlight Scope Myopia. Yusef Komunyakaa. AF; CDa; WeT

Gray brick, ash, hand-bent railings, steps so big. Cumberland Station. Dave Jeddie Smith. HCAP

Gray despair. The Old Mare. Elizabeth Jane Coatsworth. MoAmPo

Gray Folk, The. Edith Nesbit. NOBVV; PEW

Gray fur collars on a steel limb. Golgotha. X. J. Kennedy. NYBP

Gray Glove. Roo Borson. NOBC

Gray Goose and Gander. *Unknown.* OxBoLi; OxNR

Gray gray of frosty grasses, insects chirp-chirping. Village Night. Po Chü-i, *Chinese*. CoBCP, *tr. by* Burton Watson

Gray hairs, unwelcome monitors, begin. The Dial. Thomas Cole. APN-1

Gray heron flies past, A. Splitting Wood Near Morris, Oklahoma on Robbie and Lesa McMurtry's Farm. Lance Henson. HATNAP

Gray Hills Taught Me Patience, The. Allen Eastman Cross. AH

Gray maidservant lets me in, A. Matinees. James Merrill. HCAP; NOBA

Gray Mare, The. *Unknown*. AmFP

Gray mist wolf. Four Mountain Wolves. Leslie Marmon Silko. VoR

Gray mob-cap and a girl's, A. "Michael Field." CPO

Gray Moment. Momcilo Nastasijevic, *Serbo-Croatian*. HSix, *tr. by* Charles Simic

Gray Morning. Aleksandr Blok, *Russian*. TCRP, *tr. by* Geoffrey Thurley

Gray Nights. Ernest Christopher Dowson. Son

Gray of the sea, and the gray of the sky, The. Her Thought and His. Paul Laurence Dunbar. NAAAL

Gray on gray post, this silent little bird. The Spotted Flycatcher. Walter De la Mare. OxBSP

Gray owl medicine man. War Songs. Tohono O'odham, *Papago*. PaTW, *tr. by* Ruth Murray Underhill

Gray rainwater lay on the grass in the late afternoon. Wednesday. Marvin Bell. VCAP

Gray Squirrel, The. Humbert Wolfe. MoBrPo

Gray steel, cloud-shadow-stained. Watch the Lights Fade. Robinson Jeffers. CMoP; NOBA

Gray Stones and Gray Pigeons. Wallace Stevens. SAmP

Gray Thrums. Clara Doty Bates. OBCA

Gray tide flows and flounders in the rocks, The. At Sainte-Marguerite. Trumbull Stickney. APN-2; OxBA

Gray Weather. Robinson Jeffers. CMoP

Gray whale / Now that we are sending you to the end. For a Coming Extinction. W. S. Merwin. HCAP; NNaP; PoE; PoPoPo; VCAP

Gray Woods Exploding, The. Earle Birney. NoAM

Grayed in, and gray. . . . Gwendolyn Brooks. *See* Kitchenette Building.

Grazing. Chiyojo, *Japanese*. WPoS, *tr. by* Katz, Michael

Grazing. Mitsui Futabako, *Japanese*. WPJ, *tr. by* Kenneth Rexroth *and* Ikuko Atsumi

Grazing Locomotives. Archibald MacLeish. GM

GREAT. Great frog race. Ian Hamilton Finlay. KaS

Great A, little a. Pancake Day. Mother Goose. CBNP; LB; OxNR; ReMoGo

Great A was alarmed at B's bad behavior. Alphabet. *Unknown*. OxNR

Great Adventure, The. *Unknown*. *See* Love Will Find Out the Way.

Great Alexander sailing was from his true course turned. The Speaking Tree. Muriel Rukeyser. VGW

Great all-seeing burning eye of day, The. Libra, September. John Taylor. NOSC

Great and bounteous Benefactor. The Nativity of St. John the Baptist. Christopher Smart. ChIV-2 *Fr.* Hymns and Spiritual Songs for the Fasts and Festivals of the Church of England.

Great and glorious thing it is, A. Arithmetic on the Frontier. Rudyard Kipling. OBWP

Great and noble creed, A. (LL) Be True [*or* Be True Thyself]. Horatius Bonar. CTV

Great and Strong. Miroslav Holub, *Czech*. RB, *tr. by* George Theiner

Great Arbiter of Fate, The. Ch'u Yüan, *Chinese*. SuSp, *tr. by* Wu-Chi Liu

Great are the Hittites. Concerning My Neighbors, the Hittites. Charles Simic. VCAP

Great are the myths—I too delight in them. Leaves of Grass (1855). Walt Whitman. APN-1

Great Artist Reconsiders the Homeric Simile, The. John Tranter. BMAP; NOBAu; NoAM

Great Auk's ghost rose on one leg, The. Ralph Hodgson. KaS

Great-Aunt Rebecca. Elizabeth Brewster. NOBC

Great-aunts have a corner, and wrinkled skin, The. The Language of Great-Aunts. Alberto A. Ríos. UnSA

Great Bassist, The. Lawson Fusao Inada. OpBo

Great Bear, The. John Hollander. ColAP; LiTM; NYBP; NoAM; TwCP

Great Bear, come down, shaggy night. Invocation of the Great Bear. Ingeborg Bachmann, *German*. VCWP, *tr. by* Mark Anderson

Great Bear Lake Meditations, The. J. Michael Yates.
  "Again and again I go away from you." HoPM
  "I persist in a little fabric between me and the world." NOBC
  "*Legend*: The god in the sun made two men." HoPM
  "Wolves say to the dogs, The." HoPM

Great big dog. The Tale of a Dog and a Bee. *Unknown*. BoTP

Great big gawky Gumbo Cole. Big Gumbo. William Jay Smith. FuFo

Great bird landed here, A. Heptonstall Old Church. Ted Hughes. InPS-3

Great birth will come after ages, A. The Song of the Woman. *Unknown*. TIRV *Fr.* The Voyage of Bran.

Great Birthday Blaublau with Rhymework and Assonance. Paul Celan, *German*. CBNP

Great black hill, The. Pāri's Hill Is Partial to Dancers. Kapilar, *Tamil*. PLW, *tr. by* A. K. Ramanujan

Great Blue. Brendan Galvin. AFr

Great blue ceremony of the air, The. Mary and the Bramble. Lascelles Abercrombie. OBMV

Great Blue Heron, The. Carolyn Kizer. CoAP; IMW; WPE

Great blue mountain! Ghost. Mount Kearsarge. Donald Hall. LoL

Great Breath, The. "Æ." MoBrPo; OBEV; OBMV

Great Britain Through the Ice: Or, Premature Patriotism. Charles Tennyson Turner. Son

Great Brown Owl, The. Jane Euphemia Browne. OxBChV

Great buck-wagon, our 'desert ship', The. A Song of the Wagon-whip. Samuel Cron Cronwright. PeSAV

Great bumble. Sleek. In the Pinewoods, Crows and Owl. Mary Oliver. Poetr

Great captain if you will! great Duke! great Slave! Wellington. Charles Harpur. NOBAu

Great Central Railway, Sheffield Victoria to Banbury. John Betjeman. NYBP

Great Chain of Being, The. Oppian, *Greek*. OBCVT, *tr. by* William Diaper

Great Citadels whereon the Gold Sun Falls. John Berryman. *Fr.* Sonnets. Son

Great city has a hundred million rooms so any combination, The. Day at a Time. Michael Dransfield. BMAP

Great Cowley then, a mighty genius, wrote. Joseph Addison. EPCY *Fr.* An Account of the Greatest English Poets.

Great cry went up from the stockyards and, A. The Delicate, Plummeting Bodies. Stephen Dobyns. FYAP

Great cup tumbled, ringing like a bell, The. The Grail. Sidney Keyes. FaBoTw

Great Dark, The. Martin Carter. PBCV

Great dark work, The. Toward a Poetics. Onwuchekwa Jemie. PBMAP

Great Day, The. W. B. Yeats. APAD; BIrV; CMoP; OxBSP

Great Digest, The. Confucius. PFTM

Great Diocletian. Abraham Cowley. *See* The Garden.

Great-enough both accepts and subdues; the great frame takes all creatures. Phenomena. Robinson Jeffers. NOBA; OxBA

Great Escape, The. Ralph Adamo. MT

Great events grow in the shadow. Fragment. Betti Alver, *Estonian*. CEEP, *tr. by* Ivar Ivask

Great Expectations. Charles Dickens.
  Joe Gargery's Epitaph on His Father. FaBoVe

Great fame can be obtained. Autumn Thoughts. Lu Yu, *Chinese*. OHPC, *tr. by* Kenneth Rexroth

Great Farter, The. Nakasuk, *Eskimo*. STP, *tr. by* Jerome Rothenberg

"Great father Alighier, if from the skies." To Dante. Vittorio Alfieri, *Italian*. AWP, *tr. by* Lorna De' Lucchi

Great Father Eating His Children, The. Hesiod. RaBo, *tr. by* Richmond Lattimore *Fr.* Theogony.

Great Favorit Beheaded, A. Sir Richard Fanshawe. *See* The Fall.

Great Fetishes, The. Blaise Cendrars, *French*. PFTM, *tr. by* Ron Padgett

Great Figure, The. William Carlos Williams. AiP; HeIP-4; InPK-6; MoP; NoAM; SAmP; TTTS

Great fish's eyes never shut, The. Rosario Castellanos, *Spanish*. BoWoP, *tr. by* Willis Barnstone

Great Fleas [have little fleas upon their backs to / bite 'em]. Augustus De Morgan. BXAP; CTAV; FPC
  ("Still, and so on.") (LL) FPC

Great folks are of a finer mould. An Epigram on Scolding. Jonathan Swift. FaBoEE; FaBoVe

Great Foreign Writer Visits Age-Old Temple, Greeted by Venerable Abbess, 1955. Anthony Thwaite. OBCoV

Great Fortune is an hungry thing. Chorus. Aeschylus. AWP, *tr. by* Gilbert Murray *Fr.* Agamemnon. NAWM-1, *tr. by* Robert Fagles

Great Fountains, The. Anne Hébert, *French*. BoWoP, *tr. by* Willis Barnstone

Great Freight, The. Ingeborg Bachmann, *German*. PBWP, *tr. by* Bill Crisman

Great Friend. Henry David Thoreau. PoEL-4

Great friend and servant of the good. Song. Ben Jonson. *Fr.* Pleasure Reconciled to Virtue. NAEL-1; OAEL-1

Great frog race. Ian Hamilton Finlay. KaS

Great Garret, or 100 Wheels, The. James McMichael. AmPA

Great Gatsby, The. F. Scott Fitzgerald.
  Epitaph from *The Great Gatsby*. OxBM
Great Gawd, I'm Feelin' Bad. *Unknown*. AS
Great Giver has ended His disposing, The. Day of Atonement. Charles
  Reznikoff. ChIV-1; KSG
Great God accept our gratitude. Doxology. Josephine D. Henderson Heard.
  CBWP-4
Great God, attend while Zion sings. Isaac Watts. AmFP
Great God, How Frail a Thing Is Man. Mather Byles. AH
Great God, how short's mans time; each minute speaks. Meditations for July
  19, 1666. Philip Pain. SCAP
Great God I ask thee for no meaner pelf. Henry David Thoreau. NOBA
Great God, let all my tuneful pow'rs. Ottiwell Heginbothom. AmFP
Great God, our King! (LL) America. Samuel Francis Smith. AiP; CTV;
  EBEvV; FaBoBe; PoLF
Great God, Preserver of All Things. Francis Daniel Pastorius. AH
Great God, the Followers of Thy Son. Henry Ware Jr. AH
Great God, Thy Works. Mather Byles. AH
Great Goddess *Peace* does Wealth on us bestow. The Pæan of Bacchylides,
  On Peace. Bacchylides, *Greek*. OBCVT, *tr. by* Philip Ayres
Great Goddesse to whose throne in Cynthian fires. The Shadow of Night.
  George Chapman. PoEL-2
Great, good and just, could I but rate. His Metrical Vow. James Graham,
  Marquess of Montrose. NOBE; OxBS
Great-Grandfather. Freda Downie. FaBoWP
Great-grandfather at Waterloo. Limerick. Frank Richards. PeLi
Great-Grandfathers, blessed by great-grandmothers. Geneology. Bob
  Kaufman. NBV
Great grandmother / was a guinea woman. Guinea Woman. Lorna
  Goodison. HCP
Great-great-grandmother. Guy Butler. PeSAV
Great grey swollen body, A. Every Day. Günter Kunert, *German*. CEEP,
  tr. by Michael Hamburger
Great heart, who taught thee so to dye? On Sir Walter Rawleigh at His
  Execution. *Unknown*. NOSC
Great-hearted Christ, importunate and mild. Invocation. Chad Walsh. *Fr.*
  The Psalm of Christ. TrCP
Great Helmsman, The. David Woo. OpBo
Great Hogarth's honour'd Dust is here. (LL) An Epitaph on William
  Hogarth. Samuel Johnson. EBEV; OxAEP-1
Great Horse Fair, The. Desmond O'Grady. PBCIP
Great horse running in the fields. Horse. Gloria Anzaldúa. UnSA
Great humility fills me. Thank You, My Fate. Anna Swirszczynska,
  Polish. BLT, *tr. by* Czeslaw Milosz *and* Leonard Nathan (b. 1924)
Great Hunger, The. Patrick Kavanagh.
  "Clay is the word and clay is the flesh." NoAM; NoP-4; OxBTC
  "He gave himself another year." BIrV
  "Maguire is not afraid of death, the Church will light him a candle." CIP-
  2
Great Hymm. Ntsikana Gaba, *Xhosa*. PeSAV, *tr. by* John Knox Bokwe.
  PeSAV, *tr. by* Thomas Pringle
Great Ia′ kîm will rise from below, The. Song of the Ia′ kîm.
  Unknown. *Fr.* Dances and Songs of the Winter Ceremonial. APN-2, *tr.
  by* Franz Boas
Great-in-counsels made her this reply, The. Ulysses Leaves the Nymph
  Calypso. Homer. *Fr.* Odyssey. NAWM-1, *tr. by* Robert Fitzgerald
Great Industrial Centre, A. Edith Nesbit. VWP
Great Infirmities. Charles Simic. ChAP
Great Insohreckshan, Di. Linton Kwesi Johnson. FaBoPV
Great is a drink of snow. Asclepiades, *Greek*. GrAn, *tr. by* Alan Marshfield
Great is my envy of you, earth, in your greed. Petrarch. NAWM-1, *tr. by*
  Edwin Morgan *Fr.* Sonnets to Laura.
Great is the folly of a feeble brain. Joseph Hall. EBEV; FMP *Fr.*
  Virgidemiarum.
Great is the fury of these supernatural ones. Song for Pacifiying the Excited
  Nū′ LmaL. *Unknown*. *Fr.* Dances and Songs of the Winter
  Ceremonial. APN-2, *tr. by* Franz Boas
Great is the sun, and wide [*or* wise] he goes. Summer Sun. Robert Louis
  Stevenson. MoBrPo; PWR
Great is thy worke in Wildernesse, Oh man. Mr. Eliot Pastor of the Church
  of Christ at Roxbury. Edward Johnson. SCAP
Great Jehovah speaks to us, The. The Names and Order of the Books of the
  Old Testament. Thomas Russell. BLPA; ChIV-1
Great Jehova's working word effecting wondrously, The. Good News from
  New England. Edward Johnson. SCAP
Great king. Harvest of War. Kappiyarrukkappiyanar, *Tamil*. PLW, *tr. by*
  A. K. Ramanujan
Great King. Tuini Ngawai, *Maori*. PeNZ, *tr. by* Margaret Orbell
Great Lalula, The. Christian Morgenstern. CBNP

Great Lament of my Obscurity Three, The. Tristan Tzara, *French*. PFTM,
  tr. by Jerome Rothenberg
Great land and a wide land was the east land, A. *Unknown*. OBVE, *tr. by*
  Daniel G. Brinton *Fr.* Walam Olum; or, Red Score [of the Lenâpé],
  The [*or* The Wallam Olum; The Red Score or Painted History of the
  Lenni Lenape].
Great learned lady, whom I long have known. To the Lady Arabella.
  Emilia Lanier. NOSC
Great legend of the railways and reservoirs, the weariness of carriage, The.
  "Factory." Andre Breton *and* Philippe Soupault. PFTM, *tr. by* David
  Gascoyne *Fr.* The Magnetic Fields.
Great light was born in Athens when, A. Simonides, *Greek*. PGA, *tr. by*
  Kenneth Rexroth
Great little berries in the dogwood. Nice Mountain. Gerald Stern. PuP-14
Great Lord of All, Whose Work of Love. Jacob Duché. AH
Great love goes mad to be spoken: you went out. Preserves. Jack Butler.
  MT
Great love may seem like none at all. Sent in Parting. Tu Mu, *Chinese*.
  CoBCP, *tr. by* Burton Watson
Great Lover, The. Rupert Brooke. HoPM; ImPo; LiTM; MoBrPo; PoRA
Great [*or* Greate] Macedon, that out of Persia chased, The. In Praise of
  Wyatt's Psalms. Henry Howard, Earl of Surrey. AAS; SiPS
Great machete blow of red pleasure right in the face there was blood, The.
  The Miraculous Weapons. Aimé Césaire, *French*. PFTM, *tr. by*
  Clayton Eshleman *and* Annette Smith
Great / man / is / gone, A. E. E. Cummings. NYBP
Great man once said to me, A. White Paper. V. Narayana Rao, *Telugu*.
  OMIP, *tr. by* V. Narayana Rao
Great Man's Death: An Anecdote, The. Everette Maddox. MT
Great master! Boyish, sympathetic man! To Keats. Amy Lowell. Son
Great Masturbator, The. Salvador Dali, *French*. PFTM, *tr. by* Marcel Jean
Great men have been among us; hands that penned. England, 1802, III.
  Wordsworth. FaBoPV; OBEV; PoEL-4; Son
Great Merchant, Dives Pragmaticus, Cries His Wares, The. Thomas
  Newbery.
  "What lack you, sir? What seek you? What will you buy?" OxBChV
Great Monarch, whose feared hands the thunder fling. A Paraphrase Upon
  Part of the CXXXIX Psalm. Thomas Stanley. ChIV-1
Great Moth, The. Robert Gittings. OxBTC
Great Mourning. Bible, Apocrypha. TrJP *Fr.* First Maccabees.
Great Nature clothes the soul, which is but thin. The Soul's Garment.
  Margaret Lucas Cavendish, Duchess of Newcastle. WPE
Great Nature she doth clothe the soul within. Soul and Body. Margaret
  Lucas Cavendish, Duchess of Newcastle. OxBSP; PEW
Great Nebula in Andromeda, The. Hugh Seidman. AmPA
Great Northern. Dave Etter. GM
Great odes have had no revival, The. Ancient Airs. Li Po, *Chinese*. SuSp,
  tr. by Joseph J. Lee
Great One dwells, The. Isha Upanishad. Andrew Schelling. PT
Great ones on several boards / at the same time, The. Charles Simic. *See*
  Prodigy.
Great or small, you furnish your parts toward the soul. (LL) Crossing
  Brooklyn Ferry. Walt Whitman. APN-1; AmPP; ColAP; FaBoA; InPS-
  3; MoP; NAAL-1; NAAL-3; NCAP; NOBA; NoAM; NoP-4; PAR; TAP
Great Overdog, The. Canis Major. Robert Frost. KaS; MoAmPo
Great Pacific railway, The. The Railroad Cars Are Coming. *Unknown*. AS
Great Painter! to thy soul aglow with thought. Raphael. Henrietta Cordelia
  Ray. CBWP-3
Great Palaces of Versailles, The. Rita Dove. NMM-2; NoAM
Great Panjandrum [Himself], The. Samuel Foote. CBNP; FaBoCh; PoLF
Great philosopher did choke, A. Samuel Butler. FaBoEE
Great Physician, The. Sadi. AWP, *tr. by* Sir Edward Arnold *Fr.* The
  Gulistan.
Great poets are not in the language but in business, The. Poetry Paper.
  Andrei Codrescu. SPE
Great Poll-Tax Victory of '88, The. Noel Petty. UV
Great Potter works no private favors, The. Spirit Expounds. T'ao Ch'ien.
  Fr. Substance, Shadow, and Spirit. CoBCP, *tr. by* Burton Watson
Great pulsation passed. Glass lay around me, The. Rejoice in the Abyss.
  Stephen Spender. AF
Great recluse lives in market and court, The. The Half-recluse. Po Chü-i,
  Chinese. ChiP, *tr. by* Arthur Waley
Great River wraps an arm, The. On the River. Yü Hsüan-chi, *Chinese*.
  SuSp, *tr. by* Jan W. Walls
Great Sadness, The. Federico García Lorca, *Spanish*. PFTM, *tr. by* Jerome
  Rothenberg
Great Santa Barbara Oil Disaster OR, The. Conyus. AmPA; NBV
Great Scarf of Birds, The. John Updike. NYBP

Great sea has set me in motion, The. Uvavnuk, *Eskimo*. EnlH, *tr. by* Stephen Mitchell

  ("And my soul is swept up in joy.") (LL) WPoS

  ("Great sea, The.") WPoS

Great sea-roads to England, The. The Gates to England. Marjorie Wilson. BoTP

Great Serbian Migration 1690. Milorad Pavic, *Serbo-Croatian*. HSix, *tr. by* Charles Simic

Great Silkie of Sule Skerry, The. *Unknown*. ESPB; FaBoCh

Great Sir, having just had the good luck to catch. Copy of an Intercepted Despatch from His Excellency Don Strepitoso Diabolo. Thomas Moore. OBSV

Great sleeves of air, The. Between. Agnes Nemes Nagy, *Hungarian*. VCWP, *tr. by* Hugh Maxton

Great Society, The. Robert Bly. NoAM

Great Soul, from Thee. Epicurus praised. Lucretius, *Latin*. OBCVT, *tr. by* Thomas Creech

Great Soul of Friendship whither art thou fled. On Rosania's Apostasy, and Lucasia's Friendship. Katherine Philips. KTR

Great soul, thou sittest with me in my room. To the Spirit of Keats. James Russell Lowell. Son

Great South Land, The. Rex Ingamells.

  "Cook admired the native courage, made." NOBAu

  "They made impudent inspection of our coast." CBAP

Great Spaces. Howard Moss. TwCP

Great Spirit, whose dry lands thirst, help us to find. *Unknown*. FHYEP Fr. U.N. Environmental Sabbath Program.

Great Spirit's lodge—you have heard of it. I will enter it, The. Meda Songs. *Unknown, Ojibwa Native American*. APN-2, *tr. by* Henry Rowe Schoolcraft

Great spirits now on earth are sojourning. Addressed to Haydon. Keats. OBNC; Ro; Son

Great star has fallen into my lap, A. Reconciliation. Else Lasker-Schüler, *German*. PBWP, *tr. by* Robert Alter

Great stone hearth has gone, The. Fire. Dorothy Wellesley, Duchess of Wellington. OBMV

Great Streets of silence led away. Emily Dickinson. APN-2; NOCV

Great success need not be proud. Tseng Jui. SuSp, *tr. by* Wayne Schlepp Fr. Tune: "Sheep on Mountain Slope"—Lamenting the Times.

Great Summons, The. Ch'u Yüan, *Chinese*. AWP, *tr. by* Arthur Waley

Great Summons, The. *Unknown, Chinese*. ChiP, *tr. by* Arthur Waley

Great Tay of the Waves. Lewis Spence. FaBoTC

Great tempest on the Plain of Ler, A. *Unknown*. NOIV

Great thing / is not having / a mind, The. The Red Poppy. Louise Glück. AFr

Great Things. Thomas Hardy. GTBS-P; NOBE

  ("Greatest things to me!") (LL) GTBS-P

Great things are done when Men and Mountains meet. William Blake. OxBSP Fr. Gnomic Verses.

Great thrushes have not appeared this year, The. The Unremarkable Year. Roy Fuller. OxBC

Great Time, A. W. H. Davies. ImPo; MoBrPo

Great *Titanic*. *Unknown*. AmFP

Great Tom. Richard Corbet. OxBoLi

Great Unaffected Vampires and the Moon. Stevie Smith. NoAM

Great Uncle Joe. Apology. Duane Niatum. HATNAP

Great Unrestrained Sadist, The. Hans Arp, *German*. PFTM, *tr. by* Joachim Neugroschel

Great Venus, Queene [*or* Queen] of Beautie [*or* Beauty] and of grace. Address to Venus. Lucretius. AWP, *tr. by* Spenser Fr. De Rerum Natura (On the Nature of Things).

Great Wager, The. Geoffrey Anketell Studdert-Kennedy. TrCP

Great Wagon, The. Toṇṭaimāṉ Iḷantiraiyaṉ, *Tamil*. PLW, *tr. by* A. K. Ramanujan

Great Wall, The. Chu Ch'ing-yü, *Chinese*. SuSp, *tr. by* Irving Y. Lo

Great wall of china, The. The Yellow River. Nabaneeta Dev Sen, *Bengali*. OMIP, *tr. by* Nabaneeta Dev Sen

Great War, The. Vernon Scannell. NSI; OBWP

Great wave drove at him with toppling crest, A. Homer. GrIP, *tr. by* Robert Fitzgerald Fr. Ulysses Leaves the Nymph Calypso. Fr. Odyssey. NAWM-1, *tr. by* Robert Fitzgerald

Great Way has no gate, The. Wu-Men, *Chinese*. EnlH, *tr. by* Stephen Mitchell

Great Way isn't difficult, The. The Mind of Absolute Trust. Seng-ts'an, *Chinese*. EnlH, *tr. by* Stephen Mitchell

Great Way—simple as it is, The. Speaking My Mind. Chung-ch'ang T'ung, *Chinese*. CoBCP, *tr. by* Burton Watson

Great Wheel, The. "Hugh MacDiarmid." OxBS

Great white lilies in the grass, The. Pallor. Agnes Mary Frances Robinson. NOBVV; VWP

Great, wide, beautiful, wonderful [World]. The World. William Brighty Rands. BoTP; CTV; NOxBChV; OxBChV

Great wind kill my little shell with sound, The. (LL) Mount Lykaion. Trumbull Stickney. OxBA; Son

Great wind rises, A. Song of the Great Wind. Liu Pang, *Chinese*. SuSp, *tr. by* Ronald C. Miao

Great woe, fire & war come on me. Epigram. Skythinos, *Greek*. GrAn, *tr. by* Thomas Meyer

Great Women Composers, The. Gavin Ewart. OBCoV

Great Work Farm Elegy. Allen Grossman. BAP-93

Great you call Demosthenes. Self-Portrait. Moses Mendelssohn, *German*. TrJP

Greate Macedon that out of Persy chased, The. Henry Howard, Earl of Surrey. *See* In Praise of Wyatt's Psalms.

Greater cats with golden eyes, The. Vita Sackville-West. APAD; OBMV; OTCP; PC; Spl

Greater Courage. Natan Zach, *Hebrew*. PoSu, *tr. by* Peter Everwine *and* Shulamit Yasny-Starkman

Greater Friendship Baptist Church, The. Carole C. Gregory Clemmons. BlSi

Greater Gift, The. Margaret E. Bruner. PoToHe

Greater Love. Wilfred Owen. APAD; CMoP; EnLoPo; FaBoMo; GTBS-P; ImPo; LiTM; MoBrPo; MoP; NoAM; TFi

Greatest bliss, The. The Kiss. Charlotte Dacre. CABP; NOBRP

Greatest delight, I sense, the. Betrayal. Adam Zagajewski, *Polish*. VCWP, *tr. by* Gorczynski, Renata

Greatest in many things, in some the least. On a Distinguished Politician. J. E. Thorold Rogers. FaBoEE

Greatest Love, The. Anna Swirszczynska, *Polish*. PoSu, *tr. by* Czeslaw Milosz *and* Leonard Nathan

  ("Her children say: / 'Old fool'.") (LL) BLT, *tr. by* Czeslaw Milosz *and* Leonard Nathan

Greatest of These, The, *abr*. Bible, *N.T*. Fr. First Corinthians.

Greatest plumber / in all the town, The. Nursery Rhyme. Lorine Niedecker. NMM-2

Greatest saints and sinners have been made, The. Samuel Butler. FaBoEE

Greatest self-made man in the world today, The. Our Noble Booker T. Washington. Mrs. Henry Linden. CBWP-4

Greatest things to me! Thomas Hardy. *See* Great Things.

Greatly shining. Wind and Silver. Amy Lowell. BoWoP; HeIP-4; KaS; MoAmPo; Spl

Greatness in Little. Richard Leigh. NOSC

Greatness of *Mind* and *Fortune* too. Pindar. OBCVT, *tr. by* Abraham Cowley Fr. The Second Olympique Ode of Pindar.

Grecian Kindness. John Wilmot, 2d Earl of Rochester. OxBSP

Greece. Robert Browning. Fr. Cleon the poet (from the sprinkled isles). OAEL-2

Greece. Gunnar Ekelof. BLT

Greed. *Unknown*. OxNR

Greed and Aggression. Sharon Olds. DeD; RaBo

Greedy Baby / sucking the sweet tit. Alicia Ostriker. DeD

Greedy Jane. *Unknown*. OxBChV

Greedy Little Pig, The. Irene F. Pawsey. BoTP

Greedy man is he who sits, The. *Unknown*. ReMoGo

Greedy Ned. *Unknown*. FuFo

Greedy Richard. Jane Taylor. OxBChV

Greedy the people, The. E. E. Cummings. SoSe-8

Greedy Tom. *Unknown*. OxNR

Greedy young fellow named Ned, A. Greedy Ned. *Unknown*. FuFo

Greedyguts. Kit Wright. OTCP

Greek Architecture. Herman Melville. NoP-4

Greek Epigram. Ezra Pound. MoAmPo

Greek Room, The. James W. Thompson. BPo

Greek ship / Sails on the sea, A. The Couple. Sandra Hochman. NYBP

Greek summer! Peace Pillar. Otto Orban, *Hungarian*. CEEP, *tr. by* Emery E. George

"Greek Tragedy" of course is the sort of thing. Their Philistinism Considered. Robert Pinsky. NoAM Fr. Essay on Psychiatrists.

Greeks, The. Tom Clark. PoA

Greeks' chieftains, all irkèd with the war, The. The Trojan Horse. Virgil. OAEL-1, *tr. by* Henry Howard, Earl of Surrey Fr. The Second Book of Virgil's *Aeneid*. SiPS, *tr. by* Henry Howard, Earl of Surrey Fr. The Aeneid [*or* Eneados, *Aeneis*].

Greeks Like Clouds, The. Homer. OBVE, *tr. by* George Chapman Fr. The Iliad.

Green. D. H. Lawrence. GBL; LoP; MoBrPo; PoA

Green Afternoon, The. Henry Rago. VGW

Green and blue the reedy shallows. At Yuen Yang Lake. Wu Wei-yeh, *Chinese.* OHMPC, tr. by Kenneth Rexroth

Green and growing thorn-tree, A. Forgive and Forget. "Totius," *Afrikaans.* PeSA, tr. by Anthony Delius

Green and silent spot amid the hills. Fears in Solitude. Coleridge. FHYEP; OBWP; Ro

Green and the Black, The. Anthony Bailey. NYBP

Green and yellow patchwork across the country lies, A. *Unknown.* ChiPo

Green Apples. Ruth Stone. InPS-3

Green arbor that I once knew, A. Linda Beatrice Brown. GT

Green arsenic smeared on an egg-white cloth. L'Art, 1910. Ezra Pound. HeIP-4; OxBA

Green as an afterthought. (LL) Weathering Out. Rita Dove. CMAP; LCAP-2; NoAM

Green as that summer fly. Silk Robe. Jeffrey Skinner. PBCAP

Green Automobile, The. Allen Ginsberg. BB

Green Banana Leaves. Yün Shou-p'ing, *Chinese.* CoBLCP, tr. by Jonathan Chaves

Green be the turf above thee. On the Death of Joseph Rodman Drake. Fitz-Greene Halleck. APN-1; BLPA; PoEL-4

Green Bed, The. *Unknown.* AmFP

Green-blue ground, The. on Gay Wallpaper. William Carlos Williams. MeMAP; MoAmPo; TAP

Green, blue, yellow, and red. The One. Patrick Kavanagh. MoBrPo; TIRV

Green Breeks. Douglas Dunn. FaBoPV

Green Briar Shore, The. *Unknown.* AmFP

Green Broom. *Unknown.* See Broom, Green Broom.

Green bubbles—new brewed wine. A Question Addressed to Liu Shih-chiu. Po Chü-i, *Chinese.* CoBCP, tr. by Burton Watson

Green Buddhas / On the fruit stand. Watermelons. Charles Simic. OBAL; VCAP

Green bushes are bursting with giant flowers. The Asphyxiated Man. Victor Serge, *Russian.* AF, tr. by James Brook

Green Candles. Humbert Wolfe. MoBrPo

Green catalpa tree has turned, The. April Inventory. W. D. Snodgrass. CoAP; ColAP; HAP; LiTM; NoAM; NoP-4; Poetr; TAP; TRP; TwCP; VCAP

Green Chateau, The. Wendy Mulford. NBrP

Green cheese, yellow laces. *Unknown.* OxNR

Green Chile. Jimmy Santiago Baca. NAmP90

Green cockleburs, the. Richard Wright. KaS

Green Cornfield, A. Christina Rossetti. BoTP

(Skylark, The.) ACTP

Green creepers planted inside the house. What She Said. Orampokiyar. PLW *Fr.* Five on the Riverside Cane. PLW, tr. by A. K. Ramanujan

Green Dryad's Plea, The. Thomas Hood. *Fr.* The Plea of the Midsummer Fairies. OBNC

Green elm with the one great bough of gold, The. October. Edward Thomas. CABP; NoAM

Green Enravishment of Human Life. Sister Juana Inés de la Cruz, *Spanish.* WPOW, tr. by Samuel Beckett *and* Octavio Paz

Green Evening, A. Brendan Galvin. AFr

Green Eye, The. James Merrill. PoA

Green eye—and a red—in the dark, A. The Train. Mary Elizabeth Coleridge. BoTP

Green Eye of the Yellow God, The. J. Milton Hayes. BLPA; EBEvV; EBNV

Green-eyed and could not give them to her children. About this Woman. Judith Rodriguez. BMAP

Green-eyed Care. Old Cat Care. Richard Hughes. OBMV

Green Family, The. Colleen Thibaudeau. NOBC

Green fields are like constructions of the mind which have / suddenly, The. At Parting. Duoduo, *Chinese.* AF, tr. by Gregory Lee *and* John Cayley

Green figures move forward and the objects grow larger, The. North. Tony Towle. PmAP

Green fingers, green hand, by now green man. Garden, Wilderness. Michael Hamburger. OBGa

Green Frog at Roadstead, Wisconsin. James Schevill. TAP

Green garden of growing weeds, A. Playing with Fire. James Simmons. CIP-2

Green gossip of the maidenhair, The. Day 20. Bruce Beaver. BMAP *Fr.* Odes and Days.

Green grape, and you refused me. Brief Autumnal. *Unknown, Greek.* GrAn; WeW-3, tr. by Dudley Fitts

Green Grass. *Unknown.* BoTP; CH; FaBoVe; OxBoLi; OxNR

Green Grass and Yellow Balloons. Etheridge Knight. GT

Green grass is bowing, The. The Wind in the Grass. Siegfried Emerson. BoTP

Green grass tendrils like silk. The Wandering Gentleman. *Unknown, Chinese.* SuSp, tr. by Ronald C. Miao

Green gravel green gravel. *Unknown.* FaBoVe

Green, green. *Unknown.* ChiP, tr. by Arthur Waley *Fr.* Seventeen Old Poems.

Green, Green, and Green Again. Conrad Potter Aiken. *Fr.* And in the Human Heart.

Green, Green Is El Aghir. Norman Cameron. FaBoTC; MoBS; OBWP; OxBTC

(El Aghir.) FaBoTw

("Sprawled on the crates and sacks in the rear of the / truck.") FaBoTC

Green green, river bank grasses. Mei Sheng *and* Fu I, *Chinese.* ChiPo, tr. by Burton Watson *Fr.* Nineteen Old Poems of the Han. CoBCP, tr. by Burton Watson

Green green, river bank grasses. *Unknown, Chinese.* CoBCP, tr. by Burton Watson

Green green the cypress on the ridge. Mei Sheng *and* Fu I. *Fr.* Nineteen Old Poems of the Han. CoBCP, tr. by Burton Watson

Green green the cypress on the ridge. *Unknown, Chinese.* CoBCP, tr. by Burton Watson

Green grow the rashes, O; / Green grow the rashes, O; / The sweetest hours that e'er I spend. Robert Burns. AWP; CTC; ImPo; NAEL-2; NoP-4; OAEL-1; OxAEP-2; PeLV; SCGP

("There's naught but care on every hand.") PBMP

Green Grow the Rushes O. *Unknown.* See Carol of the Numbers.

Green Groweth the Holly. *Unknown.* NoSic

Green Hammock, White Magnolia Tree. Ruth Gilbert. PeNZ

Green Hell, Green Death. Jan Barry. CDa

Green hills on both banks—mounds of rice kernels. Insscribed on a Painting. Cheng Hsieh, *Chinese.* SuSp, tr. by Irving Y. Lo

Green hills sloping from the nothern wall. Seeing a Friend Off. Li Po, *Chinese.* CoBCP, tr. by Burton Watson

Green I love you green. Sleepwalkers' Ballad. Federico García Lorca, *Spanish.* WeW-3, tr. by John Frederick Nims

Green Ice. Vivienne Finch. BrRo

Green is the grass on riverbanks. *Unknown, Chinese.* SuSp, tr. by Dell R. Hales

Green is the night, green kindled and apparelled. The Candle a Saint. Wallace Stevens. PoRA

Green is the plane-tree in the square. A London Plane-Tree. Amy Levy. PEW

Green it's your green I love. Sleepwalkers' Ballad. Federico García Lorca, *Spanish.* STV, tr. by John Frederick Nims

Green Jade Plum Trees in Spring. Ou-yang Hsiu, *Chinese.* OHPC, tr. by Kenneth Rexroth

Green Knight's Farewell to Fancy, The. George Gascoigne. NoSic

Green Lady, The. Charlotte Druitt Cole. BoTP

Green lamp flares on the table, The. This Life. Rita Dove. AmPA; GT

Green lawn / a picket fence. Once. Alice Walker. BlSi

Green leaf that will outlast the winter. Louis Zukofsky. VGW

Green leaves. Tanka. Kanoko Okamoto, *Japanese.* MJT, tr. by Makoto Ueda

"Green leaves, what are you doing." The Five-Fingered Maple. Kate Louise Brown. BoTP

Green level of lily leaves, A. To Paint a Water Lily. Ted Hughes. CABP

Green Light. Kenneth Fearing. PoE; VGW

Green Light. Rolf Jacobsen. EC3

Green light floods the city square, The. Sunken Evening [in Trafalgar Square]. Laurie Lee. LiTM; NYBP

Green Linnet, The. Wordsworth. GTBS-P

Green little vaulter in the sunny grass. To the Grasshopper and the Cricket. Leigh Hunt. GSo; OBNC; OxAEP-2; Son

Green lotus leaves, a canopy on the pond. *Unknown.* *Fr.* Summer. SuSp, tr. by Michael E. Workman *Fr.* Tzu-yeh Songs of the Four Seasons.

Green Lowland of Pianos, A. Jerzy Harasymowicz, *Polish.* CBNP, tr. by Czeslaw Milosz

Green Market, New York. Julia Kasdorf. LoHu

Green Martyrs. Richard Murphy. NOIV *Fr.* The Battle of Aughrim.

Green Mistletoe! / Oh, I remember now. Winter. Walter De la Mare. OAEL-2; OBMV

Green mothering of moss knits shadow and light, The. Rain Forest. Dave Jeddie Smith. HCAP; MT

Green mountain lies beyond the north wall of the city, The. Saying Farewell to a Friend. Li Po, *Chinese.* TAL, tr. by Robert Payne

Green mountains on three sides, a bamboo fence all around. Sitting on a Rock by Mountain Stream. Ch'en Yü-i, *Chinese.* SuSp, tr. by Irving Y. Lo

Green mwold on zummer bars do show. Tokens. William Barnes. PoEL-4

Green nut tree, The. The Fruited Month. Zalman Schneour, *Hebrew.* MHP, *tr.* by Ruth Finer Mintz

Green of Jesus, The. Spring Song. Lucille Clifton. CrSp

Green of the distant meadows, lightly. HP

Green pine grows in eastern garden, A. T'ao Ch'ien. SuSp, *tr.* by Wu-chi Liu   *Fr.* Drinking Wine. CoBCP, *tr.* by Burton Watson

Green Place, A. Honor Moore. FFC

Green Plumes of Royal Palms. LeRoy V. Brant. AH

Green Rain. Dorothy Livesay. NALW; NIP-4; NOBC; NoP-4

Green Rain. Mary Webb. CH

Green Red Brown and White. May Swenson. VGW

Green Refrain, The. Avraham Huss, *Hebrew.* MHP, *tr.* by Ruth Finer Mintz

Green Revolutions. Barbara Guest. FaBoWP

Green River. William Cullen Bryant. APN-1; NOBA; OxBA

Green River, The. Lord Alfred Bruce Douglas. OBEV

Green road lies this way, The. El Camino Verde. Paul Blackburn. PmAP

Green Roads, The. Edward Thomas. NoAM

Green robe, green robe, lined with yellow, *fr. the Chinese of the* Confucian Odes. Ezra Pound. APSN

Green Rock, Winthrop Bay. Sylvia Plath. AFr

Green rushes with red shoots. Plucking The Rushes. *Unknown, Chinese.* ChiP; LoP, *tr.* by Arthur Waley; BoLoP; OBVE

Green rustlings, more-than-regal charities. Royal Palm. Hart Crane. CMoP; MoAmPo; MoP; NoAM

Green scapulars to wear over your shroud. (LL) The Strand at Lough Beg. Seamus Heaney. CIP-2; NoAM; OBWP

Green-shadowed people sit, or walk in rings. Spring. Philip Larkin. MoBrPo

Green Shepherd, The. Louis Simpson. NYBP

Green shingles of rest homes unfold revealing, The. The United States Prepare for the Permanent Revolution. George Hitchcock. SPE

Green Shutters, shut your shutters! Windyridge. Beside the Seaside. John Betjeman.

Green shutters, shut your shutters! Windyridge. John Betjeman. OxBTC *Fr.* Beside the Seaside.

Green Side, The. Jennifer Maiden. BMAP

Green sleeves and tartan ties. Robert Burns. FaBoVe

Green Snake. B. R. Lakshman Rao, *Kannada.* OMIP, *tr.* by A. K. Ramanujan

Green snake, when I hung you round my neck. To the Snake. Denise Levertov. AmPP; LiTM; NMM-2; PoA

Green soaks into the dark trees. Twilight in West Virginia: Six O'Clock Mine Report. Irene McKinney. PBCAP

Green Song. Dame Edith Sitwell. BWW

Green Spring receiveth. The Great Summons. Ch'u Yüan, *Chinese.* AWP; ChiP, *tr.* by Arthur Waley

Green Symphony. John Gould Fletcher. MoAmPo

Green Tree, The. James Reiss. AmPA

Green trees form shade, the path is covered with moss. Recording My Happiness upon Returning Home. Wen Cheng-ming, *Chinese.* CoBLCP, *tr.* by Jonathan Chaves

Green Trees that in the Forest grew. (LL) A Dialogue between the Soul and [the] Body. Andrew Marvell. ESCV; FMP; FSCP; GeHe; HAP; InPS-3; MeLP; NAEL-1; NoP-4; OAEL-1; OxAEP-1; PoEL-2; SeCP; SoSe-8; TFi

Green Valley, The. Sylvia Townsend Warner. MoBrPo

Green was the maiden, green, green! Juan Ramón Jiménez, *Spanish.* NNPT, *tr.* by J. B. Trend *and* J. L. Gili

Green Willow, The. *Unknown.* EBEvV; SCGP

Green Willow, Green Willow. *Unknown.* AmFP

Green willows are for girls to study under. Heresy for a Class-Room. Rolfe Humphries. PFE

Green willows, fragrant grass, the many-stationed road. Tune: "Spring in Jade Pavilion." Yen Shu, *Chinese.* SuSp, *tr.* by An-yan Tang

Green woodpecker flying up and down, The. The Green Woodpecker's Nest. John Clare. FaBoVe

Green Woodpecker's Nest, The. John Clare. FaBoVe

Green yellow dog up. i have not. i am. green red cat down. i is not. i is. Scraptures: 7th Sequence. B. P. Nichol. FTOS

Greenback Dollar, The. *Unknown.* AmFP

Greener Grass. Frank Steele. Poetsp

Greene's Farewell to Folly. Robert Greene.
Song: "Sweet are the thoughts that savour of content." PoEL-2; PoToHe

Greene's Groatsworth of Wit. Robert Greene.
Palinode, A.

Greene's Mourning Garment. Robert Greene.
Hexametra Alexis in Laudem Rosamundi. GBL; PoEL-2
Shepherd's Wife's Song, The. HAP; NoSic; RACG

Greene's Vision. Robert Greene.
Description of Sir Geoffrey Chaucer, The. CTC; NoSic; SCGP
(Sir Chaucer.) FaBoCh

Greenest jade for a clothes-pounding stone. Ch'ing-yang Ford. *Unknown, Chinese.* CoBCP, *tr.* by Burton Watson

Greenest of grass in the long meadow grows, The. June. Jane G. Stewart. BoTP

Greengrocer, The. Michael Longley. BiHa   *Fr.* Wreaths.

Greenhalgh's Pub. Julian Croft. NOBAu

Greenhouse Vanity, The. Les A. Murray. FaBoVe

Greenland Whale Fishery, The. *Unknown.* AmFP

Greenland Winter, A. Lucy Diamond. BoTP

Greens. David Ray. VGW

Greens. *Unknown.* AS

Greensleeves. Lady Greensleeves. *Unknown.* FaBoCh; GBL; PoEL-2; TTTS

Greensleeves was all my joy, etc. *Unknown. See* Lady Greensleeves.

Greenwich Observatory. Sidney Keyes. MoBrPo

Greenwood's. Michael Sharkey. NOBAu

Greeting, A. W. H. Davies. MoBrPo

Greeting. Henrietta Cordelia Ray. CBWP-3

Greeting to Queen Elizabeth, the Rare White Heron of Single Flight, A. Wiremu Kingi Kerekere, *Maori.* PeNZ, *tr.* by Wiremu Kingi Kerekere

Greeting to thee, O most trusty friend!, A. To My Own Face. Caroline Lindsay. VWP

Greetings, 260 thousand ccm. Murder Machine 43. Kurt Schwitters, *German.* PFTM, *tr.* by Jerome Rothenberg

Greetings from the Chateau. James Schuyler. FTOS

Greetings, great evangelist! Lines on the Return to Britain of Billy Graham. E. J. Thribb. PeLV

Greetings! you seven students of Professor Aristides. *Unknown, Greek.* GrAn, *tr.* by Peter Jay

Gregory Griggs, Gregory Griggs. *Unknown.* OxNR

Gregory's House. David Huddle. PBCAP

Greg's got custody of Sally and wants. Julia Alvarez. CrSp

Grenada. Mikhail Arkadyevich Svetlov, *Russian.* TCRP, *tr.* by Daniel Weissbort

Grenadier. A. E. Housman. OBMV; OBWP

Grenadier, The. *Unknown.* OxNR

Grendel. *Unknown. Fr.* Beowulf. OAEL-1, *tr.* by Charles W. Kennedy; ASW, *tr.* by Kevin Crossley-Holland

Gretel in Darkness. Louise Glück. AmPA; NoAM; NoP-4

Gretsch love / gretsch hate. Elvin Jones Gretsch Freak. David Henderson. SeSe

Grey already the hair at my temples. Strato, *Greek.* GrAn, *tr.* by Teddy Hogge

Grey and dankish thing, A. Theodore Weiss. DiPo   *Fr.* Every Second Thought.

Grey and Green. Arthur Symons. NOBVV; PeVV   *Fr.* At Dieppe.

Grey as a guinea-fowl is the rain. Two Kitchen Songs. Dame Edith Sitwell. CMoP

Grey as a mouse. Oliphaunt. J. R. R. Tolkien. NOxBChV

Grey beards wag, the bald heads nod, The. Miniature. Eden Phillpotts. OxBSP

Grey brick upon brick. Dublin. Louis MacNeice. CIP-2; IIP; OxBTC   *Fr.* The Closing Album.

Grey Brother. U. M. Montgomery. BoTP

Grey Cock, or, Saw You My Father?, The. *Unknown.* ESPB

Grey courtyards where the imprisoned. Via Margutta. Maria Luisa Spaziani, *Italian.* NeIt, *tr.* by Beverly Allen

Grey day, drenched, humid, the sun-, A. All the Women Caught in Flaring Light. Minnie Bruce Pratt. CPO

Grey dust runs on the ground like a mouse, The. Dust. P. A. Ropes. BoTP

Grey Eye Weeping, A. Egan O'Rahilly, *Irish.* FaBoPV; OBMV, *tr.* by Frank O'Connor

Grey-eyed King, The. "Anna Akhmatova," *Russian.* PBWP, *tr.* by Robert Tracy

Grey flies, fragile, slender-winged and slender-legged. Evening Dance of the Grey Flies. Patricia K. Page. NOBC

Grey Frock, A. Zinaida Hippius, *Russian.* PBWP, *tr.* by Temira Pachmuss

Grey girl who had not been singing stopped, The. New Year's Eve. John Berryman. LiTM

Grey goat grazed on the hill, The. Grey Brother. U. M. Montgomery. BoTP

Grey goose and gander. *Unknown.* LB

Grey-green stretch of sandy grass, The. Grey and Green. Arthur Symons. NOBVV; PeVV   *Fr.* At Dieppe.

Grey Hair, The. Judah Halevi, *Hebrew.* TrJP, *tr. by* J. Chotzner

Grey haunted eyes, absent-mindedly glaring. The Face in the Mirror. Robert Graves. CABP

Grey hills of that country fall away, The. Cadaver Politic. Tom Paulin. PNI

Grey. Intangible drops. Sea. Marie-Claire Bancquart, *French.* MFP, *tr. by* Martin Sorrell

Grey Monk, The. William Blake. PeECV

Grey mountains, sea and sky. Even the misty. The Sea Anemones. Gwen Harwood. BMAP

Grey Ones, The. Louis MacNeice. CMoP

Grey over Riddrie the clouds piled up. King Billy. Edwin Morgan. NoP-4

Grey psychopath in her season, The. Cat. Joe Rosenblatt. NOBC

Grey pussy-willows. Slumber in Spring. Elizabeth Gould. BoTP

Grey [*or* Gray] sea and the long black land, The. Meeting At Night. Robert Browning. APAD; AWP; BoLoP; CABP; CBLP; EBEvV; EnVR; FHYEP; FaBoVe; GBL; GLoP; HeIP-4; InPS-3; LoP; NAEL-2; NOBE; NOBVV; OBEV; OBNC; OPOU; OxBSP; PFE; PeVV; PoRA; SAGP; SCGP; SCV; SoSe-8; TFi; UnPo

Grey Selchie of Sule Skerry, The. *Unknown.* OxBB

Grey sky, grey city-smoke. 9th July, 1932. Mary Ursula Bethell. PeNZ

Grey the sky, and growing dimmer. Twilight. Louisa S. Guggenberger. NOBVV; PEW

Grey Time moves silently, and creeping on. *Unknown, Greek.* GrAn, *tr. by* Peter Jay

Grey, to the low grass cropping. Prisoner. Wole Soyinka. PBMAP *Fr.* Idanre and Other Poems (1967).

Grey was the morn, all things were grey. A Bit of Colour. Horace Smith. BoTP

Grey water tanks in grey mist. Bayonne Turnpike to Tuscarora. Allen Ginsberg. NNaP

Grey Wolf, The. Arthur Symons. FaBoTw

Grey Woman. Gladys Cardiff. CDW

Greyer than the tide below, the tower. Homage to Jack Yeats. Thomas MacGreevy. OBMV

Greyhound should be headed like a snake, A. The Properties of a Good Greyhound. Dame Juliana Berners. RB

Greyish yellow is the color of the dust. Love Poem. Meir Wieseltier, *Hebrew.* IP, *tr. by* Warren Bargad *and* Stanley F. Chyet

Griboyedov's Waltz. Aleksandr Bashlachov, *Russian.* TCRP, *tr. by* Sarah W. Bliumis

Grid. Mark Jarman. PuP-17

Grid Erectile. Christopher Dewdney. FTOS

Grief. Wendell Berry. MT

Grief. Elizabeth Barrett Browning. EBEvV; HeIP-4; IMW; InPK-6; NALW; NOBVV; OBEV; OBNC; PoLF; SDW; VWP; WPE

(Silent Grief.) LBC

Grief. Maureen Seaton. LoHo

Grief. Siamanto, *Armenian.* AF, *tr. by* Peter Balakian *and* Nevart Yaghlian

Grief. *Unknown, Welsh.* OBWVE, *tr. by* Aneirin Talfan Davies

Grief and Joy. Frederic Lawrence Knowles.

  "Joy is a partnership." IMW

Grief, find the words, for thou hast made my brain. Sonnet 94. Sir Philip Sidney. *Fr.* Astrophil and Stella. AAS; SiPS

Grief[e], interrupted speech [*or* speach] with tears [*or* teares] supplies [*or* supplyes]. (LL) A Pastoral[l] Dialogue. Thomas Carew. CaPo; GBL; SeCP

Grief is not apparel. Homocide. Essex Hemphill. GT

Grief: I've grieved as a solitary phoenix grieves. Kuan Han-ch'ing. SuSp, *tr. by* Jerome P. Seaton *Fr.* Tune: "Intoxication in the East Wind."

Grief now hath pacified her face;. The Widow. Walter De la Mare. LBC

Grief / o grief. Alarum. Urszula Koziol, *Polish.* WPOW, *tr. by* Czeslaw Milosz

Grief of Love, The. *Unknown, Arabic.* AWP, *tr. by* Wilfrid Scawen Blunt

Grief Plucked Me Out of Sleep. Jill King. PeSA

Grief reached across the world to get me. Carmen 65. Catullus. RaBo, *tr. by* Jacob Rabinowitz *Fr.* Carmina.

Grief Streams Down My Chest. Lance Jeffers. PoBA

Grief that began before the ancient Flood. (LL) In Death Valley. Edwin Markham. APAD; APN-2; PaTW

Grief without a pang, void, dark, and drear, A. Coleridge. IMW *Fr.* Dejection.

Griefe, killing griefe: have nott my torments binn. Sonnet 28. Mary Sidney, Countess of Montgomery Wroth. KTR *Fr.* Pamphilia to Amphilanthus.

Grief's Circle. C. S. Lewis. LBC

Griefs of Women, The. David R. Slavitt. BXAP

Grief's prodigals, where are you? Unthrifts, where? Upon Mr. Hopton's Death. Henry Halswell. NOSC

Griesly Wife, The. John Streeter Manifold. MoBS; MoBrPo

Grievance, A. James Kenneth Stephen. BXAP

Griev'd that they bound it, grieves that they are broken. (LL) Behold, O Aspasia! I Send You Verses. Walter Savage Landor. OBNC; SCGP

Grieve not, dear love, although we often part. John Digby. NOSC; OxBSP

Grieve Not for Beauty ("Grieve not for the invisible, transported brow"). Witter Bynner. PoA

Grieve Not the Holy Spirit, etc. George Herbert. ESCV

Grieved lands of Africa, The. Agostinho Neto. PBMAP

Grieving the sapless limbs, the shorn and shaken. (LL) Dead Boy. John Crowe Ransom. CMoP; FaBoMo; FuPo; MeMAP; NoAM; NoP-4; OxBA; PoE; TwCP

Grievous folly shames my sixtieth year, A. Hafiz. AWP, *tr. by* Richard Le Gallienne *Fr.* Odes.

"Grill me some bones," said the Cobbler. At the Keyhole. Walter De la Mare. MoBrPo

Grim bulwarked hatred between heart and heart! (LL) 1492. Emma Lazarus. APN-2; PAR; WPE

Grim in my tight black coat as the sleazy beetle. The Vanity of the Bright Young Men. John Crowe Ransom. FuPo *Fr.* Sixteen Poems in Eight Pairings.

Grim monarch! see, deprived of vital breath. To a Lady on the Death of Her Husband. Phillis Wheatley. TAP

Grim reader, did you ever see a ghost? Byron. OxBSn *Fr.* Don Juan.

Grim Sisters, The. Liz Lochhead. CABP; FaBoTC

Grim Town in a Steep Valley. Thomas Lux. BAP-93

Grimes Golden Greening Yellow Transparent. Counting-out Rhyme. Eve Merriam. KaS

Grin muffled but / sneaky slithering. Fitzi in the Yearbook. Lyn Lifshin. DeD

Grinder, who serenely grindest. Lines on Hearing the Organ. Charles Stuart Calverley. NOBL

Grinder's art has been known so long, The. Glimpsed through a Lens. Yevgeny Borisovich Rein, *Russian.* TCRP, *tr. by* Bernard Meares

Grinding Vibrato. Jayne Cortez. BlSi

Grinding yoke from Israel's neck he tore, The. Eulogy for Hasdai ibn Shaprut. *Unknown, Hebrew.* TrJP, *tr. by* Israel Abrahams

Griots Who Know Brer Fox, The. Colleen J. McElroy. NAAL

Grip down and begin to awaken. (LL) Spring and All. William Carlos Williams. CMoP; ChAP; ColAP; HAP; InPK-6; InPS-3; LiTM; MeMAP; MoAmPo; MoP; NAAL-2; NOBA; NoAM; OxBA; PoE; PoPoPo; TAP; TFi; TRP; UnPo

Gripe. Lincoln Kirstein. PoWW

Gripped on the shoulder of the man in front. (LL) War Blinded. Douglas Dunn. DiPo; OBWP

Grit. Geoff Page. NOBAu

Grizzel Grimme. *Unknown.* FaBoEE

Grizzly Bear. Mary Austin. CTV

Grizzly Bear is huge and wild, The. Infant Innocence. A. E. Housman. FaBoCh; ImPo; NOBL; OxBoLi; PeLV; Spl

Gro-ink. Kopita, kopita, ko-pi-ta. . . konk. Nub. Chris Wallace-Crabbe. BMAP

Grocery. Charles Simic. AFr

Grocery Store, The. Maura Stanton. NAmP90

Grodek. Georg Trakl, *German.* AF, *tr. by* Daniel S. Simko; PeFWW, *tr. by* Michael Hamburger

  ("Grandsons still unborn, The.") (LL) AF, *tr. by* Daniel S. Simko

  ("In the evening the autumn woods ring.") AF, *tr. by* Daniel S. Simko

Groin, come of age, his [']state sold out of hand. On Groin. Ben Jonson. NOSC

Groined by deep glens and walled along the west. The Glens. John Hewitt. IIP

Groins, for his fleshly burglary of late. Upon Groins: Epigram. Robert Herrick. CaPo

Grongar Hill. John Dyer. CABP; NOEC; NoP-4; OxAEP-1; PoEL-3

  Prospects. GaP

  Tenants of an Abandoned Castle. APo

Groom of the Chamber's Religion in King Henry the Eighth's Time, A. John Harington. NoSic

Groom retails the favours of his lord . ., The. (LL) Poverty in London. Samuel Johnson. NOEC; OBSV; OxAEP-1

Groome of the Chambers religion in King Henry the eights time, A. Sir John Harington. PBRV

Groping along the tunnel, step by step. The Rear-Guard. Siegfried Sassoon. MoBrPo; NAEL-2; NoAM; OBWP; PoWW; SAGP

Groping back to bed after a piss. Sad Steps. Philip Larkin. NoAM; NoP-4

"Gross, Coarse, Hideous" (Police Description of My Pictures). D. H. Lawrence. FaBoEE

Gross innocent. Pablo Neruda. TTTS *Fr.* Elephant.

Grotesque. Amy Lowell. BoWoP

Grotesque. Frederic Manning. PeFWW

Grotesque and queerly huddled. The Troop ship. Isaac Rosenberg. NSI; PoWW

Grotesques. Robert Graves. CMoP; OBCoV

"Dr. Newman with the crooked pince-nez." PeLV

"Sir John addressed the Snake-god in his temple." PeLV

Grotto, The. Francis Scarfe. PoA

Grouchy Good Night to the Academic Year, A. Ted Pauker. NOBL; PeLV

Ground beneath my feet is cracked, The. Day Twenty-three. Victor Coleman. NOBC

Ground drops back, The. Aeroplane. Pudjipangu, *Aborigine*. NOBAu, *tr. by Georg von Brandenstein*

Ground Elder. Leonard Clark. OBGa

Ground Glass. Irina Odoyevtseva, *Russian*. TCRP, *tr. by Bradley Jordan*

Ground / itself would / hint, The. Kiche Manitou. Nathaniel Mackey. FTOS

Ground-Squirrel Song. *Navajo Oral Tradition*. TTTS

Ground-Thumping Song. *Unknown, Chinese*. CoBCP, *tr. by Burton Watson*

Ground / under a maple-tree. Sigil. Hilda Doolittle.

Ground was frozen so hard, The. Dying with Amish Uncles. Julia Kasdorf. PBCAP

Groundhog, The. Richard Eberhart. CMoP; FaBoMo; ImPo; LiTM; MoAmPo; MoP; NoAM; RaBo; TAP; TFi; TRP; UnPo

Groundhog is, at best, a simple soul, The. Luci Shaw. TrCP

Groundhog we dumped in the woods, The. Middle Age. Paula Rankin. MT

Grounds of Winter. John Hollander. AFr

Group of jolly cowboys, discussing plans at ease, A. When the Work's All Done This Fall. *Unknown*. AS

Group of Musings, A. Henrietta Cordelia Ray. CBWP-3

Group of Officials, A. Yang Shih-ch'i, *Chinese*.

"Beyond the temple, a hidden cliff." CoBLCP, *tr. by Jonathan Chaves*

Group Photo from Pretoria Local on the Occasion of a Fourth Anniversary (Never Taken). Jeremy Cronin. AF; PeSAV

("Uprooted tree leaves / behind it a hole in the ground, An.") AF

Group Shot. Basil T. Paquet. CDa

Group Therapy. Carolyn M. Rodgers. ISC

Groups of God, The. The Rainmakers. Robert Kelly. PmAP

Grove, The. Edwin Muir. LiTM

Grove beyond the Barley, The. Alden Nowlan. MoCV

Groves of Blarney [they look so charming], The. Richard Alfred Millikin. OBCoV; OBGa; OxBoLi

("'Tis in every feature I would make it shine.") (LL) OBCoV

Groves of Eden, vanished now so long, The. Alexander Pope. OAEL-1 *Fr. Windsor-Forest [or Windsor Forest].*

Groves were God's first temples. Ere man learned, The. A Forest Hymn. William Cullen Bryant. APN-1; TAP

Grow high above my head. (LL) Invocation: "Let me be buried in the rain." Helene Johnson. NAAAL; SAGP

Grow old along with me! Robert Browning. ImPo; PoToHe *Fr. Rabbi Ben Ezra.* NAEL-2; OBNC

Grow old along with me! Rabbi Ben Ezra. Robert Browning. NAEL-2; OBNC

Grow to my lip, thou sacred kiss. The Kiss. Thomas Moore. NOBRP

Grow weary if you will, let me be sad. Lesbia. Richard Aldington. PoLF

Growing, The. Mongane Wally Serote. PBMAP

Growing Dark. James Schuyler. GLP

Growing Friendship. *Unknown*. CTV

Growing, he saw his friends increase. Tony White. Richard Murphy. BiHa

Growing in Grace. Jack R. Clemo. NOCV

Growing Old. Matthew Arnold. EnVR; FHYEP; NAEL-2; NOBVV; OAEL-2; PoEL-5

Growing Old. Byron. NOBE; SCV *Fr. Canto the First.* NAEL-2; OAEL-2; PoE Fr. Don Juan.

Growing Old [or Growing Older]. Rollin J. Wells. BLPA

(As We Grow Older.) PoToHe

Growing Rhyme, A. J. M. Westrup. BoTP

Growing River, The. Rodney Bennett. BoTP

Growing Smiles. *Unknown*. PoLF

Growing Tip, The. Mahadai Das. HCP

Growing Together. Joyce Carol Oates. CrSp

Growing Up. *Unknown*. CTV

Growing up in Miami any tropical fruit I ate. Frutas. Ricardo Pau-Llosa. CMAP

Growing Up Italian. Maria Gillan. UnSA

Growltiger's Last Stand. T. S. Eliot. FaBoCh; OBCA

Grown and Flown. Christina Rossetti. NOBVV

Grown old are these strong elements of tragedy. One Hundred Lines for the Coast. Kojo Laing. HBAPE

Grown old in Love from Seven till Seven times Seven. William Blake. FaBoEE; OAEL-2

Grown quiet, I looked at his pink back, and thought. (LL) Invocation: "It's crazy to think one could describe them." Robert Pinsky. NoP-4

Grown-up. Edna St. Vincent Millay. NoAM

Grown-ups. Geoffrey Holloway. OTCP

Grown-ups say things like. Chivvy. Michael Rosen. OTCP

Grown violent, do's either die, or tire. (LL) Love Me Little, Love Me Long. Robert Herrick. BLPA; CBLP; CaPo; FaBoBe; SCGP

Grows deathless by the Sacrifice. (LL) Friendship's Mystery, To My Dearest Lucasia. Katherine Philips. CPO; PBRV; PEW

Grows in weight. (LL) Son: "What I took in my hand." Robert Creeley. FTOS; PoA

Growth of Love, The. Robert Bridges.

"Man that sees by chance his picture made, A." NoAM

"My lady pleases me and I please her." Son

"O weary pilgrims, chanting of your woe." MoBrPo

"They that in play can do the thing they would." NoAM

"Whole world now is but the minister, The." Son

Grr—what's that? A dog? A poet? From a Spanish Cloister. G. K. Chesterton. UV

Grub First, Then Ethics. W. H. Auden. *See On Installing an American Kitchen in Lower Austria.*

Grudge, The. Dimitris Tsaloumas. BMAP

Grudges mend and wear and turn in winter. Household. Laura Jensen. LCAP-2

Gruesome ghoul, the grisly ghoul, The. The Ghoul. Jack Prelutsky. OBCA

Grumble Family, The. *Unknown*. PWR

Grumblers. Leonard Clark. PeP

Grunion. Wendy Rose. CDW

Gruyere—is being cleared of its forest—the mountains. An End to Myth. Charles Buckmaster. BMAP

Gryll Grange. Thomas Love Peacock.

Love and Age. NOBVV; OBEV; OBNC

Gryll's State. Roy Blount Jr. OBAL

Guadalupe, W.I. Nicolás Guillén, *Spanish*. TTY, *tr. by Anselm Hollo*

Guaranteed the canopy of the firmament above us. (LL) The Picnic, an Homage to Civil Rights. Michael S. Weaver. LTA; PoPoPo

Guard, The. Lyn Hejinian.

"Can one take captives by writing." FTOS

Guard at the Binh Thuy Bridge, The. John Balaban. AF; CDa; FYAP

Guard-Duty. August Stramm, *German*. PeFWW, *tr. by Patrick Bridgwater*

Guard me, Oh God, from hating man my brother. Shin Shalom, *Hebrew*. MHP, *tr. by Ruth Finer Mintz*

Guard me, oh God, from the cold winds that blow. A Woman's Prayer. Yehuda Karni, *Hebrew*. MHP, *tr. by Ruth Finer Mintz*

Guard picks dead leaves from plants, The. In an Urban School. Toi Derricotte. PBCAP

Guarded Wound, The. Adelaide Crapsey. WPE

Guardian-Angel, The. Robert Browning. PeECV

Guardian Angel. Rolf Jacobsen, *Norwegian*. RaBo, *tr. by Robert Bly*

Guardian Angels. Edmund Spenser. *Fr. Wood Of Error.* AEP

Guardian of heavenly gates, self-portrait, neon retort. New York Airport at Night. Andrey Andreievich Voznesensky, *Russian*. TCRP, *tr. by William Jay Smith*

Guardian of Helicon, Urania's son. Carmen 61. Catullus. OxBM, *tr. by Frederic Raphael and Kenneth McLeish Fr. Carmina.*

Guardian of the gate. Kanemasa, *Japanese*. OHPJ, *tr. by Kenneth Rexroth*

Guardian Prince of Albion burns in his nightly tent, The. A Prophecy. William Blake. *Fr. America; a Prophecy.* OAEL-2

Guardians, The. Geoffrey Hill. NoP-4

Guarding the doors of the Hispanic Society. The Spanish Lions. Phyllis McGinley. NYBP

Guard's Mistake, The. Edmund Blunden. NSI

Gubbinal. Wallace Stevens. NAAL-2

Gud Ber. *Unknown*. FaBoVe

Gude and Godlie Ballatis, The. *Unknown*.

Till Christ ("Till Christ, quhome I am haldin for to lufe"). OxBS

Gude Lord Graeme is to Carlisle gane. The Bewick and the Graeme. *Unknown*. OxBB

Gude Lord Scroop[e]'s to the huntin[g] gane. Hughie [the] Gra[e]me. *Unknown*. ESPB; IBB

Gude Wallace, *vers. A. Unknown*. ESPB

Gude Wallace. *Unknown*. ESPB

Gudewife sits i' the chimney-neuk, The. A Ballad of the Were-Wolf. Graham R. Tomson. OxBSn; VWP, *at. to Rosamund Marriott Watson*

Gudrun Laments over Sigurd. *Unknown.* OBVE *Fr.* The First Lay of Gudrun. AWP, *tr. by* William Morris *and* Eirikr Magnusson *Fr.* The Elder Edda.

Gudrun of old days. The First Lay of Gudrun. *Unknown.* AWP, *tr. by* William Morris *and* Eirikr Magnusson *Fr.* The Elder Edda.

Guerillas. Seamus Deane. BiHa

Guerrilla-Cong, The. Michael S. Harper. NBV

Guerrilla Handbook, A. Imamu Amiri Baraka. PoBA

Guerrilla War. William Daniel Ehrhart. CDa

Guerrillas. Roger McTair. PBCV

Guess Who. Fred Chappell. NBLV

Guess who is this creature. A Song to the Wind. Taliesin, *Welsh.* FaBoCh, *tr. by* A. P. Graves

Guessing. *Unknown, Burmese.* PBWP, *tr. by* U Win Pe

Guest, The. "Anna Akhmatova," *Russian.* RaBo, *tr. by* Jane Kenyon *and* Vera Dunham

Guest. D. J. Enright. OxBC

Guest, The. Rilke, *German.* FP, *tr. by* J. B. Leishman

Guest, The. *Unknown. See* Preparations.

Guest Arrives, A. Tu Fu, *Chinese.* CoBCP, *tr. by* Burton Watson

Guest Ellen at the Supper for Street People, The. David Ferry. NIP-4

Guest is inside you, and also inside me, The. Kabir, *Hindi.* RaBo, *tr. by* Robert Bly

Guests in their summer colors have fled, The. The Last Picnic. Stanley Kunitz. AF

Guests moved restless, The. The Party. Antigone Kefala. BMAP

Guests on the sea: Our visit is short. Mahmoud Darwish, *Arabic.* VCWP, *tr. by* Lena Jayyusi *and* W. S. Merwin

G'uggery G'uggery Nunc. Limerick. John Betjeman. PeLi

Guid[-]day now, bonnie Robin. Robin Redbreast's Testament. *Unknown.* NTP

Guide and Guard. Herman Melville. NCAP

Guide, and support, and cheer me to the end! (LL) Wordsworth and His Music, *identical to lines 754–860 of* The Recluse; Home at Grasmere. Wordsworth. EPCY; FHYEP; OAEL-2; PoE

Guide Me, O Thou Great Jehovah. William Williams. OBWVE

Guide to Holland, A. Peter Sirr. PBCIP

Guide to Patrons, A. Alattur Killar, *Tamil.* PLW, *tr. by* A. K. Ramanujan

Guide to the Other Gallery. Dana Gioia. RA

Guide to the Perplexed. David Malouf. NOBAu

Guide to the Stone Age, The. James Tate. WeT

Guide to the Symphony. Weldon Kees. VGW

Guide us to Thy perfect light. (LL) We Three Kings of Orient Are. John Henry Hopkins, Jr. AH; APN-2; PChr

Guided Missiles Experimental Range. Robert Conquest. OxBC

Guido, I wish that you and Lapo and I. Sonnet. Dante, *Italian.* RB; TTTS, *tr. by* Kenneth Koch

Guido, I would that Lapo, thou, and I. Sonnet: To Guido Cavalcanti. Dante, *Italian.* NNPT; AWP, *tr. by* Shelley

Guidon flags flutter gaily [*or* gayly] in the wind, The. (LL) Cavalry Crossing a Ford. Walt Whitman. AiP; AmPP; CBCWP; HeIP-4; InPK-6; InPS-3; MoP; NAAL-1; NAAL-3; NoAM; OxBA; SAmP; TAP; TFi; TRP; UnPo

Guido's Aurora. Henry David Thoreau. APN-1

Guiffre's Nightmusic. Thomas McGrath. MoNo; SeSe

Guild, The. Sharon Olds. RaBo

Guillotine's / Sharp blade?, The. "V. Ropshin," *Russian.* TCRP, *tr. by* Albert C. Todd

Guilt, Desire and Love. James Baldwin. GLP

Guilt Trip. David Lehman. PUP-18

Guilty, my Lord, what can I more declare? Edward Taylor. ChIV-1, *sect.* XXV, Division II *Fr.* Preparatory Meditations Before My Approach to the Lord's Supper.

"Guilty or Not Guilty?" *Unknown.* BLPA

Guinea. Jacques Roumain, *French.* NegPo; TTY, *tr. by* Langston Hughes

Guinea Corn. *Unknown.* PBCV

Guinea-Pig Song, A. *Unknown.* OxBChV; PeP

Guinea Woman. Lorna Goodison. HCP

Guitar. Federico García Lorca, *Spanish.* InPK-6, *tr. by* Keith Waldrop

Guitar / makes dreams cry, The. The Six Strings. Federico García Lorca, *Spanish.* RB, *tr. by* Donald Hall

Guitarist Tunes Up, The. Frances Darwin Cornford. SoSe-8

Gulf. Tudor Arghezi, *Romanian.* CEEP, *tr. by* Stavros Deligiorgis

Gulf, The. Denise Levertov. NNaP

Gulf, The. Derek Walcott. NoP-4; PoPoPo

Gulf Coast Blues. Clarence Williams. NAAAL

Gulistan, The. Sadi, *Persian.*

Alas! AWP, *tr. by* L. Cranmer-Byng

Courage. AWP, *tr. by* Sir Edwin Arnold

Dancer, The. AWP, *tr. by* Sir Edward Arnold

Friendship. AWP, *tr. by* L. Cranmer-Byng

Gift of Speech, The. AWP, *tr. by* L. Cranmer-Byng

Great Physician, The. AWP, *tr. by* Sir Edward Arnold

He Hath No Parallel. AWP, *tr. by* L. Cranmer-Byng

Help. AWP, *tr. by* Sir Edwin Arnold

Hyacinths to Feed Thy Soul. BLPA; FaBoBe

Love's Last Resource. AWP, *tr. by* L. Cranmer-Byng

Mesnevi. AWP, *tr. by* L. Cranmer-Byng

On the Deception of Appearances. AWP, *tr. by* L. Cranmer-Byng

Sooth-Sayer, The. AWP, *tr. by* Sir Edwin Arnold

Take the Crust. AWP, *tr. by* L. Cranmer-Byng

Wealth. AWP, *tr. by* Sir Edwin Arnold

Gull flies low across the darkening bay, A. Nocturne. James McAuley. BMAP

Gull'' Flight, The. Nigel Roberts. NOBAu
("Gulls' night, The.") BMAP
("They go / as shiftworkers / to the dawn.") (LL) BMAP

Gull inch-perfect over water, the busy crane, The. Louise Herlin, *French.* MFP, *tr. by* Martin Sorrell

Gull Lake set in the rolling prairie. At Gull Lake; August, 1810. Duncan Campbell Scott. NOBC

Gull, up close, A. Seagulls. John Updike. Poetsp

Gullfish. Tom Weatherly. *Fr.* Cantos. PoBA

Gulling[e] Sonnets, The. Sir John Davies. Son
"As when the bright[e] Crulean firmament." NoSic
"My case is this." NoSic
"Sacred muse that first[e] made love divine [*or* devine]." NoSic; PBRV
"What eagle can beho[u]ld her sunbright[e] eye." NoSic

Gulliver. Sylvia Plath. NOBA

Gulliver in Lilliput. Alexander Pope. FuFo

Gulliver Plays Cards. Nikolai Semionovich Tikhonov, *Russian.* TCRP, *tr. by* Michael Frayn

Gulls. William Carlos Williams. OxBA

Gull's Cry. Robert Penn Warren. FuPo *Fr.* To a Little Girl, One Year Old, in a Ruined Fortress.

Gull's Flight, The. Nigel Roberts. NOBAu

Gum has no shade, The. Robert, Viscount Sherbrooke Lowe. NOBAu *Fr.* Songs of the Squatters.

Gum-trees Stripping. Judith Wright. BMAP

Gums hurt, teeth ache—the ills and woes of age! Congratulating a Friend On His New Dentures. Tô Giang Tư', *Vietnamese.* AVP, *tr. by* Huỳnh Sanh Thông

Gun, The. Stephen Dobyns. CMAP

Gun-metal is somehow cool even in this heat. On Duty. Frederick D'Aguiar. PBCV

Gun / shells on our blk / tomorrows. (LL) Right On: White America. Sonia Sanchez. ISC

Gun Teams. Gilbert Frankau. OxBTC

Gun, the trap, the axe are borne, The. Revenge of the Hunted. Robert Arthur Douglas Ford. MoCV

Gunclick / hopesfears / lovehate. Las' Rights. Brian Meeks. PBCV

Gunga. Rachel Lyman Field. OBCA *Fr.* A Circus Garland.

Gunga Din. Rudyard Kipling. APAD; EBEvV; EBVV; MoBrPo
("You may talk o' gin and beer.") APAD

Gunned down in New York City. Exit on Feedback. Gavin Selerie. NBrP

Gunner, The. Francis Webb. BMAP; CBAP

Gunner rides on horseback, he lives in luxury, The. The Infantryman. *Unknown.* NSI

Gunny Harlabakis / Was a lifer. On Hats and Things. Mcavoy Layne. CDa

Gunpowder Plot, The. *Unknown.* OxNR

Gunpowder Plot Day. *Unknown.* FaBoPV; OxNR

Guns. Mcavoy Layne. CDa

Guns, The. William Soutar. FaBoTC

Guns, all that death-night, who would stoop to hear?, The. (LL) The Deserted Village. "Robin Hyde." PeNZ; WPE

Guns know what is what, but underneath, The. Memories of a Lost War. Louis Simpson. OBWP; VGW

Guns spell money's ultimate reason, The. Ultima Ratio Regum. Stephen Spender. AF; CMoP; ImPo; LiTM; NoP-4; OAEL-2; OBWP; PoWW; SAGP

Gunslinger. Edward Dorn.
Idle Visitation, An. NOBA; PmAP

Idle Visitation, An. NOBA

Gup, Scot! John Skelton. OxBoLi

Gurgling waters foam and play, The. On the rapids of the St. Lawrence. Henrietta Cordelia Ray. CBWP-3

Gurlie an gray the snell Fife shore. The War in Fife. Sydney Goodsir Smith. FaBoTC *Fr.* Armageddon in Albyn.

Gus: The Theatre Cat. T. S. Eliot. OBCA; OxBTC

Gut eats all day and lechers all the night. On Gut. Ben Jonson. NoP-4; PoPoPo

Gutsy bugs grabbed grub from me till disgusted, The. Parmenion of Macedon, *Greek.* GrAn, *tr. by* Peter Jay

Gutting the Salmon. Robert Adamson. BMAP

Guttural Muse, The. Seamus Heaney. NOIV

Guttural sorrow of the refugees, The. (LL) The British Museum Reading Room. Louis MacNeice. LiTM; MoBrPo; NOBE

Guvener B. is a sensible man. What Mr. Robinson Thinks. James Russell Lowell. AmPP *Fr.* The Biglow Papers.

Guy. Ralph Waldo Emerson. NOBA

Guy Fawkes '58. Fiona Kidman. PeNZ

Guy Mannering. Sir Walter Scott.

   Nativity Chant, The. FaBoCh

Guy picked me up north of Santa Fe, The. Story. John Balaban. CDa

Guy who's sitting in is not an ass, The. Mark Stern. Frederick Feirstein. RA

Guyana not Ghana. Marc Matthews. PBCV

Guyon's Voyage to the Bower of Bliss. Edmund Spenser. NoSic *Fr.* Wood Of Error. AEP

   "Two dayes now in that sea he sayled has." OxBoS

Guys and Dolls. Frank Loesser. OBAL

Gwan! Gwan! Cry the Fish Hawks. *Unknown, Chinese.* CoBCP, *tr. by* Burton Watson

G'way an' quit dat noise, Miss Lucy—. When Malindy Sings. Paul Laurence Dunbar. AAP; APN-2; ISC; NAAAL; PoBA

Gwendoline. Bayard Taylor. BXAP

Gwine find a beauty shop. Kinky Hair Blues. Una Marson. PBCV

Gwine to Run All Night; or, De Camptown Races. Stephen Collins Foster. OBAL

Gwladys Rhys. W. J. Gruffydd, *Welsh.* OBWVE, *tr. by* Myrddin Lloyd

Gyges['] ring they bear[e] about them still, A. Lovers How They Come and Part. Robert Herrick. GBL; OxBSP; OxBoLi; PoEL-3

Gym. Richard Murphy. BiHa

Gymnasiad, The, or Boxing Match. Paul Whitehead.

   "As when two monarchs of the brindled breed." NOEC

   Boxers, The. ECEV

Gymnastics Teacher, The. Automedon, *Greek.* GrAn, *tr. by* W. S. Merwin

Gypsies. John Clare. *See* Gipsies: "The Snow falls deep; the forest lies alone."

Gypsies. Rachel Lyman Field. BoTP

Gypsies. John Langhorne. NOEC *Fr.* The Country Justice.

Gypsies came to our good lord's gate, The. The Gypsy Laddie. *Unknown.* ESPB; HAP

Gypsies came to our Lord's yett, The. Johny Faa. *Unknown.* OxBB

Gypsies in the Wood. *Unknown.* BoTP; OxBSP; OxBoLi; OxNR

Gypsies Metamorphosed, The. Ben Jonson.

   Dinner for the Devil. NOSC

   Faery Beam upon You, The. BeJo

      (Song.) OxBSP

   Song: "To the old, long life and treasure." OxBSP

Gypsies on the Move. Charles Baudelaire, *French.* GS, *tr. by* Unknown

Gypsies [*or* Gipsies] they came to my Lord Cassilis' yett [*or* gate], The. The Gypsy Laddie. *Unknown.* ESPB; EnSB

Gypsy. Josephine Miles. MoP; NoAM

Gypsy, The. Susan Stewart. NAmP90

Gypsy, The. Edward Thomas. NoAM; NoP-4

Gypsy Christmas. Otto Orban, *Hungarian.* CEEP, *tr. by* Emery E. George

Gypsy Davy, The. *Unknown.* AmFP; AS

Gypsy Girl, The. Ralph Hodgson. *See* The Gipsy Girl.

Gypsy Laddie, The. *Unknown.* ESPB; HAP

   (Johnny Faa, the Lord of Little Egypt.) EnSB

Gypsy Man. Langston Hughes. NAAAL

Gypsy Music in Krakow. Tom Pickard. NBrP

Gypsy-race my pity rarely move, The. Gypsies. John Langhorne. NOEC *Fr.* The Country Justice.

Gypsy woman told my mother, The. Hoochie Coochie. Muddy Waters. NAAAL

Gypsy's Window, The. Denise Levertov. CLPP

Gyre's Galax. Norman Henry, II Pritchard. PoBA

Gyres! the gyres! Old Rocky Face look forth, The. W. B. Yeats. GTBS-P; HAP; NoAM

Gyroscope. Howard Nemerov. NoAM

H

H[oly] Communion, The. George Herbert. ChIV-1; ESCV

H ear t h. Janet Sutherland. NBrP

H. M. S. *Hero.* Michael Roberts. OxBTC

H. M. S. Pinafore. Sir William Schwenck Gilbert.

   Englishman, The. NOBL

   First Lord's Song, The. PeLV

H-óran ó a vee-ó. A Complaint about Exile. Mairi MacLeod, *Gaelic.* PBWP, *tr. by* Joan Keefe

H. Scriptures, The ("Oh Book! infinite sweetnesse! let my heart"). George Herbert. ChIV-1; ESCV; MiEL

H. Scriptures, The ("Oh that I knew how all thy lights combine"). George Herbert. GeHe

   (H. Scriptures II.) ChIV-2

H. Scriptures. Henry Vaughan. ChIV-2; ESCV

H[ome], thou return'st from Thames, whose naiads long. An Ode on the Popular Superstitions of the Highlands of Scotland. William Collins. NOEC; OAEL-1; OxAEP-1

Ha, ha, give me ale. (LL) In Praise of Ale. Thomas Bonham. FaBoCh; OBEV

Ha ha! ha ha! This world doth pass. Fara Diddle Dyno. Thomas Weelkes. CBNP; FaBoCh; OBCoV; OxBoLi; PeLV

Ha ha. You searching. Clear Channel. Lorenzo Thomas. FTOS

Ha-Kon-E-Crase, the Eagle Dance. *Unknown.* APN-2 *Fr.* War Dance. APN-2, *tr. by* George Catlin

Hā' mats'a Song Composed about Fifty Years Ago. *Unknown.* *Fr.* Dances and Songs of the Winter Ceremonial. APN-2, *tr. by* Franz Boas

Hā' mats'a Song, La' Lasiqoala. *Unknown.* *Fr.* Dances and Songs of the Winter Ceremonial. APN-2, *tr. by* Franz Boas

Hā' mats'a Song of the Koskimo. *Unknown.* *Fr.* Dances and Songs of the Winter Ceremonial. APN-2, *tr. by* Franz Boas

Hā' mats'a Song of the Lau' itsîs. *Unknown.* *Fr.* Dances and Songs of the Winter Ceremonial. APN-2, *tr. by* Franz Boas

Ha' not you seen, Camillo? Shakespeare. OxBM *Fr.* The Winter's Tale.

Ha! Original Sin! Ogden Nash. NBLV

Ha! sir, I have seen you sniffing and snoozling. The Faun. Ezra Pound. FaBoCh; FaBoTw

Ha! tott'ring Johnny strut and boast. The Creditor to His Proud Debtor. George Moses Horton. AAP; NAAAL

Ha' we lost the goodliest fere o' all. Ballad of the Goodly Fere. Ezra Pound. CMoP; ChIV-2; ImPo; LiTM; MeMAP; MoAmPo; MoBS; PoRA; TrCP

Ha! whare ye gaun, ye crowlin' [*or* crowlan] ferlie! To a Louse [On Seeing One on a Lady's Bonnet at Church]. Robert Burns. APo; BLPA; FaBoVe; NAEL-2; NOBRP; NOEC; OxBS; PBMP

Haanetjie's Morning Dialogue. Essop Patel. PeSAV

Habeas Corpus Blues, The. Conrad Potter Aiken. NYBP

Habit of Perfection, The. Gerard Manley Hopkins. ChIV-2; ImPo; MoBrPo; MoP; NoAM; OBEV; OBMV; OxAEP-2; PoRA; Poetr; RB; TFi

Habit of staring, The. David Woo. OpBo

Habitable planets are unknown or too. Native's Letter. Arthur Nortje. HBAPE; PeSAV

Habitat. Judith Wright. CBAP

Habitation. Margaret Atwood. BoWoP; FaBoWP; WeW-3

Habitation. Ralph Knevet. NOSC

Habits of the Hippopotamus. Arthur Guiterman. OBCA

Habitué of a small-town club, this man. The Ephemeral Past. Antonio Machado Ruiz, *Spanish.* NNPT, *tr. by* Charles Tomlinson *and* Henry Gifford

Habla Usted Espa~nol? James Reiss. AmPA

Haciendo Apenas la Recolección. Tino Villanueva. UnSA

Hackeysack Players, The. Cynthia Huntington. NAmP90

Hackney Coachman, The; Or, The Way to Get a Good Fare. Hannah More. WoRP

Hackney'd in business, wearied at that oar. Retirement. William Cowper.

Had a definite flavour of gin. (LL) Limerick: "From the bathing machine came a din." Edward Gorey. OBAL; OBCoV; PeLi

Had a / weed in it. (LL) Reflective. A. R. Ammons. HCAP; PiM; VCAP

Had anything been wrong, we should certainly have heard. (LL) The Unknown Citizen. W. H. Auden. HeIP-4; InPK-6; LiTM; MeMAP; NBLV; NIP-4; NOBL; NYBP; OBSV; PFE; PoRA; Poetr; SAGP; SoSe-8; TRP; UnPo

Had broken and thrown away! (LL) The Slave's Dream. Henry Wadsworth Longfellow. FaPoR; NAAL-1; NAAL-3

Had Cowley ne'er spoke, Killigrew ne'er writ. Sir John Denham. FaBoEE

Had cut grooves too deeply across our backs. (LL) Hard Rock Returns to Prison from the Hospital for the Criminal Insane. Etheridge Knight. CoAmPo; InPS-3; MoP; NAAAL; NIP-4; NNaP; PBCAP; SAGP; TAP; TRP; UnPo

Had damned him to the hell of impotence. (LL) The Disappointment. Aphra Behn. NALW; NOSC; PEW

Had died, but for now let us take some comfort. The Human Fabric. Robert Penn Warren. Fr. Fall Comes in Back-Country Vermont. NYBP; VGW

Had *Dorothea* liv'd when mortals made. Edmund Waller. See At Penshurst [Another].

Had everyone Suum. To the Archbishop of Tuam. Unknown. FaBoEE

Had Gadyaa Kid, a Kid. Unknown, Hebrew. TrJP

Had gone up to. Memory Gardens. Robert Creeley. FTOS

Had he and I but met. The Man He Killed. Thomas Hardy. CMoP; ChAP; HAP; HeIP-4; LiTM; MoBrPo; NIP-4; OBWP; PBMP; Poetr; RB; TFi; WeW-3

Had he not drank them up for you. (LL) His Saviour[']s Words, Going to the Cross[e]. Robert Herrick. ChIV-2; NOCV

Had I a man's fair form, then might my sighs. To ———: "Had I a man's fair form, then might my sighs." Keats. OxAEP-2

Had I an inn at Bethlehem. Lineage. Robert Farren. TIRV

Had I been an ox or horse. Wang An-shih. SuSp, tr. by Jan W. Walls Fr. In the Style of Han Shan and Shih Te.

Had I been mindful of my high descent. Hadewijch, Dutch. PBWP, tr. by Frans van Rosevelt

Had I but plenty of money, money enough and to spare. Up at a Villa—Down in the City. Robert Browning. FHYEP; GTBS-P; InPS-3; NOBE; PoRA

Had I but strength enough, and time. Charles Robinson. BXAP

Had I but the torrent's might. The Death of Hoel. Thomas Gray. NOEC

Had I heard my father mention. Never in My Life. Walter McDonald. MT

Had I lived till now. Poem for the Year Twenty Twenty. Alfred M. Lee. AmPA

Had I my wish I would distend my guts. The Extravagant Drunkard's Wish. Edward Ward. CBNP; NOEC

Had I not perceived so much of worth in her. The Legacy. Heinrich von Morungen, German. GePo, tr. by F. C. Nicholson

Had I, Pygmalion like, the power. The Choice. Soame Jenyns. ECEV

Had I remained in innocent security. Angellica's Lament. Aphra Behn. LW

Had I the choice to tally greatest bards. Walt Whitman. Poetr; SoSe-8 Fr. Fancies at Navesink.

Had I the heavens' embroidered cloths. He Wishes for the Cloths of Heaven. W. B. Yeats. ADE; APAD; ChAP; MoBrPo; NoAM; OBEV

Had I the wings of a bird. Thoughts. Maggie Pogue Johnson. CBWP-4

Had lasted a minute more. (LL) A Thunderstorm in Town. Thomas Hardy. APAD; BoLoP; CBLP; EnLoPo; GBL; GLoP; OxBSP

Had Life remained one whole. Unit. Mary Elizabeth Fullerton. NOBAu

Had *Lucan* hid the truth to please the time. To the Translator of Lucan [or Lucan's Pharsalia, 1614]. Sir Walter Ralegh. PBRV; SiPS

Had me a cat, the cat pleased me. Fiddle-I-Fee. Unknown. AmFP

Had mournful Ovid been to Brent condemned. William Diaper. OBSV Fr. Brent; a Poem to Thomas Palmer Esq.

Had my soul tottered off to sleep. Wondrous the Merge. James Richard Broughton. GLP

Had not plucked a handful when night came! (LL) Plucking The Rushes. Unknown, Chinese. ChiP; LoP; LP, tr. by Arthur Waley

Had not these me against myself defended. (LL) Grace. Ralph Waldo Emerson. APN-1; AmPP; NCAP

Had not thy waves forbad the rest. (LL) Upon Julia['s] Washing Herself in the River. Robert Herrick. CaPo; OBCVT

Had old Hippocrates, or Galen. Ben Jonson. Fr. Volpone. NAEL-1

Had Sacharissa liv'd when Mortals made. At Penshurst [Another]. Edmund Waller. BeJo; OAEL-1

Had she come all the way for this. The Haystack in the Floods. William Morris. CABP; EBEV; EBNV; EBVV; EnVR; HAP; NAEL-2; NoP-4; OAEL-2; OBNC; OBNV; OxAEP-2; PeVV; PoEL-5; PoRA

Had somewhere to get to and sailed calmly on. (LL) Musée des Beaux Arts. W. H. Auden. CABP; CMoP; ClHu; GS; GTBS-P; HAP; HeIP-4; ImPo; InPK-6; InPS-3; LiTM; MeMAP; MoP; NAEL-2; NOBE; NoAM; NoP-4; OxAEP-2; PBMP; PFE; PoE; PoPoPo; PoRA; Poetr; RaBo; SCV; SoSe-8; TFi; TRP; TrCP; TwCP

Had sowed these fruits, and got the harvest in. (LL) To the Immortal[l] Memory [or Memorie] and Friendship of That Noble Pair[e], Sir Lucius Cary and Sir H. [or Henry] Morison. Ben Jonson. BeJo; NAEL-1; NOBE; NOSC; NoP-4; OAEL-1; PoEL-2; SeCP

Had stayed at home behind me and / was fast asleep in bed. (LL) My Shadow. Robert Louis Stevenson. CTV; ChAP; FaBoBe; OTCP; OxBChV; PWR; UV

Had there been falsehood in my breast. Emily Jane Brontë. NOBVV

Had there been peace there never had been riven. Dedication. Drummond Allison. FaBoTw

Had this effulgence disappeared. Composed upon an Evening of Extraordinary Splendour and Beauty. Wordsworth. OAEL-2

"Had we a king," said Wallace then. Gude Wallace. Unknown. ESPB

Had we but World enough and Time. To His Coy Mistress. Andrew Marvell. APAD; AWP; BoLoP; CABP; CBLP; ClHu; EBEV; EBEvV; ESCV; EnLoPo; FHYEP; FMP; FSCP; FaBoSe; GBL; GEA; GLoP; GeHe; HAP; HeIP-4; HoPM; ImPo; InPK-6; InPS-3; LoP; MeLP; NAEL-1; NIP-4; NOBE; NOSC; NoP-4; OAEL-1; OBEV; OxAEP-1; PBMP; PBRV; PFE; PoE; PoEL-2; PoLF; PoPoPo; PoRA; Poetr; SAGP; SCGP; SCV; SeCP; TFi; TRP; UV

Had we but world enough, and time. To His Coy Mistress. Stanley J. Sharpless. BXAP

Had we but world enough, and time. To His Importunate Mistress. Peter De Vries. NBLV; NIP-4

Had We Two Met. Walter Savage Landor. FaBoEE; OxBSP

Had you been born. Ten Years Ago. Eileen Moeller. CrSp

Had your intent been to repent. Michael Wigglesworth. NAAL-3 Fr. The Day of Doom. NAAL-1; SCAP

Haddock Fishermen. George Mackay Brown. NoP-4

Hades in Manganese. Clayton Eshleman. APSN

Hadn't heard of the atom bomb. The Seals in Penobscot Bay. Daniel Gerard Hoffman. TwCP

Hadrian's Address to His Soul When Dying. Emperor Hadrian, Latin. OBVE, tr. by Byron

(Adrian's Address to His Soul When Dying). OBCVT, tr. by Byron

Hadrian's Lane. Ray DiPalma. FTOS

Haemorrhage. Padraic Flacc. CIP-2

Haere Ra. James Keir Baxter. PeNZ

Hag, The ("Hag is astride, The"). Robert Herrick. BeJo; CaPo; FaBoCh

("Call'd out by the clap of the Thunder.") (LL) OxBSn

(Hag, The.) OxBSn

Hag, The ("Staff[e] is now greased [or greas'd], The"). Robert Herrick. CaPo

Hag and the Slavies, The. Jean de La Fontaine, French. AWP; OBVE, tr. by Edward Marsh

Hag is astride, The. The Hag. Robert Herrick. BeJo; CaPo; FaBoCh; OxBSn

Hag of Béara, The. Unknown. NOIV

Hag of Beare, The. Unknown, Irish. BIrV; PBWP, tr. by John Montague; OBVE, tr. by Lady August Gregory; NOIV, tr. by Thomas Kinsella

Hag-Ridden. Robert Graves. BIrV

Hagar. Francis Lauderdale Adams. OxBS

Hagar. Elisabeth Eybers, Afrikaans. PeSA, tr. by the author

Hagar and Ishmael. Else Lasker-Schüler, German. BoWoP, tr. by Rosemarie Waldrop

Haggadah. Abraham Moses Klein. TrJP

Haggai. John Chagy. ChIV-1

Haggard daylight steer, The. (LL) The Death of a Toad. Richard Wilbur. CMoP; LiTM; MoP; NAAL-2; NoAM; PFE; PoA; Poetr

Haglets, The. Herman Melville. APN-2

Hai! daughter of the Thundercloud. Dance-Song of the Lightning. Unknown, Hottentot. PeSA

Haiku: "August heat." Gerald Vizenor. VoR

Haiku: "Autumn's bright moon." Chiyojo, Japanese. PBWP, tr. by R. H. Blyth

Haiku: "Dew of the rouge-flower, The." Chiyojo, Japanese. PBWP, tr. by R. H. Blyth

Haiku: "Dragon-fly strives patiently, The." José Juan Tablada, Spanish. PBMP, tr. by Samuel Beckett

Haiku: "Eastern guard tower." Etheridge Knight. BPo; MoP; TAP

Haiku: "Fallen flowers rise." Arakida Moritaké, Japanese. SoSe-8, tr. by Harold G. Henderson

Haiku: "Falling flower, The." Arakida Moritaké, Japanese. SoSe-8, tr. by Babette Deutsch

Haiku: "I feel a sudden chill—." Buson. IMW

Haiku: "Lightning flashes, The!" Basho, Japanese. SoSe-8, tr. by Earl Miner

Haiku: "Lightning gleam, A." Basho, Japanese. SoSe-8, tr. by Harold G. Henderson

Haiku: "Spring rain." Chiyojo, Japanese. PBWP, tr. by R. H. Blyth

Haiku: "Was it yesterday." Sonia Sanchez. FFC

Haiku: "Your voice unwrapping." Sonia Sanchez. FFC

Haiku. Sonia Sanchez. ISC

Haiku: After The Orgies. Gavin Ewart. APAD

Haiku Ambulance. Richard Brautigan. InPK-6

Haiku: The Season of Celebrity. Gavin Ewart. APAD

Hail, aged God who lookest on thy Father. He Prayeth for Ink and Palette That He May Write. *Unknown.* AWP *Fr.* Book of the Dead.

Hail and beware the dead who will talk life until you are blue. A Newly Discovered "Homeric" Hymn. Charles Olson. MoP; NeAP; NoAM; PoM

Hail and Farewell. Catullus. *See* On the Burial of His Brother.

Hail beauteous Chiswick! hail, sequestered seat! Chiswick. Thomas Maurice. OBGa *Fr.* Richmond Hill.

Hail, beauteous stranger of the grove [*or* wood]! To the Cuckoo. Michael Bruce, *rev. by* John Logan. NOEC; OBEV

Hail, blushing goddess, beauteous Spring! Esther Vanhomrigh. LW

Hail bride and bridegroom, children both of Jove. Wedding Song: Lullaby for Sleepy Lovers. Theocritus, *English.* ITG, *tr. by* John Dryden *and* Nahum Tate

Hail, Columbia. Joseph Hopkinson. FaBoBe

Hail, Comly and Clene. *Unknown. See* Haylle, Comly and Clene.

Hail, curious wights! to whom so fair. To the Virtuosos. William Shenstone. ECEV

Hail! Dawn is shining glory doing. Kilaben Bay Song. *Unknown, Aborigine.* NOBAu, *tr. by* Perce Haslam

Hail dawning Peace! Speed on thy glorious rise! The End of the Whole Matter. Albery Allson Whitman. AAP *Fr.* Not a Man and Yet a Man.

Hail, Dionysos. Dudley Randall. BPo

Hail, ever-pleasing Solitude! Hymn on Solitude. James Thomson. NOEC

Hail Flag of the Union! Hail Flag of the free! Stars and Stripes. Mary Weston Fordham. CBWP-2

Hail, forest nymphs, daughters of the river. Moiro, *Greek.* GrAn, *tr. by* Fleur Adcock

Hail, Garcia, hammer of pigeons. Paul Evans. NBrP *Fr.* The Sofa Book.

Hail! gentle youth, and do not deem me rude. Lines: To a Young Gentleman of Surpassing Beauty. Ellen Johnston. VWP

Hail Girl Burning and hail Girl Verdant. The Axion Esti. Odysseus Elytis, *Greek.* GrIP, *tr. by* Edmund Keeley *and* George Savidis *Fr.* Axion Esti.

Hail, glorious day; mayst thou be writ in gold. Simon Ford. NOSC *Fr.* London's Resurrection.

Hail, glorious day which miracles adorn. On Christmas Day. Robert Boyle, 1st Earl of Orrery. TIRV

Hᴀɪʟ graceful morning of eternal day. To the Blessed Virgin. William Alabaster. NoSic

Hail[e] great Redeemer, man, and God, all hail[e]. A Hymn[e] to Our Saviour on the Cross[e]. George Chapman. PeECV; PoEL-2

Hail, guest! We ask not what thou art. Welcome over the Door of an Old Inn. *Unknown.* PoToHe

Hail, happy bride, for thou art truly blest! On the Death of Mrs. Bowes. Lady Mary Wortley Montagu. BoWoP; LW

Hail, happy day, when smiling like the morn. To the Right Honourable William, Earl of Dartmouth[, His Majesty's Principal Secretary of State for North America]. Phillis Wheatley. AmPP; CrDW; NAAAL; NALW

Hail, happy lot of the laborious man. Poverty, in Imitation of Milton. Samuel Jones. NOEC

Hail, happy Pope, whose generous mind. Jonathan Swift. EPCY *Fr.* A Libel on the Reverend Dr. Delany.

Hail, happy saint, on thine immortal throne. On the Death of the Rev. Mr. George Whitefield, 1770. Phillis Wheatley. ColAP; NAAAL; NAAL-1; NAAL-3

Hail, happy virgin! of celestial race. To Almystrea, on her Divine Works. Elizabeth Thomas. ECWP

Hail! Ho! / Sail! Ho! A Sea-Song from the Shore. James Whitcomb Riley. BoTP; FPC

Hail, Holy Land. Thomas Tillam. *See* Upon the First Sight of New England, June 29, 1638.

Hail, holy Lead!—of human feuds the great. Lead. Ambrose Bierce. APN-2; OBAL *Fr.* The Devil's Dictionary.

Hail! home of exiles and of Seminoles! Albery Allson Whitman. AAP *Fr.* Twasinta's Seminoles; Or Rape of Florida.

Hail, May Day, dedicated to holy delights, to joy as full as unadulterated. May Morning. George Buchanan. PBRV

Hail, mediocrity, beneath whose spell. Roy Campbell. MoBrPo *Fr.* The Georgiad.

Hail, meek-eyed maiden, clad in sober grey. Ode to Evening. Joseph Warton. OxAEP-1

Hail mer- / ry, tricky, and clandestine. Ode to Pornography. Jack Anderson. PoA

Hail, Muse! et caetera.--We left Juan sleeping. Byron. OAEL-2 *Fr.* Canto the Third. *Fr.* Don Juan.

Hail, Muse! et caetera.--We left Juan sleeping. Canto the Third. Byron. *Fr.* Don Juan.

Hail O Girl prophetic and daedalic. (LL) The Axion Esti. Odysseus Elytis, *Greek.* GrIP, *tr. by* Edmund Keeley *and* George Savidis; VCWP, *tr. by* Keeley, Edmund and Philip Sherrard

Hail, O most worthy in all the world! *Unknown. Fr.* Christ 1. AnOE, *tr. by* Charles W. Kennedy

Hail, oh hail to the king who does in glory reign. Beatrice Quickenden. AH

Hail, old patrician trees, so great and good! On Solitude. Abraham Cowley. NOSC; OxAEP-1

Hail Our Incarnate God! William Duke. AH

Hail! Oure patron and lady of erthe. Salve Regina. *Unknown.* MiEL

Hail peace and joy on earth! Firecrackers snap. The French National Holiday. Nguyễn Khuyến, *Vietnamese.* AVP, *tr. by* Huỳnh Sanh Thông

Hail peaceful Shade, whose sacred verdant side. To the University. Alicia D'Anvers. KTR; NOSC *Fr.* Academia; or The Humours of the University of Oxford.

Hail, Queen of Heaven. *Unknown.* OxBSP

Hail! Richmond, hail! thy matchless beauties. Richmond Gardens: A Poem. *Unknown.* OBGa *Fr.* Richmond Gardens: A Poem.

Hail, sacred shades! cool, leafy house! Upon the Priory Grove, His Usual Retirement. Henry Vaughan. BeJo

Hail, scintillate flasher, thou jewel in the dark. To a Firefly. *Unknown.* PFE

Hail, Silimela! The Pleiades. S. E. K. Mqhayi, *Xhosa.* PeSAV, *tr. by* Jeff Opland

Hail[e], sister springs! Saint Mary Magdalene. Richard Crashaw. ESCV; GeHe; MeLP; OAEL-1; OBEV; SeCP

Hail South Australia! blessed clime. *Unknown.* NOBAu

Hail Sovereign Queen of secrets, who hast power. John Fletcher *and* Shakespeare. PoEL-2 *Fr.* The Two Noble Kinsmen.

Hail sterne superne! Hail in eterne. Ane Ballat of Our Lady. William Dunbar. OxBS

Hail, Sympathy! thy soft idea brings. William Lisle Bowles. Byron. OBNC *Fr.* English Bards and Scotch Reviewers.

Hail! the Glorious Golden City. Felix Adler. AH

Hail then ye daring few! who proudly soar. The Air Balloon. Henry James Pye. NOEC *Fr.* Aerophorion.

Hail / there is new breath here. Xango. Edward Kamau Brathwaite. HCP

Hail, thou Great God in thy Boat. He Embarketh in the Boat of Ra. *Unknown.* AWP *Fr.* Book of the Dead.

Hail, thou my native soil! thou blessed plot. The Frolic Mariners of Devon. William Browne. OxAEP-1 *Fr.* Britannia's Pastorals.

Hail, thou sole Empress of the Land of wit. A Pindarick To Mrs. Behn on her Poem on the Coronation. *Unknown.* KTR

Hail thou sweet and welcome day. The First of August in Jamaica. Joshua McCarter Simpson. AAP

Hail, thou who shinest from the moon. He Establisheth His Triumph. *Unknown.* AWP *Fr.* Book of the Dead.

Hail to the black! (LL) The Song of the Smoke. W. E. B. DuBois. ISC; SSLK

Hail to the Brightness of Zion's Glad Morning. Thomas Hastings. AH

Hail to the chief who in triumph advances. Boat Song. Sir Walter Scott. OxAEP-2; PoEL-4 *Fr.* The Lady of the Lake.

Hail to the coming time! (LL) The Fine Old English Gentleman; New Version. Charles Dickens. NOBVV; OBSV

Hail to the god who joins us; for through him. The Sonnets to Orpheus I, 12. Rilke, *German.* ITG, *tr. by* Stephen Mitchell

Hail to the Joyous Day. Royall Tyler. AH

Hail to the Queen. *Unknown.* AH

Hail to the Sabbath Day. Stephen Greenleaf Bulfinch. AH

Hail to the sage divine of Milan's plains! On Hearing That Torture Was Suppressed throughout the Austrian Dominions. John Codrington Bampfylde. Son

Hail to thee, blithe horse, bird thou never wert! Strike. Veronica Forrest-Thomson. FaBoTC

Hail to Thee, Blithe Owl. Ring Lardner. OBAL

Hail to thee, blithe roadster! To a Bicycle. *Unknown.* BXAP

Hail to thee, blithe Spirit! To a Skylark. Shelley. EBEvV; FHYEP; FaBoBe; GTBS-P; HAP; ImPo; InPS-3; NAEL-2; NOBE; NOBRP; NoP-4; OAEL-2; OBEV; OBNC; OxAEP-2; PBMP; PoLF; Ro; SCGP; TFi

Hail to thee thou holy Babe. Christmas Hymn. *Unknown, Irish.* TIRV, *tr. by* Douglas Hyde

Hail to thy puggy nose, my Darling. A Natal Address to My Child, March 19th 1844. Eliza Ogilvy. VWP

Hail to you through whom joy will shine out;. Akathistos Hymn. *Unknown, Greek.* GrIP, *tr. by* Constantine A. Trypanis

Hail, Tranquil Hour of Closing Day. Leonard Bacon. AH

Hail, tribes of Outer. North American Haiku. Gavin Ewart. APAD

Hail, universal mother! lightly rest. Meleager. Ovid. NOBRP, tr. by John Herman Merivale Fr. Metamorphoses.

Hail Wedded Love! Jay Macpherson. MoCV

Hail[e] wedded love, mysterious law, true source. Unfallen Love. Milton. NOSC Fr. Book IV. OAEL-1 Fr. Paradise Lost.

Haile from the dead, or from eternity. Lines on a Purple Cap Received as a Present from My Brother. George Alsop. SCAP

Haile gracefull morning of eternall Daye. William Alabaster. ESCV Fr. Divine Meditations. Son

Haill clanjamfrie!, The. (LL) The Bonnie Broukit Bairn. "Hugh MacDiarmid." FaBoCh; FaBoTC; FaBoVe; HAP; InPS-3

Hailstones falling like sharp blue sky chips. Crazy Horse Monument. Peter Blue Cloud. HATNAP; UnSA

Hailstorm in May. Gerard Manley Hopkins. Spl

Hain't no use to weep, hain't no use to moan. Down in the Lonesome Garden. Unknown. BPo

Hair. Rémy de Gourmont, French. AWP, tr. by Jethro Bithell

Hair, The. May Swenson. DeD Fr. Poet to Tiger. GLP

(Poet to Tiger.) CPO

("When you're not looking.") (LL) CPO

Hair: A Narrative. Cheryl Clarke. NMM-2

Hair and bacon grease, pearl button. Genie's Prayer Under the Kitchen Sink. Rita Dove. RACG

Hair beneath. Stand farther off then! go, The. (LL) Sonnet: "I lift my heavy heart up solemnly." Elizabeth Barrett Browning. NALW; PEW; VWP

Hair-bowed Rose, deep in lush grass of the river. Profile of Rose. Glyn Jones. OBWVE

Hair—braided chestnut. Portrait in Georgia. Jean Toomer. NoP-4; PFE

Hair, in my comb's teeth. Clement Hoyt. HA

Hair is heaven's water flowing eerily over us. Hair Poem. Bill Knott. SPE

Hair of fine silver, shaggy and twisted. Francesco Berni. ItIP

Hair on our shoulders dangles and shines, The. (LL) The Natives. David Mura. CDa

Hair ornament of the sun, The. Takajo Mitsuhashi, Japanese. BoWoP; WPJ, tr. by Kenneth Rexroth and Ikuko Atsumi

Hair Poem. Bill Knott. SPE

Hair—shiny black geisha hair. Portrait. Beverly Acuff Momoi. LoHo

Hair— / silver-gray. Face. Jean Toomer. NoP-4

Hair that I gloss down. Just Like the Legend. Léon Damas, French. PFTM, tr. by Norman R. Shapiro

Hair the color of. Powwow. Carroll Arnett. LTA

Hair Tonic. Gisèle Prassinos, French. PFTM, tr. by Marcel Jean

Hair-Tonic Bottle, The. Ben King. OBAL

Hair unbound, in this. Akiko Yosano, Japanese. OHMPJ, tr. by Kenneth Rexroth

Hair which boldly speaks in Bernice's despite, A. Description of Perfect Beauty. Christian Hofmann von Hofmannswaldau, German. GePo, tr. by George C. Schoolfield

Hairband, homespun, opera-hat, afghan. Motley. Peter Davison. NBLV

Haircut. Karl Shapiro. TwCP

Hairdo and ornaments all the latest fashion. Beginning of Spring—A Stroll with My Wife. Hsü Chün-ch'ien, Chinese. CoBCP, tr. by Burton Watson

Hairdresser's, The. Pierre McOrlan, French. MFP, tr. by Martin Sorrell

Hairline Fracture, A. Amy Clampitt. NoAM

Hairs less in sight, or any hairs but these!' (LL) But anxious cares the pensive nymph oppressed. Alexander Pope. EBNV; OxAEP-1

Hairy Dog, The. Herbert Asquith. PeP

(My Hairy Dog.) CTV

Hairy Toe, The. Unknown. OBSP

Hairy was here. News from the Cabin. May Swenson. NYBP

Haka: Hinemotu. Te Aomuhurangi te Maaka. PeNZ

Haka: The Blossoming. Pita Sharples, Maori. PeNZ, tr. by Pita Sharples

Haka: The Feathered Albatross. Muru Walters, Maori. PeNZ, tr. by the author

Hakeldama. Zbigniew Herbert, Polish. GI, tr. by John Carpenter and Bogdana Carpenter

Hako, The. Unknown, Pawnee.

Song of the Promise of the Buffalo. APN-2, tr. by Alice C. Fletcher

Song to the Trees and Streams. APN-2, tr. by Alice C. Fletcher

Halcyon. Hilda Doolittle.

"I'm not here." MoAmPo

Halcyon Days. Jim Barnes. CDW; VCAP

Halcyon Days. Walt Whitman. OxBA

Half a bar, half a bar. The Village Choir. Unknown. UV

Half a league, half a league. The Charge of the Light Brigade. Tennyson. APAD; BLPA; CABP; CTV; ChAP; EBEvV; EnVR; FHYEP; FaBoBe; FaPoR; HoPM; NAEL-2; NOBVV; NoP-4; OBWP; OxAEP-2; PBMP; PeVV; TFi; UV

Half a lifetime now, I've played my art on the stage. Tune: "Slow Chant." Ma Chih-yüan, Chinese. SuSp, tr. by Sherwin S. S. Fu

Half a loaf, half a loaf. The Charge the the Bread Brigade. Ezra Pound and Noel Stock. UV Fr. The Poems of Alfred Venison, the Poet of Titchfield Street.

Half afraid to break a promise. Michael Hartnett. NOIV Fr. A Farewell to English.

Half an hour north of Grand Central. In Cheever Country. Dana Gioia. GM

Half asleep. Gareth Owen. OTCP

Half asleep on the cold grass. For a Stone Girl at Sanchi. Gary Snyder. BB

Half awake in my Sunday nap. Three Green Windows. Anne Sexton. NYBP

Half-Ballad of Waterval. Rudyard Kipling. PeSAV

Half-bent Man. Richard Eberhart. NYBP

Half Black, Half Blacker. Sterling Plumpp. PoBA

Half-blown Rose, The. Samuel Daniel. Fr. To Delia.

("Look, Delia, How we 'steem the half-blown rose.") NoP-4

Half-Breed. Cherríe Moraga. UnSA

Half-bridge over nothingness. Northhanger Ridge. Charles Wright. HCAP

Half-Built Boat in a Hayfield. Norman MacCaig. FaBoTC

Half-caste. John Agard. NBrP

Half-Caste Girl. Judith Wright. NALW

Half close your eyelids, loosen your hair. He Thinks of Those Who Have Spoken Evil of His Beloved. W. B. Yeats. NoAM

"Half-cracked" to Higginson, living. I Am in Danger—Sir—. Adrienne Rich. HCAP; NALW; NOBA

Half-dead comatose, The. They Do Not Go Gentle. Basil T. Paquet. CDa

Half-door, hall door. Purgatory. W. B. Yeats. CMoP

Half-hidden by trees, the sheer roof of the barn. The Barn. Stephen Spender. CMoP

Half-hidden in a graveyard. The Stranger. Walter De la Mare. OxBTC

Half Holiday. Olive Enoch. BoTP

Half-holiday for the burial. Of course, they punish, A. Black Spring. Innokenty Fiodorovich Annensky, Russian. NNPT, tr. by Robert Lowell

Half in a dream. Kenneth Rexroth. APSN Fr. The Love Poems of Marichiko.

Half in the dim light from the hall. To ———. W. S. Braithwaite. PoBA

Half in the Family, Half Out. Po Chü-i, Chinese. CoBCP, tr. by Burton Watson

Half into the mountains—a mountain monastery. Climbing to a Mountain Monastery. Tu Hsün-ho, Chinese. SuSp, tr. by Edward H. Schafer

Half-measures / can kill. Yevtushenko, Russian. TCRP, tr. by Albert C. Todd

Half-moon hangs on sparse wu-t'ung tree. Tune: "Song of Divination." Su Shih, Chinese. SuSp, tr. by Eugene Eoyang

Half-moon westers low, my love, The. So Sound You Sleep. A. E. Housman. CBLP; LBC

Half my friends are dead. Sea Canes. Derek Walcott. FP; HeIP-4

Half of a clasping of the hands. Hawley Truax. NYBP

Half of his / body hung in. Spirits. Victor Hernandez Cruz. PoBA

Half of Life. Friedrich Hölderlin, German. OBVE, tr. by James Blair Leishman

Half Of Me. Saint Augustine. LBC

Half of my life is gone, and I have let. Mezzo Cammin. Henry Wadsworth Longfellow. APN-1; GSo; NAAL-1; NAAL-3; NCAP; PAR; PoE; TAP

Half of our borders, rivers and mountains were gone. In the Home of the Scholar Wu Su-chiang. Wu Tsao, Chinese. BoWoP; WPOW, tr. by Kenneth Rexroth and Ling Chung

Half of the minnows. J. W. Hackett. HA

Half Past Four, October. Anna Hajnal, Hungarian. BoWoP, tr. by Daniel Hoffman

Half past nine—high time for supper. In Praise of Cocoa, Cupid's Nightcap Stanley J. Sharpless. NBLV; PeLV

Half-past three in the morning! Louise on the Door-Step. Charles MacKay. EBVV

Half-recluse, The. Po Chü-i, Chinese. ChiP, tr. by Arthur Waley

Half remembering, yet not remembering, just waked up from a dream. Song on Being Too Lazy to Get Up. Shao Yung, Chinese. CoBCP, tr. by Burton Watson

Half seated on a mossy crag. The Mountain Maid. Dora Sigerson Shorter. SDW

Half-shut doors through which we heard that music, The. Multitudes Turn in Darkness. Conrad Potter Aiken. PoA

Half Sigh. Unknown. PBA, tr. by Miriam Koshland

Half spirit, the older. The Jest. Austin Clarke. BIrV

Half squatter, half tenant (no rent). Manuelzinho. Elizabeth Bishop. FaBoWP; NYBP

Half the spring has gone by since our parting. Tune: "Pure Serene Music." Li Yü, *Chinese.* SuSp, *tr. by* Daniel Bryant

Half the time they munched the grass, and all the time they lay. Cows. James Reeves. NOxBChV; NTCP; NTP

Half the women are asleep on the floor. Lies and Longing. Linda Gregg. WWSi

Half the year has hot nights, like this. Elegies for the Hot Season. Sandra McPherson. AmPA

Half-way across the racing river. Midstream. D. J. Enright. OxBC

Half-way, for one commandment broken. A. E. Housman. OxBSP

Half-Way Pause, A. D. G. Rossetti. NOBVV

Halfway Street, Sidcup. Fleur Adcock. Spl

Halibut Cove Harvest. Kenneth Leslie. NOBC

Halieutica. William Diaper, *after the Greek of* Oppian.
 "Lamprey, glowing with uncommon fires, The." ECEV; OBVE
 Sex-life of Fish, The. ECEV
  (Eels and Tortoises.) NOEC
 "When pleasing heat, and fragrant blooms inspire." BXAP
 "When they in throngs a safe retirement seek." OBVE

Halieutica. Oppian, *Greek.*
 "Dolphins were Men, (Tradition hands the Tale)." APo, *tr. by* William Diaper
 "Hermit-Fish, unarm'd by Nature left, The." OBCVT, *tr. by* William Diaper
 Loves of the Eel, The. APo, *tr. by* William Diaper
 Loves of the Tortoise, The. APo, *tr. by* William Diaper

Hall by the water where flowers grow dense, A. An Occasional Poem. Ssu-k'ung Shu, *Chinese.* SuSp, *tr. by* Irving Y. Lo

Hall of Ifor Hael, The. Evan Evans, *Welsh.* OBWVE, *tr. by* Gwyn Williams

Hall of Ocean Life. John Hollander. PoA

Hallaig. Sorley MacLean. FaBoTC

Hallaj's corpse was burnt and when the flame. Farid-uddin Attar. *Fr.* The Conference of the Birds. TOF, *tr. by* Afkham Darbandi *and* Dick Davis

Hallelujah, I'm a Bum. *Unknown.* AS
 ("Baker is dead, The.") (LL) GM
 (Hallelujah, Bum Again.) GM
 ("Oh, why don't I work like the other men do?") GM

Hallelujah! kneel and sing / Praises to the heav'nly king. Psalm 148. Bible, *O.T., Hebrew.* OBVE *Fr.* Psalms.

Hallelujah; or, Britain's Second Remembrancer. George Wither.
 Rocking Hymn, A. OxBChV
  (Hymn L: Rocking Hymn, A.)

Hallelujah! Praise the Lord. Edwin Francis Hatfield. AH

Hallelujah. Praise ye the Lord from the heavens. Bible, *O.T. See* Psalm 148.

"Hallelujah!" was the only observation. A. E. Housman. CBNP; PeLV

Hallesches Tor: Communion. Henrikas Nagys, *Lithuanian.* CEEP, *tr. by* Jonas Zdanys

Halley's Comet. Norman Nicholson. NoP-4

Hallo My Fancy. William Cleland. CH; OxBoLi

Hallow days o Yule are come, The. The Wife of Usher's Well. *Unknown.* ESPB

Hallow-Fair. Robert Fergusson. OxBS

Hallow the threshold, crown the posts anew! On the Queen's Return from the Low Countries. William Cartwright. OBEV

Hallowed be the Sabbaoth. Epitaph in St. Olave's, Southwark, on Mr. Munday. *Unknown.* OxBoLi

Hallowed Ground. Thomas Campbell. BLPA

Halloween. Robert Burns. NOBRP

Hallowe'en. Lizelia Augusta Jenkins Moorer. CBWP-3

Halloween, I ride the subway to an early evening class. A Taxi to the Flame. Vickie Karp. WWSi

Hallowe'en mask, A. Clement Hoyt. HA

Hallowe'en 1971. Michael Dennis Browne. AmPA

Hallowe'en Pumpkin, A. Dorothy Aldis. AYFP

Hallowing of Hell, The. Robin Morgan.
 "And blessed be the women who get you through." GLP

Hallucination. Arthur Symons. ADE

Halo. Ralph Nixon Currey. PeSA

Halsted Street Car. Carl Sandburg. NAAL-2

Halt, The. Edward Richard Burton Shanks. NSI

Halted against the shade of a last hill. Spring Offensive. Wilfred Owen. GTBS-P; NSI; PeFWW

Haltersick's Song. John Pickering. NoSic *Fr.* Horestes.

Hamasah. Hittan of Tayyi, *Arabic.*
 His Children. AWP

Hamatreya. Ralph Waldo Emerson. APN-1; NAAL-3; NCAP; PAR

Hambone and the Heart, The. Dame Edith Sitwell. OBMV

Hamburg: the clock hands move upon their star. Galaxies. Alan Gould. NOBAu

Hamburger. August Kleinzahler. PmAP

Hamburger Hill. Michael McClintock. HA *Fr.* Vietnam.

Hame came our goodman. Our Goodman. *Unknown.* ESPB

Hame, Hame, Hame. Allan Cunningham. CH; OBEV

Hamelin Town's in Brunswick. The Pied Piper of Hamelin. Robert Browning. EBNV; FaBoBe; FaBoCh; NOxBChV; OBNV; OBSP; OxBChV; PeLV

Hamilton Greene. Edgar Lee Masters. MoP; NoAM; OxBA *Fr.* Spoon River Anthology.

Hamlen Brook. Richard Wilbur. VCAP; WeW-3

Hamlet. Ciaran Carson. FaBoVe; PNI

Hamlet. Boris Pasternak, *Russian.* AF, *tr. by* Jon Stallworthy *and* Peter France; TCRP, *tr. by* Yakov Hornstein
 ("Buzz subsides. I have come on stage, The.") AF, *tr. by* Jon Stallworthy *and* Peter France
 ("Life is not a stroll across a field.") (LL) AF, *tr. by* Jon Stallworthy *and* Peter France

Hamlet. Boris Pasternak, *Russian.* GI, *tr. by* Nina Kossman

Hamlet. Shakespeare. NAWM-1
 "Angels and ministers of grace defend us!" EBEV; OxAEP-1; OxBSn
  ("Say, why is this? wherefore? what should we do?") (LL) OxBSn
 "As thou'rt a man."
 "Ay, marry, is 't."
 "Ay, so, God be wi' ye! Now I am alone." OxAEP-1
 Frailty, Thy Name is Woman.
  ("O, that this too too sullied flesh would melt.") IMW
 "How all occasions do inform against me." HoPM
 "Look here, upon this picture, and on this." OxAEP-1
 "Mote it is to trouble the mind's eye, A." OxAEP-1
 "My lord, as I was sewing in my closet." OxAEP-1
 "O! my offense is rank, it smells to heaven." OxAEP-1
 Ophelia's Song. EBEV; EBEvV; EnLoPo; NoSic; PoRA; SCGP
  (O's Song: ("How should I your true love know").) GBL
 "So hallow'd and so gracious is the time." OxBSn
 Song: "Tomorrow is saint valentine's day." EnLoPo; NoSic
  (Song: "Tomorrow is Saint Valentine's Day.") EBEvV; NTCP
 To Thine Own Self Be True. ImPo
 "What ceremony else?" EBEV
 "Where wilt thou lead me? Speak; I'll go no further." OxBSn
 "Why, let the strucken deer go weep." NoSic
 "Yet here, Laertes! aboard, aboard, for shame!" EBEvV

Hamlet, *limerick.* Stanley J. Sharpless. BXAP; NBLV; PeLi

Hamlet. Yevgeny Mikhailovich Vinokurov, *Russian.* TCRP, *tr. by* Daniel Weissbort

Hamlet in Russia, A Soliloquy. Boris Pasternak, *Russian.* FaBoPV, *tr. by* Robert Lowell

Hamlet's Soliloquy Imitated. Richard Jago. BXAP

Hammer and Anvil. Samuel Valentine Cole. PoLF

Hammer keeps a-ring-in' on somebody's coffin, The. Way Over in the New Buryin' Groun'. *Unknown.* AS

Hammer Man. *Unknown.* AS

Hammer, Ring. *Unknown.* AmFP

Hammer-Song. *Unknown.* FaBoVe

Hammer, The, / struck my nail. Almanac. May Swenson. NYBP

Hammers, The. Ralph Hodgson. MoBrPo; NOBE; OxBTC

Hammers pound there above. Along Galeana Street. Octavio Paz, *Spanish.* VCWP, *tr. by* Elizabeth Bishop

Hammerstroke and. The Murdered Girl Is Found on a Bridge. Jane Hayman. NYBP

Hammock was a blue cocoon, The. A Dream of Dying. Leslie Monsour. FFC

Hamnavoe Market. George Mackay Brown. FaBoTC

Hampstead Highgate Finchley Hendon Muswell hill: rage loud. William Blake. NOBRP *Fr.* Jerusalem; The Emanation of the Giant Albion.

Hampton Court. Alexander Pope. OBSV *Fr.* The Rape of the Lock[, an Heroi-Comical Poem]. FHYEP; HAP; ImPo; OAEL-1; OBNV; PeLV; PoEL-3

Hamtramck: The Polish Women. Toi Derricotte. InPS-3

Han court honors clever eunuchs, The. Inscription on a Tree atop mount Sacrifice (Ssu Shan) and Sent to Censor Ch'iao. Ch'en Tzu-ang, *Chinese.* SuSp, *tr. by* Geoffrey R. Waters

Han-shan. *Unknown, Chinese.* CoBCP, *tr.* by Burton Watson

Ha'nacker Mill. Hilaire Belloc. FaPoR; MoBrPo; OxBTC; RB

Hand, The. Brian Fawcett. NOBC

Hand, The. Howard Moss. TAP

Hand, The. Phạm Hổ, *Vietnamese.* AVP, *tr.* by Huỳnh Sanh Thông

Hand. Edouard Roditi. SPE

Hand, The. Ronald Stuart Thomas. NOCV; OxBC

Hand a shade of moonlight on the pillow, The. Non Ti Fidar. Louis Zukofsky. VGW

Hand and Foot, The [*or* Hand and the Foot, The]. Jones Very. APN-1; OxBA; PAR; PoEL-4; TAP

Hand appeared out of the earth, A. The Dream of the Quartz Pebble. Vasco [*or* Vasko] Popa. PoSu, *tr.* by Anne Pennington *Fr.* The Quartz Pebble.

Hand burns resinous in the evening sky, The. Egyptian Register. "Ern Malley." BMAP

Hand-clapping Rhyme. *Unknown.* NTCP

Hand Further, The. Clark Coolidge. PmAP

Hand Games. Marge Piercy. CrSp

Hand goes up, The. Country Greeting. Frank Steele. Poetsp

Hand in Hand; a Song. Shen Yüeh, *Chinese.* SuSp, *tr.* by Richard B. Mather

Hand in hand they dance in a row. The Clothes-Line. Charlotte Druitt Cole. BoTP

Hand in the breast pocket, The. (LL) Marriage. Marianne Moore. ColAP; NALW; NOBA

Hand Me Down Blues. Calvin Forbes. GT

Hand-Mirror, A. Walt Whitman. NAAL-1; NAAL-3; OxBA; PoPoPo

Hand Mirror. Daisy Zamora, *Spanish.* LoL, *tr.* by Barbara Paschke

Hand moves, andn the fire's whirling takes different shapes, A. Singing Image of Fire. Kukai, *Japanese.* EnlH, *tr.* by Stephen Mitchell

Hand of Art here torpid lies, The. An Epitaph on William Hogarth. Samuel Johnson. EBEV; OxAEP-1

Hand of peace you sent from Israel, The. For My Mother. Philip Schultz. FiLi; NAmP90

Hand of Solo, A. Thomas Kinsella. CIP-2; NOIV

Hand over hungry hand. (LL) Climbing. Lucille Clifton. GT; LoL

Hand reaches for the cocktail, it's in darkness, The. Glass House. Diane Ward. PmAP

Hand reaches up, A. Ruth Latta. HA

Hand-Rolled Cigarettes. Yevtushenko, *Russian.* VCWP, *tr.* by Stanley Kunitz

Hand-Shadows. Jarold Ramsey. NIP-4

Hand springs out of the earth, A. Vasco [*or* Vasko] Popa. *See* The Dream of the Quartz Pebble.

Hand swinging the loops of paint—splashes—drips. Ode to Jackson Pollock. Michael McClure. PmAP

Hand tells the bowstring, The. Japanese Archery. Aleksander Wat, *Polish.* TOF, *tr.* by Richard Lourie

Hand that made us is divine, The, *par.* by Joseph Addison. Bible, *O.T. See* Psalm 19.

Hand that made us is Divine, The. (LL) Ode: "The Spacious firmament on high." Joseph Addison. BLPA; ChIV-1; ECEV; FaBoBe; FaPoR; NOCV; NOEC; PoEL-3; TOF

Hand That Rocks the Cradle Is the Hand That Rules the World, The. William Ross Wallace. PoLF

"Hand that rocks the cradle, The"—but there is no such hand. The Modern Baby. William Croswell Doane. BLPA

Hand that rounded Peter's dome, The. Ralph Waldo Emerson. *Fr.* The Problem. APN-1; AWP; AmPP; MeMAP; NAAL-1; NAAL-3; NOBA; OxBA; PAR; TAP

Hand that signed the paper felled a city, The. Dylan Thomas. MoBrPo; MoP; NOBE; NoAM; NoP-4; OBWP; OxBoV; PBMP; RB

Hand-tinted, creamy olive skin. Taking It Back. Dixie Salazar. UnSA

Hand trembling towards hand; the amazing lights. Sonnet Reversed. Rupert Brooke. NOBL; PeLV

Hand triumphant to disaster. (LL) The Parable of the Blind. William Carlos Williams. LCAP-2; SAmP

Handbag. Ruth Fainlight. OPOU

Handbell Choir, The. Jane Flanders. PBCAP

Handbook of Versification. Gilbert Sorrentino. PoA

Handcart Song, The. *Unknown.* AmFP

Handful of Dust, A. James Oppenheim. TrJP

Handful of Pebbles, Mouthful of Stones. Pegatha Hughes. LoHo

Handful of red sand, from the hot clime, A. Sand of the Desert in an Hour-Glass. Henry Wadsworth Longfellow. NCAP

Handfuls of Wind. Yekhi'el [*or* Yehiel] Mar, *Hebrew.* MHP, *tr.* by Ruth Finer Mintz

Handing me the bread / dipped in the dish. Judas' Reproach. Nina Kossman. GI

Handing out anti-war leaflets at United Aircraft. Home Front. Bill Tremblay. CDa

Handiwork of God, The. *Unknown.* CTV

Handle for the Flutist, A. Odia Ofeimun. HBAPE

Handling Sin. Robert Mannyng.
Dancers of Colbek, The. PoE

Handloom, The. Judith Rodriguez. FaBoWP

Handmaid of Religion, The. Edgell Rickword. OBSV

Hands. Bernard Dadié, *French.* NegPo, *tr.* by Ellen Conroy Kennedy

Hands. Donald Finkel. CoAP

Hands, The. Tony Harrison. FaBoTw

Hands. Edvard Kocbek, *Slovene.* PoSu, *tr.* by Michael Scammell *and* Veno Taufer

Hands, The. Denise Levertov. NeAP; PoM

Hands. Namsu Park, *Korean.* CKP, *tr.* by Jaihiun Kim

Hands. Victor Serge, *Russian.* AF, *tr.* by James Brook

Hands are being plated, The; they'll be brass. Clock without Hands. John Frederick Nims. PoA

Hands clenched under my shawl. "Anna Akhmatova," *Russian.* PBWP, *tr.* by Robert Tracy

Hands explore tentatively, The. The Feel of Hands. Thom Gunn. EP

Hands folded to construct a church and steeple. Unholy Sonnets. Mark Jarman. BAP-94

Hands full of sun are in spring's longing for you. David Rokeah, *Hebrew.* MHP, *tr.* by Ruth Finer Mintz

Hands gripped hard on the desert, The. (LL) At the Bomb Testing Site. William Stafford. CoAP; LiTM; NIP-4; NoAM; OBWP; Poetr; RB

Hands must touch and handle many things, The. The New Man. Jones Very. APN-1; NAAL-3

Hands of God, The. D. H. Lawrence. ChIV-2

Hands of Mary Joe, The. Mary TallMountain. LoL

Hands picking a rose. Tanka. Tsukamoto Kunio, *Japanese.* MJT, *tr.* by Makoto Ueda

Hands that eased my mother's labor drew, The. Rhyme for the Child as a Wet Dog. Judith Johnson Sherwin. TAP

Hands were yours, the arms were yours, The. The Empty Body. Mark Strand. UnPo *Fr.* Elegy for My Father. HCAP; LCAP-2

Hands, wings, are found. (LL) Icarus. Stephen Spender. MoBrPo; MoP; UV

Hand's / writing the, A. Out of the Identical. Gustaf Sobin. PmAP

HANDSAWWWWWWWWWWWWWWWWW. Richard Lebovitz. KaS

Handsome and self-absorbed young man, The. True Love at Last. D. H. Lawrence. PFE

Handsome friend, charming and kind. Beatrice, Countess de Die, *Provençal.* WPOW, *tr.* by Meg Bogin

Handsome Heart, The. Gerard Manley Hopkins. FaBoVe

Handsome men wearing red ties walk past my window. Love. Grace Paley. IFJA

Handsome one, white-black checkered son of the water. The Muscovy Drake. E. A. S. Lesoro, *Sotho.* PeSA, *tr.* by Dan Kunene *and* Jack Cope

Handsome young airman lay dying, A. The Dying Airman. *Unknown.* AS; OxBoLi; PeLV; RB

Handsome young monk in a wood, A. Limerick. *Unknown.* PeLi

Handsome youth with a golden whip, A. Tune: "Mountain Hawthorns." Yen Chi-tao, *Chinese.* SuSp, *tr.* by James J. Y. Liu

Handwriting on the Wall, The. Knowles Shaw. BLPA

Handwriting on the Wall. *Unknown.* AmFP

Handy dandy. *Unknown.* OxNR

Handy Mole who plied no shovel, A. Christina Rossetti. VWP

Handy Pandy, Jack-a-Dandy. Mother Goose. ReMoGo

Hang at my hand as I write now. Verses for a First Birthday. George Barker. MoBrPo

Hang flags in the airs of July. John Heath-Stubbs. *Fr.* Two Wedding Songs. NTP

Hang-Glider's Daughter, The. Marilyn Hacker. MoLi

HANG him, base gull! I'll stab him, by the Lord. Boreas. Samuel Rowlands. NoSic

Hang it all, Robert Browning. Canto 2. Ezra Pound. AmPP; HAP; MeMAP; MoAmPo; NOBA; NoAM; OxBA; PoA *Fr.* Cantos.

Hang Me, O Hang Me, and I'll Be Dead and Gone. *Unknown.* AmFP

Hang new heavens with new birds, all is renewed. (LL) Shiva. Robinson Jeffers. NOBA; NoAM; Son

Hang out our banners on the outward walls. Shakespeare. *See* To-morrow, and to-morrow, and to-morrow.

Hang Out the Flag. James Sterling Tippett. CA

Hang sorrow, cast away care. Song. *Unknown.* NOSC

Hang that day with black, that night, sinister, moonless. Hegesippus, *Greek.* GrAn, *tr. by* Edwin Morgan

Hang up Hooks, and shears [*or* Sheers] to scare. Another Charme for Stables. Robert Herrick. BeJo

Hang Up the Baby's Stocking! *Unknown.* OBCP

Hang up those dull, and envious fools. Another. In Defense of Their Inconstancy [*or* Inconstancie]. A Song. Ben Jonson. BeJo; NAEL-1; SeCP

Hanged man, please grow wild and luminous. To Her Dead Mate: Montana, 1966. Elizabeth Libbey. AmPA

Hanging Burley. Jim Wayne Miller. MT

Hanging Fire. Audre Lorde. NIP-4; NMM-2; NoAM; NoP-4; PoPoPo; Poetr; TRP; UnSA

("Momma's in the bedroom / with the door closed.") (LL) UnSA

Hanging from the beam. The Portent. Herman Melville. APAD; APN-2; AmPP; CBCWP; ColAP; InPK-6; NAAL-1; NAAL-3; NCAP; NOBA; NoP-4; OBWP; OxBA; PAR; PoE; PoEL-5; TAP

Hanging from the branches of a green / willow tree. Lady Ise, *Japanese.* BoWoP, *tr. by* Willis Barnstone

Hanging Man, The. Sylvia Plath. HCAP; VCAP

Hanging of Sam Archer, The. *Unknown.* AmFP

Hanging on the wall, an iron face watches me. The Mask. Irma McClaurin. BlSi

Hanging on the walls. Gallery of My Heart. King D. Kuka. VoR

Hanging out of the train, I. Autumn in Sigulda. Andrey Andreievich Voznesensky, *Russian.* TCRP, *tr. by* W. H. Auden

Hanging Out the Linen Clothes. *Unknown.* AS

Hanging / out under the bridge. Getting Across. Carter Revard. VoR

Hanging raindrops, The. Jakuren, *Japanese.* OHPJ, *tr. by* Kenneth Rexroth

Hanging scroll in a swirl of colors, lacking line, A. Longing. "Shu Ting," *Chinese.* ChiPo, *tr. by* Helen F. Siu *and* Zelda Stern

Hanging, Zomba Central Prison, A. Frank Mkalawile Chipasula. PeSAV

Hangman. Ai. AmPA

Hangman / what will you do with my arms? Gunnar Ekelof, *Swedish.* PFTM, *tr. by* Muriel Rukeyser *and* Leif Sjoberg

Hangman's Love Song, The. Stanley Moss. VGW

Hangman's Room, The. János Pilinszky, *Hungarian.* PoSu, *tr. by* Peter Jay

Hangover Mass. X. J. Kennedy. DiPo

Hangs and cannot wake itself. (LL) Laser. A. R. Ammons. NAAL-2; NOBA; NoAM

Hangs on and howls, biting at air. (LL) The Vacuum. Howard Nemerov. NIP-4; RB

Hangs. / whipped / blood. Biography. Imamu Amiri Baraka. TAP

Hank Mobley's. Cornelius Eady. SeSe

Hannah. Judy Grahn. NMM-2 *Fr.* Helen you Always Were / The Factory.

Hannah, A Plaintive Tale. Robert Southey. Ro *Fr.* Monthly Magazine, 4 287.

Hannah Bantry. *Unknown.* OxNR

Hannah's Song of Thanksgiving. Bible, *O.T.* AWP *Fr.* First Samuel. (Song of Hannah, The.) TrCP, *ad. by* Michael Drayton

Hannah's Thanksgiving. Bible, *O.T.* BoWoP *Fr.* First Samuel.

Hannibal. Eugen Jebeleanu, *Romanian.* CEEP, *tr. by* Donald Eulert *and* Stefan Avadanei

Hannibal ("Produce the urn that Hannibal contains"). Juvenal. OBVE, *tr. by* William Gifford *Fr.* Satires.

Hannibal ("Put Hannibal i' th' scale"). Juvenal. OBVE, *tr. by* Henry Vaughan *Fr.* Satires.

Hannibal ("Throw Hannibal on the scales, how many pounds"). Juvenal. OBVE, *tr. by* Robert Lowell *Fr.* Satires.

Hans Breitmann as a Politician. Charles Godfrey Leland. ("There's a liddle fact of hishdory vitch few hafe oondershtand." APN-2

Hans Breitmann's Party [*or* Barty]. Charles Godfrey Leland. NOBL; OBAL; OBCoV

Hans Carvel, Impotent and Old. Matthew Prior. PeLV

Hansel and Gretel. Anne Sexton. InPS-3

Hansel, Gretel and Ruby Redlips. Anita Endrezze-Danielson. HATNAP

Hap. Thomas Hardy. AWP; CABP; CMoP; EBVV; EnVR; GSo; ImPo; MoBrPo; NAEL-2; NoAM; NoP-4; OAEL-2; PBMP; PFE; Poetr; Son

Hapless youth, whom fates averse had drove, A. The Fable of the Young Man and His Cat. Christopher Pitt. ECEV

Happen you come on your own. Seven Sides and Seven Syllables. Edouard J. Maunick, *French.* NegPo; VCWP, *tr. by* Carolyn Kizer

Happening at Sordid Creek. Peter Porter. NoAM

Happening to pass a Roman Catholic church. A Moment of Eschatological Doubt. Stanley J. Sharpless. PeLV

Happie is he, that from all Businesse cleere. Horace. *See* The Praises of a Country Life.

Happier, I would surely be. The Unfortunate Male. Kalonymos ben Kalonymos. *Fr.* The Touchstone. TrJP, *tr. by* J. Chotzner

Happiest day—the happiest hour, The. Edgar Allan Poe. AmPP; ImPo; MeMAP; OxBA

Happiest life consists in ignorance, The. Sophocles. IMW *Fr.* Ajax.

Happiest Pair, The. George Lyttelton. LBC

Happiness. William Dickey. Poetsp

Happiness. Stephen Dunn. PiM

Happiness. A. A. Milne. NOxBChV

Happiness. Carl Sandburg. OxBA

Happiness. Ruth Stone. NAmP90

Happiness amidst Troubles. Immanuel di Roma, *Italian.* TrJP, *tr. by* J. Chotzner

Happiness doesn't have any songs. Pain. Edith Södergran, *Swedish.* WPOW, *tr. by* Samuel Charters

Happiness, faintly as the excrement. Passion Shaved beneath the Grain-Silo. Peter Finch. NBrP

Happiness is like a crystal. Priscilla Leonard. BLPA; PoToHe

Happiness Is the Art of Being Broken. Bruce Dawe. NoAM

Happiness Makes Up in Height for What It Lacks in Length. Robert Frost. MoAmPo; SoSe-8

Happiness of 6 A.M. Harvey Shapiro. NYBP

Happy about Being Old. Yüan Mei, *Chinese.* CoBLCP, *tr. by* Jonathan Chaves

Happy all those who have in him their stay, *par. by* Milton. Bible, *O.T. See* Psalm 2.

Happy Arabia. Tom Matthews. PNI

Happy are men who yet before they are killed. Insensibility. Wilfred Owen. CMoP; FaBoTw; InPS-3; LiTM; NoP-4; OBWP; OxAEP-2; OxBTC; PeFWW; PoWW

Happy are they and charmed in life. Memorial on the Slain at Chickamauga. Herman Melville. CBCWP

Happy are those of simple ways who still bless the light. Song Yet Song. Amir Gilbo'a, *Hebrew.* MHP, *tr. by* Ruth Finer Mintz

Happy are you, whom Quantock overlooks. William Diaper. NOEC; OBSV *Fr.* Brent; a Poem to Thomas Palmer Esq.

Happy art thou, whom God does bless. The Garden. Abraham Cowley. OBGa *Fr.* The Garden.

Happy band on the hill slope, A. The Battle of Waun Gaseg. Llywelyn ab y Moel, *Welsh.* OBWVE, *tr. by* H. Idris Bell

Happy Birthday. Frank Bidart. HCAP; VCAP

Happy birthday, a gray day like the first one—. Alicia Ostriker. CrSp

Happy boy,—at Drury's, A. (LL) School and Schoolfellows. Winthrop Mackworth Praed. FP; OxAEP-2

Happy bridegroom, Hesper brings. Sappho. OBCVT, *tr. by* A. E. Housman *Fr.* Epithalamium.

Happy bridegroom! / Now your wedding has come true. Bridal Songs. Sappho, *Greek.* GrIP, *tr. by* Suzy Q. Groden

Happy Cat, The. Randall Jarrell. PC

Happy Child, A. Kate Greenaway. BoTP

Happy choristers of air. A Pastoral[l] Hymn[e]. John Hall. MeLP

"Happy Christmas to all, and to all a good night!" (LL) A Visit from St Nicholas. Clement Clarke Moore. APN-1; AiP; BLPA; CTV; ChAP; FaBoBe; NTCP; OBAL; OBCA; OBCP; OxBChV; PChr; PWR; TFi

Happy Countryman, The. Nicholas Breton. *See* The Merry Country Lad.

Happy Day Will Soon Appear, The. *Unknown.* AH

Happy Easter, my Lady. Sister Juana Inés de la Cruz. CPO

Happy Ending. Fleur Adcock. LW

Happy genius of my household?, The. (LL) Danse Russe. William Carlos Williams. CMoP; InPS-3; NOBA; NoP-4; PoE; Poetr; RaBo; SAGP; SAmP; TAP

Happy he whose eyes have view'd. Boethius. OBVE, *tr. by* Samuel Johnson *Fr.* Consolation of Philosophy, The ("De Consolacione Philosophie").

Happy Heart, The. Thomas Dekker *and others.* GTBS-P; RB; SCGP *Fr.* The Pleasant Comedy of Patient Grissell [*or* Grissel *or* Grissill]. (Sweet Content.) APAD; CH; OBEV ("Then hey nonny nonny, hey nonny nonny!") (LL) APAD

Happy Heart, A. Josephine D. Henderson Heard. CBWP-4

Happy insect, what can be. The Grasshopper. Abraham Cowley, *after the Greek of* Anacreon. AWP; BeJo; NOSC; OAEL-1; OBCVT; OBVE; OxAEP-1

Happy Insensibility. Keats. GTBS-P

Happy is England! I could be content. Keats. OxAEP-2

Happy [*or* Happie] is he, that from all business clear. The Praises of a Country Life. Horace, *Latin.* OBVE; SeCP, *tr. by* Ben Jonson *Fr.* Epodes.

Happy is he, that with fix'd Eyes. Boethius. OBCVT, *tr. by* Henry Vaughan *Fr.* Some Odes of the Excellent and Knowing Severinus, Englished: Metrum 12. Lib. 3.

Happy Is the Man. Bible, *O.T.* TrJP *Fr.* Proverbs.

Happy Is the Man. Bible, *O.T.* *See* Psalm 1.

Happy is the man whom Thou hast set apart. Psalm. "Yehoash," *Yiddish.* TrJP, *tr. by* Isidore Goldstick

Happy Isle. Edmund Spenser. *Fr.* Wood Of Error. AEP

Happy Life, A, Book 10, Epigram 47; *see also* "Things that make the happier life, are these, The," *by* Ben Jonson. Martial, *Latin.* FMP; OBVE, *tr. by* Sir Richard Fanshawe

("*Death* neither *wish,* nor *feare* to *see.*") (LL) OBCVT, *tr. by* Sir Richard Fanshawe

(Happy Life out of Martiall, A.) OBCVT, *tr. by* Sir Richard Fanshawe

("Things that makes a life to please, The.") OBCVT, *tr. by* Sir Richard Fanshawe

Happy Life, The. Martial, *Latin.* NAEL-1; NOBE; NoSic; OBVE; SiPS

(Means to Attain the Happy Life, The.) FaBoEE; OBEV

Happy Life, The. William Thompson. ECEV

Happy Life, A. Mildmay Fane, 2d Earl of Westmorland. BeJo

(Happy Life (Martial X. xlvii), A.) NOSC

Happy Life of a Country Parson, The, *in imitation of* Swift. Alexander Pope. BXAP; UV

Happy Life out of Martiall, A. Martial. *See* A Happy Life.

Happy lover who has come, A. Tennyson. EBVVPR; EnVR *Fr.* In Memoriam A. H. H.

Happy Man, A. Carphyllides, *Greek.* AWP, *tr. by* E. A. Robinson. *Fr.* Variations of Greek Themes.

Happy Mathematician, The. Anna Wickham. WPN

Happy moments tell me, pray. The Birth of Time. Josephine D. Henderson Heard. CBWP-4

Happy New Year, A. W. H. Auden. OBSV

Happy New Year, A. (LL) Christmas Carol: "God bless the master of this house." *Unknown.* BoTP

Happy New Year, Anyway. Joanna Cole. NTCP

Happy Nightingale, The. *Unknown.* OxBChV

Happy one, who is almost / an idiot, The. Paul Klee, *German.* PFTM, *tr. by* Anselm Hollo

Happy Pair, The. Sir Charles Sedley.
Marriage and Money. OBSV

Happy Pair, A. Priscilla Jane Thompson. CBWP-2

Happy people die whole, they are all dissolved in a moment, they have had what they wanted. Post Mortem. Robinson Jeffers. MoAmPo

Happy Returns! the children say. Grannie's Birthday. Eliza Ogilvy. VWP

Happy, Saviour, Would I Be. Edwin H. Nevin. AH

Happy shall he be, that taketh and dasheth thy little ones against the stone. (LL) Psalm 137. Bible, *O.T.* AWP; NAWM-1; OAEL-1; TrJP

Happy Sheep, The. Wilfrid Thorley. CTV

Happy, so she lived. (LL) Air: "The Love of a Woman." Robert Creeley. VCAP; VGW

Happy Swain, The. Ambrose Philips. EnLoPo

Happy that first white age! when wee. Lib. 2. Metrum 5. Boethius, *Latin.* NOSC; OBCVT; OBVE, *tr. by* Henry Vaughan *Fr.* Consolation of Philosophy, The ("De Consolacione Philosophie").

Happy the dead! Consolation in War. Lewis Mumford. NYBP

Happy, The Leper's Bride. Tennyson. CBLP

Happy the man, and happy he alone. Dryden. APAD

Happy the man, who free as air. The Widower. Royall Tyler. OBAL

Happy the Man, who his whole time doth bound. The Old Man of Verona. Claudian, *Latin.* AWP; OBCVT; OBVE, *tr. by* Abraham Cowley

Happy the man who in his pot contains. The Suet Dumpling. *Unknown.* BXAP

Happy the man who is thirsty. Epithalamion/Wedding Dawn. Michael Dennis Browne. CMAP

Happy the man who, safe on shore. The Hurricane. Philip Freneau. TAP

Happy the man, who, void of cares and strife. John Phillips. NOEC *Fr.* The Splendid Shilling. BXAP; OAEL-1

Happy the man whose wish and care. Ode on Solitude. Alexander Pope. AWP; EBEvV; FHYEP; GEA; GTBS-P; HeIP-4; ImPo; NAEL-1; NOSC; PBMP; PoRA; PoToHe; SCGP

Happy the nations of the moral North! Donna Julia. Byron. PoEL-4 *Fr.* Canto the First. NAEL-2; OAEL-2; PoE *Fr.* Don Juan.

Happy the savage of those early times. European Crimes. Charles Churchill. *Fr.* Gotham. NOEC

Happy the wild birds that can soar. Unfair to Men. *Unknown, Welsh.* OBWVE, *tr. by* Gwyn Jones

Happy the year, the month, that finds alive. To William Wordsworth on His Seventy-Fifth Birthday. Hartley Coleridge. EPCY

Happy those early days [*or* dayes]! when I. The Retreat[e]. Henry Vaughan. AWP; CABP; ClHu; ESCV; FMP; FSCP; GTBS-P; GeHe; HAP; ImPo; InPK-6; InPS-3; MeLP; NAEL-1; NIP-4; NOBE; NOCV;

NOSC; NoP-4; OAEL-1; OBEV; OBWVE; PBRV; PeECV; PoE; PoEL-2; PoRA; SCGP; SeCP; TFi; TOF

Happy Thought. Robert Louis Stevenson. BoTP; CTV; FaBoBe; OxBChV; PWR; Spl

("World is so full of a number of, The.") CTV

Happy, too happy was the world. Boethius, *Latin.* MLL, *tr. by* Helen Waddell *Fr.* Consolation of Philosophy, The ("De Consolacione Philosophie").

Happy Too Much. Boethius. CTC, *tr. by* Queen of England Elizabeth I *Fr.* Consolation of Philosophy, The ("De Consolacione Philosophie").

Happy View, A. C. Day Lewis. CMoP

Happy Warrior, The. Sir Herbert Read. NSI; PeFWW

Happy were he could finish forth his fare. Robert Devereux, 2d Earl of Essex. NoSic; OxBSP

Happy who like Ulysses, or that lord. Heureux Qui, comme Ulysse, A Fait un Beau Voyage. Joachim Du Bellay, *French.* AWP, *tr. by* G. K. Chesterton

Happy Workhouse and the Good Effects of Industry, The. John Dyer. NOEC *Fr.* The Fleece.

Happy ye leaves when as those lilly hands. Edmund Spenser. *See* Sonnet 1: "Happy ye leaves! whenas those lilly hands."

Happy ye leaves! when as those lily hands. Sonnet 1. Edmund Spenser. EBEV; GSo; NAEL-1; OAEL-1; PoE; Son *Fr.* Amoretti. AAS

Happy youth! that shalt possess[e]. To My Cousin (C.R.) Marrying My Lady (A.) Thomas Carew. SeCP

Happy ys he that may obtaine her love. (LL) From Tuscan came my lady's worthy race. Henry Howard, Earl of Surrey. AAS; SiPS

Happyer those times were, when the Flaxen clew. William Browne. PBRV *Fr.* Britannia's Pastorals Book 2.

Happy's the man whose pleasant labours with the lark. The Ploughman, in Imitation of Milton. Samuel Jones. NOEC

Har cume Christopher Columbus cumming ober t' waves. Christopher. Diane Glancy. PUP-18

Harangue on the Death of Hayyim Nahman Bialik. César Tiempo, *Spanish.* TrJP, *tr. by* Donald Devenish Walsh

Harbach 1944. János Pilinszky, *Hungarian.* AF; PoSu; HP, *tr. by* Ted Hughes *and* Janos Csokits

Harbingers are come. See, see their mark, The. The Forerunners. George Herbert. ESCV; FSCP; GeHe; NAEL-1; NoP-4; PBRV; TOF

Harbor, The. William Ellery Channing. APN-1

Harbor. Henrikas Radauskas, *Lithuanian.* CEEP, *tr. by* Jonas Zdanys

Harbor, The. Carl Sandburg. ColAP; TAP

Harbor Dawn, The. Hart Crane. AmPP; CMoP; LiTM; MoAmPo; NOBA; NoAM; OxBA *Fr.* Powhatan's Daughter. *Fr.* The Bridge. NAAL-2

Harbor Lights. Mark Doty. WWSi

Harbour. Edward Kamau Brathwaite. PBCV

Harbour, The. Winifred M. Letts. TIRV

Harbour Bridge, The. Thomas Hardy. NoAM

Harbour of Fowey, The. Sir Arthur Thomas Quiller-Couch. OBCoV

Harbour roars out, The. Creide's Lament for Cael. *Unknown.* NOIV

Hard as hurdle arms, with a broth of goldish flue. Harry Ploughman. Gerard Manley Hopkins. EnVR; FaBoMo

Hard brown bug, maybe a beetle, A. He Faces the Second Winter. Philip Levine. PoA *Fr.* Sierra Kid.

Hard, but you can polish it. Stone. Donald Justice. CRP *Fr.* Things.

Hard by the lilied Nile I saw. A Crocodile. Thomas Lovell Beddoes. APo; NOBVV; RB *Fr.* The Last Man.

Hard by the tall elms and a wooded hill. The Old Rustic Mill. George Sands Johnson. PWR

Hard captains of industry, The. Still Century. Tom Paulin. BiHa

Hard cold fire of the northerner, The. Belfast. Louis MacNeice. PeECV

Hard Country. Philip Booth. CoAP

Hard Daddy. Langston Hughes. MoLi; NAAAL

Hard energy, like the stars. (LL) My Sad Captains. Thom Gunn. CMoP; FaBoMo; LiTM; NAEL-2; NoAM; NoP-4; PoPoPo

Hard heart of a child, The. (LL) Beauty. Elinor Wylie. NAAL-2; OxBA

Hard Heart of Mine. Henry Alline. AH

Hard is my fate, thus to want bread. Between an Unemployed Artist and His Wife. *Unknown.* NOEC

Hard is the doubt, and difficult to deeme. Edmund Spenser. OAEL-1 *Fr.* Wood Of Error. AEP

Hard is the stone, but harder still. The Image-Maker. Oliver St. John Gogarty. OBEV; OBMV; PoRA

Hard it is, very hard. The Choice of the Cross. Dorothy Leigh Sayers. TrCP *Fr.* The Devil to Pay.

Hard Journey, A. Yes. Hayden Carruth. VGW

Hard knowledge to come by. The Music of the Spheres. Marvin Bell. PoA

Hard life of the young, The. (LL) Album. Josephine Miles. ColAP

Hard Listener, The. William Carlos Williams. OxBSP

Hard Lovers, The. George Dillon. PoA

Hard Road Blues. *Unknown.* FaBoVe

Hard Rock Returns to Prison from the Hospital for the Criminal Insane. Etheridge Knight. CoAmPo; InPS-3; MoP; NAAAL; NIP-4; NNaP; PBCAP; SAGP; TAP; TRP; UnPo

("Across our backs.") (LL) GT

("Had cut deep bloody grooves / Across our backs.") (LL) AF

Hard sand breaks, The. Hermes of the Ways. Hilda Doolittle. WPE

Hard shape to describe—not circular, not square, A. A Playful Poem on a Chicken Egg. Hsieh Chin, *Chinese.* CoBLCP, *tr. by* Jonathan Chaves

Hard stones! Hard stones! The Convict Song. Alfred Cruickshank. PBCV

Hard Structure of the World, The. Richard Eberhart. NoAM

Hard Times. John Ashbery. NoAM

Hard Times. *Unknown.* AmFP

Hard Times A' Coming. Nayo-Barbara Watkins. BkSV

Hard times, bad year, and a family dispossessed. On a Moonlit Night, Sent to my Brothers and Sisters. Po Chü-i, *Chinese.* SuSp, *tr. by* Irving Lo

Hard to Bear. Tudor Jenks. OBCA

Hard to imagine two men more unlike, the one. Hopkins and Whitman. Lynne McMahon. PuP-15

Hard to pronounce and play, the OBOE. Oboe. Laurence McKinney. NBLV

Hard to remember how the water went. Loch Sionascaig. Norman MacCaig. FaBoTC

Hard to say what the natural numbers are. Northwestern Mathematics. Tony Esolen. BAP-94

Hard water and square wheels. Written While Riding the Long Island Rail Road. May Swenson. GM

Hard-working Miner, The ("Hard-working miners, The"). *Unknown.* AmFP

Hard-working Miner, The. *Unknown.* AmFP

Hard-working miners, The. The Hard-working Miner. *Unknown.* AmFP

Harden now thy tyred hart, with more than flinty rage. Catullus. *See* Carmen 8 ("Break off / fallen Catullus").

Hardened in a leaf? (LL) Sea Rose. Hilda Doolittle. FaBoMo; HeIP-4; NoAM; NoP-4; OxWW; TRP

Hardening of the World, and the First Settlement of Men, The. *Unknown, Zuni.*

"That the earth be made safer for men, and more stable." APN-2, *tr. by* Frank Hamilton Cushing

Harder lesson, to learn continence, A. Cymochles and Phaedria. Edmund Spenser. *Fr.* Wood Of Error. AEP

Harder time is coming, A. The Respite. Ingeborg Bachmann, *German.* WPOW, *tr. by* Michael Hamburger

Hardest knife ill used doth lose his edge, The. (LL) Sonnet 95. Shakespeare. HeIP-4; SCGP

Hardest work I ever did, The. Bile Them Cabbage Down. *Unknown.* AmFP

Hardly a ghost left to talk with. The slavs moved on. The River Now. Richard Hugo. VCAP

Hardly a Man Is Now Alive. Ring Lardner. OBAL

Hardly a shot from the gate we stormed. Badminton. Sir Alfred Comyn Lyall. PeVV *Fr.* Studies at Delhi, 1876.

Hardly spring, with ice. Chiyojo, *Japanese.* BoWoP, *tr. by* David Ray

Hardnes[s] of her h[e]art[e] and truth of mine [*or* myne]. Sir John Davies. *Fr.* The Gulling[e] Sonnets. Son

Hardness Scale, The. Joyce Peseroff. TRP

Hardon ("Get One Today"). Ian Wedde. PeNZ

Hardship of Accounting, The. Robert Frost. FaBoCh; OBAL *Fr.* Ten Mills.

Hardweed Path Going. A. R. Ammons. HCAP; UnPo; VGW

Hardwood sheathing, A. The Great Fetishes. Blaise Cendrars, *French.* PFTM, *tr. by* Ron Padgett

Hardy Garden, The. Edna St. Vincent Millay. GaP

Hardy Perennial. Richard Eberhart. AiP

Hare, A. Walter De la Mare. EBEV

Hare-hunting. William Somervile. NOEC *Fr.* The Chase.

Hare we had run over, The. Interruption to a Journey. Norman MacCaig. RB

Harebell and Pansy. Laurence Binyon. CABP

Hares, The. Susan Miles. LW

Hares at Play. John Clare. NTP; RB

Hares on the Mountain. *Unknown.* PeLV

Hares on their forms at dusk were not so still. "Robin Hyde." PeNZ *Fr.* The Houses.

Hari helps his people. Mirabai, *Hindi.* BoWoP, *tr. by* Willis Barnstone *and* Usha Nilsson

Hari, look at me a while. Mirabai, *Hindi.* BoWoP, *tr. by* Willis Barnstone *and* Usha Nilsson

Hark! A Sacrifice. Robert Davenport. NOSC

Hark. Song: "Hark! hark! the lark at heaven's gate sings." Shakespeare. AWP; BoTP; CH; EBEvV; FaBoCh; ImPo; NIP-4; NOSC; NoSic; OBEV; PFE; TFi; UV *Fr.* Cymbeline.

Hark! ah, the nightingale. Philomela. Matthew Arnold. EBVVPR; FHYEP; OAEL-2; OBEV; UnPo

Hark, All Ye Lovely Saints. *Unknown.* OAEL-1

Hark, All You Ladies [That Do Sleep]. Thomas Campion. AAS; EBEV; NoSic; PoEL-2

Hark, and Hear My Trumpet Sounding. *Unknown.* AH

Hark! for the beetle winds his horn. The Fairies' Song. Jane Taylor. NOBRP

Hark! from the tombs a doleful sound. Plenary. *Unknown.* AmFP

Hark! from yon covert, where those tow'ring oaks. Hare-hunting. William Somervile. NOEC *Fr.* The Chase.

Hark, hark!/ Bow-wow./ The watch-dogs bark. Song. Shakespeare. *Fr.* The Tempest. OAEL-1

Hark! hark! that pig—that pig! the hideous note. Ode to a Pig while His Nose Was Being Bored. Robert Southey. NOBL

Hark, hark, the bark as Fido springs. Dawn Chorus. Mary Holtby. UV

Hark! Hark! / The dogs do bark! Hibiscus and Salvia Flowers. D. H. Lawrence. FaBoPV

Hark, hark, the dogs do bark. Mother Goose. LB; OxNR; ReMoGo

("And some in velvet gowns.") (LL) LB

Hark! Hark! with Harps of Gold. Edwin Hubbell Chapin. AH

Hark!—heard ye the signals of triumph afar? The Caffer Commando. Thomas Pringle. PeSAV

H[e]ark how she laughs aloud. Lucasta Laughing. Richard Lovelace. CavPo; PoEL-3

Hark how the Mower Damon sung. Damon the Mower. Andrew Marvell. ESCV; GeHe; NAEL-1; NOSC; OAEL-1

Hark, I hear the bells of Westgate. Westgate-on-Sea. John Betjeman. OxBoLi

Hark! My beloved! Bible, *O.T.* TrJP *Fr.* The Song of Songs. AWP

("Voice of my beloved, The.") PBMP

Hark, my Flora! Love doth call us. A Song of Dalliance. William Cartwright. NOSC

Hark, my soul! it is the Lord. Lovest Thou Me? William Cowper. ChIV-2 *Fr.* Olney Hymns.

Hark, now everything is still. The Shrouding of the Duchess of Malfi. John Webster. CH; HAP; NOBE; OBEV; SCGP *Fr.* The Duchess of Malfi. NAEL-1

Hark! now I hear them—Ding-dong, bell. (LL) Ariel's Song ("Full fathom [*or* fadom] five thy father lies"). Shakespeare. APAD; AWP; ClHu; EBEV; EBEvV; FaBoCh; GTBS-P; HAP; HoPM; ImPo; InPK-6; InPS-3; NAEL-1; NOBE; NOSC; NTP; NoP-4; NoSic; OBEV; OPOU; OxBSP; PoE; PoEL-2; PoPoPo; PoRA; TFi

H[e]ark! O h[e]ark, you guilty trees. Orpheus to Woods. Richard Lovelace. CaPo

Hark! one saith: "Proclaim!" All Flesh Is Grass. Bible, *O.T.* TrJP *Fr.* Isaiah.

Hark, reader! wilt be learn'd i' th' wars? To My Truly Valiant, Learned Friend, Who in His Book Resolved the Art Gladiatory into the Mathematics. Richard Lovelace. CaPo; PoEL-3

Hark! she is call'd, the parting houre is come. On the Assumption. Richard Crashaw. ESCV

Hark! the dogs howl! the sleetwinds blow. Tennyson. EnVR

Hark! the flow of the four rivers. Farewells from Paradise. Elizabeth Barrett Browning. OBEV

Hark! the herald angels sing / timidly. Dean Inge. Humbert Wolfe. FaBoEE

Hark, the mavis' evening sang. Robert Burns. OBEV

Hark! the tiny cowslip bell. Spring Has Come. *Unknown.* BoTP

Hark! the wood doves' moan. Lai. May Probyn. VWP

Hark! 'Tis the Saviour of Mankind. John Murray. AH

Hark to the blackbird's pleasing note. The Bullfinch in Town. Henrietta, Lady Luxborough Knight. ECWP

Hark to the whimper of the sea-gull. The Sea-Gull. Ogden Nash. ImPo

Hark, ye sighing sons of sorrow. The Mouldering Vine. *Unknown.* AmFP

Harke, al[l] you ladies that do sleep [*or* doo sleepe]. Hark, All You Ladies [That Do Sleep]. Thomas Campion. AAS; EBEV; NoSic; PoEL-2

Harlackenden, among these men of note Christ hath thee seated. Among These Troopes of Christs Souldiers, Came. . . Mr. Roger Harlackenden. Edward Johnson. SCAP

Harlech Castle. John Corben. Spl

Harlem. Jean Brierre, *French.* TTY, *tr. by* John F. Matheus

Harlem. A. E. Housman. PoPoPo

Harlem. Langston Hughes. APSN; AiP; AmPP; CrDW; GLP; GT; HCAP; HeIP-4; InPS-3; NAAAL; NoP-4; PBMP; Poetr; RaBo; SAmP; SSLK *Fr.* Lenox Avenue Mural. HoPM

(Dream Deferred.) InPK-6; LiTM; MBE; PoBA; SoSe-8

("Like a heavy load.") (LL) SSLK

Harlem. Maureen Seaton. LoHo

Harlem Dancer, The. Claude McKay. BPo; CrDW; ISC; NIP-4; NoAM; SAGP; Son; TAP

Harlem dud. For "Mr. Dudley," a Black Spy. James A. Emanuel. BPo; NBV

Harlem Freeze Frame. Lebert Bethune. GT; PoBA

Harlem Gallery. Melvin Beaunearus Tolson.

Birth of John Henry, The. BPo; NAAAL; TTY

Harlem Gallery: Book I, The Curator, The. PFTM

Sea-Turtle and the Shark, The. PoBA

Harlem Gallery: From the Inside. Larry Neal. BPo; MoNo; NBV

Harlem is vicious / modernism. BangClash. Return of the Native. Imamu Amiri Baraka. APSN; BPo; ColAP

Harlem, Montana. James Welch. CDW; HATNAP; PaTW

(Harlem, Montana: Just Off the Reservation.) PoPoPo

("Oh God, we're rich.") (LL) PaTW

Harlem, Montana: Just Off the Reservation. James Welch. *See* Harlem, Montana.

Harlem Riot, 1943. Pauli Murray. PoBA

Harlem Shadows. Claude McKay. AmPP; ColAP; NAAAL

Harlem Suite. Raymond R. Patterson. BAP-96

Harlem Sweeties. Langston Hughes. LiTM; NoP-4; TTY

("Delicious, *fine* Sugar Hill.") (LL) NoP-4

Harlequin-Horace, The. Horace, *Latin.*

"In Days of Old, when *Englishmen* were— *Men,.*" OBCVT, *tr. by* James Miller

HARLEY, the Nation's great Support. Part of the Seventh Epistle of the First Book of Horace Imitated: And Address'd to a Noble Peer. Horace. OBCVT, *tr. by* Jonathan Swift *Fr.* The Epistles.

Harlot's Catch. Robert Malise Bowyer Nichols. FaBoTw

Harlot's House, The. Oscar Wilde. ADE; EBVV; MoBrPo; NAEL-2; NoAM; PFE

Harmonics. William Vaughn Moody. APN-2

Harmonie du Soir. Charles Baudelaire, *French.* AWP, *tr. by* Lord Alfred Douglas

Harmonious powers with Nature work. Floating Island at Hawkshead. Dorothy Wordsworth. PEW; Ro

Harmony. Thomas Grant Springer. PoToHe

Harmony. *Unknown, Greek.* GrAn, *tr. by* William J. Philbin

Harnessed scorpions / before her. (LL) We have seen how the most amiable. Hilda Doolittle. BoWoP; PBWP

Harold. David Ignatow. LTA

Harold Wilson's Selected Poems. Mary Wilson.

"I went out of the conf'rence to get a pint of beer." UV

Harold's Song. Sir Walter Scott. *See* Rosabelle.

Haroun Al-Rachid for Heart's-Life. *Unknown.* AWP *Fr.* The Thousand and One Nights.

Haroun's Favorite Song. *Unknown.* AWP *Fr.* The Thousand and One Nights.

Harp, The. Ralph Waldo Emerson. APN-1

Harp, The. Ralph Knevet. ChIV-2

Harp, The. Po Chü-i, *Chinese.* TAL, *tr. by* Robert Payne

Harp of David, The. Jacob Cohen, *Hebrew.* TrJP, *tr. by* Sholom J. Kahn

Harp of David, The. "Yehoash," *Yiddish.* TrJP, *tr. by* Alter Brody

Harp of the North, farewell! The hills grow dark. Farewell Thou Minstrel Harp. Sir Walter Scott. OBNC; OxAEP-2 *Fr.* The Lady of the Lake.

Harp of the North, Farewell! The Hills Grow Dark. Sir Walter Scott. *See* Farewell Thou Minstrel Harp.

Harp Song. Lu Yu, *Chinese.* CoBCP, *tr. by* Burton Watson

Harp That Once through Tara's Halls, The. Thomas Moore. CABP; FaPoR; NAEL-2; OBNC; PoLF

Harp the monarch minstrel swept, The. Byron. ChIV-1

Harpkin gaed up t'the hill. *Unknown.* BaBoVe

Harpoonist. George Mackay Brown. FaBoTC *Fr.* Runes from a Holy Island.

Harried / earth is swept, The. The Wind Increases. William Carlos Williams. NAAL-2

Harriet. Robert Lowell. NoP-4

Harriet Beecher Stowe. Paul Laurence Dunbar. AAP; BPo; PoPoPo

Harriet Beecher Stowe. Dorothy Parker. NALW *Fr.* A Pig's-Eye View of Literature.

Harriet Beecher Stowe's Works. Frank Barbour Coffin. AAP

Harriet Feigenbaum is a Sculptor. Phyllis Koestenbaum. BAP-93

Harriet Simper Has Her Day. John Trumbull. *Fr.* The Progress of Dulness. AmPP

Harriet there was always somebody calling us crazy. Audre Lorde. BlSi

Harriet Tubman aka Moses. Samuel Allen. ISC

Harriet tubman / coming down the river. Cross Over the River. Sam Cornish. MBE

Harrow and Flanders. Robert Offley Ashburton Crewe-Milnes, Marquess of Crewe. NSI

Harrowing. Douglas Messerli. FTOS

Harry Fat and Uncle Sam. James Keir Baxter. PeLV

Harry Parry. *Unknown.* OxNR

("And dance and sing all the night.") (LL) LiLi

("Oh, rare Harry Parry.") LiLi

Harry Ploughman. Gerard Manley Hopkins. EnVR; FaBoMo

Harry Pollit Was a Bolshie. *Unknown.* OBCoV

Harry Semen. "Hugh MacDiarmid." FaBoTC

Harry, who is allergic, offered to chuck him. A Dog in the Lifeboat. Joyce Peseroff. CMAP

Harry, whose tuneful[l] and well-measured [*or* well-measur'd] song. To Mr. H. Lawes On His Airs. Milton. AWP; NOSC; NoP-4

Harsh bray and hollow, The. Two Kitchen Songs. Dame Edith Sitwell. CMoP

Harsh Climate. Charles Simic. LCAP-2

Harsh cry the crows. The Solitary. Friedrich Wilhelm Nietzsche, *German.* AWP, *tr. by* Ludwig Lewisohn

Harsh russet of dried blood, The. (LL) Buried at Springs. James Schuyler. CoAP; PoM

Harsh with salt of the sea. (LL) A Drover. Padraic Colum. AWP; MoBrPo; OBMV; RB

Hart Crane. Julian Symons. PoA

Hart he loves the high wood, The. Mother Goose. FaBoCh; OxNR; ReMoGo

Hart Loves the High Wood, The. *Unknown.* RB

Hartico. Anna Walters. VoR

Hartmanswillerkopf. Naomi Mitchison. WPN

Hartnett, the poet, might as well be dead. Michael Hartnett, *Irish.* BiHa, *tr. by* Gabriel Fitzmaurice *Fr.* The Purge.

Hart's Castle. Gawin Douglas. PoEL-1 *Fr.* King Hart.

Hartwell Gardens. A. Merrick, of Aylesbury. OBGa

Harum Scarum. Roger McGough. OTCP

Harvard, Cambridge, Mass. Julian Symons. PeLV

Harvard '61: Battle Fatigue. Robert Penn Warren. *Fr.* Two Studies in Idealism: Short Survey of American and Human History. CBCWP

Harvest. Blaise Cendrars, *French.* BLT, *tr. by* Monique Chefdor

Harvest, The. Alice Corbin. BoTP

Harvest. M. M. Hutchinson. AYFP; BoTP

Harvest. David James. CMAP

Harvest. Gary Soto. PBCAP

Harvest Bow, The. Seamus Heaney. BiHa; NoAM; PBCIP; PNI

Harvest Dawn Is Near, The. George Burgess. AH

Harvest-Home. Theocritus. HePo, *tr. by* Barbara Hughes Fowler; AWP, *tr. by* Charles Stuart Calverley *Fr.* Idylls.

("There was a time when Eucritus and I were going.") HePo, *tr. by* Barbara Hughes Fowler

Harvest Month[. A full moon]. Natan Zach, *Hebrew.* IP, *tr. by* Warren Bargad *and* Stanley F. Chyet

Harvest Moon. Jan Barry. CDa

Harvest Moon, The. Ted Hughes. AYFP

Harvest Moon, The. Henry Wadsworth Longfellow. APN-1

Harvest-mouse with caution walks, The. The Rustler. William Stroud. Spl

Harvest of Hate. Wole Soyinka. AF

Harvest of the Sea. Máire Mhac an tSaoi. PBWP

Harvest of War. Kappiyarrukkappiyanar, *Tamil.* PLW, *tr. by* A. K. Ramanujan

Harvest ripe, the farmers rejoice, The. Hastily Composed on the Mo-ling Road. Wang An-shih, *Chinese.* SuSp, *tr. by* Jan W. Walls

Harvest Sacrifice. Su Tung-p'o, *Chinese.* OHPC, *tr. by* Kenneth Rexroth

Harvest shall stop? The. (LL) Gathering Leaves. Robert Frost. RB; VGW

Harvest Song. Richard Dehmel, *German.* AWP, *tr. by* Ludwig Lewisohn

Harvest Song. Ludwig Heinrich Christoph Hölty, *German.* AWP, *tr. by* Charles T. Brooks

Harvest Song. Jean Toomer. NoP-4

Harvest Song. *Unknown.* BoTP; OxNR

Harvest Time. G. A. Watermeyer, *Afrikaans.* PeSA, *tr. by* Guy Butler, Uys Krige *and* Jack Cope

Harvest to Seduce, A. Melville Cane. NYBP

Harvesters, The. Mary Gilmore. NOBAu

Harvesting at Sunset. Anh Tho', *Vietnamese.* AVP, *tr.* by Huỳnh Sanh Thông

Harvesting of the Roses, The. Menahem ben Jacob, *Hebrew.* TrJP

Harvesting Wheat for the Public Share. Li Chü, *Chinese.* BoWoP; PBWP, *tr.* by Kenneth Rexroth *and* Ling Chung

Harvey Always Wins. Jack Prelutsky. NTCP

Harvey, the happy above happiest men. To the Right Worshipfull, My Singular Good Frend, Master Gabriell Harvey, Doctor of the Lawes. Edmund Spenser. NoSic *Fr.* Commendatory Sonnets.

Harvey, the happy above happiest men. To the Right Worshipfull, My Singular Good Friend, Master Gabriel Harvey, Doctor of the Lawes. Edmund Spenser. NoSic

Has a gold tooth, sits long hours. Black Bourgeoisie. Imamu Amiri Baraka. BPo

Has Any One Supposed It Lucky to Be Born? Walt Whitman. *Fr.* Song of Myself. AmPP; MoAmPo; NAAL-3; NOBA; OxBA

Has anyone seen the boy who used to come here? Jelaluddin Rumi, *Sanskrit.* RaBo, *tr.* by Coleman Barks and John Moyne

Has auld Kilmarnock [*or* K**********] seen the Deil? Tam Samson's Elegy. Robert Burns. PoEL-4

Has been a common day. (LL) First Sight of Her and After. Thomas Hardy. FaBoVe; PoEL-5

Has done the lover mortal hurt. (LL) Vergissmeinnicht. Keith Douglas. FaBoMo; GTBS-P; InPS-3; NAEL-2; NoAM; NoP-4; OBWP; OxBTC; PoWW; RB; SoSe-8

Has earned a night's repose. Henry Wadsworth Longfellow. *See* The Village Blacksmith.

Has Faded in Part But Magnificent Also Late for RC / Mirrors. Robert Grenier. PmAP

Has fallen away? (LL) The Moods. W. B. Yeats. CTC; EBVVPR

Has Fate sneaked in. Tanka. Ishikawa Takuboku, *Japanese.* MJT, *tr.* by Makoto Ueda

Has gladdened once our humble sphere. (LL) A Reminiscence. Anne Brontë. SDW

Has he no friend, no loving mother near? (LL) The Fruit Plucker. Coleridge. CH; FaBoCh; OBNC

Has he tempered the viol's wood. Ezra Pound. *See* Canto 81.

Has left a note saying GONE AWAY. (LL) Ending. Gavin Ewart. NBLV; OxBSP; SoSe-8

Has my life been a failure? I wonder—. "Ivan Venediktovich Elagin," *Russian.* TCRP, *tr.* by Helen Matveyeff

Has no feeling but because he has so much. (LL) The Student. Marianne Moore. NAAL-2; TwCP

Has not altered. Spenser's Ireland. Marianne Moore. FaBoWP; IIP; LiTM; MeMAP; NOBA; NoAM; OxBA; TAP

Has not changed since Thou wast young! (LL) Ex Ore Infantium. Francis Thompson. BoTP; OxBChV

Has not his flying-crooked gift. (LL) Flying Crooked. Robert Graves. FaBoMo; LiTM; OxBSP; PeLV; RB; TwCP

Has not the night been as a drunken rose. The Drunken Rose. Amarou, *Sanskrit.* AWP, *tr.* by E. Powys Mathers

Has oft'ner left me mourning. Wordsworth. *See* Simon Lee [the Old Huntsman].

Has only just / begun. (LL) Poem 143. Charles Olson. APSN; ColAP

Has painted his hands blue. The Logical Positivist. David Bromige. FTOS

Has quite escaped my mind! (LL) A Chronicle. *Unknown.* CBNP; OBSP

Has set me softly down beside you. The poem is you. (LL) Paradoxes and Oxymorons. John Ashbery. FTOS; HeIP-4; NoAM; PmAP; PoPoPo; Poetr; SAGP

Has thrust his nose under every board. Ego. Robert Siegel. PoA

Has to do with the story about the girl who didn't die. From the New World. Jorie Graham. NMM-2

Has yet caught me. (LL) King of China's Daughter, The. Dame Edith Sitwell. NOxBChV

Hasbrouck and the Rose. Howard Phelps Putnam. OxBA

Haschish, The. John Greenleaf Whittier. APN-1; NCAP; OBAL

Haskell. Witter Bynner. NoP-4

Hassan. James Elroy Flecker.

  Hassan's Serenade. OBEV

  War Song of the Saracens. EBEvV; MoBrPo

    ("We are they who come faster than fate: we are they who ride.") EBEvV

Hast broke the teeth. This help was from the Lord; / Thy blessing on thy people flows, *par.* by Milton. Bible, *O.T. See* Psalm 3.

Hast gain'd thy entrance, Virgin wise and pure. (LL) Lady That in the Prime. Milton. ChIV-2; Son

Hast never come to thee an hour. Walt Whitman. SAmP

Hast power to say the Time in terms of tone. (LL) To Richard Wagner. Sidney Lanier. APN-2; NCAP

Hast then sweet Love our wished flight. (LL) Come away, come, sweet love. John Dowland. GBL; NAEL-1; NoSic; PoEL-2

Hast thou a charm to stay the morning-star. Chamouny; the Hour Before Sunrise. A Hymn. Coleridge. Ro

Hast thou a cunning instrument of play. Preparation. Thomas Edward Brown. OBEV

Hast thou given the horse strength? Bible, *O.T.* CTAV *Fr.* Job.

Hast Thou Given the Horse Strength. Bible, *O.T. Fr.* Then the Lord Answered ("Who is this that darkeneth counsel by words without knowledge?"). AWP *Fr.* Job. NAWM-1

Hast Thou Heard It, O My Brother. Theodore Chickering Williams. AH

Hast thou named all the birds without a gun? Forbearance. Ralph Waldo Emerson. MeMAP; TAP

Hast thou no Arm for Me? (LL) At least—to pray—is left—is left. Emily Dickinson. APN-2; NCAP

Hast thou no mercy, wind, that thou should'st tear from me. The Mother's Lament. Mary E. Tucker. CBWP-1

Hast thou not wondered, *Adam,* at my stay? Eve tempts Adam. Milton. FaBoSe *Fr.* Paradise Lost.

Hast Thou seen her, great Jew. A Highland Woman. Sorley MacLean. FaBoTC

Hast thou seen reversed the prophet's miracle. Frederick Goddard Tuckerman. NOBA *Fr.* Sonnets.

"Hast thou seen that lordly castle." The Castle by the Sea. Ludwig Uhland, *German.* AWP, *tr.* by Longfellow

Hast thou seen the down i' th' air. A Song to a Lute. Sir John Suckling. BeJo; CaPo; EnLoPo

Hast thou, spirit. Shakespeare. OxAEP-1 *Fr.* The Tempest. OAEL-1

Haste. Bits of Wisdom. Benjamin Franklin. CTV

Haste thee, nymph, and bring with thee. Mirth, with Thee I Mean to Live. Milton. *Fr.* L'Allegro. AWP; FHYEP; GTBS-P; HAP; HoPM; ImPo; NOSC; NoP-4; OAEL-1; OBEV; PBRV; PoPoPo; TFi

Haste to the mighty ocean. August. Henrietta Cordelia Ray. CBWP-3

Hasten (great prince) unto thy British Isles. On the Numerous Accesse of the English to Waite upon the King in Holland. Katherine Philips. KTR; NOSC

Hasten hither, little book. Company in Loneliness. *Unknown.* NOIV

Hasten on your childhood to the hour when white in. Poems. Pablo Picasso, *French.* SPE, *tr.* by David Gascoyne

Hasten toward immense and earthly joy, the eyelids blinking as they. Waking. Tristan Tzara, *French.* AF, *tr.* by Mary Ann Caws

Hastening on, the wanderer strode. The Wanderer. "Yehoash," *Yiddish.* TrJP, *tr.* by Isidore Goldstick

Hastily Composed on the Mo-ling Road. Wang An-shih, *Chinese.* SuSp, *tr.* by Jan W. Walls

Hasty Pudding, The. Joel Barlow. AmPP; NAAL-3; NOBA; OBAL; OxBA; TAP

Hat. Tomasz Jastrun, *Polish.* AF, *tr.* by Daniel Bourne

Hat Factory, The. Paul Durcan. BiHa

Hat Given to the Poet by Li Chien, The. Po Chü-i, *Chinese.* ChiP, *tr.* by Arthur Waley

Hat Lady, The. Linda Pastan. SoSe-8

Hat pulled low at work. One of the Years. William Stafford. KaS

Hat-Tomb. Guillaume Apollinaire, *French.* CBNP

Hate. James Stephens. MoBrPo

Hate and the Love of the World, The. Max Ehrmann. PoToHe

Hate, be a faithful prop, and find. Pavel Grigoryevich Antokolsky, *Russian.* TrJP, *tr.* by Babette Deutsch

Hate is only one of many responses. Poem. Frank O'Hara. NeAP

Hate me or love, I care not, as I pass. The Unicorn. Ruth Pitter. MoBrPo

Hate-Song, A. Shelley. EnLoPo

Hate the Idle Pleasures. Shakespeare. *Fr.* King Richard III.

Hated by the Muses! B kw rm. Euenos, *Greek.* GrAn, *tr.* by Alistair Elliot

Hateful Old Age. *Unknown, Welsh.*

  "Before my back was bent I was eloquent." OBWVE, *tr.* by Gwyn Jones

Hater he came and sat by a ditch, A. A Hate-Song. Shelley. EnLoPo

Hath any loved you well, down there. Song from "Chartivel." Marie de France. AWP; EnLoPo; WPOW *Fr.* Chartivel.

Hath brought thee to be loved by none. (LL) To His Forsaken Mistress. Sir Robert Ayton. GBL; OBEV

Hath cared to look upon thy face. (LL) Eros. Robert Bridges. CABP; CMoP; NOBE; PoEL-5

Hath God, who freely gave you his own Son. To the Rev'd Mr. Jno. Sparhawk on the Birth of his Son. Samuel Sewall. SCAP

Hath melted like snow in the glance of the Lord! (LL) The Destruction of Sennacherib. Byron. APAD; BLPA; CABP; CTV; ChAP; ChIV-1; EBEvV; FHYEP; FaBoBe; FaBoCh; FaPoR; HAP; HeIP-4; InPS-3; NoP-4; OBWP; OxAEP-2; PBMP; PoLF; RB; SCGP; TFi; TrCP; WeW-3

Hath no misfortune, but that Rich she is. (LL) Sonnet 37: "My mouth doth water, and my breast doth swell." Sir Philip Sidney. NAEL-1; Son

Hath not the morning dawned with added light? Ethnogenesis. Henry Timrod. APN-2; AmPP; NOBA; OxBA

Hath oftener left me mourning. (LL) Simon Lee [the Old Huntsman]. Wordsworth. GTBS-P; NAEL-2

Hath onely Anger an Omnipotence. Upon the Asse That Bore Our Saviour. Richard Crashaw. ChIV-2; GeHe

Hath the Rain a Father? Jones Very. ChIV-1

Hath this world aught so fair as Stella is? (LL) Sonnet 21: "Your words my friend (right healthful caustics) blame." Sir Philip Sidney. NAEL-1; NoSic; PoE

Hatikvah—a Song of Hope. Naphtali Herz Imber, *Hebrew.* TrJP, *tr. by* Henry Snowman

Hating Jews. Tom Wayman. LTA

Hating the air! (LL) Poets Hitchhiking on the Highway. Gregory Corso. BB

Hatn slipped thy hold and thou art dead and gone. Sir Thomas Wyatt. *See* In mourning wise since daily I increase.

Hatred. Gwendolyn B. Bennett. BlSi; ColAP; NAAAL; PoBA; RaBo ("My hatred.") (LL) ColAP; NAAAL

Hatred and vengeance, my eternal portion. Lines Written During a Period of Insanity. William Cowper. ChIV-1; EBEV; HAP; NOEC; NoP-4; OAEL-1

Hatred of all men / —and disgust. (LL) The Raper from Passenack. William Carlos Williams. PFE

Hatred Surely Does Not Kiss. Kaspar Stieler, *German.* GePo, *tr. by* George C. Schoolfield

Hatred's swift repulsions play. (LL) The Visit. Ralph Waldo Emerson. APN-1; NOBA; PAR

Hats. Francis Stewart [or "Frank"] Flint. NSI

Hats off! / Along the street there comes. The Flag Goes By. Henry Holcomb Bennett. FaBoBe; PWR

Hatteras Calling. Conrad Potter Aiken. ColAP; NOBA; TAP

Hatters, The. Nan McDonald. NOBAu

Hattie Rice Rich. Adrienne Rich. *Fr.* Grandmothers. HCAP; NAAL-2; NoAM

Hattie Went to Market. Leslie Simon. FFC

Haud ictus sapio. (LL) Gascoigne's Good-Morrow. George Gascoigne. AAS; NOCV; NoSic

Haud ictus sapio. (LL) Gascoigne's [or Gascoygnes] Good-Night. George Gascoigne. AAS; NOCV; NoSic

Haul Away, My Rosy. *Unknown.* AmFP

Haul up the flag, you mourners. Elegy for Two Banjos. Karl Shapiro. TrJP

Hauled up from the field by obscure. The Victors. Anthony McNeill. PBCV

Hauling Over Wolf Creek Pass in Winter. Walter McDonald. CDa; MT

Haunch under the whip of douches in the slime. Spermal Chimney. Francis Picabia, *French.* PFTM, *tr. by* Jerome Rothenberg

Haunched like a hare, he hooed. Metamorphosis. Sylvia Plath. PoA

Haunt him, Mona! Haunt him, demon sister! The Brother-in-Law. Larry Rubin. MT

Haunted, The. Brad Leithauser. RA

Haunted. Edith Nesbit. VWP

Haunted. Siegfried Sassoon. CMoP

Haunted Beach, The. Mary Robinson. ECWP; Ro ("Upon a lonely desert beach.") Ro

Haunted Country. Robinson Jeffers. OxBA

Haunted House, The. Thomas Hood. EBEV

Haunted House. Edwin Arlington Robinson. MeMAP

Haunted Houses. Henry Wadsworth Longfellow. PWR

Haunted Oak, The. Paul Laurence Dunbar. AAP; ColAP; NAAAL; UnPo

Haunted Palace, The. *fr.* The Fall of the House of Usher. Edgar Allan Poe. APN-1; CH; MeMAP; NAAL-3; NOBA; OxBA; PoEL-4; TAP; TFi

Haunter, The. Thomas Hardy. NOBE

Haunting Poe's Baltimore. Allen Ginsberg. CLPP

Haunting the Western Moor. (LL) A Trampwoman's Tragedy. Thomas Hardy. NAEL-2; OBNC; OBNV

Haunts me the lugubrious shape. Half-bent Man. Richard Eberhart. NYBP

Havana Birth. Susan Mitchell. NAmP90

Havdala. Amir Gilbo'a, *Hebrew.* IP, *tr. by* Warren Bargad *and* Stanley F. Chyet

Havdolah Wine. Miriam Ulinover, *Yiddish.* CEEP, *tr. by* Seth L. Wolitz

Have a being less durable even than he. (LL) The Poplar Field. William Cowper. CH; FHYEP; HAP; NOBE; NOEC; PoEL-3

Have a Nice Day. Robert Long. NAmP90

Have a Nice Day. Jack Myers. NAmP90

Have a still shorter date, and die sooner than we. William Cowper. *See* The Poplar Field.

Have a turnip [*or* Turnep] than his [*or* a] father[?]. (LL) The Turnip Vendor. Samuel Johnson. OxNR; PeLV

Have all built their nests in my beard! Edward Lear. *See* There was an Old Man with a beard.

Have all built their nests in my /beard! beard. (LL) There was an Old Man with a beard. Edward Lear. CBNP; CTV; NOBL; NOxBChV; NTCP; OPOU; OxBChV; PeLV; PeLi; Poetr; TLR

Have certain periods set, and hidden fates. (LL) Sonnet: "Dost see how unregarded now." Sir John Suckling. BeJo; CaPo; CavPo; NOSC

Have come to court me. My Mother's Suitors. Liz Lochhead. FaBoTC

Have crawled too far! (LL) I know that He exists. Emily Dickinson. APN-2; AmPP; NCAP

Have died, the Present teaches, but in vain! (LL) Robert Gould Shaw. Paul Laurence Dunbar. CBCWP; PoPoPo; Son

Have ending. (LL) White Island. Robert Herrick. BeJo; NOSC; NoP-4; OAEL-1; TOF

Have eyes to wonder, but lack tongues to praise. (LL) Sonnet 106. Shakespeare. AWP; CTC; EBEvV; EnLoPo; FaBoCh; GLoP; GTBS-P; ImPo; NAEL-1; NOBE; NoSic; OBEV; OxAEP-1; PoRA; SCGP; Son

Have gathered them and will do never again. (LL) In Memoriam (Easter, 1915). Edward Thomas. GTBS-P; NOBE; NoP-4; OBWP; OBWVE; OxBTC; PeFWW; Spl

Have Gentlemen perhaps forgotten this? A Poet Speaks from the Visitors' Gallery. Archibald MacLeish. NYBP

Have good day, now, Mergerete. *Unknown.* MiEL

Have, have ye no regard, all ye. His Saviour[']s Words, Going to the Cross[e]. Robert Herrick. ChIV-2; NOCV

Have heard a kitten in the wilderness. (LL) Chaplinesque. Hart Crane. CMoP; HeIP-4; LiTM; MoP; NAAL-2; NOBA; NoAM; OxBA; VGW

Have I a body or have I none? *Unknown, Chinese.* CoBCP, *tr. by* Burton Watson

Have I a wife? Bedam I have! The Brewer's Man. Leonard Alfred George Strong. OBCoV; NOCV

Have I caught my heav'nly jewel. Second Song. Sir Philip Sidney. NoSic *Fr.* Astrophil and Stella. AAS; SiPS

Have I lost my liberty. Mary Sidney, Countess of Montgomery Wroth. *Fr.* Urania.

Have I no weapon-word for thee—some message brief and fierce? To the Pending Year. Walt Whitman. OxBSP

Have I not blessed thee? Then go forth; nor fear. To His Book[e]. Robert Herrick. CaPo

Have I not seen the hills of Candahar. Albery Allson Whitman. APN-2 *Fr.* Twasinta's Seminoles; Or Rape of Florida.

Have I spent all my life turning. Simon and the Tarantula. James Wright. NNaP

Have I the power to bid the frost not melt. To Barba. Edward May. FaBoEE

Have I, this moment, led thee from the beach. Walter Savage Landor. GBL

Have I told you the name of a lady? Have You Seen the Lady? John Philip Sousa. OBAL

Have mercy, Lord, on me. Lord, Have Mercy. Nahum Tate. TIRV

Have minde upon my supplicacioun. Chaucer. *See* The Complaint of Chaucer to His [Empty] Purse.

Have not yet passed the islands, I must watch them still. (LL) The Argonauts. D. H. Lawrence. GrIP; NoAM

Have once a thought to turne. (LL) Though I regarded not. Henry Howard, Earl of Surrey. AAS; SiPS

Have pity, pity, friends, have pity on me. Epistle in Form of a Ballad to His Friends. François Villon, *French.* AWP, *tr. by* Swinburne

Have power to cure all sadness—but despair. (LL) To Spring. Charlotte Smith. BWW; WPE

Have saved them from the gas. (LL) "It Out-Herods Herod. Pray You, Avoid It." Anthony Hecht. AF; CoAP; NIP-4; NOBA; NoAM; OxBC

Have Some Madeira, M'dear? Michael Flanders. OBCoV

Have stood aside and watched yourself go by. (LL) Watch Yourself Go By. Strickland W. Gillilan. BLPA; PWR; PoToHe

Have sworn to bring us low. (LL) The Town Betrayed. Edwin Muir. FaBoTC

Have the poets left a single spot for a patch to be sewn? Antar. TTY, *tr. by* A. J. Arberry *Fr.* The Mu'allaqat.

Have thou no other gods but me. The Ten Commandments. *Unknown.* OxBChV

Have to work after all. (LL) Necessity. Langston Hughes. APSN; NOBA; RaBo

Have waked marooned upon the coasts of morning. (LL) Bout with Burning. Vassar Miller. LiTM; MT; MoAmPo

Have we forgot how Raphael's numerous prose. Wentworth Dillon, 4th Earl of Roscommon. EPCY *Fr.* An Essay on Translated Verse.

Have ye beheld (with much delight). Upon the Nipples of Julia's Breast. Robert Herrick. CaPo; NAEL-1; NOSC; PeLV. *See* Lochinvar.

Have ye e'er heard of gallant like young / Lochinvar? Lochinvar? (LL) Lochinvar. Sir Walter Scott. BoTP; EBEvV; EBNV; FaBoBe; NOBE; NTP; OBNV; OxAEP-2; OxBS; PoRA; TFi.

Have ye heard of our hunting, o'er mountain and glen. The Hunters of Men. John Greenleaf Whittier. PAR

Have ye seen the morning sky. The Happy Swain. Ambrose Philips. EnLoPo

Have you a gold cup. The Question. Robert Duncan. NeAP

Have you any idea. The Mother of Michitsuna, *Japanese*. OHPJ, *tr. by* Kenneth Rexroth

Have You Anything to Say in Your Defense? César Vallejo, *Spanish*. AF, *tr. by* James Wright; RaBo

("God was sick, / gravely.") (LL) AF, *tr. by* James Wright

Have you become grass or a cloud that fades. Parting. Jure Kastelan, *Croatian*. CEEP, *tr. by* Peter Kastmiler

Have You Been at Carrick? *Unknown, Irish*. BIrV, *tr. by* Edward Walsh

Have you been in our wild west country? then. The West Country. Alice Cary. APN-2

Have you come back, then, to the promised city. In Memory of the Poet. Variant. Tomas Venclova, *Lithuanian*. CEEP, *tr. by* David McDuff

Have you come to the Red Sea place in your life. At the Place of the Sea. Annie Johnson Flint. BLPA

Have you cut off your hands yet? (LL) The Friend. Marge Piercy. CrSp; NALW; NMM-2; Poetr

Have you dug the spill. Harlem Sweeties. Langston Hughes. LiTM; NoP-4; TTY

Have you ever been ordered to strip. Solitary Confinement. Robert Walker. NOBAu

Have You Ever Faked an Orgasm? Molly Peacock. BAP-95; RA

Have you ever heard of lynching in the great United States? Lynching. Lizelia Augusta Jenkins Moorer. CBWP-3

Have you ever heard of the Sugar-[Plum Tree?] The Sugar-Plum Tree. Eugene Field. CTV; NBLV; OTCP; OxBChV

Have you ever heard that a tailor was ill? The Tailor. Joseph Leftwich. TrJP

Have you ever heard the sun in the sky. Have You Heard the Sun Singing? John Smith. AYFP

Have you ever sat by the railroad track. Empties Coming Back. Angelo de Ponciano. BLPA

Have you ever sat in crystal space, enjoying the sensations. The Call of the Air. Jeffery Day. NSI

Have you ever smelled summer? That Was Summer. Marci Ridlon. NTCP

Have you ever watched your old mother. Mother. Vladimir Holan, *Czech*. PoSu, *tr. by* Ian *and* Jarmila Milner

Have you forgotten yet? Aftermath. Siegfried Sassoon. MoBrPo; NSI; PoFWW; PoWW; TrJP

Have you had a kindness shown? Pass It On. Henry Burton. PWR

Have you heard Howard's tape? War Stories. Perry Oldham. CDa

Have you heard, my dear Anne, how my spirits are sunk? Lines by a Lady on the Loss of her Trunk. Richard Brinsley Sheridan. OBCoV

Have you heard, my friend, the slander that the Negro has to face? Immortality. Lizelia Augusta Jenkins Moorer. CBWP-3

Have you heard of a collier of honest renown. Patient Joe; or, The Newcastle Collier. Hannah More. ECWP; WoRP

Have You Heard of Artemisia? Heather McPherson. PeNZ

Have you heard of one Humpty Dumpty. The Ballad of Persse O'Reilly. James Joyce. CBNP; PeLV *Fr.* Finnegans Wake.

Have you heard of the dreadful fate. The Ashtabula Disaster. Julia A. Moore. OBAL

Have you heard of the wonderful one-hoss shay. The Deacon's Masterpiece; or, The Wonderful "One-Hoss Shay." Oliver Wendell Holmes. APN-1; AmPP; FaBoBe; NAAL-3; NOBA; OBAL; OBCA; OxBA; PoLF; PoRA; TAP; TFi *Fr.* The Autocrat of the Breakfast Table.

Have you heard the latest miser story. Nicarchus of Alexandria, *Greek*. GrAn, *tr. by* Peter Porter

Have you heard the story that gossips tell. John Burns of Gettysburg. Bret Harte. CBCWP

Have You Heard the Sun Singing? John Smith. AYFP

Have you heard the tale of the aloe plant. The Aloe Plant. Henry Harbaugh. BLPA

Have you heard? The troubles. Sulpicia, *Latin*. BoWoP, *tr. by* Aliki *and* Willis Barnstone

Have you listened for the things I have left out? Unsaid. A. R. Ammons. NOBA

Have you lived long, sir, in these parts? An Interview. K. W. Grandsen. OxBTC

Have you never seen. Bring the Wine! Li Po, *Chinese*. CoBCP, *tr. by* Burton Watson

Have you news of my boy Jack? My Boy Jack. Rudyard Kipling. APAD

Have you not in a chimney seen. A Description of Maidenhead. John Wilmot, 2d Earl of Rochester. NOBL

Have you not noted, in some family. The Birth-Bond. D. G. Rossetti. Son *Fr.* The House of Life.

Have you not seen the grasses on the riverbank? Pao Chao. SuSp, *tr. by* Irving Y. Lo *Fr.* The Weary Road.

Have you not seen (you must remember). Henry Luttrell. NOBRP *Fr.* Letter to Julia, in Rhyme.

Have you noticed. Angels. Anne Szumigalski. NOBC

Have you noticed? Ghosts. Mary Oliver. Poetr

Have you preserved time. Peace Project (5). Eric Mottram. NBrP

Have you provided for her grace's servants? Ben Jonson. *Fr.* The Alchemist. FaBoSe

Have you really come home? (LL) The Father of My Country. Diane Wakoski. NoAM; TAP

Have you seen. The Seashore. Leonid Nikolaevich Martynov, *Russian*. TCRP, *tr. by* J. R. Rowland

Have you seen a little dog anywhere about? My Dog. Emily Lewis. OTCP

Have you seen an apple orchard in the spring? An Apple Orchard in the Spring. William Martin. PWR

Have you seen but a bright lily grow. So White, So Soft, So Sweet. Ben Jonson. APAD; FaBoCh *Fr.* The Devil Is an Ass. OxBSn

"Have you seen Hugh." The King of Connacht. *Unknown, Early Irish*. IIP; NNPT, *tr. by* Frank O'Connor

Have you seen my circus? The Morning Stars. Robert Lax. KSG

Have you seen my cousin? Shakespeare. OxAEP-1 *Fr.* Troilus and Cressida.

Have you seen our LIttle Sister? To Little Sister From No. 16. *Unknown*. NSI

Have You Seen the Lady? John Philip Sousa. OBAL

Have you seen the listening snake? The Vines. John Gray. NOBVV

Have you sometimes, calm, silent let your tread aspirant rise. Heard on the Mountain. Victor Hugo. AWP, *tr. by* Francis Thompson *Fr.* Feuilles d'Automne.

Have you time for a story. Charity Overcoming Envy. Marianne Moore. GS; NYBP

Haven and last refuge of my pain, The. Michelangelo Buonarroti. *Fr.* Three Poems. AWP, *tr. by* George Santayana

Haven't I told you enough? (LL) When I Was Growing Up. Nellie Wong. OxWW; UnSA

Haven't seen my friend Li Po for some time. No Word. Tu Fu, *Chinese*. SuSp, *tr. by* Eugene Eoyang

Having a Coke with You. Frank O'Hara. GLP; VCAP

Having a crush was how I existed. A Suburban Childhood. Liz Rosenberg. IFJA; PBCAP

Having a fine new suit. Apologue. Tony Connor. BoLoP

Having after long desire. To Venus. Joachim Du Bellay, *French*. FLP; LoP, *tr. by* Alistair Elliot

Having attained success in business. Robert Whitmore. Frank Marshall Davis. BPo; PoBA

Having been born a woman. To Be a Woman. Daisy Zamora, *Spanish*. IFJA, *tr. by* Margaret Randall *and* Elinor Randall

Having been tenant long to a rich Lord. Redemption. George Herbert. CABP; ESCV; FMP; FSCP; GSo; GeHe; HAP; InPK-6; InPS-3; MeLP; NAEL-1; NOBE; NOCV; NOSC; NoP-4; PBRV; PeECV; PoE; PoPoPo; Poetr; SCGP; SCV; SeCP; SoSe-8; TFi; TrCP; WeW-3

Having Climbed to the Topmost Peak of the Incense-Burner Mountain. Po Chü-i, *Chinese*. ChiP, *tr. by* Arthur Waley

Having come to this place. This Place in the Ways. Muriel Rukeyser. AiP

Having commanded Adam to bestow. Naming the Animals. Anthony Hecht. ChIV-1

Having Completed My Fortieth Year. John Tranter. BMAP

Having confided to the heavy-lipped. A Digression. Richard Wilbur. BAP-94

Having confused me. A Voice From the Roses. Maxine W. Kumin. NMM-2

Having crowded once onto the threshold of mortality. Divinities. W. S. Merwin. PoA

Having crushed. Tanka. Kondō Yoshimi, *Japanese*. MJT, *tr. by* Makoto Ueda

Having delivered now what praises are. Edward Herbert. EPCY *Fr.* Elegy for Dr. Donne.

Having dined yesterday on a goat's foot. Automedon, *Greek*. GrAn, *tr. by* Peter Jay

Having Eaten Breakfast. David Chapman Berry. BXAP

Having endured them all. (LL) To an Artist, to Take Heart. Louise Bogan. NYBP; TRP

Having given up hope for a high-wire act. Learning to Swim at Forty-Five. Colleen J. McElroy. GT

Having gone out through the west city wall in the chilly dawn. Arriving after Rain at the Temple of Heavenly Peace. Wang Shih-chieng, *Chinese*. SuSp, *tr. by* Richard John Lynn

Having gone upstairs. A Mirror. Jean Follain, *French*. BLT, *tr. by* Czeslaw Milosz *and* Robert Hass

Having grown up. Tanka. Kondō Yoshimi, *Japanese*. MJT, *tr. by* Makoto Ueda

Having heard the instruction. One Modern Poet. Carl Sandburg. OBAL

Having hooded my face with hair. The Sibyl's Song. Michele Roberts. BrRo

Having interred [*or* interr'd] her infant-birth. Ode, upon a Question Moved, Whether Love Should Continue Forever? An. Edward Herbert, 1st Baron Herbert of Cherbury. MeLP; NOBE; OxAEP-1; SeCP

Having invented a new Holocaust. U. S. 1946 King's X. Robert Frost. CrDW; NIP-4

Having It Out With Melancholy. Jane Kenyon.

4 Often. LoL

Bottles. BAP-93

Credo. BAP-93

From the Nursery. BAP-93

(1 From the Nursery.) LoL

In and Out. BAP-93

(6 In and Out.) LoL

Once There Was Light. BAP-93; LoL

("'Ones drown!' After that, I wept for days.") (LL) LoL

Pardon. BAP-93; LoL

("To my desk, books, and chair.") (LL) LoL

Suggestion from a Friend. BAP-93

(3 Suggestion from a Friend.) LoL

Wood Thrush. BAP-93

Having just been aroused by some gurgling, rising and falling. Recognitions. David Mura. MoLi

Having Led a Charmed Life, He Had to be Hanged Twice. Mac Wellman. FTOS

Having left hard [*or* solid] ground behind. The Insular Celts. Ciaran Carson. BIrV; CIP-2; IIP

Having left the great mean city, I make. Goodbye to London. Louis MacNeice. PeECV

Having let flow. Tanka. Kanoko Okamoto, *Japanese*. MJT, *tr. by* Makoto Ueda

Having lived. Tanka. Toki Zenmaro, *Japanese*. MJT, *tr. by* Makoto Ueda

Having locked ourselves. The Space Explorer's Story. David Harmer. SpW

Having lost my leather purse. My Son. Ruth Stone. WPE

Having Lost My Sons, I Confront the Wreckage of the Moon: Christmas, 1960. James Wright. CoAP; HCAP; NAAL-2

Having molded clay in the shape of my ailing form. Masaoka Shiki, *Japanese*. MJT, *tr. by* Makoto Ueda

Having myself been scared silly when I was young. The Thief. Alden Nowlan. RaBo

Having never been. On Trying to Imagine the Kiwi Pregnant. Clarence Major. GT

Having no force to fly. (LL) Pine boat a-shift, fr. *the Chinese of the* Confucian Odes. Ezra Pound. APSN; OBVE

Having passed over the world. The Last Frontier. John Gould Fletcher. FuPo

Having power is nothing to be concerned about. Wang Fan-chih, *Chinese*. SuSp, *tr. by* Eugene Eoyang

Having put yourself on the way. Spirits, Dancing. Arthur Gregor. NYBP; VGW

Having rid Hamelin town of its vermin. Limerick. Ted Thompson. PeLi

Having seen thy salvation. (LL) A Song for Simeon. T. S. Eliot. ChIV-2; GI; NOCV

Having so rich a treasury, so fine a hoard. The Daisy. Marya Alexandrovna Zaturenska. MoAmPo

Having spelt it out in blood. National Bird. N. Pichamurti, *Tamil*. OMIP, *tr. by* Rajagopal Parthasarathy

Having spent a hard-earned sleep, you must break camp in the mountains. Breaking Camp. David Wagoner. PaTW

Having split up the chaparral. The Wide Land. A. R. Ammons. TwCP

Having sucked deep. Finis. Basho, *Japanese*. EP, *tr. by* Nobuyuki Yuasa

Having / swallowed the / water. Third Part. Leslie Scalapino. DeD *Fr.* Floating Series.

Having taken her slowly by surprise. A Pause for Breath. Ted Hughes. NYBP *Fr.* Root, Stem, Leaf.

Having the Wrong Name for Mr. Wright. Helen Barolini. UnSA

Having this day my horse, my hand, my lance. Sonnet 41. Sir Philip Sidney. AEP; HAP; NAEL-1; PoE; Son *Fr.* Astrophil and Stella. AAS; SiPS

Having to Love Something Else, The. Russell Edson. FiLi

Having traveled ten *li* from the high city walls. Traveling at Break of Day. Huang Ching-jen, *Chinese*. SuSp, *tr. by* Chang Yin-nan *and* Lewis C. Walmsley

Having tried to use the. It Is Deep. Carolyn M. Rodgers. NAAAL; SSLK

Having used every subterfuge. A Renewal. James Merrill. OxBSP; PiM; SAGP; VCAP

Having written several poems which I will not publish. Baedeker for Metaphysicians. Brian Higgins. FaBoTw

Haw Lantern, The. Seamus Heaney. NoAM; PNI

Hawaii Dantesca. Charles Wright. HCAP; LCAP-2

Hawk, The. George Mackay Brown. NoP-4; RB

Hawk, The. W. B. Yeats. PoA

Hawk and Snake. Leslie Marmon Silko. VoR

Hawk Chant of the Saginaws. *Unknown, Ojibwa Native American.* APN-2, *tr. by* Henry Rowe Schoolcraft

Hawk hovers in air, A. Loneliness. Tu Fu, *Chinese*. OHPC, *tr. by* Kenneth Rexroth

Hawk Is a Woman. Hildegarde Flanner. WPE

Hawk Nailed to a Barn Door. Peter Blue Cloud. VoR

Hawk Roosting. Ted Hughes. CMoP; GTBS-P; HAP; HeIP-4; LiTM; OxBTC; TwCP; UnPo

Hawk turns into the sun. The Net of Place. Paul Blackburn. PmAP

Hawkers. Tanka. Masaoka Shiki, *Japanese*. MJT, *tr. by* Makoto Ueda

Hawking for the Partridge. Thomas Ravenscroft. OxBoLi

Hawk's Cry in Autumn, The. Joseph Brodsky, *Russian*. TCRP, *tr. by* Alan Myers *and* Joseph Brodsky

Hawk's Eyes. Yvor Winters. PoA

Hawks turn their heads nimbly round, The. Hawk Chant of the Saginaws. *Unknown, Ojibwa Native American.* APN-2, *tr. by* Henry Rowe Schoolcraft

Hawk's Way. Ted Olson. HoPM

Hawktree. Dave Jeddie Smith. HCAP

Hawthorn, The. *Unknown*. EnVB; MiEL

Hawthorn Hedge, The. Judith Wright. WPE

Hawthorn morning moving, The. Renewal by Her Element. Denis Devlin. CIP-2; IIP

Hawthorne. Henry Wadsworth Longfellow. PoEL-5

Hawthorne. James Russell Lowell. AmPP; NOBA; OxBA; TAP *Fr.* A Fable for Critics. NAAL-1; NAAL-3

("For making him fully and perfectly man.") (LL) OxBA

Hawthorne. Robert Lowell. AFr

Hawthorne Garland, A. Richard Harter Fogle. OBAL

Hay, ay, hay, ay. *Unknown*. MiEL

Hay Fever. Alec Derwent Hope. NoAM

Hay for the Horses. Gary Snyder. BB; CoAmPo; LoL; TRP

Hay Harvest. Patrick Reginald Chalmers. BoTP

Hay has long been built into the stack, The. From Harvest to January. Charles Tennyson Turner. NOBVV

Hay, Hey, Hey, Hey! I Will Have the Whetstone and I May. *Unknown*. CBNP

Hay Hotel, The. Oliver St. John Gogarty. BIrV

Hay is for horses. *Unknown*. OxNR

Hay making. Joanna Baillie. OxAEP-2

Hay Scuttle. Robert Morgan. WeT

Hay-Time. C. M. Lowe. BoTP

Hay-Time; or, The Constant Lovers. A Pastoral. Josiah Relph. NOEC

Hayle holy-land wherein our holy lord. Upon the First Sight of New England, June 29, 1638. Thomas Tillam. AH; SCAP

Haylle, Comly and Clene. *Unknown*. OBEV; OxBoLi *Fr.* The Second Shepherd's Play. NAEL-1; PoEL-1

Haymakers, Rakers. Thomas Dekker *and others*. *See* Song.

Haymaking. E. M. Adams. BoTP

Haymaking. Alfred Percival Graves. BoTP

Haymaking. Edward Thomas. MoBrPo

Haymaking. William Carlos Williams. NoAM *Fr.* Pictures from Brueghel.

Hayseed. *Unknown*. AS

Haystack in the Floods, The. William Morris. CABP; EBEV; EBNV; EBVV; EnVR; HAP; NAEL-2; NoP-4; OAEL-2; OBNC; OBNV; OxAEP-2; PeVV; PoEL-5; PoRA

Haytime. Irene F. Pawsey. BoTP

Hazardous Waste. James Sherry. FTOS

Hazard's friend Elliot is homosexual. Wholesome. William Meredith. TAP

Haze. Henry David Thoreau. *Fr.* A Week on the Concord and Merrimack Rivers.

Haze, char, and the weather of All Souls'. In the Elegy Season. Richard Wilbur. InPK-6; NYBP

Hazed with harvest dust and heat. For the Missing in Action. John Balaban. AF; PuP-15

Hazel Stick for Catherine Ann, A. Seamus Heaney. NoAM

He. Vasco [or Vasko] Popa, *Serbian.* CBNP; PoSu *Fr.* Games. RB, *tr. by* Anne Pennington

("Some bite off the others.") NNPT, *tr. by* Anne Pennington

He Abjures Love. Thomas Hardy. CBLP; OBNC

He accepts the circle, speech and so. Anne-Marie Albiach, *French.* BoWoP, *tr. by* Keith Waldrop

He adored the desk, its brown-oak inlaid with ebony. Geoffrey Hill. HAP; NoAM; NoP-4 *Fr.* Mercian Hymns.

("He wept, attempting to mas / ter *ancilla* and *servus*.") (LL) NoP-4

He: Age doesn't matter when you're both in love. Julia Alvarez. Son *Fr.* 33.

("Where are the girls who were beautiful?") RA

He aims. At her. Then drops his aim. Idly. (LL) The Guard at the Binh Thuy Bridge. John Balaban. AF; CDa

He all that time among the sewers of Troy. Troy. Edwin Muir. CMoP

He also said to the disciples, "There was a rich man who had a steward." Luke 16:1–9; He also said to the disciples. Ernesto Cardenal. GI *Fr.* St. Luke.

He also told them a parable. Luke 6:39. William Carlos Williams. GI *Fr.* St. Matthew; He also told them a parable.

He always bathed afterwards. Bathing. Kate Daniels. NAmP90

He always comes on market days. The Balloon Man. Rose Fyleman. BoTP

He always has something to grumble about. A Chip on His Shoulder. *Unknown.* BLPA

He always took me to visit the squadron. Two Memorial Poems. David Avidan, *Hebrew.* IP, *tr. by* Warren Bargad *and* Stanley F. Chyet

He ambles along like a walking pin cushion. Hedgehog. Chu Chen Po, *Chinese.* OHMPC; PiM, *tr. by* Kenneth Rexroth

He and his, unwashed all winter. The Native. W. S. Merwin. PoRA

He and I. End of a Course. Ivor Armstrong Richards. CRP

He and She. Sir Edwin Arnold. BLPA

He and She. Eugene Fitch Ware. PoLF

He Approacheth the Hall of Judgment. *Unknown.* AWP *Fr.* Book of the Dead.

He as O, A. E. E. Cummings. InPS-3

He ascended from a lonely crag in winter. On the Death of Karl Barth. Jack R. Clemo. NOCV

He ask'd, and hoped, through Christ. Do thou the same! (LL) Epitaph: "Stop, Christian passer-by!—Stop, child of God." Coleridge. CH; NAEL-2; NOCV; OAEL-2; PeECV

He asked for bread, and he received a stone. (LL) On the Setting Up of Mr. Butler's Monument in Westminster Abbey. Samuel Wesley. NBLV; NOEC; OxBSP

He Asked Them What Did They Know & They Told Him. *Unknown, Seneca Indian.* STP, *tr. by* Jerome Rothenberg *and* Richard Johnny John

He Asketh Absolution of God. *Unknown.* AWP *Fr.* Book of the Dead.

He ate and drank the precious Words. Emily Dickinson. APN-2

He ate, drank, slept, talk'd politics, and died. (LL) On a Certain Alderman. John Cunningham, *after the Greek of* Simonides. FaBoEE; OBCoV

He ate the dormouse, / Else it was he[e]. (LL) A Catch. Ben Jonson. CBNP; OxNR

He attempted *texas red light.* Random (Re-arrangeable) Study for *Views.* Tony Towle. PmAP

He avoids the momentous rhythm. The Last Man. Thom Gunn. OxAEP-2 *Fr.* Misanthropos.

He awoke this morning from a strange dream. Chief Leschi of the Nisqually. Duane Niatum. CDW

He bade me "Be Happy," he whisper'd "Forget me." Frances Sargent Osgood. PAR

He bare him [or hym] up, he bare him [or hym] down. The Corpus Christi Carol. *Unknown.* HAP

He bathes his soul in women's wrath. The Irish Patriarch. Ruth Pitter. NALW

He beat me with the hem of a kimono. The Club. Mitsuye Yamada. LoHo; NMM-2

—He became a teetotaler out of his socialist convictions; during. About My Father. Irena Klepfisz. NMM-2

He best can paint 'em, who shall feel 'em most. (LL) Eloisa to Abelard. Alexander Pope. NAEL-1; PoEL-3; RACG

He Biddeth Osiris to Arise from the Dead. *Unknown.* AWP *Fr.* Book of the Dead.

He blinks upon the hearth-rug. On a Cat, Ageing. Sir Alexander Gray. PC

He bought an old ship's lifeboat. A Fine Day for Straw Hats. Louis Simpson. PBCV

He breathed in air, he breathed out light. Goodbye. Adrian Mitchell. OPOU

He brought a light so she could see. Strains of Sight. Robert Duncan. CMoP; PoE

He built a house, time laid it in the dust. His Monument. Sarah Knowles Bolton. PWR

He built a mud-wall'd hovel, where he kept. George Crabbe. *Fr.* Peter Grimes. EBNV; ECEV; FHYEP; OBNV; PoEL-4; Ro *Fr.* The Borough.

He built himself a house. Fairy Tale. Miroslav Holub, *Czech.* RB, *tr. by* George Theiner

He built the ranch house down a little draw. The Ranch in the Coulee. Gwendolen Haste. PaTW *Fr.* Montana Wives.

He called a conquered land his own. Wolfe Tone. Austin Clarke. CIP-2

He called her: golden dawn. Paris and Helen. Judy Grahn. CrSp

He calleth to me out of Seir, Watchman, what of the night? Watchman, What of the Night? Bible, *O.T.* AWP *Fr.* Isaiah.

He calls it their stage which echoes our first misrecognition of unity. Instances. The Swan. Mei-Mei Berssenbrugge. OpBo

He calls you in his wedding coat. The Wedding Coat. Harriet Rose. BrRo

He came, a dark youth, singing in the dawn. Paul Laurence Dunbar. James David Corrothers. NAAAL

He came all so still. Ancient Christmas Carol. *Unknown.* PChr

He came and took me by the hand. The Mystery. Ralph Hodgson. CH; MoBrPo

He came apart in the open. Martin's Blues. Michael S. Harper. HCAP; PoBA

He came at midnight, his legs cut off. War's End. Dahlia Ravikovitch, *Hebrew.* IP, *tr. by* Warren Bargad *and* Stanley F. Chyet

He came back. Dry River Bed. Andrew Salkey. PBCV

He came back and shot. He shot him. When he came. Incident. Imamu Amiri Baraka. AF; NoAM

He came from hills to comfortable plains. The Mountaineer. Robert Nathan. TrJP

He came from Malta. A Maltese Dog. Tymnes, *Greek.* FaBoCh; FaBoEE; Spl, *tr. by* Edmund Blunden; OBCVT, *tr. by* Edmund Blunden *Fr.* Epigrams.

He came in she said he had come in. Adelaide's Dream. Christopher Middleton. PeLV

He came in silver armor, trimmed with black. Sonnet. Gwendolyn B. Bennett. PoBA

He came of a sharecrop farm family. Corporal Kevin Spina, U. S. M. C. Bryan Alec Floyd. CDa

He came on the 28th of February, stood. Date. Sarah Kirsch, *German.* CEEP, *tr. by* Wayne Kvam

He came over to London and straight away strode. Dinky Di. *Unknown.* NOBAu

He came to deliver the secret of the sun. U Tam'si Tchicaya. *See* A Mat to Weave.

He came to his love's window at the dead of the night. The Little Drummer. *Unknown.* AmFP

He came to my desk with a quivering lip. New Leaf, A [or The]. Helen Field Fischer, *at. to* Kathleen Wheeler. PoToHe

He came to the desert of London town. William Blake. James Thomson. CABP; EPCY

He Came to Visit Me. Martin Seymour-Smith. FaBoTw

He can build, and once more fire. (LL) Song: "Heare ye Ladies that despise." John Fletcher. CBLP; NOBE; OBEV; PoEL-2

He can curse the God that made him for the colour of his hair. (LL) Oh who is that young sinner with the handcuffs on his wrists? A. E. Housman. FaBoTw; NOBVV; SoSe-8

He can only drink tea now, screwed and filed. Pink Slip at Tool & Dye. Dave Jeddie Smith. NoAM

He cannot his unheard skull. In Nora's House with Rilke's Apollo. Clark Coolidge. PT

He cannot imagine a doorknob. The Feeling Type and His Friends. Michael Davidson. FTOS

He carried the spit to the nearest urn. The Citizen's Way. Vladimir Burich, *Russian.* TCRP, *tr. by* Albert C. Todd

He carries shadows in his face like caves. On the Apparition of Oneself. William Burford. PoA

He cast his net at morn where fishers toiled. Failure. Kate Tucker Goode. PWR

He ceased; and Satan stayed not to reply. Satan. Milton. *Fr.* Book II. FHYEP; NAEL-1; OxAEP-1 *Fr.* Paradise Lost.

He changes into a bird, and that's. Gout. Lewis Warsh. FTOS

He clasps the crag with crookèd hands. The Eagle. Tennyson. APAD; APo; BoTP; CH; CTAV; CTV; ChAP; ClHu; FHYEP; FPC; FaBoCh;

GTBS-P; HeIP-4; InPK-6; NAEL-2; NOBVV; NTCP; NTP; NoP-4; OAEL-2; OxBSP; PFE; Poetr; SAGP; SCGP; TFi; TRP; UnPo

He climbed and, under the gray leaves. The Olive Garden. Rilke, *German*. GI, *tr. by* David Curzon *and* Will Alexander Washburn

He climbed, devoured. In her mouth. Cat in the Dovecote. Avner Trainin, *Hebrew*. MHP, *tr. by* Ruth Finer Mintz

He climbed to the treetop. Columns. Meir Wieseltier, *Hebrew*. IP, *tr. by* Warren Bargad *and* Stanley F. Chyet

He climbs the stair. Waterchew! Gregory Corso. VGW

He closes his eyes. Wink. Roger Gilbert-Lecomte, *French*. PFTM, *tr. by* Pierre Joris

He Comes Among. George Barker. OBMV

He comes down to the shadow. Heron. Ted Walker. NYBP

He comes from the north. Three for Bear. Aimé Césaire, *French*. PFTM, *tr. by* Frances Densmore

He comes from the north. *Unknown*. Fr. Sioux Metamorphoses. STP, *tr. by* James Koller

He comes home with evening: all his fleecy flock. An Eye for an Eye. Homer. *Fr.* Odyssey. NAWM-1, *tr. by* Robert Fitzgerald

He comes in the night! He comes in the night! Santa Claus. *Unknown*. BoTP

He Comes Not To-night. Josephine D. Henderson Heard. CBWP-4

He comes often. On business. Business. Miryana Basheva, *Bulgarian*. CEEP, *tr. by* Brenda Walker

He comes running. A Poem about a Wolf Maybe Two Wolves. *Unknown*, *Seneca Indian*. STP, *tr. by* Jerome Rothenberg *and* Richard Johnny John

He comes through the door. The Assassin's Fatal Error. Lawrence Raab. AmPA

He comes to brood and sit. (LL) Peace. Gerard Manley Hopkins. GTBS-P; OxBSP; TrCP

He comes to near that comes to be denied. (LL) The Lady's Resolve. Lady Mary Wortley Montagu. BoWoP; ECWP; OxBSP

He comes unknown and heard and stands there. Man into a Churchyard. Bernard Gutteridge. SPE

He comes with western winds, with evening's wandering airs. Emily Brontë. *Fr.* The Prisoner. NALW; NOBVV

He Cometh Forth into the Day. *Unknown*. AWP *Fr.* Book of the Dead.

He cometh, O bliss! Judah Halevi, *Hebrew*. TrJP, *tr. by* Emma Lazarus

He Commandeth a Fair Wind. *Unknown*. AWP *Fr.* Book of the Dead.

He Considers the Birds of the Air. Karl Kirchwey. GI

He could have come to tell us. Never Give a Bum an Even Break. James Welch. NoAM

He could not decide if the city at dusk / was the furnace of gods. The Watcher. Edward Hirsch. PUP-18

He could see the little lake. The Lake. James Stephens. MoBrPo

He could see things. Another Kind of Country. Charles Sullivan. IIP

He could sing sweetly on a string. Orpheus. Elizabeth Madox Roberts. MoAmPo

He could trimble. Oui Papa. Delano Abdul Malik de Coteau. PBCV

He couldn't remember what propelled him. Man on a Fire Escape. Edward Hirsch. WWSi

He courts her up there on the roof. The Muse Is Always the Other Woman. Constance Urdang. PBCAP

He crawls to the edge of the foaming creek. Meeting the Mountains. Gary Snyder. NoAM; TAP

He crouches, and buries his face on his knees, / And hides in the dark of his hair. The Last of His Tribe. Henry Clarence Kendall. CBAP

He, cursed with an ugly wife. Palladas, *Greek*. InMo, *tr. by* Sam Hamill

He cut a sappy sucker from the muckle rodden-tree. The Whistle. Charles Murray. OxBS

He cuts down the lakes so they appear straight. John Ashbery. CBNP

He debated whether. Arthur Ridgewood, M.D. Frank Marshall Davis. BPo

He Defendeth His Heart against the Destroyer. *Unknown*. AWP Fr. Book of the Dead.

He did his duty both by peers and peasants. King George V. Charles W. Hayward. NOBAu

He did not come / A gnostic. Incarnation Poem. John Leax. TrCP

He did not come in the dawning. He did not come at noon. Alfred Noyes. OxBoV

He did not come of a long line of stone-cutters. The Man Who Went Absent from the Native Literature. Anthony Cronin. CIP-2

He did not lie to us, that spirit, mournfully severe. The Progeny of Cain. Nikolai Stepanovich Gumilyov, *Russian*. TCRP, *tr. by* Simon Franklin

He did not think me strange or older, Nor I, him. (LL) All Souls' Night. Frances Cornford. EnLoPo; OxBSP; OxBTC

He did not wear his scarlet coat. The Condemned Man. Oscar Wilde. EBEvV; EBNV; MoBrPo; NOBE; NOBVV; NoAM; OBMV; OBNC; TFi; UV *Fr.* The Ballad of Reading Gaol. CABP; OBNV; OxAEP-2

He did not wear his swallow tail. The Gourmand. Harry Graham. UV

He didn't dare come home. Engagement. Nichita Stanescu, *Romanian*. CEEP, *tr. by* Mariana Carpinisan *and* Mark Irwin

He didn't say. Malcolm Spoke / Who Listened? Haki R. Madhubuti. NAAAL

He "Digesteth Harde Yron." Marianne Moore. CMoP; NoAM

He dines alone surrounded by reflections. Witch Doctor. Robert Earl Hayden. NoAM

He disagrees with Simone de Beauvoir. His Plans for Old Age. William Meredith. TAP

He disappeared in the dead of winter. In Memory of W. B. Yeats. W. H. Auden. CABP; CMoP; EPCY; GEA; HAP; HeIP-4; HoPM; IIP; ImPo; LiTM; MeMAP; MoBrPo; NOBE; NoAM; NoP-4; OAEL-2; OxAEP-2; OxBTC; PFE; Poetr; TFi; TRP; UnPo; WeW-3

He discovers himself on an old airfield. The Old Pilot. Donald Hall. LCAP-2

He does not come. Ono no Komachi, *Japanese*. WPJ, *tr. by* Kenneth Rexroth *and* Ikuko Atsumi

("My heart burns up.") (LL) OHMPJ, *tr. by* Kenneth Rexroth

("You do not come.") OHMPJ, *tr. by* Kenneth Rexroth

He does not think that I haunt here nightly. The Haunter. Thomas Hardy. NOBE

He doesn't like it, of course. His Body. Sandra McPherson. AmPA; LoL

He Done His Level Best. "Mark Twain." AiP

He doth sit by us and moan. (LL) On Another's Sorrow. William Blake. AWP; FHYEP; OxAEP-2; PoEL-4; Ro

He drank enough. D. H. Lawrence. Fr. A Snake came to my water-trough. CABP; CMoP; ChAP; EBEvV; EBNV; FaBoMo; HeIP-4; HoPM; LiTM; NOBE; NTP; NoAM; NoP-4; OAEL-2; PoRA; Poetr; TFi

He draws a man. Picture of a Man. Calvin Forbes. ISC

He draws memory out of me with hands of fire. Passion. Penelope Shuttle. LW *Fr.* Passion.

He dreamed first. Adam's Dying. Frederic Ridgely Torrence. FYAP

He dreamed not that the ocean would bear ships. A. J. Seymour. *Fr.* For Christopher Columbus. PBCV

He dreamed of / an open window. The Dream. Felix Pollak. RaBo

He dreamt that he saw the buffalant. Song. Thomas Hood. CBNP

He drew a circle that shut me out. Outwitted. Edwin Markham. BLPA; MoAmPo; PoToHe

He drew hundreds of women. Beauty and Sadness. Cathy Song. NoAM

He dropped, [—]more sullenly than wearily. The Dead-Beat. Wilfred Owen. PeFWW

He drowsed and was aware of silence heaped. The Death-Bed. Siegfried Sassoon. AF; LiTM; NSI; PeFWW; PoFWW

He dwelt among 'apartments let'. Jacob. Phoebe Cary. APAD; APN-2; OBAL; PAR

He dyes / his white hair black. The Compromise. Ibn al-Rumi, *Arabic*. ArPe, *tr. by* Omar S. Pound

He eats of the fruits of the great Speckle. Real Live. Ted Berrigan. FTOS *Fr.* The Sonnets.

He either fears his fate too much. The Touch. James Graham, Marquess of Montrose. *Fr.* I'll Never Love Thee More. GBL; NOBE; OBEV

He Embarketh in the Boat of Ra. *Unknown*. AWP *Fr.* Book of the Dead.

He ended and the kebars sheuk. Robert Burns. *Fr.* Love and Libery—A Cantata. NOBRP; NOEC

He ended, nor the Argicide refus'd. Homer. OBVE, *tr. by* William Cowper *Fr.* Odyssey. NAWM-1, *tr. by* Robert Fitzgerald

He entered with the authority of politeness. The Southerner. Karl Shapiro. NYBP

He Entereth the House of the Goddess Hathor. *Unknown*. AWP *Fr.* Book of the Dead.

He escape the lynch days. He survives. Wole Soyinka. HBAPE

He Establisheth His Triumph. *Unknown*. AWP *Fr.* Book of the Dead.

He Faces the Second Winter. Philip Levine. PoA *Fr.* Sierra Kid.

He fails who climbs to power and place. Failure and Success. Richard Watson Gilder. PWR

He fathers-forth whose beauty is past change: / Praise him. (LL) Pied Beauty. Gerard Manley Hopkins. APAD; AWP; CMoP; ClHu; EBEvV; EBVV; EnVR; EnlH; FaBoMo; GTBS-P; HAP; HeIP-4; HoPM; ImPo; InPK-6; InPS-3; LiTM; MoBrPo; MoP; NAEL-2; NOBF; NOBVV; NTP; NoAM; NoP-4; OAEL-2; OBEV; OBMV; OBNC; OxAEP-2; OxBSP; PBMP; PoE; PoPoPo; PoRA; Poetr; RB; RaBo; SCGP; SCV; SoSe-8; TFi; TTTS; UV; WeW-3

He feared angina from his thirtieth year. David Campbell. *See* I Starting from Central Station.

He fed them generously who were his flocks. W. D. Snodgrass. Son

He feels small as he awakens. The Awakening. Robert Creeley. NeAP

He Fell among Thieves. Sir Henry John Newbolt. EBVV; FaPoR; OBEV; OBWP; OxBTC

He fell for a beautiful. The Love of the Quartz Pebble. Vasco Popa. PoSu, *tr.* by Anne Pennington *Fr.* The Quartz Pebble.

He fell from her knees like a ball of yarn. Mother. Zbigniew Herbert, *Polish.* IFJA, *tr.* by John Carpenter *and* Bogdana Carpenter

He fell from the roof. News. Louis Dudek. *Fr.* Provincetown. MoCV

He fell in victory's fierce pursuit. The General Elliott. Robert Graves. PeLV

He fell off a barn on his head. Captains Courageous. Frank O'Hara. FTOS

He felt the wild beast in him betweenwhiles. George Meredith. EnVR; NOBVV *Fr.* Modern Love.

He finds the God there far unlike his books. (LL) Chorus Sacerdotum. Greville Fulke. HAP; NAEL-1; NOBE; NoP-4; NoSic; PoEL-1

He first deceased; [*or* deceas'd:] she for a little tried [*or* tri'd]. Upon the Death of Sir Albert [*or* us] Morton's Wife. Sir Henry Wotton. BoLoP; EnLoPo; FaBoEE; OBEV; OxBM; PBRV; SeCP; WeW-3

He flew awa in a blazing flame. (LL) Riddles Wisely Expounded. *Unknown.* CH; ESPB; OxBoLi

He followed his own mind. *Unknown, Tlingit Indian.* STP, *tr.* by James Koller

He followed me up and he followed me down. Lady Isabel and the Elf Knight (Pretty Polly). *Unknown.* AmFP

He followed their lilting stanzas. A Local Poet. John Hewitt. PNI

He found a formula for drawing comic rabbits. Epitaph on an Unfortunate Artist. Robert Graves. FaBoEE; NOBL; OBCoV

He found a fossil. Stone. Mark McWatt. HCP

He found her by the ocean's moaning verge. George Meredith. EnVR; NoP-4; OAEL-2 *Fr.* Modern Love.

He frightens all the witches and the dragons in their lair. The Black Cock. Ishmael Reed. ISC

He from the wind-bitten North with ship and companions descended. A Drifter off Tarentum. Rudyard Kipling. FaBoEE; NSI; PeFWW; PoWW *Fr.* Epitaphs of the War [1914–1918]. OBWP

He fumbles at your Soul. Emily Dickinson. APN-2; LW; NAAL-1; NAAL-3; NCAP; NOCV; PAR; TRP

("He fumbles at your spirit.") CBLP; ColAP

("That scalps your naked soul.") (LL) ColAP

He gave answers to questions they didn't ask. Dorothee Sölle. CrSp

He gave himself another year. Patrick Kavanagh. BIrV *Fr.* The Great Hunger.

He gave his strength and his loveliness for his country. On a Soldier Killed in the Great War. R. Williams Parry, *Welsh.* OBWVE, *tr.* by H. Idris Bell

He gave joy to men & more joy. Krantor. Theaitetus, *Greek.* GrAn, *tr.* by Dennis Schmitz

He gave silver shoes to the rabbit. Blake Leads a Walk on the Milky Way. Nancy Willard. OBCA

He gave the solid rail a hateful kick. The Egg and the Machine. Robert Frost. MoAmPo

He gave us all a good-bye cheerily. Messmates. Sir Henry John Newbolt. CH; EBVV; PeVV

He gave us eyes to see them, And lips that we might tell, How great is God Almighty, Who has made all things well. (LL) All things bright and beauteous. Cecil Frances Alexander. FaPoR; OxBChV; TIRV; UV

He gazed and gazed and gazed and gazed. Rhyme for a Child Viewing a Naked Venus in a Painting [of "The Judgement of Paris"]. Robert Browning. OBCoV

He gives her all the configurations. Configurations. Grace Nichols. LW

He gives me a handshake. Big Chill Variations. Reuben Jackson. UnSA

He gloried in the feats. My Father's Heroes. Allison Joseph. SeSe

He glows like a broadchested / Georgian munching a raspberry. Osip Mandelstam. *See* Poem No. 286 (On Stalin).

He gossips like my grandmother, this man. The Cleaving. Li-Young Lee. NAmP90; OpBo; PuP-16

He grew where waves ride nine feet high. In Memoriam: Roy Campbell. Ralph Nixon Currey. PeSA

He had a name. Generations 1. Sam Cornish. GT

He Had a Quality of Growth. Muriel Rukeyser. NNaP

He had been coming a very long time. For Malcolm Who Walks in the Eyes of Our Children. Quincy Troupe. PoBA

He had been free. Resurrection. Winifred Holtby. WPN

He had been long t'wards Mathematicks. Portrait of Sidrophel. Samuel Butler. PoEL-3 *Fr.* Hudibras.

He had determined to dance the presence of the dance. He had been in fact determined. The Presence of the Dance / The Resolution of the Music. Robert Duncan. FTOS

He had done with fleets and squadrons, with the restless roaming seas. Admiral Dugout. Cicely Fox-Smith. NSI

He had driven half the night. Hay for the Horses. Gary Snyder. BB; CoAmPo; LoL; TRP

He had got, finally. A Poem for Speculative Hipsters. Imamu Amiri Baraka. NOBA; NoAM

He had his Thirty-nine Articles. A Fossil. May Kendall. VWP

He had just surrendered the secret of the sun. A Mat to Weave. U Tam'si Tchicaya, *French.* NegPo, *tr.* by Ellen Conroy Kennedy

He had need of a way. Being Somebody. Edwin Honig. TAP

He had no royal palace. A Christmas Verse. "Kay." BoTP

He had not looked. When We Look Up. Denise Levertov. *Fr.* During the Eichmann Trial. HP

He "Had Not Where to Lay His Head." Frances Ellen Watkins Harper. PWR

He had smiled at us. Maximus, to Gloucester, Letter 19. Charles Olson. CMoP *Fr.* The Maximus Poems.

He had studied in private years ago. Artichoke. Henry Taylor. MT

He had to be four times cuckold. (LL) The Temperaments. Ezra Pound. BoLoP; MeMAP; NOBA; NoAM; OBCoV

He had to die they say. Heaven's Ring. Vasco Popa, *Serbian.* VCWP, *tr.* by Charles Simic

He had written praises of a regicide;. Byron on Southey. Byron. OxBoV *Fr.* The Vision of Judgment.

He halted in the wind, and—what was that. A Boundless Moment. Robert Frost. NAAL-2

He hands / down the gift. The Gift. Robert Creeley. NOBA

He hands them back when he sees they are done. (LL) The Toaster. William Jay Smith. NOxBChV; OTCP

He has a rather plain wife. My Neighbor. Roque Dalton, *Spanish.* AF, *tr.* by Richard Schaaf

He has an eye for cities. Among his rows. Lewis Mumford. George Buchanan. PNI

He has built himself a cottage in the wood. A Cottage in the Wood. Russell Edson. LCAP-2

He has chopped wood (very badly too) and carried logs for one. Caliban's Journal. Suniti Namjoshi. RACG

He has come to report himself. The Missing Person. Donald Justice. NYBP; Poetr

He has few hairs, only about the ears. Anacreon, *Greek.* OBCVT, *tr.* by David Constantine

He has gone. Last Journey. Enrique Gonzáles Martínez, *Spanish.* PBMP, *tr.* by Samuel Beckett

He has gone away again. To Her Father. Sophie Cabot Black. MoLi

He has gone into the forest. Journey to the Interior. William Jay Smith. DiPo

He has hanged himself—the Sun. November. Frederick William Harvey. OxBTC

He has held. Pereyin Muruvalar, *Tamil.* PLW, *tr.* by A. K. Ramanujan

He has lain here for a terrible, motionless. Woody Guthrie Visited by Bob Dylan: Brooklyn State Hospital, New York, 1961. David Wojahn. PBCAP *Fr.* Mystery Train: A Sequence.

He has lost him completely. And now he is seeking. In Despair. Constantine P. Cavafy, *Greek.* EP, *tr.* by Rae Dalven

He has not woo'd, but he has lost his heart. A Country Dance. Charles Tennyson Turner. NOBVV

He has solved it—Life's wonderful problem. Laurels and Immortelles. *Unknown.* BLPA

He has the sign. Portrait of Malcolm X. Etheridge Knight. PoBA

He has three singles on the charts and in. Tattoo, Corazon: Ritchie Valens, 1959. David Wojahn. PBCAP *Fr.* Mystery Train: A Sequence.

He hasn't gone to work. The Poem Circling Hamtramck, Michigan, All Night in Search of You. Philip Levine. NNaP

He Hath Need of Rest. Josephine D. Henderson Heard. CBWP-4

He Hath No Parallel. Sadi. AWP, *tr.* by L. Cranmer-Byng *Fr.* The Gulistan.

He hath no place to rest his head. Judaeus Errans. Louis Golding. TrJP

'He hears it not now, but used to notice such things'? (LL) Afterwards. Thomas Hardy. CH; CMoP; EBEV; GEA; GTBS-P; InPS-3; LiTM; MoBrPo; NOBE; NoP-4; OAEL-2; OBNC; OxAEP-2; PoEL-5; PoPoPo; TFi; TOF

He Hears the Cry of the Sedge. W. B. Yeats. OxBTC; RB

He hears the summer at a distance. Vanishing Point. Peter Cooley. AmPA

He Held Radical Light. A. R. Ammons. PoE; VCAP

He Hides within the Lily. William Channing Gannett. AH

He hie fie finger / speak in simple sound. The Man. Robert Creeley. OBAL

He hies him once more to the runlet, / To fetch her the Drake! (LL) The Little Man That Had a Little Gun. "Lewis Carroll." BXAP; CBNP

He hikes those narrow chords one more time. But, ruby my dear. Wanda Coleman. MoNo

He hoes the grain under a midday sun. Pitying the Farmer. Li Shen, *Chinese.* CoBCP, *tr.* by Burton Watson

He Hola. Keri Hulme. PeNZ

He Holdeth Fast to the Memory of His Identity. *Unknown.* AWP *Fr.* Book of the Dead.

He holds a volume open in his hands. Boy with Book of Knowledge. Howard Nemerov. NoP-4

He humbled and hewed down until at last he fell himself. *Unknown. See* The Battle of Maldon.

He imagines her. Hugh Seidman. *Fr.* The Modes of Vallejo Street, San Diego, Los Angeles. UnPo

He Intercedes with Charlemagne for His Brother in Exile. Paul the Deacon, *Latin.* MLL, *tr. by* Helen Waddell

He invented a rainbow but lightning struck it. Bushed. Earle Birney. MoCV; NOBC; NoAM; NoP-4

He is a bad sleeper and it is a joy to me. A Bad Sleeper. Paul Verlaine, *French.* EP, *tr. by* François Pirou

He is a friendly TOAD. (LL) A Friend in the Garden. Juliana Horatia Ewing. BoTP; CTAV; OxBChV; PeP

He is a god in my eyes. He is More than a Hero. Sappho, *Greek.* NNPT, *tr. by* Mary Barnard

He is a parricide to his mother's name. In Praise of Women in General. Thomas Randolph. NOSC

He is a tower unleaning. But how will he not break. Vaunting Oak. John Crowe Ransom. OxBA; VGW

He is a young knight from the south of Han-tan. Youth of Han-tan, The; a Song. Kao Shih, *Chinese.* SuSp, *tr. by* Joseph J. Lee

He is almost a god, a man beside you. Sappho, *Greek.* InMo, *tr. by* Sam Hamill

He is always right. The Interrogator. Elizabeth Jennings. WPE

He is an Englishman! The Englishman. Sir William Schwenck Gilbert. NOBL *Fr.* H. M. S. Pinafore.

He is an inharmonious note. Fragment. Sir Roger Casement. TIRV

He is an utter failure as a devil. A Devil. Zbigniew Herbert, *Polish.* RB, *tr. by* Czeslaw Milosz

He is blood, himself. The Water of the Flowery Mill (II). Jerome Rothenberg. FTOS

He is coming, Adzed-Head. *Unknown.* NOIV

He is coming, my long-desired lord. The River of Heaven. *Unknown.* AWP, *tr. by* Lafcadio Hearn *Fr.* Manyo Shu, Part 3 of 4.

He is dead, the beautiful youth. Killed at the Ford. Henry Wadsworth Longfellow. CBCWP

He Is Declared True of Word. *Unknown.* AWP *Fr.* Book of the Dead.

He Is Far. *Unknown.* OAEL-1

He is firm and strong. Oriki Erinle. *Unknown, Yoruba.* PBA; TTY, *tr. by* Ulli Beier

He is from those mountains. What She Said. Kapilar, *Tamil.* PLW, *tr. by* A. K. Ramanujan

He Is Gone. Anna Swirszczynska, *Polish.* PoSu, *tr. by* Czeslaw Milosz *and* Leonard Nathan (b. 1924)

He is gone that gray haired man. The Accordian Player. W. R. Rodriguez. EC3

He is having his hair cut. Towels are tucked. Alex at the Barber's. John Fuller. PeLV

He is knit with his doom. (LL) Exiles. "Æ." BIrV; MoBrPo

He is knit with his doom. (LL) Germinal. "Æ." BIrV; MoBrPo; OBEV; OBMV

He Is like the Lotus. *Unknown.* AWP *Fr.* Book of the Dead. (Death as a Lotus Flower.) TTY, *tr. by* Ulli Beier

He Is like the Serpent Saka. *Unknown.* AWP *Fr.* Book of the Dead.

He is lost to the small farms, lane by lane. (LL) A Day in August. Frank Ormsby. IIP; PBCIP; PNI

He is made one with Nature. Made One With Nature. Shelley. EPCY; LBC *Fr.* Adonais; An Elegy on the Death of Keats. EBEV; FHYEP; HoPM; ImPo; NOBRP; OAEL-2; OxAEP-2; PoEL-4; TFi

He is making love with his wife on the roof. The Roof of the World. Michael Dennis Browne. AmPA

He is more than a hero. Sappho, *Greek.* NNPT; PRWP, *tr. by* Mary Barnard

He is murdered upright in the day. Vaticide. Myron O'Higgins. PoBA

He Is My Countryman. Antoni Slonimski, *Polish.* TrJP, *tr. by* Frances Notley

He is my love / my sweet nutgrove. *Unknown, Irish.* BIrV, *tr. by* Michael Hartnett

He is no friend who in thine hour of pride. Friendship. Sadi. AWP, *tr. by* L. Cranmer-Byng *Fr.* The Gulistan.

He is not a brother to me. The Brother. Semion Yakovlevich Nadson, *Russian.* TrJP, *tr. by* H. Badanes

He is not dead. (LL) Frederick Douglass: 1817-1895. Langston Hughes. BPo; CBCWP

He Is Not Dead. James Whitcomb Riley. BLPA

He is not dead nor liveth. Epilogue. Dorothy, Duchess of Wellington Wellesley. OBMV *Fr.* Deserted House.

He is not de[a]d that sometime [*or* somtyme] hath a fall. Sir Thomas Wyatt. AAS; OBVE

He is not here, the old sun. No Possum, No Sop, No Taters. Wallace Stevens. HCAP; MeMAP; OxBA; TAP; VGW

He is not John the gardener. A Friend in the Garden. Juliana Horatia Ewing. BoTP; CTAV; OxBChV; PeP

He is not the man who goes over the wall. Man on the Edge. Herberto Padilla, *Spanish.* VCWP, *tr. by* Alastair Reid *and* Alexander Coleman

He is now at rest. Samuel Rogers. EPCY *Fr.* Italy. OBNC

He is old, two weeks to eighty. Blue Sparks in Dark Closets. Richard Snyder. Poetsp

He is older than the naval side of British history. Chief Petty Officer. Charles Causley. OxBTC

He is one of the prophets come back. Lawrence Ferlinghetti. NeAP; PoM

He Is Out of Heart with His Time, *sonnet.* Guerzo di Montecanti, *Italian.* AWP, *tr. by* D. G. Rossetti

He is patient, he is not angry. Invocation of the Creator. *Yoruba Oral Tradition, Yoruba.* BLT, *tr. by* Ulli Beier

He is quick, thinking in clear images. In Broken Images. Robert Graves. NoP-4; TRP

He is risen now that was so long asleep. War. Georg Heym, *German.* PeFWW, *tr. by* Patrick Bridgwater

He is rust / in moonlight. Coyote Fragments. Lance Henson. HATNAP

He is Shaka the unshakable. Shaka, King of the Zulus. *Unknown, Zulu.* PBA; TTY, *tr. by* A. C. Jordan

He is sherrier. The Thinnest Shadow. John Ashbery. TTTS

He is singing the end. Spider Webster's Declaration: He Is Singing the End of the World Again. Judy Grahn. EC2

He is stark mad, who ever says. The Broken Heart. Donne. EBEV; FSCP

He is sun-bright myth and Cosmic Light. O Lord of Light! A Mystic Sage Returns to Realms of Eternity! Askia Muhammad Touré. SeSe

He is the Great God, Who is in heaven. Great Hymm. Ntsikana Gaba, *Xhosa.* PeSAV, *tr. by* John Knox Bokwe

He Is the Lonely Greateness. Madeleine Caron Rock. CH

He is the oldest grandfather. The Memory Sire. Barney Bush. HATNAP

He is the pond's old father, its brain. The Snapper. William Heyen. AmPA

He is to weet a melancholy carle. A Portrait. Keats. BXAP; UV

He is trying to write down a book he wrote years ago in his head. South America. Tom Raworth. NBrP

He is very busy with his looking. Young Heroes. Gwendolyn Brooks. BPo; NAAAL

He is very old. At his sunken brow. Derzhavin. Georgy Arkadevich Shengeli, *Russian.* TCRP, *tr. by* Daniel Weissbort

He is wasted now. Dylan, Who Is Dead. Samuel Allen. PoBA

He jangles his keys in the rain. The Ram. Selima Hill. EP; NBrP

He jests at scars [that never felt a wound]. The Living Juliet. Shakespeare. EBEvV; ImPo *Fr.* Romeo and Juliet.

He journeys over the dark land. St Sava's Journey. Vasco Popa. PoSu, *tr. by* Anne Pennington *Fr.* St Sava's Spring.

He jumped me while I was asleep. Assailant. John Raven. BPo

He jumped, seeing an island like a hand. Hart Crane. Julian Symons. PoA

He jumps from behind, flying like a shard. The White Tiger Leaps. Sarah Gorham. FFC *Fr.* Notes From a Chinese Love Manual.

"He killed his parents." Majeski Plays the Saxophone. Martín Espada. SeSe

He [*or* When he] killed the noble Mudjokivis. The Modern Hiawatha. George A. Strong. BXAP; EBEvV; OBCoV; PeLV; UV *Fr.* The Song of Milkanwatha.

He Kindleth a Fire. *Unknown.* AWP *Fr.* Book of the Dead.

He knelt, the Savior knelt and prayed. The Agony in the Garden. Felicia Dorothea Hemans. TrCP

He knew how death hunts / at distance. Epitaph: Atticus. Paulus Silentiarius, *Greek.* GrAn, *tr. by* Andrew Miller

He knew it was waiting for him somewhere. My Father's Death. Constance Urdang. PBCAP

He knew nothing about death. Nani Worries about Her Father's Happiness in the Afterlife. Ana Castillo. MoLi

He knew what I wanted. O Dirty Bird Yr Gizzard's Too Big & Full of Sand. James Koller. PoM

"He Knoweth Not That the Dead Are Thine." Mary Elizabeth Coleridge. OBNC (Unpunished.) SAGP

He Knoweth the Souls of the East. *Unknown.* AWP *Fr.* Book of the Dead.

He knows he must explain this. Hugh Seidman. *Fr.* The Modes of Vallejo Street, San Diego, Los Angeles. UnPo

He knows he will be hurt. Night Piece. Louise Glück. FiLi

He knows how to steal / laughs in a place / where your skin / is your passport. Yusef Komunyakaa. *See* Untitled Blues.

He knows what height is, this hillside dweller. Ralph Thompson. HCP

He larved ond he larved on he merd such a nauses. The Ondt and the Gracehoper. James Joyce. BIrV *Fr.* Finnegans Wake.

He lay, and those who watched him were amazed. The Sprig of Lime. Robert Malise Bowyer Nichols. GTBS-P

He lay in the middle of the world, and twitcht. John Berryman. HCAP; PoE *Fr.* Dream Songs.

He lay on the couch night after night. Saturn. Sharon Olds. RaBo

He lay on the floor covered in shit. 999 Call. Elizabeth Bartlett. FaBoWP

He lay with quiet heart in the stern asleep. Prayer at Night. Alcuin, *Latin.* MLL, tr. by Helen Waddell

He Leadeth Me. Joseph Henry Gilmore. AH

He leans on the gate going staying. Marlene Mountain. HA

He left his pants upon a chair. The Mistake. Theodore Roethke. OBCoV *Fr.* Three Epigrams. NBLV

He left not faction, but of that was left. (LL) Zimri: The Duke of Buckingham. Dryden. AWP; NOBE; OBSV

He left the Court in mere despair. (LL) Suppose me dead; and then suppose. Jonathan Swift. NOBE; NOEC; OxBoLi; PeLV; PoEL-3

He lies / Beside me. On Death and Love. Janet Campbell Hale. VoR

He lifted up, among the actuaries. So Long? Stevens. John Berryman. HAP; HCAP; NOBA *Fr.* Dream Songs.

He lifts his small hands. Mantis. Ruth Miller. PeSAV

He lifts the heavy tube. The Elk Uncovers the Heavens. John Bensko. MT

He lighted with his golden lamp on high. Walter Savage Landor. EPCY *Fr.* Shakespeare.

He Liked the Dead. Malcolm Lowry. OxBTC

He listened at the porch that day. A Year's Spinning. Elizabeth Barrett Browning. NAEL-2

He Lived a Life. H. N. Fifer.
  "What was his creed?" PoToHe

He Lived amidst th' Untrodden Ways. Hartley Coleridge. NOBL; PFE; PeLV; UV

He lived in a small farm-house. A Refusal to Mourn. Derek Mahon. PNI

He lived so little: only forty years. "Nikolai Nikolaevich Morshen," *Russian.* TCRP, tr. by Bradley Jordan

He lives—he then unties the string. (LL) Warning to Children. Robert Graves. CBNP; FaBoCh; NOxBChV; NTP; NoP-4; OAEL-2

He lives in the sky. The Eagle above Us. Santiago Altamirano, *Cora Indian.* STP, tr. by Anselm Hollo

He lives, who last night flopped from a log. Burning. Galway Kinnell. CoAP

He liveth long who liveth well. Length of Days. Horatius Bonar. PWR

He loathed the fraud, yet would not bed alone. (LL) Ulysses. Robert Graves. CBLP; CMoP; EP; FaBoTw; MoP; NoAM

He lolls in the supermarket. Portrait of a House Detective. Hans Magnus Enzensberger, *German.* HP, tr. by Michael Hamburger; PoSu

He looked about six or seven, only much too thin. Forgiveness Dream. Jean Valentine. LCAP-2; NMM-2

He looked up to the convent. Black Spiders. Kathleen Jamie. FaBoTC

He looks back at me. The Guerrilla-Cong. Michael S. Harper. NBV

He looks back over the last metaphor. The Great Artist Reconsiders the Homeric Simile. John Tranter. BMAP; NOBAu; NoAM

He looks down to watch the river twist. Gargoyle. Thomas Rabbitt. MT

He looks into a glass. Lord, What is Man? Carl Rakosi. FTOS

He looks like a fat little old man. Dead Seal. Alfred Wellington Purdy. MoCV; MoP

He loved her, and through many years. Then and Now. Paul Laurence Dunbar. PBMP

He loved her so he wrote. Body Language. Sylvia Kantaris. LW

He loved his cabin: there. Salt Water Story. Richard Hugo. NAAL-2; NoAM

He loved peculiar plants and rare. Education's Martyr. May Kendall. VWP

He loved the brook's soft sound. The Peasant Poet. John Clare. FHYEP; OAEL-2; OBNC

He loved three things [in life]. "Anna Akhmatova," *Russian.* BoWoP, tr. by Barbara Einzig; RaBo, tr. by Jerome Bullitt

He loved to pull out his clasp-knife. Gardener. A. H. Snow. OBGa

He Loves. David Schirmer, *German.* GePo, tr. by George C. Schoolfield

He Loves and He Rides Away. Sydney Thompson Dobell. OBNC

He Loves in Vain. Christian Hofmann von Hofmannswaldau, *German.* GePo, tr. by George C. Schoolfield

He loves it when the lawyer shouts. Watching TV, the Elk Bones Up on Metaphysics. John Bensko. MT

He loves me. *Unknown.* OxNR

He made it / say itself inside our heads. Robert Kelly. *See* Newark.

He made peace with eternity. Second-Class Citizen. Slavko Mihalic. PoSu, tr. by Charles Simic

He made the whole Fleet love him, damn his eyes! (LL) 1805. Robert Graves. FaBoCh; OBCoV; OBSV; PeLV

He makes himself comfortable. 1st Dance—Making Things New—6 February 1964. Jackson Mac Low. FTOS

He Maketh Himself One with Osiris. *Unknown.* AWP *Fr.* Book of the Dead.

He Maketh Himself One with the God Ra. *Unknown.* AWP, tr. by Robert Hillyer *Fr.* Book of the Dead.

He Maketh Himself One with the Only God, Whose Limbs Are the Many Gods. *Unknown.* AWP *Fr.* Book of the Dead.

He making speedy way through spersed ayre. Edmund Spenser. NoSic *Fr.* Wood Of Error. AEP

He many waies his labouring thoughts revolves. Virgil. OBCVT, tr. by Sir John Denham *Fr.* The Passion of Dido for Aeneas.

He marvelled at her breasts, and when he'd seen them. Amaru. EP, tr. by John Brough

He may be six kinds of a liar. Loyalty. Berton Braley. BLPA

He may our prophet, and our tutor prove. Mary Sidney, Countess of Montgomery Wroth. NoP-4

He measured out his spirit tower. *Unknown, Chinese.* SuSp, tr. by Heng Kuan

He Meditates on the Life of a Rich Man. Douglas Hyde, *Irish.* OBMV, tr. by Lady Augusta Gregory

He meets, by heavenly chance express. The Lover. Coventry Patmore. OxAEP-2 *Fr.* The Angel in the House.

He met a lady. From the Hazel Bough. Earle Birney. HeIP-4

He might be weak enough to suffer woe. (LL) Spit in my face ye [or you] Jew[e]s, and pierce my side. Donne. Son; TOF

He motions me over with a question. Kidnap[p]er. Tess Gallagher. AmPA

He moves into his Hall: The Pow'rs resort. Homer. *See* Thetis Asks Jove to Revenge Her Son Achilles.

He needs you. Dorothee Sölle. CrSp *Fr.* When He Came.

He never acted well by man or woman. George IV. William Makepeace Thackeray. *Fr.* The Georges. FaBoEE

He Never Did That to Me. Noël Coward. NBLV

He Never Expected Much. Thomas Hardy. NAEL-2; NoAM; OxBTC; SCV

He never felt twice the same about the flecked river. This Solitude of Cataracts. Wallace Stevens. LCAP-2

He never learned her, quite. Year after year. Marrysong. Dennis Scott. HCP

He never lives to tell. Calenture. Alastair Reid. NYBP

He never made the dive—not while I watched. The Springboard. Louis MacNeice. PoA

He Never Said a Mumblin' Word, *see also* Crucifixion: "They crucified my Lord, an' He never said a mumbalin' word." *Unknown.* APN-2

He never spoke a word to me. Simon the Cyrenian Speaks. Countee Cullen. BPo; ChIV-2; HAP; MoAmPo; TTY; TrCP

He nice frum far, but far frum nice. Vicious Circle. Marsha Prescod. LW

He nothing common did or mean. King Charles on [or upon] the Scaffold. Andrew Marvell. *Fr.* An Horatian Ode upon Cromwell's Return from Ireland. CABP; EBEV; ESCV; FMP; GTBS-P; GeHe; HAP; IIP; InPS-3; NOBE; NOSC; OAEL-1; OBEV; OBWP; OxAEP-1; PoEL-2; SCGP; SeCP; TFi

He, of his gentleness. In the Wilderness. Robert Graves. CH; MoBrPo; PeECV

He offers, between planes. Conversation with a Fireman from Brooklyn. Tess Gallagher. CrSp; IFJA

He often came and stood outside my door. The Lonely Dog. Margaret E. Bruner. PoToHe

He often would ask us. The Choirmaster's Burial. Thomas Hardy. PeECV

He once did love with fond affection. Forsaken. *Unknown.* AmFP

He once riveted boat to whale. Harpoonist. George Mackay Brown. FaBoTC *Fr.* Runes from a Holy Island.

He only happy is, and wise. How to Ride Out a Storm. Mildmay Fane, 2d Earl of Westmorland. NOSC

He opened the car door. There was a low rumble. The Meeting. Nicki Jackowska. BrRo

He opens his eyes with a cry of delight. A Child's Christmas Day. *Unknown.* OBCP

He Overcometh the Serpent of Evil in the Name of Ra. *Unknown.* AWP *Fr.* Book of the Dead.

He overtook a cruiser in a tiny boat. Performances. Nina Cassian, *Romanian.* IFJA, tr. by Brenda Walker

He paced the length of it all day. My Father's Garden. E. K. Miller. IFJA

He Paid Me Seven. *Unknown.* BPo

He painted the mountain over and over again. Dearest Reader. Michael Palmer. FTOS

He pass'd his Journey, to the Court arriv'd. Claudian. OBCVT, *tr. by* Aaron Hill *Fr.* Claudian's Rufinus: or, The Court Favourite's Overthrow.

He paused on the sill of a door ajar. The Newcomer's Wife. Thomas Hardy. BoLoP; OxBTC

He pays the whole, and yet I am not free. (LL) Sonnet 134. Shakespeare. HeIP-4; OxAEP-1

He Perceives His Rashness in Love, but Has No Choice. Guido Guinicelli, *Italian.* AWP, *tr. by* D. G. Rossetti

He planked down sixpence and he took his drink. Henry Turnbull. Wilfrid Wilson Gibson. FaBoTw

He played by the river when he was. Washington. Nancy Byrd Turner. CTV

He plays. Advice. Lee Cataldi. BMAP

He plodded away through drifts of i / ce. Susan Howe. FTOS

He Praises the Trees. *Unknown, Irish.* BIrV, *tr. by* Robin Skelton

He prayed for patience; Care and Sorrow came. His Answer. Clara Ann Thompson. BlSi; CBWP-2

He prayeth best [*or* well], who loveth best [*or* well]. Coleridge. BoTP; CTV *Fr.* The Rime of the Ancient Mariner. CABP; CH; EBEV; EBNV; FHYEP; FaBoBe; FaBoCh; HAP; HeIP-4; HoPM; ImPo; InPS-3; NOBE; NoP-4; OAEL-2; OBEV; OBNC; OBNV; OxAEP-2; OxBoS; PeECV; PoE; PoEL-4; PoPoPo; SCGP; TFi; TOF

He Prayeth for Ink and Palette That He May Write. *Unknown.* AWP *Fr.* Book of the Dead.

He preached upon "Breadth" till it argued him narrow. Emily Dickinson. AmPP; NAWM-2; NOCV

He preaches to the crowd that power is lent. Vox Populi. Dryden. NOBE *Fr.* The Medal [*or* Medall].

He preens his plumes while strutting proud. With Reservations. Naomi Stroud Simmons. PoSu

He preferr'd Hanover to England. George I--Star of Brunswick. William Makepeace Thackeray. *Fr.* The Georges. FaBoEE

He pushes behind the words. Waiting. Robert Creeley. VGW

He put his acorn helmet on. An Elfin Knight. Joseph Rodman Drake. BoTP *Fr.* The Culprit Fay.

He put the Belt around my life. Emily Dickinson. TRP

He puts four dimes into the slot. Vending Machine. Hans Magnus Enzensberger. PoSu

He Puts Me to Rest. David Ignatow. VGW

He Raise a Poor Lazarus. *Unknown.* AH

He ran a good shop, and he died. The Greengrocer. Michael Longley. BiHa *Fr.* Wreaths.

He ran the course and as he ran he grew. Innocence. Thom Gunn. HP; LiTM

He reaches Weymouth treads the Esplanade. The Royal Tour. "Peter Pindar." OxBoLi; PeLV

He Remembers Forgotten Beauty. W. B. Yeats. CTC

  ("On her most lonely mysteries.") (LL) ADE

  (O'Sullivan Rua to Mary Lavell.) ADE

He Remembers How He Didn't Understand What Lieutenant Dawson Meant. James Whitehead. MT

He removes his glove. Raymond Roseliep. HA

He Resigns. John Berryman. OxBSP; WeW-3

He rested in the cool, that traveller. The African Tramp. Geoffrey Haresnape. PeSA

He rested through the winter, watched the rain. Death of a Gardener. Phoebe Hesketh. OBGa

He Revisits Cambridge. Tennyson. *Fr.* In Memoriam A. H. H.

He rides at their head. The College Colonel. Herman Melville. CBCWP; LiLi; NCAP; OBWP

He riseth up early in the morning. The Mighty Hunter. Mrs. J. B. Worley. PoLF

He roars in the swamp. The Alligator. Beatrice Witte Ravenel. WPE

He rode a white horse. Colonel. Kate Llewellyn. NOBAu

He rode forth armed: breast-plate and crest. A Romance. Chester Kallman. PoA

He rode into town upon a wild-eyed mountain horse. Yellowjacket. Peter Blue Cloud. HATNAP

He rose at dawn and, fired with hope. The Sailor Boy. Tennyson. OxBoS; SCGP

He rose the morrow morn. (LL) The Rime of the Ancient Mariner. Coleridge. CABP; CH; EBEV; EBNV; FHYEP; FaBoBe; FaBoCh; HAP; HeIP-4; HoPM; ImPo; InPS-3; NOBE; NOBRP; NoP-4; OAEL-2; OBEV; OBNC; OBNV; OxAEP-2; OxBoS; PeECV; PoE; PoEL-4; PoPoPo; Ro; SCGP; TFi; TOF

He rose up on his dying bed. Hope. Langston Hughes. APSN; OBAL; PFTM

He rubbed his eyes and wound the silver horn. Little Boy Blue. John Crowe Ransom. LiTM

He runs before the wise men: He. Stanley Kunitz. NoP-4; VGW

He Said. Jean Valentine. TAP

He said he would be back and we'd drink wine together. Waiting for Icarus. Muriel Rukeyser. LCAP-2; NNaP

He said—(I only give the heads)—he said. Byron. EPCY *Fr.* The Vision of Judgment. OAEL-2

He said I should try something harder. A Mask of Anger. Lyn Hejinian. FTOS

He said: "If in his image I was made." Trumbull Stickney. APN-2

He said it was like a black bird. His Depression. Patricia Dobler. CMAP

He said: / "Let's stay here." Party Piece. Brian Patten. BoLoP; FaBoSe

He said to them, Look at this: you see. The Tall Wind. K. O. Arvidson. PeNZ

He sang in another room. Montecastelli Poem. Sophie Behrens. NBrP

He sang of life, serenely sweet. The Poet. Paul Laurence Dunbar. AAP; BPo; CrDW; NAAAL

He sank beneath the Lowland sea. *Unknown. See* The Golden Vanity.

He sat at the Algonquin, smoking a cigar. At the Algonquin. Howard Moss. Poetsp

He sat at the dinner table. Just like a Man. *Unknown.* BoTP

He sat in a wheeled chair, waiting for dark. Disabled. Wilfred Owen. CMoP; InPS-3; LiTM; MoP; NAEL-2; NSI; NoAM; OBWVE; OxBTC; PeFWW; PoFWW; PoPoPo; SCGP

He sat in his cell staring. The Baboon. Rhydwen Williams, *Welsh.* OBWVE, *tr. by* R. Gerallt Jones

He sat up slowly, and around his left side. Lazarus. Agnes Nemes Nagy, *Hungarian.* GI; PoSu, *tr. by* Frederic Will

He sat upon the rolling deck. Sailor. Langston Hughes. PoA

He sate like winter o'er the wasted year. Thomas Tod Stoddart. NOBRP *Fr.* Death-Wake, The; or, Lunacy.

He saw her from the bottom of the stairs. Home Burial. Robert Frost. ColAP; IMW; NAAL-2; SoSe-8; TAP; TRP

He saw in every palm-leat something new. On the Flesh of Christ. John William Corrington. MT

He saw it first, me just the big, the. Dennis's Sky Leopard. Thylias Moss. IFJA

He saw the skull within the looping. Epitaph for a Scientist. Lex Banning. NOBAu

He saw thee Lord of all his creatures stand. (LL) The Created. Jones Very. APN-1; NOCV; PAR

He says again, 'Good fences make good neighbors'. (LL) Mending Wall. Robert Frost. AFr; AmPP; CMoP; ChAP; ClHu; EBEvV; FaBoPV; HAP; HeIP-4; HoPM; ImGa; InPS-3; LiTM; MeMAP; MoAmPo; MoP; NAAL-2; NOBA; NoAM; NoP-4; OxBA; PoE; PoPoPo; Poetr; SAmP; SCV; SoSe-8; TAP; TFi; VGW; WeW-3

He says he doesn't feel like working today. My Erotic Double. John Ashbery. LCAP-2; PoE; SAGP; VCAP

He says, / in discs, each a different color. Chitra Divakaruni. *See* Yuba City School.

He says *My reign is in peace,* so slays. A Foreign Ruler. Walter Savage Landor. OBSV; PFE

He says: / "Only the black mind can project." Moving. Helen G. Quigless. BkSV

He says the waves in the ship's wake. Leaving Forever. Denise Levertov. InPK-6

He scanned it—staggered. Emily Dickinson. PoEL-5

He scarce had ceas't [*or* ceased] when the superior fiend. Satan's Summons. Milton. NOSC *Fr.* Book I. FHYEP; NAEL-1; OAEL-1; OxAEP-1 *Fr.* Paradise Lost.

He scattered tarantulas over the roads. The Devil in Texas. *Unknown.* NBLV; RB

He scorned his land, his tongue denied. Dic Siôn Dafydd. Thomas Jacob Thomas, *Welsh.* OBWVE, *tr. by* H. Idris Bell

He scowled at the barometer: "Will it rain?" Philosopher. John Frederick Nims. PFE

He seemed to know the harbour. The Shark. Edwin John Pratt. NOBC

He seems no longer to tremble. Theodore Roethke. *See* The Meadow Mouse.

He Sees His Beloved. James I, King of Scotland. PoEL-1 *Fr.* The Kingis Quair.

He sees them pass. Once. Eric N. Batterham. CH

He sees through stone. Etheridge Knight. CoAmPo; GT; MT; NNaP; PBCAP; PoBA

He seized me by the waist and kissed my throat. Charleston in the Eighteen-Sixties. Adrienne Rich. CoAP; NAAL-2

He served his God so faithfully and well. On a Puritan. Hilaire Belloc. FaBoEE

He served his master well from youth to age. Old Stephen. Charles Tennyson Turner. EBVV

He set out and kept hunting. The Hunter. Frank O'Hara. NNaP

He shakes the dust from off his feet. Battle of Murfreesboro. Allen Tate. FaBoA

He shall feed his flock like a shepherd: he shall gather the lambs with his arm and carry them in his bosom, and shall gently lead those that are young. (LL) Comfort ye, comfort ye my people. Bible, *O.T.* OBVE, *stanzas 1–8;* TrJP

He shall not hear the bittern cry. Lament for Thomas MacDonagh. Francis Ledwidge. BIrV; NOIV

He shall parley in the gate. Bible, *O.T. See* Psalm 127.

He/She. Stephen Dunn. NAmP90

He shifted his trumpet, and only took snuff. (LL) Poem: "Of old, when Scarron his companions invited." Oliver Goldsmith. FaBoEE; NOEC; NOIV; OBCoV; OxBoLi

He shifts on the bed carefully, so as. The Man on the Hotel Room Bed. Galway Kinnell. VCAP

He Shook off the Beast. Charles Wesley. ChIV-2

He should, he could, he would, he did the best. (LL) Look[e] Home. Robert Southwell. ESCV; NOCV; NoSic

He should not have sent his son. Meditations of Mr. Cogito on Redemption. Zbigniew Herbert, *Polish.* GI, *tr. by* John Carpenter *and* Bogdana Carpenter

He shoves the .38. The Cage Walker. Yusef Komunyakaa. WWSi

He showed me hights I never saw. Emily Dickinson. PoE

He shows me tonight. Nobody. Novica Tadic, *Serbo-Croatian.* HSix; VCWP, *tr. by* Charles Simic

He shuddered briefly and stared down the long valley. The Return of Robinson Jeffers. Robert Hass. AmPA

He shudders. . . feeling on the shaven spot. Electrocution. Lola Ridge. WPE

He shuffled my file. Lilith and the Doctor. Kathleen Norris. CrSp

He Singeth a Hymn to Osiris, the Lord of Eternity. *Unknown.* AWP *Fr.* Book of the Dead.

He Singeth in the Underworld. *Unknown.* AWP *Fr.* Book of the Dead.

He sipped at a weak hock and seltzer. The Arrest of Oscar Wilde at the Cadogan Hotel. John Betjeman. CMoP; EBEV; MoBrPo; MoP; NoAM; NoP-4; OxBTC

He sits at the bar in the Alhambra. Simple. Naomi Long Madgett. GT; PoBA

He sits in front of the bright, blazing grate. The Old Freedman. Priscilla Jane Thompson. CBWP-2

He sleeps on the top of a mast. The Unbeliever. Elizabeth Bishop. NAAL-2; NoAM

He slept in my bed. Drugs. Jacquie Jones. ISC

He slept like a rock or a man that's dead. (LL) The Weary Blues. Langston Hughes. ColAP; FaBoA; ISC; MoP; NAAAL; NOBA; NoAM; NoP-4; PoPoPo; SAmP

He slew the noble Mudjekeewis. What Hiawatha Probably Did. *Unknown.* NBLV

He slid out of the skin, leaving it. Summer. Diane Wakoski. VGW

He smashed all the glass in the room (Bill:50) $50). (LL) Delirium in Vera Cruz. Malcolm Lowry. FaBoTw; NoP-4; OxBTC

He smears. John Wilkinson. NBrP

He smelled bad and was red-eyed with the miseries. Portrait from the Infantry. Alan Dugan. AF

He smiles and looks gay. (LL) The Description of a Good Boy. Henry Dixon. OxBChV; OxNR

He smorit thame with smuke. (LL) The Dance of the Sevin Deidly Synnis. William Dunbar. MiEL; OxBS; PoE

He snuggles his fingers. After Winter. Sterling Brown. GT; PoBA

He sought the mountain and the loneliest height. Jesus Praying. Hartley Coleridge. ChIV-2

He spake, to whom I, answ'ring, thus replied. Homer. *Fr.* Odyssey. NAWM-1, *tr. by* Robert Fitzgerald

He spoke; and silent tow'rd the northern sky. Joel Barlow. APN-1 *Fr.* The Columbiad.

He spoke; and Sohrab smiled on him, and took. The Death of Sohrab. Matthew Arnold. *Fr.* Sohrab and Rustum. EBNV; OBNV

He spoke, and what he spoke was soon obeyed. London Subverted by the Furies. Abraham Cowley. NOSC

He spoke of undying love. The Talker. Benjamin Appel. TrJP

He spoke while sitting on what seemed to be. Memory II. George Seferis, *Greek.* GrIP, *tr. by* Edmund Keeley *and* Philip Sherrard

He Sports by Himself. Susan Miles. BXAP

He stalks in his vivid stripes. A Tiger in the Zoo. Leslie Norris. OTCP

He stalls above me like an elephant. (LL) To Speak of Woe That Is in Marriage. Robert Lowell. MoP; NAAL-2; NoAM

He stands against what looks like the other side. David Ferry. FaBoA

He stands before a red-hot furnace. The Worker. Nikolai Stepanovich Gumilyov, *Russian.* TCRP, *tr. by* Simon Franklin

He stands beside his ancient, lovely mistress. The Old Fisherman. Emily Grosholz. RA

He stands, cold in the morning wind. Roll-Call In the Concentration Camp. Dan Pagis, *Hebrew.* PoSu, *tr. by* Robert Friend

He stands in the door. Dried Fruit. Philip Dow. BXAP

He stands, stamps a little in his boots. The Roll Call. Dan Pagis, *Hebrew.* HP, *tr. by* Stephen Mitchell

He stands with his forefeet on the drum. Two Performing Elephants. D. H. Lawrence. RB

He stared at ruin. Ruin stared straight back. Dream Song 45. John Berryman. HCAP; PoPoPo; SAGP *Fr.* Dream Songs.

He startles awake. His eyes are full of white light. The Hermit Wakes to Bird Sounds. Maxine W. Kumin. Poetsp

He starts a landslide shooting a. Rabbit Shoeshine. S. K. Kelen. BMAP

He stayed, and was imprisoned in possession. W. H. Auden. CMoP *Fr.* Sonnets from China.

He steals your whole estate. (LL) Air: "A Fox may steal your hens, sir." John Gay. NOEC; NoP-4

He stepped on a land mine. Private Ian Godwin, U. S. M. C. Bryan Alec Floyd. CDa

He steps down from the dark train, blinking; stares. Ten Days Leave. W. D. Snodgrass. MoAmPo; Poetsp; UnPo

He steps out from the others. Passion of Ravensbrück. János Pilinszky, *Hungarian.* GI, *tr. by* Janos Csokits *and* Ted Hughes; HP, *tr. by* Ted Hughes; AF; PoSu, *tr. by* Ted Hughes *and* Janos Csokits

He still believes by middle-age. The Traveler. Duane Niatum. HATNAP

He still may leave thy garland green. (LL) Love and Friendship. Emily Jane Brontë. EBVV; FP; InPK-6; LW; SDW

He still stares into the windshield. After Going Off the Road During the Snowstorm. William Meissner. CMAP

He still wore the OD tee shirt. When Chicken Man Came Home to Roost. Frank A. Cross Jr. CDa

He stirs, beginning to awake. A Field Hospital. Randall Jarrell. NoP-4

He stood, a worn-out City clerk. Peace. Charles Stuart Calverley. EBVV; NOBVV

He stood alone within the spacious square. James Thomson. NOBVV *Fr.* The City of Dreadful Night. OBNC

He stood among a crowd at Drumahair [*or* Dromahair]. The Man Who Dreamed of Faeryland. W. B. Yeats. CMoP; NAEL-2; NoAM; NoP-4

He stood and call'd / His legions, angel forms, who lay intranced. Satan's Legions and the Beech Leaves of the Casentino. Milton. *Fr.* Book I. FHYEP; NAEL-1; OAEL-1; OxAEP-1 *Fr.* Paradise Lost.

He stood, and heard the steeple. Eight O'Clock. A. E. Housman. CMoP; InPK-6; MoBrPo; MoP; NoAM; OxBSP; PFE; PoE; Poetr; SoSe-8

He stood before my heart's closed door. The Refiner's Gold. Frances Ellen Watkins Harper. PWR

He stood in his shoes / And he wondered. (LL) The Naughty Boy. Keats. BoTP; CBNP; FHYEP; FaBoCh; OBCoV; OxBChV

He stood still by her bed. The Goodnight. Louis Simpson. PBMP

He stood upon the coast of County Clare. St. Enda. Laurence David Lerner. PeSA

He stood wrapped in air. Annunciation. Anna Kamienska, *Polish.* GI, *tr. by* Curzon, David and Grażyna Drabik

He stopped: it surely was a groan. The Sailor who had Served in the Slave-Trade. Robert Southey. Ro *Fr.* Poems.

He stopped on the irreproachable sidewalk. Elysee. Larry Eigner. VGW

He strides across the grassy corn. The Scarecrow. Andrew Young. FaBoTw

He sucks with greed the treacherous attraction. Death of a Fly. Goethe, *German.* STV, *tr. by* John Frederick Nims

He sung of God—the mighty source. David's Song to Saul. Christopher Smart. KSG *Fr.* "Song to David, A."

He switched on the electric light and laughed. Intimate Supper. Peter Redgrove. FaBoMo; OxBC

He takes the long review of things. To a Certain Most Certainly Certain Critic. David McCord. OBAL

He talked of Africa. Companion—North-East Dug-Out. Ivor Gurney. FP

He talked of Delhi brothels half the night. Long Tom. Wilfrid Wilson Gibson. OxBTC

He tells many bad things. Young Training. Lawrence McGaugh. PoBA

He tells me about the time. Learning My Father's Language. Lorraine Duggin. LoHo

He tells me in Bangkok he's robbed. Baby Villon. Philip Levine. CoAP; WeT

He tells you when you've got on too much lipstick. The Perfect Husband. Ogden Nash. Poetr

He tempted me to. Akiko Yosano, *Japanese.* OHMPJ, *tr. by* Kenneth Rexroth

He tends the tree who wants to eat the fruit. Nguyễn Trãi, *Vietnamese.* AVP, *tr. by* Huỳnh Sanh Thông

He thanked me for my kindness, disagreed. William Wetmore Story. APN-1 *Fr.* A Contemporary Criticism.

He Thanks His Woodpile. Lew Welch. BB

He that can trace a ship making her way. The Heart Is Deep. Roger Wolcott. ChIV-1; SCAP

He that dwelleth in the secret place of the most High. Psalm 91. Bible, *O.T.* AWP *Fr.* Psalms.

He that for fear his Master did deny. To St. Peter and St. Paul. Henry Constable. NoSic; Son

He that had come that morning. Ballad of John Cable and Three Gentlemen. W. S. Merwin. CoAP; NOBA

He that has clean hands, and a pure heart, *sel., vv. 1–4.* Bible, *O.T. See* Psalm 24.

He that has grown to wisdom hurries not. Sonnet: Of Moderation and Tolerance. Guido Guinicelli, *Italian.* AWP, *tr. by* D. G. Rossetti

He That Hath No Mistress. *Unknown.* GBL; OxBSP

He that hath set his headlong heart. Boethius, *Latin.* MLL, *tr. by* Helen Waddell *Fr.* Consolation of Philosophy, The ("De Consolacione Philosophie").

He that heareth my word. Bible, *N.T.* CTV *Fr.* The Bible, John 5:24.

He that holds fast the golden mean. 2: Moderation. Horace. PoToHe, *tr. by* William Cowper *Fr.* Odes.

He that in youthe no vertu will yowes. *Unknown.* MiEL

He that is by Mooni now. Mooni. Henry Clarence Kendall. OBEV

He that is down, needs fear no fall. The Shepherd Boy Sings [in the Valley of Humiliation]. John Bunyan. BoTP; EBEV; EBEvV; NOBE; NTP; OBEV; OxBSP *Fr.* The Pilgrim's Progress.

He that is slow to anger is better than. The Bible, Proverbs 16:32. Bible, *O.T.* CTV *Fr.* Proverbs.

He that is weary, let him sit. Employment. George Herbert. FaBoVe; GeHe; SeCP

He that lies at the stock. Rock, Ball, Fiddle. *Unknown.* CBNP; CH; OxBoLi; OxNR

He that loves a rosy cheek. Disdain Returned. Thomas Carew. CavPo; GTBS-P; PFE *Fr.* Disdain Returned. BeJo

He That Loves a Rosy Cheek. Heinrich von Rugge, *German.* AWP, *tr. by* Jethro Bithell

He That None Can Capture. May Swenson. LW

He that of such a height hath built his mind. To the Lady Margaret, Countess [*or* Countesse] of Cumberland. Samuel Daniel. NOSC

He that owns wealth, in mountain, wold, or waste. Wealth. Sadi. AWP, *tr. by* Sir Edwin Arnold *Fr.* The Gulistan.

He That Regards the Precious Things of Earth. Moses ibn Ezra. *Fr.* The World's Illusion. TrJP, *tr. by* Solomon Solis-Cohen

He that spendes muche and getes nothing. *Unknown.* MiEL

He that to God's law doth cling. Freedom. Abraham ibn Ezra, *Hebrew.* TrJP, *tr. by* Solomon Solis-Cohen

He that will give good words to thee, will flatter. Shakespeare. FaBoPV *Fr.* Coriolanus.

He that will not love must be. Not To Love. Robert Herrick. CaPo

He that would thrive must rise at five. *Unknown.* OxNR

He that would write an epitaph for thee. An Epitaph on Dr. Donne, Dean of Paul's. Richard Corbet. BeJo; EPCY

He the Beloved. Qorratu'l-Ayn, *Farsi.*

"Cupbearer, O victorious Falcon, come!" WPOW, *tr. by* Deirdre Lashgari

He there now does enjoy eternal rest. Sleep after Toil. Edmund Spenser. *Fr.* Wood Of Error. AEP

He Thinks of His Past Greatness When a Part of the Constellations of Heaven. W. B. Yeats. PoEL-5

He Thinks of Those Who Have Spoken Evil of His Beloved. W. B. Yeats. NoAM

He thinks when we die we'll go to China. Heaven. Cathy Song. NoAM

He thought he kept the universe alone. The Most of It. Robert Frost. BLT; HAP; NAAL-2; NoP-4; TOF; TRP; WeW-3

He thought he saw an elephant [*or* a banker's clerk *or* a buffalo]. The Mad Gardener's Song. "Lewis Carroll." CBNP; OxBChV; PBMP *Fr.* Sylvie and Bruno.

He thought I thought he thought I slept. (LL) The Kiss. Coventry Patmore. BoLoP; EnLoPo; NOBVV

He thought it humanity's lot for ever to be persuading a huge rock up a mountainside. David Bromige. FTOS *Fr.* Tight Corners.

He thought to quell the stubborn hearts of oak. Buonaparte. Tennyson. Son

He threw them out and slammed the gate shut. Eden. James Simmons. PNI

He thrust his joy against the weight of the sea. The Surfer. Judith Wright. WPE

He tips his boy baby's hand in an icy. Three Sonnets for Iva. Marilyn Hacker. GLP

He tiptoes into the room almost as if he were an intruder. The Annunciation. Stephen Mitchell. GI

He told his life story to Mrs. Courtly. Autumn. Stevie Smith. FaBoWP; LW; NBLV

He told me he had spent. Shortening the Road. Michael Davitt, *Irish.* PBCIP, *tr. by* Philip Casey

He told the crowd "The devils." John Logan. CRP *Fr.* A Short Life of the Hermit.

He Told Us He Wanted a Black Coffin. Jackie Kay. CPO

He too has an eternal part to play. The Historical Judas. Howard Nemerov. NoP-4; Poetr

He too must with me wash his body, though. An Anniversary of Death. John Wieners. PoM

He took / flight. Exile. Erich Fried, *German.* AF, *tr. by* Georg Rapp

He Took Her. Tom Masson. OBAL

He took her with a sigh. (LL) Never Pain to Tell Thy Love. William Blake. CBLP; EnLoPo; GLoP; InPS-3; NAEL-2; NOBE; OAEL-2; OBNC; PoEL-4; SCGP

He tossed a life preserver to the young castaway in '55. Requiem. Otto Orban, *Hungarian.* CEEP, *tr. by* Jascha Kessler

He touched me, so I live to know. Emily Dickinson. NCAP

He touches, and the wheel of time goes round. Hurdy-Gurdy Man in Winter. Vernon Watkins. NYBP

He travels after a winter sun. Tilly. James Joyce. RB

He travels the fastest who travels alone! (LL) The Winners. Rudyard Kipling. BLPA; FaPoR; MoBrPo

He tried to / climb a / ladder of light. Written for Love of an Ascension—Coltrane. Carolyn M. Rodgers. SeSe

He Tries out the Concords Gently. "Eduard Georgievich Bagritzky," *Russian.* TrJP, *tr. by* C. M. Bowra

He trilled a carol fresh and free. The First Voice. "Lewis Carroll." *Fr.* The Three Voices. BXAP

He trudges the streets of Blantyre. Tramp. Frank Mkalawile Chipasula. HBAPE; PeSAV

He turned his field into a meeting-place. W. H. Auden. SCV *Fr.* Sonnets from China.

He turned up in benighted villages. Prince Foma. Pavel Nikolaevich Vasilyev, *Russian.* TCRP, *tr. by* David Macduff

He turns his back to dress; i've lost him. Memoirs of a Velvet Urinal. Michael Dransfield. BMAP

He turns to you, measly immortal page. Page. Sandra McPherson. PoA

He Understands the Great Cruelty of Death. Petrarch. BIrV *Fr.* Sonnets to Laura.

He unto whom thou art so partial. Post-Obits and the Poets. Martial, *Latin.* AWP; FaBoEE; OBVE; OBCVT, *tr. by* Byron

He wakens from the clover rick. The Sun-Witch to the Sun. George Howe. NYBP

He wakes; speak to him. Shakespeare. SCV *Fr.* King Lear.

He walked up and down the street 'till the shoes fell off his feet. Tramp, Tramp, Tramp, Keep on a-Tramping. *Unknown.* AS

He Walketh by Day. *Unknown.* AWP *Fr.* Book of the Dead.

He walks still upright from the root. The Hewel, or Woodpecker. Andrew Marvell. *Fr.* Upon Appleton House [To My Lord Fairfax]. FaBoPV; GeHe; SeCP

He waltzes into the lane. Makin' Jump Shots. Michael S. Harper. AFr; ISC; PoE

He wanders with his country, too. (LL) Another ("The Centaur, siren [*or* syren], I forgo[e]"). Richard Lovelace; PoEL-3

He wanted to rise up to the moment. The Poet Lied. Odia Ofeimun. HBAPE

He wanted to tell her the weekend idea was 'neat'. Sestina. James Cummins. BAP-95

He wants it back with interest. (LL) The Lady's-Maid's Song. John Hollander. LiTM; TwCP

He wants to be. Self-Portrait. Robert Creeley. NoAM; PmAP

He wants to wonder not look so. Jerome in His Study. Clark Coolidge. FTOS

He warranted no better, I don't know. (LL) Mr Bleaney. Philip Larkin. HoPM; InPS-3; OxBC; PoE; PoPoPo; TRP; UV

He was a big man, says the size of his shoes. Abandoned Farmhouse. Ted Kooser. WeW-3

He was a blessing one never prays for—. Obituary. Steve Chimombo. HBAPE

He was a farmer, he didn't think much of towns. Stephen Vincent Benét. AiP *Fr.* John Brown's Body.

He was a foe without hate. Tribute to Robert E. Lee. Benjamin H. Hill. CTV

He was a good boy. Uncle's First Rabbit. Lorna Dee Cervantes. NoAM

He Was a Man of Jokes outside Office. Oswald Basize Dube. PeSAV

He was a might poet—and. Shelley. EPCY *Fr.* Peter Bell the Third.

He was a mighty hunter in his youth. The White Cat of Trenarren. Alfred Leslie Rowse. OxBTC; PC

He was a poet he was. Poem for a Dead Poet. Roger McGough. NTP

He was a rat, and she was a rat. What Became of Them? *Unknown.* BoTP; CTAV; OBCA; OxBChV

He was a real nice man. (LL) Seumas Beg. James Stephens. FuFo; OxBTC

He was a reprobate I grant. The Deceased. Keith Douglas. FaBoTw

He was a selfish shellfish. Idyll: "He was a selfish shellfish." Stoddard King. NBLV

He was a traveler west of the river,/ only he knew how lonely he was. Tune: Eternal Longing. *Unknown. Fr.* Four *Tz'u* from Tun-huang. CoBCP, *tr. by* Burton Watson

He was a young god. Genesis. Evan Jones. PBCV

He was alive with death. Sergeant Brandon Just, U. S. M. C. Bryan Alec Floyd. CDa

He was always the same. Portrait. Leopold Staff, *Polish.* PoSu, *tr. by* Adam Czerniawski

He was an Indiana corporal. At Chancellorsville. Andrew Hudgins. CBCWP

He was an old wolf, no teeth, his tail all but bare. *Unknown. Fr.* Sioux Metamorphoses. STP, *tr. by* James Koller

He *was,* and *is* not! Graecia's trembling shore. Stanzas on the Death of Lord Byron. Elizabeth Barrett Browning. Ro *Fr.* Globe and Traveller, no. 6733.

He was arrested and detained. Soft Targets. Essex Hemphill. GT

He was as old as old could be. Danny Murphy. James Stephens. BoTP

He was at Naples writing letters home. Wallace Stevens. CMoP; MeMAP; NOBA *Fr.* Esthétique du Mal. LiTM

He was back. Said nothing. Homecoming. Wislawa Szymborska, *Polish.* PoSu, *tr. by* Adam Czerniawski

He was born as little children are. He Was One of Us. Helen Steiner Rice. CTV

He was born in Alabama. Of De Witt Williams on His Way to Lincoln Cemetery. Gwendolyn Brooks. NOBA; NoAM *Fr.* A Street in Bronzeville. BPo; BlSi; FaBoWP

He was born in Deutschland, as you would suspect. The Progress of Faust. Karl Shapiro. NYBP

He was caught in the whirlpool of dismay. The Whirlpool. *Unknown.* PoToHe

He was digging; his fingers. Of Mohenjo Daro at Oxford. Keki N. Daruwalla. OMIP

He was dreaming of the factories across the water's fog. What Cannot Be Kept. Reginald Shepherd. GT

He was dying on the cross. On the Cross*. Anna Kamienska, *Polish.* GI, *tr. by* Curzon, David and Grazyna Drabik

He was fifteen. And she, Wisconsin. Philip Booth. IFJA

He was first seen in a Louisiana bayou. Grandfather Was Queer, Too. Bob Kaufman. NAAAL

He was formidable, he was, the little booger. Robert Penn Warren. *See* Ballad: Between the Boxcars.

He was found by the Bureau of Statistics to be. The Unknown Citizen. W. H. Auden. HeIP-4; InPK-6; LiTM; MeMAP; NBLV; NIP-4; NOBL; NYBP; OBSV; PFE; PoRA; Poetr; SAGP; SoSe-8; TRP; UnPo

He was her man, and he done her wrong. *Unknown. See* Josie.

He was holding clean globes in his hands. (LL) Medgar Evers. Gwendolyn Brooks. NoP-4

He was impoverished, possessing a full island. Castaway. John Nerber. PoA

He was in logic[k] a great critic. The Metaphysical Sectarian. Samuel Butler. MeLP; OxBoLi; PeLV; PoEL-3 *Fr.* Hudibras.

He was just a young aviator. Lindbergh. *Unknown.* AmFP

He was just back. Vietnam. Clarence Major. PoBA

He was like the Lord drunk. Alcoholic. F. D. Reeve. NYBP

He was lost. Conqueror of a Forbidden Landscape. Amryl Johnson. NBrP

He was lost!—not a shade of doubt. Little Lost Pup. Arthur Guiterman. CTV

He Was Lucky. Anna Swirszczynska, *Polish.* HP; PoSu, *tr. by* Magnus J. Krynski *and* Robert A. Maguire

He was my *Friend,* the truest *Friend* on earth;. On the Death of Mr William Hervey. Abraham Cowley. FP *Fr.* On the Death of Mr. William Hervey [*or* Harvey]. EBEvV; OBEV; SeCP

He was my man, but he done me wrong. (LL) Josie. *Unknown.* AS; AmFP; EBEvV; EBNV; NIP-4; NOBA; NTP; OxBoLi; RB; UnPo

He was no good. Somewhere. Black Jess. Peter Kane Dufault. NYBP

He was no longer my father. The Mirror. Michael Davitt, *Irish.* BiHa; CIP-2; PBCIP, *tr. by* Paul Muldoon

He was not able to read or write. The Gardener. Louis MacNeice. IIP *Fr.* Novelettes.

He was not bad, as emperors go, not really—. Apology for Domitian. Robert Penn Warren. NOBA

He was not left completely alone. Red. Utrillo: "La Belle Gabrielle." Dezsö Tandori, *Hungarian.* CEEP, *tr. by* Bruce Berlind

He was not the Godric who fled from the fight. . . . (LL) The Battle of Maldon. *Unknown, Anglo-Saxon.* AnOE; OAEL-1, *tr. by* Charles W. Kennedy

He was off the road on the island. Will Work for Food. Stanley Plumly. PUP-20

He was once a tiny, helpless thing. Aaron Nicholas, Almost Ten. Janet Campbell Hale. VoR

He Was One of Us. Helen Steiner Rice. CTV

He was out of work that year. Days of 1908. Constantine P. Cavafy, *Greek.* PFTM, *tr. by* Keeley, Edmund and Phillip Sherrard

He was preparing an Ulster fry for breakfast. The Civil Servant. Michael Longley. BiHa *Fr.* Wreaths.

He was reading late, at Richard's, down in Maine. Henry's Understanding. John Berryman. MoP; NOBA; NoAM

He was standing on the edge of us. We Never Know. Yusef Komunyakaa. MT

He was still Uncle. The Empress Brand Trim: Ruby Reminisces. Sherley Anne Williams. BlSi

He was straight and strong, and his eyes were blue. A Lynmouth Widow. Amelia Josephine Burr. LW

He was strange weather, this luther. he read books, mainly poetry. Poet: What Ever Happened to Luther? Haki R. Madhubuti. UnSA

He was such a curious lover of shells. Full Fathom Five. Arthur Rex Dugard Fairburn. PeNZ

He was the best postilion. The Postilion Has Been Struck by Lightning. Patricia Beer. OxBC

He was the doctor up to Combe. Coroner's Jury. Leonard Alfred George Strong. OxBTC

He was the first always: Fortune. Envy. Adelaide Anne Procter. NOBVV; VWP

He was the first to see the snow. (LL) First Snow in Alsace. Richard Wilbur. NoP-4; OBWP

He was the only one of us. The Governor of the Ollie Street. Ahmos, II Zu-Bolton. BkSV

He was the slave of Ambition. The Mills of the Gods. *Unknown.* BLPA

He was the terror of the district. The Urchin. Konstantin Iakovlevich Vanshenkin, *Russian.* TCRP, *tr. by* Daniel Weissbort

He was their servant (some say he was blind). W. H. Auden. CMoP *Fr.* Sonnets from China.

He was there / Old Man Coyote. Medicine-Tail, *Crow Indian.* STP, *tr. by* W. S. Merwin

He was tired after his voyages. Retired. Iain Crichton Smith. SpW

He was to weet a man of full ripe years. Edmund Spenser. UV, *sect.* 4, *canto* 3 *Fr.* Wood Of Error. AEP

He was walking a frozen road. Music of Spheres. Jean Follain, *French.* BLT, *tr. by* Czeslaw Milosz *and* Robert Hass

He was walking from Bethany to Jerusalem. The Miracle. Boris Pasternak, *Russian.* GI, *tr. by* Nina Kossman

He was wilder than a wolf when he brought. With Bill Pickett at the 101 Ranch. Colleen J. McElroy. WeT

He was wise. (LL) Hunting Song. Donald Finkel. CoAP; MoBS

He was (woe worth that word!) to each well thinking mind. *Unknown.* EPCY *Fr.* Epitaph Upon the Right Honorable Sir Philip Sidney.

He watch her like a coonhound watch a tree. Balance. Marilyn Nelson Waniek. FFC; NAmP90; RA

He watched the stars and noted birds in flight. W. H. Auden. CMoP *Fr.* Sonnets from China.

He watched them as they walked towards the tree. The Tree. Dorothy Auchterlonie. NOBAu

He watched with all his organs of concern. Poem: "He watched with all his organs of concern." W. H. Auden. PoA *Fr.* The Quest.

He wears a beautiful necklace. Carlton Fisk is My Ideal. Bernadette Mayer. DeD

He welcomes us still. His Welcome. Auvaiyar, *Tamil.* PLW, *tr. by* A. K. Ramanujan

He went down to the woodshed. No One Heard Him Call. Dorothy Aldis. TLR

He went home when the new replacements arrived. Lance Corporal Purdue Grace, U. S. M. C. Bryan Alec Floyd. CDa

He went in with his fur coat flung open. Subject for a Story. Nikolai Ivanovich Glazkov, *Russian.* TCRP, *tr. by* Daniel Weissbort

He went into a grey day. For One Who Died Young. Hoffman Reynolds Hays. SPE

He went into his harvest barn. The Farmer. Mary Elizabeth Fullerton. CBAP

He went into the shop and sat down. Alien goes Shopping. Pamela Gillilan. SpW

He went off; didn't say when he'd be back. Holiday's End. Haim Guri, *Hebrew*. IP, tr. by Warren Bargad *and* Stanley F. Chyet

He went there. Poem of the Conscripted Warrior. "Rui Nogar," *Portuguese*. TTY, tr. by Dorothy Guedes *and* Philippa Rumsey

He went to fix the awning. Fixer of Midnight. Reuel Denney. OBAL

He went to the wood and caught it. Riddle. *Unknown*. OxNR

He wept, attempting to mas / ter *ancilla* and *servus*. Geoffrey Hill. *See* He adored the desk, its brown-oak inlaid with ebony.

He whispers: 'I'm not sorry. "Anna Akhmatova," *Russian*. LoP, tr. by Judith Hemschemeyer

He whittled scallops for a hardy thatch. The Thatcher. Brendan Kennelly. CIP-2

He who appointed weight to the wind. Semyon Izrailevich Lipkin, *Russian*. TCRP, tr. by Albert C. Todd

He who at first a womans mind. Inconstancy. James Harrington. PBRV

He who began from brick and lime. In Obitum Ben. Jons. Mildmay Fane, 2d Earl of Westmorland. BeJo; NOSC; OxBSP

He who beneath thy shelt'ring wing resides, *ad. by* Alexander Pope. Bible, *O.T. See* Psalm 91.

He who binds to himself a joy. Eternity . William Blake. APAD; AWP; EBEV; EnlH; FaBoEE; ImPo; NOBE; NTP; NoP-4; OBNC; OxBSP; Poetr; RB; SCGP; SoSe-8; Spl   *Fr.* Several Questions Answered.

He-who-came-forth was. The Son. FiLi; NALW

He who could pierce my grief. The Black Shawl. Lotte Moos. NBrP

He who could win the girl I love. A Girl's Hair. Dafydd ab Edmwnd, *Welsh*. OBWVE, tr. by Gwyn Williams

He who crosses a park in great and flourishing Havana. Central Park Some People (3 P.M.) Nancy Morejón, *Spanish*. PBWP, tr. by Sylvia Carranza

He who doesn't dance stIll dances   Aleksandr Semionovich Kushner, *Russian*. TCRP, tr. by Bernard Meares

He who first stretched his nerves of subtile wire. Science and Poetry. James Russell Lowell. NCAP

He who gave weight to the wind. Yury Mikhailovich Kublanovsky, *Russian*. TCRP, tr. by Yevgeny Yevtushenko

He who, grown aged in this world of woe. Byron. EPCY   *Fr.* Childe Harold's Pilgrimage.

He who has compared himself to the eye of a horse. Boris Pasternak. "Anna Akhmatova," *Russian*. TCRP, tr. by Stanley Kunitz *with* Max Hayward

He Who Has Lost All. David Diop, *French*. TTY, tr. by Anne Atik

He who has lost soul's liberty. Soul's Liberty. Anna Wickham. MoBrPo; OxBSP

He who has made his reckoning with life. Boethius, *Latin*. MLL, tr. by Helen Waddell   *Fr.* Consolation of Philosophy, The ("De Consolacione Philosophie").

He who has no hands. Orator. Ralph Waldo Emerson. OxBA   *Fr.* Quatrains.

He who has once been happy is for aye. With Esther. Wilfrid Scawen Blunt. OBEV; OBMV; OBNC   *Fr.* Esther [a Young Man's Tragedy].

He, who has so much duende—like me. Duende. Nina Zivancevic, *Serbo-Croatian*. HSix, tr. by Charles Simic

He who has toiled and bought for himself books. Proverbs. Samuel Ha-Nagid, *Hebrew*. TrJP, tr. by Israel Abrahams

He Who Knows ("He who knows not and knows not [that he knows not]"). *Unknown, Arabic*. CTV, tr. by *Unknown*; BLPA

He who knows how to shave the razor, will know how to erase the. Henri Michaux. PFTM, tr. by Pierre Joris   *Fr.* Slices of Knowledge.

He who knows not and knows not [that he knows not]. He Who Knows. *Unknown, Arabic*. CTV, tr. by *Unknown*; BLPA

He who knows not what thing is Paradise. Angelo Poliziano.   *Fr.* Three Ballate. AWP, tr. by John Addington Symonds

He Who Loved Beauty. Alec Brock Stevenson. FuPo

He who made a feast of dew, drink from a rock. Inscription in Monastic Refectory. Alcuin, *Latin*. MLL, tr. by Helen Waddell

He who misled them all—the butler, Toomes. (LL) The Feckless Dinner-Party. Walter De la Mare. FP; FaBoTw

He, who navigated with success. Death of a Young Son by Drowning. Margaret Atwood. BoWoP; NOBC

He, who once was my brother, is dead by his own hand. Justice Is Reason Enough. Diane Wakoski. AmPA; NMM-2

He Who Owns the Whistle Rules the World. Roger McGough. AYFP

He who plucked light. A Child Asleep. J. P. Clark Bekederemo. PBMAP   *Fr.* A Reed in the Tide.

He who saved Ankoma Oh nature. Prelude to Akwasidae. *Unknown, Twi*. TTY, tr. by Halim El-Dabh

He who sits from day to day. On a Similar Occasion for the Year 1790. William Cowper. NOCV

He who stole my virginity / is the same man. Silabhattarika, *Sanskrit*. WPOW, tr. by W. S. Merwin *and* J. Moussaieff Masson

He who thinks perchance to drown. Drunkenness. Friedrich von Logau, *German*. GePo, tr. by George C. Schoolfield

He who would acclaim Cleanness in becoming style. *Unknown*. NOCV, tr. by Brian Stone   *Fr.* Cleanness.

He who writ [or wrote] this, not without pains and thought. Prologue. Dryden. PeLV   *Fr.* Secret Love; or, The Maiden Queen.

He Whose Hand and Eye Are Gentle. *Unknown, Welsh*. OBWVE, tr. by Kenneth Hurlstone Jackson

He will be an uncle / if we are lucky. (LL) Game after Supper. Margaret Atwood. FaBoWP; LCAP-2

He will be your constant friend. Bible, *O.T. See* Psalm 121.

He will find out his way. *Unknown. See* Love Will Find Out the Way.

He will go over and tell the king. Over the Wall: Berlin, May 1975. Charles Hubert Sisson. OxBC

He will have turned. Old Story. Lance Henson. VoR

He will insist on. The Bath. Joel Oppenheimer. NeAP

He will sit at the bare table, reading a dictionary. Time of Waiting. Geoffrey Dutton. CBAP

He will walk in as you're sitting down to a meal. (LL) The Book of Yolek. Anthony Hecht. HP; NoP-4

He will watch the hawk with an indifferent eye. Icarus. Stephen Spender. MoBrPo; MoP; UV

He Wishes for the Cloths of Heaven. W. B. Yeats. APAD; ChAP; MoBrPo; NoAM; OBEV

(Aedh Wishes for the Cloths of Heaven.) ADE

He wishes he could hug them like big friends from home. (LL) The Stalin Epigram. Osip Emilevich Mandelstam, *Russian*. NNPT, tr. by Clarence Brown *and* W. S. Merwin; AF, tr. by W. S. Merwin *and* Clarence Brown

He with body waged a fight. The Four Ages of Man. W. B. Yeats. TrCP

He with whom I ran hand in hand. A Woman Meets an Old Lover. Denise Levertov. BLT

He woke, and wondered more: for there she /lay lay. (LL) Nuptial Sleep. D. G. Rossetti. EBVV; EnVR; NAEL-2; NOBVV

He woke at five and, unable. Physical Universe. Louis Simpson. InPS-3

He woke; the clank and racket of the train. Stretcher Case. Siegfried Sassoon. NSI

He works / stone to. Rock Painting. Carroll Arnett. VoR

He worshipped at the altar of Romance. An Epitaph. Colin Ellis. OxBTC

He would assume a seeing into the word. Notes for Echo Lake 2. Michael Palmer. PT

He would declare and could himself believe. Never Again Would Birds' Song Be The Same. Robert Frost. FYAP; HAP; InPK-6; LoP; NIP-4; NoAM; NoP-4; SoSe-8; Son; VGW

He would drink by himself. Casualty. Seamus Heaney. FaBoPV; NAEL-2; PBCIP; PoE

He would have been eleventh. (LL) A Mighty Runner. Nicarchus of Alexandria. MeMAP; OBAL

He Would Have His Lady Sing. Digby Mackworth Dolben. EBEV

He would like not to kill. He would like. The Robber Bridegroom. Margaret Atwood. LCAP-2

He would not lie uncovered. Burial of the Dog. Susan Musgrave. NoAM

He would not stay for me; and who can wonder? A. E. Housman. CBLP

He wraps himself in flames. The Tenant Who Lives in Fire. Sandor Csoori, *Hungarian*. CEEP, tr. by Nicholas Kolumban

He writes from the provinces: It is. Reply to the Provinces. Galway Kinnell. NYBP

He wrote *The I and the It*. On the Death of a German Philosopher. Stevie Smith. OBCoV

He yawned and watched the lilac horns of his island. Derek Walcott. NoP-4   *Fr.* Omeros.

He yelled at me in Greek. John Berryman. FYAP   *Fr.* Dream Songs.

Head, The. Padraic Fallon. CIP-2

Head, A. James Schuyler. PoM

Head-Ache, The; An Ode to Health. Jane Cave. "Ah! why from me art thou for ever flown." ECWP

Head bumper. *Unknown*. OxNR

Head Couples. William H. Matchett. NYBP

Head in a cloud Moses stands. Moses. Sydney Tremayne. OxBS

Head Is a Paltry Matter, The. Pier Giorgio Di Cicco. NOBC

Head Itself. Laura Riding Jackson. PoA

Head of Hair, The. Charles Baudelaire, *French*. EP, tr. by Richard Howard

Head of *Italy, Caesar* acquits, The. To the Emperour Titus, upon his Banishing Sycophants. Martial, *Latin*. OBCVT, tr. by Pecke, Thomas

Head of Medusa. Marya Alexandrovna Zaturenska. MoAmPo

Head of Medusa on a Rotella of Michelangelo da Caravaggio, in the Gallery of the Grand Duke of Tuscany, The. Giambattista Marino, *Italian*. GS, *tr. by Unknown*

Head of Tasso, The. John Skoyles. CMAP

Head or Tail—which does he lack?, A. The Hippo. Theodore Roethke. VGW

Head poking from a vermilion tower, all eight directions cramped. After Getting Drunk, I Scribble Songs and Poems. Lu Yu, *Chinese*. CoBCP, *tr. by Burton Watson*

Head pure, sinless quite of brain or soul, A. Robert Burns. FaBoEE *Fr.* Versicles on Sign-Posts.

Head the ship for England! Homeward Bound. William Allingham. FaBoBe

Head to limp head, the sunk-eyed wounded scanned. Smile, Smile, Smile. Wilfred Owen. PeFWW

Headache, The. Mary Leapor. ECWP

Heading East or West, down the. Farewell to Shen Yueh. Fan Yun, *Chinese*. OHMPC, *tr. by Kenneth Rexroth*

Headland. Brewster Ghiselin. PoA

Headlands. Jack Hirschman. CLPP

Headless bird flew back, The. Codex Minor. Rachel Hadas. EOEF

Headless fountains / running loose. The Preponderance. William Meredith. PBMP

Headless, lacking foot and hand. Unknown Female Corpse. Rudyard Kipling. PoWW *Fr.* Epitaphs of the War [1914–1918]. OBWP

Headless limbless / it appears. The Quartz Pebble. Vasco [*or Vasko*] Popa. PoSu, *tr. by Anne Pennington Fr.* The Quartz Pebble.

Headless torsos, faceless lovers, friends of mine. (LL) The Onion, Memory. Craig Raine. NAEL-2; NoAM; NoP-4

Headless young Beau, A. *Unknown, French*. CBNP

Headline History. William Plomer. OBCoV

Headline to Summarize a Passion. U Tam'si Tchicaya, *French*. NegPo, *tr. by Ellen Conroy Kennedy*

Headlined in Heaven. Paul Grano. NOBAu

Headquarters. Gilbert Frankau. NSI

Headrock. Brian Coffey. CIP-2

Heads, impenetrable / And the slow bulk, The. Oxen: Ploughing at Fiesole. Charles Tomlinson. OxBTC

Heads of strong old age are beautiful, The. Promise of Peace. Robinson Jeffers. LiTM; MoAmPo

Heads or Tails? Kit Wright. OTCP

Headstrong young lady of Ealing, A. Limerick. Edward Gorey. PeLi

Headwaters. N. Scott Momaday. NoP-4

Heal Me, My God. Judah Halevi, *Hebrew*. TOF, *tr. by David Goldstein*

Healed of My Hurt. Herman Melville. AmPP

Healer of broken bones. (LL) Elegy for Her Brother Sakhr. Al-Khansa, *Arabic*. WPOW, *tr. by Bridget Connelly; BoWoP, tr. by Willis Barnstone*

Healing. D. H. Lawrence. RaBo

Healing. Abraham Reisen, *Yiddish*. TrJP, *tr. by Joseph Leftwich*

Healing, The. Shelley White. EC2

Healing Animal. Joy Harjo. SeSe

Healing of the Leper, The. Vernon Watkins. FaBoTw

Healing Prayer to the Salmon-Berry Vines. *Kwakiutl Oral Tradition, Kwakiutl*. PaTW, *tr. by Franz Boas*

Healing Song. Etheridge Knight. BkSV *Fr.* Three Songs.

Healing Song. *Unknown*. OBVE, *tr. by Frances Densmore*

Healing Songs. Tohono O'odham, *Papago*. PaTW, *tr. by Frances Densmore*

Healing the Mare. Linda McCarriston. LoL

Healing the World from Battery Park. Tim Dlugos. BAP-93

Health, A. Edward Coote Pinkney. APN-1

Health at the Ford, A. Robert Cameron Rogers. FaBoBe

Health from the lover of the country, me. 1.1. Horace. AWP, *tr. by Abraham Cowley Fr.* Epistles.

Health! I seek thee; dost thou love. Robert Bloomfield. OBNC *Fr.* Shooter's Hill.

Health in his rags, Content upon his face. On Seeing a Bird-Catcher. Eliza Cook. VWP

Health is the first good lent to men. Four[e] Things Make Us Happy Here. Robert Herrick. CaPo; Spl

Health to great Gloucester—from a man unknown. Dedication. Charles Churchill. OBSV

Health to my fair Odelia! Some that know. To Odelia. James Shirley. BeJo

Healthy Spot, A. W. H. Auden. AiP

Heap cassia, sandal-buds and stripes. Song. Robert Browning. OBEV *Fr.* Paracelsus.

Heap earth upon it. (LL) Requiescat. Oscar Wilde. EBVV; MoBrPo; OBNC; PeVV; SAGP

Heap of Faggots, A. Andrew Young. FaBoTC

Heap of Rags, The. W. H. Davies. NSI

"Heap on more wood!--the wind is chill." Sir Walter Scott. OBCP *Fr.* Marmion.

Hear 'em exchange best wishes at New Year's! Best Wishes for the New Year. Trần Tế Xu'o'ng, *Vietnamese*. AVP, *tr. by Huỳnh Sanh Thông*

Hear father yet thou Long-Armed Lord! these latest words I say. *Unknown*. TAL, *tr. by Sir Edward Arnold Fr.* The Bhagavad-Gita.

Hear! hear! Lilian's Song. George Darley. OBNC

Hear hear hear hear. ARK 37, Prospero's Songs to Ariel (constructed in the form of a quilt snipped from Roger Tory Peterson's *A Field Guide to Western Birds*). Ronald Johnson. APSN *Fr.* Ark.

Hear! hear! hear! / Listen! the word. The Mocking-Bird. Richard Hovey. APN-2

Hear, Hear, O Ye Nations. Frederick Lucian Hosmer. AH

Hear, hear that solitary bell. Helena. Alfred de Vigny, *French*. GrIP, *tr. by Richard Stoneman*

Hear in the sea, Thetis, Memnon's alive. Asclepiodotus, *Greek*. GrAn, *tr. by Alistair Elliot*

Hear, Jehovah! / May the eternal serpent's curse be on him! Byron. NOBRP *Fr.* Cain: A Mystery.

Hear Lydiat's life, and Galileo's end. (LL) The Scholar's Life. Samuel Johnson. NOBE; OBSV

Hear me,/ helper of mankind. The Homeric Hymn to Ares. *Unknown*. RaBo, *tr. by Charles Boer Fr.* Homeric Hymns.

Hear me, my God, and hear me soon. The Petition. Thomas Beedome. NOSC

Hear me [*or* Heare mee], O God! A Hymn[e] to God the Father. Ben Jonson. BeJo; NOSC; NoP-4; OxAEP-1; Poetr; SeCP; TrCP

Hear me, whom I betrayed. Envoi. James Vincent Cunningham. VGW

Hear me, ye smokeless skies and grass-green earth. Song. Charles Mair. NOBC *Fr.* The Last Bison.

Hear my prayer, O Lord, and let my cry come unto thee. Bible, *O.T. See* Psalm 102.

Hear my voice, birds of war! Ojibwa War Songs. *Unknown, Ojibwa Indian*. AWP, *tr. by H. H. Schoolcraft*

Hear now a curious dream I dreamed last night. My Dream. Christina Rossetti. BrRo; VWP

Hear now a sound of floods. Song for Ilva Mackay and Mongane. Keorapetse Kgositsile. PBMAP

Hear, O Israel. Shema Yisrael. *Unknown*. TrJP

Hear, O Israel! and plead my cause against the ungodly nation. Adah Isaacs Menken. AAP; CBWP-1

Hear, O Israel, Jehovah, the Lord our God is one. Israel. Israel Zangwill. TrJP

Hear, O Israel, the commandments of life. The Path of Wisdom. Bible, Apocrypha. TrJP *Fr.* Baruch.

Hear, O Israel! / Will you never tire of repeating in your prayers. André Spire, *French*. TrJP, *tr. by Stanley Burnshaw*

Hear, on any night. A White Line. Art Lange. MoNo

Hear, sweet spirit, hear the spell. An Invocation. Coleridge. CH; PeECV *Fr.* Remorse.

Hear that tree-lizard singin' out. Jarrangulli. Roland Robinson. NOxBChV

Hear, the bird of day. David Campbell. NOBAu

Hear the dreary, dreary rain. Voices of the Rain. Henrietta Cordelia Ray. CBWP-3

Hear the fluter with his flute. The Amateur Flute. *Unknown*. BXAP

Hear the legend of the Admen. The Legend of the Admen. Everett W. Lord. BLPA

Hear the music, the thunder of the wings. Love the wild swan. (LL) Love the Wild Swan. Robinson Jeffers. MoAmPo; NoAM; Son

Hear the right, O Lord, attend unto my cry. Bible, *O.T. See* Psalm 17.

Hear the sledges with the bells. The Bells. Edgar Allan Poe. APN-1; ChAP; MeMAP; OBAL; OBCA; PoLF; TAP; TFi

Hear the voice of the Bard! Introduction. William Blake. APAD; ChIV-1; EBEV; FHYEP; HAP; InPS-3; NAEL-2; NAWM-2; NOBE; NOBRP; NOEC; NoP-4; OAEL-2; OBEV; PoE; PoEL-4; RB; Ro; TFi *Fr.* Songs of Experience.

Hear the Word of the Lord. Bible, *O.T.* TrJP *Fr.* Isaiah.

Hear the word that Jesus spake. A Lost Word of Jesus. Henry Van Dyke. TrCP

Hear this, and tremble, all. Upon My Lord Chief Justice's Election of My Lady Anne Wentworth [*or* A.W.] for His Mistress. Thomas Carew. CaPo

Hear[e] us, O hear[e] us Lord; to thee. Donne. *Fr.* The Litanie. PoEL-2

Hear what God the Lord hath spoken. Hymn 10. William Cowper. ChIV-1 *Fr.* Olney Hymns.

Hear, ye children, the instruction of a father. The Legacy. Bible, *O.T.* TrJP *Fr.* Proverbs.

Hear, ye ladies [that despise]. Song: "Heare ye Ladies that despise." John Fletcher. CBLP; NOBE; OBEV; PoEL-2 *Fr.* The Tragedy of Valentinian.

Hear ye not how, from all high points of Time. Henry Highland Garnet. CrDW

Hear[e] ye Virgins, and I'll [*or* Ile] teach. To Virgins. Robert Herrick. CaPo

Heard all the crickets singing, and was glad. (LL) A Prayer in Darkness. G. K. Chesterton. MoBrPo; PoLF

Heard de owl a hootin'. Gal's Cry for a Dying Lover. Langston Hughes. NAAAL

Heard him gladly. Waldere 1. *Unknown, Anglo-Saxon.* AnOE, *tr. by* Charles W. Kennedy

Heard in a Violent Ward. Theodore Roethke. HCAP

Heard in the Cougate. Robert Garioch. FaBoTC; OxBTC

Heard on a Boat. T'an Yüan-ch'un, *Chinese.* SuSp, *tr. by* Irving Y. Lo

Heard on the Mountain. Victor Hugo. AWP, *tr. by* Francis Thompson *Fr.* Feuilles d'Automne.

Heard ye eer of the silly blind harper. The Lochmaben Harper. *Unknown.* ESPB; OxBB

Heard ye o' the tree o' France. The Tree of Liberty. Robert Burns. FaBoPV

Heard ye the thunder of battle. Trafalgar. Francis Turner Palgrave. FaBoBe

Heard you that shriek. The Slave Mother. Frances Ellen Watkins Harper. APN-2; CrDW; NAAAL

Heare me. A Mistress keeps her lover on his toes. Ovid. OBCVT, *tr. by* Ben Jonson *Fr.* Catiline his Conspiracy.

Hearing. Michael McClintock. HA

Hearing. W. S. Merwin. NoAM

Hearing. Miroslav Valek, *German.* CEEP, *tr. by* Ewald Osers

Hearing a Flute at Broken Bridge. Yün Shou-p'ing, *Chinese.* CoBLCP, *tr. by* Jonathan Chaves

Hearing a Flute on the River Chi. Wen Cheng-ming, *Chinese.* CoBLCP, *tr. by* Jonathan Chaves

Hearing a low growl in your throat, you'll know that it's started. Death, the Last Visit. Marie Howe. NAmP90

Hearing a Song from My Boat. Chang Yü, *Chinese.* CoBLCP, *tr. by* Jonathan Chaves

Hearing a sound that may be thy return. Hildegarde Flanner. *Fr.* Sonnets in Quaker Language. WPE

Hearing Aid, The. Richard Jones. NAmP90

Hearing how tourists, dazed with reverence. Aldport (Mystery Tour). Kingsley Amis. NOBL *Fr.* The Evans Country.

Hearing I ask from the holy races. Voluspo. *Unknown.* AWP, *tr. by* Henry Adams Bellows *Fr.* The Elder Edda.

Hearing Impairment. Les A. Murray. OBCoV

Hearing Loom and Shuttle. Yü Chi, *Chinese.* CoBLCP, *tr. by* Jonathan Chaves

Hearing loss? Yes, loss is what we hear. Hearing Impairment. Les A. Murray. OBCoV

Hearing Men Shout at Night on MacDougal Street. Robert Bly. InPS-3

Hearing of harvests rotting in the valleys. Paysage Moralisé. W. H. Auden. MoBrPo; OAEL-2; UnPo

Hearing of past actions. John Cage. APSN *Fr.* Diary: How to Improve the World (You Will Only Make Matters Worse).

Hearing of you, I never lost a brother. Stepping Outside. Tess Gallagher. AmPA

Hearing one saga, we enact the next. Remembering the 'Thirties. Donald Davie. FaBoPV; NoP-4; OxBTC

Hearing Russian Spoken. Donald Davie. GTBS-P

Hearing Steps. Charles Simic. HCAP

Hearing That His Friend Was Coming Back from the War. Wang Chien, *Chinese.* ChiP, *tr. by* Arthur Waley; FP

Hearing that on Sunday I would leave. The Emerald. James Merrill. FiLi *Fr.* Up and Down.

Hearing the Early Oriole. Po Chü-i, *Chinese.* ChiP, *tr. by* Arthur Waley

Hearing the stones cry out under the horizons. (LL) Wind. Ted Hughes. NAEL-2, NoP-4; Poetr

Hearing, this June day, the thin thunder. Home Thoughts from Abroad. William Robert Rodgers. OBCoV

Hearing your words, and not a word among them. Edna St. Vincent Millay. CMoP; ColAP; MoP; NoAM; Poetr; VGW

Hearke, Now Every Thing Is Still. John Webster. *See* The Shrouding of the Duchess of Malfi.

Hearken all ye, 'tis the feast o' Saint Stephen. The Feast o' Saint [*or* St.] Stephen. Ruth Sawyer. OBCP

Hearken, Lady Betty, hearken. Christopher Anstey. NOEC *Fr.* The New Bath Guide.

Hearken, O blessed one, whose eternal eye sees all. To the Sun. *Unknown, Greek.* GrIP, *tr. by* Apostolos N. Athanasskis *Fr.* The Orphic Hymns.

Hearken, thou craggy ocean pyramid! To Ailsa Rock. Keats. OBNC

Hearken to me, gentlemen. King Estmere. *Unknown.* ESPB; OBNV; OxBB

Hears not my Phillis how the birds. Song. Sir Charles Sedley. EnLoPo

Hears thy voice right, now he is gone. (LL) Memorial Verses. Matthew Arnold. CABP; NAEL-2; OAEL-2

Hearse Song, The. *Unknown.* AS; OxBoLi; RB

Hearse was the oven of the crematory, The. The Funeral. "M. J.," *Polish.* TrJP, *tr. by* A. Glanz-Leyeles

Hears't thou, my soul, what serious things. Dies Irae. Thomas of Celano, *Latin.* AWP; TIRV, *tr. by* Richard Crashaw

Heart. Guillaume Apollinaire. TTTS, *tr. by* Roger Shattuck *Fr.* Heart, Crown, and Mirror.

Heart, The. Stephen Crane. APAD; HoPM; MoAmPo *Fr.* The Black Riders [and Other Lines].

Heart, The. Michael Drayton. NOSC

Heart, The. Harvey Shapiro. HoPM

Heart, The. Jakov Steinberg, *Hebrew.* TrJP, *tr. by* Harry H. Fein

Heart, The. Francis Thompson.
   All's Vast. MoBrPo; Son
   (Correlated Greatness.) GTBS-P

"Heart you hold too small and local thing, The." OBMV

Heart and Mind. Dame Edith Sitwell. LW; OxBTC; TwCP

Heart and service to you proffered, The. Sir Thomas Wyatt. SiPS

Heart asks Pleasure—*first*, The. Emily Dickinson. APN-2; AmPP; CMoP; MeMAP; MoAmPo; NAAL-1; NAAL-3; NOBA; NoP-4; OxBA; PoPoPo; SAGP; WPE

Heart Attack in the Country, A. Terry Hummer. NAmP90

Heart be content, though she be gone. Ostella forth of Town: To My Heart. John Tatham. NOSC

Heart cold in the breast with terror, grieving. Lament for Llywelyn ap Gruffudd. Gruffudd ab yr Ynad Coch, *Welsh.* OBWVE, *tr. by* Joseph P. Clancy

Heart, Crown, and Mirror. Guillaume Apollinaire, *French.*
   Heart. TTTS, *tr. by* Roger Shattuck
   "In this mirror I am enclosed." TTTS, *tr. by* Roger Shattuck
   "Kings who have died." TTTS, *tr. by* Roger Shattuck

Heart does hurt, The. It Really Is the Heart. Denise Riley. NBrP

Heart Exchange. Sir Philip Sidney. *See* The Bargain.

Heart Flies Up, Erratic as a Kite, The. Delmore Schwartz. PoA

Heart free, hand free. Sic Vita. W. S. Braithwaite. NAAAL

Heart has need of some deceit, The. Only the Polished Skeleton. Countee Cullen. VGW

Heart, heart, lie still. Ellen S. Hooper. PAR

Heart-Hungry. Josephine D. Henderson Heard. CBWP-4

Heart Is Deep, The. Roger Wolcott. ChIV-1; SCAP

Heart is hard in nature, and unfit, The. Animals Enjoying Life. William Cowper. APo *Fr.* The Task.

Heart is the Target, The. Ellen Bryant Voigt. WeT

Heart Knoweth Its Own Bitterness, The. Christina Rossetti. VWP

Heart, knowing, The. What He Said. Allur Nanmullai, *Tamil.* PLW, *tr. by* A. K. Ramanujan

Heart, let us this once reason together. Donald Justice. MT

Heart made full of thought, A. Maghnas O Domhnaill. NOIV

Heart of a Girl Is a Wonderful Thing, The. *Unknown.* BLPA

Heart of a woman [goes forth with the dawn], The. Georgia Douglas Johnson. BlSi; ISC; NAAAL; NMM-2; PoLF

Heart of All the Scene, The. Ralph Waldo Emerson. *Fr.* Woodnotes I ("For this present, hard"). AmPP; NOBA

Heart of autumn! The Chipmunk. Herman Melville. NCAP

Heart of Autumn. Robert Penn Warren. ColAP; FuPo; MT; Poetr

Heart of Herakles, The. Kenneth Rexroth. BLT *Fr.* The Lights in the Sky are Stars.

Heart of London beating warm, The. (LL) London. John Davidson. NOBE; OBNC

Heart of Midlothian, The. Sir Walter Scott.
   Madge Wildfire Sings. OBNC
   (Pride of Youth, The.) GTBS-P

Heart of Oak. David Garrick. NOEC; OxBoLi

Heart of oak etc. (LL) Heart of Oak. David Garrick. NOEC; OxBoLi

Heart of O'Leary, S.J., The. Limerick. David Phillips. PeLi

Heart of Rice Straw, A. Nellie Wong.
   "Ma, my heart must be made of rice straw." UnSA

Heart of standing is we cannot fly., The. (LL) Aubade: "Hours before dawn we were woken by the quake." William Empson. FaBoMo; FaBoTw; OxAEP-2; OxBTC

Heart of the Backlog. Robert Penn Warren. MT

Heart-of-the-Daybreak. Eugène Marais, *Afrikaans.* PeSA, *tr. by* Uys Krige *and* Jack Cope

Heart of the heartless world. To Margot Heinemann. John Cornford. BoLoP; OBWP; OxBTC

Heart of the Quartz Pebble, The. Vasco [or Vasko] Popa. PoSu, tr. by Anne Pennington Fr. The Quartz Pebble.

Heart of the World, The. Rabbi Nahman of Bratzlav, Yiddish. TrJP, tr. by Joseph Leftwich

Heart on the Hill, The. Petrarch. AWP Fr. Sonnets to Laura.

Heart oppressed [or oppress'd] with desperate thought. Sir Thomas Wyatt. SiPS

Heart that resembles a cave, A. The Guide to the Stone Age. James Tate. WeT

Heart! We [or Heart, we] will forget him! Emily Dickinson. SAmP

Heart, with what lonely fears you ached. Leda. Robert Graves. PFE

Heart without love is like, A. Abandoned Churches. Lyubomir Levchev, Bulgarian. CEEP, tr. by Ewald Osers

Heart Wounds. Claire Richcreek Thomas. PoToHe

Heart you hold too small and local thing, The. Francis Thompson. OBMV Fr. The Heart.

Heartbreak Camp. Roy Campbell. OxBTC

Heartbreak Hotel. Liz Lochhead. FaBoTC

Hearted Americans are. The Kind-. James Laughlin. CDa

Hearth and Home. Stoddard King. OBAL

Hearth Song. John Montague. PNI

Hearthstone. Harold Monro. OBMV

Heartland. Jim Barnes. HATNAP

Heartless Art, The. Tony Harrison. NoP-4

Hearts, The. Robert Pinsky. VCAP

Hearts (1983). Laurie Duggan. BMAP Fr. Three Found Poems.

Heart's Abysses, The. Walter Savage Landor. FaBoEE; OBSV

Heart's Anchor, The. William Winter. PoToHe

Heart's Content. Unknown. PoLF

Heart's Ease. Paul Hoover. PmAP

Heart's Ease. Mary E. Tucker. CBWP-1

Heart's Flag. Namjo Kim, Korean. CKP, tr. by Jaihiun Kim

Heart's Haven. D. G. Rossetti. Son Fr. The House of Life.

Hearts, like doors. Robert Louis Stevenson. CTV

Hearts, like doors, will ope with ease. Unknown. OxNR

Heart's Music. Thomas Campion. AAS; OBEV

Heart's Needle. W. D. Snodgrass. CAPP-1

    Child of My Winter Born. MoAmPo

    "Easter has come around." VCAP

    "I thumped on you the best I could." NoAM

    "Late April and you are three; today." VCAP

    "Vicious winter finally yields, The." MoLi

Hearts of men are merciless, The. (LL) Two Poems about President Harding. James Wright. CoAP; MoP; WeT

Hearts that are great beat never loud. A Thought. Abram Joseph Ryan. PWR

Hearts thus intermixed speak, The. Friendship in Emblem, or the Seal, to my Dearest Lucasia. Katherine Philips. CABP; PBRV

Heat. Hilda Doolittle. CMoP; HeIP-4; InPK-6; MoAmPo; OxBA; PiM; TAP; TRP; UnPo Fr. The Garden. NoAM

Heat. Archibald Lampman. NOBC; NTP

Heat. Kenneth Mackenzie. BMAP; CBAP

Heat. Deborah Stein. BAP-96

Heat and cold, dusk and dawn have crowded one upon the other. Po Chü-i. See The Spring River.

Heat and cold, twilight and dawn succeed each other so swiftly. The Spring River. Po Chü-i, Chinese. CoBCP, tr. by Burton Watson

Heat before the storm. Nicholas Virgilio. HA

Heat goes deep as cold. Epigram. Unknown, Irish. NOIV, tr. by Thomas Kinsella

Heat-heavy creatures. Mary Kinzie. FFC

Heat in the Room, The. Weldon Kees. SPE

Heat Lightning. Robert Penn Warren. MT

Heat lightning silhouettes the hills. Home Game. Don Allen Johnson. EC2

Heat-lightning streak. Basho, Japanese. InPK-6

Heat of Midnight Tears, The. Mirabai, Rajasthani. WPoS, tr. by Robert Bly

Heat of the oven, The. Breaded Meat, Breaded Hands. Michael S. Harper. ISC

Heathen Are Come into Thine Inheritance, The. Bible, O.T. TrJP Fr. Psalms.

Heathen Pass-ee, The. Arthur Clement Hilton. NOBL; UV

Heather Flowers. Eliseus Williams, Welsh. OBWVE, tr. by Kenneth Hurlstone Jackson

Heat's on the hooker, The. Translations from the English. George Starbuck. VGW

Heave Away. Unknown. AS

Heaven. Rupert Brooke. EBEV; HoPM; LiTM; MoBrPo; NOBE; NSI; PoRA

Heaven. Mark Doty. NAmP90

Heaven. George Herbert. ESCV; GeHe; SeCP; TTTS; TrCP

Heaven. David Lehman. PuP-15

Heaven. Philip Levine. LCAP-2

Heaven. Cathy Song. NoAM

Heaven. Arthur Seymour John Tessimond. OxBM

Heaven. Unknown. PoLF

Heaven and earth a rotating ball. Tune: "Wild Geese Have Come Down; Song of Victory"—Idle Leisure. Teng Yu-pin, Chinese. SuSp, tr. by Hellmut Wilhelm

Heaven and earth, and all that hear me plain. A Protest. Sir Thomas Wyatt. SiPS

Heaven and Earth exist for ever;. Substance, Shadow, and Spirit. Ch'ien T'ao, Chinese. ChiP, tr. by Arthur Waley

Heaven and earth go on forever, never ceasing. Substance, Shadow, and Spirit. T'ao Ch'ien. CoBCP, tr. by Watson, Burton (b. 1925) Fr. Substance, Shadow, and Spirit. CoBCP, tr. by Burton Watson

Heaven and [or &] earth to peace beguiles. (LL) A Cradle Song: "Sweet dreams form a shade." William Blake. FHYEP; OBCP

Heaven and Hell. Nalungiaq, Eskimo. STP, tr. by Edward Field

Heaven and Hell. Willie Nelson. InPK-6

Heaven and Hell. Francis Thompson. OxBSP

Heaven conserve thy course in quietness, fr. the Chinese of the Confucian Odes. Ezra Pound. APSN

Heaven creates all things. The Quarrel of the Six Beasts. Unknown, Vietnamese. AVP, tr. by Huỳnh Sanh Thông

Heaven expands, autumn arcs high, the night still long. Following the Rhymes of Autumn Night Song by Meng Tzu-chou, Signatory Official of the Board of Rites. Yü Chi, Chinese. CoBLCP, tr. by Jonathan Chaves

Heaven God bestow, The. (LL) Way I read a Letter's—this, The. Emily Dickinson. CBLP; InPS-3; WPE

Heaven-Haven. Gerard Manley Hopkins. APAD; EBEvV; HeIP-4; MoBrPo; MoP; NOBE; NOCV; NoAM; OBEV; OBNC; OxAEP-2; OxBSP; PeECV; RB; SoSe-8; TFi; TOF

Heaven, Heaven, Heaven Is the Place. Langston Hughes. AH; NOBA

Heaven in the South, earth Northward. Kuan Han-ch'ing. SuSp, tr. by Jerome P. Seaton Fr. Tune: "Intoxication in the East Wind."

Heaven Is Here. John G. Adams. AH

Heaven is inscrutable. Don't Go Out of the Door. Li Ho, Chinese. PLT, tr. by A. C. Graham

"Heaven"—is what I cannot reach! Emily Dickinson. NOCV

Heaven itself would stoop to her. (LL) Comus; a Masque Presented at Ludlow Castle. Milton. FHYEP; OAEL-1

Heaven-murdered one. Poem of Solitude at Columbia University. Federico García Lorca, Spanish. PBMP, tr. by Ben Belitt

Heaven of Animals, The. James Dickey. CoAP; ColAP; HeIP-4; LiTM; MT; NAAL-2; NOBA; NoAM; PoE; TAP; TRP; VCAP

Heaven-reflecting, usual moon, The. Coming from Evening Church. Charles Causley. NTP

Heaven rose no God in heaven could create! (LL) On Listening to the Spirituals. Lance Jeffers. SSLK

Heaven shall forgive you Bridge at dawn. Ballade D'une Grande Dame. G. K. Chesterton. OxBoLi; OxBoV

Heaven, the earth, and all the liquid main [or mayne], The. Anchises to Aeneas. Virgil, Latin. OBCVT; OBVE, tr. by Sir Walter Alexander Raleigh Fr. The Aeneid [or Eneados, Aeneis].

Heaven took my wife. Now it. Sorrow. Mei Yao Ch'en, Chinese. OHPC, tr. by Kenneth Rexroth

Heaven vows to keep him. (LL) Epitaph On Solomon Pavy, &[;Salomon or Salathiel Pavy&];, a Child of Q[ueen] El[izabeth's] Chapel. Ben Jonson. BeJo; GEA; HoPM; NAEL-1; NOBE; NOSC; OAEL-1; OBEV; PoEL-2; SCGP; SeCP; TFi; UnPo

Heaven / was only half as far that night. 21. Lawrence Ferlinghetti. CLPP

Heaven which art in Heaven Our Father in Heaven. Kay Smith. TrCP Fr. Footnote to the Lord's Prayer.

Heaven, which man's generations draws. Epilogue. Francis Thompson. MoBrPo Fr. A Judgment in Heaven.

Heavenly Aeroplane, The. Unknown. NOCV

Heavenly City, The. Stevie Smith. APAD; FaBoTw

Heavenly Eloquence. Samuel Daniel. See Poetry in England.

Heavenly Evil, holy One. Hymn to Evil. Louis Ginsberg. PoA

"Heavenly Father"—take to thee. Emily Dickinson. APN-2; PoEL-5

Heavenly Foreigner, The. Denis Devlin.

    "Spires, firm on their monster feet rose light and thin, The." CIP-2

Heavenly labials in a world of gutturals. / It will undo him. (LL) The Plot Against the Giant. Wallace Stevens. CMoP; OxBA; SAmP

Heavenly music, furred with praise, An. (LL) Upon a Wasp Chilled [*or* Child] with Cold. Edward Taylor. NAAL-1; NAAL-3; NOBA; NOCV; PoEL-3

Heavenly Rhetoric, The. Shakespeare. ImPo; Son *Fr.* Love's Labour's Lost.

Heavenly Traveler. Chech'on Park, *Korean*. CKP, *tr.* by Jaihiun Kim

Heavenly Vision. William Billings. AmFP

Heavens are wrath—the thunder's rattling peal, The. Written in a Thunder Storm July 15th, 1841. John Clare. EnVR

Heavens bright lamp, shine forth some of thy light. George Alsop. SCAP

Heavens declare the glory of God, The, *par.* by Stephen Mitchell. Psalm 19. Bible, *O.T.* AWP; NAWM-1; OBVE; TrJP *Fr.* Psalms.

Heavens Do Declare, The. *Unknown.* AH

Heavens doe declare / The majesty of God, The, *fr.* the Bay Psalm Book. Bible, *O.T. See* Psalm 19.

Heavens doe declare / The majesty of God, The. Psalm 19. *Unknown.* SCAP *Fr.* The Bay Psalm Book.

Heaven's mercy shines, wonders and glorys meet. The Mercies of the Year. John Danforth. SCAP

Heaven's mills are grinding slowly, but they grind exceeding small. Divine Revenge. Friedrich von Logau, *German.* GePo, *tr.* by George C. Schoolfield

Heavens, ocean, and all earth, rejoice! Sedulius Scottus. NOIV *Fr.* The Defeat of the Norsemen.

Heaven's power is infinite; earth, air, and sea. Ovid. OAEL-1, *tr.* by Dryden *Fr.* Philemon and Baucis. CTC, *tr.* by Arthur Golding *Fr.* Metamorphoses.

Heaven's Ring. Vasco [*or* Vasko] Popa, *Serbian.* VCWP, *tr.* by Charles Simic

Heavens' sun perfected in your eyes, The. (LL) Woman. Randall Jarrell. CBLP; NOBA

Heavensgate (1961). Christopher Okigbo.

  Bridge. PBMAP

  Eyes Watch the Stars. PBMAP

  Lustra. PBMAP

  Overture. PBMAP

  Passion Flower. PBMAP

Heavily flapping are the bustards' plumes. *Unknown, Chinese.* SuSp, *tr.* by C. H. Wang

Heavily hangs the tiger-lily. (LL) Song: "A Spirit haunts the year's last hours." Tennyson. GTBS-P; GaP; HeIP-4; LaPo; OBGa; OBNC

Heaviness of twilight at noon, The. Monsoon. Beckian Fritz Goldberg. NAmP90

Heaving roses of the hedge are stirred, The. Winter Will Follow. Richard Watson Dixon. CH; GTBS-P

Heaving the Lead Line. *Unknown.* AmFP

Heav'n it self would stoop to her. (LL) The Spirit's Epilogue. Milton. NOBE; NOSC; OBEV; OxAEP-1

Heavy and dull, the motionless clouds. Motionless Clouds. T'ao Ch'ien, *Chinese.* CoBCP, *tr.* by Burton Watson

Heavy Bear, The. Delmore Schwartz. ImPo *Fr.* The Repetitive Heart.

Heavy bear who goes with me, The. The Heavy Bear. Delmore Schwartz. ColAP; ImPo; LiTM; NOBA; NoAM; PFE; Poetr; TAP; TrJP; TwCP; UnPo *Fr.* The Repetitive Heart.

Heavy blue veins streaked across my mother's legs, some of them bunched up into dark lumps at her ankles. Luis J. Rodriguez. UnSA

Heavy dew. Thick mist. Dense grass. Passing a Ruined Palace. Wen T'ing-yün, *Chinese.* OHMPC, *tr.* by Kenneth Rexroth

Heavy glacier and the terrifying Alps, The. Long Lines. Paul Goodman. VGW

Heavy hangs the raindrop. A.E. Emily Jane Brontë. *Fr.* The Two Children. PoEL-5

Heavy hangs the raindrop. The Two Children. Emily Jane Brontë. PoEL-5

Heavy-hearted. Judah Al-Harizi, *Hebrew.* TrJP

Heavy Heavy Heavy. John Malcolm Brinnin. NYBP

Heavy, heavy, heavy, hand and heart. Tenebrae. Denise Levertov. NoP-4

Heavy mist, A. A muffled sea. Atheling Grange; or, The Apotheosis of Lotte Nussbaum. William Plomer. OBNV

Heavy rain crumbles a wall of my house, A. Night Rain: A Wall Collapses—Sent To My Neighbors. Yang Shih-ch'i, *Chinese.* CoBLCP, *tr.* by Jonathan Chaves

Heavy shower bends her to the earth, The. The Little Birch Tree. Stepan Petrovich Shchipachov, *Russian.* TCRP, *tr.* by Daniel Weissbort

Heavy smells of Spring, The. Jack. Louis Golding. TrJP

Heavy sobs which rise up and choke me, The. *Unknown, Japanese.* WPJ, *tr.* by Kenneth Rexroth *and* Ikuko Atsumi

Heavy sounds are over-sweet, The. City-Storm. Harold Monro. MoBrPo

Heavy, to hurt those sacred seeds of thee. (LL) To His Dying Brother, Master William Herrick. Robert Herrick. CaPo; CavPo; NOSC

Heavy umbrellas / aren't worth their weight, The. Crocus Night. James Schuyler. PoM

Heavy violets there is no way. Barbara Guest. FTOS

Heavy Water Blues. Bob Kaufman. NBV

  ("Radio is teaching my goldfish Jujuitsu, The.") CLPP

Heavy with salt, and warm. The Equinox. DuBose Heyward. PoA

Heavyweight champ of Seattle, The. *Unknown.* OBAL

Heavyweight champion of the world Mike Tyson. Today's News. Elizabeth Alexander. ISC

Hebrew Melodies. Heinrich Heine, *German.*

  By the Waters of Babylon. TrJP, *tr.* by Charles Godfrey Leland

Hebrew Nation did not write it, The. William Blake. OAEL-2

Hebrew of your poets, Zion, The. Charles Reznikoff. ChIV-1; VGW

Hebrews. James Oppenheim. TrJP

Hebrides, The. Michael Longley. PBCIP

Hecale. Callimachus, *Greek.*

  "As long as it was still noon and the earth." HePo, *tr.* by Barbara Hughes Fowler

  "South wind does not shed so great a cast, The." HePo, *tr.* by Barbara Hughes Fowler

  "They fell asleep but not for long, for soon." HePo, *tr.* by Barbara Hughes Fowler

Hecatompathia; or, Passionate Century of Love. Thomas Watson.

  "Some that reporte great Alexanders life." AAS

  "Speake gentle heart, where is thy dwelling place?" AAS

Hector. Valentin Iremonger. CIP-2

Hector Arms. Homer. NOSC, *tr.* by George Chapman *Fr.* The Iliad.

Hector Flees before Achilles. Homer. OBVE, *tr.* by Alexander Pope *Fr.* The Iliad.

Hector Protector was dressed all in green. Mother Goose. OxNR; ReMoGo

Hector spake to them thus, & the Trojans cheered with applauses. Homer. *See* Specimen of a Translation of the Iliad in Blank Verse.

Hector, the captain bronzed, from simple fight. Geoffrey Scott. OBMV *Fr.* The Skaian Gate.

Hector's Child and the Plume. Homer. OBVE, *tr.* by George Chapman *Fr.* The Iliad.

Hector's Defiance. Homer. NOSC, *tr.* by George Chapman *Fr.* The Iliad.

Hector's flight. Homer. OBCVT, *tr.* by Robert Fitzgerald *Fr.* The Iliad.

Hecuba. Euripides, *Greek.*

  "Ilion, o my city." OBCVT, *tr.* by Richmond Lattimore

Hecuba's Testament. Rosario Castellanos, *Spanish.* STV, *tr.* by John Frederick Nims

He'd had enough of lying in the furze. The Ghostly Father. Peter Redgrove. MoBS

Hedge before me, one behind, A. *Unknown, Irish.* BIrV, *tr.* by Flann O'Brien

Hedge Life. James Dickey. LCAP-2

Hedge Schoolmaster, A. Padraic Fallon. CIP-2

Hedgehog. Chu Chen Po, *Chinese.* OHMPC; PiM, *tr.* by Kenneth Rexroth

Hedgehog. Paul Muldoon. BIrV; NoAM; PBCIP

Hedgehog and His Coat, The. Elizabeth Fleming. BoTP

Hedgehog is a creature with four legs, and thorns, A. The Composition. Jean Kenward. PeP

Hedgehog is a little beast, The. Edith King. BoTP

Hedgerows. Stanley Plumly. NAmP90

Hedges are dazed as cock-crow, heaps of leaves, The. Departure in Middle Age. Roland Mathias. CRP; OBWVE

Hedges Freaked With Snow. Robert Graves. OxBTC *Fr.* Three Songs for the Lute.

Heed the old oracles. The Undersong. Ralph Waldo Emerson. *Fr.* Woodnotes II ("As sunbeams stream through liberal space"). NOBA

Heedless and wilful, took their knights to bed. (LL) Women have loved before as I love now. Edna St. Vincent Millay. HeIP-4; NALW; PoA

Heedless o' My Love. William Barnes. GBL

Heedless of where the next bright bolt may fall. (LL) The White Goddess. Robert Graves. MoBrPo; NAEL-2; NoP-4; OAEL-2

Heemi. Hone Tuwhare. PeNZ

Heere uninterr'd suspendes (though not to save). Feltons Epitaph. *Unknown.* PBRV

Heere we doe not lynger; thee vowd sollemnitye finnisht. Polyphemus. Virgil. NoSic, *tr.* by Richard Stanyhurst *Fr.* The Aeneid [*or* Eneados, Aeneis].

Heetum peetum penny pie. A Game on the Fingers. *Unknown.* CBNP

Heh jimmy. Six Glasgow Poems. Tom Leonard. FaBoTC

Heidi men call me when their homes I visit. Song of the Seeress. *Unknown, Norse.* NAWM-1, *tr.* by Paul B. Taylor *and* W. H. Auden

Heifer Clambers Up, A. Gary Snyder. NOBA

Heigh ho! my heart is low. *Unknown.* OxNR

Heigh ho, my heart! would God that she were mine! (LL) Rosaline. Thomas Lodge. GTBS-P; OBEV; OxAEP-1

Heigh-ho on a Winter Afternoon. Donald Davie. OxBTC

Heigh ho! says Anthony Rowley. (LL) Mr. Frog Went a-Courting. Mother Goose. AS; AmFP; OxNR

Heigho, dot and go one. (LL) The Lover's Arithmetic. *Unknown*. CBNP; OxBoLi; PeLV

Height of the Ridiculous, The. Oliver Wendell Holmes. OBAL; OBCA

Height of the Season, The. Maxine W. Kumin. FFC

Height of trees. Geese Blood. Barbara Guest. FTOS

Heights. Aleksei Eliseievich Kruchyonykh. CBNP

Heights of Macchu Picchu, The. Pablo Neruda, *Spanish*.
"Stone within stone, and man, where was he?" VCWP, *tr. by* Nathaniel Tarn

Heimkehr, Die. Heinrich Heine, *German*. AWP, *tr. by* Ezra Pound

Heine's mother was a monster. A Century Piece for Poor Heine. John Logan. NNaP

Heinrich Heine. Ludwig Lewisohn. TrJP

Heir of Linne, The. *Unknown*. ESPB

Heir to the office of a man not dead. A Miltonic Sonnet for Mr. Johnson on His Refusal of Peter Hurd's Official Portrait. Richard Wilbur. CAPP-1

Heirloom. Leonard Cohen. NOBC

Heirloom. Abraham Moses Klein. NOBC; TrJP

Heirloom. Robin Morgan. NMM-2

Heirloom. Kathleen Jessie Raine. NALW

Heirloom. Cinda Thompson. LoHo

Heirs of Stalin, The. Yevtushenko, *Russian*. TCRP
("It will seem to me / that Stalin still lives in the mausoleum.") (LL) VCWP, *tr. by* George Reavey
("Mute was the marble. / Mutely glimmered the glass.") VCWP, *tr. by* George Reavey

Hektor of Troy. Archias of Macedon, *Greek*. GrAn, *tr. by* Dudley Fitts

Hélas! Oscar Wilde. ADE; MoBrPo; NAEL-2; Son; TIRV
(Hélas¹.) GSo

Hélas¹. Oscar Wilde. *See* Hélas!

Helbatrawss, The. Kingsley Amis. NOBL

Held among wars, watching. Kollwitz, Käthe. Muriel Rukeyser. NMM-2

Held back, like a bow drawn tight. Walter Höllerer, *German*. CLPP, *tr. by* Jerome Rothenberg

Held between wars / my lifetime. Käthe Kollwitz. Muriel Rukeyser. NALW; NMM-2

Held in the two hands, you. Muriel Rukeyser. *See* Käthe Kollwitz.

Held it. Martin Shea. HA

Held prisoner in the house. (LL) Sunday Afternoons. Yusef Komunyakaa. NAmP90; NoP-4

Hélé helélé the King is a great king. Ex-Voto for a Shipwreck. Aimé Césaire, *French*. PFTM, *tr. by* Clayton Eshleman *and* Annette Smith

Heledd and Inge, when the torches are red. In Berlin, August 1945: Lehrte Bahnhof. Alun Llywelyn-Williams, *Welsh*. OBWVE, *tr. by* Joseph P. Clancy

Helen. Hilda Doolittle. BoWoP; ColAP; FaBoWP; LiTM; MoAmPo; NAAL-2; NALW; NMM-2; NOBA; NoAM; NoP-4; TAP
("White ash amid funeral cypresses.") (LL) PoPoPo

Helen. James Harrison. NBLV

Helen. Mary Lamb. NOBRP

Helen. Marlowe. ImPo *Fr.* Doctor Faustus. NAEL-1; OAEL-1
(Face of Helen, The.)

Helen. Peter Meinke. PBCAP

Helen. Paul Valéry, *French*. LoP; OBVE, *tr. by* Robert Lowell

Helen. Charles Kenneth Williams. PuP-17

Helen and the elders. Homer. OBCVT, *tr. by* George Chapman *Fr.* The Iliad.

Helen, had I known yesterday. Release. D. H. Lawrence. CMoP

Helen in Egypt. Hilda Doolittle.
"Alas, my brothers." NOBA
"Another shout from the wharves." NOBA

Helen like the Rose. Evan Lloyd. OBWVE *Fr.* The Powers of the Pen.

Helen of Kirconnell, *see also* Where Helen Lies *by* Robert Burns. *Unknown*. AWP; CH; ImPo; OBEV; SCGP
(Fair Helen.) GTBS-P
("Since my Love died for me.") (LL) GTBS-P

Helen Paints a Room (1984). John A. Scott. BMAP

Helen, the Sad Queen. Paul Valéry, *French*. AWP, *tr. by* Joseph T. Shipley

Helen, thy beauty is to me. To Helen. Edgar Allan Poe. APN-1; AWP; AmPP; BoLoP; CH; ClHu; ColAP; FaBoBe; GBL; GLoP; HAP; HeIP-4; HoPM; ImPo; InPS-3; LoP; MeMAP; NAAL-1; NAAL-3; NIP-4; NOBA; NOBE; NoP-4; OBEV; OxBA; PAR; PBMP; PoE; PoEL-4; PoLF; PoPoPo; PoRA; SAGP; TAP; TFi; WeW-3

Helen Todd: My Birthname. Sandra McPherson. LCAP-2; LoL

Helen you Always Were / The Factory. Judy Grahn.
Hannah. NMM-2

Helena. Alfred de Vigny, *French*. GrIP, *tr. by* Richard Stoneman

Helena Embarks for Palestine. Cynewulf. *Fr.* Elene. AnOE, *tr. by* Charles W. Kennedy

Helen's Burning. Laura Riding Jackson. ColAP

Helen's Lamentation. Homer. OBVE, *tr. by* Congreve *Fr.* The Iliad.

Helen's lips, as drifting dust. Consolation. Arthur Guiterman. BXAP

Helicon. John Hollander. Poetr

Heliodora's Brows. Meleager, *Greek*. GrAn
("That, flower of flowers, outfaces all.") (LL) GrIP, *tr. by* Peter Whigham

Heliogabalus. John Hollander. NBLV; OBAL

Heliotropism / of branches, now darkened. Antonin Bartusek. CEEP

Hell ("At once with him they rose"). Milton. *Fr.* Book II. FHYEP; NAEL-1; OxAEP-1 *Fr.* Paradise Lost.

Hell. Edith Södergran, *Finnish*. NNPT; PFTM, *tr. by* Stina Katchadourian

He'll be a former cat burglar. My Diamond Stud. Alice Fulton. WWSi

Hell blot black for alway the thought "Peace"! (LL) Sestina: Altaforte. Ezra Pound. CMoP; ColAP; FaBoTw; ImPo; MoAmPo; NOBA

Hell-bound Train, The. *Unknown*. BLPA

Hell freezing over. To keep sane. Mandelstam. David Young. AmPA

Hell Gate. A. E. Housman. NoAM; SCGP; UnPo

He'll grow into his sleep so sound again. (LL) Ten Days Leave. W. D. Snodgrass. MoAmPo; Poetsp; UnPo

He'll hie me, par *is* he? the God divide her. Catullus. *See* Sappho.

Hell, I love everybody. (LL) Goodtime Jesus. James Tate. LCAP-2; WeT

Hell in Texas. *Unknown*. BLPA

Hell is a city much like London. Shelley. OBSV; OxBSn *Fr.* Peter Bell the Third.

Hell is constant and eternal. (LL) Hell. Edith Södergran, *Finnish*. NNPT; PFTM, *tr. by* Stina Katchadourian

He'll labour, night and day, / To be a Pilgrim. John Bunyan. *See* The Pilgrim.

He'll never rise again but he is ready. The Ash Plant. Seamus Heaney. BiHa

Hell raised a hoarse, half-human cheer. (LL) A Ballad of Hell. John Davidson. EBVV; HoPM; MoBrPo

Hell, rising from a thousand thrones, / Shall do it reverence. Edgar Allan Poe. *See* The City in the Sea.

"Hell" said the Devil, as it might have been. Reborn. Kingsley Amis. OxBC

He'll shoot baith thy young son and me. (LL) The Great Silkie of Sule Skerry. *Unknown*. ESPB; FaBoCh; OxBB

He'll struggle, but at length comply with ease. Tibullus. *See* Elegies 1.iv: "Far from the tender Tribe of Boys remove."

Hell To Pay. Susanne Doyle. FFC

Hell, Well, Heaven. Mongane Wally Serote. PBMAP

Hell where youth and laughter go. (LL) Suicide in [the] Trenches. Siegfried Sassoon. PoFWW; PoWW

Hellas. Desmond O'Grady.
"Here, because of the shock, the sudden." PBCIP
"But Greece and her foundations are." GrIP
Chorus: "World's great age begins anew, The." EBEV; HAP; NOBE; OAEL-2; PoEL-4
(Chorus from "Hellas.") AWP
(Final Chorus, The.)
Chorus: "Worlds on worlds are rolling ever." NAEL-2

Hellenics, The. Walter Savage Landor.
Ternissa. NOBE; OBNC
(Ternissa! You Are Fled.) PoEL-4

Hellhound on My Trail. Robert Johnson. NAAAL

Hello. Gregory Corso. PoM

Hello. Naomi Shihab Nye. MT; NAmP90

Hello, daffodil, saffron-yellow exclamation. Yellow Gramophone. Sheila Cussons, *Afrikaans*. PeSAV, *tr. by the author*

Hello darkness my old friend. The Sound of Silence. Paul Simon. PBMP

Hello Death Angel, old familiar, old nemesis. Address. Lynda Hull. PUP-19

Hello, Girls. *Unknown*. AS

Hello! Hello!/ Are you there? Are you there? Telephone Message, A (To Whom it May Concern). John Oxenham. NSI

"Hello, hello, hello, sir." Jump-Rope Rhyme. *Unknown*. NTCP

Hello. Hello. What's your name? Philodemus, *Greek*. PGA, *tr. by* Kenneth Rexroth

Hello There. Brian S. Salome. BXAP

Hello There! Harvey Shapiro. WeT

—"Hello there.—" *Hello there yourself.* Philodemus, *Greek.* EP, *tr. by* Moebius, William; GrAn, *tr. by* William Moebius

Hello Ungod. Anthony McNeill. HCP

Hello Up There. Marge Piercy. NBLV

Hell's gate. Virgil, *Latin.* OBCVT, *tr. by* Sir John Harington

Helluva hard tay read theez init. Good Style. Tom Leonard. FaBoTC

Helmet and rifle, pack and overcoat. The Battle. Louis Simpson. InPS-3; OBWP; PBCV; PoWW

Helmet now an hive for bees becomes, The. The Vote. Ralph Knevet. FMP; NOSC

Helmets; a Fragment, The. Thomas Penrose. NOEC

Helmsman, The. Hilda Doolittle. CMoP; OxBA

Help! X. J. Kennedy. CA

Help. Sadi. AWP, *tr. by* Sir Edwin Arnold *Fr.* The Gulistan.

Help. John Greenleaf Whittier. Son

Help, a love, a you, a wife. (LL) Love Song: I and Thou. Alan Dugan. HoPM; InPK-6; MoP; NoAM

Help! Help! Trouble at the Farm. Ivy O. Eastwick. BoTP

Help, help all tongues to celebrate this wonder. Ben Jonson. NOSC *Fr.* The Masque of Queens.

Help! How Minne has deserted me. Friedrich von Hausen, *German.* GePo, *tr. by* Frederick Goldin

Help, Lord, because the Godly Man. Francis Rous. AH

Help make earth happy / Like the heaven above. Julia A. Fletcher Carney. *See* (Little Things).

Help me down Cemetery Road. (LL) Toads Revisited. Philip Larkin. CMoP; NOBL; OxAEP-2

Help[e] me! help[e] me! now I call. To His Mistresses. Robert Herrick. CaPo; SeCP

Help me, Lord, I'm. Black Hole. Adrian Rumble. SpW

Help me to help your life. Letter to P. Robert Friend. NYBP

Help[e] me to seek [*or* seke] for I lost it there. Sir Thomas Wyatt. AAS; SiPS

Help Me Today. Elsie Robinson. PoToHe

Help of the helpless, O, abide with me. Henry Francis Lyte. *See* Abide with me[; fast falls the eventide].

Help Thy Servant. Andrew Broaddus. AH

Help us, oh God, we're rich. (LL) Harlem, Montana. James Welch. CDW; HATNAP; PoPoPo

Help us to do the things we should. Mrs. William H. Dietz. CTV

Help Wanted. Franklin Waldheim. BLPA

Helpe, crosse, fairest of timbres three. *Unknown.* MiEL

Helping Hand, A. Miroslav Holub, *Czech.* PoSu, *tr. by* George Theiner

Helpless like this. New World A-Comin'. Edward Kamau Brathwaite. NoP-4 *Fr.* The Arrivants: A New World Trilogy.

Hemlock at Sunset, A. Alec Brock Stevenson. FuPo

Hemlock in the Furrows. Adah Isaacs Menken. CBWP-1

Hemlock shakes in the rafter, the oak in the driving keel, The. (LL) Misgivings. Herman Melville. APN-2; NAAL-1; NAAL-3; NCAP; NOBA; OxBA

Hemlocks slumped, The. Bonus. A. R. Ammons. HCAP

Hemmed-in Males. William Carlos Williams. PoRA *Fr.* A Folded Skyscraper.

Hemp. . . / A stick. Gauge. Langston Hughes. APSN

Hems gathered up, sash not yet tied. *Unknown.* CoBCP, *tr. by* Burton Watson *Fr.* Tzu Yeh Songs.

Hen, The. Christian Morgenstern, *German.* RB, *tr. by* W. D. Snodgrass *and* Lore Segal

Hen-eagle broods, sick, A. What He Said to His Heart, Arguing against Further Ambition and Travel. Ilankiranar, *Tamil.* PLW, *tr. by* A. K. Ramanujan

Hen Flower, The. Galway Kinnell. NNaP

Hen is the best example of what living constantly with humans, The. Zbigniew Herbert, *Polish.* VCWP, *tr. by* Czeslaw Milosz *and* Peter Dale Scott

Hen It Is a Noble Beast, The. William McGonagall. NBLV

Hen, one who could have brought more geese, a female, a wild one, dead, A. The Wings of a Wild Goose. "Chrystos." GLP

Hen remarked to the mooley cow, The. Art. *Unknown.* BLPA; NBLV

Hen under Bay-Tree. Ruth Pitter. OxBTC

Hen Woman. Thomas Kinsella. CIP-2; PBCIP

Hence, all you vain delights. Melancholy. John Fletcher. GTBS-P; OBEV; PoEL-2 *Fr.* The Nice Valor.

Hence Cupid! with your cheating toys. Against Love. Katherine Philips. BoWoP; WPE

Hence, heart, with her that must depart. A Bequest of His Heart. Alexander Scott. OBEV

Hence, hence, all you vain delights. Melancholy. Thomas Middleton. NOSC

Hence, loath'd vulgarity. Fashion. Horace Twiss. BXAP

Hence loathèd Melancholy. L'Allegro. Milton. AWP; FHYEP; GTBS-P; HAP; HoPM; ImPo; NOSC; NoP-4; OAEL-1; OBEV; PBRV; PoPoPo; TFi

Hence, stupid Peace! thy pride and song. The Age of War. *Unknown.* NOBRP

Hence thro' the windings of the mazy wood. Stowe, the Gardens of the Rt. Hon. Richard Lord Viscount Cobham. Gilbert West. OBGa

Hence vain deluding Joys. Il Penseroso. Milton. AWP; FHYEP; GTBS-P; HAP; HoPM; ImPo; NOSC; OAEL-1; OBEV; TFi

Hence, ye Profane; I hate ye all. Horace. OBCVT, *tr. by* Abraham Cowley *Fr.* An Ode of Horace, not exactly copyed, but rudely imitated.

Hence ye profane: mell not with holy things. Satire VIII. Joseph Hall. ChIV-2

Henceforth, from the mind. Louise Bogan. WPE

Henceforth I will not set my love. Sir Arthur Gorges. GBL

Henchman, The. John Greenleaf Whittier. OBEV

Hendecasyllabics. Tennyson. EBEV; NOBL; PeLV

Hendy hap ichabbe yhent, An. *Unknown. See* Alison.

Hengest Cyning. Jorge Luis Borges, *Spanish.* NYBP, *tr. by* Norman Thomas Di Giovanni

Henley's a special regatta. Limerick. Jim Anthony. PeLi

Henpecked Husband, A. *Unknown.* PeLV

Henry Adams / Was mortally afraid of Madams. W. H. Auden. OBAL *Fr.* Academic Graffiti.

Henry and King Pedro, clasping. The Death of Don Pedro. *Unknown, Spanish.* AWP, *tr. by* John Gibson Lockhart

Henry and Mary. Robert Graves. NOxBChV; NTP

Henry before Agincourt: October 25, 1415. John Lydgate. CH

Henry C. Calhoun. Edgar Lee Masters. LiTM *Fr.* Spoon River Anthology.

Henry got me with child. Amanda Barker. Edgar Lee Masters. NoAM *Fr.* Spoon River Anthology.

Henry Green. Mary Wyatt and Henry Green. *Unknown.* AmFP

Henry I to the Sea. Eugene Lee-Hamilton. PeVV

Henry in Ireland to Bill underground. An Elegy for W.C.W., The Lovely Man. John Berryman. NoP-4 *Fr.* Dream Songs.

Henry IV. Shakespeare. OxBSn *Fr.* Henry IV.

Henry James. Robert Louis Stevenson. OBNC

Henry James at Newport. Weldon Kees. PoA

Henry K. Sawyer. *Unknown.* AmFP

Henry King, Who Chewed Bits of String, and Was Early Cut Off in Dreadful Agonies. Hilaire Belloc. NBLV; OBCoV; OxAEP-2; PeLV

(Henry King.) FuFo

Henry Martyn. *Unknown.* ESPB

Henry Porter wore good clothes for his journey. Passage. Elizabeth Alexander. ISC

Henry sats in de bar and was odd. John Berryman. HCAP; PoPoPo; VCAP *Fr.* Dream Songs.

("Of a newborn child.") (LL) ColAP

HENRY THE GRANDFATHER. Little Books / 137 / Silence Mar 22 79. Hannah Weiner. FTOS

HENRY THE GRANDFATHER. Little Books 137 Silence Mar 22 79. Hannah Weiner. FTOS *Fr.* Little Books / Indians.

Henry Turnbull. Wilfrid Wilson Gibson. FaBoTw

Henry V before Agincourt. Shakespeare. FaPoR *Fr.* King Henry V.

Henry VI (skeleton). Shakespeare.

"Jesu preserve your royal Majesty!" OxBSn

Henry was a young king. Henry and Mary. Robert Graves. NOxBChV; NTP

Henry was every morning fed. The Boy and the Snake. Charles Lamb *and* Mary Lamb. OxBChV

Henry's Confession. John Berryman. LCAP-2; MoP; NAAL-2; NoAM; PoE; TwCP; VCAP *Fr.* Dream Songs.

Henry's Fate. John Berryman. ColAP

Henry's mind grew blacker the more he thought. John Berryman. FaBoMo; NOBA *Fr.* Dream Songs.

Henry's pelt was put on sundry walls. John Berryman. MoP; NoAM; Poetr; TRP *Fr.* Dream Songs.

Henry's Secret. Dorothy Kilner. OxBChV

Henry's Understanding. John Berryman. MoP; NOBA; NoAM

Hens, The. Elizabeth Madox Roberts. OBCA

Hen's Nest. John Clare. Son

Henyard Round, The. Donald Hall. Poetsp

Hep-Cat Chung, 'ware my town. Confucius. *Fr.* Songs of Cheng. CTC, *tr. by* Ezra Pound

Heptalogia, The. Swinburne.

Higher Pantheism in a Nutshell, The. BXAP; CABP; CBNP; EnVR; PeVV

Nephelidia. BXAP; EnVR; HoPM; PeVV

Sonnet for a Picture. BXAP; OAEL-2; UV

Heptonstall. Ted Hughes. OxAEP-2

Heptonstall Old Church. Ted Hughes. InPS-3

Her, a Statue. Thomas Tod Stoddart. OBNC

Her Accident. Thomas Hood. EBVV *Fr.* Miss Kilmansegg and Her Precious Leg.

Hēr Æthoelstān cyning, eorla drihten. *Unknown.* CABP *Fr.* Battle of Brunanburh.

Her angel looked upon God's face. The Eternal Image. Ruth Pitter. MoBrPo; OxBTC

Her Answer. John Bennett. BLPA

Her Anxiety. W. B. Yeats. OPOU

Her Apron through the Trees. Roger Weingarten. AmPA

Her arms across her breast she laid. The Beggar Maid. Tennyson. BoTP

Her arms are gravelled at the undertow. Airport. Martin Johnston. CBAP

Her arms around me—child—. From a Photograph. George Oppen. FTOS

Her arms have the beauty. What He Said. Orerulavanar, *Tamil.* PLW, *tr. by* A. K. Ramanujan

Her arms semaphore fat triangles. Momma Welfare Roll. Maya Angelou. SAGP

Her back in a line straight. Foul Line—1987. Colleen J. McElroy. LTA; NMM-2

Her bare feet tell the neurasthenic: fake moustaches on that ostrich. Metal Coughdrops. Tristan Tzara, *French.* PFTM, *tr. by* Jerome Rothenberg

Her beauty is hidden by a cloudy screen. Li Shang-yin, *Chinese.* OHMPC, *tr. by* Kenneth Rexroth

Her beauty, passive in despair. The Philanthropist and the Jelly-fish. May Kendall. VWP

Her beauty, which we talk of. Helen's Burning. Laura Riding Jackson. ColAP

Her Bed. Robert Herrick. PBRV

("See's thou that cloud, as silver clear.") PFE

Her black negligee. Hal Roth. HA

Her blacks crackle and drag. (LL) Edge. Sylvia Plath. FaBoWP; HCAP; NAAL-2; NALW; PFE; PoE; PoPoPo; TAP; VCAP

Her blows did make you blue. (LL) How Violets Came Blue. Robert Herrick. BeJo; CaPo; TTTS

Her body is not so white as. Queen-Anne's-Lace. William Carlos Williams. AmPP; MeMAP; MoAmPo; NAAL-2; NOBA; NoAM; NoP-4; TAP

Her Boreale. Richard Corbet.

Fairies' Farewell, The. BeJo; NOSC; OxAEP-1

Her boredom took her away. So simple. Ella Mi Fu Rapita! Gavin Ewart. NoAM

Her bracelets tinkle. *Unknown, Japanese.* OHMPJ, *tr. by* Kenneth Rexroth

Her breast is fit for pearls. Emily Dickinson. CPO; HeIP-4

Her breasts are the cities. Nostalgia for Titian. Ivan Krustev, *Bulgarian.* CEEP, *tr. by* Belin Tonchev

Her breasts lift with her arms. Rod Willmot. HA

Her brother is coming back tonight. Tennyson. *Fr.* Maud [A Monodrama]. EnVR

Her burning eyes on her forgetful hands. (LL) The Power of Interval. John Byrne Leicester Warren, 3d Baron De Tabley. NOBVV; OxBSP

Her charms had struck a sturdy CAIRD. Robert Burns. *Fr.* Love and Libery—A Cantata. NOBRP; NOEC

Her chaunging lookes no colour longe can holde. Medea's Frenzy. Seneca. OBVE, *tr. by* John Studley *Fr.* Medea.

Her cheek is flush'd with fever red. The Dying Child. Letitia Elizabeth Landon. VWP

Her cheeks are hot, her cheeks are white. Bianca. Arthur Symons. PeVV

Her cheeks were white, her eyes were wild. The Sea. W. H. Davies. FaBoTw

Her children say: / "Old fool." Anna Swirszczynska. *See* The Greatest Love.

Her Christening. Thomas Hood. NOBVV *Fr.* Miss Kilmansegg and Her Precious Leg.

Her cottage is next door to mine. The Girl Next Door. Nguyễn Bính, *Vietnamese.* AVP, *tr. by* Huỳnh Sanh Thông

Her cottage, then a cheerful object, wore. The Excursion. Wordsworth. OBGa *Fr.* The Excursion.

Her Dancing Days. Anna Adams. BrRo

Her darkness fell, before her day was done;. The Blind Tramp. Lilian Bowes-Lyon. WPN

Her day out from the workhouse-ward, she stands. The Ice. Wilfrid Wilson Gibson. OxBTC

Her Death. Thomas Hood. NOBVV *Fr.* Miss Kilmansegg and Her Precious Leg.

Her deceased husband's shoelace must be unknotted. Shoelace. Roger Fanning. BAP-93

Her Descending Down. Margaret Lucas Cavendish, Duchess of Newcastle. NOSC

Her Dilemma. Thomas Hardy. EnVR; NOBVV

Her door opened on the white water. The Little Lady of Ch'ing-ch'i. *Unknown, Chinese.* ChiP, *tr. by* Arthur Waley

Her drooping flowers dabble upon. Betty by the Sea. Ronald McCuaig. NOBAu

Her Education. Thomas Hood. EBVV *Fr.* Miss Kilmansegg and Her Precious Leg.

Her Elegy. *Unknown, Papago Indian.* STP, *tr. by* Armand Schwerner; BoWoP, *tr. by* Ruth Underhill

Her even lines her steady temper show. On a Lady's Writing. Anna Laetitia Barbauld. PEW

Her exquisite yellow youth. . . . (LL) Jessie Mitchell's Mother. Gwendolyn Brooks. BoWoP; ColAP; NALW; NMM-2

Her Eyes. Daniel Casper von Lohenstein, *German.* GePo, *tr. by* George C. Schoolfield

Her Eyes. John Crowe Ransom. LiTM; MeMAP; OBAL

Her eyes. What her girl friend said. Peyanar. PLW *Fr.* Nine on Happy Reunion. PLW, *tr. by* A. K. Ramanujan

Her eyes are bright as sparkling stars. Mine. Mary E. Tucker. CBWP-1

Her eyes are fixed; they seek the skies. Murillo's Magdalen. William Ellery Channing. APN-1

Her eyes are gold. Rufinus, *Greek.* GrAn, *tr. by* Alan Marshfield

Her eyes are velvet, soft and fine. My Poker Girl. Tom Masson. OBAL

Her eyes are wild, her head is bare. The Mad Mother. Wordsworth. Ro

Her eyes flood lickes his feets faire staine. Luke 7; She Began To Wash His Feet with Teares and Wipe Them with the Haires of Her Head. Bible, *N.T.* NOSC, *tr. by* Richard Crashaw *Fr.* St. Luke.

Her eyes' flood licks his feet's fair stain. On Mary Magdalene. Richard Crashaw. FMP

Her eyes glowed pale as radium. The Dream Kitchen. Sandra M. Gilbert. IFJA

Her eyes lined with kohl. Peyanar. *See* What her girl friend said ("Her eyes").

Her eyes still closed. Hal Roth. HA

Her eyes the glow-worm[e] lend thee. The Night-Piece, to Julia. Robert Herrick. BeJo; BoTP; CBLP; CH; CaPo; EBEvV; NAEL-1; NOSC; NoP-4; OAEL-1; OBEV; PoE; PoEL-3; PoRA; SAGP; SCGP; SeCP; TFi

Her eyes were gentle; her voice was for soft singing. An Old Woman Remembers. Sterling Brown. ISC; PoBA

Her [or hir] face her [or hir] tongue [or tong] her [or hir] wit. Sir Arthur Gorges. CBLP; GBL

("To serve to trust to fear.") (LL) LoP

Her face thins almost. Each Day. Sister Maura. CRP

Her face, though smaller than a child's, smaller than a flower. Death from Cancer. Edith Jay Scovell. WPN

Her face was like sad things: was like the lights. A Stranger. Lionel Pigot Johnson. NOBVV

Her Fairness, Wedded to a Star. Edward Joseph Harrington O'Brien. FaBoBe

Her father blended truth and myth. Singing down the Breadfruit. Pauline Stewart. NOxBChV

Her father had a shop for selling leather. Charles Reznikoff. *Fr.* Massacres. APSN

Her father is sick. He dozes most afternoons. Anastasia McLaughlin. Tom Paulin. PBCIP

Her father lov'd me; oft invited me. Shakespeare. EBEV; OxAEP-1; SCV *Fr.* Othello.

Her feet beneath her petticoat. The Bride. Sir John Suckling. *Fr.* A Ballad[e] [upon a Wedding]. BeJo; CaPo; EBEV; EBNV; OxBM; SeCP

Her filthie parbreake all the place defiled has. (LL) Gentle knight was pricking on the plaine, A. Edmund Spenser. EBEV; FHYEP; NAEL-1; OAEL-1; Poetr

Her fingers bore the winecup in. The Two of Them. Hugo von Hofmannsthal, *German.* STV, *tr. by* John Frederick Nims

Her fingers on the girl's bare neck, light. Timarista and Krito. Rosanna Warren. *Fr.* Funerary Portraits. NoAM

Her flames enlighten Nature, never burn thee. (LL) Sonnet: "Earth with thunder torn, with fire blasted, The." Fulke Greville. AAS; NoSic

Her flowers were exclusive blue. Exclusive Blue. Robert Francis. CRP

Her foot sparkled like silver. Rufinus Domesticus, *Greek.* InMo, *tr. by* Sam Hamill

Her for a mistress would I fain enjoy. How to Choose a Mistress. *Unknown.* NOSC

Her for a Mistris would I faine enjoy. A Mistresse. Ausonius, *Latin.* OBCVT, *tr. by Unknown*

Her fork clinks. Widow's Supper. Mary Jane Moffat. IMW

Her future, all in her, presented an avenue of gloom, as if to say Go on, do what you. Seeking Out His face in a Cup. Fanny Howe. FTOS

Her Garden. Meena Alexander. OMIP

Her Garden. Freda Downie. FaBoWP

Her Garden. Elizabeth Jennings. GaP

Her gentle limbs did she undress. Christabel and Geraldine. Coleridge. *Fr.* Christabel. FHYEP; NAEL-2; NOBRP; OAEL-2; Ro

Her God began to pulse through me. Ruth. Diane Q. Lewis. CrSp

Her grandmother called her from the playground. Legacies. Nikki Giovanni. CrSp; NMM-2; UnSA

Her grieving parents cradled here. Epitaph. Sylvia Townsend Warner. MoBrPo

Her guardian sylph prolonged the balmy rest. (LL) Sol through white curtains shot a tim'rous ray. Alexander Pope. ECEV

Her hair dense as darkness. Twin Hills. Vidyapati, *Sanskrit.* EP, *tr. by* Deben Bhattacharya

Her hair is yellow as sulphur, and her gaze. The Cat-Lady. John Barlas. ADE

Her hand a goblet bore for him. The Two. Hugo von Hofmannsthal, *German.* AWP, *tr. by* Ludwig Lewisohn

Her hand on the doorknob. Rod Willmot. HA

Her hands lift and tend King Salmon. The Hands of Mary Joe. Mary TallMountain. LoL

Her health is good. She owns to forty-one. Occupation: Housewife. Phyllis McGinley. WPE *Fr.* I Know a Village.

Her Heart. Bartholomew Griffin. *Fr.* Fidessa, More Chaste than Kind[e].

Her heart is always doing lovely things. John Masefield. SAGP

Her heart is like her garden. My Mother's Garden. Alice E. Allen. BLPA; FaBoBe

Her heart it brak in twa O. (LL) Willie and Lady Margerie [*or* Maisry]. *Unknown.* ESPB; OxBB

Her heart so stricken, Helen. Alcaeus, *Greek.* InMo, *tr. by* Sam Hamill

Her holy anger was. Non-gae. Yongno Pyon, *Korean.* CKP, *tr. by* Jaihiun Kim

Her house is become like a man dishonored. Dirge. Bible, Apocrypha. TrJP *Fr.* First Maccabees.

Her house loomed at the end of a Berkshire lane. Not at Home. Robert Graves. CABP

Her Husband. Ted Hughes. OxBC

Her Husband Asks Her to Buy a Bolt of Silk. Ch'en Tao, *Chinese.* OHMPC, *tr. by* Kenneth Rexroth

Her husband was *hors de combat.* Limerick. C. Vita-Finzi. PeLi

Her I was and her I drank. Gud Ber. *Unknown.* FaBoVe

Her imaginary playmate was a grown-up. Cinderella. Randall Jarrell. LCAP-2; NAAL-2; VCAP

Her iron beats. Domestic Scene. Michael Hartnett. BIrV

Her Justice next appears, which did support. Sixth Pearle, The: Justice. Lady Diana Primrose. KTR *Fr.* A Chain of Pearl.

Her Kind. Anne Sexton. CoAP; HCAP; HeIP-4; LiTM; NALW; PoPoPo; Poetr; SAGP; TAP; TwCP; VCAP; WPOW

Her knees and [*or* &] elbows are only glued together. (LL) When a Man has Married a Wife. William Blake. FaBoEE; OAEL-2; OxBoLi; PeLV

Her—'last Poems'. Emily Dickinson. NALW

Her last words wandered across the ceiling. Death in the Evening. Miroslav Holub, *Czech.* PoSu, *tr. by* George Theiner

Her leggings could burn. Of Three Friendly Warnings This Is the Third. *Unknown, Seneca Indian.* STP, *tr. by* Jerome Rothenberg *and* Richard Johnny John

Her Legs. Robert Herrick. PFE

    ("I fain would kiss my Julia's dainty leg.") CavPo

    ("Which is as white and hair-less as an egge.") (LL) NOSC

Her Letter. Bret Harte. PoLF

Her life is in the marble! yet a fall. Her, a Statue. Thomas Tod Stoddart. OBNC

Her Life Runs Like a Red Silk Flag. Bruce Weigl. AF

Her lily hand her rosy cheek lies under. Shakespeare. EP *Fr.* The Rape of Lucrece.

Her limp lover Maud couldn't pardon. Limerick. Kit Wright. PeLi

Her Lips Are Copper Wire. Jean Toomer. GT; NoAM

Her little boy weeping sought. (LL) The Little Boy Found. William Blake. FHYEP; NoP-4; Ro

Her long paper legs. Leroy Gorman. HA

Her long with ardent look his Eye pursu'd. Milton. UnPo *Fr.* Book IX. FHYEP; NAEL-1; NAWM-1; OAEL-1 *Fr.* Paradise Lost.

Her longer head like a swines snout doth show. Claudian. OBCVT, *tr. by* Thomas Randolph *Fr.* De histrice. Ex Claudiano.

Her Longing. Theodore Roethke. NAAL-2

Her Losses make our Gains ashamed. Emily Dickinson. NALW

Her "love" for whose dear love I rise and fall. (LL) Sonnet 151. Shakespeare. EBEV; HeIP-4; NoSic; OxAEP-1; PoE; PoEL-2

Her love hath end. (LL) The Ocean's Love to Cynthia. Sir Walter Ralegh. NoSic; PBRV; SiPS

Her love in all her honor. (LL) "A"-11 River That Must Turn Full After I Stop Dying. Louis Zukofsky. APSN; ColAP; VGW

Her Majestie resembled to the crowned piller. Ye must read upward. George Puttenham. PBRV

Her Man Described by Her Own[e] Dictamen. Ben Jonson. *Fr.* A Celebration of Charis in Ten Lyric[k] Pieces [*or* Peeces]. BeJo; OxAEP-1; SeCP

Her men's boots wore out. Portrait. Yaroslav Vasilevich Smelyakov, *Russian.* TCRP, *tr. by* Simon Franklin

Her Merriment. W. H. Davies. EnLoPo

Her mind, adorned with virtues manifold. (LL) Sonnet 15: "Ye tradeful merchants that, with weary toil." Edmund Spenser. HeIP-4; NIP-4; OAEL-1; Son

Her morning adornment finished now. Tune: "Casket of Pearls, A." Li Yü, *Chinese.* SuSp, *tr. by* Daniel Bryant

Her mother died when she was young. Kemp Owyne. Alice Cary. ESPB; EnSB

Her Mouth and Mine. W. H. Davies. CBLP

Her Muffe. Richard Lovelace. PBRV

Her name is at my tongue whene'er I speak. Ever Present. Philip Ayres. OxBSP

Her name is Helen. Beth Brant. CPO; GLP

Her Name like the Hours. Gloria Evans Davies. OBWVE

Her name was Ate, mother of debate. The House of Ate. Edmund Spenser. *Fr.* Wood Of Error. AEP

Her nerves awry, importunate. For a Violin, Somewhat Nervously. Vladimir Mayakovsky, *Russian.* InMo, *tr. by* Sam Hamill

Her own clasped hands. (LL) Preface to a Twenty Volume Suicide Note. Imamu Amiri Baraka. BB; CAPP-1; CrDW; MoLi; NAAAL; PoBA; PoM; SAGP; TTY

Her Passing. William Drummond, of Hawthornden. *See* Madrigal: "The Beauty [*or* Beautie], and the life."

Her perfect naked breast. Argentarius, *Greek.* InMo, *tr. by* Sam Hamill

Her planted eye to-day controls. Fate. Ralph Waldo Emerson. APN-1; NoP-4 *Fr.* Quatrains.

Her poets die for the mountains. After Asia. Michael Stephens. CDa

Her Precious Leg. Thomas Hood. NOBVV *Fr.* Miss Kilmansegg and Her Precious Leg.

Her pretty feet. Upon Her Feet. Robert Herrick. BeJo; CBLP; CaPo; OxBSP; PoE

Her purple shoes know the way, and the metal band on her ankle knows it. The Sacrifice. Gertrud Kolmar, *German.* AF, *tr. by* David Kipp

Her refusal to accept a room of solitude. Pieces. Duane Niatum. HATNAP

Her remembered frailty had strengthened his. Private First Class Brooks Morgenstein, U. S. M. C. Bryan Alec Floyd. CDa

Her Reply. Sir Walter Ralegh. *See* The Nimphs [*or* Nymph's] Reply to the Sheepheard [*or* Shepherd].

Her Resurrection has again with Thee. (LL) Upon M. Ben Jo[h]nson: Epigram. Robert Herrick. BeJo; CaPo

Her Reticence. Theodore Roethke. RACG

Her ringlets glistened like the gold of morn. A Picture. Henrietta Cordelia Ray. CBWP-3

Her Rival for Aziza. *Unknown.* AWP *Fr.* The Thousand and One Nights.

Her saffron gown. *Unknown, Greek.* GrAn, *tr. by* Peter Jay

Her sails are spread and colours flying. The Emigrant Ship. Henry Dalton. PBCV

Her scarf *à la* Bardot. Twice Shy. Seamus Heaney. TwCP

Her sense of humor has no gold stop. Telephonist. Janet Frame. WPE

Her Seventeenth Winter. John Leax. CRP

Her shadow races with slanting moonbeams. Written for My Neighbor. Shen Yüeh, *Chinese.* CoBCP, *tr. by* Burton Watson

Her shadow races with slanting moonbeams. Written for My Neighbor. Wang Seng-ta, *Chinese.* CoBCP, *tr. by* Burton Watson

Her shoes could burn. Of Three Friendly Warnings This Is the Second. *Unknown, Seneca Indian.* STP, *tr. by* Jerome Rothenberg *and* Richard Johnny John

Her sight is short, she comes quite near. Jenny Wren. W. H. Davies. MoBrPo

Her silence at dinner. Scott Montgomery. HA

Her silken gown rustles. Wang Chien. SuSp, *tr. by* William H. Nienhauser *Fr.* Palace Poems.

Her sins to her Saviour! (LL) The Bridge of Sighs. Thomas Hood. EBEV; FaPoR; GTBS-P; OBEV; OxAEP-2

Her Sister. "Moira O'Neill." OxBTC

Her skin, saffron toasted in the sun. Proof. Dharmakirti, *Spanish*. EP, *tr. by* Octavio Paz

Her sleeping head with its great gelid mass. Perseus. Robert Earl Hayden. NoAM

Her soft plump shoulders. What Her Girl Friend Said to Him. Ammuvanar, *Tamil*. PLW, *tr. by* A. K. Ramanujan

Her Son. Ebba M. Leaf. PWR

Her songs died on the air. (LL) Song: "She sat and sang alway." Christina Rossetti. GBL; NAEL-2

Her soul is a select district. Paysage Choisi. Francis Sparshott. MoCV

Her spirit hiding among skin and bones. Beside a Deathbed. Vassar Miller. MT

Her stockings are torn but she is beautiful. (LL) Women. Adrienne Rich. NMM-2; TRP

Her Story. Diên Nghị, *Vietnamese*. AVP, *tr. by* Huỳnh Sanh Thông

Her Story. Naomi Long Madgett. PoBA

Her story. E. A. Markham. HCP

Her strong enchantments failing. A. E. Housman. FaBoTw; NOBE; NOBVV; NTP; OAEL-2; PeVV

Her / strong / white / legs. Romp. Dave Etter. WeW-3

Her sweet Weight on my Heart a Night. Emily Dickinson. CPO

Her that I love, I hate! "How's that, do you know?" they wonder. Catullus. *See* Carmina, LXXXV.

Her thin night dress? Toi Derricotte. *See* Touching/Not Touching: My Mother.

Her thin puny little body. Clinic Day. Jo Barnes. BrRo

Her Thought and His. Paul Laurence Dunbar. NAAAL

Her Time. Theodore Roethke. NAAL-2

Her Toys. Théophile Gautier, *French*. FLP, *tr. by* Alistair Elliot

Her Triumph. Ben Jonson. CBLP; CTC; EBEV; NOSC; NoP-4; PoEL-2 *Fr.* A Celebration of Charis in Ten Lyric[k] Pieces [*or* Peeces]. BeJo; OxAEP-1; SeCP

(Triumph of Charis, The.) NOBE; TFi

Her udder shrivels and the milk goes dry. (LL) The Cow in Apple Time. Robert Frost. APo; MoAmPo; OxBSP; PoLF

Her veil blows across my face. Love-Life. Hugo Williams. CBLP

Her veil was artificial flowers and leaves. Marlowe. HoPM *Fr.* Hero and Leander. AAS

Her Voice. Barney Bush. HATNAP

Her Voice Could Not Be Softer. Austin Clarke. NOIV

Her voice did quiver as we parted. On Fanny Godwin. Shelley. OBNC

Her voice forever match to dry wood. Dirge in Jazz Time. Vassar Miller. FFC

Her voice is like some angel picking at the door. Alan Brunton. PeNZ

Her voice roosts in my memory. Route. Philippe Soupault. PFTM

Her whole life is an Epigram smack smooth & neatly pend. William Blake. FaBoEE; InPK-6; OAEL-2; PeLV

Her Word of Reproach. Sarah Morgan Bryan Piatt. NCAP

Her Words. Theodore Roethke. LoP

Her Words from the Corner. Ory Bernstein, *Hebrew*. IP, *tr. by* Warren Bargad *and* Stanley F. Chyet

Her wounds came from the same source as her power. (LL) Power. Adrienne Rich. ColAP; NALW; TAP

Her young employers, having got in late. A Summer Morning. Richard Wilbur. FaBoMo; NBLV

Hera, Hung from the Sky. Carolyn Kizer. NMM-2; WPE

Heracles. Euripides, *Greek*.
   "Against the wittie gifte of shotinge in a bowe." OBCVT, *tr. by* Roger Ascham

Heraclitus. William Johnson Cory, *par. from the Greek of* Callimachus. AWP; EBEvV; EBVV; FP; FaBoEE; FaPoR; InPK-6; NOBE; OBEV; OBNC; OxAEP-2; OxBSP; PoRA; SCGP; UV

Heraclitus at Glasgow Cross. Gerald Mangan. FaBoTC

Heraclitus by the Lake. Lucian Blaga, *Romanian*. CEEP, *tr. by* Peter Jay *and* Virgil Nemoianu

Herakles. Parrhasios, *Greek*. GrAn, *tr. by* Peter Jay

Herakles' rebuttal was too much. Philodemus, *Greek*. PGA, *tr. by* Kenneth Rexroth

Heralds of Christ. Laura S. Copenhaver. AH

Herba Santa. Herman Melville. NCAP

Herbaceous Plodd. Michael Dugan. FuFo

Herbe Féconde (1973). Joseph Miezan Bognini.
   "Suddenly an old man on the threshold of the age." PBMAP
   "We are men of the new world a tree prompts us to harmony." PBMAP

Herbert Street Revisited. John Montague. CIP-2; IIP; PBCIP; PNI

Herbert White. Frank Bidart. AmPA

Herbert's a hard and horrid man. One for the Anthologies. Gavin Ewart. OBCoV

Herbertson telephoned. For the Record. Roy McFadden. PNI

Hercules Furens. Seneca, *Latin*.
   "Let oken club now strike, and poast of might." OBVE, *tr. by* Jasper Heywood

Hercules Oetaeus. Seneca, *Latin*.
   "Learne Lordings, learne to feare and dread th'unweildy." OBCVT, *tr. by* John Studley
   "Let other mount aloft, let other sore." OBVE, *tr. by* John Studley

Herd, The. Peter Fallon. PBCIP

Herd-Boy, The. Lu Yu, *Chinese*. ChiP, *tr. by* Arthur Waley

Herdboy returns, none too early, The. Yang Shih-ch'i. CoBLCP, *tr. by* Jonathan Chaves *Fr.* A Painting of Water Buffaloes.

Herder who hailed from Terre Haute, A. Limerick. *Unknown*. PeLi

Herdmen, The. William Byrd. *See* The Quiet Life.

Herds, The. W. S. Merwin. NYBP

Herdsman's Song. *Unknown, Chinese*. ChiP, *tr. by* Arthur Waley

Herdsmen, The. Theocritus. AWP, *tr. by* Charles Stuart Calverley *Fr.* Idylls.
   "O Polyphemus, while your flocks you keep." OBCVT, *tr. by* Francis Fawkes

Here. Marvin Bell. AmPA

Here. Robert Creeley. NOBA

Here. Jane Kenyon. LoL

Here. Philip Larkin. CMoP; PoE

Here. Bob Orr. PeNZ

Here. Octavio Paz, *Spanish*. STV, *tr. by* John Frederick Nims

Here. Ronald Stuart Thomas. GTBS-P; RB

Here a false face won't help you. (LL) Racoon. Kenneth Rexroth. KaS; NNaP

Here a little child I stand. Grace for a Child. Robert Herrick. AWP; BeJo; BoTP; CTV; FaBoCh; InPS-3; NAEL-1; NOSC; NTP; OBEV; OxAEP-1; OxBChV; PFE; PoE; SCGP; TFi

Here a pretty Baby lies. Upon a child. Robert Herrick. OBEV; PBRV

Here, a sheer hulk, lies poor Tom Bowling. Poor Tom. Charles Dibdin. NOEC; OxAEP-1; OxBoLi

Here a solemn[e] fast keep[e]. An Epitaph upon a Virgin. Robert Herrick. CaPo; FaBoEE; OxBoLi; PoEL-3

Here, above, / cracks in the buildings are filled with battered moonlight. The Man-Moth. Elizabeth Bishop. CBNP; LiTM; MoAmPo; MoP; NALW; NOBA; NoAM; Poetr

Here all seeking is over. *Hawaiian Oral Tradition, Hawaiian*. ITG, *tr. by* E. S. Craighill Handy, Mary Kawena Pukui *and* Jane Hirshfield

Here, all star-paven at our Lady's well. A Heretic's Pilgrimage. Eva Gore-Booth. TIRV

Here all the passions, for their greater sway. Thomas Parnell. EPCY *Fr.* The Essay on the Different Styles of Poetry.

Here am I. Please to Remember. Walter De la Mare. NTP

Here am I, little [J]jumping Joan. Little Jumping Joan. Mother Goose. LB; NTCP; OxNR; ReMoGo

Here am I now cast down. Ex Nihilo. David Gascoyne. GTBS-P *Fr.* Miserere.

Here, Amanda, gently bending. The Garden Window. Aaron Hill. OBGa

Here among long-discarded cassocks. Diary of a Church Mouse. John Betjeman. OxBTC

Here among them the americans this baffling. [American Journal]. Robert Earl Hayden. ISC

Here and hereafter, touch a Paradise. (LL) To Ned. Herman Melville. APN-2; NAAL-1; NAAL-3; NOBA; PAR; PoEL-5

Here and in hell. (LL) The Nameless One. James Clarence Mangan. BIrV; IIP; NOIV; OBEV

Here and Now. Philip Levine. PoA

Here and now is clear so we. 20-200 on 737. Heather McHugh. NIP-4

Here and There. Anne Lauterbach. PmAP

Here are / blue teapot. Components. Roger McDonald. CBAP

Here are cakes for thy body. The Other World. *Unknown, Egyptian*. OxBSn, *tr. by* Robert Silliman Hillyer; AWP *Fr.* Book of the Dead.

Here are fine gifts, children. Sappho, *Greek*. BoWoP, *tr. by* Willis Barnstone

Here are grapes ready to turn to wine. Crinagoras, *Greek*. GrAn, *tr. by* Alistair Elliot

Here are my lady's knives and forks. *Unknown*. LB

Here are no signs of festival. African Christmas. John Press. OBCP

Here are sweet peas, on tiptoe for a flight. Sweet Peas. Keats. FHYEP *Fr.* I stood tip-toe upon a little hill.

Here are the brains here the hearts. One o'Clock. Philippe Soupault, *French*. AF, *tr. by* Schmidt, Paulette

Here are the lady's knives and forks. *Unknown*. OxNR

Here are the Schubert *Lieder*. Now begin. For M.S. Singing *Fruhlingsglaube* in 1945. Frances Darwin Cornford. BrRo

Here are those who are challenged by. The Jewish Singles Event. Stewart Florsheim. UnSA

Here are two half-grown black cats perched on a / lump. Walking beside the Kamogawa, Remembering Nansen and Fudo and Gary's Poem. Philip Whalen. BB

Here are two pictures from my father's head. Wounds. Michael Longley. FaBoPV; PBCIP; PNI

Here are weeds about his mouth. Wide Empty Landscape with a Death in the Foreground. N. Scott Momaday. CDW

"Here are your magic glasses. Ballad of the Magic Glasses. Maura Stanton. FFC

Here, as in a painting, yellow noon burns [or noon burns yellow]. Natalya Gorbanevskaya, *Russian*. BoWoP; PBWP, *tr. by* Daniel Weissbort

Here at the center of the turning year. New Year. Stephen Spender. AWP

Here at the seashore they use the clouds over and over. Rhode Island. William Meredith. NoP-4

Here at the Super Duper, in a glass tank. Lobsters. Howard Nemerov. PBMP; PFE

Here at the Vespasian-Carlton, it's just one. Boom! Howard Nemerov. LiTM; NBLV; NIP-4

Here at the wayside station, as many a morning. The Wayside Station. Edwin Muir. FaBoTw

Here at Woodlands, Moriah. Salmon Courage. Marlene Philip. PBCV

Here be dragons, and bitter. Bitter Wood. Martin Carter. HCP

Here, because of the shock, the sudden. Desmond O'Grady. PBCIP *Fr.* Hellas.

Here before the sunrise blue and in this solitude. Janine Pommy-Vega. CLPP

Here beside dwelleth. The Juggler and the baron's daughter. *Unknown.* NoSic

Here beside the threshing floor, O hardworking ant. Antipater of Sidon. HePo, *tr. by* Barbara Hughes Fowler *Fr.* Epigrams.

Here blooms the legend fed by [or with] Time and Chance. Rouen, Place de la Pucelle. Maria White Lowell. APN-2

Here bounds the gaudy, gilded chair. The Birth-Day. Mary Robinson. ECWP; WoRP

Here by a snowbound river. To Robert Nichols. Robert Graves. PeFWW

Here by the ample river's argent sweep. Two Backgrounds. Edith Wharton. APN-2

Here by the grey north sea. A Northern Vigil. Bliss Carman. OBEV

Here by the moorway you returned. Your Last Drive. Thomas Hardy. OBNC

Here, by the seashore, there lies / Archilochus. Gaetulicus, *Greek*. GrAn, *tr. by* Edward Lucie-Smith

Here, by this brook, we parted; I to the East. The Brook; An Idyl. Tennyson. OxAEP-2

Here by this crumbling wall. The Butterfly Garden. Alfred Noyes. OBGa

Here, Caelia [or Celia], for thy sake I part. To the Mutable Fair. Edmund Waller. BeJo; SeCP

Here, Charmian, take my bracelets. Cleopatra. William Wetmore Story. APN-1

Here circling trees, which form a shade. The Leasowes: Or, A Poetical Description of the Late Mr. Shenstone's Rural Retirement. Joseph Giles. OBGa *Fr.* The Leasowes: Or, A Poetical Description of the Late Mr. Shenstone's Rural Retirement.

Here Cleita sleeps. You ask her life and race? The Monument of Cleita. Edward Cracroft Lefroy. AWP *Fr.* Echoes from Theocritus.

Here come I to my own again. The Prodigal Son. Rudyard Kipling. NoAM *Fr.* Kim.

Here come real stars to fill the upper skies. Fireflies in the Garden. Robert Frost. OxBSP; SAmP

Here come the capybaras on their bikes. Wild Ones[, The]. James Fenton. PeLV *Fr.* Wild Life Studies.

Here come the line-gang pioneering by. The Line-Gang. Robert Frost. OxBSP

Here comes a cropper. That's what I said. (LL) American Lights, Seen from Off Abroad. John Berryman. LCAP-2; OBAL; OBCoV

Here Comes a Lusty Wooer. *Unknown.* CH; NTP; OxNR

Here comes / Babel, Isaak. Elderblossom. Johannes Bobrowski, *German*. AF, *tr. by* Matthew Mead

Here comes Kate Summers who, for gold. The Bird of Paradise. W. H. Davies. NSI

Here comes my lady with her little baby. *Unknown.* OxNR

Here comes Old Man Adkins with a battle-ax. Coal Loadin' Blues. *Unknown.* AmFP

Here comes one more looking pale. Man from the Death Institute. Novica Tadic, *Serbian*. VCWP, *tr. by* Charles Simic

Here comes the elephant. The Elephant. Herbert Asquith. BoTP; CTAV

Here comes the question. The Prerogative of Lieder. Ray DiPalma. FTOS

Here comes the shadow not looking where it is going. Sire. W. S. Merwin. CoAP; VGW

—Here comes the smoking Bouillabaisse! (LL) The Ballad of Bouillabaisse. William Makepeace Thackeray. APAD; OBEV; OxAEP-2

Here continueth to rot. Epitaph on Colonel Francis Chartres. John Arbuthnot. FaBoEE; OBSV

Here costive many minutes did I strain. Privy-Love for My Landlady. George Farewell. NOEC; OBCoV

Here Cupid tempers his unerring darts. Psyche; or The Legend of Love. Mary Tighe. Ro *Fr.* Psyche, with Other Poems, 3rd edition.

Here cursing swearing Burton lies. Robert Burns. FaBoEE

Here dead lie we because we did not choose. A. E. Housman. FaBoEE; NOBVV; NoP-4; OAEL-2; PoFWW; PoLF; SAGP; Spl

Here deare Iöas lies. Iöas' Epitaph. William Drummond, of Hawthornden. PoEL-2

Here, decayed, an old. Harlech Castle. John Corben. Spl

Here Delia's buried at fourscore. Hildebrand Jacob. FaBoEE

Here died St. Amand, shepherd of his sheep. Epitaph for St. Amand, Bishop of Utrecht. Alcuin, *Latin*. MLL, *tr. by* Helen Waddell

Here dock and tare. In the Grave No Flower. Edna St. Vincent Millay. NAAL-2

Here doth Dionysia lie. Epitaph of Dionysia. *Unknown.* OBEV

Here, dying for the world, the world's life hung. On the Cross. Alcuin, *Latin*. MLL, *tr. by* Helen Waddell

Here earth and sky are reduced to an ultimate simplicity. Nullarbor. William Hart-Smith. BMAP

Here ended Hall, and our last light, that long. Epic, The [Morte d'Arthur]. Tennyson. NAEL-2 *Fr.* Morte d'Arthur. EnVR

Here erect I guard the land / and Phrikon's crops and hut. Priapus the Scarecrow. Antistius Vetus, *Greek*. GrAn, *tr. by* Alistair Elliot

Here, ever since you went abroad. What News. Walter Savage Landor. DoLoP

Here everything is white and clean. In the Hospital. George Garrett. PFE

Here, five feet deep, lies on his back. On the Astrologer and Almanac Maker, John Partridge. Jonathan Swift. FaBoEE

Here followeth the unfashionable fashion, or the too too homely Worshipping of God. John Taylor.
   "Gods *Houses,* almost like *Troyes Ilion,.*" PBRV

Here Follows Some Verses upon the Burning of Our House [July 10th, 1666. Copied Out of a Loose Paper]. Anne Bradstreet. AiP; BoWoP; CoIAP; NAAL-1; NAAL-3; NALW; NoP-4; NOSC; OxBA; Poetr; SCAP; WPE

Here for a little we pause. Benicasim. Sylvia Townsend Warner. OBWP

Here for a thousand years processional. Eleusis. Trumbull Stickney. *Fr.* Sonnets from Greece. APN-1

Here. Forget. Poem. Charles Bernstein. FTOS

Here free from riot's hated noise. Inscription. William Cowper. OBGa

Here from his prominent but thankfully. Old Bachelor Brother. Brad Leithauser. NoP-4; RA

Here, from laborious art, proud towns, ye rose! On Catania and Syracuse Swallowed Up by an Earthquake, from the Italian of Filicaja. Anna Seward. Son

Here from the start, from our first of days, look. The Tally Stick. Jarold Ramsey. NIP-4

Here goes a poor old chimney sweeper. The Chimney Sweeper. *Unknown.* AmFP

Here goes my lord. *Unknown.* ReMoGo

Here has my salient faith annealed me. Key West. Hart Crane. CMoP

Here have I seen the king, when great affairs. Sir John Denham. PoE *Fr.* Cooper's Hill. BeJo; CABP; PBRV; SeCP

Here, here are our enjoyments done. Lucasia, Rosania and Orinda Parting at a Fountain, July 1663. Katherine Philips. KTR; PEW

Here, here I live with what my board. His Content in the Country. Robert Herrick. CaPo; CavPo

Here, here, oh here Eurydice [or Euridice]. Orpheus to Beasts. Richard Lovelace. CaPo

Here Hermes, says Jove who with nectar was mellow. Jupiter and Mercury. David Garrick. ECEV

Here he's at it, spading toward a. The Ditchdigger. Igor Moiseievich Irtenev, *Russian*. TCRP, *tr. by* John High

Here hills and vales, the woodland and the plain. Alexander Pope. ECEV *Fr.* Windsor-Forest [or Windsor Forest].

Here I Am. Li-Young Lee. IFJA

Here I am again, doubled over, I'm here, pretending I know what I'm doing. Prelude. Lydia Tomkiw. *Fr.* New York Love Song (Part 1—Lower East Side). WWSi

Here I am again with my sickle, spade, hoe. Weeding. Michael Hamburger. OBGa

Here I am, an industry without chimneys. The Perfection of Dentistry. Marvin Bell. AmPA; CoAP

Here I am, an old man in a dry month. Gerontion. T. S. Eliot. AmPP; CMoP; ColAP; EBEV; GTBS-P; HAP; ImPo; InPS-3; LiTM; MoP; NAAL-2; NOBA; NoAM; OAEL-2; OxAEP-2; OxBA; TAP; TFi

Here I am at 8:08 p.m. indefinable ample rhythmic frame. Red Shift. Ted Berrigan. PT

Here I am, full-grown, flourishing. Abraham Sutskever, Yiddish. TrJP, tr. by Joseph Leftwich

Here I am in Europe. The Promenade. U Tam'si Tchicaya, French. NegPo, tr. by Ellen Conroy Kennedy

Here I am launching my Second Book of Epigrams—. Lucilius, Greek. GrAn, tr. by Peter Porter

Here I am, seated, with all my words. Silence Concerning an Ancient Stone. Rosario Castellanos, Spanish. PBWP, tr. by George D. Schade

Here I am six years old in Sub B, sitting on the big rock. Imagination. Dina Uahupirapi. LoHo

Here I am, sprouted to my full height. Abraham Sutskever, Yiddish. TrJP, tr. by Joseph Leftwich

Here I am, troubling the dream coast. In California. Louis Simpson. WeT

Here I am with my rabbits. Unknown. OxNR

Here I am writing you on old newspaper against a tide of print. Cow Perserverance, The. Frederick D'Aguiar. HCP

Here I ame and fourthe I mouste. Unknown. MiEL

Here I come creeping, creeping everywhere. The Song of the Grass. Leigh Hunt. BoTP

Here I go again. Starting from San Francisco. Lawrence Ferlinghetti. CAPP-1; GM

Here I lie at the chancel door. On Elizabeth Ireland. Unknown. FaBoEE

Here I lie for the last time. Epitaph on an Irish Priest. Unknown. FaBoEE

Here i lie in chinatown. My Ship Does Not Need a Helmsman. Alan Chong Lau. OpBo

Here I ligg, Sydney Slugabed Godless Smith. Slugabed. Sydney Goodsir Smith. FaBoTC; OxBS Fr. Under the Eildon Tree.

Here I myself [or my selfe] might likewise die. Poetry Perpetuates the Poet. Robert Herrick. BeJo; FaBoEE

Here / I sing in green branch. At Pakiri Beach. David Mitchell. PeNZ

Here I sit. Bad Morning. Langston Hughes. OBAL

Here I slept with my face turned. Prospect Beach. Lou Lipsitz. VGW

Here I stand / Replacing another, who has been murdered. An End or a Beginning. Bei Dao, Chinese. AF, tr. by Bonnie S. McDougall

Here I was and here I drank. Unknown. MiEL

Here I— / What does. Epitaph. Paulus Silentiarius, Greek. GrAn, tr. by Andrew Miller

Here, if the road shall bring thee back. New Year's Eve. Boethius, Latin. MLL, tr. by Helen Waddell Fr. Consolation of Philosophy, The ("De Consolacione Philosophie").

Here in a distant place I hold my tongue. Egan O Rahilly. Unknown, Irish. EBEV; OBMV, tr. by James Stephens

Here in his lamp-lit parable, he'll scan. The Garden. Vita Sackville-West. OBGa

Here, in huge cauldrons, the rough mass they stow. The Iron Industry in Birmingham. Richard Jago. NOEC Fr. Edge-Hill; or, The Rural Prospect Delineated and Moralised.

Here in Kansas is a school. Haskell. Witter Bynner. NoP-4

Here in Katmandu. Donald Justice. CoAmPo; CoAP; HeIP-4; WeT

Here, in late spring, the summer is on us already. Hot Afternoons Have Been in West 15th Street. Paul Blackburn. VGW

Here in my bosom, and at home. (LL) To the World [A Farewell for a Gentlewoman, Virtuous and Noble]. Ben Jonson. BeJo; SeCP

Here in my curving hands I cup. This Quiet Dust. John Hall Wheelock. MoAmPo

Here in my hands a small cold-chisel. The Little Chisel. N. P. van Wyk Louw, Afrikaans. PeSA, tr. by Jack Cope and Uys Krige

Here in my head, the home that is left for you. Burning the Letters. Randall Jarrell. MoAmPo

Here in my heart I am Helen. Song of One of the Girls. Dorothy Parker. NALW

Here in Nantucket does the tiny soul. Phenomenal Survivals of Death in Nantucket. Louise Glück. AmPA

Here in Netanya. Meir Wieseltier, Hebrew. IP, tr. by Warren Bargad and Stanley F. Chyet

Here in the cool and book-infested den. Ulysses' Library. David Daiches. PoA

Here in the country's heart. The Country Faith. Norman Gale. BoTP; OBEV

Here in the dark, O heart. Second Best. Rupert Brooke. MoBrPo

Here, in the darkness, where this plaster saint. Madeleine in Church. Charlotte Mew. VWP

Here in the good old U. S. A. In the Good Old U. S. A. José Angel Villalongo Sr. UnSA

Here in the green scooped valley I walk to and fro. The Green Valley. Sylvia Townsend Warner. MoBrPo

Here in the half-darkness of a basement. Chinese Laundry. Yury Kazarnovsky, Russian. TCRP, tr. by Bradley Jordan

Here, in the hollow caverns of the rocks. The Wily Fox. Edward Davies, Welsh. OBWVE, tr. by Joseph P. Clancy

Here in the long white ward I stand. The Nurse. G. M. Mitchell. NSI

Here in the marshland, past the battered bridge. Harrow and Flanders. Robert Offley Ashburton Crewe-Milnes, Marquess of Crewe. NSI

Here in the middle of London. South African Exhibition, 1907. Kingsley Fairbridge. PeSAV

Here, in the most Unchristian basement. The Men's Room in the College Chapel. W. D. Snodgrass. MoAmPo

Here in the mountain village. Evening in the Village. Lu Yu, Chinese. OHPC, tr. by Kenneth Rexroth

Here in the newspaper—the wreck of the East Bound. It's Here In The. Russell Atkins. PoBA

Here in the North I chase an old despair. Trumbull Stickney. APN-2

Here in the quiet of my room. Prayer of an Unemployed Man. W. C. Ackerly. PoToHe

Here, in the room of my life. The Room of My Life. Anne Sexton. VCAP

Here, in the sand, where someone laid him down. Cruciform. Winifred Welles. NYBP

Here in the scuffled dust. W. D. Snodgrass. Fr. Heart's Needle. CAPP-1

Here in the self is all that men can know. Sonnet. John Masefield. AWP Fr. Lollingdon Downs.

Here in the slack of night. Camphor Laurel. Judith Wright. BMAP

Here in the uplands. Scotland. Sir Alexander Gray. FaBoTC; OxBS

Here, in the withered arbor, like the arrested wind. Statue and Birds. Louise Bogan. MoAmPo

Here in this bleak city of Rochester. Sestina d'Inverno. Anthony Hecht. NoAM

Here in this carload. Written in Pencil in the Sealed Railway-Car. Dan Pagis, Hebrew. AF, tr. by Stephen Mitchell

Here in this foreground of sunny Italian fields. Two Figures on Canvas. Gerald William Barrax. MT

Here in this great house in the barrack square. The Hambone and the Heart. Dame Edith Sitwell. OBMV

Here in this homely cabinet. Matthew Stevenson. NOSC Fr. An Elegy upon Old Freeman.

Here in this house, among photographs. From Room to Room. Jane Kenyon. LoL

Here in this leafy place. Before Sedan. Austin Dobson. PeVV

Here, in this little Bay. Magna Est Veritas. Coventry Patmore. GTBS-P; HAP; NOBE; NOBVV; OBEV; OBNC; OxBSP Fr. The Unknown Eros.

Here in this rough trench lies. Poseidippus, Greek. GrAn, tr. by Edward Lucie-Smith

Here in this sequestered close. A Garden Song. Austin Dobson. OBEV; OBGa; OBNC

Here in this simmering marsh. (LL) River Roses. D. H. Lawrence. CMoP; GBL; OAEL-2

Here in this transport. Scrawled in Pencil in a Sealed Car. Dan Pagis, Hebrew. PoSu, tr. by Robert Friend

Here in this world / I won't live. Lady Izumi, Japanese. BoWoP, tr. by Willis Barnstone

Here in West Philadelphia. A Black Man's Sonata. Michael S. Weaver. UnSA

Here is. Jean-Joseph Rabéarivelo, French. NegPo, tr. by Ellen Conroy Kennedy

("And perhaps some tasteless grains of salt.") (LL) PBMAP

("She.") PBMAP

Here is a beetle as black as my hat. E. S. Goodwill. BXAP

Here is a child who is leaning over a paper. The Mirror. John N. Morris. PoA

Here is a coast; here is a harbor. Arrival at Santos. Elizabeth Bishop. FaBoWP; OxBC

Here is a cup left empty in their. Broken Home. William Stafford. NNaP

Here is a ditch of hopelessly dead water. Dead Water. Wen Yi-tuo, Chinese. PFTM, tr. by Arthur Sze

Here is a family so little famous. Photograph in a Stockholm Newspaper for March 13, 1910. Don Coles. NOBC

Here is a famous world. There Is No Place to Hide. Gwendolyn MacEwen. Fr. The T. E. Lawrence Poems. NOBC

Here is a heart-shaped leaf. Maple Leaf. "Shu Ting," Chinese. VCWP, tr. by Carolyn Kizer

Here is a house with a pointed door. A Little Finger Game. E. J. Falconer. BoTP

Here is a piece of required reading. Terminus. Nicholas Christopher. BAP-95

Here is a place that is no place. The Patient: Rockland County Sanitarium. Calvin C. Hernton. PoBA

Here is a poem for the two of us to play. The Newly Pressed Suit. Roger McGough. MoP

Here is a rarity. Know Thyself. Kenneth Burke. OBAL

Here Is a Song. John Peck. AH

Here is a symbol in which. Rock and Hawk. Robinson Jeffers. ColAP; NOBA; NoAM; OxBA; PaTW; Poetr

Here Is a Toast That I Want to Drink. Walter Lathrop. PoLF

Here is another poem in a picture. Daryl Hine. GS; NoAM

Here is Brooklyn / here are the Anglos. Day of the Dead. Patricia Jones. WWSi

Here is fresh matter, poet. Church and State. W. B. Yeats. CMoP

Here is Grandpa, who did not want America. 1920 Photo. Patricia Dobler. CMAP

Here is Joe Blow the poet. On Being Asked for a Peace Poem. Howard Nemerov. OxBC

Here is Klito's little shack. Leonidas, Greek. GrAn; NNaP; PGA, tr. by Kenneth Rexroth

Here is much burning anger, mighty hate. Shimon Halkin, Hebrew. MHP, tr. by Ruth Finer Mintz

Here is my uncle, a rice ball in his mouth. A Nisei Picnic: From an Album. David Mura. LoL

Here is no peace, although the air has fainted. Innocent Landscape. Elinor Wylie. OxBA

Here is ouzo (she said) to try you. Ouzo Unclouded. Robert Graves. GrIP

Here is the ancient floor. The Self-Unseeing. Thomas Hardy. EBEV; HAP; MoBrPo; NOBE; NOBVV; OBNC; OxAEP-2; RB; WeW-3

Here is the black sheep, master. The Black Sheep Gojko Djogo, Serbo-Croatian. AF, tr. by Michael March and Dušan Puvaić

Here is the church, and here is the steeple. Unknown. OxNR

Here is the fern's frond, unfurling a gesture. Fern. Ted Hughes. NYBP

Here is the foreign cliff and the fabled sea. On a Picture by Michele Da Verona, of Arion as a Boy Riding upon a Dolphin. Anne Ridler. PoA

Here is the haven: pain touched with soft magic. Hospital. Wilfred John Funk. PoToHe

Here is the house, in readiness for you. To the New Owner. Lucile Hargrove Reynolds. PoToHe

Here is the long-bided hour: the labor of years is accomplished. Work. Aleksandr Sergeyevich Pushkin, Russian. AWP, tr. by Babette Deutsch and Avrahm Yarmolinsky

Here is the mother all boobed and bodicey. Victorian Family Photograph. Kit Wright. OBCoV

Here is the News from space. Michael Rosen. OBSP; SpW

Here is the phial; here I turn the key. A Minor Poet. Amy Levy. VWP

Here is the place, my lord; good my lord, enter. Shakespeare. OxAEP-1 Fr. King Lear.

Here is the place; right over the hill. Telling the Bees. John Greenleaf Whittier. APN-1; AWP; ColAP; GEA; NOBA; NoP-4; PAR; TAP

Here is the river Eurotas. Antiphilus, Greek. InMo, tr. by Sam Hamill

Here is the shadow of its joy. (LL) Monet's "Waterlilies." Robert Earl Hayden. GT; Poetr

Here is the shadow of truth, for only the shadow is true. A Way to Love God. Robert Penn Warren. NAAL-2

Here is the soundless cypress on the lawn. The Nightingale near the House. Harold Monro. MoBrPo

Here is the stream again under the rainbow. U Tam'si Tchicaya. PBA, tr. by E. S. Yntema Fr. Debout.

Here is the tale of Carrousel. The Ballad of a Barber. Aubrey Beardsley. ADE; NOBVV

Here is the train! The Holiday Train. Irene Thompson. BoTP

Here is the world's bitter end. Wind. Tribal Homeland. Evangeline Paterson. NBrP

Here is the yoke, with arrow and share near by. The Laborer. José-Maria de Heredia, French. AWP, tr. by Wilfrid Thorley

Here is this horse from a bad family, hating his burden and snaffle, not patient. Mule. Rodney Jones. NAmP90

Here it comes again, imagination of myself. International Date Line, Monday/Monday 27:XI:67. Philip Whalen. BB

Here it is, near the house. Right in the Trail. Gary Snyder. PmAP

Here it is night! I stay at the Summit Temple. The Summit Temple. Li Po, Chinese. TAL, tr. by Robert Payne

Here it is spring again. The Late Singer. William Carlos Williams. SAmP

Here it is three years since my grandmother died. The Grandmother. Gérard de Nerval, French. IMW, tr. by Barbara Howes

Here its like that. Blue Tanganyika. Lebert Bethune. PoBA

Here it's rose-time again, chick-peas in season. Philodemus, Greek. GrAn, tr. by William Moebius

Here Jack and Tom are paired with Moll and Meg. George Meredith. EnVR; PoEL-5 Fr. Modern Love.

Here Johnson lies—a sage by all allow'd. Epitaph on Dr. Johnson. William Cowper. EPCY

Here Klito spent eighty years. (LL) Here is Klito's little shack. Leonidas, Greek. GrAn; NNaP; PGA, tr. by Kenneth Rexroth

Here lapped in hallowed slumber Saon lies. Saon of Acanthus. Callimachus, Greek. AWP, tr. by John Addington Symonds

Here lay a fair fat land. Culbin Sands. Andrew Young. GTBS-P; OxBS; OxBTC

Here lay dark Pittsburgh, from whose site there broke. James Kirke Paulding. APN-1 Fr. The Backwoodsman.

Here let me rest me feet! Reverie of a Mum. Nancy Keesing. CBAP; NOBAu

Here let me sit, in this empty, cool, terraced hall. Ernest Francisco Fenollosa. APN-2 Fr. Ode on Reincarnation.

Here let my Lord hang up his conquering lance. The Celestial City. Giles, the Younger Fletcher. ChIV-2, stanzas 30–44; NOSC Fr. Christ's Victory and Triumph.

Here let the Muse perform the painter's art. Unknown. ECWP Fr. Clio's Picture.

Here let us pause:—the opening prospect view. John Pierpont. APN-1 Fr. Airs of Palestine.

Here lie a grasshopper and a / Cicada. Argentarius, Greek. GrAn, tr. by Fleur Adcock

Here lie Ciardi's pearly bones. Elegy Just in Case. John Ciardi. TwCP

Here lie I, Martin Elginbrodde. George Macdonald. FaBoEE

Here lie I, once a witty fair. An Epitaph. Samuel Wesley. NOEC

Here lie I, Timon. Timon's Epitaph. Shakespeare. AWP Fr. Timon of Athens.

Here lie John Hughes and Sarah Drew. Epitaph. Lady Mary Wortley Montagu. ECWP

Here lie my old bones: my vexation now ends. Messenger Mounsey. FaBoEE

Here lie the banes o' Tammy Messer. Tammy Messer. Unknown. FaBoEE

Here lie the bones of Elizabeth Charlotte. On an Aberdeen Favourite. Unknown. FaBoEE

Here lie two poor lovers, who had the mishap. Epitaph on the Stanton-Harcourt Lovers. Alexander Pope. FaBoEE Fr. Three Epitaphs on John Hewet and Sarah Drew. NIP-4

Here lie Willie Michie's [or M—hie's] banes. Epitaph on a Schoolmaster. Robert Burns. FaBoEE

Here lies a bard, Hipponax--honored name! The Grave of Hipponax. Edward Cracroft Lefroy. AWP Fr. Echoes from Theocritus.

Here lies a bard, let epitaphs be true. My Epitaph. H. J. Daniel. FaBoEE

Here lies a Bond under this tomb. On Bond the Usurer. Unknown. NOSC

Here lies a clerk who half his life had spent. The Volunteer. Herbert Asquith. OBWP; OxBTC

Here lies a digger, all his chips departed. Epitaph on a Diamond Digger. Albert Brodrick. PeSAV

Here lies a Doctor of Divinity. Richard Porson. FaBoEE

Here lies a dog: may every dog that dies. Epitaph on the Favourite Dog of a Politician. Hilaire Belloc. OBSV

Here lies a great sleeper, as everybody knows. Epitaph on a Great Sleeper. Sir Aston Cokayne. FaBoEE

Here lies a lady of beauty and high degree. John Crowe Ransom. AWP; CMoP; HAP; LiTM; MeMAP; MoAmPo; MoP; NAAL-2; NoAM; PoRA; RB; TAP; VGW Fr. Sixteen Poems in Eight Pairings.

Here lies a little bird. On a Little Bird. Martin Donisthorpe Armstrong. CH

Here lies a man. And here, a girl. They live. Memorial. Robert Pinsky. HCAP

Here lies a man, and still no man. Epitaph I. Unknown. Fr. Duel with Verses over a Great Man. TrJP

Here lies a man who was killed by lightning. At Great Torrington, Devon. Unknown. FaBoEE

Here lies a most beautiful lady. An Epitaph. Walter De la Mare. ImPo; LiTM; MoBrPo; OBEV; RB

Here lies a peer. Epitaph on the Duke of Grafton. Sir Fleetwood Shepherd. FaBoEE

Here lies a piece of Christ; a star in dust. An Epitaph for a Godly Man's Tomb. Robert Wild. FaBoEE

Here lies a poet—where's the great surprise! "Z. Z." FaBoEE

Here lies a poet who would not write. Voice from the Tomb (1). Stevie Smith. PoA

Here lies a poor woman who always was tired. Epitaph. Unknown. FaBoEE; OBCoV

Here Lies a Prisoner. Charlotte Mew. MoBrPo

Here lies a shoe-maker whose knife and hammer. At His Father's Grave. John Ormond. FaBoTw; OBWVE

Here lies a simple Jew. Epitaph. "Sholom Aleichem," *Yiddish.* TrJP, *tr. by* Joseph Leftwich

Here lies a true maid, deformed and old. My Own Epitaph. Mary Chandler. ECWP

Here lies Anacreon. Simonides, *Greek.* PGA, *tr. by* Kenneth Rexroth

Here lies, and none to mourn him but the sea. Edna St. Vincent Millay. HeIP-4 *Fr.* Epitaph for the Race of Man.

Here lies Arkheanassa of Kolophon. Arkheanassa. Asclepiades, *Greek.* GrAn, *tr. by* Peter Jay

Here lies Bogus, beatnik bard. Epitaph for a Beatnik Poet. Guy Owen. CRP

Here lies David Garrick, describe me who can. David Garrick. Oliver Goldsmith. NOEC *Fr.* Retaliation. OxBoLi

Here lies Dr. Keene, the good Bishop of Chester. Epitaph on Dr. Keene. Thomas Gray. FaBoEE

Here lies Fred. On Prince Frederick. *Unknown.* ACTP; FaBoEE; NOBL; NTP; OxBoLi

Here lies free from blood and slaughter. In Memory of Captain Underwood Who Was Drowned. *Unknown.* FaBoEE

Here lies Hilaire Belloc, who. Hilaire Belloc. Humbert Wolfe. FaBoEE

Here lies I, no wonder I'm dead. *Unknown.* FaBoEE

Here lies in death, who living always lied. On Rÿneveld, an Unpopular Dutch Judge. *Unknown.* FaBoEE

Here lies intombed / Beneath these bricks. Epitaph on a Willing Girl. Thomas Rowlandson. FaBoEE

Here lies John Bun. John Bun. *Unknown.* NBLV

Here lies John Dumbelow. Of One That Died of the Wind-Colic. *Unknown.* CBNP

Here lies John Hughes and Sarah Drew. Epitaph. Lady Mary Wortley Montagu. CABP; FaBoEE

Here lies John Knott. Epitaph on John Knott. *Unknown.* FaBoEE

Here lies John Trot, the Friend of all mankind. Another [Epitaph]. William Blake. FaBoEE

Here lies Jonson [*or* lyes Johnson] with the rest. Upon Ben Jo[h]nson. Robert Herrick. BeJo; CaPo; FaBoEE; NoP-4

Here lies Judge A——, he's done with legal tort. Epitaph for a Judge. Benedict Jeitteles, *Hebrew.* TrJP, *tr. by* Joseph Chotzner

Here lies Landor. Walter Savage Landor. FaBoEE

Here lies Lord Coningsby—be civil. Lord Coningsby's Epitaph. Alexander Pope. FaBoEE

Here lies magnanimous Humility. Upon the Tomb of the Most Reverend Mr. John Cotton. Benjamin Woodbridge. SCAP

Here lies Mistress Keene the Bishop of Chester. Epitaph on Dr. Keene's Wife. Thomas Gray. FaBoEE

Here lies Mr. Chesterton. G. K. Chesterton. Humbert Wolfe. TrJP

Here lies my dear wife, a sad slattern and a shrew. *Unknown.* FaBoEE

Here lies my poor wife, much lamented. *Unknown.* FaBoEE

Here lies my poor wife, without bed or blanket. *Unknown.* FaBoEE

Here lies my wife. Susannah Prout. Walter De la Mare. FaBoEE

Here lies my wife. Eternal peace. Epigram. James Vincent Cunningham. NIP-4

Here lies Nachshon, a man of great renown. An Epitaph. Isaac Benjacob, *Hebrew.* TrJP, *tr. by* Joseph Chotzner

Here lies New Critic who would fox us. Epigram. James Vincent Cunningham. MoAmPo; OBAL

Here lies Nolly Goldsmith, for shortness call'd Noll. On Oliver Goldsmith. David Garrick. FaBoEE

Here lies old Forty-five Per Cent. Old Forty-five Per Cent. *Unknown.* FaBoEE

Here lies old *Hobson,* Death hath broke his girt. On the University Carrier Who Sick'n'd in the Time of His Vacancy. John Milton. EBEV; FaBoCh; FaBoEE; NOSC; OxAEP-1

Here lies our good Edmund, whose genius was such. Edmund Burke. Oliver Goldsmith. FaBoEE; FaBoPV; NOEC *Fr.* Retaliation. OxBoLi

Here lies our Sovereign Lord the King. Epitaph on Charles II. John Wilmot, 2d Earl of Rochester. SCGP

Here lies Piron—a man of no position. Alexis Piron, *French.* FaBoEE

Here lies poor Johnson. Reader! have a care. Doctor Johnson. Soame Jenyns. FaBoEE; OBSV

Here lies resting, out of breath. Little Elegy. X. J. Kennedy. APAD; CoAP; CoAmPo; HoPM

Here lies Sam Johnson:—Reader, have a care. Epitaph on Dr Samuel Johnson. Soame Jenyns. ECEV

Here lies Sir John Plumpudding of the Grange. *Unknown.* FaBoEE

Here lies Sir Tact, a diplomatic fellow. Epitaph. Timothy Steele. InPK-6; NBLV

Here lies Stephen Pwanya. An Epitaph. Julius Chingono. PeSAV

Here lies that poet, buried in the night. On a Poet. Henry Parrot. FaBoEE

Here lies the author of the "Apparition." An Author's Epitaph, Written by Himself. Abel Evans. FaBoEE

Here lies the best and worst of fate. On the Duke of Buckingham. James Shirley. FaBoEE

Here lies the body of Daniel Saul. *Unknown.* FaBoEE

Here lies the body of Edith Bone. On Myself. Edith Bone. FaBoEE

Here lies the body of Richard Hind. Epitaph. Francis, Lord Jeffrey Jeffrey. FaBoEE; OxBoLi

Here lies the body of Sir John Guise. *Unknown.* FaBoEE

Here lies the body of W. W. On William Wilson, Tailor. *Unknown.* FaBoEE

Here lies the body of William Jones. Epitaph on William Jones. *Unknown.* FaBoEE

Here lies the corpse of Doctor Chard. *Unknown.* FaBoEE

Here lies the corpse of William Prynne. On William Prynne. Samuel Butler. FaBoEE

Here lies the dust of Timas. Sappho, *Greek.* InMo, *tr. by* Sam Hamill

Here lies the fairest flower, that stood. David's Epitaph on Jonathan. Francis Quarles. ChIV-1

Here lies the good old knight Sir Harry. Epitaph for Sir Henry Lee. *Unknown.* FaBoEE

Here lies the great. False marble, where? *Unknown.* FaBoEE

Here lies, the Lord have mercy upon her. Upon One of the Maids of Honour to Queen Elizabeth. John Hoskyns. FaBoEE

Here lies [*or* lyes] the Lord of Leicester that all the world did hate. (LL) Epitaph on the Earl of Leicester. Sir Walter Ralegh. RB; SiPS

Here lies the man that madly slain. John Hoskyns. FaBoEE

Here lies the man was born and cried. Epitaph, An: On a Man for Doing Nothing. John Hoskyns. NOSC

Here lies the man who in life. On a Contentious Companion. John Hoskyns. FaBoEE

Here lies the man who stripp'd Sin bare. Ebenezer Elliot. FaBoEE

Here lies the monstrous WHAT-A-THIRST. Epitaphs for some Space Beasts. Wes Magee. SpW

Here lies the noble flesh of Spartacus the knave. Sonnet. Daniel Casper von Lohenstein. GePo *Fr.* Arminius.

Here lies [*or* lyes] the noble warrior [*or* Warryor] that never blunted sword. Epitaph on the Earl of Leicester. Sir Walter Ralegh. RB; SiPS

Here lies the preacher, judge, and poet, Peter. On Peter Robinson. Francis, Lord Jeffrey Jeffrey. NBLV; OxBoLi

Here lies the Reverend Jonathan Doe. On the Reverend Jonathan Doe. *Unknown.* FaBoEE

Here lies Thomas Logge—a Rascally Dogge. Thomas Logge. Walter De la Mare. FaBoEE

Here lies to each her parent''s ruth. On My First Daughter. Ben Jonson. BeJo; EBEV; FaBoEE; HoPM; InPS-3; NAEL-1; NOBE; NOSC; NoP-4; PFE; PoE; SeCP

Here lies what had not birth, nor shape, nor frame. Epitaph on James Moore Smythe. Alexander Pope. FaBoEE

Here lies what's left. On Leslie Moore. *Unknown.* CTV

Here lies, whom hound did ne'er pursue. Epitaph on a Hare. William Cowper. HAP; NOEC; NoP-4; PeP; PoEL-3; PoPoPo

Here lies Wise and Valiant Dust. Epitaph on the Earl of Strafford. John Cleveland. FaBoEE; FaBoPV; NOBE; NOSC; PBRV; PeECV

Here lies with Death auld Grizzel Grimme. Grizzel Grimme. *Unknown.* FaBoEE

Here lies, within his tomb, so calm. On the Clerk of a Country Parish. William Shenstone. FaBoEE

Here lies wrapped up tight in sod. Epitaph for a Postal Clerk. X. J. Kennedy. NIP-4

Here lieth John Cruker, a maker of bellows. The Bellows Maker of Oxford. John Hoskyns. FaBoEE

Here lieth One whose name was writ on water. On Keats. Shelley. FaBoEE

Here lieth the worthy warrior / Who never bloodied sword. On the Earl of Leicester. *Unknown.* FaBoEE

Here lieth Thom Nick's body. Upon a Fool. John Hoskyns. FaBoEE

Here lieth under this marble ston. An Epitaph. *Unknown.* MiEL

Here, Lord, Retired, I Bow in Prayer. Matthew Bolles. AH

Here luxury's the common lot. The light. Grasse: The Olive Trees. Richard Wilbur. NAAL-2; NOBA; NYBP; NoAM

Here lyes a Boy y finest child from me. On My Boy Henry. Lady Jane Cavendish *and* Lady Elizabeth Brackley. KTR

Here lyeth he, who was born and cried. On One That Lived Ingloriously. John Hoskyns, *after the Greek of* Simonides. FaBoEE

Here Lysis set an empty tomb. Phanias, *Greek.* GrAn, *tr. by* Peter Porter

Here may Paulinus rest, for ever rest. Epitaph for Paulinus of Aquileia and Arno of Salzburg. Alcuin, *Latin.* MLL, *tr. by* Helen Waddell

Here men walk alone. The City. Ogden Nash. CBNP

Here morning in the ploughman's songs is met. Ploughman Singing. John Clare. EnVR

Here must wee rest; and where else should wee rest? A Serious and a Curious Night-Meditation. Thomas Traherne. SeCP

Here my chamelion [*or* or camelion] muse her self[e] doth cha[u]nge. To His Good Friend [*or* Freinde] Sir Anthony Cooke. Sir John Davies. *Fr.* The Gullinge[e] Sonnets. Son

Here, my child with fever sleeps. Caesura. Patricia Cumming. MDDM

Here my meat is, clean and dressed. Epitaph for a Meat-Packer. Guy Owen. CRP

Here, newness is all. Or almost all. And like. Day Begins at Governor's Square Mall. Leon Stokesbury. MT

Here, next the mountain, the cold comes early. Early Autumn in the Mountains. Wen T'ing-yün, *Chinese.* SuSp, *tr. by* William R. Schultz

Here no bugles sound reveille. (LL) Soldier Rest! [Thy Warfare O'er]. Sir Walter Scott. AWP; NOBE; OBNC; PoRA

Here not the flags, the rhythmic. Neutrality. Sidney Keyes. MoBrPo

Here on Earth. "Rachel," *Hebrew.* MHP, *tr. by* Ruth Finer Mintz

Here on Mondays, after the. Anglo-Saxon Comedy. Peter Rose. BMAP

Here on the earth—not in high clouds. Here on Earth. "Rachel," *Hebrew.* MHP, *tr. by* Ruth Finer Mintz

Here, on the forest's edge, I have pitched camp. In Camp. Jibanananda Das, *Bengali.* OMIP, *tr. by* Clinton B. Seely

Here on the west edge, the town turned its back on the west. City Limits. Ted Kooser. GM

Here once did sound sweet words, a-spoke. The Vield Path. William Barnes. NOBVV

Here once the evenings sobbed. The Pear-Tree. Iwan Goll, *German.* TrJP, *tr. by* Babette Deutsch *and* Avrahm Yarmolinsky

Here only the wind enters unbidden. Refuge Even Beyond Refuge. Reiner Kunze, *German.* CEEP, *tr. by* Ewald Osers

Here open'd Hell, all Hell I here implor'd. Homer. OxBSn *Fr.* The Odyssey.

Here, or not many feet from hence. Certain True Woords Spoken Concerning One Benet Corbett after Her Death. Richard Corbet. SeCP

Here penned within the human fold. The Human Fold. Edwin Muir. LiTM

Here Philip the father buried. Callimachus. HePo *Fr.* Epigrams.

Here, reader, turn your weeping eyes. The Orator's Epitaph. Henry Peter Brougham, 1st Baron Brougham and Vaux. NBLV

Here redbuds like momentary trees. Locus. Robert Earl Hayden. FYAP

Here rests his head upon the lap of earth. Epitaph. Thomas Gray. FHYEP; FaBoPV; SCGP *Fr.* Elegy Written in a Country Churchyard. APAD; AWP; CABP; ClHu; EBEV; EBEvV; FHYEP; FaBoBe; FaBoPV; FaPoR; GTBS-P; HAP; HeIP-4; ImPo; InPK-6; InPS-3; NOBE; NOEC; NoP-4; OAEL-1; OBEV; OxAEP-1; PBMP; PoEL-3; PoLF; PoPoPo; Poetr; SCGP; SCV; TFi; UV; UnPo; WeW-3

Here rests poor Stella's restless part. Stella's Epitaph. Mary Jones. ECWP

Here rests Tiosav. Epitaphs from Karansko Cemetery. Ljubomir Simovic, *Serbo-Croatian.* HSix, *tr. by* Charles Simic

Here Reynolds is laid, and to tell you my mind. Sir Joshua Reynolds. Oliver Goldsmith. FaBoEE; NOEC; OBCoV *Fr.* Retaliation. OxBoLi

Here Rhodoklea / is a garland. Rufinus, *Greek.* GrAn, *tr. by* Alan Marshfield

Here [*or* How] richly, with ridiculous display. Epitaph on the Politician Himself. Hilaire Belloc. FaBoEE; MoBrPo; NBLV; OBSV

Here Saon of Akanthos, Dikon's son. Callimachus, *Greek.* GrAn, *tr. by* Peter Jay

Here shadow[e] lie. Epitaph for Sir Lawrence Tanfield. Lady Elizabeth Tanfield. NOSC; TOF

Here she beholds the chaos dark and deep. Alexander Pope. FHYEP *Fr.* To Dr. Jonathan Swift. OxAEP-1, *book* I, *ll.* 1–330; CBNP, *book* I, *ll.* 1–84, *first edition vers.*; OBSV; PoE *Fr.* The Dunciad.

Here she lies, a pretty bud. Upon a Child That Died [*or* Dyed]. Robert Herrick. BeJo; CH; CaPo; InPK-6; NoP-4; OBEV; PFE; Poetr

Here she lies [*or* lyes] (in Bed of Spice). Upon a Maid[e]. Robert Herrick. CaPo; FaBoCh; FaBoEE; OxBoLi

Here She Stands. Jean-Joseph Rabéarivelo, *French.* PBA, *tr. by* Miriam Koshland

Here She Was Wont to Go. Ben Jonson. BeJo; OxBSP *Fr.* The Sad Shepherd.

(Aeglamour's Lament.) CH

Here should my wonder dwell, and here my praise. The Thames. Sir John Denham. NAEL-1; NOSC *Fr.* Cooper's Hill. BeJo; CABP; PBRV; SeCP

Here silken twines, there locks you see. An Ear-string. William Strode. NOSC

Here sit a shepherd and a shepherdess. The Green Shepherd. Louis Simpson. NYBP

Here sits the Lord Mayor. Forehead, Eyes, Cheeks, Nose, Mouth, and Chin. Mother Goose. FaBoVe; LB; OxNR; ReMoGo

Here, six years old, by Destiny's crime. Epitaph for Erotion. Martial, *Latin.* FaBoEE, *tr. by* James Michie

Here sleeps at length poor Col, and without screaming. Epitaph on Himself. Coleridge. FaBoEE

Here something stubborn comes. Seed Leaves. Richard Wilbur. NoP-4

Here somewhere, the world splits in two. The Man Who Decided. Slavko Mihalic, *Croatian.* CEEP, *tr. by* Peter Kastmiler

Here sparrows build upon the trees. My Early Home. John Clare. BoTP; PoLF

Here stand I, for whores as great. *Unknown.* FaBoEE

Here stands death, a bluish decoction in a cup with no saucer. Death. Rilke, *German.* PFTM, *tr. by* Pierre Joris

Here stood a lofty church—there is a steeple. Pleasant Delusion of a Sumpteous Citty. Sarah Kemble Knight. SCAP

Here stood Hypocrisy, in sober brown. Timothy Dwight. NOCV *Fr.* The Triumph of Infidelity.

Here, / Take it home and give it to your wife. The Wooden Handle. Gojko Djogo, *Serbo-Croatian.* AF, *tr. by* Michael March *and* Dušan Puvaić

Here, take my *Likeness* with you, whilst 'tis so. My Picture. Abraham Cowley. CBLP

Here take my Picture, though I bid farewell;. His Picture. Donne. FSCP; MeLP; OxAEP-1; PBRV *Fr.* Elegies.

Here tame boys fly down the long light of halls. To a Visiting Poet in a College Dormitory. Carolyn Kizer. PoA

Here the boat set me down, and I wait. Queen of the River. Elizabeth Nannestad. PeNZ

Here the crow starves, here the patient stag. Rannoch, by Glencoe. T. S. Eliot. NAEL-2 *Fr.* Landscapes. RB

Here the delicate dance of silence. Woodtown Manor. John Montague. PBCIP

Here the eye is inevitably cast. Sakhara. Robert Arthur Douglas Ford. NOBC

Here the foot prints stop;. After Twenty Years. Fadwa Tuqan, *Arabic.* AГ, PBWP, *tr. by* Unknown

Here the frailest leaves of me and yet my strongest lasting. Walt Whitman. APN-1; NAAL-1; NAAL-3; PAR

Here the hangman stops his cart. The Carpenter's Son. A. E. Housman. ChIV-2; MoBrPo; OxAEP-2; PBMP; SAGP; UV

Here the hills are earth's bones. Asian Desert. Dorothy, Duchess of Wellington Wellesley. OBMV

Here the horse-mushrooms make a fairy ring. The Fairy Ring. Andrew Young. Spl

Here the human past is dim and feeble and alien to us. Haunted Country. Robinson Jeffers. OxBA

Here the image of a child on a hill. Michael Palmer. APSN *Fr.* Baudelaire Series.

Here the jack-hammer jabs into the ocean. Colloquy in Black Rock. Robert Lowell. MoAmPo; NAAL-2

Here the picture is less gloomy. All That Glitters. Maureen Owen. PmAP

Here the round begins again. A Traveller. J. R. Rowland. CBAP

Here the savoury roast and pungent sauce. A Latrine in a Suburb of Smyrna. Agathias, *Greek.* GrAn, *tr. by* Guy Davenport

Here the trees are eight stories high. Murmuring. Judit Tóth, *Hungarian.* CEEP, *tr. by* Emery E. George

Here then is the life-giving activity given to every man: the sexual / act, vivificator. Stefan Brecht. CLPP *Fr.* Sex.

Here they all come to die. The Country of a Thousand Years of Peace. James Merrill. NoP-4

Here they are. The soft eyes open. The Heaven of Animals. James Dickey. CoAP; ColAP; HeIP-4; LiTM; MT; NAAL-2; NOBA; NoAM; PoE; TAP; TRP; VCAP

Here they lie mottled to the ground unseen. Partridges. John Masefield. OxBTC

Here they stood, whom the Kecoughtan first believed. Elegy in an Abandoned Boatyard. Dave Jeddie Smith. VCAP

Here they went with smock and crook. Forefathers. Edmund Blunden. NOBE, NoP-4; OBEV; OBMV; OxBTC

Here those of us who really understand. Manhattan. Osbert Lancaster. NOBL; PeLV *Fr.* Afternoons with Baedeker.

Here to the leisured side of life. The Lamplighter. "Seumas O'Sullivan." BIrV

Here Today. Andrew Elliott. PNI

Here Together Met. Louis Johnson. PeNZ

Here too are dreaming landscapes. In the Miscroscope. Miroslav Holub, *Czech.* PoSu, *tr. by* Ian *and* Jarmila Milner

Here too there are guys like the guys of the Volye. Mangin Street. Berysh Vaynshteyn. CEEP, *tr. by* Benjamin Harshav *and* Barbara Harshav *Fr.* New York Everywhere.

Here too, 'tis sung, of old Diana stray'd. Alexander Pope. OxAEP-1 *Fr.* Windsor-Forest [*or* Windsor Forest].

Here under leafy bowers. Under Leafy Bowers. Judah Al-Harizi, *Hebrew.* TrJP

Here, under pear-trees, on the broad verandahs. David Campbell. BMAP

Here under the radiant rays of the sun. Facing the Chair. "Hugh MacDiarmid." FaBoMo

Here used to be. The Worship of Cromm Cruaich. *Unknown.* TIRV *Fr.* The Voyage of Bran.

Here war is harmless like a monument. W. H. Auden. OBWP *Fr.* Sonnets from China.

Here was a place where none would ever come. Haunted House. Edwin Arlington Robinson. MeMAP

Here was raised. The Plain of Adoration. *Unknown, Irish.* BIrV, tr. by John Montague

Here was the sound of water falling only. The Owl. Robert Penn Warren. MoAmPo

Here, watching T.V. Hunting the Dugong. Gladys Cardiff. HATNAP

Here we are all, by day; by night we are [*or* w'are] hurled. Dream[e]s. Robert Herrick. BeJo; CaPo; HAP; KaS; NAEL-1; OPOU; OxBSP; Spl

Here we are, if you have any more. Thomas Middleton. *Fr.* The Changeling. PoEL-2

Here we are, picking the first fern-shoots. Song of the Bowmen of Shu. Ezra Pound, after the Chinese. OBVE

Here we are, see? At the Well. Paul Blackburn. APSN

Here we are, without our clothes. Sexual Couplets. Craig Raine. EP

Here we bring new water. A New Year Carol. *Unknown.* BoTP; CH; OBCP; OxBoLi

Here we broached the Christmas barrel. The House of Hospitalities. Thomas Hardy. RB

Here we can observe the superior mirages. Traveller's Guide to Antarctica. Adrien Stoutenburg. NYBP

Here We Come a-Haying. Eunice Close. BoTP

Here we come a-piping. *Unknown.* BoTP; CH

Here we come again, again, and here we come again! The Children's Carol. Eleanor Farjeon. PChr

Here we come gathering nuts an' [*or* in] May. *Unknown.* LB

Here we come looby loo. Lubin. *Unknown.* FaBoVe

Here we enact the opening of the world. An Australian Garden. Peter Porter. OBGa

Here we go a-walking, so softly, so softly. From a Walking Song. Charles Williams. BoTP

Here we go around this ring. Marriage. *Unknown.* AmFP

Here we go dancing jingo-ring. The Merry-ma-Tanzie. *Unknown.* OxNR

Here we go round ring by ring. *Unknown.* OxNR

Here we go round the mulberry bush, The. The Mulberry Bush. *Unknown.* ACTP; LB; ReMoGo

Here we go up, up, up. *Unknown.* BoTP

Here We have No Firm Dwelling-Place. Eugène Marais, *Afrikaans.* PeSAV, tr. by Hugh Finn

Here we have the sea of children; here. Geography Lesson. Carol Rumens. FaBoWP

Here we have thirst. An Egyptian Pulled Glass Bottle in the Shape of a Fish. Marianne Moore. NALW; PBWP

Here We Loved. Yehuda Amichai, *Hebrew.*
"My father was four years at their war." MHP, tr. by Ruth Finer Mintz

Here We March All Around in a Ring. *Unknown.* AmFP

Here we must rest; and where else should we rest? Sepulchrum Domus Mea Est. William Austin. NOSC

Here we part. Farewell Once More to My Friend Yen at Feng Chi Station. Tu Fu, *Chinese.* OHPC, tr. by Kenneth Rexroth

Here we're set upon the green grass. Green Grass. *Unknown.* FaBoVe

Here Where Coltrane Is. Michael S. Harper. NAAAL; PoBA

Here, where fecundity of Babel frames. Babylon and Sion (Goa and Lisbon). Luís de Camões, *Portuguese.* AWP, tr. by Richard Garnett

Here where our Lord once laid his head. Upon the Holy Sepulchre. Richard Crashaw. FaBoEE

Here, where precipitate spring with one light bound. Faesulan Idyll. Walter Savage Landor. Ro

Here, where relumed by changing seasons, burn. Roy Campbell. OxBTC *Fr.* The Golden Shower.

Here, where summer slips. The Red and the Green. Anne Wilkinson. MoCV

Here, where the baby paddles in the gutter. Lean Street. George Sutherland Fraser. FaBoTC; OxBS

Here, where the breath of the scented-gorse floats through the sun-stained air. Breton Afternoon. Ernest Christopher Dowson. OBNC

Here where the end of bone is no end of song. The Poet's Corner. Laura Riding Jackson. FuPo

Here where the fields lie lonely and untended. A Deserted Home. Sidney Royce Lysaght. CH

Here where the meadows gave ease to tired feet. On One Dying in a Convent. Stephen Lucius Gwynn. TIRV

Here where the parrots come down. Thomas and Charlie. Peter Wild. AmPA

Here, where the red man swept the leaves away. Frederick Goddard Tuckerman. NOBA; TAP *Fr.* Sonnets.

Here, where the taut wave hangs. Life's Circumnavigators. William Robert Rodgers. GTBS-P

Here where the wind is always north-north-east. New England. Edwin Arlington Robinson. HeIP-4; MeMAP; MoAmPo; NAAL-2; NOBA; OxBA; PoPoPo; TAP

Here, where the world is quiet. The Garden of Proserpine. Swinburne. CABP; GaP; NoP-4; PeVV; TFi *Fr.* The Garden of Proserpine. AWP; BLPA; FaPoR; HAP; NAEL-2; NOBE; NOBVV; OBNC; PoE; PoEL-5; PoRA; SCV

Here, where Vespasian's legions struck the sands. Embarcation. Thomas Hardy. OBWP

Here with a Loaf of Bread beneath the Bough. Omar Khayyám. UV *Fr.* The Rubáiyát of Omar Khayyám [of Naishápúr]. AWP; EBVV; FaBoBe; FaPoR; HAP; NAEL-2; PoEL-5

Here / With my beer / I sit. Beer. George Arnold. OBAL

Here with roses in bloom, with woodbine twining the laurel. Anacreon's Grave. Goethe, *German.* STV, tr. by John Frederick Nims

Here with the desert so austere that only. Burial Flags. Ralph Nixon Currey. PoWW

Here X. lies dead, but God's forgiving. J. E. Thorold Rogers. FaBoEE

Here you are beside me again. Shadow. Guillaume Apollinaire, *French.* PeFWW, tr. by Christopher Middleton

Here you are near me once more. Shadow. Guillaume Apollinaire, *French.* AF, tr. by Anne Greet

Here you are once more, sitting at a table. Trying to Begin. Robert Mezey. WeT

Here you can find joy in cloudy weather or bright, day or night. Tune: "Coda." Kuan Yün-shih. SuSp, tr. by Richard John Lynn *Fr.* Medley of Southern and Northern Tunes—Scenic Tour of West Lake.

Here you could pass your holidays. A Kyoto Garden. D. J. Enright. OBGa

Here you find no counted seeds. Right of Way. Eugene McCarthy. IIP

Here you grew up. On a land which is flat. Paul-Eerik Rummo, *Estonian.* CEEP, tr. by Ivar Ivask

Here you see old Tom Moore. The Days of 'Forty-Nine [*or* '49]. *Unknown, att. to* Charley Rhodes. APN-2

Here! You sons of the men. English Thornton. Edgar Lee Masters. OxBA *Fr.* Spoon River Anthology.

Here you've got time to think. In Line at the Supermarket. Greg Pape. PBCAP

Hereafter, The. Andrew Hudgins. RA

Hereafter, shall smell of the lamp, not thee. (LL) His Farewell [*or* Fare-well] to Sack. Robert Herrick. BeJo; CaPo; CavPo; NAEL-1; SeCP

Heredity, *limerick.* Arthur Guiterman. OBAL; PeLi

Heredity. Thomas Hardy. CTC; EBEV; RB

Heredity. Tony Harrison. *Fr.* The School of Eloquence. NAEL-2; NoAM

Heredom. Ken Irby. FTOS

Here's a ball for baby. *Unknown.* LB

Here's a body—there's a bed! Good Night. Thomas Hood. OTCP; Spl

Here's a cosy warm house for Edward and me. (LL) Address to a Child during a Boisterous Winter Evening. Dorothy Wordsworth. BoTP; NTP; OxBChV; WoRP

Here's a fine bag of meat. Bags of Meat. Thomas Hardy. RB

Here's a girl from a dangerous town. Belfast Tune. Joseph Brodsky. VCWP

Here's a good rule of thumb. Reflection on Ingenuity. Ogden Nash. RB

Here's a guessing story. What Is It? H. E. Wilkinson. BoTP

Here's a guy. Michael McClintock. HA

Here's a hand to the boy who has courage. Our Heroes. Phoebe Cary. BLPA

Here's a hotel where even the stairs. Hot Springs. Earle Birney. OxBC

Here's a jolly couple! Oh the jolly jolly cuple! *Unknown.* NOSC

Here's a large one for the lady. The Broom Squire's Song. *Unknown.* OxNR

Here's a little mouse)and. Four III. E. E. Cummings. FaBoMo; TTTS

Here's a poor widow from Babylon. *Unknown.* OxNR

Here's a song. Season Song. *Unknown, Irish.* RB, tr. by Flann O'Brien

Here's an example from / A Butterfly. The Example. W. H. Davies. MoBrPo

Here's an old lady, almost ninety-one. Two Old Ladies. Siegfried Sassoon. OxBTC

Here's another Spaniard! Welcome! Antonio Machado Ruiz, *Spanish.* STV, *tr. by* John Frederick Nims

Here's Cooper, who's written six volumes to show. Cooper. James Russell Lowell. NOBA; OxBA; TAP *Fr.* A Fable for Critics. NAAL-1; NAAL-3

Here's Dog Diogenes, you ferryman. *Unknown, Greek.* GrAn, *tr. by* Edward Lucie-Smith

Here's fine rosemary, sage, and thyme. The Cries of London. *Unknown.* OPOU

Here's Finiky Hawkes. *Unknown.* OxNR

Here's flowers for you. The Flowers of Perdita. Shakespeare. GBL *Fr.* The Winter's Tale.

Here's Looking at You Francis Bacon. Joan Retallack. FTOS

Here's no more news, than virtue, I may as well. To Sir Henry Wotton. Donne. OxAEP-1

Here's one in whom Nature feared—faint at such vying. Cardinal Bembo's Epitaph on Raphael. Thomas Hardy, *after* Pietro Bembo. FaBoEE

Here's praise to the nape of the neck. Nape. Jane Epton Seale. CrSp

Here's proof—as if one needed any. Dedicatory Epistle, with a Book of 1949. Roy Fuller. PeLV

Here's something folk tales tell. Remember Haiti, Cuba, Vietnam. Andrew Salkey. PBCV

Here's Sulky Sue. Sulky Sue. Mother Goose. OxNR; ReMoGo

Here's the garden she walked across. The Flower's Name. Robert Browning. CTC; GaP; OBGa *Fr.* Garden Fancies.

Here's to Lysidice: pour in ten ladles, boy. Argentarius, *Greek.* GrAn, *tr. by* Fleur Adcock

Here's to that bedraggled sparrow. Sparrow of Espanola. Michael Pettit. NAmP90

Here's to the maiden [*or* maid] of Bashful fifteen. Song. Richard Brinsley Sheridan. EBEvV; NOEC; NOIV; OxAEP-1; OxBoLi; PeLV; PoRA *Fr.* The School for Scandal.

Here's to the men who lose! To the Men Who Lose. George L. Scarborough. BLPA

Here's to the poor widow from Babylon. *Unknown.* BoTP

Here's to the Red of it. A Toast to the Flag. John Jay Daly. PoLF

Here's to thee, old apple tree. *Unknown.* OxNR

Here's to women for they bear such / lovely kiddies! (LL) Uncle Henry. W. H. Auden. NOBL; PeLV

Here's two or three jolly boys. *Unknown.* OxNR

Here's what I see. Dogs Gambol. Novica Tadic, *Serbian.* VCWP, *tr. by* Charles Simic

Here's where I wanted to put the streetcars. Old Postcards. Günter Eich, *German.* AF, *tr. by* Stuart Friebert

Here's witts extraction morall and divine. One Presenting a Rare Book to Madame Hull. John Saffin. SCAP

Heresy for a Class-Room. Rolfe Humphries. PFE

Heretic's Pilgrimage, A. Eva Gore-Booth. TIRV

Heretic's Tragedy, The. Robert Browning. OAEL-2

Hereto I come to view a voiceless ghost;. After A Journey. Thomas Hardy. CBLP; CMoP; EBEV; EnLoPo; GBL; GTBS-P; LoP; OBNC; OxAEP-2; OxBSn; OxBTC; PoE; PoEL-5

Heretse! Baboon. *Unknown, Hottentot.* PeSA

Hereunder Jacob Schmidt who, man and bones. Immortal Helix. Archibald MacLeish. PFE

Hereux Qui, comme Ulysse, A Fait un Beau Voyage. Joachim Du Bellay. AWP, *tr. by* G. K. Chesterton *Fr.* Regrets.

Herezsometobaccozhere. We Got Everything We Needed Here and Aint It Something. *Unknown, Seneca Indian.* STP, *tr. by* Jerome Rothenberg *and* Richard Johnny John

Heriot's Ford. Rudyard Kipling. PoRA *Fr.* The Light That Failed.

Heritage. Gwendolyn B. Bennett. BISi; ColAP; NAAAL; PoBA

Heritage. Countee Cullen. BPo; ColAP; CrDW; HeIP-4; MoAmPo; NAAAL; NAAL-2; NoAM; NoP-4; PoBA; PoPoPo; Poetr; SSLK; TTY ("Spicy grove, cinamon tree, / What is Africa to me?") (LL) ChAP

Heritage. Mary Gilmore. CBAP

Heritage. Haim Guri. HP

Heritage. Linda Hogan. UnSA

Heritage. Dorothea MacKellar. NOBAu

Heritage. Augustus Young. CIP-2; IIP

Herkeneth, lordinges, grete and smale. *Unknown.* MiEL

Herm whose length measured degrees of heat, The. William Empson. PoA *Fr.* Bacchus. NoAM

Herman Altman. Edgar Lee Masters. OxBA *Fr.* Spoon River Anthology.

Herman Melville. Conrad Potter Aiken. NoAM; TAP

Herman Melville. W. H. Auden. MeMAP; OxBA

Hermaphrodite's Song, The. Lorna Mitchell. BrRo

Hermaphroditus, a delight, a. Ovid, Meet a Metamorphodite. Jonathan Williams. PoM

Hermes came to me in a dream. I said. Sappho, *Greek.* BoWoP, *tr. by* Willis Barnstone

Hermes, god / of crossed sticks. Prayer to Hermes. Robert Creeley. PoM

Hermes, lord of the dead, look down and guard the fathers' power. The Libation Bearers. Aeschylus, *Greek.* NAWM-1, *tr. by* Robert Fagles

Hermes of the Ways. Hilda Doolittle. WPE

Hermes Trismegistus. Hilda Doolittle. NALW *Fr.* Tribute to the Angels.

Hermetic Bird. Philip Lamantia. VGW

Hermetic Silence. Edward Foster. PT

Hermit, The. Eloise Bibb. CBWP-4

Hermit, The. W. H. Davies. MoBrPo

Hermit and Politician. Po Chü-i, *Chinese.* ChiP, *tr. by* Arthur Waley

Hermit and the Soul, The. Henrietta Cordelia Ray. CBWP-3

Hermit Cackleberry Brown, on Human Vanity, The. Jonathan Williams. OBAL; PoM

Hermit Feng's Residence on the Lake. Hsü Pen, *Chinese.* CoBLCP, *tr. by* Jonathan Chaves

Hermit-Fish, unarm'd by Nature left, The. Oppian. OBCVT, *tr. by* William Diaper *Fr.* Halieutica.

Hermit Has a Visitor, The. Maxine W. Kumin. BoWoP

Hermit hoar, in solemn cell. Idyll. Samuel Johnson. NBLV; NOBL; PeLV

Hermit in his cave beside the sea, The. The Hermit and the Soul. Henrietta Cordelia Ray. CBWP-3

Hermit Li's Herb Garden Retreat at T'ung-ch'uan. Hsü Pen, *Chinese.* CoBLCP, *tr. by* Jonathan Chaves

Hermit Marbán, The. *Unknown.* NOIV

Hermit Wakes to Bird Sounds, The. Maxine W. Kumin. Poetsp

Hermitage. Donald Davidson.

Descending Chestnut Ridge. FuPo

Hermitage, The. *Unknown, Irish.* IIP, *tr. by* Frank O'Connor

Hermit's chapel, the pilgrim's prayer, The. (LL) Usk. T. S. Eliot. FaBoCh; NOCV; PeECV

Hermit's Curse, The. Richard Harteis. CMAP

Hermit's Song, A. *Unknown, Irish.* BIrV, *tr. by* James Simmons

Hermit's Song, The. *Unknown, Irish.* TIRV, *tr. by* Kuno Meyer

Hermogenes is rather short. Lucilius, *Greek.* GrAn, *tr. by* Peter Porter

Hernando De Soto. Rosemary Benét *and* Stephen Vincent Benét. NBLV

Hero. Yevgeny Aronovich Dolmatovsky, *Russian.* TCRP, *tr. by* Daniel Weissbort

Hero, The. Marianne Moore. CMoP; NOBA; OxBA; PoA *Fr.* Part of a Novel, Part of a Poem, Part of a Play.

Hero, The. Siegfried Sassoon. OBWP

Hero and Leander. Donne. FMP; NoSic; SoSe-8

Hero and Leander. Marlowe, First *and* Second Sestiads, *completed by* George Chapman. AAS

Hero and Leander. Marlowe.

Amorous Neptune. NOBE

"And now the sun that through the horizon peeps." OAEL-1

Bridal Song: "O come, soft rest of cares, come Night." NOBE; OBEV

"By this Leander being near the land." EBEV; FaBoSe

("That pulls or shakes it from the golden tree.") (LL) FaBoSe

Epithalamion Teratos. NoSic

"Her veil was artificial flowers and leaves." HoPM

Hero Feels the Shaft of Love. GBL

"Leander to the envious light." OAEL-1

Leander's Return. EBNV

Love at First Sight. NOBE

"Men of wealthy Sestos, every year, The." AEP

"New light gives new directions, Fortunes new." NoSic; OAEL-1; PBRV

"Now from Leander's place she rose, and found." EBEV

"O none but gods have power their love to hide." OxAEP-1

"On Hellespont, guilty of true love's blood." NoSic; OAEL-1; PoE; PoEL-2

"So on she goes, and in her idle flight." PoE

Who Ever Loved, That Loved Not at First Sight? ImPo

Hero and Leander. Musaeus, *Greek.*

"Amaze then tooke him." OBCVT, *tr. by* George Chapman

Hero and the Hydra, The. James McAuley.

Tomb of Heracles, The. BMAP

Hero and Thief. Kofi Anyidoho. PBMAP

Hero Feels the Shaft of Love. Marlowe. GBL *Fr.* Hero and Leander. AAS

Hero first thought it, The. Truth. "Æ." MoBrPo

Hero in the Land of Dough, A. Robert Clairmont. KaS

Hero of Our Times, The. Kiên Giang, *Vietnamese.* AVP, *tr. by* Huỳnh Sanh Thông

Herodes, thou wikked foe, wharof is thy dredinge? William Herebert. MiEL

Hérodiade. I. Hérodiade. Arthur Symons. ADE *Fr.* Stéphane Mallarmé.

Heroes. Robert Creeley. NOBA; NoP-4

Heroes. Sorley MacLean. FaBoTC

Heroes, The. Louis Simpson. OBWP

Heroes. Walt Whitman. *Fr.* Song of Myself. AmPP; MoAmPo; NAAL-3; NOBA; OxBA

Heroes, and Kings! your distance keep. Epitaph for One Who Would Not Be Buried in Westminster Abbey. Alexander Pope. FaBoEE

Heroes meet again in the underworld, The. Homer. OBCVT, *tr. by* David Constantine *Fr.* The Iliad.

Heroes never tire. General Truths. David Avidan, *Hebrew.* IP, *tr. by* Warren Bargad and Stanley Chyet *Fr.* Samson, Our Hero.

Heroes paused upon the plain, The. The Byrnies. Thom Gunn. MoP; NoAM; OxBTC

Heroes, Saints, and Neighbors. Gillian Conoley. PUP-19

Heroes screamed from my fingertips. Bard. Gavin Bantock. FaBoTw

Heroic Epistle to Sir William Chambers, An. William Mason. OBGa

Heroic Simile. Robert Hass. VCAP

Heroic Vengeance. Milton. *Fr.* Samson Agonistes. FHYEP; OAEL-1; PoEL-3

Heroides. Ovid, *Latin.*

　Dido's farewell. OBCVT, *tr. by* George Turberville

　"To Paris that was once her owne though now it be not so." OBVE, *tr. by* George Turberville

Heroin. Jim Carroll. OBCoV

Heroine in ass-skin. Book of Cordelia. Susan Howe. *Fr.* White Foolscap/Book of Cordelia. PmAP

Heron. James King Annand. NOxBChV

Heron. Philip Booth. Poetsp

Heron. Stanley Plumly. AmPA

Heron. Ted Walker. NYBP

Heron, The. Vernon Watkins. GTBS-P; TwCP; UnPo

Heron [*or* Hern] flew east, the heron [*or* hern] flew west, The. *Unknown.* EnSB

Heron stalks, The. Sunset at Twin Lake. Anita Endrezze-Danielson. HATNAP

Herons. Robin Blaser. NeAP

Hero's Portion. John Montague. NOIV

Hero's Will, A. Nguyễn Công Trú', *Vietnamese.* AVP, *tr. by* Huỳnh Sanh Thông

Herr Bruckner often wandered into church. Lives of the Great Composers. Dana Gioia. EOEF; RA

Herr Direktor, ich sent Sei ein cable. Ein Complaint. Virginia Graham. OBCoV

Herr-Knit Bunnet, The. Robert Crawford. FaBoTC

Herrick, thou art too coarse to love. (LL) The Vision. Robert Herrick. CaPo; CavPo; SCGP; SeCP

Herrick's Julia. Helen Smith Bevington. BXAP

Herring is prolific, The. Kenneth Rexroth. HoPM *Fr.* A Bestiary. OBAL

Herring loves the merry moonlight, The. The Oyster. Sir Walter Scott. FaBoCh; NTP *Fr.* The Antiquary.

Herring Weir, The. Sir Charles G. D. Roberts. NOBC *Fr.* Songs of the Common Day.

Hers could not staye for sympathie. (LL) A Song: "It is not Beauty [*or* beautie] I demand[e]." George Darley. Ro

Herself listening to herself, having no name. John Holmes. HoPM

Hersilia. William Johnson Cory. NOBVV

Hertha. Swinburne. OAEL-2

Hervé Riel. Robert Browning. FaBoBe

Hervenis, harping on the hackneyed text. Sunday: A Fragment Transcribed from a Ms. in Chatterton's Handwriting. Thomas Chatterton. ECEV

He's a dragon, see. Strato, *Greek.* GrAn, *tr. by* Tony Harrison

He's a high clear forehead. Robert Johnstone. PNI *Fr.* Every Cache.

He's a little dog, with a stubby tail, and a moth-eaten coat of tan. Bum. W. Dayton Wedgefarth. BLPA

He's an old grey horse, with his head bowed sadly. The Old Whim Horse. Edward Dyson. CBAP

He's dead / the dog won't have to. Death. William Carlos Williams. NAAL-2; OxBA; VGW

He's Doing Natural Life. Conyus. PoBA

He's driving a truck, and we know. Young Elvis. Cornelius Eady. CMAP

He's filled himself with himself. The Secret of the Quartz Pebble. Vasco [*or* Vasko] Popa. PoSu, *tr. by* Anne Pennington *Fr.* The Quartz Pebble.

He's from another time track. Another Time Track. Ilze Mueller. LoHo

He's gone, and all our plans. To His Love. Ivor Gurney. NAEL-2; NTP; NoP-4; OBWP; PeFWW; PoWW

He's Gone Away. *Unknown.* AS

He's gone to bed at last, that flaring, glaring. My Stearine Candles. James Henry. NOBVV

He's got a radio on his shoulder. Street Music. Greg Pape. PBCAP

He's had enough of the circle. The Adventure of the Quartz Pebble. Vasco [*or* Vasko] Popa. PoSu, *tr. by* Anne Pennington *Fr.* The Quartz Pebble.

He's knelt to fish her face up from the sidewalk. The Rebirth of Venus. Mary Jo Salter. FFC; WWSi

He's learning to shoot. Shirley Kaufman. CrSp *Fr.* Watts.

He's neither Chinese. A Buddhist Priest. Ho Xuan Huong, *Vietnamese.* PBWP, *tr. by* Nguyen Ngoc Bich *and* Burton Raffel

He's not from some country. What She Said about Her Unfaithful, Estranged Husband. Netumpalliyattan, *Tamil.* PLW, *tr. by* A. K. Ramanujan

He's now the ruler of the country which once exiled him. The Exile's Return. Slavko Mihalic. PoSu, *tr. by* Peter Kastmiler *and* Charles Simic

He's *only* a talented man! (LL) The Talented Man. Winthrop Mackworth Praed. CABP; NOBL; OBCoV; PeLV

He's only rich that cannot tell his store. (LL) Against Fruition. Sir John Suckling. BeJo; CaPo; CavPo; NOSC

He's out stuck in a bird's craw. Maitreya the Future Buddha. Gary Snyder. *Fr.* Burning. NeAP; PoM *Fr.* Myths and Texts.

He's played hookey to see the flick again. Buddy Holly Watching *Rebel Without a Cause*, Lubbock, Texas, 1956. David Wojahn. PBCAP *Fr.* Mystery Train: A Sequence.

He's standing here alone—a stray, a waif. A Man Has Lost His Way. Trần Tế Xu'o'ng, *Vietnamese.* AVP, *tr. by* Huỳnh Sanh Thông

He's still young—; thirty, but looks younger. Self-Portrait. Frank Bidart. HCAP

He's sure to cry. (LL) Little Boy Blue, come blow [up] your horn[!]. Mother Goose. BoTP; FaBoBe; OxNR

He's the man who climbs his barn. Man in the Moon. Linda Hogan. HATNAP

He's under the haycock fast asleep! Mother Goose. *See* Little Boy Blue, come blow [up] your horn[!].

He's up. And off, a tipsy. Son and Heir. Philip Gross. APAD

He's walked each path beneath the pines. A Little Landscape by Yen Wen-kuei. Yü Chi, *Chinese.* CoBLCP, *tr. by* Jonathan Chaves

Hesh! my baby; stop yer fuss. Aunt Chloe's Lullaby. Daniel Webster Davis. AAP

Hesiod's is the theme and his the style. Callimachus. HePo *Fr.* Epigrams.

Hesiod's style and themes: the poet from Soloi. Callimachus, *Greek.* GrAn, *tr. by* Peter Jay

Hesitant door chain, The. Into Blackness Softly. Mari E. Evans. PoBA

Hesitate to Call. Louise Glück. LW

Hesitating Veteran, The. Ambrose Bierce. CBCWP

Hesitating's my one steadiness. Steady. Blaga Dimitrova, *Bulgarian.* CEEP, *tr. by* Jascha Kessler *and* Aleksandar Shurbanov

Hesitation. "Lu Hsün," *Chinese.* SuSp, *tr. by* William R. Schultz

Hesperia. Swinburne. OBNC

Hesperia. Richard Henry Wilde.

　"Across the Prairie's silent waste I stray." APN-1

　"Beyond Vermont's green hills, against the skies." APN-1

　"Change blots out change,—their very memory dies." APN-1

　"Father of Rivers! standing by thy side." APN-1

　"If the romantic land whose soil I tread." APN-1

　"Mount Auburn! loveliest city of the dead." APN-1

　"Saint Augustine, thy praise was sung by one." APN-1

　"Where dost thou lie, great Nimrod of the West!" APN-1

Hesperides, The. Tennyson. OAEL-2

Hesperos, you bring home all the bright dawn disperses. Sappho, *Greek.* BoWoP, *tr. by* Willis Barnstone

Hesperus' Hymne[e] to Cynthia. Ben Jonson. *See* Hymn to Diana.

Hesperus the Bringer. Byron. AWP *Fr.* Canto the Third. *Fr.* Don Juan.

Hesperus! the day is gone. John Clare. EBVV; GTBS-P; NOBVV; OAEL-2

Hessian in his last letter home, The. Christmas. Steve Hassett. CDa

Hester. Charles Lamb. GTBS-P; OBEV

Hetero-sex is best for the man of a serious turn of mind. Epigram. Argentarius, *Greek.* GrAn, *tr. by* Fleur Adcock. OBCVT

Heterosexual Poem. Strato, *Greek.* GrAn, *tr. by* Teddy Hogge

Heterosexuals can get AIDS too. An Alarming New Development. Ron Schreiber. GLP

Heu Quam Precipiti. Boethius. MLL, *tr. by* Helen Waddell; OBMV, *Fr.* Consolation of Philosophy, The ("De Consolacione Philosophie").

Heureux Qui, comme Ulysse, A Fait un Beau Voyage. Joachim Du Bellay, *French.* AWP, *tr. by* G. K. Chesterton

Heven, it es a riche ture. *Unknown.* MiEL

Hewel, or Woodpecker, The. Andrew Marvell. *Fr.* Upon Appleton House [To My Lord Fairfax]. FaBoPV; GeHe; SeCP

Hexameters[; Paraphrase of Psalm XLVI], *see also* "God in our refuge and strength, a very present help in trouble." Coleridge. ChIV-1

Hexametra Alexis in Laudem Rosamundi. Robert Greene. GBL; PoEL-2 *Fr.* Greene's Mourning Garment.

Hey Betty Martin. *Unknown.* AS

Hey, boys, joint ahead. Track-lining Song. *Unknown.* AmFP

Hey, Boys! Up Go We! *Unknown.* NOBAu

Hey Cool Papa. For Cool Papa Bell. Tom Dent. ISC

Hey diddle diddle. *Unknown.* LB; OxNR

Hey [*or* Sing hey], diddle, diddle, / The cat and the fiddle. High Diddle Diddle. Mother Goose. CBNP; FaBoBe; HoPM; OxBoLi; OxNR; ReMoGo

Hey diddle dinkety, poppety, pet. The Merchants of London. Mother Goose. OxNR; ReMoGo

Hey diddle, dinkety, poppety pet. *Unknown.* BoTP

Hey diddle dout, / My candle's out. *Unknown.* OxNR

Hey ding a ding. *Unknown.* OxNR

Hey, dorolot, dorolot! *Unknown.* OxNR

Hey Father Death, I'm flying home. V. Father Death Blues. Allen Ginsberg. CLPP *Fr.* Don't Grow Old.

Hey! hey! by this day! The Unhappy Schoolboy. *Unknown.* OxBChV

Hey, hey, hey, hey! *Unknown.* MiEL

Hey-ho-day! me no care a dammee! Negro Song at Cornwall. *Unknown.* PBCV

Hey! Ho! Hurrah! Kamatari, *Japanese.* OHMPJ, *tr. by* Kenneth Rexroth

Hey ho, what shall I say? Thomas Ravenscroft. CBLP

("Come againe ho, hey.") (LL) PBRV

Hey-How for Hallowe'en. *Unknown.* FaBoCh

Hey let's fight that shaman, let's fight that ghost first & then that shaman. Ghost & Shaman. *Unknown, Bella Bella Indian.* STP, *tr. by* Franz Boas

Hey Mama, what's revolution? Bedtime Story. Nayo-Barbara Watkins. NBV

Hey, my kitten, my kitten. My Kitten. Mother Goose. OxNR; ReMoGo

Hey Nellie, / how long you been here? did you. Smokey's Getting Old. Jessica Hagedorn. OpBo

Hey Nonny No! *Unknown.* CH; EBEV; FaBoCh; OBEV

Hey! [*or* Hay!] now [*or* nou] the day dawis [*or* daunns]. The Night Is Near [*or* Neir] Gone. Alexander Montgomerie. CH; OBEV; OxBS

Hey noyney! I will love our Sir John and I love eny. *Unknown.* MiEL

Hey, pop! / Re-bop! / Mop! / Y-e-a-h! (LL) Dream Boogie. Langston Hughes. APSN; AmPP; HCAP

Hey Robin. Joseph Skipsey. EBVV

Hey Sweetie. Albert Goldbarth. IFJA

Hey there poleece. Poem to a Nigger Cop. Bobb Hamilton. TTY

Hey, this little kid gets roller skates. 74th Street. Myra Cohn Livingston. SSCS

Hey, woman in the white, transparent dress. Camelia. Igor Moiseievich Irtenev, *Russian.* TCRP, *tr. by* Bradley Jordan

Hey, Wully Wine. *Unknown.* CH

Hey, you sharp little con men! Stop Fooling. Velemir Khlebnikov, *Russian.* TCRP, *tr. by* Gary Kern

Hey, you, *you slant-eyed, luscious brown-skinned / broad,.* Words and Thoughts. John Clark Pratt. CDa

Heye Louerd, thou here my bone. *Unknown.* MiEL

Heyl, Levedy, see-sterre bright. William Herebert. MiEL

Hezekiah. Thomas Parnell.

"From the black beach and broad expanse of sea." ChIV-1

Hezekiah's Display. John Keble. ChIV-1

Hi. Gregory Corso. EC3

Hi! Walter De la Mare. PeLV

Hi! handsome hunting man. Walter De la Mare. NOxBChV

Hi, Jimmis, nagah, matty man, you deh 'pon um again. Deh 'Pon Um Again. Michael McTurk. PBCV

Hi, mawning Susie, how yuh is? yuh get de small-pox yet? Lizzie Discourses on the Small-Pox. Edward Cordle. PBCV

Hi! Miss Liza's got er banjer. Miss Liza's Banjer. Daniel Webster Davis. AAP

Hi! shoo aller birds. Bird Starver's Cry. *Unknown.* FaBoVe

Hi there. My name is George. Notes on the Peanut. June Jordan. NoAM

Hialmar Speaks to the Raven. Charles Marie René Leconte de Lisle, *French.* AWP, *tr. by* James Elroy Flecker

Hiatus. Margaret Avison. HAP

Hiawatha Revisited. George A. Strong. *See* The Modern Hiawatha.

Hiawatha's Photographing. "Lewis Carroll." BXAP; NOBL; PeLV

Hiawatha's Wooing. Henry Wadsworth Longfellow. EBNV *Fr.* The Song of Hiawatha.

Hibakusha's Letter (1955), The. David Mura. OpBo

Hibernia. Stuart Howard-Jones. NOBL

Hibernia's Helicon is dry. William Dunkin. NOEC *Fr.* An Epistle to Robert Nugent, Esq. with a Picture of Doctor Swift in Old Age.

Hibiscus, The. Nguyễn Trãi, *Vietnamese.* AVP, *tr. by* Huỳnh Sanh Thông

Hibiscus. Su Shih. SuSp, *tr. by* Irving Y. Lo On Chao Ch'ang's Flower Paintings in Wang Po-yang's Collection.

Hibiscus and Salvia Flowers. D. H. Lawrence. FaBoPV

Hibiscus Flowers. Li Shang-yin, *Chinese.* SuSp, *tr. by* Eugene Eoyang *and* Irving Y. Lo

Hibiscus is flaming and frillier. Limerick. Ruth Silcock. PeLi

Hibiscus on the Sleeping Shores. Wallace Stevens. InPS-3

Hibou et Minou allèrent à la mer. Le Hibou et la Poussiquette. Edward Lear. NYBP; PC, *tr. into French by* Francis Steegmuller

Hic, Hoc, the Carrion Crow. *Unknown.* OxBoLi

Hic jacet Tom Shorthose. *Unknown.* FaBoEE

Hic Vir, Hic Est. Charles Stuart Calverley. OxBoLi; PeLV

Hicche-Hykeres Tale, The. W. F. N. Watson. BXAP

Hiccups. Léon Damas, *French.* NegPo; PFTM, *tr. by* Ellen Conroy Kennedy

Hick-a-more, Hack-a-more. Sunshine. Mother Goose. OxNR; ReMoGo

Hickamore hackamore. Riddle. *Unknown.* FaBoVe

Hickery, dickery, 6 and 7. A Counting-out Rhyme. *Unknown.* ReMoGo

Hickety pickety i sillickety [*or* i-silicity]. *Unknown.* OxNR

Hickety, pickety, my black hen. The Black Hen. Mother Goose. BoTP; LB; OxNR; ReMoGo

Hickie, The. Liz Lochhead. LW

Hickory, dickory, dock. Mother Goose. FaBoBe; LB; OxNR; ReMoGo

Hid by the august foliage and fruit of the grape-vine. To a Chameleon. Marianne Moore. APo

"Hid! Hid!" the fish-hawk saith, fr. *the Chinese of the* Confucian Odes. Ezra Pound. APSN

Hid in a close and lowly nook. A City Garden W. S. Braithwaite. GT

Hid in its own shadow. Vasco [*or* Vasko] Popa. See The Adventure of the Quartz Pebble.

Hidden. Ron Silliman.

"Lucky my ears 'pop' at the hilltop." FTOS

Hidden. Tanka. Tsukamoto Kunio, *Japanese.* MJT, *tr. by* Makoto Ueda

Hidden beneath his hair. (LL) The Hairy Dog. Herbert Asquith. CTAV; CTV; PeP

Hidden by a minstrel-smile. (LL) Heritage. Gwendolyn B. Bennett. BlSi; ColAP; NAAAL; PoBA

Hidden dragons entice with their mysterious forms. Climbing the Tower by the Pond. Hsieh Ling-yün, *Chinese.* SuSp, *tr. by* Francis Westbrook

Hidden Essence. Henrietta Cordelia Ray. CBWP-3

Hidden Flame. Dryden. *See* Song: "I feed a flame within, which so torments me."

Hidden immortal. Near a Waterfall at Ryumon. Lady Ise, *Japanese.* BoWoP, *tr. by* Etsuko Terasaki *and* Irma Brandeis

Hidden in hidden rooms. Hide and Seek. Mudrooroo. BMAP

Hidden in wonder and snow, or sudden with summer. Laurentian Shield. Francis Reginald Scott. NOBC

Hidden language, not that of hands or eyes, a language beyond gesture. The Desert. Edmond Jabès, *French.* AF, *tr. by* Rosemarie Waldrop

Hidden Line, The. Joseph Addison Alexander. BLPA

Hidden lovers' woes. His Own True Wife. Wolfram von Eschenbach, *German.* AWP, *tr. by* Jethro Bithell

Hidden monastery garden, poppies, drowsy noontime, The. Siege. Dan Pagis, *Hebrew.* IP, *tr. by* Warren Bargad *and* Stanley F. Chyet

Hidden People and the Star People, The. *Unknown.* STP, *tr. by* Barbara Tedlock *Fr.* Ceremony of Sending.

Hidden strength, A. Chastity. Milton. *Fr.* Comus; a Masque Presented at Ludlow Castle. FHYEP; OAEL-1

Hide [*or* Hyd], Absalon, thy gilte tresses clere. Balade. Chaucer. AWP; EBEV; EnVB; GBL; HAP; ImPo; NOBE; OAEL-1; OBEV; SCGP *Fr.* The Legend of Good Women.

Hide, Absalon, thy gilte tresses clere. Chaucer. EnVB

Hide and Seek. Phyllis Drayson. BoTP

Hide and Seek. Robert Graves. KaS; NTCP

Hide and Seek. Mudrooroo. BMAP

Hide-and-Seek. Vasco [*or* Vasko] Popa. HSix, *tr. by* Charles Simic *Fr.* Games. RB, *tr. by* Anne Pennington

Hide and Seek. Vernon Scannell. NOxBChV

Hide and Seek. Sara Teasdale. NMM-2

Hide not thy love and myne shal bee. Pure Simple Love. Aurelian Townshend. SeCP

Hide not thy talent in the earth. The One Talent. William Cutler. PWR

Hide of My Mother, The. Edward Dorn. NeAP

Hide of the black cow is stretched, The. Jean-Joseph Rabéarivelo. PBMAP *Fr.* Traduits de la Nuit.

Hide this one night thy crescent, kindly Moon. To the Moon. Pierre de Ronsard, *French.* AWP, *tr. by* Andrew Lang

Hide Thou Me. *Unknown.* AmFP

Hideho Heights. Mu. Melvin Beaunearus Tolson. MoNo

Hideho Heights / and I, like the brims of old hats. The Harlem Gallery: Book I, The Curator. Melvin B. Tolson. PFTM *Fr.* The Harlem Gallery: Book I, The Curator.

Hideous hue which William is, The. Purple William or The Liar's Doom. A. E. Housman. CBNP; NOxBChV

Hideous laughter, The. Because the Wind Remembers. Frank Mkalawile Chipasula. HBAPE

Hidesong. Aig Higo. PBMAP; TTY

Hiding. Dorothy Aldis. ChAP

Hiding in the church of an abandoned stone. Confession to J. Edgar Hoover. James Wright. CAPP-1; CoAmPo

Hiding in the / cucumber garden. Vidya, *Sanskrit.* WPOW, *tr. by* W. S. Merwin *and* J. Moussaieff Masson

Hiding Place. Richard Armour. NIP-4

Hie Away, Hie Away. Sir Walter Scott. OxAEP-2 *Fr.* Waverley.

Hie, hie, says Anthony. Mother Goose. OxNR

Hie prudence, and wirking mervelous, the. The Preiching of the Swallow. Robert Henryson. EnVB; OxBS

Hie to the market, Jenny come trot. *Unknown.* OxNR

Hie upon Hielands [*or* High up on highland *or* High upon Highlands]. Bonnie [*or* Bonny] George [*or* James] Campbell. *Unknown.* AmFP; CH; ESPB; OxBB; OxBoLi; SCGP

Hiems. Shakespeare. *See* Winter.

Hierarchie of the Blessed Angells. Thomas Heywood. "Finnes and Laplands are acquainted well, The." OxBSn

Hierarchy. George Mackay Brown. FaBoTC *Fr.* Runes from a Holy Island.

Hieronymus Bosch. Pavel Grigoryevich Antokolsky, *Russian.* TCRP, *tr. by* Bernard Meares

Hiero's former Nurse. Dioscorides, *Greek.* GrAn, *tr. by* Peter Whigham

Hierusalem, my happy [*or* happie] home. *Unknown.* NOBE; OBEV; PeECV; PoEL-2; SCGP; TOF

Higgledy-piggledy / Andrea Doria. Last Words. John Hollander. OBAL

Higgledy-piggledy / Anna Karenina. The Russian Soul II. John Hollander. NBLV

Higgledy-piggledy / Archangel Raphael. Paradise Lost, Book V: An Epitome. Anthony Hecht. NBLV

Higgledy-piggledy, / Benjamin Harrison. Historical Reflections. John Hollander. OBAL; OBCoV

Higgledy-piggledy / Franklin D. Roosevelt. Danish Wit. John Hollander. NBLV

Higgledy, piggledy / Gloria Vanderbilt. Poor Kid. William Cole. OBAL

Higgledy-piggledy / Heliogabalus. Heliogabalus. John Hollander. NBLV; OBAL

Higgledy-Piggledy here we lie. Charade. *Unknown.* OxNR

Higgledy-piggledy / John Simon Guggenheim. No Foundation. John Hollander. OBAL; OBCoV

Higgledy-piggledy / Josephine Bonaparte. Appearance and Reality. John Hollander. OBAL

Higgledy-piggledy / Ludwig van Beethoven. Double Dactyls. E. William Seaman. OBCoV; WeW-3

Higgledy, piggledy, my black hen. Hickety, pickety, my black hen. Mother Goose. CTAV; FaBoBe; OxNR

Higgledy-piggledy / President Jefferson. Twilight's Last Gleaming. Arthur W. Monks. NIP-4

Higgledy-piggledy / Ralph Waldo Emerson. From the Grove Press. Anthony Hecht. OBAL; OBCoV

Higgledy-Piggledy / T. S. Eliot. Double Dactyl. Chris Wallace-Crabbe. OBCoV

Higgledy-piggledy / T. S. Eliot. Vice. Anthony Hecht. OBAL

Higglety, Pigglety, Pop! Samuel Griswold Goodrich. NOxBChV; OxNR

High above the lake a bomber flies. This Summer's Sky. Bertolt Brecht, *German.* PoSu, *tr. by* Michael Hamburger

High amid / gothic rocks the altar stands. Sub Specie Aeternitatis. Robert Earl Hayden. AmPP *Fr.* An Inference of Mexico.

High and proud on the barnyard. Chanticleer. John Chipman Farrar. CTV

High and solemn mountains guard Rioupéroux. Rioupéroux. James Elroy Flecker. OBEV

High as a star, yet lowly as a flower. Beauty. Madison Cawein. APN-2

High as the sky it flies. Riddle. *Unknown.* FaBoVe

High at the window in her cage. A Caged Bird. Sarah Orne Jewett. APN-2; ColAP

High autumn days. The Sad Birds. Harry Mathews. PmAP

High bare field, brown from the plough, and borne, A. The Potato Harvest. Sir Charles G. D. Roberts. NOBC

High-born Helen, round your dwelling. Helen. Mary Lamb. NOBRP

High Bridge above the Tagus River at Toledo, The. William Carlos Williams. CTC

High-Class Bananas, The. Gary Gildner. PBCAP

High Cliffs lashed by icy polar winds. Aleutian Islands. Blaise Cendrars, *French.* BLT, *tr. by* Monique Chefdor

High-coiffed the muse in green brocade. Remark. Charles Spear. PeNZ

High Country. Tim Thorne. BMAP

High Diddle Diddle. Mother Goose. CBNP; ReMoGo

High diddle ding, did you hear the bells ring?, *diff. vers.* The Parliament Soldiers. *Unknown.* OxNR

High diddle doubt, my candle's out. My Little Maid. *Unknown.* ReMoGo

High Dike. Li Ho, *Chinese.* PLT, *tr. by* A. C. Graham

High dome, The. Seamen's Mission. Gerald Dawe. PNI

High Fidelity. Thom Gunn. PoA

High Flight. John Gillespie Magee Jr. ImGa; PoWW; SAGP

High Germany. Edward Richard Burton Shanks. OBMV

High-hearted Surrey! I do love your ways. A Salutation. Louise Imogen Guiney. APN-2

"High heavenly priest of the White Lake" is now, The. Portrait of the Artist with Li Po. Charles Wright. ColAP

High Hills, The. Ivor Gurney. NTP

High, hollowed in green. The Quest. Denise Levertov. LW

High Holy Days. Jane Shore. NoP-4

High in the darkening heavens. Harriet Tubman aka Moses. Samuel Allen. ISC

High in the pine-tree. The Turtle-Doves' Nest. *Unknown.* BoTP

High in the woodland, on the mountain-side. The Ant-Heap. Arthur Christopher Benson. EBVV

High Island. Richard Murphy. CIP-2; NOIV

High June. Catherine A. Morin. BoTP

High King of Glory permit her to get the mange, The. (LL) A Glass of Beer. James Stephens. CMoP; InPK-6; MoBrPo; MoP; NBLV; OBCoV; OBMV; OxBS; OxBTC; PFE; RB

High King, wilt hear me plead? He Intercedes with Charlemagne for His Brother in Exile. Paul the Deacon, *Latin.* MLL, *tr. by* Helen Waddell

High-loping Cowboy, The. Curley W. Fletcher. AiP

High Midnight was garlanding her head, The. Moonlight. Jacques Tahureau, *French.* AWP, *tr. by* Andrew Lang

High Modes: Vision as Ritual: Confirmation. Michael S. Harper. NBV

High Noon at Los Alamos. Eleanor Wilner. NoP-4

High o'er his moldering castle walls. A Voice from the Invisible World. Goethe, *German.* AWP, *tr. by* James Clarence Mangan

High o'er the Hills. William Walker. AH

High on a mountain's highest ridge. Wordsworth. *Fr.* The Thorn. FaBoSe; Ro

High on a rock, coeval with the skies. The Temple of Chastity. Mary Robinson. Poetr

High on a throne of royal state, which far. Milton. OAEL-1, *ll.* 1–309; NIP-4, *ll.* 1–42 *Fr.* Book II. FHYEP; NAEL-1; OxAEP-1 *Fr.* Paradise Lost.

High on his brick cliff his garden hung. The Garden. John Hollander. GaP

High on his figured couch beyond the waves. Theseus and Ariadne. Robert Graves. HAP

High on his stockroom ladder like a dunce. Playboy. Richard Wilbur. MoP; NOBA; NoAM; SAGP

High on Nardil and June light. Wood Thrush. Jane Kenyon. BAP-93 *Fr.* Having It Out With Melancholy. BAP-93

High on some cliff, to heaven up-piled. William Collins. EPCY *Fr.* Ode on the Poetical Character.

High on the dove-cot. Doves. E. J. Falconer. BoTP

High on the mountain of sunrise where standeth the Temple of Sebek. He Knoweth the Souls of the West. *Unknown.* AWP *Fr.* Book of the Dead.

High on the upper, outermost bough. Sappho, *Greek.* InMo, *tr. by* Sam Hamill

High over Mecca Allah's prophet's corpse. Dissatisfaction with Metaphysics. William Empson. CMoP

High overhead. Thomas Edward Brown. NOBVV

High piled cumulus. Thomas A. Clark. NBrP *Fr.* Twenty Poems.

High pink wall; plaster in map shapes peeling, A. Blue Arm. Bernard Spencer. NoAM

High poetry and low. Wallace Stevens. PoA

High poets are gone, The. For the Family of Cuchonnacht O Dalaigh. David O'Bruadair, *Irish*. NOIV, *tr.* by Thomas Kinsella

High Priest, The. *Unknown, Hebrew*. TrJP, *tr.* by Arthur Davis

High Priests of telescopes and cyclotrons, The. Ode to Terminus. W. H. Auden. HAP

High Renaissance. George Starbuck. NBLV; OBAL

High Resolve. *Unknown*. PoToHe

High rock face above Flathead Lake, A. The Eye in the Rock. John Haines. PaTW

High Seas on the Caspian. Boris Petrovich Kornilov, *Russian*. TCRP, *tr.* by Bernard Meares

High sheriff tol' de deputy, "Go out an' bring me Laz'us." Poor Lazarus. *Unknown*. NAAAL

High Skip, The. *Unknown*. LB

High-speed metal snake switches its tail, A. The Chief of the West, Darkling. David Knight. MoCV

High-spirited friend, / I send not balms, nor corsives to your wound. An Ode. Ben Jonson. BeJo; OBEV

High Summer. Ebenezer Jones. NOBVV

High Summer on the Mountains. Idris Davies. OxBTC

High summer's sheen upon all things. The Web. Theodore Weiss. CoAP

High Talk. W. B. Yeats. CBNP; FaBoVe; RaBo

High tensile wire, when strained. Fencing. Anthony Lawrence. NOBAu

High the vanes of Shrewsbury gleam. The Welsh Marches. A. E. Housman. FaBoTw; SCGP

High tide. William J. Higginson. HA

High Tide. Jean Starr Untermeyer. MoAmPo

High Tide at Gettysburg, The. Will Henry Thompson. BLPA; CBCWP; FaBoBe

High Tide on the Coast of Lincolnshire, 1571, The. Jean Ingelow. EBVV; OxAEP-2

("Jetty, to the milking shed.") (LL) PEW

High time now gan it wex for Una faire. Edmund Spenser. FHYEP *Fr.* Wood Of Error. AEP

High to Low. Langston Hughes. HCAP; PoPoPo

High-toned Old Christian Woman, A. Wallace Stevens. CMoP; MoP; NAAL-2; NOBA; NoAM; Poetr; TAP

High-toned Old Fascist Gentleman, A. William Zaranka. BXAP

High up among the mountains, through a lovely grove of cedars. Bears. Arthur Guiterman. PoRA

High up, birches have a homely aspect. Stopping by Shadows. Robin Fulton. FaBoTC

High up in the courts of heaven today. A Little Dog-Angel. Norah M. Holland. PoLF

High up on a snowy peak. Ivan Alekseievich Bunin, *Russian*. TCRP, *tr.* by Simon Franklin

High upon the hillside where the shadows play. Skippets, the Bad One. Christine E. Bradley. BoTP

High walls and huge the body may confine. Freedom for the Mind. William Lloyd Garrison. FaBoBe

High waving heather'neath stormy blasts bending. Emily Jane Brontë. PEW

High Way to the Spital House, The. Robert Copland.

"To write of Sol in his exaltation." NoSic

High Wind at the Battery. Ralph Pomeroy. NYBP

High wind . . . They turn their backs to it, and push. Glasgow Schoolboys, Running Backwards. Douglas Dunn. OxBC

High Windows. Philip Larkin. FaBoMo; NAEL-2; NoAM; PoPoPo

High Wonders. Naomi Marks. BXAP

High Wood. Philip Johnstone. NSI; PoFWW

High / yellow / black / girl. To Anita. Sonia Sanchez. ISC

High-yellow of my heart, with breasts like tangerines. The Peasant Declares His Love. Emile Roumer, *French*. NegPo; TTY, *tr.* by John Peale Bishop

High Zero. Andrew Crozier.

"All of your ideas." NBrP

"All that it should be." NBrP

"In the time it takes." NBrP

"Then in the smoke." NBrP

Higher Argument. Milton. NOSC *Fr.* Book IX. FHYEP; NAEL-1; NAWM-1; OAEL-1 *Fr.* Paradise Lost.

Higher Empiricism, The. Francis C. Golffing. PoA

Higher Good, The. Theodore Parker. FaBoBe

Higher Pantheism, The. Tennyson. CABP; EnVR

Higher Pantheism in a Nutshell, The. Swinburne. BXAP; CABP; CBNP; EnVR; PeVV *Fr.* The Heptalogia.

Higher than a house, / Higher than a tree. Mother Goose. OxNR; ReMoGo

Highest Divinity. *Unknown, Hebrew*. TrJP, *tr.* by Israel Zangwill

Highest of Immortals bright. Indra, the Supreme God. *Unknown*. AWP *Fr.* Vedic Hymns.

Highest, omnipotent, good Lord. Canticle of Living Creatures. Saint Francis of Assisi. ItIP

Highest Sickness, The. Boris Pasternak, *Russian*. TCRP, *tr.* by Mark Rudman *and* Bohdan Boychuk

Highland Glen near Loch Ericht, A. Arthur Hugh Clough. *Fr.* Bothie of Tober-na-Vuolich, The [A Long-Vacation Pastoral].

Highland Harry Back Again. Robert Burns. EBEV

Highland lad my Love was born, A. Robert Burns. *Fr.* Love and Libery—A Cantata. NOBRP; NOEC

Highland Mary. Robert Burns. AWP; GTBS-P; OBEV; SAGP

Highland Mary. Mary Weston Fordham. CBWP-2

Highland Woman, A. Sorley MacLean. FaBoTC

Highlanders. Iain Crichton Smith. FaBoTC

Highlandmen hae a' come down, The. The Lady of Arngosk. *Unknown*. ESPB

Highly bored damsel called Brown, A. Limerick. *Unknown*. PeLi

Highty, tighty, paradighty, clothed [all] in green. Riddle. *Unknown*. OxNR

Highway, The. W. S. Merwin. PoA

Highway I was walking on, The. Charles Reznikoff. FTOS *Fr.* By the Well of Living and Seeing.

Highway is full of big cars, The. Come, And Be My Baby. Maya Angelou. OPOU

Highway, since you my chief Parnassus be. Sonnet 84. Sir Philip Sidney. OBEV; OxAEP-1; SCGP *Fr.* Astrophil and Stella. AAS; SiPS

Highwayman, The. Alfred Noyes. ChAP; EBEvV; EBNV; NOxBChV; NTP; OBNV; OBSP; PoLF; SAGP

Highwayman, The. *Unknown*. ECEV

Highwaymen, The. John Gay. *Fr.* The Beggar's Opera. OAEL-1

Hike on the Downs, A. John Betjeman. OBCoV

Hiking. Joseph Bruchac. CDW

Hiking a levee through the salt marsh. Wings and Seeds. Sandra McPherson. LoL

Hilaire Belloc. Humbert Wolfe. FaBoEE

Hilbert's Program. Milo De Angelis, *Italian*. NeIt, *tr.* by Lawrence Venuti

Hildegund eagerly urged him. Waldere 1. *Unknown, Anglo-Saxon*. ASW, *tr.* by Kevin Crossley-Holland

Hill, The. Rupert Brooke. MoBrPo; OxBTC; SAGP; Son

Hill, The. Robert Creeley. CRP; RaBo; TRP

("Like a hill.") (LL) CoAmPo

Hill, A. Anthony Hecht. CoAP; GEA; NYBP; NoP-4; VCAP

Hill, The. Edgar Lee Masters. CMoP; ColAP; FYAP; LiTM; NOBA; NoAM; OxBA; TAP *Fr.* Spoon River Anthology.

Hill-billy, hill-billy come to buy. Pedlar. Confucius. CTC; OBVE, *tr.* by Ezra Pound *Fr.* Wei Wind.

Hill (breeder) of Helicon. Catullus. *See* Carmen 61 ("Guardian of Helicon, Urania's son").

Hill Country. Olive Senior. HCP

Hill Daughter. Louise McNeill. MoLi

Hill Farmer Speaks, The. Ronald Stuart Thomas. GTBS-P; OBWVE

Hill full, a hole full, A. The Mist. *Unknown*. ReMoGo

Hill of Beans, A. Rita Dove. WWSi

Hill of the Graces, The. Spenser. NOBE *Fr.* Wood Of Error. AEP

Hill of Truth, The, *shorter vers*. Donne. *See* Satire 3.

Hill of Zion yields, The. Mount Zion. *Unknown*. AmFP

Hill-Side Park, The. W. H. Davies. OBGa

Hill Summit, The. D. G. Rossetti. NoP-4 *Fr.* The House of Life.

Hill Wife, The. Robert Frost. CMoP; HAP; InPS-3; LiTM; NoP-4; RACG

House Fear. NTP; VGW

Impulse, The. HoPM; RaBo

Loneliness. VGW

Oft-Repeated Dream, The. Poetr

Hillcrest. Edwin Arlington Robinson. MeMAP; OxBA

Hills, The. Frances Darwin Cornford. MoBrPo

Hills, The. D. H. Lawrence. ChIV-1

Hills, The. John Wills. HA

Hills afloat across the water are. Lamentation on Ninety-Mile Beach. Barry Mitcalfe. PeNZ

Hills and I would exchange qualities, The. Mask Series. Carol Snow. PUP-19

Hills and rivers of the lowland country, The. A Protest in the Sixth Year of Ch'ien Fu. Ts'ao Sung, *Chinese*. ChiP, *tr.* by Arthur Waley

Hills are white, but not with snow, The. An Orchard at Avignon. Agnes Mary Frances Robinson. NOBVV

Hills are wroth; the stones have scored you bitterly, The. To a Young Girl Leaving the Hill Country. Arna Bontemps. GT

Hills hunch their backs, The. A Fistful of News. Antoine-Roger Bolamba. PBMAP

Hills in emerald robes of richest dye, The. Among the Berkshire Hills. Henrietta Cordelia Ray. CBWP-3

Hills moved. I watched their shadows. Beetle on the Shasta Daylight. Shirley Kaufman. NYBP; WPE

Hills of God, Break Forth in Singing. John Wright Buckham. AH

Hills of Salt. Dahlia Ravikovitch, *Hebrew*. WPOW, tr. by Chana Bloch

Hills peep o'er hills, and Alps on Alps arise! (LL) Alps on Alps. Alexander Pope. EBEvV; HAP; HoPM; NOBE; PoLF, *ll*. 215–232

Hills picking up the / moonlight like. Nina Cassian, *Rumanian*. BoWoP, tr. by Stavros Deligiorgis

Hills sleep on in their eternity, The. (LL) To a Friend. Hartley Coleridge. FP; OBEV; OBNC; PoLF

Hills step off into whiteness, The. Sheep in Fog. Sylvia Plath. FaBoWP; HCAP; LCAP-2

Hills stirring under their woven, The. Goethe's Blues. Denise Levertov. FaBoWP

Hills turn hugely in their sleep, The. Robert Silliman Hillyer. MoAmPo *Fr*. Prothalamion.

Hills yet hills, and still the yellow town, The. Naples Again. Arthur Freeman. NYBP

Hillside Thaw, A. Robert Frost. CMoP

Hilltop, The. Richard Hugo. Poetr

Hilo: First Night Back. Garrett Kaoru Hongo. LoL

Him. Shoshone Wedding Song. Mary Austin, *Shoshone*. ITG, tr. by Robert Hass

Him, on the Bicycle. Bruce Weigl. CDa

Him rival to the gods I place. Catullus to Lesbia. Catullus. OBCVT, tr. by W. E. Gladstone

Him that I love I wish to be. Even. Anne Morrow Lindbergh. AiP

Him the Almighty Power. Satan Defiant. Milton. *Fr*. Book I. FHYEP; NAEL-1; OAEL-1; OxAEP-1 *Fr*. Paradise Lost.

("Orchid-lipped, loose-jointed, purplish, indolent.") EP

Himself. Edwin John Ellis.

"At Golgotha I stood alone." OBMV

Himself. Peter Fallon. PBCIP

Himself it was who wrote. Astræa. Ralph Waldo Emerson. APN-1

"Himself on the Wood there," says one. Cross Talk. Cyril Cusack. TIRV

Himselfe afoot before his weary'd bands. Cato in the desert. Lucan, *Latin*. OBCVT, tr. by Thomas May

Hind and the Panther, The. Dryden.

Confessio Fidei. NOBE

"Dame, said the Panther, times are mended well." PoEL-3

"One evening, while the cooler shade she sought." PoEL-3

"Portly prince, and goodly to the sight, A." OBSV

Presbyterians, The. NOSC

Hind Etin. *Unknown*. ESPB; OxBB

Hind Horn. *Unknown*. AmFP; ESPB

Hindoo: He Doesn't Hurt a Fly or a Spider Either, The. A. K. Ramanujan. OxBC

Hindu Cradle Song. Sarojini Naidu [or Nayadu]. BoTP

Hindu Sepoy in France. Rudyard Kipling. *Fr*. Epitaphs of the War [1914–1918]. OBWP

Hinge of the year, The. Nicholas Virgilio. HA

Hinged, sliding, folding or rotating structure, A. Seven Doors Away. Virginia Hooper. PT

Hinky Dinky, Parlee-Voo. *Unknown*. AS

Hint for the Incomplete Angler. Kendrick Smithyman. PeNZ

Hint from Voiture. William Shenstone. EnLoPo

Hinted Wish, A. Martial, *Latin*. AWP, tr. by Francis Lewis

Hinterland. Margaret Stanley-Wrench. OBGa

Hints from Horace. Byron.

"Peace to Swift's faults! his wit hath made them pass." EPCY

Power of song, The. OBCVT.

Hinty, minty, cuty, corn. *Unknown*. ImGa *Fr*. Counting-out Rhymes.

Hinx! minx! / The old witch winks! *Unknown*. OxNR

Hippo, The. Theodore Roethke. VGW

Hippodromania; or, Whiffs from the Pipe. Adam Lindsay Gordon. "Rest, and be thankful! On the verge." CBAP

Hippolytus. Euripides, *Greek*.

Chorus sing of escape, The. OBCVT, tr. by Hilda Doolittle

"No more, O my spirit." AWP, tr. by Hilda Doolittle

O for the Wings of a Dove. AWP, tr. by Gilbert Murray

"Oh Love! oh Love! whose shafts of fire." OBCVT, tr. by Thomas Love Peacock

Hippolytus. Seneca, *Latin*.

"Light griefs can speak." IMW

Hippolytus Temporizes. Hilda Doolittle. RACG

Hipponax. Alcaeus, *Greek*. GrAn, tr. by Alistair Elliot

Hippopotamothalamion. John Hall Wheelock. FYAP

Hippopotamus, The. Hilaire Belloc. InPK-6

Hippopotamus. Joanna Cole. NTCP

Hippopotamus, The. Georgia Roberts Durston. CTV

Hippopotamus, The. T. S. Eliot. AWP; CBNP; HoPM; ImPo; NAEL-2; OBMV; VGW

Hippopotamus had a bride, A. Hippopotamothalamion. John Hall Wheelock. FYAP

Hippopotamus is strong, The. Habits of the Hippopotamus. Arthur Guiterman. OBCA

Hipsaw! my deaa! you no do like a-me! *Unknown*. Fr. Dancing Songs. PBCV

Hiraeth. *Unknown, Welsh*. OBWVE, tr. by Aneirin Talfan Davies

Hiraeth in N.W.3. Wynford Vaughan-Thomas. NOBL

"Hiram, I think the sump is backing up." Mending Sump. Kenneth Koch. BXAP; InPK-6; MoP; NeAP; NoAM

Hiram Powers' "Greek Slave." Elizabeth Barrett Browning. GS; NALW

Hired Man's Faith in Children, The. James Whitcomb Riley. LiLi

Hired Man's Way, The. John Kendrick Bangs. OBCA

Hireling's wages to the priest are paid, A. Poet vs. Parson. Ebenezer Elliot. Son

Hiroona. Horatio Nelson Huggins. PBCV

Hiroshige. Mark Perlberg. NYBP

Hiroshima. "Agyeya," *Hindi*. OMIP, tr. by Agyeya and Leonard Nathan

Hirsute hell chimney-spouts, black thunderthroes. To My First White Hairs. Wole Soyinka. OPOU

His Age, Dedicated to His Peculiar Friend, Master John Wickes, under the Name of Posthumus. Robert Herrick. CaPo; SeCP

His all the mercy and the power. (LL) The Whale. Melville. APN-2; ChIV-1; KSG

His Ancestry. George Clinton Rowe. AAP *Fr*. Toussaint L'Overture.

His anchor, seaweed-probing, boat-securing. Philip of Thessalonica, *Greek*. GrAn, tr. by Edwin Morgan

His Answer. Clara Ann Thompson. BlSi; CBWP-2

His Answer to a Friend. Robert Herrick. CavPo

His Anthem, to Christ on the Cross. Robert Herrick. CavPo

His Apologies. Rudyard Kipling. CTAV

His Are the Thousand Sparkling Rills. Cecil Frances Alexander. TIRV

His armies love massacre. A King's Double Nature. Kākkai Pātiniyār Naccellaiyār. PLW, tr. by A. K. Ramanujan

His art is eccentricity, his aim. Pitcher. Robert Francis. OxBSP; RaBo; WeW-3

His artificial feet calumped in holy rhythm. Deacon Morgan. Naomi Long Madgett. BlSi

His baby cry. The Birth of Shaka. Mbuyiseni Oswald Mtshali. PBMAP

His ball, beautiful leaved, and his noisy boxwood rattle. Leonidas of Tarentum. HePo, tr. by Barbara Hughes Fowler *Fr*. Epigrams.

His balls: it sure was pleasant to spend a day in the country. (LL) Farm Implements and Rutabagas in a Landscape. John Ashbery. CBNP; CoAP; PmAP

His banquets cure most ills. Al-Lajjam al-Harrani, *Arabic*. ArPe, tr. by Omar S. Pound

His bare feet warmed by the thick black dust. Shelly Beach. Christopher Koch. NOBAu

His beak could open a bottle. Little Owl Who Lives in the Orchard. Mary Oliver. PuP-16

His being gone is a gift to my people. Wulf and Eadwacer. *Unknown*. BoWoP, tr. by Willis Barnstone and Elene Kolb

His best / were the two. My Father's Fights. Stuart Dybek. PBCAP

His bicycle stood at the window-sill. A Constable Calls. Seamus Heaney. FaBoPV; NOIV *Fr*. Singing School.

His black bony peasant body. Miranda. David Dabydeen. HCP

His black whiskers and his little dancing feet. Gerald Stern. *See* Behaving Like a Jew.

His blood's sweet current much more loud to be. (LL) Church-Lock and Key. George Herbert. ESCV; GeHe; OxBSP

His Body. Sandra McPherson. AmPA; LoL

His body doubled. On the Swag. Ronald Allison Kells Mason. PeNZ

His book and glasses on the kitchen table. (LL) Joseph Come Back as the Dusk. Franz Wright. CMAP; LCAP-2

His Boyhood. George Clinton Rowe. AAP *Fr*. Toussaint L'Overture.

His bride to the fair island. (LL) The Enchanted Island. Letitia Elizabeth Landon. CABP; NOBRP

His brother after dinner. Uncle Bull-Boy. June Jordan. PoBA

His brother calls to tell me. Bob Hosey Is Dead. Lloyd Davis. EC2

His Camel. Alqamah. *Fr.* The Mufaddaliyat. AWP, *tr.* by Sir Charles Lyall

His care-free swagger was a fine invention. W. H. Auden. CMoP *Fr.* Sonnets from China.

His case inspires interest. A Man of Words. John Ashbery. PoA

His cat Smut to lick. He wept, attempting to mas- / ter *ancilla* and *servus*. (LL) He adored the desk, its brown-oak inlaid with ebony. Geoffrey Hill. HAP; NoAM

His cauldrons seethe. This Man. G. S. Shivarudrappa, *Kannada.* OMIP, *tr.* by A. K. Ramanujan

His Cavalier. Robert Herrick. CaPo

    ("Ay! and a world of pikes pass through.") (LL) CavPo

His changing eyes. (LL) The Cat and the Moon. W. B. Yeats. APo; CMoP; CTAV; FaBoCh; TTTS; WHSW

His Children. Hittan of Tayyi. AWP *Fr.* Hamasah.

His children tuckered out, tucked in (three girls). Frost at Midnight. Mary Jo Salter. RA

His chosen comrades thought at school. What Then? W. B. Yeats. CMoP

His clumsy body is a golden fruit. Deaf-Mute in the Pear Tree. Patricia K. Page. NoAM; NoP-4; PoE

His collar is frayed, and his trousers unpressed. Shabby Old Dad. Anne Campbell. PoToHe

His comb was redder than the fine coral, *sels.* Chaucer. *Fr.* The Nun's Priest's Tale. FHYEP; NAEL-1; NAWM-1; OAEL-1 *Fr.* The Canterbury Tales.

His compassionate face, slightly wan. On the Street. Constantine P. Cavafy, *Greek.* BoLoP, *tr.* by Rae Dalven

His Content in the Country. Robert Herrick. CaPo; CavPo

His corpse below. (LL) Spirit of Plato. *Unknown, Greek.* OBCVT; AWP; OBVE, *tr.* by Shelley

His corpse owre a' the city lies. The Dead Liebknecht. "Hugh MacDiarmid." FaBoPV; OBVE

His corpse was returned. Captain James Leson, U. S. M. C. Bryan Alec Floyd. CDa

His country seared its conscience through its gain. William Lloyd Garrison. Joseph Cotter, Sr.. AAP

His Creed. Robert Herrick. BeJo

His cycle kerbed, the peeler found. Bigamy. Roy McFadden. PNI *Fr.* Memories of Chinatown.

His daughter Charlotte said to Mr. Brontë. Sampler from Haworth. Frances Minturn Howard. WPE

His Defence Against the Idle Critic. Michael Drayton. NOSC

His Depression. Patricia Dobler. CMAP

His Desire. Robert Herrick. OxBSP

His desires, growing. Black Man's Feast. Sarah Webster Fabio. PoBA

His dinner on the stove, Grandpa smirked at our jar. Leftover Blessings. Julia Kasdorf. PBCAP

His Discourse with Cupid. Ben Jonson. *Fr.* A Celebration of Charis in Ten Lyric[k] Pieces [*or* Peeces]. BeJo; OxAEP-1; SeCP

His dogs would follow him. They are pure. Hunter. Rosanna Warren. *Fr.* Funerary Portraits. NoAM

His Eccentricities. (LL) Bat is dun with wrinkled Wings, The. Emily Dickinson. APo; NCAP

His echoing axe the settler swung. The Settler. Alfred Billings Street. FaBoBe

His eldest son, Arradas' heir. His Boyhood. George Clinton Rowe. AAP *Fr.* Toussaint L'Overture.

His English stream so pure did flow. Sir John Denham. EPCY *Fr.* On Mr. Abraham Cowley, His Death and Burial amongst the Ancient Poets.

His Excuse for Loving. Ben Jonson. NOSC; PoEL-2 *Fr.* A Celebration of Charis in Ten Lyric[k] Pieces [*or* Peeces]. BeJo; OxAEP-1; SeCP

His eyes are green and his nose is brown. The King of the Hobbledygoblins. Laura Elizabeth Richards. OBCA

His eyes are quickened so with grief. Lost Love. Robert Graves. AWP; CBLP; CH; FaBoCh; LoP; MoBrPo

His eyes were so dilated. Georg Trakl. Else Lasker-Schüler, *German.* PFTM, *tr.* by Durchslag, Audri and Jeanette Litman-Demeestère

His face is streaked with prepared tears. The Clown. Janet Frame. PeNZ

His face is trodden deeper in the mud. (LL) Glory of Women. Siegfried Sassoon. NAEL-2; NoP-4; OBWP; OxAEP-2; PeFWW; PoFWW

His face not much older than mine. Finding a Chet Baker Album in the Dimestore 2-for-$1 Pile. David Hilton. MoNo

His face seems blinded. The Rondanini Pieta. Hilda Morley. FiLi

His face severe in clouds above the waters of childhood. Remembering My Father. Zbigniew Herbert, *Polish.* VCWP, *tr.* by John Carpenter and Bogdana Carpenter

His fair large front and eye sublime declared. Paradise. Milton. *Fr.* Book IV. OAEL-1 *Fr.* Paradise Lost.

His fame rose like a billow in the south. Elegy for Tru'o'ng Dịnh. Nguyễn Dình Chiểu, *Vietnamese.* AVP, *tr.* by Huỳnh Sanh Thông

His family roots are in the mountains. The Prosperous Villager. Li K'ai-hsien, *Chinese.* CoBLCP, *tr.* by Jonathan Chaves

His farces are physic; his physic a farce is. (LL) On Sir John Hill, M. D., Playwright. David Garrick. FaBoEE; NBLV

His Farewell [*or* Fare-well] to Sack. Robert Herrick. BeJo; CaPo; CavPo; NAEL-1; SeCP

His father and grandfather before him were coachmen. Birth of a Coachman. Paul Durcan. PBCIP

His father gave him a box of truisms. The Truisms. Louis MacNeice. IIP; NOBE; OBSV; PNI

His Father's Hands. Thomas Kinsella. PoE

His Feet are shod with Gauze. Emily Dickinson. SAmP

His Fingers Seem to Sing. Sam Cornish. GT

His fingers wake, and flutter; up the bed. Conscious. Wilfred Owen. NSI; PoWW

His first bullet is a present, a mark of intelligence that will. The Knee. Ciaran Carson. PNI

His flaggy wings when forth he did display. The Dragon. Edmund Spenser. *Fr.* Wood Of Error. AEP

His flaming *Rome,* and as it burn'd, he play'd. (LL) Of My Lady Isabella Playing on the Lute. Edmund Waller. HAP; SeCP

His footsteps in the room. Alexis Rotella. HA

His forehead was stamped with *Administrator / of the Great Mansion.* Imhotep. Yusef Komunyakaa. PUP-19

His foresworn life. Lady Ukon. *See* I am forgotten now.

His friend the watchman was still awake. A Leave-Taking. Arno Holz, *German.* AWP, *tr.* by Jethro Bithell

His friends he loved. His direst earthly foes. An Epitaph. Sir William Watson. FP; NOBVV

His gimpy leg was testimony to / some other surgeon's art. Old Doc. Mark Vinz. Poetsp

His glory and his monuments are gone. (LL) Meru. W. B. Yeats. GSo; NoAM; OAEL-2; PoA; PoPoPo

His golden locks time hath to siluer turn'd. A Farewell to Arms. George Peele. InPS-3; NIP-4; NOBE; NoSic; OBEV; OBWP; OxAEP-1; PoEL-2; PoRA; SCGP; TFi *Fr.* Polyhymnia.

His golden locks time hath to silver turned. George Peele. *See* A Farewell to Arms.

His Grace! impossible! what dead! A Satirical Elegy on the Death of a Late Famous General. Jonathan Swift. HoPM; NBLV; NoP-4; OBSV; PBMP; PFE; PoE; PoEL-3; Poetr

His Grange, or Private Wealth. Robert Herrick. BeJo; CaPo

    ("Though clock / To tell how night draws hence.") CavPo

HIS GRATEFUL OPPONENTS SET UP THIS STATUE OF APIS THE BOXER. Lucilius, *Greek.* GrAn, *tr.* by Peter Porter

His green eyes on the homestead of another man. The Snake. Andrew Suknaski. NOBC

His green garden's twytined digging fork. To Priapos. *Unknown, Greek.* GrAn, *tr.* by Guy Davenport

His hand came from the east. Homer. *See* Apollo Defeats Patroclus.

His hand came out of the east. Apollo Defeats Patroclus. Homer, *Greek.* OBVE, *tr.* by Christopher Logue *Fr.* The Iliad.

His Hand Shall Cover Us. Isaac ben Samuel of Dampière, *Hebrew.* TrJP, *tr.* by Nina Davis Salaman

His hands old edging out of time. Geraldine Monk. NBrP

His hat is rammed on. Near the School for Handicapped Children. Thomas William Shapcott. CBAP

His head appeared in the hand. Orpheus. John Kinsella. BMAP

His head like a fist rooted in his abdomen. The Agents. Robert Conquest. SPE

His head split in four parts. Promenade. David Ignatow. TrJP

His headstone said. The Funeral of Martin Luther King, Jr. Nikki Giovanni. BPo

His heart swells. Peyanar. PLW *Fr.* Seven Said by the Foster-Mother. PLW, *tr.* by A. K. Ramanujan

His heart, to me, was a place of palaces and pinnacles [and shining towers]. I Have Been Through the Gates. Charlotte Mew. MoBrPo; SAGP

His heart to the darkness and into the sadness of joy. (LL) First Song. Galway Kinnell. LiLi; LiTM; NoP-4; Poetr; TwCP

His heart unbiassed, and his mind his own. (LL) In gayer hours, when high my fancy ran. Richard Savage. NOEC; OBSV

His heart was in his garden; but his brain. Frederick Goddard Tuckerman. APN-2; NoP-4 *Fr.* Sonnets.

His high-boned, young face is so brown. White Pass Ski Patrol. John Logan. CAPP-1

His Hill. Kapilar, *Tamil.* PLW, *tr.* by A. K. Ramanujan

His holy / slowly / mulled over. Darwin. Lorine Niedecker. APSN

His Hope or Sheet-Anchor. Robert Herrick. CaPo

His Illness. Solomon ibn Gabirol, *Hebrew.* TOF, *tr.* by David Goldstein

His Immortality. Thomas Hardy. CMoP

His jacket, boots kept outside the holding cell. After Stroke. Bill Griffiths. NBrP

His kind velvet bonnet. The Cat. Dame Edith Sitwell. NTP

His kingdom is forever. (LL) Mighty Fortress Is Our God, A. Martin Luther, *German*. PWR, *tr. by* Frederick Henry Hedge; CTC, *tr. by* M. Woolsey Stryker; AWP, GePo

His Lady's Cruelty. Sir Philip Sidney. *See* Sonnet 31: "With how sad steps, O Moon, thou climb'st the skies!"

His Lady's Death. Pierre de Ronsard, *French*. AWP, *tr. by* Andrew Lang

His Lady's Eyes. Greville Fulke. *See* Caelica.

His Lady's Tomb. Pierre de Ronsard, *French*. AWP, *tr. by* Andrew Lang

His lamp, his bow, and quiver laid aside. Cupid Turned Plowman. Moschus, *Greek*. AWP, *tr. by* Matthew Prior

His last days linger in that low attic. The Old Jockey. Frederick Robert Higgins. OBMV; OxBTC

His last glimpse of the former wife. After Eden. James Simmons. PNI

His Last Request to Julia. Robert Herrick. CavPo

His last white eärms, an' they stood still. (LL) The Turnstile. William Barnes. CH; NOBVV

His left hand, in heat of noonday. Ann Griffiths, *Welsh*. WPoS, *tr. by* H. A. Hodges

His life is in the body of the living. The Soul and Body of John Brown. Muriel Rukeyser. CBCWP; MoAmPo

His lips move ceaselessly. The Humped Ox. Flavien Ranaivo, *French*. NegPo, *tr. by* Ellen Conroy Kennedy

His Litany to the Holy Spirit. Robert Herrick. BeJo; NOSC; PeECV; PoLF (Litany to the Holy Spirit.) OBEV

His little heart to cheer. (LL) Robin Redbreast. William Allingham. FaBoBe; OxBChV

His little one and his wife. (LL) Demon [*or* Daemon] Lover. *Unknown*. AmFP; ESPB; EnSB; HAP; OAEL-1; OxBB; UnPo; WeW-3

His living name. (LL) Epilogue: "Those blessèd structures, plot and rhyme." Robert Lowell. HCAP; NAAL-2; NoAM; NoP-4; PoPoPo; SAGP; VCAP

His logic unperturbed, exacting new. Metaphysician. Robert Fitzgerald. PoA

His look will flow like oil over us. (LL) Ank'hor Vat. Denis Devlin. BIrV; CIP-2; NOIV

His lordship's steed. Riding. William Allingham. OxBChV

His Lunch Bucket. Doug Cockrell. Poetsp

His Manhood. George Clinton Rowe. AAP *Fr.* Toussaint L'Overture.

His Mansion in the Pool. Emily Dickinson. OBAL

His master coming through the door. (LL) My Dog. John Kendrick Bangs. BLPA; FaBoBe

His Metrical Prayer. James Graham, Marquess of Montrose. ChIV-2; OxBS (On Himself, upon Hearing What Was His Sentence.) NOSC

His Metrical Vow. James Graham, Marquess of Montrose. OxBS (Epitaph on Charles I.) NOBE

His mind moves upon silence. (LL) Long-Legged Fly. W. B. Yeats. APAD; CMoP; FaBoMo; FaBoTw; InPS-3; LiTM; MoP; NAEL-2; NOBE; NoAM; NoP-4; PoE

His miracles abbreviated, *Lives of Saints*. St. Peregrinus' Cancer. Judith Hall. BAP-95

His Monument. Sarah Knowles Bolton. PWR

His most kind sister all his secrets knew. Repentance. George Chapman. *Fr.* Hero and Leander. AAS

His Mother. Haim Guri, *Hebrew*. IP, *tr. by* Warren Bargad *and* Stanley F. Chyet; MHP, *tr. by* Ruth Finer Mintz

His mother dear Cupid offended late. Sonnet 17. Sir Philip Sidney. *Fr.* Astrophil and Stella. AAS; SiPS

His mother weaves silk for a living. Morsel. Ali Sardar Jafri, *Urdu*. OMIP, *tr. by* Kathleen Grant Jaeger *and* Baidar Bakht

His mother wept so bitterly. The Mother of Judas. Yevgeny Mikhailovich Vinokurov, *Russian*. GI, *tr. by* Anthony Rudolf

His mother whisper my son my son. (LL) How Is He Coming Then. Lucille Clifton. CrSp; NALW

His Mother's Service to Our Lady. François Villon, *French*. AWP; CTC, *tr. by* D. G. Rossetti

His Mother's Wedding Ring. George Crabbe. *See* The Marriage Ring.

His moving likeness on the page. (LL) Lens. Anne Wilkinson. MoCV; NOBC

His naked skin clothed in the torrid mist. The Serf. Roy Campbell. GTBS-P; MoBrPo; OBMV

His Name, and when they do't be most my Joys. (LL) Hosanna. Thomas Traherne. ChIV-2; PoEL-2

His name is Jason, he's. Stud. Michael Lassell. GLP *Fr.* Times Square Poems.

His name is / Rubin. Rubin. Charles Cooper. PoBA

His name was Chance, Jack Chance, he said. Ballad of a Strange Thing. Howard Phelps Putnam. OxBA

His Necessary Darkness. Nancy Sullivan. TAP

His nights in the aunts' house, their talk and tea. A Provincial Adolescence. Michael Foley. PNI

His nose is short and scrubby. My Dog. Marchette Chute. ImGa; WHSW

His Offering, with the Rest, at the Sepulcher. Robert Herrick. ChIV-2

His old age fell on years of abundant harvest. A Felicitous Life. Czeslaw Milosz, *Polish*. PoSu, *tr. by* Czeslaw Milosz *and* Lillian Vallee

His only beauty to be / all moose. (LL) Poetry, a Natural Thing. Robert Duncan. NOBA; NoAM; PmAP; TRP

His overalls hung on the hook by his hat, and I noticed. Treasures. Claire Richcreek Thomas. PoToHe

His Own Epitaph. Robert Herrick. CaPo

His Own Epitaph, When He Was Sick. John Hoskyns. FaBoEE

His Own True Wife. Wolfram von Eschenbach, *German*. AWP, *tr. by* Jethro Bithell

His pads furring the scarp's rime. The Snow-Leopard. Randall Jarrell. APo; LiTM; TwCP

His pains so racked my heart. Sympathy. Viola Meynell. LW

His palms spotless. What She Said to Him, after Meeting His Concubine. Cakalacanar, *Tamil*. PLW, *tr. by* A. K. Ramanujan

His paper propped against the electric toaster. Daniel at Breakfast. Phyllis McGinley. OBSV; OxBM

His Parting from Her. Donne. EBEV *Fr.* Elegies.

His pendulous body tolled. A Hanging, Zomba Central Prison. Frank Mkalawile Chipasula. PeSAV

His pendulous stomach hangs a-shaking. (LL) Wagner. Rupert Brooke. FaBoTw; NOBL; PeLV

His Petition to Mr. Speaker. James Carkesse. CBNP

His Petition to Queen Anne of Denmark (1618). Sir Walter Ralegh. SiPS

His Picture. Donne. FSCP; PBRV *Fr.* Elegies. (Elegie V: His Picture.) MeLP; OxAEP-1

His piercing pince-nez. Some dim frieze. Sonnet I. Ted Berrigan. FTOS *Fr.* The Sonnets.

His Pilgrimage. Sir Walter Ralegh. *See* The Passionate Man[']s Pilgrimage.

His place, as he sat and as he thought, was not. A Quiet Normal Life. Wallace Stevens. NAAL-2; NoAM

His place is before, not in, the National Gallery. London Pavement Artist. James Schevill. TAP

His Plans for Old Age. William Meredith. TAP

His plumage is dun. Jailbird. Vernon Scannell. OxBC

His poems, yellow, torn and fading. Langston Hughes. Lew Blockcolski. VoR

His Poetry His Pillar. Robert Herrick. BeJo; CaPo; NOSC; SeCP

His pole and paddle have been with him a long time. Chang Yü. *Fr.* Paintings. CoBLCP, *tr. by* Jonathan Chaves

His poor mother gives Mikythos'. Leonidas of Tarentum, *Greek*. PGA, *tr. by* Kenneth Rexroth

His power to maintain. Mother Goose. *See* The Lion and the unicorn.

His Praises. Swidi-Nonkamfela Mhlongo, *Zulu*. PeSAV, *tr. by* Elizabeth Gunner

His praises hymned in Masses by throaty Russian priests. Paul the First. Pavel Grigoryevich Antokolsky, *Russian*. TCRP, *tr. by* Bernard Meares

His Prayer for Absolution. Robert Herrick. BeJo; CavPo

His Prayer to Ben Jo[h]nson. Robert Herrick. BeJo; CaPo; NAEL-1; NoP-4; NOSC; OxBSP; OxBoLi; PeLV

His pride / Had cast him out from Heaven, with all his host. Satan. Milton. *Fr.* Book I. FHYEP; NAEL-1; OAEL-1; OxAEP-1 *Fr.* Paradise Lost.

His Prime. George Clinton Rowe. AAP *Fr.* Toussaint L'Overture.

His Promise. Aaron Shurin. FTOS

His red-hot words can cauterize. (LL) Go softly past the graveyard where. Leonidas of Tarentum, *Greek*. GrAn; OBCVT, *tr. by* Fleur Adcock

His Remedie for Love. Michael Drayton. AAS *Fr.* Idea.

His Request. Owen Roe O'Sullivan, *Irish*. BIrV, *tr. by* Joan Keefe

His Request to Julia. Robert Herrick. BeJo; CaPo; CavPo; NOSC

His rest, and on his lips their honey made. (LL) Love Sleeping. Plato, *Greek*. AWP; FaBoEE, *tr. by* Thomas Stanley

His Return to London. Robert Herrick. BeJo; CaPo; NAEL-1

His role is to invert the fairy tale. Psychiatrist. Peter De Vries. OBAL

His Rule of Behaviour: If You Are Civil, I Am Sober. James Carkesse. NOSC

His sad and usual heart, dry as a winter leaf. (LL) Aspects of Robinson. Weldon Kees. CoAP; NYBP

His Sailing from Julia. Robert Herrick. PoEL-3

His Saviour['] Words, Going to the Cross[e]. Robert Herrick. ChIV-2; NOCV

His shadow monstrous on the palace wall. Oedipus. Thomas Blackburn. FaBoTw

His Shield. Marianne Moore. LiTM; NALW

His shoulder did I hold. Any Saint. Francis Thompson. MoBrPo

His silent laugh still shakes the hills at dawn. (LL) Small grey cloudy louse that nests in my beard, The. James Keir Baxter. NoP-4

His sins were scarlet, but his books were read. (LL) On His Books. Hilaire Belloc. FaBoEE; MoBrPo; NBLV; OxBoLi; WeW-3

His sister named [or called] Lucy O'Finner. Limerick. "Lewis Carroll." PeLi

His snout intimate with / worms and leaves. (LL) Coins handsome as Nero's; of good substance and. Geoffrey Hill. FaBoMo; HAP; NoAM

His Son. Callimachus, Greek. AWP, tr. by G. B. Grundy

His son! His son! His son! (LL) Rundown Church (Ballad of the First World War). Federico García Lorca, Spanish. AF, tr. by Robert Bly; RaBo

His Son's / A Jew. Unknown. OBCoV

His soul is gone aloft. (LL) Poor Tom. Charles Dibdin. NOEC; OxAEP-1; OxBoLi

His soul is with the saints, I trust. (LL) The Knight's Tomb. Coleridge. FaBoCh; RB

His soul stretched tight across the skies. T. S. Eliot. Fr. Preludes (I–IV). HeIP-4; OBMV; Poetr; TwCP; UnPo; VGW; WeW-3

His sovereignty is o'er my gathered throng. Kalonymos ben Moses of Lucca. TrJP, tr. by Nina Davis Salaman

His speculation he regretted. I Want a Tenant; a Satire. John O'Keefe. NOEC

His Spirit in smoke ascended to high heaven. The Lynching. Claude McKay. ColAP; CrDW; GT; PoBA

His stars eternally. (LL) Drummer Hodge. Thomas Hardy. AWP; EBEV; GTB3-P; HAP; InPS-3; MoP; NAEL-2; NOBVV; NoAM; NoP-4; OBWP; OxAEP-2; PeFWW; Poetr; WeW-3

His startled life with lead, and all went out. (LL) A Working Party. Siegfried Sassoon. AF; PoFWW

His stature was not very tall. The Description of Sir Chaucer. Robert Greene. CTC; FaBoCh; NoSic; SCGP Fr. Greene's Vision.

His Story. Sandra Cisneros. MoLi

His sullen kinsmen, by the winter sea. Santa Claus. Dom Moraes. NoAM

His sun went down in the morning. Our Ernest. "Elmo." PWR

His sun's arms and grappling. Isaac: a Poise. Peter Cole. ChIV-1

His tale anon, and seyde in this manere. (LL) The General Prologue. Chaucer. FHYEP; OAEL-1; PoE

His tale anoon, and saide as ye may heere. (LL) The General Prologue. Chaucer. NoP-4

His teare-wet Feet still drying with her Haire. (LL) For the Magdalene. William Drummond, of Hawthornden. ChIV-2; PoEL-2

His Tears to Thamesis [or Thamasis]. Robert Herrick. NOSC

His theme / over and over. Williams: An Essay. Denise Levertov. InPS-3; PmAP

His Throne Is with the Outcast. James Russell Lowell. TrCP

His tongue out with its fork. (LL) Eve. Christina Rossetti. CH; ChIV-1; GTBS-P; NALW; NIP-4; PoEL-5; Poetr

His trousers are wind. Song to a Lover. Unknown, Amharic. BoWoP, tr. by Willis Barnstone

His twelve-year-old / son. Callimachus, Greek. GrAn, tr. by Peter Jay

His Uncle came on Franklin Hyde. Franklin Hyde. Hilaire Belloc. NBLV

His vast frame splayed on an uneasy chair. Confrontation with an Artist. Elisabeth Eybers. PeSAV

His vision, from the constantly passing bars. The Panther. Rilke, German. APo; PiM, tr. by Stephen Mitchell

His vision from the passing by of bars. Rilke. See The Panther.

His voice rings loud and carries far. The Village Crier. Unknown, Vietnamese. AVP, tr. by Huỳnh Sanh Thông

His voice / went on / and on / through the leaves. Lawrence Ferlinghetti. See Pound at Spoleto.

His waiting becomes a time to hear thoughts, the sound. Picture of a Japanese Farmer, Woodland, California, May 20, 1942. Jim Mitsui. OpBo

His was a house in which the father drank. O Hero. Eve Shelnutt. CMAP

His was the first corpse I had ever seen. My Wicked Uncle. Derek Mahon. OxBC

His was the mastery of life. Conscientious Objector. Edward Davison. NSI

His Welcome. Auvaiyar, Tamil. PLW, tr. by A. K. Ramanujan

His whiskers didn't come, his mustache is gone. A Mustacheless Bard. J. Gordon Coogler. OBAL

His Wife. Shirley Kaufman. LCAP-2

His Wife. "Rachel," Hebrew. WPOW, tr. by Sholom J. Kahn

His wife looked it up in her dream book / and played it. (LL) Hope. Langston Hughes. APSN; OBAL; PFTM

His wife nods, and a secret smile. James Fenton. See A German Requiem.

His wife, that he may live. . (LL) A Reasonable Affliction. Matthew Prior. NBLV; NOEC

His wild heart beats with painful sobs. The Happy Warrior. Sir Herbert Read. NSI; PeFWW

His Winding-Sheet. Robert Herrick. CaPo; OBEV

His words were magic and his heart was true. Uncle Ananias. Edwin Arlington Robinson. MoAmPo; NIP-4

His work was done; his blessing lay. The Death of Moses. Frances Ellen Watkins Harper. AAP Fr. Moses: A Story of the Nile.

Hisperica Famina. Jack Spicer. CBNP

Hiss, hiss—the north wind blows. Commiserating with the Poor. Li K'ai-hsien, Chinese. CoBLCP, tr. by Jonathan Chaves

Hiss of flame before earth, The. H ear t h. Janet Sutherland. NBrP

Hissed offstage / mocked by the batteries. Ode on the Revolution. Vladimir Mayakovsky, Russian. TCRP, tr. by Daniel Weissbort

Hist, but a word, fair and soft! Master Hugues of Saxe-Gotha. Robert Browning. OAEL-2

Hist   whist / little ghostthings. E. E. Cummings. NOxBChV

Histoire. Harry Mathews. NIP-4; PmAP

    ("Revealed glory of sexism.") (LL) NoP-4

Historic Moment, An. William J. Harris. KaS

Historic, side-long, implicating eyes. La Gioconda. "Michael Field." ADE; CABP

Historical Judas, The. Howard Nemerov. NoP-4; Poetr

Historical Museum, Manitoulin Island. Lisel Mueller. PoA

Historical Reflections. John Hollander. OBAL; OBCoV

Historie of Squyer William Meldrum, The. Sir David Lindsay. Squire Meldrum at Carrickfergus. OxBS

Historiography. Lorenzo Thomas. MoNo; SeSe

Historiotherapy. Martin Sorescu, Romanian. CEEP, tr. by Andrei Banta

History. Kelly Cherry. FFC

History. G K. Chesterton. OBSV Fr. Songs of Education.

History. Rita Dove. FFC; NAAAL Fr Mother Love.

History. Ralph Waldo Emerson. APN-1

History. Robert Fitzgerald. FYAP

History. Arthur Gregor. TAP

History. D. H. Lawrence. RaBo

History. James Liddy, Irish. CIP-2

History. James Liddy. CIP-2 Fr. Love Songs of Corca Bascinn.

History. Herberto Padilla, Spanish. AF, tr. by Alastair Reid

History. Gary Soto. PBCAP

History. Unknown. ACTP

History among the Rocks. Robert Penn Warren. CBCWP; MoAmPo Fr. Kentucky Mountain Farm.

History and Abstraction. Thomas Lux. AmPA

History and Reality. Stephen Spender. HP

History as Apple Tree. Michael S. Harper. AFr

History as Decoration. Rosanna Warren. DiPo

History Books. Thomas Lux. PUP-20

History Classes. Tony Harrison. Fr. The School of Eloquence. NAEL-2; NoAM

History during Nocturnal Snowfall. Robert Penn Warren. DiPo

History has to live with what was here. Robert Lowell. ColAP; HCAP; TAP; VCAP

History Lesson, A. Miroslav Holub, Czech. PoSu; RB, tr. by George Theiner

History Lesson. Mark Van Doren. NYBP

History Lessons. Seamus Deane. BiHa; PBCIP; PNI

History Makers. George Campbell. PBCV

History Myth of the Coming of the A'shiwi as Narrated by 'Kiäklo. Zuni Oral Tradition.

    "Following their road of exit, they stooped over and came out." APN-2, tr. by Matilda Coxe Stevenson

History of a Literary Movement. Howard Nemerov. PoE

History of blacklife is put down in the motions, The. The Sound of Afroamerican History Chapt I. S. E. Anderson. PoBA

History of Civilization, A. Albert Goldbarth. HCAP

History of Costume, A. Michelle Cliff. OxWW

History of Education. David McCord. OBAL

History of Ideas. James Vincent Cunningham. NIP-4; VCAP

History of Lesbianism, A. Judy Grahn. GLP

History of Love, A. William Carlos Williams. VGW

History of my feeling for you (or is it the way you change), The. Kathleen Fraser. CrSp

History of Navigation, A. Nancy Eimers. BAP-96

History of New Mexico. Gaspar Pérez De Villagrá, Spanish.

"World has no such pleasing joy, The." PaTW, *tr. by* Miguel Encinias, Alfred Rodríguez, *and* Joseph P. Sánchez

History of Paisley, A. Agha Shahid Ali. PUP-20

History of Poetry, The. Peter Cooley. NAmP90

History of the Flood, The. John Heath-Stubbs. MoBS; NOxBChV; NTP; UxBTC

History of the Lyre, A. Letitia Elizabeth Landon. VWP

History of Truth, The. W. H. Auden. FaBoMo

History of World Languages. D. J. Enright. OxBC

History she (Zelda) said stops here. Inside History. Angela McCabe. AmPA

History, the angel, was stirred. Northern Ireland: Two Comments. Seamus Deane. CIP-2

History theirs whose language is the sun. (LL) An Elementary School Classroom in a Slum. Stephen Spender. FaBoMo; MoBrPo; TwCP; UnPo

Hit betidde somtime in the termes of Judé. Unknown. EnVB *Fr.* Patience.

Hit me! Jab me! Third Degree. Langston Hughes. BPo

Hit wes upon a Scere-thorsday that vre louerd aros. Judas. Unknown. ESPB

Hitch Haiku. Gary Snyder. LCAP-2

"After weeks of watching the roof leak." InPK-6; KaS

"They Didn't Hire Him." Poetr

Hitchcock Blue. Lucie Brock-Broido. EOEF

Hitchhiker. Jack Marshall. NYBP

Hitchhikers, The. Diane Wakoski. NoAM

Hither, Ardelia, I your steps pursue. Some Reflections. Anne Finch, Countess of Winchilsea. ChIV-1

Hither at Death all mortal Minds descend. Punishment in Hell. Claudian, *Latin.* OBCVT, *tr. by* Jabez Hughes

Hither, O captives, hither let you come. Boethius, *Latin.* MLL, *tr. by* Helen Waddell *Fr.* Consolation of Philosophy, The ("De Consolacione Philosophie").

Hither the heroes and the nymphs resort. Alexander Pope. ECEV *Fr.* The Rape of the Lock. FHYEP; HAP; ImPo; OAEL-1; OBNV; PeLV; PoEL-3

Hither thou com'st: the busy [*or* busie] wind all night. The Bird. Henry Vaughan. ESCV; GeHe; OBEV; PoE; PoEL-2

Hither We Come, Our Dearest Lord. Enoch W. Freeman. AH

Hither, where tangled thickets of the acacia. The Babiaantje. Frank Templeton Prince. MoBrPo

Hitler Speaks. Helen Waddell. MLL

Hit's a mighty fur ways up de Far'well Lane. My Honey, My Love. Joel Chandler Harris. FaBoBe *Fr.* Uncle Remus and His Friends.

Hittites, The. Roy Fuller. OxBSP

Hitty Pitty within the wall. Unknown. OxNR

Hmmmm. Leslie Scalapino.

"How can I help myself, as one woman said to me about wanting." DeD

Ho, all you cats in all the street. Cat's Meat. Harold Monro. OBMV

Ho, boys, ho! for California, O! The Banks of Sacramento. Unknown. AS

Ho! brother [*or* broder] Teague, dost hear de decree. Lilli Burlero [*or* Lilliburlero]. Thomas Wharton. NOIV; OxBoLi

Ho! Cupid calls, come Lovers, come. Cupid's Call. James Shirley. BeJo; NOSC

Ho, everyone that thirsteth. A. E. Housman. ChIV-1; OAEL-2

Ho, for the Pirate Don Durk of Dowdee! The Pirate Don Durk of Dowdee. Mildred Plew Meigs. ChAP

Ho, Giant! This is I! The Bean-Stalk. Edna St. Vincent Millay. NOxBChV

Ho Ho Ho Caribou. Joseph Ceravolo. PmAP

("Never / stop!") (LL) FTOS

Ho, Moeris! Whether on thy way so fast? Lycidas and Moeris. Virgil. AWP, *tr. by* Dryden *Fr.* Eclogues.

Ho, my little sparrow! For well I know. "Hugh MacDiarmid." FaBoTC

Ho! Persephone brings flowers, to them. The Old Men. Irving Feldman. TwCP

"Ho[o]!" quod the Knyght, "good sir[e], namo[o]re of this!" Chaucer. *See* The Nun's Priest's Prologue.

'Ho!' said the child, 'how fine the horses go'. The Mother. Dora Sigerson Shorter. VWP

"Ho, sailor of the sea!" "How's My Boy?" Sydney Thompson Dobell. CH

Ho, why dost thou shiver and shake. Gaffer Gray. Thomas Holcroft. NOEC; OxAEP-1

Hoar-Frost. Amy Lowell. ColAP

Hoar frost has congealed. Along the Grand Canal. Ch'in Kuan, *Chinese.* BLT, *tr. by* Kenneth Rexroth

Hoar with salt-sleet and chalkings of the birds. (LL) Sometimes I walk where the deep water dips. Frederick Goddard Tuckerman. APN-2; NOBA; PAR

Hoardings screened the landscape from his sight. The Copy-writer's Dream. Bruce Dawe. BMAP

Hoarse with fulfillment, I never made promises. (LL) Noah's Raven. W. S. Merwin. ChIV-1; HCAP

Hoatchunk' Narwoanar, or Winnebago War Song. Unknown, Winnebago Native American. APN-2, *tr. by* Caleb Atwater

Hob Gobbling's Song. James Russell Lowell. OBCA

Hob, shoe, hob; hob, shoe, hob. Unknown. OxNR

Hob the Elf. Norman M. Johnson. BoTP

Hob upon a Holiday ("Hob yawned three times and rubbed his eyes"). Unknown. NOEC

Hobart Town, Van Diemen's Land (11th June, 1837). Hal Porter. NOBAu

Hobbes clearly proves that every creature. Critics. Jonathan Swift. HAP; SCV *Fr.* On Poetry: a Rhapsody. OBSV

Hobbinol. William Somervile.

On the Village Green. ECEV

Hobie [*or* Hobbie] Noble. Unknown. ESPB; IBB; OxBB

Hobnelia seated in a dreary Vale. Thursday; or, The Spell. John Gay. PoEL-3 *Fr.* The Shepherd's Week.

Hoboken was the first stop. Homegoing. Brigitte Frase. LoHo

Hobson has supt, and's newly gon to bed. (LL) On the University Carrier Who Sick'n'd [*or* Sickened] in the Time of His Vacancy [, Being Forbid to go to London, by Reason of the Plague]. Milton. EBEV; FaBoCh; FaBoEE; NOSC; OxAEP-1

Hoc Est Corpus. Alex Comfort. LiTM

Hoccleve's Complaint. Thomas Hoccleve.

"After that harvest inned had his sheves." EnVB

Hock-Cart, or Harvest Home, The. Robert Herrick. BeJo; CaPo; EBEV; FaBoPV; NAEL-1; NOSC; OxAEP-1; SeCP

Hockney: Blue Pool. David Trinidad. WWSi

Hoddley, poddley, puddle and fogs. Unknown. OxNR

Hoddy doddy. Unknown. OxNR

Hoeing. Gary Soto. PBCAP

Hog at the Manger. Norma Farber. PChr

Hog Butcher for the World. Chicago. Carl Sandburg. AiP; AmPP; CMoP; ColAP; FaBoA; LiTM; MoAmPo; MoP; NAAL-2; NOBA; NoAM; NoP-4; OxBA; PoA; Poetr; SAGP; TAP; TFi; TRP; UnPo; VGW

Hog Drovers. Unknown. AmFP

Hog-Eye. Unknown. AS

Hog-Eye Man, The. Unknown. AS

Hog, the Sheep and Goat, Carrying to a Fair, The. Anne Finch, Countess of Winchilsea. ECWP

Hogamous, higamous. William James. OxBM

Hogger on his death-bed lay, A. The Dying Hogger. Unknown. AS

Hogwash. Robert Francis. LCAP-2; NIP-4; TRP

Hogyn cam to bowers dore. Unknown. MiEL

Hohenlinden. Thomas Campbell. CABP; CH; FaBoCh; FaPoR; GTBS-P; NOBE; NOBRP; OBNC; OBWP; TFi

Hoise up the sail, cried they who understand. A Sea-Voyage from Tenby to Bristol. Katherine Philips. WPE

Hoist up and I could lean over, A. The Bull Moses. Ted Hughes. Poetr

Hoist your burdens, get on down the road. (LL) Gravelly Run. A. R. Ammons. CoAP; NAAL-2; NoAM; PoA; VCAP

Hoisting the tuba, like a golden. Strolling Musicians. Nikolai Alekseievich Zabolotsky, *Russian.* TCRP, *tr. by* Daniel Weissbort

Hokey, pokey, whisky, thum. Unknown. OxNR

Hokku: In the Falling Snow. Richard Wright. *Fr.* Hokku Poems. PoBA

Hokku Poems. Richard Wright. PoBA

Hold a baby to your ear. Conch. Elwyn Brooks White. LiLi

Hold, are you mad? you damned [*or* damn'd] confounded dog. Epilogue to Tyrannic[k] Love. Dryden. OBCoV *Fr.* Tyrannic Love.

Hold back the hand that works the mill. A Water-mill. Antipater of Thessalonica, *Greek.* GrAn, *tr. by* Alistair Elliot

Hold back thy hours. Song: "Hold back thy hours, dark night, till we have done." Francis Beaumont *and* John Fletcher. OxBSP *Fr.* The Maid's Tragedy.

Hold Fast Your Dreams. Louise Driscoll. BLPA; ChAP; FaBoBe

Hold hard, Ned! Lift me down once more, and lay me in the shade. The Sick Stockrider. Adam Lindsay Gordon. CBAP

Hold high the woof, dear friends, that we may see. On a Piece of Tapestry. George Santayana. APN-2

Hold, Hold. T. Alan Broughton. CMAP

Hold, hold it tight. Song for a Girl on Her First Menstruation. Unknown, Boikin. BoWoP, *tr. by* Joe Prentuo

Hold, hold your hand, hold; mercy, mercy, spare. A Sonnet on Sir William Alexander's Harsh Verses after the English Fashion. James I, King of England. Son

Hold it up sternly—see this it sends back, (who is it? is it you?). A Hand-Mirror. Walt Whitman. NAAL-1; NAAL-3; OxBA; PoPoPo

Hold my rooster, hold my hen. *Unknown.* FaBoVe; TTY

Hold not your lips so close; dispense. Kiss, The 1656. To Mrs. C. Thomas Shipman. NOSC

Hold of the land. (LL) Battle of Brunanburh. *Unknown, Anglo-Saxon.* CABP; OBVE; OBWP; PeVV, *tr. by* Tennyson

"Hold the horse's head" the farmer said. The Horse's Head. Brendan Kennelly. CIP-2

Hold the pen close to your ear. The Thin Prison. Leslie Norris. OTCP

Hold them now, Earth, now hand of man cannot. The Last Survivor's Speech. *Unknown.* NAEL-1, *tr. by* Alfred David *Fr.* Beowulf. OAEL-1, *tr. by* Charles W. Kennedy; ASW, *tr. by* Kevin Crossley-Holland

Hold til there is not a breath to / take. Rite-ing. Ntozake Shange. MoNo

Hold up the universe, good girl. Hold up. Good Girl. Molly Peacock. FFC

Hold up your head. *Unknown.* OxNR

"Hold your hand, Lord Judge," she says. The Maid Freed from the Gallows. *Unknown.* ESPB

Holding a jug of wine among the flowers. Drinking Alone under Moonlight. Li Po, *Chinese.* TAL, *tr. by* Robert Payne

Holding black whips. Thoughts of Chairman Mao. David Young. AmPA

Holding Hands. Lenore M. Link. FPC; NTCP

Holding his gaze. Alexis Rotella. HA

Holding its huge life open to the sky. To My Friends. Stephen Berg. NYBP

Holding the arm of his helper, the blind. The Visitor. Gibbons Ruark. MT

Holding the feathered dancing string. Koel (Rainbird) and Effigy. *Unknown, Aborigine.* NOBAu, *tr. by* Mungayana Nundhirribala

Holding the Mirror Up to Nature. Howard Nemerov. PoA

Holding the Sky. William Stafford. GM

Holding the water. William J. Higginson. HA

Holding you. Anita Virgil. HA

Hole, The. Robert Creeley. FTOS

Hole. Leonard Nathan. PBCAP

Hole in the Floor, A. Richard Wilbur. NOBA

Hole in the Sea, The. Marvin Bell. NYBP

Hole, Where Once in Passion We Swam. Dave Jeddie Smith. NoAM

Holes, The. Stephen Berg. NYBP

Holes Commence Falling. David Huddle. PBCAP

Holes in my arms. For Real. Jayne Cortez. PoBA

Holes in the floor of the barn loft, The. Hay Scuttle. Robert Morgan. WeT

Holes, spaces—not just in the small of the back. Widower. Bible, Apocrypha. OxBM

Holiday, The. Hans Magnus Enzensberger, *German.* VCWP, *tr. by* Enzensberger, Hans Magnus and Michael Hamburger

Holiday, The. Stevie Smith. BWW

Holiday, A. Ella Wheeler Wilcox. OxBM

Holiday at Hampton Court. John Davidson. EBVV

Holiday, boys! cry holiday! (LL) Vulcan's Song. John Lyly. EBEV; NoSic

Holiday Gown. John Cunningham. ECEV

Holiday in Reality. Wallace Stevens. OxBA

Holiday Train, The. Irene Thompson. BoTP

Holidays. Eva Mylonas, *Modern Greek.* BoWoP, *tr. by* Kimon Friar

Holidays. Dara Wier. NAmP90

Holiday's End. Haim Gouri, *Hebrew.* IP, *tr. by* Warren Bargad *and* Stanley F. Chyet

Holidays, I'd look out the window for them. The Relatives. Ed Ochester. CMAP

Holiest of all holidays are those, The. Henry Wadsworth Longfellow. PoToHe

Holiness[e] on the head. Aaron. George Herbert. ChIV-1; FSCP; GeHe; MeLP; NOSC; OAEL-1; PeECV

Holland, that scarce deserves the name of land. Andrew Marvell. OBSV *Fr.* The Character of Holland. NOBL; PeLV

((((((Hollanditis)))))). Simon Vinkenoog, *Dutch.* CLPP, *tr. by* Charles McGeehan

Hollis laughed. Johnna at the Windmill. Diane Glancy. CRP

Hollo! keep it up, boys—and push around the glass. Drinking Song. Robert Fergusson. OxAEP-1

Holloe Menn, The. Harrison Everard. BXAP

Hollow, the. Robert Morgan. MT

Hollow Echo. Fazil Hüsnü Daglarca. CRP

Hollow eyes of shock remain, The. Two Years Later. John Wieners. PmAP; PoM; RaBo

Hollow Land, The. William Morris.

Song: "Christ keep the Hollow Land." PoEL-5

Hollow Men, The. T. S. Eliot. ImPo; InPS-3; LiTM; MoAmPo; NAAL-2; OAEL-2; OBMV; PBMP

Hollow sound of your hard felt hat, The. Hats. Francis Stewart [*or* "Frank"] Flint. NSI

Hollow Thesaurus, The. Roger McDonald. BMAP; CBAP

Hollow Tree, A. Robert Bly. NNaP

Hollow winds begin to blow, The. Signs of Rain. Edward Jenner. BLPA

Hollowness. Mac Wellman.

"Two hollow eyes follow a cat's crie." FTOS

Holly, The. Walter De la Mare. CMoP

Holly and Mistletoe. Eleanor Farjeon. PChr

Holly and the Ivy, The. *Unknown.* CH; PeECV; PChr

Holly and the ivy, / When they are both full grown, The. The Holly and the Ivy. *Unknown.* CH; PChr

Holly's up, the house is all bright, The. The Christmas Tree. Peter Cornelius. PChr

Hollywood. Karl Shapiro. LiTM; OxBA

Holmes. James Russell Lowell. NOBA *Fr.* A Fable for Critics. NAAL-1; NAAL-3

Holocaust. Charles Reznikoff.

"When the Second World War began." HP

Holocaust. Myra Sklarew. CRP

Holocaust 1944, *To my mother.* Anne Ranasinghe. HP

Holofernes's Letter. Shakespeare. CBNP *Fr.* Love's Labour's Lost.

Holstenwall. Sidney Keyes. FaBoTV

Holver and Hivy made a gret party. *Unknown.* MiEL

Holy, & holy. The damned are said to say. John Berryman. *Fr.* Eleven Addresses to the Lord. OxBC

Holy and mighty poet of the spirit. Shelley. Thomas Wade. EPCY

Holy angels, in envy I cast no sigh. Gaspara Stampa, *Italian.* BoWoP, *tr. by* J. Vitiello

Holy, as I suppose I dare to call you. John Berryman. *Fr.* Eleven Addresses to the Lord. OxBC

Holy Baptism (1). George Herbert. GeHe

Holy Baptism (2). George Herbert. ChIV-2; PoEL-2

Holy be the white head of a Negro. George Campbell. PBCV

Holy boy, The. Children of Love. Harold Monro. MoBrPo

Holy City, City of Night. Lynda Hull. PUP-19

Holy Communion, The. Henry Vaughan. ESCV

Holy Cross. Sir Shane Leslie. TIRV

Holy Fair, The. Robert Burns. OBSV

Holy Family. Peter Cooley. NAmP90

Holy Family. Muriel Rukeyser. ChIV-2; MoAmPo

Holy Family. Katharine Tynan. TIRV

Holy Father, Great Creator. Alexander V. Griswold. AH

Holy Ghost, The. Donne. NOCV *Fr.* The Litanie. PoEL-2

Holy God, We Praise Thy Name. Clarence A. Walworth. AH

Holy Grail, The. Jack Spicer.

Book of Gawain, The. PoM

Holy Hill, A. "Æ." AWP

Holy, holy, holy. Bible, *O.T.* CTV *Fr.* Bible, O.T., Isaiah 6:3.

Holy! Holy! Holy! Holy! Holy! Holy! [Holy! Holy! Holy! Holy! Holy!]. Footnote to Howl. Allen Ginsberg. CAPP-1; CLPP

"Holy, holy, holy!" the choir chants sweet and low. An Opening Service. Clara Ann Thompson. CBWP-2

Holy Innocents, The. Robert Lowell. CoAmPo; MoAmPo; OBCP; OxBC

Holy Is the Desire to Proclaim the Existence of God. Meir Wieseltier, *Hebrew.* IP, *tr. by* Warren Bargad *and* Stanley F. Chyet

Holy is the moon and our own Selene. *Unknown, Greek.* GrAn, *tr. by* Peter Porter

Holy Land of Walsingham, The. *Unknown, sometimes at. to* Sir Walter Ralegh. EnSB

Holy light of loneliness, The. Breaking. Cynthia Huntington. NAmP90

Holy, lion-like sleep. The Return. Angelos Sikelianos, *Greek.* GrIP, *tr. by* Edmund Keeley *and* Philip Sherrard

Holy Longing, The. Goethe, *German.* RaBo, *tr. by* Robert Bly

Holy man, ungird your gabardeen. Rest. Roots. Seymour Mayne. NOBC

Holy Mass For Relja Krilatica. Milorad Pavic.

Song: "But I'm the one from whom they stole a button from his trouser leg." HSix

Song: "But I'm the one to whom others spit in the hand when he works." HSix

Song: "But I'm the one who carries a garlic clove in the ear." HSix

Song: "Rejoice bather between two waters." HSix, *tr. by* Charles Simic

Song: "Rejoice eleventh finger reckoner of stars." HSix, *tr. by* Charles Simic

Song: "Rejoice mason of years." HSix

Song: "Rejoice singer of songs for the deaf." HSix

Song: "Rejoice you who sleep with a finger in your ear." HSix

Holy moder, that bere Crist. William Herebert MiFI

Holy Nativity, The. Richard Crashaw. *See* In the Holy Nativity of Our Lord God.

Holy Night. Lucille Clifton. CrSp; NALW

Holy Nunnery, The. *Unknown.* ESPB

Holy Office, The. James Joyce. FaBoTw; NoAM; OxBTC

Holy Ones, the Young Ones, The. Chayyim Zeldis. TrJP

Holy Rood, The. John, of Hereford Davies.

"Although we do not all the good we love." Son

Holy Rose, The. Vyacheslav Ivanovich Ivanov, *Russian.* AWP, *tr.* by Babette Deutsch *and* Avrahm Yarmolinsky

Holy Russia. Maksimilian Aleksandrovich Voloshin, *Russian.* TCRP, *tr.* by Bernard Meares

Holy Satyr. Hilda Doolittle. MoAmPo

Holy Scripture, Writ Divine. From a London Bookshop. *Unknown.* NBLV

Holy Skirts. Else Von Freytag-Loringhoven. PFTM

Holy Sonnets. Holy Sonnets *is the title often given to* Divine Meditations, *the collection of 19 sonnets comprising the second part of this longer work.* Donne. ESCV

From Holy Sonnets. NoP-4

("Thou hast made me, and shall thy work decay?") GSo; NoP-4

Holy Sonnet. OPOU

Holy Sonnet 14.

("Batter my heart, three-personed God.") FMP; FSCP; PFE; PoPoPo

("Batter my heart, three-personed God for You.") NoP-4

(Holy Sonnet 14.) PoPoPo

(Nor ever chast, except you ravish mee.) (LL) PBRV

"I am a little world made cunningly." ChIV-1; NAEL-1; NIP-4; NoP-4; PoE; SeCP; Son

"If poisonous [*or* poysonous] mineral[l]s, and if that tree." EBEV; FaBoVe; ImPo; NAEL-1; OAEL-1; OxAEP; PoEL-2; SCGP; SeCP; Son; UnPo

("If poisonous minerals, and if that tree.") NoP-4

La Corona. ChIV-2; ESCV; Son

Annunciation. TrCP

(Crown, The.) ChIV-2

Resurrection. ESCV

"Oh my black[e] soul[e]! now thou art summoned." EBEV; OAEL-1; OxAEP-1; Poetr; Son; TOF

("Oh my black soul! now thou art summonèd.") FMP

("That being red, it dyes red souls to white.") (LL) FMP

"Oh, to vex me, two contraries meet in one." ChIV-2

("Show me dear Christ, Thy Spouse so bright and clear.") FSCP; NoP-4; PeECV

("When she'is embrac'd and open to most men.") (LL) PBRV

("When she's embraced and open to most men.") (LL) NoP-4

Since she whome I lovd, hath payd her last debt. PBRV

("Least the World, fleshe, yea Devill putt thee out.") (LL) PBRV

("Since she whom I loved hath paid her last debt.") FMP; FSCP

"Spit in my face ye [*or* you] Jew[e]s, and pierce my side." Son; TOF

"This is my play's [*or* playes] last scene, here heavens appoint." EBEV; FaBoVe; MeLP; SeCP; Son

"What if this present were the world's last night?" EBEV; HeIP-4; ImPo; InPS-3; MeLP; NAEL-1; NOCV; NOSC; OxAEP-1; PeECV; PoE; Son

"Why are we[e] by all creatures waited on?" NOCV; PoE; PoEL-2; TrCP

"Wilt thou love God, as he thee? [*or* thee!] then digest." TrCP

Holy Spirit, Faithful Guide. Marcus Morris Wells. AH

Holy Spirit, / giving life to all life. Hildegard von Bingen, *German.* EnlH, *tr.* by Stephen Mitchell

Holy Spirit, Lord of light. Hymn to the Holy Spirit. Stephen Langton. TrCP

Holy Spirit, Truth Divine. Samuel Longfellow. AH

Holy stond in the hall [*or* halle]. Nay, Ivy, Nay. *Unknown.* CH

Holy the supernatural extra brilliant intelligent kindness of the / soul! soul! (LL) Footnote to Howl. Allen Ginsberg. CAPP-1; CLPP

Holy Thursday [I.] ("'Twas on a Holy Thursday, their innocent faces clean"). William Blake. CH; FHYEP; InPS-3; NAEL-2; NAWM-2; NOBE; NOBRP; NOEC; NoP-4; OAEL-2; PeECV; PoE; Ro; SCV; TFi; TrCP *Fr.* Songs of Innocence.

Holy Thursday [II.] ("Is this a holy thing to see"). William Blake. FHYEP; InPS-3; NAEL-2; NOBRP; NOEC; NoP-4; OAEL-2 *Fr.* Songs of Experience.

(Holy Thursday (Experience).) NOxBChV

("Nor poverty the mind appal.") (LL) Ro

(Holy Thursday (Innocence).) NOxBChV

Holy Tide, The. Frederick Tennyson. OBEV

Holy Was Demeter Walking th' Corn Furrow. Edward Sanders. PoM

Holy Water come and bring. The Spell. Robert Herrick. CaPo; OxBSn

Holy Well, The ("As it fell out one May morning"). *Unknown.* FaBoCh; NOCV

Holy Willie's Prayer. Robert Burns. EBEV; NOBRP; NOEC; OBCoV; OBSV; OxBS; PoE; PoEL-4; TFi

("Amen, Amen!") (LL) NoP-4

("And a' the glory shall be thine! / AMEN! AMEN!.") (LL) CABP

("O Thou, wha in the heavens dost dwell.") NoP-4

Holy Wroughte of sterres bright. William Herebert. MiEL

Holyhead. September 25, 1727. Jonathan Swift. BIrV; NOIV

Homage. Gilbert Highet. BXAP

Homage. Gustave Kahn, *French.* TrJP, *tr.* by Jethro Bithell

Homage and Lament for Ezra Pound in Captivity. Robert Duncan. NOBA

Homage: Light from the Hall. David Wojahn. PBCAP *Fr.* Mystery Train: A Sequence.

Homage to a Government. Philip Larkin. EBEV; FaBoPV; NoAM

Homage to a Hat and Uncle Guido and Eliot. Tomaz Salamun, *Slovenian.* CEEP, *tr.* by Šalamun, Tomaž *and* Anselm Hollo

Homage to Chagall. Duane Niatum. CDW

Homage to Claudius Ptolemy. Brotherhood. Octavio Paz, *Spanish.* LoL, *tr.* by Eliot Weinberger

Homage to Faiz Ahmed Faiz. Agha Shahid Ali. OpBo

Homage to Ferd. Holthausen. Gwen Harwood. NOBAu

Homage to Hieronymus Bosch. Thomas MacGreevy. BIrV; SPE

Homage to Jack Yeats. Thomas MacGreevy. OBMV

Homage to John Millington Synge. Mairtin O Direain, *Irish.* NOIV, *tr.* by Thomas Kinsella

Homage to Literature. Muriel Rukeyser. SeSe

Homage to Lucille, Dr. Lord-Heinstein. Marge Piercy. NMM-2

Homage to Mallarmé. Daniel Mark Epstein.

Barrel Organ, The. DiPo

Homage to Marcel Proust. Thomas MacGreevy. CIP-2

Homage to Mistress Bradstreet. John Berryman.

"Governor your husband lived so long, The." NOBA

"I trundle the bodies, on the iron bars." NOBA

"O all your ages at the mercy of my loves." NOBA

"When by me in the dusk my child sits down." ColAP

"Winters close, Springs open, no child stirs, The." NAAL-2; NoP-4

Homage to My Hips. Lucille Clifton. NAAAL; Poetr

Homage to Paul Cézanne. Charles Wright. VCAP

"Dead are a cadmium blue, The." HCAP

Homage to Paul Delvaux. Ramon Guthrie. PoE

Homage to René Magritte. George Melly. SPE

Homage to Ryszard Kapuściński. David Wojahn. BAP-95

Homage to Sextus Propertius. Ezra Pound.

Difference of Opinion with Lygdamus. MeMAP

Elegy VII. VGW

"Midnight, and a letter comes to me from." MeMAP

"Now if ever it is time to cleanse Helicon." VGW

"Persephone and Dis, Dis, have mercy upon her." MeMAP

"Shades of Callimachus, Coan ghosts of Philetas." CMoP; HAP; NOBA; OBVE; OxBA

"Twisted rhombs ceased their clamour of accompaniment, The." MeMAP

"When, when, and whenever death closes our eyelids." MeMAP; OBMV; PoA

"Who, who will be the next man to entrust his girl to a friend?" FaBoMo

Homage to Sextus Propertius. Propertius, *Latin.*

"Me happy, night, night full of brightness." OBCVT, *tr.* by Ezra Pound

Homage to the British Museum. William Empson. CMoP; FaBoMo; LiTM; MoBrPo; PoE

Homage to the Canal People. Andrew Sant. NOBAu

Homage to the Carracci. Thomas M. Disch. PoA

Homage to the Empress of the Blues. Robert Earl Hayden. HCAP; LCAP-2; NAAAL; PoBA

Homage to the New World. Michael S. Harper. LCAP-2

Homage to the Philosopher. Babette Deutsch. TrJP

Homage to the Tru'ng queens. *Unknown, Vietnamese.* AVP, *tr.* by Huỳnh Sanh Thông

Homage to thee, O Ra, at thy tremendous rising! The Dead Man Ariseth and Singeth a Hymn to the Sun. *Unknown.* AWP *Fr.* Book of the Dead.

Homard à Igor Stravinsky: Vernacular Variations. Hugh Haughton. CBNP

Home. Antonin Bartusek, *German.* CEEP, *tr.* by Ewald Osers

Home. Anne Brontë. VWP

Home. Henry Cuyler Bunner.

"Home, Sweet Home," with Variations ("As sea-foam blown of the winds, as blossom of brine that is drifted"). OBAL

"Home, Sweet Home," with Variations ("Brown o' San Juan"). OBAL

"Home, Sweet Home," with Variations ("Mid pleasures and palaces though we may roam"). OBAL

Home. Matilda Caroline Edwards. PWR

Home. Calvin Forbes. GT

Home. E. A. Guest. BLPA; FaBoBe; OBAL; PWR

Home. William Ernest Henley. PoLF

(Falmouth.) MoBrPo

Home! Nellie Womack Hines. PoToHe

Home. Kyudong Kim, *Korean*. CKP, *tr. by* Jaihiun Kim

Home. Frank Ormsby. PBCIP; PNI

Home. Vincent O'Sullivan. PeNZ

Home. *Unknown, Chinese*. OHMPC, *tr. by* Kenneth Rexroth

Home. Ivan Zhdanov, *Russian*. TCRP, *tr. by* John High

Home address: galaxy and star number. End of the Questionnaire. Dan Pagis, *Hebrew*. PoSu, *tr. by* Robert Friend

Home after Three Months Away. Robert Lowell. HCAP; MoLi; PBMP

Home again, home again, joggety jog [*or* jiggety-jog]. (LL) To market, to market, to buy a fat pig. *Unknown*. BoTP; FaBoBe; LB; OxNR; ReMoGo

Home and Mother. Hettye Rayburn Ramsey. PWR

Home at Grasmere. Wordsworth. *See* The Recluse; Home at Grasmere.

Home! at the word, what blissful visions rise. Home, Sweet Home, with Variations. Henry Cuyler Bunner. OBAL

Home, away home, ere the lightning floated forth again. D. H. Lawrence. *See* Lightning.

Home Burial. Robert Frost. ColAP; IMW; NAAL-2; SoSe-8; TAP; TRP

Home-coming. Léonie Adams. MoAmPo

Home-Coming. Albert Ehrenstein, *German*. TrJP, *tr. by* Babette Deutsch *and* Avrahm Yarmolinsky

Home Coming. Lenrie Peters. HBAPE; PBMAP

Home early. Gary Hotham. HA

Home for Thanksgiving. W. S. Merwin. NoAM

Home From Abroad. Laurie Lee. APAD

Home from Guatemala, back at the Waldorf. Arrival at the Waldorf. Wallace Stevens. HCAP

Home from his journey Farmer John. Farmer John. John Townsend Trowbridge. PWR

Home front, The. Aristophanes, *Greek*. OBCVT, *tr. by* Tony Harrison

Home Front. Bill Tremblay. CDa

Home Game. Don Allen Johnson. EC2

Home Greeting, A. Priscilla Jane Thompson. CBWP-2

Home Ground. Charles Brasch. PeNZ

Home, home from the horizon far and clear. At Night. Alice Thompson Meynell. CH; OxAEP-2

Home is more than just four walls. Hearth and Home. Stoddard King. OBAL

Home is mysterious: a place to die, a place to breed. Destinations. Josephine Jacobsen. WPE

Home Is So Sad. Ted Walker. LBC

Home is so sad. It stays as it was left. Philip Larkin. InPK-6; OxBSP

("Music in the piano stool. That vase, The.") (LL) LBC

Home Is Where There Is One to Love Us. Charles Swain. BLPA; FaBoBe; PoToHe

Home late. Michael Dudley. HA

Home Leave. Barbara Howes. TwCP

Home Movies. Carter Revard. VoR

Home News. Ahmed Tidjani-Cissé. PBMAP

Home no more home to me, whither must I wander? Robert Louis Stevenson. CH

Home of Aphrodite, The. Euripides. AWP, *tr. by* Gilbert Murray *Fr.* Bacchae.

Home of the Percys' high-born race. Alnwick Castle. Fitz-Greene Halleck. APN-1

Home on the Range, A. *Unknown, sometimes at. to* Brewster Higley. APN-2; FaBoBe

Home on the Range, February 1962. Edward Dorn. CoAmPo

Home Revisited: Midnight. John Ciardi. NYBP

Home Sickness. Louise Bennett. HCP

Home-Sickness. Justinus Kerner, *German*. AWP, *tr. by* James Clarence Mangan

Home-Sickness. Hedwig Lachmann, *German*. TrJP, *tr. by* Jethro Bithell

Home, Sweet Home! John Howard Payne. APN-1; BLPA; EBEvV; FaBoBe *Fr.* Clari, the Maid of Milan.

Home Sweet Home with Variations. Henry Cuyler Bunner. BXAP; OBAL *Fr.* Home.

Home, The Spare Room, The. Robert Adamson. BMAP

Home they brought her warrior dead. Tennyson. OxAEP-2 *Fr.* The Princess.

Home Thoughts. Denis Glover. PeNZ

Home Thoughts. *Unknown*. NSI

Home-Thoughts, From Abroad. Robert Browning. AWP; BoTP; CABP; ClHu; EBEvV; EBVV; FHYEP; FaBoBe; FaPoR; HeIP-4; ImPo; NAEL-2; NOBE; NOBVV; NoP-4; OBEV; OBNC; PBMP; PoLF; PoRA; TFi; UV

("O to be in England.") APAD

Home Thoughts from Abroad. William Robert Rodgers. OBCoV

Home Thoughts from Home. Alasdair Maclean. FaBoTC

Home-Thoughts, from the Sea. Robert Browning. EBEvV; NAEL-2; SCGP

Home to me is laughter. June Brown Harris. PoToHe

Home Town Elegy. George Sutherland Fraser. FaBoTC

Home Travel. Joseph Hall. CBLP

Home Truths from Abroad. *Unknown*. UV

Home when he came, he seemed not to be there. Leander's Return. Marlowe. EBNV *Fr.* Hero and Leander. AAS

Homecoming. Bruce Dawe. BMAP; CBAP

Homecoming. Ho Ch'e Ch'ang, *Chinese*. OHMPC, *tr. by* Kenneth Rexroth

Homecoming. Langston Hughes. SAmP; TRP

Homecoming. Nguyễn Ý Thuần, *Vietnamese*. AVP, *tr. by* Huỳnh Sanh Thông

Homecoming. Desmond O'Grady. IIP

Homecoming. Lenrie Peters. *See* Home Coming.

Homecoming. Sonia Sanchez. NAAL; PoBA

Homecoming. Dennis Scott. PBCV

Homecoming. Edith Södergran, *German*. WPoS, *tr. by* David McDuff

Homecoming. Wisława Szymborska, *Polish*. PoSu, *tr. by* Adam Czerniawski

Homecoming. Peter Viereck. CoAP

Homecoming. Charles Wright. WeT

Homecoming. Mitsuye Yamada. NMM-2

Homecoming—Late at Night. Tu Fu, *Chinese*. OHPC, *tr. by* Kenneth Rexroth

Homecoming—Massachusetts. John Ciardi. NYBP

Homecoming of Love Amongst Illustrious Ruins. Rafael Alberti, *Spanish*. CLPP, *tr. by* Kenneth Rexroth

Homecoming Singer, The. Jay Wright. PoBA; VCAP

Homegoing. Brigitte Frase. LoHo

Homeland. Pauline Melville. HCP

Homeland! O beloved village. My Country. Elolongue Epanya Yondo, *French*. NegPo, *tr. by* Ellen Conroy Kennedy

Homeless. Adelaide Anne Procter. VWP

Homeless! / The Living Bread. Despised and Rejected. Katharine Lee Bates. TrCP

Homely Meats. John, of Hereford Davies. *See* The Author Loving These Homely Meats.

Homeostasis finally. System oscillation over. All parameters at rest. The Middle Manager in Paradise. Michael Foley. PNI

Homeowners unite. The Firebombing. James Dickey. CAPP-1; OBWP

Homeplace, The. Lenard D. Moore. GT

Homer. Albert Ehrenstein, *German*. TrJP, *tr. by* Babette Deutsch *and* Avrahm Yarmolinsky

Homer and the Brazen Head of Rumour. George Chapman. NOSC

Homer said everything beautifully, but to call. Antipater of Thessalonica, *Greek*. GrAn, *tr. by* Alistair Elliot

Homer was poor. His scholars live at ease. Epigram. James Vincent Cunningham. VGW

Homer where born where buried of whom the son. Brian Coffey. BiHa *Fr.* The Death of Hektor.

Homeric. Richard Jackson. NAmP90

Homeric Hexameter, The. Coleridge. OxAEP-2

Homeric Hymn to Ares, The. *Unknown*. RaBo, *tr. by* Charles Boer *Fr.* Homeric Hymns.

Homeric Hymns. *Unknown, Greek*.

Homeric Hymn to Ares, The. RaBo, *tr. by* Charles Boer

Hymn to Athena. AWP

Hymn to Castor and Pollux. AWP

Hymn to Earth the Mother of All. AWP

(Hymn to the Earth.) OBCVT, *tr. by* Charles Boer

("I will remember you.") (LL) OBCVT, *tr. by* Charles Boer

("Mother of us all, The.") OBCVT, *tr. by* Charles Boer

Hymn to Mercury. OBVE

Hymn to Selene. AWP

To Demeter. GrIP, *tr. by* Thelma Sargent

Homer's Gift of Fame. Homer. NOSC, *tr. by* George Chapman *Fr.* The Iliad.

Homer's Hymn to Castor and Pollux. *Unknown*. *See* Hymn to Castor and Pollux.

Homer's Hymn to the Moon. *Unknown*. *See* Hymn to Selene.

Homer's Iliad Book 12. George Chapman.
"... Through the wall, uprore." PBRV

Homer's Iliad, To the Reader. George Chapman.
"And, for our tongue, that still is so empayr'd." PBRV

Homer's Odysseys. George Chapman.
"In meantime flew our ships, and straight we fetch'd." OxBoS

Home's not merely four square walls. Home Is Where There Is One to Love Us. Charles Swain. BLPA; FaBoBe; PoToHe

Homes of England, The. Felicia Dorothea Hemans. FaPoR; NOBRP; PEW; UV; WPE

Home's the place we head for in our sleep. Indian Boarding School: The Runaways. Louise Erdrich. HATNAP; NoAM; UnSA

Homesick. Helmut Heissenbüttel, *German*. CLPP, *tr. by* Jerome Rothenberg

Homesick. Else Lasker-Schüler, *German*. PBWP, *tr. by* Michael Hamburger

Homesick Blues. Langston Hughes. GM; MoAmPo; NAAAL

Homesickness. Kirim Kim, *Korean*. CKP, *tr. by* Jaihiun Kim

Homesickness! that long / Exposed weariness! Marina Tsvetayeva, *Russian*. TCRP, *tr. by* Elaine Feinstein

Hometown flophouse / was what she could afford, The. Hotel Nights with My Mother. Linda McCarriston. NMM-2

Hometown Piece for Messrs. Alston and Reese. Marianne Moore. OBAL

Homeward at evening through the drifted snow. Cold Pastoral. Diotimus, *Greek*. GrAn, *tr. by* Dudley Fitts

Homeward Bound. William Allingham. FaBoBe

Homeward Bound. Heinrich Heine, *German*.
And When I Lamented. TrJP, *tr. by* Emma Lazarus
Dearest Friend, Thou Art in Love. TrJP, *tr. by* Emma Lazarus
Du bist wie eine Blume. TrJP, *tr. by* Emma Lazarus; AWP, *tr. by* Kate Freiligrath Kroeker
("Thou Seemest Like a Flower.") TrJP, *tr. by* Emma Lazarus
I, a Most Wretched Atlas. TrJP, *tr. by* Emma Lazarus
Mortal, Sneer Not at the Devil. TrJP, *tr. by* Emma Lazarus
Thou Hast Diamonds. TrJP, *tr. by* Emma Lazarus

Homeward Bound. Ezekiel Mphahlele. AF

Homeward Journey, The. Leonard Aaronson. TrJP

Homework. Allen Ginsberg. NoAM

Homework. Mona Van Duyn. FFC; VCAP

Homework Assignment on the Subject of Angels. Tadeusz Rózewicz, *Polish*. VCWP, *tr. by* Magnus J. Krynski *and* Robert A. Maguire

Homework, homework. Gary Hoskins. CTV

Homework! Oh, homework! Jack Prelutsky. ChAP

Homines qouque si taceant, vocem invenient libri. Steve McCaffery. FTOS *Fr.* Panopticon.

Homing at dusk—the snow falls on them—cattle. Diotimus, *Greek*. GrAn, *tr. by* Alistair Elliot

Homing Instinct, The. Mark Jarman. WWSi

Homing Pigeons. Ted Walker. NYBP

Homo Plangens. Nichita Stanescu, *Romanian*. CEEP, *tr. by* Petru Popescu *and* Peter Jay

Homo Sapiens. John Wilmot, 2d Earl of Rochester. *See* A Satire [or Satyre] against [Reason and] Mankind.

Homo Suburbiensis, for Craig McGregor. Bruce Dawe. BMAP

Homicide. Essex Hemphill. GT

Homœopathy. Sir John Collings Squire. NSI

Homosexuality. Frank O'Hara. LCAP-2; PoA; TAP

Homunculus et la Belle Étoile. Wallace Stevens. MoAmPo

Honest Abe Lincoln. Max Shulman. OBAL

Honest Deacon, The. Isaac Hinton Brown. PWR

Honest life, The. Virgil, *Latin*. OBCVT, *tr. by* Robert Andrews

Honest lover whosoever. Ode to Lovers. Sir John Suckling. UV

Honest man was Deacon Ray, An. The Honest Deacon. Isaac Hinton Brown. PWR

Honest with Oneself. "Don Aminado," *Russian*. TCRP, *tr. by* Albert C. Todd

Honestly I wish I were dead! Sappho, *Greek*. BoWoP, *tr. by* Willis Barnstone

Honestly I'd as soon be dead! Sappho, *Greek*. STV, *tr. by* John Frederick Nims

Honesty-Stones. J. S. Harry. NOBAu

Honey. Robert Morgan. BLT

Honey Bear. Elizabeth Lang. BoTP

Honey-flowers to the honey-comb. Chimes. D. G. Rossetti. OBNC

Honey Lamb, The. Jonathan Williams. PoM

Honey-making bee loves flowers, A. A Cradlesong. Tố Hữu, *Vietnamese*. AVP, *tr. by* Huỳnh Sanh Thông

Honey-Mead: "I am valued by man, fetched from afar." Cynewulf. AnOE, *tr. by* Charles W. Kennedy *Fr.* Riddles (Exeter Book).

Honey Moon. Kathleen Leland Baker. NBLV

Honey of peace in old poems, The. (LL) To the Stone-Cutters. Robinson Jeffers. AmPP; ColAP; MoAmPo; NAAL-2; NOBA; OxBA; PoRA

Honey on the Rod. Elizabeth Major.
Authors of Confession, The. KTR

Honey peace in old poems, The. Robinson Jeffers. *See* To the Stone-Cutters.

Honey people murder mercy U.S.A. In Memoriam: Martin Luther King, Jr. June Jordan. NAAAL; PoBA

Honey, pepper, leaf-green limes. Jamaica Market. Agnes Maxwell-Hall. TTY; WHSW

Honey Stealer, The. Theocritus, *Greek*. OBCVT, *tr. by Unknown*

Honey, Take a Whiff on Me. *Unknown*. OxBoLi

Honey / When de man. Sister Lou. Sterling Brown. BkSV; GM; ISC; PoBA

Honeycomb of Bees, The. Hrubín František, *Czech*. CEEP, *tr. by* Don Mager

Honeycomb perfection of this form before me. Roberto Tejada. BAP-96

Honeyed by time. The Wooden Chamber. Anne Hébert, *French*. WPOW, *tr. by* Birgit Swenson

Honeymoon. Barry Goldensohn. NAmP90

Honeymoon, The. James Simmons. PNI

Honeymoon is over, The. Judith Viorst. LW

Honeymoon Postcard. Paul Durcan. OBCoV

Honeymooning alone / oh the food's. Heartbreak Hotel. Liz Lochhead. FaBoTC

Honeystain / the rhetoricians of blackness. The Anti-Semanticist. Everett Hoagland. BPo; NBV

Honeysuckle (Chevrefoil). Marie de France. BoWoP, *tr. by* Patricia Terry

Honeysuckle, nightshade. Poem for L. C. Peter Klappert. AmPA

"Honeysuckle Was the Saddest Odor of All, I Think." Thadious M. Davis. BISI

Honeysuckle's siege at the nerve-ends. Infamous Doctrine. Paul Evans. NBrP

Hongo Store 29 Miles Volcano Hilo, Hawaii, The. Garrett Kaoru Hongo. PoPoPo; WeT

Honi. Dan Pagis, *Hebrew*. IP, *tr. by* Warren Bargad *and* Stanley F. Chyet

Honolulu. Robert Mazzocco. WWSi

Honor (1969). Allston James. CDa

Honor a going thing, goldfinch, corporation, tree. Mechanism. A. R. Ammons. HAP

Honor Maria, I see you. Pauline Melville. HCP

Honor, riches, marriage blessing. Shakespeare. *Fr.* The Tempest. OAEL-1

"Honor," said the man. Definitions. Joseph Joel Keith. PoToHe

Honor to those who in the life they lead. Thermopylae. Constantine P. Cavafy, *Greek*. GrIP, *tr. by* Edmund Keeley *and* Philip Sherrard

Honora, should that cruel time arrive. To Honora Sneyd. Anna Seward. ECWP

Honour. Abraham Cowley. BoLoP

Honour Dishonoured. Wilfrid Scawen Blunt. OBMV

Honour is flashed off exploit, so we say. In Honour of St. Alphonsus Rodriguez. Gerard Manley Hopkins. EBEV; OxAEP-2

Honour is so sublime perfection. To the Countesse of Bedford. Donne. MeLP

Honour plays a bubble's part. John Gay. PeLV *Fr.* Polly; an Opera.

Honour, that Guardian Angel, can alone. Martha Sansom. LW *Fr.* Clio.

Honour the Light Brigade, / Noble six hundred! Tennyson. *See* The Charge of the Light Brigade.

Honour thy father and thy mother. Bible, *O.T.* CTV *Fr.* The Bible, Exodus 20:12.

Honour thy parents; but good manners call. God to Be First Served. Robert Herrick. OxBChV

Honour with Age. Walter Kennedy. OxBS

Honourable Entertainment Given to the Queen's Majesty in Progress at Elvetham, 1591, The. Nicholas Breton.
Phillida and Coridon. OBEV; TTTS
(Ploughman's Song, The.) NOBE

Honourable Winifred Wemyss, The. Limerick. *Unknown*. PeLi

Honoured I lived e'erwhile with honoured men. Honour Dishonoured. Wilfrid Scawen Blunt. OBMV

Honours that the people give always, The. The Thespians at Thermopylae. Norman Cameron. GTBS-P

Honure, joy, helthe, and plesaunce. Charles, Duc d' Orléans. MiEL

Hoochie Coochie. Muddy Waters. NAAAL

Hooded Legion, The. Gerald McCarthy. CDa

Hoofer, The. A. K. Redwing. VoR

Hook-nosed, longsighted he was, like me. Baltic Summer. Yunna Petrovna Moritz, *Russian.* TCRP, *tr. by* Bernard Meares

Hook shot kisses the rim and, A. Fast Break. Edward Hirsch. DiPo; EOEF; VCAP

Hooked for two years now on wrinkle creams. Aging. Erica Jong. CrSp

Hooking boxes of dogfish. Kapital. Frank Gaspar. BAP-96

Hooly and Fairly. Joanna Baillie. RACG; WoRP

Hoop, a rolling O, oh those have power, A. Ode on Zero. Phoebe Pettingell. PoA

Hoopoe. George Darley. OBNC *Fr.* Nepenthe.

Hoosen Johnny. *Unknown.* AS

Hoot. Marlene Mountain. HA

Hoover, in grim silence, sat, The. Limerick. David Woodsford. PeLi

Hooves drummed, / Seeming to say. On Being Kind to Horses. Vladimir Mayakovsky, *Russian.* TCRP, *tr. by* Bernard Meares

Hop hop, thump thump. Stevie Smith. WPE *Fr.* The Dedicated Dancing Bull and the Water Maid.

Hop-poles stand in cones, The. The Midnight Skaters. Edmund Blunden. FaBoTw; GTBS-P; MoBrPo; NOBE; NoP-4; PeFWW

Hop, Skip, and Jump. Gary Snyder. LCAP-2

Hope. Philip Booth. APAD

Hope. William Cowper. "Though clasp'd and cradled in his nurse's arms." PoEL-3

Hope. George Herbert. ChIV-2; FMP; PoEL-2; WeW-3

Hope. Langston Hughes. APSN; OBAL; OBCA; PFTM; TRP

Hope. Randall Jarrell. MoAmPo

Hope. F. D. Reeve. PoA

Hope. Christopher Smart. ChIV-1 *Fr.* Hymns for the Amusement of Children.

Hope. Edith Södergran. PBWP, *tr. by* Jaakko A. Ahokas

Hope. Theognis, *Greek.* AWP, *tr. by* John Hookham Frere

Hope. Clara Ann Thompson. CBWP-2

Hope. Mary E. Tucker. CBWP-1

Hope. *Unknown, Irish.* CIP-2; IIP, *tr. by* Frank O'Connor

Hope and Despair. Lascelles Abercrombie. OBMV

Hope and Faith. Isaac Leibush Peretz, *Yiddish.* TrJP, *tr. by* Henry Goodman

Hope and Fear. Swinburne. FaBoBe

Hope and Joy. Christina Rossetti. OxBChV

Hope, art thou true, or dost thou flatter me? Sonnet 67. Sir Philip Sidney. *Fr.* Astrophil and Stella. AAS; SiPS

Hope Deferred. Clara Ann Thompson. CBWP-2

Hope! Fortune! Je m'en fous! Palladas, *Greek.* GrAn, *tr. by* Tony Harrison

Hope humbly then; with trembling pinions soar. Alexander Pope. EBEvV *Fr.* An Essay on Man.

Hope I dreamed of was a dream, The. Mirage. Christina Rossetti. BoLoP; PoRA

Hope is like a harebell trembling from its birth. Comparisons. Christina Rossetti. OxBChV

"Hope" is the thing with feathers. Emily Dickinson. APN-2; AmPP; ChAP; MeMAP; MoAmPo; NOBA; NoP-4; OxBA; PFE; PiM; SAmP; TAP

Hope is what skims time always from our lives. Julius Polyaenus, *Greek.* GrAn, *tr. by* Peter Jay

Hope, like the hyaena [*or* hyena], coming to be old. Henry Constable. EnLoPo; SCGP; Son *Fr.* Diana.

Hope! Not distant is the Springtime. Hope and Faith. Isaac Leibush Peretz, *Yiddish.* TrJP, *tr. by* Henry Goodman

Hope, of all ills that men endure. In Praise of Hope. Abraham Cowley. OxAEP-1

Hope Thou in God. Josephine D. Henderson Heard. CBWP-4

Hope! Thou vain, delusive maiden. Josephine D. Henderson Heard. CBWP-4

Hope was but a timid friend. Emily Jane Brontë. NoP-4

Hope, whose weak[e] being ruined [*or* ruin'd] is. Against Hope. Richard Crashaw. MeLP; NOBE; NOSC *Fr.* The Mistress.

Hope ye, my verses, that posterity. Joachim Du Bellay. PoE *Fr.* Ruins of Rome.

Hopeful old fellow called Rousseau, A. Limerick. John Fay. PeLi

Hopeful Spiritual Athlete, The. Kabir, *Hindi.* RaBo, *tr. by* Robert Bly

Hopeless Desire Soon Withers and Dies. "A. W." NoSic

Hopeless longing of the day, The. (LL) Longing. Matthew Arnold. GLoP; PoLF; SoSe-8

Hopelessly handcuffed to a mysterious butterfly. A Lost Mohican Visits Hell's Kitchen. A. K. Redwing. VoR

Hopelessness. Li Ch'ing-chao, *Chinese.* BLT, *tr. by* Kenneth Rexroth

Hope's Okay. A. R. Ammons. HCAP

Hoping Against Hope. Christina Rossetti. CBLP

Hoping all the time. *Unknown.* AWP, *tr. by* Arthur Waley *Fr.* Kokin Shu.

Hoping for a Dog. Sophie Way. PeP

Hoping it might be so. (LL) The Oxen. Thomas Hardy. APo; BoTP; CABP; CMoP; ChAP; EBEV; HAP; InPK-6; LiTM; MoBrPo; MoP; NOBE; NTP; NoAM; OAEL-2; OBCP; OxAEP-2; OxBTC; PChr; PeECV; Poetr; RB; SoSe-8; TFi; TOF; TRP; WeW-3

Hopkins and Whitman. Lynne McMahon. PuP-15

Hopper o'ditches. A. Riddle. *Unknown.* FaBoVe

Hopping frog, hop here and be seen. Christina Rossetti. VWP

Hopping Toad Blues. Raymond R. Patterson. SeSe

Hoppity. A. A. Milne. NTCP

Hoppy. Reginald Gibbons. DiPo

Hops. Boris Pasternak, *Russian.* BoLoP; TTTS, *tr. by* Jon Stallworthy *and* Peter France

("Beneath a willow entwined with ivy.") LoP, *tr. by* Robert Lowell

(Wild Vines.) LoP, *tr. by* Robert Lowell

Hops are a menace on the moon, a nuisance crop. Moon-Hops. Ted Hughes. CABP

Hora Stellatrix. Amy Lowell. SDW

"Horae Canonicae." W. H. Auden. *See* Terce.

Lauds. TrCP

Prime. CMoP; PoE

Terce. CMoP; PoE

("After shaking paws with his dog / (Whose bark would tell the world that he is always kind).") GI

("Horae Canonicae.") GI

Vespers. FaBoMo

Horae Canonicae. Donald Davie. CRP

Horat. Carm. lib. 4. Ode 13. Horace, *Latin.* OBCVT, *tr. by* William Cartwright

Horatian Canons of Friendship, The. Horace. OBCVT, *tr. by* Christopher Smart *Fr.* The Satires.

Horatian Epode to the Duchess of Malfi. Allen Tate. FaBoMo

Horatian Ode. Joseph Warren Beach. PoA

Horat. Ode 29. Book 3. Horace. *See* To Maecenas.

Horatian Ode upon Cromwell's Return from Ireland, An. Andrew Marvell. CABP; EBEV; ESCV; FMP; GTBS-P; GeHe; HAP; IIP; InPS-3; NOBE; NOSC; OAEL-1; OBEV; OBWP; OxAEP-1; PoEL-2; SCGP; SeCP; TFi

(Horatian Ode upon Cromwel's Return from Ireland, An.) FSCP; PBRV

("Power must it maintain, A.") (LL) FMP; NoP-4; PoPoPo

("Pow'r must it *maintain,* A.") (LL) CABP; FSCP; PBRV

Horatian Variation. Leonard Bacon. NYBP

Horatians, The. W. H. Auden. NYBP

Horatio, of ideal courage vain. Feigned Courage. Yitzhak Lamdan. OxBChV

Horatius. Thomas Babington Macaulay, 1st Baron Macaulay. OBWP *Fr.* Lays of Ancient Rome. *See* Horatius at the Bridge.

Horatius at the Bridge. Thomas Babington Macaulay, 1st Baron Macaulay. FaBoCh; FaPoR; OBNV; OBWP; OxAEP-2; PoLF *Fr.* Lays of Ancient Rome.

(Horatius.) EBEvV; OxAEP-2

("Lars Porsena of Clusium.") EBNV

Horeb's mountain top of old. Mountain Tops. Lizelia Augusta Jenkins Moorer. CBWP-3

Horestes. John Pickering.

Haltersick's Song. NoSic

Song Sung by Egistus and Clytemnestra. NoSic

Vice's Song, The. NoSic

Horizon. Kevin Hart. NOBAu

Horizon Blues. David Henderson. GT

Horizon: washed ashore, The. Storm. Helga Marie Heinze, *German.* CEEP, *tr. by* Katherine Bradley

Horizons for the man Flammonde. (LL) Flammonde. Edwin Arlington Robinson. AmPP; CMoP; LiTM; MeMAP; NoAM

Horizontal in a deckchair on the bleak ward [*or* Horizontal on a deckchair in the Ward]. Ezra Pound. Robert Lowell. MoP; NAAL-2; NOBA; NoAM

Horn, The. Léonie Adams. MoAmPo

Horn, The. James Reeves. OTCP

Horn for weapon, and wool for shield. The Zodiac Song. John Ruskin. NOBVV

Horn: I am always at the aetheling's shoulder. *Unknown.* EEP, *tr. by* Michael Alexander *Fr.* Riddles (Exeter Book).

Horn: I'm loved by my lord, and his shoulder. Cynewulf. ASW, *tr. by* Kevin Crossley-Holland *Fr.* Riddles (Exeter Book).

Horn of your silver bus, The. Let Not Your Hart Be Truble. James Seay. WeT

Horn: "Time was when I was weapon and warrior." Cynewulf. AnOE, *tr. by* Charles W. Kennedy *Fr.* Riddles (Exeter Book).

Horned Snake, The. Louis Oliver. HATNAP

Horses to Rule wins Nature lends. Beauty. Anacreon, *Greek.* OBCV I, *tr. by* Thomas Stanley

Hornets occasionally build their nests near roads. Wearing Achilles' Armour, Patroclus, along with the Myrmidons, Attacks the Trojans. Homer. OBVE, *tr. by* Christopher Logue *Fr.* The Iliad.

Hornless hart carries off the harem, The. The Royal Stag. "Hugh MacDiarmid." FaBoMo

Hornpipe. Dame Edith Sitwell. FaBoMo; GTBS-P; OAEL-2 *Fr.* Façade.

"Horns of the house, hall-gables burning?, The." The Fight at Finnsburg. *Unknown, Anglo-Saxon.* EEP, *tr. by* Michael Alexander

Horns protruded from the. The Rising. Jayne Cortez. NBV

Horns [*or* Hornes] to bulls wise Nature lends. Beauty. Thomas Stanley, *after the Greek of* Anacreon. AWP; OBVE

Horny-Goloch, The. *Unknown.* FaBoCh

Horoscope. Rasa Livada, *Serbo-Croatian.* HSix, *tr. by* Charles Simic

Horoscope. Colleen J. McElroy. GT

Horrible crime was committed, A. Pearl Bryan. *Unknown.* AmFP

Horrible Decree, The. Charles Wesley.
  "Sinners, abhor the Fiend." NOCV

Horrible Today, The. Max Jacob, *French.* AF, *tr. by* Ron Padgett

Horrid Voice of Science, The. Vachel Lindsay. PoA

Horror. Peter Baum, *German.* AWP, *tr. by* Jethro Bithell

Horror. Henry Treece. SPE

Horror Comic. Robert Conquest. OxBTC

Hors de Combat. "Anvari," *Persian.* ArPe, *tr. by* Omar S. Pound

Horse. Gloria Anzaldúa. UnSA

Horse, The. Bible, *O.T. See* Hast Thou Given the Horse Strength.

Horse. Louise Glück. NALW

Horse, The. Philip Levine. CoAP; VCAP

Horse. Kenneth Rexroth. NNaP *Fr.* A Bestiary. OBAL

Horse and a flea and three blind mice, A. Whoops! *Unknown.* NTCP

Horse and His Rider, The. Joanna Baillie. ECWP; NOEC

Horse & Rider. Wey Robinson. BXAP

Horse and the Mule, The. John Huddlestone Wynne. OxBChV

Horse and Tree. Rita Dove. TRP

Horse Boyle was called Horse Boyle because of his brother Mule. Dresden. Ciaran Carson. CIP-2; PBCIP; PNI

Horse butcher, The. Pierre McOrlan, *French.* MFP, *tr. by* Martin Sorrell

Horse Calligram. Guillaume Apollinaire. PFTM

Horse can't pull while kicking, A. Horse Sense. *Unknown.* BLPA; PWR

Horse Chestnut Tree, The. Richard Eberhart. CMoP; LiTM; MoAmPo; PFE

Horse Cursed by the Sun, The. *Unknown, Hottentot.* PeSAV, *tr. by* W. H. I. Bleek

Horse Did Not Come Back, The. Veliyanar Erumai, *Tamil.* PLW, *tr. by* A. K. Ramanujan

Horse Dream. Ojars Vacietis, *Latvian.* CEEP, *tr. by* Inara Cedrins

Horse I am, whom bit, A. The Trojan Horse. William Drummond, of Hawthornden. PFE

Horse in the drugstore / wants to be admired, The. Tess Gallagher. AmPA

Horse Latitudes. Frankie Paino. NAmP90

Horse Named Bill, The. *Unknown.* AS

Horse: not one less than twenty. Isuba. Jim Barnes. *Fr.* Four Things Choctaw. HATNAP

Horse on a Fence. George Evans. PmAP

Horse on the Wall. Marcia Southwick. CMAP; NAmP90

Horse Power. Tom Raworth. NBrP

Horse Sense. *Unknown.* BLPA; PWR

Horse Show, The. William Carlos Williams. CMoP; FiLi; NOBA; TAP; VGW

Horse that carried Miss Kilmansegg, The. Her Accident. Thomas Hood. EBVV *Fr.* Miss Kilmansegg and Her Precious Leg.

Horse Thief, The. William Rose Benét. MoAmPo

Horse Trader's Song, The. *Unknown.* AmFP

Horse-Watering Hole, The. Yang Wei-chen, *Chinese.* CoBLCP, *tr. by* Jonathan Chaves

Horse Weebles. Edward Kamau Brathwaite. PBCV

Horse with a chestnut mane reflected in the green waves of the spring river. Tune: "Echoing Heaven's Everlastingness." Wang Kuo-wei, *Chinese.* SuSp, *tr. by* Ching-i Tu

Horse with birds on its mane, doubt on its tail, The. Godhorse. Kojo Laing. HBAPE

Horseback on Sunday morning. The Wild Geese. Wendell Berry. TRP

Horseman at the Roadside, The. Yang Wei-chen, *Chinese.* CoBLCP, *tr. by* Jonathan Chaves

Horseman high alone as an eagle on the spur of the mountain over Mirmas Canyon draws rein, looks down, A. The Coast-Road. Robinson Jeffers. PaTW

Horseman on the Skyline, The. Henry Lawson. CBAP

Horseman, pass by! (LL) Under Ben Bulben. W. B. Yeats. CMoP; HAP; IIP; LiTM; MoP; NAEL-2; NoAM; NoP-4; OxBTC

Horses, The ("Barely a twelvemonth after"). Edwin Muir. CABP; CMoP; FaBoTC; GEA; HAP; HeIP-4; MoBrPo; MoP; NOBE; NoAM; OAEL-2; OxBTC; PoE; Poetr; RB; TRP; WeW-3

Horses. Mahadai Das. HCP

Horses, The. Ted Hughes. NoAM

Horses. Edwin Muir. APo; CMoP; FaBoCh; OAEL-2

Horses. Gwyn Thomas, *Welsh.* OBWVE, *tr. by* Joseph P. Clancy

Horses. Dorothy, Duchess of Wellington Wellesley. OBMV; OxBTC

Horses and Men in the Rain. Carl Sandburg. PoLF

Horses and the Angels, The. Agnes Nemes Nagy, *Hungarian.* CEEP, *tr. by* Bruce Berlind

Horses at Valley Store. Leslie Marmon Silko. VoR

Horses can swim—but not well, and not far. Horses in the Sea. Boris Abramovich Slutsky, *Russian.* TCRP, *tr. by* J. R. Rowland

Horses Chawin' Hay. Hamlin Garland. OBAL

Horse's Head, The. Brendan Kennelly. CIP-2

Horses in Snow. Roberta Hill Whiteman. NoAM

Horses in the Sea. Boris Abramovich Slutsky, *Russian.* TCRP, *tr. by* J. R. Rowland

Horse's mind, The. Unity. Fazil Hüsnü Daglarca, *Turkish.* RaBo, *tr. by* Tâlat S. Halman

Horses of Marini, The. Tania Van Zyl. PeSA

Horses of the sea, The. Christina Rossetti. NTCP *Fr.* Sing-Song.

Horses on the Camargue. Roy Campbell. GTBS-P; PeSA

Horses out of their brains bored all, The. Flying Noises. Thomas Lux. LCAP-2

Horses, the pigs, The. Familiar Friends. James Sterling Tippett. BoTP

Horsewoman of charm at Uttoxeter, A. Limerick. R. D. Condon. PeLi

Hos Ego Versiculos. Francis Quarles. NOSC *Fr.* Argalus and Parthenia.

Hosanna. Thomas Traherne. ChIV-2; PoEL-2

Hosanna—musick is divine, *par. by* Christopher Smart. Bible, *O.T. See* Psalm 147.

Hosanna to Christ. Isaac Watts. NOCV

Hospice. Lynda Hull. PuP-15

Hospital. Wilfred John Funk. PoToHe

Hospital, The. Patrick Kavanagh. BIrV; CABP; CIP-2

Hospital. Geoffrey C. Millard. PeSA

Hospital. Charles North. FTOS

Hospital, The. Sofiya Iul'evna Preygel, *Russian.* TCRP, *tr. by* Bradley Jordan

Hospital. Karl Shapiro. VGW

Hospital. Boris Abramovich Slutsky, *Russian.* TCRP, *tr. by* J. R. Rowland

Hospital. / All in white. My Friends. Mikhail Kuz'mich Lukonin, *Russian.* TCRP, *tr. by* Albert C. Todd

Hospital Barge at Cérisy. Wilfred Owen. RB

Hospital Duties. *Unknown.* CBCWP

Hospital Evening. Gwen Harwood. FaBoWP

Hospital for Defectives. Thomas Blackburn. GTBS-P; OxBTC

Hospital for sick and needy Jews, A. The New Jewish Hospital at Hamburg. Heinrich Heine, *German.* TrJP, *tr. by* Charles Godfrey Leland

Hospital: it wasn't her idea, The. Darlene's Hospital. John Ashbery. ColAP

Hospital Night. Francis Webb. BMAP

Hospital/Poem. Sonia Sanchez. BPo; PoBA

Hospital Prison Ship, The. Philip Freneau. AmPP *Fr.* The British Prison Ship.

Hospital—Retrospections, The. Kenneth Mackenzie. CBAP (New Arrival.) BMAP

Hospital State, The. Betsy Sholl. PBCAP

Hospital Window, The. James Dickey. HCAP; MT; NoAM; PFE; VCAP

Hospitality in Ancient Ireland. *Unknown, Irish.* TIRV, *tr. by* Kuno Meyer

Host is riding from Knocknarea, The. The Hosting of the Sidhe. W. B. Yeats. NoAM

Host of peaks rear up into the color of cold, A. Spending the Night at a Mountain Temple. Chia Tao, *Chinese.* SuSp, *tr. by* Stephen Owen

Host of the Air, The. W. B. Yeats. CH

Hostages, The. Muriel Rukeyser. AF

Hostel, The. Herman Melville. APN-2 *Fr.* Clarel: A Poem and Pilgrimage in the Holy Land.

Hostess' Daughter, The. Ludwig Uhland, *German.* AWP, *tr. by* Margarete Münsterberg

Hostess of the Ferry Inn, The. Gwerfyl Mechain, *Welsh*. OBWVE, *tr. by* H. Idris Bell

Hostesse, The. Virgil, *Latin*. OBCVT, *tr. by* Thomas Stanley

Hosting of the Sidhe, The. W. B. Yeats. NoAM

Hot afternoon. Anita Virgil. HA

Hot Afternoons Have Been in West 15th Street. Paul Blackburn. VGW

Hot Anger stirs the soup; Grief moves the dust. The Sisters. Melissa Cannon. FFC

Hot Bath in an Old Hotel. Paula Rankin. MT

Hot Boiled Beans. *Unknown*. ReMoGo

Hot boys, she says, are sweet in the summertime. Heat. Deborah Stein. BAP-96

Hot Cake. Shu Hsi, *Chinese*. ChiP, *tr. by* Arthur Waley

Hot Codlins. *Unknown*. ReMoGo

Hot cross buns, hot cross buns / One a penny poker. *Unknown*. OxNR

Hot cross buns! Hot-cross buns! / One a penny, two a penny. Mother Goose. BoTP; OxNR; ReMoGo

Hot Day. Henrikas Radauskas, *Lithuanian*. CEEP, *tr. by* Jonas Zdanys

Hot Day at the Races. Tom Raworth. SPE

Hot Day In Sydney, A. *Unknown*. NOBAu

Hot Dog Poem, The. Jane Barnes. GLP

Hot Flame of My Grief, The. Moses ibn Ezra, *Hebrew*. TrJP, *tr. by* Solomon Solis-Cohen

Hot horn hand in my face is all. My Mother Shoots the Breeze. Fred Chappell. MT

Hot, humid, the smell of sewage. Greenhalgh's Pub. Julian Croft. NOBAu

Hot in June a narrow winged. A Nameless One. Margaret Avison. HeIP-4; NOBC

Hot midsummer night on Water Street, A. Hot Night on Water Street. Louis Simpson. TwCP

Hot night. Cor Van den Heuvel. HA

Hot night makes us keep our bedroom windows open, The. To Speak of Woe That Is in Marriage. Robert Lowell. MoP; NAAL-2; NoAM

Hot night of the ramparts. Embrace the Blade. Joyce Mansour, *French*. PBWP, *tr. by* Carol Cosman

Hot Night on Water Street. Louis Simpson. TwCP

Hot Noon in Malabar. Kamala Das. OMIP

Hot Pease Man, The. Mother Goose. OxNR; ReMoGo

Hot red rocks of Aden, The. Home Thoughts. *Unknown*. NSI

Hot-spit-and-damn of unchartable cargo flashes past. Red Letters. Mekeel McBride. CMAP

Hot Springs. Earle Birney. OxBC

Hot Summer Sunday. A. L. Hendriks. PBCV

Hot summer wind, A. Lorraine Ellis Harr. HA

Hot sun[ne], cool[e] fire, tempered with sweet air[e]. Bethsabe's Song. George Peele. ChIV-1; GBL; ImPo; NOBE; NoSic; OxBSP; OxBoLi; PoEL-2; RB *Fr.* Love of King David and Fair Bethsabe. ChIV-1

Hot sun, cool fire, tempered with sweet air. George Peele. *See* Bethsabe's Song.

Hot thme, The. Just after Michael's Death, the Game of Pool. Richard Tipping. BMAP

Hotel again! My friend Paul is a prisoner of the Germans My, The. In Search of the Traitor. Max Jacob, *French*. AF, *tr. by* Michael Brownstein

Hotel Ameridemocratogrando. Black Man, 13th Floor. James A. Emanuel. NBV

Hotel De Dream. Jane Cooper. NMM-2

Hotel de l'Univers et Portugal. James Merrill. PoA

Hotel doorman's frantic whistle, The. Theatre Hour. Ogden Nash. ImGa

Hotel Fire: New Orleans. Paul Ruffin. InPK-6

Hôtel Fraternité. Hans Magnus Enzensberger, *German*. CLPP, *tr. by* Jerome Rothenberg

Hotel in Paris. Dennis Trudell. PoA

Hotel Lautréamont. John Ashbery. FTOS

Hotel Marine. David Campbell. BMAP

Hotel Nights with My Mother. Linda McCarriston. NMM-2

Hotel Normandie Pool, The. Derek Walcott. HCP; VCWP

Hotel North. Yongt'ae Kim, *Korean*. CKP, *tr. by* Jaihiun Kim

Hotel Paradiso e Commerciale. John Malcolm Brinnin. NYBP; TwCP

Hotel Sander, The. Donald Revell. CMAP

Hôtel Transylvanie. Frank O'Hara. NeAP; PoM

Hotels. C. D. Wright. CMAP

Hothouse Flowers. Theodore Wratislaw. ADE

Hots, The. Michael Sharkey. NOBAu

Hottentot Venus. Stephen Gray. PeSAV

Hou lang we've socht. The Mankind Toun. Tom Scott. FaBoTC

Houdini. Eli W. Mandel. NIP-4; NOBC

Hough gruntough wough Thomough. Epitaph in the Bermuda Tongue, Which Must Be Pronounced With the Accent of the Grunting of a Hog. John Taylor. CBNP

Hound, The. Robert Francis. SoSe-8

Hound, The. Kaye Starbird. KaS

Hound / Could never be called refined, The. The Angry Poet. Frank O'Connor, *Irish*. CIP-2

Hound of Heaven, The. Francis Thompson. ChIV-2; EBEvV; EnVR; ImPo; LiTM; MoBrPo; NAEL-2; OBMV; PoEL-5; TFi

Hounded Lovers, The. William Carlos Williams. NYBP

Hounded slave that flags in the race, leans by the fence, The. The Wounded Person. Walt Whitman. *Fr.* Song of Myself. AmPP; MoAmPo; NAAL-3; NOBA; OxBA

Hounds, The. John Freeman. OBMV; OxBSP

Hounds are breathing at my trail, The. Can-Can. John Fuller. PeLV *Fr.* Fox-Trot.

Hounds are either the work of wind, The. Dennis Phillips. FTOS *Fr.* Means.

Hounds of Spring, The. Swinburne. AWP; CTC; EBVV; FaBoBe; HAP; NAEL-2; NOBE; OAEL-2; OBEV; PoE; SCGP; TFi; WeW-3 *Fr.* Atalanta in Calydon.

  (Chorus.) EBVVPR; EnVR; GTBS-P

Hounds of the Soul, The. Louis Ginsberg. TrJP

Hounds that heralded the rich, The. Against Paradise. Jonathan Holden. NAmP90

Hour, The. Vivian Virtue. PBCV

Hour after hour the cards were fairly shuffled. Whist. Eugene Fitch Ware. PoLF

Hour at last come round, The. The Dying Gaul. Desmond O'Grady. BIrV; PBCIP

Hour farther witch art in Heaven. Robert Desnos, *French*. MFP, *tr. by* Martin Sorrell

Hour from night to day, The. Four in the Morning. Wislawa Szymborska, *Polish*. BLT; PiM, *tr. by* Magnus J. Krynski *and* Robert A. Maguire

"Hour gets later, the times get worse, The." Preliminary Poem. John Heath-Stubbs. OxBC

Hour Glass, The ("Consider this small dust, here in the glass"). Ben Jonson. GLoP; ImPo

Hour-Glass [*or* Houre-Glasse], The. Ben Jonson. BeJo; CaPo; EnLoPo; NIP-4; OAEL-1; SeCP

Hour Glass, The. Edward Quillinan. NOBRP

Hour-glass whispers to the lion's roar, The. Our Bias. W. H. Auden. MoP; Poetr

Hour-hand and the minute-hand upon a polished dial, The. The Speed Track. "Peter." BoTP

Hour has struck, though I heard not the bell!, The. (LL) This was the woman; what now of the man? George Meredith. EnVR; Son *Fr.* Modern Love.

Hour in a Studio, An. Richard Watson Gilder. APN-2

Hour is dark. The river comes to its end, The. Mary Ursula Bethell. PeNZ *Fr.* By the River Ashley.

Hour is held deep, in the underneath of time, An. Naming Souls. Uri Zvi Greenberg, *Hebrew*. PeFWW, *tr. by* Jon Silkin *and* Ezra Spicehandler

"Hour is late, The," the shepherds said. The Shepherd Left Behind. Mildred Plew Meigs. TrCP

Hour of Death, The. Felicia Dorothea Hemans. NOBRP; OBNC

Hour of Magic, The. W. H. Davies. MoBrPo

Hour of Peaceful Rest, The. There Is an Hour of Peaceful Rest. William Bingham Tappan. AH

Hour of Sleep, The. Robert Ellis, *Welsh*. OBWVE, *tr. by* H. Idris Bell

Hour ten he rose, ten-sworded, every finger. Timoshenko. Sidney Keyes. OBWP

Hour, the spot, are here at last, The. At Harper's Ferry Just before the Attack. Edward W. Williams. AAP; CBCWP

Hour when the moon mists over. Dawn. Philippe Jaccottet, *French*. VCWP, *tr. by* W. S. Merwin

Hour with thee! When earliest day, An. Sir Walter Scott. BoLoP; GLoP

Hourglass, The. Joseph Beaumont. NOSC

Hourglass. Josephine Jacobsen. BAP-93; NoP-4

Hours, The. John Peale Bishop. OxBA

Hours, The. David Diop, *French*. NegPo, *tr. by* Ellen Conroy Kennedy

Hours, The. Paul Ramsey. CRP

Hours are viewless angels, The. Christopher Pearse Cranch. PWR

Hours before dawn we were woken by the quake. Aubade. William Empson. FaBoMo; FaBoTw; OxAEP-2; OxBTC

Hours continuing long, sore and heavy-hearted. Walt Whitman. PAR; PoPoPo

  ("Face of his hours reflected?, The.") (LL) PoPoPo

Hour's Glory, The. Henrietta Cordelia Ray. CBWP-3

Hours I spent with thee, dear heart, The. The Rosary. Robert Cameron Rogers. FaBoBe

Hour's Late, The. Abba Kovner, *Hebrew.* IP, *tr.* by Warren Bargad *and* Stanley F. Chyet

Hours of rest are over, The. To-Day. Lessie M. Drown. PWR

Hours of Sleep. *Unknown.* NBLV

Hours of Solitude. Charlotte Dacre.
  Il Trionfo del Amor. Ro

Hours of the Day, The. Richard Kenney.
  In Retrospect. Son

Hours pass / slowly as a snail. Clockface. Judith Thurman. Spl

Hours rise up putting off stars and it is, The. Impression. E. E. Cummings. MoAmPo; OxBA

Hours when nothing but the rumours. Nights in Black Valley. Gerald Mangan. FaBoTC

Hous-keping's dead, *Saturio:* wot'st thou where? Joseph Hall. PBRV *Fr.* Virgidemiarum Book 5.

House, The. George Bowering. NOBC

House. Robert Browning. NAEL-2

House, The. Robert Creeley. FTOS

House, A. Yuly Markovich Daniel, *Russian.* TCRP, *tr.* by David Burg *and* Arthur Boyars

House. Murray Edmond. PeNZ

House. Robert Hass. LoL

House, A. Libby Houston. NBrP

House. Sue May. NBrP

House across the Way, The. Ralph Hodgson. FaBoTw

House and hollow; village and valley-side. Winter Encounters. Charles Tomlinson. LiTM

House and Land. Allen Curnow. PeNZ

House Beautiful, The. Robert Louis Stevenson. NOBE

House Beside the Sea, The. Rachel Hadas. FFC

House (Blown Apart). David Shapiro. PT

House-Builders, The. Kamala Das. PBWP

House by the Side of the Road, The. Sam Walter Foss. BLPA; FaBoBe

House Cap. Bernadette Mayer. FTOS

House Carpenter, The. *Unknown.* AS

House Carpenter, The. *Unknown. See* Demon [*or* Daemon] Lover.

House cat has never seen the sea, The. Woman asleep. Marie-Claire Bancquart, *French.* MFP, *tr.* by Martin Sorrell

House Destroyed by Fire, The. Don Bogen. WeT

House Divided, A. Michael Ondaatje. MoCV

House Fear. Robert Frost. NTP; VGW *Fr.* The Hill Wife. CMoP; HAP; InPS-3; LiTM; NoP-4; RACG

House fell head-first, quietly crushing all but a child, The. Bianor, *Greek.* GrAn, *tr.* by Richard Evans

House full, a hole full, A. *Unknown.* OxNR

House full, [a] yard full, [A]. Riddle. *Unknown.* LB; NTCP

House Guest. Elizabeth Bishop. NYBP; TAP

House had gone to bring again, The. The Need of Being Versed in Country Things. Robert Frost. NOBA; NoAM; OxBA; SAmP; TRP; UnPo

House I knew not, newly cloth'd with skin. (LL) The Preparative. Thomas Traherne. ESCV; GeHe; PoEL-2

House in Broad Street, red brick, with nine rooms, The. The Things. Conrad Potter Aiken. HAP; WeW-3

House in Byzantium, A. Agathias, *Greek.* GrAn, *tr.* by Fleur Adcock

House in Spring. Wesley McNair. AFr; CMAP
  ("Of Mars Hill, Maine.") (LL) AFr

House in Taos, A. Langston Hughes. NAAAL

House in the Green Well, The. John Hall Wheelock. MoAmPo

House in the Wood, The. Randall Jarrell. LCAP-2

House Is an Enigma. Laura Jensen. LCAP-2

House is cold. It's raining, The. Joseph Come Back as the Dusk. Franz Wright. CMAP; LCAP-2

House is crammed: tier beyond tier they grin, The. Blighters. Siegfried Sassoon. CMoP; FaBoTw; MoP; NoAM; OxBSP; PoFWW; PoWW

House Is Empty, The. Yona Wallach, *Hebrew.* IP, *tr.* by Warren Bargad *and* Stanley F. Chyet

House is empty and the trough is broken, The. The House Is Empty. Yona Wollach, *Hebrew.* IP, *tr.* by Warren Bargad *and* Stanley F. Chyet

House is filled. The last heartthrob, The. Near the Ocean. Robert Lowell. NOBA

House is haunted; when the little feet, The. Haunted. Edith Nesbit. VWP

House is like a garden, The. A Holiday. Ella Wheeler Wilcox. OxBM

House Is Old, The. Ron Schreiber. GLP

House is so quiet now, The. The Vacuum. Howard Nemerov. NIP-4; RB

House is yours, The. William Carlos Williams. VGW

House leaks and leans, The. The Ancestors. John Peale Bishop. PoA

House Made of Rain, The. Naomi Shihab Nye. NAmP90

House Martins: This wind wafts little creatures. Cynewulf. AOW, *tr.* by Kevin Crossley-Holland *Fr.* Riddles (Exeter Book).

House-Mates. Leon Gellert. CBAP; NOBAu

House my earthly parent left, The. The Cottage. Jones Very. APN-1; OxBA

House Next Door, The. Douglas Dunn. OxBC

House next door has yellow windows, The. The Factory. Aleksandr Blok, *Russian.* TCRP, *tr.* by Yakov Hornstein

House of Ate, The. Edmund Spenser. *Fr.* Wood Of Error. AEP

House of Broughton Street, The. Mary Ann Larkin. AiP

House of Busyrane, The. Edmund Spenser. NoSic *Fr.* Wood Of Error. AEP

House of Christmas, The. G. K. Chesterton. MoBrPo

House of Desire, The. Sherley Anne Williams. BlSi

House of Falling Leaves, The. W. S. Braithwaite. NAAAL; PoLF

House of Fame, The. Virgil. OBCVT, *tr.* by Geoffrey Chaucer *Fr.* The Aeneid.

House of five fires, you never raised me. In the Longhouse, Oneida Museum. Roberta Hill Whiteman. NoAM

House of Geraniums, A. Peter Scupham. OxBSn

House of God, The. Alec Derwent Hope. OxBC; PFE

House of God is due to be converted, The. Development. D. J. Enright. OxBSP

House of Hospitalities, The. Thomas Hardy. RB

House of Life, The. D. G. Rossetti.
  Ardour and Memory. OAEL-2
  Autumn Idleness. GBL; OAEL-2
  Barren Spring. EBVV; IMW; NoP-4; OAEL-2; OBNC; PoEL-5
  Birth-Bond, The. Son
  Body's Beauty. OAEL-2; Son
    (Lilith.) PoEL-5
  Bridal Birth. Son
  Choice, The. GTBS-P; OBEV
  Heart's Haven. Son
  Hill Summit, The. NoP-4
  Inclusiveness. NAEL-2
  Kiss, The. NOBVV; Son
  Life-in-Love. HAP
  "Lost days of my life until to-day, The." EnVR
  Lost on Both Sides. EnVR
  Love Enthroned. OBNC
  Lovesight. EBVV; GTBS-P; NAEL-2; OBNC
  Mid-Rapture. FaBoBe
  Nuptial Sleep. EBVV; EnVR; NAEL-2; NOBVV
  One Hope, The. GSo; NAEL-2; OAEL-2
  Pride of Youth. OBNC
  Sea-Limits, The. EnVR; NAEL-2; OAEL-2
  Severed Selves. BoLoP; GLoP
  Silent Noon. EnVR; GLoP; GSo; GaP; HAP; NAEL-2; NoP-4; OBNC; PoEL-5
  Sonnet, A [*or* The: "Sonnet is a moment's monument"]. EnVR; NAEL-2; Son
  Soul's Beauty. OBEV
    (Sibylla Palmifera.) OxAEP-2
  Superscription, A. EBVV; GSo; GTBS-P; NAEL-2; NoP-4; OAEL-2; OBNC; PoEL-5
  Willowwood ("I sat with Love upon a woodside well"). CABP; NAEL-2; OAEL-2; PoEL-5
    ("Till both our heads were in his aureole.") (LL) CABP
  Willowwood ("And now love sang: but his was such a song"). NAEL-2; OAEL-2
  Willowwood ("O ye, all ye that walk in Willowwood"). NAEL-2; OAEL-2
  Willowwood ("So sang he: and as meeting rose and rose"). NAEL-2; OAEL-2
  Without Her. GBL; GLoP; OBNC; PoEL-5; Son
    ("What of her glass without her? The blank grey.") GLoP
  Woodspurge, The. CABP; EBEV; EnVR; GEA; GTBS-P; HAP; HeIP-4; NOBE; NoP-4; OAEL-2; OBEV; OBNC; PBMP; PoEL-5; SCGP; TfI; UnPo

House of Lords, The. Sir William Schwenck Gilbert. NAEL-2 *Fr.* Iolanthe.

House of Madam Juju, The. Mieko Kanai, *Japanese.* BoWoP, *tr.* by Christopher Drake

House of Mercy, A. Stevie Smith. FaBoWP

House of Mourning written by Mr Scott, The. All These Are Vile. Keats. OBCoV

House of Night, The. Philip Freneau.
 "At distance far approaching to the tomb." NAAL-1; NAAL-3
 "At last, by chance and guardian fancy led." NAAL-1; NAAL-3
 "But now this man of hell toward me turned." NAAL-1; NAAL-3
 "By some sad means, when reason holds no sway." PoEL-4
 "Much spoke he of the myrtle and the yew." NAAL-1; NAAL-3
 "Sad was his countenance, if we can call." NAAL-1; NAAL-3
 "Then up three winding stairs my feet were brought." NAAL-1; NAAL-3
 "Trembling I write my dream, and recollect." NAAL-1; NAAL-3
 "Up rushed a band, with compasses and scales." NAAL-1; NAAL-3

House of Prayer, The. William Cowper. ChIV-2 *Fr.* Olney Hymns.

House of Pride, The. William James Dawson. PoToHe

House of Red Leaves, The. Liu E, *Chinese.* CoBLCP, *tr. by* Jonathan Chaves

House of Rest. John Betjeman. OxAEP-2
 ("And all of them are near.") (LL) LBC

House of Richesse, The. Edmund Spenser. CH *Fr.* Wood Of Error. AEP

House of the Customs-Men, The. Eugenio Montale. ItIP

House of the Injured, The. John Haines. WeT

House of the mouse, The. Lucy Sprague Mitchell. NTCP

House on a Cliff. Louis MacNeice. NOIV

House on Bentalou Street, The. Beginnings. Michael S. Weaver. PBCAP

House on Buder Street, The. Gary Gildner. TAP

House on fire, A! We stumbled over the snow. Houses Burning; Quebec. Patrick Anderson. NOBC

House on Moscow Street, The. Marilyn Nelson Waniek. NMM-2; UnSA

House on the Hill, The. Edwin Arlington Robinson. APN-2; GEA; MoAmPo; NAAL-2; NCAP

House Plants. David McFadden. NOBC

House ringed round with trees and in the trees, A. Asylum. John Freeman. OBMV

House-Rules I: Reading. Alistair Elliot. CBLP

House Slave, The. Rita Dove. NoAM

House-Slave, The. Mervyn Morris. PBCV

House-snake dwells here still, The. The Closed World. Denise Levertov. NoP-4

House Song to the East. *Unknown, Navajo Indian.* TTTS

House That Fear Built: Warsaw, 1943, The. Jane Flanders. CrSp; PBCAP

House That Jack Built, The. Coleridge. CBNP *Fr.* Sonnets Attempted in the Manner of Contemporary Writers. Son

House That Jack Built, The. Mother Goose. BoTP; FaBoBe; OxBoLi; OxNR; ReMoGo

House That Jack Built, The. *Unknown.* FaBoBe; NBLV; OxBoLi

House That Was, The. Laurence Binyon. MoBrPo

House-Top, The. Herman Melville. APN-2; CBCWP; NAAL-1; NAAL-3; NCAP; NOBA

House, village, city, land, and empire harvest hurt. Women's Rule. Friedrich von Logau, *German.* GePo, *tr. by* George C. Schoolfield

House was empty and, The. Music in an Empty House. Hugh Sykes Davies. SPE

House was quiet and the world was calm, The. Wallace Stevens. AiP; HAP; NoP-4; SAmP; VGW

House was shaken by a rising wind, The. Brainstorm. Howard Nemerov. HAP; TRP

House was still—the room was still, The. Charlotte Brontë. NOBVV

House where I was born, The. The Doves. Katharine Tynan. AWP

House, with blind unhappy face, The. The Gray Folk. Edith Nesbit. NOBVV; PEW

House with coarse stuccoed, The. Tania Van Zyl. PeSA

House with Nobody in It, The. Joyce Kilmer. BLPA; ChAP

House-wreckers have left the door and a staircase, The. Charles Reznikoff. KaS

Houseboat Days. John Ashbery. FTOS

Houseboat Mouse. Charles Sullivan. ImGa

Household. Laura Jensen. LCAP-2

Household Dilemma. Angie Gilligan. NBrP

Household Fires. Indira Sant, *Marathi.* OMIP, *tr. by* Vinay Dharwadker

Household of Ruth, The. Mrs. Henry Linden. CBWP-4

Household words, no more depart. (LL) Seaweed. Henry Wadsworth Longfellow. APN-1; ColAP; OxBA; TAP

Housekeeper, The. Vincent Bourne, *Latin.* PoLF, *tr. by* Charles Lamb

Houseplant. Felicity Napier. BrRo

Houses. Agha Shahid Ali. NIP-4

Houses, The. "Robin Hyde."
 "Adolicus; that's a creeper rug, its small." PeNZ

"Hares on their forms at dusk were not so still." PeNZ
 "None of it true; for Christ's sake, spill the ink." PeNZ

Houses. Donald Justice. WeT
 (Poem.) PoA

Houses. Dan Pagis, *Hebrew.* IP, *tr. by* Warren Bargad *and* Stanley F. Chyet

Houses, The. Eden Phillpotts. OxBTC

Houses, an embassy, the hospital. Days of 1964. James Merrill. CoAP; HCAP; NAAL-2; PoE; VCAP

Houses and rooms are full of perfumes. Walt Whitman. EBEvV; UnPo *Fr.* Song of Myself. AmPP; MoAmPo; NAAL-3; NOBA; OxBA
 ("Houses and rooms are full of perfumes, the shelves are crowded with perfumes.") ColAP

Houses are faces. Aileen Fisher. NTCP

Houses are haunted, The. Disillusionment of Ten O'Clock. Wallace Stevens. CBNP; CMoP; ChAP; InPS-3; NAAL-2; NoAM; OxBA; RB; SAmP; SoSe-8; TRP; TTTS

Houses Burning; Quebec. Patrick Anderson. NOBC

Houses, churches, mixed together. A Description of London. John Bancks. NOEC; OBCoV

Houses die, and will not die, The. Heartland. Jim Barnes. HATNAP

Houses of Corr an Chait are cold, The. Seamas Dall Mac Cuarta, *Irish.* NOIV, *tr. by* Thomas Kinsella

Houses of Emily Dickinson, The. Larry Rubin. NIP-4

Houses of the city no longer hum and play, The. John Gould Fletcher. *Fr.* Irradiations. MoAmPo

Houses trot toward us. Elm Street. Alberta Turner. CMAP

Housewife. Susan Fromberg Schaeffer. CrSp

Housewife. Anne Sexton. NALW; NMM-2

Housewifery. Edward Taylor. *See* Huswifery.

Housewife's Letter: To Mary. Anne Halley. NMM-2

Housewife's Prayer on the Morning Preceding a Fete, The. Elizabeth Moody. ECWP

Housework. Amanda Berenguer, *Spanish.* WPOW, *tr. by* Priscilla Joslin

Housing. Denise Riley. NBrP

Housing conditions: number of galaxy and star. End of the Questionnaire. Dan Pagis, *Hebrew.* NNPT, *tr. by* Stephen Mitchell

Housing Shortage. Naomi Replansky. CrSp; NMM-2

Hovering at a Low Altitude. Dahlia Ravikovitch, *Hebrew.* VCWP, *tr. by* Chana Bloch *and* Ariel Bloch

Hovering clouds scatter over the islet. Arriving at North Pond by Stupid Brook on a Morning Walk after the Rain. Liu Tsung-yüan, *Chinese.* SuSp, *tr. by* Jan W. Walls

Hovering like the heron. What She Said. Orampokiyar. PLW *Fr.* Five on the Riverside Cane. PLW, *tr. by* A. K. Ramanujan

How a Girl Got Her Chinese Name. Nellie Wong. WPOW

How a Girl Was Too Reckless of Grammar [by Far]. Guy Wetmore Carryl. OBAL

How-a! How-a! / O-ta-pa! / I am proud of being at home! Wa-Sissica, the War Song. *Unknown.* APN-2 *Fr.* War Dance. APN-2, *tr. by* George Catlin

How about that! (LL) To Satch. Samuel Allen. ISC; PoBA; TTY

How all occasions do inform against me. Shakespeare. HoPM *Fr.* Hamlet. NAWM-1

How am I hitched. Suffering. Albert Ehrenstein, *German.* TrJP, *tr. by* Babette Deutsch

How amiable are thy tabernacles, O Lord of hosts! Bible, *O.T. See* Psalm 84.

How Annandale Went Out. Edwin Arlington Robinson. GSo; MoAmPo; NOBA; NoAM; PFE; SoSe-8

How Apollo's laurel sapling shakes. Hymn to Apollo. Callimachus. HePo, *tr. by* Barbara Hughes Fowler *Fr.* Hymns.

How are our Spirituall Gamesters slipt away? An Elegy upon the Death of That Holy Man of God Mr. John Allen. Edward Taylor. PoEL-3

How are the mighty fallen, and the weapons of war perished! (LL) David's Lament. Bible, *O.T.* AWP; OBVE; OBWP; TrJP

How are thy servants blest, O Lord! Ode. Joseph Addison. OxAEP-1; OxBoS

How Are You, Dear World, This Morning? Horace Logo Traubel. TrJP

How are you so smooth-faced. Girl. *Unknown, Serbian.* RB, *tr. by* Anne Pennington

How Bacchus Finds Ariadne Sleeping. Nonnus. *See* Dionysiaca.

"How bare! How all the lion-desert lies." Macrinus against Trees. "Michael Field." WPE

How beastly the bourgeois is. D. H. Lawrence. LiTM; NAEL-2; OBSV

How beautiful and calm how crimson pale. The Spirit Craft. Charles G. Ballard. VoR

How beautiful are both these nothings. (LL) Shane O'Neill's Cairn. Robinson Jeffers. NOBA; NoAM

How beautiful are thy feet with shoes. Song of Songs. *Unknown.* NNPT, *tr. by Unknown*

How beautiful, how beautiful you streamed upon my sight. Corinne's Last Love Song. Lady Jane Francesca Wilde. VWP

How beautiful is the rain! Rain in Summer. Henry Wadsworth Longfellow. AYFP; BoTP

How beautiful it was, that one bright day. Hawthorne. Henry Wadsworth Longfellow. PoEL-5

How beautiful the Buddhist statues. Imaizumi Sogetsu-Ni, *Japanese.* WPJ, *tr. by Kenneth Rexroth and Ikuko Atsumi*

How beautiful the Earth is still. Anticipation. Emily Jane Brontë. OBNC

How beautiful this hill of fern swells on! Stanzas from "Child Harold." John Clare. OBNC *Fr. Child Harold.*

How Beautiful upon the Mountains. Bible, *O.T.* TrJP *Fr. Isaiah.*

How beautiful you are, my love. A Canticle for Abba Jacob. Marilyn Nelson Waniek. FFC

How Big Was Alexander? Elijah Jones. BLPA

How bitter for these border men! Call to Arms. Tso Yen-nien, *Chinese.* CoBCP, *tr. by Burton Watson*

How bless'd the Swain of *Bethnal-green.* Felix, qui patriis. . . and c.: Imitated from Claudian. Claudian, *Latin.* OBCVT, *tr. by Stephen Duck*

How blessed is a middle rank in life! Nguyễn Trãi, *Vietnamese.* AVP, *tr. by Huỳnh Sanh Thông*

How blessed is he who leads a country life. To My Honoured [*or* Honour'd] Kinsman, John Driden [of Chesterton in the County of Huntingdon, Esquire]. Dryden.

How blessed [*or* blest] was the created state. The Fall. John Wilmot, 2d Earl of Rochester. ChIV-1; EnLoPo

How blest are lovers in disguise! A Song. George Farquhar. NOSC

How blest art thou, canst love the country [*or* countrey], Wroth. To Sir Robert Wroth. Ben Jonson. BeJo

How blest is he, who for his country dies. To the Earl of Oxford, Late Lord Treasurer. Jonathan Swift, *after the Latin of* Horace. OBVE

How blest the land that counts among. The Statesmen. Ambrose Bierce. APN-2

How blest would be Ïërne's isle. Written in Ireland. Mary Alcock. ECWP; NOEC

How blind men are! We surely cannot know. Understanding. H. W. Bliss. PoToHe

How brave the peasant who lives beside the lake. Hsü Chung-hsing. CoBLCP, *tr. by Jonathan Chaves Fr.* Song of Catching Tigers.

How brazenly new is that old moon up there. And a Star Fell. Marie Under, *Estonian.* CEEP, *tr. by Ivar Ivask*

"How brent is your brow, my Lady Elspat!" Lady Elspat. *Unknown.* ESPB

How bright this weird autumnal eve. Fires in Illinois. John James Piatt. APN-2

How brightly glistening in the sun. Home. Anne Brontë. VWP

How brittle are the Piers. Emily Dickinson. NCAP

How busie are the sonnes of men? Roger Williams. SCAP

How busied's man. My CLose-Committee. Mildmay Fane, 2d Earl of Westmorland. BeJo

How but in custom and in ceremony. W. B. Yeats. ITG

How, butler, how! bevis a tout! *Unknown.* MiEL

How calm, how beautiful, comes on. The Golden Hour. Thomas Moore. OBNC *Fr. Lalla Rookh.*

"How came that blood on thy coat-lap?" The Dead Brother. *Unknown.* EnSB

How can a girl with such a big belly be so desirable? Mrs. Loewinsohn etc. Ron Loewinsohn. NeAP

How can any man throw out. Rufinus Domesticus, *Greek.* InMo, *tr. by Sam Hamill*

How *can* he be? The words are wild. (LL) Child Is Father to the Man, The. Gerard Manley Hopkins. NOBL; NOBVV; NTP

How can I be bitter? A Second-Hand Elegy. Michael Anania. CDa

How can I blame the cherry blossoms. The daughter of Shunzei, *Japanese.* WPJ, *tr. by Kenneth Rexroth and Ikuko Atsumi*

How can I call out? How can I shout? At Night. Bella Akhatovna Akhmadulina, *Russian.* BoWoP, *tr. by Daniel Halpern and Albert Todd*

How can I care whether you sigh for me. Song: How Can I Care? Robert Graves. GBL

How can I climb the Mount of Purgatory? Cato. Charles Hubert Sisson. NOCV

How can I complain / that you have shaved your hair? Yokobue, *Japanese.* WPJ, *tr. by Kenneth Rexroth and Ikuko Atsumi*

How can I describe anything when all these interruptions keep *arriving* and then. Hannah Weiner. PmAP *Fr.* Clairvoyant Journal.

How can I give thee up, my child, my dearest, earliest born. Wail of the Divorced. Mary E. Tucker. CBWP-1

How can I help myself, as one woman said to me about wanting. Leslie Scalapino. DeD *Fr.* Hmmmm.

How can I hope a wise heart to attain. Dietmar von Aist [or Eist]. *German.* GePo, *tr. by Carroll Hightower*

How can I regret my life. The Signal. David Ignatow. NNaP

How can I say about the music, how can I. Of What The Music to Me. Clark Coolidge. MoNo

How can I say this? I Learned To Sew. Mitsuye Yamada. LoHo

How Can I See You, Love. David Vogel, *Hebrew.* HP, *tr. by* A. C. Jacobs

How Can I Show This Poem to Geraldine? Kitty Tsui. CPO

How Can I Sing. Odia Ofeimun. HBAPE

How can I sing light-souled and fancy-free. Lorenzo de' Medici. *Fr.* Two Lyrics. AWP, *tr. by John Addington Symonds*

How can I sustain. Private Pain in Time of Trouble. Kathleen Spivack. AmPA

How can I tell you. S. J. Marks. NYBP

How can I tell you of the terrible cries. The Wars. Howard Moss. VCAP

How can I thank you B, for your ear, your mind, your affection? The Inn at Kirchstetten. James Laughlin. PmAP

How can I, that girl standing there. Politics. W. B. Yeats. CBLP; CMoP; HeIP-4; InPS-3; OxBTC; PoE; SAGP; SCV

How can I turn from Africa and live? (LL) A Far Cry from Africa. Derek Walcott. HeIP-4; MoP; NAEL-2; NoAM; NoP-4; PBCV; PFE; TTY; UnPo

How can I turn this wheel that turns my life. The Wheel. Edwin Muir. NoAM

How can I, who cannot control. Blind Steersmen. Francis Ernest Kobina Parkes. PBA

How can I write about you. My True Love Hath My Heart. Naomi Mitchison. LW

How can one e'er be sure. Lady Horikawa. *Fr.* Hyaku-Nin-Isshu. AWP, *tr. by Curtis Hidden Page*

How can one make an absence flower. A Flowering Absence. John Montague. BiHa; CIP-2; PBCIP

How can one tell what Love may be about. Psychoanalysis. Gavin Ewart. NYBP

How can the tide of the river be compared to your love? Po Chü-i. SuSp, *tr. by Irving Y. Lo Fr.* Tune: "Ripples Sifting Sand."

How can the tree but waste and wither away. Death in Life. Thomas, 2d Baron Vaux of Harrowden Vaux. NoSic

How can there be heroic feelings, as in bygone days? Lamenting Yang Ch'uan. "Lu Hsün," *Chinese.* SuSp, *tr. by William R. Schultz*

How can they write or paint. Observations in a Cornish Teashop. Kenneth Rexroth. OBAL

How can we know the dancer from the dance? (LL) Among School Children. W. B. Yeats. CABP; CMoP; GTBS-P; HAP; ImPo; InPS-3; LiTM; MoBrPo; MoP; NAEL-2; NAWM-2; NIP-4; NOBE; NoAM; NoP-4; OAEL-2; OxBTC; PoE; PoPoPo; Poetr; SCGP; TFi; TRP

How can we live without the unknown in front of us? Argument. René Char, *French.* AF, *tr. by Mary Ann Caws*

How can you be quite so uncouth? After sharing. Ode to the Diencephalon. W. H. Auden. OxAEP-2

How can you live, how exist. The Likeness. Arthur Gregor. VGW

How can you look at the Neva. "Anna Akhmatova," *Russian.* BoWoP, *tr. by Stanley Kunitz and Max Hayward*

How can you set to the table a-dining? The Lost Baby. *Unknown.* AmFP

How! Canst thou see the basket wherein lay. Moses in Infancy. Jones Very. ChIV-1; KSG

How cast down is the mind that took to my Lesbia, culprit. Catullus. *See* Carmen 75 ("Reason blinded by sin, Lesbia").

How changed is here each spot man makes or fills! Matthew Arnold. *Fr.* Thyrsis. EnVR; FHYEP; NAEL-2; NOBE; NoP-4; OBEV; OBNC

How charmingly permanence strolls. From the Skein of the Straight Line. Tymoteusz Karpowicz, *Polish.* CEEP, *tr. by Zak, Ewa*

How cold the snow. *Unknown.* PChr, *tr. by Cheli Durán Fr.* Four Christmas Carols.

How come nobody is being bombed today? All Quiet. David Ignatow. CoAmPo

How Come the Truck-Loads? Judith Rodriguez. FaBoWP

How come to town she was, tied bright and prim. On a Photograph of My Mother at Seventeen. Miller Williams. MT

How comely glisten the rounded cheeks. Fatness. Alan Ansen. CoAP

How comes it, Flora, that, whenever we. The Queen of Hearts. Christina Rossetti. CBLP; PeVV

How comes that blood all over thy shirt? Edward. *Unknown.* HoPM

How comest thou, O flower so fair. The Snowdrop. Mary Weston Fordham. CBWP-2

How comforting. The Day They Cleaned Up the Border El Salvador, February, 1981. Wendy Rose. HATNAP

How comforting it is, once or twice a year. James Fenton. Fr. A German Requiem. NAEL-2; NoAM

How compare either of this grim twain? Thomas Hardy and A. E. Housman. Max Beerbohm. NBLV

How cool it feels. Basho, *Japanese*. TTTS, *tr. by* Kenneth Koch *and* Harold Henderson

How could God think of so many. Our Wonderful World. Jessie Orton Jones. CTV *Fr.* (XXI from Secrets).

How *could* I but rejoice? (LL) A Cottage in Grasmere Vale. Dorothy Wordsworth. NALW; PEW

How could I have known. Rufinus Domesticus, *Greek*. InMo, *tr. by* Sam Hamill

How could I seek the empty world again? (LL) Remembrance. Emily Jane Brontë. BoLoP; BoWoP; BrRo; CABP; CBLP; CH; EBEV; EBVV; EnLoPo; EnVR; GLoP; HAP; IMW; LBC; NAEL-2; NALW; NOBE; NOBVV; NoP-4; OBNC; OxAEP-2; PBWP; PEW; PoE; PoEL-5; PoPoPo; Poetr; TFi; VWP; WPE; WeW-3

How could my mother have known. Thinking of My Mother Who Fifteen Years Later, Has Gone East to See the Leaves. Judith Sornberger. MDDM

How could she not take pride in him. On the Marriage at Cana. Rilke, *German*. GI, *tr. by* David Curzon *and* Will Alexander Washburn

How could they do it, as though a smoky wind. The Weepers. Rodney Jones. NAmP90

How could we be so happy, now some thousand years. Note to Wang Wei. John Berryman. NYBP

How crowded and bustling it is over there. Tune: "Going Up Small Pavilion." Kuan Yün-shih. SuSp, *tr. by* Richard John Lynn *Fr.* Medley of Southern and Northern Tunes—Scenic Tour of West Lake.

How cruel is the story of Eve. Stevie Smith. NALW

How cursed that country, how severe its doom. Thomas Maurice. NOEC *Fr.* An Epistle to the Right Hon. Charles James Fox.

How daur ye ca' me "Howlet-face." Robert Burns. FaBoEE

How dear to my heart are the grand politicians. The Old Hokum Buncombe. Robert E. Sherwood. NBLV

How dear to my [*or* this the] heart are the scenes of my childhood. The Old Oaken Bucket. Samuel Woodworth. BLPA; FaBoBe

How dear to my heart is the old village drugstore. The Hair-Tonic Bottle. Ben King. OBAL

How dear to this heart are the scenes of my childhood. The Bucket. Samuel Woodworth. APN-1

How Death Came. *Unknown, Hottentot*. PeSA; TTY, *tr. by* W. H. I. Bleek

How deep we met in the sea, my love. First Love. Jean Valentine. NMM-2

How deep yon azure dyes the sky! Thomas Parnell. OxAEP-1 *Fr.* Night Piece on Death. NOEC

How delectable are the attributes of Virginity! Meditation, Followed by Excellent Advice. Eratosthenes, *Greek*. GrAn, *tr. by* Dudley Fitts

How Delicately. Joyce Carol Oates. EOEF

How delicious is the winning. Freedom and Love. Thomas Campbell. GLoP; GTBS-P

How delightful, at sunset, to loosen the boat! The Excursion. Tu Fu, *Chinese*. AWP, *tr. by* Amy Lowell *and* Florence Ayscough

How delightful to meet Mr. Hodgson! Lines to Ralph Hodgson Esqre. T. S. Eliot. NBLV; OBAL; PeLV *Fr.* Five-Finger Exercises.

How did a great Red-tailed Hawk. The Dead by the Side of the Road. Gary Snyder. HAP; InPS-3

How did he die / O if I told you. The Gangster's Death. Ishmael Reed. PoBA

How did I miss this isthmus of old bricks between the Shelter-Workshop amd the Dominion Bank. Progress Alley. Rodney Jones. WWSi

How did she leave the world? with what contempt? Ben Jonson. Fr. An Elegy [*or* Elegie] on the Lady Jane Pawlet [*or* Paulet], [Marchioness of Winton]. SeCP

How did the party go in Portman Square? Juliet. Hilaire Belloc. BoLoP; EnLoPo; GLoP

How did the stones vote. The Election. Leonard Nathan. PBCAP

How did they fume, and stamp, and roar, and chafe. Atticus. Alexander Pope. *Fr.* Epistle to Dr. Arbuthnot. FHYEP; InPS-3; NoP-4; OAEL-1; OxAEP-1; PoE; PoEL-3; TFi

How did they kill my grandmother? How They Killed My Grandmother. Boris Abramovich Slutsky, *Russian*. HP, *tr. by* Daniel Weissbort

How did you come to develop the concept of Negritude? Aime Cesaire *and* Rene Depestre. PFTM, *tr. by* Joan Pinkham *Fr.* Discourse on Colonialism.

How did you come to me, my sweet? To a Child Who Inquires. Olga Petrova. BLPA

How Did You Die? Edmund Vance Cooke. BLPA; CTV; PWR

How died my master, Strato? Shakespeare. OxAEP-1 *Fr.* Julius Caesar.

How Different! Ebenezer Elliot. EBEV

How difficult to live without you! "Naum Korzhavin," *Russian*. TCRP, *tr. by* Stanley Kunitz

How dishonest the sun. Seeing through the Sun. Linda Hogan. HATNAP

How do I enter the silence of stones. Mona Sa'udi, *Arabic*. WPOW, *tr. by* Kamal Boullata

How do I hate you? Let me count the ways. Sonnet. Stanley J. Sharpless. UV

How do I know it is not my own? (LL) A Painting of the Butterfly Dream by the Master Artist Li Tsai. Chu Yün-ming, *Chinese*. ChiPo; CoBLCP, *tr. by* Jonathan Chaves

How do I love thee? Let me count the ways. Sonnet. Elizabeth Barrett Browning. APAD; BWW; BoLoP; CABP; CTC; EBEvV; EBVV; EnVR; FaBoBe; GLoP; GSo; HeIP-4; HoPM; ImPo; InPK-6; LBC; NAEL-2; NALW; NIP-4; NoP-4; OPOU; OxAEP-2; OxBM; PFE; PoE; PoLF; PoPoPo; PoRA; PoToHe; Poetr; SAGP; Son; TFi; UV; UnPo; VWP; WPE *Fr.* Sonnets from the Portuguese.

How do I love you, beech-trees, in the autumn. Beechwoods at Knole. Vita Sackville-West. NTP

How do I pity that proud wealthy clown. My Estate. John Norris. NOSC

How do I spin my time away. On the Spirit Adulterated by the Flesh. Thomas, the Elder Warton. ChIV-1

How do I thank thee, death, and bless thy power. On the Lady Arabella. Richard Corbet. NOSC

How do people feel. Stolen Away. Joseph Ceravolo. FTOS

How do robins build their nests? What Robin Told. George Cooper. CTV

How do they do it, the ones who make love. Sex without Love. Sharon Olds. DeD; HeIP-4; NIP-4; Poetr; TRP

How do we know, by the bank-high river. The Last Lap. Rudyard Kipling *Fr.* Land and Sea Tales.

How do you begin fully to realize that somebody is not. Facing Change. Dr. Tony Lake. LBC

How do you know that the pilgrim track. The Year's Awakening. Thomas Hardy. CMoP; OxBTC

How do you like to go up in a swing. The Swing. Robert Louis Stevenson. CTV; ChAP; FPC; FaBoBe; LiLi; NOxBChV; NTCP; TLR

How do you like what you have. Gertrude Stein. AiP *Fr.* Portraits and Repetition.

How do you like your blueeyed boy / Mister Death. (LL) Portrait. E. E. Cummings. AmPP; CMoP; HeIP-4; InPK-6; NAAL-2; NIP-4; NOBA; OxBSP; PoE; RB; TAP; VGW

How do you make bread talk, this old treasure all wrapped. Bread Is Born. Anne Hébert, *French*. BoWoP, *tr. by* Maxine W. Kumin

How do you recognize death? Minor Elegy. Henriqueta Lisboa, *Portuguese*. BoWoP, *tr. by* Willis Barnstone *and* Nelson Cerqueira

How Do You Shape an Axe Handle? Gary Snyder. NoAM

How do you spell change brother like frayed slogan underwear. New York City 1970. Audre Lorde. NBV

How does a person get to be a capable liar? Golly, How Truth Will Out. Ogden Nash. MoAmPo

How does it happen, tell me. Judge Somers. Edgar Lee Masters. FaBoEE; OBSV *Fr.* Spoon River Anthology.

How does it help me if, with flawless art. Elegy 23. Louise Labé, *French*. WPOW, *tr. by* Raymond Oliver

How does my royal soul? How fares your Majesty? Shakespeare. *Fr.* He wakes; speak to him. SCV *Fr.* King Lear.

How does one get outside. Dear Miss. Herman Gladwin. PeNZ

How does one stand. The American Sublime. Wallace Stevens. FaBoA

How Does the Negative Look. . . . Jaroslaw Iwaszkiewicz, *Polish*. CEEP, *tr. by* Magnus J. Krynski *and* Robert A. Maguire

How does the sun set? Jonah. Tomaz Salamun, *Slovenian*. CEEP, *tr. by* Šalamun, Tomaž, Eliot B. Anderson, Eliot B., *and* Charles Simic

How does the Water / Come down at Lodore? The Cataract of Lodore. Robert Southey. NOxBChV *Fr.* The Cataract of Lodore. NTP; OxBChV

How doth the city sit solitary, that was full of people! The Misery of Jerusalem. Bible, *O.T.* AWP *Fr.* Lamentations.

How doth the little busy bee. Isaac Watts. CTV; EBEvV; HoPM; OxAEP-1; UV

("Some good account at last.") (LL) ChAP

How doth the little crocodile. The Crocodile. "Lewis Carroll." CBNP; CTAV; CTV; ChAP; FaBoCh; FaBoEE; HoPM; NBLV; NOBL; NOBVV; RB; TFi; TTTS; UV *Fr.* Alice's Adventures in Wonderland.

How drunk I got tonight. Drinking Spree Beneath the Open Sky. Slavko Mihalic, *Croatian*. CEEP; PoSu, *tr. by* Peter Kastmiler

How dully in the evening. Calendar of the Air. Yevgeny Borisovich Rein, *Russian*. TCRP, *tr. by* Lubov Yakovleva

How dumb before the poleaxe they sink down. Marriages. Anthony Thwaite. OxBM

How Each Thing Save the Lover in Spring Reviveth to Pleasure. Henry Howard, Earl of Surrey. *See* When Windsor Walls.

How *early* has young *Chromius* begun. Pindar. OBCVT, *tr. by* Abraham Cowley *Fr.* The First Nemeæn Ode of Pindar.

How easily the ripe grain. The Widow. W. S. Merwin. NYBP; UnPo; VGW

How easy to tell it's a man. Transvestite. Lisa Zeidner. CMAP

How empty seems the town now you are gone! From One Who Stays. Amy Lowell. BoWoP; IMW

How entrancing are the 124 ways. Larousse Gastronomique. Anne Stevenson. PeLV

How everything gets tamed. Mountain, Fire, Thornbush. Harvey Shapiro. VGW

How Everything Happens. May Swenson. HAP

How excellent is thy name in all the worlde, *par. by* Miles Coverdale. Bible, *O.T. See* Psalm 8.

How fair a flower is sown. Coventry Patmore. FaBoEE

How fair is youth that flies so fast! Then be happy, ye who may. Triumph of Bacchus and Ariadne. Lorenzo de' Medici. CTC, *tr. by* Richard Aldington *Fr.* Carnival Songs.

How far are they deceived, that hope in vain. In the Person of a Lady, to Bajazet, Her Unconstant Gallant. "Ephelia." PEW

How far is it? Getting There. Sylvia Plath. GM

How Far Is It Called to the Grave? *Unknown.* BLPA

How Far Is It to Bethlehem? Frances Alice Chesterton. BoTP; PChr

"How far is it to Bethlehem Town?" How Far to Bethlehem? Madeleine Sweeny Miller. BLPA

How far is it to you by foot? Vassar Miller. FFC

How far is St. Helena from a little child at play? A St. Helena Lullaby. Rudyard Kipling. EBEV; FaBoCh; PoEL-5

How Far to Bethlehem? Madeleine Sweeny Miller. BLPA

"How fared you when you mortal were?" After. Ralph Hodgson. MoBrPo

How fashionably sad my early poems are! About My Poems. Donald Justice. PoA

How fast thou fliest, O Time, on loves swift wings. Sonnet 32. Mary Sidney, Countess of Montgomery Wroth. NOSC *Fr.* Pamphilia to Amphilanthus.

How fetching! Somebody's husband. *Fr.* An Exchange of Poems by Tung-yang Stream. CoBCP, *tr. by* Burton Watson

How fetching! Somebody's wife. An Exchange of Poems by Tung-yang Stream. Hsieh Ling-yün, *Chinese.* CoBCP, *tr. by* Burton Watson *Fr.* An Exchange of Poems by Tung-yang Stream. CoBCP, *tr. by* Burton Watson

How fierce in its loyalties the beat of the heart. Coronary Thrombosis. William Price Turner. OxBS

How fierce was I, when I did see. Upon Julia['s] Washing Herself in the River. Robert Herrick. CaPo; OBCVT

How fine a light on. May Song. Goethe, *German.* STV, *tr. by* John Frederick Nims

How first we met do you still remember? Brussels and Oxford. William Hurrell Mallock. EBVV

How flame the glories of Belinda's hair. Thomas Parnell. EPCY *Fr.* To Mr. Pope.

How foolish men on expeditions go! On Riding to See Dean Swift in the Mist of the Morning. Alexander Pope *and* Thomas Parnell. FaBoEE; OBCoV

How found you him? Shakespeare. OxAEP-1 *Fr.* Cymbeline.

How frail is human life! How fleet our breath. On the Death of an Infant of Five Days Old. Elizabeth Boyd. CABP; ECWP

How fresh, O[h] Lord, how sweet and clean. The Flower. George Herbert. AWP; ESCV; FMP; FSCP; GeHe; NAEL-1; NOBE; NOCV; NoP-4; OBGa; PBRV; PoEL-2; SeCP

How funny you are today New York. Steps. Frank O'Hara. CoAmPo; PmAP

How funny your name would be. Myrtle. John Ashbery. BAP-94

How gaily is at first begun. Life's Progress. Anne Finch, Countess of Winchilsea. ECWP

How Glorious Are the Morning Stars. Benjamin Keach. AH

How Glorious Is Thy Name. Bible, *O.T. See* Psalm 8.

How God Answers the Soul. Mechthild von Magdeburg, *German.* WPoS, *tr. by* Oliver Davies

How God Comes to the Soul. Mechthild von Magdeburg, *German.* WPoS, *tr. by* Oliver Davies

How God speeds the tax-bribed plough. Drone v. Worker. Ebenezer Elliot. FaBoPV; OBSV

How Goes the Night? *Unknown.* AWP, *tr. by* Helen Waddell *Fr.* Shi King.

How good it would be if our surroundings always. Dinner at Le Caprice. Rachel Wetzsteon. RA

How good of Mrs. Metz! The blur. Snapshots. John Updike. NoP-4

How good that it happened. When We Wake Up in the Morning. Anna Swirszczynska, *Polish.* CEEP, *tr. by* Magnus J. Krynski *and* Robert A. Maguire

How good to lie a little while. Friends. Abbie Farwell Brown. CTV

How goodly are the tentes of Jacob and thine habitacions Israel. Balaam's Blessing. Bible, *O.T.* OBVE, *tr. by* William Tyndale *Fr.* Numbers.

How Goodly Is Thy House. Henry S. Jacobs. AH

How grace this hallowed day? Christmas. Henry Timrod. APN-2

How Great unto the Living Seem the Dead! The Dead. Charles Heavysege. NOBC

How happy a thing were a wedding. On Marriage. Thomas Flatman. EnLoPo; NOBL; PeLV

How happy are those who know. The Bible, Matthew 5:3–12, Phillips. *Unknown.* CTV *Fr.* The Bible, Matthew 5:3–12, Phillips.

How happy for us, that it is not at home! (LL) The Place of the Damned [*or* Damn'd]. Jonathan Swift. ChIV-2; FaBoEE; OBSV

How happy I can be with my love away! The Absence. Sylvia Townsend Warner. MoBrPo

How happy in his low degree. Country Life. Horace. AWP, *tr. by* Dryden *Fr.* Epodes.

How happy is he born and taught. The Character of a Happy Life. Sir Henry Wotton. EBEvV; GTBS-P; NOBE; NOSC; NTP; OBEV

How happy is the blameless vestal's lot! Life of a Nun. Alexander Pope. ECEV *Fr.* Eloisa to Abelard. NAEL-1; PoEL-3; RACG

How happy is the little Stone. Emily Dickinson. APN-2; RB

How happy to be a fish. Fish and Bird. Rosemary Brinckman. BoTP

How happy uncle us'd to be. Uncle an' Aunt. William Barnes. NOBVV

How happy you who varied joys pursue. Epistle. Lady Mary Wortley Montagu. ECWP

How hard a fate enthrals the wretched maid. Virgil. ECWP, *tr. by* Elizabeth Tollet *Fr.* The Aeneid [*or* Eneados, Aeneis].

How hard it is! To the Memory of G. N. Obolduyev. Yelena Blaginina, *Russian.* TCRP, *tr. by* Vera Dunham

How hard it is, we say. Clothes Maketh the Man. Theodore Weiss. NoAM

How hardly I concealed my tears. Song. Anne Wharton. LW

How harsh the change, since those plump halcyon days. The Egyptian Cat. D. J. Enright. PC

How have I served you? I have let you waste. John Hewitt. PNI *Fr.* Sonnets for Roberta (1954).

How he found his life long ago. How Just One Poor Man Lives. Alonzo Gonzales Mó, *Mayan.* STP, *tr. by* Allan F. Burns

How He Saved St. Michael's. Mary Anna Phinney Stansbury. BLPA

How He Saw Her. Ben Jonson. *Fr.* A Celebration of Charis in Ten Lyric[k] Pieces [*or* Peeces]. BeJo; OxAEP-1; SeCP

How He Should Like to Be Kissed. Paul Fleming, *German.* GePo, *tr. by* Harold B. Segel

How he survived them they could never understand. The Pora. W. H. Auden. MeMAP

How he thought. Drop the Wires. Hugh Seidman. AmPA

How he would drinke his Wine. Martial, *Latin.* OBCVT, *tr. by* Robert Herrick

How heavy do I journey on the way. Sonnet 50. Shakespeare. OxAEP-1 *Fr.* Sonnets.

How Her Teeth Were Pulled. *Unknown, Paiute Indian.* STP, *tr. by* Jarold Ramsey

How! hey! it is non les. Unknown. MiEL

How, hey! It is none les. A Henpecked Husband. *Unknown.* PeLV

How High the Moon. Lance Jeffers. PoBA; SeSe

How his own members bloat and shrink again. (LL) Ogres and Pygmies. Robert Graves. CMoP; FaBoMo; LiTM; MoP; NoAM

How Hong Kong Was Destroyed. Dahlia Ravikovitch, *Hebrew.* IP, *tr. by* Warren Bargad *and* Stanley F. Chyet

"How, how," he said. "Friend Chang," I said. The Chinese Nightingale. Vachel Lindsay. MoAmPo

How I am held within a tranquil shell. The Woman with Child. Freda Laughton. LiLi

How I Became a Dog. Vladimir Mayakovsky, *Russian.* TCRP, *tr. by* Bernard Meares

How I Brought the Good News from Aix to Ghent (or Vice Versa). R. J. Yeatman *and* W. C. Sellar. BXAP; UV

How I Came to Have a Man's Name. Emma Lee Warrior. HATNAP

How I Changed My Name, Felice. Felix Stefanile. UnSA

How I Come to You. Molly Peacock. RA

How I do[e] love thee, Beaumont, and thy Muse. To Francis Beaumont. Ben Jonson. BeJo

How I Escaped from the Labyrinth. Philip Dacey. CMAP

How I forsook/ Elias and Pisa after, and betook. Sir Richard Fanshawe. AWP *Fr.* Il Pastor Fido.

How I go courting a charming beauty bright. Charming Beauty Bright. *Unknown.* AmFP

How I Got That Name, An Essay on Assimilation. Marilyn Chin. LoL; PaTW; UnSA

("By all that was lavished upon her / and all that was taken away!") (LL) UnSA

How I Had to Act. Molly Peacock. FFC; NAmP90

How I hate myself, this body which is me. Eloi, Eloi, Lama Sabachthani? D. H. Lawrence. GI

How I hate you tonight! I and Thou. Chana Bloch. CrSp

How I Learned English. Gregory Djanikian. CMAP; UnSA

How I Learned to Sweep. Julia Alvarez. FFC; RA

How I long for the man who climbed Mt. Yoshino. Shizuka, *Japanese.* WPJ, *tr. by* Kenneth Rexroth *and* Ikuko Atsumi

How I love country you have heard. Lines. Samuel Alfred Beadle. AAP

How I loved one like you when I was little!—. Slug. Theodore Roethke. APo

How I miss my father. Poem at Thirty-nine. Alice Walker. CrSp

How I regret being late to see the flowers blossom. Sighing over Flowers. Tu Mu, *Chinese.* SuSp, *tr. by* Eddie Tsang

How I Sailed on the Lake till I Came to the Eastern Stream. Lu Yu, *Chinese.* ChiP, *tr. by* Arthur Waley

How I See It. Kit Wright. OTCP

How I succeed, you kindly ask. Mary Barber. ECWP *Fr.* To a Lady, Who Commanded Me to Send Her an Account in Verse.

How I wish I had known / beforehand of this journey. *Unknown, Japanese.* BoWoP, *tr. by* Kenneth Yasuda

How I wish I were able to say what I think. Gertrude Stein. PBWP *Fr.* Stanzas in Meditation.

How I wish the Argo had never reached the land. Medea. Euripides. NAWM-1; OxBM

How I would have the poem rest. The Mahogany Ship. Judith Rodriguez. BMAP

How I Wrote It. David Dooley. TRP

How ill doth he deserve a lover's name. Eternity of Love Protested. Thomas Carew. BeJo; MeLP, NOSC

How immovably they stand on the moving stairs. On the Escalator. Adam Zagajewski, *Polish.* CEEP, *tr. by* Gorczynski, Renata

How impotent a deity am I! Sir Samuel Garth. *Fr.* The Dispensary. OBSV

How Infinite Are Thy Ways. William Force Stead. OBMV *Fr.* Uriel.

How innocent their lives look. Photos of a Salt Mine. Patricia K. Page. NIP-4; NOBC; NoAM

How intelligent he looks! Changing Diapers. Gary Snyder. RaBo

How intimate was the earth in days gone by. The Earth. David Gwenallt Jones, *Welsh.* OBWVE, *tr. by* Dyfnallt Morgan

How Is He Coming Then. Lucille Clifton. CrSp; NALW

How is it all gonna turn out. "Haida Charlie," *Tlingit Indian.* STP, *tr. by* James Koller *after* John Swanton

How is it I can eat bread here and cut meat. Evening Meal in the Twentieth Century. John Holmes. AiP

How is it proved? The Great Wager. Geoffrey Anketell Studdert-Kennedy. TrCP

How is it that. Tune: "Chilly East Wind." Kuan Yün-shih. SuSp, *tr. by* Richard John Lynn *Fr.* Medley of Southern and Northern Tunes— Scenic Tour of West Lake.

How is it that I am so careless here. Meditation 62. Philip Pain. NOBA

How is it the stomach knows first. David Hall. CDa

How is it with another woman? An Attempt at Jealousy. Marina Tsvetayeva, *Russian.* WPOW, *tr. by* Robert Perelman *and* Aleksandar Petrov

How is man parcell'd out? how ev'ry hour. The Tempest. Henry Vaughan. ESCV

How Is the Night? *Unknown, Chinese.* CoBCP, *tr. by* Burton Watson

How is your life with the other one. An Attempt at Jealousy. Marina Tsvetayeva, *Russian.* TCRP, *tr. by* Elaine Feinstein

How it comes about. Larry Eigner. PmAP

How it feels to be touching. We Become New. Marge Piercy. TAP

How it goes. Severance. Kit Robinson. FTOS

How It Is. Maxine W. Kumin. IMW; NALW; NoAM; Poetr

How it is I returned. Childhood. Sherod Santos. FiLi

How It Strikes a Contemporary. Robert Browning. CTC; EnVR; FaBoPV; GTBS-P; OAEL-2

How it was in that place, how light hung in a bright pool. Wolfpen Creek. James Still. MT

How It Will Always Seem. David Rivard. PBCAP

How It's Done. Alvin Aubert. MT

How Jack Found That Beans May Go Back on a Chap. Guy Wetmore Carryl. HoPM

How joyous his neigh! Song of the Horse. *Unknown, Navajo.* AWP, *tr. by* Natalie Curtis Burlin

How Just One Poor Man Lives. Alonzo Gonzales Mó, *Mayan.* STP, *tr. by* Allan F. Burns

How keen the nights / were. Fluteplayers from Finmarken. Carl Rakosi. FTOS

How kind, how secret[ly], [now] the sun. The Garden. Robert Penn Warren. GaP; PoA

How large unto the tiny fly. The Fly. Walter De la Mare. OTCP

How larger is remembrance than desire! Ebbtide at Sundown. "Michael Field." VWP

How Late Desire Looks. Katrina Roberts. BAP-95

How Lies Grow. Maxine Chernoff. PmAP

How life and death in Thee. To Our Blessed Lord upon the Choice of His Sepulchre. Richard Crashaw. ChIV-2; GeHe; NOSC; OAEL-1

How Light Is Spent. Bin Ramke. BAP-95

How like a bolt of white silk is this water. Li Po. SuSp, *tr. by* Irving Lo *Fr.* Songs of Ch'iu-p'u.

How like a fire doth love increase in me[e]. Sonnet 48. Mary Sidney, Countess of Montgomery Wroth. NOSC *Fr.* Pamphilia to Amphilanthus.

How like a man, is Man, who rises late. Eye-Opener. Malcolm Lowry. NoP-4

How like a rich and gorgeous picture hung. A November Landscape. Sarah Helen Whitman. ColAP

How like a winter hath my absence been[e]. Sonnet 97. Shakespeare. AWP; EnLoPo; GTBS-P; HeIP-4; NAEL-1; NOBE; NoSic; OAEL-1; OBEV; OxAEP-1; PoRA; SCGP; Son; TFi *Fr.* Sonnets.

How like an angel came I down! Wonder. Thomas Traherne. CH; ESCV; GeHe; HAP; ImPo; NAEL-1; NoP-4; PoE; SeCP; TOF

How like her! But 'tis she herself. In the Mile End Road. Amy Levy. PEW; RACG

How like the leper, with his own sad cry. The Buoy-Bell. Charles Tennyson Turner. GSo; PeVV; Son

How like to threads of flax, *par. by* Francis Quarles. Psalm 119.37. Bible, *O.T.* ChIV-1 *Fr.* Psalms.

How like you this, what hath she now deserved? Sir Thomas Wyatt. *See* The Lover Showeth How He Is Forsaken of Such as He Sometime Enjoyed.

How Lillies Came White. Robert Herrick. BeJo; CaPo

How Lisa Loved the King. "George Eliot." LW

How little I know / about you finally. Margaret Atwood. CrSp *Fr.* Five Poems for Grandmothers.

How little of God's grace caresses you, Massadah. Yitzhak Lamdan. MHP, *tr. by* Ruth Finer Mintz *Fr.* In the Khamsin.

How lonely it can be in jail! Prison Thoughts. Tô Hũ'u, *Vietnamese.* AVP, *tr. by* Huỳnh Sanh Thông

How long ago Hector took off his plume. Parting in Wartime. Frances Darwin Cornford. APAD; FaBoWP; NIP-4

How long ago she planted the hawthorn hedge. The Hawthorn Hedge. Judith Wright. WPE

How long ago we dreamed. Carol of the Three Kings. W. S. Merwin. PChr

How long between the grain and the wind. Andrea Zanzotto, *Italian.* VCWP, *tr. by* Ruth Feldman *and* Brian Swann

How Long Blues. Leroy Carr. NAAAL

How long can man stare. Vertigo. Tongjip Shin, *Korean.* CKP, *tr. by* Jaihiun Kim

How long, dear Savior, O how long. Isaac Watts. AmFP

How long, great God, a wretched captive here. The Expostulation. Elizabeth Singer Rowe. PEW

How Long Has Trane Been Gone. Joe Corrie. NAAAL

How Long Has Trane Been Gone. Jayne Cortez. ISC

How long have we forgotten how to listen! Nelly Sachs, *German.* WPoS, *tr. by* Ruth and Matthew Mead

How long have you suffered from this tick? Interview with Herr Limerick. Andreas Okopenko, *German.* CBNP

How long, how long, has that evenin' train gone? How Long Blues. Leroy Carr. NAAAL

How long, how long must I regret? The Lost Tribe. Ruth Pitter. WPOW

How Long I Sailed. Hartley Coleridge. Son

How long in these empty thermals near the cold. Crinagoras, *Greek.* GrAn, *tr. by* Alistair Elliot

How long it has been since I ceased / to resemble myself! The Circle with a Hole in the Middle. Peter Kostakis. MoNo

How Long, Jehovah? Henry Ainsworth. AH

How long, long ago. Kenneth Rexroth. APSN *Fr.* The Love Poems of Marichiko.

How long must we two hide the burning gaze. United. Paulus Silentiarius, *Greek.* AWP, *tr. by* W. H. D. Rouse

How long, my heroes, shall we live in bondage. War Hymn. Rhigas Pheraios, *Greek.* GrIP, *tr. by* Rae Dalven

How long, O God! how long must I remain. The Negro's Lament. John Willis Menard. AAP

How long, O lion, hast thou fleshless lain? The Lion's Skeleton. Charles Tennyson Turner. NOBVV

How long, O lord, shall I forgotten be?, *par.* by Sir Philip Sidney. Psalm 13. Bible, *O.T.* NoSic; OBVE *Fr.* Psalms.

How long, O Lord, shall I forgotten be? Psalm 13   Sir Philip Sidney. FMR *Fr.* Psalms.

How long, oh gracious God! how long. James M. Whitfield. AAP

"How long shall fortune faile me now." The Earl of Westmoreland. *Unknown.* ESPB

How long shall this like dying life endure. Sonnet 25. Edmund Spenser. AAS *Fr.* Amoretti. AAS

How long shall you and I be bound. Water Whirligigs. D. J. Opperman, *Afrikaans.* PeSA, *tr. by* Jack Cope *and* Uys Krige

How long she waited for her executioner! Head of Medusa. Marya Alexandrovna Zaturenska. MoAmPo

How long since you left your native soil? The Banana Plant. Tongmyong Kim, *Korean.* CKP, *tr. by* Jaihiun Kim

How long this way: that everywhere. Red Sea. James Agee. *Fr.* Two Songs on the Economy of Abundance. MoAmPo

How long will it last? Lady Horikawa, *Japanese.* WPJ; WPOW, *tr. by* Kenneth Rexroth *and* Ikuko Atsumi

How long wilt thou forget me, O Lord? Bible, *O.T. See* Psalm 13.

How looks the night? There does not miss a star. Gerard Manley Hopkins. OxBSP *Fr.* Fragments.

How lovely are the tombs of the dead nymphs. Panope. Dame Edith Sitwell. MoBrPo

How lovely are thy dwellings fair!, *par.* by Milton. Bible, *O.T. See* Psalm 84.

How lovely are thy tabernacles, *sel. of diff. vers., vv. 1–4.* Psalm 84. Bible, *O.T.* TrJP *Fr.* Psalms.

How lovely is the sound of oars at night. Boats at Night. Edward Richard Burton Shanks. CH

How lovely is thy dwelling. Psalm 84. Mary Sidney Herbert, Countess of Pembroke. CABP

How lovely it is today! *Unknown. Fr.* Four Glosses. NOIV

How lovely it was, after the official fright. The Phenomenon. Karl Shapiro. CMoP; NYBP

How lovely the Imperial Mound, but when can I visit it? On the Road to Western Hill. Ch'ien Ch'ien-i, *Chinese.* SuSp, *tr. by* Irving Y. Lo

How lush, how loose, the uninhibited squash is. Squash in Blossom. Robert Francis. FYAP

How man-y roads must a man walk down be-fore you. Blowin' in the Wind. "Bob Dylan." KaS

How many a father have I seen. Tennyson. EBVVPR; EnVR *Fr.* In Memoriam A. H. H.

How many apples grow on the tree? George Barker. NOxBChV

How many bards gild the lapses of time! Keats. LaPo; OxAEP-2

How many beautiful flowers in the wilds. Casting Fragrance to the Winds. Xuân Diệu, *Vietnamese.* AVP, *tr. by* Huỳnh Sanh Thông

How many blessed groups this hour are bending. Sabbath Sonnet. Felicia Dorothea Hemans. Son

How many bullets does it take. Death in Yorkville. Langston Hughes. PoBA

How many buttons are missing today! Nobody Knows but Mother. Mary Morrison. BLPA

How many children must have come to pass. Walter Parmer. Greg Williamson. RA

How many dawns, chill from his rippling rest. To Brooklyn Bridge. Hart Crane. AiP; AmFP; AmPP; CMoP; ChIV-1; ClHu; ColAP; FaBoA; HAP; HeIP-4; ImPo; InPS-3; KSG; LiTM; MeMAP; MoAmPo; NOBA; NoAM; NoP-4; OxBA; PoE; PoPoPo; TAP; TFi; TRP; WeW-3 *Fr.* The Bridge. NAAL-2

How many days has my baby to play? Mother Goose. OxNR; ReMoGo

How Many Days Has My Baby to Play? *Unknown.* BoTP

How many doors will this man open. Death. Roy Fuller. NoAM

How many evenings in the arbor by the river. Tune: "As in a Dream; a Song." Li Ch'ing-chao, *Chinese.* BoWoP; SuSp, *tr. by* Eugene Eoyang

How many faults you might accuse me of. Sonnet. Elinor Wylie. NAAL-2

How many fires. George Reavey. SPE

How many guys are sitting at their kitchen tables. Ray. Hayden Carruth. PuP-17

How Many Heavens. Dame Edith Sitwell. TrCP

How many humble hearts have dipped. To a Post-Office Inkwell. Christopher Darlington Morley. PoLF

How many lives ago. Kenneth Rexroth. APSN *Fr.* The Love Poems of Marichiko.

How many loves had I. Doll. John Wieners. FTOS

How many men are killed by power, by power. Sejanus ("How many men are killed by power, by power"). Juvenal. OBVE, *tr. by* Robert Lowell *Fr.* Satires.

"How many miles is it to Babylon?" *Unknown.* ACTP

How many miles to Babylon? To Babylon. Mother Goose. BoTP; FaBoCh; LB; NTP; OxBSP; OxBoLi; OxNR; ReMoGo

How many moments must(amazing eachl). E. E. Cummings. PoA

How many names. Some trouble. Hedgerows. Stanley Plumly. NAmP90

How many notes written. . . . Suicide Note. Janice Mirikitani. OxWW

How many pallid Christs, with painted blood. All Around Us. Constance Urdang. PBCAP

How many paltry, foolish, painted things. Sonnet 6: 'How many paltry, foolish, painted things'. Michael Drayton. AAS; AEP; EnLoPo; GBL; HAP; HeIP-4; NAEL-1; NIP-4; NOSC; OAEL-1; SCGP *Fr.* Idea.

How many people came. Tanka. Kondō Yoshimi, *Japanese.* MJT, *tr. by* Makoto Ueda

How Many Poems Were Lost. Abba Kovner, *Hebrew.* IP, *tr. by* Warren Bargad *and* Stanley F. Chyet

How many pounds does the baby weigh. Weighing the Baby. Ethel Lynn Beers. PoToHe

How many prompters! what a chorus! (LL) Plays. Walter Savage Landor. NBLV; OxBSP; OxBoLi; PeLV

How many scenes, O sun. Ode to the Sun. Eloise Bibb. CBWP-4

How many shoelaces will they make of that! (LL) The Mad Yak. Gregory Corso. BB; PFE; PmAP

How many stolen glances can we trade. Paulus Silentiarius, *Greek.* InMo, *tr. by* Sam Hamill

How many threads have I broken with my teeth. How many. Scratch Music. C. D. Wright. CMAP; NAmP90

How Many Times. Marie Howe. MoLi

How many times, Death. O All Down within the Pretty Meadow. Kenneth Patchen. HAP; WeW-3

How many times do I love thee, dear? Song. Thomas Lovell Beddoes. ImPo; NAEL-2; PoEL-4 *Fr.* Torrismond.

How many times have I traveled. Commuter. Lisel Mueller. GM

How many times our hands will enter. Holidays. Dara Wier. NAmP90

How many times these low feet staggered. Emily Dickinson. AmPP; HAP; NAAL-1; NAAL-3; PoEL-5; WeW-3

How many ways can you bring me ten? Making Tens. M. M. Hutchinson. BoTP

How many were going to St. Ives? (LL) As I was going to St. Ives. Mother Goose. LB; NTCP; OxNR; ReMoGo

How many wise men and heroes. To the Tune "The River Is Red." Ch'iu Chin, *Chinese.* AiP; BoWoP; PBWP, *tr. by* Kenneth Rexroth *and* Ling Chung

How many years since 1619 have I been singing Spirituals? Since 1619. Margaret Abigail Walker. NoP-4

How Marigolds Came Yellow. Robert Herrick. TTTS

How massively, with what a fine stiff rise. Erucius of Cyzicus, *Greek.* GrAn, *tr. by* Peter Jay

How may one be spared the sorrow and regret of human life? Tune: "Song of Tzu-yeh." Li Yü, *Chinese.* SuSp, *tr. by* Daniel Bryant

How memory cuts away the years. Autumn. Jean Starr Untermeyer. MoAmPo

How Metaphor Can Save Your Life. Myra Sklarew. CRP

How much?—and—do you love me, kid? (LL) Threes. Carl Sandburg. CMoP; OxBA; PoLF

How much are they deceived who vainly strive. Love and Jealousy. William Walsh. BoLoP

How much better it seems now. The Next Poem. Dana Gioia. DiPo; NoP-4

How much Christian, so to speak, can I get? Jacob Glatstein, *Yiddish.* GI, *tr. by* Benjamin Harshav *and* Barbara Harshav

How much death works. Eyes Fastened with Pins. Charles Simic. VCAP

How Much Earth. Philip Levine. NNaP

How much I should like to begin. At the Edge. Denise Levertov. NAAL-2

How much I wanted them to go. The Testament. Mikhail Yuryevich Lermontov, *Russian.* NNPT, *tr. by* Cornford, Frances Darwin and Esther Polianowsky Salaman

How Much Is Not True. Kabir. RaBo

How Much Longer? Robert Mezey. OBWP

How much longer will I be able to inhabit the divine sepulcher. John Ashbery. FTOS; NeAP; PmAP; PoM

How much more / Of wind and rain? Tune: "Groping for Fish." Hsin Ch'i-chi, *Chinese.* SuSp, *tr. by* Irving Y. Lo

How much of paper's soiled! what floods of ink! An Epistle to Lady Bowyer. Mary Jones. ECWP

How much, Preventing God! how much I owe. Grace. Ralph Waldo Emerson. APN-1; AmPP; NCAP

How much regret in my dream last night? Tune: "Butterflies Lingering over Flowers." Wang Kuo-wei, *Chinese.* SuSp, *tr. by* Ching-i Tu

How much shall I love her? The Echo-Elf Answers. Thomas Hardy. CBLP

"How much," sighed the gentle Narcissus. Limerick. Stephen Sylvester. PeLi

How much the heart may bear and yet not break! Endurance. Elizabeth Akers Allen. PoToHe

How much there was of everything: kettledrums and horns and bells! Nikolai Ivanovich Tryapkin, *Russian.* TCRP, tr. by Bradley Jordan

How much wood would a woodchuck chuck? Wood-chuck. *Unknown.* ImGa; TLR

How much work. Hating Jews. Tom Wayman. LTA

How mutable is every thing that here. Meditation 29. Philip Pain. *Fr. Meditations for July 26, 1666.* NOBA; SCAP

How naked go the sometime nude! (LL) The Naked and the Nude. Robert Graves. EP; NYBP; SoSe-8

How narrow the bear trail. The Rendezvous. Maxine W. Kumin. NMM-2

How near me came the hand of Death. A Widow's Hymn. George Wither. OBEV

How neatly a cat sleeps. Cat's Dream. Pablo Neruda, *Spanish.* PC

How nice! How convenient! The Marvelous Land of Indefinitions. Lorenzo Thomas. PmAP

How nice it is to eat! Beautiful Meals. Thomas Sturge Moore. BoTP

How nice to be a local swan. Sitting Pretty. Margaret Fishback. PoLF

How nice to know Mr MacBeth. With a Presentation Copy of Verses. Martin Bell. PeLV

How no shoe fit them. My Mother's Feet. Stanley Plumly. FiLi

How noteless Men, and Pleiads, stand. Emily Dickinson. PoE

How now! is he dead? Shakespeare. OxAEP-1 *Fr. Antony and Cleopatra.*

How odd / Of God. W. N. Ewer. OBCoV

How Oft the Banshee Cried. Thomas Moore. AWP

How oft have I, my dear [or dere] and cruel[l] foe. Petrarch, *Italian.* AAS, tr. by Sir Thomas Wyatt

How oft have I with publike voyce runne on? Lady Elizabeth Carey. KTR, *act I, scene I Fr. Mariam.* WPE

How oft I dream of childhood days, of tricks we used to play. Rosie Nell. *Unknown.* AS

How Oft in Schoolboy Days. Frederick Goddard Tuckerman. APN-2; NoP-4; Son *Fr. Sonnets.*

How oft I've watch'd thee from the garden croft. Orion. Charles Tennyson Turner. GSo

How oft 'tis said, "this is a songless Land." The Songless Land. Francis Carey Slater. PeSAV

How oft we see the female sex. The School for Satire. Lady Sophia Burrell. ECWP

How oft, when thou, my music, music play'st. Sonnet 128. Shakespeare. NAEL-1; OxAEP-1; PoE *Fr. Sonnets.*

How often and often I wish. Limerick. Frances Darwin Cornford. PeLi

How often does a man need to see a woman? The Word Made Flesh. Walter James Turner. OBMV

How often, for some trivial wrong. Retaliation. Margaret E. Bruner. PoToHe

How often have I carried our family word. Quoof. Paul Muldoon. CBNP; FaBoVe; PBCIP; PNI

How often have I started out. Inspiration. Robert W. Service. WeW-3

How often have my tears. In Allusion to the French Song. Richard Lovelace. CaPo

How often have we known a dog to be. Beyond the Grave. Margaret E. Bruner. PoToHe

How Often I Feel Like You. Iain Crichton Smith. FaBoTC

How often my grandparents allude to death, now. Behind the Veil. Andrew Lansdown. NOBAu

How often should we think of this, that we. Meditations for August 1, 1666. Philip Pain. SCAP

How often we forget all time, when lone. Stanzas. Edgar Allan Poe. APN-I

How often we neglect a friend. Atonement. Margaret E. Bruner PoToHe

How often, when life's summer day. Walter Savage Landor. FaBoEE

How Old Are the People of the World. Charles Fort. CMAP

How Old Are You? H. S. Fritsch. PoLF; PoToHe

How old may Phillis [or Phyllis] be, you ask. Phillis's Age. Matthew Prior. EnLoPo; FaBoEE

How old was Mary out of whom you cast. Charlotte Mew. MoBrPo *Fr. Madeleine in Church.*

How on Solemn Fields of Space. Elizabeth Daryush. NOCV

How One Winter Came in the Lake Region. Wilfred Campbell. NOBC

How overwhelming. Topsy: Part 2. Al Young. MoNo

How Paddy Stole the Rope. *Unknown.* BLPA

How painful, dear, how strange it is. Ballad About a Smoke-Filled Railway Carriage. Aleksandr Kochetkov, *Russian.* TCRP, tr. by Lubov Yakovleva

How pitiful is her sleep. In Memory of Kathleen. Kenneth Patchen. IMW; MoAmPo

How placid, how divinely sweet. Meandering Wye. Robert Bloomfield. *Fr. The Banks of Wye.* OBNC

How placidly shine / The river, the spring, and the sun. Rosalía de Castro, *Galician.* PBWP, tr. by Benjamin M. Woodbridge, Jr.

How pleasant is Saturday night. Song. *Unknown.* CTV

How pleasant it is that always. Song. Florence Smith. BLPA

How Pleasant It Is to Have Money. Arthur Hugh Clough. NOBE *Fr. Dipsychus [and the Spirit].*

How pleasant it is to have money. (LL) Le Diner. Arthur Hugh Clough. OBCoV; OBSV

How pleasant to know Mr. Lear! Self-Portrait of the Laureate of Nonsense. Edward Lear. CBNP; EBEV; FP; FaBoCh; GTBS-P; HAP; NBLV; NOBE; NOBL; NOBVV; NTP; NoP-4; OxAEP-2; PeLV; PoPoPo; UV

How poecile and endearing is the Porch. Frank O'Hara. CBNP

How Poetry Comes to Me. Gary Snyder. LoL; PoPoPo; SAGP

How poor, how rich, how abject, how august. Edward Young. OAEL-1 *Fr. Night Thoughts.*

How poor was Jacob's motion, and how strange. On Jacob's Purchase. Francis Quarles. ChIV-1

How possibly could I. Cameo in Sudden Light. Lorenzo Thomas. FTOS

How Potchikoo Got Old. Louise Erdrich. *Fr. Old Man Potchikoo.* HATNAP

How prone we are to sin, how sweet were made. And Forgive Us Our Trespasses. Aphra Behn. EBEV

How? "Providence," and yet a Scottish crew? John Cleveland. NOSC *Fr. The Rebel [or Rebell] Scot.*

How pure the hearts of lovers as they walk. Prothalamion for an Autumn Wedding. May Sarton. ITG

"How Quick You Are!" *Unknown, Chinese.* CuBCP, tr. by Burton Watson

How quickly the postures shift. On Your Own. Tess Gallagher. NMM-2

How quickly we age. Not so the heavens. Tune: "Song of Picking Mulberry" Double-Ninth Festival. Mao Tse-tung, *Chinese.* SuSp, tr. by Eugene Eoyang

How quiet and how still to-day old Bethel's corners 'round. The Day after Conference. Josephine D. Henderson Heard. CBWP-4

How quiet is the morning in the hills! Morning in the Hills. Bliss Carman. NOBC

How red the rose that is the soldier's wound. The Soldier's Wound. Wallace Stevens. CMoP; NOBA *Fr. Esthétique du Mal.* LiTM

How rich and pleasing thou, my Julia, art. To Julia. Robert Herrick. CaPo

How rich, O Lord! how fresh thy visits are! Unprofitablenes. Henry Vaughan. ESCV; FMP; GeHe; NOSC

How rich the wave in front, impressed. Lines Written near Richmond, upon the Thames, at Evening. Wordsworth. Ro

How rich we were, to know them, exiles. Priest Lake. William Stafford. PoA

How Roses Came Red. Robert Herrick. BeJo; CaPo; SoSe-8

How rough a sea. Basho, *Japanese.* TAL, tr. by Harold G. Henderson

How sad, cold moon! Flute. Sokch'o Shin, *Korean.* CKP, tr. by Jaihiun Kim

How sad it is. Tanka. Toki Zenmaro, *Japanese.* MJT, tr. by Makoto Ueda

How sad it is to be a woman! Woman. Fu Hsüan, *Chinese.* ChiPo, tr. by Arthur Waley

How sad it is to be framed in woman's form! Woman. Fu Hsüan, *Chinese.* ChiP, tr. by Arthur Waley

How sad it must be. A Poem for My Father. Sonia Sanchez. BPo

How safe, methinks, and strong, behind. After Floods on the Wharfe. Andrew Marvell. *Fr. Upon Appleton House [To My Lord Fairfax].* FaBoPV; GeHe; SeCP

How say that by law we may torture and chase. She's Free! Frances Ellen Watkins Harper. BlSi; Son

How see you Echo? When she calls I see. Echo. Pamela Grey, Viscountess Grey of Fallodon CH

How seldom, friend, a good, great man inherits. The Good Great Man. Coleridge. PWR

"How shall I a habit break?" A Builder's Lesson. John Boyle O'Reilly. PWR; PoLF; PoToHe

How shall I array my love? The Question. Frederick Goddard Tuckerman. APN-2; ColAP

How shall I be a poet? Poeta Fit, Non Nascitur. "Lewis Carroll." OBSV

How shall I begin my song. Songs for the Four Parts of the Night. Owl Woman, *Papago Indian.* PBWP; WPoS, tr. by Frances Densmore

How shall I behold the face. Milton. TOF *Fr. Book IX.* FHYEP; NAEL-1; NAWM-1; OAEL-1 *Fr. Paradise Lost.*

How shall I forsake wisdom? In Praise of Wisdom. Solomon ibn Gabirol, *Hebrew*. TrJP, *tr.* by Solomon Solis-Cohen

How shall I guard my soul so that it be. The Song of Love. Rilke, *German*. AWP, *tr.* by Ludwig Lewisohn

How shall I report. The Commendations of Mistress Jane Scrope. John Skelton. *Fr.* Phyllyp Sparowe [*or* Philip Sparrow]. AAS; PoEL-1

How shall I speak of doom, and ours in special. Tales from a Family Album. Donald Justice. Poetr

How shall I tell the torments of that hour. The Author Consults a Critic and Sells His Manuscript. Francis Hawling. NOEC *Fr.* The Signal; or, A Satire against Modesty.

How shall I tell you. Nikolai Nikolaievich Aseyev, *Russian*. TCRP, *tr.* by Daniel Weissbort

How shall my tongue expresse that hallow'd fire. Francis Quarles. ESCV *Fr.* Emblems.

How shall the river learn. Max Schmitt in a Single Scull. Richmond Lattimore. AiP

How shall the wine be drunk, or the woman known? A Voice from under the Table. Richard Wilbur. AmPP; HAP; NOBA

How shall we adorn. Angle of Geese. N. Scott Momaday. CDW; HATNAP

How shall we bring our dying heart up. Leah Goldberg. MHP, *tr.* by Ruth Finer Mintz *Fr.* On Blossoming.

How shall we hide from the bear that is moving all around the world? Song of a Bear Dancer Named Walas Nāʼ nĕ (Great Bear). *Unknown*. *Fr.* Dances and Songs of the Winter Ceremonial. APN-2, *tr.* by Franz Boas

How shall we please this age? If in a song. To Nysus. Sir Charles Sedley. FaBoEE; OBSV

How shall we praise the magnificence of the dead. Tetélestai. Conrad Potter Aiken. LiTM; MoAmPo

How Shall We Rise to Greet the Dawn? Sir Osbert Sitwell.

"Continually they cackle thus." PoWW

How shall we speak of Canada. W. L. M. K. Francis Reginald Scott. NOBC

How shall we walk naked when. Julia Randall. CrSp *Fr.* Adam Says See.

How shall your name go down in history. To Youth. Josephine D. Henderson Heard. CBWP-4

How shalt thou bear the Cross that now. The Eternal Years. Frederick William Faber. PWR

How She Operates. Grace Caroline Bridges. LoHo

How She Resolved to Act. Merrill Moore. MoAmPo

How should I / Be so pleasant. Sir Thomas Wyatt. SiPS

How should I, even if I could. To Catulinus That He Cannot Write Him an Epithalamium Because of the Enemy Hosts. Apollinaris Sidonius, *Latin*. MLL, *tr.* by Helen Waddell

How should I love my best? Madrigal. Edward Herbert, 1st Baron Herbert of Cherbury. PoEL-2; SeCP

How should I not be glad to contemplate. Everything Is Going to Be All Right. Derek Mahon. PBCIP

How should I praise thee, Lord! how should my r[h]ymes. The Temper (1). George Herbert. ESCV; FSCP; GeHe; NOCV; NoP-4; PoEL-2

How should I your true love know. An Old Song Ended. D. G. Rossetti. BoLoP; EBVV

How should I your true love know. Ophelia's Song. Shakespeare. CH; EBEV; EBEvV; EnLoPo; GBL; NoSic; PoRA; SCGP *Fr.* Hamlet. NAWM-1

How should the world be luckier if this house. Upon a House Shaken by the Land Agitation. W. B. Yeats. CMoP

How shril are silent tears? when sin got head. Admission. Henry Vaughan. ESCV

How sick I get. Father. Paul Carroll. NeAP

How silently the years have sped away. To My Dead Brother. Clara Ann Thompson. CBWP-2

How silly that soldier is pointing his gun at the wood. Russians. Keith Douglas. OxBTC

How silly were those sages heretofore. Samuel Butler. NOBL *Fr.* Satire upon the Licentious Age of Charles II.

How simply & how strangely. Boschlog: Being a Cartulary from The Ship of Fools. B. Catling. NBrP

How sits this city, late most populous. Donne. ChIV-1 *Fr.* Lamentations of Jeremy, for the Most Part According to Tremeullius.

How sleep the brave who sink to rest. Ode Written in the Beginning of the Year 1746. William Collins. AWP; CABP; GTBS-P; HAP; NAEL-1; NOBE; NOEC; NoP-4; OBEV; OxAEP-1; OxBSP; PBMP; PoE; PoEL-3; SCGP; TFi

How slow they are awakening, these trees. Plain Fare. Daryl Hine. CoAP

How slowly glide the hours by, the minutes hours seem. The Drunkard's Wife. Mary E. Tucker. CBWP-1

How slowly learns the child at school. Citizenship; Form 8889512, Sub-Section Q. G. K. Chesterton. OxBoLi

How smooth that lake expands its ample breast! Stanzas. Ann Radcliffe. WPE

How so well a gardener be. The Feat of Gardening. John Gardner. OBGa

How Socratic is Somerset Maugham! Limerick. R. B. S. Instone. PeLi

How soft a Caterpillar steps—. Caterpillar. Emily Dickinson. APo; SAmP

How soon doth man decay! Mortification. George Herbert. ESCV; FSCP; GeHe; NOSC; SeCP

How soon hath Time the suttle [*or* subtle] theef [*or* thief] of youth. Sonnet. Milton. APAD; GSo; HeIP-4; InPS-3; NAEL-1; NOSC; NoP-4; PBMP; PFE; PoE; SCGP; Son

How splendid in the morning glows. Hassan's Serenade. James Elroy Flecker. OBEV *Fr.* Hassan.

How Spring Comes. Alice Notley. PmAP

How startling to find the portraits of the gods. Roy Fuller. Son *Fr.* Mythological Sonnets.

How still he stands as mists begin to move. The Guard at the Binh Thuy Bridge. John Balaban. AF; CDa; FYAP

How still, how happy! These [*or* Those] are words. Emily Jane Brontë. BWW; NOBVV; OBNC; SCGP

How still, / How strangely still. Sea Calm. Langston Hughes. OxBoS

How still the hawk. Charles Tomlinson. LiTM

How straight is Heaven's Way! Rights. Phan Bội Châu, *Vietnamese*. AVP, *tr.* by Huỳnh Sanh Thông

How strange. Unique? Adrian Rumble. SpW

How strange a thing a lover seems. Love's Perversity. Coventry Patmore. EnVR *Fr.* The Angel in the House.

How strange at night [*or* it is] to wake. Night and Sleep. Coventry Patmore. CH; EBVV

How strange is Love; I am not one. The Gourmet's Love-Song. P. G. Wodehouse. NOBL

How strange it seems! These Hebrews in their graves. The Jewish Cemetery at Newport. Henry Wadsworth Longfellow. APN-1; AmPP; ChIV-1; ColAP; FaBoA; HAP; HeIP-4; HoPM; MeMAP; NCAP; NOBA; NoP-4; OxBA; PAR; PoPoPo; TAP

How strange the pride of many Irishmen! The New Style. David O'Bruadair, *Irish*. BIrV, *tr.* by John Montague

How strange this ice, so motionless and still. A Dance of Death. "Michael Field." ADE

How strange to awake in a city. Hearing Men Shout at Night on MacDougal Street. Robert Bly. InPS-3

How strange to be gone in a minute? A man. A Final Sonnet. Ted Berrigan. FTOS; PmAP *Fr.* The Sonnets.

How strange will be my death, of which I've been thinking since childhood. About Death and Other Things. Aleksandar Ristovic, *Serbo-Croatian*. HSix, *tr.* by Charles Simic

How strangely blind is prejudice, the Negro's greatest foe! Prejudice. Lizelia Augusta Jenkins Moorer. CBWP-3

How strong does my passion flow. On Her Loving Two Equally. Aphra Behn. NALW; NIP-4

How strongly does my passion flow. Song. Aphra Behn. OxAEP-1

How struts my love my cavalier. Cock-a-Hoop. Isabella Gardner. WPE

How subtle-secret is your smile! Did you love none then? Nay, I know. Oscar Wilde. MoBrPo *Fr.* The Sphinx.

How sweet and innocent are country sports. James Thomson. UV *Fr.* Of a Country Life.

How sweet and lovely dost thou make the shame. Sonnet 95. Shakespeare. HeIP-4; SCGP *Fr.* Sonnets.

How sweet I roamed [*or* roam'd] from field to field. The Prince of Love. William Blake. CH; EnLoPo; GLoP; ImPo; NAEL-2; NOBE; NOEC; NoP-4; OAEL-2; OBNC; PoEL-4; Poetr; SAGP; TFi

How sweet is harmless solitude! Solitude. Mary Mollineux. NOSC

'How sweet is mortal Sovranty!' — think some. Omar Khayyám. UV *Fr.* The Rubáiyát of Omar Khayyám [of Naishápúr]. AWP; EBVV; FaBoBe; FaPoR; HAP; NAEL-2; PoEL-5

How Sweet Is the Language of Love. Oliver Holden. AH

How sweet is the Shepherd's sweet lot! The Shepherd. William Blake. BoTP; ChAP; FHYEP; Ro *Fr.* Songs of Innocence.

How sweet the answer Echo makes. Echoes. Thomas Moore. GTBS-P; NOBRP; OxAEP-2

How sweet the chime of the Sabbath bells! Creeds of the Bells. George W. Bungay. PWR

How sweet the moonlight sleeps upon this bank! Moonlight. Shakespeare. OxAEP-1 *Fr.* The Merchant of Venice.

How sweet the name of Jesus sounds. The Name of Jesus. John Newton. ECEV; NOCV; NOEC

How sweet the tuneful bells' responsive peal! Sonnet: At Ostend. William Lisle Bowles. NOEC

How Sweet Thy Precious Gift of Rest. Menahem ben Makhir of Ratisbon, *Hebrew*. TrJP, *tr.* by Herbert Loewe

How sweetly did the moments glide. The Cottager's Complaint, on the Intended Bill for Enclosing Sutton-Coldfield. John Freeth. NOEC

How sweetly doth *My Master* sound! *My Master!* The Odour. 2. Cor. 2. George Herbert. ChIV-2; ESCV

How swift along the winding way. Upon Boys Diverting Themselves in the River. Thomas Foxton. OxBChV

How swiftly it dries. Burial Songs. *Unknown, Chinese.* ChiP, tr. by Arthur Waley

How terrible it is to trust no one. *Unknown, Russian.* TCRP, tr. by Bradley Jordan

How terrifying at night is the convex face of the black. First Psalm (Posthumous). Bertolt Brecht, *German.* PFTM, tr. by Anselm Hollo

How that glory remains in remembrance. *Unknown, Old English.* NoP-4 tr. by Edward Morgan. *Fr.* Beowulf, ASW, tr. by Kevin Crossley-Holland; OAEL-1, tr. by Charles W. Kennedy

How that great work of Love enhances Nature's. (LL) Sonnet: "Yet, love, mere love, is beautiful indeed." Elizabeth Barrett Browning. BWW; CTC; OxAEP-2

How the Abbey of Saint Werewulf Juxta Slingsby Came by Brother Fabian's Manuscript. Sebastian Evans. PeVV

How the Bulls Were Begotten. *Unknown, Irish.*
  Two Bulls, The. NOIV, tr. by Thomas Kinsella

How the candle burns. Imants Ziedonis, *Latvian.* CEEP, tr. by Inara Cedrins

How the Days Passed. Who'd have believed they'd. Natan Zach, *Hebrew.* IP, tr. by Warren Bargad *and* Stanley F. Chyet

How the days went. Now That I Am Forever with Child. Audre Lorde. CrSp; NAAAL; NALW; PoBA; Poetr

How the Death of a City Is Never More than the Sum of the Deaths of Those Who Inhabit Its Spaces. Victor Coleman. NOBC

How the Doughty Duke of Albany like a Coward Knight Ran Away Shamefully. John Skelton.
  "O ye wretched Scots." OBSV

How the elements solidify! Event. Sylvia Plath. NOBA

How the First Hielandman of God Was Made. *Unknown.* OBSV

How the Great Guest Came. Edwin Markham. BLPA

How the Hen Sold Her Eggs to the Stingy Priest. Nancy Willard. LCAP-2

How the Invalids Make Love. Susan Feldman. AmPA

How the lightstruck trees change sun. Powers of Congress. Alice Fulton. NAmP90

How the Lover Perisheth in His Delight, As the Fly in the Fire. Petrarch. Son *Fr.* Sonnets to Laura.

How the majestic stellar lights of Heav'n. Compensation. Henrietta Cordelia Ray. CBWP-3

How the New Teacher Got Her Nickname. Brian Patten. NOxBChV

How the old Mountains drip with Sunset. Emily Dickinson. RB

How the red road stretched before us, mile on mile. Independence. Nancy Cato. WPE

How the river cools your blood is something you can't. Autobiography, Chapter XVII: Floating the Big Piney. Jim Barnes. HATNAP

How the Soul Speaks to God. Mechthild von Magdeburg, *German.* WPoS, tr. by Oliver Davies

How the splendour of these veils and of this dress. Phaedra. Osip Emilevich Mandelstam, *Russian.* OBVE, tr. by James Greene

How the Waters closed above Him. Emily Dickinson. PoEL-5

How the Wild South East Was Lost. Kit Wright. OBCoV

How the wind howls this morn. The End of May. William Morris. NOBVV

How the Women Will Stop War. Aristophanes. *Fr.* Lysistrata. NAWM-1, tr. by B. B. Rogers

How the World Works: An Essay. Albert Goldbarth. NAmP90

How the young attempt / and are broken. Generation. Audre Lorde. NBV; Poetr

How the youthful. William Blake. *See* London ("I wander through [*or* thro'] each chartered [*or* charter'd] street").

How these pieces of paper: lined unlined small large crinkled smooth. Joanne Burns. BMAP

How They Brought the Good News by Sea. Norma Farber. PChr

How They Brought the Good News from Ghent to Aix. Robert Browning. EBEvV; EBNV; FHYEP; FaBoBe; FaPoR; HoPM; NAEL-2; OBSP; PeVV; UV
  "Not a word to each other; we kept the great pace." Poetr

How they came into the world. A History of Lesbianism. Judy Grahn. GLP

How They Communicate. Lucretius, *Latin.* APo, tr. by Rolfe Humphries

How They Killed My Grandmother. Boris Abramovich Slutsky, *Russian.* HP, tr. by Daniel Weissbort

How They Made the Golem. John Robert Colombo. MoCV

How They Sleep. *Unknown.* CTV

How thin and sharp is the moon tonight! Winter Moon. Langston Hughes. KaS; SAmP

How Things Work. Gary Soto. NoAM

How this woman came by the courage, how she got. John Berryman. TAP *Fr.* Dream Songs.

How this year of years do I best see. May Trees in a Storm. Geoffrey Grigson. GBL

How time reverses. For My Contemporaries. James Vincent Cunningham. CoAP; VCAP

How to Be Happy. *Unknown.* BLPA

How to Be Old. May Swenson. UnPo

How to behold what cannot be held? Giovanni da Fiesole on the Sublime. Richard Howard. GS

How to Catch Aunt Harriette. Ruth Stone. NMM-2

How to Choose a Mistress. Edmond Prestwich. NOSC

How to Choose a Mistress. *Unknown.* NOSC

How to Dress Like a Femmy Dyke. Jane Barnes. GLP

How to Dress like a Scary Dyke. Jane Barnes. GLP

How to Eat a Poem. Eve Merriam. ChAP

How to Eat Corn. Dick Bakken. EC2

How to explain that on the day. Irreconcilables. Arthur Gregor. NYBP

How to Fertilize Soil. James Grainger. *See* Compost.

How to Find Love in an Instant. Michael Lassell. GLP *Fr.* Times Square Poems.

How to follow. Imamiya Middle School. Shaku Chōkū, *Japanese.* MJT, tr. by Makoto Ueda

How to Forget. Rebecca Foresman. PoToHe

How to Get Grizzly Spirit. *Unknown, Tlingit Indian.* STP, tr. by James Koller

How to Get On in Society. John Betjeman. NOBL; OBSV; OxBTC; UV

How to Get There. Frank O'Hara. NoP-4

How to honor the village, the tribe, / that floral apron. Marilyn Chin. *See* The Floral Apron.

How to Hug Your Three-Year-Old Daughter. Paul B. Janeczko. IFJA

How to keep—is there any, is there none such, nowhere known. The Leaden Echo and the Golden Echo. Gerard Manley Hopkins. CMoP; GTBS-P; ImPo; LiTM; MoBrPo; NOBVV; OBMV; OBNC

How to Kill. Keith Douglas. FaBoMo; NOBE; PoWW; RB

How to live? How be simple and literal? Vladimir Holan, *Czech.* PoSu, tr. by Ian *and* Jarmila Milner

How to Make a Sailor's Pie. Joan Aiken. NTP

How to Make Rhubarb Wine. Ted Kooser. PBCAP

How to Meditate. Jack Kerouac. BB; CLPP; PoM
  ("—lights out— / fall, hands a-clasped, into instantaneous.") CLPP

How to Obtain Her. *Unknown.* NoSic

How to Organise a Successful Small Business. Brian Chan. HCP

How to Paint a Perfect Christmas. Miroslav Holub, *Czech.* OBCP, tr. by George Theiner *and* Ian Milner

How to put it. . . without offence. Thomas Kinsella. BiHa *Fr.* A Technical Supplement.

How to Reach the Sun. . . on a Piece of Paper. Wes Magee. NOxBChV

How to Read Me. Walter Savage Landor. NOBVV

How to Read the First Line. Gabriel Preil, *Yiddish.* CEEP, tr. by Laya Firestone

How to Ride Out a Storm. Mildmay Fane, 2d Earl of Westmorland. NOSC

How to say the distance, not the difference. Black English. Richard Katrovas. LTA

How to See Deer. Philip Booth. Poetsp

How to serve you, and you trust me. Richard Lovelace. *See* To Lucasta[, from Prison].

How to Start a War. Phyllis McGinley. OBSV

How to Stuff a Pepper. Nancy Willard. CrSp

How to Tell a Camel. J. Patrick Lewis. TLR

How To Tell the Wild Animals. Carolyn Wells. NBLV

How to the invisible. Elementary Cosmogony. Charles Simic. NNaP

How to Treat Elves. Morris Gilbert Bishop. OBAL; OBCA

How to Watch Your Brother Die. Michael Lassell. GLP

How to Write a Letter. Elizabeth Turner. ACTP; OxBChV

How true it is when I am sad. Work. J. W. Thompson. PoToHe

How Tuesday Began. Kathleen Fraser. NYBP

How ugly babies are! How heedless. Vikram Seth. OBCoV *Fr.* The Golden Gate.

How unpleasant to meet Mr. Eliot! Lines for Cuscuscaraway and Mirza Murad Ali Beg. T. S. Eliot. NBLV; NTP; OBAL; OBCoV; PeLV; UV *Fr.* Five-Finger Exercises.

How unpurposed, how inconsequential. Gouzeaucourt: The Deceitful Calm. Edmund Blunden. PeFWW

How vainly men themselves amaze. The Garden. Andrew Marvell. AWP; ClHu; ESCV; FMP; FSCP; GTBS-P; GaP; GeHe; HAP; ImPo; InPS-3; MeLP; NAEL-1; NIP-4; NOBE; NOSC; OAEL-1; OBEV; OBGa; PBRV; PoE; PoEL-2; PoLF; PoPoPo; PoRA; Poetr; SCGP; SeCP; TFi; TOF; TRP

How varied the family Sen! Limerick. Roy Fuller. PoLi

How vast a world is figured by a word! A Word: Man. Washington Allston. APN-1

How vast, how dread, o'erwhelming is the thought. On a Falling Group in the Last Judgement of Michael Angelo, in the Cappella Sistina. Washington Allston. APN-1

How very much I loved you only I know. Nikos Gatsos. GrIP Fr. Amorgos.

How vigilant was Spenser. Edmund Clerihew Bentley. OBCoV Fr. Clerihews.

How Violets Came Blue. Robert Herrick. BeJo; CaPo; TTTS

How warm this woodland wild Recess! Recollections of Love. Coleridge. NAEL-2

How was I born? Where from? Why did I come. Unknown, Greek. GrAn, tr. by Peter Jay

How was thy mother a lioness. Lamentation. Bible, O.T. TrJP Fr. Ezekiel.

How We Beat the Favourite. Adam Lindsay Gordon. CBAP; PeVV

How We Carry Ourselves. Jimmy Santiago Baca. AF

How we desire desire! Joy of surcease. Epigram. James Vincent Cunningham. VGW

How we drift in the twilight of bus stations. Sleeping on the Bus. Martín Espada. BAP-96

How We Drove the Trotter. W. T. Goodge. NOBAu

How we envy their not caring. The Card-Players. David Ray. VGW

How we go on. (LL) Axe Handles. Gary Snyder. ColAP; LoL; NoAM; PmAP; PoPoPo; VCAP

How We Heard the Name. Alan Dugan. CoAP; NoAM; PFE

How We Learned about Friction. Carol J. Pierman. CMAP

How We Make Lumber Out of Trees. Crawdad Nelson. EC3

How We See. Edward Bond. HP

How well (dear Brother) art thou called Stone? To My Reverend Dear Brother, M. Samuel Stone. John Cotton. SCAP

How well do I recall that walk in state. Frederick Goddard Tuckerman. APN-2 Fr. Sonnets.

How well her name an Army doth present. Ana(Mary-Army)gram. George Herbert. ChIV-2; GeHe; OAEL-1

How well I know that fountain. Song of the Soul That Knows God by Faith. Saint John of the Cross, Spanish. TIRV, tr. by Seamus Heaney

How well I know that fountain's rushing flow. St John of the Cross: Song of the Soul That Is Glad to Know God by Faith. Roy Campbell. PeECV

How well I know what I mean to do. By the Fire-Side. Robert Browning. EBVV; OAEL-2

How well the brittle boat doth personate. On the Same [Death of My Dear Brother, Mr. H.S., Drowned]: The Boat. William Hammond. NOSC

How well you served me above ground. Spirit's Song. Louise Bogan. NYBP

How when one entered a cottage. The Answer. John Montague. CIP-2; TIRV

How white. Bacchylides, Greek. InMo, tr. by Sam Hamill

How will he hear the bell at school. Mutterings Over the Crib of a Deaf Child. James Wright. LCAP-2; LiLi

How will I hide? (LL) Question. May Swenson. LiTM; PFE; SAGP; VGW

How will I think of you. December 21st. Jean Valentine. LCAP-2

How will it go, crumbling earthquake, towering inferno, juggernaut, volcano, smashup. A New Reality Is Better Than a New Movie! Imamu Amiri Baraka. NoAM

How will our unborn children scoff at us. The Future Verdict. Ada Cambridge. NOBAu

How Will You Call Me, Brother. Mari E. Evans. BlSi

How will you crawl in to me, little one? A Bomb Victim in the Cathedral Speaks to a Child. Gunars Salis, Latvian. CEEP, tr. by Baiba Kaugara

How will you cross the autumn mountain alone? Princess Oku, Japanese. BoWoP, tr. by Willis Barnstone

How will you fill your goblet? Abraham Sutskever, Yiddish. HP, tr. by Chana Bloch

How will you manage. Princess Daihaku. AWP, tr. by Arthur Waley Fr. Manyo Shu, Part 2 of 4.

How will you your Christmas keep? Keeping Christmas. Eleanor Farjeon. OBCP

How wisely Nature did decree. Eyes and Tears. Andrew Marvell. FSCP; GeHe

How wretched is a woman's fate. Woman's Hard Fate. Unknown. ECWP

How you became a poet's a mystery! Heredity. Tony Harrison. Fr. The School of Eloquence. NAEL-2; NoAM

How You Get Born. Erica Jong. UnPo

How you go along all day, Strange. Kirby Doyle. NeAP

How your eyes dazzle down into my soul! James Thomson. EnVR Fr. Sunday at Hampstead.

"How'd I solve de Negro Problum?" Uncle Rube on the Race Problem. Clara Ann Thompson. CBWP-2

Howdy, Honey, Howdy! Paul Laurence Dunbar. PoLF

However dry and windless. Bamboo. William Plomer. PeSA

However, imperceptibly you'll grow up. Shows. Yevgeny Mikhailovich Vinokurov, Russian. TCRP, tr. by Daniel Weissbort

However, / in all their games. Margaret Atwood. Fr. The Circle Game. MoCV

However the battle is ended. Only One Way. Ella Wheeler Wilcox. PWR

However the image enters. Afterimages. Audre Lorde. LTA; VCAP

However they talk, whatever they. Unknown, German. CTV, tr. by Louis Untermeyer

However we wrangled with Britain awhile. Literary Importation. Philip Freneau. TAP

However you look at it. The Secular. Chris Wallace-Crabbe. NOBAu

Howie gave sentence of slaughter. The Desertion of the Women and Seals. George Mackay Brown. OxBC

Howl. Allen Ginsberg. SAGP Fr. Howl. AmPP; LCAP-2; PoM

("Bodies good to eat a thousand years.") (LL) NoP-4; SAGP

("Flowers! Down to the river! into the street!") (LL) TAP

("I saw the best minds of my generation destroyed by madness, starving / hysterical naked.") NoP-4; SAGP

II. CLPP

("River! into the street!") (LL) BB

Howl, Howl. Christopher Reid. OBCoV

Howl, howl, howl! O! you are men of stones. Shakespeare. OxAEP-1 Fr. King Lear.

Howling of Wolves, The. Ted Hughes. APo; OxBTC

Howling storm is brewing, A. The Storm. Heinrich Heine, German. AWP, tr. by Louis Untermeyer

Howling wind blows hard from west to east, A. Dark Night. Tản Đà, Vietnamese. AVP, tr. by Huỳnh Sanh Thông

Howres for the Hours of Matines, The. Richard Crashaw. PeECV

"How's My Boy?" Sydney Thompson Dobell. CH

Hsi-li Echoed My Poems, and I Respond to Him, Using the Same Rhymes— Also Sent to Tsung-lien. Yang Shih-ch'i, Chinese.

("Not sobered up from my muddy Kao-yang drunk.") CoBLCP, tr. by Jonathan Chaves

Hsi-shih dreams at dawn, in the cool of silk curtains. A Girl Combs Her Hair. Li Ho, Chinese. PLT, tr. by A. C. Graham

Hsi Shih received the favor of Wu. Following the Rhymes of the Six Poems "Thinking of the Past at Ku-Su and Ch'ien-t'ang." Ni Tsan, Chinese. CoBLCP, tr. by Jonathan Chaves

Hsiu-chou. T'ang Hsien-tsu, Chinese. CoBLCP, tr. by Jonathan Chaves

Hsün-yang on the Yangtze, seeing off a guest at night. Song of the Lute. Po Chü-i, Chinese. CoBCP, tr. by Burton Watson

Hub of the Universe, The. Walt Whitman. ImPo Fr. Song of Myself. AmPP; MoAmPo; NAAL-3; NOBA; OxBA

Hubert's Museum. Louis Simpson. OxBC

Huc omnes pariter. Boethius. OBMV, tr. by John Walton Fr. Consolation of Philosophy, The ("De Consolacione Philosophie").

Huck Finn at Ninety, Dying in a Chicago Boarding House Room. James Schevill. TAP

Hucksters haggle in the mart, The. For a War Memorial. G. K. Chesterton. PoWW

Hudibras. Samuel Butler.

Argument, The. EBEV; NAEL-1; OAEL-1

Arms and the Man. NOSC

"For his religion it was fit." OBSV; OBCoV

"In mathematic[k]s he was greater." NOBL

Independent Squire. NOBE

Metaphysical Sectarian, The. MeLP; PeLV

Portrait of Sidrophel. PoEL-3

Presbyterian Knight, The. NOBE; NOSC

(Canto I.) CABP

("When civil dudgeon first grew high.") CABP; OAEL-1

"Question then, to state it first, The." NOBL

"Quoth he, My faith as adamantine." OBSV

"Quoth he, to bid me not to love." NOBL

Sidrophel, the Rosicrucian Conjurer. OxBoLi

"Some were for setting up a king." EBEV

"There is a tall long-sided dame." OBSV

"This place (quoth she) they say's enchanted." NOBL

"What makes a knave a child of God." NOBL; OBSV

"What Rage, O Citizens, what fury." OBCVT

Hudibras and Milton Reconciled. William Somervile. NOEC

Hudibras, the Presbyterian Knight, abr. Samuel Butler. See The Metaphysical Sectarian.

Hudney, Sutej IX, X, XI, 7, 9, 25, 58, 60, 61, 64. Index. Paul Violi. EOEF; PmAP

Hue and Cry after Fair Amoret, A. William Congreve. NOEC; OBEV

Huelsenbeck / janko, chant / tzara. L'amiral cherche une maison à louer. Richard Huelsenbeck, Marcel Janko, and Tristan Tzara. PFTM

Huesca. John Cornford. See To Margot Heinemann.

Huey. Etheridge Knight. NNaP

Huffy Henry hid the day. John Berryman. CBNP; ColAP; HCAP; NAAL-2; NoP-4; PoE; VCAP Fr. Dream Songs.

Hug, The. Tess Gallagher. CrSp

Hug me closer, closer, mother. Little Bessie. Unknown. AmFP

Hug o' War. Shel Silverstein. NTCP

Huge car with the sad voice, The. Kojo Laing. HBAPE

Huge doll of my body, The. My Life. Mark Strand. NoAM

HUGE FIGURES FUCKING THE HUGE FIGURES / FUCKING, THE. (Fuck Ode). Michael McClure. BB Fr. Dark Brown.

Huge fish, bold and noble, A. Fish in a Painting. Ho Ching-ming, Chinese. CoBLCP, tr. by Jonathan Chaves

Huge glaring maps the walls surround. The Domestic Philosopher. Unknown. ECWP

Huge-headed oak. He Praises the Trees. Unknown, Irish. BIrV, tr. by Robin Skelton

Huge sea widens from us, mile on mile, The. Dunoon and the Holy Loch. Iain Crichton Smith. FaBoTC Fr. By the Sea.

Huge shoe mounts up from the horizon, A. The Wounded Breakfast. Russell Edson. LCAP-2

Huge upon the hazy plain. Grazing Locomotives. Archibald MacLeish. GM

Huge vapors brood above the clifted shore. Written near a Port on a Dark Evening. Charlotte Smith. NoP-4

Huge, viewless, ocean into which we cast. To Silence. Thomas Lovell Beddoes. Son

Huge with Time, a wombfruit lanced. Wole Soyinka. HBAPE

Hugging the Jukebox. Naomi Shihab Nye. NMM-2

Hugging the Shore. Mary E. Tucker. CBWP-1

Hugh of Lincoln. Unknown. EnSB; OxBB

(Sir Hugh; or, The Jew's Daughter.) ESPB

Hugh Selwyn Mauberley. (Life and Contacts). Ezra Pound. AmPP; CMoP; InPS-3; LiTM; NOBA; NoAM; TAP

"Age demanded an image, The." HAP; MoAmPo; VGW

"Beneath the sagging roof." MoAmPo

Brennbaum. MoAmPo

E. P. Ode Pour l'Election de Son Sepulchre. HAP; MoAmPo; MoP; NAAL-2; NoAM; VGW

("All things save Beauty alone.") (LL) NoP-4

(Hugh Selwyn Mauberley.) MeMAP; NoP-4

Envoi (1919). HAP; MoP; UnPo; VGW

(Envoi: "Go, dumb-born book.") MoAmPo; OxBA

Mr. Nixon. MoAmPo

Siena Mi Fe'; Disfecemi Maremma. MoAmPo

"Tea-rose tea-gown, etc." ColAP; MoAmPo; NOBE

"There died a myriad." MoAmPo; NOBE; PoE; TRP

"These fought in any case." ColAP; HeIP-4; MoAmPo; NOBE; OBWP; PoE; PoWW; TRP; VGW

("And liars in public places.") (LL) ColAP

Yeux Glauques. MoAmPo

Hugh Spencer's Feats in France. Unknown. ESPB

Hughie at the Inn. Elinor Wylie. NYBP; WPE

Hughie Graham. Robert Burns. OxBB

Hughie [the] Gra[e]me. Unknown. ESPB; IBB

Huh!—For All?. (LL) Children's Rhymes. Langston Hughes. BPo; NOxBChV

Huh uh! Chillun, let us pray! (LL) An Ante-Bellum Sermon. Paul Laurence Dunbar. AAP; APN-2; BPo; NAAAL

Hula Skirt, 1959, The. Kimiko Hahn. UnSA

Hullo, Inside. Max Fatchen. NOxBChV

Human Abstract, The. William Blake. FHYEP; NAEL-2; NOBRP; NOEC; OAEL-2; OxAEP-2; PoE; PoEL-4; Ro Fr. Songs of Experience.

Human Affection. Stevie Smith. LiLi; NALW

Human Animal, The. Jane Mayhall. TAP

Human Being Is a Lonely Creature, The. Richard Eberhart. PFE

Human contours are so easily lost, The. The Human Form Divine. Kathleen Jessie Raine. WPE

Human cunt, like the eye, dilates, The. Tryst. Olga Broumas. DeD

Human Debasement; a Fragment. Edward Rushton. NOEC

Human eye, a sphere of waters and tissue, absorbs an energy that, The. Beam 4. Ronald Johnson. APSN Fr. Ark.

Human Fabric, The. Robert Penn Warren. Fr. Fall Comes in Back-Country Vermont. NYBP; VGW

Human Fold, The. Edwin Muir. LiTM

Human Form Divine, The. Kathleen Jessie Raine. WPE

Human Geography. Gloria Fuertes, Spanish. BoWoP, tr. by Willis Barnstone

Human Greatness. Edwin Barclay. PBA

Human Heart, The. Frank Carleton Nelson. PoToHe

Human Heart its hungry Gorge, The. (LL) A Divine Image ("Cruelty has a Human heart"). William Blake. ChIV-1; NAEL-2; NoP-4; OBNC; RB; Ro

Human House. Ryuichi Tamura, Japanese. VCWP, tr. by Christopher Drake

Human Life. Matthew Prior. FaBoEE; OBCoV

Human Life. Samuel Rogers.

Another and the Same. OBNC

Man's Going Hence. OBNC

Human life does not reach a hundred. Roaming Immortal. Ts'ao Chih, Chinese. SuSp, tr. by Ronald C. Miao

Human Mind, The. Ai Shih-te, Chinese. TrJP, tr. by William C. White

Human Misery. Andreas Gryphius, German. GePo, tr. by George C. Schoolfield

Human Nature. Phan Bội Châu, Vietnamese. AVP, tr. by Huỳnh Sanh Thông

Human Qualities. Dahlia Ravikovitch, Hebrew. IP, tr. by Warren Bargad and Stanley F. Chyet

Human race is going to the cemetery, The. Etel Adnan. WPOW Fr. The Beirut-Hell Express.

Human reason is beautiful and invincible. Incantation. Czeslaw Milosz, Polish. VCWP, tr. by Czeslaw Milosz and Robert Pinsky

Human Seasons, The. Keats. GTBS-P; LaPo; PoPoPo

("Or else he would forego his mortal nature.") (LL)

Human shape is a ghost, The. Jelaluddin Rumi, Persian. LoL, tr. by Coleman Barks

Human Skull, The. Chế Lan Viên, Vietnamese. AVP, tr. by Huỳnh Sanh Thông

Human Soul. René Maran, French. TTY, tr. by Mercer Cook

Human torch / races through Prague, A. Ballad of Jan Palach, Student and Heretic. Ondra Lysohorsky, Lachian. AF, tr. by Ewald Osers

Human Touch, The. Spencer Michael Free. BLPA; FaBoBe; PoToHe

Human Wishes. Robert Hass. NAmP90

Humanities Lecture. William Stafford. NNaP; NoAM

HUMANITY, the field of miseries. Exaltatio Humanae Naturae. William Alabaster. NoSic

Humans Bought and Sold (two poems). Ōkuma Nobuyuki, Japanese. MJT, tr. by Makoto Ueda

Humble-Bee, The. Ralph Waldo Emerson. APN-1; APo; MeMAP; NCAP; NOBA; OxBB

Humble Beginnings. Thomas Lovell Beddoes. NOBVV

Humble Heart, A. Alfred Norris. PWR

Humble night. Hush after hush. Are you listening?, A. Snow Figure. David Baker. PuP-17

Humble Petition of the British Jacobins to their Brethren of France, The. Unknown. NOBRP

Humble springs of stately Plimouth Beach, The. Upon the Springs Issuing out from the Foot of Plimouth Beach. Samuel Sewall. SCAP

Humble Wish, The. B–ll M–rt–n. ECWP; LW

Humble Wish; off Porto-Sancto, March 29, 1779, An. Edward Thompson.

I've served my country nine and twenty years. NOEC

Humbly showeth: / That I went to warm myself in Lady Betty's chamber, because I was cold. Mrs. Harris's Petition. Jonathan Swift. CABP

Humiliated again. Rod Willmot. HA

Humiliation. Kaifi A'Zmi, Urdu. OMIP, tr. by Mumtaz Jahan

Humiliation in Its Disguises. Andrew Crozier. NBrP

Humility. George Herbert. NOSC

Humility. Marie Luise Kaschnitz, German. WPOW, tr. by Michael Hamburger

Humility is the eye of the needle. Yelena Rubisova, Russian. TCRP, tr. by Thomas E. Bird

Humm Tee Dim Tay. Humpty Dumpty. Michael Rosen and Susanna Steele. NOxBChV

Humming bee purrs softly o'er his flower, The. The Cricket. Frederick Goddard Tuckerman. APN-2; NCAP; NOBA; PAR

Humming-Bird. D. H. Lawrence. APo; CMoP; InPS-3; LiTM; NoAM; RB

Humming Bird, The. Richard Lewis. APo *Fr.* A Journey from Patapsko to Annapolis.

Humming-Bird, The. Mary E. Tucker. CBWP-1

Hummingbird, A. Emily Dickinson. HeIP-4; NAAL-1; PoEL-5; SoŞç-8

Hummingbird, The. Mary Howitt. CTV

Hummingbird. X. J. Kennedy. NOxBChV

Hummingbird. Harold Littlebird. VoR

Hummingbird: a Seduction, The. Pattiann Rogers. NAmP90

Hummingbird Light. Diane Wakoski. PmAP

Hummingbirds. Norman Dubie. LCAP-2

"Hummingbirds" he said, and spat. Winged tongues. In the Tool-shed. Andrew Greig. FaBoTC

Humorous Lovers, The. William Cavendish, Duke of Newcastle. Song: "We'll, placed in Love's triumphant chariot high." OxBSP

Humorous Verse. Abu Dulama, *Arabic.* TTY, *tr. by* Raoul Abdul

Humours. John Marston. NoSic *Fr.* Satires.

Humours of the King's Bench Prison, a Ballad, The. Leonard Howard. NOEC

Hump-backed flute player, The. Gary Snyder. APSN *Fr.* Mountains and Rivers without End: The Market.

Humped Ox, The. Flavien Ranaivo, *French.* NegPo, *tr. by* Ellen Conroy Kennedy

Humphy-backit heron, A. Heron. James King Annand. NOxBChV

Humpty Dump Dublin squeaks through his norse. An Advertisement for Finnegans Wake. James Joyce. CBNP; OBCoV

Humpty Dumpty. Michael Rosen *and* Susanna Steele. NOxBChV

Humpty Dumpty sat on a wall. Mother Goose. FaBoBe; LB; OxBoLi; OxNR; ReMoGo

Humpty Dumpty went to the moon. Michael Rosen. SpW

Humpty Dumpty's Song. "Lewis Carroll." GTBS-P; OBCoV; OxBChV; OxBoLi; PeLV *Fr.* Through the Looking-Glass.

(Humpty Dumpty's Recitation.) OBSP; PeVV

Hunchback, The. John Peale Bishop. PoA

Hunchback and the Dwarf, The. Marutanilanakanar, *Tamil.* PLW, *tr. by* A. K. Ramanujan

Hunchback Girl: She Thinks of Heaven. Gwendolyn Brooks. ChAP *Fr.* A Street in Bronzeville. BPo; BlSi; FaBoWP

Hunchback in the park, The. Dylan Thomas. EBEV; FaBoTw; MoBrPo; NAEL-2; NoAM; NoP-4; SAGP; TwCP

Hunchback of Dugbe, The. Wole Soyinka. VCWP

Hunchback on the corner, with gum and shoelaces, The. Pursuit. Robert Penn Warren. FuPo; HAP; MoAmPo; TwCP

Hunchback Woman. The Hunchback and the Dwarf. Marutanilanakanar, *Tamil.* PLW, *tr. by* A. K. Ramanujan

Hunchbacked / by his heart. The Life. Philip Dow. AmPA

Hunchèd camels of the night, The. An Arab Love-Song. Francis Thompson. AWP; MoBrPo

Hunched, hump-backed, gigantic. Blues. Edward Kamau Brathwaite. GT

Hunched I make my way, uncertainly. On the Back of a Photograph. János Pilinszky, *Hungarian.* NNPT; PoSu, *tr. by* Peter Jay

Hunder pipers canna blaw, A. Calvinist Sang. Alexander Scott. OxBS

Hundred buffalo, A. Bone Yard. Jim Barnes. CDW

Hundred-Fold Cord, The. Chang Yü. *Fr.* Four Poems On the Ch'ung-wu Festival. CoBLCP, *tr. by* Jonathan Chaves

Hundred-gated City! thou. Hundred-gated Thebes. George Darley. NOBE *Fr.* Nepenthe.

Hundred-gated Thebes. George Darley. NOBE *Fr.* Nepenthe.

Hundred Headless Woman, The. Max Ernst, *French.* PFTM, *tr. by* Dorothea Tanning

Hundred houses were in ruins, A. Never Again. Jaroslav Seifert, *Czech.* AF, *tr. by* Ewald Osers

Hundred is the most I ever made, A. The Figure a Poem Makes. Jim Hall. CMAP

Hundred mares, all white! their manes, A. The Mares of the Camargue. Frédéric Mistral. AWP, *tr. by* George Meredith *Fr.* Mirèio.

Hundred men shouting at once, helping to rattle the oars, A. Blue Rapids. Lu Yu, *Chinese.* CoBCP; SuSp, *tr. by* Burton Watson

Hundred rivers day and night flow on, The. Beginning of Autumn: A Poem to Send to Tzu-yu. Su Tung-p'o, *Chinese.* CoBCP, *tr. by* Burton Watson

Hundred ruddy peach-moons ring the grass, A. Under the September Peach. Robert Wallace. Son

Hundred thousand li of journey, how many dangers?, A. For the Monk San-tsang on His Return to the Western Regions. Li Tung, *Chinese.* CoBCP, *tr. by* Burton Watson

Hundred thousand million mites we go, A. Charles Hamilton Sorley. NSI; PoWW

Hundred Tongues, A. Viên Linh, *Vietnamese.* AVP, *tr. by* Huỳnh Sanh Thông

Hundred Ways of Playing Solitaire, A. Belle Randall. Mabel Woo. CRP

Hundred Years Ago, A. *Unknown.* AS

Hundred years are but a butterflys dream, A. Tune: "Sailing at Night"—A Song Sequence. Ma Chih-yüan, *Chinese.* SuSp, *tr. by* Sherwin S. S. Fu

Hundred Years from Now, A. Mary A. Ford. BLPA

Hundred years from now, dear heart, A. In a Rose Garden. John Bennett. BLPA; FaBoBe

Hundred years have passed and gone, A. Centenary's Day. Marcus Garvey. PBCV

Hundred years is a very long time, A. A Hundred Years Ago. *Unknown.* AS

Hundred years the Ark in the building was, A. Michael Drayton. ChIV-1 *Fr.* Noah's Flood.

Hundreds of houses, thousands of houses—like a great chess-board. Climbing the Terrace of Kuan-yin and Looking at the City of Ch'ang-an. Po Chü-i, *Chinese.* ChiP, *tr. by* Arthur Waley

Hundreds of migrating hawks are roosting in the hedgerows. Driving into Enid. Michael Van Walleghen. FYAP

Hundreds of stars in the pretty sky. Only One Mother. George Cooper. BoTP; CTV; FPC

Hundreds of years you Stella's feet may kiss! (LL) Sonnet 84: "Highway, since you my chief Parnassus be." Sir Philip Sidney. OBEV; OxAEP-1; SCGP

Hung be the heavens with black, yield day to night. A King Is Dead. Shakespeare. OxAEP-1 *Fr.* King Henry VI, Pt. I.

Hung between thief and thief. Improperia. Francis Sparshott. MoCV

Hung clouded in the dragon-guarded shrine. (LL) The Locomotive. Christopher Pearse Cranch. APN-1; GM

Hung midsea / Like a boat mid-air. For the Death of 100 Whales. Michael McClure. BB

Hung there in the thermal. Vultures. Margaret Atwood. LCAP-2

Hunga a twis man tripe. Pressure Drop. Onuora Oku. PBCV

Hunger. Laurence Binyon. NTP; OxBTC

Hunger. Cries From Chiapas. Muriel Rukeyser. CPO

Hunger. Adrienne Rich. NMM-2

Hunger. Rimbaud, *French.* AWP, *tr. by* Louise Varese

Hunger. Jerome Rothenberg. APSN

Hunger. Samik, *Eskimo.* STP, *tr. by* Edward Field

Hunger. Charles Simic. NNaP

Hunger. Gaspara Stampa, *Italian.* WPOW, *tr. by* Brenda Webster

Hunger. Ruth Stone. InPS-3

Hunger and Thirst. John Peale Bishop. PoA

Hunger Camp at Jaso. Wislawa Szymborska. *See* Starvation Camp near Jaslo.

Hunger drove you across. The Heart is the Target. Ellen Bryant Voigt. WeT

Hunger makes a person climb up to the ceiling. *Unknown.* PBA; TTY, *tr. by* Ulli Beier

Hunger of the Suffering Man, The. Syl Cheney-Coker. PBMAP

Hungering Hearts. *Unknown.* PoToHe

Hungering on the gray plain of its birth. A Lion Named Passion. John Hollander. NoAM

Hungry, and plucking / the fruit. (LL) O Taste and See. Denise Levertov. ChIV-1; CrSp; PBWP; TAP

Hungry and thirsty for holiness. The Life of St Sava. Vasco [*or* Vasko] Popa. PoSu, *tr. by* Anne Pennington *Fr.* St Sava's Spring.

Hungry Black Child, The. Adam David Miller. NBV; PoBA

Hungry crows sit and guard. Song of the Maidens. Yüan Hao-wen, *Chinese.* SuSp, *tr. by* Stephen West

Hungry Dead, The. Jim Wayne Miller. MT

Hungry Fox with fierce attack, An. The Fox and the Grapes. Phaedrus, *Latin.* OBCVT, *tr. by* Christopher Smart

Hungry Grass, The. Donagh MacDonagh. BIrV; IIP

Hungry Man's Wheel, The. César Vallejo, *Spanish.* PFTM, *tr. by* Clayton Eshleman *and* Jose Rubia Barcia

Hungry Mauchs, The. William Soutar. FaBoTC

Hungry winter, this winter. To Hell with It. Frank O'Hara. NeAP

Hungry / without money—. Michael McClintock. HA

Hunnish horse / Hunnish horse. Tune: "Song of Flirtatious Laughter." Wei Ying-wu, *Chinese.* SuSp, *tr. by* Hellmut Wilhelm

Hunt ceases, The. St. Eustace. Derek Mahon. BiHa

Hunt Goes By, The. Howard Nemerov. *Fr.* Epigrams. OBAL

Hunt, hunt again. If you do not find it, you. Fairy Story. Robert Penn Warren. NYBP

Hunt in the Black Forest, A. Randall Jarrell. CoAP; LCAP-2

Hunt is up, the hunt is up, The. *Unknown.* CH

Hunt not, fish not, shoot not. Bishop Blomfield's First Charge to His Clergy. Sydney Goodsir Smith. FaBoEE

Hunt Walking. Wesley McNair. AFr

Hunt was up, the hunt was up, The. The Capture of Edwin Alonzo Boyd. Peter Miller. MoCV

Hunter, The. Frank O'Hara. NNaP

Hunter. Vasco [or Vasko] Popa. HSix, *tr. by* Charles Simic *Fr.* Games. RB, *tr. by* Anne Pennington

Hunter, The. Raymond Souster. NOBC

Hunter. Rosanna Warren. *Fr.* Funerary Portraits. NoAM

Hunter Once, Now an Ascetic, A. Marippittiyar, *Tamil.* PLW, *tr. by* A. K. Ramanujan

Hunter Poems of the Yoruba. *Unknown, Yoruba.* RB, *tr. by* Ulli Beier

Hunter to the husbandman, The. A Valentine. Robert Graves. FuPo

Hunter Trials. John Betjeman. EBEvV; OBCoV

Hunters are back / from beating the winter's face, The. The Woman Thing. Audre Lorde. BlSi; GT; NMM-2

Hunters in the Snow, The. William Carlos Williams. GS; LCAP-2 *Fr.* Pictures from Brueghel.

("Over-all picture, The.") GS

Hunters in the Snow: Brueghel. Joseph Langland. LiTM

Hunter's Moon. Stephen Sandy. NYBP

Hunters mount menacing as they go, The. Saville in Trouble. Albery Allson Whitman. AAP *Fr.* Not a Man and Yet a Man.

Hunters of Kentucky; or, Half Horse and Half Alligator, The. Samuel Woodworth. AS

Hunters of Men, The. John Greenleaf Whittier. PAR

Hunters of the Deer, The. Dale Zieroth. NOBC

Hunter's Prayer. *Unknown, Hottentot.* PeSA

Hunter's Song. *Unknown, Hitchiti (Creek) Native American.* APN-2, *tr. by* Albert S. Gatschet

Hunter's Song at Nightfall, The. Goethe, *German.* STV, *tr. by* John Frederick Nims

Hunters went out with guns, The. Good Grease. Mary TallMountain. UnSA

Hunting. William Daniel Ehrhart. CDa

Hunting. Tymoteusz Karpowicz, *Polish.* PoSu, *tr. by* Jan Darowski

Hunting. "Yehoash," *Yiddish.* TrJP, *tr. by* Isidore Goldstick

Hunting a hare. Our dogs are raising a racket. Andrey Andreievich Voznesensky, *Russian.* TCRP, *tr. by* W. H. Auden

Hunting and Fishing. Alexander Pope. ECEV *Fr.* Windsor-Forest [*or* Windsor Forest].

Hunting Civil War Relics at Nimblewill Creek. James Dickey. CBCWP; CoAmPo; WeT

("And stood in his grandson's shape.") (LL) CBCWP

Hunting for Blueberries. Thomas James. AmPA

Hunting of Cupid, The. George Peele.

Love. NOBE

Hunting of the Cheviot, The. *Unknown. See* Chevy Chase.

Hunting of the Gods, The. *Unknown.* OxBoLi

Hunting of the Hare, The. Margaret Lucas Cavendish, Duchess of Newcastle. BWW; FaBoVe; KTR; NOSC

Hunting of the Snark, The. "Lewis Carroll." CBNP; OBNC; OBNV; PoEL-5

Baker's Tale, The. EBEV; NAEL-2; OxAEP-2

Fit the First: The Landing. EBEvV

Fit the Second: The Bellman's Speech. OBCoV

Fit the Sixth: The Barrister's Dream. EBNV

Vanishing, The. OxAEP-2

Hunting Pheasants in a Cornfield. Robert Bly. CoAmPo; TRP

Hunting Rabbits. Peter Skrzynecki. BMAP

Hunting season: / Once every year, the Deer catch human beings. They. Long Hair. Gary Snyder. NOBA

Hunting Song. Coleridge. *Fr.* Zapolya.

Hunting Song. Henry Fielding. OxBoLi; PeLV *Fr.* Don Quixote in England.

Hunting Song. Donald Finkel. CoAP; MoBS

Hunting Song. Sir Walter Scott. GTBS-P; SCGP

Hunting Song ("There's my war club"). *Unknown, Chippewa Indian.* STP, *tr. by* Jerome Rothenberg

Hunting Song ("This time I'll show up"). *Unknown, Chippewa Indian.* STP, *tr. by* Jerome Rothenberg

Hunting-Song. *Unknown, Navajo.* AWP, *tr. by* Natalie Curtis

Hunting Song. Paul Whitehead. OxBoLi *Fr.* Apollo and Daphne.

Hunting the Dugong. Gladys Cardiff. HATNAP

Hunting the Wren. *Unknown.* FaBoVe

Huntington sleeps in a house six feet long. Southern Pacific. Carl Sandburg. GM

Huntsman, The. Edward Lowbury. OBSP

Hurdy-Gurdy Man, The. Elizabeth Fleming. BoTP

Hurdy-Gurdy Man in Winter. Vernon Watkins. NYBP

Hurl down the nerve-gnarled body hurtling head. The Final Hunger. Vassar Miller. LiTM

Hurly, hurly, roon the table. *Unknown.* FaBoCh *Fr.* Two Graces.

Hurlygush. Maurice Lindsay. OxBS

Huron, The. Ruth Herschberger. WPE

Huron Carol, The. Jesse Edgar Middleton. OBCP

Hurra[h] for the pumpkin pie! (LL) Thanksgiving Day. Lydia Maria Child. APN-1; ImGa; NTCP; OBCA; WHSW

Hurrah! for a day with the farmer. A Day at the Farm. "L. J." BoTP

Hurrah for revolution and more cannon-shot! The Great Day. W. B. Yeats. APAD; BIrV; CMoP; OxBSP

Hurrah for the choice of the nation! Lincoln and Liberty. *Unknown.* AS

Hurrah for Thunder. Christopher Okigbo. HBAPE

Hurrahing in Harvest. Gerard Manley Hopkins. APAD; CMoP; MoBrPo; NAEL-2; PeECV; PoE; TOF

("Summer ends now; now, barbarous in beauty, the stooks arise.") APAD

Hurricane, The. Hart Crane. CMoP; MoAmPo; OxBA; TrCP

Hurricane, The. Philip Freneau. TAP

Hurricane Drummers! Self-Aid in Haggerston. Iain Sinclair. NBrP

Hurrier, The. Harold Monro. MoBrPo

Hurry, brothers, hurry. The Altar of the Fatherland. Andreas Kalvos, *Greek.* GrIP, *tr. by* Philip Sherrard

Hurry, hurry, Mary dear. N. M. Bodecker. TLR

Hurry of the Spirits, in a Fever and Nervous Disorders, The. Isaac Watts. NOEC

Hurry On, My Weary Soul. *Unknown.* AH

"Hurry!" said the leaves. A Summer Shower. *Unknown.* BoTP

Hurry the baby as fast as you can. Making a Man. Nixon Waterman. BLPA

Hurry, worry, unwary. Old Amusement Park. Marianne Moore. NYBP

Hurrying Away from the Earth. Robert Bly. PoA

Hurrying thru eternity. After the Cries of the Birds. Lawrence Ferlinghetti. CAPP-1

Hurrying to catch my Comet. Naturally the Foundation Will Bear Your Expenses. Philip Larkin. FaBoPV; PeLV

Hurt. Marcie Hans. CA

Hurt Hawks. Robinson Jeffers. AmPP; CMoP; ChAP; ColAP; FYAP; LiTM; MoAmPo; MoP; NAAL-2; NOBA; NoAM; NoP-4; OxBA; RB; SAGP; TAP; TFi; TRP; UnPo

Hurt No Living Thing. Christina Rossetti. OTCP *Fr.* Sing-Song.

"Hurt not the trees." (LL) The Trees Are Down. Charlotte Mew. BrRo; ChIV-2; MoBrPo; NTP; OxAEP-2; TrCP; VWP; WPE; WPOW

Hurt of Love, The. George Macdonald. TrCP

Hurt people crawl as if they. These Days. William Stafford. NNaP

Hurt. / U worried abt a. To All Sisters. Sonia Sanchez. PoBA

Hurtling between hedges now, I see. The Limerick Train. Brendan Kennelly. PBCIP

Hurtling past us in an old Volvo are women who speak with forked. Women who Speak with Steak Knives. Susan Hampton. BMAP

Husband, The. Cyril Dabydeen. HCP

Husband. Popati Hiranandani, *Sindhi.* OMIP, *tr. by* Popati Hiranandani

Husband and Heathen. Sam Walter Foss. OBAL

Husband and Wife. Arthur Guiterman. PoToHe

Husband and wife! No converse now ye hold. The Husband's and Wife's Grave. Richard Henry Dana. APN-1

Husband and wife we loved each other then. The Old Man's Song, about His Wife. *Unknown, Eskimo.* STP, *tr. by* Armand Schwerner

Husband, if you will be my dear. Wife to Husband. John Harington. NoSic

Husband of Poverty, The. Henry Neville Maughan.

Song: "There was a Knight of Bethlehem." BoTP

Husband of To-Day, The. Edith Nesbit. VWP

Husband, put down Spinoza, Pericles. Put Off Constricting Day. Mary Stanley. PeNZ

Husband to Wife. John Harington. NoSic

Husband who lived in Tiberias, A. Limerick. *Unknown.* PeLi

Husbandman, The. George Wither. NOSC *Fr.* A Collection of Emblemes, Ancient and Moderne.

Husband's and Wife's Grave, The. Richard Henry Dana. APN-1

Husbands and Wives. Miriam Hershenson. NTCP

Husband's Lament, The. Brian Merriman. OBVE, *tr. by* Frank O'Connor *Fr.* The Midnight Court. NOIV, *tr. by* Thomas Kinsella

Husband's Message, The ("Now shall I unseal myself to yourself alone"). *Unknown, Anglo-Saxon.* EEP, *tr. by* Michael Alexander

Husband's Message, The. *Unknown, Anglo-Saxon.* AnOE, *tr. by* Charles W. Kennedy
("Now that we are on our own I can explain this secret stave.") ASW

Husband's Return, The. Priscilla Jane Thompson. CBWP-2

Hush. David St. John. LCAP-2

Hush-a-ba birdie [*or* burdie], croon, croon. *Unknown.* OxNR

Hush-a-baa, baby / Dinna mak' a din. *Unknown.* OxNR

Hush-a-bye a baa lamb. *Unknown.* OxNR

Hush-a-bye, baby[, on the tree-top]. Mother Goose. LB; OxNR; ReMoGo

Hush-a-bye, baby, / Daddy is near. *Unknown.* ReMoGo

Hush-a-bye, baby, lie still with thy daddy. *Unknown.* ReMoGo

Hush-a-bye, baby / The beggar shan't have 'ee. *Unknown.* OxNR

Hush-a-bye, baby, they're gone to milk. *Unknown.* OxNR

Hush, baby, my dolly, I pray you don't cry. Baby Dolly. *Unknown.* ReMoGo

Hush Honey. Ruby C. Saunders. BlSi

Hush, hush, do not speak. Mani Leib, *Yiddish.* TrJP, *tr. by* Joseph Leftwich

Hush, hush, little baby. Evening. *Unknown.* BoTP

Hush, hush, / Nobody cares! John Bingham Morton. UV *Fr.* When We Were Very Silly.

Hush! Hush! Whisper who dares! A. A. Milne. UV *Fr.* Vespers.

Hush is over all the teeming lists, A. Frederick Douglass. Paul Laurence Dunbar. CBCWP; PoBA

Hush, little baby, don't say a word. *Unknown.* OxNR; TLR

Hush little Lily. Chillen Get Shoes. Sterling Brown. NoP-4

Hush, lullay. Lullaby. Léonie Adams. MoAmPo

Hush, my baby, do not cry. *Unknown.* OxNR

Hush! my dear, lie still and slumber. A Cradle Hymn. Isaac Watts. OBEV; OxBChV; PoEL-3; SCGP

Hush! not a whisper! Oars, be still! The Coracle Fishers. Robert Bloomfield. *Fr.* The Banks of Wye. OBNC

Hush of / the river, The. The Canoer. Diane Wakoski. HeIP-4

Hush! oh ye billows. Hymn. Joseph Sheridan Le Fanu. TIRV *Fr.* Beatrice.

Hush. On the edge. Rain in the Pine Wood. Gabriele D'Annunzio. ItIP

"Hush!" she says by rote under the trees. The Poor Mother. Edith Jay Scovell. WPN

Hush, Suzanne! The Mouse in the Wainscot. Ian Serraillier. OTCP

Hush thee, my babby. *Unknown.* OxNR

Hush Thee, Princeling. Anna Elizabeth Bennett. AH

Hush! 'tis a holy hour—the quiet room. Evening Prayer, at a Girls' School. Felicia Dorothea Hemans. VWP

Hush up, baby, / Don't say a word. The Mocking Bird. *Unknown.* AmFP

Hush ye, hush ye! honey, darlin'. Lullaby. Clara Ann Thompson. CBWP-2

Hush! Yo' mouth. Hush Honey. Ruby C. Saunders. BlSi

Hushaby, / Don't you cry. All the Pretty Little Horses. *Unknown.* AmFP; OxBoLi; TTTS

Hush'd be the camps to-day. Walt Whitman. SAmP *Fr.* Memories of President Lincoln.

Hushed plane, the pond. Ice-fishers' lights. Still little city. Prayer for the Little City. Sydney Lea. NAmP90

Hushed, the lake-shore's pines. O. Mabson Southard. HA

Hushed was the courtyard of the temple. The Cicada. Ou-yang Hsiu, *Chinese.* ChiP, *tr. by* Arthur Waley

Hushie ba, burdie beeton. *Unknown.* OxNR

Hushing of the Wye, The. Tennyson. *Fr.* In Memoriam A. H. H.

Huswifery. Edward Taylor. ColAP; MeMAP; NAAL-1; NAAL-3; NIP-4; NOBA; NOBE; OxBA; SCAP; TAP; TFi
(Housewifery.) NoP-4

Hut, The. Hilda Van Stockum. CTV

Hut in the bush of bark or rusty tin, The. The Hatters. Nan McDonald. NOBAu

Huts that stand like plaited baskets. Village and Factory. Alexander Ilyich Bezymensky, *Russian.* TrJP, *tr. by* Babette Deutsch

Huts under the drifts have frozen, The. Winter. Ion Caraion, *Romanian.* CEEP, *tr. by* Marguerite Dorian *and* Elliott B. Urdang

Huxley Hall. John Betjeman. CABP; OBSV

Huy Nguyen: Brothers, Drowning Cries. David Mura. CDa

Huzza! Hodgson, we are going. Lines to Mr Hodgson. Byron. NBLV; OBCoV; OxBoS

Hwaet! / A dream came to me. The Dream of the Rood. *Unknown, Anglo-Saxon.* EEP; NOCV, *tr. by* Michael Alexander

Hwæt, wē gār-dena in geardagum. Unknown. CABP *Fr.* Beowulf.

Hy-Brasail—the Isle of the Blest. Gerald Griffin. BLPA

Hyacinth. Louise Glück. NoAM

Hyacinth I wished me in her hand, A. (LL) Madrigal: "Like the Idalian Queen[e]." William Drummond, of Hawthornden. CBLP; GBL; NOBE; NOSC; OAEL-1; OBAL; OBEV; PeLV; PoEL-2; SCGP

Hyacinth is not yet used. Stonebridge Park Estate. Pauline Melville. HCP

Hyacinths to Feed Thy Soul. Sadi. BLPA; FaBoBe *Fr.* The Gulistan.

Hyacinthus. Olive Custance. ADE

Hyænas [*or* Hyenas], The. Rudyard Kipling. NAEL-2; OBSV

Hyaku-Nin-Isshu. Various authors, *Japanese.* AWP, *tr. by* Curtis Hidden Page

Hyder Iddle. *Unknown.* OxNR

Hydrologist tells me, The. You Live on a Drifting Road. Robert Ivanovich Rozhdestvensky, *Russian.* TCRP, *tr. by* J. R. Rowland

Hydromel and Rue. George Marion McClellan. AAP

Hyena. Carol Muske. AmPA

Hyena. *Unknown, Hottentot.* PeSAV, *tr. by* W. H. I. Bleek; PeSA
("Thou who makest thy escape from the tumult!") PeSAV, *tr. by* W. H. I. Bleek

Hyena. *Unknown, Hurutsche.* TTY, *tr. by* George Economou

Hyena. *Unknown, Yoruba. Fr.* Hunter Poems of the Yoruba. RB, *tr. by* Ulli Beier

Hyena Addressing Her Young Ones, The. *Unknown, Hottentot.* PeSAV, *tr. by* W. H. I. Bleek
(Hyena's Song to her Children.) PeSA

Hylas. Propertius. AWP, *tr. by* F. A. Wright *Fr.* Elegies. AWP

Hylas. Theocritus, *Greek.* HePo, *tr. by* Barbara Hughes Fowler *Fr.* Idylls.

Hylas and the Water Nymphs. Theocritus, *Greek.* OBCVT, *tr. by* Leigh Hunt

Hymen. Hilda Doolittle.
"Never more will the wind." CTC

Hymen, god of marriage bed. Epithalamium. Joseph Rutter. NOSC

Hymen hath together tied. Epithalamium. R. Hatton. NOSC

Hymeneal. Catullus. *Fr.* Carmen 61 ("Guardian of Helicon, Urania's son"). OxBM, *tr. by* Frederic Raphael *and* Kenneth McLeish *Fr.* Carmina.

Hymeneal[l] Dialogue, An. Thomas Carew. SeCP

Hymeneal Song on the Nuptials of the Lady Anne Wentworth and the Lord Lovelace, An. Thomas Carew. CaPo

Hymen's Triumph. Samuel Daniel.
Love. CBLP

Hymmnn. Allen Ginsberg. NOBA

Hymn: "And many voices marshalled in one hymn." Thomas Lovell Beddoes. NOBVV

Hymn: "Drop, drop, slow tears." Phineas Fletcher. OxBSP
(Hymn, A.) PeECV

Hymn: "For you I would put on embroidered robes." Jane King. HCP

Hymn: "Framer of the earth and sky." Saint Ambrose, *Latin.* TrCP

Hymn: "Hush! oh ye billows." Joseph Sheridan Le Fanu. TIRV *Fr.* Beatrice.

Hymn: "I know if I find you I will have to leave the earth." A. R. Ammons. CoAmPo

Hymn: "In vain the dusky night retires." Elizabeth Singer Rowe. ECWP

Hymn: "Lord, when the wise men came from far[r]." Sidney Godolphin. BeJo; HAP; MeLP; NOCV; PeECV
(Lord when the wise men came from Farr.) PBRV
(Maditation on the Nativity.) NOSC

Hymn: "Lord, within thy fold I be." Priscilla Jane Thompson. CBWP-2

Hymn: "Now the day is over." Sabine Baring-Gould. OxBChV; WHSW

Hymn: "O God of Hosts, thine Ear incline." *Unknown.* NOBRP

Hymn: "Thine are all the gifts, O God!" John Greenleaf Whittier. NOxBChV

Hymn: "Thou hidden love of God, whose height." John Wesley. NOEC
(Hymn.) ECEV

Hymn, The: "To the Almighty on his radiant throne." Anne Finch, Countess of Winchilsea. ChIV-1 *Fr.* A Pindaric Poem.

Hymn, An: "Wake, O my soul; awake, and raise." Phineas Fletcher. NOSC

Hymn: "When winds are raging." Harriet Beecher Stowe. AH
(Hymn.) PoToHe

Hymn: "Where should I seat you, where." Márton Kalász, *Hungarian.* CEEP, *tr. by* Jascha Kessler

Hymn: "Ye golden lamps of heaven, farewell." Philip Doddridge. ECEV

Hymn[e, The]. Ben Johnson. See Hymn to Diana.

Hymn. Isaac Watts. See Crucifixion to the World by the Cross of Christ.

Hymn. Jack Kerouac. CLPP

Hymn. Joseph Addison. See Ode: "How are thy servants blest, O Lord!"

Hymn. Saint Francis Xavier. ChIV-2

Hymn, a snare, and an exceeding sun. (LL) Boy Breaking Glass. Gwendolyn Brooks. AiP; MoP; NAAL-2; NoAM; NoP-4

Hymn among the Ruins. Octavio Paz, *Spanish*. PFTM, *tr. by* William Carlos Williams

Hymn Before Sleep. Prudentius, *Latin*. OBCVT, *tr. by* John Gray

Hymn for Airmen. "M. C. D. H." NSI

Hymn for Atonement Day. Judah Halevi, *Hebrew*. TrJP, *tr. by* Solomon Solis-Cohen

Hymn for Christmas Day, A. John Byrom. ECEV; NOCV; PoEL-3

Hymn for Easter Morn. John Mason Neale. TrCP

Hymn for Lanie Poo. Imamu Amiri Baraka. BB

Each Morning. PoBA

Hymn for Morning. Prudentius, *Latin*. MLL, *tr. by* Helen Waddell

Hymn for Pentecost. James Clarence Mangan. TIRV

Hymn for Saturday. Christopher Smart. *See* For Saturday.

Hymn for St. John's Eve. *Unknown, Latin*. AWP, *tr. by* Dryden

Hymn for the Close of the Week. Peter Abelard, *Latin*. TrCP

Hymn for the Eve of the New Year. Abraham Gerondi, *Hebrew*. TrJP, *tr. by* Solomon Solis-Cohen

Hymn in Adoration of the Blessed Sacrament. Richard Crashaw. MeLP

Hymn in Columbus Circle. Stephen Vincent Benét. OBAL

Hymn in Praise of Neptune, A. Thomas Campion. NOBE; OBEV

Hymn L: Rocking Hymn, A. George Wither. *See* A Rocking Hymn.

Hymn of Apollo. Shelley. OAEL-2

(Song of Apollo.) NAEL-2

Hymn of Empedocles. Matthew Arnold. OBEV *Fr.* Empedocles on Etna.

Hymn of Freedom. Michael J. Barry. TIRV

Hymn[e] of Heavenly Beauty [or Beautie], An. Edmund Spenser. PeECV

"But whoso may, thrice happy man him hold."

Hymn of Pan. Shelley. FaBoCh; OBEV; PoEL-4

Hymn of the Earth. William Ellery Channing. APN-1

Hymn of the Fairest Fair, The. William Drummond, of Hawthornden.

"In those vast fields of light, ethereal plains." NOSC

Hymn of the Magdalen. Marbod of Rennes, *Latin*. MLL, *tr. by* Helen Waddell

Hymn[e] of the Nativity, An. Richard Crashaw. *See* In the Holy Nativity of Our Lord God.

Hymn of the Patriotic War Veterans. Benjamin Péret, *French* . AF, *tr. by* Keith Hollaman

Hymn of the World Without. Bible, *O.T. See* Psalm 104.

Hymn of Trust. Oliver Wendell Holmes. *See* O Love Divine, That Stooped to Share.

Hymn of Unity. *Unknown, Hebrew*. TrJP, *tr. by* H. M. Adler

Hymn of Weeping. Amittai ben Shefatiah, *Hebrew*. TrJP, *tr. by* Nina Davis Salaman

Hymn on Froude and Kingsley, A. William Stubbs. FaBoEE

Hymn on Solitude. James Thomson. NOEC

Hymn on the Morning of Christ's Nativity [or On the Morning of Christ's Nativity]. Milton. NAEL-1; NOBE; OBEV *Fr.* On the Morning of Christ's Nativity. MeLP; NOCV; NoP-4; PBRV; PoEL-3; SCGP

"But peaceful was the night." FaBoCh

"Oracles are dumm, The." GrIP

Hymn[e] on the Nativity [or Nativitie] of My Saviour, A. Ben Jonson. BeJo; ChIV-2; TrCP

Hymn on the Seasons, A. James Thomson. CABP *Fr.* The Seasons.

Hymn[:] Sung at the Completion of the Concord Monument, April 19, 1836. Ralph Waldo Emerson. *See* Concord Hymn.

Hymn 10. William Cowper. ChIV-1 *Fr.* Olney Hymns.

Hymn To a Woman Under Interrogation. Reiner Kunze, *German*. CEEP; PoSu, *tr. by* Ewald Osers

("Bad (she said) was / the moment of.") CEEP, *tr. by* Ewald Osers

Hymn to Adversity. Thomas Gray. GTBS-P

Hymn to Aphrodite. *Unknown, Greek*.

"But *Jove* at length with just Resentment fir'd." OBCVT, *tr. by* William Congreve

Hymn to Aphrodite: Invocation. *Unknown, Greek*.

"Sing, Muse, the Force, and all-informing Fire." OBCVT, *tr. by* William Congreve

Hymn to Apollo. Callimachus. HePo, *tr. by* Barbara Hughes Fowler *Fr.* Hymns.

Hymn to Artemis. Callimachus. HePo, *tr. by* Barbara Hughes Fowler *Fr.* Hymns.

Hymn to Artemis of the Strict Observance: For a Chorus of Spartan Girls Dressed as Doves To Sing at Dawn on the Feast of the Plow, A. Alcman, *Greek*.

"Vendettas end among the gods." OBCVT, *tr. by* Guy Davenport

Hymn to Athena. *Unknown*. AWP *Fr.* Homeric Hymns.

Hymn to Castor and Pollux. *Unknown, Greek*. OBCVT, *tr. by* Shelley

Hymn to Castor and Pollux. *Unknown*. AWP *Fr.* Homeric Hymns.

(Homer's Hymn to Castor and Pollux.)

Hymn[e] to Christ, at the Author's Last Going into Germany, A. Donne. EBEV; MeLP

Hymn to Colour. George Meredith. OBNC

Hymn to Comus. Ben Jonson. NOSC; SCGP *Fr.* Pleasure Reconciled to Virtue. NAEL-1; OAEL-1

(Comus's Song.) OBCoV

Hymn to Contentment, A. Thomas Parnell. NOEC

Hymn to Cynthia. Ben Jonson. *See* Hymn to Diana.

Hymn to Demeter. Callimachus. HePo, *tr. by* Barbara Hughes Fowler *Fr.* Hymns.

Hymn to Demeter. *Unknown, Greek*.

"There Ceres, distant from the powers divine." OBCVT, *tr. by* Richard Hole

Hymn to Diana. Callimachus, *Greek*.

"Goddess, how oft you bent the silver bow." OBCVT, *tr. by* William Dodd

Hymn to Diana. Catullus. AWP, *tr. by* Richard Claverhouse Jebb *Fr.* Carmina.

Hymn to Diana. Ben Jonson. AWP; CH; GTBS-P; HAP; NOBE; OBEV; PoRA; SeCP; TFi *Fr.* Cynthia's Revels.

(Hespreus' Hymne[e] to Cynthia.)

(Hymn to Cynthia.) NOSC; PoE; SCGP

Hymn to Earth. Elinor Wylie. LiTM; MoAmPo

Hymn to Earth the Mother of All. *Unknown*. AWP *Fr.* Homeric Hymns.

(Hymn to the Earth.) OBCVT, *tr. by* Charles Boer

("I will remember you.") (LL) OBCVT, *tr. by* Charles Boer

("Mother of us all, The.") OBCVT, *tr. by* Charles Boer

Hymn to Eros. Denise Levertov. LW

Hymn to Evil. Louis Ginsberg. PoA

Hymn[e] to God My God, In My Sickness[e]. Donne. EBEV; ESCV; HeIP-4; ImPo; InPS-3; MeLP; NAEL-1; NOSC; OAEL-1; OxAEP-1; PoE; PoEL-2; SeCP; SoSe-8; TFi, TOF

("Since I am coming to that holy room.") FMP; NoP-4

("Therfore that he may raise the Lord throws down.") (LL) PBRV

Hymn to God the Father, A. Donne. AWP; EBEV; FMP; FSCP; HAP; InPK-6; MeLP; NAEL-1; NOBE; NOSC; OAEL-1; PeECV; PoEL-2; PoRA; SCGP; SCV; SeCP; SoSe-8; TFi; TOF

Hymn[e] to God the Father, A. Ben Jonson. BeJo; NOSC; NoP-4; OxAEP-1; Poetr; SeCP; TrCP

Hymn to Her Unknown. Walter James Turner. OBMV

Hymn to Hermes. *Unknown, Greek*.

"O, let not e'er this quarrel be averred!" OBCVT, *tr. by* Shelley

"Out of the lofty cavern wandering." OBCVT, *tr. by* Shelley

Hymn to Inanna. "Lady of All Powers." WPoS

Hymn to Indra, A, *ad. fr. Sanskrit*. Sir William Jones. NOBRP

Hymn to Intellectual Beauty. Shelley. FHYEP; HAP; HeIP-4; ImPo; LaPo; NAEL-2; NOBRP; NoP-4; OAEL-2; OBNC; PoE; Ro; TOF

("Like life and fear, a dark reality.") (LL) LaPo

("To fear himself, and love all humankind.") (LL) Ro

Hymn to Joy. Julia Cunningham. PChr

Hymn: To Light. Abraham Cowley. MeLP; OxAEP-1

Hymn to Love. Lascelles Abercrombie. OBEV *Fr.* Emblems of Love.

Hymn to Mercury. *Unknown*. OBVE *Fr.* Homeric Hymns.

Hymn to Moloch. Ralph Hodgson. OxBTC

Hymn to My God in a Night of My Late Sickness[e], A. Sir Henry Wotton. MeLP; NOSC

Hymn to Na'ra'yena, A, *ad. fr. Sanskrit*. Sir William Jones. NOBRP

Hymn to Night. Melville Cane. MoAmPo

Hymn to Night, A. Max Michelson. TrJP

Hymn[e] to Our Saviour on the Cross[e], A. George Chapman. PeECV; PoEL-2

Hymn to Pan. John Fletcher. NOBE; OBEV *Fr.* The Faithful Shepherdess.

Hymn to Pan. Keats. PoEL-4; Ro *Fr.* Endymion: Poetic Romance.

("Oh thou, whose mighty palace roof doth hang.") Ro

Hymn to Priapus. D. H. Lawrence. CMoP; OBMV; PoE; SCGP

Hymn to Proserpine. Swinburne. EBVV; EnVR; NAEL-2; OAEL-2; OBNC; PoEL-5

Hymn to Proust. Gavin Ewart. NYBP

Hymn to Saint Geryon. Michael McClure. PmAP

Hymn to Saint Teresa. Richard Crashaw. EBEV; ESCV; GeHe; MeLP *Fr.* A Hymn to the Name and Hono[u]r of the Admirable Saint[e] T[h]eresa. NOBE; OBEV; PoEL-2

(Hymn to Sainte Teresa, A.) HAP; NOSC

(Hymn to the Name and Honor of the Admirable Saint Teresa, A.) NoP-4

("Loue, thou art Absolute sole lord.") FSCP

("Must learn in life to die like thee.") (LL) NoP-4

("Must learn in life to dy like thee.") (LL) FSCP

Hymn to Science. Mark Akenside. ECEV; PoEL-3
Hymn to Selene. *Unknown.* AWP *Fr.* Homeric Hymns.
  (Homer's Hymn to the Moon.)
Hymn to St. Geryon. Michael McClure.
  "Gesture the gesture the gesture the gesture, The." NeAP
Hymn to Su'rya, A *ad fn Sunskii.* Sir William Jones. NOBRP
Hymn to the Creator. John Clare. NOBVV
Hymn to the Earth. *Unknown, Latin.* OBCVT, *tr. by* Shelley
Hymn to the Earth. *Unknown. See* Hymn to Earth the Mother of All.
Hymn to the Evening, An. Phillis Wheatley. WPE
Hymn to the Fallen. *Unknown, Chinese.* ChiP; OBWP, *tr. by* Arthur Waley
Hymn to the Graces, A. Robert Herrick. NOSC
Hymn to the Graveyard. Tujin Park, *Korean.* CKP, *tr. by* Jaihiun Kim
Hymn to the Guilotine. "Peter Pindar." NOBRP
Hymn to the Holy Spirit. Stephen Langton. TrCP
Hymn to the Moon. Lady Mary Wortley Montagu. ECWP
Hymn to the Morning, An. Phillis Wheatley. TAP
Hymn to the Name and Hono[u]r of the Admirable Saint[e] T[h]eresa, A.
  Richard Crashaw. NOBE; OBEV; PoEL-2
Hymn to the Night. Henry Wadsworth Longfellow. APN-1; MeMAP;
  NOBA; OxBA; PWR; TAP
Hymn to the North Star. William Cullen Bryant. NCAP
Hymn to the Orange. *Unknown, Chinese.* SuSp, *tr. by* Wu-Chi Liu
Hymn to the Pepper. Novella Nikolaevna Matveyeva, *Russian.* TCRP, *tr.
  by* Deming Brown
Hymn to the Saints, and to Marquis Hamilton[, An]. Donne. NOSC
Hymn to the Spirit of Nature. Shelley. GTBS-P *Fr.* Prometheus
  Unbound. NOBRP; OAEL-2
Hymn to the Sun, The. Akhenaton, *Egyptian.* TTY, *tr. by* J. E. Manchip
  White
Hymn to the Sun. Charles Montague Doughty. FaBoTw *Fr.* The Dawn in
  Britain.
Hymn to the Sun. Michael Roberts. FaBoCh; OxBTC
Hymn to the Sun. *Unknown.* TTTS
Hymn to the Supreme Being. Christopher Smart. ChIV-1
  "But, O immortals! What had I to plead." NOEC
Hymn to the Thousand Islands. Henrietta Cordelia Ray. CBWP-3
Hymn to the Virgin. *Unknown.* NoSic
Hymn to the Virgin Mary. Conor O'Riordan, *Irish.* TIRV, *tr. by* Eleanor
  Hull
Hymn to the Winds. Joachim Du Bellay, *French.* AWP, *tr. by* Andrew
  Lang
Hymn to Tirumāl (Viṣṇu). Kirantaiyar, *Tamil.* PLW, *tr. by* A. K.
  Ramanujan
Hymn to Tsui-Xgoa. *Unknown, Hottentot.* PeSA
Hymn to Venus, An. Sappho, *Greek.* OBCVT, *tr. by* Ambrose Philips
Hymn to Venus, The. *Unknown, formerly at. to* Homer, *Greek.*
  "Among the springs which flow from Ida's head." OBVE, *tr. by* Congreve
  "But when the golden-thron'd Aurora made." OBVE, *tr. by* Congreve
Hymn to Vishnu. Jayadeva. AWP, *tr. by* Sir Edwin Arnold *Fr.* The Gita
  Govinda.
Hymn to Zeus. Aeschylus. *Fr.* Agamemnon. NAWM-1, *tr. by* Robert
  Fagles
Hymn Tunes, The. Edward Lucie-Smith. PBCV
Hymn Written in Windsor Forest, A. Alexander Pope. NOEC; OxBSP
  (Lines Written in Windsor Forest.) EBEV
Hymne for the Epiphanie, A; Sung as by the three Kings. Richard
  Crashaw. *See* In the Glorious Epiphanie of Our [*or* Ovr] Lord God[, A
  Hymn. Svng as by the Three Kings].
Hymne of Heavenly Beautie, An. Edmund Spenser. PeECV *Fr.* Fowre
  Hymnes.
Hymne of the Nativity, Sung by the Shepheards, A. Richard Crashaw.
  PBRV
Hymne to Apollo, An. *Unknown, Greek.*
  "And you (O *Delian* Virgins) doe me grace." OBCVT, *tr. by* George
  Chapman
Hymne to Christ, at the Author's Last Going into Germany, A. Donne.
  EBEV; ESCV; MeLP; NAEL-1; NOSC; OxAEP-1; PeECV
Hymne to Love, An. Robert Herrick. NOSC
Hymns. Callimachus, *Greek.*
  Hymn to Apollo. HePo, *tr. by* Barbara Hughes Fowler
  Hymn to Artemis. HePo, *tr. by* Barbara Hughes Fowler
  Hymn to Demeter. HePo, *tr. by* Barbara Hughes Fowler
  On the Bath of Pallas. HePo, *tr. by* Barbara Hughes Fowler
Hymns and Spiritual Songs for the Fasts and Festivals of the Church of
  England. Christopher Smart.
  Ascension of Our Lord Jesus Christ, The. NOCV

Crucifixion of Our Blessed Lord. ChIV-2
Epiphany. NOCV
Nativity of Our Lord, The. EBEV; HAP; NOBE; PoFL-3; SCGP
  (Nativity of Our Lord and Saviour Jesus Christ, The.) NOCV
Christmas Day. OBCP
Nativity of St. John the Baptist, The. ChIV-2
St. Philip and St. James. NOCV; NOEC
St. Thomas. ChIV-2
Hymns for the Amusement of Children. Christopher Smart.
Conclusion of the Matter, The. ChIV-1; KSG
Elegance. NOCV
Faith. ChIV-1
For Saturday. FaBoCh; NOEC; OxBChV
  (Hymn for Saturday.) OxBChV
  (Hymns for Saturday.) NOxBChV
Fortitude. ChIV-2
Gratitude. NOEC
Hope. ChIV-1
Long-Suffering of God. NOCV
Loveliness. NOCV
Mirth. OxBChV
Moderation. NOCV
Mutual Subjection. NOCV
  (Consideration for Others.) OxBChV
Praise. OxBChV
Pray Remember the Poor. NOEC
Taste. ChIV-1; NOCV
Hymns in Darkness. Nissim Ezekiel.
  "There's only this." OMIP
Hymns of the Marshes. Sidney Lanier. APN-2
Marsh Song—At Sunset. NOBA
Marshes of Glynn, The. AmPP; ImPo; NOBA; NoP-4; OxBA
  ("On the length and the breadth of the marvellous marshes of Glynn.")
  (LL) NoP-4
Sunrise. PoEL-5
Hymns to Our Lady of Chartres. Geoffrey Hill.
  "Eia, with handbells, jews' harps, risible." DiPo
Hymnus Ad Patrem Sinensis. Philip Whalen. BB
Hymnus in Noctem. George Chapman. PoEL-2 *Fr.* The Shadow of Night.
Hypatia. Elizabeth Tollet.
  "What cruel laws depress the female kind." ECWP; NOEC
Hyperbola, The. Footnote at "Figure of Speech." Tina Darragh. FTOS
Hyperbole! Can't you arise. Prose for Des Esseintes. Donald Davie, *after
  the French of* Stéphane Mallarmé. OBVE
Hyperion. Keats. OAEL-2; Ro
  ("Celestial.") (LL) Ro
Bruised Titans, The. OBNC
Saturn. OBNC
  "So ended Saturn; and the God of the Sea." FHYEP
  "Thus in alternate uproar and sad peace." FHYEP
Hyperion and Saturn. Keats. *Fr.* Hyperion. OAEL-2; Ro
Hypnos, seeing how. Licymnios, *Greek.* InMo, *tr. by* Sam Hamill
Hypochondriacs / Spend the winter at the bottom of Florida and the summer
  on top of the Adirondriacs. Oh to Be Odd! Ogden Nash. CBNP
Hypochondriacus. Charles Lamb. BXAP
Hypochondriasis. Ambrose Bierce. APN-2 *Fr.* The Devil's Dictionary.
Hypocrisy will serve as well. Samuel Butler. FaBoEE
Hypocrite Auteur. Archibald MacLeish. AmPP
Hypocrite is strange of race, A. Kalonymos ben Kalonymos. *Fr.* The
  Touchstone. TrJP, *tr. by* J. Chotzner
Hypocrite Swift now takes an eldest daughter. Louise Bogan. PoA
Hypocrite women, how seldom we speak. Denise Levertov. NALW; NMM-
  2; PoM
Hypocrites shed tears. On Watching Politicians Perform at Martin Luther
  King's Funeral. Etheridge Knight. NNaP
Hysteria. Chu Shu-chen, *Chinese.* OHPC, *tr. by* Kenneth Rexroth
Hywell the Good Weighs the Worth of a Cat. Felicity Bast. PC

I

I. Philip Nanton. HCP
I. Kenneth Rexroth. *Fr.* A Bestiary. OBAL
I. Charles Reznikoff. FTOS *Fr.* Jews in Babylonia.
I, a boat with a bony keel. A Dentist's Window. James Keir Baxter.
  OxBC

I, a Most Wretched Atlas. Heinrich Heine. TrJP, tr. by Emma Lazarus *Fr.* Homeward Bound.

I, a princess, king-descended, decked with jewels, gilded, drest. A Royal Princess. Christina Rossetti. BrRo

I, a ship, built on the profits / from my master's amorous trade. Philip of Thessalonica, *Greek.* GrAn, tr. by Robin Skelton

I, a slave, chained to an oar of poem. Stoic. Lawrence Durrell. NYBP

I, a traveler, came from south of the river. A Traveler's Moon. Po Chü-i, *Chinese.* SuSp, tr. by Chiang Yee

I, a wanderer north of Tu-ling. Parting from the Courtier Sung. Yin Shih, *Chinese.* CoBCP, tr. by Burton Watson

I abdicate my daily self that bled. Vita Nuova. Stanley Kunitz. VGW

I abhor the slimy [or slimie] kiss [or kisse]. Kisses Loath[e]some. Robert Herrick. CBLP; CaPo; CavPo; EP; OxBSP

I abide and abide and better abide. Sir Thomas Wyatt. BoLoP; EnLoPo; SiPS

I, about to retire, profoundly happy, honoured to be of your earth, was not "sent from heaven to say hail." The Poet. Nikiphoros Vrettakos. GrIP *Fr.* Liturgy Under the Acropolis.

I admire the quixotic display of your paramountcy. On His Royal Blindness Paramount Chief Kwangala. Jack A. Mapanje. AF

I admire your felicitous phrasing. Limerick. A. M. Sayers. PeLi

I advise rest; the farmhouse. To a Print of Queen Victoria. James Keir Baxter. OxBC

I advocate a semi-revolution. A Semi-Revolution. Robert Frost. LiTM

I aim at a tree with a rifle. Mischief. Pong-gon Chon, *Korean.* CKP, tr. by Jaihiun Kim

I Ain't Going to Hurry No More. Jesse F. García. UnSA

I ain't going to hurry up for the white man no more. I Ain't Going to Hurry No More. Jesse F. García. UnSA

I ain't gonna tell no body. 34 Blues. Charlie Patton. FaBoPV

I aint jokin people, I aint playin around. Concentration Camp Blues. Henry Dumas. SeSe

I ain't superstitious. Superstitions. Maggie Pogue Johnson. CBWP-4

I almost ruined the stew and where. The Pigs for Circe in May. Joanne Kyger. PoM

I, Alphonso, live and learn. Alphonso of Castile. Ralph Waldo Emerson. NOBA

I always felt like a bird blown through the world. Stripping and Putting on. May Swenson. WeW-3

I always had such a good time, good time girl. Each and. Little Red Riding Hood. Ania Walwicz. BMAP

I always knew / you were singing! Throat Song: The Whirling Earth. Wendy Rose. HATNAP

I always like summer. Knoxville, Tennessee. Nikki Giovanni. BPo; BlSi; ISC; MBE; NOxBChV; PoBA

I always loved this solitary hill. Infinito, L'. Giacomo Leopardi, *Italian.* AWP, tr. by Lorna De' Lucchi

I always remember West Lake. Tune: "Song of the Wine Spring." P'an Lang, *Chinese.* SuSp, tr. by James J. Y. Liu

I always say I won't go back to the mountains. Sourdough Mountain Lookout. Philip Whalen. BB; NeAP; PoM

I always see, I don't know why. The Knowledgeable Child. Leonard Alfred George Strong. OBMV

I always talk of living in the mountains. For Several Years I Have Wanted To Grow a Garden, But Have Never Finished One. This Year It Is Already Halfway Through Summer, and This Has Made Me Despondent. Chu Yün-ming, *Chinese.* CoBLCP, tr. by Jonathan Chaves

I always thought if I could just. Place Where Things Got. Heather McHugh. NAmP90

I always try to dislike my poets. It's Hard to Dislike Ewart. Gavin Ewart. OBCoV

I always wanted a red balloon. Tragedy. Jill Spargur. BLPA

I always wanted to give birth. The Mother Poem (two). Jackie Kay. NBrP

I always was afraid of Somes's Pond. Atavism. Elinor Wylie. NALW; PoA

I always woke to. Carpenter's Daughter. Cathy Young Czapla. IFJA

I am. Yevgeny Yevtushenko. HP

I am a babe of royalty. Royal Education. Winthrop Mackworth Praed. OBSV

I am a bairn. De. Robert Alan Jamieson. FaBoVe

I am a Bard of no regard. Robert Burns. PoE *Fr.* Love and Liberty—A Cantata. NOBRP; NOEC

I am a bird from mountains you don't know. Foreword to a Book of Poems. Xuân Diệu, *Vietnamese.* AVP, tr. by Huỳnh Sanh Thông

I Am a Black Woman. Mari E. Evans. ISC; NAAAL

("Look / on me and be / renewed.") (LL) NAAAL

I am a blue fox on a gray farm. Monologue of a Blue Fox. Yevtushenko, *Russian.* TCRP, tr. by John Updike and Albert C. Todd

I am a bold Coachman, and drive a good hack. Hackney Coachman, The; Or, The Way to Get a Good Fare. Hannah More. WoRP

I am a bonded highwayman, Cole Younger is my name. Cole Younger. *Unknown.* AmFP

I Am a Book I neither Wrote nor Read. Delmore Schwartz. TAP

I am a book with a cover of blue. Solo with Chorus. Rose Fyleman. NOxBChV

I am a broken-hearted milkman, in grief I'm arrayed. Polly Perkins. *Unknown.* OBCoV; OxBoLi; PeLV

I am a bunch of red roses. Love Song. *Unknown, Turkish.* BoWoP, tr. by Reza Baraheni and Zahra-Soltan Kohshoohtaezeh

I Am a Cowboy in the Boat of Ra. Ishmael Reed. NAAAL; NIP-4; PoBA

I Am a Creature. Giuseppe Ungaretti, *Italian.* PeFWW, tr. by David McDuff and Jon Silkin

I am a dispossessed Ontario wood. Silverthorn Bush. Robert Finch. NOBC

I am a feather on the bright sky. The Delight Song of Tsoai-Talee. N. Scott Momaday. CDW; InPK-6; PaTW

I am a ferryboat. A traveler, you trample me down. The Ferryboat and the Traveler. Yong-un Han, *Korean.* CKP, tr. by Jaihiun Kim

I am a frog. The Frog Prince. Stevie Smith. HAP; NTP

I am a gentle Anarchist. The Gentle Anarchist. Brunton Stephens. NOBAu

—I am a gentleman in a dustcoat trying. Piazza Piece. John Crowe Ransom. BoLoP; ColAP; FuPo; GLoP; HeIP-4; MeMAP; MoAmPo; MoP; NAAL-2; NOBA; NoAM; NoP-4; OxBA; Poetr; Son; TAP; TFi

"I am a gold lock." Lock and Key. *Unknown.* ReMoGo

I Am a Hunchback. Robert Louis Stevenson. OxBSP

I am a jolly soldier. Bunker's Hill, or the Soldier's Lamentation. John Freeth. NOEC

I am a jovial collier lad, as blithe as blithe can be. Down in a Coal Mine. J. B. Geoghegan. AmFP

I am a king's daughter, you a king's wife. A Letter to Her Mother. Eristi-Aya, *Akkadian.* BoWoP, tr. by Willis Barnstone

I am a lady. Small Sad Song. Alastair Reid. NYBP

I am a lady young in beauty waiting, (LL) Piazza Piece. John Crowe Ransom. BoLoP; ColAP; FuPo; GLoP; HeIP-4; McMAP; MoAmPo; MoP; NAAL-2; NOBA; NoAM; NoP-4; OxBA; Poetr; Son; TAP; TFi

I am a lamp, a lamp that is out. She Warns Him. Frances Darwin Cornford. EnLoPo

I am a lioness. 'Aisha bint Ahmad al-Qurtubiyya, *Arabic.* WPOW, tr. by Elene Margot Kolb

I am a little church(no great cathedral). E. E. Cummings. MeMAP

I am a little girl with my pants pulled down around my ankles. Pants. Lisa Vice. GLP

I am a little orphan girl. An Orphan Girl. Mrs. Henry Linden. CBWP-4

I am a little world made cunningly. Donne. ChIV-1; NAEL-1; NIP-4; NoP-4; PoE; SeCP; Son *Fr.* Holy Sonnets. ESCV *Fr.* Holy Sonnets.

I Am a Live Man. Yehuda Amichai, *Hebrew.* IP, tr. by Warren Bargad and Stanley F. Chyet

I am a lone, unfathered chick. Orphan Born. Robert Jones Burdette. OBAL

I am a lonely being, scarred by swords. Riddles. *Unknown.* NoP-4

I am a mad mother. Projected Scenario of a Performance to Be Given Before the UN. Lawson Fusao Inada. FaBoA

I am a man defeated in his loins. Beggar to Burgher. Arthur Rex Dugard Fairburn. PeNZ

I am a man now. Here. Ronald Stuart Thomas. GTBS-P; RB

I am a man of Chiang-nan. Wang T'ing-hsiang. *Fr.* Songs of Chiang-nan. CoBLCP, tr. by Jonathan Chaves

I am a man of war and might. A Soldier. Sir John Suckling. CavPo; PoE

I am a miner. The light burns blue. Nick and the Candlestick. Sylvia Plath. CoAP; FiLi; LCAP-2; NALW; PBWP; Poetr

I am a murderer; I wring words by the rough of their necks. Judge Dreadword. Victor D. Questel. HCP

I Am a Negro. Muhammad Al-Faituri, *Arabic.* TTY, tr. by Halim El-Dabh

I am a parcel of vain strivings tied. Henry David Thoreau. APN-1; AmPP; ColAP; NCAP; OxBA; PAR; PoEL-4; TAP

("In a bare cup.") (LL) NoP-4

I am a plane-tree. I was sound and strong when the blasts. Philip of Thessalonica, *Greek.* GrAn, tr. by Edwin Morgan

I am a poet. The Uncertainty of the Poet. Wendy Cope. OPOU

I am a poet, a unanimous. Italy. Giuseppe Ungaretti, *Italian.* PeFWW, tr. by David McDuff and Jon Silkin

I am a poor pilgrim of sorrow. City Called Heaven. *Unknown.* NAAAL

I am a poor wayfaring stranger. Poor Wayfaring Stranger. *Unknown.* AmFP

I am a pretty wench. *Unknown.* OxNR

I am a prisoner in the hands of the enemy. The Other Side of the Valley. *Unknown, Chinese.* ChiP, tr. by Arthur Waley

I am a purse. Yevtushenko, *Russian.* TCRP, tr. by Albert C. Todd

I am a reaper whose muscles set at sundown. All my oats are cradled. Harvest Song. Jean Toomer. NoP-4

I am a rebel soldier and far from my home. (LL) One Morning in May [or The Nightingale]. *Unknown.* AS; AmFP; OxBoLi

I am a rich widow, I live all alone. The Rich Widow. *Unknown.* AmFP

I am a roving gambler, I've gambled all around. The Roving Gambler. *Unknown.* AS

I am a roving shanty boy, love to sing and dance. The Roving Shanty Boy. *Unknown.* AmFP

I am a roving traveler and go from town to town. The Gamboling Man. *Unknown.* AS

I am a sea-shell flung. Frutta di Mare. Geoffrey Scott. OBMV

I am a serf. I work in the sweat of my brow. Juhan Viiding, *Estonian.* CEEP, *tr. by* Ivar Ivask

I am a sincere man. José Martí. *Fr.* Simple Verses. TTY, *tr. by* Seymour Resnick

I am a sinful man of men. The Joyce's Repentance. *Unknown, Irish.* TIRV, *tr. by* Douglas Hyde

I am a skinny girl. The Skinny Girl. Anne Hébert, *French.* BoWoP, *tr. by* Willis Barnstone

I am a sleeping body. Ark Apprehensive. Jay Macpherson. NOBC *Fr.* The Ark.

I am a solitary man, not a democracy. Yehuda Amichai. PoSu, *tr. by* Ruth Nevo *Fr.* Travels of a Latter-Day Benjamin of Tudela.

I am a Son of Mars who have been in many wars. Robert Burns. *Fr.* Love and Libery—A Cantata. NOBRP; NOEC

I am a soul in the world: in. The Invention of Comics. Imamu Amiri Baraka. CAPP-1; CRP; GT; LiTM; NAAAL; PBMP; PoBA

I am a spring. The Well. Thomas Edward Brown. NOBVV

I am a stag: of seven tines. The Alphabet Calendar of Amergin. *Unknown, Irish.* BIrV, *tr. by* Robert Graves

I am a stag: of seven tines. Amergin's Charm. Amergin, *Irish.* NNPT, *tr. by* Robert Ranke Graves

I am a stranger in the land. Death. *Unknown.* BLPA

I am a sundial, and I make a botch. On a Sundial. Hilaire Belloc. FaBoEE

I am a sundial. Ordinary words. Hilaire Belloc. FaBoEE

I am a sundial, turned the wrong way round. Hilaire Belloc. FaBoEE

I am a thief. Listen. Jessica Hagedorn. WPOW

I am a very mature person. A Decision. Edith Södergran, *Swedish.* PBWP, *tr. by* Jaakko A. Ahokas

I am a very old pussy. An Old Cat's Confessions. Christopher Pearse Cranch. APN-1; OBCA

I Am a Victim of Telephone. Allen Ginsberg. NBLV

I am a wanderer roaming back and north. The Lyre of Myriad Tunes. Thế Lũ', *Vietnamese.* AVP, *tr. by* Huỳnh Sanh Thông

I am a wandering child. Women at the Crossroad / (May Elegba Forever Guard the Right Doors). Opal Palmer Adisa. GT

I am a white girl gone brown to the blood color of my mother. For the Color of My Mother. Cherríe Moraga. UnSA

I am a widow, robed in black, alone. Christine de Pisan, *French.* BoWoP, *tr. by* Willis Barnstone

I Am a Woman. Akhtar Amiri, *Farsi.* "My home is the mountain." WPOW, *tr. by* Fereshte Mahamadi

I am a woman and my poems. The Practice of Magical Evocation. Diane Di Prima. BB; PmAP; PoM

I am a woman controlled. The Scream. May Miller. Poetr

I am a woman in a red blouse. Connie Deanovich. Connie Deanovich. WWSi

I am a woman of Heng-t'ang. High Dike. Li Ho, *Chinese.* PLT, *tr. by* A. C. Graham

I am a woman with paper. Poem for a Chorus. Marie Cartier. CrSp

I am a young executive. No cuffs than mine are cleaner. Executive. John Betjeman. NOBL

I am a young girl. Motet. *Unknown, French.* PBWP, *tr. by* Carol Cosman

I am a young girl, gay. *Unknown, French.* BoWoP, *tr. by* Willis Barnstone

I am a young jolly brisk sailor. Tarpauling Jacket. *Unknown.* OxBoLi; PeVV

I am a young maiden, and I willingly. Giovanni Boccaccio. ItIP

I am accused of tending to the past. Lucille Clifton. ISC

I am afraid. Wedding Day. Seamus Heaney. OxAEP-2

I am afraid I may be Ilia. Fear. Anna Hajnal, *Hungarian.* BoWoP, *tr. by* Daniel Hoffman

I am afraid of being crushed in the pincers. Sometimes. Greg Kuzma. Poetsp

I Am Afraid of Fire. Anna Swirszczynska, *Polish.* AF, *tr. by* Czeslaw Milosz

I am afraid to own a Body. Emily Dickinson. NCAP

I am afraid to think about my death. No Coward's Song. James Elroy Flecker. OxBSP

I am alert to these letters in extraordinary numbers. Bordering Manuscript. James Applewhite. PoA

I am Alice of Daphne, and my heart clogs for John Pounden. Alice of Daphne, 1799. John Ennis. PBCIP

I am alive—I guess. Emily Dickinson. NOBA

I am all bent to glean the golden ore. To His Lady Selvaggia Vergiolesi; Likening His Love to a Search for Gold. Cino da Pistoia, *Italian.* AWP, *tr. by* D. G. Rossetti

I am all things. Some Magic. James Koller. PoM

I am almost afraid to write down. The Old WPA Swimming Pool in Martins Ferry, Ohio. James Wright. WeT

I Am Almost Asleep. Eldon Grier. MoCV

I am alone in the plains. Léopold Sédar Senghor, *French.* VCWP, *tr. by* Melvin Dixon

I am alone; / It is winter. (LL) Alone. Walter De la Mare. CBLP; EnLoPo

I am alone tonight. Report of Health. John Updike. PBMP

I am already a singing flower. The Singing Flower. "Shu Ting," *Chinese.* VCWP, *tr. by* Carolyn Kizer

I am already quite scarce. For years [or now]. The Last Ones. Dan Pagis, *Hebrew.* PoSu, *tr. by* Robert Friend

I am always aware of my mother. Mother. Kiyoko Nagase, *Japanese.* BoWoP; WPJ, *tr. by* Kenneth Rexroth and Ikuko Atsumi

I Am an American. Elias Lieberman. PoLF

I am an ancient reluctant conscript. Old Timers. Carl Sandburg. NoAM

I am an apple, tossed. Sokrates to Xanthippé. Plato, *Greek.* GrAn, *tr. by* Peter Jay

I am an arrow shot by a boy. Arrow in the Sky. Henrikas Radauskas, *Lithuanian.* CEEP, *tr. by* Jonas Zdanys

I am an earth-ling. The Earth-ling. Brian Patten. SpW

I am an end and a beginning. The Monument. Vladislav Felitsianovich Khodasevich, *Russian.* TCRP, *tr. by* Michael Frayn

"I am an owl of orders gray." The Song of the Owl. Richard Kendall Munkittrick. OBCA

I am as brisk. Keats. CBNP *Fr.* Three Undated Fragments.

"I am as brown as brown can be." The Brown Girl. *Unknown.* ESPB; OxBB

I Am As God And God As I. "Angelus Silesius." GePo, *tr. by* George C. Schoolfield *Fr.* The Cherubical Wanderer.

I Am as Happy as a Queen on Her Throne. Mrs. Henry Linden. CBWP-4

I am as I am and so will I be. Sir Thomas Wyatt. NoSiC; SiPS

I am as large as God, and God as small as I. I Am As God And God As I. "Angelus Silesius." GePo, *tr. by* George C. Schoolfield *Fr.* The Cherubical Wanderer.

I am as light as any roe. *Unknown.* MiEL

I am as old and outworn as my shoes. The Salt Sea. Chongsam Kim, *Korean.* CKP, *tr. by* Jaihiun Kim

I am ashamed before the earth. Therefore I Must Tell the Truth. Torlino, *Navajo Indian.* STP, *tr. by* Washington Matthews

I am asking about the way ahead. Lenrie Peters. HBAPE

I am asking for understanding / for the women who have not given. For the Barren Woman. Desanka Maksimovic, *Serbo-Croatian.* GI, *tr. by* Ivo Soljan

I am asking you to come back home. Jo Carson. EC3; RaBo

I am asleep, dreaming a terrible dream, so I awake. Light. Frank Bidart. *Fr.* Elegy. HCAP

I am at Deep Well where the spirit-trees. Roland Robinson. CBAP; NOBAu *Fr.* Deep Well.

I am at once source. Sleeping with Cats. Marge Piercy. *Fr.* Six Underrated Pleasures. EC2

I am Athenian, that was my city. Erucius of Cyzicus, *Greek.* GrAn, *tr. by* Peter Levi

I am Attibon Legba. Attibon Legba. René Depestre. NegPo, *tr. by* Ellen Conroy Kennedy *Fr.* Epiphanies of the Voodoo Gods.

I am away from home. The Faithful Wife. Patricia Beer. LW

I am back from up the country—very sorry that I went. Up the Country. Henry Lawson. CBAP

I am Baukis the bride's. Epitaph on a Betrothed Girl. Erinna, *Greek.* GrAn, *tr. by* Lenore Mayhew

I am become a shell of delicate alleys. Airliner. Francis Webb. CBAP; NOBAu

I Am Becoming My Mother. Lorna Goodison. OPOU ("Yellow/brown woman.") GT

I am beset by spirits, layer on layer. The Fathers. Ann Stanford. IMW

I am beset with a dream of fair woman. Maureen Duffy. LW

I am black. W. E. B. DuBois. *See* The Song of the Smoke.

I am black and I have seen black hands[, millions and millions of / them]. I Have Seen Black Hands. Richard Wright. AF; PoBA

I am bleeding. The Song of the Woman with Her Parts Coming Out. Susan Griffin. GLP

I am blessed with my location. The Lost Pictures. Hollis Spurgeon Summers. HoPM

I am both Watutsi and Pygmy. Old Man in New Country. James Berry. NBrP

I am Branson; Nature's laws. Henry Charles Beeching and John Bowyer Nichols. FaBoEE Fr. Balliol Rhymes.

I am bright with the wonder of you. Brightness. Denis Glover. PeNZ

"I am busy," said the sea. Day. Cecil Arthur Spring-Rice. BoTP

I am but a heart-broken dreamer. Love. Mogwol Park, Korean. CKP, tr. by Jaihiun Kim

I am but finite, yet thine infinitely. (LL) Artillery [or Artillerie]. George Herbert. GeHe; InPS-3; NoP-4; PoEL-2

I am, by fate, slave to your will. To My More Than Meritorious Wife. John Wilmot, 2d Earl of Rochester. OxBSP

I am called Chyldhod [or Childhoud], in play is all my mynde [or mind]. Pageant Verses. Sir Thomas More. AAS

I am Cassander come down from the Sky. Samuel Johnson. CBNP

I am Charlotte. I don't say hello. Charlotte, Her Book. Elizabeth Bartlett. FaBoWP

I Am Cherry Alive[; the little girl sang]. Delmore Schwartz. NOxBChV; NTP; TTTS

("I will always be new!") (LL) NOxBChV

I am Chiang Liang. Old Leaves from the Chinese Earth. Sadanand Rege, Marathi. OMIP, tr. by Dilip Chitre

I am climbing. Unknown, Crow Indian. STP, tr. by W. S. Merwin

I am cold and alone. The Boy Fishing. Edith Jay Scovell. FaBoWP

I am come into my garden, my sister, my spouse. Bible, O.T. OBVE; TOF Fr. The Song of Songs. AWP

I am come into my garden, my sister, my spouse. I have gathered my. Bible, O.T. See My love is white and ruddy.

I am come to make thy tomb. John Webster. Fr. The Duchess of Malfi. NAEL-1

I am constantly wounded. Unknown. PGA Fr. Carmina Burana.

I am content. The Fossil. Boynton Merrill Jr. CRP

I am content, I do not care. Careless Content. John Byrom. NOEC; OBCoV

I am content to live the patient day. Tuckanuck, I. George Cabot Lodge. APN-2

I am curiously stirred. The Courtship. Ann Beresford. LW

I am dangerous. Scissor-Man. George MacBeth. FaBoMo

I am dark, daughters of Jerusalem. Song. Bible, O.T. WPoS, tr. by Chana Bloch and Ariel Bloch Fr. The Song of Solomon.

I am dead. The Larva. Tadeusz Różewicz, Polish. PoSu, tr. by Magnus F. Krynski

I Am Dead But I Know the Dead Are Not Like This. Charles Bukowski. PmAP

I am dead, Horatio. Wretched queen, adieu! Death of Hamlet. Shakespeare. Fr. Hamlet. NAWM-1

I am dead, to be sure. A Small Fig Tree. Donald Hall. ChIV-2; GI

I am digging. Archaeology. George Ella Lyon. IFJA

I Am Disquieted When I See Many Hills. Hyam Plutzik. VGW

I am dissatisfied with my poetry. Song for Bird and Myself. Jack Spicer. MoNo

I am Drink, carved by a skilled hand. On a Ring. Asclepiades, Greek. GrAn, tr. by Alan Marshfield

I am driving; it is dusk; Minnesota. Driving toward the Lac Qui Parle River. Robert Bly. CoAmPo; LCAP-2; WeT

I am drunk of the pot. I, Lessimus, of Salt Lake City. Robert Peters. BXAP

I am Duchess of Malfy still. John Webster. OxBoV Fr. The Duchess of Malfy.

I am dying; but what of that? Nunc Dimittis. John Cowper Powys. LBC

I am dying, Egypt, dying. Antony and Cleopatra. William Haines Lytle. BLPA

I am ebbing—but not like the sea. The Hag of Béara. Unknown. NOIV

I am enamored, and yet not so much. Sonnet: He Will Not Be Too Deeply in Love. Cecco Angiolieri, da Siena, Italian. AWP, tr. by D. G. Rossetti

I am essence of Rose Solitude. Rose Solitude. Jayne Cortez. MoNo

I am Eve, great Adam's wife. Eve. Unknown, Irish. BIrV, tr. by Thomas Macdonagh

I am far away from you. After a Death. Sandra M. Gilbert. IMW

I Am Fashion's Toy. Mary E. Tucker. CBWP-1

I am fated to perform a heroic deed. "Aleksandr Iakovlevich Yashin," Russian. TCRP, tr. by Daniel Weissbort

I am featly-tripping Lee. Henry Charles Beeching. FaBoEE Fr. Balliol Rhymes.

I am fever'd with the sunset. The Sea Gypsy. Richard Hovey. ChAP

I am filthy. Lice gnaw me. Swine, when they look at me, vomit. The scabs. Comte de Lautréamont. PFTM, tr. by Alexis Lykiard Fr. Maldoror.

I am fish. Fish. Emily Townsend. NYBP

I am five. Venus's-Flytraps. Yusef Komunyakaa. FiLi; NAmP90; WeT

I am fixed in waiting. Sagimusume: The White Heron Maiden. Jonny Kyoko Sullivan. WPOW

I am forbidden to look back. Remembering Love. Aleksandr Semionovich Kushner, Russian. TCRP, tr. by Paul Graves and Carol Ueland

I am forgotten now. Lady Ukon, Japanese. WPJ, tr. by Kenneth Rexroth and Ikuko Atsumi

("His foresworn life.") (LL) OHPJ, tr. by Kenneth Rexroth

("It does not matter / That I am forgotten.") OHPJ, tr. by Kenneth Rexroth

I am fourteen / and my skin has betrayed me. Hanging Fire. Audre Lorde. NIP-4; NMM-2; NoAM; NoP-4; PoPoPo; Poetr; TRP; UnSA

I am from everywhere. Edouard J. Maunick. NegPo, tr. by Ellen Conroy Kennedy Fr. As Far as Yoruba Land.

I Am from Ireland. Unknown. HAP

("Come ant daunce wyt me, / in irlaunde.") (LL) NoP-4

(I Am from Ireland.) HAP; NoP-4

("Ich am of Irlaunde [or Irlonde].") GEA; MiEL; SCGP

I am full of grief, and the tear runs from my eye. Five Arabic Verses in Praise of Wine. Unknown, Arabic. TrJP, tr. by Hartwig Hirschfeld

I am fully qualified to work as a doorkeeper, and for this reason. Rabi'a al-Adawiyya, Persian. WPoS, tr. by Charles Upton

I am furious with myself. Elsa Tió, Spanish. BoWoP, tr. by Willis Barnstone

"I am Gaspar. I have brought frankincense." The Three Kings. "Rubén Dario," Spanish. PChr, tr. by Lysander Kemp

I am giving you the dark birds of night. Michele Murray. MDDM Fr. Dance Poem.

I am glad I'm who I am. Jessie Orton Jones. CTV Fr. (VIII from Secrets).

I am going home by sea. Derek Mahon. IIP Fr. Afterlives. CIP-2

I AM GOING ON A JOURNEY AND I WILL BRING. A Table Laid with Horrors. Forrest Gander. PT

I am going to bring back Solomon. Get to Hell Outa Here. "The Mighty Sparrow." PBCV

I am going to keep things like this. (LL) Hawk Roosting. Ted Hughes. CMoP; GTBS-P; HAP; HeIP-4; LiTM; OxBTC; TwCP; UnPo

I am going to market. Marketing. E. J. Falconer. BoTP

I / am going to rise. Vive Noir! Mari E. Evans. PoBA

I Am Going to Sleep (Suicide Poem). Alfonsina Storni, Spanish. BoWoP, tr. by Aliki and Willis Barnstone

I am Goya. Andrey Andreievich Voznesensky, Russian. OBWP; TCRP; VCWP, tr. by Stanley Kunitz

I am growing calmer. Rimma Fiodorovna Kazakova, Russian. TCRP, tr. by Lubov Yakovleva

I Am Growing Old. George Sands Johnson. PWR

I am hands. In Laddery Street Herself. Laura Riding Jackson. Fr. Forgotten Girlhood. RB

I am harum. Harum Scarum. Roger McGough. OTCP

"I am he who bursts the guarded gate." Boast of Masopha. Z. D. Mangoaela, Sotho. PeSA

I am hearing the shape of the rain. In the Mountain Tent. James Dickey. MT; WeT

I Am Here. Jimmy Santiago Baca. NAmP90

I am here, and there is nothing to say. Lecture on Nothing. John Cage. FTOS

I am here, / and will follow. (LL) For My Mother: Genevieve Jules Creeley. Robert Creeley. PoM; TRP

I am here, I have traversed the Tomb. He Cometh Forth into the Day. Unknown. AWP Fr. Book of the Dead.

I am here to worship the blue. Wild Asters. Ruth Stone. IMW

I am Hermes. I stand in the crossroads by a windy. Anyte, Greek. BoWoP, tr. by Willis Barnstone

I am his Highness' dog at Kew,. Epigram Engraved on the Collar of a Dog Given [or Which I Gave] to His Royal Highness. Alexander Pope. FaBoEE; ImPo; InPK-6; KaS; NOEC; NTCP; OxBSP; OxBoLi; SoSe-8; TTTS

I am holding this turquoise. The Serenity in Stones. Simon J. Ortiz. CDW; ColAP

I am I, old Father Fisheye that begat the ocean, the worm. The End. Allen Ginsberg. CoAmPo

I am in a desert. Bushed. Barry McKinnon. NOBC

I Am in a Novel. D. H. Lawrence. OBCoV

I Am in Danger—Sir—. Adrienne Rich. HCAP; NALW; NOBA

I am in great misery tonight. Suibne Geilt. NOIV

I am in Hong Kong. How Hong Kong Was Destroyed. Dahlia Ravikovitch, *Hebrew*. IP, *tr. by* Warren Bargad *and* Stanley F. Chyet

I am in love, meantime, you think; no doubt you would think so. Claude to Eustace. Arthur Hugh Clough. EnVR; FaBoVe *Fr.* Amours de Voyage. NOBVV

I am in love with the laughing sickness. Zizi's Lament. Gregory Corso. BB; NeAP; VGW

I am in love, you say; I do not think so exactly. (LL) Claude to Eustace: "I am in love, meantime, you think; no doubt you would think so." Arthur Hugh Clough. EnVR; FaBoVe

I am in my Eskimo-hunting-song mood. Eskimo Occasion. Judith Rodriguez. CBAP; FaBoWP; NOBAu

I am in the book. The Dream Dream. Michael Davidson. FTOS

I am in the castle, my younger brother is beyond. The Other Side of the Valley. *Unknown, Chinese.* CoBCP, *tr. by* Burton Watson

I am in the old room across from the synagogue. The Old Room. W. S. Merwin. NYBP

I am in the tub with my body. To My Body. Nancy Sullivan. TAP

I am inside someone. Agony As Now, An. Imamu Amiri Baraka. AmPP; BPo; LiTM; NAAL-2; NoP-4; UnSA

I am Ireland. Padraic Pearse, *Irish*. IIP; OBMV, *tr. by* Lady Augusta Gregory

I am Jane Addams. Jane Addams (September 6, 1860–May 21, 1935). Gwendolyn Brooks. PuP-16

I am jealous! I am jealous! which I ne'er have been before. Lines / Suggested by the Song of a Nightingale. Eliza Cook. VWP

I am Jesu that cum to fight. *Unknown.* MiEL

I am Jojo / give me the sun to eat. Giant Jojo. Michael Rosen. FuFo

I am Judas. W. B. Yeats. GI *Fr.* "Calvary."

I am just going outside and may be some time. Antarctica. Derek Mahon. PBCIP

I am keeping this diary because I am fascinating. A Fascinating Poet's Dream. *Unknown.* PFE

I am kneading my bread Winnie Mandela. The Evening News. Audre Lorde. NAAAL

I am leading a quiet life. Autobiography. Sonja [dA]kesson, *Swedish*. BoWoP, *tr. by* Ingrid Claréus

I am like a flag unfurled in space. Presaging. Rilke, *German*. AWP; TrJP, *tr. by* Jessie Lemont

I am like a jackfruit on the tree. The Jackfruit. Ho Xuan Huong, *Vietnamese*. PBWP, *tr. by* Nguyen Ngoc Bich

I Am like a Rose. D. H. Lawrence. OxBSP

I am like a sliced-up worm. Chaadayev on Basmannaya. Oleg Grigorevich Chukhonstev, *Russian*. TCRP, *tr. by* Simon Franklin

I am like a train. The City of Yes and the City of No. Yevtushenko, *Russian*. TCRP, *tr. by* Tina Tupkina-Glaessner *and* Geoffrey Dutton *and* Igor Mezhakoff-Koriakin

I am like you, Mama always said. Father. Sharon Doubiago. NMM-2

I am listening for your footsteps death. The Body Inside the Soul. Bell Hooks. ISC

I am living more alone now than I did. The Last Chapter. Walter De la Mare. CMoP; MoBrPo

I am locked in a little cedar box. Satan Says. Sharon Olds. PBCAP

I am lonely. Poem for Some Black Women. Carolyn M. Rodgers. BlSi

I am / look / ing at. You Too? Me Too—Why Not? Soda Pop. Robert Hollander. NIP-4

I am looking for a past. The Journey. David Ignatow. Poetsp

I am looking for the photo that would make all the difference in my life. Lost and Found. Maxine Chernoff. PmAP

I am looking for the women of my house. Lineage. Daisy Zamora, *Spanish*. LoL, *tr. by* Margaret Randall

"I am Lot's pillar, caught in turning." Columns and Caryatids. Carolyn Kizer. WPE

I am. . . lying here counting the stars. I am. . . Star Counting. John Rice. SpW

I am made all things to all men. At His Execution. Rudyard Kipling. ChIV-2

I am made to sow the thistle for wheat, the nettle for a nourishing dainty. Night II (Enion's Lament). William Blake. PoE; Ro *Fr.* Vala; or The Four Zoas.

I am making / a wind come here. *Unknown, Crow Indian.* STP, *tr. by* W. S. Merwin

I am Marilyn Mei Ling Chin. How I Got That Name. Marilyn Chin. LoL; PaTW; UnSA

I am master of my kite, and. Boy with Kite. Phoebe Hesketh. AYFP

"I am master of the chivalric idiom" Spenser said. Master. Brendan Kennelly. BiHa

I am mighty melancholy. Vandunk's Four Humours, in Quality and Quantity. Richard Brathwaite [*or* Brathwait]. NOSC

I am Miss Stein. Gertrude Stein at Snails Bay. Peter Porter. OxBC

I am monarch of all I survey. Verses Supposed to Be Written by Alexander Selkirk during His Solitary Abode on the Island of Juan Fernandez. William Cowper. EBEvV; GTBS-P; NOEC; PoEL-3; PoLF

I am monarch of troubles a host. Verses. Maria Jane Jewsbury. VWP

I am most honoured. Great Foreign Writer Visits Age-Old Temple, Greeted by Venerable Abbess, 1955. Anthony Thwaite. OBCoV

I am moved often, and easily. A Few Facts about Me. Charles North. PmAP

I Am My Beloved's. Bible, *O.T., Hebrew.* BoWoP, *tr. by* Willis Barnstone; TrJP *Fr.* The Song of Songs. AWP

I am my mother's daughter. Marge Piercy. MDDM *Fr.* My Mother's Novel.

I am myself at last; now I achieve. I Am like a Rose. D. H. Lawrence. OxBSP

I am nailing them up to the cathedral door. Everywoman Her Own Theology. Alicia Ostriker. CrSp

I Am New York City. Jayne Cortez. BoWoP

I am no brazen face to hale the Lord. Rabbi Yom-Tob of Mayence Petitions His God. Abraham Moses Klein. TrJP

I am no longer master of my tears. U Tam'si Tchicaya. NegPo, *tr. by* Ellen Conroy Kennedy *Fr.* Fragile.

I am no shepherd of a child's surmises. Montana Pastoral. James Vincent Cunningham. MoAmPo; VGW

I am no woman. I am a neuter. Vierge Moderne. Edith Södergran, *Swedish*. PFTM, *tr. by* Stina Katchadourian

I Am Not a Conspiracy Everything Is Not Paranoid. Susan Musgrave. NoAM

I am not a handsome man. Eclipse. Ed Roberson. GT

I am not a mechanism, an assembly of various sections. Healing. D. H. Lawrence. RaBo

I am not a metaphor or symbol. The Distant Drum. Calvin C. Hernton. GT; TTY

I am not a painter, I am a poet. Why I Am Not a Painter. Frank O'Hara. CoAmPo; HCAP; MoP; NOBA; NeAP; NoAM; NoP-4; PoE; PoM; PoPoPo; Poetr; VCAP

I am not a poet. Explanatory Note. Yevgeny Bunimovich, *Russian*. TCRP, *tr. by* Albert C. Todd

I am not a sparrow or a rat. On the Thirteenth Day of the Eleventh Month I Went to the Granary for the First Time since My Illness. Mei Yao Ch'en, *Chinese*. SuSp, *tr. by* Jonathan Chaves

I am not any of the faces. Failure of an Invention. Safiya Henderson-Holmes. UnSA

I am not blind. For Steph. Wendy Rose. CDW

I Am Not Bound to Win. Abraham Lincoln. CTV

I am not going to invite you. Blond. Joseph De Roche. HeIP-4

I am not going to turn into gold. Bassus, *Greek*. PGA, *tr. by* Kenneth Rexroth

I am not here. Hovering at a Low Altitude. Dahlia Ravikovitch, *Hebrew*. VCWP, *tr. by* Chana Bloch *and* Ariel Bloch

I am not I. Juan Ramón Jiménez, *Spanish*. RaBo, *tr. by* Robert Bly ("I am this one.") APAD, *tr. by* Robert Bly

I am not I; pity the tale of me. (LL) Sonnet 45: "Stella oft sees the very face of woe." Sir Philip Sidney. InPS-3; NAEL-1; NoSic; PoE

I am not in court for any assault. The Old Man's Case. Martial, *Latin*. OBCVT, *tr. by* Philip Murray

I am not Mahomet. Edmund Clerihew Bentley. NOBL *Fr.* Clerihews.

I am not one of those who left the land. "Anna Akhmatova," *Russian*. TCRP, *tr. by* Stanley Kunitz *with* Max Hayward

I am not one who much or oft delight. Personal Talk. Wordsworth. NOBE

I am not poor, but I am proud. Thought. Ralph Waldo Emerson. AmPP

I am not ready to die. May Sarton. CrSp *Fr.* Gestalt at Sixty.

I am not resigned to the shutting away of loving hearts in the hard ground. Dirge Without Music. Edna St. Vincent Millay. CMoP; IMW; MeMAP

I AM not suited for service in a country town;. Planting Bamboos. Po Chü-i, *Chinese*. ChiP, *tr. by* Arthur Waley

I am not sure I would always fight for my life. What Would You Fight For? D. H. Lawrence. OxBSP

I am not sure if I knew the truth. Youth. "Laurence Hope." WeW-3

I am not to be trifled with. Hoatchunk' Narwoanar, or Winnebago War Song. *Unknown, Winnebago Native American*. APN-2, *tr. by* Caleb Atwater

I am not treacherous, callous, jealous, superstitious. A Face. Marianne Moore. OxBSP

I am not what my lips explain. Utterance. Donald Davidson. FuPo

I am not yet born; O hear me. Prayer Before Birth. Louis MacNeice. AF; EBEvV; FaBoVe; GTBS-P; PBMP; PNI; TIRV; TwCP

I am not yet twenty-two and I am tired of living. Asclepiades. HePo, *tr. by* Barbara Hughes Fowler *Fr.* Epigrams.

I am not you. Africa's Plea. Roland Tombekai Dempster. TTY

I am not your God. African Easter. Abioseh Nicol. PBA

I Am Not Yours[, not lost in you]. Sara Teasdale. SAGP; VGW

I am now so weary with waiting. Gaspara Stampa, *Italian.* WPOW, *tr. by* Harold M. Priest

I am now very high upon the tree of the seasons. News of My Mother. Jean-Baptiste Tati-Loutard. PBMAP *Fr.* Poèmes de la Mer (1968).

I am of Ireland. I Am from Ireland. *Unknown.* EnVB; FaBoCh; NOBE; OBEV; OPOU; PoEL-1

I am of Ireland. W. B. Yeats. CMoP; IIP

I am of little worth and poor, apart. Song of Loneliness. Judah Halevi, *Hebrew.* TrJP, *tr. by* Nina Davis Salaman

I am of old and young, of the foolish as much as the wise. Walt Whitman. ImGa *Fr.* Song of Myself. AmPP; MoAmPo; NAAL-3; NOBA; OxBA

I Am of the Earth. Anna Walters. VoR

I am of this world. *Unknown, Japanese.* BoWoP; IMW, *tr. by* Geoffrey Bownas *and* Anthony Thwaite *Fr.* Manyo Shu, Part 2 of 4.

I am Ojistoh, I am she, the wife. Ojistoh. Emily Pauline Johnson. NOBC

I am old. Epitaph. Christopher Logue. OxBTC

I am old, sick and lonely. Verses. Su Tung-p'o, *Chinese.* TAL, *tr. by* Robert Payne

I am olde whan age doth apele. *Unknown.* MiEL

I am on my way running. Song for a Young Girl's Puberty Ceremony. *Unknown, Papago Indian.* ChAP, *tr. by* Frances Densmore

I am one-half Chinese and one-half French. Neither Fish Nor Fowl. Nguyễn Hữu Chu, *Vietnamese.* AVP, *tr. by* Huỳnh Sanh Thông

I am one of passion's asses. The Girls of Llanbadarn. Dafydd ap Gwilym, *Welsh.* OBWVE, *tr. by* Rolfe Humphries

I am one of those troubled hearts. Human Soul. René Maran, *French.* IIY, *tr. by* Mercer Cook

I am only nineteen. That Distance Apart. Jackie Kay. NBrP

I am only one. Lend a Hand. Edward Everett Hale. CTV

I am, outside. Incredible panic rules. John Berryman. VCAP *Fr.* Dream Songs.

I am outside of. Dualism. Ishmael Reed. NAAAL

I am owner of the sphere. Ralph Waldo Emerson. *Fr.* History. APN-1

I am peasant. Transfiguration. Jack Hirschman. CLPP

I am picking wild grapes last year. The Winemaker's Beat-étude. Alfred Wellington Purdy. MoCV

I am pleased with a frame of four lights. My Greenhouse. Edwin Morgan. OBGa

I am poor and old and blind. Belisarius. Henry Wadsworth Longfellow. APN-1; PoEL-5

I am poor brother Lippo, by your leave! Fra Lippo Lippi. Robert Browning. CTC; EBVV; EBVVPR; EnVR; FHYEP; NoP-4; OAEL-2; OxAEP-2

I am Priapus. I was put here according to custom. Lucian, *Greek. tr. by* Edwin Morgan GrAn; OBCVT

I am provoked. Epigram. Strato, *Greek.* GrAn, *tr. by* W. G. Shepherd

I am putting makeup on empty space. Makeup on Empty Space. Anne Waldman. PoA

I am Queen Anne, of whom 'tis said. *Unknown.* ACTP

I am quite sure he thinks that I am God. Bishop Doane on His Dog. George Washington Doane. BLPA; FaBoBe

I Am Raftery ("I am Raftery, hesitant and confused"). Derek Mahon. OxBC

I Am Raftery [*or* Raferty]. Anthony Raftery, *Modern Irish.* AWP, *tr. by* Douglas Hyde

I am Raifteiri, the poet, full of courage and love. Anthony Raftery, *Irish.* NOIV, *tr. by* Thomas Kinsella

I am rather tall and stately. *Unknown.* FaBoEE; NOBL *Fr.* Balliol Rhymes.

I am reading. The Distant Orgasm. James Tate. AmPA

I am reading a diary at night. Discovering Lasseter. Conal Fitzpatrick. NOBAu

I am related to stones. Giant Tortoise. Anthony Hecht. APo

I am reminded, by the tan man who wings. The Elevator Man Adheres to Form. Margaret Danner. PoBA

I am reminded of the vestment. I'm Not Here / Never Was. Constanța Buzea, *Rumanian.* BoWoP, *tr. by* Stavros Deligiorgis

I am resolved, this charming day. John Dyer. ECEV *Fr.* The Country Walk.

I am riding on a limited express, one of the crack trains [of the nation]. Limited. Carl Sandburg. GM; HAP; MoAmPo; OxBA; SAGP

I Am Root. Claribel Alegría, *Spanish.* VCWP, *tr. by* Carolyn Forché

I Am Rose [my eyes are blue]. Gertrude Stein. KaS; OBCA; TrJP

I am running into a new year. Lucille Clifton. CrSp

I am sad this morning. Kenneth Rexroth. APSN *Fr.* The Love Poems of Marichiko.

I am scorned by patterns which hold. Moon at Three A.M. Lance Henson. CDW

I am searching everywhere! (LL) The Snare. James Stephens. BoTP; CH; CMoP; SCGP

I am seeing this: two men are sitting on a pole. The Mitchells. Les A. Murray. BMAP

I am set off. Luxembourg Garden. Michael S. Weaver. GT

I am sick. Spring Fever. Yunsuk Hong, *Korean.* CKP, *tr. by* Jaihiun Kim

I am sick today. Labour Pains. Akiko Yosano, *Japanese.* WPJ, *tr. by* Kenneth Rexroth *and* Ikuko Atsumi

I am silver and exact. I have no preconceptions. Mirror. Sylvia Plath. FaBoWP; HAP; NIP-4; NYBP

I Am Singing Now. Luci Tapahonso. UnSA

I Am Singing the Cold Rain. Lance Henson, *Cheyenne Indian.* HATNAP; STP, *tr. by the author*; PiM, *tr. by* Lance Henson

I am singing to the heavens above. Incantations of Modoc Conjurers. *Unknown, Modoc Native American.* APN-2, *tr. by* Albert S. Gatschet

I am sitting across the table. Sunday at the State Hospital. David Ignatow. RaBo

I am sitting again on the steps of the burned out barrack. On the Far Edge of Kilmer. Gerald Stern. LoL

I am sitting here. The Poor Girl's Meditation. *Unknown, Irish.* BIrV; OBMV, *tr. by* Padraic Colum

I am sitting in a cell with a view of evil parallels. Jail Poems. Bob Kaufman. NAAAL

I am sitting in a strange room listening. Baby-Sitting. Gillian Clarke. FaBoWP; NTP

I am sitting in Mike's Place trying to figure out. One Thousand Fearful Words for Fidel Castro. Lawrence Ferlinghetti. VGW

I am sitting sad and lonely. Lines to Florence. Mary Weston Fordham. CBWP-2

I am sleepless in the glow and shadow of the lamplight. Visiting Tsan, Abbot of Ta-Yun. Tu Fu, *Chinese.* OHPC, *tr. by* Kenneth Rexroth

I am sleepy, and the oozy weeds about me twist. (LL) Billy in the Darbies. Herman Melville. APN-2; HAP; NAAL-1; NAWM-2; NCAP; NOBA; OxBoLi; PoEL-5

I am slowly dying, water evaporating. George Bowering. NOBC *Fr.* Summer Solstice.

I am so fair that wheresoe'er I wend. Beauty Accurst. Richard Le Gallienne. ADE; RACG

I am so glad and very. E. E. Cummings. CMoP

I am so lonely for the twentieth century. Survey. Donald Revell. WeT

I am so out of love through poverty. Sonnet: Of Why He Would Be a Scullion. Cecco Angiolieri, da Siena, *Italian.* AWP, *tr. by* D. G. Rossetti

I am so passing rich in poverty. Sonnet: He Jests Concerning His Poverty. Bartolomeo di Sant' Angelo, *Italian.* AWP, *tr. by* D. G. Rossetti

I am sorry to speak of death again. Poetics against the Angel of Death. Phyllis Webb. MoCV; NOBC

I am sorry you are. Roots. Charlotte Watson Sherman. ISC

I am standing above you and tide. Bridge. Christopher Okigbo. PBMAP *Fr.* Heavensgate (1961).

I am standing for peace and non-violence. The Patriot. Nissim Ezekiel. FaBoVe

I am standing / on the balcony. Night Vision. Paula Gunn Allen. NMM-2

I am standing on the threshold of eternity at last. On the Threshold. *Unknown.* BLPA

I am standing upon the seashore. The Ship. *Unknown.* PoLF

I am. . . Star Counting. John Rice. SpW

I am still bitter about the last place we stayed. Codicil. Ruth Stone. BoWoP

I am still hurt, Plin. A Letter for Allhallows. Peter Kane Dufault. NYBP; NoP-4

I am still on fire. Distance. Eugene B. Redmond. SeSe

I am still rich. Thomas Curtis Clark. PoToHe

I am strange here and often I am still trying. Evening. W. S. Merwin. NAAL-2

I am Suibne the wanderer. Suibne Geilt. NOIV

I am surprised to see. Letter Written on a Ferry While Crossing Long Island Sound. Anne Sexton. CoAP; NAAL-2; NYBP; TwCP

I Am Taliesin. I Sing Perfect Metre. *Unknown, Welsh.* OBWVE, *tr. by* Ifor Williams

I am Te-ngau-reka-a-tu. Taiaha Haka Poem. Apirana Taylor. PeNZ

I am telling you a number of half-conditioned ideas. Sunday Evening. Barbara Guest. NeAP

I am telling you this. Blue Ruth: America. Michael S. Harper. PoBA

I am tempted to think of you. A Poem of Villeneuve St Georges. Mbella Sonne Dipoko. PBMAP

I am that Dido which thou here do'st see. Ausonius, *Latin*. NoSic; OBVE, *tr. by Sir Walter Ralegh*

I am that last, that. A Final Thing. Li-Young Lee. FiLi

I am that man who with a luminous look. Brevities. Siegfried Sassoon. PoLF

I am that man with helmet made of thorn. For an Ex-Far East Prisoner of War. Charles Causley. OxBC

I am that Savior that vouchsafed to die. On the Inscription Over the Head of Christ on the Cross. Henry Colman. ChIV-2

I am that serpent-haunted cave. The Pythoness. Kathleen Jessie Raine. MoBrPo

I am that which began. Hertha. Swinburne. OAEL-2

I am that woman whose works are good. Sovereign Queen. Padeshah Khatun, *Farsi*. WPOW, *tr. by* Deirdre Lashgari

I am the acorn. Journey. Judith Nicholls. OBSP

I am the American heartbreak. American Heartbreak. Langston Hughes. AmPP; BPo; LiTM

I am the ancient Apple-Queen. Pomona. William Morris. NOBVV

I Am the Autumn. Itsik Manger, *Yiddish*. TrJP, *tr. by* Joseph Leftwich

I am the bird of the wayside. Prelude. Christine Ama Ata Aidoo. PBWP

I am the bird that flutters against your window in the. Guardian Angel. Rolf Jacobsen, *Norwegian*. RaBo, *tr. by* Robert Bly

I am the black centipede, the rusher with a black nose. Praises of the Train. Demetrius Segooa, *Sotho*. PeSA

I Am the Blood. Isaac Rosenberg. MoBrPo

I am the blossom pressed in a book. Briefly It Enters, and Briefly Speaks. Jane Kenyon. CrSp

I am the blue! I come from the lower world. Helen. Paul Valéry, *French*. LoP; OBVE, *tr. by* Robert Lowell

I am the boy with his hands raised over his head. The House That Fear Built: Warsaw, 1943. Jane Flanders. CrSp; PBCAP

I am the broken reed in this deathly organ. How We Carry Ourselves. Jimmy Santiago Baca. AF

I am the captain of my soul. Probably. Keith Preston. NBLV

I Am the Cat. Leila Usher. BLPA

I am the cat of cats. I am. The Cat of Cats. William Brighty Rands. CTAV; FPC; NOxBChV; OxBChV; PC

I am the chaunt-rann of a Singer. The Poet. Padraic Fiacc. CIP-2

I am the darker brother. I, Too, Sing America. Langston Hughes. PoLF

I am the Dean, and this is Mrs. Liddell. *Unknown*. FaBoEE *Fr.* Balliol Rhymes.

I am the Dean of Christ Church, Sir. Cecil Arthur Spring-Rice. FaBoEE; NOBL *Fr.* Balliol Rhymes.

I am the disappeared woman. Disappeared Woman I. Marjorie Agosin, *Spanish*. LoHo, *tr. by* Cola Franzen

I Am the Doore. Richard Crashaw. GeHe; NAEL-1

I am the family face. Heredity. Thomas Hardy. CTC; EBEV; RB

I am the farmer, stripped of love. The Hill Farmer Speaks. Ronald Stuart Thomas. GTBS-P; OBWVE

I am the first to drink of the blue that still looks for its eye. Paul Celan, *German*. VCWP, *tr. by* Michael Hamburger

I am the flute of Daphnis. On this wall. The Flute of Daphnis. Edward Cracroft Lefroy. AWP *Fr.* Echoes from Theocritus.

I am the freshly dead husband. Kojo Laing. HBAPE

I am the ghost of Shadwell Stair. Shadwell Stair. Wilfred Owen. FaBoTw

I Am the Gilly of Christ. Joseph Campbell. TIRV

I am the grass. / Let me work. (LL) Grass. Carl Sandburg. AWP; ColAP; MoAmPo; MoP; NAAL-2; NOBA; NoAM; OBWP; OxBA; PeFWW; PoLF; Poetr; TFi

I am the grave of Baucis the bride. Passing by. Erinna. HePo, *tr. by* Barbara Hughes Fowler *Fr.* Epigrams.

I am the Great Bassist. The Great Bassist. Lawson Fusao Inada. OpBo

I am the great learner. Learner. Mahadai Das. HCP

I Am the Great Sun[, but you do not see me]. Charles Causley. NTP; PeECV; TOF

I am the Gross National Product. William Harmon. WeT *Fr.* Treasure Holiday.

I am the Incredible Henry McHugh. The Incredible Henry McHugh. Robert Fisher. FuFo

I am the keeper of the earth and air. Keeper. Esther Iverem. GT

I am the land of their fathers. The Recall. Rudyard Kipling. PFE

I am the least. The Mite. Boynton Merrill Jr. CRP

I am the little New Year, ho, ho! The New Year. *Unknown*. BoTP

I am the living body of the Great Spirit above. Chants to the Deity. *Unknown, Ojibwa Native American*. APN-2, *tr. by* Henry Rowe Schoolcraft

I Am the Lord. Alexander Mack, *German*. AH, *tr. by* Sheema Z. Buehne

I am the Lord of Light, the self-begotten Youth. He Maketh Himself One with the God Ra. *Unknown*. AWP, *tr. by* Robert Hillyer *Fr.* Book of the Dead.

I am the magical mouse. The Magical Mouse. Kenneth Patchen. KaS

I am the maiden in bronze set over the tomb of Midas. Cleoboulos, *Greek*. GrAn, *tr. by* Richmond Lattimore

I am the man that hath seen affliction. Affliction. Bible, *O.T.* TrJP *Fr.* Lamentations.

I am the man who looked for peace and found. War Poet. Sidney Keyes. NoP-4; PoWW

I am the mighty He-she-it. Opus Nil. Hans Arp, *German*. CBNP, *tr. by* Michael Hamburger

I am the month when roses. June. Mary Weston Fordham. CBWP-2

I am the mother of sorrows. The Paradox. Paul Laurence Dunbar. AAP; PoBA

I Am the Mountainy Singer. Joseph Campbell. MoBrPo

I am the Muse who sung alway. Solution. Ralph Waldo Emerson. OBAL

I am the night watchman of rue de Flandre. The Night Watchman of Pont-au-Change. Robert Desnos, *French*. AF, *tr. by* Carolyn Forché

I am the October lady. Horoscope. Colleen J. McElroy. GT

I am the one in your dreams. The Dark Lord of Savaiki. Alistair Campbell. PeNZ

I am the one who looks the other way. The Bystander. Rosemary Dobson. CBAP

I am the one whom ringdoves see. Thomas Hardy. OxBTC

I am the one whose praise. Hildegard von Bingen, *Latin*. CrSp

I am the one whose thought. Death. William Bell Scott. NOBVV

I am the only being whose doom. Emily Jane Brontë. NALW

I am the only one, the only one left. Ki-u-nad'-dis-si's Song. *Unknown*. APN-2, *tr. by* Stephen Powers *Fr.* Sacred Songs of the Konkau.

I am the people—the mob—the crowd—the mass. Carl Sandburg. AmPP; OxBA; TAP

I am the pirate's parrot. The Parrot. *Unknown*. CTAV

I Am the Poet Davies, William. W. H. Davies. OxBSP

I am the poet of reality. Walt Whitman. BLT

I am the poet of the Body and I am the poet of the Soul. Walt Whitman. ColAP; WeW-3 *Fr.* Song of Myself. AmPP; MoAmPo; NAAL-3; NOBA; OxBA

I am the poet of the spare room. The Home, The Spare Room. Robert Adamson. BMAP

I am the Prince in the Field. He Maketh Himself One with Osiris. *Unknown*. AWP *Fr.* Book of the Dead.

I am the pure lotus. He Is like the Lotus. *Unknown*. TTY, *tr. by* Ulli Beier; AWP *Fr.* Book of the Dead.

I am the pure, the true of word, triumphant. He Defendeth His Heart against the Destroyer. *Unknown*. AWP *Fr.* Book of the Dead.

I am the pure traveler. He Entereth the House of the Goddess Hathor. *Unknown*. AWP *Fr.* Book of the Dead.

I am the rain. Grace Nichols. AYFP

I am the reaper. William Ernest Henley. OBNC *Fr.* Echoes.

I am the Red Cloud. Red Cloud's Song. *Unknown*. APN-2, *tr. by* Stephen Powers *Fr.* Sacred Songs of the Konkau.

I am the resurrection, and the life. Bible, *O.T.* CTV *Fr.* John 11:25,26.

I am the rose of Sharon, and the lily of the valleys. Bible, *O.T.* BoLoP; GBL; OBVE *Fr.* The Song of Songs. AWP

I am the ruined queen. Dido: Swarming. Kathleen Spivack. PoA

I am the self-appointed guardian of English literature. Souvenir de Monsieur Poop. Stevie Smith. NALW

I am the serpent, fat with years. He Is like the Serpent Saka. *Unknown*. AWP *Fr.* Book of the Dead.

I am the seventh son of the son. Malcolm X—an Autobiography. Larry Neal. BPo

I am the shadow in the shadow of the wicker. Home Revisited: Midnight. John Ciardi. NYBP

I am the shepherd of the heavenly flock. Ivar Ivask, *Estonian*. CEEP, *tr. by* Ivar Ivask

I am the sieve she strains from. 4 Daughters. Lucille Clifton. IFJA

I am the sister of him. Little. Dorothy Aldis. CTV; NTCP; WHSW

I am the Smoke King. The Song of the Smoke. W. E. B. DuBois. ISC; NAAAL; PoBA; SSLK; UnPo

I am the song that sings the bird. Charles Causley. NOxBChV

I am the stage, impassive, mute and cold. Nature. Alfred de Vigny, *French*. AWP, *tr. by* Margaret Jourdain

I am the stone the Persians put to bear. The Statue of Nemesis at Rhamnus. Parmenion of Macedon, *Greek*. GrAn, *tr. by* Alistair Elliot

I am the teacher of athletes. Walt Whitman. ColAP *Fr.* Song of Myself.

I am the thunder of my tribe. Warsong of the Kwakiutl. *Unknown, Kwakiutl Oral Tradition*. APN-2; PaTW, *tr. by* Franz Boas *Fr.* Songs of the Kwakiutl Indians.

I am the tomb of a shipwrecked man. Sail on. Theodoridas, *Greek.* GrAn, *tr. by Peter Jay*

I am the tomb of Crethon; here you read. The Tomb of Crethon. Leonidas of Tarentum, *Greek.* AWP, *tr. by John Hermann Merivale*

I am the tomb of Tellen, I contain. Leonidas of Tarentum, *Greek.* GrAn, *tr. by Peter Levi*

I am the true vine, and my Father is the husbandman. Bible, *N.T.* OBVE *Fr.* St. John.

I am the trumpet blown by time [*or* Time]. The Trumpet. Ilya Grigoryevich Ehrenburg, *Russian.* TCRP; TrJP, *tr. by Yakov Hornstein*

I am the Turquoise Woman's son. The War God's Horse Song. *Unknown, Navajo Indian.* RB, *tr. by Louis Watchman;* TTTS

I Am the Very Model [*or* Pattern] of a Modern Major-General. Sir William Schwenck Gilbert. NOBL *Fr.* The Pirates of Penzance.
(Modern Major-General, The.) NBLV

I am the very pattern of a modern major-gineral. Sir William Schwenck Gilbert. UV *Fr.* The Pirates of Penzance.

I am the voice that often speaks. Voice. Albie Ollivierre. NBrP

"I Am the Way." Alice Thompson Meynell. NOBVV; OBMV; OxBSP

I am the wee falorie man. The Wee Falorie Man. *Unknown.* FaBoVe

I am the wind which breathes upon the sea. The Mystery. Amergin, *Irish.* TIRV, *tr. by Douglas Hyde*

I am the woman of the great expanse of the water. The Midnight Velada. María Sabina. PFTM, *tr. by Henry Munn and Alvaro Estrada Fr.* The Midnight Velada.

I am the woman of the principal fountain. Shaman. María Sabina, *Spanish.* WPOW, *tr. by Henry Munn*

I am thinking of tents and tentage, tents through the ages. Thinking of Tents. Reed Whittemore. TAP

I am thinking of that boy who bragged about the day he threw. Boy at the Paterson Falls. Toi Derricotte. PBCAP

I am this one. Juan Ramón Jiménez. *See* I am not I.

I am thy father's spirit. Shakespeare. *Fr.* Hamlet. NAWM-1

I am thy fugitive, thy votary. To the Lord Love. "Michael Field." OBMV

I am tired of civilization. (LL) Tired. Fenton Johnson. NAAAL; PoBA; PoLF; TTY

I am tired of cursing the Bishop. Crazy Jane on the Mountain. W. B. Yeats. CMoP

I am tired of planning and toiling. The Cry of the Dreamer. John Boyle O'Reilly. BLPA

I am tired of the tundra of the mind. Inspiration. Lynn Emanuel. NAmP90

"I am tired of this barn!" said the colt. The Barn. Elizabeth Jane Coatsworth. OBCP

I am tired of work; I am tired of building up somebody else's civilization. Tired. Fenton Johnson. NAAAL; PoBA; PoLF; TTY

I am to follow her. There is much grace. George Meredith. NAEL-2; NOBVV *Fr.* Modern Love.

I am to see to it that I do not lose you. (LL) To a Stranger. Walt Whitman. APN-1; NOBA; SAmP

I am told that the best people have begun saying. War Has Been Given a Bad Name. Bertolt Brecht, *German.* NNPT; PoSu, *tr. by John Willett;* HP, *tr. by Willet, John*

I am too arid for tears, and for laughter. Song of the Maverick. Mary Austin. PaTW

I Am Too Near. Wislawa Szymborska, *Polish.* BoWoP; PBPW, *tr. by Czeslaw Milosz*

I am too near, too clear a thing for you. A Flower of Mullein. Lizette Woodworth Reese. MoAmPo

I am too young to grow a beard. Street Song. Thom Gunn. HeIP-4; OxBC

I am troubled, I'm dissatisfied, I'm Irish. (LL) Spenser's Ireland. Marianne Moore. FaBoWP; IIP; LiTM; MeMAP; NOBA; NoAM; OxBA; TAP

I am trying to decide to go swimming. The Wind Is Blowing West. Joseph Ceravolo. TTTS

I am trying to describe to you a river at first light. Ideogram. William Meredith. Poetr

I am trying to drain my mind. Prelude to Nothing. Sonia Sanchez. GT

I am trying to imagine. Re-forming the Crystal. Adrienne Rich. TAP

I am trying / to learn to walk again. Walk. Frank Horne. BPo

I am trying to pry open your casket. Dear Reader. James Tate. SPE

I am 25 years old. My Poem. Nikki Giovanni. BPo; NBV; PoBA

I am twenty-four. The Survivor. Tadeusz Rózewicz, *Polish.* HP; PoSu, *tr. by Adam Czerniawski*

I am two fool[e]s, I know. The Triple Fool[e]. Donne. FMP; FSCP; GBL; NOSC; PBRV; SoSe-8

"I am unable," yonder beggar cries. A Lame Beggar. Donne. FMP; NoSic; PeLV; PFE

I am unhappy. / I do not care what happens. Motoyoshi Prince, *Japanese.* OHPJ, *tr. by Kenneth Rexroth*

I am unhappy that I am not God. He Puts Me to Rest. David Ignatow. VGW

I am unity on high. The Moon Sings to the Stream. Leah Goldberg. MHP, *tr. by Ruth Finer Mintz Fr.* Songs of the Stream.

I am unjust, but I can strive for justice. Why I Voted the Socialist Ticket. Vachel Lindsay. MoAmPo

I am valued by men, fetched from afar. Honey-Mead: "I am valued by men, fetched from afar." Cynewulf. AnOE, *tr. by Charles W. Kennedy Fr.* Riddles (Exeter Book).

I Am Vertical. Sylvia Plath. PiM

I am waiting for my case to come up. Lawrence Ferlinghetti. AiP; PmAP *Fr.* Oral Messages.

I am waiting for news, let it come. Snow Poem. Rodolfo Di Biasio, *Italian.* NeIt, *tr. by Stephen Sartarelli*

I am walking a trail. Intimidations of an Autobiography. James Tate. NoAM

I am walking and I. Ray A. Young Bear. STP

I am walking rapidly through striations of light and dark thrown under an arcade. I Dream I'm the Death of Orpheus. Adrienne Rich. NALW

I am Walt Disney of the Kingdom of Satan. Another Catalogue Item. David Avidan. *Fr.* Traveling in the City. IP, *tr. by Warren Bargad and Stanley F. Chyet*

I am warm. The Promise. Jewel C. Latimore. BlSi

I am watching a woman swim below the surface. The Exchange. Alicia Ostriker. NMM-2

I am watching them churn the last milk. The Mad Yak. Gregory Corso. BB; PFE; PmAP

I am wearing absent-minded red. Spots of Blood. Phyllis Webb. NOBC

I am Weary, Mother. Mary E. Tucker. CBWP-1

I am weary of lying within the chase. Ballade de Marguerite. *Unknown, French.* AWP, *tr. by Oscar Wilde*

I Am Weary of Straying. Sarah E. York. AH

I am weary of the Garden. Said the Rose. George Henry Miles. BLPA

I am weary of the working. To Solitude. Alice Cary. APN-2

I am weaving a song of waters. Song. Gwendolyn B. Bennett. BlSi

I am who the trail took. Exploration. Daniel Gerard Hoffman. CoAP

I am William Bronk, have been raised to believe. The Plainest Narrative. William Bronk. APSN

I am wind on sea. Amergin. *Fr.* Amergin's Songs. NOIV

I am with thee, and *Most take all.* (LL) The Quidditie [*or* Quiddity]. George Herbert. GeHe; NOSC; PoEL-2

I Am with Those. Ingrid Jonker, *Afrikaans.* BoWoP, *tr. by Jack Cope and William Plomer*

I am wondering how I could have changed her blood. Marlow and Nancy. Sandra McPherson. AmPA

I am wondering what became of all those tall abstractions. The Death of Allegory. Billy Collins. WeW-3

I am worn out with dreams. Men Improve with the Years. W. B. Yeats. OxAEP-2

I am yesterday, to-day and to-morrow. He Walketh by Day. *Unknown.* AWP *Fr.* Book of the Dead.

I am: yet what I am none cares or knows. John Clare. APAD; CABP; EBEV; EBVV; EnVR; FHYEP; GTBS-P; HAP; NAEL-2; NOBE; NOBVV; NoP-4; OAEL-2; OBEV; OBNC; OxAEP-2; PeECV; PoEL-4; PoPoPo; Ro; TFi; TOF; TRP

I am! yet what I am who cares, or knows? Written in Northampton County Asylum. John Clare. PBMP; PFE

I am you are he she it is. Monkey. Bruce Weigl. CDa

I am your ancestor. You know next-to-nothing. Our Dust. C. D. Wright. NAmP90

I am your mother, your mother's mother. Jelaluddin Rumi, *Persian.* OBVE, *tr. by Elizabeth Daryush*

I am your servant and your thrall. (LL) Beauty clear and fair. John Fletcher. NOSC; OBEV

I am your son, white man! Mulatto. Langston Hughes. NAAL-2

I Am Your Wife. *Unknown.* PoToHe

I am yours, you are mine. Frau Ava, *German.* BoWoP, *tr. by Willis Barnstone*

I amna' fou' sae muckle as tired—deid dune. Sic Transit Gloria Scotia. "Hugh MacDiarmid." CMoP

I, an ambassador of Otherwhere. From the Embassy. Robert Graves. PoA

I an I Alone; or Goliath. Michael Smith. PBCV

I, an unwedded wandering dame. Epitaph. Sylvia Townsend Warner. MoBrPo

I and I. Khalil-ur-Rahman Azmi, *Urdu.* OMIP, *tr. by C. M. Naim and Norman H. Zide*

I and my white Pangur. The Monk and His Pet Cat. *Unknown, Old Irish.* CH

I and my zero face. Absolving You. Colette Inez. NMM-2

I and myself swore enmity. Alack. Interior. Sir John Collings Squire. OxBSP

I and Pangur Bán, my cat. Pangur Bán. *Unknown, Gaelic.* FaBoCh; RB, *tr. by* Robin Flower

I and the other intruders. Of Objects Considered as Fortresses in a Dutiful Place. Hyam Plutzik. VGW

I and Thou. Chana Bloch. CrSp

I and You. Nikolai Stepanovich Gumilyov, *Russian.* TCRP, *tr. by* Yakov Hornstein

I, Angelo, obese, black-garmented. Angelo Orders His Dinner. Bayard Taylor. BXAP

I apologize to coincidence for calling it necessity. Under a Certain Little Star. Wislawa Szymborska, *Polish.* VCWP, *tr. by* Magnus J. Krynski *and* Robert A. Maguire

I appear like a bird from nowhere. Below Hekla. Selima Hill. FaBoWP

I Applied for the Board. Jimmy Santiago Baca. LoL

I approached Moses and said to him. Moses. Amir Gilbo'a, *Hebrew.* MHP, *tr. by* Ruth Finer Mintz

I argue / that where the body is concerned. Saddle and Cell. The Three Marias, *Portuguese.* BoWoP, *tr. by* Helen R. Lane

I arise above the clouds. The Airman's Breastplate. Oliver St. John Gogarty. TIRV

I arise and unbuild it again. (LL) The Cloud. Shelley. CABP; FHYEP; NAEL-2; NoP-4; PWR; PoEL-4

I arise from dreams of thee. The Indian Serenade. Shelley. AWP; CBLP; FaBoBe; GTBS-P; HoPM; ImPo; NAEL-2; OBEV; RaBo; TTTS

I arise today. Saint Patrick's Breastplate; or, The Deer's Cry. Saint Patrick, *Irish.* TIRV, *tr. by* Kuno Meyer

I, Arnor the red poet, made. The Five Voyages of Arnor. George Mackay Brown. FaBoTC

I arose early and stepped outside. February Morning. King D. Kuka. VoR

I arose swiftly that night, for I heard a knock at my door. The Future. James Oppenheim. TrJP

I Arrive In Madrid. Al Young. GT

I arrive / in the unbearable heat. Song for My Father. Jessica Hagedorn. MoLi

I arrive /Langston Langston. Do Nothing Till You Hear from Me. David Henderson. GT; PoBA

I Arrived in that Town, Everyone Greeted Me and I Recognized no One. When I Was Going to Read My Verses, the Devil, Hidden Behind a Tree, Called Out to Me Sarcastically and Filled My Hands with Newspaper Clippings. J. V. Foix, *Catalan.* PFTM, *tr. by* David H. Rosenthal

I as in love with the word "aloha." Poem for George Helm: Aloha Week 1980. Eric Chock. OpBo

I Ask. Novica Tadic, *Serbo-Croatian.* HSix, *tr. by* Charles Simic

I ask a man in the smoker where he is going and he answers: "Omaha." (LL) Limited. Carl Sandburg. HAP; MoAmPo; OxBA; SAGP

I ask a mountain woman for a light. Brewing Tea at Moon Pond. Chang Yü. *Fr.* Seven Poems on Living in the Mountains: Seeing Off. CoBLCP, *tr. by* Jonathan Chaves

I ask all blessings. *Unknown, Navajo Indian.* EnlH, *tr. by* Stephen Mitchell

I ask but one thing of you, only one. To a Friend. Amy Lowell. PoLF

I ask but right: let her that caught me late. 1.3. Ovid. EBEV, *tr. by* Marlowe *Fr.* Elegies.

I ask for the strength to follow through my life. Time of Day. Selden Rodman. PoA

I Ask My Mother to Sing. Li-Young Lee. LoL; OpBo; UnSA

I Ask My Teachers. Sister Mary Madeleva. CRP *Fr.* Concerning Death.

I ask myself what kind of man am I. (LL) Bitter Cold, Living in the Village. Po Chü-i, *Chinese.* ChiPo; SuSp, *tr. by* Irving Lo

I ask no kind return in love. Fanny [or Frances] Macartney Greville. *See* A Prayer for Indifference.

I ask no kind return of love. A Prayer for Indifference. Fanny [or Frances] Macartney Greville. OBEV *Fr.* A Prayer for Indifference. ECWP; NOEC

I ask not of sorrow, but in wonder. (LL) Encounter. Czeslaw Milosz, *Polish.* PiM, *tr. by* Czeslaw Milosz *and* Lillian Vallee; ChAP

I ask not why Astrea fled away. Wit's Abuse. Anne Wharton. KTR

I ask not wit, nor beauty do I crave. The Humble Wish. B—ll M—rt—n. ECWP; LW

I ask not wit, nor beauty do I crave. The Wish, By a Young Lady. Laetitia Pilkington. PEW

I ask the muse about this drifting. The Muse's Answer. Gibbons Ruark. MT

I ask thee whence those ashes were. A Question. *Unknown.* NOSC

I ask thy aid, O potent rum! Resentments Composed because of the Clamor of Town Topers Outside My Apartment. Sarah Kemble Knight. AiP; SCAP

I ask, who will buy a poem? Mahon O'Heffernan, *Early Modern Irish.* NOIV, *tr. by* Thomas Kinsella

I ask you: Has the Singer sung. Non Omnis Moriar. Allen Tate. FuPo

I ask You not for victory. The Prizefighter's Prayer. Menotti Vincent Caprani. TIRV

I ask you to come back now as you were in youth. Invitation to a Ghost. Donald Justice. BAP-93

I ask'd a young Youth what it mean'd. Alicia D'Anvers. KTR *Fr.* Academia; or The Humours of the University of Oxford.

I askéd a thief to steal me a peach. The Angel. William Blake. ImPo; NAEL-2; NoP-4; OBNC; PoE

I asked an aged man, a man of cares. What Is Time? James Marsden. PWR

I asked her why she didn't. Girl with Long Dark Hair. Stephen Gray. PeSA

I asked if I got sick and died, would you. A Question. John Millington Synge. MoBrPo; NOIV; OBMV; OxBTC; SAGP

I asked if I should pray. Mohini Chatterjee. W. B. Yeats. NoAM

I asked [or askd] my Dear Friend, Orator Prigg. Orator Prigg. William Blake. OBSV

I asked my mother for fifty cents. *Unknown.* OxBoLi

I asked no other thing. Emily Dickinson. APN-2; NOBA; OxBA; PBMP

I asked professors who teach the meaning of life to tell me what is happiness. Happiness. Carl Sandburg. OxBA

I asked the heaven of stars. Night Song at Amalfi. Sara Teasdale. MoAmPo

I asked the holly, "What is your life if. . . ?" Trees. Ted Hughes. NYBP

I asked the Lord: "Sire, is this true." A Dream Question. Thomas Hardy. ChIV-1

I asked the maid in dulcet tone. Scones. *Unknown.* OBCoV

I asked [or ask't] thee oft what poets thou hast read. Upon the Same. Robert Herrick. CaPo

I asked unanswerable questions a child asks. Herbert Mason. IMW *Fr.* Gilgamesh.

I at my window sit, and see. Autumn. *Unknown.* NOEC

I, / at one time. The Self-Hatred of Don L. Lee. Don L. Lee. BPo

I ate and drank with you, fellow men. Yevgeny Mikhailovich Vinokurov, *Russian.* TCRP, *tr. by* Daniel Weissbort

I ate pancakes one night in a Pancake House. The Player Piano. Randall Jarrell. MT; NAAL-2

I ate the thornapple leaves. Datura Hunting Song. *Pima Oral Tradition.* PaTW, *tr. by* Frank Russell

I attach no importance to life. The Spectral Attitudes. André Breton, *French.* SPE, *tr. by* David Gascoyne

I attended the burial of all my rosy feelings. Transaction. A. R. Ammons. HCAP; PoA

I await his coming. Guessing. *Unknown, Burmese.* PBWP, *tr. by* U Win Pe

I awakened to dryness and the ferns were dead. The Tragedy of Leaves. Charles Bukowski. HoPM

I awoke happy, the house. The Revelation. William Carlos Williams. SAmP

I awoke in profuse sweat, arms aching. Hag-Ridden. Robert Graves. BIrV

I awoke in the midsummer not-to-call night, in the white and the walk of the morning. Moonrise. Gerard Manley Hopkins. EnVR; MoBrPo; NOBVV; RB

I awoke only to hear the dull clobbing of the wind. Night Shore. Barry O. Higgs. PeSA

I bade make ready for our guests to-night. (LL) Circe. Augusta Davies Webster. PeVV; VWP

I bargained with life for a penny. My Wage. Jessie Belle Rittenhouse. BLPA; PoToHe

I bathe in orchid water. The Lord among the Clouds. Ch'u Yüan. ChiPo, *tr. by* Burton Watson *Fr.* Nine Songs. CoBCP, *tr. by* Burton Watson

I bear a little more than I can bear. (LL) Sonnet: "I hereby swear that to uphold your house." Elinor Wylie. ImPo; MoAmPo; NAAL-2; OxBA; Son

I bear the sucker-torch to the western tree-ridge. Songs of Spirits. *Unknown, Wintu.* APN-2, *tr. by* Jeremiah Curtin

I beat like a deaf man on the door of the dead. The Son of the Bone Speaks. Roger Gilbert-Lecomte, *French.* PFTM, *tr. by* Pierre Joris

I become them, sometimes. Pure fight. Pure fantasy. Lean. (LL) The Turncoat. Imamu Amiri Baraka. NeAP; PoE

I been rebuked and I been scorned. *Unknown.* BkSV; NAAAL ("I been 'buked an' I been scorned.") OxBoLi

I been ridin' fer cattle the most of my life. The High-loping Cowboy. Curley W. Fletcher. AiP

I been scarred and battered. Langston Hughes. *See* Still Here.

I been t'inkin' 'bout de preachah; whut he said de othah night. Philosophy. Paul Laurence Dunbar. BPo; NAAAL

I befriended Mike with the good hash pipe. Robyn Selman. PUP-19

I beg death's pardon now. And mourn the dead. (LL) The Pardon. Richard Wilbur. FP; MoP; NOBA; NoAM; Poetr

I beg God's grace, guardian of the parish. In Praise of Tenby. *Unknown, Welsh.* OBWVE, tr. by Joseph P. Clancy

I began in Ohio. Stages on a Journey Westward. James Wright. LCAP-2

I begin as tradition advises. Catechism. Betsy Sholl. CrSp

I begin through the grass once again to be bound to the Lord. Reconciliation. "Æ." OBMV; TrCP

I begin with the hills. This House. Ray A. Young Bear. CDW

I beheld, and lo a great multitude, which no man could number. Heavenly Vision. William Billings. AmFP

I beheld her, on a day. How He Saw Her. Ben Jonson. *Fr.* A Celebration of Charis in Ten Lyric[k] Pieces [or Peeces]. BeJo; OxAEP-1; SeCP

I, being born a woman and distressed. Edna St. Vincent Millay. BoLoP; GLoP; LW; LoP; NALW; NIP-4; NoP-4

I Believe. Saul Tchernichowsky, *Hebrew.* TrJP, tr. by Reginald V. Feldman

I believe a leaf of grass is no less than the journey-work of the stars. Walt Whitman. SAmP *Fr.* Song of Myself. AmPP; MoAmPo; NAAL-3; NOBA; OxBA

("Boiling her iron tea-kettle and baking shortcake.") (LL) PAR

("I believe a leaf of grass is no less than the journeywork of the stars.") PAR

("I follow quickly, I ascend to the nest in the fissure of the cliff.") (LL) ColAP

I believe *all* childern's good. The Hired Man's Faith in Children. James Whitcomb Riley. LiLi

I believe if I look over my shoulder. The Fall of Light. Elizabeth Kirschner. CMAP

I believe if I should die. Creed. Mary Ashley Townsend. BLPA; FaBoBe

I believe in God above. A Child's Creed. *Unknown.* CTV

I believe in God, the Almighty Ruler. Abraham Lincoln's Creed. *Unknown.* CTV, tr. by William E. Barton

I believe in God the Father. The Apostles' Creed. *Unknown.* CTV

I believe in magic. I believe in the rights. Credo. Maxine W. Kumin. NMM-2

I believe in the brook as it wanders. The Handiwork of God. *Unknown.* CTV

I believe in the flesh and the appetites. Walt Whitman. *Fr.* Song of Myself. AmPP; MoAmPo; NAAL-3; NOBA; OxBA

I believe in the increasing of life: whatever. The Escape. Ivor Gurney. OxBSP

I believe in the sun. *Unknown.* HP

I believe in the ultimate justice of Fate. Credo. Georgia Douglas Johnson. PoBA

I believe in this stalled magnificence. The Snowbound City. John Haines. SPE

I believe in you my soul, the other I am must not abase itself to you. Walt Whitman. APAD; ColAP; PAR *Fr.* Song of Myself. AmPP; MoAmPo; NAAL-3; NOBA; OxBA

("And elder and mullen and pokeweed.") (LL) PAR Swiftly Arose. TrCP

I believe it all, and for no man's death I grieve. (LL) A Letter from Brooklyn. Derek Walcott. FP; OxBTC

I believe the dose will do. (LL) A Receipt to Cure [or for] the Vapours. Lady Mary Wortley Montagu. ECWP; NOEC; NoP-4; PBWP; PEW; PeLV

I believe the grief of Tantalus in Hell. Paulus Silentiarius, *Greek.* InMo, tr. by Sam Hamill

I believe there is no one alive who weeps for my sorrow. Heinrich von Morungen, *German.* GePo, tr. by Frederick Goldin

I bend over an old hollow cottonwood stump. A Hollow Tree. Robert Bly. NNaP

I bend over the woman. The Country Midwife: A Day. Ai. GT

I Bended unto Me. Thomas Edward Brown. NOBVV; NTCP

I Bent to Touch a Damp Cloth to Your Mouth. Sherod Santos. *Fr.* The Sheltering Ground. Son

I bequeath my notes to my successors and heirs. Hieronymus Bosch. Pavel Grigoryevich Antokolsky, *Russian.* TCRP, tr. by Bernard Meares

I, Bertold Brecht, came out of the black forests. Of Poor B.B. Bertolt Brecht, *German.* RB, tr. by Michael Hamburger

I beseech God's favour, faultless your gift. Petition for Reconciliation. Cynddelw Brydydd Mawr, *Welsh.* OBWVE, tr. by Joseph P. Clancy

I bespeak words. Introduction. Clere Parsons. FaBoTw

"I bet I can hold my breath." One-Upmanship. Miriam Chaikin. NTCP

I bet you don't wear shoulder pads in bed. Wagers. Marilyn Hacker. RA

I bind unto myself to-day. St Patrick's Breastplate. Saint Patrick, *Irish.* FaBoCh, tr. by Frances Alexander

I blame Myrtis. Korinna, *Greek.* PBWP, tr. by John Dillon

I blame old women for buying paper roses. Look, No Hands. Pearse Hutchinson. PBCIP

"I bleed by the black stream." Haemorrhage. Padraic Fiacc. CIP-2

I bless the daily labor of my hands. Marina Tsvetayeva, *Russian.* WPoS, tr. by David McDuff

I bless[e] Thee, Lord, because I GROW. Paradise. George Herbert. GaP; GeHe; ImPo; NOSC; OAEL-1; SeCP

I Bless Thee, Lord, for Sorrows Sent. Samuel Johnson. AH

I blink and half my life is over. Pete Winslow. CLPP

I block out the midday brightness with a screen depicting dark woods. Impromptu on a Hangover. P'i Jih-hsiu, *Chinese.* CoBCP, tr. by Burton Watson

I born / from / a force. Motto Vision 1971. Delano Abdul Malik de Coteau. PBCV

I bought a dollar and a half's worth of small red potatoes. The Simple Truth. Philip Levine. NoP-4

I bought a pack of Camels yesterday. Invoice No. 13, A Masque of Resignation. William Harmon. WeT

I bought a red-brick villa. Song for Straphangers. George Buchanan. PNI

I bought (I was too wealthy for my age). A Visit to the Dead. Norman Cameron. FaBoTC; OxBSn

I bowed my head, and heard the sea far off / Washing its hands. (LL) At the Slackening of the Tide. James Wright. UnPo; VGW

I break off a branch, and prod my lazy donkey. A Trip to a Mountain Village. Li K'ai-hsien, *Chinese.* CoBLCP, tr. by Jonathan Chaves

I Break the Sky. Owen Dodson. PoBA

I BREAK up cypress and make a book-box. On a Box Containing his Own Works. Po Chü-i, *Chinese.* ChiP, tr. by Arthur Waley

I breathe, sweet Gib [or Ghib], the temperate air of Wrest. To my Friend G.N. from Wrest. Thomas Carew. BeJo; CaPo

I breathe the air of another country. Australia. Gary Catalano. NOBAu

I breathed upon the aluminum microphone-stand a body's length away. Thus Crosslegged on Round Pillow Sat in Space. Allen Ginsberg. NNaP

I bring fresh showers for the thirsting flowers. The Cloud. Shelley. CABP; FHYEP; LaPo; NAEL-2; NoP-4; PWR; PoEL-4

I bring myself back from the streets that open like long. Home for Thanksgiving. W. S. Merwin. NoAM

I bring ye love. Quest. What will love do? Upon Love, by Way of Question and Answer. Robert Herrick. CBLP; CaPo

I bring you a goat. Hroswitha von Gandersheim. WPOW, tr. by Patrick Diehl *Fr.* Paphnutius.

I bring you as offering. (LL) Orchard. Hilda Doolittle. CMoP; LiTM; MoAmPo; OxBA

I bring you news. *Unknown.* NOIV

I brocht my love a cherry. Auld Sang. William Soutar. OxBS

I broke a glass, got bloodstains on the sheet. Eight Days in April. Marilyn Hacker. FFC

I broke the second part of the First Commandment. Ivar Grunthal, *Estonian.* CEEP, tr. by Ivar Ivask

I Brood about Some Concepts, for Example. Alicia Ostriker. PBCAP

I Brotachos of Gortyn lie here. This. Simonides, *Greek.* GrAn, tr. by Peter Jay

I brought a little wolf cub home. Wolf Cub. Sergey Sergeievich Narovchatov, *Russian.* TCRP, tr. by Lubov Yakovleva

I brought a lover home. Christmas in the Midwest. Maureen Seaton. LoHo

I brought my children to the mound. Anniversaries of War. Yehuda Amichai, *Hebrew.* VCWP, tr. by Benjamin Harshav *and* Barbara Harshav

I brought my life this far. Anniversary. Odysseas Elytis, *Greek.* AF; GrIP, tr. by Edmund Keeley *and* Philip Sherrard

I brush the spider webs from the dismantled sky. Housework. Amanda Berenguer, *Spanish.* WPOW, tr. by Priscilla Joslin

I Build. Tadeusz Różewicz, *Polish.* CEEP, tr. by Victor Contoski

I built a hut in a little wood. My Hut. Eileen Mathias. BoTP

I built my house near where others dwell. Written While Drunk. Ch'ien T'ao, *Chinese.* ChiPo, tr. by Cyril Birch

I built my house upon the solid rock. Here We have No Firm Dwelling-Place. Eugène Marais, *Afrikaans.* PeSAV, tr. by Hugh Finn

I built my hut in a place where people live. T'ao Ch'ien, *Chinese.* Fr. Drinking Wine. CoBCP, tr. by Burton Watson

I BUILT my hut in a zone of human habitation. Ch'ien T'ao, *Chinese.* ChiP, tr. by Arthur Waley

I built my hut near where people live. José Juan Tablada. AWP, tr. by Arthur Waley *Fr.* Two Drinking Songs.

I built my soul a lordly pleasurehouse. The Palace of Art. Tennyson. EnVR; NOBRP

I built on the sand. Foundations. Leopold Staff, *Polish.* BLT, tr. by Czeslaw Milosz

I buried Mama in her wedding dress. She Didn't Even Wave. Ai. NMM-2

I burn[e], and cruel[l] you, in vain[e]. To My Mistress [or Mistris], I
Burning in Love. Thomas Carew. SeCP

I burn no incense, hang no wreath. The Widow's Song. Edward Coote
Pinkney. APN-1

I burned my life, that I might find. The Alchemist. Louise Bogan. AWP;
MoAmPo

I burst out laughing. (LL) The Lesson. Charles Simic. AF; HCAP

I buy the dark with my last fifteen cents. Depression Days. Pat Mora.
UnSA

I, Caesar, when I learned of the fame. Limerick. *Unknown*. PeLi

I call on those that call me son. Are You Content. W. B. Yeats. IIP

I call that parent rash and wild. The Velvet Hand. Phyllis McGinley.
OBCoV

I call the land of Ireland. Amergin. *Fr.* Amergin's Songs. NOIV

I call up the handful of planets close enough. Late, Watching Television.
Del Marie Rogers. IFJA

I call up words that he may write them down. Demands of the Muse.
Vernon Watkins. PoA

I call you, we'll see the snails fall and break. Arm in Arm. Virgil
Teodorescu, *Romanian*. CEEP, *tr. by* Donald Eulert *and* Stefan
Avadanei

I call you with honest words. Bláthmac Mac Con Brettan. NOIV *Fr.* A
Poem to Mary.

I called at your. From an Afternoon Caller. Sister Mary Madeleva. CRP

I called him to come in. Evening. James Wright. NOBA; NYBP

I called one day—on Eden's strand. Emily Dickinson in Southern
California. X. J. Kennedy. NBLV; OBCoV

I called out of mine affliction. Jonah's Prayer. Bible, *O.T.* TrJP *Fr.*
Jonah.

I called today, Peter, and you were away. The Thermal Stair. W. S.
Graham. FaBoMo

I called you because I could not stand alone. Burden. Peter Kane Dufault.
NoP-4

I calls 'er Sal. My Old Dutch. Albert Chevalier. LBC

I Came a-Riding. Reinmar von Zweter, *German*. AWP, *tr. by* Jethro Bithell

I came across a little demon. The Little Demon. Zinaida Nikolayevna
Gippius, *Russian*. TCRP, *tr. by* Lubov Yakovleva

I came across these facts which, mixed with / others. Scotland in the
1890s. Robert Crawford. FaBoTC

I came, alas! to conquer—not to die! (LL) Much spoke he of the myrtle and
the yew. Philip Freneau. NAAL-1; NAAL-3

I came as a shadow. Nocturne Varial. Lewis Alexander. PoBA

I came back at last to my own house. The Substitute for Time. John
Koethe. EOEF

I came before the water. Mussel Hunter at Rock Harbor. Sylvia Plath.
NYBP

I came first through the warm grass. The Bee's Last Journey to the Rose.
Brian Patten. OTCP

I came from somewhere. Poem of the Future Citizen. José Craveirinha,
Portuguese. TTY, *tr. by* Dorothy Guedes *and* Philippa Rumsey

I came / heavy with child in the fierce sun. Waiheke 1972—Rocky Bay.
Christina Beer. PeNZ

I came here. I don't know you here. Clark Coolidge. PmAP *Fr.* At Egypt.

I came home and found a lion in my living room. The Lion for Real.
Allen Ginsberg. GLP; HCAP; RB

I came home from Vietnam. Anna Grasa. Bruce Weigl. CDa

I came in from the garden. Scales. Libby Houston. NBrP

I came/ in the blinding sweep. To Mother. Frank Horne. BPo *Fr.* Letters
[or Notes] Found near a Suicide. PoBA

I came into the City and none knew me. An Upper Chamber. Frances
Bannerman. OBEV

I came into the pasture-ground. Settlement. Ingeborg Bachmann, *German*.
PoSu, *tr. by* Daniel Huws

I came out to sit on Cold Mountain. *Unknown*, *Chinese*. CoBCP, *tr. by*
Burton Watson

I came out a winner. O Realm Bejewelled. Forugh Farrokhzad, *Farsi*.
WPOW, *tr. by* Jascha Kessler *and* Amin Banani

I came then to the city of my brethren. The Shore of Life. Robert
Fitzgerald. VGW

I came to a field. Pastoral. Charles Simic. NNaP

I came to love, I came into my own. (LL) The Dream. Theodore Roethke.
EP; NYBP; UnPo

I came to the east. I Come from a South. Ruy Duarte de Carvalho.
PBMAP

I came to the end at an inappropriate midnight. Post Operative. Thomas
William Shapcott. BMAP

I came to visit my friend. Birds of Detroit. Greg Pape. PBCAP

I came to you with a greeting. Morning Song. Afanasi Afanasievich Fet,
Russian. AWP, *tr. by* Max Eastman

I came too late to the hills: they were swept bare. The Wilderness.
Kathleen Jessie Raine. BoWoP; WPE

I came, yes, dear, dear. Kore in Hades. Kathleen Jessie Raine. NALW

I came, you know, but your gate was locked. Old Friend. Dimitris
Tsaloumas. BMAP

I Can. Ralph Waldo Emerson. CTV *Fr.* In an age of fops and toys.
PoLF *Fr.* Voluntaries. APN-1; CBCWP

I can afford to discriminate. The Discriminator. Vernon Scannell. OxBC

I can almost see. On the Rouge. Raymond Souster. NOBC

I can & do lie down with you amidst the venomous. For the Safety of
Lovers. John James. NBrP

I can break your heart. (LL) The Kid. Ai. GT; NoAM

I can climb our apple tree. Jessie Orton Jones. CTV *Fr.* (IX from
Secrets).

I can close my eyes one heartbeat. My Father's Country. Joyce Lee.
NOBAu

I can die tomorrow and I have not loved. For the Book of Love. Jules
Laforgue, *French*. NNPT, *tr. by* Vernon Watkins

I can feel my cheek / still burning. (LL) The Portrait. Stanley Kunitz.
FiLi; IMW; Poetsp; RaBo

I can feel the loneliness. Muneyuki, *Japanese*. OHPJ, *tr. by* Kenneth
Rexroth

I can feel the tug. Punishment. Seamus Heaney. FaBoPV; InPS-3; NAEL-
2; NoAM; NoP-4; OxAEP-2; PBCIP; PoPoPo; SAGP

I Can Fly. Felice Holman. NTCP

I can give myself to her. Akiko Yosano, *Japanese*. WPJ; WPOW, *tr. by*
Kenneth Rexroth *and* Ikuko Atsumi

I can hear the evening bell. Returning by Night to Lu-Men. Meng Hao Jan,
Chinese. OHMPC, *tr. by* Kenneth Rexroth

I can hear the voice of Boris Vian, which is something because of course I
never. Paris Visitation. Michael Brownstein. FTOS

I can imagine, in some otherworld. Humming-Bird. D. H. Lawrence. APo;
CMoP; InPS-3; LiTM; MoUL; RB

I can imagine someone who found. California Hills in August. Dana
Gioia. DiPo; InPK-6

I can love both fair[e] and brown[e]. The Indifferent. Donne. BoLoP;
CBLP; ESCV; NAEL-1; NAWM-1; NOSC; PBMP; SoSe-8

I can make a sandwich. Recipe. Bobbi Katz. CTV

I can make out the rigging of a schooner. North Haven. Elizabeth Bishop.
HCAP

I can manage so few of you. Persons Unknown. Aidan Carl Mathews.
BiHa

I can meet you. Reservation Love Song. Sherman Alexie. PoPoPo

I can [or kan] nam[o]ore; my tale is at an ende. (LL) The Franklin's Tale.
Chaucer. NAEL-1; OAEL-1

"I" Can Never Be a Great Man, An. Stephen Spender. OBMV

I can no longer ask how it feels. The Making of a Servant. J. J. R.
Jolobe. PeSAV

I can no longer hold, my body grows. A Lover that Durst Not Speak to His
M[istress]. James Shirley. NOSC

I can no longer remain in this building. Passing Through Doorways. Frank
Kuppner. FaBoTC

I can no longer talk to cabbages. Cabbages. Renate Wood. CMAP

I can no longer tell dream from reality. Akazome Emon, *Japanese*. WPJ,
tr. by Kenneth Rexroth *and* Ikuko Atsumi

I can no longer untangle my hair. *Unknown*, *Chinese*. OHMPC, *tr. by*
Kenneth Rexroth

I can not invent it. Hilda Doolittle. NALW *Fr.* Tribute to the Angels.

I can not see why trials come. I Can Trust. Daniel Webster Davis. AAP

I can only say I have waited for you. Time of Waiting in Amsterdam.
Ingrid Jonker, *Afrikaans*. BoWoP, *tr. by* Jack Cope *and* William Plomer

I can remember. I can remember. The Boy Actor. Noël Coward. OxBTC

I can remember our sorrow, I can remember our laughter. Memory. Helen
Hoyt. PoLF

I can remember when he was a pup. (LL) The Span of Life. Robert Frost.
HoPM; LiTM; SoSe-8

I can remember wind-swept streets of cities. Memory. Margaret Walker
Alexander. GT

I can see a picture. Pictures. F. Ann Elliott. BoTP

I can see myself years back at Sunion. Adrienne Rich. *Fr.* Twenty-one
Love Poems. GLP

I can see the stones. Masaoka Shiki, *Japanese*. OHMPJ, *tr. by* Kenneth
Rexroth

I can see the traces of old work. House (Blown Apart). David Shapiro.
PT

I can shake the wild hay, and wet seed sticks to my hand. Stalks of Wild
Hay. Harold Lenoir Davis. PoA

I can sing a true song about myself. *Unknown*. ASW, *tr. by* Kevin
Crossley-Holland *Fr.* The Seafarer.

I can sing of myself a true song. *Unknown.* PoRA, tr. by L. Iddings   Fr. The Seafarer.

I can stay awake all night, if need be. Zoo Keeper's Wife. Sylvia Plath. EP

I can support it no longer. Flower Herding on Mount Monadnock. Galway Kinnell. CoAmPo; HeIP-4; LCAP-2; NOBA; NoAM

I can take cover. The Vain Girl Jilted. Edith Jay Scovell. WPN

I can tell by the way the trees beat, after. The Man Watching. Rilke, *German.* RaBo, tr. by Robert Bly

I can tell you about this because I have held in my hand. Drawn by Stones, by Earth, by Things That Have Been in the Fire. Marvin Bell. VCAP

I can think of William of Orange. The Centaurs. Paul Muldoon. BiHa

I Can Trust. Daniel Webster Davis. AAP

I can understand the haggard eyes. Ted Hughes. NoAM   Fr. Stations.

I can use it. Song of the Crab Medicine-Bag. *Unknown, Chippewa Indian.* STP, tr. by Jerome Rothenberg

I can usually feel at home in rooms. Aleksandr Petrovich Mezhirov, *Russian.* TCRP, tr. by Deming Brown

I can wade Grief. Emily Dickinson. APN-2; ColAP; HeIP-4; NOBA

I canceled your funeral, Mother. Elegy for My Mother. Andrey Andreievich Voznesensky, *Russian.* TCRP, tr. by William Jay Smith and F. D. Reeve

I canna tell what has come ower me. Ich Weiss Nicht Was Soll es Bedeuten. Heinrich Heine, *German.* AWP, tr. by Alexander Macmillan

I cannot all the *Species* rehearse. Of Roses and Hyacinths. Rene Rapin, *Latin.* GaP, tr. by John Evelyn

I cannot be positive which. (LL) The Yak. Hilaire Belloc. CTAV; MoBrPo; NBLV; NOBL; NoAM; OxBChV; PeP

I cannot blind myself. How Can I Sing. Odia Ofeimun. HBAPE

I cannot bring a world quite round. Wallace Stevens. CMoP; RaBo   Fr. The Man with the Blue Guitar.

I cannot but ask, in the park and the streets. Parvenant. Arthur Hugh Clough. OBCoV   Fr. Spectator ab Extra. OBCoV; OxBoLi; PeLV; PeVV

I cannot but believe, though you were dead. Nurse. Frances Darwin Cornford. WPN

I cannot change as others do. Constancy. John Wilmot, 2d Earl of Rochester. OBEV

I Cannot Choose but Think upon the Time. "George Eliot." Son   Fr. Brother and Sister. NALW

I cannot cry out. A Woman and Her Dying Warrior. Vanparanar, *Tamil.* PLW, tr. by A. K. Ramanujan

I cannot dance, O Lord. Mechthild von Magdeburg, *German.* WPoS, tr. by Jane Hirshfield

I cannot dance upon my Toes. Emily Dickinson. APN-2; NCAP

I cannot disclaim that string-thin, five-year-old boy. The Naval Base (Part III). Jeremy Cronin. AF

I cannot eat but little meat. Jolly Good Ale and Old. William Stevenson *and* John Still. OBEV   Fr. Back and Side Go Bare, Go Bare. HeIP-4; NAEL-1   Fr. Gammer Gurton's Needle.

I cannot eat but little meat. *Unknown.* PFE

I cannot find my way. Credo. Edwin Arlington Robinson. AmPP; CMoP; LiTM; MeMAP; MoAmPo; NAAL-2; OxBA; PFE; TAP; TrCP

I cannot find my way to Nazareth. Fragment. Yvor Winters. OBSV

I cannot forget. Marichiko, *Japanese.* OHMPJ, tr. by Kenneth Rexroth

I cannot forget my jo. A Poor French Sailor's Scottish Sweetheart. William Johnson Cory. EBVV

I cannot forget / The perfumed dusk inside the. Kenneth Rexroth. APSN   Fr. The Love Poems of Marichiko.

I cannot forget with what fervid devotion. William Cullen Bryant. APN-1

I cannot give the reasons. Mervyn Laurence Peake. NOxBChV

I cannot give you the Metropolitan Tower. Parting Gift. Elinor Wylie. OxBA

"I cannot go to school today." Sick. Shel Silverstein. ChAP

I cannot go to you. *Unknown, Japanese.* OHMPJ, tr. by Kenneth Rexroth

I Cannot Grow. W. H. Auden. RB

I cannot hold my peace, Keats. To John Keats, Poet, at Spring Time. Countee Cullen. NAAAL

I cannot lie here anymore. Nuala Ni Dhomhnaill, *Irish.* BiHa, tr. by Michael Hartnett

I cannot live with You. Emily Dickinson. APN-2; AmPP; MoAmPo; NAAL-1; NAAL-3; NOBA; OxBA; PoEL-5; TRP

("And that White Sustenance— / Despair.") (LL) PAR

("Despair.") (LL) NCAP; NoP-4

I cannot live without thee! (LL) To His Coy Love, A Canzonet. Michael Drayton. NOSC; PBRV; SAGP

I cannot love thee as I ought. Tennyson. EBVVPR; EnVR   Fr. In Memoriam A. H. H.

I cannot move. Malcolm. Welton Smith. BPo

I cannot ope mine eyes. Mattens. George Herbert. ESCV; SCGP

I cannot praise the Doctor's eyes. On Hearing a Lady Praise a Certain Rev. Doctor's Eyes. George Outram. EBVV

I cannot praise Thee. By his instrument. Shall the Dead Praise Thee? George Macdonald. TrCP

I cannot reach it; and my striving eye. Childhood. Henry Vaughan. NOSC

I cannot recall you gentle. Black Mother Woman. Audre Lorde. CrSp; MDDM; Poetr

I cannot say. Lady Izumi, *Japanese.* WPoS, tr. by Jane Hirshfield *and* Mariko Aratani

I cannot say, and I will not say. He Is Not Dead. James Whitcomb Riley. BLPA

I cannot say the name of the city. Slavko Mihalic. PoSu, tr. by Peter Kastmiler

I cannot see him plain, that far-off sire. The Immigrant. Donald Davidson. FuPo

I cannot see the features right. Tennyson. ImPo; PoEL-5   Fr. In Memoriam A. H. H.

I cannot see the short, white curls. The Dumb World. W. H. Davies. OBWVE; OxBTC

I cannot see your face. A Sprig of Rosemary. Amy Lowell. CPO

I cannot send you back my hart. An Answeare to my Lady Alice Egdertons Songe, Of I prethy send mee back my Hart. Lady Jane Cavendish. KTR

I cannot skill of these thy ways. Justice. George Herbert. FMP

I cannot sleep at night. I cannot. Words of Old Age. Marie-Madeleine, *German.* CPO, tr. by Lillian Faderman, Brigitte Eriksson and Frankie Hucklenbroich

I cannot sleep or take the air. A Snowy Day. *Unknown, Welsh.* OBWVE, tr. by H. Idris Bell

I cannot sleep. The long, long. Night Thoughts. Lu Yu, *Chinese.* OHPC, tr. by Kenneth Rexroth

I cannot sleepe, my eyes ill neighbouring lids. John Marston. PoEL-2   Fr. The Malcontent.

I cannot spare water or wine. Mithridates. Ralph Waldo Emerson. APN-1; NCAP; NOBA

I cannot stand the man who wears. Ringless. Diane Wakoski. NALW

I cannot stay, / And if I could it would be senseless. Tune: "Paying Homage at the Golden Gate." Sun Kuang-hsien, *Chinese.* SuSp, tr. by Hellmut Wilhelm

I cannot stay at Florence, not even to wait for a letter. Arthur Hugh Clough. EBVVPR, canto 5, 7   Fr. Amours de Voyage. NOBVV

I cannot stop thinking of Srirangam. Speaking of Places. Rajagopal Parthasarathy. OMIP

I cannot tell! (LL) On the Departure Platform. Thomas Hardy. CBLP; NOBE; OBNC; OxBTC

I cannot tell for I do not know. (LL) Two Pigeons. *Unknown.* OxNR; ReMoGo

I cannot tell, not I, why she. Poem. Walter Savage Landor. GBL; OAEL-2

I cannot tell who loves the skeleton. La Bella Bona-Roba. Richard Lovelace. BeJo; CBLP; CaPo; CavPo; EBEV; NOSC; OAEL-1; PoEL-3; SeCP

I cannot tell you how it was. May. Christina Rossetti. GBL; GLoP; NOBVV

I cannot think the thing farewell. (LL) There rolls the deep where grew the tree. Tennyson. HAP; NOBE; OAEL-2

I cannot view the bloom upon the rose. Blind. Norman V. Pearce. PoToHe

I cannot walk an inch. No So. Not So. Anne Sexton. CrSp

I cannot write unless he's sent above! (LL) A Parental Ode to My Son, Aged Three Years and Five Months. Thomas Hood. OBCoV; PoLF

I can't appease Ashimbabbar, the moon god An. Crimes of Lugalanne. Enheduanna, *Sumerian.* BoWoP, ad. by Aliki and Willis Barnstone

I can't be talkin' of love, dear. Song. Esther Mathews. ImPo

I can't bear to watch your hips. Argentarius, *Greek.* InMo, tr. by Sam Hamill

I can't break with the Dark One. Mirabai, *Hindi.* BoWoP, tr. by Willis Barnstone *and* Usha Nilsson

I can't, Celinda, say, I love. To Celinda. Elizabeth Singer Rowe. PEW

I can't even remember the name of the one who fell. Ballad: Between the Boxcars. Robert Penn Warren. CRP; CAP

I can't forget / How she stood at the top of that long marble stair. Piazza di Spagna, Early Morning. Richard Wilbur. InPS-3; NoP-4; OxBSP; PFE; SAGP; VGW

I can't get him out of my mind, out of my mind. John Berryman. NoP-4   Fr. Dream Songs.

I Can't Get Started, *for Ira Hayes.* Ai. GT

I Can't Have a Martini, Dear, but You Take One, or, Are You Going to Sit There Guzzling All Night? Ogden Nash. PoRA

I can't hear myself think in America no more! Spearo's Blues (or: Ode to a Grecian Yearn). Eugene B. Redmond. NBV

I Can't Help You. Ryszard Krynicki, *Polish.* BLT, *tr.* by Stanislaw Baranczak *and* Clare Cavanagh

I can't hold it, keep it. Loke. Ronald Albert Simpson. CBAP

I can't hold you and I can't leave you. Sister Juana Inés de la Cruz, *Spanish.* PBWP, *tr.* by Judith Thurman

I can't live in this world. Further Notice. Philip Whalen. BB; PoM; VGW

I can't remember. Biology Teacher. Zbigniew Herbert, *Polish.* PoSu, *tr.* by John Carpenter *and* Bogdana Carpenter

I can't remember—. Origin. "Eduard Georgievich Bagritzky," *Russian.* TCRP, *tr.* by Vera Dunham

I can't remember how it happened. Father and Son. Robert Greacen. PNI

I can't ridge it back again from char. Death of the Kapowsin Tavern. Richard Hugo. NAAL-2

"I can't say it is love I have to offer—and it isn't love I want. It is something." D. H. Lawrence. ITG *Fr.* Women in Love.

I can't say our garden is a delight. Louisiana. Steve Crow. HATNAP

I can't stand it, said the old man. In the End. Peter Everwine, *after* Natan Sach. NNaP

I can't stand the wily magpie and all his extravagant stories! Tune: "Magpie on the Branch." *Unknown, Chinese.* CoBCP, *tr.* by Burton Watson *Fr.* Four Tz'u from Tun-huang. CoBCP, *tr.* by Burton Watson

I can't stand Willy wet-leg. Willy Wet-Leg. D. H. Lawrence. CMoP; RB

I can't tell my husband about the vacant lot. The Yellow Hills in Back. Christianne Balk. IFJA

I care not a curse though from birth he inherit. The Worker. Gerald Massey. EBVV

I care not for my Lady's soul. The Lust of the Eyes. Elizabeth Siddal. VWP

I care not for these ladies. Thomas Campion. AAS; HAP; NAEL-1; NoP-4; NoSic; PoE; SCGP

I care not what the sailors say. Crazy Jane Reproved. W. B. Yeats. CMoP

I care nothing for battle odes. "Anna Akhmatova," *Russian.* TCRP, *tr.* by Daniel Weissbort

I Carried Statues. Agnes Nemes Nagy, *Hungarian.* BoWoP; PoSu, *tr.* by Bruce Berlind

I carried you to an island. Sea-bundle. Jennifer Rankin. BMAP

I carry it on my keychain, which itself. The Ring. Diane Wakoski. PoA

I carry my black sheep back to her herd. Ljiljana Djurdjic, *Serbo-Croatian.* HSix, *tr.* by Charles Simic

I carry the ground-hog along by the tail. The Hunter. Raymond Souster. NOBC

I carry you in a glass jar. The Doll. Gregory Orr. AmPA

I carry your heart(i carry in my heart. (LL) I carry your heart with me(i carry it in). E. E. Cummings. MeMAP; TAP

I carry your heart with me(i carry it in). E. E. Cummings. MeMAP; TAP

I carve my first head. Then I carve another. Hallowe'en 1971. Michael Dennis Browne. AmPA

I carved your name on my watchband. Letters from a Man in Solitary. Nazim Hikmet, *Turkish.* AF, *tr.* by Randy Blasing *and* Mutlu Konuk

I cast from me the medications. Loneliness. Franz Werfel, *German.* TrJP, *tr.* by Edith Abercrombie Snow

I catch. John Wills. HA

I catch myself trying. Untitled Blues. Yusef Komunyakaa. GT; UnSA *Fr.* After a photograph by Yevgeni Yevtushenko.

I catch the movement of his lips. Marina Tsvetayeva, *Russian.* *Fr.* The Daughter of Jairus. BoWoP, *tr.* by Paul Schmidt

I Catcha da Plenty of Feesh. *Unknown.* AS

I caught a little ladybird / That flies far away. Christina Rossetti. FaBoVe

I caught a tremendous fish. The Fish. Elizabeth Bishop. ChAP; FaBoWP; HAP; HeIP-4; HoPM; InPK-6; LiTM; MoAmPo; MoP; NAAL-2; NALW; NOBA; NTP; NoAM; NoP-4; PoE; PoPoPo; Poetr; RB; TFi; TRP

I caught the American bull. Buffalo. Henry Dumas. PoBA

I caught this morning morning's mínion, king-. The Windhover. Gerard Manley Hopkins. APAD; CABP; CMoP; ClHu; EBEvV; EBVV; EnVR; GEA; GTBS-P; HAP; InPK-6; InPS-3; LiTM; MoBrPo; MoP; NAEL-2; NOBE; NOBVV; NoAM; NoP-4; OAEL-2; OBNC; OxAEP-2; PFE; PeECV; PoE; PoEL-5; PoPoPo; PoRA; Poetr; RB; SCGP; SCV; TFi; TOF; TRP; UnPo

I caught you grazing on my knee. To a Flea in a Glass of Water. Desmond A. Greig. PeSA

I cause great many worries to my mother. Spoons with Realistic Dead Flies on Them. Charles Simic. FiLi

I cease not from desire till my desire. Hafiz. AWP; TAL, *tr.* by Gertrude Lowthian Bell *Fr.* Odes.

I celebrate myself, / And what I assume you shall assume. Walt Whitman. *See* Song of Myself.

I celebrate Rhegion, Italy's tip. The Tomb of Ibykos. *Unknown, Greek.* GrAn, *tr.* by Peter Jay

I celebrate the personality of Jack! Jack and Jill. Charles Battell Loomis. DNAP

I celebrate thirty years. Marina Ivanovna Tsvetayeva. *See* Desk.

I celebrated this day in March. Juhan Viiding, *Estonian.* CEEP, *tr.* by Ivar Ivask

I chanced upon a new book yesterday. To Edward FitzGerald. Robert Browning. NAEL-2; OxBSP

I chanced upon an early walk to spy. The Orchard and the Heath. George Meredith. OBNC

I, Chang P'ing-tzu, had traversed the Nine Wilds and seen their wonders. The Bones of Chuang Tzu. Chang Heng, *Chinese.* AWP, *tr.* by Arthur Waley

I change, and so do women too. Written on a Looking-Glass. *Unknown.* FaBoEE

I changed a grown man's clothes on a stripped ward. In a Building Named for a Governor. Christopher L. Dornin. CRP

I charge you, O daughters of Jerusalem, if ye find my beloved, that ye tell him, that I am sick of love. (LL) I am come into my garden, my sister, my spouse. Bible, O.T. OBVE; TOF

I charge you, O winds of the West, O. Mathilde Blind. TrJP *Fr.* Love in Exile.

I charm thy life. Kehama's Curse. Robert Southey. NOBRP; OBNC *Fr.* The Curse of Kehama.

I check my parents' house while they're abroad. Julia Alvarez. CrSp

I Ching. Diane Di Prima. SeSe

I Ching, The. *Unknown, Chinese.*
   "Marrying maiden / Undertakings bring misfortune, The." PFTM, *tr.* by Cary F. Baynes *and* Richard Wilhelm

I choose a place that is unfrequented by men. (LL) Madly Singing in the Mountains. Po Chü-i, *Chinese.* BLT; ChiP, *tr.* by Arthur Waley

I choose not to walk among ghosts. Antigone VI. Herbert Martin. PoBA

I chopped down the house that you had been saving to live in next summer. Variations on a Theme by William Carlos Williams. Kenneth Koch. BXAP; KaS; NBLV; NIP-4; NoAM; NoP-4; PmAP; PoM; PoPoPo

I chose the blonde from the chemist's, thirty-six. Happening at Sordid Creek. Peter Porter. NoAM

I chose the book haphazard. Reading Aloud to My Father. Jane Kenyon. BAP-96

I clasp in the hot pit and bed. Memorial Couplets for the Dying Ego. George Barker. EBEV

I clasp them, is because they die. (LL) Mimnermus in Church. William Johnson Cory. NOBE; OBEV

I clearly hear the crowing of a rooster. I Don't Know That Man. Jan Polkowski, *Polish.* AF, *tr.* by Michael March *and* Jaroslaw Anders

I Climb That Barren Ridge. *Unknown, Chinese.* CoBCP, *tr.* by Burton Watson

I climb the black rock mountain. Where Mountain Lion Lay [*or* Laid] Down with Deer. Leslie Marmon Silko. ImGa; Poetr; TRP; VoR; WPOW

I climb the cold mountain by. View from the Cliffs. Tu Mu, *Chinese.* OHMPC, *tr.* by Kenneth Rexroth

I climb the hill: from end to end. Tennyson. EBVV; FHYEP; PoEL-5 *Fr.* In Memoriam A. H. H.

I climb the road to Cold Mountain. *Unknown, Chinese.* CoBCP, *tr.* by Burton Watson

I CLIMB to the ridge of the Pei-mang Hills. The Ruins of Lo-yang. Ts'ao Chih, *Chinese.* ChiP, *tr.* by Arthur Waley

I climbed a hill as light fell short. The Song of Honor [*or* Honour]. Ralph Hodgson. MoBrPo

I climbed through woods in the hour-before-dawn dark. The Horses. Ted Hughes. NoAM

I climbed towards you on a ray of moonlight. Fantasy under the Moon. Emmanuel Boundzekei-Dongala, *French.* PBMAP; TTY, *tr.* by Gerald Moore *and* Ulli Beier

I cling and swing. The Fifteen Acres. James Stephens. BoTP

I cling to this crippled tree. The Rivers. Giuseppe Ungaretti, *Italian.* PFTM, *tr.* by Allen Mandelbaum

I close my eyes. Tanka. Ishikawa Takuboku, *Japanese.* MJT, *tr.* by Ueda, Makoto

I close my eyes and bow my head. Talking to God. Garry Cleveland Myers. CTV

I close the book in my hands. Chang Yü. *Fr.* Paintings. CoBLCP, *tr.* by Jonathan Chaves

I close the book on *Crime and Punishment.* Crime and Punishment. Paul Lake. RA

I closed my book to listen. Church Bells. Clara Ann Thompson. CBWP-2

I closed my eyes as I sat in the jet. Day Flight. Jack Davis. CBAP

I Closed My Eyes To-Day and Saw. William Force Stead. OBMV

I collide with sun and foam, a fierce. L'Agulhas, A Walk. Wilma Stockenström, *Afrikaans.* PeSAV, *tr.* by Rosa Keet

I come alone. To surprise you. Visit. James Welch. AmPA

I come among the peoples like a shadow. Hunger. Laurence Binyon. NTP; OxBTC

I come back to the cottage in. Only Years. Kenneth Rexroth. TAP

I come back to the geography of it. Maximus, to Gloucester, Letter 27. Charles Olson. NOBA; PoE *Fr.* The Maximus Poems.

I come back to try to remember the faces she saw every day. The Mad Druggest. Robert Penn Warren. *Fr.* Tale of Time. LCAP-2

I come crying / dry leaves. Clinton. Sterling Plumpp. BkSV *Fr.* Clinton.

I come every day. It's Me Again, God. Helen Steiner Rice. CTV

I Come from a South. Ruy Duarte de Carvalho. PBMAP

I come from Alabama [with my Banjo on my knee]. Oh! Susanna. Stephen Collins Foster. APN-2; OBAL

I come from alcohol. Genealogy. Joan Larkin. LoHo

I come from far away. I have forgotten my country. Foreign Woman. Rosario Castellanos, *Spanish.* WPOW, *tr.* by J. M. Cohen

I come from haunts of coot and hern. The Brook. Tennyson. BoTP; CTV; ChAP; EBEvV; FHYEP; FaBoBe *Fr.* The Brook; An Idyl. OxAEP-2

I come from nothing. A Song of Derivations. Alice Thompson Meynell. CABP

I come from Salem County. Cowboy Song. Charles Causley. PoRA

I come from the city of Boston. Boston. John Collins Bossidy, *also at. to* Samuel C. Bushnell. FaBoEE; NBLV; OBAL; OBCoV; OxBoLi; PeLV

I Come from the Nigger Yard. Martin Carter.

"I come from the nigger yard of yesterday." PBCV

I come home at the end of four years of research. Rice. Chemmanam Chacko, *Malayalam.* OMIP, *tr.* by K. Ayyappa Paniker

I come home from you through the early light of spring. Adrienne Rich. BoWoP; CPO *Fr.* Twenty one Love Poems. GLP

I come home in the evening. Song to be Shouted Out. Nissim Ezekiel. OBCoV *Fr.* Songs for Nandu Bhende.

I come into the room The room stands waiting. Breaking Open. Muriel Rukeyser. AF

I come, my bonnie Annie! (LL) The Trumpeter of Fyvie. *Unknown.* ESPB; OxBB

I come of a mighty race. Hebrews. James Oppenheim. TrJP

I come off a little bit ventilated. Wings. John Godfrey. PmAP

I come out of a California orange grove. Smudging. Diane Wakoski. AmPA

I come quietly. Tree Stillness. Karen L. Mitchell. GT

I come the rushing wind that shook the place. The Promise. Jones Very. NCAP

I Come to Bury Caesar. Sydney Justin Harris. PoA

I come to read them poems. In White America. Lucille Clifton. LTA

I Come to Supplicate. Simeon ben, of Mainz Isaac ben Abun, *Hebrew.* TrJP, *tr.* by Nina Davis Salaman

I come to tell you that my son is dead. The Prince. Edgar Bowers. CoAmPo

I come to the fear of love. The Fear of Love. Wendell Berry. EC2

I come to the simplest things. The Retired Pilot to Himself. Walter McDonald. CDa

I come / to the White Painted Woman. Puberty Rite Dance Song (Traditional). *Unknown, Apache Indian.* BoWoP, *tr.* by Willis Barnstone

I come to the, O God long since forgot. Before the Statue of Apollo. Saul Tchernichovsky, *Hebrew.* TrJP, *tr.* by L. V. Snowman

I come to visit here this afternoon. Dropping By the Guava Graveyard in So'n-La. Trần Huy Liệu, *Vietnamese.* AVP, *tr.* by Huỳnh Sanh Thông

I come to White Painted Woman. Song for Girls' Puberty Rites. *Chiricahua Apache Oral Tradition.* PaTW, *tr.* by Morris Edward Opler

I come to you. Prayer of a Woman in Charge of Berry Picking in Knights Inlet. *Unknown.* WPoS

I come to you with the vertigoes of the source. Yvonne Caroutch, *French.* BoWoP, *tr.* by David Cloutier

I come tonight to sing you songs. Korinna, *Greek.* InMo, *tr.* by Sam Hamill

I come upon it suddenly, alone. A Country Pathway. James Whitcomb Riley. CA

I come with my pen. Island Muse. John C. M. Lyons. NBrP

I confess my ashamed desire. (LL) Why Is God Love, Jack? Allen Ginsberg. CLPP; FTOS

I confess, my friend, I am puzzled. (LL) Meditatio. Ezra Pound. FaBoCh; OBAL; PBMP

I conjour hem in the name of the Fader, and Sone. *Unknown.* MiEL

I, Conscience, know this Mother-Wit me it taught. The Age of Reason. William Langland. NOCV *Fr.* The Vision of Piers Plowman.

I consecrate to thee. (LL) Rose Aylmer. Walter Savage Landor. AWP; BoLoP; CABP; CH; EnLoPo; GBL; GLoP; HAP; HoPM; NAEL-2; NOBE; NOBRP; NoP-4; OBEV; OBNC; OxAEP-2; PoEL-4; Poetr; Ro; SCGP; TFi; UnPo; WeW-3

I consider I really am through. Limerick. Elizabeth H. Lister. PeLi

I consider myself a poet but im not reading poetry as you see. A Private Occasion in a Public Place. David Antin. PmAP

I could be eased easier than the apple Eve. A Mourning. Vassar Miller. NMM-2

I could be in Paris or Vienna. "Naum Korzhavin," *Russian.* TCRP, *tr.* by Albert C. Todd

I could become a great grinning host. Poem. Jack Kerouac. CLPP

I could bring You Jewels—had I a mind to. Emily Dickinson. TAP

I could call to my support a dozen trees. Goodbye. Virgil Teodorescu, *Romanian.* CEEP, *tr.* by Stavros Deligiorgis

I could divide a leaf. Propositions. Phyllis Webb. MoCV

I could do nothing: nothing. Do you. The Child Taken from the Mother. Minnie Bruce Pratt. GLP

I could draw its map by heart. Amor Loci. W. H. Auden. NOCV

I could go on writing like this forever. (LL) Squeal. Louis Simpson. BXAP; UnPo

I COULD have a job, but am too lazy to choose it;. Lazy Man's Song. Po Chü-i, *Chinese.* ChiP; OBVE, *tr.* by Arthur Waley

I could have been Lord Dacre or a balalaika-maker. Peter Norman. UV

I could have loved the winter. Snow. Innokenty Fiodorovich Annensky, *Russian.* TCRP, *tr.* by Lubov Yakovleva with Daniel Weissbort

I could have painted pictures like that youth's. Pictor Ignotus. Robert Browning. CTC

I could have wept and howled. Song of the Unloved. *Unknown, Sotho.* PeSA, *tr.* by Jack Cope *and* Dan Kunene

I could kill you right now. Lobo. Charles Lillard. NOBC

I could love thee till I die. The Platonic Lady. John Wilmot, 2d Earl of Rochester. NOSC

I could no deeper love. (LL) Song: Love Still Has Something of the Sea Sir Charles Sedley. GBL; NOBE; OxAEP-1

I could not dig. A Dead Statesman. Rudyard Kipling. FaBoEE; NBLV; OPOU; PoFWW; PoWW *Fr.* Epitaphs of the War [1914–1918]. OBWP

I could not hope / to touch the sky. Sappho, *Greek.* BoWoP, *tr.* by Willis Barnstone

I could not look on Death, which being known. The Coward. Rudyard Kipling. FaBoEE; FaBoTw; PeFWW *Fr.* Epitaphs of the War [1914–1918]. OBWP

I could not name a single blessing. Neither Shadow of Turning. Jack R. Clemo. NOCV

I could not sleep for thinking of the sky. John Masefield. LiTM *Fr.* Lollingdon Downs.

I could not swallow the lake. (LL) Swallow the Lake. Clarence Major. FTOS; GT; NAAAL; PmAP; PoBA; WeT

I Could Not though I Would. George Gascoigne. PoEL-1

I could resign that eye of blue. To Cloe. Martial, *Latin.* AWP; NBLV, *tr.* by Thomas Moore

I could say it's the happiest period of my life. The Ongoing Story. John Ashbery. HCAP

I could take the Harlem night. Juke Box Love Song. Langston Hughes. NAAAL; PoBA; SAmP; TTTS

I could use cool water or strong coffee. A Bullet. Sandor Csoori, *Hungarian.* CEEP, *tr.* by Nicholas Kolumban

I could wish to be dead! The Tragic Mary Queen of Scots, II. "Michael Field." OBMV

I couldn't do it again. The Garden. Louise Glück. NoP-4

I couldn't explain it to my husband. The Continental Divide. Maria Flook. WeT

I couldn't stand sitting around reading. Can't Stand It. Vladimir Mayakovsky, *Russian.* TCRP, *tr.* by Bernard Meares

I couldn't touch a stop and turn a screw. Thirty Bob a Week. John Davidson. CABP; EBEV; EBVV; FaBoPV; FaBoTw; ImPo; NOBE; NOBVV; OAEL-2; OBNC; OxBS; OxBTC

I couldn't wait. My childhood angered me. The Wise Child. Edward Lucie-Smith. PBCV

I Counsel You Beware. A. E. Housman. PFE

I count black-lipped. Come Back Blues. Michael S. Harper. PoBA

I count the years by Junes that flush our laurel. To One Who Waits. Katharine Lee Bates. CPO

I, Crank Cuffin, swear to be. The Oath of the Canting Crew. *Unknown.* CBNP

I crave an ampler, worthier sphere. Anno 1829. Heinrich Heine, *German.* AWP; OBVE, *tr.* by Charles Stuart Calverley

I craved for flash of eye and sword. Dreams. Israel Zangwill. TrJP

I crawl, I creep; my Christ, I come. To Christ. Robert Herrick. CavPo

I crawl up the couch leg feeling. Whose Scene? Ruth Stone. BoWoP

I cremated Sam McGee! (LL) The Cremation of Sam McGee. Robert W. Service. NOBC; OBCoV; OBNV; PoLF; SAGP

I cried to dream again. (LL) To Dream Again. William Shakespeare. OxAEP-1; RB

I cried unto God with my voice, even unto God with my voice. Psalm 77. Bible, O.T. AWP Fr. Psalms.

I cross a stream, cross another stream. Seeking out Hermit Hu. Kao Ch'i, Chinese. CoBLCP, tr. by Jonathan Chaves

I cross the river to pluck hibiscus. Unknown, Chinese. SuSp, tr. by Dell R. Hales

I crossed sand-hills. Euripides. OBCVT, tr. by Hilda Doolittle Fr. Iphigeneia at Aulis.

I crouch over my radio. Speech. Henry Taylor. NBLV

I crowd all earth into a traveller's eye. Shillong. Bernard Gutteridge. PoWW

I cry. The Woman's Mourning Song. Bell Hooks. ISC

I cry:/ but you want comforting. Quatrain. Jelaluddin Rumi, Persian. ArPe, tr. by Omar S. Pound

I cry I cry. No Categories! Stevie Smith. NoP-4

I cry to you beyond upon this bitter air. (LL) Immortal Autumn. Archibald MacLeish. CMoP; MoAmPo; NAAL-2

I cry your mercy, pity, love!—ay, love! To Fanny. Keats. BoLoP; EBEV; Son

I cupboard these pickled peaches in Time's despite. (LL) Homework. Mona Van Duyn. FFC; VCAP

I curse my bearing, childhood, youth. John Millington Synge. FaBoEE

I curse the optimistic views of Haig. Scribbled at a Cabinet Meeting. Sir Edward Carlson. FaBoVe

I cursed thee oft, I pity now thy case. Sonnet 46. Sir Philip Sidney. Fr. Astrophil and Stella. AAS; SiPS

I cut a stick for my love. It is too early. I Would Call It Derangement. Gerald Stern. PuP-17

I cut in two / A long November night. Hwang Chin-i, Korean. PBWP, tr. by Peter H. Lee

I cut the deck. A Valentine for Ben Franklin Who Drives a Truck in California. Diane Wakoski. NoAM

I damn such fools!—Go, go you're bit. (LL) The Day of Judgement. Jonathan Swift. BIrV; ChIV-1; NOBE; NOEC; OAEL-1; OBSV; SCGP

I dance and dance without any feet—. Spells. James Reeves. NTP

I dance on your paper. Jack o' the Inkpot. Algernon Blackwood. BoTP

I danced on "Shop Around." Boppin' is Safer than Grindin'. Thulani Davis. GT

I Danced to the Rumble of the Drum. Elevena Burbank. AiP

I dare not ask a kiss[e]. To Electra. Robert Herrick. CaPo; HoPM; OBEV

I dare not, faith I dare not pipe at Noon. Theocritus. OBCVT, tr. by Thomas Creech Fr. Idyll 1.

I, dark in light, exposed. Fr. The Blindness of Samson. ImPo Fr. Samson Agonistes. FHYEP; OAEL-1; PoEL-3

I deal in wisdom, not in dry desire. Supper with Lindsay. Theodore Roethke. FP

I declare myself. Nu-plastik Fanfare Red. Judith Rodriguez. BMAP

I dedicate this poem. Daughters. "Astra." BrRo

I defy you Wallace Stevens. Shirley Lim. UnSA

I delight in the prime of a boy of twelve. Epigram. Strato, Greek. GrAn, tr. by Thomas Meyer

I demand a thatched house. The Poet's Request. Unknown, Irish. BIrV, tr. by John Montague

I demand that the human race. Poem. Jack Kerouac. CLPP

I depend on the stars. For Sleep. Larry Eigner. FTOS

I descend on my love. How God Comes to the Soul. Mechthild von Magdeburg, German. WPoS, tr. by Oliver Davies

I desire that my body be. When I Am Dead. George MacBeth. OxBTC

I despise love. What weighty God. Alcaeus, Greek. InMo, tr. by Sam Hamill

I despise my friends more than you. To an Enemy. Maxwell Bodenheim. TrJP

I despise neo-epic verse sagas. Callimachus, Greek. GrAn, tr. by Peter Jay ("I despise neo-epic sagas: I cannot.") OBCVT, tr. by Peter Jay

I did but look and love awhile. The Enchantment. Thomas Otway. OBEV

I did but prompt the age to quit their [or thir] clogs. On the Detraction Which Followed upon My Writing Certain Treatises. Milton. FaBoPV; NoP-4; Son

I did expect a ring. (LL) Hope. George Herbert. ChIV-2; FMP; PoEL-2; WeW-3

I did my best; / farewell. (LL) The Sparrow. William Carlos Williams. InPS-3; LCAP-2; Poetr; VGW

I did my best when I was young. Fair Trade. Gary Soto. BAP-96

I did not cry, my good mother, the song in my hand burst in tears. The Silent Words. Haim Guri, Hebrew. MHP, tr. by Ruth Finer Mintz

I did not fall from the sky. The Women of Dan Dance with Swords in Their Hands to Mark the Time When They Were Warriors. Audre Lorde. NAAL-2; NALW; NoAM

I did not grow up among paintings. Nostalgia. Bin Ramke. MT

I did not know death was so strange. (LL) The Child Dying. Edwin Muir. FaBoTw; GTBS-P; PoWW; RB

I did not know she'd take it so. Under the Mistletoe. Countee Cullen. PChr

I Did Not Know the Truth of Growing Trees. Delmore Schwartz. LiTM

I did not know what I was doing. (LL) Confession to J. Edgar Hoover. James Wright. CAPP-1; CoAmPo

I did not know where you kept your heart. A "Case of Assault." Lydia Stephanou, Modern Greek. BoWoP, tr. by Kimon Friar

I did not live until this time. To My Excellent Lucasia, On Our Friendship. Katherine Philips. CPO; LW; MeLP; NALW; NOSC; NoP-4; PBRV; PEW; WPE; WPOW

I did not lose my heart in summer's even. A. E. Housman. LiTM

I did not love him for myself alone. Trinity. "Michael Field." VWP

I did not manage to save. Jerzy Ficowski, Polish. HP; PoSu, tr. by Keith Bosley and Krystyna Wandycz

I did not notice. Franz Wright. LCAP-2

I did not see Lannes at Ratisbon. Heroes. Sorley MacLean. FaBoTC

I did not see the frigate Constitution. Resurrection. Richard Palmer Blackmur. PoA

I did not stand at the altar, I stood. The Wedding Vow. Sharon Olds. ITG

I did not take the road to the capital. Tune: "Partridge Sky"—Written at the Po-shan Monastery. Hsin Ch'i-chi, Chinese. SuSp, tr. by Irving Y. Lo

I did not think that I should find them there. The Clerks. Edwin Arlington Robinson. APN-2; MoAmPo; NAAL-2; PoEL-5

I did not want to be old Mr. Uncle Dog; the Poet at 9. Robert Sward. CoAP; VGW

I did not weep my father. May Sarton. MDDM Fr. Of Grief.

I didn't come out my mummy's tummy. What Jenny Knows. Jackie Kay. NOxBChV

. . . I didn't expect you today. Letter. Iosif Pavlovich Utkin, Russian. TCRP, tr. by Lubov Yakovleva

I didn't get much sleep last night. Underwear. Lawrence Ferlinghetti. OBAL

I didn't give her a goodbye kiss. Grandmother Grace. Ronald Wallace. Poetr

I didn't have anything to think about. (LL) You ask me what I thought about. Kenneth Rexroth. APSN; PiM

I Didn't Know. Ellen Bass. NMM-2

I didn't know where the temple was. Visiting the Temple of Accumulated Fragrance. Wang Wei, Chinese. CoBCP, tr. by Burton Watson

I didn't like the way he went away. The Smile. Robert Frost. Fr. The Hill Wife. CMoP; HAP; InPS-3; LiTM; NoP-4; RACG

I didn't make you know how glad I was. A Servant to Servants. Robert Frost. CMoP; NAAL-2

I didn't mind dying—it wasn't that at all. Harvard '61: Battle Fatigue. Robert Penn Warren. Fr. Two Studies in Idealism: Short Survey of American and Human History. CBCWP

I didn't start taking myself seriously as a poet. The Bite. Gerald Stern. APAD

I didnt thing I'd. I Was Surprised to Find Myself Out Here & Acting like a Crow. Unknown, Seneca Indian. STP, tr. by Jerome Rothenberg and Johnny John

I didn't want a monument. The Invasion of Grenada. William Daniel Ehrhart. CDa

—I didn't want this, not. Marina Ivanovna Tsvetayeva. TCRP Fr. I didn't want this, not. OBVE Fr. Poem of the End.

I die, and yet not dies in me. Dhu 'l-Nún, Persian. TOF, tr. by A. J. Arberry

I Die because I Do Not Die. Saint, of Avila Theresa, Spanish. TOF, tr. by E. Allison Peers

I die for Your holy word without regret. Elegy. Antonio Enriquez Gomez, Spanish. TrJP

I die I die the Mother said. The Grey Monk. William Blake. PeECV

I die / If I but spy. Upon Julia. Ernest Radford. BXAP

I died as mineral and became a plant. Jelaluddin Rumi, Persian. TOF, tr. by R. A. Nicholson

I died for Beauty—but was scarce. Emily Dickinson. APN-2; AWP; BoWoP; ImPo; LiTM; MeMAP; MoAmPo; NAAL-2; NAAL-3; NAWM-2; NOBA; PBMP; SAmP; SDW

I Died True. Francis Beaumont and John Fletcher. See Aspatia's Song.

I died with [or at] the first blow and was buried. Autobiography. Dan Pagis, Hebrew. AF; PoSu; VCWP, tr. by Stephen Mitchell; IP, tr. by Warren Bargad and Stanley F. Chyet

I dine at Blenheim twice a week. (LL) On the Hon. George Nathaniel Curzon, Commoner of Balliol. John William Mackail *and* Cecil Arthur Spring-Rice. FaBoEE; NOBL; OBCoV; PeLV

I disapprove even of eloquent / Myrtis. Korinna, *Greek.* WPOW, *tr. by* Richmond Lattimore

I discover, remaindered from yesterday. The Strand. Michael Longley. IIP

I discovered the evidence. Crazy Horse Speaks. Sherman Alexie. UnSA

I discovered the sweet lovely lady. Albrecht von Johannsdorf, *German.* GePo, *tr. by* Sylvia Stevens

I Discuss the Past and Not the Present. What Men of Today Are Worth Discussing? May the Men of the Past Not Blame Me for My Discussion of Them. Chin Nung, *Chinese.*

"Who bought a mountain and became a hermit there?" CoBLCP, *tr. by* Jonathan Chaves

I DISMOUNT from my horse at the Hsi-lin Temple. Visiting the Hsi-lin Temple. Po Chü-i, *Chinese.* ChiP, *tr. by* Arthur Waley

I do be thinking God must laugh. Boys. Winifred M. Letts. TIRV

I do believe. (LL) Dingty diddlety. Mother Goose. FaBoVe; OxNR

I do believe that die I must. His Creed. Robert Herrick. BeJo

I do but ask that you be always fair. Edna St. Vincent Millay. Son

I do[e] but name thee Pembroke, and I find. To William, Earl[e] of Pembroke. Ben Jonson. SeCP

I do confess thou'rt smooth and fair. To His Forsaken Mistress. Sir Robert Ayton. GBL; OBEV

I do direct the night. Portrait of Myself with Arshile Gorky and Gertrude Stein. Jerome Rothenberg. FTOS

"I do guess / that's genius for you." June Jordan. *See* A Poem about Intelligence for My Brothers and Sisters.

I do in thee delight. (LL) Christ's Reply. Edward Taylor. NAAL-1; NAAL-3; PoEL-3

I do know this. The Time #? Esther Iverem. WWSi

I do like a little bit of butter to my bread! (LL) The King's Breakfast. A. A. Milne. OBCoV; OTCP; OxBChV

"I Do Like To Be Beside the Seaside." Dame Edith Sitwell. PFTM *Fr.* Façade.

I Do Love My Charlie So. Zelda Sayre Fitzgerald. AiP

I do my best to smile at spring, small flowers. White Days. Reginald Shepherd. GT

I do not ask—for you are fair. The Complaisant Swain. Ovid. AWP, *tr. by* F. A. Wright *Fr.* Amores.

I do not believe that David killed Goliath. Charles Reznikoff. ChIV-1

I do not call it his sign. Mahadevi, *Kannada.* WPoS, *tr. by* Jane Hirshfield

I do not care if. *Unknown, Japanese.* OHMPJ, *tr. by* Kenneth Rexroth

I do not catch these subtle shades of feeling. The Wife of All Ages. Edith Nesbit. VWP

I do not complain of suffering for Love. Knowing Love in Herself. Hadewijch, *Flemish.* WPoS, *tr. by* Oliver Davies

I do not consider myself worth counting. Takeko Kujo, *Japanese.* WPJ, *tr. by* Kenneth Rexroth *and* Ikuko Atsumi

I do not count the hours I spend. Waldeinsamkeit. Ralph Waldo Emerson. APN-1; NOBA; PAR

I do not doubt you would have liked. Mother's Day. Daisy Zamora, *Spanish.* LoL, *tr. by* Margaret Randall

I do not dream of Sussex downs. Home Thoughts. Denis Glover. PeNZ

I do not enjoy. Rufinus, *Greek.* GrAn, *tr. by* Alan Marshfield

I do not feel the peace of the saints. A Bird in the Hand. Vassar Miller. CRP

I do not grudge them: Lord, I do not grudge. The Mother. Padraic Pearse. TIRV

I do not hold a mirage in my hand—. What's Not in the Heart. Abba Kovner, *Hebrew.* AF, *tr. by* Shirley Kaufman

I Do Not Know. Yong-un Han, *Korean.* CKP, *tr. by* Jaihiun Kim

I do not know. Holocaust 1944. Anne Ranasinghe. HP

I do not know: I only feel it, and I'm torn in two. Catullus. *See* Carmen 85.

I do not know if the color of the day. A Poem of Attrition. Etheridge Knight. GT

I do not know more than the Sea tells me. Achilles' Song. Robert Duncan. FTOS

I do not know much about gods; but I think that the river. The Dry Salvages. T. S. Eliot. AiP; NoP-4; OxBA *Fr.* Four Quartets.

I do not know / One of my sex; no woman's face remember. Shakespeare. OxBM *Fr.* The Tempest. OAEL-1

I do not know the power of my hand. When I Know the Power of my Black Hand. Lance Jeffers. ISC; NBV

I do not know what promise it makes to him. (LL) Birth of Love. Robert Penn Warren. GEA; UnPo; VCAP

I do not know where I have been. Hell, Well, Heaven. Mongane Wally Serote. PBMAP

I do not know which god sent me. At the Gates. Kofi Awoonor. PBMAP; VCWP *Fr.* Night of My Blood (1971).

I do not like my state of mind. Symptom. Dorothy Parker. LW

I do not like the empty vocabulary. In the Dunes. Aleksandr Blok, *Russian.* TCRP, *tr. by* Geoffrey Thurley

I do not like the other sort. An Ulsterman. "Lynn Doyle." TIRV

I do not like the way you slide. Egg Thoughts. Russell Hoban. NTCP; OTCP

I do not live in the depthless cool. The Turning of the Year. Delaina Thomas. OpBo

I do not look for love that is a dream. Christina Rossetti. GBL

I do not love [or like] thee, Doctor Fell. Doctor Fell. Thomas Brown, *after the Latin of* Martial. AWP; FaBoEE; NBLV; OBCoV; OBCVT; OBVE; OxNR

I do not love thee!—no! I do not love thee! Caroline Elizabeth Norton. OBEV

I do not love to wed. The Poet Loves a Mistress, but Not to Marry. Robert Herrick. CaPo

I do not mean the symbol. The Woman Who Could Not Live With Her Faulty Heart. Margaret Atwood. LCAP-2

I do not regret, complain, or weep. Sergey Aleksandrovich Yesenin, *Russian.* TCRP, *tr. by* Daniel Weissbort

I do not sleep at night. Night-Piece. Raymond R. Patterson. PoBA

I do not thank Thee, Lord. Thanks Be to God. Janie Alford. PoToHe

I do not think Grandmother or Grandfather. Favorite Grandson Braid. Phillip William George. VoR

I do not think of you lying in the wet clay. In Memory of My Mother. Patrick Kavanagh. BIrV; CIP-2; LBC; MoP; NoAM; RaBo

I do not think that skies and meadows are. Reciprocity. John Drinkwater. PoA

I do not think the ending can be right. But That Is Another Story. Donald Justice. CoAP; NoP-4

I do not understand. The Unknown. Elmer Osborn Laughlin. BLPA

I do not visit his grave. He is not there. Peachstone. Dannie Abse. OxBC; WeW-3

I do not want a gaping crowd. When I Am Dead. James Edward Wilson. PoLF

I do not want a plain box, I want a sarcophagus. Last Words. Sylvia Plath. FYAP

I do not want only. Poem. Colleen Thibaudeau. NOBC

I do not want to be reflective any more. Wolves. Louis MacNeice. NoAM; OxBTC

I do not want to pour out my heart any more. Marcus Aurelius. Charles Hubert Sisson. OxBC

I do not want what. My Own Hallelujahs. Zack Gilbert. PoBA

I do not waste what is wild. Empty Kettle. Louis Oliver. HATNAP

I do not wear black for you. For My Neverborn. Nancy Shiffrin. EC3

I do not wish to know. After the Persian. Louise Bogan. NYBP; PoA

I do not wish you joy without a sorrow. A Birthday Wish. Dorothy Nell McDonald. PoToHe

I do remember some things. Manna. James Tate. GM

I do seem to zee Grammer as she did use. Grammer's Shoes. William Barnes. EBVV; EnVR

I do something consciously. 6th Dance—Doing Things With Pencils—17-18 February 1964. Jackson MacLow. PmAP

I do the black boot stomp. Foot Fire Burn Dance. Natasha Le Bel. BAP-96

I do tricks in order to know. With My Crowbar Key. William Stafford. CoAmPo

I done been 'roun' to evvy spot. Belle Layotte. George Washington Cable. APN-2

I Done Got So Thirsty That My Mouth Waters at the Thought of Rain. Patricia Jones. BlSi

I done try go to church, I done go for court. One Wife for One Man. Frank Aig-Imoukhuede. PBA

I don't as they put it believe in god. Dorothee Sölle. CrSp

I don't believe in becoming a Buddha. Drinking Wine. Mo Shih-lung, *Chinese.* CoBLCP, *tr. by* Jonathan Chaves

I don't believe in God and fate. Bulat Shalvovich Okudzhava, *Russian.* TCRP, *tr. by* Deming Brown

I Don't Believe in Human-tales. Brian Patten. OTCP

I don't believe there's such a thing. I Don't Believe in Human-tales. Brian Patten. OTCP

I don't belong this far north. Washington. Lorna Dee Cervantes. *Fr.* Visions of Mexico While at a Writing Symposium in Port Townsend, Washington. NoAM

I don't care. *Unknown, Japanese.* OHMPJ, *tr. by* Kenneth Rexroth

I don't care if you're married, I'll still get you. *Unknown.* STP *Fr.* Kiowa "49" Songs.

I don't care what you say. The Rain. Richard Edwards. AYFP

I don't complain that time passes too soon. Tune: "Green Jade Cup." Kung Tzu-chen, *Chinese*. SuSp, *tr. by* An-van Tang

I don't dare start thinking in the morning. Blues at Dawn. Langston Hughes. SAmP

I don't enclose the universe in my grasp. Vladimir Shchirovsky, *Russian*. TCRP, *tr. by* Albert C. Todd

I don't feel like reading another book. Yang Wan-li. SuSp, *tr. by* Jonathan Chaves *Fr.* Songs of Depression.

I don't give a damn. Croon. Langston Hughes. PFTM

I don't give a damn if some Thracian ape strut. Archilochus, *Greek*. GrAn, *tr. by* Stuart Silverman

I don't give a duck. (LL) Poem in Time of Winter. Ray Mathew. NOBAu; OBCoV

I don't go much on religion. Little Breeches. John Milton Hay. FaBoBe

I don't have any place to come up through. Shaman Song. Luswat, *Tlingit Indian*. STP, *tr. by* James Koller

I Don't Have the Energy. Artie Gold. NOBC

I don't imagine I'll manage to express Sunyata. I Fail as a Dharma Teacher. Diane Di Prima. BB

I don't know. After Seeing Paintings in a Small Book by T. C. Cannon (1946-1978). Alice Sadongei. HATNAP

I don't know. A Poem against Rats. Fred Levinson. AmPA

I don't know about you,/ but I'm sick of good poems. A. R. Ammons. HCAP *Fr.* Sphere.

I don't know any greatest treat. The Parterre. E. Harriet Palmer. NOBL; PeLV

I don't know anyone at the table except. Strange Thanksgiving. Tess Gallagher. NAmP90

I don't know anything about God but what the human record tells. Even on Sunday. Robin Blaser. FTOS

I don't know as I get what D.H. Lawrence is driving at. Poem. Frank O'Hara. LCAP-2

I don't know, but my folks say. Titanic, a Toast. *Unknown*. CBNP

I don't know how he came. Osawatomie. Carl Sandburg. CMoP; OxBA

I don't know how it was. Mystery. "Yehoash," *Yiddish*. TrJP, *tr. by* Marie Syrkin

I don't know if he is rare on these northern lakes. The Pelican. Greg Kuzma. AmPA

I don't know if I can bear this suddenly. Poem. Paul Zweig. WeT

I Don't Know if Mount Zion would recognize itself. Abba Kovner, *Hebrew*. IP, *tr. by* Warren Bargad *and* Stanley F. Chyet

I don't know if, when you were young. Twenty-Eight Lines for My Wife. Yên Ba, *Vietnamese*. AVP, *tr. by* Huỳnh Sanh Thông

I don't know man trust is a precious thing. Man in a Window. Ralph Angel. NAmP90

I don't know politics but I know the names. Introduction. Kamala Das. NALW; WPOW

I don't know somehow it seems sufficient. Gravelly Run. A. R. Ammons. CoAP; NAAL-2; NoAM; PoA; VCAP

I Don't Know That Man. Jan Polkowski, *Polish*. AF, *tr. by* Michael March *and* Jaroslaw Anders

I don't know the language. Homesick. Else Lasker-Schüler, *German*. PBWP, *tr. by* Michael Hamburger

I don't know the wisdom others seem to need. Konstantin Dmitrievich Balmont, *Russian*. TCRP, *tr. by* April FitzLyon

I don't know what it was you gave my husband to eat. The Horse butcher. Pierre McOrlan, *French*. MFP, *tr. by* Martin Sorrell

I don't know what the final buzzer means. Triple Overtime. Lucinda Roy. GT

I don't know whether the gray deer knows. The Deer. "Asya," *Yiddish*. CEEP, *tr. by* Gabriel Preil *and* Howard Schwartz

I don't know who it is. The Lovely Étan. *Unknown*. NOIV

I don't know who that man is. Pilate's Wife. Nina Kossman. GI

I don't know why. The Writing in the Fire. Eugenijus Matuzeviius, *Lithuanian*. CEEP, *tr. by* Irene Pogoželskyte Suboczewski

I don't know why I'm so crazy. Why? Myra Cohn Livingston. CA

I don't know why you tell me I'm drunk. Toxaoci, *Tlingit Indian*. STP, *tr. by* James Koller

I don't know your stories. This one here. The Feud. Sydney Lea. RA

I Don't Let the Girls Worry My Mind. *Unknown*. AmFP

I Don't Like Beetles. Rose Fyleman. OxBChV

I Don't Like No Railroad Man. *Unknown*. AS

I don't like weddings. The Wedding in the Courthouse. Kathleen Norris. CrSp

I don't love flowers / I love women. The Lilac by the Museum on St. Wenceslas Square. Vitězslau Nezval, *Czech*. AF, *tr. by* Ewald Osers

I don't love paradise. Paradise and Hell. Võ Liêm So'n, *Vietnamese*. AVP, *tr. by* Huỳnh Sanh Thông

I don't love you. Imamu Amiri Baraka. NAAAL

I don't love you as if you were the salt-rose, topaz. Sonnet XVII. Pablo Neruda, *Spanish*. TTG, *tr. by* Stephen Mitchell

I don't mind dying. As Befits a Man. Langston Hughes. PFE

I don't mind eels. The Eel. Ogden Nash. NOxBChV; NTCP

I don't mind it so much any more. Uptown Love Poem. David St. John. WWSi

I don't / pity this man, I love him. Vanzetti. Charles Buckmaster. CBAP

I don't plow my southern acre. Thinking of the Way Home, a Song. Lo Yin, *Chinese*. SuSp, *tr. by* Geoffrey R. Waters

I don't refuse that kiss. Ammianus, *Greek*. InMo, *tr. by* Sam Hamill

I Don't Remember Anything of Then. Frank O'Hara. *Fr.* Ode to Michael Goldberg's Birth and Other Births. NeAP

I don't remember the name of the story. The Mystery of the Caves. Michael Waters. CMAP

I don't remember train whistles. A Narrative of the Life and Times of John Coltrane: Played by Himself. Michael S. Harper. MoNo; SeSe

I don't remember when. The Lost Girls. Linda Hogan. IFJA

I don't see my mother dancing. Legacy. Márton Kalász, *Hungarian*. CEEP, *tr. by* Jascha Kessler

I don't seek salvation in poetry. Khikhimora. Nikolai Ivanovich Glazkov, *Russian*. TCRP, *tr. by* Daniel Weissbort

I don't sleep. All night. Mirabai, *Hindi*. BoWoP, *tr. by* Willis Barnstone *and* Usha Nilsson

I don't think it important. The Beast Section. Welton Smith. PoBA

I don't think that I believe in "gay life." Sonnet No. 22. Mark Ameen. GLP

I don't travel much in these parts. Passing Ch'ien-hsi as Military Adviser in the Third Month of the Year Yi-ssu. T'ao Ch'ien, *Chinese*. SuSp, *tr. by* Eugene Eoyang

I don't understand it myself. Too Lazy to Write Poetry. Chu Yün-ming, *Chinese*. CoBLCP, *tr. by* Jonathan Chaves

I Don't Want Any More Visitors. Ingrid Jonker, *Afrikaans*. PeSA, *tr. by* Ingrid Jonker

I Don't Want to Be a Gambler. *Unknown*. AS

I don't want to be a nun. *Unknown*, *Spanish*. BoWoP, *tr. by* Willis Barnstone

I don't want to be a soldier. *Unknown*. NSI; PoWW *Fr.* Soldiers' Songs of the First World War.

("And———my bloody life away.") (LL) OBCoV

I don't want to hear you beg. Isn't It Funny? Essex Hemphill. GLP

I don't want to say anything about. For You. Lawrence Raab. CMAP

I don't want your greenback dollar. The Greenback Dollar. *Unknown*. AmFP

I doubt if ten men in all Tilbury Town. Edwin Arlington Robinson. PoEL-5 *Fr.* Captain Craig.

I doubt if the wind in your boots. Stiles. John Pudney. NYBP

I doubt if you knew. The Rescue. John Logan. CoAP; NYBP

I doubt not God is good, well-meaning, kind. Yet Do I Marvel. Countee Cullen. BPo; CrDW; GEA; NAAAL; NAAL-2; NoAM; PBMP; PFE; PoBA; SAGP; SSLK; Son; TAP; TTY

I drag a boat over the ocean. Lal Ded, *Kashmiri*. BoWoP; WPoS, *tr. by* Willis Barnstone

I drag my shirt across the floor. Eager Street. Kendra Kopelke. AiP

I drag the lawn chair. Camellias. Linda Pastan. IFJA

I dragged my steps across a desert bare. The Prophet. Aleksandr Sergeyevich Pushkin, *Russian*. NNPT, *tr. by* Frances Darwin Cornford *and* Esther Poliabowsky Salaman

I drank cool water from the fountain. The Raisin. Donald Hall. TAP

I drank firmly. His Father's Hands. Thomas Kinsella. PoE

I drank it when we met the gas / Beyond Gesthemane! Rudyard Kipling. *See* Gethsemane [1914–18].

I draw a line from. The Landscape. James Bertolino. CMAP

I draw hats on rabbits, sew women back. The Prestidigitator 2. Al Young. NBV

I dreaded that first Robin, so. Emily Dickinson. APN-2; AmPP; HAP; MeMAP; MoAmPo; NAAL-1; NAAL-3

I Dream I'm the Death of Orpheus. Adrienne Rich. NALW

I dream in the intimate semi-darkness of an afternoon. Visit. Léopold Sédar Senghor. PBMAP

I dream my love goes riding out. Song for a Dancer. Kenneth Rexroth. TAP

I dream of. Memory of a Dream From the Year 1963. Tadeusz Rózewicz, *Polish*. PoSu

I dream of a headless man. Green Martyrs. Richard Murphy. NOIV *Fr.* The Battle of Aughrim.

I dream of a red-rose tree. Women and Roses. Robert Browning. NAEL-2

I dream of coupling. Dream of Pairing. Ntozake Shange. GT

I dream / of embroidering / new skin. Nellie Wong. *See* Dreams in Harrison Railroad Park.

I dream of Jeanie with the light brown hair. Jeanie with the Light Brown Hair. Stephen Collins Foster. APN-2

I dream of journeys repeatedly. The Far Field. Theodore Roethke. ColAP; NAAL-2; NoAM *Fr.* North American Sequence.

I dream of St. Francis. Peter Orlovsky. BB

I dream of Serenity. I'm a Dreamer. Kattie M. Cumbo. BlSi

I dream of you to wake: would that I might. Christina Rossetti. *Fr.* Monna Innominata. BWW

I dream red dreams, an oasis of fire and light. Nellie Wong. MDDM *Fr.* Red Journeys.

I dream'd I walk'd in raptures high. Thomas Baker. BXAP *Fr.* The Steam Engine; or, The Power of the Flame.

I dream'd in a dream I saw a city invincible to the attacks of the whole of the rest of the earth. Walt Whitman. APN-1

I dream'd that, as I wander'd by the way. The Question. Shelley. CH; GTBS-P; OBEV

I dreamed a dream, and in my dream, I heard. The Snapping of the Bow. James David Corrothers. NAAAL

I dreamed a dream: I dreamt that I espied. Arthur Hugh Clough. NOBVV

I dreamed [*or* dreamt] a dream the other night. Lowlands. *Unknown.* OxBoLi

I dreamed a dream the other night, when everything was still. Prospecting Dream. *Unknown.* AmFP

I dreamed a dreary dream this night. The Braes of Yarrow. *Unknown.* ESPB; OxBB

I dreamed, and saw a modern Hell, more dread. The Pessimist's Vision. Constance Naden. VWP

I dreamed I called you on the telephone. For the Dead. Adrienne Rich. NAAL 2

I dreamed I held / A sword against my flesh. Kasa no Iratsume, *Japanese.* BoWoP; OHPI; WPOW, *tr. by* Kenneth Rexroth

I dreamed I lay in a little gray boat. Waking. Katharine Pyle. OBCA

I dreamed I moved among the Elysian fields. Edna St. Vincent Millay. NoP-4

I dreamed I saw a little brook. A Vision of Children. Thomas Ashe. EBVV

I dreamed I saw Joe Hill last night. Joe Hill. Alfred Hayes. UnPo

I dreamed I stood upon a little hill. Two Loves. Lord Alfred Bruce Douglas. ADE

I dreamed I was a barber; and there went. The Barber. John Gray. ADE; NOBVV

I dreamed I was a dog in a dog show. Dog Show. Laurie Anderson. OxWW

I dreamed I was a Thing from space. My Thing from Outer Space. James Kirkup. SpW

I dreamed I was in a desert and because I was sick of myself. The Tablets. Nicanor Parra, *Spanish.* VCWP, *tr. by* W. S. Merwin

I dreamed it rose. Black Buoy. Robert H. Davis. HATNAP

I dreamed last night I dreamed, and in that sleep. Le Rêve. Edgar Bowers. CoAmPo

I Dreamed Last Night of My True Love. *Unknown.* AS

I dreamed last night / that I was married. A Journey Away. Carl Rakosi. PFTM

I dreamed of him last night, I saw his face. The Dead Poet. Lord Alfred Bruce Douglas. ADE; GSo

I dreamed of war-heroes, of wounded war-heroes. The Heroes. Louis Simpson. OBWP

I dreamed Ted Williams. Dream of a Baseball Star. Gregory Corso. BB; PmAP; VGW

I dreamed [*or* dream'd] that, as I wandered [*or* wander'd] by the way. The Question. Shelley. CH; GTBS-P; OBEV

I dreamed that, buried in my fellow clay. The Dream. *Unknown.* NOEC

I dreamed that in a city dark as Paris. Louis Simpson. CoAP; WeT

I dreamed that in a light-industry mill. In a Fever. Ernest Bryll. CEEP

I dreamed / that Leo Tolstoy. Tadeusz Rózewicz. *See* Memory of a Dream From the Year 1963.

I dreamed that one had died in a strange place. A Dream of Death. W. B. Yeats. GBL

I dreamed that overhead. The Army of the Dead. Barry Pain. NSI

I dreamed that someone's coming. Someone like No One Else. Forugh Farrokhzad, *Farsi.* WPOW, *tr. by* Deirdre Lashgari

I dreamed the heavy sky suddenly opened a gate. Dream. Vahan Tekeyan, *Armenian.* AF, *tr. by* Hovanessian, Diana Der *and* Marzbed Margossian

I dreamed the nymph that o'er my fancy reigns. Sonnet. Sir William Alexander, Earl of Stirling. NOSC *Fr.* Aurora.

I dreamed: the world had grown quiet and was awaiting the end. Dream. Novella Nikolaevna Matveyeva, *Russian.* TCRP, *tr. by* Deming Brown

I dreamed there was an Emperor Antony. Cleopatra's Lament. Shakespeare. UnPo *Fr.* Antony and Cleopatra.

I dreamed there would be Spring no more. Tennyson. NOBE *Fr.* In Memoriam A. H. H.

I dreamed this dream and I still dream of it. Arseny Aleksandrovich Tarkovsky, *Russian.* NNPT, *tr. by* Richard McKane

I dreamed [*or* dream'd] this mortal part of mine. The Vine. Robert Herrick. BeJo; CaPo; CavPo; EP; NAEL-2; NoP-4

I dreamed [*or* dream'd] we both were in bed. The Vision to Electra. Robert Herrick. SeCP

I dreamed you were my child, and I had come. The Dream. Paul Petrie. TAP

I Dreamt a Dream. Arthur Hugh Clough. NAEL-2 *Fr.* Dipsychus [and the Spirit].

I dreamt a dream the other night. Lowlands. *Unknown.* OxBoLi

I dreamt a dream tonight. Shakespeare. OxBSn *Fr.* Romeo and Juliet.

I Dreamt a Dream—What can it mean? The Angel. William Blake. CH; FHYEP; RACG; Ro *Fr.* Songs of Experience.

I dreamt about you last night. Dream. *Unknown, Eskimo.* STP, *tr. by* Armand Schwerner

I dreamt her sensual proportions. The Death of Venus. Robert Creeley. NOBA

I DREAMT I climbed to a high, high plain. The Pitcher. Yüan Chen, *Chinese.* AWP; ChiP, *tr. by* Arthur Waley

I dreamt I drank too much lemonade. Cruising. Gig Ryan. BMAP

I dreamt I dwelt in marble halls. The Palace of humbug. "Lewis Carroll." CBNP

I dreamt I held the laughter-loving girl. Macedonius, *Greek.* GrAn, *tr. by* Adrian Wright

I dreamt I saw great Venus by me stand. A Dream of Venus. Bion, *Greek.* AWP, *tr. by* Leigh Hunt

I dreamt. I saw three ladies in a tree. The Three Ladies. Robert Creeley. NeAP

I dreamt it all, from end to end, the carriageway. Dublin Girl, Mountjoy, 1984. Dermot Bolger. BiHa

I dreamt last night. The Fierce Dream. Jeffrey Wainwright. DiPo

I dreamt last night. For No Clear Reason. Robert Creeley. VGW

I dreamt last night of you, John-John. John-John. Thomas Macdonagh. AWP

I dreamt (no "dream" awake—a dream indeed). In Sleep. Alice Thompson Meynell. BrRo

I dreamt of the old house. To My Sister. Olga Fiodorovna Berggolts, *Russian.* BoWoP, *tr. by* Daniel Weissbort

I dreamt one night—it was a horrid dream. Out of the Frying Pan into the Fire. James Henry. NOBVV

I dreamt that I was God Himself. Ezra Pound, *after the German of* Heine. FaBoEE

I dreamt you stood upon the trap of the world. On the Death of Ronald Ryan. Bruce Dawe. BMAP

I dremt that madness passes like a dream. (LL) That Which We Call a Rose. Michael Dransfield. BMAP

I dressed my father in his little clothes. The Boat. Robert Pack. CoAP

I Drift in the Wind. Ingrid Jonker, *Afrikaans.* PeSA; WPOW, *tr. by* Jack Cope

I drift off in a panel van waiting for Isolda. Spread Rhythm. C. D. Wright. LCAP-2

I drink champagne early in the morning. Cordon Negro. Essex Hemphill. GLP

I drink the bitterness of primroses and autumn skies. The Feasts. Boris Pasternak, *Russian.* TCRP, *tr. by* Yakov Hornstein

I drink to military asters, to all that I'm censured about. Osip Emilevich Mandelstam, *Russian.* TCRP, *tr. by* Bernard Meares

I drink to your glory my god. The Scorner. Felix Tchicaya U'Tamsi, *French.* PBMAP; TTY, *tr. by* Gerald Moore *and* Ulli Beier

I drive home with the books that I will read. Edgar Bowers. VCAP *Fr.* Autumn Shade.

I drive my carriage from the Upper East Gate. Mei Sheng *and* Fu I. *Fr.* Nineteen Old Poems of the Han. CoBCP, *tr. by* Burton Watson

I drive my chariot up to the Eastern Gate. Years Vanish Like the Morning Dew. Mei Sheng, *Chinese.* IMW, *tr. by* Arthur Waley

I drive west from the old dump. The Drive In. Michael S. Harper. AFr

I dropped my sail and dried my dropping seines. Mass at Dawn. Roy Campbell. OxAEP-2; PeSA

I drops in to see young Ben. Chorus of a Song That Might Have Been Written by Albert Chevalier. Max Beerbohm. OBCoV; UV

I droun twa. (LL) Tweed and Till. *Unknown.* FaBoCh; FaBoVe; OBEV; OxBSP

I drove home that night in the rain. Little L.A. Villanelle. Carol Muske. WWSi

I drove to Little Hunger promontory. Little Hunger. Richard Murphy. BIrV

I drove to Oak Park, took two tours. Falling Water. John Koethe. BAP-95

I drove up to the graveyard, which. The Soul Longs to Return Whence It Came. Richard Eberhart. CMoP

I du believe in Freedom's cause. Letter Six—The Pious Editors' Creed. James Russell Lowell. APN-1; NCAP *Fr.* The Biglow Papers.

I dug a grave under an oak-tree. Amy Lowell. BoWoP *Fr.* Dreams in War Time.

I dug and dug amongst the snow. Christina Rossetti. FaBoEE

I dug, beneath the cypress shade. The Grave of Love. Thomas Love Peacock. CH; OxAEP-2; OxBSP

I dug in with all the spirit of spring. Knowing. Mary Coghill. BrRo

I dun already seen. (LL) U Name This One. Carolyn M. Rodgers. BlSi; NMM-2; PoBA

I dwell alone—I dwell alone, alone. Autumn. Christina Rossetti. BrRo; VWP

I dwell in Grace's court[e]. Content and Ri[t]ch[e]. Robert Southwell. ChIV-2; NoSic

I dwell in Possibility. Emily Dickinson. APN-2; EnIH; HeIP-4; NALW; NAWM-2; NCAP; NOBA; NoAM; OxBA; PAR; Poetr; SAGP

I dwell in this leaky Western castle. Dowager. John Montague. IIP

I. EAST TEXAS. Travels in the South. Simon J. Ortiz. UnSA

I eat alone. Michael McClintock. HA

I Eat Kids Yum Yum! Dennis Lee. TLR

I eat my peas with honey. *Unknown.* NTCP

I edged back against the night. High Tide. Jean Starr Untermeyer. MoAmPo

I embrace the purpose of God, and the doom assigned. Tennyson. *See* My life has crept so long on a broken wing.

I embraced the summer dawn. Dawn. Rimbaud. TTTS, *tr. by* Enid Rhodes Peschal *Fr.* Illuminations.

I employ the blind mandolin player. A Music. Wendell Berry. VGW

I empty myself of the names of others. I empty my pockets. The Remains. Mark Strand. NYBP

I encountered the crowd returning from amusements. Resolution of Dependence. George Barker. FaBoTw; LiTM

I end in shadow. Bob Boldman. HA

I end the only lit and waitful thing in miles of / darkened houses. (LL) After Anacreon. Lew Welch. BB

I Enter by the Darkened Door. Jenny King. BXAP

I enter, jingling hindu temple bells, deodorant ears. Blessing a Bride and Groom; a Wedding Night Poem. Robert Peters. BXAP

I enter the lit house. (LL) Parliament Hill Fields. Sylvia Plath. HCAP; NALW

I entered into unknowning. Stanzas Concerning an Ecstasy Experienced in High Contemplation. Saint John of the Cross, *Spanish.* TOF, *tr. by* K. Kavanaugh *and* O. Rodrigues

I entered it before I understood it. Spring at Nant Dywelan. Bobi Jones, *Welsh.* OBWVE, *tr. by* Joseph P. Clancy

I entered my parlor one bright summer morn. The Humming-Bird. Mary E. Tucker. CBWP-1

I entered with a torch before me. Fleance. Michael Longley. CIP-2; PNI

I envy e'en the fly its gleams of joy. Written in Prison. John Clare. EnVR; OAEL-2

I Envy Not Endymion. Sir William Alexander, Earl of Stirling. Son *Fr.* Aurora.

I envy not in any moods. 27. Tennyson. APAD; CABP; EBEvV; FHYEP; ImPo; OAEL-2; OBNC *Fr.* In Memoriam A. H. H.

I envy not the dead that rest. Mary Elizabeth Coleridge. VWP

I Epiktetos was born a slave, deformed. On Epiktetos the Stoic. *Unknown, Greek.* GrAn, *tr. by* Peter Jay

I escort. Praises of the Bantu Kings (1–10). Jerome Rothenberg. FTOS

I, even I, am he who knoweth the roads. De Aegypto. Ezra Pound. VGW

I even I know the Eastern Gate of Heaven. He Knoweth the Souls of the East. *Unknown.* AWP *Fr.* Book of the Dead.

I exchange eyes with the Mad Queen. Vision. Harry Crosby. SPE

I expect no man to understand. Madonna vs. Child. Joan Murray. FiLi

I Expect You Think This Huge Dark Coat. Christine M. Donald. GLP

I expected him to look dead in the casket. Elegy. Richard Hugo. GM

I Expected My Skin and My Blood to Ripen. Wendy Rose. WPOW

I expected this face but did not predict it. Elijah Speaking. Doug Fetherling. NOBC

I explain the silvered passing of a ship at night. Stephen Crane. APN-2 *Fr.* War Is Kind.

I face the yellow flowers. A Painting of Chrysanthemums in the Boneless Style of Hsü Ch'ung-ssu. Yün Shou-p'ing, *Chinese.* CoBLCP, *tr. by* Jonathan Chaves

I Fail as a Dharma Teacher. Diane Di Prima. BB

I fail to see the ancients before my time. A Song on Climbing the Gate Tower at Yu-chou. Ch'en Tzu-ang, *Chinese.* SuSp, *tr. by* Wu-Chi Liu

I fain would kiss my Julia's dainty leg. Robert Herrick. *See* Her Legs.

I fain would know what she hath deserved. Sir Thomas Wyatt. *See* The Lover Showeth How He Is Forsaken of Such as He Sometime Enjoyed.

I, Fan-chih, wear my socks inside out. Wang Fan-chih, *Chinese.* SuSp, *tr. by* Eugene Eoyang

I fasted for some forty days on bread and buttermilk. The Pilgrim. W. B. Yeats. RB

I fasted three canonical hours. The Maiden's Plight. Brian Merriman. BIrV, *tr. by* Frank O'Connor *Fr.* The Midnight Court. NOIV, *tr. by* Thomas Kinsella

I fear at night he will not come again. (LL) Sleep. Bartholomew Griffin. AAS; NoSic; SCGP

I fear, Mr. Lear, you're a clot. Limerick. Eric Swainson. PeLi

I fear[e] no Earthly Powers. On Himselfe. Robert Herrick. CavPo; PFE

I fear no more. (LL) A Hymn to God the Father. Donne. AWP; EBEV; FMP; FSCP; HAP; InPK-6; MeLP; NAEL-1; NOBE; NOSC; OAEL-1; PeECV; PoEL-2; PoRA; SCGP; SCV; SeCP; SoSe-8; TFi; TOF

I fear that appearances are worshipped throughout France. The Rat and the Elephant. Jean de La Fontaine, *French.* OBVE, *tr. by* Marianne Moore

I fear that I shall never make. Poet-Tree. Earle Birney. APAD; OxBC

I fear thy kisses, gentle maiden. Shelley. GTBS-P

I fear time's tumbril hurrying us. Time is. Alan Beam. APAD

I fear to love thee, Sweet, because. To Olivia. Francis Thompson. MoBrPo

I feed a flame within, which so torments me. Song. Dryden. AWP; OBEV *Fr.* Secret Love; or, The Maiden Queen.

I feed on your Name like a cockroach on a crumb—this cockroach / Is holy. (LL) PsalmIII: "To God: to illuminate all men. Beginning with Skid Road." Allen Ginsberg. CAPP-1; ChIV-1

I feel a breath from other planets blowing. Rapture. Stefan George, *German.* AWP, *tr. by* Ludwig Lewisohn

I feel a little better today. The Master Carpenter. G. Shankara Kurup, *Malayalam.* OMIP, *tr. by* K. M. George *and* A. K. Ramanujan (1929–93)

I feel a little jumpy around you. Jump City. Harryette Mullen. IFJA

I feel a newer life in every gale. May. James Gates Percival. BoTP

I feel a sudden chill—. Haiku. Buson. IMW

I feel an apparition. Wallace Stevens, *after the French of* Jean Le Roy. OBVE

I Feel Empty. Yona Wallach, *Hebrew.* IP, *tr. by* Warren Bargad *and* Stanley F. Chyet

I feel empty, empty as a swimming pool. Yona Wallach, *Hebrew.* IP, *tr. by* Warren Bargad *and* Stanley F. Chyet

I Feel I Am[, I only know I am]. John Clare. FHYEP; NOBVV; OAEL-2

I feel I know what you have worked through, you. For John Berryman. Robert Lowell. NOBA

I feel I should go to Norfolk Virginia and drink. Reality U.S.A. Mark Halliday. NAmP90

I feel / in her pockets; she wore nice cotton gloves. Secondhand Coat. Ruth Stone. NALW; NIP-4

I feel it when the game is done. Footnote to Tennyson. Gerald Bullett. UV

I feel my face being bitten by the tides. The Knowledge That Comes through Experience. Jane Cooper. NMM-2

I feel my heart melting. Dusk. Gabriela Mistral, *Spanish.* BoWoP, *tr. by* David Garrison

I feel myself in need. George Moses Horton, Myself. George Moses Horton. AAP; NAAAL

I feel, O Laudanum, thy power divine. In Praise of Laudanum. William Harrison. NOEC

I feel of others' affairs / as though they were. Murasaki Shikibu, *Japanese.* WPJ, *tr. by* Kenneth Rexroth *and* Ikuko Atsumi

I feel pity for that girl Polya. To Kolya Otrada. Mikhail Kuz'mich Lukonin, *Russian.* TCRP, *tr. by* Albert C. Todd

I feel remorse for all that time has done. Love's Remorse. Edwin Muir. OxBTC

I feel ridiculous. Put Down. Léon Damas, *French.* TTY, *tr. by* Seth L. Wolitz

I feel ridiculous / in their shoes. Sell Out. Léon Damas, *French.* NegPo, *tr. by* Ellen Conroy Kennedy

I feel such people making love behind old stairways. Evenings in the Sea. Eleanor Lerman. WeT

I feel that in the days gone by. In Days Gone By. Ida M. Mills. BoTP

I feel the cold this night for Aodh. Mag Uidhir's Winter Campaign. Eochadh O'Hussey. NOIV

I feel the coming glory of the Light. (LL) Credo. Edwin Arlington Robinson. AmPP; CMoP; LiTM; MeMAP; MoAmPo; NAAL-2; OxBA; PFE; TAP; TrCP

I feel the dead in the cold of violets. Sophia De Mello Breyner, *Portuguese*. VCWP, *tr.* by Ruth Fainlight

I feel the reasonableness of existence. Yevgeny Mikhailovich Vinokurov, *Russian*. TCRP, *tr.* by Albert C. Todd

I feel the stubborn humming. Swift Floods. Kata Szidónia Petröczi, *Hungarian*. WPOW, *tr.* by Laura Schiff

I feel the truth; so let the world surmise. (LL) Their sense is with their senses all mixed in. George Meredith. NAEL-2; NoP-4; OAEL-2; SCGP

I feel within myself a life. The Mother. Caroline Clive. VWP

I feel your steps in the hall. Karin Boye. PBWP, *tr.* by Nadia Christensen *Fr.* A Dedication.

I fell. Makeda (Queen of Sheba). WPoS

I fell asleep, and had a dream. An Unromantic Awakening. Priscilla Jane Thompson. CBWP-2

I fell asleep in the daytime. Recording a Dream. Yang Shih-ch'i, *Chinese*. CoBLCP, *tr.* by Jonathan Chaves

I fell asleep thinking of him. Ono no Komachi, *Japanese*. WPJ, *tr.* by Kenneth Rexroth *and* Ikuko Atsumi

I fell down. Three Ways to Screw Up on Your Way to The Doings Three Ways. *Unknown, Seneca Indian*. STP, *tr.* by Jerome Rothenberg *and* Richard Johnny John

I fell in love. I kissed her. *Unknown, Greek*. GrAn, *tr.* by Barriss Mills

I fell in love with a Gentile boy. The Ballad of Edie Barrow. Gwendolyn Brooks. PFE

I fell in love with Demo of Paphos. No big surprise. Philodemus. HePo, *tr.* by Barbara Hughes Fowler *Fr.* Epigrams.

I fell in love with her kisses. *Unknown, Greek*. InMo, *tr.* by Sam Hamill

I fell in love with the Lord Buddha. The Lord Buddha. Fumiko Hayashi, *Japanese*. WPJ, *tr.* by Kenneth Rexroth *and* Ikuko Atsumi

I fell in love with you, Atthis. Sappho, *Greek*. PGA, *tr.* by Kenneth Rexroth

I fell next to him. His body rolled over. Postcard (Found on His body after He Was Killed by the Nazis). Miklós Radnóti, *Hungarian*. RaBo, *tr.* by Steven Polgar, Stephen Berg, *and* S. J. Marks

I felt a cleavage in my mind. Emily Dickinson. NOBA; OxBA; TRP ("I felt a Cleaving in my Mind.") APN-2

I felt a Funeral in my Brain. Emily Dickinson. APN-2; AmPP; BoWoP; CMoP; HeIP-4; MeMAP; NAAL-1; NAAL-3; NALW; NOBA; NoP-4; OxBA; PAR; PBWP; PoE; PoEL-5; PoRA; Poetr; RaBo; SCV; SoSe-8; TAP; TFi

("And I and silence some strange race, / Wrecked, solitary, here.") (LL) ColAP

I felt a spirit of love begin to stir. Dante. AWP *Fr.* La Vita Nuova.

I felt no pain when they cut it off. Child with Six Fingers. Carol Muske. AmPA

I felt no tremor and I caught no sounds. The White Dust. Wilfrid Wilson Gibson. MoBrPo

I felt such love for you. A Poem for My Wet Nurse. Cheng Hsieh, *Chinese*. CoBLCP, *tr.* by Jonathan Chaves

I felt the lurch and halt of her heart. Lightning. D. H. Lawrence. CMoP; MoBrPo; SAGP

I felt the season changing in the yard today. The Man and the Tree. Philip Mead. NOBAu

I felt the wind soft from the land of souls. Olives and Mountains. Elizabeth Barrett Browning. *Fr.* Aurora Leigh. VWP

I fight a battle every day. The Fighter. Samuel Ellsworth Kiser. BLPA

I Fight Back. Lillian Allen. PBCV

I Fights Mit Sigel! Grant P. Robinson. BLPA

I figured / anything anybody. Mrs. Sadie Grindstaff, Weaver and Factotum. Jonathan Williams. OBAL

I fill this cup to one made up. A Health. Edward Coote Pinkney. APN-1

I fill'd [*or* filld] with woes the passing Wind. (LL) The Crystal Cabinet. William Blake. CH; FaBoCh; OAEL-2; OBNC; PoEL-4

I finally found a way of using the tree. The Beckett Kit. Linda Gregg. AmPA

I find her huddled on the bed. Rod Willmot. HA

I find him in the garden. Staked tomato-plants are what. Early Discoveries. David Malouf. CBAP

I find his feet. He is what is left of my life. (LL) The Dreadful Has Already Happened. Mark Strand. HCAP; NoAM; VCAP

I find my love fishing. *Unknown, Egyptian hieroglyphics into Italian*. BoWoP; PBWP, *tr.* by Boris de Rachewiltz; *English vers.* by Ezra Pound *and* Noel Stock

I find no fault in this just man. (LL) Eighth Air Force. Randall Jarrell. MoP; NOBA; NoAM; NoP-4; OBWP; PoWW; TRP; VCAP

I find no peace and all my war[r] is done. Description of the Contrarious Passions in a Lover. Petrarch. AAS; OAEL-1; OBVE; Poetr; SiPS, *tr.* by Sir Thomas Wyatt *Fr.* Sonnets to Laura.

I finish chanting my new poems. Yang Wan-li. SuSp, *tr.* by Jonathan Chaves *Fr.* Songs of Depression.

I Fire at the Face of the Country Where I Was Born. Kazuko Shiraishi, *Japanese*. WPJ, *tr.* by Kenneth Rexroth *and* Ikuko Atsumi

I First / met the light and shook it. Audubon *Enfant*. Pamela Alexander. WeT

I first remember you in Paris, blaze. Memoir. Honor Moore. GLP

I first tasted under Apollo's lips. Evadne. Hilda Doolittle. BoWoP; LW

I first would have him understand. On His Garden Book. Francis Daniel Pastorius. SCAP

I fish for minnows in the lake. Epigram. Su Tung-p'o. OHPC

I fish until the clouds turn blue. Shifting Colors. Robert Lowell. HCAP

I fled Him, down the nights and down the days. The Hound of Heaven. Francis Thompson. CABP; ChIV-2; EBEvV; EnVR; ImPo; LiTM; MoBrPo; NAEL-2; OBMV; PoEL-5; TFi

I flee the city, temples, and each place. Sonnet 17. Louise Labé, *French*. BoWoP, *tr.* by Willis Barnstone

I float / On the wind. Tamaki of a Hundred Lovers. Hirini Melbourne. PeNZ

I floated on a cloud one day. Cloud Fantasy. Henrietta Cordelia Ray. CBWP-3

I follow from my window down. From the Window Down. Louis O. Coxe. NYBP

I follow her down the night, begging her not to depart. (LL) Aware. D. H. Lawrence. MoBrPo; NoAM

I follow quickly, I ascend to the nest in the fissure of the cliff. Walt Whitman. *See* I believe a leaf of grass is no less than the journey-work of the stars.

I follow the army to campaign on distant roads. Joining the Army: A Song. Wang Ts'an, *Chinese*. SuSp, *tr.* by Ronald C. Miao

I follow the curve of his penis. Women of my Color. Wanda Coleman. NMM-2

I follow the moon into the mountains. In the Mountains. Wang An-shih, *Chinese*. SuSp, *tr.* by Jan W. Walls

I follow the scent of a woman. Dancing the Shout to the True Gospel; or, The Song Movement Sisters Don't Want Me to Sing. Rita Mae Brown. CrSp

I Followed a Path. Patricia Parker. BlSi

I followed her to the station, with her suitcase in my hand. Love in Vain. Robert Johnson. UnPo

I followed, o splendid season. A Poem to Show the Trouble That Befell Him When He Was at Sea. Thomas Prys, *Welsh*. OBWVE, *tr.* by Gwyn Williams

I followed the narrow cliffside trail half way up the mountain. The Deer Lay Down Their Bones. Robinson Jeffers. NoAM

I followed where they led. His Throne Is with the Outcast. James Russell Lowell. TrCP

I ford a river to play with autumn water. In Imitation of Ancient Songs. Li Po, *Chinese*. SuSp, *tr.* by Joseph J. Lee

I Forget. Sachiko Yoshihara, *Japanese*. WPJ, *tr.* by Kenneth Rexroth *and* Ikuko Atsumi

I forget everything. I forget faces. The Keeper. William Carpenter. Poetsp

I forget just why. (LL) Lament: "Listen, children: / Your father is dead." Edna St. Vincent Millay. CrSp; FiLi; IMW; MeMAP

I forgive you, Maria. Stevie Smith. BWW

I forgot that my lips. Chiyojo, *Japanese*. WPJ, *tr.* by Kenneth Rexroth *and* Ikuko Atsumi

I forgotten who. Bumi. Imamu Amiri Baraka. PoBA

I foster a Love fond of playing ball. It throws. Meleager. HePo, *tr.* by Barbara Hughes Fowler *Fr.* I'll Twine White Violets. NIP-4, *tr.* by Goldwin Smith

I fought Kenny Kinney in the 7th, 8th, and 9th grades. How We Make Lumber Out of Trees. Crawdad Nelson. EC3

I fought on foot in every quarter. Semyon Petrovich Gudzenko, *Russian*. TCRP, *tr.* by Gordon McVay

I found a ball of grass among the hay. Mouse's Nest. John Clare. InPK-6; NAEL-2; RB

I found a dimpled spider, fat and white. Design. Robert Frost. CMoP; ColAP; HeIP-4; InPK-6; InPS-3; MoP; NAAL-2; NOBA; NoAM; NoP-4; PBMP; PoPoPo; Poetr; RaBo; SAmP; SoSe-8; Son; TAP; TFi; TRP

I found a fox, caught by the leg. A Fellow Mortal. John Masefield. OxAEP-2

I Found a Horseshoe. *Unknown*. AS

I found a house in the forest. The House of the Injured. John Haines. WeT

I found a / hummingbird. The Container. Cid Corman. VGW

I found a little brown purse. Found in the Woods. Irene F. Pawsey. BoTP

I found a little fairy flute. Fairy Music. Enid Blyton. BoTP

I found a pigeon's skull on the machair. Perfect. "Hugh MacDiarmid." NoP-4; RB

I found a torrent falling in a glen. The Torrent. Edwin Arlington Robinson. APN-2

I found a / weed. Reflective. A. R. Ammons. HCAP; PiM; VCAP

I found again in the heart of a friend. (LL) The Arrow and the Song. Henry Wadsworth Longfellow. CTV; ColAP; MeMAP; PWR; PoToHe; UV

I found at daybreak yester morn. *Unknown.* *Fr.* Medieval Norman Song. AWP, *tr.* by John Addington Symonds

I found her asleep in the snows. Song of the Lonely Shepherd. Anna Wickham. WPN

I found her in the shade of spring. The Rose Wreaths. Friedrich Gottlieb Klopstock, *German.* GePo, *tr.* by J. W. Thomas

I found her out there. Thomas Hardy. CH; CMoP; NOBE; NoAM; OAEL-2; OxAEP-2; PoE; PoEL-5

I found him in the guard-room at the Base. Lamentations. Siegfried Sassoon. OBSV; OxAEP-2; PeFWW

I found his wool face, I went away. Reading Walt Whitman. Calvin Forbes. NBV; PoBA

I found in Innisfail the fair. Alfrid's Itinerary through Ireland. *Unknown, Irish.* TIRV, *tr.* by James Clarence Mangan

I found in Munster, unfettered of any. *Unknown.* BIrV, *tr.* by James Clarence Mangan *Fr.* Prince Alfrid's Itinerary.

I found it in a legendary land. On Discovering a Butterfly. Vladimir Nabokov. NYBP

I found it in the bottom drawer. The Manual. Larry Rubin. MT

I found myself, girls, early one fine day. She Finds Herself in a Garden. Angelo Poliziano, *Italian.* GaP, *tr.* by John Hollander

I found myself one day all, all alone. Angelo Poliziano *Fr.* Three Ballate. AWP, *tr.* by John Addington Symonds

I found that ivory image there. Crazy Jane Grown Old Looks at the Dancers. W. B. Yeats. CMoP; EBEV

I found the colour of your. At Castor Bay. Sam Hunt. PeNZ

I found the packets of seed in a cobwebbed drawer. Lost Seed. Patrick Williams. PNI

I found the task that I had dreaded so. The Dreaded Task. Margaret E. Bruner. PoToHe

I found the words to every thought. Emily Dickinson. APN-2; AmPP

I found them here when I came. We Call Them Greasers. Gloria Anzaldúa. GLP

I found this jawbone at the sea's edge. Relic. Ted Hughes. NAEL-2; NoP-4

I found this photograph. Returning to the Town Where We Used to Live. Susan Musgrave. NOBC

I found you in a newspaper. Idea of a Swimmer. Jean-Richard Bloch, *French.* TrJP, *tr.* by "S. P."

I found you on a rainy morning. Nansen. Gary Snyder. BB

I found your Horace with the writing in it. On First Looking into Loeb's Horace. Lawrence Durrell. FaBoMo; LiTM

I, François Villon, ta'en at last. Would I Be Shrived? John D. Swain. BLPA

I frightened a little mouse under the [*or* her] chair. (LL) Pussy-Cat, Pussy-Cat,/ where have you been? Mother Goose. BoTP; FaBoBe; LB; OxNR; ReMoGo

I, from my chamber window, mark. Autumn Thoughts. Mary E. Tucker. CBWP-1

I from my window looked at early dawning. Bereft. Josephine D. Henderson Heard. CBWP-4

I gaed to spend a week in Fife. The Annuity. George Outram. PeVV

I gat your letter, winsome Willie. To William Simpson, Ochiltree. Robert Burns. OxBS

"I gave my love a cher-ry that has no stone, I." The Riddle Song. *Unknown.* KaS

I gave myself to Him—. Emily Dickinson. APN-2; ITG

I gave myself to Love Divine. Saint, of Avila Theresa, *Spanish.* TOF, *tr.* by E. Allison Peers

I gave the jewel away to its owner. Lady Otomo no Sakanoé, *Japanese.* WPJ, *tr.* by Kenneth Rexroth *and* Ikuko Atsumi

I gave to Hope a watch of mine: but he. Hope. George Herbert. ChIV-2; FMP; PoEL-2; WeW-3

I Gaze across the Distant Hills. William Williams, *Welsh.* OBWVE, *tr. by* H. Idris Bell

I gaze at this, my hometown. Yüan Mei. *Fr.* Five Poems on Returning to Hangchou. CoBLCP, *tr. by* Jonathan Chaves

I gaze at you. The Tattooed Man. Robert Earl Hayden. NoAM

I gaze far and long. Teika, *Japanese.* OHMPJ, *tr. by* Kenneth Rexroth

I gaze upon the beauty of the stars. The Beauty of the Stars. Moses ibn Ezra, *Hebrew.* TrJP, *tr. by* Solomon Solis-Cohen

I gaze upon the roast. Pot Roast. Mark Strand. FiLi

I gaze, where August's sunbeam falls. Newark Abbey. Thomas Love Peacock. NOBE; OBNC

I gaze with grief upon our generation. A Thought. Mikhail Yuryevich Lermontov, *Russian.* AWP, *tr.* by Max Eastman

I gazed through the darkness, one very dark night. The Light in the Window. C. L. Erickson. PWR

I gently touched her hand: she gave. I Pressed Her Rebel Lips. *Unknown.* BoLoP

I get as far as the park. Veteran. Walter McDonald. CDa

I get in between the covers as quietly as I can. The Word. Mark Cox. NAmP90

I get my degree. Lawd, Dese Colored Chillum. Ruby C. Saunders. BlSi; LTA

I get so drunk, I could be called the Earl of Dissipation! Chin Nung. CoBLCP, *tr.* by Jonathan Chaves *Fr.* Thirty Poems of Longing for People.

I get tired teaching the students I have now. My Students. Lisa Lewis. PUP-19

I Get Up at Dawn. Lu Yu, *Chinese.* OHPC, *tr.* by Kenneth Rexroth

I get up. I am sick of / Rouging my cheeks. Morning. Chu Shu-chen, *Chinese.* BLT; BoWoP; OHPC, *tr.* by Kenneth Rexroth

I give my word on it. There is no way. Still and All. Burns Singer. OxBS

I give thee all, I can no more. A Sum. "Lewis Carroll." Spl

I give thee thanks, Adonai! My Soul in the Bundle of Life. *Unknown.* TrJP, *tr.* by E. Margaret Rowley *Fr.* The Dead Sea Scrolls.

I give Thee thanks, my King. Mael Isu O Brolchain. NOIV

I give you a house of snow. The Dove of New Snow. Vachel Lindsay. MoAmPo

I Give You Back. Joy Harjo. HATNAP; LoL; UnSA

("But come here, fear / I am alive and you are so afraid / of dying.") (LL) UnSA

I give you horses for your games in May. May. Folgore da San Geminiano. *Fr.* Sonnets of the Months. AWP, *tr.* by D. G. Rossetti

I give you meadow-lands in April, fair. April. Folgore da San Geminiano. *Fr.* Sonnets of the Months. AWP, *tr.* by D. G. Rossetti

I give you my sprig of lilac. Walt Whitman. *See* Spring.

I give you no greeting, Geoffrey. Marbod of Rennes, *Latin.* MLL, *tr. by* Helen Waddell

I give you now Professor Twist. The Purist. Ogden Nash. KaS; MoAmPo; NBLV; OBCA

I Give You Thanks My God. Bernard Dadié, *French.* TTY, *tr. by* Donatus Ibe Nwoga

I give you the end of a golden string. William Blake. NTP *Fr.* Epigraph. OBNC *Fr.* Jerusalem; The Emanation of the Giant Albion.

I give you the end of a golden string. Epigraph. William Blake. OBNC; Spl *Fr.* Jerusalem; The Emanation of the Giant Albion.

I give you the unhingeing sleeve. If So. Barbara Guest. BAP-95

I give you this Bible and word of a. Inscription on the Flyleaf of a Bible. Dannie Abse. TrJP

I glance and see the nameboard hanging there. The Shrine of Ts'en Yi-tung. Ho Xuan Huong, *Vietnamese.* AVP, *tr.* by Huỳnh Sanh Thông

I glance down at my shoe and—there's the lace! To Be Said Over and Over Again. György Petri, *Hungarian.* VCWP, *tr.* by Wilmer, Clive and George Gömöri

I go. Buson. ChAP

I go a road / among the upturned. In the Underworld. Muriel Rukeyser. APSN

I go back again. Hawk and Snake. Leslie Marmon Silko. VoR

I Go Back to May 1937. Sharon Olds. BLT

("Do what you are going to do, and I will tell about it.") (LL) LoL

I go back ways to hurl rooftops. In My Mind. Norman MacCaig. OxBC

I Go before, my darling. *Unknown.* NoSic

I Go by Road. Catulle Mendès, *French.* AWP; TrJP, *tr.* by Alice Meynell

I go digging for clams once every two or three years. Clamming. Reed Whittemore. NYBP; TAP

I Go Dreaming Roads in My Youth. Luis Omar Salinas. AiP

I go for voting clean. (LL) Aunt Chloe's Politics. Frances Ellen Watkins Harper. NAAAL; NALW

I go. I go. I go. Ngungalari. Archie Weller. RACG

I go on in the dark, lit from within; does day exist? Miguel Hernández, *Spanish.* AF, *tr.* by Timothy Baland

I go one step forward. Student. Cheng Min. PBWP, *tr.* by Kenneth Rexroth *and* Ling Chung

I go out. The Top of the World. Yves Bonnefoy, *French.* VCWP, *tr. by* John Naughton

I go out of darkness / Onto a road of darkness. Lady Izumi, *Japanese.* WPOW, *tr. by* Kenneth Rexroth

I go out to totem street. Knock on Wood. Henry Dumas. PoBA

I go separately. Santa Fe Trail. Barbara Guest. FTOS; NeAP; PoM

I go through hollyhocks. Las Trampas U. S. A. Charles Tomlinson. TwCP

I go tiptoe. Sunday. Ojars Vacietis, *Latvian*. CEEP, tr. by Inara Cedrins

I go to concert, party, ball. My Rival. Rudyard Kipling. OxBTC

I go to say goodbye to the Cailleach. The Wild Dog Rose. John Montague. BIrV; CIP-2; PBCIP; PoE

I go to school in the morning. Embroidery. Catherine Nomura Crystal. AiP

I go to the Turkish shop, buy a bun. The Turkish Bakery. *Unknown, Korean*. PBWP, tr. by Peter H. Lee

I go to work. Workday. Linda Hogan. HATNAP

I go westwards in the Desert. Going Westwards. Sorley MacLean. FaBoTC

I go, with your good grace, lords and kinsmen. Hartmann von Aue, *German*. GePo, tr. by Frederick Goldin

I got a brown baby. Brown Baby Blues. Una Marson. PBCV

I got a gal at the head of the creek. Cripple Creek. *Unknown*. APN-2

I Got a Gal at the Head of the Holler. *Unknown*. AS

I got a home in dat Rock. *Unknown*. BPo; CrDW

I Got a Letter from Jesus. *Unknown*. AS

I got a one-eyed wife, a headless child. Guess Who. Fred Chappell. NBLV

I got down on my knees with the little. Staff. John Engman. NAmP90

I got his name and phone. On Finding Out that the One You Slept with the Night Before Was Murdered the Next Day. Chuck Ortleb. GLP

I got me flowers to straw [*or* strew *or* strow] Thy [*or* the] way. Easter. George Herbert. BoTP; CH; FHYEP; FaBoCh; NAEL-1; NOBE; OBEV

I got navy blue eyes that apologize. From Him. Andra Davis. IFJA

I got one good look. Coon Song. A. R. Ammons. MoP; NOBA

I got out of bed. Otherwise. Jane Kenyon. LoL

I Got Rhythm. Ira Gershwin. CBLP

I got so I could take his name. Emily Dickinson. APN-2; CMoP

I Got the Blues. *Unknown*. ITY

I got to Kansas City on a Frid'y. Kansas City. Oscar, II Hammerstein. OBAL

I got to keep on dancing. Alvin Cash/Keep on Dancin'. David Henderson. GT

I got up and opened the shoji. *Unknown, Japanese*. WPJ, tr. by Kenneth Rexroth *and* Ikuko Atsumi

I got up early Sunday morning. Who and Each. Ron Padgett. PmAP

I got up in the night. The Riverman. Elizabeth Bishop. NYBP

I gotta / buy me a new. Après le Bain. William Carlos Williams. OBAL

I grant indeed that fields and flocks have charms. Rural Life. George Crabbe. NOBE *Fr.* The Village.

I grant it true, that others better tell. Horace. OBCVT, tr. by George Crabbe *Fr.* The Candidate.

I greet my love with wine and gladsome lay. Sabbath, My Love. Judah Halevi, *Hebrew*. TrJP, tr. by Solomon Solis-Cohen

I greet you, son, with joy and winter rue. Muse in Late November. Jonathan Henderson Brooks. ChIV-1

I grew / for you. The Strong Bond. Juana de Ibarbourou, *Spanish*. PBWP, tr. by Linda Scheer

I grew from the earth. *Unknown, Greek*. PGA, tr. by Kenneth Rexroth

I grew up bent over / a chessboard. Prodigy. Charles Simic. AF; VCAP

I grew up in a village: now. Paradise. Louise Glück. NAmP90

I GREW up near the town of Jung-yang. Stopping the Night at Jung-yang. Po Chü-i, *Chinese*. ChiP, tr. by Arthur Waley

I grew up on the reserve. Lenore Keeshig-Tobias. FFC

I grew up staring at the picture of him. Cousin. David Huddle. CDa

I grieve and dare not show my discontent. On Monsieur's Departure. Elizabeth I, Queen of England. CABP; LW; NAEL-1; NALW; PEW; WPE

I grieved for Buonaparté, with a vain. 1801. Wordsworth. Son

I grope to find the phrases for two thoughts. Pass it on, II. Rachel Hadas. NMM-2

I grow a white rose. José Martí. *Fr.* Simple Verses. TTY, tr. by Seymour Resnick

I grow accustomed to a new disguise. Journal. John Ciardi. PoA

I grow old under an intensity. Mirror. James Merrill. CoAP

I *guess an' fear!*. (LL) To a Mouse[, On Turning Her Up in Her Nest, with the Plough, November, 1785]. Robert Burns. APAD; APo; EBEvV; FaBoVe; GEA; GTBS-P; HAP; HeIP-4; ImPo; InPS-3; NAEL-2; NOEC; NoP-4; OAEL-1; OxAEP-2; OxBS; PoE; PoLF; Ro; SCGP; TFi; UV

I guess because it was Key West. Meeting the Reincarnation Analyst. Gary Gildner. AmPA

I guess I'll be back late. Human House. Ryuichi Tamura, *Japanese*. VCWP, tr. by Christopher Drake

I guess it is ever green. Evergreen Cemetery. Alfred Wellington Purdy. MoCV

I guess it will come suddenly. And every. Amir Gilbo'a, *Hebrew*. IP, tr. by Warren Bargad *and* Stanley F. Chyet

I guess nobody ever does. Nikki Giovanni. *See* Legacies.

I guess there is a garden named. The Mirror Perilous. Alan Dugan. LiTM; TwCP

I guess today's another day among the days. Tortoise. Thomas Rabbitt. CMAP

I guess you love me now. Songs of Divorce. Jane Green, *Ojibwa Indian*. WPOW, tr. by Frances Densmore

I guide my boat to mooring by a misty islet. Passing the Night on a River in Chien-te. Meng Hao Jan, *Chinese*. SuSp, tr. by Paul W. Kroll

I gulp down seven drinks of water. Hiccups. Léon Damas, *French*. NegPo; PFTM, tr. by Ellen Conroy Kennedy

I Had a Black Man. *Unknown*. OxBoLi

I had a cat and the cat pleased me. *Unknown*. OxNR

I had a chair at every hearth. The Lamentation of the Old Pensioner. W. B. Yeats. HAP; InPK-6; NoAM; TRP; WeW-3

I had a crisis at the supermarket, yesterday. My Androgynous Years. James Harms. CMAP

I had a dog like a love. Penny Trumpet. Raphael Rudnik. NYBP

I had a dog / Whose name was Buff. *Unknown*. OxNR

I had a Donkey, that was all right. The Donkey. Theodore Roethke. OBCA

I Had a Dove [and the Sweet Dove Died]. Keats. CH
   Song: "I had a dove, and the sweet dove died." PeP

I had a dream. Death Survey. Mongane Wally Serote. PeSAV

I had a dream / and I could see. Nightmare Boogie. Langston Hughes. APSN

I had a dream: Columbia the Great. Albery Allson Whitman. APN-2 *Fr.* An Idyll of the South.

I had a dream. I walked in a field of feather grass. Aleksey Petrovich Tsvetkov, *Russian*. TCRP, tr. by Albert C. Todd

I had a dream one winter's night. A Dream. Maggie Pogue Johnson. CBWP-4

I had a dream: that I was cast in iron. The Monument. Yaroslav Vasilevich Smelyakov, *Russian*. TCRP, tr. by Simon Franklin

I had a dream three walls stood up wherein a raven bird. Anger's Freeing Power. Stevie Smith. NTP; OxBC

I had a dream, which was not all a dream. Darkness. Byron. CABP; GEA; NAEL-2; OAEL-2; PoE; PoEL-4; Ro

I had a duck-billed platypus when I was up at Trinity. Patrick Barrington. OBCoV; PeLV

I Had a Future. Patrick Kavanagh. BIrV; NoAM

I had a hippopotamus; I kept him in a shed. Patrick Barrington. PeP

I had a little bird. The Orphan's Song. Sydney Thompson Dobell. CH; OBNC

I had a little boy. Blue Bell Boy. *Unknown*. ReMoGo

I had a little chamber in the house. Elizabeth Barrett Browning. *Fr.* Aurora Leigh. VWP

I had a little cow. *Unknown*. OxNR

I had a little dog and his name was Blue Bell. *Unknown*. OxNR

I had a little dog, and my dog was very small. A Child's Dream. Frances Darwin Cornford. NOxBChV

I had a little goldfish. O Goldfish! Robert Fisher. PeP

I had a little hen, the prettiest ever seen. The Clever Hen. *Unknown*. BoTP; LB; ReMoGo

I had a little hobby-horse. *Unknown*. BoTP; ReMoGo

I had a little hobby horse, it was well shod. Mother Goose. OxNR

I had a little horse, his name was Dappled Grey. *Unknown*. OxNR

I had a little husband. *Unknown*. BoTP; OxNR; ReMoGo

I had a little moppet. The Little Moppet. Mother Goose. OxNR; ReMoGo

I had a little mule and his name was Jack. *Unknown*. CA

I had a little nag. *Unknown*. OxNR

I had a little nut-tree, / nothing would it bear. A Nut Tree. Mother Goose. ACTP; BoTP; CH; LB; NTP; OxBoLi; OxNR; TTTS

I had a little pony. Dapple-gray. Mother Goose. BoTP; LB; OxNR; ReMoGo

I had a little pony. *Unknown*. ACTP

I had a love in soft south land. Love from The North. Christina Rossetti. CBLP

I had a Mother who read to me. The Reading Mother. Strickland W. Gillilan. BLPA

I had a pet lizard called Albert. Jasmine Pinto. PeP

I had a silver penny. Nursery Rhyme of Innocence and Experience. Charles Causley. NOxBChV; NTP

I had a son and his name was John. Rundown Church (Ballad of the First World War). Federico García Lorca, *Spanish*. AF, tr. by Robert Bly; RaBo

I had a sweet tortoise called Pye. My Tortoise. Stevie Smith. PeP

I Had a Terror—Since September. Gerald William Barrax. MT

"I had a true love but she left me." The Quaker's Wooing. *Unknown*. AS

I had a vision when the night was late. The Vision of Sin. Tennyson. EBVVPR; OAEL-2

I had almost forgotten the singing in the streets. Singing in the Streets. Leonard Clark. NOxBChV

I had ambition, by which sin. Ambition. W. H. Davies. MoBrPo

I had an uncle once who kept a rock in his pocket. I've Got a Home in That Rock. Raymond R. Patterson. MBE; PoBA

I had as lief be embraced by the porter at the hotel. Two Figures in Dense Violet Night. Wallace Stevens. MoAmPo

I had auchteen months o' the war. On Leave. John Buchan, 1st Baron Tweedsmuir. NSI

I had awakened early. Second Ode to Persephone. Robert Kelly. *Fr.* The Book of Persephone. PoM

I had become callous like most. On the Death of Lisa Lyman. Della Burt. BlSi

I had been happy, if the general camp. Shakespeare. OxBM *Fr.* Othello.

I had been hungry, all the Years. Emily Dickinson. ImPo; LiTM; MeMAP; MoAmPo; NALW; SAmP; WPoS

I had been sitting for days. Long Distance. Dana Naone. CDW

I had been thinking of Gabriel. Hilda Doolittle. NALW *Fr.* Tribute to the Angels.

I Had But Fifty Cents. *Unknown.* BLPA; NBLV; WHSW

I had come to the edge of the water. Seamus Heaney. PBCIP *Fr.* Station Island.

I had come to the house, in a cave of trees. Medusa. Louise Bogan. AWP; BoWoP; HoPM; MoAmPo; NALW; NMM-2; NoAM; NoP-4; Poetr; WPE

I had eight birds hatch [*or* hatched] in one nest. In Reference to Her Children, 23 June, 1659 [*or* 1659]. Anne Bradstreet. BoWoP; NAAL-3; TAP

I had finally obtained my goal. Recollections of the Cross. Vladimir Nikolaevich Sokolov, *Russian.* TCRP, *tr. by* Albert C. Todd

I had finished my dinner. An Easy Decision. Kenneth Patchen. PFE

I had forgot you / and the past. Hilda Doolittle. *See* So you have swept me back.

I had found out a gift for my fair. Natural Selection. Constance Naden. VWP

I had gone broke, and got set to come back. Epigram. James Vincent Cunningham. MoAmPo; OxBSP; VCAP

I had gone out to check on new lambs. Rebecca Newth. CrSp

I had good manners. Road Block: Sante Fe, New Mexico. Connie Deanovich. WWSi

I had grasped God's garment in the void. Suspended. Denise Levertov. PiM

I had heard / before, of an / American who would have preferred. Mr. Brodsky. Charles Tomlinson. MoP; NoAM; NoP-4; OxBC

I had heard the bird's name, and searched with intent. The Oyster-Eaters. John Blight. NOBAu

I had just gone to bed. Petronius Arbiter, *Greek.* PGA, *tr. by* Kenneth Rexroth

I had just turned the classic page. To A. H. James M. Whitfield. APN-2

I had long known the diverse tastes of the wood. Gift of Sight. Robert Graves. EP

I had lots of fun today. Through the Window. Vladislav Felitsianovich Khodasevich, *Russian.* TCRP, *tr. by* Yakov Hornstein

I had my good and my. *Unknown.* MiEL

I had never heard of the whiteness. Poem. David Schloss. PoA

I had never seen a cornfield in my life. In the Elementary School Choir. Gregory Djanikian. UnSA

I had no choice but to shave my hair. The Wrestler's Heart. Gary Soto. PuP-17

I had no desire for life. Writing My Feelings. Yüan Mei, *Chinese.* CoBLCP, *tr. by* Jonathan Chaves

I had no God but these. Christ and the Pagan. John Banister Tabb. TrCP

I had no thought of violets of late. Sonnet. Alice Moore Dunbar-Nelson. BlSi; PoBA; Son

I had no time to hate, because. Emily Dickinson. PoLF

I had not an evil end in view. A True Dream. Elizabeth Barrett Browning. NALW

I had not been there before where the vagina opens. The First Birth. Rodney Jones. MT

I had not fastened my sash over my gown. Tzu Yeh, *Chinese.* WPOW, *tr. by* Kenneth Rexroth *and* Ling Chung

I had not known, in friendly life attached. Death of a Friend. Witter Bynner. IMW

I had not minded—Walls. Emily Dickinson. AWP

I had not thought to have unlockt my lips. Temperance and Virginity. Milton. *Fr.* Comus; a Masque Presented at Ludlow Castle. FHYEP; OAEL-1

I Had Occasion to Tell a Visitor about an Old Trip I Took. Lu Yu, *Chinese.* CoBCP, *tr. by* Burton Watson

I had often, cowled in the slumberous heavy air. Dürer: Innsbruck, 1495. "Ern Malley." BMAP

I had over-prepared the event. Villanelle: The Psychological Hour. Ezra Pound. CTC; NAAL-2

I had seen, as dawn was breaking. La Nuit Blanche. Rudyard Kipling. MoBrPo; UV

I had soaked the old house. Zimmer and His Turtle Sink the House. Paul Zimmer. Poetsp

I had some cards printed. Madam's Calling Cards. Langston Hughes. SAmP

I had the lab science, the ecology of texts. The Other Syllabus. Chenjerai Hove. HBAPE

"I had this dream." My Dream. Lew Blockcolski. VoR

I had three friends. Three Friends. *Unknown, Yoruba.* BoWoP; PBA, *tr. by* Ulli Beier

I had to kick their law into their teeth in order to save them. "Negro" Hero. Gwendolyn Brooks. ColAP; RACG

I had two pigeons bright and gay. Two Pigeons. *Unknown.* OxNR; ReMoGo

I had walked life's way with an easy tread. I Met the Master. *Unknown.* PoLF

I had walked since dawn and lay down to rest on a bare hillside. Vulture. Robinson Jeffers. NAAL-2; NOBA; NoAM; PaTW; SAGP

I had wanted a daughter. Mothers of Sons. Lesley Saunders. BrRo

I had watched the ascension and decline of the moon. Walter James Turner. *Fr.* The Seven Days of the Sun. OBMV

I had written to Aunt Maud. Waste. Harry Graham. OBCoV; UV

I hae seen great anes and sat in great ha's. My Ain Fireside. Elizabeth Hamilton. FaBoBe

I hae stuid an hour o the lown midsimmer nicht. Sainless. Douglas Young. FaBoTC

I hailed me a woman from the street. My Madonna. Robert W. Service. BLPA

I hammer a nail. Bob Boldman. HA

I hang by my heels from the sky. Hera, Hung from the Sky. Carolyn Kizer. NMM-2; WPE

I happened once upon a time. James Hatley. *Unknown.* ESPB

I happened to come to the foot of a pine tree. In Reply to Questions. T'ai-shang, *Chinese.* CoBCP, *tr. by* Burton Watson

I happy am if well with you. (LL) In Reference to Her Children, 23 June, 1659 [*or* 1659]. Anne Bradstreet. BoWoP; NAAL-3; TAP

I hardly ever tire of love or rhyme. *Variation on Belloc's "Fatigue".* Wendy Cope. UV

I hardly hear a Woman's Clack. (LL) On His Own Deafness. Jonathan Swift. BIrV; FaBoEE

I hardly know how to speak to you now. Cambridge Elegy. Sharon Olds. IMW

I hate an easy woman. Rufinus, *Greek.* GrAn, *tr. by* Alan Marshfield

I hate and love. Why? You may ask but. Carmina, LXXXV. Catullus, *Latin.* CTC; OBVE, *tr. by* Ezra Pound *Fr.* Carmina.

I hate Eros. He is loathsome and will not. Alcaeus, *Greek.* GrAn, *tr. by* Peter Jay

I hate Fruition, now 'tis past. A Fragment of Petronius, Paraphras'd. Petronius Arbiter, *Latin.* OBCVT, *tr. by* John Oldham

I hate it when grown-ups say. The Frogologist. Brian Patten. OTCP

I Hate My Moaning. Gerald Stern. CMAP

I hate my verses, every line, every word. Love the Wild Swan. Robinson Jeffers. MoAmPo; NoAM; Son

I hate that drum's discordant sound. Ode. John Scott of Amwell. ECEV; NIP-4; NOEC; OxAEP-1; PeFWW

I hate the cyclic poem, nor do I rejoice. Callimachus. HePo *Fr.* Epigrams.

I hate the dreadful hollow behind the little wood. Tennyson. EBVVPR; FaBoPV *Fr.* Maud [A Monodrama]. EnVR

("War with a thousand battles, and shaking a hundred thrones.") (LL) FaBoPV

I hate the flower of wood or common field. Hothouse Flowers. Theodore Wratislaw. ADE

I hate the man who builds his name. The Poet and the Rose. John Gay. PeLV *Fr.* Fables.

I hate the Spring in parti-coloured vest. Sonnet. Mary Locke. ECWP

I hate these phrases: Of power absolute. Joshua Sylvester, *after the French of* Guy du Faur de Pibrac. FaBoEE

I hate to hear those crazy cocks crowing around a thatched inn. Rising Early in the Morning. Chao Yi, *Chinese.* SuSp, *tr. by* Chang Yin-nan *and* Lewis C. Walmsley

I hate to see de ev'nin' sun go down. St. Louis Blues. William Christopher Handy. BkSV; CrDW, *longer vers.*

I hate to spend the night. Thanks Just the Same. *Unknown.* PoLF

I hate wide mouth black girls. Illusion. Colleen J. McElroy. ISC

I hate you with a necessary hate. The Destroyer of a Soul. Lionel Pigot Johnson. ADE

"I hate your laces." The Teasing Toads. Michael Rosen. OTCP

I hated it, after he died, the way we left him. The Dead Body Itself. Sharon Olds. PuP-16

I hated thee, fallen tyrant! I did groan. Feelings of a Republican on the Fall of Bonaparte. Shelley. Son

"I hates to think of dyin'," says the skipper to the mate. The Worried Skipper. Wallace Irwin. BLPA

I Haue [or Have] a Yong Suster. Unknown. See I Have a Young Sister.

I have a bird in my head and a pig in my stomach. Alive for an Instant. Kenneth Koch. PmAP

I Have a Blue Piano. Else Lasker-Schüler, German. TrJP, tr. by Ralph Manheim

I have a bowl of paper whites. Window Ledge in the Atom Age. Elwyn Brooks White. NBLV; OBAL

I have a boy of five years old. Anecdote for Fathers, Showing how the Art of Lying may be Taught. Wordsworth. Ro

I have a child. A Child Shall Lead. Audre Lorde. FiLi

I have a convocation of crows. Ovulation. Lily Pond. DeD

I have a daughter / mozambique. Bocas: A Daughter's Geography. Ntozake Shange. NAAAL

I have a delicious problem. Giant Red Woman. Clarence Major. GT

I have a dog. My Doggie. C. Nurton. BoTP

I have a dream. The Dream. Lola Ridge. NMM-2

I have a fairy by my side. My Fairy. "Lewis Carroll." CBNP

I have a fifth of therapy. Interview with Doctor Drink. James Vincent Cunningham. OxBSP; VGW

I have a friend who stil believes in heaven. Celestial Music. Louise Glück. PuP-14

I have a friend who would give a price for those long fingers all of one length. Snakes, Mongooses, Snake-Charmers and the Like. Marianne Moore. CMoP

I have a garden and I have a well. Hayyim Nahman Bialik, Hebrew. MHP, tr. by Ruth Finer Mintz

I have a garden closed away. The Garden of the Sexes. Jay Macpherson. GaP

I have a garden here, shaped. Letter from an Institution: III. Michael Ryan. AmPA

I have a garden of my own. Child's Song. Sir Thomas More. ChAP

I have a gentle cock. Unknown. MiEL; NOBE; NoP-4; OBCoV; OPOU; PeLV

("In mine ladye's chaumber.") (LL) OBCoV

I have a golden ball. A Rune of Riches. Florence Converse. BoTP

I have a grief. Agitato Ma Non Troppo. John Crowe Ransom. OxBA Fr. Sixteen Poems in Eight Pairings.

I have a highbred neighbor, one who stands. The Kindly Neighbor. E. A. Guest. PoToHe

I have a life that did not become. Easter Morning. A. R. Ammons. HCAP; NAAL-2; NoAM; PoPoPo

I have a little budgie. The Fat Budgie. John Lennon. NBLV

I have a little home amidst the city's din. The Complacent Cliff-Dweller. Margaret Fishback. PoLF

I have a little house. My Little House. J. M. Westrup. BoTP

I have a little pussy. Catkin. Unknown. ACTP; CTV

I have a little rocking chair. My Rocking Chair. Doris I. Bateman. CTV

I have a little shadow that goes in and out with me. My Shadow. Robert Louis Stevenson. CTV; ChAP; FPC; FaBoBe; OTCP; OxBChV; PWR; UV

I have a little shadow that goes out sometimes with me. My Shadow. W. Hodgson Burnett. UV

I have a little sister, they call her Peep-Peep. Mother Goose. BoTP; LB; OxNR

("She has but one eye.") (LL) LB

I have a little windmill on my head. Sliding Trombone. Georges Ribemont-Dessaignes, French. SPE, tr. by David Gascoyne

I have a lover. Tuesday Night Affair. Sandra Turner Bond. ISC

I have a mackintosh shiny brown. Chestnut Buds. Evelyn M. Williams. BoTP

I have a mistress, for perfections rare. A Devout Lover. Thomas Randolph. HoPM; OBEV

I have a neighbor. Rosellen Brown. FFC

I have a new garden. Unknown. See I have a newe gardin.

I have a new home. A roaring Sparring Partner like a sunspot. The Newark Public Library Reading Room. Sotère Torregian. NBV

I have a new umbrella. My New Umbrella. M. M. Hutchinson. BoTP

I have a newe gardin. Unknown. MiEL

("But not pear Jonet!") (LL) OBGa

("I have a new garden.") OBGa

I have a pet koala. My Pet Koala. Unknown. PeP

I have a pretty little flow'r. Francis Daniel Pastorius. SCAP

I Have a Rendezvous with Death. The Rendezvous. Alan Seeger. APAD; AiP; BLPA; FaPoR; PFE; PeFWW; PoFWW

I have a room whereinto no one enters. Memory. Christina Rossetti. OBNC

I have a seamstress, making a shirt for me. The Seamstress. Harry Clifton. BiHa

I have a sister, little sister, living in Chung-li. Tu Fu, Chinese. CoBCP, tr. by Watson, Burton (b. 1925) Fr. Seven Songs Written During the Ch'ien-yüan Era. CoBCP, tr. by Burton Watson

I have a small aquarium. My Pet Goldfish. Edward Williams. PeP

I have a smiling face, she said. The Mask. Elizabeth Barrett Browning. OBNC; VWP

I have a terrible fear of being an animal. César Vallejo, Spanish. SPE, tr. by Robert Bly

I have a theory about motion. Jazz Dancer. Cornelius Eady. SeSe

I have a tree, a graft of love. Arbor Amoris. François Villon, French. AWP, tr. by Andrew Lang

I have a whim to speak in verse. Unknown. NOIV Fr. The Fortification of New Ross.

I have a white cat whose name is Moon. Moon. William Jay Smith. PC

I have a white dog. My Dog, Spot. Rodney Bennett. BoTP

I have a yong suster. I Have a Young Sister. Unknown. CH; EnVB; FaBoVe; InPS-3; MiEL; NAEL-1; OAEL-1; PeLV; PoEL-1

I have a young love. The Sailor. Sylvia Townsend Warner. OBMV

I Have a Young Sister. Unknown. CH; EBEV; FaBoVe; MiEL; NAEL-1; NoP-4; OAEL-1

(I Haue [or Have] a Yong Suster.) EnVB; InPS-3; PoEL-1

("I have a young suster.") EBEV

("She is without longinge.") (LL) NoP-4

I have a young suster. Unknown. See I Have a Young Sister.

I have all / my mother's habits. Mother's Habits. Nikki Giovanni. BlSi

I have allowed my family to scatter. Autumn. Boris Pasternak, Russian. TCRP, tr. by Henry Kamen

I have already come to the verge of. An Unborn Child. Derek Mahon. CABP; PNI

I have already grown a goitre in this drudgery. Michelangelo Buonarroti. See To Giovanni da Pistoia When the Author Was Painting the Vault of the Sistine Chapel, 1509.

I have always been sorry. To the Tune "Glittering Sword Hilts." Liu Yu Hsi, Chinese. OHMPC, tr. by Kenneth Rexroth

I have always found that Angels have the vanity to speak of themselves as the only wise; this they do with a confident insolence sprouting from systematic reasoning. Opposition Is True Friendship. William Blake. Fr. The Marriage of Heaven and Hell. NAEL-2; NOBRP; OAEL-2

I Have Always Heard of These Old Men. Unknown. AmFP

I have always known / That at last I would. Narihira, Japanese. OHPJ, tr. by Kenneth Rexroth

I have always regretted the shallowness of words. Looking at My Knife-hilt Ring, a Song. Liu Yu Hsi, Chinese. SuSp, tr. by Daniel Bryant

I Have Approached. Alan Paton. PeSA

I have armoured my feelings. Rufinus, Greek. GrAn, tr. by Alan Marshfield

I / Have Arrived. Status Symbol. Mari E. Evans. NAAAL

I have assumed a conscious sociability. Garden Party. Sir Herbert Read. OBGa

I have avoided your wide English eyes. Sweet William. "Ern Malley." BMAP

I have awakened from the unknowing to the knowing. For William Edward Burghardt Du Bois on His Eightieth Birthday. Bette Darcie Latimer. PoBA

I have baptized thee Withy, because of thy slender limbs. To ————? Richard Dehmel, German. AWP, tr. by Jethro Bithell

I have beaten him often, head and heel. Poète Manqué. Ernest Sandeen. CRP

I have beaten out my exile. (LL) The Rest. Ezra Pound. AmPP; MeMAP; MoAmPo; NOBA; NoAM; OxBA; PoA

I have been a censor for fifteen months. Censorship. Arthur Waley. OxBTC

I Have Been a Foster. Unknown. EBEV; OxBSP

I have been a movie fan. He Never Did That to Me. Noël Coward. NBLV

I have been a privileged spectator at innumerable acts of vandalism;. The Drummer. Bruce Beaver. BMAP

I have been a / way so long. Homecoming. Sonia Sanchez. NAAAL; PoBA

I have been all my lovers. Desire 1. Thulani Davis. ISC

I have been bent no less. Time's Mirror. Peyton Houston. *Fr.* Sonnet Variations. Son

I have been bitter with you, my brother. Colloquy with Keats. "Ern Malley." BMAP

I have been cherish'd and forgiven. Lines. Hartley Coleridge. FUEL-4

I have been cruel to a fat pigeon. Fly. W. S. Merwin. ChAP; NNaP

I have been faithful to thee, Cynara! in my fashion. (LL) Non Sum Qualis Eram Bonae sub Regno Cynara[e]. Ernest Christopher Dowson. ADE; APAD; AWP; BLPA; BoLoP; CABP; CBLP; ClHu; EBVV; EnLoPo; FaBoBe; GBL; GLoP; GTBS-P; HAP; HeIP-4; ImPo; MoBrPo; NAEL-2; NOBE; NoP-4; OAEL-2; OBEV; OBMV; OBNC; PeVV; PoRA; SAGP; TFi; UnPo

I have been having an affair. Affair of the Heart. Peter Porter. BMAP

I have been her kind. (LL) Her Kind. Anne Sexton. CoAP; HCAP; HeIP-4; LiTM; NALW; PoPoPo; Poetr; SAGP; TAP; TwCP; VCAP; WPOW

I have been here before. Sudden Light. D. G. Rossetti. BoLoP; CABP; CTC; EBEvV; GLoP; NOBE; NOBVV; NoP-4; OAEL-2; OBNC; PoLF

I have been here. Dispersed in meditation. Agnosco Veteris Vestigia Flammae. James Vincent Cunningham. VGW

I have been here for a half hour. The Library. Aidan Carl Mathews. CIP-2

I have been ill so long that I do not count the days. Being Visited by a Friend During Illness. Po Chü-i, *Chinese.* ChiP, *tr. by* Arthur Waley

I have been in a marine aquarium and I have seen. The Marine Aquarium. Louis Dudek. MoCV *Fr.* Atlantis.

I have been in this bar. The Man Who Married Magdalene. Anthony Hecht. ChIV-2; PeLV

I have been kissed before, she added, blushing slightly. Arthur Hugh Clough. FaBoVe *Fr.* Bothie of Tober-na-Vuolich, The [A Long-Vacation Pastoral].

I have been looking at you. Astonishment. Anna Swir, *Polish.* IFJA, *tr. by* Czeslaw Milosz *and* Leonard Nathan (b. 1924)

I have been one acquainted with the night. Acquainted with the Night. Robert Frost. CMoP; GSo; HAP; LiTM; MeMAP; MoAmPo; MoP; NOBA; NoAM; NoP-4; PoE; PoLF; Poetr; SAGP; SAmP; Son; TFi; TRP; TwCP; VGW; WeW-3

I have been playing around. An End To It. Asa Benveniste. NBrP

I have been profligate of happiness. To Olive. Lord Alfred Bruce Douglas. OBEV

I have been proud and said, "My Love, my own." (LL) Sonnet: "First time he kissed me, he but only kissed." Elizabeth Barrett Browning. BLPA; CTC; FaBoBe; LW

I have been so great a lover. The Great Lover. Rupert Brooke. HoPM; ImPo; LiTM; MoBrPo; PoRA

I have been studying how I may compare. Shakespeare. OxAEP-1 *Fr.* King Richard III.

I have been there again, and seen the backs. Again. Jon Stallworthy. OxBC

I have been there / Sicily. Exile. Theognis, *Greek.* OBCVT, *tr. by* Andrew Miller

I have been thinking. Lynn. Jeanne Foster. CrSp

I have been thinking of the difference between water. Kabir, *Hindi.* EnIH, *tr. by* Robert Bly

I Have Been Through the Gates. Charlotte Mew. MoBrPo; SAGP

I have been to my God like the iris and the anemone. Saul Tchernichowsky. MHP, *tr. by* Ruth Finer Mintz *Fr.* To the Sun.

I have been treading on leaves all day until I am autumn-tired. A Leaf-Treader. Robert Frost. MoAmPo

I have been up and down the town. Hunger. Ruth Stone. InPS-3

I have been waiting to speak to you. Eve (Rachel). Michael S. Harper. MoLi

I have been walking for hours on a street called Consolation. Night: Volcano, California. Ellery Akers. CMAP

I have been wanton, and too bold I fear. His Last Request to Julia. Robert Herrick. CavPo

I have been warned. It is more than thirty years since I wrote. But I Am Growing Old and Indolent. Robinson Jeffers. ColAP; NOBA; TAP

I have been watching the war map slammed up for advertising. Buttons. Carl Sandburg. SAGP

I have been with you, and I have thought of you. Chinese Villanelle. John Yau. PmAP

I have been wondering. A Letter. Anthony Hecht. NYBP; OxBC

I have been young, and now am not too old. Report on Experience. Edmund Blunden. FaBoTw; GTBS-P; NOBE; OBMV; OBWP; PeFWW

"I have beene all day looking after." The Witches' Song. Ben Jonson. CH

I have begun to die. The Sentry. Alun Lewis. PoWW

I have begun to live on memories. Poem. Henrikas Nagys, *Lithuanian.* CEEP, *tr. by* Jonas Zdanys

I have believed too long in one thing. March Weather. Jon Swan. NYBP

I have borne the anguish of love, which ask me not to describe. Hafiz. AWP, *tr. by* John Hindley *Fr.* Odes.

I Have Bowed before the Sun. Anna Walters. WPOW

I have braved, for want of wild beasts, steel cages. May 24, 1980. Joseph Brodsky, *Russian.* TCRP, *tr. by* Joseph Brodsky

I have broken step and faith. The Identikit. Amryl Johnson. NBrP

I HAVE brought my pillow and am lying at the northern. Folk-Songs. Chan Fang-sheng, *Chinese.* ChiP, *tr. by* Arthur Waley

I have burned ten thousand volumes. On the Day of Washing the Buddha in the Year Ting-wei (1607), I Dreamed That My Late Son Shih-ch'ü Was Holding a Book, and Appeared To Be Quite Happy. He Said That He Had Earned His Chin-shih Degree in the Underworld. After We Sighed and Laughed Together for a Long Time, I Woke Up and Wrote This Poem. T'ang Hsien-tsu, *Chinese.* CoBLCP, *tr. by* Jonathan Chaves

I have but four, the treasures of my soul. The Slave Mother. Frances Ellen Watkins Harper. ColAP

I have but one chance left,—and that is going to Florence. Claude to Eustace—*from Bellagio.* Arthur Hugh Clough. FaBoVe *Fr.* Amours de Voyage. NOBVV

I have carried it with me each day: that morning I took. A Morning. Mark Strand. HCAP

I have carried my pillow to the windowsill. Summer near the River. Carolyn Kizer. CoAP; VGW

I have cast in here a soul. War Songs. *Unknown, Sioux Native American.* APN-2, *tr. by* Alfred Longley Riggs

I have climbed all the way to the summit. An Auditor Thinks about Female Nature. Jamie Grant. NOBAu

I have come down. Prologue. Odia Ofeimun. HBAPE

I have come far to have found nothing. Cid Corman. VGW *Fr.* Three Tiny Songs.

I have come to catch birds. The Bird Catcher. *Unknown, Egyptian.* TTY, *tr. by* Ulli Beier

I have come to the borders of sleep. Lights Out. Edward Thomas. LBC; NOBE; OxAEP-2; PoWW

I have come upon the visage again. Wood Floor Dreams. Lance Henson. VoR

I have consider'd it; and find. The Resolve. Henry Vaughan. ESCV

I have considered [*or* consider'd] it, and find[e]. The Reprisal[l]. George Herbert. ESCV; GeHe

I have continued to seek her. The Constant Lover. Louis Simpson. NYBP

I have courage and hardihood. Besieged. Zalman Schneour, *Yiddish.* TrJP, *tr. by* Joseph Leftwich

I have crossed an ocean. Epilogue. Grace Nichols. HCP

I Have Cut an Eagle. James Koller. PoM

I have cut the plaintain grove. The Witch. Santal. RaBo

I have decided I'm divine. Ballade of the New God. Thomas M. Disch. RA

I have desired, and I have been desired. Soeur Louise de la Miséricorde (1674). Christina Rossetti. VWP

I have desired to go. Heaven-Haven. Gerard Manley Hopkins. APAD; EBEvV; HeIP-4; MoBrPo; MoP; NOBE; NOCV; NoAM; OBEV; OBNC; OxAEP-2; OxBSP; PeECV; RB; SoSe-8; TFi; TOF

I have discovered a country. Connais-Tu Le Pays? Richard Shelton. NYBP

I have discovered that most of. January Morning. William Carlos Williams. InPS-3

I have done all I could. The Tree and the Lady. Thomas Hardy. MoBrPo

I have done it again. Lady Lazarus. Sylvia Plath. ChIV-2; CoAmPo; FaBoWP; HCAP; MoP; NAAL-2; NALW; NIP-4; NOBA; NoAM; NoP-4; OxWW; PoPoPo; Poetr; SAGP; TAP; TRP; VCAP; VGW

I have done one braver thing. The Undertaking. Donne. FSCP; NAEL-1; NOBE

I have done the deed. Didst thou not hear a noise? Macbeth Does Murder Sleep. Shakespeare. EBEV; OxAEP-1 *Fr.* Macbeth.

I have dreamed a dream of fulfillment, of freedom. Disciples Asleep at Gethsemane. Paul Kane. GI

I have dreamt it again: standing suddenly still. Wormwood. Thomas Kinsella. CIP-2; PBCIP

I have drifted in silence. Imitations Based on the American. Frank Polite. BXAP

I have drunk ale from the Country of the Young. He Thinks of His Past Greatness When a Part of the Constellations of Heaven. W. B. Yeats. PoEL-5

I have eaten. This Is Just to Say. William Carlos Williams. ChAP; HeIP-4; InPK-6; InPS-3; KaS; NAAL-2; NIP-4; NOBA; NTP; NoAM; NoP-4; OPOU; PBMP; PoPoPo; Poetr; TAP; TRP

I have eaten the city. Manhattan. Hoffman Reynolds Hays. SPE

I have enjoyed your company. Poetry Visits an Old Lady. Aleksandar Petrov, *Serbian.* CEEP, *tr. by* Krinka Vidakovic Petrov *and* Mark Strand

I have examin'd and do find. To Mrs M. A. at Parting. Katherine Philips. CPO; FP

I have exhausted the delighted range. Michael Hartnett. CIP-2

I have fallen in love with American names. American Names. Stephen Vincent Benét. FaBoA; OBAL; OxBA

I have fastened everything within a black cloak. The Assignation. Juana de Ibarbourou, *Spanish.* PBWP, *tr. by* Brian Swann

I have fathered. Father Poem. Joel Oppenheimer. PoM

I have felt it as they've said. Larry Eigner. PoM

I have felt the swaying of the elephant's shoulders; and now you want me to climb on a jackass? Try to be serious. (LL) Why Mira Can't Go Back to Her Old House. Mirabai, *Rajasthani.* EnlH, *tr. by* Robert Bly

I have finally learned. Valerio Magrelli, *Italian.* NeIt, *tr. by* Dana Gioia

"I have finished another year," said God. New Year's Eve. Thomas Hardy. MoBrPo; NoAM

I Have Folded My Sorrows. Bob Kaufman. PoBA

I have followed to this strand the scent of their blood. Pilgrimage to Loango Strand. Jean-Baptiste Tati-Loutard. PBMAP

I have followed you model. Ode to a Model. Vladimir Nabokov. OBAL

I have forsworn[e] it whil[e] I live [*or* life]. *Unknown.* MiEL

I Have Fought the Good Fight. Jared Bell Waterbury. AH

I have found God. Discovery. Hilda Schiff. HP

I have found out a gift for my Erin. A Pastoral Ballad by John Bull. Thomas Moore. BIrV; OBSV

I have found such joy in simple things. Grace Noll Crowell. PoToHe

I have freed myself at last. From the Bridge. Claribel Alegría, *Spanish.* VCWP, *tr. by* D. J. Flakoll; AF, *tr. by* Darwin Flakoll

I have from you this red. Valerio Magrelli, *Italian.* NeIt, *tr. by* Dana Gioia

I have given my answer. (LL) Personal. Langston Hughes. NOBA; NTP

I have gone far from my beloved ones. Jerusalem the Dismembered. Uri Zvi Greenberg. TrJP, *tr. by* Charles A. Cowen *Fr.* Jerusalem.

I have gone out, a possessed witch. Her Kind. Anne Sexton. CoAP; HCAP; HeIP-4; LiTM; NALW; PoPoPo; Poetr; SAGP; TAP; TwCP; VCAP; WPOW

I have gone through life quietly. Earth. Yaroslav Vasilevich Smelyakov, *Russian.* TCRP, *tr. by* Albert C. Todd

I have got a new-born sister. Choosing a Name. Charles Lamb *and* Mary Lamb. OxBChV

I Have Got My Leave. Rabindranath Tagore. OBMV *Fr.* Gitanjali.

I have great need that the Saint grant help. Cynewulf. AnOE, *tr. by* Charles W. Kennedy *Fr.* Juliana.

I have grown past hate and bitterness. Nationality. Mary Gilmore, *Eskimo.* CBAP

I have grown used to the retreat of seasons. Lady Anne Bathing. Anthony Delius. PeSA

I have had a most rare vision. Bottom's Dream. Shakespeare. CBNP *Fr.* A Midsummer Night's Dream.

I have had asthma for a. Visitors. Tu Fu, *Chinese.* BLT; OHPC, *tr. by* Kenneth Rexroth

I have had enough. Sheltered Garden. Hilda Doolittle. NMM-2

I have had enough of women, and enough of love. Wanderer's Song. Arthur Symons. SAGP

I have had playmates, I have had companions. The Old Familiar Faces. Charles Lamb. AWP; BLPA; FP; FaBoBe; FaPoR; GTBS-P; NOBE; OBEV; OxAEP-2; RB

I have had to learn the simplest things. Maximus, to Himself. Charles Olson. CMoP; NOBA; NeAP; PmAP; PoE; PoM; VGW *Fr.* The Maximus Poems.

I have heard a mother bird. Welcome to Spring. Irene Thompson. BoTP

I have heard ingenuous Indians say. Roger Williams. SCAP

I have heard it said. To the Muse. Denise Levertov. APSN

I have heard of fish. The Sun. Anne Sexton. NYBP; PBWP

"I have heard," said a maid from Montclair. Limerick. Morris Gilbert Bishop. PeLi

I have heard some jealous women say. Romantic. George Garrett. HoPM

I have heard talk of bold Robin Hood. Robin Hood's Golden Prize. *Unknown.* ESPB

I have heard tell somewhere. The Old Dog in the Ruins of the Graves at Arles. James Wright. NNaP

I have heard that far from here. *Unknown.* ASW, *tr. by* Kevin Crossley-Holland *Fr.* The Phoenix.

I have heard that hysterical women say. Lapis Lazuli. W. B. Yeats. CABP; CMoP; EnlH; FaBoMo; FaBoTw; HeIP-4; InPS-3; LiTM; MoP; NAEL-2; NAWM-2; NOBE; NoAM; NoP-4; OAEL-2; TFi

I have heard the affairs in Ch'ang-an are like a game of chess. Tu Fu. SuSp, *tr. by* Wu-chi Liu *Fr.* Autumn Thoughts.

I have heard the curlew crying. Wild Geese. Katharine Tynan. IIP

I have heard the pigeons of the Seven Woods. In the Seven Woods. W. B. Yeats. CMoP; NoAM

I have heard them knock / on my dimension. Michael Hartnett. NOIV

I have heard what the talkers were talking, the talk of the beginning and the end. Walt Whitman. ColAP *Fr.* Song of Myself.

("Exactly the contents of one, and exactly the contents of two, and which is / ahead?") (LL) PAR

I have heard your voice floating, royal and real. To Dinah Washington. Etheridge Knight. PoBA

I have hoped, I have planned, I have striven. Unsubdued. Samuel Ellsworth Kiser. PoToHe

I have hopped, when properly wound up, the whole length. The Tin Frog. Russell Hoban. Spl

I have imagined all this. The Sleeping. Lynn Emanuel. AiP; WWSi

I have imagined the stars over Swallow Creek. Swallow Creek. Trish Rucker. CMAP

I have invented a new species of poetry, "verse without words" or sound-. Flight out of Time. Hugo Ball. PFTM, *tr. by* Pierre Joris *and* Jerome Rothenberg *Fr.* Flight out of Time.

I have it in my heart to serve God so. Of His Lady in Heaven. Jacopo da Lentino, *Italian.* AWP, *tr. by* D. G. Rossetti

I have it now. The Stone. Henry Vaughan. ChIV-1

I have it underfoot; I have found it. For a Swarm of Bees. *Unknown, Anglo-Saxon.* ASW, *tr. by* Kevin Crossley-Holland

I have just come down from my father. The Hospital Window. James Dickey. HCAP; MT; NoAM; PFE; VCAP

"I have just come from the salt, salt sea." The House Carpenter. *Unknown.* AS

I have just flown 1100 miles from Australia. Christchurch, N. Z. Earle Birney. OxBC

I have just realized that the stakes are myself. Revolutionary Letter #1. Diane Di Prima. CLPP

I have just seen a [most] beautiful thing. The Black Finger. Angelina Weld Grimké. NAAAL; PoBA

I have just seen you go down the mountain. Departure. Wang Wei, *Chinese.* TAL, *tr. by* Robert Payne

I have killed the moth flying around. Moth-Terror. Benjamin De Casseres. TrJP

I have known one bound to a bed by wrist and ankle. The Choice. Hilary Corke. NYBP

I have known the inexorable sadness of pencils. Dolor. Theodore Roethke. AmPP; CMoP; HCAP; HeIP-4; HoPM; LiTM; MoP; NoAM; OPOU; OxBSP; PBMP; PoA; SAGP; TRP

I have known the silence of the stars and of the sea. Silence. Edgar Lee Masters. MoAmPo; PoToHe

I have known the strange nurses of Kindness. But I Do Not Need Kindness. Gregory Corso. NeAP

I have known what it is to love. Love. Darwin T. Turner. SAGP

I Have Labored Sore. *Unknown.* EnVB; MiEL; WeW-3

I have lain in the sun. Nimium Fortunatus. Robert Bridges. MoBrPo

I have learn'd. Shakespeare. OxAEP-1 *Fr.* King Henry IV, Pt. I. NAEL-1

I have led a good life, full of peace and quiet. The Good Boy. *Unknown.* AS

I have led her home, my love, my only friend. Tennyson. CBLP; EBVV; NAEL-2; NOBVV *Fr.* Maud [A Monodrama]. EnVR

("Shadowing the snow-limbed Eve from whom she came.") (LL) PoEL-5

"There is none like her, none." OBNC

I have left you at last. (LL) Ireland. Dora Sigerson Shorter. IIP; OBEV; TIRV

I have lighted the candles, Mary. Kenneth Patchen. TrCP

I Have Lived and I Have Loved. *Unknown.* TTTS

I have lived between my two hands. Hands. Edvard Kocbek, *Slovene.* PoSu, *tr. by* Michael Scammell *and* Veno Taufer

I have lived in important places, times. Epic. Patrick Kavanagh. BIrV; CABP; CIP-2; NOIV; NoP-4

I have lived long enough, having seen one thing, that love hath an end. Hymn to Proserpine. Swinburne. EBVV; EnVR; NAEL-2; OAEL-2; OBNC; PoEL-5

I have lived on the lip. Jelaluddin Rumi, *Persian.* EnlH, *tr. by* Coleman Barks *and* A. J. Arberry

I Have Lived This Way for Years and Do Not Wish to Change. Michael C. Blumenthal. HCAP

I have looked at this photograph. Rescue. Dabney Stuart. NYBP

I have lost, and lately, these. Upon the Loss[e] of His Mistresses. Robert Herrick. BeJo; CaPo; CavPo; NAEL-1; NOSC; PFE; PoE

I have lost my melch Cow. 2 Antemasque, The: Two Countrye Wives, the Songe. Lady Jane Cavendish. KTR *Fr.* A Pastorall.

I have lost this wager. Time wins. Time Wins. Benoy Majumdar, *Bengali.* OMIP, *tr. by* Jyotirmoy Dutta

I Have Loved England. Alice Duer Miller. PoLF *Fr.* The White Cliffs.

I have loved flowers that fade. Robert Bridges. MoBrPo

I have loved statues. . . spangled dawns have seen. Statues. Olive Custance. ADE

I have loved the air outside Shop-Rite Liquor. Poetics. August Kleinzahler. PmAP

I have loved thirty by three. Gormley, Queen of Ireland. PBWP, *tr. by* Joan Keefe *Fr.* Gormley's Laments.

I have made a footprint, a sacred one. Planting Initiation Song. *Unknown, Osage.* WPoS, *tr. by* Francis La Flesche

I have made a mistake, someone tells me. The Beaten Track. Steve Benson. FTOS

I have made a sirventes against the city of Toulouse. Sirventes. Paul Blackburn. NeAP; PoM

I have made tales in verse, but this man made. The Waggon-Maker. John Masefield. EBEV

I have marked, as on the heather now I strayed. As on the Heather. Reinmar von Hagenau, *German.* AWP, *tr. by* Jethro Bithell

I have mentioned it by name. Edouard J. Maunick. NegPo, *tr. by* Ellen Conroy Kennedy *Fr.* As Far as Yoruba Land.

I have met them at close of day. Easter 1916. W. B. Yeats. CMoP; FaBoMo; FaBoPV; FaPoR; GEA; HAP; HeIP-4; IIP; InPS-3; LiTM; MoP; NAEL-2; NAWM-2; NIP-4; NOBE; NOIV; NoAM; NoP-4; OAEL-2; OBWP; OxAEP-2; OxBTC; PoE; PoPoPo; TFi

I have mislaid the torment and the fear. Success. William Empson. OxBTC

I have moved to Dublin to have it out with you. John Berryman. MoP; NoAM; TRP *Fr.* Dream Songs.

I have my gri-gri. Portrait. Antoine-Roger Bolamba. PBMAP

I have my heart on my fist. The Tomb of the Kings. Anne Hébert. PBWP, *tr. by* Kathleen Weaver

I have my piety too, which could. An Epitaph on Master Vincent Corbet[t]. Ben Jonson. BeJo

I have my yellow boots on to walk. The Stepping Stones. W. S. Graham. FaBoTC

I have never been rich before. To My Friend. Anne Campbell. PoToHe

I have never cut my hair. Window That Watched the Pru. Anne Sexton. Poetr

I have never returned. Alien. Gillian Allnutt. NBrP

I have never seen him, this invisible member of the panel, this thirteenth juror. The People vs. the People. Kenneth Fearing. MoAmPo

I have never seen the place where I was born. Birthplace. Tahereh Saffarzadeh, *Farsi.* WPOW, *tr. by* Deirdre Lashgari

I have never seen volcanoes. Emily Dickinson. PoEL-5

I have never soared, never soared. Bulat Shalvovich Okudzhava, *Russian.* TCRP, *tr. by* Deming Brown

I have no Brother—they who meet me now. Thy Brother's Blood. Jones Very. APN-1; NOBA; PAR; PoEL-4; TAP

I have no children / to float in the space between. Etheridge Knight. *See* The Idea of Ancestry.

I have no desire to live, but I am afraid of death. Ts'ai Yen. WPOW *Fr.* Eighteen Verses Sung to a Tatar Reed Whistle.

I have no dog, but it must be. My Dog. John Kendrick Bangs. BLPA; FaBoBe

I have no embroidered headband. Sappho, *Greek.* BoWoP, *tr. by* Willis Barnstone

I have no Life but this. Emily Dickinson. FaBoVe

I have no memories or photograph of my father. O-Bon: Dance for the Dead. Garrett Kaoru Hongo. LoL

I have no mockings or arguments.. . . I witness and wait. (LL) Trippers and askers surround me. Walt Whitman. ColAP; PAR

I have no more a golden store. The Merry Jovial Beggar. Peter Casey, *Irish.* TIRV, *tr. by* Douglas Hyde

I have no name. Fiddler Jones. Edgar Lee Masters. LiLi

I have no name. Infant Joy. William Blake. APAD; FHYEP; LiLi; NAEL-2; NTP; OxAEP-2; OxBSP; PoLF; Ro *Fr.* Songs of Innocence.

I have no name, / I am but two days old. William Blake. *See* Infant Joy.

I have no other earthly friend! (LL) Affliction of Margaret—, The. Wordsworth. GTBS-P; PoEL-4; RACG

I have no pain, dear mother, now. *Unknown.* OBCoV *Fr.* Soldiers' Songs of the First World War.

I have no rattles. *Ambo Oral Tradition. Fr.* Five Ghost Songs. TTTS

I have no seed to spread over the world. Patrizia Cavalli, *Italian.* NeIt, *tr. by* Robert McCracken

I Have No Strength for Mine. Joanne Kyger. PoM

I have no way to fight the tanks. Protest. Ioanna Tsatsos, *Greek.* GrIP, *tr. by* Jean Demos

I have no wish. Christmas. Giuseppe Ungaretti, *Italian.* NNPT, *tr. by* Michael Hamburger

I have no wish at all other than. Song for Grass Leaf. Toksu Moon, *Korean.* CKP, *tr. by* Jaihiun Kim

I have no wit, no words, no tears. A Better Resurrection. Christina Rossetti. NOBVV; VWP

I have no words that could prevail. The Silent Singer. Anna Wickham. WPN

I have not ever seen my father's grave. Father Son and Holy Ghost. Audre Lorde. MoLi; NAAAL; NoAM; PoBA

I have not ever seen my father's grave. (LL) Father Son and Holy Ghost. Audre Lorde. MoLi; NAAAL; NoAM; PoBA

I have not experienced the true. Lighthouse. Novella Nikolaevna Matveyeva, *Russian.* TCRP, *tr. by* Deming Brown

I Have Not Lingered in European Monasteries. Leonard Cohen. NOBC

I have not ridden a horse much. The Sharing. Bruce Weigl. CDa

I have not seen your writing. The Letter. Patricia Beer. OxBC

I Have Not Signed a Treaty with the United States Government. "Chrystos." UnSA

I have not spent the April of my time. Sonnet: "I have not spent the April of my time." Bartholomew Griffin. AAS *Fr.* Fidessa, More Chaste than Kind[e].

I have not used my darkness well. Squall. Stanley Moss. CoAP

I have not woken from a dream nor arrived by express train. Prague in the Midday Sun. Vítězslav Nezval, *Czech.* AF, *tr. by* Ewald Osers

I have nothing new to ask of you. Another Year Come. W. S. Merwin. NYBP

I have nothing to give you, but my anger. A Love Poem for My Country. Frank Mkalawile Chipasula. HBAPE

I have nothing to say about the war. Yehuda Amichai, *Hebrew.* IP, *tr. by* Bargad, Warren and Stanley Chyet; PoSu, *tr. by* Yehuda Amichai *and* Ted Hughes *Fr.* Patriotic Songs.

("And all of Jerusalem is the explanation for his death.") (LL) IP, *tr. by* Bargad, Warren and Stanley Chyet

I have nothing to say about the war. Yehuda Amichai. *Fr.* Songs of the Land of Zion Jerusalem. IP, *tr. by* Warren Bargod *and* Stanley F. Chyet

I have nothing to say to you, Billie Holiday. Billie in Silk. Angela Jackson. SeSe

I have often imagined that glances. Valerio Magrelli, *Italian.* NeIt, *tr. by* Dana Gioia

I have paid my price to live with myself on the terms that I willed. (LL) The Refined Man. Rudyard Kipling. FaBoEE; FaBoTw; PeFWW

I have perceiv'd that to be with those I like is enough. Walt Whitman. SAmP *Fr.* Leaves of Grass (1855). APN-1

I have pined for the sight of the sea for years. The Beautiful Sea. Mary E. Tucker. CBWP-1

I have *poetic* licence, i WriTe thE way i waNt. According to my Mood. Benjamin Zephaniah. NOxBChV

I have prayed for the end of his breath. The Stone Dolphin. Fay Zwicky. BMAP *Fr.* Three Songs of Love and Hate.

I have prepared the hibachi. *Unknown, Japanese.* WPJ, *tr. by* Kenneth Rexroth *and* Ikuko Atsumi

I Have Recently Edited My Unworthy Poems in Four Chapters, Copied Them Out in My Own Hand, and Entrusted Them to My Daughter to Keep. Five Miscellaneous Poems. Chin Nung, *Chinese.*

"In the silences between peals of the bell." CoBLCP, *tr. by* Jonathan Chaves

I have rinsed clean. The Winter Sky. So Chong-Ju, *Korean.* CKP, *tr. by* Jaihiun Kim

I have risen from your body. The Onion. John Thompson. NOBC

I have said / She 's adulteress; I have said with whom. Shakespeare. OxAEP-1 *Fr.* The Winter's Tale.

I have said that the soul is not more than the body. The Hub of the Universe. Walt Whitman. EnlH *Fr.* Song of Myself. AmPP; MoAmPo; NAAL-3; NOBA; OxBA

I have said that the soul is not more than the body. Walt Whitman. ColAP *Fr.* Song of Myself. AmPP; MoAmPo; NAAL-3; NOBA; OxBA

I have seen a court, and a dozen courts. A Christmas Revel. Dafydd Bach ap Madog Wladaidd, *Welsh.* OBWVE

I have seen a lovely thing. Blight. Arna Bontemps. ColAP

I Have Seen Black Hands. Richard Wright. AF; PoBA

I have seen bus depots. Reflecting on the Aging-Process. Robert Peters. BXAP

I have seen come on. Death. John A. Stone. MT

I have seen flowers come in stony places. Epilogue. John Masefield. FaBoEE; OxBTC

I have seen full many a sight. Dinah Kneading Dough. Paul Laurence Dunbar. NAAAL

I have seen her, wonderful! This Version of Love. Dorothy Hewett. BMAP; CBAP

I have seen lines on a paper. Borders. Michael S. Weaver. GT

I have seen mannequins. Walter James Turner. *Fr.* The Seven Days of the Sun. OBMV

I have seen men binding their brothers in chains, and crafty. The Hate and the Love of the World. Max Ehrmann. PoToHe

I have seen, O desolate one, the voice has its tower. Bell Tower. Léonie Adams. MoAmPo

I have seen old ships sail like swans asleep. The Old Ships. James Elroy Flecker. CH; MoBrPo; OBMV; PoRA

I have seen the light coming up over the town, like ash. Overture to Strangers. Phyllis Haring. PeSA

I have seen the paschal men today. Easter '68. Basil T. Paquet. CDa

I have seen the rosebud blow. On Viewing Her Sleeping Infant. Maria Frances Cecelia Cowper. ECWP

I have seen the smallest minds of my generation. Problem in Social Geometry—the Inverted Square! Ray Durem. PoBA

I have seen the soft light flicker. Message from Ohanapecosh Glacier. W. M. Ransom. CDW

I have seen the white horsemen riding to hell. Apocalypse and Resurrection. John Clifford Bayliss. SPE

I have seen them at many hours. Moths. Julia Fields. Fr. Poems: Birmingham 1962–1964. PoBA

I have seen them trying. Norman Jordan. NBV

I have seen this picture before. From Homegrown: An Asian-American Anthology of Writers. Colleen J. McElroy. LTA

I have seen you, little mouse. The Little Mouse. Unknown. ReMoGo

I have seen you, my erect morning, bare chested with tree-top tousled head. Morning in My City. Avraham Shlonsky, Hebrew. MHP, tr. by Ruth Finer Mintz

I have seen you suffer in the midst of winters. Harlem. Jean Brierre, French. TTY, tr. by John F. Matheus

I Have Set My Heart So High. Unknown. OAEL-1

I have shut my balcony door. Casida of Sobbing. Federico García Lorca, Spanish. AF, tr. by Robert Bly

I have slain none except my mother. She. An Only Son. Rudyard Kipling. Fr. Epitaphs of the War [1914–1918]. OBWP

I have smelled all the perceptible smells. Looking Back. Heinrich Heine, German. NNPT, tr. by Christopher Middleton

I have snapped off my burning. Maui. Meg Campbell. PeNZ

I have so little sorrow. Song. Patricia Jones. ISC

"I have so many women" he said inside her. Splitting the Infinite. Yona Wallach, Hebrew. IP, tr. by Warren Bargad and Stanley F. Chyet

I have so much faith in you. I believe. To Trust. Antonia Pozzi, Italian. PBWP, tr. by Lynne Lawner

I have solved the riddle. Dressing My Daughter. George Eklund. IFJA

I Have Some Friends before Me Gone. Unknown. AH

I have something to tell you. Two Friends. David Ignatow. PBMP

I have sought long with steadfastness. Sir Thomas Wyatt. SiPS

I have sought the elusive aroma. Barbecue Service. James Applewhite. MT

I have sown beside all waters in my day. A Black Man Talks of Reaping. Arna Bontemps. BPo; ColAP; NAAAL; PoBA; SSLK

I have spent my life. "Stephany." NBV

I have spread wet linen. Today. Ethel Romig Fuller. PoToHe

I have strolled the long groves of the Classics and Canons. Rhyme-Prose on the Idle Life. P'an Yüeh, Chinese. CoBCP, tr. by Burton Watson

I have studied the tight curls. Movement Song. Audre Lorde. VCAP

I have such papers that grim Cato's wife. De Libro suo. Martial, Latin. OBCVT, tr. by R. Fletcher

I have sworn ten thousand times. Kenneth Rexroth, after the Greek of Palladas. NNaP; PGA

I have taken that vow. The Red-haired Man's Wife. James Stephens. MoBrPo

I have taken the woman of beauty. The Bear's Song. Unknown, Haida. AWP, tr. by Constance Lindsay Skinner Fr. Three Songs from the Haida.

I have tasted each varied pleasure. My Childhood's Home. Caroline Elizabeth Norton. Ro Fr. The Undying One.

I have the delusion / that you are with me. Akiko Yosano, Japanese. WPJ, tr. by Kenneth Rexroth and Ikuko Atsumi

I have the eyes of a real sea calf. The Seal. Guillaume Apollinaire, French. CBNP

I have the same. December 9th. Eileen Myles. PmAP

I have thee, thou hast me. Unknown, German. GePo, tr. by Alexander Gode

I have this deal of death about my hands. Blood. Ray Bremser. NeAP

I have this large tattoo on my chest. It is like a dream I have. Confessional Poem. Louis Jenkins. RaBo

I have thought of beaches, fields. Bundles. Carl Sandburg. MoAmPo

I Have Three Daughters. Ruth Stone. InPS-3

I have thrown wide my window. Midnight. Michael Roberts. OBMV

I have to live with myself, and so. Myself. E. A. Guest. BLPA; PWR

I have to thank God I'm a woman. The Affinity. Anna Wickham. NALW

I have to write a page. Vladimir Leonovich, Russian. TCRP, tr. by Albert C. Todd

I have told you. Tenth Symphony. John Ashbery. NOBA

I have tossed hours upon the tides of fever. Bout with Burning. Vassar Miller. LiTM; MT; MoAmPo

I have traveled, I have traveled. The Consumptive. Priscilla Jane Thompson. CBWP-2

I have tried to shift the stars. The Juniper Moon Pulls at My Bones. Earle Thompson. HATNAP

I have turned into a little shrine, a favorite. A Favorite Little Shrine. Enrique Lihn. VCWP

I have turned to the landscape because men disappoint me. The Ram's Horn. John Hewitt. BIrV; PNI

I Have Twelve Oxen. The Twelve Oxen. Unknown. CH

I have twelve oxen that be faire and brown. Unknown. MiEL

I have two sicknesses, Love. Unknown, Greek. PGA, tr. by Kenneth Rexroth

I have understood nothing. Edouard J. Maunick. NegPo, tr. by Ellen Conroy Kennedy Fr. As Far as Yoruba Land.

I have walked a great while over the snow. The Witch. Mary Elizabeth Coleridge. BrRo; CABP; NALW; PFE; VWP; WPE

I have wanted excellence in the knife-throw. The Language of the Brag. Sharon Olds. NMM-2; PBCAP

I have wanted other things more than lovers. Monody to the Sound of Zithers. Kay Boyle. PoA

I have wasted my life. (LL) Lying in a Hammock at William Duffy's Farm in Pine Island, Minnesota. James Wright. CoAmPo; ColAP; HAP; HCAP; HoPM; NOBA; Poetr; SAGP; TRP; VCAP; WeT

I have watched a thousand days. Salonikan Grave. Rudyard Kipling. Fr. Epitaphs of the War [1914–1918]. OBWP

I have watched your fingers drum. The Hand. Howard Moss. TAP

I have wept with the spring storm. After the Persian. Louise Bogan. PoA

I have wished a bird would fly away. A Minor Bird. Robert Frost. CMoP; SAmP

I have with fishing-rod and line. The Wounded Hawk. Herbert Edward Palmer. FaBoTw

I have work to dream. Bill Knott. See Two Vietnam Poems: (1966).

I have wrapped my dreams in a silken cloth. For a Poet. Countee Cullen. TTY

I have written a million words. Millionaire. A. J. Seymour. HCP

I have wrought these words together out of a wryed existence. The Wife's Complaint. Unknown, Anglo-Saxon. BoLoP; EEP, tr. by Michael Alexander

I haven't a clue where I've been. Limerick. Sydney Bernard Smith. PeLi

I haven't sung your praise. To My Country. "Rachel," Hebrew. PBWP, tr. by Diane Mintz

I haveta turn my television down sometimes cuz. A Different Love Poem / We Need a Change. Ntozake Shange. UnSA Fr. Okra to Greens /.

I, having loved ever since I was a child a few things. Modern Declaration. Edna St. Vincent Millay. SAGP

I, he says, am not a warrior. Novella Nikolaevna Matveyeva, Russian. TCRP, tr. by Deming Brown

I hear a dog barking. Behind Prison Bars. No Ch'ŏn-myŏng, Korean. CKP, tr. by Jaihiun Kim

I hear a river thro' the valley wander. Trumbull Stickney. See I heard a river thro' the valley wander.

I hear a river thro' the valley wander. Variations on a Fragment by Trumbull Stickney. John Hollander. BAP-94 Fr. Variations on a Fragment by Trumbull Stickney.

I hear a river thro' the valley wander. Variations on a Fragment by Trumbull Stickney. John Hollander. NoP-4

I hear a step. A step. Ted Greenwald. FTOS

I hear a sudden cry of pain! The Snare. James Stephens. BoTP; CH; CMoP; SCGP

I hear a whistling. Emmett Till. James A. Emanuel. NIP-4; PoBA

I hear again the tread of war go thundering through the land. Albert Sidney Johnston. Kate Brownlee Sherwood. CBCWP

I hear along our street. Christmas Carols. Henry Wadsworth Longfellow. BoTP

I hear America singing, the varied carols I hear. Walt Whitman. AWP; AiP; FaBoBe; HAP; MoAmPo; PBMP; SAGP; SAmP; TFi; WeW-3

I hear an army charging upon the land. James Joyce. PFE; SAGP

I hear and behold God in every object, yet understand God not in the least. Walt Whitman. See I have said that the soul is not more than the body.

I hear and is my heart not badly shaken? (LL) Shancoduff. Patrick Kavanagh. BIrV; CIP-2; FaBoTw; IIP

I hear but my brain doesn't get the. Andrew Pacheco. CTV

I hear eating. Night Fun. Judith Viorst. TLR

I hear / he won't give horses for poems. An Insult. Unknown. NOIV

I hear her sew. Leroy Gorman. HA

I hear her voice like. Her Voice. Barney Bush. HATNAP

I hear in my heart, I hear in its ominous pulses. The Wild Ride. Louise Imogen Guiney. ColAP; RACG

I hear it in the deep heart's core. (LL) The Lake-Isle of Innisfree. W. B. Yeats. ADE; APAD; CABP; CMoP; ChAP; ClHu; EBEvV; FaPoR; HeIP-4; IIP; InPK-6; InPS-3; LiTM; MoBrPo; MoP; NAEL-2; NOBE; NTP; NoAM; NoP-4; OBEV; OxAEP-2; OxBTC; PoE; PoPoPo; PoRA; Poetr; SAGP; TFi; UV

I Hear It Said. Barbara Young. BLPA

I hear it was charged against me that I sought to destroy institutions. Walt Whitman. APN-1; MoAmPo; PBMP

I hear leaves drinking rain. The Rain. W. H. Davies. BoTP; OxBTC

I hear many voices. To Adhiambo. Gabriel Okara. PBA; PBMAP

I hear people waiting for the riot to begin in their hearts. Ray Charles at Mississippi State. Tom Dent. NBV

I hear something coming. Breathing. James Tate. LCAP-2

I Hear Something Falling, said the wind. Natan Zach, *Hebrew*. IP, *tr. by* Warren Bargad *and* Stanley F. Chyet

I hear that Andromeda. Sappho, *Greek*. PBWP, *tr. by* Mary Barnard

I HEAR THAT THE AXE HAS FLOWERED. Paul Celan, *German*. PoSu, *tr. by* Michael Hamburger

I hear that the peonies are magnificent. To Hsü Shih-t'ing. Hsü Wei, *Chinese*. CoBLCP, *tr. by* Jonathan Chaves

I hear that you have burned ten thousand of your poems. Twenty-eight Characters Sent to Tung-ts'un on the Subject of the Poems He Burned. Cheng Hsieh, *Chinese*. CoBLCP, *tr. by* Jonathan Chaves

I hear the beat. The Talking Drums. Kojo Gyinaye Kyei. PBA

I hear the halting footsteps of a lass. Harlem Shadows. Claude McKay. AmPP; ColAP; NAAAL

I hear the man downstairs slapping the hell out of his stupid wife [again]. The .38. Ted Joans. PFE; WeW-3

I hear the noise about thy keel. Tennyson. EBVV; EnVR *Fr.* In Memoriam A. H. H.

I hear the piano playing. The Strange House. Thomas Hardy. OxBSn

I hear the Shadowy Horses, their long manes a-shake. Michael Robartes Bids His Beloved Be at Peace. W. B. Yeats. MoP; NoAM

I hear the voice. Israel. Carl Rakosi. ChIV-1

I hear [or heare] the whistling ploughman [or plough-man] all day long. On the Ploughman [or Plough-Man]. Francis Quarles. NOSC

I hear they're hoping to run trips. 'Do you think we'll ever get to see Earth, sir?'. Sheenagh Pugh. SpW

I hear voices. i hear them often. I've heard them. Be Quiet, Go Away. Wanda Coleman. NAAAL

I Hear You. Shirley Kaufman. MDDM

I hear you call. The Call of the River Nun. Gabriel Okara. PBA

I hear you have gone to live among the village mounds. Visiting the Hermit Cheng. Po Chü-i, *Chinese*. TAL, *tr. by* Robert Payne

I hear you, I will come. (LL) Bredon Hill. A. E. Housman. EBVV; MoBrPo; NAEL-2; OxAEP-2; SoSe-8; UV

I hear you Trane. Afreeka Brass. Mwatabu Okantah. SeSe

I hear your voice saying *Hello* in that guarded way. Telephoning Home. Carol Ann Duffy. NBrP

I Hear You've Let Go. Rosario Ferré, *Spanish*. BoWoP, *tr. by* Willis Barnstone

I heard a bird at dawn. The Rivals. James Stephens. BoTP; OBEV; OBMV

I heard a bird sing. Oliver Herford. NTCP; PoLF

I heard a brooklet gushing. Whither? Wilhelm Müller. AWP, *tr. by* Longfellow *Fr.* The Beautiful Maid of the Mill.

I heard a/ couple of fleas. Archy, the Cockroach, Speaks. Don Marquis. *Fr.* Certain Maxims of Archy. OBAL

I heard a cow low, a bonnie cow low. *Unknown*. FaBoCh *Fr.* The Queen of Elfan's [*or* Elfland's] Nourice [*or* Nourrice]. ESPB

I heard a Fly buzz—when I died[—died]. Emily Dickinson. APN-2; AmPP; BoWoP; CMoP; ClHu; ColAP; HAP; HeIP-4; HoPM; ImPo; InPK-6; LiLi; LiTM; MeMAP; MoAmPo; MoP; NAAL-1; NAAL-3; NALW; NAWM-2; NOBA; NoAM; NoP-4; OxBA; PAR; PoE; PoPoPo; PoRA; Poetr; SAmP; SCV; SoSe-8; TAP; TFi; TOF; TRP; WeW-3

I heard a fly buzz when I died. *Unknown*. PFE

I heard a herald's note announce the coming of a king. Rex Mundi. David Gascoyne. NoP-4

I Heard a Linnet Courting. Robert Bridges. LiTM; OBEV; OBMV

I heard a mouse. The Mouse. Elizabeth Jane Coatsworth. BoTP; NOxBChV; OBCA

I heard a Noise and Wishèd for a Sight. Thomas Bateson. EBEV; HAP; OAEL-1

I heard a river thro' the valley wander. Trumbull Stickney. APN-2 *Fr.* Dramatic Fragments.

("I hear a river thro' the valley wander.") NoP-4

I Heard a Soldier. Herbert Trench. CH

I heard a thousand blended notes. Lines Written in Early Spring. Wordsworth. FHTEP; GTBS-P; LaPo; NAEL-2; NOBRP; OAEL-2; PBMP; PoLF; Ro

I heard a voice, within me, call. "Anna Akhmatova," *Russian*. TCRP, *tr. by* Daniel Weissbort

I heard a winter tree in song. Conceit. Mervyn Laurence Peake. Spl

I heard a woman's voice that wailed. In Ruin Reconciled. Aubrey Thomas De Vere. BIrV

I heard an angel speak last night. A Curse for a Nation. Elizabeth Barrett Browning. NALW; VWP; WPE; WPOW

I heard an ignorant crow call, "Life is now." Old Snapshot. Ronald G. Everson. MoCV

I heard an owl at midday. Como lo Siento. Lorna Dee Cervantes. NoAM

I heard Andrew Jackson say, as he closed his Virgil. Andrew Jackson's Speech. Robert Bly. CoAmPo

I HEARD at nights your long sighs. Dreaming of a Dead Lady. Shên Yo, *Chinese*. ChiP, *tr. by* Arthur Waley

I heard Caruso last night for the first time, I'm 28. Explaining the Evening News to Corbyn. James Harms. CMAP

I heard Christ sing quhile roond him dar. "Hugh MacDiarmid." ChIV-2

I heard from a decent man the other day. On Hearing It Has Been Ordered in the Chapterhouse of Ireland That the Friars Make No More Songs or Verses. Pádraigín Haicéad, *Irish*. NOIV, *tr. by* Thomas Kinsella

I heard him in the autumn winds. Life in Death. Ellice Hopkins. PeVV

I heard how, to the beat of some quick tune. The Dancer. Sadi. AWP, *tr. by* Sir Edward Arnold *Fr.* The Gulistan.

I heard Immanuel singing. Vachel Lindsay. HAP

I heard in the night the pigeons. No Child. Padraic Colum. OBMV

I heard last night a little child go singing. Casa Guidi Windows. Elizabeth Barrett Browning. VWP *Fr.* Casa Guidi Windows.

I heard last night a little child go singing. Part I. Elizabeth Barrett Browning. PEW *Fr.* Casa Guidi Windows.

I heard last night a lovely lute. A Summer Eve's Vision. Maria Jane Jewsbury. VWP

I heard my love was going to Yang-chou. *Unknown*. BoWoP, *tr. by* Arthur Waley *Fr.* Tzu Yeh Songs.

I heard my love was gone on garrison at Chin-wei Mountain. Tune: "Immortal at the River." Wang Kuo-wei, *Chinese*. SuSp, *tr. by* Ching-i Tu

I heard my meatless bones. Night Fear. Don Receveur. CDa

I heard my name, the day rose and disappear over the beach. the day on each breath. City of Men. Aaron Shurin. FTOS

I heard no sound where I stood. The Sleeping House. Tennyson. OBNC *Fr.* Maud has a garden of roses. FHYEP *Fr.* Maud [A Monodrama]. EnVR

I heard of gold at Sutter's Mill. When I Went Off to Prospect. *Unknown*. AmFP

I heard of poor. Poor. Myra Cohn Livingston. KaS

I heard on the meadow. Heinrich von Morungen, *German*. GePo, *tr. by* Frederick Goldin

I heard one who said: "Verily." Cassandra. Edwin Arlington Robinson. CMoP; ImPo; LiTM; MeMAP; NoAM; OxBA

I heard or seemed to hear the chiding Sea. Sea-Shore. Ralph Waldo Emerson. APN-1; ColAP; OxBA

I heard that south of the capital city. Southern Mountains. Han Yü, *Chinese*. SuSp, *tr. by* Charles Hartman

I heard the bells on Christmas Day. Christmas Bells. Henry Wadsworth Longfellow. AH; CTV; OBCP; PChr

I Heard the Byrd. Oliver Lagrone. SeSe

I heard the carping [or herde a carpyng] of a clerk. Robyn and Gandeleyn. *Unknown*. ESPB; EnSB; OxBB

I heard the Challenge "Who goes there?" The Watchers. Edmund Blunden. PoFWW

I heard the dogs howl in the moonlight night. Dream, A [or The]. William Allingham. BIrV; NOBVV

I heard the dust falling between the walls. (LL) Redeployment. Howard Nemerov. LiTM; OBWP; PoWW; TrJP

I heard the farm cocks crowing loud, and faint, and thin. Daybreak in a Garden. Siegfried Sassoon. BoTP

I heard the Indian Agent say. The Old Man's Lazy. Peter Blue Cloud. HATNAP; LTA

I heard the old, old men say. The Old Men Admiring Themselves in the Water. W. B. Yeats. CMoP; FaBoCh; KaS

I Heard the Old Song. B. W. Vilakazi, *Zulu*. PeSA

I heard the Poor Old Woman say. Lament for the Poets: 1916. Francis Ledwidge. AWP

I heard the pulse of the besieging sea. To S.C. Robert Louis Stevenson. PeVV

I heard the sighing of the reeds. By the Pool at the Third Rosses. Arthur Symons. ADE *Fr.* In Ireland.

I heard the sighing of the reeds. In Ireland: By the Pool at the Third Rosses. Arthur Symons. OBNC

I heard the snowflakes whisper in the still dark night. Snowflakes. Ruth M. Arthur. BoTP

I heard the trailing garments of the Night. Hymn to the Night. Henry Wadsworth Longfellow. APN-1; MeMAP; NOBA; OxBA; PWR; TAP

I heard the weeping of the newly born in its mother's bosom. The Circle of Weeping. Amir Gilbo'a, *Hebrew.* MHP, tr. by Ruth Finer Mintz

I heard them say I'm ugly. The Ugly Child. Elizabeth Jennings. NOxBChV

I heard this morning. Summer nineteen seventy. Lindiwe Mabuza. WPOW

I heard thy fate without a tear. Stanzas. Byron. PBMP

I heard two workers say, "This chaos / Will soon be ended." Idiom of the Hero. Wallace Stevens. AFr; OxBA

I heard you solemn-sweet pipes of the organ as last Sunday morn I pass'd the church. Walt Whitman. APN-1; OxBA; SAmP

I Held a Shelley Manuscript. Gregory Corso. BB; PmAP; VGW

I Held His Name. Alberto A. Ríos. NoAM

I held it truth, with him who sings. Tennyson. EBVV; EBVVPR; EnVR; HeIP-4; OAEL-2; OBNC *Fr.* In Memoriam A. H. H.

I held the briefcase at arm's length from me. The Briefcase. Paul Muldoon. CABP

I held the man for nothing in my arms. (LL) Saint Judas. James Wright. CoAmPo; GI; LCAP-2; NOBA; WeT

I Held the Vein, But Death. Dennis Phillips. FTOS

I held you / through all your shifts. Eventual Proteus. Margaret Atwood. MoCV

I helped a little lame dog. My Little Dog. Pearl Forbes MacEwen. BoTP

I here, thou there, yet both but one. (LL) A Letter to Her Husband, Absent upon Public[k] Employment. Anne Bradstreet. HAP; HeIP-4; KTR; NAAL-1; NAAL-3; NALW; NoP-4; PEW; PoPoPo; SCAP

I hereby swear that to uphold your house. Sonnet. Elinor Wylie. ImPo; MoAmPo; NAAL-2; OxBA; Son *Fr.* One Person.

I, Hermes, guard Cyllene's wooded slopes. Nicias, *Greek.* GrAn, tr. by Anthony Holden

I, Hermes, have been set up. Anyte, *Greek.* GrAn; OBVE; PGA, tr. by Kenneth Rexroth

I. Hérodiade. Arthur Symons. ADE *Fr.* Stéphane Mallarmé.

I hid my love when young while [*or* till] I. Secret Love. John Clare. FHYEP; GLoP; LoP; NOBVV; NTP; OAEL-2; OBNC; PoE; PoEL-4; RB; SCGP

I hit her in the face because she loved me. The Sick Assailant. Anna Wickham. WPN

I hoard a little spring of secret tears. On Shooting a Swallow in Early Youth. Charles Tennyson Turner. NOBVV

I hoed and trenched and weeded. A. E. Housman. LiTM; MoBrPo; UnPo; WeW-3

I hold a banyan of memories of home. Away. Andrew Salkey. HCP

I hold a chipped bowl in my hands. The Game. Edvard Kocbek, *Slovene.* PoSu, tr. by Michael Scammell *and* Veno Taufer

I hold a letter in my hand. A Poem for the Meeting of the American Medical Association. Oliver Wendell Holmes. PoEL-5

I Hold A Lust To See People. Out of the Wailing. Stephen Caldwell Wright. ISC

I hold a rattlesnake in my hand, gently. Victory Drive, near Fort Benning, Georgia. Bin Ramke. MT

I hold dead friends like jewels in my hand. Jewels In My Hand. Sasha Moorsom. APAD

I hold him, verily, of mean emprise. He Perceives His Rashness in Love, but Has No Choice. Guido Guinicelli, *Italian.* AWP, tr. by D. G. Rossetti

I hold it good—as who shall hold it bad? Columbia's Agony. "Orpheus C. Kerr." OBAL

I hold it towards you. (LL) To Fanny Brawne. Keats. BoLoP; FHYEP; HAP; InPK-6; InPS-3; NOBE; NoP-4; OAEL-2, OxBSP; PoPoPo; TRP

I hold it true that thoughts are things. Secret Thoughts. Ella Wheeler Wilcox. PWR

I hold it true, whate're befall. Tennyson. UV *Fr.* 27. CABP *Fr.* In Memoriam A. H. H.

I hold my honey and I store my bread. My Dreams, My Works Must Wait Till after Hell. Gwendolyn Brooks. NoP-4

I hold your head tight. Marichiko, *Japanese.* OHMPJ, tr. by Kenneth Rexroth

I hold your head tight between. Kenneth Rexroth. APSN *Fr.* The Love Poems of Marichiko.

I Hope and Fear. Thomas Lodge. Son *Fr.* Phyllis.

I hope he doesn't see me walking past his bed. Letter. Alexander Bergman. TrJP

I Hope I Don't Have You Next Semester, But. Edwin S. Godsey. HoPM

I Hope, I Fear. Sir William Alexander, Earl of Stirling. Son *Fr.* Aurora.

I hope my child'll. Lament over Love. Langston Hughes. NAAAL

I hope the old Romans. Ancient History. Arthur Guiterman. KaS; OBCA

I hope they never get a rope on you, weather. Weather. May Swenson. PaTW

I hope to feel some pity when it comes. When It Comes. John Wain. PFE

I hope when I am dead that I shall lie. Oblivion. Jessie Redmond Fauset, *fr. the French of* Massillon Coicou. NegPo

I hope when you're yourself and twice my age. Metaphor for My Son. John Holmes. ImGa

I hope you'll forgive the black paint. I Have Lived This Way for Years and Do Not Wish to Change. Michael C. Blumenthal. HCAP

I hoped that he would love me. The Kiss. Sara Teasdale. NMM-2

I HUG my pillow and do not speak a word;. Poems in Depression, at Wei Village. Po Chü-i, *Chinese.* ChiP, tr. by Arthur Waley

I hung his coat and trousers to roast before a fire. (LL) Taffy was a Welshman, Taffy was a thief. Mother Goose. OxNR; RB; ReMoGo

I hung my verses in the wind. The Test. Ralph Waldo Emerson. OBAL

I hunt among stones. (LL) The Kingfishers. Charles Olson. APSN; CMoP; InPS-3; NAAL-2; NoBA; NeAP; PoM; VCAP

"I, I, I." What a strange word he's saying! In Front of the Mirror. Vladislav Felitsianovich Khodasevich, *Russian.* TCRP, tr. by Michael Frayn

I, I, the future that mends everything. (LL) The Elementary Scene. Randall Jarrell. CMoP; PoE

I, Icarus. Alden Nowlan. NOxBChV

I idly cut a parsley stalk. On a Midsummer Eve. Thomas Hardy. FaBoVe

"I, if I perish, perish"—Esther spake. Christina Rossetti. *Fr.* Monna Innominata. BWW

I imagine a day when the children. Company. Michael Longley. IIP

I Imagine Angels. Guillaume Apollinaire, *French.* PiM, tr. by Kenneth Koch

I imagine everything wrapped in a beatific mist. Georgy Vladimirovich Ivanov, *Russian.* TCRP, tr. by Daniel Weissbort

I imagine him still with heavy brow. Beethoven's Death Mask. Stephen Spender. OxBTC

I imagine myself / a mouth. Fruit, of the Earth. Cyril Dabydeen. PBCV

I imagine the time of our meeting. Forms of the Earth at Abiquiu. N. Scott Momaday. CDW

I imagine this [*or* the] midnight moment's forest. The Thought-Fox. Ted Hughes. FaBoMo; HeIP-4; InPS-3; MoP; NTP; NYBP; NoAM; NoP-4; Poetr; SCV

I imagine where God has never been. Peter Levi. TOF

I imagined the bombs and fighters. Air Raid. Peter Wild. Poetsp

I implore Neptune to claim his child today! Anne Spencer. *See* At the Carnival.

I in a new understanding of my confusion. (LL) In Broken Images. Robert Graves. NoP-4; TRP

I, in my intricate image, stride on two levels. Dylan Thomas. SPE

I, in your frutefull woomb conceyved, born was. Nicholas Grimald. PBRV *Fr.* A Funeral Song, Upon the Decease of Annes His Mother.

I inhabit a sacred wound. Lagoonal Calendar. Aimé Césaire, *French.* VCWP, tr. by Clayton Eshleman *and* Annette Smith

I intended an ode. Urceus Exit. Austin Dobson. OBEV *Fr.* Rose-Leaves.

I invite you, child, to dance. You come. I bow my blond head. Song for a Dance. Abraham Sutskever, *Yiddish.* CEEP, tr. by Ruth Whitman

I is the ghost of Stevey Fizzlegig. The Ghost. Fitz-James O'Brien. FaBoVe; NOEC

I jiggled it. This Tooth. Lee Bennett Hopkins. TLR

I Jocky Bell o'Braikenbrow lyes under this stane. On Jocky Bell. *Unknown.* FaBoEE

I John saw. I testify. Hilda Doolittle. NALW *Fr.* Tribute to the Angels.

I journey / And the highway journeys too. Journey. Vasco Popa. PoSu *Fr.* Besieged Serenity.

I journeyed to the suburbs, and there I was told, tr. sect. 1. T. S. Eliot. UV *Fr.* Choruses from "The Rock."

I joy, dear[e] Mother, when I view. The British Church. George Herbert. ESCV; PeECV

I joy not in no earthly bliss. *Unknown.* NoSic

I joy to see how in your drawen work. Sonnet 71. Edmund Spenser. NoP-4; PBRV; PoE *Fr.* Amoretti. AAS

I just came by the prison-door. Pray Remember the Poor. Christopher Smart. NOEC *Fr.* Hymns for the Amusement of Children.

I just knew it when we swept above the old roofs of Dijon. Elizabeth Barrett Browning. PeVV *Fr.* Aurora Leigh. VWP

I Just Missed the Bus and I'll Be Late for Work. Ariel Dorfman, *Spanish.* AF, tr. by Ariel Dorfman *and* Edith Grossman

I just once want to feel. From Riot Rimes U.S.A. #78. Raymond R. Patterson. MBE

I just said I didn't know. Parachutes, My Love, Could Carry Us Higher. Barbara Guest. NeAP

I just think it will happen, soon. (LL) Going, Going. Philip Larkin. NoAM; OxAEP-2

I Just Wanna Testify. Cornelius Eady. IFJA

I keep a blue bottle. Melancholy inside Families. Pablo Neruda, *Spanish*. RaBo, *tr. by* Robert Bly *and* James Wright

I keep a TV monitor on my chest. Shorts / Excerpts. Bill Knott. PBCAP

I keep dreaming I'm dead. Qaqatcguk, *Tlingit Indian*. STP, *tr. by* James Koller

I keep falling in love. One Hundred and Forty-Ninth Chorus. Jack Kerouac. PmAP   *Fr.* Mexico City Blues.

I keep feeling all space as my image. Poem. Sanders Russell. SPE

I keep forgetting. Lily Brett. HP

I keep him waiting, tuck in the curtains. Planning the Perfect Evening. Rita Dove. GT   *Fr.* A Suite for Augustus.

I keep losing. And That Is Why. . . . Magda Bartošová, *Czech and Slovak*. CEEP, *tr. by* Magda Bartošová

I keep my parents in a garden. Eden Is a Zoo. Margaret Atwood. WPE

I keep pushing this. The Prophets. Richard Shelton. NYBP

I keep running around. Song. *Unknown, Chippewa Indian*. STP, *tr. by* Jerome Rothenberg

I keep saying. Salsabîl. Jamîl, *Arabic*. ArPe, *tr. by* Omar S. Pound

I keep the custom of the Ferry. The Hostess of the Ferry Inn. Gwerfyl Mechain, *Welsh*. OBWVE, *tr. by* H. Idris Bell

I keep the rustic gate closed. Idleness. Lu Yu, *Chinese*. OHPC; OxBM, *tr. by* Kenneth Rexroth

I keep the taste of feasting. The Epitaph of Sardanapalos. *Unknown, Greek*. PGA, *tr. by* Kenneth Rexroth

I keep thinking of you standing in Korea, in the courtyard. Solitary. Sharon Olds. NMM-2

"I Keep to Myself Such Measures. . . ." Robert Creeley. NoAM; PmAP

I ken a glog-hole. The Glog-Hole. "Hugh MacDiarmid." NTP

I ken these islands each inhabited. Harry Semen. "Hugh MacDiarmid." FaBoTC

I kenning [*or* kening] through astronomy divine. Meditation 8 (First Series). Edward Taylor. AmPP; ChIV-2; MeMAP; NAAL-1; NAAL-3; NOBA; OxBA; PoEL-3; SCAP; TAP   *Fr.* Preparatory Meditations Before My Approach to the Lord's Supper.

I kenning through astronomy divine. Meditation Eight. Edward Taylor. ChIV-2; NAAL-3

I kept my answers small and kept them near. Answers. Elizabeth Jennings. OxBSP; OxBTC

I kept singing this, and I will call it out from the grave. Julianus of Egypt, *Greek*. GrAn, *tr. by* W. S. Merwin

I kept the house on the corner of Linden and Pineapple Streets. Birdie McReynolds. Samuel Hoffenstein. BXAP; NBLV

I kept the memory, like a miracle. Good Filya. Nikolai Mikhailovich Rubtsov, *Russian*. TCRP, *tr. by* Lubov Yakovleva

I killed a man, and he was dead, *fa la la, la la la*. Tom Tell-Truth. *Unknown*. CBNP

I killed a snake this morning in the grass. The Snake. Vance Palmer. NOBAu

I killed them, but they would not die. The Immortals. Isaac Rosenberg. FaBoTw; NSI; TrJP

I killed you Malcolm. Confession to Malcolm. Conyus. NBV

I kiss these before I kiss that. Let's See If I Have It Right. Stephen Dunn. CMAP

I kiss your lips. Spring in This World of Poor Mutts. Joseph Ceravolo. FTOS

I kissed my father. (LL) The Gift. Li-Young Lee. LoL; OpBo; RaBo; UnSA

I kissed them in fancy as I came. Two Lips. Thomas Hardy. BoLoP

I Kissed You. *Unknown*. BLPA

I kissed you, bride and lost, and went. The Loser. Adrienne Rich. RACG

I kneel down to peer into a culvert. Kneeling Down to Look [*or* Peer] into a Culvert. Robert Bly. NoAM

I knew a boy who took long walks. Stalky Jack. William Brighty Rands. BoTP

I knew a cuckold once. I grieve for him. My Friend the Cuckold. Morris Gilbert Bishop. OBCoV

I knew a man, a common farmer, the father of five sons. Walt Whitman. BLT   *Fr.* "I Sing the Body Electric."

I knew a man who used to say. The Statesman. Hilaire Belloc. NOBE

I knew a simple soldier boy. Suicide in [the] Trenches. Siegfried Sassoon. PoFWW; PoWW

I knew a woman, lovely in her bones. Theodore Roethke. AmPP; BoLoP; HAP; HeIP-4; HoPM; InPK-6; LiTM; LoP; MoAmPo; MoP; NAAl.-2; NOBA, NoAM; NoP-4; PoE; Poetr; RaBo; SAGP; SoSe-8; TAP; TFi; TRP; TwCP; UnPo; VCAP

("I measure time by how a body sways.") (LL) NoP-4; SAGP

I knew a young hooker / called Jade. Jade. Janice Mirikitani. UnSA

I knew he would speak to me. Misguided. Harriet Brown. CrSp

I knew her self was not in that strange place. (LL) The Harlem Dancer. Claude McKay. BPo; CrDW; ISC; NIP-4; NoAM; SAGP; Son; TAP

I knew him as a friend: married. She was older. Rowing in Familiar January. Milo De Angelis, *Italian*. NeIt, *tr. by* Lawrence Venuti

I Knew I'd Sing. Heather McHugh. WeT

I knew it was love, and I felt it was glory. (LL) Stanzas Written on the Road between Florence and Pisa. Byron. GTBS-P; NAEL-2

I knew like a song your vows weren't strong. Mahsati, *Farsi*. WPOW, *tr. by* Deirdre Lashgari

I knew little, and what I knew. First Sex. Sharon Olds. NMM-2

I knew not 'twas so dire a crime. Last Words. Emily Brontë. WPE

I knew not who had wrought with skill so fine. Before a Painting. James Weldon Johnson. GT

I knew something was wrong. I. Slim's Song. Etheridge Knight. BkSV   *Fr.* Three Songs.

I knew that in winter it would snow. Plumbers. Susan Miles. NOxBChV

I knew the dignity of the words. My Grandfather's Funeral. James Applewhite. MT

I knew too that through them I knew too that he was through, I knew [too that he threw them]. A Valentine to Sherwood Anderson. Gertrude Stein. NoAM; PFTM

I knew you forever and you were always old. Some Foreign Letters. Anne Sexton. MoAmPo

I know. The Wall. Ismail, *Telugu*. OMIP, *tr. by* V. Narayana Rao

I know a dog called Isaac. Three Dogs. E. C. Brereton. BoTP

I know a flower of beauty rare. The Lay of the Captive Count. Goethe, *German*. AWP, *tr. by* James Clarence Mangan

I Know a Flower So Fair and Fine. Nicolai Frederik Severin Grundtvig, *Norwegian*. AH, *tr. by* Olav Lee

I know a forest and in that forest. The Pool. Hayyim Nahman Bialik, *Hebrew*. MHP, *tr. by* Ruth Finer Mintz

I know a funny little man. Mr Nobody. *Unknown*. BoTP; CTV; ChAP

I know a garden with three strange gates. The Last Gate. Stella Mead. BoTP

I know a green grass path that leaves the field. The Green River. Lord Alfred Bruce Douglas. OBEV

I know a Jew fish crier down on Maxwell Street. Fish Crier. Carl Sandburg. OxBA

I know a little. Certain Tall Buildings. Franz Wright. NAmP90

I know a little butterfly with tiny golden wings. The Butterfly. Margaret Rose. BoTP

I know a little cupboard. The Cupboard. Walter De la Mare. NTCP

I know a little garden-close. A Garden By The Sea. William Morris. CH; EBEvV; GaP; LBC; NOBE; OAEL-2; OBEV; OBNC; PoEL-5   *Fr.* The Life and Death of Jason.

I know a little language of my cat, tho Dante says. A Little Language. Robert Duncan. PoM   *Fr.* Dante.

I know a little man both ept and ert. Gloss. David McCord. OBAL

I know a little what it is like, once here at high tide. Seaweeds. Sandra McPherson. AmPA; PoA

I Know a Man. Robert Creeley. CoAmPo; InPS-3; NIP-4; NOBA; NoP-4; OxBSP; PoM; VCAP

("Out where yr going.") (LL) CoAmPo; NoP-4

I know a place that holds the Sky. The Upside-Down World. Hamish Hendry. BoTP

I know a pool where nightshade preens. Crazed. Walter De la Mare. OxBSP

I know a retired dentist who only paints mountains. Mountains. W. H. Auden. FaBoPV   *Fr.* Bucolics.

I know a solemn secret to keep between ourselves. The Elfin People Fill the Tubes. Winifred M. Letts. BoTP

I know a spot where Love delights to dream. A Sacred Grove. Edward Cracroft Lefroy. AWP   *Fr.* Echoes from Theocritus.

I Know a Village. Phyllis McGinley.

5:32, The. NMM-2; OxBM; WPE

Occupation: Housewife. WPE

I know a wasted place high in the Alps. Edgar Bowers. *Fr.* Two Poems on the Catholic Bavarians. CRP

I know a wind. Grass Leaves. Un-gyo Kang, *Korean*. CKP, *tr. by* Jaihiun Kim

I know all. He Asked Them What Did They Know & They Told Him. *Unknown, Seneca Indian*. STP, *tr. by* Jerome Rothenberg *and* Richard Johnny John

I know all about boys, I do. All about Boys and Girls. John Ciardi. NOxBChV

"I know all," you say; of incompleteness, you have enough. Palladas, *Greek*. GrAn, *tr. by* Sam Bradley

I know, although when looks meet. Crazy Jane and Jack the Journeyman. W. B. Yeats. CMoP

I know an ice handler who wears a flannel shirt. Ice Handler. Carl Sandburg. OxBA

I know—and yet I cannot share, as once. August the First; Court Martial. The Mother Speaks. Marjorie Oludhe Macgoye. HBAPE

I know, as my life grows older. Whatever Is—Is Best. Ella Wheeler Wilcox. BLPA; PWR

I know, blue modest violets. Violets. *Unknown*. BoTP

I know. But I do not approve. And I am not resigned. (LL) Dirge Without Music. Edna St. Vincent Millay. CMoP; IMW; MeMAP

I know but will not tell. Elegy. Alan Dugan. NIP-4

I know by the arrow of darkness. Momcilo Nastasijevic. HSix, *sect.* 3, *tr. by* Charles Simic *Fr.* Deaf Things.

I know de moonlight, I know de starlight. *Unknown*. BPo

I know exactly what I want to say. For J. W. Rafael Campo. RA

"I know, fair lady, how to love the lover well." Philodemus, *Greek*. GrAn, *tr. by* William Moebius

I know for I have tried. (LL) Between the form of Life and Life. Emily Dickinson. APN-2; PAR

I know her not! Her hand has been in mine. The Lady in the White Dress, Whom I Helped into the Omnibus. Nathaniel Parker Willis. APN-1

I know him, February's thrush. The Thrush in February. George Meredith. OBNC

I know him; / He'll give no horse for a poem. *Unknown, Irish*. BIrV, *tr. by* Vivian Mercier

I know how people get treated when they die. Andcyck, *Tlingit Indian*. STP, *tr. by* James Koller

I know I am but summer to your heart. Edna St. Vincent Millay. HeIP-4

I know I am poor. *Unknown, Greek*. PGA, *tr. by* Kenneth Rexroth

I know I am / The Negro Problem. Dinner Guest: Me. Langston Hughes. BPo; LTA; SSLK

I know I change / have changed. Daguerreotype Taken in Old Age. Margaret Atwood. BoWoP; NoAM

I know I dreamed again last night. At Dawn. Michael Patrick Hearn. CA

"I know I have lost my train." Joshua Lane. *Unknown*. ACTP

I know I have the best of time and space, and was never measured and never. Walt Whitman. NoAM *Fr.* Song of Myself. AmPP; MoAMPo; NAAL-3; NOBA; OxBA

I know, I know—though the evidence. Blow, West Wind. Robert Penn Warren. ColAP

I know I shall never write poems. The Drawer of My Writing Desk. Boris Petrovich Kornilov, *Russian*. TCRP, *tr. by* Bernard Meares

I know if I find you I will have to leave the earth. Hymn. A. R. Ammons. CoAmPo

I know I'll lose her. James McMichael. BAP-93 *Fr.* The Person She Is.

I Know I'm Not Sufficiently Obscure. Ray Durem. BPo; LiLi; PoBA

I Know Inside. Yüan Mei, *Chinese*. CoBLCP, *tr. by* Jonathan Chaves

I know it is my sin[ne] which locks thine ear[e]s. Church-Lock and Key. George Herbert. ESCV; GeHe; OxBSP

I know it sounds too much like poetry. For You. James Moore. PuP-14

I know / it's no easy joy. Wine. Nikolai Nikolaevich Ushakov, *Russian*. TCRP, *tr. by* Daniel Weissbort

I know lots of men who are in love and lots of men who are. I Never Even Suggested It. Ogden Nash. PoLF

I know monks masturbate at night. The Earnest Liberal's Lament. Ernest Hemingway. OBAL; OBSV

I know moon-rise, I know star-rise. *Unknown*. APN-2; CrDW; NAAAL; UnPo

I Know Moonlight. *Unknown*. AS

I know: My beloved Jonathan Swift. Unfulfilled Love. Ljiljana Djurdjic, *Serbo-Croatian*. HSix, *tr. by* Charles Simic

I know my body's of so frail a kind. Man. Sir John Davies. *Fr.* Nosce Teipsum. NoSic; SiPS

I Know My Soul. Claude McKay. BPo

I know my soul hath power to know all things. Sir John Davies. OBEV *Fr.* Man. *Fr.* Nosce Teipsum. NoSic; SiPS

I know my upper arms will grow. The Life I Led. Nikki Giovanni. GT

I Know Myself a Man. Sir John Davies. *See* Man.

I know myself linked by chains of fire. Elsa Gidlow. CrSp *Fr.* Chains of Fire.

I know no paint of poetry. On Fairford Windows. William Strode. NOSC

I know not, but I burn and feel it so. (LL) *Carmina*, LXXXV. Catullus, *Latin*. OBCVT; OBVE, *tr. by* Richard Lovelace

I know not how it falls on me. Emily Brontë. NOBVV

I know not how it may be with others. Old Furniture. Thomas Hardy. OxBTC

I know not if from uncreated spheres. Michelangelo Buonarroti. *Fr.* Three Poems. AWP, *tr. by* George Santayana

I know not if it was a dream. I viewed. The Passing Show. Ambrose Bierce. APN-2

I know not of what we ponder'd. Companions. Charles Stuart Calverley. NOBL; PeLV

I know not that the men of old. The Men of Old. Richard Monckton, 1st Baron Houghton Milnes. OBEV

I know not what I am, and what I know, I'm not. One Knows Not What One Is. "Angelus Silesius." GePo, *tr. by* George C. Schoolfield *Fr.* The Cherubical Wanderer.

I know not what spell is o'er me. Lorelei. Heinrich Heine, *German*. NAWM-2, *tr. by* Aaron Kramer; TrJP, *tr. by* Emma Lazarus

I know not what the future hath. John Greenleaf Whittier. NOCV *Fr.* The Eternal Goodness.

I know not what to do. Fragment 36. Hilda Doolittle. CMoP; CPO; NALW; OxBA; VGW

I know not when it was, I still confuse childhood and Eden. Léopold Sédar Senghor, *French*. NegPo, *tr. by* Ellen Conroy Kennedy

I know not when this tiresome man. The Sundowner. John Shaw Neilson. CBAP

I Know Not Where the Road Will Lead. Evelyn Atwater Cummins. AH

I know not who thou art, oh lovely one! To the Lady in the Chemisette with Black Buttons. Nathaniel Parker Willis. OBAL

I know not why, but all this weary day. Henry Timrod. APN-2; PAR

I know not why, but it is true—it may. Edgar Allan Poe. Timothy Thomas Fortune. AAP

I know not why my soul is rack'd [*or* racked]. Changed. Charles Stuart Calverley. NOBVV

I know nothing but this scene. James Liddy. BiHa *Fr.* Epithalamion I–IV.

I know now that once I longed to be white. When I Was Growing Up. Nellie Wong. OxWW; UnSA

I know of course. I, the Survivor. Bertolt Brecht, *German*. PoSu, *tr. by* John Willett; HP, *tr. by* Willet, John

I know some lonely Houses off the Road. Emily Dickinson. APN-2; MoAMPo; OxBA; PoRA

I Know Something Good about You. Louis C. Shimon. BLPA; PoToHe

I know that a gangster will not murder me. "Ivan Venediktovich Elagin," *Russian*. TCRP, *tr. by* Helen Matveyeff

I know that all beneath the moon decays. William Drummond, of Hawthornden. GSo; LoP; Son

("But that, oh me, I both must write and love!") (LL) Son

I know that any weed can tell. Song. Louis Ginsberg. TrJP

I know that He exists. Emily Dickinson. APN-2; AmPP; NCAP

I know that his eyes look into mine. Assurance. Josephine D. Henderson Heard. CBWP-4

I Know That I Am a Great Sinner. Swami Purohit. OBMV

I Know That I Must Die Soon. Else Lasker-Schüler, *German*. TrJP, *tr. by* Ralph Manheim

I know that I shall meet my fate. An Irish Airman Foresees His Death. W. B. Yeats. APAD; ChAP; EBEvV; FaBoCh; FaBoMo; GTBS-P; HeIP-4; HoPM; LiTM; MoBrPo; MoP; NOBE; NoAM; NoP-4; OBMV; OBWP; PoPoPo; PoWW; Poetr; SCV; TFi; WeW-3

I know that life is Jason. The Golden Fleece. Oscar Williams. PoA

I know that mind. ESP. Carter Revard. VoR

I know that peace is soon coming, and love of common object. Geranium. Edward Dorn. PmAP

I know that the sun rising. Pindar's Revenge. Edward Sanders. PoM

I know that this my crying, like the crying. Night. Hayyim Nahman Bialik, *Hebrew*. AWP, *tr. by* Maurice Samuel

I know that what our neighbours call *longueurs*. Byron. OBSV *Fr.* Canto the Third. *Fr.* Don Juan.

I know / that when a grumbling old woman. Superstition. Minji Karibo. WPOW

I know the barn where they got you. For a Woodscolt Miscarried. John William Corrington. MT

I know the bottom, she says. I know it with my great tap root. Elm. Sylvia Plath. NOBA; NYBP; NoAM; NoP-4; Poetr

I know the colour rose, and it is lovely. Pathology of Colours. Dannie Abse. NIP-4; NoAM

I know the force of words, I know their clarion call. Vladimir Mayakovsky, *Russian*. TCRP, *tr. by* Bernard Meares

I know the hedge in Briar Lane. I Must Away. May Sarton. BoTP

I know the injured pride of sleep. Night and Morning. Austin Clarke. CIP-2

I know the limitations of my body. The Realist. Carl H. Greene. NBV

I know the moon is troubling. David St. John. NAmP90

I know the new wife can't equal the old! *Unknown. See* Old Poem.

I know the reputation / of the idle ways. Lady Ki [*or*Kii], *Japanese.* WPJ; WPQW, *tr. by* Kenneth Rexroth and Ikuko Atsumi

I know the reward of the secret tear as it humbly falls. Reward. Shimon Halkin, *Hebrew.* MHP, *tr. by* Ruth Finer Mintz

I know the ships that pass by day. The Lights. J. J. Bell. BoTP

I know the sky will fall one day. Child's Song. Gerald Louis Gould. BoTP

I know the sun shines, and the lilacs are blowing. Enlisted Today. *Unknown.* CBCWP

I know the [*or* a] thing that's most uncommon. On a Certain Lady at Court. Alexander Pope. NOBE; NOEC; OBEV; OxBSP; SAGP

I know the truth—give up all other truths! Marina Tsvetayeva, *Russian.* NNPT; WPoS, *tr. by* Elaine Feinstein; OPOU, *tr. by* Elaine Feinstein *and* Angela Livingstone

I know the way[e]s of learning; both the head. The Pearl. [Matth. 13.45 *or* Matt. 13:45]. George Herbert. ChIV-2; EBEV; ESCV; FHYEP; FSCP; GeHe; HAP; NOCV; NOSC; OAEL-1; PoEL-2; SeCP

I know the white wedding dress is suicidal. Story. Larry Levis. CMAP

I know thee. My name is Tom. Archaic Song of Dr. Tom the Shaman. *Unknown, Nootka Indian.* STP, *tr. by* Jerome Rothenberg

I know there are some fools that care. The Deformed Mistress. Sir John Suckling. BXAP

I know there is a worm in the human heart. John Clare. Jon Anderson. AmPA

I know there is someone. Poem to Be Read and Sung. César Vallejo, *Spanish.* SPE, *tr. by* Robert Bly *and* James Wright

I know thou art a senseless thing. The Old Crib. Mary E. Tucker. CBWP-1

I know 'tis vain ye mountains, and ye woods. A Painter. Thomas Cole. APN-1

I know to whom I write. Here, I am sure. An Epistle to Master John Selden. Ben Jonson. BeJo; FP

I know to whom I write. Here, I am sure. Ben Jonson. *Fr.* An Epistle to Master John Selden. BeJo; FP

I know two women / and the one. The Wife. Robert Creeley. VGW

I know what the caged bird feels, alas! Sympathy. Paul Laurence Dunbar. AAP; APAD; APN-2; CrDW; GEA; GT; NAAAL; NoP-4; PoBA; SSLK

I know where I belong. Wonders. Lorenzo Thomas. MoNo

I know where I'm going. John Kitching. SpW

I Know Where I'm Going. *Unknown.* NTP

I know why, getting up in the cold dawn. To a Daughter with Artistic Talent. Peter Meinke. Poetsp

I know why the caged bird sings! (LL) Sympathy. Paul Laurence Dunbar. AAP; APAD; APN-2; CrDW; GEA; GT; NAAAL; NoP-4; PoBA; SSLK

I know you all, and will awhile uphold. Shakespeare. *Fr.* King Henry IV, Pt. I. NAEL-1

I know you are there. The sweat is, I am here. (LL) Certainty Before Lunch. John Berryman. LCAP-2; OxBC

I know you know. (LL) Carnal Knowledge. Thom Gunn. BoLoP; EP

I know you little, I love you lots. My Love For You. *Unknown.* Spl

I know you: solitary griefs. The Precept of Silence. Lionel Pigot Johnson. MoBrPo

I know you think of me when you are lonely. Plea for My Heart's Sake. Naomi Long Madgett. SeSe

I know your root. In Praise of Plants. Branko Miljkovic, *Serbian.* CEEP; HSix, *tr. by* Charles Simic *Fr.* In Praise of Plants.

I know you're down there, Plug-hole Man. The Plug-hole Man. Carey Blyton. FuFo

I knowed a man, which he lived in Jones. Thar's More in the Man than Thar Is in the Land. Sidney Lanier. NOBA

I Korinna am here to sing the courage. Korinna, *Greek.* BoWoP, *tr. by* Willis Barnstone

I lack the braver mind. Confession of Faith. Elinor Wylie. MoAmPo

I laid me down upon a bank. William Blake. EnLoPo; GBL

I laid my haffet on Elfer Hill. Elfer Hill. *Unknown, Danish.* AWP, *tr. by* Robert Jamieson

I *Lais!* once a *heavenly Whore!* An Epigram out of Plato To Madam Amara. *Unknown, Greek.* OBCVT, *tr. by* Charles Goodall

I Lais, once an arrow. Kenneth Rexroth, *after the Greek of* Sekundos. NNaP; PGA

I, Lais, who laughed disdainfully at Greece. Lais' Mirror. *Unknown, Greek.* GrAn, *tr. by* Peter Jay

I laks yo' kin' of lovin'. Long Gone. Sterling Brown. BPo; NAAAL

I lang hae thought, my youthfu' friend. Epistle to a Young Friend. Robert Burns. EBEV

I language want, to dress[e] my fancies in. Imagination. Margaret Lucas Cavendish, Duchess of Newcastle. KTR; NOSC

I lately lost a preposition. The Naughty Preposition. Morris Gilbert Bishop. NBLV; NYBP; PeLV

I laugh at each dull bore, taste's parasite. Fresco-Sonnets to Christian Sethe. Heinrich Heine, *German.* AWP, *tr. by* John Todhunter

I laugh at my failing strength in old age. Shih Te, *Chinese.* SuSp, *tr. by* James M. Hargett

I laugh at what you call dissolution, / And I know the amplitude of time. Walt Whitman. *See* Who goes there! hankering, gross, mystical, nude?

I laughed a crumbling laugh. Emily Dickinson. MeMAP

I laved my hands. Lost for a Rose's Sake. *Unknown.* AWP, *tr. by* Andrew Lang

I lay at the edge of a well. The Underground Stream. James Dickey. NOBA

I lay dear treasure for you. The Pack. Frank Prewett. HATNAP

I lay down in my grave. Elegy. Maya Angelou. CrSp

I lay down with my love and there was song. Armorial. Ralph Gustafson. MoCV

I lay face-downward on the grass. The Barrier. Louis Lavater. NOBAu

I lay i' the bosom of the sun. Palabras Grandiosas. Bayard Taylor. OBAL

I lay in my coffin under the sod. Post Mortem. Arthur Joseph Munby. NOBVV

I lay in the Holy Cross. Reginald Pugh, The Man Who Came from the Army. Emma Lee Warrior. HATNAP

I lay my harp on the curved table. The Harp. Po Chü-i, *Chinese.* TAL, *tr. by* Robert Payne

I lay paralyzed. Suppression. Jayne Cortez. NBV

I lay waiting. Bog Queen. Seamus Heaney. NoAM; RACG

I lay with an acupuncture needle. Even the Eagles Must Gather. Alma Villanueva. FFC

I lay with my heart under me. Cicada. Adrien Stoutenburg. NYBP

I lean on a lighthouse rock. Girl at the Seaside. Richard Murphy. BIrV

I lean on my rustic gate. Twilight in the River Pavilion. Chiang Shih-ch'üan, *Chinese.* OHMPC, *tr. by* Kenneth Rexroth

I lean on my staff, gaze at the sunlit snow. Evening View as the Snow Clears. Chia Tao, *Chinese.* SuSp, *tr. by* Stephen Owen

I leaned out of window, I smelt the white clover. Seven Times Three—Love. Jean Ingelow. PoLF *Fr.* Songs of Seven.

I leant [*or* leaned] upon a coppice gate. The Darkling Thrush. Thomas Hardy. APo; CABP; CMoP; ClHu; EBVV; HAP; ImPo; InPS-3; LiTM; MoBrPo; MoP; NAEL-2; NIP-4; NOBE; NOBVV; NoAM; NoP-4; OAEL-2; OBEV; OBNC; PFE; PoE; PoPoPo; Poetr; RB; SoSe-8; TFi; TOF; UnPo

I learn, as the years roll onward. Life's Lessons. *Unknown.* PoLF

I learn by going where I have to go. (LL) The Waking. Theodore Roethke. APAD; AmPP; CRP; CoAP; HAP; HCAP; HeIP-4; InPK-6; InPS-3; LiTM; MoAmPo; MoP; NAAL-2; NIP-4; NOBA; NoAM; NoP-4; PFE; PoPoPo; Poetr; RaBo; TAP; TFi; TwCP; VCAP; WeW-3

I learn to live by guile, to do without love. Book of Routh. Carolyn Beard Whitlow. FFC

I learn you were hurt my sweet and hurt again. Clotho. Hilaire Kirkland. *Fr.* Clotho, Lachesis, Atropos. PeNZ

I learned from my mother how to love. What I Learned from My Mother. Julia Kasdorf. PBCAP

I learned in my credulous youth. Why, Some of My Best Friends Are Women. Phyllis McGinley. NMM-2

I Learned That Her Name Was Proverb. Denise Levertov. CrSp

I learned to be honest. A Question of Climate. Audre Lorde. NoAM

I learned to read in the dark. Song of the Third Generation. Julia Lisella. UnSA

I Learned To Sew. Mitsuye Yamada. LoHo

I learned to shoot. Casting. Kevin Young. GT

I learned to wash in shell-holes, and to shave myself in tea. New Army Education. *Unknown.* NSI

I learned two things. Riding Lesson. Henry Taylor. NBLV

I learnt the collects and the catechism. Elizabeth Barrett Browning. EnVR *Fr.* Aurora Leigh. VWP

I leave all the scarlet flowers. Tomiko Yamakawa, *Japanese.* WPJ, *tr. by* Kenneth Rexroth *and* Ikuko Atsumi

I leave it for you to say why it is. Pietà. Allen Afterman. NOBAu

I leave me people, me land, me home. Wherever I Hang. Grace Nichols. HCP

I leave Mortality, and things below. The Extasie. Abraham Cowley. SeCP

I leave my heart in the doorway. Thank You for the Valentine. Diane Wakoski. HoPM

I leave our house, our town, familiar fields. Living Apart. Maura Stanton. FFC; NAmP90

I leave the number and a short. The Ubiquity of the Need for Love. Ron Koertge. IFJA

I leave you in your garden. To Yvor Winters, 1955. Thom Gunn. GTBS-P

I left along the distant roads, my apple tree, and now you bloom alone. The Song of the Eternal Sailor. Slavko Janevski, *Macedonian.* CEEP, *tr. by* Vasa D. Mihailovich

I left bright Venice. (LL)   Julian and Maddalo; A Conversation.   Shelley. OAEL-2

I left Cornell / with half a wit; six mismated socks.   Prayer.   Daniel Berrigan.   AF

I left my hills.   Lady Izumi, *Japanese*.   BoWoP, *tr. by* Willis Barnstone

I Left My Low amd Humble Home.   Nathaniel Hawthorne.   APN-1

I left my prayers and the kneeling pilgrims.   Fair Cassidy.   *Unknown, Irish.*   BIrV, *tr. by* Donagh MacDonagh

I left my room at last, I walked.   The Monster.   Thom Gunn.   PFE

I left old Lake Chemo a long way behind me.   Lake Chemo.   James Wilton Rowe.   AmFP

I left the farm I loved. I went.   Exile.   George Rostrevor Hamilton, *after the Greek of* Isidoros of Aigai.   FaBoEE

I left thee with a courage high.   Sir John Collings Squire.   BXAP   *Fr.* My Father's Cot.

I left those walls.   Nina Cassian, *Romanian*.   PoSu, *tr. by* Nina Cassian *and* Naomi Lazard

I left you to your adorning. (LL)   At the Draper's.   Thomas Hardy.   MoBrPo; OxBM

I lend a deck of cards to someone passing by.   Headline to Summarize a Passion.   U Tam'si Tchicaya, *French*.   NegPo, *tr. by* Ellen Conroy Kennedy

I, Lessimus, of Salt Lake City.   Robert Peters.   BXAP

I let down my long line; it went falling; I pulled.   The Angler's Story.   John Hollander.   AFr

I let the incense grow cold.   Li Ch'ing-chao, *Chinese*.   BoWoP; OHMPC, *tr. by* Kenneth Rexroth

I licked and kissed her in a bathroom stall.   Robyn Selman.   PUP-19

I lie and imagine a first light gleam in the bay.   Achill.   Derek Mahon.   BiHa; PBCIP; PNI

I lie beneath my patchwork blanket at the southern window.   Rising from Sleep.   Wang Chiu-ssu, *Chinese*.   CoBLCP, *tr. by* Jonathan Chaves

I lie down with God, and may God lie down with me.   *Unknown, Irish*.   TIRV, *tr. by* Eleanor Hull

I lie down with Thee, O Jesus.   Night Prayer.   *Unknown, Irish*.   TIRV, *tr. by* Douglas Hyde

I lie for a long time on my left side and my right side.   Dead Color.   Charles Wright.   HCAP; LCAP-2

I lie here beside you.   Mount Gilboa.   Malka Heifetz-Tussman, *Yiddish*.   PBWP, *tr. by* Marcia Falk

I lie here thinking of you.   Love Song.   William Carlos Williams.   Poetr

I lie in my crib midday this is.   Baby's Pantoum.   Anne Waldman.   FFC

I lie long abed.   Yakamochi, *Japanese*.   OHPJ, *tr. by* Kenneth Rexroth

I lie under the crust of the night singing.   Pregnant Woman.   Ingrid Jonker, *Afrikaans*.   PeSA, *tr. by* Jack Cope *and* Uys Krige

I lie under your hand—a cur.   Dog.   Ingrid Jonker, *Afrikaans*.   PBWP, *tr. by* Jack Cope *and* William Plomer

I Lift My Eyes Up to the Hills.   Cotton Mather.   AH

I lift my head and watch.   Thoughts in Exile.   Su Tung-p'o, *Chinese*.   OHPC, *tr. by* Kenneth Rexroth

I Lift My Heart to Thee.   Thomas Sternhold.   AH

I lift my heavy heart up solemnly.   Sonnet.   Elizabeth Barrett Browning.   LW; NALW; PEW; VWP   *Fr.* Sonnets from the Portuguese.

"I lift my lamp beside the golden door!" (LL)   The New Colossus.   Emma Lazarus.   APAD; APN-2; AiP; CA; FaBoA; GS; GSo; NoP-4; PAR; PoLF; SAGP; Son; WPE

I lift my songs.   Battle Song.   Macuilxochitl, *Nahuatl Indian*.   WPOW, *tr. by* Catherine Rodriguez-Nieto

I lift the boy's body.   The Good Shepherd: Atlanta, 1981.   Ai.   RACG; WWSi

I lift the Lord on high.   Père Lalement.   Marjorie Lowry Christie Pickthall.   NOBC

I lift the toilet seat.   Surprise.   Richard Brautigan.   KaS

I lift up mine eyes unto the hills.   The Hills.   D. H. Lawrence.   ChIV-1

I like a church; I like a cowl.   The Problem.   Ralph Waldo Emerson.   APN-1; AWP; AmPP; MeMAP; NAAL-1; NAAL-3; NOBA; OxBA; PAR; TAP

I like a look of Agony.   Emily Dickinson.   APN-2; HeIP-4; InPS-3; NAAL-1; NAAL-3; NoP-4; OxBSP; PAR; PoE; PoPoPo; TAP

I like a lot of woman, full grown.   Nicarchus of Alexandria, *Greek*.   InMo, *tr. by* Sam Hamill

I like a woman built on ample lines.   Nicarchus of Alexandria, *Greek*.   GrAn, *tr. by* Peter Porter

I like bars close to home and home run down.   The Hilltop.   Richard Hugo.   Poetr

I like being in your apartment, and not disturbing anything.   Staying at Ed's Place.   May Swenson.   SAGP; VCAP

I like blowing bubbles, and swinging on a swing.   Things I Like.   Marjorie H. Greenfield.   BoTP

I like hot days, hot days.   Summer.   Walter Dean Myers.   PiM

I like it here just fine.   Girl Held without Bail.   Margaret Abigail Walker.   BPo; PoBA

I Like Little Pussy.   Jane Taylor.   FaBoBe; OxNR
   ("But Pussy and I / Very gently will play.") (LL)   CTV
   ("I love little Pussy.")   CTV; FPC
   ("To be worried or teased.") (LL)   FPC

I like little pussy, her coat is so warm.   Pussy.   *Unknown*.   ACTP; PeP

I like movies because.   Why I Like Movies.   Patricia Jones.   BISi

I like my body when it is with your.   E. E. Cummings.   BoLoP; Son; VGW

I like not tears in tune, nor will [*or* do] I prize.   On the Memory of Mr. Edward King, Drowned in the Irish Seas.   John Cleveland.   HAP; OAEL-1; SeCP

I like old houses, with steps that sag.   Old Houses.   Jennie Romano.   PoToHe

I like people.   Trombone Solo.   Stoddard King.   NBLV

I like rust on a nail.   And the Same Words.   David Ignatow.   NNaP

I like sitting alone when the moon is shining.   Song of the pines.   Po Chü-i, *Chinese*.   TAL, *tr. by* Robert Payne

I like Sunday evenings after you're here.   To H.   John Wieners.   FTOS

I like the backs of houses. Fronts are smug.   Hinterland.   Margaret Stanley-Wrench.   OBGa

I like the clattering of hoof on street.   Metrics.   Rhina P. Espaillat.   FFC

I like the cold rooms of autumn, sitting.   Morning Coffee.   György Petri, *Hungarian*.   VCWP, *tr. by* Wilmer, Clive and George Gömöri

I like the fall.   The Mist and All.   Dixie Willson.   CTV

I like the hunting of the hare.   The Old Squire.   Wilfrid Scawen Blunt.   FaPoR; OBEV; SCGP

I like the story of the circus waif.   The Road.   Herbert Morris.   DiPo

I like the town on rainy nights.   Rainy Nights.   Irene Thompson.   AYFP; BoTP

I like the wind.   Wind Secrets.   Diane Wakoski.   AmPA

I Like Them Fluffy.   Sir Alan Patrick Herbert.   NBLV

I like these foreign shores and I have never.   "Ivan Venediktovich Elagin," *Russian*.   TCRP, *tr. by* Helen Matveyeff

I like to crawl around the house after my brother's wife.   *Unknown, Tlingit Indian*.   STP, *tr. by* James Koller

I like to find.   Pleasures.   Denise Levertov.   NOBA; NeAP; NoAM; PoE; Poetr

I like to get off with people.   Conviction IV.   Stevie Smith.   LW

I like to hear of wealth and gold.   Common Things.   Paul Laurence Dunbar.   GT

I like to play close by my father's den.   "Are You There?"   Strickland W. Gillilan.   PoToHe

I like to play with many boys.   (Friends).   *Unknown*.   CTV

I like to ride in a tramcar.   Travelling.   Dorothy Graddon.   BoTP

I like to see a thing I know.   New Sights.   *Unknown*.   BoTP

I like to see it lap the Miles.   Emily Dickinson.   APN-2; BoWoP; CTV; GM; InPK-6; LiTM; MoAmPo; NAAL-1; NAAL-3; NAWM-2; NOBA; NoAM; NoP-4; OBAL; OBCA; OxBA; SoSe-8; TFi

I like to think.   Snowdrops.   Mary Vivian.   BoTP

I like to think of Harriet Tubman.   Susan Griffin.   NALW; NMM-2

I like to think that ours will be more than just another story.   Wishful Thinking.   Michael C. Blumenthal.   HCAP

I like to toss him up and down.   My Cats.   Stevie Smith.   CBNP; PC

I like to walk / And hear the black crows talk.   Crows.   David McCord.   MoAmPo

I like to walk down Fisher Street.   Fisher Street.   Thylias Moss.   GT

I like to watch.   The Bath.   Robin Becker.   PBCAP

I like to watch an angleworm.   Angleworms.   Marie Louise Allen.   CTV

I like to wear boots.   Is There Life after Feminism.   Maude Meehan.   NMM-2

I like working near a door. I like to have my work-bench close by.   Monologue.   Hone Tuwhare.   PeNZ

I like you, Mrs. Fry! I like your name!   A Friendly Address.   Thomas Hood.   PoEL-4

I like your muse because she's gay and witty.   W. H. Auden.   NOBL   *Fr.* Letter to Lord Byron.

'I liked that,' said Offa, 'sing it again'. (LL)   King of the perennial holly-groves, the riven sandstone.   Geoffrey Hill.   HAP; NoAM

I likes a woman.   Preference.   Langston Hughes.   APSN; HCAP; NOBA; SAGP

I limp along, looking for feathers.   Stuffy Turkey.   Dave Etter.   SeSe

I 'listed at home for a lancer.   Lancer.   A. E. Housman.   MoBrPo; OBWP

I listen, and the mountain lakes.   Maybe Alone on My Bike.   William Stafford.   NYBP

I listen for him through the rain.   At Daybreak.   Siegfried Sassoon.   LBC

I listen for the sounds of cannon, cries.   On Lookout Mountain.   Robert Earl Hayden.   PoE

I listen hard in the kitchen. American Dream. Vern Rutsala. CMAP

I listen to a waterfall. Yün Shou-p'ing. *Fr.* On the Painting, Mist Over Ten Thousand Mountains by Shih-ku. CoBLCP, *tr. by* Jonathan Chaves

I listen to the pulse of a life / different from mine. Miyoko Goto, *Japanese.* WPJ, *tr. by* Kenneth Rexroth *and* Ikuko Atsumi

I listen to these songs. Gaelic Songs. Iain Crichton Smith. FaBoTC

I listened, there was not a sound to hear. Full Moon; Santa Barbara. Sara Teasdale. OBCA

I listened to the Phantom by Ontario's shore. The Poet. Walt Whitman. MoAmPo *Fr.* By blue Ontario's shore. APN-1

I listened to the voices that shattered. Enmeshment. Lewis Warsh. FTOS

I live a modest life. I don't suppose. The Parrot. Oleg Grigorevich Chukhonstev, *Russian.* TCRP, *tr. by* Simon Franklin

I live among the grasses. The Field-Mouse. Enid Blyton. BoTP

I live among the Pigmies and the Cranes. Pigmies and Cranes. Walter Savage Landor. NOBVV

"I live because of their help on the way." (LL) Growing Old [*or* Growing Older]. Rollin J. Wells. BLPA; PoToHe

I live between heaven and earth. A Lone Wild Goose. Lu Kuei Meng, *Chinese.* SuSp, *tr. by* Robin D. S. Yates

I live between. I stalk space of these authors shunt. This Garden Being: The Hanging of Books. Clark Coolidge. FTOS

I live but in the present,—where art thou? Today. Jones Very. TAP

I live, but not in myself. Stanzas of the Soul that Suffers with Longing to See God. Saint John of the Cross, *Spanish.* TOF, *tr. by* K. Kavanaugh *and* O. Rodrigues

I live for books. Light. Diane Wakoski. OPOU

I live for those who love me. What I Live For. George Linnaeus Banks. BLPA; FaBoBe; PWR; PoToHe

I live, I die, I burn myself and drown. Sonnet 8. Louise Labé, *French.* BoWoP, *tr. by* Willis Barnstone

I live in a doorway. Sonrisas. Pat Mora. NIP-4

I live in a room named East. Suddenly. Robin Blaser. FTOS; PoM

I live in a town. Family Jewels. Essex Hemphill. GLP; GT

I live in an orchard. Confetti of bruised petals. Postcard from the Garden. Marge Piercy. NoAM

I live in music. Ntozake Shange. ISC

I live in the city, *see also* Poema del City 2. Ron Padgett. WWSi

I live in the town. The Town Child. Irene Thompson. BoTP

I live in this house, walls being plastered. Keep Me Still, for I Do Not Want to Dream. Larry Eigner. NeAP

I live invisible (in my whole sky). Too Bright a Day. Norman MacCaig. GTBS-P

I live my life in growing orbits. Rilke, *German.* RaBo, *tr. by* Robert Bly

I live now in an ancient book. Haim Guri, *Hebrew.* IP, *tr. by* Warren Bargad *and* Stanley F. Chyet

I live on the water. Winding Up. Derek Walcott. NoAM

I live on this depraved and lonely cliff. Vittoria da, Marchesa di Pescara Colonna, *Italian.* BoWoP, *tr. by* Willis Barnstone

I live quietly and go nowhere. My Father's House. Calvin Forbes. WeT

I live underneath / the light of day. Charles Olson. *See* Chockablock Once a man was traveling through the woods, and.

I Live up Here. W. S. Merwin. CAPP-1

I live where darkness / is not. Mukta Bai, *Marathi.* BoWoP, *tr. by* Willis Barnstone

I live / with a bullet in my heart. Margarita Iosifovna Aliger, *Russian.* TCRP, *tr. by* Daniel Weissbort

I live with love encompassed round. Love's Mirror. Constance Naden. VWP

I live without inhabiting/ Myself. Saint John of the Cross. OBVE, *tr. by* Roy Campbell *Fr.* Coplas about the Soul Which Suffers with Impatience to See God.

I live, yet no true life I know. I Die because I Do Not Die. Saint, of Avila Theresa, *Spanish.* TOF, *tr. by* E. Allison Peers

I live; yet 'tis not I. He lives in me. Devotion. Paul Fleming, *German.* GePo, *tr. by* F. Warnke

I lived a life without love, and saw the being. The Mirage. Oscar Williams. LiTM

I lived alone as happy as Larry. The Husband's Lament. Brian Merriman. OBVE, *tr. by* Frank O'Connor *Fr.* The Midnight Court. NOIV, *tr. by* Thomas Kinsella

I lived among great houses. The Statesman's Holiday. W. B. Yeats. CMoP; OxBTC

I lived for many years in the bush—far out—and I starved for lack of rain. The Gravy Train. R. R. Davidson. NOBAu

I lived here nearly 5 years before I could / meet the middle western day. Chicago Poem. Lew Welch. BB; NeAP; PoM

I lived in the first century of world wars. Poem. Muriel Rukeyser. UnPo

I lived in those times. For a thousand years. Epitaph. Robert Desnos, *French.* PFTM, *tr. by* Kenneth Rexroth

I lived inside a machine. On Being a Householder. Alan Dugan. NoAM

I lived obscurely and uncertainly. Ilya Grigoryevich Ehrenburg, *Russian.* TCRP, *tr. by* Gordon McVay

I lived on drugs and understood the pushers. Passing Through Experiences. Robert Adamson. BMAP

I lived with Mr. Punch, they said my name was Judy. Variations. Randall Jarrell. VGW

I lived with Pride; the house was hung. The House of Pride. William James Dawson. PoToHe

I lived with visions for my company. Sonnet. Elizabeth Barrett Browning. BWW *Fr.* Sonnets from the Portuguese.

I loathe, abhor, detest, despise. Dried Apple Pies. *Unknown.* BLPA

I loathe [*or* lothe] that I did love. The Aged Lover Renounceth Love. Thomas, 2d Baron Vaux of Harrowden Vaux. NoSic; OAEL-1; PoEL-1; SCGP

I loathe the twin seas. *Unknown, Japanese.* OHMPJ, *tr. by* Kenneth Rexroth

I loed you for yir kindness. The Deean Tractorman, Clear. Edith Anne Robertson. OxBS

I loitered weeping with my bride for gladness. James Agee. *Fr.* Lyrics. MoAmPo

I long desired to see, I now have seen. Mt. Ida. Trumbull Stickney. *Fr.* Sonnets from Greece. APN-1

I long for the call to council. Alcaeus, *Greek.* InMo, *tr. by* Sam Hamill

I long not now, a little while at least. Protest. Countee Cullen. PFE

I long to kisse the *Image of my Death.* (LL) Sonet to Sleepe. William Drummond, of Hawthornden. NOSC; OxBS; Son

I long to spread my tiny wings. A Wreath of Holly. Joseph Cephas Holly. AAP

I long to talk[e] with some old lover's ghost. Love's Deity [*or* Deitie]. Donne. AWP; ESCV; GBL; ImPo; SeCP; SoSe-8

I longed for companionship rather. In the Night. Stevie Smith. FP

I longed to. Sappho, *Greek.* InMo, *tr. by* Sam Hamill

I look. Catharina Regina von Greiffenberg. WPoS, *tr. by* Hirshfield, Jane *and* Samuel Michael Halevi *Fr.* On the Sweet Comfort Brought by Grace.

I look after you as you go. The Weingarten Travel Blessing. *Unknown, German.* GePo, *tr. by* Carroll Hightower

I look along the valley of my gun. The Possibility That Has Been Overlooked Is the Future. Michael Hartnett. NOIV

I look at my hands, Momma. Laura Davis. MDDM *Fr.* Things You Gave Me.

I look at my shadow over and over in the lake. Looking in the Lake. Po Chü-i, *Chinese.* TAL, *tr. by* Robert Payne

I look at the crisp golden-threaded hair. Canzone: His Portrait of His Lady, Angiola of Verona. Fazio degli Uberti, *Italian.* AWP, *tr. by* D. G. Rossetti

I look at the swaling sunset. In Trouble and Shame. D. H. Lawrence. OBMV

I look at you, and I sigh. (LL) A Drinking Song. W. B. Yeats. BoLoP; GLoP; LoP; OAEL-2

I look at you from such deep graves. Aleksandr Yeryomenko, *Russian.* TCRP, *tr. by* John High

I look far off at T'ien-t'ai's summit. *Unknown, Chinese.* CoBCP, *tr. by* Burton Watson

I look for a way of writing. Valerio Magrelli, *Italian.* NeIt, *tr. by* Dana Gioia

I look for an explanation. Complaint. Alistair Paterson. *Fr.* Incantations for Warriors. PeNZ

I look in that one kind of dwindled. And in this. Album—A Runthru. Clark Coolidge. FTOS

I look into my glass. Thomas Hardy. EBEV; FaBoTw; HAP; NAEL-2; NOBE; NOBVV; NoP-4; OxAEP-2; OxBSP; SCV; WeW-3

I look into the crater of the ant. (LL) The Vantage Point. Robert Frost. MeMAP; OxBA

I look into the henyard. The Darkling Chicken. Robert Peters. BXAP

I look out at the fields. Snakes. Virgil, *Latin.* OBCVT, *tr. by* David R. Slavitt

I look out at the white sleet covering the still streets. Sleet Storm on the Merritt Parkway. Robert Bly. CoAmPo; NOBA

I look over my own shoulder. The Zen of Housework. Al Zolynas. BLT

I look up. William J. Higginson. HA

I look up and see his curtains and bed;. On the Death of his Father. Wei Wên-Ti, *Chinese.* ChiP, *tr. by* Arthur Waley

I Look Up to the Sky. Samuel Ha-Nagid, *Hebrew.* TOF, *tr. by* David Goldstein

I look upon the world—and she resembles a garden. The End of Man Is Death. Moses ibn Ezra, *Hebrew.* TrJP, *tr. by* Solomon Solis-Cohen

I looked across the water. The Loon upon the Lake. *Unknown, Ojibwa Native American.* APN-2, *tr.* by Charles Fenno Hoffman

I looked and I saw. Who But the Lord? Langston Hughes. BPo

I looked at my days and saw that. Purpose. Desmond O'Grady. PBCIP

I looked at that face, dumbfounded. Esse. Czeslaw Milosz. TOF

I looked down and saw a pit most black. Lady Elizabeth, Culross Melvill. *Fr.* A Godly Dream. WPE

I looked far back into other years, and lo, in bright array. Mary, Queen of Scots. Henry Glassford Bell. BLPA; FaBoBe

I Looked for a Sounding-Board. Henriëtte Roland-Holst, *Dutch.* WPOW, *tr.* by Jonathan Crewe

I looked for Beauty:—on a throne. Beauty and Her Visitors. Winthrop Mackworth Praed. NOBRP

I looked for that which is not, nor can be. A Pause of Thought. Christina Rossetti. NOBE; OBNC *Fr.* Three Stages.

I looked in my heart while the wild swans went over. Wild Swans. Edna St. Vincent Millay. CMoP; MoAmPo; PBWP; UnPo

I looked in the first glass. The Three Mirrors. Edwin Muir. NoAM

I looked like Abraham Lincoln. Elliott Hawkins. Edgar Lee Masters. OxBA *Fr.* Spoon River Anthology.

I looked on that prophetic land. Presences Perfected. Siegfried Sassoon. MoBrPo

I looked outside. Pools of water. Amir Gilbo'a, *Hebrew.* IP, *tr.* by Warren Bargad *and* Stanley F. Chyet

I looked over Jordan and [*or* an'] what did I see. *Unknown. See* Swing low, sweet chariot.

I looked through the window and I saw a house. A House. Yuly Markovich Daniel, *Russian.* TCRP, *tr.* by David Burg *and* Arthur Boyars

I looked to find a man who walked with God. Enoch. Jones Very. ChIV-1, IIAP

I looked to find Spring's early flowers. The Lament of the Flowers. Jones Very. APN-1; ColAP; NOBA; OxBA

I looked up from my writing. Thomas Hardy. NoAM

I lose myself within thy mind—from room. To Elizabeth Barrett Browning, in 1851. Dora Greenwell. VWP

I lost my father when I was just two. What Mother Told Me Once. Phùng Quán, *Vietnamese.* AVP, *tr.* by Huỳnh Sanh Thông

I lost my mare in Lincoln Lane. *Unknown.* OxNR

I lost my pardner, what'll I do? Skip to My Lou. *Unknown.* AmFP

I lost the love, of heaven above. A Vision. John Clare. EBVV; GTBS-P; NAEL-2; NOBVV; NTP; OAEL-2; OBNC; PoE; Ro

I lounge on the jetty in the fragrance of catalpa. Quatrain. Tu Fu, *Chinese.* SuSp, *tr.* by Jerome Seaton

I lov'd [*or* lou'd] my selfe, because my selfe lov'd [*or* lou'd] you. (LL) The Excuse. Sir Walter Ralegh. AAS; SiPS

I lov'd thee from the earliest dawn. Early Affection. George Moses Horton. AAP

I love a man who is not worth. Did This Happen to Your Mother? Did Your Sister Throw Up a Lot? Alice Walker. ISC

I love a still conservatory. Magic. Walter James Turner. OBGa

I love all beauteous things. Robert Bridges. BoTP; CMoP; EBEV; OxAEP-2; TrCP

I love all shining things. Shining Things. Elizabeth Gould. BoTP

I love all sights of earth and skies. The Flaneur. Oliver Wendell Holmes. APN-1

I love America where truth can be shouted from the housetops. Franklin E. Jordan. CTV

I love and fear him. Lady Kasa, *Japanese.* OHPJ, *tr.* by Kenneth Rexroth

I love and fear him. Kasa no Iratsume, *Japanese.* BoWoP, *tr.* by Kenneth Rexroth

I love and hate. Ah! never ask why so! Catullus. *See* Carmina, LXXXV.

I love, and he loves me again. A Nymph's Passion. Ben Jonson. BeJo; OBEV

I love at early morn from new-mown swath. Summer Images. John Clare. OBNC

I love beautiful things. The Proletariat Speaks. Alice Moore Dunbar-Nelson. NMM-2

I love breasts, hard. Breasts. Charles Simic. NNaP; RaBo

I Love But Thee. Heinrich Heine, *German.* AWP, *tr.* by Louis Untermeyer

I love calling west through time zones. Distances. Claire Bateman. WeT

I love her for her fine blue coat. The Boor's Wooing. Anna Wickham. WPN

I love her with the seasons, with the winds. Constancy. "Michael Field." CPO; VWP

I love him not; but shew no reason can. Antipathy. Martial, *Latin.* OBCVT, *tr.* by Rowland Watkyns

I love him not; but shew no reason can. Antipathy. Rowland Watkyns, *after the Latin of* Martial. FaBoEE

I love how old men carry purses for their wives. In the End We Are All Light. Liz Rosenberg. LiLi

I love it, I love it. The Old Arm-Chair. Eliza Cook. BrRo; InPK-6; Poetr; VWP

I love little Pussy. Jane Taylor. *See* I Like Little Pussy.

I love little pussy, her coat is so warm. *Unknown.* LB

I love, loved, and so doth she. Sir Thomas Wyatt. SiPS

I love / love's delicacy. Sappho, *Greek.* InMo, *tr.* by Sam Hamill

I love my enemies, those I forgive. Leonid Andreievich Zavalniuk, *Russian.* GI, *tr.* by Magda Bogin

I Love My Jesus Quite Alone. Johannes Kelpius, *German.* AH, *tr.* by Christopher Witt

I love my little gecko. My Gecko and I. Colin West. PeP

I love my little son, and yet when he was ill. The Two Parents. "Hugh MacDiarmid." FaBoTw; OxBTC

I Love My Love. Helen Adam. NeAP; WPOW

I love my Love, and my Love loves me! (LL) Answer to a Child's Question. Coleridge. BoTP; FaBoBe; NOxBChV; NTP; OxBChV

I love my neighbour. Love Thy Neighbour. D. H. Lawrence. ChIV-2

I love my work and my children. God. Ovid in the Third Reich. Geoffrey Hill. CABP; FaBoMo; HP; NoAM

I love not thy perfections. When I hear. Depreciating Her Beauty. Wilfrid Scawen Blunt. OBMV *Fr.* The Love Sonnets of Proteus.

I love nothing better than my wife. (LL) I love sixpence, jolly [*or* pretty] little sixpence. Mother Goose. LB; OxNR

I love old gardens best. A Charleston Garden. Henry Bellamann. PoLF

I love old mothers—mothers with white hair. Old Mothers. Charles Sarsfield Ross. PoToHe

I love or I don't—despair comes easily to me. She Loves Me, She Loves Me Not. Dmitry Sergeievich Merezhkovsky, *Russian.* TCRP, *tr.* by Albert C. Todd

I love roads. Roads. Edward Thomas. PeFWW

I love Russia. Mikhail Valentinovich Kulchitsky. TCRP, *tr.* by Daniel Weissbort *Fr.* That's What It's Like.

I LOVE SEAHORSES, TEDDYBEARS, AFRICAN VIOLETS. Mad Sonnet: Grace. Michael McClure. BB

I love sixpence, jolly [*or* pretty] little sixpence. Mother Goose. LB; OxNR ("And I took twopence home to my wife.") (LL) ReMoGo ("I love sixpence, a jolly, jolly sixpence.") ReMoGo

I Love Somebody. *Unknown.* AmFP

I love sweets. Ellen West. Frank Bidart. NAAL-2; PoPoPo; RACG

I love the autumn moon. To the Tune "Chieh san ch'eng" ("I love the autumn moon"). Yang Shen. *Fr.* Four Poems from the Sequence "Singing of the Moon." CoBLCP, *tr.* by Jonathan Chaves

I love the cows best when they are a few feet away. Cow Worship. Gerald Stern. IFJA; LoL

I love the days of long ago. My Africa. Michael Dei-Anang. PBA

I love the evenings, passionless and fair, I love the evens. A Sunset. Victor Hugo. AWP, *tr.* by Francis Thompson *Fr.* Feuilles d'Automne.

I love the fitful gust that shakes. Autumn. John Clare. BoTP

I love the / friday night. Realarro. Marc Matthews. HCP

I love the lit corners of your kerosine smile. Senior Lady Sells Garden Eggs. Kojo Laing. HBAPE

I love the little winding lanes. Lanes in Summer. Malcolm Hemphrey. BoTP

I Love the Lord. *Unknown.* AH

I love the man whose lofty mind. Self-Reliance. James M. Whitfield. NAAAL

I Love the Night. Matilda Caroline Edwards. PWR

I love the old melodious lays. Proem. John Greenleaf Whittier. APN-1; OxBA; TAP

I love the p'i-p'a's music in my heart. Hsü Pen. *Fr.* Five Things Sought For—In the Manner of Han Wo. CoBLCP, *tr.* by Jonathan Chaves

I love the quality of the. An Essay on William Carlos Williams. Victor Hernandez Cruz. PmAP

I love the sea. The Sea at Evening. Christopher Laird. PBCV

I love the serenity of living in the woods. Wang Chiu-ssu. CoBLCP, *tr.* by Jonathan Chaves *Fr.* Living in the Woods.

I love the silent hour of night. Night. Anne Brontë. VWP

I love the sky at night. Appassionato. Lyubomir Levchev, *Bulgarian.* CEEP, *tr.* by Jascha Kessler *and* Aleksandar Shurbanov

I love the small hours of the night. The Pleasant Joys of Brotherhood. James Simmons. OBCoV; PBCIP

I love the sound of the horn in the deep, dim woodland. The Sound of the Horn. Alfred de Vigny, *French.* AWP, *tr.* by Wilfred Thorley

I love the spring moon. To the Tune "Chieh san ch'eng" ("I love the spring moon"). Yang Shen. *Fr.* Four Poems from the Sequence "Singing of the Moon." CoBLCP, *tr.* by Jonathan Chaves

I love the stillness you leave behind you. What I Have to Tell You, Until Next Time. David Avidan, *Hebrew.* IP, *tr. by* Warren Bargad *and* Stanley F. Chyet

I love the stream flowing endlessly. Robert Bly Finds Something in New Jersey. Carol Poster. BXAP

I love the summer moon. To the Tune "Yu hu-lu" ("I love the summer moon"). Yang Shen. *Fr.* Four Poems from the Sequence "Singing of the Moon." CoBLCP, *tr. by* Jonathan Chaves

I love the way the cows go down to the water. A Knowledge of Water. Judson Mitcham. Poetr

I love the winter moon. To the Tune "Yu hu-lu" ("I love the winter moon"). Yang Shen. *Fr.* Four Poems from the Sequence "Singing of the Moon." CoBLCP, *tr. by* Jonathan Chaves

I love the word. Yes. Brendan Kennelly. CIP-2

I Love Thee. Josephine D. Henderson Heard. CBWP-4

I love Thee. (LL) "Why do I love" You, Sir? Emily Dickinson. APN-2; LW

I love thee, Betty. *Unknown.* OxNR

I love thee for thy fickleness. *Unknown.* NOSC

I love thee, I love thee, and life will depart. A Mother's Love. Ellen Johnston. VWP

I love thee more, but I esteem thee less. (LL) Carmen 92 ("Lesbia loads me night & day with her curses"). Catullus. OBCVT; OBVE; OxBSP

I love thee; never dream that I am dumb. Penetration. "Michael Field." VWP

I love these gardens, all their show. The Gardeners. Christopher Reid. DiPo

I love this body of mine that has lived a life. Celebration of the Body. Daisy Zamora, *Spanish.* LoL, *tr. by* Dinah Livingston

I love this byre. Shadows are kindly here. The Innkeeper's Wife. Clive Sansom. OBCP

I love this sunlight cold in spaces transparent turning blue. Amir Gilbo'a, *Hebrew.* IP, *tr. by* Warren Bargad *and* Stanley F. Chyet

I Love Thy Kingdom, Lord. Timothy Dwight. AH

I love to encounter you in strange cities. Edouard J. Maunick. PBMAP *Fr.* Les Manèges de la Mer (1964).

I love to go out in late September. Blackberry Eating. Galway Kinnell. InPK-6; NIP-4; PiM; SoSe-8

I love to pass my fingers. Olokun. J. P. Clark Bekedermo. PBMAP *Fr.* A Reed in the Tide.

I love to rise ere gleams the tardy light. December Morning. Anna Seward. ECWP

I love to rise in a summer morn. The School-Boy. William Blake. AYFP; CH; FHYEP; FaBoCh; OxAEP-2 *Fr.* Songs of Experience.

I love to see a lobster laugh. Fun. Leroy F. Jackson. CTV

I love to see boards lying on the ground in early spring. Old Boards. Robert Bly. CAPP-1

I love to see the little stars. The Oneness of the Philosopher with Nature. G. K. Chesterton. CBNP

I love to see the old heath's withered brake. Emmonsail's Heath in Winter. John Clare. PoEL-4

I love to see the starry flag. Our Flag. *Unknown.* CA

I love to see those loving and beloved. Lonely Love. Edmund Blunden. OxBTC

I love to see, when leaves depart. Autumn. Roy Campbell. GTBS-P; MoBrPo; OBMV; OxBTC

I Love to Steal Awhile Away. Phoebe Hinsdale Brown. AH

I love to stretch. Summer Morning. Charles Simic. IFJA

I Love to Tell the Story. Katherine Hankey. CTV

I love to wander through the woodlands hoary. October. S. W. Whitman. BoTP

I love uncertain gestures. Valerio Magrelli, *Italian.* NeIt, *tr. by* Jonathan Galassi

I love wine but have no wine to drink. On Hearing That San-p'ing's Newly Brewed Chrysanthemum Wine Is Ready to Drink—Investigating with a Poem. Pien Kung, *Chinese.* CoBLCP, *tr. by* Jonathan Chaves

I love *you.* (LL) Dance of the Infidels. Al Young. MoNo; NBV; PoBA; SeSe

I love you and the rosebush. Armando Uribe, *Spanish.* HoPM, *tr. by* Miller Williams

I love you as a sheriff searches for a walnut. To You. Kenneth Koch. CAPP-1

I love you better than I love my race. Charles Mair. NOBC *Fr.* Tecumseh.

I love you first because your face is fair. V-Letter. Karl Shapiro. NYBP; NoAM; TrJP

I love you for the grief that lurks within. Sonnet Macabre. Theodore Wratislaw. ADE

I love you for your brownness. To a Dark Girl. Gwendolyn B. Bennett. BlSi; ColAP; NAAAL; PoBA; SAGP

I love you ginger bread mama. Ginger Bread Mama. Doughtry Long. BPo; PoBA

I love you, great new Titan! Soldier: Twentieth Century. Isaac Rosenberg. PoWW

I love you in the newly born. Finger-nails. Paolo Buzzi, *Italian.* PFTM, *tr. by* Felix Stefanile

I love you, Mrs. Acorn. Would your husband mind. Song. Kath Fraser. LW

I love you, / Not only for what you are. Love. Roy Croft. BLPA; FaBoBe; PoToHe

I love you, rotten. Medlars and Sorb-Apples. D. H. Lawrence. FaBoVe; NoAM; OAEL-2

I love you, silent statue: for your sake. The White Statue. Olive Custance. ADE

I love you so, yet it's still not enough? You Must Say It. Xuân Diệu, *Vietnamese.* AVP, *tr. by* Huỳnh Sanh Thông

I love you—Titan lover. Girl to Soldier on Leave. Isaac Rosenberg. PeFWW

I love you well, my steel-white dagger. Dagger. Mikhail Yuryevich Lermontov, *Russian.* AWP, *tr. by* Max Eastman

I love you with my life—'tis so I love you. "Michael Field." VWP

"I love you," you said between two mouthfuls of pudding. A Considered Reply to a Child. Jonathan Price. BoLoP

I love your eyebrows, said one. You Must Have Been a Sensational Baby. Harold Norse. GLP

I love your hands. Your Hands. Angelina Weld Grimké. PoBA

I love your hands. Your Hands. Gevorg Emin, *Armenian.* IFJA, *tr. by* Diana Der Hovanessian

I love your lips when they're wet with wine. Ella Wheeler Wilcox. BLPA; FaBoBe

I love your throat, so fragrant, fair. You. Angelina Weld Grimké. CPO

I loved a child of this countrie. *Unknown.* GBL; PBWP

I loved a lass, a fair one. George Wither. CH; GBL; GLoP; NOBE; NOSC; OBEV

I loved booze. Clifton. Joan Larkin. GLP

I loved her softness, her warm human smell. The Lion's Bride. Gwen Harwood. BoWoP

I loved him not; and yet, now he is gone. The Maid's Lament. Walter Savage Landor. OBEV; OBNC; RACG *Fr.* The Citation and Examination of Shakespeare.

I loved him three storms ere he loved me again. Love's Flight. Else Lasker-Schüler, *German.* TrJP, *tr. by* Jethro Bithell

I loved my friend. Poem. Langston Hughes. NTCP

I loved my lord, my black-haired lord, my young love. The Magnet. Ruth Stone. MoAmPo

I loved my love from green of Spring. Grown and Flown. Christina Rossetti. NOBVV

I loved one flower too much. Mrs. Fleetwood Habergham. *See* The Seeds of Love.

I loved / secretly. *Unknown.* BoWoP *Fr.* Carmina Burana.

I loved the way it felt once, practically invincible. Outside the Depot. Betsy Sholl. LTA

I loved thee beautiful and kind. Epigram. Robert Nugent, Earl Nugent. NOEC

I loved thee long and dearly. Florence Vane. Philip Pendleton Cooke. APN-1

I loved thee once, I'll love no more. To an Inconstant One. Sir Robert Ayton. OBEV

I loved thee, though I told thee not. The Secret. John Clare. GBL; GLoP

I loved Theotormon. Visions of the Daughters of Albion. William Blake. CABP; OAEL-2

I loved to talk of home. Pacific Epitaphs. Dudley Randall. MoP

I loved you. Aleksandr Sergeyevich Pushkin, *Russian.* LoP, *tr. by* R. M. Hewitt

I LOVED you dearly, Stone Fish Lake. Stone Fish Lake. Yüan Chieh, *Chinese.* ChiP, *tr. by* Arthur Waley

I loved you; even now I may confess. I Loved You Once. Aleksandr Sergeyevich Pushkin, *Russian.* BoLoP, *tr. by* Reginald Mainwaring Hewitt

I loved you first: but afterwards your love. Christina Rossetti. LoP *Fr.* Monna Innominata. BWW

I loved you first the time I saw you last. Letting Go. Daryl Hine. NoP-4

I Loved You Once. Aleksandr Sergeyevich Pushkin, *Russian.* BoLoP, *tr. by* Reginald Mainwaring Hewitt

I lower sail at river mouth. At the Chiang-ning River Mouth. Wang An-shih, *Chinese.* SuSp, *tr. by* Jan W. Walls

I lurk on the floor of silence. Hunting. Tymoteusz Karpowicz, *Polish.* PoSu, *tr. by* Jan Darowski

I. M. Margaritae Sorori. William Ernest Henley. *See* Margaritæ Sorori [I. M.].

I made a house of houselessness. Rose Cecil O'Neill. LW

I made a posy for my love. Posies. Agnes Mary Frances Robinson. VWP

I made a posy [or posie], while the day ran by. Life. George Herbert. ESCV; FMP; FSCP; GeHe; MeLP; NOSC; NoP-4; SeCP

I made another garden, yea. Song. Arthur William Edgar O'Shaughnessy. OBEV

I made my song a coat. A Coat. W. B. Yeats. CMoP; EPCY; IIP; LiTM; NAEL-2; NoAM; OxAEP-2; OxBSP; PoEL-5

I made myself as a tree. March Hares. Andrew Young. SAmP

I made no choice / I decided nothing. Margaret Atwood. NALW Fr. Circe / Mud Poems.

I made the motions of the sacred place. Edouard J. Maunick. NegPo, tr. by Ellen Conroy Kennedy Fr. As Far as Yoruba Land.

I made the Muses sick. The Death of the Gods; an Ode Written in Imitation of Pindar. L. Ker. NOEC

I made the pilgrimage again. Derailment: A Delirium. Steve Chimombo. HBAPE

I made up my mind for to change my way. The Trail to Mexico. Unknown. AmFP

I, Maister Andro Kennedy. The Testament of Mr. Andro Kennedy. William Dunbar. OxBS

I make a pact with you, Walt Whitman. A Pact. Ezra Pound. AmPP; ColAP; MeMAP; MoP; NAAL-2; NOBA; NoAM; OxBA; TAP

I make a simple assertion. Working with Tools. A. R. Ammons. TRP

I make a trip to each clock in the apartment. Two Mornings and Two Evenings. Elizabeth Bishop. PoA

I make all the poetic pauses. Dana Naone. CDW

I make free with old albums. At the Wailing Wall. Aidan Carl Mathews. BiHa; CIP-2

I make my children promises. Teacher. Audre Lorde. MDDM

I make this dirge for you Miss Mary Binning I miss you. Dirge. Unknown, Hawaiian. BoWoP, tr. by Armand Schwerner

I make this song about me full sadly. The Wife's Lament. Unknown, Anglo-Saxon. WPE

I make this song sadly about myself. Unknown. See The Wife's Lament.

I many times thought Peace had come. Emily Dickinson. SAmP

I marched [or march'd] three miles through scorching sand. On a Curate's Complaint of Hard Duty. Jonathan Swift. OBCoV; SCGP; TIRV

I marked all kindred powers the heart finds fair. Love Enthroned. D. G. Rossetti. OBNC Fr. The House of Life.

I marked where lovely Venus and her court. Venus's Looking-Glass. Christina Rossetti. NALW

I married. Lorine Niedecker. NMM-2

I married a man of the Croydon class. Nervous Prostration. Anna Wickham. FaBoWP

I married a second time the other day. Second Marriage. Mei Yao Ch'en, Chinese. SuSp, tr. by Jonathan Chaves

I married in my youth a wife. James Vincent Cunningham. MoAmPo

I marvell'd why a simple child. Only Seven. Henry Sambrooke Leigh. BXAP

I, Maximus of Gloucester, to You ("By ear, she sd"). Charles Olson. NeAP Fr. The Maximus Poems.

I, Maximus of Gloucester, to You ("Off-shore, by islands hidden in the blood"). Charles Olson. LiTM; NOBA; NoAM; PmAP; PoM Fr. The Maximus Poems.

I may be dead to-morrow, uncaressed. For the Book of Love. Jules Laforgue, French. AWP, tr. by Jethro Bithell

I may be following you! (LL) Award. Ray Durem. BPo; PoBA; TTY

I may be smelly and I may be old. The River God. Stevie Smith. BrRo; FaBoSe; FaBoTw; FaBoWP; PBWP

I may even be. Power and Light. James Dickey. NAAL-2

I May, I Might, I Must. Marianne Moore. ChAP; FaBoWP; OBAL; OxBSP; PFE

I may live on until. Fujiwara no Kiyosuke, Japanese. OHPJ, tr. by Kenneth Rexroth

I may not touch the hand I saw. A Separation. William Johnson Cory. OBNC

I may picture her there. (LL) Thoughts of Phena. Thomas Hardy. EBVV; NOBVV; NoP-4; OxBTC

I May Reap. Patrick Kavanagh. TIRV

I mean. . . I . . . can fly / like a bird in the sky. . . . Nikki Giovanni. See Ego Tripping [(There May Be a Reason Why)].

I mean that too, but yet a hidden strength. Chastity ("I Mean That Too, But Yet a Hidden Strength"). Milton. NOSC Fr. Comus; a Masque Presented at Ludlow Castle. FHYEP; OAEL-1

I mean / the fiddleheads have forced their babies. May 10th. Maxine W. Kumin. NYBP

I mean to penetrate the particular. The Medium IV: Sights. Carl Rakosi. InPS-3

I meant to do my work today. Richard Le Gallienne. CTV

I measure. Tanka. Kanoko Okamoto, Japanese. MJT, tr. by Makoto Ueda

I measure every Grief I meet. Emily Dickinson. MoAmPo

I measure time by how a body sways. (LL) I knew a woman, lovely in her bones. Theodore Roethke. NoP-4; SAGP

I measured myself by the wall in the garden. Day Dreams, or Ten Years Old. Margaret Johnson. BLPA

I meditate upon a swallow's flight. Coole Park, 1929. W. B. Yeats. CABP; IIP; OAEL-2; OBMV

I meet two soldiers sometimes here in Hell. That Exploit of Yours. Ford Madox Ford. PeFWW; PoWW

I meet you in an evil time. An Eclogue for Christmas. Louis MacNeice. FaBoMo; NoAM; OBMV

I member we went to the hospital that day. The Killing of the Birds. Shirley Williams. BoWoP

I mend the fyre and beikit me about. Robert Henryson. EBEV; PoE Fr. The Testament of Cresseid. OxBS

I met a girl from Derrygarve. A New Song. Seamus Heaney. CABP; CIP-2; FaBoTw

I met a guy I used to know, who said. Ozymandias II. Howard Nemerov. Son

I met a King this afternoon! Emily Dickinson. ChAP

I met a lady / on a lazy street. From the Hazel Bough. Earle Birney. NIP-4

I met a little cottage-girl. Wordsworth on Lloyd George. Mary Visick. UV

I met a little cottage Girl. Wordsworth. UV Fr. We Are Seven. BLPA; NAEL-2; NOBRP; OxBChV; Ro

I met a little Elf-man [or Elfman], once. The Little Elf. John Kendrick Bangs. CTV; FPC; FaBoBe; NTCP; OBCA

I met a little Pacifist. The Rime of the Gentle Pacifist. "Pontiff." NSI

I met a man as I went walking. Puppy and I. A. A. Milne. BoTP

I met a man in South Street, tall. Cutty Sark. Hart Crane. FaBoMo Fr. The Bridge. NAAL-2

I met a man mowing. Hay Harvest. Patrick Reginald Chalmers. BoTP

I met a man with a triple-chin. The Man Who Sang the Sillies. John Ciardi. OBCA

I met a rat under a bridge. And we sat there in the mud discussing the rats's loveliness. The Rat's Legs. Russell Edson. WeT

I met a seer. The Book of Wisdom. Stephen Crane. HoPM; MoAmPo Fr. The Black Riders [and Other Lines].

I met a seer. Eidolons. Walt Whitman. APN-1

I met a traveler [or traveller] from an antique land. Ozymandias [of Egypt]. Shelley. APAD; AWP; CABP; CH; ChAP; ClHu; FaBoBe; FaBoCh; FaPoR; GSo; GTBS-P; HAP; HeIP-4; HoPM; ImPo; InPK-6; InPS-3; NAEL-2; NIP-4; NOBE; NoP-4; OAEL-2; OBNC; OPOU; PFE; PoE; PoLF; PoPoPo; PoRA; RB; Ro; SCGP; SCV; SoSe-8; Son; TFi; UV

I met a traveller from an antique land. Ozymandias Revisited. Morris Gilbert Bishop. BXAP; NBLV; UV

I met a woman, weeping by the sea. Cavour. Menella Bute Smedley. VWP

I met an elf-man in the woods. How to Treat Elves. Morris Gilbert Bishop. OBAL; OBCA

I met an honest man today. Alien. William Price Turner. OxBS

I met ayont the cairney. Empty Vessel. "Hugh MacDiarmid." FaBoTC; FaBoTw; OxBS

I Met by Chance. Heinrich Heine, German. AWP, tr. by John Todhunter

I met Death—he was a sportsman—on Cole's. Cole's Island. Charles Olson. PoM Fr. The Maximus Poems.

I met her as a blossom on a stem. The Dream. Theodore Roethke. EP; NYBP; UnPo

I Met Her in the Garden Where the Praties Grow. Unknown. AS

I met her in the leafy woods. A Dream. W. H. Davies. CBLP

I met him again, he was trudging along. I Fights Mit Sigel! Grant P. Robinson. BLPA

I met Jack on a Friday night. A Tip for Saturday. Francis Webb. BMAP

I met Louisa in the shade. Louisa; After Accompanying Her on a Mountain Excursion. Wordsworth. APAD; GBL

I met Musette / In the water-closet. Vague Lyric by G. M. Max Beerbohm. FaBoEE

I Met My Solitude[. We two stood glaring]. Naomi Replansky. BrRo; NMM-2

I met Poetry, an old prostitute walking. Moral Story II. David McKee Wright. PeSA

I met the Bishop on the road. Crazy Jane Talks with the Bishop. W. B. Yeats. BoLoP; CABP; CMoP; EBEV; InPK-6; MoP; NAEL-2; NoAM; NoP-4; OAEL-2; OxAEP-2; PFE; PoE; PoPoPo; TOF; TRP

I met the Love-Talker one eve in the glen. The Love-Talker. "Ethna Carbery." CH; WPE

I Met the Master. Unknown. PoLF

I Met This Guy Who Died. Gregory Corso. Poetsp

I met this lovely scene once before, on horseback. Gazing at Ch'ang-po Mountain. Li K'oi-hsien, *Chinese.* CoDLCP, *tr. by* Jonathan Chaves

I met with the girls coming from afar off. Love-Song of the Water Carriers. *Unknown, Zulu.* PeSA

I met wizened wood-woman. The Old Woman and the Sandwiches. Libby Houston. OBSP

I might, and yet thou goest safe, supreme. (LL) He felt the wild beast in him betweenwhiles. George Meredith. EnVR; NOBVV

I might have been born in Beirut. Curriculum Vitae. Lawrence Joseph. PBCAP

I might have sung of the world. Sara Teasdale. NMM-2

I might, unhappy word, O me, I might. Sonnet 33. Sir Philip Sidney. OAEL-1 *Fr.* Astrophil and Stella. AAS; SiPS

I mind as 'ow the night afore that show. The Chances. Wilfred Owen. OxBTC

I mind me in the days departed. The Deserted Garden. Elizabeth Barrett Browning. GaP

I mind me of a morning while the mountains yet were grey. Mooimeisjes. Perceval Gibbon. PeSAV

I mind o' the Ponnage Pule. The Ponnage Pool. Helen B. Cruickshank. FaBoTC

I mind them or the show or resonance of them—I come and I depart. Walt Whitman. SAmP *See* The Little one sleeps in its cradle.

I Minded God. Henry Ainsworth. AH

I mingle with the young and gay. I Smile, but Oh! My Heart Is Breaking. Mary E. Tucker. CBWP-1

I mingle with your bones. The One Lost. Isaac Rosenberg. MoBrPo

I miss my grandmother. Dream Poem. Mary Jo Bona. UnSA

I miss our lizards. The one who watched us. Lizards in Sardinia. Eamon Grennan. BiHa

I miss that corridor drenched in shadow. Lost Brilliance. Rita Dove. PUP-19

I miss the peace and quiet of Chicago. Poem after Apollinaire. Ira Sadoff. AmPA

I miss the toad poking up in the mud. Primarily We Miss Ourselves As Children. Gary Gildner. CMAP

I miss you in the morning, dear. Miss You. *Unknown.* PoToHe

I Missed His Book, but I Read His Name. John Updike. NoP-4; OBAL ("*M.* Anantanarayanan.") (LL) NoP-4

I missed / the last transport. The Abandoned. Zbigniew Herbert, *Polish.* PoSu, *tr. by* Michael March *and* Jaroslaw Anders

I mix my men and booze. Sally: Twelfth Street. Naomi Long Madgett. NBV

I mock thee not, though I by thee am mocked. To Flaxman. William Blake. FaBoEE; OxBoLi

I most gentle of cats through long-drawn sickness aweary. The Epitaph of Felis. John Jortin, *Latin.* PC, *tr. by* Samuel Courtauld

I mourn for Antibia the virgin. Anyte, *Greek.* GrAn, *tr. by* Sally Purcell

I mouth. The Hickie. Liz Lochhead. LW

I move a white day. Chess. Martin Sorescu, *Romanian.* CEEP, *tr. by* Donald Eulert *and* Stefan Avadanei

I move among my pots and pans. Trimming the Sails. Vassar Miller. NMM-2

I move back by shortcut. The World. Vern Rutsala. Poetsp

I move on feeling and have learned to distrust those who don't. Poem of Angela Yvonne Davis. Nikki Giovanni. PoBA

I Move that We Adjourn the Meeting. Nicanor Parra. *See* I Move the Meeting Be Adjourned.

I move the curtain back. After I Have Voted. Laura Jensen. AmPA

I Move the Meeting Be Adjourned. Nicanor Parra. HoPM, *tr. by* Miller Williams *Fr.* Manifesto.

I move through houses like a hermit crab. Living Lean. Christine E. Hemp. IFJA

I Move to Random Consolations. William Heyen. AmPA

I move to the window. Threading the Miles. Alfred Encarnacion. OpBo

I moved, to keep the moon. On Aesthetics, More or Less. Peter Kane Dufault. NYBP

I moved with the morning. (LL) A Field of Light. Theodore Roethke. LiTM; TwCP

I Mun Be Married a Sunday. Nicholas Udall. CBLP *Fr.* Ralph Roister Doister.

I Muriel stood at the altar-table. Don Baty, the Draft Resister. Muriel Rukeyser. NNaP

I muse, alone, an Ararat. (LL) Lakeshore. Francis Reginald Scott. MoCV; NOBC

I muse not that your Dog turds oft doth eate. Martial, *Latin.* OBCVT, *tr. by* Francis Davison

I mused/ Up and down, up and down, the terraced streets. Elizabeth Barrett Browning. *Fr.* Aurora Leigh. VWP

I Must Away. May Sarton. BoTP

I must be able to protect you. 'Marnia. LW

I must be careful about such things as these. Sonnet. Ed Roberson. GT

I must be dreaming through the days. Experience. Lesbia Harford. CBAP

I must be ill, of course. I've been shivering. Fever. Bella Akhatovna Akhmadulina, *Russian.* TCRP, *tr. by* Elaine Feinstein

I must be mad, or very tired. Meeting-House Hill. Amy Lowell. ColAP; MoAmPo; OxBA; PoRA

I must become a child again. (LL) Innocence. Thomas Traherne. CABP; ChIV-2; ESCV; MiEL; NOSC

I Must Become a Menace to My Enemies. June Jordan. NAAAL

I must complain, yet doe enjoy my Love. Thomas Campion. AAS

I must depart, but like to his last breath. Parted Souls. Edward Herbert, 1st Baron Herbert of Cherbury. SeCP

I must down to the seas again, to the lonely sea and the sky. John Masefield. *See* Sea-Fever.

I must eat my dinner. Shakespeare. *Fr.* The Tempest. OAEL-1

I must explain why it is that at night, in my own house. Still Life. Reed Whittemore. CoAP; CoAmPo

I must go back to winter. Two Decisions. Vernon Watkins. OxBTC

I must go down to the seas again, to [the lonely sea and the sky]. Sea-Fever. John Masefield. CABP; CTV; ChAP; EBEvV; FaBoBe; FaPoR; MoBrPo; NTP; OxAEP-2; OxBTC; OxBoS; PoLF; UV

I must go down to the seas again, where the billows romp and reel. Sea-Chill. Arthur Guiterman. BXAP; UV

I must go on, till in my tearful line. The Cross. Jones Very. NCAP

I must go too. The Departing Boat. Yongch'ol Park, *Korean.* CKP, *tr. by* Jaihiun Kim

I must go walk[e] the woods so wild. Sir Thomas Wyatt. MiEL

I must have back this breath. Dealing Scraps. Ruth Garnett. ISC

I must have been dozing in the tub. The Soap-Pig. Paul Muldoon. PBCIP

I must have passed the crest a while ago. The Long Hill. Sara Teasdale. MoAmPo

I must, I will have gin!—that skillet take. Strip Me Naked, or Royal Gin for Ever; a Picture. *Unknown.* NOEC

"I must leave here," said Lady De Vere. Limerick. *Unknown.* PeLi

I must leave you, but. Ariwara no Yukihira, *Japanese.* OHPJ, *tr. by* Kenneth Rexroth

I must lie down with them all soon and sleep. Thomas Kinsella. BIrV *Fr.* Nightwalker.

I must not grieve my love, whose eyes would read. Samuel Daniel. OBEV *Fr.* To Delia.

I must not think of thee; and, tired yet strong. Renouncement. Alice Thompson Meynell. BoLoP; GLoP; GSo; LW; MoBrPo; NOBE; OBEV; OBMV; OBNC; PEW; Son; VWP; WPE

I must / Not trust. Anacreontic. Robert Herrick. CaPo; CavPo

I must once again. Absalom. Yona Wallach, *Hebrew.* IP, *tr. by* Warren Bargad *and* Stanley F. Chyet

I must possess you utterly. Possession. Richard Aldington. MoBrPo

I must read only children's books. Osip Emilevich Mandelstam, *Russian.* TCRP, *tr. by* Albert C. Todd

I must remember. Spreading Wings on Wind. Simon J. Ortiz. HATNAP

I must remember to dismiss. Nature Study, After Dufy. Helen Smith Bevington. NYBP

I must say / Yes, sir. Porter. Langston Hughes. GM

I must stay here with my hurt. (LL) Here. Ronald Stuart Thomas. GTBS-P; RB

I must tell you. The Grass. George Bowering. MoCV

I must tell you. Young Sycamore. William Carlos Williams. TAP

I must tell you, my dear. Love in Mayfair. May Probyn. VWP

I must wait for a stranger to knock on my door. Elegy. David Ignatow. NNaP

I mustn't ask about him, Tune: "Drunk among the Flowers." Tune: Drunk among the Flowers. Mao Wen-hsi, *Chinese.* CoBCP, *tr. by* Burton Watson

I, my dear, was born to-day. On My Birthday, July 21. Matthew Prior. OBEV

(I my (self)-per-por-trait-(or). Spring Bank. Geraldine Monk. NBrP

I myself. (Invocation for Storing Corn). *Unknown, Nahuatl.* WPoS, *tr. by* Alarcón, Francisco X.

I myself am a complete orchestra / So long. (LL) Old King Cole ("Me clairvoyant"). G. K. Chesterton. BXAP; NOBL; UV

I myself am everything. Links. Ana Blandiana, *Romanian.* CEEP, *tr. by* Michael Impey

I myself and Pangur Bán. Pangur Bán. *Unknown.* NOIV

I myself have rolled the pearl screens up to their jade hooks. Tune: "Sand of Silk-washing Stream." Li Ching, *Chinese.* SuSp, *tr. by* Daniel Bryant

I myself saw furious with blood. Aeneas at Washington. Allen Tate. FYAP; FuPo; NOBA; NoAM; OxBA

I nail Picasso's girl with a mirror. Notes from an Analyst's Couch. Anita Endrezze-Danielson. CDW

I name you Evening, O ambiguous Evening, you fluttering leaf. Man and Beast. Léopold Sédar Senghor, *French.* PFTM, tr. by Melvin Dixon

I ne have joy, plesauns, nor comfort. *Unknown.* MiEL

I need a ritual to perform, / clean and sane, for this perfect washday. Domestic Tranquility. Gerald William Barrax. GT

I need but little! A crust of bread. Velemir Khlebnikov, *Russian.* TCRP, tr. by Gary Kern

I need kai kai ah. For the Poets. Jayne Cortez. PmAP

I need me a house like that. Where the Heart Is. Ntozake Shange. GT

I need not go. Thomas Hardy. NOBE; OBEV; OxBTC

I need not your needles. *Unknown.* OxNR

I need nothing but God's mercy. Question. Edith Södergran, *German.* WPoS, tr. by David McDuff

I need only fall asleep / to return. Ana Blandiana, *Rumanian.* BoWoP, tr. by Stavros Deligiorgis

I need so much the quiet of your love. At Nightfall. Charles Hanson Towne. BLPA; FaBoBe; PoToHe

I need some cover tonight from the dark. Shelter. Bruce Weigl. PUP-18

I need something easy. Honey Moon. Kathleen Leland Baker. NBLV

I need to learn a language but not english. Language. Jennifer Maiden. BMAP

I need to worship someone. Bulat Shalvovich Okudzhava, *Russian.* TCRP, tr. by Deming Brown

I needed to point to the buildings, as if they all stood. Thirty Years Rising. Olena Kalytiak Davis. BAP-95

I ne'er could any lustre see. Air. Richard Brinsley Sheridan. NOEC *Fr.* The Duenna.

I ne'er was struck before that hour. First Love. John Clare. BoLoP; EnLoPo; GBL; GLoP; HAP; NOBVV; NoP-4; PoPoPo; Ro

I never barked when out of season. On a Dog of Lord Eglinton's. Robert Burns. OxBSP

I never believed in mirages. Vladimir Semionovich Vysotsky, *Russian.* TCRP, tr. by Albert C. Todd

I never believed that in my broken life. Ts'ai Yen. BoWoP; WPOW *Fr.* Eighteen Verses Sung to a Tatar Reed Whistle.

I never bought a young gazelle. 'Twas Ever Thus. *Unknown.* BXAP

I never can forget. (LL) September [Days Are Here]. Helen Hunt Jackson. APN-2; PoLF

I never cared for Life: Life cared for me. Epitaph. Thomas Hardy. FaBoEE; LiLi

I never cast a flower away. Partings. Maria Jane Jewsbury. OxBChV

I never crossed your threshold with a grief. The Closed Door. Theodosia Pickering Garrison. BLPA; PoToHe

I never dared be radical when young. Ten Mills. Robert Frost.

I never did on cleft Parnassus dream. Prologue to the First Satire. Persius. AWP, tr. by Dryden *Fr.* Satires.

I never drank of Aganippe well. Sonnet 74. Sir Philip Sidney. NAEL-1; NoSic; Son *Fr.* Astrophil and Stella. AAS; SiPS

I Never Even Suggested It. Ogden Nash. PoLF

I never gave a lock of hair away. Sonnet. Elizabeth Barrett Browning. EBVV; HAP *Fr.* Sonnets from the Portuguese.

I never go to the plains beneath the hills. Song of the Old Man of the Hills. Meng Chiao, *Chinese.* PLT, tr. by A. C. Graham

I / never / guessed any. E. E. Cummings. NYBP

I never hear it ring without. The Door-Bell. Charlotte Becker. PoToHe

I never heard the word "escape." Emily Dickinson. CMoP; NCAP; NOBA; SAmP

I never knew. (LL) Willy Lyons. James Wright. HCAP; NNaP; PoE

I never knew a night so black. John Kendrick Bangs. PoToHe

I never knew the earth had so much gold. Feuerzauber. Louis Untermeyer. TrJP

I never knew the worth of him / Until he died. (LL) An Old Story. Edwin Arlington Robinson. MoAmPo; OxBSP

I never know what to say. A Portrait. Stevie Smith. WPN

I/ never liked/ white folks. Alice Walker. PoBA *Fr.* Once. BlSi

I never look upon the sea. Aunt Zillah Speaks. Herbert Edward Palmer. FaBoTw

I never lost as much but twice. Emily Dickinson. HeIP-4; MoAmPo; NAAL-1; NAAL-3; NCAP; NOBA; NoAM; NoP-4; PFE; TAP

I never rear'd a young gazelle. 'Twas Ever Thus. Henry Sambrooke Leigh. UV

I Never rested on the Muses bed. To William Drummond of Hawthornden. Mary Oxlie, of Morpeth. KTR

I never said I loved you, John. No, Thank You, John. Christina Rossetti. NAEL-2

I never saw a Moor. Emily Dickinson. ACTP; CTV; ChAP; HeIP-4; ImGa; ImPo; LiTM; MeMAP; MoAmPo; PoLF; SAmP; TAP; TFi; WPoS ("As if the chart were given.") (LL) ACTP; ChAP

I never saw a Purple Cow. The Purple Cow. Frank Gelett Burgess. CBNP; CTV; FPC; NBLV; NTCP; OBAL; OBCA; OBCoV; PoLF; TFi; TLR

I never saw a wild thing. Self-Pity. D. H. Lawrence. OxBTC; RB

I Never Saw You. Jyoti Lanjewar, *Marathi.* OMIP, tr. by Vinay Dharwadker

I never saw you madam, lay [or sawe my Ladye] laye apart. Complaint That His Ladie After She Knew of His Love Kept Her Face Alway Hidden from Him. Henry Howard, Earl of Surrey. AAS; PoEL-1; SiPS

I never see the colored boats of night. The Age of Sheen. Dorothy Hughes. NYBP

I never see you. The Buddha. Daya Pawar, *Marathi.* OMIP, tr. by Eleanor Zelliot *and* Jayant Karve

I never set my two eyes on a head was so fine as your head. A Translation from Walter von der Vogelweide. Walther von der Vogelweide. MoBrPo, tr. by J. M. Synge

I never shall forget thee—'tis a word. To Mrs. Norton. Frances Anne Kemble. VWP

I Never Shall Love the Snow Again. Robert Bridges. CH; CMoP

I never stoop'd so low, as they. Negative Love. Donne. FSCP

I never tasted the Pierian spring. On Her Blindness. Priscilla Pointon. ECWP *Fr.* To the Critics.

I never thought for a moment. Emily Dickinson, Bismarck and the Roadrunner's Inquiry. Ray A. Young Bear. HATNAP

I never thought to see us. Sherley Anne Williams. MDDM *Fr.* The Peacock Poems.

I never tire in my search of solitude. In Search of Solitude. Chao Yi, *Chinese.* SuSp, tr. by Chang Yin-nan *and* Lewis C. Walmsley

I never told you. What They Do to You in Distant Places. Marvin Bell. Poetsp

I never touched thy royal hand, dead queen. The Lost Light. Emily Jane Pfeiffer. VWP

I never understood the girls. The Girls. Diane Wakoski. NMM-2

I never wanted the red of fire, the black at midnight. Miracle. Wen Yi-tuo, *Chinese.* PFTM, tr. by Arthur Sze

I never wanted to be a star. On Earth. Forugh Farrokhzad, *Persian.* BoWoP, tr. by Girdhard Tikku

I never was a slave—a robber took. Albery Allson Whitman. AAP *Fr.* Twasinta's Seminoles; Or Rape of Florida.

I never was attached to that great sect. The Longest Journey. Shelley. OxBM *Fr.* Epipsychidion.

I never wash'd, that I could tell. The Prologue of Persius. Persius, *Latin.* OBCVT, tr. by Unknown

I never wholly feel that summer is high. High Summer. Ebenezer Jones. NOBVV

I never would cry, Old chairs to mend. *Unknown. See* Chairs to Mend.

I never writ, nor no man ever loved. (LL) Sonnet 116. Shakespeare. APAD; AWP; CABP; ClHu; EBEvV; EnLoPo; GBL; GTBS-P; HAP; HeIP-4; ITG; ImPo; InPS-3; LoP; NAEL-1; NIP-4; NOBE; NoSic; OAEL-1; OBEV; OxAEP-1; OxBM; PBMP; PFE; PoE; PoEL-2; PoPoPo; PoRA; Poetr; SAGP; SCGP; SCV; SoSe-8; Son; TFi; TRP; UnPo; WeW-3

I, no sense of being alive. A Diary without Dates. Chio Nakamura, *Japanese.* WPJ, tr. by Kenneth Rexroth *and* Ikuko Atsumi

I, now at Carthage. He, shot dead at Rome. *Vale* from Carthage. Peter Viereck. LiTM; MoAmPo

I now had only to retrace. Charlotte Brontë. NOBVV

I now solicit not the Muses nine. William Woty. NOEC *Fr.* A Mock Invocation to Genius.

I now think[e], Love is rather deaf[e], than [or then] blind. My Picture Left in Scotland. Ben Jonson. BeJo; CBLP; FMP; NAEL-1; PBRV; PoEL-2; SeCP

I now will throw myself down. A Dialogue. David Ignatow. NNaP

I nursed it in my bosom while it lived. Memory. Christina Rossetti. OBNC

I, Oedipus, the club-foot, made to stumble. Oedipus. Edwin Muir. CMoP

I offer my back to the silken net. An Allegory. David Ignatow. VGW

I offer you the golden flagon. Offering Wine. Yü Wu-ling, *Chinese.* CoBCP, tr. by Burton Watson

I oft have wished for Hell for Ease from Heaven. (LL) Grown old in Love from Seven till Seven times Seven. William Blake. FaBoEE; OAEL-2

I often bow; your hat you never stir. Martial, *Latin.* OBCVT, tr. by William Hay

I often meet a monster. Max Fatchen. OTCP

I often pause and wonder. *Unknown.* CTV

I often read the writings of the sages. Words from the Goblet of Wisdom. Yüan Mei, *Chinese.* CoBLCP, tr. by Jonathan Chaves

I often sit and wish that I. A Kite. Frank Dempster Sherman. CTV
I often wish'd, that I had clear. Horace. OBCVT, *tr. by* Swift, Jonathan (1667-1745) and Alexander Pope. *Fr.* An Imitation of the Sixth Satire of the Second Book of Horace.
I often wonder as the fairy-story. The Lucky Marriage. Thomas Blackburn. GTBS-P
I often wonder how it is. My Playmate. Mary I. Osborn. BoTP; OTCP
I on the sunny side of Three Rivers. For Ku Yen-hsien, A Poem for Him to Give to His Wife. Lu Yün, *Chinese.* CoBCP, *tr. by* Burton Watson
I once conjectur'd that those tygers hard. Seaconk or Rehoboths Fate. Benjamin Tompson. SCAP
I Once Did a Bamboo Painting for Somebody—Now He Wants Me To Do Another. I Have Written This To Answer Him. Hsü Wei, *Chinese.* CoBLCP, *tr. by* Jonathan Chaves
I once did court a damsel most beautiful and bright. A Lover's Lament. *Unknown.* AmFP
I once drove to Atlantic City. Zoom (The Commodores). Thulani Davis. ISC
I once had a cat called Maria. Limerick. Paul Griffin. PeLi
I once had a sweet little doll, dears. The Little Doll. Charles Kingsley. OxBChV *Fr.* The Water Babies.
I once had money and a friend. Money and a Friend. *Unknown.* BLPA
I once heard the survivors. Don Marquis. NBLV *Fr.* Certain Maxims of Archy. OBAL
I once knew a lass and I oft heard her tell. So I Let Her Go. *Unknown.* AmFP
I once knew a little girl, a charming beauty bright. The Rejected Lover. *Unknown.* AmFP
I Once Knew a Man. Lucille Clifton. Poetr
I once knew a spinster of Staines. Limerick. Plaiwon. PeLi
I once knew a woman named Benedicta, who infused everything. Which One Is Genuine? Charles Baudelaire, *French.* RaBo, *tr. by* Robert Bly
I once knowed an ole Sexion Boss but he done been laid low. The Old Section Boss. *Unknown.* BPo
I Once Loved a Young Man. *Unknown.* AmFP
I once loved a young man as dear as my life. I'm Going to Georgia. *Unknown.* AmFP
I once may see when yeares shall wreck my wrong. Samuel Daniel. AAS *Fr.* To Delia.
I once spent an evening in a village. The Man Upright. Thomas Macdonagh. BIrV
I once took my girl to Southend. Limerick. Veronica Nicolson. PeLi
I once wanted a white man's eyes upon. Lunchcounter Freedom. Thylias Moss. PoPoPo
I once wanted these walls. Remembering Walls. Robin Fulton. FaBoTC
I Once was a maid, tho' I cannot tell when. Robert Burns. NBLV; OxBoLi *Fr.* Love and Libery—A Cantata. NOBRP; NOEC ("I once was a maid, though I cannot tell when.") RACG
I once was a Pirate what sailed the 'igh seas. Cat Morgan Introduces Himself. T. S. Eliot. NOBL; PeLV
I once was a seaman stout and bold. Jolly Soldier. *Unknown.* AmFP
I once was happy, when while yet a child. Charlotte Smith. PEW; WPE *Fr.* Beachy Head.
I once would spout words like "the most," "the best." O Life I Love and Cherish Like My Wife! Việt Phu'o'ng, *Vietnamese.* AVP, *tr. by* Huỳnh Sanh Thông
I once wrote a letter as follows. The Invoice. Robert Creeley. VGW
I Only Am Escaped Alone to Tell Thee. Howard Nemerov. CoAP; HeIP-4; NoAM
I only asked my friends to be friendly and polite. Two Friends. Stevie Smith. WPN
I only knew one poet in my life. How It Strikes a Contemporary. Robert Browning. CTC; EnVR; FaBoPV; GTBS-P; OAEL-2
I only saw my father's face in butchery. The Bull-roarer. Gerald Stern. NAmP90
I open up, mop gray ice. Juana Bautista Lucero, Circa 1926, to Her Photographer. Elizabeth Libbey. CMAP
I order the carriage to stop for a while. (LL) On the Road through Chang-te. Sun Yün-feng, *Chinese.* BoWoP; WPOW, *tr. by* Kenneth Rexroth and Ling Chung
I ordered this, this clean wood box. The Arrival of the Bee Box. Sylvia Plath. FaBoMo; FaBoWP; HCAP; NALW
I owe my living to the abattoir. My father, the manager, sat in the office. The Abattoir. Ania Walwicz. BMAP
I owe nothing to winter. My Winter Past. Eldon Grier. NOBC
I owe you an apology. A Question of Form and Content. Jon Stallworthy. OxBC
I own a solace shut within my heart. Behind a Wall. Amy Lowell. SDW
I pace the sounding sea-beach and behold. Milton. Henry Wadsworth Longfellow. AWP; AmPP; GSo; TAP

I paid my 30[dc] and rode by the bus. Ten Years Old. Nikki Giovanni. MBE
I Paint What I See. Elwyn Brooks White. NBLV; NYBP
I painted my eyes with black antimony. Love Song. *Unknown, Bagirmi.* BoWoP, *tr. by* H. Gaden
I painted rouge on my lips. Lover of Love. Hagiwara Sakutaro, *Japanese.* PFTM, *tr. by* Hiroaki Sato
I painted the mailbox. That was fun. Painting the Gate. May Swenson. TLR; WeW-3
I painted the roof of a skyscraper. People Who Must. Carl Sandburg. CA
I park the car because I'm happy. Now. Christopher Gilbert. GT
I park the car half in the ditch and switch off and sit. Stealing Trout. Ted Hughes. NYBP
I parted from my life last night. On the Death of His Wife. Muireadhach Albanach O'Dalaigh, *Irish.* BIrV; CIP-2, *tr. by* Frank O'Connor
I pass the day tense, day-. Kenneth Rexroth. APSN *Fr.* The Love Poems of Marichiko.
I Pass the Night at General Headquarters. Tu Fu, *Chinese.* OHPC, *tr. by* Kenneth Rexroth
I passed along the water's edge below the humid trees. Indian upon God, The [*or* An]. W. B. Yeats. MoBrPo
I passed by the beach. Akahito, *Japanese.* HoPM; OHPJ, *tr. by* Kenneth Rexroth
I passed by the house of the young man who loves me. Love Song. *Unknown, Egyptian.* TTY, *tr. by* J. E. Manchip White
I patched my coat with sunlight. The Coat. Dennis Lee. TLR
I paused by the fence / and looked up. A Green Evening. Brendan Galvin. AFr
I paused in a garden alley of cypress and rose, resembling Paradise. Last Things. Kathleen Jessie Raine. NYBP
I peel off your plastic underwear. Visit. Chitra Divakaruni. NMM-2
I peeled bits of straw and I got switches too. Song. John Clare. NAEL-2
I peeped through the window. *Unknown.* OxNR
I peer adown a shining group. Tribute. Eloise Bibb. CBWP-4
I persist in a little fabric between me and the world. J. Michael Yates. NOBC *Fr.* The Great Bear Lake Meditations.
I phoned up the funeral director. He Told Us He Wanted a Black Coffin. Jackie Kay. CPO
I pick up your scroll of poems, read in front of the lamp. Aboard a Boat, Reading Yüan Chen's Poems. Po Chü-i, *Chinese.* CoBCP, *tr. by* Burton Watson
I picked an azalea. Lady Izumi, *Japanese.* OHMPJ, *tr. by* Kenneth Rexroth
I picked fresh mint. My Garden. Norah E. Hussey. BoTP
I picked up a leaf. Les Étiquettes Jaunes. Frank O'Hara. CAPP-1
I piece together my child. Quartet. Sherley Anne Williams. WeT
I pitched my day's leazings in Crimmercrock Lane. The Dark-Eyed Gentleman. Thomas Hardy. MoBrPo; NBLV; UnPo
I pitied him for his small strategy. (LL) The Compassionate Fool. Norman Cameron. GTBS-P; OxBSP; OxBTC; RB
I place these numbed wrists to the pane. Nightmare Begins Responsibility. Michael S. Harper. GT; HCAP; LCAP-2; LoL; PoPoPo; TAP; VCAP
I placed a jar in Tennessee. Anecdote of the Jar. Wallace Stevens. AmPP; CMoP; ColAP; FaBoA; HCAP; HeIP-4; HoPM; InPK-6; MeMAP; MoAmPo; MoP; NAAL-2; NAWM-2; NOBA; NoAM; NoP-4; OxBA; OxBSP; PoA; PoPoPo; Poetr; SAmP; TAP; TFi; UnPo
I placed my dream in a boat. Song. Cecília Meireles, *Portuguese.* WPOW, *tr. by* Eloah F. Giacomelli
I placed my hand cupped. Return of an Ikon. Dimitris Tsaloumas. BMAP
I planned to get drunk to ease my sadness. Yang Chi. *Fr.* Living in a Riverside Village—; Miscellaneous Impressions. CoBLCP, *tr. by* Jonathan Chaves
I planned to have a border of lavender. Paul Goodman. GLP; VGW
I plant beans at the foot of the southern hill. T'ao Ch'ien. SuSp, *tr. by* Wu-chi Liu *Fr.* On Returning to My Garden and Field.
I planted a hundred mulberry trees. Country House. Ch'u Ch'uang I, *Chinese.* OHMPC, *tr. by* Kenneth Rexroth
I planted a young tree when I was young. A Dumb Friend. Christina Rossetti. FP
I planted beans at the foot of the southern mountain. Returning to My Home in the Country. T'ao Ch'ien, *Chinese.* CoBCP, *tr. by* Burton Watson
I planted him in this country / like a flag. (LL) Death of a Young Son by Drowning. Margaret Atwood. BoWoP; NoBC
I planted rice before Spring Festival. Su Tung-p'o, *Chinese.* CoBCP, *tr. by* Watson, Burton (b. 1925); CoBCP *Fr.* Eastern Slope.
I play a spade:—Such strange new faces. Arrivals at a Watering-Place. Winthrop Mackworth Praed. NOBL; NOBRP; PeLV
I play for Seasons; not Eternities! George Meredith. OBNC; SCGP *Fr.* Modern Love.
I play it cool. Motto. Langston Hughes. CA; NAAAL; PoBA

I play pool. I aim toward the faces. Games. Sandra McPherson. LCAP-2

I play the Masonic Funeral March. Julia Fields. *Fr.* Poems: Birmingham 1962–1964. PoBA

I play your furies back to me at night. High Fidelity. Thom Gunn. PoA

I played piano while my daddy knelt. The Southern Crescent Was on time. Andrew Hudgins. GM

I pledge allegiance. Pledge of Allegiance to the Flag. Francis Bellamy. CTV

I pledge myself through thick and thin. Tory Pledges. Thomas Moore. OBSV

I pluck *heng*-herbs at the Chin-ling riverside. Wang T'ing-hsiang. *Fr.* Songs of Chiang-nan. CoBLCP, *tr. by* Jonathan Chaves

I pluck the clustering flowers from the wall. Tune: "Sprig of Flowers, A"—Not Bowing to Old Age. Kuan Han-ch'ing, *Chinese.* SuSp, *tr. by* Jerome P. Seaton

I plucked my soul out of its secret place. I Know My Soul. Claude McKay. BPo

I plucked pink blossoms from mine apple tree. An Apple Gathering. Christina Rossetti. NAEL-2; OBNC

I, / poet by trade. Ars Poetica. Claribel Alegría, *Spanish.* LoL, *tr. by* D. J. Flakoll

I polish your skin. It is that of a woman. A Song in Praise of a Favourite Humming-Top. Hone Tuwhare. PeNZ

I ponder on life. Max Ehrmann. PoToHe

I ponder you in clamor and in silence. Psalm. Tudor Arghezi, *Romanian.* AF, *tr. by* Andrei Bantas *and* Thomas Amherst Perry; CEEP, *tr. by* Peter Jay *and* Virgil Nemoianu

I pour out wine in a libation to the river god. Meeting My Fellow Countryman, Yü Wu-chung. Yang Chi, *Chinese.* CoBLCP, *tr. by* Jonathan Chaves

I pour the cream. (LL) Vacation. William Stafford. BLT; Poetsp

I praise a patron high-hearted in strife. In Praise of Owain Gwynedd. Cynddelw Brydydd Mawr, *Welsh.* OBWVE, *tr. by* Joseph P. Clancy

I praise God's mankind in an old woman. Lines: I Praise God's Mankind in an Old Woman. Wilfred Watson. NOBC

I praise him not. James Russell Lowell. AiP *Fr.* Ode Recited at the Harvard Commemoration (July 21, 1865). APN-1; CBCWP; NOBA; OBWP

I praise Saint Everyman, his house and home. Here Together Met. Louis Johnson. PeNZ

I praise the country women. Grit. Geoff Page. NOBAu

I praise the disk of the rising sun. Vidya. PBWP; WPOW *Fr.* The Sun.

I praise the Frenchman, his remark was shrewd. William Cowper. BLPA *Fr.* Retirement.

I praise the speech, but cannot now abide it. Of the Wars in Ireland. John Harington. NoSic

I praise the tortilla in honor of El Panzón. Praise the Tortilla, Praise the Menudo, Praise the Chorizo. Ray Gonzales. UnSA

I praise those ancient Chinamen. Hymnus Ad Patrem Sinensis. Philip Whalen. BB

I praised thee not while living; what to thee. To Elizabeth Barrett Browning, in 1861. Dora Greenwell. VWP

I Pratyng Parret am, to speake. The Parret. Martial, *Latin.* OBCVT, *tr. by* Timothy Kendall

I pray above your grave. The two small hills. The Honeycomb of Bees. Hrubín František, *Czech.* CEEP, *tr. by* Don Mager

I pray for a child-like heart. A Prayer for Love. *Unknown.* CTV

I pray from the heart a prayerbook. Amir Gilbo'a, *Hebrew.* IP, *tr. by* Warren Bargad *and* Stanley F. Chyet

I pray! My little body and whole span. Supplication of the Black Aberdeen. Rudyard Kipling. BLPA

I pray that the great world's flowering stay as it is. The Gardener to His God. Mona Van Duyn. GaP; RACG; TrCP; UnPo; WPE

I pray the Lord my soul to take. Ogden Nash. NBLV *Fr.* One from One Leaves Two.

I pray the prayer the Easterners do. Salaam Alaikum. *Unknown.* PoLF

I pray thee by the soul of her that bore thee. Iris, Her Book. Oliver Wendell Holmes. NCAP

I pray thee, Dante, shouldst thou meet with Love. To Dante: He Mistrusts the Love of Lapo Gianni. Guido Cavalcanti, *Italian.* AWP, *tr. by* D. G. Rossetti

I pray thee leave, love me no more. To His Coy Love, A Canzonet. Michael Drayton. NOSC; PBRV; SAGP

I pray thee Nymph Penaeis stay, I chase not as a fo. Ovid. OBVE, *tr. by* Arthur Golding *Fr.* Metamorphoses.

I pray Thee O Lord. A Prayer. Julian Tuwim, *Polish.* TrJP, *tr. by* Wanda Dynowska

I pray thee spare me, gentle Boy. Loves Feast. Sir John Suckling. CBLP

I pray you, be not wroth. *Unknown. Fr.* Vox Populi, Vox Dei. FaBoPV

I pray you, Christ, to change my heart. Christ's Bounty. *Unknown, Irish.* TIRV, *tr. by* Brendan Kennelly

"I pray you, cum kiss me." *Unknown.* MiEL

I pray you, forgive me in the stillness of your shoes swollen on these sands. Haim Guri, *Hebrew.* IP, *tr. by* Warren Bargad *and* Stanley F. Chyet

I pray you, let us roam no more. Thomas Moore. OBNC *Fr.* Odes to Nea.

I prayed for riches, and achieved success. Answered Prayers. Ella Wheeler Wilcox. PWR

I prefer red chile over my eggs. Green Chile. Jimmy Santiago Baca. NAmP90

I prepare the last meal. Capital Punishment. Sherman Alexie. BAP-96

I press against the emptiness. Aubade. Vassar Miller. WeT

I press[e] not to the choir [*or* quire], nor dare I greet. To My Worthy Friend Master George Sands [*or* Sandys], on His Translation of the Psalms. Thomas Carew. BeJo; CaPo; EPCY; MeLP

I press pen to paper like a pistol to the temple. Amir Gilbo'a, *Hebrew.* IP, *tr. by* Warren Bargad *and* Stanley F. Chyet

I press'd my Julia's lips, and in the kiss. Love Palpable. Robert Herrick. CavPo

I Pressed Her Rebel Lips. *Unknown.* BoLoP

I pretend to wait for you to enlarge the minutes. Patrizia Cavalli, *Italian.* NeIt, *tr. by* Judith Baumel

I prithee, daughter, do not make me mad. Shakespeare. OxAEP-1 *Fr.* King Lear.

I prithee let my heart alone. Song. Thomas Stanley. BeJo

I prithee spare me, gentle boy. Song. Sir John Suckling. BeJo; CavPo

I promise to make you more alive than you've ever been. Ordeal. Nina Cassian, *Rumanian.* PBWP, *tr. by* Michael Impey *and* Brian Swann

I promise you these days and an understanding. Tourist Death. Archibald MacLeish. NAAL-2

I promised once if I got hold of. Written in a Copy of Swift's Poems, for Wayne Burns. James Wright. NOBA

I propose to you. The Statue. Robert Creeley. LCAP-2

I prove a theorem and the house expands. Geometry. Rita Dove. CMAP; HCAP; HeIP-4; Poetr

I puff my breast out, my neck swells. Weathercock, The: "I puff my breast out, my neck swells." Cynewulf. RB, *tr. by* Geoffrey Grigson *Fr.* Riddles (Exeter Book).

I pull the huge book down from the bookcase. *Automobiles of the Asylum.* Philip Hammial. BMAP

I pulled a hummingbird out of the sky one day but let it go. Wind. Dionne Brand. NOxBChV

I pulled on a suit of mail. Precautions. Martin Sorescu, *Romanian.* VCWP, *tr. by* Muldoon, Paul *and* Joana Russell-Gebbett

I pump him full of lost watches. (LL) Birthplace Revisited. Gregory Corso. NeAP; PoM; VGW

I pumped the iron handle and watched the water. My Father Washes His Hands. Fred Chappell. MT

I push out of Customs, stumble, almost fall, legs numb from. Restroom. Chitra Divakaruni. UnSA

I put my cap in the cage. Quartier Libre. Jacques Prévert, *French.* CLPP, *tr. by* Lawrence Ferlinghetti

I put my hat upon my head. Ballad. Samuel Johnson. CBNP; KaS; NOBL; OxAEP-1; UV

I put my hat upon my head. F. A. V. Madden. BXAP

I put my hat upon my head. Ian Sainsbury. BXAP

I put my hat upon my head. A Second Stanza for Dr. Johnson. Donald Hall. KaS

I put my hat upon my head. Ian Stirling. BXAP

I put my hat upon my head. Peter Veale. BXAP; NBLV

I put on a pair of overshoes. Around My Room. William Jay Smith. TLR

I put on La Path'etique. La Pathétique. Lily Brett. HP

I put the bulb in the ground. The Spring Flower. Stanley Cook. AYFP

I put your leaves aside. The Weather-Cock Points South. Amy Lowell. CPO; NALW; NoP-4

I quail, lean to beginnings, sheath-wet. (LL) Cuttings ("This urge, wrestle, resurrection of dry sticks"). Theodore Roethke. ColAP; HCAP; LCAP-2; MoP; NAAL-2; NOBA; NoAM; OBGa; TAP; TRP; UnPo; VCAP

I quarreled with kings till the Sabbath. Song of the Sabbath. Kadya Molodovsky, *Yiddish.* PBWP; WPOW, *tr. by* Jean Valentine

I raced west away from the dawn. Thaba Bosio. S. D. R. Sutu, *Sotho.* PeSA, *tr. by* Dan Kunene *and* Jack Cope

I rage, I melt, I burn. John Gay. NAEL-1 *Fr.* Acis and Galatea.

I, Rainey Betha, 22. Plaint. Charles Henri Ford. SPE

I raise my cup and invite. Moon, Flowers, Man. Su Tung-p'o, *Chinese.* OHPC, *tr. by* Kenneth Rexroth

I raise my winecup to the flowers. To the Tune "Stopping My Horse to Listen." Yang Shen, *Chinese.* CoBLCP, *tr. by* Jonathan Chaves

I raise the curtains and go out. Alone. Chu Shu-chen, *Chinese.* BoWoP; OHPC, *tr. by* Kenneth Rexroth

I ran from the prison house but they captured me. The Prison House. Alan Paton. PeSA

I ran into the afterlife. Once, Driving West of Billings, Montana. Susan Mitchell. WeT

I ran / my neck broken I ran. Galway Kinnell. *Fr.* The Dead Shall Be Raised Incorruptible. NOBA; PoE

I ran out in the morning, when the air was clean and new. Autumn Morning at Cambridge. Frances Darwin Cornford. PoRA

I ran to the church. Journey Back to Christmas. Gwen Dunn. OBCP

I ran up and grabbed your arm, the way a man. At the Washing of My Son. David Ray. RaBo

I ran up six flights of stairs. The Whole Mess. . . Almost, The . . Almost. Gregory Corso. BB

I ran upon life unknowing, without or science or art. Tennyson. FaBoEE

I rang them up, while touring Timbuctoo. To Someone Who Insisted I Look up Someone. X. J. Kennedy. OBCoV

I reach from pain. Reuben, Reuben. Michael S. Harper. LoL; PoE

I reached that waterhole, its mud designed. Roland Robinson. CBAP *Fr.* The Wanderer.

I reached the end, but you live on. The Wind. Boris Pasternak, *Russian.* TCRP, *tr. by* Yakov Hornstein

I read. Bob Boldman. HA

I read a boy's poem called. Every Morning After Killing Thousands of Angels. Ryuichi Tamura, *Japanese.* VCWP, *tr. by* Christopher Drake

I read a novel by a friend of mine. I Am in a Novel. D. H. Lawrence. OBCoV

I read a sad poem / on the wall. Graffiti. Jane Yolen. SSCS

I read about the Blaskets and Dunquin. John Millington Synge. FaBoEE

I read how Quixote in his random ride. Parable. Richard Wilbur. OxBSP

I read in the papers about the. Freedom Train. Langston Hughes. GM

I read last night of the Grand Review. A Second Review of the Grand Army. Bret Harte. CBCWP

I read of a thousand killed. A Thousand Killed. Bernard Spencer. OBWP

I read once of a valley. After Babel. Peter Goldsworthy. NOBAu

I read or write, I teach or wonder what is truth. Apologia pro Vita Sua. Sedulius Scottus, *Latin.* BIrV, *tr. by* Helen Waddell

I read / Sand Creek massacre. Brief Wyoming Meditation. Diane Di Prima. BB

I read the marble-lettered name. A Grave in Hollywood Cemetery, Richmond. Margaret Junkin Preston. CBCWP

I read you the soft verses of antiquity. 19 January 1944. Salvatore Quasimodo, *Italian.* AF, *tr. by* Jack Bevan

I really don't want to die now. Vladimir Shchirovsky, *Russian.* TCRP, *tr. by* Bradley Jordan

I really love you, / believe me. It is something I inherited. Attila József. Attila József, *Hungarian.* AF, *tr. by* John Batki

"I really take it very kind." Domestic Asides; or, Truth in Parentheses. Thomas Hood. PeLV

I really thought that drinking here would. Knocking Around. John Ashbery. NoAM

I reason, Earth is short. Emily Dickinson. APN-2; NCAP; TAP

I recall a drinking party on the bridge, the Meridian Bridge. Tune: "Immortal at the River"—Ascending a Little Tower at Night. Ch'en Yü-yi, *Chinese.* SuSp, *tr. by* James J. Y. Liu

I recall, before the banks. By the Bridge. Ted Walker. NYBP

I recall everything, but more than all. Double Sonnet. Anthony Hecht. Son

I recall that I stood before the breaking waves. Mark Strand. BAP-93 *Fr.* Dark Harbor.

I recall the times she came. Four Recollections. Shen Yüeh, *Chinese.* SuSp, *tr. by* Richard B. Mather

I reckon—when I count at all. Emily Dickinson. APN-2; MoAmPo; NIP-4; NoP-4; PAR

I recognized her and stopped to say I owned. In the Middle of the Journey. David Keller. CMAP

I recognized him by his skips and hops. Pan and the Cherries. Paul Fort, *French.* AWP, *tr. by* Jethro Bithell

I recollect a nurse call'd [*or* called] Ann. A Terrible Infant. Frederick Locker-Lampson. NOxBChV; OBCoV

I recommend herbs for you. Conversation in Front of a Helicopter. Rosario Murillo, *Spanish.* CLPP, *tr. by* Alejandro Murguía

I recover now the time I drove. Art McCooey. Patrick Kavanagh. CIP-2

I refuse to turn into gold. Bassus, *Greek.* GrAn, *tr. by* Peter Jay

I regretted the arrival of my death. What Profit? Immanuel di Roma, *Hebrew.* TrJP, *tr. by* J. Chotzner

I rein in my horse. Teika, *Japanese.* OHMPJ, *tr. by* Kenneth Rexroth

I release you, my beautiful and terrible. I Give You Back. Joy Harjo. HATNAP; LoL; UnSA

I remain with what was not fully said. Nina Berberova, *Russian.* TCRP, *tr. by* Albert C. Todd

I Remember ("I remember / January, / 1968"). Mae Jackson. PoBA

I Remember. Anne Sexton. LW

("Door to your room was / the door to mine, The.") (LL) AFr

I Remember. Stevie Smith. BoLoP; BoWoP; FaBoWP; InPK-6; OxBC

I remember. William Carlos Williams. MeMAP *Fr.* Paterson.

I remember a dead man. Forget-Me-Nots. Yevgeny Mikhailovich Vinokurov, *Russian.* TCRP, *tr. by* Daniel Weissbort

I remember a dim evening in Kishinyov [*or* Kishinev]. "Dovid Knut," *Russian.* TCRP, *tr. by* John Glad

I remember a far tall island. The Child's Return. Phyllis Shand Allfrey. PBCV

I remember a former day when I and a friend. Coming Again to Heng-yang, I Mourn for Liu Tsung-yüan. Liu Yu Hsi, *Chinese.* SuSp, *tr. by* Daniel Bryant

I remember a grass hut. Fujiwara No Toshinari, *Japanese.* OHMPJ, *tr. by* Kenneth Rexroth

I remember a house where all were good. In the Valley of the Elwy. Gerard Manley Hopkins. EnVR; ImPo; NOBVV; NOCV; OxAEP-2; TOF

I remember a waterfall at the bottom of grottoes. Someone I knew, a. Trance Event. Robert Desnos, *French.* PFTM, *tr. by* Marcel Jean

I remember an ancient Chinese picture kept over there in Daitokuji. Ernest Francisco Fenollosa. APN-2 *Fr.* Ode on Reincarnation.

I remember at times. Scholar II. Seamus Deane. CIP-2; NOIV

I remember being ashamed of my father. Fathers and Sons. Tom Leonard. CABP; FaBoTC

I Remember Clifford. Philip Levine. APAD

I Remember Dexedrine. 1970. Pamela Brown. BMAP

I Remember Galileo. Gerald Stern. FYAP

I remember God as an eccentric millionaire. Quite Apart from the Holy Ghost. Adrian Mitchell. OBSV

I remember, gracious, graceful moon. To the Moon. Giacomo Leopardi, *Italian.* TTTS, *tr. by* Kenneth Koch

I Remember Haifa Being Lovely But. Lyn Lifshin. UnSA

I remember how I came here. Winter Evening Poem. Laura Jensen. LCAP-2

I remember how, long ago, I found. Crystals like Blood. "Hugh MacDiarmid." HAP; RB

I Remember How She Sang. Rob Penny. PoBA

I remember, I remember. Thomas Hood. ACTP; BLPA; CH; EBEvV; FaBoBe; FaPoR; GTBS-P; ImPo; NOBE; NTP; OxAEP-2; PoEL-4; TFi

I Remember, I Remember. Philip Larkin. NOBL; NTP

I remember / January, / 1968. I Remember. Mae Jackson. PoBA

I remember / Joal! Joal. Léopold Sédar Senghor, *French.* NegPo, *tr. by* Ellen Conroy Kennedy

I remember long veils of green rain. Green Rain. Dorothy Livesay. NALW; NIP-4; NOBC; NoP-4

I remember Longwood. Blind Adolphus. Angela McCabe. AmPA

I remember my father, slight. Subterfuge. Vassar Miller. NMM-2

I remember my grandmother on her hard knees. Patient. Lynn Emanuel. CMAP

I remember my mother's Aunt Rebecca. Great-Aunt Rebecca. Elizabeth Brewster. NOBC

I remember myself waiting. Prehistory. David Avidan, *Hebrew.* IP, *tr. by* Warren Bargad *and* Stanley F. Chyet

I remember now how first I knew what death was. Original Sin. Alexander Kinnan Laing. NYBP

I remember once, on a journey to the west. I Remember the River at Wu Sung. Mei Yao Ch'en. OHPC

I remember one winter-night meadow. The Doomed Spaceman. Ted Walker. SpW

I remember partly. Southwest Passage. Dudley Fitts. PoA

I remember rooms that have had their part. Rooms. Charlotte Mew. PBWP

I Remember Sharpeville. Sipho Sepamla. AF

I remember sitting together in parks. Love's Advocate. Phoebe Hesketh. LW

I remember striding through the August twilight. Calling on Peadar O'Donnell at Dungloe. John Hewitt. CIP-2

I remember that year, under the blossoms. Tune: Lotus-leaf Cup. Wei Chuang, *Chinese.* CoBCP, *tr. by* Burton Watson

I remember that year, under the blossoms. Wen T'ing-yün, *Chinese.* CoBCP, *tr. by* Burton Watson

I Remember the Blue River. Mei Yao Ch'en, *Chinese.* OHPC, *tr. by* Kenneth Rexroth

I remember the boy, pink hand. Economics. Alvin Aubert. MT

I remember the creek that ran beside the golf course. The Stream Flowing. Robert Mezey. WeT

I remember the day I arrived. Doubting. Louis Simpson. NNaP

I remember the days / When the lily. Akiko Yosano, *Japanese*. WPJ, *tr. by* Kenneth Rexroth *and* Ikuko Atsumi

I remember the dread with which I at a quarter past four. False Security. John Betjeman. CMoP; NoAM; NoP-4

I remember the evening. The Swarming Bees. James Laughlin. VGW

I remember the forehead born. Uncle. Philip Levine. NNaP

I remember the neckcurls, limp and damp as tendrils. Elegy for Jane. Theodore Roethke. AmPP; CoAP; ColAP; HAP; HCAP; IMW; InPK-6; InPS-3; LiLi; LiTM; MoAmPo; MoLi; NoP-4; PoE; PoPoPo; Poetr; SAGP; TAP; TFi; TRP; TwCP; WeW-3

I remember the old joke. The Cliff. David Rowbotham. NOBAu

I Remember the River at Wu Sung. Mei Yao Ch'en. OHPC

I remember the Roman Emperor, one of the cruellest of them. Exeat. Stevie Smith. NAEL-2; NoAM

I Remember the Room Was Filled with Light. Judith Hemschemeyer. IFJA

I remember the time. A Little Girl's Dream World. Della Burt. BlSi

I remember the way the big windows washed. Eavan Boland. PBCIP

I remember them, man and wife, in their little car. Couple. Walter Stone. NYBP

I remember, they sent. Corpse-bearing. Thomas Ashe. EBVV; NOBVV

I remember those years when we shared the joy of love. To the Tune "Heavenly Immortal." Yang Shen, *Chinese*. CoBLCP, *tr. by* Jonathan Chaves

I remember today a Quebec roadside, the crucifix. The Crucifix. Daniel Berrigan. CRP

I remember Wednesday was the day. Two Lean Cats. Myron O'Higgins. PoBA

I remember when he took me on a trip to this place. Chin Nung. CoBLCP, *tr. by* Jonathan Chaves *Fr.* On Twisting River Is the Old Home of My Father.

I remember when I was little and the world was great. Youth and Age. Richard Eberhart. AFr

I remember when I wrote The Circus. The Circus. Kenneth Koch. PmAP

I remember when the unicorns. The Days of the Unicorns. Phyllis Webb. NOBC

I remember when we first fled the rebels. Song of P'eng-ya. Tu Fu, *Chinese*. CoBCP, *tr. by* Burton Watson

I remember when we lived on 112th Street in New York City. Understanding Guyana. Marianne Ware. EC2

I remember when we made our first promises of love. Liu E, *Chinese*. CoBLCP, *tr. by* Jonathan Chaves

I remember when you shared my insomnia. The Broken Lampstand. Wu Wei-yeh, *Chinese*. CoBLCP, *tr. by* Jonathan Chaves

I remember you as you were that last autumn—. Poem. Pablo Neruda, *Spanish*. CLPP, *tr. by* Kenneth Rexroth

I remember you in young peaches like jade. Elegy for the Wife of a Friend. Yü Hsüan-chi, *Chinese*. BoWoP, *tr. by* Geoffrey Waters

I remember your strut. Toward Guinea: For Larry Neal, 1937–1981. Houston A. Baker, Jr. ISC

I remind myself that I am. Patriot. Cyril Dabydeen. HCP

I remove my court gown and part from the Emperor's precincts. Wen Cheng-ming. CoBLCP, *tr. by* Jonathan Chaves *Fr.* Improvised on Horseback to Say Good-bye to Those Who Are Seeing Me Off.

I rename the continent to suit me. Porkskin Panorama. Marie Annharte Baker. BAP-96

I resemble everyone. Self-Portrait. A. K. Ramanujan. NoP-4

I reside at Table Mountain and my name is Truthful James. The Society Upon the Stanislaus. Bret Harte. OBAL; PaTW

I resign! Song of Resignation. Yehuda Amichai, *Hebrew*. NYBP, *tr. by* Assia Gutmann

I rest in the grace of the world, and am free. (LL) The Peace of Wild Things. Wendell Berry. MT; SAGP; VGW

I return from my second T'ien-t'ai trip. On the Twenty-First Day of the Fifth Month, I Reached Home. Yüan Mei, *Chinese*. CoBLCP, *tr. by* Jonathan Chaves

I Return to the Place I Was Born. T'ao Ch'ien, *Chinese*. OHMPC, *tr. by* Kenneth Rexroth

I Return unto Zion. Bible, *O.T.* TrJP *Fr.* Zechariah.

I returned to a long strand. North. Seamus Heaney. InPS-3

I returned to my city, familiar as tears, *sl. diff. vers.* Osip Mandelstam. *See* Leningrad.

I. RICE CHILD. Mama. Claire Kageyama. UnSA

I, Richard Kent, beneath these stones. Epitaph. Sylvia Townsend Warner. MoBrPo

I Ride an Old Paint. *Unknown*. AS; AmFP

I ride / the "A" train. Riding the "A." May Swenson. GM

I ride through a dark, dark land by night. Ichabod! The Glory Has Departed. Ludwig Uhland, *German*. AWP, *tr. by* James Clarence Mangan

I ride through Queens. An Invitation to Madison County. Jay Wright. PoBA

I ring the doorbell and wait, cap on my head. The Pee Wee Coach. Walter McDonald. IFJA

I rise. Maya Angelou. *See* Still I Rise.

I rise about eight if the morning is warm. To Miss A[——]a M[——]a Tra[——]s; an Epistle from Scotland. Charlotte Brereton. ECWP

I rise at 2 a.m. these mornings, to. The Feral Pioneers. Ishmael Reed. PoBA; UnPo

I rise early with a slight nausea. Florence. Nina Zivancevic, *Serbo-Croatian*. HSix, *tr. by* Charles Simic

I rise from the depths of my resemblance. Jean Daive, *French*. MFP, *tr. by* Martin Sorrell

I rise / I rise / I rise. (LL) Still I Rise. Maya Angelou. BlSi; NAAAL

I rise in the dawn, and I kneel and blow. The Song of the Old Mother. W. B. Yeats. MoBrPo

"I rise on Sugar-loaf Mountain." Molasses River. Richard Kendall Munkittrick. OBCA

I rise to gaze upon southern hills. A Song of Wildfire. Wen T'ing-yün, *Chinese*. SuSp, *tr. by* William R. Schultz

I rise with an effort and look out. Philippe Jaccottet, *French*. VCWP, *tr. by* Derek Mahon

I roamed the woods today and seemed to hear. A Fear. Francis Ledwidge. NOIV

I rode my horse to the hostel gate. Both Less and More. Richard Watson Dixon. SCGP

I rode one evening with Count Maddalo. Julian and Maddalo; A Conversation. Shelley. FHYEP; OAEL-2

I Rode Southern, I Rode L & N. *Unknown*. AmFP

I rode till I reached the House of Wealth. Rest Only in the Grave. James Clarence Mangan. BIrV

I rode to church last Sunday. My Love She Passed Me By. *Unknown*. AmFP

I rode to Streatham Common on a tram. A Mind Reborn in Streatham Common. Richard Percival Lister. OBCoV

I rode with Geronimo. Conyus. NBV

I rode with my darling in the dark wood at night. Stevie Smith. BrRo

I roll the red cake of lipstick. Depending on the Light. Andrea Potos. IFJA

I romp with joy in the bookish dark. (LL) Eating Poetry. Mark Strand. MoP; NoAM; PFE; TAP

I room at Sodos'—in the little green room. Lola Ridge. NMM-2 *Fr.* The Ghetto.

I rose at night, and visited. The Unborn. Thomas Hardy. CMoP

I rose at the dead of night. A Chilly Night. Christina Rossetti. VWP

I rose betimes to go I knew not where. The Poor Man's Province. John Wright. NOEC

I rose from daylong desk at last. Vision. James Devaney. NOBAu

I rub my head and find a turtle shell. The Neo-Classical Urn. Robert Lowell. NAAL-2

I run, cried the fox, in circles. Cried the Fox. Tennessee Williams. PFE

I run, I run, I am gather'd to thy heart. Alice Thompson Meynell. *See* Renouncement.

I run, I run, I am gathered to thy heart. (LL) Renouncement. Alice Thompson Meynell. BoLoP; GSo; LW; MoBrPo; NOBE; OBEV; OBMV; OBNC; PEW; Son; VWP; WPE

I Run With a Pair of Compasses Stuck in the Back of My Head. Novica Tadic, *Serbo-Croatian*. HSix, *tr. by* Charles Simic

I runs falls rises stumbles on from darkness into darkness. Robert Earl Hayden. *See* Runagate Runagate.

I rush to the office when I'm in the city. Staying Overnight at T'ien-ning Ch'an Temple. Chang Yü, *Chinese*. CoBLCP, *tr. by* Jonathan Chaves

I rush to your dwelling. Pursuit. Julian Tuwim, *Polish*. TrJP, *tr. by* Watson Kirkconnell

I said a while back. Acknowledgement. Keorapetse Kgositsile. SeSe

I said, Ah! what shall I write? A, a, a, Domine Deus. David Jones. FaBoTw; NOCV

I said fate plays a game without a score. I Sit by the Window. Joseph Brodsky, *Russian*. VCWP, *tr. by* Howard Moss

I said goodbye. Autumn. Georgi Djagarov, *Bulgarian*. CEEP, *tr. by* Jascha Kessler *and* Aleksandar Shurbanov

I said, "I have shut my heart." Over the Roofs. Sara Teasdale. ColAP

I said, I will take heed to my ways. Lord, Make Me to Know Mine End. Bible, *O.T.* TrJP *Fr.* Psalms.

I said I would always live for her. Hartmann von Aue, *German*. GePo, *tr. by* Frederick Goldin

I said I'd get her a towel and ran. Girls. Kenneth Rosen. AmPA

I said in my youth. The Primer. Josephine Jacobsen. NoP-4

I said: / Now will the poets sing. Scottsboro, Too, Is Worth Its Song. Countee Cullen. PoBA

I said: On all these, Death, with gentleness, come down. (LL) Judge Not. Theodore Roethke. ChIV-2; GI

I said petals from an appletree. (LL) Portrait of a Lady. William Carlos Williams. AmPP; CMoP; MoP; NAAL-2; NOBA; NoAM; OxBA

I said, several notebooks ago, that even if I got what. An Impression. C. S. Lewis. LBC

I said, "That's good, that's enough." (LL) Each Bird Walking. Tess Gallagher. CrSp; FaBoWP; FiLi; NAmP90

"I," said the duck, "I call it fun." Who Likes the Rain? Clara Doty Bates. BoTP

I said: "The moon is obviously a boat." Nocturnal Landscape. Malcolm Cowley. PoA

I said the people come inside. Tornado Survivor. Heather McHugh. EC3

I said—Then, dearest, since 'tis so. The Last Ride Together. Robert Browning. BoLoP; FHYEP; GLoP; NAEL-2; OBEV; PoEL-5; UnPo

I said to Heart, "How goes it?" Heart replied. The False Heart. Hilaire Belloc. FaBoCh; FaBoEE; MoBrPo; OxBSP

I said to heaven that glowed above. Hafiz. AWP, *tr.* by Ralph Waldo Emerson. *Fr.* Odes.

I said to her tears: "I am fallible and hungry." Plea. John Ciardi. OxBSP

I said to Love. Thomas Hardy. GBL

I said to my baby. Same in Blues. Langston Hughes. APSN; InPS-3; SAGP; SSLK. *Fr.* Lenox Avenue Mural. HoPM

I said to my companion, this is walking. Victoria Market. Francis Brabazon. NOBAu

I Said to My Heart. Charles, Earl of Peterborough Mordaunt. NOEC

I said to the stream, Be still, and it was still. Miracles. Julia Randall. CRP

I sail over the ocean blue. I Catcha da Plenty of Feesh. *Unknown.* AS

I sailed in my dreams to the Land of Night. Fantasy. Gwendolyn B. Bennett. BlSi

I salute God, asylum's gift. Poem on His Death-Bed. Cynddelw Brydydd Mawr, *Welsh.* OBWVE, *tr.* by Joseph P. Clancy

I salute the most high lord. The Poet's Loves. Hywel ab Owain Gwynedd, *Welsh.* OBWVE, *tr.* by Gwyn Williams

I sang as one. The Conflict. C. Day Lewis. LiTM; MoBrPo; NoP-4

I sang in the sun. Race Relations. Carolyn Kizer. LTA

I sang the songs of red revenge. Homer. Albert Ehrenstein, *German.* TrJP, *tr.* by Babette Deutsch *and* Avrahm Yarmolinsky

I sang the songs of red ripped-up vengeance. The Poet and War. Albert Ehrenstein, *German.* PeFWW, *tr.* by Christopher Middleton

I sat all morning in the college sick bay. Mid-Term Break. Seamus Heaney. InPS-3; PoPoPo

I sat alone at my window. Retrospect. J. D. H. Heard. CBWP-4

I sat alone with my conscience. Conscience. Charles William Stubbs. BLPA

I sat before my glass one day. The Other Side of a Mirror. Mary Elizabeth Coleridge. BoWoP; NALW; PEW; SDW; VWP

I sat behind the glowing grate, fresh heaped. A Meditation on Rhode Island Coal. William Cullen Bryant. TAP

I sat beside the glassy evening sea. The Departure. William Vaughn Moody. APN-2

I sat beside the glowing grate, fresh heaped. William Cullen Bryant. *See* A Meditation on Rhode Island Coal.

I sat by a stream in a. Classic. A. R. Ammons. NOBA

I sat by the granite pillar, and sunlight fell. Commemoration. Sir Henry John Newbolt. FaBoTw

I sat by the wall. Talent. Tadeusz Różewicz, *Polish.* CEEP, *tr.* by Victor Contoski

I sat down in the colored section. Segregated Railway Diner—1946. Robert Winner. LTA

I sat down on a rock. Walther von der Vogelweide, *German.* GePo, *tr.* by Frederick Goldin

I SAT drinking and did not notice the dusk. Self-abandonment. Li Po, *Chinese.* ChiP, *tr.* by Arthur Waley

I sat in the café and sipped at a Coke. Greedyguts. Kit Wright. OTCP

I sat in the cold limbs of a tree. The Man in the Tree. Mark Strand. CBNP; SPE

I sat in the door of our cottage. An Autumn Day. Clara Ann Thompson. CBWP-2

I sat me down upon a green bank-side. Bronx. Joseph Rodman Drake. APN-1

I sat next to the Duchess at tea. Limerick. *Unknown.* SoSe-8

I sat on chushioned otter-skin. The Madness of King Goll. W. B. Yeats. NAEL-2

I sat on the Dogana's steps. Canto 3. Ezra Pound. MeMAP; TAP. *Fr.* Cantos.

I Sat Up One Night. Ntozake Shange. CrSp. *Fr.* For Colored Girls Who Have Considered Suicide When the Rainbow Is Enuf.

I sat with John Brown. That night moonlight framed. Narrative. Russell Atkins. GT; PoBA

I sat with Love upon a woodside well. Willowwood. D. G. Rossetti. CABP; NAEL-2; OAEL-2; PoEL-5. *Fr.* The House of Life.

I saw a band of warriors coming on. War Dance. Miidhu, *Aborigine.* NOBAu, *tr.* by Georg von Brandenstein

I saw a bird high in the tree. Spring. Pat Brennen. CTV

I saw a boy with eager eye. The Two Boys. Mary Lamb. Ro; WoRP

I saw a brown squirrel to-day in the wood. Mr. Squirrel. V. M. Julian. BoTP

I saw a Cave of sable depth profound. Thomas Cole. APN-1

I saw a chapel all of gold. William Blake. ImPo; PFE

I saw a cottage in the sky. Friends. John Ashbery. LCAP-2

I saw a dead man's finer part. His Immortality. Thomas Hardy. CMoP

I saw a dog sethying sows. Hay, Hey, Hey, Hey! I Will Have the Whetstone and I May. *Unknown.* CBNP

I saw a donkey. The Donkey. *Unknown.* PeP

I saw a famous man eating soup. Soup. Carl Sandburg. NOBA; NOBE; OBCA

I Saw a Fish-Pond All on Fire. *Unknown.* NOBL; OxNR

I saw a fly [*or* Flie] within a Bead[e]. The Amber Bead. Robert Herrick. BeJo; CaPo

I saw a frieze on whitest marble drawn. Ecstasy. Walter James Turner. CH

I saw a gardener with a watering can. The Progress of Poetry. "Christopher Caudwell." OxBTC

I saw a gold pillar from earth to heaven. The Message of King Sakis and the Legend of the Twelve Dreams He Had in One Night. *Unknown, Serbo-Croatian.* HSix, *tr.* by Charles Simic

I saw a hawk devour a screaming bird. Hawk Is a Woman. Hildegarde Flanner. WPE

I saw a headless she-mule. Good Friday: For Lack of an Orchestra. Jack Spicer. APSN

I saw a hunchback climb over a hill. The Hunchback. John Peale Bishop. PoA

I saw a jolly hunter. Charles Causley. EBNV; NOxBChV; OPOU

I saw a little tailor sitting stitch, stitch, stitching. Tailor. Eleanor Farjeon. OTCP; OxBChV

I saw a maiden, fairest of the fair. Charity. Henrietta Cordelia Ray. CBWP-3

I saw a man pursuing the horizon. Stephen Crane. APN-2; AmPP; ChAP; GEA; HoPM; LiTM; MeMAP; MoAmPo; NOBA; NoP-4; PBMP. *Fr.* The Black Riders [and Other Lines].

I saw a mesa. Leaving Port Authority for the St. Regis Rezz. Wendy Rose. HATNAP

I saw a mouth jeering. Gargoyle. Carl Sandburg. MoP; NOBA; NoAM

I saw a pale tree, the leafless boughs—but two. Ecstasy. Hélène Swarth, *Dutch.* WPOW, *tr.* by Jonathan Crewe

I saw a Peacock with a fiery tail. *Unknown.* CH; FaBoCh; NTP; OPOU; OTCP; OxBSP; OxBoLi; OxNR; RB

I saw a people rise before the sun. Yom Kippur. Israel Zangwill. TrJP

I saw a phoenix in the wood alone. Petrarch. *Fr.* Visions. AWP

I saw a proud, mysterious cat. The Mysterious Cat. Vachel Lindsay. OBCA

I saw a shadow on the ground. The Sky. Elizabeth Madox Roberts. MoAmPo

I saw a ship a-sailing. Mother Goose. FaBoBe; LB; NTCP; OxNR; ReMoGo

I saw a ship a-sailing. Romance. "Gabriel Setoun." BoTP

I Saw a Ship A-Sailing. *Unknown.* BoTP

I saw a Ship of martial build. The Berg. Herman Melville. APN-2; AmPP; ColAP; NCAP; NOBA; NoP-4; PFE; PoEL-5; PoPoPo; TAP

I saw a sky of stars that rolled in grime. To Richard Wagner. Sidney Lanier. APN-2; NCAP. *Fr.* Street Cries.

I saw / a specialist a cook. To the Heart. Tadeusz Różewicz, *Polish.* PoSu, *tr.* by Victor Contoski

I saw a stable low and very bare. Mary Elizabeth Coleridge. ChIV-2; OBCP; OxBSP; PChr

I saw a star slide down the sky. The Falling Star. Sara Teasdale. ChAP; OBCA

I saw a staring virgin stand. Two Songs from a Play. W. B. Yeats. FaBoTw; HAP; PoE, *sect.* 1; CMoP; ImPo; NOBE; OAEL-2, *sect.* 1-2. *Fr.* The Resurrection.

I saw a stately lady. The Stately Lady. Flora Sandstrom. BoTP

I saw a trash-pit, filled and topped with earth. Where Lie All the Slain. Harry Morris. CRP

I saw a tree that was greater than all the others. Edith Södergran, *Swedish.* PBWP, *tr.* by Jaakko A. Ahokas

I saw a vision yesternight. To the State of Love or The Senses' Festival. John Cleveland. CBLP; EP

I saw a vulture in the sky. Life and Death. Walter James Turner. FaBoTw

I saw a woman drag her foot. A Stranger. Edith Jay Scovell. WPN

I saw a woman sit alone. *Unknown.* EEP, *tr.* by Michael Alexander *Fr.* Riddles (Exeter Book).

I saw a woman sitting on a beast. Sonnet 13. Edmund Spenser. ChIV-2

I saw a young snake glide. Snake. Theodore Roethke. NOBA; NYBP

I saw about her spotless wrist. Upon a Black Twist, Rounding the Arm of the Countess of Carlisle. Robert Herrick. CaPo; CavPo

I saw an ugly beast come from the sea. Sonnet 12. Edmund Spenser. ChIV-2

I saw, and trembled for the day. A Warning. Coventry Patmore. EnLoPo

I saw another man die. Wang Fan-chih, *Chinese.* SuSp, *tr.* by Eugene Eoyang

I saw bleak Arrogance, with brows of brass. Arrogance. Walter De la Mare. OxBSP

I saw children at Christmas in 1945. Children at Christmas in 1945. Vladimir Holan, *Czech.* AF, *tr.* by C. G. Hanzlicek *and* Dana Habova

I saw cold thunder in the grass. Herons. Robin Blaser. NeAP

I saw dawn creep across the sky. A Summer Morning. Rachel Lyman Field. ChAP

I saw each soul as light, each single body. Night of Souls. Ann Stanford. WPE

I saw Esau sawing wood. *Unknown.* Spl

"I saw Eternity the other night." The Experience. Bruce Bennett. PeECV

I Saw Eternity the other night. World, The (1). Henry Vaughan. AWP; ChIV-2; EBEV; ESCV; FMP; FSCP; HAP; ImPo; NAEL-1; NOBE; NOCV; NOSC; OAEL-1; OBEV; OxAEP-1; PBRV; PeECV; PoEL-2; SCGP; SeCP; TFi; TrCP

I saw fair[e] Chloris [or Cloris] walk alone. Chloris in the Snow. William Strode. NOBE; NOSC; OAEL-1; OBEV; OxBSP

I saw French once—he was South Africa cavalry—. Ivor Gurney. NSI

I Saw from the Beach. Thomas Moore. OBNC

I saw God! Do you doubt it? What Thomas an Buile Said in a Pub. James Stephens. CMoP; MoBrPo; MoP; NoAM; PoRA

I Saw God Wash the World. William Leroy Stidger. BLPA

I saw her amid the dunghill debris. Tinker's Wife. Patrick Kavanagh. CIP-2; InPS-3; MoP; NoAM

I saw her first in gleams. The Spirit's Odyssey. M. Krishnamurti. InPK-6

I saw her in a cluttered basement store. The Note. Melvin B. Tolson. GT

I saw her one, one little while, and then no more. And Then No More. Friedrich Rückert, *German.* BIrV; BLPA, *tr.* by James Clarence Mangan

I saw her plucking cowslips. The Witch. Percy H. Ilott. BoTP

I saw him a squat man with red hair. Off Brighton Pier. Alan Ross. OBWP

I saw him beat the surges under him. Shakespeare. *Fr.* The Tempest. OAEL-1

I saw him comin out the N.B. Grill. Glisk of the Great. Robert Garioch. FaBoTC

I saw him dead; I saw his Body fall. Francis Quarles. PBRV *Fr.* Divine Fancies.

I saw him forging link by link his chain. The Slave. Jones Very. TAP

I saw him in the Airstrip Gardens. Betjeman, 1984. Charles Causley. NOBL; OxBTC; PeLV; UV

I saw him in the Café Royal. On Seeing an Old Poet in the Café Royal. John Betjeman. UV

I saw him leaving the hospital. Coats. Jane Kenyon. IFJA

I saw him once before. The Last Leaf. Oliver Wendell Holmes. AmPP; FaBoBe; NAAL-1; NAAL-3; PWR; PoLF

I saw him sitting in his door. The Philosopher. Sara Teasdale. PoToHe

I saw him to the last, the grey. Painting of My Father. Padraic Fallon. NOIV

I saw him yesterday. The Quarrel. J. D. H. Heard. CBWP-4

I saw his round mouth's crimson deepen as it fell. Fragment. Wilfred Owen. OAEL-2

I saw in dream a dapper mannikin. Im Traum sah ich ein Männchen klein und putzig. Heinrich Heine, *German.* AWP, *tr.* by Sir Theodore Martin

I saw in Louisiana a live-oak growing. Walt Whitman. APN-1; AWP; AiP; ColAP; ImPo; InPK-6; InPS-3; NAAL-1; NAAL-3; NCAP; NIP-4; NOBA; NoAM; NoP-4; OxBA; PAR; PoPoPo; Poetr; SAmP

I Saw It. Ilya L'vovich Selvinsky, *Russian.* TCRP, *tr.* by Daniel Weissbort

I saw it all, Polly, how when you had call'd for sop. Poor Poll. Robert Bridges. EBEV; OxBTC; OxBoLi

I saw it / I heard it. She Touched Me. Erin Mouré. DeD

I saw its periscope in the tide. Mangrove. John Blight. NOBAu

I saw magic on a green country road. Sonnet. Michael Hartnett. BIrV; PBCIP *Fr.* Thirteen Sonnets.

I Saw My Darling. Frederick Morgan. UnPo

I saw my father drowning. David Vogel, *Hebrew.* HP, *tr.* by A. C. Jacobs

I saw my grandad late last evening. Gathering in the Days. Gareth Owen. NOxBChV

I saw my grandmother grow weak. First Death. Donald Justice. IMW; MT

I Saw My Lady Weep. My Lady's Tears. *Unknown.* EBEV; EnLoPo; LoP; NOBE; NoSic; OBEV

I saw my love, younger than primroses. In a Wood. Edith Jay Scovell. GBL

I saw my mother after twenty years. Mother. Tế Hanh, *Vietnamese.* AVP, *tr.* by Huỳnh Sanh Thông

I saw my toes the other day. In Extremis. John Updike. OBCoV

I saw myself inside again I saw. Boxing the Female. Natasha Le Bel. BAP-96

I saw myself leaving. Reflections. Carl Gardner. PoBA

I saw new Earth, new Heaven, said Saint John. Sonnet 15. Edmund Spenser. ChIV-2

I saw new worlds beneath the water lie. On Leaping over the Moon. Thomas Traherne. GeHe; ImPo; NAEL-1

I saw no Way. The Heavens were stitched. Emily Dickinson. BoWoP

I saw nobody coming, so I went instead. (LL) Henry's Confession. John Berryman. LCAP-2; MoP; NAAL-2; NoAM; PoE; TwCP; VCAP

I saw old Autumn in the misty morn. Ode: Autumn. Thomas Hood. ImPo; OAEL-2; OBEV; OBNC; OxAEP-2; PoEL-4; Ro; UnPo

I saw old Duchesses with their young loves. Vanity. Anna Wickham. FaBoTw

I saw on the slant hill a putrid lamb. For a Lamb. Richard Eberhart. CMoP; ColAP; LiTM; OxBSP; RB; SoSe-8

I saw our golden years on a black gale. Sonnet for Christmas. Judith Wright. LW

I saw pale Dian sitting by the brink. Sonnet Written in Keats's *Endymion.* Thomas Hood. EPCY; Ro

I saw police biting corktip cigarettes. Mayday. Bill Tremblay. CDa

I saw prophets tearing at their pasted-on beards. What I Saw. Zbigniew Herbert, *Polish.* AF, *tr.* by John Carpenter *and* Bogdana Carpenter

I saw red evening through the rain. Robert Louis Stevenson. NOBVV

I saw Shandon steeple a needle for a tailor to sew. *Unknown.* CBNP

I saw some lovely things today. *Unknown.* CTV

I saw that the shanty town had grown over the graves and that the crowd lived among the memorials. Lines for Translation into Any Language. James Fenton. AF

I saw the best minds of my generation. Squeal. Louis Simpson. BXAP; UnPo

I saw the best minds of my generation destroyed by madness, starving / hysterical naked. Howl. Allen Ginsberg. AmPP; LCAP-2; MoP; NoAM; PmAP; PoM; TAP; VCAP

I saw the bird that can the sun endure. Joachim Du Bellay. Son *Fr.* The Visions of Bellay.

I Saw the Bird That Dares Behold the Sun. Joachim Du Bellay, *French.* Son, *tr.* by Spenser

I saw the black trees leaning. Trees and Evening Sky. N. Scott Momaday. CDW

I saw the bodies of earth's men. The Navigators. Walter James Turner. OBMV

I saw the cells on tv, as they swam. The Present Perfect. Grace Schulman. BAP-95

I saw the constellated matin choir. Prelude to *An American Anthology.* Edmund Clarence Stedman. APN-2

I saw the / dead bird on the sidewalk. The Maze. Joanne Kyger. BB

I saw the dead nodding sugar skulls. Ghost Sickness. Luis Alberto Urrea. BAP-96

I saw the early morning mist. The Dead Horse. Cecília Meireles, *Portuguese.* PBWP, *tr.* by James Merrill

I saw the farmer plough the field. Harvest. M. M. Hutchinson. AYFP; BoTP

I saw the first pear. Orchard. Hilda Doolittle. CMoP; LiTM; MoAmPo; OxBA

I saw the garden where my aunt had died. The Entertainment of War. Roy Fisher. FaBoWP

I saw the islands in a ring all round me. Letter to Pearse Hutchinson. Eiléan Ní Chuilleanáin. FaBoWP

I saw the lovely arch. The Rainbow. Walter De la Mare. CTV; NTP

I saw the midlands. Kisses in the Train. D. H. Lawrence. MoBrPo

I saw the moon / One windy night. Flying. J. M. Westrup. BoTP

I saw the moon over Plaza Espana. They Name Heaven. Bruce Weigl. NAmP90

I saw the moon, so broad and bright. Donnybrook. James Stephens. TIRV

I Saw the Object. Thomas Watson. Son *Fr.* The Tears of Fancy.

I saw the old god of war stand in a bog between chasm and rockface. The God of War. Bertolt Brecht, *German.* AF, tr. by Michael Hamburger; FaBoPV

I saw the ramparts of my native land. Sonnet: Death Warnings. Francisco de Quevedo y Villegas, *Spanish.* AWP, tr. by John Masefield

I saw the reflection in the mirror. Drunken Americans. John Ashbery. HCAP

I saw the shapes that stood upon the clouds. London Nightfall. John Gould Fletcher. MoAmPo

"I saw the Sibly at Cumæ." A Fragment. D. G. Rossetti. PeVV

I saw the silver morning mist. The Dead Horse. Cecília Meireles, *Portuguese.* PBWP, tr. by James Merrill

I saw the sky descending, black and white. Where the Rainbow Ends. Robert Lowell. HCAP; MoAmPo

I saw the spiders marching through the air. Mr. Edwards and the Spider. Robert Lowell. CMoP; CoAP; ColAP; FaBoMo; HeIP-4; InPS-3; LiTM; NAAL-2; NOBA; NoP-4; TFi; TwCP

I saw the spires of Oxford. The Spires of Oxford. Winifred M. Letts. PoLF; PoRA

I saw the spot where our first parents dwelt. The Garden. Jones Very. APN-1; OxBA; PAR; TAP

I Saw the Sun at Midnight, Rising Red. Joseph Mary Plunkett. TIRV

I saw the throng, so deeply separate. A General Communion. Alice Thompson Meynell. NOCV; WPE

I saw the virtues sitting hand in hand. Humility. George Herbert. NOSC

I saw thee weep—the big bright tear. Byron. CBLP

I saw them, caught them in the act. Paulus Silentiarius, *Greek.* GrAn, tr. by Andrew Miller

I Saw Them Lynch. Carol Freeman. PoBA

I saw these dreamers of dreams go by. The Gold-Seekers. Hamlin Garland. FaBoBe

I saw this much from the window. The Gap in the Cedar. Roy Scheele. Poetsp

I Saw Three Ships. Kevyn Arthur. PBCV

I saw three ships come sailing by. Mother Goose. LB; OxNR

I Saw Three Ships Come Sailing In. *Unknown.* BLPA

I saw three ships go sailing by. The North Ship. Philip Larkin. RB

I saw three withered women limp across. The Private Meeting Place. James Wright. NYBP

I saw two clouds at morning. John Gardiner Calkins Brainard. PoToHe

I saw two hares in the corn. The Dance. Gareth Alban Davies, *Welsh.* OBWVE, tr. by Gwyn Jones

I saw / wet clothes hanging from a clothes line dripping with. Vision from the Ghetto. Raymond Washington. NBV

I saw in the shroud did lurk. On an Infant Dying as Soon as Born. Charles Lamb. GTBS-P; IMW; OBEV

I saw with open eyes. Stupidity Street. Ralph Hodgson. CH; LiTM; MoBrPo; OxBTC

I saw you. Near Miss. Nayo-Barbara Watkins. BkSV

I / saw you. When the Spirit Spray-Paints the Sky. Sterling Plumpp. BAP-96

I saw you dance that summer before the war. Grand Ballet. Frances Darwin Cornford. WPN

I saw you fooling often in the tents. Glimpse. William Noel Hodgson. PoFWW

I saw you / on my walk last. Glimpse. Pearl Cleage Lomax. PoBA

I saw you on the street last night. In This New Year. Mary Jane Moffat. IMW

I saw you once, Medusa; we were alone. The Muse as Medusa. May Sarton. NALW

I saw you sit waiting with your sewing on your knees. A Peasant Woman. Frances Darwin Cornford. WPN

"I saw you take his kiss!" " 'Tis true." The Kiss. Coventry Patmore. BoLoP; EnLoPo; NOBVV *Fr.* The Angel in the House.

I saw you tortured on a stake. Crucifixa. Marie-Madeleine, *German.* CPO, tr. by Lillian Faderman, Brigitte Eriksson *and* Frankie Hucklenbroich

I saw you toss the kites on high. The Wind. Robert Louis Stevenson. BoTP; CTV

I saw your manager fight. He was. Elegy for Lyn James. Leslie Norris. OBWVE

I say. all you young girls waiting to live. Song No. 2. Sonia Sanchez. FFC

I Say Goodby to Fan An-ch'eng. Shen Yüeh, *Chinese.* SuSp, *tr. by* Lenore Mayhew *and* William McNaughton

I say hello to the sunshine. Alan Brunton. PeNZ

I say, I am quite done. Let Zeus Record. Hilda Doolittle.

I say, "I'll seek her side." Thomas Hardy. CBLP

I Say, Mr. A. Samuel Allen. SeSe

I say no moir. (LL) Lament of the Master of Erskine. Alexander Scott. CH; GBL

I say no more for Clavering. Clavering. Edwin Arlington Robinson. OxBA

I say now, Fernando, that on that day. Hibiscus on the Sleeping Shores. Wallace Stevens. InPS-3

I say that my sweetly prattling Heliodora will someday. Meleager. HePo, *tr. by* Barbara Hughes Fowler *Fr.* I'll Twine White Violets. NIP-4, *tr. by* Goldwin Smith

I say that words are men and when we spell. Anna Hempstead Branch. NALW *Fr.* Sonnets from a Lock Box.

I say things to myself. Phraseology. Jayne Cortez. BlSi

I say to the lead. Poem without a Title. Charles Simic. NNaP

I say to you for now, I embrace you brother. (LL) Letter to a Tormented Playwright. Syl Cheney-Coker. HBAPE; PBMAP

I say: / yes, that's why. Reiner Kunze. *See* Reply.

I, says the buzzard. From Virgil. George Oppen. NNaP *Fr.* Five Poems about Poetry.

I scarce believe [*or* beleeve] my love to be so pure. Love's Growth. Donne. ESCV; NOSC; NoP-4; PBRV

I scarcely know my worthless picture. Any Husband to Many a Wife. Emily Jane Pfeiffer. VWP

I scissor the stem of the red carnation. Salome. Ai. NoAM

I scorn all earthy dung-bred scarabies. (LL) To the Critic. Michael Drayton. NOSC, *sect.* XXXI; Son

I scorn the doubts and cares that hurt. A Garden Song. George R. Sims. NOBVV; OBCoV; OBGa

I scraped off your smile with nails. Capital Punishment. Nina Cassian, *Romanian.* PoSu, tr. by Nine Cassian

I scream as you bite. Kenneth Rexroth. APSN *Fr.* The Love Poems of Marichiko.

I Scream You Scream. Don McKay. NOBC

I scrub the long floorboards. Finding a Long Gray Hair. Jane Kenyon. LoL

I sdrive to dddeflect at a blow the blow. Trilce. César Vallejo. PFTM, *tr. by* Clayton Eshleman

I search among the plain and lovely words. Definition. Grace Noll Crowell. PoToHe

I search for new meaning. The Sun Speaks. Marcia Southwick. CMAP

I search / for the straight path. Farewell. Florence Dacey. LoHo

I search the chemistry of specific emotions. At the Electronic Frontier. Miguel Algarin. UnSA

I search the treetops, low-hung branches, for a trace of pink. Palace Song. Wang Chien, *Chinese.* CoBCP, tr. by Burton Watson

I searched for my Self. Lal Ded, *Kashmiri.* WPoS, tr. by Jane Hirshfield

I see a bear. Ted Hughes. NOxBChV; NTP

I see a beautiful gigantic swimmer swimming naked. The Beautiful Swimmer. Walt Whitman. EP

I see a blind man every day. The Blind Man. Margaret Elizabeth Sangster. PoToHe

I see a fly. The Cold Fly. Yang Wan-li, *Chinese.* SuSp, tr. by Jonathan Chaves

I see a girl climbing the mountain. The Pilgrim. Brendan Kennelly. TIRV

I see a man who is dull. An Ancient Song of a Woman of Fez. *Unknown, Arabic.* BoWoP, tr. by Willis Barnstone

I see a truck mowing down a parade. David Ignatow. LiLi

I see an empty place at the table. No Need. Raymond Carver. LBC

I see as through a skylight in my brain. Persephone. Michael Longley. PBCIP

I see before me now a traveling army halting. Bivouac on a Mountain Side. Walt Whitman. AiP; CBCWP; OxBA; PoLF

I see before me the gladiator lie. The Dying Gladiator. Byron. NOBE *Fr.* Childe Harold's Pilgrimage.

I SEE BLACK PEOPLE. Black People. Ted Joans. MBE

I see bodies in the morning kneel. Shirley Kaufman. BoWoP

I See Chano Pozo. Jayne Cortez. MoNo; PmAP

I see Chano Pozo. (LL) I See Chano Pozo. Jayne Cortez. MoNo; PmAP

I See Chile in My Rearview Mirror. Agha Shahid Ali. NoP-4

I see during the night guard. Bizerta. George Campbell Hay. FaBoTC

I see hard times. Hard Times A' Coming. Nayo-Barbara Watkins. BkSV

I see her against the pearl sky of Dublin. My Mother's Sister. C. Day Lewis. OxBTC

I see her on a lonely forest track. The Maroon Girl. Walter Adolphe Roberts. PBCV

I see her seventeen. Arizona Highways. James Welch. CDW; NoAM

I see her stand with arms a-kimbo. Hersilia. William Johnson Cory. NOBVV

I see her still, unsteadily riding the edge. My Grandmother Washes Her Feet. Fred Chappell. MT

I see her yet, that dark-eyed one. A Memory. Adah Isaacs Menken. CBWP-1

"I see herrin'."—I hear the glad cry. With the Herring Fishers. "Hugh MacDiarmid." CABP; LiTM

I see him in a sense as strapped to his chair. Art. Francis Webb. BMAP *Fr. Around Costessey.*

I see him old, trapped in a burly house. A Pauper. Allen Tate. LiTM

I See His Blood upon the Rose. Joseph Mary Plunkett. PoLF; TIRV

I see how the grasping fingers of lovers do not let go, till. Andrejs Eglitis, *Latvian.* CEEP, *tr. by* Inara Cedrins

I see in his last preached and printed booke. On John Donne's Book of Poems. John Marriot. CH

I see in my mind, surrounding God. Vittoria da, Marchesa di Pescara Colonna, *Italian.* WPoS, *tr. by* Halevi, Samuel Michael

I see in you the estuary that enlarges and spreads itself. To Old Age. Walt Whitman. Spl

I see in you the estuary that enlarges and spreads itself. Walt Whitman. *See* To Old Age.

I see in your handsome face, my Lord. Michelangelo Buonarroti. ItIP

I see it. Song for the Dead, III. *Unknown.* TTY, *tr. by* Frances S. Herskovits

I see it again, at dusk, half darkness in its brown light. There I Am Again. Lawrence Joseph. WWSi

I see it as it looked one afternoon. Long Island Sound. Emma Lazarus. APN-2

I see I've come a pilgrimage. I didn't. The *Weepers Tower* in Amsterdam. Paul Goodman. VGW

I see madmen who. Tadeusz Rózewicz, *Polish.* PoSu, *tr. by* Adam Czerniawski

I see Mike's painting, called SARDINES. (LL) Why I Am Not a Painter. Frank O'Hara. CoAmPo; HCAP; MoP; NOBA; NeAP; NoAM; NoP-4; PoE; PoM; PoPoPo; Poetr; VCAP

I see my mother's last breath. Inheritance. Cynthia MacDonald. NMM-2

I see no equivalents. The Poet at Night-Fall. Glenway Wescott. PoA

I see now I see. Resurrection. Margaret Atwood. CrSp

I see that chance hath chosen me. Sir Thomas Wyatt. SiPS

I see that there it is on the beach. Memorial Service for the Invasion Beach Where the Vacation in the Flesh Is Over. Alan Dugan. AF; TwCP

I see that wreath which doth the wearer arm. To My Dead Friend Ben: Johnson. Henry, Bishop of Chichester King. SeCP

I see the children running out of school. The Poet Laments the Coming of Old Age. Dame Edith Sitwell. NAEL-2; NoAM

I see the dawn e'en now begin to peer. *Unknown. Fr.* Popular Songs of Tuscany. AWP, *tr. by* John Addington Symonds

I see the elephants in the yard. The Elephants Are in the Yard. Indran Amirthanayagam. OpBo

I see the Four-fold Man. The Humanity in deadly sleep. William Blake. NOBRP *Fr.* Jerusalem; The Emanation of the Giant Albion.

I see the house; my heart thyself contain. Sonnet 85. Sir Philip Sidney. *Fr.* Astrophil and Stella. AAS; SiPS

I see the map of summer, lying still. Movies for the Home. Howard Moss. NYBP

I see the millet combing gold. Midsummer. Alexander L. Posey. APN-2

I See the Moon. *Unknown.* CTV; NTCP; OxNR

I see the mosquito kneeling on the soft underside of my arm, kneeling. The Mosquito. Rodney Jones. MT

I see the temple in thy pillar reared. Jacob's Pillow, and Pillar. Henry Vaughan. ChIV-1

I see the thin bell-ringer standing at corners. The Jew at Christmas Eve. Karl Shapiro. VGW

I see the usk [*or* use]: and know my blood [*or* bloud]. The Storm. Henry Vaughan. ESCV

I see the white / light / And the night / Flies. (LL) Alba ("When the nightingale to his mate"). Ezra Pound. OBVE; VGW; WeW-3

I see thee ever in my dreams. The Karamanian Exile. James Clarence Mangan. PeVV

I see thee pine like her in golden story. Coleridge. Theodore Watts-Dunton. GSo; Son

I see them coming up the road. A Happy Pair. Priscilla Jane Thompson. CBWP-2

I see them crowd on crowd they walk the earth. The Dead. Jones Very. APN-1; HAP; NOBA; NoP-4; OxBA; PAR; TAP

I see them / Puerto Ricans. You're Nothing but a Spanish Colored Kid. Felipe Luciano. PoBA

I see them standing at the formal gates of their colleges. I Go Back to May 1937. Sharon Olds. BLT; LoL

I see them working in old rectories. The Country Clergy. Ronald Stuart Thomas. GTBS-P; OxBTC; PeECV

I see these ancestors of ours. Triptych. Frank A. Collymore. PBCV

I see they worked you over. What you in for? Coming of Age in the County Jail. Carter Revard. VoR

I see 'tis folly, but I feel 'tis woe. Catullus. *See* Carmina, 85.

I see why the touched needle scents about. Mysteries Revealed after Death. John Reynolds. NOEC *Fr.* Death's Vision.

I see you, a child. The Album. C. Day Lewis. EnLoPo; OxBTC

I see You / Brown-skinned, / Neat Afro. Thank You, Lord. Maya Angelou. CrSp

I see you did not try to save. Passing the Graveyard. Andrew Young. FaBoTC

I see you displaced, condensed, within my dream. Dream. Josephine Miles. PoA

I see you in Chicago twenty-five years ago. My Brother Inside the Revolving Doors. Wesley McNair. CMAP

I see you now. Mountain Drive. Cothrai Gogan. TIRV

I see you sitting. Matmiya. Mary TallMountain. CrSp; HATNAP; LoL

I see you what you are: you are too proud. Shakespeare. OxAEP-1 *Fr.* Twelfth Night.

"I see your lights!" But ours had long died out. (LL) The Sentry. Wilfred Owen. EBNV; PeFWW; PoWW

I see'd her in de springtime. She Hugged Me and Kissed Me. *Unknown.* BPo

I seek in prayerful words, dear friend. God Bless You. *Unknown.* PoToHe

I seek mercy / for the women stoned. For All Mary Magdalenes. Desanka Maksimovic, *Croatian.* WPOW, *tr. by* Vasa D. Mihailovich

I seem to be the victim of a cruel jest. And Her Mother Came Too. Dion Titherage. OBCoV

I seem to have loved you in numberless forms, numberless times. Rabindranath Tagore, *Bengali.* LBC, *tr. by* William Radice

I send a garland to my love. The Lover's Posy. Rufinus Domesticus, *Greek.* AWP, *tr. by* W. H. D. Rouse

I send a message, my worthy chief. A Message to a Loved One Dead. Josephine D. Henderson Heard. CBWP-4

I send, I send here my supremest kiss. His Tears to Thamesis [*or* Thamasis]. Robert Herrick. NOSC

I send it over the Western Sea. Elizabeth Barrett Browning. *See* A Curse for a Nation.

I send my poisoned candies through the mail. End of the Affair. Geoffrey Grigson. GBL

I send thee myrrh, not that thou mayest be. Not of Itself but Thee. *Unknown, Greek.* AWP, *tr. by* Richard Garnett

I send to thee. (LL) Wind from the east, oh Lapwing of the day. Hafiz. AWP; TAL, *tr. by* Gertrude Lowthian Bell

I send you a box. Yakamochi, *Japanese.* OHPJ, *tr. by* Kenneth Rexroth

I send you a lock of hair. Martial, *Greek.* PGA, *tr. by* Kenneth Rexroth

I send you here a sort of allegory. To —. With the Following Poem. Tennyson. EnVR; NOBRP

I send you here a wreath of blossoms blown. Roses. Pierre de Ronsard, *French.* AWP, *tr. by* Andrew Lang

I send you my verses. Minuchihri, *Persian.* ArPe, *tr. by* Omar S. Pound

I sent a letter to my love. George Barker. FaBoTw *Fr.* The True Confession of George Barker.

I sent a letter to my love. *Unknown.* LB

I sent for Radcliffe; was so ill. The Remedy Worse than the Disease. Matthew Prior. FaBoEE

I sent my mother copies of my poems in print. Poems. Gary Gildner. Poetsp

I sent my Soul through the Invisible. Edward Fitzgerald. APAD *Fr.* The Rubáiyát of Omar Khayyám of Naishápúr.

I sent some first for sister-in-law to try. Wang Chien. *See* Words of the Newly Wed Wife.

I sent you this bluebird of the name of Joe. Happiness. William Dickey. Poetsp

I sente a ringe, a little bande. To Helene. George Darley. NOBRP

I serve a mistress whiter than snow. Fedele's Song. Anthony Munday. HAP; SCGP *Fr.* Fedele and Fortunio.

I Set Aside. Mary Morison Webster. PeSA

I set forth hopeful—cotton-blossom Lal. Lalleswari, *Kashmiri.* WPOW, *tr. by* George Grierson, *ad. by* Deirdre Lashgari

I set my table with metaphor. Passover. Linda Pastan. NMM-2

I set the bowl of raw vegetables on the table. Before You Leave. Ai. GT

I set the shorelines of the world by perpetual decrees, so. The Edge. Sandra Price. LoHo

I shake from head to foot. (LL) Friends. W. B. Yeats. FP; IIP; MoP; NoAM

I shake my hair in the wind of morning. Triumph of Love. John Hall Wheelock. MoAmPo

I shake my robe—and mists disperse, leaving clear autumn sky. Hsü Chung-hsing. CoBLCP, *tr. by* Jonathan Chaves *Fr.* At Dawn, Climbing the Heavenly Pillar Peak of Mysterious Mountain.

I shall at last sit down with thee. Henry, Bishop of Chichester King. *See* Stay For Me There.

I shall be capricious, I shall have a whim. A Man's Woman. Mary Carolyn Davies. PoLF

"I shall be careful to say nothing at all." How She Resolved to Act. Merrill Moore. MoAmPo

I shall be glad to be silent, Mother, and hear you speak. The White Thought. Stevie Smith. Spl

I shall be mad if you get smashed about. The Soldier Addresses his Body. Edgell Rickword. PeFWW; PoWW

I shall begin to forget you. A Segment. Martin Sorescu, *Romanian.* CEEP, tr. by Dan Duescu.

I shall but love thee better after death. (LL) Sonnet: "How do I love thee? Let me count the ways." Elizabeth Barrett Browning. APAD; BWW; BoLoP; CABP; CTC; EBEvV; EBVV; EnVR; FaBoBe; GLoP; GSo; HeIP-4; HoPM; ImPo; InPK-6; LBC; NAEL-2; NALW; NIP-4; NoP-4; OPOU; OxAEP-2; OxBM; PFE; PoE; PoLF; PoPoPo; PoRA; PoToHe; Poetr; SAGP; Son; TFi; UV; UnPo; VWP; WPE

I shall come back to die. In This Dark House. Edward Davison. OBMV

I shall cry God to give me a broken foot. Flash Crimson. Carl Sandburg. MoAmPo

I shall die, but that is all that I shall do for Death. Conscientious Objector. Edna St. Vincent Millay. WPOW

I shall die in Paris, in a rainstorm. Black Stone on Top of a White Stone. César Vallejo, *Spanish.* NNPT, tr. by Thomas Merton

I shall die sooner or later. When That Day Comes. Chongsam Kim, *Korean.* CKP, tr. by Jaihiun Kim

I shall ebb out with them, who homeward go. (LL) The Autumnal[l]. Donne. FSCP; InPS-3; NOSC; PoEL-2

I shall expect / you in to dine. Catullus. *See* Carmina, XIII.

I shall find in paradise that emaciated rose shoot. Maria Luisa Spaziani. NeIt, tr. by Beverly Allen Fr. The Star of Free Will.

I Shall Find You. Siegfried Sassoon. LBC

I Shall Forget You Presently, My Dear. Edna St. Vincent Millay. HeIP-4; MeMAP; TAP

I shall gather myself into myself again. The Crystal Gazer. Sara Teasdale. MoAmPo

I shall give you five words for your birthday. Five Words for Joe Dunn on His 22nd Birthday. Jack Spicer. PoM

I shall go among red faces and virile voices. Cattle Show. "Hugh MacDiarmid." FaBoMo; HAP; MoBrPo; OBMV; OxBTC

I shall go as my father went. The Tenancy. Mary Gilmore. CBAP

I shall go back again to the bleak shore. Edna St. Vincent Millay. MeMAP; MoAmPo; SAGP; UnPo

I shall go down. Geoffrey Hill. HAP Fr. The Pentecost Castle.

I shall hate you. Hatred. Gwendolyn B. Bennett. BlSi; ColAP; NAAAL; PoBA; RaBo

I shall have had my day. (LL) My Day. Tennyson. NAEL-2; NOBVV

I shall hear that grand Amen. (LL) A Lost Chord. Adelaide Anne Procter. EBEvV; SDW; UV; VWP

I shall hide myself / within the moon of the spring night. Masako Chino, *Japanese.* WPJ, tr. by Kenneth Rexroth and Ikuko Atsumi

I shall keep singing! Emily Dickinson. APN-2

I shall know why—when Time is over. Emily Dickinson. NOCV; SAmP

I Shall Laugh Purely. Robinson Jeffers. LiTM

I shall lie hidden in a hut. Prophecy. Elinor Wylie. APAD; BoWoP; FaBoWP; NTP; SAGP; VGW

I shall look at the grass. Perseverance. Martin Sorescu, *Romanian.* VCWP, tr. by Enright, D. J. and Joana Russell-Gebbett

I shall make a song like your hair. Secret. Gwendolyn B. Bennett. BlSi; FiLi

I shall make it simple so you understand. Simple Poem. Anthony Thwaite. DiPo

I shall never forget his blue eye. Dylan Thomas. UV Fr. Parachutist.

I shall never forget you, Broadway. Broadway. Carl Sandburg. AiP

I shall never get you put together entirely. The Colossus. Sylvia Plath. AFr; FaBoWP; HCAP; LiTM; NALW; NOBA; NoAM; NoP-4; Poetr; TAP; VCAP

I shall never, in the years remaining. Robert Browning. EPCY Fr. One Word More. EnVR; PoEL-5

I shall not call for help until they coffin me. Last Lines. Egan O'Rahilly, *Irish.* IIP, tr. by Frank O'Connor

I Shall Not Care. Sara Teasdale. MoAmPo; UnPo

I Shall Not Die. Nguyễn Văn Năng, *Vietnamese.* AVP, tr. by Huỳnh Sanh Thông

I Shall Not Die for Thee. *Unknown. See* O Woman, Shapely as the Swan.

I shall not fail that rendezvous. (LL) The Rendezvous. Alan Seeger. APAD; AiP; BLPA; FaPoR; PFE; PeFWW; PoFWW

I shall not forget it (that evening either). In the Restaurant. Aleksandr Blok, *Russian.* TCRP, tr. by Geoffrey Thurley

I shall not go to heaven when I die. Helen Waddell. MLL

I shall not live in Vain. (LL) If I can stop one Heart from breaking. Emily Dickinson. AH; PWR; PoLF; PoToHe

I shall not lose thee though I die. (LL) Thy voice is on the rolling air. Tennyson. EBVV; EBVVPR; FHYEP; HeIP-4; OAEL-2

I shall not pass this way again. (LL) I Shall Not Pass This Way Again. *Unknown.* BLPA; ChAP

I Shall Not Pass This Way Again. *Unknown.* BLPA; ChAP

I shall not regard my swelled head as a sign of real glory. Aimé Césaire. TTY Fr. Return to My Native Land. NegPo, tr. by Emile Snyders

I shall not repeat others' comments about me. (LL) Wet Casements. John Ashbery. NAAL-2; PoM

I shall not see thee. Dare I say. Tennyson. OxBSn Fr. In Memoriam A. H. H.

I shall not sing a May song. The Crazy Woman. Gwendolyn Brooks. NALW

I Shall Not Want: In Deserts Wild. Charles F. Deems. AH

I shall note first / the ones I loved. The Chronicler. Alexander Bergman. TrJP

I shall paint/ God in the midst. Robert Browning. Fr. Fra Lippo Lippi. CTC; EBVV; EBVVPR; EnVR; FHYEP; NoP-4; OAEL-2; OxAEP-2

I shall rejoice, and my prediction's true. (LL) The Vote. Ralph Knevet. FMP; NOSC

I shall return to heaven. Return to Heaven. Sangbyong Ch'on, *Korean.* CKP, tr. by Jaihiun Kim

"I shall rise from the dead," I am saying. (LL) In the Mountain Tent. James Dickey. MT; WeT

I shall rot here, with those whom in their day. In Death Divided. Thomas Hardy. SCGP

I shall say, Lord, "Is it music, is it morning." Resurgam. Marjorie Lowry Christie Pickthall. TrCP

I shall say what inordinat[e] love is. Inordinate Love. *Unknown.* EBEV; MiEL; OxBSP

I Shall Say What Inordinate Love Is. Robert Frost. OxBSP

I shall see justice done. Witch. Patricia Beer. OxBC

I shall sleep in white calico. Kofi Awoonor. *See* Songs of Sorrow.

I shall sleep in white calico. Song of War. Kofi Awoonor. PBMAP

I shall slough my self as a snake its skin. Louis Golding. TrJP

I shall snap off my chains and fly freely away. Elizabeth Carter. *See* A Dialogue.

I Shall Take You in Rough Weather. Frank Prewett. HATNAP

I shall tune my lute to sing your litanies as the quiet hours pass. Ode to Africa. Bernard Dadié, *French.* NegPo, tr. by Ellen Conroy Kennedy

I shall vote Centre because. Roger Woddis. UV

I shall vote Labour because. Christopher Logue. UV

I shall walk down the road. Death. Maxwell Bodenheim. TrJP

I shall weave you a wreath. A Wreath for Africa. Bernard Dadié, *French.* NegPo, tr. by Ellen Conroy Kennedy

I Shall Weep. Peretz Hirshbein, *Yiddish.* TrJP, tr. by Joseph Leftwich

I shall yet be footloose. (LL) Broken-Face Gargoyles. Carl Sandburg. AmPP; MoAmPo; OxBA

I shan't be gone long.—You come too. Robert Frost. *See* The Pasture.

I shan't forget that winter in Bắc-giang. If in a Future Life We Meet Again. Bằng Bá Lâ, *Vietnamese.* AVP, tr. by Huỳnh Sanh Thông

I shape me— / Ever / Removed! (LL) Life in a Love. Robert Browning. FHYEP; OBNC

I sha'''t be gone long—You come too. (LL) The Pasture. Robert Frost. CMoP; MoAmPo; NAAL-2; NOBA; OxBA; PoE; SAGP; SAmP; TLR; TRP; TTTS; WHSW

I sh'd think 'e'll get right again. (LL) The Collier's Wife. D. H. Lawrence. FaBoVe; OxBTC

I shelter a song for you / *Secretly.* (LL) Secret. Gwendolyn B. Bennett. BlSi; FiLi

I shipped, d'ye see, in a Revenue sloop. The Darned Mounseer. Sir William Schwenck Gilbert. NOBL Fr. Ruddigore.

I shipped on board of a Liverpool liner. Sally Brown. *Unknown.* AmFP

I shook myself awake, saw. Freak. Chandrashekhar Patil, *Kannada.* OMIP, tr. by A. K. Ramanujan

I shoot the hippopotamus. The Hippopotamus. Hilaire Belloc. InPK-6

I shop in the streets of my hometown with/ my family. Bruce Beaver. Fr. Letters to Live Poets. CBAP

I shot a rocket in the air. Enough. Tom Masson. OBAL

I shot an arrow into the air. The Arrow and the Song. Henry Wadsworth Longfellow. CTV; ColAP; MeMAP; PWR; PoToHe; UV

I shot an arrow into the air. A Shot at Random. Wyndham Lewis. UV

I shot him, and it had to be. The Target. Ivor Gurney. PoFWW

I shot my man, 'cause he done me wrong. *Unknown. See* Josie.

I should be glad I didn't get the clap. Parting Roundel. Jemal Sharah. NOBAu

I should be glad of another death. (LL) Journey of the Magi. T. S. Eliot. EBEvV; FaBoCh; FaBoMo; GI; HAP; HeIP-4; ImPo; InPK-6; LiTM; MoAmPo; NAEL-2; NIP-4; NOCV; NoP-4; OBCP; OBMV; OxBTC; PBMP; PChr; PoE; Poetr; TAP; TFi; TRP; TwCP

I should be someplace else! Not to Choose. Alan Dugan. AFr

I should have been too glad, I see. Emily Dickinson. APN-2; MeMAP; NOCV; PAR

I should have kept right on going. A Small Fat Boy Walking Backwards. Gerry Murphy. BiHa

I should have seen the sign: "Fresh paint." Fresh Paint. Boris Pasternak, *Russian.* TrJP, tr. by Babette Deutsch

I should have thought. At Baia. Hilda Doolittle. CPO; ColAP; NAAL-2; NOBA

I should know what God and man is. (LL) Flower in the crannied wall. Tennyson. BLPA; CTV; ImPo; InPK-6; NAEL-2; PBMP; TFi

'I should like,' said the vase from the china-store. The Toys Talk of the World. Katharine Pyle. NOxBChV; OBCA

I should like to creep. A Mona Lisa. Angelina Weld Grimké. BlSi

I should like to rise and go. Travel. Robert Louis Stevenson. CTV; FaBoCh; OTCP

I should like to see that country's tiled bedrooms. Keeping Their World Large. Marianne Moore. RaBo

I should like you all to know. I'm a Gigolo. Cole Porter. OBCoV

'I should never have taken the trout.' (LL) Limerick: "The Dowager Duchess of Spout." Edward Gorey. PeLV; PeLi

I should not dare to leave my friend. Emily Dickinson. MeMAP

I should not feel it to be strange. (LL) Of One Dead. Tennyson. EBVV; EnVR; FHYEP; ImPo

I should not have waited. Akazome Emon, *Japanese.* OHPJ, tr. by Kenneth Rexroth

I should not presume to express any view. Triangular Legs. Sir Alan Patrick Herbert. NBLV

I should not then thus feel this misery. (LL) The Calm[e]. Donne. NoSic; OxBoS

I shoulder my son over dead stalks. Golden Season. Kurtis Lamkin. IFJA

I shouldered a kind of manhood. Funeral Rites. Seamus Heaney. BiHa; PBCIP

I shouted for blood as I ran, brother. Janet Begbie. NSI

I show her how to put her arms around me. Sleeping with Boa. May Swenson. BAP-94

I showed her Hights she never saw. Emily Dickinson. CPO

I shudder thinking. The Cold Irish Earth. Knute Skinner. InPK-6

I shut down the lawnmower. Leroy Gorman. HA

I shut the door but can't sit down. Relaxing in the Evening in My Study. Yang Wan-li, *Chinese.* CoBCP, tr. by Burton Watson

I shut the door, hoping to drive off sorrow. Written for My Own Amusement. Wang An-shih, *Chinese.* CoBCP, tr. by Burton Watson

I shut the door on the racket. Shoe Shop. Barton Sutter. EC3; SoSe-8

I sicken of myself, my members all are shaking. To Himself. Andreas Gryphius, *German.* GePo, tr. by George C. Schoolfield

I sigh at day-dawn, and I sigh. Sappho. Christina Rossetti. VWP

I sigh for the heavenly country. The Heavenly City. Stevie Smith. APAD; FaBoTw

I sigh for the land of the Cypress and Pine. Song—Written at the North. Samuel Henry Dickson. APN-1

I sigh to myself I am traveling far. Recalling When I Was Drunk. Yüan Chen, *Chinese.* SuSp, tr. by Dell R. Hales

I sike when I singe. *Unknown.* MiEL

I sing a song of sixpence, and of rye. Ode. Anthony C. Deane. NOBL

I sing a song reluctantly. Beatrice, Countess de Die, *Provençal.* PBWP, tr. by Carol Cosman *and* Howard Bloch

I Sing an Old Song. Oscar Williams. ImPo; LiTM

I Sing for the Animals. *Teton Sioux Oral Tradition, Teton Sioux Indian.* TTTS

I sing her worth and praises hy [or high]. A Description. Edward Herbert, 1st Baron Herbert of Cherbury. SeCP

I sing, I sing, I sing. Incantation Songs of the Klamath Lake People. *Unknown, Klamath Native American.* APN-2, tr. by Albert S. Gatschet

I sing my own true story, tell my travels. The Seafarer. *Unknown.* NoP-4

I Sing No New Songs. Frank Marshall Davis. PoBA

I sing no song. I spin instead. Spider. Norma Farber. PChr

I sing of a hero, unsung, unrecorded. Crispus Attucks McCoy. Sterling Brown. BPo

I sing of a maiden. *Unknown. See* I syng of a mayden that is makeles.

I sing of brooks, of blossom[e]s, birds, and bowers. The Argument of His Book. Robert Herrick. AWP; BeJo; CaPo; CavPo; EBEV; HAP; ImPo; NAEL-1; NOSC; NoP-4; OAEL-1; OxAEP-1; PeECV; PoE; PoEL-3; PoPoPo; PoRA; SeCP; TFi; TTTS

I Sing of Change. Niyi Osundare. PBMAP

I sing of great hotels and a man. In the foyer. The Strand Hotel, Rosslare. James Liddy. CIP-2

I sing of myself, a sorrowful woman. Wife's Lament. *Unknown, Anglo-Saxon.* PBWP; PoE, tr. by Kemp Malone

I sing of Olaf glad and big. E. E. Cummings. ColAP; HeIP-4; ImPo; LiTM; MeMAP; MoP; NAAL-2; NOBA; NoAM; NoP-4; OBSV; OBWP; PoWW; VGW

("More brave then me:more blond than you.") (LL) AF

I sing of sweepers, frequent in thy streets. The Sweepers. William Whitehead. ECEV; NOEC

I sing of the Good Samaritan. The Song of the Good Samaritan. Vernon Watkins. LiTM

I sing of warfare and a man at war, *see also* "Now manhood and garbroyls I chaunt, and martial horror" *tr. by* Richard Stanyhurst, "Arms, and the Man I sing, who, forc'd by Fate" *tr. by* John Dryden, "Arms, and the Man I sing, the first" *tr. by* William Wordsworth, *and* "Battellis and the man I will descrive, The" *tr. by* Gavin Douglas. Virgil. NAWM-1, *tr. by* Robert Fitzgerald, *abr. vers.* Fr. The Aeneid

I sing th' adventures of mine worthy wights. Poem. Thomas Morton. SCAP

I sing the birth, was born[e] tonight. A Hymn[e] on the Nativity [*or* Nativitie] of My Saviour. Ben Jonson. BeJo; ChIV-2; TrCP

I sing the body electric. Walt Whitman. CTC; SAmP Fr. Leaves of Grass (1855). APN-1

"I knew a man, a common farmer, the father of five sons." BLT

I sing the civill Warres, tumultuous Broyles. Lucan. OBCVT, tr. by Samuel Daniel Fr. The Civile Wares betweene the Howses of Lancaster and Yorke.

I sing the furious battles of the spheres. Ad Johannuelem Leporem, Lepidissimum, Carmen Heroicum. *Unknown.* CBNP

I sing the glorious Power with azure eyes. Hymn to Athena. *Unknown.* AWP Fr. Homeric Hymns.

I sing the Man, by Heav'ns peculiar grace. A Poem on Elijahs Translation. Benjamin Colman. SCAP

I Sing the man, (read it who list). Virgil. OBCVT, tr. by Charles Cotton Fr. Scarronides; or, Virgile Travestie.

I sing the man that never equal knew. Alexandreis. A. Killigrew. NoP-4

I sing the NAME which None can say. On the Name of Jesus. Richard Crashaw. ESCV; FSCP

I sing the olive oil, I who lately sang. The Year of the Olive Oil. Charles North. FTOS

I sing the quality of bamboo. Bamboo. Eric Rolls. NOBAu

I sing the simplest flower. Karl Shapiro. CMoP Fr. Six Religious Lyrics.

I sing the Sofa. I, who lately sang. The Sofa. William Cowper. Fr. The Task.

I sing the tree is a heron. Merce of Egypt. Charles Olson. NoP-4

I sing thee with the stock-dove's throat. "Michael Field." VWP

I Sing This Song for Our Mothers: Ruise. Sherley Anne Williams. MDDM

I sing to him that rests below. Tennyson. OAEL-2 Fr. In Memoriam A. H. H.

I sing *tree,* making green. Last Night's Dream. Denise Levertov. NoAM

I sink in the falling snow. Monstrance. János Pilinszky, *Hungarian.* PoSu, tr. by Peter Jay

I sink into a rare luminous blindness. Blindness. Delmira Agustini, *Spanish.* PBWP, tr. by D. M. Pettinella

I sink into bed. My Imperialism. Ryuichi Tamura, *Japanese.* AF; VCWP, tr. by Christopher Drake

I sit alone late at night. An Extra Joyful Chorus for Those Who Have Read This Far. Robert Bly. SPE

I sit alone on a rock by the stream. Autumn. Chang Yü. Fr. The Four Seasons in the Mountains. CoBLCP, tr. by Jonathan Chaves

I sit alone on the rocks trying to prepare. In the Wilderness. James Simmons. GI

I sit and beat the wizard's magic drum. The Wizard's Chant. *Unknown, Passamaquoddy Native American.* APN-2, tr. by Chares Godfrey Leland *and* John Dyneley Prince

I sit and look out upon all the sorrows of the world, and upon all oppression and shame. Walt Whitman MeMAP; NAAL-1; NAAL-3; OxBA; SAmP; TAP

I sit and sew—a useless task it seems. Alice Moore Dunbar-Nelson. BlSi; NAAAL; NALW; NMM-2; WPOW

I Sit and Wait for Beauty. Mae V. Cowdery. BlSi

I sit at a gold table with my girl. At the Altar. Robert Lowell. InPK-6 Fr. Between the Porch and the Altar.

I sit at home. Hitomaro, *Japanese.* OHPJ, tr. by Kenneth Rexroth

I sit at my desk. Kenneth Rexroth. APSN Fr. The Love Poems of Marichiko.

I sit at the top of the tree. Crow Resting. "Edward Pygge." BXAP

I sit at your side. Duet for One Voice. Linda Pastan. NMM-2

I sit beside my old ship, the timbers rotting. The Old Jason, the Argonaut. Denis Glover. PeNZ

I sit beside my peaceful hearth. The Due of the Dead. William Makepeace Thackeray. OBWP

I sit beside old retired Italians. Park. David Ignatow. Poetsp

I sit by the mossy fountain; on the top of the hill of winds. James Macpherson. NOEC Fr. Fragments of Ancient Poetry, Collected in the Highlands of Scotland.

I sit by the roadside. Changing the Wheel. Bertolt Brecht, German. PoSu, tr. by Michael Hamburger

I sit by the shed. Winter Billet. Peter Huchel, German. PoSu, tr. by Michael Hamburger

I Sit by the Window. Joseph Brodsky, Russian. VCWP, tr. by Howard Moss

I sit crotch high. Under the Oak Table. Colleen J. McElroy. GT

I sit down at a table and open a book of poems. Library. Louis Jenkins. RaBo

I sit down beside my brass lamp. Peeling Pippins. Mary TallMountain. HATNAP

I sit for my portrait on the veranda. Portrait. Brenda Marie Osbey. MT

I Sit Here. Kumeroa Ngoingoi Pewhairangi, Maori. PeNZ, tr. by the author

I sit here at your edge, in your embankment's screen. Shepherd-Song. Sigmund von Birken, German. GePo, tr. by George C. Schoolfield

I sit here long, the lamp burns dim. Green Banana Leaves. Yün Shou-p'ing, Chinese. CoBLCP, tr. by Jonathan Chaves

I sit here with affection for the lingering Year. The Year Hsin-hai (Fifteen Fifty One), New Year's Eve: Keeping Watch. Wen Cheng-ming, Chinese. CoBLCP, tr. by Jonathan Chaves

I sit here with the wind is in my hair. To Helen of Troy (N.Y.). Peter Viereck. WeW-3

I sit high on this bridge in Laventille. The Spoiler's Return. Derek Walcott. PBCV

I sit in another house whose character is. The House Is Old. Ron Schreiber. GLP

I sit in Lees. At 11:40 PM with. A Poem for vipers. John Weiners. BB

I sit in my room. Jean Toomer. GT

I sit in one of the dives. September 1, 1939. W. H. Auden. AF; CMoP; ImPo; MoBrPo; OxAEP-2; OxBA; PoE

I sit in the top of the wood, my eyes closed. Hawk Roosting. Ted Hughes. CMoP; GTBS-P; HAP; HeIP-4; LiTM; OxBTC; TwCP; UnPo

I sit, in treatment, at the movies, devoted. Valerio Magrelli, Italian. NeIt, tr. by Dana Gioia

I sit musing, ten minutes from the Jap. A Letter for Marian. Thomas McGrath. VGW

I sit on horseback at Twin Bridges. Wen Cheng-ming. CoBLCP, tr. by Jonathan Chaves Fr. Improvised on Horseback to Say Good-bye to Those Who Are Seeing Me Off.

I sit on my father's porch. Homecoming. Charles Wright. WeT

I sit on the edge. The Piano. Frank Daley. NOBC

I sit thinking of a rowing-boat I saw. The Waiting-Room. Robin Fulton. PoA

I sit waiting for one of the two kinds of miracle. Stan Rice. MoLi Fr. Incanto.

I sit with Joseph Conrad in Monet's garden. Zimmer Imagines Heaven. Paul Zimmer. PBCAP

I Sit with My Dolls. Unknown, Yiddish. TrJP, tr. by Joseph Leftwich

I sit with my wine—there's no singing or dancing. Drinking. Chu Yün-ming, Chinese. CoBLCP, tr. by Jonathan Chaves

I sit within my room and joy to find. The Presence. Jones Very. HAP; PAR

I sleep alone. Unknown, Japanese. OHMPJ, tr. by Kenneth Rexroth

I Sleep, but My Heart Waketh. Bible, O.T. BoWoP, tr. by Willis Barnstone; TrJP Fr. The Song of Songs. AWP

I sleep, I sleep. Sleeping Beauty. Olga Broumas. CPO

I sleep with thee, and wake with thee. To Mary: 'I Sleep with Thee, and Wake with Thee'. John Clare. EnLoPo; GBL; GLoP

I slept and dreamed that life was Beauty. Duty. Ellen S. Hooper. BLPA; PAR

I slept in the past / that will never come back. Princess Shikishi, Japanese. WPJ, tr. by Kenneth Rexroth and Ikuko Atsumi

I slept under rhododendron. Four Poems for Robin. Gary Snyder. BB Fr. Four Poems for Robin. MoP; NNaP; NOBA; NoAM

I slept under rhododendron. Siwashing it out once in Siuslaw Forest. Miyazawa Kenji, Japanese. SAGP, tr. by Gary Snyder

I sliced my veins on sleep's sharp glass. Blood and the Storm. Jure Kastelan, Croatian. CEEP, tr. by Peter Kastmiler

I. Slim's Song. Etheridge Knight. BkSV Fr. Three Songs.

I slow down the waterfall to a chandelier. Frozen Rain. Michael Longley. PBCIP

I slumbered with your poems on my breast. To E.T. Robert Frost. FP

I slump in the bucket seat. Twink Drives Back, in a Bad Mood, from a Party in Massachusetts. George Amabile. NYBP

I smashed a hot dog into her face. The Hot Dog Poem. Mary E. Tucker. GLP

I Smile, but Oh! My Heart Is Breaking. Mary E. Tucker. CBWP-1

I smoke, stretched out face up. Solo by Moonlight. Jules Laforgue, French. FLP, tr. by Alistair Elliot

I sneaked into. Tanka. Kitahara Hakushū, Japanese. MJT, tr. by Makoto Ueda

I So Liked Spring. Charlotte Mew. OxAEP-2; OxBTC

I, Solomon, David's son, King of Jerusalem. Henry Howard, Earl of Surrey. ChIV-1 Fr. A Paraphrase of Part of the Book of Ecclesiates.

I sometimes hold it half a sin. Tennyson. EPCY; EnVR; IMW; OAEL-2; PeECV; TOF Fr. In Memoriam A. H. H.

I sometimes sleep with other girls. Cavalier Lyric. James Simmons. UV

I sometimes think about. Unspoken World. Helen Ruggieri. LoHo

I sometimes think I'd like to be. The Best of All. Margaret G. Rhodes. BoTP

I sometimes think I'd rather crow. Unknown. CTAV

I sometimes think that never blows so red. Omar Khayyám. TRP Fr. The Rubáiyát of Omar Khayyám [of Naishápúr]. AWP; CABP; EBVV; FaBoBe; FaPoR; HAP; NAEL-2; PoEL-5

I sought a theme and sought for it in vain. The Circus Animals' Desertion. W. B. Yeats. CMoP; EPCY; FaBoMo; FaBoTw; MoP; NAEL-2; NAWM-2; NIP-4; NOBE; NOIV; NoAM; NoP-4; OAEL-2; OxBTC; TFi

I sought all over the world for a present for you until I found. John Tagliabue. Poetsp

I sought, I found, she asked me what I would. Rachel Speght. Fr. A Dream. WPE

I sought instruction from my dawning years. A Cure for Poetry. Annabella Blount. ECWP

I sought of bishop and priest and judges. On Christians, Mercy Will Fall. Unknown, Welsh. OBWVE, tr. by D. Myrddin Lloyd

I sought to hear the voice of God. The Voice of God. Louis I. Newman. PoToHe

I sought to share. The Passage. "Adunis," Arabic. VCWP, tr. by Samuel Hazo

I sowed the seeds of love. The Seeds of Love. Unknown. FaBoCh; GaP

I sowed the seeds of love. The Unfortunate Damsel. Mrs. Fleetwood Habergham. LW

I span and Eve span. Eve-Song. Mary Gilmore. CBAP; LW

I speak alone that on the nerves' taut screen. The Shield of Achilles. Tomas Venclova, Lithuanian. CEEP, tr. by David McDuff

I speak directly. The Rifle. Tymoteusz Karpowicz, Polish. PoSu, tr. by Jan Darowski

I speak for Erin. The Muse of Amergin. Unknown, Irish. BIrV; IIP, tr. by John Montague

'I speak for the world of scholarship'. Happy Arabia. Tom Matthews. PNI

I speak no polite. Turf Song. Sterling Plumpp. GT

I speak now of printers and bookmen. Printers. Denis Glover. PeNZ

I speak of that great house. Beyond the Hunting Woods. Donald Justice. CoAmPo; NYBP

I speak of that lady I heard last night. The Lady's Complaint. John Heath-Stubbs. TwCP

I Speak of the City. Octavio Paz, Spanish. VCWP, tr. by Eliot Weinberger

I speak of the history of the world. Plain Song Talk. Richard Eberhart. PoA

I speak of walls and chains; of the vials. Terms of Appointment. Arthur Rex Dugard Fairburn. PeNZ

I speak this poem now with grave and level voice. Immortal Autumn. Archibald MacLeish. CMoP; MoAmPo; NAAL-2

I speak to my Lord though I am dust and ashes. Oaks and Squirrels. Anne Porter. ChIV-1

I speak to you as a friend speaks. Conversations in Crisis. Audre Lorde. Poetr

I Spend the Night in a Room by the River. Tu Fu, Chinese. SuSp, tr. by Mark Perlberg

I spent a nicht amang the cognoscenti. I Was Fair Beat. Robert Garioch. OBCoV; OxBTC

I spent a night turning in bed. The Whip. Robert Creeley. EOEF; MoP; NeAP; PoE; PoM

I spent my youth in a loony bin. Palette of Grief. Leonid Gubanov, Russian. TCRP, tr. by Bradley Jordan

I spent the morning waxing the furniture. Days of 1992. Marilyn Hacker. BAP-95

I spied a very small brown duck. Duck-chasing. Galway Kinnell. TwCP; VGW

I spied John Mouldy in his cellar. John Mouldy. Walter De la Mare. OxBChV; RB

I splashed water on my face. Scholar I. Seamus Deane. NOIV

I splintered the landscape of midday. What About You? Vladimir Mayakovsky, *Russian*. NNPT, *tr. by* Maria Enzensberger

I spoiled the day. A Wasted Day. Frances Darwin Cornford. MoBrPo

I sport with you. Lord of the River. *Unknown*. CoBCP, *tr. by* Burton Watson *Fr.* Nine Songs.

I sport with you. Lord of the River. Ch'u Yüan. *Fr.* Nine Songs. CoBCP, *tr. by* Burton Watson

I spotted these daffs by the lake. Limerick. E. O. Parrott. PeLi

I sprang to the rollocks and Jorrocks and me. How I Brought the Good News from Aix to Ghent (or Vice Versa). R. J. Yeatman *and* W. C. Sellar. BXAP; UV

I sprang to the stirrup, and Joris, and he. How They Brought the Good News from Ghent to Aix. Robert Browning. EBEvV; EBNV; FHYEP; FaBoBe; FaPoR; HoPM; NAEL-2; OBSP; PeVV; UV

I spread my game on the cracked linoleum floor. Globe. Elizabeth Spires. WeT

I Spread Out unto Thee My Hands. Henry Ainsworth. AH

I Spy. Norah E. Hussey. BoTP

I stalk with the razorblade cranes, my pinhead reeling. *Unknown*. NBrP

I stand amid the roar. A Dream Within a Dream. Edgar Allan Poe. *Fr.* A Dream within A Dream. AmPP; GBL; MeMAP; NCAP; NOBA; OxBA; TAP

I stand and listen, head bowed. Self-employed. David Ignatow. NNaP

I stand and watch the rain. Rain and the Tyrants. Jules Supervielle, *French*. NNPT, *tr. by* David Gascoyne

I stand by you The horse heaves a sigh cross the river. Psalm of Love. Tadeusz Norwalk, *Polish*. CEEP, *tr. by* Leonard Kress

I stand here, do you understand. Olav H. Hauge, *Norwegian*. RaBo, *tr. by* Robert Bly

I stand here every afternoon. The Balloon Man. E. Herbert. BoTP

I stand high in the belfry tower. On the Tower. Annette von Droste-Hülshoff, *German*. PBWP; WPOW, *tr. by* James Edward Tobin

I stand in full armor. Poem. Paul Klee, *German*. PFTM, *tr. by* Anselm Hollo

I stand in the dark light in the dark street. Birthplace Revisited. Gregory Corso. NeAP; PoM; VGW

I stand in the hall upstairs. Closed Doors. Marie Thorson. PWR

I stand in the late sun. The Reply. Philip Levine. PoA

I stand like some country crow across the street. Romania, Romania. Gerald Stern. LCAP-2

I stand on slenderness all fresh and fair. A Cut Flower. Karl Shapiro. HAP; WeW-3

I stand on the mark beside the shore. The Runaway Slave at Pilgrim's Point. Elizabeth Barrett Browning. BrRo; NALW; VWP

I stand still under an orange tree. Dialogue. Norkiko Ibaragi, *Japanese*. WPJ, *tr. by* Kenneth Rexroth *and* Ikuko Atsumi

I stand there slapping a house. The Apprentice Painter. Jack Myers. AmPA

I stand to-day on this historic ground. The National Cemetery, Beaufort, South Carolina. Josephine D. Henderson Heard. CBWP-4

I stand under a leafless tree. Rain—Birdoswald. Frances Horovitz. APAD; NBrP

I stand up. (LL) Miss Rosie. Lucille Clifton. AmPA; BlSi; NMM-2; PoBA; Poetr; TwCP

I stand upon a hill and see. A Map of the City. Thom Gunn. NAEL-2; NoP-4; PoE

I stand within the willowing shadows of Memp-ch-ton. On Hearing the Marsh Bird's Water Cry. Duane Niatum. CDW

I star in the loam. Deadsong. Don Domanski. NOBC

I stare out of the long windowed house. Returned American. Kathleen Cain. LoHo

I stared at the printed words. Printed Words. Liz Sohappy Bahe. CDW

I start awake at night afraid of death. Sonnet 21. Paul Goodman. VGW

I start out for a walk at last after weeks at the desk. After Long Busyness. Robert Bly. PoA

I started Early—Took my Dog. Emily Dickinson. APN-2; AmPP; ColAP; HAP; InPK-6; LiTM; McMAP; NAAL-1; NAAL-3; PoFL-5; WeW-3

I started on the trail of June twenty-third. The Lone Star Trail. *Unknown*. AS

I started out in the Virginia mountains. Pokeberries. Ruth Stone. IFJA; NMM-2

I started picking up the stones. Apologia pro Vita Sua. A. R. Ammons. HCAP; NOBA

I Starting from Central Station. David Campbell. BMAP *Fr.* Starting from Central Station.

I Starve My Belly for a Sublime Purpose. Anna Swirszczynska, *Polish*. BLT, *tr. by* Czeslaw Milosz *and* Leonard Nathan (b. 1924)

I stay clear. I Have No Strength for Mine. Joanne Kyger. PoM

I stayed the night for shelter at a farm. Robert Frost. *See* The Witch of Coös.

I stayed [*or* staid] the night for shelter at a farm. The Witch of Coös. Robert Frost. InPS-3; LiTM; MeMAP; MoP; NOBA; NoAM; PoE *Fr.* Two Witches. CMoP

I stem from a tremendous memory. Autobiography. Tommy Olofsson, *Swedish*. IFJA, *tr. by* Jean Pearson

I step out into the snow, my eyes shut. Summer Again. Yves Bonnefoy, *French*. VCWP, *tr. by* Lisa Sapinkopf

I stepped from black to black. Black Power. Raymond R. Patterson. NBV

I stepped from Plank to Plank. Emily Dickinson. CMoP; NOBA; NOCV; OxBSP; SAmP; SDW

I stifled in that room. We Were Sisters Weren't We. Katie Donovan. BiHa

I still get the occasional snapshot in letters. The Same Trouble with Beauty You've Always Had. Michael Atkinson. BAP-93

I still kept thinking that I was rich. Elizaveta Kuzmina-Karavayeva, *Russian*. TCRP, *tr. by* Vera Dunham

I still remember Conch-Shell Slope, west of the River Tzu. Hsieh Chin. CoBLCP, *tr. by* Jonathan Chaves *Fr.* In Grief, Lamenting for My Elder Brother Ts'ang-ch.

I still remember the half-lit meaning. Jacob Glatstein, *Yiddish*. CEEP, *tr. by* Ruth Whitman

I still remember the time at the mountain hut. A Painting of Yams. Yün Shou-p'ing, *Chinese*. CoBLCP, *tr. by* Jonathan Chaves

I still searched for your. March. Alfonsas Nyka-Niliunas, *Lithuanian*. CEEP, *tr. by* Jonas Zdanys

I still shall smile and go my careless way. Sonnet. Mamie A. Richardson. LW

I stirred wet sand and gathered myself. Seamus Heaney. NoAM *Fr.* Sweeney Redivivus.

I stole through the dungeons, while everyone slept. Alternative Endings to an Unwritten Ballad. Paul Dehn. OBCoV

I stomp about these rooms in an old overcoat. Sketch for an Aesthetic Project. Jay Wright. GT

I stood again within the garden old. The Garden Seat. Angelina Weld Grimké. NMM-2

I stood and leant upon the mast. The Voyage. Heinrich Heine, *German*. AWP, *tr. by* John Todhunter

I stood and watched him dig one hole all day. Robert Frost's Left-leaning *Trespassers Will Be Shot* Sign. William Zaranka. BXAP

I stood and watched the still, mysterious Night. Night. Augusta Cooper Bristol. APN-2

I stood as one enchanted. Entangled. Mathilde Blind. VWP

I stood aside to let the cows. Man and Cows. Andrew Young. EBEV

I stood at eve, as the sun went down, by a grave where a woman lies. 'Ostler Joe. George R. Sims. BLPA

I stood at the back of the shop, my dear. At the Draper's. Thomas Hardy. MoBrPo; OxBM *Fr.* Satires of Circumstance in Fifteen Glimpses.

I stood before it for hours in wintertime. (LL) A Hill. Anthony Hecht. CoAP; GEA; NYBP; NoP-4; VCAP

I stood beside a hill. February Twilight. Sara Teasdale. AYFP; OBCA

I stood beside thy lowly grave. The Grave of a Poetess. Felicia Dorothea Hemans. Ro; VWP

I stood by Honor and the Dean. Sahara. Coventry Patmore. EBVV *Fr.* The Angel in the House.

I stood by the bars at evening. By the Pasture Bars. George Sands Johnson. PWR

I stood during the entire journey. Please Give This Seat to an Elderly or Disabled Person. Nina Cassian, *Romanian*. PiM, *tr. by* Naomi Lazard

I Stood in the Maytime Meadows. *Unknown*. TTTS

I stood naked in the corner as my mother. The Confusion of Planes We Must Wander in Sleep. Bruce Weigl. NAmP90

I Stood on a Tower in the Wet. Tennyson. OxBSP

I stood on Brocken's sovran height, and saw. Lines Written in the Album at Elbingerode, in the Hartz Forest. Coleridge. Ro

I stood on the bridge at midnight. The Bridge. Henry Wadsworth Longfellow. APN-1

I stood once at the tip of the earth. Makeshift. Laura Riding Jackson. BAP-93

I stood still and was a tree amid the wood. The Tree. Ezra Pound. CMoP; PBMP

I stood tip-toe upon a little hill. Keats. Sweet Peas. FHYEP

I stood today on a mound of clay. Created Clay. Maimee Lee Brown. PWR

I stood upon a high place. Stephen Crane. APN-2; MeMAP *Fr.* The Black Riders [and Other Lines].

I stood watching / I the parade of floats. Preface. Ras Michael. HCP

I stood with three comrades in Parliament Square. Armistice Day. Charles Causley. NAEL-2; NoP-4; OBWP

I stood within the empty House of Youth. Helen Waddell. MLL

I stood within the heart of God. Pandora Speaks. William Vaughn Moody. AH *Fr.* The Fire-Bringer.

I stoompled oud ov a dafern. Wein Geist. Charles Godfrey Leland. APN-2

I stoop to gather a seabird's feather. The Feather. Vernon Watkins. FaBoTw

I stooped to the silent Earth and lifted a handful of her dust. A Handful of Dust. James Oppenheim. TrJP

I stop for a short rest at the wine seller's west of the city. Leaving the City. Liu K'o-chuang, *Chinese.* CoBCP, *tr. by* Burton Watson

I stop my boat on the pure Ssu. Mooring My Boat on the Ssu River and Watching the Moon. Wen Cheng-ming, *Chinese.* CoBLCP, *tr. by* Jonathan Chaves

I stop on the way. Chongno Street. Un Ko, *Korean.* CKP, *tr. by* Jaihiun Kim

I stop somewhere waiting for you. (LL) Song of Myself. Walt Whitman. APN-1; AmPP; ColAP; FaBoBe; FaBoVe; HeIP-4; MeMAP; MoAmPo; NAAL-3; NAWM-2; NCAP; NOBA; NTP; NoAM; OxBA; PoE; PoPoPo; RaBo; SAGP; SAmP

I stop to consult my diary and think how queer. Rogation Day: Portrush. James Simmons. PBCIP

I stop to listen. Arizona Zipper. HA

I Stop Writing the Poem. Tess Gallagher. NMM-2; PiM

I stopped at her door for a drink of water. The Girl by Green River. *Unknown, Chinese.* OHMPC, *tr. by* Kenneth Rexroth

I stopped deep. African in Louisiana. Kojo Gyinaye Kyei. PBA

I stopped in a sidestreet surplus shop, just south of Yorkville. The Cot. Grover Amen. NYBP

I stopped my car on Gibson Avenue. I Am Here. Jimmy Santiago Baca. NAmP90

I stopped to pick up the bagel. The Bagel. David Ignatow. CoAmPo; PiM; TwCP

I strayed, all alone, where the Autumn. A Rose in October. James Whitcomb Riley. OBAL

I strayed along the strand with mussels strewn. Along the Strand. Alfred Mombert, *German.* TrJP, *tr. by* Jethro Bithell

I stretch out flat to the horizon. Before They Made Things Be Alive They Spoke. Lucario Cuevish, *Luiseño Indian.* STP, *tr. by* Jerome Rothenberg

I stretched my hand out in front of me, into the darkness. In Darkness. Amir Gilbo'a, *Hebrew.* MHP, *tr. by* Ruth Finer Mintz

I stroked her sheek with my finger. For My Daughter's Twenty-First Birthday. Jeanne Murray Walker. MDDM

I strolled across. The Waking. Theodore Roethke. TTTS

I strolled around the zoo. Nikolai Ivanovich Glazkov, *Russian.* TCRP, *tr. by* Daniel Weissbort

I strove with all, for all were worth my strife. Epitaph for G. B. Shaw. Max Beerbohm. FaBoEE

I strove with none for none was worth my strife. Edward Morgan Forster. UV

I strove with none, for none was worth my strife. On His Seventy-Fifth Birthday. Walter Savage Landor. AWP; EBEV; EBEvV; FaBoEE; FaPoR; GTBS-P; NOBE; NOBVV; NTP; NoP-4; OAEL-2; OBEV; OBNC; OxAEP-2; PBMP; SAGP; SCGP; TFi; TRP; UV *Fr.* The Last Fruit Off an Old Tree.

I struck the board, and cried [*or* cry'd], "No more!" The Collar. George Herbert. AWP; CABP; ClHu; EBEV; FMP; FSCP; FaBoVe; GeHe; HAP; HeIP-4; ImPo; InPS-3; MeLP; NAAL-2; NIP-4; NOBE; NOCV; NOSC; NoP-4; OAEL-1; OBWVE; PBRV; PoE; PoEL-2; PoPoPo; PoRA; SCGP; SCV; SeCP; TFi; TOF; WeW-3

I struck tomorrow square in the face. Hidesong. Aig Higo. PBMAP; TTY

I studied in the hedge school. The Herd. Peter Fallon. PBCIP

I study out a dark similitude. The Swan. Theodore Roethke. VGW

I study the lives on a leaf: the little. The Minimal. Theodore Roethke. HCAP; MoP; NOBA; NoAM; RB

I Substitute for the Dead Lecturer. Imamu Amiri Baraka. PoE

I suddenly have come to love. George Buchanan. PNI

I suddenly understand—I'm watching you chop away. Life is Happy. Albert Goldbarth. BAP-93

I summon to the winding ancient stair. A Dialogue of Self and Soul. W. B. Yeats. CMoP; FaBoMo; LiTM; MoBrPo; NAEL-2; NoAM; PoE

I supped where bloomed the red rose. Supper. Walter De la Mare. NYBP

I suppose I could try if I chose. Limerick. "E. F. C." PeLi

I suppose it hasn't been easy living with me either. Poem in Praise of My Husband (Taos). Diane Di Prima. BB

I suppose it's myself that you're making allusion to. At the "Atlantic" Dinner, December 15, 1874. Oliver Wendell Holmes. OBCoV

I suppose the time will come. Emily Dickinson. FaBoVe

I suppose you just gape and let your gaspings. Ted Hughes. HAP *Fr.* Skylarks.

I surprise girlhood. I Want Aretha to Set This to Music. Sherley Anne Williams. NAAAL

I suspect he knew that trunks are metaphors. Houdini. Eli W. Mandel. NIP-4; NOBC

I swam the Huron of love, and am not ashamed. The Huron. Ruth Herschberger. WPE

I Swear. Bella Akhatovna Akhmadulina, *Russian.* TCRP, *tr. by* Albert C. Todd

I swear by desire. Meleager, *Greek.* PGA, *tr. by* Kenneth Rexroth

I swear by what the sages spoke. Crazy Bill to the Bishop. Robert Peters. BXAP

I swear I ain't done what Richard. Say Hello to John. Sherley Anne Williams. BlSi

I sweep the street and lift me hat. The Old Man at the Crossing. Leonard Alfred George Strong. OBMV

I swing the spirit like a child. Imploration for Clear Weather. *Unknown, Ojibwa Native American.* APN-2, *tr. by* W. J. Hoffman

I switch on the light. Crickets tick. Sleep in the Heat. Laura Jensen. AmPA

I swore I would go back. O Lyric Love. Winfield Townley Scott. VGW

I swore, love, by your / dominion, to rest. Maccius, *Greek.* GrAn, *tr. by* Alan Marshfield

I swore not to love you. Lady Otomo no Sakanoé, *Japanese.* WPJ, *tr. by* Kenneth Rexroth *and* Ikuko Atsumi

I swore to stab the sonnet with my pen. Karl Shapiro. PoA *Fr.* White-haired Lover.

I swore to you, son of Kronos, never. Strato, *Greek.* GrAn, *tr. by* W. G. Shepherd

I syng of a mayden that is makeles. *Unknown.* CH; ChIV-2; EBEV; FaBoCh; ImPo; InPK-6; InPS-3; MiEL; NAEL-1; NOBE; NOCV; OAEL-1; PoE; PoEL-1; SCGP; SCV; TFi; TOF

("Godes moder be.") (LL) CABP; NoP-4

("I sing of a maiden.") CABP; NoP-4

I take a jewel from a junk-shop tray. Nothing. James Fenton. APAD

I take as my theme "The Independent Woman." Two. Carolyn Kizer. FFC; NMM-2; VCAP *Fr.* Pro Femina.

I take down the old guitar from the wall. The Old Guitar. John Hollander. DiPo

I take for a change. Conflict. Kwangnim Kim, *Korean.* CKP, *tr. by* Jaihiun Kim

I take heart, breaking in. The Mud Dauber Wasp. Peter Kane Dufault. NoP-4

I take horse before cockcrow. Visit to the Monastery of Good Omen. Lu Chi, *Chinese.* OHMPC, *tr. by* Kenneth Rexroth

I take my pen in hand. The Letter. Elizabeth Riddell. LW; NOBAu

I take my son outside. What I Tell Him. Simon J. Ortiz. CDW; ChAP

I take my stand by the Ulster names. Ulster Names. John Hewitt. BiHa

I take off my shirt, I show you. Taking Off My Clothes. Carolyn Forché. AmPA; NoAM

I take the clue divine. (LL) My Cocoon tightens—Colors tease. Emily Dickinson. APN-2; NAAL-1; NAAL-3; PAR

I take the dogs into. La Bagarède. Galway Kinnell. NYBP

I take the pressure of thine hand. (LL) Doors, where my heart was used to beat. Tennyson. EnVR; FHYEP; OBNC; PoEL-5; SCV

I take the royal carriage for an evening outing. The Lotus Pond. Ts'ao P'i, *Chinese.* SuSp, *tr. by* Ronald C. Miao

I take the snap from center, fake to the right, fade back. . . I've. Football. Louis Jenkins. RaBo

I take the twist-about, empty street. The Rendezvous. Bernard Spencer. GTBS-P

I Take Thee Life. Margot Ruddock. OBMV

I take their hands. They. Ronald Stuart Thomas. OxBTC

I take you by the hand. Your eyes. Goodbye to Brigid / An Agnus Dei. Padraic Fiacc. CIP-2

I take you looking at the statue. The Statue. Kenneth Allott. SPE

I TAKE your poems in my hand and read them beside the candle. On Board Ship: Reading Yüan Chên's Poems. Po Chü-i, *Chinese.* ChiP, *tr. by* Arthur Waley

I takes and [I] paints. Poem by a Perfectly Furious Academician. Shirley Brooks. NOBVV; PeLV

I takes up for my colored men. The Generation Gap. Ruby C. Saunders. BlSi

I Talk to My Body. Anna Swirszczynska, *Polish.* BLT, *tr. by* Czeslaw Milosz *and* Leonard Nathan

I talked one midnight with the jolly ghost. All in a Garden Green. William Ernest Henley. OBMV

I talked to a farmer one day in Iowa. Iowa Farmer. Margaret Walker Alexander. GT

I talked to old Lem. Old Lem. Sterling Brown. BPo; PoBA; TTY

I taste a draught beer never brewed. Emily's Haunted Housman. David Cummings. BXAP

I taste a liquor never brewed. Emily Dickinson. APN-2; AmPP; CMoP; HeIP-4; LiTM; MeMAP; MoAmPo; NAAL-1; NAAL-3; NOBA; NoAM; OxBA; PAR; PBMP; PoEL-5; SAGP; SDW; SoSe-8; TAP; TFi; WPE ("From Manzanilla come!") (LL) PFE

I taught myself to live simply and wisely. "Anna Akhmatova," *Russian.* PBWP, *tr. by* Richard McKane

I teach German literature, and this is how it goes. Teaching German Literature. Vincent Buckley. OBCoV

I teach how we cheat the young. A 4 Part Geometry Lesson. Robin Blaser. NeAP

I tear at my belly. U Tam'si Tchicaya. PBMAP *Fr.* Le Ventre (1964).

I tell a wanderer's tale, the same. Encounter at St. Martin's. Ken Smith. OPOU

I tell her she has outlived her usefulness. Altar. Marilyn Chin. PoPoPo

I tell him, don't be mad at me. Kindergarten Curse. Nina Zivancevic, *Serbo-Croatian.* HSix, *tr. by* Charles Simic

I tell it the way it is. Letters from the Poet Who Sleeps in a Chair. Nicanor Parra, *Spanish.* AF, *tr. by* Miller Williams

I tell my daughters. Listen. Luci Tapahonso. MoLi

I tell my secret? No indeed, not I. Winter: My Secret. Christina Rossetti. BrRo; NAEL-2; NOBVV; VWP

I tell of Another Young Death. César Tiempo, *Spanish.* TrJP, *tr. by* Donald Devenish Walsh

I tell the children in school sometimes. Our Room. Molly Peacock. IFJA; NMM-2

I tell thee, Dick, where I have been. A Ballad[e] [upon a Wedding]. Sir John Suckling. BeJo; CaPo; EBEV; EBNV; NoP-4; OxBM; SeCP

I tell words that talk in trees, this hill. Pot Shot. Padraic Fallon. CIP-2

I tell ye, Sue, it ain't no use! Goin' Back T'morrer. Hamlin Garland. OBAL

I tell yeh whut! The chankin'. Horses Chawin' Hay. Hamlin Garland. OBAL

I tell you, Chickadee. S M. Alice Walker. CrSp

I tell you, hopeless grief is passionless. Grief. Elizabeth Barrett Browning. EBEvV; HeIP-4; IMW; InPK-6; LBC; NALW; NOBVV; OBEV; OBNC; PoLF; SDW; VWP; WPE

I tell you how dat hypocrite do. That Hypocrite. Unknown. BPo

I tell you I am angry. The Friendship. Toi Derricotte. IFJA; PBCAP

I tell you that I see her still. I Only Am Escaped Alone to Tell Thee. Howard Nemerov. CoAP; HeIP-4; NoAM

I tell you this across the blackened vine. (LL) Even in the moment of our earliest kiss. Edna St. Vincent Millay. HeIP-4; VGW

I tell you what I dreamed last night. Christina Rossetti. PeVV *Fr.* The Convent Threshold. NALW; NoP-4; VWP

I tell you (you needn't believe it). Parrhasios, *Greek.* GrAn, *tr. by* Richard Evans

I test my bath before I sit. Samson Agonistes. Ogden Nash. OBCoV

I tethered my horse beside the plum blossoms. From Chekiang I Went to Hsin-an . . . I Wrote These Four Lines to Make Fun of Myself. Hsü Wei, *Chinese.* CoBLCP, *tr. by* Jonathan Chaves

I' th' isle of Britain, long since famous grown. A Satire on Charles II. John Wilmot, 2d Earl of Rochester. NOSC; PeLV

I Thank God I'm Free at Las'. *Unknown.* BPo; CrDW; PBMP; TAP ("O free at last.") (LL) APN-2

I thank the, Lord so dere, that wold vowchsayf. *Unknown.* PoE *Fr.* Noah.

I thank thee and I praise thee, O thou radiant grace. Thanksgiving. "Yehoash," *Yiddish.* TrJP, *tr. by* Isidore Goldstick

I thank you, dear blessed mother. Mother's Birthday. Lydia Wagenlander. PWR

I thank you for the many steps. Dear Mother. Ebba M. Leaf. PWR

I thank you, God. Thanksgiving. Louise Driscoll. CTV

I thank You God for most this amazing. E. E. Cummings. APAD; MeMAP; NTP; TAP; TrCP

I thank You, God in Heaven, for. In Gratitude for Friends. Margaret Elizabeth Sangster. CTV

I thank you, Lord, for having made me Black. Bernard Dadié, *French.* NegPo, *tr. by* Ellen Conroy Kennedy

I that all through my early days. Lament for the Makers. W. S. Merwin. BAP-96

I, that ame of all most crost. Song. Mary Sidney, Countess of Montgomery Wroth. KTR *Fr.* Pamphilia to Amphilanthus.

I that erstwhile the world's sweet air did draw. Sonnet. George Wither. NOSC *Fr.* The Shephe[a]rd's Hunting.

I that have been a lover, and could show it. A Sonnet to the Noble Lady, the Lady Mary Wroth. Ben Jonson. BeJo; NoP-4

I that in heill [or health] wes [or was] and gladnes[s] [or gladiness]. Lament for the Makaris. William Dunbar. EBEV; EnVB; HAP; NOBE; NoP-4; OAEL-1; OBEV; OxBS; PoEL-1; SCGP

I that lived ever about you. English Girl. *Unknown, Chinese.* OBMV, *tr. by* E. Powys Mathers

I, the bosun's mate, John Reading. Death of the Bosun's Mate. Louis Johnson. PeNZ

I, the first named. Dylan Thomas. CBNP

I, the genius Severyanin. Epilogue. "Igor Severyanin," *Russian.* TCRP, *tr. by* Bernard Meares

I' the how-dumb-deid o' the cauld hairst nicht. The Eemis-Stane. "Hugh MacDiarmid." FaBoTC; NAEL-2

I, the old woman of Beare. The Old Woman of Beare Regrets Lost Youth. *Unknown, Irish.* OBMV, *tr. by* Frank O'Connor

I, the poet William Yeats. To Be Carved on a Stone at Thoor Ballylee. W. B. Yeats. FaBoEE; IIP; NoAM; NoP-4

I the poor nuttree, joyning to the way. Nux (The Walnut Tree). Ovid. OBCVT, *tr. by* R. Hatton *Fr.* Ovids Walnut-Tree transplanted.

I, the priest of Rhea, long-haired. Erucius of Cyzicus, *Greek.* GrAn, *tr. by* Robin Skelton

I, the Survivor. Bertolt Brecht, *German.* PoSu, *tr. by* John Willett; HP, *tr. by* Willet, John

I therefore pray thee, Renny dear. Ballad. Samuel Johnson. OBCoV; OxAEP-1

I, therefore, will begin. Soul of the age! Ben Jonson. NOBE *Fr.* To the Memory of My Beloved, the Author Mr William Shakespeare. BeJo; EPCY; HAP; HeIP-4; NOSC; OAEL-1; OxAEP-1; PoEL-2; SeCP

I Think. James Schuyler. TTTS

I think a lot about it. Around the Rough and Rugged Rocks the Ragged Rascal Rudely Ran. John Ashbery. InPS-3

I think a time will come when you will understand. For My Father. Paul Potts. FaBoTw

I think about you & it's like having spirits come down on me. Yuwaku, *Tlingit Indian.* STP, *tr. by* James Koller

I think all this is somewhere in myself. The Room. Merwin. NOBA

I think at a distance I hear a loud voice. The Missionary. Mrs. Henry Linden. CBWP-4

I think awhile of Love, and while I think. Friendship. Thoreau. FP

I think continually of those who were truly great. Stephen Spender. CABP; CMoP; EBEvV; HAP; HeIP-4; ImPo; LiTM; MoBrPo; NOBE; NoP-4; OAEL-2; OxBTC; PoRA; RaBo; TFi

I think he sits at that strange table. At It. Ronald Stuart Thomas. OxBC

I think I am becoming. Interior Monologue 666. Tom Marshall. NOBC

I think I could turn and live with animals, they're so placid and self- / contain'd.

I think I could turn and live awhile with animals. Animals. Walt Whitman. HAP; ImPo; SAmP; WeW-3 *Fr.* Song of Myself. AmPP; MoAmPo; NAAL-3; NOBA; OxBA

I think I grow tensions. The Flower. Robert Creeley. PmAP

I think I have no other home than this. Old Memories of Earth. Ronald Allison Kells Mason. PeNZ

I think I heard the belle. The Old Lady's Lament for Her Youth. François Villon, *French.* BoLoP, *tr. by* Robert Lowell

I Think I Know No Finer Things than Dogs. Hally Carrington Brent. BLPA

I think I must have lived. The Fox. Philip Levine. SoSe-8

I think I remember this moorland. We Have Been Here Before. Morris Gilbert Bishop. NYBP

I think I see her sitting bowed and black. Oriflamme. Jessie Redmond Fauset. BlSi; PoBA

I think I see my father's sister stand. First Book: Young Aurora's Fostermother. Elizabeth Barrett Browning. NALW; PEW *Fr.* Aurora Leigh. VWP

I think I shall end by not feeling lonesome. Street Cries. Marjorie Welish. EOEF

I think I should have loved you presently. Edna St. Vincent Millay. NAAL-2

I think I should like to die in Massachusetts. Dying in Massachusetts. Donald W. Baker. PuP-15

I think I sing that [or this] little song. Union Man. Albert Morgan. AmFP

I think I smell smoke. Il Janitoro. George Ade. OBAL

"I think I want some pies this morning." Greedy Richard. Jane Taylor. OxBChV

I think I was enchanted. Emily Dickinson. APN-2; NALW

I think I was not yet two. My First Memory, Switzerland, Circa 1947. Joan Dobbie. LoHo

I think I will not hang myself to-day. (LL) A Ballade of Suicide. G. K. Chesterton. NBLV; OBCoV

I think I wrote a poem today but I don't know well. Noon Point. Clark Coolidge. PmAP

I think if I lay dying in some land. The Harbour. Winifred M. Letts. TIRV

I think if you had loved me when I wanted. Success. Rupert Brooke. OxBTC

I think I'll get a paper. Nerves. "Sagittarius." OxBTC

"I think I'm going to have it." Poem to my Daughter. Anne Stevenson. NMM-2

I think in fours. Thought. Fazil Hüsnü Daglarca. CRP

I think it better that in times like these. On Being Asked for a War Poem. W. B. Yeats. NIP-4; OBWP; OxAEP-2; PoWW

I think it is in Virginia, that place. Low Fields and Light. W. S. Merwin. CoAmPo; LCAP-2

I think it mercy if thou wilt forget. (LL) If poisonous [or poysonous] mineral[l]s, and if that tree. Donne. EBEV; FaBoVe; ImPo; NAEL-1; NoP-4; OAEL-1; OxAEP-1; PoEL-2; SCGP; SeCP; Son; UnPo

I think it must be lonely to be God. The Preacher: Ruminates Behind the Sermon. Gwendolyn Brooks. NAAAL; PBMP Fr. A Street in Bronzeville. BPo; BlSi; FaBoWP

I think it quite a charming myth. Monkeys. Frank A. Collymore. PBCV

I think it rains. Wole Soyinka. AF

I think it was Spring—but not certain I am. Epicurean Reminiscences of a Sentimentalist. Thomas Hood. CBNP; PeLV

I think mice. (Mice). Rose Fyleman. BoTP; CTV; ChAP; NTCP

I think naught great: I am the highest thing of all. Man Is The Highest Thing. "Angelus Silesius." GePo, tr. by George C. Schoolfield Fr. The Cherubical Wanderer.

I think of a flower that no eye has ever seen. Beauty. Laurence Binyon. MoBrPo

I think of all the galloping. Johnny's Team. Eugene Field. PWR

I think of all the places I've been. Unknown, Chinese. CoBCP, tr. by Burton Watson

I think of all the things at school. Johnny's Hist'ry Lesson. Nixon Waterman. PoLF

I think of all the toughs through history. Lines for a Book. Thom Gunn. CABP

I think of corner shots, the ball. Day and Night Handball. Stephen Dunn. AmPA

I think of him overturning the tables of the money. Esta. Linda Gregg. AFr

I think of him / Who lives south of the big sea. Unknown, Chinese. BoWoP, tr. by Wai-lim Yip

I Think of Housman Who Said the Poem Is a Morbid Secretion, like a Pearl. Judith Kroll. UnPo

I think of how geologists must love. A Geologist and Millions of Years. Xuân Diệu, Vietnamese. AVP, tr. by Huỳnh Sanh Thông

I think of it as a large moment with shadows. When Skyscrapers Were Invented in Chicago. Edward Hirsch. WWSi

I think of it with wonder now. The Glass. Sharon Olds. NIP-4

I think of my wife, and I think of Lot. Marriage Couplet. William Cole. OBAL

I think of our anonymous boys. Nocturnal Visits. Claribel Alegría, Spanish. VCWP, tr. by D. J. Flakoll

I think of Plato and the limited technology. The Cave. Michael Collier. PuP-15

I think of that meadow off down in Coyne's. Coyne's. John Ennis. PBCIP

I think of the Celts as rather a whining lady. The Celts. Stevie Smith. NoP-4

I think of the days. Fujiwara no Atsutada, Japanese. OHPJ, tr. by Kenneth Rexroth

I think of the masts at Cette and the sweet rain. (LL) American Letter. Archibald MacLeish. AmPP; OxBA

I think of the razor-sharp knife. Talking of Sharp Things. Frank Mkalawile Chipasula. HBAPE

I think of the room at Bon Secours. Pilgrimage. Anna Wickham. WPN

I think of the sea changing and changing. Marina. O. B. Hardison, Jr. AiP; CRP

I think of the tribes: the women prized for fatness. The Tribes. Roy Fuller. LiTM

I think of thee!—My thoughts do twine and bud. Sonnet XXIX. Elizabeth Barrett Browning. PEW Fr. Sonnets from the Portuguese.

I think of things like the shadow of a branch. The Shadow of a Branch. Edith Marcombe Shiffert. WPE

I think of when she comes. Shen Yüeh, Chinese. Fr. Six Poems on Remembering. CoBCP, tr. by Burton Watson

I think of when she sits. Shen Yüeh. Fr. Six Poems on Remembering. CoBCP, tr. by Burton Watson

I think of when she sits. Wang Seng-ta, Chinese. CoBCP, tr. by Burton Watson

I think of when she sleeps. Shen Yüeh. Fr. Six Poems on Remembering. CoBCP, tr. by Burton Watson

I think of when she sleeps. Wang Seng-ta, Chinese. CoBCP, tr. by Burton Watson

I think of Wind and her wild ways the year we had nothing to lose. Grace. Joy Harjo. NAmP90

I think of you standing. For the Women of Poland; December 1981. June Hirshfield WeT

I think of you with nothing on. (LL) Celia Celia. Adrian Mitchell. FaBoEE; OPOU

I think, old bone, the world's not with us much. To William Wordsworth from Virginia. Julia Randall. NMM-2; WPE

I think once more he seems to die. (LL) I climb the hill: from end to end. Tennyson. EBVV; FHYEP; PoEL-5

I think she sleeps: it must be sleep, when low. George Meredith. NAEL-2 Fr. Modern Love.

I think some saint of Eirinn wandering far. Fuchsia Hedges in Connacht. Padraic Colum. TIRV

I think sometimes about. Friedrich von Hausen, German. GePo, tr. by Frederick Goldin

I think sometimes / of the fingernail slotted. Michael Hartnett. CIP-2

I think that God is proud of those who bear. Grace Noll Crowell. PoToHe

I think that I live in a street. For the Record. George Jonas. MoCV

I think that I shall never read. Poems. Thomas M. Disch. UV

I think that I shall never see / A billboard. Song of the Open Road. Ogden Nash. EBEvV; OBAL

I think that I shall never see / A poem. Trees. Joyce Kilmer. BLPA; ChAP; EBEvV; FPC; FaBoBe; PFE; UV

I think that look of Christ might seem to say. The Meaning of the Look. Elizabeth Barrett Browning. TrCP

I think that night's our balance. Suite to Fathers. James Harrison. AmPA

I think that the Root of the Wind is Water. Emily Dickinson. RB

I think that the tortoise-shell cat. Amber. Shirley Toulson. PeP

I think the dead are tender. Shall we kiss?—. She. Theodore Roethke. BoLoP

I think the dead lie hungry in the dark. The Hungry Dead. Jim Wayne Miller. MT

I think the gentle soul of him. Ilicet. Theodosia Pickering Garrison. PoLF

I think the Hemlock likes to stand. Emily Dickinson. NCAP

I think the loathed minutes one by one. Moments. Ivor Gurney. OxBSP

I think the thing you call Renown. Winthrop Mackworth Praed. OBSV Fr. The Chaunt of the Brazen Head.

I think there are most tigers in the wood. (LL) Ceremony. Richard Wilbur. CoAP; MoP; NAAL-2; NoAM

I think therefore I am not. Cogito Ergo. Jerzy Ficowski, Polish. PoSu, tr. by Frank J. Corliss, Jr., and Grazyna Sandel

I think they were about as high. The Shade-Catchers. Charlotte Mew. NTP

I think this house's mouth is full of dirt. Independence Day, 1956: A Fairy Tale. James Galvin. PoPoPo

I think this is something you should get clear. Unknown, Greek. GrAn, tr. by Peter Jay

I think this night is cold for Hugh; the heaviness of its downpour is a cause. On Maguire's Winter Campaign. Eochaidh Ó Heóghusa. PBRV

"I think," thought Sam Butler. English Liberal. Geoffrey Taylor. FaBoEE

I think to make love to a nurse would be perfect. Angel. Andrew Elliott. PNI

I think to say this / wrongly. (LL) The Whip. Robert Creeley. EOEF; MoP; NeAP; PoE; PoM

I think true love is never blind. True Love. Phoebe Cary. PoToHe

I think very well of Susan but I do not know her name. Gertrude Stein. NoP-4

I think when Judas' mother heard. Judas Iscariot. Countee Cullen. PoLF

I think you are ready. (LL) Tract. William Carlos Williams. LiTM; MeMAP; MoAmPo; MoP; NOBA; NoAM; SAmP; TAP; TwCP; VGW

I think you feel, Antoine, that of us two. The Garden of Writing. Nicolas Boileau-Despéaux, French. GaP, tr. by John Hollander

I think you're bashful. The First Date. David Avidan. Fr. Samson, Our Hero. IP, tr. by Warren Bargad and Stanley F. Chyet

I thirst, but not as once I did. My Soul Thirsteth for God. William Cowper. TrCP Fr. Olney Hymns.

I thirst for God, to Him my soul aspires. The Living God. Abraham ibn Ezra, Hebrew. TrJP, tr. by Alice Lucas

I thirst for violins, as drunkards thirst. Ideal and Reality. Joseph Campbell. BIrV

I thought. Rosy Ear. Zbigniew Herbert, Polish. EP, tr. by Czeslaw Milosz

I thought, as I wiped my eyes on the corner of my apron. An Ancient Gesture. Edna St. Vincent Millay. NALW; NMM-2

I thought he was bankrupt. Max Jacob. PFTM, tr. by Bill Zavatsky Fr. The Cock and the Pearl.

I thought he was dumb. Tortoise Shout. D. H. Lawrence. LiTM; NAEL-2; PFTM

I thought i might be in slug's. Okra to greens. Ntozake Shange. MoNo

I thought I saw an angel flying low. Nocturne at Bethesda. Arna Bontemps. ChIV-2; NAAAL

I thought I saw buffalo. *Unknown. Fr.* Sioux Metamorphoses. STP, *tr. by* James Koller

I thought I was growing wings. Seeing for a Moment. Denise Levertov. VCAP

I thought I was so tough. Tamer and Hawk. Thom Gunn. APAD; APo; FaBoTw

I thought I woke: the midnight sun. Stanzas. Paul Goodman. PoA

I thought if only I could marry. Unfair to Women. *Unknown, Welsh.* OBWVE, *tr. by* Gwyn Jones

I thought it made me look more "working class." Turns. Tony Harrison. *Fr.* The School of Eloquence. NAEL-2; NoAM

I thought it rained last night yet it's sunny this morning. Staying Overnight at the Temple of the Holy Vulture. Yang Wan-li, *Chinese.* SuSp, *tr. by* Sherwin S. S. Fu

I Thought It Was Harry. William Bronk. APSN

I thought it would last my time. Going, Going. Philip Larkin. NoAM; OxAEP-2

I thought my all was given before. Wretten by Me at the Death of My 4th Sonne and 5th Child Perigrene Payler. Mary Carey. KTR

I thought no more was needed. A Song. W. B. Yeats. CBLP

I thought of cards along the mantelpiece. December Fragments. Richmond Lattimore. PChr

I thought of Chatterton, the marvellous Boy. We Poets in Our Youth. Wordsworth. *Fr.* Resolution and Independence. EBEV; FHYEP; HAP; InPS-3; NOBE; NOBRP; NOCV; NoP-4; OAEL-2; OBNC; OxAEP-2; PoEL-4; Ro; TFi

I thought of eden. Civilization Aha. Sipho Sepamla. PBMAP

I thought of leaving her for a day. Second Thoughts. "Michael Field." LW

I thought of thee—I thought of thee The Confessional. Nathaniel Parker Willis. APN-1

I thought of Thee, my partner and my guide. After-Thought. Wordsworth. NOBE; OBEV; OBNC *Fr.* The River Duddon [A Series of Sonnets].

I thought of Troy, what we had built her for. (LL) Aeneas at Washington. Allen Tate. FYAP; FuPo; NOBA; NoAM; OxBA

I thought of walking round and round a space. Seamus Heaney. *Fr.* Clearances. CIP-2; PBCIP; PNI

I thought once how Theocritus had sung. Sonnet. Elizabeth Barrett Browning. BWW; EBVV; EnVR; GBL; GLoP; LBC; NOBE; NoP-4; OBEV; OBNC; OxAEP-2; PoPoPo; WPE *Fr.* Sonnets from the Portuguese.

I thought Silver must have snaked logs. Silver. A. R. Ammons. NoP-4

I thought so once. (LL) My Own Epitaph. John Gay. CABP; FaBoEE; LiLi; NIP-4; NOEC; PFE; PeLV

I thought that I knew all there was to know. Small, Smaller. Russell Hoban. NOxBChV

I thought that I was ravished to a height. Unum est Necessarium. Agnes Mary Frances Robinson. VWP

I thought that Love had been a boy. *Unknown.* EnLoPo

I thought that you were an anchor in the drift of the world. The World. William Bronk. APSN

I thought the chrysanthemum bloomed in autumn. Ise Tayu, *Japanese.* WPJ, *tr. by* Kenneth Rexroth *and* Ikuko Atsumi

I thought the earth / remembered me, she. Sleeping in the Forest. Mary Oliver. InPS-3

I thought the gesture was only about me. Robyn Selman. PUP-19

I thought the night without a sound was falling. How Infinite Are Thy Ways. William Force Stead. OBMV *Fr.* Uriel.

I thought these wondrous when thy soul portrayed. To Charlotte Cushman. Eliza Cook. VWP

I Thought There Were Limits. Douglas G. Jones. MoCV

I thought would ring me out about. (LL) A Narrative of the Life and Times of John Coltrane: Played by Himself. Michael S. Harper. MoNo; SeSe

I thought you always knew it well. One Way of Looking at It. Arthur Joseph Munby. NOBVV

"I thought you loved me." "No, it was only /fun." In The Orchard. Muriel Stuart. EBNV; LW; OxBTC

I thought you were good. Divorce Song. *Unknown, Tsimshian Indian.* STP, *tr. by* Carl Cary

I threw / Single die, A. Die. Novica Tadic, *Serbo-Croatian.* HSix, *tr. by* Charles Simic

I threw the inside of my gizzard out, splashing. Zimmer Drunk and Alone, Dreaming of Old Football Games. Paul Zimmer. PBCAP

I, through all chances that are given to mortals. To Ausonius. Paulinus of Nola, *Latin.* LBC; LoP; OBCVT, *tr. by* Helen Waddell

I thumped on you the best I could. W. D. Snodgrass. NoAM *Fr.* Heart's Needle. CAPP-1

I, thy King, so say! (LL) Before the Feast of Shushan. Anne Spencer. BlSi; NAAAL

I tiptoed into her sleep. Mirru. Kenneth Patchen. MoLi

I, to make myself laugh louder and longer. Velemir Khlebnikov. TCRP, *tr. by* Gary Kern *Fr.* War in a Mousetrap.

I To my Brothers. Judith Wright. BMAP *Fr.* For a Pastoral Family.

I to the hills lift up mine eyes. Psalm 121. *Unknown.* OBCA *Fr.* The Bay Psalm Book.

I to the Hills Will Lift Mine Eyes. Francis Rous. AH

I to the Lord from My Distress. *Unknown.* AH

I told everyone / your name was Arthur. Arturo. Maria Gillan. UnSA

I told her that. (LL) Soufrière. Ellsworth McGranahan Keane. HCP; PBCV

I told her: the sidewalks are muddy. Konstantin Konstantinovich Sluchevsky, *Russian.* TCRP, *tr. by* Albert C. Todd

I told her when I left one day. In the Night She Came. Thomas Hardy. OxBM

I Told Jesus. Sterling Plumpp. PoBA

I told the Sun that I was glad. The Sun. John Drinkwater. NTCP

I, too am America. (LL) I too, sing America. Langston Hughes. CrDW; HCAP; HeIP-4; NAAAL; NOxBChV; NTP; PoBA; PoLF; PoPoPo; SAGP; SSLK

I too beneath your moon, almighty Sex. Edna St. Vincent Millay. NAAL-2; NALW

I, too, but seem! (LL) In Utrumque Paratus. Matthew Arnold. OBNC; PoEL-5

I, too, dislike it: there are things that are important beyond all this / fiddle. Poetry. Marianne Moore. AmPP; BoWoP; CMoP; ColAP; FaBoWP; HAP; HeIP-4; ImGa; ImPo; LiTM; MoAmPo; MoP; NAAL-2; NALW; NIP-4; NOBA; NoAM; NoP-4; OxBA; PoE; PoPoPo; Poetr; TAP; TFi; UnPo

I too have been in love, and my sleepless. Boris Pasternak. TCRP, *tr. by* Albert C. Todd *Fr.* A Poem.

I too have encompassed a lot: a mother thrice—. Elizaveta Kuzmina-Karavayeva. TCRP, *tr. by* Vera Dunham *Fr.* Whit Monday.

I, too, have faked the glamor of gray towers. Disloyal Lines to an Alumnus. Edmund Wilson. OBCoV

I, too, have plucked a stalk of grass. Ronald Johnson. *Fr.* Letters to Walt Whitman. VGW

I, Too, Know What I Am Not. Bob Kaufman. GT

I too, on Corpus Christi Day. A Garland on the Wrist. Jaroslav Seifert, *Czech.* CEEP, *tr. by* Ewald Osers

I, too, saw God through mud. Apologia Pro Poemate Meo. Wilfred Owen. LiTM; MoBrPo; NAEL-2; NSI; PeFWW; PoFWW

I too, sing America. Langston Hughes. CrDW; HCAP; HeIP-4; NAAAL; NOxBChV; NTP; PoBA; PoLF; PoPoPo; SAGP; SSLK

I too was born out of a lion's mouth. Let Heroes Account to Love. Alan Dugan. NoAM

I took a piece of plastic clay. Sculpture. *Unknown.* PoLF; PoToHe

I took a piece of the rare cloth of Ch'i. A Present from the Emperor's New Concubine. Pan Chieh-yû, *Chinese.* BoWoP; OHMPC, *tr. by* Kenneth Rexroth

I took a walk on the railroad track. A Walk. Raymond Carver. GM

I took away three pictures. Sandhill People. Carl Sandburg. CMoP

I took him by the arm and said. F. Mullen. UV

I took love home with me. Act #2. John Weiners. BB

I took money and bought threatening trees. Planting Flowers on the Eastern Embankment. Po Chü-i, *Chinese.* ChiP; OBGa, *tr. by* Arthur Waley

I took my girl to a fancy ball. I Had But Fifty Cents. *Unknown.* BLPA; NBLV; WHSW

I took my girlfriend to your last poetry reading. Short Order. Charles Bukowski. HoPM

I took my heart in my hand. Twice. Christina Rossetti. GBL; NOBE; OBEV; OBNC; TOF; TrCP; VWP

I took my oath I would inquire. The Inquest. W. H. Davies. GTBS-P; NOBE; OxBTC; RB

I took my Power in my Hand. Emily Dickinson. ChIV-1; KSG; SAmP

I took one Draught of Life. Emily Dickinson. APN-2; NTP

I took the scroll. I could not brook. Lines Written Under a Picture of a Girl Burning a Love-Letter. Letitia Elizabeth Landon. NOBRP

I took up the burden of life anew. To My Mother. Mary Weston Fordham. CBWP-2

I took wild honey from the plants. Distribution of Poetry. Jorge de Lima, *Portuguese.* PFTM, *tr. by* John Nist

I tossed my friend a wreath of roses, wet. Gifts. Mary Elizabeth Coleridge. PBWP; VWP

I touch jig-saw fragments. A. L. Hendriks. *Fr.* D'Où Venons Nous? Que Sommes Nous? Où Allons Nous. PBCV

I touch you in the night, whose gift was you. The Science of the Night. Stanley Kunitz. ColAP; MoAmPo; TwCP

I touch you like the waves admire the weirs. The Oasis Motel. William Olsen. NAmP90

I touched the flesh with my eyes. Fish. Joe Rosenblatt. NOBC

I touched the heart that loved me as a player. A Shattered Lute. Alice Thompson Meynell. SDW

I touched up sexy Hermione. Asclepiades, *Greek*. GrAn, *tr. by* Alan Marshfield

I trained me a falcon, for more than a year. *Unknown, German*. GePo, *tr. by* Frederick Goldin

I tramp my streets into recognition. Charles Brasch. *Fr.* Home Ground. PeNZ

I tramped out hundreds of miles in the war. Ballad of the Shot Heart. Nikolai Vasil'evich Panchenko, *Russian*. TCRP, *tr. by* Daniel Weissbort

I travel day and night toward the Yangtze and the sea. Su Tung-p'o, *Chinese*. CoBCP, *tr. by* Burton Watson

I travel far in a little boat. Traveling by Boat at Shun-ch'ang. Hsü Chung-hsing, *Chinese*. CoBLCP, *tr. by* Jonathan Chaves

I traveled [*or* travell'd] among unknown men. Wordsworth. AWP; GTBS-P *Fr.* Lucy. FHYEP; NOBE; OAEL-2; OBEV; OBNC; SCGP; TFi

("I travelled among unknown men.") PFE; Ro

("That Lucy's eyes surveyed.") (LL) PFE

("Which Lucy's eyes surveyed!") (LL) Ro

I traveled [*or* travell'd] on, seeing the hill, where lay. The Pilgrimage. George Herbert. ESCV; GeHe; NAEL-1; NOSC; PoE

I traveled to the ocean. Prayer to the Pacific. Leslie Marmon Silko. CDW; NoP-4; PoPoPo; VoR; WeW-3

I Traveled with Them. Don Allen Johnson, *Arabic*. AWP, *tr. by* J. B. Trend

I travelled the land from Leap to Corbally. The Volatile Kerryman. Owen Roe O'Sullivan, *Irish*. BIrV, *tr. by* Sean O'Riada

I travelled [*or* traveld] thro' [*or* through] a land of men. The Mental Traveller. William Blake. ChIV-2; NAEL-2; OAEL-2; PoE; PoEL-4; Ro

I traversed a dominion. Mute Opinion. Thomas Hardy. CMoP

I tried each thing, only some were immortal and free. As One Put Drunk into the Packet-Boat. John Ashbery. HAP; HCAP; VCAP

I tried this play one day. My father leaves his medicines open. I take. Daredevil. Ania Walwicz. BMAP

I tried to do what I was told, made. Mama Remembers. Lawrence Joseph. FiLi

I Tried to Exchange Two Painting for Some Grain But Failed. Hsü Wei, *Chinese*. CoBLCP, *tr. by* Jonathan Chaves

I tried to live small. Housing Shortage. Naomi Replansky. CrSp; NMM-2

I tried to tell her. Offspring. Naomi Long Madgett. CrSp; GT; SoSe-8

I tried to tell the doctor. Oh, I'm 10 Months Pregnant. Ntozake Shange. GT

I tried to turn the handle, but. (LL) Humpty Dumpty's Song. "Lewis Carroll." CBNP; EBEV; GTBS-P; NOBVV; OBCoV; OBSP; OxBChV; OxBoLi; PeLV; PeVV

I tripped up his heels and he fell on his nose. (LL) Bandy Legs. Mother Goose. OxNR; ReMoGo

I trundle the bodies, on the iron bars. John Berryman. NOBA *Fr.* Homage to Mistress Bradstreet.

I trust every animal. Dogalypse. Andrey Andreievich Voznesensky, *Russian*. CLPP, *tr. by* Lawrence Ferlinghetti *et al.*

I trust I have not wasted breath. Tennyson. EnVR; FHYEP; OAEL-2 *Fr.* In Memoriam A. H. H.

I try to forget, but it is in vain. To the Distant One. Po Chü-i, *Chinese*. TAL, *tr. by* Robert Payne

I try to hold your face in my mind's million eyes. A Bride's Hours. Jean Valentine. FaBoWP

I turn the carriage, yoke and set off. Mei Sheng *and* Fu I. *Fr.* Nineteen Old Poems of the Han. CoBCP, *tr. by* Burton Watson

I turn the lea-green down. Ploughman. Patrick Kavanagh. TIRV

I turn the page and read. At the British Museum. Richard Aldington. MoBrPo

I turn to You. To the Divine Neighbor. Judah Leib Teller, *Yiddish*. CEEP, *tr. by* Gabriel Preil *and* Howard Schwartz

I turn to you high priests. Lament. Tadeusz Rózewicz, *Polish*. PoSu, *tr. by* Magnus J. Krynski

I turn to you, in the deep twilight of a cellar. To the Spirits of Shakespeare and Velázquez. Sándor Weöres, *Hungarian*. CEEP, *tr. by* Emery E. George

I turn you out of doors. Alain Chartier, *French*. BoLoP, *tr. by* Edward Lucie-Smith

I turned and gave my strength to woman. Two Generations. Leonard Alfred George Strong. OBMV

I turned aside and bowed my head and wept. (LL) The Tropics in New York. Claude McKay. CrDW; GT; NoAM; PBMP; PFE; PoBA; TTY

I turned on the TV. Tube Time. Eve Merriam. TLR

I undersign'd Lord Kitchener of Karthoum. The Proclamation, or Paper Bomb. F. W. Reitz, *Afrikaans*. PeSAV, *tr. by* F. W. Reitz

I understand. In the Restaurant. Gerald William Barrax. GT

I understand the large hearts of heroes. Heroes. Walt Whitman. SAmP *Fr.* Song of Myself. AmPP; MoAmPo; NAAL-3; NOBA; OxBA

I understand you well enough, Donne. A Letter to Donne. Charles Hubert Sisson. NOCV

I UNDERSTOOD I UNDERSTOOD. Jaan Kaplinski, *Estonian*. CEEP, *tr. by* Grabbi, Hellar

I understood that. Julian of Norwich. CrSp

I unpetalled you, like a rose. Juan Ramón Jiménez, *Spanish*. ITG, *tr. by* Stephen Mitchell

I upon the first creation. Gratitude. Christopher Smart. NOEC *Fr.* Hymns for the Amusement of Children.

I urgency, I begged. *Give me your dish,* I said, icy. Hélène Cixous. VCAP, *tr. by* Anne Liddle *and* Sarah Cornell *Fr.* Vivre L'Orange.

I used the table as a reference and just did things from there. Texas. Mei-Mei Berssenbrugge. PmAP

I used to be a drill man. Drill Man Blues. George Sizemore. AmFP

I used to be / an admissions counselor. Skin Color from the Sun. Daryl Ngee Chinn. LTA

I used to dream of Chuang Tzu. A Painting of the Butterfly Dream by the Master Artist Li Tsai. Chu Yün-ming, *Chinese*. ChiPo; CoBLCP, *tr. by* Jonathan Chaves

I used to fall. My Heart Belongs to Daddy. Cole Porter. OBAL

I used to have an old grey horse. Goin' Down to Town. *Unknown*. AS

I used to lie on my back, imagining. Childhood. Maura Stanton. CMAP

I used to make fun of you when you were a little girl & poor. Song for the Richest Woman in Wrangell. Guxnawu, *Tlingit*. STP, *tr. by* James Koller

I used to meet him at. Thunder. Pat Therese Francis. EC2

I used to prefer them and now I'm one of them. Older Men. Alfred Corn. GLP

I used to sit under trees and meditate. Buddha. Jack Kerouac. BB

I used to tell you, "Frances, we grow old." Kenneth Rexroth, *after the Latin of* Ausonius. NNaP; PGA

I used to think all poets were Byronic. Triolet. Wendy Cope. OBCoV

I used to think that grown-up people chose. Childhood. Frances Darwin Cornford. FaBoWP; KaS; OxBSP; OxBTC

I used to think you could get a boy. Foreign Exchange. Marion Winik. IFJA

I used to walk on solid gr'und. To a Sea Eagle. "Hugh MacDiarmid." MoBrPo

I used to walk the morning stream. Walk. Brian Merriman. BIrV, *tr. by* Brendan Behan *Fr.* The Midnight Court. NOIV, *tr. by* Thomas Kinsella

I used to wonder that other men and women were alive. Half Of Me. Saint Augustine. LBC

I usta wonder who i'd be. Adulthood. Nikki Giovanni. CrSp; NMM-2

I verse a settler's tale of olden times. Charles Harpur. CBAP *Fr.* The Creek of the Four Graves.

I Vision God [standing]. *Unknown*. NAAAL; TTY

I visited my distant relatives / by Lake Suwa in Shinshū. Walking-with-a-Cane-Pass. Rin Ishigaki, *Japanese*. WPJ, *tr. by* Kenneth Rexroth *and* Ikuko Atsumi

I visited Père Lachaise to look for the remains of Apollinaire. At Apollinaire's Grave. Allen Ginsberg. BB

I vow to thee, my country, all earthly things above. Cecil Arthur Spring-Rice. BoTP; NSI

I vow'd unvarying faith. Constancy Rewarded. Coventry Patmore. NOBVV; OxBSP *Fr.* The Angel in the House.

I.W. To her unconstant Lover. Isabella Whitney. PBRV

I wad ha'e gi'en him my lips tae kiss. Mary's Song. Marion Angus. LW

I wade by the edge of the sparkling stream. In the Green Shade. Brian Lee. AYFP

I wage not any feud with Death. Tennyson. ImPo *Fr.* In Memoriam A. H. H.

I wait, dear child, for you to come. You'll Never Know. Ruby Marion Wray. PWR

I wait for her who restores my fingertips. Song of Expectancy. George Hitchcock. SPE

I wait for his foot fall. Earth Trembles Waiting. Blanche Shoemaker Wagstaff. PoLF

I wait. I don't go. He will come, the one. Here I Am. Li-Young Lee. IFJA

I Wait My Lord. *Unknown*. AWP, *tr. by* Helen Waddell *Fr.* Shi King.

I wait to tangle fear around my hand. Night along the Mackinac Bridge. Roberta Hill Whiteman. CDW

I wait, with those that rest. Ark to Noah. Jay Macpherson. NOBC; PoA *Fr.* The Ark.

I waited and worked / To win myself leisure. Koheleth. Louis Untermeyer. ChIV-1; TrJP

I waited eighteen years to become a man. Basket Case. Basil T. Paquet. CDa

I Waited for Chuang Hsüan-yüan But He Never Came. Mo Shih-lung, *Chinese.* CoBLCP, *tr. by* Jonathan Chaves

I waited for my. *Unknown, Japanese.* OHPJ, *tr. by* Kenneth Rexroth

I waited for the train at Coventry. Godiva. Tennyson. EBVVPR

I waited full two hours, or more. The Tryst. Mary E. Tucker. CBWP-1

I waited in a map of dreams. In the Town With Cat-/ Shaped Maze. Mieko Kanai, *Japanese.* WPJ, *tr. by* Kenneth Rexroth *and* Ikuko Atsumi

I wake and feel the fell of dark, not day. Gerard Manley Hopkins. CABP; EnVR; FaBoVe; NoP-4; OxAEP-2; PeVV; TRP

I wake at midnight. Shellfish. Rin Ishigaki, *Japanese.* WPJ, *tr. by* Kenneth Rexroth *and* Ikuko Atsumi

I wake, but before I know it it is done. Aging. Randall Jarrell. PoA

I wake despondent. Morning. Tove Ditlevsen, *Danish.* PBWP, *tr. by* Nadia Christensen

I wake from a nap, light clouds. Waking from a Nap. Ni Tsan, *Chinese.* CoBLCP, *tr. by* Jonathan Chaves

I wake! I feel the day is near. Chanticleer. Celia Laighton Thaxter. NOxBChV

I wake in a dark flat. Derek Mahon. *Fr.* Afterlives. CIP-2

I wake in the dark and remember. Rain Travel. W. S. Merwin. ColAP

I Wake Thinking of Myself as a Man. Susan Griffin. GLP

I wake to find myself lying in an open field. Robert Bly Says Something Too. Henry Taylor. BXAP

I wake to sleep, and take my waking slow. The Waking. Theodore Roethke. APAD; AmPP; CRP; CoAP; HAP; HCAP; HeIP-4; InPK-6; InPS-3; LiTM; MoAmPo; MoP; NAAL-2; NIP-4; NOBA; NoAM; NoP-4; PFE; PoPoPo; Poetr; RaBo; TAP; TFi; TwCP; VCAP; WeW-3

I wake to the sound of a soft, low patter. Night Rain. Countee Cullen. GT

I Wake Up Alone. Li Shang-yin, *Chinese.* OHMPC, *tr. by* Kenneth Rexroth

I wake up and say: I'm through. Morning Exercises. Nina Cassian, *Romanian.* PoSu, *tr. by* Andrea Deletant *and* Brenda Walker

I wake up chasing my breath, my. Falso Brilhante. Nathaniel Mackey. NAAAL

I wake up cold, I who. The Man With Night Sweats. Thom Gunn. CABP; PoPoPo

I wake up in the bed my grandmother died in. Stove. Philip Booth. FYAP

I wake up in your bed. I know I have been dreaming. Adrienne Rich. CPO; NAAL-2; NoAM; TRP *Fr.* Twenty-one Love Poems. GLP

I wake up mumbling, "I'm." Capricorn Rising. Nathaniel Mackey. MoNo

I wake up my car. Morning Bird Songs. Tomas Tranströmer, *Swedish.* InPS-3, *tr. by* Robert Bly

I wake up standing before a scene I stood. The Phantom Light of All Our Day. Nathaniel Mackey. GT; PT

I waked [*or* wak'd], she fled, and day brought back my night. (LL) On His Deceased Wife. Milton. BoLoP; CABP; CBLP; EBEV; EnLoPo; GBL; GLoP; GSo; HAP; IMW; ImPo; LBC; NAEL-1; NOBE; NOSC; NoP-4; OAEL-1; OBEV; OxBM; PBRV; PFE; PeECV; PoE; PoEL-3; SAGP; SCGP; SCV; Son; TFi; WeW-3

I wakened my thoughts from slumber. The Sources of My Being. Moses ibn Ezra, *Hebrew.* TOF, *tr. by* David Goldstein

I wakened on my hot, hard bed. The Watch. Frances Darwin Cornford. InPK-6; MoBrPo; OxBTC; PFE; SAGP

I wakened, still a child. The Life Ahead. Philip Levine. NoAM

I walk a road—an ancient, trodden way. Another While. Morris Jacob Rosenfeld, *Yiddish.* TrJP

I walk about in the night. Magic Song. *Unknown, Ojibwa Native American.* APN-2, *tr. by* Henry Rowe Schoolcraft

I walk about in the night time. Song for the Metai Only. *Unknown. Fr.* Music and Poetry of the Indians. APN-2, *tr. by* John Tanner

I walk among men. New York. Toki Zenmaro, *Japanese.* MIT, *tr. by* Makoto Ueda

I walk among men with tall bones. Clouds on the Sea. Ruth Dallas. PeNZ *Fr.* Letter to a Chinese Poet.

I walk and I wonder. Spring. Isaac Rosenberg. TrJP

I walk and think of various things. Georgy Vladimirovich Ivanov, *Russian.* TCRP, *tr. by* Daniel Weissbort

I walk at dawn across the hollow hills. Poem. Ruthven Todd. SPE

I walk back. Getting the Mail. Galway Kinnell. UnPo

I walk before no man, a hawk in his fist. I Walk before No Man (Composed While Asleep). Jonathan Swift. CBNP

I Walk before No Man (Composed While Asleep). Jonathan Swift. CBNP

I walk behind you, hand. Days of 1956. Robin Magowan. SPE

I walk [*or* walked] beside the prisoners to the road. A Camp in the Prussian Forest. Randall Jarrell. CMoP; HP; MoAmPo; OBWP; OxBC; PoWW

I walk down a long / passage way. A Poem for Museum Goers. John Weiners. BB; NeAP

I walk down the garden paths. Patterns. Amy Lowell. AWP; BoWoP; MoAmPo; NoP-4; OxBA; PBMP; WHSW

I walk down the narrow. The Man in the Mirror. Mark Strand. NYBP

I walk in loneliness through the greenwood. *Unknown, French.* BoWoP, *tr. by* Willis Barnstone

I walk in nature still alone. Great Friend. Henry David Thoreau. PoEL-4

I Walk in the History of My People. "Chrystos." UnSA

I walk in the old street. Louis Zukofsky. VGW

I walk into the vineyard at night, into acres of cordoned vines. Revelation in the Mother Lode. George Evans. AF; PmAP

I walk on glass. I Build. Tadeusz Rózewicz, *Polish.* CEEP, *tr. by* Victor Contoski

I walk on the bridge in my white suit that I bought in Dakar. White Suit. Blaise Cendrars, *French.* NNPT, *tr. by* Hoida, Peter

I walk on the sea-shore. Voice. Zbigniew Herbert, *Polish.* PoSu, *tr. by* Czeslaw Milosz

I walk on the waste-ground for no good reason. For No Good Reason. Peter Redgrove. PoE

I Walk Out into the Country at Night. Lu Yu, *Chinese.* OHPC, *tr. by* Kenneth Rexroth

I walk the blacktop towards Center Harbor. Antique Shop. Tina Barr. EC3

I walk the purple carpet into your eye. Inside Out. Diane Wakoski. CoAP; NYBP

I walk those streets tonight, streets named for gems. Grid. Mark Jarman. PuP-17

I walk through sunlit gardens. Recollections of the Sun. A. L. Hendriks. NBrP

I walk through the long schoolroom questioning. Among School Children. W. B. Yeats. CABP; CMoP; GTBS-P; HAP, ImPo, InPS-3; LiTM; MoBrPo; MoP; NAEL-2; NAWM-2; NIP-4; NOBE; NoAM; NoP-4; OAEL-2; OxBTC; PoE; PoPoPo; Poetr; SCGP; TFi; TRP

I walk'd in the lonesome evening. William Allingham. EnLoPo

I walked a mile with Pleasure. Along the Road. Robert Browning Hamilton. BLPA

I walked abroad in [*or* on] a snowy day. Soft Snow. William Blake. SoSe-8

I walked all the way from East St. Louis. East St. Louis Blues. *Unknown.* AmFP

I walked alone and thinking. Sinner's Rue. A. E. Housman. PeVV

I walked [*or* walk'd] along a stream for pureness rare. A Fragment. Gervase Markham. CTC

I walked beside the stone. My Grandmother's Burial Ground. Elizabeth Cook-Lynn. HATNAP

I walked entranced / Through a land of Morn. A Vision of Connaught in the Thirteenth Century. James Clarence Mangan. NOIV

I walked in a desert. Stephen Crane. MeMAP; NAAL-2 *Fr.* The Black Riders [and Other Lines].

I walked in a desert. *Unknown.* PFE

I walked in loamy Wessex lanes, afar. The Pity of It. Thomas Hardy. CMoP; LiTM

I walked into a loge in the Teatro Melisso. Pound at Spoleto. Lawrence Ferlinghetti. BB; PoM

I walked into the room. To My Father. John Berryman. PoPoPo

I walked on the banks of the tincan banana dock. Sunflower Sutra. Allen Ginsberg. AmPP; CoAP; GM; HCAP; InPS-3; NAAL-2; NOBA; NeAP; PaTW; PoPoPo; VCAP

I walked on the edge of the churchyard, my shoes hurt my. At the Pauwels. Diane Glancy. CRP

I walked out into Lithuania. Sigitas Geda, *Lithuanian.* CEEP, *tr. by* Jonas Zdanys

I walked over the grave of Henry James. Richard Eberhart. VGW

I walked slowly along the river. One Hundred and Fifty Years. Jack Davis. BMAP

I walked [*or* walkt] the other day to spend my hour. Henry Vaughan. ESCV; FSCP; GeHe

I walked through Ballinderry in the spring-time. Lament for the Death of Thomas Davis. Sir Samuel Ferguson. BIrV; NOIV

I walked to the distant road. Song of the Field. Jan Bolesw Ozog, *Polish.* CEEP, *tr. by* Leonard Kress

I walked, when love was gone. A Breath of Air. James Wright. NOBA

I walked where in their talking graves. At the British War Cemetery, Bayeux. Charles Causley. NAEL-2; NoP-4; OBWP; OxBC; PoWW

I walked with a flower. Earth, Sky. Sydney Clouts. PeSA

I walked with you as far as the graineries beside the gates. Songs for a Three-String Guitar. Léopold Sédar Senghor, *French.* PBA, *tr. by* Miriam Koshland

I walked with you this eleventh in the coppice. November Poppies. Hilary Corke. NYBP

I walked you to the village where the granaries are at the threshold of Night. Léopold Sédar Senghor. NegPo, *tr. by* Ellen Conroy Kennedy *Fr.* Songs for Signare.

I wander aimless, to and fro. Aimless. Louis Palagyi, *Hungarian.* TrJP, *tr. by* Watson Kirkconnell

I wander all night in my vision. The Sleepers. Walt Whitman. APN-1; AmPP; NAAL-1; NAAL-3; PAR

I wander by the edge. He Hears the Cry of the Sedge. W. B. Yeats. OxBTC; RB

I wander more and more about the city. On Death. Aleksandr Blok, *Russian.* TCRP, *tr. by* Geoffrey Thurley

I wander through a crowd of women. At Piccadilly Circus. Vivian de Sola Pinto. OBMV

I wander through [*or* thro'] each chartered [*or* charter'd] street. London. William Blake. AWP; ClHu; FHYEP; FaBoPV; HAP; HeIP-6; InPK-6; InPS-3; NAEL-2; NAWM-2; NIP-4; NOBE; NOBRP; NOEC; OAEL-2; OBNC; OxAEP-2; PBMP; PoE; PoEL-4; Poetr; RB; SCGP; SCV; TFi; TRP; UnPo; WeW-3 *Fr.* Songs of Experience.

I wandered away from my early childhood, framed by her massive hair. Officials rob. Material's Daughter. Aaron Shurin. FTOS

I wandered forth at night alone. Lament over the Ruins of the Abbey of Teach Molaga. Unknown, *Irish.* NOIV, *tr. by* James Clarence Mangan

I wandered in a suburb of the north. James Thomson. NOBVV *Fr.* The City of Dreadful Night. OBNC

I wandered lonely as a Cloud. Daffodils. Wordsworth. APAD; BLPA; CABP; CTV; ChAP; ClHu; FaBoBe; GTBS-P; ImPo; InPK-6; InPS-3; LaPo; NAEL-2; NOBE; NOBRP; NoP-4; OAEL-2; OBEV; OBNC; PFE; PWR; PoPoPo; PoRA; Ro; SAGP; SCGP; SCV; SoSe-8; TFi; TTTS; UnPo

I wandered lonely as a cloud in Foyles. Upon Finding Dying: An Introduction, by L. E. Sissman, Remaindered at IS. Louis Edward Sissman. NoP-4

I wandered lonely as a dog. Adolescent. Joyce Peseroff. CMAP

I wandered lonely by the sea. The Goose-Girl. Edith Nesbit. VWP

I wandered out a while agone. Sonnet. George Wither. NOSC *Fr.* Fair Virtue, the Mistress of Philarete.

I wandered through the ancient wood. The Cataract Isle. Christopher Pearse Cranch. APN-1

I wandered to the surfy marge. Sea Knell. John Updike. OxBoS

I wandered up to Beaucourt; I took the river track. Beaucourt Revisited. Audrey Herbert. PoFWW

I wandering went / Among the haunts and dwellings of mankind. Shelley. *Fr.* Prometheus Unbound. NOBRP; OAEL-2

I wanna be the leader. The Leader. Roger McGough. OPOU

I want. (LL) For W.C.W ("The Rhyme is after"). Robert Creeley. FTOS; LCAP-2

I want a good lover. What Do You Want? John Newlove. NOBC

I want a hero: an uncommon want. Canto I. Byron. FHYEP *Fr.* Canto the First. NAEL-2; OAEL-2; PoE *Fr.* Don Juan.

I want / a love to hold. Defense Rests. Vassar Miller. MoAmPo

I Want-a-name-'ere La Guantanamera. Guillermo Cabrera Infante, *Spanish.* CBNP, *tr. by* Donald Gardner *and* Suzanne Jill Levine

I Want a Tenant; a Satire. John O'Keefe. NOEC

I want an egg for Easter. An Egg for Easter. Irene F. Pawsey. BoTP

I Want Aretha to Set This to Music. Sherley Anne Williams. NAAAL

I want free life and I want fresh air. Lasca. Frank Desprez. BLPA; FaBoBe

I want him to have another living summer. A 14-Year-Old Convalescent Cat in the Winter. Gavin Ewart. OPOU; OxBSP

I want me a home. Black Woman Throws a Tantrum. Nayo-Barbara Watkins. NBV

I want my funeral to include this detour. Detour. Michael Longley. CIP-2

I want no paradise only to be. The Kiwi Bird in the Kiwi Tree. Charles Bernstein. FTOS

I want nothing but your fire-side now. Hearthstone. Harold Monro. OBMV

I want something suited to my special needs. Needs. A. R. Ammons. NIP-4; OBAL; PFE

I want the sun snuffed out. In a Hurry. Xuân Diệu, *Vietnamese.* AVP, *tr. by* Huỳnh Sanh Thông

I want the world to stop and spin no more. Silk Threads of Memory. Chế Lan Viên, *Vietnamese.* AVP, *tr. by* Huỳnh Sanh Thông

I want these words / to stand. The Task. Subhash Mukhopadhyay, *Bengali.* OMIP, *tr. by* Pritish Nandy

I want things. On the Corner. Kit Robinson. FTOS

I want to be. The Last of the Fire Kings. Derek Mahon. FaBoPV; PNI

I want to be a white horse! Three Presidents. Robert Bly. LCAP-2

I want to be buried in an anonymous crater inside the moon. Unholy Missions. Bob Kaufman. TTY

I want to be in a garden with my love. Unknown, *Arabic.* BoWoP, *tr. by* Willis Barnstone

I want to be lifted, to meet the air. Wild and Blue. Laurie Duesing. DeD

I want to be / like that. Nikki Giovanni. *See* Poem for Flora.

"I want to be new," said the duckling. The New Duckling. Alfred Noyes. BoTP

I want to be with my love in a garden. Unknown, *Arabic.* BoWoP, *tr. by* Willis Barnstone

I Want to Be Your Daughter Now. Katie McBain. "I wonder why I can't remember." MDDM

I want to be your friend. The Yueh-Fu, *Chinese.* ITG, *tr. by* Arthur Waley

I want to check. After the Anti-Semitic Calls on a Local Talk Station. Lyn Lifshin. UnSA

I Want to Die While You Love Me. Georgia Douglas Johnson. BlSi; ISC; NAAAL; SAGP

("And nothing more to give.") (LL) OxWW

I want to drown in good-salt water. Miss Millay Says Something Too. Samuel Hoffenstein. BXAP; NBLV

I want to enter death. Desire. Claribel Alegría, *Spanish.* LoL, *tr. by* D. J. Flakoll

"I want to fight you," he said in a Belfast accent. Experience. James Simmons. BIrV

I want to forget my manners. Hope. Edith Södergran, *German.* PBWP, *tr. by* Jaakko A. Ahokas

I want to gather your darkness. To Drink. Jane Hirshfield. CrSp

I want to go aboard my ship, and sail and sail away. The Dream Ship. W. K. Holmes. BoTP

I want to go on. First Prelude. Francis J. Smith. CRP

I want to lament the princess who was killed. In Memory, 1978. Judith Kazantzis. BrRo

I want to learn to whistle. Whistles. Dorothy Aldis. CTV

I want to live in the shade of your face. Tinfoil. Joyce Mansour, *French.* MFP, *tr. by* Martin Sorrell

I want to live, live to distraction. Aleksandr Blok, *Russian.* TCRP, *tr. by* Jon Stallworthy *and* Peter France

I want to look at what happened. Ofay-Watcher Looks Back. Mongane Wally Serote. PBMAP

I want to love you very much. "Marnia." LW

I want to make you. Haiku. Sonia Sanchez. ISC

I want to mourn the stream. Words of Comfort. Đỗ Tấn Xuân, *Vietnamese.* AVP, *tr. by* Huỳnh Sanh Thông

I want to praise bodies. To Praise. Ellen Bass. CrSp

I want to remember the fallen palm. Oblivion. Ellis Ayitey Komey. PBA; PBMAP

I Want to Say Your Name. Léopold Sédar Senghor, *French.* TTTS, *tr. by* Kenneth Koch

I want to see it face to face. Nothing. Charles Simic. NNaP

I want to see the slim palm-trees. Heritage. Gwendolyn B. Bennett. BlSi; ColAP; NAAAL; PoBA

I want to travel the common road. The Common Road. Silas H. Perkins. BLPA; FaBoBe

I want to understand light years. Rosellen Brown. FFC

I want to understand the steep thing. Climbing You. Erica Jong. PoA

I want to wash my father's face. Last Acts. Sharon Olds. NIP-4

I want to write you. Love Poem. Linda Pastan. NIP-4

I want you when the shades of eve are falling. Arthur L. Gillom. BLPA; FaBoBe

I wanta say just gotta say something. Beautiful Black Men. Nikki Giovanni. BPo; NAAAL

I wanted . . . a guneaform, a woman's form. Diringer's *The Alphabet: A Key to the History of Mankind.* Stephanie Strickland. LoHo

I wanted a house. There Are No Such Trees in Alpine, California. John Haines. PaTW; WeT

I wanted a rib sandwich. Rib Sandwich. William J. Harris. UnSA

I wanted so ably. The World. Robert Creeley. MoP; NoP-4; PmAP; VCAP

I wanted the gold, and I sought it. The Spell of the Yukon. Robert W. Service. BLPA; FaBoBe

I wanted them over. Say Ja. Tom Mandel. PmAP

I wanted this morning to bring you a gift of roses. The Roses of Sa'adi. Marceline Desbordes-Valmore, *French.* BoWoP, *tr. by* Barbara Howes

I wanted to be a nature poet. "Honeysuckle Was the Saddest Odor of All, I Think." Thadious M. Davis. BlSi

I wanted to be sure to reach you. To the Harbormaster. Frank O'Hara. CRP; CoAP; NAAL-2; PoM; VCAP

I wanted to bring you this Jap iris. For C. Philip Whalen. NeAP; VGW

I wanted to die so I walked. Colorado Blvd. Lorna Dee Cervantes. NAmP90; PaTW

I wanted to go down to where the roots begin. Origins. Eric Ormsby. NoP-4

I wanted to harness and go. Baroness Mu Impeded in Her Wish to Help Famine Victims in Wei. Confucius. *Fr.* Yung Wind. CTC, *tr. by* Ezra Pound

I wanted to know my mother when she sat. Leroy. Imamu Amiri Baraka. BPo; PmAP; PoBA

I wanted to know what it was like before we. Waving Good-by. Gerald Stern. MoLi

I wanted to see you, / thighs showing. Leila Miccolis, *Portuguese.* BoWoP, *tr. by* Willis Barnstone *and* Nelson Cerqueira

I wanted to start *Ex Nihilo.* To an Idea. David Shapiro. PT

I wanted to start the story. We Are Going to Be Here Now. Primus St. John. GT

I wanted to take a walk. Walking Past Paul Blackburn's Apt. on 7th St. Diane Wakoski. TAP

I wanted to write. For Saundra. Nikki Giovanni. BPo; NAAAL; TTY

I wanted to write the lips of sleepers. Amir Gilbo'a, *Hebrew.* IP, *tr. by* Warren Bargad *and* Stanley F. Chyet

I wanted you here in the wards, where I am the doctor! (LL) Variations on a Theme by William Carlos Williams. Kenneth Koch. BXAP; KaS; NBLV; NIP-4; NoAM; NoP-4; PmAP; PoM; PoPoPo

I wanted you, nameless Woman of the South. Southern Cross. Hart Crane. *Fr.* Three Songs. NAAL-2 *Fr.* The Bridge. NAAL-2

"I warn ye all, ye gay ladies." Child Waters. *Unknown.* ESPB; OxBB

I was a bachelor, I lived by myself. The Weaver. *Unknown.* AS

I was a belfry and blizzard of birds. One Evening. Ljubomir Simovic, *Serbo-Croatian.* HSix, *tr. by* Charles Simic

I was a boy when I heard three red words a thousand Frenchmen. Threes. Carl Sandburg. CMoP; OxBA; PoLF

I was a boy when I left home. Homecoming. Hu Ch'c Ch'ang, *Chinese.* OHMPC, *tr. by* Kenneth Rexroth

I was a child and overwhelmed: Mozart. The Corner Knot. Robert Graves. NYBP

I was a child in a small midwestern town. On the Legends of a Dancer. Jean Garrigue. NMM-2

I was a child when first I read your books. To Elizabeth Barrett Browning. Bessie Rayner Parkes. VWP

I was a coffin, and I became a flower. Magdalene. Agnes Gergely, *Hungarian.* CEEP, *tr. by* Timea K. Szell

I was a cottage maiden. Cousin Kate. Christina Rossetti. VWP

I was a girl waiting by the roadside for my boyfriend to come. The Elwha River. Gary Snyder. NoAM

I was a god and self-enchanted. A Dream. May Swenson. NMM-2

I was a high-born gentleman. Gypsy Davy. *Unknown.* AS

I was a humble clerk. The African Trader's Complaint. Dennis C. Osadebay. PBA

I was a joke at dinners; aye, any would-be wit. Revenge to Come. Propertius. AWP, *tr. by* Kirby Flower Smith *Fr.* Elegies. AWP

I was a lady of high renown. Jamie Douglas. *Unknown.* ESPB; OxBB

I was a leather skinned harridan. Granny Crack. James Reaney. NOBC

I was a mere boy in a stone-cutter's shop. Abraham. Delmore Schwartz. ChIV-1

I was a peasant girl from Germany. Elsa Wertman. Edgar Lee Masters. MoP; NoAM; OxBA *Fr.* Spoon River Anthology.

I was a peasant of the Polish plain. Five Souls. W. N. Ewer. NSI

I was a quick-footed, long-eared hare, just snatched from my mother's. Meleager. HePo, *tr. by* Barbara Hughes Fowler *Fr.* I'll Twine White Violets. NIP-4, *tr. by* Goldwin Smith

I was a rebel, if you please. An Address by an Ex-Confederate Soldier to the Grand Army of the Republic. Maurice Thompson. CBCWP

I was a shepherd to fools. Convoy Escort. Rudyard Kipling. *Fr.* Epitaphs of the War [1914–1918]. OBWP

"I Was a Stranger and Ye Took Me In." Mary E. Tucker. CBWP-1

I was a virgin till I was 23. Then I always had more than one lover. Of Flesh and Spirit. Wang Ping. BAP-93

I was a youth of studious mind. Scientific Wooing. Constance Naden. VWP

I was all night at this. Putting On My Shoes I Hear the Floor Cry Out beneath Me. Michael Heffernan. BXAP

I was alone on a sunny shore. Forest Lake. Edith Södergran, *German.* WPoS, *tr. by* Stina Katchadourian

I was alone once, waiting. For the Marsh's Birthday. James Wright. NYBP

I was altered in the placenta. The Dead Poet. Alfred Wellington Purdy. NOBC

I was always called in early for dinner. Don't Forget. Stephen Berg. PoA

I was always fascinated. Mother, May I? Alma Villanueva. WPOW

I was an Arab. A Fantasy. Mathilde Blind. VWP

I was angry with my cow. The Cry of the Child. William Zaranka. BXAP

I was angry with my friend. A Poison Tree. William Blake. APAD; AWP; FHYEP; HAP; HoPM; ImPo; NAEL-2; NTP; NoP-4; OxAEP-2; PFE; PoEL-4; RB; Ro; SCV; SoSe-8; TFi; WeW-3 *Fr.* Songs of Experience.

I was asking for something specific and perfect for my city. Mannahatta. Walt Whitman. MoAmPo

I was asleep but my heart stayed awake. Song. Bible, *O.T.* WPoS

I was barely in my country. December, hot. Surrounding Blues on the Way Down. Bruce Weigl. CDa

I Was Before I Was, who now. Dan Pagis, *Hebrew.* IP, *tr. by* Warren Bargad *and* Stanley F. Chyet

I was born almost ten thousand years ago. *Unknown.* OBCoV

I Was Born at a Place of Pines. Geoffrey Lehmann. *Fr.* Ross's Poems. CBAP

I was born at birth of blossoms. Rosalía de Castro, *Galician.* STV, *tr. by* John Frederick Nims

I was born in a bad slum. Plot Improbable, Character Unsympathetic. Elder Olson. PFE

I was born in a time of peace. Ts'ai Yen. BoWoP; PBWP; WPOW *Fr.* Eighteen Verses Sung to a Tatar Reed Whistle.

I was born in Belfast between the mountain and the gantries. Carrickfergus. Louis MacNeice. NAEL-2; NOIV; NoAM; PNI

I was born in Boston, a city you all know well. The Boston Burglar. *Unknown.* AmFP

I was born in Bristol, and it is possible. Family Fortunes. Charles Hubert Sisson. OxBC

I was born in Mississippi;. A Poem for Myself (Or Blues for a Mississippi Black Boy). Etheridge Knight. AF; BkSV; PoPoPo

I was born in the city. Greener Grass. Frank Steele. Poetsp

I was born in the Congo. Ego Tripping [(There May Be a Reason Why)]. Nikki Giovanni. CrSp; GT; ISC; MoP; Poetsp; RaBo

I was born on a street named Joy. Lines on His Birthday. John Logan. CAPP-1

I was born on Double Creek, on a forty-acre hill. On Double Creek. James Still. MT

I was born the year of the gray pennies. 1943. Sandra McPherson. FaBoWP

I was born the year of the loon. Chronicle. Mei-Mei Berssenbrugge. OpBo

I was born under a crooked star. His Story. Sandra Cisneros. MoLi

I was born under the mudbank. Seeing You. Jean Valentine. PuP-16

I was born unto this snowy-red earth. The Song Taught to Joseph. Ray A. Young Bear. AF

I was born upon thy bank, river. Henry David Thoreau. PoEL-4

I was born with a song in my tongue. Ars. Marina Tsvetayeva, *Russian.* BoWoP, *tr. by* Willis Barnstone *and* Edward Brown

I was broke and out of a job in the city of London. Paddy, Get Back. *Unknown.* AmFP

I was brought up in Sheffield, all of a high degree. The Sheffield 'Prentice. *Unknown.* AmFP

I was brought up on old Aristotle. Limerick. C. S. Cook. PeLi

I was buried near this dyke [*or* Dike]. An Epitaph. William Blake. FaBoEE; OBCoV

I was burning incense, paying respects to my mother. The Night of the First Full Moon. Li K'ai-hsien, *Chinese.* CoBLCP, *tr. by* Jonathan Chaves

"I was but [*or* bat] seven year auld [*or* alld]." The Laily Worm and the Machrel of the Sea. *Unknown.* ESPB; OxBB; PoEL-1; SCGP

I was but what you'd brush. Seven Strophes. Joseph Brodsky, *Russian.* EP, *tr. by* Paul Graves

I was combing some long hair coming out of a tree. In the Forest. Russell Edson. LCAP-2

I was coming to that. (LL) Welsh Incident. Robert Graves. CBNP; CMoP; EBEvV; NOBE; OBSP; OxBTC

I was counting time in the heartbeat of the storm. Hero and Thief. Kofi Anyidoho. PBMAP

I Was Dancing Alone in Binh Dinh Province. D. F. Brown. CDa

I was dead and I wanted peace. A Grammar. Andrei Codrescu. SPE

I / was descending the mountain. Capriccio 9. Lyubomir Levchev, *Bulgarian.* CEEP, *tr. by* Jascha Kessler *and* Aleksandar Shurbanov

I was eighteen when I came in these gates. Words from Hell. David Helwig. NOBC

I Was Fair Beat. Robert Garioch. OBCoV; OxBTC

I was far forward on the plain, the burning swamp. The Little Girl with Bands on Her Teeth. Genevieve Taggard. VGW

I was fishing in the abandoned reservoir. Quinnapoxet. Stanley Kunitz. AFr; LoL

I was 5 years old. New York City—1935. Gregory Corso. Poetsp

I was flying over sydney. Flying. Michael Dransfield. BMAP

I was foretold that on a certain day. Sonnet XX. Louise Labé, *French.* PBWP, tr. by Joan Keefe and Richard Terdiman.; BoWoP, tr. by Willis Barnstone

I was foretold, your rebel[l] sex. A Deposition from Love. Thomas Carew. BeJo; CaPo; CavPo; MeLP

I was four in this photograph fishing. Fifth Grade Autobiography. Rita Dove. ISC; NIP-4

I was fourteen and it was my birthday party in Haiti. When they. The Mother. Gregory Orr. WeT

I was friends with all the solitudes. Bits of Silk. Ion Caraion, *Romanian.* CEEP, tr. by Marguerite Dorian and Elliott B. Urdang

I was going along a dusty highroad. Mountain Talk. A. R. Ammons. HCAP

I was going thru the big earth. A Song about a Dead Person—or Was It a Mole? *Unknown, Seneca Indian.* STP, tr. by Jerome Rothenberg and Richard Johnny John

I was going thru the big smoke. Another Song about That Same Dead Person or Mole—Whichever it Was. *Unknown, Seneca Indian.* STP, tr. by Jerome Rothenberg and Richard Johnny John

I was going to say something. Ancestor. Thomas Kinsella. BIrV; NOIV; PBCIP; PoE

I was going to the City to sell the herbs I had plucked. Hermit and Politician. Po Chü-i, *Chinese.* ChiP, tr. by Arthur Waley

I was going to the river for water. Mirabai, *Indian.* WPoS, tr. by Jane Hirshfield

I was going up to say something. Thomas Kinsella. *See* Ancestor.

I was Hermocrateia: twenty-nine / children I bore. Antipater of Thessalonica, *Greek.* GrAn, tr. by Alistair Elliot

I was, I am not; smiled, that since did weep. An Epitaph. Thomas Heywood. OxBSP

I was ill, lying on my bed of old papers. The Secret Garden. Rita Dove. NoAM

I was in a printing house in Hell & I saw the method in. A Memorable Fancy. William Blake. *Fr.* The Marriage of Heaven and Hell. NAEL-2; NOBRP; OAEL-2

I was in prison in that town. Sebastopol. Ilya L'vovich Selvinsky, *Russian.* TCRP, tr. by Daniel Weissbort

I was in the bookstore, reading the ends of mysteries. Three Songs. Rachel Wetzsteon. RA

I was in the lane and saw the car pass. A and B. Charles Hubert Sisson. OxBC

I was invested in mother-earth, the crypt of roots. Geoffrey Hill. NoAM *Fr.* Mercian Hymns.

I was jus. Bob O'Meally. MBE

I was just beginning to feel in the mood. An Old Husband Suspects Adultery. Gavin Ewart. NoAM

I was Kallimachos, age five. Lucianus, *Greek.* GrAn, tr. by Peter Jay

I was kissed once. The Kiss. Alice Walker. GT

I was kneeling with my daughter into a chaos. Jungle Gliders. Roger Weingarten. NAmP90

I was led into captivity by the bitch business. Money. Charles Hubert Sisson. APAD; OxBSP

I was looking for the powerful spring grass, how powerful. Sixty-Six Poems for a Blackfoot Bundle. *Unknown, Blackfoot Indian.* STP, tr. by Jerome Rothenberg

I Was Looking for the University. Clarence Major. GT

I Was Made Erect and Lone. Henry David Thoreau. PoEL-4

I was making my way home late one night. Aisling. Paul Muldoon. PNI

I was mindless. The Potter's Wheel. Calvin Forbes. GT

I was miserable, of course, for I was seventeen. Mingus at the Showplace. William Matthews. SeSe

I was myself blown. For My People. Wendy Rose. CDW

I was never an ascetic. "Naum Korzhavin," *Russian.* TCRP, tr. by Albert C. Todd

I was never the light lad. The Spawn of Slums. James W. Thompson. BPo

I was never the one to spot him walking. Blueberry Man. David Bergman. GLP

I was not born to Helicon, nor dare. A Gratulatory to Mr. Ben Johnson for His Adopting of Him to Be His Son. Thomas Randolph. BeJo

I was not chosen to head the dragon list. Tune: "Overtures"—On Myself. Ch'iao Chi, *Chinese.* SuSp, tr. by Sherwin S. S. Fu

I was not in safety, neither had I rest, neither was I quiet; yet trouble came. (LL) Let the Day Perish [Wherein I Was Born]. Bible, *O.T.* AWP; OBVE; TrJP

I was not; now I am—a few days hence. The Mystery. Paul Laurence Dunbar. APN-2

I was not sorrowful, I could not weep. Spleen. Ernest Christopher Dowson. ADE; APAD; MoBrPo; NOBVV

I Was Not There. Karen Gershon. HP

I was not useful? So. Fidelity Rewarded. Dora Greenwell. VWP

I was not—was born—was. Inscribed on a Statue of Hermes. *Unknown, Greek.* GrAn, tr. by Peter Jay

I was of delicate mind. I stepped aside for my needs. The Refined Man. Rudyard Kipling. FaBoEE; FaBoTw; PeFWW *Fr.* Epitaphs of the War [1914–1918]. OBWP

I Was on a Golf Course the Day John Cage Died of a Stroke. Stephen Paul Miller. BAP-94

I was on a white coast once. Canticle. David Shapiro. TTTS

I was on my high / horse then. The Thorn Merchant's Mistress. Yusef Komunyakaa. RACG

I was out in my kayak. Spring Fiord. *Unknown, Eskimo.* STP, tr. by Armand Schwerner

I was out in the country one beautiful night. The Widow's Old Broom. *Unknown.* AmFP

I was out in the early evening, taking a walk in the fields to think about this. Strange Fruit. Joy Harjo. SeSe

I was parading the Côte d'Azur. My Father's Geography. Michael S. Weaver. GT; PBCAP

I was passing through the village of mottled bamboo. Woman Tung. Wu Chia-chi, *Chinese.* CoBLCP, tr. by Jonathan Chaves

I was passionate. Lal Ded, *Kashmiri.* WPoS, tr. by Jane Hirshfield

I was playing golf the day. The Englishman's Home. Harry Graham. CBNP; PeLV *Fr.* Some Ruthless Rhymes.

I was playing, I suppose. When It Happened. Hilda Schiff. HP

I was promised a horse but what I got instead. Palladas, *Greek.* GrAn, tr. by Tony Harrison

I was pulling veronica out of the lawn when this hornet came. A. R. Ammons. NoAM *Fr.* Sphere.

I was raised up in Louisville, a town you all knew well. Frank James, the Roving Gambler. *Unknown.* AmFP

I was reading about rationalism. The Bat. Jane Kenyon. CrSp; LoL

I Was Received in an Early Audience at Heaven-Gate and Then at Noon I Was Summoned to the Yu-shun Gate. In the Evening I Withdrew, and Improvised This Poem. Yang Shih-ch'i, *Chinese.* CoBLCP, tr. by Jonathan Chaves

I was returning from a friend's one night. A Close Encounter. Adrian Rumble. SpW

I was run over by the truth one day. To Whom It May Concern. Adrian Mitchell. OBWP

I was scared to walk out / with the dough. (LL) Situation. Langston Hughes. APSN; OBAL

I was securing the pin in the diaper. A Visit. George Ella Lyon. CrSp

I was sent forth from the power. Andal. PFTM, tr. by George W. MacRae *Fr.* The Tiruppavai.

I was sent forth from the power. *Unknown.* PFTM, tr. by George W. MacRae *Fr.* The Thunder: Perfect Mind.

I was sent in to see her. Tear. Thomas Kinsella. NOIV; NoP-4

I was setting out from my house. The Dragonfly-Mother. Denise Levertov. InPS-3

I was seventy-seven, come August. The Little Old Lady in Lavender Silk. Dorothy Parker. NBLV

I was shitting 'cause the theatre lady. Kala: Saturday Night at the Pahala Theatre. Lois-Ann Yamanaka. PUP-18

I was shocked out of my dream! Impressions of Shanghai. Kuo Mo-jo, *Chinese.* ChiPo, tr. by Kai-yu Hsu

I was sick. Jesus Was Crucified or: It Must Be Deep. Carolyn M. Rodgers. BlSi; PoBA

I Was Sick and in Prison. Jones Very. ColAP; NOBA

I was sitting behind a somewhat neat old person. Concert. Josephine Miles. NALW

I was sitting in her living room. Self-Portrait. Lloyd Schwartz. WeT

I was sitting in mcsoreley's. outside it was New York and beauti- / fully snowing. E. E. Cummings. NoAM

I was sitting in my study. Papa's Letter. *Unknown.* WeW-3

I was sitting on the roof with my grandmother. Coming of Age. Michael Palma. UnSA

I was sitting there, taking my ease. Limerick. Cyril Ray. PeLi

I was sixteen years of age. Song Ballet. *Unknown.* AmFP

I was sleeping. A Translation From. Fred Levinson. AmPA

I Was Sleeping Where the Black Oaks Move. Louise Erdrich. HATNAP; NoP-4; PoPoPo

I was sleepless, I was awake all night. Sleepless. Al-Khansa, *Arabic.* BoWoP, tr. by Willis Barnstone

I was so chill, and overworn, and sad. Song. Anna Wickham. MoBrPo

I was so sick last night I. Morning After. Langston Hughes. MoP; NAAL-2; NBLV; NoAM; OBCoV

I was standing in a crap game doing no harm, Baby! You've Been a Good Old Wagon, but You've Done Broke Down. Ben Harney. OBAL

I was standing there. The Oral Tradition. Eavan Boland. NBrP; PBCIP

I was sure I would never get lost / in the tangled roads of love. Kenrei Mon-in Ukyo no Daibu, *Japanese*. WPJ, tr. by Kenneth Rexroth *and* Ikuko Atsumi

I Was Surprised to Find Myself Out Here & Acting like a Crow. *Unknown, Seneca Indian*. STP, tr. by Jerome Rothenberg *and* Johnny John

I was takin' off my bonnet. Darwinism in the Kitchen. *Unknown*. NBLV

I was talking / to a friend. Eagle in the Land of Oz. Don Receveur. CDa

I was that lonely. (LL) The Geranium. Theodore Roethke. CoAP; UnPo; WeW-3

I was the chief of the race—he had stricken my father dead. The Voyage of Maeldune. Tennyson. PoEL-5

I was the first fruits of the battle of Missionary Ridge. Knowlt Hoheimer. Edgar Lee Masters. OxBA *Fr.* Spoon River Anthology.

I was the last passenger of the day. The Bus. Leonard Cohen. HeIP-4

I was the Moor Moraima. A Lovely Young Moor. *Unknown*. BoWoP, tr. by Willis Barnstone

I was the one who found you who brought. Devils Clowns and Women. Rochelle Owens. DeD

I was the only child of Frances Harris of Virginia. Hamilton Greene. Edgar Lee Masters. MoP; NoAM; OxBA *Fr.* Spoon River Anthology.

I was the only girl under the stairs. The Big House. Paul Muldoon. NoAM

I was the patriarch of the shining land. John Sutter. Yvor Winters. MoAmPo; MoP; NOBA; NoAM; PaTW

I was the poetry editor. Poetry Editor. Yevgeny Mikhailovich Vinokurov, *Russian*. TCRP, tr. by Daniel Weissbort

I was the staunchest of our fleet. The Derelict. Rudyard Kipling. NoAM

I was there. A Yearning. Arapera Hineira Blank, *Maori*. PoNZ, tr. by the author

I was there and I remember the brown brocade. In Memory of V. R. Lang. Mac Hammond. PoA

I was thinking about her all the way from Troy. Fortunes of War. Kit Wright. PeLV

I was thinking, Mother, of that poor old horse. Reserved. Walter De la Mare. GTBS-P

I was thirsty. Epigram. Meleager, *Greek*. GrAn, tr. by Peter Whigham

I was thrashing on the couch. That Great Wingless Bird. Adrian C. Louis. UnSA

I was three-ish. The Right Arm. Paul Muldoon. NoAM

I was thrilled when I went to the Zoo. Limerick. Victor Gray. PeLi

I was thy Neighbo[u]r once, thou rugged Pile! Elegiac Stanzas Suggested by a Picture of Peele Castle, in a Storm [Painted by Sir George Beaumont]. Wordsworth. GS; GTBS-P; NAEL-2; NOBRP; NoP-4; OAEL-2; OBNC; PoE; Ro

I was tired of being a woman. Consorting with Angels. Anne Sexton. NALW; NMM-2

I was tired. So I lay down. Mnemonic. Li-Young Lee. UnSA

I was tired / When we found the place. By the River. Anna McMullen. LBC

I was too late for the most important. A Longing for Jail. Edvard Kocbek, *Slovene*. PoSu, tr. by Michael Scammell *and* Veno Taufer

I was upon the high and blessed mound. Sonnet: Of the Grave of Selvaggia, on the Monte della Sambuca. Cino da Pistoia, *Italian*. AWP, tr. by D. G. Rossetti

I was walking a mile. Tennyson. EBVV *Fr.* Maud [A Monodrama]. EnVR

I was walking along the Sea of Galilee. "Dovid Knut," *Russian*. TCRP, tr. by John Glad

I was walking down by the old / Santee. Second Carolina Said-Song. A. R. Ammons. OBAL

I was walking downtown. The Man in Black. Mark Strand. SPE

I was walking in a government warehouse. Fifteen Million Plastic Bags. Adrian Mitchell. OBSV; OxBTC

I was walking near the hotel in the evening. Southern Dawn. Pier Paolo Pasolini, *Italian*. VCWP, tr. by Norman MacAfee *and* Luciano Martinengo

I Was Washing Outside in the Darkness. Osip Emilevich Mandelstam, *Russian*. AF; FaBoPV, tr. by W. S. Merwin *and* Clarence Brown

I was welcomed here—clear gold. Settling. Denise Levertov. PaTW

I was wrong, quite wrong! Soliloquy 2. Richard Aldington. PoFWW

I wash off. (LL) For My Lover, Returning to His Wife. Anne Sexton. CBLP; HCAP; Poetr; SAGP; UnPo; WPE

I Wash the Shirt. Anna Swirszczynska, *Polish*. BLT, tr. by Czeslaw Milosz *and* Leonard Nathan

I washed a load of clothes. Alone for a Week. Dolores Kendrick. FFC

I wasn't there / when you died. To My Grandmother, Lady-Woman. Marina Ama Omowale Maxwell. HCP

I wasn't there when your body, signaling, woke you. Grandmother. Marilyn Krysl. CrSp

I wasn't with you when death came. When Death Came. Adam Zagajewski, *Polish*. VCWP, tr. by Renata Gorcyznski, Benjamin Ivry, *and* C. K. Williams

I Waste Away. Bible, *O.T.* TrJP *Fr.* Isaiah.

I waste my teeming age. I do not know. Abishag. Jacob Fichman, *Hebrew*. TrJP, tr. by Robert Friend

I wat was mony a weeping e'e. (LL) Jamie Telfer of [*or* in] the Fair Dodhead. *Unknown*. ESPB; IBB; OxBB

I watch a man in the schoolyard. Speech Against Stone. Charles Martin. RA

I watch a streak of red that might have issued from Christ's breast. (LL) Soldiers Bathing. Frank Templeton Prince. GTBS-P; ImPo; LiTM; MoBrPo; NOCV; OBWP; OxBTC; PeSA

I watch, and long have watched, with calm regret. Wordsworth. Son

I watch her in the corner there. Arachne. Rose Terry Cooke. APN-2; APo

I watch me until I disappear and we. Analogue. Marie Ponsot. CLPP

I watch the arch of her head. Caput Tuum Ut Carmelus. "Michael Field." CPO

I watch the Beast as it licks itself. War. André Breton, *French*. AF, tr. by Mary Ann Caws *and* Jean-Pierre Cauvin

I watch the happier people of the house. Neurasthenia. Agnes Mary Frances Robinson. NOBVV

I watch the Indians dancing to help the young corn at Taos [pueblo. The old men squat in a ring]. New Mexican Mountain. Robinson Jeffers. InPS-3; MoP; NoAM; SAGP

I watch you. Watching You. Simon J. Ortiz. HATNAP

I watched a laughing cloud. Evening. King D. Kuka. VoR

I watched a rosebud very long. Symbols. Christina Rossetti. NALW

I watched him breathe. (LL) The Race. Sharon Olds. MoLi; RaBo

I watched little black boys. Nayo-Barbara Watkins. NBV

I watched old squatting chimpanzee: he traced. Sporting Acquaintances. Siegfried Sassoon. OxBTC

I watched the hills drink the last color of light. Thought's End. Léonie Adams. MoAmPo

I watched the Moon around the House. Emily Dickinson. APN-2; NCAP

I watched the seeds come down this afternoon. At a Country Hotel. Howard Nemerov. PoRA

I watched the woman in the room. Between Love and Death. Frank Stanford. MT

I watched thee when the foe was at our side. Love and Death. Byron. EBEV; NOBE

I watched them float up the dark chimney. (LL) Sorrow. D. H. Lawrence. CMoP; GTBS-P; OBMV

I watched them once, at dusk, on television, run. Salmon. Jorie Graham. NAmP90

I watched them tearing a building down. Which Are You? *Unknown*. PoLF

I watcht as the flung screen door. The Envies. George Bowering. NOBC

I watered my horse at the Long Wall caves. Song. Susan Ch'en Lin, *Chinese*. CoBCP, tr. by Burton Watson

I wear a cloak of laughter. Cloak of Laughter. Abigail Cresson. PoToHe

I wear a cobra's black bonnet. Godiva. David Chapman Berry. BXAP

I wear an easy garment. Free Labor. Frances Ellen Watkins Harper. PAR

I weary of the heat of hell. Satiety. Theodore Wratislaw. ADE

I weary of these noisy nights. Away. Max Ehrmann. PoToHe

I weave the night, I cross the weft with stars. In the Flight of the Blue Heron: To Montezuma. Anita Endrezze-Danielson. CDW

I weep and weep a tear. The Tear. Martin Sorescu, *Romanian*. VCWP, tr. by Heaney, Seamus and Joana Russell-Gebbett

I weep, but with no bitterness I weep. Souvenir. Alfred de Musset, *French*. AWP, tr. by George Santayana

I weep for Adonais—he is dead! Adonais; An Elegy on the Death of Keats. Shelley. EBEV; FHYEP; HoPM; ImPo; NOBRP; NoP-4; OAEL-2; OxAEP-2; PoEL-4; Ro; TFi

I weep for Adonis, "The lovely Adonis is dead." Bion. *See* Lament for Adonis.

I weep like a child for / the past. D. H. Lawrence. *See* Piano.

I weigh 486 lbs on Jupiter. A Letter to Ron Silliman on the Back of a Map of the Solar System. Dennis Schmitz. LCAP-2

I welcome the anonymity of the middle years. Bruce Beaver. *Fr.* Letters to Live Poets. CBAP

I welcome you, silvery moon. The Early Graves. Friedrich Gottlieb Klopstock, *German*. GePo, tr. by J. W. Thomas

I welcomed the Spring in romantic Chungking. Lyric to Spring. Joseph W. Stilwell. OBAL

I well remember how some threescore years. Very Old Man. James Henry. NOBVV

I Wende to Dede. *Unknown.* HAP; MiEL

I went a roaming, maidens, one bright day. Angelo Poliziano. *Fr.* Three Ballate. AWP, *tr. by* John Addington Symonds

I went a-sailing with my dear. A Tull of the See. Elizabeth T. Corbett. OBCA

I went all around the world to find food. Hā′ mats′a Song of the Lau′ itsîs. *Unknown. Fr.* Dances and Songs of the Winter Ceremonial. APN-2, *tr. by* Franz Boas

I went back in the alley. Homecoming. Langston Hughes. SAmP; TRP

I went by footpath and by stile. Paying Calls. Thomas Hardy. FP

I went by on tiptoe. My Grandfather's Death. Vicente Aleixandre, *Spanish.* IMW, *tr. by* Stephen Kessler

I went by this building. Red Flower. Ann Turner. SSCS

I went down by Cascadilla. Cascadilla Falls. A. R. Ammons. NOBA

I went down the tree-lined street of false gods. The Marvels of the City. Charles Simic. LCAP-2

I went down to Jordan. Singing Hallelujia. Fenton Johnson. NAAAL

I went down to malcolmland. Half Black, Half Blacker. Sterling Plumpp. PoBA

I went down to my garden patch. *Unknown.* TLR

I went down to Saint James this morning. St. James Infirmary. *Unknown.* AmFP

I Went Down to the Depot. *Unknown.* AS

I went down to the railway. Willow Song. Anne Stevenson. NoP-4

I went down to the river. Life Is Fine. Langston Hughes. NBLV; SAmP

I went down to the underworld with the chief of the ghosts. Therefore I have supernatural power. Song of the Ghost Dancer. *Unknown. Fr.* Dances and Songs of the Winter Ceremonial. APN-2, *tr. by* Franz Boas

I went downtown. *Unknown.* TLR

I went for a walk over the dunes again this morning. Corsons Inlet. A. R. Ammons. CoAP; ColAP; MoP; NAAL-2; NOBA; NoAM; NoP-4; PoE; VCAP

I went into a public-'ouse to get a pint o' beer. Tommy. Rudyard Kipling. CABP; EBEV; FaPoR; MoBrPo; NoP-4; OBWP; OxAEP-2; OxBTC; PeVV; UV

I went into my garden to gather some herbs. Ditty. Sister Bertken, *Dutch.* WPOW, *tr. by* Jonathan Crewe

I went into my grandmother's garden / And there I found a farden. Swinging. *Unknown.* OxNR

I went into my grandmother's garden, / And there I found a farthing. A Farthing. *Unknown.* OxNR

I went into my mother as. To the Unborn and Waiting Children. Lucille Clifton. InPK-6

I went into the barber's and said, quite calmly. They Don't Understand a Thing. Vladimir Mayakovsky, *Russian.* TCRP, *tr. by* Bernard Meares

I went into the Maverick Bar. Gary Snyder. HCAP; NAAL-2; PoE; VCAP ("'What is to be done'.") (LL) LoL; PaTW

I went into the wood one day. Fairy Story. Stevie Smith. NOxBChV; OBSP

I went last night to a turkey feast Oh, God, don't fail your children / now! The Spiritual for Nine Voices. Kay Boyle. NMM-2

I went my Sunday mornings round. Song. John Clare. NOBVV

I went on Friday afternoons. Au Tombeau de Mon Père. Ronald McCuaig. NOBAu

I went out at daybreak and stood on Primrose Hill. Birds Waking. W. S. Merwin. NOBA

I WENT out at the eastern gate. The Eastern Gate. *Unknown, Chinese.* ChiP, *tr. by* Arthur Waley

I went out in the Spring. Tsurayuki, *Japanese.* OHMPJ, *tr. by* Kenneth Rexroth

I Went Out into the Garden. Moses ibn Ezra, *Hebrew.* TrJP, *tr. by* Solomon Solis-Cohen

I went out of the conf'rence to get a pint of beer. Mary Wilson. UV *Fr.* Harold Wilson's Selected Poems.

I went out on a frosty morning. Ice Cold. Sean O Riordain, *Irish.* NOIV, *tr. by* Thomas Kinsella

I went out on a week end. Quiet had come back—. Lost in the Centuries. William Stafford. EC2

I went out seeking love. More Stanzas Applied to Spiritual Things. Saint John of the Cross, *Spanish.* TOF, *tr. by* K. Kavanaugh *and* O. Rodrigues

I went out to a festival. I'd Rather See than Be One, But. Anne Halley. NMM-2

I went out to the hazel wood. The Song Of Wandering Aengus. W. B. Yeats. ADE; APAD; CH; CMoP; ChAP; FaBoCh; MoBrPo; NTP; OTCP; PBMP; PoEL-5; PoRA; RaBo; SAGP; TFi; TTTS

I went out to the winter sea. The Winter Sea. Namjo Kim, *Korean.* CKP, *tr. by* Jaihiun Kim

I went out walking. On Mother's Day. Grace Paley. NMM-2

"I went to a mausoleum today, and found." Lineage. Frank Bidart. *Fr.* Elegy. HCAP

I went to a party, The Rose on My Cake. Karla Kuskin. TLR

I went to bat for the Lady Chatte. A Lass in Wonderland. Francis Reginald. MoCV

I went to ch'ch, 'tother night. Sister Johnson's Speech. Maggie Pogue Johnson. CBWP-4

I Went to Death. I Wende to Dede. *Unknown.* HAP; MiEL

I went to Frankfort, and got drunk. Epigram on an Academic Visit to the Continent. Richard Porson. FaBoEE; OxBoLi; PeLV

I Went to Gold Mountain to Visit a Ch'an Master But He Was Not at Home. Mo Shih-lung, *Chinese.* CoBLCP, *tr. by* Jonathan Chaves

I went to her who loveth me no more. Song. Arthur William Edgar O'Shaughnessy. OBNC

I went to London both blithe and gay. The Highwayman. *Unknown.* ECEV

I went to ma daddy. Hard Daddy. Langston Hughes. MoLi; NAAAL

I went to market and bought me a cat. An Old Rhyme. *Unknown.* BoTP

I went to Noke. *Unknown.* OxNR

I went to play with Billy. He. What Johnny Told Me. John Ciardi. TLR

I went to river last night. Voz de la Gente. Jimmy Santiago Baca. PmAP

I went to school today. Mummy and Donor and Deirdre. Jackie Kay. CPO

I went to see. Main Character. Jimmy Santiago Baca. NAmP90

I went to see Irving Babbitt. Richard Eberhart. OBAL

I went to the animal fair. Animal Fair. *Unknown.* AS; BLPA; FaBoBe; NTCP

I went to the dances at Chandlerville. Lucinda Matlock. Edgar Lee Masters. CMoP; HAP; LiTM; MoAmPo; MoP; NOBA; NoAM; OxBA; PBMP *Fr.* Spoon River Anthology.

I went to the fields with the leisure I got. The Frightened Ploughman. John Clare. EnVR; PoEL-4

I went to the Garden of Love. The Garden of Love. William Blake. APAD; AWP; EnLoPo; FHYEP; GBL; GLoP; GaP; HAP; NAEL-2; NoP-4; OBGa; OxAEP-2; PoE; PoPoPo; RB; Ro; SCGP; TFi; TRP *Fr.* Songs of Experience.

I went to the Hotel Broog. A Difference of Zoos. Gregory Corso. VGW

I went to the river: couldn't get across. Keep It Clean. Charlie Jordan. CBNP

I went to the toad that lies under the wall. *Unknown.* OxNR

I went to the wood and got it. A Thorn. *Unknown.* ReMoGo

I went to the wood of flowers. The Wood of Flowers. James Stephens. BoTP

I went to turn the grass once after one. The Tuft of Flowers. Robert Frost. AWP; MoAmPo; NAAL-2; OxBA

I went under cover of night. Nicodemus. Howard Nemerov. GI

I went up one pair of stairs / Just like me. Just Like Me. *Unknown.* BoTP; ReMoGo

I went uptown last Saturday night. Blue Monday. *Unknown.* AmFP

I went with the Duchess to tea. Limerick. Woodrow Wilson. PeLi

I Wept as I Lay Dreaming. Heinrich Heine, *German.* AWP, *tr. by* John Todhunter

I were unkind unless that I did shed. Lines on His Companions Who Died in the Northern Seas. Thomas James. NOSC

I what I always imagined. The Face. Susan Mitchell. NAmP90

I whisk the litter from my mother's tomb. Sweeping. Leslie Monsour. FFC

I whispered, "I am too young." Brown Penny. W. B. Yeats. BoLoP; CBLP; CMoP; FaBoCh; GLoP; IIP; LiLi

I who am dead a thousand years / And wrote this crabbed post-classic screed. To a Poet a Thousand Years Hence. John Heath-Stubbs. OxBC

I who am dead a thousand years / And wrote this sweet archaic song. To a Poet a Thousand Years Hence. James Elroy Flecker. MoBrPo; PoRA

I who am nothing, and this tissue. Hoc Est Corpus. Alex Comfort. LiTM

I who by day am function of the light. Epigram. James Vincent Cunningham. VGW

I, who could have been the best of poems. Nikolai Stepanovich Gumilyov, *Russian.* TCRP, *tr. by* Simon Franklin

I, who cut off my sorrows. Akazome Emon, *Japanese.* BoWoP; WPJ; WPOW, *tr. by* Kenneth Rexroth *and* Ikuko Atsumi

I who employ a poet's tongue. Timid Lover. Countee Cullen. ColAP

I, who have been so many angels. The Photo That Watches. Carlota Caulfield, *Spanish.* LoHo, *tr. by* Carol Maier

I who have not sown. I May Reap. Patrick Kavanagh. TIRV

I, who used to score five, even nine times. Philodemus, *Greek.* GrAn, *tr. by* William Moebius

I, who used to ward off the starlings and that snatcher. Antipater of Sidon. HePo, *tr. by* Barbara Hughes Fowler *Fr.* Epigrams.

I who wait for myself. A Poetry Calendar. Chimako Tada, *Japanese.* VCWP, tr. by Naoshi Koriyama *and* Edward Lueders

I who wanted to talk. Me Again. Jacqueline Dash. BAP-96

I whole in body and in minde. Isabella Whitney. BWW *Fr.* The Manner of Her Will and What She Left to London and to All Those in It, at Her Departing. NoSic

I whom you touched am other things beside. Atropos. Hilaire Kirkland. *Fr.* Clotho, Lachesis, Atropos. PeNZ

I widow / redo my life. Homecoming. Mitsuye Yamada. NMM-2

I will accept thy will to do and be. A Bruised Reed Shall He Not Break. Christina Rossetti. OxAEP-2

I will admit freely that it hurt. Small Talk in a Garden. O. B. Hardison Jr. CRP

I will always be new! Delmore Schwartz. *See* I Am Cherry Alive[; the little girl sang].

I will arise and go now, and go to Innisfree. The Lake-Isle of Innisfree. W. B. Yeats. ADE; APAD; CABP; CMoP; ChAP; ClHu; EBEvV; FaPoR; HeIP-4; IIP; InPK-6; InPS-3; LiTM; MoBrPo; MoP; NAEL-2; NOBE; NTP; NoAM; NoP-4; OBEV; OxAEP-2; OxBTC; PoE; PoPoPo; PoRA; Poetr; SAGP; TFi; UV

I will arise and go now, and go to Inverness. The Cockney of the North. Harry Graham. UV

I will await my spring. Till The Peonies Bloom. Yongnang Kim, *Korean.* CKP, tr. by Jaihiun Kim

I will be faithful to thee; aye, I will! Thomas Hardy. *Fr.* She, to Him. EnVR

I will be home in two months and look you in the eyes. (LL) Message. Allen Ginsberg. CoAmPo; NeAP; VGW

I will be / M o ving in the Street of her. E. E. Cummings. VGW

I will be patient while my Lord. Cinderella. Ruby C. Saunders. BISi

"I will be sorry for their childishness." (LL) The Toys. Coventry Patmore. EBEV, EDVV; NORVV; OBEV; OxAEP-2; PoToHe; SoSe-8

I will be the gladdest thing. Afternoon on a Hill. Edna St. Vincent Millay BoTP; ChAP; ImGa; NTCP; OBCA; OxBA; TTTS

I will be true, despite thy scythe and thee. (LL) Sonnet 123. Shakespeare. OxAEP-1; Son

I will be your lover. The Bush Speaks. Ernest G. Moll. NOBAu

I will be your mouth now, to do your singing. A Funeral Plainsong from a Younger Woman to an Older Woman. Judy Grahn. DeD; GLP

I will begin to delineate the green family. The Green Family. Colleen Thibaudeau. NOBC

I will blame him. After Listening to Jack Teagarden. . . . James McKean. SeSe

I will build my fire today. A Charm for Lighting the Fire. *Unknown, Irish.* NOIV, tr. by Thomas Kinsella

I will call you. My Friend the Wind. King D. Kuka. VoR

I will carry my coat and not put on my belt. *Unknown.* BoWoP, tr. by Arthur Waley *Fr.* Tzu Yeh Songs.

I WILL cast out Wisdom and reject Learning. Taoist Song. Hsi K'ang, *Chinese.* ChiP, tr. by Arthur Waley

I will come to you. Yakamochi, *Japanese.* OHPJ, tr. by Kenneth Rexroth

I will confesse. An Hymne to Love. Robert Herrick. NOSC

I will consider the outnumbering dead. Merlin. Geoffrey Hill. InPK-6; TRP

I will deny everything. Reprieve. Laurie Duesing. DeD

I will die in Miami in the sun. Variations on a Text by Vallejo. Donald Justice. NoAM; VCAP

I will dream it again. (LL) Wormwood. Thomas Kinsella. CIP-2; PBCIP

I will drink to your health, sweet Amy. To Amy. J. Gordon. OBAL

I will duly pass the day O my mother, and duly return to you. (LL) The Sleepers. Walt Whitman. AmPP; NAAL-1; NAAL-3

I will enjoy thee now my *Celia,* come. A Rapture. Thomas Carew. BeJo; CABP; CaPo; NAEL-1; OAEL-1; OxAEP-1; PBRV; SeCP

I will exchange a city for a sunset. Barter. Marie Blake. PoToHe

I will find that it's still there. (LL) Mementos, 1. W. D. Snodgrass. MoAmPo; NoP-4; SAGP; UnPo; VCAP

I will follow. (LL) Grandfather. Lance Henson, *Cheyenne Indian.* CDW; HATNAP, tr. by Lance Henson

I will give my love an apple without e'er a core. *Unknown.* RB ("And she may unlock it without any key.") (LL) ITG

I will go and get my friends—I will go and get my friends. *Unknown. Fr.* Specimens of Indian Songs. APN-2, tr. by Lewis Cass

I Will Go Back to the Great Sweet Mother. Swinburne. NAEL-2 *Fr.* The Triumph of Time.
(Return, The.) OxBos

I will go home to my children. (LL) Fathers and Sons. Tom Leonard. CABP; FaBoTC

I Will Go into the Ghetto. Charles Reznikoff. VGW

I will go to P'eng Hsien in the place where he dwells. Ch'u Yüan. *See* Yüan, Ch'ü.

I will go up the mountain after the Moon. Moon Folly. Fannie Stearns Gifford. RACG *Fr.* The Songs of Conn the Fool.

I will go with the first air of morning. Fishing. Dorothy, Duchess of Wellington Wellesley. OBMV

I will grieve alone. In Response to a Rumor that the Oldest Whorehouse in Wheeling, West Virginia, Has Been Condemned. James Wright. CoAP; NNaP; NoAM; VCAP

I will haunt these States. A Vow. Allen Ginsberg. CLPP; OBWP

I will have all my beds blown up, not stuft. Ben Jonson. EBEV *Fr.* The Alchemist. FaBoSe

I will have to accept women. This Form of Life Needs Sex. Allen Ginsberg. CLPP; NNaP

I will have to ask for my slum location again. When I Lost Slum Life. Sipho Sepamla. PeSAV

I will have to tell you what it is like. What It Is Like. Gerald Stern. NAmP90

I will have you. (LL) Lilies are white. *Unknown.* BoTP; LB; OxNR

I will hold beauty as a shield against despair. Beauty as a Shield. Elsie Robinson. BLPA; PoToHe

I will in Cassio's lodging lose this napkin. Shakespeare. OxAEP-1 *Fr.* Othello.

I Will Keep Christmas. P. A. Ropes. BoTP

I will kill—I will kill—the Big Knives, I will kill. *Unknown. Fr.* Specimens of Indian Songs. APN-2, tr. by Lewis Cass

I will lament and cry. (LL) Bitter-Sweet. George Herbert. FHYEP; FMP; GeHe; NOBE; NoP-4; OxBSP

I will lay down my silk robe. The Good Old Dog. Toi Derricotte. InPS-3

I will leave this old village behind me. . . . Farewell Song. Nikolai Mikhailovich Rubtsov, *Russian.* TCRP, tr. by Bradley Jordan *and* Katya Zubritskaya

I will leave your white house and tranquil garden. "Anna Akhmatova," *Russian.* LoP, tr. by Judith Hemschemeyer

I will lift up mine eyes unto the hills. Psalm 121. Bible, *O.T.* AWP *Fr.* Psalms.

I will live in Ringsend. Ringsend. Oliver St. John Gogarty. OBMV; OxBTC

I Will Look Up. Josephine D. Henderson Heard. CBWP-4

I will look with detachment. On Being Head of the English Department. Pinkie Gordon Lane. BISi; GT

I will lose you. It is written. The Sweater. Gregory Orr. TRP

I will make love. *Unknown, Spanish.* BoWoP, tr. by Willis Barnstone

I will make you brooches and toys for your delight. The Song of a Traveller. Robert Louis Stevenson. BoTP; EBVV; ITG; MoBrPo; OBEV

I will never again. The Promise. Toi Derricotte. GT

I will never be a hero. A Name. Aleksandr Samsonovich Ginger, *Russian.* TCRP, tr. by Albert C. Todd

I will never be able to stop my tears. On the Death of His Baby Son. Su Tung-p'o, *Chinese.* OHPC, tr. by Kenneth Rexroth

"I will never eate nor drinke," Robin Hood said. Robin Hood's Death. *Unknown.* ESPB

I will never forget my only beating. The Beating. Richard Katrovas. NAmP90

I will no longer kiss. On Himselfe. Robert Herrick. CaPo; CavPo

I will no longer lightly walk behind. I Must Become a Menace to My Enemies. June Jordan. NAAAL

I will not climb these heights again. Saint Colm-Cille and the Cairn of Farewell. John Irvine. TIRV

I will not crush the world's corolla of wonders. Lucian Blaga, *Romanian.* PFTM, tr. by Andrei Codrescu

I will not die for you. *Unknown, Irish.* NOIV, tr. by Thomas Kinsella

I will not doubt, though all my ships at sea. Faith. Ella Wheeler Wilcox. PoToHe

I will not give thee all my heart. Grace Hazard Conkling. LW

I will not have you think me less. A Jewish Poet Counsels a King. Santob de Carrion. TrJP *Fr.* Consejos y Documentos al Rey Dom Pedro.

I Will Not Let Thee Go. Robert Bridges. CMoP; EnLoPo; FaBoBe; OBNC

I will not let you say a Woman's part. A Woman's Answer. Adelaide Anne Procter. VWP

I will not live without him. (LL) Liadan Laments Cuirithir. *Unknown, Irish.* BIrV; PBWP, tr. by John Montague

I will not perturbate. To the Dead Cardinal of Westminster. Francis Thompson. PeVV

I will not play at tug o' war. Hug o' War. Shel Silverstein. NTCP

I will not say to you, "This is the Way; walk in it." To My Son. *Unknown.* PoLF

I will not shut me from my kind. 108. Tennyson. CABP; EnVR; FHYEP *Fr.* In Memoriam A. H. H.

I Will Not Tell the Secrets. Wilfrid Scawen Blunt. Son *Fr.* Esther [a Young Man's Tragedy].

I will not toy with it nor bend an inch. The White City. Claude McKay. BPo; CrDW; NeAM; NaDo; TAP

I will not try to reach again. The Evenlode. Hilaire Belloc. OxAEP-2

I will not weep, for 'twere as great a sin. An Elegy upon S[ir] W[alter] R[aleigh]. Henry King, Bishop of Chichester. NOSC

I will now only believe that he has died. Now I Will Only Believe. B. W. Vilakazi. PeSAV

I will obey you to my utmost power. To a Lady, Who Desired Me Not To Be in Love with Her. John Cutts. NOSC

I will—of You—. (LL) Alter! When the Hills do—. Emily Dickinson. AmPP; CBLP; FaBoBe; ITG; SoSe-8

I will pluck from my tree a cherry-blossom wand. The Cherry-Blossom Wand. Anna Wickham. MoBrPo

I will pronounce your name, Naëtt, I will declaim you, Naëtt! Léopold Sédar Senghor. PBMAP

I will put Chaos into fourteen lines. Edna St. Vincent Millay. Son

"I will put upon you the Telephone Curse," said the witch. The Witch of East Seventy-second Street. Morris Gilbert Bishop. NYBP

I will reach into the grab-bag of unconscious things. Private Pantomime. Ruth Stone. PoA

I will read a few of these to see if they exist. The Theory of the Flower. Michael Palmer. PT

I will remember you. *Unknown. See* Hymn to Earth the Mother of All.

I will remember you on Bloom Street. Bloom Street. Angela McCabe. AmPA

I will rise. Wine Bowl. Hilda Doolittle. NoP-4

I will roar and squander. Folly's Song. Thomas Dekker *and others.* NOSC

I will sing a song of battle. The Song of Chess. Abraham ibn Ezra, *Hebrew.* TrJP, *tr. by* Nina Davis Salaman

I will sing, if ye will hearken. The Laird o' Logie. *Unknown.* CH; ESPB

I will sing no more songs! O'Bruadair. David O'Bruadair, *Irish.* BIrV, *tr. by* James Stephens

I will sing unto the Lord, because he hath dealt bountifully with me. (LL) Psalm 13. Bible, *O.T.* OBVE

I will sleep. December. Ron Padgett. SPE

I will speak about women of letters, for I'm in the racket. Three. Carolyn Kizer. NALW; NMM-2 *Fr.* Pro Femina.

I will stop dreaming now. Success. Cornelius Eady. ISC

I will take my trouble and wrap it in a blue handkerchief. Boats in the Bay. Winifred Holtby. WPN

I will teach you my townspeople. Tract. William Carlos Williams. LiTM; MeMAP; MoAmPo; MoP; NOBA; NoAM; SAmP; TAP; TwCP; VGW

I will teach you to become American, my students. Notes for a Lecture. David Ignatow. NNaP

I will tell a true tale of myself. Seafarer. *Unknown.* PoE, *tr. by* Kemp Malone

I will tell you of a fellow. Common Bill. *Unknown.* AS

I will tell you of a gallant soldier. The Soldier's Wooing. *Unknown.* AmFP

I will the devil kiss. (LL) A Small Fig Tree. Donald Hall. ChIV-2; GI

I will track you down the years. Quest. Naomi Long Madgett. BPo

I will walk into some one's dwelling. Love Song. *Unknown, Ojibwa Native American.* APN-2, *tr. by* Henry Rowe Schoolcraft

I will walk with a lover of wisdom. Little Elegy. Denis Devlin. NOIV

I will whisper your name. Eshu. Adesanya Alakoye. ISC

I will write a poem about nothing. William of Aquitaine, *French.* CBNP

I Will Write Songs against You. Charles Reznikoff. SAGP; VGW

I will write you a letter. I Think. James Schuyler. TTTS

I will write you a poem instead of bringing rice. Paying a Sick-call to Yao Ts'un-tao in the Rain. Shen Chou, *Chinese.* CoBLCP, *tr. by* Jonathan Chaves

I, Willie Wastle. *Unknown.* OxNR

I wince in self-revelation. Sincerity. Agnes Nemes Nagy, *Hungarian.* VCWP, *tr. by* Hugh Maxton

I winced. Catching fire, I shivered with cold. Marburg. Boris Pasternak, *Russian.* TCRP, *tr. by* Yakov Hornstein

I Winna Let On. James King Annand. NOxBChV

I wish a greater knowledge, then t'attaine. Francis Quarles. PBRV *Fr.* Divine Fancies.

I wish all the / mandragona. Blue Funk. Joel Oppenheimer. NeAP

I wish, God, for some end I do not will. Elizabeth Jennings. PeECV; TOF *Fr.* The Sonnets of Michelangelo.

I wish, how I wish that I had a little house. The Shiny Little House. Nancy M. Hayes. BoTP

I wish I could be. Love Isn't. Patricia Parker. NMM-2

I wish I could be. Marichiko, *Japanese.* OHMPJ, *tr. by* Kenneth Rexroth

I wish I could be. Kenneth Rexroth. APSN *Fr.* The Love Poems of Marichiko.

I wish I could be. Theophanes, *Greek.* GrAn, *tr. by* Peter Jay

I wish I could lend a coat. Akahito. AWP, *tr. by* Arthur Waley *Fr.* Manyo Shu, Part 2 of 4.

I wish I could remember the [*or* that] first day. The First Day. Christina Rossetti. BoLoP; FaBoBe; GBL; Son *Fr.* Monna Innominata. BWW

I wish I could still stay. The Peacock Poems: 1. Sherley Anne Williams. NAAAL

I wish I had an aeroplane. A Penny Wish. Irene Thompson. BoTP

I wish I had been born beside a river. The Upper Canadian. James Reaney. NOBC

I wish I had the voice of Homer. Cancer's a Funny Thing. John Burdon Sanderson Haldane. OxBTC

I wish I had two little mouths. Mouths. Dorothy Aldis. CTV

I wish I lived in a caravan. The Pedlar's Caravan. William Brighty Rands. BoTP; OxBChV

I wish I loved the human race. Wishes of an Elderly Man[, Wished at a Garden Party, June 1914]. Sir Walter Alexander Raleigh. FaBoCh; FaBoEE; NBLV; NOBL; NTP; OBCoV; PeLV

I wish I owned a Dior dress. Reflections at Dawn. Phyllis McGinley. NBLV; NOBL

I wish I thought *What Jolly Fun!* (LL) Wishes of an Elderly Man[, Wished at a Garden Party, June 1914]. Sir Walter Alexander Raleigh. FaBoCh; FaBoEE; NBLV; NOBL; NTP; OBCoV; PeLV

I Wish I Was a Grown Up Man. Maggie Pogue Johnson. CBWP-4

I Wish I Was a Little Bird. *Unknown.* AS

I Wish I Was a Mole in the Ground. *Unknown.* AmFP

I Wish I Was by That Dim Lake. Thomas Moore. PoEL-4

I wish I was in de land ob cotton. Dixie [*or* Dixie's Land]. Daniel Decatur Emmett. APN-1; CBCWP

I wish I was where I would be. John Clare. NOBVV

I wish i were. Poem For My Nephew. Nikki Giovanni. NOxBChV

I wish I were a / Elephantiaphus. *Unknown.* OxBoLi

I wish I were a wild beast. Aleksandr Ivanovich Vvedensky, *Russian.* TCRP, *tr. by* Bradley Jordan

I wish I were an Emperor. Wishes. F. Rogers. BoTP

I wish I were close. Akahito, *Japanese.* HoPM; OHPJ, *tr. by* Kenneth Rexroth

I Wish I Were in Love Again. Lorenz Hart. OBCoV

I Wish I Were [*or* Was] Single Again. *Unknown.* AS (Single Girl, The.) AmFP

I wish I were the wind, and you. *Unknown, Greek.* GrAn, *tr. by* Barriss Mills

I wish I were where Helen lies. Helen of Kirconnell. *Unknown.* AWP; CH; GTBS-P; ImPo; OBEV; SCGP

I wish, I *wish* he'd stay away! (LL) Antigonish. Hughes Mearns. CTV; FPC; NBLV; NOxBChV; PoLF

I wish I'd never been born. (LL) Po' Boy Blues. Langston Hughes. ColAP; NAAAL

I wish it soon may have a Better. (LL) Verses on the Death of Dr. Swift, D.S.P.D., Occasioned by Reading a Maxim in Rochefoucauld. Jonathan Swift. NOEC; PoEL-3; PeLV; SCV

I wish it were over the terrible pain. Introspective. Christina Rossetti. VWP

I wish my life to be led until death. The Prologue. Tongju Yun, *Korean.* CKP, *tr. by* Jaihiun Kim

I wish not Thasos rich in mines. Mimnermus Incert. Walter Savage Landor. PoEL-4

I wish, O son of the Living God. The Hermit's Song. *Unknown, Irish.* TIRV, *tr. by* Kuno Meyer

I wish sometimes, although a worthlesse thing. Giles, the Elder Fletcher. AAS *Fr.* Licia.

I wish that I could get in line. They Don't Speak English in Paris. Ogden Nash. OBAL

I wish that I could talk with her again. Mother. Bea Liu. LoHo

I wish that my room had a floor. Limerick. Frank Gelett Burgess. OBCA; PeLi

I wish that there were some wonderful place. The Land of Beginning Again. Louisa Fletcher. BLPA

I wish that when you died last May. May and Death. Robert Browning. FP; IMW; NOBE

I wish the rent. Little Lyric (of Great Importance). Langston Hughes. NBLV; OBAL; OBCoV

I wish them cramps. Wishes for Sons. Lucille Clifton. NAAAL; NMM-2

I wish there were a touch of these boats about my life. Boat Poem. Bernard Spencer. FaBoTw; OxBTC

I wish they were / Grass. (LL) Late November in a Field. James Wright. NAAL-2; NNaP

I wish they would hurry up their trip to Mars. A Projection. Reed Whittemore. AiP

I wish they'd killed you in a decent show. (LL) To Any Dead Officer. Siegfried Sassoon. NSI; PoFWW

"I wish to buy a dog," she said. On Buying a Dog. Edgar Klauber. NTCP

I wish to God I never saw you, Mag. Mag. Carl Sandburg. SAGP

I wish to God my child was born. Lullaby. Unknown. AmFP

I wish to make my sermon brief. Praise of Little Women. Juan, Archpriest of Hita Ruiz, Spanish. AWP, tr. by Longfellow

I wish to paint my eyes. Unknown, Egyptian hieroglyphics. BoWoP, tr. by Willis Barnstone

I wish to state in the first place that. SURcenSURE. Marcel Duchamp, French. PFTM, tr. by Jerome Rothenberg and Peggy Guggenheim

I wish to submit a memorial expressing my feelings. Submitting a Memorial Requesting Permission to Return Home and Care for My Parents. Yang Chi, Chinese. CoBLCP, tr. by Jonathan Chaves

I wish you, in January, the swirl of blown snow—. Wishes for the Months. John Heath-Stubbs. AYFP

I wish you triumphs that are yours already. For Marianne Moore's Birthday. Kay Boyle. NMM-2

I wish you would come. Lady Izumi, Japanese. BoWoP, tr. by Willis Barnstone

I wish your breast was made of glass. The Lover's Lament. Unknown. AS

I wished, all the mild days of middle March. John Berryman. LoP Fr. Sonnets to Chris.

I wished to be born, I was born, and after I was born I made all spirits. Song for Medicine Hunting—Rarely for the Metai. Unknown. Fr. Music and Poetry of the Indians. APN-2, tr. by John Tanner

I wished to shirk my task one day. Discovery. Benjamin Keech. PoToHe

I wist not what to wish, yet sure thought I. Anne Bradstreet. PBWP Fr. Contemplations. AmPP; NAAL-3; PoEL-3; SCAP; WPE

I with time to life ascend. Musical Pumpkin Hut. Heinrich Albert, German. GePo, tr. by George C. Schoolfield

I with uncovered head. James Russell Lowell. Fr. Ode Recited at the Harvard Commemoration (July 21, 1865). APN-1; CBCWP; NOBA; OBWP

I, with whose colors [or colours] Myra dressed [or dress'd] her head. Myra. Greville Fulke. GBL; HAP; NOBE; NoSic; OBEV Fr. Caelica.

I woke, and we were sailing on. Coleridge. OxBSn Fr. Rime of the Ancient Marine.

I woke at three; for I was bid. Going to Church. Coventry Patmore. PeVV Fr. The Angel in the House.

I woke before the day, when the night bird. Thomas Iron-Eyes. Marnie Walsh. WPOW

I woke before the morning, I was happy all the day. A Good Boy. Robert Louis Stevenson. PWR

I woke / Just about daybreak, and fell back. Poems to a Brown Cricket. James Wright. NYBP

I woke up about 2:30 this morning and thought about Philip's / hat. Philip Whalen's Hat. Joanne Kyger. BB

I woke up this mornin'. Empty Bed Blues. Bessie Smith. OBAL; UnPo

I woke up this mornin'. Sylvester's Dying Bed. Langston Hughes. NoAM; Poetr; SAmP; UnPo

I woke up this mornin' with the blues all round my bed. I Got the Blues. Unknown. TTY

I woke up this morning. Karla Kuskin. TLR

I woke up to the bleating of a lamb. Chriseaster. Molly Peacock. FFC

I wol now syngen yif I can. The House of Fame. Virgil. OBCVT, tr. by Geoffrey Chaucer Fr. The Aeneid.

I wolde witen of sum [or som] wis wight. This World Fares as a Fancy. Unknown. EnVB

I, Woman. Irma McClaurin. BlSi

I wonder about the trees. The Sound of Trees. Robert Frost. NoAM; OxBA

I wonder are there roses still. The German Graves. Sir Alan Patrick Herbert. NSI

I wonder as I Wander. Unknown. PChr

I wonder as into bed I creep. Sweet Dreams. Ogden Nash. OTCP

I wonder, by my troth, what thou and I. The Good[-]Morrow. Donne. APAD; AWP; BoLoP; CABP; CBLP; ClHu; EBEV; ESCV; EnLoPo; FHYEP; FaBoBe; FaBoVe; FMP; FSCP; HoPM; ImPo; InPS-3; ITG; LoP; MeLP; NAEL-1; NAWM-1; NoP-4; NOSC; OAEL-1; OxAEP-1; PoE; PoEL-2; PoRA; Poetr; SCV; SeCP; SoSe-8; TFi

I wonder do you feel today. Two in the Campagna. Robert Browning. APAD; EBEV; EBVV; EnVR; FHYEP; GTBS-P; NAEL-2; NOBE; NOBVV; NoP-4; OAEL-2; OBNC; OxAEP-2; OxBM; PoE; PoEL-5; SCGP; TFi; TOF

I wonder, Duddon, if you still remember. To the River Duddon. Norman Nicholson. NoP-4

I wonder how King Arthur felt. Limerick. Moss Rich. PeLi

I wonder how many old men last winter. The Minneapolis Poem. James Wright. FYAP; NoAM; UnPo

I Wonder How My Home Is. Unknown, Tewa Indian. PBMP, tr. by H. J. Spinden

I wonder how the organist. The Organist. George W. Stevens. BLPA

I wonder if Christ had a little black dog. The Little Black Dog. Elizabeth Gardner Reynolds. PoLF

I wonder if the courtiers at the Western Capital know of these things, or not? Po Chü-i. See Ease.

I wonder if the elephant. Pete at the Zoo. Gwendolyn Brooks. TLR

I wonder if the old cow died or not. The Question. Wilfrid Wilson Gibson. NSI

I wonder if the sap is stirring yet. The First Spring Day. Christina Rossetti. FaBoVe

I wonder if you really send. Together. Sarah Orne Jewett. CPO

I wonder: is there no way for us to meet again. Wallāda, Arabic. PBWP, tr. by A. R. Nykel

I wonder is there nowhere a / Do-right man? (LL) Early Evening Quarrel. Langston Hughes. SAmP; UnPo

I wonder poet, can you take it. The Muse to an Unknown Poet. Paul Potts. FaBoTw

I wonder, since we are both travelling out. The Travelling Out. Lucile Adler. NYBP

I wonder sometimes if the soldiers lying. Song for the Heroes. Alex Comfort. MoBrPo

I wonder what day of the week. An Untimely Thought. Thomas Bailey Aldrich. PWR

I wonder what eagle did to him. Gaxe, Tlingit Indian. STP, tr. by James Koller

I Wonder What It Feels Like to Be Drowned? Robert Graves. MoBrPo

I wonder what my kite can see. The Kite. Pearl Forbes MacEwen. BoTP

I wonder what to mean by sanctuary, if a real or. Triphammer Bridge. A. R. Ammons. ColAP; NAAL-2; NOBA

I wonder where julia found that strange, rather common / little boy? (LL) False Security. John Betjeman. CMoP; NoAM; NoP-4

I wonder whether / you've been avoiding. Sometimes in Winter. Marc Cohen. BAP-93

I wonder why I can't remember. Katie McBain. MDDM Fr. I Want to Be Your Daughter Now.

I wonder why that scene comes back tonight. Pilate Remembers. William E. Brooks. ChIV-2

I wonder why the grass is green. Jeannie Kirby. BoTP; OTCP

I wondered always where. The Hunchback of Dugbe. Wole Soyinka. VCWP

I wondered what had. They. Robert Creeley. FTOS

I wondered why the covers felt so cold. Night Snow. Po Chü-i, Chinese. CoBCP, tr. by Burton Watson

I won't be my father's Jack. Other Little Tune, T'. Mother Goose. OxNR; ReMoGo

I won't be reconstructed and I don't give a damn. (LL) The Rebel. Innes Randolph. NBLV; OBAL; OxBoLi

I won't go with you. I want to stay with Grandpa! My Last Afternoon with Uncle Devereux Winslow. Robert Lowell. NAAL-2; NoP-4; VGW

I Won't Sell His Love. Fadwa Tuqan, Arabic. AF, tr. by Mounah Aikhouri and Hamid Algar

I Wonta Thank Ya. Tejumola Ologboni. NBV

I work. Tanka. Ishikawa Takuboku, Japanese. MJT, tr. by Ueda, Makoto

I work all day, and get half-drunk at night. Aubade. Philip Larkin. CABP; GEA; NoP-4; SoSe-8; TRP

I work and I remember. I conceive. That's All. Lawrence Joseph. EOEF; PBCAP

I work and I remember, that's all. (LL) That's All. Lawrence Joseph. EOEF; PBCAP

I work at night, surrounded by city. Burial in the East. Pablo Neruda, Spanish. TRP, tr. by Angel Flores

I work at night, the city all around me. Funeral in the East. Pablo Neruda, Spanish. TRP, tr. by Robert Bly

I work nights at the University Bookshop. Thoughts of Jack Kerouac—& Other Things. Peter Olds. PeNZ

I work nights, in the ring of the city. Burial in the East. Pablo Neruda, Spanish. TRP, tr. by Ben Belitt

I work or play, as I think best. Emancipation. Unknown. BLPA

I work to music on the radio. The Campus. David Posner. NYBP

I work up this mornin'. Langston Hughes. See Sylvester's Dying Bed.

I worked all the winter. Tired as I Can Be. Unknown. FaBoVe

I worked for a woman. Madam and Her Madam. Langston Hughes. RACG; SAmP

I worked for a year in the cellar. One Minute of Night Sky. John Engman. NAmP90

I worship the greatest first. Hippolytus Temporizes. Hilda Doolittle. RACG

I Worship Thee, O Holy Ghost. William F. Warren. AH

I worship your fleece which is the perfect triangle. The Ninth Secret Poem. Guillaume Apollinaire, *French.* APAD, tr. by Oliver Bernard

I wot a tree XII bowes betake. *Unknown.* MiEL

I wot full well that beauty cannot last. To His Friend. George Turberville. AEP; CTC

I wot[t] what I do[o] mean[e]. (LL) Me list no more to sing. Sir Thomas Wyatt. AAS; SiPS

I would ask of you, my darling. Will You Love Me When I'm Old? *Unknown.* BLPA; FaBoBe

I would be a fool to want more children. "Alta." MDDM

I would be a soft pink rose. *Unknown, Greek.* InMo, tr. by Sam Hamill

I Would Be Clad in Christ's Skin. *Unknown.* EnVB; MiEL

I would be married, but I'd[e] have no wife. On Marriage. Richard Crashaw. FaBoEE

I would be ready, Lord. Ready. Margaret Junkin Preston. PWR

I would be true, for there are those [who trust me]. Howard Arnold Walter. PoLF; PoToHe

("And prompt and glad to do the / things I've heard.") (LL) CTV

I would be wandering in distant fields. In Bondage. Claude McKay. PoBA

I would but I can't. *Unknown, Greek.* GrAn, tr. by Thomas Meyer

("When I ask or take / what I'd give.") (LL) FP, tr. by Thomas Meyer

I Would Call It Derangement. Gerald Stern. PuP-17

"I would doubt," said the Bishop of Balham. Limerick. Terence Rattigan. PeLi

I would fain know what she hath deservèd. (LL) The Lover Showeth How He Is Forsaken of Such as He Sometime Enjoyed. Sir Thomas Wyatt. APAD; CABP; LoP; NoP-4; PFE

I would follow it, I think. (LL) So lonely am I. Ono no Komachi, *Japanese.* BoWoP; PBWP, tr. by David Keene

I would have been as great as George Eliot. Margaret Fuller Slack. Edgar Lee Masters. RACG

I would have each couple turn. The Dance. Wendell Berry. ITG

I would hold another person in my thoughts. "Eduard Veniaminovich Limonov," *Russian.* TCRP, tr. by Nina Kossman

I Would I Might Forget That I Am I. George Santayana. AWP

I would I were a bird so free. *Unknown.* Fr. Popular Songs of Tuscany. AWP, tr. by John Addington Symonds

I would I were Actaeon, whom Diana did disguise. ------ Bewe. NoSic

I would, if I could. Mother Goose. OxNR

I would immortalize these nymphs: so bright. L'Après-Midi d'un Faune. Stéphane Mallarmé, *French.* AWP, tr. by Aldous Huxley

I would in rich and golden coloured raine. Thomas Lodge. AAS *Fr.* Phyllis.

I would it were not as it is. Sir Edward Dyer. SCGP

I would lie low—the ground on which men tread. The Earth. Jones Very. APN-1; OxBA

I would like all things to be free of me. Proof. Brendan Kennelly. CIP-2; PBCIP

I would like just to be silent. Jerzy Ficowski. HP

I would like my love to die, *Author's own English vers. of his* "Je voudrais que mon amour meure." Samuel Beckett. BIrV

("Mourning her who thought she loved me.") (LL) CIP-2; IIP; NOIV

I would like to describe the simplest emotion. Zbigniew Herbert, *Polish.* PoSu, tr. by Czeslaw Milosz

I would like to dive. The Diver. W. W. Eustace Ross. NOBC

I would like to know from where. Metamorphosis. Slavko Mihalic, *Croatian.* CEEP, tr. by Peter Kastmiler

I would like to let things be. Facts of Life, Ballymoney. Eamon Grennan. PBCIP

I would like to watch you sleeping. Variation on the Word *Sleep.* Margaret Atwood. DeD; ITG; NOBC

I Would Like You for a Comrade. Edward Abbott Parry. NOxBChV; OxBChV

I would listen even again to that labouring breath. (LL) Remorse. John Betjeman. MoBrPo; OxBSP

I would live all my life in nonchalance and insouciance. Introspective Reflection. Ogden Nash. NBLV; OBCoV

I would live for a day and a night. The Song-Maker. Anna Wickham. MoBrPo

I would live in your love as the sea-grasses live in the sea. Sara Teasdale. LW

I would look up-and laugh-and love-and lift. (LL) I would be true, for there are those [who trust me]. Howard Arnold Walter. PoLF; PoToHe

I would make a crown / Of all the cities I have known. Express. Vincente Huidobro, *Spanish.* PFTM, tr. by David Guss

I would make a vessel, ship, a boat. Calvary. Padraig De Brun, *Irish.* TIRV, tr. by Máire Mhac an tSaoi

I would need a distance of a hundred years. Classic Verses. Rade Drainac, *Serbo-Croatian.* HSix, tr. by Charles Simic

I would never marry a young girl or an old woman. Honestus, *Greek.* GrAn, tr. by Edwin Morgan

I would not alter thy cold eyes. Flos Lunae. Ernest Christopher Dowson. OBMV; PeVV

I would not always reason. The straight path. The Conjunction of Jupiter and Venus. William Cullen Bryant. APN-1

I would not ask Thee that my days. A Humble Heart. Alfred Norris. PWR

I would not be the Moon, the sickly thing. In Dispraise of the Moon. Mary Elizabeth Coleridge. CH; PEW

I would not breathe, when blows thy mighty wind. The Spirit. Jones Very. NCAP

I would not, could I, make thy life as mine. A Vain Wish. Philip Bourke Marston. GSo

I would not do by thee as thou hast done! (LL) Lines on Hearing That Lady Byron Was Ill. Byron. EBEV; OxAEP-2

I would not feign a single sigh. Song. John Clare. GBL

I would not go to old Joe's house. Old Joe Clark. *Unknown.* APN-2

I would not have the risk diminished. (LL) A Map of the City. Thom Gunn. NAEL-2; NoP-4; PoE

I would not leave that land, if I were thou. To Charles Roux, of Switzerland. Nathaniel Parker Willis. APN-1

I Would Not Live Alway. William Augustus Mühlenberg. AH

I would not marry a blacksmith. Soldier Boy for Me. *Unknown.* AmFP

I would not paint—a picture. Emily Dickinson. APN-2; NAAL-1; NAAL-3; NOBA; NoP-4; TRP

I Would Not Recommend Love. Harold Norse. CLPP

I would not the good bishop be. (LL) The Problem. Ralph Waldo Emerson. APN-1; AWP; AmPP; MeMAP; NAAL-1; NAAL-3; NOBA; OxBA; PAR; TAP

I would not write a lament for you. Salt. Anne Hartigan. CIP-2

I would prefer. The Counterfeiter. Michael Davitt, *Irish.* PBCIP, tr. by Philip Casey

I would put on my coat and galoshes. (LL) White Apples. Donald Hall. LoL; TAP

I would rid myself of an old way of life. Diogenes. Arthur Rex Dugard Fairburn. PeNZ

I would set all things whatsoever front to back. Percy Wyndham Lewis. CTC *Fr.* One-Way Song.

I would sit in the center of the world. The Message of Crazy Horse. Lucille Clifton. PaTW

I would tell a marvelous vision. The Dream of the Cross. *Unknown, Anglo-Saxon.* EBEV, tr. by Sally Purcell

I would that all men my hard case would know. Behold the Deeds! Henry Cuyler Bunner. NBLV

I would that even now. Princess Shoku. Fr. Hyaku-Nin-Isshu. AWP, tr. by Curtis Hidden Page

I would that folk forgot me quite. Tess's Lament. Thomas Hardy. FaBoTw; FaBoVe

I would that I were dead! Tennyson. See Mariana.

I would that we were, my beloved, white birds on the foam. The White Birds. W. B. Yeats. ADE

I would the gift I offer here. Dedication. John Greenleaf Whittier. APN-1; OxBA

I would the God of Love would die. To His Mistress. James Shirley. BeJo

I would to heaven that I were so much clay. Fragment. Byron. CTC; NAEL-2; NOBL; OAEL-2; OxBSP *Fr. Don Juan.*

I would wait for the tunnels. Driving the Big Chrysler across the Country of My Birth. Michael S. Harper. MoNo

I would wear one by my side. (LL) If wishes were horses. Mother Goose. FaBoBe; LB; OxNR; ReMoGo

I would worship if I could. Great Spaces. Howard Moss. TwCP

I Wouldn't. John Ciardi. TLR

I wouldn't be bothered with drawers. Limerick. *Unknown.* PeLi

I wouldn't be the raven. It's Me Man. James Berry. HCP

I wouldn't coax the plant if I were you. Woman with Flower. Naomi Long Madgett. GT

I wouldn't like at all to be. Lion Thoughts. Iowna Elizabeth Banker. CTV

I wouldn't marry a bachelor. Old Maid's Song. *Unknown.* AmFP

I wouldn't marry a farmer. A Railroad Man for Me. *Unknown.* CA

I wouldn't much object, if I were black. A Negro Cemetery Next to a White One. Howard Nemerov. OxBSP

I wouldn't say I was dying for it. Feeding the ducks at the Howard Johnson Motel. Susan Mitchell. NAmP90

I wove myself of many delicious strands. Einstein's Bathrobe. Howard Moss. VCAP

I wove this garland, Rodokleia. Rufinus Domesticus, *Greek.* InMo, *tr. by* Sam Hamill

I wrastle not with rage. Robert Southwell. *Fr.* Content and Ri[t]ch[e]. ChIV-2; NoSic

I, wretched Virtue, sit. Mnasalcas, *Greek.* GrAn, *tr. by* Edward Lucie-Smith

I write a psalm in the field Corn sheds blossoms. Psalm of the Field. Tadeusz Nowak, *Polish.* CEEP, *tr. by* Leonard Kress

I write characters in lamplight. Yüan Mei. *Fr.* Miscellaneous Poems on Growing Old. CoBLCP, *tr. by* Jonathan Chaves

I write for my own kind. John Hewitt. PNI

I write, Honora, on the sparkling sand! Elegy. Anna Seward. CPO

I write in praise of the solitary act. Against Coupling. Fleur Adcock. CBLP; LW; NALW

I write my God in blue. Meta-A and the A of Absolutes. Jay Wright. TRP

I write no letters. Poem. Henrikas Nagys, *Lithuanian.* CEEP, *tr. by* Jonas Zdanys

I write of Jam, a subject stiff. On Jam. Hilaire Belloc. NBLV

I Write Poems. Gloria Fuertes, *Spanish.* WPOW, *tr. by* Philip Levine

I write this poem. For Musia's Grandchildren. Irving Layton. NOBC

I write to make people anxious and miserable and to worsen their indigestion. (LL) Serious Concerns. Wendy Cope. OBCoV

I write to make you suffer. Anne-Marie Kegels, *French.* BoWoP, *tr. by* Willis Barnstone

I write to you beneath this tent. Post Card. Guillaume Apollinaire, *French.* AF, *tr. by* Oliver Bernard

I wrote: In the dark cavern of our birth. Strange Type. Malcolm Lowry. NoP-4

I wrote some lines once on a time. The Height of the Ridiculous. Oliver Wendell Holmes. OBAL; OBCA

I wrote the postcard to you and went out. Getting Through. James Merrill. NYBP

I wrote to you to say that I'd be there. One's Correspondence. Connie Bensley. OBCoV

I wrote "Who wrote Icon Basilike?" (LL) On ["Who Wrote Icon Basilike" by Dr.] Christopher Wordsworth, Master of Trinity. Benjamin Hall Kennedy. FaBoEE; OBCoV

I wrung my hands under my dark veil. "Anna Akhmatova," *Russian.* BoLoP; RaBo, *tr. by* Max Hayward *and* Stanley Kunitz

I wud sooner sleep. (LL) Old Shepherd's Prayer. Charlotte Mew. MoBrPo; OxBTC; WPE

I, YANG TZŬ, hid from life. Poverty. Yang Hsiung, *Chinese.* ChiP, *tr. by* Arthur Waley

I Years had been from Home. Emily Dickinson. NOBA; OxBA; PoRA; SAmP

I yet SUPERIOR am to you. (LL) The Forsaken Wife. Elizabeth Thomas. ECWP; LW

I yielded myself to the perfect whole. (LL) Each and All. Ralph Waldo Emerson. APN-1; AWP; AmPP; ColAP; MeMAP; NAAL-1; NAAL-3; NCAP; NOBA; OxBA; PAR; TAP

I, you, he, she, we. Jelaluddin Rumi, *Persian.* LoL, *tr. by* Coleman Barks

I/ am going to rise. Vive Noir! Mari E. Evans. NBV

Ia Drang Valley. Yusef Komunyakaa. MT

Iago Prytherch his name, though, be it allowed. A Peasant. Ronald Stuart Thomas. OBWVE

Iambes VIII. André Marie de Chénier, *French.* FaBoPV, *tr. by* Tom Paulin

Iambic Feet Considered as Honorable Scars. William Meredith. OxBSP; PoA

Iambica. Edmund Spenser. *See* Iambicum Trimetrum.

Iambically runs. (LL) On the Imprint of the First English Edition of "The Works of Max Beerbohm." Max Beerbohm. InPK-6; OBCoV

Iambicum Trimetrum. Edmund Spenser. BoLoP; EBEV; OBEV; PoEL-1

(Iambica.) OxBoLi

Ianthe. John Lyle Donaghy. *See* Glenarm.

Ianthe. Walter Savage Landor.

Absence. CBLP; OBNC

Ianthe's Question. OBEV

Ianthe's Troubles. GBL; NOBE

(Ianthe.) OBEV

"My hopes retire; my wishes as before." GBL; OBNC

Passed Ruin'd Ilion. AWP; SCGP

(Ianthe.) PoEL-4

("One name, Ianthe, shall not die.") (LL) NAEL-2; NOBRP; NoP-4

("Past ruin'd Ilion Helen lives.") GLoP

(Verse: "Past ruin'd Ilion.") OBEV

"Proud word you never spoke, but you will speak." CBLP; EnLoPo; GBL; GLoP; OBEV

Remain, Ah Not in Youth Alone. HAP; OBNC

"Thou hast not rais'd, Ianthe, such desire." GBL

Well I Remember [How You Smiled]. HAP; OBNC

"When Helen first saw wrinkles in her face." EnLoPo

"Ye walls! sole witnesses of happy sighs." EnLoPo

Ibant Obscuræ. Thomas Edward Brown. OBNC

Ibby Damsel. *Unknown.* AmFP

Ibis. Ovid, *Latin.*

"Let th'earth deny thee fruit, and stream." OBCVT, *tr. by* Thomas Underdowne

Ibn Gabirol. Yehuda Amichai, *Hebrew.* AF, *tr. by* Gutmann, Assia

Icarus. Ronald Bottrall. GTBS-P

Icarus. Edward Field. PFE

Icarus. Valentin Iremonger. BIrV; CIP-2

Icarus. Stephen Spender. MoP

(Airman.) UV

Icarus. *Unknown.* OBEV

Icarus, by *cire* you were *perdu.* Julianus Sees a Bronze Statue of Icarus in a Public Bath. Julianus of Egypt, *Greek.* GrAn, *tr. by* Lee T. Pearcy

Icarus in November. Alec Brock Stevenson. FuPo

Icarus Schmicarus. Adrian Mitchell. OBCoV

Ice. Ai. FYAP

Ice. Walter De la Mare. AYFP; OTCP

Ice, The. Wilfrid Wilson Gibson. OxBTC

Ice. Alan Gould. NOBAu

Ice. Stephen Spender. FaBoMo; GTBS-P

Ice age is here, The. Attention. Adrienne Rich. TAP

Ice boooms. (LL) Ice. Walter De la Mare. AYFP; OTCP

Ice Cold. Sean O Riordain, *Irish.* NOIV, *tr. by* Thomas Kinsella

Ice Cream. Peter Wild. Poetsp

Ice-Cream Wars, The. John Ashbery. PoA

Ice Handler. Carl Sandburg. OxBA

Ice has been cracking all day. Spring. Michael Hogan. InPK-6

Ice honed by wind. Tracking the Siuslaw Man. Jim Barnes. HATNAP

Ice in the school-room, listen. A Schooling. Seamus Deane. CIP-2; PNI

Ice of Ladoga, The. Aleksandr Petrovich Mezhirov, *Russian.* TCRP, *tr. by* Deming Brown

Ice: On the way a miracle: water become bone. Cynewulf. ASW, *tr. by* Kevin Crossley-Holland *Fr.* Riddles (Exeter Book).

Ice Plant in Bloom. W. S. Di Piero. PaTW

Ice Skin, The. James Dickey. NYBP

Ice: The wave, over the wave, a wierd thing I saw. *Unknown.* EEP, *tr. by* Michael Alexander *Fr.* Riddles (Exeter Book).

Ice tinkled in glasses. Blues and Bitterness. Lerone Bennett Jr. PoBA

Iceberg: Curious, fair creature came floating on the waves, A. Cynewulf. ASW, *tr. by* Kevin Crossley-Holland *Fr.* Riddles (Exeter Book).

Iced with a vanilla. A Meeting of Cultures. Donald Davie. OxBC

Icehouse in Summer, The. Howard Nemerov. MoP; NoAM

Iceman, The. Gordon Challis. PeNZ

Ich am of Irlaunde [or Irlonde]. *Unknown. See* I Am from Ireland.

Ich sterbe . . . Life ebbs with an easy flow. The End of a War. Sir Herbert Read. OBMV; PeFWW

Ich Weiss Nicht Was Soll es Bedeuten. Heinrich Heine, *German.* AWP, *tr. by* Alexander Macmillan

Ichabod[!]. John Greenleaf Whittier. APN-1; NAAL-1; NAAL-3; NOBA; OxBA; PAR; PBMP; PoEL-4; TAP

Ichabod! The Glory Has Departed. Ludwig Uhland, *German.* AWP, *tr. by* James Clarence Mangan

Ichot a burde in a bour ase beryl so bright. *Unknown.* MiEL

Ichot a burde in boure bryht. Blow, Northern Wind. *Unknown.* GBL; OBEV

Ichthycide. Joe Rosenblatt. NOBC

Ichthyosaurus, The. *Unknown.* CTV

Icicle the moon drifting through it, An. Matsuo Allard. HA

Icicles, An. *Unknown. See* Riddle: "Lives in winter."

Icicles upon the pane, The. February. Henrietta Cordelia Ray. CBWP-3

Ickle ockle, blue bockle. *Unknown.* OxNR

Icon. Hugh Seidman. BAP-93

Icons. Miriam Waddington. NOBC

Icos. Charles Tomlinson. GTBS-P

Icy, empty dawn cracks in the fields, The. Pacifists. George Woodcock. NOBC

Icy evil that struck his father down, The. El-Hajj Malik El-Shabazz. Robert Earl Hayden. NAAAL; PoBA

Icy sun rises silently, The. Quail Sky. Li Ch'ing-chao, *Chinese*. OHPC, tr. by Kenneth Rexroth

Id. Harry Clifton. PBCIP

I'd a dream to-night. Mater Dolorosa. William Barnes. CH; NOBE; OBEV

I'd almost know, the nights I snuck in late. Fifteen to Eighteen. Marilyn Hacker. GLP

I'd already lost my hair. Now my sun. The Corn. Daniel David Moses. HATNAP

I'd been on duty from two till four. Stand-to: Good Friday Morning. Siegfried Sassoon. FaBoTw

I'd bury my face in my hands but. The Ruins. Marcia Southwick. CMAP

I'd Choose to Be a Daisy. *Unknown*. BoTP

I'd decided I initiate most. Sonnet 37. Phyllis Koestenbaum. FFC

I'd draw all this into a fine element,—a color. The Rug. Michael McClure. NeAP

I'd gie them a' to King Charlie'. (LL) The Bonnie House o' Airlie. *Unknown*. ESPB; OBEV; OxBB; OxBS

I'd give it five stars. Revelation: The Movie. Elton Glaser. PBCAP

I'd have to piss through my eyes to cry for you. I Just Missed the Bus and I'll Be Late for Work. Ariel Dorfman, *Spanish*. AF, tr. by Ariel Dorfman *and* Edith Grossman

I'd lay me doune and dee. (LL) Annie Laurie. William Douglas, *rev. by* Lady Jane Scott. FaBoBe; ImPo

I'd like a little love in the wine-red Afternoon. Gillian Conoley. CMAP

I'd like to be a bee. Torquato Tasso. ItIP

I'd like to be a mother. A Mother. Victoria C. Armuth. CTV

I'd like to be the sort of friend that you have been to me. A Friend's Greeting. E. A. Guest. BLPA

I'd like to live with you. Marina Tsvetayeva, *Russian*. BoWoP, tr. by Paul Schmidt

I'd like to peddle toy balloons. The Balloon Seller. Elizabeth Fleming. BoTP

I'd like to / Pull. The Intelligent Sheepman and the New Cars. William Carlos Williams. OBAL

I'd like to taste my life again in little. Return to Paris. Jules Supervielle, *French*. MFP, tr. by Martin Sorrell

I'd like us to open the cabinets and let the resin of firs out. At Night the Jellyfish Unfold Their Veils. Virgil Teodorescu, *Romanian*. CEEP, tr. by Donald Eulert *and* Stefan Avadanei

I'd Love to Be a Fairy's Child. Robert Graves. BoTP; ChAP

I'd love to give a party. A Wish. Elizabeth Gould. BoTP

I'd make a bed for you. Labasheedy (The Silken Bed). Nuala Ni Dhomhnaill, *Irish*. CIP-2, tr. by the Author

I'd meet the wise men going in. (LL) Christmas Morning. Elizabeth Madox Roberts. MoAmPo; NOxBChV; PChr

I'd not despoil the linnet's nest. The Bird's Nest. *Unknown*. ACTP

I'd oft heard tell of this Sledburn fair. Sledburn Fair. *Unknown*. CH

I'd rather be the ship that sails. The Ship That Sails. *Unknown*. PoToHe

I'd rather have fingers than toes. On Digital Extremities. Frank Gelett Burgess. PeLi

I'd rather have the thought of you. Choice. Angela Morgan. PoLF

I'd rather my fist be made of steel. The Last Word. Imamu Amiri Baraka. UnSA

I'd rather see than be one! (LL) The Purple Cow. Frank Gelett Burgess. CBNP; CTV; FPC; NBLV; NTCP; OBAL; OBCA; OBCoV; PoLF; TFi; TLR

I'd Rather See than be One, but. Anne Halley. NMM-2

I'd *rather* you'd not go unless you must. (LL) A Servant to Servants. Robert Frost. CMoP; NAAL-2

I'd rock my own sweet childie to rest in a cradle of gold on a bough of the willow. Irish Lullaby. Alfred Percival Graves. IIP

I'd run about / on the desert. Her Elegy. *Unknown, Papago Indian*. STP, tr. by Armand Schwerner; BoWoP, tr. by Ruth Underhill

I'd scratch out both his eyes. (LL) Hard Daddy. Langston Hughes. MoLi; NAAAL

I'd shoot the man who pulled up slowly in his hot car this morning. If I Had a Gun. Gig Ryan. BMAP

I'd sit inside the abandoned shack all morning. About a Year After He Got Married He Would Sit Alone in an Abandoned Shack in a Cotton Field Enjoying Himself. James Whitehead. MT

I'd smoke in the freezer. Shoplifters. Maura Stanton. CMAP

I'd stop writing at the capture of the unicorn. (LL) Ancient Airs. Li Po, *Chinese*. SuSp, tr. by Joseph J. Lee

I'd talk to them now. Gifts. Judy Ruiz. IFJA

I'd toddle safely home and die—in bed. (LL) Base Details. Siegfried Sassoon. MoBrPo; OxBSP; OxBoV; PeFWW; PoFWW; SAGP

I'd wake up starved on the day of the match. Reflections on Hillsborough in Memoriam. T. H. Naisby. NOBAu

I'd wave the gnats away and try. Crew Practice on Lake Bled, in Jugoslavla. James Scully. NYBP

I'd wed you without herds, without money, or rich array. Cashel of Munster. William English, *Irish*. BIrV; GBL; OBEV, tr. by Sir Samuel Ferguson

Idanre and Other Poems (1967). Wole Soyinka.
    Death in the Dawn. PBMAP
    Night. PBMAP
    Prisoner. PBMAP
    Season. PBMAP

Idbury bells are ringing. Country Thought. Sylvia Townsend Warner. MoBrPo

Idea. Michael Drayton.
    Another to the River Ankor. NOSC
    "As Love and I, late harboured in one inn." NoSic
      ("As Love and I, late harbour'd in one inn.") LoP
    "As other men, so I myself do muse." NOSC; NoSic; Son
    "Calling to [my] mind[e] since first my love begun." NOBE; PoEL-2; SCGP
    "Evil [or Evill] spirit, your beauty, haunts me still, An." AAS; GBL; NOBE; NoSic
    His Remedie for Love. AAS
    "If he, from heaven that filched the living fire." AAS
      ("If he from heaven that filched that living fire.") NoP-4
    "Like an adventurous seafarer am I." NOSC; Son
    "Love, in a humour, played the prodigal." NoSic
    Night and Day.
      ("Dear, why should you command me to my rest.") GSo
      (Sonnet: "Dear [or Deere], why should you command me to my rest.")
    "Nothing but no and I, and I and no." GBL; PoEL-2
    "O, why should Nature niggardly restraine!" PBRV
    Parting, The. GLoP; OBEV; SCV
      (Love's Farewell.) GTBS-P
      ("Since ther's no helpe, Come let us kisse and part.") GEA
    Since There's No Help. CABP; LoP; PFE; PoPoPo
      (Love's Farewell.) GTBS-P
      ("Since ther's no helpe, Come let us kisse and part.") GEA
    Sonnet 35: 'Some, misbelieving and profane'. AEP
    Sonnet 6: 'How many paltry, foolish, painted things'. AEP
    "There's nothing grieves me, but that age should haste." AAS; NOSC; OAEL-1
    "To nothing fitter can I Thee compare." SCGP; Son
      ("I give Thee backe, when all the rest is spent.") (LL) PBRV
    To the Critic. NOSC, sect. XXXI
    To the Reader of These Sonnets. AAS; NAEL-1; NOSC; Son
      ("Into these loves who but for passion looks.") NoP-4
      ("That cannot long one fashion entertain.") (LL) NoP-4
    "Truce, gentle love, a parley now I crave." NoSic
    "Whilst thus my pen strives to eternize thee." AAS; Son
    "Why should your fair eyes with such sovereign grace." SCGP
    "Witlesse gallant, a young wench that woo'd, A." AAS
    "You are [or You're] not alone when you are still alone." PoEL-2

Idea, The. Agnes Mary Frances Robinson. VWP

Idea of a Swimmer. Jean-Richard Bloch, *French*. TrJP, tr. by "S. P."

Idea of Ancestry, The. Etheridge Knight. AF; BPo; CoAmPo; ISC; NAAAL; NIP-4; NNaP; PBCAP; PoBA; RaBo
    ("And I have no children / to float in the space between.") (LL) ChAP
    ("I have no children / to float in the space between.") (LL) GT

Idea of Entropy at Maenporth Beach, The. Peter Redgrove. FaBoMo

Idea of illusion suggests that existences in different worlds, The. Experience. Mei-Mei Berssenbrugge. PT

Idea of justice may be precious, An. Ode. Frank O'Hara. NeAP

Idea of Order at Key West, The. Wallace Stevens. CMoP; ColAP; HAP; HCAP; HeIP-4; MeMAP; MoAmPo; MoP; NAAL-2; NAWM-2; NIP-4; NOBA; NoAM; NoP-4; OxBA; PoE; PoPoPo; Poetr; SAmP; TAP; TFi

Idea of trust, or, The. Thom Gunn. Poetsp

Ideal, The. T. R. Hummer. LTA

Ideal. Padraic Pearse, *Modern Irish*. AWP, tr. by Thomas Macdonagh

Ideal, An. Henrietta Cordelia Ray. CBWP-3

Ideal and dearly beloved voices. Voices. Constantine P. Cavafy, *Greek*. LBC, tr. by Rae Dalven

Ideal and Reality. Joseph Campbell. BIrV

Ideal Angels. John Robert Colombo. MoCV

Idealism. Ronald Arbuthnott Knox. *See* Limerick: "There once was a man who said "God.""

Ideals. Robert Greene. PoToHe

Idea's Mirrour. Michael Drayton.
    "Golden sun upon his fiery wheels, The." NoSic

Identification in Belfast (I.R.A. Bombing). Robert Lowell. OxBC

Identikit, The. Amryl Johnson. NBrP

Identity. Robert Francis. AFr

Identity A Poem. Gertrude Stein. PFTM

Identity Card. Mahmoud Darwish, *Arabic*. VCWP, *tr. by* Denys Johnson-Davies

Ideogram. William Meredith. Poetr

Idiom of the Hero. Wallace Stevens. AFr; OxBA

Idiot, The. Adèle Naudé. PeSA

Idiot, The. Dudley Randall. BPo; LTA

Idiot, The. Robert Southey. Ro *Fr.* Morning Post, no. 9198.

Idiot, The. Keith Wilson. Poetsp

Idiot-Born, The. Eliza Cook. VWP

Idiot Boy, The. Wordsworth. NOBRP; OBNV; Ro

Idiot greens the meadows with his eyes, The. Allen Tate. FaBoMo

Idiot me has ended one more day's official grind! Climbing K'uai Pavilion. Huang T'ing-chien, *Chinese*. SuSp, *tr. by* Michael E. Workman

Idiotic silence of state holidays, The. Gratitude. György Petri, *Hungarian*. VCWP, *tr. by* Wilmer, Clive and George Gömöri

"Idle as trout in light Colonel Jones." The Famine Road. Eavan Boland. FaBoWP

Idle Charon. Eugene Lee-Hamilton. NOBVV

Idle cuckoo, having made a feast, The. On the Cuckoo. Francis Quarles. NTP

Idle Droning. Po Chü-i, *Chinese*. CoBCP, *tr. by* Burton Watson

Idle Fyno. *Unknown*. PoEL-2

Idle, I enjoy only tranquillity. Replying to Hsi-mei's "Thoughts in Early Autumn." Lu Kuei Meng, *Chinese*. SuSp, *tr. by* Robin D. S. Yates

Idle Life I Lead, The. Robert Bridges. LiTM

Idle poet, here and there, An. The Revelation. Coventry Patmore. EnLoPo; GBL, GLoP, GTBS P; HAP; LoP; OBNC; OxBSP *Fr.* The Angel in the House.

Idle Pursuits. Alexander Pope. ECEV, *book IV, ll.* 565–604 *Fr.* Yet, yet a moment, one dim ray of light. NAEL-1; OAEL-1; PoEL-3 *Fr.* The Dunciad.

Idle Thoughts. Lu Yu, *Chinese*. CoBCP, *tr. by* Burton Watson

Idle Verse. Henry Vaughan. MiEL

Idle Visitation, An. Edward Dorn. NOBA; PmAP *Fr.* Gunslinger.

Idle Words. Walter Savage Landor. OBSV

Idleness. Lu Yu, *Chinese*. OHPC; OxBM, *tr. by* Kenneth Rexroth

Idler with a wand for a walking stick, An. Batyushkov. Osip Emilevich Mandelstam, *Russian*. OBVE, *tr. by* W. S. Merwin *and* Clarence Brown

Idlers, The. Edmund Blunden. BoTP; CH

Idlers. Leonid Nikolaevich Martynov, *Russian*. TCRP, *tr. by* J. R. Rowland

Idler's busy, for he loves the Muse, An. A Gaffer in Love. Y Vân Tử', *Vietnamese*. AVP, *tr. by* Huỳnh Sanh Thông

Idleset: "Ill's the airt o the Word the day." Thurso Berwick. OxBS

Idling pivot of the frigate bird, The. Man o' War Bird. Derek Walcott. TTY

Idolatry. Arna Bontemps. SAGP

Idyl. Henrietta Cordelia Ray. CBWP-3

  Sunrise. BlSi

  Sunset. BlSi

Idyl: "And my young sweetheart sat at board with me." Alfred Mombert, *German*. AWP, *tr. by* Ludwig Lewisohn

Idyll: "He was a selfish shellfish." Stoddard King. NBLV

Idyl of Harvest Time, An. John Townsend Trowbridge. APN-2

Idyl of Spring, An. Henrietta Cordelia Ray. CBWP-3

Idyll. Theocritus, *Greek*. *Fr.* Idylls.

  ("Shepheard *Paris* bore the *Spartan* Bride, The.") OBCVT, *tr. by* John Dryden

Idyll: "Hermit hoar, in solemn cell." Samuel Johnson. NOBL; PeLV

Idyll 1. Moschus, *Greek*. OBCVT, *tr. by* Francis Fawkes

Idyll 1. Theocritus, *Greek*.

  "I dare not, faith I dare not pipe at *Noon*." OBCVT, *tr. by* Thomas Creech

Idyll 14. Theocritus, *Greek*.

  "*Tom, Will,* and *Dick,* and I, a jovial Crew." OBCVT, *tr. by* Thomas Creech

Idyll of the Rose. Ausonius, *Latin*. AWP, *tr. by* John Addington Symonds

Idyll of the South, An. Albery Allson Whitman.

  "I had a dream: Columbia the Great." APN-2

Idylls. Theocritus, *Greek*.

  Cyclops, The ("And so an easier life"). AWP

  ("For love there is no other drug, Nicias.") HePo, *tr. by* Barbara Hughes Fowler

  Damoetas and Daphnis. HePo, *tr. by* Barbara Hughes Fowler

  Death of Daphnis, The. HePo, *tr. by* Barbara Hughes Fowler; AWP, *tr. by* Charles Stuart Calverley

  ("Sweet is the whispering of that pine tree, goatherd.") HePo, *tr. by* Barbara Hughes Fowler

  Enchantment, The. HePo, *tr. by* Barbara Hughes Fowler; CTC; OBVE, *tr. by* Thomas Creech

  ("Where is my bay? Bring it, Thestylis. Where are my charms?") HePo, *tr. by* Barbara Hughes Fowler

  Fishermen, The. AWP; OBVE, *tr. by* Charles Stuart Calverley

  Gorgo and Praxinoa. HePo, *tr. by* Barbara Hughes Fowler

  Harvest-Home. HePo, *tr. by* Barbara Hughes Fowler; AWP, *tr. by* Charles Stuart Calverley

  ("There was a time when Eucritus and I were going.") HePo, *tr. by* Barbara Hughes Fowler

  Herdsmen, The. AWP, *tr. by* Charles Stuart Calverley

  Hylas. HePo, *tr. by* Barbara Hughes Fowler

  Idyll.

  ("Shepheard *Paris* bore the *Spartan* Bride, The.") OBCVT, *tr. by* John Dryden

  Incantations, The. AWP, *tr. by* Charles Stuart Calverley

  Little Heracles. HePo, *tr. by* Barbara Hughes Fowler

  Neteheard. OBCVT, *tr. by* Unknown

  ("Eunica skorned me, when her I would have sweetly kist.") OBCVT, *tr. by* Unknown

  ("In cittie, nor on hill, but al the night must sleepe alone.") (LL) OBCVT, *tr. by* Unknown

Idylls of the King. Geoffrey Hill. NoAM; PoE *Fr.* An Apology for the Revival of Christian Architecture in England.

Idylls of the King, *sels.* Tennyson.

  Passing of Arthur, The. FHYEP; NAEL-2; OBNC

  "And answer made King Arthur, breathing hard." PeECV, *ll.* 330–440; EBEV

  ("Before the eyes of ladies and of kings.") (LL) EBEV

  "Then rose the King and moved his host by night." PeVV

  Pelleas and Ettarre. NAEL-2

  "Rose, but one, none other rose had I, A." PoEL-5

Iesu, swete son dere! Our Lady's Song. *Unknown*. OBEV

If. Franklin Pierce Adams. OBAL

If. Jared Angira. PBMAP

If. Blaga Dimitrova, *Bulgarian*. CEEP, *tr. by* Jascha Kessler *and* Aleksandar Shurbanov

If. Rudyard Kipling. APAD; BLPA; CTV; ChAP; EBEvV; FaBoBe; FaPoR; OxBChV; OxBTC; PFE; PWR; SAGP; UV

If. Patrick Lane. NOBC

If ("If all the land were apple-pie"). *Unknown*. FPC

If a calving cow. What Her Mother Said. *Unknown, Tamil*. PLW, *tr. by* A. K. Ramanujan

If a child of my clan should die. A King's Last Words. Ceraman Kanikkal Irumporai, *Tamil*. PLW, *tr. by* A. K. Ramanujan

If a clear [*or* cleere] fountain[e] still keeping a sad course. The Duke's Song. Mary Sidney, Countess of Montgomery Wroth. WPE *Fr.* Urania.

If a clear fountain still keeping a sad course. Mary Sidney, Countess of Montgomery Wroth. *See* The Duke's Song.

If a cuckoo comes into the village. A Theory. Charles Simic. ChAP

If a custom-tailored vet. Cole Porter. NBLV *Fr.* Always True to You in My Fashion.

If a fir tree had a foot or two like a turtle, or a wing. That Journeys Are Good. Jelaluddin Rumi, *Persian*. RaBo, *tr. by* Robert Bly

If a flame has fallen among the cedars. Haim Guri, *Hebrew*. IP, *tr. by* Warren Bargad *and* Stanley F. Chyet

If a good man were ever housed in Hell. The Good Man in Hell. Edwin Muir. MoBrPo

If a lot of people are laughing. Dennis Williams. EC2

If a Man who Turnips cries. The Turnip Vendor. Samuel Johnson. OxNR; PeLV

If a man with a shovel came down the road. The Diggers. W. S. Merwin. CBNP; SPE

If a man's drunk from morning on. Kāri Sober. Kapilar, *Tamil*. PLW, *tr. by* A. K. Ramanujan

If a monkey drives a car. Poems We Can Understand. Paul Hoover. EOEF; PmAP

If a person conceives an opinion. Poeta Loquitur. Swinburne. OAEL-2

If a pig wore a wig. Christina Rossetti. VWP

If a straight horizontal thread one meter long falls from a height of one. The 1914 Box. Marcel Duchamp. PFTM

If a Suite in Praise of the Yoruba Oracle. Awotunde Aworinde, *Yoruba*. PFTM, *tr. by* Judith Gleason *and* John Olaniyi Ogundipe

If a swan / sang. (LL) Swan and Shadow. John Hollander. InPK-6; PoA; VCAP

If a task is once begun. Always Finish. *Unknown.* BLPA; CTV; FaBoBe

If, after attaining Buddhahood, anyone in my land. Amitabha's Vow. Gary Snyder. *Fr.* Burning. NaAP; PoM *Fr.* Myths and Texts.

If, after I die they should want to write my biography. Fernando Pessoa, *Portuguese.* PeSAV, *tr. by* Jonathan Griffin

If after rude and boisterous seas. The Plaudite, or End of Life. Robert Herrick. CaPo

If, after the bombardment is over. The Discourse on Method. Herberto Padilla, *Spanish.* VCWP, *tr. by* Alastair Reid *and* Alexander Coleman

If again in the spring. Seeing the Plum Blossoms by the River. Lady Ise, *Japanese.* BoWoP, *tr. by* Etsuko Terasaki *and* Irma Brandeis

If all a top physicist knows. After Reading a Child's Guide to Modern Physics. W. H. Auden. NYBP

If all be true that I do think. A Catch. Henry Aldrich. FaBoEE; NOSC; OxBSP; PFE

If all of me is still there. Plenty-hawk, *Crow Indian.* STP, *tr. by* W. S. Merwin

If all our life were one broad glare. The Joy of Incompleteness. Albert Crowell. PoToHe

If all the answer's to be the Sinai sort. Golden Calf. Norman MacCaig. ChIV-1; OxBS

If all the good people were clever. Good and Clever. Elizabeth Wordsworth. OxBTC

If all the land were apple-pie. If. *Unknown.* FPC

If all the seas were one sea. Mother Goose. BoTP; OxNR; ReMoGo

If all the seas were one sea. *Unknown.* CTV

If all the ships I have at sea. My Ships. Ella Wheeler Wilcox. PoLF

If all the sorrows of this weary earth. Friends. Thomas Curtis Clark. PoToHe

If all the tears thou madest mine. Tears and Joys. Margaret Louisa Woods. LBC

If all the trees in all the woods were men. Cacoëthes Scribendi. Oliver Wendell Holmes. NBLV; OBCoV

If all the world. Resources. Milton. *Fr.* Comus; a Masque Presented at Ludlow Castle. FHYEP; OAEL-1

If all the world and love [*or* loue] were young. The Nimphs [*or* Nymph's] Reply to the Sheepheard [*or* Shepherd]. Sir Walter Ralegh. AAS; AEP; BoLoP; CABP; CTC; ClHu; EBEvV; GLoP; HAP; HeIP-4; HoPM; ImPo; InPK-6; InPS-3; NAEL-1; NBLV; NIP-4; NOBE; NoP-4; NoSic; OAEL-1; OBEV; PFE; PoE; PoPoPo; Poetr; RACG; RB; SAGP; SCGP; SiPS; TFi; TRP; UV; WeW-3

If all the world were apple-pie. Mother Goose. ReMoGo

If all the world were [*or* was] paper. *Unknown.* CBNP; EBEvV; NOSC; NTCP; OBCoV; OxNR; TTTS

If *Amoret*, that glorious eye. To Amoret, Walking in a Starry Evening. Henry Vaughan. BeJo; FMP

If amorous faith, a heart of guileless ways. Signs of Love. Petrarch. AWP *Fr.* Sonnets to Laura.

If an eagle be imprisoned. America. Henry Dumas. ChAP; PoBA

If an unkind word appears. On File. John Kendrick Bangs. PoToHe

If angels sung a Savior's birth. John Stephenson. AmFP

If any ask why there's no great She-Poet. Dedication of the Cook. Anna Wickham. MoBrPo; NALW

If Any Be Pleased to Walk into My Poor Garden. Francis Daniel Pastorius. SCAP

If any God should say. Rebirth. Rudyard Kipling. OBNC

If any have a stone to shy. The Pebble. Elinor Wylie. ChIV-1; MoAmPo

If any little word of mine. The Little Word. *Unknown.* PWR; PoToHe

If any man would know the very cause. Is Out of Heart with His Time. Guerzo di Montecanti, *Italian.* AWP, *tr. by* D. G. Rossetti

If any mourn us in the workshop, say. Batteries Out of Ammunition. Rudyard Kipling. *Fr.* Epitaphs of the War [1914–1918]. OBWP

If any question why we died. Common Form. Rudyard Kipling. FaBoEE; FaBoTw; PeFWW *Fr.* Epitaphs of the War [1914–1918]. OBWP

If any vision should reveal. Tennyson. OxBSn *Fr.* In Memoriam A. H. H.

If any wench Venus's girdle wear. Song. John Gay. PeLV; PoEL-3 *Fr.* The Beggar's Opera. OAEL-1

If anybody comes to I. On Dr. Lettsom. *Unknown.* FaBoEE

If anybody's friend be dead. Emily Dickinson. FP

If apples were pears. To My Valentine. *Unknown.* CTV

If art and industry should doe as much. New English Canaan; Prologue. Thomas Morton. SCAP

If art were a series of arbitrary digs. On Geoffrey Grigson. Cyril Connolly. OBCoV

If as a flower [*or* flowre] doth spread and die. Employment (1). George Herbert. GeHe

If, as Plato called them, shadows. Boethius at Cavalzero. John Macoubrie. CRP

If as the wind[e]s and waters here below. The Storm. George Herbert. ESCV

If, as well may happen. Read Me, Please! Robert Graves. NYBP

If at your coming princes disappear. Comets and Princes. Samuel Johnson. FaBoEE

If aught can teach us aught, Affliction's looks. Affliction. Sir John Davies. NOBE *Fr.* Nosce Teipsum. NoSic; SiPS

If aught [*or* ought] of oaten stop, or pastoral song. Ode to Evening. William Collins. AWP; CABP; EBEV; ECEV; FaBoBe; GTBS-P; HAP; ImPo; NAEL-1; NOBE; NOEC; NoP-4; OAEL-1; OBEV; OxAEP-1; PoE; PoEL-3; SCGP; TFi

If Auschwitz had been in Hampshire. Edward Bond. HP

If bees are few. (LL) To make a prairie it takes a clover and one bee. Emily Dickinson. BoWoP; HeIP-4; NBLV; OBCA; OxBA

If bees stay at home. *Unknown.* OxNR ("It'll be a fine day.") (LL) ACTP

If Bethlehem were here today [*or* to-day]. Christmas Morning. Elizabeth Madox Roberts. MoAmPo; NOxBChV; PChr

If Birds That neither Sow nor Reap. Roger Williams. AH

If blocked, a fart can kill a man. Nicarchus of Alexandria, *Greek.* GrAn, *tr. by* Robin Skelton

If Blood Is Black Then Spirit Neglects My Unborn Son. Conrad Kent Rivers. PoBA

If but God wearieth. (LL) Antique Harvesters. John Crowe Ransom. MoAmPo; OxBA

If but some vengeful god would call to me. Hap. Thomas Hardy. AWP; CABP; CMoP; EBVV; EnVR; GSo; ImPo; MoBrPo; NAEL-2; NoAM; NoP-4; OAEL-2; PBMP; PFE; Poetr; Son

If by dull rhymes our English must be chained. On the Sonnet. Keats. NIP-4; NoP-4; OAEL-2

If by his torturing, savage foes untraced. The Captive Escaped in the Wilds of America. Addressed to the Hon. Mrs. O'Neill. Charlotte Smith. Son

If by mischance the people in the street. George Wither. PBRV *Fr.* Britain's Remembrancer Canto 4.

If by your art, my dearest father, you have. Shakespeare. *Fr.* The Tempest. OAEL-1

If, Calvus, effects of grief. Catullus. *See* Love and Death.

"If Candlemas be fine and clear." At Candlemas. Charles Causley. OBCP

If care do cause men cry, why do not I complain. Henry Howard, Earl of Surrey. SiPS

If chance assigned [*or* assign'd]. Sir Thomas Wyatt. SiPS

If china, then only the kind. Stanislaw Baranczak, *Polish.* AF, *tr. by* Magnus J. Krynski

If Christmas brought me nothing more. A Poem for Christmas. C. A. Snodgrass. PoToHe

If Church spire be clëar. Senilio's Weather Saw. Martin Bell. PeLV

If clothed in black you tread the busy town. John Gay. ECEV *Fr.* Trivia; or, The Art of Walking the Streets of London.

If come into this world again I must. Dew on a Dusty Heart. Jean Starr Untermeyer. MoAmPo

If "compression is the first grace of style." To a Snail. Marianne Moore. APo; CMoP; FaBoMo; FaBoWP; MeMAP; NAAL-2; NALW; PoPoPo

If Cynthia be a queen, a princess, and supreme. Sir Walter Ralegh. SiPS ("Thy mind of neither needs, in both seeing it exceeds.") (LL) NoP-4

If Dante mourns, there wheresoe'er he be. To One Who Had Censured His Public Exposition of Dante. Giovanni Boccaccio. AWP *Fr.* Sonnets.

If design govern in a thing so small. (LL) Design. Robert Frost. CMoP; ColAP; HeIP-4; InPK-6; InPS-3; MoP; NAAL-2; NOBA; NoAM; NoP-4; PBMP; PoPoPo; Poetr; RaBo; SAmP; SoSe-8; Son; TAP; TFi; TRP

If doughty [*or* daughty] deeds my lady please[s]. Robert Graham. GTBS-P; OBEV

If down his throat a man should choose. An Unsuspected Fact. Edward Cannon. FPC

If dreams could dream, beyond the canon of landscapes. Psyche's Dream. Anne Lauterbach. EOEF

If, dumb too long, the drooping Muse hath stayed. To the Earl of Warwick, on the Death of Mr. Addison. Thomas Tickell. NOEC; OxAEP-1

If duty, wife, lead thee to deem. Husband to Wife. John Harington. NoSic

If dying well is courage's great test. For the Athenian Dead at Plataia. Simonides, *Greek.* GrAn, *tr. by* Peter Jay

If earthward you could wing your flight. England Expects? Sir Owen Seaman. NOBL

If e'er in thy sight I found favour, Apollo. The Poet's Prayer. *Unknown.* OBSV

If Eve hadn't eaten the apple. Limerick. Wendy Cope. PeLi

If ever against this easy blue and silver. Interruption. Robert Graves. ImPo; LiTM

If ever chance or choice thy footsteps lead. The Flying Tailor. James Hogg. BXAP

If Ever Hapless Woman Had a Cause. Mary Sidney Herbert, Countess of Pembroke. WPE

If ever I go to sea. Me—Pirate. Clive Sansom. OTCP

If ever I should condescend to prose. Poetical Commandments. Byron. OxBoLi; PeLV, *canto 1, stanzas 204–206* Fr. Canto the First. NAEL-2; OAEL-2; PoE Fr. Don Juan.

If ever love had force in huma[i]ne brest? Sonnet 42. Mary Sidney, Countess of Montgomery Wroth. BWW Fr. Pamphilia to Amphilanthus.

If ever man might him avaunt. Sir Thomas Wyatt. SiPS

If ever mercy move you murder me. To the Mercy Killers. Dudley Randall. SoSe-8

If ever there lived a Yankee lad. Darius Green and His Flying-Machine. John Townsend Trowbridge. FaBoBe; OBAL; OBCA; OxBChV; PoLF

If ever there was a beginning. Let There Be Light! D. H. Lawrence. ChIV-1; KSG

If ever two were one, then surely we. To My Dear and Loving Husband. Anne Bradstreet. AmPP; BoWoP; ColAP; HAP; HeIP-4; KTR; LW; NAAL-1; NAAL-3; NIP-4; NOBA; NOCV; NOSC; NoP-4; OxBA; OxBM; OxBSP; OxWW; PEW; PiM; PoE; PoEL-3; PoLF; SAGP; SCAP; TAP; TFi; WPE; WeW-3

If ever you go to Dublin town. Patrick Kavanagh. CMoP; IIP; InPS-3

If ever you go to the North Countree. Edenhall. "Susan Coolidge." OBCA

If ever you should go by chance. How To Tell the Wild Animals. Carolyn Wells. NBLV

If everything happens that can't be done. E. E. Cummings. ITG; SoSe-8; WeW-3

If everything tends to become real. For Example (1): Stepping Out. Anne Lauterbach. PT

If everywhere in the street. Song: "If everywhere in the street." Denis Glover. PeNZ *Fr.* Sings Harry.

If external action is effete. The Past Is the Present. Marianne Moore. MeMAP; NAAL-2

If faithful soul[e]s be alike glorified [*or* glorifi'd]. Donne. *Fr.* Holy Sonnets. ESCV *Fr.* Holy Sonnets.

If, fallen in evil days on evil tongue. Byron. EPCY *Fr.* Dedication: "Bob Southey! You're a poet—poet-laureate." CTC; OAEL-2; OBSV *Fr.* Don Juan.

If famous Apelles with his hand of art. Pietro Aretino. GS

If fancy [*or* fansy] would favour. Sir Thomas Wyatt. AAS; SiPS

If fictive music fails your lyre, confess. What's Good for the Soul is Good for Sales. Richard Wilbur. NBLV *Fr.* Flippancies.

If, finding it, he fails to find / Its master. (LL) The Snail. Vincent Bourne, *Latin.* BoTP; CTAV; OBVE, *tr. by* William Cowper

If for all the promises you regard so lightly. 2.8. Horace. STV, *tr. by* John Frederick Nims *Fr.* Odes.

If Freud was right and dreams of falling are. On Waking after Dreaming of Raoul. Lynn Emanuel. NAmP90

If from the height of that celestial sphere. To Shakespeare. Frances Anne Kemble. Son

If from the public way you turn your steps. Michael [A Pastoral Poem]. Wordsworth. FHYEP; NAEL-2; NOBRP; OAEL-2; OxAEP-2

If fruits are fed on any beast. Epitaph after Reading Ronsard's Lines from Rabelais. John Millington Synge. FaBoEE

If George Washington / had not. Diane Wakoski. MoLi *Fr.* The Father of My Country. NoAM; TAP

If girls were nice. Rufinus, *Greek.* GrAn, *tr. by* Alan Marshfield

If God had stopped work after the fifth day. The Imperfect Paradise. Linda Pastan. SoSe-8

If God kept a terrarium. Walter James Turner. *Fr.* The Seven Days of the Sun. OBMV

If Gray Had Had to Write His Elegy in the Cemetery of Spoon River Instead of in That of Stoke Poges, *parody.* Sir John Collings Squire. BXAP

If grief come early. First or Last. Thomas Hardy. CMoP

If Grief Could Burn Out. Quintin Hailsham. LBC

If grief could burn out. Philip Larkin. LBC

If grief for grief can touch thee. Emily Jane Brontë. EnLoPo; OBNC ("Beloved, again!") (LL) GLoP; VWP

If half my heart is here, doctor. Angina Pectoris. Nazim Hikmet, *Turkish.* VCWP, *tr. by* Randy Blasing *and* Mutlu Konuk

If Hart Crane played trumpet. Almost Blue. Mark Doty. SeSe

If hate is painful and if love's a pain. Euenus, *Greek.* GrAn, *tr. by* Alistair Elliot

If he could have kept. Sam. Lucille Clifton. MoLi; UnSA

If he could say it, he meant to. Supposition with Qualification. Philip Booth. AFr

If he could solve the riddle. Sphinx. Robert Earl Hayden. GT; HCAP

If he cried, he cried in private. John Kitching. SpW

If he did not come apart in her hands, he fell. Diane Di Prima. PFTM *Fr.* Loba.

If he found a little liquor. Elegy. Auvaiyar, *Tamil.* PLW, *tr. by* A. K. Ramanujan

If he, from heaven that filched the living fire. Michael Drayton. AAS *Fr.* Idea. ("If he from heaven that filched that living fire.") NoP-4

If he had a sense of identity it was probably with a stone. Sense of Identity. Zbigniew Herbert, *Polish.* CEEP, *tr. by* John Carpenter *and* Bogdana Carpenter

If he had only been a more inspiring Leader. On the Death of Ludwig Erhard. Hal Colebatch. NOBAu

If He Let Us Go Now. Shirley Williams. BoWoP

If he married a woman with nothing to wear? (LL) Nothing to Wear. William Allen Butler. OBAL; PoLF

If he roam far away. The Dilemma. Anna Wickham. WPN

If he that erst the form so lively drew. Henry Howard, Earl of Surrey. SiPS

If he were I, he would do what I did. (LL) The Hanging Man. Sylvia Plath. HCAP; VCAP

If he would come to-day, to-day, to-day. Hoping Against Hope. Christina Rossetti. CBLP

If Heaven had no love for wine. Drinking Alone in Moonlight. Li Po, *Chinese.* TAL, *tr. by* Robert Payne

If Heaven has into being deigned to call. Slavery. Hannah More. WoRP

If heaven were to do again. The Peaceful Shepherd. Robert Frost. MoAmPo

If Heaven weren't fond of wine. Li Po. SuSp, *tr. by* Irving Lo *Fr.* Drinking Alone beneath the Moon.

If heav'n the grateful liberty would give. The Choice. John Pomfret. NOEC

If Hercules' tall stature might be guessed. On a Good Leg and Foot. William Strode. NOSC

If honour to an ancient name be due. On the Welsh Language. Katherine Philips. CABP; NOSC

If hope grew on a bush, / And joy grew on a tree. Hope and Joy. Christina Rossetti. OxBChV

If Hot Flowers Come to the Street. R. Meenakshi, *Tamil.* OMIP, *tr. by* Martha Ann Selby

If I a*M inte*rupting you please excuse me. To Lady Wyatt. Edward Lear. CBNP

If I am proud, you surely know. Called Proud. Walter Savage Landor. GBL; GLoP

If I Am Too Brown or Too White for You. Wendy Rose. HATNAP

If I became. If I Became a Stone. So Chong-Ju, *Korean.* VCWP, *tr. by* David R. McCann

If I Became a Stone. So Chong-Ju, *Korean.* VCWP, *tr. by* David R. McCann

If I Blindfold You. Marjorie Welish. FTOS

If I bring back. For My Unborn and Wretched Children. Alfred B. Spellman. PoBA

If I can stop one Heart from breaking. Emily Dickinson. AH; PWR; PoLF; PoToHe

If I consider / My body like the fields. Lady Ise, *Japanese.* WPOW, *tr. by* Donald Keene

If I could be a gipsy-boy. The Caravan. Madeleine Nightingale. BoTP

If I could believe that death. Gaspara Stampa, *Italian.* PBWP, *tr. by* Lynne Lawner

If I could bestow immortality. The Objects of Immortality. Pattiann Rogers. WeT

If I could climb the garden wall. There. Rodney Bennett. BoTP

If I could drive steel like John Henry. Drivin' Steel. *Unknown.* AS

If I could have / Two things in one. Moriturus. Edna St. Vincent Millay. MeMAP

If I could have your arms tonight. Sleepless. Sara Teasdale. SAGP

If I could I surely would. Pharoah's Army Got Drownded. *Unknown.* AS

If I could, I'd write. Housewife's Letter: To Mary. Anne Halley. NMM-2

If I could just touch your ankle, he whispers, *there.* Persephone Underground. Rita Dove. FFC; NAmP90

If I could let you go as trees let go. May Sarton. PoSu *Fr.* The Autumn Sonnets.

If I could linger on his lovely chest. Sonnet 13. Louise Labé, *French.* BoWoP, *tr. by* Aliki *and* Willis Barnstone

If I could live to God for just one day. Just One Day. Susan E. Gammons. PWR

If I could only get all of you. Trying Again. Dahlia Ravikovitch, *Hebrew.* VCWP, *tr. by* Chana Bloch *and* Ariel Bloch

If I could only live at the pitch that is near madness. Richard Eberhart. AFr; LiTM

If I could raise rivers, I'd raise them. Douglas Crase. NAAL-2

If I could reach you now, in any way. Letter to a Mute. Thomas James. AmPA

If I could scratch figures. Molly. Maurice Kenny. MoLi

If I could send him only. Her Reticence. Theodore Roethke. RACG

If I Could Shut the Gate against My Thoughts. *Unknown.* NOCV

If I could tell you. Impasse. Langston Hughes. LiTM

If I could track you down to have you taste. Patterns. Roberta Hill Whiteman. HATNAP

If I could trust mine own self with your fate. Christina Rossetti. *Fr.* Monna Innominata. BWW

If I Could Walk Out into the Cold Country. Elizabeth Brewster. NOBC

If I could wish. Wish. Dorothy Brown Thompson. CTV

If i cud ever write a. To P. J. (2 Yrs Old Who Sed Write a Poem for Me in Portland, Oregon). Sonia Sanchez. CA; MBE; NOxBChV

If I describe my house. The House. George Bowering. NOBC

If I desire something, I know it not. Hadewijch II, *Flemish.* WPoS, *tr. by* Sheila Hughes

If I did come of set intent. To Archinus. Callimachus, *Greek.* AWP, *tr. by* F. A. Wright

If I did tell she. English Girl Eats Her First Mango. John Agard. HCP

If I Die a Railroad Man. *Unknown.* AS

If I die, don't take me to the cemetery. Life-Hook. Juana de Ibarbourou, *Spanish.* WPOW, *tr. by* Marti Moody

If I die here. Song of a Man About to Die in a Strange Land. Mary Austin. PaTW

If I don't go out I'll only mope. Out and Back on the Fifteenth Night of the First Month. Mei Yao Ch'en, *Chinese.* CoBCP, *tr. by* Burton Watson

If I don't strangely love her. Catullus. *See* Carmen 92 ("Lesbia loads me night & day with her curses").

If I don't take anything to the party I'll feel bad. *Unknown, Tlingit Indian.* STP, *tr. by* James Koller

If I dress up like a peacock. Equality. Nina Cassian, *Romanian.* IFJA, *tr. by* Brenda Walker

If I drink water while this doth last. Chorus. Thomas Love Peacock. NBLV *Fr.* Crotchet Castle.

If I entreat this lady that all grace. Sonnet: To a Friend Who Does Not Pity His Love. Guido Cavalcanti, *Italian.* AWP, *tr. by* D. G. Rossetti

If I esteemed you less, Envy would kill. Sonnet to Byron. Shelley. EPCY; Ro

If I ever read it. (LL) A Patch of Old Snow. Robert Frost. CMoP; OxBSP; WeW-3

If I Felt Less. Morris Wintchevsky, *Yiddish.* TrJP, *tr. by* Joseph Leftwich

If I Forget Thee. Emanuel Litvinoff. TrJP

If I forget thee, Jerusalem. Yehuda Amichai, *Hebrew.* AF, *tr. by* Gutmann, Assia

If I forget thee, O Jerusalem, may my right hand forget to play. Bible, *O.T. See* Psalm 137.

If I found you wandering round the edge. On Ballycastle Beach. Medbh McGuckian. PBCIP

If I freely may discover. Song from Poetaster, or The Arraignment. Martial, *Latin.* BeJo; OBCVT, *tr. by* Ben Jonson

If I go alone. Rod Willmot. HA

If I had a donkey that wouldn't go. *Unknown.* OxNR

If I had a Green Automobile. The Green Automobile. Allen Ginsberg. BB

If I Had a Gun. Gig Ryan. BMAP

If I had a little wife. *Unknown.* OxNR

If I had a son! A little child. Barren. "Rachel," *Hebrew.* TrJP, *tr. by* L. V. Snowman

If I had a trunk like a big elephant. John Kendrick Bangs. OBCA

If I had [*or* I'd] as much money as I could spend. Mother Goose. OxNR

If I had but one year to live. One Year to Live. Mary Davis Reed. PoToHe

If I had but two little wings. Coleridge. BoTP; CH

If I had chosen thee, thou shouldst have been. As To His Choice of Her. Wilfrid Scawen Blunt. GSo; Son *Fr.* The Love Sonnets of Proteus.

If I had clamoured at Thy Gate. The Rebel. Rudyard Kipling. *Fr.* Epitaphs of the War [1914–1918]. OBWP

If I had given you that love and care. John Hewitt. PNI *Fr.* Sonnets for Roberta (1954).

If I had known in the morning. Our Own. Margaret Elizabeth Munson Sangster. BLPA; PoToHe

If I had known what trouble you were bearing. Mary Carolyn Davies. BLPA

If I had made the world—ah me! Sarah Morgan Bryan Piatt. NCAP

If I had never known your face at all. Sir William Watson. FaBoBe *Fr.* Sonnets to Miranda.

If I had not met the red-haired boy whose father. One of the Lives. W. S. Merwin. BAP-94

If I had peace to sit and sing. The Singer. Anna Wickham. MoBrPo

If I had thought thou couldst have died. To Mary. Charles Wolfe. LBC; OBEV; OxAEP-2

If I have faltered more or less. The Celestial Surgeon. Robert Louis Stevenson. ACTP; EBVV; MoBrPo; PoToHe

If i have made, my lady, intricate. E. E. Cummings. CMoP; NOBA; PoRA; SAGP

If I have wounded any soul to-day. My Evening Prayer. Charles H. Gabriel. BLPA; FaBoBe

If I have wronged you Lord forgive me. Migrant's Lament: A Song. Alfred Temba Qabula. PeSAV

If I heard a voice from heaven say 'Live without'. Elegy 9b. Ovid, *Latin.* EP, *tr. by* Peter Green

"If I hold my breath and do not speak." Ganga. Thomas Blackburn. MoBS

If I,—instead of threatening, talking big. Robert Browning. EBVVPR *Fr.* The Ring and the Book.

If I journeyed to a suburb of a Sunday. Marbled Chuckle in the Savannahs. Kenward Elmslie. FTOS

If I knew a way, I would tell you. Magnolia. Larry Levis. CMAP

If I knew I'd bear myself proudly. Matija Beckovic, *Serbo-Croatian.* HSix, *tr. by* Charles Simic

If I knew you and you knew me. To Know All Is to Forgive All. Nixon Waterman. BLPA; PoToHe

If I lay on that beach with you. Adrienne Rich. *Fr.* Twenty-one Love Poems. GLP

If I leave all for thee, wilt thou exchange. Sonnet. Elizabeth Barrett Browning. Son *Fr.* Sonnets from the Portuguese.

If I lie naked. Confession. Pearl Cleage. ISC

If I, like Solomon. . . . O To Be A Dragon. Marianne Moore. CTC; ChIV-1; KSG; NALW; NMM-2

If I live [*or* grow] to be old, for I find I go down. The Old Man's Wish. Walter Pope. NOSC

If I lived in this place for a thousand years. Cuchulainn. Michael O'Loughlin. BiHa; PBCIP

If I love you! (LL) Madam and Her Madam. Langston Hughes. RACG; SAmP

If I Love You. Frank Prewett. HATNAP

If I love you. Thread. Catherine Lucy Czerkawska. LW

If I make it over the pass. Hauling Over Wolf Creek Pass in Winter. Walter McDonald. CDa; MT

If I make not Jerusalem the beginning of my joy. Bible, *O.T. See* Psalm 137.

If I make the lashes dark. Before the World Was Made. W. B. Yeats. CBLP; GTBS-P

If I may have it, when it's dead. Emily Dickinson. NCAP

"If I may make a point." Household Dilemma. Angie Gilligan. NBrP

If I might alter kind. The Lover Whose Mistress Feared a Mouse. George Turberville. NTP

If I Might Be an Ox. *Unknown.* RB

If I might only love my God and die! If Only. Christina Rossetti. TrCP

If I must choose which I would elevate. Robert Frost. UV *Fr.* New Hampshire.

If I must dial a number to call you. Valerio Magrelli, *Italian.* NeIt, *tr. by* Dana Gioia

If I must die young. Second Language. Christine Dumaine. LoHo

If I must of my Senses lose. Prayer. Theodore Roethke. TwCP

If I only knew. Nelly Sachs, *German.* PoSu, *tr. by* Ruth *and* Matthew Mead

If I Only Was the Fellow. Will S. Adkin. BLPA

If I owned all of Alba. Saint Columcille. NOIV

If I popped in at Downing Street. A Prayer. Max Beerbohm. UV

If I prefer not Jerusalem above my chief joy. Bible, *O.T. See* Psalm 137.

If I profane with my unworthiest hand. Shakespeare. OxAEP-1; PFE; SoSe-8; Son *Fr.* Romeo and Juliet.

If I Ride This Train. Joe Johnson. PoBA

If I said, "Little wives." The Wives. Donald Hall. CoAP

If I saw you liked that dull unhappy boy. The Road Map. Thom Gunn. CBLP

If I say Thy name, art Thou there ? It may be so. John Berryman. *Fr.* Eleven Addresses to the Lord. OxBC

If I shall enterprise to make. The Praise of Faith. John Hall. ChIV-2

If I shall ever return home. (LL) Another Spring. Tu Fu, *Chinese.* BLT; OHPC, *tr. by* Kenneth Rexroth

If I should cast off this tattered coat. Stephen Crane. APN-2; PBMP *Fr.* The Black Riders [and Other Lines].

If I should cast off this tattered coat. *Unknown.* PFE

If I should die and leave you here a while. Turn Again to Life. Mary Lee Hall. PoLF

If I Should Die Before I Wake. Robert Mezey. NYBP

If I should die, think only this of me. The Soldier. Rupert Brooke. APAD; CABP; EBEvV; FaPoR; GSo; HeIP-4; LiTM; MoBrPo; NAEL-2; NOBE; NSI; NoP-4; OBEV; OBWP; OxBTC; PeFWW; PoA; PoFWW; PoLF; PoRA; PoWW; Son; TFi; UV *Fr.* 1914.

If I Should Die To-Night. Charles Walter Brown. PWR

If I Should Die Tonight. Ben King. NBLV; OBAL; PoLF

If I Should Die Tonight. Arabella Eugenia Smith. BLPA

If I Should Ever by Chance. Edward Thomas. FaBoCh; MoBrPo; OBMV; OBWVE; OxBChV

If I should ever need to reach your heart. Understanding. Pauline E. Soroka. PoLF

If I should fall, grieve not that one so weak. To My Mother—1916. Donald S. Cox. NSI

If I should go away. Post-Script: for Gweno. Alun Lewis. BoLoP; GTBS-P

If I should go before the rest of you. The First To Go. Joyce Grenfell. LBC

If I should learn, in some quite casual way. Edna St. Vincent Millay. HeIP-4

If I should lose, think only this of me. The Doctor. Roger Woddis. UV

If I should now forget, or not remember thee. To Spencer. George Turberville. NoSic

If I should pass the tomb of Jonah. Losers. Carl Sandburg. CMoP; MoAmPo; NoAM

If I should round the corner quickly. The Mythos of Samuel Huntsman. Hyam Plutzik. LiTM

If i should sleep with a lady called death. E. E. Cummings. BoLoP; VGW

If I should treat my lady with aplomb. Ballad of Fat Margot. Augustus Young. CIP-2

If I singe, ye will me lakke. *Unknown.* MiEL

If I speek good english. Changed Mind (or the Day I Woke Up). Tejumola Ologboni. NBV

If I Stand in My Window. Lucille Clifton. BPo

If I take an acorn. Alice Todd. BoTP

If I think of a horse wandering about sleeplessly. Night. Robert Bly. WeT

If I thought I could get away. Kenneth Rexroth. APSN *Fr.* The Love Poems of Marichiko.

If I told you we could see nail polish stopping. A Small Patch of Ice. Betsy Sholl. PBCAP

If I use my forbidden hand. The Bond. Nuala Ni Dhomhnaill, *Irish.* PBCIP, *tr. by* Medbh McGuckian

If I walked straight slap. Ivor Gurney. Spl

If I was so. (LL) Bad Luck Card. Langston Hughes. NoP-4; SAmP; TRP

If I Went Away. Desmond O'Grady, *Irish.* CIP-2

If I were a cassowary. Impromptu. Samuel Wilberforce. NBLV

If I were a cinnamon peeler. The Cinnamon Peeler. Michael Ondaatje. NOBC

If I were a female hummingbird perched still. The Hummingbird: a Seduction. Pattiann Rogers. NAmP90

If I were a kite, high in the sky. A Kite. Scott Trevor. CTV

If I were a mouse. The Furry Home. J. M. Westrup. BoTP

If I Were a Pig. Elizabeth Fleming. BoTP

If I Were a Queen. Christina Rossetti. NOxBChV

If I Were an Apple. *Unknown.* BoTP

If I were but a bird. *Unknown, German.* GePo, *tr. by* Ingrid Wal[do]e-Engel

If I were called in. Water. Philip Larkin. FaBoMo; OxBSP; PeECV

If I were doing my Laundry I'd wash my dirty Iran. Homework. Allen Ginsberg. NoAM

If I were fierce and bald and short of breath. Base Details. Siegfried Sassoon. MoBrPo; OxBSP; OxBoV; PeFWW; PoFWW; SAGP

If I were fire, I'd burn the world away. Sonnet: Of All He Would Do. Cecco Angiolieri, da Siena, *Italian.* AWP, *tr. by* D. G. Rossetti

If I were French, I'd write. Breasts. Maxine Chernoff. PmAP

If I were from Timbuktu, perhaps. Dark Mirror. Calvin Forbes. GT

If I were in a fairy tale. The Duck. Edith King. BoTP

If I were in China this minute. Foreign Ways. Diana Chang. UnSA

If I Were King. Justin Huntly McCarthy, *par. fr. the French of* Villon. PoLF

If I were Lord of Tartary. Tartary. Walter De la Mare. OxBChV

If I were loved, as I desire to be. Tennyson. GSo; Son

If I were oh, so very small. P. A. Ropes. BoTP

If I were only sure. Shirome, *Japanese.* WPJ, *tr. by* Kenneth Rexroth *and* Ikuko Atsumi

If I were Pablo Neruda. My Name. Daniel Berrigan. AF

If I were rich what would I do? Why Tomas Cam Was Grumpy. James Stephens. CMoP

If I were sitting. Midnight Song. Pinkie Gordon Lane. GT

If I were stone dead and buried under. Felo de Se. Richard Hughes. OBMV

If I were the kind of man I want. Broads. David R. Slavitt. BXAP

If I were to stand. Tanka. Kanoko Okamoto, *Japanese.* MJT, *tr. by* Makoto Ueda

If I Were to Tell of Our Labours, Our Hard Lodging. Aeschylus. *Fr.* Agamemnon. NAWM-1, *tr. by* Robert Fagles

If I were used to writing verse. A First Attempt in Rhyme. Thomas Hood. OBCoV

If I weren't working, I'd sleep next to you. Bloomingdale's. Marilyn Hacker. CPO; DeD *Fr.* Love, Death and the Changing of the Seasons.

If / ice shall melt. W. W. Eustace Ross. NOBC

If I'd as much money as I could spend. Chairs to Mend. *Unknown.* LB; OxNR; ReMoGo

If "ifs" and "ans" [*or* If ifs and ands were pots and pans]. *Unknown.* FaBoBe; LB

If I'm not mistaken. Final Exam. Dan Pagis, *Hebrew.* IP, *tr. by* Warren Bargad *and* Stanley F. Chyet

If, in a fisherman's hut, you poke. Hand-Rolled Cigarettes. Yevtushenko, *Russian.* VCWP, *tr. by* Stanley Kunitz

If in a Future Life We Meet Again. Bàng Bá Lâ, *Vietnamese.* AVP, *tr. by* Huỳnh Sanh Thông

If, in an odd angle of the hutment. Eighth Air Force. Randall Jarrell. MoP; NOBA; NoAM; NoP-4; OBWP; PoWW; TRP; VCAP

If in beginning twilight of winter will stand. E. E. Cummings. NYBP

If in his study he hath so much care. Antiquary. Donne. EBEV; NOSC

If in me anger, or disdain. To Elinda. Richard Lovelace. CavPo

If in my mind I marry you every year. Late Loving. Mona Van Duyn. NMM-2

If in some far-off, future day. Epitaph for a Cat. Margaret E. Bruner. PoLF

If in that Syrian garden, ages slain. Easter Hymn. A. E. Housman. EBEV; GI

If, in the light of things, you fade. Star. Derek Walcott. PFE; PiM

If, in the month of dark December. Written After Swimming from Sestos to Abydos. Byron. NAEL-2; NBLV; NoP-4

If in the silent grave the dead. To A Friend. Catullus. LBC

If, in the silent mind of One all-pure. In Utrumque Paratus. Matthew Arnold. OBNC; PoEL-5

If in the world there be more woe. Sir Thomas Wyatt. SiPS

If in the years to come you should recall. Edna St. Vincent Millay. HeIP-4

If in this Town an unflusht Puny be. Ovid. OBCVT, *tr. by* Hoy, Thomas *Fr.* The Art of Love.

If, in well-bred society, ('hear! hear!'). Nathaniel Parker Willis. *Fr.* Lady Jane, The; a Humorous Novel in Rhyme. OBAL

If in your heart you make. It Depends on You. "Angelus Silesius," *German.* EnlH, *tr. by* Stephen Mitchell

If intercourse gives you thrombosis. Limerick. *Unknown.* PeLi

If it ain't simply this, what is it? Keep Talking. Philip Levine. WeW-3

If It Be Destined. Petrarch. AWP; SiPS, *tr. by* Edward Fitzgerald *Fr.* Sonnets to Laura.

If it be night then, when the screech-owl's call. Sonnet: "If it be night. . . ." Alec Brock Stevenson. FuPo

If it be shame to love a pretty woman. Albery Allson Whitman. AAP *Fr.* The Octoroon.

If It Be True. Esther Johnson. OxBSP

If it be true that poets, as you say. To a Friend. Oliver St. John Gogarty. FP

If it but herald death, the vision is divine! (LL) The Prisoner. Emily Jane Brontë. NOBE; NoP-4; OBEV; OBNC

If it chance your eye offend you. A. E. Housman. ChIV-2

If it could weep, it could arise and go. (LL) Grief. Elizabeth Barrett Browning. EBEvV; HeIP-4; IMW; InPK-6; LBC; NALW; NOBVV; OBEV; OBNC; PoLF; SDW; VWP; WPE

If it doesn't open up. The Naming of Things. Bahinabai Chaudhari, *Marathi.* OMIP, *tr. by* Philip Engblomb *and* Jayant Karve

It it ever is. The Invitation. Robert Creeley. FTOS

If it form the one landscape that looks as bad. Quicksands. William Zaranka. BXAP

If it form the one landscape that we, the inconstant ones. In Praise of Limestone. W. H. Auden. CMoP; FYAP; FaBoPV; HAP; MoP; NAEL-2; NoAM; NoP-4; OAEL-2

If It Is Not My Portion. Rabindranath Tagore. OBMV *Fr.* Gitanjali.

If it is unpermissible, in fact fatal. To a Giraffe. Marianne Moore. APo

If it is you, there / in the light boat on the pond. Lady Ise, *Japanese.* BoWoP, *tr. by* Etsuko Terasaki *and* Irma Brandeis

If it may stand with your most wished content. In Defence of Poetry. Ben Jonson. EPCY *Fr.* Every Man in His Humour.

If it must be; if it must be, O God! Sonnet I. David Gray. OxBS *Fr.* In the Shadows.

If it rains. What Her Girl Friend Said, Consoling Her when She Was Distressed by the Town's Gossip. Uloccanar, *Tamil.* PLW, *tr. by* A. K. Ramanujan

If it were a sea, this immense wind. Maria Luisa Spaziani, *Italian.* NeIt, *tr. by* Beverly Allen

If it were done when 'tis done, then 'twere well. Vaulting Ambition. Shakespeare. EBEvV; OxAEP-1 *Fr.* Macbeth.

If it / Were lighter touch. The Guarded Wound. Adelaide Crapsey. WPE

If it were not for the voice. Nakatsukasa. *Fr.* Shui Shu. AWP, *tr. by* Arthur Waley

If it were not your face that melts. Andrea Zanzotto, *Italian.* VCWP, *tr. by* Ruth Feldman *and* Brian Swann

If it were real / Perhaps I'd understand it. Ono no Komachi, *Japanese.* WPOW, *tr. by* Rob Swigart

If it were set anywhere else but so. Head Itself. Laura Riding Jackson. PoA

If it's ever spring again. Thomas Hardy. OxBTC

If It's Only Rhythm. Dennis Phillips. FTOS *Fr.* Etudes.

If I've a taste, it's not alone. Hunger. Rimbaud, *French.* AWP, *tr. by* Louise Varese

If, Jerusalem, I Ever Should Forget Thee. Heinrich Heine, *German.* TrJP, *tr. by* Margaret Armour

If Juan Rodriguez is alive today. Disgrace. David Hall. CDa

If life be time that here is spent. Of the Loss of Time. John Hoskyns. FaBoEE

If life were never bitter. Mortimer Collins. OBCoV

If Life's a Lousy Picture, Why Not Leave before the End. Roger McGough. OxBTC

If Light can thus deceive, wherefore not Life? (LL) To Night. Joseph Blanco White. EBEV; GSo; OBEV; OxAEP-2; Son

If, like winds semaphored by a rose. Robert Desnos, *French.* MFP, *tr. by* Martin Sorrell

If Lincoln were to come again to earth. If Lincoln Should Return. Margaret E. Bruner. PoToHe

If livelihood by knowledge were endowed. Mesnevi. Sadi. AWP, *tr. by* L. Cranmer-Byng *Fr.* The Gulistan.

If, Lord, Thy Love for Me Is Strong. Saint, of Avila Theresa, *Spanish.* AWP; PBWP, *tr. by* Arthur Symons

If Love In These Be Founded. Henry Constable. *Fr.* Diana.

If love is chaste, what bears adultery? Sonnet. Sibylla Schwarz, *German.* GePo, *tr. by* George C. Schoolfield

If love, or fear, would let me tell his name. (LL) A Nymph's Passion. Ben Jonson. BeJo; OBEV

If love should count you worthy, and should deign. Decision. *Unknown.* PoToHe

If love were what the rose is. A Match. Swinburne. CBLP; NOBVV

If lust should chase my soule, made swift by fright. Francis Quarles. ESCV *Fr.* Emblems.

If Luther's day expand to Darwin's year. Epilogue. Herman Melville. APN-2; NCAP *Fr.* Clarel: A Poem and Pilgrimage in the Holy Land.

If maiden is your soul, like Mary undefiled. The Spiritual Impregnation. "Angelus Silesius." GePo, *tr. by* George C. Schoolfield *Fr.* The Cherubical Wanderer.

If mama / could use. Lucille Clifton. NAAAL

If man him bithoghte. *Unknown.* MiEL

If Marilyn Monroe. Leo Romero. LTA

If Martin Van Buren ever swam in water. 1837. Jackson MacLow. APSN *Fr.* The Presidents of the United States of America.

If Mary came would Mary. A Penitent Considers Another Coming of Mary. Gwendolyn Brooks. NoAM; PChr

If me want for go in a Ebo. *Unknown.* *Fr.* Work-Songs. PBCV

If meat the gods give, I the steam. Steam in Sacrifice. Robert Herrick. CaPo

If medals were ordained for drinks. To a Boon Companion. Oliver St. John Gogarty. OBMV

If memory serves, we've shared together. Martial, *Latin.* FP, *tr. by* James Michie

If men be judged wise. Epigram. Joseph Solomon Del Medigo, *Hebrew.* TrJP

If mine eyes can speak to do hearty errand, *speech of Cleophila.* Sapphics. Sir Philip Sidney. *Fr.* Arcadia.

If money grew on trees. Annual Returns. Greg Williamson. RA

If more than once, as annals tell. Timoleon. Herman Melville. APN-2

If music [or musique] and sweet poetry [or poetrie] agree. To His Friend Master R.L., In Praise of Music and Poetry. Richard Barnfield. AAS; EPCY; Son

If Music be the food of love, play on. The Food of Love. Shakespeare. EBEvV *Fr.* Twelfth Night.

If my blues don't get you my jazzing must. (LL) St. Louis Blues. William Christopher Handy. CrDW

If, My Darling. Philip Larkin. EBEV; LiTM

If my darling should depart. Hafiz. *Fr.* I said to heaven that glowed above. AWP, *tr. by* Ralph Waldo Emerson *Fr.* Odes.

If my dear love were but the child of state. Sonnet 124. Shakespeare. NoSic *Fr.* Sonnets.

If my garden oak spares one bare ledge. Creed. Anne Spencer. NMM-2

If my imprisonment has no end. From Prison. Todros ben Judah Abulafia, *Hebrew.* TOF, *tr. by* David Goldstein

If my kisses wrong you, then tit for tat. Strato, *Greek.* GrAn, *tr. by* W. G. Shepherd

If my nipples were to drip milk. Sappho, *Greek.* BoWoP, *tr. by* Willis Barnstone

If my parents and your parents. Almost a Love Poem. Yehuda Amichai, *Hebrew.* HP, *tr. by* Abramson, Glenda

If my poor Harp has ever poured. To the Late William Jerdan. Eliza Cook. VWP

If my torch goes out it will be dark. Search. Claribel Alegría, *Spanish.* BoWoP, *tr. by* Aliki *and* Willis Barnstone

If Nancy Hanks / Came back as a ghost. Nancy Hanks. Rosemary Benét *and* Stephen Vincent Benét. NTCP

If nature prompts you, or if friends persuade. William Whitehead. OBSV *Fr.* A Charge to the Poets.

If neither brass, nor marble, can withstand. The Power of Time. Jonathan Swift. FaBoEE; OxBSP

If night takes the form of a whale and. Isabel Fraire, *Spanish.* BoWoP, *tr. by* Thomas Hoeksema

If nine times you your bridegroom[e] kiss[e]. The Tithe [*or* Tythe]: To the Bride. Robert Herrick. CaPo

If no love is, O God, what feele I so? The Song of Troylus. Chaucer. AWP; OAEL-1 *Fr.* Troilus and Criseyde [*or* Criseide]. EnVB

If no one ever marries me—. Laurence Alma-Tadema. ACTP; OxBChV; WHSW

If no Pain were, how judge we of Pleasure? Limerick. William Bliss. PeLi

If not a so-called Negro bought a bottle. Racist Psychotherapy. Isaac J. Black. NBV

If not enjoyed, it sighing cries, / Heigh ho! (LL) Love. Samuel Daniel. CBLP; NOBE; OBEV; PoEL-2

If not I, / if not you? (LL) The Speed of Darkness. Muriel Rukeyser. APSN; GLP; LCAP-2

If now thou seest me a wreck, worn out and minished of sight. Old Age. Al-Aswad, son of Ya'fur. *Fr.* The Mufaddaliyat. AWP, *tr. by* Sir Charles Lyall

If, O Maecenas, versed in lore antique. Horace, *Latin.* OBVE, *tr. by* Sir Theodore Martin

If, O my Lesbia, I should commit. Second Philosopher's Song. Aldous Leonard Huxley. OBCoV

If of the dead save good nought should be said. William Drummond, of Hawthornden. NOSC

If of thy mortal goods thou art bereft. Hyacinths to Feed Thy Soul. Sadi. BLPA; FaBoBe *Fr.* The Gulistan.

If on a Spring night I went by. The Prayer. John Galsworthy. UV

If one could have that little head of hers. A Face. Robert Browning. CTC

If one is judged by one's dreams. Horse Dream. Ojars Vacietis, *Latvian.* CEEP, *tr. by* Inara Cedrins

If one revolves a vine-enamored thumb. Images for the Gospel of Christ. Paul Ramsey. CRP

If one should bring me this report. Of One Dead. Tennyson. EBVV; EnVR; FHYEP; ImPo *Fr.* In Memoriam A. H. H.

If one should tell them what's clearly seen. Crumbs or the Loaf. Robinson Jeffers. CMoP

If Only. Christina Rossetti. TrCP

If only. Tanka. Maekawa Samio, *Japanese.* MJT, *tr. by* Makoto Ueda

If Only. Tennyson. *Fr.* Maud [A Monodrama]. EnVR

("O that 'twere possible.") LBC; SAGP

("What and where they be!") (LL) CBLP; LBC; OxBSn; SAGP

If only I could forget that Frenchman. The French Prisoner. János Pilinszky, *Hungarian.* PoSu, *tr. by* Janos Csokits *and* Ted Hughes

If only Life-and-Death. *Unknown, Japanese.* TAL, *tr. by* Arthur Waley

If only once the chariot of the Morn. The Glory of Nature. Frederick Tennyson. OBNC

If only that so many dead lie round. (LL) Church Going. Philip Larkin. CABP; CMoP; GTBS-P; HeIP-4; LiTM; MoBrPo; MoP; NAEL-2; NIP-4; NoAM; NoP-4; OAEL-2; Poetr; SCV; SoSe-8; TFi; TwCP; UnPo

If only the phantom would stop reappearing! Faust. John Ashbery. TwCP

If only those scraps from Aleppo, from Qumran. I Saw Three Ships. Kevyn Arthur. PBCV

If only / Under the canopy of stars. Errol Francis. NBrP *Fr.* Fragments of the Green Island.

If only, when one heard. *Unknown.* AWP, *tr. by* Arthur Waley *Fr.* Kokin Shu.

If only you'd seen if only you'd seen. The Voice of My White City. Abba Kovner, *Hebrew.* IP, *tr. by* Warren Bargad *and* Stanley F. Chyet

If orange chiffon sadness. Orange Chiffon. Jayne Cortez. BlSi

If Orpheus' voice had force to breathe such music's love. Third Song. Sir Philip Sidney. PoEL-1 *Fr.* Astrophil and Stella. AAS; SiPS

If our antagonists take me. &[;Last Poems&];. Osip Emilevich Mandelstam. PFTM

If out of a dire suspicion. Wet Hair: If Now His Mother Should Come. Robert Penn Warren. NoAM *Fr.* Penological Study: Southern Exposure.

If parting be decreed for the two of us. Parting. Judah Halevi, *Hebrew.* AWP; TrJP, *tr. by* Nina Davis Salaman

If people in this neighborhood get sick. Ballad of the Neighborhood Shaman. Kao Ch'i, *Chinese.* CoBLCP, *tr. by* Jonathan Chaves

If Pigs Could Fly. James Reeves. OTCP

If Pliny, Lord High Treasurer of all. Painture [*or* Peinture]. Richard Lovelace. CaPo

If poems are eternal occasions, then. The Marginalization of Poetry. Bob Perelman. FTOS

If poisonous [*or* poysonous] mineral[l]s, and if that tree. Donne. EBEV; FaBoVe; ImPo; NAEL-1; NoP-4; OAEL-1; OxAEP-1; PoEL-2; SCGP; SeCP; Son; UnPo *Fr.* Holy Sonnets. ESCV.

If poverty be a title to poetry, I am sure nobody can dispute mine. The Beggar's Opera. John Gay. OAEL-1

If Profit offered immortality for gold. Anacreon, *Greek.* InMo, *tr. by* Sam Hamill

If Pythias has a customer. Poseidippus, *Greek.* PGA, *tr. by* Kenneth Rexroth

If questioning could make us wise. Because She Would Ask Me Why I Loved Her. Christopher John Brennan. CBAP

If raisins grew on you from head to toe. Two Gardens. Yona Wollach, *Hebrew.* IP, *tr. by* Warren Bargad *and* Stanley F. Chyet

If rightly tuneful bards decide. Amoret. Mark Akenside. OBEV

If Rome so great, and in her wisest age. To Edward Alleyn. Ben Jonson. NOSC

If sadly thinking, with spirits sinking. The Deserter. John Philpot Curran. OxAEP-1

If Sanct Paules day be fair and cleir. *Unknown.* MiEL

If satire charms, strike faults, but spare the man;. Edward Young. EPCY *Fr.* Epistle II: To Mr. Pope, From Oxford.

If saying No. Solo for Two Voices. Octavio Paz, *Spanish.* STV, *tr. by* John Frederick Nims

If she asks why the sun. To Jann, in Her Absence. C. J. Driver. PeSA

If she be made of white and red. Shakespeare. CTC *Fr.* Love's Labour's Lost.

If she be not as kind as fair. Song. William Walsh *and* Sir George Etherege (1653–91). NOSC

If she cleared her throat. (LL) Caught. Rodney Jones. FiLi; NAmP90

If she did not love you, she would not be. Ronald David Laing. OxBM

If she should give me all I ask of her. George Henry Boker. APN-2 *Fr.* Sonnets: A Sequence on Profane Love.

If she was beautiful is uncertain the more. Legend of Lilja. Sarah Kirsch, *German.* AF, *tr. by* Wayne Kvam

If she whom I love, should love me. (LL) Love's Deity [*or* Deitie]. Donne. AWP; ESCV; GBL; ImPo; SeCP; SoSe-8

If she wishes to go I will not forgive her. (LL) The River God. Stevie Smith. BrRo; FaBoSe; FaBoTw; FaBoWP; PBWP

If Sleep and Death be truly one. Tennyson. OBNC; PeECV *Fr.* In Memoriam A. H. H.

If snow falls on the far field. Mother's Song. *Unknown.* BoWoP, *tr. by* Willis Barnstone

If So. Barbara Guest. BAP-95

If so a toad be laid. A Charme, or an Allay for Love. Robert Herrick. FaBoCh

If so it hap, this of-spring of my care. Samuel Daniel. AAS *Fr.* To Delia.

If So the Man You Are. Wyndham Lewis. OBSV

If solitaries, why so many? Monks. Palladas, *Greek.* GrAn, *tr. by* Peter Jay

If some nosey body asks "well." Poem for a "Divorced" Daughter. Horace Coleman. ISC

If somebody shot that shit Shute. (LL) General inspecting the trenches, The. Sir Alan Patrick Herbert. NSI; PoWW

If someone insults you. Autant En Emporte le Vent. Marguerite de Navarre, *French.* PBWP, *tr. by* Aline Allard

If someone said, Escape. Longface Mahoney Discusses Heaven. Horace Gregory. VGW

If someone says you're too short. Apothegms and Counsels. Colette Inez. EOEF

If someone was walking across. A Confession. Robert Mezey. AmPA; PFE

If someone's with her. Poseidippus, *Greek.* GrAn, *tr. by* Edward Lucie-Smith

If strange things happen where she is. On Portents. Robert Graves. FaBoMo

If such there were—with you, the moral of his strain! (LL) The Fatal Spell. Byron. CBLP; OBNC

If Suddenly a Clod of Earth. Harold Monro. MoBrPo *Fr.* Strange Meetings.

If sunlight fell like snowflakes. Sunflakes. Frank Asch. NTCP

If that I joy before I see / thy full deliverance past. Bible, *O.T. See* Psalm 137.

If That—indeed—redeem. (LL) Prison gets to be a friend, A. Emily Dickinson. APN-2; NCAP

If that my hand, like yours, dear George, were skilled. To G. H. B. James Bayard Taylor. Son

If the Birds Knew. John Ashbery. PoA

If the Black Frog Will Not Ring. Ed Roberson. PoBA

If the blues would let me. Miss Blues'es Child. Langston Hughes. ChAP; SAmP; TTTS

If the butterfly courted the bee. Topsy-turvy World. William Brighty Rands. OxBChV

If the deep wood is haunted, it is I. Nocturne. Robert Silliman Hillyer. FYAP, *tr. by* John Moyne *and* Coleman Barks

If the Devil don't want nothing. Bedtime Story. Paula Rankin. CMAP

If the driver is good. The Great Wagon. Toṇṭaimāṉ Iḷantiraiyaṉ, *Tamil.* PLW, *tr. by* A. K. Ramanujan

If the dull substance of my flesh were thought. Sonnet 44. Shakespeare. Son *Fr.* Sonnets.

If the egg had one spot of blood on it. White Petticoats. Chana Bloch. CrSp

If the fat butcher thinks he slays. Mutton. *Unknown.* BXAP

If the forest of her hair. Bhartrihari, *Sanskrit.* EP, *tr. by* John Brough

If the fresh trunk have sap enough to give. On Grafting. Thomas Randolph. GaP

If the great outside system—species and stars—proceeds. Across Space and Time. Charles Olson. PoM

If the heart of a man is deprest [*or* depressed] with cares. Would You Have a Young Virgin? John Gay. EnLoPo; NAEL-1 *Fr.* The Beggar's Opera. OAEL-1

If the hill overlooking our city has always been known as Adam's Grave. Vespers. W. H. Auden. FaBoMo *Fr.* Horae Canonicae.

If the lady hath any loveliness, let it die. Blackberry Winter. John Crowe Ransom. OxBA; PoRA

If the light of the sun, moon, and stars. Robert Frost. Novella Nikolaevna Matveyeva, *Russian.* TCRP, *tr. by* Deming Brown

"If the Lord Would Make windows in Heaven." Edwin Arlington Robinson. MeMAP

If the lost word is lost, if the spent word is spent. T. S. Eliot. UV *Fr.* Ash Wednesday [*or* Ash-Wednesday]. MoAmPo; OxBA; VGW

If the maiden coughs immediately after. J. H. Thomas. BXAP

If the man who turnips cries. Ballad. Samuel Johnson. CBNP; OxAEP-1

If the moon smiled, she would resemble you. The Rival. Sylvia Plath. LoP

If the muse were mine to tempt it. The Colored Soldiers. Paul Laurence Dunbar. AAP; APN-2; CBCWP; NAAAL

If the oak is out before the ash. *Unknown.* OxNR

If the old home can laugh, let's hear it now. Catullus. *See* Carmen 31 ("Apple of islands, Sirmio, & bright peninsulas, set").

If the Owl Calls Again. John Haines. CoAP; CoAmPo; HeIP-4

If the petals are shed. Falling Petals. Chi-hun Cho, *Korean.* CKP, *tr. by* Jaihiun Kim

If the quick spirits in your eye. Persuasions to Enjoy. Thomas Carew. BeJo; CaPo; NAEL-1; NOBE; NOSC; OBEV; SeCP

If the red slayer think he slays. Brahma. Ralph Waldo Emerson. APAD; APN-1; AWP; AmPP; ColAP; HAP; ImPo; MeMAP; NOBA; NoP-4; OBEV; OxBA; PAR; PoE; PoRA; TAP; TFi; UV; UnPo

If the romantic land whose soil I tread. Richard Henry Wilde. APN-1 *Fr.* Hesperia.

If the scorn of your bright eyne. Song. Shakespeare. CTC *Fr.* As You Like It.

If the soul was born with pinions. Marina Tsvetayeva, *Russian.* WPoS, *tr. by* David McDuff

If the speed is open. A Piano. Gertrude Stein. PBWP *Fr.* Tender Buttons.

If the stars fell; night's nameless dreams. Joseph. G. K. Chesterton. ChIV-2

If the Stars Should Fall. Samuel Allen. PoBA

If the time ever came. Poem for Ben Barney. Leslie Marmon Silko. CDW; VoR

If the tombstone placed over me is small to see and close. Leonidas of Tarentum. HePo, *tr. by* Barbara Hughes Fowler *Fr.* Epigrams.

If the unfortunate fate engulfing me. Farewell to My Mother. "Placido," *Spanish.* TTY, *tr. by* James Weldon Johnson

If The War Keeps On. Bernard Gilbert. NSI

If the weather breaks. Jane Cooper. *Fr.* The Weather of Six Mornings. NYBP

If the wild bowler thinks he bowls. Brahma. Andrew Lang. BXAP; NOBL; PeLV; UV

If the winds of heaven. Henjō Abbot, *Japanese.* OHPJ, *tr. by* Kenneth Rexroth

If the year is meditating a suitable gift. Request to a Year. Judith Wright. CBAP; FaBoWP; NALW; NoAM; NoP-4

If there are any heavens my mother will (all by herself) have. E. E. Cummings. MeMAP; MoAmPo; NAAL-2

("And the whole garden will bow.") (LL) FiLi

If there be a rainbow in the eve. *Unknown.* FaBoVe

If there be any lover in the world, O Moslems, 'tis I. Jelaluddin Rumi, *Persian.* TOF, *tr. by* R. A. Nicholson

If there be any one can take my place. Christina Rossetti. *Fr.* Monna Innominata. BWW

If there be none, never mind it. (LL) For every evil under the sun. Mother Goose. LB; OxNR; ReMoGo

If there be sorrow. Mari E. Evans. PBMP; SAGP

("Restrained.") (LL) SAGP

If there be truth in what you sing. On Reading Dr. Young's Satires. Jonathan Swift. EPCY

If there exists a hell—the case is clear. To Sir Toby. Philip Freneau. NAAL-1; NAAL-3; NoP-4; TAP

If there is a God. Ewa Lipska, *Polish.* CEEP, *tr. by* Magnus J. Krynski

If there is a man white as marble. Metaphor as Degeneration. Wallace Stevens. LCAP-2

If there is a Pure Land. Death Sunyata Chant: A Rite for Passing Over. Diane Di Prima. BB

If there is a scheme. Charles Reznikoff. PiM

If there is a sound before death in America. For the Evening Land. David Shapiro. BAP-96

If there is no change in the ocean. No Change in Me. *Unknown.* AmFP

If there is someone above. Double-face, *Crow Indian.* STP, *tr. by* W. S. Merwin *after* Robert Lowie

If there is something that takes you. Conjuring Against Alien Spirits. Quincy Troupe. ISC

If there is the statue of a saint. In the Badlands of Desire. Beckian Fritz Goldberg. NAmP90

If there must be a god in the house, must be. Less and Less Human, O Savage Spirit. Wallace Stevens. AFr; VGW

If there was a house with three girls in it. Céilí. Ciaran Carson. CIP-2; PBCIP

If there was a world more disturbing than this. Amnesia. Bruce Weigl. CDa

If there was only a road there. The Blue West. Dahlia Ravikovitch, *Hebrew.* PBWP, *tr. by* Chana Bloch

If there were an open way. On One Condition. Charles Madge. SPE

If there were another. Songs of an Other. Robert Duncan. PmAP

If there were any power in human love. Sonnet. Frances Anne Kemble. VWP

If there were dreams to sell. Dream-Pedlary. Thomas Lovell Beddoes. BoTP; CH; FaBoBe; HAP; NOBE; OBEV; OBNC; OxAEP-2; PoEL-4; Ro

If there were no authority on earth. Chaucer. OxBM *Fr.* The Wife of Bath's Prologue. FHYEP; NAEL-1; OAEL-1, *ll.* 1–862 *complete Fr.* The Canterbury Tales.

If there were, oh! an Hellespont of cream. The Author Loving These Homely Meats. John, of Hereford Davies. CBLP; CBNP; FaBoCh; OBCoV; Son *Fr.* The Scourge of Folly.

If there were seven blind men. XXII. Essex Hemphill. NAAAL *Fr.* Conditions.

If there's no Sun, I still can have the Moon. Philosophy. John Kendrick Bangs. PoToHe

If there's one animal that isn't a wimp, it. Let's Hear it for the Limpet. Kit Wright. AYFP

If they are mine or no. (LL) Tell me not here, it needs not saying. A. E. Housman. APAD; GTBS-P; LiTM; NOBE; NoAM; OAEL-2; OBNC; OxBTC; SCV

If they ask, who here doth lie. Epitaph on Sir Walter Pye. John Hoskyns. FaBoEE

If they can get across our garden they have eaten it. Negotium Perambulans. Peter Redgrove. OBGa

If they had cursed the man. A Part-Sequence for Change. Robert Duncan. VGW

If They Honoured Me, Giving Me Their Gifts. "Michael Field." OBMV

If they say my furred cloak. Chanson. Pernette De Guillet, *French.* PBWP, *tr. by* Joan Keefe *and* Richard Terdiman

If they say: "you must suffer both torture and burning"—. Mikhail Alekseievich Kuzmin, *Russian.* TCRP, *tr. by* Yakov Hornstein

If they show me a stone and I say stone they will say stone. Amir Gilbo'a, *Hebrew.* MHP, *tr. by* Ruth Finer Mintz

If they true bailiffs be, who for the law maintaining. On Mercenary and Unjust Bailiffs. Henricus Selyns. SCAP

If they wanted freedom. Eeva-Liisa Manner. PBWP *Fr.* Cambrian.

If they were pretty. Reign of Terror. Jim Hall. CMAP

If this be love, to draw[e] a weary [*or* wearie] breath. Samuel Daniel. AAS; GBL; GLoP; GSo *Fr.* To Delia.

If this brain's over-tempered. I've Tasted My Blood. Milton Acorn. MoCV; NOBC

If this night passes. This Night. N. Revathi Devi, *Telugu.* OMIP, *tr. by* V. Narayana Rao *and* A. K. Ramanujan (1929–93)

If this our little life is but a day. A Sonnet to Heavenly Beauty. Joachim Du Bellay, *French.* AWP; CTC, *tr. by* Andrew Lang

If this uncertain age in which we dwell. The Lesson for Today. Robert Frost. LiTM

If this was our battle, if these were our ends. To a President. Witter Bynner. OBAL

If this were a movie, the sound of sizzling would foretell disaster. Schadenfreude. Stephanie Brown. BAP-95

If This Were Faith. Robert Louis Stevenson. OBNC

If this were what Aholibah. (LL) Aholibah. Swinburne. ChIV-1; KSG

If this world's friends might see but once. The Seed Growing Secretly. Henry Vaughan. ChIV-2; ESCV; GeHe

If thou a reason dost desire to know. To Cynthia, on Her Embraces. Sir Francis Kynaston. GBL

If thou art sleeping, maiden. Song. Gil Vicente, *Spanish.* AWP; CTC, *tr. by* Longfellow

If thou beest he; but O how fall'n! how chang'd. Milton. SCV *Fr.* Book I. FHYEP; NAEL-1; OAEL-1; OxAEP-1 *Fr.* Paradise Lost.

If thou be'st ice, I do admire. The Miracle. Sir John Suckling. CaPo

If thou canst wake with me, forget to eate. John Ford. PoEL-2 *Fr.* The Lover's Melancholy.

If thou didst feed on western plains of yore. To a Goose [*or* Gosse]. Robert Southey. BXAP; NOBL; PeLV; Son

If thou dislik'st the piece thou light'st on first. To the Sour[e] Reader. Robert Herrick. NBLV; NoP-4; SeCP

If thou dost bid thy friend farewell. Parting. Coventry Patmore. PoToHe

If thou hast squander'd years to grave a gem. A Charge. Herbert Trench. OBEV

If thou indeed derive thy light from Heaven. Wordsworth. TrCP

If thou kiss not me? (LL) Love's Philosophy. Shelley. APAD; BLPA; BoLoP; FHYEP; FaBoBe; GLoP; GTBS-P; HoPM; OxAEP-2; PBMP; PoToHe; SCGP

If thou must love me, let it be for nought. Sonnet. Elizabeth Barrett Browning. BWW; CTC; GSo; HeIP-4; InPS-3; LW; OBEV; OBNC; OxAEP-2; PoToHe; SoSe-8 *Fr.* Sonnets from the Portuguese.

If thou of fortune be bereft. Not by Bread Alone. *Unknown, Greek.* PoLF, *tr. by* James Terry White

If thou shouldst ever come by choice or chance. Ginevra. Samuel Rogers. OxAEP-2; PoLF

If Thou Shouldst Return. Clara Ann Thompson. CBWP-2

If thou survive my well-contented day. Post Mortem. Shakespeare. GTBS-P *Fr.* Sonnets.

If thou wert here, these tears were tears of light! The Day-Dream. Coleridge. Ro

If thou wilt come and dwell with me at home. Richard Barnfield. *See* The Affectionate Shepherd.

If thou wilt ease thine heart. Wolfram's Dirge. Thomas Lovell Beddoes. NOBE; OBEV; OBNC; OxAEP-2; PoEL-4 *Fr.* Death's Jest Book.

If Thou Wilt Hear. John Grave. AH

If thou wilt let down thy milk to me. (LL) Cushy cow bonny, let down thy milk. Mother Goose. CTAV; OxNR; ReMoGo

If thou wilt mighty be, flee from the rage. Sir Thomas Wyatt. SiPS

If thou wouldest roses scent. Francis Daniel Pastorius. SCAP

If Thou Wouldst Know. Hayyim Nahman Bialik, *Hebrew.* TrJP, *tr. by* Harry H. Fein

If thou would'st view fair Melrose aright. Melrose Abbey. Sir Walter Scott. OBNC; OxAEP-2 *Fr.* The Lay of the Last Minstrel.

If thought can reach to Heaven. The Rabbi's Song. Rudyard Kipling. ChIV-1

If thus we needs must go. The Heart. Michael Drayton. NOSC

"If thy wife is small bend down to her and." Ian Wedde. PeNZ *Fr.* Earthly: Sonnets for Carlos.

If tired of trees I seek again mankind. The Vantage Point. Robert Frost. MeMAP; OxBA

If to be absent were to be. Song. Richard Lovelace. BeJo; CBLP; CaPo; FMP; GTBS-P; MeLP; NOSC; OBEV; OxAEP-1; SeCP

If to that place. Place of grass. Insomnia. Robert Penn Warren. *Fr.* Tale of Time. LCAP-2

If to the Pump Room in the morn we go. *Unknown.* NOEC *Fr.* The Diseases of Bath; a Satire.

If, to their time, they reason had to know the truth of this'. (LL) Laid in my quiet bed, in study as I were. Henry Howard, Earl of Surrey. CABP; CH; SiPS

If to write, rewrite, and write again. Arthur Hugh Clough. EnVR

If to your twilight land of dream. In Memoriam—Leo: A Yellow Cat. Margaret Sherwood. BLPA

If(touched by love's own secret)we, like homing. E. E. Cummings. PoA

If trees could talk. Alabama Poem. Nikki Giovanni. BkSV

If true that notion, which but few contest. *Unknown.* FaBoEE

If 'twere the time of lilies. To The Lady Radegund, With Violets. Venantius Fortunatus, *Latin.* LoP, tr. by Helen Waddell

If up's the word;and a world grows greener. E. E. Cummings. MeMAP

If waker care, if sudden [or sodayne] pale colo[u]r. Sir Thomas Wyatt. AAS; NoSic

If we all knew where. The Rainbow. Opal Palmer Adisa. GT

If we are separated I will. Travelling Together. W. S. Merwin. IFJA

If we are to cross the barriers of snow. An Ark for Lawrence Durrell. Robert Duncan. RaBo

If we are truly free, and live in a free country. Turning Away from Lies. Robert Bly. LCAP-2

If we, as we are, are dust, and dust, as it will, rises. Snow. Charles Wright. ColAP; LCAP-2

If we but knew what forces helped to mold. Plea for Tolerance. Margaret E. Bruner. PoToHe

If We Cannot Live People as People. Charles Lynch. PoBA

If we could be taken alone together in a driverless. The Possible Salvation of Continuous Motion. Pattiann Rogers. MT

If we could get the hang of it entirely. Entirely. Louis MacNeice. CMoP

If we could know. Julia Harris May. LBC

If we could know the mystery. Our Task. Henrietta Cordelia Ray. CBWP-3

If we could only push these walls. Maze Without a Minotaur. Dana Gioia. RA

If We Didn't Have to Eat. Nixon Waterman. OBAL

If we give love and sympathy. Helen King. PoToHe

If we had dope for an excuse, or love. In Memory of My First Chapatis. Diane Di Prima. PoM

If We Knew. May Riley Smith. BLPA

If we live all our lives under lies. Cuba Libre. Imamu Amiri Baraka. BB

If we meet a gorilla. We Must Be Polite. Carl Sandburg. NOxBChV

If we must die—let it not be like hogs. Claude McKay. AmPP; BPo; ColAP; CrDW; ISC; MeLP; NAAAL; NoAM; PBCV; PoBA; Poetr; SAGP; SSLK; Son; TFi; TTY; UnPo

If we must part. A Valediction. Ernest Christopher Dowson. BoLoP

If we recall your voices. The Suicides. Donald Justice. Poetr

If we shall live, we live. Meeting. Christina Rossetti. CBLP; GBL; LW

If we should ever meet again. Lines. Louisa Costello. Ro *Fr.* Songs of a Stranger (1825).

If we should fail? Shakespeare. OxBoV *Fr.* Macbeth.

If we talk, we're too tired to make love; if we. Marilyn Hacker. VCAP *Fr.* Taking Notice.

If we tell, gently, gently. Vanity. Birago Diop. PBMAP

If we, the proximate damned, presumptive blest. To Franz Kafka. Edwin Muir. FaBoTC

If we those generous sons deservedly praise. Upon My Lord Winchilsea's Converting the Mount in His Garden to a Terrace. Anne Finch, Countess of Winchilsea. OBGa

If We Try. George Sands Johnson. PWR

If we were a rock 'n' roll band. Rock 'N' Roll Band. Shel Silverstein. ImGa

If well thou viewst us with no squinted eye. Against a Rich Man Despising Poverty. Phineas Fletcher. NOSC

If we're to go on living. Wislawa Szymborska. *See* Four in the Morning.

If we've promised them aught, let us keep our promise! (LL) The Pied Piper of Hamelin. Robert Browning. EBNV; FaBoBe; FaBoCh; NOxBChV; OBNV; OBSP; OxBChV; PeLV

If what began (look far and wide) will end. Conclusion. John Frederick Nims. PoA

If what I find I do not love. Resignation. Santob De Carrion, *Spanish.* TrJP, tr. by George Ticknor

If when Don Cupid's dart. Love's Offence. Sir John Suckling. CaPo; NOSC

If when my wife is sleeping. Danse Russe. William Carlos Williams. CMoP; InPS-3; NOBA; NoP-4; PoE; Poetr; RaBo; SAGP; SAmP; TAP

If, when night comes, you bid me go away. (LL) Night and Day. Michael Drayton. AAS; GSo; NOBE; PoEL-2; Son

If when the sun at noon displays. A Beautiful Mistress. Thomas Carew. CavPo

If when the wind blows. Daniel Webster's Horses. Elizabeth Jane Coatsworth. MoAmPo; OBCA

If when they brought the good news. Gospel. Kevyn Arthur. PBCV

If, whittler and dumper, gross carver. The Arc Inside and Out. A. R. Ammons. NoAM; NoP-4

If Winter comes, can Spring be far behind? (LL) Ode to the West Wind. Shelley. AWP; CH; ClHu; EBEV; FHYEP; FaBoBe; GTBS-P; HAP; HeIP-4; ImPo; InPS-3; NAEL-2; NAWM-2; NIP-4; NOBE; NOBRP; NoP-4; OAEL-2; OBEV; OBNC; OxAEP-2; PBMP; PFE; PeECV; PoE; PoEL-4; PoLF; PoPoPo; PoRA; Poetr; Ro; SCGP; TFi; TRP; WeW-3

If wishes were horses. Mother Goose. FaBoBe; LB; OxNR; ReMoGo

If Wishing for the Mystic Joys of Love. Thomas Chatterton. OxBSP

If with complaint the pain might be expressed. Sir Thomas Wyatt. SiPS

If with light head erect I sing. Henry David Thoreau. FaBoBe *Fr.* Inspiration. APN-1; AmPP; ColAP; FaBoBe; NCAP; NOBA; OxBA

If with old love of you, dear Hills! I share. Composed at Rydal on May Morning, 1838. Wordsworth. LaPo *Fr.* Memorials of a Tour in Italy, 1837.

If with the literate, I am. Oscar Wilde. Dorothy Parker. NALW *Fr.* A Pig's-Fye View of Literature.

If within the cruel Southland you have chanced to take a ride. Jim Crow Cars. Lizelia Augusta Jenkins Moorer. CBWP-3

If women could be fair, and yet not fond. Edward, 17th Earl of Oxford De Vere. GTBS-P; NoSic

"If words could speak words should have told. . . ." Out There. Breyten Breytenbach, *Afrikaans.* VCWP

If yet I have not all thy love. Lovers' Infiniteness[e]. Donne. ESCV; MeLP; NOSC; OAEL-1; PoEL-2; SeCP

If yo' brother done you wrong. You Fight On. *Unknown.* AS

If you and I, Julius, old friend. Martial, *Latin.* FP, tr. by James Michie

If you are a gentleman. A Sure Test. *Unknown.* OxNR; ReMoGo

If you are a revolutionary. The Reactionary Poet. Ishmael Reed. GT

If you are a simple mortal, do not speak. Flux. Simonides, *Greek.* OBCVT, tr. by Willis Barnstone

If you are always kind. (LL) Mary's Lamb [or Mary and Her Lamb]. Sarah Josepha Buell Hale. CTV; FaBoBe; ImGa; OBCA; OxBChV; OxNR; PeP

If you are cold, this poem will not warm you. This Poem. Constance Urdang. PBCAP

If you are living, remember. Farewell to Maria. Tadeusz Borowski, *Polish.* HP, tr. by Tadeusz Pióro

If you are merry sing away. Mirth. Christopher Smart. OxBChV *Fr.* Hymns for the Amusement of Children.

If you are on the Gloomy Line. Get a Transfer. *Unknown.* BLPA

If you are only kind. Sarah Josepha Buell Hale. *See* Mary's Lamb [or Mary and Her Lamb].

If you are still alive when you read this. Goodbye. Bill Knott. SPE

If you are tempted to reveal. Three Gates. Beth Day. BLPA; PoToHe

If you ask me how it is. Why My Hair Is Not Gray. Picirantaiyar, *Tamil.* PLW, tr. by A. K. Ramanujan

If you ask me where I am. Gunnar Ekelof, *Swedish.* PFTM, tr. by Muriel Rukeyser and Leif Sjoberg

If you burn your scorched soul too often, Love, she'll fly. Meleager. HePo, tr. by Barbara Hughes Fowler *Fr.* I'll Twine White Violets. NIP-4, tr. by Goldwin Smith

If You But Knew. *Unknown.* BLPA; FaBoBe

If you call / I will come to you. Sokchong Shin, *Korean.* CKP, tr. by Jaihiun Kim

If You Can Hear My Hooves. Harold Littlebird. VoR

If you can keep your head when all [about you]. If. Rudyard Kipling. APAD; BLPA; CTV; ChAP; EBEvV; FaBoBe; FaPoR; OxBChV; OxBTC; PFE; PWR; SAGP; UV

If you can keep your head when all about you. Recruiting Song. Michael Foster. UV

If you can see why she feels that she kneels if you can see why he knows that he shows what he bestows. On Her Way. Gertrude Stein. PFTM

If you can sleep when those who write about you. Rewards and Fairies. Roger Woddis. UV

If you cannot on the ocean. Your Mission. Ellen M. Huntington Gates. BLPA

If you can't be a **pine** on the top of the hill. Be the Best of Whatever You Are. Douglas Malloch. BLPA

If you can't be free, be a mystery. (LL) Canary. Rita Dove. LoL; SeSe

If you can't eat you got to. E. E. Cummings. CMoP

If you come at all. Yourself and Myself. *Unknown, Irish.* NOIV, *tr. by* Thomas Kinsella

If You Come Back. Jack Cope. PeSA

If you complain your flames are hot. To Her Lover's Complaint. Jane Barker. OxBSP

If you could be there / with the rest. Hunt Walking. Wesley McNair. AFr

If You Could Come. Katharine Lee Bates. CPO

If you could crowd them into forty lines! Limitations. Siegfried Sassoon. MoBrPo

If you could know that roads are oranges. Amelia Erhardt. Amelia Erhardt, *Romanian.* CEEP, *tr. by* Stavros Deligiorgis

If you could only keep quiet [*or* quite] still and wait. (LL) Myxomatosis. Philip Larkin. CMoP; MoP; NoAM; PFE

If you could see, fair brother, how dead beat. Prolonged Sonnet: When the Troops Were Returning from Milan. Niccolò degli Albizzi, *Italian.* AWP; OBVE, *tr. by* D. G. Rossetti

If you, dear Celia, cannot bear. The Sacrifice: An Epistle to Celia. Mary Leapor. PEW

If you destroy our tongue. Curse. Kalju Lepik, *Estonian.* CEEP, *tr. by* Ivar Ivask

If you die you lose with rambling. Beneath the Radar—for the RAF and All Low Flying Aircraft. Geraldine Monk. NBrP

"If you do love me weel, Willie." Fair Janet. *Unknown.* ESPB

If you do not shake the bottle. On Tomato Ketchup. *Unknown.* NBLV; Spl

If you don't come to the mountains in autumn. Staying Overnight at Blue Cloud Temple. Mo Shih-lung, *Chinese.* CoBLCP, *tr. by* Jonathan Chaves

If-you-don't-go-down-with ME! (LL) Disobedience. A. A. Milne. NOxBChV

If you don't have a woman that lives with you. Strange Business. Jelaluddin Rumi, *Persian.* LoL, *tr. by* Coleman Barks

If you don't know how, why pretend? To the Tune "Red Embroidered Shoes." Huang O, *Chinese.* ChiPo; PBWP; WPOW, *tr. by* Kenneth Rexroth *and* Ling Chung

If you don't know the kind of person I am. A Ritual to Read to Each Other. William Stafford. RaBo

If you don't know your place, then I'll tietzsche. (LL) Limerick: "'If you're aristocratic,' said Nietzsche." Gerry Hamill. OBCoV; PeLi

If you don't like my apples. *Unknown.* OxBoLi

If you don't put your shoes on before I count fifteen then. One, Two, Three. Michael Rosen. OTCP

If you draw a bow, draw a strong one. Tu Fu. *Fr.* On the Border, First Series. CoBCP, *tr. by* Burton Watson

If you draw a bow, draw the strongest. Tu Fu. SuSp, *tr. by* Ronald C. Miao *Fr.* Frontier Songs, First Series.

"If you dream," said the eminent Freud. Limerick. Russell Miller. PeLi

If you evah go to Houston. Midnight Special. *Unknown.* AS

If you ever come to our house. Carolyn Gardner. PeP

If you ever, ever, ever meet a grizzly bear. Grizzly Bear. Mary Austin. CTV

If you ever find. Wise 1. Imamu Amiri Baraka. PFTM *Fr.* Why's / Wise.

If you feel that you're right on your beam ends. Limerick. Leslie Johnson. PeLi

If you find a man who does not receive. Cry "Infidel!" Alfred Gibbs Campbell. AAP

If you find a paddling pool. The Paddling Pool. E. M. Adams. BoTP

If you find for your verse there's no call. Limerick. *Unknown.* PeLi

If you go a-picnicking and throw your scraps about. Picnics. *Unknown.* BoTP

If you go away. The Azaleas. Sowol Kim, *Korean.* CKP, *tr. by* Jaihiun Kim

If you go away, / why should I adorn myself? *Unknown, Japanese.* BoWoP, *tr. by* Kenneth Yasuda

If you had a friend strong, simple, true. Robert Lewis. PoToHe

If you had known. Thomas Hardy. GBL; LBC

If you had lusted after something noble or decent. Sappho, *Greek.* InMo, *tr. by* Sam Hamill

If you had the insight. Sighioara 1982. Grete Tartler, *Romanian.* CEEP, *tr. by* Fleur Adcock

If You Happy Would Be. Abraham Fernández. AH

If you have a friend worth loving. Seeds of Kindness. *Unknown.* BLPA; PWR; PoToHe

If you have a tender message. Before It Is Too Late. Frank Herbert Sweet. PoToHe

If you have a word of cheer. Tell Her So. Mrs. Henry Linden. CBWP-4

If you have a word of cheer. Tell Him So. J. A. Egerton. PWR

If you have forgotten water-lilies floating. Water-Lilies. Sara Teasdale. MoAmPo; NMM-2

If you have formed [*or* formd] a Circle to go into. To God. William Blake. OAEL-2

If you have lost the radio beam, then guide yourself by the sun or the stars. Any Man's Advice to His Son. Kenneth Fearing. CMoP

If you have no time. Lady Izumi, *Japanese.* BoWoP, *tr. by* Willis Barnstone

If you have not read the Slavic poets. To Robinson Jeffers. Czeslaw Milosz, *Polish.* EC3, *tr. by* Czeslaw Milosz *and* Richard Lourie

If you have revisited the town, thin Shade. To a Shade. W. B. Yeats. NAEL-2; PoEL-5

If you have spoken something beautiful. If You Made Gentler the Churlish World. Max Ehrmann. PoToHe

If you have taken this rubble for my past. Delta. Adrienne Rich. LoL; NIP-4; PiM

If you have tears, prepare to shed them now. Shakespeare. OxAEP-1 *Fr.* Julius Caesar.

If you haven't made noise enough to warn him, singing, shouting. Meeting a Bear. David Wagoner. HAP; PaTW; WeW-3

If you hear a kind word spoken. Tell Him So. *Unknown.* BLPA

If you hear rustling in the straw. David Philips. BXAP

If You Imagine. Raymond Queneau, *French.* NNPT, *tr. by* Michael Benedikt

If you insult me in my absence. Apollinarius, *Greek.* GrAn, *tr. by* Peter Jay

If you live along with all the other people. Worm Either Way. D. H. Lawrence. NoAM

If you look for the truth outside yourself. Tung-shan, *Japanese.* EnlH, *tr. by* Stephen Mitchell

If you love me. Lady Izumi, *Japanese.* BoWoP, *tr. by* Willis Barnstone

If you loved me ever so little. Satia Te Sanguine. Swinburne. PeVV

If You Made Gentler the Churlish World. Max Ehrmann. PoToHe

If you mean to keep this appointment. Instructions for Elijah. Myra Sklarew. CRP

If you melt some lead. Valerio Magrelli, *Italian.* NeIt, *tr. by* Dana Gioia

If you mice are looking for *food.* Ariston, *Greek.* GrAn, *tr. by* W. G. Shepherd

If you must yawn, just turn aside. *Unknown.* CTV

If you never do anything for anyone else. The Immoral Proposition. Robert Creeley. LiTM; NeAP; PoM

If you never spend your money. Icarus Schmicarus. Adrian Mitchell. OBCoV

If you please, will you let the king's horses go through? Mother Goose. *See* To Babylon.

If you really care for me. *Unknown, Spanish.* BoWoP, *tr. by* Willis Barnstone

If you really imagine wisdom grows with a beard. Lucianus, *Greek.* GrAn, *tr. by* Edwin Morgan

If you really love me honey, hey- yah. *Unknown.* STP *Fr.* Kiowa "49" Songs.

If you refuse me once, and think again. Ditty. Edward Herbert. NOSC

If you ride in it, you mus' be holy, this train. (LL) This Train. *Unknown.* AmFP; OxBoLi

If You Saw a Negro Lady. June Jordan. GT

("Into surprise observing / happy birthday.") (LL) NMM-2

If you saw my little backyard, "Wot a pretty spot!" you'd cry. The Cockney's Garden. Edgar Bateman. OBGa

If You See a Fairy Ring. *Unknown.* BoTP

If you see a tall fellow ahead of a [*or* the] crowd. Forget It. *Unknown.* PoLF

If you see someone beautiful / hammer it out right then. Adaios of Macedon, *Greek.* GrAn, *tr. by* Alistair Elliot

If You See This Man. Thomas Lux. AmPA

"If you seek for Eldorado." (LL) Eldorado. Edgar Allan Poe. APN-1; AWP; AmPP; CTV; ChAP; ColAP; FPC; FaBoBe; FaBoCh; LiLi; MeMAP; NCAP; NOBA; NOxBChV; NTP; NoP-4; OxBA; TAP

If you set out in this world. The Seventh. Attila József, *Hungarian.* AF; NNPT; RB, *tr. by* John Batki

If you should be surprised, Nathan. Jacob Glatstein, *Yiddish.* CEEP, *tr. by* Ruth Whitman

If you should bid me make a choice. The Windmill. Edward Verrall Lucas. BoTP

If you should go before me, dear, walk slowly. Walk Slowly. Adelaide Love. BLPA

If you should meet a crocodile. *Unknown.* CTAV

If you should see a man. The Truth. Ted Joans. AmFP; TTY

If you sit down at set of sun. At Set of Sun. "George Eliot." PoToHe

If you sneeze on Monday, you sneeze for danger. Sneezing. *Unknown.* ReMoGo

If you stay in comfort too long. You Will Forget. Chenjerai Hove. HBAPE

If you still have bacon and eggs for breakfast. Sipho Sepamla. PeSAV

If you strike. Genuine Poem, Found on a Blackboard in a Bowling Alley in Story City, Iowa. Ted Kooser. KaS

If you strike a thorn or rose. Keep a-Goin'. Frank Lebby Stanton. PWR

If you take the moon in your hands. The Moon in Your Hands. Hilda Doolittle. BoWoP; FaBoWP; NYBP *Fr.* Sigil.

If you, that have grown old, were the first dead. The New Faces. W. B. Yeats. GTBS-P

If you think it crude to be rough and rude. Robert Swan. NSI

If You Think Kindly of Me. *Unknown, Chinese.* CoBCP, *tr. by* Burton Watson

If you think, mother. What Her Girl Friend Said to the foster-mother. Orampokiyar. PLW *Fr.* Five on the Crabs. PLW, *tr. by* A. K. Ramanujan

If you think you are beaten, you are. The Man Who Thinks He Can. Walter D. Wintle. PoLF

If you think you are beaten, you are. The Victor. C. W. Longenecker. PWR

If you try to do what's right. Lines Suggested by an Edition of Blake's Poems. Sir Walter Alexander Ralegh. OBCoV

If you wander far enough. Oh No. Robert Creeley. HeIP-4; InPK-6

If you want a game to tame you and to take your measure in. The Trucker. Will Dyson. NOBAu

If you want a thing bad enough. Success. Berton Braley. PoToHe

If you want my apartment, sleep in it. Rent. Jane Cooper. FYAP; TAP

If you want to die you will have to pay for it. (LL) Charon. Louis MacNeice. FaBoTw; PNI

If you want to find the Sergeant. *Unknown.* NSI

If you want to go to heaven. The Blood-strained Banders. *Unknown.* AmFP

If you want to have the kind of a church. It Isn't the Church—It's You. *Unknown.* BLPA

If you want to know where the privates were. Where They Were. *Unknown.* AS

If you want to live in the country you have to understand the power. The Power of Maples. Gerald Stern. APAD

If you want to live in the kind of a town. It Isn't the Town, It's You. R. W. Glover. BLPA

If you want to live, then live. . . . Georgy Vladimirovich Ivanov, *Russian.* TCRP, *tr. by* Daniel Weissbort

If you weep, I think that. Larry Eigner. FTOS

If you were an Eskimo baby. An Eskimo Baby. Lucy Diamond. BoTP

If you were an owl. That's What We'd Do. Mary Mapes Dodge. OBCA

If you were busy being kind. How to Forget. Rebecca Foresman. PoToHe

If you were coming in the Fall. Emily Dickinson. AmPP; CBLP; NOBA; OxBA; PoRA; SoSe-8

If you were exchanged in the cradle and. A Story That Could Be True. William Stafford. KaS; NTCP; RaBo

If you were going to get a pet. Robert Creeley. MoP; NOBA; NeAP; NoAM; Poetr

If you were just in keeping our pact of love. Wallāda, *Arabic.* PBWP, *tr. by* A. R. Nykel

If you were only one inch tall, you'd ride a worm to school. One Inch Tall. Shel Silverstein. OBCA

If you were riding in a coach. Oaths of Friendship. *Unknown, Chinese.* FP; ChiP, *tr. by* Arthur Waley

If you were to ask me why I dwell among green mountains. Conversations in the Mountains. Li Po, *Chinese.* RaBo; TAL, *tr. by* Robert Payne

If you were twenty-seven. Heaven. Philip Levine. LCAP-2

If you will come on such a day. The Gardener. Sidney Keyes. MoBrPo

If you will tell me why the fen. I May, I Might, I Must. Marianne Moore. ChAP; FaBoWP; OBAL; OxBSP; PFE

If you wisely invest in heaven. Frank Lloyd Wright. CTV

If you wish in this world to advance. A Thought from Ruddigore. Sir William Schwenck Gilbert. OBCoV *Fr.* Ruddigore.

If you wish to pull a cork. Lilliputian's Beer Song. Septimus Winner. OBAL

If you wonder why. No Offense. Kevin Young. LTA

If you would know the love which I you bear. Sir John Davies. *Fr.* Sonnets to Philomel. SiPS

If you would learn. The Antiquary. Joseph Campbell. OxBTC

If you would only stop to count your blessings. Count Your Blessings. Mrs. Henry Linden. CBWP-4

If you would seek us. Shakespeare. OxAEP-1 *Fr.* The Winter's Tale.

If you your lips would keep from slips. Our Lips and Ears. *Unknown.* BLPA

If you'd died I would've cut off my hair. *Unknown, Tlingit Indian.* STP, *tr. by* James Koller *after* John Swanton

If you'll listen a while, I'll sing you a song. Jim Fisk. *Unknown.* AS

If you'll listen for a moment, I will tell you now, my friends. What We Teach at Claflin. Lizelia Augusta Jenkins Moorer. CBWP-3

If your first memory was the arms of your father. Reprieve on the Stoop. Belle Waring. PBCAP

If your loved one prove unworthy, why then. Elizabeth Daryush. WPN

If your mother is a Jew, you are a Jew. A Meditation in Seven Days. Alicia Ostriker. PBCAP

If your words have become pewter. Plainsong. Gail Hanlon. BAP-96

If You're Anxious for to Shine in the High Aesthetic Line. Bunthorne's Song. Sir William Schwenck Gilbert. CABP; EBVV; OAEL-2; NAEL-2; NBLV *Fr.* Patience.

"If you're aristocratic," said Nietzsche. Limerick. Gerry Hamill. OBCoV; PeLi

If You're Ever Going to Love Me. *Unknown.* BLPA

If You're Ever in a jam. Friendship. Cole Porter. FP

If you're not home, where. Numbers, Letters. Imamu Amiri Baraka. BPo; NOBA

If you've ever stole a pheasant-egg be'ind the keeper's back. Loot. Rudyard Kipling.

If you've got a job to do. Do It Now! *Unknown.* BLPA

If you've got but fifty cents! (LL) I Had But Fifty Cents. *Unknown.* BLPA; NBLV; WHSW

If you've tried and have not won. Don't Give Up. Phoebe Cary. CTV

Iflimit iflimis haflamard foflomor meflemen toflomo. Cerveri De Girona, *Provençal.* CBNP, *tr. by* Anthony Bonner

Ifor Hael's hall, poorly it looks. The Hall of Ifor Hael. Evan Evans, *Welsh.* OBWVE, *tr. by* Gwyn Williams

Ifyi stull / huuny / wurkt oot. Tom Leonard. FaBoTC *Fr.* Unrelated Incidents.

Ignatio lived on the river. The Boat Builder. Mark McWatt. HCP

Ignorance of Death. William Empson. CMoP; LiTM; NoAM

Ignorant, in the sense. Death of an Irishwoman. Michael Hartnett. CIP-2; IIP; PBCIP

Ignorant man does well to shut his trap, The. Palladas, *Greek.* GrAn, *tr. by* Tony Harrison

Ignorant men, who disclaim. Sister Juana Inés de la Cruz. *Fr.* A Satirical Romance. PBWP, *tr. by* Judith Thurman

Ignorant of all logic and all law. Palladas, *Greek.* GrAn, *tr. by* Tony Harrison

Ignorant people so that. Brief Curriculum. Reiner Kunze, *German.* PoSu, *tr. by* Michael Hamburger

Ignore dull days; forget the showers. Lesson From a Sundial [Sun-Dial]. *Unknown.* Spl

Ignotum per Ignotius, or a Furious Hodge-Podge of Nonsense; a Pindaric. *Unknown.* CBNP; NOEC

Ijajee's Story. Charlotte DeClue. EC2

Ikhnaton looked like. Why I Often Allude to Osiris. Ishmael Reed. GT

Ikhnaton's Night. Agnes Nemes Nagy, *Hungarian.* CEEP, *tr. by* Laura Schiff

Il Capriccio Dramatico. Lorenzo Da Ponte, *Italian.*
To an Artful Theatre Manager. TrJP, *tr. by* John Mazzinghi

Il Janitoro. George Ade. OBAL

Il Pastor Fido. Sir Richard Fanshawe, *after the Italian of* Giovanni Battista Guarini.
Fall, The. NOSC
(Great Favorit Beheaded, A.) OBVE
Golden Age, The. NOSC; OAEL-1
"How I forsook/ Elias and Pisa after, and betook." AWP
"Learn women all from this housewifery." OBVE
Ode on His Majesty's Proclamation. NOBE
Of Beauty. BoLoP
(Beauty.) GBL
"Our beauty is to us that which to men." OBVE
Rose, A. OBEV; PoEL-2

(Rose of Life, The.) AWP

"Well may that kisse be sweet that's giv'n t' a sleek." OBVE

Il Penseroso. Milton. AWP, FiTVEP, OTB3-F, HAP; HOPM; ImPo; NOSC; OAEL-1; OBEV; TFi

("Hence vain deluding Joys.") NoP-4

Poetry and the Melancholy Man. EPCY

"Sweet bird that shunn'st the noise of folly." CH

Il Piccolo Rifiuto. Louis MacNeice. CMoP

Il Pleut Doucement sur la Ville. Paul Verlaine, *French.* AWP, *tr. by* Ernest Dowson

Il Trionfo del Amor. Charlotte Dacre. Ro *Fr.* Hours of Solitude.

Ilaria, thou that wert so fair and dear. The Tomb of Ilaria Giunigi. Edith Wharton. APN-2

Ile gaze no more on her bewitching face. Song: Murdring Beautie. Thomas Carew. SeCP

Ile give thee leave my love, in beauties field. Sonnet. Sir William Alexander, Earl of Stirling. OxBS *Fr.* Aurora.

Ile sooth his plots: and strow my hate with smiles. George Chapman. PoEL-2 *Fr.* Bussy d'Ambois.

Ilex Tree, The. Agnes Lee. PoA

Iliad, The. Homer, *Greek.*

Achilles kills Lycaon. OBCVT, *tr. by* Alexander Pope

Achilles Over the Trench. OBVE, *tr. by* Tennyson

("So saying, light-foot Iris pass'd away.") OBCVT Tennyson

Achilles sets out. OBCVT, *tr. by* Alexander Pope

Achilles sets out. OBCVT, *tr. by* Christopher Logue

"Achilles with wild fury in his heart." OBWP, *tr. by* Robert Fitzgerald

Ajax and his Brother. OBVE, *tr. by* Alexander Pope

"Ajax the swift swerv'd never from the side." OBVE, *tr. by* William Cowper

"All grave old men, and souldiers they had bene, but for age." OBVE, *tr. by* George Chapman

"And as in winter time when Jove his cold-sharpe javelines throwes." OBVE, *tr. by* George Chapman

"And as when with the West-wind's flawes the sea thrusts up her waves." OBVE, *tr. by* George Chapman

"And now was Paris come / From his high towres." OBVE, *tr. by* George Chapman

Andromache's Lament for Hector. OxBM

Andromache's Lamentation. OBVE, *tr. by* Congreve

Apollo Defeats Patroclus. OBVE, *tr. by* Christopher Logue

(Apollo hits Patroclus.) OBCVT, *tr. by* Christopher Logue

("His hand came from the east.") OBCVT, *tr. by* Christopher Logue

("Perhaps.") (LL) OBCVT, *tr. by* Christopher Logue

"As when an architect some palace wall." OBVE, *tr. by* William Cowper

"As when devouring flames some forest seize." OBVE, *tr. by* William Cowper

"As when of frequent bees." OBVE, *tr. by* George Chapman

"As when the winds, ascending by degrees." OBVE, *tr. by* Alexander Pope

"At her departure his disdain return'd." OBVE, *tr. by* Dryden

Battle. OBCVT, *tr. by* Tennyson

Battle. OBCVT, *tr. by* Ogilby, John

"Big with great purposes and proud, they sat." OBVE, *tr. by* William Cowper

"Bright-footed Thetis did the sphere aspire." NoSic, *tr. by* George Chapman

Briseis mourns Patroclus. OBCVT, *tr. by* Edward, Earl of Derby

"But ere sterne conflict mixt both strengths, faire Paris stept before." OBVE, *tr. by* George Chapman

"But now, no longer deaf to honour's call." OBVE, *tr. by* Alexander Pope

Clash in Arms of the Achaians and Trojans. OBCVT, *tr. by* George Meredith

Destruction of the Grecian Fort, The. OBVE, *tr. by* Alexander Pope

"Embodied close, the lab'ring Grecian train." OBVE, *tr. by* Alexander Pope

Equity in death. OBCVT, *tr. by* Alexander Pope

"Fierce they drove on, impatient to destroy." OBVE, *tr. by* Alexander Pope

"Frail as the leaves that quiver on the sprays." OBVE, *tr. by* Samuel Johnson

Goddess intervenes between Achilles and Agamemnon, The. OBCVT, *tr. by* Alexander Pope

Goddess intervenes between Achilles and Agamemnon, The. OBCVT, *tr. by* John Dryden

("Content to bid the War aloof in Peace?") (LL) OBCVT, *tr. by* John Dryden

Greeks Like Clouds, The. OBVE, *tr. by* George Chapman

Hector Arms. NOSC, *tr. by* George Chapman

Hector Flees before Achilles. OBVE, *tr. by* Alexander Pope

Hector's Child and the Plume. OBVE, *tr. by* George Chapman

Hector's Defiance. NOSC, *tr. by* George Chapman

Hector's flight. OBCVT, *tr. by* Robert Fitzgerald

Helen and the elders. OBVE, *tr. by* George Chapman

Helen's Lamentation. OBVE, *tr. by* Congreve

Heroes meet again in the underworld, The. OBCVT, *tr. by* David Constantine

Homer's Gift of Fame. NOSC, *tr. by* George Chapman

Invocation, "The Wrath of *Peleus* Son, O Muse, resound." OBVE; OBCVT, *tr. by* John Dryden

Juno seduces Jove. OBCVT, *tr. by* Alexander Pope

Killing of Lykaon, The. OBCVT, *tr. by* Robert Lowell

"Like Leaves on Trees the Race of Man is found." OBVE, *tr. by* Alexander Pope

Menelaus wounded. OBCVT, *tr. by* William Cowper

Neptune Goes to the Greeks. NOSC, *tr. by* George Chapman

Night Piece: the Trojans outside Troy. OBVE, *tr. by* Alexander Pope

Night Piece: the Trojans outside Troy. OBVE, *tr. by* George Chapman

("And all did wilfully expect the silver-throned morne.") (LL) OBCVT, *tr. by* George Chapman

(Fire-light.) OBCVT, *tr. by* George Chapman

("This speech all Troians did applaud; who from their traces losde.") OBCVT, *tr. by* George Chapman

"Nor lingered Paris in the lofty house." OBVE, *tr. by* Tennyson

Old Trojan Chiefs See Helen, The. OBVE, *tr. by* Alexander Pope

Paris and Menelaus. OBVE, *tr. by* Alexander Pope

Patroclus Spears Thestor. OBVE, *tr. by* William Cowper

Patroclus's Request to Achilles for his Arms. Imitated from the Beginning of the Sixteenth Iliad of Homer. OBCVT, *tr. by* Thomas Yalden

Phœnix pleads with Achilles. OBCVT, *tr. by* Edward, Earl of Derby

Priam and Achilles. NOSC; OBCVT, *tr. by* George Chapman

("Nor *Jove* gets the command of me.") (LL) OBCVT, *tr. by* George Chapman

"O my husband. . . / cut off from life so young! You leave me a widow." GrIP, *tr. by* Robert Fagles

Proposition and Invocation. NOSC

River Scamander Attacks Achilles. OBVE, *tr. by* Alexander Pope

Sacrifice to Apollo, The. OBVE, *tr. by* Dryden

Sarpedon's Speech. NOSC, *tr. by* George Chapman

(". . . as ye see a mountaine Lion fare.") OBCVT, *tr. by* George Chapman

(Sarpedon to Glaucus.) OBCVT, *tr. by* George Chapman

Sarpedon's Speech to Glaucus. OBVE, *tr. by* Sir John Denham

(Sarpedon's Speech to Glaucus in the 12th of Homer.) OBCVT, *tr. by* Sir John Denham

("Thus to *Glaucus* spake.") OBCVT, *tr. by* Sir John Denham

Shield of Achilles, The. NOSC, *tr. by* George Chapman

Specimen of a Translation of the Iliad in Blank Verse. OBCVT, *tr. by* Tennyson

Speech of Sarpedon (an Ally of the Trojans) to Glaucus, The. OBVE, *tr. by* Alexander Pope

Stones and Snow. OBVE, *tr. by* Alexander Pope

Thetis and the Nereids. OBCVT, *tr. by* Robert Fagles

Thetis Asks Jove to Revenge Her Son Achilles. OBVE, *tr. by* John Dryden

("He moves into his Hall: The Pow'rs resort.") OBCVT, *tr. by* John Dryden

(Olympians.) OBCVT, *tr. by* John Dryden

Two Ajaxes Compared to Oxen, The. OBVE, *tr. by* George Chapman

Vulcan Forges the Shield of Achilles. OBVE, *tr. by* Alexander Pope

("And bears the blazing Present through the Skies.") (LL) OBCVT, *tr. by* Alexander Pope

(Vulcan forges the armour of Achilles.) OBCVT, *tr. by* Alexander Pope

Wasps, The. OBVE, *tr. by* Alexander Pope

Watch and the Dogs, The. OBVE, *tr. by* Alexander Pope

Wearing Achilles' Armour, Patroclus, along with the Myrmidons, Attacks the Trojans. OBVE, *tr. by* Christopher Logue

"Why dost thou so explore." OBVE, *tr. by* George Chapman

Iliad. Humbert Wolfe. MoBrPo

Ilicet. Theodosia Pickering Garrison. PoLF

Ilicet. Swinburne. NOBVV

Ilion, o my city. Euripides. OBCVT, *tr. by* Richmond Lattimore *Fr.* Hecuba.

I'll act out a weird dream. Marie-Francoise Prager, *French.* BoWoP, *tr. by* Willis Barnstone *and* Elene Kolb

I'll always dress in black and rave. Christine de Pisan, *French*. BoWoP, *tr. by* Willis Barnstone

I'll always remember my town by the sea. (LL) Block City. Robert Louis Stevenson. CTV; NTCP

I'll ask, "Now, really, beyond the sky, / is there another sky?" Yüan Mei. *See* Finding Serenity.

I'll bark against the Dog-star. Loving Mad Tom. *Unknown*. CBNP; NOSC

I'll be an amulet, I'll be good news. Haim Gouri, *Hebrew*. IP, *tr. by* Warren Bargad *and* Stanley F. Chyet

I'll be an otter, and I'll let you swim. River-Mates. Padraic Colum. AWP

I'll be finished, if I'll survive—. Boris Alekseievich Chichibabin, *Russian*. TCRP, *tr. by* Albert C. Todd *and* Yevgeny Yevtuskenko

I'll Be Fourteen Next Sunday. *Unknown*. AmFP

I'll be polite in many ways. Lloyd E. Werth. CTV

I'll be the strongest amid you. The Strongest. "Yehoash," *Yiddish*. TrJP, *tr. by* Marie Syrkin

I'll be the Vicar of Bray, Sir. (LL) The Vicar of Bray. *Unknown*. FaBoPV; NOBE; NOBL; OBSV; OxBoLi

I'll believe then that you are dead. Then I'll Believe. B. W. Vilakazi, *Zulu*. PeSA, *tr. by* Jack Cope

I'll bequeath no goods to you when I am dead. Testament. Tudor Arghezi, *Romanian*. AF; CEEP, *tr. by* Andrei Banta *and* Thomas Amherst Perry

I'll burn my books!—Ah, Mephistophilis! (LL) The End of Doctor Faustus. Marlowe. FaBoVe; HeIP-4; PeECV; PoEL-2

I'll Buy a Peacock Bird. Modwena Sedgwick. PeP

I'll buy you a tartan bonnet. *Unknown*. OxNR

I'll chase through the gypsy camp of dark streets. Osip Emilevich Mandelstam, *Russian*. TCRP, *tr. by* Bernard Meares

I'll [*or* Ile] come to thee in all those shapes. To Electra. Robert Herrick. CaPo

I'll compare you to the outskirts of Copenhagen. Looking You In the Back of the Head. Walid Bitar. WeT

I'll descend mid other men. Freedom. Sean O Riordain, *Irish*. TIRV, *tr. by* Coslett Quin

I'll die for him tomorrow. (LL) Bonny Barbara Allan ("In Scarlet Town where I was born.") *Unknown*. AWP; BoLoP; CH; ESPB; HeIP-4; InPK-6; NAEL-1; OxBB

I'll dig with it. (LL) Digging. Seamus Heaney. BIrV; CIP-2; IIP; InPS-3; NAEL-2; NoP-4; SAGP; TwCP

I'll do what the raids suggest. A Boy. John Ashbery. NeAP

I'll dress you. Love Poem for Three for Kaye & Me. Gregory Corso. PmAP

I'll drown my book. (LL) Magic. Shakespeare. AWP; EBEV; OxAEP-1; SCV

I'll eat when I'm hungry, I'll drink when I'm dry. Rye Whisky. *Unknown*. APN-2; OxBoLi

Ill-equipped bride-to-be, I left home, An. Robyn Selman. PUP-19

I'll faint no more beneath the burden. Submission. Clara Ann Thompson. CBWP-2

Ill fares the land, to hastening ills a prey. Oliver Goldsmith. OBSV; UV *Fr.* The Deserted Village. NOEC; OAEL-1; PoEL-3

Ill fates pursue me, may I never find. Lady Mary Wortley Montagu. ECEV *Fr.* Town Eclogues. ECEV

I'll ferry you. (LL) Ferry Me across the Water. Christina Rossetti. BoTP; NTP; OxBChV; TLR

I'll follow and bring you back by force. I *will!*—. (LL) Home Burial. Robert Frost. ColAP; IMW; NAAL-2; SoSe-8; TAP; TRP

I'll Follow Thee. Clara Ann Thompson. CBWP-2

I'll forget I saw you. Tanka. Yosano Tekkan, *Japanese*. MJT, *tr. by* Makoto Ueda

I'll frame, my Heliodora! a garland for thy hair. A Garland for Heliodora. Meleager, *Greek*. AWP, *tr. by* "Christopher North"

I'll get up soon, and leave my bed unmade. The Widower in the Country. Les A. Murray. DiPo

I'll give a candle. Fair Exchange. Aileen Fisher. NOxBChV

I'll give my love an apple without a core. *Unknown*. *See* I will give my love an apple without e'er a core.

"I'll give to you a paper of pins." Paper of Pins. *Unknown*. AmFP

I'll go among the dead to save my friend. An Afternoon at the Beach. Edgar Bowers. MT; VCAP

I'll go, said I, to the woods and hills. The Apostate. Alfred Edgar Coppard. OBMV

I'll go up on the mountain top. Liza Jane. *Unknown*. AS

Ill Government. Robert Herrick. CavPo

I'll grab hold of a butt of dream. Amir Gilbo'a, *Hebrew*. IP, *tr. by* Warren Bargad *and* Stanley F. Chyet

I'll greet the sun once more. Once More. Forugh Farrokhzad. BoWoP, *tr. by* Jascha Kessler *and* Amin Banani

I'll hold my candle high, and then. High Resolve. *Unknown*. PoToHe

Ill Humor. Goethe, *German*. STV, *tr. by* John Frederick Nims

I'll keep your shirt white. Death Song. *Unknown*, *Turkish*. BoWoP, *tr. by* Reza Baraheni *and* Zahra-Soltan Shokoohtaezeh

I'll Kill you if you Quote it! (LL) Cinq Ans Après. Frank Gelett Burgess. APN-2; NBLV; OBAL; OBCoV; TFi

I'll know no more;—the heart is torn. Sir Eustace Grey. George Crabbe.

Ill lay he long, upon this last return. John Berryman. TAP *Fr.* Dream Songs.

I'll lay this halfway me, which the we body name. Martin Opitz, *German*. GePo, *tr. by* George C. Schoolfield

I'll lay you five hundred pounds. The Broomfield Hill. *Unknown*. AmFP; CH; ESPB; OxBB

I'll leave thy heart a-dying. (LL) The Cheat of Cupid; or, The Ungentle Guest. Robert Herrick. AWP; OBVE

I'll live, and as he pulls me down mount higher. (LL) Ovid, *Latin*. CABP; NoSic, *tr. by* Marlowe *Fr.* Elegies

I'll Marry Not at All. *Unknown*. AmFP

Ill Met by Zenith. Ogden Nash. NYBP

I'll mock those thoughts of yours. Prologue. Vladimir Mayakovsky. TCRP, *tr. by* Bernard Meares *Fr.* The Cloud in Trousers.

I'll never have a river of gold. Bassus, *Greek*. InMo, *tr. by* Sam Hamill

I'll Never Love Thee More. James Graham, Marquess of Montrose. GBL; NOBE; OBEV

(My Dear and Only Love.) BeJo

"I'll never reach forty," my mother would say. She'd Say. Frank Davey. NOBC

I'll never see a tree at all. (LL) Song of the Open Road. Ogden Nash. EBEvV; OBAL

I'll not forget / I swear. The Cliffs at Manzanilla. Jan Carew. PBCV

I'll not touch wood nor, fingers crossed. Favour. Robert David Fitzgerald. CDAP

I'll not weep that thou art going to leave me. Stanzas. Emily Jane Brontë. WPE

Ill Omens. Thomas Moore. PoEL-4

I'll only show your lines, and say, 'Tis this. (LL) Ode: Of Wit. Abraham Cowley. BeJo; EPCY; MeLP; NAEL-1; NOSC; OAEL-1; OxAEP-1; SeCP

I'll rest me in this sheltered bower. The Arbour. Anne Brontë. EBVV

I'll sacrifice in flames of love to Thee. Leaf[e] gold, Lord of thy golden wedge o'erlaid. Edward Taylor. NAAL-1; NAAL-3

I'll Sail upon the Dog-Star. Thomas D'Urfey. FaBoCh; OxBoLi *Fr.* A Fool's Preferment.

I'll say. So no more now, from your loving husband, Wilfred. (LL) The Jungle Husband. Stevie Smith. FaBoWP; NBLV; NIP-4; RB

I'll shoot a little bird for little brother. *Unknown, Tlingit Indian*. STP, *tr. by* James Koller *after* John Swanton

I'll sing of *Heroes*, and of *Kings*;. Love. Anacreon, *Greek*. AWP; BeJo; OBVE; OBCVT, *tr. by* Abraham Cowley

I'll sing you a good old song. The Fine Old English Gentleman. *Unknown*. CH

I'll sing you a new ballad, and I'll warrant it first-rate. The Fine Old English Gentleman; New Version. Charles Dickens. NOBVV; OBSV

I'll sing you a song. A Bar on the Piccola Marina. Noël Coward. NBLV

I'll sing you a song / and it'll be a sad one. Sioux Indians. *Unknown*. AmFP

I'll sing you a song / Nine verses long. *Unknown*. OxNR

I'll sing you a song of the world and its ways. Six Feet of Earth. *Unknown*. BLPA

I'll sing you a song / The days are long. *Unknown*. OxNR

I'll sing you a true song of Billy the Kid. Billy the Kid. *Unknown*. FaBoBe

I'll sing you [a] one-O [*or* twelve O]. Carol of the Numbers. *Unknown*. AmFP; OxBoLi

I'll sink my roots far down. Returning Spring. Pauli Murray. GT

I'll stare at something less prepoceros. (LL) The Rhinoceros. Ogden Nash. MoAmPo, OBAL

I'll still follow you, primordial. Tortoise and Badger. Cheryl Clarke. FFC

I'll still walk with the rain open and dreaming. With the Rain. Amir Gilbo'a, *Hebrew*. IP, *tr. by* Warren Bargad *and* Stanley F. Chyet

I'll still write on, and you shall rail. (LL) The Headache. Mary Leapor. ECWP; PEW

I'll teach my sons. My Sons. Ron Loewinsohn. NeAP

I'll tell it You. (LL) The Only News I know Emily Dickinson. APN-2; NOCV

I'll tell my own daddy. *Unknown*. OxNR

I'll tell thee everything I can. The White Knight's Song. "Lewis Carroll." BXAP; CBNP; FaBoCh; HAP; InPS-3; NAEL-2; NOBE; NOBL; NoAM; NoP-4; OAEL-2; OxBChV; PeLV; PoRA; TFi; UV *Fr.* Through the Looking-Glass.

I'll tell thee now (dear Love) what thou shalt do. A Valediction of the Book. Donne. NoP-4

I'll tell ye of ane great occasioun. Did Ye See Me? Robert Garioch. OBCoV

I'll tell you a story, a story anon. King John and the Bishop. *Unknown.* ESPB

I'll tell you a story / About Jack a Nory. Mother Goose. LB; OxNR; ReMoGo

I'll tell you a story / concerning John and Joan. Ballad. Peter Reading. PeLV

I'll tell you bluntly. Osip Emilevich Mandelstam, *Russian.* TCRP, *tr. by* Bernard Meares

I'll tell you how the Sun rose. Emily Dickinson. APN-2; AmPP; PoEL-5; TAP

I'll tell you of a come-lye young lady fair. Fair Phoebe and Her Dark-eyed Sailor. *Unknown.* AmFP

I'll tell you of a wild Colloina boy. The Wild Colloina Boy. *Unknown.* AmFP

I'll tell you the story of Jimmy Jet. Jimmy Jet and His TV Set. Shel Silverstein. OBCA; OBCoV

I'll tell you what you're doing: YOU. What'mmmIdoin'? slurs Lyris, feigning shock. Martial, *Latin.* OBCVT, *tr. by* Tony Harrison

I'll test my power. Song of the Man Who Succeeded. *Unknown, Chippewa Indian.* STP, *tr. by* Jerome Rothenberg *from* Frances Densmore

I'll think of the Leech-gatherer on the lonely moor[!] (LL) Resolution and Independence. Wordsworth. EBEV; FHYEP; HAP; InPS-3; NOBE; NOBRP; NOCV; OAEL-2; OBNC; OxAEP-2; PoEL-4; TFi

I'll think of thee, mine own, dear one. To a Loved One. Mary Weston Fordham. CBWP-2

I'll try to look and see how far they'll go. A Blind Poet Looks at the World Outside. Nguyễn Đình Chiểu, *Vietnamese.* AVP, *tr. by* Huỳnh Sanh Thông

I'll Twine White Violets. Meleager, *Greek.* NIP-4, *tr. by* Goldwin Smith (Epigrams.)

  "Cup takes its sweet joy and tells how it touches, The." HePo, *tr. by* Barbara Hughes Fowler

  "Did I not tell you, my soul, 'By Cypris, you will be caught'." HePo, *tr. by* Barbara Hughes Fowler

  "Flower-feasting bee, why do you touch upon." HePo, *tr. by* Barbara Hughes Fowler

  "I foster a Love fond of playing ball. It throws." HePo, *tr. by* Barbara Hughes Fowler

  "I say that my sweetly prattling Heliodora will someday." HePo, *tr. by* Barbara Hughes Fowler

  "I was a quick-footed, long-eared hare, just snatched from my mother's." HePo, *tr. by* Barbara Hughes Fowler

  "If you burn my scorched soul too often, Love, she'll fly." HePo, *tr. by* Barbara Hughes Fowler

  "I'll weave in the white violet. I'll weave in." HePo, *tr. by* Barbara Hughes Fowler

  "I'm down. Step on my neck, you savage god, with your heel." HePo, *tr. by* Barbara Hughes Fowler

  "Love fed Heliodora's fingernail and made." HePo, *tr. by* Barbara Hughes Fowler

  "Love-prone Asclepias with eyes like a summer's day." HePo, *tr. by* Barbara Hughes Fowler

  "Mosquito, may you fly, a swift courier for me." HePo, *tr. by* Barbara Hughes Fowler

  "Mosquitoes, shameless and shrill of voice, sucking the blood." HePo, *tr. by* Barbara Hughes Fowler

  "Now the white violet blooms and narcissus that loves." HePo, *tr. by* Barbara Hughes Fowler

  "Pour and say again and again and yet again." HePo, *tr. by* Barbara Hughes Fowler

  "Pour for Heliodora Persuasion and pour for Cypris." HePo, *tr. by* Barbara Hughes Fowler

  "Sell it, though it sleeps still at its mother's breast!" HePo, *tr. by* Barbara Hughes Fowler

  "Shrilling cicada, drunk on drops of dew, you sing." HePo, *tr. by* Barbara Hughes Fowler

  "Still in his mother's lap the baby Love played." HePo, *tr. by* Barbara Hughes Fowler

  "Tears beneath the earth, Heliodora, I give." HePo, *tr. by* Barbara Hughes Fowler

  "Within my heart Love himself made Heliodora." HePo, *tr. by* Barbara Hughes Fowler

  "Yes, I'd rather hear Heliodora's voice." HePo, *tr. by* Barbara Hughes Fowler

  "You're sleeping, Zenophila, my tender bloom. I wish." HePo, *tr. by* Barbara Hughes Fowler

"I'll wager, I'll wager, I'll wager with you." The Broomfield Hill. *Unknown.* ESPB

I'll wagonloads of love and glory bring. (LL) Meditation 38. Edward Taylor. MeMAP; NAAL-1; NAAL-3; NOBA; OxBA

I'll wake you and shake you. To the Laggards. Joseph Bovshover, *Yiddish.* TrJP, *tr. by* Joseph Bovshover

I'll Wear Me a Cotton Dress. *Unknown.* BPo

I'll weave in the white violet. I'll weave in. Meleager. HePo, *tr. by* Barbara Hughes Fowler *Fr.* I'll Twine White Violets. NIP-4, *tr. by* Goldwin Smith

Ill Wind, The. Jay Macpherson. MoCV

I'll [*or* Ile] write, because I'll [*or* Ile] give. To Critic[k]s. Robert Herrick. CaPo

I'll [*or* Il'e] write no more of Love; but now repent. On Himselfe. Robert Herrick. CaPo

I'll write no more verses—plague take 'em! Those Flapjacks of Brown's. Bert Leston Taylor. OBAL

Ille Terrarum. Robert Louis Stevenson. OxBS

Illegitimate Things. William Carlos Williams. MoAmPo

Illi Morituri. Mary Morison Webster. PeSA

Illicit. D. H. Lawrence. *See* On the Balcony.

Illiterate, The. William Meredith. NoP-4; VCAP

Illness. Po Chü-i, *Chinese.* ChiP, *tr. by* Arthur Waley

Illness and idleness give me much leisure. Po Chü-i, *Chinese.* ChiP, *tr. by* Arthur Waley

Ills of all the human race, The. Misunderstood. Lizelia Augusta Jenkins Moorer. CBWP-3

Ill's the airt o the Word the day. Idleset. Thurso Berwick. OxBS

Illuminated. Tanka. Masaoka Shiki, *Japanese.* MJT, *tr. by* Ueda, Makoto

Illumination. D. F. Brown. CDa

Illumination, The. Stanley Kunitz. TAP

Illumination. Jeffrey Wainwright. DiPo

Illuminations. Louise Glück. NALW

Illuminations. Rimbaud, *French.*

  Chercheuses de Poux, Les. AWP, *tr. by* T. Sturge Moore

  Dawn. TTTS, *tr. by* Enid Rhodes Peschal

  Girls Looking for Lice. FLP, *tr. by* Alistair Elliot

Illumined bright now shines the splendid dome. Mary Tighe. NOBRP *Fr.* Psyche.

Illusion. Colleen J. McElroy. ISC

Illusion works impenetrable. Maia. Ralph Waldo Emerson. APN-1; PAR

Illusions. Ralph Waldo Emerson. APN-1

  ("And to endurance.") (LL) NCAP

  (Motto to "Illusions.") NCAP

Illusions, The: they fit like an iron lung, and. Memorandum / The Accountant's Notebook. Kathleen Norris. OBAL

Illustration. John Ashbery. NAAL-2

Illustration [—a Footnote], The. Denise Levertov. PoA

Illustration / is nothing to you without the application, The. To a Steam Roller. Marianne Moore. BoWoP; CMoP; FaBoMo; MeMAP; MoAmPo; OxBA; PoPoPo; VGW

Illustrious Ancestors. Denise Levertov. AmPP; MoP; NAAL-2; NOBA; PmAP; VGW

Illustrious Holland! hard would be his lot. Byron. OBSV *Fr.* English Bards and Scotch Reviewers.

Illustrious Lady, where shall I begin. To the Countess Dowager of Huntingdon. Bathsua Pell Makin. KTR

Illustrious monarch of Iberia's soil. Columbus to Ferdinand. Philip Freneau. OBCA

Illustrious One, in whom death is the vagrom wound. Singing Death. Stan Rice. FYAP; IMW

I'm 41st in line for Plisetskaya. A Chorus of Nymphs. Andrey Andreievich Voznesensky, *Russian.* VCWP, *tr. by* Vera Dunham and H. W. Tjalsma

I'm a bad, bad man. Bad Man. Langston Hughes. NAAAL

I'm a broken-hearted miner, who loves his cup to drain. The Stringybark Cockatoo. *Unknown.* NOBAu

I'm a Dreamer. Kattie M. Cumbo. BlSi

I'm a fortunate tree. Once I stood drinking wind and bird-song, in the wood. Julianus Sees the Chair of the Sophist Craterus. Julianus of Egypt, *Greek.* GrAn, *tr. by* Lee T. Pearcy

I'm a Gigolo. Cole Porter. OBCoV

I'm a heartbroken raftsman, from Greenville I came. Jack Haggerty. *Unknown.* AmFP

I'm a lean dog, a keen dog, a wild dog and lone. Lone Dog. Irene McLeod. NOxBChV

I'm a little butterfly. *Unknown.* OxNR

I'm a little gentleman. One Little Boy. *Unknown.* NOxBChV

I'm a little husbandman. Another Little Boy. *Unknown.* NOxBChV

I'm a mad immortal between heaven and earth. To the Tune "Nan-hsiang-tzu." Shen Chou, *Chinese.* ChiPo; CoBLCP, *tr. by* Jonathan Chaves

I'm a man without a zero. I Want-a-name-'ere La Guantanamera. Guillermo Cabrera Infante, *Spanish.* CBNP, *tr. by* Donald Gardner *and* Suzanne Jill Levine

I'm a peevish old man with a penny-whistle. Beggar's Serenade. John Heath-Stubbs. BoLoP

I'm a poor little girl. The Wagoner's Lad. *Unknown.* AmFP

I'm a poor lonesome cowboy. Poor Lonesome Cowboy. *Unknown.* AS

I'm a pretty little thing. The Field Daisy. Jane Taylor. BoTP

I'm a quince, saved over from last year, still fresh. A Quince Preserved through the Winter, Given to a Lady. Antiphilus, *Greek.* GrAn, *tr. by* W. S. Merwin

I'm a rambling wretch of poverty, from Tip'ry town I came. The Son of a Gambolier. *Unknown.* AS

I'm a riddle in nine syllables. Metaphors. Sylvia Plath. HeIP-4; InPK-6; Poetr; SoSe-8

I'm a-rollin', I'm a-rollin', I'm a-rollin', through an unfriendly world. *Unknown.* NAAAL

"I'm a runaway child". The Space Between. Ana Luisa Ortiz de Montellano. LoHo

I'm a skyscraper wean; I live on the nineteenth flair. The Jelly Piece Song. Anne McNaughton. NTP

I'm a Soldier in the Army of the Lord. *Unknown.* AmFP

I'm a stable cat, a working cat. The Stable Cat. Leslie Norris. PChr

I'm a strange composition as e'er was in nature. A Prize Riddle on Herself When 24. Elizabeth Frances Amherst. ECWP

I'm a strange creature, for I satisfy women. Riddle. Cynewulf. ASW, *tr. by* Kevin Crossley-Holland. *Fr.* Riddles (Exeter Book).

I'm a stranger in your city, my name is Paddy Flynn. Portland County Jail. *Unknown.* AS

I'm a tiger in the rain. Sad Day in Berlin. Sarah Kirsch, *German.* PBWP, *tr. by* Gerda Mayer

I'm A Worker. Jayne Cortez. NBV

I'm about to go shopping. Song. James Schuyler. TTTS

I'm afraid to close my eyes. Menace of the Sick. Breyten Breytenbach, *Afrikaans.* PeSAV, *tr. by* Stephen Gray *and* A. J. Coetzee

I'm Agoing to Lay Down My Sword. *Unknown.* AH

I'm all afire and from bright blaze annealed. Concerning Himself. Paul Fleming, *German.* GePo, *tr. by* George C. Schoolfield

I'm all alone. (LL) Little Jumping Joan. Mother Goose. LB; NTCP; OxNR; ReMoGo

I'm all alone in this world, she said. 50–50. Langston Hughes. NOBA; NoAM; PoE; SAGP

I'm always alone. Mother Goose. *See* Little Jumping Joan.

I'm always / most surprised. Justice. Petra von Morstein, *German.* BoWoP, *tr. by* Rosemarie Waldrop

I'm an Old Cowhand. Johnny Mercer. OBAL

I'm an unable woman who loves to dance. Residual Paralysis. Marie Ponsot. NMM-2

I'm as free a little bird as I can be. Free Little Bird. *Unknown.* AmFP

I'm ashamed of my thoughts. *Unknown.* NOIV

I'm at no center, big and slack as I am. All (Facts, Stories, Chance). C. S. Giscombe. BAP-96

I'm at the bottom again. The baron's there. Yury Osipovich Dombrovsky, *Russian.* TCRP, *tr. by* Bradley Jordan

I'm beginning to talk to myself. But My Blood. Rose Romano. UnSA

I'm Bert, p'rhaps you've heard of me, Bert, you've had word of me. Burlington Bertie from Bow. William Hargreaves. OBCoV

I'm big for ten years old. Dumb Insolence. Adrian Mitchell. NOxBChV

I'm Black and Blue. Heinrich Heine, *German.* AWP, *tr. by* John Todhunter

"I'm bored. My cape, please." Stavrogin's Farewell. János Pilinszky. CEEP, *tr. by* Jascha Kessler. *Fr.* Three Poems.

I'm bored to extinction with Harrison. Limericks and Puns. *Unknown.* PeLi

I'm buried beneath the layered debris. Note. Meir Wieseltier, *Hebrew.* IP, *tr. by* Warren Bargad *and* Stanley F. Chyet

I'm busy! / I am building. The New Heart. Semyon Isaakovich Kirsanov, *Russian.* CLPP, *tr. by* Anselm Hollo

(Im)c-a-t(mo). E. E. Cummings. HAP

I'm called by the name of a man. *Unknown.* OxNR

I'm Callicratia / who bore / 29 children. *Unknown, Greek.* GrAn, *tr. by* Tony Harrison

I'm Captain Jinks of the Horse Marines. Captain Jinks. *Unknown.* BLPA

I'm careful of the words I say. Be Careful. *Unknown.* NBLV

I'm ceded—I've stopped being Theirs. Emily Dickinson. APN-2; NALW; PAR; TRP; WPOW; WPoS

I'm cheap and insignificant. The Soldier's Cigarette. Harold Beckh. NSI

I'm cold. I'm destitute and absurd. Konstantin Konstantinovich Kuzminsky, *Russian.* TCRP, *tr. by* Albert C. Todd

I'm coming home through the red lacquered lobby. Harbor Lights. Mark Doty. WWSi

"I'm corrupt," he said to me in the French. The Corrupt Man in the French Pub. Brian Higgins. OxBTC

I'm cross with god who has wrecked this generation. John Berryman. FaBoMo *Fr.* Dream Songs.

I'm curled into a ball. Poetry Reading. Anna Swirszczynska, *Polish.* BLT, *tr. by* Czeslaw Milosz *and* Leonard Nathan

I'm determined to be an old maid. I'll Marry Not at All. *Unknown.* AmFP

I'm digging at my father's grave. Family Plot, October. Gail Mazur. NAmP90

I'm digging holes for three wilted saplings. Noon. Perry Oldham. CDa

I'm doing it again. The Reading. Gabriel Gbadamosi. HBAPE

I'm down. Step on my neck, you savage god, with your heel. Meleager. HePo, *tr. by* Barbara Hughes Fowler. *Fr.* I'll Twine White Violets. NIP-4, *tr. by* Goldwin Smith

I'm dreaming the My Lai soldier again. Anne Sexton. SAGP

I'm driving a car in Tel Aviv. End of the Trip. David Avidan. *Fr.* Traveling in the City. IP, *tr. by* Warren Bargad *and* Stanley F. Chyet

I'm far from what I call my home. John Campbell. PeSAV

I'm five years old. The Party to which Wolves are Invited. Thylias Moss. NMM-2

I'm folding up my little dreams. My Little Dreams. Georgia Douglas Johnson. BlSi; NAAAL

I'm fond of doctors and drivers of hacks. Samuel Hoffenstein. OBCoV

I'm forty-one. I was twenty-three then. Vermont. David Huddle. CDa

I'm frightened at night. At Night. Elizabeth Jennings. OTCP

I'm full of everything I do not want. Sonnet: Of the 20th of June 1291. Cecco Angiolieri, da Siena, *Italian.* AWP, *tr. by* D. G. Rossetti

I'm getting deep lines on my forehead. Limerick. Ron Rubin. PeLi

I'm getting old and feeble and I cannot work no more. The Old Miner's Refrain. *Unknown.* AmFP

I'm getting used to not understanding. At the Protestant Museum. Hugh Maxton. CIP-2

I'm giving a party to-morrow at three. My Party. Queenie Scott-Hopper. BoTP

I'm glad our house is a little house. Song for a Little House. Christopher Darlington Morley. BoTP; CTV

"I'm glad pigs can't fly," said young Sellers. Limerick. Ron Rubin. PeLi

I'm glad that I am born to die. Shout for Joy. *Unknown.* AmFP

I'm glad the sky is painted blue. *Unknown.* CTV

I'm goin' away for to stay a little while. He's Gone Away. *Unknown.* AS

I'm goin' 'ome to Blighty—ain't I glad to 'ave the chance! Going Home. Robert W. Service. NSI

I'm goin' out West, down on the Rio Grande. Alice B. *Unknown.* AS

I'm goin' to whoop you, Sammy Taylor. A Domestic Storm. Priscilla Jane Thompson. CBWP-2

I'm goin' where de Southern crosses top de C. & O. Tin Roof Blues. Sterling Brown. NAAAL

I'm going, all along. (LL) Some keep the Sabbath going to Church. Emily Dickinson. HeIP-4; MoAmPo; PBMP

"I'm going down," she said, tying her yellow scarf. Descending. Valentin Iremonger. EnLoPo

I'm going out to clean the pasture spring. The Pasture. Robert Frost. CMoP; MoAmPo; NAAL-2; NOBA; NOxBChV; OxBA; PoE; SAGP; SAmP; TLR; TRP; TTTS; WHSW

I'm going stark, staring mad because of the guns. (LL) Repression of War Experience. Siegfried Sassoon. AF; CMoP; NSI; NoAM; PeFWW; PoE

I'm going to be just like you, Ma. A Dance For Ma Rainey. Al Young. ISC; NAAAL; NBV; UnSA

I'm going to bring you something. Conversations in Mayan. Alonzo Gonzales Mó, *Mayan.* STP, *tr. by* Allan F. Burns

I'm going to Georgia. *Unknown.* AmFP

I'm going to live without you. For My Father. Louise Glück. MoLi *Fr.* Metamorphosis. MoLi

I'm going to move ahead. Border. Taslima Nasrin, *Bengali.* VCWP, *tr. by* Carolyne Wright *and* Farida Sarkar

I'm going to murder you with love. Food of Love. Carolyn Kizer. Poetr

I'm going to pull my stinking wagon. The Refuse Man. David Ignatow. WeT

I'm going to ride old Railroad Bill. *Unknown.* *See* Railroad Bill, Railroad Bill.

I'm Going to Rocky Island. *Unknown.* AmFP

I'm going to try and overcome my limitation. Serious Concerns. Wendy Cope. NoP-4; OBCoV

I'm go'n' to lay down my sword and shield. Ain' Go'n' to Study War No Mo'. *Unknown.* AS

I'm gong to murder you with love. Food of Love. Carolyn Kizer. RaBo

I'm gonna die & won't see you all any more. Tsakak, *Tlingit Indian.* STP, *tr. by James Koller after John Swanton*

I'm gonna marry my brother's wife. *Unknown, Tlingit Indian.* STP, *tr. by* James Koller *after* John Swanton

I'm gonna walk to the graveyard. Young Gal's Blues. Langston Hughes. NAAL-2

I'm grateful for the past. (LL) False Though She Be [to me and love]. William Congreve. BoLoP; EnLoPo; GLoP; NOBE; OBEV; OxBSP

I'm grateful, really grateful. Sulpicia, *Latin.* PBWP, *tr. by* John Dillon

"I'm growing old, I've sixty years." Carcassonne. Gustave Nadaud, *French.* BLPA; FaBoBe, *tr. by* John R. Thompson

I'm happiest when most away. Emily Jane Brontë. EnVR; NAEL-2

I'm happy, Kerouac, your madman Allen's. Malest Cornifici Tuo Catullo. Allen Ginsberg. BB; NeAP

I'm Here. Theodore Roethke. CoAP; NYBP *Fr.* Meditations of an Old Woman.

I'm here an not here. Me head's. From Lucy: Holiday Reflections. James Berry. PBCV

I'm here, on the dark porch, restyled in my mother's chair. Sitting at Night on the Front Porch. Charles Wright. ColAP; LCAP-2

I'm hiding, I'm hiding. Hiding. Dorothy Aldis. ChAP

I'm Honest Abe. Honest Abe Lincoln. Max Shulman. OBAL

I'm hungry, oh so hungry. The Birds on the School Windowsill. Evelyn Dainty. BoTP

I'm in a mirrorless room. Poem No. XV. Sang Yi, *Korean.* PFTM, *tr. by* Walter Lew

I'm in love with a girl from Uttoxeter. Limerick. Gerard Benson. PeLi

I'm incorrect: the learned say. On Being Charged with Writing Incorrectly. "The Amorous Lady." ECWP

I'm introducing it as a hunchback. Yury Arabov, *Russian.* TCRP, *tr. by* John High

I'm jilted, forsaken, outwitted. The Jilted Nymph. Thomas Campbell. EnLoPo

I'm Just a Stranger Here, Heaven Is My Home. Carole C. Gregory Clemmons. PoBA

I'm just Miss Blues'es child! (LL) Miss Blues'es Child. Langston Hughes. ChAP; SAmP; TTTS

"I'm King of the cabbages green." Old King Cabbage. Richard Kendall Munkittrick. OBCA

I'm learning how to read the rocks. Indian Ruins Along Rio de Flag. Greg Pape. PBCAP; PaTW

I'm like a skiff on the ocean tost. John Gay. EnLoPo

"I'm like a vine supported on a stick." Leonidas of Tarentum, *Greek.* GrAn, *tr. by* Alistair Elliot

I'm like all lovers, wanting love to be. Poem. Lesbia Harford. NOBAu

I'm living in a cave. Song. *Unknown, Chippewa Indian.* STP, *tr. by* Jerome Rothenberg

I'm looking mighty seedy while holding down my claim. Little Old Sod Shanty. *Unknown.* AS; AmFP

I'm looking out of the window. The Invention of a Garden. Jay Wright. GT

I'm / lost / among a / maze of cans. Supermarket. Felice Holman. OTCP

Im lying there looking at her. Brandon Kershner. *Fr.* 3 Dialogues. EC2

I'm made in sport by Nature. On an Indian Tomineois, the Least of Birds. Thomas Heyrick. NOSC

I'm makin' a road. Florida Road Workers. Langston Hughes. MoAmPo

"I'm Mark's alone!" you swore. Given cause to doubt you. Contemplation. John Frederick Nims. InPK-6

I'm melted down into a black ooze. In a Remote Cloister Bordering the Empyrean. Joel Sloman. VGW

I'm middle-aged. Political Activist Living Alone. Pat Arrowsmith. BrRo

I'm mighty glad to see you, Mrs. Curtis. The Transparent Man. Anthony Hecht. FYAP

"I'm moving from Grief Street." Old Mama Saturday. Marie Ponsot. BAP-95

I'm naturally lazy, carefree. Fisherman on a Southern Stream. Lu Kuei Meng, *Chinese.* SuSp, *tr. by* Robin D. S. Yates

I'm no He-man you know, I'm not a He. Wyndham Lewis. *Fr.* If So the Man You Are. OBSV

I'm no longer the bitter girl. Love Which Frees. Gloria Fuertes, *Spanish.* WPOW, *tr. by* Philip Levine

I'm no reformer; for I see more light. Optimism. Ella Wheeler Wilcox. PWR

I'm Nobody! Who are you? Emily Dickinson. APN-2; AmPP; BoWoP; CBNP; ChAP; FPC; HeIP-4; MeMAP; NALW; NBLV; NOBA; NTP; OBCA; OBCoV; OTCP; OxBSP; PAR; PoPoPo; SAmP; TAP; WPE

I'm not a judge, I own; in short. Arthur Hugh Clough. EnVR *Fr.* Dipsychus [and the Spirit].

I'm Not a Man. Harold Norse. GLP

I'm not at all scared of the Pleiades setting, Antipater of Thessalonica, *Greek.* GrAn, *tr. by* Tony Harrison

I'm not at home if people call. (LL) Arrivals at a Watering-Place. Winthrop Mackworth Praed. NOBL; NOBRP; PeLV

I'm Not Complaining. Philip Schultz. SoSe-8

I'm not depressed, as I walk along this street. The People in These Houses. Jack Matthews. CMAP

"I'm not even a 'bus I'm a tram." (LL) Limerick: "There once was a man [or There was a young man] who said, 'Damn!'." Maurice Evan Hare. NOBL; OxBoLi; PeLV; PeLi

I'm not going to cry all the time. My Heart. Frank O'Hara. PiM

I'm not going to tell you everything. Closed Mill. Maggie Anderson. PBCAP

I'm not here. Hilda Doolittle. MoAmPo *Fr.* Halcyon.

I'm not here. Halcyon. Hilda Doolittle.

I'm Not Here / Never Was. Constanta Buzea, *Rumanian.* BoWoP, *tr. by* Stavros Deligiorgis

I'm not interested in the poverty. I Go Dreaming Roads in My Youth. Luis Omar Salinas. AiP

I'm not planning to turn into gold. Somebody else. Bassus. HePo, *tr. by* Barbara Hughes Fowler *Fr.* Epigrams.

I'm not sure at what point. Honor (1969). Allston James. CDa

I'm not the branch, only the prebranchness. Ivan Zhdanov, *Russian.* TCRP, *tr. by* John High

I'm not without you. The Place of O. Ray A. Young Bear. VoR

I'm now arriv'd the soul desired port. Edmund Davie 1682; Annagram. Benjamin Tompson. SCAP

"I'm of no use," said a little brown seed. The Little Brown Seed. Harriett Mulford Lothrop. PWR

I'm offering for sale today. A Bargain Sale. Samuel Ellsworth Kiser. PoToHe

I'm old and you're going away. Sending Tzu-lung Off to a Post in Chi-chou. Lu Yu, *Chinese.* CoBCP, *tr. by* Burton Watson

I'm Older than You, Please Listen. Arthur Rex Dugard Fairburn. PeNZ

I'm on a straight path with the sun gone down. Luigi Fontanella, *Italian.* NeIt, *tr. by* Michael Palma

I'm on My Way to Canaan. *Unknown.* AH

I'm on my way to Canada. Away to Canada. Joshua McCarter Simpson. AAP

I'm Only a Broken-down Miner. *Unknown.* AmFP

I'm only a cavalry charger. An Appeal. *Unknown.* NSI

I'm only a consumer, and it really doesn't matter. Cheer for the Consumer. Nixon Waterman. OBAL

I'm only a poor little mouse, ma'am. The Mouse. Laura Elizabeth Richards. OBCA

I'm persistent as the pink locust. The Pink Locust. William Carlos Williams. SAmP

"I'm pregnant," I wrote to her in delight. 1973. Marilyn Hacker. GLP

I'm quiet as an old leather belt lapped snakewise. Quiet. Brian Swann. AmPA

I'm quite the opposite of my clever master. Faust's Servant. Roy Fuller. OxBTC

I'm red pepper in a shaker. Sugar in the Cane. Tennessee Williams. OBAL

"I'm rich," / said / Irish. Eternities. Norman Mailer. NYBP

I'm round at Heliodorus' place—. Lucilius, *Greek.* GrAn, *tr. by* Peter Porter

I'm running on the bridge. Jonathan. Yona Wollach, *Hebrew.* IP, *tr. by* Warren Bargad and Stanley F. Chyet

I'm Sad. Forugh Farrokhzad, *Persian.* BoWoP, *tr. by* Reza Baraheni

I'm Sad and I'm Lonely. *Unknown.* AS

I'm sad and serious. A Poem with a Tilde in the Title. Nina Zivancevic, *Serbo-Croatian.* CEEP; HSix, *tr. by* Charles Simic

I'm safe—safe in a mood. "Nearer God, Nearer Realite." Joellen Kwiatek. PUP-18

I'm scared a lonely. Never see my son. John Berryman. NoP-4

I'm seated beside my phone. In the Dark. David Ignatow. WeT

I'm sensitive to what the traffic will. What You Want Means What You Can Afford. Cynthia Bond. BAP-94

I'm sick of fame—I'm gorged with it, so full. A New Canto. Lady Caroline Lamb. Ro

I'm sick of love; O let me lie. To Sycamores. Robert Herrick. CaPo

I'm sitting alone by the fire. Her Letter. Bret Harte. PoLF

I'm sitting by the hearthstone now. Twilight Musings. Mary Weston Fordham. CBWP-2

I'm sitting in the sunshine. Postponed Nightmare. Sandor Csoori, *Hungarian.* VCWP, *tr. by* Roberts, Len and László Vértes

I'm sitting on my couch saying my rosary. I haven't. Mama Rosanna's Last Bead-Clack. Laurel Speer. CrSp

I'm sitting on the stile, Mary. The Countess of Dufferin. Helen Selina Blackwood, Countess of Dufferin. OxAEP-2

I'm Smith of Stoke, aged sixty-odd. Epitaph on a Pessimist. Thomas Hardy. FaBoEE; PFE; TRP

I'm so sorry for old Adam. Old Adam. *Unknown.* AS

I'm sorry but we can't go to the immersions tonight. The Ganges. Norman Dubie. LCAP-2

I'm sorry for the Dead—Today. Emily Dickinson. SAmP

I'm sorry I done it, Major. The Deserter. Gilbert Frankau. PoFWW

I'm sorry I'm late. Apology and Explanation. John Sparrow. OBCoV

I'm sorry, officer. I didn't see the sign. First Offense. David Lehman. PmAP

I'm sorry to say my dear wife is a dreamer. Be Off! Stevie Smith. OxBC

I'm sound asleep, when a knock at the gate wakes me. Recording My Happiness. Wang Chiu-ssu, *Chinese.* CoBLCP, *tr. by* Jonathan Chaves

I'm speaking again. Speaking. Michael Ryan. AmPA; SoSe-8

I'm spending my nights in the doss house. Soup Kitchen Song. *Unknown.* NOBAu

I'm standing on this side. My Home. Yên Thao, *Vietnamese.* AVP, *tr. by* Huỳnh Sanh Thông

I'm still a man, still free to be a man. In a Canton Jail. Phan Bội Châu, *Vietnamese.* AVP, *tr. by* Huỳnh Sanh Thông

I'm still struck (as when I saw my first Pasque-flower). The Black Train. Thomas McGrath. GM

I'm straddling the top tier, my wet shirt clinging. Hanging Burley. Jim Wayne Miller. MT

I'm sure if I were a woman I should hate. Sonnet: Equality of the Sexes. Gavin Ewart. Son

I'm sure we should all be as happy as / kings. (LL) Happy Thought. Robert Louis Stevenson. BoTP; CTV; FaBoBe; OxBChV; PWR; Spl

I'm surprised by her call. We don't know each other very well. The Waif of Echo Park. Wanda Coleman. EC3

I'm talking about stillness, the hush. Morandi. Charles Wright. WeT

I'm taught P-l-o-u-g-h. O-U-G-H. Charles Battell Loomis. NBLV

I'm teaching those who will step across the line to be arrested. Passive Resistance. Enid Shomer. BAP-96

I'm Thankful That My Life Doth Not Deceive. Henry David Thoreau. PoEL-4

I'm thankful that the sun and moon. Gasbags. *Unknown.* NOBL

I'm the Beautiful Basking Shark. The Ballad of the Basking Shark. Thomas Hood Jr. CBNP

I'm the bloke that's trained to sit behind the public stamp machines. A Song of the GPO. Gerry Hamill. NOBL

I'm the great Sir William Anson. *Unknown.* FaBoEE *Fr.* Balliol Rhymes.

I'm the Kilfenora teaboy. The Kilfenora Teaboy. Paul Durcan. PBCIP

I'm the king of the castle. King of the Castle. *Unknown.* OxNR

I'm the lidded voice from limbo. New Speaker. James Berry. NBrP

I'm the pert little pimpernel. Pimpernel. Charlotte Druitt Cole. BoTP

I'm the queerest young fellow that you ever heard. The Ballad of Joking Jesus. James Joyce. ChIV-2

I'm the short one, the empty face. Spoon. Conrad Hilberry. IFJA

I'm the snow on mountains. Death Songs. *Unknown, Turkish.* BoWoP, *tr. by* Reza Baraheni *and* Zahra-Soltan Shokoohtaezeh

I'm the way I am. Jacques Prévert, *French.* STV, *tr. by* John Frederick Nims

I'm thinking about you. What else can I say? Postcard. Margaret Atwood. NoAM

I'm through with acid and with praise. Recantation. Minuchihri, *Persian.* ArPe, *tr. by* Omar S. Pound

I'm tired of Love: I'm still more tired of Rhyme. Fatigue. Hilaire Belloc. NBLV; NOBL; OxBTC; UV

I'm tired of murdering children. Two Vietnam Poems: (1966). Bill Knott. PBCAP; SPE

I'm tired of seeing sights south of the river. Climbing a Solitary Islet in the River. Hsieh Ling-yün, *Chinese.* SuSp, *tr. by* Francis Westbrook

I'm tired of symbols, of laws divine. To My Generation. Benyamin Galai, *Hebrew.* TrJP, *tr. by* Jacob Sonntag

I'm tired of town and suburb life. Tristan da Cunha. Ian D. Colvin. PeSAV

Im Traum sah ich ein Männchen klein und putzig. Heinrich Heine, *German.* AWP, *tr. by* Sir Theodore Martin

I'm trav'ling to my grave. The Traveler. *Unknown.* AmFP

I'm undecided, Samson said to the columns. For Advanced Seminar Students Only. David Avidan. *Fr.* Samson, Our Hero. IP, *tr. by* Warren Bargad *and* Stanley F. Chyet

I'm up against the wall. The Wall. William Hawkins. MoCV

"I'm very drowsy," said the Bear. Hard to Bear. Tudor Jenks. OBCA

I'm walking out on Rome. Antonio Porta, *Italian.* CLPP, *tr. by* Molino, Anthony

I'm wanton—no I've stopped that. Complaynt. Anne Waldman. FiLi

I'm watching my power and my rapture. The Sportsman. Anna Wickham. WPN

I'm way down HERE! God, Are You There? Helen Steiner Rice. CTV

I'm wearin' [*or* wearing] awa', John [*or* Jean]. The Land o' the Leal. Carolina Oliphant, Baroness Nairne. GTBS-P; NOBRP; OBEV; OxBS

I'm weary o' the rose as o' my brain. The Great Wheel. "Hugh MacDiarmid." OxBS

I'm weary of this tedious dull deceit. Sulpicia to Cerinthus. Sulpicia, *Latin.* OBCVT, *tr. by* George Lyttelton

I'm weary of towns, it seems a'most a pity. Tired of Towns. Andrew Lang. EBVV

I'm "wife"—I've finished that. Emily Dickinson. CMoP; PAR

I'm working like a dog, testing my memory. The Expulsion. Gerald Stern. LCAP-2

I'm writing just after an encounter. Whatever You Say Say Nothing. Seamus Heaney. OBWP; OxBC

I'm yours, dearest, as are the winter towns. Marceline, to Her Husband. Elizabeth Libbey. AmPA

Image, The. Roy Fuller. GTBS-P; OxBTC

Image, The. Robert Hass. BLT

Image, The. Richard Hughes. OBMV

Image. Thomas Ernest Hulme. InPK-6; OxBTC

Image. Anna de Noailles, *French.* PBWP, *tr. by* Carol Cosman

Image, as in a Hexagram. Lew Welch. BB

Image comes, An. Laser. A. R. Ammons. NAAL-2; NOBA; NoAM

Image comes down to live as fact, and turns. The Shadowgraphs. Richmond Lattimore. NYBP

Image dance of change, An. Conclusion. Siegfried Sassoon. MoBrPo

Image flickers, a firefly, The. Broadcast. Ivan V. Lalic, *Serbo-Croatian.* HSix, *tr. by* Charles Simic

Image in Lava, The. Felicia Dorothea Hemans. CABP; NOBRP ("It must, it *must* be so!") (LL) VWP

Image insists, An. Christopher Okigbo. PBMAP *Fr.* Limits (1962).

Image-Maker, The. Oliver St. John Gogarty. OBEV; OBMV; PoRA

Image-Maker, The. Stanley Kunitz. AFr

Image-Nation (the Poēsis). Robin Blaser. PoM

Image-Nation 13 (the Telephone). Robin Blaser. PoM

Image-Nation 3. Robin Blaser. PoM

Image o' God, The. Joe Corrie. ChIV-1; OxBS

Image of City. Lance Henson. VoR

Image of Leda, An. Frank O'Hara. HCAP; LCAP-2

Image of Lethe, An. The Coming of War Actaeon. Ezra Pound. CMoP; PoA; PoE

Image of the Engineer's model, An. Birdland. Allen Fisher. NBrP

Image of the frozen lake, The. Luigi Fontanella, *Italian.* NeIt, *tr. by* Michael Palma

Image the images the great games therefore the locked. The Book of Job and a Draft of a Poem to Praise the Paths of the Living. George Oppen. NNaP

Image / the pawnees, The. The Pride. John Newlove. MoCV; NOBC

Image / (the rim) / and going 'round, The. A Poem for the Sefirot as a Wheel of Light. Naftali Bacharach, *Hebrew.* PFTM, *tr. by* Jerome Rothenberg *and* Harris Lenowitz

Imagerie d'Epinal. Aleksander Wat, *Polish.* AF, *tr. by* Czeslaw Milosz *and* Leonard Nathan

Imageries of dreams reveal a gracious age. The Age of a Dream. Lionel Pigot Johnson. OBMV

Images. Richard Aldington. MoBrPo; PoA

Images. Waring Cuney. *See* No Images.

Images. Valery Larbaud, *French.* BLT, *tr. by* William Jay Smith

Images. Naomi Long Madgett. LTA

Images. Kathleen Jessie Raine. NYBP

Images. Richard Schaukal, *German.* AWP, *tr. by* Ludwig Lewisohn

Images. Marilyn Williams. IFJA

Images cast against the eternally shifting / heavens. (LL) Study Peace. Imamu Amiri Baraka. APSN; PoBA

Images drip down my back like sweat. On the Morning of the Third Night above Nisqually. W. M. Ransom. CDW

Images for the Gospel of Christ. Paul Ramsey. CRP

Images leap with him from branch to branch. His eyes. A Poet at Twenty. Donald Hall. SPE

Images of a faded world possessed me, I cannot flee! Saul Tchernichowsky. MHP, *tr. by* Ruth Finer Mintz *Fr.* To the Sun.

Images of Angels. Patricia K. Page. MoCV; NoAM

Images of J—— assail him. The Bus Trip. Joel Oppenheimer. NeAP

Images! Venerable as Druidical trees. George Barker. FaBoMo *Fr.* In Memory of David Archer.

Imaginary Conversations. Walter Savage Landor.

Regeneration. Ro
Imaginary Dialogue. Antiphilus, *Greek*. GrAn, *tr. by* Dudley Fitts
Imaginary Elegies. Jack Spicer.
"God must have a big eye to see everything." NeAP; PmAP
"God's other eye is good and gold. So bright." NeAP; PmAP
"Poetry, almost blind like a camera." NeAP; PmAP
"Yes, be like God. I wonder what I thought." NeAP
Imaginary Iceberg, The. Elizabeth Bishop. FaBoWP; ImPo; LiTM; MoAmPo; PFE
Imaginary man, go. Here is your passport. Instructions for Crossing the Border. Dan Pagis, *Hebrew*. PoSu, *tr. by* Stephen Mitchell
Imaginary Sonnets. Eugene Lee-Hamilton.
    Luther to a Bluebottle Fly. Son
Imaginary Translation. Marilyn Hacker. DiPo
Imaginary tremolo. Jean-Joseph Rabéarivelo, *French*. NegPo, *tr. by* Ellen Conroy Kennedy
Imagination. John Davidson. APAD; MoBrPo *Fr.* New Year's Eve.
Imagination. Margaret Lucas Cavendish, Duchess of Newcastle. NOSC
Imagination. Shakespeare. ImPo *Fr.* A Midsummer Night's Dream.
Imagination. Dina Uahupirapi. LoHo
Imagination of Necessity, The. Andrei Codrescu. SPE
Imagination that we spurned and crave, The. (LL) To the One of Fictive Music. Wallace Stevens. MeMAP; MoAmPo; NoP-4
Imaginative Life, The. Geoffrey Hill. NoAM
Imagine: A Town. Daphne Marlatt. NOBC *Fr.* Steveston.
Imagine a world so heavy / that even the sun is squeezed dark! The Ladder: Roger Vail's Photo of a Rockface in the Carrara (Italy) Marble Quarries. Dennis Schmitz. PUP-18
"Imagine being the first to say: *surveillance*." Inventors. Michael C. Blumenthal. DiPo; NoAM
Imagine bouncing bumping humping over a cliff. Drift. Alberta Turner. LCAP-2
Imagine father that you had a brother were. Landscape with Next of Kin. Olga Broumas. BoWoP
Imagine it, a Sophocles complete. The Fire at Alexandria. Theodore Weiss. NoAM; PoA; SAmP; TAP
Imagine living in a strange, dark city for twenty years. Foreign. Carol Ann Duffy. NBrP
Imagine or remember how the road at last led us. Nocturne Militaire. Thomas McGrath. AF
Imagine that any mind ever *thought* a red geranium! Red Geranium and Godly Mignonette. D. H. Lawrence. GTBS-P; NoAM
Imagine that July morning: Cape Henry and Virginia. The Tempest. William Jay Smith. MoAmPo
Imagine that motion, the turning and pressing. Elinor Frost's Marble-Topped Kneading Table. Pattiann Rogers. LoHo
Imagine the desert the cast of light. Jerusalem Shadow. Melanie Kaye/Kantrowitz. LoHo
Imagine the princess' surprise! The Frog Prince. Robert Pack. Poetr
Imagine the South. George Woodcock. MoCV; NOBC
Imagine them as they were first conceived. Images of Angels. Patricia K. Page. MoCV; NoAM
Imagined Description of Myself, in Another Scene, An. Ory Bernstein, *Hebrew*. IP, *tr. by* Warren Bargad *and* Stanley F. Chyet
Imagining. Tanka. Shaku Chōkū, *Japanese*. MJT, *tr. by* Makoto Ueda
Imago. Amy Clampitt. VCAP
Imamiya Middle School. Shaku Chōkū, *Japanese*. MJT, *tr. by* Makoto Ueda
Imhotep. Yusef Komunyakaa. PUP-19
Imitating the Old Poems. Pao Chao, *Chinese*. CoBCP, *tr. by* Burton Watson
Imitating the Old Poems. T'ao Ch'ien, *Chinese*.
    (Imitating the Old Poems, No. 4.) CoBCP, *tr. by* Burton Watson
Imitation. Hilaire Belloc. OBCoV
Imitation of Chaucer. Alexander Pope. OBCoV
Imitation of Christ, The. Thomas À Kempis, *Latin*.
    "Love is a great thing, a great good in every way; it alone lightens what is." ITG, *tr. by* Stephen Mitchell
Imitation of Horace. Book I, Satyr IX, Written in June, 1681, An. Horace, *Latin*.
    "As I was walking in the *Mall* of late." OBCVT, *tr. by* John Oldham
Imitation of Julia A. Moore. "Mark Twain." OBAL
Imitation of Life. Michael S. Weaver. UnSA
Imitation of Martial, Book II Ep, An 105. "Captain H——." NOEC
Imitation of Monsieur Beranger. "Naum Korzhavin," *Russian*. TCRP, *tr. by* Albert J. Todd
Imitation of Pope. A Compliment to the Ladies. William Blake. *See* A Compliment to the Ladies.

Imitation of Spenser. Keats.
    To Hope. LaPo
Imitation of the Seventeenth Epistle of the First Book of Horace. Address'd to Dr. S[wi]ft, An. Horace, *Latin*.
    "Country Parson turn'd in Years, The." OBCVT, *tr. by* William Diaper
Imitation of the Sixth Satire of the Second Book of Horace, An. Horace, *Latin*.
    "I often wish'd, that I had clear." OBCVT, *tr. by* Swift, Jonathan (1667-1745) and Alexander Pope
    "Once on a time (so runs the Fable)." OBCVT, *tr. by* Pope, Alexander (1688-1744) and Jonathan Swift
Imitation warrior. Warrior. Frank Mkalawile Chipasula. PeSAV
Imitations Based on the American. Frank Polite. BXAP
Immaculate Conception, The. Paul Eluard *and* Andre Breton, *French*.
    32 Positions of Love, The. PFTM, *tr. by* Marcel Jean
Immaculate Sir Walter Raleigh, The. Limerick. T. L. McCarthy. PeLi
Immaculate white bed. (LL) Nantucket. William Carlos Williams. HAP; InPS-3; OxBA; TAP; TRP; WeW-3
Immanent. Walter De la Mare. PoA
Immanuel Kant. Miroslav Holub, *Czech*. VCWP, *tr. by* David Young *and* Dana Hábová
Immature black eagle walks assuredly, An. Our Bird Aegis. Ray A. Young Bear. BAP-96
Immeasurable haze. To the Holy Spirit. Yvor Winters. MoAmPo; PaTW; VGW
Immeasurable pain! Po Chü-i, *Chinese*. ChiP, *tr. by* Arthur Waley
Immeasurable sadness! Sadness. Tennyson. FaBoEE
Immeasurable sea with ships in flight, An. (LL) Antony and Cleopatra. José-Maria de Heredia, *Spanish*. EP; FLP, *tr. by* Alistair Elliot
Immediate Content Recognition. Diane Ward. PmAP
Immemorial, / And after us. 29 Poems. Louis Zukofsky.
Immense architecture / building in air. Nathaniel Tarn. *Fr.* Journal of the Laguna de San Ignacio. APSN
Immense, august, like some Titanic bloom. Chartres. Edith Wharton. APN-2
Immense coldness from the Longobards, An. The Longobards. Zbigniew Herbert, *Polish*. PoSu, *tr. by* Czeslaw Milosz
Immense hope, and forbearance, The. Spring Day. John Ashbery. ColAP; NOBA
Immense pale houses! The sunshine and the snow. American Scenes (1904). Donald Justice. MT
Immense room as quiet, An. The Penn Central Station at Beacon, N.Y. Ed Ochester. GM
Immensity. Morning. Giuseppe Ungaretti. PFTM
Immensity cloistered [*or* Immensitie cloysterd] in thy dear[e] womb[e]. Nativity [*or* Nativitie]. Donne. *Fr.* La Corona. ChIV-2; ESCV; Son *Fr.* Holy Sonnets.
Immersed in your mud, can you / not believe her a sister? (LL) Eel, The. Eugenio Montale, *Italian*. PFTM, *tr. by* Cid Corman
Immigrant. Fleur Adcock. OPOU
Immigrant, The. Donald Davidson. FuPo
Immigrant. Arthur Nortje. PeSAV
Immigrant Daughter's Song. Mary Ann Larkin. IIP
Immigrants. Pat Mora. UnSA
Immigrants in Our Own Land. Jimmy Santiago Baca. AF; UnSA
Immobile, but fearless. The Hares. Susan Miles. LW
Immoderate Death that wouldst not once confer. On the Death of the Lord Treasurer. *Unknown*. FaBoEE
Immigrant. Fleur Adcock. OPOU
Immolated. Herman Melville. NCAP
Immolation. Robert Farren. TIRV
Immoral Proposition, The. Robert Creeley. LiTM; NeAP; PoM
Immorality, An. Ezra Pound. CMoP; ImPo; LiTM; MoAmPo; NOBA; OBAL
Immortal. Mark Van Doren. MoAmPo
Immortal as our Soul. (LL) To My Excellent Lucasia, On Our Friendship. Katherine Philips. CPO; LW; MeLP; NALW; NOSC; NoP-4; PBRV; PEW; WPE; WPOW
Immortal Autumn. Archibald MacLeish. CMoP; MoAmPo; NAAL-2
Immortal Bard! thou fav'rite of the Nine! The Womans Labour, an epistle. Mary Collier. PEW
Immortal[l] clothing I put on. The Transfiguration. Robert Herrick. CaPo
Immortal glories in my mind revive. Joseph Addison. *Fr.* A Letter from Italy [to the Right Honourable Charles Lord Halifax]. NOEC
Immortal Hate. Milton. NOBE *Fr.* Book I. FHYEP; NAEL-1; OAEL-1; OxAEP-1 *Fr.* Paradise Lost.
Immortal Heat, O let thy greater flame. Love (2). George Herbert. GeHe; Son
Immortal Helix. Archibald MacLeish. PFE

Immortal Imogen, crowned queen above. The Two Swans. Thomas Hood. CH

Immortal is an ample word. Emily Dickinson. NOCV

Immortal Israel. Judah Halevi, *Hebrew*. TrJP, *tr. by* Solomon Solis-Cohen

Immortal Love, author of this great frame. Love (1). George Herbert. GeHe; HoPM; Son

Immortal Love, Forever Full. John Greenleaf Whittier. AH

Immortal Newton never spoke. On Mr. Nash's Present of His Own Picture at Full Length. Philip Dormer Stanhope, 4th Earl of Chesterfield. NOEC

Immortal Part, The. A. E. Housman. MoBrPo; SCGP; SoSe-8; UnPo

Immortal praise with one accord. (LL) A Satire on London. Henry Howard, Earl of Surrey. AAS; SiPS

Immortal with his bamboo cane, The. The Cane of Ch'iung Bamboo. Hsü Chung-hsing, *Chinese*. CoBLCP, *tr. by* Jonathan Chaves

Immortality. "Æ." AWP; OBMV; TIRV

Immortality. Joseph Jefferson. BLPA

Immortality. "Nicolai Maksimovich Minsky," *Russian*. TrJP, *tr. by* Babette Deutsch

Immortality. Susan Langstaff Mitchell. TIRV

Immortality. Lizelia Augusta Jenkins Moorer. CBWP-3

Immortall love, authour of this great frame. Love. George Herbert. ESCV; HoPM; Son

Immortals, The. Isaac Rosenberg. FaBoTw; NSI; TrJP

Immortals come and assemble, The. Inscribed on a Wall Painting of Assembled Immortals. Chao Meng-fu, *Chinese*. CoBLCP, *tr. by* Jonathan Chaves

Immortals don't stay long in the world of men. Replying to a Poem by a New Graduate Lamenting the Loss of His Wife. Yü Hsüan-chi, *Chinese*. SuSp, *tr. by* Geoffrey R. Waters

Immutable as my regret. (LL) The Grave of Love. Thomas Love Peacock. CH; OxAEP-2; OxBSP

Imogene. Eloise Bibb. CBWP-4

Impact of a dollar upon the heart, The. Stephen Crane. MeMAP

Impartial Law enrolled a name, The. My Name and I. Robert Graves. NYBP; NoAM

Impasse. Langston Hughes. LiTM

Impatient all the foggy day for night. Fever. Thom Gunn. EP

Impatient as we were for all of them to join us. The Bungalows. John Ashbery. CoAP

Impatient Heart, The. Bruce Andrews. FTOS

Impatient with cripples, foreigners, children. Il Piccolo Rifiuto. Louis MacNeice. CMoP

Impatient with Desire. George, Baron Lansdowne Granville. OxBSP

Impatient with the enigmatic, Al Capone. Suite for Celery and Blind Date. Philip Dow. BXAP

Imperator Victus. Hart Crane. OxBA

Imperceptible / It withers in the world. Ono no Komachi, *Japanese*. OHPJ, *tr. by* Kenneth Rexroth

Imperceptible light / *Scintilla animae*. Kenneth Rexroth. *Fr.* The Bell. PFTM *Fr.* A Prolegomenon to a Theodicy.

Imperceptively the world became haunted by her white dress. The White Dress. Marya Alexandrovna Zaturenska. MoAmPo

Impercipient, The. Thomas Hardy. EBVV; NAEL-2

Imperfect Air. Ralph Hawkins. NBrP

Imperfect Enjoyment, The. John Wilmot, 2d Earl of Rochester. BoLoP ("To do the wronged Corinna right for thee.") EP

Imperfect Enjoyment, The. William Walsh *and* Sir George Etherege (1653–91). NOSC

Imperfect enough once for all at thirty. Last Things, Black Pines at 4 a.m. Robert Lowell. NOBA

Imperfect Paradise, The. Linda Pastan. SoSe-8

Imperfect Sestina. Phyllis Webb. NOBC

Imperial Adam, naked in the dew. Alec Derwent Hope. BMAP; CBAP; ChIV-1; HAP; KSG; NIP-4; NoAM; NoP-4

Imperial host before proud Gloucester lay, The. Powers of Darkness. Abraham Cowley. NOSC

Imperial Thumbprint. Tom Weatherly. PoBA

Imperialists in Retirement. Edward Lucie-Smith. PBCV

Imperialists jail us—we are not jailed. You Cannot Lock Up the Mind. Xuân Thủy, *Vietnamese*. AVP, *tr. by* Huỳnh Sanh Thông

Imperious bath-maid, O why. *Unknown, Greek*. GrAn, *tr. by* W. G. Shepherd

Imperious Fool! think not because you're fair. To a Proud Beauty. "Ephelia." KTR; PEW

Imperious Muse, your arrows ever strike. Japanese Beetles. X. J. Kennedy. OBAL

Imperishable creatures. The Furnace. Thomas Kinsella. BiHa

Impermanence. Lal Ded, *Kashmiri*. BoWoP

Impersonal the aim. Night of Battle. Yvor Winters. PoA

Implacable angel / Has shot his dart, The. Epitaph. Leone da Modena, *Hebrew*. TrJP

Implant. Günter Kunert, *German*. CEEP, *tr. by* Michael Hamburger

Implicated generations made, The. Celtic Cross. Norman MacCaig. FaBoTC; OxBS

Imploration for Clear Weather. *Unknown, Ojibwa Native American*. APN-2, *tr. by* W. J. Hoffman

Imploring Mecca / to achieve. Be-Bop Boys. Langston Hughes. APSN; MoNo; OBAL

Imploring to Be Resigned at Death. George Moses Horton. AAP

Imponderable the dinosaur. Cape Hatteras. Hart Crane. InPS-3; MoAmPo *Fr.* The Bridge. NAAL-2

"Important is the nation's health." The Double Standard. Franklin Pierce Adams. OBAL

Important thing is not, The. Is. Patrick Kavanagh. FaBoTw

Important Words. F. E. Elwell. CTV

Importune me no more! (LL) When I was fair and young, then [*or* and] favour graced me. Elizabeth I, Queen of England. CBLP; CTC; NIP-4; NTP; NoSic; PoRA; Poetr

Impossibilities to His Friend. Robert Herrick. OxBSP

Impossible Pictures, The. Tom Paulin. CABP; CIP-2

Impossible Poem, The. George Oppen. NNaP *Fr.* Some San Francisco Poems.

Impossible to call a lamb a lambkin. Gone Are the Days. Norman MacCaig. CABP; OxBC

Impossible to Trust Women. *Unknown*. MiEL

Imposture, The. James Shirley.
Piping Peace. NOBE
(Song: "You virgins that did late despair.") PoEL-2

Impotence. Marvin Bell. AmPA

Impotent Lover, The. Automedon, *Greek*. GrAn, *tr. by* W. S. Merwin

Impression. E. E. Cummings. MoAmPo

Impression, An. C. S. Lewis. LBC

Impression de Nuit; London. Lord Alfred Bruce Douglas. ADE; OBEV

Impression Du Matin. Oscar Wilde. ADE; EBVV; MoBrPo; NAEL-2; NoAM

Impression du Voyage. Oscar Wilde. GrIP

Impressions. Lu Yu, *Chinese*. SuSp, *tr. by* Irving Y. Lo

Impressions. Oscar Wilde.
Garden, The. PoRA
Les Silhouettes. EBVV

Impressions / of Chicago; For Howlin' Wolf. Quincy Troupe. NAAAL; NBV

Impressions of Shanghai. Kuo Mo-jo, *Chinese*. ChiPo, *tr. by* Kai-yu Hsu

Impressions of Things Encountered. Ch'en Tzu-ang, *Chinese*.
"As the crescent moon is born from the Western Sea." SuSp, *tr. by* William H. Nienhauser
"Kingfishers nest on South Sea islands." SuSp, *tr. by* Irving Y. Lo
"Orchids grow through spring and summer." SuSp, *tr. by* William H. Nienhauser

IMPRIMIS——My departed Shade I trust. Mira's Will. Mary Leapor. BWW; CABP; ECWP; NOEC; NoP-4; PEW

Imprimis, there's a table blotted. An Inventory of the Furniture of a Collegian's Chamber. John Winstanley. OBSV

Imprisoned, The. Robert Fitzgerald. TwCP

Imprisoned Recusant Writes to His Wife, An. Francis Tregian. NoSic

Imprisoned Soul, The. Walt Whitman. *See* The Last Invocation.

Imprisoned winds slumber within their caves, Th'. On the Dark, Still, Dry, Warm Weather Occasionally Happening in the Winter Months. Gilbert White. NOEC

Impromptu. Mary Elizabeth Coleridge. VWP

Impromptu. Márton Kalász, *Hungarian*. CEEP, *tr. by* Jascha Kessler

Impromptu. Frances Anne Kemble. APN-1

Impromptu. Mary Kinzie. CMAP

Impromptu. Meng Chiao, *Chinese*. PLT, *tr. by* A. C. Graham

Impromptu. Phan Van Trinh, *Vietnamese*. AVP, *tr. by* Huỳnh Sanh Thông

Impromptu. Alexander Pope. NoP-4

Impromptu. Samuel Wilberforce. NBLV

Impromptu. Wu Wei-yeh, *Chinese*. CoBLCP, *tr. by* Jonathan Chaves

Impromptu Inspirations. Yang Wei-chen, *Chinese*. CoBLCP, *tr. by* Jonathan Chaves

Impromptu; Late Spring at Pan-shan. Wang An-shih, *Chinese*. CoBCP, *tr. by* Burton Watson

Impromptu on a Hangover. P'i Jih-hsiu, *Chinese*. CoBCP, *tr. by* Burton Watson

Impromptu on Charles II. John Wilmot, 2d Earl of Rochester. FaBoEE; NBLV; NOBL; NTP; OBSV; OxAEP-1; PeLV

Impromptu Poems. Li K'ai-hsien, *Chinese*. CoBLCP, *tr.* by Jonathan Chaves

Impromptu: The Suckers. William Carlos Williams. FaDoA

Improperia. Francis Sparshott. MoCV

Improved Binoculars, The. Irving Layton. NOBC

Improvement too, the idol of the age. The Task. William Cowper. OBGa *Fr.* The Task.

Improvisation for Piano, after *Mood Indigo*. Michael S. Weaver. UnSA

Improvisations. Chu Yün-ming, *Chinese*. CoBLCP, *tr.* by Jonathan Chaves

Improvisations on a Sentence by Poe. Jack Spicer. APSN

Improvisations on Aesop. Anthony Hecht. OBAL

Improvisatrice and Other Poems, The. Letitia Elizabeth Landon.
    Sappho's Song. VWP
    "When should lovers breathe their vows?" Ro

Improvised on Horseback to Say Good-bye to Those Who Are Seeing Me Off. Wen Cheng-ming, *Chinese*.
    "All of you are seeing me off, east of the Emperor's city." CoBLCP, *tr.* by Jonathan Chaves
    "Beneath the Shrine of the Three Loyal Ones." CoBLCP, *tr.* by Jonathan Chaves
    "Floating clouds and worldly affairs." CoBLCP, *tr.* by Jonathan Chaves
    "For three years I sadly listened." CoBLCP, *tr.* by Jonathan Chaves
    "I remove my court gown and part from the Emperor's precincts." CoBLCP, *tr.* by Jonathan Chaves
    "I sit on horseback at Twin Bridges." CoBLCP, *tr.* by Jonathan Chaves
    "In the past when I saw friends off." CoBLCP, *tr.* by Jonathan Chaves
    "This man of leisure for twenty years." CoBLCP, *tr.* by Jonathan Chaves
    "Wine of parting flowed and flowed, The." CoBLCP, *tr.* by Jonathan Chaves
    "Wishing to try retirement, I requested release from duty." CoBLCP, *tr.* by Jonathan Chaves

Impulse, The. Robert Frost. HoPM; RaBo *Fr.* The Hill Wife. CMoP; HAP; InPS-3; LiTM; NoP-4; RACG

In. G. S. Giscombe. Bro Duncanson. GT

In 1944. Statistic. Michelle Parkerson. ISC

In a back alley, on the cracked pavement, slick with the strewn waste. Four Chinatown Figures. Garrett Kaoru Hongo. NAmP90

In a bare cup. Henry David Thoreau. *See* I am a parcel of vain strivings tied.

In a basement just off Saint-Michel. 104 Boulevard Saint-Germain. Kenneth Pitchford. NYBP

In a Bath Teashop. John Betjeman. CBLP; EnLoPo

In a beaker sits a beetle. The Beetle. Nikolai Makarovich Oleynikov, *Russian*. TCRP, *tr.* by Anatoly Liberman

In a Bed-Sitter. Hal Porter. NOBAu

In a big wind, in a ruined house. Man: 1961. Pranabendu Dasgupta, *Bengali*. OMIP, *tr.* by Buddhadeva Bose

In a blind corner jolly *Bacchus* taught. Being half foxt he praiseth Bacchus. Horace, *Latin*. OBCVT, *tr.* by Thomas Flatman

In a Blind Garden. David Shapiro. ChIV-1

In a boat, Getting Up at Night. Su Shih, *Chinese*. SuSp, *tr.* by Irving Y. Lo

In a Boat, Getting Up at Night. Su Tung-p'o, *Chinese*. ChiPo, *tr.* by Irving Yucheng Lo

In a Boat on a Summer Evening. Lu Yu, *Chinese*. CoBCP, *tr.* by Burton Watson

In a Boat on the Cha River. Chang Yü, *Chinese*. CoBLCP, *tr.* by Jonathan Chaves

In a Book-Box I Found the Lost Manuscript of a Poem Sent to Me by the Late Kao [Ch'i]. Chang Yü, *Chinese*. CoBLCP, *tr.* by Jonathan Chaves

In a bowl to sea went wise men three. Three Men of Gotham. Thomas Love Peacock. BXAP; CBNP; CH; FaBoCh; OBEV; OxAEP-2 *Fr.* Nightmare Abbey.

In a branch of a willow hid. To a Caty-did. Philip Freneau. TAP

In a Building Named for a Governor. Christopher L. Dornin. CRP

In a Bye-Canal. Herman Melville. APN-2; NCAP

In a cabin, in a canon. Percy Montross. *See* Oh, My Darling Clementine.

In a Café. Rosemary Dobson. CBAP

In a cafe under a lazy fan. Country Nun. Geoff Page. CBAP

In a Canton Jail. Phan Bội Châu, *Vietnamese*. AVP, *tr.* by Huỳnh Sanh Thông

In a Cathedral City. Thomas Hardy. EnLoPo
    ("Spot's unconsciousness of you!, The.") (LL) GLoP

In a cavern, in a canyon. Clementine. *Unknown*. CTV; KaS

In a cavern, in a canyon. Paul Dehn. KaS *Fr.* Rhymes for a Modern Nursery.

In a cavern, in a canyon [excavating for a mine]. Oh, My Darling Clementine. Percy Montross. AmFP; FaBoBe; OBAL

In a certain sense, they are not serious. Their Seriousness, with Further Comparisons. Robert Pinsky. NoAM *Fr.* Essay on Psychiatrists.

In a chain reaction. Atomic Pantoum. Peter Meinke. WeW-3

In a Chain-Store Cafeteria. Paul Grano. NOBAu

In a childhood of hats. The Hat Lady. Linda Pastan. SoSe-8

In a Christian Churchyard. James Thomson. NOBVV

In a Church of Padua. Herman Melville. APN-2

In a Churchyard. Richard Wilbur. HeIP-4

In a circle of thaw. Virginia Brady Young. HA

In a city, Trieste or Udine. The Day of My Death. Pier Paolo Pasolini, *Italian*. VCWP, *tr.* by Lawrence Ferlinghetti *and* Francesca Valente; GI, *tr.* by Max Hayward *and* Lawrence R. Smith

In a Classroom. Adrienne Rich. LoL

In a climate where. Intuition. Anthony Delius. PeSA

In a coign of the cliff between lowland and highland. A Forsaken Garden. Swinburne. EBEV; EBEvV; GTBS-P; GaP; NOBE; NOBVV; NoP-4; OAEL-2; OBGa; OBNC; OxAEP-2; SCGP

In a Convent Garden. Alan Brownjohn. OBGa

In a cool curving world he lies. The Fish. Rupert Brooke. APo

In a Copy of More's (or Shaw's or Wells's or Plato's or Anybody's) Utopia. Max Beerbohm. OBCoV

In a Copy of Omar Khayyám. James Russell Lowell. NCAP

In a corner of blue sky. Daily Wages. Amrita Pritam, *Punjabi*. PBWP, *tr.* by the author and Charles Brasch

In a Corner of the Sky. Federico García Lorca. PFTM

In a cottage in Fife. Two Comical Folk. Mother Goose. OxNR; ReMoGo

In a Country Church. Ronald Stuart Thomas. FaBoMo; TOF

In a Country Museum. Patricia Beer. FaBoWP

In a country of drifting spectacles. The Old Lady Across the Hall Has Gone to Live Behind the Door. Colette Inez. CMAP

In / a / cove. The Signs. Norman Henry, II Pritchard. NBV

In a dark, dark wood, there was a dark, dark house. The Dark House. *Unknown*. NTCP

In a dark hour (there are more and more of them now). Jovan Hristic, *Serbo-Croatian*. HSix, *tr.* by Charles Simic

In a Dark Time. Theodore Roethke.
    "In a dark time, the eye begins to see." HAP; HeIP-4; MoAmPo; MoP; NAAL-2; NOBA; NYBP; NoAM; NoP-4; PBMP; PaTW; PeECV; PoE; Poetr; RaBo; TAP; TFi; VCAP
    ("And one is One, free in the tearing wind.") (LL) NoP-4; PBMP; PaTW

In a Day. Li Shang-yin, *Chinese*. SuSp, *tr.* by Eugene Eoyang *and* Irving Y. Lo

In a day or two the chairs will fall to pieces. Little House, Big House. Medbh McGuckian. PNI

In a dear little home of tarpaulin and boards. No Thoroughfare. Ruth Holmes. BoTP

In a desert land, this pearl-studded city. Jaisalmer, 1. Ghulam Mohammed Sheikh, *Gujarati*. OMIP, *tr.* by Saleem Peeradina *and* Ghulam Mohammed Sheikh

In a dingy kitchen / Facing a Ghetto backyard. Lamentations. Alter Brody. TrJP

In a disingenuous letter. The Oranges Returned. Gilbert Sorrentino. FTOS

In a dismal air; a light of breaking summer. Lament. George Sutherland Fraser. PoWW

In a Double Rainbow. Harold Littlebird. VoR

In a Dream. David Ignatow. PoA

In a Dream. Lu Yu, *Chinese*. SuSp, *tr.* by Irving Y. Lo

In a dream he fled the house. Coleridge. Medbh McGuckian. CIP-2

In a dream I bought a. Dream May 18, 1958. Peter Orlovsky. BB

"In a dream I never exactly dreamed." Another Life. Frank Bidart. HCAP; VCAP

In a dream I returned to the river of bees. The River of Bees. W. S. Merwin. HeIP-4; LCAP-2; VCAP

In a Dream I Traveled among Ten Thousand Acres of Lotuses. Lu Yu, *Chinese*. SuSp, *tr.* by Irving Y. Lo

In a dream you came. Mother's Letter from the North. Kyudong Kim, *Korean*. CKP, *tr.* by Jaihiun Kim

In a dreamlike fall, the long. Apis Mellifica. Roger McDonald. NOBAu

In a drear-nighted December. Happy Insensibility. Keats. CH; GTBS-P; NOBE; OBEV; OBNC; PBMP

In a drugstore north of Ft. Lauderdale. The Story I Like to Tell. Robin Becker. PBCAP

In a Duplex Near the San Andreas Fault. Dionisio D. Martinez. NoP-4

In a Eweleaze near Weatherbury. Thomas Hardy. EnVR

In a far-away northern county in the placid pastoral region. The Ox-Tamer. Walt Whitman. RB

In a far off hamlet near the sea. Uranne. Mary Weston Fordham. CBWP-2

In a fashionable suburb of Santa Barbara. In Montecito. Randall Jarrell. CoAP; NYBP; VGW

In a Fever. Ernest Bryll. CEEP

In a few moments. The Death of a Negro Poet. Conrad Kent Rivers. BPo

In a field. Keeping Things Whole. Mark Strand. CAPP-1; CoAP; HCAP; HeIP-4; LCAP-2; PoPoPo; TAP; VCAP

In a field. (LL) Marriage. William Carlos Williams. ITG; PoA

In a field of swaying grain. Death Seed. Ricarda Huch, German. PBWP, tr. by Susan C. Strong

In a fit, Philaenion bit me. Asclepiades, Greek. InMo, tr. by Sam Hamill

In a foreign land in an old foreign house. Before the Map of Russia. "Teffi," Russian. TCRP, tr. by Albert C. Todd

In a forest of frost, in a dawn of cornflowers. (LL) Poppies in October. Sylvia Plath. FaBoWP; HCAP; LCAP-2; NoAM

In a frith as I con fare fremede. Unknown. MiEL

In a frosty sunset. Winter: East Anglia. Edmund Blunden. OxBTC

In a Garden. Elizabeth Jennings. NOCV

In a Garden in the Grounds of Coleorton, Leicestershire. Wordsworth. OBGa

In a garden shady this holy lady. W. H. Auden. FaBoTw; TwCP Fr. Anthem for St. Cecilia's Day.

In a garden where the whitethorn spreads her leaves. Alba Innominata. Unknown, French. AWP, tr. by Ezra Pound

In a Garret. Herman Melville. OBAL

In a Garret. Nguyễn Nhưọc Pháp, Vietnamese. AVP, tr. by Huỳnh Sanh Thông

In a gay jar upon his shoulder. The Amphora. Fyodor Kuz'mich Sologub, Russian. AWP, tr. by Babette Deutsch and Avrahm Yarmolinsky

In a ghost town. Little Picture Catalogue. Novica Tadic, Serbo-Croatian. HSix; VCWP, tr. by Charles Simic

In a Glass-Window for Inconstancy. Edward Herbert, 1st Baron Herbert of Cherbury. OxBSP; SeCP

In a glove shop. The Rose. Novica Tadic, Serbo-Croatian. HSix, tr. by Charles Simic

In a Gondola. Robert Browning. ("Moth's kiss first!, The.") APAD

In a gorge titanic. Ula Masondo's Dream. William Plomer. MoBS

In a grass hut lodged at the end of the narrow lane. In the Year with the Cyclical Sign Mou-shen. T'ao Ch'ien, Chinese. CoBCP, tr. by Burton Watson

In a Grave-Yard. W. S. Braithwaite. PoBA

In a great steep-banked ravine. The Pit of Cologne. Boris Abramovich Slutsky, Russian. TCRP, tr. by J. R. Rowland

In a greatbig. . . night . . . big . . . night. (LL) Sylvester's Dying Bed. Langston Hughes. NAAAL; NoAM; Poetr; SAmP; UnPo

In a Green Night. Derek Walcott. PFE

In a green place lanced through. The Blue Heron. Theodore Goodridge Roberts. NOBC

In a grove. Tanka. Tsukamoto Kunio, Japanese. MJT, tr. by Makoto Ueda

In a grove most rich of shade. Eighth Song. Sir Philip Sidney. NoSic; PBRV Fr. Astrophil and Stella. AAS; SiPS

In a gust of wind the white dew. Bunya no Asayasu, Japanese. OHPJ, tr. by Kenneth Rexroth

In a hard intellectual light / I will kill all delight. Richard Eberhart. CMoP; LiTM

In a heavy light like yellow onions. (LL) Yellow Light. Garrett Kaoru Hongo. InPS-3; OpBo; WWSi; WeT

In a herber [or a harbour or an arbour] green [or grene], asleep [or aslepe] whereas [or where as or where] I lay. In Youth Is Pleasure. Robert Wever. CBLP; NOBE; OBEV Fr. Lusty Juventus.

In a hidden spot on the northern mountain. Yün Shou-p'ing. CoBLCP, tr. by Jonathan Chaves Fr. On the Day of the Mid-Autumn Festival of the Year Ping-yin (1686), Together with Chang Han-chan, Ching-fan, and Ching-t'ien, I Saw the Kuei Blossoms at the Northern Garden of Jade Peak.

In a high wind, on a rock in the back paddock. One. One. Laurie Duggan. BMAP Fr. The Ash Range.

In a highly classified report smuggled. Wings. Maureen Seaton. FFC

In a hollow of the forest. The Bomber. "Brian Vrepont." NOBAu

In a home for incurables. A Visit. Anna Swirszczynska, Polish. PoSu, tr. by Czeslaw Milosz and Leonard Nathan (b. 1924)

In a Hospital Garden, after Henrikas Radauskas. Randall Jarrell. OBGa

In a Hot Country. Wendy Mulford. NBrP

In a hotel in Tashkent. Political Relations. Audre Lorde. GLP

In a Hotel Writing-Room. John Cowper Powys. OxBTC

In a house of empty rooms. A Closing. May Miller. ISC

In a Hundred Years. Elizabeth Doten. BLPA

In a Hurry. Xuân Diệu, Vietnamese. AVP, tr. by Huỳnh Sanh Thông

In a Japanese Moss Garden. Brad Leithauser. OBGa

In a land whose prosperity constantly grows. Olga Beshenkovskaya, Russian. TCRP, tr. by Anatoly Liberman

In a Late Hour. James McAuley. BMAP

In a Letter to A.R.C. on Her Wishing to Be Called Anna. Matilda Barbara Betham-Edwards. ECWP; WoRP

In a liftship near Hue. Him, on the Bicycle. Bruce Weigl. CDa

In a light fantastic round. (LL) Comus' Summons. Milton. FaBoCh; NOBE; NOSC; OBEV

In a lit-tle bed a wo-man was born, In a. Turkey in the Corn. Woody Guthrie. KaS

In a little house keep I pictures suspended, it is not a fix'd house. My Picture-Gallery. Walt Whitman. NAAL-1; NAAL-3

In a long forgotten snow. (LL) Song: "Let it be forgotten, as a flower is forgotten." Sara Teasdale. MoAmPo; PoA

In a loose robe of tinsel forth [or tynsell foorth] she came. Corinna Bathes. George Chapman. OxAEP-1 Fr. Ovid's Banquet of Sense.

In a lovely garden, filled with fair and blooming flowers. The Mission of the Flowers. Frances Ellen Watkins Harper. BlSi

In a Lovely Garden Walking. Ludwig Uhland, German. AWP, tr. by George Macdonald

In a maiden-time professed. Song. Thomas Middleton. OxBSP Fr. The Witch.

In a Meadow. John Swinnerton Phillimore. OBEV

In a meadow/ Beside the chapel three boys were playing football. Patrick Kavanagh. CIP-2; PoE Fr. Father Mat. CMoP

In a mean abode in [or on] the Shankill Road. The Ballad of William Bloat. Unknown. NOBL; PeLV

In a melancholly studdy. Robert Wild. PBRV Fr. Alas poore Scholler, whither wilt thou goe.

In a milkweed cradle. Baby Seeds. Unknown. CTV

In a mirror of bronze. To the Fortuneteller Hsüeh T'ieh-yai. Hsieh Chin, Chinese. CoBLCP, tr. by Jonathan Chaves

In a modern love poem. Tadeusz Rózewicz. See Draft of a Modern Love Poem.

In a Monotonous Dream. Elaine Equi. PmAP

In a Moonlight Wilderness. S. T. Coleridge. See The Fruit Plucker.

In a more hostile view, the psychiatrists. Dionysus as Psychiatrist. Robert Pinsky. HCAP Fr. Essay on Psychiatrists.

In a Motel on Lake Erie. James Tate. LCAP-2

In a Mucker fog. (LL) Kerr's Ass. Patrick Kavanagh. NOIV; RB

In a museum, I ask. Tutankhamen. William Dickey. Poetsp

In a Museum in the Capital. William Stafford. LCAP-2

In a Music-Hall. John Davidson. EBVV

In a Myrtle [or Mirtle] Shade. William Blake. ChIV-1

In a Naples Bar. Andrejs Eglitis, Latvian. CEEP, tr. by Inara Cedrins

In a narrow road where there was not room to pass. Meeting in the Road. Unknown, Chinese. ChiP, tr. by Arthur Waley

In a nation of one hundred fine, mob-hearted, lynching, relenting, repenting millions. Vachel Lindsay. Fr. Bryan, Bryan, Bryan, Bryan. CMoP; MeMAP; OxBA; OxBoLi

In a neighborhood of tinkling jade. Ballad of the Deserted Mansion. Kao Ch'i, Chinese. CoBLCP, tr. by Jonathan Chaves

In a Net of Blue and Gold. Jane Hirshfield. WeT

In a night hour this is how the things are written. And now night. Amir Gilbo'a, Hebrew. IP, tr. by Warren Bargad and Stanley F. Chyet

In a nook. In May. John Millington Synge. MoBrPo; SAGP

In a package of minutes there is this We. An Aspect of Love, Alive in the Ice and Fire. Gwendolyn Brooks. BPo; CAPP-1; TAP

In a Park, in Siena, at Twilight. Ory Bernstein, Hebrew. IP, tr. by Warren Bargad and Stanley F. Chyet

In a Parlor Containing a Table. Galway Kinnell. NBLV; OxBSP

In a plain pleasant cottage, conveniently neat. The Miller. John Cunningham. ECEV

In a Plantation. Basil T. Paquet. CDa

In a poem, one line may hide another line. One Train May Hide Another. Kenneth Koch. BAP-94

In a post-coach and four, with postillions as fine. Priscilla Pointon. ECWP Fr. Letter to a Sister, Giving an Account of the Author's Wedding-Day.

In a posture. Tanka. Nakajō Fumiko, Japanese. MJT, tr. by Makoto Ueda

In a Prominent Bar in Secaucus [One Day]. X. J. Kennedy. AiP; CoAmPo; FYAP; HoPM; NBLV; NIP-4; OBAL; TRP

In a Provincial Capital Sick in Bed. Hsieh T'iao, Chinese. CoBCP, tr. by Burton Watson

In A Queen's Domain. Sarah Morgan Bryan Piatt. NCAP

In a quiet water'd land, a land of roses. The Dead at Clonmacnois [or Clonmacnoise]. Angus O'Gillan, Irish. OBEV; OBMV, tr. by Thomas William Rolleston

In a quiet water'd land, a land of roses. The Dead at Clonmacnois. Thomas William Hazen Rolleston. APAD

In a red winter hat blue. Self-Portrait. William Carlos Williams. LCAP-2 *Fr.* Pictures from Brueghel.

In a red winter hat blue. William Carlos Williams. *See* The Parable of the Blind.

In a redwood grove, on a low hill facing east. Run My Hand Under. Andrew Schelling. PT

In a Remote Cloister Bordering the Empyrean. Joel Sloman. VGW

In a Roman tram, where the famous Roman mob. The Thief. Stanley Kunitz. MoAmPo; VGW

In a room on a shelf away from everything else. I Held His Name. Alberto A. Ríos. NoAM

In a Rose Garden. John Bennett. BLPA; FaBoBe

In a salt lake of moonlight. Moorings. Norman MacCaig. OxBTC

In a scented wood. The Night. Helen Leuty. BoTP

In a Season of Unemployment. Margaret Avison. MoCV; NOBC

In a sense. Life. Artie Gold. NOBC

In a shoe box stuffed in an old nylon stocking. The Meadow Mouse. Theodore Roethke. ChAP; HeIP-4; PeP; RB; TRP

In a sick shade of spruce, moss-webbed, rock-fed. As It Looked Then. Edwin Arlington Robinson. CMoP; MeMAP

In a small city at dusk. Martin Carter. HCP

In a small grove I met a little shepherdess. Guido Cavalcanti. *See* Ballata: Concerning a Shepherd-Maid.

In a small theodolite of paper. Soluble Noughts and Crosses; or, California, Here I Come. Roger Roughton. SPE

In a snug little cot lived a fat little mouse. The Country Mouse and the City Mouse. Richard Scrafton Sharpe *and* Mrs. Pearson. OxBChV

In a solitude of the sea. The Convergence of the Twain. Thomas Hardy. CABP; FaBoTw; HeIP-4; InPK-6; InPS-3; LiTM; MoBrPo; MoP; NAEL-2; NIP-4; NoAM; NoP-4; OAEL-2; OxBTC; PBMP; PFE; PeVV; PoPoPo; Poetr; SCGP; TFi

In a South African Museum. Evangeline Paterson. NBrP

In a Southern garden Lucinda sits. The Bones of Incontention. Robert David Cohen. NYBP

In a spathe of silence. The Messenger. Frances Horovitz. BrRo

In a spiral of lights. (LL) Banneker. Rita Dove. LCAP-2; NoAM

In a Spring Still Not Written Of. Robert Wallace. CMAP

In a springtime, before noon, the kitchen door. Till Eulenspiegel. "Eduard Georgievich Bagritzky," *Russian.* TCRP; *tr. by* Vera Dunham

In a stable of stones I lie still. The Lifeguard. James Dickey. NYBP; NoP-4; SoSe-8

In a Station of the Metro. Ezra Pound. AmPP; ChAP; ColAP; HAP; HeIP-4; InPK-6; MeMAP; MoAmPo; MoP; NAAL-2; NIP-4; NOBA; NoAM; NoP-4; OxBA; PFE; PoE; PoPoPo; Poetr; TAP; TFi; UnPo; VGW; WeW-3

In a Storm. Antoine-Roger Bolamba, *French.* NegPo, *tr. by* Ellen Conroy Kennedy

In a story called. Brothers. Marcia Southwick. NAmP90

In a summer [*or* somer] season, when soft[e] was the sun[ne] [*or* sonne]. Prologue: "In a summer season, when soft was the sun." William Langland. EBVV; OAEL-1; PoE; PoEL-1 *Fr.* The Vision of Piers Plowman.

In a swaying boat drifting along with the stream. Seeking Hsin E in the Western Hills. Meng Hao Jan, *Chinese.* SuSp, *tr. by* Daniel Bryant

In a Tavern. Louis Jenkins. RaBo

In a terrible fog I once lost my way. Lost. James Godden. OBSP

In a thick stand of trees in a forest. So Terrifyingly Melancholy. Hagiwara Sakutaro, *Japanese.* PFTM, *tr. by* Hiroaki Sato

In a thin cloud of cool and glowing muslin. The Palanquin. Charles Marie René Leconte de Lisle, *French.* FLP; LoP, *tr. by* Alistair Elliot

In a thousandth of a second. Asymmetry of the Universe. Fabio Doplicher, *Italian.* NeIt, *tr. by* Stephen Sartarelli

In a Time of Sickness. Orpingalik, *Eskimo.* STP, *tr. by* Edward Field

In a town with a name as beautiful. Dogknotting in Quezaltenango. Vincent O'Sullivan. PeNZ

In a Train. Robert Bly. TTTS

In a U-Haul North of Damascus. David Bottoms. FYAP; MT

In a valley [*or* the vale *or* the vaile] of this restless [*or* restles] mind. Quia Amore Langueo. *Unknown.* ImPo; NOBE; NOCV; OBEV; PoEL-1, *tr. by* Helen Gardner

In a Warm Bath. Carl Rakosi. TAP

In a wee, twee cul-de-sac. The Fruit of Knowledge. Robert Johnstone. PNI

In a weird, forlorn voice. The President Slumming. James Tate. OBAL

In a wheat field. A Conversation. Gisèle Prassinos, *French.* PFTM, *tr. by* Pierre Joris

In a while they rose and went out aimlessly riding. Merlin Enthralled. Richard Wilbur. CMoP; NYBP

In a white gully among fungus red. Native Born. Eve Langley. WPE

In a Wood. Thomas Hardy. OBNC ("Pale beech and pine so blue.") EnVR

In a Wood. Edith Joy Scovell. GBL

In a wooden room, surrounded by lights and / Faces. The Killing. George MacBeth. FaBoMo

In a Year. Robert Browning. CBLP

In a year the nightingales were said to be so loud. The Kingfisher. Amy Clampitt. HCAP

In / ability to love, The. Ghost Song. Jack Spicer. APSN

In Adam's fall/ We sinned all. An ABC. *Unknown.* OBCA *Fr.* The New England Primer.

In Adam's house, in Paradise, the room is still. Great Work Farm Elegy. Allen Grossman. BAP-93

In Æsop's tales an honest wretch we find. A Fable. Matthew Prior. NoP-4

In aeternum I was once determed. Sir Thomas Wyatt. NoSic

In Africa. Roy Fuller. PoWW

In Africa the wine is cheap, and it is. A Certain Slant of Sunlight. Ted Berrigan. PT

In After Days. Austin Dobson. OBEV

In after times when strength or courage fail. Buffel's Kop. Roy Campbell. PeSA

In Age. William Lisle Bowles. *Fr.* Milton: On the Busts of Milton, in Youth and Age. Son

In age I boast not many scores of years. Officialdom. Nguyễn Công Trú', *Vietnamese.* AVP, *tr. by* Huỳnh Sanh Thông

In Agrigentum, earlier in Olympia. Empedocles on Etna. Herbert B. Mallalieu. PoA

In Egypt's land contaygious to the Nile. Pharao's Daughter. Michael Moran. BIrV; ChIV-1

In Air. Peter Clarke. PBA

In air hard as sand. Mary Kinzie. FFC

In Aix. Grace Paley. NMM-2

In Aku Aku is there double. Oh, Noa, Noa! William Cole. NBLV

In Alaska an Eskimo girl. The Eskimo Girl. David Ray. LTA

In Albion then, with equal lustre bright. Walter Harte. EPCY *Fr.* An Essay on Satire, Particularly on The Dunciad.

In all ages, always, everywhere, and everywhere. Yuliya Vladimirovna Drunina, *Russian.* TCRP, *tr. by* Albert C. Todd

In all my Emma's beauties blest. Translation of a South American Ode. Oliver Goldsmith. NOIV

In all ten directions of the universe. Ryokan, *Japanese.* EnlH, *tr. by* Stephen Mitchell

In All the Days of My Childhood. Russell Edson. AmPA

In all the Eastern hemisphere. The Fall of J. W. Beane. Oliver Herford. OBAL

In all the good Greek of Plato. Survey of Literature. John Crowe Ransom. FaBoCh; MeMAP; NBLV; OBAL; TAP; TwCP; VGW

In all the land no women found so fair. (LL) The Beauty of Job's Daughters. Jay Macpherson. ChIV-1; MoCV; NOBC

In All the Magic of Christmas-Tide. John Jacob Niles. AH

In all the old paintings. Annunciation. Kay Smith. NIP-4

In all the windows / of stone. (LL) The Path among the Stones. Galway Kinnell. NNaP; NOBA

In all the world. Fujiwara No Toshinari, *Japanese.* OHPJ, *tr. by* Kenneth Rexroth

In all the world one cage holds this small bird. The Bird in a Cage. *Unknown, Vietnamese.* AVP, *tr. by* Huỳnh Sanh Thông

In all these rotten shops, in all this broken furniture. The Dancing. Gerald Stern. LCAP-2; LoL; UnSA

In all those stories the hero. Heroes. Robert Creeley. NOBA; NoP-4

IN) all those who got. E. E. Cummings. FaBoEE

In all thy humors, whether grave or mellow. Temperament. Martial, *Latin.* AWP, *tr. by* Joseph Addison

In Allusion to the French Song. Richard Lovelace. CaPo

In Alsace, during the war. George Oppen. APSN *Fr.* Route.

In america. Bow to Allah. Brian G. Gilmore. ISC

In america. XXIV. Essex Hemphill. NAAAL *Fr.* Conditions.

"In America," began / the lecturer, "everyone must have a." The Student. Marianne Moore. NAAL-2; TwCP

In America, there is an answer for everything. Tomorrow, We'll Dance in America. James Harms. PUP-18

In America we don't say things straight. The Congressman Visits the Grade School. James B. Hathaway. IFJA

In Ampezzo. Trumbull Stickney. APN-2; ColAP

In Amsterdam there dwelt a maid. The Fair Maid of Amsterdam. *Unknown.* OxBoLi; PeLV; RB

In an Abandoned Garden. Han-shan, *Chinese.* GaP, *tr. by* Burton Watson

In an African folk tale, the rain. The Rain's Marriage. Marcia Southwick. NAmP90

In an age of fops and toys. Ralph Waldo Emerson. PoLF *Fr.* Voluntaries. APN-1; CBCWP

I Can. CTV

In an Album. James Russell Lowell. OBAL

In an ancient overgrown park. Duckweed. Leopold Staff, *Polish.* PoSu, *tr. by* Adam Czerniawski

In An Artist's Studio. Christina Rossetti. NAEL-2; NALW; NoP-4; PEW; Poetr; VWP

("One face looks out from all his canvases.") NoP-4; PEW

In an Emergency. (LL) "Faith" is a fine invention. Emily Dickinson. APN-2; AmPP; MeMAP; NAAL-1; NAAL-3; NCAP; NOBA; NoP-4; OxBA; PAR; TAP

In an envelope marked. Personal. Langston Hughes. NOBA; NTP

In an eternal night. (LL) The Garden of Proserpine. Swinburne. CABP; GaP; NoP-4; PeVV; TFi

In an exciting world of love-bites, nipple-nipping. The Lovesleep. Gavin Ewart. OxBC

In an idle hour I thought of former days. Thinking of the Past. Po Chü-i, *Chinese,* tr. by Arthur Waley

In an Indian ditch lies. The World's Last Unnamed Poem. A. K. Redwing. VoR

In an instant, by instinct, I apprehended. An Act. Kenneth Rosen. AmPA

In an Iridescent night. Ruth Stone. MoAmPo; NALW; NMM-2; OxWW

In an Irish Churchyard. "Violet Fane." VWP

In an ocean, 'way out yonder. The Dinkey-Bird. Eugene Field. FPC

In an old, dark house. Fly in December. Robert Wallace. NYBP

In an Old House. Spencer Brown. NYBP

In an Old Orchard. Peter Kane Dufault. NYBP

In an orchard a little fountain flows. Song of the Ill-Married. *Unknown, French.* BoWoP, *tr. by* Patricia Terry

In an orchard soft with rot. (LL) Never May the Fruit Be Plucked. Edna St. Vincent Millay. NAAL-2; OxBSP

In an uncumbered clime / Minute inductons wake. (LL) Coffee. James Vincent Cunningham. MoAmPo; VGW

In an upper room at midnight. The Love Feast. W. H. Auden. OBCoV; PFE

In an upstairs room. John Wills. HA

In an Urban School. Toi Derricotte. PBCAP

In ancient days there lived a Turk. Kafoozalum. *Unknown.* BLPA

In ancient days, when God cast down his page. Words. Nikolai Stepanovich Gumilyov, *Russian.* TCRP, *tr. by* Simon Franklin

In ancient times, as story tells. Baucis and Philemon. Jonathan Swift. NOEC; OAEL-1

In ancient times, no matter where. Little Britain. *Unknown.* NOEC

In ancient times—'twas no great loss. On a Nomination to the Legion of Honour. *Unknown.* FaBoEE

In and Out. Jane Kenyon. BAP-93 *Fr.* Having It Out With Melancholy. BAP-93

(6 In and Out.) LoL

In and Out. Louis Edward Sissman. NYBP

(Severance of Connections, 1946.) TwCP

In and out among the narrow little ways of the town. Good Friday. Christy Brown. TIRV

In and out the bushes, up the ivy. The Chipmunk's Day. Randall Jarrell. OBCA

In and out the slipping slates. (LL) Ireland with Emily. John Betjeman. GTBS-P; OxBTC

In Andrea's Garden. Susan Hampton. BMAP

In anguish we uplift. War Song. John Davidson. OBNC

In another being, at last. (LL) Words for the Wind. Theodore Roethke. CoAP; NOBA

In Answer of an Elegiacal[l] Letter, Upon the Death of the King of Sweden [from Aurelian Townsend, Inviting Me to Write on That Subject]. Thomas Carew. BeJo

In Answer to a Question From P. W. Lew Welch. BB

In Answer to Their Questions. Giovanna (Janet) Capone. UnSA

In Answer to Your Query. Naomi Lazard. NBLV

In antient Times, as Story tells. Ovid. OBCVT, *tr. by* Jonathan Swift *Fr.* Baucis and Philemon, Imitated, From the Eighth Book of Ovid's Metamorphose.

In April / Come he will. The Cuckoo. *Unknown.* BoTP

In April now I think upon the rain. The Rain. Alasdair Maclean. FaBoTC

In April one seldom feels cheerful. Waste Land Limericks. Wendy Cope. FaBoWP

In April [or Aprill], the koocoo can sing her song by rote. The Koocoo. *Unknown.* TTTS

In April / the ponds / open / like black blossoms. Blossom. Mary Oliver. CrSp

In April we will pierce his body. Letters to a Stranger. Thomas James. AmPA

In April when the flowers spring. Heinrich von Veldeke, *German.* GePo, *tr. by* Frederick Goldin

In Aprile at the hicht of noon. On Seein an Aik-Tree Sprent Wi Galls. Robert Garioch. OxBS

In Arabia. Gertrude Gerard. PeLi

In Arabia's book of fable. Princess Sabbath. Heinrich Heine, *German.* TrJP, *tr. by* Charles Godfrey Leland

In Arcadia. Lawrence Durrell. MoBrPo

In Arden. Charles Tomlinson. OxBC

In Arizona / (how many years in the mountains). Louis Zukofsky. TRP *Fr.* 29 Songs.

In Armorik, that is called Britayne [*or* Britaine]. The Franklin's Tale. Chaucer. NAEL-1; OAEL-1 *Fr.* The Canterbury Tales.

In at our windows, blinking, summer peers. Lines in Honor of Natalya. Pavel Nikolaevich Vasilyev, *Russian.* TCRP, *tr. by* David Macduff

In August. Hamlin Garland. APN-2

In August we carried the old horsehair mattress. Green Apples. Ruth Stone. InPS-3

In August, when the air of love was peeled. Bible Story. Charles Causley. TOF

In autumn. Absentia Animi. Gunnar Ekelof, *Swedish.* PFTM, *tr. by* Muriel Rukeyser *and* Leif Sjoberg

In Autumn. Jon Anderson. AmPA

In Autumn. Charles Hubert Sisson. PeECV

In autumn moonlight the face turns icy. Meng Chiao. SuSp, *tr. by* Stephen Owen *Fr.* Autumn Meditations.

In autumn moonlight, when the white air wan. Robert Bridges. GSo

In autumn, the bats. The Bat. Roberta Spear. AmPA

In autumn the falling leaves. Gathering Leaves. Stanley Cook. AYFP

In autumn when the woods are red. Robert Louis Stevenson. NOBVV

In Autumpne, whan the sonne in Vyrgyne. The Bowge of Courte. John Skelton. AAS

In Autumpne, whan the sonne in vyrgyne. The Bowge of Courte. John Skelton. AAS

In back of our town. Gasco. Günter Grass, *German.* CLPP, *tr. by* Jerome Rothenberg

In Back of the Real. Allen Ginsberg. AmPP; HeIP-4

In balance with this life, this death. (LL) An Irish Airman Foresees His Death. W. B. Yeats. APAD; ChAP; EBEvV; FaBoCh; FaBoMo; GTBS-P; HeIP-4; HoPM; LiTM; MoBrPo; MoP; NOBE; NoAM; NoP-4; OBMV; OBWP; PoPoPo; PoWW; Poetr; SCV; TFi; WeW-3

In Ball's Market after surfing till noon. The Supremes. Mark Jarman. CMAP

In Barracks. Siegfried Sassoon. FaBoTw

In *Bath* a wanton wife did dwell. *Unknown.* PBRV *Fr.* The Wanton Wife of Bath.

In Bayreuth once. Mary Desti's Ass. Frank O'Hara. FTOS

In Beatle light. For Craig Who Leapt Off a Cliff into Hummingbird Light. Diane Wakoski. PmAP

In beauty at my feet. (LL) Rainy Nights. Irene Thompson. AYFP; BoTP

In beauty may I walk. *Unknown, Navajo Indian.* RB, *tr. by* Jerome K. Rothenberg

In bed, asleep, I dream. Leaving the Monastery Early in the Morning. Lu Yu, *Chinese.* OHPC, *tr. by* Kenneth Rexroth

In bed, dull man[?] Upon My Lord Brohall's Wedding. Sir John Suckling. CaPo

In bed I muse on Tenier's [*or* Teniers'] boors. The Bench of Boors. Herman Melville. APN-2; NAAL-1; NAAL-3; NoP-4; OBAL; SoSe-8

In bed we laugh, in bed we cry. Translation of Lines by Benserade. Samuel Johnson, *after the French of* Isaac Benserade. FaBoEE

In bed with our bodies so completely intertwined. The Love Poem. Andrew Elliott. PNI

In bed with the stranger who had picked him up. A Bride. Harry Fainlight. BoLoP

In Belfast, Europe, your man. The British Connection. Padraic Fiacc. PNI

In Berlin. Ōkuma Nobuyuki, *Japanese.* MJT, *tr. by* Makoto Ueda

In Berlin, August 1945: Lehrte Bahnhof. Alun Llywelyn-Williams, *Welsh.* OBWVE, *tr. by* Joseph P. Clancy

In Bertram's Garden. Donald Justice. BoLoP; MT; SAGP; VGW

In Bethlehem / On Christmas morn. Christus Natus Est. Countee Cullen. ChIV-2

In between. Langston Hughes. *See* Advice.

In between mud pies and the cultivated gardens. The Snake's Destiny. Hy Sobiloff. PFE

In bible times heavenly messengerss, disguised as beggars. The Unforseen. Amy Gerstler. DeD

In black core of night, it explodes. African Dream. Bob Kaufman. GT; PoBA

In Blackwater Woods. Mary Oliver. OlOp

In Blanco County. Russell T. Fowler. NOBC

In Bloemfontein. Alan Ross. BoLoP

In Blue. David Chapman Berry. BXAP

In blue jeans & a sweater. I sat down & wrote. (LL) Sonnet 115: "All we were going strong last night this time." John Berryman. APAD; FaBoMo

In Blue-Stocking Hollow. Donald Davidson. FuPo

In Body healthy, and compos'd in Mind. Mary Leapor. See Mira's Will.

In body healthy, and composed in mind. (LL) Mira's Will. Mary Leapor. BWW; ECWP; NOEC; NoP-4; PEW

In bold letters. (LL) Can't Tell. Nellie Wong. LTA; OpBo

In Bondage. Claude McKay. PoBA

In bounty and peace remain. (LL) Kilcash. Unknown, Irish. BIrV; IIP; OBMV, tr. by Frank O'Connor

In bower and field he sought, where any tuft. Adam and Eve in the Garden. Milton. ITG, tr. by Robert Hass Fr. Book IX. FHYEP; NAEL-1; NAWM-1; OAEL-1 Fr. Paradise Lost.

In bowler hats and Sunday suits. Orange March. Richard Murphy. NOIV Fr. The Battle of Aughrim.

In boyhood's days we read with keen delight. The Printing-Press. Christopher Pearse Cranch. APN-1 Fr. Seven Wonders of the World.

In Breughel's great picture, The Kermess. William Carlos Williams. See The Dance.

In Brief. Angel Cuadra, Spanish. AF, tr. by Katherine Rodriguez Nieto

In bright succession raise, her Ornament and Guard! (LL) The Cotter's Saturday Night inscribed to Robert Aiken [or R. A****], Esq. Robert Burns. FaBoBe; NOBRP; PoLF

In brilliant gas light. Good Night. William Carlos Williams. SAmP

In Britain's isles, as Heylyn notes. Matthew Prior. NOEC Fr. Alma; or, The Progress of the Mind.

In broad daylight. Lament for Kepa Anaha Ehau. Arapeta Awatere, Maori. PeNZ, tr. by the author

In broad daylight I dream I. A Dream at Night. Mei Yao Ch'en, Chinese. BLT; OHPC, tr. by Kenneth Rexroth

In Broad Daylight I Dream of My Dead Wife. Mei Yao Ch'en, Chinese. OHPC, tr. by Kenneth Rexroth; OxBM

In Broken Images. Robert Graves. NoP-4; TRP

In Brueghel's great picture, The Kermess. The Dance. William Carlos Williams. AmPP; CMoP; HAP; HeIP-4; InPK-6; LiTM; MeMAP; MoP; NAAL-2; NIP-4; NOBA; NoAM; OxBA; PoE; Poetr; SAmP; SoSe-8; TAP; TFi

In Bruton Town there lived a farmer. Bruton Town. Unknown. EnSB

In bulging heads that crowd for miles the dazzling south. (LL) April, 1885. Robert Bridges. OxBSP; OxBTC

In Ca Mau. Horace Coleman. CDa

In cabin'd ships at sea. Walt Whitman. OxBoS

In cabinets of amethyst and frost. (LL) The Laurel Axe. Geoffrey Hill. NAEL-2; NoAM; PoE

In California. Donald Davie. NoAM

In California. Louis Simpson. WeT

In California / ankle-high animals occupy the tablelands. Report from California. Lois Moyles. NYBP

In California During the Gulf War. Denise Levertov. BAP-93

In California, north of the Golden Gate. Mendocino Rose. Garrett Kaoru Hongo. WeW-3

In calm and cool and silence, once again. First-Day Thoughts. John Greenleaf Whittier. APN-1; AmPP; TrCP

In calm fellowship they sleep. In a Grave-Yard. W. S. Braithwaite. PoBA

In came her sister. Lady Maisry. Unknown. ESPB; OxBB

In Camp. Jibanananda Das, Bengali. OMIP, tr. by Clinton B. Seely

In canary grass insects. Ethan Boldt. Roger Weingarten. AmPA

In candent ire the solar splendor flames. Aestivation [an Unpublished Poem, by My Late Latin Tutor]. Oliver Wendell Holmes. NOBL; OBAL Fr. The Autocrat of the Breakfast Table.

In Carmel Bay the people say. Abalone. Unknown. AS

In Carrowdore Churchyard. Derek Mahon. CIP-2; NoP-4; PBCIP; PNI

In Case. James Sherry.
"What should be the title of a king. Too, how also to include. What happened when." FTOS

In casual simplicity. (LL) How happy is the little Stone. Emily Dickinson. APN-2; RB

In catholic school. For Talking. Denise Nico Leto. UnSA

In caves with a single purpose. Fish and Chips on the Merry-Go-Round. K. O. Arvidson. PeNZ

In Ceaseless Rosemary. (LL) Essential oils—are wrung. Emily Dickinson. APN-2; AmPP; PBMP

In Celebration. Ellen Bass. NMM-2

In Celebration. Mark Strand. NoAM

In Celebration of My Uterus. Anne Sexton. CrSp; NALW

In Celebration of Spring. John Balaban. CDa

In Celia's face a question did arise. Lips and Eyes. Giovanni Battista Marino, Italian. OBVE; OxBSP, tr. by Thomas Carew

In Cemeteries. D. J. Enright. OxBC

In certain descriptions I notice certain words occur. Certainly Metaphysics. Asa Benveniste. NBrP

In Chalk Rooms. Aina Kraujiete, Latvian. CEEP, tr. by Inara Cedrins

In chamber low and scored by time. The Hostel. Herman Melville. APN-2 Fr. Clarel: A Poem and Pilgrimage in the Holy Land.

In Chapman's day poets had to write about Gods. On First Looking into Chapman's Homer II. Peter Peterson. BXAP

In chariot like an hibiscus flower at his side. Confucius. Fr. Songs of Cheng. CTC, tr. by Ezra Pound

In Cheever Country. Dana Gioia. GM

In Ch'i-an, on a Chance Theme. Tu Mu, Chinese.
"Setting sun is two rods high on the bridge over the brook, The." PLT, tr. by A. C. Graham

In Chicago, it is snowing softly. The Legend. Garrett Kaoru Hongo. LoL; NAmP90; OpBo; TRP; WWSi

In Chicago near the lake, on the North Shore. That Winter. Ruth Stone. BAP-93

In childhood it's easy to feel. Limerick. Nigel Andrew. PeLi

In childhood, never believed till now. (LL) The Snowfall. Donald Justice. CRP; Poetr; VGW

In childhood's sunny day my heart was taught to love. To Whittier. Josephine D. Henderson Heard. AAP; CBWP-4

In childhood's unsuspicious hours. Epicurean. William James Linton. EBVV

In China, / even the peasants. Lost Sister. Cathy Song. NoAM; PiM

In Choker's Lane, the doors appear. Choker's Lane. Kenneth Slessor. BMAP

In Chota Nagpur and Bengal. Tree Marriage. William Meredith. GLP

In Christ Church, Bristol, on Thomas Turner, Twice Master of the Company of Bakers. Francis, Lord Jeffrey Jeffrey. NBLV
(Epitaph in Christ Church, Bristol, on Thomas Turner, Twice Master of the Company of Bakers.) OxBoLi

In Chu hai, dead machine guns lie frozen in the sun. Chrome Babies Eating Chocolate Snowmen in the Moonlight. A. K. Redwing. VoR

In Church. Thomas Hardy. InPK-6; MoBrPo; SCV Fr. Satires of Circumstance in Fifteen Glimpses.

"In churches," said the Pardoner, "when I preach." Chaucer. See The Pardoner's Prologue.

In churches, when the infirmity [or the'infirmitie]. Donne. Fr. The Litanie. PoEL-2

In cinemas we sought. Sing, Brothers, Sing! William Robert Rodgers. MoBrPo

In Cipres springes [or Cyprus springs] (wheras [or whereas] dame Venus dwelt). Henry Howard, Earl of Surrey. AAS; SiPS

In cittie, nor on hill, but al the night must sleepe alone. Theocritus. See Neteheard.

In classic beauty, cold, immaculate. Mnemosyne. Madison Cawein. APN-2

In classical environs. Goliardic Song. Anthony Hecht. OBCoV

In clear stars bringing silver corn. Night Visits. "Chrystos." CPO

In climes beyond the solar road. Thomas Gray. OxAEP-1 Fr. The Progress of Poesy. AWP; GTBS-P; NOEC; OBEV

In cloaks of snow, hairs snow-white, and beaks of blue jade. Egrets. Tu Mu, Chinese. SuSp, tr. by Irving Y. Lo; APo, tr. by Irving Yucheng Lo

In Cloe's chamber, she and I. A Fragment. John Bancks. NOEC

In clouded Majesty here Dullness shone. Alexander Pope. See To Dr. Jonathan Swift.

In clouds drew on the evening's close. Evening, Gertrude. Anne Batten Cristall. ECWP

In Cnidus born, the consort I became. By Heraclides. Heraclitus of Halicarnassus, Greek. OBCVT; OBVE, tr. by William Cowper

In cock-wattle sunset or grey. Nostalgia. Louis MacNeice. OxAEP-2

In cold hell, in thicket, how. Charles Olson. PmAP; PoM

In cold rain at Kao-yu. Mooring at Night at Kao-yu. Wang Shih-chieng, Chinese. CoBLCP, tr. by Jonathan Chaves

In cold stiff soils the bleaters oft complain. Treating Sheep Ailments. John Dyer. ECEV Fr. The Fleece.

In Cold Storm Light. Leslie Marmon Silko. NoAM; VoR

In Colón I searched for my. Searching for Grandfather. Olive Senior. HCP

In colour, with their eyelids shut. (LL) A Martian Sends a Postcard Home. Craig Raine. NAEL-2; NoAM; NoP-4

In coming to the feast I found. The Horn. Léonie Adams. MoAmPo

In Commendation of George Gascoigne's Steel Glass. Sir Walter Ralegh. SiPS

  (Walter Rawley [*or* Ralegh *or* Rawely] of the Middle Temple, in Commendation of the Steel[e] Glass[e].) AAS

In Commendation of Music. William Strode. OBEV

In considering things gastronomic. Limerick. *Unknown.* PeLi

In Consort to Wednesday, Jan. 1st. 1701. Richard Henchman. SCAP

In contact, lo! the flint and steel. Alone. Ambrose Bierce. APN-2 *Fr.* The Devil's Dictionary.

In converse with the mountains, moors, and fens. (LL) Prelude: "Still south I went and west and south again." John Millington Synge. AWP; IIP; MoBrPo; OBMV

In Cool, Green Haunts. Mahlon Leonard Fisher. WeW-3

In cool seas of September click the stones. Reculver Bay. Vicki Raymond. NOBAu

In copious gulps of potent ale expires. (LL) The Birth of the Squire; an Eclogue. John Gay. NAEL-1; NOEC; PoEL-3

In corduroy trousers and seedy black coats. W. H. Auden. *Fr.* A Happy New Year. OBSV

In corridor and cubicle. Spring Song of A Civil Servant. James Keir Baxter. PeLV

In countless upward-striving waves. Nominalist and Realist. Ralph Waldo Emerson. APN-1

In court to serve, decked with fresh array. The Courtier's Life. Sir Thomas Wyatt. FaBoEE; NoSic

In Creve Coeur, Missouri. Rosanna Warren. PoPoPo

In Crisis. Lawrence Durrell. LiTM

In crisis you may know me. October Poem. Tamura Ryuichi, *Japanese.* AF, *tr. by* Christopher Drake

In Danger from the Outer World. Robert Bly. CAPP-1

In danger of which. Poem. Ray DiPalma. FTOS

In Dante's Hell. Geoff Page. OBCoV

In Darkness. Amir Gilbo'a, *Hebrew.* MHP, *tr. by* Ruth Finer Mintz

In daylight, even. The Countershadow. Philip Booth. NYBP

In Days Gone By. Hera Katene-Horvath. PeNZ

In Days Gone By. Ida M. Mills. BoTP

In days, my Lord, when mother Time. Soame Jenyns. OBSV *Fr.* An Epistle Written in the Country to the Right Honourable the Lord Lovelace.

In days of old, / So I've been told. The Feast of the Monkeys. John Philip Sousa. OBAL

In Days of Old, when *Englishmen* were— *Men,*. Horace. OBCVT, *tr. by* James Miller *Fr.* The Harlequin-Horace.

In days of old, when our fond mother earth. The Negro Meets to Pray. Daniel Webster Davis. AAP

In days of peace my fellow-men. From a Full Heart. A. A. Milne. NSI

In days of summer let me go. In Ampezzo. Trumbull Stickney. ColAP

In de dead of night I sometimes. The Old Cabin. Paul Laurence Dunbar. PoLF

In de Vinter Time. *Unknown.* AS

In dealing with time it is found. Limerick. V. R. Ormerod. PeLi

In Death Divided. Thomas Hardy. SCGP

In death I know well enough all things end in emptiness. To Show My Sons. Lu Yu, *Chinese.* CoBCP, *tr. by* Burton Watson

In Death Valley. Edwin Markham. APAD; APN-2; PaTW

In Death's Field. Al-Khansa, *Arabic.* BoWoP, *tr. by* Willis Barnstone

In Debtor's Yard the stones are hard. Oscar Wilde. NOBVV *Fr.* The Ballad of Reading Gaol. CABP; OBNV; OxAEP-2

In December, when the days draw to be short. Little John Nobody. *Unknown.* CBNP; OxBoLi

In deep distress, I cried to God. George Dyer. Ro

In deep Siberian mines retain. Message to Siberia. Aleksandr Sergeyevich Pushkin, *Russian.* AWP; TTY, *tr. by* Max Eastman

In Defence of Humanism. David Gascoyne. *See* Salvador Dali.

In Defence of Metaphysics. Charles Tomlinson. MoBrPo

In Defence of Poetry. Mafika Pascal Gwala. PeSAV

In Defence of Poetry. Ben Jonson. EPCY *Fr.* Every Man in His Humour.

In Defense of Black Poets. Conrad Kent Rivers. BPo

In Defense of Superficiality. Elder Olson. NYBP

In deference to the cloud parade. The Cloud Parade. Laura Jensen. LCAP-2

In degenerate times, people love extravagance. To Ch'eng Fei-t'ao. Wu Chia-chi, *Chinese.* CoBLCP, *tr. by* Jonathan Chaves

In Derision of a Country Life. Edward Ravenscroft. NOSC

In dese hard times. (LL) Negro Soldier's Civil War Chant. *Unknown.* BPo; TAP

In Despair. Constantine P. Cavafy, *Greek.* EP, *tr. by* Rae Dalven

In despair at not being able to rival the creations of God. Hymn to Her Unknown. Walter James Turner. OBMV

In detention / in concentration camps. Intifada. June Jordan. NAAAL

In Deya when the mist. The Island. Carolyn Forché. NMM-2

In dim green depths rot ingot-laden ships. Sunken Gold. Eugene Lee-Hamilton. GSo; NOBVV

In Dispraise of the Moon. Mary Elizabeth Coleridge. CH; PEW

In distant countries I have been. The Last of the Flock. Wordsworth. Ro

In distress, in the dark. Holy Is the Desire to Proclaim the Existence of God. Meir Wieseltier, *Hebrew.* IP, *tr. by* Warren Bargad *and* Stanley F. Chyet

In Distrust of Merits. Marianne Moore. ColAP; LiTM; MeMAP; MoAmPo; NAAL-2; OBWP; OxBA

In Divés' Dive. Robert Frost. GI; VGW *Fr.* Ten Mills.

In-doors and out,—summer and winter—Mirth. (LL) To the Grasshopper and the Cricket. Leigh Hunt. GSo; OBNC; OxAEP-2; Son

In drab derelict marsh near the madhouse. Charles Brasch. *Fr.* Home Ground. PeNZ

In dread, all that the clergy teach the young. (LL) The Straying Student. Austin Clarke. BIrV; CIP-2; NOIV

In dream I saw two Jews that met by chance. Moses and Jesus. Israel Zangwill. TrJP

In dream / the beavers come to. Seneca Journal 1: "A Poem of Beavers." Jerome Rothenberg. APSN

In Dream: The Privacy of Sequence. Ray A. Young Bear. CDW

In dreams I crossed a barren land. Ballade of Broken Flutes. Edwin Arlington Robinson. APN-2

In Dreamy Swoon. George Darley. OBNC *Fr.* Nepenthe.

In drear-nighted December. Keats. PoPoPo

In due course of course you will [all] be issued with. Unarmed Combat. Henry Reed. *Fr.* Lessons of the War. HeIP-4; OBWP

In due season the amphibious crocodile. Amphibious Crocodile. John Crowe Ransom. FuPo; OBAL

In Earliest Spring. William Dean Howells. APN-2; FaBoBe

  (Earliest Spring.) OBEV

In early days / If kings were made by men. Human Debasement; a Fragment. Edward Rushton. NOEC

In early morning twilight, raw and chill. The Eviction. William Allingham. BIrV; NOIV *Fr.* Laurence Bloomfield in Ireland.

In Early Summer Lodging in a Temple to Enjoy the Moonlight. Po Chü-i, *Chinese.* ChiP, *tr. by* Arthur Waley

In early youth's unclouded scene. Thirty-eight: Addressed to Mrs H—y. Charlotte Smith. ECWP; NALW; PEW; WPOW

In earth, air, water, plants, and other men. (LL) Large glooms were gathered in the mighty fane. James Thomson. EBEV; OAEL-2

In eastern sky. (LL) Wolfram's Dirge. Thomas Lovell Beddoes. NOBE; OBEV; OBNC; OxAEP-2; PoEL-4

In eastern village and western village. Silkworm Song of Torchlit Fields. Kao Ch'i, *Chinese.* CoBLCP, *tr. by* Jonathan Chaves

In eaves sole sparrow[e] sit[t]s not more alone. David's Peccavi. Robert Southwell. ChIV-1

In Ecclesiastes I read, "That which is far off and exceeding deep". J. P. White. ChIV-1

In Egypt they worshiped me. I Am the Cat. Leila Usher. BLPA

In Egypt we had the best time. World War II. Jeni Couzyn. PeSAV

In 8 is alle my love. *Unknown.* MiEL

In eighteen hundred and eighty nine. Obituary. Conrad Potter Aiken. OBAL

In eighteen hundred and forty-one. Working on the Railway. *Unknown.* APN-2

In 1898 Tahirassawichi went to Washington. Tahirassawichi in Washington. Ernesto Cardenal, *Spanish.* VCWP, *tr. by* Carlos Altschul *and* Monique Altschul; EC2

In 1861, George Hew sailed in a rowboat. The Network. Arthur Sze. AiP; OpBo

In elderis dayis, as Esope can declair. The Taill of the Foxe, That Begylit the Wolf, in the Schadow of the Mone. Robert Henryson. OxBS

In Emulation of Mr Cowleys Poem Call'd The Motto. Mary Astell. KTR; NOSC

In encampments. What the Servants Said to Him, as He Returned Home. Maturaittamilkkuttan Katuvan Mallanar, *Tamil.* PLW, *tr. by* A. K. Ramanujan

In encampments. What the Servants Said to him, as he returned home. Virrūrru Mūteyinanār, *Tamil.* PLW, *tr. by* A. K. Ramanujan

In England from the train you see. From the Train. Marjorie Wilson. BoTP

In England now I hear the window shake. At Home the Green Remains. John Figueroa. PBCV

In England's green and pleasant bowers. (LL) Epigraph. William Blake. OBNC; Spl

In England's green & pleasant Land. (LL) Jerusalem. William Blake. AWP; BoTP; CABP; ChIV-1; ClHu; EBEvV; FHYEP; FaBoCh; FaBoPV; FaPoR; HAP; HeIP-4; ImPo; InPS-3; NAEL-2; NAWM-2; NOBE; NOBRP; NOCV; OAEL-2; OBEV; ORNC; OnAEP-2, PoECV, PoE; PoEL-4; PoRA; RB; Ro; SCGP; TFi; UV

In Epping Forest. John Clare. *See* Stanzas from "Child Harold."

In Eternum ("In eternum I was once determed"). Sir Thomas Wyatt. AAS; NOBE; SiPS

In ethics class so many years ago. Ethics. Linda Pastan. InPK-6

In Europe, you can't move without going down into history. In the Yukon. Ralph Gustafson. MoCV; NoP-4

In even Will Hunter's hands. (LL) The Weepies. Paul Muldoon. NoAM; PNI

In Evening Air. Theodore Roethke. NYBP; TAP

In every dream thy lovely features rise. Sonnet. William Barnes. BoLoP; LBC

In every meanest face I see. Sons of Promise. Thomas Curtis Clark. PoToHe

In every old lady I chance to meet. Old Ladies. Will Allen Dromgoole. WeW-3

In every one be her great glory famed. (LL) In Honour of That High and Mighty Princess Queen Elizabeth of Happy Memory. Anne Bradstreet. NALW; NoP-4

In every part of every living thing. Lake Superior. Lorine Niedecker. FaBoWP

In everything you do. *Unknown.* CTV

In evil hour, and with unhallow'd voice. William Crowe. NOBRP

In evrich mart that stands on British ground. The School-Mistress. William Shenstone. NOEC

In ev'ry race, in ev'ry clime. Lines to a Graduate. Lizelia Augusta Jenkins Moorer. CBWP-3

In ev'ry town where Thamis rolls his tide. The Alley; an Imitation of Spenser. Alexander Pope. NOEC

In Exile. Emma Lazarus. APN-2

In Extremis. John Updike. OBCoV

In fact, what change? The chimney of the spine. In Retrospect. Richard Kenney. Son *Fr.* The Hours of the Day.

In fair Worcester City and in Worcestershire. The Gosport Tragedy. *Unknown.* AmFP

In faith, good Histor, long is your delay. Geron and Histor. Sir Philip Sidney. SiPS *Fr.* Arcadia.

In faith, I do[e] not love thee with mine eyes. Sonnet 151. Shakespeare. HeIP-4; OxAEP-1; PoEL-2 *Fr.* Sonnets.

In faith I not [well] what to say. Sir Thomas Wyatt. SiPS

In faith, Squier, thou hast thee wel yquit. Introduction to the Franklin's Prologue and Tale. Chaucer. NAEL-1 *Fr.* The Canterbury Tales.

In faith thou shalt haue mine. Robin Hood Rescuing Three Squires. *Unknown.* ESPB; EnSB

In fall we raked. The Winter Before the War. Walter McDonald. CDa

In fall, when afternoons begin. Near-Sightedness. Edmond Yi-teh Chang. OpBo

In fallow college days, Tom Harland. The Ballad of Lager Bier. Edmund Clarence Stedman. OBAL

In far-off England, years ago. Destiny. Eloise Bibb. CBWP-4

In Fargo, North Dakota, a man. To Flood Stage Again. James Wright. NOBA

In fascination of her brightness. (LL) Dome of Sunday, The [or A]. Karl Shapiro. CMoP; CoAP; LiTM; MoAMPo; NoAM; OxBA

In Favor of One's Time. Frank O'Hara. NeAP; PoA

In fear and trembling, I think I would fulfill my life. A Task. Czeslaw Milosz, *Polish.* AF, *tr. by* Czeslaw Milosz

In fear of the rich mouth. The Frightened Man. Louise Bogan. FaBoWP

In Februar come foul days, flee them gin ye may. The Anatomy of Winter. Hesiod, *Greek.* OBCVT, *tr. by* Robert Garioch

In February. P. A. Ropes. BoTP

In February I give you gallant sport. February. Folgore da San Geminiano. *Fr.* Sonnets of the Months. AWP, *tr. by* D. G. Rossetti

In feeling I was but a child. One Year Ago. Adah Isaacs Menken. CBWP-1

In Ferrara. John Jenkins *and* Ken Bolton. BMAP

In Festubert. Edmund Blunden. OBMV

In Fields of Summer. Galway Kinnell. VGW

In 15 minutes. California Peninsula: El Camino Real. Al Young. GT

In 'fifty, Congress passed a Bill. Elymas Payson Rogers. CBCWP *Fr.* A Poem on the Fugitive Slave Law.

In fire, on are the heat. Tirumal. Katuvan Ilaveyinanar, *Tamil.* PLW, *tr. by* A. K. Ramanujan

In fire-script. Thou Shalt Not. Malka Heifetz-Tussman, *Yiddish.* AWP, *tr. by* Marcia Falk

In First People's sky there is no moon. Raven/Moon. Anita Endrezze-Danielson. VoR

In flame and a clamorous breath known to the eye-pecking gulls. (LL) A Drifter off Tarentum. Rudyard Kipling. FaBoEE; NSI; PeFWW; PoWW

In Flanders fields in Northern France. A Square Dance. Roger McGough. NSI

In Flanders Fields the cannons boom. Another Reply to "In Flanders Fields." J. A. Armstrong. BLPA

In Flanders Fields the poppies blow. John McCrae. BLPA; CTV; ChAP; FaPoR; NOBC; NoP-4; OBWP; PeFWW; PoFWW; PoWW; SAGP

("In Flanders Fields.") (LL) CTV; ChAP; NoP-4; PoFWW; SAGP

In Fla[u]ndres whylom [or whilom] was a compa[ig]nye. The Pardoner's Tale. Chaucer. FHYEP; NAEL-1; OAEL-1; PoE *Fr.* The Canterbury Tales.

In Flaundres whilom was a compaignye. The Three Rioters. Chaucer. EBNV *Fr.* The Pardoner's Tale. FHYEP; NAEL-1; NAWM-1; OAEL-1; PoE *Fr.* The Canterbury Tales.

In Flavia's eyes is every grace. On Miss Eleanor Ambrose, a Celebrated Beauty in Dublin. Philip Dormer Stanhope, 4th Earl of Chesterfield. FaBoEE

In Flight. Jennifer Regan. CrSp

In flight in escape. Nelly Sachs, *German.* BoWoP, *tr. by* Arthur Wensinger

In-flight Note. Judith Rodriguez. BMAP

In flowed [or flow'd] at once a gay embroidered [or embroider'd] race. A Young Traveller Is Presented to the Goddess Dulness. Alexander Pope. NOEC *Fr.* Yet, yet a moment, one dim ray of light. NAEL-1; OAEL-1; PoEL-3 *Fr.* The Dunciad.

In fond delusion once I left thy side. A Sonnet to My Mother. Heinrich Heine. TrJP, *tr. by* Emma Lazarus

In Fond du Lac, Bronxville, Butte, Chicago. Last Year's Discussion: The Nobel Russian. Phyllis McGinley. FaBoEE

In forest shade my infant years trained up. Natural Religion. Robert Southey. Ro *Fr.* Joan of Arc.

In forgiving mood, this sultry July afternoon. Goodbye to Regal. Daniel Huws. NYBP

In form and feature, face and limb. The Twins. Henry Sambrooke Leigh. CTV

In former days we'd both agree. Bhartrihari, *Sanskrit.* BoLoP; LoP, *tr. by* John Brough

In former years I passed this city. Sha-ch'eng, "Sand City." Yang Shih-ch'i, *Chinese.* CoBLCP, *tr. by* Jonathan Chaves

In Fourteen Hundred and Ninety-. Adams Franklin Pierce. CTV

In fragrance. I can / eat as I go. (LL) Stepping Westward. Denise Levertov. CrSp; NALW; Poetr; VGW

In fragrant Dixie's arms. Church Burning: Mississippi. James A. Emanuel. PoBA

In Francum. Sir John Davies. FaBoEE
(Francus.) OBCoV

In Freedom's War, of "Thirty Years" and more. Enfant perdu. Heinrich Heine, *German.* AWP, *tr. by* Lord Houghton

In from the fields they come. The Harvesters. Mary Gilmore. NOBAu

In from the night. Answer Me. Adah Isaacs Menken. CBWP-1

In front of. Marlowe. *See* Doctor Faustus.

In Front of a Large Number of People. John Godfrey. FTOS

In front of Hua-yang cave, autumns pass like sleet. Drinking at the Cave Mouth. Tsung Ch'en, *Chinese.* CoBLCP, *tr. by* Jonathan Chaves

In front of me, the palings of a fence. For Signs. Thom Gunn. PoE

In front of my horse's head, I see Red Heart Station. Red Heart Station. Yang Shih-ch'i, *Chinese.* CoBLCP, *tr. by* Jonathan Chaves

In front of our mouths, wherever we swim. Goldfish on the Writing Desk. Max Brod, *German.* TrJP, *tr. by* Babette Deutsch *and* Avrahm Yarmolinsky

In front of the City Hotel in Kumasi. A Rock Thrown into the Water Does Not Fear the Cold. Audre Lorde. NAAL-2

In Front of the Landscape. Thomas Hardy. OBNC

In Front of the Mirror. Vladislav Felitsianovich Khodasevich, *Russian.* TCRP, *tr. by* Michael Frayn

In front / of the public housing project. Waiting for the Cops. Martín Espada. EC2

In front of the sombre mountains. On the Balcony. D. H. Lawrence. GBL; PoA

In full glare [or flare] I came here, man-tall but thin. The Roundhouse Voices. Dave Jeddie Smith. MT; NoAM; VCAP

In Fury and Terror. The Storm. Elizabeth Jane Coatsworth. OBCA

In Fuscum. Sir John Davies. FaBoEE

In futurity / I prophetic see. The Little Girl Lost. William Blake. FHYEP; NOBRP *Fr.* Songs of Experience.

In Gaetam. Thomas Bastard. FaBoEE

In gayer hours, when high my fancy ran. Richard Savage. NOEC; OBSV *Fr.* The Bastard.

In Genesis, Adam's the winner. Limerick. Bill Greenwell. PeLi

In Genesis, the world was made. Old Testament Contents. *Unknown.* BLPA

In Germany once lived a censor. The Ballad about the German Censor. "David Samuilovich Samoylov," *Russian.* TCRP, *tr. by* Lubov Yakovleva

In ghostlier demarcations, keener sounds. (LL) The Idea of Order at Key West. Wallace Stevens. CMoP; ColAP; HAP; HCAP; HeIP-4; MeMAP; MoAmPo; MoP; NAAL-2; NAWM-2; NIP-4; NOBA; NoAM; NoP-4; OxBA; PoE; PoPoPo; Poetr; SAmP; TAP; TFi

In Glasgow, in 'Eighty-four. In a Music-Hall. John Davidson. EBVV

In Glencullen. John Millington Synge. OBMV

In God alone my confidence do stay. (LL) It was the time, when rest, soft sliding downe. Joachim Du Bellay. AWP; Son

In God's Eternity. Hosea, I Ballou. AH

In going to my naked bed, as one that would have slept. Amantium Irae Amoris Redintegratio. Richard Edwards. OBEV; SCGP

In gold sandals. Sappho, *Greek.* BoWoP, *tr. by* Willis Barnstone

In Golden Gate Park that day. Lawrence Ferlinghetti. PmAP; RB

In gonia once which was Pata. Limerick. Arthur Shaw. PeLi

In good King Charles's golden days. The Vicar of Bray. *Unknown.* FaBoPV; NOBE; NOBL; OBCoV; OBSV; OxBoLi

In good old Stalin's early days. Garland for a Propagandist. Ted Pauker. NOBL

In gorgeous plumage, azure, gold and green. Peacocks: A Mood. Olive Custance. ADE

In Gosport of late a young damsel did dwell. The Gosport Tragedy. *Unknown.* AmFP

In Goya's greatest scenes we seem to see. Lawrence Ferlinghetti. HeIP-4; LiTM; NeAP; NoAM; PBMP; PmAP; PoM; TAP

In grade school I wondered. Zimmer in Grade School. Paul Zimmer. KaS; PBCAP

In Gratitude for Friends. Margaret Elizabeth Sangster. CTV

In graves where drips the winter rain. The Song of the Graves. *Unknown.* OBMV, *tr. by* Ernest Rhys *Fr.* The Black Book of Carmarthen.

In gray, battle-scarred Leningrad. The Enemy. Alice Walker. GT

In grey-haired Celia's withered arms. A Paraphrase from the French. Matthew Prior. OxBoLi; PeLV

In grief and anguish of my heart, my voice I did extend. The Song of Jonah in the Whale's Belly. Michael Drayton. ChIV-1

In Grief, Lamenting for My Elder Brother Ts'ang-ch. Hsieh Chin, *Chinese.* "I still remember Conch-Shell Slope, west of the River Tzu." CoBLCP, *tr. by* Jonathan Chaves

In grievous deity my cat. Startled into Life Like Fire. Charles Bukowski. PmAP

In grimy winter dusk / We slowed for a concrete platform. Stop. Richard Wilbur. LCAP-2

In haist ga hy thee to sum hoill. John Rolland. OxBS *Fr.* The Seven Seages.

In Hans' old mill his three black cats. Five Eyes. Walter De la Mare. PC

In hard / country. Hard Country. Philip Booth. CoAP

In Hardwood Groves. Robert Frost. HAP

In Harlem wandering from street to street. (LL) Harlem Shadows. Claude McKay. ColAP; NAAL

In Harmony with Kao "The Second" Ch'i's Poem "On Hearing a P'i-p'a Played Next Door." Hsü Pen, *Chinese.* CoBLCP, *tr. by* Jonathan Chaves

"In harmony with Nature?" Restless fool. Matthew Arnold. CABP

In harmony would you excel. A Cantata. Jonathan Swift. CBNP

In Hässelby. Evening Walk. Sonja [dA]kesson, *Swedish.* WPOW, *tr. by* Joanna Bankier

In haste one evening while making dinner. Potato. Jane Kenyon. AFr

In haste poste haste, when first my wandering [*or* wandring] mind[e]. No Hast But Good. George Gascoigne. AAS; NoSic; Son *Fr.* Gascoigne's Memories.

In Havenpool Harbour the ebb was strong. The Mongrel. Thomas Hardy. APo

In Hayden's Collage. Michael S. Harper. NAAAL

In he 50s, we drove each month to my uncle's house. Gambling. Vince Gotera. OpBo

In hearts at peace, under an English heaven. (LL) The Soldier. Rupert Brooke. APAD; CABP; EBEvV; FaPoR; GSo; HeIP-4; LiTM; MoBrPo; NAEL-2; NOBE; NSI; NoP-4; OBEV; OBWP; OxBTC; PeFWW; PoA; PoFWW; PoLF; PoRA; PoWW; Son; TFi; UV

In hearts like thine ne'er may I hold a place. Answer to ——'s Professions of Affection. Byron. OxBSP

In heart's space hath Eros. Meleager, *Greek.* GrAn, *tr. by* Peter Whigham

In Heaven. Ssu-k'ung Shu, *Chinese.* SuSp, *tr. by* Irving Y. Lo

In Heaven a spirit doth dwell. Israfel. Edgar Allan Poe. APN-1; AWP; AmPP; ImPo; MeMAP; NAAL-1; NAAL-3; NOBA; OxBA; PAR; PoE; PoEL-4; TAP

In heaven-high musings and many. The Strength of Fate. Euripides. *Fr.* Alcestis.

In heaven soaring up, I dropped [*or* dropt] an ear[e]. The Joy of Church Fellowship Rightly Attended. Edward Taylor. AH; AmPP; MeMAP; NAAL-1; NAAL-3; OxBA; SCAP *Fr.* God's Determinations [touching his Elect].

In Heaven / Some little blades of grass. The Blades of Grass. Stephen Crane. MoAmPo *Fr.* The Black Riders [and Other Lines].

In Heaven [*or* Heav'n], their earthy [*or* earthly] bodies left behind. (LL) Song: "If to be absent were to be." Richard Lovelace. BeJo; CBLP; CaPo; CavPo; FMP; GTBS-P; MeLP; NOSC; OBEV; OxAEP-1; SeCP

In heaven, too. Heard in a Violent Ward. Theodore Roethke. HCAP

In heavenly realms of hellas dwelt. E. E. Cummings. NOBA; OBSV

In heav'n above, in earth and air, / And in the vast profound!, *par. by* Christopher Smart. Bible, *O.T. See* Psalm 8.

In heavy drink and in love. Atlantis. Slavko Mihalic. PoSu, *tr. by* Charles Simic

In Heavy Mind. James Agee. MoAmPo

In hell, maximum sea. Fresco. Martin Sorescu, *Romanian.* VCWP, *tr. by* Enright, D. J. and Joana Russell-Gebbett

In hell the sinners. Fresco. Martin Sorescu, *Romanian.* CEEP, *tr. by* Irina Livezeanu

In hell, which has / an easy chair. (LL) What Hell Is. Heather McHugh. CrSp; WeT

In her boudoir, the young lady—unacquainted with grief. *Unknown, Chinese.* OBVE, *tr. by* Arthur Waley

In her cloak and hat. Elizabeth Anna Hart. *See* Mother Tabbyskins.

In her gnarled sleep it. The Cherry Tree. Thom Gunn. GLP; Poetsp

In her hand the knife, brisk, brilliant as moon-claw. Cleaning a Fish. Dave Jeddie Smith. NoAM

In her old voice the mountains. Marlene Mountain. HA

In Her Only Way. Robert Graves. OxBSP *Fr.* Three Songs for the Lute.

In her ornate tower by bright moonlight always she thinks of him, Tune: "Deva-like Barbarian." Tune: Deva-like Barbarian. Wen T'ing-yün, *Chinese.* CoBCP, *tr. by* Burton Watson

In Her Own Image. Eavan Boland. PBCIP

In her own isle's remotest grove. The Temple of Venus. Soame Jenyns. NOEC

In Her Praise. Robert Graves. BIrV

In Her Prison. Sarah Morgan Bryan Piatt. NCAP

In her room at the prow of the house. The Writer. Richard Wilbur. HCAP; ImGa; MoLi; NoAM; OxBC; PoPoPo; Poetr; SoSe-8

In Her Song She Is Alone. Jon Swan. NYBP

In her storefront living room. The Palm Reader. Nicholas Christopher. NoP-4

In her tomb by the sounding sea. (LL) Annabel Lee. Edgar Allan Poe. AWP; AiP; BLPA; CH; ChAP; EBEvV; GEA; GLoP; HeIP-4; ImPo; NAAL-1; NAAL-3; NCAP; OBCA; OBSP; TFi

'In here,' our teacher said. Owl. Ted Walker. NOxBChV

In hermetic enclosure. Jacques Rabémanganjara. NegPo, *tr. by* Ellen Conroy Kennedy *Fr.* Lamba.

In hermit's robe, clean and simple. Ch'ien Ch'ien-i. *Fr.* Miscellaneous Feelings at West Lake. CoBLCP, *tr. by* Jonathan Chaves

In Hexameter sings serenely a Harvard Professor. Couplet: February 24, 1847. Henry Wadsworth Longfellow. APN-1

In Heytesbury Wood. Siegfried Sassoon. OBGa

In High Places. Harriet Monroe. PoA

In high school I had a friend. Domingo Limón. Alberto A. Ríos. BAP-96

In high spirits a gang. Maple Leaves. Yun-gi Hong, *Korean.* CKP, *tr. by* Jaihiun Kim

In highest walk of heav'n the sun did ride. Sonnet 22. Sir Philip Sidney. Son *Fr.* Astrophil and Stella. AAS; SiPS

In Him We Live [& Move & Have Our Being]. Jones Very. APN-1; OxBA

In his blue suit, an Oxford Standard Authors. Study in Blue. Evan Jones. NOBAu

In his country. What She Said. Orampokiyar, *Tamil.* PLW, *tr. by* A. K. Ramanujan

In his country. What She Said to Her Girl Friend. Kapilar, *Tamil.* PLW, *tr. by* A. K. Ramanujan

In his country of cool seas, they say. What She Said. Ceyti Valluvan Peruncattan, *Tamil.* PLW, *tr. by* A. K. Ramanujan

In His face they spit their icy scorn. New Negro Sermon. Jacques Roumain, *French.* NegPo, *tr.* by Ellen Conroy Kennedy

In his father's face flying. Icarus. Ronald Bottrall. GTBS-P

In his fields. What She Said ("In his fields"). Orampokiyar. *Fr.* Five on the Crabs. PLW, *tr.* by A. K. Ramanujan

In his fields, mother. What Her Girl friend Said to the Foster-Mother. Orampokiyar. PLW *Fr.* Five on the Crabs. PLW, *tr.* by A. K. Ramanujan

In his great tidal movements round the earth. (LL) Ireland. John Hewitt. CIP-2; IIP

In his grief. While at Prayer. Abba Kovner, *Hebrew.* IP, *tr.* by Warren Bargad *and* Stanley F. Chyet

In his low-ceilinged oaken room. The Silent Room. Kingsley Amis. OxBC

In his own image the Creator made. On Man. Walter Savage Landor. OBNC

In his place, mother / field-crabs cut into the pink. What She Said. Orampokiyar. PLW *Fr.* Five on the Crabs. PLW, *tr.* by A. K. Ramanujan

In his place, mother, / mud-spattered spotted crabs. What She Said. Orampokiyar, *Tamil.* PLW, *tr.* by A. K. Ramanujan *Fr.* Five on the Crabs. PLW, *tr.* by A. K. Ramanujan

In his portrait of Carlyle, Whistler builds. After Whistler. Stanley Plumly. LCAP-2

In his private derelict sandlorry / named *Albion.* Geoffrey Hill. *See* Gasholders, russet among fields. Mildams, marpools.

In his sea-lit / distance, the pitcher winding. The Double-Play. Robert Wallace. CMAP; PFE

In his tall senatorial. The Drum; the Narrative of the Demon of Tedworth. Dame Edith Sitwell. FaBoTw

In his unweeting way. (LL) New Year's Eve. Thomas Hardy. MoBrPo; NoAM

In his vast miscellaneous works we find. *Unknown.* EPCY

In his voice that made my nipples stand out straight. (LL) At Sixteen. Ann Darr. DeD; LW

In his wedding band watching the clouds pass. Alexis Rotella. HA

In his winged collar. Japanese Jokes. Peter Porter. OBCoV

In history's mysteries vast. Limerick. *Unknown.* PeLi

In holiday gown, and my new-fangled hat. Holiday Gown. John Cunningham. ECEV

In honey essenced bliss of sleep's deceit. The Garden of Joy. Isaac Rosenberg. GaP

In honnour of this heghe fest, of custume yere by yere. A Lover's New Year's Gift. John Lydgate. PoEL-1

In Honor of David Anderson Brooks, My Father. Gwendolyn Brooks. MoLi

In Honor of that High and Mighty Princess, Queen Elizabeth, of Most Happy Memory. Anne Bradstreet. *See* In Honour of That High and Mighty Princess Queen Elizabeth of Happy Memory.

In Honour of Dorian and his Creator. Lionel Pigot Johnson, *Latin.* ADE, *tr.* by Ian Fletcher

In Honour of St. Alphonsus Rodriguez. Gerard Manley Hopkins. EBEV; OxAEP-2

In Honour of St. David's Day. *Unknown.* OBWVE

In Honour of Taffy Topaz. Christopher Darlington Morley. WHSW

In Honour of That High and Mighty Princess Queen Elizabeth of Happy Memory. Anne Bradstreet. NALW

(In Honor of that High and Mighty Princess, Queen Elizabeth, of Most Happy Memory.) NoP-4

In Honour of the Holy Spirit. Hildebert, *Latin.* MLL, *tr.* by Helen Waddell

In horse latitudes sailors once lashed. Horse Latitudes. Frankie Paino. NAmP90

In Hospital. James Elroy Flecker. OxBTC

In Hospital. William Ernest Henley.

Before. MoBrPo

Waiting. NAEL-2; NOBVV

In Hospital. Frank O'Hara. LCAP-2

In Hospital: Poona (1). Alun Lewis. OBWVE

In hospital where windows meet. A Lady of Quality. Thomas Kinsella. PBCIP

In Hsü-chou, in the District of Ku-fêng. Chu Ch'ên Village. Po Chü-i, *Chinese.* ChiP, *tr.* by Arthur Waley

In Hung-fu Monastery we brush off the dust from purple window gauze. Passing Hung-fu Monastery with Yüan-ming: Inscribed in Jest. Huang T'ing-chien, *Chinese.* SuSp, *tr.* by Michael E. Workman

In idle August, while the sea soft. Derek Walcott. NoP-4

In Illness, Dismissing My Singing Girl. Ssu-k'ung Shu, *Chinese.* CoBCP, *tr.* by Burton Watson

("Ten thousand things wound my heart when you're before my eyes.") CoBCP, *tr.* by Burton Watson

In Illyria, the love-sick Orsino. Limerick. Stanley J. Sharpless. PeLi

In Imitation. Larry Eigner. FTOS

In Imitation of Anacreon. Matthew Prior. FaBoEE

In Imitation of Ancient Songs. Li Po, *Chinese.* SuSp, *tr.* by Joseph J. Lee

In Imitation of Ancient-style Poetry. Pao Chao, *Chinese.* SuSp, *tr.* by Daniel Bryant

In Imitation of Horace. Aphra Behn. KTR; NOSC

In Imitation of Hsü Kan ("Since you went away"). Liu Chün, *Chinese.* SuSp, *tr.* by Jan W. Walls

In Imitation of T'ao P'eng-tse. Wei Ying-wu, *Chinese.* SuSp, *tr.* by Irving Y. Lo

In Imitation of "The King of Huai-nan." Pao Chao, *Chinese.* CoBCP, *tr.* by Burton Watson

In India. Karl Shapiro. NYBP

In India lives a bird that is unique. Farid-uddin Attar. *Fr.* The Conference of the Birds. TOF, *tr.* by Afkham Darbandi *and* Dick Davis

In innocence I said. James Vincent Cunningham. OxBSP

In Ireland [or Irlaunde or Irlonde]. (LL) I Am from Ireland. *Unknown.* EnVB; FaBoCh; GEA; HAP; IIP; MiEL; NOBE; OBEV; OPOU; PoEL-1; SCGP

In Ireland. Arthur Symons.

By the Pool at the Third Rosses. ADE; OBNC

In Ireland: By the Pool at the Third Rosses. Arthur Symons. OBNC

In Ireland, we're all of us just. The Deadly Seven. Sydney Bernard Smith. PeLi

In it there is a dream. A Girl's Head. Katherine Gallagher. NOBAu

In it there is a space-ship. A Boy's Head. Miroslav Holub, *Czech.* CBNP, *tr.* by Ian Milner *and* George Theiner

In Italy a man's name, here a woman's. How I Changed My Name, Felice. Felix Stefanile. UnSA

In Italy, where this sort of thing can occur. A Hill. Anthony Hecht. CoAP; GEA; NYBP; NoP-4; VCAP

In its absence it has become beautiful. The Glove. Harold Bond. NYBP

In its first dumb form. Susan Howe. FTOS *Fr.* Secret History of the Dividing Line.

In its going down, the moon. Poem. Robert Hoggra. MoCV

In-itself and for-itself, The. Song for the In-Itself and For-Itself. Henry Weinfield. BAP-94

In January, 1962. Ted Kooser. Poetsp

In Jazz Rhythms. Janina Degutyte, *Lithuanian.* CEEP, *tr.* by M. G. Slavenas

In Jersey City where I did dwell. The Butcher Boy. *Unknown.* AmFP

In Jimmy's Garden. Quincy Troupe. GT

In jolly "hans around." (LL) October's Party. George Cooper. BoTP; PoLF

In joy, that our lives / are so familiar. (LL) Return of the Native. Imamu Amiri Baraka. APSN; BPo; ColAP

In joye withouten hende. / Amen. *Unknown.* See Ubi Sunt Qui ante Nos Fuerunt? [or Contempt of the World].

In joyous Summer, when the exulting earth. The Lament of the Forest. Thomas Cole. APN-1

In Judgment of the Leaf. Kenneth Patchen. CLPP; VGW

("In the earth of your eyes, in easy wonder building a new god.") (LL) CLPP

In July month, ae bonny morn. My Winsome Dear. Robert Fergusson. VGW *Fr.* Leith Races.

In jumping and tumbling. Tumbling. *Unknown.* ACTP; OxBChV

In June, amid the golden fields. The Groundhog. Richard Eberhart. CMoP; FaBoMo; ImPo; LiTM; MoAmPo; MoP; NoAM; RaBo; TAP; TFi; TRP; UnPo

In June and Gentle Oven. Anne Wilkinson. MoCV; NOBC

In June, examiners. The Grand Central Hotel. Roy McFadden. PNI

In June I give you a close-wooded fell. June. Folgore da San Geminiano. *Fr.* Sonnets of the Months. AWP, *tr.* by D. G. Rossetti

In June the sun is a bonnet of light. Sun. Gary Soto. TRP

In June was a jar had. Robert Kelly. FTOS

In just a Country Town. (LL) There's been a Death, in the Opposite House. Emily Dickinson. APN-2; InPS-3; MeMAP; SAmP; SoSe-8

In just an instant mist and cloud. Inscribed on "Drunk in the Autumn Woods." Tao-chi, *Chinese.* CoBLCP, *tr.* by Jonathan Chaves

In Just- / spring when the world is mud-. E. E. Cummings. AmPP; FaBoVe; HeIP-6; InPK-6; MoAmPo; NAAL-2; NIP-4; NoP-4; Poetr; SoSe-8; WeW-3

("BalloonMan whistles / far / and / wee.") (LL) NOxBChV; NoP-4

("Far / and / wee.") (LL) PoPoPo

("Spring when the world is mud.") NOxBChV; PoPoPo

In Kansas. Carter Revard. HATNAP

In Kenscoff Market the breeze brought spices. Kenscoff. Lorna Goodison. GT

In Kensington Gardens. Arthur Symons. EnLoPo

In Kerry. John Millington Synge. GBL; MoBrPo

In Köhln [Köln], a town of monks and bones. Cologne. Coleridge. FaBoEE; NBLV; PBMP

In kraals of slanting shade the herd. Buffalo. Charles Eglington. PeSA

In La Mancha he mopeth. The Rusty Man. Herman Melville. NCAP

In Laddery Street Herself. Laura Riding Jackson. *Fr.* Forgotten Girlhood. RB

In Lady Lusher's drawing-room, where float the strains of Brahms. The Martyred Democrat. C. J. Dennis. CBAP

In lamplight, I open your book, and start to weep. Lamenting for Kao Ch'ing-ch'iu, Chi-ti. Chang Yü, *Chinese.* CoBLCP, *tr. by* Jonathan Chaves

In Lamplight, Watching My Wife Preparing a Flower Arrangement—Playfully Inscribing Four Poems. Ch'ien Ch'ien-i, *Chinese.* CoBLCP, *tr. by* Jonathan Chaves

In Language. Eugene Gloria. OpBo

In Lantana Street's mid-morning. At the Nature-Strip. Judith Rodriguez. CBAP

In Larch Wood. Larch Wood Secrets. Ivy O. Eastwick. BoTP

In Late Spring of the Year *Keng-hsü* (1790), I Stayed at the Sun Family's Gemstone Mountain Villa at West Lake. Before Leaving, I Wrote These Poems as Mementos. Yüan Mei, *Chinese.* CoBLCP, *tr. by* Jonathan Chaves

In late sun, the beauty of river and hill. Chüeh-chü. Tu Fu, *Chinese.* CoBCP, *tr. by* Burton Watson

In late winter. The Bear. Galway Kinnell. CoAP; ColAP; InPS-3; NNaP; TAP; TRP; VCAP; VGW

In late years, I love only the stillness. To Subprefect Chang. Wang Wei, *Chinese.* SuSp, *tr. by* Irving Y. Lo

In leaf after leaf we seem to hear the sighing of the wind. Wu Chen. *Fr.* Poems Inscribed on Paintings of Bamboo. CoBLCP, *tr. by* Jonathan Chaves

In length of days and soundness of limb you and I are one. To Liu Yü-hsi. Po Chü-i, *Chinese.* ChiP, *tr. by* Arthur Waley

In Lesbiam. Martial, *Latin.* OBCVT, *tr. by* R. Fletcher

In letters of gold on T'ang's bathtub. The Great Digest. Confucius. PFTM *Fr.* The Great Digest.

In Librum. Sir John Davies. FaBoEE

In Lieu. Louis MacNeice. CMoP

In life I stroll the capital city. Poem in the Form of a Coffin-Puller's Song. Miu Hsi, *Chinese.* CoBCP, *tr. by* Burton Watson

In life three ghostly friars were we. The Ghosts. Thomas Love Peacock. OBCoV

In life's rough-and-tumble. To Margo. Gavin Ewart. APAD

In light, and nothing else, awake. (LL) At the San Francisco Airport. Yvor Winters. AiP; HeIP-4; InPK-6; NIP-4; NOBA

In Light of Time. Heather McHugh. CMAP

In lily ponds, the plump colorful buds. What the Concubine Said When She Heard the Wife Complain about the Concubine's Wiles. Villakaviralinar, *Tamil.* PLW, *tr. by* A. K. Ramanujan

In Limbo. Richard Wilbur. AFr

In Line at the Supermarket. Greg Pape. PBCAP

In little hands she holds an open book. Mani Leib, *Yiddish.* CEEP, *tr. by* Keith Bosley

In Little Rock the people bear. The Chicago *Defender* Sends a Man to Little Rock. Gwendolyn Brooks. CrDW; NAAAL; PoBA; Poetr

In London city was Bicham born. Young Beichan. *Unknown.* ESPB

In London City where I once did dwell, there's where I got my learning. Barbra Allen. *Unknown.* AS

In London / every now and then. Like a Beacon. Grace Nichols. OPOU

In London here the streets are grey, an' grey the sky above. Irish Skies. Winifred M. Letts. TIRV

In London I never know what to be at. Country and Town. Charles Morris. NOEC

In London stands a famous pile. A South Sea Ballad. Edward Ward. OBCoV

In London there I was bent. London Lickpenny. *Unknown.* OBSV

In London Town. Mary Elizabeth Coleridge. VWP

In looking o'er the prospects. The Prospect of the Future. Mrs. Henry Linden. CBWP-4

In Lord Carpenter's Country. Barry O. Higgs. PeSA

In Los Angeles / while the mountains cleared of smog. Tongue-tied in Black and White. Michael S. Harper. HCAP

In Love. David Wevill. MoCV

In love are we made visible. In Love Made Visible. May Swenson. NMM-2

In Love For Long. Edwin Muir. BoLoP; LiTM; LoP; MoBrPo

In love longing / I listen to the monk's bell. At the Sutra Chanting of Her Dead Daughter. Lady Izumi, *Japanese.* WPJ, *tr. by* Kenneth Rexroth *and* Ikuko Atsumi

In Love Made Visible. May Swenson. NMM-2

In love to be sure what disasters we meet. The Lover's Arithmetic. *Unknown.* CBNP; OxBoLi; PeLV

In love with none, but me. (LL) A Conjuration, to Electra. Robert Herrick. GBL; PoEL-3

In Love with the Bears. Greg Kuzma. NYBP

In Love with Wholes. Alberta Turner. LCAP-2

In Love with You. Kenneth Koch. CAPP-1

In Love's name you are charged: oh, fly [*or* charged hereby]. Love's Hue and Cry. James Shirley. BeJo

In love's name, Your emissary. (LL) The Gift. Louise Glück. FaBoWP; FiLi

In love's rubber armor I come to you. Love Sonnet. John Updike. Son

In loving, each one hath free choice. Isabella Whitney. *Fr.* Sweet Nosegay, A, or Pleasant Posy. WPE

In loving thee thou know'st I am forsworn. Sonnet 92. Shakespeare. HeIP-4 *Fr.* Sonnets.

In lowly dale, fast by a river's side. The Land of Indolence. James Thomson. NOEC *Fr.* The Castle of Indolence.

In lungs fresh like honeycomb. Indian. Laura Jensen. AmPA

In Lupum. Martial, *Latin.* OBCVT, *tr. by* William Cartwright

In lurid cartoon colors, the big baby. Eden. Emily Grosholz. FFC; RA

In Magic Words. Merrill Moore. Son

In man, ambition is the common'st thing. Ambition. Robert Herrick. CaPo

In Manchester there are a thousand puddles. Watch Your Step—I'm Drenched. Adrian Mitchell. RB

In Manchester today a man was seen. Here is the News. Michael Rosen. OBSP

In man's cannot be right. (LL) A Double Standard. Frances Ellen Watkins Harper. AAP; BlSi; CrDW; NAAAL; PWR

In Mantua-territory half is slough. Robert Browning. EBVVPR *Fr.* Sordello.

In many a village churchyard's simple grave. Obscurity of Woman's Worth. Caroline Elizabeth Norton. VWP

In marble walls [*or* halls] as white as milk. Mother Goose. OxNR

In March and April, thereabout. Alison. *Unknown.* HAP

In March birds couple, a new birth. The Leaves Come Again. Henry Vaughan, *sometimes at.* to Thomas Stanley. FaBoEE

In March I give you plenteous fisheries. March. Folgore da San Geminiano. *Fr.* Sonnets of the Months. AWP, *tr. by* D. G. Rossetti

In March the seed. Mater Dei. Padraic Fallon. NOCV

In Marion, the honey locust trees are falling. Two Poems about President Harding. James Wright. CoAP; MoP; WeT

In martial sports I had my cunning tried. Sonnet 53. Sir Philip Sidney. NAEL-1; NoSic *Fr.* Astrophil and Stella. AAS; SiPS

In math I was the whiz kid, keeper. Flash Cards. Rita Dove. LoL; PoPoPo

In mathematic[k]s he was greater. Samuel Butler. NOBL *Fr.* Hudibras.

In matters of commerce the fault of the Dutch. The Dutch. George Canning. OxBoLi; PeLV

In May. John Millington Synge. MoBrPo; SAGP

In May, approaching the city, I. The Ritualists. William Carlos Williams. NYBP

In May I go a-walking. *Unknown.* BoTP

In May it muryeth when it dawes. *Unknown.* MiEL

In May, that moder is of monthes glade. Chaucer. EnVB *Fr.* Troilus and Criseyde [*or* Criseide]. EnVB

In May, when sea-winds pierced our solitudes. Rhodora, The [On Being Asked Whence Is the Flower]. Ralph Waldo Emerson. APN-1; AWP; AmPP; GEA; MeMAP; NAAL-1; NAAL-3; NOBA; NoP-4; OxBA; PAR; PFE; PWR; PoE; TAP; TFi

In Me, Past, Present, Future Meet. Siegfried Sassoon. OBEV; OxBSP

In me something glimpsed its occasion. Passing Through. Patrick Williams. PNI

In me there is a vast and lonely place. Zora Cross. *Fr.* Love Sonnets. CBAP

In meantime flew our ships, and straight we fetch'd. George Chapman. OxBoS *Fr.* Homer's Odysseys.

In meetin' come nex' Sunday. (LL) The Courtin'. James Russell Lowell. AmPP; NOBA; OBAL

In melancholic fancy. Hallo My Fancy. William Cleland. CH; OxBoLi

In Memorial. J. Gordon Coogler. OBAL

In Memoriam. Bernard Dadié, *French.* NegPo, *tr. by* Ellen Conroy Kennedy

In Memoriam. W. J. Gruffydd, *Welsh.* OBWVE, *tr. by* R. Gerallt Jones

In Memoriam. A. B. L. Hodgson. NSI

In Memoriam. Martin Johnston. BMAP; NOBAu

In Memoriam. Michael Longley. PNI

In Memoriam[, Private D. Sutherland]. Ewart Alan Mackintosh. PoWW

In Memoriam. Léopold Sédar Senghor. PBMAP

In Memoriam. John Skoyles. CMAP
In Memoriam [Easter 1915]. Edward Thomas. *See* In Memoriam (Easter, 1915),
In Memoriam: A. C., R. J. O., K. S. John Betjeman. *Fr.* Old Friends. FP
In Memoriam A. H. H. Tennyson.
   "And bask'd and batten'd in the woods." (LL) CABP
   "Oh yet we trust that somehow good.) CABP
   "That reach thro' nature, moulding men." (LL) CABP
   "Again at Christmas did we weave." EBVV; IMW; OAEL-2; PChr; PeECV
   ("And calmly fell our Christmas-eve.") (LL) PChr
"And all is well, though [*or* tho'] faith and form." EBVVPR; OAEL-2
And buds and blossoms like the rest. EBVV; FHYEP; GTBS-P; NOBE; OBNC
"And was the day of my delight." OAEL-2
"As sometimes in a dead man's face." ImPo
"By night we lingered [*or* linger'd] on the lawn." EBVV; EnVR; FHYEP; HAP; OAEL-2; OBNC; PeECV; PoEL-5; TOF
   "Till now the doubtful dusk reveal'd." GTBS-P
"Contemplate all this work of Time." EBVV; EnVR; OAEL-2
"Dark house, by which once more I stand." EBEV; EBVV; EBVVPR; EnVR; FHYEP; GTBS-P; HAP; HeIP-4; ImPo; NOBE; OAEL-2; OBNC; PoEL-5; SCGP; SCV; SoSe-8; UnPo
"Dear friend, far off, my lost desire." EBVVPR; FHYEP; OAEL-2
"Dip down upon the northern shore." EBVV
"Do we indeed desire the dead." EBVVPR; EnVR; OAEL-2
"Doors, where my heart was used to beat." EnVR; FHYEP; OBNC; PoEL-5; SCV
"Fair ship, that from the Italian shore." EBVV; EBVVPR; EnVR; OAEL-2
"From art, from nature, from the schools." OAEL-2
"Happy lover who has come, A." EBVVPR; EnVR
"How many a father have I seen." EBVVPR; EnVR
"I cannot love thee as I ought." EBVVPR; EnVR
"I cannot see the features right." ImPo; PoEL-5
"I climb the hill: from end to end." EBVV; FHYEP; PoEL-5
"I dreamed there would be Spring no more." NOBE
"I hear the noise about thy keel." EBVV; EnVR
"I held it truth, with him who sings." EBVV; EBVVPR; EnVR; HeIP-4; OAEL-2; OBNC
"I shall not see thee. Dare I say." OxBSn
"I sing to him that rests below." OAEL-2
"I sometimes hold it half a sin." EPCY; EnVR; IMW; OAEL-2; PeECV; TOF
"I trust I have not wasted breath." EnVR; FHYEP; OAEL-2
"I wage not any feud with Death." ImPo
"If any vision should reveal." OxBSn
"If Sleep and Death be truly one." OBNC; PeECV
In Memoriam.
   ("From all the circle of the hills.") (LL) OBGa
"In those sad words I took farewell." EnVR
"Is it, then, regret for buried time." FHYEP
"It is the day when he was born." EBVV; FHYEP
"Love that rose on stronger wings, The." EBVVPR
"More than my brothers are to me." OAEL-2
"My own dim life should teach me this." EnVR; FHYEP; OAEL-2
"O days and hours, your work is this." PeECV
"O Sorrow, cruel fellowship." EBVVPR; EnVR; HAP; OAEL-2
"O thou that after toil and storm." PeECV
"O true and tried, so well and long." OAEL-2
   "O happy hour, and happier hours." EnVR
Of One Dead. ImPo
"Old warder of these buried bones." PeECV; PoEL-5
"Old yew, which graspest at the stones." EBVV; EBVVPR; EnVR; GTBS-P; NOBE; OAEL-2; OBNC; PoEL-5; UnPo
"On that last night before we went." EBVV; OAEL-2; PoEL-5
"One writes, that 'Other friends remain'." EnVR; PoEL-5
"Path by which we twain did go, The." EBVV; PeECV; SCV
"Peace; come away: the song of woe." EBVV; EBVVPR; EnVR; FHYEP; IMW
Ring Out the Old, Ring In the New.
"Risest thou thus, dim dawn, again." EBVV; OBNC; PeECV; PoEL-5
"Sad Hesper o'er the buried sun." EBVV; EnVR
"'So careful of the type?' but no." EBVV; EBVVPR; EnVR; FHYEP; HAP; OAEL-2; OBNC; TOF
Somersby, Lincolnshire; after Leaving the Refectory.
   ("Unwatched, the garden bough shall sway.") GaP

"Strong Son of God, immortal Love." EBVV; EBVVPR; EnVR; HAP; NAWM-2; OAEL-2; TrCP
"Sweet after showers, ambrosial air." EBVV
"There rolls the deep where grew the tree." HAP; NOBE; OAEL-2
"Thou comest, much wept for: such a breeze." EBVV; PeECV
"Though truths in manhood darkly join." OAEL-2
"Thy voice is on the rolling air." EBVV; EBVVPR; FHYEP; HeIP-4; OAEL-2
"Time draws near the birth of Christ, The." EBVV; EBVVPR; FHYEP; NOCV; OAEL-2; PChr; SoSe-8
   ("Peace and goodwill, to all mankind.") (LL) PChr
"Time draws near the birth of Christ, The." EBVV; OAEL-2
"'Tis well, 'tis something; we may stand." EBVV
To-night the Winds Begin. EBVV; GTBS-P; ImPo; NOBE; OAEL-2; OBNC; PeECV; PoEL-5
"To Sleep I give my powers away." EnVR
"Tonight ungathered let us leave." EBVV; FHYEP; OAEL-2
"Urania speaks with darkened brow." OAEL-2
"We leave the well-beloved place." EBVV; FHYEP; PoEL-5
"What hope is here for modern rhyme." EnVR
"What words are these have fallen from me?" EBEV
"When Lazarus left his charnel-cave." EBVV; FHYEP; OAEL-2; PeECV; TOF
"When on my bed the moonlight falls." OAEL-2; PeECV; SCGP
"When rosy plumelets tuft the larch." FHYEP; OBNC
"Wish, that of the living whole, The." EBVV; EBVVPR; EnVR; FHYEP; HAP; OAEL-2; OBNC; TOF
"With such compelling cause to grieve." EBVV
"With trembling fingers did we weave." EBVV; FHYEP; OAEL-2
In Memoriam Akbar Babool. Wopko Jensma. PeSAV
In Memoriam. Alphonse Campbell Fordham. Mary Weston Fordham. AAP; CBWP-2
In Memoriam Ben Zwane. Wopko Jensma. PeSAV
In Memoriam (Easter, 1915). Edward Thomas. GTBS-P; NOBE; NoP-4; OBWP; OBWVE; OxBTC; PeFWW; Spl
In Memoriam: Ernst Toller. W. H. Auden. NYBP
In Memoriam F.M. Dostoevsky. János Pilinszky. CEEP, *tr.* by Jascha Kessler *Fr.* Three Poems.
In Memoriam Francis Ledwidge. Seamus Heaney. CIP-2; NoAM
In Memoriam Frederick Douglass. Eloise Bibb. CBWP-4
In Memoriam Frederick Douglass. Henrietta Cordelia Ray. CBWP-3
In Memoriam, J.A.R., Drowned, East London. Guy Butler. PeSAV
In Memoriam J.H.H. C. J. Ronald. NSI
In Memoriam James Joyce. "Hugh MacDiarmid."
   In the Fall. FaBoMo; InPS-3
   "It was Landor who first said." FaBoPV
   We Must Look at the Harebell. NAEL-2
   "We must look at the harebell as if." NoP-4
In Memoriam John Coltrane. Michael Stillman. InPK-6
In Memoriam Krishna Menon. E. J. Thribb. OBCoV
In Memoriam Larry Parnes ("Mr Parnes Shillings and Pence"). E. J. Thribb. OBCoV
In Memoriam—Leo: A Yellow Cat. Margaret Sherwood. BLPA
In Memoriam: Martin Luther King, Jr. June Jordan. NAAAL; PoBA
In Memoriam of E. B. Clark. Lizelia Augusta Jenkins Moorer. CBWP-3
In Memoriam Paul Laurence Dunbar. Henrietta Cordelia Ray. CBWP-3
In Memoriam: Roy Campbell. Ralph Nixon Currey. PeSA
In Memoriam S. L. Akintola. David Knight. MoCV
In Memoriam Salvador Dali. E. J. Thribb. OBCoV
In Memoriam. Susan Eugenia Bennett. Mary Weston Fordham. CBWP-2
In Memoriam the Master—Noel Coward (1900-1973). E. J. Thribb. PeLV
In Memory. Lionel Pigot Johnson.
   "Ah! fair face gone from sight." OBNC; PoEL-5
In Memory, 1978. Judith Kazantzis. BrRo
In Memory of a Black Union Leader. Aimé Césaire, *French.* VCWP, *tr.* by Clayton Eshleman *and* Annette Smith
In Memory of a Friend. George Barker. OxBTC
In Memory of Arthur Clement Williams. Eloise Bibb. CBWP-4
In Memory of Arthur Winslow. Robert Lowell.
   Death from Cancer. TwCP
In Memory of Basil, Marquess of Dufferin and Ava. John Betjeman. OBWP
In Memory of Bryan Lathrop. Edgar Lee Masters. PoA
In Memory of Captain Underwood Who Was Drowned. *Unknown.* FaBoEE
In Memory of David Archer. George Barker.
   "Images! Venerable as Druidical trees." FaBoMo

In Memory of Edward Wilson. James Clerk Maxwell. *See* Rigid Body Sings.

In Memory of Elizabeth Kearney, Blasket-Islander. Michael Davitt, *Irish.* BiHa, *tr. by the author*

In Memory of Eva Gore-Booth and Con Markievicz. W. B. Yeats. FaBoPV; NoAM; OAEL-2; OBMV; OxBTC

In Memory of Gerard Dillon. Michael Longley. BiHa; PBCIP

In Memory of James M. Rathel. Josephine D. Henderson Heard. CBWP-4

In Memory of Jane Fraser [*or* Frazer]. Geoffrey Hill. MoP; NAEL-2; NoAM; OxBTC

In Memory of Kathleen. Kenneth Patchen. IMW; MoAmPo

In Memory of Major Robert Gregory. W. B. Yeats. EBEV; OAEL-2; SCGP

In Memory of My Arab Grandmother. Evelyn Arcad Zerbe. WPOW

In Memory of My Dear Grandchild Anne Bradstreet Who Deceased June 20, 1669, Being Three Years and Seven Months Old. Anne Bradstreet. BoWoP; NAAL-1; NAAL-3; TrCP

In Memory of My Dear Grandchild Elizabeth Bradstreet Who Deceased August, 1665, Being a Year and Half Old. Anne Bradstreet. ColAP; NAAL-1; NAAL-3; NOCV; SCAP; WPE

In Memory of My Feelings. Frank O'Hara. APSN; ColAP; NAAL-2; NeAP; PoM

In Memory of My First Chapatis. Diane Di Prima. PoM

In Memory of My Mother. Patrick Kavanagh. BIrV; CIP-2; MoP; NoAM; RaBo

  (Memory of His Mother, A.) LBC

In Memory of Radio. Imamu Amiri Baraka. BB; NAAAL; NAAL-2; NeAP; NoP-4; PoM; Poetr

  ("This Love.") (LL) NoP-4

In Memory of Sigmund Freud. W. H. Auden. HAP; NoAM; OAEL-2; OxBA

In Memory of the Poet. Variant. Tomas Venclova, *Lithuanian.* CEEP, *tr. by David McDuff*

In Memory of the Unknown Poet, Robert Boardman Vaughn. Donald Justice. DiPo; NoAM

In Memory of the Utah Stars. William Matthews. Poetsp

In Memory of Titian Tabidze. Yunna Petrovna Moritz, *Russian.* TCRP, *tr. by J. R. Rowland*

In Memory of V. R. Lang. Mac Hammond. PoA

In Memory of W. B. Yeats. W. H. Auden. CMoP; EPCY; GEA; HAP; HeIP-4; HoPM; IIP; ImPo; LiTM; MeMAP; MoBrPo; NOBE; NoAM; NoP-4; OAEL-2; OxAEP-2; OxBTC; PFE; Poetr; TFi; TRP; UnPo; WeW-3

  (In Memory of W. B. Yeats (D. January 1939).) CABP

  ("Pardons him for writing well.") (LL) CABP

  "Earth, receive an honoured guest." FaBoTw

In Memory of Walter Savage Landor. Swinburne. PoEL-5

In memory we are walking. Maria Gillan. UnSA

In Mem'ry's fairest court a shrine is set. To Laura. Henrietta Cordelia Ray. CBWP-3

In Men Whom Men Condemn as Ill. Joaquin Miller. PoLF *Fr.* Byron.

In Merche, after the first C. *Unknown.* MiEL

In Mercy, Lord, Incline Thine Ear. Isaac M. Wise. AH

In Merioneth, over the sad moor. Dead. Lionel Pigot Johnson. OBNC; PoEL-5

In merry Scotland, in merry Scotland. Henry Martyn. *Unknown.* ESPB

In mery May, quhen medis springis. Prologue to the Avowis of Alexander. John Barbour. OxBS *Fr.* The Buik of Alexander.

In Mexico, I met myself one day. El Día de los Muertos. Rafael Campo. RA

In Mexico I'll finish the novel I'll write. In Answer to a Question From P. W. Lew Welch. BB

In mid-river we join the ancient force. Baptism. Dale Zieroth. NOBC

In middle life when the skin slackens. Ambulando. Charles Brasch. PeNZ

In midnight sadness and tobacco fumes. Epistle to Baron Delvig. Oleg Grigorevich Chukhonstev, *Russian* TCRP, *tr. by Simon Franklin*

In midnight sleep of many a face of anguish. Old War-Dreams. Walt Whitman. OxBSP

In midnights of November. A. E. Housman. PeVV

In Minako Wada's House. Brad Leithauser. NoP-4

In Mind. Denise Levertov. NALW; NMM-2

In mine ladye's chaumber. *Unknown. See* I have a gentle cock.

In mine one [*or* own] monument I lie [*or* lye]. Song. Richard Lovelace. CBLP; OxBSP

In Missing. Ray A. Young Bear. CDW

In Mississippi / balloons of hunger. No New Music. Stanley Crouch. GT; PoBA

In Modern Dress. Craig Raine. NoAM

In mole-blue indolence the sun. The Jungle. Alun Lewis. OBWVE

In Moncur Street. Dorothy Hewett. NOBAu

In Montecito. Randall Jarrell. CoAP; NYBP; VGW

In moonlight, we would enjoy these flowers together. Looking at Chrysanthemums And Remembering Meng-tsai and Yu-wen. Chang Yü. *Fr.* Seven Poems on Living in the Mountains: Seeing Off. CoBLCP, *tr. by Jonathan Chaves*

In Morfudd's Arms. Dafydd ap Gwilym, *Welsh.* OBWVE, *tr. by Rolfe Humphries*

In morning light my damson show'd [*or* showed]. The Plum Tree by the House. Oliver St. John Gogarty. OBEV; PoRA

In most things I did as my father had done. George II. H. J. Daniel. *Fr.* The Georges. FaBoEE

In mothers womb thy fingers did me mak. A Thankful Acknowledgment of God's Providence. John Cotton. SCAP

In Mourning for His Dead Wife. P'an Yüeh, *Chinese.* IMW; OHMPC, *tr. by Kenneth Rexroth*

In mourning for your second son. Consoling Wu Te-cheng on the Death of His Son. Shen Chou, *Chinese.* CoBLCP, *tr. by Jonathan Chaves*

In mourning wise since daily I increase. Sir Thomas Wyatt. NoSi

  ("Hatn slipped thy hold and thou art dead and gone.") (LL) PeECV

In moving-slow he has no Peer. The Sloth. Theodore Roethke. ChAP; OBAL; OBCA; PiM; TRP

In mud lodges, below, I have conversed with the Mothers. The Man with Exploded Eyes. Stefan Aug. Doinas, *Romanian.* CEEP, *tr. by Peter Jay and Virgil Nemoianu*

In Murasaki's time. Tale of Genji. Hugh Seidman. AmPA

In my Autumn garden I was fain. An October Garden. Christina Rossetti. GaP; OBGa

In my bed at night. Bible, *O.T. See* On My Bed I Sought Him.

In my beginning is my end. In succession. East Coker. T. S. Eliot. HAP; VGW *Fr.* Four Quartets.

In my Bìnu shrine, the sogo altars pull me home. 19. Jay Wright. MoNo

In My Boat, Painting a Picture of Going Home by Boat. Yün Shou-p'ing, *Chinese.*

  "Essence of ink, The." CoBLCP, *tr. by Jonathan Chaves*

In my boat that goes. Saigyo, *Japanese.* AWP, *tr. by Arthur Waley*

In my body you search the mountain. Counterparts. Octavio Paz, *Spanish.* EP, *tr. by Eliot Weinberger*

In my breast are stored weapons of every description. Inscribed on My Grass-script Calligraphy Written While Drunk. Lu Yu, *Chinese.* SuSp, *tr. by Irving Y. Lo*

In my broken heart's disdain! (LL) The Runaway Slave at Pilgrim's Point. Elizabeth Barrett Browning. BrRo; NALW; VWP

In my childhood trees were green. Autobiography. Louis MacNeice. NOIV; PNI; RB

In my city / dinosaurs are not extinct. Ode to Chicago. Elaine Equi. WWSi

In my craft or sullen art. Dylan Thomas. BoLoP; CMoP; GTBS-P; HAP; HeIP-4; LiTM; MoP; NIP-4; NoAM; NoP-4; OPOU; PFE; PoE; PoPoPo; Poetr; RaBo; WeW-3

In my dark cell, low prostrate on the ground. Abelard to Eloisa. Judith Madan. RACG

In my dream, children. Jerusalem. Adrienne Rich. FiLi

In my dream I take. Kemo Sabe. Diane Glancy. LTA

In my dream I was catching the vanishing shadows. Vanishing Shadows. Konstantin Dmitrievich Balmont, *Russian.* TCRP, *tr. by April FitzLyon*

In my dream of the hydroplane. Sailing to Bien Hoa. Bruce Weigl. CDa

In my dream you're wearing an old trenchcoat. Tower. Deborah Woodard. CDa

In my dreams I am always saying goodbye and riding away. Stevie Smith. FaBoWP

In my dry cell. The Riven Quarry. Gloria C. Oden. GT; PoBA

In my family. People in My Family. Grace Paley. EC3

In my family there are two famous paintings. I Tried to Exchange Two Painting for Some Grain But Failed. Hsü Wei, *Chinese.* CoBLCP, *tr. by Jonathan Chaves*

In My Fashion. Dannie Abse. OxBM

In My Father's House. Bruce Smith.

  Address. Son

In My Father's House. *Unknown.* AS

In my father's house are many cobwebs. Portrait of the Artist as an Old Man. Michael Dransfield. BMAP; CBAP

In my first gentle days. Nicholas Kilmer. PeECV *Fr.* Petrarch.

In My First Hard Springtime. James Welch. AmPA; CDW

In My Garden. *Unknown.* BoTP

In my garden grows a tree. The Apple Rhyme. Madeleine Nightingale. BoTP

In my garden three ways meet. Ralph Waldo Emerson. GaP

In my grandmother's house there was always chicken soup. A Story About Chicken Soup. Louis Simpson. NNaP; PoE; PoWW; TAP; UnSA

In my heart. Tanka. Kitahara Hakushū, *Japanese*. MJT, *tr. by* Makoto Uéda

In my heart's depth. Akazome Emon, *Japanese*. WPJ; WPOW, *tr. by* Kenneth Rexroth *and* Ikuko Atsumi

In my house is my book collection, filled with book-worms. Li K'ai-hsien. *Fr.* Impromptu Poems. CoBLCP, *tr. by* Jonathan Chaves

In my house we had an elephant named Italy. Autobiography. Robert Viscusi. UnSA

In my innermost vein I must hide him. The Totem. Léopold Sédar Senghor, *French*. NegPo, *tr. by* Ellen Conroy Kennedy

In my lady's chamber. (LL) I have a gentle cock. *Unknown*. MiEL; NOBE; NoP-4; OPOU; PeLV

In my land there are no distinctions. Poem for the Young White Man Who Asked Me How I, An Intelligent, Well-Read Person Could Believe in the War Between Races. Lorna Dee Cervantes. LTA; NMM-2; PBCAP; PoPoPo; UnSA; WPOW

In my last poem. Erratum. E. J. Thribb. PeLV

In my left pocket a Chickasaw hand. The Truth Is. Linda Hogan. HATNAP; LTA; NMM-2; UnSA

In my life / As in the twilight. Issa, *Japanese*. OHPJ, *tr. by* Kenneth Rexroth

In My Lifetime. James Welch. CDW

In my little garden. In My Garden. *Unknown*. BoTP

In my medicine cabinet. Jack Kerouac. HA

. . . In my melodious city cupolas burn. Marina Ivanovna Tsvetayeva. AF, *tr. by* Mary Maddock *Fr.* The Cycle Akhmatova.

In My Mind. Norman MacCaig. OxBC

In my mind. Tanka. Yosano Tekkan, *Japanese*. MJT, *tr. by* Makoto Uéda

In my mother's lost language. Bee Mother. Meredith Stricker. LoHo

In My Mother's Room, (for Vanessa). Colleen J. McElroy. GT; NMM-2

In my narrow room, I throw. Mist. Li Ch'ing-chao, *Chinese*. OHPC, *tr. by* Kenneth Rexroth

In my native province when I was young. From the Tibetan. John Hewitt. PNI

In My Own Back Yard. David Young. WeT

In My Own Backyard. James Tate. BAP-93

In my own twentieth century. Natalya Gorbanevskaya, *Russian*. PBWP, *tr. by* Daniel Weissbort

In my photograph of the Sphinx. Mouth of the Wolf. Susan Stewart. NAmP90

In my possession. Tanka. Fumi Saito, *Japanese*. MJT, *tr. by* Ueda, Makoto

In my room, on the whitewashed wall. The Fishing-Tackle. Bertolt Brecht, *German*. PoSu, *tr. by* Lee Baxendall

In my rose-wet cave—whatever happens, this is. (LL) The Floating Poem, Unnumbered. Adrienne Rich. CPO; NALW; NMM-2; NoAM

In my rudyard-kipling-simple years I read. The Thrifty Elephant. John Holmes. NYBP

In my sad soul entertain / Mirth, till thou rejoice again!, *par. by* Thomas Carew. Bible, *O.T. See* Psalm 137.

In my season as red as the red-breasted. The Reality of Autumn. Duane Niatum. HATNAP

In my sky at twilight you are like a cloud. Pablo Neruda, *Spanish*. LoP, *tr. by* W. S. Merwin

In my sleep I was fain of their fellowship, fain. Sunrise. Sidney Lanier. PoEL-5 *Fr.* Hymns of the Marshes. APN-2

In my solitary house, I am drunk again. (LL) One Night. Constantine P. Cavafy, *Greek*. EP; LoP, *tr. by* Rae Dalven

In my stars there's three times ten. Antipater of Thessalonica, *Greek*. GrAn, *tr. by* Alistair Elliot

In my stone eyes I see. What Riddle Asked the Sphinx. Archibald MacLeish. HoPM

In My Study in Monastery, Rising after a Nap. Huang T'ing-chien, *Chinese*. "Peach and plum blossoms, speechless, keep swaying in the wind." SuSp, *tr. by* Michael E. Workman

"Short on brains, long on stupidity, the mantis seizes the cicada." SuSp, *tr. by* Michael E. Workman

In My Thirtieth Year. Archibald MacLeish. *See* L'An Trentiesme de Mon Eage.

In My Time, at Your Place. Yehuda Amichai, *Hebrew*. IP, *tr. by* Warren Bargad *and* Stanley F. Chyet

In my village, another year has gone floating by. Sitting by Myself. K'ang Hai, *Chinese*. CoBLCP, *tr. by* Jonathan Chaves

In my wicker basket. (LL) A Wicker Basket. Robert Creeley. HAP; MoP; NoAM; Poetr

In my young days I drank a / Lot of wine. A Friend Advises Me to Stop Drinking. Mei Yao Ch'en, *Chinese*. HoPM; OHPC, *tr. by* Kenneth Rexroth

In my young days I never. To an Old Tune. Hsin Ch'i-chi, *Chinese*. OHMPC, *tr. by* Kenneth Rexroth

In my younger years. Dreams. Nikki Giovanni. PoDA

In my youth. Opposition. Kaneko Mitsuharu, *Japanese*. NNPT, *tr. by* Geoffrey Bownas *and* Anthony Thwaite

In my youth the growls. Tennyson. FaBoEE

In my youth's summer I did sing of One. Byron. NOBRP *Fr.* Childe Harold's Pilgrimage Canto III. Ro *Fr.* Childe Harold's Pilgrimage.

In nameless warmth, sun light in every corner. Edgar Bowers. VCAP *Fr.* Autumn Shade.

In Nara, the ancient capital. Ise Tayu, *Japanese*. WPJ, *tr. by* Kenneth Rexroth *and* Ikuko Atsumi

In Nara (two poems). Mori Ōgai, *Japanese*. MJT, *tr. by* Makoto Ueda

In narrow room nature's whole wealth, yea more. Paradise. Milton. NOSC *Fr.* Book IV. OAEL-1 *Fr.* Paradise Lost.

In nature apt to like when I did see. Sonnet 16. Sir Philip Sidney. NAEL-1 *Fr.* Astrophil and Stella. AAS; SiPS

In Nature There Is Neither Right nor Left nor Wrong. Randall Jarrell. CBLP; EP; OxBC

In "nature" there's no choice. Beyond the End. Denise Levertov. NeAP; VGW

In Nature's pieces still I see. A Divine Mistress. Thomas Carew. BeJo; CavPo

In Neglect. Robert Frost. OxBSP; VGW

In New Orleans dwelt a young Creole. Limerick. Alben Barkley. PeLi

In New South Wales, as I plainly see. William Forster. CBAP *Fr.* The Devil and the Governor.

In Nick Ray's "Bigger Than Life." 1956. Maxine Scates. PBCAP

In night, when colors [*or* colours] all to black[e] are cast. Greville Fulke. AAS; OAEL-1; Son *Fr.* Caelica.

In Nine Sleep Valley. James Merrill. "Geode, the troll's melon." HCAP

In 1915 my grandfather's. Grandfather. Michael S. Harper. LCAP-2; NAAAL; TAP; VCAP

In 1945, when the keepers cried kaput. The Gift. John Ciardi. LiTM

In 1944 the fitting room was a fluoroscope where bones. For Want of a Male a Shoe Was Lost. Colleen J. McElroy. WeT

In 1943 Althea was a welder. Of Althea and Flaxie. Cheryl Clarke. GLP

In nineteen hundred and twenty-two. Mr. Vachel Lindsay Discovers Radio. Samuel Hoffenstein. BXAP

In nineteen hundred they preferred. Upper Family. Maxwell Bodenheim. OBAL

In 1910 a royal princess. English. Osbert Lancaster. NOBL; PeLV *Fr.* Afternoons with Baedeker.

In 1935 Hitler said / "The Third Reich." Distances. Otto René Castillo, *Spanish*. AF, *tr. by* Margaret Randall

In 1939 the skylark had nothing to say to me. The Ninth of July. John Hollander. CoAP

In nineteen years, we have parted, and met. To Hsiao Shih-ying. Hsieh Chin, *Chinese*. CoBLCP, *tr. by* Jonathan Chaves

In no country. No Offence. D. J. Enright. OxBTC

In No Strange Land. Francis Thompson. HAP; MoBrPo; NOBE; OBEV; TrCP

(Kingdom of God, The.) FaPoR; GTBS-P; NOCV

In no such winter can survive alone. (LL) Midcentury Love Letter. Phyllis McGinley. LW; OxBM

In no wise is the pillar-of-fire. Hilda Doolittle. WPoS *Fr.* The Walls Do Not Fall.

In Nora's House with Rilke's Apollo. Clark Coolidge. PT

In North Great George's Street. "Seumas O'Sullivan." BIrV

In North Ward they do many strange dances. Juan Chi. CoBCP, *tr. by* Watson, Burton (b. 1925) *Fr.* Singing of Thoughts.

In Norway land there lived a maid. The Grey Selchie of Sule Skerry. *Unknown*. OxBB

In Nottamun Town not a soul would look up. Nottamun Town. *Unknown*. CBNP; OxBoLi

In Nottingham there lives a jolly tanner. Robin Hood and the Tanner. *Unknown*. ESPB

In November. Archibald Lampman. NOBC

In November, in the days to remember the dead. St. Malachy. Thomas Merton. VGW

In No. 64 Von Tempsky has his picture up. Von Tempsky's Dance. Murray Edmond. PeNZ

In Number, Weight, and Measure, needs not *Rhime*. Andrew Marvell. *See* On Mr Milton's "Paradise Lost."

In number, weight, and measure, needs not rhyme. (LL) On Mr Milton's "Paradise Lost." Andrew Marvell. CABP; EPCY; NOSC

In Nunhead Cemetery. Charlotte Mew. FaBoWP; NoP-4

In Obitum Ben. Jons. Mildmay Fane, 2d Earl of Westmorland. OxBSP

(On Ben Jonson.) BeJo

In October. Claire Malroux, *French.* VCWP, *tr. by* Marilyn Hacker

In October marching, taking the sweet air. Towards Lillers. Ivor Gurney. NAEL-2; NoP-4

In October of the year. Ox Cart Man. Donald Hall. FYAP; InPS-3; LCAP-2; LoL

In o'er-strict calyx lingering. To Beethoven. Sidney Lanier. NCAP

In Ohio. James Wright. NNaP

In Ohio, where these things happen. The Breathers. James Reiss. AmPA

In Oklahoma, / Bonnie and Josie. Life Is Motion. Wallace Stevens. SAmP

In old age / I'm back. The Pond in a Bowl. Han Yü, *Chinese.* SuSp, *tr. by* Kenneth O. Hanson

In old days / driving through soft waters. Carmen 64. Catullus. APSN, *tr. by* Louis Zukofsky *and* Celia Zukofsky *Fr.* Carmina.

In old days those who went to fight. Hearing That His Friend Was Coming Back from the War. Wang Chien, *Chinese.* ChiP, *tr. by* Arthur Waley

In old Kentuck in de arternoon. Clare de Kitchen. *Unknown.* BLPA

In old Minako Wada's house. In Minako Wada's House. Brad Leithauser. NoP-4

In old stories the jungle was busy. The Sun-Hunters. Mark O'Connor. NOBAu

In olden times we oft have heard. The Natal Hunters. Allen F. Gardiner. PeSAV

In One Battle. Imamu Amiri Baraka. BPo

In one corner. George Swede. HA

In 100% surefire arsenic. Shake'nbake Ballad. Peter Van Toorn. NOBC

In one of the three pots. Viaticum. Birago Diop. PBMAP

In one of those excursions (may they ne'er). Conclusion. Wordsworth. OAEL-2; OBNC *Fr.* The Prelude; Growth of a Poet's Mind [1850 vers.]

In one of those excursions (may they ne'er). Wordsworth. EBEV, *book* 14, *ll.* 1–119 *Fr.* Conclusion: "In one of those excursions (may they ne'er)." OAEL-2; OBNC *Fr.* The Prelude; Growth of a Poet's Mind [1850 vers.]

In one of your earlier letters, the one you wrote in response to Song of the. Song of the Andoumboulou: 6. Nathaniel Mackey. FTOS

In One Place. Robert Wallace. Poetsp

In one place, flying clubs. Hsü Wei. *Fr.* Inscribed on Paintings for the People of Hangchow. CoBLCP, *tr. by* Jonathan Chaves

In only thee, my timid, fleet gazelle. The Timid Gazelle. Kasmuneh, *Arabic.* TrJP

In Orangeburg My Brothers Did. Alfred B. Spellman. BPo; PoBA

In Orbit. Henry Taylor. BXAP

In orchard under the hawthorne. Vergier. *Unknown, Provençal.* GBL, *tr. by* Ezra Pound

In order to blow what it's like being born. (LL) Lester Leaps In. Al Young. MoNo; SeSe

In order to perfect all readers. Wall, Cave, and Pillar Statements, after Asōka. Alan Dugan. CoAP

In order to play one needs magic and Rousseau and must remember play. Magic (or Rousseau). Carla Harryman. FTOS

In order to revitalize the roaring of phosphenes. In Order to Speak. Aimé Césaire, *French.* VCWP, *tr. by* Clayton Eshleman *and* Annette Smith

In order to snuff out two candles. Addition to the Opposition. Aleksandr Yeryomenko, *Russian.* TCRP, *tr. by* Albert C. Todd

In Order to Speak. Aimé Césaire, *French.* VCWP, *tr. by* Clayton Eshleman *and* Annette Smith

In Orknay. William Fowler. OxBS

In other days. (LL) Fare Well. Walter De la Mare. EBEvV; GTBS-P; NOBE; NoP-4; OBEV

In other days, I was poor enough to suit. Cold Mountain Poem No. 158. Han-shan, *Chinese.* PC, *tr. by* Brooks, E. Bruce

In other places! (LL) Coming Back to America. James Dickey. NYBP; WeT

In other years I would say, how pretty they are. The Metronomic Moon. Michael Young. APAD

In our community everything was kept quiet. A Kiss in the Dark. Thomas Sayers Ellis. GT

In our content, before the autumn came. Elinor Wylie. NAAL-2; NALW *Fr.* One Person.

In our heart of hearts believing. Thomas Hardy. *See* Men Who March Away.

In our house every floor was a wailing wall. My Guardian Angel Stein. Philip Schultz. InPS-3

In our kitchen. The Truth About Karen. Kenneth Carroll. ISC

In our midst, on a wooden stick. Tricks. Daniil Kharms, *Russian.* TCRP, *tr. by* Bradley Jordan

In our monotonous sublime. (LL) Waking Early Sunday Morning. Robert Lowell. FaBoMo; HCAP; NOBA; OxBC; VCAP

In our old shipwrecked days there was an hour. Love Dies. George Meredith. BoLoP; EnVR; NOBVV *Fr.* Modern Love.

In our place. Relief. Charles Vildrac, *French.* PeFWW, *tr. by* Christopher Middleton

In our souls everything. Antonio Machado Ruiz, *Spanish.* EnlH, *tr. by* Robert Bly

In our town, people live in rows. The Fired Pot. Anna Wickham. FaBoTw; FaBoWP; LW; OxBTC

In Oxford there lived a merchant by trade. The Crafty Farmer. *Unknown.* AmFP; ESPB

In pain she bore the son who her embrace. Elegy. Moses ibn Ezra, *Hebrew.* TrJP, *tr. by* Solomon Solis-Cohen

In Painswick Churchyard. Frances Horovitz. NBrP

In painting bamboo, the spirit must be transmitted. A Painting of Bamboo by Ni Yün-lin. Yang Chi, *Chinese.* CoBLCP, *tr. by* Jonathan Chaves

In pairs / as if to illustrate their sisterhood. For the Sisters of the Hôtel Dieu. Abraham Moses Klein. NoP-4

In paper case. Epitaph on a Dormouse. *Unknown.* OxBChV

In Parenthesis. David Jones.

  "And the place of their waiting a long burrow." FaBoMo

  "And to Private Ball it came." OBWVE

  "But sweet sister death has gone debauched today and stalks." OBWP; OxAEP-2; PeFWW

  "But why is Father Larkin talking to the dead?" PoE

  "Every one of these, stood, separate, upright, above ground." PeECV

  Five Unmistakable Marks, The. NAEL-2

  "Across upon this undulated board of verdure chequered bright." NoAM

  King Pellam's Launde. OAEL-2

  "So thus he sorrowed till it was day." NoAM

  "You can hear the silence of it." FaBoMo

In Paris, at the Opera. Temptation. Arthur Hugh Clough. PeLV *Fr.* Dipsychus [and the Spirit].

In Paris with You. James Fenton. NoP-4

In Parliament, the Minister. Just Another Autumn Day. Roger McGough. AYFP

In part these nightly terrors to dispel. Moonlight. . . Scattered Clouds. Robert Bloomfield. OBNC *Fr.* The Farmer's Boy.

In parts, through prospects scattered far and near. Birmingham and Wolverhampton. James Woodhouse. *Fr.* The Life and Lucubrations of Crispinus Scriblerus. NOEC

In paschall feast, the end of a[u]ncient rite. Of the Blessed Sacrament of the Altar [or Aulter]. Robert Southwell. OBEV

In pasture where the leaf and wood. The Quest. James Wright. NYBP

In paths untrodden. Walt Whitman. APN-1; NOBA; OxBA

In peace, and reck'ns thee her eldest son. (LL) To Sir Henry Vane the Younger. Milton. PBRV; Son

In peace the aleph. Aleph Poem. Jerome Rothenberg. FTOS

In Peblis town sum tyme, as I heard tell. John, of Stobo Reid. OxBS *Fr.* The Thre Prestis of Peblis.

In Père La Chaise. Joaquin Miller. APN-2

In Perspective. Robert Graves. OxBSP

In Peterborough Churchyard. Paulus Silentiarius, *Greek.* FaBoEE; NOBL

In petticoat of green. Of Phyllis. William Drummond, of Hawthornden. CBLP

In Piam Memoriam. Geoffrey Hill. OxBC

In pilgrim life our rest. Edwin Sandys. AH; ChIV-1

In Pin-up Ruffles now she flaunts. Mary Evelyn. KTR *Fr.* Mundus Muliebris.

In Pinter's new play that's now running. Limerick. Frank Richards. PeLi

In pinup ruffles now she flaunts. Mundus Muliebris. Mary Evelyn. NOSC

In pious times ere [or e'r] priest-craft did begin. Dryden. EBEvV; FHYEP; FaBoPV; HAP; NOSC; OAEL-1; PoE *Fr.* Absalom and Achitophel, Pt. I. EBEvV; FHYEP; FaBoPV; HAP; NOSC; OAEL-1; PoE

In Piranezi's rarer prints. Prelusive. Herman Melville. AmPP *Fr.* Clarel: A Poem and Pilgrimage in the Holy Land.

In placid hours well-pleased we dream. Art. Herman Melville. AmPP; APN-2; ColAP; NAAL-1; NAAL-3; NCAP; NOBA; PAR

In Plague Time. Thomas Nashe. *See* A Litany in Time of Plague.

In plazas calcined pure white, bulls charge. Interludes. Fabio Doplicher, *Italian.* NeIt, *tr. by* Stephen Sartarelli

In Pleasant Lands Have Fallen the Lines. James Flint. AH

In poesy's spells some all their raptures find. John Clare. EPCY *Fr.* Shadows of Taste.

In Pompano Beach, Florida. Robin Becker. PBCAP

In Ponticum. Martial, *Latin.* OBCVT, *tr. by* R. Fletcher

In Portugal, 1912. Alice Thompson Meynell. NOCV

In Prague. Paul Celan, *German.* VCWP, *tr. by* Michael Hamburger

In Prais of Wemen. William Dunbar. NoP-4

In Praise of a Cremation Ground. Kaṭaiyaṉ Kaṇṇaṉār, *Tamil*. PLW, *tr. by* A. K. Ramanujan

In Praise of a Girl. Huw Morus, *Welsh*, OBWVF, *tr. by* Gwyn Williams

In Praise of Ale. Thomas Bonham. FaBoCh

  (Pipe and Can II.) OBEV

  ("When that the chill charocco blows.") FaBoCh

In Praise of Ale. William Stevenson *and* John Still. *See* Back and Side Go Bare, Go Bare.

In Praise of Antonioni. Stephen Holden. NYBP

In Praise of Carnations. Wang Chi, *Chinese*. SuSp, *tr. by* Hellmut Wilhelm

In Praise of Cocoa, Cupid's Nightcap. Stanley J. Sharpless. NBLV; PeLV

In Praise of Drainage. Anne Wilson. ECWP *Fr.* Teisa, a Descriptive Poem of the River Tees, Its Towns and Antiquities.

In Praise of Fidelia. Mildmay Fane, 2d Earl of Westmorland. BeJo; NOSC; OxBSP

In Praise of His Loving and Best-beloved Fawnia. Robert Greene. *See* Fawnia.

In Praise of Hope. Abraham Cowley. OxAEP-1

In Praise of Isabel Pennell. John Skelton. *See* To Mistress [*or* Maystres] Isabell Pennell.

In Praise of Laudanum. William Harrison. NOEC

In Praise of Limestone. W. H. Auden. CMoP; FYAP; FaBoPV; HAP; MoP; NAEL-2; NoAM; NoP-4; OAEL-2

In Praise of Marriage. Christine de Pisan, *French*. OxBM

In Praise of My Sister. Wislawa Szymborska, *Polish*. PoSu, *tr. by* Adam Czerniawski; BLT, *tr. by* Magnus J. Krynski *and* Robert A. Maguire

  ("Everything, / everything.") (LL) BLT, *tr. by* Magnus J. Krynski *and* Robert A. Maguire

  ("My sister does not write poems.") BLT, *tr. by* Magnus J. Krynski *and* Robert A. Maguire

In Praise of New York. Thomas M. Disch. WWSi

In Praise of Old Women. Marya Fiamengo. WPOW

In Praise of Owain Gwynedd. Cynddelw Brydydd Mawr, *Welsh*. OBWVE, *tr. by* Joseph P. Clancy

In Praise of Plants. Branko Miljkovic, *Serbian*.

  ("And my blood that weaves oxygen and time.") (LL) CEEP, *tr. by* Charles Simic

In Praise of Poor Scholars. T'ao Ch'ien, *Chinese*. SuSp, *tr. by* Eugene Eoyang

In Praise of Self-Deprecation. Wislawa Szymborska, *Polish*. BLT, *tr. by* Magnus J. Krynski *and* Robert A. Maguire

In Praise of Tenby. *Unknown, Welsh*. OBWVE, *tr. by* Joseph P. Clancy

In Praise of the Broom. *Unknown, Vietnamese*. AVP, *tr. by* Huỳnh Sanh Thông

In Praise of the Hat. *Unknown, Vietnamese*. AVP, *tr. by* Huỳnh Sanh Thông

In Praise of the Sun. "A. W." CTC

In Praise of Three Young Men. Lochlann Og O Dalaigh. NOIV

In Praise of Virginity. Hroswitha von Gandersheim, *Latin*. PBWP, *tr. by* John Dillon

In Praise of Wine. *Unknown, Latin*. MLL, *tr. by* Helen Waddell

In Praise of Wisdom. Solomon ibn Gabirol, *Hebrew*. TrJP, *tr. by* Solomon Solis-Cohen

In Praise of Women. William Dunbar. CABP

In Praise of Women in General. Thomas Randolph. NOSC

In Praise of Wyatt's Psalms. Henry Howard, Earl of Surrey. SiPS

  (Great Macedon that out of Persy chased, The.) AAS

In Princes Street Gairdens. Robert Garioch. FaBoTC

In Prison. William Morris. PeVV

In Prison. Michael Smith. PWR

In prison joys, fettered [*or* fetter'd] with chains of gold. (LL) The Courtier's Life. Sir Thomas Wyatt. FaBoEE; NoSic

In prison you put on your clothes. Rehabilitative Report: We Can Still Laugh. Daniel Berrigan. AF

In Procession. Robert Graves. TwCP

In Progress. Christina Rossetti. BoWoP; NAEL-2; WPE

In Prospect Street, outside the Splendid Bar. Sweeney to Mrs. Porter in the Spring. Louis Edward Sissman. NYBP

In Protest. Li Ho, *Chinese*. SuSp, *tr. by* Maureen Robertson

In proving that one has had the experience / of carrying a stick? (LL) Critics and Connoisseurs. Marianne Moore. AmPP; CMoP; FaBoWP; MeMAP; NOBA; NoAM; OxBA; Poetr

In purest song one plays the constant fool. Infirmity. Theodore Roethke. CoAP; NAAL-2; NYBP

In Pusseyville, where pussies live. Cats and Dogs. Howard Moss. OBAL

In Queen Victoria's early days. The New Vicar of Bray. Colin Ellis. NOBL

In raging fires of Love. (LL) Walking Parker Home. Bob Kaufman. MoNo; NAAAL

In raging winds the arrows' cries continue without end. Following the Rhymes of Wang An-shih's Poem "Inscribed on the Wall of the Temple of Western Great Unity." Huang T'ing-chien, *Chinese*. SuSp, *tr. by* Michael E. Workman

In railway halls, on pavements near the traffic. Stephen Spender. FaBoMo

In Re Conferences. Vladimir Mayakovsky, *Russian*. TCRP, *tr. by* Albert C. Todd

In re Solomon Warshawer. Abraham Moses Klein. MoCV

In Reading Gaol by Reading Town. Oscar Wilde. *Fr.* The Ballad of Reading Gaol. CABP; OBNV; OxAEP-2

In reality the barn wasn't clean, ninety men. Trakl. Norman Dubie. NAmP90

In Recompense. Eda Lou Walton. LW

In rectangular vertigo the balepress. Making Hay. Philip Hodgins. NOBAu

In red weather. Wallace Stevens. *See* Disillusionment of Ten O'Clock.

In red wool jacket and earflaps. The Week-End Indian. Anita Endrezze-Danielson. VoR

In Reference to Her Children, 23 June, 1659 [*or* 1659]. Anne Bradstreet. BoWoP; NAAL-3; TAP

In Remembrance of the Forgotten. "Lu Hsün," *Chinese*. SuSp, *tr. by* William R. Schultz

In Reply to Questions. T'ai-shang, *Chinese*. CoBCP, *tr. by* Burton Watson

In Reply When Lesser Officials of Chung-tu Brought a Pot of Wine and Two Fish to My Inn as Gifts. Li Po, *Chinese*. CoBCP, *tr. by* Burton Watson

In Residence: A Worst Case View. Sean O'Brien. OBCoV

In respect of riches, then, just or unjust. Unrighteous Mammon (Luke 16:9). Ernesto Cardenal, *Spanish*. GI, *tr. by* Robert Pring-Mill

In Respect of the Elderly. Thomas Love Peacock. VoR

In Response to a Rumor that the Oldest Whorehouse in Wheeling, West Virginia, Has Been Condemned. James Wright. CoAP; NNaP; NoAM; VCAP

In Response to Executive Order 9066: All Americans of Japanese Descent Must Report to Relocation Centers. Dwight Okita. UnSA

In restaurants we argue. They Eat Out. Margaret Atwood. NoAM

In Retrospect. Richard Kenney. Son *Fr.* The Hours of the Day.

In Return. (LL) Motto. Langston Hughes. CA; NAAAL

In rice fields of Ch'ang-ku, by the fifth month. Ch'ang-ku. Li Ho, *Chinese*. SuSp, *tr. by* Maureen Robertson

In roaring he shall rise and on the surface die. (LL) The Kraken. Tennyson. APo; EnVR; NAEL-2; NoP-4; OAEL-2; OBNC; OxBSn; PeECV; PoEL-5; TOF

In Rome, on Campo dei Fiori. Campo dei Fiori. Czeslaw Milosz. HP

In Romney Marsh. John Davidson. EBVV; OxBTC

In rosy-fingered dawn they go. Jersey Cattle. Ralph Nixon Currey. OxBTC

In rosy morn I saw Aurora red. Shortness of Life. Thomas Fairfax, Baron Fairfax of Cameron. NOSC

In Rough Weather. Paul Lake. RA

In royal Anna's golden days. Given to a Lady Who Asked Me to Write a Poem. Janet Little. ECWP

In Ruin Reconciled. Aubrey Thomas De Vere. BIrV

In ruling well what guerdon? Life runs low. The Two Old Kings. John Byrne Leicester Warren, 3d Baron De Tabley. OBEV

In Saba, as by one consent. The Medallion. Herman Melville. APN-2 *Fr.* Clarel: A Poem and Pilgrimage in the Holy Land.

In Sabbath quiet, a street. The Grace-Note. Denise Levertov. CoAmPo

In sable clad, Urania come. Ode on the Passion. Thomas, the Elder Warton. ChIV-2

In sad and ashy weeds. The Good Shepherd's Sorrow for the Death of His Beloved Son. Anne, Duchess of Arundel Howard. NOSC; WPE

In Saginaw, in Saginaw. The Saginaw Song. Theodore Roethke. NBLV; RB

In Saigon heat I suddenly felt so cool. The Dress of Hà-Đông silk. Sa Nguyên, *Vietnamese*. AVP, *tr. by* Huỳnh Sanh Thông

In Salem. Lucille Clifton. AmPA

In Salem dwelt a glorious king. Thomas Traherne. ChIV-1

In Salem seasick spindrift drifts or skips. Salem. Robert Lowell. AiP; Son

In San Juan I wonder how my home is. I Wonder How My Home Is. *Unknown, Tewa Indian*. PBMP, *tr. by* H. J. Spinden

In Santa Maria del Popolo. Thom Gunn. CMoP; FaBoMo; GTBS-P; OxBC; PoE

In Saram. John Cotton. SCAP

In Saturday Market, there's eggs a-plenty. Saturday Market. Charlotte Mew. WPE

In Saturn's reign, at Nature's early birth. Juvenal. OAEL-1; OBSV; OBVE, *tr. by* Dryden *Fr.* Satires.

In Scarlet town, where I was born [*or* bound]. Barbara Allen. *Unknown.* EBEvV; EBNV; OBEV

In scenes like these, which, daring to depart. William Collins. EPCY *Fr.* An Ode on the Popular Superstitions of the Highlands of Scotland. NOEC; OAEL-1; OxAEP-1

In scenes paternal, not beheld through years. Anna Seward. NOEC *Fr.* Eyam.

In schomer, when the leves spryng. Robin Hood and the Potter. *Unknown.* ESPB

In School-Days. John Greenleaf Whittier. BLPA; FaBoBe; OBCA

In school I was taught the names. Columbus Day. Jimmie Durham. HATNAP; LTA

In science today we learned. Stars. Nikki Giovanni. KaS

In Scotland there was a babie born. Hind Horn. *Unknown.* ESPB

In Scotland town where I was borned. Hind Horn. *Unknown.* AmFP; ESPB

In *Scythia's* Realms, no Herbage on the Fields. Scythian winters. Virgil, *Latin.* OBCVT, *tr. by* Joseph Trapp

In sea-cold Lyonesse. Sunk Lyonesse. Walter De la Mare. FaBoCh; LiTM

In sealed box cars travel. Still. Wislawa Szymborska, *Polish.* AF, *tr. by* Robert A. Maguire *and* Magnus Jan Krynski

In search of a shore. Tanka. Nakajō Fumiko, *Japanese.* MJT, *tr. by* Makoto Ueda

In Search of her Son, to the listening Crowd. Idyll 1. Moschus, *Greek.* OBCVT, *tr. by* Francis Fawkes

In Search of Solitude. Chao Yi, *Chinese.* SuSp, *tr. by* Chang Yin-nan *and* Lewis C. Walmsley

In Search of the Traitor. Max Jacob, *French.* AF, *tr. by* Michael Brownstein

In search of wisdom, far from wit I fly. Wit and Wisdom. Ambrose Philips. OxAEP-1

In secret place, this hyndir [*or* hindir] nycht [*or* nicht]. William Dunbar. MiEL

In secret place where once I stood. The Flesh and the Spirit. Anne Bradstreet. AmPP; ChIV-2; NAAL-1; NAAL-3; NOBA; OxBA; OxWW; SCAP; TAP

In secret sorrow, and sad pensiveness. (LL) Sonnet 34: "Like as a ship, that through the ocean wide." Edmund Spenser. NAEL-1; PoE

In seed time learn, in harvest teach, in winter enjoy. Proverbs of Hell. William Blake. *Fr.* The Marriage of Heaven and Hell. NAEL-2; NOBRP; OAEL-2

In sensuous coil. Kings. *Unknown. Fr.* The Panchatantra. AWP, *tr. by* Arthur Ryder

In Sepia. Jon Anderson. PoA

In September, at falling of the leaf. The Assembly of Ladies. Unknown. OBGa

In September 1939. Bernard Gutteridge. PoWW

In seventeen hundred and forty-four. The Kilruddery Hunt. Thomas Mozeen. BIrV

In Shadow. Hart Crane. NOBA

In Shame and Humiliation. James Wright. CAPP-1

In shantung suits we whites are cool. The Devil-Dancers. William Plomer. PeSA; PeSAV

In shaping the snow into blossoms. "Ping Hsin." BoWoP; WPOW *Fr.* Spring Waters.

In shards the sylvan vases lie. The Ravaged Villa. Herman Melville. APN-2; CTC; GaP; NCAP; NOBA; PoEL-5

In Siberia's wastes. Siberia. James Clarence Mangan. BIrV; NOBVV; NOIV

In Sickness. Jonathan Swift. NOEC

(In Sickness. Written Soon after the Author's Coming to Live in Ireland, upon the Queen's Death, October 1714.) CABP

In signe of favor stedfast still. To His Darrest Freind. John Steward of Baldynneis. OxBS

In silence I must take my seat. Table Rules for Little Folk[s]. *Unknown.* OxBChV

In silence / The overloaded canoe leaves our shores. Exile. Mbella Sonne Dipoko. PBMAP

In silent night when rest I took. Here Follows Some Verses upon the Burning of Our House [July 10th, 1966. Copied Out of a Loose Paper]. Anne Bradstreet. AiP; BoWoP; ColAP; NAAL-1; NAAL-3; NALW; NOBA; NOSC; NoP-4; OxBA; PEW; Poetr; SCAP; TAP; WPE

In silks and satins the ladies went. Chemin Des Dames. Crosbie Garstin. NSI

In simmer, whan aa sorts foregether. Embro to the Ploy. Robert Garioch. FaBoTC; OxBS

In sixth grade Mrs. Walker. Persimmons. Li-Young Lee. NIP-4; NoP-4

In Sleep. Alice Thompson Meynell. BrRo

In sleep before me *Venus* seem'd to stand. Bion, *Greek.* OBCVT, *tr. by* Thomas Stanley

In sleep the other night I met you, seventeen. Marge Piercy. MDDM *Fr.* My Mother's Body.

In sleep when an old man's body is no longer aware of its boundaries. A Journey through the Moonlight. Russell Edson. LCAP-2

In slow procession, one by one, silently. From Far Away. Delmira Agustini, *Spanish.* PBWP, *tr. by* D. M. Pettinella

In small backyards old men's long underwear. The Patricians. Douglas Dunn. OxBC

In small green cup an acorn grew. The Acorn. *Unknown.* BoTP

In sober mornings, doe [*or* do] not thou reherse [*or* rehearse]. When He Would Have His Verses Read. Robert Herrick. BeJo; CaPo; CavPo; NOBE; NOSC; SCGP

In soft hanging coils, she embroiders her hair. Tune: "Southern Song, A." Wen T'ing-yün, *Chinese.* SuSp, *tr. by* William R. Schultz

In Solitary Confinement, Sea Point Police Cells. C. J. Driver. PeSA

In solitude. Without a hand to hold. (LL) The Preacher: Ruminates Behind the Sermon. Gwendolyn Brooks. NAAL; PBMP

In some cool room in college after. We Could Have Met. Lee Cataldi. BMAP

In some Havana of the heart I still. Train Whistles in the Wind and Rain. Henry Carlile. PuP-17

In Some Seer's Cloud Car. Christopher Middleton. TwCP

In some small town, one indifferent summer. (LL) Syringa. John Ashbery. APSN; HCAP; NoAM; VCAP

In some unused lagoon, some nameless bay. The Dismantled Ship. Walt Whitman. AmPP; OxBA

In Some Way or Other the Lord Will Provide. Mrs. M. A. W Cook. AH

In somer when the shawes be sheyne. May in the Green-Wood. *Unknown.* OBEV

In somer, when the shawes be sheyne. Robin Hood and the Monk. *Unknown.* EBNV; ESPB; OBNV

In something you have written in school, you say. Serpent Knowledge. Robert Pinsky. ColAP *Fr.* An Explanation of America.

In sooth, I know not why I am so sad. Shakespeare. OxAEP-1 *Fr.* The Merchant of Venice.

In Soto's bosom you may find. Soto, a Character. Mary Leapor. ECWP

In South Oregon the Klamath play. The Woyi. Lew Blockcolski. VoR

In Spanish he whispers there is no time left. The Visitor. Carolyn Forché. FYAP; OPOU

In Spanishburg there are boys in tight jeans. Spitting in the Leaves. Maggie Anderson. PBCAP

In Sparkhill buried lies that man of mark. Local Note. Arthur Guiterman. NBLV

In Spayn. Sir Thomas Wyatt.
("Of myghty love the winges for this me gyve.") (LL) PBRV
("Tagus fare well that westward with thy strems.") PBRV

In Spite. Rufinus, *Greek.* GrAn, *tr. by* Alan Marshfield

In spite of all the learned have said. The Indian Burying Ground. Philip Freneau. AmPP; ColAP; HAP; NAAL-1; NAAL-3; NOBA; NoP-4; OxBA; PoEL-4; PoLF; TAP; TFi

In spite of ice, in spite of snow. On Observing a Large Red-Streak Apple. Philip Freneau. ColAP; NAAL-1; NAAL-3

In spite of love. Family Pictures. Mervyn Morris. PBCV

In spite of what the quarrymen said. Clearsightedness. Andrew Salkey. PBCV

In spotted globes, that have resembled all. Greatness in Little. Richard Leigh. NOSC

In spring and fall there are many fine days. Moving House. T'ao Ch'ien, *Chinese.* CoBCP, *tr. by* Burton Watson

In spring during spring. Jaan Kaplinski, *Estonian.* CEEP, *tr. by* Ivar Ivask

In Spring I look gay. *Unknown.* BoTP; OxNR

In spring if there are dogs they will bark. Ballade of Sayings. W. S. Merwin. NNaP

In Spring of the Year *Ping-shen* Ch'ien Ch'ien-i, *Chinese.*
"Pavilions of dance, terraces of song." CoBLCP, *tr. by* Jonathan Chaves
"Willow catkins beyond the garden wait for evening tides." CoBLCP, *tr. by* Jonathan Chaves

In spring of youth it was my lot. The Lake: To———. Edgar Allan Poe. APN-1; MeMAP; NAAL-1; NAAL-3

In Spring, quince trees. Ibycus, *Greek.* GrIP, *tr. by* Diane J. Rayor

In Spring we gather mulberry leaves. *Unknown, Chinese.* OHMPC, *tr. by* Kenneth Rexroth

In Springtime. Coleridge. *See* Work Without Hope.

In springtime the violets. Springtime. Nikki Giovanni. TLR

In St. Lucie's distant isle. The Sorrows of Yamba, or the Negro Woman's Lamentation. Hannah More. Ro

In stained barn drenched. Paysagesque. Norman Henry, II Pritchard. GT

In State. Forceythe Willson. APN-2
"O Keeper of the Sacred Key."

In stature the Manlet was dwarfish. The Little Man That Had a Little Gun. "Lewis Carroll." BXAP; CBNP *Fr.* Sylvie and Bruno Concluded.

In steaming tubs, / Huge, unblushing. (LL) Dreams of Water. Donald Justice. LCAP-2; NYBP

In steeps and sighs. Charles Wright. *Fr.* Homage to Paul Cézanne. VCAP

In still transparency, the water pools. Waterfall. Greg Williamson. RA

In stone settlements when the moon is stone. Peter Levi. EBEV; TOF

In streets east, streets west, they expound the Buddhist canon. The Girl of Mt. Hua. Han Yü, *Chinese.* CoBCP, *tr.* by Burton Watson

In subsequent waves. Sleeplessness. Luigi Fontanella, *Italian.* NeIt, *tr.* by W. S. Di Piero

In subtler webs than finest summer haze. Henry David Thoreau. *See* On fields oer which the reaper's hand has passed.

In such a night, when every louder wind. A Nocturnal Reverie. Anne Finch, Countess of Winchilsea. BWW; CABP; EBEV; ECEV; ECWP; GEA; NAEL-1; NALW; NOEC; NoP-4; OxAEP-1; PBWP; PoE; PoEL-3; Poetr; WPE

In such an armor he may rise and raid. Bronzeville Man with a Belt in the Back. Gwendolyn Brooks. PoBA

In such luxurious plentie of all pleasure. Edmund Spenser. OAEL-1 *Fr.* Wood Of Error. AEP

In such white robes heav'n's angels used to be. Donne. OxBSn *Fr.* Elegies.

In sullen Humour one Day Jove. Mercury and Cupid. Matthew Prior. PeLV

In sullen silence. Tanka. Toki Zenmaro, *Japanese.* MJT, *tr.* by Makoto Ueda

In summer elms are made for me. Dilemma of the Elm. Genevieve Taggard. MoAmPo

In summer I am very glad. Playgrounds. Laurence Alma-Tadema. BoTP

In summer, in the open air. Summer Sabbath. Jessie E. Sampter. TrJP

In summer, like the theaters, I close up. Valerio Magrelli, *Italian.* NeIt, *tr.* by Dana Gioia

In summer-time, when all the sky was blue. A Song Out of Season. May Probyn. VWP

In summer time, when leaves grew green and birds were singing. King Edward the Fourth and a Tanner of Tamworth. *Unknown.* ESPB

In summer time, when leaves grow green and flowers are fresh and gay. Robin Hood and the Curtal Friar. *Unknown.* ESPB

In summer time, when leaves grow green / Down a down a down. Robin Hood and the Tinker. *Unknown.* ESPB

In summer time, when leaves grow green, when they doe grow both green and long. The Noble Fisherman; or, Robin Hood's Preferment. *Unknown.* ESPB

In summer, when the days were long. Summer Days. Wathen Mark Wilks Call. EBVV

In summer when the woods are green. In the Fair Forest. *Unknown.* BoTP

In summer's heat and mid-time of the day. 1.5. Ovid, *Latin.* BoLoP; CABP; EBEV; EP; GBL; NNPT; NoSic; OBVE; OxAEP-1, *tr.* by Marlowe *Fr.* Elegies.

In summer's heat and mid-time of the day. Elegies. Marlowe. LoP

In summers heate and mid-time of the day. Ovid. *See* Elegies, 1.5.

In summer's mellow midnight. The Night Wind. Emily Jane Brontë. EBVV; NAEL-2; NALW; VWP

In summer's twilight wind that parries. A Message for Summer in the Suburbs. Richard Behm. EC2

In summertime it was a paradise. The Seaside: In and Out of the Season. Charles Tennyson Turner. Son

In summertime on Bredon. Bredon Hill. A. E. Housman. EBVV; MoBrPo; NAEL-2; OxAEP-2; SoSe-8; UV

In sun and snow slumbers. Photo at the Bridge. Dan Pagis, *Hebrew.* IP, *tr.* by Warren Bargad and Stanley F. Chyet

In sun or cold the weather picks scarecrow bones clean. The Long Blues. Calvin C. Hernton. GT

In sunburnt parks where Sundays lie. Cobb Would Have Caught It. Robert Fitzgerald. HAP; TwCP

In sunlight on the Avenue. Galway Kinnell. LiTM *Fr.* The Avenue Bearing the Initial of Christ into the New World.

In Syros' harbor abandoned merchant ships lay idle. Syros. Tomas Tranströmer, *Swedish.* BLT, *tr.* by Swenson, May and Leif Sjöberg

In t' other hundred, o'er yon swarthy moor. The Country Curate. Henry Taylor. NOEC

In Taihang born, in Taihang bred. *Unknown.* ChiPo

In "taking charge of your possessions when you saw them" you became a golden jay. To the Peacock of France. Marianne Moore. MeMAP

In Tall Grass. Carl Sandburg. PoA

In Teesdale. Andrew Young. OxBSP

In Temptation. Charles Wesley. NOEC; PoEL-3

In ten seconds' time. The Launch. Stanley Cook. SpW

In ten thousand pine trees. A Painting of People Strolling through a Pine Forest. Hsü Wei, *Chinese.* CoBLCP, *tr.* by Jonathan Chaves

In tender May when the sweet laugh of Christ. The Puritan. Karl Shapiro. MoAmPo

In Tenebris. Thomas Hardy. NOBE
    "There have been times when I well might have passed and the ending have come." OAEL-2
    "When the clouds' swoln bosoms echo back the shouts of the many and strong." CMoP; ChIV-1; LiTM; NoAM; OxBTC
    "Wintertime nighs." NoAM; OAEL-2; SCGP

In Teos and in Samos. Anacreon. Friedrich von Hagedorn, *German.* GePo, *tr.* by George C. Schoolfield

In Texas Grass. Quincy Troupe. GT; NAAAL; PoBA; UnSA
    ("Waiting for rusted trains / silent in texas grass.") (LL) UnSA

In Thai Binh (Peace) Province. Denise Levertov. AF

In that age when being was believing. The History of Truth. W. H. Auden. FaBoMo

In that ancient time—in eternity. Words Spoken by Pasternak during a Bombing. Bella Akhatovna Akhmadulina, *Russian.* BoWoP, *tr.* by Jean Valentine and Olga Carlisle

In that awful hour when I'm on my deathbed. Repentance. Brendan Behan, *Irish.* TIRV, *tr.* by Ulick O'Conner

In that bad year and city of your birth. For an Emigrant. Randall Jarrell. OxBA

In that building, long and low. The Ropewalk. Henry Wadsworth Longfellow. MeMAP; NCAP

In that café crowded with fools we stood. Paul Verlaine, *French.* NNPT, *tr.* by Alistair Elliot

In that city we were perfect. Los Angeles. Mark Jarman. WWSi

In that country of thresholds we move like vandals. Papermill Graveyard. Ben Belitt. NYBP

In that country pallor was from the ground. Journey To Barcelona. Sylvia Townsend Warner. WPN

In that country the animals. The Animals in That Country. Margaret Atwood. NALW; NoAM

In that delightful land which is washed by the Delaware's waters, *sels.* Henry Wadsworth Longfellow. *Fr.* Part the Second. *Fr.* Evangeline, a Tale of Acadie.

In that empty house. Clement Hoyt. HA

In that great day. The Judgment Day. James Weldon Johnson. ChIV-2

In that hotel my life. The Illumination. Stanley Kunitz. TAP

In that icy heart one voice; My Lady weeps. Table of Contents. Henry Lawes, *Italian.* CBNP, *tr.* by Peggy Forsyth

In that it falls her sacrifice. (LL) Sonnet: "Tell me[e] no more how fair[e] she[e] is." Henry, Bishop of Chichester King. EnLoPo; GLoP; MeLP; SeCP

In that land all is and nothing's ought. Neither Here nor There. William Robert Rodgers. ImPo; LiTM; MoBrPo

In that land, in that land. Southern Paiute Poetry. *Unknown, Southern Paiute Native American.* APN-2, *tr.* by John Wesley Powell

In that land we tried to speak. Siren. Anna Semionovna Prismanova, *Russian.* TCRP, *tr.* by Bradley Jordan

In that lightning flash. Clement Hoyt. HA

In that lost Caucasian garden. The Naming of the Beasts. Francis Sparshott. NOBC

In that new country mountains won't have a name. Preservation. William Stafford. CMAP

In that November off Tehuantepec. Sea Surface Full of Clouds. Wallace Stevens. AmPP; CMoP; MoAmPo; VGW

In that, O Queen of queens, thy birth was free. To Our Blessed Lady. Henry Constable. NoSic

In that old house of many generations. First Travels of Max. John Crowe Ransom. NTP

In that particular temple. Suniti Namjoshi and Gillian Hanscombe. CPO

In That proud port, which her so goodly graceth. Sonnet 13. Edmund Spenser. Son *Fr.* Amoretti. AAS

In that same gardin all the goodly flowres. Edmund Spenser. NOBE *Fr.* The Garden of Adonis. NOBE; OBGa; PoEL-1 *Fr.* Wood Of Error. AEP

In that shop which deals exclusively in forests sawn into. The Wood merchant's parlour. Pierre McOrlan, *French.* MFP, *tr.* by Martin Sorrell

In that so sudden summer storm they tried. Summer Storm. Louis Simpson. OxBC

In that state I came return. (LL) The Retreat[e]. Henry Vaughan. AWP; CABP; CIHu; ESCV; FMP; FSCP; GTBS-P; GeHe; HAP; ImPo; InPK-6; InPS-3; MeLP; NAEL-1; NIP-4; NOBE; NOCV; NOSC; NoP-4; OAEL-1; OBEV; OBWVE; PBRV; PeECV; PoE; PoEL-2; PoRA; SCGP; SeCP; TFi; TOF

In that town I was twenty. Snow there lay. Yunna Petrovna Moritz, *Russian.* TCRP, *tr. by* J. R. Rowland

In that town were hard spaces. Town I Left. Helen Sorrells. CrSp

In that world as it may be, newborn and haunted, what with solitude mean? (LL) Yom Kippur 1984. Adrienne Rich. GLP; NoAM

In the Absence of Bliss. Maxine W. Kumin. NoAM

In the absence of light. The Seed Is the Light of the Earth. Christina Pacosz. LoHo

In the Acadian land, on the shores of the Basin of Minas. Part the First. Henry Wadsworth Longfellow. *Fr.* Evangeline, a Tale of Acadie.

In the afternoon. (LL) A Poem for the Insane. John Weiners. NeAP; PmAP; PoM

In the afternoon sun. Beams. Audre Lorde. NoAM

In the afternoon, while the wind. Views from the High Camp. W. S. Merwin. CoAmPo

In the Age of Postcapitalism. Lawrence Joseph. PBCAP

In the air of your name, Lord / in your house / in my life, *par. by* David Rosenberg. Bible, *O.T. See* Psalm 23.

In the air to aggravate the truly menacing. (LL) Chez Jane. Frank O'Hara. CoAP; ColAP; NOBA; NeAP; NoAM; PoA; PoE

In the airconditioned drone. Monsoon Girl. Harry Clifton. BiHa; PBCIP

In the almond—what dwells in the almond? Mandorla. Paul Celan, *German.* PoSu, *tr. by* Michael Hamburger

In the America of the dream. The Lonesome Dream. Lisel Mueller. CoAP

In the American schoolyard. The Air Base at Châteauroux, France. Sherod Santos. NAmP90

In the Amorite City. Haim Guri, *Hebrew.* IP, *tr. by* Warren Bargad *and* Stanley F. Chyet

In the Ancient Manner. Chao Meng-fu, *Chinese.* CoBLCP, *tr. by* Jonathan Chaves

In the antique forest dreary. Rhyme of the Antique Forest. Henrietta Cordelia Ray. CBWP-3

In the April Rain. Mary Anderson. BoTP

In the Ashtray. Vasco [*or* Vasko] Popa, *Serbian.* VCWP, *tr. by* Anne Pennington

In the attention it pays to each detail. Love. Kelly Cherry. CRP

In the Autumn, on Retreat at a Mountain Temple. Lady Izumi, *Japanese.* WPoS, *tr. by* Jane Hirshfield *and* Mariko Aratani

In the autumn when words sound. Akiko Baba, *Japanese.* WPJ, *tr. by* Kenneth Rexroth *and* Ikuko Atsumi

In the back bedroom, laughing when you pull. First Time: 1950. Honor Moore. FFC; GLP

In the back of the dark Chinese store. The Thrashing Doves. Jack Kerouac. PmAP

In the back of the nunnery. Monastic Outhouse. Aleksandar Ristovic, *Serbo-Croatian.* HSix, *tr. by* Charles Simic

In the Backs. Frances Darwin Cornford. BrRo

In the Backs. James Kenneth Stephen. NOBVV

In the backyard of our house on Norwood. The Minks. Toi Derricotte. NAmP90; PuP-15

In the bad old days a bewigged country Squire. Wigs and Beards. Robert Graves. NOBL

In the Badlands. David Wagoner. UnPo

In the Badlands of Desire. Beckian Fritz Goldberg. NAmP90

In the banana zone, in the poinciana tropics. Louvres. Les A. Murray. BMAP

In the barn the tenant cock. Morning. John Cunningham. NOEC

In the baroque style of coral, India. The Coral Reef. John Blight. NOBAu

In the basement of the museum finery is on display; a history of costume. A History of Costume. Michelle Cliff. OxWW

In the bath I look up and see the brown moth. Now That I Am Never Alone. Tess Gallagher. NAmP90

In the Bavarian steeple, on the hour. The Spire. Ellen Bryant Voigt. NoAM

In the Bay. Arthur Symons. OBNC *Fr.* Amoris Exsul.

In the Bay of Naniwa—. The Woes of the Crab. *Unknown Fr* Manyo Shu, Part 2 of 4.

In the Bay of Sumi. Toshiyuki, *Japanese.* OHPJ, *tr. by* Kenneth Rexroth

In the beauty of the lilies Christ. Julia Ward Howe. CTV

In the beginnin o aa things the Wurd wis there ense. Bible, *N.T.* FaBoVe *Fr.* St. John.

In the Beginning. Laura Riding Jackson. KSG

In the Beginning. Valerie Sinason. BrRo

In the beginning, at every step, he turned. The Sickness of Adam. Karl Shapiro. CRP *Fr.* Adam and Eve.

In the beginning God created the heaven. To the New Moon. Salvatore Quasimodo, *Italian.* SpW, *tr. by* Jack Bevan

In the beginning God created the heaven and the earth. Bible, *O.T.* NAWM-1 *Fr.* Genesis.

In the beginning God made thee. Aholibah. Swinburne. ChIV-1; KSG

In the beginning, God, the great schoolmaster. The Autograph on the Soul. Adah Isaacs Menken. CBWP-1

In the beginning he merely marked. West Coast Indian. George Clutesi. HATNAP

In the beginning I stood by the window. Windows in Providence. Aliki Barnstone. BoWoP

In the beginning, in the wet. War Memoir: Jazz, Don't Listen to It at Your Own Risk. Bob Kaufman. MoNo; NAAAL

In the beginning Love satisfies us. Love's Maturity. Hadewijch, *Flemish.* WPoS, *tr. by* Oliver Davies

In the beginning of time. Wilderness. Yuksa Yi, *Korean.* CKP, *tr. by* Jaihiun Kim

In the beginning the light And the first hour. Odysseus Elytis. GrIP, *tr. by* Edmund Keeley *and* George Savidis *Fr.* Axion Esti.

In the beginning, the word. You Bet Your Life. Nancy Vieira Couto. PBCAP

In the beginning there were transports. Genesis. Jules Alan Wein. TrJP

In the Beginning Was a Word. Robert Graves. PoA

In the beginning was the three-pointed star. Dylan Thomas. ChIV-2

In the beginning / was the Word. Hilda Doolittle. *See* From The Walls Do Not Fall.

In the beginning was the Word. John 1:1 and 14. Gail Holst-Warhaft. GI *Fr.* St. John.

In the bend of your mouth soft murder. Lion. May Swenson. LiTM

In the big library scholars sit and read books. Jovan Hristic, *Serbo-Croatian.* HSix, *tr. by* Charles Simic

In the Big Rock Candy Mountains. (LL) The Big Rock Candy Mountains. *Unknown.* AmFP; FaBoA; OBAL; TTTS

In the Bistro. Gwen Harwood. FaBoWP

In the bitter year of 1988 I was banished to San Diego. Song of the Sad Guitar. Marilyn Chin. WWSi

In the black winter morning. Bereft. Thomas Hardy. BoLoP; NoAM

In the bleak mid-winter. A Christmas Carol. Christina Rossetti. ACTP; InPS-3; NOBVV; VWP

In the blizzard / while chopping wood. From the Spotted Night. Ray A. Young Bear. AF; HATNAP

In the bloodstained warmth of the barns. Celebration of Nadir. János Pilinszky, *Hungarian.* CEEP, *tr. by* Emery E. George

In the Blooming Time o'th' year. Silvio's Complaint: A Song, To a Fine Scotch Tune. Aphra Behn. KTR

In the blossom-land Japan. An Old Song. "Yehoash," *Yiddish.* AWP, *tr. by* Marie Syrkin

In the blue air. Bats. Mary Oliver. HeIP-4

In the blue distance. Nelly Sachs, *German.* BoWoP, *tr. by* Ruth Mead *and* Matthew Mead

In the blue-green shadows. On a Landscape by Myself. Yün Shou-p'ing, *Chinese.* CoBLCP, *tr. by* Jonathan Chaves

In the blue hubbub of the same-through-wealth sky. Geography. Kenneth Koch. NoAM

In the blue night. Pine Tree Tops. Gary Snyder. NOBA

In the blue rays. Tanka. Miyazawa Kenji, *Japanese.* MJT, *tr. by* Makoto Ueda

In the bluebell forest. Bluebells. Olive Enoch. BoTP

In the blurring low-blood-pressure. The Judgment. Kathleen Spivack. BoWoP

In the Bodies of Words. May Swenson. NMM-2

In the bonds of Death He lay. Martin Luther. CTV

In the Borghese Gardens. Charles Tomlinson. OBGa

In the *Boston Sunday Herald* just three lines. To an American Poet Just Dead. Richard Wilbur. HCAP; NBLV

In the bottom of my mind. (LL) The Goat Paths. James Stephens. AWP; CH; SCGP; UnPo

In the Bottomless Pit. Maksimilian Aleksandrovich Voloshin, *Russian.* TCRP, *tr. by* Yakov Hornstein

In the Bower of Bliss. Edmund Spenser. GaP *Fr.* Wood Of Error. AEP ("O horrible enchantment, that him so did blend.") (LL) FaBoSe

In the bramble bush shelley slowly eats a lark's heart. Hot Day at the Races. Tom Raworth. SPE

In the brave days of old. (LL) Horatius at the Bridge. Thomas Babington Macaulay, 1st Baron Macaulay. CABP; EBEvV; EBNV; FaBoCh; FaPoR; OBNV; OBWP; OxAEP-2; PoLF

In the Breeze. Boris Pasternak, *Russian.* TrJP, *tr. by* C. M. Bowra

In the bright bay of your morning, O God. Prayer. Claire Goll, *German.* TrJP, *tr. by* Babette Deutsch *and* Avrahm Yarmolinsky

In the bright broad Swiss glare I stand listening. Recessional. Thomas MacGreevy. CIP-2

In the broken light, in owl weather. Colloquy. Weldon Kees. NYBP

In the brutal nights we used to dream. Reveille. Primo Levi, *Hebrew*. HP, *tr. by* Ruth Feldman *and* Brian Swann

In the bulb / of its / voices are buoyant among Gustaf Sobin. *See* What the music.

In the burgeoning age of Arnaut when for God and man to be. A Fit of Something against Something. Alan Ansen. WeT

In the burned house I am eating breakfast. Morning in the Burned House. Margaret Atwood. BAP-96

In the cabin. . . . Three Dimensions. José Craveirinha. PBMAP

In the Cafe. Iain Crichton Smith. FaBoTC *Fr.* By the Sea.

In the Cage. Robert Lowell. NOBA; Son

In the Camp There Was One Alive. Randall Jarrell. HP

In the Canyon of Echo, there's a railroad begun. Echo Canyon. *Unknown*. AmFP

In the capital Spring comes late. Buying Flowers. Po Chü-i, *Chinese*. TAL, *tr. by* Robert Payne

In the Carolinas. Wallace Stevens. SAmP; VGW

("White iris beautifies me, The.") (LL) FiLi

In the Case of Lobsters. Petra von Morstein, *German*. BoWoP, *tr. by* Rosemarie Waldrop

In the casket of the Hours. *Unknown*. TAL, *stanzas* I–XX, *tr. by* Reynold A. Nicholson *Fr.* The Meditations.

In the Cathedral. Patricia Beer. OxBC

In the Cathedral Close. Edward Dowden. EBVV; IIP

In the cathedral the acolytes are praying. The Habeas Corpus Blues. Conrad Potter Aiken. NYBP

In the cave she will claw out of— / a woman giving birth to herself. Liz Lochhead. *See* Mirror's Song.

In the cedar canoe gliding and paddling. Geese Gone Beyond. Gary Snyder. NoAM

In the cedar-limbs. Wallace Stevens. *See* Thirteen Ways of Looking at a Blackbird.

In the Cemetery. Thomas Hardy. InPK-6; Son *Fr.* Satires of Circumstance in Fifteen Glimpses.

In the censer the coals are high. Final Prayer. Enheduanna, *Sumerian*. BoWoP, *tr. by* Aliki *and* Willis Barnstone

In the centre of the poster, Napoleon. A Poster of Our Dazzling Victory at Saarbrucken. Rimbaud. FaBoPV; OBWP, *tr. by* Robert Lowell *Fr.* Eighteen-Seventy.

In the chamber. Margaret Witter Fuller. CrSp *Fr.* Memoirs, I.

In the chaos of the autumn sun. The Smell of Old Newspapers Is Always Stronger after Sleeping in the Sun. Mike Lowery. Poetsp

In the cherry blossom's shade. Issa, *Japanese*. EnlH, *tr. by* Stephen Mitchell

In the *chih-yüan* period, the being *hsin-mao*. Poem of Prefectural Judge Yang T'ien-jui Righting a Wrong. Chao Meng-fu, *Chinese*. CoBLCP, *tr. by* Jonathan Chaves

In the childhood of April, while purple woods. The Dead to the Living. Edith Nesbit. VWP

In the Children's Hospital. "Hugh MacDiarmid." NAEL-2

In the chorus of memories a blessing in disguise. Declension. Stephen Sandy. PoA

In the church fallen like dancers. Enfidaville. Keith Douglas. PoWW

In the Church of I AM she hears there is a time to heal. Do What You Can. Lawrence Joseph. PBCAP; WWSi

In the Churchyard. Eleanor Ross Taylor. UnPo

In the Churchyard at Cambridge. Henry Wadsworth Longfellow. AmPP; PoEL-5; TAP

In the citadel of Jade Gate Pass, elm leaves early scatter yellow. Wang Ch'ang-ling. SuSp, *tr. by* Ronald C. Miao *Fr.* Following the Army on Campaign.

In the city of Marseilles, there lived a beautiful lady. The Lowly Peasant. *Unknown*. PBWP, *tr. by* Rina Benmayor

In the city of St. Francis they have taken down the statue of St. Francis. Afterwards, They Shall Dance. Bob Kaufman. TwCP; VGW

In the City Park. Bulat Shalvovich Okudzhava, *Russian*. TCRP, *tr. by* Deming Brown

In the clear light that confuses everything. The Laurel Tree. Louis Simpson. NNaP

In the clear water by the beach. Bianor, *Greek*. GrAn, *tr. by* Robin Skelton

In the Clearing. Donald Finkel. BAP-95

In the clearing stands. Missionaries in the Jungle. Linda Piper. BlSi

In the cliff over the frog pond. The Fossils. Galway Kinnell. NYBP

In the close covert of a grove. The Geranium. Richard Brinsley Sheridan. BoLoP; EP

In the closet. Lucille and Ernie's Master Bedroom. Dara Wier. CMAP

In the Cloud Chamber. Roger Weingarten. PUP-18

In the cloud-gray mornings. Hoar-Frost. Amy Lowell. ColAP

In the Cloud of Unknowing. Carol Rumens. DiPo

In the Coach. Thomas Edward Brown.

"Conjergal rights! conjergal rights!" PeVV

In the coffin. Walt Whitman. *See* Reconciliation.

In the cold Camp'ea, where ridges. Campèa. Andrea Zanzotto, *Italian*. VCWP, *tr. by* Ruth Feldman *and* Brian Swann (b. 1940)

In the cold, cold parlor. First Death in Nova Scotia. Elizabeth Bishop. CoAP; FaBoWP; LCAP-2; NOBA; NYBP

In the cold dome of the college observatory. Conjunctions. Eamon Grennan. PBCIP

In the cold my voice grew hoarse. Song. Gunars Salis, *Latvian*. CEEP, *tr. by* Laris Salinš

In the cold shed sharpening saws. Sixth-Month Song in the Foothills. Gary Snyder. HCAP

In the cold snows of a dream. (LL) The Road at My Door. W. B. Yeats. BIrV; NOBE; PoE

In the convent vegetable garden the nuns. In a Convent Garden. Alan Brownjohn. OBGa

In the cool light / In the darkness. (LL) Tenzone. Ezra Pound. MeMAP; PoA

In the cool of morning Andrew Jackson came. Twilight on Union Street. Donald Davidson. FuPo

In the cool waters of the river. Woman. Valente Goenha Malangatana, *Portuguese*. PBA; PeSAV; TTY, *tr. by* Dorothy Guedes *and* Philippa Rumsey

In the copper marsh. Heron. Philip Booth. Poetsp

In the corner of a flower-shop. Twelve. Rossana Ombres, *Italian*. NeIt, *tr. by* Ruth Feldman

In the corner the fire made a place. Two Women. Tania Van Zyl. PeSA

In the cornfield and the thirsty grass. (LL) July. Alexander L. Posey. APAD; APN-2

In the Counselor's Waiting Room. Bettie M. Sellers. InPK-6

In the Country. Lu Yu, *Chinese*. OHMPC, *tr. by* Kenneth Rexroth

In the Country. Ssu-k'ung Shu, *Chinese*. SuSp, *tr. by* Hellmut Wilhelm

In the county of El Carmen. El Corrido de Gregorio Cortez. *Unknown*, *Spanish*. PaTW, *tr. by* Paredes, Américo

In the County Tyrone, in [*or* near] the town of Dungannon. The Old [*or* Ould] Orange Flute. *Unknown*. OBCoV; OxBoLi

In the Course of Time the original. Natan Zach, *Hebrew*. IP, *tr. by* Warren Bargad *and* Stanley F. Chyet

In the court of examinations. Spring Vista from the Tower of Illuminated Distance. Li Meng-yang, *Chinese*. CoBLCP, *tr. by* Jonathan Chaves

In the Courtyard. Miriam Ulinover, *Yiddish*. CEEP, *tr. by* Seth L. Wolitz

In the courtyard a poor blind man is repairing a concertina. Part of a Novel. Gyula Illyés, *Hungarian*. CEEP, *tr. by* Emery E. George

In the courtyard is a marvelous tree. *Unknown*, *Chinese*. SuSp, *tr. by* Charles Hartman

In the courtyard where the cooing of pigeons. The Courtyard. Eddy Van Vliet, *Flemish*. VCWP, *tr. by* John Van Tiel

In the covenant's radiance that moment had come. Uri Zvi Greenberg, *Hebrew*. MHP, *tr. by* Ruth Finer Mintz

In the cowslip's [*or* cowslip] peeps I lie [*or* lye]. Clock-A-Clay [The Lady Bug]. John Clare. APo; EBEV; EBVV; EnVR; NAEL-2; NOxBChV; OAEL-2; OBNC; PoEL-4

In the cream gilded cabin of his steam yacht. Mr. Nixon. Ezra Pound. MoAmPo *Fr.* Hugh Selwyn Mauberley. (Life and Contacts). AmPP; CMoP; InPS-3; LiTM; NOBA; NoAM; TAP

In the crimson of the morning, in the whiteness of the noon. The Coming of His Feet. Lyman Whitney Allen. BLPA

In the cross field. Out West. Gary Snyder. NNaP

In the crystal sky / of the fresco. The Pope in Ancona. Jaroslaw Iwaszkiewicz. CEEP

In the curious phenomenon of your occipital horn. (LL) To a Snail. Marianne Moore. APo; CMoP; FaBoMo; FaBoWP; MeMAP; NAAL-2; NALW; PoPoPo

In the daily space. Daily Space. João Cabral de Melo Neto, *Portuguese*. VCWP, *tr. by* W. S. Merwin

In the daisied lap of summer. The Season's Lovers. Miriam Waddington. MoCV

In the damp places. Nijole Miliauskaite, *Lithuanian*. VCWP, *tr. by* Jonas Zdanys

In the dank halls of Buchenwald. Juliek's Violin. Michael C. Blumenthal. CMAP

In the dark. The Black Jewel. W. S. Merwin. LCAP-2

In the Dark. David Ignatow. WeT

In the Dark. James Merrill. LCAP-2

In the dark. Train. Ken Smith. SPE

In the Dark. Patrick Williams. PNI

In the Dark Again. C. G. Hanzlicek. CMAP

In the dark and narrow street. When the Night and Morning Meet. Dora Greenwell. EBVV

In the dark at first, we see things in their sleep. Girandole. Dorothy Donnelly. NYBP

In the dark church of music. Vivaldi. Delmore Schwartz. NYBP

In the dark house, the cry of a child. Teething. Tom Wayman. CDa

In the dark lobby. L. A. Davidson. HA

In the Dark None Dainty. Robert Herrick. CaPo; CavPo

In the dark sky there. Lyn Hejinian. FTOS *Fr.* The Cell.

In the dark womb where I began. C. L. M. John Masefield. LiTM; MoBrPo; OxBTC

In the dark woods. To our baby that died[1]. Yosano Tekkan, *Japanese*. MJT, *tr. by* Makoto Ueda

In the darkening church. Rufus Prays. Leonard Alfred George Strong. MoBrPo

In the darkness east of Chicago. A Valedictory to Standard Oil of Indiana. David Wagoner. NYBP

In the dating bar, the potted ferns lean down. A History of Civilization. Albert Goldbarth. HCAP

In the dawn. Sakanoe No Korenori, *Japanese*. OHMPJ, *tr. by* Kenneth Rexroth

In the dawn, although I know. Fujiwara no Michinobu, *Japanese*. OHPJ, *tr. by* Kenneth Rexroth

In the dawn-dirty light, in the biggest snow of the year. Roe-Deer. Ted Hughes. NOxBChV; NoAM; OxAEP-2

In the days before the high tide. A Sea Song. Digby Mackworth Dolben. EBVV

In the days of Caesar Augustus. Christmas Day; the Family Sitting. John Meade Falkner. ChIV-2; NOCV; OxBTC

In the days of mild Jerry Hall. Limerick. *Unknown*. PeLi

In the days of old. Thomas Love Peacock. NOBRP

In the days of old Rameses, are you on, are you on? *Unknown*. AS; OBCoV

In the Days of Prismatic Color. Marianne Moore. MeMAP

In the Days of Socrates. Friedrich Hölderlin, *German*. PFTM, *tr. by* Richard Sieburth

In the days of the Prince's glory. The Palace of Prince Ma—Now It Is a Buddhist Temple. Yang Shih-ch'i. *Fr.* Three Poems on Ch'ang-sha. CoBLCP, *tr. by* Jonathan Chaves

In the days that tried our fathers. "Orpheus C. Kerr." *Fr.* The Rejected "National Hymns." OBAL

In the days when it was still stupendous. The Wisdom Tooth. Jonathan Holden. NAmP90

In the days when moles still held their general meetings. Brief Thoughts on cats Growing on Trees. Miroslav Holub, *Czech*. PoSu, *tr. by* Ian *and* Jarmila Milner

In the days when they were first planted before the Calyx Tower. Willow Branch Song. Liu Yu Hsi, *Chinese*. SuSp, *tr. by* Daniel Bryant

In the daytime. Ono no Komachi, *Japanese*. WPJ, *tr. by* Kenneth Rexroth *and* Ikuko Atsumi

In the daytime. Tanka. Kitahara Hakushū, *Japanese*. MJT, *tr. by* Makoto Ueda

In the dead hour of night. The Silent Night. Mrs. Henry Linden. CBWP-4

In the dead night we walk behind a hearse. Abel. John Wheelwright. ChIV-1

In the Dead of the Night. Norman Dubie. AmPA

In the Dean's porch a nest of clay. In the Cathedral Close. Edward Dowden. EBVV; IIP

In the death mask by Gherardi. Keats' Lips. Michael Waters. CMAP

In the december of my springs. The December of My Springs. Nikki Giovanni. GT

In the Deep Channel. William Stafford. RB

In the Deep Museum. Anne Sexton. MoAmPo

In the deep night, that all is well. (LL) My Lord and King. Tennyson. EBVVPR; NOBE; NOCV; OBEV; OBNC; PeECV

In the depths of the parasol I see the marvelous prostitutes. A Man and Woman Absolutely White. André Breton, *French*. PFTM, *tr. by* David Antin

In the desert. The Desert Has Many Teachings. Mechthild von Magdeburg, *German*. WPoS, *tr. by* Jane Hirshfield

IN THE DESERT. The Heart. Stephen Crane. APAD; APN-2; ColAP; FaBoEE; HoPM; LiTM; MeMAP; MoAmPo; NOBA; NoP-4; OxBSP; TAP *Fr.* The Black Riders [and Other Lines].

In the Desert. Semyon Izrailevich Lipkin, *Russian*. TCRP, *tr. by* Albert C. Todd

In the Desert. Herman Melville. NCAP

In the desert of Itabira. Travelling in the Family. Carlos Drummond de Andrade, *Portuguese*. NNPT, *tr. by* Elizabeth Bishop

In the deserted village, sunken down. The Deserted Village. "Robin Hyde." PeNZ; WPE

In the dimly lit room. Vision of Your Body. Daisy Zamora, *Spanish*. LoL, *tr. by* Dinah Livingston

In the Distress upon Me. Henry Ainsworth. AH

In the ditch. Galway Kinnell. *Fr.* The Dead Shall Be Raised Incorruptible. NOBA; PoE

In the Dock. Walter De la Mare. LiTM

In the doll's. Bob Boldman. HA

In the Dome Car of the "Canadian." Sid Marty. NOBC

In the Doorway. Robert Browning. SCGP *Fr.* James Lee's Wife.

In the Dordogne. John Peale Bishop. OBWP; PeFWW; PoWW; VGW

In the downhill of life, when I find I'm declining. Tomorrow. John Collins. GTBS-P

In the Downtown Tombs of long long ago. Partial Luetic History of an Individual at Risk. J. M. Regan. GLP

In the dream I am burning the rice. Offering. Sharan Strange. BAP-94; GT

In the dream I became 2 men my age. (1980). C. S. Giscombe. GT

In the dream I enter the house. Bone-Flower Elegy. Robert Earl Hayden. NoAM

In the dreamy silence. Autumn. Alexander L. Posey. APN-2

In the dreamy silence after bath. The Mother. Sharon Olds. PBCAP

In the Dresden Gallery. Yevgeny Mikhailovich Vinokurov, *Russian*. TCRP, *tr. by* Albert C. Todd

In the drifting rain the cows in the yard are as black. Milking before Dawn. Ruth Dallas. NTP; PeNZ

In the drinking-well. Aunt Eliza. Harry Graham. FPC

In the Due Honor of the Author Master Robert Norton. John Smith. SCAP

In the Dumps. *Unknown*. CBNP

In the Dunes. Aleksandr Blok, *Russian*. TCRP, *tr. by* Geoffrey Thurley

In the dungeon-crypts, idly did I stray. The Prisoner. Emily Jane Brontë. NALW; NOBVV

In the dusk of the evening. Old Mountain Road. Charles Simic. FYAP

In the dusk the path. Lady Izumi, *Japanese*. OHMPJ; WPOW, *tr. by* Kenneth Rexroth

In the dusk the path. Lady Izumi, *Japanese*. WPOW, *tr. by* Kenneth Rexroth

In the Dusky Path of a Dream. Rabindranath Tagore. *Fr.* The Gardener. OBMV

In the dust. . . in the cool / tombs. Carl Sandburg. *See* Cool Tombs.

In the dusty light of an attic room he woke. Ballad of the Swimming Angel. Jeffrey Skinner. WeT

In the early evening, as now, a man is bending. Poem. Louise Glück. HCAP; Poetr

In the early evening, the suspended bowls. The Specter. "Anna Akhmatova," *Russian*. TCRP, *tr. by* Daniel Weissbort

In the early hours / the lovebirds. Paraguay. Carl Rakosi. FTOS

In the early morning / when the light and the sea smell come stumbling in. In Solitary Confinement, Sea Point Police Cells. C. J. Driver. PeSA

In the early springtime, after their tea. En Famille. Dame Edith Sitwell. NALW

In the earnest path of duty. Poem. Charlotte Forten. BlSi

In the earth of your eyes, in easy wonder building a new god. Kenneth Patchen. *See* In Judgment of the Leaf.

In the earth, the earth, thou shalt be laid. Warning and Reply. Emily Jane Brontë. WPE

In the East. Georg Trakl, *German*. PeFWW, *tr. by* Michael Hamburger ("Dark wrath of people, The.") AF, *tr. by* Daniel S. Simko ("Wild wolves have broken through the gates.") (LL) AF, *tr. by* Daniel S. Simko

In the East Central State of Nigeria, four years. Epilogue to Casualties. J. P. Clark Bekederemo. HBAPE

In the East, in the East is my heart. My Heart Is in the East. Judah Halevi, *Hebrew*. TrJP

In the eastern quarter dawn breaks, the stars flicker pale;. Cock-crow Song. *Unknown, Chinese*. ChiP, *tr. by* Arthur Waley

In the Egg. Günter Grass, *German*. AF, *tr. by* Michael Hamburger *and* Christopher Middleton

In the eggs. John Corben. Spl

In the eggshell after the chick has hatched. Michael Segers. HA

In the Egyptian Museum. Janet Lewis. NYBP

In the elbow of a macaroni. A Blue Jeaned Rock Queen in Search of Happiness on a Blind Thursday at 1/3 Speed and Crying. A. K. Redwing. VoR

In the Elegy Season. Richard Wilbur. InPK-6; NYBP

In the Elementary School Choir. Gregory Djanikian. UnSA

In the embankment's mad roar. On the Railway. Aleksandr Blok, *Russian*. TCRP, *tr. by* Geoffrey Thurley

In the Emptied Rest Home. Bella Akhatovna Akhmadulina, *Russian*. BoWoP, *tr. by* Jean Valentine *and* Olga Carlisle

In the empty church. Nicholas Virgilio. HA

In the empty city a morning horn. Tune: "Pale-golden Willows." Chiang K'uei, *Chinese*. SuSp, *tr. by* Chiang Yee

In the empty lot—a place. The Wild. Wendell Berry. VGW

In the empty mountains. Hitomaro, *Japanese*. OHPJ, *tr. by* Kenneth Rexroth

In the empty mountains after the new rain. Autumn Twilight in the Mountains. Wang Wei, *Chinese*. OHMPC, *tr. by* Kenneth Rexroth

In the encyclopedia. Fact. Kenneth Rexroth. OBAL

In the End. Peter Everwine, *after* Natan Sach. NNaP

In the end he was light enough. The Dead Father. Bernd Jentzsch, *German*. CEEP, *tr. by* Ewald Osers

In the end is the body—what we know. Gail Holst-Warhaft. GI

In the End of Days. Bible, *O.T.* TrJP *Fr.* Isaiah.

In the end of the sabbath, as it began to dawn toward the first day of the week. Bible, *N.T.* NAWM-1 *Fr.* St. Matthew.

In the End We Are All Light. Liz Rosenberg. LiLi

In the end you are tired of those places. Locations. James Harrison. AmPA

In the endless night, having deserted me, where have you gone? Tune: "Telling of Innermost Feelings." Ku Hsiung, *Chinese*. SuSp, *tr. by* James J. Y. Liu

In the Enola Gay. August 6, 1945. Alison Fell. NBrP

In the Environs of the Funeral Home. The Funeral Home. Robert Mezey. LiTM

In the eternal / Light of the spring day. Ki no Tomonori, *Japanese*. OHPJ, *tr. by* Kenneth Rexroth

In the Evening. "Anna Akhmatova," *Russian*. TCRP, *tr. by* Daniel Weissbort

In the evening. At Sunset. Ivy O. Eastwick. BoTP

In the evening. Siv Cedering Fox. CA

In the Evening. Adrienne Rich. ColAP

In the evening / as far as the eye can see. A Green Lowland of Pianos. Jerzy Harasymowicz, *Polish*. CBNP, *tr. by* Czeslaw Milosz

In the evening gusts of wind and rain. Tune: "Song of Picking Mulberry." Li Ch'ing-chao, *Chinese*. SuSp, *tr. by* Eugene Eoyang

In the evening / haze darkening on the hills. Another Night in the Ruins. Galway Kinnell. AF; CoAP

In the Evening I Walk by the River. Ou-yang Hsiu, *Chinese*. OHPC, *tr. by* Kenneth Rexroth

In the evening land, a woman. The Going Under of the Evening Land. Mekeel McBride. CMAP

In the evening the autumn woods ring. Georg Trakl. *See* Grodek.

In the evening the dusk. The Poet Is Dead. William Everson. NoAM

In the evening / The mists trail. *Unknown, Chinese*. TAL, *tr. by* Arthur Waley

In the evening / The rice leaves in the garden. Minamoto no Tsunenobu, *Japanese*. OHPJ, *tr. by* Kenneth Rexroth

In the evening there is a snail. Talking to the Mule. Laura Jensen. AmPA

In the evening there were flocks of nighthawks. September 2. Wendell Berry. PoA

In the Evening, Walking in the Western Fields. Chang Yü, *Chinese*. CoBLCP, *tr. by* Jonathan Chaves

In the evening when the light is dim. Valerio Magrelli, *Italian*. NeIt, *tr. by* Dana Gioia

In the evening wind. Tanka. Maekawa Samio, *Japanese*. MJT, *tr. by* Makoto Ueda

In the evening your vision widens. Nelly Sachs, *German*. WPoS, *tr. by* Michael Roloff

In the evenings they listen to the same. The Intruder. Frank Stanford. MT

In the eye of seafaring man. The Winds of Change. Charles G. Ballard. VoR

In the eye of the king there was a postage stamp. The Way to Finish it Off. E. L. T. Mesens, *French*. CBNP

In the eyes of the cat. The Cat's Eye. Yorie. PC

In the faint blue light. Vincent Buckley. BMAP *Fr.* Stroke.

In the Fair Forest. *Unknown*. BoTP

In the Fall. "Hugh MacDiarmid." FaBoMo; InPS-3 *Fr.* In Memoriam James Joyce.

In the fall, I believe again in poetry. Still. Aila Meriluoto, *Finnish*. PBWP, *tr. by* Jaakko A. Ahokas

In the fall-out of daisies on the rockland. Absent Daughter. Barend Toerien, *Afrikaans*. PeSA, *tr. by the author*

In the Falling Deer's Mouth. Michael Levien. PoRA

In the falling snow. Hokku: In the Falling Snow. Richard Wright. *Fr.* Hokku Poems. PoBA

In the far corner. The Blackbird. Humbert Wolfe. BoTP; NOxBChV

In the far spaces of eternity. Harmony. Thomas Grant Springer. PoToHe

In the Far West. Cow Boy. Vicente Huidobro, *Spanish*. PFTM, *tr. by* David Guss

In the few warm weeks. A Christmas Message. Gavin Ewart. FaBoMo

In the Field. Richard Wilbur. NAAL-2; NYBP

In the Fields. Charlotte Mew. MoBrPo; NTP; OxAEP-2

In the fields, the silos open their mouths. Hangman. Ai. AmPA

In the final hour, dear. "Valery Frantsevich Pereleshin," *Russian*. TCRP, *tr. by* Thomas E. Bird

In the fine land, the west land, the land where I belong. (LL) The West Wind. John Masefield. CABP; LiTM; MoBrPo

In the Fire Lane. Thulani Davis. WWSi

In the first Autumn night. First Autumn Night. Katie Donovan. BiHa

In the first cage. Aisle of Dogs. Chase Twichell. BAP-96

In the first country. Bright after Dark. Pearse Hutchinson. PBCIP

In the first negative, a shape presages. Sound Waves. Mary Kinzie. FFC

In the first rank of these did Zimri stand. In the first rank of These did Zimri stand. Dryden. HAP *Fr.* Absalom and Achitophel, Pt. I. EBEvV; FHYEP; FaBoPV; NOSC; OAEL-1; PoE

In the first ruder age, when love was wild. Love's Force. Thomas Carew. CaPo

In the first taxi he was alone tra-la. The Taxis. Louis MacNeice. OxBTC; PNI

In the first year of freedom's second dawn. George III. Byron. *Fr.* The Vision of Judgment. OAEL-2

In the first year of the last disgrace. News of the World II. George Barker. FaBoTw

In the 5 a.m. dusk. Dionne Brand. PBCV *Fr.* Military Occupations.

In the flash of that explosion. Wedding Day at Nagasaki. Rodney Hall. CBAP

In the Flight of the Blue Heron: To Montezuma. Anita Endrezze-Danielson. CDW

In the Flowering Season. Michael Roberts. FaBoTw

In the Fog. Lilian Moore. TLR

In the fog we drift hither. Rain on the River. Lu Yu, *Chinese*. OHPC, *tr. by* Kenneth Rexroth

In the Footsteps of Genghis Khan. Jan Barry. CDa

In the footsteps of the walking air. Kenneth Patchen. SPE

In the Ford plant. The Foundations of American Industry. Donald Hall. CA

In the Forest. George Bowering. NOBC

In the Forest. Russell Edson. LCAP-2

In the forest, in unexplored. Michael Dransfield. CBAP *Fr.* Geography.

In the Formal Garden. Peter Jones. OBGa

In the foul rag-and-bone shop of the heart. (LL) The Circus Animals' Desertion. W. B. Yeats. CMoP; EPCY; FaBoMo; FaBoTw; MoP; NAEL-2; NAWM-2; NIP-4; NOBE; NOIV; NoAM; NoP-4; OAEL-2; OxBTC; TFi

In the frayed apple leaves a grin of copper. The Child is Revenant to the Man. Vincent Buckley. BMAP

In the frontroom I dance. Impromptu. Mary Kinzie. CMAP

In the full river. What She Said. Orampokiyar. PLW *Fr.* Five on the Riverside Cane. PLW, *tr. by* A. K. Ramanujan

In the furrows of the world. Nation. Charlie Cobb. PoBA

In the Gallery. John Hollander. CBLP

In The Gallery Where the Fat Men Go. Louis Golding. PoFWW

In the garbage bin. Alexis Rotella. HA

In the Garden. Walter De la Mare. FP

In the garden. Garden. Michael Bullock. OBGa

In the garden a strange tree grows. *Unknown, Chinese*. CoBCP, *tr. by* Burton Watson

In the Garden at Swainston. Tennyson. OBEV; OBNC

In the Garden City Café with its murals on the wall. Huxley Hall. John Betjeman. CABP; OBSV

In the Garden of Eden lay Adam. Limerick. *Unknown*. PeLi

In the garden of Shut-Eye Town. (LL) The Sugar-Plum Tree. Eugene Field. CTV; NBLV; OTCP; OxBChV

In the garden on a summer night. Brazen Image. Anne Hartigan. CIP-2

In the garden pool. O. Mabson Southard. HA

In the garden. Summer's end. Evening. On a bench. Verses Written on Sand. "Melech Ravitch," *Yiddish*. CEEP, *tr. by* Seymour Mayne *and* Rivka Augenfeld

In the garden there strayed. *Unknown*. SoSe-8

In the Garden: Villa Cleobolus. Lawrence Durrell. OBGa

In the garret under the sloping eaves. The Wedding Gift. Minna Irving. BLPA

In the gathering dew. Lady Sagami, *Japanese*. BoWoP, *tr. by* Willis Barnstone

In the gathering gloom they lie. Terror. "Yehoash," *Yiddish.* TrJP, *tr. by* Isidore Goldstick

In the Giant's Castle. Ruth Dallas. PeNZ

In the girdered dark. A Drink of Milk. John Montague. PNI

In the glassed-in jazz club acres above. Night above the Town. Thomas Lux. SeSe

In the Gloaming. Jennifer Maiden. BMAP

In the gloaming to be roaming[, where the crested waves are foaming]. Charles Stuart Calverley. BXAP; NOBL; OBCoV; PeLV

In the gloom of whiteness. Snow. Edward Thomas. FaBoTw; NTP; OPOU; PFE

In the Glorious Epiphanie of Our [*or* Ovr] Lord God[, A Hymn. Svng as by the Three Kings]. Richard Crashaw. FSCP; PoEL-2

(Hymne for the Epiphanie, A; Sung as by the three Kings.) ESCV

In the Gold Mines. B. W. Vilakazi. TTY

(On the Gold Mines.) PeSA

In the golden air, the risky autumn. Piazzas. Barbara Guest. NeAP

In the golden reign of Charlemaign the king. Rhotruda. Frederick Goddard Tuckerman. NCAP

In the golden twilight the rain. The Terrace in the Snow. Su Tung-p'o, *Chinese.* OHPC, *tr. by* Kenneth Rexroth

In the Good Old U. S. A. José Angel Villalongo Sr. UnSA

In the Grass. Annette von Droste-Hülshoff, *German.* PBWP, *tr. by* James Edward Tobin

In the grassy fields I lie. (LL) The Sheep. Ann Taylor. BoTP; CTAV; OxBChV

In the grave. (LL) Dirge: "Swallow leaves her nest, The." Thomas Lovell Beddoes. NOBE; OBNC; PoEL-4

In the Grave No Flower. Edna St. Vincent Millay. NAAL-2

In the Graveyard. Macdonald Clarke. PWR

In the great gardens, after bright spring rain. The Innocent Spring Dame Edith Sitwell. NOBE; OxBTC *Fr.* The Sleeping Beauty.

In the Great House, and in the House of Fire. He Holdeth Fast to the Memory of His Identity. *Unknown.* AWP *Fr.* Book of the Dead.

In the Great Metropolis. Arthur Hugh Clough. EnVR

In the great night my heart will go out. Owl Woman's Death Song. *Unknown, Papago.* BoWoP, *tr. by* Ruth Underhill

In the great place the great house is gone from in the sun. Slave Quarters. James Dickey. CAPP-1; NYBP

In the great shade of August, under the sycamores. A Valediction. Julia Randall. NMM-2

In the great snowfall before the bomb. Lorine Niedecker. NMM-2

In the great world—which, being interpreted. Byron. OxBoLi; PeLV *Fr.* Canto the Eleventh. NOBRP *Fr.* Don Juan.

In the green light of water, like the day. The Swans. Dame Edith Sitwell. CMoP; WPE

In the Green Shade. Brian Lee. AYFP

In the greenest of our valleys. The Haunted Palace. Edgar Allan Poe. APN-1; CH; MeMAP; NAAL-3; NOBA; PoEL-4; TAP; TFi

In the greenhouse lives a wren. *Unknown.* OxNR

In the Greenwood. Desmond O'Grady, *Irish.*
 "My darling, my love." CIP-2, *tr. by* Desmond O'Grady

In the grey evening. The Garden Hose. Beatrice Janosco. NTCP

In the grey summer garden I shall find you. I Shall Find You. Siegfried Sassoon. LBC

In the grey wastes of dread. Horses on the Camargue. Roy Campbell. GTBS-P; PeSA

In the Grounds. Douglas Dunn. NoP-4

In the groves of Africa from their natural wonder. An African Elegy. Robert Duncan. NoAM

In the guard towers. Charles Simic. *See* Begotten of the Spleen.

In the guest room. Alexis Rotella. HA

In the half-light / And. (LL) Canto 2. Ezra Pound. AmPP; HAP; MeMAP; MoMaP; NOBA; NoAM; OxBA; PoA

In the hallway above the pit of the stairwell. Indictment of Senior Officers. Sharon Olds. PBCAP

In the harbour, in the island, in the Spanish Seas. Trade Winds. John Masefield. FaBoCh; OBMV

In the harvest too. And Then the Water. Milo De Angelis, *Italian.* NeIt, *tr. by* Lawrence Venuti

In the Heart of the Desert. Al-Tirimmah, *Arabic.* ArPe, *tr. by* Omar S. Pound

In the heart of the Hills of Life, I know. My Springs. Sidney Lanier. UnPo

In the heart of the Indian territory of Oklahoma. Go For Broke. André Breton, *French.* PFTM, *tr. by* David Antin

In the heart of winter and a boy running. (LL) History Lessons. Seamus Deane. BiHa; PBCIP; PNI

In the heat. Bob Boldman. HA

In the heat of noon. Consolation to Empty Pitchers. K. S. Narasimhaswami, *Kannada.* OMIP, *tr. by* A. K. Ramanujan

In the Heat of the Morning. Anne Szumigalski. FaBoWP

In the heaven of the god I hope for (call him X). Heaven. Arthur Seymour John Tessimond. OxBM

In the heights of heaven is the throne of your dwelling. Sanctification. Joseph Ibn Abithur, *Hebrew.* TOF, *tr. by* David Goldstein

In the hellish heat and thick smoke. Food-Factory Kitchen. Vladimir Salimon, *Russian.* TCRP, *tr. by* Vera Dunham

In the heydays of 'forty-five. For George Santayana. Robert Lowell. CMoP; NAAL-2; VGW

In the hickory scent. The Smokehouse. Yusef Komunyakaa. NoP-4

In the high corridors. Corridor. Federico García Lorca, *Spanish.* CBNP

In the high, high grass of Guinea. Country Graveyard. Charles Pressoir, *French.* NegPo, *tr. by* Edna Worthley Underwood

In the high jungle where Assam meets Tibet. Moschus Moschiferus. Alec Derwent Hope. CBAP

In the high seat, before-dawn dark. Why Log Truck Drivers Rise Earlier Than Students of Zen. Gary Snyder. LoL; NNaP

In the high wilderness. Coplas. Antonio Machado Ruiz, *Spanish.* AF, *tr. by* Robert Bly

In the highlands, in the country places. Robert Louis Stevenson. FaBoCh; OBEV; OxBS; SCGP

In the Hills. Wang Wei, *Chinese.* TAL, *tr. by* Robert Payne

In the Holy Nativity of Our Lord God. Richard Crashaw. GeHe; PoEL-2
(Hymn[e] of the Nativity, An.) HAP; MeLP
(In the Holy Nativity of Our Lord God A Hymn Sung as by the Shepheards.) FSCP
("Our selves become our own best SACRIFICE.") (LL) FSCP
Shepherds' Hymn, The. NOBE
Verses from the Shepherd's Hymn. OBEV

In the home of mysterious life I lie. Songs of the Sacred Mysteries. *Unknown, Sioux Native American.* APN-2, *tr. by* Alfred Longley Riggs

In the Home of the Scholar Wu Su-chiang. Wu Tsao, *Chinese.* BoWoP; WPOW, *tr. by* Kenneth Rexroth *and* Ling Chung

In the hometown tonight. A Castle in Lynn. Linda McCarriston. LoL; NMM-2

In the Hospital. George Garrett. PFE

In the Hospital. Laura Jensen. AmPA

In the Hospital Near the End. Sharon Olds. NIP-4

In the hospital of life. Anywhere Out of the World. Charles Baudelaire, *French.* PT, *tr. by* David Rosenberg

In the hot gold sunlight. Brown Girl. Angelina Weld Grimké. CPO

In the Hotel. Jorie Graham. BAP-94

In the hottest time, when all is still and windless. *Unknown.* CoBCP, *tr. by* Burton Watson *Fr.* Tzu Yeh Songs.

In the hour of death, after this life's whim. Dominus Illuminatio Mea. Richard Doddridge Blackmore. OBEV

In the hour [*or* houre] of my distress [*or* distresse]. His Litany to the Holy Spirit. Robert Herrick. BeJo; NOSC; OBEV; PeECV; PoLF

In the house. Tanka. Masaoka Shiki, *Japanese.* MJT, *tr. by* Ueda, Makoto

In the House Blues. Bessie Smith. NAAAL

In the house east of here lives an old woman. *Unknown, Chinese.* CoBCP, *tr. by* Burton Watson

In the house in Detroit. Sand Nigger. Lawrence Joseph. LTA; WWSi

In the house made of dawn. The Night Chant. *Navajo Oral Tradition, Navajo.* ITG, *tr. by* Matthews, Washington *and* Robert Hass

In the house of life. (LL) Pax. D. H. Lawrence. EnIH; PeECV; TrCP

In the house of red leaves are the most beautiful dances. The House of Red Leaves. Liu E, *Chinese.* CoBLCP, *tr. by* Jonathan Chaves

In the House of the Aylors. Albery Allson Whitman. AAP *Fr.* Not a Man and Yet a Man.

In the House of the Dying. Jane Cooper. CrSp

In the house of the hangman. The Hangman's Love Song. Stanley Moss. VGW

In the house of the Red Rock. Tsĕ' ni Gisí' n, or Song in the Rock. *Unknown.* *Fr.* The Night Chant. APN-2, *tr. by* Washington Matthews

In the house that has died. Water Song. Michael S. Weaver. ISC

In the house with the tortoise chair. Poem to Ease Birth. *Unknown, Aztec Indian.* BoWoP; STP, *tr. by* Anselm Hollo

In the huge, rectangular room, the ceiling. My Mother, Who Came from China, Where She Never Saw Snow. Laureen Mar. CrSp; WPOW

In the huge, wide-open, sleeping eye of the mountain. The Bear. Ted Hughes. APo; FaBoMo

In the human cities, never again to. Despisals. Muriel Rukeyser. CPO; NMM-2

In the hummingbird house. Hummingbird Light. Diane Wakoski. PmAP

In the hungry kitchen. Kitchen Poem. Francis Scarfe. SPE

In the Huon Valley. James Philip McAuley. CBAP

In the Inner City. Lucille Clifton. HeIP-4; SSCS; UnSA

In the interim, how the children should be educated. Allen Curnow. *Fr.* A Small Room with Large Windows. PeNZ

In the Isle of Dogs. John Davidson. OBNC

In the Jackdaw folder of "Historical Genitalia." Politics of Envy. Duncan Forbes. PeLV

In the Jeta Pavilion of the Setting Sun. Drinking at Night in the Western Pavilion of the Fa-hua Temple. Liu Tsung-yüan, *Chinese*. SuSp, *tr. by* Jan W. Walls

In the Khamsin. Yitzhak Lamdan, *Hebrew*.
   "Distant soughing of pine forests caresses my ear, The." MHP, *tr. by* Ruth Finer Mintz
   "How little of God's grace caresses you, Massadah." MHP, *tr. by* Ruth Finer Mintz
   "On roads beyond the camp the Khamsin struck me." MHP, *tr. by* Ruth Finer Mintz
   "Why did Hagar weep over Ishmael when he thirsted." MHP, *tr. by* Ruth Finer Mintz

In the King's Rooms. Timothy Steele. RA

In the Kitchen. Mary Leapor. ECWP *Fr.* Crumble Hall.

In the kitchen as the toast browns. At My Father's House. Nancy Travis. ISC

In the knot there's no untying. (LL) Freedom and Love. Thomas Campbell. GLoP; GTBS-P

In the Laboratory. Dan Pagis, *Hebrew*. PoSu, *tr. by* Robert Friend

In the laboratory waiting room. Through a Glass Eye, Lightly. Carolyn Kizer. BoWoP

In the Ladies' Room at the Bus Terminal. William Zaranka. BXAP

In the Lake District. Joseph Brodsky, *Russian*. BLT, *tr. by* Kline, George L.

In the lamplight falling. Night. Peter Everwine. NNaP

In the land o' the leal. (LL) The Land o' the Leal. Carolina Oliphant, Baroness Nairne. GTBS-P; NOBRP; OBEV; OxBS

In the land of dwarfs. Forugh Farrokhzad, *Persian*. BoWoP, *tr. by* Girdhard Tikku

In the land of God. Cecil County. Ron Welburn. PoBA

In the Land of the Lotus Eaters. Tony Hoagland. PUP-18

In the land of turkeys in turkey weather. Dance of the Macabre Mice. Wallace Stevens. CMoP; NOBA; OxBA; PFTM

In the language of the spirit. Leap Year. Charles North. FTOS

In the last days. Apocalypse. Francis Ernest Kobina Parkes. PBA

In the last low cottage in Blackthorn Lane. The Wise-Woman. Agnes Mary Frances Robinson. VWP

In the last minutes he said more to her. Seamus Heaney. PNI *Fr.* Clearances. CIP-2; PBCIP; PNI

In the last storm, when hawks. The Epitaph Ending in And. William Stafford. LCAP-2

In the late evening. Iain Crichton Smith. SpW

In the late night listening from bed. Thinking for Berky. William Stafford. MoLi

In the laundermat. Sydell Rosenberg. HA

In the Lecture Room. James Keir Baxter. PeLV *Fr.* Cressida.

In the Library. Michael Patrick Hearn. NTCP

In the Library. Ed Ochester. Poetsp

In the licorice fields at Pontefract. The Licorice Fields at Pontefract. John Betjeman. CABP; CMoP

In the life we live [or lead] together every paradise is lost. Against Botticelli. Robert Hass. AmPA

In the light falling from old growth trees. Renewal. Diane Averill. CMAP

In the little courtyard, by the side window. Li Ch'ing-chao. SuSp, *tr. by* Eugene Eoyang *Fr.* Tune: "Sand of Silk-washing Stream."

In the little port half hidden by the headlines of Pentire. War. S. S. Hunt. NSI

In the little red house by the river. Wilderspin. Mary Elizabeth Coleridge. VWP

In the lives of their friends. (LL) Beware: Do Not Read This Poem. Ishmael Reed. BPo; NIP-4; PoBA

In the Local Museum. Walter De la Mare. HAP

In the log dugout hidden by osiers. The Sighs of the Gunner from Dakar. Guillaume Apollinaire, *French*. PeFWW, *tr. by* Anne Hyde Greet

In the lonesome latter years. The Promissory Note. Bayard Taylor. BXAP

In the long ago. (LL) An End. Christina Rossetti. CBLP; GBL; SDW

In the long journey out of the self. Journey to the Interior. Theodore Roethke. DiPo *Fr.* North American Sequence.

In the long journey out of the self. Journey to the Interior. Theodore Roethke. LCAP-2; NYBP; TRP; VGW

In the long run we must fix our compass. Respected, Feared, and Somehow Loved. Marjorie Welish. PmAP

In the long, sleepless watches of the night. The Cross of Snow. Henry Wadsworth Longfellow. APN-1; ColAP; GSo; HeIP-4; MeMAP; NOBA; NoP-4; OxBA; TAP

In the Longhouse, Oneida Museum. Roberta Hill Whiteman. NoAM

In the Looking Glass. "Anna Akhmatova," *Russian*. TCRP, *tr. by* Daniel Weissbort

In the Lord's eyes. (LL) This Place Rumord to Have Been Sodom. Robert Duncan. NOBA; NeAP; PoM

In the Lost Province. Tom Paulin. PBCIP

In the love his beauty bringeth. (LL) The Singing Cat. Stevie Smith. OxBTC; PC

In the love of home and country and the flag of Uncle Sam. Loyalty to the Flag. Lizelia Augusta Jenkins Moorer. CBWP-3

In the Lungs. Milo De Angelis, *Italian*. NeIt, *tr. by* Lawrence Venuti

In the Lybian desert I. Modo and Alciphron. Sylvia Townsend Warner. MoBrPo

In the Madison Zoo. Roberta Hill Whiteman. CDW

In the main square of Berdyansk. The Sky. Vladimir Nikolaevich Kornilov, *Russian*. TCRP, *tr. by* Daniel Weissbort

In the mandolin air of pistons. Couch Fantasy. Adrian C. Louis. NAmP90

In the manger of course were cows[s] and the Child Himself / Was like unto a lamb. Pig. Anthony Hecht. APo; GI; OxBC

In the Marble Quarry. James Dickey. NoP-4

In the market, in the cloister—only God I saw. Baba Kuhi of Shiraz, *Persian*. TOF, *tr. by* R. A. Nicholson

In the marketplace where St Florian. She Looked At the Sun. Tadeusz Różewicz, *Polish*. PoSu, *tr. by* Magnus F. Krynski

In the Meadow There's a Dead Deer. *Unknown, Chinese*. CoBCP, *tr. by* Burton Watson

In the meal-bin. (LL) Mossbawn Sunlight. Seamus Heaney. APAD

In the Memory of the Most Worthy Benjamin Jonson. William Cartwright.
   "Where shall we find a Muse like thine, that can." EPCY

In the Menagerie. Oleg Grigorevich Chukhonstev, *Russian*. TCRP, *tr. by* Simon Franklin

In the men's room at the office today. Found Parable. J. D. McClatchy. BAP-94

In the merry month of May. Phillida and Coridon. Nicholas Breton. EBEvV; NOBE; NoSic; OBEV; TTTS *Fr.* The Honourable Entertainment Given to the Queen's Majesty in Progress at Elvetham, 1591.

In the middle. Black Love Black Hope. Doughtry Long. SeSe

In the middle of a tiny spot and nearly bare there is a nice thing to say that. A Leave. Gertrude Stein. PFTM

In the middle of our times. Middle. Jimmie Durham. HATNAP

In the middle of the harbour. Derek Walcott. TTY *Fr.* A Sea-Chantey. RB

In the Middle of the Journey. David Keller. CMAP

In the middle of the journey of our life. The Dark Wood. Dante, *Italian*. BiHa; PiM, *tr. by* Seamus Heaney *Fr.* Inferno. NAWM-1, *tr. by* John Ciardi *Fr.* Divina Commedia.

In the middle of the night. Philodemus, *Greek*. PGA, *tr. by* Kenneth Rexroth

In the middle of the night he started up. Silver Wedding. Ralph Hodgson. CBLP; OxBTC

In the middle of the night I slipped away from my husband. Philodemus. HePo, *tr. by* Barbara Hughes Fowler *Fr.* Epigrams.

In the middle of the night in the next room. The Cell of Himself. Arthur Freeman. TwCP

In the Middle of the Party. Carl Dennis. CBNP

In the middle of the road there was a stone. Carlos Drummond de Andrade, *Portuguese*. BLT, *tr. by* Elizabeth Bishop

In the middle of the sea. Song. *Unknown, Chippewa Indian*. STP, *tr. by* Jerome Rothenberg

In the middle of the wood I set sail. Amhrán na mBréag. Pearse Hutchinson. PBCIP

In the Middle of Things, Begin. Beckian Fritz Goldberg. NAmP90

In the middle silences of this night's course the blackthorn. David Jones. OxAEP-2 *Fr.* Mabinog's Liturgy.

In the Midst of Life. Tadeusz Rózewicz, *Polish*. PoSu, *tr. by* Adam Czerniawski
   ("It was a voice of another man.") (LL) HP

In the midst of my garden. The Palm Tree. Abd-ar-Rahman I, *Arabic*. AWP, *tr. by* J. B. Trend

In the midst of the hall. Tennyson. *See* The Mermaid.

In the midst of wilderness there stands a flower tree. Flower-tree. Sang Yi, *Korean*. CKP, *tr. by* Jaihiun Kim

In the midst of words your wordless image. The Heart. Harvey Shapiro. HoPM

In the mighty British Army. Rumour. Owen Rutter. NSI *Fr.* The Song of Tiadatha.

In the Mile End Road. Amy Levy. PEW; RACG

In the Mirror. Elizabeth Fleming. BoTP

In the mirror. Penny Harter. HA

In the Miscroscope. Miroslav Holub, *Czech.* PoSu, *tr.* by Ian *and* Jarmila Milner

In the misty night humming to themselves like morons. Troll's Courtship. Louis MacNeice. AF *Fr.* The Trolls.

In the Moldavian Steppe. Aleksandr Vertinsky, *Russian.* TCRP, *tr.* by Daniel Weissbort

In the month of April, at night. Lied. Alfonsas Nyka-Niliunas, *Lithuanian.* CEEP, *tr.* by Jonas Zdanys

In the month of Averil. The Cuckoo. *Unknown.* FaBoVe

In the month of February. *Unknown.* BoTP

In the month of June the grass grows high. Reading the Book of Hills and Seas. Ch'ien T'ao, *Chinese.* ChiP, *tr.* by Arthur Waley

In the month of May when all leaves open. Robert Bly. ITG

In the Moonlight. Thomas Hardy. NoAM *Fr.* Satires of Circumstance in Fifteen Glimpses.

In the Morgue. Israel Zangwill. TrJP

In the Morning. Jayne Cortez. BlSi

In the Morning. Paul Laurence Dunbar. BPo

In the morning. Steve Kowit. BLT

In the morning and at night. T'ao Ch'ien. SuSp, *tr.* by Eugene Eoyang *Fr.* The Seasons Come and Go.

In the morning, as he was returning to the city. Matthew 21:18–22; In the morning. Donald Hall. GI *Fr.* St. Matthew.

In the morning he steps out. The Crier. Philip Kahclamet, *Wishram Chinook Indian.* STP, *tr.* by Dell Hymes

In the Morning I Look for You. Solomon ibn Gabirol, *Hebrew.* TOF, *tr.* by David Goldstein

In the Morning I Will Pray. William Henry Furness. AH

In the morning in the blue snow. Annual Gaiety. Wallace Stevens. MoAmPo

In the morning, in the morning. A. E. Housman. CBLP

In the morning light a line. The Morning Light. Louis Simpson. NNaP

In the morning of life, when its cares are unknown. Thomas Moore. Ro

In the morning one often feels. Chris Tysh. DeD *Fr.* Porné.

In the morning part. Did John's Music Kill Him? Alfred B. Spellman. NAAAL; SeSe

In the morning sow thy seed, and in the evening withhold not thine hand: for thou knowest not whether shall prosper, either this or that, or whether they both shall be alike good. (LL) Cast thy bread upon the waters. Bible, *O.T.* AWP, *stanzas* 1–6; OBVE

In the morning the bitch whelped. The Bitch. Sergey Aleksandrovich Yesenin, *Russian.* TCRP, *tr.* by Daniel Weissbort

In the morning the city. City. Langston Hughes. SSCS

In the morning the Jews were lined up by an officer. Charles Reznikoff. *See* Jews from Holland, France, and Hungary, and later from.

In the morning, the water fed the sky. Commentary Text Commentary Text Commentary Text. David Shapiro. PmAP

In the morning they build embankments against floods. Wu Chia-chi. CoBLCP, *tr.* by Jonathan Chaves *Fr.* Returning to the Alluvial Fields.

In the morning when I leave my hogan. Mother's Lace. Shonto Begay. NOxBChV

In the morning when ye rise. Another Charme (variant). Robert Herrick. OxBSn

In the mornings we're in the dark. More Blues and the Abstract Truth. C. D. Wright. NAmP90

In the most obscure of streets in the shadow of architectural ribs, where. Zurich Chronicle February 1916. Tristan Tzara, *French.* PFTM, *tr.* by Ralph Manheim

In the mountain rain. Death Poems in September. Diane Di Prima. BB

In the mountain temple they beat the Dharma Drum. Dawn at Chiao Mountain, Seeing Off K'un lun on His Way Back to Ching-k'ou. Wang Shih-chieng, *Chinese.* SuSp, *tr.* by Richard John Lynn

In the Mountain Tent. James Dickey. MT; WeT

In the mountain village. Kanemori, *Japanese.* OHMPJ, *tr.* by Kenneth Rexroth

In the Mountain Village. Wang Hung Kung, *Chinese.* OHMPC, *tr.* by Kenneth Rexroth

In the mountain village. Minamoto no Morotada, *Japanese.* OHPJ, *tr.* by Kenneth Rexroth

In the mountain where you are unworshiped. Inanna and Ebih. Enheduanna, *Sumerian.* BoWoP, *ad.* by Aliki *and* Willis Barnstone

In the Mountains. Agha Shahid Ali. WeT

In the Mountains. Lucian Blaga, *Romanian.* CEEP, *tr.* by Peter Jay *and* Virgil Nemoianu

In the Mountains. Ssu-k'ung Shu, *Chinese.* SuSp, *tr.* by Edward H. Schafer

In the Mountains. Wang An-shih, *Chinese.* SuSp, *tr.* by Jan W. Walls

In the Mountains as Autumn Begins. Wen T'ing-yün, *Chinese.* OHMPC, *tr.* by Kenneth Rexroth

In the mountains o' the west. The Maid o' the West. John Clare. OAEL-2

In the Mountains on a Summer Day. Li Po, *Chinese.* AWP, *tr.* by Arthur Waley

("Wind from the pine-tree trickles on my bare head, A.") (LL) ChiP, *tr.* by Arthur Waley

In the Mountains on a Summer Day. Li Po, *Chinese.* TAL, *tr.* by Robert Payne

In the Mountains, Parting from Master Ning as I Return to West Bank. Kao Ch'i, *Chinese.* CoBLCP, *tr.* by Jonathan Chaves

In the Mourning. Keorapetse Kgositsile. PBMAP *Fr.* The Present is a Dangerous Place to Live.

In the Mourning Time. Robert Earl Hayden. BPo

In the mud of the Cambrian main. A Ballade of Evolution. Grant Allen. EBVV

In the multitude of counsellors. Kyrielle: Party Politics. Frederick Thomas Bennett Macartney. NOBAu

In the Museum. Isabella Gardner. NYBP; SoSe-8

In the music of the morns. A Call. Thomas Holley Chivers. Poetr

In the Naked Bed, in Plato's Cave. Delmore Schwartz. LiTM; MoAmPo; NOBA; NoAM; PoA; VGW

In the name of Love. (LL) Sirventes. Paul Blackburn. NeAP; PoM

In the name of the Father full of virtue. Exodus to Connacht. Fear Dorcha O'Meallain, *Irish.* FaBoPV; TIRV, *tr.* by Thomas Kinsella

In the name of the God of strangers, we beg you. Damagetus, *Greek.* GrAn, *tr.* by John Heath-Stubbs *and* Carol A. Whiteside

In the name of the Lord put I my trust. Bible, *O.T. See* Psalm 11.

In the name of the people. Chorus. Matsemela Manaka. PeSAV *Fr.* Pula.

In the nation of rainy days. Pluvia. Donald Hall. BAP-93

In the nativity of time. Love Made in the First Age[: To Chloris]. Richard Lovelace. BeJo; CaPo; NAEL-1; OAEL-1; SeCP

In the natural year come two thanksgivings. The Sabbath of Mutual Respect. Marge Piercy. CrSp

In the Neolithic Age savage warfare did I wage. Rudyard Kipling. NOBVV

In the network, in the ruin. Trope Market. Jackson MacLow. PmAP

In the New Sun. Philip Levine. NNaP

'In the New World Happiness is Allowed'. Peter Porter. BMAP

In the night. Blues. Sonia Sanchez. GT

In the Night. Elizabeth Jennings. NYBP

In the night. (LL) My Love's Guardian Angel. William Barnes. GBL; PoEL-4

In the Night. Stevie Smith. FP

In the Night. James Stephens. OBMV

In the Night. *Unknown.* FPC; NBLV

In the night after the azalea. Thunder. Yun-gi Hong, *Korean.* CKP, *tr.* by Jaihiun Kim

In the night, in the wind, at the edge of the rain. Irises. Li-Young Lee. BLT

In the Night of the Full Moon. Carl Busse, *German.* AWP, *tr.* by Jethro Bithell

In the Night She Came. Thomas Hardy. OxBM

In the night she told a story. A Story. Jean Ingelow. VWP

In the night the house is thin and blue. House. Sue May. NBrP

In the night there was a murder in the street. Of Autumn. Veronica Porumbacu, *Rumanian.* BoWoP, *tr.* by Willis Barnstone *and* Matei Calinescu

In the nighttime someone in my place. Luigi Fontanella, *Italian.* NeIt, *tr.* by Michael Palma

In the Nine Provinces there is not room enough;. A Vision. Ts'ao Chih, *Chinese.* ChiP, *tr.* by Arthur Waley

In the north-west there is a high house. *Unknown.* ChiP, *tr.* by Arthur Waley *Fr.* Seventeen Old Poems.

In the northern hemisphere. Kangaroo. D. H. Lawrence. EBEV; InPS-3; OxBTC

In the northwest there is a drifting cloud. Ts'ao P'i, *Chinese.* SuSp, *tr.* by Ronald C. Miao

In the northwestern pond there is a dragon-ox. Hsü Wei. *Fr.* Songs of Yen-ching. CoBLCP, *tr.* by Jonathan Chaves

In the numb, numberless days. The Burning. N. Scott Momaday. HATNAP

In the Nuptial Chamber. Thomas Hardy. InPK-6 *Fr.* Satires of Circumstance in Fifteen Glimpses.

In the Ocean. Patricia Goedicke. NMM-2

In the ocean there's a very sad turtle. 229th Chorus. Jack Kerouac. PoM *Fr.* Mexico City Blues.

In the office is Mrs. Apostolacos; the bus driver is Ray. (LL) The Questions. Robert Pinsky. ColAP

In the offing scatterest foam, thy white sails crowding. (LL) A Passer-by. Robert Bridges. CMoP; EBeVV; ImPo; LiTM; MoBrPo; OAEL-2; OBEV; OBNC; OxBTC; SCGP

In the old accents I will sing, my Glory, my Delight. Fellowship. "Michael Field." VWP

In the old age black was not counted fair. Sonnet 127. Shakespeare. OxAEP-1 *Fr.* Sonnets.

In the old back streets o' Pimlico. The Rambling Sailor. Charlotte Mew. PoRA

In the Old City. Jacob Fichman, *Hebrew.* TrJP, *tr. by* Sholom J. Kahn

In the old days (a custom laid aside). Abraham Davenport. John Greenleaf Whittier. AmPP; NoP-4

In the old days back when. Death Crown. Robert Morgan. MT

In the old days I had no wine to drink. Poem in the Form of a Coffin-Puller's Song. T'ao Ch'ien, *Chinese.* CoBCP, *tr. by* Burton Watson

In the old days with married women's stockings. The Libertine. Louis MacNeice. MoP; NoAM

In the old neighborhood, each funeral parlor. Teach Us to Number Our Days. Rita Dove. NoAM

In the old, old days when the West was young. The Texas Ranger. Margie B. Boswell. AiP

In the old park, deserted in the frost. An Exchange Of Feelings. Paul Verlaine, *French.* FLP; LoP, *tr. by* Alistair Elliot

In the old stone pool. Basho, *Japanese.* InPK-6, *tr. by* Cid Corman

In the old testament. Bible Study. Gloria C. Oden. GT

In the old time, by the forks of the Santiam. A Kalapuya Prophecy. *Unknown, Kalapuya Indian.* STP, *tr. by* Jarold Ramsey

In the old time women's cunts had teeth in them. How Her Teeth Were Pulled. *Unknown, Paiute Indian.* STP, *tr. by* Jarold Ramsey

In the one cool room of [or in] the house. Developing a Wife. Andrew Taylor. BMAP; CBAP

In the one light on. First Aid at 4 A.M. Christopher Bursk. InPK-6

In the one-two domestic goose one-two one-two step. Henry Beissel. MoCV *Fr.* New Wings for Icarus.

In the only free. In the Ladies' Room at the Bus Terminal. William Zaranka. BXAP

In the open light. (LL) Coal. Audre Lorde. BlSi; NALW; NBV; NoAM; PoBA; VCAP

In the open sea. *Unknown, Japanese.* OHMPJ, *tr. by* Kenneth Rexroth

In the opening / and shutting of an eye. Winter Song. Lucha Corpi. NMM-2

In the Operating Room. Alden Nowlan. NOBC

In the Orchard. Henrik Ibsen, *Norwegian.* AWP, *tr. by* Sir Edmund Gosse

In the orchard. Plume. Richard Kenney. NoP-4

In the Orchard. Anne Stevenson. ColAP

In The Orchard. Muriel Stuart. EBNV; LW; OxBTC ("'Good night.'. . . "Good night."") (LL) LW

In The Orchard. Swinburne. BoLoP; LoP

In the orchard at twilight. Gevorg Emin, *Armenian.* IFJA, *tr. by* Diana Der Hovanessian

In the orchard grass, through the daisies and clover. Blossom. May Probyn. VWP

In the orchard rooms. Fruit. Philippe Jaccottet, *French.* MFP, *tr. by* Martin Sorrell

In the other gardens. Autumn Fires. Robert Louis Stevenson. NOxBChV; NTP

In the Outhouse. Mitsuye Yamada. *Fr.* Camp Notes. WPOW

In the painkilling cold that wrapped. Snow. David Wevill. MoCV

In the painting. Up against the Wall. David Chapman Berry. BXAP

In the Palace of the President this morning. Easter Sunday, 1985. Charles Martin. RA

In the Palais Royal Garden I stood listening to-day. Christopher Pearse Cranch. APN-1; PAR

In the palm. A Guerrilla Handbook. Imamu Amiri Baraka. PoBA

In the Pantry. "Hugh MacDiarmid." NOAM

In the pantry the dear dense cheeses, Cheddars and harsh. O Cheese. Donald Hall. DiPo

In the parading square. Medusa on Skyros. Alison Fell. NBrP

In the Park. Judith Beveridge. BMAP

In The Park. Gwen Harwood. BMAP; CBAP; GEA

In the Park. Peter Jones. OBGa

In the Park. Iain Crichton Smith. FaBoTC *Fr.* By the Sea.

In the park a crow awakes. Kenneth Rexroth. APSN *Fr.* The Love Poems of Marichiko.

In the parking lot. Cor Van den Heuvel. HA

In the parlour of the Marchioness of Dufferin and Ava. (LL) Notes for a Revised Sonnet. "Edward Pygge." BXAP; OBCoV

In the parlour of the shanty where the lives have all gone wrong. Will Yer Write It Down for Me? Henry Lawson. CBAP

In the Past. Trumbull Stickney. ColAP; NOBA; OxBA

In the past I brought trouble upon myself when I sought rank and honor. Tune: "Wild Geese Have Come Down; Song of Victory." *Unknown, Chinese.* SuSp, *tr. by* Sherwin S. S. Fu

In the past when I saw friends off. Wen Cheng-ming. CoBLCP, *tr. by* Jonathan Chaves *Fr.* Improvised on Horseback to Say Good-bye to Those Who Are Seeing Me Off.

In the Pasture of Dead Horses. Julia Wendell. PUP-20

In the Pauper's Turnip-Field. Herman Melville. OxBSP; PoEL-5

In the pause. Wallflower to a Moonbeam. Louis Untermeyer. BXAP

In the penetrating damp. A Restless Night in Camp. Tu Fu, *Chinese.* OHPC, *tr. by* Kenneth Rexroth

In the Person of a Lady, to Bajazet, Her Unconstant Gallant. "Ephelia." PEW

In the Person of Womankind [A Song Apologetic]. Ben Jonson. BeJo; SeCP

In the Person of Womankind (In Defense of Their Inconstancy). Ben Jonson. *See* Another. In Defense of Their Inconstancy [*or* Inconstancie]. A Song.

In the "phoenix ranks" I was granted the Purple Robe. Selling My Official Robe. Yang Chi, *Chinese.* CoBLCP, *tr. by* Jonathan Chaves

In the photograph he stands alone. Chinese Camp, Kamloops (circa 1883). Andrew Suknaski. NOBC

In the pinch of time, facing. Victorian Grandmother. Margo Lockwood. Poetsp

In the Pines. Bill Monroe. GM

In the Pines. *Unknown.* AmFP

In the Pinewoods, Crows and Owl. Mary Oliver. Poetr

"In the Pink." Siegfried Sassoon. CMoP

In the place where. Judy Grahn. NALW *Fr.* Edward the Dyke and Other Poems.

In the placid summer midnight. Street Scene. William Ernest Henley. BoTP

In the play Amy didn't want to be. First Grade. William Stafford. PiM

In the pleasant pastime of temple viewing. Manners. Edith Marcombe Shiffert. WPE

In the Poppy Field. James Stephens. PoRA

In the Potting Shed. Sir Osbert Sitwell. OBGa

In the Praise of Music. Humphrey Gifford. NoSic

In the premises of the tongue. A Mouth Is Always Muzzled. Martin Carter. HCP

In the Prison Pen. Herman Melville. PoEL-5; TAP

In the *Proceedings of the Royal Institute of Anthropophagy.* A Perversion. Christopher Reid. OBCoV

In the prose version. Helen Paints a Room (1984). John A. Scott. BMAP

In the Public Garden. Marianne Moore. NOBA

In the Public Gardens. John Betjeman. NYBP

In the Public Theater lobby, I wait for Marie. Marilyn Hacker. VCAP *Fr.* Taking Notice.

In the Purple Bar. Gig Ryan. BMAP

In the purple light, heavy with redwood, the slopes drop seaward. Apology for Bad Dreams. Robinson Jeffers. AmPP; MoAmPo; NOBA; OxBA

In the quarter of the Negroes. Cultural Exchange. Langston Hughes. BPo; PoBA

In the Queen Anne's lace a toad. Alexis Rotella. HA

In the Queen's Room. Norman Cameron. OxBTC *Fr.* Three Love Poems. FaBoTW; GTBS-P

In the quiet before cockcrow when the cricket's. Dear Men and Women. John Hall Wheelock. IMW; NYBP

In the quiet glades of Eden. (LL) The Quiet Glades of Eden. Robert Graves. BoLoP; EP

In the quiet of the morning I heard a knock at my door;. Ch'ien T'ao, *Chinese.* ChiP, *tr. by* Arthur Waley

In the R-Mitage. Great Birthday Blaublau with Rhymework and Assonance. Paul Celan, *German.* CBNP

In the railroad yards, leaving the city of darkness. And as for Man. Loren C. Eiseley. GM

In the rain in a yard in Cessnock. Limerick. Ruth Silcock. PeLi

In the rain that has passed by. Lost City. Ingrid Jonker, *Afrikaans.* PeSA, *tr. by* Jack Cope *and* Ruth Miller

In the rain, the naked old father is dancing, he will get wet. Natural History. Robert Penn Warren. NAAL-2

In the rains of winter the pa children. The Dark Welcome. James Keir Baxter. PeNZ *Fr.* Five Sestinas.

In the rat race he won by a whisker. Lifelines. Gavin Ewart. SPE

In the Reading-Room of the British Museum. Louise I. Guiney. APN-2

In the realms of the good and great. (LL)　Emmeline Grangerford's "Ode to Stephen Dowling Bots, Dec'd." "Mark Twain." APN-2; NBLV; OBAL; Poetr

In the rear-view mirror suddenly. Auto Mirror. Adam Zagajewski, *Polish.* BLT, *tr. by* Czeslaw Milosz *and* Robert Hass

In the recurring dream. Stanley Kunitz. *Fr.* The Testing-Tree. FYAP; UnPo

In the Red Grove. Andrew Duncan. NBrP

In the Refectory. Alcuin, *Latin.* MLL, *tr. by* Helen Waddell

In the Restaurant. Gerald William Barrax. GT

In the Restaurant. Aleksandr Blok, *Russian.* TCRP, *tr. by* Geoffrey Thurley

In the Restaurant. Thomas Hardy. MoBrPo *Fr.* Satires of Circumstance in Fifteen Glimpses.

In the Ringwood. Thomas Kinsella. CMoP; PBCIP

In the ripest days of August, sunflowers. The Whisper. Eugene Gloria. OpBo

In the river bank, an empty sandpit. Frankfurt. János Pilinszky, *Hungarian.* AF; PoSu, *tr. by* Ted Hughes *and* Janos Csokits

In the Room. James Thomson. NOBVV; PeVV

In the Room of the Bride-Elect. Thomas Hardy. InPK-6 *Fr.* Satires of Circumstance in Fifteen Glimpses.

In the room's corner the shadow played its little flute. The Flute. Sophia De Mello Breyner, *Portuguese.* VCWP, *tr. by* Ruth Fainlight

In the Root Cellar. Maxine W. Kumin. FaBoWP

In the rose creeping into the tower of exiles. A Winter Day. Philip Lamantia. CLPP

In the Royal City spring is almost over;. The Flower Market. Po Chü-i, *Chinese.* ChiP, *tr. by* Arthur Waley

In the rubbish dumps, a concrete dam far off in the mountain. (LL) Summer Holiday. Robinson Jeffers. MoAmPo; OxBA

In the rude age when scyence was not so rife. Another Tribute to Wyatt. Henry Howard, Earl of Surrey. AAS; SiPS

In the Rue Monsieur le Prince. Song for "Buvez les Vins du Postillion"—Advt. Jean Garrigue. TAP

In the rush odour of Danish meadows. Peter Huchel, *German.* PoSu, *tr. by* Michael Hamburger

In the salt warp / was the plasma. Origins. Carl Rakosi. FTOS

In the same post, the Old Fox receives. Negotiation. Alan Brownjohn. PeLV

In the same sweet eternity of love. (LL) Love What It Is. Robert Herrick. FaBoEE; GBL

In the same way. (LL) Apology. William Carlos Williams. OxBA; SAmP

In the sand I grew, by the rocky sea-wall. The Husband's Message. *Unknown, Anglo-Saxon.* AnOE, *tr. by* Charles W. Kennedy

In the Sangre de Cristos near Santa Fe. Modern Times. Janet Sylvester. BAP-94

In the satin shade of an olive tree. Achilles and the Tortoise. Miroslav Holub, *Czech.* PoSu, *tr. by* Stuart Friebert *and* Dana Hábová

In the scented bud of the morning—O. The Daisies. James Stephens. AWP

In the school auditorium. Bully. Martín Espada. LTA; UnSA

In the Sea. Brendan Kennelly. BiHa

In the sea. (LL) Little Fish. D. H. Lawrence. AYFP; OxBTC; RB; Spl; TTTS

In the sea at Ashkelon stand the amphoras of Rome. Decline of an Empire. Dan Pagis, *Hebrew.* IP, *tr. by* Warren Bargad *and* Stanley F. Chyet

In the sea, Biscayne, there prinks. Homunculus et la Belle Étoile. Wallace Stevens. MoAmPo

In the sea of ivy clothed Iwami. Hitomaro, *Japanese.* OHPJ, *tr. by* Kenneth Rexroth *Fr.* Manyo Shu, Part 2 of 4.

In the sea of life. Epigraph. Gu Cheng, *Chinese.* ChiPo, *tr. by* Helen F. Siu *and* Zelda Stern

In the Sea of Tears. Naomi Replansky. BrRo

In the sea, sunset. O. Mabson Southard. HA

In the season of late August star-fall. Amazing Grace in the Back Country. Robert Penn Warren. ColAP

In the season when the world leafs and flowers. Compiuta Donzella, *Italian.* ItIP

In the Second Month of Summer, Taking My Family to the Villages East of the City. Li K'ai-hsien, *Chinese.* CoBLCP, *tr. by* Jonathan Chaves

In the Secret House. Christopher Middleton. FaBoMo

In the sedge beyond Chalco. The Flowering War. *Unknown, Aztec Indian.* STP, *tr. by* Jerome Rothenberg

In the semi-dark we take everything off. Hotels. C. D. Wright. CMAP

In the Seminole darkness of your singing eyes. Poem to a Redskin. Wendy Rose. CDW

In the Servants' Quarters. Thomas Hardy. FaBoVe; MoBrPo

In the Seven Woods. W. B. Yeats. CMoP; NoAM

In the seventh month the Fire-star declines. *Unknown, Chinese.* SuSp, *tr. by* Irving Y. Lo

In the shabby train no seat is vacant. The Refugees. Randall Jarrell. MoAmPo

In the shade of a metaphor. Patrizia Cavalli, *Italian.* Nelt, *tr. by* Robert McCracken *with* Patrizia Cavalli

In the shade of a plane tree with our shopping. City Park. Christine Crow. SSCS

In the Shadows. David Gray.
　Sonnet I: "If it must be; if it must be, O God!" OxBS

In the shaking of the sieve, the refuse. The Test of Men. Bible, Apocrypha. TrJP *Fr.* Ecclesiasticus.

In the shambles of love, they kill only the best. Jelaluddin Rumi. RaBo, *tr. by* Coleman Barks *and* John Moyne *Fr.* Four Quatrains.

In the shape of this night, in the still fall. At the New Year. Kenneth Patchen. LiTM *Fr.* Eight Early Poems.

In the shoal of wind. Birds. Namsu Park, *Korean.* CKP, *tr. by* Jaihiun Kim

In the shop in the muceque. Note on a Shop in the Muceque. Geraldo Bessa Victor, *Portuguese.* PeSAV, *tr. by* Donald Burness

In the shoppes. Gemwood. Marvin Bell. CMAP

In the shower, at the shaving mirror or beach. My Mammogram. J. D. McClatchy. BAP-95

In the shower naked. Breast Examination. Wanda Coleman. GT

In the Shreve High football stadium. Autumn Begins in Martins Ferry, Ohio. James Wright. ColAP; HCAP; HeIP-4; InPK-6; InPS-3; NoAM; SAGP; VCAP; WeT; WeW-3

In the sightless air I dwell. Song of a Spirit. Ann Radcliffe. ECWP

In the Silence. Stephany Fuller. BPo

In the silence and the gloom. (LL) Aftermath. Henry Wadsworth Longfellow. APN-1; NAAL-1; NAAL-3; NOBA; PAR; PoPoPo; TAP

In the silence that prolongs the span. Black Jackets. Thom Gunn. HeIP-4; NAEL-2; NoP-4; TwCP

In the silences between peals of the bell. Chin Nung. CoBLCP, *tr. by* Jonathan Chaves *Fr.* I Have Recently Edited My Unworthy Poems in Four Chapters, Copied Them Out in My Own Hand, and Entrusted Them to My Daughter to Keep. Five Miscellaneous Poems.

In the Silent Night. Isaac Leibush Peretz, *Yiddish.* TrJP, *tr. by* Joseph Leftwich

In the singed breath of London. Liberty and Ten Years of Return. Christopher Howell. CDa

In the six-acre field. Lost. Millen Brand. NYBP

In the sixth month, deep in the mountains. Summer. Chang Yü. *Fr.* The Four Seasons in the Mountains. CoBLCP, *tr. by* Jonathan Chaves

In the sixth month, outside the gate. Wen Cheng-ming. CoBLCP, *tr. by* Jonathan Chaves *Fr.* The Chung-i Temple.

In the sixth month the angel Gabriel was sent from God. Luke 1:26–38; In the sixth month the angel Gabriel. Anna Kamienska. GI *Fr.* St. Luke.

In the sixty-three years. Summing Up. Claribel Alegría, *Spanish.* LoL, *tr. by* D. J. Flakoll

In the sky, not a sliver of cloud. On the Night of the Sixteenth of the Eighth Month: Watching the Moon from the Deck of the Ship, Aimomaru in the Black Water Sea. Liu E, *Chinese.* CoBLCP, *tr. by* Jonathan Chaves

In the sky the Milky Way turns. Tune: "Southern Song, A." Li Ch'ing-chao, *Chinese.* SuSp, *tr. by* Eugene Eoyang

In the sky there is a moon and stars. Proportion. Amy Lowell. BoWoP

In the sludge drawer of animals in arms. Rules of Sleep. Howard Moss. VCAP

In the Slums. George Campbell. PBCV

In the small beauty of the forest. Psalm. George Oppen. NNaP

In the small hours, several rounds. C'est Plus Qu'en Crime, C'est une Faute. David Trinidad. WWSi

In the small old barn. The Eternal Landscape. Lenard D. Moore. GT

In the small town where the hero was born. Pietà. Wislawa Szymborska, *Polish.* VCWP, *tr. by* Magnus J. Krynski *and* Robert A. Maguire

In the Smoking-Car. Richard Wilbur. CoAmPo; GM; LiTM; MoAmPo

In the Snake Park. William Plomer. NYBP; OxBTC

In the Snowfall. Gwerfyl Mechain, *Welsh.* BoWoP, *tr. by* Willis Barnstone

In the soft air perfumed with blooming May. Lines to Mount Glen. George Marion McClellan. AAP

In the soft armchair sprawls the boy unmoving. The Limits of Physics. Dan Pagis, *Hebrew.* IP, *tr. by* Warren Bargad *and* Stanley F. Chyet

In the Soul Hour. Robert Mezey. AmPA

In the South. His Fingers Seem to Sing. Sam Cornish. GT

In the South be drooping trees. Chou and the South. *Unknown.* CTC, *tr. by* Ezra Pound *Fr.* Shi King.

In the South be drooping trees. Confucius. CTC, *tr.* by Ezra Pound *Fr.* Chou and the South.

In the south of the city on a cold rainy February day. Doing Time in Baltimore. Judith Baumel. WWSi

In the south, sleeping against. Legacy. Imamu Amiri Baraka. ColAP; MoP; NOBA; NoAM; PoBA

In the South there is a saying. Why Are Daddies So Mean? Jane Chambers. GLP

In the southern land many birds sing;. The South. Wang Chien, *Chinese.* AWP; BLT; ChiP, *tr.* by Arthur Waley

In the southern village the boy who minds the ox. The Herd-Boy. Lu Yu, *Chinese.* ChiP, *tr.* by Arthur Waley

In the space where the poem has happened. (LL) The Double-Play. Robert Wallace. CMAP; PFE

In the Spring. William Barnes. GBL

In the Spring. Meleager, *Greek.* AWP, *tr.* by Andrew Lang

In the Spring. Tennyson. *Fr.* Locksley Hall. EBEV; EBVVPR; EnVR; FaBoBe; ImPo; NAEL-2; OAEL-2

In the spring, by the big shuck-pile. Burning the Cat. W. S. Merwin. NIP-4

In the Spring Garden. Geoffrey Grigson. OBGa

In the Spring, on the trees. Fluttering Leaves. Rodney Bennett. BoTP

In the spring ravine. Onoe No Shibafune, *Japanese.* OHMPJ, *tr.* by Kenneth Rexroth

In the Spring the quince and the. Ibycus, *Greek.* PGA, *tr.* by Kenneth Rexroth

In the spring woods, how good it is to see. Aspects of the World like Coral Reefs. William Bronk. VGW

In the Springtime I am always. Old Age. Ou-yang Hsiu, *Chinese.* OHPC, *tr.* by Kenneth Rexroth

In the square of a lighted window. Observation of a Bee. Leah Goldberg, *Hebrew.* WPOW, *tr.* by Stephen Mitchell

In the squdgy river. The Hippopotamus. Georgia Roberts Durston. CTV

In the state of old Kentucky. The Death of Samuel Adams. *Unknown.* AmFP

In the State of "Old Palmetto," from the town of Eutawville. The Eutawville Lynching. Lizelia Augusta Jenkins Moorer. CBWP-3

In the States. Robert Louis Stevenson. AiP

In the steel room. Birth. George Ella Lyon. CrSp

In the still-blistering late afternoon. The Farmer. Ellen Bryant Voigt. MT; WeW-3

In the still morning when you move. Tropics. Ellen Bryant Voigt. WeT

In the stillness. Expectant Mother. Penelope Shuttle. BrRo

In the stillness after dawn we two. Equinox 1980. Peter Davison. NoP-4

In the Storm of Roses. Ingeborg Bachmann, *German.* AF, *tr.* by Mark Anderson

In the strange city of life. Nostalgia. Walter De la Mare. LiTM

In the strange house. The Father. Jean Valentine. MoLi *Fr.* The Messenger. LCAP-2

In the Stravinsky book by Lillian Libman. Reading in the Night. Roy Fuller. OxBC

In the Street. John Shaw Neilson. CBAP

In the street of the sky night walks scattering poems. (LL) Impression. E. E. Cummings. MoAmPo; OxBA

In the street two children sharpen. East Bronx. David Ignatow. CoAmPo

In the streetcar conductor's uniform. Portrait: The Freedom Fighter. George Jonas. NOBC

In the stump of the old tree, where the heart has rotted out. Poem. Hugh Sykes Davies. SPE

In the Style of Han Shan and Shih Te. Wang An-shih, *Chinese.*
"Had I been an ox or horse." SuSp, *tr.* by Jan W. Walls
"Wind blew, a tile fell from the roof, The." SuSp, *tr.* by Jan W. Walls

In the Suburbs. Louis Simpson. TRP; WeT

In the suburbs, the nativity scene. Lost Child. Lee Upton. CMAP

In the summer heat and fever crackling. The Boy; or, Son of Rip-off. Malcolm Glass. BXAP

In the summer of the first year of Chia-yu (A.D. 1056). The Cicada. Ou-yang Hsiu, *Chinese.* AWP, *tr.* by Arthur Waley

In the sun-glad nakedness. Costis Palamas. GrIP, *tr.* by Philip Sherrard *Fr.* Life Immovable.

In the sunny orchard closes. In the Orchard. Henrik Ibsen, *Norwegian.* AWP, *tr.* by Sir Edmund Gosse

In the sun's path. Dawn in the Valley. Fily-Dabo Sissoko, *French.* NegPo, *tr.* by Ellen Conroy Kennedy

In the swamp in secluded recesses. Walt Whitman. *Fr.* Spring. LBC *Fr.* Memories of President Lincoln.

In the sweet shire of Cardigan. Simon Lee [the Old Huntsman]. Wordsworth. GTBS-P; NAEL-2; Ro

In the swollen head of the nation. (LL) Up Rising. Robert Duncan. APSN; NNaP

In the Tail of the Scorpion. Genevieve Taggard VGW

In the tall quiet pines of Washington. For Tom Numkena, Hopi/Spokane. Harold Littlebird. VoR

In the Tank. Thom Gunn. NoAM

In the tattered wallpaper I see a butterfly dying. Poem No. X. Sang Yi. PFTM

In the teashop's ingle-nook. (LL) In a Bath Teashop. John Betjeman. CBLP; EnLoPo

In the temple. Bob Boldman. HA

In the Tenth Month of the Year Jen-tzu (1672) the Imperial Censor Tan Chiang-shang, Mountain Man Wang Shih-ku and I Traveled by Boat to Pi-ling and Moored There. We Lingered Among the Frosty Trees and Red Leaves. Wang Was Entrusted with the Task of Painting a Picture, and We Each Wrote Twelve Poems to Record Our Delightful Experience. Yün Shou-p'ing, *Chinese.*
"Scorpion's tails, silver hooks." CoBLCP, *tr.* by Jonathan Chaves

In the terrible night, natural substance of all nights. Fernando Pessoa, *Portuguese.* NNPT, *tr.* by Jonathan Griffin

In the terrible years of Yezhovism I spent seventeen months standing in. Instead of a Preface. "Anna Andreyevna Akhmatova." PFTM

In the Theatre. Dannie Abse. NoAM

In the third-class seat sat the journeying boy. Midnight on the Great Western. Thomas Hardy. CH; NOBE; OxAEP-2

In the third day of May. The Boy and the Mantle. *Unknown.* ESPB; OxBB

In the Third Month. David Ray. RaBo

In the third month, a sudden flow of blood. The Vow. Anthony Hecht. CoAmPo; InPK-6

In the time it takes. Andrew Crozier. NBrP *Fr.* High Zero.

In the time of old sin without sadness. Variations on [*or of*] an Air: After [Algernon Charles] Swinburne. G. K. Chesterton. NOBL

In the Time of Revolution. Julius Lester. PoBA

In the tiny village. What She Said. Vayilanrevan, *Tamil.* PLW, *tr.* by A. K. Ramanujan

In the tombs. The Tombs. Latif Asad Abdullah. BAP-96

In the Tool-shed. Andrew Greig. FaBoTC

In the top and front of a bus, eager to meet his fate. Figure of Eight. Louis MacNeice. OxBSP

In the touch of this bosom there worketh a spell. Coleridge. RB *Fr.* Christabel and Geraldine. *Fr.* Christabel. FHYEP; NAEL-2; NOBRP; OAEL-2; Ro

In the tower the bell. The Bell. Richard Jones. NAmP90

In the Town. *Unknown, French.* OBCP; PChr, *tr.* by Eleanor Farjeon

In the town dump I find a still-beating heart. George Swede. HA

In the town of Athy one Jeremy Lanigan. Lanigan's Ball. *Unknown.* OxBoLi

In the town of Bardez where Armenians. The Dance. Siamanto, *Armenian.* AF, *tr.* by Peter Balakian *and* Nevart Yaghlian

In the town of Odessa. Dvonya. Louis Simpson. NNaP; NOBA

In the town where every man is king. Josephine Miles. NALW

In the Town With Cat-/ Shaped Maze. Mieko Kanai, *Japanese.* WPJ, *tr.* by Kenneth Rexroth *and* Ikuko Atsumi

In the Tradition / (Not a White Shadow but Black People Will Be Victorious). Imamu Amiri Baraka. MoNo

In the Train. James Thomson. BoTP; OBEV *Fr.* Sunday at Hampstead.

In the tranced dancing of men. (LL) The Bear on the Delhi Road. Earle Birney. HeIP-4; MoCV; NOBC; NYBP; NoAM; NoP-4

In the Tree-Top. Lucy Larcom. OBCA

In the Trenches. Richard Aldington. PeFWW

In the tunnel of woods, as the road. Last Things. William Meredith. NoAM

In the twelfth month of this Eighth Year. Bitter Cold, Living in the Village. Po Chü-i, *Chinese.* SuSp, *tr.* by Irving Lo

In the Twentieth Century. James Philip McAuley. ChIV-2

In the Twentieth Century of my trespass on earth. Galway Kinnell. *Fr.* The Dead Shall Be Raised Incorruptible. NOBA; PoE

In the Twenty-Fifth Year of Marriage, It Goes On. Alicia Ostriker. PBCAP

In the twenty-fifth year of my age. Petit Testament. "Ern Malley." BMAP

In the Underworld. Muriel Rukeyser. APSN

In the universal Sun. (LL) The Invitation. Shelley. CH; GTBS-P; NAEL-2; OBEV

In the unmade light I can see the world. West Wall. W. S. Merwin. RaBo

In the unnavigable dusk, when. Owl. Peter Kane Dufault. NYBP

In the unsigned print. Two Japanese Prints. Pat Matsueda. EC3

In the usual way of the young / we made appointments. I Say Goodby to Fan An-ch'eng. Shen Yüeh, *Chinese.* SuSp, *tr.* by Lenore Mayhew *and* William McNaughton

In the vale [or vaile] of restless mind. Quia Amore Langueo. *Unknown, Middle English.* NOBE; NOCV; PoEL-1, *tr.* by Helen Gardner

In the Valley. Priscilla Jane Thompson. CBWP-2

In the Valley of Cauteretz. Tennyson. BoLoP; NAEL-2; NOBE (Two and Thirty Years Ago.) LBC

In the Valley of the Elwy. Gerard Manley Hopkins. EnVR; ImPo; NOBVV; NOCV; OxAEP-2; TOF

In the valley of the Pegnitz, where across broad meadowlands. Nuremberg. Henry Wadsworth Longfellow. AmPP

In the valleys of the future we shall walk. Desmond O'Grady. PBCIP *Fr.* Lines in a Roman Schoolbook.

In the vase. Tanka. Masaoka Shiki, *Japanese.* MJT, *tr.* by Ueda, Makoto

In the vaulted way, where the passage turned. Thomas Hardy. CBLP

In the very earliest time. Magic Words. *Eskimo Oral Tradition, Inuit.* BLT, *tr.* by Edward Field

In the very earliest time. Magic Words. *Unknown, Eskimo.* ImGa; PiM, *tr.* by Edward Field; RaBo; STP

In the very midst of life. Martin Luther, *German.* GePo, *tr.* by F. Samuel Janow

In the vestibule behind the church I saw the parson. Parson's Pleasure. Barry O. Higgs. PeSA

In the village churchyard she lies. In the Churchyard at Cambridge. Henry Wadsworth Longfellow. AmPP; PoEL-5; TAP

In the Village of My Forefathers. Vasco [or Vasko] Popa. PoSu, *tr.* by Anne Pennington *Fr.* Raw Flesh.

In the vine-shadows on the veranda. The Sisters. Judith Wright. NALW

In the violent day. (LL) This Morning. Muriel Rukeyser. BoWoP; CrSp

In the visions of sailors. Between Rivers and Seas. Lance Henson. VoR

In the Waiting Room. Elizabeth Bishop. FaBoWP; HeIP-4; InPS-3; LCAP-2; LiLi; NAAL-2; NALW; NOBA; NoAM; PoE; VCAP

("And it was still the fifth / of February, 1918.") (LL) AFr

("It was still the fifth / of February, 1918.") (LL) NoP-4

("Stranger could ever happen.") (LL) ColAP

In the Waiting Room. Patricia Goedicke. NMM-2

In the waiting room of the railway. The Hen. Christian Morgenstern, *German.* RB, *tr.* by W. D. Snodgrass *and* Lore Segal

In the wake. Gustave Keyser. HA

In the Wake of Home. Adrienne Rich. LCAP-2

In the waking night. The Cage. David Gascoyne. SPE

In the War they made a celestial cave. Transgressing the Real. Robert Duncan. APSN *Fr.* Passages.

In the Ward. Robert Lowell. NAAL-2

In the waters, blue and permanent. (LL) The Drowned Children. Louise Glück. HCAP; VCAP

In the Way Back. Debi Kang Dean. UnSA

In the Week When Christmas Comes. Eleanor Farjeon. PChr

In the west cloud masses swelled, but even the wind was powerless to breathe. Idlers. Leonid Nikolaevich Martynov, *Russian.* TCRP, *tr.* by J. R. Rowland

In the west you're still asleep. You Who Sleep. Philippe Soupault, *French.* AF, *tr.* by Schmidt, Paulette

In the western village the day grows long. Feelings in Nature ("In the western village the day grows long"). Ma Chih-yüan. *Fr.* Four Poems to the Tune "Ch'ing-chiang yin." CoBLCP, *tr.* by Jonathan Chaves

In the white house in Rutherford. The Canaries in Uncle Arthur's Basement. Ed Ochester. CMAP

In the white of my thought. For Robert Desnos. Tristan Tzara, *French.* AF, *tr.* by Mary Ann Caws

In the white of noon-day's brightness the city seems blotted out. In the Old City. Jacob Fichman, *Hebrew.* TrJP, *tr.* by Sholom J. Kahn

In the white snowflakes of a blizzard. Dance of the Soul. Vladimir Shchirovsky, *Russian.* TCRP, *tr.* by Bradley Jordan

In the white-washed medical-smelling milkhouse. My Grandmother Washes Her Vessels. Fred Chappell. MT

In the wide womb of possibility. Sir Richard Blackmore. Poetr *Fr.* Possibilities. Poetr

In the wild October night-time, when the wind raved round the land. The Night of Trafalgar. Thomas Hardy. CH; FaBoCh; MoBrPo; OBMV *Fr.* The Dynasts.

In the Wilderness. Robert Graves. CH; ChIV-2; MoBrPo; PeECV

In the Wilderness. James Simmons. GI

In the wilds there is a dead doe. *Unknown, Chinese.* SuSp, *tr.* by Wu-Chi Liu

In the wind that blows. The Dead. René Arcos, *French.* PeFWW, *tr.* by Christopher Middleton

In the wind that ripples over them. Last Scene in the First Act. Marge Piercy. NoAM

In the Winter. Sir Osbert Sitwell. OBGa

In the winter dusk. Surveillances. Tom Paulin. CIP-2; PNI

In the Winter of My Thirty-eighth Year. W. S. Merwin. NOBA

In the winter stadium, picturing. What You Can't See. Karen Chase. SeSe

In the winter time we go. White Fields. James Stephens. OTCP

In the wintertime. Toe'osh; a Laguna Coyote Story. Leslie Marmon Silko. CDW; NoAM; VoR

In the wintertime my father wears a hat. Clock on Hancock Street. June Jordan. FaBoWP

In the wondrous light of a pair of brown eyes. Admiration. Josephine D. Henderson Heard. CBWP-4

In the Wood. Eileen Mathias. BoTP

In The Wood. Boris Pasternak, *Russian.* LoP, *tr.* by J. M. Cowen

In the Woods. Dorothy Baker. BoTP

In / the / woods. Marlene Mountain. HA

In the Woods. Heinz Piontek, *German.* CLPP, *tr.* by Jerome Rothenberg

In the woods I came on an old friend fishing. Finding a Teacher. W. S. Merwin. NNaP

In the woodyard were green and dry. The Rick of Green Wood. Edward Dorn. NeAP; PmAP; PoM

In the words of Phokylides: the tribes of women. On the Problem of Choosing a Wife. Phocylides, *Greek.* OBCVT, *tr.* by Willis Barnstone

In the Workhouse. George R. Sims. *See* Christmas Day in the Workhouse.

In the world. (LL) The World. Robert Creeley. MoP; NoP-4; PmAP; VCAP

In the world are distant roads. The Wanderer. "Andrey Platonov," *Russian.* TCRP, *tr.* by Albert C. Todd

In the world are millions and millions of men, and each man. Angel and Stone. Howard Nemerov. NYBP

In the world which He has created. Hymmnn. Allen Ginsberg. NOBA

In the world's heart burns a torch of fire. Shin Shalom, *Hebrew.* MHP, *tr.* by Ruth Finer Mintz

In the worst inn's worst room, with mat half-hung. The Duke of Buckingham. Alexander Pope. NOBE *Fr.* Epistle III, to Allen Lord Bathurst.

In the wracks of Walsingham. A Lament for Our Lady's Shrine at Walsingham. *Unknown.* NoSic; PoEL-2

In the Yard of the Policlinic. Vladimir Holan, *Czech.* AF, *tr.* by C. G. Hanzlicek *and* Dana Habova

In the yard the autumn moon shines white. The Rats. Georg Trakl, *German.* APo, *tr.* by John Hollander

In the Year Chi-hai (1299), While Returning by Way of Purple Fungus Mountain at Springmouth, I Lamented for Lecture Master Chin. Tai Piao-yüan, *Chinese.* CoBLCP, *tr.* by Jonathan Chaves

In the year 1910—and I give the date without uncertainty. Versos de Montalgo. *Unknown.* AS, *tr.* by Frank J. Dobie

In the year *tan-o.* Rhyme-Prose on the Owl. Chia Yi, *Chinese.* CoBCP, *tr.* by Burton Watson

In the Year with the Cyclical Sign *Mou-shen.* T'ao Ch'ien, *Chinese.* CoBCP, *tr.* by Burton Watson

In the years of her age the most beautiful. Petrarch. OBMV, *tr.* by J. M. Synge *Fr.* Sonnets to Laura.

In the yellow pickup. The Weekend Equestrian. Michael S. Weaver. GT

In the Yukon. Ralph Gustafson. MoCV; NoP-4

In the zero of the night, in the lipping hour. The Approach to Thebes. Stanley Kunitz. PoA

In the zócalo. Three Portraits. George Hitchcock. VGW

In the Zoo. A. K. Ramanujan. VCWP

In the zunsheen ov our zummers. The Geate A-Vallen To. William Barnes. EnVR

In Thee! (LL) Wild Nights—Wild Nights! Emily Dickinson. APAD; ITG; NCAP; NoP-4; PoPoPo; SDW; WPoS

In thee must ever find a foe. (LL) O Memory, Thou Fond Deceiver. Oliver Goldsmith. OBEV; OxBSP

In their ascent from the pavement. The Soul. Peter Cooley. NAmP90

In their congealed light. Through Binoculars. Charles Tomlinson. OAEL-2

In their homes, much glass and steel. Their cars. Those Who Want Out. Denise Levertov. LoHo

In their long hair they lie. Tombs of the Hetaerae. Rilke, *German.* PFTM, *tr.* by Pierre Joris

In their purple hearts. (LL) Pear Tree. Hilda Doolittle. BoWoP; CMoP; ColAP; MoAmPo; NOBA; PoE; UnPo

In their religion they are so unev'n. Daniel Defoe. OBSV *Fr.* The True-born Englishman.

In their small, queer houses. Ant-Hills. "Marian Douglas." OBCA

In their workclothes. (LL) Crossing Kansas by Train. Donald Justice. AiP; NYBP

In them days / they won't hardly no way to know if. First Carolina Said-Song. A. R. Ammons. OBAL

In there, furtively watching, crying. Charles Kenneth Williams. *See* Alzheimer's: The Wife.

In these cold evenings, when the rain. Fear of the Earth. Alex Comfort. MoBrPo

In these days, every mother's son or daughter. Ebenezer Elliot. Son

In these days of indigestion. Some Little Bug. Roy Atwell. PoLF

IN these deep solitudes and awful cells. Eloisa to Abelard. Alexander Pope. NAEL-1; PoEL-3; RACG

In These Dissenting Times. Alice Walker. InPS-3; PoBA Women. NMM-2; WPOW ("Of it / Themselves.") (LL) NAAAL

In these few years. Mother's Voice. Robert Creeley. FiLi; Poetr

In These Houses of Swift Easy Women. Brenda Marie Osbey. MT

In th'Heaven of Mary's eye, a Teare. (LL) The Tear[e]. Richard Crashaw. ImPo; SeCP

In things a moderation keep[e]. Moderation. Robert Herrick. FaBoEE

In 'thirty-nine, in Poland. Children's Crusade 1939. Bertolt Brecht, German. MoBS, tr. by Michael Hamburger

In this age of decadence people love antiques. Collecting Antiques. Cheng Hsieh, Chinese. CoBLCP, tr. by Jonathan Chaves

In This Age of Hard Trying, Nonchalance Is Good and. Marianne Moore. MeMAP

In this bath Cypris once was bathed by Love, her son. Marianus, Greek. GrAn, tr. by Anthony Holden

In this big house—. Saturn. Günter Grass, German. AF, tr. by Michael Hamburger and Christopher Middleton

In this blue light. San Sepolcro. Jorie Graham. HCAP; PoPoPo; VCAP

In this book I see your face and in your face. Frontispiece. May Swenson. CoAP; WPE

In this café Durruti. The Midget. Philip Levine. WeT

In this café they have solved the problem of names. The Café of Situations. Martin Johnston. BMAP Fr. In Transit: A Sonnet Square.

In this city how many masters are clouds. Amsterdam. Jean Garrigue. TAP

In this cold monument lies one. An Epitaph on M. H. Charles Cotton. EBEV; FaBoEE

In this cold room. Samuel Hearne in Wintertime. John Newlove. NOBC

In this cool corner where dark stars of ivy. Destroying Angel. Hilary Corke. NYBP

In this country I planted not one seed. Sailing from the United States. Stanley Moss. VGW

In this country lightning quickens stone. Mineral Kingdom. Jacques Dupin, French. VCWP, tr. by Paul Auster

In this country there is neither measure nor balance. Two Campers in Cloud Country. Sylvia Plath. NYBP

In This Dark House. Edward Davison. OBMV

In this dark I rest. Eye Mask. Denise Levertov. BLT

In this deep valley of wastes more than forlorn. Solitude. Andreas Gryphius, German. GePo, tr. by George C. Schoolfield

In this desolation. The Soldier. Uys Krige, Afrikaans. PeSA, tr. by the author

In this earthly configuration. Concentration Constellation. Lawson Fusao Inada. PaTW

In this factory, here the axe-grinders. University Curriculum. William Price Turner. OxBS

In this fair stranger's eyes of grey. Absence. Matthew Arnold. EnVR; GLoP Fr. Switzerland.

In this glass palace are flowers in golden baskets. The Lovers. Conrad Potter Aiken. NYBP

In this grave age, when comedies are few. Joseph Addison. OxBSn Fr. The Drummer, or the Haunted House.

In this green month when resurrected flowers. Memorial Wreath. Dudley Randall. CBCWP; PoBA

In this high pasturage, the Blunden time. The Archaeological Picnic. John Betjeman. EnLoPo

In This His Suit. Mark Cox. NAmP90

In this house (in a dying orchard. Margaret Atwood. CrSp Fr. Solstice Poem.

In this house, she said, in this high second storey. Under. Sir John Collings Squire. FaBoTw

In this image of my friend's studio. Chariot. Stanley Kunitz. BAP-93

In this land vague malevolence. Van Diemen's Land. Allen Afterman. NOBAu

In this little room. Slave Cabin, Sotterly Plantation, Maryland, 1989. Lucille Clifton. LoL

In this little Urn[e] is laid. Upon Prue [or Prew], His Maid. Robert Herrick. BeJo; CaPo; NAEL-1; NoP-4

In this lone, open glade I lie. Lines Written in Kensington Gardens. Matthew Arnold. GaP; OBGa; FHYEP

In this long summer wilderness. What He Said in the Desert. Otalantaiyar, Tamil. PLW, tr. by A. K. Ramanujan

In this meadow starred with spring. Morning Glory. Siegfried Sassoon. TrCP

In this meantime the Trachin king sore vexed in his thought. Ceyx and Alcyone. Ovid, Latin. NoSic, tr. by Arthur Golding Fr. Metamorphoses.

In this merry morn of May. Unknown. Fr. Medieval Norman Song. AWP, tr. by John Addington Symonds

In this mirror. I Imagine Angels. Guillaume Apollinaire, French. PiM, tr. by Kenneth Koch

In this mirror I am enclosed. Guillaume Apollinaire. TTTS, tr. by Roger Shattuck Fr. Heart, Crown, and Mirror.

In This Motherless Geography. Elaine Orr. CrSp

In This New Year. Mary Jane Moffat. IMW

In this odd life will tarnish or pass away. (LL) Moonrise. D. H. Lawrence. LiTM; PoA

In this old house. (LL) Sadie and Maud. Gwendolyn Brooks. InPK-6; MoP; NAAAL; NOBA; NoAM; TAP

In this parable of vengeance. The Impossible Pictures. Tom Paulin. CABP; CIP-2

In This Place. Robert C. Fuentes. BAP-96

In this place an Irishman should feel at home. November in Boston. Thomas McCarthy. BiHa

In this place God leaves His morsels unguarded. For the Woman at the Fast-Food Fish Place Who Called Me Pig. Gary Margolis. IFJA

In this place they make small gardens bloom. And after a Long While. Ory Bernstein, Hebrew. IP, tr. by Warren Bargad and Stanley F. Chyet

In this place years ago. At the Door of the Native Studies Director. Robert H. Davis. HATNAP

In this road that I must take. Journey. Roy Daniells. MoCV

In this room. No One. Lilian Moore. TLR

In this room, holding hands. All Day We've Longed for Night. Sarah Webster Fabio. BlSi

In this season of brief arrivals. Listening to September. Brendan Galvin. CMAP

In this season, through the clear tears. August, on the Rented Farm. Dave Jeddie Smith. ColAP

In this short Life. Emily Dickinson. NTP; SAmP

In this small character is sent. Upon a Braid of Hair in a Heart. Henry, Bishop of Chichester King. EnLoPo

In this small fort, besieged with snow. Lines Written on a Window at The Leasowes. William Shenstone. OxBSP

In this squalid, dirty dooryard. The Pear Tree. Edna St. Vincent Millay. MoAmPo

In this State's Twenty-eighth. Doing Justice. Bruce Cutler. EC2

In this stoned and. Definition of Nature. Eugene B. Redmond. NBV; PoBA

In This Strange Labyrinth How Shall I Turn? Mary Sidney Wroth. NAEL-1 Fr. A Crown of Sonnets Dedicated to Love.

In this sweet book, the treasury of wit. To His Lady. Sir John Davies. SiPS

In This Theayter they has plays. An Old Woman, Outside the Abbey Theater. Leonard Alfred George Strong. MoBrPo

In this time of rain and thunder. What He Said. Peyanar, Tamil. PLW, tr. by A. K. Ramanujan Fr. Nine on Happy Reunion. PLW, tr. by A. K. Ramanujan

In this town, in the blurred and snowy dawn. Geneva. Alastair Reid. NYBP

In this vain, busy world, where the good and the gay. Stanzas. Mary Robinson. ECWP; WoRP

In this war the Hun has brought us. Owen Rutter. NSI Fr. The Song of Tiadatha.

In This Way. Gertrude Stein. PFTM

In this weedy field somewhere inside marriage. Wild Strawberries. Ronald Wallace. IFJA

In this world. Flannery O'Connor. Dorothy Walters. PoRA

In this world, (the Isle of Dreames) [or dreams]. White Island. Robert Herrick. BeJo; NOSC; NoP-4; OAEL-1; TOF

In this worlds raging sea. Regrat. William Drummond, of Hawthornden. PoEL-2

In this year of executioners' songs. Let the Midnight Special. Joseph Bruchac. GM

In tholde [or th'olde] dayes of the king Arthour. The Wife of Bath's Tale. Chaucer. FHYEP; NAEL-1; OAEL-1 Fr. The Canterbury Tales.

In those days a decree went out from Caesar Augustus. Luke 2:1–7; In those days a decree went out from Caesar Augustus. Louise Glück. GI Fr. St. Luke.

In those days, I couldn't tell if I was strong. Working Construction. Eric Chock. OpBo

In those days, in a place where dentists thrive. In the Lake District. Joseph Brodsky, Russian. BLT, tr. by Kline, George L.

In those days it was haughty and proud. Louse. Wolf Ehrlich, *Russian.* TCRP, *tr. by* Daniel Weissbort

In those days Mary arose and went with haste into the hill. Luke 1:39–56: In those days Mary arose. Rilke. GI *Fr.* St. Luke.

In those days said Hiawatha. Picture-Writing. Henry Wadsworth Longfellow. APN-1 *Fr.* The Song of Hiawatha.

In those days the oatfields. Stacking the Straw. Amy Clampitt. VCAP

In those days / When civilization kicked us in the face. The Vultures. David Diop, *French.* PBA; TTY, *tr. by* Ulli Beier; PBMAP

In those days when my father was still big. Johnson Brothers Ltd. Rutger Kopland, *Dutch.* VCWP, *tr. by* James Brockway

In those far years of inertia. Aleksandr Blok. TCRP, *tr. by* Jon Stallworthy *and* Peter France *Fr.* Retribution.

In those first days. Thomas A. Clark. NBrP *Fr.* Twenty Poems.

In those freckles live their savours. (LL) Fairy Land, 1. Shakespeare. NOBE; OBEV

In those hours I'm home among the still things. Letting the Parakeet Fly. Judith W. Steinbergh. IFJA

In those painful days, we knew. Yesterday's Illusion *or* Remembering the Thirties. Alun Llywelyn-Williams, *Welsh.* OBWVE, *tr. by* R. Gerallt Jones

In those sad words I took farewell. Tennyson. EnVR *Fr.* In Memoriam A. H. H.

In those vast fields of light, ethereal plains. William Drummond, of Hawthornden. NOSC *Fr.* The Hymn of the Fairest Fair.

In those years, people will say, we lost track. Adrienne Rich. LoL

In those years when our sense, desire and wit. Greville Fulke. NOCV *Fr.* Caelica.

In Three Days. Robert Browning. CBLP

In thrice 10,000 seasons, I will come back to this world. Domestic Mysticism. Lucie Brock-Broido. PoPoPo

In through the porch and up the silent stair. The Old House. Amy Levy. PEW; VWP

In thy own self's perennial masterdom. (LL) At Sainte-Marguerite. Trumbull Stickney. APN-2; OxBA

In till this tyme that I of tell. Macbeth. Andrew of Wyntoun. OxBS

In Time. Kathleen Jessie Raine. WPE

In time all undertakings are made good. Robert Graves. FaBoEE

In time inferred, the deep beneath this calm crest. Counter Play. Ion Barbu, *Romanian.* CEEP, *tr. by* Thomas Amherst Perry *and* George Preda

In time it came round, the time. Christmas Ballad. Saint John of the Cross, *Spanish.* STV, *tr. by* John Frederick Nims

In Time Like Air. May Sarton. NYBP

In Time like Glass. Walter James Turner. MoBrPo; OBMV

In time of daffodils(who know. E. E. Cummings. MeMAP

In Time of Famine. Helen Hunt Jackson. PAR

In Time of Gold. Hilda Doolittle. PoA

In Time of Grief. Lizette Woodworth Reese. APN-2

In Time of Need. William Stafford. UnPo

In Time of Pestilence. Thomas Nashe. *See* A Litany in Time of Plague.

In Time of Plague. Thomas Nashe. *See* A Litany in Time of Plague.

In time of silver rain. Langston Hughes. SAmP

In Time of "The Breaking of Nations." Thomas Hardy. BoLoP; CMoP; ChIV-1; EBEV; EBEvV; HAP; LiTM; MoBrPo; MoP; NAEL-2; NOBE; NoAM; NoP-4; OAEL-2; OBEV; OBWP; OPOU; OxAEP-2; PoWW; Poetr; RB; TFi; WeW-3

In time of yore when shepherds dwelt. Nicholas Breton. NoSic

In time the Princess playing with the child. Michael Drayton. ChIV-1 *Fr.* Moses His Birth and Miracles.

In time [*or* tyme] the strong and stately [*or* statelie] turrets fall. Time. Giles, the Elder Fletcher. AAS; EBEV *Fr.* Licia.

In time to come, if such a crime should be. Horace. *See* To Maecenas.

In time we rode that trail. Thanksgiving at Snake Butte. James Welch. AiP

In time, we will not kiss. In Your Words. Edward Foster. PT

In Times and Places. Umberto Piersanti, *Italian.* NeIt, *tr. by* Stephen Sartarelli

In time's assembly line. Assembly Line. "Shu Ting," *Chinese.* VCWP, *tr. by* Carolyn Kizer

In Time's concatenation and. After Night Flight Son Reaches Bedside of Already Unconscious Father, Whose Right Hand Lifts in a Spasmodic Gesture, as Though Trying to Make Contact: 1955. Robert Penn Warren. NOBA *Fr.* Mortmain.

In times like these, when widows, orphans weep. To a Friend in Love during the Riots. William Parsons. NOEC

In times of stormy weather. Strange Hurt. Langston Hughes. GT

In to thir dirk and drublie days. Meditatioun in Wyntir. William Dunbar. EnVB; OxBS

In today's mail I found the chain letter you've been sending for. Avant-Dernières Pensées. Dionisio D. Martinez. BAP-94

In Tolouse or Ankara, in Hungary or Scotland. All. Antoni Slonimski, *Polish.* TrJP, *tr. by* Wanda Dynowska

In tombs of gold and lapis lazuli. Oil and Blood. W. B. Yeats. OxBSn

In tottering row, like shadows, silently. By the Sea. Richard Watson Dixon. OBNC

In Transit: A Sonnet Square. Martin Johnston.

   Café of Situations, The. BMAP

   Drinking Sappho Brand Ouzo. BMAP

In trellised shed with clustering roses gay. Wordsworth. EPCY

In trellised shed with clustering roses gay. Wordsworth. EPCY *Fr.* White Doe of Rylstone, The; or, The Fate of the Nortons.

In tropical climes there are certain times of day. Mad Dogs and Englishmen. Noël Coward. NBLV; NOBL; PeLV

In troth, I do myself persuade [*or* perswade]. Love Enthroned. Richard Lovelace. CaPo

In Trouble and Shame. D. H. Lawrence. OBMV

In truth how glorious was the High Priest. The High Priest. *Unknown, Hebrew.* TrJP, *tr. by* Arthur Davis

In truth it was a landscape wildly gay. James Kirke Paulding. APN-1 *Fr.* The Backwoodsman.

In truth, O Love, with what a boyish kind. Sonnet 11. Sir Philip Sidney. CBLP; PoE *Fr.* Astrophil and Stella. AAS; SiPS

In Trying Times. Herberto Padilla, *Spanish.* AF, *tr. by* Alastair Reid

In tse'gíhi, / In the house made of the dawn. Prayer of First Dancers. *Unknown. Fr.* The Night Chant. APN-2, *tr. by* Washington Matthews (After Bitahatini.) PFTM

In Tupelo, Mississippi. The Tupelo Destruction. *Unknown.* AmFP

In turns therefrom sipped lovers' wine. (LL) Under the Waterfall. Thomas Hardy. BoLoP; CTC; NAEL-2; NoP-4

In twenty minutes he forgot the sirens. (LL) The Sirens. John Streeter Manifold. LiTM; MoBrPo; Son

In Two Fields. Waldo Williams, *Welsh.* OBWVE, *tr. by* Gwyn Jones

In two large columns on thy motley page. Verses Addressed to the Imitator of the First Satire of the Second Book of Horace: An Attack on Pope. Lady Mary Wortley Montagu. CABP; ECEV

In twos and threes and fives. Porpoises. Norman MacCaig. FaBoTC

In Uganda an early king chose. Alice Walker. InPS-3

In undetected trains we left our land. Embarkation, 1942. John Jarmain. PoWW

In unexperienced [*or* unexperienc'd] infancy. Shadows in the Water. Thomas Traherne. CABP; GeHe; HAP; NoP-4; OAEL-1; PoEL-2; SCGP; SeCP

In unplowed Maine he sought the lumberers' gang. Ralph Waldo Emerson. MeMAP; TAP *Fr.* Woodnotes I ("For this present, hard"). AmPP; NOBA

In us and into us and ours. For Eusi, Ayi Kwei and Gwen Brooks. Keorapetse Kgositsile. PoBA

In using there are always two. Song of the Fucked Duck. Marge Piercy. BoWoP; LW

In Utrumque Paratus. Matthew Arnold. OBNC; PoEL-5

In utter chaos no sooner were you born. Lamenting for My Late Daughter. Wu Wei-yeh, *Chinese.* CoBLCP, *tr. by* Jonathan Chaves

In Vain. Adah Isaacs Menken. CBWP-1

In vain, dear Madam, yes, in vain you strive. An Epistle to a Lady. Mary Leapor. BWW; BWWP; ECWP; NOEC

In Vain Earth Decks Herself. Moses ibn Ezra. *Fr.* The World's Illusion. TrJP, *tr. by* Solomon Solis-Cohen

In vain, fair sorceress, thy eyes speak charms. William Habington. BeJo *Fr.* Castara.

In vain[e] fair[e] sorceress[e], thy eyes speak[e] charm[e]s. To a Wanton. William Habington. NOSC; SeCP

In vain her veins incised—jagged boulders. Spokane Falls. Phillip William George. VoR

In vain I gather up these stars from the ground. Meng Chiao. SuSp, *tr. by* Stephen Owen *Fr.* Apricots Die Young.

In vain I see the morning rise. The Poet's Delay. Henry David Thoreau. PAR

In vain, in vain it is, I find. The Necessity of Fate. Jane Barker. BWW

In vain! In vain! My pleading all in vain! Arria to Poetus. Mary E. Tucker. CBWP-1

In vain, in vain—the all-composing Hour. The Reign of Chaos. Alexander Pope. EBEV; FaBoPV; NOBE; NoP-4; SCV *Fr.* Yet, yet a moment, one dim ray of light. NAEL-1; OAEL-1; PoEL-3 *Fr.* The Dunciad.

In vain, mine eyes, you labour to amend. Sir Philip Sidney. SiPS *Fr.* Arcadia.

In vain, or else in vain his wings. (LL) Persuasions to Enjoy. Thomas Carew. BeJo; CaPo; NAEL-1; NOBE; NOSC; OBEV; SeCP

In vain, poor nymph, to please our youthful sight. An Elegy, to an Old Beauty. Thomas Parnell. ECEV; NOEC

In vain the dusky night retires. Hymn. Elizabeth Singer Rowe. ECWP

In vain / They shook their garments. Irony of God. Eva Warner. TrCP

In vain thou bid'st me strike the lyre. The Misanthropist. James M. Whitfield. AAP

In vain to me the smiling [or smileing] Mornings shine. Sonnet [on the Death of Mr. Richard West]. Thomas Gray. GSo; NOBE; NOEC; NoP-4; PoE; PoEL-3; Son

In vain you boast poetic names of yore. Impromptu. Alexander Pope. NoP-4

In vain your bangles cast. Abiku. Wole Soyinka. PBA; PBMAP

In valleys green and still. A. E. Housman. FaBoTw; OAEL-2; SCV

In vaulted place where shadows flit. In a Church of Padua. Herman Melville. APN-2

In Velvet. Ann Chandonnet. EC3

In Vietnam. Militerotics. Chuck Ortleb. GLP

In Vietnam I was always afraid of mines. Mines. Bruce Weigl. CDa

In Vietnam, poets brushed on printed silk. For Mrs. Cam, Whose Name Means "Printed Silk." John Balaban. CDa

In Virgyne the sweltrie sun gan sheene. An Excelente Balade of Charitie. Thomas Chatterton. EBEV; NOEC; OxAEP-1

In Vorkuta no disciple of the Lord. Vorkuta. Horst Bienek, *German*. AF, *tr. by* Matthew Mead

In Waka Bay when. Akahito, *Japanese*. OHMPJ, *tr. by* Kenneth Rexroth

In *Wakefield* there lives a jolly Pinder. The Jolly Pinder of Wakefield. *Unknown*. ESPB

IN Wales there is a borough town. A Tale of a Friar and A Shoemaker's Wife. Thomas Churchyard. NoSic

In walking naked. (LL) A Coat. W. B. Yeats. CMoP; EPCY; IIP; LiTM; NAEL-2; NoAM; OxAEP-2; OxBSP; PoEL-5

In warm war-sun they erupt. Mules. Ted Walker. NYBP

In Waste Places. James Stephens. MoBrPo; SCGP

In water-heavy nights behind grandmother's porch. Adolescence—I. Rita Dove. ISC; NoAM; PiM

In water nothing is mean. The fugitive. Patience. Elaine Feinstein. BrRo; FaBoWP

In waters still as a burnished mirror's face. Fishing in the Wei River. Po Chü-i, *Chinese*. ChiP, *tr. by* Arthur Waley

In waters where no charts avail. The Island. Herman Melville. NCAP

In waves still as the skillful yachts pass over. (LL) The Yachts. William Carlos Williams. AmPP; CMoP; HeIP-4; ImPo; LiTM; MeMAP; MoAmPo; MoP; NOBA; NoAM; NoP-4; OxBA; PoE; SAmP; TFi

In Weather. Robert Hass. AmPA

In Wee-John-Boo the bellies of bloodhounds. Orange Jews. Ted Berrigan *and* Ron Padgett. SPE

In Western Massachusetts, Sixteen Months Sober. Joan Larkin. LoHo

In western skies. Sunset. Henrietta Cordelia Ray. BlSi *Fr.* Idyl. CBWP-3

In Westminster Abbey. John Betjeman. CMoP; InPK-6; NBLV; NIP-4; NOBL; NoAM; OAEL-2; OBSV; OxAEP-2; TOF

In Westminster not long ago. The Ratcatcher's Daughter. *Unknown*. OxBoLi

In wet May, in the months of change. An Exequy. Peter Porter. NoAM; NoP-4; OxBC

In what dark silent grove. Cogitabo Pro Peccato Meo. William Habington. ChIV-1

In what estate so ever I be. Timor Mortis. *Unknown*. NoP-4

In what house, the jade flute that sends these dark notes drifting. Spring Night in Lo-Yang—Hearing a Flute. Li Po, *Chinese*. CoBCP; TTTS, *tr. by* Burton Watson

In what I do, I speak. The City Worker. Edith Jay Scovell. WPN

In What Manner the Soule Is United to the Body. Sir John Davies. *See* The Soul and the Body.

In what place in years to come. Sitting Alone in the Courtyard. Yü Chi, *Chinese*. CoBLCP, *tr. by* Jonathan Chaves

In what recesses of the brain. Memory, a Poem. Laetitia Pilkington. ECWP

In what rich harmony, what polished lays. John Pierpont. APN-1 *Fr.* Airs of Palestine.

In what soft language shall my thoughts get free. Upon the Death of Her Husband. Elizabeth Singer Rowe. ECWP

In what torn ship soever I embark. A Hymn[e] to Christ, at the Author's Last Going into Germany. Donne. EBEV; MeLP

In what torn [or torne] ship soever I embark [or embarke]. A Hymne to Christ, at the Author's Last Going into Germany. Donne. EBEV; ESCV; MeLP; NAEL-1; NOSC; OxAEP-1; PeECV

In Wheeling, West Virginia, inmates riot. Legacy. Joy Harjo. WeT

In which being there together is enough. (LL) Final Soliloquy of the Interior Paramour. Wallace Stevens. ColAP; HAP; HCAP; LCAP-2

In which if they turn and twist, it is neither with volition nor /consciousness consciousness. (LL) A Grave. Marianne Moore. CMoP; FaBoWP; HAP; HeIP-4; MeMAP; MoP; NAAL-2; NOBA; NoAM; NoP-4; OxBoS; PoE; Poetr; TAP; TFi; TRP; UnPo; WPE; WeW-3

In Which Names. Ilse Aichinger, *German*. AF, *tr. by* Chappel, Allen H.

In Which Roosevelt Is Compared to Saul. Vachel Lindsay. ChIV-1

In Which She Satisfies a Fear with the Rhetoric of Tears. Sister Juana Inés de la Cruz. BoWoP, *tr. by* Aliki *and* Willis Barnstone

In White. Robert Frost. TRP

In White America. Lucille Clifton. LTA

In white tulips. Raymond Roseliep. HA

In Whitman's day there were the secret bathers. Devolution of the Nude. Lynne McMahon. NAmP90

In whom the *Lord of Hosts* did pitch his tent! (LL) Ana(Mary-Army)gram. George Herbert. ChIV-2; GeHe; OAEL-1

In whose will is our peace? Thou happiness. Epigram. James Vincent Cunningham. VGW

In wild flight. *Unknown. Fr.* Sioux Metamorphoses. STP, *tr. by* James Koller

In wind from Asia and a wanton rain. (LL) The Way a Ghost Dissolves. Richard Hugo. NAAL-2; NoAM; NoP-4

In wind o wet rapid a scribble reported in water. Catullus. *See* Carmen 70 ("Lesbia says she'ld rather marry me").

In wind or water streame do require to be writ. Catullus. *See* Carmen 70 ("Lesbia says she'ld rather marry me").

In Windsor Castle. Henry Howard, Earl of Surrey. NOBE ("So cruel prison how could betide, alas.") CABP; NoP-4

In wings and starched. Chana Bloch. CrSp *Fr.* The Sacrifice.

In Winter. Saigyo. GaP, *tr. by* Burton Watson *Fr.* Sixty-four Tanka.

In winter I get up at night. Bed in Summer. Robert Louis Stevenson. ACTP; NBLV; OTCP; OxBChV

In Winter in my Room. Emily Dickinson. APN-2; AmPP; MoP; NAAL-1; NAAL-3; NALW; NCAP; NOBA; NoAM; OxBA; Poetr

In winter in the woods alone. Robert Frost. HeIP-4

In winter it darkens the moment lunch is over. Eclogue IV: Winter. Joseph Brodsky, *Russian*. TCRP, *tr. by* Joseph Brodsky

In winter my mothers goes away. Desert. Del Marie Rogers. MDDM

In winter on her hearth lighting some coal. Antipater of Thessalonica, *Greek*. GrAn, *tr. by* Alistair Elliot

In winter, those first mornings after my father died. The Pier. Garrett Kaoru Hongo. OpBo

In winter, when the fields are white. Humpty Dumpty's Song. "Lewis Carroll." CBNP; EBEV; GTBS-P; NOBVV; OBCoV; OBSP; OxBChV; OxBoLi; PeLV; PeVV *Fr.* Through the Looking-Glass.

In winter when the rain rain'd cauld. Tak' Your Auld Cloak about Ye. *Unknown*. OxBS

In winter's just return, when Boreas gan his reign. Henry Howard, Earl of Surrey. AAS; SiPS

In wiser days, my darling rosebud, blown. To My Daughter Betty. Thomas Michael Kettle. TIRV

In wit, as nature, what affects our hearts. Alexander Pope. HAP *Fr.* An Essay on Criticism. NAEL-1; PoEL-3; TFi

In with the big stack of advertisements for Pain, Mole finds. Dossier of the Torturer. Michael Benedikt. WeT

In with them, and tore down the slaughterhouse [or slaughter-house]. (LL) Reuben Bright. Edwin Arlington Robinson. APN-2; MeMAP; MoAmPo; NOBA; Son; TAP

In wonted walkes. Sir Philip Sidney. PoEL-1

In Worcester, Massachusetts. In the Waiting Room. Elizabeth Bishop. AFr; ColAP; FaBoWP; HeIP-4; InPS-3; LCAP-2; LiLi; NAAL-2; NALW; NOBA; NoAM; NoP-4; PoE; VCAP

In Word and Will I am a friend to you. On Himself. William Oldys. FaBoEE

In wrath and grief away the Paynims fly. *Unknown*. OBWP, *tr. by* Dorothy L. Sayers *Fr.* The Song of Roland. NAWM-1, *tr. by* Frederick Goldin, *abr.*

In wyndes or waters stremes do require to be writt. Catullus. *See* Carmen 70 ("Lesbia says she'ld rather marry me").

In Xanadu did Kubla Khan. Kubla Khan; or, A Vision in a Dream. Coleridge. APAD; AWP; CABP; CH; EBEvV; FHYEP; FaBoBe; FaBoCh; GEA; HAP; HeIP-4; HoPM; ImPo; InPK-6; InPS-3; NAEL-2; NAWM-2; NIP-4; NOBE; NOBRP; NoP-4; OAEL-2; OBEV; OBGa; OBNC; OxAEP-2; PBMP; PoE; PoEL-4; PoPoPo; PoRA; Poetr; Ro; SAGP; SCGP; SCV; SoSe-8; TFi; TOF; TRP; WeW-3

In yellow meadows no delight. Sir Thomas Browne. FaBoEE

"In yonder fields" (with that directs her eye. The Bad Landlord. William Chamberlayne. NOSC *Fr.* Pharonnida.

In yonder grave a Druid lies. Ode Occasioned by the Death of Mr. Thomson. William Collins. EPCY; NAEL-1; NOEC; PoE

In yonder Grave Your Druid lies! (LL) Ode Occasioned by the Death of Mr. Thomson. William Collins. EPCY; NAEL-1; NOEC; PoE

In younger years I stayed away from the world. On Being Assigned as Military Adviser to the Garrison Army. T'ao Ch'ien, *Chinese.* CoBCP, *tr. by* Burton Watson

In Your Absence. Elizabeth Baxter. PoToHe

In Your Bad Dream. Richard Hugo. LCAP-2

In your dream you met Demeter. Demeter. Genevieve Taggard. NMM-2

In your ears my song. You Laughed and Laughed and Laughed. Gabriel Okara. PBA

In your hollow, hoary olive tree. Olive Tree. Lorenzo Mavilis, *Greek.* GriP, *tr. by* Rae Dalven

In Your Mind. Carol Ann Duffy. FaBoTC

In your next letter I wish you'd say. Letter to N.Y. Elizabeth Bishop. LiLi; TwCP

In your own secret sins and terrors! (LL) In the Churchyard at Cambridge. Henry Wadsworth Longfellow. AmPP; PoEL-5; TAP

In your palm, the ripe weight. (LL) Persimmons. Li-Young Lee. NIP-4; NoP-4

In your panties. Hiroaki Sato. HA

In your presence I rediscovered my name. Your Presence. David Diop, *French.* PBA, *tr. by* Ulli Beier

In your silence sank as into a deep sea. Dialogue. Leah Goldberg, *Hebrew.* MHP, *tr. by* Ruth Finer Mintz

In your twenties you knew with elegiac certainty. A Lifetime Devoted to Literature. Judith Rodriguez. NOBAu

In Your Words. Edward Foster. PT

In Your Young Dream. Richard Hugo. InPK-6

In Youth. William Lisle Bowles. *Fr.* Milton: On the Busts of Milton, in Youth and Age. Son

In youth, gay scenes attract our eyes. The Vanity of Existence. Philip Freneau. AmPP

In youth I couldn't sing to the common tune. Returning to My Home in the Country. T'ao Ch'ien, *Chinese.* CoBCP, *tr. by* Burton Watson

In youth I loved the adventurous race. When the Prince of Lang-yeh's Poem in the Old Style. Wang Seng-ta, *Chinese.* CoBCP, *tr. by* Burton Watson

In Youth Is Pleasure. Robert Wever. NOBE; OBEV *Fr.* Lusty Juventus. (Of Youth He Singeth.) CBLP

In youth is pleasure, in youth is pleasure. (LL) In Youth Is Pleasure. Robert Wever. CBLP; NOBE; OBEV

In youth, it was a way I had. Indian Summer. Dorothy Parker. NIP-4

In youth we dream of death. Hardy Perennial. Richard Eberhart. AiP

In youth's spring, it was my lot. Edgar Allan Poe. *See* The Lake: To——.

In yr absence / i. Max Factor Pink. Nigel Roberts. BMAP

In Yüeh Viewing the Past. Li Po, *Chinese.* CoBCP, *tr. by* Burton Watson

In zummer, leate at evenen tide. The Rwose in the Dark. William Barnes. NOBVV

Ina Unique TracethatRemovesBeforeandAfterLeftandRight. Poem No. V. Sang Yi. PFTM

INAMORATAS, with an approbation. The Sundays of Satin-Legs Smith. Gwendolyn Brooks. NAAAL; Poetr; SeSe

Inanna and An. Enheduanna, *Sumerian.* BoWoP, *ad. by* Aliki *and* Willis Barnstone

Inanna and Ebih. Enheduanna, *Sumerian.* BoWoP, *ad. by* Aliki *and* Willis Barnstone

Inanna and Enlil. Enheduanna, *Sumerian.* BoWoP, *ad. by* Aliki *and* Willis Barnstone

Inanna and Ishkur. Enheduanna, *Sumerian.* BoWoP, *ad. by* W. W. Hallo *and* J. J. A. van Dijk

Inanna and the Anunna. Enheduanna, *Sumerian.* BoWoP, *ad. by* Aliki *and* Willis Barnstone

Inanna and the City of Uruk. Enheduanna, *Sumerian.* BoWoP, *ad. by* Aliki *and* Willis Barnstone

Inanna and the Divine Essences. Enheduanna, *Sumerian.* BoWoP, *ad. by* Aliki *and* Willis Barnstone

Inanna Exalted. Enheduanna, *Sumerian.*
 "O lady of all truths bright light going forth." WPOW, *tr. by* Anne Draffkorn Kilmer

Inanna sang. *Ancient Sumerian Oral Tradition.* ITG, *tr. by* Diane Wolkstein *and* Samuel Noah Kramer *Fr.* The Courtship of Inanna and Dumuzi.

Inapprehensiveness. Robert Browning. CBLP; NOBVV

Inattentive, suborned, betrayed, and shiftless. Young Prince of Tyre. "Ern Malley." BMAP

Inauguration. Lorenzo Thomas. NBV

Inca Tupac Upanqui, The. William Hart-Smith. NOBAu

Incantation. Bella Akhatovna Akhmadulina, *Russian.* TCRP, *tr. by* Albert C. Todd

Incantation, An. Byron. LaPo

Incantation. Czeslaw Milosz, *Polish.* VCWP, *tr. by* Czeslaw Milosz *and* Robert Pinsky

Incantation. Alistair Paterson. *Fr.* Incantations for Warriors. PeNZ

Incantation by Laughter. Velemir Khlebnikov, *Russian.* CBNP, *tr. by* Gary Kern

Incantation Songs of the Klamath Lake People. *Unknown, Klamath Native American.* APN-2, *tr. by* Albert S. Gatschet

Incantations, The. Theocritus. AWP, *tr. by* Charles Stuart Calverley *Fr.* Idylls.

Incantations for Warriors. Alistair Paterson. PeNZ

Incantations of Modoc Conjurers. *Unknown, Modoc Native American.* APN-2, *tr. by* Albert S. Gatschet

Incanto. Stan Rice.
 "Enough is never enough—That voice comes back—Suave." MoLi
 "I sit waiting for one of the two kinds of miracle." MoLi

Incarnate devil in a talking snake. Dylan Thomas. KSG

Incarnate One, The. Edwin Muir. PeECV

Incarnatio Est Maximum Dei Donum [*or* Donum Dei]. William Alabaster. NoSic

Incarnation, The. William Langland. OBEV; PoEL-1 *Fr.* The Vision of Piers Plowman.

Incarnation, The. Charles Wesley. NOCV

Incarnation and Passion, The. Henry Vaughan. GeHe; TrCP

Incarnation Poem. John Leax. TrCP

Incautious—of the Sun. (LL) Before I got my eye put out. Emily Dickinson. APN-2; LiTM; MeMAP; PAR; PoE

Incautious young woman named Venn, An. Limerick. Edward Gorey. PeLV; PeLi

Incautious *Youth,* why do'st thou so mis-place. To My Young Lover. Jane Barker. LW

Incendiary. Vernon Scannell. OxBC

Incense, and flesh of swine, and this year's grain. To Phidyle ("Caelo supinas si tuleris"). Horace. AWP, *tr. by* Austin Dobson *Fr.* Odes.

Incense of the Lucky Virgin. Robert Earl Hayden. AmPP

Incessant now their hollow sides they pound. The Boxers. Paul Whitehead. ECEV *Fr.* Gymnasiad, The, or Boxing Match.

Inchcape Rock, The. Robert Southey. EBEvV; EBNV; FaBoBe; OBNV; OBSP; OxAEP-2

Incidence. Rae Armantrout. FTOS

Incident. Imamu Amiri Baraka. AF; NoAM

Incident. Countee Cullen. BPo; ChAP; KaS; NAAAL; NAAL-2; NOxBChV; NTCP; NoAM; NoP-4; OBCA; PFE; PoBA; PoPoPo; Poetr; SSLK; VGW

Incident. Eamon Grennan. BiHa

Incident, An. Douglas Le Pan. MoCV; NoP-4

Incident at Imuris. Alberto A. Ríos. NIP-4; PuP-14

Incident here and there, An. The Walls Do Not Fall. Hilda Doolittle. AF; NoP-4; OBWP; NAAL-2

Incident in a Rose Garden. Donald Justice. CRP

Incident in the Early Life of Ebenezer Jones, Poet, 1828, An. John Betjeman. CMoP; MoP; NoAM

Incident in Transylvania. Roger McDonald. BMAP

Incident of the French Camp. Robert Browning. FaPoR; OBWP

Incident on a Front Not Far from Castel di Sangro. Harry Brown. NYBP

Incidents in the Life of My Uncle Arly. Edward Lear. CBNP; OAEL-2; OBCoV; OxBoLi
 ("O my agèd Uncle Arly!") NOxBChV

Incline Thine ear, O God. Therefore, We Thank Thee, God. Reuben Grossman, *Hebrew.* TrJP, *tr. by* L. V. Snowman

Inclusiveness. D. G. Rossetti. NAEL-2 *Fr.* The House of Life.

Incognita. Austin Dobson. EBVV

Incomparable treasure, heart's blood spilt. The Poetry of Gerard Manley Hopkins. Monk Gibbon. TIRV

Incompleteness. Henrietta Cordelia Ray. CBWP-3

Inconclusive Evening, An. Frances Bellerby. FaBoTw

Inconstancy. James Harrington. PBRV

Inconstancy Reproved. Sir Robert Ayton. *See* To His Forsaken Mistress.

Inconstancy's the Greatest of Sins. Edward Herbert. OxBSP

Inconstant Dawn, thou tak'st thy time. Meleager, *Greek.* GrAn, *tr. by* Peter Whigham

Incontestably sang, and the people were beautiful. (LL) The Unpredicted. John Heath-Stubbs. BoLoP; OxBC

Inconvenience, An. John Raven. BPo; CRP

Incorrigible, brash. Nature Notes: Dandelions. Louis MacNeice. FP *Fr.* Nature Notes.

Incorrigible, brash, / They brightened the cinder path of my childhood. Louis MacNeice. *See* Nature Notes: Dandelions.

Incredible Henry McHugh, The. Robert Fisher. FuFo

Incredible: that pretty finch of E's. E's Finch. Paul Verlaine, *French.* FLP, *tr. by* Alistair Elliot

Incrusted in his island home that lies beyond the sea. The Neutral British Gentleman. "Orpheus C. Kerr." OBAL

Indecent, self-soiled, bilious. Geocentric. Pattiann Rogers. NAmP90

Indeed, good Sir, you're quite mistaken. Verses Designed to Be Sent to Mr. Adams. Elizabeth Frances Amherst. ECWP

Indeed I have sought thee too long, O Apollo. A Search for Apollo. Agnes Mary Frances Robinson. VWP

Indeed I must confess. Platonic[k] Love. Abraham Cowley. BeJo; NoP-4 *Fr.* The Mistress.

Indeed indeed, I cannot tell. Henry David Thoreau. RaBo

Indeed indeed it is growing very sultry. The Cubical Domes. David Gascoyne. SPE

Indeed, it will soon be over, I shall be done. Intimations of Mortality. Stanley Kunitz. MoAmPo

Indeed, Sir Peter, I could wish, I own. On Clergymen Preaching Politics. John Byrom. ECEV

Indeed then, it was your own courage. Anyte, *Greek.* GrAn, *tr. by* John Heath-Stubbs *and* Carol A. Whiteside

Indefiniteness is an element of the true music. Improvisations on a Sentence by Poe. Jack Spicer. APSN

Independance wid a vengeance. Louise Bennett. FaBoVe; PBCV

Independence. Nancy Cato. WPE

Independence. Adebayo Faleti, *Yoruba.* PBA, *tr. by* Bakare Gbadamosi *and* Ulli Beier

Independence Bell—July 4, 1776. *Unknown.* BLPA; FaBoBe

Independence Day. Phan Trọng Quảng, *Vietnamese.* AVP, *tr. by* Huỳnh Sanh Thông

Independence Day. William Jay Smith. TwCP

Independence Day, 1956: A Fairy Tale. James Galvin. PoPoPo

Independence Day (while for us the bugle sounds retreat). In the Clearing. Donald Finkel. BAP-95

Independence tun Big-Smady! Independence Twenty-One. Louise Bennett. PBCV

Independence Twenty-One. Louise Bennett. PBCV

Independent, The. Phyllis McGinley. FaBoEE

Independent Man, The. Gwendolyn Brooks. *Fr.* A Street in Bronzeville. BPo; BlSi; FaBoWP

Independent Squire. Samuel Butler. NOBE *Fr.* Hudibras.

Index. Paul Violi. EOEF; PmAP

India. Walter James Turner. MoBrPo

India Guide, The; or, Journal of a Voyage to the East Indies in 1780. Sir George Dallas.
    Miss Emily Brittle Sails for India. NOEC

Indian. Laura Jensen. AmPA

Indian at the Burial-Place [*or* Burying-Place] of His Fathers, An. William Cullen Bryant. APN-1

Indian Bagman's Toast. *Unknown.* FaBoVe

Indian Blood. Mary TallMountain. LoL; UnSA

Indian Boarding School: The Runaways. Louise Erdrich. HATNAP; NoAM; UnSA

Indian Burying Ground, The. Philip Freneau. AmPP; ColAP; HAP; NAAL-1; NAAL-3; NOBA; NoP-4; OxBA; PoEL-4; PoLF; TAP; TFi

Indian Cave Jerry Ramsey Found, The. William Stafford. NoAM

Indian College Blues. Adrian C. Louis. NAmP90; PaTW

Indian Convert, The. Philip Freneau. TAP

Indian Emperor, The. Dryden.
    Song from The Indian Emperor. NoP-4
    (Song).

Indian Girl.) Lenard D. Moore. GT

Indian Gone!, The. Josiah D. Canning. APN-1

Indian Hunter, The. Eliza Cook. BLPA

Indian Love Song. Lew Blockcolski. VoR

Indian maid the demararie october twenty seven seventeen eighty one. Edward Thompson. NOEC

Indian Movie, New Jersey. Chitra Divakaruni. UnSA

Indian Names. Lydia Huntley Sigourney. APN-1; ColAP; PAR

("Though ye destroy their dust.") (LL) OBCA; PoLF

Indian Princess, The. The Pet Deer. James Tate. SPE

Indian Reservation: Caughnawaga. Abraham Moses Klein. LiTM; NOBC; NoP-4

Indian Rock, Bainbridge Island, Washington. Duane Niatum. CDW

Indian Ruins Along Rio de Flag. Greg Pape. PBCAP; PaTW

Indian Serenade, The. Shelley. AWP; CBLP; HoPM; ImPo; OBEV; RaBo; TTTS
    (Lines to an Indian Air.) FaBoBe; GTBS-P

Indian Singing in 20th Century America. Gail Tremblay. HATNAP; LTA

Indian Song: Survival. Leslie Marmon Silko. CDW; VoR

Indian Student; or, Force of Nature, The. Philip Freneau. OxBA

Indian Summer. Wilfred Campbell. NOBC

Indian Summer. Emily Dickinson. MoAmPo

Indian Summer. Hamlin Garland. APN-2

Indian summer. Lorraine Ellis Harr. HA

Indian Summer. Dorothy Parker. NIP-4

Indian Summer: Montana, 1956. W. M. Ransom. CDW

Indian to His Love, The. W. B. Yeats. PBMP

Indian upon God, The [*or* An]. W. B. Yeats. MoBrPo

Indian weed [now] withered quite, The. A Religious Use of [Taking] Tobacco. Robert Wisdome. OBCoV; OBEV; SCGP

Indian, who lived at Muskingum, remote, An. The Indian Convert. Philip Freneau. TAP

Indian Woman's Death-Song, The. Felicia Dorothea Hemans. PEW; Ro
    ("One moment, and that realm is ours. On, on, dark rolling stream!") (LL) NoP-4

Indiana. Hart Crane. *Fr.* Powhatan's Daughter. *Fr.* The Bridge. NAAL-2

Indians. John Fandel. NYBP

Indians at the Guthrie. Gerald Vizenor. VoR

Indians count of men as dogs, The. Roger Williams. SCAP

Indians have mostly gone, The. Like Ghosts of Eagles. Robert Francis. LCAP-2

Indians must be the loneliest people on Earth—. We Exist. Janice Gould. UnSA

Indians prize not English gold, The. Roger Williams. SCAP

Indian's Retort, The. Jones Very. NCAP

Indians stole fair Annie, The. Fair Annie. *Unknown.* CH; ESPB; OxBB

Indictment of Senior Officers. Sharon Olds. PBCAP

Indies, The. Edouard Glissant, *French.*
    "Child climbs to the island's highest point, The." NegPo, *tr. by* Ellen Conroy Kennedy
    "O Sun! O age-old labor mutely mixed with ocean." NegPo, *tr. by* Ellen Conroy Kennedy
    "One of them, taking advantage of the crew's momentary carelessness." NegPo, *tr. by* Ellen Conroy Kennedy
    "They fastened a people to merchant ships." NegPo, *tr. by* Ellen Conroy Kennedy

Indifference. Harry Graham. NBLV

Indifference. Geoffrey Anketell Studdert-Kennedy. TrCP

Indifference— / A house. Dmitry Vasil'evich Bobyshev, *Russian.* TCRP, *tr. by* Albert C. Todd

Indifferences and success had crowned them all. (LL) On First Looking into Loeb's Horace. Lawrence Durrell. FaBoMo; LiTM

Indifferent, The. Donne. BoLoP; CBLP; ESCV; NAEL-1; NAWM-1; NOSC; PBMP; SoSe-8

Indifferent, flippant, earnest, but all bored. The Conscript. Wilfrid Wilson Gibson. PoFWW

Indifferent glimmer of distant stars, The. The Garden of Gethsemane. Boris Pasternak, *Russian.* GI, *tr. by* Nina Kossman

Indigestion. Wendy Cope. *See* Serious Concerns.

Indignant at the fumbling wits, the obscure spite. Paudeen. W. B. Yeats. HAP; OxBSP; PoEL-5

Indignation Dinner, An. James David Corrothers. NAAAL

Indigo. Chitra Divakaruni. OpBo

Indigo Glass in the Grass, The. Wallace Stevens. PoA

Individualist Speaks, The. Louis MacNeice. OBMV

Indolence. Vernon Watkins. FaBoTw

Indolent Housewife—in Daisies—lain! (LL) How many times these low feet staggered. Emily Dickinson. AmPP; HAP; NAAL-1; NAAL-3; PoEL-5; WeW-3

Indolent vicar of Bray, An. Limerick. Langford Reed. PeLi

Indoors. George Johnston. PoA

Indoors the tang of a tiny oil lamp. Outdoors. House on a Cliff. Louis MacNeice. NOIV

Indra, the Supreme God, *fr.* Rig Veda. *Unknown.* AWP *Fr.* Vedic Hymns.

Induction, The. Milton. *See* Invocation.

Induction to "A Mirror for Magistrates." Thomas Sackville. AAS
    (Complaint of Henry Duke of Buckingham, The.) PoEL-1

Induction, The. NoSic

Midnight ("Midnight was come, when every vital thing"). CH
    ("Midnight was come, and every vital thing.") AEP
    ("'When Fortune frown'd, the feller made my fall'.") (LL) AEP

Indulge thy smiling scorn, if smiling still. The Fish Turns Into a Man, and Then Into a Spirit, and Again Speaks. Leigh Hunt. *Fr.* The Fish, the Man, and the Spirit. HAP; NOBL; NTP; OBEV; PoEL-4

Indulgent Nature on each kind bestows. On Dr. Evans Cutting Down a Row of Trees. *Unknown.* FaBoEE

Industrial City. Antigone Kefala. BMAP

Industrial Evils. Joseph Cottle. NOEC *Fr.* Malvern Hills.

Industrious young obstetrician, An. Limerick. Isaac Asimov. PeLi

Inebriety. George Crabbe. BXAP

Ineffable Dou, The. Sydney Goodsir Smith. OxBS

Inept young person, Miss Muffet, The. Limerick. Dean Walley. PeLi

Inertia. Kirti Chaudhari. WPOW, *tr. by* Leonard Nathan

Inertia. Vivienne Finch. BrRo

Inevitability. Imants Ziedonis, *Latvian.* CEEP, *tr. by* Inara Cedrins

Inevitable. John Betjeman. MoBrPo

Inexhaustible. Israel Zangwill. TrJP

Inexorable. William Drummond, of Hawthornden. *See* Madrigal: "My thoughts hold mortal[l] strife."

Inextinguishable Blaze. Charles Wesley. NOEC

Infamous Doctrine. Paul Evans. NBrP

Infancy! fearless, lustful, happy, nestling for delight. William Blake. OxAEP-2 *Fr.* Visions of the Daughters of Albion. CABP; OAEL-2; Ro

Infant and the Pearl, The. Douglas Oliver.
  "We followed the river to Fortune's Wheel." NBrP

Infant Boy at Midcentury. Robert Penn Warren.
  "When the century dragged, like a great wheel stuck at dead center." MoAmPo

Infant Innocence. A. E. Housman. FaBoCh; ImPo; NOBL; OxBoLi; PeLV; Spl

Infant Joy. William Blake. APAD; FHYEP; LiLi; NAEL-2; NTP; OxAEP-2; OxBSP; PoLF; Ro *Fr.* Songs of Innocence.
  ("I have no name, / I am but two days old.") PoPoPo

Infant quirk of a pine, An. Navidad, St. Nicholas Ave. Alfred Corn. NoP-4

Infant Song. Charles Causley. NOxBChV; OxBC

Infant Sorrow. William Blake. APAD; EBEvV; FHYEP; InPS-3; NAEL-2; OBNC; OxAEP-2; OxBM; OxBSP; PoEL-4; RB *Fr.* Songs of Experience.
  ("And grey hairs are on my head.") (LL) PFE
  ("My mother groaned, my father wept!") PoPoPo; Ro

Infant—wailing in maneless fear, An. Life. Ella Wheeler Wilcox. PoToHe

Infantry. Alun Lewis. PoWW

Infantryman, The. *Unknown.* NSI

Infatuation. Frederick Goddard Tuckerman. NCAP

Infelice. Stevie Smith. LW

Infelix. Adah Isaacs Menken. AAP; CBWP-1; PAR

Inference of Mexico, An. Robert Earl Hayden.
  Sub Specie Aeternitatis. AmPP

Inferno. Dante. NAWM-1, *tr. by* John Ciardi *Fr.* Divina Commedia.
  "And now we walked along the solid mire." OBVE, *tr. by* Robert Lowell
  Dark Wood, The. BiHa, *tr. by* Seamus Heaney
    (Inferno, Canto I, The.) PiM, *tr. by* Seamus Heaney
    ("Where the straight road had been lost sight of.") (LL) PiM, *tr. by* Seamus Heaney
  "Middle of life's journey; I, The." STV, *tr. by* John Frederick Nims
  Pier delle Vigne. HoPM, *tr. by* John Ciardi
  Ugolino. FaBoPV, *tr. by* Seamus Heaney
Inferno, Canto I, The. Dante. *See* The Dark Wood.

Infidel Reclaimed, The. Edward Young. NOEC *Fr.* Night Thoughts.

Infidelity. Olga Fiodorovna Berggolts, *Russian.* BoWoP; IMW, *tr. by* Daniel Weissbort

Infidelity. Stanley Plumly. NAmP90

Infidelity. Louis Untermeyer. TrJP

Infield Outfield. Asa Benveniste. NBrP

Infinite, The. Giacomo Leopardi, *Italian.* ItIP

Infinite, The. John Boyle O'Reilly. TIRV

Infinite a sudden Guest, The. Emily Dickinson. WPoS

Infinite consanguinity it bears. Hart Crane. ColAP; OxBA *Fr.* Voyages. CMoP; MeMAP; NOBA; NoAM; TAP

Infinite grief! amazing woe! Look on Him Whom They Pierced, and Mourn. Isaac Watts. NOCV

"Infinite task of the human heart," The. (LL) For the One Who Would Take Man's Life in His Hands. Delmore Schwartz. LiTM; MoAmPo; VGW

"Infinite", The. Word horrible! at feud. Legem Tuam Dilexi. Coventry Patmore. PoEL-5 *Fr.* The Unknown Eros.

Infinitely far. Tanka. Saitō Mokichi, *Japanese.* MJT, *tr. by* Ueda, Makoto

Infinito, L'. Giacomo Leopardi, *Italian.* AWP, *tr. by* Lorna De' Lucchi

Infinity. Walt Whitman. *Fr.* Song of Myself. AmPP; MoAmPo; NAAL-3; NOBA; OxBA

Infinity Effect at the Hôtel Soubise. Alfred Corn. EOEF

Infinity, when all things it beheld. The Preface. Edward Taylor. AmPP; HAP; MeMAP; NAAL-1; NAAL-3; NOBA; NOSC; OxBA; SCAP *Fr.* God's Determinations [touching his Elect].

Infir Taris. *Unknown.* OxNR

Infirm and aged, doth he sit. The Old Year. Priscilla Jane Thompson. CBWP-2

Infirmity. Theodore Roethke. CoAP; NAAL-2; NYBP

Inflammable Woman, The. James Keir Baxter. OxBC

Inflation. Charles O. Hartman. PoA

Inflation. Heather McHugh. NAmP90

Inflation. Nicanor Parra, *Spanish.* AF, *tr. by* Miller Williams

Influence. Sarah Knowles Bolton. PWR

Influence of Local Attachment, The. Richard Polwhele.
  Visit to the Author's Paternal Seat, A. NOEC

Influence of Natural Objects, The. James Simmons. PNI

Influence of Natural Objects [in Calling Forth and Strengthening the Imagination in Boyhood and Early Youth]. Wordsworth. AWP *Fr.* Introduction—Childhood and School-Time. FHYEP *Fr.* The Prelude; Growth of a Poet's Mind [1850 vers.]

Informer, art thou in the tree. On the Meetings of the Scotch Covenanters. *Unknown.* FaBoEE

Infusion Room, The. Jane Cooper. BAP-95

Ingenious god was old Zeus, An. Deus "Sex" Machina. Harriet Mandelbaum. PeLi

Ingenious insect, but of ruthless mold. To the Spider. Thomas Russell. Son

Ingenious *L——* were a Picture drawn. Horace. OBCVT, *tr. by* William King *Fr* The Art of Cookery, In Imitation of Horace's Art of Poetry. To Dr. Lister.

Ingenuity too astonishing, An. The Sun Underfoot Among the Sundews. Amy Clampitt. NoP-4

Inglorious Milton, The. Francis Letters. NOBAu

Ingmar Bergman's "Seventh Seal." Robert Duncan. PoE

Ingoldsby Legends, The. "Thomas Ingoldsby."
  Jackdaw of Rheims, The. EBNV; OBCoV; OBNV; OBSP

Ingrateful[l] Beauty Threatened. Thomas Carew. BeJo; CaPo; MeLP; OBEV; SeCP
  ("Knew her themselves through all her veils.") (LL) CavPo; PBRV

Ingratitude, how deadly is the smart. Sonnet: Ingratitude. Anna Seward. ECWP; NOEC

Ingrown. James Berry. PBCV

Inhabitants of Old Jerusalem, The. The Popish Plot. Dryden. *Fr.* Absalom and Achitophel, Pt. I. EBEvV; FHYEP; FaBoPV; HAP; NOSC; OAEL-1; PoE

Inheritance. Cynthia MacDonald. NMM-2

Inheritances. Jane Cooper. *Fr.* Dispossessions. FaBoWP

Inheritors, The. Gary Geddes. NOBC

Inheritors, The. William Peskett. PNI

Inhuman Henry. A. E. Housman. NBLV

Inimitably quick. Static Autumn. Yvor Winters. PoA

Iniquity of the Fathers upon the Children, The. Christina Rossetti. FaBoVe

Inis Fal. Egan O'Rahilly, *Irish.* BIrV; OBMV, *tr. by* James Stephens

Initial, Dæmonic, and Celestial Love. Ralph Waldo Emerson.
  Dæmonic and the Celestial Love, The. APN-1

Initiate, The. W. S. Merwin. NNaP

Initiation. Jayne Cortez. PoBA

Initiation. Monifa Atungaye Love. ISC

Initiation. Rilke, *German.* TrJP, *tr. by* C. F. MacIntyre

Initiations. Paul Niger, *French.*
  "What?/ a rhythm." NegPo, *tr. by* Ellen Conroy Kennedy

Injian Ocean sets an' smiles, The. For to Admire. Rudyard Kipling. MoBrPo

Injoy such Liberty. Richard Lovelace. *See* To Althea, from Prison.

Injure Tinglit. Busk, Pierce. Maggie O'Sullivan. NBrP

Injured Maple. Ronald G. Everson. NOBC

Injustice of the Courts. Lizelia Augusta Jenkins Moorer. CBWP-3

Ink runs from the corners of my mouth. Eating Poetry. Mark Strand. MoP; NoAM; PFE; TAP

Ink-specked sheets feel like cigar leaf;, The. Opening Le Ba Khon's Dictionary. John Balaban. CDa

Inkstone Inscription for the Blind Scholar Ho Yung-kuang, An. Chin Nung, *Chinese.* CoBLCP, *tr. by* Jonathan Chaves

Inky, dinky spider. *Unknown.* CTV

Inky gloss of your mane, The. *Unknown, Greek.* GrAn, *tr. by* W. G. Shepherd

Inland City. John Crowe Ransom. CMoP

Inland, / far inland go my thoughts. Song of the Rejected Woman. Kibkarjuk, *Eskimo into Danish.* WPOW, *tr. by* Knud Rasmussen; *English vers. by* Tom Lowenstein

Inland, inland, inland, inland. Oxaitoq's Song. *Unknown, Eskimo.* APN-2, *tr. by* Franz Boas

Inland Lighthouse, The. James McMichael. AmPA

Inmate, An. Peter Kocan. NOBAu

Inn. Pierre Reverdy, *French.* PFTM, *tr. by* Patricia Terry

Inn at Kirchstetten, The. James Laughlin. PmAP

Inn That Missed Its Chance, The. Amos Russel Wells. TrCP

Inn towers impressively on the bank of the ancient river, The. To the Innkeeper at Five Rivers, Sun Pen. Chang Yü, *Chinese.* CoBLCP, *tr. by* Jonathan Chaves

Innate Deception of Unspoiled Beauty, The. Dara Wier. CMAP

Innately reserved. Tanka. Kanoko Okamoto, *Japanese.* MJT, *tr. by* Makoto Ueda

Inner Ear. T. R. Hummer. MT

Inner greet. Greenberg said it. Columbus. Muriel Rukeyser. AF

Inner Man, The. Charles Simic. IFJA

Inner Mongolia—The Grasslands. Sibyl James. LoHo

Inner Part, The. Louis Simpson. PBCV; PBMP; RaBo

Inner Realm, The. Priscilla Jane Thompson. CBWP-2

Inner Temple Masque, The. William Browne.
Sirens' Song, The. NOBE; OBEV
(Syrens' Song, The.) GBL

Inner Tube. Michael Ondaatje. NoAM

Inner Vision, The. Wordsworth. GTBS-P *Fr.* Poems Composed or Suggested During a Tour, in the Summer of 1833.

Inniskeen Road: July Evening. Patrick Kavanagh. CIP-2; MoP; NoAM; Poetr

Innkeeper's Wife, The. Clive Sansom. OBCP

Innocence, The. Robert Creeley. NeAP

Innocence, *(to Tony White).* Thom Gunn. HP; LiTM

Innocence. Patrick Kavanagh. RB

Innocence. Wislawa Szymborska, *Polish.* PoSu, *tr. by* Jan Darowski

Innocence. Thomas Traherne. CABP; ChIV-2; ESCV; MiEL; NOSC

Innocence? / In a sense. A Life. Howard Nemerov. OBCoV; PBMP

Innocence of her, The. The Innocent Breasts. Joel Oppenheimer. PoM

Innocence? Soon as you try putting your finger on it. 1966. David Rivard. PBCAP

Innocent, The. Denise Levertov. KaS

Innocent Breasts, The. Joel Oppenheimer. PoM

Innocent bride from the Mission, An. Limerick. *Unknown.* PeLi

Innocent decision: to enjoy. Triple Feature. Denise Levertov. NoP-4

Innocent England. D. H. Lawrence. OBCoV

Innocent Landscape. Elinor Wylie. OxBA

Innocent maiden of Gloucester, An. Limerick. *Unknown.* PeLi

Innocent Mistress, The. Mary Pix.
Song by Mrs. P—, A. KTR

Innocent Play. Isaac Watts. NOEC

Innocent Spring, The. Dame Edith Sitwell. NOBE *Fr.* The Sleeping Beauty.

Innocent's Song. Charles Causley. GTBS-P; OBCP

Inns are not residences. (LL) Silence. Marianne Moore. CMoP; FaBoMo; FaBoWP; InPS-3; NALW; NOBA; TRP

Innsbruck, now I must depart. *Unknown, German.* GePo, *tr. by* Ingrid Waløe-Engel

Innumerable Beauties, thou white haire. Sonnet. Edward Herbert. PoEL-2

Innumerable Christ, The. "Hugh MacDiarmid." EBEV; OxAEP-2; OxBS

Innumerable the images. Documentary Film. "Ern Malley." BMAP

Innumerable worlds! We dream of them. Contemplation of the Heavens. Bill Manhire. PeNZ

Inordinate Love. *Unknown.* EBEV; OxBSP

Inpatient. Dolores Kendrick. FFC

Inquest, The. W. H. Davies. GTBS-P; NOBE; OxBTC; RB

Inquietude. Pauli Murray. BlSi

Inquietude of a Particular Matter, The. Alberto A. Ríos. NAmP90

Inquiring about the Health of Li Te-hua. Hsü Chung-hsing, *Chinese.* "Who would have thought that a disease of the ordinary world." CoBLCP, *tr. by* Jonathan Chaves

(Inquiry before snow. (LL) Silence / .is / a / looking. E. E. Cummings. CMoP; PoE

Inquisition. Gloria Wade-Gayles. ISC

Inquisitive Bridegroom, The. William Somervile. ECEV

Inquisitors, The. Robinson Jeffers. MoAmPo

Insane thought, An. Tanka. Mori Ōgai, *Japanese.* MJT, *tr. by* Makoto Ueda

Insatiable Priest, The. Matthew Prior. OxBSP

Insatiableness. Thomas Traherne. NOSC

Insccribed on a Painting. Cheng Hsieh, *Chinese.* SuSp, *tr. by* Irving Y. Lo

Inscribed in Melrose Abbey. *Unknown.* FaBoEE

Inscribed in the Silver of the Sea. Ivan V. Lalic, *Serbian.* CEEP, *tr. by* C. W. Truesdale

Inscribed on a Landscape by Mi Yüan-hui. Chao Meng-fu, *Chinese.* CoBLCP, *tr. by* Jonathan Chaves

Inscribed on a Lichen-Covered Wall in My Hut. Chin Nung, *Chinese.* "Three lines of 'clerk script' calligraphy." CoBLCP, *tr. by* Jonathan Chaves

Inscribed on a Painting ("At the country inn, thousands of peach trees"). T'ang Yin, *Chinese.* CoBLCP, *tr. by* Jonathan Chaves

Inscribed on a Painting. Hsü Wei, *Chinese.* CoBLCP, *tr. by* Jonathan Chaves

Inscribed on a Painting ("Little boat floats by the dock, The"). Tao-chi, *Chinese.* CoBLCP, *tr. by* Jonathan Chaves

Inscribed on a Painting ("Magic mists twirl around the sky"). Yün Shou-p'ing, *Chinese.* CoBLCP, *tr. by* Jonathan Chaves

Inscribed on a Painting. Ni Tsan, *Chinese.* CoBLCP, *tr. by* Jonathan Chaves

Inscribed on a Painting ("On the mountain, old trees, still green in autumn"). T'ang Yin, *Chinese.* CoBLCP, *tr. by* Jonathan Chaves

Inscribed on a Painting ("Places I go, leaning on my bramble cane, The"). T'ang Yin, *Chinese.* CoBLCP, *tr. by* Jonathan Chaves

Inscribed on a Painting. Shen Chou, *Chinese.* SuSp, *tr. by* Daniel Bryant

Inscribed on a Painting. Shen Chou, *Chinese.* SuSp, *tr. by* Irving Y. Lo

Inscribed on a Painting. T'ang Yin, *Chinese.* SuSp, *tr. by* Chiang Yee

Inscribed on a Painting ("Thatched hut among the pines, door open near a cliff") T'ang Yin, *Chinese.* CoBLCP, *tr. by* Jonathan Chaves

Inscribed on a Painting ("Who needs a raft that can invade the stars?"). Yün Shou-p'ing, *Chinese.* CoBLCP, *tr. by* Jonathan Chaves

Inscribed on a Painting. Yü Chi, *Chinese.* CoBLCP, *tr. by* Jonathan Chaves

Inscribed on a Painting by Myself. Ni Tsan, *Chinese.* CoBLCP, *tr. by* Jonathan Chaves

Inscribed on a Painting by Shih-ku. Yün Shou-p'ing, *Chinese.* "Through the windy valley." CoBLCP, *tr. by* Jonathan Chaves

Inscribed on a Painting: Cultivating Leisure. Wen Cheng-ming, *Chinese.* "Volumes of books, tea and incense." CoBLCP, *tr. by* Jonathan Chaves

Inscribed on a Painting of a Cock. T'ang Yin, *Chinese.* SuSp, *tr. by* Chiang Yee

Inscribed on a Painting of a Fisherman. T'ang Yin, *Chinese.* CoBLCP, *tr. by* Jonathan Chaves

Inscribed on a Painting of a Wu-t'ung Tree by Myself. Tao-chi, *Chinese.* CoBLCP, *tr. by* Jonathan Chaves

Inscribed on a Painting of Bamboo. T'ang Yin, *Chinese.* CoBLCP, *tr. by* Jonathan Chaves

Inscribed on a Painting of Bamboo. Wu Chen, *Chinese.* CoBLCP, *tr. by* Jonathan Chaves

Inscribed on a Painting of Bamboo Presented to Lecturer Ch'en Upon His Departure to Resume His Duties at Nanking. Yang Shih-ch'i, *Chinese.* "Even ordinarily, parting is difficult." CoBLCP, *tr. by* Jonathan Chaves

Inscribed on a Painting of Dragons by Ch'en So-weng. Hsieh Chin, *Chinese.* CoBLCP, *tr. by* Jonathan Chaves

Inscribed on a Painting of Sailboats on the River—Seeing Off Yen-chi on His Journey to Ch'ang-an. Yün Shou-p'ing, *Chinese.* CoBLCP, *tr. by* Jonathan Chaves

Inscribed on a Painting of Windy Bamboo, to Be Presented to Tzu-kan. Hsü Wei, *Chinese.* SuSp, *tr. by* Chiang Yee

Inscribed on a Plantain Leaf To Show to a Certain Person. Liu Ling-hsien, *Chinese.* CoBCP, *tr. by* Burton Watson

Inscribed on a Scroll "Plum Blossoms by the Water." Huang T'ing-chien, *Chinese.* SuSp, *tr. by* Michael E. Workman

Inscribed on a Snowscape. Yün Shou-p'ing, *Chinese.* CoBLCP, *tr. by* Jonathan Chaves

Inscribed on a Statue of Hermes. *Unknown, Greek.* GrAn, *tr. by* Peter Jay

Inscribed on a Wall Painting of Assembled Immortals. Chao Meng-fu, *Chinese.* CoBLCP, *tr. by* Jonathan Chaves

Inscribed on an Album Leaf Painted by Dr. Lin. Pien Kung, *Chinese.* CoBLCP, *tr. by* Jonathan Chaves

Inscribed on Byron's Poetic Works. Su Man-shu, *Chinese.* SuSp, *tr. by* Wu-chi Liu

Inscribed on "Drunk in the Autumn Woods." Tao-chi, *Chinese.* CoBLCP, *tr. by* Jonathan Chaves

Inscribed on My Grass-script Calligraphy Written While Drunk. Lu Yu, *Chinese.* SuSp, *tr. by* Irving Y. Lo

Inscribed on My Ink Landscape Painting. Tao-chi, *Chinese.* CoBLCP, *tr. by* Jonathan Chaves

Inscribed on My Large Landscape Hanging Scroll "Listening to a Waterfall." Tao-chi, *Chinese.* CoBLCP, *tr. by* Jonathan Chaves

Inscribed on My Little Painting of Plum Blossom and Bamboo. Tao-chi, *Chinese.* CoBLCP, *tr. by* Jonathan Chaves

Inscribed on Paintings for the People of Hangchow. Hsü Wei, *Chinese.* CoBLCP, *tr. by* Jonathan Chaves

Inscribed on Sun An-chih's "Painting of Pines and Catalpas." Chao Meng-fu, *Chinese.* CoBLCP, *tr. by* Jonathan Chaves

Inscribed on the Arbor of the Old Drunkard (Tsui-weng-t'ing) at Ch'u-chou. Ou-yang Hsiu, *Chinese.* SuSp, *tr. by* Irving Y. Lo

Inscribed on the Fan of a Wealthy Old Man. Shen Chou, *Chinese.* SuSp, *tr. by* Irving Y. Lo

Inscribed on the Painting "Meaning of a Poem by Wang Wei." Li Tung-yang, *Chinese.* CoBLCP, *tr. by* Jonathan Chaves

Inscribed on the Painting of "Garden for Retirement": Pavilion of Sincerity, on Rocky Mountain. Chu Yi-tsun, *Chinese.* SuSp, *tr. by* Chang Yin-nan *and* Lewis C. Walmsley

Inscribed on the Painting "Pleasures of the Lute by the River." Lin Hung, *Chinese.* SuSp, *tr. by* Irving Y. Lo

Inscribed on the Painting, "River in Autumn." Ni Tsan, *Chinese.* CoBLCP, *tr. by* Jonathan Chaves

Inscribed on the Painting, "Solitary Crane," in the Collection of Jao Shih-ying. Yü Chi, *Chinese.* CoBLCP, *tr. by* Jonathan Chaves

Inscribed on the Painting "Spring Dawn at Peach Blossom Spring" by Scholar Shang Te-fu. Chao Meng-fu, *Chinese.* CoBLCP, *tr. by* Jonathan Chaves

Inscribed on the Painting, "Stabbing a Tiger," by Chao Tzu-ang, in the Collection of Scholar Yang. Yang Shih-ch'i, *Chinese.* CoBLCP, *tr. by* Jonathan Chaves

Inscribed on the Wall at the Temple of the Auspicious Talisman. Tao-chi, *Chinese.* CoBLCP, *tr. by* Jonathan Chaves

Inscribed on the Wall of a Rice Cake Shop. Chin Nung, *Chinese.* CoBLCP, *tr. by* Jonathan Chaves

Inscriptio. Alexander Pope. OxBSP

Inscription. William Cowper. OBGa

Inscription: "For one long term, or e'er her trial came." George Canning. FaBoEE

Inscription: Terence, *Latin.* OBCVT, *tr. by* Frank Lawrence Lucas

Inscription: "To them who crossed the flood." Herman Melville. UnPo

Inscription, The: "While yet Rolfe's foot in stirrup stood." Herman Melville. APN-2 *Fr.* Clarel: A Poem and Pilgrimage in the Holy Land.

Inscription: "Whoe'er thou art whose path, in summer lies." Mark Akenside. NOEC

(Tragedy of a Shepherd.) ECEV

Inscription at Villers-Bretonneux. Geoff Page. NOBAu

Inscription by the Sea, An. Glaukos. AWP; FaBoEE *Tr. by* Edwin Arlington Robinson *Fr.* Variations of Greek Themes.

Inscription for a Graveyard. Yvor Winters. CRP

Inscription for a Grotto. Mark Akenside. NOEC; OBGa; PoEL-3

Inscription for a Headstone. Austin Clarke. BIrV; CIP-2; IIP

Inscription for a Mirror in a Deserted Dwelling. William Rose Benét. MoAmPo

Inscription for a Monument in Crossthwaite Curch, in the Vale of Keswick. Wordsworth. EPCY

Inscription for a Portrait of Dante. Giovanni Boccaccio. AWP *Fr.* Sonnets.

Inscription for a Statue of Pan. *Unknown, Greek.* GrAn, *tr. by* Dudley Fitts

Inscription for a War, 'Stranger, go tell the Spartans we died here obedient to their commands.' Simonides of Keos, for the Spartan Dead at Thermopylae. Alec Derwent Hope. BMAP; NoP-4

Inscription for a Wayside Spring. Frances Darwin Cornford. BrRo

Inscription for an Old Bed. William Morris. *See* Lines for a Bed at Kelmscott Manor.

Inscription for the Entrance to a Wood. William Cullen Bryant. APN-1; AmPP; OxBA; TAP

Inscription for the Moss-Hut at Dove Cottage. Wordsworth. OBGa

Inscription for the Tank. James Wright. TwCP

Inscription in a Beautiful Retreat Called Fairy Bower. Hannah More. ECWP; NoP-4

Inscription in Monastic Refectory. Alcuin, *Latin.* MLL, *tr. by* Helen Waddell

Inscription on a Statue. Hermocreon, *Greek.* GrAn, *tr. by* Alistair Elliot

Inscription on a Tree atop mount Sacrifice (Ssu Shan) and Sent to Censor Ch'iao. Ch'en Tzu-ang, *Chinese.* SuSp, *tr. by* Geoffrey R. Waters

Inscription on Monument of Dorothy, Lady Hubert. Anne King. KTR

Inscription on the Flyleaf of a Bible. Dannie Abse. TrJP

Inscription on the Liberty Bell. Bible, *O.T.* CA

Inscription on the Tomb of the Lady Mary Wentworth, The. Thomas Carew. *See* Maria Wentworth.

Inscriptions: "About holiday rooms there can be." Eavan Boland. PuP-17

Inscriptions at the City of Brass. *Unknown.* AWP *Fr.* The Thousand and One Nights.

Inscriptions on Greek tombstones intrigued him. Ronald Wyn. Robert Bagg. TwCP

Insect, An. Tanka. Kanoko Okamoto, *Japanese.* MJT, *tr. by* Makoto Ueda

Insect Kitchen, The. Nicki Jackowska. BrRo

Insects. Isidor Schneider. TrJP

Insects, The. Nancy Willard. LCAP-2

Insensibility. Wilfred Owen. CMoP; FaBoTw; InPS-3; LiTM; NoP-4; OBWP; OxAEP-2; OxBTC; PeFWW; PoWW

Inseparable. Philip Bourke Marston. BoLoP

Inseparable from the fire. Coda. William Carlos Williams. NOBA

Insert, The. R. L. Barth. CDa; InPK-6

Inserting the Mirror. Rosemarie Waldrop.

"To explore the nature of rain I opened the door because inside the workings of language clear vision is impossible." PmAP

Inside. Andrew Salkey. HCP

Inside Diameter. Clarence Major. PmAP

Inside History. Angela McCabe. AmPA

Inside, it is bare but dimly alive. Thomas Kinsella. CIP-2 *Fr.* The Messenger.

Inside / (jittery / burned language). Re:searches (Fragments, after Anakreon, for Emily Dickinson). Kathleen Fraser. PmAP

Inside Language. Charles Borkhuis. PT

Inside my father's close. My Father's Close. *Unknown, French.* AWP, *tr. by* D. G. Rossetti

Inside my heart it's changed, what spring once meant. A Fighter's Thoughts of Spring. Lê Đùc Thọ, *Vietnamese.* AVP, *tr. by* Huỳnh Sanh Thông

Inside My Zulu Hut. Mbuyiseni Oswald Mtshali. PDMAP

Inside of King's College Chapel, Cambridge. Wordsworth. OBNC *Fr.* Ecclesiastical Sonnets.

(Within King's College Chapel, Cambridge.) GTBS-P

Inside of the shell, The. Evening. Beatrice Hawley. MoLi

Inside or out, the key is pain. It holds. Hospital. Karl Shapiro. VGW

Inside Out. Diane Wakoski. CoAP; NYBP

Inside the brain they are holding a mass funeral for the dead brain cells. The Brain Cells. Donald Hall. TAP

Inside the catalytic mine field. Explosive Decibel Journeys. Will Alexander. PT

Inside, the church lights up today's rain. [Poem 2]. Fernando Pessoa. PFTM, *tr. by* Edwin Honig *and* Susan M. Brown *Fr.* Oblique Rain.

Inside the coconut is Katerina's baby. A Coconut for Katerina. Sandra McPherson. LCAP-2

Inside the hollowness that is bone. Blue. Michael C. Blumenthal. CMAP

Inside the house is warm. Brian Coffey. IIP *Fr.* Nightfall, Midwinter, Missouri. CIP-2 *Fr.* Missouri Sequence.

Inside the light of a three-way lamp. The Fire Burns Low. John Leax. TrCP

Inside the lunchroom the travelling nuns wove. Feathered Dances. Kenward Elmslie. PmAP

Inside the nighttime of the storm. The Enormous Hand. Jorge de Lima, *Portuguese.* PFTM, *tr. by* June Jordan

Inside the River. James Dickey. PoA

Inside the skull the wakeful brain. The Camera Obscura. John Addington Symonds. NOBVV

Inside the tower not a broken tower two. Image-Nation (the Poésis). Robin Blaser. PoM

Inside the Tulip. George Bowering. MoCV

Inside the veins there are navies setting forth. Waking from Sleep. Robert Bly. NOBA; NoP-4; Poetr; SPE

Inside / The wireless is irritable with static. Dog Fight. Eric Rolls. NOBAu

Inside the Wolf's fang, the mountain of heather. Amulet. Ted Hughes. NOxBChV

Inside this clay jar there are meadows and groves and the One who made them. Kabir, *Hindi.* EnlH, *tr. by* Czeslaw Milosz *and* Robert Hass (b. 1941)

Inside this music there is someone. Listening to Bach. Robert Bly. *Fr.* Six Winter Privacy Poems. LCAP-2

Inside this pencil. The Unwritten. W. S. Merwin. IFJA

Insidious in ways no gunfire touches, revolution. Revolutionary Revolution. George Buchanan. IIP

Insincere Wish Addressed to a Beggar, An. Mary Elizabeth Coleridge. NOBVV; PEW; VWP

Insistent as a whistle, her voice up. Claiming Kin. Ellen Bryant Voigt. WeT

Insistently through sleep—a tide of voices. The Harbor Dawn. Hart Crane. AmPP; CMoP; LiTM; MoAmPo; NOBA; NoAM; OxBA *Fr.* Powhatan's Daughter. *Fr.* The Bridge. NAAL-2

Insolvent—every Noon—. (LL) I gave myself to Him—. Emily Dickinson. APN-2; ITG

Insomnia. Timothy Geiger. PuP-17

Insomnia. Ivan V. Lalic, *Serbo-Croatian.* HSix, *tr. by* Charles Simic

Insomnia. Lu Yu, *Chinese.* OHMPC, *tr. by* Kenneth Rexroth

Insomnia. Wyatt Prunty. RA

Insomnia. Marina Tsvetayeva, *Russian.*
"Black as[—] the centre of an eye, the centre, a blackness." PBWP

Insomnia. Robert Penn Warren. *Fr.* Tale of Time. LCAP-2

Insomnia I. Howard Nemerov. DiPo

Insomnia: The Distances. Sydney Lea. RA

Insomnia the Gem of the Ocean. John Updike. NBLV

Insomniac Poem. Ron Loewinsohn. NeAP

Insomniac Sleeps Well for Once and, The. Hayden Carruth. NNaP

Insomniac trees rattle silken little. Unholy Spring. John Godfrey. FTOS

Insomniacs, The. Adrienne Rich. NYBP

Inspector Hsü Claims He Has Found the Secret of Youth. T'ang Hsien-tsu, *Chinese.* CoBLCP, *tr. by* Jonathan Chaves

Inspiration. Lynn Emanuel. NAmP90

Inspiration, The. James Montgomery. *Fr.* The West Indies. PBCV

Inspiration. Sherod Santos. NAmP90

Inspiration. Robert W. Service. WeW-3

Inspiration. Henry David Thoreau. APN-1; AmPP; ColAP; NCAP; NOBA; OxBA
"If with light head erect I sing." FaBoBe

Inspire our sons to seek their man-shadows. If We Cannot Live People as People. Charles Lynch. PoBA

Instability. Henrietta Cordelia Ray. CBWP-3

Instans Tyrannus. Robert Browning. EBEV

"Instant coffee with slightly sour cream." Poem. Frank O'Hara. LiLi

Instead of a Journey. Michael Hamburger. NYBP

Instead of a Preface. "Anna Andreyevna Akhmatova." PFTM

Instead of a solemn wedding and marriage-bed. Anyte, *Greek.* GrAn, *tr. by* Sally Purcell

Instead of becoming the empress of joined kingdoms. End of the Game. Artur Miedzyrzecki, *Polish.* PoSu, *tr. by* Artur Miedzyrzecki *and* John Batki

Instead of coin and money. John Skelton. NoSic *Fr.* Elinour Rumming.

Instead of pearls—a wrought clasp. The Gift. Hilda Doolittle. CPO

Instead of thought, true pleasure be begun / And never ended. (LL) Get Hence Foule Griefe. Sir Philip Sidney. PoEL-1; SiPS

Instead of two cats, there weren't any. (LL) The Cats of Kilkenny. *Unknown.* ChAP; PeLi; ReMoGo

Instead of wisdom—experience, a flat. "Anna Akhmatova," *Russian.* LoP, *tr. by* Judith Hemschemeyer

Instinct. Edith Södergran, *Swedish.* PFTM, *tr. by* Stina Katchadourian

Instructed by the fiery dead. (LL) The Cross. Allen Tate. AWP; ChIV-2; MoAmPo; OxBA

Instructed in love. Ingeborg Bachmann. WPOW, *tr. by* Daniel Huws *Fr.* Songs in Flight.

Instructed to speak of God with emphasis. Memorial to a Missionary. Keith Sinclair. PeNZ

Instruction. Hazel Hall. NMM-2

Instruction from Bly. Cynthia MacDonald. NMM-2

Instruction Manual, The. John Ashbery. HAP; InPS-3; NOBA; NeAP; NoAM; PoM; Poetr

Instructions for a Waitress. Yehuda Amichai, *Hebrew.* PoSu, *tr. by* Harold Schimmel

Instructions for Building Straw Huts. Yusef Komunyakaa. GT

Instructions for Crossing the Border. Dan Pagis, *Hebrew.* PoSu, *tr. by* Stephen Mitchell

Instructions for Elijah. Myra Sklarew. CRP

Instructions for the Erection of a Statue to Myself in Central Park. Colette Inez. CMAP

Instructions for the Waitress. Yehuda Amichai, *Hebrew.* IP, *tr. by* Warren Bargad *and* Stanley F. Chyet

Instructions for Your New Osiris. Lorenzo Thomas. PmAP

Instructions From England 1936. Valentine Ackland. WPN

Instructions of King Cormac. Cormac, King of Cashel. PoToHe

Instructions of King Cormac, The. *Unknown, Irish.*
"'O Cormac, grandson of Conn,' said Carbery." BIrV, *tr. by* Kuno Meyer

Instructions on landscaping. Richard Jago. OBGa *Fr.* Edge-Hill.

Instructions, Supposed to Be Written in Paris, for the Mob in England. Mary Alcock. ECWP
("Of liberty, reform, and rights I sing.") Ro

Instructions to a Celebrated Laureat. "Peter Pindar."
George III Visits Whitbread's Brewery. NOEC

Instructions to a Princess. Ishmael Reed. PoBA

Instructions to a Seed. David Curzon. GI

Instructions to the Double. Tess Gallagher. FaBoWP; NMM-2

Instructive poison, something he could use. (LL) The Farmer. Ellen Bryant Voigt. MT; WeW-3

Instructor said, The. Theme for English B. Langston Hughes. ColAP; FaBoA; HCAP; MoP; NIP-4; NOBA; NoAM; NoP-4; PoPoPo; Poetr; SSLK

Instrument, The. Kathleen Jessie Raine. PoA

instruments of music are made ready, The. The Dancers of Huai-nan. Chang Heng, *Chinese.* ChiP, *tr. by* Arthur Waley

Instrumentum Vocale. Kevin Magee. PT

Insular Celts, The. Ciaran Carson. BIrV; CIP-2; IIP

Insult, An. *Unknown.* NOIV

Insult before Gift-Giving. Frank Bolton, *Tsimshian Indian.* STP, *tr. by* Armand Schwerner

Insulted. Priscilla Jane Thompson. CBWP-2

Insurance salesman named Flint, An. Limerick. Charles Barsotti. PeLi

Insusceptibles, The. Adrienne Rich. CoAmPo; HeIP-4; Son

Integrity. Adrienne Rich. ColAP

Intellect. Ralph Waldo Emerson. APN-1; NoP-4

Intellect of man is forced to choose, The. The Choice. W. B. Yeats. CMoP; NoAM; OxBSP; OxBTC

Intellectual, The. Karl Shapiro. CMoP

Intellectual cautious-/ ly creeping cat. (LL) Bird-witted. Marianne Moore. CMoP; NAAL-2

Intellectuals, The. Dudley Randall. PoBA

Intelligent beings must have been living there. (LL) Earth ("'Planet doesn't explode of itself, A,' said drily"). John Hall Wheelock. LiTM; SAGP; SoSe-8

Intelligent Sheepman and the New Cars, The. William Carlos Williams. OBAL

Intelligible sun of Justice and you, gloryfying myrtle. Odysseus Elytis. GrIP, *tr. by* Edmund Keeley *and* George Savidis *Fr.* Axion Esti.

Intemperate torch grazed, The. Night-piece. "Ern Malley." BMAP

Intendant Yao Shan Has Requested Six Poems on Living in the Mountains, The. Yang Shih-ch'i, *Chinese.*
White Stone Slope. CoBLCP, *tr. by* Jonathan Chaves

Intended for Sir Isaac Newton. Alexander Pope. ECEV; InPK-6; WeW-3
(Epitaph Intended for Sir Isaac Newton.) PFE

Intense and terrible beauty, how has our race with the frail naked nerves. Gale in April. Robinson Jeffers. MoAmPo

Intensive Care. Carol Muske. PBCAP

Intent ear hears the silence hears silence and then the pen, The. Pen Vine and Scroll. John Taggart. FTOS

Intent gets blocked by noise. Hand Games. Marge Piercy. CrSp

Intent to consider. Kit Robinson. FTOS *Fr.* Up Early.

Inter, mitzy, titzy, tool. *Unknown.* FaBoVe; OxNR

Intercede for us dear saint we beseech thee. Prayer to Saint Grobianus. Roger McGough. NOxBChV

Intercessors. Austin Clarke. CMoP

Interchange of display. Horse Power. Tom Raworth. NBrP

Interesting case, the progress of a bird. When, An. Will to Will. Keith Waldrop. PmAP

Interests of a black man in a cellar, The. Black Tambourine. Hart Crane. InPK-6; InPS-3; MeMAP; NoAM; OxBA; OxBSP; TAP

Interface. Gloria Anzaldúa. GLP

Interferon. Miroslav Holub, *Czech.* VCWP, *tr. by* David Young *and* Dana Hábová

Interim. Frank Ormsby. CIP-2

Interim, The. Robert Penn Warren. *Fr.* Tale of Time. LCAP-2

Interior. Padraic Colum. MoBrPo

Interior. Sir John Collings Squire. OxBSP

Interior at Petworth: From Turner. Rosanna Warren. NoAM

Interior Landscape. Gloria Fuertes, *Spanish.* BoWoP, *tr. by* Willis Barnstone

Interior Monologue 666. Tom Marshall. NOBC

Interior Prisoner, The. Geoffrey O'Brien. BAP-95

Interior (With Jane). Frank O'Hara. LCAP-2

Interlinked is truth to duty, have you had the precious thought. Duty, or Truth at Work. Lizelia Augusta Jenkins Moorer. CBWP-3

Interlude, An. Robert Duncan. CMoP

Interlude. Walter Savage Landor. GTBS-P

Interlude. Amy Lowell. NMM-2

Interlude. Karl Shapiro. PBMP

Interlude. Dame Edith Sitwell. MoBrPo

Interlude. Welton Smith. PoBA

Interludes. Fabio Doplicher, *Italian.* NeIt, tr. by Stephen Sartarelli

Internal Migration: On Being on Tour. Alan Dugan. NoAM

International Chainpoem. *Unknown.* SPE

International Conference. Colin Ellis. FaBoEE

International Date Line, Monday/Monday 27:XI:67. Philip Whalen. BB

International Hymn. George Huntington. PoLF

International Solidarity. Phan Trọng Quảng, *Vietnamese.* AVP, tr. by Huỳnh Sanh Thông

Interpone tuis, interdum gaudia curis. Cato Uticensis. OBCVT, tr. by Sir Richard Baker *Fr. Catoes Morall Distichs: Translated and Paraphras'd, with variations of Expressing, in English verse.*

Interpretation of a Poem by Frost. Thylias Moss. PuP-14

Interpreters, The. Swinburne. PoEL-5

Interracial. Georgia Douglas Johnson. TTY

Interred [*or* Interr'd] beneath this marble stone. An Epitaph. Matthew Prior. FaBoEE; NAEL-1; OAEL-1; OBCoV; OBSV; PoEL-3

Interrogated by / the whips of my own imperfection. Confession and Salute to the Fire. Lyubomir Levchev, *Bulgarian.* CEEP, tr. by Ewald Osers

Interrogation. Sophie Cabot Black. BAP-93

Interrogation, The. Li-Young Lee. PoPoPo

Interrogation, The. Edwin Muir. CMoP; PoWW

Interrogations of the Sparrow. Elizabeth Spires. FFC

Interrogator, The. Elizabeth Jennings. WPE

Interrupt this Ground. (LL) Ample make this Bed. Emily Dickinson. MoAmPo; NAAL-1; NAAL-3; OxBA; PoEL-5

Interrupted Reproof, The. Priscilla Jane Thompson. CBWP-2

Interruption. Robert Graves. ImPo; LiTM

Interruption to a Journey. Norman MacCaig. RB

Intersection in the Sky. Mcavoy Layne. CDa

Interstices. William J. Higginson. HA

Interval. Joseph Auslander. FYAP

Interview, An. K. W. Grandsen. OxBTC

Interview. Sara Henderson Hay. OBCA

Interview near Florence, An. Samuel Rogers. *Fr.* Italy. OBNC

Interview with a Child. Wislawa Szymborska, *Polish.* CEEP, tr. by Tadeusz Swek

Interview with a Guy Named Fawkes, U.S. Army. Walter McDonald. CDa

Interview with Doctor Drink. James Vincent Cunningham. OxBSP; VGW

Interview with Herr Limerick. Andreas Okopenko, *German.* CBNP

Intery, mintery, cutery corn. Mother Goose. FaBoVe; OxNR; ReMoGo

Intifada. June Jordan. NAAAL

Intil the pit-mirk nicht we northwart sail. Arctic Convoy. James King Annand. OxBS

Intimate Letter 1973. Padraic Fiacc. PNI

Intimate Parnassus. Patrick Kavanagh. MoBrPo

Intimate Supper. Peter Redgrove. FaBoMo; OxBC

Intimates. D. H. Lawrence. BoLoP; CBLP; NBLV; OxBSP; RaBo

Intimations of Immortality. Wordsworth. *Fr.* Ode: Intimations of Immortality [from Recollections of Early Childhood]. AWP; FHYEP; HAP; HeIP-4; NOBE; NOBRP; OAEL-2; OBEV; OBNC; PBMP; PoE; PoEL-4

Intimations of Mortality. Stanley Kunitz. MoAmPo

Intimidations of an Autobiography. James Tate. NoAM

Into a dark and lonely wood. (LL) The Villain. W. H. Davies. MoBrPo; OxBSP; OxBTC; SAGP

Into a little close of mine I went. Lorenzo de' Medici. *Fr.* Two Lyrics. AWP, tr. by John Addington Symonds

Into a pair of stars. Tanka. Akiko Yosano, *Japanese.* MJT, tr. by Ueda, Makoto

Into a sweet May morning. John of Hazelgreen. *Unknown.* ESPB

Into a ward of the whitewashed walls. Somebody's Darling. Marie La Coste. BLPA; UnPo

Into a world where children shriek like suns. On a Child Who Lived One Minute. X. J. Kennedy. HoPM; NYBP; Poetr

Into an empty space. (LL) The Ballad of Reading Gaol. Oscar Wilde. CABP

Into azure cloudland searching. To My Distant Beloved. Alois Jeitteles, *German.* TrJP, tr. by the Reverend Dr. Troutbeck

Into Battle. Julian Grenfell. FaPoR; OBEV; OBMV; OBWP; OxBTC; PeFWW; PoFWW

Into Blackness Softly. Mari E. Evans. PoBA

Into blossom. James Wright. *See* A Blessing.

Into concrete mixer throw. Barbara Roe. UV

Into each other's gaze. (LL) Judas Iscariot. Stephen Spender. MoBrPo; NIP-4

Into Hell's cave stepped a new guest. Arrival in Hell. Ricarda Huch, *German.* PBWP, tr. by Susan C. Strong

Into her mother's bedroom to wash the ballooning body. Jessie Mitchell's Mother. Gwendolyn Brooks. BoWoP; ColAP; NALW; NMM-2

Into her secret eyes. Nobody dared. "Anna Andreyevna Akhmatova." *See* Crucifixion.

Into Hey nonny, nonny. Shakespeare. *See* Song: "Sigh no more, ladies, sigh no more."

Into hey nony nony. (LL) Song: "Sigh no more, ladies, sigh no more." Shakespeare. AWP; CTC; NoSic; PoEL-2; UV

Into his kit when sent to the front he had tucked. Favorite Iraqi Soldier. Stephen Dobyns. BAP-93

Into his rosy chamber stepped the Sun. At Sunset. Henrietta Cordelia Ray. CBWP-3

Into irrelevance. Yvor Winters. *See* To the Holy Spirit.

Into Laddery Street. Laura Riding Jackson. *Fr.* Forgotten Girlhood. RB

Into Mexico. Mona Van Duyn. VCAP

Into my empty head there come. Morning Swim. Maxine W. Kumin. Poetr; WPE

Into my eyes he loving looked. The Mirror. Judah Halevi, *Hebrew.* TrJP, tr. by Emma Lazarus

Into My Heart an Air that Kills. The Land of Lost Content. A. E. Housman. CMoP; EBEV; GEA; LBC; LiTM; MoBrPo; NOBE; NOBVV; NTP; NoAM; OAEL-2; OPOU; OxAEP-2; OxBTC; TFi

Into nothing. Nothing. Tom Raworth. NBrP

Into one of three pots. Viaticum. Birago Diop, *French.* NegPo, tr. by Ellen Conroy Kennedy

Into our empty room. Their Party, Our House. Jon Swan. NYBP

Into ourselves / who (look). ,startled. (LL) Four III. E. E. Cummings. FaBoMo; TTTS

Into Prison. Bill Griffiths. NBrP

Into—Renown! (LL) Read—Sweet—how others—strove. Emily Dickinson. AH; NOCV

Into small waves and sparkle as he comes. (LL) Summer Wind William Cullen Bryant. APN-1; PoEL-4

Into Suburbia between eight and nine. Three-handed Fugue. Phyllis Gotlieb. NOBC

Into that house whose tenants do not love. (LL) The Things. Conrad Potter Aiken. HAP; WeW-3

Into that pit / I had to climb down. Burning Shit at An Khe. Bruce Weigl. AF; CDa

Into that pit when I did enter in. Elizabeth, Lady Culross Melvill. *Fr.* A Godly Dream. WPE

Into the Ark. John Blight. BMAP

Into the atmosphere, out of this world. Tune: "The Charm of Nien-nu"— Kunlun Mountains. Mao Tse-tung, *Chinese.* SuSp, tr. by Eugene Eoyang

Into the blinding sun. Nicholas Virgilio. HA; InPK-6

Into the blue river hills. Sunset from Omaha Hotel Window. Carl Sandburg. AiP

Into the clouds, and never more return! (LL) Ode on Indolence. Keats. NAEL-2; OBNC; Ro

Into the common death beyond the mousetrap. (LL) Funeral Oration for a Mouse. Alan Dugan. HAP; Poetr

Into the Dark. Paul Monette. AmPA

Into the darkness and the hush of night. Night. Henry Wadsworth Longfellow. APN-1

Into the Depths. Adah Isaacs Menken. CBWP-1

Into the destination of the wind! (LL) To the Lacedemonians. Allen Tate. NAAL-2; NoAM

Into the Dusk-Charged Air. John Ashbery. APSN

Into the enormous sky flew. Boris Pasternak. ITG, tr. by Hass, Robert and Stephen Mitchell *Fr.* A Wedding.

Into the furnace let me go alone. Baptism. Claude McKay. PBCV

"Into the future. Let what will be, be." (LL) Acceptance. Robert Frost. CMoP; GSo; OxBA

Into the Glacier. John Haines. CoAP

Into the gloom of the deep, dark night. The Engine. Ella Wheeler Wilcox. APN-2

Into the Glories of th' Almighty Sun. (LL) *see also* Ros. Andrew Marvell. ESCV; FSCP; GeHe; HAP; MeLP; NOSC; SCGP; SeCP

Into the grave. (LL) To Blossoms. Robert Herrick. BeJo; CaPo; GTBS-P; NAEL-1; NOSC; OBEV; SCGP; SeCP

Into the haven where they would be. (LL) Love at Large. Coventry Patmore. EBVV; NOBVV

Into the inmost temple thus I came. The Temple of Venus. Edmund Spenser. *Fr.* Wood Of Error. AEP

Into the last dream of Offa the King. (LL) Not strangeness, but strange likeness. Obstinate. Geoffrey Hill. HAP; NoAM

Into the light of the sea. (LL) Songs for the Four Parts of the Night. Owl Woman, *Papago Indian.* WPoS, tr. by Frances Densmore

Into the Mead he comes, nor (seen) doth fright. Moschus. OBCVT, *tr.* by Thomas Stanley *Fr.* Europa.

Into the mid[d]le temple of my h[e]art[e]. Sir John Davies. *Fr.* The Gulling[e] Sonnets. Son

Into the night. The Inland Lighthouse. James McMichael. AmPA

Into the Park a-maying! (LL) Sister, Awake! *Unknown.* BoTP; CH; NOBE; OBEV

Into the pit of / the empty / flowerpot. William Carlos Williams. *See* Poem: "As the cat / climbed over."

Into the pool of silence our tears made. The Ancient Couple on Lu Mountain. Mark Van Doren. VGW

Into the quiet of this room. The Room. William Soutar. EBEV

Into the rapt, imperious, seagoing river. (LL) The Son. Denise Levertov. FiLi; NALW

Into the rescued world newcomer. Beyond Knowledge. Alice Thompson Meynell. ChIV-1

Into the scented woods we'll go. Green Rain. Mary Webb. CH

Into the Silent Land! Song of the Silent Land. Johann Gaudenz von Salis-Seewis, *German.* AWP, *tr.* by Longfellow

Into the silver night. Revelation. Sir Edmund William Gosse. OBEV

Into the sixties / a trane / came. Don't Cry, Scream. Haki R. Madhubuti. SeSe

Into the skies, one summer's day. The Thought. William Brighty Rands. OBEV

Into the slain tons of needles. By Canoe through the Fir Forest. James Dickey. NYBP *Fr.* On the Coosawattee.

Into the slain tons of needles. On the Coosawattee. James Dickey.

Into the soil a seed is sown. Mors et Vita. James Edwin Campbell. AAP

Into the street the Piper stept. Robert Browning. BoTP; OxAEP-2 *Fr.* The Pied Piper of Hamelin. EBNV; FaBoBe; FaBoCh; NOxBChV; OBNV; OBSP; OxBChV; PeLV

Into the sunshine. The Fountain. James Russell Lowell. BoTP; OBCA

Into the towering gulfs of air. (LL) Veni Coronaberis. Geoffrey Hill. DiPo; NoP-4

Into the underneath—. Recessional. Robert Kelly. FTOS

Into the unforgiving new day. (LL) The Man with the Saxophone. Ai. NMM-2; SeSe; WWSi

Into the void behold my shuddering flight. Anna Hempstead Branch. NALW *Fr.* Sonnets from a Lock Box.

Into the woods my Master went. A Ballad of Trees and the Master. Sidney Lanier. APAD; APN-2; ChIV-2; ColAP; NOBA; OxBA; PoEL-5; PoLF

Into these loves, who but for passion look[e]s. To the Reader of These Sonnets. Michael Drayton. AAS; NAEL-1; NOSC; Son *Fr.* Idea.

Into thir inmost bower. Milton. TOF, *ll.* 738–775 *Fr.* Book IV. OAEL-1 *Fr.* Paradise Lost.

Into this place whereas the elfin knight. The Nymphs and Graces Dancing. Edmund Spenser. *Fr.* Wood Of Error. AEP

Into this pleasant Shadow all the weak & weary. William Blake. NOBRP *Fr.* Milton.

Into this wild abyss. Satan's Journey. Milton. NOSC *Fr.* Book II. FHYEP; NAEL-1; OxAEP-1 *Fr.* Paradise Lost.

Into what fictive worlds can imagination. The Horatians. W. H. Auden. NYBP

Into your arms I came. To the Anxious Mother. Valente Goenha Malangatana, *Portuguese.* PBA, *tr.* by Dorothy Guedes *and* Philippa Rumsey

Intoxicatingly. To a Dancer. Arthur Symons. ADE

Intoxication of final loneliness. (LL) Medlars and Sorb-Apples. D. H. Lawrence. FaBoVe; NoAM; OAEL-2

Intra-Political. Margaret Avison. MoCV

Intramural Aestivation, or Summer in Town, by a Teacher of Latin. Oliver Wendell Holmes. *See* Aestivation [an Unpublished Poem, by My Late Latin Tutor].

Intrepid Ricardo, The. Edmund Clerihew Bentley. OBCoV *Fr.* Clerihews.

Intricate ship. Alice Ordered Me to be Made. Alice Notley. FTOS

Intriguing thought—what artists dyed the flowers? Ode to All Flowers. Nguyễn Công Trứ', *Vietnamese.* AVP, *tr.* by Huỳnh Sanh Thông

Introduced / to the Upanishads / by T. S. Eliot;. Situation. Kaa Naa Subramanyam, *Tamil.* OMIP, *tr.* by Kaa Naa Subramanyam

Introduction. "Anna Akhmatova," *Russian.* PFTM, *tr.* by Lenore Mayhew *and* William McNaughton

Introduction: "Clear transparent sea with light, The." Horatio Nelson Huggins. *Fr.* Hiroona. PBCV

Introduction, The: "Did I, my lines intend for public[k] view." Anne Finch, Countess of Winchilsea. BWW; NAEL-1; NALW; NoP-4; WPOW

Introduction: "Hear the voice of the Bard!" William Blake. APAD; ChIV-1; EBEV; FHYEP; HAP; InPS-3; NAEL-2; NAWM-2; NOBE; NOBRP; NOEC; NoP-4; OAEL-2; PoE; PoEL-4; RB; Ro; TFi *Fr.* Songs of Experience.

(Bard, The.)

Introduction: "I bespeak words." Clere Parsons. FaBoTw

Introduction: "I don't know politics but I know the names." Kamala Das. NALW; WPOW

Introduction: "Joy of the poor knocked on the door, The." Nathan Alterman. MHP, *tr.* by Ruth Finer Mintz *Fr.* The Joy of the Poor.

Introduction, The. Louis MacNeice. PNI

Introduction. William Morris. *See* Prologue: The Wanderers.

Introduction: "Piping down the valleys wild." William Blake. NOBRP; Ro *Fr.* Songs of Innocence.

(From Songs of Innocence.) NoP-4

(Reeds of Innocence.) ImPo; OBEV

Introduction: "Should you ask me, whence these stories?" Henry Wadsworth Longfellow. ColAP; MeMAP; NOBA; PoE; Poetr *Fr.* The Song of Hiawatha.

Introduction and Anecdotes. "Peter Pindar." PoEL-3 *Fr.* Bozzy and Piozzi.

Introduction—Childhood and School-Time. Wordsworth. FHYEP *Fr.* The Prelude; Growth of a Poet's Mind [1850 vers.]

"Dust as we are, the immortal spirit grows." SCV

"Ere I had told / Ten birthdays when among the mountain-slopes." TOF

"Fair seed time had my soul, and I grew up." HAP; PoE; PoEL-4

("Did summon us in his delightful round.") (LL) PoEL-4

("Work like a sea?") (LL) HAP

Influence of Natural Objects [in Calling Forth and Strengthening the Imagination in Boyhood and Early Youth]. AWP

Lines: "One summer evening (led by her) I found."

"O there is blessing in this gentle breeze." OAEL-2

Skating. CH

Introduction of a refrain, The. 'Twixt Cup and Lip. Mark Hollis. NBLV

INTRODUCTION TO A DESERT. Artistic Copy. Tymoteusz Karpowicz, *Polish.* CEEP, *tr.* by Zak, Ewa

Introduction to a Poem. Nikolai Ivanovich Glazkov, *Russian.* TCRP, *tr.* by Daniel Weissbort

Introduction to Poetry. Paul Lake. RA

Introduction to the Beyond. Blaga Dimitrova, *Bulgarian.* CEEP, *tr.* by Jascha Kessler *and* Aleksandar Shurbanov

Introduction to the Franklin's Prologue and Tale. Chaucer. NAEL-1 *Fr.* The Canterbury Tales.

Introduction to the Nun's Priest's Tale, The, *see* Prologue of the Nun's Priest's Tale, The. Chaucer. *See* The Nun's Priest's Prologue.

Introduction to the Pardoner's Prologue and Tale. Chaucer. FHYEP; NAEL-1; PoE *Fr.* The Canterbury Tales.

Introduction to the Parson's Tale, The. Chaucer. NAEL-1 *Fr.* The Canterbury Tales.

Introductory to Second Edition. Alfred Islay Walden. AAP

Introit. Padraic Fiacc. CIP-2

Introspective. Christina Rossetti. VWP

Introspective Reflection. Ogden Nash. NBLV; OBCoV

Intruder. Susan Feldman. AmPA

Intruder, The. Carolyn Kizer. BoWoP; InPK-6

Intruder, The. Frank Stanford. MT

Intruder in a Set Scene. Norman MacCaig. FaBoTC

Intrusion. Denise Levertov. VCAP

Intuition. Anthony Delius. PeSA

Inundation, The. Howard Sergeant. SPE

Inupiat Christmas Pageant, The. Peggy Shumaker. PBCAP

Invades, and drowns them all in tears. (LL) A Foreign Ruler. Walter Savage Landor. OBSV; PFE

Invalid Dawn. Elizabeth Daryush. WPN

Invalid girl asked, An. Those Who Do Not Dance. Gabriela Mistral, *Spanish.* WPoS, *tr.* by Maria Giachetti

Invalid's Song. Harata Tangikuku, *Maori.* PeNZ, *tr.* by Margaret Orbell

Invariably when wine redeems the sight. The Wine Menagerie. Hart Crane. NOBA; NoAM; OxBA; VGW

Invasion. Eileen Duggan. PeNZ

Invasion Exercise on the Poultry Farm. John Betjeman. NOBL

Invasion of Grenada, The. William Daniel Ehrhart. CDa

Invasion Summer. Laurie Lee. OxBSP

Invasions. Jimmy Santiago Baca. PaTW

Invective against Ibis. Ovid, *Latin.*

"While Thracians shal with arrowes war, Iaziges with bowe." OBVE, *tr.* by Thomas Underdowne

Invent it now. Your own place. Your Own Place. Edward Lucie-Smith. PBCV

Inventing a story with grass. A Birth. James Dickey. FiLi; NOBA

Inventing Sin. George Ella Lyon. CrSp

Inventing the Filipino. Fatima Lim-Wilson. PUP-19

Invention, The. Paul Éluard, *French.* NNPT, *tr.* by Samuel Beckett

Invention begs from door to door in the indescribable darkness. Kissing Natalia. Eldon Grier. NOBC

Invention of a Garden, The. Jay Wright. GT

Invention of Comics, The. Imamu Amiri Baraka. CAPP-1; CRP; GT; LiTM; NAAAL; PBMP; PoBA

Invention of Fire, The. Andrew Taylor. CBAP

Invention of New Jersey, The. Jack Anderson. EC2

Invention of Pittsburgh, The. Maggie Anderson. PBCAP

Invention of the Telephone, The. Peter Klappert. AmPA

Invention of White People, The. Leslie Marmon Silko. STP

Inventions. Miroslav Holub, Czech. PoSu, tr. by George Theiner

Inventor of the geodesic domes. Air. Philip Dow. BXAP

Inventors. Michael C. Blumenthal. DiPo; NoAM

Inventor's Wife, The. E. R. Corbett. PoLF

Inventory. Günter Eich, German. AF, tr. by David Young

Inventory. Dorothy Parker. NBLV

Inventory. Jacques Prévert, French. STV, tr. by John Frederick Nims

Inventory. Frank Stanford. MT

Inventory of Places Propitious for Love. Angel González, Spanish. VCWP, tr. by Steven Ford Brown and Revuelta Gutierrez

Inventory of the Furniture of a Collegian's Chamber, An. John Winstanley. OBSV

Inverey cam doun Deeside, whistlin and playin. The Baron of Brackley. Unknown. ESPB

Inversnaid. Gerard Manley Hopkins. APAD; CMoP; EnVR; FaBoVe; GTBS-P; ImPo; LiTM; MoBrPo; NoAM; OAEL-2; PeVV; PoRA; RB; SAGP; SCGP; TFi; UnPo

Investment, The. Robert Frost. CMoP; OxBA

Invictus. William Ernest Henley. APAD; BLPA; CABP; EBEvV; FaBoBe; FaPoR; HoPM; ImPo; MoBrPo; NOBE; OBEV; OBMV; OBNC; SAGP Fr. Echoes.

Invincible begetters, assorted Scutzes. Saga. Maxine W. Kumin. AFr

Invisibility Poem: Lesbian. Ilze Mueller. LoHo

Invisible Autumn. Joseph Ceravolo. FTOS

Invisible Boundaries. Maureen Hurley. LoHo

Invisible, chimerical. Riddle. Daryl Hine. NoP-4

Invisible hand, An. Sierra. Alfonsina Storni, Spanish. PBWP, tr. by Rachel Benson

Invisible History. Walta Borawski. GLP

Invisible, indivisible Spirit. Hilda Doolittle. BoWoP Fr. Tribute to the Angels.

Invisible King, The. Goethe, German. RaBo, tr. by Robert Bly

Invisible Men, The. Nakasuk, Eskimo. RaBo, tr. by Edward Field

Invisible Playmate, The. Margaret Widdemer. CTV

Invisible woman in the asylum corridor, The. Robin Morgan. NMM-2

Invisible Work. Margaret Gibson. MT

Invitation. Marion Angus. LW

Invitation, The. Robert Creeley. FTOS

Invitation, The. George Herbert. ChIV-1; ESCV

Invitation, The. Robert Herrick. CaPo

Invitation, The. Charles Kingsley. NOBVV

Invitation. Myra Cohn Livingston. TLR

Invitation, The. Goronwy Owen, Welsh. OBWVE, tr. by George Borrow

Invitation, The. Shelley. GTBS-P; OBEV

(Invitation, to Jane, The.) CH

Invitation. Solomon ibn Gabirol, Hebrew. TrJP, tr. by Israel Zangwill

Invitation, The. Leonard Welsted. NOEC

Invitation from a Country Cottage, The. Martha Sansom. ECWP

Invitation in It, from American Citizen, The. Kay Boyle. NMM-2

Invitation Standing. Paul Blackburn. VGW

Invitation to a Ghost. Donald Justice. BAP-93

Invitation to Dalliance. Unknown. FaBoEE

Invitation to Eternity. John Clare. See Invite to Eternity.

Invitation to Hsiao Ch'u-shih. Po Chü-i, Chinese. ChiP; OBVE, tr. by Arthur Waley

Invitation, to Jane, The. Shelley. See The Invitation.

Invitation To Juno. William Empson. CBLP; CMoP; FaBoMo; LoP

("Graft annual upon perennial trees?") (LL) LoP

Invitation to Madison County, An. Jay Wright. PoBA

Invitation to Mary. Mairtin O Direain, Irish. TIRV, tr. by the author

Invitation to Miss Marianne Moore. Elizabeth Bishop. NALW

Invitation to the Bee. Charlotte Smith. OxBChV

Invitation to the Dance. Apollinaris Sidonius, Latin. AWP, tr. by Howard Mumford Jones

Invitation to the Dance. Pentti Saarikoski, Finnish.

"No, Quetzalcoatl, don't come back." VCWP, tr. by Herbert Lomas

Invite to Eternity, An. John Clare. NAEL-2; NOBVV; OAEL-2; OBNC; Ro

Invite to Eternity. John Clare. NAEL-1; NOBVV; OAEL-2; OBNC (Invitation to Eternity.) PoEL-4

Invited guests in silent order sat, Th'. Animal Magnetism; the Pseudo-Philosopher Baffled. Laurence Hynes Halloran. NOEC

Invites His Nymph to His Cottage. Philip Ayres. EnLoPo

Invites Poets and Historians to Write in Cynthia's Praise. Philip Ayres. Son

Inviting a Friend to Supper. Ben Jonson, after Martial. AWP; BeJo; FP; NOBE; NOSC; NoP-4; OAEL-1; OxBoLi; PeLV; PoEL-2; SeCP

("Libertie, that wee'll enjoy to night, The.") (LL) PBRV

("To night, grave sir, both my poore house, and I.") PBRV

Inviting a Friend to Supper. Martial, Latin. OBCVT, tr. by Ben Jonson

Invocation: "Almighty God, who fillest the recesses of the heavens." Bishop Patrick, Latin. NOIV, tr. by Thomas Kinsella

Invocation: "Appear, O Mother, was the perpetual cry." Wilfred Watson. MoCV

Invocation: "As pools beneath stone arches take." John Drinkwater. PoA

Invocation: "Come down from heaven to meet me when my breath." Siegfried Sassoon. MoBrPo

Invocation: "Come, lovely Muse, desert for me." Samuel Hoffenstein. BXAP

Invocation. Maria Elena Cruz Varela, Spanish. VCWP, tr. by Mairym Cruz-Bernal and Deborah Digges

Invocation: "Dolphin plunge, fountain play." Louis MacNeice. NTP

Invocation: "Earth, ocean, air, belovèd brotherhood!" Shelley. NAEL-2 Fr. Alastor; or, The Spirit of Solitude. OAEL-2; Ro

Invocation: "Great-hearted Christ, importunate and mild." Chad Walsh. Fr. The Psalm of Christ. TrCP

Invocation, An: "Hear, sweet spirit, hear the spell." Coleridge. CH; PeECV Fr. Remorse.

(Voice Sings, A.) CH

Invocation. Samuel Hoffenstein.

"Come, live with me and be my love." NBLV

Invocation: "It's crazy to think one could describe them." Robert Pinsky. NoAM Fr. Essay on Psychiatrists.

(Lakeside Identification, A.) NoP-4

("Yes, crazy to suppose one could describe them.") NoP-4

Invocation: "Last night my soul departed." Muireadhach Albanach O'Dalaigh. NOIV

Invocation: "Let me be buried in the rain." Helene Johnson. NAAAL; SAGP

Invocation. Milton. NOSC; PoEL-3, ll. 1–26 Fr. Book I. FHYEP; NAEL-1; OAEL-1; OxAEP-1 Fr. Paradise Lost.

(Induction, The.) PoE, ll. 1–26

Invocation, An: "My claw is tired of scribing!" Saint Columcille. NOIV

Invocation: "Pheobus, arise! / And paint the sable skies." William Drummond, of Hawthornden. OBEV

Invocation: "Senator Smoot (Republican, Ut.)" Ogden Nash. OBAL

Invocation. Shelley. See Song: "Rarely, rarely, comest thou."

Invocation: "Silent, about-to-be-parted-from house." Denise Levertov. PoA

Invocation: "Ten bloody years with this quill lying." Valentin Iremonger. BIrV

Invocation. Virgil, Latin. OBCVT, tr. by John Dryden Fr. The Aeneid [or Eneados, Aeneis].

Invocation: "Wasp, climbing the window pane." Howard Nemerov. Fr. Epigrams. OBAL

Invocation, The: "Wrath of Peleus Son, O Muse, resound, The." Homer, Greek. OBVE, tr. by Dryden; OBCVT, tr. by John Dryden Fr. The Iliad.

Invocation and Prelude. Stefan George, German. AWP, tr. by Ludwig Lewisohn

(Invocation for Storing Corn). Unknown, Nahuatl. WPoS, tr. by Alarcón, Francisco X.

Invocation: "Maidens young and virgins tender." Horace. See 1.21: To Apollo and Diana ("Dianam tenerae dicite virgines").

Invocation of Comus, The. Milton. See Comus' Summons.

Invocation of Death. Kathleen Jessie Raine. Fr. Two Invocations of Death.

Invocation of Peace. "Fiona Macleod."

"Deep peace, pure white of the moon to you." BoTP

Invocation of Silence. Richard Flecknoe. NOSC; OxBSP

Invocation of the Creator. Yoruba Oral Tradition, Yoruba. BLT, tr. by Ulli Beier

Invocation of the Great Bear. Ingeborg Bachmann, German. VCWP, tr. by Mark Anderson

Invocation To Dsilyi N'Eyani. Unknown. APN-2, tr. by Washington Matthews Fr. The Mountain Chant.

Invocation. To Horror. Hannah Cowley. NOBRP

Invocation to Melancholy, An. Henry Headly.

"Child of the potent spell and nimble eye." ECEV

Invocation to Saint Bride. John Irvine. TIRV

Invocation, To the Genius of Slumber Written Oct. 1787. Anna Seward. PEW

Invocation to the Muse. Richard Hughes. MoBrPo

Invocation to the Muse. Henrietta Cordelia Ray. CBWP-3

Invocation to the Social Muse. Archibald MacLeish. LiTM

Invocation to the U' wannami. *Unknown, Zuni.* APN-2, *tr. by* Matilda Coxe Stevenson

Invocation to the U'wannami (Rain-Makers). *Zuni Oral Tradition, Zuni.* PaTW, *tr. by* Stevenson, Matilda Coxe

Invocation to Youth. Laurence Binyon. OBEV

Invoice, The. Robert Creeley. VGW

Invoice No. 13, A Masque of Resignation. William Harmon. WeT

Involuntary, / I may live on. Sanjō Emperor, *Japanese.* OHPJ, *tr. by* Kenneth Rexroth

Inward Conversation. Charles Baudelaire, *French.* InPK-6, *tr. by* Robert Bly

Inward Morning, The. Henry David Thoreau. AmPP; PAR

Io! Paean! Io! sing. Charles Lamb. OxAEP-2 *Fr.* The Triumph of the Whale.

Io recovers her shape. Ovid, *Latin.* OBCVT, *tr. by* George Sandys

Iöas' Epitaph. William Drummond, of Hawthornden. PoEL-2

Iolanthe. Sir William Schwenck Gilbert.

    House of Lords, The. NAEL-2

    Nightmare, [A *or* The]. NOBL; NTP; OBCoV; OxBoLi; PBMP; PeLV; PoRA

    (Chancellor's Nightmare, The.) CBNP

Ion. Euripides.

    Delphic Dawn. GrIP, *tr. by* Ronald Frederick Willetts

Iowa. Michael Dennis Browne. NYBP

Iowa Farmer. Margaret Walker Alexander. GT

Iowa, June. Michael Dennis Browne. AmPA

Iphigeneia at Aulis. Euripides, *Greek.*

    "Blessed are they." ITG, *tr. by* Merwin, W. S. and George E. Dimock Jr.

    "I crossed sand-hills." OBCVT, *tr. by* Hilda Doolittle

Iphigenia [*or* Iphigeneia] in Aulis. Euripides, *Greek.*

    "And Pergamos, / City of the Phrygians." AWP; OBVE, *tr. by* Hilda Doolittle

Iphione. Thomas Caulfield Irwin. EnLoPo

Ipsey Wipsey spider. *Unknown.* OxNR

Ipsissimus. Eugene Lee-Hamilton. PeVV

IpsofactopaperAnswerallquesti. Headrock. Brian Coffey. CIP-2

Iram indeed is gone with all his rose. Omar Khayyám. OBVE *Fr.* The Rubáiyát of Omar Khayyám [of Naishápúr]. AWP; EBVV; FaBoBe; FaPoR; HAP; NAEL-2; PoEL-5

Ire. Ronald Stuart Thomas. OxBSP

Ireland. John Hewitt. CIP-2; IIP

Ireland. Paul Muldoon. PBCIP

Ireland. Richard Ryan. CIP-2

Ireland. Dora Sigerson Shorter. IIP; OBEV; TIRV

Ireland. Jonathan Swift. FaBoPV

Ireland never was contented. Walter Savage Landor. FaBoEE; GTBS-P; OBCoV; OxBSP; OxBoLi; PeLV

Ireland 1972. Paul Durcan. PBCIP

Ireland with Emily. John Betjeman. GTBS-P; OxBTC

Iris. Herman Melville. NCAP

Iris. Muriel Rukeyser. APSN; ColAP

Iris. David St. John. LCAP-2

    ("And you remain.") (LL) GM

Iris. William Carlos Williams. InPS-3; LCAP-2; WeW-3

Iris, Her Book. Oliver Wendell Holmes. NCAP

Irises, The. Jeanne Foster. CrSp

Irises. Li-Young Lee. BLT

Irises. Gustaf Sobin. APSN

Irish. Paul Celan, *German.* OBVE, *tr. by* Michael Hamburger

Irish Airman Foresees His Death, An. W. B. Yeats. ChAP; EBEvV; FaBoCh; FaBoMo; GTBS-P; HeIP-4; HoPM; LiTM; MoBrPo; MoP; NOBE; NoAM; NoP-4; OBMV; OBWP; PoPoPo; PoWW; Poetr; SCV; TFi; WeW-3

    (Irish Airman Forsees His Death, An.) APAD

Irish Airman Foresees His Death, An. W. B. Yeats. *See* An Irish Airman Foresees His Death.

Irish-American Dignitary. Austin Clarke. BIrV

Irish Antiquities. Thomas Moore. FaBoEE

Irish Childhood in England: 1951, An. Eavan Boland. CIP-2

Irish Cliffs of Moher, The. Wallace Stevens. NOBA; RaBo; TOF; VGW

Irish Fairy lost her way, An. Menella Bute Smedley. VWP

Irish for No, The. Ciaran Carson. PNI

Irish Harp: Fragment I, The. Sydney, Lady Morgan Owenson. Ro *Fr.* The Lay of an Irish Harp, or Metrical Fragments.

Irish Harper and His Dog, The. Thomas Campbell. CH

Irish have the thickest ankles in the world, The. John Berryman. TAP *Fr.* Dream Songs.

Irish Hierarchy Bans Colour Photography. Paul Durcan. BiHa; PBCIP

Irish Hotel. David Wevill. NYBP

Irish lady can say, that to-day is every day, The. Cézanne. Gertrude Stein. TAP

Irish Lake, An. William Robert Rodgers. BIrV

Irish Lamentation, An. Goethe, *German.* AWP, *tr. by* James Clarence Mangan

Irish Love Song, An. John Todhunter. IIP

Irish Lullaby. Alfred Percival Graves. IIP

Irish Marriage Night, An. Brian Merriman. BIrV, *tr. by* Frank O'Connor *Fr.* The Midnight Court. NOIV, *tr. by* Thomas Kinsella

Irish Patriarch, The. Ruth Pitter. NALW

Irish Peasant to His Mistress, The. Thomas Moore. TIRV

Irish Picture, An. J. Stanyan Bigg. NOBVV

Irish poets, learn your trade. W. B. Yeats. OxAEP-2 *Fr.* Under Ben Bulben. CMoP; HAP; IIP; LiTM; MoP; NAEL-2; NoAM; NoP-4; OxBTC

Irish Reaper's Harvest Hymn. John Keegan. TIRV

Irish Requiem, An. Michael O'Loughlin. PBCIP

Irish Schoolmaster, The. Thomas Hood. BXAP

Irish Skies. Winifred M. Letts. TIRV

Irish Song [Rosie O'Grady]. Noël Coward. NBLV; OBCoV

Irish Sweaters. Shirley Graves Cochrane. IIP

Irishman in Coventry, An. John Hewitt. BIrV; CIP-2; IIP; PNI

Iroko. Onwuchekwa Jemie. PBMAP

Iron. Walter De la Mare. NOBL

Iron Age, The. Hesiod, *Greek.* OBCVT, *tr. by* Thomas Cooke

Iron bells toll, The. Van Gogh. David Mitchell. PeNZ

Iron chains and silver cangues: crowds of prisoners. The Prisons Are Full of Convicts. Yang Yi, *Chinese.* SuSp, *tr. by* Jonathan Chaves

Iron Heaven. Betti Alver. BoWoP, *tr. by* Willis Barnstone *and* Felix Oinas

Iron horse draweth nigh, with its smoke nostrils high, The. The Utah Iron Horse. *Unknown.* AmFP

Iron Horse is rusting, The. The End of the Line. Thomas McGrath. GM

Iron Industry in Birmingham, The. Richard Jago. NOEC *Fr.* Edge-Hill; or, The Rural Prospect Delineated and Moralised.

Iron Landscapes (and the Statue of Liberty). Thom Gunn. FaBoA; FaBoPV

Iron Lung, The. Stanley Plumly. AmPA; LCAP-2

"Iron Man" sat with open eyes / a witnessing body, The. Rogue and Jar: 4/27/77. Thulani Davis. MoNo; SeSe

Iron Nerves. Betti Alver, *Estonian.* CEEP, *tr. by* Ivar Ivask

Iron queen of uncreations. The Gardens of Proserpine. Turner Cassity. PoA

Iron scallops border the path, barely. Earliest Spring. Denise Levertov. LCAP-2

Iron Spike. Seamus Heaney. TRP

Iron thing coming from Pompi, from the round-house. The Train. *Unknown.* TTY, *tr. by* D. F. van der Merwe

Ironing. Nellie Wong. FFC

Ironing Their Clothes. Julia Alvarez. CrSp

Irony. Louis Untermeyer. TrJP

Irony of God. Eva Warner. TrCP

Irradiations. John Gould Fletcher. MoAmPo

    "As I wandered over the city through the night."

    "Flickering of incessant rain."

    "Houses of the city no longer hum and play, The."

    "Morning is clean and blue and the wind blows up the clouds, The."

    "My stiff-spread arms / Break into sudden gesture."

    "O seeded grass, you army of little men."

    "Over the roof-tops race the shadows of clouds."

    "Spattering of the rain upon pale terraces, The."

    "Trees, like great jade elephants, The."

Irreconcilables. Arthur Gregor. NYBP

Irregular continuity of discrete particles blasted into the atmosphere: writing, The. Radiant. James Sherry. FTOS

Irregular rattle (shutters) and, An. The Master of the Golden Glow. James Schuyler. FTOS

Irresponsive silence of the land, The. Aloof. Christina Rossetti. NOBE; OBEV; OBNC; PEW *Fr.* The Thread of Life.

Irthing Valley. Frances Horovitz. NBrP

Irving. James Russell Lowell. TAP *Fr.* A Fable for Critics. NAAL-1; NAAL-3

Is. Patrick Kavanagh. FaBoTw

I's a broken-hearted keelman, and I's over head in love. Cushie Butterfield. George Ridley. NTP

Is a caterpillar ticklish? Only My Opinion. Monica Shannon. CTV

Is a cave, there are bones at the hearth. (LL) Abel's Bride. Denise Levertov. FaBoWP; NALW; VGW

Is a little wind. Four Bird Songs. Simon J. Ortiz. HATNAP

Is a mildewed tent. Under the center pole. Despair. Maxine W. Kumin. FFC

Is a monstrance, / the blue dogs bay. The Moon Is the Number 18. Charles Olson. CMoP; PoE

Is a mouth. Robert Creeley. *See* The Language.

Is a question of strength. Oppression. Jimmy Santiago Baca. AF

Is a short life of trouble. (LL) The Other Side of the River. Charles Wright. MT; VCAP

Is a short string of beautiful. My Past. Dennis Cooper. GLP

Is a son born into this world of woe? Charles Churchill. OBSV *Fr.* The Times.

Is a stately thing. (LL) The Stranger. Jean Garrigue. LiTM; NOBA; TwCP

Is all overrun with rue? (LL) The Seeds of Love. Mrs. Fleetwood Habergham. FaBoCh; OxBoLi

Is all the light of all their day. (LL) The Revelation. Coventry Patmore. EnLoPo; GBL; GLoP; GTBS-P; HAP; LoP; OBNC; OxBSP

Is all the rest I knew! (LL) Went up a year this evening! Emily Dickinson. HAP; WeW-3

Is all this sorrow? I don't know. Yehuda Amichai, *Hebrew*. IP, *tr. by* Bargad, Warren and Stanley Chyet; IP; PoSu *Fr.* Laments on the War Dead.

Is almost more than I can bear. (LL) A Young Wife. D. H. Lawrence. MoBrPo; PBMP

Is also great / And would suffice. Robert Frost. *See* Fire and Ice.

Is *also* Stewart Granger. (LL) The Prisoner of Zenda. Richard Wilbur. NBLV; OBCoV

Is an astonishingly slim. Opener. Chris Wallace-Crabbe. BMAP *Fr.* The Bits and Pieces.

Is an enchanted thing. The Mind Is an Enchanting Thing. Marianne Moore. CMoP; HeIP-4; InPK-6; MeMAP; MoAmPo; NAAL-2; NoP-4; OxBA; PoE; WPOW

Is anyone waiting for you at the end of the road? Traveling Star. Ljubomir Simovic, *Serbo-Croatian*. HSix, *tr. by* Charles Simic

Is anything central? The One Thing That Can Save America. John Ashbery. AiP; FaBoA; NOBA; NoAM; PmAP

Is Aristocracy. (LL) Pedigree of Honey, The, vers. 2. Emily Dickinson. MoP; SAmP

Is at hand, and so farewell. (LL) Bridal Song to Amala. Thomas Lovell Beddoes. GBL; NOBVV; OBNC; PoEL-4

Is back upon your mouth these thousand years. (LL) To Jesus on His Birthday. Edna St. Vincent Millay. ChIV-2; HeIP-4; TrCP

Is best from age to age. (LL) The Shepherd Boy Sings [in the Valley of Humiliation]. John Bunyan. BoTP; EBEV; EBEvV; NOBE; NTP; OBEV; OxBSP

Is better for man and for woman than cycles of blossoming Spring. (LL) Magdalen Walks. Oscar Wilde. EBVV; MoBrPo

Is blisse with immortalitie. Her Majestie resembled to the crowned piller. Ye must read upward. George Puttenham. PBRV

Is breaking in despair. (LL) The Slave Mother. Frances Ellen Watkins Harper. NAAAL; PAR

Is broken, be admitted in. (LL) Shadows in the Water. Thomas Traherne. CABP; GeHe; HAP; NoP-4; OAEL-1; PoEL-2; SCGP; SeCP

Is buried with the pole. (LL) Astronomy. A. E. Housman. NoP-4; OBWP

Is burning, burning the unbired grain. (LL) Children of Light. Robert Lowell. CMoP; NAAL-2; OxBA

Is—Bury me not in a land of slaves!. (LL) Bury Me in a Free Land. Frances Ellen Watkins Harper. AAP; BPo; ColAP; CrDW; ISC; NAAAL; PAR

Is but a child's balloon, forgotten after play. (LL) Above the Dock. Thomas Ernest Hulme. FaBoMo; GTBS-P; NTP

Is but its longing for the tomb. (LL) The Wheel. W. B. Yeats. GTBS-P; Poetr

Is by admitting / or opening away. The Way Things Work. Jorie Graham. NMM-2

Is by His hand alone that guides nature and fate. (LL) In Memory of My Dear Grandchild Elizabeth Bradstreet Who Deceased August, 1665, Being a Year and Half Old. Anne Bradstreet. ColAP; NAAL-1; NAAL-3; NOCV; SCAP; WPE

Is Cathleen, the daughter of Houlihan. (LL) Red Hanrahan's Song about Ireland. W. B. Yeats. CMoP; FaBoCh; NOIV

Is come, my love is come to me. (LL) A Birthday. Christina Rossetti. AWP; CABP; CH; EBEvV; GLoP; ITG; ImPo; LW; NAEL-2; NALW;

NOBE; NOBVV; OAEL-2; OBEV; PEW; PFE; PeVV; PoE; SDW; TFi; TTTS; UV; VWP; WPE

Is coming, and makes noise. (LL) The Approach of the Storm. *Unknown, Chippewa*. OBVE; TTTS, *tr. by* Frances Densmore

Is cruel to thy cruelty. (LL) Limits. Ralph Waldo Emerson. APN-1; OxBSP; PoEL-4

Is each neat niplet of her breast. (LL) Upon the Nipples of Julia's Breast. Robert Herrick. CaPo; NAEL-1; NOSC; PeLV

Is even more fun than going to San Sebastian, Irún, Hendaye, Biarritz, Bayonne. Having a Coke with You. Frank O'Hara. GLP; VCAP

Is fair and wise [*or* bonny and blithe] and good and gay. (LL) Birthdays. Mother Goose. BLPA; BoTP; FaBoBe; FaBoCh; LB; NBLV; OTCP; OxNR; ReMoGo

Is far too good for thee'. (LL) Jellon Grame. *Unknown*. EBEV; ESPB; OxBB

Is Friends fled, or Love grown cold? An Epistle. Mary Mollineux. KTR

Is gazing at the moon again. The Selenologist. Bill Manhire. PeNZ

Is given in outline and no more. (LL) I sometimes hold it half a sin. Tennyson. EPCY; EnVR; IMW; OAEL-2; PeECV; TOF

Is giv'n thee till the break of day. (LL) Introduction: "Hear the voice of the Bard!" William Blake. APAD; ChIV-1; EBEV; FHYEP; HAP; InPS-3; NAEL-2; NAWM-2; NOBE; NOBRP; NOEC; NoP-4; OAEL-2; OBEV; PoE; PoEL-4; RB; Ro; TFi

Is God mad? Was Christ. Third Person Neuter. Heather McHugh. NAmP90

Is heaven a place where pearly streams. What Is Heaven? Philip James Bailey. PWR

Is hows to hump a cows. (LL) Way to hump a cow is not, The. E. E. Cummings. NOBA; NoAM; OxBA

Is immortal diamond. (LL) That Nature Is a Heraclitean Fire and of the Comfort of the Resurrection. Gerard Manley Hopkins. EnVR; EnlH; FaBoMo; FaBoVe; GTBS-P; NoP-4; OAEL-2; PFTM; PoE; PoEL-5

Is inverted, slow and gay. (LL) The Operation. W. D. Snodgrass. InPK-6; TAP

Is it a dream, and nothing more—this faith. Geoffrey Anketell Studdert-Kennedy. PoToHe

Is It a Month. John Millington Synge. BIrV

Is it a road at the world's edge? (LL) Six Variations. Denise Levertov. AmPP; CoAmPo; LCAP-2

Is It a Sin to Love Thee? *Unknown*. BLPA

Is it an idle fantasy. The Mist Maiden. Henrietta Cordelia Ray. CBWP-3

Is it anxiety, nausea. Self-Portrait of the Other. Herberto Padilla, *Spanish*. VCWP, *tr. by* Alastair Reid *and* Andrew Hurley

Is it any better in Heaven, my friend Ford. To Ford Madox Ford in Heaven. William Carlos Williams. AmPP; ColAP; NOBA

Is it bad to have come here. Gallant Château. Wallace Stevens. MoAmPo

Is It Because of Some Dear Grace. Louis Golding. TrJP

Is it because your sable hair. La Belle Juive. Henry Timrod. APN-2

Is it birthday weather for you, dear soul? Birthday Poem for Thomas Hardy. C. Day Lewis. EBEvV; EPCY

Is it calm after midnight on its rocky slope. Phlox Diffusa: A Poem for My Fiftieth Birthday. Sandra McPherson. PUP-20

Is it enough? I'm Here. Theodore Roethke. CoAP; NYBP *Fr.* Meditations of an Old Woman.

Is it foolhardy to hope. Zeugma. Christopher Reid. CBLP

Is it for now or for always. Philip Larkin. ITG

Is it illusion? or does there a spirit from perfecter ages. Spirit from Perfecter Ages. Arthur Hugh Clough. EBEV; OBNC; OxAEP-2 *Fr.* Amours de Voyage. NOBVV

Is it ironical, a fool enigma. Dartmoor: Sunset at Chagford. Thomas Edward Brown. NOBVV

Is it just like picking a lock. The Bomb Disposal. Ciaran Carson. CIP-2; IIP

Is it merely an image that keeps haunting me? (LL) Gold Glade. Robert Penn Warren. CRP; Poetr; TRP

Is it my clothes, my way of walking. Disembarking at Quebec. Margaret Atwood. PoE

Is it no dream that I am he. Walter Savage Landor. GBL

Is it not fine to fling against loaded dice. Hughie at the Inn. Elinor Wylie. NYBP; WPE

Is it not fit the mold and frame. A Dedication of My First Son. Mildmay Fane, 2d Earl of Westmorland. BeJo

Is it not lovely, while the day flows on. By the Swanannoa. William Gilmore Simms. APN-1

Is it not so, my Tory, ultra-Julian? (LL) Dedication: "Bob Southey! You're a poet—poet-laureate." Byron. CTC; OAEL-2; OBSV

Is it not strange that men can die. Reflection. Walter James Turner. OBMV

Is it not sure a deadly pain. *Unknown*. EnLoPo

Is it not sweet to die? for, what is death. Death Sweet. Thomas Lovell Beddoes. NOBVV

Is It Not You, Lord! Padraig De Brun. TIRV

"Is It Nothing to You?" May Probyn. OBEV

Is it poetry I'm after those moments when. Vocation. Carol Rumens. DiPo

Is it possible. Sir Thomas Wyatt. CABP; GBL; NoP-4; NoSic; SiPS

Is it raining. Mary, can you see? Wildflowers. Richard Howard. NoAM

Is it really so very unthinkable. Limerick. Basil Ransome-Davies. PeLi

Is It Really Worth the While? *Unknown.* BLPA

Is it serious, or funny. B. Larry Eigner. NeAP

Is it the palm, the cocoa-palm. The Palm-Tree. John Greenleaf Whittier. NCAP

Is it the wind of the dawn that I hear. Duet. Tennyson. APAD; GBL *Fr.* Becket.

Is it, then, regret for buried time. Tennyson. FHYEP *Fr.* In Memoriam A. H. H.

"Is it thou?" "Ay," cries Fra Lippo Lippi. Limerick. Gerard Benson. PeLi

Is it thy will thy image should keep open. Sonnet 61. Shakespeare. PoEL-2 *Fr.* Sonnets.

Is it time now to go away? Death of a Vermont Farm Woman. Barbara Howes. MoAmPo

Is it to me, this sad lamenting strain? An Answer to a Love-Letter in Verse. Lady Mary Wortley Montagu. ECWP; LW

Is It True? Sarah Williams. BLPA

Is it true that after this life of ours we shall one day be awakened. Resurrection. Vladimir Holan, *Czech.* PoSu, *tr. by* George Theiner

Is it true that black birds infinitely dispersed. To Krishna Haunting the Hills. Andal, *Tamil.* BoWoP, *tr. by* Willis Barnstone

Is it true, ye gods, who treat us. Arthur Hugh Clough. EnVR

Is it Ulysses that approaches from the east. The World as Meditation. Wallace Stevens. HeIP-4; LCAP-2

Is it wise. Stevie Smith. NAEL-2

Is it worth while, dear, now. Long Plighted. Thomas Hardy. NOBVV

Is it you standing among the olive trees. Mark Strand. BAP-93 *Fr.* Dark Harbor.

("Is it you standing among the olive trees.") NoP-4

Is it your command. Lady Ise, *Japanese.* OHPJ, *tr. by* Kenneth Rexroth; WPJ, *tr. by* Kenneth Rexroth *and* Ikuko Atsumi

Is John Smith within? Mother Goose. OxNR; ReMoGo

Is Joy's insuring quality. (LL) Go not too near a House of Rose. Emily Dickinson. MoAmPo; NIP-4

"Is jy klaar." Haanetjie's Morning Dialogue. Essop Patel. PeSAV

Is king of glory crown'd. Bible, *O.T. See* Psalm 24.

Is large, bald, beakless and blind. (LL) Fork. Charles Simic. AmPA; ChAP; ColAP; HCAP; LCAP-2; PoPoPo; TRP; WeW-3

Is less ta'en up wi't. (LL) Empty Vessel. "Hugh MacDiarmid." FaBoTC; FaBoTw; OxBS

Is Life itself but many ways of thought. Substitution. Anne Spencer. BlSi

Is life so dear, or peace so sweet. Patrick Henry. CTV

Is Life Worth Living? Alfred Austin. PWR

Is, Listen, listen, I am a man like you. (LL) The Hill Farmer Speaks. Ronald Stuart Thomas. GTBS-P; OBWVE

Is love a light for me? A steady light. Secret Flowers. Katherine Mansfield. LW

Is love so prone to change and rot. A Bed of Forget-Me-Nots. Christina Rossetti. VWP

Is made up of reservoirs. The Hard Structure of the World. Richard Eberhart. NoAM

Is manhood less because man's face is black? Albery Allson Whitman. AAP; APN-2 *Fr.* Twasinta's Seminoles; Or Rape of Florida.

Is melting an old frost moon. Dawn's Rose. Ted Hughes. *Fr.* Crow. PoE

Is memory most of miseries miserable. Memory. D. G. Rossetti. OxBSP

Is merry glory. Langston Hughes. Gwendolyn Brooks. ColAP

Is more than ever slave! (LL) A Servant When He Reigneth. Rudyard Kipling. ChIV-1; KSG

Is mother of silences. (LL) Seasons of the Soul. Allen Tate. FuPo; OxBA

Is music is men. Eddie Priest's Barbershop and Notary. Kevin Young. ISC

Is my friend, O daughters of Jerusalem. Bible, *O.T. See* My love is white and ruddy.

Is my sweet, bonie Lady! (LL) Geordie [An Old Ballad]. *Unknown.* ESPB; OxBB

Is my team ploughing. A. E. Housman. CBLP; CMoP; EBEvV; EBVV; LiTM; MoBrPo; NoAM; NoP-4; OBEV; Poetr

("Is my team plowing.") SAGP

Is my team plowing. A. E. Housman. *See* Is my team ploughing.

Is/Not / Not. Margaret Atwood. LW

Is not one of the seven deadly sins. Self-Pity. Philip Hodgins. NOBAu

Is not the woman moulded by your wish. Pastiche. Elinor Wylie. NALW

Is not thilke the mery moneth of May. Edmund Spenser. PBRV *Fr.* The Shepheardes Calender.

Is not unlike building a poem: the pure. Building an Outhouse. Ronald Wallace. PBCAP

Is nothing to the Dead. (LL) My Triumph lasted till the Drums. Emily Dickinson. APN-2; OBWP

Is of the slightest bondage made aware. (LL) The Silken Tent. Robert Frost. AmPP; ColAP; ImPo; InPK-6; NOBA; NoP-4; Son; TAP; TRP; TwCP; WeW-3

Is of your maidenhood. (LL) To Mistress Margery Wentworth. John Skelton. EBEV; EnLoPo; NOBE; OAEL-1; OBEV

Is only there. (LL) Peace. George Herbert. AWP; ESCV; GeHe; NOCV; NOSC

Is oppression as old as the moss around ponds? The World's One Hope. Bertolt Brecht, *German.* AF, *tr. by* John Willett, Ralph Manheim *and* Erich Fried

Is our love over? The Mother of Michitsuna, *Japanese.* WPJ, *tr. by* Kenneth Rexroth *and* Ikuko Atsumi

Is out at elbows, why should I repine? (LL) The Power of Time. Jonathan Swift. FaBoEE; OxBSP

Is palpable—and Love. (LL) A Song: "The World is young today." Digby Mackworth Dolben. NOBVV; OBNC

Is pounding and pounding, and the mouth answering. (LL) Gargoyle. Carl Sandburg. MoP; NOBA; NoAM

Is powerless to our Western Cotton! (LL) The Haschish. John Greenleaf Whittier. APN-1; NCAP; OBAL

Is prettier far than these. (LL) The Rainbow. Christina Rossetti. ACTP; OxBChV

Is quicker. (LL) Reflections on Ice-breaking. Ogden Nash. AiP; ImPo; LiTM; NBLV; NoP-4; OBAL; PeLV

Is / red beans. Energy. Victor Hernandez Cruz. PoBA

Is rounded with a sleep. (LL) "Be cheerful, sir." Shakespeare. APAD; EnlH

Is rounded with a sleep. (LL) Epilogue. Shakespeare. ImPo; RB; SAGP; UV

Is saved today, tomorrow to be slain. (LL) Disdain Punished. Dryden. EBNV; NOSC

Is scarcely right; this red should have been much duller. (LL) Vlamertinghe. Edmund Blunden. NoP-4; OBWP; PeFWW

Is scented with White Heliotrope. (LL) White Heliotrope. Arthur Symons. GLoP; LoP

Is she dead? Confessional. Frank Bidart. GLP

Is she too quiet or am I. Fet Walks Melody Home. Gary Hyland. IFJA

Is shut / 22 hours a day and all day Sunday. The Pitt-Rivers Museum, Oxford. James Fenton. FaBoMo *Fr.* Exempla.

Is sick, by nature. (LL) A Far Cry after a Close Call. Richard Howard. NYBP; UnPo

Is sicklied o'er with the pale cast of thought. (LL) Hamlet's Soliloquy. Shakespeare. EBEvV; HoPM; ImPo; OxAEP-1; UV

Is slender and her red hair lights the wall. (LL) Degrees of Gray in Philipsburg. Richard Hugo. CoAP; NAAL-2; NoAM; TRP; VCAP

Is so long she ehn see de man. Gifts. Amryl Johnson. HCP

Is something like the rest. The Politics of Rich Painters. Imamu Amiri Baraka. VGW

Is spread any more. (LL) The Mouse. Elizabeth Jane Coatsworth. BoTP; NOxBChV; OBCA

Is still the pleasant'st jest. (LL) Lucasta Laughing. Richard Lovelace. CavPo; PoEL-3

Is tell you my mind, Annes Tayliur: Dame. *Unknown.* MiEL

Is that an attitude for a flower, to stand. Hyacinth. Louise Glück. NoAM

Is that dance slowing in the mind of man. The Dance. Theodore Roethke. *Fr.* Four for Sir John Davies. MoAmPo; NOBA; NoAM

Is that dance slowing in the mind of man. Four for Sir John Davies. Theodore Roethke. MoAmPo; NOBA; NoAM

Is that foolish youth still sawing. Ancient Autumn. Charles Simic. ColAP

Is that you have your slaves, and the Greek had his helot. (LL) Cooper. James Russell Lowell. NOBA; OxBA; TAP

Is that you sistah Harris? An Afternoon Gossip. Priscilla Jane Thompson. CBWP-2

Is the Ahkond of Swat! (LL) The A[h]kond of Swat. Edward Lear. CBNP; FaBoCh; PeLi

Is the alphabet responsible. Learning to Write. Audre Lorde. GT

Is the applause always plausible that applauds the bosses'. The Tasty 'Tanjarines' of Inhambane. José Craveirinha, *Portuguese.* PeSAV, *tr. by* Michael Wolfers

Is the ball very stupid *ma mignonne*? At the Ball! Charles Henry Webb. OBAL

Is the burden of my song. *Unknown. See* Love me little, love me long!

Is the clock wound up, is it wound? The Insect Kitchen. Nicki Jackowska. BrRo

Is the / dinner / ready. I Ask. Novica Tadic, *Serbo-Croatian.* HSix, *tr. by* Charles Simic

Is the ending of my song. (LL) The Seven Virgins. *Unknown.* CH; OBEV

Is the fish ready? You're a tedious while. Dialogue between a Squeamish Cotting Mechanic and His Sluttish Wife, in the Kitchen. Edward Ward. NOEC *Fr.* Nuptial Dialogues.

Is the kitchen tap still dripping? Guest. D. J. Enright. OxBC

Is the man bigger than a fly's wing? what pleasure! Tablet V. Armand Schwerner. PFTM

Is the moon tired? she looks so pale. Christina Rossetti. BoTP; OTCP

Is the one gift you cannot give. (LL) At the British War Cemetery, Bayeux. Charles Causley. NAEL-2; NoP-4; OBWP; OxBC; PoWW

Is the orange and black / oriole's swinging nest! (LL) Fall 1961. Robert Lowell. OBWP; VGW

Is the prayer of the Red River girl. *Unknown. See* Red River Valley.

Is the property of space. The Property of Density. Sarah Lindsay. EC3

Is the slim curved crook of the moon tonight! (LL) Winter Moon. Langston Hughes. KaS; SAmP

Is the snow on Kurakake mountain. (LL) The Snow on Saddle Mountain. Miyazawa Kenji, *Japanese.* ColAP; NOBA; NoAM, *tr. by* Gary Snyder

Is the soul solid, like iron? Some Questions You Might Ask. Mary Oliver. ColAP

Is the struggle and strife. Let the Rest of the World Go By. J. Keirn Brennan. UnPo

Is the total black, being spoken. Coal. Audre Lorde. BlSi; NAAAL; NALW; NBV; NoAM; NoP-4; PoBA; VCAP

Is the turf that has cover'd my Willy frae me! Susanna Blamire. *See* Auld Robin Forbes.

Is the university of hunger the wide waste. University of Hunger. Martin Carter. PBCV

Is the world's wonder. (LL) Winter's thunder. *Unknown.* FaBoVe; LB

Is there a great green commonwealth of Thought. John Masefield. LiTM; MoBrPo *Fr.* Sonnets.

Is there a solitary wretch who hies. On Being Cautioned against Walking on an Headland Overlooking the Sea, because It Was Frequented by a Lunatic. Charlotte Smith. ECWP; WoRP

Is There a Voice. Philip Appleman. BXAP

Is there an imagination that sits enthroned. Wallace Stevens. HCAP *Fr.* The Auroras of Autumn.

Is there any reward? Hilaire Belloc. OBCoV

"Is there anybody there?" said the Traveller. The Listeners. Walter De la Mare. AWP; CMoP; ClHu; EBEvV; HAP; HeIP-4; HoPM; ImPo; InPK-6; LiTM; MoBrPo; MoP; NOBE; NOxBChV; NTP; NoAM; NoP-4; OBEV; OBMV; OBSP; OxAEP-2; PoRA; Poetr; SoSe-2; TFi

Is there anything as I can do ashore for you. A Valediction (Liverpool Docks). John Masefield. OBMV

Is there anything in Spring so fair. Apple Blossoms. Henry Adams Parker. BoTP

Is there for honest Poverty. For A' That and A' That ["Is there, for honest poverty"]. Robert Burns. CABP; FaBoBe; FaBoPV; FaPoR; ImPo; NAEL-2; NOEC; OAEL-1; OxAEP-2; OxBS; TFi; UV

Is, there is not a word of fear. (LL) Death Stands above Me[, whispering low]. Walter Savage Landor. NOBE; NoP-4; OAEL-2; OBNC; OxBSP; PFE; PoEL-4

Is There Life after Feminism. Maude Meehan. NMM-2

Is there never a man in all *Scotland.* Johnie Armstrong. *Unknown.* ESPB; PBRV

Is There No Balm in Christian Lands? *Unknown.* AH

Is there no secret place on the face of the earth. The Moneyless Men. Henry T. Stanton. BLPA

Is there no vision in a lovely place? William Montgomerie. OxBS *Fr.* Kinfauns Castle.

Is there nothing to be said about the cockroach which is kind? Cockroach. Mary Ann Hoberman. *Fr.* Bugs. OBCA

Is there one room at your head, Saunders? *Unknown. Fr.* Clerk Saunders. EBNV

Is there really a new Mr. Nixon. Limerick. T. Griffiths. PeLi

Is there still any shadow there, on the rainwet window of the coffee pot. Memo. Kenneth Fearing. CMoP; PoE

Is there when I get home from work but allows me silence. Dream Lesbian Lover. "Chrystos." CPO

Is this a dagger which I see before me. Shakespeare. EBEvV *Fr.* Macbeth.

Is this a fast, to keep. To Keep a True Lent. Robert Herrick. TrCP

Is this a holy thing to see. Holy Thursday [II.] William Blake. FHYEP; InPS-3; NAEL-2; NOBRP; NOEC; NOxBChV; NoP-4; OAEL-2; Ro *Fr.* Songs of Experience.

Is This Africa. Roland Tombekai Dempster. PBA

Is this darkness the night of Power, or the black falling of your hair? Bibi Hayati, *Persian.* WPoS, *tr. by* Jane Hirshfield

Is this happening. Ark 34, Spire on the Death of L.Z. Ronald Johnson. FTOS

Is this man turning angel as he stares. The Messenger. Thom Gunn. PoA

Is this my tomb, this humble stone. Charlotte Brontë. VWP

Is this peace? Kayaking through. Peace #3. Alma Villanueva. FFC

Is this rapture that your rums have filled me with. Marie Galante. Guy Tirolien, *French.* NegPo, *tr. by* Ellen Conroy Kennedy

'Is this, saith one, the Nation that we read'. Andrew Marvell. PBRV *Fr.* The First Anniversary of the Government under O.C.

Is this the Lake, the cradle of the storms. Written on the Banks of Wastwater During a Calm. John Wilson. LaPo

Is this the monument of Leonato? Shakespeare. OxAEP-1 *Fr.* Much Ado about Nothing.

Is this the object. Sestina. Judith Kroll. AmPA

Is this the region, this the soil, the clime. Satan as Rebel-Liberator. Milton. *Fr.* Book I. FHYEP; NAEL-1; OAEL-1; OxAEP-1 *Fr.* Paradise Lost.

Is this the self I thought I knew, within. Reflections. Vivian Smith. CBAP

Is this the street? Never a sign of life. Stormy Night. William Robert Rodgers. PNI

Is this the ultimate exile no man born. Ultimate Exile IV. Ralph Nixon Currey. PeSA

Is this—the way? (LL) Title divine—is mine! Emily Dickinson. APN-2; NALW; NOBA; PAR

Is this the way my Father. Matin Hymn. Josephine D. Henderson Heard. CBWP-4

Is this where idealism ends. Guerrillas. Roger McTair. PBCV

Is this where people are buried? In Painswick Churchyard. Frances Horovitz. NBrP

Is this where Tasso walked? Old Sant'Onofrio. Pure Dust. Maria Luisa Spaziani, *Italian.* NeIt, *tr. by* Beverly Allen

Is this your special light. Six Nations Museum Onchiota, New York—January. Wendy Rose. HATNAP

Is thy face like thy mother's, my fair child! Byron. OAEL-2 *Fr.* Childe Harold's Pilgrimage.

Is thy face like thy mother's, my fair child. Childe Harold's Pilgrimage Canto III. Byron. Ro *Fr.* Childe Harold's Pilgrimage.

Is thy sun obscured to-day. My Grace Is Sufficient. Josephine D. Henderson Heard. CBWP-4

Is too precise in every part. (LL) Delight in Disorder. Robert Herrick. APAD; AWP; BeJo; CABP; CaPo; CavPo; ClHu; EBEvV; EBEvV; EP; EnLoPo; FaBoSe; GTBS-P; HAP; HeIP-4; ImPo; InPK-6; InPS-3; NAEL-1; NIP-4; NOBE; NOSC; NoP-4; OAEL-1; OBEV; OxAEP-1; PBMP; PBRV; PeLV; PoE; PoRA; Poetr; SAGP; SCGP; SeCP; TFi; TRP; WeW-3

Is vanity and woe. Elizabeth Carter. *See* Ode to Wisdom.

Is waiting for his Old Dutch? (LL) The Fat White Woman Speaks. G. K. Chesterton. OBCoV; UV

Is wetter water, slimier slime! (LL) Heaven. Rupert Brooke. EBEV; HoPM; LiTM; MoBrPo; NOBE; NSI; PoRA

Is what it feels like. (LL) Before the [*or* a] Cashier's Window in a Department Store. James Wright. CoAP; NYBP

Is what the sea-birds know. (LL) An Inscription by the Sea. Edwin Arlington Robinson, *after* Glaucus. AWP; FaBoEE

Is what the sea-birds know. (LL) An Inscription by the Sea. Glaukos. AWP; FaBoEE

Is what to make of a diminished thing. (LL) The Oven Bird. Robert Frost. APo; AWP; AmPP; GSo; HeIP-4; MeMAP; MoP; NAAL-2; NOBA; NoAM; NoP-4; OxBA; PoE; Son; TAP

Is what you first see, stepping off the train. Welcome to Hiroshima. Mary Jo Salter. DiPo; NIP-4; NMM-2; RA

Is with me at thy farewell, joyous Bark! (LL) Where lies the Land to which yon Ship must go? Wordsworth. OBNC; PoEL-4

Is with us, for He loves us all. (LL) Evening. Thomas Miller. ACTP; NOxBChV

Is without world. The Howling of Wolves. Ted Hughes. APo; OxBTC

Is worth an age without a name. (LL) Sound, Sound the Clarion. Thomas Osbert Mordaunt. EBEV; FaBoEE; FaPoR; NOBE; NOEC; OBEV

Is yo eye so empty. Signals. Jewel C. Latimore. PoBA

Is your crop of millet. What Her Friend Said to Her, before the Rains. Kapilar, *Tamil.* PLW, *tr. by* A. K. Ramanujan

Isaac. Amir Gilbo'a, *Hebrew.* MHP, *tr. by* Ruth Finer Mintz

Isaac: a Poise. Peter Cole. ChIV-1

Isaac and Archibald were two old men. Edwin Arlington Robinson. OxBA

Isaac Singer (you probably know). Limerick. Peter Brookes. PeLi

Isaac's Marriage. Henry Vaughan. ChIV-1

Isabel met an enormous bear. Adventures of Isabel. Ogden Nash. ChAP; MoAmPo; NOxBChV; NTCP; OBAL; OBCA

Isabella; or, The Morning. Sir Charles Hanbury Williams. "Monkey, lap-dog, parrot, and her Grace, The." NOEC

Isabella spits at Spain. Bourbons. Walter Savage Landor. OBSV

Isabelle. James Hogg. BXAP

Isaiah. Bible, *O.T. See also* Bible, Isaiah.
All Flesh Is Grass. TrJP
And He Shall Judge Among Nations. PBMP
"Comfort ye, comfort ye my people." OBVE, *stanzas* 1–8; TrJP
For Zion's Sake. TrJP
Hear the Word of the Lord. TrJP
How Beautiful upon the Mountains. TrJP
I Waste Away. TrJP
In the End of Days. TrJP
Israel, My Servant. TrJP
Let Me Sing of My Well-beloved. TrJP
Messiah, The. AWP
My Thoughts Are Not Your Thoughts. TrJP
Rod of Jesse, The. AWP; OBVE; TrJP
Song of the Harlot. TrJP
Song of The Suffering Servant, The. NAWM-1
Watchman, What of the Night? AWP
Whom Shall One Teach. TrJP
"Wildernesse and the solitaire place shall be glad for them, The." OBVE

Isaiah by Kerosene Lantern Light. Robert Harris. ChIV-1; NOBAu

Isaiah: Chapter 66. David Rosenberg. ChIV-1

Isaiah said would be the serpent's meat. William Meredith. *See* On Falling Asleep by Firelight.

Isaiah 66.11. Francis Quarles. ChIV-1

Isatou died. Lenrie Peters. HBAPE; PBMAP

I'se been upon de karpet. Old Maid's Soliloquy. Maggie Pogue Johnson. CBWP-4

I'se got a gal in the Sourwood Mountain. Sourwood Mountain. *Unknown.* AmFP

I'se wild Nigger Bill. Wild Negro Bill. *Unknown.* BPo; NAAAL

Isha Upanishad. Andrew Schelling. PT

Ishmael. Herbert Edward Palmer. OBEV

Ishtar. Judith Wright. NALW; NoAM

Isiah said would be the serpent's. (LL) On Falling Asleep by Firelight. William Meredith. ChIV-1; NYBP; NoAM

Isias my love, with your scented breath. Argentarius, *Greek.* GrAn, *tr. by* Fleur Adcock

Isidor. Louis Simpson. NNaP

Isis Wanderer. Kathleen Jessie Raine. NALW; OxBS

Island, The. Carolyn Forché. NMM-2

Island. Langston Hughes. HCAP *Fr.* Lenox Avenue Mural. HoPM

Island, The. Brendan Kennelly. PBCIP

Island. Mai Th(stilde;a)o, *Vietnamese.* AVP, *tr. by* Huỳnh Sanh Thông

Island, The. Herman Melville. NCAP

Island, The. Edwin Muir. OAEL-2

Island. Meredith Stricker. LoHo

Island, The. George Woodcock. MoCV

Island and the Cattle, The. Nicholas Moore. SPE

Island Celebration. Kenward Elmslie. FTOS

Island dreams under the dawn, The. The Indian to His Love. W. B. Yeats. PBMP

Island Funeral. Frank Stanford. MT

Island in the Evening, The. Fairfield Porter. PoA

Island Mary. Lucille Clifton. NALW

Island Muse. John C. M. Lyons. NBrP

Island of Mirrors, The. Ricardo Pau-Llosa. CMAP

Island of the Three Marias. Alberto A. Ríos. NoAM

Island off the main, An. Tycoon, Poet, Saint. Abdur-Rahman Slade Hopkinson. PBCV

Island School. George Mackay Brown. FaBoTC

Island that had flowered to the sun, The. The Coming of Dusk upon a Village in Haiti. Henry Rago. HoPM

Island was a word he woke upon, The. Settler. Stewart Lindh. PoA

Island Waters. Tony Beyer. PeNZ

Island / what shall I say of you, your peat-bogs. Remembering an Island. Robin Fulton. FaBoTC

Island within Island. Henry Dumas. GT

Island Women of Paris, The. Rita Dove. LoL

Islanders, Inlanders. Michael Mott. PoA

Islandman. Brenda Chamberlain. OBWVE

Islands, The. Hilda Doolittle. MoAmPo

Islands, The. Randall Jarrell. SPE

Islands are green. Alaskan Fragments June 1981—Summer Solstice. Wendy Rose. HATNAP

Islands move inward. The Name of Our Country. Dennis Schmitz. AmPA

Islands scars of the water. Aimé Césaire. PFTM, *tr. by* Clayton Eshleman *and* Annette Smith *Fr.* Notebook of a Return to the Native Land.

Islands Where I Was Born, The. Gloria Rawlinson. PeNZ

Islands which have. Nicholas Hasluck. NOBAu

Isle!/ Island of the syllables of flame! Song. Jacques Rabémanganjara, *French.* NegPo, *tr. by* Ellen Conroy Kennedy

Isle Juan Fernandez off Valparaiso Bay, The. Battle of the Falkland Isles. "I. C." NSI

Isle of Arran. Alastair Reid. FaBoTC

Isle of Man Shore, The. *Unknown.* AmFP

Isle of Palms and Other Poems, The. John Wilson.
Sonnet III. Written at Midnight, on Helm Crag. Ro

Isle of Portland, The. A. E. Housman. MoBrPo

Isle of Streams; or, the Jamaica Hermit, The. William Hosack. PBCV

Isle of Ulung, The. Ch'ihwan Yu, *Korean.* CKP, *tr. by* Jaihiun Kim

Isles of Greece, The. Demetrios Capetanakis. GTBS-P

Isles of Greece, the isles of Greece!, The. Byron. AWP; FaPoR; NOBE; OBEV; OxAEP-2 *Fr.* Canto the Third. *Fr.* Don Juan.

ISM, The. Wanda Coleman. PmAP

Isn't It Funny? Essex Hemphill. GLP

Isn't it good she asked (as. Rhyme. James Laughlin. WeW-3

Isn't it nice that everyone has a grocery list. Population. Mark Halliday. NAmP90; PUP-18

Isn't it plain the sheets of moss, except that. Landscape. Mary Oliver. HeIP-4

Isn't it strange. A Bag of Tools. R. L. Sharpe. BLPA; PoToHe

Isn't it strange some people make. Some People. Rachel Lyman Field. ChAP; NTCP

Isn't it wonderful, when you think. Wonderful. Julian S. Cutler. PWR

Isn't ligature—or is it ligament?—a lovely word? Fragment. Rupert Brooke. NSI

Isn't the secret intent. Rilke. ITG, *tr. by* Stephen Mitchell *Fr.* The Seventh Duino Elegy.

"Isn't the violet a dear little flower? And the daisy, too." The Lay Preacher Ponders. Idris Davies. OxBTC

Isolate. Clarence Major. PmAP

Isolate *and.* Barrett Watten. FTOS *Fr.* Progress.

Isolate and full, the moon. Full Moon. Tu Fu. OHPC

Isolation. Arthur Symons. OxBSP

Isolation of exile is a gutted, The. Waiting. Arthur Nortje. HBAPE

Isolation: To Marguerite. Matthew Arnold. *See* To Marguerite.

Isope [*or* Aesoe] myn auctor makis mencioun. Robert Henryson. *See* The Tale of the Upland Mouse and the Burgess Mouse.

Israeal in ancient days. Old-Testament Gospel. William Cowper. ChIV-2; TrCP *Fr.* Olney Hymns.

Israel. Yitzhak Lamdan, *Hebrew.* MHP, *tr. by* Ruth Finer Mintz

Israel. Carl Rakosi. ChIV-1

Israel. Israel Zangwill. TrJP

Israel II. Charles Reznikoff. ChIV-1

Israel, My Servant. Bible, *O.T.* TrJP *Fr.* Isaiah.

Israel's Duration. Judah Halevi, *Hebrew.* TrJP, *tr. by* Nina Davis Salaman

Israfel. Edgar Allan Poe. APN-1; AWP; AmPP; ImPo; MeMAP; NAAL-1; NAAL-3; NOBA; OxBA; PAR; PoE; PoEL-4; TAP

Isreal I. Charles Reznikoff. ChIV-1

Issue of great Jove, draw near you Muses nine, The. The Garden. Nicholas Grimald. GaP; OAEL-1; OBGa

'Issues from the hand of God, the simple soul'. Animula. T. S. Eliot. CRP; GEA

Is't here the fairies haunt the place. On a Nook Called Fairyland. Henrietta Cordelia Ray. CBWP-3

Istanbul. 21 March. I woke today. The Thousand and Second Night. James Merrill. NYBP

Isuba. Jim Barnes. *Fr.* Four Things Choctaw. HATNAP

It. Gary Snyder. LCAP-2

It adds itself to the list of other places. Exiles: Ends. Leonard Schwartz. PT

It ain't forever, *Gimme!* (LL) Preference. Langston Hughes. APSN; HCAP; NOBA; SAGP

It ain't gonna rain, it ain't gonna snow. Ain't Gonna Rain. *Unknown.* AS

It Ain't Neccessarily So. Ira Gershwin. OBAL

It aint no. Bob O'Meally. MBE

It ain't the failures he may meet. The Quitter. *Unknown.* BLPA

It ain't the guns nor armament. Co-operation. J. Mason Knox. BLPA

It All Comes Together Outside the Restroom in Hogansville. James Seay. MT

It all happened on the water. Miracle. Susan Griffin. CrSp

It all happened so fast. Fenya was in the straight chair. Pastoral. Norman Dubie. AmPA

It all returns. (LL) For Love. Robert Creeley. CoAmPo; NOBA; PmAP; VCAP

It all wears out. I keep telling myself this, but. Down by the Station, Early in the Morning. John Ashbery. HCAP

It always felt to me—a wrong. Emily Dickinson. ChIV-1

It Always Seems. A. M. Sayers. BXAP

It asked a crumb—of Me. (LL) "Hope" is the thing with feathers. Emily Dickinson. APN-2; AmPP; ChAP; MeMAP; MoAmPo; NOBA; NoP-4; OxBA; PFE; PiM; SAmP; TAP

It asked for bread and butter first. The Perfect Child. Adrian Porter. NBLV

It baffles the foreigner like an idiom. Drug Store. Karl Shapiro. CMoP; OxBA; TwCP

It be as short as yours. (LL) Life. George Herbert. ESCV; FMP; FSCP; GeHe; MeLP; NOSC; NoP-4; SeCP

It befell at Martynmas. Captain Car; or, Edom o Gordon. Unknown. ESPB

It began as a joke: she did not like to leave the house. Another Poem about the Madness of Women. Tom Wayman. NOBC

It began in her pram. The Renaming. Valerie Sinason. BrRo

It began / When God popped His head. Noah's Ark. Roger McGough. OBSP

It begins again, the nocturnal pulse. The Assassination. Donald Justice. VCAP

It begins with my dog, now dead, who all his long life. The Retrieval System. Maxine W. Kumin. FaBoWP; WeW-3

It begins with one or two soldiers. Truce. Paul Muldoon. PBCIP; PNI

It bends far over Yell'ham Plain. The Comet at Yell'ham. Thomas Hardy. CMoP; GBL

It blows and rains enough to make you sick. The State of the World. T(tilde;a)n Đà, Vietnamese. AVP, tr. by Huỳnh Sanh Thông

It breaks the heart, don't ask. Ni Tsan. Fr. Two Poems to the Tune "Jen-yüeh yüan." CoBLCP, tr. by Jonathan Chaves

It breaks up green moss ground. Pond in a Basin. Tu Mu, Chinese. SuSp, tr. by Eddie Tsang

It burn me, it burn me for true! (LL) The Carpenter's Complaint. Edward Baugh. HCP; OBCoV; PBCV

It burns in the void. The World. Kathleen Jessie Raine. OxBTC

It came into her mind, seeing how the snow. Edna St. Vincent Millay. Fr. Sonnets from an Ungrafted Tree. NALW

It came to his palms. The Fifty Gunner. Frank A. Cross Jr. CDa

It came to me that all this time. Days and Nights. Kenneth Koch.

It came today to visit. The Visitor. Jack Prelutsky. OTCP

It came upon the midnight clear. Edmund Hamilton Sears. AH; APN-1; PWR

It came upon the noontide air. Bishop James A. Shorter. Josephine D. Henderson Heard. CBWP-4

It Can Be Done. Unknown. PoToHe

It can kill a man. (LL) Poetry Is a Destructive Force. Wallace Stevens. MeMAP; OxBA; RaBo

It cannot be/ reasoned with. Julius Lester. Fr. In the Time of Revolution. PoBA

It cannot be. Where is that mighty joy. The Temper (2). George Herbert. GeHe

It cannot come / except you make it. Balboa, the Entertainer. Imamu Amiri Baraka. AF; NoAM

It can't keep a-goin'. If The War Keeps On. Bernard Gilbert. NSI

It caught his image as he flew. (LL) L'Oiseau Bleu. Mary Elizabeth Coleridge. BoTP; CH; VWP

It ceased to hurt me, though so slow. Emily Dickinson. SAmP

It chanced his lips did meet her forehead cool. George Meredith. CBLP; EnVR; NOBVV Fr. Modern Love.

It chaunced me on day beside the shore. The Ruines of Time. Edmund Spenser. OxAEP-1

It comes about that the drifting of these curtains. The Curtains in the House of the Metaphysician. Wallace Stevens. PoA

It comes back. Deceased. Cid Corman. VGW

It comes blundering over the. How Poetry Comes to Me. Gary Snyder. LoL; PoPoPo; SAGP

It comes to this. Revelations. David Meltzer. NeAP

It Couldn't Be Done. E. A. Guest. BLPA; FaBoBe

It crawls, the underground snake. Readers of Newspapers. Marina Tsvetaeva, Russian. TCRP, tr. by Elaine Feinstein and Angela Livingstone

It cries and cries. Tanka. Yosano Tekkan, Japanese. MJT, tr. by Makoto Ueda

It darted across the pond. The Catch. Stanley Kunitz. MoLi

It Depends on You. "Angelus Silesius," German. EnlH, tr. by Stephen Mitchell

It Did. Robert Lowell. NoAM

It did not condemn. (LL) Bible is an antique Volume, The. Emily Dickinson. APN-2; ChIV-1; NAAL-1; NAAL-3; NoP-4; PAR

It did not last; the Devil howling Ho. Sir John Collings Squire. FaBoEE

It didn't require great character at all. The Power of Taste. Zbigniew Herbert, Polish. PoSu, tr. by John Carpenter and Bogdana Carpenter

It dissipated suspected. Epitaph. Marie-Claire Bancquart, French. MFP, tr. by Martin Sorrell

It does, it does, I have seen it. America Bleeds. Angelo Lewis. PoBA

It does not happen. That love, removes. Audubon, Drafted. Imamu Amiri Baraka. TTY

It does not matter / That I am forgotten. Lady Ukon. See I am forgotten now.

It does not worry me that this verse has three stresses. The Eumenides at Home. James Agate. BXAP

It doesn't always do to let a mug know everything. Charlie Piecan. L. Murray and F. Leigh. OxBoLi

It doesn't do to do much talking. Not Much Talking. Unknown. PWR

It doesn't exist, I know, but I love. The Buddy Bolden Cylinder. William Matthews. SeSe

It doesn't look like a finger it looks like a feather of broken glass. Poem. Hugh Sykes Davies. SPE

It doesn't matter if you are late or early. The Pendulum. Michael Cuddihy. CMAP

It doesn't really matter if I met him in a bar, picked him up or was. Future. Vicki Viidikas. BMAP

It doesn't speak and it isn't schooled. Desire. Molly Peacock. RA

It Don't Mean a Thing (If It Ain't Got That Swing). Unknown. NAAAL

It dropped so low—in my Regard. Emily Dickinson. CMoP; HAP; HeIP-4; InPK-6; OxBA; OxBSP; PRMP; PFE

It drowned the amber-colored flesh with blood. (LL) The Jewels. Charles Baudelaire, French. NAWM-2, tr. by David Paul; BoLoP; tr. by Roy Campbell

It ended, and the morrow brought the task. George Meredith. EnVR Fr. Modern Love.

It ended when he popped one of the three of the order. Rock, Scissors, Paper. Deborah Digges. NAmP90

It faces west, and round the back and sides. Domicilium. Thomas Hardy. GaP; OBGa

It faded on the crowing of the cock. Hamlet. Shakespeare. PeECV, sect. I, i; OxBSn; TOF Fr. Hamlet. NAWM-1

It falles me here to write of Chastity. The Legend of Britomartis, or of Chastitie. Edmund Spenser. NAEL-1 Fr. Wood Of Error. AEP

It falls over the upright cliff. A Waterfall. Suyong Kim, Korean. CKP, tr. by Jaihiun Kim

It feels like a bear eating me. Divorce. Adam Koehn. AiP

It fell about the Lambmass tide. Bonny Lizie Baillie. Unknown. ESPB

It fell about the Lammas time. Lord Livingston. Unknown. ESPB; OxBB

It fell about the Martinmas. Jamie Telfer of [or in] the Fair Dodhead. Unknown. ESPB; IBB; OxBB

It fell about the Martinmas[s] time. Edom o' Gordon. Unknown. ESPB; OxBB

It fell about the Martinmas time. Get Up and Bar the Door. Unknown. ESPB; HeIP-4; NoP-4; OxBS; PBMP

It fell in the ancient periods. Uriel. Ralph Waldo Emerson. APN-1; NAAL-1; NAAL-3; NOBA; OxBA; PAR

It fell on a day, and a bonnie simmer [or bonny summer] day. The Bonnie House o' Airlie. Unknown. ESPB; OBEV; OxBB; OxBS

It fell on a summer's [or sommers] day. Thomas Campion. HAP

It fell upon a Wodensday [or Wednesday]. Brown Robyn's [or Robin's] Confession. Unknown. CH; ESPB

It fell upon the Lammas time. Young Ronald. Unknown. ESPB

It fell when I was sleeping. In my dream. The Land-Mine. George MacBeth. OBWP

It felt like the zero in brook ice. The Funeral. Norman Dubie. InPK-6; NoAM

It finds a home amid the woods and brooks. The Old Banyan Tree. Nguyễn Trãi, Vietnamese. AVP, tr. by Huỳnh Sanh Thông

It first began when sitting in the huge auditorium. On Having Been an Experimental Sacred Cow for Four Years, and a Token African on Faculty. Kofi Awoonor. HBAPE

It flows through old hushed Egypt and its sands. The Nile. Leigh Hunt. EBEV; GSo; NOBE; OBNC

It follows now you are to prove. Ben Jonson. Fr. Pleasure Reconciled to Virtue. NAEL-1; OAEL-1

It fortuned (as faire it then befell). Edmund Spenser. OAEL-1 Fr. Wood Of Error. AEP

It gets awful lonely. Lonely. Bloke Modisane. PBA

It gets harder to walk. The Jewish Cemetery in Prague. Daniel S. Simko. CEEP

It gives a lovely light! (LL) First Fig. Edna St. Vincent Millay. APAD; AiP; ChAP; EBEvV; FaBoWP; NALW; NoAM; NoP-4; PoA; PoLF; TAP

It gives such divine materials to men, and accepts such leavings from / them at last. (LL) This Compost. Walt Whitman. AWP; MoAmPo; NAAL-1; NAAL-3; PFTM

It glimmers like a wakeful lake in the dusk narrowing room. The Mirror. Isaac Rosenberg. NoAM

It goes away from you suddenly, doesn't it surely first? Saturday Night. Clark Coolidge. FTOS

It goes easier with rabbits than with dogs or cats. An. Experimental Animals. Miroslav Holub, *German.* CEEP, *tr. by* Simko, Daniel

It got me up. The Monster. Karen L. Mitchell. GT

It grows cold in the forest. Choosing a Stone. John Haines. WeT

It had a velvet cap. John Skelton. FP *Fr.* Phyllyp Sparowe [*or* Philip Sparow]. AAS; PoEL-1

It had gotten so bad. By the 5th Generation Louisiana, After Slavery. Ahmos, II Zu-Bolton. BkSV

It had pleased God to form poor Ned. The Idiot. Robert Southey. Ro *Fr.* Morning Post, no. 9198.

It hangs from heaven to earth. Tapestry. Charles Simic. LCAP-2; VCAP

It happened in Jacksboro in the year of 'seventy-three. The Buffalo Skinners. *Unknown.* AmFP

It happened in some peasant land. Bloody Fable. Desanka Maksimovic, *Serbo-Croatian.* HSix, *tr. by* Charles Simic

It happened in Vallen-Koski. Innokenty Fiodorovich Annensky, *Russian.* TCRP, *tr. by* Lubov Yakovleva *with* Daniel Weissbort

It happened, it happened all on a Saturday night. Johnny Dyers. *Unknown.* AmFP

It happened not far away. Clonfeacle. Paul Muldoon. CIP-2

It happened once upon a time. James Hatley. *Unknown.* ESPB

It happens lonely—no one. The Moment. William Stafford. NNaP

It happens through the blond window, the trees. Ascension. Denis Devlin. BIrV; ChIV-2

It happens. Will it go on? Paralytic. Sylvia Plath. FaBoWP

It happens working. Richard E. McMullen. IFJA

It has a head like a cat, feet like a cat. Riddle. *Unknown.* NTCP

It has all. From Gloucester Out. Edward Dorn. NOBA; PmAP; PoM

It has been a month since I gave up shaving. House Plants. David McFadden. NOBC

It has been raining now since. Rain Downriver. Philip Levine. VCAP

It has circles of light fragments. Cartography of the Subtle Heart. Jeni Couzyn. NBrP

It has for ages been observed. Vladimir Uflyand, *Russian.* TCRP, *tr. by* Daniel Weissbort

It has gone with me as with a child. Heinrich von Morungen, *German.* GePo, *tr. by* Frederick Goldin

It has happened / and it goes on happening. What Happens. Tadeusz Rózewicz, *Polish.* AF, *tr. by* Robert A. Maguire *and* Magnus Jan Krynski

It has happened suddenly. Je Suis une Table. Donald Hall. SPE

It has hardened. Momcilo Nastasijevic, *Serbo-Croatian.* HSix, *sect.* 2, *tr. by* Charles Simic *Fr.* Deaf Things.

It has never been confined to one locality. (LL) England. Marianne Moore. MeMAP; MoAmPo

It has no wings. Loneliness and July Ninth. Claribel Alegría, *Spanish.* BoWoP, *tr. by* Aliki *and* Willis Barnstone

It Has Snowed Repeatedly and We Can Count On a Good Crop of Wheat and Barley. Lu Yu, *Chinese.* SuSp, *tr. by* Burton Watson

It has taken me. Leaving You. Lily Brett. HP

It has taken me three years. Lines Written in a Pittsburgh Skyscraper. Diane Ackerman. WWSi

It has the unassuming face of a burnt-out candle. Velemir Khlebnikov, *Russian.* AF, *tr. by* Paul Schmidt

It has to be a hill. The Person as Dreamer: We Talk about the Future. Michael Hartnett. PBCIP *Fr.* Notes on My Contemporaries.

It has to be the end of the day. Surf-casting. W. S. Merwin. NOBA

It has turned cold. Autumn. Wang Wei, *Chinese.* OHMPC, *tr. by* Kenneth Rexroth

It hath been said of old that plays are feasts. To the Reader of Master William Davenant's Play [*The Wits*]. Thomas Carew. CaPo

It hunches / with a brittle black spine. Mrs. Baez Serves Coffee on the Third Floor. Martín Espada. EC3

It hurries down to wither on the strand. (LL) Memory. Walter Savage Landor. EBEV; NOBVV; OAEL-2

It is a beauteous Evening, calm and free. By the Sea. Wordsworth. AWP; FHYEP; GSo; GTBS-P; HeIP-4; ImPo; NAEL-2; NIP-4; NOBRP; NoP-4; OAEL-2; OBEV; OxAEP-2; PoEL-4; PoLF; SCGP; Son; TFi

It is a being somewhat like a well. Woman. Rumiko Kora, *Japanese.* WPJ, *tr. by* Kenneth Rexroth *and* Ikuko Atsumi

It is a boring song / but it works every time. (LL) Siren Song. Margaret Atwood. HAP; NIP-4; PoA; WeW-3

It is a bright house. Bright House. Sumako Fukao, *Japanese.* WPJ, *tr. by* Kenneth Rexroth *and* Ikuko Atsumi

It is a clearing deep in a forest: overhanging boughs. Johnson's Cabinet Watched by Ants. Robert Bly. MoP; NOBA

It is a cold and snowy night. The main street is deserted. Driving to Town Late to Mail a Letter. Robert Bly. HeIP-4; InPK-6; VGW

It is a cramped little state with no foreign policy. Shame. Richard Wilbur. CoAmPo; FaBoMo; OBCoV; OxBC

It is a dreary evening. My Journal. Adelaide Anne Procter. VWP

It is a fearful thing to be. The Pope. A. E. Housman. OBCoV

It is a fearful thing to fall into the hands of the living God. The Hands of God. D. H. Lawrence. ChIV-2

It is a flower. On this mountainside it is dying. (LL) Flower Herding on Mount Monadnock. Galway Kinnell. CoAmPo; HeIP-4; LCAP-2; NOBA; NoAM

It is a funny thing, but true. Folks and Me. Lucile Crites. PWR

It is a God-damned lie to say that these. Another Epitaph on an Army of Mercenaries. "Hugh MacDiarmid." InPK-6; MoP; NAEL-2; NSI; NoAM; NoP-4; OBWP; RB

It is a good thing to give thanks. Bible, *O.T.* CTV *Fr.* The Bible, Psalm 92:1.

It is a great day. (LL) Today Is a Day of Great Joy. Victor Hernandez Cruz. LoL

It is a hive. Inside My Zulu Hut. Mbuyiseni Oswald Mtshali. PBMAP

It is a hollow garden, under the cloud. Winter Swan. Louise Bogan. ColAP

It is a huge spider, which can no longer move. The Spider. César Vallejo, *Spanish.* RaBo, *tr. by* Robert Bly

It is a kind of shadow. The Umbrella. Ann Stanford. NYBP

It is a land with neither night nor day. Cobwebs. Christina Rossetti. CABP; NAEL-2; NALW; VWP

It is a long time since I flapped my wings. The Angels of 1912 and 1972. Richard Jackson. NAmP90

It is a lost road into the air. An Airstrip in Essex, 1960. Donald Hall. LCAP-2; LiTM

"It is a month, and isna mair." The White Fisher. *Unknown.* ESPB

It is a new America. Brown River, Smile. Jean Toomer. PoBA *Fr.* The Blue Meridian.

It is a pilgrim coming from the East. The Pilgrim from the East. Gustave Kahn, *French.* TrJP, *tr. by* Jethro Bithell

It is a place where poets crowned may feel the heart's decaying. Cowper's Grave. Elizabeth Barrett Browning. OxAEP-2

Is Is a Pleasant Day. *Unknown.* BoTP

It is a simple ritual. My Brother. Patricia Parker. CPO; GLP

It is a small plant. William Carlos Williams. ColAP

It is a solemn evening, golden-clear. The After-Glow. Mathilde Blind. OBNC

It is a strange bird. A Strange Bird. Michael Dransfield. BMAP

It is a stubble field, where a black rain is falling. De Profundis. Georg Trakl, *German.* PFTM, *tr. by* James Wright

It is a sultry day; the sun has drank [*or* drunk]. Summer Wind. William Cullen Bryant. APN-1; PoEL-4

It is a Sunday morning a few minutes before noon and. Sunday Morning. Susan Griffin. NMM-2

It is a terror. Perspectives on the Second World War. Irena Klepfisz. NMM-2

It is a test you have to pass. Essie Parrish in New York. Elsie Parrish, *Kashia Pomo Indian.* STP, *tr. by* George Quasha

It is a theatre floating through the clouds. Wallace Stevens. HCAP *Fr.* The Auroras of Autumn.

It is a thought breaking the granite heart. On the Death of Her Body. James Keir Baxter. PeNZ

It is a thousand sunsets since I lay. The Carse. Lewis Spence. FaBoTC

It is a very curious fact. Lines for a Worthy Person Who Has Drifted by Accident into a Chelsea Revel. Sir Alan Patrick Herbert. NOBL

It is a voiceless shouting. Flag. Ch'ihwan Yu, *Korean.* CKP, *tr. by* Jaihiun Kim

It is a warm grey afternoon in August. Out of Control; the Quarry. Christopher Dewdney. NOBC

It is a water hand, this right one. Look to the Back of the Hand. Judith Minty. PoA

It is a willow when summer is over. Willow Poem. William Carlos Williams. NAAL-2

It is a winter night. Fever and chill. A Winter's Tale. Robert Patrick Dana. NYBP

It is a winter's tale. A Winter's Tale. Dylan Thomas. CMoP

It is a wonder foam is so beautiful. Spray. D. H. Lawrence. AYFP

It is a year of good harvest. Harvesting Wheat for the Public Share. Li Chü, *Chinese.* BoWoP; PBWP, *tr.* by Kenneth Rexroth *and* Ling Chung

It is again. "Stephany." NBV

It is all a rhythm. The Rhythm. Robert Creeley. LiTM

It is all right. All they do. To the Muse. James Wright. NAAL-2; NNaP

It is All Souls' Day, then, a reverential day in Portugal. Lisbon. Russell Atkins. GT

IT IS ALMOST BEAUTIFUL when fraud and hypocrisy. Senate Hearings. Michael McClure. BB

It is almost time to grow up. Movin' with Nancy. David Trinidad. PmAP

It is almost too long ago to remember. That Moment. Sharon Olds. Poetr

It is already so late at night. Ise Tayu, *Japanese.* WPJ, *tr.* by Kenneth Rexroth *and* Ikuko Atsumi

It is always a temptation to an armed and agile nation. Dane-Geld. Rudyard Kipling. OxBTC

It is always difficult to measure. Our World Is Less Full Now That Mr. Fuller Is Gone. Kalamu ya Salaam. ISC

It is always easy to sentimentalize old lovers. They are distant. To H.N. David Mura. UnSA

It is always night here. Star & Garter Theater. Dennis Schmitz. LCAP-2

It is always so: the declining. Returning from Harvest. Vernon Watkins. NYBP

It is always the quiet ones. Rite de Passage. Michele Roberts. NBrP

It is an ancestral castle. Life in the Castle. Anne Hébert, *French.* BoWoP, *tr.* by Aliki *and* Willis Barnstone

It is an ancient Mariner. The Rime of the Ancient Mariner. Coleridge. CABP; CH; EBEV; EBNV; FHYEP; FaBoBe; FaBoCh; HAP; HeIP-4; HoPM; ImPo; InPS-3; NOBE; NoP-4; OAEL-2; OBEV; OBNC; OBNV; OxAEP-2; OxBoS; PeECV; PoE; PoEL-4; PoPoPo; Ro; SCGP; TFi; TOF

It is an antique carcass eaten up by rust. Frisco-City. Blaise Cendrars, *French.* BLT, *tr.* by Monique Chefdor

It is an auncient waggonere. The Rime of the Auncient Waggonere. William Maginn. BXAP; ClHu

It is an honorable Thought. Emily Dickinson. NOCV

It is an image of irreversible loss. The Sorrow Garden. Thomas McCarthy. BiHa

It is as if they are ashamed. The Elephants Dying. Michael C. Blumenthal. NoAM

It is at moments after i have dreamed. E. E. Cummings. LoP; OxBA

It is at morning, twilight they expire. After Midnight. Charles Vildrac, *French.* AWP, *tr.* by Jethro Bithell

It is because you always hope, my heart. Akiko Yosano, *Japanese.* WPJ, *tr.* by Kenneth Rexroth *and* Ikuko Atsumi

It is because you were my friend. Mortal Combat. Mary Elizabeth Coleridge. VWP

It Is Becoming Now to Declare My Allegiance. C. Day Lewis. LiTM

It is beginning to grow light. (LL) The Sun. Marge Piercy. WPOW

It is better. Abandoning Your Car in a Snowstorm: Rosslyn, Virginia. Michael C. Blumenthal. NoAM

It Is Better. Bible, *O.T.* TrJP *Fr.* Ecclesiastes.

It is better this year. If the Birds Knew. John Ashbery. PoA

It Is Better to Be Together. Ruth Miller. PeSA

It is blood. It is not hail, battering my temples. July 18, 1936–July 18, 1938. Miguel Hernández, *Spanish.* AF, *tr.* by Timothy Baland

It is blue. (LL) Blue Monday. Diane Wakoski. NALW; PmAP

It is borne in upon me that pain. The Human Being Is a Lonely Creature. Richard Eberhart. PFE

It is building music. (LL) Then. Muriel Rukeyser. GLP; LCAP-2

It is, but hadn't ought to be. (LL) Mrs. Judge Jenkins[; Being the Only Genuine Sequel to "Maud Muller"]. Bret Harte. APN-2; BXAP

It is calm work, remembering their names. A House of Geraniums. Peter Scupham. OxBSn

It is Christmas Day in the workhouse, and the cold, bare walls are bright. Christmas Day in the Workhouse. George R. Sims. BLPA; EBNV; OBCP

It is clear that Napoleon's Queen. Limerick. Moss Rich. PeLi

It is cold, bitter as a penny. Who Will Know Us? Gary Soto. GM

It is cold dark midnight, yet listen. Homeless. Adelaide Anne Procter. VWP

It is cold here. The Moths. W. S. Merwin. HeIP-4

It is cold. I am / drawing my life around me to get warm. "Love is not Love." Marie Ponsot. NMM-2

It is colder now, / there are many stars. Epistle to Be Left in the Earth. Archibald MacLeish. CMoP; MoAmPo; NOBA; SAGP

It is common knowledge to every schoolboy and even every Bachelor of Arts. Portrait of the Artist as a Prematurely Old Man. Ogden Nash. ImPo; InPS-3; LiTM

It is dangerous for a woman to defy the gods;. Letter to My Sister. Anne Spencer. BlSi; NAAAL; NMM-2; PoBA

It Is Dangerous to Read Newspapers. Margaret Atwood. CrSp; HeIP-4; OBWP

It is dark. The Last Bus. Mark Strand. TwCP

It is dark, now, and grave. Melting Pot. Michael Echeruo. PBMAP; TTY

It is daybreak everywhere. (LL) The Bells of San Blas. Henry Wadsworth Longfellow. APN-1; MeMAP; OxBA; PAR

It is December in Wicklow. Exposure. Seamus Heaney. PBCIP; PNI

It is decided, dear Theramenes. Phaedra. Jean Racine, *French.* NAWM-2, *tr.* by Kenneth Muir

It Is Deep. Carolyn M. Rodgers. NAAAL

It Is Deep. Carolyn M. Rodgers. SSLK

It is difficult now to speak of poetry. George Oppen. NNaP *Fr.* Of Being Numerous.

It is difficult to imagine how vulnerable they are. The Birds. David Posner. NYBP

It is difficult to keep sane in it. Rain Forest. Eric Rolls. NOBAu

It is disastrous to be a wounded deer. Hello. Gregory Corso. PoM

It is done! Laus Deo! John Greenleaf Whittier. AmPP; CBCWP

It is done by us all, as God disposes[, from]. The Excrement Poem. Maxine W. Kumin. AFr; FaBoWP

It is early dawn. The city forty miles away draws airplanes. Written Forty Miles South of a Spreading City. Robert Bly. NNaP

It is early, yet. The Grand Canyon. James Merrill. TAP

It is earnest. Scenes from the Door. Gertrude Stein. AF

It is easier to forgive an enemy than to forgive a friend. William Blake. OAEL-2 *Fr.* Jerusalem; The Emanation of the Giant Albion.

It is easily forgotten, year to. Memorial Day. Michael Anania. NoAM

It is easy enough to be pleasant. Worthwhile. Ella Wheeler Wilcox. BLPA; EBEvV; PoToHe

It is easy enough to love flowers but these. Giant Decorative Dahlias. Molly Holden. OxBTC

It is easy to be young. (Everybody is). How to Be Old. May Swenson. UnPo

It is eating me. A Fly on the Water. Paul Zweig. WeT

It is enough for me. Old Man Told Me. Lance Henson. VoR

It is enough! My feeble sense. Dying Song. Anton Ulrich, *German.* GePo, *tr.* by George C. Schoolfield

It is enough; time presses, we are thrifty. Philip Appleman. BXAP

It is equal to living in a tragic land. Dry Loaf. Wallace Stevens. MeMAP; NOBA; OxBA; PoRA; RaBo

It is essential I remember. Man White, Brown Girl and All That Jazz. Gloria C. Oden. GT; PoBA

It is essential that the U. S. A. standard of hygiene and inspection. Hearts (1983). Laurie Duggan. BMAP *Fr.* Three Found Poems.

It is eternal life.. . it is happiness. Walt Whitman. *See* There is that in me.. . I do not know what it is.. . but I know it is in me.

It is eternally winter. Asclepiades, *Greek.* InMo, *tr.* by Sam Hamill

It is evening. One bat dances. A Soul. Randall Jarrell. CMoP

It is Everywhere. Jean Toomer. GT

It is far from just between us. *Unknown.* NOIV

It is far to Assisi. The Mental Hospital Garden. William Carlos Williams. CRP

It is finished. The enormous dust-cloud over Europe. Armistice. Paul Dehn. OxBTC

'It is finished.' The last nail. Tenebrae. David Gascoyne. PeECV

It is fitting that you be here. On Seeing Two Brown Boys in a Catholic Church. Frank Horne. PoBA; TTY

It is 5:15 a.m. Dear Chris, hello. (LL) A Final Sonnet. Ted Berrigan. FTOS; PmAP

It is for us / to praise the Lord of all. The Kingdom of God. Rab, *Hebrew.* TrJP

It is for you, my mother fair. For You. James Harvey Spencer. PWR

It is four in the afternoon. Time still for a poem. Public Journal. Phyllis McGinley. NBLV

"It is four times as big as the bush!" (LL) Limerick: "There was an Old Man who said, 'Hush!'." Edward Lear. KaS; NOBL; OxBChV; OxBoLi; PeLV; PeLi

It is friday. The Coming of John. Amus Mor. MoNo

It is friday / the eagle has flown. The Coming of John. Amus Mor. SeSe

It is from the ideas of you that you emerge. Correspondences. Robert Duncan. PoM

It is fun to ride the horse. Horse. Kenneth Rexroth. NNaP *Fr.* A Bestiary. OBAL

It is going to be a splendid summer. Future Work. Fleur Adcock. DiPo

It is going to rain. She Thinks of Her Beloved. Lu Chi, *Chinese.* OHMPC, *tr.* by Kenneth Rexroth

It is good to be out on the road, and going one knows not where. Tewkesbury Road. John Masefield. BoTP

It is graceful to see one. Fallen Petals. Hyonggi Yi, *Korean.* CKP, *tr. by* Jaihiun Kim

It is growing dark. L. A. Davidson. HA

It is hanging / in the edge of sunshine. *Unknown.* Fr. Poems for the Game of Silence. STP, *tr. by* Frances Densmore

It is hard as diamonds; it wants to destroy us all. (LL) The Unbeliever. Elizabeth Bishop. NAAL-2; NoAM

It is hard going to the door. The Door. Robert Creeley. NeAP; NoAM; PoM; VGW

It is hard to beat a good meal. Thomas Kinsella. CIP-2 *Fr.* A Technical Supplement.

It is hard to believe of the world that there should be. The Nature of Musical Form. William Bronk. PT

It is hard / To make a poem in prison. To Make a Poem in Prison. Etheridge Knight. AF

It is hard to remember parents at their loving. Train Song. Fiona Kidman. PeNZ

It Is Her Cousin's Death. Gail Fox. NOBC

It is her eyes. In Her Own Image. Eavan Boland. PBCIP

It is here that music / resists the division. The Loom. Robert Kelly. PT *Fr.* The Loom.

It is I, lads, who look after this place. Virgil. OBCVT, *tr. by* John Heath-Stubbs *Fr.* Three Inscriptions for Statues of Priapus.

It is I who travel in the winds. George Copway's Dream Song. *Unknown, Ojibwa Native American.* APN-2, *tr. by* George Copway

It Is Important. Gail Tremblay. WeW-3

It is important to do something meaningless. First Thing. Kit Robinson. FTOS

It is in captivity. The Bull. William Carlos Williams. LiTM; TwCP

It is in dying that we are born to / eternal life. Saint Francis of Assisi. *See* Prayer of St. Francis of Assisi for Peace.

It is in vain, the sorrow. Paul Fleming, *German.* GePo, *tr. by* J. W. Thomas

It is irrevocable. Not like marriage. Yes, But. Rachel Hadas. NMM-2

It is Isis the mystery. Don Juan. D. H. Lawrence. PoA

It is June, it is June. Andraitx—Pomegranate Flowers. D. H. Lawrence. NoP-4

It is late at night and still I am losing. In Divés' Dive. Robert Frost. GI; VGW *Fr.* Ten Mills.

It is late in the day of the world. Latter Day Lysistrata. Lauris Edmond. PeNZ

It is late in the Winter night. Winter Night. Yüan Mei, *Chinese.* OHMPC, *tr. by* Kenneth Rexroth

It is late in the year. Night in the House by the River. Tu Fu, *Chinese.* OHPC, *tr. by* Kenneth Rexroth

It is late January and at last the snow. The Winter Climbing. Andrew Greig. FaBoTC

It is late last night the dog was speaking of you. Donal Og. *Unknown, Irish.* RB, *tr. by* Lady Augusta Gregory

It is Leviathan, mountain and world. History. Robert Fitzgerald. FYAP

It is like the first and last time I tried a Coleman. Falling in Love at Sixty-Five. Mona Van Duyn. NoP-4

It is like the plot of an ol / novel. Instructions to a Princess. Ishmael Reed. PoBA

It is likely enough that lions and scorpions. Ante Mortem. Robinson Jeffers. MoAmPo

It is little I repair to the matches of the Southron folk. At Lord's. Francis Thompson. EBVV; OPOU; OxBSP; PeLV

It is lovely to walk fields of tall grass. Anacreon, *Greek.* InMo, *tr. by* Sam Hamill

It is made to be rolled down. A Poem Like a Grenade. John Haines. SPE

It is Margaret you mourn for. (LL) Spring and Fall. Gerard Manley Hopkins. CABP; CMoP; ClHu; EBEV; GTBS-P; HAP; HeIP-4; HoPM; IMW; ImPo; InPK-6; InPS-3; LiLi; LiTM; NAEL-2; NIP-4; NOBE; NoAM; NoP-4; OPOU; OxAEP-2; PFE; PeVV; PoE; PoEL-5; PoPoPo; Poetr; RB; SAGP; SCGP; SCV; TFi; TOF; TRP

It is May on every hand. Bird Song. William Carlos Williams. SAmP

It is midday; the deep trench glares. Noon. Robert Malise Bowyer Nichols. PoFWW

It is midnight. Poem at Thirty. Sonia Sanchez. BPo; BlSi; NAAAL; NMM-2; NTP; PoBA

It is midnite. The room is blue. Death Songs. L. V. Mack. PoBA

It is miserable. Líadan and Cuirithir. *Unknown.* NOIV

It is Monday morning. The Goldfish Wife. Sandra Hochman. NYBP; UnPo

It Is Monsoon at Last. Basil T. Paquet. CDa

It is morning because the sun has risen. Concerning the Afterlife, the Indians of Central California Had Only the Dimmest Notions. Robert Hass. LoL

It is morning, Chrysilla. Some time ago the clarion cock. Antipater of Thessalonica, *Greek.* GrAn, *tr. by* W. G. Shepherd

It is morning darling look the sun. Aubade: N.Y.C. Robert Wallace. HoPM

It is morning, Senlin says, and in the morning. Morning Song of Senlin. Conrad Potter Aiken. CMoP; ImPo; LiTM; MoAmPo; NoAM; OxBA *Fr.* Senlin; a Biography.

It is most true that eyes are formed to serve. Sonnet 5. Sir Philip Sidney. NAEL-1; NoSic; OAEL-1; Son *Fr.* Astrophil and Stella. AAS; SiPS

It is most true that God to Israel, *par. by* Countess of Pembroke, Mary Sidney Herbert. Psalm 73. Bible, *O.T.* NoSic *Fr.* Psalms.

It is much like ocean the way it opens. Open Country. Richard Hugo. LCAP-2

It is my desire, it is my wish. Elias Lönnrot. PFTM, *tr. by* Francis Peabody Magoun, Jr. *Fr.* The Kalevala.

It is my first Scotch tinkling. Christmas Party. Kate Daniels. NAmP90

It is my joy in life to find. Make Me Worthy of My Friends. *Unknown.* CTV

It is my nature that makes me love you often. How God Answers the Soul. Mechthild von Magdeburg, *German.* WPoS, *tr. by* Oliver Davies

It is my only description. (LL) "I Keep to Myself Such Measures. . . ." Robert Creeley. NoAM; PmAP

It is myself. To a Dog Injured in the Street. William Carlos Williams. LCAP-2; LiTM; SAmP

It Is Near Toussaints'. Ivor Gurney. PeFWW

It is necessary that things. Anaximander, *Greek.* PGA, *tr. by* Kenneth Rexroth

It is never enough to know what you want. The Wish to Be Believed. Mona Van Duyn. PoA

It is new. Al-Hutay'a, *Arabic.* ArPe, *tr. by* Omar S. Pound

It is New Year's Day. Best Loved of Africa. Margaret Danner. PoBA

It is night again. Tzu Yeh, *Chinese.* WPOW, *tr. by* Kenneth Rexroth *and* Ling Chung

It is night and the barbarians have not come. Poem Beginning with a Line by Cavafy. Derek Mahon. PNI

It is night like a red rag. A Moment of War. Laurie Lee. OBWP

It is no dream of mine. Henry David Thoreau. ImGa

It is no fault to be deformed. To a Hunchback. Ibn al-Rumi, *Arabic.* ArPe, *tr. by* Omar S. Pound

It is no madness to say. Hilda Doolittle. FaBoMo *Fr.* The Flowering of the Rod.

It is no vulgar nature I have wived. George Meredith. NAEL-2 *Fr.* Modern Love.

It Is Not. Valerie Martinez. BAP-96

It is not a range of a mountain. Gertrude Stein. NoP-4

It Is Not Always May. Henry Wadsworth Longfellow. PWR

It is not bad. Let them play. The Bloody Sire. Robinson Jeffers. CMoP; ImPo; LiTM; PoA

It is not Beauty [or beautie] I demand[e]. A Song. George Darley. GTBS-P; NOBRP; OAEL-2; OBNC; OxAEP-2; Ro

It is not, Celia, in our power. To a Lady Asking Him How Long He Would Love Her. Sir George Etherege. OBEV; SAGP

It is not clear what they love. Two Lovers on Bridge in Winter. Paula Rankin. CMAP

It is not cosy to live. From the Chinese. Michael Smith. CIP-2; PBCIP

It is not death, that sometime in a sigh. Sonnet. Thomas Hood. GSo; OBNC

It is not enough. The Prophet's Warning or Shoot to Kill. Ebon Dooley. PoBA

It is not enough to drink. "When the Wild Goose Finds Food He Calls His Comrades"—I Ching. Jan Kemp. PeNZ

It is not far beyond the Village church. Walden. William Ellery Channing. APN-1; PAR

It is not far to my place. Visit. A. R. Ammons. CoAP; TwCP

It is not grief or pain;. After Soufrière. "Michael Field." VWP

It is not growing like a tree. The Noble Nature. Ben Jonson. GTBS-P; ImPo; OBEV *Fr.* To the Immortal[l] Memory [*or* Memorie] and Friendship of That Noble Pair[e], Sir Lucius Cary and Sir H. [*or* Henry] Morison. BeJo; NAEL-1; NOBE; NOSC; OAEL-1; PoEL-2; SeCP

It is not gunfire I hear but a hunting horn. (LL) Aristocrats. Keith Douglas. FaBoMo; NAEL-2; NoAM; NoP-4; OBWP

It is not I, ever or now. (LL) The Pebble. Elinor Wylie. ChIV-1; MoAmPo

It is not—I swear it by every fiery omen to be seen these nights. Readings, Forecasts, Personal Guidance. Kenneth Fearing. MoAmPo

It is not in yr service that I wear myself out. Loba Addresses the Goddess, The / or The Poet as Priestess Addresses the Loba-Goddess. Diane Di Prima. PmAP

It is not just. Harriet Jacobs. ISC

It Is Not, Lord, the Sound of Many Words. Henry Lok. *Fr.* Sundry Christian Passions Contained in Two Hundred. Son

It is not mine to run, with eager feet. Not Mine. Julia Caroline Ripley Dorr. PWR

It is not right to judge a man. First Impressions. Alfred Grant Walton. PoToHe

It is not safe to know. (LL) Lover and Philosopher. Sir William Davenant. GEA; NOBE; OBEV

It is not so much. Outrage. Lucille Iverson. CrSp

It is not so much the image of the man. Photograph of Haymaker, 1890. Molly Holden. OxBTC

It is not the earth that I worship. Earth Song. Thomas Love Peacock. VoR

It is not the hunter who is cunning. First Lessons. Marilyn Chin. LoHo

It is not the moon, I tell you. Mock Orange. Louise Glück. NoAM; PoPoPo; SAGP; VCAP

It is not the still weight. The Jungle. William Carlos Williams. PFE

It is not the weight of the jewel or plate. The Perfect Gift. Edmund Vance Cooke. PChr

It is Not Time Yet to Light the Candle. Sokchong Shin, *Korean.* CKP, *tr.* by Jaihiun Kim

It is not to be thought of. England, 1802. Wordsworth. FaPoR

It is not vertue, wisdom, valour, wit. Woman. Milton. *Fr.* Samson Agonistes. FHYEP; OAEL-1; PoEL-3

It is not what they built. It is what they knocked down. James Fenton. HP *Fr.* A German Requiem. NAEL-2; NoAM

It is not wine that makes me reel / Not juice of grape I crave. Agathias, *Greek.* GrAn, *tr.* by Peter Whigham

It is not words could pay you what I owe. (LL) Apology for Understatement. John Wain. OxBTC; PFE

It is nothing to me, the beauty said. Nothing and Something. Frances Ellen Watkins Harper. PWR

It is now nearly forty years, I guess. The Mother's Lament. Helen Selina Blackwood, Countess of Dufferin. VWP

It is now 24 years since I rode in a stranger's funeral. Riding in a Stranger's Funeral. Robert Wallace. CMAP

It is—Occasionally. (LL) We do not play on Graves. Emily Dickinson. NIP-4; PoEL-5

It is of a fearless Irishman a story I will tell. Brennan on the Moor. *Unknown.* AmFP

It is, of course, the wrong house. The Houses of Emily Dickinson. Larry Rubin. NIP-4

It is often said that something may survive of a person. My True Love Hath My Heart. Marcel Proust, *French.* LBC, *tr.* by Charles Kenneth Michael Scott Moncrieff

It is one that most people should be prepared to be blank upon. (LL) Ignorance of Death. William Empson. CMoP; LiTM; NoAM

It is only a door. (LL) Prospective Immigrants Please Note. Adrienne Rich. AiP; PoPoPo; VGW

It is other people who have separated. Lady Otomo no Sakanoé, *Japanese.* TAL, *tr.* by Arthur Waley

It is out in the flimsy suburbs. Sunday in Glastonbury. Robert Bly. CoAmPo

It is over. What is over? Amen. Christina Rossetti. WPoS

It is overdue time. Ron Welburn. NBV

It is passing strange to be in the company. Hair: A Narrative. Cheryl Clarke. NMM-2

It is past midnight in a thick fog when sirens. Street Fire. Daniel Halpern. AmPA

It is perfectly natural for the Sun to shine initially in the upper / lefthand corner of the first page of this book. The Sun as a Spinning Top (I). Francis Ponge, *French.* AF, *tr.* by Serge Gavronsky

It is plain now what you are. Your head has dropped. Carrion. Harold Monro. NSI; PeFWW *Fr.* Youth in Arms.

It is pleasant to hang out. Elizabeth Daryush. WPN

It is portentous, and a thing of state. Abraham Lincoln Walks at Midnight. Vachel Lindsay. AmPP; CBCWP; CMoP; MeMAP; MoAmPo; NOBA; OxBA; TAP; TFi; VGW

It is possible the heights of this view are a museum. The Flight from Manhattan. Les A. Murray. BMAP *Fr.* The Sydney Highrise Variations.

It is raining in my heart, but I don't believe that it is raining. Sentences. David Shapiro. PT

It is raining softly. The Front Window. Rae Desmond Jones. BMAP

It is rather strange to be speaking, but I know you are there. A Voice at a Seance. Anthony Hecht. OxBSn

It is really the most miniscule thing. Shaving. Stephen Dobyns. NAmP90

It is reported. Sharks in Shallow Water. Fred Levinson. AmPA

It is right. Planting Onions. Jane Flanders. CrSp

It is said that certain orientational concepts of. Maxim. Josephine Miles. CrSp

It is said that that western land is of Earth the best. The Land Called Scotia. Saint Donatus, *Latin.* NOIV

It is said there are those who can never be sane. Bill. Peter Kocan. CBAP

It is scribbled along the body. Eighth Sky. Michael Palmer. FTOS

It is senseless for any man. Praise of God. *Unknown.* NOIV

It is she alone that matters. Bouquet of Belle Scavoir. Wallace Stevens. MoAmPo

It is so hard for one who has known your love. Penelope. Judita Vaiiunaite, *Lithuanian.* CEEP, *tr.* by Irene Pogoželskyte Suboczewski

It is so hard to be earth bound. Ornithology. Laini Mataka. ISC

It is so long gone by, and yet. A Reminiscence. Amy Levy. VWP

It is so much easier to forget than to have been Mr. Whittier. Mr. Whittier. Winfield Townley Scott. VGW

It is so peaceful on the Ceiling! Sleeping on the Ceiling. Elizabeth Bishop. OBGa; TTTS

It is so sad. The Loneliness. John Wieners. PmAP

It is so small a thing. Hymn of Empedocles. Matthew Arnold. OBEV *Fr.* Empedocles on Etna.

It is so still in the house. The Mother's Song. *Unknown, Eskimo.* OBCP, *tr.* by Peter Freuchen

It is so thin a splinter of singing. (LL) Splinter. Carl Sandburg. KaS; OBCA; SoSe-8; Spl

It is some picture on the margin wrought. (LL) The Book. William Drummond, of Hawthornden. CH; ChIV-1; GTBS-P; KSG

It is some time since I have been. The Hill. Robert Creeley. CRP; CoAmPo; RaBo; TRP

It is Soul Brother Number One, James Brown. Homage: Light from the Hall. David Wojahn. PBCAP *Fr.* Mystery Train: A Sequence.

It is Spring in the mountains. Written on the Wall at Chang's Hermitage. Tu Fu, *Chinese.* EOEF; EnlH; HoPM; OHPC, *tr.* by Kenneth Rexroth

It is Spring on the lake and. Sailing on the Lake to the Ching River. Lu Yu, *Chinese.* OHPC, *tr.* by Kenneth Rexroth

It is strange to think of the Annas, the Vronskys, the Pierres, all the Tolstoyan lot wiped out. Fate and the Younger Generation. D. H. Lawrence. OxBoLi

It is subtle, and weary, and wide. A Doubt. Sarah Morgan Bryan Piatt. NCAP

'It is such a beautiful day I had to write you a letter'. Thoughts of a Young Girl. John Ashbery. CoAmPo; MoLi; TAP; VGW

It is summer, city summer. Chicago, Summer Past. Richard Snyder. Poetsp

It is Sunday. In Memoriam. Léopold Sédar Senghor. PBMAP

It is Sunday afternoon. At the End of the Weekend. Ted Kooser. PBCAP

It is sweet in summer to slake. Asclepiades, *Greek.* PGA, *tr.* by Kenneth Rexroth

It is talked the warld all over. Sheath and Knife. *Unknown.* ESPB

It is Tet. Night Flare Drop, Tan Son Nhut. Horace Coleman. CDa

It is that hour when listening ones will weep. John Neal. APN-1 *Fr.* The Battle of Niagara.

It is the awaited hour. Friendship. Octavio Paz, *Spanish.* FP, *tr.* by Charles Tomlinson

It is the bare and leafless Tree. Holy Cross. Sir Shane Leslie. TIRV

It is the best thing. Pregnancy. Sandra McPherson. BoWoP; LoL; NMM-2

It is the black God, Kali. The Coming of Kali. Lucille Clifton. NMM-2

It is the box from which no jack will spring. The Funeral. Donald Hall. Son

It is the catkin summer. Mild February. Hal Summers. AYFP

It is the cause, it is the cause, my soul. Othello and Desdemona. Shakespeare. EBEV *Fr.* Othello.

It is the clay that makes the earth stick to his spade. In Nunhead Cemetery. Charlotte Mew. FaBoWP; NoP-4

It is the day of all the year. *Unknown.* OxNR

It is the day when all the sons of God. Hellas. Shelley.

It is the day when he was born. Tennyson. EBVV; FHYEP *Fr.* In Memoriam A. H. H.

It is the easiest thing, sir, to be done. The Devil Is an Ass. Ben Jonson. OxBSn

It is the effort of the lie. Upon the Intimation of Love's Mortality. Jean Garrigue. NMM-2

It is the endless dance of the dead. Dirge. Quincy Troupe. PoBA

It is the eve of battle. The Reason Why. George Clinton Rowe. AAP

It is the evening. Nativity Poem. Louise Glück. GI

It is the evening hour. To Mary: 'It Is the Evening Hour'. John Clare. BoLoP; EnLoPo; GBL; GLoP; LBC

It is the fashion now to wave aside. Edna St. Vincent Millay. HeIP-4

It is the first death that seems so open. An Early Death. Daniel Halpern. FiLi

It is the first mild day of March. A Change in the Year. Wordsworth. AYFP; BoTP; OAEL-2; Ro

It is the football season once more. Autumn. Vernon Scannell. OxBTC

It is the gentle poet's art. Iron. Walter De la Mare. NOBL

It is the Harvest Moon! On gilded vanes. The Harvest Moon. Henry Wadsworth Longfellow. APN-1

It is the heart of the night. Curfew. Teresa de Jesús, *Spanish.* AF, *tr. by* Maria Proser, Arlene Scully *and* James Scully

It is the last of the ninth, two down, bases loaded. The Lady Pitcher. Cynthia MacDonald. Poetsp

It is the little girl. Depiction of Childhood. Franz Wright. BLT   *Fr. After Picasso.*

It is the little stone of unhappiness. What I Have Written I Have Written. Peter Porter. BMAP; NOBAu

It is the middle of October. The First Dimension of Skunk. Ray A. Young Bear. HATNAP

It is the miller's daughter. The Miller's Daughter. Tennyson. OBEV

It is the nature of man that puzzles me. The Nature of Man. Charles Hubert Sisson. FaBoTw

It is the Negro's tragedy I feel. The Negro's Tragedy. Claude McKay. BPo

It is the Old Man through the sleeping town. The Fall Again. Howard Nemerov. CoAmPo

It is the pain, it is the pain, endures. Villanelle. William Empson. CBLP; CMoP; EnLoPo; LoP; MoP; NAM; OAEL-2; PoE; TRP; UV

It is the picnic with Ruth in the spring. The Picnic. John Logan. CoAmPo; TRP

It is the purest of cups. U Tam'si Tchicaya. *See* A Mat to Weave.

It is the roots from all the trees that have died. Across the Swamp. Olav H. Hauge, *Norwegian.* RaBo, *tr. by* Robert Bly

It is the sea's edge lubbers love. Sailing, Sailing. Gray Burr. NYBP

It Is the Season. Josephine Jacobsen. TAP

It is the season of the sweet wild rose. George Meredith. GBL; PoEL-5   *Fr. Modern Love.*

It is the silver seeking salvation. The Plight. James W. Thompson. BPo

It is the sinners' dust-tongued bell claps me to churches. Dylan Thomas. OxBTC

It is the soul that sees; the outward eyes. George Crabbe. OxAEP-1   *Fr. The Lover's Journey.*

It is the sound of lions lapping. Bush. Josephine Jacobsen. NoP-4

It is the spot I came to seek. An Indian at the Burial-Place [*or* Burying-Place] of His Fathers. William Cullen Bryant. APN-1

It Is the Stars That Govern Us. Michael Magee. PoA

It is the thirty-first of March. Peter Bell. John Hamilton Reynolds. OBNC

It is the time of rain and snow. Lady Izumi, *Japanese.* OHMPJ; WPOW, *tr. by* Kenneth Rexroth

It is the time when. Kenneth Rexroth. APSN   *Fr.* The Love Poems of Marichiko.

It is the unremarkable that will last. To a Wren on Calvary. Larry Levis. PuP-17

It is the way of a pleasant path. Green Frog at Roadstead, Wisconsin. James Schevill. TAP

It is the wolf running. Yellow Wolf Spirit. Ron Welburn. BAP-96

It is the year's end, the winds are blasting, and I. December 30th. Ivor Gurney. NAEL-2

It is their way to find the surface. Poem by the Charles River. Robin Blaser. NeAP

It is this deep blankness is the real thing strange. Let It Go. William Empson. FaBoMo; OxBSP; OxBTC

It Is This Way with Men. Charles Kenneth Williams. RaBo; SAGP; VCAP

It is three o'clock in the morning. Trials of a Tourist. Anne Tibble. NBLV

It is 3:17 a.m. in New York city, yes, it is. Sonnet LXXVII. Ted Berrigan. FTOS   *Fr.* The Sonnets.

It is Thursday, October 23rd. Ocean of the Streams of Story. Primus St. John. GT

It is time for all the heroes to go home. Allegiances. William Stafford. PaTW

It is time for the others to come. The Magus. James Dickey. GI

It is time to be old. Terminus. Ralph Waldo Emerson. APN-1; AWP; AmPP; MeMAP; NCAP; NOBA; OxBA; PoEL-4; PoLF; SAGP; TAP

It is time to say good-bye, adios, sayonara. Edificio Sayonara. John Yau. PT

It is to a goodly child well fitting. A Goodly Child. *Unknown.* OxBChV

It is tomorrow now. Morning Star. Thomas Hornsby Ferril. VGW

It is too late! Ah, nothing is too late. Too Late? Henry Wadsworth Longfellow. PoLF   *Fr. Morituri Salutamus.*

It is true, as someone has said, that in. Mark Strand. NoP-4   *Fr.* Dark Harbor.

It is true--/ I've always loved. Alice Walker. PoBA   *Fr.* Once. BlSi

It is true, Martin Heidegger, as you have written. The Envelope. Maxine W. Kumin. CrSp; NALW

It is true, modern life is complicated. For the Market. Jane Mayhall. TAP

It is true, that even in the best-run state. The Murder of William Remington. Howard Nemerov. CMoP; CoAP

It is true that I held Thero fair. Epigram. Meleager, *Greek.* GrAn, *tr. by* Peter Whigham

It is true that, older than man and ages to outlast him, the Pacific surf. Gray Weather. Robinson Jeffers. CMoP

It is trying to be autumn in South Texas. The Weather of Invention. Leslie Adrienne Miller. CMAP

It is 12:20 in New York a Friday. The Day Lady Died. Frank O'Hara. HCAP; LCAP-2; MoNo; MoP; NAAL-2; NeAP; NoAM; NoP-4; PmAP; PoE; PoM; Poetr; RaBo; TRP; VCAP

It is twenty years. The Piper. W. S. Merwin. NAAL-2

It is two o'clock. The pin-head spider. From The Bramble Hedge. Joan Downar. AYFP

It is unreasonable to ask my tears. The daughter of Shunzei, *Japanese.* WPJ, *tr. by* Kenneth Rexroth *and* Ikuko Atsumi

It is very early now, no light yet, nor. La Brea. Richard Kenney. DiPo

It is very nice to think. A Thought. Robert Louis Stevenson. CTV

It is waking in the night. Fix. Michael Dransfield. NOBAu

It is well for small birds that can rise up on high. *Unknown, Irish.* NOIV, *tr. by* Thomas Kinsella

It is well the widow is gone, for here winter's. The Bear and the Last Person to Remember. Robert Penn Warren. *Fr.* Fall Comes in Back-Country Vermont. NYBP; VGW

It is what he does not know. On a Squirrel Crossing the Road in Autumn, in New England. Richard Eberhart. AFrc; HeIP-4; LiTM; Poetsp

It is what, to tell the truth, you sometimes feel. History. Kelly Cherry. FFC

It is whatever day, whatever time it is. Sunday Morning. Wayne Moreland. PoBA

It is when gulfs and bays of blood. Punishments. Rafael Alberti, *Spanish.* AF, *tr. by* Geoffrey Connell

It is when I hear Mozart. Deafness. Richard Ryan. BIrV; PBCIP

It is windy today. A wall of wind crashes against. Cloudy Day. Jimmy Santiago Baca. InPS-3; LoL

It is wine-harvest, summer, the year's heart. A Poem for Maurice O'Shea. Geoffrey Lehmann. NOBAu

It is winter again. Stopping to Take Notes. Michael Smith. PBCIP

It is winter and the new year. The New Year. Mark Strand. UnPo   *Fr.* Elegy for My Father. HCAP; LCAP-2

It Is Winter, I Know. Merrill Moore. MoAmPo

It is winter in California, and outside. California Winter. Karl Shapiro. AiP

It is with me, as erst with you. On Reading Wordsworth's Lines on Peele Castle. Mary Wollstonecraft Shelley. Ro

It is worthless to write a line. Chantars No Pot Gaire Valer. Bernard de Ventadour, *Provençal.* APSN, *tr. by* Paul Blackburn

It is written in the Book of Usable Minutes. Train Rising Out of the Sea. John Ashbery. ColAP

It is written in the skyline of the city. Pact. Kenneth Fearing. CMoP

It is written that a hurricane holds the power. An Antipastoral Memory of One Summer. Dave Jeddie Smith. MT

It is your last day and hour and you are alone. Who. Edwin Honig. TAP

It is yourself you seek. Man Alone. Louise Bogan. NYBP; NoP-4

"It isn't a game for girls." Reaching Yellow River. Roberta Hill Whiteman. HATNAP

It isn't a very big cake. Poets. Gavin Ewart. PeLV

It isn't any worse than what. Anxiety about Dying. Alicia Ostriker. CrSp

It isn't as if I never enjoyed good wine. I'm Not Complaining. Philip Schultz. SoSe-8

It isn't fair is another way. Barely There. Dara Wier. CMAP

It isn't [*or* is not] raining rain to me. (April Rain). Robert Loveman. BoTP; CTV; TrJP

It isn't that the threat of the bomb is great. Cocoon. Rin Ishigaki, *Japanese.* WPOW, *tr. by* Ayusawa Takako

It isn't that you were ignorant. From the Meadow. Peter Everwine. PuP-17

It isn't the body. The Inner Man. Charles Simic. IFJA

It Isn't the Church—It's You. *Unknown.* BLPA

It isn't the poppies. Toward Umbria. Stanley Plumly. NAmP90

It isn't the thing you do, dear. The Sin of Omission. Margaret Elizabeth Munson Sangster. BLPA; PWR; PoToHe

It Isn't the Town, It's You. R. W. Glover. BLPA

It isn't true about the lambs. The Necessity. Alice B. Fogel. BAP-93

It isn't winter that brings it. Earth. Margaret Atwood. PoE

It just so happens that I'm tired of being a man. Pablo Neruda. *See* Walking [*or* Walkin'] Around.

It keeps eternal whisperings around. On the Sea. Keats. NoP-4; OAEL-2; OxBoS

It knows nothing whatever about Thee. Ronald Arbuthnott Knox. *See* O God, for as much as without Thee.

It later befell in the years that followed. The Fire-Dragon and the Treasure. *Unknown.* AnOE, *tr. by* Charles W. Kennedy *Fr.* Beowulf. OAEL-1, *tr. by* Charles W. Kennedy; ASW, *tr. by* Kevin Crossley-Holland

It lay, dark in the corner of the field. Suicide Pond. Kathy McLaughlin. PoA

It lies not in our power to love, or hate. Who Ever Loved, That Loved Not at First Sight? Marlowe. EBEvV; ImPo *Fr.* Hero and Leander. AAS

It lies not on the sunlit hill. The White Peace. "Fiona Macleod." FaBoBe

It lieth, gazing on the midnight sky. On the Medusa of Leonardo da Vinci in the Florentine Gallery. Shelley. GS

It little profits that an idle king. Ulysses. Tennyson. APAD; AWP; CABP; ClHu; EBEV; EBVVPR; EnVR; FHYEP; FaPoR; HAP; HeIP-4; HoPM; ImPo; InPK-6; InPS-3; NAEL-2; NAWM-2; NIP-4; NOBE; NOBVV; NoP-4; OAEL-2; OxAEP-2; PFE; PoE; PoPoPo; PoRA; Poetr; SAGP; SCGP; SCV; SoSe-8; TFi; TRP; UnPo; WeW-3

It looked extremely rocky for the Mudville nine that day. Casey at the Bat. Ernest Lawrence Thayer. BLPA; ChAP; FaBoBe; PoRA

It makes a Change. Mervyn Laurence Peake. OTCP

It makes me sick, the state of schooling now. Lamenting the State of Confucian Scholarship. Trần Tế Xu'o'ng, *Vietnamese.* AVP, *tr. by* Huỳnh Sanh Thông

It matters little where I was born. What Does It Matter? Noah Barker. PWR

It matters not if the pasture is far. The Cowherd, a Song. Ch'u Kuang-hsi, *Chinese.* SuSp, *tr. by* Joseph J. Lee

It may be good like it who list. Sir Thomas Wyatt. FaBoPV; SiPS ("For dred to fall I stond not fast.") (LL) PBRV

It may be these things never did occur. Kinnereth. "Rachel," *Hebrew.* TrJP, *tr. by* A. M. Klein

It may be / they dare to. Whitewash. Léon Damas, *French.* NegPo, *tr. by* Ellen Conroy Kennedy

It may be when the sunlight strikes the sill. In Your Absence. Elizabeth Baxter. PoToHe

It may happen again—this much. The Flight. John Haines. SPE

It may indeed be phantasy, when I. To Nature. Coleridge. OAEL-2

It may not always be so; and i say. E. E. Cummings. BoLoP

It may not be forever, but. The Argument Resumed; Or, Up Through Tribeca. Thomas M. Disch. WWSi

It means everything. Sizeline. Felix Mnthali. PeSAV

It midnights, not a moon is out. The Midnightmouse. Christian Morgenstern, *German.* CBNP; RB, *tr. by* W. D. Snodgrass *and* Lore Segal

It might be any night. These Days. Andrew Motion. DiPo

It might be lonelier. Emily Dickinson. APN-2; SAmP

It might have been a neurotic's paradise. Cana. Peter Steele. GI

It Might Have Been Worse. G. J. Russell. PoToHe

It might seem matter for regret. The Lower Life. May Kendall. VWP

It mounts at sea, a concave wall. From the Wave. Thom Gunn. NAEL-2; NoP-4; OxBoS

It moves across and over / across the ground. Bernadette Mayer. PT

It must acknowledge the spiritual forces which have made it. (LL) When I Buy Pictures. Marianne Moore. ColAP; OxBA

It must be / deeeeep. (LL) Jesus Was Crucified or: It Must Be Deep. Carolyn M. Rodgers. BlSi; PoBA

It must be done, my soul, but 'tis a strange. The Meditation. John Norris. NOSC

It must be mine! no other heart could prove. The Returned Heart. Sarah Dixon. ECWP

It must have been a Friday. I could hear. Katherine's Dream. Robert Lowell. CoAmPo

It must have been a single thread of tears. Meng Chiao. SuSp, *tr. by* Stephen Owen *Fr.* Apricots Die Young.

It must have been a year. Fire, Hair, Meat and Bone. Fred Johnson. PoBA

It must have been for one of us, my own. Not Thou but I. Philip Bourke Marston. BLPA

It must have been one or one-thirty. To Remain. Constantine P. Cavafy, *Modern Greek.* BoLoP, *tr. by* Nikos Stangos *and* Stephen Spender

It must have been something like. Jazz to Jackson to John. Jerry W. Ward Jr. BkSV

It must have seemed the apex of dreams. Adonis Theater. Mark Doty. NAmP90

It must, it *must* be so! Felicia Dorothea Hemans. *See* The Image in Lava.

It nearly cancels my fear of death, my dearest said. Cremation. Robinson Jeffers. BLT

It needn't have ribaldry's taint. Limerick. Don Marquis. PeLi

It never has failed, and it never will. God's Plan for Spring. Nancy Byrd Turner. CTV

It never occurred to me, never. The Meeting. Howard Moss. NYBP

It not easy to reach where she live. Getting There. Edward Baugh. HCP

It occurred on the evening before Waterloo. Old Sam. Stanley Holloway. OBCoV

It occurred when she crossed the Atlantic. Limerick. *Unknown.* PeLi

It occurs to me now. The Lesson. Charles Simic. AF; HCAP

It often falss (as here it erst befell). Edmund Spenser. *Fr.* Wood Of Error. AEP

It ofttimes has been told, that the British seamen bold. The *Constitution* and the *Guerriére. Unknown.* AmFP

It once might have been, once only. Youth and Art. Robert Browning. CTC; NAEL-2; NOBVV

"It Out-Herods Herod. Pray You, Avoid It." Anthony Hecht. AF; CoAP; NIP-4; NOBA; NoAM; OxBC

It piles up, thick and formidable, on the marble terrace. The Shadow of Flowers. Su Tung-p'o, *Chinese.* OHPC, *tr. by* Kenneth Rexroth

It pours. Night Rain. Karen L. Mitchell. GT

It put forth buds at the end of the Nine Splendors. The Fragrant Tree. Shen Yüeh, *Chinese.* SuSp, *tr. by* Richard B. Mather

It puts itself right. (LL) Cat and the Weather. May Swenson. HAP; WeW-3

It puzzles much the sages' brains. On Lord Cobham's Garden. Nathaniel Cotton. OBGa

It quickened [*or* quickned] next a toyful[l] ape, and so. Donne. PoEL-2 *Fr.* The Progress[e] of the Soul[e].

It raindrops on the cold. Introit. Padraic Fiacc. CIP-2

It rained all night on the remaining elms. April soaked. Another Elegy. Donald Hall. BAP 94

It rained in my sleep. September. Linda Pastan. Poetsp

It rained quite a lot, that spring. You woke in the morning. Metropolitan Nightmare. Stephen Vincent Benét. NYBP

It rained toward day. The morning came sad and white. Colder Fire. Robert Penn Warren. FuPo; LiTM; MoLi *Fr.* To a Little Girl, One Year Old, in a Ruined Fortress.

It Rains ("It rains, and nothing stirs within the fence"). Edward Thomas. OxBTC; PoE

It rains across the country I remember. (LL) Mnemosyne. Trumbull Stickney. APN-2; GEA; NOBA; OxBA

It rains, and nothing stirs within the fence. It Rains. Edward Thomas. OxBTC; PoE

It reaches to Gold Fish Dike. Blue Mud Shoal. Yang Shih-ch'i. *Fr.* Ten Scenes at the Hsiao Family Stone Ridge. CoBLCP, *tr. by* Jonathan Chaves

It really irks me to think I'm afraid of heights. Abyss. Diane Di Prima. BB

It Really Is the Heart. Denise Riley. NBrP

"It relaxes me," he said. Six Reasons for Drinking. Vernon Scannell. OxBC

It rests me to be among beautiful women. Tame Cat. Ezra Pound. OBAL

It rises over the lake, the farms. The Kite. Mark Strand. ColAP; NYBP

It rose dark as a stack of peat. Suilven. Andrew Young. OxBS

It said "Come home, here is an end, a goal." Woodrow Wilson. Robinson Jeffers. FaBoPV

It said welcome. The Second Coming. John William Corrington. HoPM

It sat between my husband and my children. Seele im Raum. Randall Jarrell. LCAP-2

It scares me the genius we have. The Business of Love is Cruelty. Dean Young. BAP-93

It seconds the crickets of the province[. Heard]. The Rocking Chair. Abraham Moses Klein. HeIP-4; NoP-4

It seemed as though. The Spirit of the Mountain. Ch'u Yüan, *Chinese.* ChiPo, *tr. by* Rewi Alley

It seemed corrival of the world's great prime. A Fallen Yew. Francis Thompson. MoBrPo

It seemed that out of battle I escaped. Strange Meeting. Wilfred Owen. CMoP; EBEvV; FP; FaBoMo; GTBS-P; HeIP-4; HoPM; ImPo; MoBrPo; MoP; NAEL-2; NOBE; NoAM; NoP-4; OAEL-2; OBWP; OxAEP-2; PeFWW; PoE; PoFWW; PoWW; RB; SCV; TFi

It seemed the kind of life we wanted. Clouds Gathering. Charles Simic. ColAP

It seems a certain time ago: a-maybe. One Time. Douglas Livingstone. NoP-4; PeSA

It seems a day. Nutting. Wordsworth. NAEL-2; NOBRP; OAEL-2; Poetr; RB

It seems a flower, but not a flower. A Flower. Po Chü-i, *Chinese.* TAL, *tr. by* Robert Payne

It seems a stage. The Gypsy's Window. Denise Levertov. CLPP

It seems a trick of lighting, his legs lost. Legless Boy Climbing In and Out of Chair. Michael Pettit. NAmP90

It seems, for a moment, the river ceases flowing. (LL) Summer near the River. Carolyn Kizer. CoAP; VGW

It seems high time / I challenged you to song-contest! A Dispute between Women. Unknown, Eskimo. STP, tr. by Tom Lowenstein

It seems I have no tears left. They should have fallen. Tears. Edward Thomas. GTBS-P; NAEL-2

It seems I impregnated Marge. Limerick. Unknown. PeLi

It seems like a dream. An Autumn Morning. Unknown. BoTP

It seems like a dream—that sweet wooing of old. Bachelor Hall. Eugene Field. BLPA

It seems no day passes now. A Family Procession. J. P. Clark Bekederemo. HBAPE

It seems no work of man's creative hand. Pedra. John William Burgon. BLPA

It seems now far off and foolish, a memory. Lot Later. Howard Nemerov. HoPM

It seems our days are shaped by conflagration. Fire. Luis J. Rodriguez. UnSA

It Seems That God Bestowed Somehow. Amanda Benjamin Hall. AH

It seems to be a flower, yet not a flower. Tune: "Water Dragon's Chang" After Chang Chi-fu's Lyric on the Willow Catkin. Su Shih, Chinese. SuSp, tr. by James J. Y. Liu

It seems to me I'd like to go. Far from the Madding Crowd. Nixon Waterman. BLPA; FaBoBe

It seems to me I'm resurrected. Leonid Nikolaevich Martynov, Russian. TCRP, tr. by J. R. Rowland

It seems to me I'm watching over walls. Haim Gouri, Hebrew. IP, tr. by Warren Bargad and Stanley F. Chyet

"It seems to me, O King," he said "that a." A Sparrow's Flight. The Venerable Bede. LBC

"It seems to me," said Booker T. Booker T. and W. E. B. Dudley Randall. MoP; NoAM

It seems too enormous just for a man to be. The Highway. W. S. Merwin. PoA

It seems vainglorious and proud. The Conquerors. Phyllis McGinley. PBMP

It seems wrong that out of this bird. A Blackbird Singing. Ronald Stuart Thomas. OBWVE

It semes white and is red. The Sacrament of the Altar. Unknown. NoP-4

It shall suffice that they were breathed, and died for her delight [or breath'd, and dyed, for her delight]. (LL) Follow your saint, follow with accents sweet. Thomas Campion. AAS; EBEV; EnLoPo; HAP; NOBE; NOSC; NoSic; OAEL-1; OBEV; OxAEP-1; PoE

It shines in the garden. The Garden. Mark Strand. ColAP; NoAM

It should have a woman's name. The Lake in Central Park. Jay Wright. GT

It should not have ended with letters. The Swallows of Capistrano. Trish Rucker. CMAP

It sifts from Leaden Sieves. The Snow. Emily Dickinson. ACTP; SoSe-8; WHSW

It singeth low in every heart. The Abiding Love. John White Chadwick. BLPA; FaBoBe

It sinks; and I am ready to depart. (LL) On His Seventy-Fifth Birthday. Walter Savage Landor. AWP; EBEV; EBEvV; FaBoEE; FaPoR; GTBS-P; NOBE; NOBVV; NTP; NoP-4; OAEL-2; OBEV; OBNC; OxAEP-2; PBMP; SAGP; SCGP; TFi; TRP; UV

It sleeps among the thousand hills. The Unnamed Lake. Frederick George Scott. NOBC

It slides into a cloud over Point Lobos. (LL) Phenomena. Robinson Jeffers. NOBA; OxBA

It smiles to see me. Lethargy. Donald Justice. CRP

It snows on this place. Wednesday at North Hatley. Ralph Gustafson. NOBC

It so happens I am sick of being a man. Walking [or Walkin'] Around. Pablo Neruda, Spanish. RaBo; SPE, tr. by Robert Bly

It sometimes happens. Curse of the Cat Woman. Edward Field. WeW-3

It soothes the savage doubts. Apocalypse. D. J. Enright. OBSV

It Sounded. Larry Eigner. FTOS

It sounded as if the Streets were running. Emily Dickinson. NAAL-1; NAAL-3; OxBSP; PBWP

It sounds unconvincing to say "When I was young." In the Winter of My Thirty-eighth Year. W. S. Merwin. NOBA

It speaks in voices varying with the wind. Africa. Adèle Naudé. PeSA

It spreads, the campaign—carried on. Glory. Marianne Moore. NYBP

It stands. Tanka. Kanoko Okamoto, Japanese. MJT, tr. by Makoto Ueda

It Started. Jimmy Santiago Baca. LoL

It started before Christmas. Now our son. The Red Hat. Rachel Hadas. RA

It started. First the salts. The Geyser. Agnes Nemes Nagy, Hungarian. PoSu, tr. by Bruce Berlind

It starts: a white girl in a dark house. Alternatives. Kingsley Amis. OxBC

It starts in the small hours. An interlude. James Merrill. NoAM Fr. Mirabell: Books of Number.

It starts on the Lower East Side. Lower East Side: The George Bernstein Story. Edward Field. OBCoV

It starts, somehow, in the hot damp. Barn Fire. Thomas Lux. CMAP; LCAP-2

It starts with the picture of my grandfather. The Cloud Unfolding. Ernesto Trejo. LTA

It steals the time! To business now. (LL) The Italian in England. Robert Browning. FaBoPV; OBNV

It stepped into my room. Elegy and Flame. Horace Gregory. FYAP

It stoops to labor at the lord's behest—. In Praise of the Broom. Unknown, Vietnamese. AVP, tr. by Huỳnh Sanh Thông

It stops the town we come through. Troop Train. Karl Shapiro. OxBA

It storms in Amherst five days. Winter Bouquet. Lewis Turco. EOEF

It sushes. Cynthia in the Snow. Gwendolyn Brooks. TLR

It swings upon the leafless tree. The Snow-filled Nest. Rose Terry Cooke. OBCA

It takes a fast car. Lost Parents. Lawrence Ferlinghetti. PoM

It takes a heap o' children to make a home that's true. Edgar A. Guest Considers "The Old Woman Who Lived in a Shoe" and the Good Old Verities at the Same Time. Louis Untermeyer. MoAmPo; OBAL Fr. Mother Goose Up-to-Date.

It takes a heap o' livin' in a house t' make it home. Home. E. A. Guest. BLPA; FaBoBe; OBAL; PWR

It takes a long time to forget an iron man. (LL) Washington Monument by Night. Carl Sandburg. CMoP; ImGa

It takes a long time to hear what the sands. The Bones. W. S. Merwin. CoAmPo; LiTM

It takes a mighty fire. H. D. Carberry. CA

It takes all sorts of in- and outdoor schooling. Robert Frost. SoSe-8

It takes awhile, recovering. You confess. For Alexis Christa von Hartmann: Proved Not Guilty. William Stafford. CMAP

It takes faith—this tripping through the mixed blessings. The Wreckage Entrepreneur. Alice Fulton. WWSi

It takes life to love Life. (LL) Lucinda Matlock. Edgar Lee Masters. CMoP; HAP; LiTM; MoAmPo; MoP; NOBA; NoAM; OxBA; PBMP

It takes time, and there are setbacks. A Difficult Adjustment. Lauris Edmond. FaBoWP

It takes time to make. Time to Myself. Paulette Jiles. NOBC

It tells you what you do but never why. Gentleman Aged Five before the Mirror. John Wain. PFE

It took at least a morning. Sandpile Town. Aileen Fisher. CTV

It took generations to mature. Liberace. Jonathan Holden. CMAP

It took the sea to prove a magnitude agreed on. Sensible Qualities. Fred Muratori. BAP-94

It Took TV to Civilize Our Village. Richard Moore. Son Fr. Word from the Hills.

It took 27 years to write this poem. Ruth. Colleen J. McElroy. BlSi

It trails always behind me. Jamaica 1980. Lorna Goodison. GT

It trembled so the wind swept it away. The Poplar Leaf. George Seferis, Greek. PFTM, tr. by George Economou

It tried to get from out the cage. The Cage. James Stephens. OxBTC

It turned out / that the bombs he had thrown. After His Death. Norman MacCaig. CBNP

It turns out / You can kill them. Redwings. James Wright. NNaP; WeT

It Used to Be. Ciaran Carson. See Céilí.

It wants to be somewhere else. Looking at Henry Moore's Elephant Skull Etchings in Jerusalem during the War. Shirley Kaufman. LCAP-2

It was 1918 and Louis and Sidney Bechet were walking. The Funky Butt Legacy Song (An Epic in Progress). Kofi Natambu. MoNo

It was a bad sign I was born under. The Judas Goat. Susan Musgrave. NOBC

It was a bash! I Heard the Byrd. Oliver Lagrone. SeSe

It was a beauty that I saw. A Vision of Beauty. Ben Jonson. BeJo; NOSC Fr. The New Inn.

It was a bird of Paradise. In London Town. Mary Elizabeth Coleridge. VWP

It was a blue fly with wings of pomegranate gold. Blue Fly. Joaquim Maria Machado de Assis, Portuguese. TTY, tr. by Frances Ellen Buckland

It was a Borgia-pot, he told me. The Curiosity-Shop. Peter Redgrove. OxBC

It was a bow-legged conductor of a Twopenny Bus. (LL) Polly Perkins. *Unknown.* OBCoV; OxBoLi; PeLV

It was a bowl of roses. A Bowl of Roses. William Ernest Henley. MoBrPo

It was a bright and cheerful afternoon. Summer and Winter. Shelley. OxAEP-2; SCGP

It was a bright day and all the trees were still. Silence. Walter James Turner. MoBrPo

It was a chilly winter's night. A Winter Night. William Barnes. NOBE; OBNC

It was a chosen plot of fertile land. Edmund Spenser. *See* The Legend of the Knight of the Red Crosse, or of Holinesse.

It was a close, warm, breezeless summer night. Wordsworth. PoEL-4 *Fr.* Conclusion: "In one of those excursions (may they ne'er)." OAEL-2; OBNC *Fr.* The Prelude; Growth of a Poet's Mind [1850 vers.]

It was a damp mild day of clinging mists that we met. Meeting at a Salesyard. John Ennis. CIP-2

It was a dark, dank, dreadful night. The Malfeasance. Alan Bold. OBSP

It was a day peculiar to this piece of the planet. Scotland. Alastair Reid. FaBoTC

It was a dim October day. Thomas Caulfield Irwin. BIrV *Fr.* Swift.

It was a dismal and a fearful night. Abraham Cowley. BeJo; NOBE; OxAEP-1 *Fr.* On the Death of Mr. William Hervey [*or* Harvey]. EBEV; OBEV; SeCP

It was a dismal day when chilling rain. The Greater Gift. Margaret E. Bruner. PoToHe

It was a distant winter. On the edge of the flatlands. On Guard. Meir Wieseltier, *Hebrew.* IP, *tr. by* Warren Bargad *and* Stanley F. Chyet

It was a dreadful day when late I passed. Sonnet VII. Written on Skiddaw, during a Tempest. John Wilson. Ro

It was a feather of paint. An Urban Guerrilla. Allen Curnow. PeNZ *Fr.* More Assassinato

It was a' for our rightfu' king. Farewell, A [*or* The]. Robert Burns. CH; IIP; OBEV; PoEL-4

It was a friar of orders gray [*or* grey]. The Friar of Orders Gray. *Unknown.* NOEC

It was a funky deal. Etheridge Knight. BPo; NBV; PoBA

It was a glorious May morning. Victor Garibaldi. Melvin B. Tolson. GT

It was a good word once, a little sparkler. Protest Poem. Vernon Scannell. OBCoV

It was a goodly co. E. E. Cummings. LiTM

It was a graveyard scene. The crescent moon. Great Unaffected Vampires and the Moon. Stevie Smith. NoAM

It was a hand. God looked at it. The Hand. Ronald Stuart Thomas. NOCV; OxBC

It was a hard thing to undo this knot. Gerard Manley Hopkins. NOBVV

It was a heartfelt game, when it began. Portrait. Judith Wright. OxBSP; SoSe-8

It was a house of female habitation. A House of Mercy. Stevie Smith. FaBoWP

It was a kind and northern face. Praise for an Urn. Hart Crane. AWP; CMoP; HAP; LiTM; MeMAP; MoAmPo; NOBA; NoAM; OxBA; WeW-3

It was a Knight in Scotland borne. The Fair Flower of Northumberland. *Unknown.* ESPB; OxBB

It was a lady of the north she lov'd a gentleman. Room for a Jovial Tinker: Old Brass to Mend. *Unknown.* OxBB

It was a little captive cat. The Singing Cat. Stevie Smith. OxBTC; PC

It was a long time ago. As I Grew Older. Langston Hughes. AmPP; ColAP

It Was a Long Time Before. Leslie Marmon Silko. NoAM

It was a lovely night. William Robert Rodgers. PNI *Fr.* Resurrection: An Easter Sequence.

It was a lover and his lass. Song. Shakespeare. APAD; AWP; CBLP; CH; CTC; EBEvV; GBL; GTBS-P; ImPo; InPS-3; NAEL-1; NOBE; NoSic; OBEV; OxAEP-1; RB; SCGP; TFi; TTTS *Fr.* As You Like It.

It was a Maine lobster town. Water. Robert Lowell. AFr; CMoP; HeIP-4; LCAP-2; NOBA; NoP-4; PoE

It was a melancholy, a kind of sadness. Evocation. Nichita Stanescu, *Romanian.* CEEP, *tr. by* Irina Livezeanu

It was a mighty monarch's child. Mir träumte von einem Königskind. Heinrich Heine, *German.* AWP, *tr. by* Richard Garnett

It was a miniature country once. Japan. Anthony Hecht. LiTM

It was a mother and a maid. The Milk White Doe. *Unknown, French.* AWP, *tr. by* Andrew Lang

It was a navy boy, so prim, so trim. Wilfred Owen. NSI

It was a night in winter. Clive Sansom. PChr *Fr.* The Witnesses.

It was a night of early spring. Wisdom. Sara Teasdale. MoAmPo

It was a night when the planets. Perspective Lovesong. "Ern Malley." BMAP

It was a Phrygian king. Telestes, *Greek.* InMo, *tr. by* Sam Hamill

It was a Phrygian, Pelops. Telestes, *Greek.* InMo, *tr. by* Sam Hamill

It was a place where apples sprouted teeth. Childhood. Chitra Divakaruni. OpBo

It was a poignant moment. Howl, Howl. Christopher Reid. OBCoV

It was a quiet way—. Emily Dickinson. ITG; NCAP

It was a rainbow impossibly. Prisms. Philip Dacey. Poetsp

It was a real well, real. Old Wives' Tales. Constance Urdang. PBCAP

It was a rich merchant man. The Merchant and the Fidler's Wife. *Unknown.* OxBB

It was a summer [*or* summer's] evening. The Battle of Blenheim. Robert Southey. CABP; FaBoPV; FaPoR; GTBS-P; OBNC; OBWP; OxAEP-2; PBMP; PoLF; Ro; TFi; UV

It was a summer evening. Sentences While Remembering Hiraethog. T. Glynne Davies, *Welsh.* OBWVE, *tr. by* R. Gerallt Jones

It was a summer evening in an Alabama city. Prelude. René Depestre. NegPo, *tr. by* Ellen Conroy Kennedy *Fr.* Epiphanies of the Voodoo Gods.

It was a testimony. Gregory's House. David Huddle. PBCAP

It was a tortoise aspiring to fly. Improvisations on Aesop. Anthony Hecht. OBAL

It was a trance: thieves, clowns, and the blind girl. Clamor. Anne Lauterbach. PmAP

It was a violent time. Wheels, racks, and fires. A Mirror for Poets. Thom Gunn. LiTM

It was a voice of another man. Tadeusz Rózewicz. *See* In the Midst of Life.

It was a warm September night. Gettin' Straight. Mcavoy Layne. CDa

It was a wasp or an imprudent bee. The Wasp. Daryl Hine. APo; NYBP

It was a way of punishing the house, setting it a blaze. Interior at Petworth: From Turner. Rosanna Warren. NoAM

It was a winter's morning. Harry Graham. UV *Fr.* The Battue of Berlin.

It was about the deep of night. A Ballad of Christmas. Walter De la Mare. OBCP

It was about the Martinmas time. Barbara Allan. *Unknown.* EnSB

It was after vespers one evening. Low Church. Stanley J. Sharpless. NBLV; OBCoV; PeLV

It was afternoon or later. Jaroslav Seifert. EC2

It was afterwards. Another Love Affair/Another Poem. E. Ethelbert Miller. ISC

It was all different; that, at least, seemed sure. Mutability. W. D. Snodgrass. DiPo

It was all like a childhood picture. Cuckoo. Robert Desnos, *French.* PFTM, *tr. by* Armand Schwerner

It was all so different from what she'd expected. At Thirty-three. Hans Magnus Enzensberger, *German.* VCWP, *tr. by the author* and Michael Hamburger

It Was All Very Tidy. Robert Graves. OxBTC; RB

It was almost Christmas and the pink lights of the avenue. At a Motel. Brenda Hillman. PuP-14

"It was an accident." (LL) The Dolls. W. B. Yeats. CMoP; NoAM; PoE

It was an August evening and, in snowy garments clad. Municipal. Rudyard Kipling. BXAP

It was an awful day. Troubles. Bozhidar Bozhilov, *Bulgarian.* CEEP, *tr. by* Jascha Kessler *and* Aleksandar Shurbanov

It was an evening in November. The Pig. *Unknown.* FaBoEE; OBCoV

It was an hill placed in an open plain. The Dance of the Graces. Edmund Spenser. *Fr.* Wood Of Error. AEP

It was an icy day. Complete Destruction. William Carlos Williams. SAmP

It was an old, old, old, old lady. One, Two, Three. Henry Cuyler Bunner. PoLF

It was announced in the *Daily Times*, the *New Nigerian.* Launching Our Community Developement Fund. Tanure Ojaide. HBAPE

It was April in the year Kuei-mao. The Lament of the Lady of Ch'in. Wei Chuang, *Chinese.* SuSp, *tr. by* Robin D. S. Yates

It was as if. Spring Song. Peter Fallon. CIP-2; PBCIP

It was as if the devil of evil had got. García Lorca. Louis Dudek. MoCV; NOBC

It was as though it had begun to rain lightly. The Day the Perfect Speakers Left. Leonard Nathan. WeT

It was at dinner as they sat. The Laird of Wariston. *Unknown.* ESPB

It was at the very date to which we have come. An Anniversary. Thomas Hardy. OxBTC

It was august, i was inner city. Friendly Town #1. Safiya Henderson-Holmes. UnSA

It was autumn. the day insistent. A Poem for my Most Intelligent 10:30 AM Class/Fall 1985. Sonia Sanchez. NMM-2

It Was Beginning Winter. Theodore Roethke. NAAL-2 *Fr.* The Lost Son. HAP; HCAP; LiTM; VGW

It was better when we were. For My Mother. Louise Glück. UnPo

It was born to become the imperial capital. Leningrad. "Naum Korzhavin," *Russian*. TCRP, *tr. by* Albert C. Todd

It was boss cook's fault. He left. The Tip. Belle Waring. PBCAP

It was but a little thing. The Peace-Offering. Thomas Hardy. OxBSP

It was by such a state of logical perpendiculars. Thinking the Alps. Michael Davidson. PmAP

It was cold, and all they gave him to wear. Back in the States. Louis Simpson. PBCV

It was cold then in the cautious hours. Curtain. Lance Henson. VoR

It was dark and frosty, pain congealed into ice. Deportation. "M. B.," *Polish*. TrJP, *tr. by* A. Glanz-Leyeles

It was deep April, and the morn. Prologue. "Michael Field." CPO; VWP

It was distant, as usual, drops still on the windowpane. A Poem Too Late. Natan Zach, *Hebrew*. IP, *tr. by* Warren Bargad *and* Stanley F. Chyet

It was down in old Joe's barroom. Those Gambler's Blues. *Unknown*. AS

It was early, early in the spring. The Croppy Boy. *Unknown*. AmFP; NOIV; OxBoLi

It was early, early one mornin'. Stagolee. *Unknown*. TTY

It was early in the morning. Goodhousekeeping #17. Safiya Henderson-Holmes. ISC

It was early in the season, the fall of 'sixty-three. Michigan-I-O. *Unknown*. AmFP

It was early last December. The Drunkard and the Pig. *Unknown*. OBAL

It was early Monday morning Willie Leonard arose. Willie Leonard; or, The Lake of Cold Finn. *Unknown*. AmFP

It was early Saturday, dawn. Meat. Michael Van Walleghen. NAmP90

It was early Sunday mornin. Stagolee. *Unknown*. OxBoLi; TTY

It was Easter as I walked in the public gardens. 1929. W. H. Auden. OxAEP-2

It was easy. How I Escaped from the Labyrinth. Philip Dacey. CMAP

It was easy enough. Circe. Hilda Doolittle. PoRA

It was $8,000 with a GI loan. Floor Plans. Maxine Scates. PBCAP

It was everything to me to think well of one man. Euripides. *Fr.* Medea. NAWM-1; OxBM

It was exactly eleven. Pawiak 1943. Jerzy Ficowski, *Polish*. PoSu, *tr. by* Frank J. Corliss, Jr., *and* Grazyna Sandel

It was far in the night and the bairnies grat. Gerry Hamill. BXAP

It was far in the sameness of the wood. The Demiurge's Laugh. Robert Frost. OxBA

It was fever that made the world. Jim Powell. NIP-4

It was for you that the mountains shook at Sinai. Epitaph. *Unknown*. TrJP

It was for your sake, was it not. Holy Russia. Maksimilian Aleksandrovich Voloshin, *Russian*. TCRP, *tr. by* Bernard Meares

It was general conflagration. (LL) The Devil's Thoughts. Coleridge. CBNP; OBSV; OxBoLi; PeLV

It was good for the virgin mary. Poem for Unwed Mothers. Nikki Giovanni. OBAL

It was high summer. Gran's Green Parrot. Wes Magee. PeP

It was his Mid-Western sensibilities which first. Tornado Warning. Georgia Sine. CMAP

It was his story. It would always be his story. In Memory of the Unknown Poet, Robert Boardman Vaughn. Donald Justice. DiPo; NoAM

It was hot. A size too large. High Holy Days. Jane Shore. NoP-4

It was iMpossible. 25 Mesostics Re and Not Re Mark Tobey. John Cage. PmAP

It was impossible for one to read. Holy Was Demeter Walking th' Corn Furrow. Edward Sanders. PoM

It was in Abomey that I felt. Dahomey. Audre Lorde. NAAL-2

It was in an empty lot. How I Learned English. Gregory Djanikian. CMAP; UnSA

It was in and about the Martinmas time. Bonny Barbara Allan ("In Scarlet Town where I was born"). *Unknown*. AWP; BoLoP; CH; ESPB; HeIP-4; InPK-6; NAEL-1; OxBB

It was in and about the Martinmas time. *Unknown*. *See* Barbara Allan ("It was about the Martinmas time").

It was in autumn that I met. A Picture. Dora Greenwell. EBVV

It was in June the eight and thirtieth day. John Taylor. CBNP; NOSC *Fr.* Sir Gregory Nonsense's News from No Place.

It was in October, a favorite season. Elegy for a Nature Poet. Howard Nemerov. HoPM

It was in October the woe began. The Fire of Frendraught. *Unknown*. ESPB

It was in the city of Expert. The Oxford Girl; or, Expert Town. *Unknown*. AmFP

It was in the lovely month of May. The Troubled Soldier. *Unknown*. AS

It was in the merry month of May. The Trail to Mexico. *Unknown*. AS

It was in the month of January the hills. Month of January. Frankie Armstrong. BrRo

It was in the Spring of 1825. Noel Petty. UV

It was in the year of eighteen hundred and sixty-one. Stackalee. *Unknown, comp. by* Onah L. Spencer. CrDW

It was in winter. Steeples, spires. The Fortunate Traveller. Derek Walcott. NoAM

It was insane. I thought it myself. The winter. The First Reader Santee Training School, 1873. Diane Glancy. LTA

It was intill a pleasant time. The Earl of Mar's Daughter. *Unknown*. CH; ESPB

It was Ips, Gips, and Johnson, as I've heard many say. The Three Butchers. *Unknown*. PeVV

It was just before the last fierce charge, two soldiers drew a-rein. The Last Fierce Charge. *Unknown*. AmFP

It was Landor who first said. "Hugh MacDiarmid." FaBoPV *Fr.* In Memoriam James Joyce.

It was last year. Fox Glove Song. Christina Beer. PeNZ

It was late in the night when the Squire came home. The Gipsy Laddie. *Unknown*. FaBoCh; OxBoLi

It was late last night when my lord came home. Cyril Connolly. OBCoV *Fr.* Where Engels Fears to Tread.

It was late last night when my lord come home. The Gypsy Davy. *Unknown*. AmFP

It was late, we. Man and Wife. Mitchell Goodman. SAGP; VGW

It was like a church to me. The Moor. Ronald Stuart Thomas. OBWVE

It was like a stream. Mahadevi, *Kannada*. WPoS, *tr. by* A. K. Ramanujan

It was like silver, like an ending. Testimonies. Yehuda Amichai, *Hebrew*. IP, *tr. by* Warren Bargad *and* Stanley F. Chyet

It was like the moment when a bird decides not to eat from your hand. Part of Eve's Discussion. Marie Howe. NAmP90

It was long since she could sleep in that wooden home of hers. Ballad of the Wondrous Moment. Pavel Grigoryevich Antokolsky, *Russian*. TCRP, *tr. by* Bernard Meares

It was Mabbie without the grammar school gates. The Ballad of Chocolate Mabbie. Gwendolyn Brooks. CAPP-1 *Fr.* A Street in Bronzeville. BPo; BlSi; FaBoWP

It was many and many a year ago. Annabel Lee. Edgar Allan Poe. APN-1; AWP; AiP; AmPP; BLPA; CH; ChAP; ColAP; EBEvV; GEA; GLoP; HeIP-4; ImPo; MeMAP; NAAL-1; NAAL-3; NCAP; NOBA; NoP-4; OBCA; OBSP; OxBA; PAR; PoPoPo; TAP; TFi

It was many and many a year ago. A Poe-'em of Passion. Charles Fletcher Lummis. BXAP

It was many and many a year ago. Samuel Brown. Phoebe Cary. APN-2; OBAL

It was Murupaenga who brought me here. Slave Girl's Song. *Unknown, Maori*. PeNZ, *tr. by* Margaret Orbell

It was my bridal night I remember. I Remember. Stevie Smith. BoLoP; BoWoP; FaBoWP; InPK-6; OxBC

It was my choice, it was no chance. Sir Thomas Wyatt. SiPS

It was my fate to help Billy Redanz learn how to read. The Story of My Life. Liz Rosenberg. PBCAP

It was my fifth year to heaven. Christopher Robin Changes Guard with Dylan Thomas. Bill Greenwell. UV

It was my thirtieth year to heaven. Poem in October. Dylan Thomas. EBEvV; ImPo; NAEL-2; NoAM; OxAEP-2; PoA; PoRA; RB; SoSe-8; UV

IT was near a thicky shade. The Description of the Shepherd and His Wife. Robert Greene. NoSic

It was near evening, the room was cold. The Oath. Allen Tate. FaBoMo; LiTM; OxBA; VGW

It was near midnight when I entered. Ivan Alekseievich Bunin, *Russian*. TCRP, *tr. by* Simon Franklin

It was near the Coliseum, RKO, / in the Bronx. Laughing Gas. Ruth Whitman. UnSA

It was nearly eleven. Words Read by Lightning. Elaine Equi. WWSi

It was night-time! God, the Father Good. What the Devil Said. James Stephens. CMoP

It was 1912 when the awful news got around. Shine and the Titanic. *Unknown*. CrDW; NAAAL

It was no costume jewellery I sent. With a Gift of Rings. Robert Graves. GBL

It was no vast dynastic fate. A Father's Death. John Hewitt. PNI

It was not a heart, beating. Night Shift. Sylvia Plath. AFr

It was not a very formal affair but. A Chinese Banquet. Kitty Tsui. CPO; GLP

It was not Death, for I stood up. Emily Dickinson. APN-2; MeMAP; NAAL-1; NAAL-3; NOBA; PAR; SAmP

It was not dying: everybody died. Losses. Randall Jarrell. HCAP; LCAP-2; LiTM; OxBA; PoA; SAGP; TAP; UnPo

It was not I who began it. Eve to Her Daughters. Judith Wright. NALW; NoP-4

It was not in their power to stop what the rabble they designed. (LL) The Boyne Water. *Unknown.* FaPoR; IIP; NOIV

It was not like your great and gracious ways. Departure. Coventry Patmore. NOBE; OBEV; OBNC *Fr.* The Unknown Eros.

It was not long e're he perceiv'd the skies. Michael Drayton. PoEL-2 *Fr.* The Moone-Calfe.

It was not meant for human eyes. The Combat. Edwin Muir. CMoP; FaBoTC; MoBrPo; NOBE

It was not our duty to question but to guard. Bread and a Pension. Louis Johnson. PeNZ

It was not that I lost direction. Martha Sansom. ECWP

It Was Not You. André Spire, *French.* TrJP, *tr.* by Jethro Bithell

It was nothing more than a Neapolitan Christmas creche. The light. The Horrible Today. Max Jacob, *French.* AF, *tr.* by Ron Padgett

It was October. It was the Depression. Money. What Happened. Robert Penn Warren. *Fr.* Tale of Time. LCAP-2

It was on a cold winter's night. When Poor Mary Came Wandering Home. *Unknown.* AS

It was on a May, on a midsummer's day. Sir Hugh; or, The Jew's Daughter. *Unknown.* AmFP; ESPB

It was on a Wednesday night, the moon was shining bright. Jesse James. *Unknown.* AS; FaBoBe; UnPo

It was on an evning sae saft and sae clear. The Broom of Cowdenknows. *Unknown.* ESPB

It was on one Monday morning, / All in the month of May. Lisbon. *Unknown.* AmFP

It was on one Monday morning just about one o'clock. The *Titanic.* *Unknown.* AmFP

It was on the twenty-first day of December. Ella Speed. *Unknown.* AmFP

It was one Sunday morning of June the eighth day. Henry K. Sawyer. *Unknown.* AmFP

It was only a small place and they had cheered us too much. St. Aubin d'Aubigne. Paul Dehn. OBWP

It was only a tiny seed. Only a Little Thing. M. P. Handy. PoToHe

It was only important. The Moss of His Skin. Anne Sexton. CoAP; NALW; SAGP

It was over Target Berlin the flak shot up our plane. World War II. Edward Field. GLP

It was plain to see the sense of being a woman. The Inflammable Woman. James Keir Baxter. OxBC

It was planted early. Boundary. A. L. Hendriks. PBCV

It was pneumonia. Lament of the Virtues and Verses on Account of the Death of Don Guido. Antonio Machado Ruiz, *Spanish.* OBVE, *tr.* by Charles Tomlinson *and* Henry Gifford

It was proper for them, awaking in ordered houses. Apology. Anthony Cronin. CIP-2

It was quiet. The yardman could see. The Accordionist. Vasily Vasilevich Kazin, *Russian.* TCRP, *tr.* by Daniel Weissbort

It was quite a sight for a boy from Tennessee. A Nun in Ninh Hoa. Jan Barry. CDa

It was quite simple. Lucifer Broods. D. J. Enright. OxBoV

It was roses, roses, all the way. The Patriot [An Old Story]. Robert Browning. FHYEP; PBMP

It was said at the / flirting creekwater's birth. To an Imaginary Father. Wendy Rose. CDW

It was shattered. The Battle of Maldon. *Unknown, Anglo-Saxon.* ASW; OBWP, *tr.* by Kevin Crossley-Holland

It was shattered. *Unknown. See* The Battle of Maldon.

It was Sir Christopher Gardiner. The Rhyme of Sir Christopher. Henry Wadsworth Longfellow. NCAP

It was six men of [H]industan. The Blind Men and the Elephant. John Godfrey Saxe. BLPA; BoTP; CTV; FaBoBe; OBCA; OTCP; PoToHe

It was something to see that their white was different. Holiday in Reality. Wallace Stevens. OxBA

It was spring, saturday. To Hell and Back, with Cake. Safiya Henderson-Holmes. UnSA

It was still the fifth / of February, 1918. Elizabeth Bishop. *See* In the Waiting Room.

It was sudden. The Sea Fog. Josephine Jacobsen. NYBP

It was summer. Summer or Its Ending. Yehuda Amichai, *Hebrew.* PoSu, *tr.* by Dennis Silk

It was Sunday morning, I had the *New York Times.* First Love. Sharon Olds. FYAP

It was supposed to be Arts & Crafts for a week. At the Smithville Methodist Church. Stephen Dunn. NAmP90

It was taken some time ago. This Is a Photograph of Me. Margaret Atwood. NALW; NoAM; NoP-4; Poetr

It was the arrival of the kings. The Adoration of the Magi. Christopher Pilling. OBCP

It was the Bastot Maulion. Orthone. Philip Pendleton Cooke. APN-1

It was the dead who groaned within! (LL) The Sleeper. Edgar Allan Poe. AmPP; MeMAP; NAAL-1; NAAL-3; NCAP; NOBA; OxBA; PAR; PoEL-4; TAP

It was the departure, the sun was risen. Farewell Voyaging World! Conrad Potter Aiken. NYBP

It was the dingiest bird / you ever saw. Robin Redbreast. Stanley Kunitz. AFr; NoP-4

It was the first gift he ever gave her. The Black Lace Fan My Mother Gave Me. Eavan Boland. BiHa

It was the frog in the well. The Marriage of the Frog and the Mouse. *Unknown.* EBEV

It was the frosty early hours when finally. The Weakness. Bernard O'Donoghue. NoP-4

It was the garden of the golden apples. The Long Garden. Patrick Kavanagh. OBGa

It was the generosity of delight. Love's Anniversaries. Maurice Lindsay. OxBM

It was the hole for looking in. It All Comes Together Outside the Restroom in Hogansville. James Seay. MT

It Was the Last of the Parades. Louis Simpson. NYBP

It was the month of May. Far down the Beautiful River. Henry Wadsworth Longfellow. *Fr.* Part the Second. *Fr.* Evangeline, a Tale of Acadie.

It was the morning of January 10, in the seventh year of Bonzo. Third Dungeness Spit Apocalypse. Nelson Bentley. PuP-16

It was the morning of that blessed day. Petrarch. NAWM-1 *Fr.* Sonnets to Laura.

It was the morning of the first of May. *Unknown. Fr.* Popular Songs of Tuscany. AWP, *tr.* by John Addington Symonds

It was the Rainbow gave thee birth. The Kingfisher. W. H. Davies. NOBE; OBEV; OBWVE

It was the rustle of nurses that brought him back. The Prisoner of Camau. Henry Hart. BAP-96

It was the schooner *Hesperus.* The Wreck of the *Hesperus.* Henry Wadsworth Longfellow. APN-1; BLPA; CTV; EBEvV; EBNV; FaBoBe; OBCA; OBNV; PAR

It was the season, when through all the land. Birds of Killingworth, The (The Poet's Tale). Henry Wadsworth Longfellow. MeMAP; OxBA *Fr.* Tales of a Wayside Inn.

It was the Southern drifting over the flats on a hundred low trestles. (Recent Past, The). C. S. Giscombe. GT

It was the stage-driver's story, as he stood with his back to the wheelers. The Stage-Driver's Story. Bret Harte. EBNV

It was the *Stately Southerner,* that carried the Stripes and Stars. The *Stately Southerner. Unknown.* AmFP

It Was the Time. Joachim Du Bellay, *French.* Son, *tr.* by Spenser

It Was the Time of Roses. Thomas Hood. *See* Ballad: Time of Roses.

It was the time of year. A Prehistoric Camp. Andrew Young. FaBoTC

It was the time when, granted from the gods. Virgil. *Fr.* The Second Book of Virgil's *Aeneid.* SiPS, *tr.* by Henry Howard, Earl of Surrey *Fr.* The Aeneid [*or* Eneados, *Aeneis*].

It was the time when lilies blow. Lady Clare. Tennyson. PBMP

It was the time, when rest, soft sliding downe. Joachim Du Bellay. AWP; Son *Fr.* The Visions of Bellay.

It was the virgin Zennora, who dwelt. John Heath-Stubbs. *Fr.* Artorius. EBEV

It was the west wind caught her up, as. The Ring of. Charles Olson. NOBA; VGW

It was the wind. Autumn Evening. George Anthony. SPE

It was the winter I had to get away. Men Talk. Stephen P. Dunn. NIP-4

It was the winter wild[e]. Hymn on the Morning of Christ's Nativity. Milton. NAEL-1; NOBE; OBEV *Fr.* On the Morning of Christ's Nativity. MeLP; NOCV; NoP-4; PBRV; PoEL-3; SCGP

It was the [*or* a] worthy Lord of Lorn [*or* Learne]. The Lord of Lorn and the False [*or* Fals] Steward. *Unknown.* ESPB; OxBB

It was the year the Icondic. Ballad of the Icondic. John Ciardi. OBAL

It was then night, the sound[e] and quiet sleep [*or* slepe]. The Night-Piece. Virgil. PoEL-1, *tr.* by Henry Howard, Earl of Surrey *Fr.* The Aeneid [*or* Eneados, *Aeneis*].

It was then that destiny decided to take me by the hand. Destiny. Maria Luisa Spaziani, *Italian.* NeIt, *tr.* by Beverly Allen

It was three slim does and a ten-tined buck in the bracken lay. The Revenge of Hamish. Sidney Lanier. APN-2; EBNV; NCAP; PoEL-5

It was too lonely for her there. The Impulse. Robert Frost. HoPM; RaBo *Fr.* The Hill Wife. CMoP; HAP; InPS-3; LiTM; NoP-4; RACG

It was too long ago—that Company which we served with. To One Who Was with Me in the War. Siegfried Sassoon. NSI

It was up there. An Accident. Frank A. Cross Jr. CDa

It was upon a Cristemesse night. The Dancers of Colbek. Robert Mannyng. PoE *Fr.* Handling Sin.

It was upon a Lammas night. Song. Robert Burns. BoLoP; NOBRP; OxBS; PeLV

It was upon a Shere [*or* Scere] Thorsday that vre [*or* oure] Loverd [*or* Lord] aros. Judas. *Unknown.* MiEL; PoE

It was upon the twilight of that day. Samuel Daniel. OBWP *Fr.* The Civil Wars.

It was war and leprosy, men dying in the town. Memory. Ion Caraion, *Romanian.* CEEP, *tr. by* Marguerite Dorian *and* Elliott B. Urdang

It was water I was trying to think of all the time. Appoggiatura. Donald Jeffrey Hayes. PoBA

It was, we thought, blue. Goodbye to the Bay of Naples. Wendy Mulford. NBrP

It was, when scarce had rang the morning bells. An Almanack for the Year of Our Lord, 1657. Samuel Bradstreet. SCAP

It was when we were living. When My Grandmother Said "Pussy." Carole Bernstein. UnSA

It was wild. Assassination. Don L. Lee. PoBA

It was wild. Assassination. Haki R. Madhubuti. GT

It Was Winter. Czeslaw Milosz. PaTW

It was winter. Boris Pasternak. *See* Christmas Star.

It was winter, / there was snow. We Were Three. Claribel Alegría, *Spanish.* AF, *tr. by* Carolyn Forché

"It Was Wrong to Do This" Said the Angel. Stephen Crane. MeMAP *Fr.* The Black Riders [and Other Lines].

It was years ago, at the end of Deborah's Song. His Mother. Haim Gouri, *Hebrew.* IP, *tr. by* Warren Bargad *and* Stanley F. Chyet

It was yesterday morning. Little Old Letter. Langston Hughes. SAmP

It was you: / I could have crawled. Watching Salmon Jump. Simon J. Ortiz. CDW

It was your vision of the pilot. Adrienne Rich. *Fr.* Twenty-one Love Poems. GLP

It wasn't by chance that Marpessa preferred Idas over Apollo. Marpessa's Choice. Yannis Ritsos, *Greek.* VCWP, *tr. by* Edmund Keeley

It wasn't easy, inventing the wheel. Poem for Men Only. Tony Hoagland. NAmP90

It wasn't Ernest; it wasn't Scott. Song for the Squeeze-Box. Theodore Roethke. NBLV

It wasn't in my time, or so I suppose. Responses to Montale. Brian Turner. PeNZ

It wasn't our battalion, but we lay alongside it. Sergeant-Major Money. Robert Graves. OBWP

It wasn't that she didn't recognize him in the light from the [hearth; it wasn't]. Penelope's Despair. Yannis Ritsos, *Greek.* GrIP; VCWP, *tr. by* Edmund Keeley

It wasn't the money or their silly. Delilah. Ellen Bryant Voigt. CrSp

It well bespeaks a man beheaded, quite. Division of an Estate. George Moses Horton. NAAAL

It went many years. The Lockless Door. Robert Frost. NOBA

It were best to sleep. November 1956. Evan Jones. PBCV

It were my soul's desire. The Soul's Desire. *Unknown, Irish.* TIRV, *tr. by* Eleanor Hull

It wes upon a Shere [*or* Scere] Thorsday that ure [*or* oure] Louerd [*or* Lord] aros. *Unknown.* MiEL

It will be all the same in a hundred years. In a Hundred Years. Elizabeth Doten. BLPA

It will be as it is in this life, the same room. Strophes. O. V. de L. Milosz, *French.* NNPT, *tr. by* Ezra Pound

It will be February there. The Afterlife. Ted Kooser. CMAP

It will be looked for, book[e], when some but see. To My Book. Ben Jonson. BeJo; FaBoVe; NAEL-1

It will be strange. When the Vacation Is Over for Good. Mark Strand. NYBP

It will do. It's not. John Ashbery. BAP-93 *Fr.* Baked Alaska. BAP-93

It will not be able to help us. (LL) The New Poem. Charles Wright. HCAP; WeT

It will not be heard. Tanka. Mori Ōgai, *Japanese.* MJT, *tr. by* Makoto Ueda

"It will not be long, love, till our wedding day." (LL) She Moved through the Fair. Padraic Colum. BIrV; NOIV

It will not be simple, it will not be long. Final Notations. Adrienne Rich. NMM-2

It will not hurt me when I am old. Moonlight. Sara Teasdale. APAD; VGW

It will not resemble the sea. The New Poem. Charles Wright. HCAP; WeT

It will not shine again. Emily Jane Brontë. NOBVV

It will rain tonight. New Life. Joseph E. Kariuki. TTY

It will seem to me / that Stalin still lives in the mausoleum. Yevtushenko. *See* The Heirs of Stalin.

It will undo him. Wallace Stevens. *See* The Plot Against the Giant.

"It would be / a mercy if." Phone Call to Rutherford. Paul Blackburn. PoM

It would be Eddie. The Treacherous Death of Jesse James. Ann Carrel. CMAP

It would be nice to simply melt away. Leavings. Gerard Benson. BXAP

It would be ordinary enough to live. After Christopher Wood. John James. NBrP

It would be painful to interfere. Memo. Charles G. Ballard. VoR

It would be summer, Saturday—the only day. Witness. Susan Wood. EC2

It would be very pleasant to die with a wolf woman. Yoldugu, *Tlingit Indian.* STP, *tr. by* James Koller

It would be wrong for us. It is not right. Sappho, *Greek.* BoWoP, *tr. by* Willis Barnstone

It would have been better than this. (LL) Waiting for Icarus. Muriel Rukeyser. LCAP-2; NNaP

It would have been better that I slept. Akazome Emon, *Japanese.* WPJ, *tr. by* Kenneth Rexroth *and* Ikuko Atsumi

It would have been, I think, summer—it would have been August, I think. Mississippi 1955 Confessional. Terry Hummer. NAmP90

It would have starved a Gnat. Emily Dickinson. NCAP

It would melt. Basho. ChAP

It would never be Common—more—I said. Emily Dickinson. APN-2

It woz in April nineteen eighty-wan. Great Insohreckshan, Di. Linton Kwesi Johnson. FaBoPV

It wuz one day, I believe in May, when old Si Hubbard to me did say. Si Hubbard. *Unknown.* AS

Italia, Io Ti Saluto! Christina Rossetti. VWP; WPE

Italia! Oh Italia! thou who hast. Italy. Vincenzo da Filicaia, *Italian.* AWP, *tr. by* Byron

Italian. In Answer to Their Questions. Giovanna (Janet) Capone. UnSA

Italian, The. Mikhail Arkadyevich Svetlov, *Russian.* TCRP, *tr. by* Daniel Weissbort

Italian dust covers a Libyan. Antipater of Thessalonica, *Greek.* GrAn, *tr. by* Alistair Elliot

Italian Garden, The. William Carlos Williams. OBGa

Italian in England, The. Robert Browning. FaBoPV; OBNV

Italian Music in Dakota. Walt Whitman. APN-1

Italian soldier shook my hand, The. George Orwell. OBWP; OxAEP-2

Italic. Roger McGough. OBCoV

Italics. Anselm Hollo. PmAP

Italy. Byron. *See* Italy versus England.

Italy. Vincenzo da Filicaia, *Italian.* AWP, *tr. by* Byron

Italy. Edward Coote Pinkney. APN-1

Italy. Samuel Rogers. OBNC
   "He is now at rest." EPCY

Italy. Giuseppe Ungaretti, *Italian.* PeFWW, *tr. by* David McDuff *and* Jon Silkin

Italy, my Italy? Robert Browning. *Fr.* De Gustibus. FHYEP; InPS-3; SCGP

Italy of the South. Robert Browning. *Fr.* De Gustibus. FHYEP; InPS-3; SCGP

Italy versus England. Byron. NOBE *Fr.* Beppo; a Venetian Story. NOBL; OBNV; OBSV

Itanami. *Unknown.* PBCV

Itch, The. K. Ayyappa Paniker, *Malayalam.* OMIP, *tr. by* K. Ayyappa Paniker

Itchin, when I behold thy banks again. To the River Itchin, near Winton. William Lisle Bowles. OAEL-2; Ro

Ité. Ezra Pound. HAP; MoAmPo

Item. E. E. Cummings. MoAmPo

Ithaca last night, Syracuse at noon, Cedar Rapids tonight. Seeing Auden Off. Philip Booth. PoA

Ithaca: The Palace at Four A.M. Richard Howard.
   Last Words. DiPo

Ithaka. Constantine P. Cavafy, *Greek.* GrIP, *tr. by* Edmund Keeley *and* Philip Sherrard

Itherness. Ellie McDonald. CABP

'Ithin the woodlands, flow'ry gleaded. My Orcha'd in Linden Lea. William Barnes. EBVV; FaBoVe; NOBVV

Itinerant astrologers of no great wealth. Professionals. Turner Cassity. MT

Itinerant clarinet. Dragonfly. J. D. McClatchy. APo

Itinerary. Edwin Morgan. OBCoV

It'll be a fine day. *Unknown. See* If bees stay at home.

It's. Are You Ready? Wes Magee. AYFP

It's a Bit Rich. Max Fatchen. OTCP

It's a comfort to me in life's battle. The Little Child's Faith. Louis E. Thayer. PoToHe

"It's a '49," Rhinehardt said, and slammed. Making Money: Drought Year in Minkler, California. Gary Soto. NoAM

It's a funny thing. Poem for Sigmund. Lorna Crozier. LW

It's a funny thing, but true. *Unknown.* CTV

It's a good thing Dad deserted Mom. How I Came to Have a Man's Name. Emma Lee Warrior. HATNAP

It's a grand thing when you're old, love. Life's Golden Sunset. Mrs. Henry Linden. CBWP-4

It's a Great Big Shame. Edgar Bateman. OBCoV

It's a hell / creeping back into. Back into the Garden. Sarah Webster Fabio. BlSi

It's a hot day, and I'm sweating. Goodbye. Robert Long. IFJA

It's a kind of blindness. The Painter's Daughter. Carol Muske. MoLi

It's a kind of reflex, taking the fall. Capitalism. Mark Levine. PUP-19

It's a long step round by the Crucifix for a man with a mighty load. Dead-Mule Tree: A Song of Wisdom. Sir Alan Patrick Herbert. NSI

It's a long walk in the dark. John's Song. Joan Aiken. TLR

It's a long way to Tipperary. Tipperary. Desmond O'Grady. BiHa

It's a Low Down Dirty Shame. Ollie Shepard. NAAAL

It's a madman, I said. Dream. Nana Issaia, *Modern Greek.* BoWoP, *tr. by* Helle Tzalopoulou Barnstone

It's a nightmare that horrifies hakes. Limerick. Allan M. Laing. PeLi

It's a Party (1959). Baron Wormser. SeSe

It's a pity that Casabianca. Limerick. Victor Gray. PeLi

It's a Queer Time. Robert Graves. MoBrPo

It's a question of altitude, or latitude. Brute Image. John Ashbery. NoP-4

It's a real old-fashioned butcher's shop. The Crafty Butcher. Susan Hampton. BMAP; NOBAu

It's a real rock. Wobbly Rock. Lew Welch. PoM

It's a rheumatic world if you ever stop to listen. What Happens in Shakzpeare. Alan Brunton. PeNZ

It's a scientific toy for children. Battery woman. Pierre McOrlan, *French.* MFP, *tr. by* Martin Sorrell

It's a sign of the times when even barbers. Phanias, *Greek.* GrAn, *tr. by* Peter Porter

It's a singular thing that Ned. Ned. Eleanor Farjeon. OTCP

It's a slow, slow process. On Watching a Caterpillar Become a Butterfly. Clarence Major. NAAAL

It's a slow warmth I find once more. Luigi Fontanella, *Italian.* NeIt, *tr. by* Michael Palma

It's a south wind that drives you back. Hardon ("Get One Today"). Ian Wedde. PeNZ

It's a strange courage. El Hombre. William Carlos Williams. CMoP; SAmP

It's a sunny pleasant anchorage, is Kingdom Come. Port of Many Ships. John Masefield. OBMV

It's a Terrible Thing! Everett Hoagland. BPo

It's a very odd thing. Miss T. Walter De la Mare. FaBoBe; FuFo; NTCP

It's a warm wind, the west wind, full of birds' cries. The West Wind. John Masefield. CABP; LiTM; MoBrPo

It's a weary life, it is. From the Antique. Christina Rossetti. PEW

It's a white nest! A Small Bird's Nest Made of White Reed Fiber. Robert Bly. NNaP

It's a Woman's World. Eavan Boland. CIP-2

It's about style. The Place Where He Arose. George Barlow. GT

It's about / the ball, / the bat, / and the mitt. Analysis of Baseball. May Swenson. ImGa; KaS

It's aesthetically lovely, but pangs the mind. A Still Life, Symbolic of Lines. Albert Goldbarth. BAP-95

It's after one. Last Statement. Vladimir Mayakovsky, *Russian.* FaBoPV; PBCIP, *tr. by* Tom Paulin

It's all. Young Girl Peeling Apples. Mary Jo Salter. FFC

It's all familiar. A Dream. Bella Akhatovna Akhmadulina, *Russian.* BoWoP, *tr. by* Jean Valentine *and* Olga Carlisle

It's all go to Claridges, it's all go to the champers. More Bagpipe Music. E. O. Parrott. UV

It's All in the Heart. Xuân Diệu, *Vietnamese.* AVP, *tr. by* Huỳnh Sanh Thông

It's all over. . . . Andrey Dmitrievich Dementyev, *Russian.* TCRP, *tr. by* Albert C. Todd

It's All the Same. Thadious M. Davis. BlSi

It's all the same to me what time it is. Paradise Lost, Book IV, lines 639—654. Leslie Johnson. UV

It's all the same to morning what it dawns on. Aubade. Nuala Ni Dhomhnaill, *Irish.* BiHa; PBCIP, *tr. by* Michael Longley

It's all / Too much to bear! How I Became a Dog. Vladimir Mayakovsky, *Russian.* TCRP, *tr. by* Bernard Meares

It's all very well for preachin'. The Pledge at Spunky Point. John Milton Hay. OBAL

It's all very well to dream of a dove that saves. Birdwatchers of America. Anthony Hecht. HoPM; NOBA; NoAM

It's all very well to write reviews. Lasca. Frank Desprez. BLPA; FaBoBe

It's already past one. You'll have gone to bed. Vladimir Mayakovsky, *Russian.* TCRP, *tr. by* Daniel Weissbort

It's Alright, Ma (I'm Only Bleeding). "Bob Dylan." FiLi

It's altogether something else with shrapnel. Proverbs. Teresa de Jesús, *Spanish.* AF, *tr. by* Maria Proser, Arlene Scully *and* James Scully

It's always. The Dark. Myra Cohn Livingston. TLR

It's always there, like the drone. Exchange. Dabney Stuart. HoPM

It's an easy game, this reviewin'—the editor sends yer a book. The Ballad of George R. Sims. John Betjeman. OBCoV; UV

It's an old box camera. Camera. Ted Kooser. Poetsp

It's an overcome sooth for age an' youth. Robert Louis Stevenson. NOBVV

It's any kid's most exquisite fantasy. At Graceland with a Six Year Old, 1985. David Wojahn. PBCAP *Fr.* Mystery Train: A Sequence.

It's autumn in the country I remember. Mnemosyne. Trumbull Stickney. APN-2; GEA; NOBA; OxBA

It's awf'lly bad luck on Diana. Hunter Trials. John Betjeman. EBEvV; OBCoV

It's bad luck with a coughing baby. John Tranter. CBAP *Fr.* Crying in Early Infancy.

It's been a hard winter, but summer is here and the fields. Tomas Tranströmer. RaBo, *tr. by* Robert Bly *Fr.* Standing Up.

It's been a long day's drive through a landscape. Cinema Point. Philip Mead. BMAP

It's been a long time. Joanne Kyger. BB

It's been almost thirty-five years. Valentino's Hair. Yvonne Sapia. PeVV; TRP

It's been going on a long time. A Way of Life. Howard Nemerov. NIP-4

It's been like fixing a clock, jamming the wheels. Making Up for a Soul. David Wagoner. VGW

It's been pelting down. Sheltering Places. Gerald Dawe. PNI

It's been so long. ALONE/december/night. Victor Hernandez Cruz. PBMP

It's been so long since I headed for East Mountain. Thinking of East Mountain. Li Po, *Chinese.* CoBCP; TTTS, *tr. by* Burton Watson

It's been suggested there's another sex. Preannual Poem. Yona Wallach, *Hebrew.* IP, *tr. by* Warren Bargad *and* Stanley F. Chyet

It's been suggested there's another sex. Preannual Poem. Yona Wollach. IP, *tr. by* Warren Bargad *and* Stanley F. Chyet *Fr.* Two Gardens (1969).

It's been ten years since you tried to kill me. Clearing the Air. Nancy Willard. CrSp

It's been this way for some time. New Jersey Turnpike. Richard Cumbie. NBLV

It's best to be best. Best? Siv Widerberg, *Swedish.* NTCP, *tr. by* Verne Moberg

Its bloom finished. Tanka. Miya Shūji, *Japanese.* MJT, *tr. by* Makoto Ueda

Its body in a rag-tag army. (LL) And I remember Spain. Louis MacNeice. OBWP; OxAEP-2

It's bright the icy foam as it flows. From Exile. Dafydd Benfras, *Welsh.* OBWVE, *tr. by* Anthony Conran

It's Christmas Day. I did not get. Otto. Gwendolyn Brooks. PChr

"Its claws have struck through the clouds." Wolfram von Eschenbach, *German.* GePo, *tr. by* Frederick Goldin

It's clear, Trojan cried out to Greek. Why They Waged War. John Peale Bishop. NYBP

It's cold at last and cautious winds creep. Grandfather at the Indian Health Clinic. Elizabeth Cook-Lynn. HATNAP; UnSA

It's common as / well as comic. Catullus. *See* Carmen 10 ("Varus, whom I chanced to meet").

It's common to say of bad acting, or family photos like these. Family Grove. Albert Goldbarth. HCAP

Its country and its God! (LL) The Homes of England. Felicia Dorothea Hemans. FaPoR; NOBRP; PEW; UV; WPE

It's crazy to think one could describe them. Invocation. Robert Pinsky. NoAM *Fr.* Essay on Psychiatrists.

Its Curtains. Ted Joans. PoBA

It's dark in the garage. The mechanic. The Mechanic. Richard Jones. NAmP90

It's dark in this wood, soft mocker. Praise to the End! Theodore Roethke. InPS-3

It's dark on purpose. Visiting the Oracle. Lawrence Raab. AmPA

It's dark out, Jack. All the Roary Night. Kenneth Patchen. LiTM

Its dark pages. (LL) To the Reader. Denise Levertov. AmPP; PFE; PoM; SAGP; VGW

It's dark. . . / The bastard street lamp's run away. A Drunkard's Nocturnes. "Sasha Chorny," *Russian.* TCRP, *tr. by* Bernard Meares

Its dearest changed to bores. (LL) The Summer Malison. Gerard Manley Hopkins. CMoP; PoEL-5

It's devilishly hot. Poem Seen in a Motel Fan. Alberto Blanco, *Spanish.* CLPP, *tr. by* John Oliver Simon

It's disturbing that it's not a surprise. Undertakers. Robert Johnstone. PNI

It's doing your job the best you can. That's Success! Berton Braley. PoToHe

It's drinks time, and we're gulping gin. Someone Else. Sophie Behrens. NBrP

Its drop comes from my heart, that's all. (LL) May and Death. Robert Browning. FP; IMW; NOBE

It's Easy. Lee Cataldi. BMAP

It's easy to be witty in French. For the Common Market. Michael Burn. OBCoV

It's easy to invent a Life. Emily Dickinson. APN-2

It's easy / to live on. Sky Full of Swallows. Hanns Cibulka, *German.* CEEP, *tr. by* Ewald Osers

It's easy to talk of the patience of Job. Humph! Job hed nothin' to try him! The Inventor's Wife. E. R. Corbett. PoLF

Its edges foamed with amethyst and rose. The Great Breath. "Æ." MoBrPo; OBEV; OBMV

It's 8:54 a.m. in Brooklyn it's the 28th [*or* 26th] of July [and]. Personal Poem #9. Ted Berrigan. PmAP *Fr.* The Sonnets.

It's either the Prize or a terminal worry. A Memory. Heinrich Heine, *German.* PC, *tr. by* Francis C. Golffing

Its eyes falling back against the interior of their cylinders, opened—thus laying—. Forward or Back. Aaron Shurin. FTOS

It's fading. By an Unknown Poet from Eastern Europe, 1955. György Petri, *Hungarian.* VCWP, *tr. by* Wilmer, Clive and George Gömöri

It's fifty miles to Sittingen's Rocks. Prince Robert. *Unknown.* AmFP; ESPB; OxBB

Its former green is blue and thin. The Garden Seat. Thomas Hardy. GaP; HAP; RB

It's four long years since I reached this land. Lousy Miner. *Unknown.* AmFP

It's fun to take speed. Speed, a Pastoral. John Forbes. BMAP

It's funny how beetles. Upside Down. Aileen Fisher. OTCP

It's funny to look at a hurrying hound. The Hound. Kaye Starbird. KaS

It's Gardena, late Saturday afternoon. Winnings. Garrett Kaoru Hongo. OpBo

It's getting late—the watchman's drum beats fast. A Woman Lies Alone. Ho Xuan Huong, *Vietnamese.* AVP, *tr. by* Huỳnh Sanh Thông

It's getting / to be a thing. Be You. Norman Jordan. NBV

It's going on now. Note: The Sea Grinds Things Up. Alan Dugan. AFr

It's going to be a thick night tonight. Officers' Mess. Gavin Ewart. OxBTC

It's going to come out all right—do you know? Caboose Thoughts. Carl Sandburg. CMoP

It's going to rain. The Watchers. Paul Blackburn. NYBP

It's good, my child, you often wash your hair. Pope Alexander VI. Geoffrey Lehmann. NOBAu

"It's good to be at home," you said. (LL) The Blue Bowl. Blanche Bane Kuder. BLPA; FaBoBe

Its grandest lesson: "On! sail on!" (LL) Columbus. Joaquin Miller. APN-2; CTV; EBEvV; FaBoBe

It's great to be alive and be. It's Simply Great. Sidney Warren Mase. PoToHe

It's half over. You vow. From the Waitress Papers. Sharon Doubiago. NMM-2

It's Halloween. Jack Prelutsky. NTCP

Its Happenin / But You Dont Know Abt It. Ntozake Shange. NMM-2

It's hard to credit, but. Pawntickets. John C. Ryan. IIP

It's Hard to Dislike Ewart. Gavin Ewart. OBCoV

It's hard to know if you're alive or dead. It's a Queer Time. Robert Graves. MoBrPo

It's hard to make clothes fit a miserable man. Aphorisms. Joel Chandler Harris. CrDW *Fr.* Uncle Remus: His Songs and His Sayings.

It's hard to see but think of a sea. Louis Zukofsky. VGW

It's hard to tell what bird it is. After Frost. Brian Patten. EBEV

It's hard to understand how one can leave. Stanislav Iurievich Kunyayev, *Russian.* TCRP, *tr. by* Lubov Yakovleva

It's hazardous. Tanka. Toki Zenmaro, *Japanese.* MJT, *tr. by* Makoto Ueda

It's Here In The. Russell Atkins. PoBA

It's here we took him alive. As he fought well we offered him. Mongol Libation. Victor Segalen, *French.* NNPT, *tr. by* Nathaniel Tarn

Its huge numbers include us, our cars, houses, and substantial goods. Grand Projection. Rodney Jones. BAP-93

It's in the Egg. Joe Rosenblatt. NOBC

It's in the Name. Kitty Tsui. CPO

It's in the perilous boughs of the tree. Childhood's Retreat. Robert Duncan. NoAM

It's in Your Face. *Unknown.* PoLF

It's just as well that now you save your breath. (LL) To an American Poet Just Dead. Richard Wilbur. HCAP; NBLV

It's just begun. (LL) To a Child Trapped in a Barber Shop. Philip Levine. InPK-6; MoP; NOBA; NoAM; Poetr; TAP; VGW; WeT

It's just no use. Execution. James A. Randall Jr. BPo

It's just the little homely things. Little Things. *Unknown.* PoToHe

It's just the wind, but on a gentle breeze. It's All in the Heart. Xuân Diệu, *Vietnamese.* AVP, *tr. by* Huỳnh Sanh Thông

It's Lamkin was a mason good. Lamkin. *Unknown.* ESPB; OxBB

It's late, the children come home from school. Farm Families. Lu Yu. ChiPo, *tr. by* Watson, Burton *Fr.* Farm Families. CoBCP, *tr. by* Burton Watson

It's law they ask of me and not grace. The Law and the Grace. Iain Crichton Smith. FaBoTC

It's leaving thee, my bonnie [*or* bony] Mary! (LL) The Silver Tassie. Robert Burns. NOBE; OBEV

It's like a jungle sometimes, it makes me wonder. The Message. Grandmaster Flash and the Furious Five. NAAAL

It's like a story. Alive or Not. Alfred Wellington Purdy. NOBC

It's like the Light. Emily Dickinson. FaBoVe

It's like the riddle Tolstoy. Slow Dance. David St. John. AmPA; LCAP-2

It's like the sweet must that wasps. When Slow October Changes Color. Umberto Piersanti, *Italian.* NeIt, *tr. by* Stephen Sartarelli

It's like violence done to the atmosphere. Swans in Flight. Miroslav Holub, *Czech.* FaBoPV, *tr. by* Ewald Osers

It's little I care what path I take. Departure. Edna St. Vincent Millay. MoAmPo

Its love from living. (LL) The Decoys. W. H. Auden. CMoP; PoE

It's Me Again, God. Helen Steiner Rice. CTV

It's me / bathed and ashy. Me, in Kulu Se and Karma. Carolyn M. Rodgers. PoBA

It's me, Cassandra. Monologue for Cassandra. Wislawa Szymborska, *Polish.* PoSu, *tr. by* Grazyna Drabik *and* Sharon Olds

It's me—I am a War Eagle!" Ha-Kon-E-Crase, the Eagle Dance. *Unknown.* APN-2 *Fr.* War Dance. APN-2, *tr. by* George Catlin

It's Me Man. James Berry. HCP

It's Me, Your Son. Hồng Chu'o'ng, *Vietnamese.* AVP, *tr. by* Huỳnh Sanh Thông

It's mere child's play to die—who'd care to try? Trần Cao Vân, *Vietnamese.* AVP, *tr. by* Huỳnh Sanh Thông

Its metal top refused my father's twisting. The Soup Jar. Dabney Stuart. MT

It's midnight and a light rain falls. Ghosts. Dorianne Laux. EC3

It's midnight in a drizzling fog. North of Santa Monica. Carter Revard. VoR

It's Midsummer Day. Haytime. Irene F. Pawsey. BoTP

Its "mild wild head doth lie." (LL) Sea Unicorns and Land Unicorns. Marianne Moore. NALW; PFTM

It's more than just an easy word for casual good-bye. Aloha Oe. Don Blanding. PoToHe

It's morning and the line has formed. A Cow of Our Time. Thomas M. Disch. EOEF

Its music moves, as if always back to a first love. (LL) The Rocking Chair. Abraham Moses Klein. HeIP-4; NoP-4

"It's my custom," said dear Lady Norris. Limerick. *Unknown.* PeLi

It's my lunch hour, so I go. A Step Away from Them. Frank O'Hara. CoAmPo; HCAP; InPS-3; NAAL-2; VCAP; VGW

"It's narrow, narrow, make your bed." Fair Annie. *Unknown.* ESPB

It's natural the Boys should whoop it up for. Moon Landing. W. H. Auden. OxAEP-2

It's never *now* it's always *wait until.* . . . And Now. Alan Bold. AYFP

It's nice that though you are casual about me. Sulpicia, *Latin.* BoWoP, *tr. by* Aliki *and* Willis Barnstone

It's night—I'm dangling here beneath the sky. My Shadow and I. Phan Bội Châu, *Vietnamese.* AVP, *tr. by* Huỳnh Sanh Thông

It's 1962 March 28th. Things I Didn't Know I Loved. Nazim Hikmet, *Turkish.* AF; VCWP, *tr. by* Randy Blasing *and* Mutlu Konuk

It's no coincidence / this is a used. Tricks With Mirrors. Margaret Atwood. NIP-4

It's no go the merry-go-round, [*or* merrygoround], it's no go the rickshaw. Bagpipe Music. Louis MacNeice. CABP; CMoP; EBEvV; GTBS-P; ImPo; LiTM; MoP; NAEL-2; NBLV; NOBE; NOBL; NoAM; NoP-4; OAEL-2; OBSV; OxBTC; PeLV; RB; TFi; UV

It's no good, the women are in eruption. D. H. Lawrence. InPS-3

It's no great step for a poor man to the grave. Palladas, *Greek*. GrAn, *tr. by* Tony Harrison

It's no more peculiar. The Love of Water Faucets. David James. CMAP

It's no use clamouring for hellebore when your flesh is already sick. Unwelcome advice. Persius, *Latin*. OBCVT, *tr. by* Rudd, Niall (fl. 20th cent)

"It's no use," he says, "she's left me." This is after several. In a Tavern. Louis Jenkins. RaBo

It's No Use Raising a Shout. W. H. Auden. OBMV

It's Nostalgia Week at Frank 'n' Helen's. At Frank 'n' Helen's. Constance Urdang. PBCAP

It's not a bit windy. Toadstools. Elizabeth Fleming. BoTP

It's not always easy. Face the Animal. Jean Follain, *French*. BLT, *tr. by* Heather McHugh

It's not as if we never played at cards. Playing at Cards. Belle Randall. CRP

It's not because I'm now too old. No. Lady Ki No Washika, *Japanese*. NNPT, *tr. by* Graeme Wilson

It's not celestial music it's the girl in the bathroom singing. Ode on Celestial Music. Brian Patten. OxBTC

It's not hard to forget what they ate. Place on a Grave. Frank Stanford. MT

It's not just Schüpfen she's looking for. Searching for Schüpfen. Dona Luongo Stein. LoHo

It's not much of a choice. Troth. Michael Davidson. FTOS

It's not my world, I grant, but I made it. Ride. Josephine Miles. FaBoWP

It's not only my lights that hum in this city. Nightscape. Donna Masini. WWSi

It's Not so Good to be Born a Girl/ Sometimes. Ntozake Shange. SSLK

It's not so much what you say. The Tone of Voice. *Unknown*. PoToHe

It's not surprising. Pan Cogito on Virtue. Zbigniew Herbert, *Polish*. PoSu, *tr. by* Adam Czerniawski

It's not that the Muse feels like clamming up. Folk Tune. Joseph Brodsky. EP

It's not that you were present. Mourning. Daniel Weissbort. GI

It's Not the Same. Tomoko Fukunaka, *Japanese*. WPJ, *tr. by* Kenneth Rexroth *and* Ikuko Atsumi

It's not you I've lost, / but the world. Ingeborg Bachmann. *See* A Kind of Loss.

It's nothing personal when she slips in. The Maid and I. Andrew Greig. FaBoTC

It's nothing really, and really, it could have been worse, and of course, he's. Grandfather-in-law. David Mura. LoL

It's of a blind beggar, and he lost his sight. The Blind Beggar. *Unknown*. AmFP

It's of a rich squire in Bristol doth dwell. Squire and Milkmaid; or, Blackberry Fold. *Unknown*. OxBB

It's of a young lord o' the Hielands. Lizie Lindsay. *Unknown*. ESPB; OxBB

It's of flash packet, a packet of fame. The *Dom Pedro*. *Unknown*. AmFP

It's of three rioters I have to tell. Chaucer. SCV *Fr.* The Pardoner's Tale. FHYEP; NAEL-1; NAWM-1; OAEL-1; PoE *Fr.* The Canterbury Tales.

It's off in the distance. A Song of My Song, in Three Parts. *Unknown*, *Seneca Indian*. STP, *tr. by* Jerome Rothenberg *and* Richard Johnny John

It's old, inadequate, and flourishing. (LL) Ménage à Trois. Howard Moss. GEA; VCAP

It's on this railroad bank I stand. Careless Love. *Unknown*. UnPo

It's once I courted as pretty a lass. *Unknown*. OxNR

It's only a trickle. Laocoon/Serpent. Novica Tadic, *Serbian*. VCWP, *tr. by* Charles Simic

It's only at Christmas and New Year. Fitzroy. Andrew Taylor. BMAP

It's only common sense (not that they know the score). The River Has No Hair to Hold Onto. Ralph Angel. NAmP90

It's only her version of what you were trying to do. This Book Belongs to Susan Someone. David Clewell. NAmP90

It's only whiskey that makes you pity me. Kagank, *Tlingit Indian*. STP, *tr. by* James Koller

It's over a(see just). E. E. Cummings. OxBA; VGW

It's over now; I've known it all. Emily Jane Brontë. NOBVV

Its own identity. (LL) This Consciousness that is aware. Emily Dickinson. NAAL-1; NAAL-3; PAR

Its pale tendrilous horn. (LL) Cuttings ("Sticks-in-a-drowse droop over sugary loam"). Theodore Roethke. ColAP; HCAP; LCAP-2; MoP; NAAL-2; NOBA; NOAM; OBGa; TAP; UnPo

Its pecked-at ripeness that scans you, then moves on. (LL) The Haw Lantern. Seamus Heaney. NoAM; PNI

It's pleasant to board the ferry in the sunscape. Dejeuner Sur L'Herbe. Tu Fu, *Chinese*. BLT, *tr. by* Carolyn Kizer

It's practically impossible. Guerrilla War. William Daniel Ehrhart. CDa

Its presence is not impeded by visible form. The Human Mind. Ai Shih-te, *Chinese*. TrJP, *tr. by* William C. White

Its pristine bloom. (LL) On Receiving News of the War. Isaac Rosenberg. MoBrPo; NSI; OBWP; OxAEP-2; PeFWW; PeSAV; PoWW

It's prized more than my best dancing. (LL) The First Tooth. Charles Lamb *and* Mary Lamb. ACTP; OxBChV; WoRP

It's probably the year her marriage. Satin Doll. David Wojahn. PBCAP

Its quick soft silver bell beating, beating. Auto Wreck. Karl Shapiro. CMoP; LiTM; NIP-4; RB; VGW

It's quiet for me, now that I have buried the child. Ritual Three. David Ignatow. CoAmPo

It's quiet here among the haunted tenses. The Last of England. Peter Porter. GS

It's quiet in Hell just now, it's very tame. Lament of an Idle Demon. Richard Percival Lister. NOBL

Its radiance bursts forth in summer's bright light. Sunflower. Kao Ch'i, *Chinese*. SuSp, *tr. by* Irving Y. Lo

Its rails and the Main Chance gone to scrap. Rights of Way. Thomas Reiter. GM

It's Raining. Guillaume Apollinaire, *French*. TTTS, *tr. by* Kenneth Koch

It's raining, it's pouring. *Unknown*. ACTP; OxNR

It's raining, it's raining. *Unknown*. OxNR

Its rancid saliva can't fill up a shell. On a Snail. Su Shih. SuSp, *tr. by* Irving Y. Lo *Fr.* Two Poems on Insect Painting by Candidate Yin.

It's really something, the onion. Onion. Wislawa Szymborska, *Polish*. PoSu, *tr. by* Grazyna Drabik *and* Sharon Olds

Its retributions work like clockwork. Under the Eyes. Tom Paulin. CIP-2; PNI

It's right to call you son. That cursing alcoholic. Letter to an Absent Son. Madeline DeFrees. FiLi

It's round, full round, yet not a hollow thing. In Praise of the Hat. *Unknown*, *Vietnamese*. AVP, *tr. by* Huỳnh Sanh Thông

It's run an' jump an' hop an' skip. Owdham Footbo'. Ammon Wrigley. FaBoVe

It's sad / To be the Mayor of Jerusalem. Mayor. Yehuda Amichai, *Hebrew*. PoSu, *tr. by* Assia Gutmann

It's said you take a long time over a bath. Lucilius, *Greek*. GrAn, *tr. by* Peter Porter

It's Saturday afternoon at the edge of the world. Laguna Blues. Charles Wright. PoPoPo

It's Saturday night, and I'm feeling reckless. Saturday Night. Sir Alan Patrick Herbert. NBLV

Its savage eyes, at whom do they glare? On A Toad. Su Shih, *Chinese*. SuSp, *tr. by* Irving Y. Lo; APo, *tr. by* Lo, Irving Y. *Fr.* Two Poems on Insect Painting by Candidate Yin.

It's Simply Great. Sidney Warren Mase. PoToHe

Its skirt of rain and wind and snow. Second Rondeau. Johann Nikolaus Götz, *German*. GePo, *tr. by* George C. Schoolfield

It's smoke, the star, a broom. Smoke. Rubén Bonitaz Nuño, *Spanish*. STV, *tr. by* John Frederick Nims

It's / snowing defective. Self-Pity Is a Kind of Lying, Too. James Schuyler. PoM

It's snowing hard enough that the taxis aren't running. The Rites of Manhood. Alden Nowlan. RaBo

It's so dark now. The Tip. Albert Goldbarth. HCAP

It's so hard to say in a son's words. Prayer to My Mother. Pier Paolo Pasolini, *Italian*. VCWP, *tr. by* Norman MacAfee *and* Luciano Martinengo

It's spring and Jake toddles to the garden. Jake Addresses the World from the Garden. Jack Myers. NAmP90

It's Spring Returning, It's Spring and Love. *Unknown*. HAP

It's spring; the City, wrapped. To His Chi Mistress. George Starbuck. NYBP

It's step her to your weev'ly wheat. Weevily Wheat. *Unknown*. AS

It's still a good idea. To Friends Who Have Also Considered Suicide. Phyllis Webb. NOBC

It's still here. It's still here-er. Be ready. Be ready. Mothering. Carla Harryman. FTOS

It's still inside me. My Mother's Death. Judith Hemschemeyer. MDDM

Its strength, and struck. (LL) Eight O'Clock. A. E. Housman. CMoP; InPK-6; MoBrPo; MoP; NoAM; OxBSP; PFE; PoE; Poetr; SoSe-8

It's such a / Bore. Ennui. Langston Hughes. OBAL; OBCA

It's such a little thing to weep. Emily Dickinson. RB

It's such a shock, I almost screech. Two Sad. William Cole. CTV

It's summer—softly blows a southeast wind. A Girl Caught Napping By Day. Ho Xuan Huong, *Vietnamese*. AVP, *tr. by* Huỳnh Sanh Thông

It's Sunday evening. Pomp holds the receipts. Chopin. Marilyn Nelson Waniek. RA

It's ten. Evening. The room is in half light. My Sister. Alfonsina Storni, *Spanish*. BoWoP, *tr. by* Aliki *and* Willis Barnstone

It's the anarchy of poverty. The Poor. William Carlos Williams. MoAmPo

It's the broken phrases, the fury inside him. Art Pepper. Edward Hirsch. NAmP90; SeSe

It's the country of childhood. Jardin des Colombières. Lauris Edmond. OBGa

It's the Enobarbus Complex. *Unknown, Greek*. GrAn, *tr. by* Peter Porter

It's the first night, I suppose. A First Night. Peter Kane Dufault. DiPo; NoP-4

It's the high kick they wait for, not quite allowing. Tingel-Tangel. Rosalind Pace. CMAP

It's the last snow of the season. The All, the Nothing. Yves Bonnefoy, *French*. VCWP, *tr. by* Lisa Sapinkopf

It's the long road to Guinea. Guinea. Jacques Roumain, *French*. NegPo; TTY, *tr. by* Langston Hughes

It's the old rule that drunks have to argue. The New Rule. Jelaluddin Rumi, *Persian*. RaBo, *tr. by* Robert Bly *and* Coleman Barks

It's the poor first light of morning. The Obscure. Norman Dubie. NoAM

It's the ragged source of memory. The House on Moscow Street. Marilyn Nelson Waniek. NMM-2; UnSA

It's the same thing with me. (LL) Mutual Problem. William Cole. OBAL; OBCoV

It's the stillness that fills me with peace. (LL) The Spell of the Yukon. Robert W. Service. BLPA; FaBoBe

It's the story that counts. Margaret Atwood. NALW *Fr.* Circe / Mud Poems.

It's the Syme the Whole World Over. *Unknown*. AS

It's the torque of a spring Sunday. Blues in "C." Ron Overton. SeSe

It's the willingness to sing. Mrs. Schneider in Church. Kathleen Norris. CrSp

It's the world's longest car, I swear. Longmobile. Shel Silverstein. AiP

It's there / in the hole of the sea. The Hole in the Sea. Marvin Bell. NYBP

It's there you'll see confectioners with sugar sticks and dainties. Galway Races. *Unknown*. OxBoLi

Its thi lang / wij a thi / guhtr thaht hi. Tom Leonard. FaBoTC *Fr.* Unrelated Incidents.

It's this crazy weather we've been having. Crazy Weather. John Ashbery. ColAP; PoE

It's those helmets we remember. Trainride, Vienna—Bonn. Margaret Atwood. LCAP-2

'It's three No Trumps,' the soldier said. Guy Innes. UV

It's thus he does it of a winter night. (LL) An Old Man's Winter Night. Robert Frost. AFr; AWP; HAP; MoAmPo; NAAL-2; NoAM; OxBA; VGW

It's time again. Earth's Holocaust. James Schuyler. FTOS

It's time I told you why. The Hindoo: He Doesn't Hurt a Fly or a Spider Either. A. K. Ramanujan. OxBC

It's time to get back to the car. Already, at half-past three. Sunday in Great Tew. Peter McDonald. PNI

It's time to go, but still we sit. Tides. John Fuller. AYFP

It's time to make love. Douse the glim. Limerick. Conrad Aiken. NBLV; PeLV; PeLi

It's time to say words of good omen. The Peace: A Wedding Song. Aristophanes, *Greek*. ITG, *tr. by* Robert Hass

It's time to sit down. Rest. Slave Gorgo Dimoski, *Yugoslav*. CEEP, *tr. by* Ewald Osers

It's too dark to see black. A Mother Speaks: The Algiers Motel Incident, Detroit. Michael S. Harper. AmPA; BPo; NBV

"It's too easy." Malaria. Paolo Ruffilli, *Italian*. NeIt, *tr. by* Felix Stefanile

It's too good for them. Sex and the Over Forties. Peter Porter. BMAP; CBLP

It's true I got caught in / the world. After Lalon. Allen Ginsberg. BB

It's true I make books, but not often. Why I Never Answered Your Letter. Nancy Willard. CrSp

It's True I Went to the Market. Mirabai, *Rajasthani*. WPoS, *tr. by* Robert Bly

It's true I will die. So what do I care. Nicarchus of Alexandria, *Greek*. InMo, *tr. by* Sam Hamill

Its trunk as of dead silver cast. The Felled Plane Tree. Anna Hajnal, *Hungarian*. BoWoP, *tr. by* William Jay Smith

It's 12:21 in New York a Thursday. In Blue. David Chapman Berry. BXAP

It's twenty years ago and more. In Moncur Street. Dorothy Hewett. NOBAu

It's up the spout and Charley Wag. The Moral. William Ernest Henley. OxAEP-2

It's very cold, Catherine is bundled in a coat, a poncho on top of that, / high boots, gloves. Snow: II. Charles Kenneth Williams. NoP-4

Its wednesday night baby. Master Charge Blues. Nikki Giovanni. OBAL

It's when things seem worst that you mustn't quit. (LL) Don't Quit. *Unknown*. BLPA; PoToHe

Its whistle shrieks and rips the veil of mists. The Night Train. Trần Gia Thoại, *Vietnamese*. AVP, *tr. by* Huỳnh Sanh Thông

It's wise to make the most. *Unknown, Greek*. InMo, *tr. by* Sam Hamill

It's with glasses. A Pair of Glasses. Savithri Rajeevan, *Malayalam*. OMIP, *tr. by* K. Ayyappa Paniker *and* Arlene Zide

It's wonderful how I jog. Animals Are Passing from Our Lives. Philip Levine. CoAP; ColAP; NOBA; Poetr; RaBo; TAP; WeT

It's wrang indeed now, Jenny, white. The 8th Ode of Book I. of Horace imitated in the Cumberland Manner and Dialect. Horace, *Latin*. OBCVT, *tr. by* Josiah Relph

Its wrinkled foreskin, twisting open, opens. Morning Glory. Howard Moss. DiPo

Its youth. The sea grows old in it. (LL) The Fish. Marianne Moore. AmPP; ColAP; FaBoWP; MeMAP; MoAmPo; MoP; NAAL-2; NoAM; NoP-4; OxBA; PBMP; Poetr

Itself, too vast, for interrupting—more. (LL) I got so I could take his name. Emily Dickinson. APN-2; CMoP

ITT Alcan Kaiser. I Fight Back. Lillian Allen. PBCV

Itylus. Swinburne. EBVVPR; UV

IV. Allen Ginsberg. *Fr.* Kaddish.

("With your eyes / with your Death full of Flowers.") (LL) CLPP

Ivan and the Serf. "David Samuilovich Samoylov," *Russian*. TCRP, *tr. by* Lubov Yakovleva

Ivan, do not kill your son! Sketches from History. Sergey Drofenko, *Russian*. TCRP, *tr. by* Lubov Yakovleva

Ivan paces his chamber at night. Ivan and the Serf. "David Samuilovich Samoylov," *Russian*. TCRP, *tr. by* Lubov Yakovleva

Ivanhoe. Sir Walter Scott.

Rebecca's Hymn.

Ivanovs, The. Nikolai Alekseievich Zabolotsky, *Russian*. TCRP, *tr. by* Daniel Weissbort

I've always been going somewhere—Vancouver. The Madwoman on the Train. Alfred Wellington Purdy. NoAM

I've always done so. And Then. Ōkuma Nobuyuki, *Japanese*. MJT, *tr. by* Makoto Ueda

I've always known that old age would arrive. Feeling Old Age. Liu Tsung-yüan, *Chinese*. SuSp, *tr. by* Jan W. Walls

I've always loved (your) Grace in 14 lines, sometimes. Birthday Sonnet for Grace. Bernadette Mayer. PmAP

I've always thought Polonius a dry. Lines to His Son on Reaching Adolescence. John Logan. CAPP-1

I've always wanted one. Wanting a Mummy. Sandra McPherson. AmPA; LCAP-2

I've always wished that I could ask that question. Late Night Tête-à-Tête with a Moon in Transit. Jacqueline Osherow. BAP-95

I've an empty stomach. The Ballad of Biddy Early. Nancy Willard. FFC

I've been a gangrel bodie, I've been to Sicilie. Theognis. OBCVT, *tr. by* Douglas Young *Fr.* Fowr Epigrams frae Theognis o Megara.

I've been a moonshiner for seventeen long years. Kentucky Moonshiner. *Unknown*. AS; OBAL

I've been after the exotic. The Ethnic Life. Daniel Halpern. AmPA

I've been blue all day, my gal's gone away. Gulf Coast Blues. Clarence Williams. NAAAL

I've been called sway. It's in the Name. Kitty Tsui. CPO

I've been chanting poems for forty years. Chanting Poems. Wang Chiu-ssu, *Chinese*. CoBLCP, *tr. by* Jonathan Chaves

I've been cherishing. A Room with a View. Noël Coward. PeLV

I've been digging a hole in sunlight. Four Seasons of His Discontent. Roger Weingarten. NAmP90

I've been driving for hours. Looking for a Rest Area. Stephen Dunn. AmPA

I've been giving a lot of thought. Sea Things. Gwendolyn MacEwen. FaBoWP

I've been in an open field. A Day in the Life of. . . . Conyus. GT

I've been in jail from slander. The Rocky Mountains. *Unknown*. AmFP

I've been in love for long. In Love For Long. Edwin Muir. BoLoP; LiTM; LoP; MoBrPo

I've been in love. Who hasn't? I went out and got drunk. Philodemus. HePo, *tr. by* Barbara Hughes Fowler *Fr.* Epigrams.

I've been in the storm so long. Been in the Storm So Long. *Unknown*. NAAAL

I've been scarred and battered. Still Here. Langston Hughes. SAmP

I've been smoking steadily all morning. Mathios Paskalis among the Roses. George Seferis, *Greek*. PFTM, *tr. by* Edmund Keeley *and* Philip Sherrard

I've been sweating again, a symptom. Storms. Dean Young. NAmP90

I've Been to a Marvelous Party. Noël Coward. NBLV

I've been to Palestine. John Brown. Vachel Lindsay. MoAmPo *Fr.* The Booker Washington Trilogy.

I've been trying to fashion a wifely ideal. A Plea for Trigamy. Sir Owen Seaman. NOBL; PeLV

I've been watchin' of 'em, parson. Deacon Jones' Grievance. Paul Laurence Dunbar. AAP

I've blown up your chest for thirty minutes. Morning—A Death. Basil T. Paquet. CDa

I've brewed myself a whole bunch of trouble. To the Tune "Moon Over West River." Yang Shen, *Chinese.* CoBLCP, *tr. by* Jonathan Chaves

I've brought you nuts and hops. October. Christina Rossetti. BoTP

I've built a castle in the sand. Castles in the Sand. Dorothy Baker. BoTP

I've changed stations: autumn remained behind and my bags. Leaf. Rade Drainac, *Serbo-Croatian.* HSix, *tr. by* Charles Simic

I've cleaned house. Saturday Afternoon, When Chores Are Done. Harryette Mullen. ISC

I've combed out my beard and I've found. Limerick. Pauline Phillips. PeLi

I've come back all skin and bone. The Diggins-Oh. *Unknown.* NOBAu

I've come back many times today. Gift from Kenya. May Miller. BlSi

I've come back to my city. These are my own old tears. Leningrad. Osip Emilevich Mandelstam, *Russian.* AF; FaBoPV, *tr. by* W. S. Merwin *and* Clarence Brown

I've come back to the country where I was happy. Adult. Linda Gregg. BLT

I've come this far to freedom and I won't turn back. Midway. Naomi Long Madgett. BPo; BlSi

I've come to close your door, my handsome, my darling. Frances Bellerby. FaBoWP

I've come to give you fruit from out [of] my orchard. The Crossed Apple. Louise Bogan. HeIP-4; NALW; RACG

I've come to see a stranger. Sunday Afternoon at the State Hospital. Marilyn J. Boe. LoHo

I've come to see Miss Jennian Jones. Miss Jennian Jones. *Unknown.* AmFP

I've come to tell you of things dear to me. Skin / Meat / BONES. Anne Waldman. PmAP

I've come to the house of the Immortals. At Home in the Summer Mountains. Yu Xuanji, *Chinese.* WPoS, *tr. by* Jane Hirshfield

I've Come to the Simplest Words. Amir Gilbo'a, *Hebrew.* IP, *tr. by* Warren Bargad *and* Stanley F. Chyet

I've cracked the blue bowl! China Maniacs. May Probyn. VWP

I've cropped the black hair Diego loves. Painting / (Frida Kahlo). Elizabeth Alexander. GT

I've decided to return to the emperor's court. The Return of the Proconsul. Zbigniew Herbert, *Polish.* CEEP; FaBoPV; PoSu, *tr. by* Czeslaw Milosz

I've decided to study agriculture. Li K'ai-hsien. *Fr.* Pleasures among the Fields during the Four Seasons. CoBLCP, *tr. by* Jonathan Chaves

I've discovered a way to stay friends forever. Friendship. Shel Silverstein. NTCP

"I've done my bits of mindless aggro too." Tony Harrison. FaBoVe

I've drawn a salary in the capital for forty years now. Yang Shih-ch'i. CoBLCP, *tr. by* Jonathan Chaves *Fr.* Sent to All My Nephews and Nieces at Tung-ch'eng.

I've dreamed of my first love, the subtle serpent. (LL) In Nature There Is Neither Right nor Left nor Wrong. Randall Jarrell. CBLP; EP; OxBC

I've dreamed such dreams of you that you're losing / your reality. Robert Desnos, *French.* MFP, *tr. by* Martin Sorrell

I've dropped me swag in many camps. The Search. Charles Shaw. NOBAu

I've dug up all my garden. Sowing Seeds. Ursula Cornwall. BoTP

I've eaten handfuls of fire. Back Then. Yusef Komunyakaa. GT

I've followed the billowing dust as a traveler too long. Li K'ai-hsien. *Fr.* Pleasures among the Fields during the Four Seasons. CoBLCP, *tr. by* Jonathan Chaves

I've found out why, that day, that suicide. John Berryman. PoF. *Fr.* Sonnets to Chris.

I've gathered more data on a towered city. Northern Romance. Haim Gouri, *Hebrew.* IP, *tr. by* Warren Bargad *and* Stanley F. Chyet

I've given up poetry—I have no new manuscripts. Yang Chi. *Fr.* Living in a Riverside Village—Miscellaneous Impressions. CoBLCP, *tr. by* Jonathan Chaves

I've gone and done. (LL) Hay for the Horses. Gary Snyder. BB; CoAmPo; LoL; TRP

I've got a bow and arrow. Robin Hood. Rachel MacAndrew. BoTP

I've got a dog as thin as a rail. Thin Dog. *Unknown.* PeP

I've got a home in-that Rock. Got a Home in That Rock. *Unknown.* APN-2

I've Got a Home in That Rock. Raymond R. Patterson. MBE; PoBA

I've got a lovely home. Best of All. J. M. Westrup. BoTP

I've got a mule and her name is Sal. The Erie Canal. William S. Allen. AS

I've got a pony. The Pony. Rachel MacAndrew. BoTP

I've Got an Apple Ready. John Walsh. NOxBChV

I've got an old mule and her name is Sal. William S. Allen. *See* The Erie Canal.

I've Got No Use for the Women. *Unknown.* AmFP

I've got to keep moving. Hellhound on My Trail. Robert Johnson. NAAAL

I've gotten a rock, I've gotten a reel. Susanna Blamire. ECWP

I've gotten used to this window. Glimpse from the Past. Ilse Aichinger, *German.* AF, *tr. by* Allen H. Chappel

I've grown a goitre by dwelling in this den. To Giovanni da Pistoia When the Author Was Painting the Vault of the Sistine Chapel, 1509. Michelangelo Buonarroti, *Italian.* NNPT, *tr. by* John Addington Symonds

I've grown distant from my grandfather. War Confession. Natan Zach, *Hebrew.* IP, *tr. by* Warren Bargad *and* Stanley F. Chyet

I've had enough. The Bridge Poem. Kate Rushin. GLP

I've had enough of your baseness, and I haven't killed myself. To the Enemies. Vladimir Holan, *Czech.* AF, *tr. by* C. G. Hanzlicek *and* Dana Habova

I've Had Many an Aching Pain. John Clare. NOBVV

I've had tangled feelings lately. Breakthrough. Carolyn M. Rodgers. BPo

I've had the wagon hauled out. *Unknown, Chinese.* SuSp, *tr. by* C. H. Wang

I've heard that holy madness is a state. Buzzard. George Garrett. MT

I've heard the case for clarity. I know. Giant Killer. George Garrett. CRP

I've heard the[m] lilting at our [or the] ewe-milking [or yowe-milking or yewe-milking]. The Flowers of the Forest. Jane Elliot. CH; ECWP; FaBoCh; GTBS-P; NoP-4, OBEV, OxB3, 3CGP, WPE

I've heard them lilting at loom and belting. C. Day Lewis. OBMV *Fr.* Two Songs. HAP; NoAM; NoP-4

I've just come up. Naito Joso, *Japanese.* TTTS, *tr. by* Kenneth Koch *and* Harold Henderson

I've just had an astounding dream as I lay in the straw. Minstrel's Song. Ted Hughes. OBCP

I've kept a haughty heart thro' grief and mirth. To My Mother. Heinrich Heine, *German.* TrJP, *tr. by* Emma Lazarus; AWP, *tr. by* Matilda Dickson

I've kept a place for Steven Pudenz. Steven Pudenz. Paul Bonin-Rodriguez. IFJA

I've kissed thee, sweetheart, in a dream at least. Sleep. Theophile De Viau, *French.* AWP, *tr. by* Sir Edmund Gosse

I've knocked about the world, worn out my legs. Prison Life. Du'o'ng Bá Trạc, *Vietnamese.* AVP, *tr. by* Huỳnh Sanh Thông

I've known a Heaven, like a Tent. Emily Dickinson. NCAP

I've known; all fading past me into peace. (LL) Falling Asleep. Siegfried Sassoon. MoBrPo; OxBTC

I've known ere now an interfering branch. The Axe-Helve. Robert Frost. OxBA

I've known him so long I've almost forgotten the first photo he showed. The Man Struck Twenty Times by Lightning. Maxine Chernoff. PmAP

I've known rivers. The Negro Speaks of Rivers. Langston Hughes. AiP; BPo; ColAP; CrDW; HAP; HCAP; HeIP-4; ISC; NAAAL; NAAL-2; NIP-4; NOBA; NoAM; NoP-4; OBCA; PoBA; Poetr; RaBo; SSLK; TAP; TFi; TTY; WeW-3

I've led you by my garrulous banks, babbling. What The Pool Said, On Midsummer's Day. Liz Lochhead. FaBoSe

I've left my own old home of homes. The Flitting. John Clare. FaBoPV; OxAEP-2

I've long desired dawn. Wishes. Philippe Jaccottet, *French.* MFP, *tr. by* Martin Sorrell

I've lost my Love, I know not where. Madness. Robert Merry. NOBRP

I've lost my man—I lie bereft of joy. The Widow's Reply to a Matchmaker. Nguyễn Khuyến, *Vietnamese.* AVP, *tr. by* Huỳnh Sanh Thông

I've lost my rifle and bayonet. *Unknown.* NSI; PoWW

I've lost pal, 'e's the best in all the tahn. It's a Great Big Shame. Edgar Bateman. OBCoV

I've moved here to the Immortal's place. Staying in the Mountains in Summer. Yü Hsüan-chi, *Chinese.* BoWoP, *tr. by* Geoffrey Waters

I've never been to Australia. Walking the Places I've Never Been. Yury Arabov, *Russian.* TCRP, *tr. by* John High *and* Katya Olmsted

I've never felt so knifed loose from the world. Short Wave In Shanghai. Sibyl James. LoHo

I've never kissed a man yet. My voice is like a wave. Nausicaa. Judita Vaiiunaite. CEEP, *tr. by* Irene Pogoželskyte Suboczewski *Fr.* Four Portraits.

I've never really understood Samson's hair.   Samson's Hair.   Natan Zach, *Hebrew.*   IP, *tr. by* Warren Bargad *and* Stanley F. Chyet

I've no tooth to sing you the song.   Pat Cloherty's Version of *The Maisie.*   Richard Murphy.   RB

I've not much of my own, lady, mistress, but I.   Gifts to a Lady.   Antiphilus, *Greek.*   GrAn, *tr. by* W. S. Merwin

I've now forgotten when it started, but.   Tall Trees.   Phạm Hổ, *Vietnamese.*   AVP, *tr. by* Huỳnh Sanh Thông

I've oft been told by learned friars.   An Argument.   Thomas Moore.   BoLoP; EnLoPo; GLoP; OxBSP

I've often heard my mother say.   The Unknown Color.   Countee Cullen.   OBCA

I've often on a Sabbath day.   Sabbath Bells.   John Clare.   FHYEP

I've often wish'd that I could write a book.   John Hookham Frere.   NOBRP *Fr.* Prospectus and Specimen of an Intended National Work by William and Robert Whistlecraft. Relating to King Arthur and His Round Table.

I've paid thee what I promised; that's not all.   To His Peculiar Friend Master Thomas Shapcott, Lawyer.   Robert Herrick.   NOSC

I've peeled off the shiny green bark.   New Bamboo in the North Garden at Ch'ang-ku.   Li Ho, *Chinese.*   SuSp, *tr. by* Irving Y. Lo

I've plucked the berry from the bush, the brown nut from the tree.   William Motherwell.   OxAEP-2

I've pulled the last of the year's young onions.   Eating Alone.   Li-Young Lee.   TRP; WeW-3

I've quenched my lamp, I struck it in that start.   Pilate's Wife's Dream.   Charlotte Brontë.   VWP

I've rambled and gambled all my money away.   Rabble Soldier.   *Unknown.*   AS

I've Reached the Land of Corn and Wine.   Edgar P. Stites.   AH

I've read that Luther said (it's come to me).   The Author to the Reader.   Randall Jarrell.   OxBC

I've rode the Southern, I've rode the L. & N.   I Rode Southern, I Rode L & N.   *Unknown.*   AmFP

I've seen a Dying Eye.   Emily Dickinson.   APN-2; AmPP; BoWoP; NAAL-3; NCAP; NOBA; PoEL-5; PoLF

I've seen Babylon's walls wide enough to take traffic.   The Temple of Artemis at Ephesos.   Antipater of Thessalonica, *Greek.*   GrAn, *tr. by* Tony Harrison

I've seen caravans.   Caravans.   Irene Thompson.   BoTP

I've seen fox, deer, wild turkey, pheasant, skunk.   In My Own Backyard.   James Tate.   BAP-93

I've seen him many times before.   Towards Delhi.   Kunwar Narain, *Hindi.*   OMIP, *tr. by* Vinay Dahrwadker *and* Aparna Dharwadker

I've seen one in a fairground.   The Bearded Woman, by Ribera.   Paul Muldoon.   BiHa

I've seen the grey-haired lyrists come down from the hills.   Grand Finale.   Irving Layton.   NOBC

I've seen the lights of gay Broadway.   Beale Street Blues.   William Christopher Handy.   CrDW; NAAAL

I've seen the moonbeam's shining light.   Life.   *Unknown.*   PoToHe

I've seen the smiling of Fortune beguiling.   The Flowers of the Forest.   Alison Rutherford Cockburn.   ECWP

I've seen the Thousand Islands.   Tadoussac.   Charles Bancroft.   BLPA

I've served my country nine and twenty years.   Edward Thompson.   NOEC *Fr.* An Humble Wish; off Porto-Santo, March 29, 1779.

I've six good men waitin' within half a mile'.   (LL)   Sweet Betsey from Pike.   *Unknown, sometimes att. to* John A. Stone ("Old Put").   AS; AmFP; OBAL; OxBoLi

I've smelled the barracks and live by rules.   Continuation of Life.   Boris Petrovich Kornilov, *Russian.*   TCRP, *tr. by* Bernard Meares

I've stayed in the front yard all my life.   A Song in the Front Yard.   Gwendolyn Brooks.   NAAAL; NAAL-2; NOBA; NOxBChV; NoAM; PoBA *Fr.* A Street in Bronzeville.   BPo; BlSi; FaBoWP

I've stitched my dress with continents.   Knowledge.   Nina Cassian, *Rumanian.*   BoWoP, *tr. by* Michael Impey *and* Brian Swann

I've swallowed a fly, cried Marjorie Fry.   The Cure.   Alfred Noyes.   FuFo

I've swept away.   Tanka.   Tsukamoto Kunio, *Japanese.*   MJT, *tr. by* Makoto Ueda

I've taken my fun where I've found it.   The Ladies.   Rudyard Kipling.   MoBrPo; NAEL-2

I've taken the last drag.   The City, Evening, and an Old Man: Me.   "Dhoomil," *Hindi.*   OMIP, *tr. by* Vinay Dharwadker

I've taken you to your own tomb.   A Prisoner's Funeral.   Nguyễn Ngọc Thuận, *Vietnamese.*   AVP, *tr. by* Huỳnh Sanh Thông

I've talked (remember).   Alba.   Imamu Amiri Baraka.   FTOS

I've Tasted My Blood.   Milton Acorn.   MoCV; NOBC

I've Thirty Months.   John Millington Synge.   OBMV

I've tossed an apple at you; if you can love me.   The Apple.   Plato, *Greek.*   WeW-3

I've touch each string, each muse I have invok't.   A Pindarick, to the Athenian Society.   Elizabeth Singer.   KTR

I've tried to seal it in.   The Knot.   Stanley Kunitz.   HAP

I've two teenage daughters, a decent.   Fear of Shoplifting.   Maureen Seaton.   FFC

I've used up all my film on bombed hospitals.   In Thai Binh (Peace) Province.   Denise Levertov.   AF

I've ventured it of purpose free.   Ulrich von Hutten's Song.   Ulrich von Hutten, *German.*   GePo, *tr. by* Catherine Winkworth

I've walked through their town.   Nobody Thinks Hard Enough for Poetry.   Kelvin Corcoran.   NBrP

I've waltzed my friends.   Sleepless Night.   Léon Damas, *French.*   NegPo, *tr. by* Ellen Conroy Kennedy

I've wandered to the village, Tom, I've sat beneath the tree.   Twenty Years Ago.   A. J. Gault *and* Dill Armor Smith.   BLPA

I've watched you now a full half-hour.   To a Butterfly.   Wordsworth.   ACTP; NTP   *Fr.* To a Butterfly.

I've wined and dined on Mulligan stew.   The Lady Is a Tramp.   Lorenz Hart.   OBAL

I've written you a song.   Blah, Blah, Blah.   Ira Gershwin.   OBAL

Ivied Tree-Top, An.   *Unknown.*   NOIV

Ivory in her black, and all intent.   Jesu, Joy of Man's Desiring.   Robert Fitzgerald.   NYBP

Ivory Masks in Orbit.   Keorapetse Kgositsile.   PoBA

Ivory Tower, The.   Robert Silliman Hillyer.   NYBP

Ivy, chefe of trees it is.   *Unknown.*   MiEL

Ivy Compton-Burnett's irritations.   Limerick.   *Unknown.*   PeLi

Ivy Crown, The.   William Carlos Williams.   NAAL-2; NoAM

Ivy o'er the mouldering wall, The.   The Sun-Dial.   Thomas Love Peacock.   OBNC   *Fr.* Melincourt.

I'yehe! my children.   *Unknown.*   STP   *Fr.* Ghost-Dance Songs.

Izaac Walton, Cotton, and William Oldways.   Walter Savage Landor.   PoEL-4

J

J. Alfred Prufrock to.   Said.   George Starbuck.   OBAL

J. C. Lawson / my great-grandfather.   Town History, 1917.   David Huddle.   PBCAP

J. M. W. Turner on Switzerland.   Consolations of Art.   Roy Fuller.   OxBC

J. S. Mill.   Edmund Clerihew Bentley.   OxBoLi; PeLV   *Fr.* Clerihews.

J. V. Cunningham Gets Hung Up on a Dirty, of All Things, Joke.   Henry Taylor.   BXAP

Jaan Oks.   Aleksis Rannit, *Estonian.*   CEEP, *tr. by* Henry Lymann

Jabberwocky.   "Lewis Carroll."   APAD; CABP; CBNP; CTV; ChAP; ClHu; EBEV; EBEvV; EBVV; FPC; FaBoBe; HeIP-4; HoPM; ImPo; InPK-6; InPS-3; NAEL-2; NBLV; NOBE; NOBL; NOBVV; NOxBChV; NTCP; NoAM; NoP-4; OAEL-2; OBSP; OxAEP-2; OxBChV; PFE; PeLV; PeVV; PoRA; Poetr; RB; SAGP; TFi; TRP; TTTS; UV   *Fr.* Through the Looking-Glass.

Jacaranda.   Roo Borson.   NOBC

Jack.   Louis Golding.   TrJP

Jack.   Charles Henry Ross.   ACTP; NOxBChV; OxBChV; Spl

Jack and Dinah Want Freedom.   *Unknown.*   BPo; NAAAL

Jack and Gill [*or* Jill] went up the hill.   Mother Goose.   CBNP; FaBoBe; OxBoLi; OxNR; PeLV

   ("With vinegar / and brown paper.")   (LL)   LB

Jack and Gye.   *Unknown.*   OxNR

Jack and His Fiddle.   Mother Goose.   ReMoGo

Jack and Jill.   A. E. Housman.   UV

Jack and Jill.   Charles Battell Loomis.   BXAP

Jack and Jill.   Charles Powell.   BXAP

Jack and Jill went up the hill/ To fetch some heavy water.   Paul Dehn.   ReMoGo   *Fr.* Rhymes for a Modern Nursery.

Jack and Joan they think no ill.   Thomas Campion.   FaBoCh; FaPoR

   ("*Jacke* and *Jone*, they thinke no ill.")   AAS

Jack and Roger.   Benjamin Franklin.   NOBL

   (Sampson Imitated.)   FaBoEE

Jack Barrett went to Quetta.   The Story of Uriah.   Rudyard Kipling.   NOBVV; PeVV; SCV

Jack be nimble.   Mother Goose.   LB; OxNR; ReMoGo

Jack, eating rotten cheese, did say.   Jack and Roger.   Benjamin Franklin.   FaBoEE; NOBL

Jack Ellyat Heard the Guns.   Stephen Vincent Benét.   PoLF   *Fr.* John Brown's Body.

"Jack fell as he'd have wished," the Mother said.   The Hero.   Siegfried Sassoon.   OBWP

Jack finds his wife a perfect beauty. (LL) The Double Transformation. Oliver Goldsmith. OBCoV; OBNV

Jack Frost. Cecily E. Pike. BoTP

Jack Frost. "Gabriel Setoun." BoTP

Jack Frost. Celia Laighton Thaxter. OBCA

Jack Frost. Fay Zwicky. BMAP

Jack Frost in the Garden. John P. Smeeton. BoTP

Jack Giantkiller took and struck. Driving Cross-Country. X. J. Kennedy. TwCP

Jack Haggerty. *Unknown.* AmFP

Jack Hall. Thomas Hood. NOBRP

Jack hammer! brain chiseller! come out! Men at Work. Richard Tipping. NOBAu

Jack-in-the-Box is faithful. John Mole. NOxBChV

Jack in the Pulpit. *Unknown.* OxNR

Jack Jelf. *Unknown.* ReMoGo

Jack Jingle. *Unknown.* ReMoGo

Jack johnson licked. White Hope. Ishmael Reed. ISC

Jack jump over / The candlestick. (LL) Jack be nimble. Mother Goose. LB; OxNR; ReMoGo

Jack London once told the story. Johnny. Vladimir Nikolaevich Kornilov, *Russian.* TCRP, *tr. by* Daniel Weissbort

Jack Monroe. *Unknown.* AmFP

Jack o' Diamonds. *Unknown.* AmFP

Jack o' the Inkpot. Algernon Blackwood. BoTP

Jack of the North. *Unknown.*

   "Now for that slawnders sake." PBRV

Jack Sprat could eat no fat. Mother Goose. FaBoBe; LB; OxNR; ReMoGo

Jack Sprat / Had a cat. Jack Sprat's Cat. *Unknown.* OxNR

Jack Steeplejack. Tall Story for Fred Dibnah. Geoffrey Summerfield OTCP

Jack Tar. Emile Jacot. BoTP

Jack the Giant-Killer. James Whitcomb Riley. NOxBChV

Jack the Giant Queller; an Antique History. Henry Brooke. NOEC

Jack the Jolly Tar. *Unknown.* AmFP

Jack was a swarthy, swaggering son-of-a-gun. Carl Sandburg. SAGP

Jack Would Speak Through the Imperfect Medium of Alice. Alice Notley. PT; PmAP

Jackdaw of Rheims, The. Richard Harris Barham. CABP

Jackdaw of Rheims, The. *Unknown.* EBNV; OBCoV; OBNV; OBSP *Fr.* The Ingoldsby Legends.

Jackdaw sat on the Cardinal's chair, The. The Jackdaw of Rheims. *Unknown.* EBNV; OBCoV; OBNV; OBSP *Fr.* The Ingoldsby Legends.

Jacke and *Jone*, they thinke no ill. Thomas Campion. *See* Jack and Joan they think no ill.

Jacket Notes. Ishmael Reed. UnSA

Jacket of Gray, The. Caroline Augusta Ball. CBCWP

Jackey Jackey gallops on a horse like a swallow. A Bushranger. Kenneth Slessor. CBAP; NOBAu

Jackfruit, The. Ho Xuan Huong, *Vietnamese.* PBWP, *tr. by* Nguyen Ngoc Bich

Jackie. King D. Kuka. VoR

Jackie and I cross-legged. Brown Girl, Blonde Okie. Gary Soto. NOxBChV

Jackie's gone a-sailing with trouble on his mind. Jack Monroe. *Unknown.* AmFP

Jackknife swandive gainer twist. Elegy for a Diver. Peter Meinke. Poetsp

Jacklight. Louise Erdrich. HATNAP; WeW-3

Jack's Postcards. Ken Smith. NBrP

Jackson is on sea, Jackson is on shore. *Unknown.* AS

Jackson Pollock had a quaint. Squeeze Play. Phyllis McGinley. FaBoEE; OBCoV; OBSV *Fr.* Spectator's Guide to Contemporary Art.

Jacky, come give me thy fiddle. Jack and His Fiddle. Mother Goose. OxNR; ReMoGo

Jacob. Phoebe Cary. APAD; APN-2; OBAL; PAR

Jacob. George Garrett. CRP

Jacob. Ruth Gilbert. PeNZ *Fr.* Leah.

Jacob. Delmore Schwartz. ChIV-1

Jacob: a bull among his herd. Jacob. Else Lasker-Schüler. BoWoP, *tr. by* Rosemarie Waldrop

Jacob and Esau. Else Lasker-Schüler, *German.* BoWoP, *tr. by* Rosemarie Waldrop

Jacob, hear! Jacob's Destiny. Richard Beer-Hofmann. TrJP, *tr. by* Ida Bension Wynn *Fr.* Jacob's Dream.

Jacob Wrestling with the Angel. Jones Very. ChIV-1

Jacobite Toast. John Byrom. *See* Extempore [Verses] Intended to Allay the Violence of Party-Spirit.

Jacobite's Epitaph, A. Thomas Babington Macaulay. FaPoR; NOBE; OBEV; OBNB

   (Epitaph on a Jacobite.) EBEV; NOBVV; OxAEP-2

Jacob's Dream. Richard Beer-Hofmann, *German.*

   Jacob's Destiny. TrJP, *tr. by* Ida Bension Wynn

Jacob's Ladder, The. Denise Levertov. APSN; AmPP; ChIV-1; KSG; PoM

Jacob's Pillow, and Pillar. Henry Vaughan. ChIV-1

Jacques s'apprête. Luis d'Antin Van Rooten. OBCoV *Fr.* Mots d'Heures: Gousses, Rames.

Jade. Janice Mirikitani. UnSA

Jade cave, ten thousand flowering peach trees, A. Painting. Chang Yü, *Chinese.* CoBLCP, *tr. by* Jonathan Chaves

Jade dews deeply wilt and wound the maple woods. Tu Fu. SuSp, *tr. by* Wu-chi Liu *Fr.* Autumn Thoughts.

Jade faces of the girls on Yüeh Stream, The. The Girls of Yüeh. Li Po, *Chinese.* TAL, *tr. by* Robert Payne

Jade Flower Palace. Tu Fu, *Chinese.* ChiPo; OHPC, *tr. by* Kenneth Rexroth

Jade Stairs Resentment. Li Po, *Chinese.* ChiPo, *tr. by* Greg Whincup

Jade Steps Plaint. Hsieh T'iao, *Chinese.* SuSp, *tr. by* Ronald C. Miao

Jade trees from the rear courtyard of the empire of Ch'en. Li K'ai-hsien. CoBLCP, *tr. by* Jonathan Chaves *Fr.* On Snow.

Jagg'd mountain peaks and skies ice-green. Brueghel's Winter. Walter De la Mare. GS

Jagged head. King & Queen. John Montague. PBCIP

Jaguar, The. Ted Hughes. LiTM

Jaguar is Getting Ready, The. Anna Hajnal, *Hungarian.* CEEP, *tr. by* Juliette Victor-Rood

Jah Son / Another Way. Kendel Hippolyte. PBCV

Jahr der Seele, Das. Stefan George, *German.*

   "No way too long--no path too steep." AWP, *tr. by* Daisy Broicher

Jail, Flames--Jersey, 1971. Lynda Hull. PUP-19

Jail Poems. Bob Kaufman. NAAAL

Jailbird. Vernon Scannell. OxBC

Jain Bird Hospital in Delhi, The. William Meredith. VCAP

Jaisalmer, 1. Ghulam Mohammed Sheikh, *Gujarati.* OMIP, *tr. by* Saleem Peeradina *and* Ghulam Mohammed Sheikh

Jake Addresses the World from the Garden. Jack Myers. NAmP90

Jake Balokowsky, my biographer. Posterity. Philip Larkin. OxBC

Jake's Wharf. Philip Booth. NYBP

Jalan Thamrin in Denpasar. Walking down Jalan Thamrin. Robert Francis Brissenden. CBAP

Jalapeña Gypsies. Jay Wright. NBV

Jam Fish, The. Edward Abbott Parry. OxBChV

Jam on Gerry's Rock, The. *Unknown.* AS; AmFP

Jam Session. Langston Hughes. MoNo

Jam Trap, The. Charles Tomlinson. MoBrPo

Jamaica. Louis Simpson. PBCV

Jamaica 1980. Lorna Goodison. GT

Jamaica, a Poem in Three Parts, Written in That Island in the Year 1776. *Unknown.*

   "And can the muse reflect her tear-stain'd eye." PBCV

Jamaica Market. Agnes Maxwell-Hall. TTY; WHSW

Jamaica oman cunny sah! Louise Bennett. HCP

Jamaican Bus Ride. Arthur Seymour John Tessimond. OxBTC

Jamaican Fisherman. Philip Sherlock. PBCV

Jamaican Small Gal. A. L. Hendriks. HCP

Jamal's Lamentation. Reuben Jackson. GT

James A. Wright, my difficult older brother. Elevens. Marilyn Hacker. RA

James Alan Park / Came naked stark. Thomas Erskine. FaBoEE

James Bird. *Unknown.* AmFP

James Bond Movie, The. May Swenson. FaBoWP

James Bottle's Year. Alastair Reid. FaBoTC

James Dean. Rae Desmond Jones. BMAP

James Grant. *Unknown.* ESPB

James Harris (The Daemon Lover). *Unknown.* ESPB

James Hatley. *Unknown.* ESPB

James Honeyman was a silent child. W. H. Auden. MoBS

James Hugo Johnston. Maggie Pogue Johnson. CBWP-4

James James. Disobedience. A. A. Milne. NOxBChV; NTCP; OTCP; TLR; UV

James Lee's Wife. Robert Browning.

   Among the Rocks. OxBSP

   In the Doorway. SCGP

James Madison's hand cd lead an ox to water. 1809. Jackson MacLow. APSN *Fr.* The Presidents of the United States of America.

James Monroe / laid a hand. 1817. Jackson MacLow. APSN *Fr.* The Presidents of the United States of America.

James Powell on Imagination. Larry Neal. BPo

James Rigg. James Hogg. BXAP

James Wetherell. Edwin Arlington Robinson. MoAmPo

James Whaland. *Unknown.* AS

James Wright, Richard Hugo, the Vanishing Forests of the Pacific Northwest. Campbell McGrath. PaTW

Jamesian. Thom Gunn. PiM

Jameson's Ride. Alfred Austin.
"Wrong! Is it wrong? Well, may be." UV

Jamie Douglas. *Unknown.* ESPB
(Lord Douglas.) OxBB

Jamie Douglas. *Unknown. See* Waly, Waly [Love Be Bonny].

Jamie Telfer of [*or* in] the Fair Dodhead. *Unknown.* ESPB; IBB; OxBB

Jamila. Nazik Al-Mala'ika, *Arabic.* WPOW, *tr. by* Kamal Boullata

Jan van Hogspeuw staggers to the door. The Card-Players. Philip Larkin. BLT; OxBC

Jane. Philip Hammial. BMAP

Jane Addams (September 6, 1860–May 21, 1935). Gwendolyn Brooks. PuP-16

Jane Austen. Patricia Beer. CABP

Jane Austen at the Window. Patricia Beer. FaBoWP

Jane, Jane, / Tall as a crane. Aubade. Dame Edith Sitwell. BWW; CMoP; MoBrPo; MoP; NALW; NoAM; PoRA; Poetr

Jane looks down at her organdy skirt. In Bertram's Garden. Donald Justice. BoLoP; MT; SAGP; VGW

Janet Waking. John Crowe Ransom. CMoP; ColAP; FuPo; InPK-6; MeMAP; MoAmPo; MoP; NAAL-2; NoAM; PBMP; PoE; Poetr; RB; TAP

Janitor's Boy, The. Nathalia Crane. PoLF

Jankin, the Clerical Seducer. *Unknown. See* Jolly Jankin.

Janna. King D. Kuka. VoR

Januar: by this fire [*or* thys fyre] I warme my handes. *Unknown.* EBEV

Januaries, Nature greets our eyes. Brazil, January 1, 1502. Elizabeth Bishop. BLT; FaBoWP; NoAM; PoPoPo; VCAP

January. John Clare. Ro *Fr.* The Shepherd's Calendar.

January. William Virgil Davis. IFJA

January. Cornelius Eady. IFJA

January. Douglas Gibson. OBCP

January. Hoffman Reynolds Hays. SPE

January. John Heath-Stubbs. OBCP

January. Weldon Kees. CoAP

January. Henrietta Cordelia Ray. CBWP-3

January. Folgore da San Geminiano. *Fr.* Sonnets of the Months. AWP, *tr. by* D. G. Rossetti

January. John Updike. NOxBChV

January. William Carlos Williams. MoAmPo

January, 1795. Mary Robinson. ECWP; WoRP

January brings the snow. The Garden Year. Sara Coleridge. ACTP; CTV; ChAP; FaBoBe; OTCP; OxBChV

January Dandelion, A. George Marion McClellan. AAP

January falls the snow. Calendar Rhyme. Flora Willis Watson. BoTP

January 15 as a National Holiday. Carter Revard. VoR

JANUARY FIRST. Bob Boldman. HA

January 1st. Anne Sexton. HCAP

January first isn't New Year's. Happy New Year, Anyway. Joanna Cole. NTCP

January jumps about. George Barker. AYFP

January Morning. William Carlos Williams. InPS-3

January night, A. Moonlight. Significant Fevers. Alison Fell. BrRo

January 1940. Roy Fuller. LiTM
(War Poet.) HoPM

January 1965, Looking on. Ken Irby. FTOS

January 1939. Ilya Grigoryevich Ehrenburg, *Russian.* TCRP, *tr. by* Cathy Porter

January 1939. Dylan Thomas. SPE

January of a Gnat, The. Carl Rakosi. FTOS

January 1, 1829. Nathaniel Parker Willis. APN-1

January played. One Year. N. M. Bodecker. TLR

January. Snow. For days I have craved / watermelons. Watermelon Tales. Khaled Mattawa. PUP-19

January 3, 1970. Mae Jackson. PoBA

January White Sale. William Dickey. EC2

January wind and the sun. He Who Owns the Whistle Rules the World. Roger McGough. AYFP

January wraps up the wound of his arm. Charles Henri Ford. SPE

Janus. Laurence Perrine. InPK-6

Janus am I; oldest of potentates. The Poet's Calendar. Henry Wadsworth Longfellow. APN-1

Japan. Maxine Chernoff.
Amble. PmAP
Black. PmAP

Japan. Anthony Hecht. LiTM

Japanese Archery. Aleksander Wat, *Polish.* TOF, *tr. by* Richard Lourie

Japanese Beetles. X. J. Kennedy. OBAL

Japanese City. Kenward Elmslie. PmAP

Japanese have funny things, The. A Rhyme Sheet of Other Lands. Hugh Chesterman. BoTP

Japanese Jokes. Peter Porter. OBCoV

Japanese Lovers, The. *Unknown.* BLPA

Japanese paragraph, The. Annotations Tropes and Lacunae of the Itoku Master. Ray DiPalma. FTOS

Japanese Presentation I and II. Joan Retallack. FTOS

Japanese Print. Austin Clarke. NOIV

Jar containing vermilion, The. Forgive Me. Shakti Chattopadhyay, *Bengali.* OMIP, *tr. by* Prithvindra Chakravarty *and* Ulli Beier

Jar is where the month is unclear. by stamping, by inscription, The. Agora. Aaron Shurin. PT

Jar of cider and my pipe, A. The Sluggard. W. H. Davies. OBMV

Jardin des Colombières. Lauris Edmond. OBGa

Jarrangulli. Roland Robinson. NOxBChV

Jarring the air with rumour cool. Small Fountains. Lascelles Abercrombie. CH *Fr.* Epilogue: "What shall we do for Love these days?" CH; MoBrPo *Fr.* Emblems of Love.

Jasbo Brown. DuBose Heyward. SeSe

Jasmattie live in bruk. Coolie Mother. David Dabydeen. HCP; NBrP

Jasmine. Claude McKay. GT

Jasmine. E. Ethelbert Miller. GT

Jason. Anthony Hecht. ColAP

Jaunty crop-haired graying, The. Poem about People. Robert Pinsky. VCAP

Jaunty traveller that comes to peer, The. Llyn y Gadair. T. H. Parry-Williams, *Welsh.* OBWVE, *tr. by* Anthony Conran

Javanese Dancers. Arthur Symons. ADE

Jawbone is a platter for the face, The. Dog. David Chapman Berry. BXAP

Jay a-Pass'd. William Barnes. NOBVV

Jay Gould's Daughter. *Unknown.* AS

Jay: I've one mouth but many voices. Cynewulf. ASW, *tr. by* Kevin Crossley-Holland *Fr.* Riddles (Exeter Book).

Jaybird a-sitting on a hickory limb. *Unknown.* CTV

Jays, The. John Heath-Stubbs. NOxBChV

Jazz at the Intergalactic Nightclub. Michael McClure. SeSe

Jazz Band. Frank Marshall Davis. SeSe

Jazz Band in a Parisian Cabaret. Langston Hughes. MoAmPo

Jazz Dancer. Cornelius Eady. SeSe

Jazz Fantasia. Carl Sandburg. AiP; MoAmPo; Poetr
("On the humps of the low river hills. . . go to it, O jazzmen.") (LL) SAGP

Jazz of This Hotel, The. Vachel Lindsay. SeSe

Jazz poetry was not discovered by. Words and Music in America. Kofi Natambu. MoNo

Jazz Station. Michael S. Harper. NoAM

JAZZ, the Sane Man said. Week Seven. Ellsworth McGranahan Keane. HCP

Jazz to Jackson to John. Jerry W. Ward Jr. BkSV

Jazzonia. Langston Hughes. ColAP
("O, silver tree!") NAAAL

Je ne veux de personne aupres de ma tristesse. Henri De Regnier, *French.* AWP, *tr. by* "Seumas O'Sullivan"

Je Suis une Table. Donald Hall. SPE

Je T'Adore. Thomas Kinsella. MoP; NoAM

Jealosie. Donne. CBLP; ESCV *Fr.* Elegies.

Jealous Adam. Itsik Manger, *Yiddish.* TrJP, *tr. by* Jacob Sonntag

Jealous Brothers, The. *Unknown.* AmFP

Jealous girls these sometimes were. How Marigolds Came Yellow. Robert Herrick. TTTS

Jealous Lovers, The. Donald Hall. NYBP

Jealous Man, A. Robert Graves. CMoP

Jealousy. Mei-Mei Berssenbrugge. OpBo; PmAP

Jealousy. Mary Elizabeth Coleridge. CH; EnLoPo; LW; OBNC; WPE

Jealousy. Donne. *See* Jealosie.

Jealousy. Esther Johnson. OxBSP
("O shield me from his rage, celestial Powers!") LW

(On Jealousy.) LW

Jealousy. Tristan l'Hermite, *French*. FLP, *tr. by* Alistair Elliot

Jean, death comes close to us all. The Child Bearers. Anne Sexton. BoWoP

Jean! Jean! Gin she's no' here it's no' oor bed. "Hugh MacDiarmid." FaBoTC *Fr.* A Drunk Man Looks at the Thistle.

Jean Richepin's Song. Herbert Trench. OBMV

Jeanie, come tie my. *Unknown.* BoTP

Jeanie with the Light Brown Hair. Stephen Collins Foster. APN-2

Jeanne d'Arc. Susan Bartels Ludvigson. MT

Jeanne was on bread and water in a dark room. Victor Hugo, *French*. FLP, *tr. by* Alistair Elliot

Jeannette. Otto Julius Bierbaum, *German*. AWP, *tr. by* Jethro Bithell

Jeannette and Jeannot. Charles Jefferys. BLPA

Jeannot's Answer. Charles Jefferys. BLPA

Jeat Ring Sent, A. Donne. *See* A Jet Ring Sent.

Jehovah, God, Who Dwelt of Old. Lewis R. Amis. AH

Jehovah, Lord and Majesty. Conrad Weiser, *German*. AH, *tr. by* Sheema Z. Buehne

Jehovah Our Righteousness. William Cowper. NOCV *Fr.* Olney Hymns.

Jehu. Louis MacNeice. LiTM

Jellicle Cats are black and white. The Song of the Jellicles. T. S. Eliot. EBEvV; FaBoCh; ImGa; OxBChV

Jellon Grame. *Unknown.* EBEV; ESPB; OxBB

Jelly-Fish, A. Marianne Moore. APo; ChAP

(Jellyfish, A.) OxBSP

Jelly Piece Song, The. Anne McNaughton. NTP

Jellyfish, The. Difference. Mark Doty. BAP-94

Jemima. *Unknown.* ACTP

Jemmy Ball, a lucky digger. Moggy's Wedding. Charles Robert Thatcher. NOBAu

Jengiz to Chang Chun: China. Basil Bunting. *See* Vestiges.

Jennie Jenkins. *Unknown.* AmFP

Jennie Lubell is In a Nursing Home in Provincetown. Adeline Naiman. "My mother has died, but I visit her weekly." MDDM

Jennie McGrew. Edgar Lee Masters. RACG

Jennifer Gentle and Rosemary. *Unknown. See* Riddles Wisely Expounded.

Jenny. D. G. Rossetti. EnVR; PoEL-5

Jenny and Johnny. Dorothy King. BoTP

Jenny come tie my. The Bonny Cravet. Mother Goose. OxNR

Jenny gay and Johnny grim. Jenny and Johnny. Dorothy King. BoTP

Jenny hit me when we met. John Clarke. UV

Jenny kiss'd me when we met. Paul Dehn. CBLP *Fr.* A Leaden Treasury of English Verse.

Jenny kiss'd [*or* kissed] me when we met. Rondeau: Jenny Kiss'd [*or* Kissed] Me. Leigh Hunt. BLPA; CABP; FaBoBe; ImPo; LoP; NBLV; NTCP; OBEV; OxAEP-2; PFE; PeLV; PoRA

Jenny out from Hwome. William Barnes. SCGP

Jenny Towler turned up lately. Bertolt Brecht. OxBoV, *tr. by* Ralph Manheim *and* John Willett *Fr.* The Threepenny Opera.

Jenny White and Johnny Black. Eleanor Farjeon. CTV

Jenny Wren. W. H. Davies. MoBrPo

Jenny Wren. Mother Goose. ReMoGo

Jenny Wren fell sick. Ungrateful Jenny. Mother Goose. OxNR

Jenny Wren's got a house. The Secret. Elizabeth Fleming. BoTP

Jenny, your mind commands. Reading the Brothers Grimm to Jenny. Lisel Mueller. NYBP

Jephthah's Daughter. "Yehoash," *Yiddish*. TrJP, *tr. by* Alter Brody

Jephtha's Daughter. Byron. ChIV-1

Jerboa, The. Marianne Moore. FYAP; NALW

Too Much. CMoP

Jeremiah. Bible, *O.T.*

As Fowlers Lie in Wait. TrJP

But Fear Thou Not, O Jacob. TrJP

Cry of the Daughter of My People, The. TrJP

Cursed Be the Day. TrJP

"For Thus saith The Lord to the men of Judah and Jerusalem." OBVE

O Lord, Thou Hast Enticed Me. TrJP

Oh That I Were in the Wilderness. TrJP

Jeremiah. Stefan Zweig, *German*. TrJP, *tr. by* Eden *and* Cedar Paul

Jeremiah, blow the fire. *Unknown.* OxNR

Jeremiah Obadiah, puff, puff, puff. *Unknown.* OTCP

Jeremie 17. Bible, Apocrypha. ChIV-1

Jeremy Hobbler. *Unknown.* BoTP

Jericho. Haim Guri, *Hebrew*. IP, *tr. by* Warren Bargad *and* Stanley F. Chyet

Jerking and twitching as he walks. Mightier than the Pen. Kingsley Amis. OBCoV

Jerome in His Study. Clark Coolidge. FTOS

Jerome Lallier said to ride in his sleigh. March. Judy Page Heitzman. CMAP

Jerry, Go an' Ile That Car. *Unknown.* AS

Jerry Hall, / He is so small. Mother Goose. OxNR; ReMoGo

Jerry's Plains, 1848. Geoff Page. BMAP

Jersey Cattle. Ralph Nixon Currey. OxBTC

Jersey Marsh, The. David Galler. NYBP

Jerusalem. William Blake. BoTP; FHYEP; FaPoR; NOBE; NOCV; OxAEP-2; RB; UV *Fr.* Milton.

("In England's green and pleasant Land.") (LL) APAD; CABP; NoP-4; SAGP

(New Jerusalem, The.) ImPo

(Preface.) CABP

Jerusalem. Uri Zvi Greenberg, *Hebrew*.

Jerusalem the Dismembered. TrJP, *tr. by* Charles A. Cowen

Jerusalem. Judah Halevi, *Hebrew*. TOF, *tr. by* David Goldstein

Jerusalem. Adrienne Rich. FiLi

Jerusalem. David Rokeah, *Hebrew*. MHP, *tr. by* Ruth Finer Mintz

Jerusalem be not the ground. Bible, *O.T. See* Psalm 137.

Jerusalem, my happy home. *Unknown.* PoE

Jerusalem 1967. Yehuda Amichai, *Hebrew*. IP, *tr. by* Warren Bargad *and* Stanley F. Chyet

Jerusalem Shadow. Melanie Kaye/Kantrowitz. LoHo

Jerusalem Sonnets. James Keir Baxter.

"Bees that have been hiving above the church pond, The." PeNZ

"Colin, you can tell my words are crippled now." PeNZ

"Small grey cloudy louse that nests in my beard, The." PeNZ

("Small gray cloudy louse that nests in my beard, The.") NoP-4

"Yesterday I planted garlic." PeNZ

Jerusalem the Dismembered. Uri Zvi Greenberg. TrJP, *tr. by* Charles A. Cowen *Fr.* Jerusalem.

Jerusalem; The Emanation of the Giant Albion. William Blake.

"But still the thunder of Los peals loud and thus the thunder's cry." OAEL-2

Epigraph. OBNC

"I give you the end of a golden string." NTP

"Fearing that Albion should turn his back against the Divine Vision." OAEL-2

Fields from Islington to Marybone, The. FaBoPV; OBNV

(Prelude: "Fields from Islington to Marybone, The.") OBNC

"Hampstead Highgate Finchley Hendon Muswell hill: rage loud." NOBRP

"I see the Four-fold Man. The Humanity in deadly sleep." NOBRP

"It is easier to forgive an enemy than to forgive a friend." OAEL-2

Male & Female Loves in Beulah. OBNC

Prelude: "England! awake! awake! awake!" OBNC

"Shuddring the Spectre howls, his howlings terrify the night." OAEL-2

Jesse James. *Unknown.* AS; FaBoBe; UnPo

Jesse James was a lad who [*or* that] killed many a man. *Unknown, sometimes att. to* Billy LaShade *or* Gashade. APN-2; AmFP

Jesse James was a two-gun man. William Rose Benét. FYAP; MoAmPo

Jessie Mitchell's Mother. Gwendolyn Brooks. BoWoP; ColAP; NALW; NMM-2

Jest, The. Austin Clarke. BIrV

Jest 'fore Christmas. Eugene Field. PoLF

Jester or a buffoon might play with demons and not pay, A. Courting the Famous Figures at the Grotto of Improbable Thought. Brigit Pegeen Kelly. BAP-94

Jester walked in the garden, The. The Cap and Bells. W. B. Yeats. MoBrPo; NoAM; RB

Jesu, Come on Board. Johann C. Pyrlaeus, *German*. AH, *tr. by* Sheema Z. Buehne

Jesu Crist, heovene king. *Unknown.* MiEL

Jesu, for thy muchele might. *Unknown.* MiEL

JESU is in my heart, his sacred name. George Herbert. GeHe; MeLP

Jesu, Joy of Man's Desiring. Robert Fitzgerald. NYBP

Jesu, no more! is full tide. Richard Crashaw. *Fr.* Upon the Bleeding Crucifix. SeCP

Jesu, no more, it is full tide. Upon the Bleeding Crucifix. Richard Crashaw.

Jesu our raunsoun. William Herebert. MiEL

Jesu preserve your royal Majesty! Shakespeare. OxBSn *Fr.* Henry VI.

Jesu, sweete sone dear. The Virgin's Song. *Unknown.* NOBE

Jesu that is most of might. *Unknown.* MiEL

Jesu, thie love within mee is soe maine. William Alabaster. ESCV *Fr.* Divine Meditations. Son

JESU, thy love within me is so main. A Divine Sonnet. William Alabaster. NoSic

Jesu, to Thee My Heart I Bow. Nikolaus Ludwig, Graf von Zinzendorf, *German.* AH, *tr. by* John Wesley

Jesukin. Saint Ita, *Irish.* TIRV, *tr. by* George Sigerson

Jesus. Francis Lauderdale Adams. OxBS

Jesus. James Philip McAuley. CBAP; ChIV-2

Jesus. Novica Tadic, *Serbo-Croatian.* HSix; VCWP, *tr. by* Charles Simic

Jesus a Child His Course Begun. Margaret Fuller. AH

Jesus and His Mother. Thom Gunn. OxBC

Jesus before Pilate said nothing. René Daumal, *French.* GI, *tr. by* Washburn, Katharine

Jesus Borned in Bethlea. *Unknown.* AmFP

Jesus Dies. Anne Sexton. CrSp; RACG

Jesus, Enthroned and Glorified. Zachary Eddy. AH

Jesús, Estrella, Esperanza, Mercy. Middle Passage. Robert Earl Hayden. BPo; ColAP; InPS-3; NoAM; PoBA; TRP; VCAP

Jesus, friend of little children. Walter J. Mathams. CTV

Jesus got up one day a little later than usual. Goodtime Jesus. James Tate. LCAP-2; WeT

Jesus, grant us all a blessing. Shouting Song. *Unknown.* AmFP

Jesus had gone far up the dark slope, when he looked back. Quetzalcoatl Looks Down on Mexico. D. H. Lawrence. PeECV

Jesus, I Come to Thee. Nathan S. S. Beman. AH

Jesus, I Live to Thee. Henry Harbaugh. AH

Jesus, in Sickness and in Pain. Thomas H. Gallaudet. AH

Jesus, Keep Me Near the Cross. Fanny Crosby. AH

Jesus, look with pitying eye. (LL) Evening Contemplation. George Washington Doane. AH; BLPA; FaBoBe

Jesus, Lover of My Soul. In Temptation. Charles Wesley. NOEC; PoEL-3

Jesus Loves Me, This I Know. Anna Bartlett Warner. AH

Jesus, Master, O Discover. *Unknown.* AH

Jesus, Merciful and Mild! Thomas Hastings. AH

Jesus, my Light. They Shall Look on Him. "Michael Field." VWP

Jesus! my Shepherd, Husband, Friend. John Newton. *Fr.* The Name of Jesus. ECEV; NOEC

Jesus on the Sabbath. *Unknown, Irish.* TIRV, *tr. by* Brendan Kennelly

Jesus, our brother, kind [*or* strong] and good. The Friendly Beasts. *Unknown.* PChr

Jesus Praying. Hartley Coleridge. ChIV-2

Jesus Saviour, Pilot Me. Edward Hopper. AH

Jesus, Shepherd of Thy Sheep. George Washington Bethune. AH

Jesus, son of the living God. Jesus on the Sabbath. *Unknown, Irish.* TIRV, *tr. by* Brendan Kennelly

Jesus Spreads His Banner o'er Us. Roswell Park. AH

Jesus, These Eyes Have Never Seen. Ray Palmer. AH

Jesus, thou art the sinner's friend. 'Tis Sweet to Rest in Lively Hope. *Unknown.* AmFP

Jesus, Thou Divine Companion. Henry Van Dyke. AH

Jesus Was Crucified or: It Must Be Deep. Carolyn M. Rodgers. BlSi; PoBA

Jesus, Won't You Come B'm-By? *Unknown.* AS

Jet Ring Sent, A. Donne. CBLP; OxBSP

(Jeat Ring Sent, A.) PoEL-2

Jet Set Melodrama. Michael Brownstein. FTOS

Jetty, to the milking shed. Jean Ingelow. *See* The High Tide on the Coast of Lincolnshire, 1571.

Jetty with its old wormeaten planks, The. Re-encounter. Joaquim Paço D'Arcos, *Portuguese.* PeSAV, *tr. by* Roy Campbell

Jew. James A. Randall Jr. BPo

Jew, The. Isaac Rosenberg. ChIV-1; MoBrPo

Jew at Christmas Eve, The. Karl Shapiro. VGW

Jew Walks in Westminster Abbey, A. Aubrey Hodes. TrJP

Jewel, The. James Wright. CoAP; NAAL-2

Jewel of the almost islands and the isles. Catullus. *See* Carmen 31 ("Apple of islands, Sirmio, & bright peninsulas, set").

Jewel of the secret treasury, The. Hafiz. AWP, *tr. by* Gertrude Lowthian Bell *Fr.* Odes.

Jewel Stairs' Grievance, The. Li Po, *Chinese.* NOBA; OBVE, *tr. by* Ezra Pound

Jewelers' windows have been muted with, The. Natural History. Karl Kirchwey. WWSi

Jewelled steps are already quite white with dew, The. The Jewel Stairs' Grievance. Li Po, *Chinese.* NOBA; OBVE, *tr. by* Ezra Pound

Jewels, The. Charles Baudelaire, *French.* NAWM-2, *tr. by* David Paul; BoLoP; LoP, *tr. by* Roy Campbell

Jewels In My Hand. Sasha Moorsom. APAD

Jewish Arabic Liturgies. *Unknown, Arabic.* TrJP, *tr. by* Hartwig Hirschfeld

Jewish Bride, The. Paul Durcan. BiHa

Jewish Cemetery at Newport, The. Henry Wadsworth Longfellow. APN-1; AmPP; ChIV-1; ColAP; FaBoA; HAP; HeIP-4; HoPM; MeMAP; NCAP; NOBA; NoP-4; OxBA; PAR; PoPoPo; TAP

Jewish Cemetery at Olsany, Kafka's Grave, April, Sunny Weather, The. Miroslav Holub, *Czech.* PoSu, *tr. by* David Young *and* Dana Hábová

Jewish Cemetery in Prague, The. Daniel S. Simko. CEEP

Jewish Conscript, The. Florence Kiper Frank. TrJP

Jewish May, The. Morris Jacob Rosenfeld, *Yiddish.* TrJP, *tr. by* Rose Pastor Stokes *and* Helena Frank

Jewish Poet Counsels a King, A. Santob de Carrion. TrJP *Fr.* Consejos y Documentos al Rey Dom Pedro.

Jewish Singles Event, The. Stewart Florsheim. UnSA

Jews at Haifa. Randall Jarrell. MoAmPo

Jews from Holland, France, and Hungary, and later from. Charles Reznikoff. HP *Fr.* Mass Graves.

Jews in Babylonia. Charles Reznikoff.

I. FTOS

Jews in Hell. Tom Mandel. PmAP

Jews in the Land of Israel. Yehuda Amichai, *Hebrew.* IP; PoSu, *tr. by* Warren Bargad *and* Stanley F. Chyet

Jews Speak in Heaven, The. Gary Catalano. NOBAu

Jezrael. Avraham Shlonsky, *Hebrew.* MHP, *tr. by* Ruth Finer Mintz

Jig, A. Robert Greene. *See* Doron's Jigge.

Jig Tune: Not for Love. Thomas McGrath. VGW

Jigsaw Puzzle. Russell Hoban. NTCP

Jill, A Pindaric Ode. Elizabeth Thomas.

"Nine times the sun his yearly course had run." ECWP

Jill's Death. George Buchanan. PNI

Jilted Nymph, The. Thomas Campbell. EnLoPo

Jim. Hilaire Belloc. *See* Jim Who Ran Away from His Nurse, and Was Eaten by a Lion.

Jim Bludso of the Prairie Belle. John Milton Hay. APN-2; FaBoBe

Jim Crack Corn; or The Blue Tail Fly. *Unknown, sometimes at. to* Daniel Decatur Emmett. APN-2

Jim Crow Car. Langston Hughes. GM

Jim Crow Cars. Lizelia Augusta Jenkins Moorer. CBWP-3

Jim Desterland. Hyam Plutzik. RB; VGW; WeT

Jim Dumps was a most unfriendly man. Force. *Unknown.* OBCoV *Fr.* Advertising Rhymes.

Jim Fisk. *Unknown.* AS

Jim, give me your paw! For luck! To Kachalov's Dog. Sergey Aleksandrovich Yesenin, *Russian.* TCRP, *tr. by* Daniel Weissbort

Jim Hall's guitar walking around. From Rich Uneasy America to My Friend Christopher Logue. Adrian Mitchell. SeSe

Jim Jay. Walter De la Mare. CBNP

Jim Jones. *Unknown.* CBAP

Jim says a sailor man. When We Are Men. Stella Mead. BoTP

Jim Who Ran Away from His Nurse, and Was Eaten by a Lion. Hilaire Belloc. EBNV; NOxBChV; OBSP; OxAEP-2; OxBChV

(Jim.) NoAM; PeLV

Jiminy Whillikers / Admiral Samuel. Monarch of the Sea. George Starbuck. OBAL

Jimmy Jet and His TV Set. Shel Silverstein. OBCA; OBCoV

Jimmy Judge. *Unknown.* AmFP

Jimmy the Mowdy. Greedy Tom. *Unknown.* OxNR

Jimmy's Enlisted; or, The Recruited Collier. *Unknown.* EBEV

Jingle bells! jingle, bells! *Unknown.* OxNR

Jingle in a broken tongue, A. (LL) The Poet. Paul Laurence Dunbar. AAP; BPo; CrDW; NAAL

Jingling her moon of parchment. Preciosa and the Wind. Federico García Lorca, *Spanish.* STV, *tr. by* John Frederick Nims

Jinny. *Unknown.* NOSC

Jinny the Just. Matthew Prior. NOBE; NOEC; OBEV; PoEL-3

Jist Ti Let Yi No. Tom Leonard. FaBoTC

Jitterbugging in the Streets. Calvin C. Hernton. PoBA

Jittery Jim. William Jay Smith. FuFo

Jo Jo, My Child. *Unknown, Hebrew.* TrJP, *tr. by* Immanuel Olsvanger

Joal. Léopold Sédar Senghor, *French.* NegPo, *tr. by* Ellen Conroy Kennedy

Joan / did you never hear. To Joan. Lucille Clifton. CrSp

Joan Miró ("After that war, when death had gone away"). Ruthven Todd. SPE

Joan Miró ("Once there were peasant pots and a dry brown hare"). Ruthven Todd. SPE

Joan of Arc. Benjamin Péret, *French.* PFTM, *tr. by* Keith Hollaman

Joan of Arc. Robert Southey.

Natural Religion. Ro

Joan of Arc / Built an ark. Hisperica Famina. Jack Spicer. CBNP

João was young like us. The Poem of João. Noémia da Sousa, *Portuguese*. PeSAV, *tr. by* Margaret Dickinson

Job. Bible, *O.T.* NAWM-1

  "Hast thou given the horse strength?" CTAV

  Job's Entreaty. AWP

  Let the Day Perish [Wherein I Was Born]. OBVE; TrJP (Job's Curse.) AWP

  "Moreover the Lord answered Job, and said." OBVE

  Out of the Whirlwind. AWP

  Not Flesh of Brass. TrJP

  Then the Lord Answered ("Who is this that darkeneth counsel by words without knowledge?"). AWP

  "Knowest thou the time when the wild goates of the rocke bring forth?" OBVE

  "Then the Lord answered Job out of the whirlewind, and sayd." AWP; OBVE

Job. Elizabeth Sewell. ChIV-1

Job Complaineth of Life. Bible, *O.T. Fr.* Job. NAWM-1

Job Davies, eighty-five. Lore. Ronald Stuart Thomas. NoP-4; OxBC; RB

Job. I. John Hall. ChIV-1

Job in certain lives has been to find a, The. The Spell. Molly Peacock. FFC

Job Militant. Francis Quarles.

  Meditatio Tertia Decima. ChIV-1

Job sat in a corner of the dump eating asparagus. Cæsura. John Ashbery. ChIV-1; KSG

Job Speaks. David Rosenberg. PT

Job the Father. Richard Shelton. PBCAP

Job Triumphant. Joshua Sylvester.

  Leviathan. KSG

Job's Comforters. Bible, *O.T. Fr.* Job. NAWM-1

Job's Curse. Bible, *O.T. See* Let the Day Perish [Wherein I Was Born].

Job's Entreaty. Bible, *O.T.* AWP *Fr.* Job. NAWM-1

Job's Epitaph. Joshua Sylvester. ChIV-1

Job's Wife. Betsy Sholl.

  "Yes, I said it." CrSp

Jocelyn, my Dragon. Colin West. PeP

Jock o' Dreams. Rose Fyleman. BoTP

Jock o' the Side. *Unknown.* ESPB; IBB; OxBB

Jock of Hazeldean. Sir Walter Scott. GTBS-P; NAEL-2; NOBRP; OxBS

Jock the Leg and the Merry Merchant. *Unknown.* ESPB

Jock, to the First Army. Violet Jacob. NSI

Jocund my Muse was; but his Life was chast. (LL) The Pillar of Fame. Robert Herrick. BeJo; CaPo; NIP-4; SeCP

Joe Bowers. *Unknown.* AmFP

Joe Brickhouse saw his dog. A Dog and a Boy. Richard Katrovas. NAmP90

Joe Gargery's Epitaph on His Father. Charles Dickens. FaBoVe *Fr.* Great Expectations.

Joe Hill. Alfred Hayes. UnPo

Joe Turner. *Unknown.* CrDW

Joe Turner Blues. W. C. Handy. CrDW

Joe Turner Blues. *Unknown.* AS

Joe's Luck. Albert Brodrick. PeSAV

Joe's No Saint. John D. Sheridan. TIRV

Jog On, jog on, the footpath way. Song: "Jog on, jog on, the footpath way." Shakespeare. BoTP; FaBoCh; NoSic; OxBSP *Fr.* The Winter's Tale.

Johann Joachim Quantz's Five Lessons. W. S. Graham. FaBoMo; FaBoTC

Johannes Agricola in Meditation. Robert Browning. TOF

Johannes Milton, Senex. Robert Bridges. CMoP; PeECV; PoEL-5

John, Gospel according to. *See also* St. John *and* Bible, John.

John. Jones Very. ChIV-2

John 1:1–14. Gail Holst-Warhaft. GI *Fr.* St. John.

John 1:14 (1964). Jorge Luis Borges, *Spanish*. GI, *tr. by* David Curzon *and* Sarah Recalde

John 1:14 (1969). Jorge Luis Borges, *Spanish*. GI, *tr. by* Norman Thomas Di Giovanni

John 1:14; And the Word became flesh and dwelt among us. Jorge Luis Borges. GI *Fr.* St. John.

John 2:1–12; On the third day there was a marriage. Rilke. GI *Fr.* St. John.

John 3; But Men Loved Darknesse Rather than Light. Bible, *N.T.* ChIV-2, *tr. by* Richard Crashaw *Fr.* St. John.

John 3:1–15; Now there was a man. Howard Nemerov. GI *Fr.* St. John.

John, 8:21. Bible, *N.T.*

  Christ's Promise. LBC

John 11:25,26.

  "I am the resurrection, and the life." CTV

John 11:30–44; Now Jesus had not yet come to the village. Rilke. GI *Fr.* St. John.

John 12:24–25; Truly, truly, I say to you. Pier Paolo Pasolini. GI *Fr.* St. John.

John 13:21–30; When Jesus had thus said, he was troubled. Nina Kossman. GI *Fr.* St. John.

John 14:1–2. Mary Elizabeth Fullerton. GI *Fr.* St. John.

John 20:11–18; But Mary stood weeping outside the tomb. Rilke. GI *Fr.* St. John.

John Adams knew the hand. 1797. Jackson MacLow. APSN *Fr.* The Presidents of the United States of America.

John Adams lies here, of the parish of Southwell. On a Carrier Who Died of Drunkenness. Byron. NBLV

John Adkins' Farewell. *Unknown.* AmFP

John and Peter and Robert and Paul. The Chemistry of Character. Elizabeth Dorney. BLPA

John Anderson, my jo, John, / I wonder what ye mean. Robert Burns. FaBoVe; OxBS

John Anderson my jo, John / When we were first acquent. Robert Burns. AWP; BoLoP; CBLP; GTBS-P; HelP-4; ImPo; InPK-6; NOBE; NOBRP; NOEC; OBEV; OxBM; PoE; PoToHe; TFi; TRP

John Armstrongs last good night. *Unknown. See* Johnie Armstrong.

John B. Sails, The. *Unknown.* AS

John Barley-Corn, My Foe. Charles Follen Adams. OBAL

John Barleycorn [a Ballad]. Robert Burns. FaBoCh; RB

John Berryman asked me to write a poem about roosters. A Poem with Capital Letters. Jane Cooper. FaBoWP

John Berryman Listening to Robert Johnson's "King of the Delta Blues," January 1972. David Wojahn. SeSe

John Bird, a laborer, lies here. Epitaph. Sylvia Townsend Warner. MoBrPo

John Brown. Vachel Lindsay. MoAmPo *Fr.* The Booker Washington Trilogy.

John Brown, glowing far and down. The Smell of Coal Smoke. Les A. Murray. NOBAu

John Brown of Ossawatomie spake on his dying day. Brown of Ossawatomie. John Greenleaf Whittier. NCAP

John Brown's Body. Stephen Vincent Benét.

  "Congressmen came out to see Bull Run, The." CBCWP

  "He was a farmer, he didn't think much of towns." AiP

  Jack Ellyat Heard the Guns. PoLF

  John Brown's Prayer. CBCWP

  Love Came By from the Riversmoke. MoAmPo

  Song of the Riders. MoAmPo

John Brown's body lies a-mould'ring in the grave. *Unknown.* CBCWP

John Bun. *Unknown.* NBLV

John Burns of Gettysburg. Bret Harte. CBCWP

John Cabot, out of Wilma, once a Wycliffe. Riot. Gwendolyn Brooks. BPo; CAPP-1; NAAAL; NALW; NBV; PoBA; TAP

John Chapman. Richard Wilbur. OxBC

John Clare. Jon Anderson. AmPA

John Coltrane: An Impartial Review. Alfred B. Spellman. PoBA (John Coltrane.) SeSe

John Coltrane Arrived with an Egyptian Lady. Nathaniel Mackey. MoNo; PT

John Coltrane died this morning, LeRoi's in jail. Newark. Robert Kelly. MoNo; SeSe

John Connu Rider. Andrew Salkey. NTP

John Cook had a little grey mare. Mother Goose. OxNR

  Donne. James Simmons. CIP-2

John Dory. *Unknown.* ESPB

John Evereldown. Edwin Arlington Robinson. APN-2; CMoP; ColAP; MeMAP; NCAP; OxBA

John Fane Dingle. Glaucopis. Richard Hughes. OBMV

John, founder of towns, - dweller in none;. Bread-Word Giver. John Wheelwright. ChIV-2

John Gilbert was a bushranger. *Unknown.* NOBAu

John Gilpin was a citizen. The Diverting History of John Gilpin. William Cowper. EBNV; FaBoBe; OBNV

John Gorham. Edwin Arlington Robinson. MoAmPo

John Grumlie. Allan Cunningham. PoLF

John had. Happiness. A. A. Milne. NOxBChV

John Hardy. *Unknown.* AmFP

John Hardy was a desp'rate man. *Unknown.* APN-2

John Harralson, John Harralson, you are a wretched creature. Two Appeals to John Harralson, Agent. *Unknown.* OBAL

John Henry. *Unknown.* CrDW

John Henry tol' his cap'n. *Unknown. See* John Henry was a lil [*or* little] baby.

John Henry was a lil [*or* little] baby. *Unknown.* NOBA; OxBoLi
 ("John Henry tol' his cap'n.") AS
 ("Lawd, Lawd, an' I don' need no man.") (LL) APN-2
 ("When John Henry was a little babe [*or* fellow].") AmFP; BPo; NAAAL

John. In the sound of that rebellious word. Ebenezer Elliot. Son

John J. Curtis. Joseph Gallagher. AmFP

John-John. Thomas Macdonagh. AWP

John Keats. Byron. FaBoEE; UV

John Keats. D. G. Rossetti. EPCY

John Keats rose at dawn. Nick Enright. PeLi

John Kinsella's Lament for Mrs. Mary Moore. W. B. Yeats. CMoP; LiTM; OAEL-2; RB

John Knox. Iain Crichton Smith. OxBS

John L. Sullivan Enters Heaven. Robert Frost. BXAP

John Landless Leads the Caravan. Iwan Goll, *French.* TrJP

John, look what Mis' Nelson give me. The Easter Bonnet. Clara Ann Thompson. CBWP-2

John Marr. Herman Melville.
 "Since as in night's deck-watch ye show." APN-2

John Masefield Relates the Story of Tom, Tom, the Piper's Son. Louis Untermeyer. MoAmPo *Fr.* Mother Goose Up-to-Date.

John Maydew *or* The Allotment. Charles Tomlinson. OBGa

John Maynard. Horatio Alger Jr. BLPA; FaBoBe

John Mouldy. Walter De la Mare. OxBChV; RB

John Muir on Mt. Ritter. Gary Snyder. NOBA *Fr.* Burning. NeAP; PoM *Fr.* Myths and Texts.

John of Hazelgreen. *Unknown.* ESPB

John of Tours. *Unknown, French.* AWP, *tr. by* D. G. Rossetti

John Peel. John Woodcock Graves. CH; OxBoLi

John Percy / Said to his nursy. John Bingham Morton. UV

John Quincy Adams. Rosemary Benét *and* Stephen Vincent Benét. OBCA

John Quincy Adam's right hand. 1825. Jackson MacLow. APSN *Fr.* The Presidents of the United States of America.

John Rabbit, by Dame Eagle chased. The Eagle and the Beetle. Jean de La Fontaine, *French.* OBVE, *tr. by* Elizur Wright

John Rogers' Exhortation to His Children. *Unknown.* OBCA *Fr.* The New England Primer.

John Smith and his son, John Smith. Wallace Stevens. TLR

John Smith, fellow fine. *Unknown.* OxNR

John Smith of His Friend Master John Taylor. John Smith. SCAP

John spared his patient labouring ox. Adaios of Macedon, *Greek.* GrAn, *tr. by* Robin Skelton

John Stuart Mill. J. S. Mill. Edmund Clerihew Bentley. OxBoLi; PeLV *Fr.* Clerihews.

John Sutter. Yvor Winters. MoAmPo; MoP; NOBA; NoAM; PaTW

John Thomson and the Turk. *Unknown.* ESPB

John, Tom, and James. Charles Henry Ross. NBLV; OxBChV

John was a bad boy, and beat a poor cat. John, Tom, and James. Charles Henry Ross. NBLV; OxBChV

John Webster. Swinburne. *Fr.* Sonnets of English Dramatic Poets. Son

John Wesley's Rule. *Unknown.* CTV

John while swimming in the ocean. Brats. X. J. Kennedy. NBLV

John, you were figuring in the gay career. To John Lamb, Esq.: Of the South-Sea House. Charles Lamb. Son

Johnie Armstrang. *Unknown.* IBB; OxBB

Johnie Armstrong. *Unknown.* ESPB; HoPM
 (John Armstrongs last good night.) PBRV

Johnie Blunt. Robert Burns. OxBB

Johnie Cock. *Unknown.* ESPB

Johnie o' Cocklesmuir. *Unknown. See* Johnie Cock.

Johnie Scot. *Unknown.* ESPB

Johnna at the Windmill. Diane Glancy. CRP

Johnnie Cope. Adam Skirving. OxBS

Johnnie Crack and Flossie Snail. Dylan Thomas. OTCP *Fr.* Under Milk Wood.

Johnnie get your gun, get your gun, get your gun. Over There. George M. Cohan. FaBoA

Johnnie Norrie. *Unknown.* OxNR

Johnny. Vladimir Nikolaevich Kornilov, *Russian.* TCRP, *tr. by* Daniel Weissbort

Johnny and Jane and Jack and Lou. Children's Ball-Bouncing Song. *Unknown.* NOBAu

Johnny Armstrong killed a calf. *Unknown.* OxNR

Johnny Carroll's Camp. *Unknown.* AmFP

Johnny Cock, in a May morning. Johnie Cock. *Unknown.* ESPB

Johnny come down de hollow. *Unknown.* APN-2

Johnny Crow. Johnny Crow's Garden. L. Leslie Brooke. NOxBChV

Johnny Dow [*or* Doo]. *Unknown.* FaBoEE

Johnny Dyers. *Unknown.* AmFP

Johnny Faa, the Lord of Little Egypt. *Unknown.* EnSB

Johnny Gallagher. *Unknown.* AmFP

Johnny German. *Unknown.* AmFP

Johnny had a little dove. Johnny's Farm. H. M. Adams. BoTP

Johnny he's risen up in the morn. Johnny of Cockley's Well. *Unknown.* EnSB

Johnny, I Hardly Knew Ye. *Unknown.* BIrV; IIP; OxBoLi

Johnny of Cockley's Well. *Unknown.* EnSB

Johnny Sands ("There was a man named Johnny Sands, who married Betty Hague"). *Unknown.* AmFP

Johnny shall have a new bonnet. Mother Goose. OxNR; ReMoGo

Johnny Tek Away Mi Wife. "Slim" Beckford *and* Sam Blackwood. PBCV

Johnny Thomson, so they say. Mrs. Vickers' Daughter. *Unknown.* AmFP

Johnny Weissmuller Dead in Acapulco. Clive James. NOBAu

Johnny's Farm. H. M. Adams. BoTP

Johnny's Hist'ry Lesson. Nixon Waterman. PoLF

Johnny's into England gane. McNaughtan. *Unknown.* OxBB

Johnny's Pet Superstition. Clara Ann Thompson. CBWP-2

Johnny's so long at the fair. (LL) O, Dear! What Can the Matter Be? *Unknown.* CBLP; CH; OxNR

Johnny's Team. Eugene Field. PWR

Johnny's the Lad I Love. *Unknown.* OxBoLi

John's efforts to extract a thorn / failed miserably. Ammianus, *Greek.* GrAn, *tr. by* Robin Skelton

John's Song. Joan Aiken. TLR

Johnson Brothers Ltd. Rutger Kopland, *Dutch.* VCWP, *tr. by* James Brockway

Johnson-Jinkson. *Unknown.* AmFP

Johnson's Cabinet Watched by Ants. Robert Bly. MoP; NOBA

Johny Faa. *Unknown.* OxBB

Johny he has risen up i' the morn. Johnie Cock. *Unknown.* ESPB

Join me in celebrating. James Simmons. PNI

Join with the noble-hearted. Distich. Shuraikh, *Arabic.* TrJP

Joining Sir Ulick's at the river's bend. Lord Crashton: The Absentee Landlord. William Allingham. NOIV *Fr.* Laurence Bloomfield in Ireland.

Joining the Army: A Song. Wang Ts'an, *Chinese.* SuSp, *tr. by* Ronald C. Miao

Joining the Colours. Katharine Tynan. APAD

Joke, A. Aleksander Wat, *Polish.* BLT, *tr. by* Czeslaw Milosz *and* Leonard Nathan

Joke the size of a small moon headed, A. For Stuart Porter, Who Asked for a Poem That Would Not Depress Him Further. Jeffrey Skinner. PBCAP

Jolly Beggar, The. James V, King of Scotland. OxBB

Jolly Beggars, The. Robert Burns. *See* Love and Libery—A Cantata.

Jolly fat widows, The. Julia Fields. GT

Jolly Good Ale and Old. William Stevenson *and* John Still. OBEV *Fr.* Back and Side Go Bare, Go Bare. HeIP-4; NAEL-1 *Fr.* Gammer Gurton's Needle.

Jolly Jankin. *Unknown.* OxBoLi; PeLV; PoE
 (Jankin, the Clerical Seducer.) FaBoSe
 ("Kyrieleyson.") (LL) FaBoSe

Jolly Miller, The. *Unknown.* ACTP

Jolly old sow once lived in a sty, A. The Three Little Pigs. Sir Alfred Scott Gatty. ACTP; BoTP; OxBChV

Jolly Pinder of Wakefield, The. *Unknown.* ESPB; PBRV

Jolly Plowboy, The. *Unknown.* AmFP

Jolly Shepherd, The. *Unknown.* NOBE

Jolly Soldier, The. *Unknown.* AmFP

Jolly Thresherman, The. *Unknown.* AmFP

Jolly young fellow from Yuma, A. Limerick. Ogden Nash. PeLi

Jolly Young Waterman, The. Charles Dibdin. NOEC; OxAEP-1

Jollymerry / hollyberry. The Computer's First Christmas Card. Edwin Morgan. NOxBChV; PChr

Jonah. Bible, *O.T.*
 Jonah's Prayer. TrJP

Jonah. Randall Jarrell. ChIV-1

Jonah. Tomaz Salamun, *Slovenian.* CEEP, *tr. by* Šalamun, Tomaž, Eliot B. Anderson, and Charles Simic

Jonah and the Whale. Gareth Owen. OBSP

Jonah and the Whale. *Unknown.* BLPA

Jonah had his whale but we had sedans. Big Cars. Jane Flanders. PBCAP

Jonah was an immigrant, so runs the Bible tale. Darky Sunday School. *Unknown.* OxBoLi

Jonah's Prayer. Bible, *O.T.* TrJP *Fr.* Jonah.

Jonas Kindred's Household. George Crabbe. OBNC *Fr. Tales.*

Jonathan. "Rachel," *Hebrew.* TrJP, *tr. by* L. V. Snowman

Jonathan. Yona Wollach, *Hebrew.* IP, *tr. by* Warren Bargad *and* Stanley F. Chyet

Jonathan Bing. Beatrice Curtis Brown. NOxBChV

Jonathan Houghton. Edgar Lee Masters. OxBA *Fr.* Spoon River Anthology.

Jonathan Swift Somers. Edgar Lee Masters. OBAL *Fr.* Spoon River Anthology.

Jone o' Grinfilt. Joseph Lees. NOBRP

Jones! as from Calais southward you and I. Composed Near Calais on the Road Leading to Ardres, August 7, 1802. Wordsworth. FaBoPV

Jonquils and violets smelling sweet. Before Spring. P. A. Ropes. BoTP

Jordan. George Herbert. FHYEP; FSCP; GeHe; HAP; InPS-3; MeLP; NAEL-1; NOCV; NOSC; NoP-4; OAEL-1; PeECV; PoE; PoEL-2; Poetr; SeCP; TFi; TrCP

Jordan (II): "When first my lines [*or* verse] of heavenly [*or* heav'nly] joy[e]s made mention." George Herbert. ESCV; GeHe; NAEL-1; NOSC; OAEL-1; OBWVE; SeCP

　("Copie out onely that, and save expense.") (LL) FSCP; PBRV

　("Copy out only that, and save expense.") (LL) CABP; FMP

Jorge the Church Janitor Finally Quits. Martín Espada. LTA

Jorkyns was great; he labored in the City. The Tale of Jorkyns and Gertie; or, Vice Rewarded. Richard Percival Lister. NYBP

José Cruz. Mel Glenn. LiLi

José, the wind is just the restless walking of air. Wind. Tim Seibles. NAmP90

Joseph. G. K. Chesterton. ChIV-2

Joseph. Timothy Steele. RA

Joseph and Mary walked one day. The Cherry-Tree Carol. *Unknown.* AmFP

Joseph, being seventeen years old, was feeding the flock with his brethren. Bible, *O.T.* NAWM-1 *Fr.* Genesis.

Joseph Ben Tachfin came from the Sahara. Marrakech. Ralph Nixon Currey. PeSA

Joseph Come Back as the Dusk. Franz Wright. CMAP; LCAP-2

Joseph Conrad. Malcolm Lowry. CLPP

Joseph, honoured from sea to sea. The Man of the House. Katharine Tynan. TIRV

Joseph, i afraid of stars. Holy Night. Lucille Clifton. CrSp; NALW

Joseph in Carcere: or, the Innocent Prisoner. Sir Francis Hubert. ChIV-1; KSG *Fr.* Egypt's Favorite.

Joseph Joseph breathed slower. Then. Lawrence Joseph. PBCAP

Joseph of Arimathaea. Mervyn Morris. HCP

Joseph was an old man. The Cherry-Tree Carol. *Unknown.* AmFP; EBEV; ESPB; EnSB; HeIP-4; OAEL-1; OBCP; OxBB; OxBSn; OxBoLi; PeECV; SCGP; TFi

Joseph were a young man, a young man were he. The Cherry-Tree Carol. *Unknown.* AmFP

Joseph, you are crying, but you have cried enough! Song for Joseph. *Unknown, Maori. tr. by* Margaret Orbell

Joseph's Coat. George Herbert. ChIV-1; GeHe; KSG

Joseph's Suspicion. Rilke, *German.* TrCP, *tr. by* J. B. Leishman

Joshua. X. J. Kennedy. ChIV-1

Joshua at Schechem. Charles Reznikoff. ChIV-1

Joshua fit de battle of Jericho [*or* ob Jerico]. *Unknown.* APN-2; BPo; CrDW; NOBA; TAP

Joshua Lane. *Unknown.* ACTP

Josie. *Unknown.* AS

　("Frankie and Johnny were lovers.") FaBoA; NAAAL

　("He was her man, and he done her wrong.") (LL) FaBoA

　("I shot my man, 'cause he done me wrong.") (LL) NAAAL

Journal. John Ciardi. PoA

Journal. Gayl Jones.

　3-31-70. BlSi

Journal of Society, The. Godfrey Turner. NOBL; PeLV

Journal of the Laguna de San Ignacio. Nathaniel Tarn. APSN

Journal of the Storm. Greg Kuzma. AmPA

Journal of the Thousand Choices. Susan Wheeler. PUP-19

Journal to Stella. Morton Dauwen Zabel. PoA

Journalist, The. Cornelius Mathews. APN-1 *Fr.* Poems on Man in His Various Aspects under the American Republic.

Journalists. Rudyard Kipling. *Fr.* Epitaphs of the War [1914–1918]. OBWP

Journey, The. Igor Bobrowsky. CDa

Journey, The. Eavan Boland. BiHa

Journey. Breyten Breytenbach, *Afrikaans.* AF, *tr. by* Denis Hirson

Journey. Constance Carrier. AFr

Journey, The. Aidan Clarke. BoTP

Journey. Elizabeth Cook-Lynn. HATNAP

Journey. Roy Daniells. MoCV

Journey, A. Edward Field. BLT

Journey. Rodney Hall. NOBAu

Journey, The. David Ignatow. Poetsp

Journey, The. Maxine W. Kumin. MDDM

Journey, The. Judith Nicholls. OBSP

Journey, The. Mary Oliver. CrSp

Journey. Vasco [*or* Vasko] Popa. PoSu *Fr.* Besieged Serenity.

Journey, The. Franz Wright. LCAP-2

Journey, The. James Wright. NoAM; PoE; WeT

Journey and Observations of a Countryman, The. John Hawthorn. Deathbed, A. NOEC

Journey, and the struggles of the moon, The. (LL) Ajanta. Muriel Rukeyser. LiTM; MoAmPo; NNaP

Journey Away, A. Carl Rakosi. PFTM

Journey Back to Christmas. Gwen Dunn. OBCP

Journey from Patapsko to Annapolis, A. Richard Lewis.

　Humming Bird, The. APo

　Mocking Bird, The. APo

Journey in the Orient. Maria Luisa Spaziani, *Italian.* BoWoP, *tr. by* Ruth Feldman

Journey is never what's expected, The. Transit Authority. Tony Sanders. BAP-95

Journey, 1966. Anselm Hollo. PmAP

Journey North. Tu Fu, *Chinese.* SuSp, *tr. by* Hugh M. Stimson

Journey of the Magi. T. S. Eliot. EBEvV; FaBoCh; FaBoMo; GI; HAP; HeIP-4; ImPo; InPK-6; LiTM; MoAmPo; NAEL-2; NIP-4; NOCV; NoP-4; OBCP; OBMV; OxBTC; PBMP; PChr; PoE; Poetr; TAP; TFi; TRP; TwCP

Journey Onwards, The. Thomas Moore. GTBS-P; OxAEP-2

Journey Out. Rachel Hadas. RA

Journey round the World. Ingrid Jonker, *Afrikaans.* PBWP, *tr. by* Jack Cope *and* William Plomer

Journey: the North Coast. Robert Gray. BMAP

Journey through the Moonlight, A. Russell Edson. LCAP-2

Journey to a Village. Wang Yü-ch'eng, *Chinese.* CoBCP, *tr. by* Burton Watson

Journey To Barcelona. Sylvia Townsend Warner. WPN

Journey to Hell, A; or, A Visit Paid to the Devil. Edward Ward. Parish Poor-Officers, The. NOEC

Journey to Iceland. W. H. Auden. PoA

Journey to the Interior. Theodore Roethke. DiPo; LCAP-2; NYBP; TRP; VGW *Fr.* North American Sequence.

Journey to the Interior. William Jay Smith. DiPo

Journey to the Place of Ghosts. Jay Wright. GT; VCAP

Journey toward Evening. Phyllis McGinley. NYBP

Journeying by Stream: Following Chin-chu Torrent I Cross the Mountains. Hsieh Ling-yün, *Chinese.* SuSp, *tr. by* Francis Westbrook

Journeying over many seas and through many countries. Catullus. *See* On the Burial of His Brother.

Journeying to Hsiang-yi. Ch'en Yü-yi, *Chinese.* SuSp, *tr. by* Irving Y. Lo

Journeying to the Village. Wang Yü-ch'eng, *Chinese.* SuSp, *tr. by* Irving Y. Lo

Journeys. Meg Campbell. PeNZ

Journey's End. Humbert Wolfe. TrJP

Jove descends in sleet and snow. The Storm. Alcaeus, *Greek.* AWP, *tr. by* John Hermann Merivale

Jove, for Europa[e]s love took[e] shape of bull. Would I were Changed. Barnabe Barnes. AAS *Fr.* Parthenophil and Parthenophe.

Jove grant large space of life, and length of days. Juvenal. OBCVT, *tr. by* Thomas Shadwell *Fr.* The Tenth Satyr of Juvenal.

Jove send me more such afternoons as this. (LL) Elegies: 1.5. Ovid, *Latin.* BoLoP; CABP; EBEV; EP; GBL; NNPT; NoSic; OBVE; OxAEP-1, *tr. by* Marlowe

Jovial Beggar, The. *Unknown.* BoTP

Jovial Shepheard's Song, The. Michael Drayton. *See* The Trent.

Joy. Gavin Bantock. OxBTC

Joy. Robinson Jeffers. CMoP

Joy. Carl Sandburg. SAGP

Joy—a beginning. Anguish, ardor. Relearning the Alphabet. Denise Levertov. NOBA

Joy a fix'd state—a tenure, not a start! Sydney, Lady Morgan Owenson. NOBRP

Joy! a heart so overflowing. Bernard de Ventadour, *French.* STV, *tr. by* John Frederick Nims

Joy and anger are not caused by outside things. Miscellaneous Feelings in the Sui Garden. Yüan Mei, *Chinese.* CoBLCP, *tr. by* Jonathan Chaves

Joy and Peace in Believing. William Cowper. NOCV *Fr.* Olney Hymns.

Joy and Pleasure. W. H. Davies. OBMV

Joy and Temperance and Repose. *Unknown.* SoSe-8

Joy and the soul are mates, as heart and sorrow. The Cruse. Louise Townsend Nicholl. NYBP

Joy, did I [*or* I did] lock thee up; but some bad man. The Bunch of Grapes. George Herbert. ChIV-1; ESCV; GeHe; NAEL-1; NOSC; TOF

Joy-fulfiller / fruit provider / many-skilled cook of the whole year. On the Fruit-Providing Autumn Season. Catharina Regina von Greiffenberg, *German.* WPoS, *tr. by* Michael Hamburger

Joy has round eyes and terror has—. In the City Park. Bulat Shalvovich Okudzhava, *Russian.* TCRP, *tr. by* Deming Brown

Joy is a partnership. Frederic Lawrence Knowles. IMW *Fr.* Grief and Joy.

Joy is a trick in the air. Birth-Dues. Robinson Jeffers. MoAmPo

Joy May Kill. Michelangelo Buonarroti, *Italian.* AWP, *tr. by* John Addington Symonds

Joy of Church Fellowship Rightly Attended, The. Edward Taylor. AmPP; MeMAP; NAAL-1; NAAL-3; OxBA; SCAP *Fr.* God's Determinations [touching his Elect].

Joy of Cooking, The. David Mus.

    Conserves. PoA

Joy of Incompleteness, The. Albert Crowell. PoToHe

Joy of Knowledge. Isidor Schneider. TrJP

Joy of Life. Moses ibn Ezra. TrJP, *tr. by* Solomon Solis-Cohen *Fr.* The Book of Tarshish.

Joy of my life, full oft for loving you. Sonnet 82. Edmund Spenser. HeIP-4 *Fr.* Amoretti. AAS

Joy of My Life! While Left Me Here. Henry Vaughan. FMP; GeHe

Joy of the Poor, The. Nathan Alterman, *Hebrew.*

    Convert Comes to the City, A. MHP, *tr. by* Ruth Finer Mintz

    Introduction: "Joy of the poor knocked on the door, The." MHP, *tr. by* Ruth Finer Mintz

    Song to the Wife of His Youth, The. MHP, *tr. by* Ruth Finer Mintz

Joy of the poor knocked on the door, The. Introduction. Nathan Alterman. MHP, *tr. by* Ruth Finer Mintz *Fr.* The Joy of the Poor.

Joy of Union, The. Yang Fang, *Chinese.* CoBCP, *tr. by* Burton Watson

Joy precedes it, sudden joy. Fragment from the Golden Age. János Pilinszky, *Hungarian.* CEEP, *tr. by* Emery E. George

Joy, shipmate, joy! Walt Whitman. MeMAP; MoAmPo; TAP

Joy so short alas, the pain so near, The. Sir Thomas Wyatt. SiPS

Joy to Philip, he this day. Going into Breeches. Charles Lamb *and* Mary Lamb. OxBChV

Joy to the bridegroom and the bride. The Milkmaid's Epithalamium. Thomas Randolph. BoLoP; EP

Joyce was afraid of thunder. Volcano. Derek Walcott. OxBC

Joyce's Repentance, The. *Unknown, Irish.* TIRV, *tr. by* Douglas Hyde

Joyful at length may be my fare. (LL) Consolation. Henry Howard, Earl of Surrey. AAS; EBEV; EnLoPo; NOBE; NoSic; SiPS

Joyful Noise, A. Donald Finkel. CoAP

Joyful Sound It Is, A. George Strebeck. AH

Joyfully, Joyfully Onward I Move. William Hunter. AH

Joyless / what I have done. Liadan Laments Cuirithir. *Unknown, Irish.* BIrV; PBWP, *tr. by* John Montague

Joyous birds, hid under greenewoode shade, The. Torquato Tasso. OBVE *Fr.* Godfrey of Bulloigne; or, The Recoverie of Jerusalem.

Joys. James Russell Lowell. BoTP

Joys of Mary, The. *Unknown.* AmFP

Joys of the Country: Seven Poems. Wang Wei, *Chinese.*

    "Lush, lush, fragrant grasses in autumn green." CoBCP, *tr. by* Burton Watson

Joys Once Shared. C. S. Lewis. LBC

Joze was born in the village of Loski Potok. Yugoslav Story. Susan Hampton. BMAP

J's the jumping Jay-walker. Phyllis McGinley. SSCS *Fr.* All around the Town.

Juan de Juni the priest said. Aodh Ruadh O'Domhnaill. Thomas MacGreevy. CIP-2; OBMV

Juan in England. Byron. FaBoVe, *canto* 11, *stanza* 8–20 *Fr.* Canto the Eleventh. NOBRP *Fr.* Don Juan.

Juan knew several languages—as well. Byron. OAEL-2 *Fr.* Canto the Eleventh. NOBRP *Fr.* Don Juan.

Juan, the moron next door. Report from the Correspondent They Fired. David McElroy. AmPA

Juana. Alfred de Musset, *French.* AWP, *tr. by* Andrew Lang

Juana Bautista Lucero, Circa 1926, to Her Photographer. Elizabeth Libbey. CMAP

Juan's Song. Louise Bogan. NYBP; NoP-4

Jubilate Agno, *sels.* Christopher Smart.

    Fragment A.

    "Let Anaiah bless with the Dragon-fly, who sails over the pond by the wood-side and feedeth on the cresses." FaBoVe, *ll.* 100–113

    "Rejoice in God, O ye Tongues; give the glory to the Lord, and the Lamb." FaBoVe, *ll.* 1–22

    Fragment B.

    "For I bless the PRINCE of PEACE and pray that all the guns may be nail'd up, save such as are for the rejoicing days." InPS-3

    "For man is between the pinchers while his soul is shaping and purifying." ChIV-1

    "For the doubling of flowers is the improvement of the gard'ner's talent." ChIV-2; NOEC

    "For the spiritual musick is as follows." NOEC

    "Let Elizur[e] rejoice with the Partridge, who is a prisoner of state and is proud of his keepers." PoEL-3

    "Let Ephah rejoice with Buprestis, the Lord endue us with temperance and humanity, till every cow have her mate!" NOEC

    "Let Peter rejoice with the Moon Fish who keeps up the life in the waters by night." ChIV-2

    "Let Shobi rejoice with the Kastrel—blessed be the name JESUS in falconry and in the MALL." NOEC

    My Cat Jeoffry. APo; CABP; FaBoCh; PeP; PoE; RB

    ("For he purrs in thankfulness, when God tells him he's / a good Cat.") (LL) PeP

    (From Jubilate Agno.) NoP-4; PoPoPo

Jubilate Herbis. Norma Farber. PChr

Jubilate Matteo. Gavin Ewart. UV

Jubilation T. Cornpone. Johnny Mercer. OBAL; OBCoV

Jubilee before Revolution. Andrew Lang. BXAP

Juce of lekes with gotes galle. *Unknown.* MiEL

Judaeus Errans. Louis Golding. TrJP

Judah in exile wanders. George Sandys. AH; ChIV-1

Judas. Vassar Miller. ChIV-2; MoAmPo

Judas. *Unknown.* ESPB; PoE

Judas and the Profiteer. Sir Osbert Sitwell. NSI

Judas descended to this lower Hell. Judas and the Profiteer. Sir Osbert Sitwell. NSI

Judas Goat, The. Susan Musgrave. NOBC

Judas Iscariot. Countee Cullen. PoLF

Judas Iscariot. Stephen Spender. MoBrPo; NIP-4

Judas Iscariot looks down from heaven. April 1939. Dorothy, Duchess of Wellington Wellesley. WPN

Judas Iscariot / sat in the upper. Ronald Allison Kells Mason. PeNZ

Judas Maccabeus. Bible, Apocrypha. TrJP *Fr.* First Maccabees.

Judas' Reproach. Nina Kossman. GI

Judas Touch, The, for J.M. David Malouf. BMAP

Judeebug's Country. Joe Johnson. PoBA

Judge, The. Yaroslav Vasilevich Smelyakov, *Russian.* TCRP, *tr. by* Simon Franklin *and* Albert C. Todd

Judge Dreadword. Victor D. Questel. HCP

JUDGE GIVES NEGRO 90 DAYS IN COUNTY JAIL. (LL) Ballad of the Landlord. Langston Hughes. HCAP; NAAAL; NOBA

Judge Gorba. "Mikhail Semionovich Golodny," *Russian.* TCRP, *tr. by* Simon Franklin

Judge, judge, tell the judge. *Unknown.* OxBoLi

Judge Me, O God. Joel Barlow. AH

Judge Not. Josephine D. Henderson Heard. CBWP-4

Judge Not. Theodore Roethke. ChIV-2; GI

Judge not a Princess' worth impeached hereby. Queen Katherine to Owen Tudor. Michael Drayton. NoSic *Fr.* England's Heroical Epistles.

Judge not, that you be not judged. Theodore Roethke. GI *Fr.* St. Matthew.

Judge not the preacher; for He is thy Judge. George Herbert. OxAEP-1

Judge of an abnormal stone. The Narrator. Milo De Angelis, *Italian.* NeIt, *tr. by* Lawrence Venuti

Judge said "Stand up, boy, and dry up your tears," The. Twenty-one Years. *Unknown.* AmFP

Judge Somers. Edgar Lee Masters. FaBoEE; OBSV *Fr.* Spoon River Anthology.

Judge, who lives impeccably upstairs, The. Upstairs Downstairs. Hervey Allen. PoA

Judge with the Sore Rump, The. St. George Tucker. OBAL

Judged by my goddess' doom to endless pain. William Percy. Son *Fr.* Coelia.

Judged by the Company One Keeps. *Unknown.* BLPA; NBLV

Judgement. Ciaran Carson. PBCIP

Judgement. George Herbert. ESCV; GeHe; SeCP

Judgement Day. Rooplall Monar. HCP

Judgement Day. Odia Ofeimun. HBAPE

Judgement of God, The. William Morris. PeVV

Judgement of Tiresias, The. Hildebrand Jacob. NOEC

Judges. Bible, *O.T.*

    "And the Lord discomfited Sisera, and all his chariots, and all his host." OxBoV

    Song of Deborah, The. AWP; BoWoP; PBWP

    (Then Sang Deborah and Barak.) TrJP

    "Blessed above women/ shall Jael the wife of Heber the Kenite be." WPOW

Judges of the Little Box, The. Vasco [*or* Vasko] Popa, *Serbo-Croatian.* HSix, *tr. by* Charles Simic

Judges, who rule the world by laws. Psalm 58. Isaac Watts. NoP-4

Judging by Appearances. Emilie Poulsson. FPC

Judging Distances. Henry Reed. BoLoP; GTBS-P; NIP-4; NOBE; PoWW; Poetr *Fr.* Lessons of the War. HeIP-4; OBWP

    (2. Judging Distances.) NoP-4

Judging Lear. Libby Houston. NBrP

Judgment, The. Kathleen Spivack. BoWoP

Judgment Day. Robert Garioch, *after the Italian of* Giuseppe Belli. OBVE

Judgment Day, The. James Weldon Johnson. ChIV-2

Judgment Day. Ronald Stuart Thomas. CRP

Judgment in Heaven, A. Francis Thompson.

    Epilogue: "Heaven, which man's generations draws." MoBrPo

Judgment of Paris, The. W. S. Merwin. NAAL-2; NNaP

Judgment of Paris, The. Ralph Schomberg. TrJP

Judgment of the May, The. Richard Watson Dixon. OBNC

Judicious Observation of That Dreadful Comet, A. Ichabod Wiswall. SCAP

Judith. Lascelles Abercrombie.

    Song: "Balkis was in her marble town." MoBrPo

Judith. Eloise Bibb. CBWP-4

Judith. Bible, Apocrypha.

    With Timbrels. TrJP

Judith. Gertrud Kolmar, *German.* AF, *tr. by* David Kipp

Judith. Adah Isaacs Menken. APN-2; CBWP-1; PAR

Judith dances on my wall. The Dance She Does. Harryette Mullen. ISC

Judith of Bethulia. John Crowe Ransom. FYAP; FaBoMo; LiTM; MeMAP; NOBA; NoAM

Judith Recalls Holofernes. Maura Stanton. AmPA

Judy-One. Don L. Lee. TAP

Judy Sugden! Judy, I made you caper. Barnsley and District. Donald Davie. NoAM; OxBC

Jug Brook. Ellen Bryant Voigt. MT

Jug of water in the hand, and on, A. Dawn. "Rachel," *Hebrew.* TrJP, *tr. by* A. M. Klein

Juggler. Richard Wilbur. CMoP; LiTM; NYBP; TAP

Juggler and the baron's daughter, The. *Unknown.* NoSic

Juggy's Christening. *Unknown.* NOEC

Jugs, The. Paul Celan, *German.* HP; OBVE, *tr. by* Christopher Middleton

Juice of apples climbs in me, The. The Forbidden. Phyllis Haring. PeSA

JuJu. Askia Muhammad Touré. PoBA; SeSe

Juju of My Own, A. Lebert Bethune. PoBA

Juke Box Love Song. Langston Hughes. NAAAL; PoBA; SAmP; TTTS

Julia Disdainful: or, The Frozen Zone. Robert Herrick. *See* The Frozen Zone; or, Julia Disdainful.

Julia, how Irishly you sacrifice. Reproach to Julia. Robert Graves. FaBoEE

Julia, I bring. A Ring Presented to Julia. Robert Herrick. PeLV

Julia, if I chance to die. His Request to Julia. Robert Herrick. BeJo; CaPo; CavPo; NOSC

Julia, when thy Herrick dies. To Julia. Robert Herrick. CaPo; NOSC

Julian and Maddalo; A Conversation. Shelley. FHYEP; OAEL-2

    ("They learn in suffering what they teach in song.") (LL) FHYEP

Juliana. Cynewulf, *Anglo-Saxon.*

    "I have great need that the Saint grant help." AnOE, *tr. by* Charles W. Kennedy

Julianus Sees a Bronze Statue of Icarus in a Public Bath. Julianus of Egypt, *Greek.* GrAn, *tr. by* Lee T. Pearcy

Julianus Sees a Magistrate's Axe. Julianus of Egypt, *Greek.* GrAn, *tr. by* Lee T. Pearcy

Julianus Sees the Chair of the Sophist Craterus. Julianus of Egypt, *Greek.* GrAn, *tr. by* Lee T. Pearcy

Julia's Petticoat. Robert Herrick. BeJo; CaPo

    (Upon Julia's Petticoat.) CavPo

Juliek's Violin. Michael C. Blumenthal. CMAP

Juliet. Hilaire Belloc. BoLoP; EnLoPo; GLoP

Juliet: Good-night, good-night! as sweet repose and rest. Shakespeare. ITG *Fr.* Romeo and Juliet.

Juliet's Garden. Charles Tomlinson. OBGa

Julius Caesar. Shakespeare.

    "Calphurnia here, my wife, stays me at home." OxBSn

    "Friends, Romans, countrymen, lend me your ears." OxAEP-1

    "How died my master, Strato?" OxAEP-1

    "If you have tears, prepare to shed them now." OxAEP-1

    "Let me see, let me see; is not the leaf turned down." OxBSn

    Mark Antony Addresses the Mob. FaPoR

    "O mighty Cæsar! dost thou lie so low?" OxAEP-1

    "O, pardon me, thou bleeding piece of earth." EBEvV; OxAEP-1

    "Since Cassius first did whet me against Cæsar." OxAEP-1

    "Who ever knew the heavens menace so?" OxAEP-1

Julius Caesar. *Unknown.* InPK-6

July. John Clare. AYFP

July. John Heath-Stubbs. AYFP

July. Alexander L. Posey. APAD; APN-2

July. Henrietta Cordelia Ray. CBWP-3

July. Folgore da San Geminiano. *Fr.* Sonnets of the Months. AWP, *tr. by* D. G. Rossetti

July. Sonia Sanchez. GT

July 18, 1936–July 18, 1938. Miguel Hernández, *Spanish.* AF, *tr. by* Timothy Baland

July, August, suspense. / Wall Street lost to sense. Vachel Lindsay. *Fr.* Bryan, Bryan, Bryan, Bryan. CMoP; MeMAP; OxBA; OxBoLi

July Evening. Norman MacCaig. FaBoTC

July 4, 1984: For Buck. June Jordan. NoAM

July 4th. May Swenson. PoA

July, I'm dozing in sun on the deck. In My Own Back Yard. David Young. WeT

July in Indiana. Robert Fitzgerald. AiP; NYBP

July in Washington. Robert Lowell. LCAP-2; NAAL-2

July 1914. "Anna Akhmatova," *Russian.* PeFWW, *tr. by* Stanley Kunitz *and* Max Hayward; WPOW, *tr. by* Stanley Kunitz, (*Pt. I only*)

July the First. Robert Currie. Poetsp

July the first, of a morning clear, one thousand six hundred and ninety. The Boyne Water. *Unknown.* FaPoR; IIP; NOIV

July 31. Norman Jordan. PoBA

July 27. Norman Jordan. NBV

Jumbled in the Common Box. W. H. Auden. PoRA

Jumblies, The. Edward Lear. CABP; CBNP; CTV; EBEV; EBEvV; FaBoBe; ImPo; NAEL-2; NOxBChV; OxBChV; OxBoLi; PeLV; PeVV; PoRA; TFi; UV

Jump back, honey, jump back. (LL) A Negro Love Song. Paul Laurence Dunbar. AAP; APAD; APN-2; ColAP; CrDW; NAAAL; SSLK

Jump Cabling. Linda Pastan. InPK-6

Jump City. Harryette Mullen. IFJA

Jump down, turn around to pick a bale of cotton. Pick a Bale of Cotton. *Unknown.* NAAAL

Jump he went over. (LL) Leg over leg. Mother Goose. LB; OxNR; ReMoGo

'Jump over the moon?' the cow declared. Max Fatchen. SpW

Jump-Rope Rhyme. *Unknown.* NTCP

Jump stone leaf shadow sun. The Fire. Robert Duncan. APSN; VGW *Fr.* Passages.

Jump stop shake. (LL) Blackberry Sweet. Dudley Randall. HAP; ISC; InPS-3; KaS; PoBA; SAGP; SoSe-8; WeW-3

Jumping Joan. Mother Goose. *See* Little Jumping Joan.

June. John Clare. Ro

June. Elaine Feinstein. BrRo

June. Mary Weston Fordham. CBWP-2

June. Francis Ledwidge. BIrV; NOIV

June. Irene F. Pawsey. BoTP

June. Henrietta Cordelia Ray. CBWP-3

June. Folgore da San Geminiano. *Fr.* Sonnets of the Months. AWP, *tr. by* D. G. Rossetti

June. Jane G. Stewart. BoTP

June 1967 at Buchenwald. Alan Bold. FaBoTC

June at Truro Beach the joyous bathers. Kite-Flying. Christopher Gilbert. GT

June Bracken and Heather. Tennyson. EnLoPo

June Fugue. Thomas William Shapcott. NOBAu

June in her eyes, in her heart *January*. (LL) The Spring. Thomas Carew. BeJo; CaPo; CavPo; NoP-4; PBRV; PoE; PoEL-3

June, 1915. Charlotte Mew. OxAEP-2

June of the iris and the rose. The Rose. Vita Sackville-West. GaP

June ("Over his keys the musing organist"). James Russell Lowell. *See* Prelude to Part the First.

June sun in an orchard, A. My Mother's Burying. Sean O Riordain, *Irish.* TIRV, *tr. by* Valentine Iremonger

June 10. Magdalena de Rodriguez, *Spanish.* WPOW, *tr. by* Nina Serrano

June Thunder. Louis MacNeice. CMoP

Jungle, The. Diane Di Prima. PoM

Jungle. Phyllis Haring. PeSA

Jungle, The. Alun Lewis. OBWVE

Jungle, The. Randolph Stow. *Fr.* Thailand Railway. CBAP

Jungle, The. William Carlos Williams. PFE

Jungle Café, The. Gary Soto. NoAM

Jungle Gliders. Roger Weingarten. NAmP90

Jungle Husband, The. Stevie Smith. FaBoWP; NBLV; NIP-4; RB

Jungle Mammy Song. *Unknown.* AS

Jungle night—it rains and rains, roofs leak, A. Nguyễn Chí Thiện, *Vietnamese.* VCWP, *tr. by* Huynh Sanh Thông

Jungle spreads, The. In Praise of a Cremation Ground. Kataiyan Kannanār, *Tamil.* PLW, *tr. by* A. K. Ramanujan

Jungle Trees, The. Marjorie Wilson. BoTP

Jungle Warfare. Jack Spicer. APSN

Junglegrave. S. E. Anderson. PoBA

Junior Addict. Langston Hughes. BPo

Junior High Dance. Allison Joseph. UnSA

Juniper. Eileen Duggan. PChr

Juniper. Robert Francis. VGW

Juniper, aspen, blue spruce, just thawing snow. The Call of Nature. Tony Harrison. NoAM

Juniper, juniper. *Unknown.* BoTP

Juniper Moon Pulls at My Bones, The. Earle Thompson. HATNAP

Junk. Richard Wilbur. HAP; WeW-3

("From my neighbor's ashcan.") NoP-4

Junk Man passed the house today, The. Ol' Clothes. *Unknown.* PoToHe

Junk Shop, The. Henri Coulette. NYBP

Junker-Lied. Turner Cassity. WeT

Junkies loved Charles Parker and the sports, The. Historiography. Lorenzo Thomas. MoNo; SeSe

Junkyard dog, The. Nicholas Virgilio. HA

Juno seduces Jove. Homer. OBCVT, *tr. by* Alexander Pope *Fr.* The Iliad.

Jupiter and Ganimede. Thomas Heywood. FaBoSe

Jupiter and Mercury. David Garrick. ECEV

Jupiter and Ten. James Thomas Fields. OBAL

Jurgis Petrakas, the Workers' Angel, Organizes the First Miners' Strike in Exeter, Pennsylvania. Anthony Petrosky. FYAP

Just. Judith Johnson Sherwin. TAP

Just a few feet away, a temple from the Six Dynasties. Yang Chi. *Fr.* Living in a Riverside Village—Miscellaneous Impressions. CoBLCP, *tr. by* Jonathan Chaves

Just a herd of Negroes. Share-Croppers. Langston Hughes. SAmP

Just a line of posts along the baymouth. Jack's Postcards. Ken Smith. NBrP

Just a line to remind my friends that after much trouble. Dear Folks. Patrick Kavanagh. FaBoTw

Just a little white with the dust. (LL) Break of Day in the Trenches. Isaac Rosenberg. CABP; FaBoMo; GTBS-P; MoBrPo; NAEL-2; NOBE; NSI; NoAM; NoP-4; OAEL-2; OBWP; OxAEP-2; PeFWW; PoA; PoFWW; PoWW; TFi

Just a Smack at Auden. William Empson. LiTM; MoBrPo; PeLV; UV; UnPo

("Waiting for the end, boys, waiting for the end.") (LL) OBCoV

Just about at the triple-barreled pistol. Armor. Sharon Olds. InPS-3

Just after Michael's Death, the Game of Pool. Richard Tipping. BMAP

Just after Noon with Fierce Shears. Tram Combs. TwCP

Just an Old Sweet Song. Donagh MacDonagh. CIP-2

Just and fit actions, Ptolemy (he saith). A Speech out of Lucan. Lucan. OBVE, *tr. by* Ben Jonson *Fr.* Pharsalia.

Just Anger, A. Marge Piercy. CrSp

Just Another Autumn Day. Roger McGough. AYFP

Just Another Gig. Baron James Ashanti. SeSe

Just are the ways of God. The Transcendence of God. Milton. *Fr.* Samson Agonistes. FHYEP; OAEL-1; PoEL-3

Just as a year might end. Nightsong. Louis O. Coxe. FYAP

Just as Clay became a world champion. Homage to a Hat and Uncle Guido and Eliot. Tomaz Salamun, *Slovenian.* CEEP, *tr. by* Šalamun, Tomaž and Anselm Hollo

Just as fear never kills. This Strange Calculation of Roots. Edouard J. Maunick, *French.* NegPo, *tr. by* Teo Savory

Just as Gisors had placed. *Unknown, French.* CBNP

Just as he gets a beard. Statilius Flaccus, *Greek.* GrAn, *tr. by* Thomas Meyer

Just as He spoke it from his Hands. Emily Dickinson. APN-2

Just as I joy at noble autumn. To the Tune "Partridge Sky." Yang Shen, *Chinese.* CoBLCP, *tr. by* Jonathan Chaves

Just as my fingers on these keys. Peter Quince at the Clavier. Wallace Stevens. AmPP; CMoP; HeIP-4; InPK-6; InPS-3; LiTM; MeMAP; MoAmPo; NAWM-2; NOBA; NoAM; NoP-4; OxBA; PoE; SAmP; TAP; TFi; TwCP

Just as soon as the average type. Salute, Friends! Vladimir Salimon, *Russian.* TCRP, *tr. by* Albert C. Todd

Just as that monkey would, poor Polly, have done for you. (LL) Poor Poll. Robert Bridges. EBEV; OxBTC; OxBoLi

Just as the earth puckered its mouth. The Abortion. Anne Sexton. NMM-2

Just as the signal tower lights flash. Night at an Airport. David Ignatow. NNaP

Just as the twilight's holy hour. To an Infant. Mary Weston Fordham. CBWP-2

Just as the winged energy of delight. Rilke. RaBo

Just as Thou Art. Russell Sturgis Cook. AH

Just as we were amazed to learn. The Psychopathology of Everyday Life. William Matthews. NIP-4

Just as you'd expect. Daytrip to Paradox. Dara Wier. CMAP

Just at the self-same beat of Time's wide wings. The Bruised Titans. Keats. OBNC *Fr.* Hyperion. OAEL-2; Ro

Just back from a beach of sand and shells. The Old Lobsterman. John Townsend Trowbridge. APN-2

Just because I forget. Letter for Duncan. Larry Eigner. FTOS; PoM

Just because I smile and smile. Because. B. W. Vilakazi, *Zulu.* PeSA

Just because I turn on the light. To the House Ghost. Paula Rankin. CMAP

Just because it perished? (LL) Passer Mortuus Est. Edna St. Vincent Millay. CMoP; FaBoWP; MoAmPo; OxBA

Just because some teachers go away. Brain Drain. "The Mighty Chalkdust." PBCV

Just because there is music. Maybe I'm Amazed. Jim Carroll. PmAP

Just because your cousins perjured themselves. Loss. Carl Dennis. PUP-20

Just before dawn. Alan Pizzarelli. HA

Just before night darkens to total night. Dog-Day Night. Robert Francis. WeT

Just before the storm. Alan Pizzarelli. HA

Just before their divorce, still living. The Daughter's Brooch. Jeannine Savard. CMAP

Just before winter. Pushing Forty. Alison Fell. FaBoTC

Just broke from school, pert, impudent, and raw. Soame Jenyns. ECEV; OBSV *Fr.* The Modern Fine Gentleman.

Just controls their operations: the Napoleon of Crime! (LL) Macavity: The Mystery Cat. T. S. Eliot. ChAP; InPS-3; NBLV; NOBL; OBCA; OxBChV; OxBoV; PeLV; PoRA; RB; UV

Just days after the vet came. Healing the Mare. Linda McCarriston. LoL

Just drop a tear for the Croppy Boy. (LL) The Croppy Boy. *Unknown.* AmFP; NOIV; OxBoLi

Just for a handful of silver he left us. The Lost Leader. Robert Browning. EBEvV; EnVR; FHYEP; FaBoPV; NAEL-2; PBMP; PWR; SCGP

Just for a space that I met her. Incognita. Austin Dobson. EBVV

Just for fun. Tanka. Ishikawa Takuboku, *Japanese.* MJT, *tr. by* Makoto Ueda

Just for the fun of it, he burned down Rome. The Monk's Tale. Geoffrey Chaucer, *Old English.* OxBoV, *tr. by* David Wright

Just for To-Day. Ernest R. Wilberforce. PWR

Just four miles to go and the frontier ahead. The German Frontier at Basel: 1942 and 1992. Hilda Schiff. HP

Just Friends. Robert Creeley. NeAP

Just God! and these are they. Clerical Oppressors. John Greenleaf Whittier. NAAL-1

Just How Crazy Brenda Is. Melinda Goodman. GLP

Just How It Happened. Priscilla Jane Thompson. CBWP-2

Just Jumbo. Eileen Mathias. BoTP

Just last friday. Jamal's Lamentation. Reuben Jackson. GT

Just like a jovial hunter. (LL) Sir Lionel. *Unknown.* AmFP; ESPB

Just like a Man. *Unknown.* BoTP

Just like dropped leaves in wind! (LL) Fantasy of an African Boy. James Berry. HCP; NTP; PBCV

Just Like Me. *Unknown.* BoTP; ReMoGo

Just like that. When he brings the new bike home. The Bicycle Rider. Thomas William Shapcott. CBAP

Just Like the Legend. Léon Damas, *French.* PFTM, tr. by Norman R. Shapiro

Just like the Travels of Captain Cook! (LL) The Pedlar's Caravan. William Brighty Rands. BoTP; OxBChV

Just Like This. D. A. Olney. BoTP

Just like unto a nest of boxes round. Of Many Worlds in This World. Margaret Lucas Cavendish, Duchess of Newcastle. NOSC

Just look at them, the shameless well-to-do. Palladas, *Greek.* GrAn, tr. by Tony Harrison

Just look, Manetto, at that wry-mouth'd minx. Sonnet: Of an Ill-Favored Lady. Guido Cavalcanti, *Italian.* AWP, tr. by D. G. Rossetti

Just look, 'tis a quarter past six, love. The Coming Woman. Mary Weston Fordham. CBWP-2

Just Looking, Thank You. Leonard Nathan. EC2

Just lost, when I was saved! Called Back. Emily Dickinson. AmPP; MoAmPo; NOBA; NOCV

Just man followed then his angel guide, The. Lot's Wife. "Anna Akhmatova," *Russian.* BoWoP; PBWP, tr. by Richard Wilbur

Just missed him! (LL) On a Squirrel Crossing the Road in Autumn, in New England. Richard Eberhart. AFr; HeIP-4; LiTM; Poetsp

Just now I had a funny sensation. Galway Kinnell. *Fr.* Ruins under the Stars. LCAP-2

Just now / Out of the strange. The Warning. Adelaide Crapsey. Spl; WPE; WeW-3

Just now the lilac is in bloom. The Old Vicarage, Grantchester. Rupert Brooke. EBEvV; MoBrPo; NoP-4; OxBTC; PoRA

Just off his motorbike. Going to Mass after Fifteen Years. Maxine Scates. PBCAP

Just off the highway to Rochester, Minnesota. A Blessing. James Wright. ChAP; CoAmPo; ITG; InPK-6; InPS-3; NAAL-2; NOBA; NoAM; NoP-4; PoE; PoPoPo; Poetr; RaBo; TRP; TwCP; VCAP; WeT

Just One Day. Susan E. Gammons. PWR

Just one hundred poems in this little book. Reading the Poetry Collection of Lü Fang-ch'ing. Chang Yü, *Chinese.* CoBLCP, tr. by Jonathan Chaves

Just one more time. Only one. The Needle: For a Friend Who Disappeared. Franz Wright. CMAP; NAmP90

Just out of San Francisco one cold December day. The Dying Hobo. *Unknown.* AmFP

Just past sunset. Bob Boldman. HA

Just Quartering a Tree. (LL) Wind begun to knead the Grass, The, First Version. Emily Dickinson. NAAL-1; NAAL-3; WeW-3

Just quartering a tree. (LL) Wind begun to rock the Grass, The. Emily Dickinson. APN-2; HAP; NAAL-1; NCAP; WeW-3

Just short of danger the camcorder stops;. The Storm Chasers. William Olsen. PUP-20

Just sitting around smoking, drinking and telling stories. And with March a Decade in Bolinas. Joanne Kyger. BLT

Just smiling. (LL) Try Smiling. *Unknown.* BLPA; PWR

Just so it goes: the day, the night. An Ordinary Evening in Cleveland. Lewis Turco. NYBP

Just so long and long enough. (LL) As freedom is a breakfastfood. E. E. Cummings. CMoP; LiTM; NOBA; OxBA; TAP; VGW

Just-So Stories. Rudyard Kipling.
  Merrow Down. NOxBChV

Just stand aside and watch yourself go by. Watch Yourself Go By. Strickland W. Gillilan. BLPA; PWR; PoToHe

Just the lessons given you now. Maxims in Rhyme for the Young. J. Clark. PWR

Just the other day. José Montoya. PaTW *Fr.* Faces at the First Farmworkers Constitutional Convention.

"Just the place for a Snark!" the Bellman cried. Fit the First: The Landing. "Lewis Carroll." EBEvV *Fr.* The Hunting of the Snark. CBNP; OBNC; OBNV; PoEL-5

Just the Two of Us. Kate Jennings. BMAP

Just the Two of Us. Taeko Tomioka, *Japanese.* WPOW, tr. by Harry and Lynn Guest *and* Kajima Shozo

Just then, forgetful of the strict command. Homer. OBVE, tr. by William Cowper *Fr.* Odyssey. NAWM-1, tr. by Robert Fitzgerald

Just there, in a corner of the whin-field. Our Lady of Ardboe. Paul Muldoon. BiHa; PBCIP

Just think how amazing! someone getting up and walking on the water. (LL) Galilee Shore. Allen Ginsberg. ChIV-2; FTOS

Just think how it's improved her French. (LL) Compensation. Harry Graham. CBNP; PeLV

Just This. István Vas, *Hungarian.* CEEP, tr. by Jascha Kessler

Just this one day in all the year. The Skeleton in the Cupboard. Dora Sigerson Shorter. VWP

Just to Be Needed. Mary Eversley. PoToHe

Just to be tender, just to be true. God's Will for You and Me. *Unknown.* SoSe-8

Just to keep her from the foggy, foggy dew. (LL) The Foggy, Foggy Dew. *Unknown.* AS; OxBoLi; PeLV

Just too late to save the stamp. (LL) Waste. Harry Graham. OBCoV; UV

Just us. / In our little house. Kenneth Rexroth. APSN *Fr.* The Love Poems of Marichiko.

Just Walking Around. John Ashbery. NAAL-2

Just when Thou wilt, O Master, call! Frances Ridley Havergal. VWP

Just when you're able to admit. Corps d'Esprit. Heather McHugh. AmPA

Justice. Agathias, *Greek.* PC, tr. by Peter Whigham

Justice. George Chapman. NOSC *Fr.* Euthymiae Raptus; or, The Teares of Peace.

Justice. George Herbert. FMP

Justice. Langston Hughes. BPo

Justice. Petra von Morstein, *German.* BoWoP, tr. by Rosemarie Waldrop

Justice Denied in Massachusetts. Edna St. Vincent Millay. AiP; MoAmPo

Justice is Done. Oumar Ba. PBMAP

Justice Is Reason Enough. Diane Wakoski. AmPA; NMM-2

Justice of the Peace, The. Hilaire Belloc. NOBVV; OBSV

Justice to Scotland, at. to Robert Burns. *Unknown.* NBLV

Justice without Passion. Jane Hirshfield. WeT

Justification. William Strode. NOSC

Justified mother of men[!], The. (LL) Faces. Walt Whitman. APN-1; PoEL-5

Justified—through Calvaries of Love. (LL) Renunciation. Emily Dickinson. APN-2; MoAmPo; NAAL-1; NAAL-3; NOBA

Justify all those renowned generations. The Renowned Generations. W. B. Yeats. OxBoLi

Justiniano Lamé Has Been Killed. Jimmie Durham. HATNAP

Justly might Female *Tortoises* complain. The Loves of the Tortoise. Oppian. APo, tr. by William Diaper *Fr.* Halieutica.

Juvenal's tenth Satyre Translated. Juvenal, *Latin.*
  "What then should man pray for? what is't that he." OBCVT, tr. by Henry Vaughan

Juxtaposition is great,—but, you tell me, affinity greater. Claude to Eustace. Arthur Hugh Clough. CBLP *Fr.* Amours de Voyage. NOBVV

K

K for the Klondyke, a country of gold. Hilaire Belloc. NoAM *Fr.* A Moral Alphabet.

K. H. Astride Ivaska, *Latvian.* CEEP, tr. by Inara Cedrins

Kĭʹ nqalaLala Song. *Unknown.* *Fr.* Dances and Songs of the Winter Ceremonial. APN-2, tr. by Franz Boas

K k k k k. Marlene Mountain. HA

Ka 'Ba. Imamu Amiri Baraka. BPo; CAPP-1; CrDW; ISC; NBV; PmAP; TAP
  ("What will be / the sacred words?") (LL) UnSA

Kabul town's by Kabul river. Ford o' Kabul River. Rudyard Kipling. FaBoTw; PeVV

Kaddish. Allen Ginsberg. HCAP; NAAL-2; NOBA; NeAP; PmAP; PoM
  ("With your eyes / with your Death full of Flowers.") (LL) CLPP

Kaddish. David Ignatow. RaBo

Kaddish. Levi-Yitzhok of Berditchev, *Yiddish.* TrJP, tr. by Joseph Leftwich

Kadia the Young Mother Speaks. Jessie E. Sampter. TrJP

Kafka Poem. Lisa Zeidner. CMAP

Kafoozalum. *Unknown.* BLPA

Kagwa hunted the lion. The Huntsman. Edward Lowbury. OBSP

Kaiser Bill went up the hill. *Unknown.* NSI

Kala: Saturday Night at the Pahala Theatre. Lois-Ann Yamanaka. PUP-18

Kalahari Bushman fires flowing. Firebowl. Sydney Clouts. PeSAV

Kalaloch. Carolyn Forché. AmPA; NoAM

Kalapuya Prophecy, A. *Unknown, Kalapuya Indian.* STP, tr. by Jarold Ramsey

Kaleidoscope. Maria Elena Cruz Varela, *Spanish.* VCWP, tr. by Mairym Cruz-Bernal *and* Deborah Digges

Kaleidoscope, The. Douglas Dunn. LBC

Kaleidoscope. Rachel Hadas. WeT

Kaleidoscope. G. K. Page. NoAM

Kaleidoscope, A. Sunfish Races. James Preston. InPK-6

Kalevala, The. Elias Lönnrot, *Finnish.*
  "It is my desire, it is my wish." PFTM, tr. by Francis Peabody Magoun, Jr.

Kali. Lucille Clifton. CrSp
  ("Kali / queen of fatality, she.") NAAAL

Kali Ma tottering up steps to shelter tin roof, feeling her way to curb, around. Describe: The Rain on Dasaswamedh Ghat. Allen Ginsberg. FTOS

Kali / queen of fatality, she. Lucille Clifton. *See* Kali.

Kallignotos swore to Ionis—no one. Callimachus, *Greek.* GrAn, *tr. by* Peter Jay

Kallirrhoê: A Dedication. Agathias, *Greek.* GrAn, *tr. by* Dudley Fitts

Kallistion the wife of Kritias. Callimachus, *Greek.* GrAn, *tr. by* Peter Jay

Kama Sutra of Kindness: Position No. 2, The. Mary Mackey. DeD

Kangaroo. D. H. Lawrence. EBEV; InPS-3; OxBTC

Kangaroo is standing up, and dwindling like a plant, A. The Dusk. Robert Gray. BMAP

Kangaroo, Kangaroo! Barron Field. NOBAu

Kanheri Caves. Dom Moraes. NoP-4

Kanonentext. Wolfgang Amadeus Mozart, *German.* CBNP, *tr. by* Hugh Haughton

Kansas Boys. *Unknown.* AS

Kansas City. Oscar, II Hammerstein. OBAL

Kansas City West Bottoms. Edward Dahlberg. PoA

Kanyariri, Village of Toil. The Village. Marina Gashe. PBA

Kapital. Frank Gaspar. BAP-96

Karamanian Exile, The. James Clarence Mangan. PeVV

Karazah to Karl. Adah Isaacs Menken. CBWP-1

Kāri Sober. Kapilar, *Tamil.* PLW, *tr. by* A. K. Ramanujan

Karl Heinrich Marx. Hans Magnus Enzensberger, *German.* FaBoPV, *tr. by* Michael Hamburger

Karl Marx. Alfred M. Lee. AmPA

Karma. Edwin Arlington Robinson. AmPP; CMoP; FP; HeIP-4; MoAmPo; TrCP

Karma of meringue, The. Anaerobics: Elaine Powers, Wheeling, West Virginia. Linda Mizejewski. CMAP

Karoo Town. Robert Dederick. PeSA

Karshish, the picker-up of learning's crumbs. An Epistle Containing the Strange Medical Experience of Karshish, the Arab Physician. Robert Browning. ChIV-2; NAEL-2

Kashmiri Song. "Laurence Hope." BLPA; FaBoBe

Kaspar Is Dead. Hans Arp, *German.* PFTM, *tr. by* Jerome Rothenberg

Kassak. Birago Diop, *French.* NegPo, *tr. by* Ellen Conroy Kennedy

"Kat" can play ball, Man, The. Funky Football. Ruby C. Saunders. BlSi

Kate and the Cowhide. *Unknown.* AmFP

Kate Kearney. Sydney, Lady Morgan Owenson. BLPA; FaBoBe

Kathaleen Ny-Houlahan [*or* Kathleen-Ni-Houlahan]. William Heffernan, *Irish.* IIP; NOIV, *tr. by* James Clarence Mangan

Katharine Jaffray. *Unknown.* ESPB

Käthe Kollwitz. Muriel Rukeyser. NALW
  ("Held in the two hands, you.") (LL) NMM-2
  (Kollwitz, Käthe.) NMM-2

Katherine is warm. Why? Melba Joyce Boyd. BlSi

Katherine Jaffray. *Unknown.* OxBB

Katherine's Dream, From *Between the Porch and the Alta.* Robert Lowell. CoAmPo

Kathleen Mavourneen. Louisa Macartney Crawford. FaBoBe

Katie Lee and Willy [*or* Willie] Grey. Josie R. Hunt *and* J. H. Pixley. BLPA

Katisje's Patchwork Dress. Pauline Smith. PeSAV

Katori Maru, October 1920. Jim Mitsui. OpBo
  ("Rain feels heavy / on the gray sidewalks of America, The.") (LL) UnSA

Katrina on the Porch. Alice Cary. APN-2

Katydids. Amy Lowell. PBWP

Katzenjammer Kids, The. James Reaney. MoCV

Kaunas 1941. Johannes Bobrowski, *German.* AF, *tr. by* Matthew Mead

Kaya-Magan am I! the first person. Léopold Sédar Senghor, *French.* PFTM, *tr. by* Melvin Dixon

Kayak Song, A. Lucy Diamond. BoTP

Kayenta Times Yet Dreaming On. Nia Francisco. HATNAP

Ke-uk, ke-uk, ke-uk, ki-kwaik. Farmer's Death. "Hugh MacDiarmid." FaBoVe

Keats. Walter Savage Landor. EPCY

Keats. Henry Wadsworth Longfellow. Son; TAP

Keats' Lips. Michael Waters. CMAP

Keats to Fanny Brawne. Edgar Lee Masters. PoA

Keelhauled across the star-wrecked death of God. George Barker. PoA *Fr.* Sonnets of the Triple-headed Manichee.

Keen as the blade of the guillotine, grey as its steel. The Execution of Madame du Barry. J. J. Bray. NOBAu

Keen, fitful gusts are whispering here and there. Keats. PoEL-4; Son

Keen stars were twinkling, The. To Jane. Shelley. APAD; FHYEP

Keen Thyself, Poor Wight. Geoffrey Keating, *Irish.* TIRV, *tr. by* Padraic Pearse

Keening of Mary, The. *Unknown, Irish.* TIRV, *tr. by* Padraic Pearse

Keep a-Goin'. Frank Lebby Stanton. PWR

Keep a hand on your dream. X. J. Kennedy. CA; Poetsp

Keep away from asps and toads. *Unknown, Greek.* GrAn, *tr. by* Alistair Elliot

Keep away from roads' webs, they always lead. Directions to a Rebel. William Robert Rodgers. LiTM

Keep away from sharp swords. Impromptu. Meng Chiao, *Chinese.* PLT, *tr. by* A. C. Graham

Keep away from sitting in the shade or lying in bed till the sun's up. Summer. Hesiod. GrIP, *tr. by* Richard Lattimore *Fr.* Works and Days.

Keep bees and. Advice to the Young. Miriam Waddington. NIP-4; NOBC

Keep conscience clear. Bits of Wisdom. Benjamin Franklin. CTV

Keep Cool. Marcus Garvey. PBCV

Keep fresh the grass upon his grave. Wordsworth's Grave. Matthew Arnold. *Fr.* Memorial Verses. CABP; NAEL-2; OAEL-2

Keep from me all that I might comprehend! Keep Hidden from Me. Rachel Korn, *Yiddish.* PBWP, *tr. by* Carolyn Kizer

Keep in God's way; keep pace with evry hour. To Be Engraven on a Dial. Samuel Sewall. SCAP

Keep in the heart the journal nature keeps. Prelude XLII. Conrad Potter Aiken. CMoP; OxBA *Fr.* Preludes for Memnon; or, Preludes to Attitude.

Keep It Clean. Charlie Jordan. CBNP

Keep It Dark. *Unknown, Zezuru.* PBA, *tr. by* Hugh Tracey

Keep me as your servant, O Girdhar. Mirabai, *Medieval Hindi.* PBWP, *tr. by* Usha Nilsson

Keep Me Still, for I Do Not Want to Dream. Larry Eigner. NeAP

Keep not thou silence, O God. Bible, *O.T. See* Psalm 83.

Keep off your thoughts from things that are past and done. Resignation. Po Chü-i, *Chinese.* ChiP, *tr. by* Arthur Waley

Keep on Pushing. David Henderson. PoBA

Keep on walkin and walkin talkin to mysel. Hard Road Blues. *Unknown.* FaBoVe

Keep ourselves warm. (LL) Lavender's Blue. *Unknown.* ACTV; LB

Keep pushing—'tis wiser than sitting aside. Never Say Fail. *Unknown.* PWR

Keep silent the sacred voices which we hear proceeding from your body. A Song of the Ts'ē' k'ois. *Unknown. Fr.* Dances and Songs of the Winter Ceremonial. APN-2, *tr. by* Franz Boas

Keep Talking. Philip Levine. WeW-3

Keep the commandments, Trapp, and go no further. Abel Evans. FaBoEE

Keep the dream alive and growing always. Song. Edwin Rolfe. TrJP

Keep the season: let the hive. James McAuley. BMAP

Keep their feet, mount their tails, and away! (LL) An Appeal to Cats in the Business of Love. Thomas Flatman. APAD; EnLoPo; GBL; HAP; OBCoV; PC

Keep thinkin' I won't be lonely / By and by. (LL) Hope. Langston Hughes. OBAL; OBCA; TRP

"Keep this for me." Faith. *Unknown.* PoToHe

Keep this in mind, and all will go. *Unknown.* CTV

Keep to the one path. Bacchylides, *Greek.* InMo, *tr. by* Sam Hamill

Keep to yourself your kisses. Taisigh Agat Fein Do Phog. *Unknown, Irish.* BIrV, *tr. by* Maire Cruise O'Brien

Keep walking, though there's no place to get to. Jelaluddin Rumi, *Persian.* LoL, *tr. by* Coleman Barks

Keep Ye Holy Sabbath Rest. *Unknown, Hebrew.* TrJP, *tr. by* Herbert Loewe

Keep Your Eyes on the Prize. *Unknown.* CrDW

Keep your kiss to yourself. *Unknown, Irish.* NOIV, *tr. by* Thomas Kinsella

Keep your voice down, my husband. Peace. Leslie Ullman. IFJA

Keep your whiskers crisp and clean. The King of Cats Sends a Postcard to His Wife. Nancy Willard. OBCA; PC

Keeper, The. William Carpenter. Poetsp

Keeper. Esther Iverem. GT

Keeper of the Midnight Gate, The. George Mackay Brown. OxBC

Keeper who worked at the zoo, A. Limerick. Frank Richards. PeLi

Keeping Christmas. Eleanor Farjeon. OBCP

Keeping Hair. Ramona Wilson. CrSp; VoR

Keeping their difficult balance. Richard Wilbur. *See* Love Calls Us to the Things of This World.

Keeping Their World Large. Marianne Moore. RaBo

Keeping Things Whole. Mark Strand. CAPP-1; CoAP; HCAP; HeIP-4; LCAP-2; PoPoPo; TAP; VCAP

Keepsake for 1829 (1828), The. Mary Lamb.
  What is Love? Ro

Kehama's Curse. Robert Southey. *Fr.* The Curse of Kehama. ("For ever and ever.") (LL) OBNC

Keine Lazarovitch, 1870-1959. Irving Layton. NIP-4

Keith Jarrett—Rainmaker. Lorna Goodison. HCP

Keith of Ravelston. Sydney Thompson Dobell. *See* The Ballad of Keith of Ravelston.

Kelly on a Mountain. The Man from Strathbogie. Olive Mary Finnin. NOBAu

Kelly sharpened is powerful, asexual and yawns. Anorexia. Jennifer Maiden. BMAP

Kellyburnbraes. Robert Burns. OxBB

Kelly's kept an unlicensed bull, well away. The Outlaw. Seamus Heaney. MoP; OxBC

Kelp. Nora Dauenhauer. HATNAP

Kemo Sabe. Diane Glancy. LTA

Kemp Owyne. Alice Cary. ESPB; EnSB

Kemp Owyne. *Unknown.* ESPB; EnSB
  (Kempion.) OxBB

Ken. Charlotte Mew. VWP

Keng-tzu (1180), First Month, Fifth Day, Dawn. Yang Wan-li, *Chinese.* CoBCP, *tr. by* Burton Watson

Kenscoff. Lorna Goodison. GT

Kensington Gardens. Muriel Spark. OBGa

Kent. Thom Gunn. *See* Breaking Ground.

Kentish landscape all about, The. Kentish Sestinas. Bozhidar Bozhilov, *Bulgarian.* CEEP, *tr. by* Ewald Osers

Kentucky Belle. Constance Fenimore Woolson. BLPA; CBCWP; FaBoBe

Kentucky Moonshiner. *Unknown.* AS; OBAL

Kentucky Mountain Farm. Robert Penn Warren.
  History among the Rocks. CBCWP; MoAmPo

Kentucky water, clear springs: a boy fleeing. The Swimmers. Allen Tate. FuPo; InPS-3; MoAmPo; NOBA; NoAM

Kenyatta Listening to Mozart. Imamu Amiri Baraka. PmAP

Kepe well X, and flee fro VII. Ten Commandments, Seven Deadly Sins, and Five Wits. *Unknown.* FaBoEE; MiEL

Kept Waiting in the Boat at Chiu-K'ou Ten Days by an Adverse Wind. Po Chü-i, *Chinese.* ChiP, *tr. by* Arthur Waley

Kéramos. Henry Wadsworth Longfellow. APN-1
  Potter's Song, The. PoEL-5

Kerria roses. The First of May. Masaoka Shiki, *Japanese.* MJT, *tr. by* Makoto Ueda

Kerr's Ass. Patrick Kavanagh. NOIV; RB

Kettle descants in a cosy drone, The. Satires of Circumstance in Fifteen Glimpses. Thomas Hardy.

Kettle sang the boy to a half-sleep, The. Halibut Cove Harvest. Kenneth Leslie. NOBC

Kevin Barry. *Unknown.* AS

Kevin of the N.E. Crew. Elizabeth Alexander. FFC

Kew. Erasmus Darwin. OBGa *Fr.* The Botanic Garden.

Key: nnnn N N gahn. The 13th Horse Song of Frank Mitchell. María Sabina, *Mazatec.* PFTM, *tr. by* Jerome Rothenberg *and* David P. McAllester

Key of Water, The. Octavio Paz, *Spanish.* VCWP, *tr. by* Elizabeth Bishop

Key: Swings by his thigh a thing most magical! *Unknown.* EEP, *tr. by* Michael Alexander *Fr.* Riddles (Exeter Book).

Key. The door. Open, A. Tom. James Schuyler. GLP

Key West. Hart Crane. CMoP

Keys lids acid and speed. (LL) Street Song. Thom Gunn. HeIP-4; OxBC

Keys of Canterbury, The. *Unknown.* AmFP

Keys please. In This Way. Gertrude Stein. PFTM

Keys turning. The Liberator. Emily Holmes Coleman. SPE

Khaldeyev, Naldeyev, and Peppermaldeyev. Daniil Kharms, *Russian.* TCRP, *tr. by* Bradley Jordan

Khikhimora. Nikolai Ivanovich Glazkov, *Russian.* TCRP, *tr. by* Daniel Weissbort

Khrushchev is coming on the right day! Poem. Frank O'Hara. NeAP; PoM

Ki-u-nad'-dis-si's Song. *Unknown.* APN-2, *tr. by* Stephen Powers *Fr.* Sacred Songs of the Konkau.

Kiche Manitou. Nathaniel Mackey. FTOS

Kick a Little Stone. Dorothy Aldis. TLR

Kick at the rock, Sam Johnson, break your bones. Epistemology. Richard Wilbur. CRP; NOBA; NoAM; OxBSP

Kicked myself out of paradise. Lilith. Enid Dame. EC3

Kicking his mother until she let go of his soul. Mundus et Infans. W. H. Auden. LiTM; MeMAP; MoBrPo; NoAM

Kicking Mule, The. *Unknown.* AmFP

Kicking the Habit. Lawson Fusao Inada. PUP-19

Kid, The. Ai. GT; NoAM

Kid Has Gone to the Colors, The. William M. Herschell. PoLF

Kid on Her Way, A. Marge Piercy. WeT

Kid Stuff. Frank Horne. NOxBChV; PChr; PoBA

Kid wanders, dazzled by the crowd, The. A Kid on Her Way. Marge Piercy. WeT

Kidnap Poem. Nikki Giovanni. BPo; Poetr; TAP

Kidnap[p]er. Tess Gallagher. AmPA

Kidnapping. Tanka. Shaku Chōkū, *Japanese.* MJT, *tr. by* Makoto Ueda

'Kids make a home,' he said, the family man. The Family Man. Bruce Dawe. BMAP

Kilaben Bay Song. *Unknown, Aborigine.* NOBAu, *tr. by* Perce Haslam

Kilbarchan now may say alas! The Life and Death of [Habbie Simson] the Piper of Kilbarchan. Robert Sempill. OxBS

Kilcash. *Unknown, Irish.* BIrV; IIP; OBMV, *tr. by* Frank O'Connor

Kilfenora Teaboy, The. Paul Durcan. PBCIP

Kill me not every [or ev'ry] day. Affliction. George Herbert. NOSC

Kill me with spite; yet we must not be foes. (LL) Sonnet 40. Shakespeare. HeIP-4; OxAEP-1; SCGP

Kill that crowing cock. *Unknown, Chinese.* OHMPC, *tr. by* Kenneth Rexroth

Kill yourselves with knives and poisoned gas. Strangers Are We All upon the Earth. Franz Werfel, *German.* TrJP, *tr. by* Edith Abercrombie Snow

Killdeer, The. Larry Gates. HA

Killed at the Ford. Henry Wadsworth Longfellow. CBCWP

Killed by an omnibus—why not? On a Man Run Over by an Omnibus. Henry Luttrell. FaBoEE

Killed by the Elevator, C—e Factory, Dundee. Nelly's Lament for the Pirnhouse Cat. Ellen Johnston. VWP

Killed in Action. Joseph Leftwich. NSI

Killer, The. A'yunini, *Cherokee Indian.* STP, *tr. by* Jerome Rothenberg

Killer, The. Judith Wright. BMAP

Killers said. Synagogue in Prague. Alan Sillitoe. HP

Killers that run, The. Leonard Cohen. NOBC

Killigrew Wood, The. Norman Dubie. AmPA

Killing, The. George MacBeth. FaBoMo

Killing, The. Edwin Muir. GI

Killing No Murder. Sylvia Townsend Warner. MoBrPo

Killing of Lykaon, The. Homer. OBCVT, *tr. by* Robert Lowell *Fr.* The Iliad.

Killing of the Birds, The. Shirley Williams. BoWoP

Kilmeny. James Hogg. OBEV; OxAEP-2 *Fr.* The Queen's Wake.

Kilmeny. Alfred Noyes. NSI

Kilroy. Peter Viereck. MoAmPo
  (Kilroy Was Here.) PoRA

Kilroy is gone. Eugene McCarthy. AiP

Kilruddery Hunt, The. Thomas Mozeen. BIrV

Kiltartan Legend. Padraic Fallon. NOIV

Kim. Rudyard Kipling.
  Prodigal Son, The. NoAM

Kim-San. Steve Denning. CDa

Kimono, The. James Merrill. ColAP

Kin. Michael S. Harper. LCAP-2

Kind-, The. James Laughlin. CDa

Kind are her answers. Thomas Campion. BoLoP; CBLP; PoEL-2

Kind Deeds. Isaac Watts. BoTP

Kind friends, you must pity my horrible tale. The Dreary Black Hills. *Unknown.* AmFP

Kind gentlemen, will you be patient awhile? Robin Hood's Birth, Breeding, Valor, and Marriage. *Unknown.* ESPB

Kind lovers, love on. Song. John Crowne. OxBSP *Fr.* Calisto.

Kind Miss. *Unknown.* AS

Kind Mousie, The. Natalie Joan. BoTP

Kind o'er the kinderbank leans my Myfanwy. Myfanwy. John Betjeman. BoLoP

Kind of Act Of, The. Robert Creeley. NeAP

Kind of an Ode to Duty. Ogden Nash. APAD

Kind of change came in my fate, A. Byron. NOBE *Fr.* The Prisoner of Chillon. PoLF

Kind of empty in the way it sees everything, the earth gets to its feet. For John Clare. John Ashbery. FYAP

Kind of Faith, A. J. C. Hall. OxBSn

Kind of Hope, A. Reiner Kunze, *German.* CEEP, *tr. by* Ewald Osers

Kind of Loss, A. Ingeborg Bachmann, *German.* VCWP, *tr. by* Mark Anderson
("It's not you I've lost, / but the world.") (LL) AF, *tr. by* Mark Anderson

Kind of rain we knew is a thing of the past, The. Kinsale. Derek Mahon. BiHa

Kind of rose she wants called John F. Kennedy, The. Fourth Ode to Persephone. Robert Kelly. *Fr.* The Book of Persephone. PoM

Kind pity chokes my spleen brave scorn forbids. Satire 3. Donne. EBEV; ESCV; FHYEP; MeLP; NAEL-1; NoSic; OAEL-1; OxAEP-1; PoE; PoEL-2; SeCP *Fr.* Satires.

Kind Saint! who loved the garden flowers. Saint Fiacre. John Irvine. TIRV

Kind voice, A, calls, "Come, little ones." Crocuses. Anna M. Platt. BoTP

Kind was the hand that at the last. The Death Mask of John Clare. Edmund Blunden. EPCY

Kind Words Can Never Die. Abby Hutchinson. AH

Kindely is now my coming. *Unknown.* MiEL

Kindergarten children first come forth, The. The May Day Dancing. Howard Nemerov. NYBP; Poetr

Kindergarten Curse. Nina Zivancevic, *Serbo-Croatian.* HSix, *tr. by* Charles Simic

Kindertotenlieder. Michael Longley. CIP-2

Kindest thing of all is to comply, The. Martial, *Latin.* OBCVT, *tr. by* William Hay

Kindle the Taper. Emma Lazarus. AH

Kindly Deed, A. Priscilla Jane Thompson. CBWP-2

Kindly I envy thy song's [*or* songs] perfection. To Mr. R. W. Donne. ESCV

Kindly Neighbor, The. E. A. Guest. PoToHe

Kindly Vision. Otto Julius Bierbaum, *German.* AWP, *tr. by* Jethro Bithell

Kindly watcher by my bed, lift no voice in prayer. Music. George Du Maurier, *after the French of* Sully-Prudhomme. OBEV; SAGP

Kindly word and a tender tone, A. A Gentle Word. *Unknown.* PoToHe

Kindness. Catherine Davis. NYBP

Kindness. Thomas Sturge Moore. OBMV

Kindness. Mary E. Tucker. CBWP-1

Kindness glides about my house. Sylvia Plath. FaBoWP

Kindness in another's trouble, / Courage in our own. Adam Lindsay Gordon. *See* Question not, but live and labor.

Kindness is a language which the. Christina Rossetti. CTV

Kindness to Animals. Laura Elizabeth Richards. NTCP

Kindness to Animals. Christina Rossetti. CTV

Kindness to Animals. *Unknown.* BoTP; WHSW

Kinds of Shel-fish. William Wood. SCAP

Kinds of Trees to Plant. Edmund Spenser. *Fr.* Wood Of Error. AEP

Kineo Mountain. Celeste Turner Wright. Poetsp

Kinfauns Castle. William Montgomerie.
"Is there no vision in a lovely place?" OxBS

King, The. Anthony Kellman. HCP

King, The. Rudyard Kipling. CABP

King, a pope, and a kaiser, A. The Ship. Charles MacKay. BLPA

King Alfred and the Peasant Woman. Anna Wickham. WPN

King and No King, A. Robert Herrick. PBRV

King & Queen. John Montague. PBCIP

King and Queen of the Pelicans we. The Pelican Chorus. Edward Lear. CTAV; OBSP

King and Subjects. *Unknown, Vietnamese.* AVP, *tr. by* Huỳnh Sanh Thông

King and the Singer, The. Ivan V. Lalic, *Serbian.* CEEP, *tr. by* C. W. Truesdale

King: April 4, 1968. Gerald William Barrax. GT

King Arthur. Dryden.
Song of Venus. OxBoLi; PoEL-3

King Arthur. Mother Goose. NTP

King Arthur. *Unknown.* FPC

King Arthur and King Cornwall. *Unknown.* ESPB

King Arthur made new knights to fill the gap. Pelleas and Ettarre. Tennyson. NAEL-2 *Fr.* Idylls of the King.

King Arthur's Waes-hael. Robert Stephen Hawker. OBEV

King asked, The. The King's Breakfast. A. A. Milne. OBCoV; OTCP; OxBChV; UV

King Balak sat on his gaudy throne. Balaam. Charles Causley. EBNV

King Berdok. *Unknown.* OxBS

King Billy. Edwin Morgan. NoP-4

King Bruce of Scotland flung himself down. Try Again. Eliza Cook. BoTP

King but an' his nobles a', The. Brown Robin. *Unknown.* ESPB; OxBB

King Canute. Stanley J. Sharpless. BXAP

King Charles on [*or* upon] the Scaffold. Andrew Marvell. *Fr.* An Horatian Ode upon Cromwell's Return from Ireland. CABP; EBEV; ESCV; FMP; GTBS-P; GeHe; HAP; IIP; InPS-3; NOBE; NOSC; OAEL-1; OBEV; OBWP; OxAEP-1; PoEL-2; SCGP; SeCP; TFi

King Charles the First walked and talked. *Unknown.* OxNR

King Christian. Johannes Evald, *Danish.* AWP, *tr. by* Longfellow

King Cobra as Political Assassin, The. Ray A. Young Bear. HATNAP

King David. Stephen Vincent Benét. ChIV-1

King David and King Solomon. Authorship. James Ball Naylor. NBLV

King David Dances. John Berryman. ChIV-1; KSG; OxBC; OxBSP

King Duffus. Sylvia Townsend Warner. FaBoWP

King Easter has courted her for her gowd. Fause Foodrage. *Unknown.* ESPB; OxBB

King Edward the Fourth and a Tanner of Tamworth. *Unknown.* ESPB

King Enjoys His Own Again, The. Martin Parker. FaBoCh; OxBoLi
(Upon Defacing of White hall.) NOSC; PBRV

King Estmere. *Unknown.* ESPB; OBNV; OxBB

King Ethelred the Unready. Bill Greenwell. BXAP

King-Fisher [*or* King-Fisher's] Song, The. "Lewis Carroll." CBNP; CTAV *Fr.* Sylvie and Bruno Concluded.

King George V. Charles W. Hayward. NOBAu

King Harald's Trance. George Meredith. EBNV; PeVV

King Hart. Gawin Douglas.
Hart's Castle. PoEL-1

King Hart, into his cumlye castell strang. Hart's Castle. Gawin Douglas. PoEL-1 *Fr.* King Hart.

King has written a braid letter, The. Lord Derwentwater. *Unknown.* ESPB

King he hath been a prisoner, The. Willie o Winsbury. *Unknown.* ESPB

King he reigns on a throne of gold, The. The Leveller. "Barry Cornwall." OxAEP-2

King he wrote a love-letter, The. Lord Derwentwater. *Unknown.* AmFP

King Henry. *Unknown.* ESPB; OxBB

King Henry Fifth's Conquest of France. *Unknown.* ESPB

King Henry IV, Pt. I. Shakespeare. NAEL-1
"I have learn'd." OxAEP-1
"O, Harry! thou hast robb'd me of my youth." OxAEP-1
"So shaken as we are, so wan with care." OxAEP-1

King Henry IV, Pt. II. Shakespeare.
"But wherefore did he take away the crown?" OxAEP-1
"This new and gorgeous garment, majesty." OxAEP-1

King Henry the Eighth was a Tudor. Limerick. Kirkham Talbot. PeLi

King Henry V. Shakespeare.
Before Agincourt. EBEV
Epilogue: "Thus far, with rough and all-unable pen." CTC
Henry V before Agincourt. FaPoR
"King is full of grace and fair regard, The." OxAEP-1
"Once more unto the breach, dear friends, / once more." SAGP
"Thus with imagin'd wing our swift scene flies." EBEV; OxAEP-1
"We few, we happy few, we band of brothers." UnPo
Yon Island Carrions Desperate of Their Bones. RB

King Henry VI, Pt. III. Shakespeare.
"Owl shriek'd at his birth, an evil sign, The." OxAEP-1

King Henry VIII. John Fletcher *and* Shakespeare.
Music. FaBoCh
(Song: "Orpheus with his Lute made Trees.") PoEL-2

King I saw who walked a cloth of gold, The. Cloth of Gold. Francis Reginald. MoCV

King in May, The. Michael Dennis Browne. NYBP

King in Thule, The. Goethe, *German.* STV, *tr. by* John Frederick Nims

King is full of grace and fair regard, The. Shakespeare. OxAEP-1 *Fr.* King Henry V.

King is out a-hunting, The. The King's Wood. C. S. Holder. BoTP

King is Quair, The. James I, King of Scotland.
("Now was there made fast by the touris wall.") OBGa

King James and Brown. *Unknown.* ESPB

King Jamie hath made a vow. Flodden Field. *Unknown.* ESPB

King John. Shakespeare.
"Must you with hot irons burn out both mine eyes?" OxAEP-1
"This England never did, nor never shall." OxAEP-1
To Gild Refinèd Gold. ImPo
What Answer Can I Give?
("*King Philip:* You are as fond of grief as of your child.") LBC
("Then have I reason to be fond of grief.") (LL) LBC

King John and the Abbot of Canterbury. *Unknown.* BoTP; EnSB

King John and the Bishop. *Unknown.* ESPB

King Kiḷḷi in Combat. Cattantaiyar, *Tamil*. PLW, *tr. by* A. K. Ramanujan

King Lear. Peter Huchel, *German*. PoSu, *tr. by* Michael Hamburger

King Lear. Shakespeare.

"As flies to wanton boys are we to the gods." PFE

"Blow, winds, and crack your cheeks! Rage." SAGP

Fool's prophecy, The. CBNP

"He wakes; speak to him." SCV

"Here is the place, my lord; good my lord, enter." OxAEP-1

"Howl, howl, howl! O! you are men of stones." OxAEP-1

"I prithee, daughter, do not make me mad." OxAEP-1

Lear's Madness. CBNP

Lear's Speech to the Storm.

"O my dear father! Restoration, hang." OxAEP-1

"Please you, draw near.--Louder the music there!" EBEV

"This is the excellent foppery of the world." OxBoV

King Lear Bewildered. Patricia Storace. FFC

King lear in a mr. whippy van. Revisionism. Joanne Burns. BMAP

King Lear's Wife. Gordon Bottomley.

"Ah, you have always been a friend to me." NSI

King Lot's Envoys. Drummond Allison. OxBSP

King Louis gave lessons in Class. Limerick. *Unknown*. PeLi

King Louis on his bridge is he. Le Père Sévère. *Unknown, French*. AWP, *tr. by* Andrew Lang

King luikit owre his castle wa', The. Sir Colin. *Unknown*. OxBB

King Mark, Tristram, and Palamede. Swinburne. EBNV *Fr.* Tristram of Lyonesse.

King Midas. Howard Moss. CoAP; TAP

(King's Speech, The.) PoA

King Midas. Ovid. CTC, *tr. by* Arthur Golding *Fr.* Metamorphoses.

King must rule kingdom. Clues are seen from afar. Maxims (Cotton MS.) *Unknown, Anglo-Saxon*. AnOE, *tr. by* Charles W. Kennedy

King, observing with judicious eyes, The. Epigram. Joseph Trapp. FaBoEE

King of Ai, The. Hyam Plutzik. LiTM

King of Brentford's Testament *abr*, The. William Makepeace Thackeray. OBNV

King of Cats Sends a Postcard to His Wife, The. Nancy Willard. OBCA; PC

King of Ch'in Drinks Wine, The. Li Ho, *Chinese*. PLT, *tr. by* A. C. Graham

King of China's Daughter, The. Dame Edith Sitwell. BoTP; FaBoMo; MoBrPo

("Has yet caught me.") (LL) NOxBChV

King of Comforts! King of life! Praise. Henry Vaughan. ESCV

King of Connacht, The. *Unknown, Early Irish*. IIP; NNPT, *tr. by* Frank O'Connor

King of France, the king of France / with forty thousand men, The. Mother Goose. OxNR

("King of France went up the hill, The.") ReMoGo

King of Glory, King of Peace. Praise (2). George Herbert. ChIV-1; ESCV

King of glory [or glorie], king of peace, / With the one make war[re] to cease. L'Envoy. George Herbert. ESCV

King of Glory sends his Son, The. Miracles at the Birth of Christ. Isaac Watts. NOCV

King of honour, louder than of England, The. Lament for the Country Soldiers. Les A. Murray. BMAP

King of Huai-nan, The. In Imitation of "The King of Huai-nan." Pao Chao, *Chinese*. CoBCP, *tr. by* Burton Watson

King of Ireland's Cairn, The. "Ethna Carbery." WPE

King of Mercy, King of Love. Begging. Henry Vaughan. ESCV

King of Oo-Rinktum-Jing, The. James Whitcomb Riley. NOxBChV

King of Owls, The. Louise Erdrich. NoAM

King of stars. The Open Door. *Unknown, Irish*. IIP, *tr. by* Frank O'Connor

King of the Beasts, deep in the wood, The. The Lion and the Echo. Brian Patten. OBSP

King of the Castle. *Unknown*. OxNR

King of the Cats is Dead, The. Peter Porter. NoAM

King of the Hobbledygoblins, The. Laura Elizabeth Richards. OBCA

King of the perennial holly-groves, the riven sandstone. Geoffrey Hill. HAP; NoAM *Fr.* Mercian Hymns.

King of Thulé, The. Goethe, *German*. AWP, *tr. by* James Clarence Mangan

King of waters, the sea shouldering whale, The. The Sea's Abundant Progeny. William Wood. NOSC; SCAP

King of Yellow Butterflies, The. Vachel Lindsay. OBCA

King of Yvetot, The. Pierre Jean de Béranger, *French*. AWP, *tr. by* William Toynbee

King Oliver of New Orleans. Satchmo. Melvin Beaunearus Tolson. BPo; NAAAL

King, once summoned his favorites, A. The King's Favorites. Priscilla Jane Thompson. CBWP-2

King Orfeo. *Unknown*. ESPB; OxBB; OxBoLi

King over Israel. Dahlia Ravikovitch, *Hebrew*. IP, *tr. by* Warren Bargad *and* Stanley F. Chyet

King Pellam's Launde. David Jones. OAEL-2 *Fr.* In Parenthesis.

"So thus he sorrowed till it was day." NoAM

King Philip had vaunted his claims. A Ballade of the Armada. Austin Dobson. FaPoR

King Philip: You are as fond of grief as of your child. Shakespeare. *See* What Answer Can I Give?

"King Rear was foorish man his girls make crazy." A Girdle round the Earth. Anthony Thwaite. PeLV

King Richard hearing of the pranks. The King's Disguise, and Friendship with Robin Hood. *Unknown*. ESPB

King Richard II. Shakespeare.

"Draw near, / And list what with our council we have done." OxAEP-1

Let's Talk of Graves. FaBoBe

Death of Kings, The. TRP

"For God's sake, let us sit upon the ground." HoPM

Richard II. OBGa

("Go bind thou up young dangling apricocks.") GaP

This England. BoTP

King Richard III. Shakespeare.

"I have been studying how I may compare." OxAEP-1

Methought That I Had Broken from the Tower. RB

"Now is the winter of our discontent." OxBoV

"Where is the duke my father with his power?" OxAEP-1

"Why looks your Grace so heavily today?" OxAEP-1

King Richard, in one of his rages. Limerick. Amanda Benjamin Hall. PeLi

King Saul and I. Yehuda Amichai, *Hebrew*. PoSu, *tr. by* Assia Gutmann

King Saul was disconcerted. David and Goliath. Priscilla Jane Thompson. CBWP-2

King scrapes the sweat, The. When a King Asks for a Chieftain's Daughter. Maturai Marutan Iḷanākaṉār, *Tamil*. PLW, *tr. by* A. K. Ramanujan

King sent for his wise men all, The. W. James Reeves. NOxBChV; NTCP

King sent his lady on the first Yule day, The. The Yule Days. *Unknown*. NTP

King Shall Reign in Righteousness, A. Sebastian Streeter. AH

King [he] sits in Dumferline [or Dumferling] town [or toune], The. Sir Patrick Spens [or Spence]. *Unknown*. AWP; AmFP; BXAP; CH; ClHu; EBEV; ESPB; EnSB; FaBoCh; FaPoR; GEA; HAP; HoPM; InPK-6; InPS-3; NAEL-1; NIP-4; NOBE; NoP-4; OAEL-1; OBEV; OBSP; OxBB; OxBS; PBMP; PoE; PoEL-1; PoPoPo; RB; SCGP; TFi; UnPo; WeW-3

King Solomon and the Ants. John Greenleaf Whittier. ChIV-1

King Solomon, before his palace gate. The Spanish Jew's Tale: Azrael. Henry Wadsworth Longfellow. APN-1 *Fr.* Tales of a Wayside Inn.

King Solomon Vistas. Ian Wedde. PeNZ

King Solomon's Camel is a hypocritical creature. Natan Zach, *Hebrew*. PoSu, *tr. by* Jon Silkin

King Solomon's Magnetic Quiz. John Wieners. FTOS

King then left his coach, The. Priam and Achilles. Homer, *Greek*. NOSC; OBCVT, *tr. by* George Chapman *Fr.* The Iliad.

King to Oxford sent a troop of horse, The. Epigram. Sir William Browne. FaBoEE

King was sick, The. His cheek was red. The Enchanted Shirt. John Milton Hay. BLPA

King Wen's Park Divine. *Unknown, Chinese*. ChiPo, *tr. by* Ezra Pound

King William Was King George's Son. *Unknown*. AmFP

King William's Dispatch to Queen Augusta. Coventry Patmore. FaBoEE

King Winter sat in his Hall one day. Outside. Hugh Chesterman. AYFP; BoTP

Kingcups. Sacheverell Sitwell. MoBrPo

Kingdom, The. Louis MacNeice.

"Over the roofs and cranes, blistered cupola and hungry smokestack." LiTM

"Under the surface of flux and of fear there is an underground movement." LiTM

Kingdom. Leopold Staff, *Polish*. PoSu, *tr. by* Adam Czerniawski

Kingdom, The. Jon Swan. NYBP

Kingdom Coming. Henry Clay Work. APN-2

Kingdom of God, The. Rab, *Hebrew*. TrJP

Kingdom of God, The. Francis Thompson. *See* In No Strange Land.

Kingdom of Heaven. Léonie Adams. MoAmPo

Kingdom of Heaven Compared to a Grain of Mustard-Seed, The. Henry Vaughan. ChIV-2

Kingdom of heaven is likened unto a man which sowed good seed in his field, The. The Parable of the Good Seed. Bible, *N.T.* InPK-6 *Fr.* St. Matthew.

Kingdom of Silence. Amir Gilbo'a, *Hebrew.* IP, *tr. by* Warren Bargad *and* Stanley F. Chyet

Kingdom or a cottage or a grave, A. (LL) Poem: "Were I a king, I could command content." Edward, 17th Earl of Oxford De Vere. FaBoEE; NTP; NoSic; OxBSP; PBRV

Kingdoms fall in sequence, like the waves on the shore, The. The Sparrow's Skull. Ruth Pitter. FaBoWP

Kinge Arthur lives in merry Carleile. The Marriage of Sir Gawain. *Unknown.* ESPB

Kinged. Shalin Hai-Jew. UnSA

Kinges baneres beth forth ilad, The. *Unknown.* MiEL

Kingfisher, The. Amy Clampitt. HCAP

Kingfisher, The. W. H. Davies. NOBE; OBEV; OBWVE

Kingfisher, The. John Heath-Stubbs. NOxBChV

Kingfisher, The. Dyneley Hussey. NSI

Kingfisher. Norman MacCaig. NoP-4

Kingfisher, The. Andrew Marvell. *Fr.* Upon Appleton House [To My Lord Fairfax]. FaBoPV; GeHe; SeCP

Kingfisher blue along a tangled bank. Poem to the Tune "Riverbank Willows." Yü Hsüan-chi. BoWoP, *tr. by* Geoffrey Waters

Kingfisher Flat. William Everson. PoM

Kingfisher green lines the deserted shore. Composed on the Theme "Willows by the Riverside." Yü Hsüan-chi, *Chinese.* SuSp; WPOW, *tr. by* Jan W. Walls

Kingfisher rises out of the black wave, The. Mary Oliver. BLT

Kingfishers, The. Charles Olson. APSN; CMoP; InPS-3; NAAL-2; NOBA; NeAP; PoM; VCAP

Kingfisher's Boxing Gloves, The. James Fenton. NoAM

Kingfishers frolic among the orchid blossoms. Poem on the Wandering Immortal. Kuo P'o, *Chinese.* CoBCP, *tr. by* Burton Watson

Kingfisher's naked arc alight, A. Allen Curnow. *Fr.* A Small Room with Large Windows. PeNZ

Kingfishers nest on South Sea islands. Ch'en Tzu-ang. SuSp, *tr. by* Irving Y. Lo *Fr.* Impressions of Things Encountered.

Kingis Quair, The. James I, King of Scotland.
    He Sees His Beloved. PoEL-1
    King is Quair, The.
    ("Now was there made fast by the touris wall.") OBGa

Kingly lyon, and the strong arm'd beare, The. William Wood. SCAP

Kings. *Unknown. Fr.* The Panchatantra. AWP, *tr. by* Arthur Ryder

Kings and Stars. John Erskine. TrCP

King's Breakfast, The. A. A. Milne. OBCoV; OTCP; OxBChV; UV
    ("Like marmalade / Instead.") (LL) UV

Kings Came Riding. Charles Williams. OBCP

Kings cast wreaths at your feet and fall upon their faces. At Your Feet, Jerusalem. Uri Zvi Greenberg, *Hebrew.* MHP, *tr. by* Ruth Finer Mintz

King's College Chapel. Charles Causley. PeECV; TOF

King's Daughter! / Wouldst thou be all fair. Everymaid. John Oxenham. TrCP

Kings' Daughters, Home for Unwed Mothers, 1948. C. D. Wright. NAmP90

King's Disguise, and Friendship with Robin Hood, The. *Unknown.* ESPB

King's Dochter Lady Jean, The. *Unknown.* AmFP; ESPB

Kings don't touch doors. The Delights of the Door. Francis Ponge, *French.* RaBo, *tr. by* Robert Bly

King's Double Nature, A. Kākkai Pāṭiṇiyār Naccelḷaiyār. PLW *tr. by* A. K. Ramanujan

King's Favorites, The. Priscilla Jane Thompson. CBWP-2

King's Garden World, A. Saba, *Arabic.* GaP, *tr. by* Wilbur Donald Newton

Kings go by with jeweled crowns, The. The Choice. John Masefield. MoBrPo *Fr.* Lollingdon Downs.

King's Highway to the Dare-Not-Know, The. "Dreams Are the Royal Road to the Unconscious." Paul Goodman. PoA

King's Horses, The. John Hewitt. IIP

King's Last Words, A. Ceraman Kanaikkal Irumporai, *Tamil.* PLW, *tr. by* A. K. Ramanujan

Kings / like golden gleams. A History Lesson. Miroslav Holub, *Czech.* PoSu; RB, *tr. by* George Theiner

King's Men, The. William Heyen. PoA

Kings of France. Mary W. Lincoln. BLPA

Kings of Peru were the Incas, The. Limerick. *Unknown.* PeLi

King's poet was his captain of horse in the wars, The. Mount Badon. Charles Williams. FaBoTw

King's Portrait, A. King Lê Thánh–tông, *Vietnamese.* AVP, *tr. by* Huỳnh Sanh Thông

Kings River Canyon. Kenneth Rexroth. *Fr.* Andrée Rexroth. APSN; VGW

King's Son, The. Thomas Boyd. OBMV

King's Speech, The. Howard Moss. *See* King Midas.

Kings who have died. Guillaume Apollinaire. TTTS, *tr. by* Roger Shattuck *Fr.* Heart, Crown, and Mirror.

King's Wood, The. C. S. Holder. BoTP

King's X—no fairs to use it anymore! (LL) U. S. 1946 King's X. Robert Frost. CrDW; NIP-4

King's young dochter was sitting in her window, The. The King's Dochter Lady Jean. *Unknown.* ESPB

Kinkaiders, The. *Unknown.* AS

Kinky Hair Blues. Una Marson. PBCV

Kinky young girl from Uttoxeter, A. Limerick. Herbert Kretzmer. PeLi

Kinmont Willie. *Unknown.* ESPB; IBB; OxBB

Kinnereth. "Rachel," *Hebrew.* TrJP, *tr. by* A. M. Klein

Kinsale. Derek Mahon. BiHa

Kinshasa. Walid Bitar. WeT

Kinshasa, we feel, is not the place to reach. The Flight of the White South Africans. Christopher Hope. PeSAV

Kinu the milkman's alley. Flute-music. Rabindranath Tagore, *Bengali.* OMIP, *tr. by* William Radice

Kiowa "49" Songs. *Unknown, Kiowa Indian.*
    "I don't care if you're married, I'll still get you." STP
    "If you really love me honey, hey- yah." STP
    "She said she don't love me anymore because I drink whiskey." STP
    "Since the narcissus bud." STP
    "You know that I love you, sweatheart, but every time I come around." STP

Kiph. Walter De la Mare. CBNP

Kirk Bell, The. John, 1st Baron Tweedsmuir Buchan. NSI

Kirk Lonegren's Home Movie Taking Place Just North of Prince George, with Sound. Sharon Thesen. NOBC

Kirk's Alarm, The. Robert Burns. OxBoLi

Kirkyaird by the Sea, The. Douglas Young, *after the French of* Paul Valéry.
    "Steekit, consecrat, fou o fire but fuel." OBVE

Kirkyard. George Mackay Brown. FaBoTC

Kirsten. Ted Berrigan. TTTS

Kisimiso. Musaemura Bonus Zimunya. HBAPE

Kiss, The. Charlotte Dacre. CABP; NOBRP

Kiss[e], A. Robert Herrick. CaPo

Kiss, The. Thomas Moore. EnLoPo; NOBRP

Kiss, The. Edith Nesbit. LW

Kiss, The. Ned O'Gorman. FYAP

Kiss, The. Coventry Patmore. BoLoP; EnLoPo; NOBVV *Fr.* The Angel in the House.

Kiss, The. Plato, *Greek.* STV, *tr. by* John Frederick Nims

Kiss, The. D. G. Rossetti. NOBVV; Son *Fr.* The House of Life.

Kiss, The. Sara Teasdale. NMM-2

Kiss, The. Alice Walker. GT

Kiss. Al Young. PoBA

Kiss? A. Pray tell me, what is in a kiss. Mary E. Tucker. CBWP-1

Kiss from her! Her mouth, coming even close to your own, how, A. Rufinus Domesticus, *Greek.* STV, *tr. by* John Frederick Nims

Kiss has nothing to do with sex, A. Bulimia. Denise Duhamel. BAP-94

Kiss I begged; but, smiling, she, A. Weeping and Kissing. Sir Edward Sherburne. NOSC

Kiss I never had, The. (LL) Midsummer. Sydney King Russell. BLPA; FaBoBe

Kiss in the Dark, A. Thomas Sayers Ellis. GT

Kiss in the Rain, A. Samuel Minturn Peck. OBAL

Kiss in the Ring. *Unknown.* OxBoLi

Kiss me again, re-kiss and kiss me whole. Sonnet 18. Louise Labé, *French.* WPOW, *tr. by* Raymond Oliver; BoWoP, *tr. by* Willis Barnstone

Kiss me and hug me. *Unknown, Spanish.* BoWoP, *tr. by* Willis Barnstone

Kiss[e] me, sweet: the wary [or warie] Lover, *after* Catullus, Carmina 5 and 7, *passim.* To the Same [Celia]. Ben Jonson. AWP; BeJo; NOSC; OAEL-1; OBVE; SeCP *Fr.* Volpone. NAEL-1

Kiss me then, my merry May. *Unknown, French.* AWP, *tr. by* John Addington Symonds

Kiss me there where pride is glittering [or glistening]. Aria. Delmore Schwartz. EP *Fr.* Two Lyrics from Kilroy's Carnival: A Masque.

Kiss me there where pride is glittering. Two Lyrics from Kilroy's Carnival: A Masque. Delmore Schwartz.

Kiss my grey hair, oh, my love. Healing. Abraham Reisen, *Yiddish.* TrJP, *tr. by* Joseph Leftwich

Kiss my lips. Gertrude Stein. PFTM *Fr.* Lifting Belly.

Kiss my mother left there when she died, The. (LL) Sonnet: "I never gave a lock of hair away." Elizabeth Barrett Browning. EBVV; HAP

Kiss, The 1656. To Mrs. C. Thomas Shipman. NOSC

Kiss Tomorrow Goodbye. Marjorie Welish. FTOS

Kiss'd yestreen, and kiss'd yestreen. *Unknown.* LW

Kisse me, sweet: The warie lover. Catullus, *Latin.* OBCVT, *tr. by* Ben Jonson

Kisses. William Strode. FaBoEE; NOSC

Kisses, Corpse Revivers. (LL) Cocktails. Ciaran Carson. BiHa; PBCIP

Kisses Desired. William Drummond, of Hawthornden. EnLoPo

Kisses in the Train. D. H. Lawrence. MoBrPo

Kisses Loath[e]some. Robert Herrick. CBLP; CaPo; CavPo; EP; OxBSP

Kisses upon the doors! The houses fall. Poeta Fui. Julia Budenz. FFC

Kissie Lee. Margaret Abigail Walker. BlSi; NALW

Kissing. Edward Herbert. EnLoPo; NOSC

Kissing Agathon, I found. Sokrates to Agathon. Plato, *Greek.* GrAn, *tr. by* Peter Jay

Kissing and bussing differ both in this. Robert Herrick. BeJo; CBLP

Kissing Helena, together. Plato, *Greek.* OBVE, *tr. by* Shelley

Kissing her hair, I sat against her feet. Swinburne. FaBoBe

Kissing Hippomenes, I crave. Epigram. Paulus Silentiarius, *Greek.* GrAn, *tr. by* Andrew Miller

Kissing Natalia. Eldon Grier. NOBC

Kissing of My Dame. *Unknown.* OxNR

Kissing Stieglitz Goodbye. Gerald Stern. LCAP-2

Kit Carson came to old Fort Lyons. Kit Carson's Last Smoke. "Stanley Vestal." PaTW

Kitchen. Laura Jensen. LCAP-2

Kitchen Door Blues. Tennessee Williams. OBAL

Kitchen fire that wakes so soon, The. Fires. Elizabeth Fleming. BoTP

Kitchen patio in snowy, The. One A.M. Denise Levertov. CAPP-1

Kitchen Poem. Francis Scarfe. SPE

Kitchen Sink. Ofelia Zepeda. PaTW

Kitchenette Building. Gwendolyn Brooks. BPo; FaBoWP; NAAAL; NAAL-2; NoP-4; PoE; PoPoPo; Poetr; UnPo *Fr.* A Street in Bronzeville. BPo; BlSi; FaBoWP

("Grayed in, and gray. . . .") (LL) GT

Kitchens. Eric Nelson. IFJA

Kitchen's old-fashioned planter's clock portrays, The. Nightfishing. Gjertrud Schnackenberg. WeW-3

Kitchie-Boy, The. *Unknown.* ESPB

Kite, The. Aleksandr Blok, *Russian.* PeFWW, *tr. by* David McDuff *and* Jon Silkin

Kite, A. Hsü Wei, *Chinese.* CoBLCP, *tr. by* Jonathan Chaves

Kite. Laura Jensen. LCAP-2

Kite. John Robert Lee. PBCV

Kite, The. Pearl Forbes MacEwen. BoTP

Kite, The. Adelaide O'Keeffe. NOxBChV; OxBChV

Kite, A. Frank Dempster Sherman. CTV

Kite, The. Mark Strand. ColAP; NYBP

Kite, A. Scott Trevor. CTV

Kite!/ Summon not me to enter: there's no doubt. For a Lady's Summons of Non-Entry. William Drummond, of Hawthornden. NOSC

Kite, completed thus, is borne along, The. Samuel Bowden. NOEC *Fr.* The Paper Kite.

Kite-Flying. Christopher Gilbert. GT

Kite Is a Victim, A. Leonard Cohen. NOBC

Kite Poem. James Merrill. TwCP

Kithairon sang of cunning Kronos. Korinna, *Greek.* BoWoP, *tr. by* Willis Barnstone

Kittatinny Tunnel in that holy place you let me hit. Cheryl Clarke. CPO

Kitten, The. Ogden Nash. PC

Kitten and [the] Falling Leaves, The. Wordsworth.

Kitten at Play, The. ChAP

Kitten at Play, The. Wordsworth. ChAP *Fr.* The Kitten and [the] Falling Leaves.

Kitten on, A. Where Knock Is Open Wide. Theodore Roethke. HAP; VGW

Kitten, writes the mousy boy in his neat. In-flight Note. Judith Rodriguez. BMAP

Kitty. Elizabeth Payson Prentiss. BoTP

Kitty Alone. *Unknown.* CBNP

Kitty and I. W. H. Davies. CBLP

Kitty-Cat Bird, he sat on a fence, The. Theodore Roethke. OBAL

Kitty Kline. *Unknown.* AmFP

Kitty Morey. *Unknown.* AmFP

Kiwi Bird in the Kiwi Tree, The. Charles Bernstein. FTOS

Kleomedes. David Wright. MoP

Kleptomaniac, The. Roger McGough. NOxBChV

Kleson's goat snorted all night through the dark. Erucius of Cyzicus, *Greek.* GrAn, *tr. by* Peter Levi

Klockius so deeply hath sworn[e], ne'er more to come. Donne. PeLV

Klupzy Girl, The. Charles Bernstein. PmAP

Knave of darkness, limber in the leaves, The. Death for the Dark Stranger. Thomas McGrath. VGW

Kneading Bread. Teresa Anderson. LoHo

Knedneuch land. In the Pantry. "Hugh MacDiarmid." NoAM

Knee, The. Ciaran Carson. PNI

Knee, The. Christian Morgenstern, *German.* CBNP; RB, *tr. by* W. D. Snodgrass *and* Lore Segal

Kneegrows niggas. Be Cool, Baby. Rob Penny. PoBA

Kneel, and thank Heaven they are not yours. (LL) William Gifford. Walter Savage Landor. FaBoEE; GTBS-P

Kneeling. Gertrude Stein. PFTM

Kneeling Camel, The. Anna Temple Whitney. BLPA

Kneeling Down to Look [or Peer] into a Culvert. Robert Bly. NoAM

Knees collapsing. Tanka. Nakajō Fumiko, *Japanese.* MJT, *tr. by* Makoto Ueda

Knees garnished with impetigo. (LL) Princes of Mercia were badger and raven, The. Geoffrey Hill. HAP; NAEL-2; NoAM; PoE

Knees of a Natural Man, *(for Jay Wright).* Henry Dumas. GT

Knell, The. Muhammad Al-Faituri, *Arabic.* TTY, *tr. by* Samir M. Zoghby

Knew her themselves, through all her veils [or vailes]. (LL) Ingrateful[l] Beauty Threatened. Thomas Carew. BeJo; CaPo; MeLP; OBEV; SeCP

Knicht had two sons o sma fame. Sir Lionel. *Unknown.* ESPB

Knickerbocker Knockabout. Clyde Watson. NOxBChV

Knife, The. Keith Douglas. NoAM

Knife, The. Milton Kaplan. TrJP

Knife, The. Richard Tillinghast. MT; WeT

Knife All Blade, A. João Cabral de Melo Neto, *Portuguese.* VCWP, *tr. by* Galway Kinnell

Knife blade of cold air keeps prying, A. Upstate. Derek Walcott. GT

Knife like a precious bond, The. Journey. Rodney Hall. NOBAu

Knife / That has learned its trade again, A. No Picture. Lutz Rathenow, *German.* CEEP, *tr. by* Boria Sax

Knife's edge, moon's edge, water's edge. Edge. Robert David Fitzgerald. CBAP

Knifing deep. Anita Virgil. HA

Knight and a lady, A. *Unknown.* BoTP

Knight and Shepherd's Daughter, The, *vers.* A. *Unknown.* ESPB; NoP-4

("But your face I coud never see.") (LL) NoP-4

(Shepherd's Dochter, The.) OxBB

("There was a shepherd's dochter.") NoP-4

Knight and the Lady, The. William Cornish. *See* You and I and Amyas.

Knight and the Shepherd's Daughter, The. *Unknown.* AmFP

Knight, Death, and the Devil, The. Randall Jarrell. ColAP; GS; WeW-3

("Of that old fox; a sheep-dog bounding at his stirrup.") (LL) ColAP

Knight Errant, The. Louise Imogen Guiney. RACG

Knight Fallen on Evil Days, The. Elinor Wylie. MoAmPo

Knight from the world's end, The. A Dream of Governors. Louis Simpson. NYBP

Knight in the Wood, The. John Warren. NOBVV; PeVV

Knight knocked at the castle gate, The. You and I and Amyas. William Cornish. NOBE; NoSic

Knight of Liddesdale, The. *Unknown.* ESPB

Knight of My Maiden Love. Priscilla Jane Thompson. CBWP-2

Knight of "silver tongue" and stately grace, A. Wendell Phillips. Henrietta Cordelia Ray. CBWP-3

Knight of the Burning Pestle, The. Francis Beaumont *and* John Fletcher. "Nose, nose, jolly red nose." FaBoCh; OxNR

Knight of the Grail, The. *Unknown. See* The Corpus Christi Carol.

Knight stands in the stable-door, The. Young Johnstone. *Unknown.* ESPB

Knight went down to the river's rim, A. Ballad. Gerda Mayer. OBSP

Knight with starry shield, The. Sir Roland; a Fragment. Robert Merry. NOEC

Knighthood, The. Chaucer. UV, *ll.* 43–72 *Fr.* The General Prologue. FHYEP; NAEL-1; NAWM-1; OAEL-1; PoE *Fr.* The Canterbury Tales.

Knight's Ghost, The. *Unknown.* ESPB

Knight's Prayer, The. *Unknown.* BoTP

Knight's Tomb, The. Coleridge. FaBoCh; RB

Knitted Things. Karla Kuskin. KaS

Knitting. Mary E. Tucker. CBWP-1

Knock at a star with my exalted head. (LL) The Bad Season Makes the Poet Sad. Robert Herrick. BeJo; CaPo; CavPo; NAEL-1; SCGP

Knock at the doorie. *Unknown.* OxNR

Knock on Wood. Henry Dumas. PoBA

Knocker, A. Zbigniew Herbert, *Polish.* PoSu, *tr.* by Czeslaw Milosz

Knocking Around. John Ashbery. NoAM

Knocking Donkey Fleas off a Poet from the Southside of Chi. Haki R. Madhubuti. SeSe

Knole. Charles Hubert Sisson. NOCV

Knolege, aquayntance, resort, favour with grace. Knowledge, Acquaintance. John Skelton. AAS; CABP

Knot, The. Vinda Karandikar, *Marathi.* OMIP, *tr.* by Vinay Dharwadker

Knot, The. Stanley Kunitz. HAP

Knot, The. Henry Vaughan. MiEL

Knot which first my heart did strain, The. Sir Thomas Wyatt. SiPS

Know. (LL) Nature. Henry Wadsworth Longfellow. FaBoBe; PoLF; TAP

Know *Celia,* (since thou art so proud,). Ingrateful[l] Beauty Threatened. Thomas Carew. BeJo; CaPo; CavPo; MeLP; OBEV; PBRV; SeCP

Know er thou knitte; prove er thou preise it. *Unknown.* MiEL

Know him for a white man. Passing into Storm. Patrick Lane. NOBC

Know me? I am the ghost of Ganesvoort Pier. Among the Missing. Richard Howard. WWSi

Know, that I would accounted be. To Ireland in the Coming Times. W. B. Yeats. NOIV; NoAM

Know that one soldier has not died in vain. (LL) Elegy for a Dead Soldier. Karl Shapiro. HAP; LiTM; OBWP; OxBA

Know the pinetrees. Know the orange dryness of sickness. The Runes. Denise Levertov. SAGP

Know then, I was born in a strange country. To My People. Edwin Seaver. TrJP

Know then, the only joy of an anchor—to be strong. The Anchor. John Blight. BMAP

Know then thyself, presume not God to scan. Know Thyself. Alexander Pope. ECEV; NOBE; NOEC; OAEL-1, *ll.* 1–18; TFi, *ll.* 1–42; ImPo, *ll.* 1–66; EBEvV; FHYEP; NAEL-1; PoEL-3 *Fr.* An Essay on Man.

Know then: / Toward summer when the sun is in Hyades. Ezra Pound, *after the Chinese* Book of Rites. OBVE

Know Thyself. Kenneth Burke. OBAL

Know Thyself. Alexander Pope. NOBE, *ll.* 1–18 *Fr.* An Essay on Man.
 (Paragon of Animals, The.)
 (Riddle of the World.)

Know what I'll promise you? Song. *Unknown, Chippewa Indian.* STP, *tr.* by Jerome Rothenberg

Know what I'm like? Some captain moors his ship. Ausiàs March, *Catalan.* STV, *tr.* by John Frederick Nims

Know! What's "know"? I *feel.* Ask any crucified man. Catullus. *See* Carmen 85.

Know ye the man whom God has blessed. Lines to the Hon. George L. Knox. Eloise Bibb. CBWP-4

Know you fair[e], on what you look[e]? On Mr. G. Herberts Booke, The Temple. Richard Crashaw. CABP; EPCY; ESCV; FSCP; GeHe; OxAEP-1

Know Yourself. John Arbuthnot. ECEV

Knowes what was first, and what shall be the end. (LL) Sonnet: "Man, dream[e] no more of curious mysteries." Greville Fulke. NOSC; NoSic

Knowest thou the land where bloom the lemon trees. Goethe. *See* Mignon.

Knowest thou the time when the wild goates of the rocke bring forth? Bible, O.T. OBVE *Fr.* Then the Lord Answered ("Who is this that darkeneth counsel by words without knowledge?"). AWP *Fr.* Job. NAWM-1

Knowing. Mary Coghill. BrRo

Knowing, The. Sharon Olds. BAP-94; ITG
 ("Beyond the body itself, we are making / love.") (LL) ITG

Knowing About Horses. Virgil. APo, *tr.* by John Dryden *Fr.* The Georgics.

Knowing how many times we kiss. Catullus. *See* Carmen 5 ("My sweetest Lesbia, let us live and love").

Knowing I Live in a Dark Age. Milton Acorn. NOBC

Knowing Love in Herself. Hadewijch, *Flemish.* WPoS, *tr.* by Oliver Davies

Knowing nothing shuts the iron gates; the new love opens them. Kabir, *Hindi.* RaBo, *tr.* by Robert Bly

Knowing that the music knows. *Unknown.* *Fr.* Tepehua Thought-Songs. STP, *tr.* by Charles Boilès

Knowingness. John Hughes. PNI

Knowledge. Louise Bogan. PoA

Knowledge. Nina Cassian, *Rumanian.* BoWoP, *tr.* by Michael Impey *and* Brian Swann

Knowledge. John Greenleaf Whittier. PoToHe *Fr.* Miriam.

Knowledge, Acquaintance. John Skelton. AAS
 (Knowledge, Acquaintance, Resort, Favour, with Grace.) CABP

Knowledge, I know, is sure, of gradual thought. Young Knowledge. "Robin Hyde." PeNZ

Knowledge not of sorrow, you were, The. Discrete Series 1929–1933. George Oppen. PFTM

Knowledge of Light, The. Henry Rago. VGW

Knowledge of Water, A. Judson Mitcham. Poetr

Knowledge That Comes through Experience, The. Jane Cooper. NMM-2

Knowledgeable Child, The. Leonard Alfred George Strong. OBMV

Knowlt Hoheimer. Edgar Lee Masters. OxBA *Fr.* Spoon River Anthology.

Known to the boys in his Latin class as "Sir." The Mysteries of Caesar. Anthony Hecht. NoP-4

Knows dat Cap'n sure is bound to die. *Unknown.* *See* No more auction block for me.

Knows he that never took a pinch. To My Nose. Alfred A. Forrester. BLPA

Know'st thou the land which lovers ought to choose? Italy. Edward Coote Pinkney. APN-1

Knoxville, Tennessee. Nikki Giovanni. BPo; BlSi; MBE; PoBA
 ("And sleep.") (LL) ISC; NOxBChV

Knuckles over the flame. Paradigms of Fire. Brian Swann. AmPA

Ko-Ishin-Mit Goes Fishing. George Clutesi. HATNAP

Ko-jin goes west from Ko-kaku-ro [*or* Ko-keku-to]. Separation on the River Kiang. Li Po, *Chinese.* InPS-3; UnPo, *tr.* by Ezra Pound

Ko-Ko's Song. Sir William Schwenck Gilbert. ImPo *Fr.* The Mikado. (Titwillow.) NoP-4

Kob Antelope. *Unknown, Yoruba.* *Fr.* Hunter Poems of the Yoruba. RB, *tr.* by Ulli Beier

Koel (Rainbird) and Effigy. *Unknown, Aborigine.* NOBAu, *tr.* by Mungayana Nundhirribala

Koheleth. Louis Untermeyer. ChIV-1; TrJP

Koker. Rooplall Monar. HCP

Kokin Shu. Various authors, *Japanese.*
 "Although it is not plainly visible to the eye." AWP, *tr.* by Arthur Waley
 "Beloved person must I think, The." AWP; TAL, *tr.* by Arthur Waley
 "Did I ever think." AWP, *tr.* by Arthur Waley
 "Hoping all the time." AWP, *tr.* by Arthur Waley
 "If only, when one heard." AWP, *tr.* by Arthur Waley
 "My love/ Is like the grasses." AWP, *tr.* by Arthur Waley
 "O Cuckoo." AWP, *tr.* by Arthur Waley
 "Since I heard." AWP, *tr.* by Arthur Waley
 "Thing which fades, A." AWP; BoWoP; PBWP, *tr.* by Arthur Waley
 "When the dawn comes." AWP, *tr.* by Arthur Waley

Kol Nidra. Joseph Leiser. TrJP

Kollwitz, Käthe. Muriel Rukeyser. NMM-2

Kolohe or Communication. Carolyn Lei-Lanilau. BAP-96

Kommunalka. Rider-rider-rider. Along a wall / crawls a spider. Communal Krakovyak. Vladimir Druk, *Russian.* TCRP, *tr.* by Albert C. Todd

Komsomol Song. Iosif Pavlovich Utkin, *Russian.* TCRP, *tr.* by Lubov Yakovleva

Koocoo, The. *Unknown.* TTTS

"Kookoorookoo! kookoorookoo!" / Crows the cock before the morn. Christina Rossetti. FaBoVe

Kopis'taya. Paula Gunn Allen. HATNAP
 ("Dance of feathers, the dance of birds, The.") (LL) OxWW

Kora in Hell. William Carlos Williams.
 "There is neither beginning nor end to the imagination." CLPP

Kore. Robert Creeley. InPS-3; RaBo
 ("Me now?") (LL) CoAmPo

Kore in Hades. Kathleen Jessie Raine. NALW

Korean Mums. James Schuyler. PmAP; VCAP

Korean Woman Seated by a Wall, A. William Meredith. Poetr

Korf a kind of clock invents. Korf's Clock. Christian Morgenstern, *German.* CBNP, *tr.* by Max Knight

Korf gets a police chief's questionnaire. The Police Inquiry. Christian Morgenstern, *German.* CBNP, *tr.* by Max Knight

Korf invents some jokes of a new sort. Delayed Action. Christian Morgenstern, *German.* RB, *tr.* by W. D. Snodgrass *and* Lore Segal

Korf's Clock. Christian Morgenstern, *German.* CBNP, *tr.* by Max Knight

Korosta Katzina Song. Koianimptiwa, *Hopi.* AWP, *tr.* by Natalie Curtis Burlin

Kosmos. Julia Ward Howe. ColAP

Kottenheide where you. Diary Page 69. Reiner Kunze, *German.* CEEP, *tr.* by Lori Fisher

Kou-chien, king of Yüeh, came back from the broken land of Wu. In Yüeh Viewing the Past. Li Po, *Chinese.* CoBCP, *tr.* by Burton Watson

Kraken, The. Tennyson. APo; EnVR; NAEL-2; NoP-4; OAEL-2; OBNC; PeECV; PoEL-5; TOF
 (Kracken, The.) OxBSn

Krakow and the Girl of Twelve. Marianne Boruch. WeT

Kral Majales. Allen Ginsberg. BB; PoM

Krankenhaus of Leutkirch, The. Richmond Lattimore. NYBP

Krantor. Theaitetus, *Greek*. GrAn, *tr. by* Dennis Schmitz

Kremenez. Hanns Cibulka, *German*. CEEP, *tr. by* Ewald Osers

Kreutzer Sonata, A. "Sasha Chorny," *Russian*. TCRP, *tr. by* Bernard Meares

Kreutzer Sonata. Ted Hughes. FaBoMo

Krĭk'ıt. Marlene Mountain. HA

Krismas Dinnah. Maggie Pogue Johnson. CBWP-4

Kroklokwafzi? Sĕmemēmi! The Great Lalula. Christian Morgenstern. CBNP

Kropotkin Poems, The. Phyllis Webb.
"Syllables disintegrate ingrate alphabets." NOBC

Kruger sets his feet. Brass Knuckles. Stuart Dybek. PBCAP

Ku Klux. Langston Hughes. BPo

Ku Li. "Robin Hyde." PeNZ

Ku'nXulaL, Thunder Bird Dance. *Unknown*. *Fr.* Dances and Songs of the Winter Ceremonial. APN-2, *tr. by* Franz Boas

Ku-ring-gai Rock Carvings. David Campbell.
Lovers, The. BMAP

Kū'siut Song. *Unknown, Bella Coola Native American*. APN-2, *tr. by* Franz Boas

Kubla Khan; or, a Vision in a Dream. Coleridge. AWP; CH; EBEvV; FHYEP; FaBoBe; FaBoCh; GEA; HAP; HeIP-4; HoPM; ImPo; InPK-6; InPS-3; NAEL-2; NAWM-2; NIP-4; NOBE; NOBRP; OAEL-2; OBEV; OBNC; OxAEP-2; PBMP; PoE; PoEL-4; PoRA; Poetr; SCGP; SCV; SoSe-8; TFi; TOF; TRP; WeW-3

("And drank the milk of paradise.") (LL) Ro

("Enfolding sunny spots of greenery.") (LL) OBGa

Kudzu Spreads Till It Darkens the Brier, The. *Unknown, Chinese*. CoBCP, *tr. by* Burton Watson

Kuks. Hanns Cibulka, *German*. CEEP, *tr. by* Ewald Osers

Kumara / Nich, nich, pasalam, bada. Bald Mountain Zaum-Poems. *Unknown*. PFTM

Kumquat for John Keats, A. Tony Harrison. NoP-4

Kundry was Wagner's creation. And they brought Tefnut back, from her wilderness. Structure of Rime XVIII. Robert Duncan. FTOS

Kung walked / by the dynastic temple. Canto 13. Ezra Pound. CMoP; FaBoMo; PoE *Fr.* Cantos.

Kupris bears trophies away. Sophocles. CTC *Fr.* Women of Trachis.

Kwela for Tomorrow. Rui Knopfli, *Portuguese*. PeSAV, *tr. by the author*

Kʏe ho! Wonderful! Kambala, *Tibetan*. WPoS, *tr. by* Miranda Shaw

Kʏe ho! Wonderful! Dakini Lion-Face, *Tibetan*. WPoS, *tr. by* Miranda Shaw

Kyoto Born in Spring Song. Gary Snyder. MoLi

Kyoto Garden, A. D. J. Enright. OBGa

Kypris keeps this spot. Anyte, *Greek*. PGA, *tr. by* Kenneth Rexroth

Kypros! Andromache's Wedding. Sappho, *Greek*. BoWoP, *tr. by* Willis Barnstone

Kyrie Eleison! The Funeral of Philip Sparrow. John Skelton. *Fr.* Phyllyp Sparowe [*or* Philip Sparrow]. AAS; PoEL-1

Kyrie eléison. (LL) Jolly Jankin. *Unknown*. EnVB; MiEL; NOBE; OxBoLi; PeLV; PoE

Kyrie, so kyrie. Jolly Jankin. *Unknown*. EnVB; FaBoSe; MiEL; NOBE; OxBoLi; PeLV; PoE

Kyrielle. May Probyn. VWP

Kyrielle: Party Politics. Frederick Thomas Bennett Macartney. NOBAu

L

[L(a.] E. E. Cummings. NIP-4; TRP

L.E.L. E. L. Christina Rossetti. VWP

L.E.L.'s Last Question. Elizabeth Barrett Browning. Ro; VWP

L M F B R. Gary Snyder. PoM

"L" may stand for fifty, Lais. Myrinos, *Greek*. GrAn, *tr. by* Adrian Wright

La Bagarède. Galway Kinnell. NYBP

La Bella Bona-Roba. Richard Lovelace. BeJo; CBLP; CaPo; EBEV; NOSC; OAEL-1; PoEL-3; SeCP

("Pass rascal deer, strike me the largest doe.") (LL) CavPo

La Belle Confidente. Thomas Stanley. BeJo; MeLP

La Belle Dame sans Merci. T. Griffiths. BXAP

La Belle Dame Sans Merci. Keats. AWP; BLPA; CH; ClHu; EBEvV; FHYEP; FaBoBe; FaBoCh; GTBS-P; HAP; HeIP-4; ImPo; InPS-3; NAEL-2; NAWM-2; NOBE; NOBRP; NTP; OAEL-2; OBEV; OBNC; OBSP; OxAEP-2; OxBSn; PBMP; PoE; PoEL-4; PoRA; Poetr; RB; SCGP; SCV; SoSe-8; TFi; TRP; UV; UnPo

(La Belle Dame Sans Merci: A Ballad.) Ro

("O what can ail thee Knight-at-arms.") APAD; CABP; FaBoSe; LaPo; NoP-4; OxBSn; PFE; PoPoPo; SAGP

La Belle Juive. Henry Timrod. APN-2

La Bourbon, A. Richard Lovelace. CaPo; CavPo

La Brea. Richard Kenney. DiPo

La Chute. Charles Olson. InPK-6

La Condition Botanique. Anthony Hecht. GaP

La Corona (*a title also given sometimes to the first sonnet in this collection of seven sonnets*). Donne. ChIV-2; ESCV; Son *Fr.* Holy Sonnets.
Annunciation. TrCP
La Corona. ESCV; Son
(Crown, The.) ChIV-2
Resurrection. ESCV

La Cucaracha. *Unknown*. AS

La Dolce Culpa. Cherríe Moraga. CPO

La Donna E Perpetuum Mobile. Irwin Edman. NYBP

La Figlia Che Piange. T. S. Eliot. CBLP; FaBoTw; GBL; HeIP-4; LoP; OxBTC; PoA; UnPo; VGW

La Fontaine de Vaucluse. Marilyn Hacker.
"Azure striation swirls beyond the stones." Son
"We may be learning how to tell the truth." Son

La Gialletta Gallante, or the Sunburned Exotic Beauty. Edward Herbert. NOSC

La Gioconda. "Michael Field." ADE; CABP
("Historic, sidelong, implicating eyes.") PeVV
(La Gioconda, by Leonardo Da Vinci, in the Louvre.) PeVV

La Gorgue. Ivor Gurney. FP

La Gueule. Erin Mouré. DeD

La, La, La! Thomas M. Disch. NBLV

La Llorona. Greg Pape. AnPA

La lupe on the dick cavett show. Natural Death. Jessica Hagedorn. WWSi

La Madonna dell' Acqua. John Ruskin. NOBVV

La Máquina a Houston. Edward Dorn. PoM

La Mélinite: Moulin-Rouge. Arthur Symons. ADE; PeVV

La Migra. Pat Mora. PaTW; UnSA

La Misère. Philip Appleman. BXAP

La Nuit Blanche. Rudyard Kipling. MoBrPo; UV

La Pathétique. Lily Brett. HP

La Plata, Missouri: Clear November Night. Jim Barnes. HATNAP

"La Pologne? La Pologne? It's very cold over there, isn't it?" the lady. Words. Wislawa Szymborska, *Polish*. PoSu, *tr. by* Krystof Zarzecki

La Préface. Charles Olson. PoM

la Promenade, A. Paul Verlaine. AWP; OBVE, *tr. by* Arthur Symons

La Promessa Sposa. Walter Savage Landor. NOBVV

La Quinque Rue. Edmund Blunden. PeFWW

La Selva. Cid Corman. VGW

La Sequia. Alberto A. Ríos. IFJA

La Toilette. Seamus Heaney. CBLP

La Une, A. Marie Ponsot. CLPP

La Vita Nuova (*see also* Dante, *Vita Nuova, tr. by* Ralph Waldo Emerson(. Dante, *Italian*.
"All ye that pass along Love's trodden way." AWP
"At whiles (yea oftentimes) I muse over." AWP
"Beyond the sphere which spreads to widest space." AWP; CTC
"Canst thou indeed be he that still would sing." AWP
"Day agone, as I rode sullenly, A." AWP
"Death, always cruel, Pity's foe in chief." AWP
"Even as the others mock, thou mockest me." AWP
"Eyes that weep for pity of the heart, The." AWP
"For certain he hath seen all perfectness." AWP
"Gentle thought there is will often start, A." AWP
"I felt a spirit of love begin to stir." AWP
"Ladies that have intelligence in love." AWP
"Love hath so long possessed me for his own." AWP
"Love's pallor and the semblance of deep ruth." AWP
"Mine eyes beheld the blessed pity spring." AWP
"My lady carries love within her eyes." AWP
"My lady looks so gentle and so pure." AWP
"Song, 'tis my will that thou do seek out Love." AWP
Sonnet: "All my thoughts always speak to me of love." AWP
Sonnet: "Love and the gentle heart are one same thing." AWP
"Stay now with me, and listen to my sighs." AWP
"That lady of all gentle memories." AWP
"That she hath gone to Heaven suddenly." CTC
"Thoughts are broken in my memory, The." AWP

"To every heart which the sweet pain doth move." AWP

"Very bitter weeping that ye made, The." AWP

"Very pitiful lady, very young, A." AWP; CTC

"Weep, Lovers, with Love's very self doth weep." AWP

"Whatever while the thought comes over me." AWP

"Woe's me! by dint of all these sighs that come." AWP

"Ye pilgrim-folk, advancing pensively." AWP; CTC

"You that thus wear a modest countenance." AWP

La Vita Nuova. Weldon Kees. VGW

Laban, I curse you for this trick you played! Jacob. Ruth Gilbert. PeNZ *Fr.* Leah.

Labasheedy (The Silken Bed). Nuala Ni Dhomhnaill, *Irish.* CIP-2, *tr. by the Author*; CABP

Label, the labor, the color, the shade. The shirt, The. (LL) Shirt. Robert Pinsky. ColAP; NAmP90

Labor Day. Louise Glück. NoAM

Labor Day, lazy flags drooping in the heat. Day of the Two Bodies. Jim Daniels. PUP-19

Labor Day (four poems). Ōkuma Nobuyuki, *Japanese.* MJT, *tr. by* Makoto Ueda

Labor raises honest sweat. The Dignity of Labor. Robert Bersohn. NBLV

Laboratory Poem. James Merrill. InPK-6; TwCP

Laboratory, The [Ancien Régime]. Robert Browning. EnVR; NAEL-2; OBEV

Laborer, The. Richard Dehmel, *German.* AWP, *tr. by* Jethro Bithell

Laborer, The. José-Maria de Heredia, *French.* AWP, *tr. by* Wilfrid Thorley

Laborers of Christ! Arise. Lydia Huntley Sigourney. AH

Laborie, Choiseul, Vieuxfort, Dennery. Sainte Lucie. Derek Walcott.

Laboring and Heavy Laden. Jeremiah Eames Rankin. AH

Laboring men, please all attend. Free Silver. *Unknown.* AmFP

Labors of Hercules, The. Marianne Moore. MeMAP; OxBA

Labour of day hath ceased to plod. Hymn Before Sleep. Prudentius, *Latin.* OBCVT, *tr. by* John Gray

Labour Pains. Akiko Yosano, *Japanese.* WPJ, *tr. by* Kenneth Rexroth *and* Ikuko Atsumi

Labourer, The. Iolo Goch, *Welsh.* OBWVE, *tr. by* Gwyn Williams

Labourer's Wife, A. John Davidson. EBVV *Fr.* To the Street Piano.

Labouring man, that tills the fertile soil, The. Edward De Vere. NoSic

Labouring poor, in spite of double pay, The. Daniel Defoe. NOBL *Fr.* The True-born Englishman.

Labours of Idleness by Guy Penseval, The. George Darley.

"My bower is in a green dell." Ro

Labyrinth. Yojong Kim, *Korean.* CKP, *tr. by* Jaihiun Kim

Labyrinth, The. Edwin Muir. CMoP; FaBoTC; MoBrPo

Labyrinth of byways, A. Forever Parted: Graveyard. Gu Cheng, *Chinese.* VCWP, *tr. by* J. P. Seaton *and* Mu Yi

Lace. Dean Young. NAmP90

Lace curtain self-destructs, A. Stéphane Mallarmé, *French.* NNPT, *tr. by* Christopher Reid

Lace Pedlar, The. Catherine A. Morin. BoTP

Lachesis. Victor James Daley. CBAP

Lachesis. Hilaire Kirkland. *Fr.* Clotho, Lachesis, Atropos. PeNZ

Lachesis. Kathleen Jessie Raine. NYBP

Lachin y Gair. Byron. OxBS

Lachrimae; or Seven Tears Figured in Seven Passionate Pavans. Geoffrey Hill.

Lachrimae Amantis. NOCV

Lachrimae Verae. NAEL-2; NoAM

Masque of Blackness, The. NoAM

Lack of Balance but not Fatal, A. Jackson Mac Low. FTOS

Lack of Steadfastness. Chaucer. PBMP

Lackamercyme, this is none of I! Mother Goose. *See* The Old Woman and the Pedlar.

Lackawanna. Galway Kinnell. GM

Lackawanna Elegy. Iwan Goll, *German.* AF, *tr. by* Galway Kinnell

lackblockblackb. Ian Hamilton Finlay. TRP

Lacking grace / beauty. Capito, *Greek.* GrAn, *tr. by* Peter Jay

Lacking my love, I go from place to place. Sonnet 78. Edmund Spenser. NoSic *Fr.* Amoretti. AAS

Lacking rich acres, thick grape-crops. Apollonides, *Greek.* GrAn, *tr. by* Peter Whigham

Lacking Sense, The. Thomas Hardy. CMoP; PoEL-5

Laconic as anglers and, like them, submissive. At the Ferry. U. A. Fanthorpe. FaBoWP

Lacquer dust and powdered bone and red cinnabar grains. An Arrowhead from the Ancient Battlefield of Ch'ang-p'ing. Li Ho, *Chinese.* PLT, *tr. by* A. C. Graham

Lacrimas or There Is a Need to Scream. K. Curtis Lyle. NBV; PoBA

Lacy mobile changing lazily, A. Watching a Cloud. Dannie Abse. OxBC

Lad came to the door at night, The. The True Lover. A. E. Housman. EBNV; OxBSn

Lad, come kiss me. Invitation. Marion Angus. LW

Lad I lo'e dearly, Tam Glen, The. (LL) Tam Glen. Robert Burns. AWP; OxBS

Lad of Athens, faithful be. Emily Dickinson. FaBoEE

Lad of the brainier kind, A. Limerick. Hymie Sneak. PeLi

Lad Philisides, The. A Country Song. Sir Philip Sidney. SiPS *Fr.* Arcadia.

Ladakh Buddhess Biker. Lawrence Ferlinghetti. BB

Ladakh Buddhess is watching me, The. Ladakh Buddhess Biker. Lawrence Ferlinghetti. BB

Ladder: Roger Vail's Photo of a Rockface in the Carrara (Italy) Marble Quarries, The. Dennis Schmitz. PUP-18

Ladders. Elizabeth Alexander. FFC

Laddie, little laddie, come with me over the hills. A Cry from the Canadian Hills. Lilian Leveridge. BoTP

Laddy tell I day, tell I do, laddy laddy tell I day. (LL) The Crafty Farmer. *Unknown.* AmFP; ESPB

Ladie stude in her bour-door, The. Young Hunting. *Unknown.* ESPB

Ladie [*or* Lady], that in the prime of earliest youth. Lady That in the Prime. Milton. ChIV-2; Son

Ladies, The. Rudyard Kipling. MoBrPo; NAEL-2

Ladies' Aid, The. *Unknown.* PoLF

"Ladies and gentlemen." Irish Sweaters. Shirley Graves Cochrane. IIP

Ladies and gentlemen come to supper. Hot Boiled Beans. *Unknown.* ReMoGo

Ladies and Gentlemen: / I am going to ask just one question. I Move the Meeting Be Adjourned. Nicanor Parra. HoPM, *tr. by* Miller Williams *Fr.* Manifesto.

Ladies and gentlemen, that is the end of the programme. Epilogue to a Poetry Reading. M. K. Joseph. PeNZ

Ladies and gentlemen:/ This broadcast comes to you from the city. Voice of the Studio Announcer. Archibald MacLeish. HoPM *Fr.* The Fall of the City.

Ladies and gentlemen, this is High Wood. High Wood. Philip Johnstone. NSI; PoFWW

Ladies and gentlemen this little girl. E. E. Cummings. CMoP; PoE

Ladies and gents, you are here assembled. James Joyce. IIP *Fr.* Gas from a Burner.

Ladies bow, and partners set, The. Soliloquy of a Maiden Aunt. Dollie Radford. NOBVV

Ladies Defence Or, the Bride-Woman's Counsellor Answered, The. Mary Lee, Lady Chudleigh.

"Unhappy they, who by their duty led." PEW

Ladies' Home Journal, the, *sonnet.* Sandra M. Gilbert. NIP-4

Ladies, I crave your indulgence for. The Young Laundryman. William Carlos Williams. SAmP

Ladies, I do here present you. A Present to a Lady. *Unknown.* PeLV

Ladies of St. James's, The. Austin Dobson. PoRA

Ladies of the morning gauze their mouths, The. Canonical Hours. William Dickey. CoAP

Ladies Prayer to Cupid, A. Thomas Carew. *See* A Lady's Prayer to Cupid.

Ladies that have intelligence in love. Dante. AWP *Fr.* La Vita Nuova.

Ladies, though to your conquering eyes. Song. Sir George Etherege. OxBSP *Fr.* The Comical Revenge.

Ladies, to this advice give heed. A Maxim Revised. *Unknown.* BLPA; NBLV

Ladies, you see time flieth. *Unknown.* NoSic

Lads and lasses gathering. The Willow-Boughs. Alexander Block. BoTP

Lads in their hundreds to Ludlow come in for the fair, The. A. E. Housman. MoBrPo; OxBTC

Lads of the village, we read in the lay, The. Stevie Smith. OxBSP

Lads of Wamphray, The. *Unknown.* ESPB; IBB

Lady, A. Amy Lowell. MoAmPo

Lady A. L., The. Richard Lovelace. *See* The Lady A. L., My Asylum [in a Great Extremity].

Lady A. L., My Asylum [in a Great Extremity], The. Richard Lovelace. CaPo

(Lady A. L, The.) CavPo

("With that delight the royal captive's brought.") CavPo

Lady Adeline Amundeville. Byron. PoEL-4 *Fr.* Don Juan.

Lady Again Complains, The. Henry Howard, Earl of Surrey. SiPS

Lady Alice ("George Collins came home last Saturday night"). *Unknown.* AmFP

Lady Alice ("George Collins come home last Friday night"). *Unknown.* AmFP

Lady Alice ("Giles Collin he said to his mother one day"). *Unknown.* ESPB

Lady Alice ("Giles Collins he said to his old mother"). *Unknown.* ESPB

Lady Alice ("She says the coffin to be opened"). *Unknown.* AmFP

Lady Alice was sitting in her bower-window. *Unknown.* ESPB

Lady and gentlemen fays, come buy! The Elfin Pedlar. George Darley. BoTP

Lady and the Bear, The. Theodore Roethke. ChAP; NBLV

Lady and the Doctor, The. Helen Leigh. WoRP

Lady and the Magpie, The. *Unknown, Chinese.* ChiP, *tr. by* Arthur Waley

Lady Anne Bathing. Anthony Delius. PeSA

Lady asks me / I speak in season, A, *shorter vers.* Canto 36. Ezra Pound. CTC; OBVE *Fr.* Cantos.

Lady at the Castle, The. John Hollander. NoAM

Lady, / baby. *Unknown.* OxNR

Lady Byron's Reply to Lord Byron's "Fare Thee Well." *Unknown.* BLPA

Lady came to a Bear by a Stream, A. The Lady and the Bear. Theodore Roethke. ChAP; NBLV

Lady Cicely Wemyss. James I, King of England. NOSC

Lady Clare. Tennyson. PBMP

Lady Comes to an Inn, A. Elizabeth Jane Coatsworth. MoAmPo

Lady Diamond. *Unknown.* ESPB

Lady Eleanor Butler. Anna Seward. CPO

Lady Elspat. *Unknown.* ESPB

Lady Erskine sits in her chamber. Child Owlet. *Unknown.* ESPB

Lady Eva Brackwell, the most lovely debutante. Charles Augustus Milverton. Gavin Ewart. OxBoV

Lady, farewell, whom[e] I in silence serve. A Poem Put into My Lady Laiton's Pocket. Sir Walter Ralegh. SiPS

Lady feeds Her little Bird, The. Emily Dickinson. CPO

Lady Fortune is both friend and foe, The. Fortune. *Unknown.* HeIP-4

Lady Freedom Among Us. Rita Dove. LoL

Lady from near Rising Sun, A. Ogden Nash. PeLi

Lady from Vanity Fair, A. Limerick. W. F. N. Watson. PeLi

Lady Greensleeves. *Unknown.* GBL; PoEL-2

Lady Greensleeves. *Unknown.* GBL; PoEL-2

(Greensleeves.) EBEvV

("Greensleeves was all my joy, etc.") (LL) PBRV

(New Courtly Sonnet of the Lady Greensleeves, A.) NoSic

Lady Hsi. Lady Wang Wei, *Chinese.* CoBCP, *tr. by* Burton Watson

Lady I Know, A. Countee Cullen. *See* For a Lady I Know.

Lady! I would that verse of mine. Stanzas. Edgar Allan Poe. NCAP

Lady in a Distant Face. James Welch. AmPA

Lady in Kicking Horse Reservoir, The. Richard Hugo. CoAP; LCAP-2; NAAL-2; NoAM; NoP-4; VCAP

Lady in the Barbershop, The. Raphael Rudnik. NYBP

Lady in the Moon, The. Li Shang-yin, *Chinese.*

"First calls of the migrant geese, no more cicadas." PLT, *tr. by* A. C. Graham

"Lamp glows deep in the mica screen." PLT, *tr. by* A. C. Graham

Lady in the Pink Mustang, The. Louise Erdrich. HATNAP

Lady in the White Dress, Whom I Helped into the Omnibus, The. Nathaniel Parker Willis. APN-1

Lady Is a Tramp, The. Lorenz Hart. OBAL

Lady is smarter than a gentleman, maybe, A. Trial and Error. Phyllis McGinley. PeLV

Lady Isabel. ("I was early on a May morning"). *Unknown.* ESPB

Lady Isabel and the Elf-Knight ("Fair lady Isabel sits"). *Unknown.* ESPB

Lady Isabel and the Elf-Knight ("May Collin"). *Unknown.* ESPB

Lady Isabel and the Elf-Knight [*or* The Elfin Knight] ("My plaid away"). *Unknown.* CH

Lady Isabel and the Elf-Knight ("There came a bird"). *Unknown.* ESPB

Lady Isabel and the Elf Knight (Pretty Polly). *Unknown.* AmFP

Lady Jane. Sir Arthur Thomas Quiller-Couch. PeLV

Lady Jane, The; a Humorous Novel in Rhyme. Nathaniel Parker Willis. OBAL

Lady, Lady, I saw your face. Anne Spencer. BlSi; NAAAL; NMM-2; PoBA

Lady, lady, lady fair. The Suffolk Miracle. *Unknown.* AmFP

Lady, lady should you meet. Social Note. Dorothy Parker. LW *Fr.* Some Beautiful Letters.

Lady Laments for Her Lost Lover, by Similitude of a Falcon, A. *Unknown, Italian.* AWP, *tr. by* D. G. Rossetti

Lady Lazarus. Sylvia Plath. ChIV-2; CoAmPo; FaBoWP; HCAP; MoP; NAAL-2; NALW; NIP-4; NOBA; NoAM; NoP-4; OxWW; PoPoPo; Poetr; SAGP; TAP; TRP; VCAP; VGW

Lady lived in Lancaster, A. Kate and the Cowhide. *Unknown.* AmFP

Lady Lost. John Crowe Ransom. MoAmPo; NoP-4; UnPo

("This morning, there flew up the lane.") MoAmPo

Lady Love. Paul Éluard, *French.* OBVE, *tr. by* Samuel Beckett

Lady, lovely lady. Vain and Careless. Robert Graves. NOxBChV; NTP

Lady loves her will, The. (LL) Hart he loves the high wood, The. Mother Goose. FaBoCh; OxNR; ReMoGo

Lady Lowbodice. *Unknown.* PeLV; PeLi

Lady Macbeth. Nikolai Ushakov, *Russian.* TCRP, *tr. by* Daniel Weissbort

Lady Maisdry was a lady fair. Lord Ingram and Chiel Wyet. *Unknown.* ESPB; OxBB

Lady Maisry. *Unknown. See* Lord Ingram and Chiel Wyet.

Lady Maisry ("Young lords o' the north country, The"). *Unknown.* ESPB; OxBB

Lady Maisry lives intill a bower. Thomas o Yonderdale. *Unknown.* ESPB

Lady Margaret sat in her bower-door. Prince Heathen. *Unknown.* ESPB

Lady Margaret sat in her bowry all alone. Sweet William's Ghost. *Unknown.* AWP; ESPB

Lady Margaret sits in her bower door. Hind Etin. *Unknown.* ESPB

Lady Margery May sits in her bower. Prince Heathen. *Unknown.* ESPB

Lady Mary Vill[i]ers lies, The. Epitaph on the Lady Mary Vill[i]ers. Thomas Carew. BeJo; CaPo; CavPo; FaBoEE; NOBE; OBEV

Lady Moon is sailing, The. Kate Louise Brown. BoTP

Lady Moon, Lady Moon, where are you roving? Richard Monckton, 1st Baron Houghton Milnes. BoTP; NOxBChV; OxBChV

Lady Murasaki says. Murasaki Shikibu. BoWoP; WPJ *Fr.* The Tale of Genji.

Lady My Treasure. Sir Philip Sidney. GBL

Lady Northcote. Mark McWatt. HCP

Lady of all powers. From The Hymn to Inanna. Enheduanna. WPoS

Lady of all the essences, full light. Inanna and the Divine Essences. Enheduanna, *Sumerian.* BoWoP, *ad. by* Aliki *and* Willis Barnstone

Lady, of anonymous flesh and face. James Vincent Cunningham. HoPM

Lady of Arngosk, The. *Unknown.* ESPB

Lady of Carlisle, The. *Unknown.* AmFP

Lady of dusk-wood fastnesses. First Praise. William Carlos Williams. VGW

Lady of features cherubic, A. Limerick. *Unknown.* PeLi

Lady of Heaven and earth, and therewithal. His Mother's Service to Our Lady. François Villon, *French.* AWP; CTC, *tr. by* D. G. Rossetti

Lady of Heaven, queen terrestrial. Ballade which Villon Made. Donagh MacDonagh. TIRV

Lady of High Degree, A. *Unknown, French.* AWP, *tr. by* Andrew Lang

Lady of Miracles. Nina Cassian, *Romanian.* WPOW, *tr. by* Laura Schiff

Lady of Quality, A. Thomas Kinsella. PBCIP

Lady of Shalott, The. Tennyson. EBEvV; EBVVPR; FHYEP; InPS-3; NAEL-2; NOBE; NOBRP; NoP-4; OAEL-2; OBEV; OBNV; OBSP; OxAEP-2; PoE; TFi; TOF

Lady of shrouding hair. *Unknown.* NOIV

Lady of the bright coils and curlings. Eire. David O'Bruadair, *Irish.* BIrV, *tr. by* Austin Clarke

Lady of the Ferry Inn. Gwerfyl Mechain, *Welsh.* BoWoP, *tr. by* Willis Barnstone

Lady of the house is on her benders, The. Five Domestic Interiors. Vernon Scannell. OxBC

Lady of the Lake, The. Sir Walter Scott.

Ballad: Alice Brand. OxAEP-2

Farewell Thou Minstrel Harp. OBNC

(Harp of the North, Farewell! The Hills Grow Dark.)

Flowers and Trees. OxAEP-2

Gathering, The. OBNC

"Now, yield thee, or by Him who made." OxBS

Soldier Rest! [Thy Warfare O'er]. AWP; NoBRP; PoRA

(Song: "Soldier rest! thy warfare o'er.") OBNC

Western Waves of Ebbing Day, The. PoEL-4

Lady of the legless world I have. Notes after Blacking Out. Gregory Corso. NeAP

Lady of the Manor, The. George Crabbe. NOBE; OBNC *Fr.* Burials. OAEL-1 *Fr.* The Parish Register.

Lady of the Night star-breathed. The Night-Blooming Jasmine. Audre Lorde. ColAP

Lady of the Pearls, The. Alexandre Dumas, *French.*

"We set out yesterday upon a winter drive." TTY

Lady of Trees, The. Mary Elizabeth Coleridge. VWP

Lady on a Bus. Jeanne Lohmann. CrSp

Lady on climbing Mount Shasta, A. Limerick. *Unknown.* PeLi

Lady on Streetcar. Sandro Penna, *Italian.* STV, *tr. by* John Frederick Nims

Lady Picking Flowers, A. Shen Chou, *Chinese.* ChiPo; CoBLCP, *tr. by* Jonathan Chaves

Lady Pitcher, The. Cynthia MacDonald. Poetsp

Lady: please don't throw rocks at my window. To the Madwoman in My Yard. Olive Senior. HCP

Lady Poverty was fair, The. Alice Thompson Meynell. NOBVV; OBMV; PeVV

Lady Prayeth the Return of Her Lover Abiding on the Seas, The. *Unknown.* GBL

(To Her Sea-faring Lover.) OBEV

Lady Queen Anne she sits in the sun. *Unknown.* OxNR

Lady Ralegh's Lament. Robert Lowell. OxBSP

Lady "Rogue" Singleton. Stevie Smith. FaBoWP; OPOU; OxBSP

Lady Sings, The. Milton. *See* Echo.

Lady stands in her bower door, The. The Twa Magicians. *Unknown.* ESPB; OAEL-1; OxBB; OxBoLi

Lady Stood, A. Dietmar von Aist [or Eist], *German.* AWP, *tr. by* Jethro Bithell; GePo, *tr. by* J. W. Thomas

Lady T-rc----l's Ring. *Unknown.* NOBRP

Lady Tactics. Anne Waldman. PoM

"Lady, take this garland." Walther von der Vogelweide, *German.* GePo, *tr. by* Frederick Goldin

Lady, tell me, will you, pray. Found—Who Lost? Mary E. Tucker. CBWP-1

Lady that hast my heart within thy hand. Hafiz. AWP, *tr. by* Gertrude Lowthian Bell *Fr.* Odes.

Lady That in the Prime. Milton. ChIV-2; Son

Lady, the shepherds have all gone. Ya Se Van Los Pastores. Dudley Fitts. FYAP

Lady there was in Antigua, A. Limerick. *Unknown.* PeLi

Lady, there's fragrance in your sighs. Lines Written for a Blank Page of "The Keepsake." Winthrop Mackworth Praed. CBLP

Lady, this is my sonnet to your eyes. (LL) Modern Love: Sonnet 30. George Meredith. CABP; GBL; HAP; NoP-4; PoEL-5

Lady, those cherries plenty. *Unknown.* NoSic

Lady, thy face is very beautiful. Letitia Elizabeth Landon. NOBRP

Lady walked by the ocean strand, The. Strand-Thistle. Gustav Falke, *German.* AWP, *tr. by* Jethro Bithell

Lady walked down a roadbed, A. A Gentle Heart: Two. Judith Johnson Sherwin. BoWoP

Lady, we would behold thee moving bright. To Christina Rossetti. "Michael Field." VWP

Lady who lies beneath this stone. Elegy in a Kensington Churchyard. Muriel Spark. FaBoTC

Lady Who Offers Her Looking-Glass to Venus, The. Matthew Prior, *after the Greek of* Plato. FaBoEE; NOEC; OBEV; OxBSP

(Farewell, A: "Venus, take my votive glass.") AWP

Lady who rules Fort Montgomery, A. Limerick. Morris Gilbert Bishop. PeLi

Lady, who signs herself "Vexed," A. Limerick. Edward Gorey. OBAL; PeLi

Lady, whom my belovéd loves so well! A Petition. Frances Anne Kemble. LW

Lady with a Falcon on Her Fist, A. Richard Lovelace. CaPo

Lady with the Unicorn, The. Vernon Watkins. TwCP

Lady with thine eyes of beauty. The Valentine. Mary Weston Fordham. CBWP-2

Lady without Paragon, A. Chaucer. *See* Balade: "Hide [or Hyd], Absalon, thy gilte tresses clere."

Lady, you think too much of speeds. Statistics. Stephen Spender. MoBrPo

LADY, you think you spite me. *Unknown.* NoSic

Lady, your art or wit could ne'er devise. To a Lady Who Sent Me a Copy of Verses at My Going to Bed. Henry, Bishop of Chichester King. CBLP

Ladybird. *Unknown.* FaBoVe

Ladybird, Ladybird fly away home. Mother Goose. FaBoVe; LB; OxNR; ReMoGo

("And she crept under the pudding-pan.") (LL) CTAV

Ladybug. Raymond Souster. MoCV

Ladybug's Christmas. Norma Farber. PChr

Lady's Complaint, The. John Heath-Stubbs. TwCP

Lady's Days. Larry Neal. NBV; SeSe

Lady's Diary, The. Charles Dibdin. NOEC

Lady's Dressing Room, The. Jonathan Swift. NoP-4

Lady's love is gained, A. The Price of Disrespect. Lizelia Augusta Jenkins Moorer. CBWP-3

Lady's-Maid's Song, The. John Hollander. LiTM; TwCP

Lady's Prayer to Cupid, A. Thomas Carew, *after* Giovanni Battista Guarini. CaPo; OBVE

Lady's Resolve, The. Lady Mary Wortley Montagu. BoWoP; OxBSP

(Resolve, The.) ECWP

Lady's Third Song, The. W. B. Yeats. FaBoTw

Lady's Way. Reuben Jackson. GT

Laertes. Hesiod, *Greek.* OBCVT, *tr. by* Michael Longley

Lafayette. Dolley Madison. AiP

Lago Maggiore. Thomas Cole. APN-1

Lagoonal Calendar. Aimé Césaire, *French.* VCWP, *tr. by* Clayton Eshleman *and* Annette Smith

Lagoons, Hanlan's Point. Raymond Souster. NOBC

L'Agulhas, A Walk. Wilma Stockenström, *Afrikaans.* PeSAV, *tr. by* Rosa Keet

Laguna Blues. Charles Wright. PoPoPo

Laguna man said. Wind and Glacier Voices. Simon J. Ortiz. HATNAP

Lai. May Probyn. VWP

Laid-by. Donald Hall. *See* "Reclining Figure."

Laid in my quiet bed, in study as I were. Henry Howard, Earl of Surrey. CABP; CH; SiPS

("From boy to man, from man to boy, would chop and change degree. . . .") (LL) PBMP

Laid like weights on the table. (LL) The Garden. Louise Glück. AmPA; HCAP; NAAL-2; VCAP

Laid me in earth and wrote these lines on my tomb. (LL) Epitaph of a Dog. *Unknown, Greek.* FP; GrAn, *tr. by* Dudley Fitts

Laid Off. Francis Webb. BMAP

Laid out for dead, let thy last kindness be. To Robin Redbreast. Robert Herrick. PoE

Laid with papyrus to catch fire. Martial, *Latin.* FaBoEE, *tr. by* James Michie

Laila Boasting. Laila Akhyaliyya, *Arabic.* BoWoP, *tr. by* Willis Barnstone

Laily Worm and the Machrel of the Sea, The. *Unknown.* ESPB; OxBB; PoEL-1; SCGP

Laïque, says the Frenchman to the Frenchman, and the. Like. Robert Desnos, *French.* MFP, *tr. by* Martin Sorrell

Lair, The. Rachel Hadas. FFC

Laird, a lord, A. *Unknown.* OxNR

Laird o' Cockpen, he's proud an' he's great, The. Carolina Oliphant, Baroness Nairne. NOBRP; WPE

Laird o Drum, The. *Unknown.* ESPB

Laird o' Logie, The. *Unknown.* CH; ESPB

Laird o' Ochiltree Wa's, The. *Unknown.* OxBB

Laird of Bristoll's daughter was in the woods walking, The. Captain Wedderburn's Courtship. *Unknown.* ESPB

Laird of Leys is on to Edinbrugh [or Edinburgh], The. The Baron o [or of] Leys. *Unknown.* ESPB; OxBB

Laird of Wariston, The. *Unknown.* ESPB

Lais. Hilda Doolittle. MoAmPo

Lais, courtesan of Corinth, why has. Elaine Feinstein. FaBoWP

Lais' Mirror. Julianus of Egypt, *Greek.* GrAn, *tr. by* Robin Skelton

Lais' Mirror. *Unknown, Greek.* GrAn, *tr. by* Peter Jay

Lais now old, that erst attempting lass. *Unknown, after the Greek of* Plato. FaBoEE

Lais to Aphrodite. Edwin Arlington Robinson, *after* Plato. FaBoEE *Fr.* Variations of Greek Themes.

Lais, who was a lovely flower. Pompeius, *Greek.* GrAn, *tr. by* Dennis Schmitz

Lak of Stedfastnesse. Chaucer. AWP

Lake, The. Matthew Arnold. EnVR *Fr.* Switzerland.

Lake, The. Louis O. Coxe. NYBP

Lake, The. Ted Hughes. FaBoTw; NYBP

Lake, The. Edgar Allan Poe. *See* The Lake: To———.

Lake, The. Barry Seiler. PT

Lake. Ronald Albert Simpson. CBAP

Lake, The. James Stephens. MoBrPo

Lake Baskunchak. Andrey Alekseievich Amalrik, *Russian.* TCRP, *tr. by* John Glad

Lake blue below the hill, The. Mary Elizabeth Coleridge. *See* L'Oiseau Bleu.

Lake Bud. Ishmael Reed. MoNo

Lake Chemo. James Wilton Rowe. AmFP

Lake comes in view, A. Landscape I. Yongt'ae Kim, *Korean.* CKP, *tr. by* Jaihiun Kim

Lake Drummond Dream. Dave Jeddie Smith. VCAP

Lake in Central Park, The. Jay Wright. GT

Lake / Is a river curled and asleep like a snake, A. Thomas Lovell Beddoes. NOBVV

Lake is blue with morning, The; and the sky. Morning on the Shore. Wilfred Campbell. NOBC

Lake is deserted now, The. The Dispossessed. Thomas Kinsella. NOCV

Lake is known as West Branch Pond, The. The Ballad of Blossom. Mona Van Duyn. EOEF

Lake is sharp along the shore, The. Lakeshore. Francis Reginald Scott. MoCV; NOBC

Lake Isle, The. Ezra Pound. OBCoV; OxBSP; PoA

Lake-Isle of Innisfree, The. W. B. Yeats. ADE; APAD; CABP; CMoP; ChAP; ClHu; EBEvV; FaPoR; HeIP-4; IIP; InPK-6; InPS-3; LiTM; MoBrPo; MoP; NAEL-2; NOBE; NTP; NoAM; NoP-4; OBEV; OxAEP-2; OxBTC; PoE; PoPoPo; PoRA; Poetr; SAGP; TFi; UV

Lake lay blue below the hill, The. L'Oiseau Bleu. Mary Elizabeth Coleridge. CH; VWP

Lake Leman woos me with its crystal face. Byron. InPS-3; NOBRP; PoEL-4 *Fr.* Childe Harold's Pilgrimage Canto III. Ro

Lake lies blind and glinting in the sun, The. Virginia Lake. James Keir Baxter. PeNZ

Lake marsh grass like two eels who were caught, The. (LL) Twilight Polka Dots. Barbara Guest. NoP-4; PmAP

Lake Merritt is Bud Powell's piano. Lake Bud. Ishmael Reed. MoNo

Lake Morning in Autumn. Douglas Livingstone. NoP-4

Lake Murry. Pinkie Gordon Lane. GT

Lake of Gaube, The. Swinburne. CABP; NAEL-2; OAEL-2

Lake of night is still in the valley, The. The Pine. Saunders Lewis, *Welsh.* OBWVE, tr. by Gwyn Morgan

Lake of pain, an absence, A. But What Is the Reader to Make of This? John Ashbery. InPS-3

Lake of the Dismal Swamp, The. Thomas Moore. BLPA

Lake of the Returned Sword, The. *Unknown, Vietnamese.* AVP, tr. by Huỳnh Sanh Thông

Lake of the Woods, The. Richard Ryan. PBCIP

Lake of Zurich, The. Friedrich Gottlieb Klopstock, *German.* GePo, tr. by George C. Schoolfield

Lake Song. Jean Starr Untermeyer. TrJP

Lake Success. Robert Conquest. OxBC

Lake sunken among, A. Woman Skating. Margaret Atwood. FaBoWP

Lake Superior. Lorine Niedecker. FaBoWP

Lake, The; Or, Modern Improvement in Landscape. Anna Seward. OBGa

Lake: To———, The. Edgar Allan Poe. APN-1; MeMAP
   ("In youth's spring, it was my lot.") NAAL-1; NAAL-3

Lake was covered all over, The. Dorothy Wordsworth. KaS

Lake was filled with distinguished fish, The. Twilight Polka Dots. Barbara Guest. PmAP

Lakefront, Cleveland. Russell Atkins. GT

Lakes. David Donnell. NoAM

Lakeshore. Francis Reginald Scott. MoCV; NOBC

Lakeside. Edmund Wilson. OBCoV *Fr.* Easy Exercises in the Use of Difficult Words.

Lakeside Identification, A. Robert Pinsky. See Invocation: "It's crazy to think one could describe them."

Lakeside Incident. Robin Skelton. NOBC

Lakeward. Trumbull Stickney. APN-2

Lakota Sister/Cherokee Mother. Victoria Lena Manyarrows. UnSA

Lakshmi. Padraic Fallon. NOIV

Lala: The Dressmaker. Honor Ford-Smith. HCP

Lalai (Dreamtime). Sam Woolagoodjah. NOBAu

Lalela Zulu. *Unknown, Zulu.* PeSA

Lalla Halima! Protect abandoned girls! Like Smoke. Mririda n'Ait Attik, *French.* PBWP, tr. by Daniel Halpern and Paula Paley

Lalla Rookh. Thomas Moore.
   "Fly to the desert, fly with me." BIrV
   Golden Hour, The. OBNC
   "Oh! ever thus from childhood's hour." UV
   Peri's Lament for Hinda, The. OBNC

L'Allée. Paul Verlaine, *French.* GaP; OBGa, tr. by Arthur Symons
   (Dans l'Allée.) AWP, tr. by Arthur Symons

L'Allegro. Milton. AWP; FHYEP; GTBS-P; HAP; HoPM; ImPo; NOSC; NoP-4; OAEL-1; OBEV; PBRV; PoPoPo; TFi
   Mirth and Poetry. EPCY

Lama, The. Ogden Nash. FaBoCh

Lama of Outer Mongolia, A. Limerick. Ogden Nash. PeLi

Lamb, The. William Blake. BoTP; CH; ChIV-2; EBEvV; FHYEP; FaBoBe; FaBoCh; HeIP-4; ImPo; InPS-3; NAEL-2; NAWM-2; NIP-4; NOBRP; NOEC; OAEL-2; OxAEP-2; OxBChV; PoE; Poetr; SoSe-8; TFi; TRP; TrCP; UnPo *Fr.* Songs of Innocence.
   ("Little Lamb, who made thee?") CTAV; NoP-4; PoPoPo; Ro; SAGP

Lamb. Michael Dennis Browne. RaBo

Lamb, The. Keith Wilson. Poetsp

Lamb indestructible lamb. Song to the Lamb. Novica Tadic, *Serbo-Croatian.* HSix, tr. by Charles Simic

Lamb of the shepherds, Child, how still you lie. (LL) The Holy Innocents. Robert Lowell. CoAmPo; MoAmPo; OBCP; OxBC

Lamb Was Bleating Softly, The. Juan Ramón Jiménez, *Spanish.* PChr, tr. by Robert Bly

Lamba. Jacques Rabémanganjara, *French.*
   "In hermetic enclosure." NegPo, tr. by Ellen Conroy Kennedy

Lambeth Lyric. Lionel Pigot Johnson. NOBVV

Lambs at Play. Christina Rossetti. BoTP
   ("On the grassy banks.") CTAV

Lambs that learn to walk in snow. First Sight. Philip Larkin. NTCP

Lame Beggar, A. Donne. FMP; NoSic; PeLV; PFE

Lament: "Blue, so blue that eye of sky." Jacques Rabémanganjara, *French.* NegPo, tr. by Ellen Conroy Kennedy

Lament: "Farewell Mercy, farewell thy piteous grace." John Lydgate. PoEL-1 *Fr.* Court of Sapience.

Lament: "Gizzard and some ruby inner parts, A." Margaret Avison. HAP

Lament: "I turn to you high priests." Tadeusz Różewicz, *Polish.* PoSu, tr. by Magnus J. Krynski

Lament: "In a dismal air; a light of breaking summer." George Sutherland Fraser. PoWW

Lament: "Listen, children: / Your father is dead." Edna St. Vincent Millay. CrSp; FiLi; IMW; MeMAP

Lament: "My man is a bone ringèd with weed." Brenda Chamberlain. WPE; WPOW

Lament, A: "O world! O life! O time!" Shelley. GTBS-P; NAEL-2; NOBE; PoRA

Lament: "Oh, everything is far." Rilke, *German.* TrJP, tr. by C. F. MacIntyre

Lament: "One sore thing is the way." Gibbons Ruark. MT

Lament: "Sleep and death, the dusky eagles." Georg Trakl, *German.* PeFWW, tr. by Michael Hamburger

Lament: "Someone is dead." Anne Sexton. CoAmPo; WPE

Lament: "Spell, treasure-bearing spell, prop up the sky standing above." *Unknown, Maori.* PeNZ, tr. by Margaret Orbell

Lament: "We who are left, how shall we look again." Wilfrid Wilson Gibson. NSI; OxBTC

Lament: "What face, in the water." William Carlos Williams. VGW

Lament, The: "What shall I send you, my dear one, there in the underworld?" *Unknown, Greek.* GrIP, tr. by Margaret Alexiou

Lament: "Young men of the world, The." Francis Stewart [or "Frank"] Flint. PeFWW

Lament: "Your dying was a difficult enterprise." Thom Gunn. GLP

Lament after Her Husband Bishr's Murder. Al-Khirniq, *Arabic.* BoWoP, tr. by Willis Barnstone

Lament City. Thomas Lux. AmPA

Lament, 1547, A, , abr. Alexander Scott. See Lament of the Master of Erskine.

Lament for a Brother. Al-Khansa, *Arabic.* ArPe, tr. by Omar S. Pound

Lament for a Cricket Eleven. Kenneth Allott. OxBTC

Lament for a Husband. *Unknown, Papuan.* BoWoP, tr. by Don Laycock

Lament for a Leg. John Ormond. NoP-4; OBWVE

Lament for a Warrior. *Unknown, Sotho.* PeSA, tr. by Dan Kunene and Jack Cope

Lament for Adonis. Bion, *Greek.* AWP, tr. by John Addington Symonds
   ("I weep for Adonis, 'The lovely Adonis is dead'.") HePo, tr. by Barbara Hughes Fowler

Lament for an Arab Encampment. Abid ibn al-Abras, *Arabic.* ArPe, tr. by Omar S. Pound

Lament for an Old Woman. Albert Huffstickler. IFJA

Lament for Aquileia Destroyed, and Never to be Built Again. Paulinus of Aquileia, *Latin.* MLL, tr. by Helen Waddell

Lament for Art O Laoghaire, The. Eibhlin Dubh O'Connell, *Irish.*
   "My steadfast love!" NOIV, tr. by Thomas Kinsella

Lament for Arthur O'Leary, The. *Unknown, Irish.*
   "My love forever!" BIrV; PBWP, tr. by Eilis Dillon

Lament for Banba. Egan O'Rahilly. AWP, tr. by James Clarence Mangan

Lament for Bion, see also translations by Shelley ("Ye Dorian woods and waves") and Wordsworth ("Ah me! the lowliest children"). Moschus, *Greek.* HePo, tr. by Barbara Hughes Fowler; AWP, tr. by George Chapman
   "Ah! when the mallow in the croft dies down." OBCVT, tr. by Walter Savage Landor
   ("Sing me 'Woe,' you glades and Dorian water.") HePo, tr. by Barbara Hughes Fowler

Lament for Chaucer. Thomas Hoccleve. OBEV *Fr.* De Regimine Principum.

Lament for Damon. John Milton, *Latin.* MLL, tr. by Helen Waddell

Lament for Fearghal Ruadh. Tadhg Og O'Huiginn. NOIV

Lament for Five Sons Lost in a Plague. Abu Dhu'ayb al-Hudhali, *Arabic*. ArPe, *tr. by* Omar S. Pound

Lament for Flodden, The. Jane Elliot. *See* The Flowers of the Forest.

Lament for Glasgerion. Elinor Wylie. PoA

Lament for Hathimoda, Abbess of Gandesheim. *Unknown, Latin*. MLL, *tr. by* Helen Waddell

Lament for Hsieh T'iao. Shen Yüeh, *Chinese*. SuSp, *tr. by* Lenore Mayhew *and* William McNaughton

Lament for Ignacio Sánchez Mejías. Federico García Lorca, *Spanish*. OBVE, *tr. by* A. L. Lloyd; NAWM-2, *tr. by* Stephen Spender *and* J. L. Gili

Lament for Kepa Anaha Ehau. Arapeta Awatere, *Maori*. PeNZ, *tr. by the author*

Lament for Lleucu Llwyd. Llywelyn Goch ap Meurig Hen, *Welsh*. OBWVE, *tr. by* Joseph P. Clancy

Lament for Llywelyn ap Gruffudd. Gruffudd ab yr Ynad Coch, *Welsh*. OBWVE, *tr. by* Joseph P. Clancy

Lament for Lost Lodgings. Phyllis McGinley. NYBP

Lament for Lu Yin. Meng Chiao, *Chinese*. SuSp, *tr. by* Stephen Owen

Lament for Maurice Bishop. Howard Fergus. PBCV

Lament for Myself, A. Yün Shou-p'ing, *Chinese*.
("As old age approaches." CoBLCP, *tr. by* Jonathan Chaves

Lament for Our Lady's Shrine at Walsingham, A. *Unknown*. PoEL-2
("In the wracks of Walshingham.") NoP-4
(Ruins of Walsingham, The.) NoSic
("Walsingam oh farewell.") (LL) PBRV

Lament for Pasiphaë. Robert Graves. FaBoTw

Lament for Siôn y Glyn. Lewis Glyn Cothi, *Welsh*. OBWVE, *tr. by* Joseph P. Clancy

Lament for Tadhg Cronin's Children. Michael Hartnett. PBCIP; RB

Lament for Tawhiao. *Unknown, Maori*. PeNZ, *tr. by* Margaret Orbell

Lament for Te Heuheu Herea. Te Heuheu Tukino, *Maori*. PeNZ, *tr. by* Margaret Orbell

Lament for Te Iwi—ika. *Unknown, Maori*. PeNZ, *tr. by* Margaret Orbell

Lament for the Country Soldiers. Les A. Murray. BMAP

Lament for the Cuckoo. Alcuin, *Latin*. NAWM-1, *tr. by* Helen Waddell

Lament for the Death of Eoghan Ruadh O'Neill. Thomas Osborne Davis. NOIV

Lament for the Death of Thomas Davis. Sir Samuel Ferguson. BIrV; NOIV

Lament for the Dorsets. Alfred Wellington Purdy. NoAM

Lament for the Drowned Country. Mary Durack. NOBAu

Lament for the Graham. Henry the Minstrel. OxBS *Fr.* The Wallace.

Lament for the Great Music. "Hugh MacDiarmid."
("Yet there is no great problem in the world today." OxBTC

Lament for the Makaris. William Dunbar. EBEV; HAP; NoP-4; OxBS
(Lament for the Makers.) OAEL-1; OBEV; PoEL-1; SCGP
(Lament: When He Wes Sek.) EnVB

Lament for the Makers. William Dunbar. *See* Lament for the Makaris.

Lament for the Makers. W. S. Merwin. BAP-96

Lament for the Makers: "No call upon anyone but the timber drifting in the waves." Jack Spicer. FTOS

Lament for the O'Neills. John Montague. CIP-2

Lament for the People of Lung. P'i Jih-hsiu, *Chinese*. SuSp, *tr. by* William H. Nienhauser

Lament for the Poets: 1916. Francis Ledwidge. AWP

Lament for the Two Brothers Slain by Each Other's Hand. Aeschylus, *Greek*. AWP *Fr.* The Seven against Thebes.

Lament for the Willows outside the City Walls, A. Yün Shou-p'ing, *Chinese*. CoBLCP, *tr. by* Jonathan Chaves

Lament for the Woodlands. *Unknown, Irish*. IIP, *tr. by* Frank O'Connor

Lament for Thomas MacDonagh. Francis Ledwidge. BIrV
(Thomas MacDonagh.) NOIV

Lament for Timoleague. Sean O'Coilean, *Irish*. TIRV, *tr. by* Sir Samuel Ferguson

Lament for Troy. Hugh, Primate of Orleans, *Latin*. MLL, *tr. by* Helen Waddell

Lament for Urien, The. *Unknown*. OBMV, *tr. by* Ernest Rhys *Fr.* The Red Book of Hergest.

Lament for Ying, A. Ch'u Yüan, *Chinese*. SuSp, *tr. by* Wu-Chi Liu

Lament him, Mauchline husbands a'. Epitaph for James Smith. Robert Burns. EBEV

Lament in Spring. "Jan Struther." WPN

Lament, lament, Sir Isaac Heard. Epitaph on Tuft-Hunter. Thomas Moore. FaBoEE

Lament my loss[e], my labo[u]r, and my pain [*or* payne]. Sir Thomas Wyatt. AAS

Lament of a Man for His Son. *Unknown, Paiute Indian*. AWP; IMW, *tr. by* Mary Austin

Lament of a Soldier's Wife. Kao Ch'i, *Chinese*. SuSp, *tr. by* Irving Y. Lo

Lament of a Subwayite. Eugene O'Neill. UV

Lament of a Woman Acorn-gatherer. P'i Jih-hsiu, *Chinese*. SuSp, *tr. by* William H. Nienhauser

Lament of an Idle Demon. Richard Percival Lister. NOBL

Lament of Edward Blastock, The. Dame Edith Sitwell. OBMV

Lament of Hsi-ch'un. Hsi-chün, *Chinese*. BoWoP, *tr. by* Arthur Waley

Lament of Hsi-Ch'un. *Unknown, Chinese*. ChiP, *tr. by* Arthur Waley

Lament of Maev Leith-Dherg, The. *Unknown, Middle Irish*. OBWP, *tr. by* Thomas W. H. Rolleston

Lament of Swordy Well, The. John Clare. FaBoVe

Lament of the Banana Man, The. Evan Jones. PBCV

Lament of the Border Widow, The. *Unknown*. OxBB
(Bonnie Bower, The.) CH

Lament of the Captive, The. Richard Henry Wilde. APN-1; ColAP

Lament of the Drums (1964). Christopher Okigbo.
"Lion-hearted cedar forest, gonads for our thunder." PBMAP

Lament of the Farm Wife of Wu. Su Tung-p'o, *Chinese*. CoBCP, *tr. by* Burton Watson

Lament of the Flowers, The. Jones Very. APN-1; ColAP; NOBA; OxBA

Lament of the Flutes. Christopher Okigbo. PBA

Lament of the Forest, The. Thomas Cole. APN-1

Lament of the Frontier Guard. Li Po, *Chinese*. OBVE; OBWP; VGW, *tr. by* Ezra Pound

Lament of the Lady of Ch'in, The. Wei Chuang, *Chinese*. SuSp, *tr. by* Robin D. S. Yates

Lament of the Master of Erskine. Alexander Scott. GBL

Lament of the Red Knight. Anna Wickham. WPN

Lament of the Unmarried Girl, The. Brian Merriman. OBVE, *tr. by* Frank O'Connor *Fr.* The Midnight Court. NOIV, *tr. by* Thomas Kinsella

Lament of the Virtues and Verses on Account of the Death of Don Guido. Antonio Machado Ruiz, *Spanish*. OBVE, *tr. by* Charles Tomlinson *and* Henry Gifford

Lament of Toby the Learned Pig, The. Thomas Hood. CBNP

Lament over Love. Langston Hughes. NAAAL

Lament over the Ruins of the Abbey of Teach Molaga. *Unknown, Irish*. NOIV, *tr. by* James Clarence Mangan

Lament Upon the Waters, The. John Ashbery. FTOS

Lament: When He Wes Sek. William Dunbar. *See* Lament for the Makaris.

Lament while Descending a Shaft. *Unknown*. AmFP

Lamentation. Bible, *O.T.* TrJP *Fr.* Ezekiel.

Lamentation, A. Thomas Campion. CH

Lamentation, The. Ts'ai Yen, *Chinese*. SuSp, *tr. by* Yi-T'ung Wang

Lamentation during His Most Painful Illness. Simon Dach, *German*. GePo, *tr. by* Ingrid Wal[do]e-Engel

Lamentation for Celin, The. *Unknown, Spanish*. AWP, *tr. by* John Gibson Lockhart

Lamentation of Enion, The. William Blake. OBNC *Fr.* Vala; or The Four Zoas.

Lamentation of Queen Elizabeth, A. Sir Thomas More. *See* A Rueful Lamentation on the Death of Queen Elizabeth.

Lamentation of the Old Pensioner, The. W. B. Yeats. HAP; InPK-6; LiLi; NoAM; PeVV; TRP; WeW-3

Lamentation on My Dear Son Simon, A. John Saffin. SCAP

Lamentation on Ninety-Mile Beach. Barry Mitcalfe. PeNZ

Lamentations. Bible, *O.T.*
Affliction. TrJP
Desolation in Zion. TrJP
Misery of Jerusalem, The. AWP

Lamentations. Alter Brody. TrJP

Lamentations. Norman Dubie. NoAM

Lamentations. Louise Glück. BoWoP; HCAP; VCAP

Lamentations. Siegfried Sassoon. OBSV; OxAEP-2; PeFWW

Lamentations of an Au Pair Girl. Susan Feldman. AmPA

Lamentations of Jeremy, for the Most Part According to Tremeullius. Donne.
"How sits this city, late most populous." ChIV-1

Lamentations of the Bronze Camels. Li Ho, *Chinese*. SuSp, *tr. by* Irving Lo

Lamentations of the Fallen Angels. *Unknown*. AnOE, *tr. by* Charles W. Kennedy *Fr.* Christ and Satan.

Lamenting all her fallen sons! (LL) The High Tide at Gettysburg. Will Henry Thompson. BLPA; CBCWP; FaBoBe

Lamenting for Kao Ch'ing-ch'iu, Chi-ti. Chang Yü, *Chinese*. CoBLCP, *tr. by* Jonathan Chaves

Lamenting for My Late Daughter. Wu Wei-yeh, *Chinese*. CoBLCP, *tr. by* Jonathan Chaves

Lamenting for My Wife. Wang Shih-chieng, *Chinese*. CoBLCP, *tr. by* Jonathan Chaves

Lamenting Life. Ma Chih-yüan. *Fr.* Three Poems to the Tune "Ssu-k'uai yü." CoBLCP, *tr. by* Jonathan Chaves

Lamenting Noble Scholar Chu. Ni Tsan, *Chinese.* CoBLCP, *tr. by* Jonathan Chaves

Lamenting Tauba. Laila Akhyaliyya, *Arabic.* BoWoP, *tr. by* Willis Barnstone

Lamenting the Dead. P'an Yüeh, *Chinese.* CoBCP, *tr. by* Burton Watson

Lamenting the Inevitable. Alicia Ostriker. UnSA

Lamenting the State of Confucian Scholarship. Trần Tế Xu'o'ng, *Vietnamese.* AVP, *tr. by* Huỳnh Sanh Thông

Lamenting the Taoist Wei Kung-yüan. Chao Meng-fu, *Chinese.* CoBLCP, *tr. by* Jonathan Chaves

Lamenting thru gipsies his fast suicide. (LL) Political Poem. Imamu Amiri Baraka. AF; CoAP; MoP; NAAL-2; NoAM; PmAP

Lamenting Yang Ch'uan. "Lu Hsün," *Chinese.* SuSp, *tr. by* William R. Schultz

Laments of the Gorges. Meng Chiao, *Chinese.*

  "Edges of the gorges hack up sun and moon, The." SuSp, *tr. by* Stephen Owen

  "Owls mimic human speech." SuSp, *tr. by* Stephen Owen

Laments on the War Dead. Yehuda Amichai, *Hebrew.*

  "Is all this sorrow? I don't know." IP, *tr. by* Bargad, Warren and Stanley Chyet; IP; PoSu

Lamia. Keats. FHYEP

  "Left to herself, the serpent now began." FaBoSe

  "Upon a time, before the faery broods." NOBRP

L'amiral cherche une maison à louer. Richard Huelsenbeck, Marcel Janko, *and* Tristan Tzara. PFTM

Lamisca, who breathed her last in lamentable pangs of labor. Dioscorides. HePo, *tr. by* Barbara Hughes Fowler *Fr.* Epigrams.

L'Amitié et l'Amour. John Swanwick Drennan. BIrV

L'Amitie: To Mrs. M. Awbrey. Katherine Philips. KTR; NOSC

  ("Soul of my Soul, my Joy, my Crown, my Friend.") CPO

  (To Mrs. Mary Awbrey.) CPO

  ("Which they and all the factious World have lost.") (LL) CPO

Lamkin. *Unknown.* AmFP; ESPB; OxBB

Lamp[e], The. Henry Vaughan. ChIV-2; ESCV

Lamp, The. Charles Whitehead. OBEV

Lamp are you, above all stars of night, A. The Pole Star. Coslett Coslett, *Welsh.* OBWVE, *tr. by* Kenneth Hurlstone Jackson

Lamp burns blue, everyone asleep, The. Sharing Lodging with Hsieh Shih-hou. Harry Mathews, *Chinese.* CoBCP, *tr. by* Burton Watson

Lamp burns blue, everyone asleep, The. Sharing Lodging with Hsieh Shih-hou. Mei Yao Ch'en, *Chinese.* CoBCP, *tr. by* Burton Watson

Lamp Flower, The. Margaret Cecilia Furse. BoTP

Lamp glows deep in the mica screen. Li Shang-yin. PLT, *tr. by* A. C. Graham *Fr.* The Lady in the Moon.

Lamp lit, A. Roberto Juarroz. VCWP, *tr. by* W. S. Merwin *Fr.* Third Vertical Poetry.

Lamp must be replenish'd, but even then, The. Byron. NAEL-2; NOBRP

  ("*Manfred* The lamp must be replenished, but even then.") Ro

  "Stars are forth, the moon above the tops, The." OAEL-2

Lamplight. May Wedderburn Cannan. NSI

Lamplight from our kitchen window-pane. Again. Glyn Jones. OBWVE

Lamplighter, The. "Seumas O'Sullivan." BIrV

Lamplighter, The. Robert Louis Stevenson. EBVV; OxBChV

Lamplighter, if you can't set two equally. Rufinus Domesticus. HePo, *tr. by* Barbara Hughes Fowler *Fr.* Epigrams.

Lamprey, glowing with uncommon fires, The. William Diaper. ECEV; OBVE *Fr.* Halieutica.

Lampriskos, the dear Muses allow you. The Schoolmaster. Herodas, *Greek.* HePo, *tr. by* Barbara Hughes Fowler

Lamps Are Burning, The. Charles Reznikoff. TrJP

Lamps burn all the night. The Fifth Sense. Patricia Beer. MoBS

Lamps now glitter down the street, The. Armies in the Fire. Robert Louis Stevenson. EBVV; FPC

L'An Trentieseme de Mon Eage. Archibald MacLeish. LiTM; MoP; NOBA

  (In My Thirtieth Year.) MoAmPo

Lana Turner has collapsed! Poem. Frank O'Hara. CLPP; FTOS; PmAP; VGW

Lancashire Winter. Tony Connor. OxBTC

Lance Corporal Purdue Grace, U. S. M. C. Bryan Alec Floyd. CDa

Lancer. A. E. Housman. MoBrPo; OBWP

Lancet, The. Denis Devlin. NOIV

Land. Carroll Arnett. VoR

Land, The. Rudyard Kipling. MoBrPo

Land, The. Vita Sackville-West. OBGa

Land and Sea Tales. Rudyard Kipling.

  Last Lap, The. OxBTC

  Nurses, The. NoAM

Land between us, The. Honesty-Stones. J. S. Harry. NOBAu

Land breaks yellow south below, pale squares. A View from Cortona. Richard Hugo. AF

Land Called Scotia, The. Saint Donatus, *Latin.* NOIV

Land Dirge, A. John Webster. *See* A Dirge: "Call for the robin-redbreast and the wren."

Land Donation. Thomas Erwin, *German.* CEEP, *tr. by* A. Leslie Willson

Land floats by under us—The The. Love Making. James Tate. SPE

Land, / I have half-forgotten. Kremenez. Hanns Cibulka, *German.* CEEP, *tr. by* Ewald Osers

Land is cold and its men gather earth for no reason, The. A Woman's Song. Colleen J. McElroy. BlSi

Land Is Gone, The. *Unknown, Maori.* PeNZ, *tr. by* Margaret Orbell

Land is lonely now, The: Anathema. Robert Stephen Hawker. EBVV *Fr.* The Quest of the Sangraal.

Land Laws, The. Merimeri Penfold, *Maori.* PeNZ, *tr. by* Margaret Orbell

Land lies in water; it is shadowed green. The Map. Elizabeth Bishop. ColAP; NOBA

Land-Mine, The. George MacBeth. OBWP

Land not mine, still, A. "Anna Akhmatova," *Russian.* WPoS, *tr. by* Jane Kenyon

Land o' the Leal, The. Carolina Oliphant, Baroness Nairne. GTBS-P; NOBRP; OBEV; OxBS

Land of Beginning Again, The. Louisa Fletcher. BLPA

Land of blue skies, and sunlight, A. Limerick. Ruth Silcock. PeLi

Land of Cokaygne, The. *Unknown.* NOIV

Land of Cotton. Gilbert Sorrentino. FTOS

Land of Counterpane, The. Robert Louis Stevenson. CTV; ChAP; EBEV; FaBoBe; NBLV; NTCP; OxBChV; PWR; TLR; WHSW

Land of Dreams, The. William Blake. CH

Land of Dreams, The. Felicia Dorothea Hemans. Ro *Fr.* Songs of the Affections, with Other Poems.

Land of Flowering Azaleas, The. Tong-yop Shin, *Korean.* CKP, *tr. by* Jaihiun Kim

Land of Heart's Desire, The. W. B. Yeats.

  Wind Blows out of the Gates of the Day, The. RB

  (Fairy Song.) MoBrPo

Land of Hope and Glory. Arthur Christopher Benson. FaPoR

Land of Indolence, The. James Thomson. *Fr.* The Castle of Indolence.

Land of leaning ice, A. North Labrador. Hart Crane. CMoP; FaBoMo

Land of Little Sticks, 1945. James Tate. LCAP-2; WeT

Land of Lost Content, The. A. E. Housman. LBC

Land of my fathers and blood, oh my fathers, whatever. Hill Daughter. Louise McNeill. MoLi

Land of Nod, The. Robert Louis Stevenson. ACTP; FPC; PWR

Land of our Birth, we pledge to thee. The Children's Song. Rudyard Kipling. BoTP *Fr.* Puck of Pook's Hill.

Land of Pharoah. Whichway. Ron Welburn. NBV

Land of spices. (LL) Prayer (I). George Herbert. EBEV; ESCV; FSCP; GSo; GeHe; InPS-3; NAEL-1; NOBE; NOSC; OAEL-1; OBWVE; OxAEP-1; PeECV; PoE; PoEL-2; TFi; TOF

Land of Story-Books, The. Robert Louis Stevenson. ACTP; CTV; ChAP; FaBoBe; PWR

Land of the Ching tribes is not my home, The. Wang Ts'an. SuSp, *tr. by* Ronald C. Miao *Fr.* Seven Poems of Lament.

Land of the ding-dong doorbell and trim hedges. Costa Geriatrica. Stanley J. Sharpless. PeLV

Land of the Free. Arthur Nicholas Hosking. BLPA

Land of Whipperginny, The. Robert Graves. NTP

Land that, from the rule of kings, The. The Bartholdi Statue. John Greenleaf Whittier. GS

Land that is lonelier than ruin, A. Swinburne. PoEL-5 *Fr.* By the North Sea.

Land wants me to come back, The. Dust Bowl. Langston Hughes. PoA

Land was ours before we were the land's, The. The Gift Outright. Robert Frost. AiP; AmPP; CMoP; ColAP; FaBoA; LiTM; MeMAP; MoAmPo; MoP; NAAL-2; NOBA; NoAM; NoP-4; OxBA; PoPoPo; Poetr; TFi; TRP

Land was theirs after we were the land's, The. The Big Rock-Candy Mountain. Louis Edward Sissman. GM

Land was there before us, The. Inauguration. Lorenzo Thomas. NBV

Land was white, The. Riddle. *Unknown.* FaBoVe; OxNR

Land where I was born sits by the seas, The. Francesca of Rimini. Dante. *Fr.* Inferno. NAWM-1, *tr. by* John Ciardi *Fr.* Divina Commedia.

Land Which No Mortal May Know, The. Bernard Barton. PWR

Landcrab I. Margaret Atwood. LCAP-2; NIP-4

Landcrab II. Margaret Atwood. NIP-4

Landed: A Valentine. Richard Howard. PoA

Landed Fish. Marge Piercy. WeT

[There Douglas] landed Lord Percye. (LL) Northumberland Betray[e]d by Douglas [or Dowglas]. *Unknown.* ESPB; OxBB

Landfall, The. John Blight. BMAP

Landfall, The. James Dickey. PoA

Landfall. Homer. OBCVT, *tr. by* George Chapman *Fr.* The Odyssey.

Landfall. Randolph Stow. BMAP

Landfall in Unknown Seas. Allen Curnow. NoP-4

Landfill. Michael S. Harper. LCAP-2

Landing, The. Daniel Halpern. AmPA

Landing of Rochambeau, The. Michael Davidson. FTOS

Landing of the Pilgrim Fathers [in New England], The. Felicia Dorothea Hemans. BLPA; FaBoBe; WPE

  (Pilgrim Fathers, The.) BoTP

Landing on the Moon. May Swenson. TAP

Landlady, The. Margaret Atwood. NALW

Landlady says he lived here, The. The Previous Occupant. Agha Shahid Ali. IFJA

Landlord, landlord. Ballad of the Landlord. Langston Hughes. HCAP; NAAAL; NOBA

Landlord's coat is tulip red, The. Wild Sports of the West. John Montague. CABP

Landmarch by camel and shipsail we take. Cargoes of the Radanites. Harry Alan Potamkin. TrJP

Landrecie. Stevie Smith. WPN

Lands which leap very high. On the Islands of All Winds. Aimé Césaire, *French.* VCWP, *tr. by* Clayton Eshleman *and* Annette Smith

Landscape, The. James Bertolino. CMAP

Landscape, The. George Daniel. NOSC

Landscape. Rade Drainac, *Serbo-Croatian.* HSix, *tr. by* Charles Simic

Landscape. David Gascoyne. FaBoMo

Landscape, The. Richard Payne Knight. OBGa

Landscape. Eve Merriam. KaS

Landscape, A. Margaret Lucas Cavendish, Duchess of Newcastle. NOSC

Landscape. Mary Oliver. HeIP-4

Landscape. A. Chaesam Park, *Korean.* CKP, *tr. by* Jaihiun Kim

Landscape. Octavio Paz, *Spanish.* OBVE, *tr. by* Charles Tomlinson

Landscape. Yün Shou-p'ing, *Chinese.*

  "Brush in rocks, draw a stream." CoBLCP, *tr. by* Jonathan Chaves

Landscape Beyond Warsaw. Peter Huchel, *German.* PoSu, *tr. by* Michael Hamburger

  ("March strikes the ice of the sky.") AF, *tr. by* Daniel S. Simko

Landscape, Dense with Trees. Ellen Bryant Voigt. MT

Landscape for the Disappeared. Yusef Komunyakaa. WeT

Landscape / full of holes, A. Loose Woman Poem. Sharon Thesen. NOBC

Landscape Gardeners, The. Geoffrey Grigson. OBGa

Landscape Heard, A. Filippo Tommaso Marinetti. PFTM

Landscape I. Yongt'ae Kim, *Korean.* CKP, *tr. by* Jaihiun Kim

Landscape I. Charles Madge. SPE

Landscape near an Aerodrome, The. Stephen Spender. LiTM; MoBrPo; NoAM; OxBTC

Landscape of Screams. Nelly Sachs, *German.* NNPT; NYBP, *tr. by* Michael Roloff

Landscape of the Capibaribe River. João Cabral de Melo Neto, *Portuguese.* VCWP, *tr. by* Richard Zenith

Landscape of Violence. Ralph Nixon Currey. PeSA

Landscape Painted on a Fan—Echoing a Poem by Wen Cheng-ming, A. Chu Yün-ming, *Chinese.* CoBLCP, *tr. by* Jonathan Chaves

Landscape (the landscape!) again: Gloucester, The. The Librarian. Charles Olson. PmAP

Landscape was, The. Coon Fire. Tom Weatherly. *Fr.* Cantos. PoBA

Landscape With Apparition. Justinas Marcinkeviius, *Lithuanian.* CEEP, *tr. by* Irene Pogoželskyte Suboczewski

Landscape with Barns. Louis Simpson. WeT

Landscape with Figures. Frank Ormsby. PBCIP

Landscape with Leaves and Figure. Olga Broumas. BoWoP

Landscape with Little Figures. Donald Justice. LCAP-2

Landscape with Next of Kin. Olga Broumas. BoWoP

Landscape with Nymphs and Satyrs. Norman Henry, II Pritchard. GT

Landscape with the Fall of Icarus. William Carlos Williams. LCAP-2; NAAL-2; NoAM *Fr.* Pictures from Brueghel.

  ("According to Breughel.") PoPoPo

Landscapeople. John Ashbery. HCAP

Landscapes. T. S. Eliot. RB

Cape Ann. NAEL-2; NoAM

New Hampshire. FaBoCh; GTBS-P; NoAM; WeW-3

Rannoch, by Glencoe. NAEL-2

Usk. FaBoCh; NOCV; PeECV

Virginia. FaBoA; InPK-6

Landscapes. Herberto Padilla, *Spanish.* VCWP, *tr. by* Alastair Reid *and* Andrew Hurley

Landscapes. Husein Tahmisic, *Serbian.* CEEP, *tr. by* Ewald Osers

Lane County Bachelor, The. *Unknown. See* Starving to Death on a Government Claim.

Lane hills and the mune, The. Omens. Sydney Goodsir Smith. FaBoTC

Lane with mud and moss—a garret flat, A. In a Garret. Nguyễn Nhu'o'c Pháp, *Vietnamese.* AVP, *tr. by* Huỳnh Sanh Thông

Lanes in Summer. Malcolm Hemphrey. BoTP

Lang Johnny More. *Unknown.* ESPB

Lang Mountain Monastery. Yang Yi, *Chinese.* SuSp, *tr. by* Jonathan Chaves

Langston Blues. Dudley Randall. SeSe

Langston Hughes. Lew Blockcolski. VoR

Langston Hughes. Gwendolyn Brooks. ColAP

Language, The. Robert Creeley. PmAP; TAP

  ("Is a mouth.") (LL) FTOS

Language. Jennifer Maiden. BMAP

Language. Jack Spicer.

  Thing Language. APSN

  ("Love.") (LL) FTOS

Language / created the landscape, The. In a Monotonous Dream. Elaine Equi. PmAP

Language Event Two. Robert Desnos, *French.* PFTM, *tr. by* Marcel Jean

Language has not the power to speak what love indites. Fragment. John Clare. FaBoEE; OAEL-2; OBNC; OxBSP; PoEL-4

Language is the first perversion of the senses. Genesis. Brian Higgins. FaBoTw

Language Mesh. Paul Celan, *German.* VCWP, *tr. by* Michael Hamburger

Language of Fossils, The. Anita Endrezze-Danielson. HATNAP

Language of Great-Aunts, The. Alberto A. Ríos. UnSA

Language of Love. Rae Armantrout. PmAP

Language of the Brag, The. Sharon Olds. NMM-2; PBCAP

Language of the howling wind allows an endless, The. Grounds of Winter. John Hollander. AFr

Language of Weather, The. Ray A. Young Bear. HATNAP

Language on which the sun flows, a. Epos. Harold Rosenberg. PoA

Language that but sparely flooers, The. The Thistle's Characteristics. "Hugh MacDiarmid." FaBoTC *Fr.* A Drunk Man Looks at the Thistle.

Language wasn't any. Inflation. Heather McHugh. NAmP90

Languages. Carl Sandburg. ColAP

Langue d'Oc. Ezra Pound, *after the Provençal of* Arnaut Daniel.

  Alba ("When the nightingale to his mate"). OBVE; VGW; WeW-3

Languedocienne. Marilyn Hacker. DeD

Languid, lethargic, listless and slow. The Complacent Tortoise. Brian Patten. OBSP

Languishing Moon, The. Sir Philip Sidney. *See* Sonnet 31: "With how sad steps, O Moon, thou climb'st the skies!"

Langwell. Kingsley Amis. NOBL; OxBC *Fr.* The Evans Country.

Lanigan's Ball. *Unknown.* OxBoLi

Lank potato, darkening. Breaking Ground. Thom Gunn. OBGa *Fr.* Breaking Ground.

Lank poverty, dank poverty. The Tin Wash Dish. Les A. Murray. BMAP

Lanky hank of a she in the inn over there, The. A Glass of Beer. James Stephens. CMoP; InPK-6; MoBrPo; MoP; NBLV; OBCoV; OBMV; OxBS; OxBTC; PFE; RB

Lantern-ceiling and quiet, A. Presbyterian Study. Tom Paulin. PBCIP

Lantern Out of Doors, The. Gerard Manley Hopkins. CMoP; TrCP

Lao Tzŭ. Po Chü-i, *Chinese.* ChiP, *tr. by* Arthur Waley

Laocoön. Wilson Harris. PBCV

Laocoön. Virgil. OBVE, *tr. by* Henry Howard, Earl of Surrey *Fr.* The Second Book of Virgil's *Aeneid.* SiPS, *tr. by* Henry Howard, Earl of Surrey *Fr.* The Aeneid [*or* Eneados, *Aeneis*].

Laocöon! thou great embodiment. Josiah Gilbert Holland. APN-1 *Fr.* The Marble Prophecy.

Laocoon/Serpent. Novica Tadic, *Serbian.* VCWP, *tr. by* Charles Simic

Lapis Lazuli. W. B. Yeats. CABP; CMoP; EnlH; FaBoMo; FaBoTw; HeIP-4; inPS-3; LiTM; MoP; NAEL-2; NAWM-2; NOBE; NoAM; NoP-4; OAEL-2; TFi

Laplander's Song to His Mistress, A. Elizabeth Singer Rowe. ECWP

Lapping of lake water, The. Lake Song. Jean Starr Untermeyer. TrJP

Laprairie Hunger Strike. Ronald G. Everson. MoCV

L'Après-Midi d'un Faune. Stéphane Mallarmé, *French.* AWP, *tr.* by Aldous Huxley

"Between the reeds I saw their bodies gleam." EP, *tr.* by Aldous Huxley

Lapse of time and rivers is the same, The. A Comparison. William Cowper. OxBSP

Lapsus Linguae. Keith Preston. NBLV; OBAL; OBCoV

Lapwing's wavering flight, The. Kathleen Jessie Raine. *Fr.* By the River Eden. NYBP

L'Arc Musical (1970). U Tam'si Tchicaya.

Epitaph. PBMAP

Larch Wood Secrets. Ivy O. Eastwick. BoTP

Large Bad Picture. Elizabeth Bishop. NYBP; OxBC

Large glooms were gathered in the mighty fane. James Thomson. EBEV; OAEL-2 *Fr.* The City of Dreadful Night. OBNC

Large Grieving Women. Slavko Mihalic. PoSu, *tr.* by Charles Simic

Large kitchen is almost dark, The. The Acolyte. Denise Levertov. CrSp

Large, low, whirring block of perfectly white, perfectly flat marble, on chrome legs. Hospital. Charles North. FTOS

Large Red Man Reading. Wallace Stevens. HAP; LCAP-2

Large Room with Wood Floor. Clarence Major. GT

Large thing comes in, A. Russell Edson. WeT

Large, yellow sky. A mountain ridge. Pinetree. Agnes Nemes Nagy, *Hungarian.* CEEP; PoSu, *tr.* by Bruce Berlind

Large yellow wings, black-fringed, The. Butterfly on Rock. Irving Layton. NOBC; NoAM

Larger. John Wills. HA

Larger Hope, The. Tennyson. CABP *Fr.* In Memoriam A.H.H.

Largest stock of armaments allows me, The. Civilian. Josephine Miles. WPE

Largo. Paul Celan, *German.* PoSu, *tr.* by Michael Hamburger

Lariat snaps, the cowboy rolls, The. The Closing of the Rodeo. William Jay Smith. AiP; TwCP

Lark, The. Bernard de Ventadour, *Provençal.* CTC; NNPT, *tr.* by Ezra Pound

Lark, The. *Unknown, Irish.* TIRV, *tr.* by Robin Flower

Lark, The. *Unknown.* NOSC

Lark begins to go up, The. Ted Hughes. HAP *Fr.* Skylarks.

Lark drives invisible pitons in the air. Movements. Norman MacCaig. OxBC

Lark now leaves his watery nest, The. Aubade. Sir William Davenant. AWP; CH; GBL; MeLP; NOBE; NOSC; OBEV; OxBSP; PoRA; TFi

Larkin. Gibbons Ruark. DiPo

Larkin Automatic Car Wash, The. Gavin Ewart. NoAM

Lark's Song, The. William Blake. *Fr.* Milton.

("Thou hearest the Nightingale begin the Song of.") APo

(Vision of Beulah, The ("Thou hearest the nightingale begin the song of spring").) NOBE

Larousse Gastronomique. Anne Stevenson. PeLV

Lars Porsena of Clusium. Horatius at the Bridge. Thomas Babington Macaulay, 1st Baron Macaulay. EBEvV; FaBoCh; FaPoR; OBNV; OBWP; OxAEP-2; PoLF *Fr.* Lays of Ancient Rome.

L'Art, 1910. Ezra Pound. HeIP-4; OxBA

L'Art Poetique. Nicolas Boileau-Despéaux.

"Waller came last, but was the first whose art." EPCY

"You, then, that would the comic laurels wear." EPCY, *tr.* by Sir William Soames *and* John Dryden

Larva, The. Tadeusz Rózewicz, *Polish.* PoSu, *tr.* by Magnus F. Krynski

Las casitas near the gray cannery. Freeway 280. Lorna Dee Cervantes. NoAM; PaTW; WeW-3

'Las, how long shall I. John Lyly. NoSic *Fr.* Midas.

Las manos abiertas de Mongo. Dándole la mano a Mongo. Martín Espada. SeSe

Las' Rights. Brian Meeks. PBCV

Las Trampas U. S. A. Charles Tomlinson. TwCP

Lasca. Frank Desprez. BLPA; FaBoBe

Laser. A. R. Ammons. NAAL-2; NOBA; NoAM

Lashed to the wheel of night. Paris. Ingeborg Bachmann, *German.* VCWP, *tr.* by Mark Anderson

Lashes of my eye are clipped away, The. Cataract. Margoret Smith. NYBP

Lass A-Laundering. *Unknown, Spanish.* STV, *tr.* by John Frederick Nims

Lass from Bally-na-Lee, The. Anthony Raftery, *Irish.* BIrV, *tr.* by Desmond O'Grady

Lass in the Female Factory, The. *Unknown.* NOBAu

Lass in Wonderland, A. Francis Reginald. MoCV

Lass, I've heard tell. The Wishing-Well. Wilfrid Wilson Gibson. NTP

Lass of Aughrim, The. Paul Muldoon. NoAM; PBCIP

Lass of curvacious physique, A. Limerick. Douglas Catley. PeLi

Lass of Patie's Mill, The. Allan Ramsay. OxAEP-1

Lass of Roch Royal, The. *Unknown.* AmFP; ESPB

Lass of the Hill, The. Mary Jones. ECWP

Lass, when they talk of love, laugh in their face. Love. Francis Jammes, *French.* AWP, *tr.* by Jethro Bithell

Lass with a Lump of Land. Allan Ramsay. NOEC

Lasses, like nuts at bottom brown. Epigram. Allan Ramsay. FaBoEE

Lassie, can ye say. For a Wife in Jizzen. Douglas Young. FaBoTC; OxBS

Lassie, What Mair Wad You Hae? Heinrich Heine, *German into Scottish.* OxBS, *tr.* by Alexander Gray

Lassie, with the lips sae rosy. Mädchen mit dem rothen Mündchen. Heinrich Heine, *German.* AWP, *tr.* by Sir Theodore Martin

Last Acts. Sharon Olds. NIP-4

Last Affair: Bessie's Blues Song. Michael S. Harper. HCAP; LCAP-2

Last All Saints' holy-day, even now gone by. Sonnet: Of Beatrice de' Portinari, on All Saints' Day. Dante, *Italian.* AWP, *tr.* by D. G. Rossetti

Last and greatest herald of Heaven's King, The. Saint John Baptist. William Drummond, of Hawthornden. ChIV-2; GTBS-P; NOBE; OBEV; OxAEP-1; SCGP; TrCP

Last and greatest Herauld of Heavens King, The. For the Baptiste. William Drummond of Hawthornden. PBRV

Last and the first tree, The. (LL) Children Playing Checkers at the Edge of the Forest. Adrienne Rich. LCAP-2; WeW-3

Last Atlantean, The. David Henson. EC2

Last autumn / The three of us tossed acorns. Akiko Yosano, *Japanese.* WPJ, *tr.* by Kenneth Rexroth *and* Ikuko Atsumi

Last, best-loved daughter of old Hsieh, you who foolishly ran off. An Elegy. Yüan Chen, *Chinese.* OxBM

Last Bison, The. Charles Mair.

Song: "Hear me, ye smokeless skies and grass-green earth." NOBC

Last bridge I won't, *shorter vers.* The Poem of the End. Marina Tsvetayeva, *Russian.* BrRo; PFTM

Last Buccaneer, The. Charles Kingsley. EBEvV; EBVV; FaBoBe

(Last Buccanier, The.) PeVV

Last Bus, The. Edmund George Valpy Knox. BXAP

Last Bus, The. Mark Strand. TwCP

Last carpenter feelie pocket guru. Twenties 27. Jackson MacLow. PmAP

Last Chance, The. Andrew Lang. NOBVV; OxBSn

Last Chantey, The. Rudyard Kipling. FaBoCh; MoBrPo

Last Chapter, The. Walter De la Mare. CMoP; MoBrPo

Last Child. X. J. Kennedy. OxBSP

Last Christmas, when Puss was in Boots. Limerick. Gina Berkeley. PeLi

Last Chrysanthemum, The. Thomas Hardy. CMoP

Last Class, The. Ellen Bryant Voigt. CrSp; MT

Last Confession, A. (LL) A Woman Young and Old. W. B. Yeats. BoLoP; CBLP; CMoP; HAP; NIP-4; OAEL-2

Last Conqueror, The. James Shirley. *See* Song: "Victorious men of earth, no more."

Last Cry of the Damp Fly, The. Dennis Lee. NTCP

Last Dance, The. May Riley Smith. SAGP

Last dark violet, The. Poetry. Abraham Sutskever, *Yiddish.* CEEP, *tr.* by Ruth Whitman

Last Dawn. Octavio Paz, *Spanish.* EP, *tr.* by Eliot Weinberger

Last Day, The. Bible, *N.T.* LBC *Fr.* 1 Corinthians, 15:51.

Last Day, The. Kevin Hart. BMAP

Last Day, The. George Seferis, *Greek.* AF, *tr.* by Edmund Keeley *and* Philip Sherrard

Last Day, The. Wen I-to, *Chinese.* ChiPo, *tr.* by Kai-yu Hsu

Last Day and the First, The. Theodore Weiss. TwCP; VGW

Last Day of the Year, The. Su Tung-p'o, *Chinese.* OHPC, *tr.* by Kenneth Rexroth

Last Day of the Year (New Year's Eve), The. Annette von Droste-Hülshoff, *German.* BoWoP, *tr.* by Willis Barnstone

Last Day of the Year; or, New Year's Eve, The. Mrs. Henry Linden. CBWP-4

Last Daybreak Song. *Unknown.* APN-2, *tr.* by Washington Matthews *Fr.* The Mountain Chant.

Last Days. Richard Hugo. PoA

Last Days at Teddington. Thom Gunn. OBGa

Last Days of Alice. Allen Tate. FuPo; NAAL-2; NOBA; OxBA; UnPo

Last days of November, and everything so green, The! The Volunteer's Thanksgiving. Lucy Larcom. OBCA

Last Deaths, The. Charles Kenneth Williams. MoLi

Last decent man alive, The. Across to the Peloponnese. James Welch. CDW

Last Defile, The. Amy Carmichael. TrCP

Last Drink, A. *Unknown.* MiEL

Last Easter I was married, that night I went to bed. The Lowlands of Holland. *Unknown.* AmFP

Last eve I passed beside of a blacksmith's door. The Anvil—God's Word. John Clifford. BLPA; PoToHe

Last Evening. Rilke, *German.* OBWP, *tr. by* J. B. Leishman

Last Fierce Charge, The. *Unknown.* AmFP

Last Fight, The. Lewis Frank Tooker. FaBoBe

Last, for December, houses on the plain. December. Folgore da San Geminiano. *Fr.* Sonnets of the Months. AWP, *tr. by* D. G. Rossetti

Last Friday, in the big light of last Friday night. Reality Is an Activity of the Most August Imagination. Wallace Stevens. NoAM

Last from the *Volscians* fair *Camilla* came. Camilla goes to war. Virgil, *Latin.* OBCVT, *tr. by* John Dryden

Last Frontier, The. John Gould Fletcher. FuPo

Last Fruit Off an Old Tree, The. Walter Savage Landor.
On His Seventy-Fifth Birthday. AWP; EBEV; NTP; OAEL-2; OxAEP-2; PBMP; SCGP

Last Galway Hooker, The. Richard Murphy. PBCIP

Last Gate, The. Stella Mead. BoTP

Last geat Englishman is low, The. Tennyson. *See* Bury the Great Duke.

Last Giustiniani, The. Edith Wharton. APN-2

Last Gods. Galway Kinnell. RaBo

Last Hiding Places of Snow, The. Galway Kinnell. IMW
("Any longer, only its stilled shapes.") (LL) FiLi

Last Hill in a Vista. Louise Bogan. FaBoWP

Last Hunt, The. William Roscoe Thayer. FaBoBe

Last Hymn, The. "Marianne Farningham." BLPA

Last Installment, The. Don Bogen. WeT

Last Instructions. Garth Tate. ISC

Last Instructions to a Painter, The. Andrew Marvell.
"After two sittings, now our Lady State." OBSV
"Paint Castlemaine in colours that will hold." OBSV

Last Invocation, The. Walt Whitman. MoAmPo; OxBA; PAR; PoEL-5; SAGP
(Imprisoned Soul, The.) OBEV

Last Journey. Enrique Gonzáles Martínez, *Spanish.* PBMP, *tr. by* Samuel Beckett

Last Journey, The. Leonidas of Tarentum, *Greek.* AWP, *tr. by* Charles Merivale

Last Journey. John Montague. CIP-2; PBCIP; PNI

Last Judgment. John Gould Fletcher. AWP

Last Judgment, The. *Unknown.* AnOE, *tr. by* Charles W. Kennedy *Fr.* Christ 3.

Last July 4th, like every July 4th for four years. Triple Trouble. Assotto Saint. GLP

Last Lap, The. Rudyard Kipling. OxBTC *Fr.* Land and Sea Tales.

Last Lauch. Douglas Young. NBLV; OxBS

Last Laugh. Robert Penn Warren. MT

Last Leaf, The. Thomas Hardy. CBLP

Last Leaf, The. Oliver Wendell Holmes. AmPP; FaBoBe; NAAL-1; NAAL-3; PWR; PoLF

Last leaves fell like notes from a piano, The. Forest of Europe. Derek Walcott. PBCV

Last Lesson of the Afternoon. D. H. Lawrence. NoAM

Last Letter to Pablo. Pat Lowther. NOBC

Last Lie, The. Bruce Weigl. AF

Last Light. Robert Kelly. VGW

Last light has gone out of the world, except, The. Liberty. Edward Thomas. OAEL-2

Last light muffles itself in cloud and goes, The. Mise en Scène. Robert Fitzgerald. NYBP; VGW

Last lighted torch of the century. . . , The. Christopher Okigbo. *See* Come Thunder.

Last lighted torch of the century. . . , The. (LL) Come Thunder. Christopher Okigbo. HBAPE; PBMAP

Last Lines. X. J. Kennedy. OBAL

Last Lines. Pamela Mordecai. HCP

Last Lines. Egan O'Rahilly, *Irish.* IIP, *tr. by* Frank O'Connor

Last Lines on a Wrestler. X. J. Kennedy. CRP

Last Look at La Plata, Missouri. Jim Barnes. CDW

Last Love. Fyodor Tyutchev, *Russian.* LoP, *tr. by* Vladimir Nabokov; BoLoP

Last Love. Nikolai Zabolotsky, *Russian.* TCRP, *tr. by* Daniel Weissbort

Last Man, The. Thomas Lovell Beddoes.
Crocodile, A. APo; NOBVV; RB

Last Man, The. Thomas Campbell. NOBRP

Last Man, The. Thom Gunn. OxAEP-2 *Fr.* Misanthropos.

Last Mass in Hagia Sophia, The. *Unknown, Greek.* GrIP, *tr. by* Richard Stoneman

Last May-day fair I search'd to find a snail. John Gay. *Fr.* Thursday; or, The Spell. PoEL-3 *Fr.* The Shepherd's Week.

Last meal together, Leeds, the Queen's Hotel. The Queen's English. Tony Harrison. DiPo

Last Meeting. Robert Penn Warren. DiPo

Last Men on Mars. Alan Bold. SpW

Last Merchant, The. Wolf Ehrlich, *Russian.* TCRP, *tr. by* Daniel Weissbort

Last Month. John Ashbery. CAPP-1; CoAP

Last month of the year, grass roots taste sweet. Li Ho. SuSp, *tr. by* Irving Y. Lo *Fr.* About Horse.

Last News about the Little Box. Vasco [or Vasko] Popa, *Serbo-Croatian.* HSix, *tr. by* Charles Simic

Last Night, The. Alfred Austin. PeVV

Last Night. Loving Again. Gloria Wade-Gayles. ISC

Last Night. Onuora Oku. PBCV

Last night a baby gargled in the throes. A Widow in Wintertime. Carolyn Kizer. IMW

Last night, after five pints of wine. Martial, *Latin.* FP, *tr. by* James Michie

Last night, again, I dreamed. Waking in March. Philip Levine. PaTW

Last night, ah, yesternight, betwixt her lips and mine. Non Sum Qualis Eram Bonae sub Regno Cynara[e]. Ernest Christopher Dowson. ADE; APAD; AWP; BLPA; BoLoP; CABP; CBLP; ClHu; EBVV; EnLoPo; FaBoBe; GBL; GLoP; GTBS-P; HAP; HeIP-4; ImPo; MoBrPo; NAEL-2; NOBE; NoP-4; OAEL-2; OBEV; OBMV; OBNC; PeVV; PoRA; SAGP; TFi; UnPo

Last night, among his fellow roughs. Private of the Buffs; or, The British Soldier in China. Sir Francis Hastings Doyle. OBEV

Last night, as half asleep I dreaming lay. Ode 44. Hafiz, *Persian.* EP, *tr. by* Richard Le Gallienne

Last night as I lay beside you all the desire had gone out of me. House. Murray Edmond. PeNZ

Last night, as I was sleeping. Antonio Machado Ruiz, *Spanish.* RaBo, *tr. by* Robert Bly

Last night, as I was washing up. The General. G. K. Menzies. NSI

Last night at black midnight I woke with a cry. The Ghosts of the Buffaloes. Vachel Lindsay. MeMAP; MoAmPo

Last night at midnight. Tune: The Taoist Priestess. Wei Chuang, *Chinese.* CoBCP, *tr. by* Burton Watson

Last night at midnight. Wen T'ing-yün, *Chinese.* CoBCP, *tr. by* Burton Watson

Last night blonde spitfire Angie Dickinson beat steel-eyed. Brute Strength. Wanda Coleman. PmAC

Last night I danced alone. Moneylight. Diane Wakoski. NMM-2

Last night I did not fight for sleep. In Hospital: Poona (1). Alun Lewis. OBWVE

Last night I dreamed a ghastly dream. Ballad of the Flood. Edwin Muir. MoBS

Last night, I dreamed of America. More. Ai. GT

Last night I dreamed we parted once again. Frederick Goddard Tuckerman. GSo

Last night I dreamed you drank coffee. One More Sign. Roberta Hill Whiteman. HATNAP

Last night I dreamt in Chinese. Modern Secrets. Shirley Lim. OPOU; UnSA

Last night I had a horrid dream. The Pantry Ghosts. Frederic Richardson. FPC

Last night I heard him in the woods. The Woodpecker. Joyce Sambrook. BoTP

Last night I licked. In Celebration. Ellen Bass. NMM-2

Last night I rode a tightrope. Wheelchairs That Kneel Down Like Elephants. Karen Fiser. IFJA

Last night I saw a silver road. The Silver Road. Hamish Hendry. BoTP

Last night I saw the savage world. Song for a Birth or a Death. Elizabeth Jennings. EBEV

Last night I saw you in my sleep. Bad Dreams. Robert Browning. GLoP

Last night I saw your corpse. Joyce Mansour, *French.* BoWoP, *tr. by* Willis Barnstone

Last night I slew my wife. Necessity. Harry Graham. PeLV *Fr.* Some Ruthless Rhymes.

Last night I spoke to a dead woman with green face. David Ignatow. VGW

Last night I supped on lobster; it nearly drove me mad. The Dream. *Unknown.* OxBoLi

Last night I tell you, I do not lie. Osip Emilevich Mandelstam, *Russian.* TCRP, *tr. by* Bernard Meares

Last night I was coming back home alone. Lyubomir Levchev, *Bulgarian.* CEEP, *tr. by* Atanas Slavov

Last night I watched my brothers play. The Brothers. Edwin Muir. GTBS-P; HeIP-4; NTP

Last night in a dream I returned to my old home. *Unknown, Chinese.* CoBCP, *tr. by* Burton Watson

Last Night in Calcutta. Allen Ginsberg. FTOS; NoAM

Last night in dream so clear I saw her. To the Tune "Child at Play." Yang Shen, *Chinese.* CoBLCP, *tr. by* Jonathan Chaves

Last Night in Elvisville. Lydia Tomkiw. WWSi

Last night in Fall River in Lafayette Park. How It Will Always Seem. David Rivard. PBCAP

Last night in La Plata an avalanche of stars. La Plata, Missouri: Clear November Night. Jim Barnes. HATNAP

Last night in London Airport. London Airport. Christopher Logue. OPOU

Last night in stomped. Dardanelles 1916. Padraic Fallon. CIP-2

Last night in swirling colour we daced again. Dermot Bolger. BiHa *Fr.* The Stardust Sequence.

Last night in the open shippen. Christmas Day. Andrew Young. OBCP

Last night Joan Sutherland was nuancing. Something Like Happiness. Stephen Dunn. PUP-20

Last night, late, a light rain. Pavlov's Dog. Michael Pettit. NAmP90

Last night my boy [*or* little boy] confessed to me. Two Prayers. Andrew Gillies. PoToHe

Last night my color-blind chainsmoking father. My Father's Neckties. Maxine W. Kumin. AFr

Last night my friend—he says he is my friend. I Hear It Said. Barbara Young. BLPA

Last night my soul departed. Invocation. Muireadhach O'Dalaigh. NOIV

Last night my soul witihin a dream. Tune: "Gazing at the South." Li Yü, *Chinese.* SuSp, *tr. by* Daniel Bryant

Last Night of the Third Moon, The. Chia Tao, *Chinese.* CoBCP, *tr. by* Burton Watson

(Last Night of the Third Month, The.) CoBCP, *tr. by* Burton Watson

Last night of the visit, the youngest put his head. A Waving Hand. Minnie Bruce Pratt. CPO; FiLi

Last night returning from my twilight walk. A Ballad of Past Meridian. George Meredith. OAEL-2; PeVV

Last Night that She lived, The. Emily Dickinson. BoWoP; CMoP; HeIP-4; MeMAP; NAAL-1; NAAL-3; OxBA; PoEL-5

("Our faith to regulate.") (LL) ColAP

Last night the carol-singers came. The Carol Singers. Margaret G. Rhodes. BoTP

Last night the cold wind and the rain blew. Sunday at the End of Summer. Howard Nemerov. ImGa

Last night the first light frost, and now sycamore. Long Walks in the Afternoon. Margaret Gibson. AFr

Last night the gypsies came. Gypsies. Rachel Lyman Field. BoTP

Last night the rainbow. Moon Shadow. George Bowering. MoCV

Last night thin rain, gusty wind. Li Ch'ing-chao, *Chinese.* BoWoP, *tr. by* Willis Barnstone *and* Sun Chu-chin

Last night thou didst invite me home to eat[e]. Upon Showbread [*or* Shewbread]: Epigram. Robert Herrick. CaPo

Last night watching the Pleiades. An Autumn Morning in Shokoku-ji. Gary Snyder. HAP; VGW; WeW-3 *Fr.* Four Poems for Robin. MoP; NNaP; NOBA; NoAM

Last night we had a thunderstorm in style. Robert Louis Stevenson. NOBVV

Last night we sailed, my love and I. Barcarolle. May Probyn. VWP

Last night we sat with the stereopticon. Readings of History. Adrienne Rich. CoAmPo

Last night went walking with a woman that I know. Trap Door. Vitězslau Nezval, *Czech.* PFTM, *tr. by* Jerome Rothenberg *and* Milos Sovak

Last night when the yellow moon. Wadasa Nakamoon, Vietnam Memorial. Ray A. Young Bear. CDa; HATNAP

Last night, while I lay thinking here. Whatif. Shel Silverstein. OTCP

Last night, within my dreaming. Pine Music. Kate Louise Brown. BoTP

Last night you were a river. Conquest. Pauli Murray. GT

Last night you would not come. Love Poem. John Logan. CAPP-1

Last Night's Dream. Denise Levertov. NoAM

Last night's planets and stars, last night's wind. Li Shang-yin, *Chinese.* CoBCP, *tr. by* Burton Watson

Last night's stars, last night's winds. Li Shang-yin, *Chinese.* PLT, *tr. by* A. C. Graham

Last o' the Tinkler, The. Violet Jacob. OxBS

Last of England, The. Peter Porter. GS

Last of England! O'er the sea, my dear, The. Ford Madox Brown. GS

Last of His Tribe, The. Henry Clarence Kendall. CBAP

Last of His Tribe. Oodgeroo of the tribe Noonuccal. BMAP

Last of last words spoken is Good-bye, The. Good-bye. Walter De la Mare. SAGP

Last of the Courtyard, The. Emily Grosholz. FFC

Last of the Fire Kings, The. Derek Mahon. FaBoPV; PNI

Last of the Flock, The. Wordsworth. Ro

Last of the Poet's Car. Tony Connor. OxBTC

Last of the poets, first of the undead. The Mole. Dennis Schmitz. AmPA

Last of the Princes, The. A. K. Ramanujan. OxBC

Last of thy unhappy Mothers Verse, The. (LL) On the Death of My First and Dearest Childe, Hector Philipps. Katherine Philips. KTR; PBRV

Last on legs, last on sax. "Bird Lives": Charles Parker [in St. Louis]. Michael S. Harper. AmPA

Last One, The. W. S. Merwin. ChAP; LCAP-2; NoAM; VGW

Last one / to die here, The. Nelly Sachs, *German.* BoWoP, *tr. by* Arthur Wensinger

Last Ones, The. "Robin Hyde." PeNZ

Last Ones, The. Dan Pagis, *Hebrew.* PoSu, *tr. by* Robert Friend

Last pale rank of poplar-trees, The. Aubade Triste. Agnes Mary Frances Robinson. NOBVV

Last Passenger Pigeon in the Cincinnati Zoo, The. Lucie Brock-Broido. WWSi

Last Picnic, The. Stanley Kunitz. AF

Last Poem. Margaret Atwood. LCAP-2

Last Poem. Charles Donnelly. *See* Poem: "Between rebellion as a private study and the public."

Last Poem, The. Jiri Orten, *Czech.* AF, *tr. by* Lyn Coffin

Last Poem. Po Chü-i, *Chinese.* ChiP, *tr. by* Arthur Waley

[Last Poems]. Osip Mandelstam. PFTM

Last pose flickered, failed, The. Rain after a Vaudeville Show. Stephen Vincent Benét. MoAmPo

Last Prayer. Evelyn Poole. WPN

Last Quatrain of the Ballad of Emmett Till, The. Gwendolyn Brooks. LCAP-2; PoBA; WPE

Last Refuge, The. Augustus Young. BIrV

Last Republicans, The. Austin Clarke. CIP-2

Last Ride Together, The. Robert Browning. BoLoP; FHYEP; GLoP; NAEL-2; OBEV; PoEL-5; UnPo

Last Ride Together (from Her Point of View), The. James Kenneth Stephen. BXAP; UnPo

Last Rites. Christina Rossetti. OxBChV

Last river leaves for desolation, The. Iwan Goll, *German.* AF, *tr. by* Galway Kinnell

Last Round, The. Anna Wickham. MoBrPo

Last Scene in the First Act. Marge Piercy. NoAM

Last screech owl cry. Foster Jewell. HA

Last sea-thing dredged by sailor Time from Space. Australia. Bernard O'Dowd. APAD

Last settlement scraggled out with a barbed wire fence, The. The Flight in the Desert. William Everson. ChIV-2; VGW

Last Snow. Andrew Young. OxBTC

Last Song of Sappho, The. Felicia Dorothea Hemans. VWP

Last Song of the Exploding Stick. *Unknown.* APN-2, *tr. by* Washington Matthews *Fr.* The Mountain Chant.

Last Songs. Galway Kinnell. VCAP

Last spell cast came late one afternoon in a brown study. I was studying my-, The. Michael Brownstein. FTOS

Last Statement. Vladimir Mayakovsky, *Russian.* FaBoPV; PBCIP, *tr. by* Tom Paulin

Last Statement for a Last Oracle. Alan Dugan. NoAM

Last Still Days in a Bunker, The. Walter McDonald. AF

Last Stop. George Seferis, *Greek.* AF, *tr. by* Edmund Keeley *and* Philip Sherrard

Last stroke tells of the decline of the sugar house, The. Step Seven. Albert Mobilio. PT

Last summer. Eleanor Schick. CA

Last summer, harvests washed away with floods. Summer Drought. Phạm Quý Thích, *Chinese.* AVP, *tr. by* Huỳnh Sanh Thông

Last summer, in the blue heat. La Vita Nuova. Weldon Kees. VGW

Last sunbeam, The. Dirge for Two Veterans. Walt Whitman. APN-1; BLT; CBCWP; MoAmPo; PoEL-5

Last Supper, The. Jacques Prévert, *French.* CLPP, *tr. by* Lawrence Ferlinghetti

Last Supper, The. Rilke, *German.* GI, *tr. by* David Curzon *and* Will Alexander Washburn

Last Supper, The. Oscar Williams. ImPo; LiTM

Last Survivor's Speech, The. *Unknown.* NAEL-1, *tr. by* Alfred David *Fr.* Beowulf. OAEL-1, *tr. by* Charles W. Kennedy; ASW, *tr. by* Kevin Crossley-Holland

Last Testaments. Lorna Crozier. LW

Last thin acre of stalks that stood, The. Immortal. Mark Van Doren. MoAmPo

Last Things. William Meredith. NoAM

Last Things. Kathleen Jessie Raine. NYBP

Last Things, Black Pines at 4 a.m. Robert Lowell. NOBA

Last things/ the turning leaves slip in the wind. Vincent O'Sullivan. PeNZ Fr. Brother Jonathan, Brother Kafka.

Last time around the forest floor. Rainier. Jim Tollerud. VoR

Last time I saw Donald Armstrong, The. The Performance. James Dickey. CoAP; CoAmPo; LiTM; MoP; PoE; SAGP; WeT

Last time I slept with the Queen, The. Limerick. Dylan Thomas. PeLi

Last time i was home, The. Mothers. Nikki Giovanni. UnPo

Last Train, The. Linda Pastan. GM

Last trainees are climbing the diving tower, The. The Naval Trainees Learn How to Jump Overboard. David Wagoner. VCAP

Last Trains, The. C. G. Hanzlicek. GM

Last Trams. Kenneth Slessor. BMAP

Last truly foolish thing I did was some years ago, The. The Void. Gwendolyn MacEwen. Fr. The T. E. Lawrence Poems. NOBC

Last Tsě' ni Gisl' n, or Song in the Rock. Unknown. Fr. The Night Chant. APN-2, tr. by Washington Matthews

Last twist of the knife, The. (LL) Rhapsody on a Windy Night. T. S. Eliot. CMoP; HeIP-4; InPS-3; PoE

Last two Februarys have passed, The. St. Bridget's Cross. Anne Hartigan. CIP-2

Last Utterance of the Delphic Oracle, The. Unknown, Greek. OBVE, tr. by Kenneth Rexroth

Last Vision of Eoghan Rua Ó Súilleabháin, The. Michael Hartnett. PBCIP

Last Visit. Robert Finch. NOBC

Last, walking with stiff legs as if they carried bundles. At Last the Women are Moving. Genevieve Taggard. NMM-2

Last Waltz in Santiago. Ariel Dorfman, Spanish. AF, tr. by Ariel Dorfman and Edith Grossman

Last War, The. Kingsley Amis. OBSV; OxBC; SAGP

Last war was my favourite picture story, The. In September 1939. Bernard Gutteridge. PoWW

Last white sawdust on the floor was grown, The. Edna St. Vincent Millay. Fr. Sonnets from an Ungrafted Tree. NALW

Last Will and Testament. Hans Magnus Enzensberger. PoSu

Last Will and Testament, A. John Winstanley. FaBoVe; OBSV

Last Wish, The. "Owen Meredith." OxBSP

Last wolf hurried toward me, The. Mary TallMountain. LoL; UnSA

Last Word, The. Matthew Arnold. APAD; NOBE; OAEL-2; OBNC; PBMP; PFE; PoEL-5; SCGP

Last Word, The. Imamu Amiri Baraka. UnSA

Last Word, The. Peter Davison. InPK-6

Last Word, A. Ernest Christopher Dowson. ADE; GSo; MoBrPo

Last Word of a Bluebird, The. Robert Frost. NOxBChV

Last word this one spoke, The. Two Friends. Norman MacCaig. FP

Last Words, sl. diff. Emily Jane Brontë. WPE

Last Words. John Hollander. OBAL

Last Words. Richard Howard. DiPo Fr. Ithaca: The Palace at Four A.M.

Last Words. Helen Hunt Jackson. SDW

Last Words, The. Maurice Maeterlinck, French. AWP, tr. by Frederick York Powell

Last Words. James Merrill. TAP

Last Words. Sylvia Plath. FYAP

Last Words. Unknown, Vietnamese. AVP, tr. by Huỳnh Sanh Thông

Last Words before Winter. Louis Untermeyer. MoAmPo

Last Words, 1968. Lance Henson. CDW

Last Words of Don Henriquez, The. Zalman Schneour, Yiddish. TrJP, tr. by Joseph Leftwich

Last Words of My English Grandmother, The. William Carlos Williams. RB; RaBo; SAmP

Last Words of the Prophet. Unknown. APN-2, tr. by Washington Matthews Fr. The Mountain Chant.

Last Words To a Dumb Friend. Thomas Hardy. APo; FP; PC

Last Words to Miriam. D. H. Lawrence. CBLP

Last World, A. John Ashbery. PoM

Last year among the flowers I saw you off. To Send to Li Tan and Yüan Hsi. Wei Ying-wu, Chinese. CoBCP, tr. by Burton Watson

Last year at the Feast of Lanterns. Lost. Chu Shu-chen, Chinese. BoWoP; OHMPC, tr. by Kenneth Rexroth

Last year he drew the harvest home. Commandeered. Lucy Gertrude Moberley. NSI

Last year I lost an incisor. Poem on Losing One's Teeth. Han Yü, Chinese. SuSp, tr. by Kenneth O. Hanson

Last year in the spring when the birds were calling. Unknown, Chinese. CoBCP, tr. by Burton Watson

Last year, Orlando. The Political Orlando. George MacBeth. NOBL

Last year, scarce one short season back. In Memoriam J.H.H. C. J. Ronald. NSI

Last year the child died. Epitaph. Olive Senior. PBCV

Last year we fought. They Fought South of the Walls. Li Po, Chinese. SuSp, tr. by Joseph J. Lee

Last year we fought by the springs of Sankan river. Fighting on the South Frontier. Li Po, Chinese. TAL, tr. by Robert Payne

Last year we parted as the flowers began to bloom. A Lady Picking Flowers. Shen Chou, Chinese. ChiPo; CoBLCP, tr. by Jonathan Chaves

Last year when I accompanied you. To a Traveler. Su Tung-p'o, Chinese. HoPM; OHPC, tr. by Kenneth Rexroth

Last year, with jade hands, you offered cups of tea. Liu E. Fr. Poems for Yukiko of Tamba. CoBLCP, tr. by Jonathan Chaves

Last year's decencies. Odysseus. Padraic Fallon. CIP-2

Last Year's Discussion: The Nobel Russian. Phyllis McGinley. FaBoEE

Last year's sunflower stalks blacken. Spring Planting. Gail Mazur. NAmP90

Last years we only met, The. For John Berryman. Robert Lowell. FP

Lastly came Winter cloathèd all in frize. Winter. Edmund Spenser. Fr. Wood Of Error. AEP

Lastly, stood war, in glittering arms yclad. The Shield of War. Thomas, 1st Earl of Dorset Sackville. Fr. Induction to "A Mirror for Magistrates." AAS

Lastly, with friends t' enjoy our day[e]s. (LL) Four[e] Things Make Us Happy Here. Robert Herrick. CaPo; Spl

Lastness. Galway Kinnell. NNaP

"Black bear sits alone, A." RaBo

Lat never a man a wooing wend. King Henry. Unknown. ESPB; OxBB

Late. Benjamin Paul Blood. APN-2

Late. Louise Bogan. PBWP; VGW

Late afternoon in July, too early to begin, A. The Gypsy. Susan Stewart. NAmP90

Late Afternoon, Late in the Twentieth Century. Jeffrey Skinner. PBCAP

Late afternoon light slices through the dormer window. The Gun. Stephen Dobyns. CMAP

Late afternoon rain of a postponed summer. Dusk: July. Marilyn Hacker. FFC

Late Annie in her bower lay. The Ballad of Late Annie. Gwendolyn Brooks. ColAP Fr. Notes from the Childhood and the Girlhood. LCAP-2

Late April and you are three; today. W. D. Snodgrass. VCAP Fr. Heart's Needle. CAPP-1

Late April. Taking stock. Generalities. Robert Conquest. OxBC

Late Arrivals. Sybil Kollar. FFC

Late at een, drinkin' the wine. The Dowie Houms o' Yarrow. Unknown. ESPB; OBEV; OxBS

Late at Night. Vern Rutsala. WeT

Late at Night. William Stafford. NNaP

Late at Night During a Visit of Friends. Robert Bly. InPS-3

Late at night I stood on a battlement. Der von Kürenberg, German. GePo, tr. by Frederick Goldin

Late at night in the kitchen. Tanka. Shaku Chōkū, Japanese. MJT, tr. by Makoto Ueda

Late Aubade, A. Richard Wilbur. Poetr; SoSe-8

Late August. Margaret Atwood. DeD

Late August. Alexis Rotella. HA

Late August, given heavy rain and sun. Blackberry-Picking. Seamus Heaney. ChAP

Late Autumn. Hanmo Chong, Korean. CKP, tr. by Jaihiun Kim

Late Autumn. May Sarton. CrSp

Late autumn. Cor Van den Heuvel. HA

Late-born and woman-souled I dare not hope. Echoes. Emma Lazarus. APN-2; GSo; PAR

Late Bus (After a Series of Hold-Ups). Russell Atkins. LTA

Late Dandelions. Ben Belitt. NYBP

Late Express, The. Barbara Giles. OTCP

Late-Flowering Lust. John Betjeman. CMoP; EP

Late Flowers. Helga Marie Heinze, German. CEEP, tr. by Katherine Bradley

Late Flowers, Wind, Sea, Sand and Fish. Bernard Kangro, Estonian. CEEP, tr. by Ivar Ivask

Late for Breakfast. Mary Dawson. TLR

Late Fourth, A. John Hollander. AFr

Late Fragment. Raymond Carver. APAD; LBC

Late Gothic. Phyllis Gotlieb. NOBC

Late Hour, The. Mark Strand. HCAP

Late in an evening forth as I went. Archie o Cawfield. *Unknown.* ESPB

Late in Fall. Ramona Wilson. VoR

Late in my life I come to you. Yehuda Amichai, *Hebrew.* IP, *tr. by* Warren Bargad *and* Stanley F. Chyet

Late in the afternoon. Spring Burning. Patrick Roland. PeSA

Late in the afternoon the light. Crepuscular. Richard Howard. TwCP

Late in the evening. Alan Pizzarelli. HA

Late in the fall. For a Woman Murdered While Running at Land's End, October 1979. Patricia Kirkpatrick. LoHo

Late in the Forest I did Cupid See. Sonnet 2. Mary Sidney, Countess of Montgomery Wroth. KTR; LW; PBRV *Fr.* Pamphilia to Amphilanthus.

Late in the Night. Eugenio Montale, *Italian.* NNPT, *tr. by* G. Singh

Late in the season the world digs in, the fat blossoms. Over and Over Stitch. Jorie Graham. HCAP; VCAP

Late in the Year K'uei-yu (1333), Staying at the Temple of the Upper Regions. Yü Chi, *Chinese.* CoBLCP, *tr. by* Jonathan Chaves

Late Indian summer's. Sun Bu-er, *Chinese.* WPoS, *tr. by* Jane Hirshfield

Late Lamented Fame of the Giant City of New York. Bertolt Brecht. FaBoA, *tr. by* Frank Jellinek

Late lark twitters from the quiet skies, A. Margaritæ Sorori [I. M.]. William Ernest Henley. CABP; MoBrPo; NOBE; OBEV; OBNC; PoRA *Fr.* Echoes.

Late Last Night. Arthur Gregor. VGW

Late last night, a girl came. *Unknown, Greek.* InMo, *tr. by* Sam Hamill

Late last night, I decided to / stop using English. Kicking the Habit. Lawson Fusao Inada. PUP-19

Late last night I was a-making my rounds. Bad Man Ballad. *Unknown.* AmFP

Late, Last Rook, The. Ralph Hodgson. MoBrPo

Late, late in the gloaming Kilmeny came hame! James Hogg. *See* Kilmeny.

Late lies the wintry sun a-bed. Winter Time [*or* Winter-Time]. Robert Louis Stevenson. ACTP; EBVV; MoBrPo; OxBChV

Late Light. Edmund Blunden. EnLoPo

Late Light. Barbara Bellow Watson. NYBP

Late light allows us to begin. 59th Light Poem: for La Monte Young and Marian Zazeela—6 November 1982. Jackson MacLow. PmAP

Late Lights in Minnesota. Ted Kooser. BLT

Late Loving. Mona Van Duyn. NMM-2

Late Miss H. came to us Wednesday at four, The. Swansong. Carol Muske. AmPA

Late Mother, The. Cynthia MacDonald. Poetsp

Late night over the Neva. Over the Neva. Wilgelm Aleksandrovich Zorgenfrey, *Russian.* TCRP, *tr. by* Sophie Lund

Late Night Radio. Geoff Page. BMAP

Late Night Tête-à-Tête with a Moon in Transit. Jacqueline Osherow. BAP-95

Late night, with my bundle of new straws. The Burden of Decision. Peter Everwine. NNaP

Late November. Sherod Santos. Son

Late November in a Field. James Wright. NAAL-2; NNaP

Late October Camping in the Sawtooths. Gary Snyder. BLT

Late October sun. White Earth. Gerald Vizenor. HATNAP

Late one night I hear his breath. Coltrane and My Father. Ralph Sneeden. SeSe

Late Passenger, The. C. S. Lewis. TrCP

Late Reflections. Babette Deutsch. NYBP

Late repentance, and the long despair, The. To George Sand on her Interview with Elizabeth Barrett Browning. Isa Blagden. VWP

Late Return. E. A. Markham. PBCV

Late Rising on Spring Days. Wei Chuang, *Chinese.* CoBCP, *tr. by* Burton Watson

Late Sewing. Hazel Hall. PaTW

Late Singer, The. William Carlos Williams. SAmP

Late singer of a sunless day. The Linnet in November. Francis Turner Palgrave. EBVV

Late snowfall;. Lorraine Ellis Harr. HA

Late Sonnet. Hayden Carruth. Son

Late Spring. Fan Ch'eng-ta. SuSp, *tr. by* Irving Y. Lo *Fr.* Seasonal Poems on Fields and Gardens.

Late Spring. Robert Hass. BLT

Late Spring, A. James Scully. NYBP

Late Spring. James Thomson. GaP

Late Spring. Yüan Chen, *Chinese.* SuSp, *tr. by* Dell R. Hales

Late Spring: Eastport, A. Philip Booth. Poetsp

Late spring has snatched away the blossoms. Impromptu; Late Spring at Pan-shan. Wang An-shih, *Chinese.* CoBCP, *tr. by* Burton Watson

Late Spring—Traveling through the Mountains. Chu Yün-ming, *Chinese.* CoBLCP, *tr. by* Jonathan Chaves

Late summer, and at midnight. The Guttural Muse. Seamus Heaney. NOIV

Late summer day. Tanka. Tsukamoto Kunio, *Japanese.* MJT, *tr. by* Makoto Ueda

Late sun, the stream and the hills; the beauty. Quatrain. Tu Fu, *Chinese.* SuSp, *tr. by* Jerome Seaton

Late that summer. Surrendered Names. Gerald Vizenor. HATNAP

Late tired with woe, e'en ready to to pine. Sonnet 62. Sir Philip Sidney. *Fr.* Astrophil and Stella. AAS; SiPS

Late Tuesday afternoon the romantic self weaves. Seventh Avenue. Mark Halliday. NAmP90

Late Twentieth-Century Prayer, A. Ernest Sandeen. WeW-3

Late Victorian Girl, The. Bill Manhire. PeNZ

Late, Watching Television. Del Marie Rogers. IFJA

Late, when it returns from the city wall. The Crow Cries at Night. Po Chü-i, *Chinese.* SuSp, *tr. by* Irving Y. Lo

Late Winter. James McAuley. BMAP

Late Wisdom. George Crabbe. OBEV *Fr.* Reflections.

Lately his haunch has grown stiff. Father. Jean Lipkin. PeSA

Lately I saw a sight most quaint. "Gross, Coarse, Hideous" (Police Description of My Pictures). D. H. Lawrence. FaBoEE

Lately, I think of my love for you and the rose. The Rose Growing into the House. Gibbons Ruark. InPK-6

Lately, I've become accustomed to the way. Preface to a Twenty Volume Suicide Note. Imamu Amiri Baraka. BB; CAPP-1; CrDW; MoLi; NAAAL; PoBA; PoM; SAGP; TTY

Lately I've become religious about atoms. Metamorpho I. Joe Rosenblatt. MoCV

Lately I've felt a grave concern. Beatrice, Countess de Die, *Provençal.* DoWoP, *tr. by* Willis Barnstone

Lately my neighbor wheezes. Running. Leslie Ullman. PBCAP

Lately on yonder swelling bush. The Budd. Edmund Waller. PBRV

Lately Our Poets [loitered in green lanes]. Walter Savage Landor. FaBoEE; GTBS-P; OAEL-2; PoEL-4

Lateness. David Shapiro. PT

Later, back in my cell, back in the thick stench. Between the Lines. Michael Hamburger. HP

Later History. David Rivard. NAmP90

Later Life: A Double Sonnet of Sonnets. Christina Rossetti. WPoS
  "Before the mountains were brought forth, before." Son
  "Something this foggy day, a something which." NAEL-2
  Sonnet 26: "This Life is full of numbness and of balk." VWP
  "To love and to remember; that is good." Son

Later, she met Joyce. Cherríe Moraga. CPO

Later Still. Philip Levine. ColAP

Later, the firecat closed his bright eyes / And slept. (LL) Earthy Anecdote. Wallace Stevens. CMoP; RB; SAmP

Laterna Obscura. Henrikas Nagys, *Lithuanian.* CEEP, *tr. by* Jonas Zdanys

Latest Decalogue, The. Arthur Hugh Clough. ChIV-1; EBEV; EBVV; EBVVPR; EnVR; FaBoEE; GTBS-P; HAP; HoPM; NAEL-2; NOBE; NOBVV; NoP-4; OAEL-2; OBNC; OBSV; PeECV; SCGP; TFi; WeW-3
  ("Approves all forms of competition.") (LL) PBMP
  ("*More* than thyself to love thy neighbour.") (LL) CABP; PFE

Latest Injury, The. Sharon Olds. FiLi

Latet Anguis. William Cornish. OBEV

Latin harsh with Aramaicisms, A. Pilate at Fortingall. Edwin Morgan. FaBoTC *Fr.* Sonnets from Scotland.

Latin is a dead tongue. *Unknown.* FaBoVe

Latin Music in New York. Jessica Hagedorn. PmAP; WWSi

Latin Night at the Pawnshop. Martín Espada. TRP; WWSi

Latitude, Longitude. George Oppen. CAPP-1

Latrine in a Suburb of Smyrna, A. Agathias, *Greek.* GrAn, *tr. by* Guy Davenport

Latter-day Geography Lesson. Ronald Allison Kells Mason. PeNZ

Latter Day Lysistrata. Lauris Edmond. PeNZ

Latter Day Psalms. Cliff Ashby. NOCV

Latter-Day Warnings. Oliver Wendell Holmes. NCAP

Latter rain, it falls in anxious haste, The. Jones Very. APN-1; OxBA

Lattice at "Split." Tina Darragh. FTOS

Lattice at/of (Com)pare (Dis)pair. Tina Darragh. FTOS

Latvian Autumn, The. Johannes Bobrowski, *German.* PoSu; CEEP, *tr. by* Ruth Mead *and* Matthew Mead

Latvian Songs. Johannes Bobrowski, *German.* AF, *tr. by* Matthew Mead

Laudanum. *Unknown.* NOEC

Laudate Dominum, *par. by* Mary Sidney Herbert. Bible, *O.T.* ChIV-1 *See* Psalm 148.

Lauds. W. H. Auden. TrCP *Fr.* Horae Canonicae.

Lauds. John Berryman. HAP

Laugh aloud, then pass by, with a kind. Nossis, *Greek.* GrAn, *tr. by* Peter Jay

Laugh and Be Merry. John Masefield. MoBrPo

Laugh, and the world laughs with you. Solitude. Ella Wheeler Wilcox. EBEvV; PWR; PoLF; SDW

Laugh is just like sunshine, A. Sunshine and Music. *Unknown.* PoToHe

Laugh, my firends, and without blame. To My Friends, Who Ridiculed a Tender Leave-Taking. Matthew Arnold. EnVR *Fr.* Switzerland.

Laugh on, laugh on at all the dreams. I Believe. Saul Tchernichowsky, *Hebrew.* TrJP, *tr. by* Reginald V. Feldman.

Laughed every goblin. Christina Rossetti. BrRo *Fr.* Goblin Market. CPO; EBEV; FaBoSe; NAEL-2; NALW; NOBVV; NOxBChV; OBNV; OxAEP-2; VWP

Laughed in our furnished room. (LL) Heavy Water Blues. Bob Kaufman. CLPP; NBV

Laughing, before the lamps, we pour each other. The Year I-mao (Fifteen Fifty Five), New Year's Eve. Wen Cheng-ming, *Chinese.* CoBLCP, *tr. by* Jonathan Chaves

Laughing eyes followed. Asante Sana, Te Te. Thadious M. Davis. BlSi

Laughing Gas. Ruth Whitman. UnSA

Laughing Hyena, after [*or* by] Hokusai, The. D. J. Enright. TwCP

Laughing, merry, childish voices, woke us in their eager glee. Christmas, South, 1866. Mary E. Tucker. CBWP-1

Laughing Place, The. Minnie Bruce Pratt. CPO

Laughing softly. Anita Virgil. HA

Laughing Song. William Blake. BoTP; FHYEP; NAEL-2; Ro *Fr.* Songs of Innocence.
   ("When the green woods laugh with the voice of.") FPC

Laughing through clouds, his milk-teeth still unshed. R.A.F. (Aged Eighteen). Rudyard Kipling. LiLi; PoWW *Fr.* Epitaphs of the War [1914–1918]. OBWP

Laughingly dash with your hair. Walt Whitman.

Laughs a child of seven. (LL) A Child's Laughter. Swinburne. NTP; PoLF

Laughter. Olive Enoch. BoTP

Laughter. Wislawa Szymborska, *Polish.* PoSu, *tr. by* Magnus F. Krynski

Laughter of a Faun, The. Novella Matveyeva, *Russian.* TCRP, *tr. by* Deming Brown

Laughter of children brings. Early Supper. Barbara Howes. WeT

Laughter pours from a thousand homes, as the water clock drips and drips. Sentiments on New Year's Eve in the Year Kuei-ssu. Huang Ching-jen, *Chinese.* SuSp, *tr. by* Chang Yin-nan *and* Lewis C. Walmsley

Laughter tumbled over laughter. Spring. Helen G. Quigless. BkSV *Fr.* Childhood Scenes in Four Seasons.

Launch, The. Stanley Cook. SpW

Launch, The. Alice Thompson Meynell. PeVV; WPE

Launched into an opposing wind, hangs. The Atlantic. Charles Tomlinson. OxBoS

Launching Our Community Developement Fund. Tanure Ojaide. HBAPE

Laundry. Bruce Smith. Son

Laundry so near the ocean bothered Frank. Duo-Tang. Kenward Elmslie. FTOS

Laura. Thomas Campion. NOBE; OBEV *Fr.* Observations in the Art of English Poesie.
   ("Ever perfect, ever in them- / Selves eternal.") (LL) CABP
   ("Ever perfet, ever in them- / selves eternall.") (LL) PBRV
   (Rose-cheeked Laura.) NoP-4
   ("Rose-cheek *Lawra* come.") AAS; PBRV
   ("Selves eternal.") (LL) NoP-4

Laura. Robert Tofte.
   Unto Thy Favor. Son
   When She Was Born. Son

Laura and Lizzie Asleep. Christina Rossetti. *Fr.* Goblin Market. CPO; EBEV; FaBoSe; NAEL-2; NALW; NOBVV; NOxBChV; OBNV; OxAEP-2; VWP

Laura was lightsome, gay, and free from guile. Caroline Elizabeth Norton. VWP *Fr.* Marriage and Love.

Laureate, The. William Edmonstoune Aytoun. BXAP; UV

Laureate, The. Robert Graves. BIrV; FaBoTw; OBSV

Laurel Axe, The. Geoffrey Hill. NAEL-2; NoAM; PoE *Fr.* An Apology for the Revival of Christian Architecture in England.
   ("Crystals kissed / in cabinets of amethyst and frost.") (LL) NoP-4

Laurel in bloom. John Wills. HA

Laurel of Liberty. A Poem, The. Robert Merry.
   "Genius, or Muse, whate'er thou art! whose thrill." NOBRP

Laurel Tree, The. Louis Simpson. NNaP

Laurels and Immortelles. *Unknown.* BLPA

Laurence Bloomfield in Ireland. William Allingham.
   Eviction, The. BIrV; NOIV
   Lord Crashton: The Absentee Landlord. NOIV

Laurentia. Medbh McGuckian. BiHa

Laurentian Shield. Francis Reginald Scott. NOBC

Laus Deo! John Greenleaf Whittier. AmPP; CBCWP

Laus Mariae. Sidney Lanier. Son

Laus Virginitatis. Arthur Symons. EnLoPo

Lausanne: In Gibbon's Old Garden: 11–12 p.m. Thomas Hardy. FaBoTw

Lava. Adam Zagajewski. PuP-16

Lava-flow. *Unknown.* OBCVT, *tr. by* Jabez Hughes *Fr.* Aetna.

Lavatory Attendant, The. Wendy Cope. UV

Lavender Bush, The. Elizabeth Fleming. BoTP

Lavender Woman, The. Lizette Woodworth Reese. APN-2

Lavender's Blue. *Unknown.* CH; NTP
   ("Keep ourselves warm.") (LL) ACTP; LB
   ("Lavender's blue, dilly, dilly.") ACTP
   ("'Lavender's blue, dilly, dilly, lavender's green'.") ITG; LB
   ("'You shall be King, dilly, dilly, when I am Queen'.") (LL) ITG

Lavinia is polite, but not profane. On Women ("Lavinia is polite"). Edward Young. ECEV *Fr.* Satires. ECEV

Law, The. Abraham ibn Ezra, *Hebrew.* TrJP, *tr. by* Alice Lucas

Law, The. Aleksandar Ristovic, *Serbo-Croatian.* HSix, *tr. by* Charles Simic

Law, The. Ella Wheeler Wilcox. PWR

Law against Lovers, The. Sir William Davenant.
   Viola's Song. NOSC

Law and the Grace, The. Iain Crichton Smith. FaBoTC

Law can take a purse in open court, The. Samuel Butler. NBLV

Law firm commanding, A. Help Wanted. Franklin Waldheim. BLPA

Law Given at Sinai, The. Isaac Watts. ChIV-1

Law like Love. W. H. Auden. PBMP

Law makes long spokes of the short stakes of men. Legal Fiction. William Empson. CMoP; FaBoMo; ImPo; LiTM; MoP; NoAM; NoP-4

Law of Fall, The. Jaihiun Kim, *Korean.* CKP, *tr. by* Jaihiun Kim

Law of God be to thee thy rest, The. *Unknown.* MiEL

Law said Dale Booth died of falling, The. For Those Who Will Live Forever. Thomas Rabbitt. CMAP

Law, say the gardeners, is the sun. Law like Love. W. H. Auden. PBMP

Law should have ear-plugs, not bandaged eyes, The. Nicarchus of Alexandria, *Greek.* GrAn, *tr. by* Peter Porter

Law that says, The. Sipho Sepamla. AF

Law there is of ancient fame, A. Tit for Tat; a Tale. John Aikin. OxBChV

Law! what is law? The wise and sage. Elymas Payson Rogers. AAP *Fr.* A Poem on the Fugitive Slave Law.

Lawd, Dese Colored Chillum. Ruby C. Saunders. BlSi; LTA

Lawd, I'm broke and hungry, ragged and dirty, too. Ragged and Dirty. *Unknown.* AmFP

Lawd Zambesi! For Singing In Good Mood. Lebert Bethune. GT

Lawde and Prayse Made for Our Sovereigne Lord the Kyng, A. John Skelton.
   "Rose both white and Rede, The." PBRV

Lawlands o' Holland, The. *Unknown.* CH *See also* The Lowlands o' [*or* of] Holland.

Lawn as white as driven snow. Autolycus as Peddler. Shakespeare. CH; NoSic; OAEL-1 *Fr.* The Winter's Tale.

Lawn of Excluded Middle. Rosemarie Waldrop. FTOS

Lawn Roller, The. Robert Layzer. OBGa

Lawns darken, evening broods in the black, The. Tennyson. Alan Ansen. CoAP

Lawrence here for ever blames. D. H. Lawrence and James Joyce. Humbert Wolfe. FaBoEE

Lawrence—not the bearded one—the one. Any Complaints? Vernon Scannell. OxBTC

Lawrence of virtuous [*or* vertuous] Father virtuous [*or* vertuous] Son. To Mr. Lawrence. Milton. AWP; GTBS-P; NOSC; OBEV; OxAEP-1; PBRV; PoE

Laws-a-massey, what have you done? Negro Reel. *Unknown.* AS

Laws are the secret avengers, The. The Avengers. Edwin Markham. MoAmPo

Laws of God, the Laws of Man, The. A. E. Housman. MoBrPo; NOBVV; NTP; OBSV; OxBoLi

Lawwwwwd have mercy. Michael Smith. *See* Black and White.

Lawyer had a legal mouse, A. A Legal Mouse. Lizelia Augusta Jenkins Moorer. CBWP-3

Lawyers, Bob, know too much, The. The Lawyers Know Too Much. Carl Sandburg. CMoP; PoE

Lawyer's Invocation to Spring, The. Henry Howard Brownell. PoLF

Lawyers Know Too Much, The. Carl Sandburg. CMoP; PoE

Lawyers may revere that tree, The. Epigram on a Lawyer's Desiring One of the Tribe to Look with Respect to a Gibbet. Robert Fergusson. OxBS

Lawyers—tell me why a hearse horse snickers hauling a lawyer's bones. (LL) The Lawyers Know Too Much. Carl Sandburg. CMoP; PoE

Lawyers themselves uphold the commonweal. *Unknown.* OBCoV

Lay a garland on my hearse. Aspatia's Song. Francis Beaumont *and* John Fletcher. AWP; CH; GBL; HAP; NOBE; OBEV; SCGP *Fr.* The Maid's Tragedy.

Lay aside phrases; speak as in the night. This Is Not Death. Humbert Wolfe. MoBrPo

Lay busily hid. (LL) A Grasshopper. Richard Wilbur. HAP; HoPM

Lay clear, unfathomed, taken as they came. (LL) Walking to Sleep. Richard Wilbur. NYBP; VCAP

Lay down, boys, and take a little nap / Lay down, boys, and take a little nap. Cumberland Gap. *Unknown.* APN-2

Lay down the red carpet—My dowry is death. (LL) The Streets of Laredo. Louis MacNeice. MoBS; OBWP

Lay down their life; they do not hate. (LL) At a Calvary near the Ancre. Wilfred Owen. ChIV-2; GI

Lay down these words. Riprap. Gary Snyder. HCAP; NAAL-2; NOBA; NeAP; NoAM; PmAP; PoM; PoPoPo; VCAP

Lay her and lea her here like a gantan grund. The Shepherd's Dochter. Douglas Young. FaBoTC

Lay in the house mostly living. Madness. James Dickey. NYBP

Lay lightly down, and slept. (LL) After Love. Maxine W. Kumin. CrSp; NMM-2; TAP

Lay me down beneaf de willers in de grass. Death Song[, A]. Paul Laurence Dunbar. PoLF

Lay me in yon place, lad. The Last o' the Tinkler. Violet Jacob. OxBS

Lay me on an anvil, O God. Prayers of Steel. Carl Sandburg. CMoP; MoAmPo; SAGP; SSCS; TrCP

Lay me on my true Love's body. (LL) Deirdre's [*or* Deidre's] Lament for the Sons of Usnach. *Unknown, Irish.* IIP; NOIV, *tr. by* Sir Samuel Ferguson

Lay neither the scrawny. Rufinus, *Greek.* GrAn, *tr. by* Alan Marshfield

Lay not up for yourselves treasures. Bible, *O.T.* CTV *Fr.* The Bible, Matthew 6:19–21.

Lay of an Irish Harp, or Metrical Fragments, The. Sydney, Lady Morgan Owenson.

Irish Harp: Fragment I, The. Ro

Lay of Finn, The. *Unknown.* AnOE, *tr. by* Charles W. Kennedy *Fr.* Beowulf. OAEL-1, *tr. by* Charles W. Kennedy; ASW, *tr. by* Kevin Crossley-Holland

Lay of Ike, The. John Berryman. LCAP-2 *Fr.* Dream Songs.

Lay [*or* Short Lay] of Sigurd, The. *Unknown.* AWP, *tr. by* William Morris *and* Eirikr Magnusson *Fr.* The Elder Edda.

"And now one prayer." OBVE

Lay of the Captive Count, The. Goethe, *German.* AWP, *tr. by* James Clarence Mangan

Lay of the Ettercap, The. John Leyden. BXAP

Lay of the Honeysuckle, The. Marie de France, *French.* WPE, *tr. by* Robin Johnson

Lay of the Last Minstrel, The, *sels.* Sir Walter Scott.

Caledonia. OBEV; PBMP

("Bard may draw his parting groan, The.") (LL) Ro

("Breathes there the man, with soul so dead.") Ro

(Patriot, The.) FaPoR; OBNC

(Patriotism.) CTV; NOBE; OxAEP-2

("Unwept, unhonoured, and unsung.") (LL) CTV

Father's Notes of Woe, A. OBNC

Love. OxAEP-2

Melrose Abbey. OxAEP-2

(Sir William of Deloraine at the Wizard's Tomb.) OBNC

Minstrel, The. OxAEP-2

Minstrel Responds to Flattery, The. OBNC

(Nature's Sympathy with the Poet.) OxAEP-2

Rosabelle. GTBS-P

Lay of the Last Survivor, The. *Unknown.* EEP, *tr. by* Michael Alexander *Fr.* Beowulf.

Lay of the Trilobite, The. May Kendall. VWP

Lay Preacher Ponders, The. Idris Davies. OxBTC

Lay to Eliza, The. Edmund Spenser. NOBE *Fr.* Aprill. NAEL-1; OBEV; PoEL-1 *Fr.* The Shepheardes [*or* Shepeards *or* Shepherd's] Calender.

Lay wreaths upon the stone. Wreaths. Requiescat. Haim Guri, *Hebrew.* MHP, *tr. by* Ruth Finer Mintz

Lay Your Arms Aside. Pierce Ferriter, *Irish.* BIrV, *tr. by* Eiléan Ní Chuilleanáin

Lay your head on a block of butter and chop. Lakshminkara, *Tibetan.* WPoS, *tr. by* Miranda Shaw

Lay your sleeping head, my love. Lullaby. W. H. Auden. BoLoP; CMoP; EBEvV; EnLoPo; GLP; HAP; LoP; MoP; NAEL-2; NOBE; NoAM; NoP-4; OAEL-2; OxAEP-2; OxBTC; PiM; PoE; SAGP; TFi; UnPo; WeW-3

Lay your weapons down, young lady. Piaras Feiritear, *Irish.* NOIV, *tr. by* Thomas Kinsella

Layer on layer of hemp leaves, jute leaves shining. Tune: Sand of Silk-washing Stream. Su Tung-p'o, *Chinese.* CoBCP, *tr. by* Burton Watson

Laying Down the Tower. Marge Piercy.

Seven of Pentacles, The. CrSp

Sun, The. WPOW

(Total Influence of Outcome of the Matter: The Sun, The.) WPOW

Laying the pen aside, when he had signed. Faustus. Alec Hope. NOBAu

Lays of Ancient Rome. Thomas Babington Macaulay.

Horatius. EBEvV; OBWP; OxAEP-2

Horatius at the Bridge. EBNV; FaBoCh; FaPoR; OBNV; OBWP; OxAEP-2; PoLF

("Lars Porsena of Clusium.") EBNV

Lazarus. Agnes Nemes Nagy, *Hungarian.* PoSu, *tr. by* Frederic Will

("Rising was as hard as having died.") (LL) GI, *tr. by* Frederic Will

Lazarus / don't come forth from the grave. The Anti-Lazarus. Nicanor Parra, *Spanish.* GI, *tr. by* Edith Grossman

Lazarus, kindling at the breath of pain. The Second Life of Lazarus. Gwen Harwood. CBAP

Lazily I stir a white feather fan. In the Mountains on a Summer Day. Li Po, *Chinese.* TAL, *tr. by* Robert Payne

Lazy. Lu Yu, *Chinese.* OHMPC, *tr. by* Kenneth Rexroth

Lazy are slaughtered, The. The Measures Taken. Erich Fried, *German.* NNPT, *tr. by* Michael Hamburger

Lazy-bones, lazy-bones, wake up and peep! Nonsense Verses. Charles Lamb. CBNP; OBCoV

Lazy deuks that sit i' the coal-neuks. *Unknown.* OxNR

Lazy dog (a bomb containing ten), The. John Cage. APSN *Fr.* Diary: How to Improve the World (You Will Only Make Matters Worse).

Lazy laughing languid Jenny. Jenny. D. G. Rossetti. EnVR; PoEL-5

Lazy Man's Song. Po Chü-i, *Chinese.* ChiP; OBVE, *tr. by* Arthur Waley

Lazy Marcus once dreamed. Lucilius, *Greek.* GrAn, *tr. by* Peter Porter

Lazy Mary. *Unknown.* AmFP

Lazy People, The. Shel Silverstein. NTCP

Lazy Pussy, The. Palmer Cox. OBCA

Lazy sheep, pray tell me why. The Sheep. Ann Taylor. BoTP; CTAV; OxBChV

Lazy Thought, A. Eve Merriam. SSCS

Lazy Witch. Myra Cohn Livingston. NOxBChV

Le Balcon. Charles Baudelaire, *French.* AWP, *tr. by* Lord Alfred Douglas

Le Chariot. John Wieners. VGW

Le Diner. Arthur Hugh Clough. OBCoV *Fr.* Spectator ab Extra. OBCoV; OxBoLi; PeLV; PeVV

Le Hibou et la Poussiquette. Edward Lear. NYBP; PC, *tr. into French by* Francis Steegmuller

Le Jardin. Oscar Wilde. *See* The Garden.

Le Jardin des Tuileries. Oscar Wilde. GaP

Le Jazz Hot. Anselm Hollo. PoM; SeSe

Le Livre. Stéphane Mallarmé, *French.*

"End / conscience." PFTM, *tr. by* Pierre Joris

Le Livre Est sur la Table. John Ashbery. SPE

Le loupgarou. Derek Walcott. OxBSn

Le Médecin Malgré Lui. William Carlos Williams. PoA

Le Monocle de Mon Oncle. Wallace Stevens. LiTM; MeMAP

Le Père Sévère. *Unknown, French.* AWP, *tr. by* Andrew Lang

Le Rêve. Edgar Bowers. CoAmPo

Le Revenant. Stevie Smith. OxBSn

Le Roy, you're earning too much money now. (LL) Washing hangs upon the line, A. Elizabeth Bishop. FaBoVe; FaBoWP

Le Tombeau de Pierre Falcon. James Reaney. MoCV

Le Ventre (1964). U Tam'si Tchicaya.

"'Congo is myself' (Lumumba), The." PBMAP

"I tear at my belly." PBMAP

Le Voyage À Cythère. John Gray. ADE

Lea we go pun. Come Come. Marc Matthews. HCP

Leaba Shíoda. Nuala Ni Dhomhnaill. CABP

Lead. Ambrose Bierce. APN-2; OBAL *Fr.* The Devil's Dictionary.

Lead. Jayne Cortez. PoBA

Lead & zinc company, The. Holes Commence Falling. David Huddle. PBCAP

Lead disc composed of black stuff for marking, A. Damocharis of Kos, *Greek*. GrAn, *tr.* by John Heath-Stubbs *and* Carol A. Whiteside

Lead, Kindly Light, amid the encircling gloom. The Pillar of the Cloud. John Henry, Cardinal Newman. ChIV-1

Lead me away with my eyes blindfolded. From "The Blue Notebook" No. 12. Daniil Kharms, *Russian*. TCRP, *tr.* by Bradley Jordan

Lead On, O King Eternal. Ernest W. Shurtleff. AH

Lead the black bull to slaughter, with the boar. Upon Master Walter Montagu's Return from Travel. Thomas Carew. CaPo

Lead us, Evolution, lead us. Evolutionary Hymn. C. S. Lewis. NOBL

Lead Us, O Father, in the Paths of Peace. William Henry Burleigh. AH

Leadbelly Gives an Autograph. Imamu Amiri Baraka. PmAP

Leaden Echo and the Golden Echo, The. Gerard Manley Hopkins. CMoP; GTBS-P; ImPo; LiTM; MoBrPo; NOBVV; OBMV; OBNC

Leaden-eyed, The. Vachel Lindsay. APAD; CMoP; FaBoEE; ImPo; OxBSP; PBMP; PoE; RB

Leaden eyelids of wan twilight close, The. George Henry Boker. APN-2 *Fr.* Sonnets: A Sequence on Profane Love.

Leaden Treasury of English Verse, A. Paul Dehn. "Jenny kiss'd me when we met." CBLP

Leader. Bruce Bennett. InPK-6

Leader, The. J. P. Clark Bekederemo. PBMAP

Leader, The. Dorothy Livesay. MoCV

Leader, The. Roger McGough. OPOU

Leaders of the Crowd, The. W. B. Yeats. EBEV; MoBrPo; OxAEP-2

Leading him in. Alexis Rotella. HA

Leading liot act to foriage is activity. On Autumn Lake. John Ashbery. LCAP-2

Leads it through the Grave to thee. (LL) Rearrange a "Wife's" affection! Emily Dickinson. NALW; PoEL-5

Leaf. Rade Drainac, *Serbo-Croatian*. HSix, *tr.* by Charles Simic

Leaf falls softly at my feet, A. Ludwig Uhland, *German*. AWP, *tr.* by John S. Dwight

Leaf floats in endless space, A. Seeking a Mooring. Wang Wei, *Chinese*. BoWoP; ChiPo; WPOW, *tr.* by Kenneth Rexroth *and* Ling Chung

Leaf for hand in hand, A. Walt Whitman. APN-1

Leaf-fringed fountain, The. In the Cafe. Iain Crichton Smith. FaBoTC *Fr.* By the Sea.

Leaf from freedom's golden chaplet fair, A. To My Father. Henrietta Cordelia Ray. AAP; BlSi; CBWP-3; Son

Leaf from the Devil's Jest-Book, A. Edwin Markham. APN-2

Leaf[e] gold, Lord of thy golden wedge o'erlaid. Edward Taylor. NAAL-1; NAAL-3 *Fr.* Preparatory Meditations Before My Approach to the Lord's Supper.

Leaf in His Ear, The. Mahadai Das. HCP

Leaf in Love and War, A. Veṟipāṭiya Kāmakkaṇṇiyār, *Tamil*. PLW, *tr.* by A. K. Ramanujan

Leaf knows sorrow in this time of thorns, The. Anglo-American Chainpoem. *Unknown*. SPE

Leaf of a light boat, A. Tune: "Joy of Eternal Union"—Passing the Seven-league Shallows. Su Shih, *Chinese*. SuSp, *tr.* by Irving Y. Lo

Leaf on the grey sand-path, A. The Unreturning Spring. Laurence Binyon. NSI

Leaf-picking, The. Frédéric Mistral, *French*. AWP, *tr.* by Harriet Waters Preston

Leaf Pile, The. Alicia Ostriker. FiLi

Leaf this boat, its light sail rolled, A. Tune: "Prelude to Allure Goddesses." Liu Yung, *Chinese*. SuSp, *tr.* by Jerome P. Seaton

Leaf-Treader, A. Robert Frost. MoAmPo

Leaf, treeless, A. Paul Celan, *German*. PoSu, *tr.* by Michael Hamburger

Leaf, Treeless for Bertolt Brecht, A. Paul Celan, *French*. AF, *tr.* by Michael Hamburger

Leaf unhooked from the branch, A. Ode to Fallen Leaves. Toksu Moon, *Korean*. CKP, *tr.* by Jaihiun Kim

Leaf will wrinkle to decay, The. The Crest Jewel. James Stephens. MoBrPo

Leafbud straggles forth, The. Upper Broadway. Adrienne Rich. HCAP; InPS-3

Leafless are the trees; their purple branches. The Golden Mile-Stone. Henry Wadsworth Longfellow. NCAP; PoEL-5

Leafless buoyancy. Sukhanovo. Natalya Gorbanevskaya, *Russian*. AF, *tr.* by Daniel Weissbort

Leafless there by my door, trembled a sense of the rose. (LL) In Earliest Spring. William Dean Howells. AP-2; FaBoBe; OBEV

Leafshade stirring on lichened bark. Culture and Anarchy. Adrienne Rich. NALW

Leafy-with-love banks and the green waters of the canal. Canal Bank Walk. Patrick Kavanagh. CIP-2; CMoP; FaBoTw; MoBrPo; NoAM; NoP-4

League and a league from the trenches, A—from the traversed maze of the lines. Headquarters. Gilbert Frankau. NSI

Leaguered in fire. An Autumn Sunset. Edith Wharton. APN-2

Leah. Ruth Gilbert.

Jacob. PeNZ

Leak in the Dike, The. Phoebe Cary. CTV

Leaks on the Chinese carpet. (LL) The Alligator Bride. Donald Hall. CoAmPo; SPE

Lean back, and get some minutes' peace. Faustine. Swinburne. EBVVPR

Lean Gaius, who was thinner than a straw. Lucilius, *Greek*. FP; GrAn; OBVE, *tr.* by Peter Porter

Lean is the ghost of Molly Means. (LL) Molly Means. Margaret Abigail Walker. BlSi; NALW; NMM-2

Lean Street. George Sutherland Fraser. FaBoTC; OxBS

Lean-to of tin. Robert Spiess. HA

Leander. Hugh Henry Brackenridge *and* Philip Freneau. *Fr.* The Rising Glory of America. AiP

Leander Stormbound. Sydney Goodsir Smith. OxBS

Leander to the envious light. George Chapman. OAEL-1 *Fr.* Hero and Leander. AAS

Leander's Return. Marlowe. EBNV *Fr.* Hero and Leander. AAS

Leane, The. William Barnes. EBVV

Leaning against the golden undertow. Kenneth Slessor. CBAP *Fr.* Out of Time.

Leaning into the hill. Fyllr. *Unknown*. NBrP

Leaning on clouds, hugging rocks, slanting every way. Wu Chen. *Fr.* Poems Inscribed on Paintings of Bamboo. CoBLCP, *tr.* by Jonathan Chaves

Leaning / on the parapet. My Father Spoke with Swans. Patrick Galvin. BiHa

Leaning over the wall at Trafalgar Square. Cosmos in London. Arthur Nortje. HBAPE; PeSAV

Leans listening on the gate, in all respect. (LL) Middle of the World. D. H. Lawrence. HAP; NoAM

Leap, The. James Dickey. NIP-4; Poetr; WeT

Leap Before You Look. W. H. Auden. NoAM

Leap-Centuries. Paul Celan, *German*. OBVE, *tr.* by Michael Hamburger

Leap in the Dark. Roberta Hill Whiteman. WPOW

Leap into the light, ye living Forms! The Sculptor. Cornelius Mathews. APN-1 *Fr.* Poems on Man in His Various Aspects under the American Republic.

Leap of Faith. David St. John. NAmP90

Leap of the salmon, The. The Shannon Estuary Welcoming the Fish. Nuala Ni Dhomhnaill, *Irish*. CIP-2, *tr.* by the author

Leap out, chill water, over reeds and brakes. The River God. Sacheverell Sitwell. MoBrPo

Leap then, and come down on the line that draws to the earth's deep, heavy center. (LL) Kangaroo. D. H. Lawrence. EBEV; InPS-3; OxBTC

Leap Yeah Party, De. Maggie Pogue Johnson. CBWP-4

Leap Year. Charles North. FTOS

Leaped at the caribou. Ho Ho Ho Caribou. Joseph Ceravolo. FTOS; PmAP

Leaped like the roe, when he hears in the woodland the voice of the huntsman? Henry Wadsworth Longfellow. See From Evangeline.

Leaping Fire, The. John Montague. Little Flower's Disciple, The. TIRV

Leaping from oak to oak, tangled-up in the woods. Sacrifice of a Red Squirrel. Joseph Langland. NYBP

Leaping into the Gulf. Patricia Beer. OxBC

Leaping Laughers, The. George Barker. OBMV

Leaping wind from England, A. Back to Rest. William Hodgson. PoFWW

Leaps over the Aisle of Syllogism. David Chapman Berry. BXAP

Lear. William Carlos Williams. MeMAP; NAAL-2; NOBA; PoA

Learn from me, Son of Kunti! also this. *Unknown*. TOF, *tr.* by Sir Edwin Arnold *Fr.* The Bhagavad-Gita.

Learn, lads and lasses, of my garden. Francis Daniel Pastorius. SCAP

Learn now, dear Prince! how, if thy soul be set. *Unknown*. TAL, *tr.* by Sir Edward Arnold *Fr.* The Bhagavad-Gita.

Learn to conform the order of our lives. (LL) A Forest Hymn. William Cullen Bryant. APN-1; TAP

Learn to Count. *Unknown*. NAAAL

Learn to labor and to wait. (LL) A Psalm of Life. Henry Wadsworth Longfellow. APN-1; CTV; EBEvV; FaBoBe; NAAL-1; NAAL-3; OBCA; PAR; PWR; PoLF; TAP

"Learn to live, and live and learn." The Saturday Review. Dora Greenwell. EBVV

Learn to mak your bed, Annie. Fair Annie. *Unknown*. OxBB

Learn to speak this little word. "No!" Eliza Cook. PoToHe

Learn to wait—life's hardest lesson. *Unknown.* PoToHe

Learn women all from this housewifery. Sir Richard Fanshawe. OBVE *Fr. Il Pastor Fido.*

Learn'd lapidaries say the diamond. To Cynthia. Sir Francis Kynaston. CBLP

Learne Lordings, learne to feare and dread th'unweildy. Seneca. OBCVT, *tr. by* John Studley *Fr. Hercules Oetæus.*

Learned and a happy ignorance, A. Eden. Thomas Traherne. ChIV-1; ESCV; GeHe; PoEL-2

Learned, full of inward pride, The. The Two Monkeys. John Gay. OBCoV

Learned in music sings the lark. The Lark. *Unknown, Irish.* TIRV, *tr. by* Robin Flower

Learned Man [Came to Me Once], A. Stephen Crane. MeMAP; MoAmPo *Fr. The Black Riders [and Other Lines].*

Learned Mistress, A. Isobel Campbell, *Irish.* NNPT, *tr. by* Frank O'Connor

Learned Mistress, A. *Unknown, Irish.* OBMV, *tr. by* Frank O'Connor

Learner. Mahadai Das. HCP

Learning a New Language. Margaret Gibson. AFr

Learning by Doing. Howard Nemerov. HAP; Poetr; TwCP; WeW-3

Learning Destiny. Herman Charles Bosman. PeSA

Learning Experience. Marge Piercy. NoAM; WeT

Learning My Father's Language. Lorraine Duggin. LoHo

Learning ("So Learned Men in Controversies Spend"). George Chapman. NOSC *Fr. Euthymiae Raptus; or, The Teares of Peace.*

Learning the Spells; a Diptych. Anita Endrezze-Danielson. CDW

Learning the Trees. Howard Nemerov. VCAP

Learning to Count. Sara Berkeley. BiHa

Learning to love differently is hard. To Have without Holding. Marge Piercy. CrSp; NIP-4

Learning to Read. Frances Harper. AAP; BlSi; NAAAL; NALW

Learning to Speak. Peter Everwine. NNaP

Learning to Swim at Forty-Five. Colleen J. McElroy. GT

Learning to Write. Audre Lorde. GT

Lear's Madness. Shakespeare. CBNP *Fr. King Lear.*

Lear's Speech to the Storm. Shakespeare. *Fr. King Lear.*

Leasowes: Or, A Poetical Description of the Late Mr. Shenstone's Rural Retirement, The. Joseph Giles. OBGa

Least her own captive else should her subdue. Katherine Philips. *See* On the Welsh Language.

Least the World, fleshe, yea Devill putt thee out. Donne. *See* Since she whome I lovd, hath payd her last debt.

Leather: I travel by foot, trample the ground. Cynewulf. ASW, *tr. by* Kevin Crossley-Holland *Fr. Riddles (Exeter Book).*

Leather-skinned wrinkled old man, A. Rock Painting. Jack Cope. PeSA

Leave, A. Gertrude Stein. PFTM

Leave Crete. Song for the Goddess of Love. Sappho, *Greek.* ITG, *tr. by* Jane Hirshfield

Leave go my hands, let me catch breath and see. In The Orchard. Swinburne. BoLoP; LoP

Leave Helen to her lover. Draw away. The White Isle of Leuce. Sir Herbert Read. FaBoTw

Leave him alone, sweet enemy. The Lonely Traveller. Kwesi Brew. PBA; TTY

Leave him: he's quiet enough: and what matter. Here Lies a Prisoner. Charlotte Mew. MoBrPo

Leave It to Me Blues. Joel Oppenheimer. VGW

Leave Krete and come to this holy temple. Sappho, *Greek.* BoWoP, *tr. by* Willis Barnstone

Leave me, all sweet refrains my lip hath made. Sonnet. Luis de Camões, *Spanish.* AWP, *tr. by* Richard Garnett

Leave me alone! my tears would make you laugh. Solo. Mary Elizabeth Coleridge. VWP

Leave me, autumn, my green trees. Song. Ana Blandiana, *Romanian.* CEEP, *tr. by* Irina Livezeanu

Leave me but love and sherry. (LL) A Loose Saraband ("Nay, prethee [*or* prithee] dear, draw nigher"). Richard Lovelace. BeJo; CaPo; PoEL-3

'Leave Me, O Love'. Sir Philip Sidney. *See* Splendidis longum valedico nugis.

Leave me: oh! leave me. Dying. Adah Isaacs Menken. CBWP-1

Leave my tomb. Employ your pick. Gregory of Nazianzus, Saint, *Greek.* GrAn, *tr. by* Robin Skelton

Leave off, good Beroe, now. To an Old Gentlewoman That Painted Her Face. George Turberville. OxBSP

Leave-Taking. Frank Gelett Burgess. OBCoV

Leave-Taking, A. Arno Holz, *German.* AWP, *tr. by* Jethro Bithell

Leave-taking, A. Swinburne. CBLP; CH; NOBE; NOBVV; OBNC; PoEL-5; PoLF

Leave the bars lying in the grass. Fall. Robert Francis. VGW

Leave the rags, you tiny lusts. Asclepiades, *Greek.* GrAn, *tr. by* Alan Marshfield

Leave the window open. Death Song. *Unknown.* BoWoP, *tr. by* Reza Baraheni *and* Zahra-Soltan Shokoohtaezeh

Leave the Word Alone. Edward Marshall. NeAP

Leave Them Alone. Patrick Kavanagh. OxBSP

Leave them to the *black* folks! (LL) Hiccups. Léon Damas, *French.* NegPo; PFTM, *tr. by* Ellen Conroy Kennedy

Leave thine own home, O youth, seek distant shores! Encouragement to Exile. Petronius Arbiter, *Latin.* AWP, *tr. by* Howard Mumford Jones

Leave this gaudy gilded stage. Song. John Wilmot. OxBSP

Leave what is white for whiter use. Stone For A Statue. Sarah Morgan Bryan Piatt. NCAP

Leave your home behind, lad. The Recruit. A. E. Housman. FaPoR

Leaves. Frank Asch. NTCP

Leaves. Countee Cullen. GT

Leaves. W. H. Davies. MoBrPo

Leaves. "Michael Field." VWP

Leaves. Sam Hamod. UnSA

Leaves. Ted Hughes. AYFP; OxBC

Leaves. Frederic Manning. NOBAu

Leaves. Katharine Tynan. BoTP

Leaves a-Vallen. William Barnes. NOBVV

Leaves and flowers are never rated the same. For Lotus Flower. Li Shang-yin, *Chinese.* SuSp, *tr. by* Eugene Eoyang *and* Irving Y. Lo

Leaves are fading and falling, The. November. Alice Cary. AYFP; OBCA

Leaves are sere, The. November. Henrietta Cordelia Ray. CBWP-3

Leaves are storm-rattled jester's bells, The. King Lear Bewildered. Patricia Storace. FFC

Leaves blowing into a sentence. Bob Boldman. HA

Leaves Come Again, The. Henry Vaughan, *sometimes at. to* Thomas Stanley. FaBoEE

Leaves Compared with Flowers. Robert Frost. NOBA

Leaves fall, fall as if from far away, The. Autumn. Rilke, *German.* TrJP, *tr. by* C. F. MacIntyre

Leaves fall from my fingers, The. October. Charles Wright. MT

Leaves fall, slanting sun lights the river. Tune: Palace of Night Revels. Chou Pang-yen, *Chinese.* CoBCP, *tr. by* Burton Watson

Leaves fall turning to the ground. Han Yü, *Chinese.* CoBCP, *tr. by* Burton Watson *Fr. Autumn Thoughts.*

Leaves floated down picturesquely, The. Words. "David Samuilovich Samoylov," *Russian.* TCRP, *tr. by* Lubov Yakovleva

Leaves from eternity are simple things. The Eternity of Nature. John Clare. EBEV

Leaves had a wonderful frolic, The. *Unknown.* BoTP

Leaves have the lightest footfall. Leaves in the Yard. Hal Summers. AYFP

Leaves have their time to fall. The Hour of Death. Felicia Dorothea Hemans. NOBRP; OBNC

Leaves have yellowed like, The. Vytautas Bloze, *Lithuanian.* CEEP, *tr. by* Irene Pogoželskyte Suboczewski

Leaves in the Yard. Hal Summers. AYFP

Leaves like Fish. Gladys Cardiff. CDW

Leaves looked at the window, The. The House across the Way. Ralph Hodgson. FaBoTw

Leaves moil in the yard. Clement Hoyt. HA

Leaves / Murmuring by myriads in the shimmering trees. From My Diary, July 1914. Wilfred Owen. FaBoMo; LiTM; MoBrPo

Leaves must be green in Spring. (LL) Malvern Hill. Herman Melville. APN-2; AmPP; CBCWP; ColAP; PAR; TAP

Leaves of a Dream Are the Leaves of an Onion, The. Arthur Sze. OpBo

Leaves of Grass (1855). Walt Whitman. APN-1 *See also* A Boston Ballad [1854]; Faces; The Sleepers; Song of Myself

("Bodies of men and women engirth me, and I engirth them, The.") APN-1

"I have perceiv'd that to be with those I like is enough." SAmP

"I sing the body electric." SAmP

"Man's body at auction, A." SAmP

("O I say now these are the soul!") (LL) CTC

"This is the female form." EP

"Will you seek afar off? you surely come back at last." ChIV-1

Leaves of heaven, The. Edward Sanders. RaBo

Leaves of Hypnos. René Char, *French.*

"Poet, conserver of the infinite faces of the living, The." PFTM, *tr. by* Cid Corman

Leaves of Hypnos No. 128. René Char, *French.* AF, *tr. by* Cid Corman

Leaves of the bush clover rustle in the wind, The. Kenrei Mon-in Ukyo no Daibu, *Japanese.* WPJ, *tr. by* Kenneth Rexroth *and* Ikuko Atsumi

Leaves of the summer, lovely summer's pride. Sonnet: Leaves. William Barnes. OBNC

Leaves rusted in the late winds, The. Snails. Philip Levine. PaTW

Leaves should be lush and the petals frail, The. (LL) Tune: "As in a Dream; a Song." Li Ch'ing-chao, *Chinese.* BoWoP; SuSp, *tr.* by Eugene Eoyang

Leaves though thick are falling; one by one, The. Autumn Leaves. Jones Very. APN-1; PAR

Leaves throng thick above, The. The Last Leaf. Thomas Hardy. CBLP

Leaves turned red and brown as my Father, The. Autumn. Helen G. Quigless. BkSV *Fr.* Childhood Scenes in Four Seasons.

Leaves were already on the trees, the fruit blossoms, The. With Janice. Kenneth Koch. PmAP

Leaves without trees. Yehuda Amichai, *Hebrew.* MHP, *tr.* by Ruth Finer Mintz

Leaving. Rae Armantrout. FTOS

Leaving. Pamela Brown. BMAP

Leaving, The. Margot Fortunato. LoHo

Leaving, The. Brigit Pegeen Kelly. APAD

Leaving. Cathy Song. NoAM

Leaving. Richard Wilbur. FP

Leaving all his wisdom standing. The Hots. Michael Sharkey. NOBAu

Leaving all the morning glories closed. Elizabeth Searle Lamb. HA

Leaving Barra. Louis MacNeice. EBEV

Leaving behind for ever the thundering Aegean. Plato. GrAn, *tr.* by Peter Jay *Fr.* Two Poems on the Eretrians Taken Prisoner by the Persians.

Leaving behind us the alien, foreign city of Dublin. Going Home to Mayo, Winter, 1949. Paul Durcan. CIP-2; PBCIP

Leaving Buffalo. Charles Martin. PoA

Leaving Crete, come visit again our temple. Sappho, *Greek.* STV; WeW-3, *tr.* by John Frederick Nims

Leaving for the Front. Alfred Lichtenstein, *German.* PeFWW, *tr.* by Patrick Bridgwater

Leaving Forever. Denise Levertov. InPK-6

Leaving Inishmore. Michael Longley. IIP

Leaving kids alone is no problem. Fire the Babysitter. David Avidan, *Hebrew.* IP, *tr.* by Warren Bargad *and* Stanley F. Chyet

Leaving Los Angeles. Quincy Troupe. MoNo

Leaving my loneliness inside her. George Swede. HA

Leaving on the freeway eye thought. Leaving Los Angeles. Quincy Troupe. MoNo

Leaving Port Authority for the St. Regis Rezz. Wendy Rose. HATNAP

Leaving Rattle Bar. Clark Coolidge. FTOS

Leaving Something Behind. David Wagoner. CoAP

Leaving the Atocha Station. John Ashbery. PmAP

Leaving the Boys Behind. Rufinus, *Greek.* GrAn, *tr.* by Alan Marshfield

Leaving the capital / to return to my fief in the East. Rhyme-Prose on the Goddess of the Lo. Ts'ao Chih, *Chinese.* CoBCP, *tr.* by Burton Watson

Leaving the City. Liu K'o-chuang, *Chinese.* CoBCP, *tr.* by Burton Watson

Leaving the city where new houses, new inhabitants, / and the newly rich reign. Seven Beginnings. Olesya Nikolayeva, *Russian.* TCRP, *tr.* by Vera Dunham

Leaving the door of the whitewashed house ajar. A Couple Waiting. Matthew Sweeney. BiHa

Leaving the island, she believes, to go to the child. Monique Laederach. *Fr.* Penelope. BoWoP, *tr.* by Charles Guenther

Leaving the Monastery Early in the Morning. Lu Yu, *Chinese.* OHPC, *tr.* by Kenneth Rexroth

Leaving the Motel. W. D. Snodgrass. NIP-4

Leaving the Peloponnese. Alcaeus, *Greek.* InMo, *tr.* by Sam Hamill

Leaving the viaduct on the left, and coming over the hill. St. Ursanne. Michael Roberts. LiTM

Leaving the white glow of filling stations. The Strand at Lough Beg. Seamus Heaney. CIP-2; NoAM; OBWP

Leaving them dumbstruck also with an ache / Nothing can satisfy. (LL) Hamlen Brook. Richard Wilbur. VCAP; WeW-3

Leaving thine outgrown shell by life's unresting sea! (LL) The Chambered Nautilus. Oliver Wendell Holmes. APN-1; APo; AmPP; ColAP; FaBoBe; HoPM; ImPo; NAAL-3; NCAP; NOBA; NoP-4; PAR; PoEL-5; PoLF; TFi

Leaving Town after the Funeral. Richard Jones. NAmP90

Leaving us behind. After the Death of Her Daughter in Child-birth. Lady Izumi, *Japanese.* PBWP, *tr.* by Edwin A. Cranston

Leaving West Archery Hall at Dusk. Hsieh Ling-yün, *Chinese.* SuSp, *tr.* by Francis Westbrook

Leaving You. Lily Brett. HP

Leaving you. A Courtesy, A Trenchant Grace. Cyrus Cassells. GT

Leavings. Gerard Benson. BXAP

Leavings from them at last. Walt Whitman. *See* This Compost.

Lebanon Bologna and meat loaf, two sandwiches. American Lunch. Bruce Smith. FiLi

Lecherous young Lilliputian, A. Limerick. C. Vita-Finzi. PeLi

Lecture had ended when I came in, The. The Deconstruction of Emily Dickinson. Galway Kinnell. PUP-20

Lecture Hall. Patrick Kavanagh. FaBoTw

Lecture on Nothing. John Cage. FTOS

Lecture upon the Shadow, A. Donne. AWP; ESCV; ImPo; NAEL-1; NoSic; SCGP; SeCP; UnPo

Lectured by Pa and Ma o'er night. The Lady's Diary. Charles Dibdin. NOEC

Lecturer's impartial prose, The. In the Lecture Room. James Keir Baxter. PeLV *Fr.* Cressida.

Lecturing on the Theme of Motherhood. Michael S. Harper. FiLi

Led by a blind and teachit by a bairn. (LL) Sonnet: "Fra bank [*or* banc] to bank [*or* banc], fra wood [*or* wod] to wood [*or* wod] I rin." Mark Alexander Boyd. EBEV; HAP; InPK-6; OBEV; Son

Led by the powre of griefe, to wailings brought. Sonnet 9. Mary Sidney. PEW *Fr.* Pamphilia to Amphilanthus.

Led on the eternal spring. (LL) Eden. Milton. GaP; OBGa

Leda. Lilian Bowes-Lyon. FaBoSe

Leda. Hilda Doolittle. NAAL-2

Leda. Robert Graves. PFE

Leda. Rilke, *German.* RaBo, *tr.* by Robert Bly

Leda. Mona Van Duyn. NMM-2

Leda and the Swan. Oliver St. John Gogarty. EBNV; HAP ("Though her Mother told her.") PFE

Leda and the Swan. W. B. Yeats. CABP; CMoP; ClHu; EBEV; FaBoSe; GSo; GTBS-P; HAP; HeIP-4; ImPo; InPK-6; LiTM; MoBrPo; MoP; NAEL-2; NAWM-2; NIP-4; NOBE; NoAM; NoP-4; OAEL-2; OxAEP-2; OxBoV; PFE; PoE; PoPoPo; Poetr; SAGP; SCV; SoSe-8; Son; TFi; TRP; WeW-3

Leda in Stratford, Ont. Anne Wilkinson. MoCV

Leda Reconsidered. Mona Van Duyn. NMM-2

Leda's Sister and the Geese. Katharyn Machan Aal. SoSe-8

Leda's Version. James Harrison. NIP-4

Lede guiterriste was a craftie ladde, The. The Probatioun Officeres Tale. Gerard Benson. BXAP; NBLV

Lee. Rose Cecil O'Neill. CPO

Lee in the Mountains. Donald Davidson. CBCWP; FuPo

Lee Morgan. David Henderson. SeSe

Lee to the Rear. John Randolph Thompson. CBCWP

Leeburn Mill. William Barnes. EnVR

Leesome Brand. *Unknown.* ESPB

Leezie Lindsay. *Unknown.* FaBoCh

Left alone. Tanka. Miyazawa Kenji, *Japanese.* MJT, *tr.* by Makoto Ueda

Left and right, I toss about my bed. Crinagoras, *Greek.* InMo, *tr.* by Sam Hamill

Left Bank Jazz Society, The. Michael S. Weaver. UnSA

Left Behind. Amy Lowell. CPO

Left by his friend to breakfast alone on the white. Edward Lear. W. H. Auden. OxAEP-2

Left Eye of Odin, The. Regina DeCormier-Shekejian. LoHo

Left hand holding distaff and wool retained on it (ah mixture). Catullus. *See* Carmen 64 ("In old days / driving through soft waters").

Left in the field / among big-bellied ewes. Naayawva Taawi. Wendy Rose. UnSA

Left leg flung out, head cocked to the right. Poet. Karl Shapiro. CMoP; LiTM; MoAmPo; NoAM

Left like an unknown's breath on mirrors. Visitations. Lawrence Durrell. MoBrPo *Fr.* Eight Aspects of Melissa.

Left like water in glasses overnight. Love from My Father. Carole C. Gregory Clemmons. PoBA

Left on for hours, / Burning, burning. (LL) Bus Stop. Donald Justice. FYAP; LCAP-2; WeT

Left on the beach. Akiko Yosano, *Japanese.* OHMPJ, *tr.* by Kenneth Rexroth

Left shoe / and the right one with its white foot, The. Linda Hogan. *See* The Truth Is.

Left side of her world is gone, The. Strokes. William Stafford. CoAmPo

Left, the golden leaf bears from his ear. The Leaf in His Ear. Mahadai Das. HCP

Left to herself, the serpent now began. Keats. FaBoSe *Fr.* Lamia.

Left to the wind. Alexis Rotella. HA

Left-wing young lady from Wick, A. Limerick. Gerry Hamill. PeLi

Leftover Blessings. Julia Kasdorf. PBCAP

Leg, The. Karl Shapiro. HAP; MoAmPo; UnPo; WeW-3

Leg in a Plaster Cast, A. Muriel Rukeyser. MoAmPo

Leg in the Subway, The. Oscar Williams. LiTM

Leg over leg. Mother Goose. LB; OxNR; ReMoGo

Legacies. Nikki Giovanni. CrSp; NMM-2

　("I guess nobody ever does.") (LL) UnSA

Legacies. Emily Grosholz. FFC

Legacies. Léon Laleau. NegPo, tr. by Ellen Conroy Kennedy. Fr. Black Music.

Legacy. Imamu Amiri Baraka. ColAP; MoP; NOBA; NoAM; PoBA

Legacy, The. Bible, O.T. TrJP Fr. Proverbs.

Legacy [or Legacie], The. Donne. FMP; SeCP

Legacy. Joy Harjo. WeT

Legacy, The. Heinrich von Morungen, German. GePo, tr. by F. C. Nicholson

Legacy. Márton Kalász, Hungarian. CEEP, tr. by Jascha Kessler

Legacy. Maurice Kenny. HATNAP

Legacy: My South. Dudley Randall. PoBA

Legacy of a Brother. Renaldo Fernandez. NBV

Legal Fiction. William Empson. CMoP; FaBoMo; ImPo; LiTM; MoP; NoAM; NoP-4

Legal Mouse, A. Lizelia Augusta Jenkins Moorer. CBWP-3

Legem Tuam Dilexi. Coventry Patmore. PoEL-5 Fr. The Unknown Eros.

Legend. Charles Causley. TOF

Legend. Hart Crane. InPS-3; OxBA

Legend, The. Garrett Kaoru Hongo. LoL; NAmP90; OpBo; TRP; WWSi

Legend. Sydney Tremayne. FaBoTC

Legend. Judith Wright. NOBAu; NTP; RB

Legend is whispered, The. Shapeshifter Poems. Lucille Clifton. LoL

Legend lives on from the Chippewa on down, The. The Wreck of the Edmund Fitzgerald. Gordon Lightfoot. NoP-4

Legend of Britomartis, or of Chastitie, The. Edmund Spenser. NAEL-1 Fr. Wood Of Error. AEP

Legend of Felix is ended, the toiling of Felix is done, The. Envoy. Henry Van Dyke. BLPA Fr. The Toiling of Felix.

Legend of Good Women, The. Chaucer.

　"Alas, that I ne had English, rhyme or prose." EPCY

　"And as for me, though that I konne [or can] but [or my wit be] lyte." CH; HeIP-4

　Balade: "Hide [or Hyd], Absalon, thy gilte tresses clere." AWP; EBEV; EnVB; GBL; HAP; ImPo; NOBE; OAEL-1; OBEV; SCGP

Legend of Hell, The. C. D. Wright. LCAP-2

Legend of Lilja. Sarah Kirsch, German. AF, tr. by Wayne Kvam

Legend of Provence, A. Adelaide Anne Procter. VWP

Legend of Rabbi Ben Levi, The. Henry Wadsworth Longfellow. NCAP

Legend of St. Gingulph's Relict, The. Thomas Lovell Beddoes. See The New Cecilia.

Legend of Success, The Salesman's Story, The. Louis Simpson. NYBP

Legend of the Admen, The. Everett W. Lord. BLPA

Legend of the Crossing-Sweeper. May Kendall. VWP

Legend of the Hive, A. Robert Stephen Hawker. EBVV

Legend of the Knight of the Red Crosse, or of Holinesse, The. Edmund Spenser. EPCY; FHYEP; NAEL-1; OAEL-1 Fr. Wood Of Error.

　("It was a chosen plot of fertile land.") AEP

　(Phaedria's Island: The Faerie Queene II.vi. 12–17.) AEP

　("Refuse such fruitless toil, and present pleasures choose.") (LL) AEP

Legend of the Northland, A. Phoebe Cary. OBCA; OBSP

Legend of the Organ-Builder, The. Julia Caroline Ripley Dorr. BLPA; FaBoBe

Legend of the raindrop, The. Helen Steiner Rice. CTV

Legend of their youth into the noon, The. (LL) Legend. Hart Crane. InPS-3; OxBA

Legend of Versailles, A. Melvin Beaunearus Tolson. BPo; NAAAL

Legend: The god in the sun made two men. J. Michael Yates. HoPM Fr. The Great Bear Lake Meditations.

Legendary. James McAuley. BMAP

Legendary darkness in the dayshine. The Gold in the Mud. Gerrit Lansing. PT

Legendary muscle that wants and grieves, The. The Hearts. Robert Pinsky. VCAP

Legion: Civic Choruses. William Harmon.

　Ceremon(y)(ies) of Mutability, The. WeT

Legion Club, The. Jonathan Swift.

　"As I strole the city, oft I." BIrV

"Legion" to "Lent" for "R." Tina Darragh. FTOS

Legless Boy Climbing In and Out of Chair. Michael Pettit. NAmP90

Legree's big house was white and green. Simon Legree—A Negro Sermon. Vachel Lindsay. MeMAP; MoAmPo; TAP Fr. The Booker Washington Trilogy.

Legs, The. Robert Graves. ImPo; LiTM; PeLV; RB

Legs are locked; the sky is dead, The. (LL) The Distant Runners. Mark Van Doren. LiTM; MoAmPo

Legs! / How we have suffered each other. Poem in Which My Legs Are Accepted. Kathleen Fraser. AmPA

Legs of the elk punctured the snow's crust, The. To Christ Our Lord. Galway Kinnell. HeIP-4; TwCP

Lehayyim, my brethren, Lehayyim, I say. Simhat Torah. Judah Leib Gordon, Hebrew. TrJP, tr. by Alice Lucas and Helena Frank

Lehmann does well with Largactil. Laprairie Hunger Strike. Ronald G. Everson. MoCV

Leisure. W. H. Davies. APAD; AWP; BoTP; CH; CTV; EBEvV; FaBoBe; LiTM; MoBrPo; NOBE; NTP; OBEV; OBMV; PoRA; TFi

Leisurely Stroll, A. Hsü Pen, Chinese.

　"Mountain of green trees and orioles everywhere!" CoBLCP, tr. by Jonathan Chaves

Leisurely talk in low voices. Tune: "Wu-t'ung" Leaves"—Written in Jest at a Banquet. Lu Chih, Chinese. SuSp, tr. by Hellmut Wilhelm

Leith police dismisseth us, The. Unknown. OxNR

Leith Races. Robert Fergusson.

　My Winsome Dear. VGW

Lela's Charms. Lizelia Augusta Jenkins Moorer. CBWP-3

"Lem" cuts a figure around "le ma" and "le me." "Legion" to "Lent" for "R." Tina Darragh. FTOS

L'Embarquement pour Cythère. John Streeter Manifold. CBAP

Lemme be wid Casey Jones. Odyssey of Big Boy. Sterling Brown. NAAAL

Lemmings, The. John Masefield. CMoP

Lemmings die every year. Over the cliff. Patricia Beer. CABP

Lemon Pie. E. A. Markham. OBAL

Lemon rind rubbed on the rim. Espresso. Carol Lee Saffoti. UnSA

Lemon Trees, The. Eugenio Montale, Italian. PFTM, tr. by Irma Brandeis

Lemonade Stand. Myra Cohn Livingston. TLR

Lemons. Ted Walker. NYBP

Lemoshl: for example. A Few Words in the Mother Tongue. Irena Klepfisz. CPO; LoHo

Lemuel's Blessing. W. S. Merwin. CAPP-1; NYBP

Lena Lovelace. Melvin B. Tolson. GT

Lend a Hand. Edward Everett Hale. CTV

Lend me, a little while, the key. The Pedlar. Charlotte Mew. NOxBChV

Lend me cruel light. To an Angry God. X. J. Kennedy. CRP

Lend me your arm. Little Song of the Maimed. Benjamin Péret, French. OBWP; PeFWW, tr. by David Gascoyne

Lend me your precious toys. To W.S.—On his Wonderful Toys. Walter Davies. NOxBChV

"Lend my thy mare to ride a mile." Money and the Mare. Unknown. ReMoGo

L'Enfant Glace. Harry Graham. CBNP; NBLV; OBCoV; PeLV

Length o' days ageän do shrink, The. The Fall. William Barnes. PoEL-4

Length of Days. Horatius Bonar. PWR

Length of Life, The. Amos Russel Wells. PWR

Length of Moon. Arna Bontemps. LiTM

Lengthening Days. Unknown. ReMoGo

Lenin. Nikolai Alekseievich Klyuyev, Russian.

　"Lenin has the spirit of an Old Believer." TCRP, tr. by Bernard Meares

Lenin. Dorothy, Duchess of Wellington Wellesley.

　"So I came down the steps to Lenin." OBMV

Lenin has the spirit of an Old Believer. Nikolai Alekseievich Klyuyev. TCRP, tr. by Bernard Meares Fr. Lenin.

Leningrad. "Naum Korzhavin," Russian. TCRP, tr. by Albert C. Todd

Leningrad. Osip Emilevich Mandelstam, Russian. TCRP, tr. by Bernard Meares; AF; FaBoPV, tr. by W. S. Merwin and Clarence Brown

Leningrad brimming with rivers and canals. Leningrad: Picture Postcard. Meir Wieseltier, Hebrew. IP, tr. by Warren Bargad and Stanley F. Chyet

Leningrad Cemetery, Winter of 1941. Sharon Olds. NIP-4

Leningrad: Picture Postcard. Meir Wieseltier, Hebrew. IP, tr. by Warren Bargad and Stanley F. Chyet

Lennie Tristano, No Wind. Jim Brodey. MoNo

Lennox Island. David McFadden. NOBC

Lenore. Edgar Allan Poe. APN-1; AmPP; PAR

Lenox Avenue is a big street. Keep on Pushing. David Henderson. PoBA

Lenox Avenue Mural. Langston Hughes. HoPM

　Comment on Curb. APSN

　"Good morning, daddy!" APSN; MBE

Harlem. APSN; AiP; AmPP; CrDW; GLP; GT; HCAP; HeIP-4; InPS-3; NAAAL; NoP-4; PBMP; Poetr; RaBo; SAmP; SSLK

   (Dream Deferred.) InPK-6; LiTM; MBE; PoBA; SoSe-8

   ("Like a heavy load.") (LL) SSLK

Island. HCAP

Letter. PoE

Same in Blues. APSN; InPS-3; SAGP; SSLK

Lens. Anne Wilkinson. MoCV; NOBC

Lent. William Robert Rodgers. PNI

Lent in a Year of War. Thomas Merton. SPE

Lenten Is Come with Love to Toune. *Unknown.* HAP; MiEL; OBEV

   ("Lenten is come with love to towne.") EBEV

Lentinus! thou dost nought but fume, and fret. Martial, *Latin.* OBVE, *tr. by* Sir Edward Sherburne

L'Envoi. Edwin Arlington Robinson. TrCP

L'Envoi: "What is the moral? Who rides may read." Rudyard Kipling. *See* The Winners.

L'Envoy. George Herbert. ESCV

Leo to His Mistress. Henry Dwight Sedgwick. BLPA

Leon, A? No. Chippewa Love Song. *Unknown, Chippewa Indian.* BoWoP, *tr. by* Frances Densmore, *ad. by* Willis Barnstone

Leona, dear, twelve months ago. Eloise Bibb. CBWP-4

Leonardo Da Vinci's. Marianne Moore. NYBP

Leonardo's "Mona Lisa." Edward Dowden. GSo

Leonardo's Secret. Robert Bly. NNaP

Leopard. *Unknown. Fr.* Hunter Poems of the Yoruba. RB, *tr. by* Ulli Beier

Leopard in Eden, The. Gail White. FFC

Leopard lives in a Muu tree, A. Jonathan Kariara. PBMAP

Leopard Skin. Douglas Stewart. NOBAu

Lepanto. G. K. Chesterton. EBEvV; EBNV; FaPoR; MoBrPo; OBMV; OBNV; RB

Leper, The. Swinburne. GBL; NOBVV

Lepers Cry. Peter Orlovsky. GLP

Lepidoptery. James Sherry. FTOS

Leprechaun, The—the omadhaun!—that lives in County Clare. Of Certain Irish Fairies. Arthur Guiterman. PoLF

Leroy. Imamu Amiri Baraka. BPo; PmAP; PoBA

Les Anges Sont Blancs. George Seferis, *Greek.* PFTM, *tr. by* George Economou

Les Ballons. Oscar Wilde. NOBVV

Les Demoiselles de Sauve. John Gray. NOBVV; PeVV

Les Estreines. Matthew Prior. OxBSP

Les Étiquettes Jaunes. Frank O'Hara. CAPP-1

Les Fleurs du Mal. Charles Baudelaire, *French.*

   Femmes Damnées. CPO, *tr. by* Carlyle Ferren MacIntyre

Les Hiboux. Charles Baudelaire. AWP, *tr. by* Arthur Symons

Les Luths. Frank O'Hara. NOBA; NoAM

Les Manèges de la Mer (1964). Edouard J. Maunick.

   "Further off is the measured force the word of the sea." VCWP, *tr. by* Gerald Moore

   ("Never say no when I speak to you from afar. . . .") (LL) VCWP, *tr. by* Gerald Moore

   "I love to encounter you in strange cities." PBMAP

Les Millwin. Ezra Pound. OBCoV

Les Planches-en-Montagnes. Michael Roberts. OBMV

Les Racines Congolaises (1968). Jean-Baptiste Tati-Loutard.

   Noonday in Immaturity. PBMAP

Les Silhouettes. Oscar Wilde. EBVV *Fr.* Impressions.

Les Sylphides. Louis MacNeice. BoLoP *Fr.* Novelettes.

Les Vaches. Arthur Hugh Clough. CBLP

Lesbia. Richard Aldington. PoLF

Lesbia. William Congreve. OxBSP

Lesbia, but with friendless intention. (LL) Carmen 72. Catullus. OBVE, *tr. by* Richard Lovelace; OxBSP, *tr. by* William Walsh

Lesbia forever on me rails. Catullus. *See* Carmen 92 ("Lesbia loads me night & day with her curses").

Lesbia from Catullus—Jul. 18th 1736. Catullus. *See* Carmen 92 ("Lesbia loads me night & day with her curses").

Lesbia! I must love you still. Catullus. *See* Carmen 75 ("Reason blinded by sin, Lesbia").

Lesbia, live to love and pleasure. Catullus, *Latin.* OBCVT, *tr. by* John Langhorne

Lesbia / live with me. Catullus. *See* Carmen 5 ("My sweetest Lesbia, let us live and love").

Lesbia loads me night & day with her curses. Carmen 92. Catullus. AWP; OBVE, *tr. by* Jonathan Swift; BoLoP, *tr. by* Peter Whigham; OxBSP *Fr.* Carmina.

Lesbia may dicker simper maul or nag talk at whom, come. Catullus. *See* Carmen 92 ("Lesbia loads me night & day with her curses").

Lesbia, my love, let's be and enjoy ourselves. Catullus. *See* Carmen 5 ("My sweetest Lesbia, let us live and love").

Lesbia, our Lesbia, the same old Lesbia. Catullus. *See* Carmen 58 ("My Lesbia, Caelius, that same Lesbia").

Lesbia Railing. Catullus. *See* Carmen 92 ("Lesbia loads me night & day with her curses").

Lesbia says she'ld rather marry me. Carmen 70. Catullus, *Latin.* OBVE, *tr. by* Richard Lovelace *Fr.* Carmina.

Lesbia thou seemst my *Thomas* to command. In Lesbiam. Martial, *Latin.* OBCVT, *tr. by* R. Fletcher

Lesbia, why are your amours. Epigram 34. Martial, *Latin.* EP, *tr. by* James Michie

Lesbian girl of Khartoum, A. Limerick. *Unknown.* NOBL; PeLV

Lesbos. Lawrence Durrell. EBEV

Lesotho. Bennett Makalo Khaketla, *Sotho.* PeSA, *tr. by* Dan Kunene *and* Jack Cope

Less and Less Human, O Savage Spirit. Wallace Stevens. AFr; VGW

Less[e] loss[e] to let her go[e]. (LL) Content and Ri[t]ch[e]. Robert Southwell. ChIV-2; NoSic

Less Nonsense. Sir Alan Patrick Herbert. OxBTC

Less pub than brothel, and you, the regulars. Catullus, *Latin.* NNPT, *tr. by* Sisson, C. H.

Less said about Edward's slut the better, The. Bliss. George Johnston. NOBC

Less said the better. Missing. John Pudney. OxBTC

Less than a day in paradise. The Stones Where the Haft Rotted. Meng Chiao, *Chinese.* PLT, *tr. by* A. C. Graham

Less than a golden one it cannot be. (LL) To His Mistress. Abraham Cowley. NOSC; OxAEP-1

Less than total is a bucketful of radiant toys. (LL) Cut the Grass. A. R. Ammons. HAP; Poetr; TAP; WeW-3

Less than two hours it took the Iroquois. Edwin John Pratt. *See* The Martyrdom of Brébeuf and Lalemant, 16 March 1649.

Lesser proof than old Voltaire's, yet greater, A. Orange Buds by Mail from Florida. Walt Whitman. NAAL-1; NAAL-3

Lesson, The. Kathleen Cain. LoHo

Lesson, The. Miroslav Holub, *Czech.* PoSu, *tr. by* Ian *and* Jarmila Milner

Lesson, The. Robert Lowell. CMoP; LCAP-2

Lesson, The. Edward Lucie-Smith. APAD; IMW; OxBTC; TwCP

Lesson, The. Charles Simic. AF; HCAP

Lesson, A. Wordsworth. GTBS-P

Lesson, The. C. D. Wright. CMAP

Lesson for Beautiful Women, A. Alastair Reid. FaBoTC

Lesson for Mamma, A. Sydney Dayre. OBCA; OxBChV

Lesson for Today, The. Robert Frost. LiTM

Lesson From a Sundial [Sun-Dial]. *Unknown.* Spl

Lesson in a Picture, A. Sarah Morgan Bryan Piatt. NCAP

Lesson in Handwriting, A. Alastair Reid. NYBP

Lesson in Love, A. Philip Hobsbaum. OxBTC

Lesson in Observation, A. Dan Pagis, *Hebrew.* AF, *tr. by* Stephen Mitchell

Lesson of Silence, A. Tymoteusz Karpowicz, *Polish.* PoSu, *tr. by* Czeslaw Milosz

Lesson of the Flowers, The. Hafiz, *Persian.* GaP, *tr. by* E. Harriet Palmer

Lesson of the Water Mill, The. Sarah Doudney. *See* The Water Mill.

Lessons. Jan Barry. CDa

Lessons from a Mirror. Thylias Moss. LTA

Lessons of Nature, The. William Drummond, of Hawthornden. *See* The Book.

Lessons of the War. Henry Reed. HeIP-4; OBWP

   Judging Distances. BoLoP; GTBS-P; NIP-4; NOBE; PoWW; Poetr

   (2. Judging Distances.) NoP-4

   Naming Of Parts. EBEvV; HoPM; ImPo; InPS-3; MoBrPo; NOBE; OxBTC; PFE; PoPoPo; PoRA; Poetr; RaBo; SAGP; SoSe-8; TFi; UV; UnPo

   ("For to-day we have naming of parts.") (LL) PFE

   (Lessons of the War.) NoP-4

   ("Today we have naming of parts. Yesterday.") APAD; NoP-4; PoPoPo; SAGP

Lest anybody spy the blood / And "You're hurt" exclaim! Emily Dickinson. *See* A Wounded Deer—leaps highest.

Lest anybody spy the blood / And "You're hurt" exclaim! (LL) Wounded Deer—leaps highest, A. Emily Dickinson. ColAP

Lest her own captive else should her subdue. (LL) On the Welsh Language. Katherine Philips. NOSC; NoP-4

Lest I fail! Ernest Christopher Dowson. *See* O Mors! Quam Amara Est Memoria Tua Homini Pacem Habenti In Substantiis Suis.

Lest it may more quarrels breed. Twelve Articles. Jonathan Swift. NBLV; OBCoV

Lest men suspect your tale to be untrue. The Devil's Advice to Story-Tellers. Robert Graves. LiTM; MoP; NAEL-2; NoAM

Lest one touch of this heart convey its grief. (LL) Sonnet: "And wilt thou have me fashion into speech." Elizabeth Barrett Browning. BWW; BrRo; CABP; EnVR; VWP

Lest sluggards loaf in bed and oversleep. The Alarm Clock. Phan Bội Châu, *Vietnamese*. AVP, *tr. by* Huỳnh Sanh Thông

Lest the fair cheeks begin their shrivelling. Homework. Mona Van Duyn. FFC; VCAP

Lest the ripple deceive us. Winter Pond. Ben Belitt. NYBP

Lest the world, flesh, yea Devil put thee out. (LL) Since she whome I lovd, hath payd her last debt. Donne. FMP; FSCP; NAEL-1; NOSC; Son

Lest thou forget in the years between. William Leroy Stidger. PoToHe

Lest you should think that verse shall die. 4.9. Alexander Pope, *Latin*. AWP; EPCY *Fr.* Odes.

Lestenyt, lordynges, both elde and yinge. Of a Rose, a Lovely Rose. *Unknown*. OBEV

Lester Leaps In. Al Young. MoNo; SeSe

Lester Young! why are you playing that clarinet. String of Pearls. Ted Berrigan. MoNo

Let *a* be taken as. . . . The Project of Linear Inquiry. Michael Palmer. PmAP

Let a joy keep you. Joy. Carl Sandburg. SAGP

Let a poem be. Tanka. Mori Ōgai, *Japanese*. MJT, *tr. by* Makoto Ueda

Let a race of men now rise and take control. Margaret Abigail Walker. *See* For my people [everywhere singing their slave songs repeatedly: their].

Let age approve of youth, and death complete the same! (LL) Rabbi Ben Ezra. Robert Browning. NAEL-2; OBNC

Let Age no longer toil with feeble strife. The Poor. John Langhorne. NOEC *Fr.* The Country Justice.

Let all be well, be well. (LL) I have led her home, my love, my only friend. Tennyson. CBLP; EBVV; NAEL-2; NOBVV

Let all chaste matrons, when they chance to see. Upon a Young Mother of Many Children. Robert Herrick. CaPo

Let All Created Things. Artis Seagrave. AH

Let all the family gather. Light Another Candle. Miriam Chaikin. NTCP

Let all the little poets be gathered together in classes. To School! Stevie Smith. FaBoEE

Let all the nation judge it. (LL) I'll Sail upon the Dog-Star. Thomas D'Urfey. FaBoCh; OxBoLi

Let all the walls. In Chalk Rooms. Aina Kraujiete, *Latvian*. CEEP, *tr. by* Inara Cedrins

Let all the world in ev'ry corner sing / My God and King. Antiphon. George Herbert. PeECV

Let all who will. Militant. Langston Hughes. PoBA

Let Allen's eyes be a jukebox of light plugged into the navel of Whitman's verb. Leaps over the Aisle of Syllogism. David Chapman Berry. BXAP

Let America Be America Again. Langston Hughes. AF; AiP

Let Anaiah bless with the Dragon-fly, who sails over the pond by the wood-side and feedeth on the cresses. Christopher Smart. FaBoVe, *ll.* 100–113 *Fr.* Fragment A. *Fr.* Jubilate Agno.

Let Aphrodite herself. Manifesto. Agathias, *Greek*. GrAn, *tr. by* Dudley Fitts

Let Archimedes loud his glasses' glory roar. Her Eyes. Daniel Casper von Lohenstein, *German*. GePo, *tr. by* George C. Schoolfield

Let baths and wine-butts be November's due. November. Folgore da San Geminiano. *Fr.* Sonnets of the Months. AWP, *tr. by* D. G. Rossetti

Let be a blind and teichit be a bairn. Mark Alexander Boyd. *See* Sonet: "Fra bank [*or* banc] to bank [*or* banc], fra wood [*or* wod] to wood [*or* wod] I rin."

Let but the son of earth. The Ages of Man. Abraham ibn Ezra, *Hebrew*. TrJP, *tr. by* Nina Davis Salaman

Let but thy voice engender with the string. Upon Her Voice. Robert Herrick. CaPo

Let by Rain. Edward Taylor. *See* An Address to the Soul Occasioned by a Rain.

Let Christian Hearts Rejoice Today. *Unknown, French*. AH, *tr. by* Francis X. Curley

Let Christmas celebrate greenly. For the fir is king. Jubilate Herbis. Norma Farber. PChr

Let clownish Cymon, in fond rustic strains. St. Anthony and His Pig; a Cantata. Frederick Forrest. NOEC

Let dainty wits cry on the sisters nine. Sonnet 3. Sir Philip Sidney. NoSic; OAEL-1; Son *Fr.* Astrophil and Stella. AAS; SiPS

Let day, let night, come no more. Elegy. Auvaiyar, *Tamil*. PLW, *tr. by* A. K. Ramanujan

Let dirty streets be paved with flow'ry green. *Unknown*. NOEC *Fr.* The Comparison.

Let due civilities be strictly paid. John Gay. OAEL-1 *Fr.* Trivia; or, The Art of Walking the Streets of London.

Let each fair maid, who fears to be disgraced. Soame Jenyns. ECEV *Fr.* The Art of Dancing.

Let each man first seek out his proper totem. A Joyful Noise. Donald Finkel. CoAP

Let Elizur[e] rejoice with the Partridge, who is a prisoner of state and is proud of his keepers. Christopher Smart. PoEL-3 *Fr.* Fragment B. *Fr.* Jubilate Agno.

Let 'em censure: what care I? In Imitation of Anacreon. Matthew Prior. FaBoEE

Let Ephah rejoice with Buprestis, the Lord endue us with temperance and humanity, till every cow have her mate! Christopher Smart. NOEC *Fr.* Fragment B. *Fr.* Jubilate Agno.

Let Evening Come. Jane Kenyon. LoL

Let[t] folly praise that fancy [*or* phancy] loves, I praise and love that Child[e]. A Child[e] My Choice [*or* Choyse]. Robert Southwell. PeECV

Let fools great Cupid's yoke disdain. Song: The Willing Prisoner to His Mistress. Thomas Carew. CaPo

Let foreign [*or* forrain] nations of their language boast. The Son[ne]. George Herbert. GeHe; PeECV; SeCP

Let gleaming motes of hayseed in the barn. Moments of Summer. Rachel Hadas. RA

Let go of the present and death. Once Again. Liz Sohappy Bahe. CDW

Let go the whore of Babylon. Miles Coverdale. ChIV-2

Let Grace conduct thee to the paths of peace. Francis Quarles. ESCV *Fr.* Emblems.

Let Happiness smile, as she wings their sweet hours. (LL) The Stolen White Girl. John Rollin Ridge. PAR; PaTW

Let her lie naked here, my hand resting. News of the World III. George Barker. FaBoTw; LiTM

Let her who walks in Paphos. Lais. Hilda Doolittle. MoAmPo

Let Heroes Account to Love. Alan Dugan. NoAM

Let him answer as he will. The Companion. Edwin Arlington Robinson. NoAM

Let him kiss me with the kisses of his mouth. The Song of Songs. Bible, *O.T.* AWP

Let Him Return. Leona Hill. PoToHe

Let him who may. To Be Recited to Flossie on Her Birthday. William Carlos Williams. VGW

Let him with kisses of his mouth. *Unknown*. AH; ChIV-1

Let it be alleys. Let it be a hall. A Lovely Love. Gwendolyn Brooks. BPo; NAAAL

Let it be forgotten, as a flower is forgotten. Song. Sara Teasdale. MoAmPo; PoA

Let it be Sabbath, Sabbath! Eternal Sabbath. Isaac Leibush Peretz, *Yiddish*. TrJP, *tr. by* Joseph Leftwich

Let it disturb no more at first. Fountain. Elizabeth Jennings. WPE

Let it end here where the blueprint. Making Chicago. Dennis Schmitz. LCAP-2

Let It Go. William Empson. FaBoMo; OxBSP; OxBTC

Let it no longer be a forlorn[e] hope. On the Baptized Ethiopian. Richard Crashaw. ChIV-2; FaBoEE; NoP-4

Let it not come near me, let it not. Fragment for the Dark. Elizabeth Jennings. FaBoWP

Let it not come unto you, all ye that pass by. Desolation in Zion. Bible, *O.T.* TrJP *Fr.* Lamentations.

Let it not your wonder move. His Excuse for Loving. Ben Jonson. NOSC; PoEL-2 *Fr.* A Celebration of Charis in Ten Lyric[k] Pieces [*or* Peeces]. BeJo; OxAEP-1; SeCP

Let kings command, and do[e] the best they may. The Power in the People. Robert Herrick. CaPo

Let love come under your roof. Carol for Advent. John Heath-Stubbs. OxBC

Let Man toil to win his living. A Song for the Workers. Eliza Cook. VWP

Let man's [*or* mans] soul [*or* Soule] be a sphere [*or* Spheare], and then, in this. Good Friday [*or* Goodfriday], 1613. Riding Westward. Donne. ChIV-2; ESCV; FSCP; InPS-3; MeLP; NAEL-1; NOCV; NOSC; NoP-4; OAEL-1; PBRV; PeECV; PoE; PoEL-2; SeCP; TFi

Let Me Be a Giver. Mary Carolyn Davies. PoToHe

Let me be a little kinder[, let me be a little blinder]. (My Daily Creed). *Unknown*. CTV; PFE; PWR

Let me be a mummy. Wake me up. Some Futureplans. David Avidan, *Hebrew*. IP, *tr. by* Warren Bargad *and* Stanley F. Chyet

Let me be at the place of the castle. Psalm Concerning the Castle. Denise Levertov. TwCP; WPE

Let me be buried as flesh, not burned, I say. Earth Buried. Kenneth Mackenzie. CBAP

Let me be buried in the rain. Invocation. Helene Johnson. NAAAL; SAGP

Let me be formed with stone. Instructions for the Erection of a Statue to Myself in Central Park. Colette Inez. CMAP

Let Me Be Held When the Longing Comes. Stephany Fuller. BPo

Let me be my own fool. A Counterpoint. Robert Creeley. NeAP

Let me be the great nail holding a skyscraper through blue nights into / white stars. (LL) Prayers of Steel. Carl Sandburg. CMoP; MoAmPo; SSCS; TrCP

Let me be what I am, as Virgil cold. An Elegy [*or* Elegie]. Ben Jonson. PoEL-2; SeCP

Let me call a ghost. Song of Three Smiles. W. S. Merwin. CoAP; NOBA; VGW

Let me confess. I'm sick of these sestinas. My Confessional Sestina. Dana Gioia. RA

Let me confess that we two must be twain. Sonnet 36. Shakespeare. HeIP-4; PBRV *Fr.* Sonnets.

Let me die a youngman's death. Roger McGough. PeLV

Let me die and not tremble at death. Imploring to Be Resigned at Death. George Moses Horton. AAP

Let me die in the Spring, said a sweet young girl. The Time to Die. Matilda Caroline Edwards. PWR

Let me do my work each day. A Prayer. Max Ehrmann. BLPA; FaBoBe; PoToHe

Let me enjoy the earth no less. Thomas Hardy. AWP; NoAM

Let me feed full, till that I fart, say[e]s Jill. (LL) Upon Jack and Jill: Epigram. Robert Herrick. CaPo; NAEL-1

Let me gallop, let me go. *Unknown, Chinese*. SuSp, *tr. by* C. H. Wang

Let me give something!—as the years unfold. Frederick Goddard Tuckerman. APN-2 *Fr.* Sonnets.

Let me give something!—though my spring be done. Frederick Goddard Tuckerman. APN-2 *Fr.* Sonnets.

Let me go forth, and share. Ode in May. Sir William Watson. OBEV

Let Me Go Warm. Luis de Góngora y Argote, *Spanish*. AWP, *tr. by* Longfellow

Let Me Go Where Saints Are Going. Lewis Hartsough. AH

Let me go where'er I will. Music. Ralph Waldo Emerson. CTV

Let Me Grow Lovely. Karle Wilson Baker. BLPA; FaBoBe

Let me hide myself in thee. (LL) A Living and Dying Prayer for the Holiest Believer in the World. Augustus Montague Toplady. ECEV; FaPoR; NOCV; NOEC; SCGP

Let Me Hold Your Hand. Kalju Lepik, *Estonian*. CEEP, *tr. by* Ivar Ivask

Let me lament the exodus of so many men from their. Recitative. Iwan Goll. PeFWW, *tr. by* Patrick Bridgwater *Fr.* Requiem for the Dead of Europe.

Let me lay it to you gently, Mr. Gone! Ray Bremser. NeAP *Fr.* Poem of Holy Madness.

Let me make the songs for the people. Songs for the People. Frances Ellen Watkins Harper. AAP; NAAAL; PWR

Let me move slowly through the street. The Crowded Street. William Cullen Bryant. NCAP

Let me no more, my love, be what I've seemed to you. Sulpicia to Cerinthus. Sulpicia, *Latin*. OBCVT, *tr. by* Allen Tate

Let me not die for ever, when I'm gone. A Wish. Frances Anne Kemble. WPE

Let me not live, if I not love. On Himselfe. Robert Herrick. CaPo

Let me not love thee, if I love thee not. (LL) Affliction (1). George Herbert. ESCV; FHYEP; FMP; FSCP; GeHe; MeLP; NAEL-1; NOBE; NOSC; NoP-4; SeCP

Let me not thirst with this Hock at my Lip. Emily Dickinson. WPoS

Let me not to the marriage of true minds. Sonnet 116. Shakespeare. AEP; APAD; AWP; CABP; ClHu; EBEvV; EnLoPo; GBL; GLoP; GSo; GTBS-P; HAP; HeIP-4; ITG; ImPo; InPS-3; LoP; NAEL-1; NIP-4; NOBE; NoSic; OAEL-1; OBEV; OxAEP-1; OxBM; PBMP; PFE; PoE; PoEL-2; PoPoPo; PoRA; Poetr; SAGP; SCGP; SCV; SoSe-8; Son; TFi; TRP; UnPo; WeW-3 *Fr.* Sonnets.

Let me obtain forgiveness of thee, Samson. Milton. EBEV *Fr.* Samson Agonistes. FHYEP; OAEL-1; PoEL-3

Let me open mama your 3 corner box. Blues for Franks Wooten. Tom Weatherly. GT; NBV

Let me out in the dark, let me go, let me go! (LL) Divorce. Anna Wickham. SAGP

Let me play to you tunes without measure or end. Bagpipe Music. "Hugh MacDiarmid." OAEL-2

Let me pour [*or* powre] forth. A Valediction: Of Weeping. Donne. ESCV; FHYEP; FSCP; HAP; HeIP-4; InPS-3; MeLP; NAEL-1; NOSC; NoP-4; OAEL-1; PBRV; PoE; SCGP; SeCP; WeW-3

Let me pray alone in autumn. Prayer in Autumn. Hyonsung Kim, *Korean*. CKP, *tr. by* Jaihiun Kim

Let me retell a story, rather old. The Two Wooden Men. Huy Cận, *Vietnamese*. AVP, *tr. by* Huỳnh Sanh Thông

Let me ryke up to dight that tear. Robert Burns. *Fr.* Love and Liberty—A Cantata. NOBRP; NOEC

"Let me see if Philip can." The Story of Fidgety Philip. Heinrich Hoffmann, *German*. ACTP; OxBChV

Let me see, let me see; is not the leaf turned down. Shakespeare. OxBSn *Fr.* Julius Caesar.

Let me see you. Mirabai, *Hindi*. BoWoP, *tr. by* Willis Barnstone *and* Usha Nilsson

Let me send you some words, a little wish. A New Year's Wish for a Little Refugee. Trần Mộng Tú, *Vietnamese*. AVP, *tr. by* Huỳnh Sanh Thông

Let me show you my love. Webern. Thomas William Shapcott. *Fr.* Piano Pieces. CBAP

Let Me Sing of My Well-beloved. Bible, *O.T.* TrJP *Fr.* Isaiah.

Let me sleep this night away. Upon Himselfe Being Buried. Robert Herrick. PBRV

Let me strap / the baby in the seat. If He Let Us Go Now. Shirley Williams. BoWoP

Let me take this other glove off. In Westminster Abbey. John Betjeman. CMoP; InPK-6; NBLV; NIP-4; NOBL; NoAM; OAEL-2; OBSV; OxAEP-2; TOF

Let me tell to you the story. Edith Agnew. PChr

Let me tell you a little story. Miss Gee. W. H. Auden. EBNV; OxBTC; UV

Let me tell you a little story / About Miss Edith Gee. A Moral Tale. Roger Woddis. UV

Let me tell you the story of how I began. Song: Lift-Boy. Robert Graves. NTP; OxAEP-2

Let me thy Angell bee, bee thou my Lord. (LL) Am I thy gold? Or purse, Lord, for thy wealth. Edward Taylor. MeMAP; NOSC; OxBA; TAP

Let me today do something that will take. A Morning Prayer. Ella Wheeler Wilcox. PoToHe

Let me work. Carl Sandburg. *See* Grass.

Let me yet hold your hand. Let Me Hold Your Hand. Kalju Lepik, *Estonian*. CEEP, *tr. by* Ivar Ivask

Let men take note of her, touching her shyness. The Gift of Song. Anthony Hecht. NYBP

Let Mine Eyes See Thee. Saint Theresa of Avila. *Spanish*. AWP, *tr. by* Arthur Symons

Let Mother Earth now deck herself in flowers. Long Their Coupled Joys Maintain. Sir Philip Sidney, *English*. ITG, *tr. by* Robert Hass; OxAEP-1; SiPS *Fr.* Arcadia.

"Let my people go!" (LL) Go down, Moses. *Unknown*. AH; BPo; BkSV; CrDW; NAAAL; NOBA; NoP-4; PeECV

Let My People Go, *see also* Go Down, Moses. *Unknown*. APN-2

Let my sweet song be pleasing unto Thee. Love Song. Judah Halevi, *Hebrew*. TrJP, *tr. by* Nina Davis Salaman

Let my words. Prayer. Joseph Bruchac. UnSA

Let no blasphemer till the sacred earth. Benediction. Mark Turbyfill. PoA

Let No Charitable Hope. Elinor Wylie. ColAP; LiLi; LiTM; MoAmPo; NAAL-2; NALW; NMM-2; OxBA; OxBSP; PiM; VGW

Let no girl wait on you on that day when you bind your wild. The Alchemy of Day. Anne Hébert, *French*. BoWoP, *tr. by* A. Poulin, Jr.

Let no man deem that he is free! (LL) The Storm Cone. Rudyard Kipling. NoAM; OxBTC

Let no tempest subside no rock stagger. In Memory of a Black Union Leader. Aimé Césaire, *French*. VCWP, *tr. by* Clayton Eshleman *and* Annette Smith

Let no word with its thinking threat. A La Une. Marie Ponsot. CLPP

Let Noah build an ark out of the old lady's shoe and. Third Psalm. Anne Sexton. NALW *Fr.* O Ye Tongues.

Let none look at *me*! (LL) Mother and Poet. Elizabeth Barrett Browning. NAEL-2; NALW; VWP

Let not a star suspect the mystery! Embalmment. "Michael Field." VWP

Let not Death boast his conquering power. On Eleanor Freeman, Who Died 1650, Aged 21. *Unknown*. OBEV

Let not his humble vesture make thee blind. The Poor Scholar. Abraham ibn Chasdai, *Hebrew*. TrJP, *tr. by* J. Chotzner

Let not my titles, crowns, and worldly honors. (To the Virgin). Maria De' Medici, *Italian*. WPoS, *tr. by* Laura Anna Stortoni *and* Mary Prentice Lillie

Let not old age disgrace my high desire. Old Age. Sir Philip Sidney. SiPS *Fr.* Arcadia.

Let not one sparke of filthy lustfull fyre. Sonnet 83. Edmund Spenser. *Fr.* Amoretti. AAS

Let not our naive labours have been in vain! (LL)   A Disused Shed in Co. Wexford. Derek Mahon. BiHa; CABP; CIP-2; FaBoPV; NOIV; NoP-4; OxBC; PBCIP; PNI

Let not the rugged brow the rhymes accuse. From Psyche. Mary Tighe. NoP-4 *Fr.* Psyche, with Other Poems, 3rd edition.

Let not the sluggish sleep. Song. *Unknown.* OxBSP

Let not the title of my verse offend. The Natural Child. Helen Leigh. ECWP; WoRP

Let not thy beauty make thee proud. Aurelian Townshend. NOSC

Let not young souls be smothered out before. The Leaden-eyed. Vachel Lindsay. APAD; CMoP; FaBoEE; ImPo; OxBSP; PBMP; PoE; RB

Let Not Your Hart Be Truble. James Seay. WeT

Let not your heart be troubled. John 14:1–2. Mary Elizabeth Fullerton. GI *Fr.* St. John.

Let nothing disturb thee. Bookmark. Saint of Theresa Avila. *Spanish.* AWP, tr. by Longfellow

Let nothing disturb thee. (Lines Written on a Bookmark Found in Her Breviary). Teresa de Cepeda Y Ahumada, *Spanish.* WPoS, tr. by Henry Wadsworth Longfellow

Let now thy power be great O Lord. Numeri XIII. John Hall. ChIV-1

Let Observation, shuddering the While. F. Mullen. UV

Let Observation with extensive View. The Vanity of Human Wishes [The Tenth Satire of Juvenal Imitated]. Samuel Johnson. CABP; EBEV; ECEV; NOEC; NoP-4; OAEL-1; OBCVT; OxAEP-1; PoEL-3; TFi; UV

Let oken club now strike, and poast of might. Seneca. OBVE, tr. by Jasper Heywood. *Fr.* Hercules Furens.

Let other mount aloft, let other sore. Seneca. OBVE, tr. by John Studley *Fr.* Hercules Oetaeus.

Let other people come as streams. Charles Reznikoff. VGW

Let other poets raise a fracas. Scotch Drink. Robert Burns. ChIV-1

Let others cheer the winning man. A Smile. *Unknown.* BLPA

Let others creep by timid steps, and slow. A Certain Type of Scientist Speaks. Alexander Pope. ECEV *Fr.* Yet, yet a moment, one dim ray of light. NAEL-1; OAEL-1; PoEL-3 *Fr.* The Dunciad.

Let others draw from smiling skies their theme. The Vision of the Night. Philip Freneau. NAAL-1; NAAL-3 *Fr.* The House of Night.

Let others from the town retire. Nonpareil. Matthew Prior. EnLoPo

Let others hail the holidays with laughter. Ausiàs March, *Catalan.* STV, tr. by John Frederick Nims

Let others pile their swelling ingots high. A Pastoral Elegy. Tibullus, *Latin.* AWP, tr. by Sir Charles Abraham Elton

Let others pray for the passenger pigeon. Elegy for the Giant Tortoises. Margaret Atwood. BoWoP

Let others probe the mystery if they can. The Right Thing. Theodore Roethke. PeECV

Let others sing of knights and paladins [or palladines]. 46. Samuel Daniel. AAS; NOBE; NoSic; OBEV; SCGP *Fr.* To Delia.

Let others to the Printing Presse run fast. Posting to Printing. Robert Herrick. PBRV

Let passion's swelling tide my senses drown! Ibnu 'l-Farid, *Persian.* TOF, tr. by R. A. Nicholson

Let peace lie on lulled lips: I will not say. (LL) The Contretemps. Thomas Hardy. CMoP; LiTM

Let Peter rejoice with the Moon Fish who keeps up the life in the waters by night. Christopher Smart. ChIV-2 *Fr.* Fragment B. *Fr.* Jubilate Agno.

Let poetry be like a key. Ars Poetica. Vincente Huidobro, *Spanish.* PFTM, tr. by David Guss

Let poets praise the blossom of wild Spring. Spring in London. John Bingham Morton. OBCoV

Let poets praise the softer winds of spring. John Bingham Morton. FaBoEE

Let rigid Cato read these lines of mine. (LL) When He Would Have His Verses Read. Robert Herrick. BeJo; CaPo; CavPo; NOBE; NOSC; SCGP

Let sailors watch the waning Pleiades. Cleonicos. Edward Cracroft Lefroy. AWP *Fr.* Echoes from Theocritus.

Let school-masters puzzle their brain. Song. Oliver Goldsmith. BIrV; NOIV; PoRA *Fr.* She Stoops to Conquer.

Let scoffers mock, let unbelief deny. Albery Allson Whitman. AAP *Fr.* The Octoroon.

Let Shobi rejoice with the Kastrel—blessed be the name JESUS in falconry and in the MALL. Christopher Smart. NOEC *Fr.* Fragment B. *Fr.* Jubilate Agno.

Let shrieking steel and gray stone be set. Psalmodist. Mani Leib, *Yiddish.* CEEP, tr. by David G. Roskies *and* Hillel Schwartz

Let sleep take her, let sleep take her, let sleep. Fourth Song the Night Nurse Sang. Robert Duncan. VGW

Let Sol his annual journeys run. Hint from Voiture. William Shenstone. EnLoPo

Let some sad trumpeter stand. 'Back on Times Square, Dreaming of Times Square'. Allen Ginsberg. CLPP; PiM; PoE

Let Sporus tremble--A What? that thing of silk. Sporus. Alexander Pope. AWP; NOBE; OBSV; SCV *Fr.* Epistle to Dr. Arbuthnot. FHYEP; InPS-3; NoP-4; OAEL-1; OxAEP-1; PoE; PoEL-3; TFi

Let the ascetics sing of the garden of Paradise. Asadullah Khan Ghalib, *Urdu.* EnlH, tr. by Jane Hirshfield

Let the bells ring, and let the boys sing. John Fletcher. SCGP *Fr.* The Spanish Curate.

Let the bird of loudest [or lowdest] lay. The Phoenix and the Turtle. Shakespeare. CABP; ImPo; NOBE; NoP-4; NoSic; OAEL-1; OBEV; OxAEP-1; PBRV; PeECV; PoEL-2; SCGP

Let the boy try along this bayonet-blade. Arms and the Boy. Wilfred Owen. CMoP; HAP; ImPo; LiTM; MoBrPo; OAEL-1; OAEL-2; OxBSP; PBMP; PFE; PoE; Poetr; SAGP; WeW-3

Let the crows go by hawking their caw and caw. River Roads. Carl Sandburg. VGW

Let the damned ride their earwigs to Hell, but let me not join them. Rock Pilgrim. Herbert Edward Palmer. OxBTC

Let the Day Perish [Wherein I Was Born]. Bible, O.T. OBVE; TrJP *Fr.* Job. NAWM-1

(Job's Curse.) AWP

Let the Deep Organ Swell. Constantine Pise. AH

Let the eugenist reach for his gun! Limerick. Stanley J. Sharpless. PeLi

Let the fire of my body. Prayer for a Tenspeed Heart. Barbara Hendryson. CrSp

Let the flowers make a journey. The Fury of Flowers and Worms. Anne Sexton. BoWoP

Let the four-clustered ivy flourish about you, Anacreon. Antipater of Sidon. HePo, tr. by Barbara Hughes Fowler *Fr.* Epigrams.

Let the greater praise belong. (LL) Lament for the Death of Thomas Davis. Sir Samuel Ferguson. BIrV; NOIV

Let the hardened by a sharp soldier's life. Horace. *See* 3.2.

Let the Light Enter! Frances Ellen Watkins Harper. PAR

Let the light of late afternoon. Let Evening Come. Jane Kenyon. LoL

Let the limited years of life do nothing for the limitless years of death! (What do you suppose death will do, then?). (LL) Respondez! Respondez! / (The war is completed—the price is paid—the title is settled beyond recall). Walt Whitman. APN-1; NoAM; PoEL-5

Let the lover be disgraceful, crazy. Jelaluddin Rumi. RaBo, tr. by John Moyne *and* Coleman Barks *Fr.* Three Quatrains.

Let the male Poets their male *Phoebus* chuse. To the Excellent Orinda. "Philo-Philippa." KTR

Let the memorial hill remember, instead of me. Yehuda Amichai. PoSu, tr. by Yehuda Amichai *and* Ted Hughes *Fr.* Patriotic Songs.

Let the Midnight Special. Joseph Bruchac. GM

Let the night keep. Night. William Rose Benét. MoAmPo

Let the Nile cloak his head in the clouds, and defy. On the Discoveries of Captain Lewis. Joel Barlow. AmPP

Let the only consistency. In the Fall. "Hugh MacDiarmid." FaBoMo; InPS-3 *Fr.* In Memoriam James Joyce.

Let the pines rock in torment of the storm. Horatian Ode. Joseph Warren Beach. PoA

Let the Priests of the Raven of dawn, no longer in deadly black. Chorus. William Blake. *Fr.* The Marriage of Heaven and Hell. NAEL-2; NOBRP; OAEL-2

Let the rain come. Prayer. Ioan Alexandru, *Romanian.* CEEP, tr. by Dan Duescu

Let the rain embrace me from my temples to my ankles. Dance in the Rain. Ana Blandiana, *Romanian.* CEEP, tr. by Irina Livezeanu

Let the rain kiss you. April Rain Song. Langston Hughes. AYFP; ImGa; NOxBChV; NTCP; OBCA

Let the rain plunge radiant. The Way Through. Denise Levertov. NeAP; PoM

Let the Rest of the World Go By. J. Keirn Brennan. UnPo

Let the rich man fill his belly. Antonio Machado Ruiz. *Fr.* Spanish Folk Songs. AWP, tr. by Havelock Ellis

Let the snake wait under. A Sort of a Song. William Carlos Williams. HoPM; NAAL-2; NoP-4; OxBSP; TAP

Let the speckled hens praise her. The Speckled Hen's Morning Song to Biddy Early. Nancy Willard. FFC

Let the superstitious wife. Another. Robert Herrick. BeJo

Let the tale's sailor from a Christian voyage. Dylan Thomas. CMoP; FaBoMo; OAEL-2 *Fr.* A Sequence of Sonnets.

Let the wick burn low: and suddenly I remember. The Sleepers. Randolph Stow. *Fr.* Thailand Railway. CBAP

Let the wind blow, for many a man shall die. (LL) Nostalgia. Karl Shapiro. CMoP; CoAP; TrJP; TwCP

Let the wood be pulled. Surprised by Me. Walter Darring. NYBP

Let the world's sharpness, like a clasping knife. Sonnet. Elizabeth Barrett Browning. NOBVV *Fr.* Sonnets from the Portuguese.

Let th'earth deny thee fruit, and stream. Ovid. OBCVT, *tr. by* Thomas Underdowne. *Fr.* Ibis.

Let them bestow on every airt[h] a limb. His Metrical Prayer. James Graham, Marquess of Montrose. ChIV-2; FaBoEE; NOSC; OxBS

Let them bury your big eyes. Elegy. Edna St. Vincent Millay. CMoP; MoAmPo; OxBA; PoRA *Fr.* Memorial to D. C.

Let Them Choose Paths. Odia Ofeimun. HBAPE

("To see the asphalt in the chaste forest.") (LL) PBMAP

Let them count scalps under the barroom wall. Lying in a Yuma Saloon. Jim Barnes. CDW

Let them grow afraid. Warning. Alicia Ostriker. DeD

Let them keep it. And Was Not Improved. Lerone Bennett Jr. PoBA

Let them lie perilous and beautiful. (LL) The Equilibrists. John Crowe Ransom. CMoP; FuPo; HAP; LiTM; MeMAP; MoP; NAAL-2; NOBA; NoAM; OxBA; TAP

Let them not make me a stone and let them not spill me / Otherwise kill me. (LL) Prayer Before Birth. Louis MacNeice. EBEvV; FaBoVe; GTBS-P; PBMP; PNI; TIRV; TwCP

Let them rest peacefully in ice. A Feather Plucked from the Tail of the Fiery Hen. Novica Tadic, *Serbo-Croatian.* HSix, *tr. by* Charles Simic

Let them return, saying you blush again for the great Great-grandmother. The Mango Tree. Hart Crane. PFTM

Let them say to my lover. Amor Mysticus. Sister Marcela de Carpio de San Felix, *Spanish.* AWP, *tr. by* John Hay

Let there be commerce between us. (LL) A Pact. Ezra Pound. AmPP; ColAP; MeMAP; MoP; NAAL-2; NOBA; NoAM; OxBA; TAP

Let there be laid, when I am dead. Posthumous Coquetry. Théophile Gautier, *French.* AWP; PeVV, *tr. by* Arthur Symons

Let there be life, said God. And what He wrought. The Power and the Glory. Siegfried Sassoon. OBMV

Let There Be Light! D. H. Lawrence. ChIV-1; KSG

Let There Be Light. William M. Vories. AH

Let there be many windows to your soul. Progress. Ella Wheeler Wilcox. BLPA

Let There Be New Flowering. Lucille Clifton. PiM

Let there be no flowery banks. A Garden of Situations. Jack Anderson. PoA

Let there be within these phantom walls. Dream House. Catherine Parmenter-Newell. PoToHe

Let this life of worry. Palladas, *Greek.* PGA, *tr. by* Kenneth Rexroth

Let those grasses. Tanka. Yosano Tekkan, *Japanese.* MJT, *tr. by* Makoto Ueda

Let those toil for gold who please. Solitude: An Ode. James Grainger. ECEV

Let those who are in favour with their stars. Sonnet 25. Shakespeare. OxAEP-1; SCGP *Fr.* Sonnets.

Let those with cost deck their ill-fashioned clay. To ———. Thomas Rymer. OxBSP

Let Thy Kingdom. *Unknown.* AH

Let thy tears, Le Vayer, let them flow. To Monsieur de la Mothe le Vayer. Molière, *French.* AWP, *tr. by* Austin Dobson

Let Tyrants Shake Their Iron Rod. William Billings. AH

Let uh revolution come. U Name This One. Carolyn M. Rodgers. BlSi; NMM-2; PoBA

Let us abandon then our gardens and go home. Justice Denied in Massachusetts. Edna St. Vincent Millay. AiP; MoAmPo

Let us await the great American novel! Critical Observations. Archibald MacLeish. OBAL

Let Us Be Frank. Alfred Cruickshank. PBCV

Let us be guests in one another's house. Any Wife or Husband. Carol Haynes. BLPA; PoToHe

Let us be honest; the lady was not a harlot until she married a. Soiled Dove. Carl Sandburg. SAGP

Let us be still. To Usward. Gwendolyn B. Bennett. BlSi

Let us become the overhanging day. Shelley. OAEL-2 *Fr.* Epipsychidion.

Let us begin and carry up this corpse. A Grammarian's Funeral. Robert Browning. NAEL-2; NOBVV; PeECV

Let Us Believe. Hildegarde Flanner. WPE

Let Us Break Bread Together. *Unknown.* AH

Let us bribe the Moon God. Prince Yuhara, *Japanese.* OHMPJ, *tr. by* Kenneth Rexroth

Let us but out those heavy dice. Birth. Gabriela Melinescu, *Romanian.* BoWoP, *tr. by* Willis Barnstone *and* Matei Calinescu

Let us celebrate the single-cloaked beings. Psalm to the Creatures. Gwilym R. Jones, *Welsh.* OBWVE, *tr. by* Joseph P. Clancy

Let Us Cheer the Weary Traveler. *Unknown.* AH

Let Us Consider Where the Great Men Are. Delmore Schwartz. MoAmPo *Fr.* Shenandoah.

Let us dance and let us sing. The Fairy Ring. *Unknown.* BoTP

Let us describe how they went. It was a very windy night and the road. Gertrude Stein. PFTM

Let us do, or die! (LL) Scots, wha hae wi' Wallace bled. Robert Burns. EBEvV; FaBoCh; FaPoR; NAEL-2; OAEL-1; OxBS

Let Us Drink. Alcaeus, *Greek.* AWP, *tr. by* John Hermann Merivale

Let us drink and be merry, dance, joke, and rejoice [*or* rejoyce]. The Careless Gallant. Thomas Jordan. HAP; NOBE; OBEV; OxBoLi; PeLV

Let us drink, and pledge the night, *see also* "Why wait we for the torches lights?" An Evening Song. Alcaeus, *Greek.* GrIP, *tr. by* James S. Easby-Smith

Let us effect a moratorium on things. Scalpel in Hand. Marjorie Welish. FTOS

Let us exchange thoughts. Carnival. Martin Sorescu, *Romanian.* CEEP, *tr. by* Dan Duescu

Let us forgive Ty Kendricks. Southern Cop. Sterling Brown. SoSe-8

Let us gather hand in hand. A Medieval Poem of the Nativity. *Unknown.* TrCP

Let us give thanks to God above. Thanksgiving. Lizelia Augusta Jenkins Moorer. CBWP-3

Let us give up our trips. Direction. Barbara Guest. WPE

Let us go and make our visit. T. S. Eliot. *See* The Love Song of J. Alfred Prufrock.

Let us go hence, my songs; she will not hear. A Leave-taking. Swinburne. CBLP; CH; NOBE; NOBVV; OBNC; PoEL-5; PoLF

Let us go hence: the night is now at hand. A Last Word. Ernest Christopher Dowson. ADE; GSo; MoBrPo

Let us go into the temple. Nossis, *Greek.* PGA, *tr. by* Kenneth Rexroth

Let us go on then. Free Radicals. James Sherry. FTOS

Let us go then, you and I. T. S. Eliot. *Fr.* The Love Song of J. Alfred Prufrock. AWP; AmPP; CMoP; ClHu; ColAP; EBEV; EBEvV; HAP; HeIP-4; HoPM; InPK-6; InPS-3; LiTM; MoAmPo; MoP; NAAL-2; NAEL-2; NAWM-2; NOBA; NOBE; NoAM; NoP-4; OAEL-2; OxBTC; PFE; PiM; PoA; PoE; PoPoPo; PoRA; Poetr; SAGP; SoSe-8; TAP; TFi; TRP; TwCP; UV; WeW-3

Let us go to the temple. Nossis, *Greek.* GrAn, *tr. by* Sally Purcell

Let us have a rest about the sunset. To the Poets. *Unknown.* PeNZ

Let Us Have Peace. Nancy Byrd Turner. PoToHe

Let us have winter loving that the heart. Winter Love. Elizabeth Jennings. BoLoP

Let us honour if we can. Dedication. W. H. Auden. PeLV *Fr.* Shorts [1927–1932].

Let us leave our island woods grown dim and blue. Prayer. "Æ." TIRV

Let us leave talking of angelic hosts. Sonnet. Elinor Wylie. OxBA *Fr.* One Person.

Let us make the test. Say God wants you. Gnostics on Trial. Linda Gregg. EC2

Let us move the stone gentleman to the toadstool wood. The Stone Gentleman. James Reeves. OxBSP

Let us not speak, for the love we bear one another. In a Bath Teashop. John Betjeman. CBLP; EnLoPo

"Let Us Now Praise Famous Men." C. Day Lewis. CMoP

Let us now praise famous men. Our Fathers. Bible, Apocrypha. OBVE; TrJP *Fr.* Ecclesiasticus.

Let us pause to consider the English. England Expects. Ogden Nash. PeLV

Let us play, and dance, and sing. The Vision of Delight. Ben Jonson. PoEL-2

Let us praise our Maker, with true passion extol Him. Anthem. W. H. Auden. NOCG

Let us put on appropriate galoshes, letting them flap open. Walking in the Snow. David Wagoner. Poetr

Let us rejoice on our cots, for His nocturnal miracles. Lauds. John Berryman. HAP

Let us save the babies. The Babies. Mark Strand. NYBP

Let us say good-bye. Bags Packed and We Expected This. Ramona Wilson. VoR

Let us see, is this real. Pawnee War-Song. *Unknown, Pawnee Native American.* APN-2, *tr. by* Daniel Garrison Brinton

Let us sing of Federation. Federation. W. T. Goodge. NOBAu

Let us sing the sacred songs. (LL) Carriers of the Dream Wheel. N. Scott Momaday. ColAP

Let us sit by the hissing steam radiator a winter's day, grey wind pattering. Horses and Men in the Rain. Carl Sandburg. PoLF

Let us sleep now. (LL) Strange Meeting. Wilfred Owen. CMoP; EBEvV; FP; FaBoMo; GTBS-P; HeIP-4; HoPM; ImPo; MoBrPo; MoP; NAEL-2;

NOBE; NoAM; NoP-4; OAEL-2; OBWP; OxAEP-2; PeFWW; PoE; PoFWW; PoWW; RB; SCV; TFi

Let us sleep together here tonight. Kenneth Rexroth. APSN *Fr.* The Love Poems of Marichiko.

Let Us Strive to Do Something. Mrs. Henry Linden. CBWP-4

Let us synge unto the Lorde, for he is become glorious. Bible, *O.T.* OBVE, *tr. by* William Tyndale *Fr.* Exodus.

Let us take the road. The Highwaymen. John Gay. *Fr.* The Beggar's Opera. OAEL-1

Let us take to our hearts a lesson. The Tapestry Weavers. Anson G. Chester. BLPA

Let us thank Almighty God. Creatrix. Anna Wickham. MoBrPo

Let us tunnel. Ronald Johnson. *Fr.* Letters to Walt Whitman. VGW

Let us two a burden try. (LL) Robin Hood. Keats. AWP; SCGP

Let us use it while [*or* whilst] we may. Of Beauty. Sir Richard Fanshawe. BoLoP; GBL; OxBSP *Fr.* Il Pastor Fido.

Let us walk in the white snow. Velvet Shoes. Elinor Wylie. CH; MoAMpo; WHSW

Let us walk with this cone of light. Clair de Lune. Gwen Harwood. BMAP

Let us wash each other's body. Rufinus, *Greek.* GrAn, *tr. by* Alan Marshfield

Let us with a gladsome mind, *par. by* Milton. Bible, *O.T.* *See* Psalm 136.

Let who so lyst with might mace to raygne. Seneca. *See* Senec. Traged. ex Thyeste Chor. 2.

Let who will think[e] us dead, or wish our death. (LL) Begging Another, on Colour of Mending the Former. Ben Jonson. CBLP; PoEL-2

Let wits contest. The Posy [*or* Posie]. George Herbert. ChIV-1; NOSC

Let Words and Sense be set by thee. (LL) To Mr. Henry Lawes, Who Had Then Newly Set a Song of Mine in the Year 1635. Edmund Waller. BeJo; CTC; SeCP

Let Y stand for you who says. You. Kenneth Rexroth. HoPM *Fr.* A Bestiary. OBAL

Let you drag me here, without demurring. To Belinda. Goethe, *German.* STV, *tr. by* John Frederick Nims

Let your eyes look at old people. In Respect of the Elderly. Thomas Love Peacock. VoR

Let your longing for me, my love. Sulpicia, *Latin.* PBWP, *tr. by* John Dillon

Let your wandering fingers. The Sand Seer. Niyi Osundare. PBMAP

Let Zeus Record. Hilda Doolittle.
   "Stars wheel in purple, yours is not so rare." MoAMpo; NOBA; TAP

Lethargic vs violence of each other for los americanos, The. Anecdotes of the Late War. Charles Olson. CBCWP

Lethargy. Donald Justice. CRP

Lethargy of evil in her eyes—The, The. A Dying Viper. "Michael Field." ADE; CABP

Lethe. Hilda Doolittle. CMoP; FaBoWP; LiTM; MoAMpo; PoRA; VGW

Lethe had passed those lips, and he knew all. (LL) He found her by the ocean's moaning verge. George Meredith. EnVR; NoP-4; OAEL-2

Let's All Hear It for Mildred Bailey! James Schuyler. MoNo

Let's Be Merry. Christina Rossetti. TLR *Fr.* Sing-Song.

Let's build bridges here and there. Interracial. Georgia Johnson. TTY

Let's call for Hymen if agreed thou art. To Anthea. Robert Herrick. EP

LET'S CALL IT THE / COLLECTIVE CONSCIOUSNESS (WE'VE GOT). John Cage. APSN *Fr.* Diary: How to Improve the World (You Will Only Make Matters Worse).

Let's celebrate the yoyo-makers. Inventing the Filipino. Fatima Lim-Wilson. PUP-19

Let's contend no more, Love. A Woman's Last Word. Robert Browning. BLPA; FaBoBe; NAEL-2; RACG

Let's count the bodies over again. Counting Small-Boned Bodies. Robert Bly. CDa; SPE

Let's Do It. Noël Coward.
   "Mr. Irving Berlin." UV

Let's Do It, Let's Fall in Love. Cole Porter. PeLV; UV
   (Let's Do It.) OBAL

Let's dress up in grown-up clothes. Mary Ann Hoberman. TLR

Let's drink up: with wine, what original. Hedylos, *Greek.* GrAn, *tr. by* William Moebius

Let's enjoy, while the season invites us. "Giovinette, Che Fate All'Amore." Lorenzo Da Ponte. TrJP, *tr. by* Natalie MacFarren *Fr.* Don Giovanni.

Let's enter the literary scene. Limerick. *Unknown.* PeLi

Let's forget the many troubles. Charles L. H. Wagner. PoToHe

Let's get going. Leylâ Hanim, *Turkish.* PBWP, *tr. by* Tâlat S. Halman

Let's Get the Coachman Drunk. Vesna Parun, *Croatian.* CEEP, *tr. by* Peter Kastmiler

Let's go—much as that dog goes. Overland to the Islands. Denise Levertov. CoAMpo; PmAP; UnPo

Let's go rolling, rolling. Getting Dirty. Dorthi Charles. TLR

Let's go see Old Abe. Lincoln Monument: Washington. Langston Hughes. CBCWP

Let's go to the wood, says this pig. *Unknown.* OxNR

Let's go up to the hillside today. Play Song. Peter Clarke. PBA

Let's have a look at another five. (LL) In Divés' Dive. Robert Frost. GI; VGW

Let's have less nonsense from the friends of Joe. Less Nonsense. Sir Alan Patrick Herbert. OxBTC

Let's hear it for Dwayne Coburn, who was small. Body Bags. R. S. Gwynn. RA

Let's Hear it for the Limpet. Kit Wright. AYFP

Let's live, my Lesbia, and love. Catullus. *See* Carmen 5

Let's make a bureaucracy. On The Empress's Mind. John Ashbery. RACG

Let's not fool ourselves. Sentences. Nicanor Parra, *Spanish.* AF, *tr. by* Miller Williams

Let's not use eyes anymore. Dialogue—2 Dollmakers. Gregory Corso. NeAP

Let's play *La Migra.* La Migra. Pat Mora. PaTW; UnSA

Let's praise whoever planted those eight posts! Swinging. Ho Xuan Huong, *Vietnamese.* AVP, *tr. by* Huỳnh Sanh Thông

Let's put the cranes in an insane asylum for observation! George Marrow's 1011th Dream. Juhan Viiding, *Estonian.* CEEP, *tr. by* Ivar Ivask

Let's radio opinions, koorie side effects in death. No Grudge. Lionel Fogarty. BMAP

Let's Say. Bob Perelman. PmAP

Let's say it was Jesus. Who is Jesus? Why should Jesus be the name. Visions of Jesus. Jerome Rothenberg. APSN

Let's say that what I miss. What Happens. Robert Long. NAmP90

Let's See If I Have It Right. Stephen Dunn. CMAP

Let's see now. The idea of reverse seeing. Quartz Tractate. Brenda Hillman. Wel

Let's skip a few short years of hollow peace. George the Third. Byron. *Fr.* The Vision of Judgment. OAEL-2

Let's spit the two of us let's spit. Poem to Shout in the Ruins. Louis Aragon, *French.* PFTM, *tr. by* Geoffrey Young

"Let's start from Zeus." Strato, *Greek.* GrAn, *tr. by* Thomas Meyer

Let's step on daddy's head shout. Step on His Head. James Laughlin. IFJA; VGW

Let's sup before we go. (LL) Come, let's to bed. Mother Goose. LB; OxBoLi; OxNR

Let's take the train. One Fine Day. E. E. Cummings. GM

Let's Talk of Graves. Shakespeare. FaBoBe *Fr.* King Richard II.
   Death of Kings, The. TRP
   "For God's sake, let us sit upon the ground." HoPM

Let's talk of graves, of worms, and epitaphs. The Death of Kings. Shakespeare. TRP *Fr.* Let's Talk of Graves. FaBoBe *Fr.* King Richard II.

Let's talk to the swallows visiting us in summer. Talk to the Peach Tree. Sipho Sepamla. PBMAP

Let's tell the story of the man. Found and Lost. Robert Long. NAmP90

Let's to the Prado and make the most of time. (LL) How It Strikes a Contemporary. Robert Browning. CTC; EnVR; FaBoPV; GTBS-P; OAEL-2

Let's try the present hour. Eunuch Unique. Francis Picabia. PFTM, *tr. by* Tom Mandel

Let's write a poem about lazy people. The Lazy People. Shel Silverstein. NTCP

Letter. Yehuda Amichai, *Hebrew.* VCWP, *tr. by* Ted Hughes *and* Yehuda Amichai

Letter, The. W. H. Auden. FaBoTw; MoP; NoAM

Letter, The. Patricia Beer. OxBC

Letter. Alexander Bergman. TrJP

Letter, The. John Blight. CBAP

Letter. Wayne Dodd. CMAP

Letter. William Daniel Ehrhart. CDa

Letter. Janet Frame. PeNZ

Letter, A. Albert Goldbarth. PuP-15

Letter, A. Anthony Hecht. NYBP; OxBC

Letter. Langston Hughes. PoE *Fr.* Lenox Avenue Mural. HoPM

Letter, The. Lynda Hull. PUP-19

Letter. Amy Lowell. CPO; NALW

Letter. W. S. Merwin. HAP

Letter. Leonard Nathan. PBCAP

Letter, A. Dan Pagis, *Hebrew.* IP, *tr. by* Warren Bargad *and* Stanley F. Chyet

Letter, The. Po Chü-i, *Chinese.* ChiP, *tr. by* Arthur Waley

Letter, The. Elizabeth Riddell. LW; NOBAu

Letter. Mark Strand. NoAM

Letter, The. Tanka. Tawara Machi, *Japanese.* MJT, *tr. by* Makoto Ueda

Letter, The. Tennyson. TTTS

Letter. Iosif Pavlovich Utkin, *Russian.* TCRP, *tr. by* Lubov Yakovleva

Letter 5. Michael Palmer. FTOS *Fr.* Letters to Zanzotto.

Letter, A ("This kind o' sogerin' ain't a mite like our October trainin' "). James Russell Lowell. OxBA *Fr.* The Biglow Papers.

Letter, A ("Thrash away, you'll hev to rattle"). James Russell Lowell. AmPP; OxBA *Fr.* The Biglow Papers.

(Mr. Hosea Biglow Speaks.)

Letter: Blues. Elizabeth Alexander. RA

Letter comes from the city today, A. The Ballet of Happiness. James Seay. WeT

Letter Following. Aidan Carl Mathews. PBCIP

Letter for Allhallows, A. Peter Kane Dufault. NYBP

(Letter for All-Hallows (1949), A.) NoP-4

Letter for Duncan. Larry Eigner. FTOS; PoM

Letter for Marian, A. Thomas McGrath. VGW

Letter from a Black Soldier. Bill Anderson. VGW

Letter from a Captain in Country Quarters to his Corinna in Town, A. Isaac Hawkins Browne. ECEV

Letter from a Contract Worker. Antonio Jacinto, *Portuguese.* PBMAP

Letter from a Coward to a Hero. Robert Penn Warren. MoAmPo

Letter from a Girl to Her Own Old Age, A. Alice Thompson Meynell. MoBrPo; VWP

Letter, From a Lady in London to a Lady at Lausanne, A. Winthrop Mackworth Praed. *See* The Talented Man.

Letter from An Hoc (4), by a Seedbed. R. L. Barth. CDa

Letter from an Institution: III. Michael Ryan. AmPA

Letter from an Island. John Malcolm Brinnin. TAP

Letter from Aragon, A. John Cornford. OBWP

Letter from Artemisa in the Town, to Chloe [*or* Cloe], in the Country, A. John Wilmot, 2d Earl of Rochester. PoE

Letter from Berlin, A. Jon Stallworthy. MoP; OBWP; OxBC

Letter from Brooklyn, A. Derek Walcott. FP; OxBTC

Letter from Charles Lamb to Thomas Manning, 22 August 1801. Charles Lamb.

On Mackintosh. Ro

Letter from Chicago. May Sarton. NALW

Letter from Ephesos. Rufinus, *Greek.* GrAn, *tr. by* Alan Marshfield

Letter from Italy [to the Right Honourable Charles Lord Halifax], A. Joseph Addison. NOEC

Letter from Li Po, A. Conrad Potter Aiken.

"Winds of doctrine blow both ways at once, The." VGW

Letter from Mama Dot. Frederick D'Aguiar. PBCV

Letter from Mr Crashaw to the Countess of Denbigh. Richard Crashaw. *See* To the Noblest and Best of Ladies, the Countess of Denbigh, Perswading her to Resolution in Religion, and to render her selfe without further delay into the Communion of the Catholick Church.

Letter from my brother, A. Surroundings. Joseph A. Soldati. CDa

"Letter from my love today, A!" A Ballad of Hell. John Davidson. EBVV; HoPM; MoBrPo

Letter from Phillis Wheatley, A. Robert Earl Hayden. NAAL; NoAM

Letter from Pretoria Central Prison. Arthur Nortje. HBAPE

Letter from the Alpes-Maritimes. Marilyn Hacker. EOEF

Letter from the Blackstock Road. Robert Sheppard.

"Robin once lunched with Herbert Read at his club." NBrP

Letter from the Caribbean, A. Barbara Howes. CoAP; IMW; UnPo

Letter from the Pygmies, A. Theodore Weiss. VGW

Letter from Underground. Ronald G. Everson. MoCV

Letter I. George Crabbe. CABP *Fr.* The Borough.

Letter II. W. S. Graham. FaBoTC

Letter in Winter. Raymond R. Patterson. PoBA

Letter lies unanswered, thus free of lies, The. Correspondence. Henri Coulette. DiPo

Letter of a Mother. Robert Penn Warren. MoAmPo

Letter of Advice, A. Winthrop Mackworth Praed. NOBL; OxBoLi; PeLV

Letter of the 26th June. Philippe Jaccottet, *French.* MFP, *tr. by* Martin Sorrell

Letter 1. Thomas Moore. NOBRP *Fr.* The Fudge Family in Paris.

Letter said you had to speak to me, The. Alan Shapiro. BAP-94

Letter Sent by the Mayor and Inhabitants of the, A. *Unknown.*

"O thow archbishop and metropolitan." NOIV

Letter Six—The Pious Editors' Creed. James Russell Lowell. APN-1 *Fr.* The Biglow Papers.

Letter 3. Charles Olson. PmAP *Fr.* The Maximus Poems.

Letter to a Benedictine Monk. Marilyn Nelson Waniek. GT

Letter to a Boy at School. Anna Wickham. NOxBChV

Letter to a Brother of the Pen in Tribulation, A. Aphra Behn. KTR

Letter to a Chinese Poet. Ruth Dallas.

Autumn Wind. PeNZ

Clouds on the Sea. PeNZ

Letter to a Cretan Flute-Maker. Justin Vitiello. UnSA

Letter to a Dead Father. Richard Shelton. PBCAP

Letter to a Friend. Jon Stallworthy. NoAM

Letter to a Friend. Husein Tahmisic, *Serbian.* CEEP, *tr. by* Ewald Osers

Letter to a Friend. Robert Penn Warren. MoAmPo

Letter to a Friend: Who Is Nancy Daum? James Schuyler. PmAP

Letter to a Lady in London, A. Esther Lewis.

"You midst gay crowds reside, I, hid in shades." ECWP

Letter to a Mute. Thomas James. AmPA

Letter to a Sister, Giving an Account of the Author's Wedding-Day. Priscilla Pointon.

"In a post-coach and four, with postillions as fine." ECWP

Letter to a Son, A. Charles Mungoshi. PeSAV

Letter to a Son at Exam Time. Linda Pastan. FiLi

Letter to a Substitute Teacher. Gary Gildner. Poetsp

Letter to a Tormented Playwright, (for *Yulisa Amadu Maddy).* Syl Cheney-Coker. HBAPE; PBMAP

Letter to a Young Father in Exile. John Logan. CAPP-1

Letter to Alex Comfort. Dannie Abse. FaBoTw; TwCP

Letter To America. Francisco Alarcon. LTA

Letter to an Absent Son. Madeline DeFrees. FiLi

Letter to an American Visitor. Alex Comfort. OxBTC

Letter to an Imaginary Friend, Part One. Thomas McGrath. NNaP

". . . All that winter, in the black cold, the buzz-saw screamed and whistled." PaTW

Letter to an Imaginary Friend, Part Two. Thomas McGrath. NNaP

Letter to Anne Ridler. George Sutherland Fraser. OxBS

Letter to be Disguised as a Gas Bill. Marge Piercy. WPE

Letter to Bee. Emily Dickinson. SAmP; TLR; TTTS

Letter to Bell from Missoula. Richard Hugo. NNaP

Letter to Ben Jonson, A. Francis Beaumont. BeJo

Letter to Breyten Breytenbach from Hong Kong. C. J. Driver. PeSAV

Letter to Daphnis, A. Anne Finch. EnLoPo; LW; NALW; PEW

(Letter to Daphnis, April 2, 1685, A.) NOSC

Letter to Derek Mahon. Michael Longley. CIP-2; IIP

(To Derek Mahon.) CABP

Letter to E. Franklin Frazier. Imamu Amiri Baraka. BPo; PoBA

Letter to Ellen Conroy Kennedy. Edouard J. Maunick, *French.* NegPo, *tr. by* Ellen Conroy Kennedy

Letter to Her Father, A. Inib-sarri, *Akkadian.* BoWoP, *tr. by* Willis Barnstone

Letter to Her Husband, Absent upon Public[k] Employment, A. Anne Bradstreet. HAP; HeIP-4; KTR; NAAL-1; NAAL-3; NALW; NoP-4; PoPoPo; SCAP

Letter to Her Mother, A. Eristi-Aya, *Akkadian.* BoWoP, *tr. by* Willis Barnstone

Letter to His Friend Isaac, A. Judah Halevi, *Hebrew.* TrJP, *tr. by* Emma Lazarus

Letter to Jeanne (at Tassajara). Diane Di Prima. BB

Letter to John Donne, A. Charles Hubert Sisson. NOCV

Letter to John Dryden, A. James Philip McAuley.

"Dear John, whoever now takes pen to write." CBAP

Letter to Julia, in Rhyme. Henry Luttrell.

"Have you not seen (you must remember)." NOBRP

"London, within thy ample verge." NOBRP

Letter to Kafka. Maura Stanton. AmPA

Letter to Lady Margaret Cavendish Holles-Harley, When a Child, A. Matthew Prior. *See* A Letter to the Honourable Lady Miss Margaret Cavendish Holles-Harley.

Letter to Levertov from Butte. Richard Hugo. NNaP

Letter to Logan from Milltown. Richard Hugo. NNaP

Letter to Lord Byron. W. H. Auden.

"England, my England--you have been my tutrix." OBSV

"I like your muse because she's gay and witty." NOBL

"Now for the spirit of the people. Here." FaBoPV

"Ottava Rima would, I know, be proper." NOBL

"Thought of writing came to me today, The." NOBL

"You lived and moved among the best society." OBSV

Letter to Maria Gisborne. Shelley.

To Maria Gisborne, from Italy. NOBE

"You are now / In London, that great sea." EBEV

"You will see Coleridge, he who sits obscure." EPCY

Letter to Miguel Otero Silva, in Caracas. Pablo Neruda, *Spanish*. AF, *tr. by* Robert Bly

Letter to Miss E.B. at Bath. Mary Savage. ECWP

Letter to Miss E. B. on Marriage. Mary Savage. LW

Letter to My Daughter at the End of Her Second Year. Donald Finkel. CoAP

Letter to My Future Child, A. Trần Đức Uyển, *Vietnamese*. AVP, *tr. by* Huỳnh Sanh Thông

Letter to My Love—All Alone, Past 12, in the Dumps, A. "The Amorous Lady." ECWP

Letter to My Mother. John Holmes.
  "When I married, I caught up." ImGa

Letter to My Mother. Sergey Aleksandrovich Yesenin, *Russian*. TCRP, *tr. by* Geoffrey Thurley

Letter to My Sister. Anne Spencer. BlSi; NAAAL; NMM-2; PoBA

Letter to My Wife. Miklós Radnóti, *Hungarian*. AF, *tr. by* Emery E. George

Letter to N.Y. Elizabeth Bishop. LiLi; TwCP

Letter to P. Robert Friend. NYBP

Letter to Pearse Hutchinson. Eiléan Ní Chuilleanáin. FaBoWP

Letter to Peter Levi, A. Elizabeth Jennings. OxAEP-2

Letter to Reed from Lolo. Richard Hugo. NNaP

Letter to Robert Fergusson. Alexander Scott. OxBS

Letter to Robert Frost, A. Robert Silliman Hillyer. MoAmPo

Letter to Ron Silliman on the Back of a Map of the Solar System, A. Dennis Schmitz. LCAP-2

Letter to Scanlon from Whitehall. Richard Hugo. NNaP

Letter to the Academy. Langston Hughes. AF

Letter to the Actor Charles Laughton concerning the Work on the Play "The Life of Galileo." Bertolt Brecht, *German*. PoSu, *tr. by* Michael Hamburger

Letter to the Front. Muriel Rukeyser.
  "Even during war, moments of delicate peace." TrJP
  "To be a Jew in the twentieth century." NALW; NMM-2; TrJP

Letter to the Honourable Lady Miss Margaret Cavendish Holles-Harley, A. Matthew Prior. NOEC; NoAM; OxBC; OxBSP
  (Letter to Lady Margaret Cavendish Holles-Harley, When a Child, A.) NOBE; OBEV

Letter to the Immigration Officer. Jan Kemp. PeNZ

Letter to Three Irish Poets, A. Michael Longley. BIrV

Letter to Wagoner from Port Townsend. Richard Hugo. NNaP

Letter to Welch from Browning. Richard Hugo. NNaP

Letter to William Carlos Williams, A. Kenneth Rexroth. NNaP

Letter to Youki. Robert Desnos, *French*. AF, *tr. by* Carolyn Forché

Letter V. W. S. Graham. OxBTC

Letter VI. W. S. Graham. FaBoMo; FaBoTC

Letter Written on a Ferry While Crossing Long Island Sound. Anne Sexton. CoAP; NAAL-2; NYBP; TwCP

Letters. Ralph Waldo Emerson. OxBSP

Letters. Rilke, *German*.
  "Marriage is in many ways a simplification of life, and it naturally combines." ITG, *tr. by* Stephen Mitchell
  "Once the realization is accepted that even between the closest people." ITG, *tr. by* Stephen Mitchell

Letters and Other Worlds. Michael Ondaatje. NOBC; NoAM; NoP-4

Letters at School, The. Mary Mapes Dodge. OBCA

Letters Come to Prison. Shahid. GLP

Letters [*or* Notes] Found near a Suicide. Frank Horne. PoBA
  To "Chick." BPo
  To James. BPo
  To Mother. BPo
  To You. BPo

Letters from a Father. Mona Van Duyn. FYAP; NoP-4

Letters from a Man in Solitary. Nazim Hikmet, *Turkish*. AF, *tr. by* Randy Blasing *and* Mutlu Konuk

Letters from a Married Man. Don Mager.
  "Beloved,/ What does it take to put a house in order?" GLP

Letters from Chankiri Prison. Nazim Hikmet, *Turkish*. PFTM, *tr. by* Randy Blasing *and* Mutlu Konuk

Letters from Home. Faustin Charles. HCP
  "Sun sends me wires of blue rain, The." HCP
  "Wind writes to me, The." HCP

Letters from Poston Relocation Camp (1942–45). David Mura. LTA

Letters from the Ming Dynasty. Joseph Brodsky, *Russian*. TCRP, *tr. by* Derek Walcott

Letters from the Poet Who Sleeps in a Chair. Nicanor Parra, *Spanish*. AF, *tr. by* Miller Williams

Letters of Mina Harker, The. Dodie Bellamy. PT

Letters of the Jews as strict as flames, The. The Alphabet. Karl Shapiro. NoAM; PoA

Letters she left to clutter up the desk. A Gesture by a Lady with an Assumed Name. James Wright. CoAmPo; LiTM

Letters to a Stranger. Thomas James. AmPA

Letters to a Young Poet. Rilke, *German*.
  "For one human being to love another human being: that is perhaps the." ITG, *tr. by* Stephen Mitchell
  "Most people have turned their solutions toward what is easy and toward." ITG, *tr. by* Stephen Mitchell
  "Someday there will be girls and women whose name will no longer mean." ITG, *tr. by* Stephen Mitchell

Letters to Live Poets. Bruce Beaver. CBAP
  (Frank O'Hara). BMAP
  "Three images of dying stick in my mind like morbid transfers." NOBAu

Letters to Martha. Dennis Brutus. PeSAV

Letters to Walt Whitman. Ronald Johnson. VGW

Letters to Zanzotto. Michael Palmer.
  Letter 5. FTOS

Lettie Walker was 71. The Older American. Cheryl Clarke. GLP

Letting. Gary Hotham. HA

Letting down the isinglass curtains. Parent. Josephine Miles. NALW

Letting Go. Daryl Hine. NoP-4

Letting midnight / out on bail. Jam Session. Langston Hughes. MoNo

Letting My Feelings Out. Yü Hsüan-chi, *Chinese*. BoWoP, *tr. by* Geoffrey Waters

Letting my tongue. Michael McClintock. HA

Letting the beat go. Robert Duncan. FTOS

Letting the Parakeet Fly. Judith W. Steinbergh. IFJA

Letting us know for certain you didn't want that kind of Jew. Fairy Straighttalk. Carl Morse. GLP

Letty's Globe. Charles Tennyson Turner. NOBVV; OBEV; PeVV

Levantine, A. William Plomer. OBMV

Levedy Fortune is bothe frend and fo, The. *Unknown*. MiEL

Levedy, ic thonke thee. Thanks and a Plea to Mary. *Unknown*. FaBoVe; MiEL

Levee Moan. *Unknown*. AS

Level and the Square, The. Robert Morris. BLPA

Level fields expand into lakes. Inscribed on the Painting "Meaning of a Poem by Wang Wei." Li Tung-yang, *Chinese*. CoBLCP, *tr. by* Jonathan Chaves

Level forest stretching far and wide, A. Wu Chen, *Chinese*. CoBLCP, *tr. by* Jonathan Chaves

Level mind in crooked times, A. Aequam Memento. Horace, *Latin*. OBCVT, *tr. by* Louis MacNeice *Fr.* Three Odes of Horace.

Level ocean lies immeasurably blind, The. The Flying Fish. Jack Cope. PeSA

Level slope of colored sea, The. Metaphysical. Robert Fitzgerald. PoA

Levelled Churchyard, The. Thomas Hardy. NOBL

Leveller, The. "Barry Cornwall." OxAEP-2

Leviathan, XLI: 1–21. Bible, O.T. *Fr.* Job. NAWM-1

Leviathan. Jay Macpherson. MoCV

Leviathan. W. S. Merwin. APo; ChIV-1; CoAmPo; MoP; NOBA; NoAM

Leviathan. Peter Quennell.
  "Music met Leviathan returning, A." MoBrPo

Leviathan. Joshua Sylvester. KSG *Fr.* Job Triumphant.

Levin, on his way to Kitty's love. Secular Games. Richard Howard. PoA

Levitation with Baby. Marilyn Nelson Waniek. NMM-2

Levivot. Saul Tchernichowsky, *Hebrew*. MHP, *tr. by* Ruth Finer Mintz

Lewesdon Hill. William Crowe.
  "Up to thy summit, Lewesdon, to the brow." NOEC

Lewis 1928–45. Iain Crichton Smith. FaBoTC *Fr.* A Life.

Lewis Carroll. Eleanor Farjeon. OxBChV

Lewis Mumford George Buchanan. PNI

L'Homme Moyen Sensuel. Ezra Pound. OBSV

Li Fu-Jên. Emperor Wu of Han, *Chinese*. ChiP, *tr. by* Arthur Waley

Li Hsü of Ch'ien-chou is an old friend of mine. Yang Shih-ch'i. *Fr.* Rhymed Words Sent to My Eldest Son. CoBLCP, *tr. by* Jonathan Chaves

Li Po on board, ready to push off. Presented to Wang Lun. Li Po, *Chinese*. CoBCP, *tr. by* Burton Watson

Li Po put it in a poem, this West-of-the-Waters Abbey. Tu Mu. PLT, *tr. by* A. C. Graham *Fr.* Recalling Former Travels.

Li Po Who? "Everybody's Reading Li Po" Silkscreened on a Purple T-Shirt. Yusef Komunyakaa. WWSi

Li Sao. Ch'u Yüan, *Chinese*.

"Oftentimes, I grew dejected and sobbed." SuSp, *tr. by* Wu-chi Liu

Yüan, Ch'ü. ChiPo, *tr. by* Burton Watson

("I am a descendant of Emperor Kao-yang.") ChiPo, *tr. by* Burton Watson

("I will go to P'eng Hsien in the place where he dwells.") (LL) ChiPo, *tr. by* Burton Watson

Liadain. *Unknown.* WPOW, *tr. by* Frank O'Connor

Líadan and Cuirithir. *Unknown.* NOIV

Liadan Laments Cuirithir. *Unknown, Irish.* BIrV; PBWP, *tr. by* John Montague

Liang Family Pool. Yang Shih-ch'i. *Fr.* Ten Scenes at the Hsiao Family Stone Ridge. CoBLCP, *tr. by* Jonathan Chaves

Liang Terrace, The. Li Ho, *Chinese.* PLT, *tr. by* A. C. Graham

Liao-ling[, sheer patterned silk—what is it like?]. Po Chü-i, *Chinese.* CoBCP, *tr. by* Burton Watson

Liar, The. Imamu Amiri Baraka. AmPP; NOBA

'Lias! 'Lias! Bless de Lawd! In the Morning. Paul Laurence Dunbar. BPo

Lib. 2. Metrum 5. Boethius, *Latin.* OBCVT, *tr. by* Henry Vaughan *Fr.* Consolation of Philosophy, The ("De Consolacione Philosophie").

Libation Bearers, The. Aeschylus, *Greek.* NAWM-1, *tr. by* Robert Fagles

Libation. / Hey sisters, we the color of our men. Ceremony. Jewel C. Latimore. BlSi

Libationer Hu Became Ill from Eating Sunflowers. These Poems Are Playfully Presented to Him and Are Also Intended to Thank Him for the Vegetables He Sent Me. Yang Shih-ch'i, *Chinese.*

"After the rain, the vegetables from your garden." CoBLCP, *tr. by* Jonathan Chaves

Libel on the Reverend Dr. Delany, A. Jonathan Swift.

"Hail, happy Pope, whose generous mind." EPCY

Liber doth vaunt how chastely he hath liv'd. In Librum. Sir John Davies. FaBoEE

Liberace. Jonathan Holden. CMAP

Liberal arts lie eastward of this shore, The. The Seven Sleepers. Mark Van Doren. FYAP

Liberal, or Innocent by Definition. James Philip McAuley. NOBAu

Liberation. Ruth Stone. BoWoP

Liberation / Poem. Sonia Sanchez. NBV

Liberator, The. Emily Holmes Coleman. SPE

Liberia?/ No micro-footnote in a bunioned book. On the Founding of Liberia. Melvin Beaunearus Tolson. UnPo *Fr.* Libretto for the Republic of Liberia.

Libertine, The. Louis MacNeice. MoP; NoAM

Liberty, The. Sarah Fyge Egerton. KTR; PEW

("With what reluctance they endure restraints.") (LL) PEW

Liberty. Paul Éluard, *French.*

"On my school notebooks." TTTS

Liberty. Emile Ologoudou. PBMAP

Liberty. Edward Thomas. OAEL-2

Liberty and Peace. Phillis Wheatley. AiP

"Lo! Freedom comes. Th' prescient Muse foretold." BlSi

Liberty and Ten Years of Return. Christopher Howell. CDa

Liberty Bell in Philadelphia, The. Crazy Quilt. Jane Wilson Joyce. CrSp

Liberty [or Libertie], that we'll [or wee'll] enjoy tonight, The. (LL) Inviting a Friend to Supper. Ben Jonson, *after* Martial. AWP; BeJo; FP; NOBE; NOSC; NoP-4; OAEL-1; OxBoLi; PeLV; PoEL-2; SeCP

Liberty to be defended on. Poem in Defense of Children. Joel Oppenheimer. CDa

Libido portion goes haywire, The. Century of Hands. Michael Davidson. FTOS

Libra, September. John Taylor. NOSC

Librarian, The. Charles Olson. PmAP

Library. Louis Jenkins. RaBo

Library, The. Aidan Carl Mathews. CIP-2

Library, The. Timothy Steele. RA

Library book, The. Gary Hotham. HA

Library closing—. Sydell Rosenberg. HA

Library in a Garden, A. Richard Le Gallienne. OBGa

Libretto for the Republic of Liberia. Melvin Beaunearus Tolson. On the Founding of Liberia. UnPo

Lice Seekers, The. Rimbaud. *See* Girls Looking for Lice.

Licentious Person, A. Donne. PeLV

Lich Gate, The. Clayton Eshleman. PmAP

Licia. Giles, the Elder Fletcher.

"Are those two stars, her eyes, my life's light gone." Son

First Did I Fear. Son

"I wish sometimes, although a worthlesse thing." AAS

"Sad, All Alone, Not Long I Musing Sat." Son

Time.

Lick your lips, X. darling, it may be the last. The Summer Ending. Glenway Wescott. PoA

Licorice Chronicles. Ted Greenwald.

"Coordinating cities gulls still gull, and, arms binged with wine, as wine." FTOS

Licorice Fields at Pontefract, The. John Betjeman. CABP; CMoP

Lid smashed into a likeness of the mad English king, George the / Third. Kenneth Koch. *See* You were wearing your Edgar Allan Poe printed cotton blouse.

Liddell and Scott. Thomas Hardy. OBCoV; OxBoLi; PeLV

Liddesdale Crosiers hae ridden a race, The. The Death of Parcy Reed. *Unknown.* ESPB

Lie, The. Rudyard Kipling. NOBL *Fr.* The Naulahka.

Lie, The. Alfred M. Lee. AmPA

Lie, The. Howard Moss. LiTM

Lie, The. Sir Walter Ralegh. AAS; CTC; EBEV; FaBoPV; GEA; HAP; ImPo; NAEL-1; NOBE; NoSic; PBRV; PoEL-2; RB; SCGP; SCV; SiPS; TFi

("No stab the soul can kill.") (LL) NoP-4; PoPoPo

Lie back, daughter, let your head. First Lesson. Philip Booth. TwCP

Lie bedridden. Spring. Clinton. Sterling Plumpp. BkSV *Fr.* Clinton.

Lie closed, my lately loved, in the far bed. John Woods. CoAmPo

Lie down with us and wait. (LL) Gathering Mushrooms. Paul Muldoon. BiHa; CIP-2; NoP-4; PBCIP; PNI

Lie for lie! (LL) The Goddess. Denise Levertov. LiTM; NALW; NOBA; NeAP; PoM

Lie on your back on stone. Canyon de Chelly. Simon J. Ortiz. PaTW

Lie one night in my arms and give me peace. (LL) News of the World III. George Barker. FaBoTw; PaTW

"Lie still, my newly married wife." The Griesly Wife. John Streeter Manifold. MoBS; MoBrPo

Lie still now. This Room and Everything in It. Li-Young Lee. OpBo

Lie, that we come from water, A. Landcrab I. Margaret Atwood. LCAP-2; NIP-4

Lie up nearer, brother, nearer, for my limbs are growing cold. The Dying Californian. *Unknown.* AmFP

Lie where you fell and longed. Letter V. W. S. Graham. OxBTC

Lied. Alfonsas Nyka-Niliunas, *Lithuanian.* CEEP, *tr. by* Jonas Zdanys

Lieh Mountain. Wang Shih-chieng, *Chinese.* SuSp, *tr. by* Richard John Lynn

Lien-ch'ang Palace was overgrown with bamboo. On Lien-ch'ang Palace. Yüan Chen, *Chinese.* SuSp, *tr. by* Angela Jung Palandri

Lies. Christopher Bursk. CDa

Lies a dead deer on younder plain, fr. *the Chinese of the* Confucian Odes. Ezra Pound. APSN

Lies About Love. D. H. Lawrence. CBLP

Lies and Longing. Linda Gregg. WWSi

Lies in flawed words and stubborn sounds. (LL) The Poems of Our Climate. Wallace Stevens. MeMAP; NoP-4; OxBA; SoSe-8; TwCP

Lies like a rod of rippled jade. (LL) Symphony in Yellow. Oscar Wilde. ADE; EBVV; MoBrPo; NOBVV; NoAM; OPOU; OxBSP; PFE

Lies on her chest of drawers. Lucille's Kumquat Colored Kimono. Dara Wier. CMAP

Lies on one hip by the fire. The Girl Writing Her English Paper. Robert Wallace. Poetsp

Lies rusting, mouldering. (LL) The Dismantled Ship. Walt Whitman. AmPP; OxBA

Lieth there so cold? [or cold!]. (LL) What the Bullet Sang. Bret Harte. APAD; APN-2; OBEV

Lieutenant, The. Konstantin Mikhailovich Simonov, *Russian.* TCRP, *tr. by* Lubov Yakovleva

Lieutenant Dawson said he'd known the girl. He Remembers How He Didn't Understand What Lieutenant Dawson Meant. James Whitehead. MT

Lieutenant Gilbert took us down the hill. P.O.W.s. R. L. Barth. CDa

Life. Francis Bacon. GTBS-P; OxAEP-1

(Life of Man, The.) NoSic

Life. "Sasha Chorny," *Russian.* TCRP, *tr. by* Bernard Meares

Life, The. Philip Dow. AmPA

Life. Artie Gold. NOBC

Life. George Herbert. ESCV; FMP; FSCP; GeHe; MeLP; NOSC; NoP-4; SeCP

Life. Henry Wadsworth Longfellow. *Fr.* A Psalm of Life. APN-1; CTV; EBEvV; FaBoBe; NAAL-1; NAAL-3; OBCA; PAR; PWR; PoLF; TAP

Life, A. Howard Nemerov. OBCoV; PBMP

Life, A. Sylvia Plath. NOBA

Life. Henrietta Cordelia Ray. CBWP-3

Life. Nan Terrell Reed. BLPA

Life, A. Iain Crichton Smith.
  Lewis 1928–45. FaBoTC
  Oban 1955–82. FaBoTC
Life. Mary E. Tucker. CBWP-1
Life. *Unknown.* PoToHe
Life. Ella Wheeler Wilcox. PoToHe
Life, The. James Wright. LCAP-2
Life. Ch'ihwan Yu, *Korean.* CKP, *tr. by* Jaihiun Kim
Life after Death. Richard W. Thomas. PoBA
Life again. John Banister Tabb. *See* Evolution.
Life Ahead, The. Philip Levine. NoAM
Life and Character of Dean Swift, The. Jonathan Swift.
  "Day will come, when't shall be said, The." NOIV
Life and Death. Sir William Davenant. *Fr.* The Christian's Reply to the
  Philosopher. MeLP
Life and Death. Walter James Turner. FaBoTw
Life and Death of Edward II, The. Sir Francis Hubert.
  "This highest scholar in the school of sin." NOSC
Life and Death of Jason, The. William Morris.
  Garden By The Sea, A. CH; EBEvV; GaP; LBC; NOBE; OAEL-2;
    OBNC; PoEL-5
    ("Anigh the murmuring of the sea.") (LL) GaP; LBC
    (Nymph's Song to Hylas, The.) OBEV
Life and Death of [Habbie Simson] the Piper of Kilbarchan, The. Robert
  Sempill. OxBS
Life and Genuine Character of Dr Swift, The. Jonathan Swift.
  From The Life and Character of Dean Swift. NOBL
Life: and I will dwell in the house of the Lord forever. Bible, *O.T. See*
  Psalm 23.
Life and Impellance. William Frederick Stevenson. NOBVV
Life and Literary Remains of L.E.L. Letitia Elizabeth Landon.
  Poet's Love, A. Ro
Life and Lucubrations of Crispinus Scriblerus, The. James Woodhouse.
  NOEC
Life and the Universe show spontaneity. The Positivists. Mortimer Collins.
  EBVV
Life As a Book That Has Been Put Down. John Ashbery. FTOS
Life / At fifteen. For a Black Child. David Diop, *French.* NegPo, *tr. by*
  Ellen Conroy Kennedy
Life at last I know is terrible. What Is Terrible. Roy Fuller. PoWW
Life at Richkings. Frances, Countess of Hertford Seymour. ECWP
Life at War. Denise Levertov. NMM-2; VGW
Life brings everything, time's length can shift. Plato the Younger, *Greek.*
  GrAn, *tr. by* Peter Jay
Life can hold such lovely things! Thank You, God. Nina Stiles. PoToHe
Life comes under no other / propositions than mountain decrees. A Little
  Thing Like That. A. R. Ammons. PUP-20
Life contracts and death is expected. The Death of a Soldier. Wallace
  Stevens. OBWP; OxBSP; SAmP; SoSe-8
Life Cycle of Common Man. Howard Nemerov. NBLV
Life/Death. Ian McDonald. HCP
Life death does end and each day dies with sleep. (LL) Sonnet: "No worst,
  there is none. Pitched past pitch of grief." Gerard Manley Hopkins.
  APAD; CMoP; EBVV; EnVR; FaBoMo; GSo; GTBS-P; HeIP-4; InPS-3;
  LiTM; MoBrPo; MoP; NAEL-2; NOBE; NOBVV; NoAM; NoP-4;
  OAEL-2; OBNC; OxAEP-2; PeVV; PoE; PoEL-5; PoPoPo; Poetr; TFi
Life did not bring me silken gowns. Red Geraniums. Martha Haskell
  Clark. BLPA
Life Doesn't Frighten Me. Maya Angelou. ChAP
Life Drawing. Richard Foerster. BAP-94
Life eternal--useless to talk of that. Shadow Replies to Substance. T'ao
  Ch'ien. *Fr.* Substance, Shadow, and Spirit. CoBCP, *tr. by* Burton
  Watson
Life flows to death as rivers to the sea. Epigram. James Vincent
  Cunningham. VGW
Life for a Life. Mary E. Tucker. CBWP-1
Life-Force, afflicted with doubt, The. Limerick. Thomas Thorneley. PeLi
Life, friends, is boring. We must not say so. John Berryman. ColAP; HAP;
  HCAP; HeIP-4; LiTM; MoP; NAAL-2; NOBA; NoAM; NoP-4; TAP;
  TRP; TwCP; VCAP *Fr.* Dream Songs.
Life from a heart of stone / and from bitter tears / a sweet land, *par. by*
  David Rosenberg. Bible, *O.T. See* Psalm 114.
LIfe from its ghost. (LL) "He Knoweth Not That the Dead Are Thine."
  Mary Elizabeth Coleridge. OBNC; SAGP
Life from the Lifeless. Robinson Jeffers. CMoP
Life had become a sort of gorgeous elegy. Chanel No. 5. Chase Twichell.
  NAmP90

Life has conquered, the wind has blown away. Hope. *Unknown, Irish.*
  CIP-2; IIP, *tr. by* Frank O'Connor
Life has dark secrets; and the hearts are few. Secrets. Letitia Elizabeth
  Landon. VWP *Fr.* Fragments.
Life has just begun. 'S Wonderful. Ira Gershwin. CBLP
Life has loveliness to sell. Barter. Sara Teasdale. SoSe-8
Life holds no sweeter thing than this—to teach. Life-Hook. Juana de
  Ibarbourou, *Spanish.* WPOW, *tr. by* Marti Moody
Life-Hook. Juana de Ibarbourou, *Spanish.* WPOW, *tr. by* Marti Moody
Life, hope, they conquer death, generally, always. After the Convention.
  Robert Lowell. NoAM
Life I do love, and still in pain protest. Extract from Solitude. Vita
  Sackville-West. WPN
Life! I know not what thou art. Anna Laetitia Barbauld. BLPA; GTBS-P;
  NoP-4; OBEV; OxAEP-1; PWR
Life I Led, The. Nikki Giovanni. GT
Life Immovable. Costis Palamas, *Greek.*
  "In the sun-glad nakedness." GrIP, *tr. by* Philip Sherrard
Life impaled him high on a cliff. Biography of an Agnostic. Louis
  Ginsberg. TrJP
Life in a day: he took his girl to the ballet. Les Sylphides. Louis
  MacNeice. BoLoP *Fr.* Novelettes.
Life in a Love. Robert Browning. FHYEP; OBNC
Life in Death. Ellice Hopkins. PeVV
Life-in-Love. D. G. Rossetti. HAP *Fr.* The House of Life.
Life in the Boondocks. A. R. Ammons. HAP
Life in the Castle. Anne Hébert, *French.* BoWoP, *tr. by* Aliki *and* Willis
  Barnstone
Life in the City: In Memoriam Edward Gibbon. Philip Whalen. PoM
Life is a bitter aspic. We are not. Wallace Stevens. CMoP *Fr.* Esthétique
  du Mal. LiTM
Life Is a Dream. Pedro Calderón de la Barca, *Spanish.* NAWM-1, *tr. by*
  Arthur Symons
  "We live, while we see the sun." AWP
Life is a game with a glorious prize. Playing the Game. *Unknown.* PWR
Life is a glass wherein we dimly see. Life's Boundary. Henrietta Cordelia
  Ray. CBWP-3
Life is a jest. My Own Epitaph. John Gay. CABP; FaBoEE; LiLi; NIP-4;
  NOEC; PFE; PeLV
Life Is a Killer. John Giorno. PmAP
Life is a long discovery, isn't it? Discovery. Joseph Belloc. OxBSP
Life Is a Platform. Peter Levi.
  "Smoke when the sun fell and when it rose." FaBoTw
Life is a Shylock; always it demands. The Law. Ella Wheeler Wilcox.
  PWR
Life is a stream. Petals. Amy Lowell. SDW
Life Is Fine. Langston Hughes. NBLV; SAmP
Life is full of mirth and pleasure. Adieu. Mary E. Tucker. CBWP-1
Life Is Happy. Albert Goldbarth. BAP-93
Life is in the rice-field, wealth in the wheat. Grace before Meat. Robert
  David Fitzgerald. NOBAu
Life is inadequate, but there are many real. Independence Day. William Jay
  Smith. TwCP
Life is like a jagged tooth. Grace Treasone. InPK-6
Life Is Long. *Unknown, Chinese.* OHMPC, *tr. by* Kenneth Rexroth
Life is long that loathsomely doth last, The. John Harington. ChIV-2
Life is made up of vanities—so small. Stern Truth. Letitia Elizabeth
  Landon. VWP
Life Is Motion. Wallace Stevens. SAmP
Life is *not* a horse with a winner's garland. Look Sheila Seeing You've
  Asked Me. Vincent O'Sullivan. PeNZ
Life is not a stroll across a field. Boris Pasternak. *See* Hamlet.
Life is not made for meetings. Presented to Wei Pa, Gentleman in
  Retirement. Tu Fu, *Chinese.* CoBCP, *tr. by* Burton Watson
Life is ours in vain. Song. Oodgeroo of the tribe Noonuccal. APAD
Life is ours like the real. Theme One: The Variations. August Wilson.
  PoBA
Life is porous enough. Permissive Entry: A Sermon on Fame. Lawrence
  Goldstein. BAP-95
Life is real, life is earnest. A Parody on "A Psalm of Life." Oliver Wendell
  Holmes. BLPA
Life is sad and so slow and so cold. Limerick. Gavin Ewart. PeLi
Life is simple and easy. For the Moment. Pierre Reverdy, *French.* TTTS,
  tr. by Ron Padgett
Life is the body's [*or* Bodies] light, which once declining. Robert Herrick.
  BeJo
  ("And dismal darkness then doth smutch the face.") (LL) CavPo
  ("Life is the body's light; which once declining.") CavPo

Life it asks of us is a dog's life, The. (LL) The Victor Dog. James Merrill. NoAM; NoP-4

Life keeps me alive: all its tubes. Life Supports. William Bronk. APSN

Life lasts the course of a kiss. Aleksandr Makarov, *Russian*. TCRP, *tr. by* Albert C. Todd

"Life! length of life!" for this, with earnest cries. Juvenal. OBVE, *tr. by* William Gifford *Fr*. Satires.

Life-Lesson, A. James Whitcomb Riley. PoLF

Life, like a marble block, is given to all. Edith Wharton. APN-2

Life, like a thread piercing through jewels. Princess Shikishi, *Japanese*. WPJ, *tr. by* Kenneth Rexroth *and* Ikuko Atsumi

Life like the periodical not yet. James Merrill. HCAP *Fr*. The Book of Ephraim.

Life, looking out attentive from the eyes of the doe. (LL) The Buck in the Snow. Edna St. Vincent Millay. ColAP; NALW; NoP-4

Life Mask. Charles Brasch. PeNZ

Life of. . . , The. Theodore Weiss. NYBP

Life of a Nun. Alexander Pope. ECEV *Fr*. Eloisa to Abelard. NAEL-1; PoEL-3; RACG

Life of a Salesman. Emily Grosholz. RA

Life of Ages, Richly Poured. Samuel Johnson. AH

Life of Hubert, The. Thomas Cole. NOEC

Life of Ideas, The. Chris Wallace-Crabbe. OBGa

Life of Intimate Fleeing, A. Robert Kelly. FTOS

Life of life! thy lips enkindle. Hymn to the Spirit of Nature. Shelley. CH; GTBS-P; NOBE; PoE; PoEL-4 *Fr*. Prometheus Unbound. NOBRP; OAEL-2

Life of Lincoln West, The. Gwendolyn Brooks. NoAM

Life of Man, The. Francis Bacon. *See* Life.

Life of Man, The. Barnabe Barnes. *Fr*. A Divine Century of Spiritual Sonnets.

Life of my life, take not so soon thy flight. To His Dying Brother, Master William Herrick. Robert Herrick. CaPo; CavPo; NOSC

Life of sabbaths here beneath!, A. Thomas Traherne. ESCV *Fr*. The Third Century.

Life of Service, The. Donald Davie. NYBP

Life of significant soil, The. (LL) The Dry Salvages. T. S. Eliot. AiP; NoP-4; OxBA

Life of St Sava, The. Vasco [*or* Vasko] Popa. PoSu, *tr. by* Anne Pennington *Fr*. St Sava's Spring.

Life of the Blessed, The. Luís De León, *Spanish*. AWP, *tr. by* Bryant

Life of the nameless foetus, the. Birthmarks. Rajani Parulekar, *Marathi*. OMIP, *tr. by* Vinay Dharwadker

Life of the Wolf, The. Gary Gildner. AmPA

Life of This World. *Unknown, Latin*.

"Life of this world, woe betide thee!" MLL, *tr. by* Helen Waddell

Life of writing, unless wondrous short, A. William Whitehead. ECEV *Fr*. A Charge to the Poets.

Life on Earth. Frank O'Hara.

"Shine, 'O world!' don't weary the gulping Pole." UnPo

Life on the Ocean Wave, A. Epes Sargent. FaBoBe

Life owes me nothing. Let the years. *Unknown*. PoToHe

Life Plastic. "Michael Field." VWP

Life pours out images, the accidental. The Rokeby Venus. Robert Conquest. GS; MoP

Life (priest and poet say) is but a dream. The Dragon-Fly. Walter Savage Landor. OBEV; OBNC

Life-Saving Medal. Philippe Soupault. PFTM

Life Sculpture. George Washington Doane. BLPA

Life Story. Taeko Tomioka, *Japanese*. WPOW, *tr. by* Harry Guest, Lynn Guest, *and* Kajima Shozo

Life Story. *Unknown*. *See* A Chronicle.

Life Story. Tennessee Williams. GLP

Life Supports. William Bronk. APSN

Life that I have is all that I have, The. Code Poem for the French Resistance. Leo Marks. APAD

Life the hound. The Hound. Robert Francis. SoSe-8

Life, the story goes. Anna Liffey. Eavan Boland. PUP-20

Life throbb'd in the sweet baby's bosom no more. Goethe. *See* The Erl-King.

Life today is hectic. What's Going to Happen to the Tots? Noël Coward. NBLV

Life was back lanes, therefore out of bounds. Elise. Alan Wearne. BMAP *Fr*. The Nightmarkets.

Life we find is nevermore. Deception. Josephine D. Henderson Heard. CBWP-4

Life which now I lead is as a perfect death, The. Love Is Life and Death. Georg Rudolph Weckherlin, *German*. GePo, *tr. by* George C. Schoolfield

Life whirls past like drunken wildfire. (LL) Winter Dawn. Tu Fu, *Chinese*. BLT; OHPC, *tr. by* Kenneth Rexroth

Life will keep hammering the grass blades into the ground. Force. Derek Walcott. OxBC

Life without Passion, The. Shakespeare. *See* Sonnet 94.

Life would be an easy matter. Nixon Waterman. *Fr*. If We Didn't Have to Eat. OBAL

Lifeguard, The. James Dickey. NYBP; NoP-4; SoSe-8

Lifeguards have gone in for the season, The. *Cleave* and *Cleave*. Brenda Hillman. WeT

Lifeguard's parallel simian arms, The. Death at Pocono Lake Preserve. Robert Bagg. WeT

Lifeguard's whistle organized our swimming, The. The River. Dabney Stuart. NYBP

Lifeless solitude—an angry waste, A. On the Telescopic Moon. John Swanwick Drennan. BIrV

Lifelines. Gavin Ewart. SPE

Lifers file into the hall, The. In the Cage. Robert Lowell. NOBA; Son

Life's a Funny Proposition after All. George M. Cohan. PoLF

Life's a Game. *Unknown*. BLPA

Life's a performance. Either join in. Palladas, *Greek*. GrAn, *tr. by* Tony Harrison

Life's an ocean crossing where winds howl. Palladas, *Greek*. GrAn, *tr. by* Tony Harrison

Life's Boundary. Henrietta Cordelia Ray. CBWP-3

Life's Chequer-Board. Edward Fitzgerald. LBC

Life's Circumnavigators. William Robert Rodgers. GTBS-P

Life's Golden Sunset. Mrs. Henry Linden. CBWP-4

Life's Handicap. Rudyard Kipling.

   Dedication, A: "My new-cut ashlar takes the light." PoEL-5

Life's Journey. Ella Wheeler Wilcox. PWR

Life's Lessons. *Unknown*. PoLF

Life's made up of little things. Mary R. Hartman. PoToHe

Life's Mirror. "Madeline Bridges." BLPA; FaBoBe; PWR; PoToHe

Life's Morning. Howell Elvet Lewis, *Welsh*. OBVVE, *tr. by* H. Idris Bell

Life's Parallels, A. Christina Rossetti. NAEL-2; PoEL-5

Life's pathway to me is dreary. The Opium-Eater. Mary E. Tucker. CBWP-1

Life's Progress. Anne Finch, Countess of Winchilsea. ECWP

Life's Scars. Ella Wheeler Wilcox. BLPA

Life's smallest miseries are, perhaps, its worst. Small Miseries. Letitia Elizabeth Landon. VWP

Life's sorrows and regrets—who can escape them?, Tune: "Song of Tzu-yeh." Tune: Song of Tzu-yeh. Li Yü, *Chinese*. CoBCP, *tr. by* Burton Watson

Life's spent guarding. What there is to guard, A. August the First: The Watchman Speaks. Marjorie Oludhe Macgoye. HBAPE

Life's stormy surge had scarcely touched. The Grafted Bud. Mary Weston Fordham. CBWP-2

Lifetime. Narayan Surve, *Marathi*. OMIP, *tr. by* Vinay Dharwadker

Lifetime Devoted to Literature, A. Judith Rodriguez. NOBAu

Lifetime's teaching grammar come to this, A. Palladas, *Greek*. GrAn, *tr. by* Tony Harrison

Lift every [*or* ev'ry] voice and sing. James Weldon Johnson. ISC; NAAAL ("True to our God, true to our native land.") (LL) CrDW

Lift latch, step in, be welcome, Sir. A Luncheon. Max Beerbohm. NOBL; OBSV; OxBTC; PeLV; UV

Lift Me Higher. Mary E. Tucker. CBWP-1

Lift not the painted veil which those who live. Sonnet. Shelley. FHYEP; GSo; NOBRP; OBNC; Son

Lift up thine eyes, sweet Psyche! What is she. Psyche, Before the Tribunal of Venus. Nathaniel Parker Willis. APN-1

Lift up, ye poor! your everlasting prayer! The Poor of London. William Forster. CBAP

Lift up your eyes on high. Erige Cor Tuum ad Me in Caelum. Hilda Doolittle. CMoP

Lift Up Your Heads. Bible, *O.T. See* Psalm 24.

Lift Up Your Heads, Rejoice! Thomas Toke Lynch. TrCP

Lift your arms to the stars. Love and Liberation. John Hall Wheelock. MoAmPo

Lift your feet and you sink deeper in the mud! Ruinous Rains. Fu Hsien, *Chinese*. CoBCP, *tr. by* Burton Watson

Lift your Glad Voices in Triumph on High. Henry Ware Jr. AH

Lifted by a little breeze. Lucilius, *Greek*. GrAn, *tr. by* Alistair Elliot

Lifted by its tufts. The Shroud. Galway Kinnell. LCAP-2

Lifting and Leaning. Ella Wheeler Wilcox. BLPA

   (Two Kinds of People.) PoToHe

Lifting Belly. Gertrude Stein.

"Kiss my lips." PFTM

"Lifting belly. Are you. Lifting." OxWW

Lifting, both hands pulling whitely. Grandpa's .45. W. M. Ransom. CDW

Lifting his slowly trickling jaws. Tête-à-Tête. Edwin Honig. NoAM

Lifting Illegal Nets by Flashlight. James Wright. NNaP

Lifting my fingers. Frozen Hands. Joseph Bruchac. CDW

Lifting of the Cloud, The. Thomas Macdonagh. TIRV

Light. Frank Bidart. *Fr.* Elegy.

Light. Cricketer. R. C. Scriven. AYFP

Light. Fireflies. Paul Fleischman. NOxBChV

Light. Richard Kenney. Son

Light. Michael Ondaatje. NIP-4

Light? Milan Richter, *Czech and Slovak.* CEEP, tr. by Ewald Osers

Light. Diane Wakoski. OPOU

Light across the courtyard. Saint's Bridge. Lola Ridge. WPE

Light along the hills in the morning, The. Notice What This Poem Is Not Doing. William Stafford. LCAP-2

Light and Rejoicing to Israel. *Unknown, Hebrew.* TrJP, tr. by Israel Abrahams

Light, angelic and black. The Wreck "Thrush." George Seferis. GrIP, tr. by Edmund Keeley and Philip Sherrard *Fr.* Thrush.

Light Another Candle. Miriam Chaikin. NTCP

Light at Equinox. Léonie Adams. ColAP

Light became her grace and dwelt among, The. Ballatetta. Ezra Pound. VGW

Light Behind the Rain. Michael Longley. CBLP

Light breaks where no sun shines. Dylan Thomas. CMoP; FaBoMo; ImPo; MoBrPo; OxAEP-2; OxBTC

Light breeze rustles the reeds, A. Night Thoughts While Travelling. Tu Fu, *Chinese.* OHPC, tr. by Kenneth Rexroth

Light brush of dawn, A. Louise Herlin, *French.* MFP, tr. by Martin Sorrell

Light chill on the knees, A. Poema del City 2. Ron Padgett. WWSi

Light do I see within my Lady's eyes. Ballata 5. Guido Cavalcanti, *Italian.* CTC, tr. by Ezra Pound

Light drizzle falling off, A. Taking a Captive / 1984. Barney Bush. HATNAP

Light exists in Spring, A. Emily Dickinson. APN-2; BoWoP; NCAP; NOBA; OxBA

Light Exists In The Fire, The. "Angelus Silesius." GePo, tr. by George C. Schoolfield *Fr.* The Cherubical Wanderer.

Light, falling / with a curve. Sanctuary. Johannes Bobrowski, *German.* CEEP, tr. by Ruth Mead and Matthew Mead

Light fell from the window and the day was done, The. The Truth is Blind. David Gascoyne. SPE

Light-fingered Dio takes after the God of Thieves. Lucilius, *Greek.* GrAn, tr. by Peter Porter

Light flickers on my shadow and myself. Back In Prison. Nguyễn Đình Kiên, *Vietnamese.* AVP, tr. by Huỳnh Sanh Thông

Light flooding both banks. A Death in Spring. Amir Gilbo'a, *Hebrew.* IP, tr. by Warren Bargad and Stanley F. Chyet

Light flows our war of mocking words, and yet. The Buried Life. Matthew Arnold. CBLP; EnVR; FHYEP; NAEL-2; OAEL-2

Light foot hears you and the brightness begins, The. A Poem Beginning with a Line by Pindar. Robert Duncan. CoAmPo; NNaP; NeAP; PmAP; PoM; VCAP

Light from the kitchen-door window comes through in a special way, The. Kitchen Sink. Ofelia Zepeda. PaTW

Light Furs, Fat Horses. Po Chü-i, *Chinese.* CoBCP, tr. by Burton Watson

Light going out in the forehead, A. Swimming By Night. James Merrill. ColAP; NYBP; VGW

Light griefs can speak. Seneca. IMW *Fr.* Hippolytus.

Light grows, and grows less tender. A Song of Blood. Sidney Walter Powell. NSI *Fr.* Gallipoli.

Light growth of green dreams drying, A. (LL) Losing Track. Denise Levertov. HeIP-4; MoP; NOBA; PoE; PoM

Light-hearted Fairy, The. *Unknown.* BoTP

Light-hearted I walked into the valley wood. Conversion. Thomas Ernest Hulme. FaBoMo; OxBSP

Light Hotel. Peter Redgrove. PoE

Light I don't have slanting through broken walls. Air. John Godfrey. FTOS

Light in Darkness. Mary E. Tucker. CBWP-1

Light, in light breezes and a favoring sun. Watching Tennis. John Heath-Stubbs. Son

Light in my heart, O Saviour, is Thy heart, The. A Poem to the Heart of Jesus. Teig Gaelach O'Sullivan, *Irish.* TIRV, tr. by Thomas Kinsella

Light in the skull of the bird, The. Section: America (2): Seen as a Bird. Nathaniel Tarn. APSN *Fr.* Lyrics for the Bride of God.

Light in the Window, The. C. L. Erickson. PWR

Light in the window seemed perpetual, The. The Room above the Square. Stephen Spender. NOBE

Light into the olive entered. After Greece. James Merrill. CoAmPo; ColAP; NOBA; NYBP; TRP

Light is around the petals, and behind them. Looking at Some Flowers. Robert Bly. NOBA

Light is burning late, A. Herbert Street Revisited. John Montague. CIP-2; IIP; PBCIP; PNI

Light is on in my father's study, A. Working late. Louis Simpson. PBCV

Light is on my body also, The. Lilith. Linda Gregg. WPOW

Light is the inside, The. Girl Powdering Her Neck. Cathy Song. NoP-4

Light, joy, and leisure; but shall they persever? / Echo. Ever. (LL) Heaven. George Herbert. ESCV; GeHe; SeCP; TTTS; TrCP

Light-Keeper, The. Robert Louis Stevenson. "Brilliant kernel of the night, The." EBVV

Light, Late Song for Solo Voice Without Piano, A. Olafs Stumbrs. CEEP

Light, light, light, my little Scotch-ee. Little Scotch-ee. *Unknown.* AS

Light Listened. Theodore Roethke. EP; MoAmPo

Light listened when she sang. (LL) Light Listened. Theodore Roethke. EP; MoAmPo

Light little zephyr came flitting, A. Morning Compliments. Sydney Dayre. OxBChV

Light looks from a dazzled leaf. Dazzle. Dorothy Roberts. NOBC

Light. Love. Freedom. Like a Blessing. Stanley Crouch. GT

Light mist girdles the mountain. Inscribed on a Painting. T'ang Yin, *Chinese.* SuSp, tr. by Chiang Yee

Light mist, then dense fog. Li Ch'ing-chao, *Chinese.* BoWoP; OHMPC, tr. by Kenneth Rexroth

Light! more light! the shadows deepen. Let the Light Enter! Frances Ellen Watkins Harper. PAR

Light of evening, Lissadell, The. In Memory of Eva Gore-Booth and Con Markievicz. W. B. Yeats. FaBoPV; NoAM; OAEL-2; OBMV; OxBTC

Light of Life, The. "Hugh MacDiarmid." CMoP

Light of our cigarettes, The. Pastel: Masks and Faces. Arthur Symons. NOBVV

Light of the moon illumines only, The. What Is Repeated, What Abides. Barbara Hendryson. CrSp

Light of the World, The. B. Alquit, *Yiddish.* CEEP, tr. by Howard Schwartz

Light on his pins. Roethke Plain. John Malcolm Brinnin. TAP

Light on his thigh was like, The. The King of the Cats is Dead. Peter Porter. NoAM

Light on the pool suddenly hides behind the wall, The. To Tzŭ-chih: among the "Flowers." Li Shang-yin, *Chinese.* PLT, tr. by A. C. Graham

Light on the Tower of David, light on the Church of St. Mary. Yehuda Amichai. *Fr.* Jerusalem 1967. IP, tr. by Warren Bargad and Stanley F. Chyet

Light oppresses and the darkness frees, The. Childhood of a Voice. Martin Carter. HCP

Light or Sheade. William Barnes. NOBVV

Light painted the sky, some months ago, The. Painting the Eaves. Tony Towle. PmAP

Light passes, The. Evening. Hilda Doolittle. CMoP; FaBoMo; VGW; WPE

Light projected lifetimes ago. Telescope. Sydney Lea. RA

Light pulling away from trees, The. Distance. Peter Everwine. NNaP

Light rain, and I'm carbound. In the Pasture of Dead Horses. Julia Wendell. PUP-20

Light rain doesn't slick the road. Tu Fu. SuSp, tr. by William H. Nienhauser *Fr.* Rain, Four Poems.

Light Reading. Vassar Miller. FFC

Light river wind, A. Robert Spiess. HA

Light rustle of rain laid down now, A. Afterglow. Jack Butler. MT

Light Shining out of Darkness. William Cowper. CABP; EBEV; ECEV; FHYEP; FaBoCh; ImPo; NOBE; NOCV; NOEC; PWR; PoEL-3; SCGP; TFi; TOF *Fr.* Olney Hymns.

(From Olney Hymns.) NoP-4

Light shivering on its tightrope. Breakfast with Jerome. Elaine Equi. WWSi

Light, so low upon earth. Marriage Morning. Tennyson. GBL

Light splashed this morning. The Round. Stanley Kunitz. PiM *Fr.* The Round.

Light-spring, oh sun, in light our wedding joys immure. Sonnet. Daniel Casper von Lohenstein. GePo *Fr.* Arminius.

Light stands over me, The. Descartes at Daybreak. Aidan Mathews. CIP-2

Light starts in a promising street, The. A Capriccio of Roman Ruins and Sculpture with Figures. J. D. McClatchy. GS

Light strikes and withdraws. Three Scenes: Todmorden. Jeff Nuttall. NBrP

". . . Light that cannot fade. . . , The." William Daniel Ehrhart. CDa

Light That Failed, The. Rudyard Kipling.

Heriot's Ford. PoRA

Light that fills heaven and earth, The. Bible, *O.T. See* Psalm 148.

Light that labored to an early fall, The. The Lake. Louis O. Coxe. NYBP

Light, that out of the west looked back once more. Night Thoughts in Age. John Hall Wheelock. NYBP

Light that shone when Hope was born, The. (LL) With trembling fingers did we weave. Tennyson. EBVV; FHYEP; OAEL-2

Light that streams into the grass. White Day's Death. Hazel Hall. PaTW

Light the first light of evening, as in a room. Final Soliloquy of the Interior Paramour. Wallace Stevens. ColAP; HAP; HCAP; LCAP-2

Light the Lamps Up, Lamplighter! Eleanor Farjeon. CH

("Light They Make, The"). Debra Bruce.
  Sonnet 2: "Deep in her seventh month, my sister dozes." FFC
  Sonnet 4: "Wet streets, black trees, a gold leaf smacked." FFC

Light up My world for Me. God to Man. *Unknown. Fr.* The Talmud. TrJP

Light up thy halls! 'Tis closing day. F. de Samara to A. G. A. Emily Jane Brontë. NALW

Light was out; the sky was down, The. Gnostic Prelude. James McAuley. BMAP

Light, water, salt, bread. Xenia. Petri Gyorgy, *Hungarian.* CEEP, *tr. by* Robert Austerlitz

Light white, a disgrace, an ink spot, a rosy charm, A. A Petticoat. Gertrude Stein. TTTS *Fr.* Tender Buttons.

Light-winged Smoke, Icarian bird. Smoke. Henry David Thoreau. APN-1; AWP; ColAP; NOBA; NoP-4; OxBA; TAP *Fr.* Walden.

Light Woman, A. Robert Browning. FP

Light Woman's Song, The. Judith Johnson Sherwin. TAP

Light Years and the Love Lost in the Oleanders. Alane Rollings. WeW-3

Light you give off, The. Jelaluddin Rumi, *Persian.* RaBo, *tr. by* Coleman Barks *and* John Moyne

Light young man lay with a lighter woman, A. On Tom Holland and Nell Cotton. *Unknown.* FaBoEE

Lighten up. Prayer. Lucille Clifton. NAAAL

Lightening / is the future brightening. Mabrak. "Bongo Jerry." PBCV

Lightheartedly breathing of the silvery winter. Hero. Yevgeny Aronovich Dolmatovsky, *Russian.* TCRP, *tr. by* Daniel Weissbort

Lighthouse. Novella Matveyeva, *Russian.* TCRP, *tr. by* Deming Brown

Lighthouse, The. Marjorie Wilson. BoTP

Lighthouse in the Night. Alfonsina Storni, *Spanish.* BoWoP, *tr. by* Aliki *and* Willis Barnstone

Lighthouse invites the storm and lights it, The. Malcolm Lowry. NOBC *Fr.* The Roar of the Sea and the Darkness.

Lighthouses. Dorothy, Duchess of Wellington Wellesley. WPE

Lighting a Fire. X. J. Kennedy. NOxBChV

Lighting a spill late in the afternoon. A Winter Talent. Donald Davie. OAEL-2

Lighting the Night Sky. Kenneth O. Hanson. FYAP

Lighting up, lest all our hearts should break. Words for Jazz Perhaps. Michael Longley. SeSe

Lightly Bound. Stevie Smith. NALW

Lightly forsaking / the spring mist as it rises. Seeing the Returning Geese. Lady Ise. BoWoP, *tr. by* Etsuko Terasaki *and* Irma Brandeis

Lightly he laughed, as one that read my thought. The Gardener's Daughter. Tennyson. OBGa

Lightly, lightly o'er [or ore] the dead. (LL) Upon a Maid[e]. Robert Herrick. CaPo; FaBoCh; FaBoEE; OxBoLi

Lightly she turns back her long red sleeves. Kuan Han-ch'ing. SuSp, *tr. by* Jerome P. Seaton *Fr.* Tune: "Green Jade Flute."

Lightly stepped a yellow star. Emily Dickinson. MoAmPo; OxBA; SAmP

Lightning, The. Judah Al-Harizi, *Hebrew.* BLT, *tr. by* T. Carmi

Lightning. Will Alexander. PT

Lightning. D. H. Lawrence. CMoP; MoBrPo; SAGP

Lightning. Mary Oliver. Poetr

Lightning. Tanka. Miyazawa Kenji, *Japanese.* MJT, *tr. by* Makoto Ueda

Lightning and the gale!, The. (LL) Old Ironsides. Oliver Wendell Holmes. APAD; APN-1; AiP; BLPA; CTV; EBEvV; FaBoBe; NAAL-1; NAAL-3; NCAP; PAR; PWR; TAP; TFi

Lightning Flash, The. *Unknown.* AmFP

Lightning flashes soar like rain before your eyes. When You're Not a Poet. Yona Wallach, *Hebrew.* IP, *tr. by* Warren Bargad *and* Stanley F. Chyet

Lightning flashes, The! Haiku. Basho, *Japanese.* SoSe-8, *tr. by* Earl Miner

Lightning gleam, A. Haiku. Basho, *Japanese.* SoSe-8; TAL, *tr. by* Harold G. Henderson

Lightning hits the roof. Woman to Man. Ai. NoAM

Lightning in the clouds! Basho, *Japanese.* WeW-3

Lightning is a yellow Fork, The. Emily Dickinson. InPK-6; NCAP

Lightning is angry in the night. Michael Is Afraid of the Storm. Gwendolyn Brooks. NOxBChV

Lightning Rod Salesman, The. M. L. Hester. CRP

Lightning scratched our sugar maple, blood. Injured Maple. Ronald G. Everson. NOBC

Lightning waked me, The.It slid under. May Swenson. ImGa

Lights, The. J. J. Bell. BoTP

Lights are all on, though it's just past midday, The. Rain. Brian Lee. AYFP

Lights are burning / In quiet rooms. Bus Stop. Donald Justice. FYAP; LCAP-2; WeT

Lights are going out, The. Larry Gates. HA

Lights extinguished, by the hearth I leant, The. A Legend of Provence. Adelaide Anne Procter. VWP

Lights from the parlour and [kitchen shone out], The. Escape at Bedtime. Robert Louis Stevenson. CTV; OTCP

Light's glittering morn bedecks the sky. Hymn for Easter Morn. John Mason Neale. TrCP

Lights in the hallway, The. James Wright. CAPP-1

Lights in the Sky are Stars, The. Kenneth Rexroth.
  Heart of Herakles, The. BLT
  Sword in a Cloud of Light, A. MoLi

Lights in the theater fail, The. The long racks. A Dancer's Life. Donald Justice. LCAP-2

Lights. Not the histrionic reds and golds. Port Phillip Night. Francis Webb. BMAP

Lights of Dublin, The. Patrick O'Connor. TIRV

Lights of London, The. Louise Imogen Guiney. APN-2

Lights off, the clock glowing 2:10, The. The Soup. Gary Soto. NoP-4

Lights on the shore. Planting. Okogbule Wonodi. PBMAP

Lights out. How to Meditate. Jack Kerouac. BB; PoM

Lights out. Ed Edward Thomas. NOBE; OxAEP-2; PoWW
  ("And myself.") (LL) LBC
  (Forest, The.) LBC

—lights out— / fall, hands a-clasped, into instantaneous. Jack Kerouac. *See* How to Meditate.

Lights out. Shades up. Girl in a Nightgown. Wallace Stevens. OxBA

Lights shining above the Neva. Yury Konstantinovich Terapiano, *Russian.* TCRP, *tr. by* Bradley Jordan

Lights shoot off the windows. With Lee Remick at Midnight. Ron Padgett. WWSi

Lights up her love-torch. Coleridge. *See* The Nightingale.

Like. Robert Desnos, *French.* MFP, *tr. by* Martin Sorrell

Like a Beacon. Grace Nichols. OPOU

Like a bird in the sky. (LL) Ego Tripping [(There May Be a Reason Why)]. Nikki Giovanni. CrSp; ISC; MoP; Poetsp; RaBo

Like a black hedgehog. Jaan Kaplinski, *Estonian.* CEEP, *tr. by* Ivar Ivask

Like a blaze of summer straw, in winter's nick. (LL) Unhappy people in a happy world, An. Wallace Stevens. CMoP; PoE

Like a Blessing. Stanley Crouch. GT

Like a bolt of silk, the rippled course of this southern river. Evening Scene at Twin Forests. Chin Nung, *Chinese.* CoBLCP, *tr. by* Jonathan Chaves

Like a bread without the spreadin'. Smile. *Unknown.* BLPA

Like a bullet. A Knife All Blade. João Cabral de Melo Neto, *Portuguese.* VCWP, *tr. by* Galway Kinnell

Like a bulwark against fate. At Rest in the Blast. Marianne Moore. MoAmPo

Like a calm hamlet at a mountain's feet. (LL) The Giantess. Charles Baudelaire, *French.* EP; FLP, *tr. by* Alistair Elliot

Like a caravan of nursing camels with humps in the sky. Jezrael. Avraham Shlonsky, *Hebrew.* MHP, *tr. by* Ruth Finer Mintz

Like a child's cut-out, she holds her weight. Dark Horse. Phillis Levin. FFC

Like a cloud the feathered albatross. Haka: The Feathered Albatross. Muru Walters, *Maori.* PeNZ, *tr. by the author*

Like a convalescent, I took the hand. Seamus Heaney. FaBoPV; NAEL-2; NoAM; TOF *Fr.* Station Island.

Like a coy maiden, ease, when courted most. Ease. William Cowper. *Fr.* The Sofa. *Fr.* The Task.

Like a dead man's grave. (LL) Brave New World. Archibald MacLeish. NOBA; OxBA

Like a deserted beach. The Man Closing Up. Donald Justice. CoAP

Like a Dog with a bottle, fast ti'd to his tail. The Batchelor's Song. Thomas Flatman. OxBM

Like a dragon you have filled the land. Inanna and An. Enheduanna, *Sumerian.* BoWoP, *ad. by* Aliki *and* Willis Barnstone

Like a dream through sleep she glided. The Chorus recall Helen's flight. Aeschylus, *Greek.* OBCVT, *tr.* by Edward Fitzgerald

Like a drop of water is my heart. Sarah Williams. LW

Like a drummer's brush. Rain. Emanuel DiPasquale. InPK-6; KaS

Like a drunk treading on his trouser cuffs. Convalescing in London. Thomas M. Disch. RA

Like a dry fish flung inland far from shore. Lost Anchors. Edwin Arlington Robinson. CMoP

Like a falling star / Excelsior! Henry Wadsworth Longfellow. *See* Excelsior.

Like a fawn from the arrow, startled and wild. Eliza Harris. Frances Ellen Watkins Harper. AAP; NAAAL

Like a fine *what* shirt I put it on. The House Beside the Sea. Rachel Hadas. FFC

Like a first coat of whitewash when it's wet. Twelfth Morning; or What You Will. Elizabeth Bishop. CBNP

Like a flat sea. Population. George Oppen. PoA

Like a flight of arrows the wind. Stormy Night in Autumn. Chu Shu-chen, *Chinese.* BoWoP; OHPC, *tr.* by Kenneth Rexroth

Like a Flower. Fily-Dabo Sissoko, *French.* NegPo, *tr.* by Ellen Conroy Kennedy

Like a fruit wine with earth. Cider and Vesalius. John Peck. AmPA

Like a funeral bell. (LL) Afternoon in February. Henry Wadsworth Longfellow. APN-1; ColAP

Like a gaunt, scraggly pine. Lincoln. John Gould Fletcher. CBCWP; MoAmPo

Like a gondola of green scented fruits. Images. Richard Aldington. MoBrPo; PoA

Like a great rock, far out at sea. Lady Sanuki. *Fr.* Hyaku-Nin-Isshu. AWP, *tr.* by Curtis Hidden Page

Like a grey wall around Europe. Recitative. Iwan Goll. PeFWW, *tr.* by Patrick Bridgwater *Fr.* Requiem for the Dead of Europe.

Like a guest on the threshold, was the Christmas Star. (LL) Christmas Star. Boris Pasternak, *Russian.* TCRP, *tr.* by Yakov Hornstein

Like a heavy load. Langston Hughes. *See* Harlem.

Like a hidden spring. My Love-Song. Else Lasker-Schüler, *German.* TrJP, *tr.* by Jethro Bithell

Like a hill. Robert Creeley. *See* The Hill.

Like a hot stone your cock weighs on mine, young man. Long Lines: Youth and Age. Paul Goodman. GLP

Like a hound with nose to the trail. Michaelmas. Norman Nicholson. MoBrPo

Like a hungry fledgeling that watches and hears. Vittoria da Colonna, Marchesa di Pescara, *Italian.* PBWP, *tr.* by Lynne Lawner

Like a hunted deer. Relations. Orerulavanar, *Tamil.* PLW, *tr.* by A. K. Ramanujan

Like a huntsman after weary chase. Sonnet 67. Edmund Spenser. GBL; HeIP-4; NAEL-1; PoE; PoEL-1; Son *Fr.* Amoretti. AAS

Like a lit-up Christmas Tree. The Lover and the Syringa-Bush. Herman Melville. OBAL

Like a lizard in the sun, though not scuttling. The Laureate. Robert Graves. BIrV; FaBoTw; OBSV

Like a long. Tanka. Miya Shūji, *Japanese.* MJT, *tr.* by Makoto Ueda

Like a long line of high-flying herons. A Parade. Peruṅkun̮rūr Kiḷr̮, *Tamil.* PLW, *tr.* by A. K. Ramanujan

Like a long step. Dance. Haim Guri, *Hebrew.* IP, *tr.* by Warren Bargad *and* Stanley F. Chyet

Like a loose island on the wide expanse. To a Deaf and Dumb Little Girl. Hartley Coleridge. PoEL-4

Like a mad lion, like a wild bull. The Race. Nuala Ni Dhomhnaill, *Irish.* CIP-2; PBCIP, *tr.* by Michael Hartnett

Like a madwoman and almost alone. Interior Landscape. Gloria Fuertes, *Spanish.* BoWoP, *tr.* by Willis Barnstone

Like a man anointing himself. (LL) At a March against the Vietnam War. Robert Bly. CDa; SPE

Like a map blanketing a bed. Patches of Sky. Debora Greger. ImGa

Like a miner, into sleep. (LL) Roger the Dog. Ted Hughes. ChAP; PeP

Like a miracle song. Another Me. Api, *Tamil.* OMIP, *tr.* by A. K. Ramanujan

Like a mountain whirlwind. Sappho, *Greek.* BoWoP, *tr.* by Willis Barnstone

Like a Mourningless Child. Kenneth Patchen. MoAmPo

Like a painting it is set before one. The View from the Window. Ronald Stuart Thomas. NoP-4

Like a pair of companionable porcupines. Baucis and Philemon. Katherine Hoskins. PoA

Like a pot turned on the straw. How Is He Coming Then. Lucille Clifton. CrSp; NALW

Like a quail. Clinton. Sterling Plumpp. BkSV *Fr.* Clinton.

Like a rainstorm, he said, the braided colors. Worsening Situation. John Ashbery. NOBA

Like a ravaged sea / this bed. Lady Ise, *Japanese.* BoWoP, *tr.* by Etsuko Terasaki *and* Irma Brandeis

Like a relentless milkman up the stairs. (LL) Living in Sin. Adrienne Rich. NIP-4; NYBP; NoP-4; Poetr; SoSe-8; TAP; UnPo

Like a rising Blackening sun. (LL) The Woman Thing. Audre Lorde. BlSi; GT; NMM-2

Like a river she was. The Memory. Robert Creeley. VGW

Like a root growing. (LL) Eleven. Archibald MacLeish. HAP; MeMAP; WeW-3

Like a round loaf, that's how small you were. To the Newborn. Judit Tóth, *Hungarian.* WPOW, *tr.* by Laura Schiff

Like a sailor in the ship's rigging he slid over the tropic of Cancer and the / tropic of Capricorn. Les Anges Sont Blancs. George Seferis, *Greek.* PFTM, *tr.* by George Economou

Like a scared rabbit running over and. Jack Spicer. *Fr.* Graphemics. VGW

Like a Scarf. James Tate. BAP-94

Like a shell, and as it opens, cuts. (LL) Earliness at the Cape. Babette Deutsch. FYAP; NYBP

Like a shipwreck'd Sailor tost. Lucretius, *Latin.* OBCVT, *tr.* by William Wordsworth *Fr.* De Rerum Natura (On the Nature of Things).

Like a silkworm weaving. Mahadevi, *Kannada.* PBWP, *tr.* by A. K. Ramanujan

Like a skein of loose silk blown against a wall. The Garden. Ezra Pound. AWP; HeIP-4; MoAmPo; NIP-4; NoP-4; OxBSP; PoPoPo; TwCP

Like a small gray / coffee-pot. The Gray Squirrel. Humbert Wolfe. MoBrPo

Like a soldier from Anders's army. Natalya Gorbanevskaya, *Russian.* TCRP, *tr.* by Albert C. Todd

Like a stone dropping down a well. In the Dark Again. C. G. Hanzlicek. CMAP

Like a sweet apple reddening on the high. Sappho, *Greek.* BoWoP, *tr.* by Willis Barnstone

Like a tea-tray in the sky. (LL) The Mad Hatter's Song. "Lewis Carroll." CTV

Like a veiled dream thy memory comes. To a Loved One of Other Days. Matilda Caroline Edwards. PWR

Like a wave crest. Uda Emperor, *Japanese.* OHPJ, *tr.* by Kenneth Rexroth

Like a white candle through a shuttered hand. The Sisters. Roy Campbell. BoLoP; EP; FaBoTw; NoP-4; OBMV

Like a white lotus. Tanka. Ishikawa Takuboku, *Japanese.* MJT, *tr.* by Ueda, Makoto

Like a woman you've longed to make love to, and finally did. Pennsylvania Winter Indian 1974. Harold Littlebird. VoR

Like a wounded bear. Dark Blue Hussars. Nikolai Nikolaievich Aseyev, *Russian.* TCRP, *tr.* by Lubov Yakovleva *with* Daniel Weissbort

Like Achilles you had a goddess for mother. On Looking into E. V. Rieu's Homer. Patrick Kavanagh. NOIV

Like air on skin, coolness of yachts at mooring. Yachts on the Nile. Bernard Spencer. NoAM

Like an adventurous seafarer am I. Michael Drayton. NOSC; Son *Fr.* Idea.

Like an adversity. (LL) Drowning is not so pitiful. Emily Dickinson. CMoP; NCAP; OxBSP

Like an Animal. Jimmy Santiago Baca. AF

Like an arrow shot / To Death from Birth. Wine. Micah Joseph Lebensohn, *Hebrew.* TrJP, *tr.* by A. M. Klein

Like an elephant. Mahadevi, *Kannada.* PBWP, *tr.* by A. K. Ramanujan

Like an enfranchised bird, who wildly springs. Sonnet 7. Caroline Elizabeth Norton. VWP

Like an home-reared animal in a quiet nook. King Pellam's Launde. David Jones. OAEL-2 *Fr.* In Parenthesis.

Like an old stone tree. (LL) The Moss of His Skin. Anne Sexton. CoAP; NALW; SAGP

Like an otter, but warm. Pastoral. Rita Dove. NAAAL

Like an ox streaming saliva, yoked to the plough. Jules Supervielle, *French.* MFP, *tr.* by Martin Sorrell

Like Ana. Nina Cassian, *Romanian.* PoSu, *tr.* by Nina Cassina

Like ankle-rings, this music. Gunnar Ekelof, *Swedish.* PFTM, *tr.* by Muriel Rukeyser *and* Leif Sjoberg

Like any summer day. (LL) The Voice. Theodore Roethke. EP; VGW

Like as a ship, that through the ocean wyde. Sonnet 34. Edmund Spenser. NAEL-1; PoE *Fr.* Amoretti. AAS

Like as a ship, that through the ocean wyde. Edmund Spenser. *Fr.* Wood Of Error. AEP

Like as the armèd knight. The Ballad Which Anne Askew[e] Made and Sang When She Was in Newgate. Anne Askew. CABP; NoP-4; NoSic; WPE

Like as the bird in the cage enclosed. Sir Thomas Wyatt. SiPS

Like as the culver on the bared bough. Sonnet 89. Edmund Spenser. GBL; PoE *Fr.* Amoretti. AAS

Like as the damask rose you see. Man's Mortality. Simon Wastell. FaBoCh *Fr.* Microbiblion.

Like as the divers-fretchled Butterfly. The Muse Reviving. Sir John Davies. SiPS

Like as the dove which seeled-up doth fly. Sir Philip Sidney. SiPS

Like as the fountain[e] of all light created. Incarnatio Est Maximum Dei Donum [*or* Donum Dei]. William Alabaster. NoSic

Like as the swan towards her death. Sir Thomas Wyatt. SiPS

Like as the tide that comes from th' Ocean main. Edmund Spenser. HoPM *Fr.* Wood Of Error. AEP

Like as the waves make towards the pebbled shore. Sonnet 60. Shakespeare. CABP; EBEV; GTBS-P; ImPo; NIP-4; NOBE; NoSic; OxAEP-1; PoRA; SCGP; Son; TFi; UnPo *Fr.* Sonnets.

Like as, to make our appetites more keen. Sonnet 118. Shakespeare. SCGP *Fr.* Sonnets.

Like Attracts Like. Emmett Williams. WeW-3

Like Balls—upon a Floor. (LL) I felt a cleavage in my mind. Emily Dickinson. APN-2; NOBA; OxBA; TRP

Like battered old millhands, they stand in the orchard—. Old Apple Trees. W. D. Snodgrass. FYAP

Like Birds of a Feather. Ralph Schomberg. *Fr.* The Judgment of Paris. TrJP

Like birds when first light breaks. Children Waking: Indian Hill Station. Ralph Nixon Currey. PeSA

Like bodiless water passing in a sigh. Fog. Louise Imogen Guiney. APN-2

Like butterflies but lately come. Beautiful Creatures Brief as These. Douglas G. Jones. MoCV

Like cat down cellar wit' nohole mouse. (LL) Scottsboro. *Unknown.* APAD

Like Chopin, not even showing my puss. Impromptu. Márton Kalász, *Hungarian.* CEEP, tr. by Jascha Kessler

Like cities, like storms. August Kleinzahler. MoNo

Like Coleridge, I waltz. Under the Ice. Stewart Conn. FaBoTC

Like Coleridge into a metaphysician. Byron. *See* Young Juan wandered by the glassy brooks.

Like Coney Island in winter. (LL) Ladies and gentlemen this little girl. E. E. Cummings. CMoP; PoE

Like costumes grandsires wore. (LL) We outgrow love like other things. Emily Dickinson. GLoP; NOBA; SoSe-8

Like courtiers contending for honours, sat down. (LL) Poem on the Supposition of an Advertisement, A; Appearing in a Morning Paper, of the Publication of a Volume of Poems, by a Servant-Maid. Elizabeth Hands. ECWP; WoRP

Like cracks. Tanka. Miyazawa Kenji, *Japanese.* MJT, tr. by Makoto Ueda

Like Crusoe with the bootless gold we stand. Experience. Edith Wharton. APN-2

Like cutting the dry rot out of a potato. Dark Conclusions. Ruth Stone. BoWoP

Like death-row prisoners, they have till the morning stars to live. Mayakovsky. Mikhail Kulchitsky, *Russian.* TCRP, tr. by Bradley Jordan

Like Deer Our Bodies. Wayne Dodd. CMAP

Like Deity—to keep. (LL) I think I was enchanted. Emily Dickinson. APN-2; NALW

Like diligence requires the courser's race. Knowing About Horses. Virgil. APo, tr. by John Dryden *Fr.* The Georgics.

Like dives in the deeps of hell. Save the Boys. Frances Ellen Watkins Harper. AAP; PWR

Like dolmens round my childhood, the old people. John Montague. EBEV; IIP; NoP-4; PBCIP; PNI

Like easy conversation / rambling, obliquely arranged. 64 Panoramic Way. Carol Moldaw. WWSi

Like Etna's dread volcano see the ample forge. The Anchorsmiths. Charles Dibdin. NOEC

Like Eyes that looked on Wastes. Emily Dickinson. CPO

Like far-off conflagrations: roses of Anjou. (LL) The Lilacs and the Roses. Louis Aragon, *French.* NNPT; OBWP, tr. by Louis MacNeice

Like fire-flies that the peasant on the hill. Dante. *Fr.* Inferno. NAWM-1, tr. by John Ciardi *Fr.* Divina Commedia.

Like foxgloves in the school of the grass moon. The Flower Master. Medbh McGuckian. PNI

Like fragments of an uncompleted world. Sierras. Joaquin Miller. APN-2

Like garden gods—and not so decent either. (LL) Sagest of women, even of widows, she. Byron. NOBL; PeLV

Like gentle swells. The Fisherman's Whore. Dave Jeddie Smith. CMAP

Like Ghosts of Eagles. Robert Francis. LCAP-2

Like God's attention. Where nothing is diminished by perspective. (LL) Equanimity. Les A. Murray. NOBAu

Like goldenrod ready to bloom. (LL) Woman in the ordinary pudgy downcast girl, The. Marge Piercy. CrSp; NMM-2

Like Grandpa Paul / The water is all of my mind. Louis Zukofsky. ChIV-1 *Fr.* "A-12."

Like gript stick. The Sermon. Richard Hughes. OBMV

Like Groping Fingers. Abraham Sutskever, *Yiddish.* TrJP, tr. by Joseph Leftwich

Like Gulliver pulling a hundred ships, *see also* "Like Gulliver who towed a hundred ships." Nina Cassian, *Romanian*, Petre Solomon. BoWoP, tr. by Willis Barnstone *and* Matei Calinescu

Like her,—because they love him. (LL) In School-Days. John Greenleaf Whittier. BLPA; FaBoBe; OBCA

Like hibiscus. Like a Flower. Fily-Dabo Sissoko, *French.* NegPo, tr. by Ellen Conroy Kennedy

Like his hand, in fever, on my forehead. (LL) Out-of-the-Body Travel. Stanley Plumly. AmPA; LCAP-2

Like hooved up ground / thats what. (LL) The Hermit Cackleberry Brown, on Human Vanity. Jonathan Williams. OBAL; PoM

Like it used to be, not even the future. (LL) Ö. Rita Dove. HCAP; WeW-3

Like John on Patmos, brooding on the Four. A Commination. Alec Derwent Hope. ChIV-2

Like Jonah in the green belly of the whale. Emily Carr. Wilfred Watson. MoCV; NOBC

Like killer kings on an Etruscan cup. (LL) Beyond the Alps. Robert Lowell. LCAP-2; NOBA

Like Leaves. Lâm thị Mỹ Dạ, *Vietnamese.* AVP, tr. by Huỳnh Sanh Thông

Like Leaves on Trees the Race of Man is found. Homer. OBVE, tr. by Alexander Pope *Fr.* The Iliad.

Like life and fear, a dark reality. Shelley. *See* Hymn to Intellectual Beauty.

Like liquid gold the wheat-field lies. A Dakota Wheat-Field. Hamlin Garland. OBCA

Like Lise, moreover, my mother was white. The Black Man's Son. Oswald Durand, *French.* TTY, tr. by Edna Worthley Underwood

Like Loving Chekhov. Denise Levertov. InPS-5

Like lust in the chill of the grave. (LL) Hamatreya. Ralph Waldo Emerson. APN-1; NAAL-3; NCAP; PAR

Like many a one, when you had gold. The Old Story. Argentarius. AWP, tr. by E. A. Robinson *Fr.* Variations of Greek Themes.

Like many of us, born too late. Shut In. Robert B. Shaw. SoSe-8

Like marmalade / Instead. A. A. Milne. *See* The King's Breakfast.

Like medals given the brave. (LL) The Field Hospital. Paul Muldoon. CIP-2; PNI

Like [*or* Lyke] Memnons rock, touched [*or* rocke toucht] with the rising sun[ne]. Sonnet: "Like Memnon's rock, touched with the rising sun." Giles Fletcher, the Elder. AAS *Fr.* Licia.

Like men riding. Nelly Trim. Sylvia Townsend Warner. MoBrPo

Like Michinoku. Minamoto no Tōru, *Japanese.* OHPJ, tr. by Kenneth Rexroth

Like milk. What She Said. Kollan Alici, *Tamil.* PLW, tr. by A. K. Ramanujan

Like moody beasts they lie along the sands. Femmes Damnées. John Gray. ADE

Like moss on water. What She Said. Paranar, *Tamil.* PLW, tr. by A. K. Ramanujan

Like Mother, like Son. Margaret Johnston Grafflin. *See* To My Son.

Like music come back to life—. Small Variation. Octavio Paz, *Spanish.* VCWP, tr. by Mark Strand

Like musical instruments. Tom Clark. CoAmPo; PmAP; TRP

Like Noah's Weary Dove. William Augustus Mühlenberg. AH

Like nothing else in Tennessee. (LL) Anecdote of the Jar. Wallace Stevens. AmPP; CMoP; ColAP; FaBoA; HCAP; HeIP-4; HoPM; InPK-6; MeMAP; MoAmPo; MoP; NAAL-2; NAWM-2; NOBA; NoAM; NoP-4; OxBA; OxBSP; PoA; PoPoPo; Poetr; SAmP; TAP; TFi; UnPo

Like Odysseus under the ram. Archilochus, *Latin.* OBVE, tr. by Guy Davenport

Like old women knitting, breathless / to tell their tales. (LL) Necessities of Life. Adrienne Rich. HCAP; NOBA; Poetr

Like one who brings an important letter to the counter after office hours: the counter is already closed. When Evil-Doing Comes Like Falling Rain. Bertolt Brecht, *German.* AF, tr. by John Willett

Like one who brought news from far. Agnes Nemes Nagy, *Hungarian.* VCWP, tr. by Hugh Maxton

Like one who in [*or* who'in] her third widowhood [*or* widdowhood] doth profess[e]. To Mr. Roland Woodward. Donne. ESCV

Like other things. Girl in the Kitchen. "Vaidehi," *Kannada.* OMIP, tr. by A. K. Ramanujan

Like others I get drunk in my blood. The Road to Exile Thinking of Vallejo. Syl Cheney-Coker. PBMAP

Like our bodies' imprint. Yehuda Amichai, *Hebrew*. AF, *tr. by* Gutmann, Assia

Like our hearts too hardened for tears. Christmas. Jonggil Kim, *Korean*. CKP, *tr. by* Jaihiun Kim

Like Oxford colledge bells, to supp. (LL) On Westwall Downes [*or* On Westwell Downs]. William Strode. NOSC; PoEL-2

Like pain of fire runs down my body my love to you, my dear! Love Song. *Unknown*. APN-2, *tr. by* Franz Boas *Fr.* Songs of the Kwakiutl Indians.

Like plump green floor plans. Rotation. Julian Bond. PFE

Like priceless treasures sinking in the sand. (LL) America. Claude McKay. MoP; NAAAL; NIP-4; NoAM; PoBA; TAP; TTY

Like Rachel. Dahlia Ravikovitch, *Hebrew*. IP, *tr. by* Warren Bargad *and* Stanley F. Chyet

Like Rain it sounded till it curved. Emily Dickinson. NCAP; RB

Like Rousseau. Imamu Amiri Baraka. PoA

Like Sand. Natan Zach, *Hebrew*. IP, *tr. by* Warren Bargad *and* Stanley F. Chyet

Like silver dew are the tears of love. Epitaph. Alfred Edgar Coppard. OBMV

Like Smoke. Mririda n'Ait Attik, *French*. PBWP, *tr. by* Daniel Halpern *and* Paula Paley

Like smoke in a bottle, like. Poem for the Name Mary. Mark Cox. NAmP90

Like so much weather / out of the west. Towards the Blanched Alphabets. Gustaf Sobin. PT

Like some ill-fated butterfly, the literalists. John Hollander. VCAP *Fr.* Powers of Thirteen.

Like some weak lords, neighboured by mighty kings. Sonnet 29. Sir Philip Sidney. *Fr.* Astrophil and Stella. AAS; SiPS

Like South Sea stock, expressions rise and fall. Time's Changes. James Bramston. NOEC *Fr.* The Art of Politics.

Like Stephen Vincent Benét, I have fallen in love with American names. Ill Met by Zenith. Ogden Nash. NYBP

Like sticks in a fire. (LL) Variations on an Air: After W. B. Yeats. G. K. Chesterton. BXAP; NOBL

Like Stone—. (LL) Soul selects her own Society—The, The. Emily Dickinson. NoP-4; OxWW; PoPoPo; SAGP

Like tall men with a battering-plank—the colt. Letter from Underground. Ronald G. Everson. MoCV

Like tatters of the *Morpho* butterfly. (LL) Under the Window: Ouro Prêto. Elizabeth Bishop. NYBP; VCAP

Like that. (LL) Poem for Flora. Nikki Giovanni. BPo; CrSp; PoBA

Like that dying woman in Mexico. If. Patrick Lane. NOBC

Like the beat beat beat of the tom-tom. Night and Day. Cole Porter. CBLP

Like the buffalo. To You. Elolongue Epanya Yondo, *French*. NegPo, *tr. by* Ellen Conroy Kennedy

Like the cadence of an old love song. Child Life. Mary E. Tucker. CBWP-1

Like the city skyline they. Commuters. Betsy Hearne. SSCS

Like the crash of the thunder. Zionist Marching Song. Naphtali Herz Imber, *Hebrew*. TrJP, *tr. by* Israel Zangwill

Like the dark germs across the filter clean. Loss. Charles Madge. FaBoMo

Like the Eyes of Wolves. Nachum Yud, *Yiddish*. TrJP, *tr. by* Joseph Leftwich

Like the fairest of all looking into her mirror. (LL) Feminism. Denise Duhamel. BAP-93; IFJA

Like the fey goose-girl in the enchanted wood. Horror. Henry Treece. SPE

Like the fish of the bright and twittering fin. Song from *Mardi*. Herman Melville. APN-2

Like the foghorn that's all lung. Syrinx. Amy Clampitt. NoP-4

Like the golden scale that emerges. Personae Separatae. Eugenio Montale, *Italian*. AF, *tr. by* William Arrowsmith

Like the heaven above. . (LL) (Little Things). Julia A. Fletcher Carney. ACTP; BLPA; FaBoBe; OxBChV

Like the high fanning tufts on swift horses. What She Said. Orampokiyar. PLW *Fr.* Five on the Riverside Cane. PLW, *tr. by* A. K. Ramanujan

Like the honeycomb dropping honey. Hildegard von Bingen, *Latin*. WPOW, *tr. by* Patrick Diehl

Like the Idalian queen. Madrigal. William Henry Drummond. EP

Like the Idalian Queen[e]. Madrigal. William Drummond, of Hawthornden. CBLP; GBL; NOBE; NOSC; OAEL-1; OBAL; OBEV; PeLV; PoEL-2; SCGP

Like the inflatable palm tree I gave to my lover. In Pompano Beach, Florida. Robin Becker. PBCAP

Like the last Gazette, or the last Address. (LL) The Art of Satire. Alexander Pope. ECEV; EPCY; NOBE; NOEC; OBSV

Like the red flame. Peyanar. PLW *Fr.* Seven Said by the Foster-Mother. PLW, *tr. by* A. K. Ramanujan

Like the stalks of wheat in the fields. Epilogue. Heinrich Heine. TrJP, *tr. by* Emma Lazarus; AWP, *tr. by* Louis Untermeyer *Fr.* The North Sea.

Like the stench and smudge of the old dump-heap. Dream, Dump-Heap, and Civilization. Robert Penn Warren. AFr

Like the steps of footsore armies. Waiting for Death. Mordecai Gebirtig, *Yiddish*. TrJP, *tr. by* Joseph Leftwich

Like the sweet apple which reddens upon [the topmost bough]. One Girl. Sappho, *Greek*. AWP; LoP; OBCVT, *tr. by* D. G. Rossetti

Like the swell of Summer's ocean. (LL) Stanzas for Music ("There be none of Beauty's daughters"). Byron. AWP; CBLP; GTBS-P; HAP; LaPo; NAEL-2; OAEL-2; PoRA

Like the tides' flood. *Unknown, Japanese*. OHMPJ, *tr. by* Kenneth Rexroth

Like the Touch of Rain [she was]. Edward Thomas. BoLoP; EnLoPo; GBL; GLoP

Like the unicorn, Uncle. Uncle Sam. Kenneth Rexroth. *Fr.* A Bestiary. OBAL

Like the universe. Science as Art. Hugh Seidman. AmPA

Like the very gods in my sight is he. Sappho, *Greek*. WPOW, *tr. by* Richmond Lattimore

Like the waters. (LL) The Old Men Admiring Themselves in the Water. W. B. Yeats. CMoP; FaBoCh; KaS

Like the white whale, born black, myself grows brighter. Pervigilium Veneris. Suzanne Noguere. PoA

Like the wild organs of the winter storm. In the East. Georg Trakl, *German*. PeFWW, *tr. by* Michael Hamburger

Like thee I once have stemm'd the sea of life. An Epitaph. James Beattie. OBEV

Like they had never been. (LL) The Tryst [*or* Trysting Place]. William Soutar. BoLoP; EBEV; FaBoTC; OxBS

Like They Say. Robert Creeley. BLT

Like this before you, just as I am. Yocheved Bat-Miriam, *Hebrew*. MHP, *tr. by* Ruth Finer Mintz

Like this stone of. I Am a Creature. Giuseppe Ungaretti, *Italian*. PeFWW, *tr. by* David McDuff *and* Jon Silkin

Like This Together. Adrienne Rich. VGW

Like this. . . You wouldn't hang me? I thought not. (LL) How Annandale Went Out. Edwin Arlington Robinson. GSo; MoAmPo; NOBA; NoAM; PFE; SoSe-8

Like those boats which are returning. Saigyo, *Japanese*. AWP, *tr. by* Arthur Waley

Like those flailing flames. Ted Hughes. HAP, *sect. 7 Fr.* Skylarks.

Like those jars that women put out to catch the dew of night. Gabriela Mistral. WPoS, *tr. by* Langston Hughes *Fr.* Prayer.

Like thousands, I took just pride and more than just. Reading Myself. Robert Lowell. HCAP; NAAL-2; TAP; VCAP

Like tiny golden. Akiko Yosano, *Japanese*. OHMPJ, *tr. by* Kenneth Rexroth

Like to a baker's oven is the grave. In Christ Church, Bristol, on Thomas Turner, Twice Master of the Company of Bakers. Francis, Lord Jeffrey Jeffrey. FaBoEE; NBLV; OxBoLi

Like to a *Feavers pulse* my *heart* doth beat. The Poetresses Petition. Margaret Lucas Cavendish, Duchess of Newcastle. KTR

Like to a fever's pulse my heart doth beat. Margaret Lucas Cavendish, Duchess of Newcastle. *See* The Poetresses Petition.

Like to a god he seems to me. Sappho. Catullus, *Latin*. AWP, *tr. by* William Ellery Leonard *Fr.* Carmina.

Like to a hermit[e] poor[e][,] in place obscure. Sir Walter Ralegh. GBL

Like to a ring without a finger. *Unknown*. NoSic

Like to Diana in her summer weed[e]. Samela. Robert Greene. GBL; NOBE; OBEV; PoEL-2 *Fr.* Menaphon.

Like to the arctic needle, that doth guide. I Am My Beloved's, and His Desire Is towards Me. Francis Quarles. EBEV; NOCV; OAEL-1; OxAEP-1 *Fr.* Emblems.

Like to the clear [*or* cleere] in highest sphere [*or* spheare]. Rosaline. Thomas Lodge. GTBS-P; OBEV; OxAEP-1 *Fr.* Rosalynde; or Euphues' Golden Legacy.

Like to the damaske rose you see. Hos Ego Versiculos. Francis Quarles. NOSC *Fr.* Argalus and Parthenia.

Like to the falling of a star. Sic Vita. Henry, Bishop of Chichester King. NOBE; NOSC; OxBSP; SCGP; SeCP

Like to the Grass That's Green Today. Peter, the Younger Bulkeley. AH

Like to the Indians, scorched with the sun[ne]. Sonnet 22. Mary Sidney Wroth. NOSC *Fr.* Pamphilia to Amphilanthus.

Like to the marigold, I blushing close. Edward Taylor. ChIV-2; SCAP *Fr.* Preparatory Meditations Before My Approach to the Lord's Supper.

Like to the sentinel stars, I watch all night. To Lucasta. Richard Lovelace. NOSC

Like to the Thundering Tone. Nonsense [*or* Nonsence]. Richard Corbet. CBNP; FaBoVe

Like to these unme[a]surable montains [*or* mountayns]. Jacopo Sannazaro, *Italian.* AAS; PoE, *tr. by* Sir Thomas Wyatt

Like Trains of Cars on Tracks of Plush. The Bee. Emily Dickinson. MoAmPo

Like / treasure hidden in the ground. Mahadevi, *Kannada.* WPOW, *tr. by* A. K. Ramanujan

Like tree shadows into the polished windscreen. (LL) From the Frontier of Writing. Seamus Heaney. CABP; PoPoPo

Like truthles[s] dream[e]s, so are my joys expired. Farewell to the Court. Sir Walter Ralegh. NoSic; SiPS; Son

Like two cathedral towers these stately pines. My Cathedral. Henry Wadsworth Longfellow. PBMP

Like two proud armies marching in the field. *Unknown.* NoSic

Like two somnambulists we entered the dawn sun. Hunting for Blueberries. Thomas James. AmPA

Like unto Them That Dream. Bible, *O.T.* TrJP *Fr.* Psalms. (Psalm 126).

Like us he had his. Ulumbo, a Cat. Rutger Kopland, *Dutch.* VCWP, *tr. by* James Brockway

Like voices on the gale. (LL) Stanzas: "Black absence hides upon the past." John Clare. EnLoPo; NOBVV

Like wanderers in elevated meekness. In the Desert. Semyon Izrailevich Lipkin, *Russian.* TCRP, *tr. by* Albert C. Todd

Like Water down a Slope. Zalman Schneour, *Hebrew.* TrJP, *tr. by* Harry H. Fein

Like wet cornstarch, I slide. Refugee Ship. Lorna Dee Cervantes. PoPoPo

Like whispers round the body of the dead! (LL) I know not why, but all this weary day. Henry Timrod. APN-2; PAR

Like widow'd turtle still her loss complain. (LL) To His Lute. William Drummond, of Hawthornden. GSo; GTBS-P; NOSC; SCGP; Son

Like wolf—and black bull or goblin hound. Charlotte Brontë. VWP

Like Yellowstone National Park. (LL) Further Notice. Philip Whalen. PoM; VGW

Like you, I belong to yesterday. Emily Dickinson. Lucha Corpi. NMM-2

Like yours may sweeten and perfume my death. (LL) A Contemplation upon Flowers. Henry, Bishop of Chichester King. MeLP; OBEV; SCGP; SeCP

Likelihood is, The. Children. Bill Manhire. PeNZ

Likelihood of Snow, The/ The Danger of Fire. Gerald Dawe. PNI

Likeness, A. Robert Browning. CTC

Likeness, The. Arthur Gregor. VGW

Likeness has made them animal and shy. The Twins. Karl Shapiro. MoAmPo; TrJP

Likeness, one of the race of fathers, A: earth / And sea and air. (LL) The Irish Cliffs of Moher. Wallace Stevens. NOBA; RaBo; TOF; VGW

LIKES to a hermit poor in place obscure. Sir Walter Ralegh. NoSic

Likkle seed / of her love fe a man, A. Belly Woman's Lament. Lillian Allen. PBCV

Lilac by the Museum on St. Wenceslas Square, The. Vitězslav Nezval, *Czech.* AF, *tr. by* Ewald Osers

Lilac ice cream! Lilac ice cream! "Igor Severyanin," *Russian.* TCRP, *tr. by* Bernard Meares

Lilac ribbon is unbound, A. Country of No Lack. Jean Starr Untermeyer. MoAmPo

Lilacs. Amy Lowell. MoAmPo; OxBA; PoRA

Lilacs and the Roses, The. Louis Aragon, *French.* NNPT; OBWP, *tr. by* Louis MacNeice

Lilacs blowing across his face glad he brought you. (LL) The Tennis Court Oath. John Ashbery. NoAM; TAP; WeT

Lilacs lift in generous bloom, The. At Home from Church. Sarah Orne Jewett. APAD; APN-2; ColAP

Lilacs on Brattle Street. Gail Mazur. PUP-19

Lilacs wither in the Carolinas, The. In the Carolinas. Wallace Stevens. FiLi; SAmP; VGW

Lilian's Second Letter. Bessie Rayner Parkes. VWP *Fr.* Summer Sketches.

Lilian's Song. George Darley. OBNC

Lilies. Bozhidar Bozhilov, *Bulgarian.* CEEP, *tr. by* Jascha Kessler *and* Aleksandar Shurbanov

Lilies, The. Richard Emil Braun. NoAM

Lilies are white. *Unknown.* BoTP; LB; OxNR

Lilies of his love appear!, The. (LL) The Revival. Henry Vaughan. NOCV; PoEL-2

Lilies of the Valley. Jon Silkin. NoAM

Lilies swinging censers fair. Easter Carol. Henrietta Ray. CBWP-3

Lilies that fester smell far worse than weeds. (LL) Sonnet 94. Shakespeare. CABP; CBLP; GTBS-P; ImPo; InPS-3; NAEL-1; NOBE; NoP-4; NoSic; OAEL-1; OBEV; OxAEP-1; OxBoV; PoE; PoEL-2; SCGP; SCV; Son; TRP

Lilith. Enid Dame. EC3

Lilith. Linda Gregg. WPOW

Lilith. D. G. Rossetti. *See* Body's Beauty.

Lilith and the Doctor. Kathleen Norris. CrSp

Lilith to Eve. Michelene Wandor. NBrP

Lilli Burlero [*or* Lilliburlero]. Thomas Wharton, 1st Marquess of Wharton. NOIV; OxBoLi

Lilliputian Ode on Their Majesties' Accession, A. Henry Carey. FaBoVe; NOEC; OBCoV

Lilliputian's Beer Song. Septimus Winner. OBAL

Lilly in a Christal, The. Robert Herrick. *See* The Lily in a Crystal.

Lilt Your Johnnie. *Unknown.* BXAP

Lily, The. William Blake. FHYEP; NOBRP; Ro *Fr.* Songs of Experience.

Lily, The. Vadim Shefner, *Russian.* TCRP, *tr. by* Albert C. Todd

Lily. Nicholas Virgilio. HA

Lily Adair. Thomas Holley Chivers. APN-1; OBAL

Lily Events. *Unknown.* PFTM

Lily in a Crystal, The. Robert Herrick. BeJo; NAEL-1; NOSC; PoEL-3; SCGP; SeCP

Lily of the West, The. *Unknown.* AmFP

Lily on liquid roses floating. Champagne Rosée. John Kenyon. OBEV

Lily's withered chalice falls, The. The Garden. Oscar Wilde. PoRA *Fr.* Impressions.

Limb of forests rises up, The. Yvonne Caroutch, *French.* BoWoP, *tr. by* David Cloutier

Limb snaps, the hive is smashed, and the survivors, A. The Crumbling Infrastructure. Thomas M. Disch. EC3

Limberick: "It's time to make love. Douse the glim." Conrad Potter Aiken. *See* Limerick: "It's time to make love. Douse the glim."

Limbo. Coleridge. OAEL-2

Limbo. Seamus Heaney. CIP-2; NoAM; OxBC

Limbo. Husein Tahmisic, *Serbian.* CEEP, *tr. by* Ewald Osers

Limbo Dancer, The. Josephine Jacobsen. FFC; PuP-16

Limejuice Tub, The. *Unknown.* NOBAu

Limeraiku. Ted Pauker. NOBL; PeLi

Limeratomy, The. Anthony Euwer.

 Face, The. OBAL; PeLi

 (My Face). PoLF

Limerick. W. H. Auden. *See* The Aesthetic Point of View.

Limerick: "According to old Sigmund Freud." *Unknown.* PeLi

Limerick: "'Active balls?' said an old man of Stoneham." C. D. Cudmore. PeLi

Limerick: "After lunch the old Duchess of Teck." *Unknown.* PeLi

Limerick: "Albert Einstein's the man we must credit." Stanley J. Sharpless. PeLi

Limerick: "All his life, Mr. George Bernard Shaw." Audrey Herbert. PeLi

Limerick: "Amoeba named Sam, and his brother, An." *Unknown.* PeLi

Limerick: "Amorous maiden antique, An." *Unknown.* PeLi

Limerick: "Ancient biologist, Heine, An." Carol Rumens. PeLi

Limerick: "Angry young husband called Bicket, An." John Galsworthy. PeLi

Limerick: "Angst, poetry, urbanized fret." Sydney Bernard Smith. PeLi

Limerick: "Ankle's chief end is exposiery, The." Anthony Euwer. PeLi

Limerick: "April. Bad month. Visit spa." Stanley J. Sharpless. PeLi

Limerick: "Archimedes, the early truth-seeker." Stanley J. Sharpless. PeLi

Limerick: "Argentine gaucho named Bruno, An." *Unknown.* NOBL

Limerick: "Arnolfinis both sat to Van Eyck." Sir Robert Witt. PeLi

Limerick: "Artist who lived in St. Ives, An." A. G. Prys-Jones. PeLi

Limerick: "Artist who lived near Montmartre, An." Sir John Waller. PeLi

Limerick: "As dull as the life of the cloister." *Unknown.* PeLi

Limerick: "As he filled up his order book pp." *Unknown.* PeLi

Limerick: "As Mozart composed a sonata." *Unknown.* PeLi

Limerick: "As played by the phantoms of Shrule." Tony Butler. PeLi

Limerick: "As the elevator car left our floor." *Unknown.* PeLi

Limerick: "As the natives got ready to serve." Ed Cunningham. PeLi

Limerick: "As tourists inspected the apse." Edward Gorey. PeLV; PeLi

Limerick: "Ascetic art student named Josh, An." D. H. Cudmore. PeLi

Limerick: "Astute Melanesians on Munda." *Unknown.* PeLi

Limerick: "At Harvard a randy old Dean." *Unknown.* PeLi

Limerick: "At last I've seduced the *au pair*." Cyril Ray. PeLi

Limerick: "At spirit séances in Queen's." Morris Gilbert Bishop. PeLi

Limerick: "At the orgy I humped twenty-two." *Unknown.* PeLi

Limerick: "Authoress, armed with a skewer, An." *Unknown.* PeLi

Limerick: "Babe, with a cry brief and dismal, The." Edward Gorey. OBAL; PeLi

Limerick: "Ballistical student named Raffity, A." D. H. Cudmore. PeLi

Limerick: "Bashful young fellow of Brighton, A." E. O. Parrott. PeLi

Limerick: "Bather whose clothing was strewed, A." *Unknown.* PeLi

Limerick: "Bells from the steeple resound, The." John Stanley. PeLi

Limerick: "Big cities are reeking with grief." *Unknown.* PeLi

Limerick: "Binary mathematician, A." *Unknown.* PeLi

Limerick: "Boadicea often would goad." Douglas Catley. PeLi

Limerick: "Boastful young fellow of Neath, A." Frank Richards. PeLi

Limerick: "Book and a jug and a dame, A." *Unknown.* PeLi

Limerick: "Both Keats and Boccaccio tell a." Joyce Johnson. PeLi

Limerick: "Bottle of perfume that Willie sent, The [*or* A]." *Unknown.* PeLi

Limerick: "Breasts of a barmaid of Crale, The." *Unknown.* NOBL

Limerick: "Brickie who had a fine tool, A." E. O. Parrott. PeLi

Limerick: "Budding young playwright named Coward, A." Doris Pulsford. PeLi

Limerick: "Business-like harlot named Draper, A." *Unknown.* PeLi

Limerick: "By Loch Ness they can toss, like confetti." Bill Greenwell. PeLi

Limerick: "Calculus fit to compute on, A." Gina Berkeley. PeLi

Limerick: "Candid Professor confesses, A." Thomas Thorneley. PeLi

Limerick: "Canner, Exceedingly Canny, A." Carolyn Wells. PeLi

Limerick: "Careless explorer named Blake, A." Ogden Nash. PeLi

Limerick: "Careless old cook of Salt Ash, A." *Unknown.* PeLi

Limerick: "Carpenter living in Crewe, A." E. O. Parrott. PeLi

Limerick: "Cassandra declining to follow." Basil Ransome-Davies. PeLi

Limerick: "Certain young chap named Bill Beebee, A." *Unknown.* PeLi

Limerick: "Certain young gourmet of Crediton, A." Charles Inge. PeLi

Limerick: "Certain young man of Hilgay, A." Ida Thurtle. PeLi

Limerick: "Certain young pate who was addle, A." Arthur Shaw. PeLi

Limerick: "Certain young sheik I'm not namin', A." *Unknown.* PeLi

Limerick: "Chap was so pose that was adi, A." Arthur Shaw. PeLi

Limerick: "Charlotte Brontë said, 'Wow, sister! *What* a man!'." Victor Gray. NOBL; PeLi

Limerick: "Chief Stewardess on a Boeing, The." Paul Alexander. PeLi

Limerick: "Cleric once heard with dismay, A." Joan Dare. PeLi

Limerick: "Come and see our French goods—you can try 'em." *Unknown.* PeLi

Limerick: "'Come now,' said Bell, 'this is choice'." Frank Richards. PeLi

Limerick: "Come to Noah's for wine and strong waters." *Unknown.* PeLi

Limerick: "Comely young widow named Ransom, A." *Unknown.* PeLi

Limerick: "Complacent old Don of Divinity, A." *Unknown.* PeLi

Limerick: "Conception, an Archbishop said, The." "L. E. J." PeLi

Limerick: "Concerning the bees and the flowers." *Unknown.* PeLi

Limerick: "Concert conductor in Rio, A." *Unknown.* PeLi

Limerick: "Conclusion I reach at the Tate, The." "Tallis." PeLi

Limerick: "Connoisseurs of coition aver." *Unknown.* PeLi

Limerick: "Consider the Emperor Nero." *Unknown.* PeLi

Limerick: "Consider the lowering Lynx." Langford Reed. PeLi

Limerick: "Consistent disciples of Marx." A. Cinna. PeLi

Limerick: "Couple from old Aberystwyth, A." Stuart Woods. PeLi

Limerick: "Couple there was in Blefuscu, A." W. F. N. Watson. PeLi

Limerick: "Couturier from Haverford West, A." E. O. Parrott. PeLi

Limerick: "Creature of charm is the gerbil, A." *Unknown.* PeLi

Limerick: "Cried the maid: 'You must marry me, Hume!'." P. W. R. Foot. PeLi

Limerick: "Crusader's wife slipped from the garrison, A." Ogden Nash. PeLi

Limerick: "Cryptic philosopher, Kant, The." "E. F. C." PeLi

Limerick: "Cute secretary, none cuter, A." Ogden Nash. PeLi

Limerick: "Cynic says: Now that we know, A." Thomas Thorneley. PeLi

Limerick: "Cynical sage with a kink, A." Hassall Pitman. PeLi

Limerick: "Dad waited while Mum bought the ham." Coral E. Copping. PeLi

Limerick: "Daring young lady of Guam, A." *Unknown.* PeLi

Limerick: "Dear Albert, of Saxe-Coburg-Gotha." W. F. N. Watson. PeLi

Limerick: "Dear Sir, You're quite wrong about me." M. Trench. PeLi

Limerick: "Decrepit old gas man named Peter, A." *Unknown.* SoSe-8

Limerick: "Democracy works (*entre nous*)." W. Stewart. PeLi

Limerick: "Desperate spinster of Clare, A." *Unknown.* PeLi

Limerick: "Devil, who plays a deep part, The." "Little Billee." PeLi

Limerick: "Devil's no longer a myth, The." "Little Billee." PeLi

Limerick: "Dickensian borough of Coketown, The." Martin Fagg. PeLi

Limerick: "Did Ophelia ask Hamlet to bed?" A. Cinna. PeLi

Limerick: "Divine by the name of McWhinners, A." *Unknown.* PeLi

Limerick: "Don't thee think, Zurrr, I be zo amazin'." Elizabeth H. Lister. PeLi

Limerick: "Don't think it will fall to your lot." Leslie Johnson. PeLi

Limerick: "Dowager Duchess of Spout, The." Edward Gorey. PeLV; PeLi

Limerick: "Dr. Johnson, when sober or pissed." A. Cinna. PeLi

Limerick: "Each Lon was a notable man." L. G. Udall. PeLi

Limerick: "Each night father fills me with dread." Edward Gorey. PeLi

Limerick: "Earnest young leftie named Tariq." Bernard Levin. PeLi

Limerick: "Elderly bride of Port Jervis, An." Ogden Nash. PeLi

Limerick: "Emperor Marcus Aurelius, The." "Yorick." PeLi

Limerick: "English professor named Brooks, An." D. H. Cudmore. PeLi

Limerick: "Enjoyment of sex, although great, The." *Unknown.* PeLi

Limerick: "Epicure, Dining at Crewe, An." *Unknown.* NTCP; PeLi; PeLV (Waiter, Please.) NBLV

Limerick: "Ethnologists up with the Sioux." *Unknown.* PeLi

Limerick: "Evangelical vicar in want." Ronald Arbuthnott Knox. PeLi

Limerick: "Example of Kant's sterling wit, An." Victor Gray. PeLi

Limerick: "Exposing his plate to the air." Joyce Johnson. PeLi

Limerick: "Exquisite bartender at Sweeney's, The." *Unknown.* PeLi

Limerick: "Fabulous Wizard of Oz, The." *Unknown.* PeLi

Limerick: "Fact of the matter is, Jack, The." John Stanley. PeLi

Limerick: "Famed big-hitter in cricket, A." Douglas Catley. PeLi

Limerick: "Famous philosopher, Kant, The." C. S. Cook. PeLi

Limerick: "Famous theatrical actress, A." *Unknown.* PeLi

Limerick: "Far beyond all the girls of Pirelli." I. D. M. Morley. PeLi

Limerick: "Fascist, erect and irate, A." Thomas Thorneley. PeLi

Limerick: "Fat-tailed Dwarf Lemur, in bed, A." Gerry Hamill. PeLi

Limerick: "Fellow from far Erewhon, A." W. F. N. Watson. PeLi

Limerick: "Fellow who fucked but as few can, A." *Unknown.* PeLi

Limerick: "Feminine mouth in Utopia, The." W. F. N. Watson. PeLi

Limerick: "Fencing instructor named Fisk, A." *Unknown.* PeLi

Limerick: "Few people could hope to compare." J. Endersby. PeLi

Limerick: "Few things to desire can so prod us." W. F. N. Watson. PeLi

Limerick: "Figure is not anatomical, The." Thomas Thorneley. PeLi

Limerick: "Filthy young fellow called Lawrence, A." Bill Greenwell. PeLi

Limerick: "Finding God's taboos totalitarian." Basil Ransome-Davies. PeLi

Limerick: "First chap to fuck little Sophie, The." Victor Gray. PeLi

Limerick: "Flighty young lady from Loddon, A." Ida Thurtle. PeLi

Limerick: "For his Campbell's Soup screen-prints, society's." Bill Greenwell. PeLi

Limerick: "For hours my wife says 'Goodbye'." Frank Burgess. PeLi

Limerick: "For the tenth time, dull Daphnis,' said Chloe." *Unknown.* PeLi

Limerick: "For Travelers Going Sidereal." Robert Frost. OBAL; PeLi

Limerick: "For Widower—wanted, house-keeper." *Unknown.* PeLi

Limerick: "French are a race among races, The." *Unknown.* PeLi

Limerick: "French poodle espied in the hall, A." *Unknown.* PeLi

Limerick: "From the bathing machine came a din." Edward Gorey. OBCoV

Limerick: "From the crypt of the church of St. Giles." *Unknown.* PeLi

Limerick: "From the elephant paddock one day." Frank Richards. PeLi

Limerick: "From the west to the fabulous east." *Unknown.* PeLi

Limerick: "G. B. Shaw wrote to Yeats: 'P'raps it's mad of me'." W. A. Rathkey. PeLi

Limerick: "Gamekeeper of Lady Chatterley, The." Gerry Hamill. PeLi

Limerick: "Gay soccer spectator from Wix, A." Cyril Mountjoy. PeLi

Limerick: "General once lived named de Gaulle, A." Paul Bristow. PeLi

Limerick: "George Stephenson said: 'These repairs'." Frank Richards. PeLi

Limerick: "George Washington said to his dad." Frank Richards. PeLi

Limerick: "Giraffes, yes, even the strongest." Frank Davies. PeLi

Limerick: "Girl who was touring Zambesi, A." *Unknown.* PeLi

Limerick: "'Given faith,' sighed the vicar of Deneham." *Unknown.* PeLi

Limerick: "Glib little beer-buff from Troon, A." Bill Greenwell. PeLi

Limerick: "God brought perfect man to fruition." Douglas Catley. PeLi

Limerick: "Goddess capricious is Fame, A." Langford Reed. PeLi

Limerick: "God's plan made a hopeful beginning." *Unknown.* PeLi

Limerick: "Goliath was known for ferocity." Frank Richards. PeLi

Limerick: "Good mechanics are all of one mind." Douglas Catley. PeLi

Limerick. Edward Gorey. OBCoV

Limerick: "Great-grandfather at Waterloo." Frank Richards. PeLi

Limerick: "G'uggery G'uggery Nunc." John Betjeman. PeLi

Limerick: "Handsome young monk in a wood, A." *Unknown.* PeLi

Limerick: "Having rid Hamelin town of its vermin." Ted Thompson. PeLi

Limerick: "Headstrong young lady of Ealing, A." Edward Gorey. PeLi

Limerick: "Heart of O'Leary, S.J., The." David Phillips. PeLi

Limerick: "Henley's a special regatta." Jim Anthony. PeLi

Limerick: "Her husband was *hors de combat*." C. Vita-Finzi. PeLi

Limerick: "Her limp lover Maud couldn't pardon." Kit Wright. PeLi

Limerick: "Herder who hailed from Terre Haute, A." *Unknown.* PeLi

Limerick: "Hibiscus is flaming and frillier." Ruth Silcock. PeLi

Limerick: "Highly bored damsel called Brown, A." *Unknown.* PeLi

Limerick: "His sister named [*or* called] Lucy O'Finner." "Lewis Carroll." PeLi

Limerick: "Honourable Winifred Wemyss, The." *Unknown.* PeLi

Limerick: "Hoover, in grim silence, sat, The." David Woodsford. PeLi

Limerick: "Hopeful old fellow called Rousseau, A." John Fay. PeLi

Limerick: "Horsewoman of charm at Uttoxeter, A." R. D. Condon. PeLi

Limerick: "'How much,' sighed the gentle Narcissus." Stephen Sylvester. PeLi

Limerick: "How often and often I wish." Frances Darwin Cornford. PeLi

Limerick: "How Socratic is Somerset Maugham!" R. B. S. Instone. PeLi

Limerick: "How varied the family Sen!" Roy Fuller. PeLi

Limerick: "Husband who lived in Tiberias, A." *Unknown.* PeLi

Limerick: "I admire your felicitous phrasing." A. M. Sayers. PeLi

Limerick: "I, Caesar, when I learned of the fame." *Unknown.* PeLi

Limerick: "I consider I really am through." Elizabeth H. Lister. PeLi

Limerick: "I fear, Mr. Lear, you're a clot." Eric Swainson. PeLi

Limerick: "'I have heard,' said a maid from Montclair." Morris Gilbert Bishop. PeLi

Limerick: "I haven't a clue where I've been." Sydney Bernard Smith. PeLi

Limerick: "'I must leave here,' said Lady De Vere." *Unknown.* PeLi

Limerick: "I once had a cat called Maria." Paul Griffin. PeLi

Limerick: "I once knew a spinster of Staines." Plaiwon. PeLi

Limerick: "I once took my girl to Southend." Veronica Nicolson. PeLi

Limerick: "I sat next to the Duchess at tea." *Unknown.* SoSe-8

Limerick: "I spotted these daffs by the lake." E. O. Parrott. PeLi

Limerick: "I suppose I could try if I chose." "E. F. C." PeLi

Limerick: "I was brought up on old Aristotle." C. S. Cook. PeLi

Limerick: "I was sitting there, taking my ease." Cyril Ray. PeLi

Limerick: "I was thrilled when I went to the Zoo." Victor Gray. PeLi

Limerick: "I went with the Duchess to tea." Woodrow Wilson. PeLi

Limerick: "I wish that my room had a floor." Frank Gelett Burgess. OBCA; PeLi

Limerick: "I wonder how King Arthur felt." Moss Rich. PeLi

Limerick: "'I would doubt,' said the Bishop of Balham." Terence Rattigan. PeLi

Limerick: "I wouldn't be bothered with drawers." *Unknown.* PeLi

Limerick: "If Eve hadn't eaten the apple." Wendy Cope. PeLi

Limerick: "If intercourse gives you thrombosis." *Unknown.* PeLi

Limerick: "If no Pain were, how judge we of Pleasure?" William Bliss. PeLi

Limerick: "'If you dream,' said the eminent Freud." Russell Miller. PeLi

Limerick: "If you feel that you're right on your beam ends." Leslie Johnson. PeLi

Limerick: "If you find for your verse there's no call." *Unknown.* PeLi

Limerick: "'If you're aristocratic,' said Nietzsche." Gerry Hamill. OBCoV

Limerick: "I'm getting deep lines on my forehead." Ron Rubin. PeLi

Limerick: "I'm glad pigs can't fly,' said young Sellers." Ron Rubin. PeLi

Limerick: "I'm in love with a girl from Uttoxeter." Gerard Benson. PeLi

Limerick: "Immaculate Sir Walter Raleigh, The." T. L. McCarthy. PeLi

Limerick: "In childhood it's easy to feel." Nigel Andrew. PeLi

Limerick: "In considering things gastronomic." *Unknown.* PeLi

Limerick: "In dealing with time it is found." V. R. Ormerod. PeLi

Limerick: "In Genesis, Adam's the winner." Bill Greenwell. PeLi

Limerick: "In gonia once which was Pata." Arthur Shaw. PeLi

Limerick: "In history's mysteries snout." *Unknown.* PeLi

Limerick: "In Illyria, the love-sick Orsino." Stanley J. Sharpless. PeLi

Limerick: "In New Orleans dwelt a young Creole." Alben Barkley. PeLi

Limerick: "In Pinter's new play that's now running." Frank Richards. PeLi

Limerick: "In the days of mild Jerry Ford." *Unknown.* PeLi

Limerick: "In the Garden of Eden lay Adam." *Unknown.* PeLi

Limerick: "In the rain in a yard in Cessnock." Ruth Silcock. PeLi

Limerick: "Incautious young woman named Venn, An." Edward Gorey. PeLV; PeLi

Limerick: "Indolent vicar of Bray, An." Langford Reed. PeLi

Limerick: "Industrious young obstetrician, An." Isaac Asimov. PeLi

Limerick: "Inept young person, Miss Muffet, The." Dean Walley. PeLi

Limerick: "Innocent bride from the Mission, An." *Unknown.* PeLi

Limerick: "Innocent maiden of Gloucester, An." *Unknown.* PeLi

Limerick: "Insurance salesman named Flint, An." Charles Barsotti. PeLi

Limerick: "Is it really so very unthinkable." Basil Ransome-Davies. PeLi

Limerick: "'Is it thou?' 'Ay,' cries Fra Lippo Lippi." Gerard Benson. PeLi

Limerick: "Is there really a new Mr. Nixon." T. Griffiths. PeLi

Limerick: "Isaac Singer (you probably know)." Peter Brookes. PeLi

Limerick: "It is clear that Napoleon's Queen." Moss Rich. PeLi

Limerick: "It needn't have ribaldry's taint." Don Marquis. PeLi

Limerick: "It occurred when she crossed the Atlantic." *Unknown.* PeLi

Limerick: "It seems I impregnated Marge." *Unknown.* PeLi

Limerick: "It's a nightmare that horrifies hakes." Allan M. Laing. PeLi

Limerick: "It's a pity that Casabianca." Victor Gray. PeLi

Limerick: "'It's my custom,' said dear Lady Norris." *Unknown.* PeLi

Limerick: "It's time to make love. Douse the glim." Conrad Potter Aiken. NBLV; PeLi

(Limerick: "It's time to make love. Douse the glim.") PeLV

Limerick: "I've combed out my beard and I've found." Pauline Phillips. PeLi

Limerick: "Ivy Compton-Burnett's irritations." *Unknown.* PeLi

Limerick: "Jolly young fellow from Yuma, A." Ogden Nash. PeLi

Limerick: "Keeper who worked at the zoo, A." Frank Richards. PeLi

Limerick: "King Henry the Eighth was a Tudor." Kirkham Talbot. PeLi

Limerick: "King Louis gave lessons in Class." *Unknown.* PeLi

Limerick: "King Richard, in one of his rages." Amanda Benjamin Hall. PeLi

Limerick: "Kings of Peru were the Incas, The." *Unknown.* PeLi

Limerick: "Kinky young girl from Uttoxeter, A." Herbert Kretzmer. PeLi

Limerick: "Lad of the brainier kind, A." Hymie Sneak. PeLi

Limerick: "Lady from Vanity Fair, A." W. F. N. Watson. PeLi

Limerick: "Lady of features cherubic, A." *Unknown.* PeLi

Limerick: "Lady on climbing Mount Shasta, A." *Unknown.* PeLi

Limerick: "Lady there was in Antigua, A." *Unknown.* PeLi

Limerick: "Lady who rules Fort Montgomery, A." Morris Gilbert Bishop. PeLi

Limerick: "Lady, who signs herself 'Vexed,' A." Edward Gorey. OBAL; PeLi

Limerick: "Lama of Outer Mongolia, A." Ogden Nash. PeLi

Limerick: "Land of blue skies, and sunlight, A." Ruth Silcock. PeLi

Limerick: "Lass of curvacious physique, A." Douglas Catley. PeLi

Limerick: "Last Christmas, when Puss was in Boots." Gina Berkeley. PeLi

Limerick: "Last time I slept with the Queen, The." Dylan Thomas. PeLi

Limerick: "Lecherous young Lilliputian, A." C. Vita-Finzi. PeLi

Limerick: "Left-wing young lady from Wick, A." Gerry Hamill. PeLi

Limerick: "Lesbian girl of Khartoum, A." *Unknown.* NOBL; PeLV

Limerick: "Let the eugenist reach for his gun!" Stanley J. Sharpless. PeLi

Limerick: "Let's enter the literary scene." *Unknown.* PeLi

Limerick: "Life-Force, afflicted with doubt, The." Thomas Thorneley. PeLi

Limerick: "Life is sad and so slow and so cold." Gavin Ewart. PeLi

Limerick: "Lisping young lady called Beth, A." *Unknown.* PeLi

Limerick: "Lissom psychotic named Jane, A." *Unknown.* PeLi

Limerick: "Lonely old maid named Loretta, A." *Unknown.* PeLi

Limerick: "Lonely young fellow of Eton, A." *Unknown.* PeLi

Limerick: "Lord, since it's hard to explain." J. E. Press. PeLi

Limerick: "Maiden at college called Breeze, A." Mrs. Mercy Warren. PeLi

Limerick: "Man called Andronicus (Titus), A." Paul Wigmore. PeLi

Limerick: "Man from Maputo and so on, A." J. H. Lee. PeLi

Limerick: "Man from the *Washington Post*, A." Anthony Burgess. PeLi

Limerick: "Man hired by John Smith and Co., A." "Mark Twain." InPK-6; PeLi

Limerick: "Man in the Land of the Houyhnhnms, A." W. S. Brownlie. PeLi

Limerick: "Man who had lately declared, A." Thomas Thorneley. PeLi

Limerick: "Man who was asked out to dinner, A." Spike Milligan. PeLi

Limerick: "Marconi, whose ardour was tireless." Stanley J. Sharpless. PeLi

Limerick: "Marquis de Sade and Genet, The." W. H. Auden. PeLi

Limerick: "Meanwhile, back home at the ranch." Victor Gray. PeLi

Limerick: "Mechanical marvel was Bill, A." *Unknown.* PeLi

Limerick: "Menagerie came to Cape Race, A." *Unknown.* PeLi

Limerick: "Millionaire, filled with elation, A." Thomas Thorneley. PeLi

Limerick: "Minister up in Vermont, A." *Unknown.* PeLi

Limerick: "Miranda, remember that Inn?" John Stanley. PeLi

Limerick: "Mr. Alan Jay Lerner (with by-play)." J. A. Lindon. PeLi

Limerick: "Mr Lear, I'm the Akond of Swat." Ethel Talbot Scheffauer. PeLi

Limerick: "Mr. Rochester's wife's pyromania." Gina Berkeley. PeLi

Limerick: "Mr. Wells of the big cerebellum." H. G. Wells. PeLi

Limerick: "Mrs. Whitehouse, mixed bathing at Deal." T. L. McCarthy. PeLi

Limerick: "Modern composer called Cage, A." Peter Alexander. PeLi

Limerick: "Modern young curate called Hyde, A." D. W. Pain. PeLi

Limerick: "Modest young maiden of Rennes, A." A. C. Cossins. PeLi

Limerick: "Monkey exclaimed with great glee, A." Frank Richards. PeLi

Limerick: "Monsieur Gauguin? 'E's gone to Tahiti." Stanley J. Sharpless. PeLi

Limerick: "Mordant and decadent Youth, A." Thomas Thorneley. PeLi

Limerick: "Mosquito was heard to complain, A." *Unknown.* PeLi

Limerick: "Most women get married, 'tis true." Barney Blackley. PeLi

Limerick: "Much-worried mother once said, A." *Unknown.* PeLi

Limerick: "Musical maiden from Frome, A." Cyril Bibby. PeLi

Limerick: "My beard's overcrowded. Now that." Richard Unwin. PeLi

Limerick: "My demands upon life are quite modest." Robert Conquest. PeLi

Limerick: "My purpose was purely corrective." Leslie Johnson. PeLi

Limerick: "Naïve young lady of Bude, A." C. Chevallier. PeLi

Limerick: "Naïve young lady of Cork, A." Reg Yearley. PeLi

Limerick: "Near-sighted fellow named Walter, A." Unknown. PeLi

Limerick: "New cinematic emporium, The." Unknown. PeLi

Limerick: "Nice pot of gold that was mari, A." Arthur Shaw. PeLi

Limerick: "Night's bible-black darkness prevails." V. R. Ormerod. PeLi

Limerick: "Ninety summers—and never a platitude." Stanley J. Sharpless. PeLi

Limerick: "No, listen, there's this albatross." Bill Greenwell. PeLi

Limerick: "'No more mistresses,' King Edward said." Frank Richards. PeLi

Limerick: "No Portuguese Lady is Nautical." Sydney Hoffman. PeLi

Limerick: "None could better our sex limousine." Unknown. PeLi

Limerick: "Not that it always transpired." Cyril Ray. PeLi

Limerick: "Novelist, flushed with success, A." Thomas Thorneley. PeLi

Limerick: "Novelist of the Absurd, A." Ogden Nash. PeLi

Limerick: "O Great Queen Whom I idolize." Jeffery Littman. PeLi

Limerick: "O, I yearn to go back to the Cam!" E. O. Parrott. PeLi

Limerick: "O sage of the stage, Shaw of Shaws!" Harold Ellis. PeLi

Limerick: "Oedipus said to the Sphinx." Victor Gray. PeLi

Limerick: "Of a sudden, the great prima donna." Unknown. PeLi

Limerick: "Of all God's jokes none is bluer." A. Cinna. PeLi

Limerick: "Of attractions the Sabines ain't stinted." D. W. Barker. PeLi

Limerick: "Of my husband I do not ask much." Unknown. PeLi

Limerick: "'Oh, halt!' cried Virginia, 'Enough!'." Otto Watteau. PeLi

Limerick: "Old archaeologist, Throstle, An." Unknown. PeLi

Limerick: "Old Danish jester named Yorick, An." Ogden Nash. PeLi

Limerick: "Old East End worker called Jock, An." Victor Gray. NOBL

Limerick: "Old gourmet who's grown somewhat stout, An." "Yorick." PeLi

Limerick: "Old Indian chief, Running B'ar, An." Mary Rita Hurley. PeLi

Limerick: "Old poet called Omar cried: 'Now', An." "J. E. C." PeLi

Limerick: "Old Woman who lived in the Shoe, The." Joyce Johnson. PeLi

Limerick: "On a date with a charming young bird." Unknown. PeLi

Limerick: "On an outing with seventeen Czechs." Unknown. PeLi

Limerick: "On May Day, the girls of Penzance." Unknown. PeLi

Limerick: "On Saturn the sexes are three." Unknown. PeLi

Limerick: "'On the beach,' said John sadly, 'there's such'." Isaac Asimov. PeLi

Limerick: "On the chest of a barmaid in Sale." Unknown. PeLi

Limerick: "One-day-old baby in Wallabout, A." Morris Gilbert Bishop. PeLi

Limerick: "One midnight, old D. G. Rossetti." Victor Gray. PeLi

Limerick: "One morning old Wilfrid Scawen Blunt." Victor Gray. NOBL

Limerick: "One morning the Monarch said: 'When'." D. W. Barker. PeLi

Limerick: "Orgy was held on the lawn, The." Unknown. PeLi

Limerick: "Othello loved Desdemona." A. Cinna. PeLi

Limerick: "Our existence would be that much grimmer ex-." Robert Conquest. PeLi

Limerick: "Our novels get longa and longa." H. G. Wells. PeLi

Limerick: "Painter, encumbered with cash, A." Thomas Thorneley. PeLi

Limerick: "Pansy who lived in Khartoum, A." Unknown. PeLi

Limerick: "Patriot living at Ewell, A." Langford Reed. PeLi

Limerick: "People the Churches love best, The." Patrick Braybrook. PeLi

Limerick: "Philosopher Berkeley once said, The." P. W. R. Foot. PeLi

Limerick: "Platinum blonde, Goldilocks, A." Fiona Pitt-Kethley. PeLi

Limerick: "Plumber from Lowater Creek, A." Unknown. PeLi

Limerick: "Poet from Cheltenham Spa, A." Betty Morris. PeLi

Limerick: "Policeman from Nottingham Junction, A." Unknown. PeLi

Limerick: "'Political women,' thought Yeats." R. K. R. Thornton. PeLi

Limerick: "Poor Ophelia sighed: 'I deplore'." Frank Richards. PeLi

Limerick: "Pop's tops!" Bill Greenwell. PeLi

Limerick: "Postmaster-General cried: 'Arschole!', The." Victor Gray. PeLi

Limerick: "Precede us, O Lord, with Thy Grace." Frank R. McManus. PeLi

Limerick: "Prince Charles in his Welsh principality." Bernard Levin. PeLi

Limerick: "'Princess,' said the Frog, 'Do not wince'." Gina Berkeley. PeLi

Limerick: "Professor of Ethical Culture, A." Unknown. PeLi

Limerick: "Prostitute living in London, A." Douglas Catley. PeLi

Limerick: "Prudish old lady called Muir, A." Unknown. PeLi

Limerick: "Psychiatrist fellow from Rye, A." Stephen Cass. PeLi

Limerick: "Psychic researcher's elation, A." Cyril Mountjoy. PeLi

Limerick: "Publisher went off to France, A." Unknown. PeLi

Limerick: "Pulmonary tuberculosis." L. G. Udall. PeLi

Limerick: "Pushing young man in Patchogue, A." Morris Gilbert Bishop. PeLi

Limerick: "Quadratic function, ambitious, A." Leo Moser. PeLi

Limerick: "Quirky old gent, name of Freud, A." Martin Fagg. PeLi

Limerick: "Quoth a cow in the marshes of Glynne." Conrad Potter Aiken. PeLi

Limerick: "Randy young girl called Miranda, A." Peter Alexander. PeLi

Limerick: "Rapist, who reeked of cheap booze, A." Unknown. PeLi

Limerick: "Rascal far gone in treachery, A." Unknown. PeLi

Limerick: "Rather extreme vegetarian, A." "Sagittarius." PeLi

Limerick: "Reason we're asked to endure, The." Bill Greenwell. PeLi

Limerick: "Rebuke by the Bishop of London, A." Victor Gray. PeLi

Limerick: "Remarkable race are the Persians, A." Unknown. PeLi

Limerick: "Remember when you are bemusing." Cyril Hughes. PeLi

Limerick: "Retired Civil Servant from Gateley, A." Ida Thurtle. PeLi

Limerick: "Revelations—we've come to the lewd." Unknown. PeLi

Limerick: "Reverend Henry Ward Beecher, The." Oliver Wendell Holmes. PeLi

Limerick: "Reverend Mr. Uprightly, The." Unknown. PeLi

Limerick: "Riverrun where can you guess?" Unknown. PeLi

Limerick: "Ronald Reagan screamed out in dismay." Frank Richards. PeLi

Limerick: "Rose gives a tremulous glance, The." Anne Norris. PeLi

Limerick: "Round-bottomed babe from Mobile, A." Unknown. PeLi

Limerick: "Rupert Murdoch, with glee, shouted: 'What'." Frank Richards. PeLi

Limerick: "Said a boastful young student from Hayes." Frank Richards. PeLi

Limerick: "Said a diffident lady named Drood." Unknown. PeLi

Limerick: "Said a dreadfully literate cat." Conrad Potter Aiken. PeLi

Limerick: "Said a fair-headed maiden of Klondike." Langford Reed. PeLi

Limerick: "Said a famous old writer called Fender." Victor Gray. PeLi

Limerick: "Said a fervent young lady of Hammels." Morris Gilbert Bishop. PeLi

Limerick: "Said a foolish young lady of Wales." Langford Reed. PeLi

Limerick: "Said a girl in green Mansfield Park." E. O. Parrott. PeLi

Limerick: "Said a gloomy young fellow called Fart." Victor Gray. PeLi

Limerick: "Said a God-fearing lady called Whitehouse." Roger Woddis. PeLi

Limerick: "Said a herring one day to a sole." Stanley J. Sharpless. PeLi

Limerick: "Said a luscious young lady called Wade." Unknown. PeLi

Limerick: "Said a Marxist who stood on the pier." W. H. G. Price. PeLi

Limerick: "Said a medical student, unmanned." Allan M. Laing. PeLi

Limerick: "Said a parson, addressing his flock." W. J. Strachan. PeLi

Limerick: "Said a practical thinker: 'One should.'" Frank Watson. PeLi

Limerick: "Said a pupil of Einstein: 'It's rotten.'" C. F. Best. PeLi

Limerick: "Said a Tripper: 'O joy, to have found.'" Thomas Thorneley. PeLi

Limerick: "Said a wife to her husband near Scole." Ida Thurtle. PeLi

Limerick: "Said an ape as he swung by his tail." Unknown. PeLi

Limerick: "Said an elderly Bishop called Greville." "Little Billee." PeLi

Limerick: "Said an eminent, erudite ermine." Unknown. PeLi

Limerick: "Said an erudite sinologue: 'How.'" R. J. P. Hewison. OBCoV

Limerick: "Said Arnold to Arthur Hugh Clough." Victor Gray. PeLi

Limerick: "Said Freud: 'I've discovered the Id.'" Frank Richards. PeLi

Limerick: "Said Isolde to Tristan: 'How curious!'" Conrad Potter Aiken. PeLi

Limerick: "Said Marlowe: 'Bay City's a drag.'" Peter Alexander. PeLi

Limerick: "Said Mars when entangled with Venus." Mary Holtby. PeLi

Limerick: "Said Miss Farrow, on one of her larks." Unknown. PeLi

Limerick: "Said Nelson at his most la-di-da-di." A. Cinna. PeLi

Limerick: "Said Old Father William: 'I'm humble.'" Conrad Potter Aiken. PeLi

Limerick: "Said Old Nick: 'Mister Lewis and me.'" M. Cassell. PeLi

Limerick: "Said Orville to Wilbur 'Hold tight!'" Stanley J. Sharpless. PeLi

Limerick: "Said Paisley: 'I've given up hope.'" Frank Richards. PeLi

Limerick: "Said philosopher-physicist Jeans." R. C. Owen. PeLi

Limerick: "Said Plato: 'The things that we feel.'" Basil Ransome-Davies. PeLi

Limerick: "Said Powell: 'Don't call me insane.'" Roger Woddis. PeLi

Limerick: "Said Queen Isabella of Spain." Unknown. PeLi

Limerick: "Said Tebbitt: 'I don't understand 'em.'" Gerry Hamill. PeLi

Limerick: "Said Tennyson: 'Yes, Locksley Hall's.'" Victor Gray. PeLi

Limerick: "Said the boy driving home towards Clere." Ida Thurtle. PeLi

Limerick: "Said the Chinese philosopher, Lin." Len. PeLi

Limerick: "Said the Duchess of Alba to Goya." Unknown. PeLi

Limerick: "Said the famous philosopher, Russell." Victor Gray. PeLi

Limerick: "Said the mythical King of Algiers." Unknown. PeLi

Limerick: "Said the newly-weds staying near Kitely." Unknown. PeLi

Limerick: "Said the Queen to her favourite ghillie." A. Cinna. PeLi

Limerick: "Said the Stoic, tormented by gout." Thomas Thorneley. PeLi

Limerick: "Said the vet as he looked at my pet." Frank Richards. PeLi

Limerick: "Said Wellington: 'What's the location'." Frank Richards. PeLi

Limerick: "Said Wilbur Wright, 'Oh, this is grand.'" Frank Richards. PeLi

Limerick: "Said Wittgenstein: 'Don't be misled!'" Peter Alexander. PeLi

Limerick: "Salopian student of Greek, A." Martin Fagg. PeLi

Limerick: "Salvation lassie named Claire, A." Unknown. PeLi

Limerick: "Sardines seem to get out of hand." Leslie Johnson. PeLi

Limerick: "Scion of Boston society, A." Conrad Potter Aiken. PeLi

Limerick: "Scribe, to the vulgar inclined, A." Douglas Catley. PeLi

Limerick: "Sculptor remarked: 'I'm afraid,' A." Unknown. PeLi

Limerick: "Señorita who strolled on the Corso, A." Unknown. PeLi

Limerick: "Sensitive girl called O'Neill, A." Unknown. PeLi

Limerick: "Serious young lady from Welwyn, A." C. Armstrong Gibbs. PeLi

Limerick: "Sermon our Pastor, Rt. Rev., The." Unknown. PeLi

Limerick: "Sexy young student once toyed, A." Richard Taylor. PeLi

Limerick: "She was caught, a young girl of Uttoxeter." Tim Hopkins. PeLi

Limerick: "Shed a tear for the WREN named McGinnis." Unknown. PeLi

Limerick: "Shelley's death—was it really his wish." Bill Greenwell. PeLi

Limerick: "Shepherd who lived up in Gwent, A." E. O. Parrott. PeLi

Limerick: "Shiftless young fellow of Kent, A." Unknown. PeLi

Limerick: "Sighed a dear little shipboard divinity." Conrad Potter Aiken. OBAL; PeLi

Limerick: "Sigmund Freud says that one who reflects." Peter Alexander. PeLi

Limerick: "Sign your name in the book. It's just ink." Sydney Bernard Smith. PeLi

Limerick: "Simple living was clearly the nub." Joyce Johnson. PeLi

Limerick: "Since my overdraft threatens to be." S. Tonkin. PeLi

Limerick: "Sir John Shagbag (Conservative, Nore)." Victor Gray. PeLi

Limerick: "Sky's are a pitiful lot, The." Bob Scott. PeLi

Limerick: "Slow-footed stockman called Beales, A." Cyril Mountjoy. PeLi

Limerick: "Smile on the famed Mona Lisa, The." Stanley J. Sharpless. PeLi

Limerick: "So obese is my cousin from Hendon." A. H. Baynes. PeLi

Limerick: "Solipsist with triplets said: 'Though,' A." Lupellus. PeLi

Limerick: "Some Harvard men, stalwart and hairy." Edward Gorey. OBCoV

Limerick: "Some lives are so odd—you agree?" Unknown. PeLi

Limerick: "Some people may think I'm a bit la-di." C. Vita-Finzi. PeLi

Limerick: "Sometimes there are airs grave and gentle." Unknown. PeLi

Limerick: "Southern hill-billy named Hollis, A." Unknown. PeLi

Limerick: "Staid schizophrenic named Struther, A." Unknown. NIP-4

Limerick: "'Strip,' Leofric said, 'and you'll find.'" Harry Thomas. PeLi

Limerick: "Student from Pembroke once said, A." Andrew Stoker. PeLi

Limerick: "Student of nuclear fission, A." W. Bernard Wake. PeLi

Limerick: "T. S. Eliot is quite at a loss." W. H. Auden. PeLi

Limerick: "Taxi-cab whore out at Iver, A." Victor Gray. NOBL; PeLi

Limerick: "Teacher of tots at Uttoxeter, A." Kate McPower. PeLi

Limerick: "Texan Rhodes Scholar named Fred, A." Lyndon T. Mole. PeLi

Limerick: "That fine English poet, Donne." Wendy Cope. PeLi

Limerick: "That smasher of shams, Bernard Shaw." Frank Buckland. PeLi

Limerick: "Then scorn not the limerick either." Robert Conquest. PeLi

Limerick: "Ther once was this ladye from Tyre." Tim Hopkins. PeLi

Limerick: "There is a creature called God." D. G. Rossetti. PeLi

Limerick: "There is an old he-wolf named Gambart." D. G. Rossetti. FaBoEE; PeLi

Limerick: "There isn't a shadow of doubt." Unknown. PeLi

Limerick: "There once was a bard of Hong Kong." Gerard Benson. OBCoV

Limerick: "There once was a couple named Mound." Unknown. PeLi

Limerick: "There once was a doctor who said." Towanbucket. PeLi

Limerick: "There once was a fellow called Hyde." E. J. Jackson. PeLi

Limerick: "There once was a Fellow of Trinity." Unknown. PeLi

Limerick: "There once was a Fellow of Wadham / Who approved of the doings of Sodom." Unknown. PeLi

Limerick: "There once was a flock of wild geese." B. Semeonoff and C. Semeonoff. PeLi

Limerick: "There once was a girl from St. Paul." Unknown. NIP-4

Limerick: "There once was a girl from the Congo." George Seferis, Greek. CBNP, tr. by Hugh Haughton

Limerick: "There once was a judge of Assize." Unknown. PeLi

Limerick: "There once was a lady called Lily." Unknown. PeLi

Limerick: "There once was a lass of Shalott." Mary Holtby. PeLi

Limerick: "There once was a man [or There was a young man] who said, 'Damn!'." Maurice Evan Hare. NOBL; OxBoLi; PeLi; PeLV

Limerick: "There once was a man who said "God."'" Ronald Arbuthnott Knox. NOBL; PeLi

Limerick: "There once was a monarch of Spain." Unknown. PeLi

Limerick: "There once was a painter named Scott." D. G. Rossetti. PeLi

Limerick: "There once was a person of Chiswick." J. M. Ross. PeLi

Limerick: "There once was a plesiosaurus." Unknown. PeLi

Limerick: "There once was a Scot who said: 'Evil'." "H. M." PeLi

Limerick: "There once was a sculptor named Phidias." Unknown. PeLi

Limerick: "There once was a vicar of Ryhill." Unknown. PeLi

Limerick: "There once was a wicked young minister." Conrad Potter Aiken. OBAL; PeLi

Limerick: "There once was a wise politician." A. M. Sayers. PeLi

Limerick: "There once was a writer called James." R. K. R. Thornton. PeLi

Limerick: "There once was an artist called Pat." Margaret Galbreath. PeLi

Limerick: "There once was an eccentric of Metz." Leslie Johnson. PeLi

Limerick: "There once was an eccentric old boffin." Unknown. PeLi

Limerick: "There once was monarch called Harry." Mary Holtby. PeLi

Limerick: "There once were two Babes in the Wood." Roger Woddis. PeLi

Limerick: "There was a black girl from Pretoria." George Seferis, Greek. CBNP, tr. by Hugh Haughton

Limerick: "There was a collection of schemers." Basil Ransome-Davies. PeLi

Limerick: "There was a crusader of Parma." Unknown. PeLi

Limerick: "There was a faith-healer of Deal." Unknown. PeLi

Limerick: "There was a fat lady of Clyde." Unknown. PeLi

Limerick: "There was a French bard who said: 'Hell'." Towanbucket. PeLi

Limerick: "There was a good Canon of Durham." William Ralph Inge. PeLi

Limerick: "There was a great German Grammarian." Thomas Thorneley. PeLi

Limerick: "There was a great Marxist called Lenin." Ted Pauker. PeLi

Limerick: "There was a kind lady called Gregory." James Joyce. FaBoEE; PeLi

Limerick: "There was a rash fellow called Weir." Unknown. PeLi

Limerick: "There was a sick man of Tobago." Unknown. OxBChV; PeLi

Limerick: "There was a small boy of Quebec." Rudyard Kipling. PeLi

Limerick: "There was a trombonist called Herb." Ron Rubin. PeLi

Limerick: "There was a wee lassie of Ulva." David Fisher. PeLi

Limerick: "There was a young artist called Saint." Unknown. PeLi

Limerick: "There was a young boy, Jack Horner." Fiona Pitt-Kethley. PeLi

Limerick: "There was a young bride named McWing." Unknown. PeLi

Limerick: "There was a young critic of King's." Arthur Clement Hilton. PeLi

Limerick: "There was a young curate called Lloyd." Duncan Campbell McGregor. PeLi

Limerick: "There was a young curate of Hants." Edmund George Valpy Knox. PeLi

Limerick: "There was a young curate of Kew." Unknown. PeLi

Limerick: "There was a young curate of Salisbury." Unknown. PeLi

Limerick: "There was a young faggot called Willy." Kenneth Petchenik. PeLi

Limerick: "There was a young fellow called Baker." Unknown. PeLi

Limerick: "There was a young fellow called Bliss." Unknown. PeLi

Limerick: "There was a young fellow called Cager." Unknown. PeLi

Limerick: "There was a young fellow called Chubb." Unknown. PeLi

Limerick: "There was a young fellow called Clyde." Unknown. PeLi

Limerick: "There was a young fellow called Crouch." Victor Gray. NOBL; PeLi

Limerick: "There was a young fellow called Hall." Unknown. PeLi

Limerick: "There was a young fellow called Lancelot." Unknown. PeLi

Limerick: "There was a young fellow called Price." Unknown. PeLi

Limerick: "There was a young fellow called Shit." Victor Gray. PeLi

Limerick: "There was a young fellow called Wyatt." Unknown. PeLi

Limerick: "There was a young fellow from Tyne." Unknown. PeLi

Limerick: "There was a young fellow named Fisher." Unknown. PeLi

Limerick: "There was a young fellow named Fonda." Ogden Nash. PeLi

Limerick: "There was a young fellow named Menzies." Unknown. PeLi

Limerick: "There was a young fellow named Skinner." Norman Douglas. PeLi

Limerick: "There was a young fellow named Sydney." Don Marquis. PeLi

Limerick: "There was a young fellow of Burma." Aldous Leonard Huxley. PeLi

Limerick: "There was a young Fellow of Caius." Unknown. NOBL

Limerick: "There was a young fellow of Ceuta." Unknown. PeLi

Limerick: "There was a young Fellow of King's." Unknown. NOBL

Limerick: "There was a young fellow of Lyme." Unknown. PeLi

Limerick: "There was a young fellow of Perth." Unknown. PeLi

Limerick: "There was a young fellow of Trinity." *Unknown.* PeLi

Limerick: "There was a young Fellow of Wadham." *Unknown.* NOBL

Limerick: "There was a young Fellow of Wadham / Who asked for a ticket to Sodom." *Unknown.* PeLi

Limerick: "There was a young genius of Queens'." Arthur Clement Hilton. PeLi

Limerick: "There was a young girl called Bianca." *Unknown.* PeLi

Limerick: "There was a young girl from a Mission." A. H. Baynes. PeLi

Limerick: "There was a young girl from Uttoxeter / Who kept hens, but refused to have cocks. It a." Alastair Chambre. PeLi

Limerick: "There was a young girl from Uttoxeter / Who made passing oarsmen gape through locks at her." L. W. Bailey. PeLi

Limerick: "There was a young girl from Uttoxeter / Who one dreary night had a fox at her." George Cowley. PeLi

Limerick: "There was a young girl from Uttoxeter / Who out on a date with two Jocks at a." Bob Scott. PeLi

Limerick: "There was a young girl from Uttoxeter / Who sported a tight-fitting baroque sweater." Stanley J. Sharpless. PeLi

Limerick: "There was a young girl of Aberystwyth." Swinburne. PeLi

Limerick: "There was a young girl of Australia." *Unknown.* PeLi

Limerick: "There was a young girl of Bahari." R. P. M. Lehmann. PeLi

Limerick: "There was a young girl of Cape Cod." *Unknown.* PeLi

Limerick: "There was a young girl of Darjeeling." *Unknown.* PeLi

Limerick: "There was a young girl of East Anglia." Aldous Leonard Huxley. PeLi

Limerick: "There was a young girl of La Plata." *Unknown.* PeLi

Limerick: "There was a Young Girl of Majorca." Edward Lear. PeLi

Limerick: "There was a young girl of Mauritius." Victor Gray. PeLi

Limerick: "There was a young girl of old Natchez." Ogden Nash. PeLi

Limerick: "There was a young girl of Penzance." *Unknown.* PeLi

Limerick: "There was a young girl of Shanghai." Bertrand Arthur William Russell, 3d Earl Russell. PeLi

Limerick: "There was a young girl of Siam." *Unknown.* PeLi

Limerick: "There was a young girl of St. Cyr." *Unknown.* PeLi

Limerick: "There was a young girl of Tralee." *Unknown.* PeLi

Limerick: "There was a young girl of Trebarwith." R. J. P. Hewison. PeLi

Limerick: "There was a young girl of Uttoxeter / Who noticed that men waved their cocks at her." D. Kartun. PeLi

Limerick: "There was a young girl of Uttoxeter / Who worked nine to five as a choc-setter." Stanley J. Sharpless. PeLi

Limerick: "There was a young girl whose frigidity." *Unknown.* PeLi

Limerick: "There was a young girl with a hernia." Heywood Broun. PeLi

Limerick: "There was a young gourmand of John's." Arthur Clement Hilton. PeLi

Limerick: "There was a young Jap on a syndicate." *Unknown.* PeLi

Limerick: "There was a young Japanese geisha." Ron Rubin. PeLi

Limerick: "There was a young lady at court." D. H. Cudmore. PeLi

Limerick: "There was a young lady called Alice." *Unknown.* PeLi

Limerick: "There was a young lady called Clarice." H. A. C. Evans. PeLi

Limerick: "There was a young lady called Etta." *Unknown.* PeLi

Limerick: "There was a young lady called Flynn." *Unknown.* PeLi

Limerick: "There was a young lady called Gloria." *Unknown.* PeLi

Limerick: "There was a young lady called Harris." Ogden Nash. PeLi

Limerick: "There was a young lady called Hilda." *Unknown.* PeLi

Limerick: "There was a young lady called Kate." *Unknown.* PeLi

Limerick: "There was a young lady called Maud." *Unknown.* PeLi

Limerick: "There was a young lady called Muffet." *Unknown.* PeLi

Limerick: "There was a young lady called Smith." *Unknown.* PeLi

Limerick: "There was a young lady called Starky." *Unknown.* PeLi

Limerick: "There was a young lady from Pecking." *Unknown.* PeLi

Limerick: "There was a young lady from Ulva." Russell Lucas. PeLi

Limerick: "There was a young lady named [*or* called] Bright." Arthur Buller. NOBL; OxBoLi; PeLV; PeLi

Limerick: "There was a young lady named Kent." *Unknown.* PeLi

Limerick: "There was a young lady of Acnos." *Unknown.* PeLi

Limerick: "There was a young lady of Brabant." *Unknown.* PeLi

Limerick: "There was a young lady of Chichester." *Unknown.* PeLi

Limerick: "There was a young lady of Chiswick." *Unknown.* PeLi

Limerick: "There was a young lady of Ealing." *Unknown.* PeLi

Limerick: "There was a young lady of Ealing / And her lover before her was kneeling." Isaac Asimov. PeLi

Limerick: "There was a young lady of fashion." *Unknown.* PeLi

Limerick: "There was a young lady of Florence." *Unknown.* PeLi

Limerick: "There was a young lady of Graz." George Seferis, *Greek.* CBNP, *tr. by* Peter Levi

Limerick: "There was a young lady of Joppa." *Unknown.* PeLi

Limerick: "There was a young lady of Kew." *Unknown.* PeLV

Limerick: "There was a young lady of Leicester." Alan Clark. PeLi

Limerick: "There was a young lady of Limerick." Andrew Lang. PeLi

Limerick: "There was a young lady of Louth." Norman Douglas. PeLi

Limerick: "There was a Young Lady of Lucca." *Unknown.* CBNP

Limerick: "There was a young lady of Lundy." W. F. N. Watson. PeLi

Limerick: "There was a young lady of Nantes." S. Littman. PeLi

Limerick: "There was a young lady of Nîmes." "Little Billee." PeLi

Limerick: "There was a Young Lady of Norway, / Who casually sat in a doorway." Edward Lear. PeLi

Limerick: "There was a young lady of Norway / Who hung by her toes in a doorway." Swinburne. PeLi

Limerick: "There was a young lady of Riga." Cosmo Monkhouse. PeLi

Limerick: "There was a young lady of Ryde, / Who ate some green apples and died." *Unknown.* PeLi

Limerick: "There was a young lady of Ryde / Who was carried too far by the tide." *Unknown.* PeLi

Limerick: "There was a young lady of Ryde / Whose shoe-strings were seldom untied." Edward Lear. OxBoLi; PeLV; PeLi

Limerick: "There was a young lady of Rye." *Unknown.* PeLi

Limerick: "There was a young lady of Slough." *Unknown.* PeLi

Limerick: "There was a young lady of Spain." *Unknown.* PeLi

Limerick: "There was a young lady of station." "Lewis Carroll." PeLi

Limerick: "There was a young lady of Sweden." Edward Lear. CBNP; EBEV; PeVV

Limerick: "There was a young lady of Tottenham." *Unknown.* PeLi; WeW-3

Limerick: "There was a young lady of Trent." *Unknown.* PeLi

Limerick: "There was a young lady of Ulva / Who drunkenly said: 'What a hulva'." Bill Greenwell. PeLi

Limerick: "There was a young lady of Ulva / Who kept a pet bee in her hand-bag." T. Johnston. PeLi

Limerick: "There was a young lady of Ulva / Who said: 'I have granted a culver'." T. Griffiths. PeLi

Limerick: "There was a young lady of Ulva / Who was famed far and wide for her vulva." Gavin Ewart. PeLi

Limerick: "There was a young lady of Ulva / Whose boy-friend said: 'Look, I will pulver'." Stanley J. Sharpless. PeLi

Limerick: "There was a young lady of Ulva / Whose sexual feelings were null. Va." Barbara E. Goff. PeLi

Limerick: "There was a young lady of Wantage." *Unknown.* PeLi

Limerick: "There was a young lady of Where?" *Unknown.* PeLi

Limerick: "There was a young lady of Whitby." "Lewis Carroll." PeLi

Limerick: "There was a young lady. . . tut, tut!" Stanley J. Sharpless. PeLi

Limerick: "There was a Young Lady whose chin." Edward Lear. PeLi

Limerick: "There was a young lady whose eyes." Edward Lear. NOBVV

Limerick: "There was a young lass of Pitlochry." *Unknown.* PeLi

Limerick: "There was a young lawyer called Rex." *Unknown.* PeLi

Limerick: "There was a young maid of Peru." Isaac Asimov. PeLi

Limerick: "There was a young maid who said, 'Why'." *Unknown.* SoSe-8

Limerick: "There was a young maiden from Multerry." *Unknown.* PeLi

Limerick: "There was a young maiden of Devon." *Unknown.* PeLi

Limerick: "There was a young man from Darjeeling." *Unknown.* PeLi

Limerick: "There was a young man named Racine." *Unknown.* PeLi

Limerick: "There was a young man of Australia." *Unknown.* PeLi

Limerick: "There was a young man of Belgrade." Isaac Asimov. PeLi

Limerick: "There was a young man of Calcutta." *Unknown.* PeLi

Limerick: "There was a young man of Cape Horn." Swinburne. PeLi

Limerick: "There was a young man of Cape Race." *Unknown.* PeLi

Limerick: "There was a young man of Devizes." Archibald Marshall. PeLi

Limerick: "There was a young man of Dumfries." *Unknown.* PeLi

Limerick: "There was a young man of Ghent." *Unknown.* PeLi

Limerick: "There was a young man of Japan." *Unknown.* PeLi

Limerick: "There was a young man of Madras." *Unknown.* PeLi

Limerick: "There was a young man of Montrose." Arnold Bennett. OxBoLi; PeLi

Limerick: "There was a young man of Nepal." *Unknown.* PeLi

Limerick: "There was a young man of Newcastle." Terence Melican. PeLi

Limerick: "There was a young man of Ostend." E. O. Parrott. PeLi

Limerick: "There was a young man of Porthcawl." A. G. Prys-Jones. PeLi

Limerick: "There was a young man of St John's." *Unknown.* PeLV

Limerick: "There was a young man of Wood's Hole." *Unknown.* PeLi

Limerick: "There was a young man so benighted." Frances Parkinson Keyes. PeLi

Limerick: "There was a young man who said: 'Ayer'." *Unknown.* PeLi

Limerick: "There was a young monarch called Ed." *Unknown.* PeLi

Limerick: "There was a young monk from Siberia." *Unknown.* PeLi

Limerick: "There was a young outlaw named Hood." E. O. Parrott. PeLi
Limerick: "There was a young peasant named Gorse." *Unknown.* PeLi
Limerick: "There was a young person called Tate." Carolyn Wells. PeLi
Limerick: "There was a Young Person of Kew." Edward Lear. CBNP
Limerick: "There was a young person of Leigh." Basil Ransome-Davies. PeLi
Limerick: "There was a young person of Smyrna." Edward Lear. OxBoLi; PeLV
Limerick: "There was a young plumber of Leigh." *Unknown.* PeLi
Limerick: "There was a young poet of Kew." *Unknown.* PeLi
Limerick: "There was a young poet of Thusis." *Unknown.* OxBoLi; PeLi
Limerick: "There was a young priest of Dun Laoghaire." *Unknown.* PeLi
Limerick: "There was a young princess, Snow-White." Gerard Benson. PeLi
Limerick: "There was a young student called Fred." V. R. Ormerod. PeLi
Limerick: "There was a young student called Jones." *Unknown.* PeLi
Limerick: "There was a young student of John's." *Unknown.* PeLi
Limerick: "There was a young woman called Myrtle." *Unknown.* PeLi
Limerick: "There was a young woman called Starky." *Unknown.* NOBL
Limerick: "There was a young woman named Plunnery." Edward Gorey. OBAL
Limerick: "There was a young woman of Dee." *Unknown.* PeLi
Limerick: "There was a young woman who said." Frances Darwin Cornford. PeLi
Limerick: "There was an archdeacon who said." *Unknown.* OBCoV
Limerick: "There was an old Bey of Calcutta." *Unknown.* PeLi
Limerick: "There was an old cynic who said." Allan M. Laing. PeLi
Limerick: "There was an old dame from Jerusalem." George Seferis, *Greek.* CBNP, *tr. by* Hugh Haughton
Limerick: "There was an old dame of Toulouse." A. M. Sayers. PeLi
Limerick: "There was an old Doctor called Coué." Bob Scott. PeLi
Limerick: "There was an old drunk called Hieronymus." Ron Rubin. PeLi
Limerick: "There was an old drunkard of Devon." Ron Rubin. PeLi
Limerick: "There was an old fellow named Hewing." *Unknown.* PeLi
Limerick: "There was an old fellow of Fife." *Unknown.* PeLi
Limerick: "There was an old fellow of Kaber." Philip Larkin. OBCoV
Limerick: "There was an old fellow of Kaber." Philip Larkin. OBCoV
Limerick: "There was an old fellow of Trinity." Arthur Clement Hilton. PeLi
Limerick: "There was an old gossip called Baird." Ogden Nash. PeLi
Limerick: "There was an old housewife of Staines." E. O. Parrott. PeLi
Limerick: "There was an old lady of Leicester." Ian T. MacKenzie. PeLi
Limerick: "There was an old madam called Rainey." *Unknown.* PeLi
Limerick: "There was an old maid of Duluth." *Unknown.* PeLi
Limerick: "There was an old man called Dupree." "R. I." PeLi
Limerick: "There was an Old Man in a boat." Edward Lear. CBNP; EBEV
(Limericks, I (i).) OBCoV
Limerick: "There was an Old Man in a tree." Edward Lear. CBNP; OxBChV; PeLi; Poetr
Limerick: "There was an old man in a trunk." Ogden Nash. PeLi
Limerick: "There was an old man of Bengal." "F. Anstey." PeLi
Limerick: "There was an old man of Boulogne." *Unknown.* PeLi
(Limerick.) PeLV
Limerick: "There was an old man of Cape Horn." Edward Lear. CBNP; EBEV; PeLi
Limerick: "There was an old man of Dunblane." Edward Lear. EBEV
Limerick: "There was an old man of Dundee." *Unknown.* PeLi
Limerick: "There was an old man of Ibreem." Edward Lear. EBEV
Limerick: "There was an old man of Kamschatka." Edward Lear. NOBL
Limerick: "There was an old man of Khartoum." William Ralph Inge. NOBL; PeLi
Limerick: "There was an old man of Lugano." Victor Gray. PeLi
Limerick: "There was an old man of [or from] Peru / Who dreamt [or dreamed] he was eating his shoe." *Unknown.* SoSe-8
("And—good grief! it was perfectly true!") (LL) KaS
(Old Man from Peru, An.) NTCP
Limerick: "There was an old man of the Cape." Robert Louis Stevenson. PeLi
Limerick: "There was an old man of the coast." Edward Lear. PeLi
Limerick: "There was an old man of Thermopylae." Edward Lear. EBEV; NOBL; OxAEP-2; PeLi
Limerick: "There was an old man of Whitehaven." Edward Lear. CBNP; EBEV; OxAEP-2
Limerick: "There was an old man on some rocks." Edward Lear. NOBVV; PeLi
Limerick: "There was an old man on the Border." Edward Lear. EBEV
Limerick: "There was an Old Man on whose nose." Edward Lear. PeLi
Limerick: "There was an old man who averred." *Unknown.* PeLi

Limerick: "There was an old man who said: 'How'" Edward Lear. OxBChV; PeLi
Limerick: "There was an Old Man who said, 'Hush!'" Edward Lear. NOBL; OxBChV; OxBoLi; PeLV; PeLi
Limerick: "There was an Old Man who said: 'Well!'." Edward Lear. PeLi
Limerick: "There was an old man who screamed out." Edward Lear. CBNP; EBEV; NOBVV; OxAEP-2
Limerick: "There was an Old Man who supposed." Edward Lear. NAEL-2; NOBVV; PeLi; Poetr
Limerick: "There was an Old Man with a Beard / Who said: 'I demand to be feared'." Roger Woddis. PeLi
Limerick: "There was an old Member called Bevan." Barbara Leigh. PeLi
Limerick: "There was an old mickey called Cassidy." Conrad Potter Aiken. PeLi
Limerick: "There was an old miser at [or of] Reading." *Unknown.* OxBChV; PeLi
Limerick: "There was an old person of Basing." Edward Lear. CBNP; EBEV; OxAEP-2; PeLi
(Limericks, I (iii).) OBCoV
Limerick: "There was an old person of Bow." Edward Lear. CBNP; EBEV; OxAEP-2
Limerick: "There was an Old Person of Bree." *Unknown.* CBNP
Limerick: "There was an Old Person of Brigg." Edward Lear. CBNP
Limerick: "There was an Old Person of Cadiz." *Unknown.* CBNP
Limerick: "There was an Old Person of Cromer." Edward Lear. PeLi
Limerick: "There was an Old Person of Ems." *Unknown.* CBNP
Limerick: "There was an old person of Fratton." *Unknown.* PeLi
Limerick: "There was an old person of Grange." Edward Lear. CBNP
Limerick: "There was an old person of Gretna." Edward Lear. OxBChV
(Limericks, I (iv).) OBCoV
Limerick: "There was an Old Person of Hurst." Edward Lear. PeLi
Limerick: "There was an old person of Persia." William Plomer. PeLi
Limerick: "There was an Old Person of Philae." Edward Lear. CBNP
Limerick: "There was an Old Person of Slough." George Robey. PeLi
Limerick: "There was an Old Person of Slough." *Unknown.* CBNP
Limerick: "There was an old sage of New Delhi." Joyce Parr. PeLi
Limerick: "There was an old Scot called McTavish." *Unknown.* PeLi
Limerick: "There was an old Welshman called Morgan." Ron Rubin. PeLi
Limerick: "There was an Old Woman of Gloster." *Unknown.* PeLi
Limerick: "There was an Old Woman of Lynn." *Unknown.* PeLi
Limerick: "There was an old woman of Wales." George Seferis, *Greek.* CBNP, *tr. by* Peter Levi
Limerick: "There was once a young man of Oporta." "Lewis Carroll." PeLi
Limerick: "There we was, and wanting our tea." "P. E. A." PeLi
Limerick: "There were once two young people of taste." Monica Curtis. PeLi
Limerick: "There's a combative artist named Whistler." D. G. Rossetti. FaBoEE; PeLi
Limerick: "There's a fortunate priest of St. Paul's." Douglas Catley. PeLi
Limerick: "There's a notable family named Stein." *Unknown.* NOBL
Limerick: "There's a Portuguese person named Howell." D. G. Rossetti. PeLi
Limerick: "There's a publishing party named Ellis." D. G. Rossetti. PeLi
Limerick: "There's a sensitive type in Tom's River." *Unknown.* PeLi
Limerick: "There's a slow tolling bell in the dark." Gavin Ewart. PeLi
Limerick: "There's a tiresome young man of Bay Shore." Morris Gilbert Bishop. PeLi
Limerick: "There's a very prim girl called McDrood." *Unknown.* PeLi
Limerick: "There's a wonderful family called Stein." *Unknown.* PeLi
Limerick: "There's an emerald frog down the loo." Ruth Silcock. PeLi
Limerick: "These days, the ubiquitous db." A. P. Cox. PeLi
Limerick: "They say that I was in my youth." *Unknown.* PeLi
Limerick: "Thomas Hobbes of Malmesbury thought." Peter Alexander. PeLi
Limerick: "Though clerical errors are fun." *Unknown.* PeLi
Limerick: "Though his plan, when he gave her a buzz." *Unknown.* PeLi
Limerick: "Though Sir James (God's-a-Formula) Jeans." R. J. P. Hewison. PeLi
Limerick: "Though the limerick can not be deaded." *Unknown.* PeLi
Limerick: "Though your dreams may seem normal and right." J. C. B. Date. PeLi
Limerick: "Three Aldis, not one of them dim." Joyce Johnson. PeLi
Limerick: "Three scribblers whose names end in Bert." C. Vita-Finzi. PeLi
Limerick: "Three wonderful people called Ley." Tim Hopkins. PeLi
Limerick: "Three wonderful people called Wick." A. M. Sayers. PeLi
Limerick: "Throughout the whole world, experts say." *Unknown.* PeLi
Limerick: "Thus spake an old Chinese mandarin." *Unknown.* PeLi
Limerick: "'Tis strange how the newspapers honour." Eugene Field. PeLi

Limerick: "To Algebra God is inclined." J. C. B. Date. PeLi

Limerick: "To avoid matrimonial disasters." Martin Fagg. PeLi

Limerick: "To her friends, said the Bright one, in chatter." Arthur Buller. PeLi

Limerick: "To her gardener, a lady named Liliom." *Unknown.* PeLi

Limerick: "To his bride said a numbskull named Clarence." *Unknown.* PeLi

Limerick: "To his club-footed child said Lord Stipple." Edward Gorey. OBCoV

Limerick: "To his Queen said the circumspect Burleigh." A. Cinna. PeLi

Limerick: "To his wife said the lynx-eyed detective." Langford Reed. PeLi

Limerick: "Tone-deaf old person of Tring, A." *Unknown.* PeLi

Limerick: "Toper who spies in the distance, A." Leslie Johnson. PeLi

Limerick: "Traveller to Timbuktu, A." *Unknown.* PeLi

Limerick: "Trouble with General Sherman, The." Basil Ransome-Davies. PeLi

Limerick: "Truth about truth is elusive, The." *Unknown.* PeLi

Limerick: "Try our Rubber Girl-Friend (air-inflatable)." *Unknown.* PeLi

Limerick: "Tutor who tooted a flute, A." Carolyn Wells. PeLi; SoSe-8

Limerick: "Two earnest young fellows named Wright." Basil Ransome-Davies. PeLi

Limerick: "Two middle-aged ladies from Fordham." *Unknown.* PeLi

Limerick: "Two playwrights called Beaumont and Fletcher." Fiona Pitt-Kethley. PeLi

Limerick: "Two she-camels spied on a goat." *Unknown.* PeLi

Limerick: "Undressing a maiden called Sue." Brian Allgar. PeLi

Limerick: "Unfortunate lad from Madrid, An." *Unknown.* PeLi

Limerick: "United States Constitution, The." Peter Alexander. PeLi

Limerick: "Unperson from West Oceania, An." C. Vita-Finzi. PeLi

Limerick: "Unpopular man of Cologne, An." *Unknown.* PeLi

Limerick: "Up the street sex is sold by the piece." *Unknown.* PeLi

Limerick: "Vain old Professor of Greek, A." Ron Rubin. PeLi

Limerick: "Van Gogh, feeling devil-may-care." "Pibwob." PeLi

Limerick: "Very apt question struck me, A." Sydney Bernard Smith. PeLi

Limerick: "Vice most obscene and unsavoury, A." *Unknown.* NOBL; PeLV

Limerick: "Victoria said: 'We've no quarrel.'" Frank Richards. PeLi

Limerick: "Victoria was bitterly short." Cyril Mountjoy. PeLi

Limerick: "Victorian gent said: 'This dance,' A." Frank Richards. PeLi

Limerick: "Viscount Stansgate, or Wedgwood, or Benn." Tim Hopkins. PeLi

Limerick: "Wanting children a couple once sat." G. W. Hanney. PeLi

Limerick: "Wanton young lady of Wimley, A." *Unknown.* PeLi

Limerick: "Watt's dream was the cream of steam engines." Bill Greenwell. PeLi

Limerick: "We all place a great deal of reliance." *Unknown.* PeLi

Limerick: "Wee Jamie, a canny young Scot." Joyce Johnson. PeLi

Limerick: "Well-buggered boy named Delpasse, A." *Unknown.* PeLi

Limerick: "'Well, I took your advice, Doc,' said Knopp." *Unknown.* PeLi

Limerick: "Well, if it's a sin to like Guinness." Cyril Ray. PeLi

Limerick: "Well, it's partly the shape of the thing." *Unknown.* SoSe-8

Limerick: "'We're not amused,' said Victoria." Stanley J. Sharpless. PeLi

Limerick: "We've got a new maid called Chrysanthemum." *Unknown.* PeLi

Limerick: "We've socially-conscious biography." *Unknown.* PeLi

Limerick: "'What have I done?' said Christine." *Unknown.* PeLi

Limerick: "What led to the crassness of Custer." Bill Greenwell. PeLi

Limerick: "What! Parted! Not even a kiss?" "X. A. M." PeLi

Limerick: "'What's the matter, old chap?' 'Well, I came.'" Joyce Johnson. PeLi

Limerick: "When a feverish groom in Armenia." Morris Gilbert Bishop. PeLi

Limerick: "When a friend said to Leda: 'Come on'." Peter Alexander. PeLi

Limerick: "When a friend told a typist called Eve." Gordon Harper. PeLi

Limerick: "When a man's too old even to toss off, he." Robert Conquest. PeLi

Limerick: "When an amorous youth from Atlantis." C. Vita-Finzi. PeLi

Limerick: "When an obstinate fellow of Fife." Allan M. Laing. PeLi

Limerick: "When approached by a person from Porlock." Richard Leighton Greene. PeLi

Limerick: "When Gauguin was visiting Fiji." Victor Gray. NOBL

Limerick: "When he raped a young maid in a train." *Unknown.* PeLi

Limerick: "When I sit in the Churchyard at Stoke." A. M. Sayers. PeLi

Limerick: "When I thought of this Duchess affair." *Unknown.* PeLi

Limerick: "When Ireland was bloody and leaderless." Gina Berkeley. PeLi

Limerick: "When Jael crept in to see Sisera." Bill Greenwell. PeLi

Limerick: "When Keats was at work on *Endymion*." Victor Gray. PeLi

Limerick: "When Lazarus came back from the dead." *Unknown.* PeLi

Limerick: "When our dean took a pious young spinster." Victor Gray. NOBL; PeLi

Limerick: "When Pegotty found Barkis was willing." Douglas Catley. PeLi

Limerick: "When the census man called upon Gail." George McWilliam. PeLi

Limerick: "When the judge with his wife having sport." *Unknown.* PeLi

Limerick: "When the Prince, who was terribly smit." Joyce Johnson. PeLi

Limerick: "When your capitalist boss takes his toll." Dominic Fitzpatrick. PeLi

Limerick: "Whenever he got in a fury, a." *Unknown.* PeLi

Limerick: "While Dubliner leopold bloom sought solace." Gerard Benson. PeLi

Limerick: "While Titian was grinding rose madder." *Unknown.* NOBL

Limerick: "While visiting Arundel Castle." Victor Gray. NOBL

Limerick: "Whilst Titian was mixing rose madder." *Unknown.* PeLi

Limerick: "Widow (conscious that time's on the wing)." Stanley J. Sharpless. PeLi

Limerick: "Wily Napoleon Bonaparte, The." Douglas Catley. PeLi

Limerick: "Wily old writer called Maugham, A." Martin Fagg. PeLi

Limerick: "Winter is here with his grouch." *Unknown.* PeLi

Limerick: "Wonderful bird is the pelican, A." Dixon Lanier Merritt. PeLi

Limerick: "Yogi from far-off Beirut, A." *Unknown.* PeLi

Limerick: "Young bride and groom of Australia, A." *Unknown.* PeLi

Limerick: "Young couple who lived at 'The Laurels', A." W. F. N. Watson. PeLi

Limerick: "Young engine-driver called Hunt, A." Victor Gray. NOBL

Limerick: "Young girl in remote Samarkand, A." George Seferis, *Greek.* CBNP, *tr. by* Peter Levi

Limerick: "Young girl of English nativity, A." *Unknown.* PeLi

Limerick: "Young girl who was no good at tennis, A." *Unknown.* PeLi

Limerick: "Young Irish servant in Drogheda, A." *Unknown.* PeLi

Limerick: "Young Joseph's new coat was real nice." Cyril Mountjoy. PeLi

Limerick: "Young lady, whose life-style the malicious, A." Gavin Ewart. PeLi

Limerick: "Young man by a girl was desired, A." *Unknown.* PeLi

Limerick: "Young man who lived on Holme Hale, A." Ida Thurtle. PeLi

Limerick: "Young man with passions quite gingery, A." *Unknown.* PeLi

Limerick: "Young men who frequent picture palaces." *Unknown.* PeLV

Limerick: "Young Oedipus learned from the Sphinx." Basil Ransome-Davies. PeLi

Limerick: "Young things who frequent picture-palaces, The." Philip Heseltine. NOBL; OBCoV; PeLi

(Picture-Palaces.) OBCoV

Limerick: "Youth and a maiden from Costessey, A." S. C. Turner. PeLi

Limerick. Edward Lear. PeLi

Limerick. *Unknown.* NOBL

Limerick. *Unknown.* OBCoV

Limerick. *Unknown.* PeLi

Limerick: For Travelers Going Sidereal. Robert Frost. *See* Limerick: "For Travelers Going Sidereal."

Limerick Is Furtive and Mean, The. Morris Gilbert Bishop. NBLV; PeLi

Limerick issued from Lear, The. J. A. Lindon. PeLi

Limerick lacks the precision, The. *Unknown.* PeLi

Limerick packs laughs anatomical, The. *Unknown.* PeLi

Limerick realm now prepares, The. *Unknown.* PeLi

Limerick Train, The. Brendan Kennelly. PBCIP

Limericks. Cosmo Monkhouse. PFE

Limericks and Puns. *Unknown.* PeLi

Limerick's birth is unclear, The. *Unknown.* PeLi

Limerick's callous and crude, The. *Unknown.* PeLi

Limericks, I (i). Edward Lear. *See* Limerick: "There was an Old Man in a boat."

Limericks, I (ii). Edward Lear. OBCoV

Limericks, I (iii). Edward Lear. *See* Limerick: "There was an old person of Basing."

Limericks, I (iv). Edward Lear. *See* Limerick: "There was an old person of Gretna."

Limericks, I (v). Edward Lear. OBCoV

Limericks, II (i). Edward Lear. OBCoV

Limericks, II (ii). Edward Lear. OBCoV

Limericks, II (iii). Edward Lear. OBCoV

Limericks, II (iv). Edward Lear. OBCoV

Limericks, II (v). Edward Lear. OBCoV

Limit. Diane Ward. FTOS

Limitation, / limp, / simply. (LL) A Little Tumescence. Jonathan Williams. NeAP; PoM

Limitations. Henrietta Cordelia Ray. CBWP-3

Limitations. Siegfried Sassoon. MoBrPo

Limited. Carl Sandburg. GM; HAP; MoAmPo; OxBA; SAGP
("Omaha.") (LL) GM

Limited, The. Robert Penn Warren. PoA

Limited air drafts. The Occurrences. George Oppen. FTOS

Limits. Ralph Waldo Emerson. OxBSP; PoEL-4

Limits (1962). Christopher Okigbo.
"Banks of reed." PBMAP
"For he was a shrub among the poplars." PBMAP
"Image insists, An." PBMAP
"Suddenly becoming talkative." PBMAP

Limits of Physics, The. Dan Pagis, *Hebrew*. IP, *tr. by* Warren Bargad *and* Stanley F. Chyet

Limits of Submission, The. Faarah Nuur, *Somali*. TTY, *tr. by* B. W. Andrzejewski *and* I. M. Lewis

Limp as unwatered flowers, the grey limbs. Homage to the Carracci. Thomas M. Disch. PoA

Limpid river / rippling in dawn light. Inscribed on a Landscape by Mi Yüan-hui. Chao Meng-fu, *Chinese*. CoBLCP, *tr. by* Jonathan Chaves

Limping past the Guthrie theater. Indians at the Guthrie. Gerald Vizenor. VoR

Limpopo. Walter Battiss. PeSAV

Limpopo and Tugela churned. The Scorpion. William Plomer. OBMV; PeSAV

L'Imprévisibilité. Zinaida Hippius, *Russian*. PBWP, *tr. by* Temira Pachmuss

Lincoln. John Gould Fletcher. CBCWP; MoAmPo

Lincoln. Henrietta Cordelia Ray. CBWP-3

Lincoln and Liberty. *Unknown*. AS

Lincoln at Gettysburg. Bayard Taylor. *Fr.* Gettysburg Ode. CBCWP

Lincoln Monument: Washington. Langston Hughes. CBCWP

Lincoln, the Man of the People. Edwin Markham. MoAmPo

Lincoln's Grave. Maurice Thompson. CBCWP

Lincolnshire Poacher, The. *Unknown*. CH; OxBoLi; PeLV

Lincolnshire Shores ("Still salt pool locked in with bars of sand, A"). Tennyson. *Fr.* The Palace of Art. EnVR; NOBRP

Lincolnshire Wolds and Lincolnshire Sea. Tennyson. *Fr.* In Memoriam A. H. H.

Linda, Linda, slender and pretty. John Fuller. PeLV

Lindamira's Complaint. Mary Sidney, Countess of Montgomery Wroth. *Fr.* Urania.

Lindbergh. *Unknown*. AmFP

Linden blossomed, the nightingale sang, The. Farewell. Heinrich Heine, *German*. AWP, *tr. by* John Todhunter

Lindie, chile, fo' Lawd sake, tell me. After the Quarrel. Priscilla Jane Thompson. CBWP-2

Line. Milo De Angelis, *Italian*. NeIt, *tr. by* Lawrence Venuti

Line. Cole Swenson. WWSi

Line coils seeking extension, The. Where the Honey Speech's Hedge. Peter Cole. PT

Line-Gang, The. Robert Frost. OxBSP

Line in long array where they wind betwixt green islands, A. Cavalry Crossing a Ford. Walt Whitman. AiP; AmPP; BLT; CBCWP; FaBoA; HeIP-4; InPK-6; InPS-3; MoP; NAAL-1; NAAL-3; NCAP; NoAM; NoP-4; OxBA; PAR; SAmP; TAP; TFi; TRP; UnPo

Line Like. Nelly Sachs, *German*. BoWoP, *tr. by* Michael Hamburger

Line of Beauty, The. Arthur William Edgar O'Shaughnessy. TIRV

Line-Storm Song, A. Robert Frost. SAGP

Line the inside of the little box. The Owners of the Little Box. Vasco [*or* Vasko] Popa, *Serbo-Croatian*. HSix, *tr. by* Charles Simic

Line through the hold in the dank, The. Bellrope. Robert Morgan. BLT

Line to Heaven by Christ Was Made, The. *Unknown*. BXAP

Lineage. Frank Bidart. *Fr.* Elegy. HCAP

Lineage. Robert Farren. TIRV

Lineage. Margaret Abigail Walker. BlSi; CrSp; NALW; NMM-2; OxWW; PBWP; PoBA

Lineage. Daisy Zamora, *Spanish*. LoL, *tr. by* Margaret Randall

Lineaments of a plummet-measured face, The. (LL) The Statues. W. B. Yeats. NoAM; OAEL-2; WeW-3

Lineaments of Gratified Desire, The. (LL) Question Answered, The [*or* A]. William Blake. FaBoEE; GBL; ITG; NoP-4; OAEL-2; OxBM

Lined coat, warm cap and easy felt slippers. Ease. Po Chü-i, *Chinese*. ChiP; Spl, *tr. by* Arthur Waley

Linen Industry, The. Michael Longley. CBLP; CIP-2; NoP-4; PBCIP; PNI

Linen Weaver, The. *Unknown*. NOEC

Linen Workers, The. Michael Longley. BiHa; CIP-2 *Fr.* Wreaths.

Lines: "At the Portals of the Future." Frances Ellen Watkins Harper. APN-2; PAR

Lines: "From fair Jamaica's fertile plains." "Ada." BlSi

Lines: "Gather the sacred dust." Abram Joseph Ryan. APN-2

Lines: "How I love country you have heard." Samuel Alfred Beadle. AAP

Lines: "I have been cherish'd and forgiven." Hartley Coleridge. PoEL-4

Lines: "If we should ever meet again." Louisa Costello. Ro *Fr.* Songs of a Stranger (1825).

Lines: "Loud is the Vale! the Voice is up." Wordsworth. LaPo

Lines: "One summer evening (led by her) I found." Wordsworth. *Fr.* Introduction—Childhood and School-Time. FHYEP *Fr.* The Prelude; Growth of a Poet's Mind [1850 vers.]

Lines: "Other day I was loving a sweet little fruitpie-and-cream, The." Gavin Ewart. SPE

Lines: "Repressive desublimation." David Bromige. FTOS

Lines: "Singularly and in pairs the decade has been ripped by bullets." Herbert Martin. PoBA

Lines: "Wake not again the cannon's thrundous voice." Alfred Gibbs Campbell. AAP

Lines: "When the lamp is shattered [*or* shatter'd]." Shelley. CBLP; CH; ImPo; NAEL-2; OBEV; OBNC; PoEL-4
(Flight of Love, The.) GTBS-P

Lines: "When youthful faith hath fled." John Gibson Lockhart. OBEV; Ro

Lines. "Ada." BlSi
(Lines Suggested on Reading "An Appeal to Christian Women of the South," by A. E. Grimke.) NAAAL
("My spirit leaps in joyousness tow'rd thine.") NAAAL

Lines. Frances Anne Kemble. VWP

Lines. Tennyson. *See* For I Dipped [*or* Dipt] into the Future.

Lines. Henry Timrod. *See* Ode: "Sleep sweetly in your humble graves."

Lines. Wordsworth. *See* Lines Composed a Few Miles Above Tintern Abbey on Revisiting the Banks of the Wye During a Tour.

Lines about a Little Boy. Aleksandr Petrovich Mezhirov, *Russian*. TCRP, *tr. by* Deming Brown

Lines are cast and the nets are set and waiting, The. *Unknown, Greek*. PGA, *tr. by* Kenneth Rexroth

Lines by a Lady on the Loss of her Trunk. Richard Brinsley Sheridan. OBCoV

Lines Composed a Few Miles Above Tintern Abbey on Revisiting the Banks of the Wye During a Tour. Wordsworth. EBEvV; FHYEP; HeIP-4; InPS-3; NoP-4; OAEL-2; OBNC; OxAEP-2; PoEL-4; Poetr; SCGP; TFi
("Five years have passed; five summers, with the length.") NoP-4; PoPoPo; Ro
(Lines.) CABP
(Lines Written a Few Miles above Tintern Abbey.) NOBRP
(Lines Written a Few Miles above Tintern Abbey, on Revisiting the Banks of the Wye during a Tour, 13 July 1798.) Ro

Lines: Composed at the Old Temples of Maralipoor. Charles Timothy Brooks. APN-1

Lines Composed in a Wood on a Windy Day. Anne Brontë. EBVV
("And hear the wild roar of their thunder today!") (LL) VWP
(Windy Day, A.) SDW

Lines Descriptive of Thomson's Island. Benjamin Lynde. SCAP

Lines for a Bed at Kelmscott Manor. William Morris. CH; NTP
(Inscription for an Old Bed.) OBEV

Lines for a Book. Thom Gunn. CABP

Lines for a Painter. Anthony Cronin. PBCIP

Lines for a Tomb. Donald Davidson. FuPo

Lines for a Worthy Person Who Has Drifted by Accident into a Chelsea Revel. Sir Alan Patrick Herbert. NOBL

Lines for a Young Wanderer in Mexico. John Logan. PoA

Lines for an Interment. Archibald MacLeish. CMoP; NOBA

Lines for an Old Man. T. S. Eliot. FaBoTW; RB; RaBo

Lines for Cuscuscaraway and Mirza Murad Ali Beg. T. S. Eliot. NBLV; NTP; OBAL; OBCoV; PeLV; UV *Fr.* Five-Finger Exercises.

Lines for Marking Time. Roberta Hill Whiteman. BoWoP; CDW

Lines for Michael in the Picture. John Logan. CAPP-1

Lines for Roethke Twenty Years after His Death. Duane Niatum. HATNAP

Lines for Translation into Any Language. James Fenton. AF

Lines from Catullus. Catullus, *Latin*. SiPS, *tr. by* Sir Walter Raleigh

Lines from Love Letters. *Unknown*. OBEV

Lines from Love Letters, I. *Unknown*. OBEV

Lines from the Testament. Pier Paolo Pasolini, *Italian*. VCWP, *tr. by* Norman MacAfee *and* Luciano Martinengo

Lines: I Praise God's Mankind in an Old Woman. Wilfred Watson. NOBC

Lines in a Roman Schoolbook. Desmond O'Grady.
"In the valleys of the future we shall walk." PBCIP
"This introspective exile here today." PBCIP

Lines in Honor of Natalya. Pavel Nikolaevich Vasilyev, *Russian*. TCRP, *tr. by* David Macduff

Lines in Memory of My Father. Basil Payne. IIP

Lines in the Corner of a Manuscript. *Unknown.* FaBoVe

Lines Left at Mr Theodore Hook's House in June, 1834. "Thomas Ingoldsby." OBCoV

Lines Left upon a Seat in a Yew-Tree which Stands near the Lake of Esthwaite, on a Desolate Part of the Shore, yet Commanding a Beautiful Prospect. Wordsworth. Ro

Lines Occasioned by the Burning of Some Letters. Sarah Dixon. ECWP; NOEC

Lines of a poem, long, short: each joined to the end decreed for it. Outside the Line. Dan Pagis, *Hebrew.* IP, *tr. by* Warren Bargad *and* Stanley F. Chyet

Lines of Life. Letitia Elizabeth Landon. NOBRP

Lines of this new song are nothing, The. Louis Zukofsky. VGW

Lines of your arteries, The. Robert. Wendy Rose. HATNAP

Lines on a Boer War Pin-up Girl Seen in the Falcon Hotel, Bude. Christopher Hope. PeSAV

Lines on a Dead Girl. Priscilla Jane Thompson. CBWP-2

Lines on a Purple Cap Received as a Present from My Brother. George Alsop. SCAP

Lines on a Young Lady's Photograph Album. Philip Larkin. EnLoPo; HAP; OAEL-2

Lines on Carmen Sylva. Emma Lazarus. TrJP

Lines on Hearing That Lady Byron Was Ill. Byron. EBEV; OxAEP-2

Lines on Hearing the Organ. Charles Stuart Calverley. NOBL

Lines on His Birthday. John Logan. CAPP-1

Lines on His Companions Who Died in the Northern Seas. Thomas James. NOSC

Lines on Leaving a Scene in Bavaria. Thomas Campbell. OBNC

Lines on Receiving His Mother's Picture. William Cowper. CH *Fr.* On the Receipt of My Mother's Picture out of Norfolk [the Gift of My Cousin Ann Bodham]. NOEC; OxAEP-1

Lines on Receiving My Mother's Picture Out of Norfolk. William Cowper. *See* On the Receipt of My Mother's Picture out of Norfolk, the Gift of My Cousin Ann Bodham.

Lines on Swinburne. Robert Browning. EPCY

Lines on the Award "Pipe Man of the Year" to Magnus Magnusson. E. J. Thribb. OBCoV

Lines on the Back of a Confederate Note. Samuel Alroy Jonas. BLPA

Lines on the Death of Bismarck. John Jay Chapman. PoEL-5
  (Bismark.) APN-2

Lines on the Death of the Rev. S. K. Talmage. Mary E. Tucker. CBWP-1

Lines on the Hundredth Anniversary of the Birth of W. Somerset Maugham. E. J. Thribb. PeLV

Lines on the Mermaid Tavern. Keats. FHYEP; PoRA; SCGP
  (Mermaid Tavern, The.) FaBoBe; GTBS-P

Lines on the Rambam. Gabriel Preil, *Yiddish.* CEEP, *tr. by* Linda Zisquit

Lines on the Return to Britain of Billy Graham. E. J. Thribb. PeLV

Lines on the Sea. Dilys Bennett Laing. NYBP

Lines on the Tombs in Westminster. Francis Beaumont. CH; FaPoR; GTBS-P; NOBE; OBEV; SCGP *Fr.* On the Tombs in Westminster Abbey.
  ("Buried in dust, once dead by fate.") (LL) GTBS-P
  (On the Tombs in Westminster Abbey.) GTBS-P; OxAEP-1

Lines on Thomas Warton's Poems. Samuel Johnson. EPCY; FaBoEE
  (Lines Written in Ridicule of Certain Poems.) SCGP

Lines parallel. The Room. De Leon Harrison. PoBA

Lines Printed under the Engraved Portrait of Milton [In Tonson's Folio of the "Paradise Lost"]. Dryden. InPK-6; OxAEP-1
  (Epigram on Milton.) EPCY

Lines Rhymed in a Letter from Oxford. Keats. *See* On Oxford.

Lines Suggested by an Edition of Blake's Poems. Sir Walter Alexander Raleigh. OBCoV

Lines Suggested by Hearing Music on the Boston Common at Night. Thomas Cole. APN-1

Lines / Suggested by the Song of a Nightingale. Eliza Cook. VWP

Lines Suggested on Reading "An Appeal to Christian Women of the South," by A. E. Grimke. "Ada." *See* Lines.

Lines to——. Mary Weston Fordham. CBWP-2

Lines to a Don. Hilaire Belloc. MoBrPo; OBSV

Lines to a Dragon-Fly. Walter Savage Landor. *See* The Dragon-Fly.

Lines to a Graduate. Lizelia Augusta Jenkins Moorer. CBWP-3

Lines to a Movement in Mozart's E-Flat Symphony. Thomas Hardy. NoAM

Lines to a Reviewer. Shelley. OxBSP

Lines to a Tree. Judah Leib Teller, *Yiddish.* CEEP, *tr. by* Gabriel Preil *and* Howard Schwartz

Lines to a World-famous Poet Who Failed to Complete a World-famous Poem; or, Come Clean, Mr. Guest! Ogden Nash. OBAL

Lines: To a Young Gentleman of Surpassing Beauty. Ellen Johnston. VWP

Lines to Accompany Flowers for Eve. Carolyn Kizer. BoWoP

Lines to an Indian Air. Shelley. *See* The Indian Serenade.

Lines to an Old Dress. Mary E. Tucker. CBWP-1

Lines to an Old School-House. Priscilla Jane Thompson. CBWP-2

Lines to Caste. Samuel Alfred Beadle. AAP

Lines to Do with Youth. Witter Bynner. PoA

Lines to Ellen, the Factory Girl. Ellen Johnston. VWP

Lines to Emma. Priscilla Jane Thompson. CBWP-2

Lines to Florence. Mary Weston Fordham. CBWP-2

Lines to His Son on Reaching Adolescence. John Logan. CAPP-1

Lines to Lord Byron. Shelley. *See* Sonnet to Byron.

Lines to Mr Hodgson. Byron. OBCoV
  (Lisbon Packet, The.) NBLV

Lines to Mother. Rose M. Stein. PWR

Lines to Mount Glen. George Marion McClellan. AAP

Lines to Mrs. Isabel Peace. Mary Weston Fordham. CBWP-2

Lines to Mrs. M. C. Turner. Eloise Bibb. CBWP-4

Lines to My Grandfathers. Tony Harrison. *Fr.* The School of Eloquence. NAEL-2; NoAM

Lines to Ralph Hodgson Esqre. T. S. Eliot. NBLV; OBAL; PeLV *Fr.* Five-Finger Exercises.

Lines to Ratclif. Henry Howard, Earl of Surrey. *See* Exhortation to Learn of Others' Trouble.

Lines to the Black Oak. Oliver La Grone. NBV

Lines to the Blessed Sacrament. *Unknown, Irish.* TIRV, *tr. by* Jeremiah J. Callanan

Lines to the Hon. George L. Knox. Eloise Bibb. CBWP-4

Lines Where Beauty Lingers. Franklin Pierce Adams. OBAL

Lines Written a Few Miles above Tintern Abbey, on Revisiting the Banks of the Wye during a Tour, 13 July 1798. Wordsworth. *See* Lines Composed a Few Miles Above Tintern Abbey on Revisiting the Banks of the Wye During a Tour.

Lines Written among the Euganean Hills. Shelley. OxBoS; PoEL-4
  ("To the haven of the grave.") (LL) OxBoS
  (Written in the Euganean Hills, North Italy.) GTBS-P

Lines Written at Bridgewater, 27 July 1797. John Thelwall.
  "Day of my double birth, if such the year." NOEC

Lines written at Bridgewater in Somersetshire, on 27 July 1797, during a Long Excursion in Quest of a Peaceful Retreat. John Thelwall. Ro *Fr.* Poems Written Chiefly in Retirement.

Lines Written beneath a Picture. Byron. OxBSP
  (Written Beneath a Picture.) Ro

Lines Written During a Period of Insanity. William Cowper. EBEV; HAP; NOEC; NoP-4; OAEL-1
  (Lines Written Under the Influence of Delerium.) ChIV-1

Lines Written for a Blank Page of "The Keepsake." Winthrop Mackworth Praed. CBLP

Lines Written for Allen Tate on His Sixtieth Anniversary. Donald Davidson. FuPo

Lines Written for Gene Kelly to Dance To. Carl Sandburg. AiP

Lines Written Immediately after Parting from a Lady. Sir Samuel Egerton Brydges. NOEC

Lines Written in a Blank Leaf of the Prometheus Unbound. Thomas Lovell Beddoes. EPCY; OAEL-2

Lines Written in a Pittsburgh Skyscraper. Diane Ackerman. WWSi

Lines Written in Early Spring. Wordsworth. FHYEP; LaPo; NAEL-2; NOBRP; OAEL-2; PBMP; PoLF; Ro
  (Written in Early Spring.) GTBS-P

Lines Written in Her Breviary. Saint, of Avila Theresa. *See* Bookmark.

Lines Written in Kensington Gardens. Matthew Arnold. FHYEP
  Lines Written in Kensington Gardens. GaP; OBGa

Lines Written in Oregon. Vladimir Nabokov. NYBP

Lines Written in Ridicule of Certain Poems. Samuel Johnson. *See* Lines on Thomas Warton's Poems.

Lines Written in the Album at Elbingerode, in the Hartz Forest. Coleridge. Ro

Lines Written in the Bay of Lerici. Shelley. NAEL-2; OAEL-2

Lines Written in the Dog-Days. William Woty. NOEC

Lines Written in Windsor Forest. Alexander Pope. *See* A Hymn Written in Windsor Forest.

Lines Written near Linton, on Exmoor. Daniel Gerard Hoffman. BXAP

Lines Written near Richmond, upon the Thames, at Evening. Wordsworth. Ro

(Lines Written on a Bookmark Found in Her Breviary). Teresa de Cepeda Y Ahumada, *Spanish.* WPoS, *tr. by* Henry Wadsworth Longfellow

Lines Written on a Farewell View of the Franconia Mountains at Twilight. Henrietta Cordelia Ray. CBWP-3

Lines Written on a Seat on the Grand Canal, Dublin. Patrick Kavanagh. BIrV; CMoP; InPS-3; NOIV

Lines Written on a Very Boisterous Day in May, 1844. John Clare. OxBSP

Lines Written on a Window at The Leasowes. William Shenstone. OxBSP

Lines Written on New Year's Day—In the Manner of Liu Hou-ts'un [Liu K'o-chuang (1187–1269)]. Wen Cheng-ming, *Chinese*.
  "There was no reason to expect sadness." CoBLCP, *tr. by* Jonathan Chaves

Lines, / Written on Seeing My Husband's Picture, painted when he was young: "Those are the features, those the smiles." Anna Sawyer. ECWP; LW

Lines Written to Console Those Ladies Distressed by the Lines 'Men Never Make Passes, etc'. Ogden Nash. PeLV

Lines Written Under a Picture of a Girl Burning a Love-Letter. Letitia Elizabeth Landon. NOBRP

Lines Written Under the Influence of Delerium. William Cowper. *See* Lines Written During a Period of Insanity.

Lines Written upon a Window-Shutter at Weston. William Cowper. NOEC

Lingam and the Yoni, The. Alec Derwent Hope. NoAM

Linger not, stranger; shed no tear;. Inscription for a War. Alec Derwent Hope. BMAP; NoP-4

Lingering clouds, rolling, rolling, The. Flood. Ch'ien T'ao, *Chinese*. ChiP, *tr. by* Arthur Waley

Lingering the rays of daylight, and the listening air is chilly. Philip and Mildred. Adelaide Anne Procter. VWP

Linguist parrot flicked his flowery wings, The. Crinagoras, *Greek*. GrAn, *tr. by* Alistair Elliot

Linin' ub De Hymns, De. Daniel Webster Davis. AAP

Lining Track. *Unknown*. AmFP

Links. Ana Blandiana, *Romanian*. CEEP, *tr. by* Michael Impey

Linnet in November, The. Francis Turner Palgrave. EBVV

Linnet in the rocky dells, The. Song. Emily Jane Brontë. HAP; OBNC; OxAEP-2; RACG; VWP

Linnet who had lost her way, A. Tenebris Interlucentem. James Elroy Flecker. MoBrPo

Linnets. Larry Levis. LCAP-2

Linstead Market. *Unknown*. FaBoVe; PBCV

Lint. Rita Dove. TRP

Lintie in a Cage. Alice V. Stuart. OxBS

Lion, The. Ogden Nash. TLR; WHSW

Lion. May Swenson. LiTM

Lion, The. Walter James Turner. MoBrPo

Lion. *Unknown, Hottentot*. PeSA

Lion and Albert, The. Marriott Edgar. OBNV

Lion and his shadow the lioness, The. Girl with Pitcher. Ruth Dallas. PeNZ

Lion and the Echo, The. Brian Patten. OBSP

Lion and the unicorn, The. Mother Goose. ACTP; BoTP; CTAV; LB; OxBoLi; OxNR; ReMoGo
  ("And drummed them out of town.") (LL) LB; OxNR
  ("His power to maintain.") (LL) OxBoLi

Lion ane his tamer, The. The Crunch. Gerda Mayer. OBSP

Lion dishonoured bids death come, The. Reversionary. Stevie Smith. FaBoEE

Lion, even when full of mud, with burrs, The. Birds. Ruth Miller. PeSA

Lion for Real, The. Allen Ginsberg. GLP; HCAP; RB

Lion-hearted cedar forest, gonads for our thunder. Christopher Okigbo. PBMAP *Fr.* Lament of the Drums (1964).

Lion-House, The. John Hall Wheelock. PFE

Lion Hunts. Patricia Beer. OxBTC

Lion is called the king, The. Kenneth Rexroth. HoPM *Fr.* A Bestiary. OBAL

Lion is never a lion in a royal hunt, A. Lion Hunts. Patricia Beer. OxBTC

Lion is the [*or* a] beast to fight, The. Sage Counsel. Sir Arthur Thomas Quiller-Couch. NBLV

Lion Named Passion, A. John Hollander. NoAM

Lion of Winter, The. Shakespeare. *See* The Fairy Blessing.

Lion over the Tomb of Leonidas, The. *Unknown, Greek*. AWP, *tr. by* Walter Leaf

Lion Tamer, The. Paul Durcan. IFJA

Lion tamers wrestle with the lions in a cage, The. Apex. Nate Salsbury. NBLV

Lion, the Lion, he dwells in the waste, The. Hilaire Belloc. CTAV; MoBrPo; NBLV; WHSW
  ("And a good little child will not play with him.") (LL) CTAV

Lion Thoughts. Iowna Elizabeth Banker. CTV

Lion's Bride, The. Gwen Harwood. BoWoP

Lions of Babylon, The. Daniela Crsnaru, *Romanian*. CEEP, *tr. by* Fleur Adcock

Lions of fire, The. Kenneth Patchen. VGW

Lions of the hill are gone, The. Deirdre's [*or* Deirdre's] Lament for the Sons of Usnach. *Unknown, Irish*. IIP; NOIV, *tr. by* Sir Samuel Ferguson

Lion's Skeleton, The. Charles Tennyson Turner. NOBVV

Lions who ate the Christians on the sands of the arena, The. Sunt Leones. Stevie Smith. NoAM

Lip was a man who used his head. James Vincent Cunningham. OBAL *Fr.* Five Epigrams.

Lip which had once been stolid, now moving, A. Divine Love. Michael Benedikt. AmPA; CoAP; CoAmPo

Lipman and Cohen, butchers, Hercules Lane. At the Jaffé Memorial Fountain, Botanic Gardens. Frank Ormsby. CIP-2

Lipper folk to Cresseid than can draw, The. Robert Henryson. *Fr.* The Testament of Cresseid. OxBS

Lips and Eyes. Giovanni Battista Marino, *Italian*. OBVE; OxBSP, *tr. by* Thomas Carew

Lips and Nose. Rodney Hall. *Fr.* The Owner of My Face. CBAP

Lips and tongue. A Hand of Solo. Thomas Kinsella. CIP-2; NOIV

Lips. / Eyes behind your neck. Silences. Agnes Gergely, *Hungarian*. CEEP, *tr. by* Timea K. Szell

Lips of that Evangelist, The. (LL) When Lazarus left his charnel-cave. Tennyson. EBVV; FHYEP; OAEL-2; PeECV; TOF

Lips of the one I love are my perpetual pleasure, The. Hafiz, *Persian*. BoLoP, *tr. by* Peter Avery *and* John Heath-Stubbs

Lips of the Wise, The. Bible, *O.T. See* The Bible, Proverbs 15:1.

Lips pressed against my heart. (LL) Evening Song. Jean Toomer. BPo; GT

Lips That Touch Liquor. George W. Young. NBLV

Lips Tongueless[e]. Robert Herrick. CaPo

Liquidity's a mystery; it's very rarely seen. The Accounting Cat. John Clarke. UV

Lisa, Leona, Loretta? Salt. Yusef Komunyakaa. UnSA

Lisa's Ritual, Age 10. Grace Caroline Bridges. LoHo

Lisbon. Russell Atkins. GT

Lisbon. *Unknown*. AmFP

Lisbon Packet, The. Byron. *See* Lines to Mr Hodgson.

Lisping young lady called Beth, A. Limerick. *Unknown*. PeLi

Lissom psychotic named Jane, A. Limerick. *Unknown*. PeLi

List all you Californ'y boys. California Trail. *Unknown*. PaTW

List, I hear the church bells ring. The Church Bells. Mrs. Henry Linden. CBWP-4

List! list! the sleigh bells peal across the snow. December. Henrietta Cordelia Ray. CBWP-3

List of the Delusions of the Insane / What They Are Afraid Of, A. David Antin. APSN

List the harp in window wailing. The Aeolian Harp. Herman Melville. AmPP; NCAP

List to me while I tell you. The Spaniard That Blighted My Life. Billy Merson. OBCoV

List to the sad wind, drearily moaning. Autumn. Priscilla Jane Thompson. CBWP-2

List while the poet trolls. The Rival Curates. Sir William Schwenck Gilbert. PeLV

Listen. Marylin Butler. CDa

Listen. Jessica Hagedorn. WPOW

Listen. Vladimir Mayakovsky, *Russian*. PFTM, *tr. by* Jack Hirschman *and* Victor Ehrlich

Listen. Linda Lancione Moyer. CrSp

Listen. Spectacular. Lilian Moore. KaS

Listen. Luci Tapahonso. MoLi

Listen. Yeshe Tsogyel. WPoS

Listen. . . / With faint dry sound. November Night. Adelaide Crapsey. FPC; Spl

Listen, and when thy hand this paper presses. A Letter from a Girl to Her Own Old Age. Alice Thompson Meynell. MoBrPo; VWP

Listen Children. Lucille Clifton. ISC; NOxBChV; PoBA

Listen, children: / Your father is dead. Lament. Edna St. Vincent Millay. CrSp; FiLi; IMW; MeMAP

Listen, comrades of the flaming centuries. David Diop, *French*. NegPo, *tr. by* Ellen Conroy Kennedy
  ("Listen comrades of the struggling centuries.") PBMAP
  ("Sign of brotherhood which comes to nourish the dreams of men, The.") (LL) PBMAP

Listen first, and show what you're made of. Sophocles. OBCVT, *tr. by* Ezra Pound *Fr.* The Women of Trachis.

Listen, for example, to the thudding of the winter stream. An Inconclusive Evening. Frances Bellerby. FaBoTw

Listen, good people, and you shall hear. The Ballad of Barnaby. W. H. Auden. OBNV *Fr.* Six Commissioned Texts.

Listen—help me! Ears. Sonja [dA]kesson, *Swedish.* WPOW, *tr. by* Joanna Bankier

Listen here, Joe. Without Benefit of Declaration. Langston Hughes. TTY

Listen, / how man has murdered the earth. The Sky. Un Ko, *Korean.* CKP, *tr. by* Jaihiun Kim

Listen I am just like. *Unknown, Japanese.* WPJ, *tr. by* Kenneth Rexroth *and* Ikuko Atsumi

Listen, I have flown through darkness towards joy. Iain Crichton Smith. FaBoTC

Listen! I will describe the best of dreams. The Dream of the Rood. *Unknown, Anglo-Saxon.* ASW, *tr. by* Kevin Crossley-Holland

Listen, / if stars are lit. Vladimir Mayakovsky, *Russian.* CLPP, *tr. by* Maria Enzensberger

Listen! In the April rain. In the April Rain. Mary Anderson. BoTP

Listen! I've a big surprise! Invitation. Myra Cohn Livingston. TLR

Listen, listen! The small song bird. Song to Imogen [in Basic English]. Richard Leighton Greene. BXAP

Listen! Listen to shopkeepers talking. Shopkeepers at the Party Meeting. Thomas McCarthy. BiHa

Listen! / Listen to the witch! Lilian Moore. ImGa; NTCP

Listen, lively lordings all. The Rising in the North. *Unknown.* ESPB

Listen, Lord—[a Prayer]. James Weldon Johnson. BPo

Listen, mad girl! for giving ear. Walter Savage Landor. CBLP

Listen more often. Breaths. Birago Diop, *French.* TTY, *tr. by* Anne Atik

Listen Mr Oxford Don. John Agard. NBrP

Listen my children, and you shall hear. Paul Revere's Ride (The Landlord's Tale). Henry Wadsworth Longfellow. APN-1; AiP; BLPA; ChAP; ColAP; EBEvV; EBNV; FaBoBe; FaBoTw; FaPoR; ImGa; NOxBChV; OBAL; OBCA; OBNV; PWR; SAGP; TFi *Fr.* Tales of a Wayside Inn.

Listen, my Dearest, hear the sweet night march! (LL) Meditation. Charles Baudelaire, *French.* InPK-6; NAWM-2, *tr. by* Robert Lowell

Listen, my dearest, once this flesh of mine. Two Hearts Divided. R. Williams Parry, *Welsh.* OBWVE, *tr. by* Joseph P. Clancy

Listen / My friend. What the Girl Friend Said to the Foster-Mother. Kapilar, *Tamil.* PLW, *tr. by* A. K. Ramanujan

Listen, my friend, this road is the heart opening. The Heat of Midnight Tears. Mirabai, *Rajasthani.* WPoS, *tr. by* Robert Bly

Listen, my love, to music's fragrant tune. Magic. Xuân Diệu, *Vietnamese.* AVP, *tr. by* Huỳnh Sanh Thông

Listen natives of a dry place. The Old Boast. W. S. Merwin. NOBA

Listen, nephew / When I opened the cantina. The Tale of Sunlight. Gary Soto. NoAM

"Listen, now, verse should be as natural." Poetry for Supper. Ronald Stuart Thomas. OxBC

Listen old man listen. Sweat-House Ritual No. 1. *Unknown, Omaha Indian.* STP, *tr. by* Jerome Rothenberg *from* Alia Fletcher *and* Francis La Flesche

Listen. Put on Morning. W. S. Graham. FaBoTw; LiTM

Listen sweet Dove unto my song. Whitsunday. George Herbert. GeHe

Listen! The fame of Danish kings. Beowulf. *Unknown, Anglo-Saxon.* ASW, *tr. by* Kevin Crossley-Holland

Listen! The garbage pouring down the chutes. For David Shapiro. David Lehman. PoA

Listen, the hay-bells tinkle as the cart. The Holy Innocents. Robert Lowell. CoAmPo; MoAmPo; OBCP; OxBC

Listen! The night-raven's song. Nicarchus of Alexandria, *Greek.* GrAn, *tr. by* Peter Porter

Listen; the poets laureate. The Lemon Trees. Eugenio Montale, *Italian.* PFTM, *tr. by* Irma Brandeis

Listen: / There roams, far away, by the waters of Clead. Nikolai Stepanovich Gumilyov. *Fr.* The Giraffe. TCRP, *tr. by* Yakov Hornstein

Listen: there was a goat's head hanging by ropes in a tree. Song. Brigit Pegeen Kelly. PUP-19 *Fr.* The Southern Review.

Listen to me and you shall hear. The World is Turned Upside Down. *Unknown.* NOSC

Listen to me, as when ye heard our father. Canadian Boat Song. John Galt *and* "Christopher North." BLPA; FaBoCh; FaPoR; OBEV; OBNC

Listen to the coal. In Memoriam John Coltrane. Michael Stillman. InPK-6

Listen to the exhortation of the dawn! The Salutation of the Dawn. *Unknown.* PoLF

Listen to the Kitchen Clock. The Old Kitchen Clock. Ann Hawkshawe. BoTP

Listen to the MUSTN'TS, child. Shel Silverstein. PiM

Listen to the phone calls they do not. Metaphor as Illness. Chuck Ortleb. GLP

Listen to the Rock Island train. Riding the Rock Island Through Kansas. Dave Etter. GM

Listen to the sea. Guillaume Apollinaire. PFTM, *tr. by* David Antin *Fr.* Victoire.

Listen to the song. Wandering Jack. Emile Jacot. BoTP

Listen to the sound of my horn. . . . Rita Dove. SeSe

Listen to the story of Willie the Weeper. Willie the Weeper. *Unknown.* BLPA; OBAL

Listen to the tale. Slim Greer. Sterling Brown. NAAAL

Listen to the water-mill. The Water Mill. Sarah Doudney. BLPA; PoToHe

Listen to Things. Spirits. Birago Diop, *French.* NegPo, *tr. by* Ellen Conroy Kennedy

Listen to this story. This Island Mopsy. Victor D. Questel. PBCV

Listen, / when i found there was no safety. To my Friend, Jerina. Lucille Clifton. NMM-2

Listen, you drawing men. Snapshots of the Cotton South. Frank Marshall Davis. PoBA

Listen! you shouldn't be so hopelessly severe. Plot with Bitterness. Vadim Gabrielevich Shershenevich, *Russian.* TCRP, *tr. by* Daniel Weissbort

Listen Zulus. Lalela Zulu. *Unknown, Zulu.* PeSA

Listenen to Big Black at S. F. State. Sonia Sanchez. BPo

Listeners, The. Walter De la Mare. AWP; CMoP; ClHu; EBEvV; HAP; HeIP-4; HoPM; ImPo; InPK-6; LiTM; MoBrPo; MoP; NOBE; NOxBChV; NTP; NoAM; NoP-4; OBEV; OBMV; OBSP; OxAEP-2; PoRA; Poetr; SoSe-8; TFi

Listener's Guide to the Birds, A. Elwyn Brooks White. NYBP

Listening. Aileen Fisher. NTCP

Listening. David Mura. PuP-15

Listening. Rod Willmot. HA

Listening closely to the noises of the earth. The Hospital. Sofiya Iul'evna Preygel, *Russian.* TCRP, *tr. by* Bradley Jordan

Listening for the sound. Nocturne. Pinkie Gordon Lane. BlSi

Listening in heaven. (LL) To Mark Anthony in Heaven. William Carlos Williams. NOBA; SAmP

Listening, listening; it is never still. The Märchen. Randall Jarrell. CMoP

Listening Macaws, The. Hazel Hall. PaTW

Listening Nydia. Henrietta Cordelia Ray. CBWP-3

Listening to a Monk from Shu Playing the Lute. Li Po, *Chinese.* SuSp, *tr. by* Joseph J. Lee

Listening to a Wanderer's "Water Melody." Wang Ch'ang-ling, *Chinese.* SuSp, *tr. by* Joseph J. Lee

Listening to a White Man Play the Blues. Silvia Curbelo. MoLi

Listening to Bach. Robert Bly. *Fr.* Six Winter Privacy Poems. LCAP-2

Listening to Beethoven on the Oregon Coast. Henry Carlile. Poetsp

Listening to Grownups Quarreling. Ruth Whitman. KaS; NTCP ("Standing in the hall against the.") KaS

Listening to September. Brendan Galvin. CMAP

Listening to Sonny Rollins at the Five-Spot. Paul Blackburn. MoNo

Listening to that lonesome whistle blow. . . . (LL) The Globe in North Carolina. Derek Mahon. BiHa; PBCIP

Listening to the Köln Concert. Robert Bly. RaBo

Listening to the Rain. K'ang Hai, *Chinese.* CoBLCP, *tr. by* Jonathan Chaves

Listening-to-the-Rain Studio. Chu Yi-tsun, *Chinese.* SuSp, *tr. by* Chang Yin-nan *and* Lewis C. Walmsley

Listening to the River. Su Tung-p'o, *Chinese.* TAL, *tr. by* Robert Payne

Listening to the Washblock in the Moonlight. Liu Ch'ang-ch'ing, *Chinese.* SuSp, *tr. by* Dell R. Hales

Listeth, lordes, in good entent. The Tale of Sir Thopas. Chaucer. BXAP, *ll.* 1–248; NAEL-1, *ll.* 1–252 *Fr.* The Canterbury Tales.

Listing Attic, The. Edward Gorey. ("Gift was delivered to Laura, A." CBNP

Listless beauty of the hour, The. History. D. H. Lawrence. RaBo

Listless he eyes the palisades. In the Prison Pen. Herman Melville. PoEL-5; TAP

Listless the silent ladies sit. Music. William Bell Scott. NOBVV

Listn the male chauvinist in mi dad. Girls Can We Educate We Dads? James Berry. NOxBChV

Lists became shorter, The. Making Lists. Gladys Cardiff. HATNAP

Lit-elle messe, moffette. Luis d'Antin Van Rooten. OBCoV *Fr.* Mots d'Heures: Gousses, Rames.

Litanie, The. Donne. PoEL-2 ("Father of heaven, and him, by whom." NOCV Holy Ghost, The. NOCV Son, The. NOCV

Litanies of Julia Pastrana (1832-1860), The. Thomas William Shapcott. CBAP; NOBAu

Litany. Carolyn Creedon. BAP-93

Litany, A. Donne. *See* The Litanie.

Litany. Elise Paschen. FFC

Litany: "From a ruler that's a curse." Charles Cotton. OBSV

Litany, A: "Ring out your bells." Sir Philip Sidney. *See* Dirge: "Ring out your bells [*or* belles], let mourning shows [*or* shewes] be spread."

Litany for Dictatorships. Stephen Vincent Benét. OxBA

Litany for Survival, A. Audre Lorde. NAAAL

Litany in Time of Plague, A. Thomas Nashe. ClHu; GEA; NAEL-1; NIP-4; OAEL-1; PoPoPo; PoRA *Fr.* Summer's Last Will and Testament.

("Adieu, farwell earth's bliss.") PeECV

(In Plague Time.) FaBoCh; FaPoR

(In Time of Pestilence.) PeECV

(In Time of Plague.)

(Lord, Have Mercy on Us.)

(Song in Time of Plague.) SCV

Litany of Sleep. Tristan Corbière, *French.*

"You who snore with your sleeping wife so near." OBVE, *tr. by* Christopher Pilling

Litany of the Dark People, The. Countee Cullen. ChIV-2

Litany of the Rooms of the Dead. Franz Werfel, *German.* TrJP, *tr. by* Edith Abercrombie Snow

Litany of Time Past. Muriel Spark. FaBoTC

Litany to Our Lady. *Unknown, Irish.* TIRV, *tr. by* Eugene O'Curry

Litany to Satan. Charles Baudelaire, *French.* AWP, *tr. by* James Elroy Flecker

Litany to the Holy Spirit. Robert Herrick. *See* His Litany to the Holy Spirit.

Literally thin-skinned, I suppose, my face. Weathering. Fleur Adcock. DiPo

Literary Dinner, A. Vladimir Nabokov. OBAL; PeLV

Literary Excellence. Robert Harris. BMAP

Literary Importation. Philip Freneau. TAP

Literature: The God, Its Ritual. Merrill Moore. FuPo

Lithe poppies ran like torchmen with the wheat. (LL) Poppies on the Wheat. Helen Hunt Jackson. APN-2; ColAP; PAR; SDW

Lithuanian autumn is no longer a boy, The. Memory of Autumns at Springtime. Gabriel Preil, *Yiddish.* CEEP, *tr. by* Laya Firestone

Lithuanian Well, The. Johannes Bobrowski, *German.* CEEP, *tr. by* Juliette Victor-Rood

Litrajure of Everyday Life, The. Michael C. Blumenthal. NoAM

Litterbox / litterbox. Concrete Cat. Dorthi Charles. KaS

Littered now the streets with light. At Christmas. Anne Ridler. WPN

Little. Dorothy Aldis. NTCP; WHSW

("Too little to look.") (LL) CTV

Little Ah Sid. *Unknown.* AS

Little airplanes of the heart, The. Sandinista Avioncitos. Lawrence Ferlinghetti. PiM

Little and Great. Charles MacKay. PoLF

Little Aster. Gottfried Benn, *German.* PFTM, *tr. by* Babette Deutsch

Little babe, while burns the west. Jean Ingelow. VWP

Little bat, little bat. To the Bat. Edith King. BoTP

Little Beauty That I Was Allowed, The. Elinor Wylie. Son *Fr.* One Person.

Little Bell. Mary E. Tucker. CBWP-1

Little Benny sat one evening. Misplaced Sympathy. Charles Follen Adams. OBAL

Little Bessie. *Unknown.* AmFP

Little Betty Blue. Betty Blue. Mother Goose. OxNR; ReMoGo

Little Betty Blue. Agnes Grozier Herbertson. ·BoTP

Little Betty Pringle [*or* Winckle] she had a pig. Betty Pringle's Pig. Mother Goose. CBNP; OxNR

Little Billee. William Makepeace Thackeray. FaBoCh; NOBL; OxAEP-2

(Three Sailors, The.) OxBB

Little Billy Breek. *Unknown.* OxNR

Little Birch Tree, The. Stepan Petrovich Shchipachov, *Russian.* TCRP, *tr. by* Daniel Weissbort

Little Bird, The. Mother Goose. ReMoGo

Little bird, The. *Unknown. Fr.* Four Glosses. NOIV

Little bird, The. *Unknown.* PBA, *tr. by* Rolf Italiaander

Little bird, a tender bird, A. The Siren Bird. Henrietta Cordelia Ray. CBWP-3

Little bird flew through the dell, A. Autumn Song. Johann Ludwig Tieck, *German.* AWP, *tr. by* James Clarence Mangan

Little bird of paradise. *Unknown.* OxNR

Little bird with tuneful throat. My Canary. Josephine D. Henderson Heard. CBWP-4

Little Birds are dining. "Lewis Carroll." *Fr.* Sylvie and Bruno Concluded. Pig-Tale, The.

Little Birds are dining. The Pig-Tale. "Lewis Carroll." *Fr.* Little Birds are dining. *Fr.* Sylvie and Bruno Concluded.

Little birds aren't on rollers, The. Joan of Arc. Benjamin Péret, *French.* PFTM, *tr. by* Keith Hollaman

Little birds in a row. Jacob Sternberg, *Yiddish.* TrJP, *tr. by* Joseph Leftwich

Little birds of the night. Stephen Crane. APN-2; APo

Little birds sit in their nest and beg, The. *Unknown.* NTCP

Little Bird's Song, A. Margaret Rose. BoTP

Little birds warble their song in the tree, The. The Bird Song. Mrs. Henry Linden. CBWP-4

Little bit, more or less each day, A. Beethoven's Sixth Symphony. Steve Benson. FTOS

Little bit of blowing, A. Thoughts for a Cold Day. *Unknown.* BoTP

Little Black Boy, The. William Blake. AWP; CABP; CH; ChAP; FHYEP; HeIP-4; NAEL-2; NAWM-2; NOBRP; NOEC; NoP-4; OAEL-2; OBEV; OBNC; OxBChV; PeECV; PoE; PoEL-4; PoPoPo; Ro; SCGP; TFi *Fr.* Songs of Innocence.

Little Black Boy's Prayer, A. Guy Tirolien, *French.* NegPo, *tr. by* Ellen Conroy Kennedy

Little Black Bug. Margaret Wise Brown. NTCP

Little black bull kem down de medder, De. Hoosen Johnny. *Unknown.* AS

Little Black Dog, The. Elizabeth Gardner Reynolds. PoLF

Little black dog ran round the house, The. *Unknown.* OxNR

Little Black Rose. *Unknown, Irish.* NOIV, *tr. by* Thomas Kinsella

Little Black Rose shall be red at last!, The. The Song: Little Black Rose. Aubrey Thomas De Vere. BIrV

Little black thing among the snow, A. The Chimney Sweeper. William Blake. EBEvV; FHYEP; NAEL-2; NAWM-2; NOEC; OAEL-2; RB; Ro *Fr.* Songs of Experience.

Little Black Train, The. *Unknown.* AmFP

Little Black Train Is A-Comin'. *Unknown.* GM

Little blessed Earth that turns, The. O Earth, Turn! George Johnston. MoCV

Little blood, more or less, he said, A. Great and Strong. Miroslav Holub, *Czech.* RB, *tr. by* George Theiner

Little Blue Apron. *Unknown.* BoTP

Little Blue Ben, who lives in the glen. *Unknown.* OxNR

Little Blue Betty lived in a den. *Unknown.* OxNR

Little Bo-Peep, / Had lost her sheep. The Fairy Sleep and Little Bo-Peep. *Unknown.* BoTP

Little Bo-Peep has lost her sheep. Mother Goose. FaBoBe; WHSW

("For they'd left all their tails behind 'em.") (LL) CTAV

("That each tail should be properly placed.") (LL) ReMoGo

("To tack again each to its lambkin.") (LL) OxNR

("To tack to each sheep its tail.") (LL) LB

Little boat floats by the dock, The. Inscribed on a Painting. Tao-chi, *Chinese.* CoBLCP, *tr. by* Jonathan Chaves

Little boat, tied up at the dock, The. Painting a Picture, The Tranquil Boat—Sent to Ko Ju-ching. Wen Cheng-ming, *Chinese.* CoBLCP, *tr. by* Jonathan Chaves

Little boat—untie the line. To the Tune, "Ch'ing-p'ing Yüeh." Yang Shen, *Chinese.* CoBLCP, *tr. by* Jonathan Chaves

Little boat with stubby oars, and West Lake's good, A. Tune: "Song of Picking Mulberry"—Recollections of West Lake. Ou-yang Hsiu, *Chinese.* SuSp, *tr. by* Jerome P. Seaton

Little Bob Robin. Bob Robin. Mother Goose. OxNR

Little Bobby Snooks was fond of his books. Bobby Snooks. *Unknown.* ReMoGo

Little Books / Indians. Hannah Weiner.

Little Books 137 Silence Mar 22 79. FTOS

Little box grows [gets] her first teeth, The. Vasco Popa, *Serbo-Croatian.* CBNP; HSix, *tr. by* Anne Pennington *and* Charles Simic

Little box which [that] contains the world, The. Last News about the Little Box. Vasco Popa, *Serbo-Croatian.* HSix, *tr. by* Charles Simic

Little boy, The. Junior Addict. Langston Hughes. BPo

Little Boy Blue. Eugene Field. CTV; ChAP; FPC; OBAL; OBCA; PoLF; SoSe-8

Little Boy Blue. John Crowe Ransom. LiTM

Little Boy Blue, come blow [up] your horn[!]. Mother Goose. BoTP; FaBoBe; OxNR

("He's under the haycock fast asleep!") (LL) LB

Little Boy Found, The. William Blake. FHYEP; NoP-4; Ro *Fr.* Songs of Innocence.

Little boy kneels at the foot of the bed. Vespers. A. A. Milne. OxBChV

Little boy, laid sick and low, A. The Dying Child's Request. Hannah Flagg Gould. OBCA

Little boy lived on the outskirts of Kolpino, A. Lines about a Little Boy. Aleksandr Petrovich Mezhirov, *Russian.* TCRP, *tr. by* Deming Brown

Little Boy Lost, The ("Father, father, where are you going?"). William Blake. FHYEP; Ro *Fr.* Songs of Innocence.

("And away the vapor flew.") (LL) NoP-4

Little Boy Lost, A ("Nought loves another as itself"). William Blake. FHYEP; PeECV; Ro *Fr. Songs of Experience.*

Little Boy Lost. Stevie Smith. FaBoTw

Little boy lost in the lonely fen, The. The Little Boy Found. William Blake. FHYEP; NoP-4; Ro *Fr. Songs of Innocence.*

Little boy once played so loud, A. Extremes. James Whitcomb Riley. FPC

Little Boy, to show his might and power, The. The Metamorphosis. Sir John Suckling. CaPo; FaBoEE

Little boy was looking for his voice, The. The Little Mute Boy. Federico García Lorca, *Spanish.* RB, *tr. by* W. S. Merwin

Little boy went into a barn, A. The Boy in the Barn. *Unknown.* ReMoGo

Little breast. Flower Market. Pierre Reverdy, *French.* PFTM, *tr. by* Kenneth Rexroth

Little Breeches. John Milton Hay. FaBoBe

Little Britain. *Unknown.* NOEC

Little Brother, The. James Reeves. OxBTC

Little brown baby wif spa'klin' eyes. Paul Laurence Dunbar. APN-2; NAAAL; NoP-4

Little brown boy. Poem. Helene Johnson. NAAAL; PoBA

Little Brown Bulls, The. *Unknown.* AmFP

Little Brown Jug. Joseph E. Winner. OBAL

Little Brown Seed. Rodney Bennett. BoTP

Little Brown Seed, The. Harriett Mulford Lothrop. PWR

Little brown squirrel hops in the corn, The. "Orpheus C. Kerr." *Fr.* The Rejected "National Hymns." OBAL

Little buoy said, A, "Mother, deer." A Misspelled Tail. Elizabeth T. Corbett. OBCA

Little by little. Fiery Declarations (two poems). Ōkuma Nobuyuki, *Japanese.* MJT, *tr. by* Makoto Ueda

Little by Little. *Unknown.* PWR

Little by little, wean yourself. Jelaluddin Rumi, *Persian.* BLT, *tr. by* Coleman Barks

Little Cape Cod Landscape. Charles North. FTOS

Little Car, The. Guillaume Apollinaire, *French.* AF, *tr. by* Oliver Bernard
("And although we were both grown men / We had just been born.") (LL) PFTM, *tr. by* Ron Padgett
("31st day of August 1914, The.") PFTM, *tr. by* Ron Padgett

Little cares that fretted me, The. A Song from Sylvan. Elizabeth Barrett Browning. BLPA

Little Carol of the Virgin, A. Félix Lope de Vega Carpio. PChr

Little cart jolting and banging through the yellow haze of dusk, The. Ch'en Tzu-lung, *Chinese.* ChiP, *tr. by* Arthur Waley

Little Cat Angel, The. Leontine Stanfield. BLPA

Little caterpillar creeps, The. Cocoon. David McCord. OBCA

Little Chap Who Follows Me, The. *Unknown.* PoToHe

Little child, A. Puer Aeternus. Kathleen Jessie Raine. NYBP

Little child, I counsel you that ye. Customs Change. *Unknown.* OxBChV

Little child sat on the floor, A. Where Do School Days End? Josephine D. Henderson Heard. CBWP-4

Little child she, half defiant came, A. Augusta Davies Webster. VWP *Fr.* Sonnets from Mother and Daughter.

Little children here ye may lere. Manners at Table When Away from Home. *Unknown.* OxBChV

Little children, never give. Kindness to Animals. *Unknown.* BoTP; CTV; WHSW

Little children you will all go. Song of Man Chipping an Arrowhead. W. S. Merwin. InPK-6

Little Child's Faith, The. Louis E. Thayer. PoToHe

Little Chisel, The. N. P. van Wyk Louw, *Afrikaans.* PeSA, *tr. by* Jack Cope *and* Uys Krige

Little church was glowing, The. Funeral Service. Cecil Gray. HCP

Little churches wake up in the half light, The. Nuns Go Walking. Aldo Palazzeschi, *Italian.* PFTM, *tr. by* Jerome Rothenberg

Little Clan, The. Frederick Robert Higgins. OBMV

Little Clotilda. *Unknown.* BoTP

Little cock sparrow sat on a green tree, A. Boy and the Sparrow. Mother Goose. OxNR; ReMoGo

Little cock sparrow sat on a tree, A. *Unknown.* ACTP; BoTP

Little colt—broncho, loaned to the farm, A. The Broncho That Would Not Be Broken. Vachel Lindsay. MeMAP

Little country box you boast, A. Martial, *Latin.* OBCVT, *tr. by Unknown*

Little cousin is dead, by foul subtraction, The. Dead Boy. John Crowe Ransom. CMoP; FaBoMo; FuPo; MeMAP; NoAM; NoP-4; OxBA; PoE; TwCP

Little Cradle Rocks Tonight in Glory, The. *Unknown.* AmFP

Little cramped words scrawling all over the paper. The Letter. Amy Lowell. CPO; NALW

Little crystal globe. Earth. Jules Supervielle, *French.* MFP, *tr. by* Martin Sorrell

Little cullud boys with beards. Flatted Fifths. Langston Hughes. MoNo

Little Dame Crump. *Unknown.* BoTP

Little Dancers, The. Laurence Binyon. BoTP; CH; MoBrPo; OxBTC

Little dark Cape girl why is it you roam. Wordspinning. Olga Kirsch, *Afrikaans.* PeSA, *tr. by* Jack Cope

Little Death. Gwyn Thomas, *Welsh.* OBWVE, *tr. by* Joseph P. Clancy

Little Demon, The. Zinaida Nikolayevna Gippius, *Russian.* TCRP, *tr. by* Lubov Yakovleva

Little Dicky Dilver. *Unknown.* OxNR

Little Diodoros is so skinny. Nicarchus of Alexandria, *Greek.* InMo, *tr. by* Sam Hamill

Little do folks the heav'nly Powers mind. Juvenal. OBCVT, *tr. by* John Oldham *Fr.* The Thirteenth Satyr of Juvenal, Imitated.

Little Dog-Angel, A. Norah M. Holland. PoLF

Little Dog that wags his tail, A. Emily Dickinson. NOxBChV

Little Dog under the Wagon, The. *Unknown.* PoLF

Little Doll, The. Charles Kingsley. OxBChV *Fr.* The Water Babies.

Little Donkey, The. Francis Jammes, *French.* PChr, *tr. by* Lloyd Alexander

Little Dove, The. *Unknown.* AmFP

Little drops of water. Kind Deeds. Isaac Watts. BoTP

Little drops of water. (Little Things). Julia A. Fletcher Carney. ACTP; BLPA; CTV; FaBoBe; OxBChV

Little drum. Bonguemba. Antoine-Roger Bolamba, *French.* NegPo, *tr. by* Ellen Conroy Kennedy

Little Drummer, The. Richard Henry Stoddard. AmFP

Little Drummer, The. *Unknown.* AmFP

Little East of Jordan, A. Emily Dickinson. ChIV-1; NoP-4

Little Eclogue. Elinor Wylie. NMM-2

Little Elegy. Denis Devlin. NOIV

Little Elegy. X. J. Kennedy. APAD; CoAP; CoAmPo; HoPM

Little Elegy. Elinor Wylie. IMW

Little Elegy for the Age. Lynne McMahon. NAmP90

Little Elf, The. John Kendrick Bangs. CTV; FPC; FaBoBe; NTCP; OBCA

Little Ellie sits alone. The Romance of the Swan's Nest. Elizabeth Barrett Browning. VWP

Little Exercise. Elizabeth Bishop. CoAP; ColAP; MoAmPo; NYBP
(Little Exercise at 4. A.M.) UnPo

Little fairy comes at night, A. The Dream Fairy. Thomas Hood. BoTP

Little Falls. Robert Hogg. MoCV

Little Fay's Thanksgiving. Henrietta Cordelia Ray. CBWP-3

Little Finger Game, A. E. J. Falconer. BoTP

Little Fir Tree, The. Margaret Rose. BoTP

Little Fish. D. H. Lawrence. AYFP; OxBTC; RB; Spl; TTTS

Little fish swim in the river, big fish swim in the sea. I Don't Let the Girls Worry My Mind. *Unknown.* AmFP

Little fishes in a brook. *Unknown.* OxNR

Little flame mouths. Dragon Night. Jane Yolen. OTCP

Little flocks of peaceful clouds. The Black Cloud. W. H. Davies. RB

Little Flower's Disciple, The. John Montague. TIRV *Fr.* The Leaping Fire.

Little Fly / Thy summer's play. The Fly. William Blake. CTAV; FHYEP; NAEL-2; NBLV; NOBRP; NOxBChV; OxAEP-2; PBMP *Fr.* Songs of Experience.

Little fogs were gathered in every hollow. The Country Wedding. Thomas Hardy. UnPo

Little Fred. *Unknown.* ReMoGo

Little French Lawyer, The. John Fletcher, *Sometimes at. to* Francis Beaumont.
Song in the Wood. NOSC

Little General Monk. *Unknown.* OxNR

Little Gidding. T. S. Eliot. FaBoMo; FaBoPV; GTBS-P; MoP; NAEL-2; NAWM-2; NOBA; NOBE; NoAM; OAEL-2; OxAEP-2; OxBTC; PeECV; TAP; TFi *Fr.* Four Quartets.
(From The Four Quartets.) CABP
"Ash on an old man's sleeve." FaBoTw

Little Giffen. Francis Orrery Ticknor. CBCWP

Little girl. Another Rhythm. Akasha (Gloria) Hull. ISC

Little girl, be careful what you say. Carl Sandburg. NOxBChV

Little girl called Silé Javotte. Christmas 1970. Spike Milligan. OBCP

Little girl dressed, The. Celebration. Ray A. Young Bear. CDW

Little Girl Found, The. William Blake. FHYEP; NOBRP; Ro *Fr.* Songs of Experience.

Little girl I was, The. Laughter. Wislawa Szymborska, *Polish.* PoSu, *tr. by* Magnus F. Krynski

Little girl is shy, The. Dream Come True. Molly Peacock. RA

Little girl knew, The. Girl, Prince, Lizard. Heather Ross Miller. MT

Little girl, little girl. *Unknown.* BoTP

Little girl, little girl, / Where have you been? Mother Goose. OxNR; ReMoGo

Little Girl Lost, A. William Blake. FHYEP; Ro *Fr.* Songs of Experience.

Little Girl Lost, The. William Blake. FHYEP; NOBRP; Ro *Fr.* Songs of Experience.

Little girl marched around her Christmas tree, A. Ogden Nash. PChr *Fr.* The New Nutcracker Suite.

Little Girl, My String Bean, My Lovely Woman. Anne Sexton. NYBP

Little girl, put your hands on my knees. The Soul of the Village. Lucian Blaga, *Romanian.* CEEP, *tr. by* Don Eulert, Stefan Avădanei, *and* Mihail Bogdan

Little girl riding the fallen tree like a spindly horse, The. Light Hotel. Peter Redgrove. PoE

Little girl saw her first troop parade and asked, "What are those?," The. Carl Sandburg. PBMP

Little Girl Wakes Early. Robert Penn Warren. PoE

Little girl was traveling unattached, as they say, The. Travelers. Josephine Miles. KaS

Little Girl with Bands on Her Teeth, The. Genevieve Taggard. VGW

Little girl with scarlet enameled fingernails, A. Melodic Trains. John Ashbery. GM; NoP-4

Little girl won't eat her sandwich, The. Blasting from Heaven. Philip Levine. CoAP; WeT

Little Girl's Dream World, A. Della Burt. BlSi

Little girl's heart must be wide and, A. R. Ernest Holmes. CTV

Little girls smearing. Schoolyard in April. Kenneth Koch. PoA

Little gold in law will make, A. Isabella Whitney. *Fr.* Sweet Nosegay, A, or Pleasant Posy. WPE

Little Good Fellows, The. Herman Melville. NCAP

Little green blackbird decided to study, The. Because His Sister Saw Shakespeare in the Moon. Kenneth Patchen. CBNP

Little green frog lived under a log, A. Strange Talk. L. E. Yates. BoTP

Little green frog once lived in a pool, A. The Frog. Rose Fyleman. BoTP

Little grey hill-glade, close-turfed, withdrawn, A. Marsyas. G. D. Roberts. NoP-4

Little group above the foreign wood, A. (LL) The Byrnies. Thom Gunn. MoP; NoAM; OxBTC

Little Hans. Steve McCaffery. FTOS

Little head, and no eyes. (LL) Tongs. Mother Goose. LB; OxNR; ReMoGo

Little health, A. *Unknown.* FP *Fr.* The Diary of Francis Kilvert.

Little heart, little heart. Robin Morgan. CrSp *Fr.* The Network of the Imaginary Mother.

Little Hearts, where light-wing'd Passion raignes, The. Sonnet 78. Greville Fulke. PBRV *Fr.* Cælica.

Little hedgerow birds, The. An Old Man [Travelling]. Wordsworth. FaBoCh; OBWP; Ro

Little Heracles. Theocritus, *Greek.* HePo, *tr. by* Barbara Hughes Fowler *Fr.* Idylls.

Little Herd-Boy's Song, The. Robert Williams Buchanan. BoTP

Little hiders hide in the hills and groves. Refuting the "Invitation to Hiding." Wang K'ang-chü, *Chinese.* CoBCP, *tr. by* Burton Watson

Little hiss of white, A, / enjoying it. (LL) Don't Talk to Me about Bread. E. A. Markham. HCP; PBCV

Little hours: two lovers herd upstairs, The. Almost Aubade. Marilyn Hacker. NoAM

Little House, Big House. Medbh McGuckian. PNI

Little house there stood within a glen, A. A Deathbed. John Hawthorn. NOEC *Fr.* The Journey and Observations of a Countryman.

Little Hundred. *Unknown.* OxNR

Little Hunger. Richard Murphy. BIrV

Little I ask; my wants are few. Contentment. Oliver Wendell Holmes. APN-1; AmPP; OxBA; PWR *Fr.* The Autocrat of the Breakfast Table.

Little Indian, Sioux, or Crow. Foreign Children. Robert Louis Stevenson. BoTP; GoJo-1

Little Infinite Poem. Federico García Lorca, *Spanish.* AF; RaBo, *tr. by* Robert Bly

("We will have to get down on all fours and eat the grasses of the cemeteries forever.") (LL) AF, *tr. by* Robert Bly

Little ink more or less!, A. Stephen Crane. APN-2; MeMAP *Fr.* War Is Kind.

Little inmate, full of mirth. The Cricket. Vincent Bourne, *Latin.* PoLF, *tr. by* William Cowper

Little island whispered over his shoulder. A Wound. Brendan Kennelly. BiHa

Little Jack Dandy-prat. *Unknown.* OxNR

Little Jack Horner/ Sat in a corner. Mother Goose. LB; OxNR; ReMoGo; SoSe-8

Little Jack Jelf. Jack Jelf. *Unknown.* ReMoGo

Little Jack Jingle. Jack Jingle. *Unknown.* ReMoGo

Little Jack Sprat / Once had a pig. *Unknown.* OxNR

Little Jenny Wren. *Unknown.* BoTP; ReMoGo

Little Jesus came to town, The. A Christmas Folk-Song. Lizette Woodworth Reese. OBCA; TrCP

Little Jesus wast Thou shy. Ex Ore Infantium. Francis Thompson. BoTP; OxBChV

Little Jew lived in a little straw hut, A. Biography. Abraham Moses Klein. TrJP

Little Jock Elliot. *Unknown.* IBB

Little joe gould has lost his teeth and doesn't know where. E. E. Cummings. NoAM

Little John a Begging. *Unknown.* ESPB

Little John Jiggy Jag. *Unknown.* OxNR

Little John Nobody. *Unknown.* CBNP; OxBoLi

Little Johnny-jump-up said. Wise Johnny. Edwina Fallis. CTV

Little Johnny wants to play. (LL) Rain, rain, go away. *Unknown.* OxNR; ReMoGo

Little Josie buried under the bright moon. Half-Caste Girl. Judith Wright. NALW

Little Jumping Joan. Mother Goose. ReMoGo

("I'm always alone.") (LL) LB

(Jumping Joan.) OxNR

Little King Boggen, he built a fine hall. *Unknown.* ReMoGo

Little King Pippin. Mother Goose. OxNR

Little Kingdom I Possess, A. Louisa May Alcott. AH

Little Kings and Queens of May. Little Kings and Queens of the May. Juliana Horatia Ewing. BoTP

Little Kings and Queens of the May. Juliana Horatia Ewing. BoTP

Little L.A. Villanelle. Carol Muske. WWSi

Little lad, little lad. *Unknown.* OxNR

Little ladies, white and green. Snowdrops. Laurence Alma-Tadema. BoTP

Little lady coyly shy. Caprichosa. Angelina Weld Grimké. NMM-2

Little lady lairdie, The. *Unknown.* OxNR

Little Lady of Ch'ing-ch'i, The. *Unknown, Chinese.* ChiP, *tr. by* Arthur Waley

Little lady, you are not going to like this. Lorenzo Da Ponte. OxBoV, *tr. by* Amanda Holden *and* Anthony Holden *Fr.* Don Giovanni.

Little Lamb, A. *Unknown.* OBCoV

Little Lamb God bless thee! (LL) The Lamb. William Blake. BoTP; CH; CTAV; ChIV-2; EBEvV; FHYEP; FaBoBe; FaBoCh; HeIP-4; ImPo; InPS-3; NAEL-2; NAWM-2; NIP-4; NOBRP; NOEC; NoP-4; OAEL-2; OxBChV; PoE; PoPoPo; Poetr; Ro; SAGP; SoSe-8; TFi; TRP; TrCP; UnPo

Little Lamb, who made thee? / Dost thou know who made thee. The Lamb. William Blake. BoTP; CH; ChIV-2; EBEvV; FHYEP; FaBoBe; FaBoCh; HeIP-4; ImPo; InPS-3; NAEL-2; NAWM-2; NIP-4; NOBRP; NOEC; OAEL-2; OxAEP-2; OxBChV; PoE; Poetr; SoSe-8; TFi; TRP; TrCP; UnPo *Fr.* Songs of Innocence.

Little lambs, little lambs. Baby Beds. *Unknown.* BoTP

Little Landscape, A. Chu Yün-ming, *Chinese.* CoBLCP, *tr. by* Jonathan Chaves

Little Landscape by Chao Ch'ien-li, A. Yü Chi, *Chinese.* CoBLCP, *tr. by* Jonathan Chaves

Little Landscape by Yen Wen-kuei, A. Yü Chi, *Chinese.* CoBLCP, *tr. by* Jonathan Chaves

Little Language, A. Robert Duncan. FTOS *Fr.* Dante.

Little late rain, A. Sarah's Choice. Eleanor Wilner. NMM-2

Little learning is a dangerous [or dang'rous] thing, A. Alps on Alps. Alexander Pope. EBEvV; HAP; HoPM; NOBE; PoLF, *ll.* 215–232; ImPo, *ll.* 215–252 *Fr.* An Essay on Criticism. NAEL-1; PoEL-3; TFi

Little less returned for him each spring, A. Anglais Mort à Florence. Wallace Stevens. SAmP

Little Libbie. Julia A. Moore. OBAL

Little Light. Jim Brodey. MoNo

Little light is going by, A. Firefly. Elizabeth Madox Roberts. NTCP

Little lonely child am I, A. The Moon-Child. "Fiona Macleod." CH

Little Lost Pup. Arthur Guiterman. CTV

Little Love-God, The. Meleager, *Greek.* AWP, *tr. by* Walter Headlam

Little loving / in between, A. (LL) Advice. Langston Hughes. NBLV; SAmP

Little Lucy Lavender. Lucy Lavender. Ivy O. Eastwick. BoTP

Little Lucy Lester. M. Steel. BoTP

Little Lullaby. Irving Feldman. NYBP

Little lute, when I am gone. Richard Corbet. FaBoEE

Little Lyric (of Great Importance). Langston Hughes. NBLV; OBAL; OBCoV

Little Madness in the Spring, A. Emily Dickinson. TAP

Little Maid, The. Anna Maria Wells. OBCA

Little Maid and the Cowslips, The. John Clare. BoTP

Little maid, pretty maid, / Whither goest thou? Mother Goose. OxNR; ReMoGo

Little Man and Maid, The. *Unknown.* ACTP

Little man in coal pit. Putting On Nightgown. *Unknown.* OxNR

Little Man That Had a Little Gun, The. "Lewis Carroll." CBNP *Fr.* Sylvie and Bruno Concluded. (Manlet, The.) BXAP

Little Man Who Wasn't There, The. Hughes Mearns. *See* Antigonish.

Little Marg'et sitting in her high hall door. Fair Margaret and Sweet William. *Unknown.* AmFP

Little marsh-plant, yellow green, A. The Sundew. Swinburne. OBNC; PeVV

Little Mary Bell had a fairy in a nut. Long John Brown & Little Mary Bell. William Blake. ECEV; RB

Little Men, The. Flora Fearne. BoTP

Little Millwins attend the Russian Ballet, The. Les Millwin. Ezra Pound. OBCoV

Little Miss and Her Parrot. John Marchant. OxBChV

Little Miss Muffet. W. S. Brownlee. PeLi

Little Miss Muffet, *parody. Unknown.* BXAP

Little Miss Muffet discovered a tuffet. The Embarrassing Episode of Little Miss Muffet. Guy Wetmore Carryl. OBCA

Little Miss Muffet / Sat on a tuffet. Mother Goose. FaBoBe; LB; OxNR; ReMoGo

Little Mistress Comfort got up early one fine day. Mistress Comfort. Elizabeth Gould. BoTP

Little Mohea, The. *Unknown.* AmFP

Little monkey goes like a donkey that means to say, A. A Dog. Gertrude Stein. PFTM; TTTS *Fr.* Tender Buttons.

Little months little smokes. Comrade. Philippe Soupault, *French. tr. by* Pat Nolan

Little Moon, The. Henry Wadsworth Longfellow. BoTP

Little Moppet, The. Mother Goose. ReMoGo

Little More Cider, A. *Unknown.* KaS

Little more kindness and a little less creed, A. World Needs, the. *Unknown.* PoToHe

Little more tired at the close of the Day, A. Growing Old [*or* Growing Older]. Rollin J. Wells. BLPA; PoToHe

Little More Traveling Music, A. Al Young. NBV

Little Morning Music, A. Delmore Schwartz. NYBP

Little moth round candle turning, The. Similie. Charlotte Dacre. NOBRP

Little moths are creeping, The. Interior. Padraic Colum. MoBrPo

Little Mouse, The. *Unknown.* ReMoGo

Little Mr. Browny Bee. Browny Bee. Irene F. Pawsey. BoTP

Little Musgrave and Lady Barnard. *Unknown.* AmFP; ESPB; OxBB

Little Mute Boy, The. Federico García Lorca, *Spanish.* RB, *tr. by* W. S. Merwin

Little Nancy [*or* Nanny] Etticoat. A Candle. Mother Goose. LB; OxNR; ReMoGo

Little nearer, this time, A. After the Second Operation. Patricia Goedicke. TAP

Little night: when you. Paul Celan, *German.* VCWP, *tr. by* Michael Hamburger

Little noises of the house, The. During a Bombardmant by V-Weapons. Roy Fuller. OxBSP

Little Ode. Paul Goodman. PoA

Little of myself do I remember. Patrizia Cavalli, *Italian.* NeIt, *tr. by* Robert McCracken

Little old-fashioned girl, The. At Grandfather's. Clara Doty Bates. OBCA

Little Old Lady, The. Rodney Bennett. BoTP

Little Old Lady in Lavender Silk, The. Dorothy Parker. NBLV

Little Old Letter. Langston Hughes. SAmP

Little old man of Derby, A. *Unknown.* OxNR; ReMoGo

Little Old Sod Shanty. *Unknown.* AS; AmFP

Little old woman, A. Bramble Jam. Irene F. Pawsey. BoTP

Little one sleeps in its cradle, The. Walt Whitman. SAmP *Fr.* Song of Myself. AmPP; MoAmPo; NAAL-3; NOBA; OxBA

("Has any one supposed it lucky to be born?") ColAP

("I mind them or the show or resonance of them—I come and I depart.") (LL) ColAP

Little Ones' A. B. C, The. Noël Coward.

"A. Stands for Absolutely Anything." NBLV

Little onion lay by the fireplace, A. Song. Nicholas Moore. SPE

Little onward lend thy guiding hand, A. Samson before the Prison in Gaza. Milton. FaBoPV; OxAEP-1 *Fr.* Samson Agonistes. FHYEP; OAEL-1; PoEL-3

Little Orphant Annie's come to our house to stay. James Whitcomb Riley. APN-2; ChAP; FPC; NBLV; OBAL; OBCA; OxBChV

Little owl flew through the night, The. On the Adequacy of Landscape. Wallace Stevens. SAmP

Little Owl Who Lives in the Orchard. Mary Oliver. PuP-16

Little, passionately, not at all, A? Villanelle of Marguerites. Ernest Christopher Dowson. MoBrPo

Little path dotted with red. Tune: "Treading on Grass." Yen Shu, *Chinese.* SuSp, *tr. by* James J. Y. Liu

Little Peach, The. Eugene Field. OBAL

Little Peach Blossoms in the Garden. Li Shang-yin, *Chinese.* SuSp, *tr. by* Eugene Eoyang *and* Irving Y. Lo

Little People. Isaac Leibush Peretz, *Yiddish.* TrJP, *tr. by* Joseph Leftwich

Little Pets of Saint Mochua, The. John Irvine. TIRV

Little picks of the roosters, The. Ballad of Black Grief. Federico García Lorca, *Spanish.* STV, *tr. by* John Frederick Nims

Little Picture Catalogue. Novica Tadic, *Serbo-Croatian.* HSix; VCWP, *tr. by* Charles Simic

Little Piece of Sky, A. Sharif Elmusa. IFJA

Little Pig. *Unknown.* OxNR

Little pig lived in a sty, A. The Greedy Little Pig. Irene F. Pawsey. BoTP

Little Piggies, The. Thomas Hood. BoTP

Little Pin: Fragment, The. George Oppen. FTOS

Little plum / said the mother to her son. Hansel and Gretel. Anne Sexton. InPS-3

Little Poll Parrot. *Unknown.* OxNR

Little Polly Flinders. Mother Goose. LB; OxNR; ReMoGo

Little poppies, little hell flames. Poppies in July. Sylvia Plath. FaBoWP; LCAP-2, RD

Little Pretty Bonny Lass, A. *Unknown.* CBLP

Little pretty Nancy girl. *Unknown.* OxNR

Little priest of Felton, The. Priest of Felton. *Unknown.* OxNR

Little prince of long ago, A. Sons of the King. Joan Agnew. BoTP

Little Pudding. Mary M. Roberts. BXAP

Little ragged girl, our ball-boy, A. A Game at Salzburg. Randall Jarrell. NoAM

Little Raindrops. Jane Euphemia Browne. BoTP; OxBChV

Little Random Creatures, The. *Unknown, Fox Indian.* STP, *tr. by* Armand Schwerner

Little red lark, The. Morning. Ivy O. Eastwick. BoTP

Little Red Riding Hood. Ania Walwicz. BMAP

Little red wagon for d black bureaucrat, A. Catechism of d Neoamerican Hoodoo Church. Ishmael Reed. NBV

Little roads to happiness, they are not hard to find, The. Wilhelmina Stitch. PoToHe

Little robin grieves, The. When the Snow is on the Ground. *Unknown.* ReMoGo

Little Robin Red-breast. *Unknown.* ACTP

Little Robin Redbreast / Came to visit me. Visitor. *Unknown.* OxNR

Little Robin Redbreast / Sat upon a rail. Niddle Noddle. Mother Goose. OxNR

Little Robin Redbreast sat upon a tree. Catch. Mother Goose. BoTP; LB; OxNR; ReMoGo

Little Robin Redbreast [*or* Red-breast] sat upon a tree. *Unknown.* BoTP; CTV

Little room, depressing, old, A. The Tailor. "S. Ansky," *Yiddish.* TrJP, *tr. by* Joseph Leftwich

Little Rosebud Girl. Anson Gonzalez. HCP

Little Ruth. Yehuda Amichai, *Hebrew.* VCWP, *tr. by* Benjamin Harshav *and* Barbara Harshav

Little Saint best fits a little Shrine, A. A Ternarie of Littles, upon a Pipkin of Jellie [*or* Jelly] Sent to a Lady. Robert Herrick. BeJo; BoTP; FaBoCh; PoEL-3

Little Sally Waters. *Unknown.* AmFP

Little Sam Clemens, one night back in Hannibal, The. Last Laugh. Robert Penn Warren. MT

Little sandpiper and I, The. (LL) The Sandpiper. Celia Laighton Thaxter. ImGa

Little Scotch-ee. *Unknown.* AS

Little Shoes That Died, The. Mary Gilmore. NOBAu

Little Shon a [*or* Johnny] Morgan, shentleman [*or* gentleman] of Wales. Shon a Morgan. *Unknown.* OxNR

Little Shrub Growing By, A. Ben Jonson. BeJo

Little sleeping and much grieving—the traveller. On the Way to Hangchow: Anchored on the River at Night. Po Chü-i, *Chinese.* ChiP, *tr. by* Arthur Waley

Little Sleep's-Head Sprouting Hair in the Moonlight. Galway Kinnell. InPS-3; LCAP-2

Little slender lad, toad-headed. The Ambrosia of Dionysus and Semele. Robert Graves. NYBP

Little snow people are hurrying down, The. Putting the World to Bed. Esther W. Buxton. NOxBChV

Little Song. Langston Hughes. TLR

Little Song of Life, A. Lizette Woodworth Reese. OBCA

Little Song of the Maimed. Benjamin Péret, *French*. OBWP; PeFWW, *tr. by David Gascoyne*

Little soul so sleek and smiling. Animula, vagula, blandula: The Emperor Hadrian to his soul. Emperor Hadrian, *Latin*. OBCVT; OBVE, *tr. by Stevie Smith*

Little Sparrow. *Unknown*. AmFP

Little sparrows, The. Pastoral. William Carlos Williams. SAmP; TwCP

Little state-funded barrack, A. It Started. Jimmy Santiago Baca. LoL

Little stream used to cross my land, A. Su Tung-p'o, *Chinese*. CoBCP, *tr. by Watson, Burton (b. 1925)*; CoBCP *Fr.* Eastern Slope.

Little sycamore, The. Love Song. *Unknown, Egyptian*. TTY, *tr. by J. E. Manchip White*

Little sympathy, who kicks beneath my ribs. Eighteenth-Century Medical Illustration: The Infant in its Little Room. Ann Townsend. PUP-20

Little Tee-wee. *Unknown*. OxNR

Little Testament. Eugenio Montale, *Italian*. PFTM, *tr. by Cid Corman*

Little Thing Like That, A. A. R. Ammons. PUP-20

(Little Things). Julia A. Fletcher Carney. ACTP; BLPA; FaBoBe; OxBChV ("Help make earth happy / Like the heaven above.") (LL) CTV

Little Things, The. Elizabeth Isler. PoToHe

Little Things. Eileen Mathias. BoTP

Little Things. John Orrick. PoToHe

Little Things. *Unknown*. PoToHe

Little Things That Happen, The. Marjorie Wilson. BoTP

Little things, that run, and quail. James Stephens. MoBrPo; PoRA

Little thinkest thou, poor aint, who there. The Ant. Richard Flecknoe. NOSC

Little thinks, in the field, yon red-cloaked clown. Each and All. Ralph Waldo Emerson. APN-1; AWP; AmPP; ColAP; MeMAP; NAAL-1; NAAL-3; NCAP; NOBA; OxBA; PAR; TAP

Little think'st thou, poor [or poore] flower. The Blossom [or Blossome]. Donne. AWP; ESCV; ImPo; MeLP; NAEL-1; SCGP; SeCP; UnPo

Little Tim Sprat. *Unknown*. CTAV

Little time for laughter, A. After. Philip Bourke Marston. NOBVV

Little toe, big toe, three toes between. Close Quarters. John Banister Tabb. OBAL

Little toe is attractive, The. The Time of Man. Phyllis Webb. MoCV

Little Tom Tittlemouse / Lived in a bell-house. *Unknown*. OxNR

Little Tommy Tacket. *Unknown*. OxNR

Little Tommy Tiddler. Paul Edmonds. BoTP

Little Tommy Tittlemouse / Lived in a little house. Tommy Tittlemouse. Mother Goose. OxNR; ReMoGo

Little Tommy [or Tom] Tucker. Tommy Tucker. Mother Goose. LB; OxNR; ReMoGo

Little Tooth, A. Thomas Lux. MoLi

Little touch of Harry in the night, A (LL) Before Agincourt. William Shakespeare. EBEV; OxAEP-1; RB

Little toy dog is covered with [dust], The. Little Boy Blue. Eugene Field. CTV; ChAP; FPC; OBAL; OBCA; PoLF; SoSe-8

Little tree / little silent Christmas tree. E. E. Cummings. NTCP; OBCP; PChr

Little trotty hetty coat. Riddle. *Unknown*. FaBoVe

Little trotty wagtail [he went in the rain]. John Clare. BoTP; CTAV; ChAP; NOxBChV; NTP; RB; SCGP; UnPo

Little Tumescence, A. Jonathan Williams. NeAP; PoM

Little Turtle, The. Vachel Lindsay. CTV; NOxBChV; NTCP; OBAL; OBCA; OBSP

Little twig that Byron planted here, The. Byron's Oak at Newstead Abbey. Timothy Thomas Fortune. AAP

Little Vagabond, The. William Blake. FHYEP; NBLV; OBSV; Ro *Fr.* Songs of Experience.

Little Village, A. Mei Yao Ch'en, *Chinese*. SuSp, *tr. by Jonathan Chaves*

Little wanderer, hie thee home. (LL) A Dream. William Blake. CH; FHYEP; NOBRP; Ro

Little while, a little while, A. Emily Jane Brontë. EnVR; OBNC; VWP

Little while spring will claim its own, A. My Heart has Known its Winter. Arna Bontemps. GT

Little white clouds are racing over the sky, The. Magdalen Walks. Oscar Wilde. EBVV; MoBrPo

Little white lilies, The. Widows' Rice. Okkūr Mācāttanar, *Tamil*. PLW, *tr. by A. K. Ramanujan*

Little white mermaidens live in the sea, The. The Mermaidens. Laura Elizabeth Richards. OBCA

Little wild bird sometimes at my ear, A. Ballata: Of True and False Singing. *Unknown, Italian*. AWP, *tr. by D. G. Rossetti*

Little wild birds have come flying, The. Love-Song. *Unknown, Russian*. AWP, *tr. by W. R. S. Ralston*

Little Willie, in the best of sashes. Harry Graham. *See* Tender-Heartedness.

Little wind, blow on the hilltop. *Unknown*. CTV

Little Word, The. *Unknown*. PWR

(Good Creed, A.) PoToHe

Little word in kindness spoken, A. Daniel C. Colesworthy. CTV

Little Words. Benjamin Keech. PoToHe

Little Work, A. George Du Maurier. FaBoBe; PoLF *Fr.* Trilby.

Little work, a little play, A. *Unknown*. PoToHe

Little Wren, A. Priscilla Jane Thompson. CBWP-2

Little Wren of tender mind, The. The Wren. *Unknown*. OxBChV

Little yellow buttercup, A. A Buttercup. *Unknown*. BoTP

Little young lambs, oh! why do you stay. The Wolf and the Lambs. Ivy O. Eastwick. BoTP

Littleblood. Ted Hughes. *Fr.* Crow. PoE

Littles. Robert Herrick. *See* A Ternarie of Littles, upon a Pipkin of Jellie [or Jelly] Sent to a Lady.

Liturgy Under the Acropolis. Nikiphoros Vrettakos, *Greek*. Poet, The. GrIP

Liu Ch'e. Ezra Pound. OBVE; VGW

Live all thy sweet life thro'. A Summer Wish. Christina Rossetti. OBNC

Live, alterable cry against my breast. (LL) Filling the Gap. Lawson Fusao Inada. MoNo; OpBo

Live / , bird which. Larry Eigner. FTOS

Live blindly and upon the hour. The Lord. Trumbull Stickney. APN-2

Live, Evil Veil. John Wheelwright. ChIV-1

Live fish—someone's New Year's gift to me. On New Year's Day of the Year Kuei-ssu (1533), Releasing Live Creatures. Wang T'ing-hsiang, *Chinese*. CoBLCP, *tr. by Jonathan Chaves*

Live fowl squatting on the grapefruit and bananas, The. Jamaican Bus Ride. Arthur Seymour John Tessimond. OxBTC

Live here, great heart; and love and dy and kill. Richard Crashaw. *Fr.* The Flaming Heart. CABP; NAEL-1; OAEL-1; PoEL-2

Live in Texas, so the country song says and no excuses. Mr. X. Catherine Bowman. BAP-95

Live in these conquering leaves; live all the same. Richard Crashaw. OxAEP-1 *Fr.* The Flaming Heart. CABP; NAEL-1; OAEL-1; PoEL-2

Live, lads, and I will die. (LL) The Carpenter's Son. A. E. Housman. ChIV-2; MoBrPo; OxAEP-2; PBMP; SAGP; UV

Live large, man, and dream small. (LL) Lore. Ronald Stuart Thomas. NoP-4; OxBC; RB

"Live like the wind," he said, "unfettered." The Wind Bloweth Where It Listeth. Countee Cullen. GT

Live, win, with me, and thou shalt see. To Phyllis to Love and Live with Him. Robert Herrick. CaPo

Live so that you. Certain Maxims of Archy. Don Marquis. OBAL

Live storm went through last night, The. Glad at the Cold (1955). Alan Dugan. NoAM

Live there at least when any are at home. (LL) First Travels of Max. John Crowe Ransom. MoAmPo; NTP

Live thy life. The Oak. Tennyson. CTV

Live to that point I will, for which I am man. Ben Jonson. FP *Fr.* An Epistle Answering to One That Asked to Be Sealed of the Tribe of Ben.

Lived to see you throwing. Hesitate to Call. Louise Glück. LW

Lively lark stretched forth her wing, The. Edward, 17th Earl of Oxford De Vere. NoSic

Liverpool. *Unknown*. AmFP

Lives. Derek Mahon. PBCIP

Lives and Times of John Keats, Shelley, and George Gordon Noel, Lord Byron, The. Dorothy Parker. NALW *Fr.* A Pig's-Eye View of Literature.

Lives and times of Oedipus and Elektra, The. This One's on Me. Phyllis Gotlieb. MoCV; NOBC

Lives but in its own excess. (LL) A Song: "For mercy, courage, kindness, mirth." Laurence Binyon. BoTP; MoBrPo

Lives in eternity's sun rise. (LL) Eternity. ("He who binds to himself a joy"). William Blake. APAD; AWP; EBEV; EnlH; FaBoEE; ImPo; NOBE; NTP; NoP-4; OBNC; OxBSP; Poetr; RB; SCGP; SoSe-8; Spl

Lives in winter. Riddle. *Unknown*. NTCP; ReMoGo

Lives, of all that ever breathed [or breath'd], most worthy the envying. (LL) First Love. Thomas Campion. GBL; OxBoLi

Lives of great men all remind us. Life. Henry Wadsworth Longfellow. *Fr.* A Psalm of Life. APN-1; CTV; EBEvV; FaBoBe; NAAL-1; NAAL-3; OBCA; PAR; PWR; PoLF; TAP

Lives of great men all remind us / As their pages o'er we turn. After Longfellow. *Unknown*. NOBL

Lives of many men are, The. To Wei Pa, a Retired Scholar. Tu Fu, *Chinese*. OHPC, *tr. by* Kenneth Rexroth

Lives of the Great Composers. Dana Gioia. EOEF; RA

Lives of the Saints. Debora Greger.

"Notre Dame, Sainte Chapelle, Sacré Coeur by foot—." NoP-4

Lives of thomas—episodes and prayers, The. John High. PT

Lives there on Earth to whom I am unknown. Gilbert West. ECEV *Fr.* The Triumphs of the Gout.

Livid sky on London, A. The Old Song. G. K. Chesterton. FaBoTw

Livid to lurid switched the sky. Sky. Robert Penn Warren. AFr

Living. Denise Levertov. BLT; OPOU; VGW; WPE

Living. Harold Monro. ImPo

Living, The. Robert Pinsky. NoAM

Living. *Unknown*. BLPA; FaBoBe

Living alone in a sad-looking house. Jerry's Plains, 1848. Geoff Page. BMAP

Living alone is like floating on blue. So, When I Swim to the Shore. Molly Peacock. NMM-2

Living Alone with Jesus—. Maxine W. Kumin. UnSA

Living along the path. North Corridor. Michael Collier. GM

Living and dying. (LL) A Grammarian's Funeral. Robert Browning. NAEL-2; NOBVV; PeECV

Living and Dying Prayer for the Holiest Believer in the World, A. Augustus Montague Toplady. NOEC

Living Apart. Maura Stanton. FFC; NAmP90

("To watch the angels fall from fiery mountains.") (LL) FFC

Living at a time. Turbid current. Fumi Saito, *Japanese*. MJT, *tr. by* Ueda, Makoto

Living between heaven and earth. Tune: "Sprig of Flowers, A"—Written for My "Ugly Studio." Chung Ssu-ch'eng, *Chinese*. SuSp, *tr. by* Sherwin S. S. Fu

Living by the Red River. James Wright. NNaP

Living God, The. Abraham ibn Ezra, *Hebrew*. TrJP, *tr. by* Alice Lucas

Living God O magnify and bless, The. Daniel ben Judah, *Hebrew*. TrJP, *tr. by* Israel Zangwill

Living Heaven thy prayers respect, The. Spiritual Laws. Ralph Waldo Emerson. APN-1

Living in a Riverside Village—mdash;Miscellaneous Impressions. Yang Chi, *Chinese*. CoBLCP, *tr. by* Jonathan Chaves

Living in a wide landscape are the flowers. Desert Flowers. Keith Douglas. FaBoTw

Living in Exile at Ch'ien-nan. Huang T'ing-chien, *Chinese*. SuSp, *tr. by* Michael E. Workman

Living in Master Fang's Garden. Yang Chi, *Chinese*. CoBLCP, *tr. by* Jonathan Chaves

Living in Retirement at Te-ch'ing. Chao Meng-fu, *Chinese*. CoBLCP, *tr. by* Jonathan Chaves

Living in retirement beyond the World. The Valley Wind. Lu Yün, *Chinese*. ChiP, *tr. by* Arthur Waley

Living in Sin. Adrienne Rich. NIP-4; NYBP; NoP-4; Poetr; SoSe-8; TAP; UnPo

Living in the Country at Kou-ch'ü in Autumn—mdash;Miscellaneous Impressions. Yang Chi, *Chinese*. CoBLCP, *tr. by* Jonathan Chaves

Living in the earth-deposits of our history. Power. Adrienne Rich. ColAP; NALW; TAP

Living in the La Brea Tar Pits. Nancy Vieira Couto. PBCAP

Living in the Mountains. Tai Shu-lun, *Chinese*. SuSp, *tr. by* William H. Nienhauser

Living in the Woods. Wang Chiu-ssu, *Chinese*.

"I love the serenity of living in the woods." CoBLCP, *tr. by* Jonathan Chaves

Living Juliet, The. Shakespeare. *Fr.* Romeo and Juliet.

Living Lean. Christine E. Hemp. IFJA

Living long is containing. Rosina Alcona to Julius Brenzaida. Judith Wright. NALW

Living man is blind and drinks his drop, A. W. B. Yeats. RaBo *Fr.* A Dialogue of Self and Soul.

Living Memory. Adrienne Rich. TRP

Living mother-of-pearl of a salmon, The. A Hazel Stick for Catherine Ann. Seamus Heaney. NoAM

Living Near the Plaza of Thieves. Leslie Ullman. PBCAP

Living or having lived. Flush / a Play. Leslie Scalapino. PmAP

Living paradise of flowers, land of honey. Merioneth. John Machreth Rees, *Welsh*. OBWVE, *tr. by* Kenneth Hurlstone Jackson

Living Pearl, A. Kenneth Rexroth. LiTM

Living quality of, The. Haymaking. William Carlos Williams. NoAM *Fr.* Pictures from Brueghel.

Living Room, The. Gjertrud Schnackenberg. FYAP

Living someplace else is wrong. The Spring Offensive of the Snail. Marge Piercy. TAP

Living Temple, The. Oliver Wendell Holmes. APN-1 *Fr.* The Autocrat of the Breakfast Table.

Living Tenderly. May Swenson. OBCA

Living Together. Jean Valentine. LCAP-2

Living Truth, The. Sterling Plumpp. PoBA

Living with the Boss. Ken Smith. NBrP

Livings. Philip Larkin.

Seventy Feet Down. RB

Living's getting harder day by day. My Village Home. Lu Yu, *Chinese*. CoBCP, *tr. by* Burton Watson

Liza! call dat chile. Meal Time. Maggie Pogue Johnson. CBWP-4

Liza in the Summer Time (She Died on the Train). *Unknown*. AS

Liza Jane. *Unknown*. AS

Lizard, The. Rona Murray. NOBC

Lizard, The. Lydia Pender. NOxBChV

Lizard, The. Theodore Roethke. NOxBChV

Lizard inching, A. Elizabeth Searle Lamb. HA

Lizard ran out on a rock and looked up, listening, A. D. H. Lawrence. NTP; RB

Lizards and Snakes. Anthony Hecht. FaBoMo; TwCP

Lizard's heart throbs, The. Hilda Morley. PmAP

"Lizards," he'd say, dispensing with local men, and then resheath. Contempt. Rodney Jones. BAP-94

Lizards in Sardinia. Eamon Grennan. BiHa

Lizard's Tango, The. Lucia Casalinuovo. IFJA

Lizie Lindsay. *Unknown*. ESPB

Lizie Lindsay. *Unknown*. ESPB

Lizie Wan sits at her father's bower door. *Unknown*. *See* Fair Lucy was sitting in her own cabin door.

Lizzie. Nancy Vieira Couto. PBCAP

Lizzie and Joe Catch a Thief. Edward Cordle. PBCV

Lizzie and Joe in Court. Edward Cordle. PBCV

Lizzie Discourses on the Small-Pox. Edward Cordle. PBCV

Llama, The. Hilaire Belloc. FaBoCh

Lloyd George and Woodrow Wilson and Clemenceau—. A Legend of Versailles. Melvin Beaunearus Tolson. BPo; NAAAL

Llyn y Gadair. T. H. Parry-Williams, *Welsh*. OBWVE, *tr. by* Anthony Conran

Lo! above the mournful chanting. Kol Nidra. Joseph Leiser. TrJP

Lo! an old song, yellow with centuries! Love, Weeping, Laid This Song. Lizette Woodworth Reese. APN-2

Lo & behold. Yes, peat bogs. Landscape for the Disappeared. Yusef Komunyakaa. WeT

Lo! as a careful housewife runs to catch. Sonnet 148. Shakespeare. SCGP *Fr.* Sonnets.

Lo as I pause in the alien vale of the airport. Twenty-third Flight. Earle Birney. HeIP-4; OxBC

Lo! As the Potter Mouldeth. *Unknown*, *Hebrew*. TrJP, *tr. by* Elsie Davis

Lo, between the Myrtles Standing. Ann Griffiths, *Welsh*. OBWVE, *tr. by* H. Idris Bell

Lo, Colin, here the place whose pleasant site. The Shepherd's Calendar, "June." Edmund Spenser. AEP

Lo! Death has reared himself a throne. The City in the Sea. Edgar Allan Poe. APN-1; AmPP; ColAP; KSG; MeMAP; NAAL-1; NAAL-3; NCAP; NOBA; NoP-4; OxBA; PAR; PoE; PoEL-4; SCV; TAP; TFi; TRP

Lo, Della Crusca! In his closet pent. William Gifford. NOBRP *Fr.* The Baviad.

Lo! down yon steep of vales proud Deva borne. Speech of the Nymph. Anna Seward. NOBRP

Lo, for I to myself am unknown, now in God's name what must I do? Jelaluddin Rumi, *Persian*. TOF, *tr. by* R. A. Nicholson

Lo! Freedom comes. Th' prescient Muse foretold. Phillis Wheatley. BlSi *Fr.* Liberty and Peace. AiP

Lo[e] here a little volume, but great [*or* large] book[e]. An Ode, which Was Prefixed to a Little Prayer-Book Givin to a Young Gentlewoman. Richard Crashaw. ESCV

Lo here hath been dawning. Morning. Thomas Carlyle. PWR

Lo here I am lord, whither wilt thou send me? To Christ. William Alabaster. NoSic

Lo here I sit at Holyhead. Holyhead. September 25, 1727. Jonathan Swift. BIrV; NOIV

Lo! here the gentle lark, weary of rest. The Death of Adonis. Shakespeare. NoSic *Fr.* Venus and Adonis.

Lo, here the state of every mortal wight. Respice Finem. Thomas Proctor. NoSic

Lo here, within the waters liquid womb. Third Day. Thomas Traherne. ChIV-1 *Fr.* Meditations on the Six Days of the Creation.

Lo, how a rose is growing. *Unknown, German.* GePo, *tr. by* Gracia Grindal

Lo, how I seek and sue to have. Sir Thomas Wyatt. SiPS

Lo how the sailor in a stormy night. Sonnet: on Loss. Sir Robert Ayton. NOSC

Lo! Hymen passes through th' admiring crowds. Epithalamium. *Unknown.* ECWP

Lo! I am come to autumn. Gold Leaves. G. K. Chesterton. OxBTC

Lo, I Am Stricken Dumb. *Unknown.* TrJP, *tr. by* Theodor H. Gaster *Fr.* The Dead Sea Scrolls.

Lo! I have learned of the loveliest of lands. *Unknown.* AnOE; OAEL-1, *tr. by* Charles W. Kennedy *Fr.* The Phoenix.

Lo, I have opened unto you the wide gates of my being. Fullfillment. Eunice Tietjens. PoToHe

Lo, I the Man. William Browne. *Fr.* Caelia. Son

Lo I the man, whose Muse whilome [*or* whylome] did maske. The Legend of the Knight of the Red Crosse, or of Holinesse. Edmund Spenser. EPCY; FHYEP; NAEL-1; OAEL-1 *Fr.* Wood Of Error. AEP

Lo! I will tell the dearest of dreams. A Dream of the Rood. Cynewulf, *Old English.* AnOE; OAEL-1, *tr. by* Charles W. Kennedy

Lo-Imi, Lo-Imi! Third Song. T. Carmi. MHP, *tr. by* Ruth Finer Mintz *Fr.* René's Songs.

Lo! in the mute, mid wilderness. The Unicorn. George Darley. OBNC; PoEL-4 *Fr.* Nepenthe.

Lo! in the painted oriel of the West. The Evening Star. Henry Wadsworth Longfellow. APN-1

Lo! in the West, fast fades the ling'ring light. Henry Kirke White. OBNC *Fr.* Clifton Grove.

Lo, Lord, Thou ridest! The Hurricane. Hart Crane. CMoP; MoAmPo; OxBA; TrCP

Lo, my loved is dying, and the call. "Michael Field." VWP

Lo now he shineth yonder. Epitaph on Prince Henry. Hugh Holland. FaBoEE

Lo! now with red rent cloak and bonnet black. George Crabbe. EBEV *Fr.* The Parish Register.

Lo Que Digo. *Unknown.* AS

Lo! smoking in the stubborn plough, the ox. The Dead Ox. Virgil, *Latin.* OBCVT, *tr. by* Charles Stuart Calverley

Lo! some we loved, the loveliest and the best. Some We Loved. Edward Fitzgerald. LBC

Lo! sun and moon, these minister for aye. Israel's Duration. Judah Halevi, *Hebrew.* TrJP, *tr. by* Nina Davis Salaman

Lo! the glorious dawn is breaking. Easter Morn. Josephine D. Henderson Heard. CBWP-4

Lo, the moon's self! Phases of the Moon. Robert Browning. *Fr.* One Word More. EnVR; PoEL-5

Lo, the Winter Is Past. Bible, *O.T.* *Fr.* The Song of Songs. AWP

Lo, then would I wander far off. / And remain in the wilderness. Bible, *O.T.* *See* Psalm 55.

Lo, thou, my Love, art fair. Christ to His Spouse [*or* The Beloved to the Spouse]. William Baldwin. NOCV

Lo, thus, as prostrate, "In the dust I write." Proem. James Thomson. NOBE; OxBS *Fr.* The City of Dreadful Night. OBNC

Lo! 'tis a gala night. The Conqueror Worm. Edgar Allan Poe. APN-1; AWP; ImPo; MeMAP; NCAP; NOBA

Lo! we have listened to many a lay. *Unknown.* *See* Beowulf.

Lo, What Enraptured Songs of Praise. Sebastian Streeter. AH

Lo! what [*or* quhat] it is to love [*or* lufe]. A Rondel of Luve [*or* Love]. Alexander Scott. BoLoP; OBEV; OxBS

Lo where a wounded heart with bleeding eyes conspire. Saint Mary Magdalene the Weeper. Richard Crashaw. ChIV-2

Lo, where envy and where lies. Written on the Walls of His Dungeon. Luís De León, *Spanish.* TrJP, *tr. by* Thomas Walsh

Lo, where left 'mid the sheaves, cut down by the iron-fanged /reaper fanged reaper. On a Forsaken Lark's Nest. Mathilde Blind. VWP

Lo! where the four mimosas blend their shade. For an Epitaph at Fiesole. Walter Savage Landor. FaBoEE; OBNC

Lo! where the rosy-bosomed [*or* bosom'd] Hours. Ode on the Spring. Thomas Gray. GTBS-P; NOEC

Lo, where with flowery head and hair all brightsome. *Unknown.* NoSic

Lo, Who Could Stand. *Unknown, Hebrew.* TrJP, *tr. by* Israel Zangwill

Lo worms enjoy the seat of bliss. Robert Burns. FaBoEE

Lo-yang. Emperor Ch'ien Wen-ti, *Chinese.* AWP, *tr. by* Arthur Waley

Lo-yang. Wen-Ti Chien, *Chinese.* ChiP, *tr. by* Arthur Waley

Lo! ye children of men and the Mother. *Unknown.* APN-2, *tr. by* Frank Hamilton Cushing *Fr.* The Generation of the Seeds, or the Origin of Corn.

Loaded on an ox cart. (LL) Starlight Scope Myopia. Yusef Komunyakaa. AF; CDa

Loaded on an oxcart. Yusef Komunyakaa. *See* Starlight Scope Myopia.

Loads of trash and we light the match. Landfill. Michael S. Harper. LCAP-2

Loadstone beckons to the long needle, The. The Joy of Union. Yang Fang, *Chinese.* CoBCP, *tr. by* Burton Watson

Loathsome life away, A. (LL) The Haunted Beach. Mary Robinson. ECWP; Ro

Loba. Diane Di Prima.

　Ave. BB

　"If he did not come apart in her hands, he fell." PFTM

Loba Addresses the Goddess, The / or The Poet as Priestess Addresses the Loba-Goddess. Diane Di Prima. PmAP

Loba's acid breast. San Fransisco. Miguel Algarin. PmAP

Lobbed ball plops, then dribbles to the cup, The. Ford Madox Ford. Robert Lowell. OxBC; TwCP

Lobe of opalescent glass. Heredom. Ken Irby. FTOS

Lobo. Charles Lillard. NOBC

Lobotomy. Kenneth Pitchford. PoA

Lob's Courtship. Elizabeth Hands. ECWP

Lobster, The. "Lewis Carroll." OxBChV *Fr.* Alice's Adventures in Wonderland.

Lobster. Anne Sexton. ChAP

Lobster Quadrille, A. "Lewis Carroll." BoTP; OxBChV; UV *Fr.* Alice's Adventures in Wonderland.

　(Mock Turtle's Song, The.) CBNP

　("'Will you walk a little faster?' said a whiting to a snail.") APAD; CTAV

　("Will you, won't you, will you, won't you, will you / join the dance?") (LL) CTAV

Lobsters. Howard Nemerov. PBMP; PFE

Lobsters in the Window. W. D. Snodgrass. NYBP; TAP; TRP

Local Contractor Flees His Winter Trouble and Saves Some Lives in a Knoxville Motel Room, A. James Whitehead. MT

Local groceries are all out of broccoli, The. Against Broccoli. Roy Blount, Jr. NBLV; OBAL

Local I'll bright my tale on, how. The Children of Greenock. W. S. Graham. FaBoTC; FaBoTw

Local Man Goes to the Killing Ground, A. James Whitehead. MT

Local Man Remembers Betty Fuller, A. James Whitehead. MT

Local Note. Arthur Guiterman. NBLV

Local Poet, A. John Hewitt. PNI

Local row. Gods make their own importance, A. (LL) Epic. Patrick Kavanagh. BIrV; CABP; CIP-2; NOIV; NoP-4

Locale. Penelope Shuttle. BrRo

Locate I / love you some-[where in]. The Language. Robert Creeley. FTOS; PmAP; TAP

Locations. James Harrison. AmPA

Loch Ness Monster's Song, The. Edwin Morgan. OPOU

Loch Sionascaig. Norman MacCaig. FaBoTC

Lochinvar. Sir Walter Scott. BoTP; EBEvV; EBNV; FaBoBe; NOBE; OxAEP-2; OxBS; PoRA; TFi *Fr.* Marmion.

　("Have ye e'er heard of gallant like young Lochinvar?") (LL) ChAP; Ro

　("O, Young Lochinvar come out of the west.") ChAP

　(Young Lochinvar.) NTP; OBNV

Lochmaben Harper, The. *Unknown.* ESPB; OxBB

Lock and Key. *Unknown.* ReMoGo

Lock dreaming within the door, The. Saturday Night. Anne Hussey. WeT

Lock the dairy door. *Unknown.* OxNR

　(What the Farmyard Fowl are Saying.) CTAV

Lock the door, Lariston, lion of Liddesdale. James Hogg. IBB; OxBS

Lock up, fair lids, the treasure of my heart, *speech of Musidorus.* Sleep. Sir Philip Sidney. SiPS *Fr.* Arcadia.

Locke sank into a swoon. Fragments. W. B. Yeats. NoAM

Locked arm in arm they cross the way. Tableau. Countee Cullen. NAAAL; PoBA

Locked House, A. W. D. Snodgrass. VCAP

Locked in Hippomenes' kisses. Paulus Silentiarius, *Greek.* InMo, *tr. by* Sam Hamill

Locked up in mother's chamber. (LL) Yankee Doodle. Richard Shuckburg *and* Edward Bangs. AmFP; OBAL; OxBoLi; OxNR

Locker Room, The. Nora Mitchell. IFJA

Locket, The. John Montague. BiHa; PBCIP

Lockless Door, The. Robert Frost. NOBA

Locks. Kenneth Koch. CoAP

Locksley Hall. Tennyson. EBEV; EBVVPR; EnVR; FaBoBe; ImPo; NAEL-2; OAEL-2

For I Dipped [*or* Dipt] into the Future. PoLF

Locomotive, The. Christopher Pearse Cranch. APN-1; GM *Fr.* Seven Wonders of the World.

Locomotives' graveyard, The. Yaroslav Vasilevich Smelyakov, *Russian.* TCRP, *tr. by* Simon Franklin

Locus, The. Cid Corman. VGW

Locus. Robert Earl Hayden. FYAP

Locust, The. *Unknown, Malagasy.* RB, *tr. by* A. Marre *and* Willard R. Trask

(Coyote and the Locust, The.) AWP

Locust, locust, playing a flute. The Coyote and the Locust. *Unknown.* AWP

Locust Swarm, The. Hsu Chao, *Chinese.* OHPC, *tr. by* Kenneth Rexroth

Locust Tree in Flower, The. William Carlos Williams. PFTM; Spl; TTTS

Locusts a-wing, multiply, fr. *the Chinese of the* Confucian Odes. Ezra Pound. APSN

Locusts laid their eggs in the corpse. The Locust Swarm. Hsu Chao, *Chinese.* OHPC, *tr. by* Kenneth Rexroth

Locusts, or Appolyonists, The. Phineas Fletcher.

"Say Muses, say; who now in those rich fields." ChIV-1

Lodestoned salmon, hurtling, The. Weir Bridge. Padraic Fallon. CIP-2

Lodging-House Fuchsias, The. Thomas Hardy. OBGa; OxBSP

Lodging with the Old Man of the Stream. Po Chü-i, *Chinese.* AWP; BLT; ChiP, *tr. by* Arthur Waley

Loe! formest of a rout that followd him. Laocoön. Virgil. OBVE, *tr. by* Henry Howard, Earl of Surrey *Fr.* The Second Book of Virgil's Aeneid. SiPS, *tr. by* Henry Howard

Loe here the precious dust is laid. Epitaph on Maria Wentworth. Thomas Carew. PoEL-3

Loew's Bridge: A Broadway Idyl. Mary E. Tucker. CBWP-1

"Our City rulers pass in grand array."

Loft. Michael Dransfield. CBAP

Lofty trees, ten thousand or more trunks. Enjoying Coolness. Wang Wei, *Chinese.* SuSp, *tr. by* Hugh M. Stimson

Lofty young squire from Portsmouth he came, A. The Golden Glove. *Unknown.* AmFP

Log. David Bromige. FTOS

Log Jam, The. William Henry Drummond. NOBC

Logan Braes. John Mayne. OxBS

Logbook. Dan Pagis, *Hebrew.* IP, *tr. by* Warren Bargad *and* Stanley F. Chyet

Logbook of a Lost Caravan. Gyula Illyés, *Hungarian.* PFTM, *tr. by* William Jay Smith

Logic does well at school. Scholars. Walter De la Mare. NoAM; Poetr

Logic is logic. That's all I say. (LL) The Deacon's Masterpiece; or, The Wonderful "One-Hoss Shay." Oliver Wendell Holmes. APN-1; AmPP; FaBoBe; NAAL-3; NOBA; OBAL; OBCA; OxBA; PoLF; PoRA; TAP; TFi

Logical Positivist, The. David Bromige. FTOS

Logic's hard lines have pressed. Judging Lear. Libby Houston. NBrP

Logs, at the door, by the fence; broadcast over the paddock. Blanche Edith Baughan. PeNZ *Fr.* A Bush Section.

Logs of wool jersey plastered with labels, The. Threads. Stephen Sandy. BAP-95

L'Oiseau Bleu. Mary Elizabeth Coleridge. BoTP; CH; VWP

("Lake blue below the hill, The.") BoTP

Loitering with a vacant eye. A. E. Housman. SoSe-8

Lola. Yona Wallach, *Hebrew.* IP, *tr. by* Warren Bargad *and* Stanley F. Chyet

Lola, are you still getting whatever you want. Yona Wallach, *Hebrew.* IP, *tr. by* Warren Bargad *and* Stanley F. Chyet

Lolek. John Jordan. TIRV

Lollay, lollay, littel child, why wepestow so sore? *Unknown.* EnVB

Lollies Noir. Dorothy Porter. BMAP

Lollingdon Downs. John Masefield.

Choice, The. MoBrPo

"I could not sleep for thinking of the sky." LiTM

Night on the Downland. MoBrPo

Sonnet: "Here in the self is all that men can know." AWP

Lollipop lady. John Agard. OTCP

Lollipops of the Pomeranian Baroque. James Fenton. PeLV

Lollocks. Robert Graves. RB

London. John Davidson. NOBE; OBNC

London. Daniel Defoe. NOEC *Fr.* Reformation of Manners.

London ("I wander through each chartered street"). William Blake. APAD; AWP; ClHu; FHYEP; FaBoPV; HAP; HeIP-4; InPS-3; NAEL-2; NAWM-2; NIP-4; NOBE; NOBRP; NOEC; OAEL-2; OBNC; OxAEP-2; PBMP; PoE; PoEL-4; Poetr; RB; Ro; SAGP; SCGP; SCV; TFi; TRP; UnPo; WeW-3 *Fr.* Songs of Experience.

("I wander thro' each charter'd street.") CABP; NoP-4; PFE; PoPoPo

London. Juvenal, *Latin.*

"Prepare for Death, if here at Night you roam." OBCVT, *tr. by* Sir Robert Stapylton

London. Charles Lloyd. Ro *Fr.* Blank Verse by Charles Lloyd and Charles Lamb.

London. John Oldham. NOSC *Fr.* A Satyr.

London. J. R. Rowland. CBAP

London: A Poem. Samuel Johnson. PoEL-3

London: A Poem in Imitation of the Third Satire of Juvenal. Samuel Johnson. PoEL-3

"Prepare for death, if here at night you roam." OAEL-1

London after the Great Fire, 1666. Dryden. *See* The New London.

London Airport. Christopher Logue. OPOU

London Bells, *see also* The Bells of London *and* London Bells: "Gay go up and gay go down." *Unknown.* OPOU

London Bells, *see also* London Bells: "Two sticks and an Apple." *Unknown. See* The Bells of London.

London Birds: a Lollipop. John Heath-Stubbs. *Fr.* Two Wedding Songs. NTP

London Bridge Is a-Burning Down. *Unknown.* AmFP

London Bridge is broken down. Mother Goose. CBNP; CH; FaBoVe; LB; OxBoLi; OxNR; ReMoGo

London Bridge was built. Stranger than the Worst. Babette Deutsch. WPE

London City. *Unknown.* AS

London Despair. Frances Darwin Cornford. OBMV

London 1802. Wordsworth. AWP; EBEvV; EPCY; FaBoPV; HAP; HeIP-4; NAEL-2; NIP-4; NOBRP; NoP-4; OBNC; OxAEP-2; PBMP; PFE; PoEL-4; PoRA; Ro; SCGP; Son; TFi; UV

(England, 1802, II.) OBEV

London Fete, A. Coventry Patmore. EBVV; EnVR; HAP; PeVV

London, from Hampstead Heath. Wordsworth. *Fr.* Extempore Effusion upon the Death of James Hogg. EBEV; NOBE; OAEL-2; SCV

London, hast thou [*or* thow] accused me. A Satire on London. Henry Howard, Earl of Surrey. AAS; SiPS

London is full of chickens, on electric spits. Peter Porter. OxBTC *Fr.* Annotations of Auschwitz.

London is painted round them: burly railings. Street Performers, 1851. Terence Tiller. GTBS-P

London: John Lane, The Bodley Head. On the Imprint of the First English Edition of "The Works of Max Beerbohm." Max Beerbohm. InPK-6; OBCoV

London Lickpenny. *Unknown, Middle English.* OBSV

London Lickpenny. *Unknown.* OBSV

London Magazine, 3 526. John Taylor.

Sonnet on the Death of the Poet J. Keats. Ro

London Magazine, 6 151. John Clare.

To Elia (unsigned). Ro

London, MDCCCII ("O friend! I know not which way I must look"). Wordsworth. GTBS-P

London Nightfall. John Gould Fletcher. MoAmPo

London Pavement Artist. James Schevill. TAP

London Plane-Tree, A. Amy Levy. PEW

London Poets. Amy Levy. PEW

London Rain. Louis MacNeice. NoP-4; Poetr

London Rurality. George, the Younger Colman, OBGa

London Snow. Robert Bridges. CH; CMoP; EBEV; EBEvV; EBVV; GTBS-P; LiTM; MoBrPo; MoP; NOBE; NOBVV; NoAM; OAEL-2; OBNC; OxAEP-2; OxBTC; PoEL-5; TFi

London Spring. Antoni Slonimski, *Polish.* TrJP, *tr. by* Frances Notley

London Street, A. Donne. NoSic *Fr.* Satires.

London Subverted by the Furies. Abraham Cowley. NOSC

London, thou art of townes. To the City of London [*or* In Honour of the City of London]. William Dunbar. EBEV; OBEV

London, thou art the flour [*or* flower] of Cities all. (LL) To the City of London [*or* In Honour of the City of London]. William Dunbar. EBEV; OBEV; OPOU

London to Folkestone. D. G. Rossetti. EnVR

London Trees. Beryl Netherclift. BoTP

London, within thy ample verge. Henry Luttrell. NOBRP *Fr.* Letter to Julia, in Rhyme.

Londonderry Air, The. Nicolas Bentley. OBCoV

London's Resurrection. Simon Ford.

"Hail, glorious day; mayst thou be writ in gold." NOSC

London's Summer Morning. Mary Robinson. ECWP; WoRP

Lone and forgotten / Through a long sleeping. The Lonely. "Æ." AWP

Lone and level sands stretch far away, The. (LL) Ozymandias [of Egypt]. Shelley. APAD; AWP; CABP; CH; ChAP; ClHu; FaBoBe; FaBoCh; FaPoR; GSo; GTBS-P; HAP; HeIP-4; HoPM; ImPo; InPK-6; InPS-3;

NAEL-2; NIP-4; NOBE; NoP-4; OAEL-2; OBNC; OPOU; PFE; PoE; PoLF; PoPoPo; PoRA; RB; SCGP; SCV; SoSe-8; Son; TFi; UV

Lone and weary as I wander'd by the bleak shore of the sea. Lament for Timoleague. Sean O'Coilean, *Irish.* TIRV, *tr. by* Sir Samuel Ferguson

Lone Bather. Abraham Moses Klein. HeIP-4

Lone boat, a sliver of moon facing the maple woods, A. Listening to a Wanderer's "Water Melody." Wang Ch'ang-ling, *Chinese.* SuSp, *tr. by* Joseph J. Lee

Lone Dog. Irene McLeod. NOxBChV

Lone figure is waving, A. A Postcard from North Antrim. Seamus Heaney. PBCIP; PNI

Lone heart, learning. Vigils. Siegfried Sassoon. CMoP

Lone Kauri Road ("First time I looked seaward, westward"). Allen Curnow. *Fr.* Trees, Effigies, Moving Objects. PeNZ

Lone Kauri Road ("Too many splashes, too many gashes"). Allen Curnow. *Fr.* Trees, Effigies, Moving Objects. PeNZ

Lone listener to my spirit wild. (LL) On the Tower. Annette von Droste-Hülshoff, *German.* PBWP; WPOW, *tr. by* James Edward Tobin

Lone, lone, and lone I stand. The Myall in Prison. Mary Gilmore. CBAP

Lone Performer, The. Velemir Khlebnikov, *Russian.* TCRP, *tr. by* Gary Kern

Lone red-winged blackbird. Nicholas Virgilio. HA

Lone Star Trail, The. *Unknown.* AS

Lone Wild Fowl, The. H. R. MacFayden. AH

Lone Wild Goose, A. Lu Kuei Meng, *Chinese.* SuSp, *tr. by* Robin D. S. Yates

Loneliness. Ivan Bunin, *Russian.* TCRP, *tr. by* Yakov Hornstein

Loneliness. Robert Frost. VGW *Fr.* The Hill Wife. CMoP; HAP; InPS-3; LiTM; NoP-4; RACG

Loneliness, A. Haki R. Madhubuti. GT

Loneliness. Mekeel McBride. CMAP

Loneliness. Tanka. Tawara Machi, *Japanese.* MJT, *tr. by* Makoto Ueda

Loneliness. Tu Fu, *Chinese.* OHPC, *tr. by* Kenneth Rexroth

Loneliness. Franz Werfel, *German.* TrJP, *tr. by* Edith Abercrombie Snow

Loneliness, The. John Wieners. PmAP

Loneliness. Al Young. PoBA

Loneliness and July Ninth. Claribel Alegría, *Spanish.* BoWoP, *tr. by* Aliki *and* Willis Barnstone

Loneliness chases me. Aleksandr Petrovich Mezhirov, *Russian.* TCRP, *tr. by* Deming Brown

Loneliness comes out of his mattress face. Elegy for 6 So Far. Gig Ryan. BMAP

Loneliness leapt in the mirrors, but all week. Departure's Girl-friend. W. S. Merwin. CoAmPo

Lonely, The. "Æ." AWP

Lonely. Bloke Modisane. PBA

Lonely. André Spire, *French.* AWP; TrJP, *tr. by* Jethro Bithell

Lonely Affair, A. Reuben Jackson. GT

Lonely and bare and desolate. From Albert to Bapaume. Alec Waugh. NSI

Lonely and big. First Pregnancy. "Alta." NMM-2

Lonely and by myself—she with her fellow. Délie. Maurice Scève, *French.* FLP, *tr. by* Alistair Elliot

Lonely and dreary was the day. Heart's Ease. Mary E. Tucker. CBWP-1

Lonely Beauty. Samuel Daniel. CTC *Fr.* The Complaint of Rosamond.

Lonely courtyard, / once more slanting wind, misty rain. Tune: "Charm of Nien-nu, The." Li Ch'ing-chao, *Chinese.* SuSp, *tr. by* Eugene Eoyang

Lonely, desolate, the new literary scene. Hesitation. "Lu Hsün," *Chinese.* SuSp, *tr. by* William R. Schultz

Lonely Dog, The. Margaret E. Bruner. PoToHe

Lonely Eagles. Marilyn Nelson Waniek. NAmP90

Lonely Farmer, The. Ronald Stuart Thomas. NoP-4

Lonely Hearts. Wendy Cope. OBCoV

Lonely in the Regent Palace. The Flight from Bootle. John Betjeman. PeLV

Lonely Isle, The. Claudian, *Latin.* AWP, *tr. by* Howard Mumford Jones

Lonely Lady, The. Charlotte Brontë. VWP

Lonely Land, The. Arthur James Marshall Smith. NOBC

Lonely Love. Edmund Blunden. OxBTC

Lonely Man, The. Randall Jarrell. FP; OxBC

Lonely moon loiters above the village, The. Sailing at Dusk from T'u-sung. Wu Wei-yeh, *Chinese.* SuSp, *tr. by* Chang Yin-nan *and* Lewis C. Walmsley

Lonely Mother, The. Fenton Johnson. NAAAL

Lonely Night in Early Autumn. Po Chü-i, *Chinese.* TAL, *tr. by* Robert Payne

Lonely old maid named Loretta, A. Limerick. *Unknown.* PeLi

Lonely pond in age-old stillness sleeps, A. Basho, *Japanese.* AWP, *tr. by* Curtis Hidden Page

Lonely Road. Peter Abrahams. PBA

Lonely rock above a midnight plain, A. Te Whetu Plains. Edward Tregear. PeNZ, *tr. by* Alan Myers

Lonely, save for a few faint stars, the sky. The Little Dancers. Laurence Binyon. BoTP; CH; MoBrPo; OxBTC

Lonely season in lonely lands, when fled, The. November. Robert Bridges. OBNC; PoEL-5

Lonely Settler, The. Oliver, the Younger Goldsmith. NOBC *Fr.* The Rising Village.

Lonely Street, The. William Carlos Williams. PoA; TwCP

Lonely stretch, in the bind of poor fishing and drouth, A. Daydreaming on the Trail. Miyazawa Kenji, *Japanese.* PFTM, *tr. by* Gary Snyder

Lonely task it is to plow, A. Plowing: A Memory. Hamlin Garland. ChAP

Lonely the Sea-Bird Lies at Her Rest. W. B. Yeats. RB

Lonely Traveller, The. Kwesi Brew. PBA; TTY

Lonely wanderer, wounded with iron, A. Shield: "Lonely wanderer, wounded with iron, A." Cynewulf. AnOE, *tr. by* Charles W. Kennedy *Fr.* Riddles (Exeter Book).

Lonely way, and as I went my eyes, A. Two Infinities. Edward Dowden. GSo

Lonely Woman, The. Valentine Ackland. WPN

Lonely Woman. Jayne Cortez. NBV

Lonely World. Mrs. Henry Linden. CBWP-4

Lonely young fellow of Eton, A. Limerick. *Unknown.* PeLi

Lonesome Dove, The. *Unknown.* AmFP

Lonesome Dove. *Unknown.* AmFP

Lonesome Dream, The. Lisel Mueller. CoAP

Lonesome scenes of winter incline to frost and snow, The. The Rejected Lover. *Unknown.* AmFP

Lonesome Valley. *Unknown.* APN-2

Lonesome Water. Roy Helton. MoAmPo

Long after hours. (LL) Hamlet. Ciaran Carson. FaBoVe; PNI

Long after it was heard no more. (LL) The Solitary Reaper. Wordsworth. APAD; AWP; CABP; CH; ClHu; EBEvV; FHYEP; FaBoCh; FaPoR; GTBS-P; HAP; HeIP-4; ImPo; InPS-3; NAEL-2; NOBE; NOBRP; NoP-4; OAEL 2; OBEV; OBNC; OxAEP-2; PoEL-4; PoPoPo; PoRA; Poetr; Ro; SCGP; SCV; SoSe-8; TFi; UnPo; WeW-3

Long after Ovid's story of Philomela. Night Singing. W. S. Merwin. PUP-19

Long after there were none of them alive. Recalled. Edwin Arlington Robinson. MeMAP

Long after you have swung back. Losing Track. Denise Levertov. HeIP-4; MoP; NOBA; PoE; PoM

Long afterward, Oedipus, old and blinded. Myth. Muriel Rukeyser. CrSp; FaBoWP; NALW; NNaP

Long afterwards. The Judgment of Paris. W. S. Merwin. NAAL-2; NNaP

Long Ago, The. Benjamin Franklin Taylor. BLPA

Long ago a brown alighted story was told. Remember Something Like This. Lionel Fogarty. BMAP

Long ago, at fourteen or fifteen. Juan Chi. *Fr.* Singing of Thoughts. CoBCP, *tr. by* Burton Watson

Long ago at the end of Deborah's song. His Mother. Haim Guri, *Hebrew.* MHP, *tr. by* Ruth Finer Mintz

Long ago her mother. What the Informant Said to Franz Boas in 1920. *Unknown, Keresan Indian.* STP, *tr. by* Armand Schwerner

Long ago, his skin itches as men enter his pores. Song Thirty-Four. Mudrooroo. BMAP *Fr.* The Song Cycle of Jacky.

Long ago I learned how to sleep. Wind Song. Carl Sandburg. MoAmPo

Long ago I lived in the country. Su Tung-p'o, *Chinese.* CoBCP, *tr. by* Burton Watson

Long ago I made that journey, fall rain coming down lightly. I Had Occasion to Tell a Visitor about an Old Trip I Took. Lu Yu, *Chinese.* CoBCP, *tr. by* Burton Watson

Long ago, I was wounded. I lived. First Memory. Louise Glück. PiM

Long ago, in Kentucky, I, a boy stood. Tell Me a Story. Robert Penn Warren. FuPo; MT *Fr.* Audubon.

Long ago, in the forests of southern Europe. The Stillness, the Dancing. Linda Bierds. NAmP90

Long ago, the Empress Wu Tse-t'ien. The Empress's Cat. Felicity Bast. PC

Long ago there was a mighty snake, and beings evil to men, *see also* The Deluge. *Unknown.* APN-2, *tr. by* Daniel Garrison Brinton *Fr.* Walam Olum.

Long ago there was an immortal man. Juan Chi. SuSp, *tr. by* Charles Hartman *Fr.* Poems Expressing My Feelings.

Long ago to a white-haired gentleman. The Hat Given to the Poet by Li Chien. Po Chü-i, *Chinese.* ChiP, *tr. by* Arthur Waley

Long ago, when Emperor Shun of Kuei was still minister to Yao of T'ang. Rhyme-Prose on the Sea. Mu Hua, *Chinese*. CoBCP, *tr.* by Burton Watson

Long ago you were perhaps. To the Waters of the Chia-ling. Yüan Chen, *Chinese*. SuSp, *tr.* by William H. Nienhauser

Long and Lazy. Robert Herrick. FaBoEE

Long are the hours the sun is above. Going Home. Robert Bridges. LBC

Long as I can call to mind. A Childish Game. Reinmar von Hagenau, *German*. AWP, *tr.* by Jethro Bithell

Long as the Darkening Cloud Abode. George Richards. AH

Long as we run up a goodly amount? Catullus. *See* Carmen 5.

Long autumn grass under my body, The. Field Manoeuvres. Richard Aldington. PeFWW; PoFWW

Long Barren. Christina Rossetti. PBWP; TrCP

Long before I hear it, Naples bright. Napoli Again. Richard Hugo. AF; LCAP-2

Long before the adult flora of. The Grace of Animals. Richard Harteis. GLP

Long before the father died. Himself. Peter Fallon. PBCIP

Long black night, The. Dusk in My Backyard. Keith Wilson. BLT

Long Blues, The. Calvin C. Hernton. GT

Long bound in ice and horrid hills of snow. After a Storm, Going a Hawking. George Daniel. NOSC

Long Branch Song, A. Robert Pinsky. NoP-4

Long canoe, The. Lullaby. Robert Silliman Hillyer. ImGa

Long closed door, oh open it again, The. Love Song. Judah Al-Harizi, *Hebrew*. TrJP, *tr.* by Emma Lazarus

Long desired the dead return. They Return. Jay Macpherson. NOBC; PoA *Fr.* The Way Down.

Long desired, the journey is begun. The suppliants. Landscapeople. John Ashbery HCAP

Long, Disconsolate Lines. Jane Cooper. PuP-16

Long Distance. Tony Harrison. NAEL-2

Long Distance. Dana Naone. CDW

Long Distance Calls. Marylee Skwirz. IFJA

Long-expected one and twenty. A Short Song of Congratulation [*or* To a Young Heir]. Samuel Johnson. EBEV; HAP; InPK-6; InPS-3; LiLi; NOBE; NOEC; OBCoV; OBSV; OxAEP-1; PFE; PeLV; PoE; PoEL-3; SCGP; TFi; UnPo

Long farewell to all you universe-swivelling optics, A. Philip of Thessalonica, *Greek*. GrAn, *tr.* by Edwin Morgan

Long Feud. Louis Untermeyer. MoAmPo

Long Garden, The. Patrick Kavanagh. OBGa

Long Gone. Sterling Brown. BPo; NAAAL

Long had this nation been amused in vain. The Spanish Descent. Daniel Defoe.

Long Hair. Gary Snyder. NOBA

Long hair, endless curls trained by the devoted. Epigram. Strato, *Greek*. GrAn, *tr.* by Teddy Hogge

Long-haired preachers come out every [*or* ev'ry] night. The Preacher and the Slave. Joe Hill. AS

Long Handscroll of Bamboo by Wang Meng-tuan, The. Li Tung-yang, *Chinese*. CoBLCP, *tr.* by Jonathan Chaves

Long Harbour, The. Mary Ursula Bethell. PeNZ

Long hast thou, friend! been absent from thy soil. Mr. Pope's Welcome from Greece. John Gay. EBEV; OxAEP-1; OxBoLi; PoEL-3

Long hast thou slumber'd, O my sounding Lyre! Daniel Alexander Payne. AAP *Fr.* The Pleasures.

Long have I beat with timid hands upon life's leaden door. The Suppliant. Georgia Douglas Johnson. PoBA

Long have I looked for my lost child. The Lost Child. James Reaney. NOBC

Long have I lov'd this bonny Lasse. Thomas Deloney. PBRV

Long have I sighed for a calm; God grant I may find it at last! Tennyson. EBVVPR *Fr.* Maud [A Monodrama]. EnVR

Long have I yearned and sought for beauty. I Sit and Wait for Beauty. Mae V. Cowdery. BlSi

Long Hill, The. Sara Teasdale. MoAmPo

Long hoe, long hoe, handle of white wood. Tu Fu, *Chinese. Fr.* Seven Songs Written During the Ch'ien-yüan Era. CoBCP, *tr.* by Burton Watson

Long Hot Summer. Archibald MacLeish. AFr

Long I followed [*or* follow'd] happy guides. Forerunners. Ralph Waldo Emerson. APN-1; OBEV; OxBA

Long I Thought That Knowledge Alone Would Suffice. Walt Whitman. NOBA

Long in thy shackles, liberty / I ask not from these walls, but thee. To Lucasta[, from Prison]. Richard Lovelace. BeJo; CaPo; CavPo

Long is the night. Curriculum Vitae. Ingeborg Bachmann, *German*. BoWoP, *tr.* by Jerome Rothenberg

Long Island Sound. Emma Lazarus. APN-2

Long Island sound, the pitiless clamor, The. The Penitential Cries of Jupiter Hammond. Gary Smith. GT

Long Island Springs. Howard Moss. UnPo

Long John Brown & Little Mary Bell. William Blake. ECEV; RB

Long Kiang, reaching heaven, The. (LL) Separation on the River Kiang. Li Po, *Chinese*. InPS-3; UnPo, *tr.* by Ezra Pound

Long lay the ocean-paths from man conceal'd. The Inspiration. James Montgomery. *Fr.* The West Indies. PBCV

Long-Legged Fly. W. B. Yeats. APAD; CMoP; FaBoMo; FaBoTw; InPS-3; LiTM; MoP; NAEL-2; NOBE; NoAM; NoP-4; PoE

Long legs, crooked thighs. Tongs. Mother Goose. LB; OxNR; ReMoGo

Long lifetime, A. Kenneth Rexroth. BLT

Long line of blood, The. Tapestry. Grace Nichols. HCP

Long line of web, A. J. W. Hackett. HA

Long Lines. Paul Goodman. VGW

Long lines, clean and syllabic as knotted bamboo. / Yes! (LL) Poetics against the Angel of Death. Phyllis Webb. MoCV; NOBC

Long Lines: Youth and Age. Paul Goodman. GLP

Long live the people! How they lived! and boiled. Part II. Elizabeth Barrett Browning. PEW

Long live the weeds and the wilderness yet. (LL) Inversnaid. Gerard Manley Hopkins. APAD; CMoP; EnVR; FaBoVe; GTBS-P; ImPo; LiTM; MoBrPo; NoAM; OAEL-2; PeVV; PoRA; RB; SAGP; SCGP; TFi; UnPo

Long live the weeds that overwhelm. Theodore Roethke. NOBA; NoAM; PoA

Long live Vietnam! Long live Vietnam! The Day of Mourning at Yên-Báy. Dặng Phu'o'ng, *Vietnamese*. AVP, *tr.* by Huỳnh Sanh Thông

Long long ago. Gorby and the Rats. Obeyd-i-Zàkàni, *Persian*. PC, *tr.* by Omar Pound

Long, long ago. (LL) Long, Long Ago. *Unknown*. BoTP; PChr

Long, Long Ago. Katherine Parker. CTV

Long, Long Ago. *Unknown*. PChr

(Christmas Song, A.) BoTP

Long, long ago, beyond the misty space. The Celts. Thomas D'Arcy Magee. TIRV

Long, long ago, when Nature had some zest. The Giantess. Charles Baudelaire, *French*. EP; FLP, *tr.* by Alistair Elliot

Long long ago when the world was a wild place. Bedtime Story. George MacBeth. MoP; SoSe-8

Long, Long Be My Heart with Such Memories Filled. Thomas Moore. FaBoBe

Long, long between your hands you held the warrior's black face. Léopold Sédar Senghor. NegPo, *tr.* by Ellen Conroy Kennedy *Fr.* Songs for Signare.

Long, long river, The. Boncho, *Japanese*. OHPJ, *tr.* by Kenneth Rexroth

Long[e] love that in my thought do[e]th [*or* I] harbour [*or* harber *or* harbar], The. The Lover for Shamefastness[e] Hideth His Desire Within His Faithful[l] Heart [*or* Hart]. Petrarch. NAEL-1; OAEL-1; OBVE; SCGP, *tr.* by Sir Thomas Wyatt *Fr.* Sonnets to Laura.

("Alas, so all things do hold their peace.") NoSic, *sect.* CIX, *tr.* by the Earl of Surrey

(Sonnet: "The long love.") AEP, *tr.* by Sir Thomas Wyatt

Long now ward, now tidy for the night, The. Off Duty. Elizabeth Daryush. WPN

Long March, The. Mao Tse-tung, *Chinese*. ChiPo, *tr.* by Rewi Alley

Long May. Rosalía de Castro, *Galician*. PBWP, *tr.* by Benjamin M. Woodbridge, Jr.

Long may the lonely one wait for comfort. The Wanderer. *Unknown, Anglo-Saxon*. AnOE; OAEL-1, *tr.* by Charles W. Kennedy

Long may this happy heaven-tied band. Epithalamion. Richard Crashaw. ITG, *tr.* by Robert Hass

Long Mountain, rise. Pocomania. Philip Sherlock. PBCV

Long my dull Muse in heavy slumbers lay. To My Lord Colrane, in Answer to His Complemental Verses Sent Me under the Name of Cleanor. Anne Killigrew. KTR

Long Nature travailed, till at last she bore. Nature's Travail. *Unknown, Greek*. AWP, *tr.* by Goldwin Smith

Long neglect has worn away. Emily Jane Brontë. NOBVV; NoP-4; PoE

Long net, tasselled with corpses, came, The. Drifter. Norman MacCaig. FaBoTC

Long night, The. Martin Shea. HA

Long Night, The. Tù' Diễn Dồn, *Vietnamese*. AVP, *tr.* by Huỳnh Sanh Thông

Long night drags on and on—, The. In the Ancient Manner. Chao Meng-fu, *Chinese*. CoBLCP, *tr.* by Jonathan Chaves

Long night of linden trees, your honey hands. The Figurehead. Maria Luisa Spaziani, *Italian*. NeIt, *tr.* by Beverly Allen

Long night succeeds thy little day. Margaret Love Peacock, for Her Tombstone, 1826. Thomas Love Peacock. OBNC

Long night, the short sleep, and La Gorgue / to wander, The. La Gorgue. Ivor Gurney. FP

Long nights when he neglects me—where's he gone? Tune: "Telling of Innermost Feelings." Ku Hsiung, *Chinese*. CoBCP, *tr.* by Burton Watson

Long Nook. John Wieners. FTOS

Long over whatever edge. The Edge. Robert Creeley. FTOS

Long past midnight I sit here. Forsaken. Zalman Schneour, *Yiddish*. TrJP, *tr.* by Joseph Leftwich

Long, perfect loveliness of sow, The. (LL) Saint Francis and the Sow. Galway Kinnell. AFr; ChAP; FYAP; InPK-6; RB

Long Person. Gladys Cardiff. CDW

Long Picnic, The. Russell Edson. LCAP-2

Long placid evening. Tune: The Butterfly Woos the Blossoms. Li Ch'ing-chao. PBWP, *tr.* by C. H. Kwock *and* Vincent McHugh

Long Plighted. Thomas Hardy. NOBVV

Long rain falls on the empty forest. Smoke rises, The. After Long Rain. Wang Wei, *Chinese*. TAL, *tr.* by Robert Payne

Long Reality, The. Haki R. Madhubuti. NAAAL

Long River, The. Donald Hall. CoAmPo; LCAP-2

Long road and a village, A. Holy Family. Muriel Rukeyser. ChIV-2; MoAmPo

Long robes, or short. Yüan Mei. *Fr.* Miscellaneous Poems on Growing Old. CoBLCP, *tr.* by Jonathan Chaves

Long rolling, The. The Main-Deep. James Stephens. MoBrPo; OBMV; UnPo

Long sea, how short-lasting, The. There Is No Land Yet. Laura Riding Jackson. ChIV-1

Long Shadow of Lincoln: A Litany, The. Carl Sandburg. CBCWP

Long Sigh. Lu Yu, *Chinese*. CoBCP, *tr.* by Burton Watson

Long since I'd ceased to care. The Parrot. Wilfrid Wilson Gibson. OBMV

Long since, it was by me desir'd. To the Queen of Bohemiah. "Eliza." KTR

Long Since Last. Ruth Miller. PeSA

Long since, there lived a boatman named Tru'o'ng Chi. Tru'o'ng Chi, the Lovelorn Boatman. *Unknown, Vietnamese*. AVP, *tr.* by Huỳnh Sanh Thông

Long since we were a family, a people. The Ring. Edwin Muir. FaBoTC

Long slick black feller. Riddle. *Unknown*. FaBoVe

Long steel grass. Trio for Two Cats and a Trombone. Dame Edith Sitwell. NAEL-2; PBWP *Fr.* Façade.

Long-Suffering of God. Christopher Smart. NOCV *Fr.* Hymns for the Amusement of Children.

Long summer day. Michael McClintock. HA

Long sunny lane and pike, white, delicate. Blackberry Blossoms. Lizette Woodworth Reese. SDW

Long-tailed pig, A. Mother Goose. OxNR

Long Tale, A. "Lewis Carroll." NoAM; OBCoV *Fr.* Alice's Adventures in Wonderland.

("con- / demn / you to / death.") (LL) NOxBChV

("Fury said to / a mouse.") NOxBChV

(Mouse's Tale, The.) CBNP; NOxBChV

Long the flimsy skirts. Wang Chien. SuSp, *tr.* by William H. Nienhauser *Fr.* Palace Poems.

Long the loose wits of a degenerate age. Verses to Mr. Richardson on his History of Sir Charles Grandison. Anna Williams. ECWP

Long Their Coupled Joys Maintain. Sir Philip Sidney, *English*. ITG, *tr.* by Robert Hass *Fr.* Arcadia.

Long they pine in weary woe, the nobles of our land. Kathaleen Ny-Houlahan [*or* Kathleen-Ni-Houlahan]. William Heffernan, *Irish*. IIP; NOIV, *tr.* by James Clarence Mangan

Long Time a Child. Hartley Coleridge. OBNC; PoEL-4; Son

("Long time a child, and still a child, when years.") GSo; LaPo; Ro

Long time ago, A. Ch'ien T'ao, *Chinese*. ChiP, *tr.* by Arthur Waley

Long Time Ago. Leslie Marmon Silko. NoAM

Long time ago, A. T'ao Ch'ien, *Chinese*. FaBoCh, *tr.* by Arthur Waley

Long Time Ago, A. *Unknown*. AmFP

Long time ago / in the beginning. The Invention of White People. Leslie Marmon Silko. STP

Long time hath Christ, long time I must confess. Of the Reed That the Jews Set in Our Saviour's Hand. William Alabaster. NoSic

Long time he lay upon the sunny hill. Childhood. Edwin Muir. CMoP; FaBoTC; HeIP-4; NoP-4

Long time in one place and I always think of moving, A. Cold Night. Ch'en Shih-tao, *Chinese*. CoBCP, *tr.* by Burton Watson

Long time in some forgotten churchyard earth of Warwickshire. Who Were before Me. John Drinkwater. OBMV

Long time I've wanted to live in the southern village, A. Moving House. T'ao Ch'ien, *Chinese*. CoBCP, *tr.* by Burton Watson; CoBCP

Long time Plain Dealing in the haughty town. Plain Dealing's Downfall. *Unknown*. OBSV

Long time since it seems today, A. W. H. Auden. FaBoA *Fr.* New Year Letter.

Long time yet, because you're strong as a mule, A. (LL) George. Dudley Randall. BPo; CoAmPo; NoAM

Long time's gone, A. On a Phrase from Southern Ohio. James Wright. LTA

Long Tom. Wilfrid Wilson Gibson. OxBTC

Long Tour: The Country Music Star Explains Why He Put off the Bus and Fired a Good Lead Guitar in West Texas. James Whitehead. MT

Long Track Blues. Sterling Brown. GM

Long tyme hathe Christ (long tyme I must confesse). On the Reed of Our Lord's Passion. William Alabaster. PoEL-2

Long Voyage, The. Malcolm Cowley. SoSe-8

Long Walks in the Afternoon. Margaret Gibson. AFr

Long war had ended, The. The Next War. Sir Osbert Sitwell. NSI; PoWW

Long was Society o'er-run. Hannah More. PEW *Fr.* The Bas Bleu; Or, Conversation.

Long was the night of error, nor dispelled. Some Early gardenists. William Mason. OBGa *Fr.* The English Garden.

Long Waters, The. Theodore Roethke. NYBP *Fr.* North American Sequence.

Long Way After Ronsard, A. James Simmons. PBCIP

Long way from the whorehouse. Solo: The Good Blues. Dolores Kendrick. FFC

Long Way Outside Yellowstone, A. Thomas McGrath. VGW

Long Way Round, The. Denise Levertov. NMM-2

Long ways, A. A Remembrance of a Color inside a Forest. Ray A. Young Bear. CDW

Long ways from home, A. *Unknown*. *See* Sometimes I feel like a motherless child.

Long wedge of geese, A. Robert Spiess. HA

Long White Seam, The. Jean Ingelow. NOBVV; SDW

Long wind coming from beyond the horizon. Commandeering the Wind. Su Shun-ch'in, *Chinese*. SuSp, *tr.* by Irving Y. Lo

Long window stretches her face, A. The Descent of Fire. Jeannine Savard. CMAP

Long years ago I wandered here. On Recrossing the Rocky Mountains after Many Years. John Charles Frémont. AiP

Long years ago the envoy of Han departed. Tune: "Pacifying the Western Barbarians." Wen T'ing-yün, *Chinese*. SuSp, *tr.* by William R. Schultz

Long years have left their writing on my brow. "George Eliot." SDW *Fr.* Brother and Sister. NALW

Long years have passed since first a merry child. To One Who Sleepeth. Mary E. Tucker. CBWP-1

Long years of pleasant friendship may be broken. True to the Best. Benjamin Keech. PoToHe

Longer to muse. Sir Thomas Wyatt. SiPS

Longer we are together, The. Ripening. Wendell Berry. RaBo

Longest and much the dearest. Book Review. Russell Davies. FaBoEE

Longest Journey, The. Shelley. OxBM *Fr.* Epipsychidion.

Longest night, The. David Lloyd. HA

Longest train I ever saw, The. In the Pines. Bill Monroe. GM

Longface Mahoney Discusses Heaven. Horace Gregory. VGW

Longfellow. Henrietta Cordelia Ray. AAP; CBWP-3

Longfellow's Visit to Venice. John Betjeman. NOBL; OBCoV

Longing. Matthew Arnold. GLoP; PoLF; SoSe-8

Longing. Ina Coolbrith. PaTW

Longing. Judah Halevi, *Hebrew*. TrJP, *tr.* by Nina Davis Salaman

Longing. George Herbert. ESCV; UV

("Which dyes.") (LL) FSCP

("With sick and famisht eyes.") FSCP

Longing. "Shu Ting," *Chinese*. ChiPo, *tr.* by Helen F. Siu *and* Zelda Stern

Longing for Eternal Life, The. Liz Rosenberg. PBCAP

Longing for Jail, A. Edvard Kocbek, *Slovene*. PoSu, *tr.* by Michael Scammell *and* Veno Taufer

Longing for Jerusalem. Judah Halevi, *Hebrew*. TrJP, *tr.* by Emma Lazarus

Longing for you. Princess Nukada, *Japanese*. WPJ, *tr.* by Kenneth Rexroth *and* Ikuko Atsumi

Longing in My Heart. Wei Ying-wu, *Chinese*. SuSp, *tr.* by Irving Y. Lo

Longmobile. Shel Silverstein. AiP

Longobards, The. Zbigniew Herbert, *Polish*. PoSu, *tr.* by Czeslaw Milosz

Longon lights are far abeam, The. Old Australian Ways. Andrew Barton Paterson. NOBAu

Longshore Intellectual. Sean Lucy. CIP-2

Longsight Market. Valerie Bloom. NBrP

Longterm Hatred. David Avidan, *Hebrew*. IP, *tr.* by Warren Bargad *and* Stanley F. Chyet

Loo! loo! Lulu! lulu! Loo! loo! Loot! loot! Rudyard Kipling. UV *Fr.* Loot.

Loo-wit. Wendy Rose. HATNAP

Look, The. Elizabeth Barrett Browning. TrCP

Look, The. Elizabeth Daryush. PoA

Look, The. Sara Teasdale. LW

Look Ahead—Look South. C. S. Giscombe.

(1962 at the edge of town). PUP-19

Look, among the boughs. Those stars are men. The Star-Tribes. *Aborigine Oral Tradition*. NOBAu, *tr.* by Fred Biggs

Look and remember. Look upon this sky. Travelogue for Exiles. Karl Shapiro. MoAmPo; TrJP

Look, and you will see that the furniture is fading. For Adrian. Derek Walcott. AFr

Look at him, over there. Disillusion. Maureen Burge. BrRo

Look at him there in his stovepipe hat. American Primitive. William Jay Smith. InPK-6; MoAmPo; OxBSP; RaBo; TwCP

Look at it well. This was the good town once. The Good Town. Edwin Muir. CMoP

Look at Jonah embarking from Joppa, deterred by. Tom Fool at Jamaica. Marianne Moore. NYBP

Look at me, and you will see a slave of that intensity. (LL) To Be a Slave of Intensity. Kabir, *Hindi*. APAD; RaBo, *tr.* by Robert Bly

Look at me 8th. Poem. Sonia Sanchez. PoDA

Look at me: my mouth unlearned complaining early. Mother of Fishermen. Henriëtte Roland-Holst. PBWP, *tr.* by Ria Leigh-Loohuizen

Look at me sleeping I am somewhat disfigured. Lachesis. Hilaire Kirkland. *Fr.* Clotho, Lachesis, Atropos. PeNZ

Look at Mr. Snowman. Mister Snowman. Joleen Urriola. CTV

Look at my continent containing. Human Geography. Gloria Fuertes, *Spanish*. BoWoP, *tr.* by Willis Barnstone

Look at my knees. I Wonder What It Feels Like to Be Drowned? Robert Graves. MoBrPo

Look at some baseball / On TV. John Updike. *See* May.

Look at That Gal. Julian Bond. TTY

Look at the aeroplane. The Aeroplane. Jeannie Kirby. BoTP

Look at the horned goat of Dionysus. Anyte, *Greek*. GrAn, *tr.* by Sally Purcell

Look at the leaves. Like Leaves. Lâm thị Mỹ Dạ, *Vietnamese*. AVP, *tr.* by Huỳnh Sanh Thông

Look at the stars! look, look up at the skies! The Starlight Night. Gerard Manley Hopkins. APAD; EnVR; GTBS-P; InPS-3; LiTM; MoBrPo; NAEL-2; PoE

Look at these most wretched remains of a man. Philip of Thessalonica, *Greek*. GrAn, *tr.* by Edwin Morgan

Look at this, golden-horned moon. Argentarius, *Greek*. GrAn, *tr.* by Fleur Adcock

Look at those clouds Vera why are you so silent. Approaching Storm. Slavko Mihalic, *Croatian*. CEEP, *tr.* by Peter Kastmiler

Look Away child. Susan Cavin. GLP

Look away! Look away! Look away! Dixie Land. (LL) Dixie [*or* Dixie's Land]. Daniel Decatur Emmett. APN-1; CBCWP; FaBoA

Look back with longing eyes and know that I will follow. The Flight. Sara Teasdale. LW

Look between the bow and the bowstring, beneath. Backgrounds to Italian Paintings: Fifteenth Century. Anne Ridler. WPE

Look closely at the letters. Can you see. Body. James Merrill. BAP-96

Look, Delia, how we [e]steem the half-blown rose. The Half-blown Rose. Samuel Daniel. NoSic; SCGP *Fr.* To Delia.

Look down on me, a little one. A Child's Morning Prayer. Jeannie Kirby. BoTP

Look for You Yesterday, Here You Come Today. LeRoi Jones *and* Imamu Amiri Baraka. SSLK

Look for your other half. Antonio Machado Ruiz. RaBo, *tr.* by Robert Bly *Fr.* Moral Proverbs and Folk Songs.

Look forth and tell me what they do. Hammer and Anvil. Samuel Valentine Cole. PoLF

Look forward, truant, to your second childhood. The Death Room. Robert Graves. NYBP

Look! From my window there's a view. There Is. Louis Simpson. CoAmPo

Look, God, I have never spoken to You. Conversion. Frances Angermayer. PoLF

Look he trusts again It's good. Warning. Tadeusz Rózewicz, *Polish*. PoSu, *tr.* by Magnus F. Krynski

Look: Here our bodies lie in a long, long line. But We Shall Bloom. Haim Guri, *Hebrew*. TrJP, *tr.* by David Kuselewitz

Look here, Petah! whut's dis here. The Examination. Priscilla Jane Thompson. CBWP-2

Look here, upon this picture, and on this. Shakespeare. OxAEP-1 *Fr.* Hamlet. NAWM-1

Look him. As quiet as a July river- / bed. Grampa. Dennis Scott. NTP; PBCV

Look[e] Home. Robert Southwell. ESCV; NOCV; NoSic

Look how evening descends and around us the barbed-wire-hemmed, wild. Seventh Eclogue. Miklós Radnóti, *Hungarian*. AF, *tr.* by Emery E. George

Look how handsome I am. Hymn of the Patriotic War Veterans. Benjamin Péret, *French*. AF, *tr.* by Keith Hollaman

Look! how the clouds are flying south! The Snow-Man. "Marian Douglas." OBCA

Look how the lark soars upward and is gone. False Poets and True. Thomas Hood. EPCY

Look[e] how the pale Queen[e] of the silent night. A Sonnet of the Moon. Charles Best. CH

Look how yon lecher's legs are worn away. Epigram. John Taylor. NOSC

Look in my face and see. (LL) A Denial. Elizabeth Barrett Browning. GBL; OBNC

Look in my face; my name is Might-have-been. A Superscription. D. G. Rossetti. EBVV; GSo; GTBS-P; NAEL-2; NoP-4; OAEL-2; OBNC; PoEL-5 *Fr.* The House of Life.

Look in the dark alcove under the stairs. Under the Stairs. Frank Ormsby. PBCIP

Look, in the Labyrinth of Memory. Delmore Schwartz. TrJP

Look in the Past, A. Jared Angira. PBMAP

Look in thy glass and tell the face thou viewest. Sonnet 3. Shakespeare. ImPo; NAEL-1; NoP-4; SCGP *Fr.* Sonnets.

Look into thought and say what thou dost see. Diving. Charlotte Brontë. PEW

Look! It is there! (LL) Not Marble nor the Gilded Monuments. Archibald MacLeish. BoLoP; CMoP; HoPM; MeMAP; PoRA; TwCP

"Look! It's a wedding!" At the ice cream shop's. What Do Women Want? Mary Jo Salter. FFC; RA

Look it's clear. Michael McClintock. HA

Look, Loig, behind. The Only Jealousy of Emer. *Unknown, Irish*. BIrV, *tr.* by John Montague

Look, look! rejoice and wonder! The Return of Astraea. Ben Jonson. NOBE

Look! look! the spring is come. First Spring Morning. Robert Bridges. BoTP

Look lovelier still compared to the angry children. (LL) Cythera. David Ferry. GS

Look, my Samsons are coming back, the gates of Gaza on their shoulders. My Samsons. Haim Guri, *Hebrew*. IP, *tr.* by Warren Bargad *and* Stanley F. Chyet

Look, my Samsons are coming back, the gates of Gaza on their shoulders. My Samsons. Haim Guri, *Hebrew*. IP, *tr.* by Warren Bargad *and* Stanley F. Chyet

Look. New sprouts push through the fields. Prayer on the Threshold of Tomorrow. Vahan Tekeyan, *Armenian*. AF, *tr.* by Hovanessian, Diana Der and Marzbed Margossian

Look, No Hands. Pearse Hutchinson. PBCIP

Look not in my eyes, for fear. A. E. Housman. PoEL-5

Look not on the infinite wave. The Governante. Dame Edith Sitwell. BWW *Fr.* The Sleeping Beauty.

Look not thou on beauty's charming. Lucy Ashton's Song. Sir Walter Scott. NOBE; OBEV; OxAEP-2; OxBS; OxBSP; Ro *Fr.* The Bride of Lammermoor.

Look now, bride of God. In Praise of Virginity. Hroswitha von Gandersheim, *Latin*. PBWP, *tr.* by John Dillon

Look now the child. Children's Hospital. Olive Senior. HCP

Look, now the sun's burning chariot comes. Delphic Dawn. Euripides, *Greek*. GrIP, *tr.* by Ronald Frederick Willetts *Fr.* Ion.

Look of sympathy, the gentle word, The. These Are Not Lost. Richard Metcalf. PoToHe

Look off, dear Love, across the sallow sand. Evening Song. Sidney Lanier. UnPo

Look on Him Whom They Pierced, and Mourn. Isaac Watts. NOCV

Look / on me and be / renewed. (LL) I Am a Black Woman. Mari E. Evans. NAAAL

Look on that form, once fit for the sculptor! Working and Waiting. Adah Isaacs Menken. CBWP-1

Look—on the topmost branches of the world. Sunday Evening in the Common. John Hall Wheelock. MoAmPo

Look on these waters, with how soft a kiss. An Aestuary. George Croly. NOBRP

Look on this statue, traveller; look well. Theocritus, *Greek*. GrAn, *tr. by* Anthony Holden

Look one way and the sun is going down. The Mockingbird. Randall Jarrell. NYBP

Look, our Spaniard's yawning. Antonio Machado Ruiz, *Spanish*. STV, *tr. by* John Frederick Nims

Look out how you use proud words. Primer Lesson. Carl Sandburg. MoAmPo

Look out! look out! Jack Frost. Cecily E. Pike. BoTP

Look out there. *Unknown*. NOIV

Look out upon the stars, my love. Serenade. Edward Coote Pinkney. APN-1

Look round, brown moon, brown bird, as you rise to fly. God is Good. It Is a Beautiful Night. Wallace Stevens. SAmP

Look round our world; behold the chain of love. Alexander Pope. FHYEP *Fr.* An Essay on Man.

Look round: You see a little supper room. De Cœnatione Micae. Martial, *Latin*. FaBoCh, *tr. by* Robert Louis Stevenson

Look! she is dead: no cover can cover her: look. Stan Rice. IMW

Look! she said you can see. Kris Hemensley. BMAP *Fr.* A Mile from Poetry.

Look Sheila Seeing You've Asked Me. Vincent O'Sullivan. PeNZ

Look sour, and hum a tune—as you may now. (LL) Epistle to Miss [*or* Miss Teresa] Blount, on Her Leaving the Town after the Coronation. Alexander Pope. BoLoP; EBEV; FHYEP; LoP; NAEL-1; NOBE; NOEC; NoP-4; PoEL-3

Look, stranger, on this island now. On This Island. W. H. Auden. CMoP; GTBS-P; MoBrPo; NAEL-2; PoE

Look that is that uninvited. Vasco [*or* Vasko] Popa. PoSu, *tr. by* Anne Pennington *Fr.* Far Within Us.

Look the builders of ruins are working. November 1936. Paul Éluard, *French*. AF, *tr. by* Gilbert Bowen

Look. The land ends up. Some Grand River Blues. Daniel David Moses. HATNAP

Look: the lute sounds in the girl's arms. The Lute. Judah Al-Harizi, *Hebrew*. BLT, *tr. by* T. Carmi

"Look," the ocean said (it was tumbled, like our sheets), "look in my eyes." (LL) The Crystal Lithium. James Schuyler. PmAP; PoM; VCAP

Look, the raft, a signal flying. Far Off-Shore. Herman Melville. OxBoS

Look: the sun has spread its wings. The Sun. Judah Al-Harizi, *Hebrew*. BLT, *tr. by* T. Carmi

Look, the trees / are turning / their own bodies. In Blackwater Woods. Mary Oliver. CrSp

Look there at the star! Shepherd's Song at Christmas. Langston Hughes. PChr

Look, *there:* one just ran past the corner. The Lost People. Michael Spence. EC2

Look / There / The smiling infant. Cold. Brian Coffey. CIP-2

Look, thoughts and dreams weave over us. Yehuda Amichai, *Hebrew*. IP, *tr. by* Warren Bargad *and* Stanley F. Chyet

Look thy last on all things shitty. Shitty. Kingsley Amis. OxBC

Look to the Back of the Hand. Judith Minty. PoA

Look to this day! Salutation to the Dawn. Kalidasa, *Sanskrit*. PoToHe

Look up and not down. Look Up *or* Lend a Hand. Edward Everett Hale. FaBoBe

Look up, and swear by the green of the spring that you'll never forget. Siegfried Sassoon. *See* Aftermath.

Look up, and swear by the slain of the War that you'll never forget! (LL) Aftermath. Siegfried Sassoon. MoBrPo; NSI; PoWW; TrJP

Look up, dear one, nor be cast down. Truth. Josephine D. Henderson Heard. CBWP-4

Look up into the dome. Altitudes. Richard Wilbur. CMoP

Look Up *or* Lend a Hand. Edward Everett Hale. FaBoBe

Look up, you men. Men there at the fire. Rilke. PChr, *tr. by* M. D. Herter Norton *Fr.* Annunciation over the Shepherds.

Look wha' happen las' week at de Oval! Edward Kamau Brathwaite. FaBoVe *Fr.* Rites.

Look what I have!—And these are all for you. (LL) Not in a silver casket cool with pearls. Edna St. Vincent Millay. CMoP; VGW

Look you child, I signify three hundred years in swarm. Policeman Cleared in Jaywalking Case. Claire Harris. PBCV

Look you, my simple friend, 'tis one of those. Arthur Hugh Clough. EnVR

Looka here. (LL) Song No. 3: "Cain't nobody tell me any different." Sonia Sanchez. FFC; NOxBChV

Looke how the woods, where enterlaced trees, *par. by* Countess of Pembroke, Mary Sidney Herbert. Psalm 72. Bible, *O.T.* OBVE *Fr.* Psalms.

Looked after him thro' happy tears. (LL) An Athenian Garden. Trumbull Stickney. APN-2; GaP; NoP-4

Looked in like tall and sheeted ghosts. John Greenleaf Whittier. *See* Snow-Bound [*or* Snow-Bound; a Winter Idyl].

Looking. Robert Kelly. FTOS

Looking and lusting is not love. Argentarius, *Greek*. InMo, *tr. by* Sam Hamill

Looking as I've looked before, straight down the heart. The Stranger. Adrienne Rich. NNaP

Looking as though. Tanka. Tawara Machi, *Japanese*. MJT, *tr. by* Makoto Ueda

Looking at a Dead Wren in My Hand. Robert Bly. NNaP

Looking at a Dry Canadian Thistle Brought In from the Snow. Robert Bly. NNaP

Looking at Chrysanthemums And Remembering Meng-tsai and Yu-wen. Chang Yü. *Fr.* Seven Poems on Living in the Mountains: Seeing Off. CoBLCP, *tr. by* Jonathan Chaves

Looking at Each Other. Muriel Rukeyser. CPO; GLP; NNaP

Looking at Henry Moore's Elephant Skull Etchings in Jerusalem during the War. Shirley Kaufman. LCAP-2

Looking at Models in the Sears Catalogue. Philip Dacey. CMAP

Looking at Mt. Mudung. So Chong-Ju, *Korean*. CKP, *tr. by* Jaihiun Kim

Looking at My Knife-hilt Ring, a Song. Liu Yu Hsi, *Chinese*. SuSp, *tr. by* Daniel Bryant

Looking at New-Fallen Snow from a Train. Robert Bly. GM

Looking at Pictures to Be Put Away. Gary Snyder. NNaP

Looking at Some Flowers. Robert Bly. NOBA

Looking at the clouds. Inscribed on a Painting. Shen Chou, *Chinese*. SuSp, *tr. by* Irving Y. Lo

Looking at the post love world. Immediate Content Recognition. Diane Ward. PmAP

Looking at the Sea. Pamela Kircher. BAP-93

Looking Back. Heinrich Heine, *German*. NNPT, *tr. by* Christopher Middleton

Looking back in my mind I can see. The Elementary Scene. Randall Jarrell. CMoP; PoE

Looking back, the language scribbles. Rereading Old Writing. David Ferry. DiPo

Looking Before and After. Carter Revard. HATNAP

Looking Both Ways Before Crossing. John Woods. CoAmPo

Looking by chance in at the open window. The Foreboding. Robert Graves. GBL; PoA

Looking deeper. John Wills. HA

Looking down into my father's / dead face. Good Night, Willie Lee, I'll See You in the Morning. Alice Walker. CrSp; IMW; ISC; NAAAL; WeW-3

Looking Down on Glen Canisp. Norman MacCaig. FaBoTC

Looking Down on Nether Stowey. Coleridge. *Fr.* Fears in Solitude. FHYEP; OBWP

Looking Far Ahead. Trần Tế Xu'o'ng, *Vietnamese*. AVP, *tr. by* Huỳnh Sanh Thông

Looking for a Country under Its Original Name. Colleen J. McElroy. BISi

Looking for a Recluse but Failing to Find Him. Chia Tao, *Chinese*. CoBCP, *tr. by* Burton Watson

Looking for a Rest Area. Stephen Dunn. AmPA

Looking for a shrine that would not fall. Aristophanes. Plato, *Greek*. GrAn, *tr. by* Peter Jay

Looking for Camels. Selima Hill. NBrP

Looking For Her. Tạ Hữu Thiện, *Vietnamese*. AVP, *tr. by* Huỳnh Sanh Thông

Looking for Him. Patty Turner. IFJA

Looking for love, she read cookbooks. The Woman Who Loved to Cook. Erica Jong. TAP

Looking for Lu Hung-chien but Failing To Find Him. Chiao-jan, *Chinese*. CoBCP, *tr. by* Burton Watson

Looking for Mountain Beavers. David Wagoner. VGW

Looking for Mushrooms at Sunrise. W. S. Merwin. NOBA

Looking for myself. Reflections. Carole Satyamurti. IFJA

Looking for Poetry. Carlos Drummond de Andrade, *Portuguese*. ChAP, *tr. by* Mark Strand

Looking for something in the Sunday paper. The Sunday News. Dana Gioia. WeW-3

Looking for the Melungeon. Dave Jeddie Smith. HCAP

Looking for you and me, my dear, looking for you and me. (LL) Refugee Blues. W. H. Auden. HP; LiTM

Looking for your light. For the Lord of Caves. Allama Prabhu, *Kanaada*. PFTM, *tr. by* A. K. Ramanujan

Looking Forward. Robert Louis Stevenson. ACTP; NBLV; OxBChV

Looking Forward to Retirement. Nguyễn Công Trứ', *Vietnamese*. AVP, *tr. by* Huỳnh Sanh Thông

Looking from the Pavilion Over the Lake. Su Tung-p'o, *Chinese*. OHPC, *tr. by* Kenneth Rexroth

Looking-Glass, A. Thomas Carew. CaPo

Looking Glass, The. Rudyard Kipling. FaBoTw; NTP; OBMV

Looking-Glass for Smokers, A. Lawrence Spooner. *On Giving Up Smoking*. NOEC

Looking in a Mirror the Day before the Advent of Autumn. Li Yi, *Chinese*. SuSp, *tr. by* William H. Nienhauser

Looking in the Lake. Po Chü-i, *Chinese*. TAL, *tr. by* Robert Payne

Looking into a Face. Robert Bly. NOBA

Looking into History. Richard Wilbur. VCAP; VGW

Looking into my daughter's eyes I read. For My Daughter. Weldon Kees. CoAP; MoLi

Looking into the blue. Horizon Blues. David Henderson. GT

Looking out from death you will always see. Duoduo, *Chinese*. AF, *tr. by* Gregory Lee *and* John Cayley

Looking out toward the stars. A. L. Hendriks. *Fr.* D'Où Venons Nous? Que Sommes Nous? Où Allons Nous. PBCV

Looking thru the commercial. A Loneliness. Haki R. Madhubuti. GT

Looking to the sea, it is a line. The Innocence. Robert Creeley. NeAP

Looking up at the stars, I know quite well. The More Loving One. W. H. Auden. HoPM; TOF

Looking West. William Stafford. NYBP

Looking You in the Back of the Head. Walid Bitar. WeT

Lookout on a Rock on the Heights of Mount Hermon. Abba Kovner, *Hebrew*. IP, *tr. by* Warren Bargad *and* Stanley F. Chyet

Looks not unnavigable to me. (LL) The Narrow Sea. Robert Graves. FaBoEE; FaBoMo

Looks thy fair face and makes it still. (LL) I cannot see the features right. Tennyson. ImPo; PoEL-5

Loom, The. Peter Cooley. CMAP

Loom, The. Robert Kelly. PT

Loom of Time, The. *Unknown*. BLPA

Looming bastion fringed with fire, A. (LL) To-night the Winds Begin. Tennyson. EBVV; GTBS-P; ImPo; NOBE; OAEL-2; OBNC; PeECV; PoEL-5

Loon Call, A. Richard Eberhart. ColAP

Loon I Thought It Was, A. *Unknown, Chippewa Indian*. OBVE, *tr. by* Frances Densmore

Loon? No, A. Chippewa Love Song. *Unknown*. BoWoP, *tr. by* Frances Densmore, *ad. by* Willis Barnstone

Loon on Forrester's Pond, The. Hayden Carruth. AFr

Loon upon the Lake, The. *Unknown, Ojibwa Native American*. APN-2, *tr. by* Charles Fenno Hoffman

Loon's Egg, The. Peter Dale Scott. MoCV

Loon's long night call, A. Three Seasons. Francis Sparshott. NOBC

Loons Mating. David Wagoner. BLT

Loose as clouds, the curled hair. Tune: "Sheep on Mountain Slope"—Boudoir Thoughts. *Unknown, Chinese*. SuSp, *tr. by* Hellmut Wilhelm

Loose, drifting in pools. Chestnuts for Verdi. Roberta Spear. WeT

Loose ghostly mouths / Breathing. (LL) Orchids. Theodore Roethke. CMoP; ColAP; TRP

Loose heady laughter shook the humid night. Jasbo Brown. DuBose Heyward. SeSe

Loose in the brush pines. Tango. Ntozake Shange. GT

Loose Saraband, A. Richard Lovelace. BeJo; CaPo; PoEL-3

Loose Shoes. Charles Bernstein. FTOS

Loose stonework and an outdated sense of freedom, The. New Dark Ages. Donald Revell. WeT

Loose to the wind her golden tresses stream'd. Petrarch. *See* She used to let her golden hair fly free.

Loose Woman. X. J. Kennedy. WeW-3

Loose Woman Poem. Sharon Thesen. NOBC

Loosed from its bonds my spirit fled away. A Dream, or the Type of the Rising Sun. Jean Adams. ECWP; NOEC

Loosed from Winter's prison. *Unknown, Japanese*. TAL, *tr. by* Arthur Waley

Loot. Rudyard Kipling. "Loo! loo! Lulu! lulu! Loo! loo! Loot! loot!" UV

Loppèd tree in time may grow again [*or* againe *or* agayne], The. Times [*or* Tymes] Go[e] By Turn[e]s. Robert Southwell. ChIV-1; NTP; NoSic; PoEL-2

Lord. The Prayer of the Cat. Carmen Bernos de Gasztold, *French*. PC, *tr. by* Rumer Godden

Lord. Troparion. Kassiane, *Greek*. WPoS, *tr. by* Liana Sakelliou

Lord, aid my work this day. Morning Prayer. Geoffrey Mac Briain Mac an Bhaird, *Irish*. TIRV, *tr. by* the Earl of Longford

Lord, all I am and hope to be. An Offering. Eloise Bibb. CBWP-4

Lord among the Clouds, The. Ch'u Yüan. ChiPo, *tr. by* Burton Watson *Fr.* Nine Songs. CoBCP, *tr. by* Burton Watson

Lord, art thou at the table head above. The Reflexion. Edward Taylor. ChIV-1, *sect.* IV, (*Division* I); AmPP; ColAP; MeMAP; OxBA *Fr.* Preparatory Meditations Before My Approach to the Lord's Supper.

Lord, as the grain which once on upland acres. Communion Hymn. George Seaver. TIRV

Lord, at This Closing Hour. Eleazar Thompson Fitch. AH

Lord, at thy voice, my heart for fear hath trembled. A Song of the Faithful. Michael Drayton. ChIV-1

Lord Barrenstock and Epicene. Stevie Smith. NALW; NBLV; OBSV; OxBoV

"Lord, being dark," I said, "I cannot bear." The Shroud of Color. Countee Cullen. NAAAL

Lord, bless Africa. Enoch Sontonga, *Xhosa*. PeSAV, *tr. by* D. D. T. Jabava

Lord bless thee and keep thee, The. Benediction. Bible, *O.T.* TrJP *Fr.* Numbers.

Lord, blow the Coal: Thy Love Enflame in mee. (LL) What love is this of thine, that cannot be. Edward Taylor. AmPP; NOCV; PoEL-3; SCAP

Lord Buddha, The. Fumiko Hayashi, *Japanese*. WPJ, *tr. by* Kenneth Rexroth *and* Ikuko Atsumi

Lord, but *how* much beauty was there / Back in 1955! (LL) Betjeman, 1984. Charles Causley. NOBL; OxBTC; PeLV; UV

Lord, by thy sweet and saving sign. The Howres for the Hours of Matines. Richard Crashaw. PeECV

Lord Byron. John Clare. EPCY

"Lord Byron" was an Englishman. Sketch of Lord Byron's Life. Julia A. Moore. OBAL

Lord, can a crumb of dust the earth outweigh. Prologue. Edward Taylor. NAAL-1; NAAL-3 *Fr.* Preparatory Meditations Before My Approach to the Lord's Supper.

Lord Christ, we pray thy mercy on our table spread. In the Refectory. Alcuin, *Latin*. MLL, *tr. by* Helen Waddell

Lord Clive. Edmund Clerihew Bentley. PeLV *Fr.* Clerihews.

Lord, confound this surly sister. The Curse. John Millington Synge. FaBoEE; NOIV; OBCoV

Lord Coningsby's Epitaph. Alexander Pope. FaBoEE

Lord Cozens Hardy. John Betjeman. OxBTC

Lord Crashton: The Absentee Landlord. William Allingham. NOIV *Fr.* Laurence Bloomfield in Ireland.

Lord, Dear God! to Thy Attending. Heinrich Otto, *German*. AH, *tr. by* Sheema Z. Buehne

Lord decided suddenly, The. The Tale of the Cyclopses. Nikolai Ivanovich Glazkov, *Russian*. TCRP, *tr. by* Daniel Weissbort

Lord Delamere. *Unknown*. ESPB

Lord, Deliver, Thou Canst Save. Eliza Lee Cabot Follen. AH

Lord Derwentwater. *Unknown*. AmFP; ESPB

Lord Descended from Above, The. Thomas Sternhold. AH

Lord Douglas. *Unknown*. *See* Jamie Douglas.

Lord Elderley, Lord Borrowmere, Lord Sickert and Lord Camp. The Stately Homes of England. Noël Coward. OBCoV

Lord Erlinton had ae daughter. Erlinton. *Unknown*. ESPB

Lord Finchley tried to mend the Electric Light. Hilaire Belloc. FaBoEE; NBLV; NOBL; NoAM; OxAEP-2; OxBoLi; PeLV

Lord Fluting Dreams of America on the Eve of His Departure from Liverpool. Paul Zimmer. VGW

Lord, for the year's apprehension. Prayer in a Pestilent Time. Anne Ridler. WPN

Lord, for to-morrow and its needs. Just for To-Day. Ernest R. Wilberforce. PWR

Lord / forgive me / if I twist the sunset. The Hungry Black Child. Adam David Miller. NBV; PoBA

Lord Galloway. Robert Burns. OxBoLi *Fr.* Epigrams on Lord Galloway.

Lord gie you chile de spirit. Gettin de Spirit. Una Marson. PBCV

Lord, give me Love! give me the silent bliss. Love, Death, and Art. Agnes Mary Frances Robinson. VWP

Lord, give me vision that shall see. Beyond the Profit of Today. *Unknown*. PoToHe

Lord God, / a tiny soul has just left. Prayer. Kumch'an Hwang, *Korean*. CKP, *tr. by* Jaihiun Kim

Lord God, forgive white Europe! Léopold Sédar Senghor. TTY, *sect.* II, *tr. by* John Reed *and* Clive Wake *Fr.* Prayer for Peace.

Lord God, I saw the son-of-a-bitch uncoil. The Rural Carrier Stops to Kill a Nine-Foot Cottonmouth. T. R. Hummer. Poetr

Lord God of Heaven, who only are. The Prayer of Nehemiah. George Wither. ChIV-1

Lord God of Hosts. Shepherd Knapp. AH

Lord God of Hosts incline thine ear. The Century Prayer. James Ephriam McGirt. AAP

Lord God of trajectory and blast. Man unto His Fellow Man. Norman Corwin. TrJP Fr. On a Note of Triumph.

Lord God Planted a Garden, The. Dorothy Frances Gurney. BLPA; EBEvV; FaBoBe

Lord God! this was a stone. The Stone. Thomas Vaughan. OBWVE

Lord God's jealous of yourself and me, The. (LL) Dread. John Millington Synge. BoLoP; MoBrPo; OxBSP; PFE

Lord Gorbals. Harry Graham. PeLV

Lord, guard and guide the men who fly. Hymn for Airmen. "M. C. D. H." NSI

Lord Harry has written a novel. A Novel of High Life. Thomas Haynes Bayly. OxAEP-2

Lord has a child, The. Langston Hughes. AH

Lord has raised and nursed it all along, The. Ode to the Betel Palm. Unknown, Vietnamese. AVP, tr. by Huỳnh Sanh Thông

Lord, Have Mercy. Nahum Tate. TIRV

Lord, have mercy on us! (LL) A Litany in Time of Plague. Thomas Nashe. CH; ClHu; EBEV; FaBoCh; FaPoR; GEA; HAP; HeIP-4; HoPM; NAEL-1; NIP-4; NOBE; NoP-4; NoSic; OAEL-1; OBEV; PFE; PeECV; PoEL-2; PoPoPo; PoRA; SCV; TFi; TRP

Lord, Have Mercy on Us. Thomas Nashe. See A Litany in Time of Plague.

Lord He lays / it on Martha's Sons!, The. Rudyard Kipling. See The Sons of Martha.

Lord, he thought he'd make a man. Dese Bones Gwine to Rise Again. Unknown. AS; OxBoLi

Lord hear [or here] my prayer [or prayre] and let my cry[e] pass[e]. Psalm 102. Bible, O.T. OBVE Fr. Psalms.

Lord, hear my prayer when trouble glooms. John Clare. ChIV-1; NOCV; TrCP

Lord Heygate had a troubled face. Hilaire Belloc. OBCoV; OxBoLi

Lord Hippo. Joseph Belloc. NoAM

Lord, how are they increased that trouble me! Psalm 3. Bible, O.T. OBVE Fr. Psalms.

Lord, how can man preach thy eternal[l] word? The Windows. George Herbert. ESCV; FMP; GeHe; MeLP; NAEL-1; NOCV; NoP-4; PFE; PeECV; PoE; SeCP; TrCP

Lord, how delightful 'tis to see. For the Lord's Day Evening. Isaac Watts. OxBChV

Lord how many are my foes. par. by Milton. Bible, O.T. See Psalm 3.

Lord Hsieh's youngest, his favorite child. Airing Painful Memories. Yüan Chen, Chinese. CoBCP, tr. by Burton Watson

Lord, hush this ego as one stops a bell. Vassar Miller. MT Fr. Love's Bitten Tongue.

Lord, I also want to meet you, see. Second Coming. Adam Small, Afrikaans. PeSAV, tr. by Carrol Lasker

Lord, I am lonely. A Stranger in This Land. Cliff Ashby. NOCV

Lord I am not entirely selfish. Prayer. Gavin Ewart. OxBC

Lord, I Am Thine. Samuel Davies. AH

Lord, I Know Thy Grace Is nigh Me. Hervey Doddridge Ganse. AH

Lord, I remember, and am sore amazed. Hymn of Weeping. Amittai ben Shefatiah, Hebrew. TrJP, tr. by Nina Davis Salaman

Lord I sleep and I sleep. David Shapiro. ChIV-1

Lord, I Want to Be a Christian. Unknown. AH

Lord, if I loved her, count it not my shame. (LL) Of the Gentle Heart. Guido Guinicelli, Italian. AWP; CTC; OBVE, tr. by D. G. Rossetti

Lord, I'm tired. A Little Black Boy's Prayer. Guy Tirolien, French. NegPo, tr. by Ellen Conroy Kennedy

Lord, in my silence how do I despise. Frailty. George Herbert. NOCV

Lord in thine anger do not reprehend me. par. by Milton. Bible, O.T. See Psalm 6.

Lord, in Thy Presence Here. Jesse L. Holman. AH

Lord Ingram and Chiel Wyet. Unknown. ESPB

(Lady Maisry.) OxBB

Lord into His Garden Comes, The. Unknown. AH

Lord Is King, The. Unknown, Hebrew. TrJP, tr. by Carrol Lasker

Lord is my shepherd. Psalm 23. Bible, O.T. AWP; ChIV-1; CTV; FaBoBe; NAWM-1; NIP-4; PoLF; SAGP; TFi; TRP; TrJP Fr. Psalms.

Lord is my shepherd, I shall not, The. Neo-Thomist Poem. Ernest Hemingway. OBAL

Lord is my shepherd; I shall not want, The. Psalm 23. Patricia Benton. APAD

Lord is not merciful to reapers and gardeners, The. "Anna Akhmatova," Russian. LoP, tr. by Judith Hemschemeyer

Lord, it is my chief complaint. William Cowper. Fr. Lovest Thou Me? ChIV-2 Fr. Olney Hymns.

Lord, it is time. The summer was too long. Autumn Day. Rilke, German. TrJP, tr. by C. F. MacIntyre

Lord Jesus, at the end of this book which I offer you. Léopold Sédar Senghor. NegPo, tr. by Ellen Conroy Kennedy Fr. Prayer for Peace.

Lord Jesus Christ, in whose hand is the breath. Unknown, Latin. MLL, tr. by Helen Waddell

Lord Jesus Christ, We Humbly Pray. Henry Eyster Jacobs. AH

Lord Jesus, who would think that I am Thine? Christina Rossetti. NOBVV

Lord Jesus! with what sweetness and delights. Ascension-Day. Henry Vaughan. ESCV

Lord, knights, and squires, the num'rous band. To a Child of Quality of Five Years Old, the Author Supposed Forty. Matthew Prior. NOEC

Lord! Lead the Way the Saviour Went. William Croswell. AH

Lord, let me be the torch that springs to light. The Torch. Theodosia Pickering Garrison. BLPA

Lord, let me live like a Regular Man. A Prayer. Berton Braley. BLPA

Lord, let me live to serve and make a loan. Hydromel and Rue. George Marion McClellan. AAP

Lord, let me make this rule. School Days. Maltbie Davenport Babcock. PWR

Lord let me suffer much. A Prayer That Will Be Answered. Anna Kamienska, Polish. BLT, tr. by Stanislaw Baranczak and Clare Cavanagh

Lord, let the angels praise thy name. Misery [or Miserie]. George Herbert. PoEL-2

Lord Livingston. Unknown. ESPB; OxBB

Lord Lovel. Unknown. ESPB

Lord Lovel he stands at his stable-door. Unknown. AS; AmFP; BLPA; ESPB; NOBL

Lord Lovel he stood at his castle gate. Lord Lovel. Unknown. AS; AmFP; BLPA; ESPB

Lord Lovell he stood at his own front door. The Tale of Lord Lovell. Unknown. NOBL; PeLV

Lord Lucky. Hilaire Belloc. NBLV

Lord Lundy from his earliest years. Hilaire Belloc. OBSV; OxBoLi; PeLV

Lord, Make a Regular Man out of Me. E. A. Guest. BLPA

Lord, make me an instrument of [Thy Peace]. Prayer of St. Francis of Assisi for Peace. Saint Francis of Assisi, Latin. CTV; PoLF; PoToHe

Lord, make me coy and tender to offend. Unkindness. George Herbert. FP; NOSC

Lord, make me free. The Christian's Prayer. Unknown. CTV

Lord, Make Me to Know Mine End. Bible, O.T. TrJP Fr. Psalms. (Psalm 39.)

Lord, Many Times Thou Pleased Art. George Wither. AH

Lord Maxwell's Last Goodnight ("Good lord of the land, will you stay thane."). Unknown. ESPB; OxBB

Lord, may it be my choice. My Choice. Unknown. CTV

Lord, may there be no moment in her life. Prayer of Any Husband. Mazie V. Caruthers. PoToHe

Lord, mine eye offended. Matthew V. 29-30. Derek Mahon. CIP-2

Lord, my heart is not haughty, nor mine eyes lofty. Bible, O.T. See Psalm 131.

Lord, my mind is not noisy with desires, par. by Stephen Mitchell. Psalm 131. Bible, O.T. EnlH Fr. Psalms.

Lord my shepherd, me His sheep, The. par. by George Sandys. Bible, O.T. See Psalm 23.

Lord, My Weak Thought in Vain Would Climb. Ray Palmer. AH

Lord of All Being, Throned Afar. Oliver Wendell Holmes. AH Fr. The Professor at the Breakfast Table. (Sun-Day Hymn.)

Lord of Dreams. Abba Kovner, Hebrew. IP, tr. by Warren Bargad and Stanley F. Chyet

Lord of Each Soul. Paul Engle. AH

Lord of Heaven and Earth has made a feast, The. On a Feast. Francis Quarles. ChIV-2

Lord of Hosts, and God of Israel! The Prayer of Hezekiah. George Wither. ChIV-1

Lord of Life, All Praise Excelling. Clement Clarke Moore. AH

Lord of Lorn and the False [or Fals] Steward, The. Unknown. ESPB; OxBB

Lord of My Heart's Elation. Bliss Carman. AH; NOBC

Lord of my love, to whom in vassalage. Sonnet 26. Shakespeare. HeIP-4 Fr. Sonnets.

Lord of Nature. Leonid Nikolaevich Martynov, Russian. TCRP, tr. by J. R. Rowland

Lord of Rosslyn's daughter gaed through the wud her lane, The. Captain Wedderburn's Courtship. Unknown. ESPB

Lord of Sea and Earth and Air. Prayer for a Pilot. Cecil Edric Mornington Roberts. CTV

Lord of the bucket in the well. (LL) The Foot-Washing. George Ella Lyon. CrSp; OxWW

Lord of the Isle, The. Stefan George, *German*. AWP, tr. by Ludwig Lewisohn

Lord of the pots and pipkins, since I have not time to be. The Divine Office of the Kitchen. Cecily Hallack. PoLF

Lord of the River. Ch'u Yüan. *Fr.* Nine Songs. CoBCP, tr. by Burton Watson

Lord of the River. *Unknown*. CoBCP, tr. by Burton Watson *Fr.* Nine Songs.

Lord of the River Hsiang. Ch'u Yüan, *Chinese*. SuSp, tr. by Wu-Chi Liu

Lord of the throne. Al-Tirimmah, *Arabic*. ArPe, tr. by Omar S. Pound

Lord of the World. *Unknown, Hebrew*. TrJP, tr. by D. A. de Sola

Lord of the Worlds Below! James Freeman. AH

Lord Our God Alone Is Strong, The. Caleb T. Winchester. AH

Lord over all! whose power the sceptre swayed. Lord of the World. *Unknown, Hebrew*. TrJP, tr. by D. A. de Sola

Lord over life and all the ways of breath. Ernest Christopher Dowson. *Fr.* De Amore. OBNC

Lord, pity such sinners. Monday afternoon. A Devotional Sonnet. Timothy Steele. CRP

Lord Rameses of Egypt sighed. Birthright. John Drinkwater. CH; OxBTC

Lord Randal[l]. *Unknown*. AWP; AmFP; EBEV; EBEvV; EBNV; EnSB; ESPB; HAP; HeIP-4; HoPM; ImPo; NTP; OAEL-1; OxBB; OxBS; Poetr; SCGP; TFi; TRP; WeW-3

("For I'm sick at the heart, and I fain wad lie down.") (LL) NoP-4; PoPoPo

(Lord Randal.) NoP-4; PoPoPo

("O where ha' you been, Lord Randal, my son?") NoP-4; PoPoPo

Lord, receive my prayer / Sweet as incense smoke. Evening Prayer. Thomas Merton. ChIV-1

Lord, Remember Me! *Unknown*. APN-2

Lord safely guide from danger brought. (LL) O Lord, Thou Hast Searched and Known Me. Mary Sidney Herbert, Countess of Pembroke. KSG; PEW

Lord, safely guide from danger brought. (LL) Psalm 139. Bible, *O.T.* NOCV; NoSic; WPE

Lord Saltoun and Auchanachie. *Unknown*. ESPB

Lord, shall I find it in Thy Holy Church. Truth. Claude McKay. BPo

Lord shall preserve thy going out and thy coming in from this time forth, and even for evermore, The. (LL) Psalm 121. Bible, *O.T.* AWP

Lord she's gone done left me done packed/up and split. Feeling Fucked Up. Etheridge Knight. GT; NNaP; PBCaP; RaBo

Lord, since it's hard to explain. Limerick. J. E. Press. PeLi

Lord speaks / this way, The. Isaiah: Ch. 66. David Rosenberg. ChIV-1

Lord, stand up for the Soviets. Prayer. Nikolai Ivanovich Glazkov, *Russian*. TCRP, tr. by Daniel Weissbort

Lord survives the rainbow of His will, The. (LL) The Quaker Graveyard in Nantucket. Robert Lowell. CMoP; ColAP; HAP; LiTM; MoP; NAAL-2; NOBA; NoAM; NoP-4; OxBA; OxBoS; PeECV; Poetr; TAP; UnPo; VCAP

Lord Tennyson and Lord Melchett. Lawrence. FaBoEE

Lord, the Lord my shepherd is, The. Sir Philip Sidney. KSG

Lord, the Roman hyacinths are blooming in bowls [and]. A Song for Simeon. Eliot. ChIV-2; GI; NOCV

Lord, the snowful sky. Sailor's Carol. Charles Causley. OBCP; PeECV

Lord, Thine humble servants hear. Hymn for Atonement Day. Judah Halevi, *Hebrew*. TrJP, tr. by Solomon Solis-Cohen

Lord, this woman who fell into many sins. Kassia. BoWoP, tr. by Aliki, Willis Barnstone, and Elene Kolb

Lord Thomas and Fair Annet. *Unknown*. ESPB

Lord Thomas and Lady Margaret. *Unknown*. ESPB

Lord Thomas is to the hunting gone. Lord Thomas and Lady Margaret. *Unknown*. ESPB

Lord Thomas Stuart. *Unknown*. ESPB

Lord, Thou art mine, and I am Thine. Clasping of Hands. George Herbert. PoEL-2

Lord, Thou Clepedest Me. *Unknown*. OxBSP

Lord, thou hast been our dwelling place in all generations. Psalm 90. Bible, *O.T.* AWP *Fr.* Psalms.

Lord, Thou hast given me a cell. A Thanksgiving to God for His House. Robert Herrick. BeJo; CavPo; FaBoBe; HAP; NOSC; PeECV; PoRA; PoToHe; SeCP; TrCP

Lord, Thou hast made this world below the shadow of a dream. McAndrew's Hymn. Rudyard Kipling. OxBTC; PoEL-5

Lord, Thou Hast Promised. Samuel K. Cox. AH

Lord, Thou who art like the sea. The Night Prayer of Glückel of Hameln. Edouard Roditi. CRP

Lord, thus I sin, repent, and sin again. A Sinner's Lament. Edward Herbert, 1st Baron Herbert of Cherbury. SeCP

Lord 'tis midnight. Three Phases of Africa. Francis Ernest Kobina Parkes. PBA

Lord to me a shepherd is, The. Psalm 23. *Unknown*. OBCA *Fr.* The Bay Psalm Book.

Lord Ullin's Daughter. Thomas Campbell. BoTP; FaPoR; GTBS-P; NOBRP

Lord, very fair my lot and beautiful my story. Very Fair My Lot. Jacob David Kamzon, *Hebrew*. TrJP, tr. by Sholom J. Kahn

Lord Walter's Wife. Elizabeth Barrett Browning. HAP; VWP

Lord, we look to once for all, The. The Heretic's Tragedy. Robert Browning. OAEL-2

Lord! what a busy [or busie], restles[s] thing. The Pursuit[e]. Henry Vaughan. GeHe; NOSC; SeCP; TrCP

Lord, what a change within us one short hour. The Power of Prayer. Richard Chenevix Trench. PoToHe

Lord! what a goodly thing is want of shirts. John Cleveland. OBSV *Fr.* The Rebel [or Rebell] Scot.

Lord, / What a menagerie! Noah's Prayer. Carmen Bernos de Gasztold, *French*. TrCP, tr. by Rumer Godden

Lord, what a thoughtless wretch was I. *Unknown*. AmFP

Lord, what am I, that, with unceasing care. To-Morrow. Félix Lope de Vega Carpio, *Spanish*. AWP, tr. by Longfellow

Lord, what are the sins. In a U-Haul North of Damascus. David Bottoms. FYAP; MT

Lord, What is Man? Carl Rakosi. FTOS

Lord, what is man? why should he cost[e] thee [or you]. C[h]aritas Nimia; or, The Dear[e] Bargain. Richard Crashaw. ESCV; NOCV; NOSC

Lord, what these weders ar cold. The Second Shepherd's Play. *Unknown*. NAEL-1; OAEL-1; PoEL-1

Lord, when I look at lovely things which pass. In the Fields. Charlotte Mew. MoBrPo; NTP; OxAEP-2

Lord, when I think. *Unknown*. CBLP

Lord, when the clock strikes. The Reader. Thomas Merton. CRP

Lord, when the sense of Thy sweet grace. An Ecstacy. Richard Crashaw. OxAEP-1

Lord, when the wise men came from far[r]. Hymn. Sidney Godolphin. BeJo; HAP; MeLP; NOBE; NOCV; NOSC; PBRV; PeECV

Lord when the wise men came from Farr. Sidney Godolphin. See Hymn: "Lord, when the wise men came from far[r]."

Lord! when thou didst thy self undress. The Incarnation and Passion. Henry Vaughan. GeHe; TrCP

Lord, Where Shall I Find Thee? Judah Halevi, *Hebrew*. TrJP, tr. by Nina Davis Salaman

Lord, who createdst man in wealth and store. Easter-Wings. George Herbert. CABP; ChIV-1; ESCV; FHYEP; FMP; FSCP; GeHe; HAP; HeIP-4; InPK-6; InPS-3; MeLP; NAEL-1; NIP-4; NOSC; NoP-4; OAEL-1; PBRV; PFE; PoE; PoEL-2; PoPoPo; Poetr; SeCP; TFi; TOF; TRP; TrCP; WeW-3

Lord, who hast formed me out of mud. Trinity Sunday. George Herbert. OxBSP

Lord, Who's the Happy Man. Nahum Tate *and* Nicholas Brady. AH

Lord will happiness divine, The. The Contrite Heart. William Cowper. NOCV *Fr.* Olney Hymns.

Lord William; or, Lord Lundy. *Unknown*. ESPB

Lord, with what care hast thou begirt us round! Sin (1). George Herbert. GeHe; NoP-4; OxAEP-1

Lord, with what glory [or glorie] wast thou served [or serv'd] of old. Sion. George Herbert. ChIV-1; ESCV

Lord, within thy fold I be. Hymn. Priscilla Jane Thompson. CBWP-2

Lord, you are my lover. How the Soul Speaks to God. Mechthild von Magdeburg, *German*. WPoS, tr. by Oliver Davies

Lord, you have ripped away from me what I loved most. Antonio Machado Ruiz, *Spanish*. GI, tr. by Robert Bly

Lord, You may not recognize me. The Gift. Louise Glück. FaBoWP; FiLi

Lord! You saved me from Ur-Germany as I fled. Uri Zvi Greenberg, *Hebrew*. MHP, tr. by Ruth Finer Mintz

Lord, you visited Paris on the day of your birth. Paris in the Snow. Léopold Sédar Senghor, *French*. PBA, tr. by Ulli Beier

Lorde blesse and kepe the, The. Bible, *O.T.* See Benediction.

Lorde is my shepherde, The; therefore can I lack nothing, *par.* by Miles Coverdale. Bible, *O.T. See* Psalm 23.

Lordinges, listen, and hold you still. Durham Field. *Unknown*. ESPB

"Lording[e]s," [or Lordynges] quod he, "in chirches whan I preche." The Pardoner's Prologue. Chaucer. FHYEP; NAEL-1; OAEL-1; PoE *Fr.* The Canterbury Tales.

Lordly and Isolate Satyrs, The. Charles Olson. CoAP; NeAP; PoM

Lordly Hudson, The. Paul Goodman. CoAP; VGW

Lords are lordliest in their wine. As Lords. Milton. *Fr.* Samson Agonistes. FHYEP; OAEL-1; PoEL-3

Lord's Chameleons, The. Peter Klappert. AmPA

Lord's Day, The. Kwangnim Kim, *Korean.* CKP, *tr. by* Jaihiun Kim

Lords do crave all, The. A Postscript to Verses on the History of France. *Unknown.* NOIV

Lords have been made whose hired robes have hidden. On the Relinquishment of a Title. Geoffrey Grigson. FaBoEE

Lords, knights, and squires, the numerous band. To a Child of Quality [Five Years Old, the Author Supposed Forty]. Matthew Prior. NOBE; NOEC; OBEV; PoEL-3

Lord's lost Him His mockingbird. Mourning Poem for the Queen of Sunday. Robert Earl Hayden. HCAP; NAAAL; NoAM; NoP-4; PoBA; PoPoPo

Lord's name be praised, The. The Litanies of Julia Pastrana (1832-1860). Thomas William Shapcott. CBAP; NOBAu

Lords of Creation, The. *Unknown.* PoLF

Lords of life, the lords of life, The. Experience. Ralph Waldo Emerson. APN-1; MeMAP; PoEL-4; TAP

Lord's Prayer, The. Massillon Coicou, *French.* NegPo, *tr. by* Ellen Conroy Kennedy

Lord's Prayer. Lawrence. PeECV ("For thine is the kingdom / the power.") GI

Lord's Prayer. Nicanor Parra, *Spanish.* GI, *tr. by* Miller Williams

Lord's Prayer, The. *Unknown.* CTV *Fr.* The Bible, Matthew 6:9–13.

Lore. Ronald Stuart Thomas. NoP-4; OxBC; RB

Lore and Language of Schoolchildren. Various authors. "Masculine, Feminine, Neuter." CBNP

Lorelei. "Alta." CrSp

Lorelei. Heinrich Heine, *German.* TrJP, *tr. by* Emma Lazarus (Loreley, The.) NAWM-2, *tr. by* Aaron Kramer

Loreley, The. Heinrich Heine. *See* Lorelei.

Lorena. H. D. L. Webster. BLPA

Lorenzo! Such the glories of the world! The Consolation. Edward Young. NOEC *Fr.* Night Thoughts.

Lorn, bold, as if saluting with her fist. (LL) Iron Landscapes (and the Statue of Liberty). Thom Gunn. FaBoA; FaBoPV

Lorry made the windows shake, A. Bar Room Conversation. James Keir Baxter. PeLV *Fr.* Cressida.

Los Angeles. Mark Jarman. WWSi

Los Angeles, 1980. Paula Gunn Allen. NMM-2

Los Angeles, / California: / a summer afternoon. Hockney: Blue Pool. David Trinidad. WWSi

Los Mineros. Edward Dorn. PoM

"Lose and love" is love's first art. A Song by the Shore. Richard Hovey. APN-2

Lose This Day Loitering. Goethe. PoLF, *tr. by* John Anster *Fr.* Faust.

Loser, The. Adrienne Rich. RACG

Losers. Jonathan Holden. CMAP

Losers. Carl Sandburg. CMoP; MoAmPo; NoAM

Losing a Language. W. S. Merwin. NoP-4

Losing a Slave-Girl. Po Chü-i, *Chinese.* AWP; ChiP, *tr. by* Arthur Waley ("Around my courtyard the little wall is low.") ChiP, *tr. by* Arthur Waley

Losing altitude, you can see below you the flames. Death of Thomas Merton. Harry Clifton. PBCIP

Losing its gust, and my ambition blind! (LL) To Fanny. Keats. BoLoP; EBEV; Son

Losing the Marbles. James Merrill. DiPo

Losing Track. Denise Levertov. HeIP-4; MoP; NOBA; PoE; PoM

Loss. Carl Dennis. PUP-20

Loss. Charles Madge. FaBoMo

Loss. Yevtushenko, *Russian.* TCRP, *tr. by* James Reagan *and* Yevgeny Yevtushenko

Loss[e] in Delay[e]. Robert Southwell. NoSic

Loss is an unintentional decline in or disappearance of. Definitions for Mendy. David Antin. APSN

Loss of an Oil Tanker. Charles Causley. OxBC

Loss of our learning brought darkness, weakness and woe. Epigram. *Unknown, Greek.* NOIV, *tr. by* Thomas Kinsella

Loss of something never felt I, A. Emily Dickinson. ChIV-2; NALW; NCAP

Loss of the *Due Dispatch*, The. *Unknown.* AmFP

Loss of the *New Columbia*, The. *Unknown.* AmFP

Loss of the Royal George. William Cowper. *See* On the Loss of the *Royal George.*

Losses. Randall Jarrell. HCAP; LCAP-2; LiTM; OxBA; PoA; SAGP; TAP; UnPo

Lost. Millen Brand. NYBP

Lost. Hayden Carruth. AFr

Lost. Chu Shu-chen, *Chinese.* BoWoP; OHMPC, *tr. by* Kenneth Rexroth

Lost. Jacob Glatstein, *Yiddish.* CEEP, *tr. by* Ruth Whitman

Lost. James Godden. OBSP

Lost. Carl Sandburg. AmPP; CMoP

Lost, The. Jones Very. APAD; APN-1; NOBA; NoP-4; PAR

Lost. David Wagoner. PaTW; PoA

Lost Acres. Robert Graves. NoAM

Lost Anchors. Edwin Arlington Robinson. CMoP

Lost, and all mine, alll mine, forever. (LL) Dear Men and Women. John Hall Wheelock. IMW; NYBP

Lost and bewildered in the thickening mist. On the Great Fog in London, December 1762. James Eyre Weeks. NOEC

Lost and Found. Maxine Chernoff. PmAP

Lost Angel, The. Philip Levine. NOBA

Lost Art, A. Richard Howard. BAP-94

Lost Baby, The. *Unknown.* AmFP

Lost Baby Poem, The. Lucille Clifton. BlSi; FiLi; ISC; WPE ("My body breaking.") (LL) NAAAL

Lost Bay. Erich Arendt, *German.* CEEP, *tr. by* David Scrase

Lost Bee, The. Phillis Levin. RA

Lost Bird. Chenjerai Hove. HBAPE

Lost Bride, The. Antiphanes, *Greek.* GrAn, *tr. by* Dudley Fitts

Lost bride and her groom, The. Lawrence. *See* Bavarian Gentians.

Lost Brilliance. Rita Dove. PUP-19

Lost Cat, The. Emile Victor Rieu. PC

Lost Child, The. James Reaney. NOBC

Lost Child. Lee Upton. CMAP

Lost Children, The. Randall Jarrell. CoAP; PBMP; TAP

Lost Chord, The. Wyndham Lewis. UV

Lost Chord, A. Adelaide Anne Procter. EBEvV; SDW; UV; VWP ("Seated one day at the Organ.") VWP

Lost City. Harold Farmer. PeSAV

Lost City. Ingrid Jonker, *Afrikaans.* PeSA, *tr. by* Jack Cope *and* Ruth Miller

Lost Continent, The. Jenny Joseph. BrRo

Lost! Cupid!/ One lost Cupid! Meleager, *Greek.* GrAn, *tr. by* Peter Whigham ("Lost! Cupid!") OBCVT, *tr. by* Peter Whigham

Lost Dancer, The. Jean Toomer. PoBA

Lost days of my life until to-day, The. D. G. Rossetti. EnVR *Fr.* The House of Life.

Lost Desire. Meleager, *Greek.* AWP, *tr. by* William M. Hardinge

Lost Doll, The. Charles Kingsley. *See* The Little Doll.

Lost for a Rose's Sake. *Unknown.* AWP, *tr. by* Andrew Lang

Lost Fugue for Chet. Lynda Hull. PuP-17; SeSe

Lost Girls, The. Linda Hogan. IFJA

Lost Heifer, The. Austin Clarke. BIrV

Lost Illusions. Georgia Douglas Johnson. NAAAL

Lost in contemplation of its end. Jean Daive, *French.* MFP, *tr. by* Martin Sorrell

Lost in glass gullies, searching for a suitcase. Hotel Marine. David Campbell. BMAP

Lost in Heaven. Robert Frost. MoAmPo

Lost in the Centuries. William Stafford. EC2

Lost in the Desert. Clarence Major. FTOS

Lost in the distance, the peaceful time when the green palanquin passed. Crooked River. Li Shang-yin, *Chinese.* PLT, *tr. by* A. C. Graham

Lost in the Galleries. Virginia Hooper. PT

Lost in the ground. (LL) Miners. Wilfred Owen. MoBrPo; NAEL-2; NOBE; NSI; OBWVE; OxAEP-2; PeFWW

Lost in the valley of her arm. Catullus. *See* Sappho.

Lost in Translation. James Merrill. FYAP; HCAP; LCAP-2; NAAL-2; NoAM; NoP-4; VCAP *Fr.* The Book of Ephraim.

Lost Jewel, A. Robert Graves. EnLoPo; NYBP

Lost Jimmie Whalen. *Unknown.* AmFP

Lost Johnny. *Unknown.* AmFP

Lost Lady, The. Sir William Berkeley. Song: "Where did you borrow that last sigh." OxBSP

Lost Lane. Dorothy, Duchess of Wellington Wellesley. WPE

Lost Leader, The. Robert Browning. EBEvV; EnVR; FHYEP; FaBoPV; NAEL-2; PBMP; PWR; SCGP

Lost Letter to James Wright, with Thanks for a Map of Fano. Gibbons Ruark. MT

Lost Light, The. Emily Jane Pfeiffer. VWP

Lost Little Sister, The. William Barnes. PoEL-4

Lost! lost! lost! Anne Boleyn. Eloise Bibb. CBWP-4

Lost—lost—lost! Into the Depths. Adah Isaacs Menken. CBWP-1

Lost Love. Dick Allen. NIP-4

Lost Love. Robert Graves. AWP; CBLP; CH; FaBoCh; LoP; MoBrPo

Lost Love, The. Wordsworth. *See* Song: "She dwelt among the untrodden ways."

Lost Lover, The. Mary de la Rivière Manley.
  Prologue: "First Adventurer for her fame I stand, The." KTR
  Song, A: "Ah Dangerous Swain, tell me no more." KTR; LW

Lost manor where I walk continually. The Pier-Glass. Robert Graves. CMoP; NoAM

Lost Mistress, The. Robert Browning. BoLoP; LoP; NOBE; OBEV; OBNC; SAGP

Lost Mohican Visits Hell's Kitchen, A. A. K. Redwing. VoR

Lost Moment. Hoyt W. Fuller. PoBA

Lost Name Woman. Shirley Lim. UnSA

Lost Occasion, The. John Greenleaf Whittier. NOBA

Lost on a fog-bound spit of sand. W. H. Auden. FaBoEE *Fr.* Shorts I.

Lost on Both Sides. D. G. Rossetti. EnVR *Fr.* The House of Life.
  (91. Lost on Both Sides.) NoP-4

Lost on September Trail, 1967. Alberto A. Ríos.
  "There was a roof over our heads." ImGa

Lost Opportunities. Henrietta Cordelia Ray. CBWP-3

Lost Orchard, The. Edgar Lee Masters. CMoP; ColAP

Lost Parasol, The. Sándor Weöres, *Hungarian*.
  "Where metalled road invades light thinning air." OBVE

Lost Parents. Lawrence Ferlinghetti. PoM

Lost People, The. Michael Spence. EC2

Lost Pictures, The. Hollis Spurgeon Summers. HoPM

Lost Pilot, The. James Tate. CoAP; NoAM; OBWP; TwCP; UnPo; WeT
  ("Goodbye, goodbye. Here come the cows.") ColAP

Lost Pleiad, The. Felicia Dorothea Hemans. NOBRP

Lost Pleiad, The. William Gilmore Simms. APN-1

Lost Seed. Patrick Williams. PNI

Lost Shoe, The. *Unknown*. ReMoGo

Lost Silvertip. J. D. Reed. NYBP

Lost Sister. Cathy Song. NoAM; PiM

Lost Son, The. Theodore Roethke. HAP; HCAP; LiTM; VGW
  Flight, The. NAAL-2; RB; TRP
    (Lost Son, The.) NoP-4
  Gibber, The. NAAL-2
  It Was Beginning Winter. NAAL-2
  Pit, The. NAAL-2
  Return, The. NAAL-2

Lost Songs. Vladimir Alekseievich Soloukhin, *Russian*. TCRP, *tr. by* Daniel Weissbort

Lost Soul, A. Jay Macpherson. NOBC; NoP-4

Lost Teddy Bear, The. Maggie Pogue Johnson. CBWP-4

Lost: The Original, Its Reason and Its Rhyme. Translation. Rika Lesser. PoA

Lost to the world; lost to myself; alone. On Himself. Robert Herrick. BeJo

Lost Tradition, A. John Montague. CIP-2; PBCIP

Lost Travellers Dream under the Hill, The. (LL) Epilogue: "Truly my Satan thou art but a dunce." William Blake. FHYEP; HAP; ImPo; OAEL-2; OBNC; OxBSP; PeECV; PoE; SCGP; WeW-3

Lost Tribe, The. Ruth Pitter. WPOW

Lost Word of Jesus, A. Henry Van Dyke. TrCP

Lost World, A. Robert Graves. NYBP

Lost, yesterday, somewhere. *Unknown*. CTV

Lost Youth. Sir Roger Casement. TIRV

Lot. David Helwig. NIP-4

Lot and His Daughters I. Alec Derwent Hope. ChIV-1

Lot and His Daughters II. Alec Derwent Hope. ChIV-1

Lot and his two daughters and their sons: Man sat sozzled with his two wives, A. Cynewulf. ASW, *tr. by* Kevin Crossley-Holland *Fr.* Riddles (Exeter Book).

Lot Later. Howard Nemerov. HoPM

Lot of love along the way, A. (LL) A Day. William Leroy Stidger. PoToHe; SoSe-8

Lot of love is chosen, The. I learnt that much. Chosen. W. B. Yeats. BoLoP; CMoP

Lot of Night Music, A. Anthony Hecht. OxBC; Poetr

Lot of the old folks here, A—all that's left. Reflections in a Slum. "Hugh MacDiarmid." FaBoTw

Lotos-Eaters, The. Tennyson. *See* The Lotus-Eaters.

Lotos Eating. Mortimer Collins. NOBVV

Lots of truisms don't have to be repeated. The Anatomy of Happiness. Ogden Nash. TAP

Lot's Wife. "Anna Akhmatova," *Russian*. BoWoP; PBWP, *tr. by* Richard Wilbur

Lot's Wife. Albert Goldbarth. KSG

Lot's Wife. Cherra S. Ransom. CrSp

Lottery & Requiem. Maggie O'Sullivan. NBrP

Lotus. Hsü Wei, *Chinese*. SuSp, *tr. by* Irving Y. Lo
  "Fifth day of the fifth month." CoBLCP, *tr. by* Jonathan Chaves

Lotus-Eaters, The. Tennyson. EnVR; NAEL-2; OAEL-2; PoEL-5; SCGP
  (Lotos-Eaters, The.) EBEvV; EBVVPR; FHYEP; NoP-4
  Song of the Lotus-Eaters. NOBE; OBEV
    (Choric Song.) HeIP-4; OBNC
    (Choric Song of the Lotus-Eaters.)

Lotus-flower doth languish, The. Die Lotusblume ängstigt. Heinrich Heine, *German*. AWP, *tr. by* James Thomson

Lotus Flowers, The. Ellen Bryant Voigt. MT

Lotus-gatherer's Song. Po Chü-i, *Chinese*. SuSp, *tr. by* Irving Y. Lo

Lotus Lake. Ts'ao P'i, *Chinese*. CoBCP; GaP, *tr. by* Burton Watson

Lotus Pond, The. Ts'ao P'i, *Chinese*. SuSp, *tr. by* Ronald C. Miao

Lotus Viewing. Su Tung-p'o, *Chinese*. CoBCP, *tr. by* Burton Watson

Lotuses have withered, they put up no umbrellas to the rain. Presented to Liu Ching-wen. Su Tung-p'o, *Chinese*. CoBCP, *tr. by* Burton Watson

Lotuses on the Crooked Pond. Lu Chao-lin, *Chinese*. SuSp, *tr. by* Paul W. Kroll

Loud complaints being made, in these quick-reading times. Announcement of a New Grand Acceleration Company for the Promotion of the Speed of Literature. Thomas Moore. OBCoV

Loud deep calls me home even now to feed it, The. Shelley. *Fr.* Prometheus Unbound. NOBRP; OAEL-2

Loud is the Summer's busy song. July. John Clare. AYFP

Loud is the Vale! the Voice is up. Lines. Wordsworth. LaPo

Loud niggers talkin more than shit. Thelonious Sphere Monk. David Henderson. MoNo

Loud Report through Lybian Cities goes, The. Fame. Virgil. OBVE, *tr. by* John Dryden *Fr.* The Aeneid [*or* Eneados, *Aeneis*].

Loud roars the wind that shakes this wall. Ghost of Edward. Joanna Baillie. ECWP *Fr.* Night Scenes of Other Times.

Loud Song, Mother, A. Isabella Gardner. FiLi

Loud sung the wind in the ruins above. Love in a Storm. Thomas Moore. Ro *Fr.* The Poetical Works of the Late Thomas Little Esq.

Loud talk in the overlighted house. Ends. Robert Frost. TRP

Loud voice, A. Tanka. Maekawa Samio, *Japanese*. MJT, *tr. by* Makoto Ueda

Loud were they, loud, as they rode o'er the hill. Charms for a Sudden Stitch. *Unknown, Anglo-Saxon*. AnOE, *tr. by* Charles W. Kennedy

Loud wind. Leroy Gorman. HA

Loud wind never reached the ship, The. Coleridge. OxBSn *Fr.* The Rime of the Ancient Mariner. CABP; CH; EBEV; EBNV; FHYEP; FaBoBe; FaBoCh; HAP; HeIP-4; HoPM; ImPo; InPS-3; NOBE; NoP-4; OAEL-2; OBEV; OBNC; OBNV; OxAEP-2; OxBoS; PeECV; PoE; PoEL-4; PoPoPo; SCGP; TFi; TOF

Loud without the wind was roaring. Emily Jane Brontë. VWP

Loudens the sea-wind, downward plunge the bows. To D'Annunzio: Lines from the Sea. Robert Malise Bowyer Nichols. OBMV

Louder than gulls the little children scream. The Beach. Robert Graves. OxBSP

Loudon Hill; or, Drumclog. *Unknown*. ESPB

Loue, thou art Absolute sole lord. Richard Crashaw. *See* Hymn to Saint Teresa.

Louerd, thu clepedest me. *Unknown*. MiEL

Lough Derg. Denis Devlin. BIrV; CIP-2

Louis Armstrong. Ernst Moerman. SeSe

Louis B. Russell. Bruce Guernsey. InPK-6

Louis i'm trying to understand what you were here. For Lil Louis. Tom Dent. BkSV

Louis, Louis, Louis, Louis. For Louis Armstrong, A Ju-Ju. Sarah Webster Fabio. SeSe

Louisa; After Accompanying Her on a Mountain Excursion. Wordsworth. GBL
  (Louisa.) APAD

Louise Bourgeois Exhibit. Maxine W. Kumin. NMM-2

Louise, have you forgotten yet. Old Loves. Henry Murger, *French*. AWP, *tr. by* Andrew Lang

Louise on the Door-Step. Charles MacKay. EBVV

Louisiana. Steve Crow. HATNAP

Louisiana Perch. Ron Padgett. FTOS

Louisiana Weekly #4, The. David Henderson. PoBA

Lounge in the shade of the luxuriant laurel's. Anyte, *Greek*. BoWoP, *tr. by* Willis Barnstone

Lourd on my hert as winter lies. "Hugh MacDiarmid." CABP

Lourenço Marques. Charles Eglington. PeSA; PeSAV

Louse. Wolf Ehrlich, *Russian*. TCRP, *tr. by* Daniel Weissbort

Louse Hunting. Isaac Rosenberg. EBEV; NAEL-2; NSI; NoAM; NoP-4; OxAEP-2; OxBTC; PeFWW

Loushan Pass. Mao Tse-tung, *Chinese*. ChiPo, *tr. by* Kai-yu Hsu

Lousy Miner. *Unknown*. AmFP

Lout, The: "For Sunday's play he never makes excuse." John Clare. EnVR

Louvres. Les A. Murray. BMAP

Lov'd I not Honour more. Richard Lovelace. *See* Song: To Lucasta, Going to the War[re]s.

Love. "Anna Akhmatova," *Russian*. TCRP, *tr. by* Daniel Weissbort

Love. Al-Abbas ibn al-Ahnaf, *Arabic*. ArPe, *tr. by* Omar S. Pound

Love. Anacreon, *Greek*. AWP; BeJo; OBCVT; OBVE, *tr. by* Abraham Cowley

Love. Robert Browning. EnLoPo; GLoP *Fr.* Earth's Immortalities.

Love. Kelly Cherry. CRP

Love. Coleridge. GTBS-P; OBEV

Love. Roy Croft. BLPA; FaBoBe

  (Why Do I Love You?) PoToHe

Love. Samuel Daniel. CBLP *Fr.* Hymen's Triumph.

Love. Ralph Waldo Emerson.

  "Personal beauty is then first charming and itself when it dissatisfies us." ITG

Love. George Herbert. HoPM; Son

  (Love.) ESCV

Love. Thomas Hood. CBLP

Love. Francis Jammes, *French*. AWP, *tr. by* Jethro Bithell

Love. "Hugh MacDiarmid." CMoP; PoE

Love. Grace Paley. IFJA

Love. Mogwol Park, *Korean*. CKP, *tr. by* Jaihiun Kim

Love. George Peele. NOBE *Fr.* The Hunting of Cupid.

Love. Samuele Romanelli, *Hebrew*. TrJP, *tr. by* A. B. Rhine

Love. Sir Walter Scott. FaBoEE; OxAEP-2 *Fr.* The Lay of the Last Minstrel.

Love. Shakespeare. *See* Song: "Tell me where is fancy [*or* Fancie] bred."

Love. Edmund Spenser. *Fr.* Wood Of Error. AEP

Love. Jack Spicer. *See* Thing Language.

Love ("Thou art too hard for me in Love"). George Herbert. PeECV

Love. Thomas Traherne. GeHe

Love. Darwin T. Turner. SAGP

Love. *Unknown, Irish*. BIrV, *tr. by* John Montague

Love. *Unknown*. SoSe-8

Love. Elolongue Epanya Yondo, *French*. NegPo, *tr. by* Ellen Conroy Kennedy

Love a child is ever criing [*or* crying]. Song. Mary Sidney, Countess of Montgomery Wroth. KTR; NOSC *Fr.* Pamphilia to Amphilanthus.

Love a Life can show Below, The. Emily Dickinson. LoP

Love a woman? You're [*or* Y'are] an ass. Song. John Wilmot, 2d Earl of Rochester. GBL; NBLV; NOBL; NOSC; PeLV

Love Affair, A. Arnold Bennett. OxBTC

Love Affair 36. Jennifer Rankin. BMAP

Love alone to him is ever pleasing. (LL) Heart's Music. Thomas Campion. AAS; OBEV

Love among the Ruins. Robert Browning. EnVR; FHYEP; HAP; NAEL-2; NOBE; OAEL-2; OBEV; PoEL-5; SCGP

Love and a Question. Robert Frost. MoBS

Love and Age. Walter Savage Landor. GBL

Love and Age. Thomas Love Peacock. NOBVV; OBEV; OBNC *Fr.* Gryll Grange.

Love and Death. Byron. EBEV; NOBE

Love and Death. Catullus. AWP, *tr. by* H.W. Garrod *Fr.* Carmina.

Love and Death. John Frederick Nims. HoPM

Love and Debt Alike Troublesome. Sir John Suckling. CavPo

Love and Discipline. Henry Vaughan. GeHe

Love and Folly. Jean de La Fontaine, *French*. AWP, *tr. by* Bryant

Love and forgetting might have carried them. Two Look at Two. Robert Frost. MoAmPo

Love and Friendship. Emily Jane Brontë. EBVV; FP; InPK-6; LW; SDW

Love and How It Becomes Important in Our Day to Day Lives. Miller Williams. MT

Love and Jealousy. Robert Greene. CBLP

Love and Jealousy. Sir Philip Sidney. SiPS *Fr.* Arcadia.

Love and Jealousy. William Walsh. BoLoP

Love and Language. Louisa S. Guggenberger. NOBVV

Love and Liberation. John Hall Wheelock. MoAmPo

Love and Libery—A Cantata. Robert Burns. NOBRP; NOEC

  (Jolly Beggars, The.) PoEL-4

Drinking Song.

  ("Who have character to lose.") (LL) NBLV

"I am a Bard of no regard." PoE

"I Once was a maid, tho' I cannot tell when." NBLV; OxBoLi

  ("I once was a maid, though I cannot tell when.") RACG

"Poor Merry-andrew, in the [*or* a] neuk." OBCoV

"So sung the BARD—and Nansie's waws." PoE

Love And Life. John Wilmot, 2d Earl of Rochester. BoLoP; EnLoPo; GBL; HAP; NOBE; OBEV; PoEL-3

(Love and Life: A Song.) NOSC

  ("'Tis all that heaven allows.") (LL) LoP

Love and Life. Grace Buchanan Sherwood. NoP-4

Love and Life of Women, The. Night Café. Gottfried Benn, *German*. PFTM, *tr. by* Michael Hamburger

Love and Lust. Isaac Rosenberg. TrJP

Love and Murder. Roy Fuller. CBLP

Love and Philosophy. George Chapman. *Fr.* A Coronet for His Mistress Philosophy.

Love and Reason. Sir Philip Sidney. SiPS *Fr.* Arcadia.

Love And Sleep. Swinburne. APAD; BoLoP; CBLP; GLoP; GSo; LoP

Love and the Creatures. Virgil, *Latin*. EP, *tr. by* John Dryden

Love and the gentle heart are one same thing. Sonnet. Dante. AWP *Fr.* La Vita Nuova.

Love, and the Gout invade the idle Brain. Remedia Amoris. Elizabeth Thomas. LW

Love and the Lady Lagia, Guido and I. Sonnet: On the Detection of a False Friend. Guido Cavalcanti, *Italian*. AWP, *tr. by* D. G. Rossetti

Love, and the thoughts that yearn for human kind. (LL) Fears in Solitude. Coleridge. FHYEP; OBWP

Love and Time. Sir Walter Ralegh. SiPS

Love Armed. Aphra Behn. *See* Song: Love Armed.

Love at First Sight. Marlowe. NOBE *Fr.* Hero and Leander. AAS

"Love at first sight," some say, misnaming. At First Sight. Robert Graves. FaBoEE; OxBSP

Love at Large. Coventry Patmore. EBVV; NOBVV *Fr.* The Angel in the House.

Love at Sea. Swinburne. AWP

Love at the closing of our days. Last Love. Fyodor Ivanovich Tyutchev, *Russian*. LoP, *tr. by* Vladimir Nabokov; BoLoP

Love at the Door. Meleager, *Greek*. AWP, *tr. by* John Addington Symonds

Love at the lips was touch. To Earthward. Robert Frost. ImPo; MeMAP; MoAmPo; MoP; NOBA; NoAM; NoP-4; OxBA; RaBo; TAP; TRP

Love bade me welcome[: yet my soul drew back]. George Herbert. APAD; AWP; CABP; CH; ChIV-2; ClHu; EBEV; ESCV; EnlH; FHYEP; FMP; FSCP; FaBoVe; GEA; GeHe; HeIP-4; ITG; ImPo; InPK-6; MeLP; NAEL-1; NOBE; NOCV; NOSC; NoP-4; OAEL-1; OBEV; OBWVE; OxAEP-1; PBMP; PBRV; PoEL-2; PoLF; PoPoPo; SCV; SeCP; TFi; TOF; TrCP; WeW-3

Love Bit, The. Joel Oppenheimer. PoM

Love—bittersweet, irrepressible. Sappho, *Greek*. BoWoP, *tr. by* Willis Barnstone

Love, born in Greece, of late fled from his native place. Sonnet 8. Sir Philip Sidney. *Fr.* Astrophil and Stella. AAS; SiPS

Love, brave vertue's younger brother. Love's Horoscope. Richard Crashaw. MeLP

Love brought by night a vision to my bed. Lost Desire. Meleager, *Greek*. AWP, *tr. by* William M. Hardinge

Love brought me to a silent Grove. Upon Love. Robert Herrick. BeJo

Love built a stately house; where *Fortune* came. The World. George Herbert. GeHe; NOSC

Love buries itself in me, up to the hilt. (LL) A Renewal. James Merrill. OxBSP; PiM; SAGP; VCAP

Love, by sure proof I may call thee unkind. Sonnet 65. Sir Philip Sidney. Son *Fr.* Astrophil and Stella. AAS; SiPS

Love Calls Us to the Things of This World. Richard Wilbur. AmPP; CMoP; ColAP; HAP; HeIP-4; InPS-3; MoAmPo; NIP-4; NoAM; NoP-4; PoE; PoRA; Poetr; SAGP; TAP; TFi; UnPo; VCAP; VGW

Love Came By from the Riversmoke. Stephen Vincent Benét. MoAmPo *Fr.* John Brown's Body.

Love cast! Meleager, *Greek*. GrAn, *tr. by* Peter Whigham

Love Charm, The, *song*. *Unknown, Chippewa Indian*. STP, *tr. by* Jerome Rothenberg

Love-charm, A. Virgil, *Latin*. OBCVT, *tr. by* Abraham Fleming

Love Child—a Black Aesthetic. Everett Hoagland. BPo

Love comes back to his vacant dwelling,—. The Wanderer. Austin Dobson. PFE

Love Constraining to Obedience. William Cowper. NOCV *Fr.* Olney Hymns.

Love dances with yellow-haired April. Temptation. Dionysios Solomos. GrIP, *tr.* by Rae Dalvin *Fr.* The Free Beseiged.

Love, Death, and Art. Agnes Mary Frances Robinson. VWP

Love, Death and the Changing of the Seasons. Marilyn Hacker.

    Another Sunday. DeD

    Bloomingdale's. DeD

    (Bloomingdale's I.) CPO

    Future Conditional. CPO; DeD

    Gramercy Park. DeD

    Noces. DeD

    Sources. DeD

Love Deposed. Thomas Stanley. NOSC

Love. Desire is stronger than age. (LL) Bitto gives to Athena. Antipater of Sidon, *Greek.* GrAn; PGA, *tr.* by Kenneth Rexroth

Love Dies. George Meredith. *Fr.* Modern Love.

Love Divine, All Loves Excelling. Charles Wesley. NOCV

Love doth again. Sir Thomas Wyatt. SiPS

Love, drunk the other day, knocked at my breast. The Dual. Richard Lovelace. CaPo

Love Enthroned. Richard Lovelace. CaPo

Love Enthroned. D. G. Rossetti. OBNC *Fr.* The House of Life.

Love essential unto youth. Ninety. Mary Elizabeth Fullerton. CBAP

Love farewell I now discover. Mary Sidney, Countess of Montgomery Wroth. *Fr.* Urania.

Love Feast, The. W. H. Auden. OBCoV; PFE

Love fed Heliodora's fingernail and made. Meleager. HePo, *tr.* by Barbara Hughes Fowler *Fr.* I'll Twine White Violets. NIP-4, *tr.* by Goldwin Smith

Love flies with bow unstrung when Time appears. Love and Age. Walter Savage Landor. GBL

Love Flows from God. Mechthild von Magdeburg, *German.* WPOW, *tr.* by Lucy Menzies

Love Flows Not from My Liver. George Chapman. Son *Fr.* A Coronet for His Mistress Philosophy.

Love for a Hand. Karl Shapiro. CoAP; NYBP

Love for an Island. Phyllis Shand Allfrey. PBCV

Love for Enjoying. James Shirley. BeJo

Love from My Father. Carole C. Gregory Clemmons. PoBA

Love from The North. Christina Rossetti. CBLP

Love, give me leave to serve thee, and be wise. An Elegy. Thomas Randolph. BeJo; NOSC

Love God— / my mother said. The Will's Love. Besmilr Brigham. CrSp

Love-goddess, saviour / Of the sea-wrecked. *Unknown, Greek.* GrAn, *tr.* by Edward Lucie-Smith

Love growne proud with victory. Mary Sidney, Countess of Montgomery Wroth. *Fr.* Urania.

Love grows alone (though I my brain for counsel harrow). He Loves in Vain. Christian Hofmann von Hofmannswaldau, *German.* GePo, *tr.* by George C. Schoolfield

Love Guards [*or* Guides] the Roses of Thy Lips. Phillis 2. Thomas Lodge. AEP; NoSic; OBEV; Son *Fr.* Phyllis.

Love Has Eyes. William Forster. CBAP

Love has found out how to mix. Asclepiades, *Greek.* GrAn; PGA, *tr.* by Kenneth Rexroth

Love has gone and left me and the days are all alike. Ashes of Life. Edna St. Vincent Millay. FaBoBe

Love has its morn, its noon, its eve, and night. Too Late. Philip Bourke Marston. OBNC

Love has its secrets, joy has its revealings. The Love Secret. *Unknown, Arabic.* AWP, *tr.* by Wilfrid Scawen Blunt

Love has never read the Ave Maria. Immanuel di Roma, *Italian.* TrJP, *tr.* by J. Chotzner

Love has seven names. Hadewijch, *Dutch.* BoWoP, *tr.* by Willis Barnstone *and* Elene Kolb

Love has stained my body. Mirabai, *Rajasthani.* WPoS, *tr.* by Jane Hirshfield

Love has subjugated me. Hadewijch, *Flemish.* WPoS, *tr.* by Mother Columba Hart

Love hath so long possessed me for his own. Dante. AWP *Fr.* La Vita Nuova.

Love he tomorrow, who lov'd never. *Unknown.* AWP, *tr.* by Thomas Stanley *Fr.* The Vigil of Venus. GBL, *tr.* by Allen Tate; OBVE, *tr.* by Thomas Stanley

Love heeds no more the sighing of the wind. The Garden of Shadow. Ernest Christopher Dowson. OBNC

Love held a harp between his hands, and, lo! Love's Music. Philip Bourke Marston. GSo

Love her he doesn't but the thought he puts. John Berryman. FaBoMo *Fr.* Dream Songs.

Love, how thou'rt tired out with rhyme! Margaret Lucas Cavendish, Duchess of Newcastle. EnLoPo

Love, I am sick for thee, sick with an absolute grief. The Grief of Love. *Unknown, Arabic.* AWP, *tr.* by Wilfrid Scawen Blunt

Love, I have lain awake by night. J. V. Cunningham Gets Hung Up on a Dirty, of All Things, Joke. Henry Taylor. BXAP

Love, I have warmed the car. News from the House. Michael Dennis Browne. NYBP

Love. I, in mine, celebrate the love-choir. (LL) Ovid in the Third Reich. Geoffrey Hill. CABP; FaBoMo; HP; NoAM

Love I love whose lips I love, A. The Accomplices. Conrad Potter Aiken. NOBA

Love, I think, is a disease. Maghnas O Domhnaill. NOIV

Love, in a humour, played the prodigal. Michael Drayton. NoSic *Fr.* Idea.

Love in a Life. Robert Browning. CBLP; EBVVPR; FHYEP; NOBE; NOBVV; OBNC

Love in a Storm. Thomas Moore. Ro *Fr.* The Poetical Works of the Late Thomas Little Esq.

Love in a Village. Isaac Bickerstaffe.

    "There was a jolly miller once." EBEvV; LB; OxNR

Love in a Warm Room in Winter. James Wright. OBAL

Love in America. Marianne Moore. AiP

Love in Exile. Mathilde Blind.

    "Dost thou remember ever, for my sake." OBNC

    "I charge you, O winds of the West, O." TrJP

Love in fantastic [*or* fantastique] triumph sat [*or* sate *or* satt]. Song: Love Armed. Aphra Behn. NALW; NOBE; NOSC; OBEV; OxAEP-1; Poetr; WPE; WeW-3 *Fr.* Abdelazer.

Love in her sunny eyes does basking play. The Change. Abraham Cowley. CBLP; MeLP; SeCP *Fr.* The Mistress.

Love in July. Ivan V. Lalic, *Serbo-Croatian.* HSix, *tr.* by Charles Simic

Love in Labrador. Carl Sandburg. VGW

Love in May. Jean Passerat, *French.* AWP, *tr.* by Andrew Lang

Love in Mayfair. May Probyn. VWP

Love in my bosom[e] like a bee. Rosalind's [*or* Rosalynd's] Madrigal[l]. Thomas Lodge. CBLP; NOBE; NoSic; OBEV; PoEL-2; SCGP *Fr.* Rosalynde; *or* Euphues' Golden Legacy.

Love in silence shall. Meleager, *Greek.* GrAn, *tr.* by Peter Whigham

Love in the Classroom. Al Zolynas. BLT; EC3; LTA

Love in the Museum. Adrienne Rich. NYBP

Love in the peaceful u.s.a. Love U.S.A. Kathleen Spivack. BoWoP; LW

Love in the Valley. George Meredith. EBVV; EnVR; NOBE; OAEL-2; OBEV

    "This I may know: her dressing and undressing." EP

Love in Vain. Robert Johnson. UnPo

Love Indestructible. Sir Walter Ralegh. LBC

Love Indestructible. Robert Southey. OBNC *Fr.* The Curse of Kehama.

Love in's first infant days had's wardrobe full. To His Scornful Mistress. William Hammond. CBLP

Love: Intimacy. Charles Kenneth Williams. CBLP

Love is a circle that doth restless[e] move. Love What It Is. Robert Herrick. FaBoEE; GBL

Love is a flame that burns with sacred fire. George Marion McClellan. AAP

Love is a funny thing. *Unknown.* TTY

Love is a great thing, a great good in every way; it alone lightens what is. Thomas À Kempis. ITG, *tr.* by Stephen Mitchell *Fr.* The Imitation of Christ.

Love is a green girl. Song. Michael Stillman. TLR

Love Is a Keeper of Swans. Humbert Wolfe. MoBrPo

Love Is a Law. John Webster *and* William Rowley. GBL *Fr.* The Thracian Wonder.

Love is a place. E. E. Cummings. FaBoEE

    ("(skilfully curled) / all worlds.") (LL) PiM

Love is a region full of fires. A Description of Love. Sir John Beaumont. NOSC

Love is a secret feeding fire that gives all creatures. *Unknown.* OxBSP

Love is a sickness full of woes. Love. Samuel Daniel. CBLP; NOBE; OBEV; PoEL-2 *Fr.* Hymen's Triumph.

Love is a twin to death; it makes my senses dead. "Angelus Silesius." GePo, *tr.* by George C. Schoolfield *Fr.* The Cherubical Wanderer.

Love is a universal migraine. Symptoms Of Love. Robert Graves. BoLoP; LoP

Love is a word, another kind of open. Audre Lorde. *See* Coal.

"Love is all / Unsatisfied ." Crazy Jane on the Day of Judgment. W. B. Yeats. CMoP

Love is and was my Lord and King. My Lord and King. Tennyson. EBVVPR; NOBE; NOCV; OBEV; OBNC; PeECV *Fr.* In Memoriam A. H. H.

Love—is anterior to Life. Emily Dickinson. CBLP

Love is begot by fancy, bred. George, Baron Lansdowne Granville. BoLoP

Love is believable. "Alta." CrSp *Fr.* 7 : 3.

Love is best. (LL) Love among the Ruins. Robert Browning. EnVR; FHYEP; HAP; NAEL-2; NOBE; OAEL-2; OBEV; PoEL-5; SCGP

Love Is Bitter. *Unknown.* PeSA

Love is boring and passe, all the old baggage. Blond Bombshell. Lynn Emanuel. NAmP90

Love Is Enough. William Morris.
    "Love is enough: though the World be a-waning." GLoP; OBEV; PoEL-5

Love is gone, gone is my love. The Silence of Love. Yong-un Han, *Korean.* CKP, *tr. by* Jaihiun Kim

Love Is Kind. Benjamin Keech. PoToHe

Love is Life. Richard Rolle of Hampole. PoEL-1 *Fr.* A Song of the Love of Jesus. PoEL-1

Love Is Life and Death. Georg Rudolph Weckherlin, *German.* GePo, *tr. by* George C. Schoolfield

Love is like butter, Evans mused, and stuck. Pendydd. Kingsley Amis. NOBL *Fr.* The Evans Country.

Love is like the lion's tooth. (LL) Crazy Jane Grown Old Looks at the Dancers. W. B. Yeats. CMoP; EBEV

Love is like the wild rose-briar. Love and Friendship. Emily Jane Brontë. EBVV; FP; InPK-6; LW; SDW

Love is Love. Sir Edward Dyer. APAD
    ("Lowest trees haue topps, the ante her gall, The.") GEA

Love is more thicker than forget. E. E. Cummings. ITG

Love is no more. Amor Vincit Omnia. Edgar Bowers. VCAP

Love is not a profession. Is/Not / Not. Margaret Atwood. LW

Love Is Not All. Edna St. Vincent Millay. Son *Fr.* Fatal Interview.

Love is not all: it is not meat nor drink. Edna St. Vincent Millay. CMoP; GSo; HAP; HeIP-4; InPS-3; MeMAP; NoAM; OxBA; TAP
    ("Love is not all: it is not meat or drink.") SAGP

Love is not concerned. Alice Walker. CrSp; SAGP

Love is not just a function of the eyes. Argentarius, *Greek.* GrAn; LoP, *tr. by* Fleur Adcock

"Love is not Love." Marie Ponsot. NMM-2

Love is not mocked whatever use. Jack Spicer. *Fr.* Graphemics. VGW

Love is not worth so much. Coda. James Tate. AmPA; NYBP

Love is soft, love is swete, love is goed sware. *Unknown.* MiEL

Love is soft, love is swete, love is good sware. Love Is Wele, [*or* Weal] Love Is Wo. *Unknown.* CBLP

Love—is that later Thing than Death. Emily Dickinson. LoP

Love Is That Orbit. George Henry Boker. Son

Love is the center and circumference. What Love Is. Ella Wheeler Wilcox. PWR

Love is the lesson which the Lord us taught. (LL) Sonnet 68: "Most glorious Lord of Life that on this day." Edmund Spenser. AEP; ChIV-2; GSo; HAP; InPS-3; NAEL-1; NOBE; NOCV; NoP-4; NoSic; OBEV; PeECV; PoE; Son

Love is the passion which endureth. What is Love? Mary Lamb. Ro *Fr.* The Keepsake for 1829 (1828).

Love is the peace, whereto all thoughts do[e] strive. Sonnet: "Love is the peace, whereto all thoughts do strive." Greville Fulke. AAS; NoSic *Fr.* Caelica.

Love is the plant of peace and most precious of virtues. Et Incarnatus Est. William Langland. NOBE *Fr.* The Vision of Piers Plowman.

Love is too young to know what conscience is. Sonnet 151. Shakespeare. EBEV; HeIP-4; NoSic; OxAEP-1; PoE; PoEL-2 *Fr.* Sonnets.

Love Is Wele, [*or* Weal] Love Is Wo. *Unknown.* CBLP

Love is what lacks then: but what does it mean to you? A Remonstrance. James Kenneth Stephen. NOBVV

Love Isn't. Patricia Parker. NMM-2

Love, it is night. The orb of day. The Passionate Professor. Bert Leston Taylor. NBLV

Love, it was good to talk to you tonight. Rondeau after a Transatlantic Telephone Call. Marilyn Hacker. ColAP; NoAM

Love itself shall slumber on. (LL) To————: "Music, when soft voices die." Shelley. AWP; CBLP; CH; EBEvV; FHYEP; GTBS-P; HeIP-4; ImPo; LBC; LoP; NOBE; OBEV; OBNC; OxAEP-2; OxBSP; PFE; PoEL-4; Poetr; TFi

Love-Joy. George Herbert. OAEL-1

Love leave to urge, thou know'st thou hast the hand. Sonnet 7. Mary Sidney, Countess of Montgomery Wroth. Son *Fr.* Pamphilia to Amphilanthus.

Love-Lesson, A. Clément Marot, *French.* AWP, *tr. by* Leigh Hunt

Love, let us live as we have lived, nor lose. To His Wife. Ausonius, *Latin.* OxBM, *tr. by* Helen Waddell

Love Letter. W. H. Auden. CBLP

Love Letter. Louise Bennett. HCP

Love Letter. Carole C. Gregory Clemmons. BlSi

Love Letter. Sylvia Plath. LW; NOBA

Love Letter. Karl Shapiro. *See* V-Letter.

Love-letter, A. Mary E. Tucker. CBWP-1

Love-Letter, A: Ruth Arbeiter to Major Paul Maxwell. Anne Stevenson. OxBM *Fr.* Correspondences.

Love-Letter-Burning. Daniel Hall. NoP-4

Love Letter to Elizabeth Thatcher, A. Thomas Thatcher. SCAP

Love Letters. Josephine D. Henderson Heard. CBWP-4

Love Letters to Her Who Lives [Alas!] Away. Nell Altizer.
    Sonnet 2: "My own heart let me have. More pity on." FFC

Love Lies Here. Walter De la Mare. LBC

Love-Life. Hugo Williams. CBLP

Love like a heavy wave. Meleager, *Greek.* InMo, *tr. by* Sam Hamill

Love, like a mountain-wind upon an oak. Sappho, *Greek.* AWP, *tr. by* William Ellery Leonard

Love lives beyond. Loves Lives Beyond the Tomb. John Clare. FHYEP; NoP-4

Love, loneliness and the face of death. (LL) Pain. Edith Södergran, *Swedish.* PBWP; WPOW, *tr. by* Jaakko A. Ahokas

Love long dormant showing itself. Palais des Arts. Louise Glück. VCAP

Love-lorn microbe met by chance, A. The Microbe's Serenade. George Ade. OBAL

Love, love. What His Friend Said, Teasing the Man in Love. Milaipperun Kantan, *Tamil.* PLW, *tr. by* A. K. Ramanujan

Love, love, a lily's my care. Words for the Wind. Theodore Roethke. CoAP; NOBA

Love, love today, my dear. Song. Charlotte Mew. MoBrPo

Love ("Love was before the light began"). *Unknown.* AWP *Fr.* The Thousand and One Nights.

Love, love! What nonsense it is. Natalya Gorbanevskaya, *Russian.* WPOW, *tr. by* Daniel Weissbort

Love, love, what wilt thou with this heart of mine? Rondel. Jean Froissart. AWP, *tr. by* Longfellow

Love-Lowe. Alan Bold. FaBoTC

Love Made in the First Age[: To Chloris]. Richard Lovelace. BeJo; CaPo; NAEL-1; OAEL-1; SeCP

Love Making. James Tate. SPE

Love may return, but never lover. (LL) Of Beauty. Sir Richard Fanshawe. BoLoP; GBL; OxBSP

Love, Maybe. Audre Lorde. Poetr

Love Me. Maria Wine, *Swedish.* PBWP, *tr. by* Nadia Christensen

Love me at last, or if you will not. Alice Corbin. LW

Love me broughte. *Unknown.* MiEL

(*Love me for ever!*). (LL) Love. Robert Browning. EnLoPo; GLoP

"Love me, for I love you"—and answer me. Christina Rossetti. Son *Fr.* Monna Innominata. BWW

Love Me - I Love You. Christina Rossetti. BoTP

Love Me Little, Love Me Long. Robert Herrick. BLPA; CBLP; CaPo; FaBoBe; SCGP

Love me little, love me long! *Unknown.* BLPA; CBLP; FaBoBe
    ("Is the burden of my song.") (LL) NoP-4

Love me, Love me, I cried to the rocks and the trees. Stevie Smith. OxBSP

Love me no more, now let the god depart. Edna St. Vincent Millay. HeIP-4

Love Me Not [for Comely Grace]. *Unknown.* CH; GTBS-P; ImPo; OBEV; OxBSP; PoLF

Love me, O Love. Sir Philip Sidney. HeIP-4

Love me, Sweet, with all thou art. A Man's Requirements. Elizabeth Barrett Browning. RACG

Love me with the left hand. The Light Woman's Song. Judith Johnson Sherwin. TAP

Love Medicine, A. Louise Erdrich. HATNAP

Love, meet me in the green glen. Meet Me in the Green Glen. John Clare. SCGP

Love mocks us all. Then cast aside. 1.33: Albi, Ne Doleas. Horace. AWP, *tr. by* Austin Dobson *Fr.* Odes.

Love much. Earth has enough of bitter in it. Ella Wheeler Wilcox. PoToHe

"Love my heart for an hour, but my bone for a day." Street Song. Dame Edith Sitwell. CMoP

Love Necessitates. Eugene B. Redmond. ISC

Love, never conquered in battle. Chorus. Sophocles, *Greek.* PiM, *tr. by* Robert Fagles; GrIP *Fr.* Antigone. NAWM-1, *tr. by* Robert Fagles

Love never lets you go. (LL) An Ever-Fixed Mark. Kingsley Amis. MoP; NoAM

Love not a loveliness too much. Ownership. Lizette Woodworth Reese. MoAmPo

Love not me for comely grace. Love Me Not [for Comely Grace].
  Unknown. CH; GTBS-P; ImPo; OBEV; OxBSP; PoLF
Love Notes. Jennifer Strauss. BMAP
Love now no fire hath left him. Out of the Italain. Giovanni Battista
  Marino, *Italian.* OBVE, *tr. by* Richard Crashaw
Love of a woman, The. Air: "The Love of a Woman." Robert Creeley.
  VCAP; VGW
Love of Fame, the Universal Passion. Edward Young. OBSV
Love of Hell, The. Abraham Burstein. TrJP
Love of King David and Fair Bethsabe. George Peele. ChIV-1
  Bethsabe's Song. GBL; NOBE; NoSic; OxBSP; OxBoLi; PoEL-2; RB
  (Bathsheba's Song.) ImPo
  (Bethsabe Bathing.)
  ("Hot sun, cool fire, tempered with sweet air.") KSG; NoP-4
Love of Moses for his race soon found, The. Flight into Midian. Frances
  Ellen Watkins Harper. AAP *Fr.* Moses: A Story of the Nile.
Love of my life, you. Vespers: Parousia. Louise Glück. PuP-17
Love of Nature. Mark Akenside. NOEC *Fr.* The Pleasure of Imagination.
Love of praise, howe'er concealed by art, The. Edward Young. *Fr.* Love of
  Fame, the Universal Passion. OBSV
Love of the Flesh, The. Janet Holmes. BAP-94
Love of the Quartz Pebble, The. Vasco [*or* Vasko] Popa. PoSu, *tr. by*
  Anne Pennington *Fr.* The Quartz Pebble.
Love, of this clearest, frailest Glass. In a Glass-Window for Inconstancy.
  Edward Herbert, 1st Baron Herbert of Cherbury. OxBSP; SeCP
Love of Travellers, The. Angela Jackson. PuP-14
Love of Water Faucets, The. David James. CMAP
Love, oh love, oh careless love. Careless Love. *Unknown.* AS; UnPo
Love on a day (wise poets tell). How Violets Came Blue. Robert Herrick.
  BeJo; CaPo; TTTS
Love On the Farm. D. H. Lawrence. CABP; CBLP; CMoP; MoBrPo;
  NAEL-2; NoAM; NoP-4; SAGP; SCGP
Love (1). George Herbert. GeHe; HoPM; Son
Love one another, but make not a bond of love. Kahlil Gibran. OxBM *Fr.*
  The Prophet.
Love only reading unto me this art. (LL) Sonnet 28: "You that with
  allegory's curious frame." Sir Philip Sidney. NoSic; OAEL-1
Love opened a vista rare with stars. Love's Vista. Henrietta Cordelia Ray.
  CBWP-3
Love or Fame. Caroline Lindsay. VWP
Love, or hate: a woman knows no mind. Sententiae: Maxims. Publilius
  Syrus, *Latin.* OBCVT, *tr. by* Gilbert Highet
Love Overgrows a Rock. Eric Roach. PBCV
Love Palpable. Robert Herrick. CavPo
Love plays a lute, and Thought an organ grand. The Two Musicians.
  Henrietta Cordelia Ray. CBWP-3
Love Poem, A. John Ashbery. HCAP
Love Poem. Roque Dalton, *Spanish.* AF, *tr. by* Richard Schaaf
Love Poem, The. Andrew Elliott. PNI
Love-Poem. Fêng Mêng-lung, *Chinese.* ChiP, *tr. by* Arthur Waley
Love Poem. John Forbes. BMAP
Love Poem: "Greyish yellow is the color of the dust." Meir Wieseltier,
  Hebrew. IP, *tr. by* Warren Bargad *and* Stanley F. Chyet
Love Poem. August Kleinzahler. MoNo
Love Poem. John Logan. CAPP-1
Love Poem. Audre Lorde. GLP; NoAM
  ("Speak earth and bless me.") CPO
Love Poem: "My clumsiest dear, whose hands shipwreck vases." John
  Frederick Nims. HoPM; InPK-6; SAGP
Love Poem. Linda Pastan. NIP-4
Love Poem. Norman Henry, II Pritchard. GT
Love Poem: "Rain smell comes with the wind." Leslie Marmon Silko.
  UnPo; VoR
Love-Poem: "Yours is the face that the earth turns to me." Kathleen Jessie
  Raine. LW; MoBrPo
Love Poem for a Wife, 2. A. K. Ramanujan. OMIP
Love Poem for My Country, A. Frank Mkalawile Chipasula. HBAPE
Love Poem for Three for Kaye & Me. Gregory Corso. PmAP
Love Poem No. 2. Yona Wallach, *Hebrew.* IP, *tr. by* Warren Bargad *and*
  Stanley F. Chyet
Love Poems. Jack Spicer.
  6. FTOS
Love Poems of Marichiko, The. Kenneth Rexroth.
  "As I came from the." APSN
  "As the wheel follows the hoof." APSN
  "Come to me, as you come." APSN
  "Did you take me because you loved me?" APSN
  "Every morning, I / Wake alone, dreaming my." APSN

"Fires / Burn in my heart." APSN
"Frost covers the reeds of the marsh." APSN
"Half in a dream." APSN
"How long, long ago." APSN
"How many lives ago." APSN
"I am sad this morning." APSN
"I cannot forget / The perfumed dusk inside the." APSN
"I hold your head tight between." APSN
"I pass the day tense, day-." APSN
"I scream as you bite." APSN
"I sit at my desk." APSN
"I wish I could be." APSN
"If I thought I could get away." APSN
"In the park a crow awakes." APSN
"It is the time when." APSN
"Just us. / In our little house." APSN
"Let us sleep together here tonight." APSN
"Lying in the meadow, open to you." APSN
"Night without end. Loneliness." APSN
"Now the fireflies of our youth." APSN
"Oh the anguish of these secret meetings." APSN
"On the bridges / And along the banks." APSN
"Once I shone afar like a." APSN
"Scorched with love, the cicada." APSN
"Some day in six inches of." APSN
"Spring is early this year." APSN
"This flesh you have loved." APSN
"Two flowers in a letter." APSN
"Uguisu sleeps in the bamboo grove, The." APSN
"Who is there? Me." APSN
"Without me you can only." APSN
"You ask me what I thought about." APSN; PiM
"You wake me, / Part my thighs, and kiss me." APSN
"Your tongue thrums and moves." APSN
Love poems they read. Uses of Poetry. Winfield Townley Scott. PoA
Love poured her beauty into my warm veins. (LL) Fragment of a Sonnet.
  Pierre de Ronsard, *French.* AWP; OBVE, *tr. by* Keats
Love-prone Asclepias with eyes like a summer's day. Meleager. HePo, *tr.*
  by Barbara Hughes Fowler *Fr.* I'll Twine White Violets. NIP-4, *tr. by*
  Goldwin Smith
Love ran with me, then walk'd, then sate. Walter Savage Landor. CBLP
Love, Reason, Hate, did once bespeak. A Barley-Break. Sir John Suckling.
  CaPo; CavPo
Love Redeemed. "William Baylebridge."
  "Quiet moon, immaculate of face, The." CBAP
Love Rejected. Lucille Clifton. BPo
Love rises up some days. "Michael Field." VWP
Love Secret, The. *Unknown, Arabic.* AWP, *tr. by* Wilfrid Scawen Blunt
"Love seeketh not Itself to please." The Clod and [*or* &] the Pebble.
  William Blake. APAD; EnLoPo; FHYEP; GLoP; InPS-3; NAEL-2;
  NOBE; NoP-4; OBNC; OxAEP-2; OxBSP; PoE; RB; Ro; SCGP; SCV;
  TFi *Fr.* Songs of Experience.
Love Serviceable. Coventry Patmore. EnLoPo *Fr.* The Angel in the
  House.
Love set you going like a fat gold watch. Morning Song. Sylvia Plath.
  BoWoP; ColAP; HCAP; HeIP-4; InPK-6; InPS-3; LCAP-2; NAAL-2;
  NIP-4; NOBA; NTP; NoP-4; PoPoPo; SAGP; VCAP
Love Should Grow Up like a Wild Iris in the Fields. Susan Griffin. CrSp
Love should intend realities: good-bye! Exit Line. John Ciardi. WeW-3
Love: Shyness. Charles Kenneth Williams. CBLP
Love signed the contract blithe and leal. Epigram. John Swanwick
  Drennan. BIrV
Love Sleeping. Plato, *Greek.* AWP; FaBoEE, *tr. by* Thomas Stanley
Love so alike, that none do slacken, none can die. (LL) The
  Good[-]Morrow. Donne. AWP; BoLoP; CBLP; ClHu; EBEV; ESCV;
  EnLoPo; FHYEP; FaBoBe; FaBoVe; FMP; FSCP; HoPM; ImPo; InPS-3;
  ITG; LoP; MeLP; NAEL-1; NAWM-1; NOSC; OAEL-1; OxAEP-1; PoE;
  PoEL-2; PoRA; Poetr; SCV; SeCP; SoSe-8; TFi
Love Somebody, Yes I Do. *Unknown.* AS
Love-song: "Beautiful, delicate bright gazelle, The." Walter James Turner.
  OBMV
Love Song: "Beautiful is she, this woman." *Unknown, Haida.* AWP, *tr. by*
  Constance Lindsay Skinner *Fr.* Three Songs from the Haida.
Love Song: "By the fierce flames of love I'm in a sad taking." Royall
  Tyler. TAP
Love Song: "Come to me in the night—we shall sleep closely together [*or*
  Let us sleep entwined]." Else Lasker-Schüler, *German.* BoWoP; TrJP,
  tr. by Michael Gillespie

Love Song: "Do not love me, my friend." Flavien Ranaivo, *French*. PBA

(Common Lover's Song, The.) NegPo, *tr.* by Ellen Conroy Kennedy

("Do not love me, cousin.") NegPo, *tr.* by Ellen Conroy Kennedy

Love Song: "Early I rose." *Unknown, Papago Indian*. AWP, *tr.* by Mary Austin

Love Song: "For what as easy." W. H. Auden. PeLV *Fr.* Five Songs.

Love Song ("I am a bunch of red roses"). *Unknown, Turkish*. BoWoP, *tr.* by Reza Baraheni *and* Zahra-Soltan Shokoohtaezeh

Love Song: "I lie here thinking of you." William Carlos Williams. Poetr

Love Song: "I passed by the house of the young man who loves me." *Unknown, Egyptian*. TTY, *tr.* by J. E. Manchip White

Love Song: "I will walk into some one's dwelling." *Unknown, Ojibwa Native American*. APN-2, *tr.* by Henry Rowe Schoolcraft

Love Song: "Let my sweet song be pleasing unto Thee." Judah Halevi, *Hebrew*. TrJP, *tr.* by Nina Davis Salaman

Love Song: "Like pain of fire runs down my body my love to you, my dear!" *Unknown*. APN-2, *tr.* by Franz Boas *Fr.* Songs of the Kwakiutl Indians.

Love Song: "Little sycamore, The." *Unknown, Egyptian*. TTY, *tr.* by J. E. Manchip White

Love-Song: "Little wild birds have come flying, The." *Unknown, Russian*. AWP, *tr.* by W. R. S. Ralston

Love Song: "Long closed door, oh open it again, The." Judah Al-Harizi, *Hebrew*. TrJP, *tr.* by Emma Lazarus

Love Song: "My boat sails downstream." *Unknown, Egyptian*. TTY, *tr.* by J. E. Manchip White

Love Song: "My love is a lotus blossom." *Unknown, Egyptian*. TTY, *tr.* by J. E. Manchip White

Love Song: "My loved one is unique, without a peer." *Unknown, Egyptian*. TTY, *tr.* by J. E. Manchip White

Love Song: "On the hill tops I visit the snares." *Unknown, Maori*. PeNZ, *tr.* by Margaret Orbell

Love Song: "One with eyes the fairest." Euripides. AWP *Fr.* The Cyclops.

Love Song: "Our roofs are adjacent". *Unknown, Turkish*. BoWoP, *tr.* by Reza Baraheni *and* Zahra-Soltan Shokoohtaezeh

Love Song: "Out of the blackthorn hedges." Ivor Gurney. EnLoPo

Love Song: "See'st thou o'er my shoulders falling." Judah Halevi, *Hebrew*. TrJP, *tr.* by Emma Lazarus

Love Song: "She is a reed swaying in blue." Earle Thompson. HATNAP

Love Song: "Sweep the house clean." William Carlos Williams. LoP; MoAmPo; SAmP

Love Song: "That haughty tyranny of thine." Luís De León, *Spanish*. TrJP, *tr.* by Thomas Walsh

Love Song: "There is a strong wall about me to protect me." Mary Carolyn Davies. LW

Love Song: "Though to think / Rejoiceth me." Margot Ruddock. OBMV

Love Song: "Tiny children." Yityangu Ejong, *Yindjibarndi*. CBAP, *tr.* by Frank Wordick

Love Song: "Your handkerchief should be blue." *Unknown, Turkish*. BoWoP, *tr.* by Reza Baraheni *and* Zahra-Soltan Shokoohtaezeh

Love Song: "You've got nice knees." Gavin Ewart. OxBTC

Love Song. Antonin Bartusek, *German*. CEEP, *tr.* by Ewald Osers

Love-Song. Else Lasker-Schüler, *German*. TrJP, *tr.* by Jethro Bithell

Love Song. Rilke, *German*.

"Everything that touches us, me and you." ITG, *tr.* by Stephen Mitchell

Love Song. *Unknown, Bagirmi*. BoWoP, *tr.* by H. Gaden

Love Song During Riot with Many Voices. Lynda Hull. NAmP90

Love Song: First Version, 1915, A. William Carlos Williams. Poetr

Love Song for Difficult Times. Maria Elena Cruz Varela, *Spanish*. VCWP, *tr.* by Mairym Cruz-Bernal *and* Deborah Digges

Love Song: I and Thou. Alan Dugan. HoPM; InPK-6; MoP; NoAM

Love Song of J. Alfred Prufrock, The. T. S. Eliot. AWP; AmPP; CMoP; ClHu; ColAP; EBEV; EBEvV; HAP; HeIP-4; HoPM; InPK-6; InPS-3; LiTM; MoAmPo; MoP; NAAL-2; NAEL-2; NAWM-2; NOBA; NOBE; NoAM; NoP-4; OAEL-2; OxAEP-2; OxBTC; PFE; PoA; PoE; PoPoPo; PoRA; Poetr; SAGP; SoSe-8; TAP; TFi; TRP; TwCP; WeW-3

("Let us go and make our visit.") (LL) PiM

"Let us go then, you and I." UV

Love Song of J. Alfred Prufrock, The. J. Walker. BXAP; PeLi

Love-Song of the Water Carriers. *Unknown, Zulu*. PeSA

Love Song of Tommo Frogley. Roger Crawford. UV

Love Song to Eohippus. Peter Viereck. MoAmPo

Love Song to King Shu-Suen. Kubatum, *Sumerian*. WPOW, *tr.* by Thorkild Jacobsen

Love Songs. Mina Loy. VGW; WPE

Love-Songs, at Once Tender and Informative. Samuel Hoffenstein. OBAL

"Your little hands." NBLV; OBCoV; TrJP

Love Songs of Corca Bascinn. James Liddy.

History. CIP-2

Love Sonnet. John Updike. Son

Love Sonnets. Zora Cross. CBAP

Love Sonnets of Proteus, The. Wilfrid Scawen Blunt.

As To His Choice of Her. GSo; Son

Depreciating Her Beauty. OBMV

St. Valentine's Day. EnLoPo

("Today, all day, I rode upon the Down.") GLoP

Woman with a Past, A. Son

Love steered my course, while yet the sun rode high. Of Fiammetta Singing. Giovanni Boccaccio. AWP *Fr.* Sonnets.

Love still a boy, and oft a wanton is. Sonnet 74. Sir Philip Sidney. Son *Fr.* Astrophil and Stella. AAS; SiPS

Love still has something of the sea. Song: Love Still Has Something of the Sea. Sir Charles Sedley. GBL; NOBE; OxAEP-1

Love Story, A. Robert Graves. CMoP; FaBoTw; NAEL-2

Love, strong as Death, is dead. An End. Christina Rossetti. CBLP; GBL; SDW

Love supreme, a love supreme, A. (LL) Dear John, Dear Coltrane. Michael S. Harper. AmPA; ISC; NIP-4; VCAP

Love-Talker, The. "Ethna Carbery." CH; WPE

Love that breeds, The. Unbosoming. "Michael Field." CPO; VWP

Love, That Doth Reign [*or* Raine] and Live Within My Thought. Complaint of a Lover Rebuked. Petrarch. AAS; GSo; HeIP-4; NAEL-1; NoP-4; OAEL-1; OBVE, *tr.* by the Earl of Surrey *Fr.* Sonnets to Laura.

Love, that drained her, drained him she'd loved, though each. The Turtle Dove. Geoffrey Hill. FaBoTw

"Love that I hae chosen, The." The Lawlands o' Holland. *Unknown*. CH

Love that is alone with love. Love and Language. Louisa S. Guggenberger. NOBVV

Love that is hoarded, moulds at last. Song. Harold C. Sandall. PoToHe

Love that is not pardoned, A. Doors. Tom Clark. CoAmPo

Love that liveth and reigneth in my thought. Complaint of a Lover Rebuked. Petrarch. AWP; PFE; SiPS; Son, *tr.* by the Earl of Surrey

Love that rose on stronger wings, The. Tennyson. EBVVPR *Fr.* In Memoriam A. H. H.

Love That's Pure, Itself Disdaining. Johann A. Gruber, *German*. AH, *tr.* by Sheema Z. Buehne

Love / The archipelago. Of the Aegean. Odysseus Elytis. GrIP, *tr.* by Kimon Friar *Fr.* Orientations.

Love the beautiful. Every Day. Felix Mendelssohn. CTV

Love, the delight of all well-thinking minds. Greville Fulke. GBL *Fr.* Caelica.

Love, the great master of true eloquence. Torquato Tasso, *Italian*. AWP, *tr.* by John Hermann Merivale

Love, the Light-Giver [*or* To Tommaso de' Cavalieri]. Michelangelo Buonarroti, *Italian*. AWP, *tr.* by John Addington Symonds. LoP

Love, the sole Goddess fit for swearing by. Friday Night. Robert Graves. LoP

Love the unholy, that frost which quickens summer. Didactic Sonnet. Melvin Walker La Follette. PoA

Love the Wild Swan. Robinson Jeffers. MoAmPo; NoAM; Son

Love thee? Yes, I'm sure I love thee. The City by the Sea. Josephine D. Henderson Heard. CBWP-4

Love, thou art Absolute sole lord. Hymn to Saint Teresa. Richard Crashaw. EBEV; ESCV; GeHe; HAP; MeLP; NOSC; NoP-4 *Fr.* A Hymn to the Name and Hono[u]r of the Admirable Saint[e] T[h]eresa. NOBE; OBEV; PoEL-2

Love—thou art high. Emily Dickinson. LoP

Love thou but me; all other realms I'll give thee. Tess. Vita Sackville-West. WPN

Love Thy Neighbour. D. H. Lawrence. ChIV-2

Love to be saved for it, proffered to, spent on! (LL) Misconceptions. Robert Browning. EnVR; OBEV

Love, to give law unto his subject hearts. Prologue. Sir Thomas Wyatt. ChIV-1 *Fr.* Penitential Psalms.

Love to *Hermes, Aphrodite* the Friend, The. (LL) To the Fair Clarinda, Who Made Love to Me, Imagin'd More Than Woman. Aphra Behn. CABP; CPO; EP; NALW; NoP-4; PEW

Love Token, A. Adelaide Anne Procter. SDW

Love? Too dangerous. Fourth Wish. Alberta Turner. LCAP-2

Love Triumphant. Dryden.

"As, when some treasurer lays down the stick." NOSC

Prologue to "Love Triumphant." OxBoLi

Love tunes my Heart just to my strings. (LL) Love. Abraham Cowley, *after the Greek of* Anacreon. AWP; BeJo; OBVE

Love, 20 Cents the First Quarter Mile. Kenneth Fearing. HAP

Love twists. The Pressures. Imamu Amiri Baraka. BPo

Love (2). George Herbert. GeHe; Son

Love U.S.A. Kathleen Spivack. BoWoP; LW

Love Under the Republicans (Or Democrats). Ogden Nash. PBMP

Love Unexpressed. Constance Fenimore Woolson. APN-2

Love Unfeigned. Chaucer. NOBE; OBEV *Fr.* Troilus and Criseyde [*or* Criseide]. EnVB

Love unreturn[e]d, howe'er [how ere] the flame. Constancy[e]. Sidney Godolphin. BeJo; NOSC

Love Versus Learning. Constance Naden. VWP

Love was alone with love. And there was nothing I could do about it. Love was. Matter. Carla Harryman. FTOS

Love was before the light began. Love ("Love was before the light began"). *Unknown.* AWP *Fr.* The Thousand and One Nights.

Love was holy hunger, and it kept my soul narrow. A Married Romantic. Olafs Stumbrs. CEEP

Love, we curve downwards, we are set to night. After Midsummer. Edith Jay Scovell. OxBTC

Love we define for ourselves, The. Prothalamion. Michael Ryan. AmPA

Love? We should smother it. Aspects of Love. Ruth Miller. LW *Fr.* Aspects of Love.

Love we thought would never stop, The. Ending. Gavin Ewart. NBLV; OxBSP; SoSe-8

Love, Weeping, Laid This Song. Lizette Woodworth Reese. APN-2

Love What It Is. Robert Herrick. FaBoEE; GBL

Love Which Frees. Gloria Fuertes, *Spanish.* WPOW, *tr. by* Philip Levine

Love, which is least sure and most dared, the pure, keen. Canzone. Peyton Houston. *Fr.* Sonnet Variations. Son

Love who will, for I'll love none. William Browne. NOSC

Love, Whose Month Was Ever May. Ulrich von Liechtenstein, *German.* AWP, *tr. by* Jethro Bithell

Love, why have you led me here. The Young Cordwainer. Robert Graves. MoBS

Love will expire; the gay, the happy dream. Procrastination. George Crabbe. NOBRP

Love Will Find Out the Way. *Unknown.* FaBoCh; GBL; OBEV (Great Adventure, The.) GTBS-P ("He will find out his way.") (LL) GTBS-P

Love will not have me cry. Canzonette. He Will Neither Boast nor Lament to His Lady. Jacopo da Lentino, *Italian.* AWP, *tr. by* D. G. Rossetti

Love winged my hopes and taught me how to fly. Icarus. *Unknown.* OBEV

Love without hope, as when the young bird-catcher. Robert Graves. BoLoP; FaBoEE; GBL; GTBS-P; NAEL-2; NOxBChV; NTP; NoP-4; OAEL-2; OPOU; PFE; Spl

Love without Hope is like Breath without Air. To Colindra. Elizabeth Thomas. LW

Love you. Tess Gallagher. *See* Conversation with a Fireman from Brooklyn.

Love you dare but look I find, The. To Cleon's Eyes. Martha Sansom. ECWP

Love, you were dying and one came and drew. A Picture. "Michael Field." VWP

Love Your Enemy. Yusef Iman. GI; BPo; TTY

"Love, / your mother" / Which is Naomi. (LL) Kaddish. Allen Ginsberg. HCAP; NAAL-2; NOBA; NeAP; PmAP; PoM

Love your toys, my darling. Toys. Abraham Sutskever, *Yiddish.* CEEP, *tr. by* Seymour Levitan

Love, You've Been a Villain. James Robinson Planché. NOBL

Loved by thee. (LL) A Woman's Last Word. Robert Browning. BLPA; FaBoEE; NAEL-2; RACG

Loved I am, and yet complain[e] of Love, *speech of Cleophila.* Complaint of Love. Sir Philip Sidney. *Fr.* Arcadia.

Loved [*or* Lov'd] I not Hono[u]r more. (LL) Song: To Lucasta, Going to the War[re]s. Richard Lovelace. AWP; BeJo; CBLP; CaPo; ClHu; EBEvV; EnLoPo; GBL; GTBS-P; HAP; HoPM; ImPo; InPK-6; InPS-3; MeLP; NAEL-1; NIP-4; NOBE; NOSC; OAEL-1; OBEV; OBWP; OxAEP-1; OxBSP; PBMP; PoE; PoEL-3; PoRA; Poetr; SCGP; SCV; SeCP; TFi; UV; WeW-3

Loved of My Soul. Israel Najara, *Hebrew.* TrJP, *tr. by* Nina Davis Salaman

Loved, on a sudden thou didst come to me. "Michael Field." VWP

Loved One, The. Joseph Hansen. NYBP

Loved One, The. Evelyn Waugh. "They told me, Francis Hinsley, they told me you were hung." OBCoV

Loved stream, that meanders along. Memories of Childhood. Sir John Carr. NOEC *Fr.* Derwent; an Ode.

Loveliest flowers, though crooked in their border. Gardener. Robert Graves. GaP; OBGa

Loveliest girl in Vienna, The. Alma. Tom Lehrer. NBLV

Loveliest lynchee was our Lord, The. (LL) The Chicago *Defender* Sends a Man to Little Rock. Gwendolyn Brooks. CrDW; NAAL; PoBA; Poetr

Loveliest of Counties, Shropshire Now. Ian Sainsbury. BXAP

Loveliest of Pies. Peter De Vries. OBAL

Loveliest of trees, the cherry now. A. E. Housman. AWP; CMoP; ChAP; ClHu; EBEvV; FaBoBe; HAP; ImPo; InPK-6; LiTM; MoBrPo; MoP; NTP; NoAM; NoP-4; OAEL-2; OxBTC; PFE; PoE; PoLF; PoPoPo; Poetr; RB; SCGP; SoSe-8; TFi; WeW-3

Loveliest of what I leave. Adonis, Dying. Praxilla, *Greek.* PBWP; WPOW, *tr. by* Richard Lattimore

Loveliness. Christopher Smart. NOCV *Fr.* Hymns for the Amusement of Children.

Loveliness of Love, The. George Darley. *See* A Song: "It is not Beauty [*or* beautie] I demand[e]."

Lovel's Song. Ben Jonson. *See* A Vision of Beauty.

Lovely! all the essential parts. These Purists. William Carlos Williams. OBAL

Lovely body of the dead, The. Lament for Glasgerion. Elinor Wylie. PoA

Lovely cheeks, or lips or eyes. Thomas Carew. *See* Disdain Returned.

Lovely cherries on the tree. Adjectives. Moishe Nadir, *Yiddish.* TrJP, *tr. by* Joseph Leftwich

Lovely Childhood. Gottfried Benn, *German.* PFTM, *tr. by* Babette Deutsch

Lovely courier of the sky. Anacreon's Dove. Samuel Johnson. AWP

Lovely Étan, The. *Unknown.* NOIV

Lovely fairy! Charming sprite! An Ode Composed in Sleep. Judith Madan. ECWP

Lovely Fia was the summer queen. A Mare. Kate Barnes. NYBP

Lovely girl, you look at me through the window. Praxilla, *Greek.* PBWP, *tr. by* John Dillon

Lovely grapes and apples. A Tabernacle Thought. Israel Zangwill. TrJP

Lovely Green Lady, A. The Green Lady. Charlotte Druitt Cole. BoTP

Lovely hill-torrents are. Song. Walter James Turner. MoBrPo

Lovely is the modest girl. *Unknown, Chinese.* SuSp, *tr. by* Wu-Chi Liu

Lovely lady, fairest of the time. Tu Fu, *Chinese.* CoBCP, *tr. by* Burton Watson

Lovely lass o' Inverness, The. Robert Burns. GTBS-P; OBEV

Lovely, lasting peace of mind! A Hymn to Contentment. Thomas Parnell. NOEC

Lovely Leda. Yaroslav Vasilevich Smelyakov, *Russian.* TCRP, *tr. by* Simon Franklin *and* Albert C. Todd

Lovely Love, A. Gwendolyn Brooks. BPo; NAAL

Lovely Maya, Hermes' mother. Barnabe Barnes. NoSic *Fr.* Parthenophil and Parthenophe.

Lovely Pamela, who found. Epitaph on a Party Girl. Richard Usborne. FaBoEE; OBCoV

Lovely Rivers and Lakes of Maine, The. George B. Wallis. BLPA

Lovely Rose Is Sprung, A. *Unknown, German.* AWP, *tr. by* Margarete Münsterberg

Lovely Shall Be Choosers, The. Robert Frost. MoAmPo; NOBA; OxBA; PoE

Lovely spot which thou dost see, The. Upon a Mole in Celia's Bosom. Thomas Carew. BeJo

Lovely Spring breeze has come, The. Spring Day on West Lake. Ou-yang Hsiu, *Chinese.* OHPC, *tr. by* Kenneth Rexroth

Lovely Stuff. Diane Ward. PmAP

Lovely the young peach tree. *Unknown, Chinese.* ChiPo, *tr. by* Burton Watson

Lovely Things. H. M. Sarson. BoTP

Lovely to be. A Bouquet of Objects. Elaine Equi. PmAP

Lovely viper, haste not on. A Song of the Cannibals. Anne Finch, Countess of Winchilsea. PoE

Lovely whore though. Cathleen. *Unknown, Irish.* BIrV, *tr. by* Thomas MacIntyre

Lovely Young Moor, A. *Unknown.* BoWoP, *tr. by* Willis Barnstone

Lovelye William. *Unknown.* AmFP

Lover, The. "Eliza." KTR

Lover. Lady Mary Wortley Montagu. *See* Lover, The; a Ballad.

Lover, The. Coventry Patmore. OxAEP-2 *Fr.* The Angel in the House.

Lover and Philosopher. Sir William Davenant. NOBE; OBEV (Philosopher and Lover; To a Mistress Dying, The.) GEA

Lover and the Syringa-Bush, The. Herman Melville. OBAL

Lover Compareth Himself to the Painful Falconer, The. *Unknown.* NoSic

Lover Compareth His State to a Ship in Perilous Storm Tossed on the Sea, The. Petrarch. *See* The Galley.

Lover Complaineth the Unkindness of His Love, The. Sir Thomas Wyatt. AAS; EBEV; GBL; HAP; InPS-3; NAEL-1; OAEL-1; PoEL-1; SiPS ("My lute awake performe the last.") PBRV

(To His Lute.) BoLoP; NOBE; OBEV

Lover for Shamefastness[e] Hideth His Desire Within His Faithful[l] Heart [or Hart], The. Petrarch. AAS; Son *Fr.* Sonnets to Laura.

Lover Having Dreamed Enjoying of His Love, Complaineth That the Dreame Is Not either Longer or Truer, The. Sir Thomas Wyatt. AAS

Lover in Winter Plaineth for the Spring, The. *Unknown.* OBEV

("Westron wynde when wyll thou blow.") FaBoVe; GBL

Lover is a slender, glowing urn, A. A Fantastic Simile. Thomas Lovell Beddoes. Son

Lover Man. James Cushing. SeSe

Lover Mourns for the Loss of Love, The. W. B. Yeats. WeW-3

Lover of Love. Hagiwara Sakutaro, *Japanese.* PFTM, *tr. by* Hiroaki Sato

Lover of swamps. To the Snipe. John Clare. FaBoPV; OBNC

Lover of the Lord. *Unknown.* AmFP

Lover of the moorland bare, A. To K. de M. Robert Louis Stevenson. OBNC

Lover Proved False, The. *Unknown.* AmFP

Lover Rejoiceth the Enjoying of His Love, The. Sir Thomas Wyatt. AAS; BoLoP; SiPS

Lover, secretly behind your smile. Paul Éluard, *French.* EP, *tr. by* Derek Parker

Lover Showeth How He Is Forsaken of Such as He Sometime Enjoyed, The. Sir Thomas Wyatt. AAS; HoPM; InPS-3; PoEL-1; PoRA

("How like you this, what hath she now deserved?") (LL) NoP-4

("I fain would know what she hath deserved.") (LL) GLoP; PoPoPo

("I would fain know what she hath deservèd.") (LL) APAD; CABP; LoP; NoP-4; PFE

("I would fain knowe what she hath deserued.") (LL) GEA

("I would fain knowe what she hath deserved.") (LL) PBRV

("They flee from me that sometime did me seek.") APAD; CABP; GLoP; LoP; NoP-4; PFE; PoPoPo

Lover Tells of the Rose in His Heart, The. W. B. Yeats. CMoP

(Aedh Tells of the Rose in His Heart.) MoBrPo

Lover that Durst Not Speak to His M[istress], A. James Shirley. NOSC

Lover, The; a Ballad. Lady Mary Wortley Montagu. ECWP; NAEL-1

("And as Ovid has sweetly in parables told, / We harden like trees, and like rivers are cold.") (LL) PEW

(Lover.) LW; PEW

("We harden like trees, and like rivers grow cold.") (LL) LW

Lover to His Lady, The. Plato, *Greek.* CTC; FaBoEE; NoSic; PFE, *tr. by* George Turberville

Lover, under burthen of his mistress' love, The. Sir John Davies. *Fr.* The Gulling[e] Sonnets. Son

Lover, upon an Accident Necessitating His Departure, Consults with Reason, A. Thomas Carew. CaPo

Lover Whose Mistress Feared a Mouse, The. George Turberville. NTP

Loverd, thou clepedest me. Wait a Little! *Unknown.* EnVB; NOCV

Lovers, The. Conrad Potter Aiken. NYBP

Lovers, The. David Campbell. BMAP *Fr.* Ku-ring-gai Rock Carvings.

Lovers, The. Alex Comfort. PoA

Lovers. Russell Edson. WeT

Lovers, The. William Robert Rodgers. BIrV; OxBSP; PNI

Lovers, The. William Jay Smith. MoAmPo

Lovers, The. Marya Alexandrovna Zaturenska. MoAmPo

Lovers and madmen have such seething brains. Imagination. Shakespeare. ImPo *Fr.* A Midsummer Night's Dream.

Lover's Appeal, The. Sir Thomas Wyatt. GTBS-P

(Appeal, The.) GLoP

Lover's Arithmetic, The. *Unknown.* CBNP; OxBoLi; PeLV

Lover's death, how regular, The. Stark Major. Hart Crane. FuPo; MeMAP

Lovers' Debouchment. William Zaranka. BXAP

Lover's eyes will gaze an eagle blind, A. Shakespeare. APAD; GBL *Fr.* Love's Labour's Lost.

Lover's Farewell, The. George Moses Horton. NAAAL

Lovers, fresh plighting lovers in our age. "Michael Field." CPO

Lovers Go Fly a Kite, The. W. D. Snodgrass. NYBP

Lovers, gratified in each other, I am asking *you.* Rilke. ITG, *tr. by* Stephen Mitchell *Fr.* The Second Duino Elegy.

Lovers How They Come and Part. Robert Herrick. GBL; OxBSP; OxBoLi; PoEL-3

Lovers in Fall. Yehuda Amichai, *Hebrew.* IP, *tr. by* Warren Bargad *and* Stanley F. Chyet

Lovers in ladies' magazines. Song. Thomas McGrath. VGW

Lovers in Summer. Vern Rutsala. WeT

Lovers in the act dispense. The Thieves. Robert Graves. BoLoP; CMoP; GTBS-P; LiTM; LoP; OAEL-2

Lovers in Winter. Robert Graves. FaBoEE; NYBP

Lovers' Infiniteness[e]. Donne. ESCV; MeLP; NOSC; OAEL-1; PoEL-2; SeCP

Lover's Journey, The. George Crabbe.

"It is the soul that sees; the outward eyes." OxAEP-1

Lover's Lament, A. *Unknown.* AmFP

Lover's Lament, The. *Unknown.* AS

Lover's Lament for Her Sailor, The. *Unknown.* AmFP

Lover's Lament *or* The Willows by the Water Side, A ("My little breath, under the willows by the water-side we used to sit"). *Unknown, Tewa Indian.* AWP, *tr. by* H. J. Spinden

Lover's Lane. Paul Laurence Dunbar. ColAP

Lover's Leap; a Tale, The. Andrew Macdonald. NOEC

Lovers' Litany, The. Rudyard Kipling. CBLP

Lovers may find similitudes. The Cascade. Edgell Rickword. FaBoTw

Lover's Meeting. Ray Mathew. CBAP

Lover's Melancholy, The. John Ford.

Dawn. OBEV

"If thou canst wake with me, forget to eate." PoEL-2

"Minutes are numbered by the fall of sands." PoEL-2

Lover's New Year's Gift, A. John Lydgate. PoEL-1

Lovers of pleasure more than God. Lover of the Lord. *Unknown.* AmFP

Lovers of the Poor, The. Gwendolyn Brooks. LCAP-2; LTA; MoP; NAAAL; NAAL-2; NOBA; NoAM; Poetr; SSLK

Lover's Posy, The. Rufinus Domesticus, *Greek.* AWP, *tr. by* W. H. D. Rouse

Lover's Progress, The. John Fletcher.

Dead Host's Welcome, The. OxAEP-1

Lovers' Quarrel, A. Robert Browning. EBVVPR

Lover's quarrel will never rest his roots, A. (LL) Cosmos in London. Arthur Nortje. HBAPE; PeSAV

Lover's Question, A. James Baldwin. GLP

Lover's Reply to Good Advice. Richard Hughes. MoBrPo

Lover's Resolution, A. George Wither. *See* The Author's Resolution.

Lover's Return. Langston Hughes. SAmP

Lovers, scholars—the fervent, the austere. Cats. Charles Baudelaire, *French.* APo, *tr. by* Richard Howard

Lovers' Song. Kofi Awoonor. PBMAP *Fr.* Three poems from Rediscovery (1964).

(Lovers think of death, The). (LL) Blindman's Buff. Peter Viereck. LiTM; MoAmPo

Lovers, we write in rapids streams and wind. Catullus. *See* Carmen 70 ("Lesbia says she'ld rather marry me").

Lovers who are young indeed, and wish to know the sort of life. Love, You've Been a Villain. James Robinson Planché. NOBL

Lovers whose lifted hands are candles in winter. For a Child Expected. Anne Ridler. LiTM

Love's Advocate. Phoebe Hesketh. LW

Love's Alchemy [or Alchemie]. Donne. ESCV; NAEL-1; OAEL-1; PoE; SeCP

("Some that have deeper digged love's mine than I.") NoP-4

("Sweetness and wit they're but mummy possessed.") (LL) NoP-4

Love's an headstrong wild desire. Henry Baker. NOEC

Loves and sorrows of those who lose an orchard. The Lost Orchard. Edgar Lee Masters. CMoP; ColAP

Love's Anniversaries. Maurice Lindsay. OxBM

Love's as Warm as Tears. C. S. Lewis. TIRV

Love's Bitten Tongue. Vassar Miller.

"Lord, hush this ego as one stops a bell." MT

Love's Clock. Sir John Suckling. CaPo; NOSC

Love's Consolation. Richard Watson Dixon.

"All who have loved, be sure of this from me." OBNC

Love's Constancy. Hadewijch, *Flemish.* WPoS, *tr. by* Oliver Davies

Love's Cure. Francis Beaumont and John Fletcher.

Song: "Turn, turn thy beauteous face away." NOSC; PoEL-2

Love's Deity [or Deitie]. Donne. AWP; ESCV; GBL; ImPo; SeCP; SoSe-8

Love's Despair. Dryden. *Fr.* The Spanish Friar [or Fryar].

("Farewell, ungrateful traitor!") GLoP; RACG

(Song.)

("When loving is a pain.") (LL) RACG

Love's domain, supernal Zion. Brynbwrla. Kingsley Amis. NOBL *Fr.* The Evans Country.

Love's Emblem. John Clare. NIP-4

Love's Emblems. John Fletcher. BoLoP; NOBE; NOSC *Fr.* The Tragedy of Valentinian.

Loves End. Edward Herbert, 1st Baron Herbert of Cherbury. SeCP

Love's Entreaty. Michelangelo Buonarroti, *Italian.* AWP

Love's Epitaph. William Cavendish, Duke of Newcastle. OxBSP

Love's Fancy. Dryden. *See* After the Pangs of a Desperate Lover.

Love's Farewell. Michael Drayton. *See* Since There's No Help.

Loves Feast. Sir John Suckling. CBLP

Love's Fidelity. Petrarch. AWP *Fr.* Sonnets to Laura.

Love's First Approach. "Ephelia." KTR

Love's Flight. Else Lasker-Schüler, *German.* TrJP, *tr. by* Jethro Bithell

Love's Force. Thomas Carew. CaPo

Love's Garden. Chaucer. GaP

Love's Glory. Greville Fulke. *Fr.* Caelica.

Love's Grave. George Meredith. OBEV *Fr.* Modern Love.

Love's Growth. Donne. ESCV; NOSC; NoP-4; PBRV

Love's Guerdons. Edith Nesbit. NOBVV

Love's hidden pearl is shining yet. Hafiz, *Persian.* TOF, *tr. by* R. A. Nicholson

Love's Horoscope. Richard Crashaw. MeLP

Love's Hue and Cry. James Shirley. BeJo

Love's Immaturity. Edith Jay Scovell. GBL

Love's Innocence. Thomas Stanley. BeJo

Love's Justification. Michelangelo Buonarroti, *Italian.* AWP; CTC (To the Marchesana of Pescara.) CTC

Love's Labour's Lost. Shakespeare.

    Blossom, The. OBEV

    (Love's Perjuries.) GTBS-P

    Heavenly Rhetoric, The. ImPo; Son

    Holofernes's Letter. CBNP

    "If she be made of white and red." CTC

    "Lover's eyes will gaze an eagle blind, A." APAD; GBL

    "O! And I forsooth in love!" OBCoV

    Spring. HAP; ImPo; InPK-6; NAEL-1; NBLV; NIP-4; NOBE; NoSic; OAEL-1; OBEV; PoEL-2; PoRA; TFi; UnPo

    ("Now daisies pied, and violets blue.") BoTP

    (Ver.)

    Winter. GTBS-P; HAP; ImPo; NIP-4; NoP-4; OAEL-1; OBEV; SCGP; TFi; UnPo; WeW-3

    (Hiems.) FaBoCh

    (Tu-Whit To-Who.) CH

Love's Last Resource. Sadi. AWP, *tr. by* L. Cranmer-Byng *Fr.* The Gulistan.

Love's Martyrs. John Ford. NOBE *Fr.* The Broken Heart.

    (Song: "Oh no more, no more, too late.") OxBSP

Love's Matrimony. William Cavendish, Duke of Newcastle. NOSC

Love's Maturity. Hadewijch, *Flemish.* WPoS, *tr. by* Oliver Davies

Love's memories haunt my footsteps still. John Clare. NOBVV

Love's Mirror. Constance Naden. VWP

Love's Mourner. Augusta Davies Webster. VWP

Love's multitudinous boneyard. 230th Chorus. Jack Kerouac. NeAP *Fr.* Mexico City Blues.

Love's Music. Philip Bourke Marston. GSo

Love's Mystery. Joseph Beaumont. NOSC

Love's night and a lamp. Meleager, *Greek.* BoLoP; GrAn, *tr. by* Peter Whigham

Loves of a little while ago, The. *Unknown, Japanese.* WPJ, *tr. by* Kenneth Rexroth *and* Ikuko Atsumi

Loves of Dido and Aeneas, The. Virgil, *Latin.*

    "But she who Love long since had swallowed down." OBCVT, *tr. by* Sir Richard Fanshawe

Loves of the Eel, The. Oppian. APo, *tr. by* William Diaper *Fr.* Halieutica.

Loves of the Puppets. Richard Wilbur. OxBC

Loves of the Tortoise, The. Oppian. APo, *tr. by* William Diaper *Fr.* Halieutica.

Love's Offence. Sir John Suckling. CaPo; NOSC

Love's Old Sweet Song. G. Clifton Bingham. FaBoBe

Love's Pains. John Clare. NOBVV

Love's pallor and the semblance of deep truth. Dante. AWP *Fr.* La Vita Nuova.

Love's Perjuries. Shakespeare. *See* The Blossom.

Love's Perversity. Coventry Patmore. EnVR *Fr.* The Angel in the House.

Love's Philosophy. Shelley. APAD; BLPA; BoLoP; FHYEP; FaBoBe; GLoP; GTBS-P; HoPM; OxAEP-2; PBMP; PoToHe; SCGP

Love's Primal Want. William Ellery Leonard. *Fr.* Two Lives. Son

Love's Progress. Donne. OAEL-1 *Fr.* Elegies.

Love's Rebel. Henry Howard, Earl of Surrey. SiPS

Love's Remorse. Edwin Muir. OxBTC

Love's Résumé. Heinrich Heine. TrJP, *tr. by* J. F. C.

Love's Secret. William Blake. *See* Never Pain to Tell Thy Love.

Love's Siege. Sir John Suckling. CBLP; CaPo

("'Tis now, since I sate down before.") CavPo

Love's Stratagems. Donald Justice. NYBP

Love's Sun. William Cavendish, Duke of Newcastle. NOSC

Loves that ended long ago. Streets. Henrik Nordbrandt, *Danish.* VCWP, *tr. by* Henrik Nordbrandt and Alexander Taylor

Love's the boy stood on the burning deck. Casabianca. Elizabeth Bishop. APAD; FaBoWP; OxBSP; PiM

Love's Triumph must be Honour's Funeral. (LL) Loving and Beloved. Sir John Suckling. BeJo; CaPo; CavPo; NAEL-1

Love's twilight wanes in heaven above. Before Sunset. Swinburne. CBLP

Loves Victory. Aurelian Townshend. *See* To the Countesse of Salisbury.

Love's Vista. Henrietta Cordelia Ray. CBWP-3

Love's Votary. George Augustus Simcox. NOBVV

Loves who many years held all my mind, The. Walter Savage Landor. GBL

Love's Witness. Aphra Behn. BoWoP; LW

Love's worshipers alone can know. Love and Folly. Jean de La Fontaine, *French.* AWP, *tr. by* Bryant

Lovesickness is like a creditor. Tune: "Clear River, a Prelude"—Lovesickness. Hsü Tsai-ssu, *Chinese.* SuSp, *tr. by* Sherwin S. S. Fu

Lovesickness— / What is the cure? Ma Chih-yüan. SuSp, *tr. by* Sherwin S. S. Fu *Fr.* Tune: "Song of Shou-yang."

Lovesight. D. G. Rossetti. EBVV; GTBS-P; NAEL-2; OBNC *Fr.* The House of Life.

Lovesleep, The. Gavin Ewart. OxBC

Lovest Thou Me? William Cowper. ChIV-2 *Fr.* Olney Hymns.

Lovin wasn easy all de time. Jean Binta Breeze. HCP

Loving Again. Gloria Wade-Gayles. ISC

Loving and Beloved. Sir John Suckling. BeJo; CaPo; CavPo; NAEL-1

Loving and Liking [Irregular Verses Addressed to A Child]. Dorothy Wordsworth. OxBChV; WoRP

Loving Henry. *Unknown.* AmFP

Loving in the War Years. Cherríe Moraga. CPO; NMM-2

Loving in truth, and fain[e] in verse my love to show. Sonnet 1. Sir Philip Sidney. AWP; EBEV; EPCY; GBL; HAP; ImPo; InPS-3; NAEL-1; NoSic; OAEL-1; OxAEP-1; PoE; Poetr; SCGP; Son; TFi *Fr.* Astrophil and Stella. AAS; SiPS

Loving is a journey with water and with stars. Pablo Neruda. ITG, *tr. by* Stephen Mitchell *Fr.* Sonnet XII.

Loving kindenes of the Lord / They clearly shall discerne, The. Bible, *O.T. See* Psalm 107.

Loving looks the large-eyed cow. A Christmas Prayer. George Macdonald. PChr

Loving Mad Tom. *Unknown.* CBNP; NOSC

Loving she is, and tractable, though wild. Characteristics of a Child Three Years Old. Wordsworth. LaPo

Loving the rituals that keep men close. Palladas, *Greek.* OBVE, *tr. by* Tony Harrison

Loving this man who is far away. Like Loving Chekhov. Denise Levertov. InPS-3

Loving You. Frances Horovitz. LW

Loving you is like living. Loving in the War Years. Cherríe Moraga. CPO; NMM-2

Loving you less than life, a little less. Edna St. Vincent Millay. NAAL-2

Loving your neighbor is all very fine when you have nice. "Alta." CrSp *Fr.* 2 : 7.

Lovingly I turn me down. After Mass. "Michael Field." WPE

Low-anchored cloud. Mist. Henry David Thoreau. AWP; AmPP; NCAP; OxBA *Fr.* A Week on the Concord and Merrimack Rivers.

Low and brown barns thatched and repatched and tattered. The Wife of Flanders. G. K. Chesterton. NSI

Low and mournful be the strain. Voluntaries. Ralph Waldo Emerson. APN-1; CBCWP

Low Barometer. Robert Bridges. CABP; CMoP; MoP; NOCV; NoAM; OBNC; Poetr; SCGP

Low beating of the tom-toms, The. Danse Africaine. Langston Hughes. NAAL

Low Bridge, Everybody Down. William S. Allen. *See* The Erie Canal.

Low Church. Stanley J. Sharpless. NBLV; OBCoV; PeLV

Low clouds yellow in a mist wind. First Movement. Padraic Fiacc. PNI

Low Fields and Light. W. S. Merwin. CoAmPo; LCAP-2

Low huts, groans muffled. The Midwives. Celia Gilbert. ChIV-1

Low in the eastern sky. To the Maiden in the East. Henry David Thoreau. OxBA

Low in thy grave with thee. David's Lament for Jonathan. Peter Abelard, *Latin.* NAWM-1, *tr. by* Helen Waddell

Low-Level Cross-Country. Howard Nemerov. GM

Low river flows like smoked glass, The. Prayer for My Son. James Applewhite. BLT

Low Road, The. Marge Piercy. CrSp

Low sandy beach and the thin scrub pine, The. Cape Cod. George Santayana. APN-2

Low sun whitens on the flying squalls, The. Rounding the Cape. Roy Campbell. PeSA

Low tide. Anita Virgil. HA

Low Tide on Grand Pré. Bliss Carman. NOBC

Low Trick, A. Frank Gelett Burgess. OBCA

Low Volume. Reiner Kunze, German. PoSu, tr. by Michael Hamburger

Low was our pretty Cot. Reflections on Having Left a Place of Retirement. Coleridge. Ro

Low winter moon. Ruth Yarrow. HA

Low ye hills in ocean lie. My Heart Is in Merioneth. Unknown, Welsh. OBWVE, tr. by Richard Llwyd

Lowdown Dirty Blues. Unknown. AmFP

Lowell. James Russell Lowell. AmPP; NOBA; OxBA; TAP Fr. A Fable for Critics. NAAL-1; NAAL-3

Lower East Side: The George Bernstein Story. Edward Field. OBCoV

Lower leaves of the trees, The. Sone Yoshitada, Japanese. OHMPJ, tr. by Kenneth Rexroth

Lower Life, The. May Kendall. VWP

Lower New York. George Cabot Lodge. APN-2

Lower the flags. Special Bulletin. Langston Hughes. PoBA

Lower the Standard: That's My Motto. Karl Shapiro. MoP; NoAM

Lower them and dream of home. (LL) Still Night Thoughts. Li Po, Chinese. CoBCP; TTTS, tr. by Burton Watson

Lowering the Coffin. Mogwol Park, Korean. CKP, tr. by Jaihiun Kim

Lowery Cot. Leonard Alfred George Strong. MoBrPo

Lowest circle of hell. Contrary to prevailing opinion is inhab-, The. What Mr. Cogito Thinks About Hell. Zbigniew Herbert, Polish. VCWP, tr. by John Carpenter and Bogdana Carpenter

Lowest Place, The. Christina Rossetti. NOBVV

Lowest trees have tops, the ant her gall, The. Love is Love. Sir Edward Dyer. APAD; NoSic; OxBSP; RB; SCGP

Lowlands. William Reed Huntington. APN-2

Lowlands. Unknown. OxBoLi

Lowlands o' [or of] Holland, The. Unknown. AmFP; CH; OxBB

Lowliest duties on herself [or itself] did lay, The. (LL) London 1802. Wordsworth. AWP; EBEvV; EPCY; FaBoPV; FaPoR; GTBS-P; HAP; HeIP-4; NAEL-2; NIP-4; NOBRP; NoP-4; OBEV; OBNC; OxAEP-2; PBMP; PFE; PoEL-4; PoRA; Ro; SCGP; Son; TFi; UV

Lowly Peasant, The. Unknown. PBWP, tr. by Rina Benmayor

Lowveld, The. Charles Eglington. PeSA

Loyal Horse, The. Nguyễn Đình Chiểu, Vietnamese. AVP, tr. by Huỳnh Sanh Thông

Loyal Housewife. Daisy Zamora, Spanish. LoL, tr. by Margaret Randall

Loyal subject, thou, to that bright Queen, A. To W. L. G. on Reading His "Chosen Queen." Charlotte Forten. BlSi

Loyalty. Berton Braley. BLPA

Loyalty to the Flag. Lizelia Augusta Jenkins Moorer. CBWP-3

Lu wine like amber. In Reply When Lesser Officials of Chung-tu Brought a Pot of Wine and Two Fish to My Inn as Gifts. Li Po, Chinese. CoBCP, tr. by Burton Watson

Luanda, you are like a white seagull. We Shall Return, Luanda. Ngudia Wendel. PBMAP

Lubber Breeze. Thomas Sturge Moore. CH

Lubin. Unknown. FaBoVe

Luca Signorelli to His Son. Eugene Lee-Hamilton. PeVV

Lucan's Pharsalia Book 1. Marlowe.
"This said, the restles generall through the darke." PBRV

Lucasia, Rosania and Orinda Parting at a Fountain, July 1663. Katherine Philips. KTR; PEW

Lucasta, frown and let me die. To Lucasta: Her Reserved Looks. Richard Lovelace. CaPo

Lucasta Laughing. Richard Lovelace. CavPo; PoEL-3

Lucasta Replies to Lovelace. G. K. Chesterton. UV

Lucasta's Fan[ne], with a Looking-Glass[e] in It. Richard Lovelace. CaPo
("If hence she dress herself but in his eyes.") (LL) CavPo

Lucasta's World. Richard Lovelace. BeJo; CaPo; SeCP

Lucent lake was lit with sheen, The. A Thought of Lake Ontario. Henrietta Cordelia Ray. CBWP-3

Lucifer Broods. D. J. Enright. OxBoV

Lucifer has bad habits. Ljiljana Djurdjic, Serbo-Croatian. HSix, tr. by Charles Simic

Lucifer in Starlight. George Meredith. AWP; CH; ChIV-1; EBVV; EnVR; HAP; ImPo; InPK-6; NAEL-2; NOBE; NOBVV; OAEL-2; OBEV; OBNC; PBMP; PoE; PoEL-5; SCGP; Son; TFi; UnPo

("On a starred night Prince Lucifer uprose.") CABP; GSo; NoP-4; PFE

Lucifer in the Train. Adrienne Rich. GM

Lucilia, wedded to Lucretius, found. Lucretius. Tennyson. EnVR; OAEL-2

Lucilius the poet has informed me. Howard Nemerov. Fr. Epigrams. OBAL

Lucille among the flamingos. Cameos. Rita Dove. NAmP90

Lucille and Ernie's Master Bedroom. Dara Wier. CMAP

Lucille's Kumquat Colored Kimono. Dara Wier. CMAP

Lucina, Care. Perses, Greek. GrAn, tr. by Peter Whigham

Lucinda Matlock. Edgar Lee Masters. CMoP; HAP; LiTM; MoAmPo; MoP; NOBA; NoAM; OxBA; PBMP Fr. Spoon River Anthology.

Lucindy, who you 'spose I seed. A Common Occurrence. Priscilla Jane Thompson. CBWP-2

Luck. Wilfrid Wilson Gibson. OBMV

Luck. Langston Hughes. PiM; SAmP

Luck has no songs, luck has no thoughts, luck has nothing. Pain. Edith Södergran, Swedish. PBWP; WPOW, tr. by Jaakko A. Ahokas

Luck? I am upset. My dog is ill. A Rune for C. Barbara Howes. NYBP

Luck of Edenhall, The. Ludwig Uhland, German. AWP, tr. by Longfellow

Luck, we've had it; our character the public's. It Did. Robert Lowell. NoAM

Luckes, my faire falcon, and your fellowes all. Sir Thomas Wyatt. See Lux, my fair falcon, and your fellowes all.

Luckily for us. (LL) Humming-Bird. D. H. Lawrence. APo; CMoP; InPS-3; LiTM; NoAM; RB

Luck's Shining Child. George Garrett. MT

Lucky. Patricia Goedicke. NMM-2

Lucky Chance, The. Aphra Behn.
Song: "Oh! Love, that stronger art than wine." LW; WPE; WPOW

Lucky Eugene. Michael Foley. PNI

LUCKY magpie, holy bird, what hateful lies you tell! The Lady and the Magpie. Unknown, Chinese. ChiP, tr. by Arthur Waley

Lucky Marriage, The. Thomas Blackburn. GTBS-P

Lucky my ears 'pop' at the hilltop. Ron Silliman. FTOS Fr. Hidden.

Lucky One, The. Reginald Shepherd. GT

Lucky shepherd, if only on the hill. Crinagoras, Greek. GrAn, tr. by Alistair Elliot

Lucky Strikes. Ron Padgett. FTOS

Lucky the husband. Mabel Kelly. Turlough Carolan, Irish. BIrV; CIP-2, tr. by Austin Clarke

Lucky with day approaching, with leaning dawn. (LL) The Wanderer. W. H. Auden. CMoP; GTBS-P; MeMAP; MoP; NoAM; RB; WeW-3

Luco is borne around the neighb'ring isles. A Poem on the Inhumanity of the Slave Trade. Ann Yearsley. Ro

Lucrece's Death. Shakespeare. NoSic Fr. The Rape of Lucrece.

Lucretius. Tennyson. EnVR; OAEL-2

Lucretius. Book the Fifth. Lucretius, Latin.
"Thus like a Sayler by the Tempest hurl'd." OBCVT, tr. by John Dryden

Lucretius could not credit centaurs. Invitation To Juno. William Empson. CBLP; CMoP; FaBoMo; LoP

Lucretius felt the change of the world in his time, the great republic. Prescription of Painful Ends. Robinson Jeffers. MoAmPo; OxBA

Lucretius knew. De Natura Rerum. Yves Bonnefoy, French. VCWP, tr. by Lisa Sapinkopf

Lucretius Paraphrased. Lucretius, Latin. OBCVT, tr. by Thomas Flatman

Lucretius versus the Lake Poets. Robert Frost. OBCoV

Lucy. Walter De la Mare. CMoP

Lucy. Wordsworth. FHYEP; NOBE; OAEL-2; OBEV; OBNC; SCGP; TFi
Education of Nature, The. GTBS-P
"I traveled [or travell'd] among unknown men." AWP; GTBS-P
("I travelled among unknown men.") PFE; Ro
("That Lucy's eyes surveyed.") (LL) PFE
("Which Lucy's eyes surveyed!") (LL) Ro
Lucy. GLoP
"Slumber did my spirit seal, A." AWP; EBEvV; EnLoPo; FaBoCh; GTBS-P; HAP; HeIP-4; ImPo; InPK-6; InPS-3; NOBRP; PBMP; PFE; PoEL-4; PoRA; SCV; UnPo; WeW-3
("With rocks and stones and trees!") (LL) LaPo; NoP-4; PFE; PoPoPo; Ro
Song: "She dwelt among the untrodden ways." NOBRP
(Lost Love, The.) GTBS-P
("She dwelt among th' untrodden ways.") Ro

Lucy Ashton's Song. Sir Walter Scott. NOBE; OBEV; OxAEP-2; OxBS; Ro Fr. The Bride of Lammermoor.

Lucy goes down the celestial escalator in light. Lucy Taking Birth. Diana Scott. BrRo

Lucy Gray; or, Solitude. Wordsworth. CH; GEA; NAEL-2; NOBRP; OAEL-2; OxAEP-2; OxBChV

Lucy Lake. Newton Mackintosh. BXAP

Lucy Lavender. Ivy O. Eastwick. BoTP

Lucy Locket lost her pocket. Mother Goose. LB; OxBoLi; OxNR; ReMoGo

Lucy Taking Birth. Diana Scott. BrRo

Lucy, you brightness[e] of our sphere [or spheare], who are. To Lucy, Countess[e] of Bedford, with Mr. Donnes Satire's [or Satyres]. Ben Jonson. BeJo; EPCY; PBRV

Lucy's Letter. James Berry. FaBoVe; HCP

Lud! what a group the motley scene discloses! Oliver Goldsmith. OBSV Fr. Epilogue to "The Sister."

Luf es lif that lastes ay, thar it in Christe es feste. A Song of the Love of Jesus. Richard Rolle of Hampole. PoEL-1

Lufthansa. John Tranter. BMAP; NOBAu

Lug us back lifeward—bone by infant bone. (LL) National Winter Garden. Hart Crane. EP; InPS-3; LiTM; NAAL-2; OxBA

Lui et Elle. D. H. Lawrence. NoAM

Luini in porcelain! Ezra Pound. Fr. Mauberley (1920). Fr. Hugh Selwyn Mauberley. (Life and Contacts). AmPP; CMoP; InPS-3; LiTM; NOBA; NoAM; TAP

Luis de Camões. Roy Campbell. FaBoTw; OxAEP-2; PeSA

Luke, Gospel according to. See also St. Luke and Bible, Luke.

Luke 10:25–37; And behold, a lawyer. Bible, N.T. GI, tr. by Stephen Mitchell. Fr. St. Luke.

Luke 10:38–42; Now as they went on their way. Bible, N.T. GI, tr. by Anna Kamienska. Fr. St. Luke.

Luke 11; Blessed Be the Paps Which Thou Hast Sucked. Bible, N.T. See Blessed be the Paps which Thou hast Sucked.

Luke 1:26–38; In the sixth month the angel Gabriel. Bible, N.T. GI, tr. by Anna Kamienska. Fr. St. Luke.

Luke 1:39–56; In those days Mary arose. Bible, N.T. GI, tr. by Rilke. Fr. St. Luke.

Luke 15:11–19; And he said, "There was a man." Bible, N.T. GI, tr. by Rilke. Fr. St. Luke.

Luke 15:20–32; And he arose and came. Bible, N.T. GI, tr. by Edwin Arlington Robinson. Fr. St. Luke.

Luke 16:1–9; He also said to the disciples. Bible, N.T. GI, tr. by Ernesto Cardenal. Fr. St. Luke.

Luke 16:19–26; "There was a rich man." Bible, N.T. GI, tr. by Robert Frost. Fr. St. Luke.

Luke 2:1–7; In those days a decree went out from Caesar Augustus. Bible, N.T. GI, tr. by Louise Glück. Fr. St. Luke.

Luke 2:21–40; And at the end of eight days, when he was circumcised. Bible, N.T. GI, tr. by T. S. Eliot. Fr. St. Luke.

Luke 23:26–38; And as they led him away. Bible, N.T. GI, tr. by W. H. Auden. Fr. St. Luke.

Luke 23:39–43; One of the criminals. Bible, N.T. GI, tr. by Jorge Luis Borges. Fr. St. Luke.

Luke: 24:13–32; That very day two of them. Bible, N.T. GI, tr. by Eric Pankey. Fr. St. Luke.

Luke 24:36–49; As they were saying this, Jesus. Bible, N.T. GI, tr. by Alec Derwent Hope. Fr. St. Luke.

Luke 2:8–20; And in that region there were shepherds. Bible, N.T. GI, tr. by Bertolt Brecht. Fr. St. Luke.

Luke 5:1–11; While the people pressed upon him. Bible, N.T. GI, tr. by Czeslaw Milosz. Fr. St. Luke.

Luke 6.25. Francis Quarles. ChIV-2

Luke 6:39. Bible, N.T. GI, tr. by William Carlos Williams. Fr. St. Matthew; He also told them a parable.

Luke 7; She Began To Wash His Feet with Teares and Wipe Them with the Haires of Her Head. Bible, N.T. NOSC, tr. by Richard Crashaw Fr. St. Luke.

Luke and John. Handwriting on the Wall. Unknown. AmFP

Luke Havergal. Edwin Arlington Robinson. APN-2; AWP; AmPP; GBL; LiTM; MeMAP; MoAmPo; NAAL-2; NCAP; NOBA; NoAM; PoEL-5; TFi; UnPo

Luke Preach-Ill admires what we laymen can mean The Insatiable Priest Matthew Prior. OxBSP

Luke XXIII. Jorge Luis Borges, Spanish. GI, tr. by David Curzon

Lula Vires. Unknown. AmFP

Lulee, lullay. Lullaby. Janet Lewis. NOCV

Lulla, la lulla, lulla lullaby. Lulla, My Sweet Little Baby. William Byrd. ChIV-2

Lulla, My Sweet Little Baby. William Byrd. ChIV-2

Lullaby: "Beloved, may your sleep be sound," fr. Words for Music Perhaps. W. B. Yeats. BoLoP; FaBoTw; LoP; OBMV

Lullaby: "But who killed Johannes, mama. . . ?" Jeremy Cronin. PeSAV

Lullaby: "Din of work is subdued, The." W. H. Auden. FaBoMo; GLP; NoAM

Lullaby, A: "For wars his life and half a world away." Randall Jarrell. HCAP; OxBC

Lullaby: "Golden slumbers kiss your eyes." Thomas Dekker and others. Fr. The Pleasant Comedy of Patient Grissell [or Grissel or Grissill].

Lullaby: "Hush, lullay." Léonie Adams. MoAmPo

Lullaby: "Hush ye, hush ye! honey, darlin'." Clara Ann Thompson. CBWP-2

Lullaby: "I wish to God my child was born." Unknown. AmFP

Lullaby: "Lay your sleeping head, my love." W. H. Auden. CMoP; EBEvV; GLP; HAP; LoP; MoP; NAEL-2; NOBE; NoAM; NoP-4; OAEL-2; OxAEP-2; OxBTC; PoE; SAGP; TFi; UnPo; WeW-3

("Entirely beautiful, The.") (LL) PiM

(Song XI: "Lay your sleeping head, my love.") EnLoPo

Lullaby: "Long canoe, The." Robert Silliman Hillyer. ImGa

Lullaby: "Lullee, lullay." Janet Lewis. CRP; NOCV

Lullaby: "My little baby sleeps, the little birds sleep." Unknown, Greek. GrIP, tr. by Philip P. Argenti and H.N. Rose

Lullaby: "My mother's an expert at one thing." Louise Glück. NAmP90

Lullaby: "Nocturnal, my panther, has eyes that spark, The." Tuvia Rivner, Hebrew. MHP, tr. by Ruth Finer Mintz

Lullaby: "O! hush thee, my darling, sleep soundly my son." Unknown, Yiddish. TrJP, tr. by Alice Lucas

Lullaby: "Puva, puva, puva." Unknown, Hopi Indian. TTTS, tr. by Natalie Curtis

Lullaby: "Sleep, baby, sleep." Unknown, Japanese. NOBE, tr. by Geoffrey Bownas and Anthony Thwaite

(Nurse's Song.) OTCP

Lullaby: "Sleep, my little baby, sleep." Samuel Hoffenstein. TrJP

Lullaby: "Someone would like to have you for her child." Unknown. TTTS

Lullaby: "Sweet and low, sweet and low." Tennyson. CTV; PoLF Fr. The Princess.

Lullaby: "Though the world has slipped and gone." Dame Edith Sitwell. CMoP; LiTM; NALW

Lullaby: "Upon my lap my sovereign sits." Richard Verstegan. CH; OBEV; SCGP

Lullaby: "Wide as this night, old as this night is old and young as it is young." Kenneth Fearing. CMoP

Lullaby: "Wind whistled loud at the window-pane, The." William Brighty Rands. BoTP

Lullaby. William Barnes. SCGP

Lullaby. Breyten Breytenbach, Afrikaans. VCWP, tr. by Breyten Breytenbach

Lullaby, The. Laura Riding Jackson. MoLi

Lullaby, A. "Lewis Carroll." See The Duchess's Lullaby.

Lullaby. Elolongue Epanya Yondo, French. NegPo, tr. by Ellen Conroy Kennedy

Lullaby. / Adult and child. Elizabeth Bishop. Fr. Songs for a Colored Singer. RB

Lullaby for a Daughter. James Harrison. MoLi

Lullaby for Ann-Lucian. Calvin Forbes. NBV; PoBA

Lullaby for My Dead Child. Denise Jallais, French. BoWoP; IMW, tr. by Maxine W. Kumin and Judith Kumin

Lullaby for Rachael. James Simmons. PNI

Lullaby for Suzanne. Michael Stillman. TLR

Lullaby for the Cat. Elizabeth Bishop. PC

Lullaby, lullaby. Phyllis L. Garlick. BoTP

Lullaby, lullaby. / It is daybreak. Lullaby. Last Daybreak Song. Unknown. APN-2, tr. by Washington Matthews Fr. The Mountain Chant.

"Lullaby, O, lullaby!" A Serenade. Thomas Hood. NBLV Fr. Domestic Poems.

Lullaby [or Lullabie] of a Lover, The. George Gascoigne. AAS; EBEV; HAP; NAEL-1; SCGP

(Gascoigne's Lullaby [or Lullabie].) NoSic; PoEL-1

("Remember Gascoigne's lullaby.") (LL) NoP-4

("Remember then this Lullabye.") (LL) GEA

("Sing lullaby, as women doe.") GEA

Lullaby of an Infant Chief. Sir Walter Scott. OxBChV

Lullaby of the Onion. Miguel Hernández, Spanish. AF, tr. by Robert Bly

Lullaby "Purple." Eve Merriam. NOxBChV

Lullaby, sweet baby mine! A Danish Cradle Song. Unknown. BoTP

Lullaby Town. John Irving Diller. BLPA

"Lullay, by-by, lullay." (LL) This Endris Night. Unknown. EBEV; NOCV

Lullay, Lullay, Like a Child. John Skelton. SCGP Fr. The Garland [or Garlande or Garlands] of Laurel[l].

(Lullay, Lullay.) ImPo

Lullay, lullay, litel child, child reste thee a throwe. Unknown. MiEL

Lullay, lullay, litel child, why wepest thu so sore? Unknown. MiEL

Lulled, at silence, the spent attack. Baggot Street Deserta. Thomas Kinsella. CIP-2; CMoP; NoAM

Lulled by rumble, babble, beep. Manhattan Lullaby. Norma Farber. SSCS; TLR

Lullee, lullay. Lullaby. Janet Lewis. CRP; NOCV

Lulling me to sleep. Michael Dudley. HA

Lulls swears he is all heart, but you'l suppose. Upon Lulls. Robert Herrick. CaPo

Lully, lulla, thou little tiny child. Coventry Carol. *Unknown.* PChr; TTTS

Lully, lullay, lully, lullay. The Corpus Christi Carol. *Unknown.* CH; EBEV; EnVB; HAP; ImPo; MiEL; NAEL-1; NOBE; NoP-4; OAEL-1; OBEV; SCV

Lumber of a London-going dray, The. An Incident in the Early Life of Ebenezer Jones, Poet, 1828. John Betjeman. CMoP; MoP; NoAM

Lumber of Spring. Anne Ridler. NYBP

Lumbering tractor rolls its panting round, The. The Agricultural Show, Flemington, Victoria. Suzanne Gardinier. CBAP

Lumberman's Alphabet, The. *Unknown.* AmFP

Lumberyard, The. Ruth Herschberger. WPE

Luminous, The. Barbara Guest. PoM

Luminous blaze! An Ode on Gas. *Unknown.* OBAL

Luminous pyrophorus / in latin letters. Beacon of Hope. Linton Kwesi Johnson. HCP

Luminous winds flicker in the moonrise. *Unknown.* SuSp, *tr. by* Michael E. Workman *Fr.* Spring. SuSp *Fr.* Tzu-yeh Songs of the Four Seasons.

"Luminously indiscreet; / Complete; continuous." (LL) The Sermon on the Warpland. Gwendolyn Brooks. BPo; LiTM; NOBA; PoBA

Lumpety, lumpety, lump! (LL) The Mischievous Raven. *Unknown.* BoTP; OxNR; ReMoGo

"Lumpish trollop, The !" Pastoral. Wyndham Lewis. UV

Lunar Baedeker. Mina Loy. VGW

Lunar Eclipse. Mei Yao Ch'en, *Chinese.* CoBCP, *tr. by* Burton Watson

Lunar Games, The. Eeva-Liisa Manner, *Finnish.* WPOW, *tr. by* Jaakko A. Ahokas

Lunar Paraphrase. Wallace Stevens. SAmP

Lunar Stanzas. Henry Coggswell Knight. CBNP

Lunatic of Lindley Meadow, The. August Kleinzahler. PmAP

Lunatic, the lover, and the poet, The. Asleep, My Love? Shakespeare. CTC; EBEvV *Fr.* A Midsummer Night's Dream.

Lunch at the Coq d'Or. Peter Davison. TwCP

Lunchcounter Freedom. Thylias Moss. PoPoPo

Luncheon, A. Max Beerbohm. NOBL; OBSV; OxBTC; PeLV
    (Luncheon (Thomas Hardy Entertains the Prince of Wales), A.) UV

Luncheon of the Boating Party, The. Leon Stokesbury. MT

Lunchroom bus boy who looked like Orson Welles, The. They Were All like Geniuses. Horace Gregory. NYBP *Fr.* The Passion of M'Phail.

Lunchtime. David Ignatow. IFJA

Lundys Letter, The. Gerald Dawe. BiHa

Lung Massif stands tens of thousands of feet. Lament for the People of Lung. P'i Jih-hsiu, *Chinese.* SuSp, *tr. by* William H. Nienhauser

Lungs draw in the air and rattle it out again, The. Remorse. John Betjeman. MoBrPo; OxBSP

Lupercalia. Ted Hughes. CMoP

Lure, The. John Boyle O'Reilly. TIRV

Lure of the Cascadura. John C. M. Lyons. NBrP

Lure of the night's dædalian sea-born breath. On an Æolian Harp. George Cabot Lodge. APN-2

Lurid Confessions. Steve Kowit. EC2

Lurking under the maple trees. The Jewish Cemetery at Olsany, Kafka's Grave, April, Sunny Weather. Miroslav Holub, *Czech.* PoSu, *tr. by* David Young *and* Dana Hábová

Lusca. John Robert Lee. HCP

Luscious and Sorrowful. Christina Rossetti. PoEL-5

Luscious lobster, with the crabfish raw, The. Kinds of Shel-fish. William Wood. SCAP

Lush grow the leaves on green stems. In Praise of Carnations. Wang Chi, *Chinese.* SuSp, *tr. by* Hellmut Wilhelm

Lush, lush, fragrant grasses in autumn green. Wang Wei. CoBCP, *tr. by* Burton Watson *Fr.* Joys of the Country: Seven Poems.

Lusiads, The. Luis de Camões, *Portuguese.* OBVE, *tr. by* Sir Richard Fanshawe
    "Rev'rend Father stood inculcating, The." PeSAV

Luss! be for ever sunk beneath. Mercury; on Losing My Pocket Milton at Luss near Ben Lomond, and Other Mountains. Robert Andrews. NOEC

Lust. Roo Borson. DeD

Lust it comes out, that gluttony went in. (LL) On Gut. Ben Jonson. NoP-4; PoPoPo

Lust of Gold, The. James Montgomery. *Fr.* The West Indies. PBCV

Lust of the Eyes, The. Elizabeth Siddal. VWP

Lustra. Christopher Okigbo. PBMAP *Fr.* Heavensgate (1961).

Lustra. Ezra Pound.
    Further Instructions. TwCP
    Rest, The. AmPP; MoAmPo; NOBA; NoAM; OxBA

Lust's too genteel to let the weather in. In a Bed-Sitter. Hal Porter. NOBAu

Lusty Juventus. Charles Madge. FaBoMo

Lusty Juventus. Robert Wever.
    In Youth Is Pleasure. NOBE; OBEV
    (Of Youth He Singeth.) CBLP

Lusty May. *Unknown.* OBEV
    (Four May Poems.) OxBS

Lusty wench as nimble as an eel, A. Epigram. John Taylor. NOSC

Lute, The. Judah Al-Harizi, *Hebrew.* BLT, *tr. by* T. Carmi

Lute and the pear are your half sisters, The. A Flock of Guinea Hens Seen from a Car. Eudora Welty. NYBP

Lute, companion of my calamity. Sonnet 12. Louise Labé, *French.* BoWoP, *tr. by* Aliki *and* Willis Barnstone

Lute Music. Kenneth Rexroth. TAP

Lute of Afric's Tribe, The. Albery Allson Whitman. APN-2

Lute Song, The. Kung Tzu-chen, *Chinese.* SuSp, *tr. by* An-yan Tang

Lute without strings, A. Without You I Am. Diana Der Hovanessian. LoHo

Lutel wot it any mon. *Unknown.* MiEL

"Luteous" to "Lymph" for "F." Tina Darragh. FTOS

Luther, they say, was unwise; he didn't see how things were going. Arthur Hugh Clough. FaBoVe *Fr.* Amours de Voyage. NOBVV

Luther to a Bluebottle Fly. Eugene Lee-Hamilton. Son *Fr.* Imaginary Sonnets.

Lutheran, Popish, Calvinistic, all of these confessions three. Faith. Friedrich von Logau, *German.* GePo, *tr. by* George C. Schoolfield

Lutra, the Fisher. James McMichael. AmPA

Luttrell, Master of Luttrellstown. Richard Murphy. PBCIP *Fr.* The Battle of Aughrim.

Luvin' wumman is a licht, A. Love. "Hugh MacDiarmid." CMoP; PoE

Lux Est Umbra Dei. John Addington Symonds. GSo

Lux, my fair falcon, and your fellows all. Sir Thomas Wyatt. FP; OxBSP; SiPS
    ("Luckes, my faire falcon, and your fellowes all.") AAS

Luxembourg 1939. Léopold Sédar Senghor. PBMAP

Luxembourg Garden. Michael S. Weaver. GT

Luxurious Man, to bring his Vice in use. The Mower Against Gardens. Andrew Marvell. CABP; EBEV; ESCV; FaBoPV; GaP; NAEL-1; NOSC; NoP-4; OAEL-1; OBGa; OxAEP-1; PBRV; PoE; PoEL-2

Luxurious room, evening.—A large lighted chandelier. Open French win. They are Coming. Filippo Tommaso Marinetti. PFTM

Luxury. Yehuda Amichai, *Hebrew.* PoSu, *tr. by* Assia Gutmann

Luxury. Donald Justice. HeIP-4

Luxury, then, is a way of. Political Poem. Imamu Amiri Baraka. AF; CoAP; MoP; NAAL-2; NoAM; PmAP

Lwonesomeness. William Barnes. NOBVV

Lyce. William Walsh. BoLoP

Lychee, The. Wang I, *Chinese.* FaBoCh, *tr. by* Arthur Waley
    (Lychee-tree, The.) ChiP, *tr. by* Arthur Waley

Lychees. Medbh McGuckian. PBCIP

Lycidas. Milton. AWP; ClHu; EBEV; EBEvV; FHYEP; GTBS-P; HAP; ImPo; InPS-3; NOBE; NOSC; OAEL-1; OBEV; OxAEP-1; PoEL-3; Poetr; SCGP; TFi; UnPo
    ("To morrow to fresh Woods, and Pastures new.") (LL) PBRV
    ("Tomorrow to fresh woods, and pastures new.") (LL) CABP; NoP-4; PFE; PoPoPo
    "But now my oat proceeds." OxBoS
    "Return Alpheus, the dread voice is past." PeECV

Lycidas and Moeris. Virgil. AWP, *tr. by* Dryden *Fr.* Eclogues.

Lycoris darling, once I burned for you. Martial, *Latin.* BoLoP, *tr. by* Peter Porter

Lydia, in Heavens Name. 1.8. Horace. OBVE, *tr. by* Sir Richard Fanshawe *Fr.* Odes.

Lydia Is Gone This Many a Year. Lizette Woodworth Reese. CH

Lydia Pinkham. *Unknown.* AS; OBCoV

Lyell's Hypothesis Again. Kenneth Rexroth. APSN

Lyf So Short, The. Palladas, *Greek.* GrAn, *tr. by* Dudley Fitts

Lying. Richard Wilbur. DiPo; HCAP; PeVV; Poetr

Lying amber of the histories, The. (LL) A Lullaby: "For wars his life and half a world away." Randall Jarrell. HCAP; OxBC

Lying apart now, each in a separate bed. One Flesh. Elizabeth Jennings. FaBoWP; LW; NoP-4; OxAEP-2; OxBTC; PBWP

Lying asleep between the strokes of night. Love And Sleep. Swinburne. APAD; BoLoP; CBLP; GLoP; GSo; LoP

Lying at Leisure during Rain. Kao Ch'i, *Chinese.* CoBLCP, *tr. by* Jonathan Chaves

Lying Awake. Thomas Hardy. FaBoVe

Lying Awake. W. D. Snodgrass. HoPM; MoAmPo; NYBP

Lying between your sheets, I challenge. The Death Grapple. Robert Graves. EP

Lying close to your heart-beat, my lips. Before Sleep. Fleur Adcock. PeNZ *Fr.* Night-Piece.

Lying Dear, The. W. S. Graham. FaBoTC

Lying disconsolate in new spring white wadded robes. Spring Rain. Li Shang-yin, *Chinese.* CoBCP, *tr. by* Burton Watson

Lying Down. Kate Daniels. FiLi

Lying Down. *Unknown, Bella Bella Indian.* STP, *tr. by* Franz Boas

Lying down I lift my legs. Troubles with the Soul at Morning Calisthenics. Anna Swirszczynska, *Polish.* BLT, *tr. by* Czeslaw Milosz *and* Leonard Nathan (b. 1924)

Lying down in the frugality of sleep. (LL) Märchenbilder. John Ashbery. LCAP-2; NOBA

Lying full length. A Morality Play: Preface. George Oppen. APSN; NNaP *Fr.* Some San Francisco Poems.

Lying Hare's lip to this day, The. (LL) How Death Came. *Unknown, Hottentot.* PeSA; TTY, *tr. by* W. H. I. Bleek

Lying here alone. Lady Izumi, *Japanese.* WeW-3

Lying in a Hammock at William Duffy's Farm in Pine Island, Minnesota. James Wright. CoAmPo; CoLAP; HAP; HCAP; HoPM; NOBA; Poetr; SAGP; TRP; VCAP; WeT

Lying in a Yuma Saloon. Jim Barnes. CDW

Lying in bed in the dark, I hear the bray. Weather Ear. Norman Nicholson. OxBSP

Lying in the dark music. The Enigma Variations. Paul Petrie. NYBP

Lying in the dark together. One, Two. Mervyn Morris. PBCV

Lying in the Grass. Sir Edmund William Gosse. EBVV

Lying in the meadow, open to you. Kenneth Rexroth. APSN *Fr.* The Love Poems of Marichiko.

Lying in the wet grass. Alexis Rotella. HA

Lying is an occupation. A Song. Laetitia Pilkington. PEW; WPE

Lying like broken sticks among the stones. (LL) Wiltshire Downs. Andrew Young. GTBS-P; NTP; OxBTC

Lying mouldering away. (LL) The Death of Queen Jane. *Unknown.* AmFP; ESPB

Lying on a Bridge. Van K. Brock. MT

Lying on my pillow, I am startled to see. New Year's Day—Following the Rhymes of Inspector Luan-chiang. Pien Kung, *Chinese.* CoBLCP, *tr. by* Jonathan Chaves

Lying so primly propped. (LL) Bells for John Whiteside's Daughter. John Crowe Ransom. CMoP; ColAP; FuPo; HAP; HeIP-4; HoPM; IMW; InPK-6; InPS-3; LiTM; MeMAP; MoAmPo; MoLi; MoP; NAAL-2; NIP-4; NOBA; NoAM; NoP-4; OxBA; PFE; PoE; Poetr; RB; SAGP; TAP; TFi; UnPo; VGW; WeW-3

Lying under the olive tree[s], O world, O death? (LL) Ultima Ratio Regum. Stephen Spender. CMoP; ImPo; LiTM; OAEL-2; OBWP; PoWW

Lying under the stars. The Heart of Herakles. Kenneth Rexroth. BLT *Fr.* The Lights in the Sky are Stars.

Lyk as the dum. The Solsequium. Alexander Montgomerie. OxBS

Lyke as a huntsman after weary chace. Edmund Spenser. *See* Sonnet 67: "Like a huntsman after weary chase."

Lyke as the armed knyght. Anne Askew. *See* The Ballad Which Anne Askew[e] Made and Sang When She Was in Newgate.

Lyke as the Culver on the barèd bough. Edmund Spenser. *See* Sonnet 89: "Like as the culver on the bared bough."

Lyke-Wake Dirge, The [*or* A]. *Unknown.* CH; EBEvV; FaBoCh; HAP; HoPM; NOBE; NTP; OBEV; PeECV; PoEL-1; TFi; WeW-3

("And Christ receive thy saul.") (LL) NoP-4

(Cleveland Lyke Wake Dirge, The.) EnSB

("This ae night, this ae night.") NoP-4

Lyle Donaghy, Poet, 1902-1949. George Buchanan. PNI

Lynch—strip of unplowed land. "Luteous" to "Lymph" for "F." Tina Darragh. FTOS

Lynched / the lakes. Our Earth Will Not Die. Niyi Osundare. HBAPE

Lynching, The. Claude McKay. ColAP; CrDW; GT; PoBA

Lynching. Lizelia Augusta Jenkins Moorer. CBWP-3

Lynching, The. Thylias Moss. GT

Lynching and Burning. Primus St. John. ISC; PoBA

Lynmouth Widow, A. Amelia Josephine Burr. LW

Lynn. Jeanne Foster. CrSp

Lynn Schmidt says. Epiphany. Pem Kremer. CrSp

Lynx, The. Charles Edward Eaton. DiPo

Lynx-eyed, cat-quiet, sleepy mild. Tintype of a Private in the Fifteenth Georgia Infantry. Paul Horgan. CBCWP

Lyre neglected, and the tuneful lay, The. To Lysander. Judith Madan. ECWP

Lyre of Myriad Tunes, The. Thế Lữ, *Vietnamese.* AVP, *tr. by* Huỳnh Sanh Thông

Lyre of the sonnet, that fully many a time. Written December 1790. Anna Seward. Son

Lyric: "The Embodiment of what." Arthur Gregor. TAP

Lyric. T. Alan Broughton. CMAP

Lyric Afterwards, A. Tom Paulin. PNI

Lyric by Nine. *Unknown.* SPE

Lyric Can Snare, The. Lee Ann Brown. PT

Lyric[k] for Legacies. Robert Herrick. BeJo

Lyric night of the lingering Indian Summer. September Midnight. Sara Teasdale. PoA

Lyric on the Lyric, A. Lizette Woodworth Reese. APN-2

Lyric Poem. Semyon Isaakovich Kirsanov, *Russian.* TCRP, *tr. by* April FitzLyon

Lyric to Mirth, A. Robert Herrick. CaPo

Lyric to Spring. Joseph W. Stilwell. OBAL

Lyricism of an Autumn Day. Kwanggun Kim, *Korean.* CKP, *tr. by* Jaihiun Kim

Lyrics. James Agee. MoAmPo

Lyrics for the Bride of God. Nathaniel Tarn.
Section: America (2): Seen as a Bird. APSN

Lyrics shimmy like. Ron Welburn. NBV

Lysidice dedicated to you, Cypris. Asclepiades. HePo, *tr. by* Barbara Hughes Fowler *Fr.* Epigrams.

Lysidice, I'm anxious to find out the meaning. Antipater of Sidon, *Greek.* GrAn, *tr. by* Tony Harrison

Lysidike dedicates. Kenneth Rexroth, *after the Greek of* Asklepiades. NNaP; PGA

Lysimachus' cushion caught Antiochus' eye. Lucilius, *Greek.* GrAn, *tr. by* Alistair Elliot

Lysistrata. Aristophanes, *Greek.* NAWM-1, *tr. by* B. B. Rogers
"Repeat after me." OBCVT, *tr. by* Douglass Parker

Lyth and listen, gentlemen. Robin Hood and the Beggar, II. *Unknown.* ESPB

Lythe and listin, gentilmen. Gest of Robyn Hode. *Unknown.* ESPB; OxBB

Lyve thowe gladly, yff so thowe may. Sir Thomas Wyatt. AAS

M

M. Anantanarayanan. John Updike. *See* I Missed His Book, but I Read His Name.

M. [*or* Mr.] Crashaw's Answer for Hope. Richard Crashaw. *See* Answer for Hope.

M. François le Vaillant Recalls His Travels to the Interior Parts of Africa. Patrick Cullinan. PeSAV

M is for Marx. Cyril Connolly. OBCoV *Fr.* Where Engels Fears to Tread.

M. le professeur in prominent senility. My Neighbor in the Mirror. Louise Glück. Son

M. l'Epicier in his white hat. Soissons. Keith Douglas. NoAM

M., Singing. Louise Bogan. ColAP; NoAM

Ma. Paul Muldoon. PNI

Ma / I never saw you. I Never Saw You. Jyoti Lanjewar, *Marathi.* OMIP, *tr. by* Vinay Dharwadker

Ma lass by munelicht fesht me frae the fail. The Deean Tractorman, Deleerit. Edith Anne Robertson. OxBS

Ma man's a gypsy. Gypsy Man. Langston Hughes. NAAAL

Ma, my heart must be made of rice straw. Nellie Wong. UnSA *Fr.* A Heart of Rice Straw.

Ma people, come an get ready. In Memoriam Ben Zwane. Wopko Jensma. PeSAV

Ma Rainey. Sterling Brown. ISC; NAAAL

Ma-wei. Li Shang-yin, *Chinese.* PLT, *tr. by* A. C. Graham

Ma-wei. Yüan Mei, *Chinese.* CoBLCP, *tr. by* Jonathan Chaves

Mabel Kelly. Turlough Carolan, *Irish.* BIrV; CIP-2, *tr. by* Austin Clarke

Mabel was married last week. Emily Writes Such a Good Letter. Stevie Smith. OBCoV

Mabel Woo. Belle Randall. CRP *Fr.* A Hundred Ways of Playing Solitaire.

Mabinog's Liturgy. David Jones.
"In the middle silences of this night's course the blackthorn." OxAEP-2

Mabrak. "Bongo Jerry." PBCV

Mac Flecknoe. Dryden. *See* MacFlecknoe; or, A Satire [*or* Satyr] upon the True-Blue [*or* -Blew] Protestant Poet T. S.

Macadam, gun-grey as the tunny's belt. Van Winkle. Hart Crane. AmPP; MoAmPo *Fr.* Powhatan's Daughter. *Fr.* The Bridge. NAAL-2

Macao. W. H. Auden. MeMAP *Fr.* A Voyage.

Macavity: The Mystery Cat. T. S. Eliot. ChAP; InPS-3; NBLV; NOBL; OBCA; OxBChV; OxBoV; PeLV; PoRA; RB; UV

Macaw preens upon a branch outspread, A. Decoration. Louise Bogan. MoAmPo

Macbeth. Andrew of Wyntoun. OxBS

Macbeth. Shakespeare.
　　"Give sorrow words; the grief that does." IMW
　　"Glamis thou art, andd Cawdor; and shalt be." OxAEP-1
　　"If we should fail?" OxBoV
　　"Is this a dagger which I see before me." EBEvV
　　"Now o'er the one half-world." OxAEP-1
　　"Raven himself is hoarse, The." EBEvV
　　"Scale of dragon, tooth of wolf." UV
　　"Seyton!—I am sick at heart." OxAEP-1
　　Thrice the Brinded Cat Hath Mewed. RB
　　Thunder. Enter the three Witches. OxBSn
　　"To-morrow, and to-morrow, and to-morrow." EBEvV; ImPo
　　　　("Hang out our banners on the outward walls.") EBEV; OxAEP-1
　　Vaulting Ambition.
　　　　("If it were done when 'tis done, then 'twere well.") UnPo

Macbeth. Horace Smith. BXAP

Macduff. Charles Tomlinson. OxBC

MacFlecknoe; or, A Satire [*or* Satyr] upon the True-Blue [*or* -Blew] Protestant Poet T. S. Dryden. CBNP; FHYEP; HAP; OAEL-1; OBSV; OxBoLi; PeLV; Poetr; TFi
　　(Mac Flecknoe.) NAEL-1; NoP-4; OxAEP-1; PoE
　　Crown Prince of Dullness, The. NOBE
　　　　("Thou last great prophet of tautology.") (LL) NOSC
　　"This is thy province, this thy wonderous way." EPCY

MacGregor's Gathering. Sir Walter Scott. OxBS

Machberoth. Immanuel di Roma, *Hebrew.* TrJP, *tr. by* J. Chotzner

Macheath and Polly. John Gay. *See* Song: "Were I laid on Greenland's coast."

Machine-gun bullets, The. Mexico, August 20, 1940. Ai. NoAM

Machine gunner aims, A. El Alamein. Steve Crow. HATNAP

Machines waited for me, The. "Antler." CLPP *Fr.* Factory.

Machines whir underground. In the unseen above towers. Twentieth Century. Lucian Blaga, *Romanian.* CEEP, *tr. by* Mihail Bogdan

"Machines will raid at dawn," they say. Dawn. Jeffery Day. NSI

Mackerel-man drives down the street, The. A Pretty Ambition. Mary Eleanor Wilkins Freeman. OBCA

Mackerel sky. *Unknown.* OxNR

MacKerral, that was one hard winter. Malcolm MacKerral. Angus Martin. FaBoTC

Macleod's Lament. Neil Munro. NSI

Macon Prairie, (Nebraska). Willa Silbert Cather. PaTW

Macrinus against Trees. "Michael Field." WPE

Macrocarpas. Michael Jackson. PeNZ

Macular Degeneration. Peter Cooley. BAP-93

Macumba Word. Aimé Césaire, *French.* PFTM, *tr. by* Clayton Eshleman *and* Annette Smith

Mad, The. Robert Pinsky. NoAM *Fr.* Essay on Psychiatrists.

Mad are predators. Too often lately they harbour, The. Geoffrey Hill. NoP-4 *Fr.* Mercian Hymns.

Mad as the Mist and Snow. W. B. Yeats. RaBo

Mad Day in March. Philip Levine. NYBP

Mad Dogs and Englishmen. Noël Coward. NBLV; NOBL; PeLV

Mad Druggest, The. Robert Penn Warren. *Fr.* Tale of Time. LCAP-2

Mad Fight Song for William S. Carpenter, 1966, A. James Wright. NoAM

Mad flight of a butterfly, The. Nazi Song. Paul Éluard, *French.* AF, *tr. by* Lloyd Alexander

Mad Gardener's Song, The. "Lewis Carroll." CBNP; OxBChV; PBMP *Fr.* Sylvie and Bruno.

Mad girl with the staring eyes and long white fingers, The. Cassandra. Robinson Jeffers. HeIP-4; LiTM

Mad Hatter's Song, The. "Lewis Carroll." NOBL *Fr.* Alice's Adventures in Wonderland.
　　("Like a tea-tray in the sky.") (LL) CTV
　　(Mad Hatter's Concert Song, The.) CBNP

Mad is the poet men call Kit. Christopher Smart. Stanley Shaw. UV

Mad Lover, The. John Fletcher.
　　"O divine star of heaven." GBL

"Orpheus I am, come from the deeps below." GBL

Mad Maid's Song, The. Robert Herrick. AWP; CH; CaPo; EnLoPo; GEA; OAEL-1; OBEV; RACG

Mad Maudlin is Come. *Unknown.* CBNP

Mad Meg on my mantelpiece. Liz Lochhead. FaBoTC *Fr.* The Furies.

Mad monsters of no kind? (LL) Hide and Seek. Robert Graves. KaS

Mad Mother, The. Wordsworth. Ro

Mad Negro Soldier Confined at Munich, A. Robert Lowell. FaBoMo; OxBC

Mad Patsy said, he said to me. In the Poppy Field. James Stephens. PoRA

Mad Poem Addressed to My Nephews and Nieces, A. Po Chü-i, *Chinese.* ChiP; NNPT, *tr. by* Arthur Waley

Mad Potter, The. John Hollander. ColAP; VCAP

Mad Queen Aeronautical Corporation . . Cyclone . 3030. Telephone Directory. Harry Crosby. SPE

Mad Scene, The. James Merrill. CoAP; NOBA; PoA; PoE; TAP

Mad sculptor in our park, A. Helen. Peter Meinke. PBCAP

Mad Song. William Blake. NAEL-2; NOEC; OAEL-2; PoE; PoEL-4

Mad Song. Denise Levertov. TAP

Mad Sonnet 1. Michael McClure. PoM

Mad Sonnet: Fame. Michael McClure. BB

Mad Sonnet: Grace. Michael McClure. BB

Mad Wolf in Lunar Web, Mad Crow on the Beach. Mac Wellman. FTOS

Mad Woman of Punnet's Town, The. Leonard Alfred George Strong. MoBrPo

Mad Yak, The. Gregory Corso. BB; PFE; PmAP

Madam and Her Madam. Langston Hughes. RACG; SAmP

Madam and the Census Man. Langston Hughes. SAmP

Madam and the Minister. Langston Hughes. NOBA

Madam and the Rent Man. Langston Hughes. SAmP

Madam and the Wrong Visitor. Langston Hughes. SAmP

Madam[e], had all antiquity [*or* antiquitie] been lost. To Mary, Lady Wroth. Ben Jonson. NOSC

MADAM, / I hope you'll think it's true. Strephon to Celia. Mary Leapor. ECWP; RACG

Madam I praise you, 'cause you'r free. To a Friend for Her Naked Breasts. "Eliza." KTR

Madam Life's a piece in bloom. To W. R. William Ernest Henley. APAD; EBVV; MoBrPo; NAEL-2; NOBVV; PeVV

Madam Mouse Trots. Dame Edith Sitwell. FaBoCh

Madam! permit a Muse, that has been long. To Madam Bhen. "Ephelia." KTR

Madam, / Reason is our soul's left hand, Faith her right. To the Countess of Bedford. Donne. NOSC

Madam, the Lady Valeria is come to visit you. Shakespeare. OxAEP-1 *Fr.* Coriolanus.

Madam to you. (LL) Madam's Past History. Langston Hughes. MoP; NoAM; SAmP

Madam, twice through the Muses' Grove I walked. Upon Mrs. Anne Bradstreet, Her Poems, Etc. John Rogers. SCAP

Madam, / Were you but only great, there are some men. To the Excellent Pattern of Beauty and Virtue, Lady Elizabeth, Countess of Ormonde. James Shirley. BeJo

Madam, withouten Many Words. Sir Thomas Wyatt. EnLoPo; NAEL-1; NoP-4; NoSic; OxBSP; SiPS

Madam would speak with me. So, now it comes. George Meredith. NOBVV *Fr.* Modern Love.

Madam, your beauty and your lovely parts. Platonic Love. Edward Herbert, 1st Baron Herbert of Cherbury. NOSC

Madam, your grace so private? Cyril Tourneur. FaBoSe *Fr.* The Revenger's Tragedy.

Madame d'Albert's Laugh. Clément Marot, *French.* AWP, *tr. by* Leigh Hunt

Madame Eglantine. Chaucer. NOBE *Fr.* The General Prologue. FHYEP; NAEL-1; NAWM-1; OAEL-1; PoE *Fr.* The Canterbury Tales.

Madame, his grace will not be absent long. Cyril Tourneur. PoEL-2 *Fr.* The Revenger's Tragedy.

Madame, I Have Come a-Courting. *Unknown.* AmFP

Madame Maynard of the hard pebble. Stranded in My Ontario. Ronald G. Everson. NOBC

Madame, / Whilst that, for which, all virtue now is sold. Epistle to Elizabeth, Countess of Rutland. Ben Jonson. BeJo

Madame, withouten Many Wordes. Madam, withouten Many Words. Sir Thomas Wyatt. AAS; EnLoPo; NAEL-1; NoSic; OBVE; OxBSP; SiPS

Madame, ye be[e]n of al[le] beaute[e] shryne [*or* shrine]. To Rosamounde. Chaucer. CBLP; EnVB; NoP-4; OAEL-1; PoE

Madam's Calling Cards. Langston Hughes. SAmP

Madam's Past History. Langston Hughes. MoP; NoAM; SAmP

Madarika. Vince Gotera. OpBo

Madboy's Song. Muriel Rukeyser. MoAmPo; TrJP

Mädchen mit dem rothen Mündchen. Heinrich Heine, *German.* AWP, *tr.* by Sir Theodore Martin

Maddening moon, A. Niyi Osundare. HBAPE, *sect.* XIX *Fr.* Moonsongs.

Made for your hands to read, your mouth to use. (LL) Future Conditional. Marilyn Hacker. CPO; DeD

Made him take up his shirt, lay down his sword. (LL) Upon Pagget. Robert Herrick. CaPo; FaBoCh

Made in Sweden: carts are my trade. (LL) A Carriage from Sweden. Marianne Moore. HAP; LiTM; TwCP

Made it for ever after red. (LL) How Roses Came Red. Robert Herrick. CaPo; SoSe-8

Made me dance with you. Latin Music in New York. Jessica Hagedorn. PmAP; WWSi

Made One With Nature. Shelley. *Fr.* Adonais; An Elegy on the Death of Keats. EBEV; FHYEP; HoPM; ImPo; NOBRP; OAEL-2; OxAEP-2; PoEL-4; TFi

("Sustains it from beneath, and kindles it above.") (LL) LBC

Made Out of Links. Hilda Morley. PmAP

Made Shine. Josephine Miles. NoAM

Made to Order Smile, The. Paul Laurence Dunbar. GT

Madeleine in Church. Charlotte Mew. VWP

"'Find rest in Him!' One knows the parsons' tags." ChIV-2

"How old was Mary out of whom you cast." MoBrPo

Madge Wildfire Sings. Sir Walter Scott. OBNC *Fr.* The Heart of Midlothian.

(Madge Wildfire's Death Song.) HAP

(Pride of Youth, The.) GTBS-P

Madison Square. A. Glanz-Leyeles, *Yiddish.* CEEP, *tr.* by Keith Bosley

Meditation on the Nativity. Sidney Godolphin. *See* Hymn: "Lord, when the wise men came from far[r]."

Madly Singing in the Mountains. Po Chü-i, *Chinese.* BLT; ChiP, *tr.* by Arthur Waley

Madman, The. S. J. Pretorius, *Afrikaans.* PeSA, *tr.* by Uys Krige *and* Jack Cope

Madman and the Lethargist, The. Coleridge. CBNP

Madman has threatened my life, A. I mean. Blue Lights. Thomas Rabbitt. NAmP90

Madman saith He said so: it is strange, The. (LL) An Epistle Containing the Strange Medical Experience of Karshish, the Arab Physician. Robert Browning. ChIV-2; NAEL-2

Madman's Song, The. John Webster. *Fr.* The Duchess of Malfi. NAEL-1

Madman's Song. Elinor Wylie. MoAmPo; PoRA

Madness. John Armstrong. NOEC *Fr.* The Art of Preserving Health.

Madness. James Dickey. NYBP

Madness. Robert Merry. NOBRP

Madness. Sachiko Yoshihara, *Japanese.* BoWoP, *tr.* by James Kirkup *and* Shozo Tokunaga

Madness of King Goll, The. W. B. Yeats. NAEL-2

Madness of love, The. Hadewijch, *Flemish.* WPoS, *tr.* by Oliver Davies

Madonna of the Evening Flowers. Amy Lowell. CPO; NALW

Madonna vs. Child. Joan Murray. FiLi

Madras, / 1965, and rain. Some Indian Uses of History on a Rainy Day. A. K. Ramanujan. OxBC

Madre Sofía. Alberto A. Ríos. NAmP90; NoAM

Madrid. Frank O'Hara. FTOS

Madrid. "Pai Wei," *Chinese.* PBWP, *tr.* by Kenneth Rexroth *and* Ling Chung

Madrid—1937. Langston Hughes. AF

Madrigal: "Astrea in this time." William Drummond, of Hawthornden. NOSC *Fr.* Urania, or Spiritual Poems.

Madrigal: "Ay me, alas, heigh ho, heigh ho!" Thomas Weelkes. FaBoCh; OxBoLi

Madrigal: "Beauty [or Beautie], and the life, The." William Drummond, of Hawthornden. PoEL-2

(Her Passing.) OBEV

Madrigal: "Come let's begin to revel't out." *Unknown.* BoTP

Madrigal, A: "Crabbed age and youth cannot live together." Shakespeare. GTBS-P; InPS-3 *Fr.* The Passionate Pilgrim.

(Age and Youth.)

Madrigal: "Daedal of my death, A." William Drummond of Hawthornden. NOSC

Madrigal: "How should I love my best?" Edward Herbert, 1st Baron Herbert of Cherbury. PoEL-2; SeCP

Madrigal: "Like the Idalian Queen[e]." William Drummond, of Hawthornden. CBLP; GBL; NOSC; OAEL-1; OBAL; PeLV; PoEL-2; SCGP

Madrigal: "My Love in her attire doth show her wit." *Unknown.* BoLoP; NAEL-1; NOBE; OBEV

Madrigal: "My mistress frowns when she should play." John Hilton. OxBoLi

(Fa La La.) CH

Madrigal: "My mistress is as fair as fine." Thomas Ravenscroft. CH; OxBoLi

Madrigal: "My thoughts hold mortal[l] strife." William Drummond, of Hawthornden. GTBS-P; NOSC; OxBSP

(Inexorable.) NOBE; OBEV

Madrigal: "This life, which seems so fair." William Drummond, of Hawthornden. OAEL-1

("Because it erst was nought, it turns to nought.") (LL) GTBS-P

Madrigal: "This world a hunting is." William Drummond, of Hawthornden. OxBSP; SAGP

Madrigal: "Unhappie [or Unhappy] Light." William Drummond, of Hawthornden. NOSC

Madrigal: "Your love is dead, lady, your love is dead." Ronald Stuart Thomas. BoLoP; EnLoPo

Madrigal. Charles Cotton. FaBoEE

Madrigal. Nicolás Guillén, *Spanish.* CLPP, *tr.* by Kenneth Rexroth

Madrigal. Sir Philip Sidney. SiPS *Fr.* Arcadia.

Madrigal. Thomas Weelkes. *See* Fara Diddle Dyno.

Madrigal. William Henry Drummond. EP

Madwoman at Rodmell. Michele Roberts. BrRo

Madwoman in the Park, The. Dame Edith Sitwell. PFTM

Madwoman of Cork, The. Patrick Galvin. BiHa

Madwoman of Papine, The. Abdur-Rahman Slade Hopkinson. PBCV

Madwoman on the Train, The. Alfred Wellington Purdy. NoAM

Madwomen of the Plaza de Mayo, The. Eli W. Mandel. NOBC

Mae West. Edward Field. FYAP

Mæcenas, you, beneath the myrtle shade. To Mæcenas. Phillis Wheatley. NAAAL

Mæg ic be me sylfum sodgied wrecan. *Unknown.* CABP *Fr.* The Seafarer (c. 10th century).

Maenads on Cithaeron, The. Euripides, *Greek.* OBCVT, *tr.* by William Arrowsmith

Maesia's Song. Robert Greene. CTC; UnPo *Fr.* Farewell to Folly.

(Song: "Sweet are the thoughts that savour of content.") PoEL-2

Maestro, extinguish the candle, serious times have come. Slavko Mihalic, *Croatian.* CEEP, *tr.* by Peter Kastmiler

Maestro has been with us since not long ago. Interview with a Child. Wislawa Szymborska, *Polish.* CEEP, *tr.* by Tadeusz Swek

Mafioso. Sandra M. Gilbert. UnSA

Mag. Carl Sandburg. SAGP

Mag Uidhir's Winter Campaign. Eochadh O'Hussey. NOIV

Magalu. Helene Johnson. BlSi; PoBA

Magda Goebbels ("This is the needle that we give"). W. D. Snodgrass. HP

Magdalen. Amy Levy. VWP

Magdalen at Michael's gate. At Glastonbury. Henry Kingsley. PoRA

Magdalen Walks. Oscar Wilde. EBVV; MoBrPo

Magdalene. Agnes Gergely, *Hungarian.* CEEP, *tr.* by Timea K. Szell

Magdalene. Marina Tsvetayeva, *Russian.* GI, *tr.* by Michael M. Naydan *and* Slava Yastremski

Magdalene (I). Boris Pasternak, *Russian.* GI, *tr.* by Nina Kossman

Maggie. Duane Niatum. HATNAP

Maggie. *Unknown.* PeP

Maggie and milly and molly and may. E. E. Cummings. AYFP; ChAP; ImGa; MeMAP; NOBA; NOxBChV; NoAM; RB

Maggie Lauder. Francis Sempill. OxBS

Maggie Mac. *Unknown.* AmFP

Maggot Song. *Unknown.* NOBAu

Magi, The. Jeffrey Fiskin. GI

Magi, The. George Garrett. MT

Magi, The. Louise Glück. PoA

("Barn / blazing in darkness, all they wish to see, The.") (LL) GI

Magi, The. Ramon Guthrie. GI; PoE

Magi, The. Milton. *Fr.* On the Morning of Christ's Nativity. MeLP; NOCV; NoP-4; PBRV; PoEL-3; SCGP

Magi. Sylvia Plath. GI

Magi, The. W. B. Yeats. CMoP; ChIV-2; GI; HAP; InPK-6; NoAM; OAEL-2; OxAEP-2; PChr; PoA; PoE; TRP; TrCP

Magic. Aimé Césaire, *French.* NegPo, *tr.* by Clayton Eshleman *and* Denis Kelly

Magic. Ovid. AWP, *tr.* by Shakespeare *Fr.* Metamorphoses. Medea's Incantation. OBVE, *tr.* by Arthur Golding

Magic. Shakespeare. AWP *Fr.* The Tempest. OAEL-1

Magic. Walter James Turner. OBGa

Magic. Xuân Diệu, *Vietnamese.* AVP, *tr. by* Huỳnh Sanh Thông

Magic and mystery, spells Circæan. Thomas Love Peacock. NOBRP   *Fr.* Rhododaphne.

Magic Apple Tree, The. Elaine Feinstein. BrRo

Magic Composer. Gilbert Sorrentino. FTOS

Magic dance, The. After the Ball. Imamu Amiri Baraka. NAAL-2

Magic dragon may hibernate in here, A. Cutstone Pond. Chao Meng-fu.   *Fr.* Twenty-Eight Poems Inscribed on T'ien-kuan Mountain. CoBLCP, *tr. by* Jonathan Chaves

Magic Flute, The. W. D. Snodgrass. NYBP

Magic Formula. *Unknown.* CA

Magic Fox. James Welch. CDW; HATNAP; NoAM

Magic Glass, The. Felicia Dorothea Hemans. NOBRP

"Magic," like the sho-nuff spaceman, you am. (LL) A Poem for "Magic." Quincy Troupe. ISC

Magic Mist, A. Owen Roe O'Sullivan, *Irish.* NOIV, *tr. by* Thomas Kinsella

Magic mists twirl around the sky. Inscribed on a Painting. Yün Shou-p'ing, *Chinese.* CoBLCP, *tr. by* Jonathan Chaves

Magic / my man. Black Magic. Sonia Sanchez. BPo

Magic of the day is the morning, The. Ballad of the Morning Streets. Imamu Amiri Baraka. TTTS

Magic (or Rousseau). Carla Harryman. FTOS

Magic Piper, The. E. L. Marsh. BoTP

Magic Problems. Lawrence Raab. BAP-93

Magic Song. *Unknown, Ojibwa Native American.* APN-2, *tr. by* Henry Rowe Schoolcraft

Magic Strings. Li Ho, *Chinese.* PLT, *tr. by* A. C. Graham

Magic Whistle, The. Margaret Rose. BoTP

Magic Wood, The. Henry Treece. SPE

Magic Words. *Unknown, Eskimo.* BLT; ImGa; PiM, *tr. by* Edward Field; RaBo; STP

Magic Words for Hunting Caribou. *Unknown, Eskimo.* STP, *tr. by* Jerome Rothenberg *and* Johnny John

Magic Words for Hunting Seal. *Unknown, Eskimo.* STP, *tr. by* Edward Field

Magic Words to Feel Better. Nakasuk, *Eskimo.* STP, *tr. by* Jerome Rothenberg

Magical Mouse, The. Kenneth Patchen. KaS

Magician, A. Eunice Ward. FPC

Magician saws a women in half, The. Magic Problems. Lawrence Raab. BAP-93

Magna Est Veritas. Coventry Patmore. GTBS-P; HAP; NOBE; NOBVV; OBEV; OBNC; OxBSP   *Fr.* The Unknown Eros.

(Truth.)

Magna Est Veritas. Stevie Smith. OxBC

Magnet, The. Thomas Stanley. NOBE

Magnet, The. Ruth Stone. MoAmPo

Magnet. Valerie Worth. KaS

Magnetic Fields, The. Andre Breton *and* Philippe Soupault, *French.* "Factory." PFTM, *tr. by* David Gascoyne

Magnetic Mountain, The. C. Day Lewis.

Nearing Again the Legendary Isle. FaBoTw; MoBrPo

Tempt Me No More. MoBrPo; OBMV; PoA

Magnets. Countee Cullen. PBMP

Magnificat, The. Bible, *N.T.* BoWoP   *Fr.* St. Luke.

("And Marie said, My soule doth magnifie the Lord.") OBVE

Magnificat. Chana Bloch. CrSp

Magnificat. Michele Roberts. APAD; BrRo; NBrP

Magnificence. John Skelton.

"Stow, birde, stow, stow!" NoSic

"Unto this process briefly compiled." NoSic

Magnificent Bull, The. *Dinka Oral Tradition.* PeP; TTTS

Magnolia. Mary Weston Fordham. CBWP-2

Magnolia. Larry Levis. CMAP

Magnolia. Tanka. Kitahara Hakushū, *Japanese.* MJT, *tr. by* Makoto Ueda

Magnum Vectigal Parsimonia. George Gascoigne. NoSic

Magpie and Pines. Louis Johnson. PeNZ

Magpie, magpie, flutter and flee. *Unknown.* OxNR

Magpie screams loudly and up his tail goes, The. *Unknown.* ChiPo

Magpies, The. Denis Glover. NTP; PeNZ

Magpies in Picardy, The. T. P. Cameron Wilson. NSI; PoFWW

Magryme, The. William Dunbar. FaBoVe

Mag's Song. *Unknown.* AS

Maguire is not afraid of death, the Church will light him a candle. Patrick Kavanagh. CIP-2   *Fr.* The Great Hunger.

Magus, The. James Dickey. GI

Magwere, Who Waits Wondering. Kingsley Fairbridge. PeSAV

Mahabharata, The. *Unknown, Sanskrit.*

Sâvitrî; or, Love and Death. TAL, *tr. by* Sir Edwin Arnold

Mahler. Jonathan Williams.

Symphony No. 3, in D Minor. VGW

Mahogany men. Uncles. Nikky Finney. ISC

Mahogany Ship, The. Judith Rodriguez. BMAP

Mahratta Ghats, The. Alun Lewis. OBWVE; PoWW

Maia. Ralph Waldo Emerson. APN-1; PAR

Maid, The. Nathan Alterman, *Hebrew.* MHP, *tr. by* Ruth Finer Mintz

Maid and I, The. Andrew Greig. FaBoTC

Maid and the Palmer, The. *Unknown.* ESPB

Maid comes into the hall, The. Lunar Eclipse. Mei Yao Ch'en, *Chinese.* CoBCP, *tr. by* Burton Watson

Maid Freed from the Gallows, The. *Unknown.* AS; AWP

("O good Lord Judge, and sweet Lord.") ESPB

Maid in the Mill, The. John Fletcher *and others.*

"Now having leisure, and a happy wind." GBL

Maid Marian. Thomas Love Peacock.

Over, Over. OxAEP-2

Robin Hood and the Grey Friars. OxAEP-2

Maid Marjory sits at the castle gate. *Unknown.* *Fr.* Medieval Norman Song. AWP, *tr. by* John Addington Symonds

Maid o' the West, The. John Clare. OAEL-2

Maid of Athens, ere we part. Byron. EBEV; FHYEP

Maid of Ehrenthal, The. Henrietta Cordelia Ray. CBWP-3

Maid of Kent, A. *Unknown.* CBLP; OxBoLi

Maid of Monterey, The. *Unknown.* AmFP

Maid of Neidpath, The. Thomas Campbell. GTBS-P

Maid of Neidpath, The. Sir Walter Scott. GTBS-P

Maid of Orleans, The. Johann Christoph Friedrich von Schiller, *German.* AWP, *tr. by* James Clarence Mangan

Maid of the Moor, The; or, The Water-Fiends. George, the Younger Colman. "Cold blows the blast--the night's obscure." NOEC

Maid she[e] went to the well to wash[e], The. The Maid and the Palmer. *Unknown.* ESPB

Maid, where's my lawrel? Oh my rageing soul! The Enchantment. Theocritus. CTC; OBVE, *tr. by* Thomas Creech   *Fr.* Idylls.

Maid Who Becomes a Bear sought the gods and found them. Last Song of the Exploding Stick. *Unknown.* APN-2, *tr. by* Washington Matthews   *Fr.* The Mountain Chant.

Maid Who Becomes a Bear walks far around, The. One of the Awl Songs. *Unknown.* APN-2, *tr. by* Washington Matthews   *Fr.* The Mountain Chant.

Maiden, The. Peter Hille, *German.* AWP, *tr. by* Jethro Bithell

Maiden. Márton Kalász, *Hungarian.* CEEP, *tr. by* Jascha Kessler

Maiden, and mistress of the months and stars. Swinburne. PoEL-5   *Fr.* Atalanta in Calydon.

Maiden and River. Mary Weston Fordham. CBWP-2

Maiden at college called Breeze, A. Limerick. Mrs. Mercy Warren. PeLi

Maiden caught me in the wild, The. The Crystal Cabinet. William Blake. CH; FaBoCh; OAEL-2; OBNC; PoEL-4; Ro

Maiden in the mor lay. A Maiden in the Moor [*or* Mor]. *Unknown.* EnVB; MiEL; PoEL-1; PoEL-5

Maiden Lies in Her Chamber, A. Heinrich Heine, *German.* AWP, *tr. by* Louis Untermeyer

Maiden moder milde. *Unknown.* MiEL

Maiden Name. Philip Larkin. GTBS-P

Maiden, not to be greeted unbenignly. (LL) Hendecasyllabics. Tennyson. EBEV; NOBL; PeLV

Maiden, there is something more. To Hersa. Forceythe Willson. APN-2

Maiden There Lived, A. *Unknown.* NOBL; PeLV

Maiden, thou wert thoughtless once. A Fragment. Anne Brontë. VWP

Maiden to the Delphic temple came, A. Love or Fame. Caroline Lindsay. VWP

Maidenhead. "Ephelia." KTR; WPE

(Maidenhead Written at the Request of a Friend.) NOSC; PEW

Maiden's Best Adorning, The. *Unknown.* OxBChV

Maidens Blush, The. Joshua Sylvester.

"But, fair Iëmpsar (wife of Potiphar)." ChIV-1

Maidens Came, The. The Bailey Beareth the Bell Away. *Unknown.* GBL; PoEL-1

Maidens, kilt your skirts and go. Celia's Home-Coming. Agnes Mary Frances Robinson. OBEV; VWP

Maidens of London's Brave Adventures, Or, a Boon Voyage Intended for the Sea, The. Laurence Price. NOSC

Maiden's Plight, The. Brian Merriman. BIrV, *tr. by* Frank O'Connor   *Fr.* The Midnight Court. NOIV, *tr. by* Thomas Kinsella

Maidens shall weep at merry morn. The Summer Malison. Gerard Manley Hopkins. CMoP; PoEL-5

Maidens who this bursting [or burning] May. A Young Man's Song. William Bell. FaBoTw

Maidens young and virgins tender. Horace. *See* Odes 1.21: To Apollo and Diana ("Dianam tenerae dicite virgines").

Maides to bed, and cover coale. A Belmans Song. Thomas Ravenscroft. PBRV

Maids. Aleksandar Ristovic, *Serbo-Croatian.* HSix, *tr. by* Charles Simic

Maid's Husband, The. Henry Carey. ECEV

Maid's Lament, The. Walter Savage Landor. OBEV; OBNC *Fr.* The Citation and Examination of Shakespeare.

    ("And, oh! pray too for me!") (LL) RACG

Maids, not to you my mind doth change. "Michael Field." VWP *Fr.* Variations on Sappho.

Maid's Thought, The. Robinson Jeffers. EP

Maids to bed and cover coal. The Bellman's Song. *Unknown.* EBEV; SCGP

Maid's Tragedy, The. Francis Beaumont *and* John Fletcher.

    Aspatia's Song. AWP; HAP; NOBE; OBEV

    (I Died True.) CH

    Bridal Song: "Cynthia, to thy power." OBEV

    Song: "Hold back thy hours, dark night, till we have done." OxBSP

Mail. Sarah Kirsch, *German.* AF, *tr. by* Wayne Kvam

Mail Has Come, The. Mary E. Tucker. CBWP-1

Mail on the counter. Rod Willmot. HA

Maim[e]'d Debauchee, The. John Wilmot, 2d Earl of Rochester. *See* The Disabled Debauchee.

Maimonides never saw the snow. Lines on the Rambam. Gabriel Preil, *Yiddish.* CEEP, *tr. by* Linda Zisquit

Main bridge of Constitution, The. Matthew XXV:30. Jorge Luis Borges, *Spanish.* GI, *tr. by* David Curzon

Main Character. Jimmy Santiago Baca. NAmP90

Main cook lies sick on a banquette, and his assistant, The. Restaurant. Maxine Hong Kingston. OpBo

Main-Deep, The. James Stephens. MoBrPo; OBMV; UnPo

Main Street. "Demyan Bedny," *Russian.* TCRP, *tr. by* Lubov Yakovleva *with* Daniel Weissbort

Main Temple Street, Puri. Jayanta Mahapatra. VCWP

Main-Truck; or, A Leap for Life, The. George Pope Morris. PoLF

Maine Lake at Night. Harry Morris. CRP

Maine Vastly Covered with Much Snow. John Tagliabue. InPK-6

Mainly I was led to them, the casinos of aluminium. Painting Mount Taranaki. David Eggleton. PeNZ

Maintrunk Country Roadsong. Sam Hunt. PeNZ

Maisie. James Merrill. HeIP-4

Maison Aragon. Tristan Tzara, *French.* PFTM, *tr. by* Jerome Rothenberg

Maitreya the Future Buddha. Gary Snyder. *Fr.* Burning. NeAP; PoM *Fr.* Myths and Texts.

Majeski Plays the Saxophone. Martín Espada. SeSe

Majestic, from the most distant time. From the Most Distant Time. Emperor Wu of Han, *Chinese.* OHMPC, *tr. by* Kenneth Rexroth

Majestic Valley. Chu Yi-tsun, *Chinese.* SuSp, *tr. by* Chang Yin-nan *and* Lewis C. Walmsley

Major André. *Unknown.* AmFP

Major Bowes' Diary. Imamu Amiri Baraka. NAAL-2

Major Macroo. Stevie Smith. NBLV

Major Work, A. William Meredith. Poetr

Majuba Hill. Roy Macnab. PeSA

Makar, The. William Soutar. FaBoTC; OxBS

Make a joyful noise unto the Lord, all ye lands. Psalm 100. Bible, *O.T., Hebrew.* NOCV *Fr.* Psalms.

Make a most infernal clatter, here the dinner comes! (LL) Going In to Dinner. Edward Richard Burton Shanks. OBMV; OxBTC

Make all your sorrow neat. The Young Wife. Derek Walcott. DiPo

Make Belicve. Gareth Owen. SpW

Make bright the arrows. Edna St. Vincent Millay. ChIV-1

Make clay ascend more quick than light. (LL) Ascension Hymn ("Dust and clay"). Henry Vaughan. ESCV; GeHe; NOSC; TrCP

Make company break. Advice of Housewives. Thomas Tusser. NoSic *Fr.* Five Hundred Points of Good Husbandry.

Make friendship with the stars. The Stars. Lydia Huntley Sigourney. ColAP

Make haste away, and let one be. To His Book[e]. Robert Herrick. NOSC

Make heathens at your doors! (LL) Bible Defence of Slavery. Frances Ellen Watkins Harper. APAD; APN-2; PAR

Make me a Bowl, a mighty Bowl. An Ode of Anacreon, Paraphras'd / The Cup. Anacreon, *Greek.* AWP; OBCVT, *tr. by* John Oldham

Make me a grave wher[e]'er you will. Bury Me in a Free Land. Frances Ellen Watkins Harper. AAP; BPo; ColAP; CrDW; ISC; NAAAL; PAR

Make me a handle as straight as the mast of a ship. To the Blacksmith with a Spade. Owen Roe O'Sullivan. IIP

Make me a heaven, and make me there. The Eye. Robert Herrick. CaPo

Make me a long coat of heavy cloth, tailor. Gingerbread Heart. Aleksandar Ristovic, *Serbo-Croatian.* HSix, *tr. by* Charles Simic

Make me chaste, Lord, but not yet. (LL) The Love Feast. W. H. Auden. OBCoV; PFE

Make me feel the wild pulsation that I felt before the strife. Tennyson. *Fr.* Locksley Hall. EBEV; EBVVPR; EnVR; FaBoBe; ImPo; NAEL-2; OAEL-2

Make me, O Lord, thy spinning wheel complete. Huswifery. Edward Taylor. ColAP; MeMAP; NAAL-1; NAAL-3; NIP-4; NOBA; NOBE; NoP-4; OxBA; SCAP; TAP; TFi

Make me too brave to lie or be unkind. A Prayer for Every Day. Mary Carolyn Davies. BLPA; FaBoBe; PoToHe

Make Me Worthy of My Friends. *Unknown.* CTV

Make men beleeve no Paradice. (LL) To Cynthia, on Concealment of Her Beauty. Sir Francis Kynaston. MeLP; NOBE

Make miniatures of the once-monstrous theme. A Short History of British India. Geoffrey Hill. OxBC

Make my cup with clay. Zonas, *Greek.* InMo, *tr. by* Sam Hamill

Make my grave shape of heart so like a flower be free aired. Snail Poem. Peter Orlovsky. BB

Make my heart as powerful as your own. Lead me to conquer. Song of the Bear. *Unknown.* APN-2 *Fr.* Minnetare Songs.

Make/n My Music. Angela Jackson. SeSe

Make new friends, but keep the old. New Friends and Old Friends. Joseph Parry. BLPA; PoToHe

Make no mistake: if He rose at all. Seven Stanzas at Easter. John Updike. TrCP

Make no mistake; there will be no forgiveness. Easter Hymn. Alec Derwent Hope. ChIV-2; GI

Make no sound, do not speak. Reading. Jean-Joseph Rabéarivelo, *French.* NegPo, *tr. by* Ellen Conroy Kennedy

Make once more my heart thy home. (LL) Song: "Rarely, rarely, comest thou." Shelley. CH; FHYEP; GTBS-P; LaPo; OBNC

Make one place ev'rywhere [or everywhere or ev'ry where]. (LL) The Temper (1). George Herbert. ESCV; FSCP; GeHe; NOCV; NoP-4; PoEL-2

Make sure that they are thoroughly cremated. (LL) Shipment to Maidanek. Ephim G. Fogel. OBWP; TrJP

Make the rhyme you're reading now. (LL) Do It Yourself. Joan Aiken. KaS; NOxBChV

Make three fourths of a cross, and a circle complete. *Unknown.* OxNR

Make thyself known, Sibyl, or let despair. Leonardo's "Mona Lisa." Edward Dowden. GSo

Make-Up. Geraldine Monk. NBrP

Make us Thy mountaineers. The Last Defile. Amy Carmichael. TrCP

Make way! From the Noisy ceilings of workshops. Ada Negri, *Italian.* PBWP, *tr. by* Lynne Lawner

Make way, make way. The Stream's Song. Lascelles Abercrombie. OBMV

Make way, make way, give leave to rove. The Little Good Fellows. Herman Melville. NCAP

Make we mery bothe more and lasse. *Unknown.* MiEL

Make Ye a Joyful Sounding Noise. *Unknown.* AH

Make yourself pure before you purify others. Tune: "As in a Dream; a Song." Su Shih, *Chinese.* SuSp, *tr. by* Irving Y. Lo

Maken pilgrimage to herself, walken. Sonia Sanchez. *See* Present.

Maker-of-Sevens in the scheme of things. The Wife-Woman. Anne Spencer. NAAAL

Makers, The. David Galler. NYBP

Makers, The. Howard Nemerov. DiPo; FYAP

Makes a man healthy, wealthy and wise. (LL) Early to bed and early to rise. *Unknown.* CTV; FaBoBe

Makes him to his own blood strange. (LL) Intellect. Ralph Waldo Emerson. APN-1; NoP-4

Makes me writhe. Tanka. Masaoka Shiki, *Japanese.* MJT, *tr. by* Makoto Ueda

Makes summer's welcome thrice more wish'd, more rare. (LL) Sonnet 56. Shakespeare. PoLF; SCGP

Makes the Little Ones Dizzy. Samuel Hoffenstein. BXAP

Makes Time so vicious in his reaping. (LL) For a Dead Lady. Edwin Arlington Robinson. CMoP; FYAP; HeIP-4; HoPM; LiTM; MoAmPo; MoP; NOBA; NoAM; OxBA; PoEL-5; PoRA; TFi

Makeshift. Laura Riding Jackson. BAP-93

Makeup on Empty Space. Anne Waldman. PoA

akhno's Philosophers. John Streeter Manifold. CBAP; NOBAu

Makin' Jump Shots. Michael S. Harper. ISC; PoE
("Gliding / as he sinks two into the chains.") (LL) AFr

Makin' Whoopee. Gustave Kahn. OBCoV

Making a Door. Dennis Schmitz. LCAP-2

Making a Great Space Small. Greg Pape. PaTW

Making a Man. Nixon Waterman. BLPA

Making Camp. David Wagoner. VCAP

Making Chicago. Dennis Schmitz. LCAP-2

Making Contact. John Streeter Manifold. CBAP

Making Feet and Hands. Benjamin Péret, *French*. SPE, *tr. by* David Gascoyne

Making Fun of the Well at the Inn below the Mountain. Chu Yün-ming, *Chinese*. CoBLCP, *tr. by* Jonathan Chaves

Making Hay. Philip Hodgins. NOBAu

Making his advances. Tortoise Gallantry. D. H. Lawrence. APo; CMoP; MoP

Making It Simple December 8, 1969. David McElroy. AmPA

Making Lists. Gladys Cardiff. HATNAP

Making love down through the centuries. Here Today. Andrew Elliott. PNI

Making love for ten thousand years on a rockledge. The Lovers. David Campbell. BMAP   *Fr.* Ku-ring-gai Rock Carvings.

Making Love to Myself. James L. White. GLP

Making Money: Drought Year in Minkler, California. Gary Soto. NoAM

Making of a Servant, The. J. J. R. Jolobe. PeSAV

Making of Birds, The. Katharine Tynan. TIRV

Making of Color, The. Hugh Seidman. AmPA

Making of Poems, The. Lucille Clifton. CrSp

Making of the Cross, The. William Everson. VGW

Making Old Bones. Alberta Turner. LCAP-2

Making Our Clowns Martyrs. Jack A. Mapanje. HBAPE

Making pilgrimage to herself. walking. (LL) Present. Sonia Sanchez. NAAAL; UnSA

Making Poetry. Anne Stevenson. DiPo

Making Samosas. Chitra Divakaruni. NMM-2

Making Tens. M. M. Hutchinson. BoTP

Making the batter understand too late. (LL) Pitcher. Robert Francis. OxBSP; RaBo; WeW-3

Making the Children Behave. William Daniel Ehrhart. CDa

Making the green one red. (LL) Macbeth Does Murder Sleep. Shakespeare. EBEV; OxAEP-1

Making the Jam without You. Maxine W. Kumin. NALW

Making the marmalade this year, I carve. Preserving. Roy Fuller. CBLP

Making the Move. Paul Muldoon. NoAM

Making the Snowshoes. R. T. Smith. EC2

Making the woods reëcho with his song. (LL) The Fair Morning. Jones Very. GSo

Making Up for a Soul. David Wagoner. VGW

Makings of Happiness, The. Ronald Wallace. PBCAP

Malacoda. Samuel Beckett. CIP-2

Malady of Love Is Nerves, The. Petronius Arbiter, *Latin*. AWP, *tr. by* Howard Mumford Jones

Malady smote the earth one year, A. The Animals Sick of the Plague. Marianne Moore, *ad. fr.* La Fontaine. InPS-3

Malaga. Pearse Hutchinson. BIrV; PBCIP

Malapert March is parent to all these. Pruning in March. Vita Sackville-West. GaP

Malaria. Paolo Ruffilli, *Italian*. NeIt, *tr. by* Felix Stefanile

Malcolm. Lucille Clifton. NAAAL

Malcolm. Welton Smith. BPo

Malcolm Is 'Bout More Than Wearing a Cap. Michael Warr. UnSA

Malcolm Lowry. Epitaph. Malcolm Lowry. OBCoV

Malcolm MacKerral. Angus Martin. FaBoTC

Malcolm Mooney's Land. W. S. Graham. FaBoTC

Malcolm Spoke / Who Listened? Haki R. Madhubuti. NAAAL

Malcolm X. Gwendolyn Brooks. PoBA; TTY
("Original.") NAAAL

Malcolm X—an Autobiography. Larry Neal. BPo

Malcontent, The. John Marston.
"I cannot sleepe, my eyes ill neighbouring lids." PoEL-2

Malcontents, The. Dryden. *Fr.* Absalom and Achitophel, Pt. I. EBEvV; FHYEP; FaBoPV; HAP; NOSC; OAEL-1; PoE

Maldive Shark, The. Herman Melville. APN-2; APo; AmPP; ColAP; GEA; NAAL-1; NAAL-3; NCAP; NOBA; NoP-4; OxBA; PAR; PFE; PoE; PoEL-5; RB; TAP

Maldoror. Comte de Lautréamont, *French*.

"I am filthy. Lice gnaw me. Swine, when they look at me, vomit. The scabs." PFTM, *tr. by* Alexis Lykiard

Male, The. Carla Harryman. PmAP

Male & Female Loves in Beulah. William Blake. OBNC   *Fr.* Jerusalem; The Emanation of the Giant Albion.

Male child—ox abandoned to the vultures!, A. A War Song of the Basotho. *Unknown*. PeSAV, *tr. by* Daniel P. Kunene

Male Rage Poem. Pier Giorgio Di Cicco. NOBC

Malediction Upon Myself. Elinor Wylie. ColAP

Malefic Return, The. Ramón López Velarde, *Spanish*. OBVE, *tr. by* Samuel Beckett

Malemute Dog, A. Pat O'Cotter. BLPA

Malepractice and maleabsence issue is loneliness & limiting to-. Men and Birth: the Unexplainable. Don L. Lee. RaBo

Malest Cornifici Tuo Catullo. Allen Ginsberg. BB; NeAP

Malfeasance, The. Alan Bold. OBSP

Malice of Innocence, The. Denise Levertov. NNaP

Malicious Envy rode. Envy. Edmund Spenser. *Fr.* Wood Of Error. AEP

Malignant growth of ivy. The Garden of Old People. Miroslav Holub, *German*. CEEP, *tr. by* Stuart Friebert *and* Dana Hábová

Malignant planets! do ye still combine. The Sow of Feeling. Robert Fergusson. NOEC

Malines. James Kenneth Stephen. OBCoV

Malta. John Forbes. NOBAu

Malte Laurids, peevish: *And one has*. Inheritances. Jane Cooper. *Fr.* Dispossessions. FaBoWP

Maltese Dog, A. Tymnes, *Greek*. FaBoCh; FaBoEE; Spl, *tr. by* Edmund Blunden   *Fr.* Epigrams.
(Dog from Malta.) OBCVT, *tr. by* Edmund Blunden; GrAn

Maltese Goat. Nigel Dennis. PFE

Malvern Hill. Herman Melville. APN-2; AmPP; CBCWP; ColAP; PAR; TAP

Malvern Hills. Joseph Cottle.
Industrial Evils. NOEC

Malvern Water, says Dr. John Wall. Malvern Waters. *Unknown*. FaBoEE

Mam, we're playing funerals now. (LL) Take One Home for the Kiddies. Philip Larkin. OxBTC; PeP

Mama. Claire Kageyama. UnSA

Mama and Daughter. Langston Hughes. UnPo

Mama & I / & Rosa, we hope never to meet. At Coueron. My First Gun. Pamela Alexander. WeT

Mama, come back. Nellie Wong. UnSA

Mama Dot's Treatise. Frederick D'Aguiar. HCP

Mama / eats death / tastes like fish. Monogram 4. Martina Werner, *German*. BoWoP, *tr. by* Rosemarie Waldrop

Mama Have You Heard the News. *Unknown*. AS

Mama / I wish I were silver. Silly Song. Federico García Lorca, *Spanish*. TTTS, *tr. by* M. D. Herter Norton

Mama is mending / my underwear. The Night Before Good-Bye. Mitsuye Yamada. NMM-2

Mama Julinda is let down into a hole. Island Funeral. Frank Stanford. MT

Mama, lying so far down. Unveiling. Hilary Sametz Lloyd. MDDM

Mama Mary's counting them. Birds on a Powerline. Herbert Asquith. NAAAL

Mama, / papa, / and us. An Inconvenience. John Raven. BPo; CRP

Mama, please brush off my coat. Mama and Daughter. Langston Hughes. UnPo

Mama Remembers. Lawrence Joseph. FiLi

Mama Rosanna's Last Bead-Clack. Laurel Speer. CrSp

Mama spent pennies. Portrait. Carolyn M. Rodgers. MBE

Mama's Report. Michael S. Harper. FiLi

MAME was singing. Queen of the Blues. Gwendolyn Brooks. NALW; SeSe

Mamma! Frank Horne. BPo

Mamma sent me to the spring, she told me not to stay. Chewing Chawing Gum. *Unknown*. AmFP

Mammon Marriage. George Macdonald. BoLoP; EBVV

Mammoth morning moved grey flanks and groaned, A. Walking Wounded. Vernon Scannell. OBWP

Mams, pig-sick of oilstains in the wash, The. Breaking the Chain. Tony Harrison. UV

Man. Ioan Alexandru, *Romanian*. CEEP, *tr. by* Andrei Banta *and* Thomas Amherst Perry

Man, The. Robert Creeley. OBAL

Man. Sir John Davies. *Fr.* Nosce Teipsum. NoSic; SiPS
"I know my soul hath power to know all things." OBEV

Man. George Herbert. ESCV; FSCP; GeHe; ImPo; NAEL-1; NoP-4; PoEL-2; SeCP

Man, The. Man and Woman Go Through the Cancer Ward. Gottfried Benn, *German*. PFTM, *tr. by* Babette Deutsch

Man. Kenneth Rexroth. *Fr.* A Bestiary. OBAL

Man. Swinburne. *See* Chorus: "Before the beginning of years."

Man. Archana Varma, *Hindi*. OMIP, *tr. by* Aruna Sitesh *and* Arlene Zide

Man. Henry Vaughan. ESCV; FMP; GeHe; MeLP; NOBE; NOCV; OBEV; PoEL-2; SCGP

Man. Humbert Wolfe. MoBrPo

Man: 1961. Pranabendu Dasgupta, *Bengali*. OMIP, *tr. by* Buddhadeva Bose

Man, I think it is a man. My Dream About the Poet. Lucille Clifton. TRP

Man, a man, a kingdom for a man!, A. A Cynic Satire. John Marston. NoSic *Fr.* Satires.

Man, a woman, an old man. They are in a hut. The man holds a news-, A. Hair Tonic. Gisèle Prassinos, *French*. PFTM, *tr. by* Marcel Jean

Man, a woman, straighten up from where, A. Vincent Buckley. BMAP

Man adrift on a slim spar, A. Stephen Crane. APN-2; NAAL-2 ("God is cold.") (LL) NoP-4

Man against the Sky, The. Edwin Arlington Robinson. AmPP; CMoP; OxBA

Man All Grown Up Is Supposed To, A. Terry Stokes. AmPA

Man Alone. Louise Bogan. NYBP; NoP-4

Man alone at the third-floor window, The. West Strand Visions. James Simmons. PBCIP

Man and a woman recite their dreams, A. Tracing of an Evening. David Shapiro. PmAP

Man and a woman sit near each other, and they do not long, A. A Third Body. Robert Bly. LoL

Man and Bat. D. H. Lawrence. RB

Man and Beast. Léopold Sédar Senghor, *French*. PFTM, *tr. by* Melvin Dixon

Man and Cows. Andrew Young. EBEV

Man and Dog. Edward Thomas. PeFWW

Man and God Distinguished. Michael Echeruo. PBMAP

Man and Height. John Rice. SpW

Man and His Image, The. Jean de La Fontaine, *French*. OBVE, *tr. by* Elizur Wright

Man and his wife are estranged, A. Estrangements. William Pitt Root. IFJA

Man and the Infinite. "Hugh MacDiarmid." FaBoTC *Fr.* A Drunk Man Looks at the Thistle.

Man and the Tree, The. Philip Mead. NOBAu

Man and the Weasel, The. Phaedrus, *Latin*. AWP, *tr. by* Christopher Smart

Man and Wife. Mitchell Goodman. SAGP; VGW

Man And Wife. Robert Lowell. AmPP; BoLoP; CoAmPo; ColAP; LoP; NAAL-2; SAGP; VCAP

Man-and-Wife Mountain, The. Ho Xuan Huong, *Vietnamese*. AVP, *tr. by* Huỳnh Sanh Thông

Man and Woman. Robert Conquest. OxBTC

Man and woman, A. The Woman's Dream. Frances Horovitz. BrRo

Man and Woman Absolutely White, A. André Breton, *French*. PFTM, *tr. by* David Antin

Man and woman are like the earth, that brings forth flowers. D. H. Lawrence. *See* Fidelity and love are two different things, like a flower and a gem.

Man and woman Go Through the Cancer Ward. Gottfried Benn, *German*. PFTM, *tr. by* Babette Deutsch

Man and woman walking, A. The Feather. Lilian Bowes-Lyon. LW

Man Arrested in Hacking Death Tells Police He Mistook Mother-in-Law for Raccoon. Susan Bartels Ludvigson. MT

Man at the moment of departure, turning, A. Ritual of Departure. Thomas Kinsella. CIP-2; CMoP

Man Awakened by a Song Above His Roof, The. Tomas Tranströmer, *Swedish*. SPE, *tr. by* Robert Bly

Man behind the book may not be man, The. The Intellectual. Karl Shapiro. CMoP

Man bent over his guitar, The. Wallace Stevens. CMoP; NoAM; RaBo *Fr.* The Man with the Blue Guitar.

Man, bewar of thine wowing. *Unknown.* MiEL

Man blew away, A. The Blizzard. Roger McDonald. NOBAu

Man-brained and man-handed ground-ape, physically, The. Original Sin. Robinson Jeffers. MoAmPo

Man called Andronicus (Titus), A. Limerick. Paul Wigmore. PeLi

Man came into the store, A. Inventory. Frank Stanford. MT

Man Can Complain, Can't He?, A. Ogden Nash. NBLV

Man Cannot Name Himself. Luci Shaw. TrCP

Man Carrying Bale. Harold Monro. MoBrPo

Man Closing Up, The. Donald Justice. CoAP

Man comes home in the morning and finds himself waiting, A. Three Self-Plagiarisms. David Avidan, *Hebrew*. IP, *tr. by* Bargad, Warren and Stanley Chyet *Fr.* Traveling in the City. IP, *tr. by* Warren Bargad *and* Stanley F. Chyet

Man, could you in yourself the vermin all behold. The Abomination Of Evil. "Angelus Silesius." GePo, *tr. by* George C. Schoolfield *Fr.* The Cherubical Wanderer.

Man Cursing the Sea. Miroslav Holub, *Czech*. VCWP, *tr. by* Stuart Friebert *and* Dana Hábová

Man dances with twelve girls, A. Kelvin Corcoran. NBrP

Man dear, did you never hear of buxom Molly Bloom at all. Post Ulixem Scriptum. James Joyce. OBCoV

Man differs more from Man, than Man from Beast. (LL) A Satire against Reason and Mankind. John Wilmot, 2d Earl of Rochester. CABP; SCV

Man, dream[e] no more of curious mysteries. Sonnet: "Man, dream[e] no more of curious mysteries." Greville Fulke. NOSC; NoSic *Fr.* Caelica.

Man-Fate, The. William Everson. NoAM

MAN FEARED THAT HE MIGHT FIND AN ASSASSIN, A. Stephen Crane. APN-2; MeMAP; NAAL-2; NoP-4 *Fr.* The Black Riders [and Other Lines].

Man Flammonde, from God knows where, The. Flammonde. Edwin Arlington Robinson. AmPP; CMoP; LiTM; MeMAP; NoAM

Man flees suffocation. René Char, *French*. AF, *tr. by* Mary Ann Caws

Man! Foolish Man! On Exodus 3: 14: "I am that I am." Matthew Prior. ChIV-1; NOCV

Man fools about with self-analysis. The Collective Portrait. Robert Finch. MoCV

Man, for whom everything is past. Remembrance of Five Loaves. Mikhail Pozdnyayev, *Russian*. TCRP, *tr. by* Vladimir Lunis *and* Albert C. Todd

Man Frail, and God Eternal. Isaac Watts. ECEV

Man from Changi, The. Graeme Hetherington. NOBAu

Man from Maputo and so on, A. Limerick. J. H. Lee. PeLi

Man from Snowy River, The. Andrew Barton Paterson. CBAP

Man from Strathbogie, The. Olive Mary Finnin. NOBAu

Man from the Crowd, The. Sam Walter Foss. PoLF

Man from the Death Institute. Novica Tadic, *Serbian*. VCWP, *tr. by* Charles Simic

Man from the *Washington Post*, A. Limerick. Anthony Burgess. PeLi

Man from Washington, The. James Welch. CDW; HATNAP; NoAM; PoPoPo; RaBo

Man grows old and indolent, A. (LL) But I Am Growing Old and Indolent. Robinson Jeffers. ColAP; NOBA; TAP

Man had just married an automobile, A. The Automobile. Russell Edson. LCAP-2; RaBo

Man has been standing, A. The Tunnel. Mark Strand. HeIP-4; TwCP

Man has created death. (LL) Death. W. B. Yeats. OxAEP-2; OxBSP

Man has forgot his Origin; in vain. The Origin of Man, I. Jones Very. APN-1; PAR

Man has found no comfort in the grave, The. (LL) The Man Who Dreamed of Faeryland. W. B. Yeats. CMoP; NAEL-2; NoAM; NoP-4

Man Has Lost His Way, A. Trần Tế Xu'o'ng, *Vietnamese*. AVP, *tr. by* Huỳnh Sanh Thông

Man has no roots, A. T'ao Ch'ien, *Chinese*. SuSp, *tr. by* Eugene Eoyang

Man has nought so much his own. The Bonds of Friendship. Simon Dach, *German*. GePo, *tr. by* Ingrid Wal[ø]e-Engel

Man He Killed, The. Thomas Hardy. CMoP; ChAP; HAP; HeIP-4; LiTM; MoBrPo; NIP-2; OBWP; PBMP; Poetr; RB; TFi; WeW-3

Man hired by John Smith and Co., A. Limerick. "Mark Twain." InPK-6; PeLi

Man. His Bowl. His Raspberries, The. Claudia Rankine. GT

Man, husband existence: ne'er launch on the sea. Epitaph of Cleonicus. Theocritus, *Greek*. FaBoEE, *tr. by* Charles Stuart Calverley

Man I had a love for, The. An Old Woman's Lamentations. François Villon, *French*. MoBrPo; OBMV, *tr. by* J. M. Synge

Man I saw in the forest, The. Dream 2: Brian the Still-Hunter. Margaret Atwood. BuWuP; CrSp

Man, if I said once, 'I know'. The Islands. Randall Jarrell. SPE

Man, if you God as balm, as light, and sweetness take. Take Therefore That You May Have. "Angelus Silesius." GePo, *tr. by* George C. Schoolfield *Fr.* The Cherubical Wanderer.

Man, if your heart is gold, and if your soul is pure. The Spiritual Ark And The Manna-Vessel. "Angelus Silesius." GePo, *tr. by* George C. Schoolfield *Fr.* The Cherubical Wanderer.

Man I'm telling you about brought himself back alive, The. The Zodiac. James Dickey.

Man in a restaurant shook hands with someone, A. Considering How Exaggerated Music Is. Leslie Scalapino. FTOS

Man in a Window. Ralph Angel. NAmP90

Man in Black, The. Mark Strand. SPE

Man in Blue, A. James Schuyler. FTOS; PmAP

Man in Hangchou Spread Word that I Had Died. Chen-chü Heard of This and Was Upset, So I Have Written This To Send Him, A. Ni Tsan, *Chinese.* CoBLCP, *tr. by* Jonathan Chaves

Man in his life has no time to have, A. Yehuda Amichai, *Hebrew.* VCWP, *tr. by* Benjamin Harshav *and* Barbara Harshav

Man in his secret shrine. Hymn in Columbus Circle. Stephen Vincent Benét. OBAL

Man in Love, A. Lady Mary Wortley Montagu. LW

Man in Our Town. *Unknown.* ReMoGo

Man in righteousness arrayed, The. Horace. *See* Odes 1.22.

Man in righteousness arrayed [*or* array'd], The. To Sally. John Quincy Adams. APN-1; AWP; OBAL

Man in terror of impotence, A. The Ninth Symphony of Beethoven Understood at Last as a Sexual Message. Adrienne Rich. TAP

Man in the black suit delivers a eulogy, The. The Eulogy. Carol Muske. PBCAP

Man in the feed store called them mountain beavers, The. Looking for Mountain Beavers. David Wagoner. VGW

Man in the Honeysuckle, The. David Campbell. BMAP

Man in the House, A. Mark McWatt. HCP

Man in the Land of the Houyhnhnms, A. Limerick. W. S. Brownlie. PeLi

Man in the middle of the street. Petronius Arbiter, *Latin.* OBCVT, *tr. by* Tim Reynolds

Man in the Mirror, The. Mark Strand. NYBP

Man in the Moon. Linda Hogan. HATNAP

Man in the Moon ("Man in the moon came tumbling down"). *Unknown.* OxBoLi; ReMoGo

Man in the Moon ("Man in the moon was caught in a trap, The"). *Unknown.* OxNR

Man in the Moon ("Mon in the mone stond and strit"). *Unknown.* MiEL

Man in the Moon, The. Margaret Stanley-Wrench. WPN *Fr.* The Newdigate Prize Poem 1937.

Man in the moon, The. *Unknown.* CBNP; LB; OxBoLi; OxNR

Man in the Moon, as he sails the sky, The. *Unknown.* OTCP

Man in the moon came tumbling down. Man in the Moon. *Unknown.* OxBoLi; ReMoGo

Man in the moon drinks claret / But he is a dull jack-a-dandy, The. Man in the Moon. *Unknown.* OxNR

Man in the Moon looked out of the moon, The. Bedtime. *Unknown.* ReMoGo

Man in the Moon Stayed up To Late, The. J. R. R. Tolkien. OBSP

Man in the moon was caught in a trap, The. Man in the Moon. *Unknown.* OxNR

Man in the mune / is making shune, The. *Unknown.* OxNR

Man in the next bed died just after eating lunch, The. We Are All Vultures. John Yau. PT

Man in the Rain, The. Van K. Brock. MT

Man in the red scarf comes—from five split places, The. The Raspberry in the Pudding. Philip O'Connor. SPE

Man in the Street. Robert Penn Warren. OBAL

Man in the street is fed, The. Carl Sandburg. OxBA

Man in the Tree, The. Mark Strand. CBNP; SPE

Man in the wilderness asked [of] me [*or* said to me], The [*or* A]. Mother Goose. BoTP; CBNP; FaBoCh; LB; OxNR; ReMoGo; Spl

Man in the wilderness asked of me, The. *Unknown.* ACTP; FPC

Man in this Lapst Estate at very best. Edward Taylor. *See* God's Selecting Love in the Decree.

Man into a Churchyard. Bernard Gutteridge. SPE

Man, introverted man, having crossed. Science. Robinson Jeffers. OxBA

Man is a spirit. This the poor flesh knows. Stevie Smith. OxBC

Man Is a Weaver. Moses ibn Ezra, *Hebrew.* TrJP, *tr. by* Emma Lazarus

Man is bending his wife, A. Conjugal. Russell Edson. PmAP

Man Is Born in Tao. Chuang Tzu, *Chinese.* BLT, *tr. by* Thomas Merton

Man is clothed, The. And When the Green Man Comes. John Haines. CoAmPo

Man is dear to man: the poorest poor. Wordsworth. PoToHe

Man is following me, A. Jennifer Rankin. BMAP

Man is immortal. Eternity. Bozhidar Bozhilov, *Bulgarian.* CEEP, *tr. by* Jascha Kessler *and* Aleksandar Shurbanov

Man Is in Pain. Philip Lamantia. NeAP

Man is leaning on a cold iron rail, A. The Man Who Loved Islands. Derek Walcott. NoAM

Man is no microcosm, and they detract. The Habitation. Ralph Knevet. NOSC

Man is pictured in the photo—, A. My Photograph. Vadim Konstantinovich Strelchenko, *Russian.* TCRP, *tr. by* Lubov Yakovleva

Man is singing on the bus, A. An Ordinary Morning. Philip Levine. WWSi

Man is still alive, The. Amnesty. "Ivan Venediktovich Elagin," *Russian.* TCRP, *tr. by* Bertram D. Wolfe

Man Is The Highest Thing. "Angelus Silesius." GePo, *tr. by* George C. Schoolfield *Fr.* The Cherubical Wanderer.

Man Is What He Wills to Be. Mrs. Henry Linden. CBWP-4

Man knocked three times, A. Madam and the Wrong Visitor. Langston Hughes. SAmP

Man know[e]s where first he ships himself[e], but he. Man's Dying-Place Uncertain. Robert Herrick. CaPo

Man Leavens the Batch. Mildmay Fane, 2d Earl of Westmorland. BeJo

Man leaves the world, A. Streets. Naomi Shihab Nye. NAmP90

Man, like others, formed by God, A. The Saxons of Flint. *Unknown, Welsh.* OBWVE, *tr. by* Mary C. Llewelyn

Man lives his life in a dust bowl. Han-shan, *Chinese.* SuSp, *tr. by* Eugene Eoyang

Man lives in the wide world, A. Aleksandr Petrovich Mezhirov, *Russian.* TCRP, *tr. by* Deming Brown

Man looking into the sea. A Grave. Marianne Moore. CMoP; FaBoWP; GEA; HAP; HeIP-4; MeMAP; MoP; NAAL-2; NOBA; NoAM; NoP-4; OxBoS; PoE; Poetr; TAP; TFi; TRP; UnPo; WPE; WeW-3

Man Lost by a River, A. Michael C. Blumenthal. RaBo

Man Lying on a Wall. Michael Longley. PNI

Man-made bay, its fat weeds, The. Mission Bay. John Koethe. PoA

Man may make a Remark, A. Emily Dickinson. SAmP

Man Meeting Himself. Howard Sergeant. SPE

Man Meets a Woman in the Street, A. Randall Jarrell. NoP-4

Man meye longe him lives wene. *Unknown.* MiEL

Man-Moth, The. Elizabeth Bishop. CBNP; LiTM; MoAmPo; MoP; NALW; NOBA; NoAM; Poetr

Man, my friend, whose conscious heart, The. To Aristius Fuscus. Horace. OBVE *Fr.* Odes.

Man never knows precisely what is right. Essay on Man. *Unknown.* PoToHe

Man o' War Bird. Derek Walcott. TTY

Man of Bombay, The. *Unknown.* ReMoGo

Man of bone confirms his throne, The. The New Ancient of Days. Herman Melville. OBAL

Man of Calvary, The. "Sin-Killer" Griffin.

"Roman soldiers come singing in full speed." AmFP

Man of firm and noble soul, The. Translation from Horace. Horace, *Latin.* OBCVT, *tr. by* Byron

Man of God is drunken without wine, The. Jelaluddin Rumi. TAL, *sect.* I–IX, *tr. by* Reynold A. Nicholson *Fr.* Dīvāni Shamsi Tabrīz.

Man of Green Hill. The Song of the Man of Green Hill. Kao Ch'i, *Chinese.* CoBLCP, *tr. by* Jonathan Chaves

Man of independent means, A. No Occupation. George Rostrevor Hamilton. FaBoEE

Man of life upright, The. Thomas Campion. AAS; NoSic; PoRA

Man of marble holds the throne, A. The Roman Stage. Lionel Pigot Johnson. NOBVV

Man of massive meditation, A. Analogue of Unity in Multeity. Richard Eberhart. Poetr

Man of My Time. Salvatore Quasimodo, *Italian.* ItIP

("Black birds, the wind, cover over their hearts, The.") (LL) AF, *tr. by* Jack Bevan

Man of Mystery. Dahlia Ravikovitch, *Hebrew.* IP, *tr. by* Warren Bargad *and* Stanley F. Chyet

Man of numbers, The. Numerology. Jerome Rothenberg. FTOS

Man of Prayer, The. Christopher Smart. *See* Strength.

Man of Sense in Bedlam, I recount, A. His Petition to Mr. Speaker. James Carkesse. CBNP

Man of Tao-his iron flute plays music, The. Yang Wei-chen. *Fr.* Songs of Lake Tung-t'ing. CoBLCP, *tr. by* Jonathan Chaves

Man of Taste, The. James Bramston.

"Whoe'er he be that to a taste aspires." NOEC

Man of the House, The. Katharine Tynan. TIRV

Man of the House, The. David Wagoner. NoAM

Man of Thessaly, [The]. *Unknown. See* Alexander's Song.

Man of Tyre went down to the sea, The. D. H. Lawrence. TOF

Man-of-war enchanted, A. Press-Gang. George Mackay Brown. FaBoTC *Fr.* Runes from a Holy Island.

Man-of-War Hawk, The. Herman Melville. APN-2; APo

Man of Words, A. John Ashbery. PoA

Man of Words [and not of deeds], A. *Unknown.* CBNP; CTV; OTCP

Man on a Fire Escape. Edward Hirsch. WWSi

Man on his own in a car, A. Meditation on the A30. John Betjeman. RB

Man on the dubious waves of error toss'd. William Cowper. NOCV *Fr.* Truth.

Man on the Dump, The. Wallace Stevens. HAP; NAWM-2; NoAM

Man on the Edge. Herberto Padilla, *Spanish.* VCWP, *tr. by* Alastair Reid *and* Alexander Coleman

Man on the Flying Trapeze, The. George Leybourne. BLPA; FaBoBe

Man on the Flying Trapeze, The. Jack Prelutsky. FuFo

Man on the Flying Trapeze, The. *Unknown.* BLPA; OxBoLi

Man on the Hotel Room Bed, The. Galway Kinnell. VCAP

Man on the Moon, The. Judy Turner. CTV

Man on the phone says he is blind, The. The Power of Faith. Thomas Rabbitt. NAmP90

Man on the porch is only the man, The. At the Lakehouse. Brighde Mullins. BAP-94

Man once married who hunts wife once more, A. *Unknown, Greek.* GrAn, *tr. by* Alistair Elliot

Man one time became dementedly fond of his cat, A. The Cat Changed to a Woman. Jean de La Fontaine, *French.* PC, *tr. by* Marianne Moore

Man—pitiful insect. Ch'i-yü-ko. *Unknown, Chinese.* CoBCP, *tr. by* Burton Watson

Man points with his umbrella, A. Paul Evans. NBrP *Fr.* The Sofa Book.

Man pulling radishes, The. Issa, *Japanese.* EnlH, *tr. by* Robert Hass

Man Rapes 25 in fight. Up, Up, Home & Away. John Forbes. NOBAu

Man Root, The. Kazuko Shiraishi, *Japanese.* WPJ, *tr. by* Kenneth Rexroth *and* Ikuko Atsumi

Man said, The. An Historic Moment. William J. Harris. KaS

Man said to the universe, A. Stephen Crane. APN-2; AmPP; FaBoEE; LiTM; NAAL-2; OBAL; OBSV; PiM; TAP; WeW-3 *Fr.* War Is Kind.

Man sat in the felon's tank, alone, A. In the Tank. Thom Gunn. NoAM

Man Saw a Ball of Gold [in the Sky], A. Stephen Crane. MeMAP *Fr.* The Black Riders [and Other Lines].

Man, seated high on Learning's awful throne. Women of the Future. Mary Scott. ECWP

Man Seeking Experience Enquires His Way of a Drop of Water, The. Ted Hughes. OxAEP-2

Man sees a tiny couple in the distance, and thinks they might be his mother and father, A. The Optical Prodigal. Russell Edson. PmAP

Man sees the stars. Man and God Distinguished. Michael Echeruo. PBMAP

Man shot himself, A. Leader. Bruce Bennett. InPK-6

Man should have no thought for property, A. Property. Robert Garioch. FaBoTC

Man should seek great glory, and not broad, A. (LL) To John Donne ("Who shall doubt, Donne, where [*or* whe'er] I a poet be[e]"). Ben Jonson. BeJo; EPCY; NoP-4; SeCP

Man sits in a timelessness, The. The Rescue. Robert Creeley. CRP; VCAP

Man Splitting Wood in the Daybreak, The. Galway Kinnell. VCAP

Man, standing in the shadows of a, A. For H. W. Fuller. Carolyn M. Rodgers. BPo

Man standing next to molten steel, The. 29. "Alta." CrSp

Man stands tall upon Poulo Condore, A. Breaking Rocks on Poulo Condore. Phan chu Trinh, *Vietnamese.* AVP, *tr. by* Huỳnh Sanh Thông

Man still lacks a scheme to save the world, A. The Barber. Tản Đà, *Vietnamese.* AVP, *tr. by* Huỳnh Sanh Thông

Man still light of foot, but ageing, took, A. Thinking of Mr. D. Thomas Kinsella. NoAM

Man stole fire, and Zeus created flame. Palladas, *Greek.* GrAn, *tr. by* Tony Harrison

Man stood in the laurel tree, A. Things. Louis Simpson. OxBC

Man Struck Twenty Times by Lightning, The. Maxine Chernoff. PmAP

Man that had six mortal wounds, a man, A. Cuchulain Comforted. W. B. Yeats. CMoP; LiTM; OAEL-2; TOF

Man that had a handsome wife, The. Things Forbidden. *Unknown.* NoSic

Man, that is borne of a woman is of a few dayes, and full of trouble. Job's Entreaty. Bible, *O.T.* AWP; OBVE *Fr.* Job. NAWM-1

Man that is open of heart to his neighbour, The. Neighbours. Rudyard Kipling. FP

Man that mates wi' Poverty, The. Comfort in Puirtith. Helen B. Cruickshank. OxBS

Man that never will declare his thought, The. On the Deception of Appearances. Sadi. AWP, *tr. by* L. Cranmer-Byng *Fr.* The Gulistan.

Man that sees by chance his picture made, A. Robert Bridges. NoAM *Fr.* The Growth of Love.

Man, the egregious egoist. Cold-blooded Creatures. Elinor Wylie. OxBSP

Man the hare has met, The. The Names of the Hare. *Unknown, Middle English.* RB, *tr. by* Seamus Heaney

Man the Monarch. Mary Leapor. ECWP

Man. The Woman, The. Hans Arp, *German.* PFTM, *tr. by* Joachim Neugroschel

Man Then Suddenly Stops Moving, A. Alberto A. Ríos. NoAM

Man (they say), A. Paulus Silentiarius, *Greek.* GrAn, *tr. by* Andrew Miller

Man Thinking about Woman. Don L. Lee. MoP

Man too bad you don't notice that my eyes. Mississippi. Aimé Césaire, *French.* NegPo, *tr. by* Clayton Eshleman *and* Denis Kelly

Man under the Bed, The. Erica Jong. AmPA

Man United. *Unknown.* FaBoVe

Man unto His Fellow Man. Norman Corwin. TrJP *Fr.* On a Note of Triumph.

Man upon mold, whatsoever thou be. *Unknown.* MiEL

Man Upright, The. Thomas Macdonagh. BIrV

Man walks beside them, A. White Oxen. Louis Simpson. NoAM

Man walks calmly on his legs in the grass, A. We Shall Overcome. Breyten Breytenbach, *Afrikaans.* PeSAV, *tr. by* Ernst van Heerden

Man walks into a room, A. There is a corpse on the floor. Gorg, a Detective Story. B. P. Nichol. NOBC

Man walks on the bridge and gives away the change in his, A. Sri Sri. OMIP, *tr. by* V. Narayana Rao *and* A. K. Ramanujan. *Fr.* Some People Laugh, Some People Cry.

Man walks towards town, A. The Late Hour. Mark Strand. HCAP

Man wants but little here below. The Wants of Man. John Quincy Adams. APN-1; OBAL; PoLF

Man was given one kiss, one, A. One kiss. Tess Gallagher. BAP-93

Man was made of social earth. The Dæmonic and the Celestial Love. Ralph Waldo Emerson. APN-1 *Fr.* Initial, Dæmonic, and Celestial Love.

Man Was Made to Mourn, a Dirge. Robert Burns. Ro

  Man's Inhumanity to Man. BLPA

Man was sitting underneath a tree, A. Seumas Beg. James Stephens. FuFo; OxBTC

Man Watching, The. Rilke, *German.* RaBo, *tr. by* Robert Bly

Man waxy, The--he jogs along the fields. Napoleon after Sedan. Rimbaud. FaBoPV; OBWP, *tr. by* Robert Lowell *Fr.* Eighteen-Seventy.

Man went a-hunting at Reigate, A. *Unknown.* BoTP; ReMoGo

Man went forth one day at eve, A. Tragedy. "Æ." MoBrPo

Man went forth with gifts, A. Martin Luther King, Jr. Gwendolyn Brooks. PoBA

Man White, Brown Girl and All That Jazz. Gloria C. Oden. PoBA

  (Man White, Brown Girl and All That Jazz / Upon the Occasion of His Marriage.) GT

Man Who Became Old, The. Alberto A. Ríos. NoAM

Man who buries his house in the sand, The. Houses. Agha Shahid Ali. NIP-4

Man who came down the street, The. The Triumph of Children. Eve Shelnutt. CMAP

Man who changed the paths of earth and sea, The. Thermopylai. Parmenion of Macedon, *Greek.* GrAn, *tr. by* Peter Jay

Man Who Closed Shop, The. Stephen Dunn. NIP-4

Man Who Decided, The. Slavko Mihalic, *Croatian.* CEEP, *tr. by* Peter Kastmiler

Man Who Dreamed of Faeryland, The. W. B. Yeats. CMoP; NAEL-2; NoAM; NoP-4

Man who feels not, more or less, somewhat, The. Sonnet: Of Love in Men and Devils. Cecco Angiolieri, da Siena, *Italian.* AWP, *tr. by* D. G. Rossetti

Man who feels the dear disease, The. A Man in Love. Lady Mary Wortley Montagu. LW

Man who fiercest charged in fight, The. Stonewall Jackson. Herman Melville. NCAP

Man Who Finds That His Son Has Become a Thief, The. Raymond Souster. NOBC

Man who first built up with good strong words, The. Antipater of Thessalonica, *Greek.* GrAn, *tr. by* Alistair Elliot

Man who found the aardvark, The. Aardvark. Kenneth Rexroth. *Fr.* A Bestiary. OBAL

Man who had fallen among thieves, A. E. E. Cummings. ChIV-2; HAP; LiTM; MeMAP; MoP; NOBA; NoAM; OxBA; TAP

Man who had lately declared, A. Limerick. Thomas Thorneley. PeLi

Man, who had no rivals in the love, A. The Man and His Image. Jean de La Fontaine, *French.* OBVE, *tr. by* Elizur Wright

Man who hated the spring was cold and narrow, The. Winifred Holtby. WPN

Man who, having collapsed, rises, takes steps, is insane. Forced March. Miklós Radnóti, *Hungarian.* AF, *tr. by* Emery E. George

Man who in his life trusts in this world, A. Epitaph. *Unknown.* TrJP

Man who invented the plastic rose, The. Sonnet on the Death of the Man Who Invented Plastic Roses. Peter Meinke. PBCAP

Man who keeps a diary, pays, A. Writing. William Allingham. NOBVV

Man who lies on his back under huge trees, The. Breathing Space July. Tomas Tranströmer, *Swedish.* RB, *tr.* by Robert Bly

Man who lives by the sea tells of a young boy who, preparing to, A. Hsü Wei. *Fr.* A Kite. CoBLCP, *tr.* by Jonathan Chaves

Man Who Loved Islands, The. Derek Walcott. NoAM

Man who loves hiking, A. Hiking. Joseph Bruchac. CDW

Man Who Makes Brooms, The. Naomi Shihab Nye. LoL

Man Who Married Magdalene, The. Anthony Hecht. ChIV-2; PeLV

Man Who Married Magdalene, The. Louis Simpson. MoP; NoAM; TAP

Man who misses the fun, The. It Can Be Done. *Unknown.* PoToHe

Man who mops the floor of the luncheonette, The. After Hours. Nicholas Christopher. WWSi

Man Who Sang the Sillies, The. John Ciardi. OBCA

Man who seemed, A. Regulation equipment. Joyce Mansour, *French.* MFP, *tr.* by Martin Sorrell

Man Who Sleeps Out in the Fields, The. Bùi Khải Nguyễn, *Vietnamese.* AVP, *tr.* by Huỳnh Sanh Thông

Man who sold his lawn to standard oil, The. The War against the Trees. Stanley Kunitz. HAP

Man who stood beside me, The. Sweet Will. Philip Levine. LCAP-2; VCAP

Man who tells you which is the whiter wash, The. Love and How It Becomes Important in Our Day to Day Lives. Miller Williams. MT

Man Who Thinks He Can, The. Walter D. Wintle. PoLF

Man who waits at the bus stop every night for his wife, The. On M. Butterfly. Wing Tek Lum. IFJA

Man who was asked out to dinner, A. Limerick. Spike Milligan. PeLi

Man Who Went Absent from the Native Literature, The. Anthony Cronin. CIP-2

Man whose height his fear improved he, The. Medgar Evers. Gwendolyn Brooks. NoP-4; PoBA

Man will keep a horse for prestige, A. Gateposts. Medbh McGuckian. BiHa; PBCIP

Man will put a large-headed nail, The. Of Green Steps and Laundry. Ralph Gustafson. NoP-4

Man with a marvelous mug, A. A Ballad in "G." Eugene Fitch Ware. PoLF

Man with a scythe: the torrent of his swing. Gardens No Emblems. Donald Davie. GaP; LiTM; OAEL-2; OBGa

Man with a thousand hearts, The. Image-Nation 13 (the Telephone). Robin Blaser. PoM

Man with Exploded Eyes, The. Stefan Aug. Doinas, *Romanian.* CEEP, *tr.* by Peter Jay *and* Virgil Nemoianu

Man with his lion under the shed of wars, The. The Song of the Borderguard. Robert Duncan. NeAP; PoM

Man With Night Sweats, The. Thom Gunn. CABP; PoPoPo

Man with No Family to Take Leave of, The. Tu Fu, *Chinese.* CoBCP, *tr.* by Burton Watson

Man with One Small Hand. Patricia K. Page. MoCV

Man with the anaconda around his neck / seems proud, The. The Anaconda. Dennis Sampson. PUP-20

Man with the big mouth, The. And Again. Alison Fell. LW

Man with the Blue Guitar, The. Wallace Stevens.
  "I cannot bring a world quite round." CMoP; RaBo
  "Man bent over his guitar, The." CMoP; NoAM; RaBo
  "Tom-tom, c'est moi. The blue guitar." CMoP
  "Tune beyond us as we are, A." CMoP

Man with the camera comes, The. Reservation Special. Lew Blockcolski. VoR

Man with the Hoe, The. Edwin Markham. APN-2; BLPA; GS; MoAmPo; PaTW; TFi
  ("And pillared the blue firmament with light?") (LL) PaTW

Man with the Hollow Breast, The. Tania Van Zyl. PeSA

Man with the red hat, The. Glazunoviana. John Ashbery. LCAP-2; VCAP

Man with the Saxophone, The. Ai. SeSe; WWSi
  ("New York. 5 A.M. / The sidewalks empty.") NMM-2

Man without Sense of Direction. John Crowe Ransom. LiTM; MeMAP; OxBA

Man you / are / a liar. Insult before Gift-Giving. Frank Bolton, *Tsimshian Indian.* STP, *tr.* by Armand Schwerner

Man you know, assured and kind, The. Almost Human. C. Day Lewis. NoAM

Man, you too, aren't you, one of these rough followers of the criminal? In the Servants' Quarters. Thomas Hardy. FaBoVe; MoBrPo

Managed as they say about such men. Peter Porter. PeLV *Fr.* Nine Points of the Law.

Management is pleased to announce, The. Jazz at the Intergalactic Nightclub. Michael McClure. SeSe

Manchán's Prayer. Saint Manchán. NOIV

Mandalay. Rudyard Kipling. EBEvV; MoBrPo; NOBE; OxAEP-2; PBMP

Mandarin Duck Lake is at Chia-ho. Ni Tsan Poem Following Rhyme-Words of Wu Chen. Wu Chen, *Chinese.* CoBLCP, *tr.* by Jonathan Chaves

Mandarin / in a silent film. The Yellow Bird. James W. Thompson. PoBA

Mandelstam. David Young. AmPA

Mandolin. Jordan Smith. WeT

Mandoline. Paul Verlaine, *French.* AWP; OBMV, *tr.* by Arthur Symons

Mandorla. Paul Celan, *German.* PoSu, *tr.* by Michael Hamburger

Mandrake Hert, The. Sydney Goodsir Smith. OxBS

Mandrakes for Supper. James Keir Baxter. OxBC

M'Andrew's Hymn. *See* McAndrew's Hymn.

Maner of Her Wyll, & What She Left to London, And to All Those in it, The. Isabella Whitney. *See* The Manner of Her Will and What She Left to London and to All Those in It, at Her Departing.

Manfred The lamp must be replenished, but even then. Byron. *See* The Lamp must be replenish'd, but even then.

Mangin Street. Berysh Vaynshteyn. CEEP, *tr.* by Benjamin Harshav *and* Barbara Harshav *Fr.* New York Everywhere.

Mango. John Robert Lee. HCP

Mango on the mango tree, The. Robert Penn Warren. MoP; NoAM *Fr.* Mexico Is a Foreign Country: Four Studies in Naturalism.

Mango Tree, The. Hart Crane. PFTM

Mangoes are not cigarettes. Richard Tipping. NOBAu

Mangos y limones. Pat Mora. BAP-96

Mangosteens. Daniel Hall. NoP-4

Mangrove. John Blight. NOBAu

Manhattan. Lorenz Hart. OBAL

Manhattan. Hoffman Reynolds Hays. SPE

Manhattan. Osbert Lancaster. NOBL; PeLV *Fr.* Afternoons with Baedeker.

Manhattan Lullaby. Norma Farber. SSCS; TLR

Manhattan Lullaby. Rachel Lyman Field. TLR

Manhole Covers. Karl Shapiro. NoAM

Mani-Mani Gatha. Jackson Mac Low. PFTM

Maniac's Song, The. Ann Taylor. NOBRP

Manichaeans, the. Gary Snyder. VGW

Manichean Geography I. Tom Paulin. PNI

Manicheans did no idols make, The. Greville Fulke. NOCV *Fr.* Caelica.

Manifest Destiny. Anita Endrezze-Danielson. CDW

Manifest Destiny. Pearse Hutchinson. CIP-2

Manifesto. Agathias, *Greek.* GrAn, *tr.* by Dudley Fitts

Manifesto. Gloria Frym. DeD

Manifesto. D. H. Lawrence. CBLP

Manifesto. Nicanor Parra, *Spanish.*
  I Move the Meeting Be Adjourned. HoPM, *tr.* by Miller Williams

Manifesto of Futurism, The. Filippo Tommaso Marinetti.
  "We had stayed up all night, my friends and I, under hanging mosque lamps." PFTM

Manifesto of Surrealism (1924). André Breton, *French.*
  Three Excerpts. PFTM, *tr.* by Richard M. Seaver *and* Helen R. Lane

Manifesto of the Presidents of the Terrestrial Globe. Velemir Khlebnikov, *Russian.* TCRP, *tr.* by Gary Kern

Manifesto on Ars Poetica. Frank Mkalawile Chipasula. HBAPE

Manila Bay. Eugene Fitch Ware. OBCoV

Mankind should hope. Letter to Miss E. B. on Marriage. Mary Savage. ECWP; LW *Fr.* Letter to Miss E.B. on Marriage.

Mankind Toun, The. Tom Scott. FaBoTC

Manless Society, The. Pierre Unik, *French.* SPE, *tr.* by David Gascoyne

Manlet, The. "Lewis Carroll." *See* The Little Man That Had a Little Gun.

Manlius to Coeymans. Clark Coolidge. FTOS

Manly Ferry. John Philip. NOBAu

Manly Man, The. *Unknown.* BLPA

Manna. Jared Angira. PBMAP

Manna. James Tate. GM

Mannahatta ("I was asking for something specific and perfect for my city"). Walt Whitman. MoAmPo

Mannequins. Laurie Sheck. PuP-17

Manner of Her Will and What She Left to London and to All Those in It, at Her Departing, The. Isabella Whitney. NoSic
  (Maner of Her Wyll, & What She Left to London, And to All Those in it, The.) BWW
  "And now let mee dispose such things." BWW
  "And (though I am perswade) that I." BWW
  "For Women shall you Taylors have." BWW
  "I whole in body and in minde." BWW
  "Now for the people in thee left." BWW
  "Now London have I (for thy sake)." BWW
  "Now when thy folke are fed and clad." BWW

"Rejoice in God that I am gon." BWW

"Yf they that keepe what I you leave." BWW

Manner of the World Nowadays, The. John Skelton.

"So many cloisters closed." PeECV

Mannerly Margery Mylk and Ale. John Skelton. AAS; NAEL-1 (Mannerly Margery Milk and Ale.) NoP-4

Manners. Elizabeth Bishop. NOxBChV; OxBC; RB

Manners. Howard Nemerov. NBLV

Manners. Edith Marcombe Shiffert. WPE

Manners are the happy way of doing things. Ralph Waldo Emerson. CTV

Manners at Table When Away from Home. Unknown. OxBChV

Manners in the dining-room. Unknown. OxNR

Manon Lescaut. Yaroslav Vasilevich Smelyakov, Russian. TCRP, tr. by Simon Franklin

Manor Garden, The. Sylvia Plath. FaBoWP; LCAP-2

Manos Karastefan´is. James Merrill. TAP

"Man's a man, A," says Robert Burns. For A' That and A' That. Unknown. BXAP

Man's a poor deluded bubble. Song. Robert Dodsley. OxBSP

Man's and woman's bodies lay without souls. A Childish Prank. Ted Hughes. CABP; OAEL-2; OxBC

Man's body at auction, A. Walt Whitman. SAmP Fr. Leaves of Grass (1855). APN-1

Man's boots with a woman in them, A. Crofter's Kitchen, Evening. Norman MacCaig. FaBoTC

Man's Civil[l] War[re]. Robert Southwell. NoSic

Man's Days. Eden Phillpotts. OBEV; OxBTC

Man's Dying-Place Uncertain. Robert Herrick. CaPo

Mans Fall, and Recovery. Henry Vaughan. ESCV

Man's Going Hence. Samuel Rogers. OBNC Fr. Human Life.

Man's Inhumanity to Man Robert Burns BLPA Fr. Man Was Made to Mourn, a Dirge. Ro

Man's life is a hundred years' constant vexation, A. Sent to Recluse Ch'eng. Wang Chi, Chinese. SuSp, tr. by Hellmut Wilhelm

Man's life is death. Yet Christ endured to live. Wednesday in Holy Week. Christina Rossetti. TrCP

Man's life is laid in the loom of time. The Loom of Time. Unknown. BLPA

Man's life is like a rose that in spring. Meditation 9. Philip Pain. Fr. Meditations for July 26, 1666. NOBA; SCAP

Man's life is well compared to a feast. A Comparison of the Life of Man. Richard Barnfield. NoSic; OxBSP

Man's life's a tragedy: his mother's womb. De Morte. Sir Henry Wotton. NOSC; OxBSP

Man's makeshift days would flash past at the best. Antiphanes, Greek. GrAn, tr. by Edwin Morgan

Man's Mortality. Simon Wastell. FaBoCh Fr. Microbiblion.

Man's mother is very sick, A. Nicanor Parra, Spanish. VCWP, tr. by W. S. Merwin

Man's nature shows no shape. Character. Phan Bội Châu, Vietnamese. AVP, tr. by Huỳnh Sanh Thông

Man's own resinous heart has fed. (LL) Two Songs from a Play. W. B. Yeats. FaBoTw; HAP; PoE, sect. 1; CMoP; ImPo; NOBE; OAEL-2, sect. 1-2

Man's Requirements, A. Elizabeth Barrett Browning. RACG

Mans restlesse soule hath restlesse eyes and ears. Roger Williams. SCAP

Man's [a] Sliding Mood, A. Mary Elizabeth Fullerton. CBAP; NOBAu

Man's Song, about His Daughter, A. Unknown, Eskimo. STP, tr. by Armand Schwerner

Man's Woman, A. Mary Carolyn Davies. PoLF

Man's years fall short of a hundred. Mei Sheng and Fu I. Fr. Nineteen Old Poems of the Han. CoBCP, tr. by Burton Watson

Man's years fall short of a hundred. Unknown, Chinese. CoBCP, tr. by Burton Watson

Manservants on the last trains. North to Milwaukee. Gerald Vizenor. VoR

Mantanza to Welcome Spring. Jimmy Santiago Baca. PmAP

Mantatee Horde, The. Mtutuzeli Matshoba. PeSAV

Mantelpiece of Shells, A. Ruthven Todd. NYBP

Mantis. David McCord. OBAL

Mantis. Ruth Miller. PeSAV

Mantle So Green, The. Unknown. AmFP

Mantova. James Wright. NNaP
(First Days, The.) TRP

Manual, The. Larry Rubin. MT

Manuelzinho. Elizabeth Bishop. FaBoWP; NYBP

Manufacturing. Alan Shapiro. BAP-95

Manuscripts don't burn. Burning Leaves. Ojars Vacietis, Latvian. CEEP, tr. by Inara Cedrins

Manwolf, worse; and their packs infest the age. (LL) Tom's Garland: Upon the Unemployed. Gerard Manley Hopkins. EnVR; FaBoPV; Son

Many a cuckoo on many a mountain peak. The Cuckoo on Mt. Chiri*. Sugwon Song, Korean. CKP, tr. by Jaihiun Kim

Many a green isle needs must be. Lines Written among the Euganean Hills. Shelley. GTBS-P; OxBoS; PoEL-4; Ro

Many a legend I have meditated. On the Death of Countess Luise Schwerin. Rilke, German. FP, tr. by J. B. Leishman

Many a long, long year ago. The Alarmed Skipper. James Thomas Fields. NBLV

Many a man gets bewitched by the elves. Heinrich von Morungen, German. GePo, tr. by Frederick Goldin

Many a poet in his lay. May. Dafydd ap Gwilym. CABP

Many a soldier's kiss dwells on these bearded lips. (LL) The Wound-Dresser. Walt Whitman. APN-1; AmPP; CBCWP; ColAP; NAAL-1; NOBA; OBWP; TAP

Many a summer is dead and buried, A. Spirits Everywhere. Ludwig Uhland, German. AWP, tr. by James Clarence Mangan

Many a swan-white breast. (LL) The Dead at Clonmacnois [or Clonmacnoise]. Angus O'Gillan, Irish. OBEV; OBMV, tr. by Thomas William Rolleston

Many a weary year had passed since the burning of Grand-Pré. Part the Second. Henry Wadsworth Longfellow. Fr. Evangeline, a Tale of Acadie.

Many a year has fled away. My Old Palette. Christopher Pearse Cranch. APN-1

Many American flags, The. The Grand Entry. Gary Snyder. NoAM

Many and many a happy year. (LL) To the Rev. F. D. Maurice. Tennyson. GTBS-P; NOBVV; PeECV

Many and More. Maya Angelou. LW

Many and sharp the num'rous Ills. Man's Inhumanity to Man. Robert Burns. BLPA Fr. Man Was Made to Mourn, a Dirge. Ro

Many Are Called. Edwin Arlington Robinson. GI; MeMAP; OxBA

Many are making love. Privilege of Being. Robert Hass. NAmP90; NIP-4

Many are the sayings of the wise. Consolation. Milton. LBC Fr. Samson Agonistes. FHYEP; OAEL-1; PoEL-3

Many are thy tones, O Ocean. Sea Cadences. Henrietta Cordelia Ray. AAP; CBWP-3

Many as noticed by the one, The. De Imagine Mundi. John Ashbery. FaBoMo

Many believe one day the ship. Straight Seeking. Anthony McNeill. HCP

Many Birds. Anne Welsh. PeSA

Many colors will take you to themselves. Never Seek to Tell Thy Love. John Ashbery. HCAP; InPS-3

Many desire, but few or none deserve. The Advice. Sir Walter Ralegh. AAS; SiPS

Many desperate arms about us and the things we know. (LL) The Character of Love Seen as a Search for the Lost. Kenneth Patchen. CLPP; VGW

Many Die Here. Gayl Jones. BlSi

Many husbands are missing tonight. The Beautiful Urinals of Paris. Charles David Wright. MT

Many in aftertimes will say of you. From Monna Innominata. Christina Rossetti. CABP; LoP; OBNC Fr. Monna Innominata. BWW

Many Indeed Must Perish in the Keel. Hugo von Hofmannsthal, German. AWP; TrJP, tr. by Jethro Bithell

Many ingenious lovely things are gone. W. B. Yeats. BIrV; PoE Fr. Nineteen Hundred and Nineteen.

Many long years ago. (LL) Old Gray Mare. Unknown. AS

Many long years ago, I loved a youth. The Blight of Love. Mary E. Tucker. CBWP-1

Many-maned scud-thumper, tub. Winter Ocean. John Updike. InPK-6; Poetr

Many, many things. Basho, Japanese. TAL, tr. by Harold G. Henderson

Many marvels walk through the world. Sophocles. OBCVT, tr. by Richard Emil Braun Fr. Antigone.

many, monstrous, scattered gray rocks, The. You Were Shattered. Giuseppe Ungaretti. ItIP

Many, monstrous, tumbled, dun-gray boulders, The. You Were Broken. Giuseppe Ungaretti, Italian. STV, tr. by John Frederick Nims

Many paths in the woods have chos- / en me. Lost. Hayden Carruth. AFr

Many people have been frighted & died in cemeteries. My Gang. Jack Kerouac. PoM

Many people have gathered together. Foot Race Song. Unknown, Pima. OBVE, tr. by Frank Russell

Many poets great and gifted whom the muse's touch had blessed. My Childhood's Happy Days. Daniel Webster Davis. AAP

Many policemen wear upon their shoulders. Sergeant Brown's Parrot. Kit Wright. OPOU

Many red devils ran from my heart. Stephen Crane. MeMAP; TAP Fr. The Black Riders [and Other Lines].

Many setups. At least as many falls. Breaking and Entering. Ralph Angel. NAmP90

Many sewing days ago. The Listening Macaws. Hazel Hall. PaTW

Many shapes of wings. Environs. Larry Eigner. FTOS; NeAP

Many Sisters to Many Brothers. Rose Macaulay. NSI

Many strange mountains in Shu and Han. Imitating the Old Poems. Pao Chao, *Chinese*. CoBCP, *tr. by* Burton Watson

Many the shadowless under the rose leaves. The Elect. Peter Cooley. CMAP

Many Things. Oliver Wendell Holmes. PoToHe

Many things have come and gone. The Breezing Dawn of the New Day. Mongane Wally Serote. PeSAV

Many things I might have said today. Aprons of Silence. Carl Sandburg. NOBA

Many things to absorb I teach to help you become eleve of mine. To a Western Boy. Walt Whitman. APN-1

Many think Quintia's beautiful. She's tall. Catullus, *Latin*. EP, *tr. by* James Michie

Many thousand gone. (LL) No more auction block for me. *Unknown*. APN-2; BPo; ISC; NAAAL; RaBo

Many Thousand Gone. *Unknown*. CrDW

Many times I wait there for my father. Buffalo. Molly Peacock. MoLi; WWSi

Many Wagons Ago. John Ashbery. HCAP

Many weary weeks divide me. The Ship's Cook, a Captive Sings. Hugo von Hofmannsthal, *German*. TrJP, *tr. by* Charles Wharton Stork

Many who have only dreamed of me. Trumbull Stickney. *Fr.* Pandora's Songs. APN-2 *Fr.* Prometheus Pyrphoros.

Many without Elegy. W. S. Graham. OxBS

Many workmen / Built a hugh ball of masonry. Stephen Crane. PFE *Fr.* The Black Riders [and Other Lines].

Many Worlds Are Walked Once. Kojo Laing. HBAPE

Many years and many days ago. Manon Lescaut. Yaroslav Vasilevich Smelyakov, *Russian*. TCRP, *tr. by* Simon Franklin

Many years have passed, mica. Accomplices. Bei Dao, *Chinese*. AF, *tr. by* Bonnie S. McDougall

Manyo Shu, Part 1 of 4. *Unknown, Japanese*.
"Because he is young." AWP, *tr. by* Arthur Waley
"By way of pretext." AWP, *tr. by* Arthur Waley
"Dress that my brother has put on is thin, The." AWP, *tr. by* Arthur Waley
"Even a flaming fire can be snatched." WPJ, *tr. by* Kenneth Rexroth *and* Ikuko Atsumi
"For my sister's sake." AWP, *tr. by* Arthur Waley
Manyo Shu, Part 4 of 4. *Unknown*.
"Thousand years, you said, A." BoLoP, *tr. by* Geoffrey Bownas *and* Anthony Thwaite
"Unknown love/ Is as bitter a thing." AWP; PBWP, *tr. by* Arthur Waley
("Unknown love/ is bitter.") BoWoP, *tr. by* Willis Barnstone
"What am I to do with my sister?" AWP, *tr. by* Arthur Waley
"When evening comes." AWP, *tr. by* Arthur Waley
"When, loosened from the winter's bonds." PBWP
"When she was still alive." OHPJ, *tr. by* Kenneth Rexroth
Manyo Shu, Part 3 of 4. *Unknown, Japanese*.
"My heart, thinking." AWP, *tr. by* Arthur Waley
"O boy cutting grass." AWP, *tr. by* Arthur Waley
"O pine-tree standing." AWP; TAL, *tr. by* Arthur Waley
"On the moor of Kasuga." AWP, *tr. by* Arthur Waley
"On the shore of Nawa." AWP, *tr. by* Arthur Waley
"Over the Spring fields." OHMPJ, *tr. by* Kenneth Rexroth
"Plum-blossom, The." AWP; TAL, *tr. by* Arthur Waley
River of Heaven, The. AWP, *tr. by* Lafcadio Hearn
"Shall we make love." AWP, *tr. by* Arthur Waley
Sudden Appearance of Cherry Blossoms, The. WPJ, *tr. by* Kenneth Rexroth *and* Ikuko Atsumi
Manyo Shu, Part 2 of 4. *Unknown*.
"How will you manage." AWP, *tr. by* Arthur Waley
"I am of this world." BoWoP; IMW, *tr. by* Geoffrey Bownas *and* Anthony Thwaite
"I wish I could lend a coat." AWP, *tr. by* Arthur Waley
"In the sea of ivy clothed Iwami." OHPJ, *tr. by* Kenneth Rexroth
"May the men who are born." AWP; TAL, *tr. by* Arthur Waley
("May those who are born after me.") OHPJ, *tr. by* Kenneth Rexroth
("Never travel such roads of love.") (LL) OHPJ, *tr. by* Kenneth Rexroth
"Men of valor, The." AWP; TAL, *tr. by* Arthur Waley
Woes of the Crab, The. APo
Manzanita, The. Yvor Winters. VGW

Manzini; Escape Artist. Gwendolyn MacEwen. NOBC

Mao Yen-shou, your painter's brush seems to move the gods. Wang Chao-chün. Li Shang-yin, *Chinese*. SuSp, *tr. by* Irving Y. Lo

Map, The. Elizabeth Bishop. ColAP; NOBA

Map. Linda Hogan. PaTW

Map. Martin Sorescu, *Romanian*. VCWP, *tr. by* Longley, Michael and Joana Russell-Gebbett

Map, The. Gary Soto. NoAM

Map, The. Mark Strand. NYBP

Map of Montana in Italy, A. Richard Hugo. LCAP-2

Map of My Country, A. John Holmes. AiP
("Map of my native country is all edges, A.") CA

Map of the City, A. Thom Gunn. NAEL-2; NoP-4; PoE

Map of the Western Part of the County of Essex in England, A. Denise Levertov. CoAP; CoAmPo; NAAL-2
("Something forgotten twenty years: though my fathers.") CoAmPo

Map of the world is felt from the inside. Rough around the, The. Anna Couani. BMAP

Map shows me where it is you are. I, The. A Private Letter to Brazil. Gloria C. Oden. GT

Maple and Sumach. C. Day Lewis. FaBoMo; Son

Maple Leaf. "Shu Ting," *Chinese*. VCWP, *tr. by* Carolyn Kizer

Maple Leaves. Yun-gi Hong, *Korean*. CKP, *tr. by* Jaihiun Kim

Maple leaves fill the emerald mountain. Boiling Falls. Liu E, *Chinese*. CoBLCP, *tr. by* Jonathan Chaves

Maples. Philip Appleman. BXAP

Maples have turned, The. Fire snaps on my tongue. On a Recent Protest against Social Conditions. David Posner. NYBP

Mapmaker on His Art, The. Howard Nemerov. NYBP

Mapooram. *Aborigine Oral Tradition*. NOBAu, *tr. by* Fred Biggs

Mapping. Robert Kelly. BAP-93

Maps. Susan Mitchell. MoLi

Maquillage. Arthur Symons. ADE; OxBSP

Marathon. Louise Glück.
Song of Obstacles. LW

Marathon runner's legs, A. Mikajo Yagi, *Japanese*. WPJ, *tr. by* Kenneth Rexroth *and* Ikuko Atsumi

Marban, a Hermit Speaks. *Unknown, Irish*. BIrV; CIP-2, *tr. by* Michael Hartnett

Marble Floor. Karol Wojtyla. CRP

"Marble I thought thee, and brickwork I find thee!" the Tourist may answer. (LL) Dear Eustatio, I write that you may write me an answer. Arthur Hugh Clough. EBVV; EBVVPR; FaBoVe; OxAEP-2

Marble mausoleum solemnly holds the rich, A. Quatrains. Salah Jahin, *Arabic*. TTY, *tr. by* Samir M. Zoghby

Marble Nor Monuments whereof Then We Spoke. John Berryman. *Fr.* Sonnets. Son

Marble one so warmed would speak, A. (LL) To a Fair Lady Playing with a Snake. Edmund Waller. CABP; CBLP; EBEV; HoPM; NOSC; PoE; PoEL-3

Marble Prophecy, The. Josiah Gilbert Holland.
"Laocöon! thou great embodiment." APN-1

Marble surfaces. Joanne Burns. BMAP

Marble-Top. Elwyn Brooks White. OBAL

Marble, weep [*or* weepe], for thou dost cover. On Margaret Ratcliffe. Ben Jonson. SeCP

Marble women in gardens used to. The Last Atlantean. David Henson. EC2

Marbled Chuckle in the Savannahs. Kenward Elmslie. FTOS

Marblehead's a rocky place. Royall Tyler. NAAL-3 *Fr.* The Contrast.

Marburg. Boris Pasternak, *Russian*. TCRP, *tr. by* Yakov Hornstein

Marcelia; or, Treacherous Friend, The. Frances Boothby.
Song: "Oh, you powerful Gods, if I must be." KTR
"What strange effects of Fortune do I prove!" KTR

Marceline, to Her Husband. Elizabeth Libbey. AmPA

March. Elizabeth Jane Coatsworth. AYFP; Spl

March. Jane Cooper.
El Sueño de la Razón. FaBoWP

March. Judy Page Heitzman. CMAP

March. Daryl Hine.
"Once when I was coming from art class they surprised me." GLP

March. A. E. Housman. FaBoCh

March. Roy McFadden. TIRV

March. Alfonsas Nyka-Niliunas, *Lithuanian*. CEEP, *tr. by* Jonas Zdanys

March. Henrietta Cordelia Ray. CBWP-3

March. Folgore da San Geminiano. *Fr.* Sonnets of the Months. AWP, *tr. by* D. G. Rossetti

March. Marina Tsvetayeva, *Russian*.

"O what tears in eyes now." TCRP, *tr.* by Elaine Feinstein

("They took quickly, they took hugely.") AF, *tr.* by Elaine Feinstein

"They took quickly, they took hugely." TCRP, *tr.* by Elaine Feinstein

March 1, The. Robert Lowell. PoPoPo

March beyond green outskirts. Girls' School. Alan Moore. BiHa

March comes, / and Eastern bluebird shows himself. This Year's Drive to Appomattox. Eleanor Ross Taylor. CBCWP

March Day in London, A. Amy Levy. VWP

March Evening. Leonard Alfred George Strong. MoBrPo

March 1st. Kathleen Spivack. NYBP

March 4th Anno 1698/9; a Charracteristicall Satyre, *diff. vers.* John Saffin. *See* A Satyretericall Charracter of a Proud Upstart.

March Hares. Andrew Young. SAmP

March has come to the bridge head. Poem by the Bridge at Ten-shin. Li Po, *Chinese.* OBVE, *tr.* by Ezra Pound

March in the ranks hard-prest, and the road unknown, A. Walt Whitman. AmPP; CBCWP; NAAL-1; NAAL-3; OxBA

MARCH ingorders. Roger McGough. AYFP

March into Virginia, The. Herman Melville. CBCWP; ColAP; HAP; ImPo; NAAL-1; NAAL-3; NCAP; NoP-4; PoE; PoPoPo; TAP

("Preparations of fate.") (LL) PoPoPo

("Throe of Second Manassas share, The.") (LL) CBCWP; ColAP; NAAL-3; NoP-4

March Journal. Charles Wright. LCAP-2

March, march, Ettrick and Teviotdale. Blue Bonnets over the Border. Sir Walter Scott. OxBS *Fr.* The Monastery.

March, march, head erect. Mother Goose. OxNR

March of the Women, The. Cicely Hamilton. BrRo

March 1, The. Robert Lowell. HCAP

March Snow. Don McKay. NOBC

March . . . Someone has walked across the snow. Vacancy in the Park. Wallace Stevens. LCAP-2, SAmP

March Storm, Poquoson, Virginia, 1963. Dave Jeddie Smith. CMAP

March strikes the ice of the sky. Peter Huchel. *See* Landscape Beyond Warsaw.

March strongly forth, my Muse, whilst yet the temperate air. Michael Drayton. NOSC *Fr.* Polyolbion.

3-31-70. Gayl Jones. BlSi *Fr.* Journal.

March toward the Front, The. Odysseas Elytis, *Greek.* AF, *tr.* by Edmund Keeley *and* George Savidis

March, Upstate. William Bronk. NYBP

March Weather. Jon Swan. NYBP

March Wind, The. E. H. Henderson. BoTP

March winds and April showers. *Unknown.* ACTP; FaBoBe; LB; OxNR; ReMoGo

March with its sharp pick. Landscape Beyond Warsaw. Peter Huchel, *German.* PoSu, *tr.* by Michael Hamburger

Marchant was ther with a forked berd, A. Chaucer. CTC *Fr.* The General Prologue. FHYEP; NAEL-1; NAWM-1; OAEL-1; PoE *Fr.* The Canterbury Tales.

Märchen, The. Randall Jarrell. CMoP

Märchenbilder. John Ashbery. LCAP-2; NOBA

Marching. Isaac Rosenberg. NSI; PeFWW

Marching armies of the past, The. Confederate Memorial Day. *Unknown.* CBCWP

Marching on Tanga, marching the parch'd plain. The Gift. Francis Brett Young. NSI

Marching 'round the Levee. *Unknown.* AmFP

Marching Song. Robert Louis Stevenson. BoTP

Marching Still. Minna Irving. CBCWP

Marching through Georgia. Henry Clay Work. APN-2; CBCWP; FaPoR

Marching to Quebec. *Unknown.* AmFP

Marching to Utah. *Unknown.* AmFP

Marcia and I went over the curve. Millions of Strawberries. Genevieve Taggard. NOxBChV

Marcia Thompane was light and compact. Dancing School. Jonathan Holden. Poetsp

Marco Bozzaris. Fitz-Greene Halleck.

"At midnight, in his guarded tent." APN-1; HoPM

Marconi, whose ardour was tireless. Limerick. Stanley J. Sharpless. PeLi

Marcus Antoninus Cui Cognomen Erat Aurelius. Burns Singer. OxBS

Marcus Aurelius. Charles Hubert Sisson. OxBC

Marcus Curtius. Oliver St. John Gogarty. OBMV

Marcus in the armed hoplites' race. Lucilius, *Greek.* GrAn, *tr.* by Peter Porter

Mare, A. Kate Barnes. NYBP

Mare lies down in the grass where the nest of the skylark is hidden, The. Vernon Watkins. OBWVE

Mare, my head cocking back, A. At Fifty in the Crystal-Dead Eye of the Center. Anne S. Perlman. CMAP

Mare Nostrum. Joel Oppenheimer. NeAP

Mares of the Camargue, The. Frédéric Mistral. AWP, *tr.* by George Meredith *Fr.* Mirèio.

Mare's skeleton in the clearing: another sign of life, The. Adrienne Rich. FaBoWP *Fr.* Shooting Script.

Margaret. Charles Cotton. *See* Two Rural Sisters.

Margaret Are You Drug. George Starbuck. InPK-6

Márgarét, áre you gríeving. Spring and Fall. Gerard Manley Hopkins. CABP; CMoP; ClHu; EBEV; GTBS-P; HAP; HeIP-4; HoPM; IMW; ImPo; InPK-6; InPS-3; LiLi; LiTM; NAEL-2; NIP-4; NOBE; NoAM; NoP-4; OPOU; OxAEP-2; PFE; PeVV; PoE; PoEL-5; PoPoPo; Poetr; RB; SAGP; SCGP; SCV; TFi; TOF; TRP

Margaret Fuller. Lorine Niedecker. NMM-2

Margaret Fuller Slack. Edgar Lee Masters. RACG

Margaret Grady—I fear she will burn. The Witch. Katharine Tynan. NOBVV

Margaret Love Peacock, for Her Tombstone, 1826. Thomas Love Peacock. OBNC

Margaret mentioned Indians. Indians. John Fandel. NYBP

Margaret Whiting Tearfully Sings. Eleanor Lerman. WeT

Margaret wrote a letter. The Dusty Miller. *Unknown.* ReMoGo

Margarita first possest [*or* possessed]. The Chronicle; a Ballad. Abraham Cowley. OxAEP-1

Margaritæ Sorori [I. M.]. William Ernest Henley. MoBrPo; NOBE; OBEV; OBNC *Fr.* Echoes.

(I. M. Margaritae Sorori.) CABP

Margery Mutton-pie. Mother Goose. OxNR

Marginal Field, The. Stephen Spender. PoA

Marginalia. W. H. Auden.

"Dead man, A/ who never caused others to die." OAEL-2

Marginalia. Richard Wilbur. CMoP; PoA

Marginalization of Poetry, The. Bob Perelman. FTOS

Marg'ret of humbler stature by the head. Two Rural Sisters. Charles Cotton. BoLoP; EnLoPo *Fr.* Resolution in Four Sonnets, of a Poetical Question Put to Me by a Friend, Concerning Four Rural Sisters. PoEL-3; Son

Mari Magno II. Arthur Hugh Clough. *Fr.* Songs in Absence.

Maria intended a letter to write. How to Write a Letter. Elizabeth Turner. ACTP; OxBChV

Maria! Maria! Maria! Vladimir Mayakovsky. TCRP, *tr.* by Bernard Meares *Fr.* The Cloud in Trousers.

Maria now I'll cease to sing. Verses Written in a London Churchyard. Christopher Smart. CBNP

Maria, she said. No city river. The Scuba Diver Recovers the Body of a Drowned Child. Gerald William Barrax. GT; NBV

Maria to Henric. *Unknown.* KTR

Maria Wentworth. Thomas Carew. CaPo; MeLP; PeECV

(Epitaph for Maria Wentworth.) BeJo

("Frail as our flesh crumble to dust.") (LL) CavPo

(Inscription on the Tomb of the Lady Mary Wentworth, The.) CavPo

Mariachi beckon, their guitars, The. On Plaza Garibaldi. Nellie Wong. OpBo

Mariam. Lady Elizabeth Carey. WPE

Chorus: "Those mindes that wholy dote upon delight." KTR

"How oft have I with publike voyce runne on?" KTR, *act* I, *scene* 1

Mariana. Tennyson. AWP; CBLP; CH; EBVVPR; EnVR; FHYEP; InPS-3; NAEL-2; NOBE; NOBRP; NoP-4; OAEL-2; OBEV; OBNC; OxAEP-2; PeVV; PoE; PoEL-5; Ro; SCGP; TFi; UnPo

("I would that I were dead!") (LL) EP

("With blackest moss the flower-plots.") EP; NoP-4

Marie antoinette / slice, The. After / the Moratorium Reading. Nigel Roberts. NOBAu

Marie Galante. Guy Tirolien, *French.* NegPo, *tr.* by Ellen Conroy Kennedy

Marie Hamilton's to the kirk gane. The Queen's Marie. *Unknown.* OBEV

Marie Lucille. Gwendolyn Brooks. TLR

Marie [*or* Mary] Magdalens Complaint at Christs Death. Robert Southwell. ChIV-2; ESCV

Marigold, The. George Wither. NOSC *Fr.* A Collection of Emblemes, Ancient and Moderne.

Marigolds. Louise Driscoll. BoTP

Marigolds in a white box. No love. Teel St. Trailer Court. Anne C. Bromley. CMAP

Marin. Philip Booth. AiP; NYBP

Marina. T. S. Eliot. CABP; CMoP; FaBoMo; GTBS-P; HeIP-4; MoLi; NAEL-2; NOBE; NOCV; PoE; TOF

("My daughter.") (LL) PoPoPo

Marina. O. B. Hardison Jr. AiP; CRP

Marina. Nichita Stanescu, *Romanian.* CEEP, *tr. by* Mariana Carpinisan *and* Mark Irwin

Marine Aquarium, The. Louis Dudek. MoCV   *Fr.* Atlantis.

Mariner that on smooth waves doth glide, The. Anne Bradstreet. WPOW *Fr.* Contemplations. AmPP; NAAL-3; PoEL-3; SCAP; WPE

Marionette. Dahlia Ravikovitch, *Hebrew.* IP, *tr. by* Warren Bargad *and* Stanley F. Chyet

Maritae Suae. William Philpot. OBEV

Maritime Ode. Fernando Pessoa. "Ah, pirates, pirates, pirates!" PFTM

Maritimes. Penelope Shuttle. BrRo

Mark, Gospel according to. *See also* St. Mark.

Mark 14:26–42; And when they had sung. Bible, *N.T.* GI, *tr. by* Boris Pasternak. *Fr.* St. Mark.

Mark 16:19–20; So then the Lord Jesus, after. Bible, *N.T.* GI, *tr. by* A. E. Housman.

Mark 5:21–43; And when Jesus had crossed. Bible, *N.T.* GI, *tr. by* Czeslaw Milosz. *Fr.* St. Mark.

Mark Antony. John Cleveland. CBLP

Mark Antony Addresses the Mob. Shakespeare. FaPoR *Fr.* Julius Caesar.

Mark[e] but this flea, and mark[e] in this. The Flea. Donne. APo; BoLoP; EBEV; EP; ESCV; FMP; FSCP; HoPM; ImPo; InPK-6; InPS-3; NAEL-1; NBLV; NIP-4; NoP-4; NoSic; OAEL-1; OxAEP-1; PFE; PoE; Poetr; SCV; SeCP; TFi

Mark finished it himself, choosing midnight. John Tranter. NoAM

Mark how the bashful morn in vain. Boldness[e] in Love. Thomas Carew. CaPo; CavPo

Mark how the feathered tenants of the flood. Water Fowl. Wordsworth. APo

Mark[e] how the lanterns cloud [or clowd] mine eyes! A Non Sequitor [*or* Sequitur]. Richard Corbet. CBNP

Mark how this polished [*or* polish'd] Eastern sheet. A Fancy. Thomas Carew. BeJo; NOSC

Mark, how yond eddy steals away. To My Mistress Sitting by a River's Side; an Eddy. Thomas Carew. BeJo; CaPo

Mark of success in this painful discrimination, A. Horace, *Latin.* OBCVT, *tr. by* Charles Hubert Sisson

Mark Stern. Frederick Feirstein. RA

Mark Stern Wakes Up. Frederick Feirstein. RA

Mark the dark rook, on pendent branches hung. George Canning *and* William Gifford (1756–1826). *Fr.* The Progress of Man. NOBRP

Mark time in front! Rear fours cover! Company—halt!. The Halt. Edward Richard Burton Shanks. NSI

Mark when she smiles with amiable cheer. Sonnet 40. Edmund Spenser. *Fr.* Amoretti. AAS

Mark, when the Evening's cooler wings. To Amoret, of the Difference 'twixt Him and Other Lovers, and What True Love Is. Henry Vaughan. BeJo; FMP; SeCP

Mark where the pressing wind shoots javelin-like. Love's Grave. George Meredith. EnLoPo; EnVR; GBL; NOBE; OBEV; OBNC; PoEL-5; SCGP *Fr.* Modern Love.

Mark yon round parson, fat and sleek. Robert Lloyd. ECEV, *ll.* 1–60; OBSV *Fr.* A Familiar Epistle to J. B. Esq.

Mark you the floor[e]? that square and speckled stone. The Church-Floor[e]. George Herbert. EBEV; ESCV; MeLP; NOSC; OAEL-1; PeECV

Marke how this polish't Easterne sheet. Thomas Carew. *See* A Fancy.

Marked by no fence. 1801. Jackson MacLow. APSN *Fr.* The Presidents of the United States of America.

Marked with D. Tony Harrison. NAEL-2 *Fr.* The School of Eloquence. NAEL-2; NoAM

Marker at Auschwitz, The. Rational Man. Muriel Rukeyser. AF

Marker slants, flowerless, day's almost done, The. Dream Song 384. John Berryman. CAPP-1; HCAP; PoPoPo; VCAP *Fr.* Dream Songs.

Market Basket in the Car, A. Thomas MacDermot. PBCV

Market breaks at sound of Western guns, The. Fleeing From Bandits. Nguyễn Đình Chiểu, *Vietnamese.* AVP, *tr. by* Huỳnh Sanh Thông

Market Day. Mary Webb. CH

Market day it was, more deserted, A. Visiting a Rural Town. Kyongnim Shin, *Korean.* CKP, *tr. by* Jaihiun Kim

Marketing. E. J. Falconer. BoTP

Marking of Folders. Anne Anderton. UV

Marking Time. Peter Steele. NOBAu

Markings. Frank Steele. Poetsp

Markings on a shitter wall. Legacy of a Brother. Renaldo Fernandez. NBV

Marks. Linda Pastan. NIP-4

Marl white road, the Dorée rushing cool, The. Tales of the Islands. Derek Walcott. OxBTC

Marlburyes Fate. Benjamin Tompson. SCAP

Marlene Dietrich is singing a lament. The Blue Angel. Allen Ginsberg. BB

Marlow and Nancy. Sandra McPherson. AmPA

Marm Grayson's Guests. Mary Eleanor Wilkins Freeman. OBCA

Marmion. Sir Walter Scott.

    Battle, The ("By this, though deep the evening fell"). PoEL-4

    Fitz-Eustace's Song. CH; GTBS-P

    (Song.) NOBRP; PoEL-4

    "'Heap on more wood!--the wind is chill'." OBCP

    Lochinvar. BoTP; ChAP; EBEvV; EBNV; FaBoBe; NOBE; OBNV; OxAEP-2; OxBS; PoRA; Ro; TFi

       ("Have ye e'er heard of gallant like young Lochinvar?") (LL) ChAP; Ro

       ("O, Young Lochinvar is come out of the west.") ChAP

       (Young Lochinvar.) NTP; OBNV

    Nelson, Pitt, Fox. OBEV

       ("Oh, what a tangled web weave.") CIV

Maroon Girl, The. Walter Adolphe Roberts. PBCV

Marpessa's Choice. Yannis Ritsos, *Greek.* VCWP, *tr. by* Edmund Keeley

Marquis de Sade and Genet, The. Limerick. W. H. Auden. PeLi

Marrakech. Ralph Nixon Currey. PeSA

Marrakech. Richard Eberhart. LiTM

Marrano, The. Barry Goldensohn. NAmP90

Marriage, A. Michael C. Blumenthal. PoPoPo

Marriage. Austin Clarke. BIrV; GTBS-P

Marriage. Mary Elizabeth Coleridge. LW; NALW; PEW; VWP

Marriage. Gregory Corso. CBLP; CoAP; LiTM; MoP; NeAP; NoP-4; OBAL; PeLV; PmAP; TAP; TRP

Marriage. PiM

Marriage, A. Robert Creeley. LiTM; NeAP; PoPoPo; RaBo

Marriage. Mary Weston Fordham. CBWP-2

Marriage. Amy Gerstler. PmAP

Marriage. Joan Logghe. IFJA

Marriage. Marianne Moore. ColAP; NALW; NOBA

    ("'Hand in the breast-pocket, The'.") (LL) NMM-2

    ("This institution.") NMM-2

Marriage. Mary Ellen Solt. BoWoP

Marriage, The. Anne Stevenson. NALW

Marriage, The. Mark Strand. LiLi; NoAM; SPE

Marriage. Walter James Turner. NOBAu

Marriage. *Unknown.* AmFP

Marriage. William Carlos Williams. ITG; PoA

Marriage à la Mode. Dryden.

    Whil'st Alexis Lay Prest [*or* Press'd]. PeLV

       (Song: "Whilst Alexis lay pressed.") BoLoP

    Why Should a Foolish Marriage Vow. CBLP; NAEL-1; NIP-4; OxBM

       (Song: "Why should a foolish marriage vow.") AWP

Marriage and Love. Caroline Elizabeth Norton.

    "Laura was lightsome, gay, and free from guile." VWP

Marriage and Money. Sir Charles Sedley. OBSV *Fr.* The Happy Pair.

Marriage betwixt Scrape, Monarch of the Maunders, and Blobberlips, Queen of the Gypsies, A. Alexander Pennecuik.

    "Below fair Peebles, on the river's side." NOEC

Marriage Couplet. William Cole. OBAL

Marriage I think. Stevie Smith. OxBM; WPN

Marriage in Eden, The. William Williams. OBWVE, *tr. by* Lewis Saunders *and* Gwyn Jones *Fr.* A View of Christ's Kingdom.

Marriage is a lovely thing. Christine de Pisan, *French.* WPOW, *tr. by* Joanna Bankier

Marriage is a sweet state. In Praise of Marriage. Christine de Pisan, *French.* OxBM

Marriage is in many ways a simplification of life, and it naturally combines. Rilke. ITG, *tr. by* Stephen Mitchell *Fr.* Letters.

Marriage is not / a house or even a tent. Habitation. Margaret Atwood. BoWoP; FaBoWP; WeW-3

Marriage Morning. Tennyson. GBL

Marriage of a Virgin, The. Dylan Thomas. ChIV-2

Marriage of Heaven and Earth, The. Howard Nemerov. NYBP

Marriage of Heaven and Hell, The. William Blake. NAEL-2; NOBRP; OAEL-2

    Marriage of Heaven and Hell, The. Ro

    Proverbs of Hell.

       "Pride of the peacock is the glory of God, The." RaBo

Marriage of Hector and Andromache, The. Sappho, *Greek*. OBVE, *tr. by* Guy Davenport

Marriage of Sir Gawain, The. *Unknown*. ESPB

Marriage of the Frog and the Mouse, The. *Unknown*. EBEV

Marriage of True Minds, The. Edward Foster. PT

Marriage of True Minds, The. Shakespeare. *See* Sonnet 116.

Marriage of two murderers in the gloom, The. Terrible Love. John Barlas. ADE

Marriage Portrait. James Applewhite. MT

Marriage Prospect, A. William Hurrell Mallock. NOBVV

Marriage Ring, The. George Crabbe. BoLoP; EnLoPo; OBEV; OxBM
(His Mother's Wedding Ring.) OBNC
(Wedding Ring, The.) LBC

Marriage Song. Judah Halevi, *Hebrew*. TrJP, tr. by Alice Lucas

Marriage Vow, The. Letitia Elizabeth Landon. VWP

Marriage Vow. Mrs. Henry Linden. CBWP-4

Marriage, which might have been a mateship sweet. Elizabeth Wolstenholme-Elmy. BrRo *Fr.* Woman Free.

Marriages. Anthony Thwaite. OxBM

Marrie dear. When in Rome. Mari E. Evans. SoSe-8

Married and Single Life. *Unknown*. AmFP

Married for one year. Making It Simple December 8, 1969. David McElroy. AmPA

Married life for a poor man. Cillactor, *Greek*. GrAn, tr. by Barriss Mills

Married Love. Kuan Tao Shêng, *Chinese*. OxBM, tr. by Kenneth Rexroth *and* Ling Chung

Married Love. Sherod Santos. Son; WeT

Married Lover, The. Coventry Patmore. OBEV; OxAEP-2 *Fr.* The Angel in the House.

Married man comes nearest to the dead, A. Samuel Butler. FaBoEE

Married, poor soul! your empire's over. Jane West. ECWP *Fr.* To a Friend on her Marriage.

Married Romantic, A. Olafs Stumbrs. CEEP

Married to a Soldier. John Clare. SCGP

Marrog, The. R. C. Scriven. SpW

Marrow, The. Theodore Roethke. NYBP; PeECV

Marrow of My Bone. Mari E. Evans. BPo

Marrow of time; eternity in brief. Church Festivals. Christopher Harvey. NOSC

Marrows. Louis Johnson. PeNZ

Marry late and the next question. Naming the Unborn. Daniel Halpern. MoLi

Marry state affords but little Ease, A. Katherine Philips. KTR

Marrying Again. Harry Mathews, *Chinese*. CoBCP, tr. by Burton Watson

Marrying Again. Mei Yao Ch'en, *Chinese*. CoBCP, tr. by Burton Watson

Marrying is like somebody. Meaning Well. Jack Gilbert. IFJA

Marrying left your maiden name disused. Maiden Name. Philip Larkin. GTBS-P

Marrying maiden / Undertakings bring misfortune, The. *Unknown*. PFTM, tr. by Cary F. Baynes *and* Richard Wilhelm *Fr.* The I Ching.

Marrying the Hangman. Margaret Atwood. NOBC

Marrysong. Dennis Scott. HCP

Mars and Venus. Rachel Hadas. GS

Mars and Venus. Homer. OBCVT, tr. by William Broome *Fr.* The Odyssey.

Mars is braw in crammasy. The Bonnie Broukit Bairn. "Hugh MacDiarmid." FaBoCh; FaBoTC; FaBoVe; HAP; InPS-3

Marsh bank, lotus rank. Confucius. *Fr.* Songs of Ch'en. CTC, tr. by Ezra Pound

Marsh Leaf. David Wagoner. PoA

Marsh marigold. Robert Spiess. HA

Marsh, New Year's Day, The. Peter Everwine. NNaP

Marsh Song—At Sunset. Sidney Lanier. NOBA *Fr.* Hymns of the Marshes. APN-2

Marshes, The. Jane Mayhall. TAP

Marshes of Glynn, The. Sidney Lanier. AmPP; ImPo; NOBA; NoP-4; OxBA *Fr.* Hymns of the Marshes. APN-2
("On the length and the breadth of the marvellous marshes of Glynn.") (LL) NoP-4

Marshlands. Emily Pauline Johnson. NOBC

Marston, dropping it in the grate, broke his pipe. Stephen Spender. FaBoTw

Marsyas. G. D. Roberts. NoP-4

Marta we found the little box. Protect Me, My Talisman. Milo De Angelis, *Italian*. NeIt, tr. by Lawrence Venuti

Martha. Walter De la Mare. MoBrPo

Martha and Mary. Gabriela Mistral, *Spanish*. GI, tr. by Dana, Doris

Martha Blake. Austin Clarke. TIRV

Martha Blake at Fifty-one. Austin Clarke. CIP-2; NOIV

Martha is not so tall, nor yet so fair. Charles Cotton. *Fr.* Resolution in Four Sonnets, of a Poetical Question Put to Me by a Friend, Concerning Four Rural Sisters. PoEL-3; Son

Martha / Mary passed this morning. Mary Passed This Morning. Owen Dodson. PoBA

Martial. Thom Gunn, *Latin*. OBGa, tr. by Peter Porter

Martial Cadenza. Wallace Stevens. AFr; MeMAP; OxBA; VGW

Martial's Favourites. Martial, *Latin*. OBCVT, tr. by Hill, Brian

Martian Sends a Postcard Home, A. Craig Raine. NAEL-2; NoAM; NoP-4

Martin and His Man. *Unknown*. CBNP

Martin and My Father. David Hernandez. UnSA

Martin Buber in the Pub. Max Harris. NOBAu

Martin Luther King, Jr. Gwendolyn Brooks. PoBA

Martin sat young upon his bed. St. Martin and the Beggar. Thom Gunn. MoBS

Martin to His Man. Martin and His Man. *Unknown*. CBNP

Martin was too peaceful for me. Martin and My Father. David Hernandez. UnSA

Martin's Blues. Michael S. Harper. HCAP; PoBA

Martyr. Mary Elizabeth Fullerton. CBAP

Martyr, The. Herman Melville. CBCWP; ColAP; NCAP; PoEL-5; TAP

Martyr Poets—did not tell, The. Emily Dickinson. APN-2

Martyrdom. "Rufus Learsi." TrJP

Martyrdom. Richard W. Thomas. PoBA

Martyrdom of Brébeuf and Lalemant, 16 March 1649, The. Edwin John Pratt. NOBC *Fr.* Brébeuf and His Brethren.

Martyrdom of St. Theresa, The. Alec Derwent Hope. CBAP

Martyrdom of Two Pagans. Philip Whalen. NeAP

Martyred Democrat, The. C. J. Dennis. CBAP

Martyred Earth, The. Ewart Milne. BIrV

Martyrs, The. Donne. *Fr.* The Litanie. PoEL-2

Martyrs, The. Jay Macpherson. MoCV

Martyr's Death, A. Menahem ben Jacob, *Hebrew*. TrJP

Maru Mori brought me. Ode to My Socks. Pablo Neruda, *Spanish*. RaBo; TRP, tr. by Robert Bly

Marvel, The. Keith Douglas. RB

Marvel, A. Carolyn Wells. OBCA

Marvel [*or* Marvaill] no more although [*or* all tho]. Fortune. Sir Thomas Wyatt. AAS; SCGP; SiPS

Marvel of marvels, if I myself shall behold. Christina Rossetti. NOBE

Marveling today at the Safeway's abundance. A Little Piece of Sky. Sharif Elmusa. IFJA

Marvell! I think you'd neither seen nor smelt. Hibernia. Stuart Howard-Jones. NOBL

Marvellous Grass. Nuala Ni Dhomhnaill, *Irish*. PBCIP, tr. by Michael Hartnett

Marvellous Martin. Charles Harpur. CBAP

Marvelous Encounter at Blue Creek, The. *Unknown, Vietnamese*. AVP, tr. by Huỳnh Sanh Thông

Marvelous four-cylindered beast. The Mechanical Cow. Robley Wilson Jr. PBCAP

Marvelous Land of Indefinitions, The. Lorenzo Thomas. PmAP

Marvelous Truth, confront us. Denise Levertov. CrSp, *stanza vii Fr.* Matins.

Marvels of the City, The. Charles Simic. LCAP-2

Marx the Sign Painter. Edgar Lee Masters. NoAM; TAP *Fr.* The New Spoon River.

Mary. Philip Appleman. GI

Mary. Bertolt Brecht, *German*. GI, tr. by Michael Hamburger *and* Max Hayward

Mary. John Clare. *See* To Mary: 'It Is the Evening Hour'.

Mary. Lucille Clifton. CrSp

Mary and Gabriel. Rupert Brooke. ChIV-2

Mary and *mare*, anagrammatized. Epigram, A Supposed Construction. John Taylor. NOSC

Mary and the Baby, Sweet Lamb. *Unknown*. AmFP

Mary and the Bramble. Lascelles Abercrombie. OBMV

Mary at Peace with the Risen Lord. Rilke, *German*. GI, tr. by David Curzon *and* Will Alexander Washburn

Mary Cassatt has her in a striped dress with a. How to Catch Aunt Harriette. Ruth Stone. NMM-2

Mary Celeste. Judith Nicholls. OBSP

Mary Desti's Ass. Frank O'Hara. FTOS

Mary Gravely Jones. Adrienne Rich. MDDM *Fr.* Grandmothers. HCAP; NAAL-2; NoAM

Mary Gulliver to Capt. Lemuel Gulliver. John Gay *and* Alexander Pope. OAEL-1

Mary had a little bird. The Canary. Elizabeth Turner. OxBChV; PeP

Mary had a little lamb. A Little Lamb. *Unknown.* OBCoV

Mary had a little lamb. Mary's Lamb [*or* Mary and Her Lamb]. Sarah Josepha Buell Hale. CTV; FPC; FaBoBe; ImGa; OBCA; OxBChV; OxNR

Mary had a little lamb. *Unknown.* LB

Mary had a pretty bird. Mary's Canary. *Unknown.* ReMoGo

Mary Had a William Goat. *Unknown.* AS

Mary Hamilton. *Unknown.* AmFP; ESPB; NoP-4; SCGP

("Word has come from the kitchen.") AmFP

Mary [*or* Marie] Hamilton. *Unknown.* ESPB; NoP-4

Mary Hamilton. *Unknown.* NOBE; OxBB

Mary! I want a lyre with other strings. To Mary Unwin. William Cowper. GTBS-P; OBEV

Mary is black, and taller than the last. Charles Cotton. *Fr.* Resolution in Four Sonnets, of a Poetical Question Put to Me by a Friend, Concerning Four Rural Sisters. PoEL-3; Son

Mary laid her Child among. Carol. Norman Nicholson. OBCP

Mary lay in jizzen. The Problem Child. "Hugh MacDiarmid." FaBoTC *Fr.* A Drunk Man Looks at the Thistle.

Mary Lifted from the Dead. William Alfred. AH

Mary [*or* Marie] Magdalene. George Herbert. ESCV

("When blessèd Mary wiped her Saviour's feet.") FMP

Mary Magdalene. Saunders Lewis, *Welsh.* OBWVE, *tr. by* Gwyn Morgan

Mary Magdalene (I). Boris Pasternak, *Russian.* AF, *tr. by* Lydia Pasternak Slater

Mary Magdalene, that easy woman. Lent. William Robert Rodgers. PNI

Mary, Mary, quite contrary. Mother Goose. LB; OxNR; ReMoGo

Mary, Mary, quite contrary. *Unknown.* ACTP

Mary mild, good maiden. Saint Columcille. NOIV

Mary Morelle Show, The. Denise Nico Leto. UnSA

Mary Morison. Robert Burns. GTBS-P; OBEV; OxBS

(Song: Mary Morison.) AWP

"Mary mother, dost thou sleep?" Mary's Dream. *Unknown, Welsh.* OBWVE, *tr. by* C. C. Bell

Mary, Mother of Christ. Countee Cullen. PChr

Mary Passed This Morning. Owen Dodson. PoBA

Mary, pray for Paris. Dumb Oxen. Sister Mary Madeleva. CRP *Fr.* Of Mary.

Mary prevents the day; she rose to weep. The Gardener. Rowland Watkyns. NOSC

Mary, Queen of Scots. Henry Glassford Bell. BLPA; FaBoBe

Mary sat musing on the lamp-flame at the table. The Death of the Hired Man. Robert Frost. AmPP; CMoP; HeIP-4; HoPM; MoAmPo; NAAL-2; NoP-4; OxBA; SAGP; SAmP

Mary stood in the kitchen. Ballad of the Bread Man. Charles Causley. RB

Mary Stuart. Edwin Muir. RB

Mary, the Blessed Virgins name. Profit and Loss: An Elegy upon the Decease of Mrs. Mary Gerrish. John Danforth. SCAP

Mary, the Christ long slain, passed silently. Motherhood. Agnes Lee. BLPA

Mary the Cook-Maid's Letter to Dr. Sheridan. Jonathan Swift. OxBoLi; PeLV

Mary, The Mother of Jesus. Ada Belle Gardner. PWR

Mary Trevellyn to Miss Roper. Arthur Hugh Clough. FaBoVe *Fr.* Amours de Voyage. NOBVV

Mary was Mother of the Lord. Hymn of the Magdalen. Marbod of Rennes, *Latin.* MLL, *tr. by* Helen Waddell

Mary Weeps for Her Child. *Unknown.* OxBoLi

Mary, will you ever grow? Water, blessed by bishops. Song for Healing. Roberta Hill Whiteman. CDW

Mary Wyatt and Henry Green, *with 3 add. sts. Unknown.* AmFP

Mary Wyatt and Henry Green. *Unknown.* AmFP

Marye, maide, milde and fre. William of Shoreham. MiEL

Maryland, my Maryland! (LL) My Maryland. James Ryder Randall. APN-2; CBCWP; FaBoBe

Maryland Virginia Caroline. Emblems. Allen Tate. AWP; VGW

Mary's Canary. *Unknown.* ReMoGo

Mary's Dream. Lucille Clifton. NALW

Mary's Dream. *Unknown, Welsh.* OBWVE, *tr. by* C. C. Bell

Mary's gone a-milking. Milking Pails. *Unknown.* CH

Mary's Lamb [*or* Mary and Her Lamb]. Sarah Josepha Buell Hale. FaBoBe; ImGa; OBCA; OxBChV; OxNR

("If you are only kind.") (LL) FPC

(Mary's Lamb.) CTV; FPC; PeP

Mary's Song. Marion Angus. LW

Mary's Song. Charles Causley. OBCP

Mary's Song. Sylvia Plath. ChIV-2; FaBoMo; FaBoWP

Mary's Visitation. Rilke, *German.* GI, *tr. by* David Curzon *and* Will Alexander Washburn

Mas' Charley. *Unknown.* PBCV

Mas-Soñer / Restaurat—Any. The House. Robert Creeley. FTOS

Masai warrior is not, The. Outbreak. Bill Anderson. VGW

Masculine, Feminine, Neuter. Michael Wulff. CBNP *Fr.* Lore and Language of Schoolchildren.

Mashed potatoes cannot hurt you, darling. Giving Potatoes. Adrian Mitchell. NBLV; RB

Mask, The. Elizabeth Barrett Browning. OBNC; VWP

Mask, The. Patty L. Harjo. VoR

Mask, The. Irma McClaurin. BlSi

Mask, A. Milton. OxAEP-1 *Fr.* Comus; a Masque Presented at Ludlow Castle. FHYEP; OAEL-1

Mask, A. Milton. *See* Comus' Summons.

Mask, A. Milton. *See* Comus; a Masque Presented at Ludlow Castle.

"Nay, lady, sit; if I but wave this wand." OxAEP-1

Mask. Stephen Spender. MoBrPo

Mask for Lydia, A. Thomas Randolph. BeJo

Mask-Maker. Michael Jackson. PeNZ

Mask [*or* Masque] of Anarchy, The. Shelley. FHYEP; OBSV; OxAEP-2; RB; SCV

(Mask of Anarchy. Written on the Occasion of the Massacre at Manchester.) Ro

Mask of Anger, A. Lyn Hejinian. FTOS

Mask of Cupid, The. Edmund Spenser. *Fr.* Wood Of Error. AEP

"First was Fancy, like a lovely boy, The." NOBE

"Noble Mayde, still standing, all this vewd, The." PoEL-1

Mask of Evil, The. Bertolt Brecht, *German.* PoSu, *tr. by* H. R. Hayes

Mask of Gaiety, The. Letitia Elizabeth Landon. VWP

Mask of Love. Thomas Kinsella. CMoP

Mask of Mutability, The. Edmund Spenser. *See* The Pageant of the Seasons and the Months.

Mask Series. Carol Snow. PUP-19

Masked Angel Costume / The Sayings of Mantan Moreland. Imamu Amiri Baraka. EC3

Masked dancers in the Dance of life. The Masquerade. Olive Custance. ADE

Masked Woman's Song. Louise Bogan. NMM-2

Masks. Judit Tóth, *Hungarian.* CEEP, *tr. by* Emery E. George

Masks! O Masks! Prayer to the Masks. Léopold Sédar Senghor, *French.* NegPo, *tr. by* Ellen Conroy Kennedy

Masochist, The. Maxine W. Kumin. PoA

Mason Abraham Knupfer is singing, trowel in hand, scaffolded, The. Aloysius Bertrand, *French.* BLT, *tr. by* E. D. Hartley

Mason lives, The. Symbolum. Goethe, *German.* FaBoPV, *tr. by* Tom Paulin

Mason's Trick. James Hayford. InPK-6

Masons, when they start upon a building. Scaffolding. Seamus Heaney. ChAP

Masque of Alfred, The. James Thomson *and* David Mallet. *See* Alfred: A Masque.

Masque of Blackness, The. Geoffrey Hill. NoAM *Fr.* Lachrimae; or Seven Tears Figured in Seven Passionate Pavans.

Masque of Christmas, The. Ben Jonson. OxBoLi

Masque of Cupid, The. Edmund Spenser. *See* The Mask of Cupid.

Masque of Queens, The. Ben Jonson.

"Help, help all tongues to celebrate this wonder." NOSC

Masque of the Inner Temple and Gray's Inne, The. Francis Beaumont.

Fourth Song, The. NOSC

Song for a Dance. FaBoCh

Masque of the Middle Temple and Lincoln's Inn, The. George Chapman.

Bridal Song: "Now sleep, bind fast the flood of air." OxBSP

Masque of the Virtues against Love. Mary Monck. ECWP; NOEC

Masquerade, The. Olive Custance. ADE

Masquerade. Carolyn M. Rodgers. BlSi

Masquerading. May Probyn. VWP

Mass at Dawn. Roy Campbell. OxAEP-2; PeSA

Mass for the Day of St. Thomas Didymus. Denise Levertov.

"God then." CrSp

"Powers and principalities—all the gods." CrSp

Mass Graves. Charles Reznikoff.

"Jews from Holland, France, and Hungary, and later from." HP

Mass hysteria, wave after breaking wave. Willowware Cup. James Merrill. VCAP

Mass is over, they have gone in peace, The. Sara Berkeley. PBCIP

Mass of hill is rammed down at dawn, The. The Bulldozer. Songbu Yi, *Korean*. CKP, *tr. by* Jaihiun Kim

Massacre, October '66. Wole Soyinka. AF; PBMAP

Massacre of the Boys. Tadeusz Rózewicz, *Polish*. HP, *tr. by* Adam Czerniawski; AF, *tr. by* Robert A. Maguire *and* Magnus Jan Krynski

("Vertical / dead tree / with no star in its crown, A.") (LL) GI, *tr. by* Adam Czerniawski

Massacre of the Innocents. Alec Derwent Hope. GI

Massacre of the Innocents, The. Giovanni Battista Marino, *Italian*.

"Yet on the other side, faine would he start." OBVE, *tr. by* Richard Crashaw

Massacre of the Macpherson, The. William Edmonstoune Aytoun. BXAP

Massacres. Charles Reznikoff. APSN

Massenet / Never wrote a Mass in A. Antony Butts. OBCoV

Masses, The. Cornelius Mathews. APN-1 *Fr.* Poems on Man in His Various Aspects under the American Republic.

Masses. César Vallejo. RB, *tr. by* Robert Bly *Fr.* España, Aparta de me Este Caliz.

Masses of flowers and plants envelop the riverbanks. Tu Fu. SuSp, *tr. by* Irving Y. Lo *Fr.* Strolling along the Riverbank, Looking for Flowers.

Massive engines lift beautifully from the deck. The Teeth Mother Naked at Last. Robert Bly. CLPP; NNaP

Massive hills, numberless valleys, all point to Ching-men. Thoughts on Historical Sites: Wang Chao-chün. Tu Fu, *Chinese*. SuSp, *tr. by* Irving Lo

Massive rains darken the marshes and slopes. Dreaming of Master Chung-lu. K'ang Hai, *Chinese*. CoBLCP, *tr. by* Jonathan Chaves

Mast Year, The. Medbh McGuckian. CIP-2

Mastectomy. Wanda Coleman. NAAAL

Master. Brendan Kennelly. BiHa

Master, The. Edwin Arlington Robinson. CBCWP; LiTM; MoAmPo

Master and Guest. Mary Elizabeth Coleridge. VWP

Master and mage, our prince of song, whom Time. To Lord Tennyson. Sir William Watson. EPCY

Master and Man. Mother Goose. OxNR; ReMoGo

Master and Man. Sir Henry John Newbolt. OxBTC

Master and the slave go hand in hand, The. Sonnet. Edwin Arlington Robinson. APN-2

Master Brunetto, this my little maid. Sonnet: To Brunetto Latini. Dante, *Italian*. AWP, *tr. by* D. G. Rossetti

Master, by Styx—which is the poets' oath. Bounce to Pope. Alec Derwent Hope. FP

Master Carpenter, The. G. Shankara Kurup, *Malayalam*. OMIP, *tr. by* K. M. George *and* A. K. Ramanujan

Master Charge Blues. Nikki Giovanni. OBAL

Master Cheng is thirty—and doesn't have a job! Cheng Hsieh. *Fr.* Seven Songs. CoBLCP, *tr. by* Jonathan Chaves

Master dragon-tamer has fled the world, The. Li Ho. SuSp, *tr. by* Irving Y. Lo *Fr.* About Horse.

Master Francesco, I have come to thee. Petrarch. Giosuè Carducci, *Italian*. AWP, *tr. by* William Dudley Foulke

"Master has come over Jordan, The." Christ and the Little Ones. Julia Gill. BLPA

Master Hugues of Saxe-Gotha. Robert Browning. OAEL-2

Master I have, and I am his man. Master and Man. Mother Goose. OxNR; ReMoGo

Master Jen has long been famous. Thanking Doctor Jen. Li K'ai-hsien, *Chinese*. CoBLCP, *tr. by* Jonathan Chaves

Master knows what he want, The. Paul Klee, *German*. CBNP

Master Liu Painted a Portrait of Me in My Old Age and Asked Me to Write a Poem About the Picture. Yang Wan-li, *Chinese*. SuSp, *tr. by* Jonathan Chaves

Master-Mistress, The. Rose Cecil O'Neill. CPO

Master Mo Tzu and Master Lao Tzu. Inspector Hsü Claims He Has Found the Secret of Youth. T'ang Hsien-tsu, *Chinese*. CoBLCP, *tr. by* Jonathan Chaves

Master, No Offering. Edwin Pond Parker. AII

Master of Auschwitz, angel of death. For the Bones of Josef Mengele, Disinterred June 1985. Robert Bringhurst. NIP-4

Master of beauty, craftsman of the snowflake. John Berryman. UnPo *Fr.* Eleven Addresses to the Lord. OxBC

Master of blood I am yours. Nocturnal Heart. Anne-Marie Kegels, *French*. BoWoP, *tr. by* W. S. Merwin

Master of human destinies am I! Opportunity. John James Ingalls. PoLF

Master of the Golden Glow, The. James Schuyler. FTOS

Master of *The Monarch of the Glen*, The. An Unsagacious Animal. David Gascoyne. PeLV

Master Shih's medical fame, because of Master Ch'en. Sent to the Master Physician, "Almond Orchard" Shih. Li K'ai-hsien, *Chinese*. CoBLCP

Master-songs are ended, and the man, The. Walt Whitman. Edwin Arlington Robinson. APN-2; NCAP; OxBA

Master Speed, The. Robert Frost. ITG

Master stood in His garden, The. For the Master's Use. *Unknown*. BLPA

Master stood upon the mount, and taught, The. Progress. Matthew Arnold. ChIV-2

Master, the swabber, the boatswain and I, The. A Sea Song. Shakespeare. NBLV; NOBL; OBCoV; OxBSP; PFE; PeLV *Fr.* The Tempest. OAEL-1

Master, the tempest is raging. Peace Be Still. *Unknown*. NAAAL

Master, then This—I crossed my father's gate. Moving on in the Dark Like Loaded Boats at Night, Though There is No Course, There is Boundlessness. Lucie Brock-Broido. MoLi

Master, they say that when I seem. Prayer. C. S. Lewis. TIRV; TrCP

Master, this is Thy Servant. He is rising eight / weeks old. His Apologies. Rudyard Kipling. CTAV

Master Tung-p'o, in raising children, was afraid of their being clever. Rebuttal of Tung-p'o's Poem on "Bathing the Infant," A. Ch'ien Ch'ien-i, *Chinese*. SuSp, *tr. by* Irving Y. Lo

Masterful units of his siesta, and always did, The. (LL) The Perfection of Dentistry. Marvin Bell. AmPa; CoAP

Masters, be kind to the old house that must fall. Rockland. Julia Randall. WPE

Masts at Dawn. Robert Penn Warren. NAAL-2; NoP-4; VCAP

Mat to Weave, A. U Tam'si Tchicaya, *French*. NegPo, *tr. by* Ellen Conroy Kennedy; PBMAP

("He came to deliver the secret of the sun.") PBMAP

("It is the purest of cups.") (LL) PBMAP

Matadors, The. Josephine Jacobsen. TAP

Match, The. Andrew Marvell. EBEV

Match, A. Swinburne. CBLP; NOBVV

Match, The. Henry Vaughan. ESCV

Match-bark of the younger dog sets fire to, The. Table-Birds. Kenneth Mackenzie. BMAP; NOBAu

Match me such marvel save in college port. William Basil Tickell Jones. UV

Match me such marvel save in Eastern clime. John William Burgon. UV *Fr.* Petra.

Match with the Moon, A. D. G. Rossetti. NOBVV

Matches among other things that were not allowed. The Burnt Child. W. S. Merwin. NoAM

Matching a Poem by Secretary Kuo. Ch'ien T'ao, *Chinese*. ChiPo, *tr. by* Burton Watson

Matching a Poem by Secretary Kuo. T'ao Ch'ien, *Chinese*.

(Matching a Poem by Secretary Kuo, No. 1.) CoBCP, *tr. by* Burton Watson

Mater Dei. Padraic Fallon. NOCV

Mater Dei. Katharine Tynan. TIRV

Mater Dolorosa. William Barnes. CH; NOBE; OBEV

Material voluptuousness vexed you. To a Nigerian Friend. Jaihiun Kim, *Korean*. CKP, *tr. by* Jaihiun Kim

Materialism. R. P. Dickey. Poetr

Materialism. C. E. M. Joad. PeLi

Materialization of Soap 1947, The. Robert Sheppard. NBrP

Material's Daughter. Aaron Shurin. FTOS

Maternal Despotism; or, The Rights of Infants. Richard Graves. NOEC

Maternal Earth stirs redly from beneath. Roy Campbell. MoBrPo *Fr.* The Flaming Terrapin.

Maternal Love Triumphant or Song of the Virtuous Female Spider. Ruth Pitter. WPN

Maternity. Alice Thompson Meynell. OxBSP; PEW; SDW; VWP

("'mother, a mother was born,' A.") (LL) SDW

Maternity Gown. David Holbrook. OxBTC

Matey. Patrick MacGill. NSI; PoWW

Mathematicians take a huge area like a whole world. To Myself. Abba Kovner, *Hebrew*. AF, *tr. by* Shirley Kaufman

Mathematics. Hanns Cibulka, *German*. CEEP, *tr. by* Ewald Osers

Mathematics of Breathing, A. Carl Phillips. BAP-94

Mathenge. Marjorie Oludhe Macgoye. HBAPE

Mathios Paskalis among the Roses. George Seferis, *Greek*. PFTM, *tr. by* Edmund Keeley *and* Philip Sherrard

Mathmid, The. Hayyim Nahman Bialik, *Hebrew*. AWP, *tr. by* Maurice Samuel

Matière de Bretagne. Paul Celan, *German*. VCWP, *tr. by* Michael Hamburger

Matilda Maud Mackenzie frankly hadn't any chin. How a Girl Was Too Reckless of Grammar [by Far]. Guy Wetmore Carryl. OBAL

Matilda told such Dreadful Lies. Hilaire Belloc. EBEvV; FaBoCh; NOBE; OxBChV

Matin Hymn. Josephine D. Henderson Heard. CBWP-4

Matin Pandemoniums, The. Richard Eberhart. NYBP

Matin Song. Thomas Heywood. GLoP; OBEV *Fr.* The Rape of Lucrece.
(Good Morrow.) CH

("Pale clouds, away! and welcome, day!") ITG

Matinee. Susan Clements. UnSA

Matinees. James Merrill. HCAP; NOBA

Mating Answer. Ronald Bottrall. PoA

Mating the Goats. Aliki Barnstone. BoWoP

Matins. George Herbert. *See* Mattens.

Matins. Denise Levertov. AmPP; FaBoWP; MoP; NOBA; NoAM; Poetr
"Marvelous Truth, confront us." CrSp, *stanza* vii

"Stir the holy grains, set." APAD

Matins and Lauds. Marie Ponsot. CLPP

Matins: James Brown and His Famous Flames Tour the South, 1958. David
Wojahn. NAmP90; PBCAP *Fr.* Mystery Train: A Sequence.

Matins [*or* Mattens], or Morning Prayer. Robert Herrick. CaPo

Matisse: "The Red Studio." W. D. Snodgrass. GS

Matlock Bath. John Betjeman. NYBP

Matmiya. Mary TallMountain. CrSp; HATNAP; LoL

Matrimony. John Williams. NOEC

Matrix. Dorothy Wellesley.
"Spiritual, the carnal, are one, The." OBMV

Matt Casey formed a social club that beat the town for style. The Band
Played On. John F. Palmer. OBAL

Mattens. George Herbert. ESCV
(Matins.) SCGP

Matter. Carla Harryman. FTOS

Matter is palsy: the land heaving, water. From Heraclitus. Alan Dugan.
PoA

Matters of Policy. Charles Bernstein. FTOS

Matthew, Gospel according to. *See also* St. Matthew *and* Bible, Matthew.

Matthew 1:18–25; Now the birth of Jesus Christ took place. Bible, N.T.
GI, *tr. by* Philip Appleman. *Fr.* St. Matthew.

Matthew 2:1–12; Now when Jesus was born. Bible, N.T. GI, *tr. by* T. S.
Eliot. *Fr.* St. Matthew.

Matthew 2:16–18; Then Herod, when he saw. Bible, N.T. GI, *tr. by* Julia
Hartwig. *Fr.* St. Matthew.

Matthew 4:1–11; Then Jesus was led up by the spirit. Bible, N.T. GI, *tr.
by* Czeslaw Milosz. *Fr.* St. Matthew.

Matthew 5:1–12; Seeing the crowds, he went up on the mountain. Bible,
N.T. GI, *tr. by* Jorge Luis Borges. *Fr.* St. Matthew.

Matthew 5:13; You are the salt of the earth. Bible, N.T. GI, *tr. by* Gail
Holst-Warhaft. *Fr.* St. Matthew.

Matthew 5:27–30; You have heard that it was said. Bible, N.T. GI, *tr. by*
Gail Holst-Warhaft. *Fr.* St. Matthew.

Matthew V. 29-30. Derek Mahon. CIP-2

Matthew 5:38–48; "You have heard that it was said, 'An eye'." Bible, N.T.
GI, *tr. by* Jacob Glatstein. *Fr.* St. Matthew.

Matthew 6:7–15; "And in praying do not heap up empty." Bible, N.T. GI,
tr. by D. H. Lawrence. *Fr.* St. Matthew.

Matthew 7:1–2; "Judge not, that you be not." Bible, N.T. GI, *tr. by*
Theodore Roethke. *Fr.* St. Matthew.

Matthew 8:20; And Jesus said to him. Bible, N.T. GI, *tr. by* Karl
Kirchwey. *Fr.* St. Matthew.

Matthew VIII, 28 ff. Richard Wilbur. GI

Matthew 8:28–34; And when he came to the other side. Bible, N.T. GI, *tr.
by* Richard Wilbur. *Fr.* St. Matthew.

Matthew 9.12. Francis Quarles. ChIV-2

Matthew 10:25–26. Bible, *N.T.* PBMP

Matthew X. 28. Roger Wolcott. SCAP

Matthew 13:1–9; That same day Jesus. Bible, N.T. GI, *tr. by* Stephen
Mitchell. *Fr.* St. Matthew.

Matthew 19:16–24; And behold, one came up to him. Anna Kamienska.
GI *Fr.* St. Matthew.

Matthew 21:1–11. Bible, N.T. GI, *tr. by* Boris Pasternak. *Fr.* St. Matthew.

Matthew 21:18–22; In the morning. Bible, N.T. GI, *tr. by* Donald Hall.
Fr. St. Matthew.

Matthew 22:1–14; And again Jesus spoke to them. Bible, N.T. GI, *tr. by*
Edwin Arlington Robinson. *Fr.* St. Matthew.

Matthew 22:15–22; Then the Pharisees went and. Bible, N.T. GI, *tr. by*
Desanka Maksimovic. *Fr.* St. Matthew.

Matthew 24:15–31. Bible, N.T. GI, *tr. by* W. B. Yeats. *Fr.* St. Matthew.

Matthew 25:14–30; "For it will be as when a man." Bible, N.T. GI, *tr. by*
Jorge Luis Borges. *Fr.* St. Matthew.

Matthew XXV:30. Jorge Luis Borges, *Spanish.* GI, *tr. by* David Curzon

Matthew 26:17–29. Bible, N.T. GI, *tr. by* Rilke. *Fr.* St. Matthew.

Matthew 26:47–56; While he was still speaking, Judas came. Bible, N.T.
GI, *tr. by* Boris Pasternak. *Fr.* St. Matthew.

Matthew 27:11–24; Now Jesus stood before. Bible, N.T. GI, *tr. by* René
Daumal. *Fr.* St. Matthew.

Matthew 27:3–10; When Judas, his betrayer, saw. Bible, N.T. GI, *tr. by*
Zbigniew Herbert. *Fr.* St. Matthew.

Matthew 27:45–56; Now from the sixth hour there was darkness. Bible,
N.T. GI, *tr. by* Ted Hughes. *Fr.* St. Matthew.

Matthew 27:57–61; When it was evening, there came a rich man. Bible,
N.T. GI, *tr. by* Rilke. *Fr.* St. Matthew.

Matthew 28:1–6; Now after the sabbath. Bible, N.T. GI, *tr. by* Czeslaw
Milosz. *Fr.* St. Matthew.

Matthew 28:16–20; Now the eleven disciples went to Galilee. Bible, N.T.
GI, *tr. by* W. B. Yeats. *Fr.* St. Matthew.

Matthew and Mark and Luke and holy John. Epi-Strauss-ium. Arthur Hugh
Clough. EnVR; NAEL-2

Matthew, and Mark, and Luke, and John. N.T. Charles Wesley. ChIV-2

Matthew, Mark, Luke and John. *Unknown.* ACTP

Matthew, Mark, Luke, and John / Bless the bed that I lie on. Before
Sleeping. *Unknown.* CH; FaBoCh; NTP; OxBoLi; OxNR

Matthew, Mark, Luke and John, / Hold the horse till I leap on. *Unknown.*
OxNR

Matthias. Matthew Arnold. PC *Fr.* Poor Matthias. PoEL-5

Mattock heavier than the hoe, A. (LL) In the Pauper's Turnip-Field.
Herman Melville. OxBSP; PoEL-5

Mattress Fire. Penny Harter. IFJA

Mauberly (1920). Ezra Pound. *Fr.* Hugh Selwyn Mauberley. (Life and
Contacts). AmPP; CMoP; InPS-3; LiTM; NOBA; NoAM; TAP

Maud [A Monodrama]. Tennyson. EnVR

Maud. Tennyson. *See* Song: "Come into the garden, Maud."
"Birds in the high Hall-garden." EBVVPR; NAEL-2; PeVV
"Catch not my breath, O clamorous heart." NAEL-2
"Cold and clear-cut face, why come you so cruelly meek." EBVVPR
"Dead, long dead." EBVVPR; OAEL-2
("As the churches have killed their Christ.") (LL) OAEL-2
"Go not, happy day." EBVV
"I hate the dreadful hollow behind the little wood." EBVVPR; FaBoPV
("War with a thousand battles, and shaking a hundred thrones.") (LL)
FaBoPV
"I have led her home, my love, my only friend." CBLP; EBVV; NAEL-2;
NOBVV; PoEL-5
("Shadowing the snow-limbed Eve from whom she came.") (LL) PoEL-
5
"There is none like her, none." OBNC
"I was walking a mile." EBVV
If Only. LBC
("O that 'twere possible.") LBC; SAGP
("What and where they be!") (LL) CBLP; LBC; OxBSn; SAGP
"Long have I sighed for a calm; God grant I may find it at last!"
EBVVPR
"Maud has a garden of roses." FHYEP
Sleeping House, The. OBNC
"Morning arises stormy and pale." EBVVPR
"Ah, what shall I be at fifty." NAEL-2
My Day. NAEL-2; NOBVV
"My life has crept so long on a broken wing." OAEL-2; OBWP
"She came to the village church." EBVV; NAEL-2
Song: "Come into the garden, Maud." AWP
("And the lily whispers, 'I wait'.") (LL) GaP

Maud Fitzgerald. *Unknown.* PeLi
Sleeping House, The. OBNC

Maud Muller, all that summer day. Mrs. Judge Jenkins[; Being the Only
Genuine Sequel to "Maud Muller"]. Bret Harte. APN-2; BXAP

Maud Muller on a summer's day. John Greenleaf Whittier. APN-1;
FaBoBe; PoLF; TAP

Saddest Words, The. ImPo

Maud went to college. Sadie and Maud. Gwendolyn Brooks. InPK-6;
MoP; NAAAL; NOBA; NoAM; TAP *Fr.* A Street in Bronzeville.
BPo; BlSi; FaBoWP

Maude Clare. Christina Rossetti. EBVV

Maudgalyâyana Saw Hell. Gary Snyder. *Fr.* Burning. NeAP; PoM *Fr.*
Myths and Texts.

Maudle-in Ballad, A. *Unknown.* BXAP

Maugre thee my love shall stay. (LL) Marie [*or* Mary] Magdalens Complaint
at Christs Death. Robert Southwell. ChIV-2; ESCV

Maui. Meg Campbell. PeNZ

Maui's Fish. Blanche Edith Baughan.
"Toward the dawn." PeNZ

Maunder's Praise of His Strowling Mort, The. *Unknown.* CBNP; OxBoLi; PeLV

Maureen Dean, wearing persimmon summer silk. On the Watergate Women. Robin Morgan. GLP

Maureen in England, Joseph in Guelph. The Wishbone. Paul Muldoon. CIP-2; PBCIP

Maurice. Rita Dove. *See Dusting.*

Maurice was in an Exhibition Hall. Austin Clarke. PoE *Fr.* Mnemosyne Lay in Dust.

Maurus. Palladas, *Greek.* GrAn, *tr. by* Tony Harrison

Mauve. Leslie Ullman. NAmP90

Mauve summer rain, The. Dame Edith Sitwell. BWW *Fr.* The Sleeping Beauty.

Mauve, the ocher of canned tamales, the dark silt, The. What Ely Was. Lynn Emanuel. PaTW

Mavis, mavis. James King Annand. NOxBChV

Mavrone. Arthur Guiterman. BXAP

Max Factor Pink. Nigel Roberts. BMAP

Max is dead and his sons. Natan Zach, *Hebrew.* IP, *tr. by* Warren Bargad *and* Stanley F. Chyet

Max Schmitt in a Single Scull. Richmond Lattimore. AiP

Maxfield Parrish. Eileen Myles. PT

Maxie Allen [always taught her]. Gwendolyn Brooks. NAAAL; NAAL-2

Maxim. Josephine Miles. CrSp

Maxim Revised, A. *Unknown.* BLPA; NBLV

Maxims (Cotton MS.) *Unknown, Anglo-Saxon.* AnOE, *tr. by* Charles W. Kennedy

Maxims (Exeter Book). *Unknown, Anglo-Saxon.* AnOE, *tr. by* Charles W. Kennedy

    ("Frost shall freeze / fire eat wood.") EEP, *tr. by* Michael Alexander

(Gnomic Verses (Exeter Book).) EEP, *tr. by* Michael Alexander

Maxims in Rhyme for the Young. J. Clark. PWR

Maximus. D. H. Lawrence. BLT; TOF

Maximus Poems, The. Charles Olson.

Celestial Evening, October 1967. PoM

    "Chockablock Once a man was traveling through the woods, and." FTOS

Cole's Island. PoM

    "Colored pictures." NoAM

I, Maximus of Gloucester, to You ("By ear, she sd"). NeAP

I, Maximus of Gloucester, to You ("Off-shore, by islands hidden in the blood"). LiTM; NOBA; NoAM; PmAP; PoM

Letter 3. PmAP

Maximus, to Gloucester, Letter 2. NoAM

Maximus, to Gloucester, Letter 19. CMoP

Maximus, to Gloucester, Letter 27. NOBA; PoE

Maximus, to Gloucester, Sunday, July 19. NAAL-2; TRP

Maximus to Himself. CMoP; NOBA; NeAP; PmAP; PoE; PoM; VGW

Poem 143. APSN; ColAP

Songs of Maximus. NeAP

    All/ wrong. NoAM

    "Colored pictures/ of all things to eat: dirty." NeAP; NoAM

Maxixe. Sir Osbert Sitwell. PoA

Maxwell[l] ton['s] braes are bonnie. Annie Laurie. William Douglas, *rev. by* Lady Jane Scott. FaBoBe; ImPo

May. Dafydd ap Gwilym. CABP

May. Thomas Dekker *and others. Fr.* The Shoemaker's Holiday. (Maytime.)

May. Yongnang Kim, *Korean.* CKP, *tr. by* Jaihiun Kim

May. Mrs. Henry Linden. CBWP-4

May. Roger McGough. AYFP

May. John Shaw Neilson. NOBAu

May. James Gates Percival. BoTP

May. Henrietta Cordelia Ray. CBWP-3

May. Christina Rossetti. GBL; GLoP; NOBVV

May. Folgore da San Gemmiano. *Fr.* Sonnets of the Months. AWP, *tr. by* D. G. Rossetti

May. Edmund Spenser. *Fr.* Wood Of Error. AEP

May. John Updike. AYFP; OBCA *Fr.* A Child's Calendar.

    ("Look at some baseball / On TV.") (LL) NOxBChV

May 1970. Stephen Berg. CDa

May again / and poems leaf out. Letter to a Son at Exam Time. Linda Pastan. FiLi

May All Earth Be Clothed in Light. George Hitchcock. VGW

May all selfishness disappear from me, / and may you always shine from my heart. Bible, *O.T. See* Psalm 104.

May all that dread the cruel feind of night. Warning to Travailers Seeking Accomodations at Mr. Devills Inn. Sarah Kemble Knight. SCAP

May all your tears, wanderer. Song of the Wanderer. Wang T'ing-hsiang, *Chinese.* CoBLCP, *tr. by* Jonathan Chaves

May, and among the miles of leafing. Mary Oliver. Poetr

May and Death. Robert Browning. FP; IMW; NOBE

May, and the wall was warm again. For miles. Winter's Cold. William Robert Rodgers. EnLoPo

May at his peril[l] further go. (LL) Superliminare. George Herbert. ESCV; NOSC; SeCP

May be as great as I. (LL) Mutual Subjection. Christopher Smart. NOCV; OxBChV

May be refin'd, and join th'angelic train. (LL) On Being Brought from Africa to America. Phillis Wheatley. CrDW; NAAL-1; NAAL-3; NALW; NOBA; NOEC; TAP; TTY; WPE

May! be thou never graced with birds that sing. [Epitaph] In Obitum M.S., X° Maij [or Maii], 1614. William Browne. FaBoBe; NOBE; OBEV

May begin, and in doing so be undone. (LL) And "Ut Pictura Poesis" Is Her Name. John Ashbery. InPS-3; VCAP

May blaze the virtue [or vertue] of their sires. (LL) A Nuptiall Song, or Epithalamie, on Sir Clipseby Crew and His Lady. Robert Herrick. BeJo; CBLP; CaPo; PoEL-3; SeCP

May Collin. Lady Isabel and the Elf-Knight. *Unknown.* ESPB

May Colven [or May Colvin]. *Unknown.* OxBB; PBMP

May come up with bird-din. Nuts in May. Louis MacNeice. MoBrPo

May crown Thy Feet, that could not crown Thy Head. (LL) The Coronet. Andrew Marvell. ESCV; FHYEP; FMP; FSCP; GeHe; MeLP; NAEL-1; NOCV; NOSC; NoP-4; PBRV; PoE; SCGP; TOF

May-Day. Aaron Hill. NOEC

May Day. *Unknown.* CTV

May Day, A. Sir Henry Wotton. *See* On a Bank [or Banck] as I Sate [or Sat] a-Fishing; a Description of the Spring.

May Day Dancing, The. Howard Nemerov. NYBP; Poetr

May Day Rounds. Renfrew County. Joan Finnigan.

    "Stoop on the log-house is brown with sweet rain-rot, The." WPE

May de Devil Preach 'is funer'l song. (LL) Promises of Freedom. *Unknown.* CrDW; NAAAL

May fifteenth. Raymond Souster. MoCV

May find you planting lentils on my grave. (LL) The Prodigal Son. Edwin Arlington Robinson. GI

May God be praised for woman. On Woman. W. B. Yeats. CMoP; ChIV-1

May God bless your home. Marriage Vow. Mrs. Henry Linden. CBWP-4

May God grant me the memory to recall my life. Sergey Gondlevsky, *Russian.* TCRP, *tr. by* Sarah W. Bliumis *and* Albert C. Todd

"May Grace be with you all" said the bishop. *Unknown, Greek.* GrAn, *tr. by* Peter Jay

May has come out from the showers. The Jewish May. Morris Jacob Rosenfeld, *Yiddish.* TrJP, *tr. by* Rose Pastor Stokes *and* Helena Frank

May have killed the cat; more likely. Curiosity. Alastair Reid. PC; SoSe-8

May he fall in with beasts that scatter fire. Ballad against the Enemies of France. François Villon, *French.* AWP, *tr. by* Swinburne

May he have new life like the fall. John Coltrane: An Impartial Review. Alfred B. Spellman. PoBA; SeSe

May he lose his way on the cold sea. Archilochus, *Latin.* OBVE, *tr. by* Guy Davenport

May his Counsels Sweet uphold you. God Be with You. *Unknown.* PoToHe

May, Home after a Year Away. Gail Mazur. NAmP90

May I be there to see! (LL) The Diverting History of John Gilpin. William Cowper. EBNV; FaBoBe; OBNV

May I come in? May I come in? Jean-Joseph Rabéarivelo, *French.* NegPo, *tr. by* Ellen Conroy Kennedy

May i feel said he. E. E. Cummings. BoLoP; HeIP-4; NBLV; NOBE; OBCoV; OxBM; PeLV; PoPoPo; SAGP

May I for my own self song's truth reckon. The Seafarer. Ezra Pound, *fr. the Anglo-Saxon.* CABP; CTC; FaBoTw; HeIP-4; NoP-4; OxBA; OxBoS

May I forever a Muse. Vow. John Updike. NYBP; PeLV

May I learn the shape of that hurt. Don. Anthony McNeill. PBCV

May I say, "It is Nestus Gurley." (LL) Nestus Gurley. Randall Jarrell. HeIP-4; TwCP

May in like Chains of Darknesse lie. (LL) Upon a Black Twist, Rounding the Arm of the Countess of Carlisle. Robert Herrick. CaPo

May in the Green-Wood. *Unknown.* OBEV

May is a pious fraud of the almanac. James Russell Lowell. APN-1 *Fr.* Under the Willows.

May is Mary's month, and I. The May Magnificat. Gerard Manley Hopkins. PeECV

May is the moneth maist amene. Of May. Alexander Scott. OxBS

May It Be. Boris Pasternak, *Russian.* TrJP, *tr. by* C. M. Bowra

May-June, 1940. Robinson Jeffers. MoAmPo

(Battle.) LiTM

May lay my burden down. (LL) In the Town. *Unknown, French.* OBCP; PChr, *tr. by* Eleanor Farjeon

May lift itself in homage of the God. (LL) Sonnet to Byron. Shelley. EPCY

May look to heaven as I depart. (LL) To the Fringed Gentian. William Cullen Bryant. APN-1; AWP; FaBoBe; PAR; PoLF; TAP

May Magnificat, The. Gerard Manley Hopkins. PeECV

May Margret stood in her bouer door. Hind Etin. *Unknown.* ESPB; OxBB

May Morn. Michael McClure. SPE

May Morning. George Buchanan. PBRV

May move, in time, the stones themselves to sing. Ronald Johnson. *See* Beam 7.

May my heart always be open to little. E. E. Cummings. OxBSP

May, 1945. Peter Porter. HP; OxBC

May 1968. Sharon Olds. NAmP90; NIP-4

May no man slepe in youre halle. *Unknown.* MiEL

May not be this poem. (LL) The Man in the Tree. Mark Strand. CBNP; SPE

May nothing evil cross this door. Prayer for This House. Louis Untermeyer. PoLF; PoToHe

May nothing I own be stolen or concealed. For the Theft of Cattle. *Unknown, Anglo-Saxon.* ASW, *tr. by* Kevin Crossley-Holland

May one who fought in honor for the South. Lincoln's Grave. Maurice Thompson. CBCWP

May peace be established throughout the land. Te Atairangikaahu. Kingi M. Ihaka, *Maori.* PeNZ, *tr. now* Kingi M. Ihaka

May-pole is up, The. Robert Herrick. CavPo

May poverty, without offence, approach. Nicholas James. NOEC *Fr.* The Complaints of Poverty.

May Queen, The. Tennyson.

"You must wake and call me early, call me early, mother." EBEvV

May! queen of blossoms. Edward, 2d Baron Thurlow Hovell-Thurlow. OBEV

May rain. Rod Willmot. HA

May rains! Sanpu, *Japanese.* TTTS, *tr. by* Kenneth Koch *and* Harold Henderson

May say Alas but cannot help or pardon. (LL) Spain 1937. W. H. Auden. AF; FaBoPV; NAEL-2; NoP-4; OBWP

May say their lords have built, but thy lord dwells. (LL) To Penshurst. Ben Jonson. AWP; BeJo; CABP; NOSC; NoP-4; OAEL-1; PBRV; PoEL-2; SeCP; TFi

May seven tears in every week. A Wish. John Millington Synge. FaBoEE

May Song. Goethe, *German.* STV, *tr. by* John Frederick Nims

May steale a heart or two from you. (LL) To the Countesse of Salisbury. Aurelian Townshend. MeLP; SeCP

May sun—whom, The. The Tulip Bed. William Carlos Williams. GaP; OBGa

May supple-footed theatre-growing ivy. Erucius of Cyzicus, *Greek.* GrAn, *tr. by* Peter Levi

May 10th. Maxine W. Kumin. NYBP

May that lovely young body of yours. Maiden. Márton Kalász, *Hungarian.* CEEP, *tr. by* Jascha Kessler

May that vast motive wash and wash our own. (LL) On the Marginal Way. Richard Wilbur. CAPP-1; CoAP; NOBA

May the Babylonish curse. A Farewell to Tobacco. Charles Lamb. OxBoLi

May the dust be light on your grave. (LL) Partridge. Agathias, *Greek.* FP; GrAn, *tr. by* Guy Davenport

May the grace of the Holy Ghost be gained by us. The Graces of the Holy Ghost. *Unknown, Irish.* TIRV, *tr. by* Douglas Hyde

May the hide of the earth split beneath my feet. Death and Rebirth. Jean-Baptiste Tati-Loutard. PBMAP

May the Lord in His mercy be kind to Belfast. (LL) Ballad to a Traditional Refrain. Maurice James Craig. BIrV; TIRV

May the maiden. Song for "The Jacquerie." Sidney Lanier. NCAP

May the man who gained my trust yet did not come. Ryojin Hisho. BoWoP

May the man who has cruelly murdered his sire. A Counterblast against Garlic. Horace. NBLV, *tr. by* Roswell Martin Field *Fr.* Epodes.

May the man who are born. Hitomaro, *Japanese.* AWP; TAL, *tr. by* Arthur Waley *Fr.* Manyo Shu, Part 2 of 4.

("May those who are born after me.") OHPJ, *tr. by* Kenneth Rexroth

("Never travel such roads of love.") (LL) OHPJ, *tr. by* Kenneth Rexroth

May the Saddest Memory. Birthday Wishes to a Husband. Lizelia Augusta Jenkins Moorer. CBWP-3

May the soil cover / your interred corpse. Ammianus, *Greek.* GrAn, *tr. by* Peter Jay

May the whole world judge me! But the dark laughter of a faun. The Laughter of a Faun. Novella Nikolaevna Matveyeva, *Russian.* TCRP, *tr. by* Deming Brown

May the will come from Thee. Annul Wars. Rabbi Nahman of Bratzlav, *Hebrew.* TrJP, *tr. by* Jacob Sloan

May the wind put out everything for you. Curses. Ljubomir Simovic, *Serbo-Croatian.* HSix, *tr. by* Charles Simic

May there always be sun! Kostya Barannikov, *Russian.* TCRP, *tr. by* Albert C. Todd

May they come, may they come. Song of the Highest Tower. Rimbaud, *French.* AWP, *tr. by* Edgell Rickword

May they stumble [*or* wander], stage by stage. Travel[l]er's Curse after Misdirection[, The]. Robert Graves. CMoP; HoPM; LiTM; MoBrPo; NBLV; OBCoV; PFE

May those who are born after me. Hitomaro. *See* May the men who are born.

May thre[a]t thy cruel[l] he[a]rt. (LL) What rage is this? What furo[u]r of what kind [*or* kynd]? Sir Thomas Wyatt. AAS; EnLoPo; SiPS

May-Time. Christina Rossetti. BoTP

May-Time. *Unknown.* AYFP

May toss him to My breast. (LL) The Pulley. George Herbert. AWP; ChIV-1; EBEvV; FHYEP; FMP; GTBS-P; GeHe; HAP; HeIP-4; ImPo; InPK-6; InPS-3; NAEL-1; NOBE; NOCV; NOSC; NoP-4; OAEL-1; OBEV; OxAEP-1; PFE; SCGP; SeCP; TFi

May Trees in a Storm. Geoffrey Grigson. GBL

May 24, 1980. Joseph Brodsky, *Russian.* TCRP, *tr. by* Joseph Brodsky

May very well cost you your life. (LL) Poem About My Rights. June Jordan. ISC; NAAAL; NMM-2

May we now venture to be kind. (LL) Exit. Edwin Arlington Robinson. MoAmPo; OxBSP

May with its light behaving. W. H. Auden. EBEV

May you be reborn in the supreme lotus, the realm of truth. Mourning My Son. Yüan Chen, *Chinese.* SuSp, *tr. by* Angela Jung Palandri

May you drink beer, or that adult' rate wine. To a Friend, Inviting Him to a Meeting upon Promise. William Habington. BeJo *Fr.* Castara.

May you live forever. In that eternity. A Curse on Herod. Amy Witting. ChIV-2; NOBAu

May you not be long on the way! (LL) Thoughts of a Young Girl. John Ashbery. CoAmPo; MoLi; TAP; VGW

May you rejoice, Paeon lord, who rule. Women at the Temple. Herodas, *Greek.* HePo, *tr. by* Barbara Hughes Fowler

Maya in the city has a dream. The Book of Ephraim. James Merrill. *Fr.* The Changing Light at Sandover. NAAL-2

Mayakovsky. Mikhail Valentinovich Kulchitsky, *Russian.* TCRP, *tr. by* Bradley Jordan

Mayakovsky was right. Kiss. Al Young. PoBA

Mayakovsky's hat worn by a horse. (LL) Answer to Voznesensky and Evtushenko. Frank O'Hara. LCAP-2; NNaP; PoM

Mayakovsky's Suicide Note. Vladimir Mayakovsky, *Russian.* PFTM, *tr. by* Jack Hirschman *and* Victor Ehrlich

Mayan Glyphs Unread, The. William Bronk. APSN

Mayan Ruins. Ory Bernstein. *Fr.* Poems from Mexico. IP, *tr. by* Warren Bargad *and* Stanley F. Chyet

Maybe all I saw was the mirror. Vision. Delmira Augustini, *Spanish.* WPOW, *tr. by* Marti Moody

Maybe Alone on My Bike. William Stafford. NYBP

Maybe because I was married and felt secure and dead. Visiting My Gravesite: Talbott Churchyard, West Virginia. Irene McKinney. PBCAP

Maybe Dats Your Pwoblem Too. Jim Hall. CMAP; MT

Maybe elegies have ruined me. Sandor Csoori, *Hungarian.* CEEP, *tr. by* Jascha Kessler

Maybe half a mile offshore the surface darkening. The Sighting. Jonathan Aaron. WeT

Maybe he dreamed of / new snow. Retired Farmer. David Allan Evans. Poetsp

Maybe I am what she always wanted. Why My Mother Made Me. Sharon Olds. Poetr

Maybe I should live here, maybe I should know things—. Lydia Tomkiw. *Fr.* New York Love Song (Part 1—Lower East Side). WWSi

"Maybe I'm a king." (LL) A Story That Could Be True. William Stafford. KaS; NTCP; RaBo

Maybe I'm Amazed. Jim Carroll. PmAP

Maybe I'm seven in the open field—. Sudden Journey. Tess Gallagher. NIP-4

Maybe it is the shyness of the pride. The Surge. Molly Peacock. NAmP90

Maybe it is true we have to return. Obsessions. Denise Levertov. LiTM

Maybe it was the Bichot. Poetry Makes Rhythm in Philosophy. Ishmael Reed. MoNo

Maybe morning lightens over. For My Grandmother, Bridget Halpin. Michael Hartnett. BIrV; IIP; PBCIP

Maybe that is what he was after. Sweet Rain. Tony Hoagland. NAmP90; PuP-16

Maybe the street is tired of being a street. New Year. Naomi Shihab Nye. LoL; MT

Maybe There's a God Around. Aleksandr Ivanovich Vvedensky, *Russian.* TCRP, tr. by Bradley Jordan.

Maybe we knew each other better. Coda. Louis MacNeice. CBLP

Maybe what Thomas means when he says grace. Reading Aquinas. Michael Heffernan. WeW-3

Maybe you ranted in the grove. Ezry. Archibald MacLeish. NOBA

Maybe Zizi is right. Venice Beach: Brief Song. Dorothy Barresi. SeSe

Maybrick trial is over now, there's been a lot of jaw, The. Penal Servitude for Mrs. Maybrick. *Unknown.* OxBoLi

Mayday. Ed Roberson. PoBA

Mayday. Bill Tremblay. CDa

Mayde ther was, y-clept Joan Hunter Dunn, A. The Summonee's Tale. Stanley J. Sharpless. BXAP

Mayde's Metamorphosis, The. John Lyly *and* Thomas Ravenscroft.
By the Moon ("By the moon we sport and play"). CH
(Urchin's Dance, The.) BoTP
Elves' Dance, The. CH

Mayflower, The. Erastus Wolcott Ellsworth. FaBoBe

Mayombe-bombe-mayombé! Sensemayá. Nicolás Guillén, *Spanish.* PFTM, tr. by Langston Hughes

Mayor. Yehuda Amichai, *Hebrew.* PoSu, tr. by Assia Gutmann

Mayor couldn't be here, but he sends his grand whereases, The. State Poetry Day. Ronald Wallace. PBCAP

Mayor has angrily banished the seven deadly, The. The Exiles. Paul Ramsey. *Fr. Three Epigrams.* CRP

Mayor of Scuttleton burned his nose, The. Mary Mapes Dodge. FPC

Maypole is up, The. Robert Herrick. BeJo

May's Invocation after a Tardy Spring. Henrietta Cordelia Ray. CBWP-3

Mayst [*or* May'st *or* Mayest] find thy darling in an urn. (LL) Epitaph on the Lady Mary Vill[i]ers. Thomas Carew. BeJo; CaPo; CavPo; FaBoEE; NOBE; OBEV; PBRV

Mayst thou die desp'rate in some dirty pool. An Adieu to My Landlady. George Farewell. NOEC

Maytide's evenen wer a-dyen, A. Light or Sheade. William Barnes. NOBVV

Maytime. Thomas Dekker *and others. See* May.

Maytime. *Unknown.* AWP, tr. by L. Cranmer-Byng *Fr.* Shi King.

Maytime, loveliest season. Sadness in Spring. *Unknown, Welsh.* OBWVE, tr. by Gwyn Jones

Mazatlan: Sea. Robert Creeley. APSN

Maze, The. Joanne Kyger. BB

Maze of Blood, A. N. C. G. Mathema. PeSAV

Maze Without a Minotaur. Dana Gioia. RA

Mbaye Dyôb! I want to say your name and your honor. Taga for Mbaye Dyôb. Léopold Sédar Senghor. PFTM, tr. by Melvin Dixon

Mbizo. Art Lange. MoNo

Mbuyazi of the Bay! Mbuyazi (Henry Francis Fynn). *Unknown.* PeSAV

McAfee's Confession. *Unknown.* AmFP

McAndrew's Hymn. Rudyard Kipling. OxBTC
(M'Andrew's Hymn.) PoEL-5

McDonald's, New Hartford, NY. Valerie Worth. AiP

McLean's Welcome. James Hogg. OxBS

McNaughton. *Unknown.* OxBB

Me. Walter De la Mare. CTV

Me. (LL) There Once Was a Puffin. Florence Page Jaques. CTV

Me a poet! My daughter with maimed limb. Self Justification. Tony Harrison. *Fr.* The School of Eloquence. NAEL-2; NoAM

Me abandonastes, mujer, porque soy muy pobre. El Abandonado. *Unknown, Spanish.* AS, tr. by Frank J. Dobie

Me Again. Jacqueline Dash. BAP-96

Me against the world. Charles Bukowski. BAP-94

Me an my captain don't agree. Me and My Captain. *Unknown.* NAAAL

Me and Marlene sit tight in her truck. Our Lady of the Laundromat. Belle Waring. PBCAP

Me, and more in my meditations, than you might suppose. Walt Whitman. *See* Crossing Brooklyn Ferry.

Me and my brother would jump off the porch. Pushing. Christopher Gilbert. LTA; SoSe-8

Me and My Captain. *Unknown.* NAAAL

Me and the Mule. Langston Hughes. PoPoPo

Me clairvoyant. G. K. Chesterton. BXAP; UV *Fr.* Variations on an Air Composed on Having to Appear in a Pageant as Old King Cole. NOBL

Me, Colored. Peter Abrahams. PBA *Fr.* Tell Freedom.

Me—come! My dazzled face. Emily Dickinson. APN-2

Me dah dead fi drink some coaknut water. Home Sickness. Louise Bennett. HCP

Me darlin love, me lickle dove. Love Letter. Louise Bennett. HCP

Me! dutiful son going back to South Wales, this time afraid. Down the M4. Dannie Abse. OxBC

Me, for example. Say Girls in Shoe Ads: "I Go for a Man Who's Tall!" Robley Wilson Jr. PBCAP

Me from Myself—to banish. Emily Dickinson. NALW; TRP

Me from the womb the midwife Muse did take. Abraham Cowley. EPCY *Fr.* Destinie.

Me go to Morant Bay. Morant Bay. *Unknown.* FaBoVe

Me happy, night, night full of brightness. Elegy VII. Propertius. MeMAP; OBCVT; VGW, tr. by Ezra Pound *Fr.* Homage to Sextus Propertius.

Me! he says, hand on his chest. Myself I Sing. George Oppen. FTOS

Me, I like to putz in the kitchen and regard. Breeze in Translation. Belle Waring. NAmP90; PBCAP

Me? / I never could keep my edges and kitchen. For Sistuhs Wearin' Straight Hair. Carolyn M. Rodgers. NAAAL

Me I will throw away. The Self-slaved. Patrick Kavanagh. MoBrPo

Me impervture, standing at ease in Nature. Walt Whitman. NOBA

Me, in Kulu Se and Karma. Carolyn M. Rodgers. PoBA

Me list no more to sing. Sir Thomas Wyatt. AAS; SiPS

Me Lord? can'st Thou mispend. Phineas Fletcher. TOF *Fr.* The Divine Wooer.

Me lover gone a Colon Bay. Colon Bay. *Unknown.* FaBoVe

"Me loving subjects," sez she. The Queen's After-Dinner Speech. William Percy French. OBCoV

Me miserable! which way shall I fly. Milton. PoE *Fr.* Book IV. OAEL-1 *Fr.* Paradise Lost.

Me 'n' Dunbar. James David Corrothers. NAAAL

Me naw disown dis-ya talk. A Go Blow Fire. Michael Smith. HCP

Me not no Oxford don. Listen Mr Oxford Don. John Agard. NBrP

Me now? Robert Creeley. *See* Kore.

Me—of Me? (LL) Me from Myself—to banish. Emily Dickinson. NALW; TRP

Me on the floor / lizard on the wall. Next Page. Atmanam, *Tamil.* OMIP, tr. by A. K. Ramanujan

Me one, way out in the crowd. Valley Prince. Mervyn Morris. PBCV

Me—Pirate. Clive Sansom. OTCP

Me rueth, Mary, thy son and thee. (LL) Now Goeth Sun under Wood. *Unknown.* MiEL; NAEL-1

Me so oft my fancy drew. The Choice. George Wither. OBEV

Me sooner starve, than those can kill. (LL) The Frozen Zone; or, Julia Disdainful. Robert Herrick. CaPo; CavPo

Me take my cutacoo. A Negro Song. *Unknown.* PBCV

Me Tarzan. Tony Harrison. *Fr.* The School of Eloquence. NAEL-2; NoAM

Me that 'ave been what I've been. Chant-Pagan. Rudyard Kipling. FaBoPV

Me thinks I heare some Cavillers object. John Taylor. PBRV *Fr.* A Comparison betwixt a Whore and a Booke.

Me thinks I see him looking on his hands. Joseph in Carcere: or, the Innocent Prisoner. Sir Francis Hubert. KSG *Fr.* Egypt's Favorite.

Me thinks I see our mighty monarch stand. *Unknown.* OBSV *Fr.* The Royal Angler.

Me thinks [*or* Methinks], I see, with what a busie [*or* busy] hast[e]. On Zacheus [*or* Zacchaeus]. Francis Quarles. HAP

Me to climb on a jackass? Try to be serious. Mirabai. *See* Why Mira Can't Go Back to Her Old House.

Me to love more, yet wish thee well much lesse. Catullus. *See* Carmina, LXXII.

Me to strike for your life's blood, and you to strike for mine. (LL) D.G.C. to J.A. Emily Jane Brontë. BrRo; EnLoPo

Me to You. Alastair Reid. NYBP

Me up at does. E. E. Cummings. NYBP; OxBSP; Poetr; WeW-3

Meadow, The. Peter Fallon. PBCIP

Meadow and the mountain with desire, The. Attraction. Ella Wheeler Wilcox. LW

Meadow Bug. Rossana Ombres, *Italian.* NeIt, tr. by Ruth Feldman

Meadow Mouse, The. Theodore Roethke. ChAP; HeIP-4; PeP; RB; TRP
("He seems no longer to tremble.") (LL) PeP

Meadows, The. Ann Taylor. BoTP

Meadows again!, The. (LL) Old Song. Edward Fitzgerald. OBEV; OxAEP-2

Meadowsweet. William Allingham. OBNC

Meal Time. Maggie Pogue Johnson. CBWP-4

Meamwhile with Vine there, Clarel stood. Symphonies. Herman Melville. APN-2 *Fr.* Clarel: A Poem and Pilgrimage in the Holy Land.

Mean Drunk Poem. Sharon Thesen. NOBC

Mean mean mean to be free. (LL) Runagate Runagate. Robert Earl Hayden. BPo; GM; ISC; InPS-3; LCAP-2; NAAAL; PoBA; SSLK

Mean old Hermon. Lucilius, *Greek.* GrAn, *tr. by* Peter Porter

Mean time, in Shades of Night Æneas lies. Morning after shipwreck. Virgil, *Latin.* OBCVT, *tr. by* John Dryden

Mean-time the Bard alternate to the strings. Mars and Venus. Homer. OBCVT, *tr. by* William Broome *Fr.* The Odyssey.

Mean wind wanders through the backcourt trash, A. Glasgow Sonnets. Edwin Morgan. FaBoTC

Meandering abroad in the Lincolnshire meadows day. Section VI. George Barker. SPE *Fr.* Calamiterror.

Meandering River. Tu Fu, *Chinese.*

"Returning from court day after day, I pawn my spring clothes." SuSp, *tr. by* Irving Y. Lo

"Single petal swirling diminishes the spring, A." SuSp, *tr. by* Irving Y. Lo

Meandering Wye. Robert Bloomfield. *Fr.* The Banks of Wye. OBNC

Meanest trick I ever knew, The. A Low Trick. Frank Gelett Burgess. OBCA

Meaning a context or vision to confer with this which could be a book. Approximately. Diane Ward. FTOS

Meaning of a Letter, The. *Unknown.* PoToHe

Meaning of Africa, The. Abioseh Nicol. PBA

Meaning of marriage begins in the giving of words. We cannot join, The. Wendell Berry. ITG *Fr.* Poetry and Marriage.

Meaning of the Look, The. Elizabeth Barrett Browning. TrCP

Meaning Well. Jack Gilbert. IFJA

Means. Dennis Phillips.

"Hounds are either the work of wind, The." FTOS

Means only those who broke—in life—thy peace. (LL) The Timber. Henry Vaughan. GeHe; OBEV; SeCP

Means to Attain the Happy Life, The. Martial. *See* The Happy Life.

Meanwhile, back home at the ranch. Limerick. Victor Gray. PeLi

Meanwhile surely there must be something to say. The Constructed Space. W. S. Graham. PoA

Meanwhile [*or* Mean while] the Adversary of God and Man. Sin and Death. Milton. EBEV, *ll.* 629–734; OBNV, *ll.* 629–889 *Fr.* Book II. FHYEP; NAEL-1; OxAEP-1 *Fr.* Paradise Lost.

Meanwhile the heinous [*or* hainous] and despiteful [*or* despightfull] act. Book X. Milton. FHYEP *Fr.* Paradise Lost.

Meanwhile the Troops beneath Patroclus' Care. The Wasps. Homer. OBVE, *tr. by* Alexander Pope *Fr.* The Iliad.

Measles in the Ark. "Susan Coolidge." OxBChV

Measure, The. Patrick Lane. NOBC

Measure for Measure. Sipho Sepamla. AF; PeSAV

Measure for Measure. Shakespeare.

At the Moated Grange. NOBE

"Ay[e], but to die, and go we know not where." RB

"Most pernicious purpose!—Seeming, seeming!" OxBoV

"'Tis one thing to be tempted, Escalus." OxBM

"When I would pray and think, I think and pray." FaBoSe

Measure me for a burial. Dimensions. Laura Riding Jackson. FuPo

Measure of a Man, The. *Unknown.* PoLF

Measured blood beats out the year's delay, The. Simple Autumnal. Louise Bogan. MoAmPo; Son

Measured rise. Robert Earl Hayden. *See* The Diver.

Measurements. Louisa Sarah Bevington. VWP

Measures Taken, The. Erich Fried, *German.* NNPT, *tr. by* Michael Hamburger

Meat. Michael Van Walleghen. NAmP90

Meat ants, meat-coloured, greet each other. The Anguish of Ants. David Campbell. BMAP

Mechanic, The. Richard Jones. NAmP90

Mechanic, The. Diane Wakoski. AmPA

Mechanical Cow, The. Robley Wilson Jr. PBCAP

Mechanical digger wrecks the drill, A. At a Potato Digging. Seamus Heaney. CIP-2

Mechanical marvel was Bill, A. Limerick. *Unknown.* PeLi

Mechanical / Oracles dot the sky. Gods in Vietnam. Eugene B. Redmond. PoBA

Mechanism. A. R. Ammons. HAP

Med Building. Gerald McCarthy. CDa *Fr.* War Story.

Meda Songs. *Unknown, Ojibwa Native American.* APN-2, *tr. by* Henry Rowe Schoolcraft

Medal [*or* Medall], The. Dryden.

Vox Populi. NOBE

Medallion, The. Herman Melville. APN-2 *Fr.* Clarel: A Poem and Pilgrimage in the Holy Land.

Medallion. Sylvia Plath. HeIP-4

Meddlesome Matty. Ann Taylor. OxBChV

Medea. Euripides. NAWM-1; OxBM

Chorus: "Sweet are the ways of death to weary feet." OBEV, *tr. by* John Byrne Leicester Warren, Lord de Tabley

"Of all things which are living and can form a judgment." GrIP, *tr. by* Rew Warner

Medea. Seneca, *Latin.*

Deaths of Orpheus and Hercules, The. OBVE

Medea's Frenzy. OBVE, *tr. by* John Studley

Medea in Athens. Augusta Davies Webster.

"Oh smooth adder/ who with fanged kisses changedst my natural blood." BrRo

Medea rejuvenates Aeson. Ovid, *Latin.* OBCVT, *tr. by* John Gower

Medea's Frenzy. Seneca. OBVE, *tr. by* John Studley *Fr.* Medea.

Medea's Incantation. Ovid. OBVE, *tr. by* Arthur Golding *Fr.* Magic. AWP, *tr. by* Shakespeare *Fr.* Metamorphoses.

Medea's invocation. Ovid, *Latin.* OBCVT, *tr. by* Arthur Golding

Medgar Evers. Gwendolyn Brooks. NoP-4; PoBA

Media. Howard Nemerov. PuP-16

Mediatrix. David Haynes. NBrP

Medical Aid. Walter Hard. BXAP

Medical Science. Robin Becker. PBCAP

Medicina pro morbo caduco et le fevre. *Unknown.* MiEL

Medicine. Alice Walker. CrSp

Medicine Bearer. Gail Tremblay. HATNAP

Medicine Formula. *Unknown, Takelma.* SAGP, *tr. by* Edward Sapir

Medicine Song of an Indian Lover. *Unknown, Ojibwa Native American.* APN-2, *tr. by* Charles Fenno Hoffman

Medicine Songs. *Unknown, Omaha Native American.* APN-2, *tr. by* Francis La Flesche

Medieval Norman Song. *Unknown, French.* AWP, *tr. by* John Addington Symonds

Medieval Poem of the Nativity, A. *Unknown.* TrCP

Medieval town, with frieze, The. What Is Poetry. John Ashbery. LCAP-2

Mediocrity in Love Rejected. Thomas Carew. BeJo; NoP-4

Meditating at midnight. Zhou Xuanjing, *Chinese.* WPoS, *tr. by* Jane Hirshfield

Meditating on Star Light While Traveling Highway. Anita Endrezze-Danielson. HATNAP

Meditatio. Ezra Pound. FaBoCh; OBAL; PBMP

Meditatio Septima. Francis Quarles. ChIV-1

Meditatio Tertia Decima. Francis Quarles. ChIV-1 *Fr.* Job Militant.

Meditation. Charles Baudelaire, *French.* InPK-6; NAWM-2, *tr. by* Robert Lowell

Meditation. Anthony Hecht. EOEF

Meditation. Reiner Kunze, *German.* CEEP, *tr. by* Lori Fisher

Meditation. The. John Norris. NOSC

Meditation. Palladas, *Greek.* GrAn, *tr. by* Dudley Fitts

Meditation 8. Philip Pain. NOBA; NOSC; OxBSP

Meditation 8 (First Series). Edward Taylor. ChIV-2; NAAL-3; *Fr.* Preparatory Meditations Before My Approach to the Lord's Supper.

("I kenning through astronomy divine.") ColAP; NoP-4

Meditation 9. Philip Pain. *Fr.* Meditations for July 26, 1666. NOBA; SCAP

Meditation 10. Philip Pain. NOBA

Meditation 12. Edward Taylor. KSG

Meditation 29. Philip Pain. *Fr.* Meditations for July 26, 1666. NOBA; SCAP

Meditation 26. Edward Taylor. NAAL-3 *Fr.* Preparatory Meditations Before My Approach to the Lord's Supper.

Meditation 38. Edward Taylor. NAAL-3 *Fr.* Preparatory Meditations Before My Approach to the Lord's Supper.

Meditation 42. Edward Taylor. NAAL-3 *Fr.* Preparatory Meditations Before My Approach to the Lord's Supper.

Meditation 62. Philip Pain. NOBA

Meditation 150 (Second Series). Edward Taylor. ColAP *Fr.* Preparatory Meditations Before My Approach to the Lord's Supper.

Meditation among Trees. Marbod of Rennes, *Latin.* MLL, *tr. by* Helen Waddell

Meditation at Kew. Anna Wickham. FaBoTw; MoBrPo; NALW

("But frankly, gaily shall we get the gods.") (LL) SAGP

Meditation at Lagunitas. Robert Hass. ColAP; NoP-4; VCAP

Meditation at Oyster River. Theodore Roethke. CMoP; MoAmPo; NYBP; PaTW *Fr.* North American Sequence.

("Shining, A.") (LL) PaTW

Meditation at Oyster River. Theodore Roethke. CMoP; MoAmPo; NYBP

Meditation at Pearl Street. Bruce Weigl. NAmP90

Meditation, Followed by Excellent Advice. Eratosthenes, *Greek.* GrAn, *tr. by* Dudley Fitts

Meditation for a Pickle Suite. Richard H. W. Dillard. HoPM; MT

Meditation for Christmas, A. Selwyn Image. OBEV

Meditation for His Mistress[e], A. Robert Herrick. CaPo; NOBE; NOSC; OBEV; SeCP

Meditation for this Day. Antonio Machado Ruiz, *Spanish.* CLPP, *tr. by* Kenneth Rexroth

Meditation Hall. Liu Tsung-yüan, *Chinese.* SuSp, *tr. by* Jan W. Walls

Meditation in Seven Days, A. Alicia Ostriker. PBCAP

Meditation of a Mariner. Dorothy Auchterlonie. CBAP

Meditation on a Bone. Alec Derwent Hope. NoAM

Meditation on a News Item. John Updike. PeLV

Meditation on Communion with God. Judah Halevi, *Hebrew.* TrJP, *tr. by* Solomon Solis-Cohen

Meditation on Rhode Island Coal, A. William Cullen Bryant. TAP

("I sat beside the glowing grate, fresh heaped.") NCAP

Meditation on Statistical Method. James Vincent Cunningham. CoAP; VGW

Meditation on the A30. John Betjeman. RB

Meditation Rock, The. Mo Shih-lung, *Chinese.* CoBLCP, *tr. by* Jonathan Chaves

Meditation Upon Ought. Alberta Turner. CMAP

Meditations. Solomon ibn Gabirol, *Hebrew.* TrJP, *tr. by* Emma Lazarus

Meditations, The. *Unknown, Arabic.*

"In the casket of the Hours." TAL, *stanzas I XX, tr. by* Reynold A. Nicholson

Meditations for August 1, 1666. Philip Pain. SCAP

Meditations for July 19, 1666. Philip Pain. SCAP

Meditations for July 25, 1666. Philip Pain. SCAP

Meditations for July 26, 1666. Philip Pain. NOBA; SCAP

Meditations in an Emergency. Frank O'Hara. PmAP; TAP; VCAP

Meditations in Time of Civil War. W. B. Yeats.

Ancestral Houses. OAEL-2; OBGa

Road at My Door, The. BIrV; NOBE; PoE

Stare's Nest by My Window, The. BIrV; GTBS-P; InPS-3; NOBE

("Bees in the crevices, The.") FaBoPV

Meditations of a Parrot. John Ashbery. TTTS

Meditations of an Old Woman. Theodore Roethke.

First Meditation. LCAP-2; NOBA

I'm Here. CoAP; NYBP

What Can I Tell My Bones? AmPP; NOBA

Meditations of Man's Mortalitie; or, A Way to True Blessedness. Alice Sutcliffe.

"Bacchus that drunken God from Hell comes forth." KTR

"Of all the Trees that in the Garden grew." KTR

Meditations of Mr. Cogito on Redemption. Zbigniew Herbert, *Polish.* GI, *tr. by* John Carpenter *and* Bogdana Carpenter

Meditations on the Moon. Paula Gunn Allen. HATNAP

Meditations on the Sepulchre in the Garden. Philip Doddridge. NOCV; NOEC; OBGa

Meditations on the Six Days of the Creation. Thomas Traherne.

Third Day. ChIV-1

Meditatioun in Wyntir. William Dunbar. EnVB; OxBS

Mediterranean, The. Allen Tate. FaBoMo; FuPo; HAP; ImPo; LiTM; MoAmPo; VGW

Medium, The. Elaine Feinstein. BrRo

Medium IV: Sights, The. Carl Rakosi. InPS-3

Medlars and Sorb-Apples. D. H. Lawrence. FaBoVe; NoAM; OAEL-2

Medley of Southern and Northern Tunes—Scenic Tour of West Lake. Kuan Yün-shih, *Chinese.*

Tune: "Butterflies." SuSp, *tr. by* Richard John Lynn

Tune: "Chilly East Wind." SuSp, *tr. by* Richard John Lynn

Tune: "Coda." SuSp, *tr. by* Richard John Lynn

Tune: "Going Up Small Pavilion." SuSp, *tr. by* Richard John Lynn

Tune: "Happy Events Approaching." SuSp, *tr. by* Richard John Lynn

Tune: "Moth Fluttering Against Lamp." SuSp, *tr. by* Richard John Lynn

Tune: "Pomegranate Blossoms." SuSp, *tr. by* Richard John Lynn

Tune: "Squabbling Quails." SuSp, *tr. by* Richard John Lynn

Medoro's Inscription Book XXIII. Ludovico Ariosto, *Italian.* NOBRP, *tr. by* William Parsons *Fr.* Orlando Furioso.

Medusa. Louise Bogan. AWP; BoWoP; HoPM; MoAmPo; NALW; NMM-2; NoAM; NoP-4; Poetr; WPE

Medusa. Amy Clampitt. NMM-2; VCAP

Medusa. Sylvia Plath. CAPP-1; NALW

Medusa Cement. Alise Alousi. IFJA

Medusa on Skyros. Alison Fell. NBrP

Mee-ow, mee-ow. Pussy-Cat and Puppy-Dog. Lilian McCrea. BoTP

Mee thinks mount Aetna with his force is closed in my brest. (LL) Cyclops. Ovid. CTC; OBVE, *tr. by* Arthur Golding

Meek and the Proud, The. Abraham ibn Chasdai, *Hebrew.* TrJP, *tr. by* J. Chotzner

Meek dew shone, the grass lay prostrate, The. The Tree. Ilya Grigoryevich Ehrenburg, *Russian.* TrJP, *tr. by* Babette Deutsch

Meek Francis lies here, friend, without stop or stay. Epitaph. Matthew Prior. FaBoEE

Meek, sang the crickets, wheat, meet, creek. A Small Score. Delmore Schwartz. PBMP

Meek twilight! soften the declining day. Sonnet to Twilight. Helen Maria Williams. Ro *Fr.* Poems.

Meet. Audre Lorde. CPO

Meet Me in St. Louis, Louis. Andrew B. Sterling. OBAL

Meet Me in the Green Glen. John Clare. SCGP

Meet me to-night, lover, meet me. Moonlight. *Unknown.* AS

Meet me tonight. Jackie. King D. Kuka. VoR

Meet-on-the-Road. *Unknown.* OBSP; OTCP; TTTS

Meet Rabbi Shatz in his correct black homburg. Tales of Shatz. Dannie Abse. OxBC

Meet was at "The Cock and Pye," The. John Masefield. OxBTC *Fr.* Reynard the Fox.

Meeting. Matthew Arnold. *See* The Lake.

Meeting, The. Louise Bogan. NYBP; NoAM

Meeting. George Crabbe. OBEV

Meeting. Peter Huchel, *German.* CEEP, *tr. by* Michael Hamburger

Meeting, The. Nicki Jackowska. BrRo

Meeting, The. Henry Wadsworth Longfellow. FP

Meeting, The. Katherine Mansfield. LW

Meeting, The. Howard Moss. NYBP

Meeting. Boris Pasternak, *Russian.* FP, *tr. by* Henry Kamen

Meeting. Christina Rossetti. CBLP; GBL

(Worth Dying For.) LW

Meeting, The. Muriel Rukeyser. MoAmPo; TrJP

Meeting, The. Ramona Wilson. VoR

Meeting a Bear. David Wagoner. HAP; PaTW; WeW-3

Meeting a lovely boy face to face. Strato, *Greek.* GrAn, *tr. by* W. G. Shepherd

Meeting after Separation. Marula, *Sanskrit.* BoWoP, *tr. by* Tambimuttu *and* G. V. Vaidya

Meeting and Passing. Robert Frost. GLoP; OxBA

Meeting at a Salesyard. John Ennis. CIP-2

Meeting At Night. Robert Browning. APAD; AWP; BoLoP; CABP; CBLP; EBEvV; EnVR; FHYEP; FaBoVe; GBL; GLoP; HeIP-4; InPS-3; LoP; NAEL-3; NOBE; NOBVV; OBEV; OBNC; OPOU; OxBSP; PFE; PeVV; PoRA; SAGP; SCGP; SCV; SoSe-8; TFi; UnPo

Meeting Bida. Fily-Dabo Sissoko, *French.* NegPo, *tr. by* Ellen Conroy Kennedy

Meeting by chance and speaking. The Judas Touch. David Malouf. BMAP

Meeting his mother makes him lose ten years. Between the Porch and the Altar. Robert Lowell.

Meeting-House Hill. Amy Lowell. ColAP; MoAmPo; OxBA; PoRA

Meeting-house is not what it used to be, The. Elegy in a Presbyterian Burying-Ground. Robert Noble Denison Wilson. BIrV

Meeting in a Lift. Vladimir Holan, *Czech.* EP, *tr. by* Miher, Jarmila and Ian Miher

Meeting in the Road. *Unknown, Chinese.* ChiP, *tr. by* Arthur Waley

Meeting Like This. Paul Willis. BAP-96

Meeting Mescalito at Oak Hill Cemetery. Lorna Dee Cervantes. PBCAP

Meeting Mick Jagger. Robert Peters. BXAP

Meeting My Fellow Countryman, Yü Wu-chung. Yang Chi, *Chinese.* CoBLCP, *tr. by* Jonathan Chaves

Meeting of Cultures, A. Donald Davie. OxBC

Meeting of Friends, A. Phillis Levin. RA

Meeting of the Waters, The. Thomas Moore. IIP; NOIV; OxBoLi; PoEL-4

Meeting Point. Louis MacNeice. CBLP; EP; PNI

Meeting the British. Paul Muldoon. BiHa; CIP-2; FaBoPV; NoAM; NoP-4; PNI

Meeting, the Departure, The. Goethe, *German.* STV, *tr. by* John Frederick Nims

Meeting the first time for many years. C. Day Lewis. NYBP

Meeting the Gulf, hosannas silently below. (LL) The River. Hart Crane. AmPP; CMoP; GM; MoAmPo; NOBA; OxBA

Meeting the Herdsmen. Mei Yao Ch'en, *Chinese.* SuSp, *tr. by* Jonathan Chaves

Meeting the Mountains. Gary Snyder. NoAM; TAP

Meeting the Reincarnation Analyst. Gary Gildner. AmPA

Meeting Together of Poles & Latitudes: In Prospect. Margaret Avison. NOBC

Meeting Trappers on the Road in Heavy Snow. Li K'ai-hsien, *Chinese.* CoBLCP, *tr. by* Jonathan Chaves

Meeting when all the world was in the bud. Loves of the Puppets. Richard Wilbur. OxBC

Meeting with Time, slack thing, said I. Time. George Herbert. FMP; NAEL-1

Meeting with Vilakazi, the Great Zulu Poet, A. Raymond Mazisi Kunene, *Zulu.* PeSAV, *tr. by the author*

Meetings. Paul Éluard, *French.* AF, *tr. by* Lloyd Alexander

[These] meetings in dreams. Yakamochi, *Japanese.* TAL, *tr. by* Arthur Waley

Meetings meetings meetings. Yuh Lookin Good. Carolyn M. Rodgers. BPo

Meets our bouquet of death-and turns sharp right. (LL) Unseen Fire. Ralph Nixon Currey. OBWP; OxBTC; PoWW

Meg Merrilies [*or* Merrilees]. Keats. BoTP; FaBoCh; OxBChV

   ("Old Meg she was a gipsy.") NOxBChV

Megaceph, chosen to serve the State. Egotist. Ambrose Bierce. APAD; APN-2; OBAL   *Fr.* The Devil's Dictionary.

Mehinaku Girl in Seclusion, A. Cathy Song. OpBo

Mein Breast, mein Corset und mein Legs. Palladas, *Greek.* GrAn, *tr. by* Tony Harrison

Mein Herz, mein Herz Ist Traurig. Heinrich Heine, *German.* AWP, *tr. by* James Thomson

Mein Kind, wir waren Kinder. Heinrich Heine, *German.* AWP; TrJP

Mein Liebchen, wir sassen zusammen. Heinrich Heine, *German.* AWP, *tr. by* James Thomson

Mek me tell you wha me Mudder do. Wha Me Mudder Do. Grace Nichols. NOxBChV

Melampus. George Meredith. PoEL-5

Melancholia. Robert Bridges. CMoP

Melancholy. John Fletcher. GTBS-P; OBEV   *Fr.* The Nice Valor.

   (Song.) PoEL-2

Melancholy. Thomas Middleton. NOSC

Melancholy Conceit. Samuel Rowlands. OxBSP

   Sir Eglamour. FaBoCh

Melancholy days are come, the saddest of the year, The. The Death of the Flowers. William Cullen Bryant. OBCA; PoLF

Melancholy days come once a year, The. A View on Death. Roy W. Watson. PWR

Melancholy days have come, The. Autumn Leaves. Charles Henry Webb. OBAL

Melancholy desire of ancient things, A. On an Air of Rameau. Arthur Symons. OBNC

Melancholy face Charles Carville had, A. Charles Carville's Eyes. Edwin Arlington Robinson. CMoP; MeMAP; OxBA; TAP

Melancholy inside Families. Pablo Neruda, *Spanish.* RaBo, *tr. by* Robert Bly *and* James Wright (1927–80)

Melancholy Knight, The. Samuel Rowlands. *See* Melancholy Conceit.

Melancholy Lay, A. Marjory Fleming. FaBoCh; NBLV

Melancholy remembrances and vesperal. (LL) The Church of a Dream. Lionel Pigot Johnson. ADE; CABP; OAEL-2; OBMV

Melancholy year is dead with rain, The. Trumbull Stickney. APN-2

Melanie. Nathaniel Parker Willis.

   "Calm and lovely paradise, A." APN-1

Melbourne or the Bush. Philip Mead. BMAP

Meleager. Ovid. CTC, *tr. by* Arthur Golding; NOBRP, *tr. by* John Herman Merivale   *Fr.* Metamorphoses.

Melhill Feast. William Barnes. OBNC

Meliboeus. O fortunate old man! Virgil. OBCVT, *tr. by* Samuel Palmer   *Fr.* The Eclogues.

Melincourt. Thomas Love Peacock.

   Sun-Dial, The. OBNC

Melinna herself! It *is*—see how kindly. Nossis, *Greek.* GrAn, *tr. by* Sally Purcell

Melissa means honeybee; yes, you're true. Argentarius, *Greek.* GrAn, *tr. by* Fleur Adcock

Melissa where is the golden. In Spite. Rufinus, *Greek.* GrAn, *tr. by* Alan Marshfield

Melissias denies her love, but her body screams. Rufinus Domesticus. HePo, *tr. by* Barbara Hughes Fowler   *Fr.* Epigrams.

Melissias denies she's in love. Rufinus, *Greek.* GrAn; OBCVT, *tr. by* Alan Marshfield

Mellifluous as bees, these brittle men. On First Looking in on Blodgett's Keats's "Chapman's Homer." George Starbuck. OBAL

Mellisandra. Harriet Rose. BrRo

Mellow. Celia Laighton Thaxter. *See* August.

Mellow as the glory roses. (LL) Gloire de Dijon. D. H. Lawrence. CMoP; EnLoPo; GBL; GLoP; NoAM

Mellow moon hangs golden in the sky, The. October. Henrietta Cordelia Ray. CBWP-3

Mellow year is hasting to its close, The. November. Hartley Coleridge. LaPo; OBNC   *Fr.* Sonnets to the Seasons.

Melodic Trains. John Ashbery. GM; NoP-4

Melodies. "Lewis Carroll." CBNP

Melodies of Time, The. Thomas Hood. *Fr.* The Plea of the Midsummer Fairies. OBNC

Melon Girl. Mei Yao Ch'en, *Chinese.* OHPC, *tr. by* Kenneth Rexroth

Melon-Slaughterer; or, A Sick Man's Praise for a Well Woman. Robert Peters. BXAP

Melons. Moshe Yungman, *Yiddish.* CEEP, *tr. by* Gabriel Preil *and* Howard Schwartz

Melpomene. Peter Huchel, *German.* CEEP, *tr. by* Michael Hamburger

Melpomene (at whose mischeifous tove). Carmen Elegiacum. Thomas Morton. SCAP

Melrose Abbey. Sir Walter Scott. OxAEP-2   *Fr.* The Lay of the Last Minstrel.

   (Sir William of Deloraine at the Wizard's Tomb.) OBNC

Melt all the butter. What Her Girl Friend Said to Her lover on His Return. Kākkai Pāṭiṉiyār Naccellaiyār, *Tamil.* PLW, *tr. by* A. K. Ramanujan

Melting, flowing into one. (LL) Gnosis. Christopher Pearse Cranch. APN-1; ColAP; PAR

Melting in thin mist and heavy clouds. Li Ch'ing-chao, *Chinese.* BoWoP, *tr. by* J. P. Seaton

Melting melodious words to lutes of amber. (LL) Upon Julia's Voice. Robert Herrick. InPK-6; NOBE; SeCP; SoSe-8

Melting Milk. Bill Berkson. PmAP

Melting Pot. Michael Echeruo. PBMAP; TTY

Melting Pot, The. Dudley Randall. BPo; NBV

Melton Mowbray Pork Pie, A. Richard Le Gallienne. BXAP

Member of the modern great, A. Epigram. John Cunningham. FaBoEE

Members of the Orchestra, The. Kevin Hart. NOBAu

Memento. Stephen Spender. HP

Memento of Roads. Nathan Alterman, *Hebrew.* MHP, *tr. by* Ruth Finer Mintz

Mementos, 1. W. D. Snodgrass. MoAmPo; NoP-4; SAGP; UnPo; VCAP

Memo. Charles G. Ballard. VoR

Memo. Kenneth Fearing. CMoP; PoE

Memo. Hildegarde Flanner. NYBP

Memo. Charles Lynch. PoBA

Memo from the Desk of X. Donald Justice. TwCP

Memo: you have only 16 lifetimes. More than 9 Lives. Bruce Beaver. BMAP

Memoir. Honor Moore. GLP

Memoirs, The. Carl Rakosi. PoA

Memoirs, I. Margaret Witter Fuller.

   "In the chamber." CrSp

Memoirs in Oxford. Frank Templeton Prince.

   "Somewhere in Mauriac a plum." PeSAV

Memoirs of a Turcoman Diplomat. Denis Devlin.

   "Evenings ever more willing lapse into my world's evening." NOIV

Memoirs of a Velvet Urinal. Michael Dransfield. BMAP

Memoirs of American Speech. Colleen J. McElroy.

   "You will learn to speak." EC2

Memorabilia. Robert Browning. FHYEP; GEA; NAEL-2; NOBVV; NoP-4; OAEL-2; OBNC; PoE; PoPoPo; RB

Memorable Fancy, A ("Angel came to me and said, An"). William Blake. *Fr.* The Marriage of Heaven and Hell. NAEL-2; NOBRP; OAEL-2

Memorable Fancy, A ("As I was walking among the fires of hell"). William Blake. *Fr.* The Marriage of Heaven and Hell. NAEL-2; NOBRP; OAEL-2

Memorable Fancy, A ("I was in a printing house in Hell & I saw the method in"). William Blake. *Fr.* The Marriage of Heaven and Hell. NAEL-2; NOBRP; OAEL-2

Memorable Fancy, A ("Once I saw a Devil in a flame of fire"). William Blake. *Fr.* The Marriage of Heaven and Hell. NAEL-2; NOBRP; OAEL-2

Memorable Fancy, A ("Prophets Isaiah and Ezekiel dined with me, and, The"). William Blake. *Fr.* The Marriage of Heaven and Hell. NAEL-2; NOBRP; OAEL-2

Memorandum. William Stafford. NYBP

Memorandum / The Accountant's Notebook. Kathleen Norris. OBAL

Memoriae Matris Sacrum. George Herbert.

  "Ah Mater, quo te deplorem fonte? Dolores." PBRV

Memoriae Positum R. G. Shaw. James Russell Lowell. CBCWP

Memorial. Robert Pinsky. HCAP

Memorial. Sonia Sanchez. BISi

Memorial Couplets for the Dying Ego. George Barker. EBEV

Memorial Day. Michael Anania. NoAM

Memorial Day. Clara Ann Thompson. CBWP-2

Memorial for Trane. Sam Greenlee. SeSe

Memorial for Two Young Seamen. George Barker. ImPo *Fr.* Pacific Sonnets.

Memorial on the Slain at Chickamauga. Herman Melville. CBCWP

Memorial Poem. Roy Fuller. OxBSP

Memorial Rain. Archibald MacLeish. AmPP; CMoP; MeMAP; MoAmPo; OBWP

Memorial Service for the Invasion Beach Where the Vacation in the Flesh Is Over. Alan Dugan. AF; TwCP

Memorial Tablet. Siegfried Sassoon. PoWW

Memorial to a Missionary. Keith Sinclair. PeNZ

Memorial to D. C. Edna St. Vincent Millay.

  Elegy: "Let them bury your big eyes." CMoP; MoAmPo; OxBA; PoRA

  "O, loveliest throat of all sweet throats." OxBA

Memorial Verses. Matthew Arnold. CABP; NAEL-2; OAEL-2

  "And Wordsworth! Ah, pale ghosts, rejoice!" EPCY

  "When Byron's eyes were shut in death." EPCY

Memorial Wreath. Dudley Randall. CBCWP; PoBA

Memorials of a Tour in Italy, 1837. Wordsworth.

  Composed at Rydal on May Morning, 1838. LaPo

Memories of a Dorset Childhood in the 1730's. Thomas Cole. *Fr.* The Life of Hubert. NOEC

Memories of a Lost War. Louis Simpson. OBWP; VGW

Memories of Aunt Maria-Martha. William Zaranka. BXAP

Memories of Childhood. Sir John Carr. NOEC *Fr.* Derwent; an Ode.

Memories of Chinatown. Roy McFadden.

  Bigamy. PNI

Memories of Her Friend Who Died. Ory Bernstein, *Hebrew.* IP, *tr. by* Warren Bargad *and* Stanley F. Chyet

Memories of Mess Duty and the War. Christopher Howell. CDa

Memories of My Father. Galway Kinnell.

  "When I come back to my father's house." RaBo

Memories of President Lincoln. Walt Whitman.

  "Hush'd be the camps to-day." SAmP

  "O Captain! my Captain! our fearful trip is done." APAD; APN-1; CBCWP; ChAP; EBEvV; FaBoBe; FaBoCh; FaPoR; ImPo; InPK-6; MeMAP; MoAmPo; OBCA; PBMP; PoLF; SAGP; SAmP; TAP; TFi

  Spring. LBC

  ("And thought of him I love.") (LL) LBC

Memories of Verdun. Alan Dugan. OxBSP; RB

Memories of West Street and Lepke. Robert Lowell. AF; AmPP; CMoP; CoAmPo; InPS-3; NAAL-2; NOBA; NoAM; PoE; SAGP; VCAP

  ("Of lost connexions.") (LL) CoAmPo

Memories open. Tanka. Maekawa Samio, *Japanese.* MJT, *tr. by* Makoto Ueda

Memoriter. Charles Spear. PeNZ

Memory. Thomas Bailey Aldrich. CTV; PoLF

Memory. Margaret Walker Alexander. GT

Memory. Anne Brontë. EBVV

Memory. William Browne. OBEV *Fr.* Britannia's Pastorals.

Memory. Ion Caraion, *Romanian.* CEEP, *tr. by* Marguerite Dorian *and* Elliott B. Urdang

Memory. Elizabeth Cook-Lynn. *Fr.* Journey. HATNAP

Memory, The. Robert Creeley. VGW

Memory. Babette Deutsch. PoA

Memory. Ralph Waldo Emerson. APN-1 *Fr.* Quatrains.

Memory. Federico García Lorca. PFTM

Memory. Oliver Goldsmith. *See* O Memory, Thou Fond Deceiver'.

Memory. Nikolai Stepanovich Gumilyov, *Russian.* TCRP, *tr. by* Yakov Hornstein

Memory. Michael Hamburger. OxBTC

Memory, A. Heinrich Heine, *German.* PC, *tr. by* Francis C. Golffing

Memory. Helen Hoyt. PoLF

Memory. Walter Savage Landor. EBEV; NOBVV; OAEL-2

Memory. Abraham Lincoln. BLPA; FaBoBe

Memory, A. Adah Isaacs Menken. CBWP-1

Memory. Christina Rossetti. OBNC

Memory. D. G. Rossetti. OxBSP

Memory. Eve Shelnutt. CMAP

Memory. Erik Johann Stagnelius, *Swedish.* AWP, *tr. by* Sir Edmund Gosse

Memory, A. Leonard Alfred George Strong. NOBL

Memory. W. B. Yeats. APAD; BIrV; PoE

Memory, a Poem. Laetitia Pilkington. ECWP

Memory at last has what it sought. Wislawa Szymborska, *Polish.* PoSu, *tr. by* Magnus F. Krynski

Memory Cabinet of Mrs. K. 1960. Susan Stewart. NAmP90

Memory, committed to the page, had broke. (LL) Passage. Hart Crane. CMoP; NOBA; PoE

Memory draws me towards death. (LL) A Dream at Night. Mei Yao Ch'en, *Chinese.* BLT; OHPC, *tr. by* Kenneth Rexroth

Memory: farfields of morning. Persephone. Robert Duncan. NOBA

Memory feeds us on a prison diet. Mandrakes for Supper. James Keir Baxter. OxBC

Memory Gardens. Robert Creeley. FTOS

Memory Gardens. Allen Ginsberg. NNaP

Memory has no end here and no beginning. Rehearsing for Death. Angelos Sikelianos, *Greek.* GrIP, *tr. by* Edmund Keeley *and* Philip Sherrard

Memory has power as real as thine. (LL) All hushed and still within the house. Emily Jane Brontë. FaBoCh; NOBVV

Memory, hither come. Song. William Blake. NAEL-2; PoEL-4

Memory: I can take my head and strike it on a wall on Cumberland Island. The Shark's Parlor. James Dickey. MT; NYBP

Memory II. Vladimir Holan, *German.* CEEP, *tr. by* Bronislava Volek *and* Andrew Durkin

Memory II. George Seferis, *Greek.* GrIP, *tr. by* Edmund Keeley *and* Philip Sherrard

Memory in sea-green with sea-weed grain. The Oracle of the Drowned. Douglas Oliver. NBrP

Memory is as narrow. Angel's Flight. Maxine Scates. PBCAP

Memory lifts her smoky mirror: 1943. Adrienne Rich. NoP-4 *Fr.* Eastern War Time.

Memory, magnesium flare, you single. Circus at the Barber's Shop. Kendrick Smithyman. PeNZ

Memory of a Dream from the Year 1963. Tadeusz Rózewicz, *Polish.* PoSu

  ("Burst into flame.") (LL) CEEP, *tr. by* Victor Contoski

  ("I dreamed / that Leo Tolstoy.") CEEP, *tr. by* Victor Contoski

  (Remembrance from a Dream in 1963.) CEEP, *tr. by* Victor Contoski

Memory of Autumns at Springtime. Gabriel Preil, *Yiddish.* CEEP, *tr. by* Laya Firestone

Memory of Elena, The. Carolyn Forché. LoL; NoAM

Memory of Hills. Rex Ingamells.

  "There are rock-rooted ranges to dominate." CBAP

Memory of His Father, A. Frederick Robert Higgins. *See* Father and Son.

Memory of His Mother, A. Patrick Kavanagh. *See* In Memory of My Mother.

Memory of Lincoln and the Yankees. James Ephriam McGirt. AAP

Memory of love, you are painful! "Anna Akhmatova," *Russian.* LoP, *tr. by* Judith Hemschemeyer

Memory of my dead, black hole through everything / gaping on the Sea of Vertigos. Persephone That Is to Say Double Issue. René Daumal, *French.* PFTM, *tr. by* Pierre Joris

Memory of my Father. Patrick Kavanagh. InPS-3; RB

Memory of my father is wrapped in white paper, The. My Father. Yehuda Amichai, *Hebrew.* IP, *tr. by* Warren Bargad *and* Stanley F. Chyet

Memory of the Dead, The. John Kells Ingram. IIP

Memory of the Hill, A. Kapilar, *Tamil.* PLW, *tr. by* A. K. Ramanujan

Memory of your profile on the pillow, The. (LL) The Profile on the Pillow. Dudley Randall. BPo; PoBA; TAP

Memory pales in the face of the moon. On Leaving Baltimore. Duane Niatum. CDW

Memory persists, I cannot shake it, The. Midwinter Tourists. Albinas Žukauskas, *Lithuanian.* CEEP, *tr. by* Irene Suboczewski

Memory Sire, The. Barney Bush. HATNAP

Memory System, A. *Unknown.* PWR

Memory, why torment me? Autumn skimmed. Nevermore. Paul Verlaine, *French.* FLP; LoP, *tr. by* Alistair Elliot

Memory's branch quivers. Postcard from Trakl. John Yau. OpBo

Memory's wedge / makes a valley. Ray DiPalma. PmAP

Memphian Temple, The. John Barlas. ADE

Memphis Blues. Sterling Brown. NAAAL

Memphite Recension. Nathaniel Mackey. PT

Memres of Alfred Stoker. Christopher Reid.

  "Firs / born Xmas day." FaBoVe

Men, The. E. Ethelbert Miller. UnSA

Men, a word of wisdom. Give. Bernard de Ventadour, *French.* STV, *tr. by* John Frederick Nims

Men and beasts of the zodiac, The. Winter Dawn. Tu Fu, *Chinese.* BLT; OHPC, *tr. by* Kenneth Rexroth

Men and Birth: the Unexplainable. Don L. Lee. RaBo

Men and Women. David Dabydeen. PBCV

Men are ashamed to eat shepherd's-purse. Eating Shepherd's-purse. Mei Yao Ch'en, *Chinese.* SuSp, *tr. by* Jonathan Chaves

Men Are Children of This World. Moses ibn Ezra, *Hebrew.* TrJP, *tr. by* Solomon Solis-Cohen

Men Are Coming Back! The. Barry Cole. OxBTC

Men are different this year in, The. January White Sale. William Dickey. EC2

Men are drawn to my ass by. Being Aware. Dennis Cooper. GLP; PmAP

Men are running across a field. Letter. Mark Strand. NoAM

Men are what they are, and what they do. Intimate Parnassus. Patrick Kavanagh. MoBrPo

Men are what they do, women are what they are. In Nature There Is Neither Right nor Left nor Wrong. Randall Jarrell. CBLP; EP; OxBC

Men at forty / Learn to close softly. Donald Justice. LiLi; MT; NoAM; NoP-4; Poetr; SAGP; VCAP; WeT

Men at Work. Richard Tipping. NOBAu

Men behind the Guns, The. John Jerome Rooney. BLPA; FaBoBe

Men, brother men, that after us yet live. The Epitaph in Form of a Ballad. François Villon, *French.* CTC; OxBoV, *tr. by* Swinburne

Men call you fayre, and you doe credit it. Sonnet 79: Edmund Spenser. AWP; FaBoBe; NAEL-1; Son *Fr. Amoretti.* AAS

Men cannot guess the things they do. The Little Things. Elizabeth Isler. PoToHe

Men choose a crystal goblet filled with wine. God's Ways, Not Our Ways. Henrietta Cordelia Ray. AAP; CBWP-3

Men claim the easiest spots. Fishing the White Water. Audre Lorde. GT

Men eat of it and die. (LL) Fame is a fickle food. Emily Dickinson. SAmP; TAP

Men err and idly mourn a fallen flower. The River. Đông Hồ, *Vietnamese.* AVP, *tr. by* Huỳnh Sanh Thông

Men Fade Like Rocks. Walter James Turner. OBMV

Men Folks ob Today, De. Maggie Pogue Johnson. CBWP-4

Men grew sae cauld, maids sae unkind. The Blind Boy's Pranks. William Thom. OBEV

Men have made them gods of love. Pain. "Æ." MoBrPo

Men heard this roar of parleying starlings, saw. February Afternoon. Edward Thomas. NoAM; PeFWW; PoWW

Men hope to last a hundred years. To an Old Tune. Lu Kuei Meng, *Chinese.* OHMPC, *tr. by* Kenneth Rexroth

Men, if you love us, play no more. In the Person of Womankind [A Song Apologetic]. Ben Jonson. BeJo; SeCP

Men Improve with the Years. W. B. Yeats. OxAEP-2

Men in Green. David Campbell. BMAP

Men in New Mexico. D. H. Lawrence. PaTW

Men in overalls the same color as earth rise from a ditch. Outskirts. Tomas Tranströmer, *Swedish.* BLT, *tr. by* Robert Bly

Men in stout uniforms, helmets like tortoise / shells. Wars. Margaret Gibson. AFr

Men in the City. Alfonsina Storni, *Spanish.* PBWP, *tr. by* Rachel Benson

Men in their prime. Battlefield. Lilian Bowes-Lyon. WPN

Men jostle and men fight with labored breath. Nguyễn Bỉnh Khiêm, *Vietnamese.* AVP, *tr. by* Huỳnh Sanh Thông

Men laughed and baaed like sheep, The. Memories of Verdun. Alan Dugan. OxBSP; RB

Men lean toward the wood. Lynching and Burning. Primus St. John. ISC; PoBA

Men led me to him, blindfold and alone. (LL) The Coward. Rudyard Kipling. FaBoEE; FaBoTw; PeFWW

Men love papers, The. They love to sign them, file them and. Larry Mitchell. GLP

Men loved wholly beyond wisdom. Louise Bogan. ColAP; LiTM; VGW

Men Made Out of Words. Wallace Stevens. MeMAP; NOBA; OxBSP; TAP; VGW

Men May Talk of Country-Christmasses. Philip Massinger. OBCP

Men o' Crowdieknowe!, The. (LL) Crowdieknowe. "Hugh MacDiarmid." InPS-2; OxBS

Men / occupying bedrooms and unemployment lines, on corners, in bars, The. Empty Warriors. Don L. Lee. RaBo

Men of Cleveland, had a vulture. To the Union Savers of Cleveland. Frances Ellen Watkins Harper. AAP

Men of England, wherefore plough. Song to the Men of England. Shelley. CABP; InPS-3; NAEL-2; PBMP

Men of Old, The. Richard Milnes. OBEV

Men of old time, The. (LL) O pine-tree standing. Hakutsu, *Japanese.* AWP; TAL, *tr. by* Arthur Waley

Men of the older, gentler soil. The Plainsmen. Charles Badger Clark, Jr. PaTW

Men of the Rocks. Joseph Gordon MacLeod. OxBS

Men of valor, The. Akahito, *Japanese.* AWP; TAL, *tr. by* Arthur Waley *Fr. Manyo Shu*, Part 2 of 4.

Men of wealthy Sestos, every year, The. Marlowe. AEP *Fr. Hero and Leander.*

Men openly call you the enemy, call you the swine. Take Down the Fiddle, Karl! John Shaw Neilson. CBAP

Men plow, and know everything about "late" and "early," The. Li K'ai-hsien. *Fr. Pleasures among the Fields during the Four Seasons.* CoBLCP, *tr. by* Jonathan Chaves

Men rent me on rode. *Unknown.* MiEL

Men Roofing. Eamon Grennan. PBCIP

Men say they know things. Walden. Thoreau. NAAL-3 *Fr. Walden*

Men seem as alike as the leaves on the trees. The Man from the Crowd. Sam Walter Foss. PoLF

Men seldom make passes. News Item. Dorothy Parker. NALW; OBAL *Fr. Some Beautiful Letters.*

Men share perceptions. The Switch Blade; or, John's Other Wife. Jonathan Williams. NeAP

Men sleep. The cassia blossoms fall. Bird and Waterfall Music. Wang Wei. OHMPC

Men, some to bus'ness, some to pleasure take. The Ghosts of Beauty. Alexander Pope. OBSV *Fr. Epistle [II,] to a Lady[: Of the Characters of Women].* NAEL-1; NOEC

Men spread disease among the faggots, one of the things they, The. Larry Mitchell. GLP

Men Talk. Stephen P. Dunn. NIP-4

Men talking, The. Eclogue. George Oppen. FTOS

Men that are safe, and sure, in all they do[e]. An Epistle Answering to One That Asked·to Be Sealed of the Tribe of Ben. Ben Jonson. BeJo

Men That Don't Fit In, The. Robert W. Service. BLPA

Men That Once Were, The. Owen Gruffydd, *Welsh.*

"Old, old/ To live on, wretched to behold." OBWVE, *tr. by* Anthony Conran

Men that worked for England, The. Elegy in a Country Churchyard. G. K. Chesterton. FaPoR; MoBrPo; NSI; OBWP; OxBSP; PoFWW

Men went to Catraeth, keen their war-band. Aneirin. OBWVE, *tr. by* Joseph P. Clancy *Fr. The Gododdin.*

Men went to Gododdin, laughter-loving. Aneirin. OBWP, *tr. by* Joseph P. Clancy *Fr. The Gododdin.*

Men who are quite humane. Epitaph for My Dog. Phan Bội Châu, *Vietnamese.* AVP, *tr. by* Huỳnh Sanh Thông

Men Who Come Behind, The. Henry Lawson. NOBAu

Men Who March Away. Thomas Hardy. CH; OBWP; PoWW *Fr. The Dynasts.*

("In our heart of hearts believing.") PoFWW

Men who march away. (LL) Men Who March Away. Thomas Hardy. OBWP; PoFWW; PoWW

Men with much toil, and time, and pain. Female Wits, The: A Song by a Lady of Quality. *Unknown.* NOSC

Men with picked voices chant the names. Overture to a Dance of Locomotives. William Carlos Williams. GM

Men with the heads of eagles. Margaret Atwood. NoAM *Fr. Circe / Mud Poems.*

Men with ventilators of black straw, The. Confab. Kenneth Rosen. AmPA

Men would never have come to need an attic. Up There. W. H. Auden. OxBTC *Fr. Thanksgiving for a Habitat.*

Men would often go hunting rabbits, The. Hunting Rabbits. Peter Skrzynecki. BMAP

Mena, deena, deina, duss. *Unknown.* LB

Menace of the Sick. Breyten Breytenbach, *Afrikaans.* PeSAV, *tr. by* Stephen Gray *and* A. J. Coetzee

Menacing machine turns on and off, The. Terror Conduction. Philip Lamantia. NeAP

Menage, The. Carl Rakosi. FTOS

Ménage à Trois. Howard Moss. GEA; VCAP

Menagerie came to Cape Race, A. Limerick. *Unknown.* PeLi

Menaphon. Robert Greene.

   Doron's Jigge. PoEL-2

   Samela. GBL; NOBE; OBEV

   (Doron's Description of Samela.) PoEL-2

   ("For beautie, wit, and matchlesse dignitie / yeeld to *Samela*.") (LL) PBRV

   ("Like to *Diana* in her Summer weede.") PBRV

Sephestia's Song to Her Child[e]. NoSic; OxAEP-1; PoEL-2

(Sephestia's Lullaby.) NOBE; OBEV

Mendacity. Alfred Edgar Coppard. OBMV

Mending Crab Pots. Dave Jeddie Smith. MT

Mending his broken *tabi* without becoming a Nora. Hisajo Sugita, *Japanese*. WPJ, *tr. by* Kenneth Rexroth *and* Ikuko Atsumi

Mending Sump. Kenneth Koch. BXAP; InPK-6; MoP; NeAP; NoAM

Mending the Adobe. Hayden Carruth. Poetsp

Mending Wall. Robert Frost. AFr; AmPP; CMoP; ChAP; ClHu; EBEvV; FP; FaBoPV; HAP; HeIP-4; HoPM; ImGa; InPS-3; LiTM; MeMAP; MoAmPo; MoP; NAAL-2; NOBA; NoAM; NoP-4; OxBA; PoE; PoPoPo; Poetr; SAmP; SCV; SoSe-8; TAP; TFi; VGW; WeW-3

Mendocino Rose. Garrett Kaoru Hongo. WeW-3

Mene Mene. Ory Bernstein, *Hebrew*. IP, *tr. by* Warren Bargad *and* Stanley F. Chyet

Menelaus wounded. Homer. OBCVT, *tr. by* William Cowper *Fr. The Iliad.*

Meng-ch'eng Hollow. Wang Wei. *Fr.* Twenty Views of Wang-ch'uan. CoBCP, *tr. by* Burton Watson

Mennonites. Julia Kasdorf. LoHo; PBCAP

Menodotis. Leonidas of Alexandria, *Greek*. AWP, *tr. by* Richard Garnett

Menoitas of Lyktos. Callimachus, *Greek*. GrAn, *tr. by* Peter Jay

Menopause—word used as an insult. Something to Look Forward To. Marge Piercy. NMM-2

Men's bodies resinous with sweat. Woodcutting. Gleb Iakovlevich Gorbovsky, *Russian*. TCRP, *tr. by* Lubov Yakovleva

Men's can at Café Society Uptown, The. Let's All Hear It for Mildred Bailey! James Schuyler. MoNo

Men's hearts love gold and jade;. Lodging with the Old Man of the Stream. Po Chü-i, *Chinese*. AWP; BLT; ChiP, *tr. by* Arthur Waley

Men's loving is a false affection. *Unknown*. NOIV

Men's Room in the College Chapel, The. W. D. Snodgrass. MoAmPo

Men's Voices. Inger Christensen, *Danish*. BoWoP, *tr. by* Nadia Christensen

Menses. Edna St. Vincent Millay. NMM-2; RACG

Menshikov. Yaroslav Vasilevich Smelyakov, *Russian*. TCRP, *tr. by* Lubov Yakovleva

Menstrual cramps. Michael Dudley. HA

Mental Cases. Wilfred Owen. CMoP; FaBoMo; NoAM; PeFWW

Mental Hospital Garden, The. William Carlos Williams.

"It is far to Assisi." CRP

Mental hospital my shadow stays outside. George Swede. HA

Mental Traveller, The. William Blake. ChIV-2; NAEL-2; OAEL-2; PoE; PoEL-4; Ro

Mental Traveller's Landfall, The. Chris Wallace-Crabbe. BMAP

Mentorides, please tell us who. Antipater of Thessalonica, *Greek*. GrAn, *tr. by* Alistair Elliot

Meow! There's a cat in my blood he roars he runs. Cat. Sutardji Calzoum Bachri, *Malay*. PC, *tr. by* Harry Aveling

Mer-Man, and Marstig's Daughter, The. *Unknown, Danish*. AWP, *tr. by* Robert Jamieson

Mercado. Greg Pape. AmPA

Merce of Egypt. Charles Olson. NoP-4

Merced. Adrienne Rich. NOBA

Merchant and the Fidler's Wife, The. *Unknown*. OxBB

Merchant Marine. Josephine Miles. TAP; VGW

(Merchant of Venice, The). Shakespeare.

Merchant of Venice, The. Shakespeare.

  All That Glisters Is Not Gold. CTC

  "Beshrew me but I love her heartily;." CTV

  Fire Seven Times Tried This, The. CTC

  "Go, draw aside the curtain, and discover." OxAEP-1

  "In sooth, I know not why I am so sad." OxAEP-1

  Song: "Tell me where is fancy [*or* Fancie] bred." CTC; EBEvV; PoEL-2

  (Love.) OBEV

Merchant, to secure his treasure, The. An Ode. Matthew Prior. AWP; EnLoPo; GLoP; GTBS-P; NOEC; NoP-4; OBEV; PoRA

Merchants. (King) Lê Thánh-tông, *Vietnamese*. AVP, *tr. by* Huỳnh Sanh Thông

Merchant's boat is piled high with goods, The. Ballad of the Merchant. Hsü Pen, *Chinese*. CoBLCP, *tr. by* Jonathan Chaves

Merchants from Cathay. William Rose Benét. MoAmPo

Merchants have multiplied more than the stars of heaven. The Executive's Death. Robert Bly. CoAP

Merchant's Joy, The. Chang Yü, *Chinese*. CoBLCP, *tr. by* Jonathan Chaves

Merchant's Joy, The. Lu Yu, *Chinese*. CoBCP, *tr. by* Burton Watson

Merchants of London, The. Mother Goose. ReMoGo

Mercian Hymns. Geoffrey Hill.

  "And it seemed, while we waited, he began to walk towards us." NoAM

  ("And it seemed, while we waited, he began to walk to / wards us.")

NoP-4

"Brooding on the eightieth letter of *Fors Clavigera*." HAP; PoE

"Clash of salutation. As keels thrust into shingle." NoAM

  ("Wine, urine and ashes.") (LL) NoP-4

"Coins handsome as Nero's; of good substance and." FaBoMo; HAP; NoAM

"Dismissing reports and men, he put pressure on the." HAP

"Gasholders, russet among fields. Mildams, marpools." HAP; NoAM; NoP-4

  ("In his private derelict sandlorry / named *Albion*.") (LL) NoP-4

"He adored the desk, its brown-oak inlaid with ebony." HAP; NoAM; NoP-4

  ("He wept, attempting to mas / ter *ancilla* and *servus*.") (LL) NoP-4

"I was invested in mother-earth, the crypt of roots." NoAM

"King of the perennial holly-groves, the riven sandstone." HAP; NoAM

"Mad are predators. Too often lately they harbour, The." NoP-4

"Not strangeness, but strange likeness. Obstinate." HAP; NoAM

"On the morning of the crowning we chorused our." HAP

"Pet-name, a common name. Best-selling brand, curt, A." NoAM

"Princes of Mercia were badger and raven, The." HAP; NAEL-2; NoAM; PoE

  ("Princes of Mercia were badger and raven. Thrall, The.") NoP-4

  ("Wrists and / knees garnished with impetigo.") (LL) NoP-4

"Processes of generation; deeds of settlement." NoP-4

"So much for the elves' wergild, the true governance." NoAM

"Strange church smelled a bit 'high,' of censers, The." PoE

"Their spades grafted through the variably-resistant." PoE

"Trim the lamp; polish the lens; draw, one by one, rare." FaBoMo

"We ran across the meadow scabbed with cow-dung, past." HAP

Mercies of the Year, The. John Danforth. SCAP

Merciful Shore, The. Maria Luisa Spaziani, *Italian*. NeIt, *tr. by* Beverly Allen

Merciless Beauty, *mod. vers.* Chaucer. BoLoP; EnVB; NAEL-1; SCGP *Fr.* Merciles[s] Beaute [*or* Beautée *or* Beauty]. CTC; EBEV; EnLoPo; HAP

Merciless love, whom nature hath denied. John Fletcher. GBL *Fr. The Chances.*

Mercury and Cupid. Matthew Prior. PeLV

Mercury Bay Eclogue. M. K. Joseph. PeNZ

Mercury; on Losing My Pocket Milton at Luss near Ben Lomond, and Other Mountains. Robert Andrews. NOEC

Mercury shew'd Apollo, Bartas Book. Nathaniel Ward. SCAP

Mercury, Venus, / Jupiter——. Planets. Jean Kenward. SpW

Mercury's Song [to Phaedra]. Dryden. NOSC; OxBSP; PBMP; PoEL-3 *Fr. Amphitryon.*

  (Song.) AWP

Mercy. Andrew Lansdown. NOBAu

Mercy. Bruce Smith. MoLi

Mercy. Bruce Weigl. CDa

Mercy abid and loke all day. *Unknown*. MiEL

Mercy is whiter than laundry. Angels in Winter. Nancy Willard. ColAP; LCAP-2

Mercy on Maryanne who through a hole beneath her collarbone. The Infusion Room. Jane Cooper. BAP-95

Mere, The. *Unknown*. EEP, *tr. by* Michael Alexander *Fr. Beowulf.*

Mere ants and gnats and trivia with stings. Palladas, *Greek*. GrAn, *tr. by* Tony Harrison

Mere chance that the patterned lute has fifty strings. The Patterned Lute. Li Shang-yin, *Chinese*. PLT, *tr. by* A. C. Graham

Merely the landscape of a vanished whim. Versailles. Adrienne Rich. OBGa

Merely to know. On the Spirit of the Heart as Moon-Disk. Kojijū, *Japanese*. WPoS, *tr. by* Edwin A. Cranston

Merida, 1969. William Matthews. EOEF

Meridian. Amy Clampitt. GEA

Meridian. David St. John. NAmP90

Merie sungen the muneches binnen Ely. Cnut's Song. *Unknown*. PoE *Fr. Canute at Ely.*

Merioneth. John Machreth Rees, *Welsh*. OBWVE, *tr. by* Kenneth Hurlstone Jackson

Merit of True Passion, The. Sir Robert Ayton. *See* Wrong Not, Sweete Empress of My Heart.

Merit will live, though parties disagree! (LL) To Wordsworth. John Clare. OAEL-2; Son

Merl. Jean Toomer. GT

Merlin. Ralph Waldo Emerson. APN-1; AmPP; NAAL-1; NAAL-3; NOBA; PAR

Merlin I. NCAP

Merlin. Geoffrey Hill. InPK-6; TRP

Merlin. Edwin Muir. FaBoTw; OxBS; RB

Merlin and the Gleam. Tennyson. FHYEP; NTP; OAEL-2

Merlin and the Snake's Egg. Leslie Norris. OBSP

Merlin Enthralled. Richard Wilbur. CMoP; NYBP

Mermaid, The. Ben King. OBAL

Mermaid, The. Lisel Mueller. CrSp

Mermaid, The. Ogden Nash. Spl

Mermaid, The. Tennyson. BoTP

  ("In the midst of the hall.") (LL) ACTP

Mermaid, The. *Unknown.* AmFP

Mermaid, The. *Unknown.* CH; ESPB

Mermaid Tavern. Keats. *See* Lines on the Mermaid Tavern.

Mermaiden, A. Thomas Hennell. FaBoTw

Mermaidens, The. Laura Elizabeth Richards. OBCA

Mermaidens' Vesper-Hymn, The. George Darley. GBL; NAEL-2; OBNC; PoEL-4 *Fr.* Syren Songs.

  (Siren Chorus.) BIrV

Mermaids, The. Edmund Spenser. *Fr.* Wood Of Error. AEP

Mermaid's / privacy, The. (LL) Necromance. Rae Armantrout. FTOS; PmAP

Merman, The. Tennyson. BoTP; UV

Merops. Ralph Waldo Emerson. APN-1; OxBA

Merorial Day: a collaboration. Anne Waldman *and* Ted Berrigan.

  "& Now the book is closed." SPE

Merrily, merrily, / All the spring. Merry Birds. Rodney Bennett. BoTP

Merrily, Merrily we welcome in the Year. (LL) Spring. William Blake. BoTP; FHYEP; FaBoCh; NOxBChV; NTP; Ro; TTTS

Merrily swinging on brier and weed. Robert of Lincoln. William Cullen Bryant. FaBoBe; OBCA

Merritt Parkway. Denise Levertov. AmPP; NeAP; PoM

Merrow Down. Rudyard Kipling. NOxBChV *Fr.* Just-So Stories.

Merry Birds. Rodney Bennett. BoTP

Merry Country Lad, The. Nicholas Breton. NoSic *Fr.* The Passionate Shepherd.

Merry cuckoo, messenger of spring, The. Sonnet 19. Edmund Spenser. *Fr.* Amoretti. AAS

Merry-Go-Round. Rachel Lyman Field. CTV

Merry-Go-Round. Langston Hughes. SAmP

Merry-go-round. James Philip McAuley. CBAP

Merry-go-round, The. Michael McClintock. HA

Merry-go-round, The. Rilke, *German.* WeW-3, tr. by C. F. MacIntyre

Merry have we met. A Party Song. *Unknown.* BoTP

Merry Heart, A. Shakespeare. *See* Song: "Jog on, jog on, the footpath way."

Merry It Is. *Unknown. See* Mirie it is, while sumer ilast.

Merry it is in the good greenwood. Ballad: Alice Brand. Sir Walter Scott. OxAEP-2 *Fr.* The Lady of the Lake.

Merry Jovial Beggar, The. Peter Casey, *Irish.* TIRV, tr. by Douglas Hyde

Merry Little Men. Kathleen M. Chaplin. BoTP

Merry-ma-Tanzie, The. *Unknown.* OxNR

Merry March wind is a boisterous fellow, The. The March Wind. E. H. Henderson. BoTP

Merry Margaret. To Mistress [or Maystres] Margaret Hussey. John Skelton. AAS; EBEV; EnLoPo; FaBoCh; HoPM; InPS-3; NAEL-1; NBLV; NOBE; NTP; NoSic; OAEL-1; OBEV; PeLV; PoE; PoEL-1; PoRA; SCGP; SCV; TFi *Fr.* The Garland [or Garlande or Garlands] of Laurel[1].

Merry mate amongst the rest, of cloisterers thus told, A. A Tale of the Beginning of Friars and Cloisterers. William Warner. NoSic *Fr.* Albion's England.

Merry merry bells of Yule, The. (LL) Time draws near the birth of Christ, The. Tennyson. EBVV; EBVVPR; FHYEP; NOCV; OAEL-2; SoSe-8

Merry, Merry Is My Lord. *Unknown, Chinese.* CoBCP, tr. by Burton Watson

Merry Merry Sparrow! The Blossom. William Blake. CTAV; FHYEP; Ro *Fr.* Songs of Innocence.

Merry the green, the green hill shall be merry. Another Song. Donald Justice. CoAmPo; NYBP; VGW

Merry wind danced over the hill, A. Such a Blustery Day! Elizabeth Gould. BoTP

Merry Window, The. Francis Scarfe. SPE

Merry [or Merrie] World did on a day, The. The Quip. George Herbert. GeHe; NOSC; OxAEP-1; SeCP

Merthe of all this land, The. God Speed the Plough! *Unknown.* EnVB

Mertill though my heart should break. To Mertill Who Desired Her to Speak to Clorinda of His Love. Elizabeth Taylor. KTR

Meru. W. B. Yeats. GSo; NoAM; OAEL-2; PoA; PoPoPo

Merulius Lacrymans. Robert Garioch. FaBoTC

Mery Gest How a Sergeaunt Wolde Lerne to Be A Frere, A. Sir Thomas More. AAS

Mery it is in May morning. *Unknown.* MiEL

Mery it was in grene forest. Adam Bell, Clim of the Clough, and William of Cloudesly. *Unknown.* ESPB; OxBB

Mescalito. Anselm Hollo. PT

Meseem'd that Love, with swifter feet than fire. An Utter Passion Uttered Utterly. John Todhunter. BXAP

Meseemeth I heard cry and groan. The Complaint of the Fair Armoress [or Armouress]. François Villon, *French.* AWP; CTC; OBVE, *tr. by* Algernon Charles Swinburne

Mesh cast for mackerel. Fishermen. Basil Bunting. PoA

Meshed in a glow of nickel, glass. Ballad of the Drinker in His Pub. N. P. van Wyk Louw, *Afrikaans.* PeSA, tr. by Uys Krige, Jack Cope, *and* Ruth Miller

Mesnevi. Sadi. AWP, tr. by L. Cranmer-Byng *Fr.* The Gulistan.

Mesopotamia. Rudyard Kipling. PoWW

Mess Deck. Alan Ross. PoWW

Mess of Love, The. D. H. Lawrence. CBLP; OAEL-2

Message, A. Fleur Adcock. DiPo

Message, The. Donne. MeLP

Message. Allen Ginsberg. CoAmPo; NeAP; VGW

Message, The. Grandmaster Flash *and* the Furious Five. NAAAL

Message, The. Michael Heffernan. RACG

Message, The. Heinrich Heine, *German.* AWP, tr. by Kate Freiligrath Kroeker

Message. Yon-gyun Kim, *Korean.* CKP, tr. by Jaihiun Kim

Message. Renata Pallottini, *Portuguese.* WPOW, tr. by Monique *and* Carlos Altschul

Message, The. Jacques Prévert, *French.* WeW-3, tr. by John Frederick Nims

Message. Dorothy M. Richardson. PoA

Message came to Joab saying "Behold, the king is weeping," A. Duty. Bible, *O.T.* LBC *Fr.* 2 Samuel, 19.

Message for Langston, A. "Kush." NBV

Message for Summer in the Suburbs, A. Richard Behm. EC2

Message from a Cross. Max Harris. NOBAu

Message from her set his brain aflame, A. George Meredith. EnVR; NOBVV *Fr.* Modern Love.

Message from Home. Kathleen Jessie Raine. WPE

Message from Ohanapecosh Glacier. W. M. Ransom. CDW

Message of Crazy Horse, The. Lucille Clifton. PaTW

Message of King Sakis and the Legend of the Twelve Dreams He Had in One Night, The. *Unknown, Serbo-Croatian.* HSix, tr. by Charles Simic

Message of Peace, A. Henry Wadsworth Longfellow. *Fr.* The Arsenal at Springfield. AmPP

Message of the March Wind, The. William Morris. OBNC

Message of the men is linear, The. Jeni Couzyn. NBrP

Message of the Rain, The. Norman H. Russell. ChAP

Message on Cape Cod, The. Michael S. Weaver. GT; PBCAP

Message to a Loved One Dead, A. Josephine D. H. Heard. CBWP-4

Message to Siberia. Pushkin, *Russian.* AWP; TTY, tr. by Max Eastman

Message Understood. Gareth Owen. SpW

Messages. Jack A. Mapanje. HBAPE

Messages. Francis Thompson. CH

Messages come through at last, The. Fort Wayne. Jack Spicer. CBNP

Messalonghi. January 22, 1824. Byron. *See* On This Day I Complete My Thirty-sixth Year.

Messe of Nonsense, A. *Unknown.* CBNP; NOSC

Messenger, The. Thom Gunn. PoA

Messenger, The. Frances Horovitz. BrRo

Messenger, The. Thomas Kinsella.

  "Inside, it is bare but dimly alive." CIP-2

Messenger, The. Jean Valentine. LCAP-2

Father, The. MoLi

Messenger from Rome. A Defence of Poetry. Giolla Brighde Mac Con Midhe. NOIV

Messenger, hear what I say. Reinmar der Alte, *German.* GePo, tr. by J. W. Thomas

Messenger of Sympathy and Love. The Meaning of a Letter. *Unknown.* PoToHe

Messengers, The. Steve Chimombo. HBAPE

Messengers. Louise Glück. ColAP; HCAP; VCAP

Messengers, The. Henrietta Cordelia Ray. CBWP-3

Messengers finally arrived and said, The. The Barbarians. Jovan Hristic, *Serbo-Croatian.* HSix, tr. by Charles Simic

Messerschmidts still tear one's heart, The. Hospital. Boris Abramovich Slutsky, *Russian.* TCRP, tr. by J. R. Rowland

Messiah, The. Bible, *O.T.* AWP *Fr.* Isaiah.

Messiah, The. Virgil. AWP, *tr.* by Dryden *Fr.* Eclogues.

("Sicilian Muses, sing we greater things.") OBVE, *tr.* by Sir John Beaumont

Messiah: A Sacred Eclogue in Imitation of Virgil's Pollio. Alexander Pope. ChIV-1

Messmates. Sir Henry John Newbolt. CH; EBVV; PeVV

Met in the milder shades of Purgatory. (LL) To Mr. H. Lawes On His Airs. Milton. AWP; NOSC; NoP-4

Meta-A and the A of Absolutes. Jay Wright. TRP

Metal Coughdrops. Tristan Tzara, *French.* PFTM, *tr.* by Jerome Rothenberg

Metal I, the soul the hearth, the blaze that warms, The. The Spiritual Alchemy. "Angelus Silesius." GePo, *tr.* by George C. Schoolfield *Fr.* The Cherubical Wanderer.

Metal of the footpath is, The. On Leaving the Footpath. John James. NBrP

Metal smokestack, The. Exercise No. 2. William Carlos Williams. SAmP

Metallic mammal. Nocturnal, A. Moon. Nicolás Guillén, *Spanish.* PFTM, *tr.* by Robert Marquez

Metamorpho I. Joe Rosenblatt. MoCV

Metamorphoses. Roy Fuller. OxBTC

Metamorphoses. Howard Nemerov. HCAP

Metamorphoses. Ovid, *Latin.*

Acteon. CTC, *tr.* by Arthur Golding

"And from the Citie Tegea there came the Paragone." OBVE, *tr.* by Arthur Golding

Baucis and Philemon. NOSC, *tr.* by Dryden

Ceyx and Alcyone. NoSic, *tr.* by Arthur Golding

Conclusion. OBCVT, *tr.* by Arthur Golding; CTC

("Now have I brought a woork too end which neither *Joves* fierce wrath.") OBCVT, *tr.* by Arthur Golding

Cyclops. CTC, *tr.* by Arthur Golding

Daedalus. CTC; OBVE, *tr.* by Arthur Golding

Daphne and Apollo. NOEC, *tr.* by Matthew Prior

"Floods, by nature enemies to land, The." OBVE, *tr.* by Dryden

Flood, The.

Golden Age, The. OAEL-1

(Before Gardens: The Golden Age.) GaP, *tr.* by Golding, Arthur

("From ech greene tree whereon the rayes of firie *Phebus* glowde.") (LL) OBCVT, *tr.* by Golding, Arthur

("Then sprang up first the golden age, which of itself.") GaP, *tr.* by Golding, Arthur

("Whereon the rayes of fiery / *Phœbus* glowed.") (LL) GaP, *tr.* by Golding, Arthur

"I pray thee Nymph Penaeis stay, I chase not as a fo." OBVE, *tr.* by Arthur Golding

King Midas. CTC, *tr.* by Arthur Golding

Magic. AWP, *tr.* by Shakespeare

Medea's Incantation. OBVE, *tr.* by Arthur Golding

Meleager. CTC, *tr.* by Arthur Golding

Meleager. NOBRP, *tr.* by John Herman Merivale

"My intention is to tell of bodies changed." NAWM-1, *tr.* by Rolfe Humphries

"Near the Cymmerians, in his dark abode." OBVE, *tr.* by Dryden

"Neare Enna walles there standes a Lake Pergusa is the name." OBVE, *tr.* by Arthur Golding

"Northern breath, that freezes floods, he binds, The." OBVE, *tr.* by Dryden

"Not Pallas, not ev'n Spleen it self could blame." OBVE, *tr.* by John Gay

"Now whyle Hippomenes/ Debates theis things." OBVE, *tr.* by Arthur Golding

Of the Pythagorean Philosophy. OBVE, *tr.* by Dryden

"This let me further add, that nature knows." OBVE

Philemon and Baucis. CTC, *tr.* by Arthur Golding

"Heaven's power is infinite; earth, air, and sea." OAEL-1, *tr.* by Dryden

"Then Lelex rose, an old experienced man." AWP; OBVE, *tr.* by Dryden

"Pygmalion seeing these to spend their times." OAEL-1, *tr.* by George Sandys

Pygmalion's Statue Comes to Life. OAEL-1, *tr.* by Arthur Golding

"Seeing as the father saw the rosy morn." OBVE, *tr.* by Joseph Addison

"Stones (a miracle to mortal view), The." OBVE, *tr.* by Dryden

"There was a man here, Samian born, but he." NAWM-1, *tr.* by Rolfe Humphries

"To thee obeyeth all the East as far as Ganges goes." OBVE, *tr.* by Arthur Golding

Metamorphoses. Yevtushenko, *Russian.* TCRP, *tr.* by Arthur Boyars *and* Simon Franklin

Metamorphosis. Louise Glück. MoLi

For My Father. MoLi

Night. MoLi

Metamorphosis. Slavko Mihalic, *Croatian.* CEEP, *tr.* by Peter Kastmiler

Metamorphosis. Sylvia Plath. PoA

Metamorphosis. Peter Porter. OxBTC

Metamorphosis. Wallace Stevens. InPK-6; VGW

Metamorphosis, The. Sir John Suckling. CaPo; FaBoEE

Metamorphosis of Pigmalions Image, The. John Marston.

"*Pigmalion,* whose hie love-hating minde." PBRV

Metamorphosis of Pygmalion's Image, The. John Marston.

"O gracious gods, take compassion." OAEL-1

Metaphor, The. Robert Graves. EP

Metaphor as Degeneration. Wallace Stevens. LCAP-2

Metaphor as Illness. Chuck Ortleb. GLP

Metaphor for My Son. John Holmes. ImGa

Metaphor of Grass in California. Charles Martin. RA

Metaphors. Sylvia Plath. HeIP-4; InPK-6; Poetr; SoSe-8

Metaphysic of Snow. Donald Finkel. PoA

Metaphysical. Robert Fitzgerald. PoA

Metaphysical Amorist, The. James Vincent Cunningham. VGW

Metaphysical Paintings, The. John Perreault. SPE

Metaphysical Sectarian, The. Samuel Butler. MeLP; PeLV *Fr.* Hudibras.

Metaphysician. Robert Fitzgerald. PoA

Metaphysics. Oliver Herford. CBNP

Metempsychosis. Kenneth Slessor. NOBAu

Meteor. Alan Pizzarelli. HA

Meteor of the war, The. (LL) The Portent. Herman Melville. APAD; APN-2; AmPP; CBCWP; ColAP; InPK-6; NAAL-1; NAAL-3; NCAP; NOBA; NoP-4; OBWP; OxBA; PAR; PoE; PoEL-5; TAP

Meteor's arc of quiet; a voiceless rain, The. Faint Music. Walter De la Mare. FaBoCh

Metevsky said to the one side. The Profiteer. Ezra Pound. NSI

Methinks all things have travelled since you shined. On the Sun Coming Out in the Afternoon. Henry David Thoreau. OxBSP; PoEL-4

Methinks already, from this chymick flame. The New London. Dryden. FaBoCh; NOBE *Fr.* Annus Mirabilis.

Methinks, dear Tom, I see thee stand demure. To the Revd. Mr. ——— on His Drinking Sea-Water. John Winstanley. NOEC

Methinks Death like one laughing lyes. Epitaph. Caecil. Boulstr. Edward Herbert, 1st Baron Herbert of Cherbury. SeCP

Methinks How Dainty Sweet It Were. Charles Lamb. Son

Methinks I see great Diocletian walk. Abraham Cowley. *See* The Garden.

Methinks I see some crooked mimic jeer. To the Critic. Michael Drayton. NOSC, *sect.* XXXI; Son *Fr.* Idea.

Methinks I see with what a busy haste. On Zacchaeus [*or* Zacheus]. Francis Quarles. NOSC; OxBSP

Methinks I spy Almighty holding in. Edward Taylor. HAP *Fr.* Preparatory Meditations Before My Approach to the Lord's Supper.

Methinks it is no journey. (LL) Tom o' Bedlam. *Unknown.* CH; FaBoCh; PoRA

Methinks my love to thee doth grow. "Michael Field." CPO

Methinks 'Tis Pretty Sport [to Hear a Child]. De Puero Balbutiente. Thomas Bastard. NoSic; OxBSP

Methinks, 'tis strange you can't afford. The Forsaken Wife. Elizabeth Thomas. ECWP; LW

Metho Drinker. Judith Wright. BMAP

Method, The. J. D. McClatchy. EOEF

Method must be purest meat, The. On Burroughs' Work. Allen Ginsberg. NAAL-2; NOBA

Methodist, The. Thomas Chatterton. ECEV

Methodist, The. Evan Lloyd.

Religion and the Lower Classes. NOEC

"Sons of War sometimes are known, The." OBSV

Methodology. Bruce Andrews. FTOS

Methought I lived in the icy times forlorn. Great Britain Through the Ice: Or, Premature Patriotism. Charles Tennyson Turner. Son

Methought I saw (as I did dream[e] in bed). The Vision. Robert Herrick. CaPo; NOSC

Methought I saw / Life swiftly treading over endless space. The Sea of Death. Thomas Hood. OBNC; PoEL-4

Methought [*or* Mee thought] I saw my late espousèd saint. On His Deceased Wife. Milton. BoLoP; CABP; CBLP; EBEV; EnLoPo; GBL; GLoP; GSo; HAP; IMW; ImPo; LBC; NAEL-1; NOBE; NOSC; NoP-4; OAEL-1; OBEV; OxBM; PBRV; PFE; PeECV; PoE; PoEL-3; SAGP; SCGP; SCV; Son; TFi; WeW-3

Methought I saw the grave where Laura lay. A Vision upon This Concei[p]t of the Faerie [*or* Faery] Queen[e]. Sir Walter Ralegh. NAEL-1; NoP-4;

NoSic; SCGP; SiPS; Son *Fr.* Commendatory Verses to Edmund Spenser's Fairy Queen.

Methought I stood where trees of every clime. A Garden-Dream. Keats. GaP *Fr.* A Dream. OBNC *Fr.* The Fall of Hyperion. OAEL-2

Methought, one night, I saw, in trance sublime. A Vision of Sunday in Heaven. Victor James Daley. ChIV-2

Methought That I Had Broken from the Tower. Shakespeare. RB *Fr.* King Richard III.

Methuselah ate what he found on his plate. Methuselah. *Unknown.* BLPA; FaBoBe

Meticulous, past midnight in clear rime. Hart Crane. ColAP; NAAL-2; PoE *Fr.* Voyages. CMoP; MeMAP; NOBA; NoAM; TAP

Metonymy as an Approach to a Real World. William Bronk. APSN; VGW

Metre Colombian, The. *Unknown.* BXAP; UV

Metric Figure. William Carlos Williams. MoAmPo

Metrical Feet. Coleridge. FHYEP; NIP-4; OxBChV; Poetr

Metrics. Rhina P. Espaillat. FFC

Metronomic Moon, The. Michael Young. APAD

Metropolitan / Museum of / Art, The. Miss Pimberton Of. Siv Cedering Fox. PBCAP

Metropolitan Nightmare. Stephen Vincent Benét. NYBP

Metropolitan Railway, The. John Betjeman. EBEV; OxAEP-2; OxBTC

Mevlana. Simon Pettet. PT

Mews Flat Mona. William Plomer. FaBoTw

Mexican dwarfs can dance for miles, The. Maxixe. Sir Osbert Sitwell. PoA

Mexican Loneliness. Jack Kerouac. CLPP

Mexicans Begin Jogging. Gary Soto. LTA

México. Lorna Dee Cervantes. *Fr.* Visions of Mexico While at a Writing Symposium in Port Townsend, Washington. NoAM

Mexico. Robert Lowell.
  "Difficulties, the impossibilities, The." HCAP
  "South of Boston, south of Washington." HCAP

Mexico, 1940. Ai. NoAM

Mexico, August 20, 1940. Ai. NoAM

Mexico City Blues. Jack Kerouac.
  113th Chorus. NeAP; PmAP
  127th Chorus. NeAP; PmAP
  146th Chorus. NeAP
  One Hundred and Forty-Ninth Chorus. PmAP
  179th Chorus. NeAP
  182nd Chorus. NeAP
  One Hundred and Eighty-Third Chorus. NeAP
  211th Chorus. NeAP; PmAP; PoM
  Two Hundred and Nineteenth Chorus. NeAP
  221st Chorus. NeAP
  225th Chorus. NeAP
  Two Hundred and Twenty-Eighth Chorus. NeAP; PmAP
  229th Chorus. PoM
  230th Chorus. NeAP
  239th Chorus: "Charley Parker Looked like Buddha." BB

Mexico Is a Foreign Country: Four Studies in Naturalism. Robert Penn Warren.
  "Mango on the mango tree, The." MoP; NoAM

Mezzo Cammin. Henry Wadsworth Longfellow. APN-1; GSo; NAAL-1; NAAL-3; NCAP; PAR; PoE; TAP
  ("Written at Boppard on the Rhine, August 25, 1842, just before.") ColAP

Mezzo Forte. William Carlos Williams. SAmP

M'Fingal. John Trumbull.
  "At once with resolution held." AmPP

Mi Abuelo. Alberto A. Ríos. PoPoPo

Mi tunge cleve to my chekis, if I bithenke not on thee. Bible, *O.T. See* Psalm 137.

Mi Vida: Wings of Fright. Martín Espada. AFr

Mia Carlotta. Thomas Augustin Daly. NBLV

Mica flask moves layout hasty. The Tab. Clark Coolidge. FTOS

Mica, if you peel carefully. Earth Angel. Jeffrey Skinner. PBCAP

Mica shines on the beach. Extract. Paul Bowles. PoA

Micah. Bible, *O.T.*
  Woe Is Me! TrJP

(Mice). Rose Fyleman. BoTP; CTV; ChAP; NTCP
  ("Are nice.") (LL) ChAP
  ("But *I* think mice.") (LL) CTV

Mice. David Marsh.

Mice are small. Mice Are Pets? Diana Taufer. CTV

Mice in the eaves, and breathe well my dear. Chess Piece Cornered. John Kinsella. BMAP

Mice in the garbage. For Rosa Yen, Who Lived Here. Greg Pape. AmPA

Mice in the Hay. Leslie Norris. NOxBChV; OBCP; PChr

Mice prepare for battle, The. *Unknown.* OBCVT, *tr. by* William Cowper *Fr.* Batrachomyomachia (The Battle of the Frogs and Mice).

Michael [A Pastoral Poem]. Wordsworth. FHYEP; NAEL-2; NOBRP; OAEL-2; OxAEP-2

Michael, Archangel of the King of Kings. A Sequence for Saint Michael. Alcuin, *Irish.* TIRV, *tr. by* Helen Waddell

Michael Is Afraid of the Storm. Gwendolyn Brooks. NOxBChV

Michael Met a Duck. J. Dupuy. BoTP

Michael Robartes and the Dancer. W. B. Yeats. OAEL-2

Michael Robartes Bids His Beloved Be at Peace. W. B. Yeats. MoP; NoAM

Michael row the [*or* de] boat ashore. *Unknown.* APN-2

Michaelmas. Norman Nicholson. MoBrPo

Michael's Song. Wilfrid Wilson Gibson. BoTP; NTP

Michal her modest flames sought to conceal. Abraham Cowley. ChIV-1 *Fr.* Davideis.

Micheál Mac Liammóir. Paul Durcan. PBCIP

Michigan-I-O. *Unknown.* AmFP

Micmac woman's body has been disinterred and her, The. Report on Her Remains. Daniel David Moses. HATNAP

Microbe's Serenade, The. George Ade. OBAL

Microbiblion, *see also* Hos Ego Versiculos, *sl. diff. vers. by* Francis Quarles, *fr.* Argalus and Parthenia. Simon Wastell.
  Man's Mortality. FaBoCh

Microcosmos. Susan Miles. OxBTC

Micromutations. James Wright. NYBP

Microscope. Gwyn Thomas, *Welsh.* OBWVE, *tr. by* Joseph P. Clancy

Microscope in Winter, The. Sandra McPherson. LCAP-2; VCAP

Mid-August at Sourdough Mountain Lookout. Gary Snyder. ColAP; HAP; InPK-6; LoL; NoP-4; PaTW; TAP; VCAP

Mid-Autumn Moon. Su Tung-p'o, *Chinese.* CoBCP, *tr. by* Burton Watson

Mid-Channel. Gwen Harwood. BMAP

Mid-day and a heat haze over all. Bruce Beaver. *Fr.* Letters to Live Poets. CBAP

Mid-Day Moon, The. John Banister Tabb. APN-2

Mid-October, Massachusetts. We drive. Incident. Eamon Grennan. BiHa

'Mid pleasures and palaces though we may roam. Home, Sweet Home! John Howard Payne. APN-1; BLPA; EBEvV; FaBoBe *Fr.* Clari, the Maid of Milan.

'Mid pleasures and palaces though we may roam. "Home, Sweet Home," with Variations. Henry Cuyler Bunner. OBAL *Fr.* Home.

Mid-Rapture. D. G. Rossetti. FaBoBe *Fr.* The House of Life.

Mid-Term Break. Seamus Heaney. InPS-3; PoPoPo

'Mid the half-lit air, and the lonely place. In the Graveyard. Macdonold Clarke. PWR

'Mid the thick covert of that woodland shade. Mary Tighe. NOBRP *Fr.* Psyche.

Mid-West, The. *Unknown.* OBCoV

Mid Winter. Hubert Witheford, *Maori.* PeNZ, *tr. by* Sam Karetu

Midafternoon in Norfolk. At the Swings. Henry Taylor. MT

Midas. John Lyly.
  "'Las, how long shall I." NoSic
  Pan's Song. OxAEP-1
  Syrinx. CBLP

Midas, they say, possessed the art of old. Epigram. "Peter Pindar." NIP-4

Midcentury Love Letter. Phyllis McGinley. LW; OxBM

Middelerd for mon wes mad. *Unknown.* MiEL

Midden of rotting bodies of men, A. Corpses in the Wood. Ernst Toller, *German.* TrJP, *tr. by* E. Ellis Roberts

Middle. Jimmie Durham. HATNAP

Middle Age. Patricia Beer. FaBoWP

Middle Age. Paula Rankin. MT

Middle-Age Enthusiasms. Thomas Hardy. LiLi

Middle age—I grow somewhat fond of the way. At My Country Home in Chung-nan. Wang Wei, *Chinese.* CoBCP, *tr. by* Burton Watson

Middle-Aged, The. Adrienne Rich. HCAP; PoPoPo

Middle   aged / couple   playing. 40—   Love. Roger McGough. OBCoV; Poetr

Middle-aged life is merry, and I love to lead it. Peekaboo, I Almost See You. Ogden Nash. EBEvV; PeLV; PoLF

Middle-aged white man in a beat-up blue Pinto, The. The Lucky One. Reginald Shepherd. GT

Middle Ages draw near. Do you hear, sensitive man, do you feel, The. Zalman Schneour, *Hebrew.* MHP, *tr. by* Ruth Finer Mintz

Middle-Class Blues. Hans Magnus Enzensberger, *German.* VCWP, *tr. by* Enzensberger, Hans Magnus and Michael Hamburger

Middle-elderly have wrinkled necks, The. Sonnet from Below the Age Gap. Keith Sinclair. PeNZ

Middle Manager in Paradise, The. Michael Foley. PNI

Middle of a War, The. Roy Fuller. OBWP; PoWW

Middle of life's journey; I, The. Dante. STV, *tr. by* John Frederick Nims *Fr.* Inferno. NAWM-1, *tr. by* John Ciardi *Fr.* Divina Commedia.

Middle of May, when the iris blows. Iris. Muriel Rukeyser. APSN; ColAP

Middle of the night, she's wide awake, carefully lying as far away as, The. The Question. Charles Kenneth Williams. NoP-4

Middle of the Way. Galway Kinnell.

"Coals go out, The." RaBo

Middle of the World. D. H. Lawrence. HAP; NoAM

Middle Passage. Frederick Douglass. CrDW

Middle Passage. Robert Earl Hayden. BPo; ColAP; InPS-3; NoAM; PoBA; TRP; VCAP

("Sails falshing to the wind like weapons.") NAAAL

Middle Passage and After, The. Larry Neal. NBV

Middle Years, The. Anthony Cronin. CIP-2

Middleaged Man, The. Louis Simpson. NNaP

Middleness of the Road, The. Robert Frost. NOBA

Middlesex. John Betjeman. OxBTC

Midget, The. Philip Levine. WeT

Midnight. Mary Ursula Bethell. PeNZ

Midnight. Louisa Sarah Bevington. PEW

Midnight. Jacob Fichman, *Hebrew.* MHP, *tr. by* Ruth Finer Mintz

Midnight. Andreas Gryphius, *German.* GePo, *tr. by* George C. Schoolfield

Midnight. Gabriela Mistral, *Spanish.* BoWoP, *tr. by* David Garrison

Midnight. Henrietta Cordelia Ray. *Fr.* Idyl. CBWP-3

Midnight. Michael Roberts. OBMV

Midnight. Tu Fu, *Chinese.* PLT, *tr. by* A. C. Graham

Midnight. Henry Vaughan. ChIV-2; ESCV

Midnight, and a letter comes to me from. Ezra Pound. MeMAP *Fr.* Homage to Sextus Propertius.

Midnight Court, The. Brian Merriman, *Modern Irish.* NOIV, *tr. by* Thomas Kinsella

Country's Crisis, The. BIrV, *tr. by* David Marcus

Husband's Lament, The. OBVE, *tr. by* Frank O'Connor

Irish Marriage Night, An. BIrV, *tr. by* Frank O'Connor

Lament of the Unmarried Girl, The. OBVE, *tr. by* Frank O'Connor

Maiden's Plight, The. BIrV, *tr. by* Frank O'Connor

Now God Stand Up for Bastards. BIrV, *tr. by* Arland Ussher

Old Man's Tale, The. BIrV, *tr. by* David Marcus

Solution, The. BIrV, *tr. by* Arland Ussher

Walk. BIrV, *tr. by* Brendan Behan

Midnight Diner by Edward Hopper, A. David Ray. WeT

Midnight Elegy. Léopold Sédar Senghor, *French.* NegPo, *tr. by* Ellen Conroy Kennedy

Midnight has come, and the great Christ Church Bell. All Souls' Night. W. B. Yeats. OxAEP-2 *Fr.* A Vision.

Midnight: I still haven't gotten to sleep. At Night, Hearing Someone Singing in the House Next Door. Mei Yao Ch'en, *Chinese.* CoBCP, *tr. by* Burton Watson

Midnight in Bonnie's Stall. Siddie Joe Johnson. PChr

Midnight is past, and it is time to go. The Last Dance. May Riley Smith. SAGP

Midnight Lamentation. Harold Monro. OxBTC

"When you and I go down." OBMV

Midnight, Lochinver. Norman MacCaig. OxBoS

Midnight ("Midnight was come, when every vital thing"). Thomas Sackville. CH *Fr.* Induction to "A Mirror for Magistrates." AAS

("Midnight was come, and every vital thing.") AEP

("'When Fortune frown'd, the feller made my fall'.") (LL) AEP

Midnight. No waves. On the Treasury of the True Dharma Eye. Dogen. EnlH

Midnight on Front Street. Roberta Hill Whiteman. CDW

Midnight on the Great Western. Thomas Hardy. CH; NOBE; OxAEP-2

Midnight or after, and the little lights. Train. Donald Justice. GM

Midnight Prayer. Hayyim Nahman Bialik, *Hebrew.* TrJP, *tr. by* Helena Frank

Midnight Ramble, The. Charles Woodward. NOEC

Midnight Ride of Paul Revere, The. Henry Wadsworth Longfellow. *See* Paul Revere's Ride (The Landlord's Tale).

Midnight Show. Karl Shapiro. OxBA

Midnight Skaters, The. Edmund Blunden. FaBoTw; GTBS-P; MoBrPo; NOBE; NoP-4; PeFWW

("And let him hate you through the glass.") (LL) NoP-4

Midnight Song. Pinkie Gordon Lane. GT

Midnight Special, The. "Leadbelly." GM

Midnight Special. Kenneth Patchen. VGW

Midnight Special. *Unknown.* AS

Midnight storm. Trees walking off across the fields in fury. Light. Michael Ondaatje. NIP-2

Midnight sun with phantom glare, The. The Russian Student's Tale. Mathilde Blind. VWP

Midnight Tennis Match, The. Thomas Lux. AmPA

Midnight. The wind yawing nor-east. Haddock Fishermen. George Mackay Brown. NoP-4

Midnight Thought, A [on the Death of Mrs. *E. H.* and Her Little Daughter]. Elizabeth Thomas. KTR; NOSC

Midnight Train, The. *Unknown.* AS

Midnight Trolleybus. Bulat Shalvovich Okudzhava, *Russian.* TCRP, *tr. by* Albert C. Todd

Midnight Vapor Light Breakdown. Betsy Sholl. LTA

Midnight Velada, The. María Sabina, *Mazatec.* PFTM, *tr. by* Henry Munn *and* Alvaro Estrada

Midnight was come, when every vital thing. Midnight. Thomas Sackville. CH *Fr.* Induction to "A Mirror for Magistrates." AAS

Midnightmouse, The. Christian Morgenstern, *German.* CBNP; RB, *tr. by* W. D. Snodgrass *and* Lore Segal

Midnights of consciousness, still, and even. Endsight. Michael Dransfield. BMAP

Midst all the dark and knotty snares. Neither Durst Any Man From That Day Ask Him Any More Questions. Richard Crashaw. ChIV-2

Midst the fair range of buildings which, new-reared. George Keate. NOEC *Fr.* A Burlesque Ode, on the Author's Clearing a New House of Some Workmen.

Midstream. D. J. Enright. OxBC

Midstream. Mao Tse-tung, *Chinese.* MoCV, *tr. by* Earle Birney

Midsummer. William Cullen Bryant. GSo

Midsummer. Robert Fitzgerald. PoA

Midsummer. Alexander L. Posey. APN-2

Midsummer. Sydney King Russell. BLPA; FaBoBe

Midsummer. James Scully. NYBP; TwCP

Midsummer. Derek Walcott.

"Certain things here are quietly American." NAEL-2; NoP-4

Gauguin. NoAM

Midsummer: XXX. AFr

"Oak inns creak in their joints as light declines, The." NoAM

"Rest, Christ! from tireless war. See, it's midsummer." TOF

Midsummer Apple Tree, The. Naomi Mitchison. WPN

Midsummer Day in France. Alexander Hume. *Fr.* Of the Day Estivall. NOCV; OxBS

Midsummer LIV. Derek Walcott. HCP

Midsummer Moon. "E. M. G. R." BoTP

Midsummer Night. Elizabeth Gould. BoTP

Midsummer Night's Dream, A. Shakespeare.

Asleep, My Love? CTC

Bottom's Dream. CBNP

Bottom's Song. CTC

"Either I mistake your shape and making quite." OxBSn

Fairy Blessing, The. OxBoLi

Fairy Land, 1. OBEV

(Fairy Song ("Over hill, over dale").) NOBE

Fairy Land, 2. OBEV

Flower of This Purple Dye. CTC

Imagination. ImPo

"Ousel cock, so black of hue, The." NoSic

Poetic Frenzy. EPCY

Through the Forest Have I Gone. CTC

Through the House. CTC

(Oberon and Titania to the Fairy Train.)

Up and Down. CTC

Yet but Three? CTC

Midsummer sea, the hot pitch road, this grass, these shacks. Midsummer LIV. Derek Walcott. HCP

Midsummer stretches before me with a cat's yawn. Port of Spain. Derek Walcott. NoAM

Midsummer, Tobago. Derek Walcott. OPOU; VCWP

Midsummer: XXX. Derek Walcott. AFr *Fr.* Midsummer.

Midsummer: XXXI. Derek Walcott. AFr

Midway. Robert Desnos, *French.* PFTM, *tr. by* Quasha, George

Midway. Naomi Long Madgett. BPo; BlSi

Midway between Mecca and Medina. To a Hero Dead at al-Safra. Hind bint Uthatha, *Arabic*. WPOW, *tr.* by Bridget Connelly *and* Deirdre Lashgari

Midway in our life's journey, I went astray. Inferno. Dante. NAWM-1, *tr.* by John Ciardi *Fr.* Divina Commedia.

Midway the hill of science, after steep. To Mr. S. T. Coleridge. Anna Laetitia Barbauld. CABP; ECWP; NOBRP; NOEC; NoP-4; Ro; WoRP

Midways of a walled garden. The Ancient Castle. William Morris. *Fr.* Golden Wings. OBNC

Midwest is Full of Vibrators, The. Lyn Lifshin. DeD

Midwest, Midcentury. Sharyn Jeanne Skeeter. ISC

Midwest Town. Ruth Delong Peterson. CA

Midwife puts a rag in the dead woman's hand, The. Obedience of the Corpse. C. D. Wright. LCAP-2; MT

Midwife's Invocation, A. *Unknown, Nahuatl*. WPoS, *tr.* by Coe, Michael D. and Gordon Whittaker

Midwife's Story; Two, A. Anne Szumigalski. NOBC

Midwinter. Margaret E. Bruner. PoToHe

Midwinter Day. Bernadette Mayer. PT

Midwinter spring is its own season. Little Gidding. T. S. Eliot. CABP; FaBoMo; FaBoPV; FaBoTw; GTBS-P; MoP; NAEL-2; NAWM-2; NOBA; NOBE; NoAM; OAEL-2; OxAEP-2; OxBTC; PeECV; TAP; TFi *Fr.* Four Quartets.

Midwinter Tourists. Albinas Žukauskas, *Lithuanian*. CEEP, *tr.* by Irene Pogoželskyte Suboczewski

Midwives, The. Celia Gilbert. ChIV-1

Might and Right. Clarence Day. NBLV

Might as well. Blues for Dan Morin. Lawson Fusao Inada. MoNo

Might have been. Certainly these ashes might have been pleasures. This Place Rumord to Have Been Sodom. Robert Duncan. NOBA; NeAP; PoM

Might have known it. Song. *Unknown, Chippewa Indian*. STP, *tr.* by Jerome Rothenberg

Might I but moor—Tonight!— / In Thee! Emily Dickinson. *See* Wild Nights—Wild Nights!

Might I, if you can find it, be given. Saint Nicholas. Marianne Moore. NYBP; WPE

Might Is Right. Israel Zangwill. TrJP

Might live invisible and dim! Henry Vaughan. *See* The Night.

Might of this pagoda seems to erupt upwards, The. On Climbing the Pagoda of the Temple of Gracious Benevolence with Kao Shih and Hsüeh Chü. Ts'en Shen, *Chinese*. SuSp, *tr.* by Daniel Bryant

Might rise from where they slept and go away. (LL) The Sheaves. Edwin Arlington Robinson. AWP; CMoP; HAP; ImGa; MoAmPo; MoP; NOBA; NoAM; OxBA; Poetr; SoSe-8; TAP

Might speak them. Then we heard them, every word. (LL) Charles Carville's Eyes. Edwin Arlington Robinson. CMoP; MeMAP; OxBA; TAP

Mightier than the Pen. Kingsley Amis. OBCoV

Mightier than the sword thou art. The Pen. Mary Weston Fordham. CBWP-2

Mighty bell is six o'clock, A. Six to Six. *Unknown, Xhosa*. PBA, *tr.* by A. C. Jordan

Mighty change it is, and ominous, A. The Winter Shore. Thomas Wade. OAEL-2

Mighty creature is the germ, A. The Germ. Ogden Nash. RB

Mighty Forms. Brenda Hillman. PuP-16; WeT

Mighty Fortress Is Our God, A. Martin Luther, *German*. PWR, *tr.* by Frederick Henry Hedge; CTC, *tr.* by M. Woolsey Stryker; AWP; GePo

Mighty God, even the Lord, hath spoken, The. Psalm 50. Bible, *O.T.* BrRo *Fr.* Psalms.

Mighty growth! The county side, A. The Old Oak Tree at Hatfield Broadoak. Frederick Locker-Lampson. OxAEP-2

Mighty Heart, The. Ralph Waldo Emerson. *Fr.* Woodnotes II ("As sunbeams stream through liberal space"). NOBA

Mighty Hunter, The. Mrs. J. B. Worley. PoLF

Mighty Love. John Fletcher. *See* Song: "Heare ye Ladies that despise."

Mighty Mary, hear me. Muireadhach Albanach O'Dalaigh. NOIV

Mighty Mother, and her son who brings, The. To Dr. Jonathan Swift. Alexander Pope. OxAEP-1, *book* I, *ll.* 1–330; OBSV; PoE *Fr.* The Dunciad.

Mighty Ocean, The. Ilya L'vovich Selvinsky, *Russian*. TCRP, *tr.* by Daniel Weissbort

Mighty One, before Whose Face. William Cullen Bryant. AH

Mighty, praised beyond compare. Rock of My Salvation. Mordecai ben Isaac, *Hebrew*. TrJP, *tr.* by Solomon Solis-Cohen

Mighty river flowing dark and deep, The. James Thomson. EBVV; EnVR *Fr.* The City of Dreadful Night. OBNC

Mighty Runner, A. Edwin Arlington Robinson. MeMAP; OBAL

Mighty spirit, and its power, which stains, The. Inebriety. George Crabbe. BXAP

Mighty Tropicale Orchestra, The. Sean Harvey. SeSe

Mighty wave rush'd o'er him as he spoke, A. Homer. OBVE, *tr.* by Pope *Fr.* Odyssey. NAWM-1, *tr.* by Robert Fitzgerald

Mighty you are, dark mouth. Dejection. Georg Trakl, *German*. PeFWW, *tr.* by Michael Hamburger

Mignon. Goethe. AWP, *tr.* by James Elroy Flecker; STV, *tr.* by John Frederick Nims *Fr.* Wilhelm Meister's Apprenticeship.

("Knowest thou the land where bloom the lemon trees.") AWP, *tr.* by James Elroy Flecker

Mignon. Henrietta Cordelia Ray. CBWP-3

Migrant, The. A. L. Hendriks. PBCV

Migrant's Lament: A Song. Alfred Temba Qabula. PeSAV

Migrating Birds. James Thomson. APo

Migration. Carole C. Gregory Clemmons. *See* Ghetto Lovesong—Migration.

Migration. Pinkie Gordon Lane. BlSi

Migration of the Grey Squirrels, The. William Howitt. OxBChV

Migratory Bird ("One day he perched on a tree with dew"). Chenjerai Hove. HBAPE

Migratory bird flew with mirth. Lost Bird. Chenjerai Hove. HBAPE

Migratory Noon. Joseph Ceravolo. FTOS

Mikado, The. Sir William Schwenck Gilbert.

Ko-Ko's Song. ImPo

(Titwillow.) NoP-4

Mike Howe's head with frozen frown. Hobart Town, Van Diemen's Land (11th June, 1837). Hal Porter. NOBAu

Mike 65. Lennox Raphael. PoBA

Mild and peaceful spring glow, Cold Food Day. Li Ch'ing-chao. SuSp, *tr.* by Eugene Eoyang *Fr.* Tune: "Sand of Silk-washing Stream."

Mild and slow and young. Girl Help. Janet Lewis. HeIP-4; InPK-6

Mild February. Hal Summers. AYFP

Mild is the parting year, and sweet. Autumn. Walter Savage Landor. EnLoPo *Fr.* Ianthe.

Mild, of sweet / countenance. Paulus Silentiarius, *Greek*. GrAn, *tr.* by Andrew Miller

Mild offspring of a dark and sullen sire! To an Early Primrose. Henry Kirke White. OBNC

Mild parochial talk was ours, A. In the Garden. Walter De la Mare. FP

Mild the mist upon the hill. Emily Jane Brontë. NOBVV

Mildmay Grove. Sue May. NBrP

Mildred's Doves. Henrietta Cordelia Ray. CBWP-3

Mile an' a bittock, a mile or twa, A. Robert Louis Stevenson. NOBVV

Mile and mile and mile; but no one would gather. The Sea. Francis Webb. CBAP

Mile behind is Gloucester town, A. Gloucester Moors. William Vaughn Moody. APN-2; NOBA; OxBA

Mile from Eden, A. Anne Ridler. WPN

Mile from Poetry, A. Kris Hemensley.

"Look! she said you can see." BMAP

"My poem's in the oven where." BMAP

"Place was famed for, The." BMAP

"Poem by John Thorpe, A." BMAP

Mile Hill. Dennis Schmitz. LCAP-2

Mile more down the flat fast road, the homestead, A. Serpent Knowledge. Robert Pinsky. NAAL-2 *Fr.* An Explanation of America.

Mile out in the marshes, under a sky, A. The Town Dump. Howard Nemerov. CMoP

Mile with Me, A. Henry Van Dyke. BLPA

"Miles," and "John Alden" were Synonym. (LL) God is a distant—stately Lover. Emily Dickinson. APN-2; NCAP

Miles go sliding by, The. Walking Song. Ivor Gurney. NTP

Miles of pram in the wind and Pam in the gorse track. Potpourri from a Surrey Garden. John Betjeman. CBLP; NOBL

Miles Weeping. Michael Waters. CMAP; PuP-15

Militance of a Photograph in the Passbook of a Bantu under Detention, The. Michael S. Harper. VCAP

Militant. Langston Hughes. PoBA

Military Harpist, The. Ruth Pitter. FaBoTw; NALW

Military-Industrial Complex, The. Robley Wilson Jr. PBCAP

Military Occupations. Dionne Brand.

"In the 5 a.m. dusk." PBCV

Militerotics. Chuck Ortleb. GLP

Militia, The. Dryden. OBSV *Fr.* Cymon and Iphigenia. EPCY; OBNV

Milk[e] all the way. (LL) To the Infant Martyrs. Richard Crashaw. ChIV-2; GeHe; NAEL-1; NoP-4; OxBSP

Milk and honey. Salt. Viktor Fiodorovich Bokov, *Russian*. TCRP, *tr.* by Bernard Meares

Milk Bottle, The. Galway Kinnell. Poetr

Milk for the Cat. Harold Monro. BoTP; FaBoBe; MoBrPo; OBMV; PC

Milk jugs, cups. Iain Crichton Smith. FaBoTC

Milk Maid, The. Mother Goose. OxNR

Milk-spray glitters along our newborn's cheek, The. The Poem of my Heart. Liz Rosenberg. FiLi

Milk White Doe, The. *Unknown, French.* AWP, *tr. by* Andrew Lang

Milk-white hair-lace wound up all her hairs, A. A Woman drest by Age. Margaret Lucas Cavendish, Duchess of Newcastle. PEW

Milk white Hind, immortal and unchang'd, A. The Churches of Rome and of England. Dryden. UV *Fr.* The Hind and the Panther.

Milk-white moon, put the cows to sleep. Carl Sandburg. ImGa

Milk-white mouse immortal and unchang'd, A. The Town Mouse and the Country Mouse. Matthew Prior. BXAP

Milkers lace their boots up at the farms, The. (LL) Cock-Crow. Edward Thomas. GTBS-P; MoBrPo; NTP; OxBSP; RB

Milkfish. Eugene Gloria. OpBo

Milking before Dawn. Ruth Dallas. NTP; PeNZ

Milking Pails. *Unknown.* CH

Milking Shed, The. John Clare. CH

Milking Time. Elizabeth Madox Roberts. OBCA

Milkmaid. Laurie Lee. APAD; BoLoP; FaBoTw

Milkmaid, The. *Unknown.* AmFP

Milkmaid's Epithalamium, The. Thomas Randolph. BoLoP; EP

Milkman, The. Clive Sansom. BoTP

Milkman and His Son, The. Thomas Lux. LCAP-2

Milkweed. Philip Levine. LCAP-2

Milkweed. James Wright. ColAP; LCAP-2; NOBA; RaBo

Milkweed and Monarch. Paul Muldoon. NoP-4

Milky in the spring grotto stone fattens, sprouts goose-quills. Tu Mu. PLT, *tr. by* A. C. Graham *Fr.* Red Slope.

Milky Way above, The. Fire Island. May Swenson. PoA; TAP

Milky Way / Milky Way, Tune: "Flirtatious Laughter." Wei Ying-wu, *Chinese.* CoBCP, *tr. by* Burton Watson

Milky Way's silver river, The. Song of the Waterfall at Mount Lu. Yang Wei-chen, *Chinese.* CoBLCP, *tr. by* Jonathan Chaves

Mill, A. William Allingham. FaBoEE; OxBSP

Mill, The. Richard Wilbur. FP; Poetsp

Mill-Doors. Carl Sandburg. SAGP

Mill Garden, The. Swinburne. EP

Mill-Pond, The. Edward Thomas, *German.* RB

Mill-Race, The. Anne Winters. BAP-96

Mill-stream, now that noises cease, The. A. E. Housman. GBL

Milla, the glory of whose beauteous rays. *Unknown.* NOSC

"Millennium," yes; "pandemonium"! Hometown Piece for Messrs. Alston and Reese. Marianne Moore. OBAL

Miller, The. John Cunningham. ECEV

Miller Canyon Trail No. 106. Michael Bowden. PuP-15

Miller, Miller. Ivy O. Eastwick. BoTP

Miller was a chap of sixteen stone, The. Chaucer. *See* The Miller's [*or* Milleres] Tale.

Miller was a stout carl, for the nones, The. Seven Pilgrims: A Miller. Chaucer. *Fr.* The General Prologue. FHYEP; NAEL-1; NAWM-1; OAEL-1; PoE *Fr.* The Canterbury Tales.

Miller's daughter, The. Spinning Song. Dame Edith Sitwell. MoBrPo

Miller's Daughter, The. Tennyson. OBEV

Miller's mill-dog lay at the mill-door, The. Bingo. *Unknown.* CH; TTTS

Miller's Prologue, The. Chaucer. NAEL-1; OAEL-1 *Fr.* The Canterbury Tales.

("There's no sense making earnest out of game.") (LL) NAWM-1

("When the knight had finished, no one, young or old.") NAWM-1

Miller's [*or* Milleres] Tale, The. Geoffrey Chaucer, *Middle English.* NAEL-1; NAWM; OAEL-1; OxBoLi; PeLV *Fr.* The Canterbury Tales.

("God save this troop! That's all I have to tell.") (LL) NAWM-1

("There used to be a rich old oaf.") NAWM-1

"Fair was this yonge wyf, and therwithal." EBEV

Miller's wife had waited long, The. Edwin Arlington Robinson. CMoP; HAP; MeMAP; NAAL-2; NoAM; NoP-4; Poetr; TAP; WeW-3

Millery, millery, dustipole. *Unknown.* OxNR

Million, The. Peter Redgrove. OxBC

Million billion trillion stars, A. (LL) Man who had fallen among thieves, A. E. E. Cummings. ChIV-2; HAP; LiTM; MeMAP; MoP; NOBA; NoAM; OxBA; TAP

Million butterflies rose up from South America, A. Annual Legend. Winfield Townley Scott. CoAP; LiTM

Million emeralds break from the ruby-budded lime, A. Tennyson. *Fr.* Maud [A Monodrama]. EnVR

Million million spermatozoa, A. Fifth Philosopher's Song. Aldous Leonard Huxley. OBCoV

Million years of death some star, A. Micromutations. James Wright. NYBP

Millionaire. A. J. Seymour. HCP

Millionaire, filled with elation, A. Limerick. Thomas Thorneley. PeLi

Millionaires, presidents—even kings. Everyday Things. Jean Ayer. BoTP

Millionbillionwillion miles from home, A. First Day at School. Roger McGough. NOxBChV

Millions o' wimmen bring forth in pain. Repetition Complex. "Hugh MacDiarmid." FaBoTC *Fr.* A Drunk Man Looks at the Thistle.

Millions of Strawberries. Genevieve Taggard. NOxBChV

Mills of the Gods, The. *Unknown.* BLPA

Milltown Union Bar, The. Richard Hugo. NoAM

Milne's Bar. Norman MacCaig. FaBoTw

Milo's from home; and, Milo being gone. Epigram. Martial, *Latin.* OBVE, *tr. by* Elijah Fenton

Milton. William Blake.

"And every Space that a Man views around his dwelling-place." BLT

"But the Wine-press of Los is eastward of Golgonooza, before the Seat." NOBRP

"But turning toward Ololon in terrible majesty Milton." OxAEP-2

"Daughters of Beulah! Muses who inspire the Poets Song." PeECV

"Into this pleasant Shadow all the weak & weary." NOBRP

Jerusalem. BoTP; FHYEP; FaPoR; NOBE; NOCV; OBEV; OxAEP-2; RB; UV

("In England's green and pleasant Land.") (LL) APAD; CABP; NoP-4; SAGP

Lark's Song, The. APo

("Thou hearest the Nightingale begin the Song of.") APo; NOBE

(Vision of Beulah, The.) NOBE

"Then Milton rose up from the heaven of Albion ardorous!" OAEL-2

"There is a place where Contrarities are equally True." NOBRP

Vision of Beulah, The ("There is a place where contrarieties are equally true"). OAEL-2

Milton[! thou shouldst be living at this hour]. London 1802. Wordsworth. AWP; EBEvV; EPCY; FaBoPV; FaPoR; GTBS-P; HAP; HeIP-4; NAEL-2; NIP-4; NOBRP; NoP-4; OBEV; OBNC; OxAEP-2; PBMP; PFE; PoEL-4; PoRA; Son; SCGP; Son; TFi; UV

Milton. Henry Wadsworth Longfellow. AWP; AmPP; GSo; TAP

Milton. Henrietta Cordelia Ray. BlSi; CBWP-3

Milton. John Banister Tabb. APN-2

Milton [Alcaics]. Tennyson. EPCY; PeECV

Milton by Firelight. Gary Snyder. BB; CoAP; CoAmPo; InPS-3; NAAL-2; SAGP

Milton: On the Busts of Milton, in Youth and Age. William Lisle Bowles. Son

Milton, our noblest poet, in the grace. In Youth. William Lisle Bowles. *Fr.* Milton: On the Busts of Milton, in Youth and Age. Son

Milton, the airport driver, retired now. Becoming Milton. Coleman Barks. RaBo

Miltonic Sonnet for Mr. Johnson on His Refusal of Peter Hurd's Official Portrait, A. Richard Wilbur. CAPP-1

Milton's strong pinion now not heaven can bound. Alexander Pope. EPCY *Fr.* The First Epistle of the Second Book of Horace Imitated.

Milton's the prince of poets—so we say. Byron. NOBL *Fr.* Canto the Third. *Fr.* Don Juan.

Milwaukee Fire, The. *Unknown.* AmFP

Mimetic. Anne Lauterbach. PmAP

Mimic Muse, The. Samuel Hoffenstein.

"With rue my heart is laden." NBLV

Mimikòs. Luigi Fontanella, *Italian.* NeIt, *tr. by* Michael Palma

Mimnermus in Church. William Johnson Cory. NOBE; OBEV

Mimnermus Incert. Walter Savage Landor. PoEL-4

Mimosas. Louis Aragon, *French.* CBNP

Mimshi Maiden, The. Hugh Raymond McCrae. NOBAu

Mina Bell's Cows. Wesley McNair. TRP

Mince-Python, The. Carolyn Wells. *Fr.* A Baker's Dozen of Wild Beasts. OBCA

Mincemeat. Elizabeth Gould. BoTP

Mind. Jorie Graham. HCAP; Poetr

Mind and environment—you have quieted both. Wu Shan-yang. Yang Chi. CoBLCP, *tr. by* Jonathan Chaves *Fr.* Thinking of My Friends at Kou-jung Subprefecture.

Mind at peace, cassia flowers fall. Birdsong Brook. Wang Wei, *Chinese.* SuSp, *tr. by* Irving Y. Lo

Mind / becomes an / oil-slicked pool, The. Doper's Dream. Don Receveur. CDa

Mind content both crown and kingdom is, A. (LL) Maesia's Song. Robert Greene. CTC; PoEL-2; UnPo

Mind Flying Afar. Edgar Lee Masters. PoA

Mind has shown itself at times, The. Hart Crane. *Fr.* For the Marriage of Faustus and Helen. InPS-3; NOBA; NoAM

Mind in its [*or* the] purest play is like some bat. Richard Wilbur. CMoP; ColAP; HCAP; HoPM; OxBSP; SoSe-8; VCAP

Mind, Intractable Thing, The. Marianne Moore. LiTM; NYBP

Mind is a city like London, The. The Mind Is an Ancient and Famous Capital. Delmore Schwartz. NoAM; TAP

Mind Is an Ancient and Famous Capital, The. Delmore Schwartz. NoAM; TAP

Mind Is an Enchanting Thing, The. Marianne Moore. CMoP; HeIP-4; InPK-6; MeMAP; MoAmPo; NAAL-2; NoP-4; OxBA; PoE; WPOW

Mind is his Wife, The. / So be it. (LL) Prayer for the Great Family. Gary Snyder. HAP; WeW-3

Mind is not, The. The Perishing Bird. Douglas G. Jones. MoCV

Mind is stifled. The horizon's, The. Cape Mootch. Boris Pasternak, *Russian.* LoP, *tr. by* J. M. Cowen

Mind knows no death. Life is the "first and last." Albery Allson Whitman. AAP *Fr.* The Octoroon.

Mind of Absolute Trust, The. Seng-ts'an, *Chinese.* EnlH, *tr. by* Stephen Mitchell
    ("For the mind in harmony with the Tao.") ITG, *tr. by* Stephen Mitchell

Mind of man is this world's true dimension, The. Greville Fulke. NOSC *Fr.* A Treaty of Human Learning.

Mind of the Frontispiece to a Book, The. Ben Jonson. GS

Mind of the people is like mud, The. Talking with Soldiers. Walter James Turner. MoBrPo

Mind Pictures. Beatrice Hastings. PeSAV

Mind-Reader, The. Richard Wilbur. LCAP-2; NAAL-2; NoAM
    "What should I tell them?" CRP

Mind Reborn in Streatham Common, A. Richard Percival Lister. OBCoV

Mind returns to it always, The. Paul Blackburn. APSN *Fr.* The Selection of Heaven.

Mind to taste, the nerve to feel!, The. (LL) Departed Youth. Hannah Cowley. CABP; ECWP

Mind, with its own eyes and ears, The. The Mind's Liberty. W. H. Davies. MoBrPo

Minde through thee divines on endlesse things, The. Thomas Lodge. PBRV *Fr.* Scillaes Metamorphosis.

Minde well all this, nor let it fly thy powrs. Against sloth. Hesiod, *Greek.* OBCVT, *tr. by* George Chapman

Mindes of men are ever so affected, The. Homer. *Fr.* Odyssey. NAWM-1, *tr. by* Robert Fitzgerald

Mindful of the shambles of the day. Nightwalker. Thomas Kinsella.

Minding Ruth. Aidan Carl Mathews. BiHa; CIP-2; PBCIP

Minds awake in bodies that were asleep. Pandora and the Moon. Merrill Moore. MoAmPo

Mind's aches from Henry James, The. Satie, at the End of Term. Simon Curtis. NOBL; PeLV

Minds I admired, the strong-bodied, The. Robyn Selman. PUP-19

Mind's immortal, but the man is dead, The. (LL) Time and the Garden. Yvor Winters. GaP; MoAmPo; NoAM; VGW

Mind's Liberty, The. W. H. Davies. MoBrPo

Mine. Frank Polite. NYBP

Mine. Mary E. Tucker. CBWP-1

Mine and the sea-wind's. (LL) The Rose. Theodore Roethke. NOBA; NYBP; TRP

Mine angry and defrauded young? (LL) A Dead Statesman. Rudyard Kipling. FaBoEE; NBLV; OPOU; PoFWW; PoWW

Mine are the night and morning. Song of Nature. Ralph Waldo Emerson. APN-1

Mine be a cot beside the [*or* a] hill. A Wish. Samuel Rogers. FaPoR; GTBS-P; NOBE; OBEV; OxAEP-2

Mine be thy love and thy love's use their treasure. (LL) Sonnet 20. Shakespeare. HeIP-4; NAEL-1; NoP-4; NoSic; OAEL-1; OxAEP-1; PBRV

Mine—by the Right of the White Election! Emily Dickinson. APN-2; CBLP; NAAL-1; NAAL-3; NALW; NoP-4; PAR; WPoS

Mine Enemy is growing old. Emily Dickinson. RaBo

Mine eye and heart are at a mortal war. Sonnet 46. Shakespeare. HeIP-4 *Fr.* Sonnets.

Mine eye, mine [*or* myne] ear[e], my will, my wit[t], my h[e]art[e]. Sir John Davies. *Fr.* The Gulling[e] Sonnets. Son

Mine eyes beheld the blessed pity spring. Dante. AWP *Fr.* La Vita Nuova.

Mine eyes have seen the glory of the [coming of the Lord]. The Battle Hymn of the Republic. Julia Ward Howe. AH; APAD; APN-1; BLPA;

CBCWP; CH; CTV; ColAP; EBEvV; FaBoA; FaBoBe; FaPoR; ImPo; NOBA; NOCV; NoP-4; OBWP; PAR; PWR; SAGP; SCV; TAP; TFi; WPE

Mine eyes, like clouds, were drizzling rain. The Rainbow; or Curious Covenant. Robert Herrick. ChIV-1

Mine high estate, power and auctority. Sir Thomas More. NoSic

Mine—long as Ages steal! (LL) Mine—by the Right of the White Election! Emily Dickinson. APN-2; CBLP; NAAL-1; NAAL-3; NALW; NoP-4; PAR; WPoS

Mine only died. (LL) [Epitaph] In Obitum M.S., X° Maii, 1614. William Browne. FaBoEE; NOBE; OBEV

Mine own enough betray me. (LL) A Song: "Oh do[e] not wanton with those eyes." Ben Jonson. CBLP; SeCP

Mine [*or* Myne] own[e] John Poyntz [*or* Poins], since [*or* sins] ye delight to know. Myn owne John poyntz sins ye delight to know. Sir Thomas Wyatt. *See* Of the Courtier's Life. AAS; NoSic; OBSV; OBVE; PoEL-1; SCGP; SiPS *Fr.* Satires.

Mine owne good Bat, before thou hoyse up saile. Councell Given to Master Bartholmew Withipoll. George Gascoigne. AAS

Mine-Sweeping Trawlers. Edward Hilton, 1st Baron Kennet of the Dene Young. NSI

Mine was a midwest home—you can keep your world. One Home. William Stafford. CoAP; VGW

Miner Boy, The. *Unknown.* AmFP

Miner thus through perils digs his way, The. Thomas Yalden. ECEV *Fr.* To Sir Humphry Mackworth.

Mineral Kingdom. Jacques Dupin, *French.* VCWP, *tr. by* Paul Auster

Minerals of Cornwall, Stones of Cornwall. Peter Redgrove. FaBoMo

Miners. Branko Miljkovic, *Serbo-Croatian.* HSix, *tr. by* Charles Simic

Miners. Wilfred Owen. MoBrPo; NAEL-2; NOBE; NSI; OBWVE; OxAEP-2; PeFWW

Miners. James Wright. CoAmPo

Miner's Doom, The. *Unknown.* AmFP

Miner's Helmet, The. George MacBeth. OxBTC

Miner's Lament, The. *Unknown.* AmFP

Miners' Response, The. Dugald Sutherland MacColl. NSI

Miners' Wives. Joe Corrie. OxBS

Mines. Bruce Weigl. CDa

Minesweeper Sunk, A. Edward Davison. NSI

Ming will be over to make way for the Ch'ing, The. Barbarian Suite. Marilyn Chin. OpBo

Mingled / breath and smell. Subway Rush Hour. Langston Hughes. InPK-6; KaS

Mingled the moonlight with daylight—the last in the narrowing west. Thomas Hardy. Walter De la Mare. NoAM

Mingled Yarns. X. J. Kennedy. OBCA

Mingling my prayer. Saigyo, *Japanese.* AWP, *tr. by* Arthur Waley

Mingus. Bob Kaufman. PoBA

Mingus at the Showplace. William Matthews. SeSe

Mingus Speaks: Found Poems. George Barlow. ISC

Miniature. Eden Phillpotts. OxBSP

Miniature. Yannis Ritsos, *Greek.* VCWP, *tr. by* Edmund Keeley

Miniature Dialogue. Edmund Wilson. OBCoV

Minimal, The. Theodore Roethke. HCAP; MoP; NOBA; NoAM; RB

Mining in Killdeer Alley. Dabney Stuart. MT

Minister of birds, islands, and pools. Cortège for Colette. Jean Garrigue. NYBP

Minister said it wad [*or* wald] dee, The. Last Lauch. Douglas Young. NBLV; OxBS

Minister up in Vermont, A. Limerick. *Unknown.* PeLi

Minister's Death, The. Wesley McNair. AFr

Miniver Cheevy, child of scorn. Edwin Arlington Robinson. AWP; AmPP; CMoP; ChAP; ClHu; EBEvV; FaBoCh; HeIP-4; ImPo; LiTM; MoAmPo; MoP; NAAL-2; NOBA; NoAM; NoP-4; OBSV; OxBA; PFE; PeLV; PoEL-5; PoLF; PoRA; Poetr; RaBo; SCV; SoSe-8; TAP; TFi
    ("Miniver coughed, and called it fate, / And kept on drinking.") (LL) ColAP

Miniver Cheevy, Jr. David Fisher Parry. BXAP; NBLV

Minks, The. Toi Derricotte. NAmP90
    (Captivity: The Minks.) PuP-15

Minneapolis Poem, The. James Wright. FYAP; NoAM; UnPo

Minnetare Songs. *Unknown, Hidatsa (Crow).*
    Song of the Bald Eagle. APN-2
      ("We want what is real.") STP
    Song of the Bear. APN-2
    Song of the Elk. APN-2
    Song of the Gun. APN-2
    Song of the Pheasant. APN-2

Song of the Weasel. APN-2

Song of the White Man. APN-2

Minnie and Mrs. Hoyne. Kenneth Fearing. PoRA

Minnie and Winnie. Tennyson. FPC; OxBChV; TTTS

Minnie, I canna caa my wheel. Douglas Young, *after the Greek of* Sappho. OBVE

Minnow, go to sleep and dream. Lullaby for the Cat. Elizabeth Bishop. PC

Minor Bird, A. Robert Frost. CMoP; SAmP

Minor Elegy. Henriqueta Lisboa, *Portuguese.* BoWoP, *tr. by* Willis Barnstone *and* Nelson Cerqueira

Minor Elegy, A. "Igor Severyanin," *Russian.* TCRP, *tr. by* Bernard Meares

Minor Key. Judah Leib Teller, *Yiddish.* CEEP, *tr. by* Gabriel Preil *and* Howard Schwartz

Minor Mythology. David Avidan, *Hebrew.* IP, *tr. by* Warren Bargad *and* Stanley F. Chyet

Minor Poet, A. Amy Levy. VWP

Minor Things. Heather Ross Miller. MT

Minor Van Gogh (He Speaks), A. Alicia Ostriker. RACG

Minotaur Next Door, The. Greg Pape. PBCAP

Minotaur Poems. Eli W. Mandel.

"My father was always out in the garage." MoCV

Minott, Lee, Willard, Hosmer, Meriam, Flint. Hamatreya. Ralph Waldo Emerson. APN-1; NAAL-3; NCAP; PAR

Minstrel, The. James Beattie.

Youth of a Poet, The. NOEC

Minstrel. Michael Dransfield. BMAP

Minstrel, The. Goethe, *German.* AWP, *tr. by* James Clarence Mangan

Minstrel, The. Sir Walter Scott. OxAEP-2 *Fr.* The Lay of the Last Minstrel.

Minstrel and Genius, to whose songs or sighs. Autumnal Ode. Aubrey Thomas De Vere. OBNC

Minstrel Boy, The. Thomas Moore. FaBoBe; OxAEP-2

Minstrel Boy to the war is gone, The. Sir Thomas More. ChAP

Minstrel Responds to Flattery, The. Sir Walter Scott. OBNC *Fr.* The Lay of the Last Minstrel.

(Nature's Sympathy with the Poet.) OxAEP-2

Minstrel stirred, murmuring to the god, and soon, The. Demodocus sings the fall of Troy. Homer. OBCVT, *tr. by* Robert Fitzgerald *Fr.* The Odyssey.

Minstrels and Maids. William Morris. *See* The Outlanders.

Minstrel's Last Lay, The. John Barth. OBAL

Minstrels' Marriage-Song. Thomas Chatterton. *See* There Lackethe Somethynge Style.

Minstrels sing the jasmine songs. Peyanar. PLW *Fr.* Seven Said by the Foster-Mother. PLW, *tr. by* A. K. Ramanujan

Minstrel's Song. Thomas Chatterton. *See* Mynstrelle's Songe ("O! synge untoe mie roundelaie").

Minstrel's Song. Ted Hughes. OBCP

Mint bed is in / bloom: lavender haze, The. Sunday. James Schuyler. TTTS

Minted flesh of leaves, The. A Town Garden. Tony Lucas. OBGa

Minuet on Reaching the Age of Fifty, A. George Santayana. ImPo

Minukha, Minukha, here comes your Faigl's Rukhl. Poem for My Grandmother's Grandmother. Lesléa Newman. LoHo

Minute flowers harden. Depend. Lilies of the Valley. Jon Silkin. NoAM

Minute I heard my first love story, The. Jelaluddin Rumi, *Persian.* ITG, *tr. by* Coleman Barks; LoL, *tr. by* Coleman Barks

Minute of Consciousness, The. Imamu Amiri Baraka. APSN

Minutes are numbered by the fall of sands. John Ford. PoEL-2 *Fr.* The Lover's Melancholy.

Minutes grow tedious, Time too slowly moves. Maria to Henric. *Unknown.* KTR

Minutes of Gold. *Unknown.* PoToHe

Mips and ma the mooly moo. Theodore Roethke. CBNP; NBLV; RB *Fr.* Praise to the End! InPS-3

Mir träumte von einem Königskind. Heinrich Heine, *German.* AWP, *tr. by* Richard Garnett

Mir träumte wieder der alte Traum. Heinrich Heine, *German.* AWP, *tr. by* James Thomson

Mira, as they dear Edward's senses grow. Ann Yearsley. ECWP *Fr.* To Mira, On the Care of her Infant.

Mira is dancing with bells tied on her ankles. Mirabai, *Hindi.* BoWoP, *tr. by* Willis Barnstone *and* Usha Nilsson

Mira to Octavia. Mary Leapor. ECWP

Mirabeau Bridge, The. Guillaume Apollinaire, *French.* BoLoP, *tr. by* Quentin Stevenson; OBVE, *tr. by* W. S. Merwin

Mirabell: Books of Number. James Merrill.

"It starts in the small hours. An interlude." NoAM

"World was everything that was the case?, The." HCAP

Mirabell's Books of Number. James Merrill. *Fr.* The Changing Light at Sandover. NAAL-2

Miracle, The. Walter De la Mare. UnPo

Miracle, The. Carl Dennis. CMAP

Miracle. Susan Griffin. CrSp

Miracle, The. Boris Pasternak, *Russian.* GI, *tr. by* Nina Kossman

Miracle, The. Sir John Suckling. CaPo

Miracle. Wen Yi-tuo, *Chinese.* PFTM, *tr. by* Arthur Sze

Miracle Ice Cream. Adrienne Rich. BAP-93 *Fr.* Not Somewhere Else, But Here. BAP-93

Miracle Indeed, A. Swami Purohit. OBMV

Miracle Mart. Wislawa Szymborska, *Polish.* PoSu, *tr. by* Adam Czerniawski

Miracle of the Burd and the Fishes, The. Tom Leonard. FaBoTC

Miracle of the children the brilliant. Exodus. George Oppen. ChIV-1; KSG; MoLi

Miracle of the world, I never will deny. Henry Constable. SCGP *Fr.* Diana.

Miracle, this massive, drab constant of experience. (LL) The Constant. A. R. Ammons. HAP; WeW-3

Miracle Workers. Oleg Khlebnikov, *Russian.*

"From three sources, / vital sources flowing in dull shades of red." TCRP, *tr. by* Bradley Jordan

Miracles. Conrad Potter Aiken. MoAmPo

Miracles. Arna Bontemps. NAAAL

Miracles. Julia Randall. CRP

Miracles. Walt Whitman. PBMP; SAmP

Miracles at the Birth of Christ. Isaac Watts. NOCV

MIRACLES'S truck comes down the little avenue. Miracle Ice Cream. Adrienne Rich. BAP-93 *Fr.* Not Somewhere Else, But Here. BAP-93

Miraculous Dawn. R. Williams Parry, *Welsh.* OBWVE, *tr. by* Joseph P. Clancy

MIRACULOUS love's wounding! *Unknown.* NoSic

Miraculous Weapons, The. Aimé Césaire, *French.* PFTM, *tr. by* Clayton Eshleman *and* Annette Smith

Mirage. Richard Harteis. CMAP

Mirage. Christina Rossetti. BoLoP; PoRA

Mirage, The. Oscar Williams. LiTM

Miramar Beach. James Vincent Cunningham. PoA *Fr.* To What Strangers, What Welcome. NoAM

Miramichi Fire, The. *Unknown.* AmFP

Miranda. David Dabydeen. HCP

Miranda, remember that Inn? Limerick. John Stanley. PeLi

Mira's Picture, a Pastoral. Mary Leapor.

Portrait of the Artist, A. ECWP

Mira's Will. Mary Leapor. BWW; ECWP; NOEC; NoP-4; PEW

("In Body healthy, and compos'd in Mind.") (LL) CABP

Mirèio. Frédéric Mistral, *Provençal.*

Mares of the Camargue, The. AWP, *tr. by* George Meredith

Miriam. John Greenleaf Whittier.

Knowledge. PoToHe

Miriam and Horlick spend a great deal of time putting off going to bed. Goodnight. Stevie Smith. FaBoWP

Mirie it is, while sumer ilast. *Unknown.* MiEL

("Merry It Is.") HAP

Mirra Lokhvitskaia's ashes are now entombed. Prologue. "Igor Severyanin," *Russian.* TCRP, *tr. by* Bernard Meares

Mirror, The. Michael Davitt, *Irish.* BiHa; CIP-2; PBCIP, *tr. by* Paul Muldoon

Mirror. Peter De Vries. PoA

Mirror, A. Jean Follain, *French.* BLT, *tr. by* Czeslaw Milosz *and* Robert Hass

Mirror, The. Judah Halevi, *Hebrew.* TrJP, *tr. by* Emma Lazarus

Mirror, The. Mark Jarman. CMAP

Mirror. James Merrill. CoAP

Mirror, The. John N. Morris. PoA

Mirror. Sylvia Plath. FaBoWP; HAP; NIP-4; NYBP

Mirror, The. Isaac Rosenberg. NoAM

Mirror. Chimako Tada, *Japanese.* BoWoP; WPJ, *tr. by* Kenneth Rexroth *and* Ikuko Atsumi

Mirror, The. Sang Yi, *Korean.* CKP, *tr. by* Jaihiun Kim

Mirror copies everything it sees, A. Reflections on Mirrors. Elder Olson. CRP

Mirror for Detractors, A. Esther Lewis. ECWP

Mirror for Poets, A. Thom Gunn. LiTM

Mirror for the Barnyard. Jack Myers. AmPA

Mirror for the Twentieth Century, A. "Adunis," *Arabic*. AF, *tr. by* Abdullah Al-Udhari

Mirror in February. Thomas Kinsella. CIP-2; GTBS-P; NoAM

Mirror in hand. Tanka. Ishikawa Takuboku, *Japanese*. MJT, *tr. by* Ueda, Makoto

Mirror in the Deserted Hall, The. Felicia Dorothea Hemans. NOBRP

Mirror in Which Two Are Seen as One, The. Adrienne Rich. NAAL-2; NNaP

Mirror mirror tell me. Robert Graves. NOxBChV; NTP

Mirror, mirror, tell me. *Unknown*. ACTP

Mirror of a Day Chiming Marigold, The. Diane Wakoski. NALW

Mirror of Matsuyama, The. Sharon Hashimoto. OpBo

Mirror of men's eyes delights me less, The. Laus Virginitatis. Arthur Symons. EnLoPo

Mirror of poets, mirror of our age. Upon Ben Jonson [*or* Johnson]. Edmund Waller. BeJo; EPCY; NOSC

Mirror of the pond gleams, The. Thoughts While Reading. Chu Hsi, *Chinese*. OHPC, *tr. by* Kenneth Rexroth

Mirror Perilous, The. Alan Dugan. LiTM; TwCP

Mirror Poem. Rachel Blau DuPlessis. DeD

Mirrored by the spring. O. Mabson Southard. HA

Mirrors, The. Sophia de Mello Breyner Andresen, *Portuguese*. PBWP, *tr. by* Allan Francovich

Mirror's Song. Liz Lochhead. FaBoTC; NBrP

    ("In the cave she will claw out of— / a woman giving birth to herself.") (LL) FaBoTC

Mirrors, Without Song. Keorapetse Kgositsile. PBMAP   *Fr.* The Present is a Dangerous Place to Live.

Mirru. Kenneth Patchen. MoLi

Mirth. Christopher Smart. OxBChV   *Fr.* Hymns for the Amusement of Children.

Mirth and Melancholy. Margaret Lucas Cavendish, Duchess of Newcastle. WPE

Mirth and Poetry. Milton. EPCY   *Fr.* L'Allegro. AWP; FHYEP; GTBS-P; HAP; HoPM; ImPo; NOSC; NoP-4; OAEL-1; OBEV; PBRV; PoPoPo; TFi

Mirth, Spring, to linger in a garden fair. Hafiz. TAL, *tr. by* Gertrude Lowthian Bell   *Fr.* Odes.

Mirth with thee I mean to live. (LL) L'Allegro. Milton. AWP; FHYEP; GTBS-P; HAP; HoPM; ImPo; NOSC; NoP-4; OAEL-1; OBEV; PBRV; PoPoPo; TFi

Mirthful Lunacy. Thomas Tod Stoddart. OBNC   *Fr.* Death-Wake, The; or, Lunacy.

Mis Mai. Dafydd ap Gwilym, *Medieval Welsh*.

    "Duw gwyddiad mai da y gweddai." CABP, *tr. by* Arthur James Johnes

Mis-shapen Time, copesmate of ugly Night. Shakespeare. OAEL-1   *Fr.* The Rape of Lucrece.

Mis' Smith. Albert Bigelow Paine. PoLF

Misanthropist, The. James M. Whitfield. AAP

Misanthropos. Thom Gunn.

    Elegy on the Dust. NoAM

    Last Man, The. OxAEP-2

Misapprehension. Paul Laurence Dunbar. BPo

Miscellaneous Feelings. T'ang Yin, *Chinese*.

    "Galloping around, north and south." CoBLCP, *tr. by* Jonathan Chaves

Miscellaneous Feelings at West Lake. Ch'ien Ch'ien-i, *Chinese*. CoBLCP, *tr. by* Jonathan Chaves

Miscellaneous Feelings in the Sui Garden. Yüan Mei, *Chinese*. CoBLCP, *tr. by* Jonathan Chaves

Miscellaneous Impressions of T'an-chou. Yang Chi, *Chinese*.

    "Up at the prow, I wash my mouth, dripping water on my robe." CoBLCP, *tr. by* Jonathan Chaves

Miscellaneous Poems on Growing Old. Yüan Mei, *Chinese*. CoBLCP, *tr. by* Jonathan Chaves

Miscellaneous Poems on Lake Biwa. Liu Ya-tzu, *Chinese*.

    "Beyond the stream at Seta stretches an endless view." SuSp, *tr. by* Wu-chi Liu

    "By Flower-and-Moon Pavilion, I stay my carriage." SuSp, *tr. by* Wu-chi Liu

    "Cataracts flying down a thousand fathoms roll up a raging billow." SuSp, *tr. by* Wu-chi Liu

Miscellaneous Poems on Living in the Woods—In the Manner of Han Shan. Wang Chiu-ssu, *Chinese*.

    "Total failure——Master Han Shan, A." CoBLCP, *tr. by* Jonathan Chaves

Miscellaneous Poems on Spirit-Valley Temple. Wang T'ing-hsiang, *Chinese*. CoBLCP, *tr. by* Jonathan Chaves

Miscellaneous Poems Written in My Studio on an Autumn Day. Chu Yün-ming, *Chinese*. CoBLCP, *tr. by* Jonathan Chaves

Miscellaneous Poems Written in the Snow. Wang T'ing-hsiang, *Chinese*. CoBLCP, *tr. by* Jonathan Chaves

Miscellaneous Poems Written While in Jail. Ch'ien Ch'ien-i, *Chinese*. CoBLCP, *tr. by* Jonathan Chaves

Miscellaneous Words on the Lake. Tsung Ch'en, *Chinese*. CoBLCP, *tr. by* Jonathan Chaves

Miscellanies of the Year Chi-hai. Kung Tzu-chen, *Chinese*. SuSp, *tr. by* Irving Y. Lo

Mischief. Pong-gon Chon, *Korean*. CKP, *tr. by* Jaihiun Kim

Mischievous Raven, The. *Unknown*. OxNR

    ("Bumpety, bumpety, bump!") (LL) LB

    (Farmer and the Raven, The.) ReMoGo

Misconception, A. James Russell Lowell. OBAL

Misconceptions. Robert Browning. EnVR; OBEV

Mise en Scène. Robert Fitzgerald. NYBP; VGW

Miserable. Hyon-jong Chong, *Korean*. CKP, *tr. by* Jaihiun Kim

Miserable change now at my end, The. Shakespeare. EBEV   *Fr.* Antony and Cleopatra.

Miserere. David Gascoyne.

    Ecce Homo. ChIV-2; LiTM; NoP-4; OBWP; PeECV

    Ex Nihilo. GTBS-P

Miserere Domine! (LL) An Invocation: "Hear, sweet spirit, hear the spell." Coleridge. CH; PeECV

Miserere, My Maker. *Unknown*. NOCV

Miserere Nobis. Ioan Alexandru, *Romanian*. CEEP, *tr. by* Peter Jay *and* Virgil Nemoianu

Misericordia! James Lipton. NBLV

Misericordia. Margaret Mead. PoA

Miserimus. Adah Isaacs Menken. CBWP-1

Misery [*or* Miserie]. George Herbert. PoEL-2

Misery and Splendor. Robert Hass. VCAP

Misery is a good thing if misery is spread. John Holmes. NYBP

Misery o de Englishman, De. (LL) A Song for England. Andrew Salkey. HCP; PBCV

Misery of Jerusalem, The. Bible, *O.T.* AWP   *Fr.* Lamentations.

Misfortunes, insults—nothing ever rankled. Farewell to Autumn. Oleg Grigorevich Chukhonstev, *Russian*. TCRP, *tr. by* Simon Franklin

Misfortunes of Elphin, The. Thomas Love Peacock.

    War Song of Dinas Vawr, The. AWP; CABP; EBEvV; FaBoCh; FaPoR; HAP; NAEL-2; NOBE; NOBRP; NTP; OAEL-2; OxAEP-2

    ("And his overthrow, our chorus.") (LL) CABP; NOBRP

Misgivings. Herman Melville. APN-2; NAAL-1; NAAL-3; NCAP; NOBA; OxBA

Misguided. Harriet Brown. CrSp

Mishka [is poet among the beasts]. John Gray. ADE; NOBVV

Misled me to my ruin. Christina Rossetti. *See* The Queen of Hearts.

Misplaced Sympathy. Charles Follen Adams. OBAL

Misplacing—Mistaking. On Sir Nathaniel Wraxall the Historian. George, the Younger Colman. FaBoEE

Miss Bailey's Ghost. George, the Younger Colman. OxBoLi

Miss Beale and Miss Buss. (LL) Miss Buss and Miss Beale. *Unknown*. FaBoEE

Miss Betty's Singing-Bird. John Winstanley. NOEC

Miss Bitter. N. M. Bodecker. NTCP

Miss Blues'es Child. Langston Hughes. ChAP; SAmP; TTTS

Miss Buss and Miss Beale. *Unknown*. FaBoEE

    ("Are Miss Beale and Miss Buss.") (LL) OBCoV

Miss Carney handed us out blank paper and marla. Model School, Inchicore. Thomas Kinsella. CIP-2

Miss Cho Composes in the Cafeteria. James Tate. WeW-3

Miss Clement's Second Grade. Maryfrances Cusumano Wagner. UnSA

Miss Dinah when she goes to church. A Little More Cider. *Unknown*. KaS

Miss Edith's Modest Request. Bret Harte. NOxBChV

Miss Emily Brittle Sails for India. Sir George Dallas. NOEC   *Fr.* India Guide, The; or, Journal of a Voyage to the East Indies in 1780.

Miss Euphemia. John Crowe Ransom. CMoP

Miss Flora McFlimsey, of Madison Square. Nothing to Wear. William Allen Butler. OBAL; PoLF

Miss Florence Jackson. David Huddle. PBCAP

Miss F[——]ny M[——]t[——]ly to Miss P[——]y B[——]s. Fanny Macartney Greville. ECWP

Miss Foggerty's Cake. *Unknown*. BLPA; NBLV

Miss Gee. W. H. Auden. EBNV; OxBTC; UV

Miss Grant. Freda Downie. FaBoWP

Miss Helen Slingsby was my maiden aunt. Aunt Helen. T. S. Eliot. OBAL; PoA

Miss Ivy, tell me supmn. Wha Fe Call I'. Valerie Bloom. FaBoVe

Miss J. Hunter Dunn, Miss J. Hunter Dunn. A Subaltern's Love-Song. John Betjeman. APAD; BoLoP; EBEvV; HAP; NOBL; NoAM; OxAEP-2; OxBTC; TwCP

Miss Jennian Jones. *Unknown.* AmFP

Miss Kilmansegg and Her Precious Leg. Thomas Hood.

"Born in wealth and wealthily nursed." EBVV

Her Accident. EBVV

Her Christening. NOBVV

Her Death. NOBVV

Her Education. EBVV

Her Precious Leg. NOBVV

Miss Kilmansegg's Birth. OxBoLi; PeLV

Miss Lavender. Jon Stallworthy. OxBC

Miss Liza's Banjer. Daniel Webster Davis. AAP

Miss Loo. Walter De la Mare. CMoP; OxBTC

Miss Millay Says Something Too. Samuel Hoffenstein. BXAP; NBLV

Miss Muffett in a runaway ugly machine. I mean. Like that. (LL) W. W. Imamu Amiri Baraka. HeIP-4; NOBA; PoBA

Miss Nancy Ellicott. Cousin Nancy. T. S. Eliot. OBAL; OxBSP

Miss One, Two, and Three. *Unknown.* OxNR

Miss Own. Edward Kamau Brathwaite. HCP

Miss Pimberton Of. Siv Cedering Fox. PBCAP

Miss R. looks at the mantel-piece, which must mean something. (LL) Evening in the Sanitarium. Louise Bogan. FYAP; FaBoWP; NALW; TwCP

Miss Rafferty wore taffeta. The Private Dining Room. Ogden Nash. NYBP; OBCoV; PFE

Miss Riley stands above me, fading fast. Bailey Gatzert: The First Grade, 1945. Lonny Kaneko. LTA

Miss Rosie. Lucille Clifton. AmPA; BlSi; NMM-2; PoBA; Poetr; TwCP

Miss T. Walter De la Mare. FaBoBe; FuFo; NTCP

Miss Tourist. "Lord Kitchener." PBCV

Miss Tristram's *poulet* ended thus: 'Nota bene'. Mr. Placid's Flirtation. Frederick Locker-Lampson. PeVV

Miss Twye. Gavin Ewart. NOBL

Miss Universe, for Thy Name's Sake, Amen. (LL) Boom! Howard Nemerov. LiTM; NBLV; NIP-4

Miss Wilson's eyes, opaque. Public School No. 18: Paterson, New Jersey. Maria Gillan. UnSA

Miss You. David Cory. BLPA; FaBoBe

Miss You. *Unknown.* PoToHe

Missed Opportunity, A. James Tate. IFJA

Misses Norman lived on Marine Square, The. Cecil Gray. HCP

Missing, The. Thom Gunn. NoP-4

Missing. John Pudney. OxBTC

Missing, The. Yannis Ritsos, *Greek.* AF, *tr. by* Edmund Keeley

Missing a kick. Jack Kerouac. HA

Missing All—prevented Me, The. Emily Dickinson. APN-2

Missing Dates. William Empson. CMoP; HAP; LiTM; MoBrPo; MoP; NOBE; NoAM; OAEL-2; PoE; UnPo

Missing France. Jules Supervielle, *French.* MFP, *tr. by* Martin Sorrell

Missing from the map, the abandoned roads. Old Roads. Eiléan Ní Chuilleanáin. CIP-2; IIP

Missing head tells yet of the sacred day, The. The Victory of Samothrace. "Rubén Darío," *Spanish.* GS, *tr. by Unknown*

Missing Link. Sean Lucy. BiHa

Missing My Daughter. Stephen Spender. GTBS-P

Missing Patriarch, The. Michael S. Weaver. PBCAP

Missing Person, The. Donald Justice. NYBP; Poetr

Missing so much and so much? (LL) To a Fat Lady Seen from the Train. Frances Darwin Cornford. APAD; BLPA; EBEvV; FaBoWP; MoBrPo; OBMV; UV; WeW-3

Missing You. "Shu Ting," *Chinese.* VCWP, *tr. by* Carolyn Kizer

Mission. *Unknown.* AmFP

Mission Bay. John Koethe. PoA

Mission of the Flowers, The. Frances Ellen Watkins Harper. BlSi

Mission Street Manifesto. Juan Felipe Herrera. PaTW

Mission Work-Boat. *Unknown, Aborigine.* NOBAu, *tr. by* Mungayana Nundhirribala

Missionaries in the Jungle. Linda Piper. BlSi

Missionary, The. Mrs. Henry Linden. CBWP-4

Missionary Hymn. James Burke. TIRV

Mississippi. Aimé Césaire, *French.* NegPo, *tr. by* Clayton Eshleman *and* Denis Kelly

Mississippi. E. Ethelbert Miller. GT

Mississippi Blues. *Unknown.* AmFP

Mississippi China woman, / why do you wear blue jeans in the city? Lost Name Woman. Shirley Lim. UnSA

Mississippi 1955 Confessional. Terry Hummer. NAmP90

Mississippi Sawyer. *Unknown.* AmFP

Mississippi steamed in July. Civil Rights. Ira Sadoff. LTA

Missouri Sequence. Brian Coffey.

Nightfall, Midwinter, Missouri. CIP-2

"Inside the house is warm." IIP

Missouri, she's a mighty river. Shenandoah. *Unknown.* APN-2

Misspelled Tail, A. Elizabeth T. Corbett. OBCA

Misspelt scrawl, upon the wall, The. In an Album. James Russell Lowell. OBAL

Misstrums me, or tries a new tune. (LL) Player Piano. John Updike. PFE; Poetr; WeW-3

Mist. Bob Boldman. HA

Mist. Li Ch'ing-chao, *Chinese.* OHPC, *tr. by* Kenneth Rexroth

Mist. Henry David Thoreau. AWP; AmPP; OxBA *Fr.* A Week on the Concord and Merrimack Rivers.

Mist, The. *Unknown.* ReMoGo

Mist and All, The. Dixie Willson. CTV

Mist and water of Five Lakes, this body not gone home. Ni Tsan. *Fr.* Two Poems to the Tune "Hsiao-t'iao hung." CoBLCP, *tr. by* Jonathan Chaves

Mist clears and the cavities, The. Derry Morning. Derek Mahon. IIP; NOIV

Mist enfolding the mountainsides, The. The Law of Fall. Jaihiun Kim, *Korean.* CKP, *tr. by* Jaihiun Kim

Mist floats on the Spring meadow. Yakamochi, *Japanese.* OHPJ, *tr. by* Kenneth Rexroth

Mist Forms. Carl Sandburg. CMoP

Mist in the palace willows, The. Echoing Old Man Mu's Poem, "Inscribed on Shen Lang-ch'ien's Little Landscape, Autumn Willows at Stone Cliff." Wang Shih-chieng, *Chinese.* CoBLCP, *tr. by* Jonathan Chaves

Mist Maiden, The. Henrietta Cordelia Ray. CBWP-3

Mist of pain has covered my dour old heart, A. Valentine Browne. Egan O'Rahilly, *Irish.* NOIV, *tr. by* Thomas Kinsella

Mist rauk is hanging, The. Song. John Clare. NOBVV

Mist where Genesis begins, The. (LL) To the Man after the Harrow. Patrick Kavanagh. CIP-2; GTBS-P

Mistah Berrybones, you daid? Ode. William Zaranka. BXAP

Mistake, A. Aleksandr Arkadevich Galich, *Russian.* TCRP, *tr. by* Albert C. Todd

Mistake. Haim Guri, *Hebrew.* IP, *tr. by* Warren Bargad *and* Stanley F. Chyet

Mistake, The. Theodore Roethke. OBCoV *Fr.* Three Epigrams. NBLV

Mistaken bird, ah whither hast thou strayed? Elegy on a Young Thrush Which Escaped from the Writer's Hand. Helen Maria Williams. ECWP

Mistaken fair, lay Sherlock by. Verses Written in a Lady's Sherlock "Upon Death." Philip Stanhope. EBEV; NOEC

Mistakes. Ella Wheeler Wilcox. PoToHe

Mistakes are dredged up again. Unalterables. Arthur Gregor. NYBP

Mister B. Rajan, diamond buyer. Fellow Passenger. Valerie Gillies. FaBoTC

Mister Backlash, Mister Backlash. The Backlash Blues. Langston Hughes. BPo

Mister Beers. Hugh Lofting. FuFo

Mister Brown. Rodney Bennett. BoTP

Mister East gave a feast. The Winds. *Unknown.* ReMoGo

Mister Johnson. Ben Harney. OBAL

Mister Lizard is Crying. Federico García Lorca, *Spanish.* TTTS, *tr. by* William Bryant Logan

Mister MacCall at Cleveland Hall. James Thomson. NOBVV

Mister Snow Man. Bertha Wilcox Smith. CTV

Mister Snowman. Joleen Urriola. CTV

Mister Socrates Snooks, a lord of creation. Socrates Snooks. Fitz Hugh Ludlow. BLPA

Mister Williams / lets youn me move. Uncle Iv Surveys His Domain from His Rocker. Jonathan Williams. NBLV; OBAL

Mister Winkler Winkler oh. Devil and the Princess. *Unknown.* FaBoVe

Mistletoe. Mary E. Tucker. CBWP-1

Mistletoe Bough, The. Thomas Haynes Bayly. BLPA

Mistletoe hung in the castle hall, The. The Mistletoe Bough. Thomas Haynes Bayly. BLPA

Mistral. Barbara Howes. NYBP

Mistral blows, the plane leaves, The. On the Eve of the Plebiscite. Kenneth Rexroth. NNaP

Mistress, The. Joan Barton. OxBTC

Mistress, The. Abraham Cowley.

Against Fruition. BeJo; NOSC

Against Hope. MeLP; NOSC

("Hope, whose weak being ruin'd is.") CABP

(On Hope.) CABP; NOBE

Change, The. CBLP; MeLP; SeCP

Platonic[k] Love. BeJo; NoP-4

Spring, The. BeJo; HAP; MeLP; OxAEP-1

Welcome, The. BoLoP

Wish, The. NOBE; NOSC; NoP-4; OBEV; OxAEP-1; PBRV

Written in Juice of Lem[m]on. SeCP

("Yet like them when they're burnt in sacrifice.") (LL) CABP

Mistress, The. John Wilmot, 2d Earl of Rochester. *See* Mistress, The: A Song.

Mistress allows an average lover, A. To His Coy Mistress. John Flood. BXAP

Mistress, Behold, in This True-Speaking Glass. Barnabe Barnes. Son *Fr.* Parthenophil and Parthenope.

Mistress Comfort. Elizabeth Gould. BoTP

Mistress Indiarubber Duck. D. Carter. BoTP

Mistress Jenny Wren. Rodney Bennett. BoTP

Mistress keeps her lover on his toes, A. Ovid. OBCVT, *tr.* by Ben Jonson *Fr.* Catiline his Conspiracy.

Mistress Macintosh. Rodney Hall. CBAP

Mistress Malone. Eleanor Farjeon. OxBChV

Mistress Margaret Hussey. John Skelton. *See* To Mistress [*or* Maystres] Margaret Hussey.

"Mistress Mary is dead and gone!" (LL) Telling the Bees. John Greenleaf Whittier. APN-1; AWP; ColAP; GEA; NOBA; NoP-4; PAR; TAP

Mistress of all my senses can invite. To Caelia. Richard Duke. NOSC

Mistress of green in flowers arrayed. Acrostics. George Moses Horton. AAP

Mistress of Vision, The. Francis Thompson. CH

Mistress Peck-Pigeon. Eleanor Farjeon. NTCP

Mistress Severin. Winfield Townley Scott. InPK-6

("Mrs. Severin came home from the Methodist Encampment.") SAGP

Mistress [*or* Mistris], since you so much desire. Mistris [*or* Mistress] Since You So Much Desire. Thomas Campion. OAEL-1

Mistress, The: A Song. John Wilmot, 2d Earl of Rochester. EBEV; NOBE; NOSC

(Mistress, The.) OxAEP-1; PFE

Mistress Towl. *Unknown.* OxBChV

Mistresse, A. Ausonius, *Latin.* OBCVT, *tr.* by *Unknown*

Mistris [*or* Mistress] Since You So Much Desire. Thomas Campion. OAEL-1

Mistrustful minds be moved. Sir Thomas Wyatt. SiPS

Mists Over the River. William Carlos Williams. ColAP

Mists rise over, The. Akahito, *Japanese.* HoPM; OHPJ, *tr.* by Kenneth Rexroth

Misunderstood. Lizelia Augusta Jenkins Moorer. CBWP-3

Mitchells, The. Les A. Murray. BMAP

Mitching. Michael Smith. CIP-2

Mite, The. Boynton Merrill, Jr. CRP

Mither's Lament, The. Sydney Goodsir Smith. FaBoTC; OxBS

("Whit care I for the leagues o sand.") FaBoTC

Mithridates. Ralph Waldo Emerson. APN-1; NCAP; NOBA

("Vein and artery, though ye kill me!") (LL) NOBA

Mithridates, he died old. (LL) Terence, this is stupid stuff. A. E. Housman. CABP; CMoP; HeIP-4; InPK-6; LiTM; MoBrPo; MoP; NAEL-2; NoAM; NoP-4; PFE; Poetr; TFi

Mitten Song, The. Marie Louise Allen. NTCP

Mix a Pancake. Christina Rossetti. NTCP *Fr.* Sing-Song.

(Pancake, The.) BoTP

Mix a pancake, / Stir a pancake. Christina Rossetti. BoTP; NTCP

Mix up. Callaloo. Merle Collins. NBrP

Mixed Emotions. Huang Ching-jen, *Chinese.* SuSp, *tr.* by Chang Yin-nan *and* Lewis C. Walmsley

Mixed Feelings. John Ashbery. HAP; WeW-3

Mixed Marriage, The. Paul Muldoon. PNI

Mixed Sketches. Don L. Lee. BPo; TAP

Mixed with age, she could foresee the future. Paul Evans. NBrP *Fr.* Two Sonnets.

Mixed with quartz grains, rose and amethyst. (LL) Sandpiper. Elizabeth Bishop. AFr; AiP; HeIP-4; NYBP; RB; TOF

Mixed with the shanties of the deep-sea men. (LL) Exotic Scent. Charles Baudelaire, *French.* EP; FLP, *tr.* by Alistair Elliot

Mixer, The. Louis MacNeice. FP; FaBoTw

Mixing fresher Air. (LL) It sounded as if the Streets were running. Emily Dickinson. NAAL-1; NAAL-3; OxBSP; PBWP

Mixtures of this garden, The. In the Garden: Villa Cleobolus. Lawrence Durrell. OBGa

Mizpah. Julia Aldrich Baker. BLPA; FaBoBe

Mmenson. Edward Kamau Brathwaite. OPOU

Mnasylla, the daughter you lament. Perses, *Greek.* GrAn, *tr.* by Peter Whigham

Mnemonic. Li-Young Lee. UnSA

Mnemosyne. Madison Cawein. APN-2

Mnemosyne. Trumbull Stickney. APN-2; GEA; NOBA; OxBA

Mnemosyne Lay in Dust. Austin Clarke.

"Maurice was in an Exhibition Hall." PoE

"One night he heard heart-breaking sound." CIP-2; CMoP

"Past the house where he was got." CMoP; PoE

"Rememorised, Maurice Devane." CMoP

"Straight-jacketing sprang to every lock." CMoP

Moanish Lady. *Unknown.* AS

Mob, The. Mcavoy Layne. CDa

Mob of dressing-tables is grazing, A. Duchesses. David Campbell. NOBAu

Mobile-Buck. James Edwin Campbell. AAP

Möbius Strip-Tease. Alec Derwent Hope. OBCoV

Moby Dick. Herman Melville.

Whale, The.

Mock Charon, A. Richard Lovelace. CaPo

Mock-Epic Satire. Walter Harte. EPCY

Mock Invocation to Genius, A. William Woty.

"I now solicit not the Muses nine." NOEC

Mock on, Mock on Voltaire, Rousseau. William Blake. ChIV-1; HAP; ImPo; NAEL-2; NAWM-2; NoP-4; OAEL-2; OBNC; OxBSP; PFE; PeECV; PoE; PoEL-4; SCGP; TFi; UnPo

Mock Orange. Louise Glück. NoAM; PoPoPo; SAGP; VCAP

Mock Song, A. Richard Lovelace. BeJo; CaPo

Mock Turtle's Song, The. "Lewis Carroll." *See* A Lobster Quadrille.

Mock up again, summer, the sooty altars. Spectacular Blossom. Allen Curnow. PeNZ

Mocking-Bird, The. Joseph Rodman Drake. APN-1

Mocking-Bird, The. Richard Hovey. APN-2

Mocking Bird, The. Sidney Lanier. APN-2

Mocking Bird, The. Richard Lewis. APo *Fr.* A Journey from Patapsko to Annapolis.

Mocking Bird, The. *Unknown.* AmFP

Mocking-bird on a branch, A. Wyncote, Pennsylvania: A Gloss. Thomas Kinsella. NOIV

Mocking-Bird's Song, The. *Unknown, Tigua Native American.* APN-2, *tr.* by Alice C. Fletcher

Mocking Fairy, The. Walter De la Mare. MoBrPo

Mocking taunt, See then whether you shall be master!, The. (LL) Walt Whitman, a kosmos, of Manhattan the son. Walt Whitman. ColAP; NoP-4

Mocking the charm of death. O God, it knows! (LL) A Dying Viper. "Michael Field." ADE; CABP

Mockingbird, The. Randall Jarrell. NYBP

Mockingbird had been following the cat, The. Charles Bukowski. PmAP

Mode of France, The. *Unknown.* PBRV

Model, The. May Probyn. VWP

Model children of the regime, The. Nguyễn Chí Thiện, *Vietnamese.* VCWP, *tr.* by Huynh Sanh Thông

Model Church, The. John H. Yates. PWR

Model for the Laureate, A. W. B. Yeats. CMoP

Model School, Inchicore. Thomas Kinsella. CIP-2

Model stands in the pale composure of his nakedness, The. Life Drawing. Richard Foerster. BAP-94

Models. Howard Nemerov. AF

Moder Phoebe. *Unknown.* FaBoVe

Moderation. Robert Herrick. FaBoEE

Moderation. Christopher Smart. NOCV *Fr.* Hymns for the Amusement of Children.

Modern Baby, The. William Croswell Doane. BLPA

Modern circus, The. Pierre McOrlan, *French.* MFP, *tr.* by Martin Sorrell

Modern composer called Cage, A. Limerick. Peter Alexander. PeLi

Modern Critics. Coleridge. FaBoEE

Modern Declaration. Edna St. Vincent Millay. SAGP

Modern delinquents. Vices of the Modern World. Nicanor Parra, *Spanish.* CLPP, *tr.* by Jorge Elliott

Modern Female Fashions. Mary Robinson. NOBRP

Modern Fine Gentleman, The. Soame Jenyns.
  "Just broke from school, pert, impudent, and raw." ECEV; OBSV
Modern Fine Lady, The. Soame Jenyns. NOEC
  "But soon th'endearments of a husband cloy." ECEV
  "For love no time has she, or inclination." OBSV
Modern Hiawatha, The. George A. Strong. EBEvV; OBCoV; PeLV; UV
  Fr. The Song of Milkanwatha.
  (Hiawatha Revisited.) BXAP
Modern Love. Keats. CBLP; OBNC; SCGP
Modern Love. George Meredith.
  30. CABP
  "All other joys of life he strove to warm." EnVR
  "Along the garden terrace, under which." NOBVV
  "At dinner, she is hostess, I am host." EnVR; NOBVV; PoE; Son
  "But where began the change; and what's my crime?" PoEL-5
  Dusty Answer, A.
  "He felt the wild beast in him betweenwhiles." EnVR; NOBVV
  "He found her by the ocean's moaning verge." EnVR; NoP-4; OAEL-2
  "Here Jack and Tom are paired with Moll and Meg." EnVR; PoEL-5
  "I am to follow her. There is much grace." NAEL-2; NOBVV
  "I play for Seasons; not Eternities!" OBNC; SCGP
  "I think she sleeps: it must be sleep, when low." NAEL-2
  "It chanced his lips did meet her forehead cool." CBLP; EnVR; NOBVV
  "It ended, and the morrow brought the task." EnVR
  "It is no vulgar nature I have wived." NAEL-2
  "It is the season of the sweet wild rose." GBL; PoEL-5
  Love Dies.
  Love's Grave. OBEV
  "Madam would speak with me. So, now it comes." NOBVV
  "Message from her set his brain aflame, A." EnVR; NOBVV
  Modern Love. GLoP; NoP-4
  (End of Love, The.) HoPM
  "My lady unto Madam makes her bow." NOBVV
  "Not solely that the Future she destroys." GBL
  "Out in the yellow meadows, where the bee." GBL
  "She issues radiant from her dressing-room." EnVR; NOBVV
  Sonnet 29: "Am I failing? For no longer can I cast." PFE
  "Their sense is with their senses all mixed in." NAEL-2; NoP-4; OAEL-2; SCGP
  "This golden head has wit in it. I live." NOBVV
  "This was the woman; what now of the man?" EnVR; Son
  "'Tis Christmas weather, and a country house." NAEL-2; NOBVV
  "We saw the swallows gathering in the sky." EnLoPo; GTBS-P; NOBE; NOBVV; OAEL-2; OBNC
  "We three are on the cedar-shadowed lawn." NOBVV
  "Yet it was plain she struggled, and that salt." EnVR
  "You like not that French novel? Tell me why." EnVR; NOBVV
Modern Love Songs. Unknown, Somali. TTY, tr. by B. W. Andrzejewski and I. M. Lewis
Modern Major-General, The. Sir William Schwenck Gilbert. See I Am the Very Model [or Pattern] of a Modern Major-General.
Modern malady of love is nerves, The. Nerves. Arthur Symons. CABP; FaBoTw
Modern Male Fashions. Mary Robinson. NOBRP
Modern Manners. Mary Alcock. ECWP
Modern Moses, or "My Policy" Man. James Madison Bell. AAP
Modern Mother, The. Alice Thompson Meynell. VWP
Modern on the Surface. Nia Francisco. HATNAP
Modern Poet, The. Mary Davys.
  "Behind the moth-eaten curtain, 'stead of press." ECWP
Modern Secrets. Shirley Lim. OPOU; UnSA
Modern Theologian, A. Paul Ramsey. Fr. Three Epigrams. CRP
Modern Times. Nicanor Parra, Spanish. AF, tr. by Miller Williams
Modern Times. Janet Sylvester. BAP-94
Modern World, The. Colin Ellis. FaBoEE
Modern young curate called Hyde, A. Limerick. D. W. Pain. PeLi
Modes of Pleasure. Thom Gunn. EP
Modes of the court, The. John Gay. Fr. The Beggar's Opera. OAEL-1
Modes of Vallejo Street, San Diego, Los Angeles, The. Hugh Seidman. UnPo
Modest chair people painted grey. People. Hans Arp, German. PFTM, tr. by Rosemarie Waldrop
Modest Proposal, A. Ted Hughes. CABP
Modest rose puts forth a thorn, The. The Lily. William Blake. FHYEP; NOBRP; Ro Fr. Songs of Experience.
Modest sinner stood behind, The. Navigation. Ralph Knevet. NOSC

Modest Wit, A. Selleck Osborn. BLPA
Modest young maiden of Rennes, A. Limerick. A. C. Cossins. PeLi
Modestly we violets cower. Violets. P. A. Ropes. BoTP
Modesty. Aaron Hill. OxBSP
Modo and Alciphron. Sylvia Townsend Warner. MoBrPo
Mœurs Contemporaines. Ezra Pound and Noel Stock.
  "They will come no more." UV
Moggy's Wedding. Charles Robert Thatcher. NOBAu
Mohawk lover who told her he stripped all his clothes, The. Deer Cloud. Susan Clements. UnSA
Mohini Chatterjee. W. B. Yeats. NoAM
Moiré. Michael McClure. SPE
Moishele, Moishele / Moses Maimonides. Double Dactyls. Eric Salzman. OBCoV
Moist Moon People. Carl Sandburg. MoAmPo
Moist with one drop of thy blood, my dry soul. Donne. See Resurrection.
Mokau roars, Tamaki roars. Lament for Tawhiao. Unknown, Maori. PeNZ, tr. by Margaret Orbell
Molasses River. Richard Kendall Munkittrick. OBCA
Mole, The. Al-Muntafil. RaBo, tr. by Robert Bly
Mole, The. Dennis Schmitz. AmPA
Mole and the Eagle, The. Sarah Josepha Buell Hale. OBCA
Mole Catcher. Edmund Blunden. OBMV
Mole-Catcher, The. John Clare. EnVR
Mole is blind, and under ground, The. The Mole and the Eagle. Sarah Josepha Buell Hale. OBCA
Mole makes his pole redhot. Alonzo Gonzales, Navajo Indian. STP, tr. by Jerome Rothenberg
Mole who knows. Back to Base. Jenny Joseph. BrRo
Moles. Aileen Fisher. CTV
Moles. William Stafford. NYBP
Moll-in-the-wad and I fell out. Unknown. OxNR
Mollis Abuti. As Sonata in Praes o Molli. Jonathan Swift. CBLP
Molly. Maurice Kenny. MoLi
Molly Means. Margaret Abigail Walker. BlSi; NALW; NMM-2
Molly Mog [or The Fair Maid of the Inn]. John Gay. OBCoV
Molly Moor. George Farewell. NOEC
Molly, my sister and I fell out. Coffee and Tea. Unknown. ReMoGo
Molly raised shy eyes to me. A Triolet. Angelina Weld Grimké. CPO
Moly. Thom Gunn. CABP; HAP; MoP; NoAM; Poetr
Mom made me dust the living room while. Telepathy. Linda Besant. IFJA
Moment, A. Mary Elizabeth Coleridge. LW; PEW
Moment. John Daniel. PaTW
Moment, The. Sharon Olds. CrSp
Moment, The. Theodore Roethke. NYBP
Moment. Tadeusz Różewicz, Polish. CEEP, tr. by Victor Contoski
Moment, The. William Stafford. NNaP
Moment, The. Tanka. Kondō Yoshimi, Japanese. MJT, tr. by Makoto Ueda
Moment Ago, A. David Avidan, Hebrew. IP, tr. by Warren Bargad and Stanley F. Chyet
Moment ago the shrill flute whistled in the bridal chamber, A. Philip of Thessalonica, Greek. GrAn, tr. by Edwin Morgan
Moment an object falls, The. Hands. Namsu Park, Korean. CKP, tr. by Jaihiun Kim
Moment comes to me, A. This Bridge Across. Christopher Gilbert. GT
MOMENT IN A SIDE AISLE, *A. Artistic Copy. Tymoteusz Karpowicz, Polish. CEEP, tr. by Zak, Ewa
Moment in the box of jade, A. Bob Boldman. HA
Moment of battle, The. Publius Papinius Statius, Latin. OBCVT, tr. by William S. Lewis
Moment of Eschatological Doubt, A. Stanley J. Sharpless. PeLV
Moment of My Father's Death, The. Sharon Olds. NAmP90; NIP-4
Moment of Parting. Stefan Aug. Doinas, Romanian. CEEP, tr. by Peter Jay and Petru Popescu
Moment of silence, first, then there it is, A. The Dial Tone. Howard Nemerov. NYBP
Moment of Truth. Rowley Habib. PeNZ
Moment of Truth, The. David Lehman. WWSi
Moment of Waking, The. John Tranter. BMAP
Moment of War, A. Laurie Lee. OBWP
Moment Please, A. Samuel Allen. PoBA; SSLK
Moment the children climb, The. From the Temple of Longing. Roger Weingarten. NAmP90
Moment the wild swallows like a flight, A. A Thunderstorm. Archibald Lampman. NOBC
Moment to / moment the / body seems. Time. Robert Creeley. LCAP-2

Moment yellow, just as four years later when, A. Lyn Hejinian. PmAP
Fr. My Life.
Moments. Ivor Gurney. OxBSP
Moments. Jane King. HCP
Moments. Marcel Schwob, French. TrJP, tr. by William Brown Meloney
Moments He Remembers, The. Mark Van Doren. NYBP
Moment's memory to that laurelled head, A. (LL) Coole Park, 1929. W. B. Yeats. CABP; IIP; OAEL-2; OBMV
Moments of Fullfillment——Writing Down Miscellaneous. Yüan Mei, Chinese. CoBLCP, tr. by Jonathan Chaves
Moments of Summer. Rachel Hadas. RA
Moments of Vision. Thomas Hardy. OAEL-2
Momentum and wash of the undefined. Platonic Subject. Anne Lauterbach. PmAP
Momma a carrot grows underground. Potlicker Blues. Calvin Forbes. GT
Momma dear, and Poppa dear. Questions and Answers (a ballad). James Kirkup. SpW
Momma had words for us. Momma Sayings. Harryette Mullen. IFJA; ISC
Momma Momma Momma. Getting Down to Get Over. June Jordan. TAP
Momma Sayings. Harryette Mullen. IFJA; ISC
Momma Welfare Roll. Maya Angelou. SAGP
Momma's in the bedroom / with the door closed. Audre Lorde. See Hanging Fire.
"Mommy, take me home. I'm a changed boy!" Ontogeny. Jarold Ramsey. NIP-4
Mom's in the kitchen telling stories. Vesta's Father. Julia Kasdorf. PBCAP
Momus' Song to Mars. Dryden. OxBSP Fr. The Secular Masque. NAEL-1; OxAEP-1; PoE; PoEL-3; SCGP
Mon in the mone stond and strit. Man in the Moon. Unknown. MiEL
Mon that wist for raine, The. Amedie Eva List. BXAP
Mona Lisa, A. Angelina Weld Grimké. BlSi
Mona Lisa. Walter Pater. OBMV
Mona Lisa. Edith Wharton. GS
Mona Lisa Tea Towel, The. Nigel Roberts. BMAP
Monadnoc. Ralph Waldo Emerson.
    "Every morn I lift my head." APN-1
Monadnock, The. John Gould Fletcher. PoA
Monangamba. Antonio Jacinto, Portuguese. TTY, tr. by Alan Ryder ("—Monangambee.. . . .") (LL) PBMAP
Monarch of Gods and Dæmons, and all Spirits. Shelley. NAEL-2; OAEL-2 Fr. Prometheus Unbound. NOBRP; OAEL-2
Monarch of the Sea. George Starbuck. OBAL
Monarche, The. Sir David Lindsay.
    After the Flood. ChIV-1; OxBS
Monarchs. Sharon Olds. LoHo
Monastery, The. Sir Walter Scott.
    Blue Bonnets over the Border. OxBS
    Book of Books, The. ChIV-1
Monastery on Mount Hill-and-Stream, The. Unknown, Vietnamese. AVP, tr. by Huỳnh Sanh Thông
Monastic Outhouse. Aleksandar Ristovic, Serbo-Croatian. HSix, tr. by Charles Simic
Mond ist aufgegangen, Der. Heinrich Heine, German. AWP, tr. by James Thomson
Monday. Vijaya Mukhopadhyay, Bengali. OMIP, tr. by Sunil B. Ray and Carolyne Wright and Vijaya Mukhopadhyay
Monday. Space-Shuttle. Judith Nicholls. SpW
Monday. William Stafford. NYBP
Monday I found a boot. Beachcomber. George Mackay Brown. FaBoTC; NTP; OxBC
Monday mornings Grandma rose an hour early to make rye. Pumpernickel. Philip Schultz. NAmP90
Mondays are meshed with Tuesdays. Too Many Names. Pablo Neruda, Spanish. VCWP, tr. by Alastair Reid
Monday's child is fair of face. Birthdays. Mother Goose. BLPA; BoTP; FaBoBe; FaBoCh; LB; NBLV; OTCP; OxNR; ReMoGo
Monday's child is fair of face. Unknown. ACTP; CTV
Mondays my aunt awoke with the first cockrow, in the orange dawn. Those Rainy Mornings. Frank Mkalawile Chipasula. HBAPE
Monet: 'Les Nymphéas'. W. D. Snodgrass. CoAP; CoAmPo
Monet never knew. Monet's Lilies Shuddering. Lawrence Ferlinghetti. PmAP
Monet Refuses the Operation. Lisel Mueller. FYAP
Monet's Lilies Shuddering. Lawrence Ferlinghetti. PmAP
Monet's "Waterlilies." Robert Earl Hayden. GT; Poetr
Money. Richard Armour. NBLV
Money. W. H. Davies. OBEV; OBMV

Money. Howard Nemerov. OxBC; VCAP; WeW-3
Money. Bob Perelman. FTOS
Money. Charles Hubert Sisson. APAD; OxBSP
Money. Unknown. AS
Money and a Friend. Unknown. BLPA
Money and the Mare. Unknown. ReMoGo
Money burns the pocket, pocket hurts. Seventh Street. Jean Toomer. NAAL-2
Money Cry, The. Peter Davison. FYAP
Money Gets the Mastery [or Masterie]. Robert Herrick. CaPo
Money Isn't Everything! Oscar Hammerstein, II. OBAL
Money Makes the Mirth. Robert Herrick. CaPo
Money men collect in high rise, The. Thumbing Old Magazines. Gerald Vizenor. VoR
Money, money, now hay goode day! Unknown. CABP; MiEL
Money thou ow'st me; prithee fix a day. Upon Bunce: Epigram. Robert Herrick. CaPo
Moneyless Men, The. Henry T. Stanton. BLPA
Moneylight. Diane Wakoski. NMM-2
Mongol Libation. Victor Segalen, French. NNPT, tr. by Nathaniel Tarn
Mongoloid boy is astounded, The. In the Dome Car of the "Canadian." Sid Marty. NOBC
Mongoloid Child Handling Shells on the Beach, A. Richard Snyder. InPK-6
Mongo's open hands. Shaking Hands with Mongo. Martín Espada. SeSe
Mongrel, The. Thomas Hardy. APo
Monk. John Taggart. FTOS
Monk and His Pet Cat, The. Unknown, Old Irish. CH
Monk and the Peasant, The. Margaret E. Bruner. PoToHe
Monk Arnulphus uncorked his ink, The. The Court Historian. George Walter Thornbury. PeVV
Monk at the Five Spot. Crepuscule with Nellie. Charles Simic. SeSe
Monk does own a frock—a bonnet too, The. The Bonze Got Stung By a Bee. Ho Xuan Huong, Vietnamese. AVP, tr. by Huỳnh Sanh Thông
Monk from Shu, carrying a precious lute. Listening to a Monk from Shu Playing the Lute. Li Po, Chinese. SuSp, tr. by Joseph J. Lee
Monk in the Kitchen, The. Anna Hempstead Branch. MoAmPo
Monk of Auspicious Fortune Monastery Asking Me to Name a Pavilion, A. Su Shih, Chinese. SuSp, tr. by Chiang Yee
Monk of Casal-Maggiore, The (The Sicilian's Tale). Henry Wadsworth Longfellow. AmPP; OxBA Fr. Tales of a Wayside Inn.
Monk sat in his den, The. The Weak Monk. Stevie Smith. BoWoP; FaBoTw
Monk, step further off. Unknown. NOIV
Monk there was, a monk of mastery [or a fair for the maistrye] [or maistrie], A. Seven Pilgrims: A Monk. Chaucer. OBCoV Fr. The General Prologue. FHYEP; NAEL-1; NAWM-1; OAEL-1; PoE Fr. The Canterbury Tales.
Monkey, The. Avianus, Latin. OBCVT, tr. by David R. Slavitt
Monkey. Vladislav Felitsianovich Khodasevich, Russian. TCRP, tr. by Michael Frayn
Monkey. Josephine Miles. LiTM
Monkey. Bruce Weigl. CDa
Monkey and the Lion, The. The Signifying Monkey. Unknown. CrDW; NAAAL
Monkey exclaimed with great glee, A. Limerick. Frank Richards. PeLi
Monkey, lap-dog, parrot, and her Grace, The. Sir Charles Hanbury Williams. NOEC Fr. Isabella; or, The Morning.
Monkey married the Baboon's sister, The. The Monkey's Wedding. Unknown. AS; BLPA
Monkeyland. Sándor Weöres, Hungarian. RB, tr. by Edwin Morgan
Monkeys. Frank A. Collymore. PBCV
Monkeys. Padraic Colum. OxBTC
Monkeys, The. Marianne Moore. CMoP; MeMAP; NOBA; OxBA
Monkeys and the Crocodile, The. Laura Elizabeth Richards. CTV
Monkeys in a forest. Where. Walter De la Mare. NYBP
Monkeys looked from their cages, The. Alien at the Zoo. Pamela Gillilan. SpW
Monkeys on Mt. Hiei. Edith Marcombe Shiffert. WPE
Monkey's Pride. John Forbes. BMAP
Monkey's Wedding, The. Unknown. AS; BLPA
Monkeys winked too much and were afraid of snakes, The. Marianne Moore. OxBA
Monks. Palladas, Greek. GrAn, tr. by Peter Jay
Monk's dissonant hat. Bandstand. Michael S. Harper. SeSe
Monk's Dream. Dave Etter. SeSe
Monk's robe hangs in a cloister in the hills, A. Paying a Visit to Monk Yung's Cloister. Meng Hao Jan, Chinese. SuSp, tr. by Joseph J. Lee

Monk's Tale, The. Geoffrey Chaucer, *Old English*. OxBoV, *tr. by* David Wright

Monna Innominata. Christina Rossetti. BWW
  First Day, The. BoLoP; FaBoBe; GBL; GLoP
  ("I wish I could remember that first day.") LBC; LW; LoP
  (Sonnet.) LW
  From Monna Innominata. CABP
  "I loved you first: but afterwards your love." LoP
  "'Love me, for I love you'—and answer me." Son
  "Youth gone, and beauty gone if ever there." GBL; GSo; OBNC; Son

Monody. Herman Melville. APN-2; NAAL-1; NAAL-3; NoP-4; OxBSP; PAR; PoE; PoEL-5; PoPoPo

Monody on the Death of Chatterton, *1796 vers*. Coleridge.
  "Elate of heart and confidence of fame." EPCY

Monody to the Sound of Zithers. Kay Boyle. PoA

Monogamy. Gerald Louis Gould.
  "You were young--but that was scarcely to your credit." OxBTC

Monogram 4. Martina Werner, *German*. BoWoP, *tr. by* Rosemarie Waldrop

Monogram 29. Martina Werner, *German*. BoWoP, *tr. by* Rosemarie Waldrop

Monogram 23. Martina Werner, *German*. BoWoP, *tr. by* Rosemarie Waldrop

Monologue. Gottfried Benn, *German*. AF, *tr. by* Christopher Middleton

Monologue. Hone Tuwhare. PeNZ

Monologue for Cassandra. Wislawa Szymborska, *Polish*. PoSu, *tr. by* Grazyna Drabik *and* Sharon Olds

Monologue in a Rand Hospital. William Elijah Hunter. PeSAV

Monologue of a Blue Fox. Yevtushenko, *Russian*. TCRP, *tr. by* John Updike *and* Albert C. Todd

Monologue of a Dying Beast. Mark Ameen. GLP

Monologue of the Crazed Mastodon. Paul Scheerbart. CDNP

Monosyllabic European called Sax / Invents a horn, A. Ginza Samba. Robert Pinsky. PUP-18

Monotones. B. P. Nichol. FTOS

Monotony Song, The. Theodore Roethke. ChAP

Monsieur Étienne de Silhouette. Some Frenchmen. John Updike. NBLV

Monsieur Ezra Pound croit que. Another Canto. John Bingham Morton. UV

Monsieur Gaston. Abraham Moses Klein. MoCV

Monsieur Gauguin? 'E's gone to Tahiti. Limerick. Stanley J. Sharpless. PeLi

Monsieur Naso, verolè, A. Martial, *Latin*. OBCVT, *tr. by* Francis Davison

Monsieur Qui Passe. Charlotte Mew. CPO

Monsoon. Beckian Fritz Goldberg. NAmP90

Monsoon. David Wevill. NYBP

Monsoon Day Fable, A. Jayanta Mahapatra. VCWP

Monsoon Girl. Harry Clifton. BiHa; PBCIP

Monster, The. Thom Gunn. PFE

Monster, The. Greg Kuzma. AmPA

Monster, The. Karen L. Mitchell. GT

Monster, The. Henry Rago. PoA

Monster, in a course of vice grown old, A. The Monument. Samuel Wesley. OxBSP

Monstering horror swallows, A. Thanksgiving (1956). E. E. Cummings. FaBoPV

Monstrance. János Pilinszky, *Hungarian*. PoSu, *tr. by* Peter Jay

Monstrous crying of wind? The. (LL) To a Child Dancing in the Wind. W. B. Yeats. IIP

Mont Blanc. Shelley. InPS-3; NAEL-2; NIP-4; NOBRP; NoP-4; OAEL-2
  (Mont Blanc. Lines Written in the Vale of Chamouni.) Ro

Montague Michael. *Unknown*. OTCP

Montalbert. Charlotte Smith.
  On Passing Over a Dreary Tract of Country, and Near the Ruins of a Deserted Chapel, During a Tempest. BoWoP; WPE

Montana Eclogue. William Stafford. NYBP; PaTW

Montana Pastoral. James Vincent Cunningham. MoAmPo; VGW

Montana Ranch Abandoned. Richard Hugo. PaTW

Montana Wives. Gwendolen Haste.
  Ranch in the Coulee, The. PaTW

Montanus' Sonnet. Thomas Lodge. PoEL-2 *Fr.* Rosalynde; or Euphues' Golden Legacy.

Montauk Highway. Harvey Shapiro. LiLi

Montcalm and Wolfe. *Unknown*. AmFP

Montecastelli Poem. Sophie Behrens. NBrP

Monterey. Charles Fenno Hoffman. FaBoBe

Montezuma. Diane Di Prima. BB

Montgomery. Sam Cornish. MBE; PoBA; Poetsp

Month of great men. February. Lolly Quinones. IMW

Month of January. Frankie Armstrong. BrRo

Month of leaves. June. Irene F. Pawsey. BoTP

Month of the drowned dog. After long rain the land, The. November. Ted Hughes. CMoP; GTBS-P

Month or twain to live on honeycomb, A. Before Parting. Swinburne. CBLP; EP; NOBVV

Monthly Magazine, 4 287. Robert Southey.
  Hannah, A Plaintive Tale. Ro

Months, The. Sara Coleridge. *See* The Garden Year.

Months, The. *Unknown*. ACTP

Months after the Muse. The Illustration [—a Footnote]. Denise Levertov. PoA

Months and days, like birds, are flying off, The. Self-Portrayal. Nguyễn Khuyến, *Vietnamese*. AVP, *tr. by* Huỳnh Sanh Thông

Months go by like water in a waterfall, The. *Unknown*, *Chinese*. OHMPC, *tr. by* Kenneth Rexroth

Montreal. Abraham Moses Klein. MoCV

Monument, The. Elizabeth Bishop. HCAP; NOBA; NoAM; Poetr; TRP

Monument, The. Vladislav Felitsianovich Khodasevich, *Russian*. TCRP, *tr. by* Michael Frayn

Monument, A. Charles Madge. FaBoMo

Monument, The. Yaroslav Vasilevich Smelyakov, *Russian*. TCRP, *tr. by* Simon Franklin

Monument, The. Samuel Wesley. OxBSP

Monument in Black. Vanessa Howard. MBE

Monument of Cleita, The. Edward Cracroft Lefroy. AWP *Fr.* Echoes from Theocritus.

Monumental. Tanka. Maekawa Samio, *Japanese*. MJT, *tr. by* Makoto Ueda

Monumental Memorial of Marine Mercy, A. Richard Steere. SCAP

Monuments for a Friendly Girl at a Tenth Grade Party. William Stafford. NoAM

Monuments of Hiroshima, The. D. J. Enright. OxBSP

Monuments to the Not Yet Lived. Leonard Schwartz. PT

Monumentum Aere, Etc. Ezra Pound. NOBA

Mony ane talks o the grass, the grass. Willie and Earl Richard's Daughter. *Unknown*. ESPB

Mony klyf he overclambe in contrayes straunge. *Unknown*. FaBoVe *Fr.* Sir Gawain and the Green Knight. OAEL-1, *tr. by* Brian Stone

Moo! Robert Silliman Hillyer. OBAL

Moochie likes to keep on playing. Moochie. Eloise Greenfield. NTCP

Mood, The. Quandra Prettyman. PoBA

Mood Apart, A. Robert Frost. OxBSP

Mood comes on—I want to cross Hsi-ling, The. Tao-chi, *Chinese*. CoBLCP, *tr. by* Jonathan Chaves

Mood Indigo. William Matthews. WeW-3

Mood of men, the world's career, The. (LL) Imagination. John Davidson. APAD; MoBrPo

Mood of Vichy, The. Hildebert, *Latin*. MLL, *tr. by* Helen Waddell

Moods. Leyb Kvitko, *Yiddish*. TrJP, *tr. by* Joseph Leftwich

Moods, The. W. B. Yeats. CTC; EBVVPR

Moody child and wildly wise, A. Motto to "The Poet." Ralph Waldo Emerson. NCAP

Mooimeisjes. Perceval Gibbon. PeSAV

"Mooly cow, mooly cow, home from the wood." The Cow-Boy's Song. Anna Maria Wells. OBCA

Moon. Nathan Alterman, *Hebrew*. MHP, *tr. by* Ruth Finer Mintz

Moon. Alan Bold. SpW

Moon, The. Robert Creeley. VGW

Moon, The. W. H. Davies. MoBrPo

Moon, The. Emily Dickinson. BoTP

Moon, The. Robert Duncan. APSN, *sect. 5 Fr.* Passages.

Moon. Nicolás Guillén, *Spanish*. PFTM, *tr. by* Robert Marquez

Moon. Frances Horovitz. BrRo

Moon, The. Hsüeh T'ao, *Chinese*. SuSp, *tr. by* Eric W. Johnson

Moon. Jean Kenward. SpW

Moon. Peggy Lyles. HA

Moon, The. Wendy Mulford. NBrP

Moon. Henry Rowe. OBEV

Moon, The. Shelley. *See* The Waning Moon.

Moon. William Jay Smith. PC

Moon. Derek Walcott. MoP

Moon, a sweeping scimitar, dipped in the stormy straits, The. Winged Man. Stephen Vincent Benét. MoAmPo

Moon above the milky field, The. Night-Piece. Léonie Adams. MoAmPo

Moon and a Cloud, The. W. H. Davies. RB

Moon and Candle-light. William Renton. NOBVV

Moon and clouds are the same. Wu-Men. EnlH

Moon and seven Pleiades have set, The. Alone. Sappho, *Greek*. AWP, *tr. by* William Ellery Leonard

Moon and Sun: A curious and wonderful creature I saw. *Unknown*. EEP, *tr. by* Michael Alexander *Fr*. Riddles (Exeter Book).

Moon and the Night and the Men, The. John Berryman. CoAP; GEA; VCAP; VGW

Moon and the Nightingale, The. Milton. *See* Evening in Paradise.

Moon and the Salt Flats, The. Mary Di Michele. NOBC

Moon and the satellite orbit, The. The Travelers. Patricia Hubbell. CTV

Moon and the Yew Tree, The. Sylvia Plath. CoAP; FaBoMo; FaBoWP; NYBP; VGW; WPE; WPOW

Moon appears from the mouth of the sheer bluff, The. Aboard a Boat at Night, Drinking with My Wife. Mei Yao Ch'en, *Chinese*. CoBCP, *tr. by* Burton Watson

Moon at dawn, The. John Wills. HA

Moon at the full. Europe has burst its banks. The Inundation. Howard Sergeant. SPE

Moon at the window. Rosamond Haas. HA

Moon at Three A.M. Lance Henson. CDW

Moon behind High Tranquil Leaves, The. Robert Malise Bowyer Nichols. OBMV

Moon blackens, geese fly high. Lu Lun. SuSp, *tr. by* Ronald C. Miao *Fr*. Frontier Songs.

Moon-Bone Song [*or Cycle*]. *Aborigine Oral Tradition*. CBAP, *tr. by* R. M. Berndt

Moon Bound. Raymond Washington. NBV

Moon-Child, The. "Fiona Macleod." CH

Moon comes from the blue sky, The. The Moon in a Winecup. Shen Chou, *Chinese*. CoBLCP, *tr. by* Jonathan Chaves

Moon cuts through, The. Somewhere Near Phu Bai. Yusef Komunyakaa. CDa

Moon does shine as bright as day. (LL) Namby-Pamby. Henry Carey. CBNP; NOEC; OBSV; UV

Moon drops one or two feathers into the field, The. Beginning. James Wright. ColAP; SAGP; VCAP

Moon Eclipse Exorcism. *Unknown, Alsea Indian*. STP, *tr. by* Armand Schwerner

Moon fades into dawn. J. W. Hackett. HA

Moon falls in shape of little metal plates against my face. Remembrance of the Founts of Night. Theo Van Doesburg, *Dutch*. PFTM, *tr. by* Jerome Rothenberg

Moon Festival. Tu Fu, *Chinese*. OHPC, *tr. by* Kenneth Rexroth

Moon Fishing. Lisel Mueller. CoAP

Moon, Flowers, Man. Su Tung-p'o, *Chinese*. OHPC, *tr. by* Kenneth Rexroth

Moon Folly. Fannie Stearns Gifford. RACG *Fr*. The Songs of Conn the Fool.

Moon had climbed the highest hill, The. The Banks of Dee. *Unknown*. AmFP

Moon had risen an hour or more, The. Crescent Moon. William Renton. NOBVV

Moon had risen on the eastern hill, The. The Sailor and His Bride. *Unknown*. AmFP

Moon hangs in the air, A. I Starting from Central Station. David Campbell. BMAP *Fr*. Starting from Central Station.

Moon hangs on a clouded sky, The. Clouded Sky. Miklós Radnóti, *Hungarian*. HP, *tr. by* Polgar, Steven, S. Berg, and S. J. Marks

Moon has a face like the clock in the hall, The. Robert Louis Stevenson. NOxBChV; PWR; TLR

("Till up in the morning the sun shall rise.") (LL) NOxBChV

Moon has a halo, there will be wind, The. I Remember the Blue River. Mei Yao Ch'en, *Chinese*. OHPC, *tr. by* Kenneth Rexroth

Moon has fallen on her back, The. Night-Piece. Frances Horovitz. LW

Moon has gone to her rest, The. Nocturne. Wilfrid Scawen Blunt. OBMV

Moon Has Set, The. Sappho, *Greek*. PGA

Moon has set above High Dike, The. Dawn in Stone City. Li Ho, *Chinese*. PLT, *tr. by* A. C. Graham

Moon has veil'd her Silver Light, The. Sappho, *Greek*. OBCVT, *tr. by* John Addison

Moon-Hops. Ted Hughes. CABP

Moon hung low 'mid clouds enshrined, The. The Fading Skiff. Henrietta Cordelia Ray. CBWP-3

Moon in a Winecup, The. Shen Chou, *Chinese*. CoBLCP, *tr. by* Jonathan Chaves

Moon, in her pride, once glanced aside, The. The Moon Sings. *Unknown*. OxBoLi

Moon in the pond, The. Missing France. Jules Supervielle, *French*. MFP, *tr. by* Martin Sorrell

Moon in your eyes is best, The. Tracking Rabbits: Night. Jim Barnes. CDW

Moon in Your Hands, The. Hilda Doolittle. BoWoP; NYBP *Fr*. Sigil.

Moon is a furnace, The. A Fresco of Swans and Bears. Robert Wallace. CMAP

Moon is a poor woman, The. Sidney Keyes. NoP-4; OBWP *Fr*. The Foreign Gate.

Moon is a sow, The. Song for Ishtar. Denise Levertov. MoP; NALW; NoAM; PoM

Moon is a white sliver, The. I Am Singing Now. Luci Tapahonso. UnSA

Moon is able to command the valley tonight, The. Moist Moon People. Carl Sandburg. MoAmPo

Moon Is Always Female, The. Marge Piercy. NoAM

Moon is an exile, The. Niyi Osundare. HBAPE, *sect*. XVIII *Fr*. Moonsongs.

Moon is an ivory tusk in the Utah sky, The. The Moon and the Salt Flats. Mary Di Michele. NOBC

Moon is at her full, and, riding high, The. The Tides. William Cullen Bryant. TAP

Moon is coming up the blue sky, The. Wine Cup and Bright Moon. Shen Chou, *Chinese*. SuSp, *tr. by* Irving Y. Lo

Moon is eaten and renewed, The. The Lunar Games. Eeva-Liisa Manner, *Finnish*. WPOW, *tr. by* Jaakko A. Ahokas

Moon is full, The. *Unknown, Japanese*. OHMPJ, *tr. by* Kenneth Rexroth

Moon is fully risen, The. Mond ist aufgegangen, Der. Heinrich Heine, *German*. AWP, *tr. by* James Thomson

Moon is like a lamp, The. The Weathercock. Rose Fyleman. BoTP

Moon is loose in the gutter tonight, The. Woman Kills Sweetheart with Bowling Ball. Laura Kasischke. PUP-18

"Moon is nailed to the 'river,' The." Ohio Is the Iroquois Word for Beautiful. Helen Ruggieri. LoHo

Moon is not green cheese, The. Night Light. Nancy Willard. LCAP-2

Moon is one, The. Teaching Numbers. Gary Soto. NOxBChV

Moon is out this morning, The. P. M. T. Dorothy Porter. BMAP

Moon Is Rising, The. *Unknown, Chinese*. TAL, *tr. by* Robert Payne

Moon is so high it is, The. I Walk Out into the Country at Night. Lu Yu, *Chinese*. OHPC, *tr. by* Kenneth Rexroth

Moon is the companion, The. To the Tune "The Southerner." Yang Shen, *Chinese*. CoBLCP, *tr. by* Jonathan Chaves

Moon is the mother of pathos and pity, The. Lunar Paraphrase. Wallace Stevens. SAmP

Moon Is the Number 18, The. Charles Olson. CMoP; PoE

Moon is tied to a few strings, The. The Cardplayers. Jack Spicer. APSN

Moon Is to Blood. Richard Duerden. NeAP

Moon Landing. W. H. Auden. OxAEP-2

Moon-like Is All Other Love. *Unknown, Middle English*. NOCV, *tr. by* Donald Davie

Moon lives in all the alone places, The. Meditations on the Moon. Paula Gunn Allen. HATNAP

Moon-Man. Dorothy Hewett. CBAP

Moon, moon / Mak' me a pair o'shoon. *Unknown*. OxNR

Moon Now Rises to Her Absolute Rule, The. Henry David Thoreau. PoEL-4

Moon of Huckleberries. Phillip William George. VoR

Moon of Id came, The. Nur, Empress Jahan, *Persian*. BoWoP, *tr. by* Willis Barnstone

Moon of Mobile, The. Thomas Holley Chivers. OBAL

Moon of the First Communion. Kathleen Norris. CrSp

Moon on the one hand, the dawn on the other, The. The Early Morning. Hilaire Belloc. BoTP; OxBSP; Spl; TLR

Moon over Mountain Pass. Li Po, *Chinese*. SuSp, *tr. by* Joseph J. Lee

Moon over Prague. Vitězslau Nezval, *Czech*. AF, *tr. by* Ewald Osers

Moon over the Mountain Pass, The. Li Po, *Chinese*. TAL, *tr. by* Robert Payne

Moon penny bright as silver. *Unknown*. FaBoVe

Moon plays horn, leaning on the shoulder of the dark universe, The. Bird. Joy Harjo. SeSe

Moon Poem. Max Jacob, *French*. AF, *tr. by* Michael Brownstein

Moon Poems. John Wieners. VGW

Moon Rises, The. Federico García Lorca, *Spanish*. TTTS, *tr. by* William Bryant Logan

Moon rises, a vengeance on anguish, The. Sleepwalkers. Bella Akhatovna Akhmadulina, *Russian*. BoWoP, *tr. by* Barbara Einzig

Moon Rocks, Moon in the Man. David Byrne. CBNP

Moon sets. A crow caws, The. Night at Anchor by Maple Bridge. Chang Chi, *Chinese*. OHMPC, *tr. by* Kenneth Rexroth

Moon setting, crows cawing, frost filling the sky. Tying Up for the Night at Maple River Bridge. Chang Chi, *Chinese.* CoBCP, *tr. by* Burton Watson

Moon Shadow. George Bowering. MoCV

Moon shines bright, The. *Unknown.* OxNR

Moon shines bright, The. In such a night as this. In Such a Night. Shakespeare. GBL *Fr.* The Merchant of Venice.

Moon shines clear as silver, The. Sun and Moon. Charlotte Druitt Cole. BoTP

Moon shrinks behind a row of shriveled trees, The. A Different Cereal. John Yau. PT

Moon Sings, The. *Unknown.* OxBoLi

Moon Sings to the Stream, The. Leah Goldberg. MHP, *tr. by* Ruth Finer Mintz *Fr.* Songs of the Stream.

Moon Song. Chuba Nweke. PBA

Moon spits fire, The. Sad Love. Vidyapati, *Sanskrit.* EP, *tr. by* Deben Bhattacharya

Moon, Sun, Sleep, Birds, Live. Kenneth Patchen. WeW-3

Moon takes on the glint of sun, The. When the Hindu Woman Sings Calypso. Rajandaye Ramkissoon-Chen. HCP

Moon, that peeped as she came up, The. Nailsworth Hill. W. H. Davies. OTCP

Moon, they say, called Mantis, The. How Death Came. *Unknown, Hottentot.* PeSA; TTY, *tr. by* W. H. I. Bleek

Moon-transport. Ted Hughes. SpW

Moon upon her fluent Route, The. Emily Dickinson. APN-2

Moon was shining brightly upon the battle plain, The. The Maid of Monterey. *Unknown.* AmFP

Moon-wind. Ted Hughes. SpW

Moon Window, The. Chang Yü. *Fr.* Twelve Miscellaneous Poems on the Fang Garden. CoBLCP, *tr. by* Jonathan Chaves

Moone-Calfe, The. Michael Drayton.
    "It was not long e're he perceiv'd the skies." PoEL-2

Mooni. Henry Clarence Kendall. OBEV

Moonless darkness stands between. Gerard Manley Hopkins. OBCP

Moonlight. Walter De la Mare. EnLoPo

Moonlight, The. Ann Hawkshawe. BoTP

Moonlight. Rajasekhara, *Sanskrit.* PC, *tr. by* Henry Heifetz

Moonlight. Shakespeare. *Fr.* The Merchant of Venice.

Moonlight. Jacques Tahureau, *French.* AWP, *tr. by* Andrew Lang

Moonlight, The. Tanka. Sasaki Yukitsuna, *Japanese.* MJT, *tr. by* Makoto Ueda

Moonlight. Sara Teasdale. APAD; VGW

Moonlight. *Unknown.* AS

Moonlight among the Pines. "Hugh MacDiarmid." OAEL-2

Moonlight and Gas. Constance Naden. VWP

Moonlight Bay. Wu Chen, *Chinese.* CoBLCP, *tr. by* Jonathan Chaves

Moonlight, clear as water. Deliverance. "Ping Hsin," *Chinese.* ChiPo, *tr. by* Kai-yu Hsu

Moonlight, harsh and clear, floods the high pavilion. The Small Garden. Cheng Hsieh, *Chinese.* SuSp, *tr. by* Wu-chi Liu

Moonlight in front of my bed. Still Night Thoughts. Li Po, *Chinese.* CoBCP; TTTS, *tr. by* Burton Watson

Moonlight is good, good for solitary sitting, The. Pine Sounds. Po Chü-i, *Chinese.* CoBCP, *tr. by* Burton Watson

Moonlight Night. Tu Fu, *Chinese.* CoBCP, *tr. by* Burton Watson

Moonlight Night: Carmel. Langston Hughes. GT

Moonlight of a former time, The. Tune: "Dim Fragrance"—Plum Blossoms. Chiang K'uei, *Chinese.* SuSp, *tr. by* An-yan Tang

Moonlight Ride, A. Harriet Hamilton King. VWP

Moonlight ripples, ripples, The. Moonlight Bay. Wu Chen, *Chinese.* CoBLCP, *tr. by* Jonathan Chaves

Moonlight. . . Scattered Clouds. Robert Bloomfield. OBNC *Fr.* The Farmer's Boy.

Moonlight shines cold on white bones, The. (LL) Travelling Northward. Tu Fu, *Chinese.* BLT; OHPC, *tr. by* Kenneth Rexroth

Moonlight, The: Juice flowing from an overripe pomegranate. Enchantment. Lewis Alexander. PoBA

Moonlight through my gauze curtains. The Skein. Carolyn Kizer. VGW

Moonlight washes the west side of the house. Winter Verse for His Sister. William Meredith. NYBP; TAP

Moonlit Apples. John Drinkwater. BoTP; EBEvV; OBMV; OxBTC; PoRA

Moonlit Night at Fragrant Mountain Temple. Wang Shih-chieng, *Chinese.* SuSp, *tr. by* Richard John Lynn

Moonlit nights on the Atlantic Ocean! Ion Gheorghe, *Romanian.* CEEP, *tr. by* Donald Eulert *and* Stefan Avadanei

Moonlit sleet. David Lloyd. HA

Moonmoth and grasshopper that flee our page. A Name for All. Hart Crane. VGW

Moonrise. Hilda Doolittle. PoA

Moonrise. Gerard Manley Hopkins. EnVR; MoBrPo; NOBVV; RB

Moonrise. D. H. Lawrence. LiTM; PoA

Moonrise Over Battlefield. Edgell Rickword. NSI; PoWW

Moonrise white cat eating the cardinal. Scott Montgomery. HA

Moons. Peter Fallon. BiHa

Moon's a devil jester, The. The Traveler. Vachel Lindsay. MoAmPo

Moon's a little arch, The. A Classic Case. Gilbert Sorrentino. NeAP

Moon's a path, The. Hansel, Gretel and Ruby Redlips. Anita Endrezze-Danielson. HATNAP

Moon's dropped child!, The. (LL) Fame. Charlotte Mew. VWP

Moon's glow by seven fold multiplied, turned red. After Reading St. John the Divine. Gene Derwood. ImPo; LiTM; WPE

Moon's left town. Moon's clean gone. (LL) Arizona Nature Myth. James Michie. FaBoA

Moon's little skullcap, The. Front Street. Howard Moss. NYBP

Moon's my constant mistress, The. Tom o' Bedlam. *Unknown.* CH; FaBoCh; PoRA

Moon's on the lake, and the mist's on the brae, The. MacGregor's Gathering. Sir Walter Scott. OxBS

Moon's the North Wind's cooky, The. Vachel Lindsay. FPC; NOxBChV; OBCA; PiM
    ("North. . . Wind. . . ???. . . again!") (LL) NOxBChV

Moon's up-riding makes a line, The. Night Scenes. Robert Duncan. VGW

Moonscape. Judith Nicholls. SpW

Moonset. Sir Henry John Newbolt. EBVV

Moonsheep stands on the huge lawn, The. Christian Morgenstern, *German.* CBNP, *tr. by* Hugh Haughton

Moonshine. Walter De la Mare. OBCoV

Moonshot, A. Giant Rocket. Wes Magee. NOxBChV

Moonshot Sonnet. Mary Ellen Solt. BoWoP

Moonsongs. Niyi Osundare.
    "Frantic as a prentice poet." HBAPE, *sect.* V
    "Maddening moon, A." HBAPE, *sect.* XIX
    "Moon is an exile, The." HBAPE, *sect.* XVIII
    "We called the statue." HBAPE

Moonstruck. "Hugh MacDiarmid." NAEL-2

Moontan. Mark Strand. NYBP

Moor, The. Ralph Hodgson. MoBrPo

Moor, The. Ronald Stuart Thomas. OBWVE

Moorhen. William Logan. DiPo

Mooring at Hsia-k'ou at Night. Li Meng-yang, *Chinese.* CoBLCP, *tr. by* Jonathan Chaves

Mooring at K'ou-ch'üeh—Sent to Dr. Lin. Pien Kung, *Chinese.* CoBLCP, *tr. by* Jonathan Chaves

Mooring at Night at Kao-yu. Wang Shih-chieng, *Chinese.* CoBLCP, *tr. by* Jonathan Chaves

Mooring at Night at the River Mouth, I Heard a Flute—Sent to My Elder Brother Hsi-ch'iao. Wang Shih-chieng, *Chinese.* CoBLCP, *tr. by* Jonathan Chaves

Mooring in the Rain at Sung-ling. Chin Nung, *Chinese.* CoBLCP, *tr. by* Jonathan Chaves

Mooring My Boat on the Ssu River and Watching the Moon. Wen Cheng-ming, *Chinese.* CoBLCP, *tr. by* Jonathan Chaves

Mooring Our Boat at Tan-yang Harbor. Kao Ch'i, *Chinese.* CoBLCP, *tr. by* Jonathan Chaves

Moorings. Norman MacCaig. OxBTC

Moorland fires are gathered up, The. Tune: "Big String of Words A"—The Great Wall. Na-lan Hsing-te, *Chinese.* SuSp, *tr. by* Lenore Mayhew *and* William McNaughton

Moors, The. John Clare. EnVR

Moose, The. Elizabeth Bishop. DiPo; FaBoWP; NAAL-2; NALW
    ("Acrid / smell of gasoline, An.") (LL) NoP-4

Moose in the Morning, Northern Maine. Mona Van Duyn. ColAP

Mop-eyed I am, as some have said. Upon Himself. Robert Herrick. OxBSP

Moral, The. David Avidan. *Fr.* Samson, Our Hero. IP, *tr. by* Warren Bargad *and* Stanley F. Chyet

Moral, The. William Ernest Henley. OxAEP-2

Moral Alphabet, A. Hilaire Belloc.
    "A stands for Archibald who told no lies." NoAM
    "B stands for Bear. When bears are seen." NoAM
    "Dreadful Dinotherium he, The." NOBL
    "E stands for egg." NoAM
    "K for the Klondyke, a country of gold." NoAM
    "R the reviewer, reviewing my book." NoAM

Moral climbs whose name should be a wreath, A. (LL) Mr. Pope. Allen Tate. ColAP; FuPo; NOBA; NoAM; TwCP; VGW

Moral is—Take care how you light, The. (LL) Darius Green and His Flying-Machine. John Townsend Trowbridge. FaBoBe; OBAL; OBCA; OxBChV; PoLF

Moral Poem, A. James Vincent Cunningham. VGW

Moral Proverbs and Folk Songs. Antonio Machado Ruiz, *Spanish.*
   "But look in your mirror for the other one." RaBo, *tr. by* Robert Bly
   "Don't trace out your profile." RaBo, *tr. by* Robert Bly
   "Look for your other half." RaBo, *tr. by* Robert Bly
   "Narcissism / is an ugly fault." RaBo, *tr. by* Robert Bly

Moral Story II. David McKee Wright. PeSA

Moral Tale, A. Roger Woddis. UV

Moral Taxi Ride, The. Erich Kästner, *German.* EP, *tr. by* Jerome Rothenberg

Moral Tetrastich, A. Sir William Jones. *See* Epigram: "On parent knees, a naked new-born child."

Morality Play: Preface, A. George Oppen. APSN; NNaP *Fr.* Some San Francisco Poems.

Morality, thou deadly bane. Robert Burns. OBSV *Fr.* A Dedication to G**** H******* Esq.

Morandi. Charles Wright. WeT

Morant Bay. *Unknown.* FaBoVe

Morbidezza. Arthur Symons. ADE

Mordant and decadent Youth, A. Limerick. Thomas Thorneley. PeLi

More. Ai. GT

More. Gertrude Stein. PBWP *Fr.* Tender Buttons.

More Abandoned, The More Divine, The. "Angelus Silesius." GePo, *tr. by* George C. Schoolfield *Fr.* The Cherubical Wanderer.

More Ancient Mariner, A. Bliss Carman. OBAL

More and / more. (LL) In Memoriam: Martin Luther King, Jr. June Jordan. NAAAL

More and more frequently the edges. Margaret Atwood. LW

More and more lately, as, not even minding the slippages yet, the aches / and sad softenings. Repression. Charles Kenneth Williams. NoP-4

More Bagpipe Music. E. O. Parrott. UV

More Ballads! here's a spick and span new Supplication. A Free Parliament Litany. *Unknown.* OxBoLi

More beautiful and soft than any moth. The Landscape near an Aerodrome. Stephen Spender. LiTM; MoBrPo; NoAM; OxBTC

More beautiful than any gift you gave. The Token. Frank Templeton Prince. FaBoTw; OxBTC

More Blues and the Abstract Truth. C. D. Wright. NAmP90

More brave then me:more blond than you. (LL) I sing of Olaf glad and big. E. E. Cummings. AF

More bright and large than this. (LL) An Answer to Another Persuading a Lady to Marriage. Katherine Philips. HAP; LW; OBEV; WeW-3

More dear, both for themselves and for thy sake! (LL) Lines Composed a Few Miles Above Tintern Abbey on Revisiting the Banks of the Wye During a Tour. Wordsworth. CABP; EBeVV; FHYEP; HeIP-4; ImPo; InPS-3; NoP-4; OAEL-2; OBNC; OxAEP-2; PoEL-4; PoPoPo; Poetr; Ro; SCGP; TFi

More delicate than the historians' are the map-makers' colors. (LL) The Map. Elizabeth Bishop. ColAP; NOBA

More discontents I never had. Discontents in Devon. Robert Herrick. BeJo; CaPo; OxBSP

More distant than the dead sea. Nadia Tuéni, *French.* PBWP, *tr. by* Carol Cosman

More essential thing, A. (LL) Pedigree of Honey, The, vers. 1. Emily Dickinson. MoP; NOBA

More for asparagus than asparagus does. Angry with China. Douglas Messerli. FTOS

More for tea! (LL) Animal crackers, and cocoa to drink. Christopher Darlington Morley. CTV

More gaily, dance. Quick-Step. Robert Creeley. VGW

More geese than swans now live, more fools than wise. (LL) Silver swan, who living had no note, The. Orlando Gibbons. FaBoCh; HAP; HeIP-4; IMW; InPK-6; NAEL-1; OPOU; OxBSP; PoEL-2; RB

More grotesque than a row of laundromats. The Novelty Shop. Duane Niatum. CDW

More had she spoke, but yawn'd—All nature nods. Alexander Pope. FHYEP *Fr.* Yet, yet a moment, one dim ray of light. NAEL-1; OAEL-1; PoEL-3 *Fr.* The Dunciad.

More hard than any ghost there is or any man there was! (LL) The Looking Glass. Rudyard Kipling. FaBoTw; NTP; OBMV

More harmless vanity?, A. (LL) On an Infant Dying as Soon as Born. Charles Lamb. GTBS-P; IMW; OBEV

More haughty than the rest, the wolfish race. The Presbyterians. Dryden. NOSC *Fr.* The Hind and the Panther.

More hopeless the more comforting, The. Autumn. Yunna Petrovna Moritz, *Russian.* TCRP, *tr. by* J. R. Rowland *with* Odile Taliani

More I beat my wife, The. (LL) Occasional Poem. A. E. Housman. NOBL; PeLV

More intricate. William J. Higginson. HA

More It Snows, The. A. A. Milne. NTCP

More Joy in Heaven. Howard Nemerov. NoAM

More kicks than pence. To Hell with Commonsense. Patrick Kavanagh. APAD; FaBoTw

More light / asked Goethe as he died. Light? Milan Richter, *Czech and Slovak.* CEEP, *tr. by* Ewald Osers

'More Light! More Light!' Anthony Hecht. AF; CoAP; CoAmPo; HAP; HP; NOBA; NoAM; NoP-4; OBWP; Poetr; RB; TwCP; UnPo; VCAP; VGW

More like a stock than like a vine. (LL) The Vine. Robert Herrick. BeJo; CaPo; CavPo; EP; NAEL-2; NoP-4

More liked by her, or loved by me. (LL) To the Most Fair and Lovely Mistress Anne Soame, Now Lady Abdie. Robert Herrick. CaPo; NOBE; NOSC

More Love. *Unknown.* AH

More love or more disdain I crave. Against Indifference. Charles Webbe. OBEV

More Love to Thee, O Christ. Elizabeth Payson Prentiss. AH

More Lovely than Antiquity. Witter Bynner. NoP-4

More Loving One, The. W. H. Auden. HoPM; TOF

More Luck to Honest Poverty. Shirley Brooks. BXAP; NOBL

More luck to honest poverty. For A' That and A' That. Shirley Brooks. UV

More of a Corpse Than a Woman. Muriel Rukeyser. NALW; NMM-2

More of the fathers are dying each day. Robert Bly. *Fr.* Six Winter Privacy Poems. LCAP-2

More oft than once Death whispered in mine ear. Redeem Time Past. William Drummond. OxAEP-1

More Power. Egan O'Rahilly, *Modern Irish.* BIrV, *tr. by* John Montague

More Questions. Ory Bernstein, *Hebrew.* IP, *tr. by* Warren Bargad *and* Stanley F. Chyet

More Reformation. Daniel Defoe.
   "To sin's a vice in nature, and we find." OBSV

More rich than Cleopatra's tomb. (LL) The Amber Bead. Robert Herrick. BeJo; CaPo

More song. birds follow the sun. Lady's Days. Larry Neal. SeSe

More Sonnets at Christmas. Allen Tate. LiTM

More sound in France—that, too, he secret keeps. (LL) A Private. Edward Thomas. GTBS-P; NSI; PeFWW

More Stanzas Applied to Spiritual Things. Saint John of the Cross, *Spanish.* TOF, *tr. by* K. Kavanaugh *and* O. Rodrigues

More Strong Than Time. Victor Hugo, *French.* AWP, *tr. by* Andrew Lang

More surprising than a moving statue. The Apparition. Bernard O'Donoghue. NoP-4

More than 9 Lives. Bruce Beaver. BMAP

More than a king's my word does rule today. To a Young Lady that Desired a Verse of My Being Servant One Day, and Mistress Another. Elizabeth Tipper. NOSC

More than a King's my Word dos rule to day. To a Young Lady That Desired a Verse of My Being Servant One Day and Mistress Another. Elizabeth Tipper. KTR *Fr.* Pilgrim's Viaticum; or, The Destitute, But Not Forlorn.

More than Apollo's golden lyre. Meleager, *Greek.* GrAn, *tr. by* Peter Whigham

More than leaves, more than flakes. Philip Appleman. BXAP

More than Morgan, I desire to eat people. Morgan. John Blight. CBAP

More than most fair [*or* fayre], full of the living fire [*or* fyre]. Sonnet 8. Edmund Spenser. PoE; Son *Fr.* Amoretti. AAS

More Than Most People. Eldon Grier. MoCV

More than my brothers are to me. Tennyson. EBVV; EBVVPR; EnVR; OAEL-2 *Fr.* In Memoriam A. H. H.

More than myself (estate, degree). Junker-Lied. Turner Cassity. WeT

More than novelty crooked its finger—silent, austere. Melissa Green. DiPo

More than of either's manners, wit, or face! (LL) An Elegy [*or* Elegie]: "Let me be what I am, as Virgil cold." Ben Jonson. PoEL-2; SeCP

More than polished stone. I Am Root. Claribel Alegría, *Spanish.* VCWP, *tr. by* Carolyn Forché

More than Suspect. André Breton, *French.* AF, *tr. by* Mary Ann Caws *and* Jean-Pierre Cauvin

More than the gems / locked away and treasured. Sent from the Capital to Her Elder Daughter. Lady Otomo no Sakanoé, *Japanese.* BoWoP; MDDM; WPOW, *tr. by* Geoffrey Bownas *and* Anthony Thwaite

More than the Grave is closed to me. Emily Dickinson. APN-2

More than the shortest distance. A Barbed Wire Fence Meditates upon the Goldfinch. Don McKay. NOBC

More than They that Watch for the Morning. May Probyn. VWP

More than thirty years have rushed. On His Thirty-Third Birthday. Ch'ang Kuo Fan, *Chinese*. OHMPC, *tr. by* Kenneth Rexroth

More than thyself to love thy neighbor. (LL) The Latest Decalogue. Arthur Hugh Clough. ChIV-1; EBEV; EBVV; EBVVPR; EnVR; FaBoEE; GTBS-P; HAP; HoPM; NAEL-2; NOBE; NOBVV; NoP-4; OAEL-2; OBNC; OBSV; PeECV; SCGP; TFi; WeW-3

More then most faire, full of the living fire. Edmund Spenser. *See* Sonnet 8: "More than most fair [*or* fayre], full of the living fire [*or* fyre]."

More things are wrought by prayer. Prayer. Tennyson. *Fr.* Morte d'Arthur. EBNV; EBVVPR; FaBoBe; NIP-4; NOBVV; OAEL-2; OBNV; OxAEP-2; PoEL-5 *Fr.* Morte d'Arthur. EnVR

More Thoughts on Nguyễn. Chế Lan Viên, *Vietnamese*. AVP, *tr. by* Huỳnh Sanh Thông

More times than you'll wake. (LL) Letter for Duncan. Larry Eigner. FTOS

More touching is the deathbed than the bier! (LL) Old Ruralities: A Regret. Charles Tennyson Turner. EBVV; Son

More voice was in her cough tonight: its first harsh, stripping sound would weaken abruptly. Helen. Charles Kenneth Williams. PuP-17

More we live, more brief appear, The. The River of Life. Thomas Campbell. GTBS-P; ImPo; OBNC

More wealth brings in than all those three. (LL) The Four Sweet Months. Robert Herrick. AYFP; BoTP

More whyght thou art than primrose leaf my Lady Galatee. Cyclops. Ovid. CTC; OBVE, *tr. by* Arthur Golding *Fr.* Metamorphoses.

More worthy I to be belov'd of thee. (LL) Sonnet 150. Shakespeare. OxAEP-1; SCGP

More ye desire her, the sooner ye miss, The. How to Obtain Her. *Unknown*. NoSic

Morels. William Jay Smith. NYBP

Moreover the Lord answered Job, and said. Bible, *O.T.* OBVE *Fr.* Job. NAWM-1

    Out of the Whirlwind. AWP

Moreover, there with them appear. Michael Wigglesworth. *See* Thus everyone before the throne.

Moreton Bay. *Unknown*. CBAP

Morgan. John Blight. CBAP

Morituri Salutamus. Henry Wadsworth Longfellow.

    "For age is opportunity no less." PoToHe

    Too Late?

Moriturus. Edna St. Vincent Millay. MeMAP

Morley's light went out. Power Failure. Michael Dennis Browne. AmPA

Mormons, led by Colonel Cooke, The. On the Road to California; or, The Buffalo Bullfight. *Unknown*. AmFP

Morn. Josephine D. Henderson Heard. CBWP-4

Morn hath risen clear and bright, The. The Expulsion of Hagar. Eloise Bibb. CBWP-4

Morning. Joanna Baillie. ECWP *Fr.* A Winter Day.

Morning. Louisa Sarah Bevington. PEW

Morning. William Blake. FaBoCh; OAEL-2

Morning. William Browne. NOSC *Fr.* Britannia's Pastorals.

Morning. Thomas Carlyle. PWR

Morning. Chu Shu-chen, *Chinese*. BLT; BoWoP; OHPC, *tr. by* Kenneth Rexroth

Morning. John Cunningham. NOEC

Morning. Charles D'Ambrosio. PUP-19

Morning. Tove Ditlevsen, *Danish*. PBWP, *tr. by* Nadia Christensen

Morning. Ivy O. Eastwick. BoTP

Morning. Edward Foster. PT

Morning, A. Mark Strand. HCAP

Morning. Giuseppe Ungaretti. PFTM

Morning. *Unknown*. NOEC

Morning. Wang Wei, *Chinese*. TAL, *tr. by* Robert Payne

Morning—A Death. Basil T. Paquet. CDa

Morning: a polished knifeblade. Jelaluddin Rumi, *Persian*. EnlH, *tr. by* Coleman Barks with *A. J.* Arberry

Morning After, The. Heinrich Heine, *German*. EP, *tr. by* Louis Untermeyer

Morning After. Langston Hughes. MoP; NAAL-2; NBLV; NoAM; OBCoV

Morning After, The. Dorothy, Duchess of Wellington Wellesley. OBMV

Morning after is the first day, The. (LL) Apple Blossom. Louis MacNeice. NTP; PeECV; RB

Morning after. . . Love, The. Kattie M. Cumbo. BlSi

Morning after shipwreck. Virgil, *Latin*. OBCVT, *tr. by* John Dryden

Morning again, nothing has to be done. Second Poem. Peter Orlovsky. NeAP

Morning and evening. Goblin Market. Christina Rossetti. CPO; EBEV; FaBoSe; NAEL-2; NALW; NOBVV; NOxBChV; OBNV; OxAEP-2; VWP

Morning and Evening. Antoni Slonimski, *Polish*. TrJP, *tr. by* Watson Kirkconnell

Morning and evening. Worrying Fruit. Christina Rossetti. BoTP; EBEvV *Fr.* Goblin Market. CPO; EBEV; FaBoSe; NAEL-2; NALW; NOBVV; NOxBChV; OBNV; OxAEP-2; VWP

Morning and evening, drunk and singing. For Kuo Hsiang. Yü Hsüan-chi, *Chinese*. BoWoP, *tr. by* Geoffrey Waters

Morning and evening in the corn. (LL) Country Summer. Léonie Adams. LiTM; MoAmPo

Morning and evening, sleep she drove away. The Spinning Woman. Leonidas of Tarentum. AWP, *tr. by* Andrew Lang *Fr.* Epigrams.

Morning and Evening Star. Plato. *See* To Stella.

Morning and night I bring. Cottage Song. John Drinkwater. UV

Morning and night I found. Same Cottage—But Another Song, of Another Season. Max Beerbohm. UV

Morning, and streaks of heavenly blue. London Spring. Antoni Slonimski, *Polish*. TrJP, *tr. by* Frances Notley

Morning, and the poet up again and out and about. The Poet's Day. Richard Weber. CIP-2

Morning and the snow might fall forever. Going to Remake This World. James Welch. CDW

Morning arises stormy and pale. Tennyson. EBVVPR *Fr.* Maud [A Monodrama]. EnVR

    "Ah, what shall I be at fifty." NAEL-2

Morning at nine, seven ultra-masculine men. In Your Bad Dream. Richard Hugo. LCAP-2

Morning at Point Dume. May Swenson. DiPo

Morning at the Window. T. S. Eliot. AWP; PoA

Morning Baking, The. Carolyn Forché. LoL

Morning bath. Anita Virgil. HA

Morning Becomes Electric. Bruce Dawe. BMAP

Morning Bell at Tiêu Monastery, The. Mạc Thiên Tích, *Chinese*. AVP, *tr. by* Huỳnh Sanh Thông

Morning Bird Songs. Tomas Tranströmer, *Swedish*. InPS-3, *tr. by* Robert Bly

Morning: blue, cold, and still. January. Weldon Kees. CoAP

Morning breaks like a pomegranate, The. Wedding Morn. D. H. Lawrence. MoBrPo

Morning Bright, with Rosy Light, The. Thomas O. Summers. AH

Morning broke like an egg. Eggs. Susan Wood. SoSe-8

Morning / broods. Strawberrying. Maurice Kenny. HATNAP

Morning Call. Richard Murphy. BiHa

Morning Chronicle, 2 436. Leigh Hunt.

    Rondeau: "Nelly kissed me when we met." Ro

Morning Coffee. György Petri, *Hungarian*. VCWP, *tr. by* Clive Wilmer and George Gömöri

Morning comes, and thickening clouds prevail, The. The Clouded Morning. Jones Very. GSo; NOBA

Morning comes; not slow, with reddening gold, the. Frederick Goddard Tuckerman. APN-2 *Fr.* Sonnets.

Morning comes, the night decays, the watchmen leave their stations, The. Empire Is No More. William Blake. *Fr.* America; a Prophecy. OAEL-2

Morning comes. The old woman, a spot, The. Grief. Wendell Berry. MT

Morning comes to consciousness, The. T. S. Eliot. *Fr.* Preludes (I–IV). HeIP-4; OBMV; Poetr; TwCP; UnPo; VGW; WeW-3

Morning Compliments. Sydney Dayre. OxBChV

Morning drum-call on my eager ear, The. Robert Louis Stevenson. NOBVV

Morning Exercises. Nina Cassian, *Romanian*. PoSu, *tr. by* Andrea Deletant *and* Brenda Walker

Morning / five thousand years ago, A. The Lions of Babylon. Daniela Crsnaru, *Romanian*. CEEP, *tr. by* Fleur Adcock

Morning fog. Gary Hotham. HA

Morning glories. Clinton. Sterling Plumpp. BkSV *Fr.* Clinton.

Morning glory!, The. Chiyojo, *Japanese*. WPoS, *tr. by* Robert Aitken

Morning Glory. Howard Moss. DiPo

Morning Glory. Ruth Pitter. FaBoWP

Morning-Glory, The. Raymond Roseliep. HA

Morning Glory. Siegfried Sassoon. TrCP

Morning Glory, The. *Unknown*. AWP, *tr. by* Helen Waddell *Fr.* Shi King.

Morning-Glory, The. Sarah Helen Whitman. ColAP

Morning glory, climbing the morning long, The. Indiana. Hart Crane. *Fr.* Powhatan's Daughter. *Fr.* The Bridge. NAAL-2

Morning. Good luck! Among the houses! Gray Morning. Aleksandr Blok, *Russian*. TCRP, *tr. by* Geoffrey Thurley

Morning Harvest. Gerald Stern. LCAP-2

Morning has its flat first light, its blaze, The. New. Jennifer Maiden. BMAP

Morning he had gone. My Face Is My Own, I Thought. Tom Raworth. SPE

Morning Hours. Rossana Ombres. NeIt *Fr.* Excursion to Ravenna of A Young Girl with Her Parents.

Morning Hymn. Thomas Ken. NOSC

Morning Hymn, A. Christopher Smart. OxBChV

Morning Hymn. Charles Wesley. TOF

Morning, if this late withered light can claim. The Zonnebeke Road. Edmund Blunden. OBWP; PeFWW

Morning in My City. Avraham Shlonsky, *Hebrew.* MHP, *tr. by* Ruth Finer Mintz

Morning in the Burned House. Margaret Atwood. BAP-96

Morning in the Hills. Bliss Carman. NOBC

Morning in the Islands. John Hollander. ColAP

Morning Inscription. Miodrag Pavlovic, *Serbo-Croatian.* HSix, *tr. by* Charles Simic

Morning is clean and blue and the wind blows up the clouds, The. John Gould Fletcher. *Fr.* Irradiations. MoAmPo

Morning is lost in a maze. We're OK. Gloria Fuertes, *Spanish.* WPOW, *tr. by* Philip Levine

Morning Jitters. John Ashbery. FTOS

Morning Joy. Marie Under, *Estonian.* CEEP, *tr. by* Ivar Ivask

Morning Letter, A. Robert Duncan. PoA

Morning Light. Mary Effie Lee Newsome. PoBA

Morning Light, The. Louis Simpson. NNaP

Morning light﹐ creaks down again!, The. (LL) Aubade: "Jane, Jane, / Tall as a crane." Dame Edith Sitwell. BWW; CMoP; MoBrPo; MoP; NALW; NoAM; PoRA; Poetr

Morning Light Is Breaking, The. Samuel Francis Smith. AH

Morning Light Song. Philip Lamantia. NeAP

Morning, May rain. The city is silent still. The Man Awakened by a Song Above His Roof. Tomas Tranströmer, *Swedish.* SPE, *tr. by* Robert Bly

Morning moon is round and gold, The. April Poem. Gerda Mayer. AYFP

Morning muezzin in orange and a mosquito. Clark Coolidge. FTOS *Fr.* At Egypt.

Morning, Noon, And. Hawley Truax. NYBP

Morning of evanescent shadow, of laughter, A. What She Wanted to Be. Ory Bernstein, *Hebrew.* IP, *tr. by* Warren Bargad *and* Stanley F. Chyet

Morning of our rest has come, The. The Poor Man's Sunday Walk. Charles MacKay. EBVV

Morning, on a beach. A man & woman sitting by fire. Moon Is to Blood. Richard Duerden. NeAP

Morning on the St. John's. Jane Cooper. NYBP

Morning on the Shore. Wilfred Campbell. NOBC

Morning ought not. Pas de Deux for Lovers. Michael Dransfield. CBAP

Morning-Piece; or, An Hymn for the Hay-Makers, A. Christopher Smart. NOEC

Morning Post, no. 10,614. Coleridge.
Spots in the Sun. Ro

Morning Post, no. 9198. Robert Southey.
Idiot, The. Ro

Morning Prayer. Geoffrey Mac Briain Mac an Bhaird, *Irish.* TIRV, *tr. by* the Earl of Longford

Morning Prayer. Ogden Nash. OxBChV

Morning Prayer. *Unknown.* PoToHe

Morning Prayer, A. Ella Wheeler Wilcox. PoToHe

Morning Quatrains, The. Charles Cotton. NOSC; PeECV

Morning quiet. Gary Hotham. HA

Morning rain, evening rain, little plums turned yellow. Feeling Sorry for Myself. Lu Yu, *Chinese.* CoBCP, *tr. by* Burton Watson

Morning rain of Wei city wets the white dust, The. A Song for Wei City. Wang Wei, *Chinese.* TAL, *tr. by* Robert Payne

Morning Roar of the City, The. Slavko Mihalic. PoSu, *tr. by* Charles Simic

Morning, Rosamonde. Anne Batten Cristall. ECWP

Morning-Selah. Amir Gilbo'a, *Hebrew.* IP, *tr. by* Warren Bargad *and* Stanley F. Chyet

Morning service! parson preaches. The House of God. Alec Derwent Hope. OxBC; PFE

Morning sky glitters, The. De Civitate Hominum. Thomas MacGreevy. CIP-2

Morning Song. Afanasi Afanasievich Fet, *Russian.* AWP, *tr. by* Max Eastman

Morning Song. Edith Nesbit. SDW

Morning Song. Sylvia Plath. BoWoP; ColAP; HCAP; HeIP-4; InPK-6; InPS-3; LCAP-2; NAAL-2; NIP-4; NOBA; NTP; NoP-4; PoPoPo; SAGP; VCAP

Morning Song. Solomon ibn Gabirol, *Hebrew.* TrJP, *tr. by* Nina Davis Salaman

Morning Song of Senlin. Conrad Potter Aiken. ImPo; MoAmPo; OxBA
Fr. Senlin; a Biography.
(Morning Song.) CMoP

Morning space expands the building's. Louise Herlin, *French.* MFP, *tr. by* Martin Sorrell

Morning spent looking for my calendar. Losing the Marbles. James Merrill. DiPo

Morning spreads over. May All Earth Be Clothed in Light. George Hitchcock. VGW

Morning Star. Thomas Hornsby Ferril. VGW

Morning Star, The. Primus St. John. PoBA

Morning star goes under cover, The. Der von Kürenberg, *German.* GePo, *tr. by* Frederick Goldin

Morning Star, O Cheering Sight! *Unknown.* AH

Morning Stars, The. Robert Lax. KSG

Morning stretched calm, beautiful, and warm, The. A Doctor's Journal Entry for August 6, 1945. Vikram Seth. OMIP

Morning Sun. Louis MacNeice. MoBrPo; TwCP

Morning sun, The. Poem for Myself and Mei: Abortion. Leslie Marmon Silko. VoR

Morning sun climbs the eastern peak, The. Pien Kung. *Fr.* Paintings. CoBLCP, *tr. by* Jonathan Chaves

Morning sun shines, The. Emperor Wu of Liang, *Chinese.* OHMPC, *tr. by* Kenneth Rexroth

Morning Swim. Maxine W. Kumin. Poetr; WPE

Morning Thanksgiving. John Drinkwater. BoTP

Morning: the soft release. Meditation for a Pickle Suite. Richard H. W. Dillard. HoPM; MT

Morning. The sun gleams wickedly on chrome. Rogue Hydrant, August. Karl Kirchwey. WWSi

Morning they set out from home, The. I Was Not There. Karen Gershon. HP

Morning They Shot Tony Lopez, Barber and Pusher Who Went Too Far, 1958, The. Gary Soto. PBCAP

Morning to Remember, A; or, E Pluribus Unum. Edward Dorn. NoAM

Morning Track, The. Edward Parone. NYBP

Morning trickles over the bruised vegetables. The Manless Society. Pierre Unik, *French.* SPE, *tr. by* David Gascoyne

Morning. / Two sparrows sit on the tin roof. Finding the Way Back. Gerald McCarthy. CDa

Morning uptown, quiet on the street. Song Form. Imamu Amiri Baraka. ChAP; TTTS

Morning Vigil. Phillip William George. VoR

Morning-Watch, The. Henry Vaughan. ESCV; FMP; GeHe; NOSC; NTP; PeECV

Morning Watch, The. Jones Very. APN-1

Morning when the things again come back, The. Thanks to the Things. Rutger Kopland, *Dutch.* VCWP, *tr. by* James Brockway

Morning Work. D. H. Lawrence. MoBrPo

Mornings and eggshells crack, the eggshells scatter. Toward a 44th Birthday. Nellie Wong. NMM-2

Mornings are his, The. Waterwings. Cathy Song. NoAM

Morning's at seven. Pippa Passes, But I Can't Get Around This Truck. Margaret Blaker. NBLV

Mornings / before the sun's liquid. Lagoons, Hanlan's Point. Raymond Souster. NOBC

Mornings / I got up early. The Way It Was. Lucille Clifton. NMM-2; WPE

Mornings I see the Wu Mountain recumbent. At the Heng-ts'ui Pavilion of Fa-hui Monastery. Su Shih, *Chinese.* SuSp, *tr. by* Irving Y. Lo

Mornings run their course, clear and deserted, The. Grappa in September. Cesare Pavese, *Italian.* RaBo, *tr. by* William Arrowsmith

Mornings the sparrow twitters seeking food. Han Yü, *Chinese.* SuSp, *tr. by* Kenneth Hanson

Mornings up before the rooster calls. Autumn Thoughts. Lu Yu, *Chinese.* CoBCP, *tr. by* Burton Watson

Mornings when sky is white as dried gristle. The Onion. Margaret Gibson. MT

Mornin's Mornin, The. Gerald Brennan. BLPA

Morns are meeker than they were, The. Emily Dickinson. ChAP; ImGa; OBCA; SAmP

Moro Assassinato. Allen Curnow.
Urban Guerrilla, An. PeNZ

Moroccans with the carpets, The. Patrizia Cavalli, *Italian.* NeIt; VCWP, *tr. by* Kenneth Koch

Morphemes in section. Morphemics. Jack Spicer. PmAP

Morphemics. Jack Spicer. PmAP

Morpheus, the humble god, that dwells. A Song. Sir John Denham. NOSC

Morpheus, the lively son of deadly sleep. Sonnet 32. Sir Philip Sidney. *Fr.* Astrophil and Stella. AAS; SiPS

Morrigan, The. *Unknown, Irish.* BIrV, *tr. by* Thomas Kinsella

Morrissey and the Russian Sailor. *Unknown.* AS

Morrow every listen. Colloam. P. Inman. FTOS

Mors et Vita. James Edwin Campbell. AAP

Morse. Les A. Murray. NTP; NoP-4

Morsel. Ali Sardar Jafri, *Urdu.* OMIP, *tr. by* Kathleen Grant Jaeger *and* Baidar Bakht

Mort aux Chats. Peter Porter. OxBC

Mortal Combat. Mary Elizabeth Coleridge. VWP

Mortal flesh is full of grief. The Vanity of the World. Siôn Cent, *Welsh.* OBWVE, *tr. by* Joseph P. Clancy

Mortal Lease, The. Edith Wharton. LW

Mortal mixed of middle clay. Guy. Ralph Waldo Emerson. NOBA

Mortal my mate, bearing my rock-a-heart. To His Watch. Gerard Manley Hopkins. MoBrPo

Mortal never won to view thee. Hafiz, *Persian.* TOF, *tr. by* R. A. Nicholson

Mortal, Sneer Not at the Devil. Heinrich Heine. TrJP, *tr. by* Emma Lazarus *Fr.* Homeward Bound.

Mortal splendor: meteors are not needed less than mountains: shine, / perishing republic, A. Robinson Jeffers. *See* Shine, Perishing Republic.

Mortal though I bé, yea ephemeral, if but a moment. From the Greek. Ptolemy, *Greek.* OBCVT, *tr. by* Bridges, Robert; GrAn, *tr. by* Robert Bridges

Mortality. Naomi Long Madgett. PoBA

Mortality [*or* Mortalitie], behold and fear[e]! Lines on the Tombs in Westminster. Francis Beaumont. CH; FaBoCh; FaPoR; GTBS-P; HAP; NOBE; OBEV; OxAEP-1; SCGP *Fr.* On the Tombs in Westminster Abbey.

Mortar. Elizabeth Robinson. PT

Mortars are / the devil coughing. Remembrance of Things Past. Horace Coleman. CDa

Morte Arthur. *Unknown.*

  Sir Gawain Encounters Sir Priamus. PoEL-1

Morte d'Arthur, incorporated in Idylls of the King *with changes, as* The Passing of Arthur. Tennyson. EBNV; EBVVPR; FaBoBe; NIP-4; NOBVV; OAEL-2; OBNV; OxAEP-2; PoEL-5 *Fr.* Morte d'Arthur. EnVR

  Epic, The [Morte d'Arthur]. NAEL-2

  Passing of King Arthur, The. APAD

  "Then loudly cried the bold Sir Bedivere." TOF

Mortgage. Angie Gilligan. NBrP

Mortification. George Herbert. ESCV; FSCP; GeHe; NOSC; SeCP

Mortified Genius, The. James Graeme. NOEC

Mortmain. Robert Penn Warren.

  After Night Flight Son Reaches Bedside of Already Unconscious Father, Whose Right Hand Lifts in a Spasmodic Gesture, as Though Trying to Make Contact: 1955. NOBA

Moschus Moschiferus. Alec Derwent Hope. CBAP

Moscow. December. Nineteen fifty-one. A Simple Man. Nikolai Ivanovich Glazkov, *Russian.* TCRP, *tr. by* Daniel Weissbort

Moscow: Summer '86. Yevgeny Bunimovich, *Russian.* TCRP, *tr. by* Bradley Jordan *and* Albert C. Todd

Moselle, The. Ausonius, *Latin.*

  "No fish has ever told another of danger." OBCVT, *tr. by* Isbell, Harold

Moses. Amir Gilbo'a, *Hebrew.* MHP, *tr. by* Ruth Finer Mintz

Moses. Isaac Rosenberg.

  "Fine! Fine!" PeFWW

Moses. Sydney Tremayne. OxBS

Moses: A Story of the Nile. Frances Ellen Watkins Harper.

  Death of Moses, The. AAP

  Flight into Midian. AAP

Moses and Jesus. Israel Zangwill. TrJP

Moses and the Princess. Peter Dickinson. NOxBChV

Moses, from whose loins I sprung. The Jew. Isaac Rosenberg. ChIV-1; MoBrPo

Moses His Birth and Miracles. Michael Drayton.

  "In time the Princess playing with the child." ChIV-1

Moses in Infancy. Jones Very. ChIV-1; KSG

"Moses" of Michael Angelo, The. Robert Browning. GS

Moses supposes his toeses are roses. *Unknown.* FuFo; OxNR

Moses, who spake with God as with his friend. The Death of Moses. "George Eliot." ChIV-1

Mosquito, The. Rodney Jones. MT

Mosquito, The. D. H. Lawrence. *See* The Mosquito Knows.

Mosquito at my ear. Issa, *Japanese.* PiM, *tr. by* Robert Hass

Mosquito at my ear—. Avedik Issahakian. ChAP

Mosquito Kingdom. Ernesto Cardenal, *Spanish.* VCWP, *tr. by* Donald D. Walsh

Mosquito Knows, The. D. H. Lawrence. FaBoEE; OxBTC

  (Mosquito, The.) RB

Mosquito, may you fly, a swift courier for me. Meleager. HePo, *tr. by* Barbara Hughes Fowler *Fr.* I'll Twine White Violets. NIP-4, *tr. by* Goldwin Smith

Mosquito was heard to complain, A. Limerick. *Unknown.* PeLi

Mosquito, you are blessed with all nice things! Phan Văn Trị, *Vietnamese.* AVP, *tr. by* Huỳnh Sanh Thông

Mosquitoes. P'i Jih-hsiu, *Chinese.* SuSp, *tr. by* William H. Nienhauser

Mosquitoes. Franz Wright. LCAP-2

Mosquitoes / Are the fattest. Mama Dot's Treatise. Frederick D'Aguiar. HCP

Mosquitoes, shameless and shrill of voice, sucking the blood. Meleager. HePo, *tr. by* Barbara Hughes Fowler *Fr.* I'll Twine White Violets. NIP-4, *tr. by* Goldwin Smith

Moss below the Stairs. Kao Ch'i, *Chinese.* CoBLCP, *tr. by* Jonathan Chaves

Moss covered paths between scarlet peonies. Visit to the Hermit Ts'ui. Ch'ien Ch'i, *Chinese.* OHMPC, *tr. by* Kenneth Rexroth

Moss covers his stone bed fresh. Weeping for the Zen Master Po-yen. Chia Tao, *Chinese.* SuSp, *tr. by* Stephen Owen

Moss-Gathering. Theodore Roethke. BLT; PaTW; VGW

  ("As if I had committed, against the whole scheme of life, a desecration.") (LL) PaTW

Moss in the gratings / of a sewer vent. January 1965, Looking on. Ken Irby. FTOS

Moss of His Skin, The. Anne Sexton. CoAP; NALW; SAGP

Mossbawn. Seamus Heaney. CIP-2; PNI

  Mossbawn Sunlight. BIrV

  (Sunlight.) APAD

  Seed Cutters, The. PNI

Most alluring clouds that mount the sky, The. Wordsworth. NOBVV

Most are innocent, shy, will not undress. Angels. Dannie Abse. PoA

Most at home with what is Real. (LL) Doggerel by a Senior Citizen. W. H. Auden. NBLV; NOBL

Most Beautiful, The. Guido Gozzano, *Italian.* TTTS, *tr. by* Victoria Pesce

Most Beautiful Girl in the World, The. Lorenz Hart. OBAL

Most beautiful of things I leave is sunlight. Praxilla, *Greek.* BoWoP, *tr. by* Willis Barnstone

Most beautiful! the red-flowering eucalyptus. The Torso / Passages 18. Robert Duncan. PmAP

Most Beautiful Woman at My Highschool Reunion, The. Ellen Marie Bissert. GLP

Most Beds are Beds. Sylvia Plath. ChAP *Fr.* The Bed Book.

Most brightly of all burned the hair of my evening loved one. Night Ray. Paul Celan, *French.* AF, *tr. by* Michael Hamburger

Most Excellent Song Which Was Solomon's, The. Michael Drayton.

  "By night within my bed, I roamed here and there." ChIV-1

Most explicit— / the sense of trap. Age. Robert Creeley. PmAP

Most glorious Lord of Life that on this day. Sonnet 68. Edmund Spenser. AEP; ChIV-2; GSo; HAP; InPS-3; NAEL-1; NOBE; NOCV; NoSic; OBEV; PoE; Son *Fr.* Amoretti. AAS

Most Gracious Queen, we thee implore. On Queen Caroline. *Unknown.* FaBoEE; OBCoV

Most gunmen. Cowboy Sayings. *Unknown.* CA

Most happy letters framed by skilfull trade. Sonnet 74. Edmund Spenser. NAEL-1 *Fr.* Amoretti. AAS

Most he dared, the. Thomas. Gábor Görgey, *Hungarian.* CEEP, *tr. by* Jascha Kessler

Most high, all-powerful sweet Lord. Canticle of the Sun. Saint Francis of Assisi, *Italian.* EnlH, *tr. by* Stephen Mitchell

Most high Lord. Cantico del Sole. Saint Francis of Assisi, *Italian.* CTC, *tr. by* Ezra Pound

Most Holy Night, that still dost keep. The Night. Hilaire Belloc. OBEV

Most holy Satyr. Holy Satyr. Hilda Doolittle. MoAmPo

Most honoured Hera, who descends from heaven. Nossis, *Greek.* GrAn, *tr. by* Sally Purcell

Most I riden by Ribbesdale. *Unknown.* MiEL

Most is your name the name of this dark stone. Rainy Mountain Cemetery. N. Scott Momaday. CDW; HATNAP

Most Lovely Shade. Dame Edith Sitwell. FaBoTw; GTBS-P

Most magnificent of sights, The. Sky Seasons. John Rice. SpW

Most men know love but as a part of life. Henry Timrod. Son

Most men use / their eyes. The Mechanic. Diane Wakoski. AmPA

Most modern nature lovers have a personal scale of values that tells them. William Wordsworth (1770-1850). Gavin Ewart. NoAM

Most musical of mourners, weep again! Shelley. EPCY *Fr.* Adonais; An Elegy on the Death of Keats. EBEV; FHYEP; HoPM; ImPo; NOBRP; OAEL-2; OxAEP-2; PoEL-4; TFi

Most near, most dear, most loved and most far. To My Mother. George Barker. FaBoMo; ImPo; LiTM; OxAEP-2; OxBTC; PFE; PoWW; RaBo; SAGP; Son; TwCP

Most needy aren oure neighebores, The. The Poor. William Langland. PoEL-1 *Fr.* The Vision of Piers Plowman.

Most noble empress, you have heard of me? Shakespeare. OxAEP-1 *Fr.* Antony and Cleopatra.

Most, O maid's child, thy choice and worthy the winning. (LL) Spring. Gerard Manley Hopkins. APAD; EBVV; GSo; HAP; LiTM; MoBrPo; NAEL-2; NOBE; NOBVV; NoAM; OAEL-2; OBMV; OBNC; RB; TFi; TrCP

Most of all. (LL) The Secret. Denise Levertov. CrSp; PBMP; Poetr

Most of his friends, as expected. As Expected. Thom Gunn. GLP

Most of It, The. Robert Frost. BLT; HAP; NAAL-2; NoP-4; TOF; TRP; WeW-3

Most of it's too dreary. Outsider Art. Kay Ryan. BAP-95

Most of my days are passed away, yet my heart is still impure. The Worthless Heart. Immanuel di Roma, *Hebrew.* TrJP

Most of the mornings here, when we awaken. For a Suicide, a Little Early Morning Music. Gibbons Ruark. MT

Most of the past is lost. Switchblade. Michael Ryan. NAmP90

Most open of rooms. Kitchens. Eric Nelson. IFJA

Most people expect their sons to be clever. Bathing the Infant. Su Shih, *Chinese.* SuSp, *tr. by* Irving Y. Lo

Most people from Idaho are crazed rednecks. Carolyn Kizer. PaTW *Fr.* Running Away from Home.

Most people have turned their solutions toward what is easy and toward. Rilke. ITG, *tr. by* Stephen Mitchell *Fr.* Letters to a Young Poet.

Most people in the world stumble. Conversation Overheard. Quincy Troupe. NAAAL

Most pernicious purpose!—Seeming, seeming! Shakespeare. OxBoV *Fr.* Measure for Measure.

Most poets to a muse that is stone-deaf cry. On the Oxford Book of Victorian Verse. "Hugh MacDiarmid." MoBrPo

Celestial Alphabet Event. Jacques Gaffarel. PFTM

Most precious treasure is never fully known, The. Bubbles on the Water. Yang Wan-li, *Chinese.* SuSp, *tr. by* Jonathan Chaves

Most present of all the watchers where we camped, The. When We Looked Back. William Stafford. NYBP

Most Quietly at Times. Cäsar Flaischlen, *German.* AWP, *tr. by* Jethro Bithell

Most reverend Father, I have borne all wrong. Two Souls. Marjorie Lowry Christie Pickthall. NOBC

Most Saturday afternoons. The Weepies. Paul Muldoon. NoAM; PNI

Most souls, 'tis true, but peep out once an age. Dull, Sullen Prisoners. Alexander Pope. CH *Fr.* Elegy to the Memory of an Unfortunate Lady. ECEV; NOBE; NOEC; OAEL-1; OBEV; SCGP

Most sweet it is with unuplifted eyes. The Inner Vision. Wordsworth. GTBS-P *Fr.* Poems Composed or Suggested During a Tour, in the Summer of 1833.

Most terrible was our hero in battle blows. From the Irish. James Simmons. PBCIP; PNI

Most that can be said, The. Parade's End. Barbara Guest. PoM

Most that I know but one. Care. Josephine Miles. NYBP

Most truly hono[u]red, and as truly dear. To Her Father, with Some Verses. Anne Bradstreet. NAAL-3; NALW

Most Unloving One, The. Samuel Daniel. *Fr.* To Delia.

Most Vital Thing in Life, The. Grenville Kleiser. PoToHe; SoSe-8

Most weeds, whilst young. Francis Daniel Pastorius. SCAP

Most women get married, 'tis true. Limerick. Barney Blackley. PeLi

Most wounds can Time repair. At Ease. Walter De la Mare. GTBS-P

Most wretched heart, most miserable. Sir Thomas Wyatt. SiPS

Mostly, the men. Western Trail Cook, 1880. Sharyn Jeanne Skeeter. ISC

Mot eran dous miei cossir. Arnaut Daniel. AWP, *tr. by* Harriet Waters Preston

Mote it is to trouble the mind's eye, A. Shakespeare. OxAEP-1 *Fr.* Hamlet. NAWM-1

Motel. William Mills. MT

Motet: "I am a young girl." *Unknown, French.* PBWP, *tr. by* Carol Cosman

Motet: "Stranger here, as all my fathers were, A." John Amner. OxBSP

Motet. *Unknown, Old French.* PBWP, *tr. by* Carol Cosman

Moth, A. Henry Bellyse Baildon. NOBVV

Moth. Lance Henson. VoR

Moth ate a word. To me it seemed, A. Book Moth. Cynewulf. AnOE, *tr. by* Charles W. Kennedy *Fr.* Riddles (Exeter Book).

Moth ate words; a marvellous event, A. *Unknown.* NoP-4

Moth flew a bee-line, The. Mothy Monologue. Ralph Gustafson. NOBC

Moth-force a small town always has. The Strength of Fields. James Dickey. VCAP

"Moth has got into it, The." Vernon Scannell. OxBC

Moth, I thought, munching a word, A. Old English Riddle. Cynewulf. OPOU, *tr. by* Gerard Benson *Fr.* Riddles (Exeter Book).

Moth-Terror. Benjamin De Casseres. TrJP

Moth under the eaves, The. Prelude to Winter. William Carlos Williams. SAmP

Mothball Fleet: Benicia, California. John Haines. WeT

Mother, A. Victoria C. Armuth. CTV

Mother, The. Gwendolyn Brooks. CrDW; CrSp; ISC; MDDM; NAAAL; NALW; NMM-2; PoPoPo *Fr.* A Street in Bronzeville. BPo; BlSi; FaBoWP

("All.") (LL)　ISC

Mother. Hayden Carruth.

Death, The. FiLi

Mother, The. Caroline Clive. VWP

Mother, The. Nikolai Ivanovich Dementyev, *Russian.* TCRP, *tr. by* Lubov Yakovleva *and* Max Hayward

Mother. Sharon Doubiago.

"My mother is a poem I'll never be able to write." MDDM

Mother. Max Ehrmann. PoToHe

Mother. Hermann Hagedorn. PoToHe

Mother. Josephine D. Henderson Heard. CBWP-4

Mother. Zbigniew Herbert, *Polish.* IFJA, *tr. by* John Carpenter *and* Bogdana Carpenter

Mother. Vladimir Holan, *Czech.* PoSu, *tr. by* Ian *and* Jarmila Milner

Mother. P. Lankesh, *Kannada.* OMIP, *tr. by* A. K. Ramanujan

Mother. Bea Liu. LoHo

Mother, The. Catulle Mendès, *French.* TrJP, *tr. by* W. J. Robertson

Mother. Kiyoko Nagase, *Japanese.* BoWoP; WPJ, *tr. by* Kenneth Rexroth *and* Ikuko Atsumi

Mother, The. Sharon Olds. PBCAP

Mother, The. Gregory Orr. WeT

Mother, The. Padraic Pearse. TIRV

Mother. Poem for a Militant. Jorge Rebelo. PBMAP

Mother. Hettye Rayburn Ramsey. PWR

Mother. River. Tanikawa Shuntaro, *Japanese.* VCWP, *tr. by* Harold Wright

Mother, The. Dora Sigerson Shorter. VWP

Mother. Abraham Sutskever, *Yiddish.* "Friday evening coos up in the attic." CEEP, *tr. by* Seymour Mayne

Mother. Tê Hanh, *Vietnamese.* AVP, *tr. by* Huỳnh Sanh Thông

Mother. *Unknown.* PoToHe

Mother. Dorothy, Duchess of Wellington Wellesley. WPN

Mother. John Greenleaf Whittier. *Fr.* Snow-Bound [*or* Snow-Bound; a Winter Idyl]. APN-1; AiP; AmPP; NAAL-3; NOBA; OxBA; TAP; TFi

Mother, a father, a boy child, two maybe, A. Holy Family. Peter Cooley. NAmP90

Mother, a mother was born, A. (LL) Maternity. Alice Thompson Meynell. PEW; VWP

Mother, among the dustbins and the manure. Stevie Smith. PBWP

Mother and father are in heaven— / Amen. Chronica. Else Lasker-Schüler, *German.* PFTM, *tr. by* Durchslag, Audri *and* Jeanette Litman-Demeestère

Mother and listener she is, but she does not listen. The Question. Muriel Rukeyser. WPOW

Mother and Poet. Elizabeth Barrett Browning. NAEL-2; NALW; VWP

Mother and Son. Alden Nowlan. RaBo

Mother and Son. Allen Tate. MoAmPo

Mother asks what I'm put to, that means men. Julia Alvarez. Son *Fr.* 33.

Mother at Shannon, waving to her young, A. Throwing the Beads. Sean Dunne. BiHa

Mother Bombie. John Lyly.

O Cupid! Monarch over Kings. CBLP

Mother Cat, The. John Montague. NOIV; PC

Mother confused with earth. The Bounty, II. Myung Mi Kim. PT

Mother Country, The. Benjamin Franklin. AiP

Mother Crab and Her Family, The. L. T. Manyase, *Xhosa.* PeSA, *tr. by* Jack Cope *and* C. M. Mcanyangwa

Mother Dark. Francesca Yetunde Pereira. PBA

Mother darling, I cannot work the loom. Sappho, *Greek.* BoWoP, *tr. by* Willis Barnstone

"Mother dear, may I go downtown." Ballad of Birmingham. Dudley Randall. BPo; HeIP-4; ISC; InPK-6; MoP; NIP-4; NoAM; NoP-4; Poetr; SoSe-8

Mother Dear, O! Pray for Me. *Unknown.* AH

Mother / Deer / Lady. Harold Littlebird. VoR

Mother does knitting, The. Familial. Jacques Prévert, *French.* CLPP, tr. by Lawrence Ferlinghetti

Mother Doesn't Want a Dog. Judith Viorst. NBLV

Mother, don't, please don't. To Mother. S. Usha, *Kannada.* OMIP, tr. by A. K. Ramanujan

Mother Doorstep. Victor James Daley. NOBAu

Mother Duck. *Unknown.* BoTP

Mother Earth: Her Whales. Gary Snyder. LCAP-2

Mother, for months a mist has been before me. Light in Darkness. Mary E. Tucker. CBWP-1

Mother Goblin's Lullaby. Jack Prelutsky. NOxBChV

Mother Goose Up-to-Date. Louis Untermeyer.
  Archibald MacLeish Suspends the Five Little Pigs. MoAmPo
  Edgar A. Guest Considers "The Old Woman Who Lived in a Shoe" and the Good Old Verities at the Same Time. OBAL
  (Edgar A. Guest Syndicates the Old Woman Who Lived in a Shoe.) MoAmPo
  Edna St. Vincent Millay Exhorts Little Boy Blue. MoAmPo
  John Masefield Relates the Story of Tom, Tom, the Piper's Son. MoAmPo
  Walter de la Mare Tells the Listener about Jack and Jill. MoAmPo

Mother Goose's Garland. Archibald MacLeish. OBAL

Mother has lupus. Dear World. Paula Gunn Allen. HATNAP

Mother, Home, Heaven. William Goldsmith Brown. FaBoBe

Mother, how wrinkled and old must you become. David Ignatow. FiLi

Mother Hubbard's Tale. Edmund Spenser.
  Fox and the Ape Go to Court, The. NoSic

Mother, I Am Still Here With You. Bàng Bá Lâ, *Vietnamese.* AVP, tr. by Huỳnh Sanh Thông

Mother, I Cannot Mind My Wheel. Walter Savage Landor. AWP; BoLoP; GBL; NAEL-2; NOBE; OBEV; OBVE; PFE

Mother, I have taken your boots. Apology. Anne Stevenson. WeT

Mother, I know that now you're suffering much. It's Me, Your Son. Hồng Chu'o'ng, *Vietnamese.* AVP, tr. by Huỳnh Sanh Thông

Mother, I long to get married. Whistle, Daughter, Whistle. *Unknown.* AmFP; OxNR; ReMoGo

Mother, I love you so. Human Affection. Stevie Smith. LiLi; NALW

Mother, I may do violence to you. Sharon Mayer Libera. CrSp

Mother, I want to go. *Unknown, Spanish.* BoWoP, tr. by Willis Barnstone

Mother, I will have a husband. Thomas Vautor. CBLP *Fr.* Songs of Divers Airs and Natures.

Mother, / If I am where I am. From an Asylum; Kathy Chattle to Her Mother, Ruth Arbeiter. Anne Stevenson. BrRo

Mother II. Marilyn Hacker. NMM-2

Mother, I'm hungry. Yu Kuang-chung, *Chinese.* ChiPo, tr. by Yu Kuang-chung

Mother in gladness, Mother in sorrow. W. Dayton Wedgefarth. PoToHe

Mother-in-Law. Adrienne Rich. PoPoPo

Mother-in-Law Is Cruel. Cheng Hsieh, *Chinese.* CoBLCP, tr. by Jonathan Chaves

Mother-in-Law of the Marquis de Sade, The. Jennifer Maiden. NOBAu

Mother is drinking to forget a man. Frying Trout While Drunk. Lynn Emanuel. NAmP90

Mother, is this the darkness of the end. For "Our Lady of the Rocks." D. G. Rossetti. EBEV; GS

Mother, it pains me that I must confide. Winter Offerings. Frank Ormsby. PNI

Mother Jackson Murders the Moon. Gloria Escoffery. HCP

Mother Land / Long lain asleep. Mother Dark. Francesca Yetunde Pereira. PBA

Mother, let me go! (LL) A Frosty Night. Robert Graves. CH; MoBS; MoBrPo; OxBTC

Mother lies in travail bed, The. Newly Dead and Newly Born. Eliza Ogilvy. VWP

Mother Love. Rita Dove.
  Demeter Mourning. NAAAL
  Demeter's Prayer to Hades. NAAAL
  History. NAAAL
  Persephone Abducted. NAAAL
  Statistic: The Witness. NAAAL
  "Who can forget the attitude of mothering?" NAAAL

Mother love is a mighty benefaction. Stevie Smith. Spl

Mother, May I? Alma Villanueva. WPOW

Mother, May I Go Out to Swim? *Unknown.* OxNR

Mother might have drowned me. The Bath. Ira Sadoff. NAmP90

Mother mortgaged the piano. Mortgage. Angie Gilligan. NBrP

Mother, Mother, Are You All There? Felicia Lamport. NBLV

Mother Mother shave me. Song. *Unknown, Nyasa.* BoWoP, tr. by Ulli Beier

Mother, mother, what illbred aunt. The Disquieting Muses. Sylvia Plath. NALW; NMM-2

Mother, mother, / Why is it not you? The One Who Struggles. Ernst Toller, *German.* TrJP, tr. by E. Ellis Roberts

Mother Nature gave bulls horns. Anacreon, *Greek.* InMo, tr. by Sam Hamill

Mother Nature, how fair has your invention's grace. The Lake of Zurich. Friedrich Gottlieb Klopstock, *German.* GePo, tr. by George C. Schoolfield

Mother, never mourn'. (LL) Mater Dolorosa. William Barnes. CH; NOBE; OBEV

Mother Night. James Weldon Johnson. Son

Mother of Fishermen. Henriëtte Roland-Holst. PBWP, tr. by Ria Leigh-Loohuizen

Mother of God, The. W. B. Yeats. ChIV-2
  ("Three-fold terror of love, The.") GI

Mother of God! no lady thou. Our Lady. Mary Elizabeth Coleridge. OBEV; OBMV; WPE

Mother of God! Our Lady! For Eleanor and Bill Monahan. William Carlos Williams. CRP; VGW

Mother of God that's Lady of the Heavens. Prayer of the Old Woman. François Villon, *French.* MoBrPo; PeECV, tr. by J. M. Synge

Mother of gods. Meleager, *Greek.* GrAn, tr. by Peter Whigham

Mother of heaven, regina of the clouds. Le Monocle de Mon Oncle. Wallace Stevens. LiTM; MeMAP

Mother of Hermes! and still youthful Maia! Fragment of an Ode to Maia Written on May Day, 1818. Keats. OAEL-2; OBEV; PoEL-4

Mother of Judas, The. Yevgeny Mikhailovich Vinokurov, *Russian.* GI, tr. by Anthony Rudolf

Mother of Man. Vesna Parun, *Croatian.* PBWP, tr. by Mary Coote

Mother of memories! O mistress-queen! Le Balcon. Charles Baudelaire, *French.* AWP, tr. by Lord Alfred Douglas

Mother of my birth, for how long were we together. Kaddish. David Ignatow. RaBo

Mother of the Groom. Seamus Heaney. OxBSP; PiM

Mother of the muses, we are taught, The. Memory. Walter Savage Landor. EBEV; NOBVV; OAEL-2

Mother of us all, The. *Unknown. See* Hymn to Earth the Mother of All.

"Mother, oh mother! where shall we hide us?" Others. James Reeves. Spl

Mother Poem. Joel Oppenheimer. PoM

Mother Poem (two), The. Jackie Kay. NBrP

Mother presses her head to her hand, already, The. Rosanna Warren. *Fr.* Funerary Portraits. NoAM

Mother, R.I.P. Barbara L. Greenberg. WeT

Mother said: Come now, say your prayers, The. The Lord's Prayer. Massillon Coicou, *French.* NegPo, tr. by Ellen Conroy Kennedy

Mother said if I wore this hat. My Hat. Stevie Smith. BrRo; CBNP

Mother said thirty years ago. Miss Florence Jackson. David Huddle. PBCAP

Mother said to call her if the H bomb exploded. Belief. Josephine Miles. ColAP; FaBoWP; MoP; NoAM; TAP

Mother Sarah rocks the cradle. Mother Sarah's Lullaby. Itsik Manger, *Yiddish.* TrJP, tr. by Jacob Sonntag

Mother sat / with hunger on her hands. Child's Parliment. Chenjerai Hove. HBAPE

Mother, saying Anne good night. William Empson. CBNP

Mother shake the cherry-tree. Let's Be Merry. Christina Rossetti. TLR

Mother Shipton's Prophecies. Charles Hindley. BLPA

Mother shouts for her child Billy, A. The Debt. Lee Upton. CMAP

Mother slew her unborn babe, A. But Murderous. Stevie Smith. PFE

Mother Speaks: The Algiers Motel Incident, Detroit, A. Michael S. Harper. AmPA; BPo; NBV

Mother Tabbyskins. Elizabeth Anna Hart. NOxBChV; OxBChV
  ("In her cloak and hat.") NOxBChV

Mother—that was (the violence that was done). Zirkus. Andrew Joron. PT

Mother, the Nurse, and the Fairy, The. John Gay. PeLV *Fr.* Fables.

Mother then must suck the Son, The. (LL) Blessed be the Paps which Thou hast Sucked. Bible, *N.T.* BXAP; ChIV-2; NOSC, tr. by Richard Crashaw

Mother-thought. Jaihiun Kim, *Korean.* CKP, tr. by Jaihiun Kim

Mother, throughout her life, took pride in me. Mother's Faith. Thù'a Phong, *Vietnamese.* AVP, tr. by Huỳnh Sanh Thông

Mother throws her voice in loops, The. Two Couples. Debra Bruce. FFC

Mother to Her Waking Infant, A. Joanna Baillie. ECWP; NOEC; NoP-4; WoRP

("Now in thy dazzled half-oped eye.") CABP

Mother to Son. Langston Hughes. ChAP; FiLi; ISC; NAAAL; NAAL-2; NTCP; OBCA; SAmP; TTY

Mother Tongue, The. Carolina Hospital. LoHo

Mother Tongue. Jon Stallworthy. NoAM

Mother, unroll the bolts and name. Naming the Fabrics. Julia Alvarez. FFC

Mother was a crack of light. Three Floors. Stanley Kunitz. LoL

Mother was a washcloth. Touch. Kathryn Kerr. IFJA

Mother Wept. Joseph Skipsey. EBVV

Mother, what trick of light. The Mirror of Matsuyama. Sharon Hashimoto. OpBo

Mother, while you were at the shops. The Snowman. Roger McGough. OTCP

Mother who gave me life. Gwen Harwood. BMAP

Mother with Child. Lenore Keeshig-Tobias. FFC

Mother wrote to say: "Stay / in Europe. Soak up as much beauty as you." John Cage. APSN *Fr.* Diary: How to Improve the World (You Will Only Make Matters Worse).

Mother, / You did not leave me an inheritance of necklaces for a wedding. Mother's Inheritance. Fawziyya Abu Khalid, *Arabic.* WPOW, *tr. by* Kamal Boullata

"Mother, you know there is a place somewhere called Paris." The Right Meaning. César Vallejo, *Spanish.* RaBo, *tr. by* Robert Bly

Motherhood. Rita Dove. NAAAL

Motherhood. Agnes Lee. BLPA

Motherhood. May Swenson. CoAP; NoP-4

Mothering. Carla Harryman. FTOS

Mothers. Auvaiyar, *Tamil.* PLW, *tr. by* A. K. Ramanujan

Mothers. Nikki Giovanni. UnPo

Mothers. Maturaipputan Ilanakanar, *Tamil.* PLW, *tr. by* A. K. Ramanujan

Mothers. Maturaiputan Ilanakanar, *Tamil.* PLW, *tr. by* A. K. Ramanujan

Mothers. Kākkai Pāṭiṇiyār Naccellaiyār, *Tamil.* PLW, *tr. by* A. K. Ramanujan

Mothers. Kakkai Patiniyar Naccellaiyar, *Tamil.* PLW, *tr. by* A. K. Ramanujan

Mothers. Kavarpentu, *Tamil.* PLW, *tr. by* A. K. Ramanujan

Mothers. Punkanuttiraiyar, *Tamil.* PLW, *tr. by* A. K. Ramanujan

Mother's Advice. Unknown. AmFP

Mothers and Daughters. David Campbell. BMAP

Mothers are hardest to forgive. The Adversary. Phyllis McGinley. FaBoEE; OBCA; OxBSP; SoSe-8

Mother's Birthday. Lydia Wagenlander. PWR

Mother's Choice, The. Unknown. OxBoLi

Mothers / cranking the machine. The Greater Friendship Baptist Church. Carole C. Gregory Clemmons. BlSi

Mothers, Daughters. Shirley Kaufman. BoWoP; CrSp; NMM-2

Mother's Day. Edwin Becker. PWR

Mother's Day. Steve Hassett. CDa

Mother's Day. Daisy Zamora, *Spanish.* LoL, *tr. by* Margaret Randall

Mother's Day Proclamation of 1870. Julia Ward Howe. CrSp

Mother's face looked tired and worn, The. The Skeptic. Clara Ann Thompson. CBWP-2

Mother's Faith. Thù a Phong, *Vietnamese.* AVP, *tr. by* Huỳnh Sanh Thông

Mother's father. Big Zeb Johnson. Everett Hoagland. GT

Mother's Habits. Nikki Giovanni. BlSi

Mother's Hands. W. Dayton Wedgefarth. PoToHe

Mother's Inheritance. Fawziyya Abu Khalid, *Arabic.* WPOW, *tr. by* Kamal Boullata

Mother's Joy, A. Ruth Fortney Maxwell. PWR

Mother's Lace. Shonto Begay. NOxBChV

Mother's Lament, The. Helen Selina Blackwood, Countess of Dufferin. VWP

Mother's Lament, The. Mary E. Tucker. CBWP-1

Mother's Lament for the Death of Her Son, A. Robert Burns. HoPM

Mother's Letter from the North. Kyudong Kim, *Korean.* CKP, *tr. by* Jaihiun Kim

Mother's List of Duties, A. Ponmutiyar, *Tamil.* PLW, *tr. by* A. K. Ramanujan

Mother's Love, A. Josephine D. Henderson Heard. CBWP-4

Mother's Love, A. Ellen Johnston. VWP

Mother's Malison; or, Clyde's Water, The. Unknown. ESPB

Mother's Nerves. X. J. Kennedy. ChAP

Mothers of America / let your kids go to the movies! Ave Maria. Frank O'Hara. CLPP; HCAP; LiLi; NAAL-2; NNaP; NoP-4; PmAP; PoM; PoPoPo; VCAP

Mothers of sailors, I hope you will draw nigh. Johnny Gallagher. Unknown. AmFP

Mothers of Sons. Lesley Saunders. BrRo

Mother's Recall. Mary Weston Fordham. CBWP-2

Mother's Song, The. Unknown, Eskimo. OBCP, *tr. by* Peter Freuchen

Mother's Song. Unknown. BoWoP, *tr. by* Willis Barnstone

Mother's Songs. Frank Barbour Coffin. AAP

Mother's Tale, The. Ai. FiLi

Mothers, / That hope of yours, your joyful burden. To the Mothers. Ernst Toller, *German.* TrJP, *tr. by* E. Ellis Roberts

Mother's Voice. Robert Creeley. FiLi; Poetr

Motho Ke Motho Ka Batho Babang (A Person Is a Person Because of Other People). Jeremy Cronin. AF

Moths. Julia Fields. *Fr.* Poems: Birmingham 1962–1964. PoBA

Moths, The. Michael Jackson. PeNZ

Moths, The. W. S. Merwin. HeIP-4

Moths, The. Sean O Riordain, *Irish.* NOIV, *tr. by* Thomas Kinsella

Moth's kiss first!, The. Robert Browning. *See* In a Gondola.

Moth's kiss, first, The! In a Gondola. Robert Browning. BoLoP; GBL; OBEV *Fr.* In a Gondola.

Moths watched us through. Adam Zagajewski, *Polish.* BLT, *tr. by* Renata Gorcyznski, Benjamin Ivry, *and* C. K. Williams

Mothy Monologue. Ralph Gustafson. NOBC

Motion, The. Josephine Jacobsen. NMM-2

Motion guided a lotion, A. A Lack of Balance but not Fatal. Jackson Mac Low. FTOS

Motion of the Cypher. Ray DiPalma. FTOS

Motion was passed, The. (LL) Wilfred Owen's Photographs. Ted Hughes. FaBoPV; OxBC

Motionless Clouds. T'ao Ch'ien, *Chinese.* CoBCP, *tr. by* Burton Watson

Motionless Faces. Carlos Drummond de Andrade, *Portuguese.* PFTM; VCWP, *tr. by* Mark Strand

("And everyone.") (LL) VCWP, *tr. by* Mark Strand

Motionless—His sons. Death Bed. Thomas Kinsella. CIP-2; PBCIP

Motionless on the Dark Side of the Light. Minnie Bruce Pratt. NMM-2

Motionless sat the shadow at the helm. Thomas Westwood. PeVV *Fr.* The Quest of the Sancgreall.

Motionless under the moon-beam. "Calvary." W. B. Yeats. GI; PeECV

Motions and Means, on land and sea at war. Steamboats, Viaducts and Railways. Wordsworth. NAEL-2 *Fr.* Poems Composed or Suggested During a Tour, in the Summer of 1833.

Motion's Holdings. A. R. Ammons. NoAM

Motion's the dead giveaway. Viable. A. R. Ammons. TAP

Motive. Muriel Rukeyser. PoA

Motive for Mayhem, A. Abigail Child. FTOS

Motive for Metaphor, The. Wallace Stevens. MoAmPo

Motley. Peter Davison. NBLV

Motley. Walter De la Mare. HoPM; PoWW

Motley's the Only Wear. Shakespeare. OBCoV *Fr.* As You Like It.

Motor Bus. Alfred Denis Godley. NOBL

(On the Motor Bus.) NBLV

Motor stops, the boat thuds mud—the river's bed, The. After the Flood. John Foulcher. NOBAu

Motorbike, A. Ted Hughes. InPS-3

Motorbike breaks down near Sanna in torrential / rain, A. Rain. Robert Crawford. FaBoTC

Motorcycle roaring in the distance—, A. Aunt Toni's Heart. Rafael Campo. RA

Motorcyclists, The. James Tate. NoAM

Mots d'Heures: Gousses, Rames. Luis d'Antin Van Rooten.

"Jacques s'apprête." OBCoV

"Lit-elle messe, moffette." OBCoV

"Polis poutre catalane." OBCoV

"Pousse y gâte, pousse y gâte." OBCoV

Motto, The. Abraham Cowley. BeJo; NOSC; SeCP

Motto. Langston Hughes. CA; NAAAL; PoBA

("Dig And Be Dug / In Return.") (LL) PoBA

Motto for a Sundial. Unknown. FaBoEE

Motto Tell me, thou skilful shepherd's swain. Roundelay. Michael Drayton. AEP *Fr.* The Shepherd's Garland.

Motto to "Illusions." Ralph Waldo Emerson. *See* Illusions.

Motto to "Nature." Ralph Waldo Emerson. *See* Nature [1836].

Motto to Richard Lovelace, Lucasta. Posthume Poems. Martial, *Latin.* OBCVT, *tr. by* Unknown

Motto to "The Poet." Ralph Waldo Emerson. NCAP

Motto Vision 1971. Delano Abdul Malik de Coteau. PBCV

Mottoes to "History." Ralph Waldo Emerson. *Fr.* History. APN-1

Mought them awake out of their sinful sleep. (LL) In Praise of Wyatt's Psalms. Henry Howard, Earl of Surrey. AAS; SiPS

Mould of Castile. Jack R. Clemo. NOCV

Mouldering Vine, The. *Unknown.* AmFP

Mound, The. Thomas Hardy. OxBTC

Mounds from the yolk. (LL) Abiku. Wole Soyinka. PBMAP

Mounds of Human Heads Are Wandering into the Distance. Osip Emilevich Mandelstam, *Russian.* AF; FaBoPV, *tr. by* W. S. Merwin *and* Clarence Brown

Mount, The. Léonie Adams. MoAmPo

Mount Ararat. Louise Glück. ColAP

Mount Auburn! loveliest city of the dead. Richard Henry Wilde. APN-1 *Fr.* Hesperia.

Mount Badon. Charles Williams. FaBoTw

Mount Eagle. John Montague. BiHa; IIP

Mount Gilboa. Malka Heifetz-Tussman, *Yiddish.* PBWP, *tr. by* Marcia Falk

Mount Kearsarge. Donald Hall. LoL

Mount. Leave your living to the wise. Where the Sun Ends. Peter Davison. ChIV-1

Mount Lykaion. Trumbull Stickney. OxBA; Son *Fr.* Sonnets from Greece. APN-1

Mount, not wearisome and bare and steep, A. Coleridge. *See* To a Young Friend, [on His Proposing to Domesticate with the Author].

Mount of Olives ("Sweet, sacred hill! on whose fair brow"). Henry Vaughan. GeHe; ESCV

Mount of the Muses, The. Robert Herrick. CaPo

Mount rides into the seething alcove. (LL) The Women of Rubens. Wisława Szymborska, *Polish.* PoSu, *tr. by* Magnus F. Krynski; VCWP, *tr. by* Magnus J. Krynski *and* Robert A. Maguire

Mount Shasta. John Rollin Ridge. APN-2; PAR

Mount T'ai P'ing. Ch'ien Ch'i, *Chinese.* OHMPC, *tr. by* Kenneth Rexroth

Mount Vernon. *Unknown.* AmFP

Mount Wu Is High. Lu Chao-lin, *Chinese.* SuSp, *tr. by* Robin D. S. Yates

Mount Zion. *Unknown.* AmFP

Mountain, The. Hayden Carruth. AFr

Mountain, The. Louise Glück. NoAM

Mountain, The. Mikhail Yuryevich Lermontov, *Russian.* AWP, *tr. by* Max Eastman

Mountain, The. W. S. Merwin. VGW

Mountain, The. Jones Very. NCAP

Mountain after mountain / Fold by fold. Tune: "Remembering the Lady of Ch'in—At the Mouth of Dragon Pool." Na-lan Hsing-te, *Chinese.* SuSp, *tr. by* Lenore Mayhew *and* William McNaughton

Mountain Afterglow, The. James Laughlin. VGW

Mountain Altar, The. Brian O'Higgins. TIRV

Mountain and lake. I Ching. Diane Di Prima. SeSe

Mountain and the squirrel, The. Fable. Ralph Waldo Emerson. APN-1; AmPP; BoTP; CTAV; CTV; FaBoBe; ImPo; MeMAP; NBLV; OBAL; OBCA; TFi

Mountain Bride. Robert Morgan. MT

Mountain Cemetery, The. Edgar Bowers. CoAmPo

Mountain Chant, The. *Unknown, Navajo.*

First Daylight Song. APN-2, *tr. by* Washington Matthews

First Song of the Exploding Stick. APN-2, *tr. by* Washington Matthews

First Song of the Thunder. APN-2, *tr. by* Washington Matthews

Invocation To Dsilyi N'Eyani. APN-2, *tr. by* Washington Matthews

Last Daybreak Song. APN-2, *tr. by* Washington Matthews

Last Song of the Exploding Stick. APN-2, *tr. by* Washington Matthews

Last Words of the Prophet. APN-2, *tr. by* Washington Matthews

One of the Awl Songs. APN-2, *tr. by* Washington Matthews

Sixth Song of the Holy Young Men. APN-2, *tr. by* Washington Matthews

Song of the Prophet. APN-2, *tr. by* Washington Matthews

Song of the Rising Sun Dance. APN-2, *tr. by* Washington Matthews

Twelfth Song of the Holy Young Men. APN-2, *tr. by* Washington Matthews

Twelfth Song of the Thunder. APN-2; AWP, *tr. by* Washington Matthews

Mountain colors, whether near or far. Distant Mountains. Ou-yang Hsiu, *Chinese.* CoBCP, *tr. by* Burton Watson

Mountain Corral. Helen Sorrells. WPE

Mountain Drive. Cothrai Gogan. TIRV

Mountain, Fire, Thornbush. Harvey Shapiro. VGW

Mountain Forest. " Aleksandr Borisovich Kusikov," *Russian.* TCRP, *tr. by* Albert C. Todd

Mountain Greenery. Lorenz Hart. OBAL

Mountain in Labor, The. Aesop, *Greek.* AWP, *tr. by* William Ellery Leonard

Mountain is the father of the clouds, The. A Painting in the Style of Secretary Kao. Yün Shou-p'ing, *Chinese.* CoBLCP, *tr. by* Jonathan Chaves

Mountain Lion. D. H. Lawrence. FaBoVe; OxBTC; RB

Mountain looks gaunt, The. Tune: "Celebration in the Eastern Plain"—Replying to a Lyric Song by the Senior Poet Ma Chih-yüan. *Unknown, Chinese.* SuSp, *tr. by* Sherwin S. S. Fu

Mountain Maid, The. Dora Sigerson Shorter. SDW

Mountain Men. Tom Clark. IFJA

Mountain moon shines on a cloudless sky, The. Written at Mauve Garden: Pine Wind Terrace. Chu Yi-tsun, *Chinese.* SuSp, *tr. by* Chang Yin-nan *and* Lewis C. Walmsley

Mountain of gods and river of fair nymphs. The Monastery on Mount Hill-and-Stream. *Unknown, Vietnamese.* AVP, *tr. by* Huỳnh Sanh Thông

Mountain of green trees and orioles everywhere! Hsü Pen. CoBLCP, *tr. by* Jonathan Chaves *Fr.* A Leisurely Stroll.

Mountain pavilion is silent—few people visit me here, The. T'ang Yin. *Fr.* Poems Inscribed on Paintings. CoBLCP, *tr. by* Jonathan Chaves

Mountain Residence of Secretary Cheng Ching-ssu, The. Hsü Pen, *Chinese.* CoBLCP, *tr. by* Jonathan Chaves

Mountain Retreat of a Recluse, The. Chang Yü, *Chinese.* CoBLCP, *tr. by* Jonathan Chaves

Mountain road ends here, The. Lyell's Hypothesis Again. Kenneth Rexroth. APSN

Mountain road is steep, the stone steps are dangerous, The. Spring Thoughts Sent to Tzu-an. Yü Hsüan-chi. BoWoP, *tr. by* Geoffrey Waters

Mountain shadow. Foster Jewell. HA

Mountain sheep are sweeter, The. The War Song of Dinas Vawr. Thomas Love Peacock. AWP; CABP; EBEvV; FaBoCh; FaPoR; HAP; NAEL-2; NOBE; NOBRP; NTP; OAEL-2; OxAEP-2 *Fr.* The Misfortunes of Elphin

Mountain snow. Seasons in Santa Fe. Gerald Vizenor. HATNAP

Mountain Spirit, The. Ch'u Yüan. *Fr.* Nine Songs. CoBCP, *tr. by* Burton Watson

Mountain Spring, A. Ch'u Ch'uang I, *Chinese.* OHMPC, *tr. by* Kenneth Rexroth

Mountain Stream, The. John Ceiriog Hughes, *Welsh.* OBWVE, *tr. by* Kenneth Hurlstone Jackson

Mountain Study. Peter Van Toorn. NOBC

Mountain-summits sleep, glens, cliffs and caves, The. Fragment: "Mountain summits sleep, glens, cliffs, and caves, The." Alcman, *Greek.* OBCVT, *tr. by* Thomas Campbell

Mountain Talk. A. R. Ammons. HCAP

Mountain teeth, tips of anemious rippled stone. On the Subject of Waves. Eldon Grier. MoCV

Mountain temple dim and far away, its back against the setting sun, A. Tune: "Sand of Silk-washing Stream." Wang Kuo-wei, *Chinese.* SuSp, *tr. by* Ching-i Tu

Mountain Tops. Lizelia Augusta Jenkins Moorer. CBWP-3

Mountain Town—Mexico. Eldon Grier. NOBC

Mountain was in great distress and loud, A. The Mountain in Labor. Aesop, *Greek.* AWP, *tr. by* William Ellery Leonard

Mountain Wind, A. "Æ." AWP

Mountaineer, The. Robert Nathan. TrJP

Mountains. W. H. Auden. FaBoPV *Fr.* Bucolics.

Mountains and cold places on the earth. The Cloud Factory. John Haines. SPE

Mountains and houses, may be also men. (LL) Far from a cultural centre he was used. W. H. Auden. CMoP; NoAM

Mountains and rivers lie in the opening sun. Spring. Tu Fu, *Chinese.* TAL, *tr. by* Robert Payne

Mountains and Rivers without End: The Market. Gary Snyder.

Earrings Dangling and Miles of Desert. APSN

"Hump-backed flute player, The." APSN

Mountains and seas. Whip-the-World. "Hugh MacDiarmid." FaBoVe

Mountains, and the lonely death at last, The. To a Traveler. Lionel Pigot Johnson. MoBrPo

Mountains are moving, rivers. The Redwoods. Louis Simpson. CoAP

Mountains are steadfast but the mountain streams. Hwang Chin-i, *Korean.* PBWP, *tr. by* Peter H. Lee

Mountains bare next the southwest, The. (LL) After the Flood. Sir David Lindsay. ChIV-1; OxBS

Mountains beyond the city fade to nothingness, The. Bamboo Branch Song of Han-chia. Wang Shih-chieng, *Chinese.* CoBLCP, *tr. by* Jonathan Chaves

Mountains blanket-wrapped. Men in New Mexico. D. H. Lawrence. PaTW

Mountains by the seaside—sharp pointed swords. A Poem to Send to Friends in the Capital. Liu Tsung-yüan, *Chinese.* CoBCP, *tr. by* Burton Watson

Mountains cannot block this dreamlike song, The. Hearing a Flute on the River Chi. Wen Cheng-ming, *Chinese.* CoBLCP, *tr. by* Jonathan Chaves

Mountains crackle, The. Her Garden. Meena Alexander. OMIP

Mountains face each other; distrusting eyes look at each other. The True Line. Pong-u Park, *Korean.* CKP, *tr. by* Jaihiun Kim

Mountain's giddy height I sought, A. The Lay of the Trilobite. May Kendall. VWP

Mountain's green and shining, The. Summer Solstice. Alan Garner. NOxBChV

Mountains grow—unnoticed, The. Emily Dickinson. MoAmPo

Mountains loom upon the path we take. Song to the Mountains. *Unknown, Pawnee.* AWP, *tr. by* Alice C. Fletcher

Mountains of Mourne, The. William Percy French. OBCoV

Mountains ring, the wild wind comes, The. Wild Wind. Li Meng-yang, *Chinese.* CoBLCP, *tr. by* Jonathan Chaves

Mountains rubbed by light clouds. Tune: "Courtyard Full of Fragrance." Ch'in Kuan, *Chinese.* SuSp, *tr. by* James J. Y. Liu

Mountains shine through forest breaks, bamboo hides the wall, Tune: "Partridge Sky." Tune: Partridge Sky. Su Tung-p'o, *Chinese.* CoBCP, *tr. by* Burton Watson

Mountains surround the ancient kingdom in a massive circle. Chin-ling. Liu Yu Hsi, *Chinese.* SuSp, *tr. by* Paul Kroll

Mountains that I like, The. Homeward Bound. Ezekiel Mphahlele. AF

Mountains they knew, and jungle, the sun, the stars—. At Tikal. William Bronk. APSN

Mounted horse will stop, The. Pegasus. Varlam Tikhonovich Shalamov, *Russian.* TCRP, *tr. by* Bradley Jordan

Mounting on high I begin to realize the smallness of Man's. Climbing the Ling-ying Terrace and Looking North. Po Chü-i, *Chinese.* ChiP, *tr. by* Arthur Waley

Mounting on high I begin to realize the smallness of Man's / Domain;. Climbing the Ling-Ying Terrace and Looking North. Po Chü-i, *Chinese.* BLT, *tr. by* Arthur Waley

Mounting the Pile she unsheaths the Trojan sword. Virgil. OBCVT, *tr. by* Anne Wharton *Fr.* A Paraphrase on the last speech of Dido in Virgil's Æneas.

Mounts through all the spires of form. (LL) Nature [1836]. Ralph Waldo Emerson. APN-1; AWP; NCAP

Mourn for the living through the livelong night. (LL) Consolations of Philosophy. Derek Mahon. BIrV; CIP-2

Mourn for Yourself. Geoffrey Keating, *Irish.* BIrV, *tr. by* Sean Lucy

Mourn, hapless Caledonia, mourn. The Tears of Scotland. Tobias Smollett. ECEV; NOEC

Mourn, mourn, ye Muses, all your loss deplore. On the Death of the Late Earl of Rochester. Aphra Behn. NoP-4

Mourn No More. John Fletcher. *See* Weep No More.

Mourn Not for Adonais. Shelley. *See* An Elegy on the Death of Keats.

Mourn not, friends, mourn not, bereaved. Lines on the Death of the Rev. S. K. Talmage. Mary E. Tucker. CBWP-1

Mourned by scholars who dream of the ghosts of Greek boys. (LL) The Funeral. Stephen Spender. CMoP; MoBrPo; NoAM

Mournful Dove, The. *Unknown.* AmFP

Mournful gift is mine, oh friends!, A. Second Sight. Felicia Dorothea Hemans. Ro

Mournful strain was in thyself alone, The. (LL) The Pines and the Sea. Christopher Pearse Cranch. ColAP; PAR

Mourning. Andrew Marvell. FMP; SeCP

Mourning, A. Vassar Miller. NMM-2

Mourning. Daniel Weissbort. GI

Mourning a Hero. Nhu'ọ'ng Tống, *Vietnamese.* AVP, *tr. by* Huỳnh Sanh Thông

Mourning Bride, The. William Congreve.
  "Music has charms to soothe a savage breast." OxAEP-1

Mourning cloak, A. John Wills. HA

Mourning for Lü Hui-chiu. Yün Shou-p'ing, *Chinese.*
  "Facing you, on the wall, across from your bed." CoBLCP, *tr. by* Jonathan Chaves

Mourning for My Son Jun-erh. Cheng Hsieh, *Chinese.* CoBLCP, *tr. by* Jonathan Chaves

Mourning for My Wife. Mei Yao Ch'en, *Chinese.* SuSp, *tr. by* Jonathan Chaves

Mourning her who thought she loved me. Samuel Beckett. *See* I would like my love to die.

Mourning Letter from Paris, A. Conrad Kent Rivers. BPo

Mourning Letter, March 29 1963. Edward Dorn. CoAmPo

Mourning My Son. Yüan Chen, *Chinese.* SuSp, *tr. by* Angela Jung Palandri

Mourning Nguyễn Thái Học and Nguyễn Thị Giang. Phan Bội Châu, *Vietnamese.* AVP, *tr. by* Huỳnh Sanh Thông

Mourning Pablo Neruda. Robert Bly. LCAP-2

Mourning Picture. Adrienne Rich. CoAP

Mourning Poem for the Queen of Sunday. Robert Earl Hayden. HCAP; NAAAL; NoAM; NoP-4; PoBA; PoPoPo

Mourning Song. Robert Pearl, *Tsimshian Indian.* STP, *tr. by* Armand Schwerner

Mourning the Death, by Hemorrhage, of a Child from Honai. Basil T. Paquet. CDa

Mourning the first and last to love me. (LL) I would like my love to die, *Author's own English vers. of his* "Je voudrais que mon amour meure." Samuel Beckett. BIrV; CIP-2; IIP; NOIV

Mourns to the city in its gloom. (LL) Derry Morning. Derek Mahon. IIP; NOIV

Mouse, The. Elizabeth Jane Coatsworth. BoTP; NOxBChV; OBCA

Mouse, The. Jean Garrigue. TwCP

Mouse, The. Laura Elizabeth Richards. OBCA

Mouse, The. Thirza Wakley. BoTP

Mouse and the Cake, The. Eliza Cook. ACTP; OxBChV; VWP

Mouse-brown foal that fain had fed, The. The Foal. William Renton. NOBVV

Mouse crawled through it, The. Hole. Leonard Nathan. PBCAP

Mouse Dinner. Aileen Fisher, *Armenian.* TLR, *tr. by* Aileen Fisher

Mouse Dinners. Russell Edson. SoSe-8

Mouse doesn't dine, A. Mouse Dinner. Aileen Fisher, *Armenian.* TLR, *tr. by* Aileen Fisher

Mouse found a beautiful piece of plum-cake, A. The Mouse and the Cake. Eliza Cook. ACTP; OxBChV; VWP

Mouse in her room woke Miss Dowd, A. *Unknown.* TLR

Mouse in the cupboard repeats himself, The. A Ritual Mouse. William Meredith. PBMP

Mouse in the Wainscot, The. Ian Serraillier. OTCP

Mouse, The Frog and The Little Red Hen, The. *Unknown.* BoTP

Mouse the trap had slapped on, but not caught, A. Ballad of the Mouse. Robert Wallace. NYBP

Mouse whose name is Time, The. Robert Francis. TLR

Mouse)Won / derfully is. E. E. Cummings. MeMAP

Mousemeal. Howard Nemerov. TwCP

Mouse's Lullaby, The. Palmer Cox. NOxBChV; OBCA; TLR

Mouse's Nest. John Clare. InPK-6; NAEL-2; RB

Mouse's Petition, The. Anna Laetitia Barbauld. ECWP; OxBChV

Mouse's Tale, The. "Lewis Carroll." *See* A Long Tale.

Mousetrap, The. Callimachus, *Greek.* HePo, *tr. by* Barbara Hughes Fowler

Mousie, mousie. Conversation. Rose Fyleman. NYBP

Mousōnios built this solid, windproof mansion, and built it well. A House in Byzantium. Agathias, *Greek.* GrAn, *tr. by* Fleur Adcock

Mouth, The. Ciaran Carson. PNI

Mouth. Dennis Scott. PBCV

Mouth and the Ears, The. Shem-Tob ben Joseph Palquera, *Hebrew.* TrJP, *tr. by* J. Chotzner

Mouth. Can blow or breathe, A. Cardinal Ideograms. May Swenson. NoP-4; OBCA

Mouth Is Always Muzzled, A. Martin Carter. HCP

Mouth like old silk soft with use, A. A Levantine. William Plomer. OBMV

Mouth of a girl who had long lain among the reeds looked, The. Lovely Childhood. Gottfried Benn, *German.* PFTM, *tr. by* Babette Deutsch

Mouth of the Hudson, The. Robert Lowell. AiP; VCAP

Mouth of the Wen River—240 feet wide, The. On Board a Boat at Chi-ning. Yüan Hung-tao, *Chinese.* CoBLCP, *tr. by* Jonathan Chaves

Mouth of the Wolf. Susan Stewart. NAmP90

Mouthful of language to swallow, A. Peaches. Donald Hall. NoP-4

Mouths. Dorothy Aldis. CTV

Move. Lucille Clifton. NAAAL

Move, and then / stop. (LL) The Turn. Robert Creeley. FTOS; LCAP-2

Move Continuing, The. Al Young. PoBA

Move in with the sun. Futility. Wilfred Owen. APAD; CMoP; FaBoMo; GTBS-P; MoBrPo; NAEL-2; NSI; NoAM; NoP-4; OBWP; PeFWW; RB

Move into / the past tense. Grammar Lesson. Linda Pastan. Poetsp

Move my home on board a fishing boat. (LL) To the Tune "Nan-hsiang-tzu." Shen Chou, *Chinese.* ChiPo; CoBLCP, *tr. by* Jonathan Chaves

Move over, ham. Hiding Place. Richard Armour. NIP-4

Moved on. None heeded, and few heard. (LL) Cassandra. Edwin Arlington Robinson. CMoP; ImPo; LiTM; MeMAP; NoAM; OxBA

Movement. Nikolai Alekseievich Zabolotsky, *Russian.* TCRP, *tr. by* Daniel Weissbort

Movement of air northward, The. Sacramento. Luke Breit. EC2

Movement of Fish, The. James Dickey. NYBP; VGW

Movement, she explained, would bring poetry to the rich, The. Ralph Hodgson. *Fr.* Flying Scrolls. FaBoTw

Movement Song. Audre Lorde. VCAP

Movements. Norman MacCaig. OxBC

Moves small beyond it. (LL) The Door. Robert Creeley. NeAP; NoAM; PoM; VGW

Moves the calm spirit, but disturbs it not. (LL) The Ocean. Moschus, *Greek.* OBCVT, *tr. by* Shelley; AWP; OBVE, *tr. by* Shelley

Movie, The. Steve Denning. CDa

Movie Actors Scribbling Letters Very Fast in Crucial Scenes. Jean Garrigue. TAP

Movie-Going. John Hollander. CoAP

Movie House. John Updike. PeLV

Movie of Robert, A. Bresson's Movies. Robert Creeley. NoP-4; PmAP

Movies and the magazines are all of them liars, The. Love Letter. W. H. Auden. CBLP

Movies are badder. Saturday Afternoon at the Movies. John Logan. NNaP

Movies for the Home. Howard Moss. NYBP

Movies, Left to Right. Howard Moss. NYBP

Movies you wouldn't let them see when they were young. (LL) Ave Maria. Frank O'Hara. HCAP; LiLi; NAAL-2; NNaP; NoP-4; PmAP; PoM; PoPoPo; VCAP

Movin' with Nancy. David Trinidad. PmAP

Moving. Jeanne Foster. CrSp

Moving. Sam Hamod.
"So we move now." UnSA

Moving. Helen G. Quigless. BkSV

Moving. Martin Shea. HA

Moving along Main St. One Day. Bobbi Sykes. BMAP

Moving deep. "Stephany." NBV

Moving finger writes; and, having writ, The. Omar Khayyám. TRP *Fr.* The Rubáiyát of Omar Khayyám [of Naishápúr]. AWP; EBVV; FaBoBe; FaPoR; HAP; NAEL-2; PoEL-5

Moving Finger writes; and, having writ, The. 71. Edward Fitzgerald. CABP

Moving from Cheer to Joy, from Joy to All. Next Day. Randall Jarrell. HAP; HCAP; MoP; NAAL-2; NYBP; NoAM; NoP-4; Poetr; VCAP; WeW-3

Moving from the bus at the Loop it's possible suddenly. Seeing St. James's. Ray Mathew. NOBAu

Moving grass, the Indian in his glade, The. (LL) This is where the serpent lives, the bodiless. Wallace Stevens. CMoP; PoE

Moving House. Ch'ien T'ao, *Chinese.* ChiP, *tr. by* Arthur Waley

Moving House ("In spring and fall there are many fine days"). T'ao Ch'ien, *Chinese.* CoBCP, *tr. by* Burton Watson

(Moving House, No. 2.) CoBCP, *tr. by* Burton Watson

Moving House ("Long time I've wanted to live in the southern village, A"). T'ao Ch'ien, *Chinese.* CoBCP

(Moving House, No. 1.) CoBCP, *tr. by* Burton Watson

Moving In. Paul Engle. PoA

Moving in a restless exhaustion. The Field of the Caribou. John Haines. WeT

Moving in her radiant care. Catullus. *See* Hymn to Diana.

Moving like women: Justice, Truth, such figures. (LL) Another September. Thomas Kinsella. BIrV; CABP; CIP-2; NoP-4

Moving Object. Jean Day. FTOS

Moving on in the Dark Like Loaded Boats at Night, Though There is No Course, There is Boundlessness. Lucie Brock-Broido. MoLi

Moving on or going back to where you came from. A Procession at Candlemas. Amy Clampitt. FaBoWP; HCAP; PoPoPo; Poetr

Moving out. Thing Poem. Petra von Morstein, *German.* BoWoP, *tr. by* Rosemarie Waldrop

Moving over the hills, crossing the irrigation. George Oppen. APSN; NNaP *Fr.* Some San Francisco Poems.

Moving shadows, The. Virgil Hutton. InPK-6

Moving sun-shapes on the spray, The. Going and Staying. Thomas Hardy. CMoP; NoAM

Moving through the silent crowd. Unemployed. Stephen Spender. NOBE

Moving van zooms, A. Alan Pizzarelli. HA

Mower Against Gardens, The. Andrew Marvell. CABP; EBEV; ESCV; FaBoPV; GaP; NAEL-1; NOSC; NoP-4; OAEL-1; OBGa; OxAEP-1; PBRV; PoE; PoEL-2

Mower to the Glow-Worms [*or* Glowworms *or* Glo-Worms], The. Andrew Marvell. AWP; CBLP; ESCV; EnLoPo; FHYEP; FMP; FSCP; GeHe; GLoP; NAEL-1; NOBE; OAEL-1; OxBoLi; PBRV; PeLV; PoEL-2; SCGP; SeCP; TFi

("Be reckoned but with herbs and flowers?") (LL) NoP-4

Mowers: An Anticipation of the Cholera, 1848, The. Charles MacKay. EBVV

Mower's Song, The. Andrew Marvell. CBLP; ESCV; FMP; NAEL-1; NOSC; PoEL-2; SeCP

Mowing. Robert Frost. CMoP; ColAP; HoPM; NAAL-2; NOBA; OxBA; TRP; VGW

Mowing, The. Sir Charles G. D. Roberts. NOBC

Mowing his three acres with a tractor. On the Turning Up of Unidentified Black Female Corpses. Toi Derricotte. NAmP90; NMM-2

Mown under / like a corpse / or a loose seed. (LL) Freeway 280. Lorna Dee Cervantes. PaTW

Moyst with one drop of thy blood, my dry soule. Resurrection. Donne. ESCV *Fr.* La Corona. ChIV-2; ESCV; Son *Fr.* Holy Sonnets.

Mozart. John Heath-Stubbs. EBEV

Mozart, Goethe, and the Duke of Wellington. The Augsburg Adoration. Randall Jarrell. NYBP

Mozart's Requiem. Felicia Dorothea Hemans. Ro

Mr. Alan Jay Lerner (with by-play). Limerick. J. A. Lindon. PeLi

Mr. and Mrs. Wendy Mulford. NBrP

Mr. and Mrs. Spikky Sparrow. Edward Lear. OxBChV

Mr. and Mrs. Vite's Journey. *Unknown.* NOBL

Mr. Aplinio Morales has reported this. Incident at Imuris. Alberto A. Ríos. NIP-4; PuP-14

Mr. Apollinax. T. S. Eliot. PoA

Mr. Artesian's Conscientiousness. Ogden Nash. NBLV

Mr. Beetle. Emily Hover. BoTP

Mr. Bidery's Spidery Garden. David McCord. OTCP

Mr Bleaney. Philip Larkin. HoPM; InPS-3; OxBC; PoE; PoPoPo; TRP; UV

—Mr Bones: there is. (LL) Dream Song 4. John Berryman. BoLoP; CAPP-1; ColAP; HAP; HCAP; NoP-4; OBAL; PoPoPo; VCAP

Mr. Brodsky. Charles Tomlinson. MoP; NoAM; OxBC

("To be merely an Indian") (LL) NoP-4

Mr. Coggs. Edward Verrall Lucas. BoTP

(Mr. Coggs, Watchmaker.) FPC

Mr. Cogito Meditates on Suffering. Zbigniew Herbert, *Polish.* VCWP, *tr. by* John Carpenter *and* Bogdana Carpenter

Mr. Cogito Tells about the Temptation of Spinoza. Zbigniew Herbert, *Polish.* GI, *tr. by* John Carpenter *and* Bogdana Carpenter

Mr. Cooper. Anthony Thwaite. OxBTC

Mr. Cromek [*or* On Cromek]. William Blake. FaBoEE

Mr Cromek to Mr Stothard. William Blake. FaBoEE

Mr. Davis's Experience. *Unknown.* AmFP

Mr. Edward Fordham. Mary Weston Fordham. CBWP-2

Mr. Edwards and the Spider. Robert Lowell. CMoP; CoAP; ColAP; FaBoMo; HeIP-4; InPS-3; LiTM; NAAL-2; NOBA; NoP-4; TFi; TwCP

Mr. Eliot Pastor of the Church of Christ at Roxbury. Edward Johnson. SCAP

Mr. Eliot's Day. Robert Francis. NYBP

Mr. Finney had a turnip. Mr. Finney's Turnip. *Unknown.* FPC

Mr Flood's Party. Edwin Arlington Robinson. AWP; AmPP; CMoP; ClHu; ColAP; EBNV; FP; HAP; HeIP-4; HoPM; LiTM; MeMAP; MoAmPo; MoP; NAAL-2; NIP-4; NOBA; NoAM; NoP-4; OxBA; PoE; PoRA; Poetr; SoSe-8; TAP; TFi; TRP; UnPo; WeW-3

Mr. Frog Went a-Courting. Mother Goose. AS

Mr. Frost Goes South to Boston. Firman Houghton. UV

Mr. 'Gator. N. M. Bodecker. NTCP

Mr. Geomethel liked to hold Saturday afternoon parties. Funny Man. Charles Bukowski. EC2

Mr. Hansen, the cop at the campus gate. Officers. Josephine Miles. FaBoWP

Mr. Heath-Stubbs as you must understand. Epitaph. John Heath-Stubbs. OxBTC

Mr. Hosea Biglow Speaks. James Russell Lowell. *See* Letter, A ("Thrash away, you'll hev to rattle").

Mr. Housman's Message. Ezra Pound. FaBoEE

Mr. Hughes. David Campbell. CBAP

Mr. Ibister, and Betsy his sister. *Unknown.* OxNR

Mr. Irving Berlin. Noël Coward. UV *Fr.* Let's Do It.

Mr Jones. Harry Graham. PeLV *Fr.* Some Ruthless Rhymes.

Mr Kartoffel's a whimsical man. James Reeves. FuFo

Mr. Leach made a speech. Forensic Jocularities. Sir George Rose. OxBoLi

Mr Lear, I'm the Akond of Swat. Limerick. Ethel Talbot Scheffauer. PeLi

Mr L'Estrange's Verses in the Prison at Lynn. Sir Roger L'Estrange. NOSC

Mr. McGregor's Garden. Medbh McGuckian. CIP-2; PNI

Mr Mistoffelees. T. S. Eliot. CBNP; NOxBChV

Mr. Mine. Anne Sexton. AFr

Mr. Molony's Account of the Crystal Palace. William Makepeace Thackeray. PeVV

Mr. Moon. Bliss Carman. FPC

Mr. Murple's got a dog that's long. Noctambule. George Johnston. MoCV

Mr. Muscle-On. Faye Kicknosway. DeD

Mr. Nehru. Tanka. Miya Shūji, *Japanese.* MJT, tr. by Makoto Ueda

Mr. Nixon. Ezra Pound. MoAmPo *Fr.* Hugh Selwyn Mauberley. (Life and Contacts). AmPP; CMoP; InPS-3; LiTM; NOBA; NoAM; TAP

Mr Nobody. *Unknown.* BoTP; CTV; ChAP

Mr. Pennycomequick. Phyllis M. Stone. BoTP

Mr. Petty-Pie. Portrait. Stevie Smith. WPN

Mr. Pierce the butcher. The Butcher's Son. Thom Gunn. BAP-93

Mr. Placid's Flirtation. Frederick Locker-Lampson. PeVV

Mr. Pope. Allen Tate. ColAP; FuPo; NOBA; NoAM; TwCP; VGW

Mr. Pope's Welcome from Greece. John Gay. EBEV; OxAEP-1; OxBoLi; PoEL-3

Mr. Punchinello. *Unknown. See* To Mr. Punchinello.

Mr. Rochester's wife's pyromania. Limerick. Gina Berkeley. PeLi

Mr. Rockefeller's Hat. Helen Smith Bevington. OBAL

Mr. Roosevelt Regrets. Pauli Murray. PoBA

Mr. Scarecrow. Sheila Braine. BoTP

Mr. Slatter. N. M. Bodecker. TLR

Mr. Squirrel. V. M. Julian. BoTP

Mr. Strugnell. Wendy Cope. UV

Mr T. / bareheaded. The Artist. William Carlos Williams. InPS-3; LCAP-2; NYBP; RB; SAGP; SAmP

Mr. Teodoro Luna in his later years had taken to kissing. Teodoro Luna's Two Kisses. Alberto A. Ríos. PoPoPo

Mr. Thomas Shepeard. Edward Johnson. SCAP

Mr. Tom Narrow. James Reeves. OBSP

Mr. Tut's House A Recollection. Julia Fields. BkSV

Mr u will not be missed. E. E. Cummings. FaBoEE; OBCoV; VGW

Mr. Vachel Lindsay Discovers Radio. Samuel Hoffenstein. BXAP

Mr. Vanessa took the phone. Parallax. Maxwell Anderson. NYBP

Mr. Wakeville on Interstate 90. Donald Hall. AFr

Mr. Ward of Anagrams Thus. Nathaniel Ward. SCAP

Mr. Wells. Elizabeth Madox Roberts. KaS

Mr. Wells of the big cerebellum. Limerick. H. G. Wells. PeLi

Mr. Whittier. Winfield Townley Scott. VGW

Mr. X. Catherine Bowman. BAP-95

Mr. Z. M. Carl Holman. PFE; SoSe-8

Mririda. Mririda n'Ait Attik, *Berber into French.* WPOW, tr. by René Euloge; *English vers. by* Daniel Halpern *and* Paula Paley

Mrs. Albion You've Got a Lovely Daughter. Adrian Henri. OxBTC

Mrs. Alfred Uruguay. Wallace Stevens. TwCP

Mrs. Baez Serves Coffee on the Third Floor. Martín Espada. EC3

Mrs. Brown. Rose Fyleman. BoTP; OxBChV

Mrs. Bubb was gay and free, fair, fat and forty-three. The One Horse Chay. *Unknown.* OxBoLi

Mrs. Busk. Sir Osbert Sitwell. OxBTC

Mrs. Chub was rich and portly. Jupiter and Ten. James Thomas Fields. OBAL

Mrs. Coley's three-flat brick. The Vacant Lot. Gwendolyn Brooks. NAAAL; NAAL-2; NOBA; NoAM *Fr.* A Street in Bronzeville. BPo; BlSi; FaBoWP

Mrs. Conti was the first. The First. Grace Cavalieri. UnSA

Mrs. E. Cohrs Brown. Mary Weston Fordham. CBWP-2

Mrs. Evans Fach, You Want Butter Again. Idris Davies. OBWVE

Mrs. Francis Ellen Harper. George Clinton Rowe. AAP

Mrs. Harris's Petition. Jonathan Swift. CABP

Mrs. Hopley, on Seeing Her Children Say Goodnight to Their Father. Gerard Manley Hopkins. FaBoEE

Mrs. Johnson Objects. Clara Ann Thompson. BlSi; CBWP-2

Mrs. Judge Jenkins[; Being the Only Genuine Sequel to "Maud Muller"], *see also* "Maud Muller on a summer's day" *by* Whittier. Bret Harte. APN-2; BXAP

Mrs. Kriss Kringle. Edith Matilda Thomas. OBCA

Mrs. Loewinsohn etc. Ron Loewinsohn. NeAP

Mrs. Louise B. Weston. Mary Weston Fordham. CBWP-2

Mrs. Lorris was a fusser. Mrs. Lorris, Who Died of Being Clean. Barbara Giles. OTCP

Mrs. MacQueen (*or* The Lollie-Shop). Walter De la Mare. BoTP

Mrs. Marmaduke Moore, at the age of ten. The Seven Spiritual Ages of Mrs. Marmaduke Moore. Ogden Nash. MoAmPo

Mrs. Mary Furman Weston Byrd. Mary Weston Fordham. CBWP-2

Mrs. Mason bought a basin. Mrs. Mason's Basin. *Unknown.* OxNR

Mrs. Mason's Basin. *Unknown.* OxNR

Mrs. Masters's fuchsias hung. The Lodging-House Fuchsias. Thomas Hardy. OBGa; OxBSP

Mrs. Myrick's Lecture. Mary E. Tucker. CBWP-1

Mrs Nightingale. Martin Fagg. UV

Mrs. Noah in the Ark. The Ballad of Mrs. Noah. Robert Duncan. MoP; NOBA; NoAM

Mrs. Pappadopoulos, and thanks. (LL) So-and-So Reclining on Her Couch. Wallace Stevens. AmPP; LiTM; NOBA

Mrs. Rebecca Weston. Mary Weston Fordham. CBWP-2

Mrs Robinson to the Poet Coleridge. Mary Robinson. Ro

Mrs. Sadie Grindstaff, Weaver and Factotum. Jonathan Williams. OBAL

Mrs. Saunder's Experience. *Unknown.* AmFP

Mrs. Schneider in Church. Kathleen Norris. CrSp

Mrs Simpkins never had very much to do. Stevie Smith. OBCoV

Mrs. Small went to the kitchen for her pocketbook. Gwendolyn Brooks. GT

Mrs. Snipkin and Mrs. Wobblechin. Laura Elizabeth Richards. OxBChV

Mrs. Snow. Donald Justice. NoP-4

Mrs. Trollope in America. Helen Smith Bevington. NBLV; OBAL

Mrs. Trollope took a doleful view. Mrs. Trollope in America. Helen Smith Bevington. NBLV; OBAL

Mrs. Vickers' Daughter. *Unknown.* AmFP

Mrs. Whitehouse, mixed bathing at Deal. Limerick. T. L. McCarthy. PeLi

Mrs Worthingtion. Noël Coward.

"Regarding yours, dear Mrs Worthington." UV

Mt. Ida. Trumbull Stickney. *Fr.* Sonnets from Greece. APN-1

Mu. Melvin Beaunearus Tolson. MoNo

Mu Tío Baca el Poeta de Socorro. Jimmy Santiago Baca. PmAP

Mu'allaqat, The. Various authors.

Abla. AWP, tr. by E. Powys Mathers

"Have the poets left a single spot for a patch to be sewn?" TTY, tr. by A. J. Arberry

Ode: "Weep, ah weep love's losing, love's with its dwelling place." AWP; TAL, tr. by Lady Anne Blunt *and* Wilfrid Scawen Blunt

Pour Us Wine. AWP, tr. by E. Powys Mathers

Much Ado about Nothing. Shakespeare.

Epitaph: "Done to death by slanderous tongues." CTC

(Claudio's Lament: "Done to death by slanderous tongues.")

"Is this the monument of Leonato?" OxAEP-1

"O! good my lord, tax not so bad a voice." OxAEP-1

"Pardon, goddess of the night." NoSic

Song: "Pardon, goddess of the night." CTC

Song: "Sigh no more, ladies, sigh no more." PoEL-2

("Into Hey nonny, nonny.") (LL) APAD

("Sigh no more, ladies, sigh no more.") APAD

Much Ado about Nothing in the City. *Unknown.* UV

Much Ado About Nothing, Thanksgiving, 1972. Ann Hayes. CMAP

Much as a man who takes delight in dreaming. Ausiàs March, *Catalan.* STV, tr. by John Frederick Nims

Much as he left it when he went from us. Why He Was There. Edwin Arlington Robinson. CMoP; NOBA

Much did I rage when young. Youth and Age. W. B. Yeats. FaBoEE

Much-discerning public hold, A. La Nuit Blanche. Rudyard Kipling. MoBrPo

Much Distressed. *Unknown.* CBAP

Much Doctrine lyes under this little Stone. (LL) The Fall. Sir Richard Fanshawe. NOSC; OBVE

Much earlier than most he found. Childhood of a Spy. Dick Davis. DiPo

Much had passed/ Since last we parted. Byron Recollected at Bologna. Samuel Rogers. *Fr.* Italy. OBNC

Much happens when we're not there. Window-Blind. Denise Levertov. LCAP-2

Much has been said of the. Three Songs. Rachel Wetzsteon. RA

Much have I labored, much read o'er. Alas for Youth. Firdausi, *Persian.* AWP, tr. by R. A. Nicholson

Much have I travell'd [*or* travelled *or* traveled] in the realms of gold. On First Looking into Chapman's Homer. Keats. APAD; BLPA; CABP; CH; ClHu; EBEvV; EPCY; FHYEP; FaBoBe; FaBoCh; GSo; GTBS-P; HAP; HeIP-4; HoPM; ImPo; InPK-6; NAEL-2; NAWM-2; NIP-4; NOBE; NOBRP; NoP-4; OAEL-2; OBAL; OBEV; OBNC; OPOU; OxAEP-2; PFE; PoE; PoEL-4; PoPoPo; Poetr; Ro; SCGP; SoSe-8; Son; TFi; TRP; UV

Much have I travelled in East Lothian and Dundee. On First Looking into Chapman's Homer. W. S. Brownlie. UV

Much have I travelled in those realms of old. On First Looking into Krafft-Ebing's *Psychopathosexualis* [*or* Psychopathia Sexualis]. Oliver St. John Gogarty. UV

Much Knowledge, Little Reason. Sir John Davies. *See* What Is This Knowledge?

Much Madness is divinest Sense. Emily Dickinson. APN-2; AmPP; BoWoP; CMoP; HeIP-4; LiTM; MeMAP; NAAL-1; NAAL-3; NALW;

NAWM-2; NCAP; NOBA; NoAM; NoP-4; OPOU; OxBA; PAR; PBMP; PFE; PoPoPo; Poetr; RaBo; SAGP; SAmP; SoSe-8; TFi; TRP; WPE

Much more than there was time for him to be. (LL) El-Hajj Malik El-Shabazz. Robert Earl Hayden. NAAAL; PoBA

Much spoke he of the myrtle and the yew. Philip Freneau. NAAL-1; NAAL-3 *Fr.* The House of Night.

Much suspected by me. Written with a Diamond On Her Window at Woodstock. Elizabeth I, Queen of England. PBWP; PEW; WPE

Much that well may be thought cannot wisely be said. (LL) The Priest and the Mulberry-Tree. Thomas Love Peacock. BoTP; OxAEP-2

Much wine had passed, with grave discourse. A Ramble in St. James's Park. John Wilmot, 2d Earl of Rochester. PeLV

Much-worried mother once said, A. Limerick. *Unknown.* PeLi

Mud ("Mud is very nice to feel"). Polly Chase Boyden. NTCP

Mud Dauber Wasp, The. Peter Kane Dufault. NoP-4

Mud is very nice to feel. Mud. Polly Chase Boyden. NTCP

Mud-stained and rain-sodden, a sport for flies and lice. Au Champ d'Honneur. Charles Kenneth Michael Scott Moncrieff. NSI

Mud turkle settin' on de end of a log. The Turtle's Song. *Unknown.* BPo

Mud Turtle, The. Howard Nemerov. NYBP

Mud Vision, The. Seamus Heaney. PBCIP

Mud Water Shango. Tom Weatherly. GT; NBV; SeSe

Muddling up the wooden stairs one night, in my socks. Spiders. David Wevill. MoCV

Muddy Kid Comes Home. Sandra Cisneros. FFC

Muddy-wheeled cart goes lurching, A. The Plain. Sándor Weöres, *Hungarian.* BLT, *tr. by* J. Kessler

Mudfish are the lowest of all fish. Chiang Lin-chi Treats Me to Mudfish. Mei Yao Ch'en, *Chinese.* SuSp, *tr. by* Jonathan Chaves

Muertes. Robert Mazzocco. WWSi

Mufaddaliyat, The. Various authors, *Arabic.* AWP, *tr. by* Sir Charles Lyall

Muffin Man, The. Ann Croasdell. BoTP

Muffin-Man's Bell, The. Ann Hawkshawe. BoTP

Muffled drum's sad roll has beat, The. The Bivouac of the Dead. Theodore O'Hara. BLPA

Mufti and their spiritual jurisdictions, The. Chorus Primus of Bashaws or Cadis. Greville Fulke. NOSC *Fr.* Mustapha.

Mugging. Allen Ginsberg. NoAM

"Tonite I walked out of my red apartment door on East tenth street's dusk." HCAP

Mugsy, what happened to you? The Search. Nancy Peterson. LoHo

Muhammedan Call to Prayer. Bilal, *Arabic.* TTY, *tr. by* Raoul Abdul

Mujer. William Carlos Williams. PC; SAmP

Mulatta as Penelope, The. Lorna Goodison. PBCV

Mulatto. Langston Hughes. NAAL-2

Mulberry Bush, The. *Unknown.* ACTP; ReMoGo

("On a cold and frosty morning.") (LL) ReMoGo

Mulberry by the Path. *Unknown, Chinese.* SuSp, *tr. by* Hans H. Frankel

Mulberry Garden, The. Sir Charles Sedley.

Child and Maiden. GTBS-P

(To Chloris.) OBEV

Mulberry Mountain. *Unknown.* AmFP

Mulch. Adam David Miller. NBV

Mulciber. Milton. NOSC *Fr.* Book I. FHYEP; NAEL-1; OAEL-1; OxAEP-1 *Fr.* Paradise Lost.

Mule. Rodney Jones. NAmP90

Mule, The. Boynton Merrill Jr. CRP

Mule Skinner's Song. *Unknown.* AS

Mule Team and Poster. Donald Justice. VCAP

Mule that lived on the road, The. Young Wife's Lament. Brigit Pegeen Kelly. NAmP90

Mules. Ted Walker. NYBP

Mules, I think, will not be here this hour, The. Empedocles on Etna. Matthew Arnold.

Mullabinda. David Rowbotham. CBAP

Mullein. Anita Virgil. HA

Mullins Farm, The. Richard H. W. Dillard. MT

Multi-colored chart without a boundary, A. Missing You. "Shu Ting," *Chinese.* VCWP, *tr. by* Carolyn Kizer

Multipara: Gravida 5. Marie Ponsot. CLPP; VGW

Multiplication is vexation. Arithmetic. *Unknown.* ACTP; ReMoGo

Multitude in haste convened, uprose, The. The Mice prepare for battle. *Unknown.* OBCVT, *tr. by* William Cowper *Fr.* Batrachomyomachia (The Battle of the Frogs and Mice).

Multitudes Turn in Darkness. Conrad Potter Aiken. PoA

Multitudinous Stars. "Ping Hsin," *Chinese.*

"Void only." PBWP

Mum and the Sothsegger. *Unknown.*

"Thenne wax I wounder wroth, as I well might." EnVB

Mum, I'll be a fireman! The Ambition. Robert Harris. BMAP

Mum won't let me keep a rabbit. Brian Patten. PeP

Mum, you would have loved the way you went! Going. Bruce Dawe. BMAP

Mumbo. . . Jumbo. . . will. . . hoo-doo. . . you. (LL) The Congo. Vachel Lindsay. CMoP; MeMAP; MoAmPo; NOBA; OxBA; PoRA; TAP

Mummer. Jack Spicer. APSN

Mummies, The. Maxine W. Kumin. Poetsp

Mummy and Donor and Deirdre. Jackie Kay. CPO

Mummy Invokes his Soul, The. "Michael Field." VWP

Mummy is singing at breakfast and dancing!/ So big! (LL) Eskimo Occasion. Judith Rodriguez. CBAP; FaBoWP; NOBAu

Mummy of a Lady Named Jemutesonekh XXI Dynasty. Thomas James. AmPA

Mumpaty, mumpaty, mump. (LL) Roger and Dolly. Henry Carey. CBNP; NOEC; OxNR; ReMoGo

Munching a plum on. To a Poor Old Woman. William Carlos Williams. BLT; ColAP; MeMAP; OBAL; PiM; TAP; TTTS

Mundus et Infans. W. H. Auden. LiTM; MeMAP; MoBrPo; NoAM

Mundus Muliebris. Mary Evelyn. NOSC

"In Pin-up Ruffles now she flaunts." KTR

Mundus Qualis. Joshua Sylvester. FaBoEE

Municipal. Rudyard Kipling. BXAP

Municipal Gallery Revisited, The. W. B. Yeats. GTBS-P; OxBTC

Muppim and Huppim! Strike blows on your drums! The Dance of Despair. Hayyim Nahman Bialik, *Hebrew.* TrJP, *tr. by* A. M. Klein

Murder in the Cathedral. T. S. Eliot.

Chorus: "We do not wish anything to happen." OxBTC

Chorus: "We have not been happy, my Lord, we have not been so happy." OxBTC

Murder Machine 43. Kurt Schwitters, *German.* PFTM, *tr. by* Jerome Rothenberg

Murder of Goins, The. *Unknown.* AmFP

Murder of Maria Marten by W. Corder, The. *Unknown.* OxBoV

Murder of William Remington, The. Howard Nemerov. CMoP; CoAP

Murder on the Downs, The. William Plomer. OxBoV

Murder Trial, The. Perseus Adams. PeSA

Murdered Girl Is Found on a Bridge, The. Jane Hayman. NYBP

Murdered himself, to show some manful deed. (LL) Sardanapalus. Henry Howard, Earl of Surrey. AAS; NoSic; SiPS

Murdered, I went, risen. The Life. James Wright. LCAP-2

Murderer, The. Paul Petrie. NYBP

Murderer, The. Stevie Smith. FaBoWP; OxBSP

Murderer & Sarapis, The. Palladas, *Greek.* GrAn, *tr. by* Tony Harrison

Murderer spread his palliasse, A. The Murderer & Sarapis. Palladas, *Greek.* GrAn, *tr. by* Tony Harrison

Murderers, The. Paul Van Ostaijen, *Dutch.* PFTM, *tr. by* Hidde van Ameyden Van Duym

Murderers / of Emmett Till. Salute. Oliver Pitcher. PoBA

Murderous middle age is my engine. Montauk Highway. Harvey Shapiro. LiLi

Murge with your white stones and green olives. Second Image Sequence. Umberto Piersanti, *Italian.* NeIt, *tr. by* Stephen Sartarelli

Murillo's Magdalen. William Ellery Channing. APN-1

Murk was the night: nor star, nor moon. Young Man Naughty's Adventure. Charlotte Brontë. VWP

Murmur. Esther Iverem. GT

Murmur of a Bee, The. Emily Dickinson. MoAmPo

Murmur of the city sounded on, The. A Day-dream. Mary Elizabeth Coleridge. VWP

Murmur of the mourning ghost, The. The Ballad of Keith of Ravelston. Sydney Thompson Dobell. CH; OBEV *Fr.* A Nuptial Eve. OBNC

Murmuring. Judit Tóth, *Hungarian.* CEEP, *tr. by* Emery E. George

Murmuring, in her sleep as it seemed, the ancient slogan / Noblesse oblige. (LL) Belief. Josephine Miles. FaBoWP; MoP; NoAM; TAP

Murmuring of Bees, has ceased, The. Emily Dickinson. APN-2

Murry, on finding le Bon Dieu. On Reading "God." G. K. Chesterton. OBCoV

Murukan̲: His Places. Nakkiranar, *Tamil.* PLW, *tr. by* A. K. Ramanujan

Murukan̲, the Red One. Nakkiranar, *Tamil.* PLW, *tr. by* A. K. Ramanujan

Muscovy Drake, The. E. A. S. Lesoro, *Sotho.* PeSA, *tr. by* Dan Kunene *and* Jack Cope

Muse, The. "Anna Akhmatova," *Russian.* TCRP, *tr. by* Stanley Kunitz *with* Max Hayward

Muse, The. Abraham Cowley. CABP; EPCY; PBRV

Muse. Donald Revell. WeT

Muse. David Wagoner. PoA

Muse and Drudge. Harryette Mullen. BAP-94

Muse and Poet. Robert Bridges. OBMV

Muse as Medusa, The. May Sarton. NALW

Muse, bid the morne awake. To His Valentine. Michael Drayton. PoEL-2

Muse bumped / against my window this morning, The. Levitation with Baby. Marilyn Nelson Waniek. NMM-2

Muse, disgusted at an age and clime, The. On the Prospect of Planting Arts and Learning in America. George Berkeley. AiP; FaBoA; ImPo; NOEC

Muse forgot, and thou beloved [*or* belov'd] no more!, The. (LL) Elegy to the Memory of an Unfortunate Lady. Alexander Pope. ECEV; NOBE; NOEC; OAEL-1; OBEV; SCGP

Muse in Late November. Jonathan Henderson Brooks. ChIV-1

Muse in the New World, The. Walt Whitman. MoAmPo *Fr.* Song of the Exposition.

Muse Is Always the Other Woman, The. Constance Urdang. PBCAP

Muse, June, Related. Brian Coffey.
"Blooms such as wither at finger-touch." BIrV

Muse! Lament away, complain away. The Reader of Poetry. Ilya L'vovich Selvinsky, *Russian.* TCRP, *tr. by* Daniel Weissbort

Muse of Amergin, The. *Unknown, Irish.* BIrV; IIP; *tr. by* John Montague

Muse of my Spenser, who so well could sing. George Crabbe. EPCY *Fr.* The Birth of Flattery.

Muse of Poetry came down one day, The. In Memoriam Paul Laurence Dunbar. Henrietta Cordelia Ray. CBWP-3

Muse of the fields, oft have I said farewell. John Clare. EPCY *Fr.* To the Rural Muse.

Muse of the Golden Throne. Sappho, *Greek.* InMo, *tr. by* Sam Hamill

Muse of the many-twinkling feet! whose charms. Byron. OBSV *Fr.* The Waltz.

Muse of Water, A. Carolyn Kizer. FFC; VCAP

Muse Reviving, The. Sir John Davies. SiPS

Muse should be sprightly, The. A Skeltoniad. Michael Drayton. PoEL-2

Muse, sing the stir that happy Whitbread made. George III Visits Whitbread's Brewery. "Peter Pindar." NOEC *Fr.* Instructions to a Celebrated Laureat.

Muse teach me the song. Sophia De Mello Breyner, *Portuguese.* VCWP, *tr. by* Ruth Fainlight

Muse, / tell me of this man of wit. Homer. *Fr.* Odyssey. NAWM-1, *tr. by* Robert Fitzgerald

Muse that stirs my blood, The. Bird and the Muse. Marya Alexandrovna Zaturenska. PoA

Muse to an Unknown Poet, The. Paul Potts. FaBoTw

Musée des Beaux Arts. W. H. Auden. CABP; CMoP; ClHu; GS; GTBS-P; HAP; HeIP-4; ImPo; InPK-6; InPS-3; LiTM; MeMAP; MoP; NAEL-2; NOBE; NoAM; NoP-4; OxAEP-2; PBMP; PFE; PoE; PoPoPo; PoRA; Poetr; RaBo; SCV; SoSe-8; TFi; TRP; TrCP; TwCP

Muses, The. Marilyn Hacker. NMM-2

Muse's Answer, The. Gibbons Ruark. MT

Muses are turned gossips; they have lost, The. Washing-Day. Anna Laetitia Barbauld. ECWP; PEW; WoRP

Muses Elizium, The. Michael Drayton.
"Paradice on earth is found, A." PBRV

Muses' Elysium [*or* Elizium]. Michael Drayton.
Description of Elizium, The. OAEL-1

Muses' Elysium X, The. Michael Drayton.
"*Satyr* O never ask how I came to this place." AEP

Muses' evening, as their morning-star[re], The. (LL) To Lucy, Countess[e] of Bedford, with Mr. Donnes Satire's [*or* Satyres]. Ben Jonson. BeJo; EPCY; PBRV

Muses' fairest light in no dark time, The. On Ben Jonson. Sidney Godolphin. BeJo; EPCY

Muse's Favor, The. Priscilla Jane Thompson. AAP; CBWP-2

Muses' friend, The (grey-eyed Aurora), yet. Morning. William Browne. NOSC *Fr.* Britannia's Pastorals.

Muses' garden, with pedantic weeds, The. On the Death of Donne. Thomas Carew. NOBE *Fr.* An Elegie upon the Death of the Deane of Pauls, Dr. Donne. MeLP; PBRV; SeCP

Muses, help me; sorrow swarmeth. The Shepherd's Sorrow, Being Disdained in Love. Thomas Lodge. NoSic

Muses, hold not invoked your holy aid. Sonnet 55. Sir Philip Sidney. *Fr.* Astrophil and Stella. AAS; SiPS

Muses kidnapped Eros, they bound him, The. Anacreon, *Greek.* InMo, *tr. by* Sam Hamill

Muses that sing love's sensual empery. Love and Philosophy. George Chapman. SCGP; Son *Fr.* A Coronet for His Mistress Philosophy.

Museum. Sydney Lea. NAmP90

Museum, The. Wislawa Szymborska, *Polish.* PoSu, *tr. by* Magnus F. Krynski

Museum Attendant, The. Archibald MacLeish. *See* Empire Builders.

Museum Man! / I wish he'd take Pa's spitbox!, The. Lorine Niedecker. MoLi

Museum of Man. Earle Birney. OxBC

Museum of Modern Art on West Fifty-third Street, The. Tulips and Addresses. Edward Field. NYBP; Poetsp

Museum of the Second Creation, The. Sandra McPherson. LCAP-2

Museum Piece. Angela Sorby. BAP-95

Museum Piece. Richard Wilbur. APAD; CMoP; CoAMP; FaBoMo; InPK-6; NIP-4; TAP; TRP

Museum Street. Judita Vaiiunaite, *Lithuanian.* CEEP, *tr. by* Jonas Zdanys

Museums and Journeys. Robin Fulton. FaBoTC

Museums and stockmarkets protect me, The. Four Stanzas Written in Anxiety. George Jonas. MoCV

Museums offer us, running from among the buses. Louis MacNeice. MoBrPo

Musgrove. *Unknown.* AmFP

Mushroom Clouds. John Engman. NAmP90

Mushroom Gatherer Deep in the Mountains Among the White Clouds, A. Hsü Wei, *Chinese.* CoBLCP, *tr. by* Jonathan Chaves

Mushroom, Soft Ear, Old Memory. Bring the North. William Stafford. LCAP-2

Mushrooms. Yury Kuznetsov, *Russian.* TCRP, *tr. by* Lubov Yakovleva

Mushrooms. Sylvia Plath. FaBoWP; PBMP; PFE; RB; WPOW
("Overnight, very / Whitely, discreetly.") PFE

Mushrooms grew near the tree. Peter Rabbit. Sandra McPherson. LCAP-2

Mushrooms grew / Overnight. Mike Evans. PFE

Music. Eugenio de Andrade, *Portuguese.* VCWP, *tr. by* Alexis Levitin

Music, A. Wendell Berry. VGW

Music. Bible, Apocrypha. TrJP *Fr.* Ecclesiasticus.

Music. Madison Cawein. APN-2

Music. Abraham Cowley. *See* A Supplication.

Music. Christopher Pearse Cranch. APN-1

Music. George Du Maurier, *after the French of* Sully-Prudhomme. OBEV; SAGP

Music. Ralph Waldo Emerson. CTV

Music. John Fletcher *and* Shakespeare. FaBoCh *Fr.* King Henry VIII.
(Song: "Orpheus with his Lute made Trees.") PoEL-2

Music. Caroline Halliday. NBrP

Music. Josephine D. Henderson Heard. CBWP-4

Music. Namjo Kim, *Korean.* CKP, *tr. by* Jaihiun Kim

Music. Amy Lowell. ColAP

Music. William Bell Scott. NOBVV

Music. Henry David Thoreau. APN-1; PAR

Music and its harmony, The. The Design. Clarence Major. PoBA

Music and Poetry. Abraham Cowley. EPCY *Fr.* Davideis.

Music and Poetry of the Indians. *Unknown, Ojibwa.* APN-2, *tr. by* John Tanner

Music divides the evening. Tu Do Street. Yusef Komunyakaa. LTA

Music first and foremost of all! Art Poétique. Paul Verlaine, *French.* AWP, *tr. by* Arthur Symons

"Music for a while." Song at Night. Norman Nicholson. FaBoTw

Music for Brass. Günter Grass, *German.* AF, *tr. by* Christopher Middleton

Music had the heat of blood, The. During Music. Arthur Symons. NOBVV

Music has charms to soothe a savage breast. William Congreve. OxAEP-1 *Fr.* The Mourning Bride.

Music I heard with you was more than music. Bread and Music. Conrad Potter Aiken. AWP; CMoP; ImPo; LiTM; MoAmPo; NOBA; OxBA; PoRA *Fr.* Discordants.

Music in an Empty House. Hugh Sykes Davies. SPE

Music in Camp. John Reuben Thompson. BLPA; CBCWP

Music in the Age of Iron. Alberto Blanco, *Spanish.* CLPP, *tr. by* Julian Palley

Music in the piano stool. That vase, The. (LL) Home is so sad. It stays as it was left. Philip Larkin. LBC

Music in Venice. Louis Simpson. NYBP

Music is played. Play, The. Celebration. Joseph Ceravolo. FTOS

Music Is Unevennesses. Geoffrey Lehmann. *Fr.* Ross's Poems. CBAP

Music it was I heard, and music too. Lines Suggested by Hearing Music on the Boston Common at Night. Thomas Cole. APN-1

Music, *jazz*, comes in. (LL) Reuben, Reuben. Michael S. Harper. LoL; PoE

Music lifting and falling. Aria. Rolfe Humphries. NYBP

Music! Lilting, soft and languorous. Alice Moore Dunbar-Nelson. BlSi

Music met Leviathan returning, A. Peter Quennell. MoBrPo *Fr.* Leviathan.

Music my rampart, and my only one. (LL) On Hearing a Symphony of Beethoven. Edna St. Vincent Millay. LiTM; MoAmPo

Music of a Tree, The. Walter James Turner. MoBrPo

Music of Astronomy, The. Martín Espada. AFr

Music of Colours—White Blossom. Vernon Watkins. LiTM

Music of His Steps, The. Samuel Wakefield. AH

Music of Spheres. Jean Follain, *French*. BLT, *tr. by* Czeslaw Milosz *and* Robert Hass

Music of the Spheres, The. Marvin Bell. PoA

Music on the Water. George Johnston. MoCV

Music stirs me, for you. Ricarda Huch, *German*. PBWP, *tr. by* Susan C. Strong

Music Swims Back to Me. Anne Sexton. ColAP; VCAP

Music[k], thou queen of heaven, care-charming spell. To Music: A Song. Robert Herrick. CaPo

Music, thou queen of souls, get up and string. A Song. Thomas Randolph. OxBSP

Music, thou soul of heaven, care-charming spell. Robert Herrick. CaPo

Music[k] to hear[e], why hear'st thou music[k]. Sonnet 8. Shakespeare. PoEL-2 *Fr.* Sonnets.

Music was going on, The. At the Fillmore. Philip Levine. NNaP

Music, when soft voices die. Shelley. LaPo *Fr.* Rose Leaves, When The Rose is Dead.

Music, when soft voices die. To———. Shelley. AWP; CBLP; CH; EBEvV; FHYEP; GTBS-P; HeIP-4; ImPo; LBC; NOBE; OBEV; OBNC; OxAEP-2; OxBSP; PFE; PoEL-4; Poetr; TFi

Musica No. 3. Richard Duerden. NeAP

Musical Instrument, A. Elizabeth Barrett Browning. CABP; EBEvV; EBVV; FaBoBe; NAEL-2; NoP-4; OAEL-2; OBEV; PEW; PoE; PoPoPo; Poetr; VWP; WPE

Musical Lion, The. Oliver Herford. OBCA

Musical maiden from Frome, A. Limerick. Cyril Bibby. PeLi

Musical man is walking along the shore, A. Telemachus with a Transistor. Ruth Dallas. PeNZ

Musical monkey is dressed like a flunkey, The. John Mole. OBCoV *Fr.* Penny Toys.

Musical Orchard, The. Douglas Dunn. FaBoMo

Musical Pumpkin-Hut. Heinrich Albert, *German*. GePo, *tr. by* George C. Schoolfield

Musical Strife; in a Pastoral Dialogue, The. Ben Jonson. BeJo

Musical Wine-Jar, A. Hedylos, *Greek*. GrAn, *tr. by* William Moebius

Musicall Consort, A. Thomas Churchyard.
  "That humor now, declines for age drawes on." PBRV

Musician. Louise Bogan. NYBP

Musicians wrestle everywhere. Emily Dickinson. APN-2

Music[k]'s Duel[l], *ad. fr. the Latin of* Strada. Richard Crashaw. GeHe; OAEL-1; SeCP

Musidora's Vision. Henrietta Cordelia Ray. CBWP-3

Musing. Li Ho, *Chinese*.
  "Ssŭ-ma Hsiang-ju pondered Leafy Mound." PLT, *tr. by* A. C. Graham

Musing on roses and revolutions. Roses and Revolutions. Dudley Randall. BPo; CoAmPo; TAP

Musing upon the restless bisinesse. Prologue. Thomas Hoccleve. PoEL-1 *Fr.* De Regimine Principum.

Musings. William Barnes. HAP; NOBE; OBNC

Musk-ox smells, The. The Long River. Donald Hall. CoAmPo; LCAP-2

Musketaquid. Ralph Waldo Emerson. APN-1; PAR

Muskrats rose from the marsh. After the Storm. Edmond Yi-teh Chang. OpBo

Musophilus; or, Defence of All Learning. Samuel Daniel.
  "Behold how every man, drawn with delight." NoSic
  "But yet in all this interchange of all." EPCY
  "O blessed letters, that combine in one." EPCY
  Poetry in England. EPCY; NoSic
  (Heavenly Eloquence.) NOBE
  "Sacred Religion, mother of form and fear." NoSic

Muspilli. *Unknown, German*. GePo, *tr. by* Carroll Hightower

Mussel Hunter at Rock Harbor. Sylvia Plath. NYBP

Mussel Rock/Lowtide—Santa Cruz, California 1959. Jeff Tagami. OpBo

Musselburgh Field. *Unknown*. ESPB

Mussels. David Keller. CMAP

Mussels. Ingrid Wendt. NMM-2

Must all successful rebels grow. 1912–1952, Full Cycle. Peter Viereck. OBAL

Must Be Freed. Lizelia Augusta Jenkins Moorer. CBWP-3

Must be some girl from the villages. Sappho, *Greek*. InMo, *tr. by* Sam Hamill

Must bear alone the weary strife. (LL) On the Death of Anne Brontë. Charlotte Brontë. VWP

Must both remain as strangers still to you. (LL) Yourself. Jones Very. APN-1; NOBA; OxBA; PAR; PoEL-4; Son

Must gulp it down at Closing Time. (LL) To His Not-so-coy Mistress. Wynford Vaughan-Thomas. BXAP; NOBL

Must hapless man, in ignorance sedate. Celestial Wisdom. Juvenal. AWP, *tr. by* Samuel Johnson *Fr.* Satires.

Must have dreamed itself. The Cocoon. Larry Levis. CMAP

Must I die now? Is this a part of life? (LL) A Cut Flower. Karl Shapiro. HAP; WeW-3

Must I lament the time that's gone because I've been cast aside? Ch'ien Ch'ien-i. SuSp, *tr. by* Irving Y. Lo *Fr.* Willow Branch Songs.

Must I shoot the. Watts. Conrad Kent Rivers. PoBA

Must I tell again. The Daemon. Louise Bogan. NYBP

Must I then see, alas! eternal night. Elegy over a Tomb. Edward Herbert, 1st Baron Herbert of Cherbury. MeLP; NOBE; OBEV; OBWVE; PoEL-2

Must I, who walk alone. Yellow Clover. Katharine Lee Bates. CPO

Must learn in life to die like thee. Richard Crashaw. *See* Hymn to Saint Teresa.

Must pine neglected and alone. (LL) The Captive Dove. Anne Brontë. EBVV; VWP

Must plough the wave no more. (LL) On the Loss of the *Royal George*. William Cowper. EBEV; FaPoR; GTBS-P; NOBE; OxAEP-1

Must quiet a heart accused by its own tears. (LL) At Cooloolah. Judith Wright. BMAP

Must soon partake his grave. (LL) Epitaph on a Hare. William Cowper. HAP; NOEC; NoP-4; PeP; PoEL-3; PoPoPo

Must sound. Mechthild von Magdeburg. *See* Effortlessly, / Love flows from God into man.

Must we part, Von Hügel, though much alike. W. B. Yeats. OBMV *Fr.* Vacillation. NoAM

Must you alone then, happy flowers. To a Nosegay in Pancharilla's Breast. Soame Jenyns. ECEV

Must you deny me a bite of your raisin? (LL) Brief Autumnal. *Unknown, Greek*. GrAn; WeW-3, *tr. by* Dudley Fitts

Must you have a part in everything? (LL) Smell. William Carlos Williams. MoAmPo; RaBo; SAmP; TAP

Must you leave, John Holmes, with the prayers and psalms. Somewhere in Africa. Anne Sexton. NALW

Must you with hot irons burn out both mine eyes? Shakespeare. OxAEP-1 *Fr.* King John.

Mustacheless Bard, A. J. Gordon Coogler. OBAL

Mustaches on the last Russian Czar. (LL) Grandparents. Robert Lowell. ColAP; LiTM

Mustapha. Fulke Greville.
  Chorus Primus of Bashaws or Cadis. NOSC
  Chorus Sacerdotum. HAP; NAEL-1; NOBE; OAEL-1; PoEL-1
  (Chorus of Priests.) NoSic; OxAEP-1
  ("O wearisome condition of humanity!") NoP-4

Musty shed. Rod Willmot. HA

Mutability. Shelley. NAEL-2; NoP-4; OBNC
  (Flower that Smiles Today, The.) LaPo

Mutability. W. D. Snodgrass. DiPo

Mutability. Edmund Spenser. AEP; PoEL-1 *Fr.* Wood Of Error. AEP
  ("And death instead of life have quicked and quit from our Nurse.") (LL) AEP
  ("What man that sees the ever-whirling wheel.") AEP

Mutability. Wordsworth. EBEV; HeIP-4; InPK-6; LaPo; NOBE; NoP-4; OAEL-2; OBEV; PoEL-4 *Fr.* Ecclesiastical Sonnets.

Mutability Claims to Rule the World. Edmund Spenser. NoSic *Fr.* Wood Of Error. AEP

Mutation. William Cullen Bryant. NCAP

Mutations of the Phoenix. Sir Herbert Read.
  "Phoenix, bird of terrible pride." FaBoTw

Mute is thy wild harp, now, O Bard sublime! To the Shade of Burns. Charlotte Smith. NoP-4

Mute Opinion. Thomas Hardy. CMoP

Mute Phenomena, The. Gérard de Nerval, *French*. NNPT, *tr. by* Derek Mahon

Mute was the marble. The Heirs of Stalin. Yevtushenko, *Russian*. TCRP, *tr. by* George Reavey

Muted Screen of Graham Greene, The. Phyllis McGinley. FaBoEE

Muted season evanescent. An Early Spring. Stephen Sartarelli. PT

Mutes, The. Denise Levertov. NALW; NOBA

Mutilated choir boys, The. Heinrich Heine. *Fr.* Heimkehr, Die. AWP, *tr. by* Ezra Pound

Mutilator of souls, The. (LL) From the Nursery. Jane Kenyon. BAP-93; LoL

Mutineer's Ballad, The. Peter Kocan. NOBAu

Mutoscope. Elizabeth Spires. NAmP90

Muttering thunder. Robert Spiess. HA

Mutterings Over the Crib of a Deaf Child. James Wright. LCAP-2; LiLi

Mutton. *Unknown.* BXAP

Mutton Bird Man. Rhyll McMaster. NOBAu

Mutual Congratulations of the Poets Anna Seward and Hayley, The. Richard Porson. FaBoEE; OBSV

Mutual forgiveness of each vice. The Gates of Paradise. William Blake. PoEL-4

Mutual Problem. William Cole. OBAL; OBCoV

Mutual Subjection. Christopher Smart. NOCV   *Fr.* Hymns for the Amusement of Children.

    (Consideration for Others.) OxBChV

Muu's Way; or Pictures from the Uterine World. *Unknown, Cuna Indian.* STP, *tr. by* Jerome Rothenberg

Muvver was barfin' 'er biby one night, A. Dahn the Plug'ole. *Unknown.* RB, *tr. by* Robert Bly

Muzik of blood. Bass Culture. Linton Kwesi Johnson. PBCV

Muzzle and jowl and beastly brow. Fearful Symmetry. Basil Bunting. OxBoS; PoA

Muzzy with drink, I let my humor recline. The Ghost of an Education. James Michie. NYBP

My Acts. William Meredith. VCAP   *Fr.* Consequences.

My adored statue. The Arid Husband. E. L. T. Mesens. SPE

My Africa. Michael Dei-Anang. PBA

My age fallen away like white swaddling. Age. Philip Larkin. CMoP

My age is three hundred and seventy-two. The Sleepy Giant. Charles Edward Carryl. NOxBChV; OTCP

My aged friend, Miss Wilkinson. The Bards. Walter De la Mare. NOBL

My Aim. A. J. Seymour. CTV

My Ain Fireside. Elizabeth Hamilton. FaBoBe

My Alba. Allen Ginsberg. CLPP; NOBA

My ancestor, a man. Snowmen. Agha Shahid Ali. IFJA

My ancestor was called on to go out. The Wind at Your Door. Robert David Fitzgerald. NOBAu

My ancestors are nearer. Ancestral Poem. Olive Senior. PBCV

My ancestors weren't hippies, cotton. Botanical Fanaticism. Thylias Moss. TRP

My Androgynous Years. James Harms. CMAP

My Angeline. Harry Bache Smith. NBLV

My animals are made of wool and glass. Elizabeth Jennings. PeP

My Answer. Ralph Adamo. MT

My answer would be music. The Medium. Elaine Feinstein. BrRo

My apparition rose from the fall of lead. Civilian and Soldier. Wole Soyinka. AF; PBMAP

My ardours for emprize nigh lost. On an Invitation to the United States. Thomas Hardy. AWP; AiP; FaBoA

My Arkansas. Maya Angelou. BlSi; NAAAL

My arm sweeps down. Gesture. Donald Finkel. InPK-6

My arms. Tanka. Nakajō Fumiko, *Japanese.* MJT, *tr. by* Makoto Ueda

My arms are given. Absolution. Diane Ward. FTOS

My arms are round you, and I lean. To the Oaks of Glencree. John Millington Synge. MoBrPo; NOIV

My arms have mutinied against me—brutes! Wild with All Regrets. Wilfred Owen. SCGP

My arms smell good. Think. Please Forward. James Welch. CDW

My army cross over. *Unknown.* CrDW

My ash spear is my barley bread. Archilochus, *Greek.* GrAn, *tr. by* Guy Davenport

My aspens dear, whose airy cages quelled. Binsey Poplars (Felled 1879). Gerard Manley Hopkins. APAD; EBVV; EnVR; InPS-3; NAEL-2; NoAM; RB

My attention is a wild. Pet Panther. A. R. Ammons. NoP-4

My Atthis, although our dear Anaktoria. Sappho, *Greek.* BoWoP, *tr. by* Willis Barnstone

My attire is noiseless when I tread the earth. Cynewulf. AnOE, *tr. by* Charles W. Kennedy   *Fr.* Riddles (Exeter Book).

My Aunt Bebe. The Aga Khan. Steve Orlen. Poetsp

My Aunt Jane she took me in. *Unknown.* FaBoVe

My Aunt Maria. The Mary Morelle Show. Denise Nico Leto. UnSA

My aunt! my dear unmarried aunt! Oliver Wendell Holmes. AmPP; TAP

My aunt she died a month ago. Death of My Aunt. *Unknown.* OxBoLi

My aunt was an herb doctor, one-eyed with crooked yellow teeth. To-ta Ti-om. Peter Blue Cloud. HATNAP

My aunts washed dishes while the uncles. Paper Matches. Paulette Jiles. IFJA; NIP-4; NOBC

My author and disposer, what thou biddest. Thus Eve to Adam. Milton. *Fr.* Book IV. OAEL-1   *Fr.* Paradise Lost.

My baby dear. Edith Nesbit. *See* Song: "Oh, baby, baby, baby dear."

My baby has no name yet. Namjo Kim, *Korean.* PBWP, *tr. by* Ko Won

My baby is sleeping overhead. A Dream Maiden. Harriet Hamilton King. VWP

My baby / loves flowers. William J. Harris. NBV

My bakelite mantel set pulled him in. Whatever Happened to Conway Twitty? Tim Thorne. BMAP

My bands of silk and miniver. Full Moon. Elinor Wylie. NALW; NoP-4

My Baptismal Birthday [or Birth-Day]. Coleridge. ChIV-2; NOCV

My beak is bent downward, I burrow below. Cynewulf. AnOE   *Fr.* Riddles (Exeter Book).

My bean-pod boat you see here. Catullus. *See* The Yacht.

My beard's overcrowded. Now that. Limerick. Richard Unwin. PeLi

My beautiful! my beautiful! that standest meekly by. The Arab's Farewell to His Horse. Caroline Elizabeth Norton. BLPA

My beautiful one gave it to me when we parted. Feelings Wakened by a Mirror. Po Chü-i, *Chinese.* CoBCP, *tr. by* Burton Watson

My beautiful picture of pirates and treasure. Jigsaw Puzzle. Russell Hoban. NTCP

My beautiful trembler! how wildly she shrinks! Ellen Learning to Walk. Frances Sargent Osgood. ColAP

My beauty is not wine to me. The Song of the Narcissus. *Unknown.* AWP   *Fr.* The Thousand and One Nights.

My bed concealed by a folding screen. Lying at Leisure during Rain. Kao Ch'i, *Chinese.* CoBLCP, *tr. by* Jonathan Chaves

My Bed Is a Boat. Robert Louis Stevenson. PWR; PeVV

My bed is like a little boat. My Bed Is a Boat. Robert Louis Stevenson. PWR; PeVV

My bed is so empty that I keep on waking up;. Winter Night. Wen-Ti Chien, *Chinese.* ChiP, *tr. by* Arthur Waley

My being not yet done. Ancient Song. Amir Gilbo'a, *Hebrew.* IP, *tr. by* Warren Bargad *and* Stanley F. Chyet

My beloved hath a vineyard. The Vineyard of My Beloved. Priscilla Jane Thompson. AAP; CBWP-2

My Beloved Is Mine, and I Am His; He Feedeth among the Lillies. Francis Quarles. MeLP; NOBE   *Fr.* Emblems.

    (Divine Rapture, A.) GLoP; OBEV

    ("E'en like two little bank-dividing brooks.") GLoP

    ("World's but theirs; but my Beloved's mine, The.") (LL) GLoP

My beloved little billiard balls. Poem to Some of my Recent Poems. James Tate. NoAM

My beloved spake, and said unto me. Song of Songs. Bible, *O.T.* OPOU   *Fr.* The Song of Songs. AWP

My beloved was laundering. Yevgeny Mikhailovich Vinokurov, *Russian.* TCRP, *tr. by* Daniel Weissbort

My Ben! Robert Herrick. BeJo

My best belovit brother of the band. To R. Hudson. Alexander Montgomerie. OxBS

My biggest worry is this. In a Time of Sickness. Orpingalik, *Eskimo.* STP, *tr. by* Edward Field

My Birds. Solomon Mutswairo, *Shona.* PeSAV, *tr. by* Solomon Mutswairo *and* Donald E. Herdeck

My birth was a suicide. Bach. Lisa Zeidner. CMAP

My Birthday. George Crabbe. OxBSP

My birthday is coming tomorrow. Growing Up. *Unknown.* CTV

My black cat doesn't know. Savoir Faire. Claribel Alegría, *Spanish.* VCWP, *tr. by* D. J. Flakoll

My black-eyed lover broke my back. The Masochist. Maxine W. Kumin. PoA

My black face fades. Facing It. Yusef Komunyakaa. MT; NAAAL; PoPoPo; TRP

My black hills have never seen the sun rising. Shancoduff. Patrick Kavanagh. BlrV; CIP-2; FaBoTw; IIP

My black mothers I hear them singing. Black Star Line. Henry Dumas. PoBA

My black self. Another. Vers Negre. Richard Caddel. NBrP

My Blackness Is the Beauty of This Land. Lance Jeffers. ISC; PoBA

My Blessed Lord, how doth thy Beautious Spouse. Meditation 150 (Second Series). Edward Taylor. ColAP; SCAP   *Fr.* Preparatory Meditations Before My Approach to the Lord's Supper.

My Blood Brother. Frank Mkalawile Chipasula. HBAPE

My blood sits upright in a chair. Blood. Franz Wright. LCAP-2

My blood so red. The Call. *Unknown.* OBEV

My bloodstream chokes on gall and spleen. Quatrain. Barend Toerien, *Afrikaans.* PeSA, *tr. by the author*

My blueveined child. (LL) A Flower Given to My Daughter. James Joyce. OBMV; RB; RaBo

My boat goes west, yours east. Farewell. Ch'ao Li-houa, *Chinese*. BoWoP, *tr. by* J. P. Seaton

My Boat Moored on a River. Yen Yü, *Chinese*. SuSp, *tr. by* Irving Y. Lo

My boat sails downstream. Love Song. *Unknown, Egyptian*. TTY, *tr. by* J. E. Manchip White

My boddy [*or* body] in the walls captived. My Body in the Walls Captived. Sir Walter Ralegh. CABP; SiPS

My body. Tanka. Miya Shūji, *Japanese*. MJT, *tr. by* Makoto Ueda

My body. What She Said. Ammuvanar, *Tamil*. PLW, *tr. by* A. K. Ramanujan

My body a rounded stone. Living Tenderly. May Swenson. OBCA

My body being dead, my limbs [*or* lims] unknown. The Preparative. Thomas Traherne. ESCV; GeHe; PoEL-2

My body breaking. Lucille Clifton. *See* The Lost Baby Poem.

My body had no entrance, and the black. Maria Shkapskaya, *Russian*. TCRP, *tr. by* Vladimir Markov *and* Merrill Sparks

My body holds its shape. The genius is intact. Mummy of a Lady Named Jemutesonekh XXI Dynasty. Thomas James. AmPA

My Body in the Walls Captived. Sir Walter Ralegh. CABP; SiPS

My body is a mystery. Instinct. Edith Södergran, *Swedish*. PFTM, *tr. by* Stina Katchadourian

My body is a torn mattress. Would You Wear My Eyes? Bob Kaufman. GT

My body is both white and round. The Cake-That-Drifts-in-Water. Ho Xuan Huong, *Vietnamese*. AVP, *tr. by* Huỳnh Sanh Thông

My body is like / a field wasted by winter. On Seeing the Field Being Singed. Lady Ise, *Japanese*. BoWoP, *tr. by* Etsuko Terasaki *and* Irma Brandeis

My body is opaque to the soul. Prayer. Jean Toomer. NAAAL

My body is weary to death of my mischievous brain. Nebuchadnezzar. Elinor Wylie. ChIV-1; KSG; MoAmPo

My body knows it will never bear children. Waiting. Jane Cooper. Ci3p, NMM-2; TAP

My body, you are an animal. I Talk to My Body. Anna Swirszczynska, *Polish*. BLT, *tr. by* Czeslaw Milosz *and* Leonard Nathan (b. 1924)

My body's self deserts me now. Muireadhach Albanach O'Dalaigh. LBC

My bones turn to dark emeralds. (LL) The Jewel. James Wright. CoAP; NAAL-2

My bonie lass I work in brass. Robert Burns. *Fr.* Love and Libery—A Cantata. NOBRP; NOEC

My book is largely growing. Introductory to Second Edition. Alfred Islay Walden. AAP

My books, my sword, the wind-swept curtain. Remembering My Late Wife. Chu Yün-ming, *Chinese*. CoBLCP, *tr. by* Jonathan Chaves

My boss did not like me. The Boss. Boris Abramovich Slutsky, *Russian*. TCRP, *tr. by* J. R. Rowland

My bower is in a green dell. George Darley. Ro *Fr.* The Labours of Idleness by Guy Penseval.

My Boy Jack. Rudyard Kipling. APAD

My Boy Tammy. Hector MacNeill. CH

My boy was scarcely ten years auld. Leesome Brand. *Unknown*. ESPB

My boy, what do you think that I can tell you? Oom Gert's Story. C. Louis Leipoldt, *Afrikaans*. PeSAV, *tr. by* C. J. D. Harvey

My brain blistered. (LL) The End of an Ethnic Dream. Jay Wright. MoNo; SeSe

My brain burns with hate of you. Paradox. Anna Wickham. LW

My brain dried like spread turf, my stomach. Seamus Heaney. CIP-2 *Fr.* Station Island.

My brain is like the ravaged shores—the sand. At Night. Frances Darwin Cornford. MoBrPo

My brethren all attend. The Zealous Puritan. *Unknown*. NOSC

"My bride is not coming, alas!" says the groom. At the Altar-Rail. Thomas Hardy. MoBrPo *Fr.* Satires of Circumstance in Fifteen Glimpses.

My bright and beauteous Bride. (LL) Love. Coleridge. GTBS-P; OBEV

My Brother. Patricia Parker. GLP

(Brother.) CPO

My Brother Bert. Ted Hughes. FuFo

("And what, oh what, would the neighbors say!") (LL) ChAP

My brother Cain, the wounded, liked to sit. Abel. Demetrios Capetanakis. GTBS-P

My brother comes home from work. You Can Have It. Philip Levine. NoP-4; VCAP

My brother flies. Those Who Wrestle with the Angel for Us. Brigit Pegeen Kelly. NAmP90

My brother, good morning: my sister, good night. (LL) The Early Morning. Hilaire Belloc. BoTP; OxBSP; Spl; TLR

My brother has a little flute. The Fairy Flute. Rose Fyleman. BoTP

My brother has on / a thin robe. Lady Otomo no Sakanoé, *Japanese*. BoWoP, *tr. by* Willis Barnstone

My Brother Inside the Revolving Doors. Wesley McNair. CMAP

My brother is homemade. Sam Cornish. MBE

My brother is skull and skeleton now. Epitaph. William Montgomerie. OxBS

My brother Jamie lost me all. Mary Stuart. Edwin Muir. RB

My brother Roger said to me. A Magician. Eunice Ward. FPC

My Brother Running: V. Wesley McNair. AFr

My brother was not a camel driver. On Her Brother. Al-Khansa, *Arabic*. BoWoP, *tr. by* Willis Barnstone

My brother you flash your teeth in response to every hypocrisy. The Renegade. David Diop. PBMAP

My Brothers. Anna Walters. VoR

My brother's always in the gully. One of the Longest Times. Alice Notley. BAP-96

My brothers are big, so much bigger than I. Second Song. T. Carmi. MHP, *tr. by* Ruth Finer Mintz *Fr.* René's Songs.

My brothers i will not tell you. Haki R. Madhubuti. ISC

My brothers playing on the green. (LL) The Brothers. Edwin Muir. GTBS-P; HeIP-4; NTP

My brothers, you would have me give a toast. The Polish Eagle. Kornel Ujejski, *Polish*. MLL, *tr. by* Helen Waddell

My brudder sittin' on de tree of life. Roll, Jordan, Roll. *Unknown*. APN-2

My brunette with the golden eyes, your ivory body, your amber. Roses Rising. René Vivien. CPO

My Buddy. Richard Hugo. SeSe

My bull is white like [the] silver fish in the river. The Magnificent Bull. *Dinka Oral Tradition*. PeP; TTTS

My Buried Friends. *Unknown*. AmFP

My cabinets are oyster-shells. Song: "My cabinets are oyster-shells." Margaret Cavendish. OxBoS; WPE *Fr.* The Convent of Pleasure.

My camel kneels at Ibn Marwan's door. Camel. Laila Akhyaliyya, *Arabic*. BoWoP, *tr. by* Willis Barnstone

My Camping Ground. Morris Jacob Rosenfeld, *Yiddish*. TrJP, *tr. by* Aaron Kramer

My Canary. Josephine D. Henderson Heard. CBWP-4

My candle burned alone in an immense valley. Valley Candle. Wallace Stevens. SAmP

My candle burns at both ends. First Fig. Edna St. Vincent Millay. APAD; AiP; ChAP; EBEvV; FaBoWP; NALW; NoAM; NoP-4; PoA; PoLF; TAP

My candle burns up lank and fair. Resurrection. Margiad Evans. OBWVE

My Captain. Dorothea Day. BLPA

My Care. Peter Fallon. CIP-2

My careful life says: "No surrender." Frank Ormsby. PBCIP

My cares comen ever anew. *Unknown*. MiEL

My Carol. Mildmay Fane. BeJo

My case is this. Sir John Davies. NoSic *Fr.* The Gulling[e] Sonnets. Son

My cassia boat, adrift and free. The Fishing Rod. Shen Yüeh, *Chinese*. SuSp, *tr. by* Richard B. Mather

My Cat and I. Roger McGough. OxBTC

My cat has got no name. Cat. Vernon Scannell. PeP

My Cat Jeoffry. Christopher Smart. APo; CABP; FaBoCh; PoE; RB *Fr.* Fragment B. *Fr.* Jubilate Agno.

("For he purrs in thankfulness, when God tells him he's / a good Cat.") (LL) PeP

(From Jubilate Agno.) NoP-4; PoPoPo

My Cathedral. Henry Wadsworth Longfellow. PBMP

My Cats. Stevie Smith. CBNP

("That sit on tombstones for your mats.") (LL) PC

My cat's tail. Cat. Judith Nicholls. PeP

My ceramic lake in dawn, water settled clear. Han Yü, *Chinese*. *Fr.* A Pond in a Jardiniere. CoBCP, *tr. by* Burton Watson

My Chakabuku Mama. Jewelle Gomez. GLP

My cheap toy lamp. Child's Song. Robert Lowell. RB

My child and I hold hands on the way to school. September, the First Day of School. Howard Nemerov. OxBC

My child, I do this for you. I give this to you. Song of the Pheasant. *Unknown*. APN-2 *Fr.* Minnetare Songs.

My child perished like the sky when it broke. Kū' siut Song. *Unknown, Bella Coola Native American*. APN-2, *tr. by* Franz Boas

My child, the Duck-billed Plat-y-pus. The Platypus. Oliver Herford. PeLV

My child, we were two children. Mein Kind, wir waren Kinder. Heinrich Heine, *German*. OBVE, *tr. by* Elizabeth Barrett Browning

My child won't stir. Woman from Chianciano. Rika Lesser. FiLi

My childhood all a myth. The Myth. Edwin Muir. CMoP

My childhood-home I see again. Memory. Abraham Lincoln. APN-1; BLPA; FaBoBe

My childhood is all memories of a patio in Sevilla. Portrait. Antonio Machado Ruiz, *Spanish*. RaBo; STV, tr. by Robert Bly

My Childhood's Happy Days. Daniel Webster Davis. AAP

My Childhood's Home. Caroline Elizabeth Norton. Ro *Fr.* The Undying One.

My childhood's trees stand rejoicing around me: O human! Homecoming. Edith Södergran, *German*. WPoS, tr. by David McDuff

My children, my little dears. The Mother Crab and Her Family. L. T. Manyase, *Xhosa*. PeSA, tr. by Jack Cope *and* C. M. Mcanyangwa

My children! speak not ill of one another. To Poets. Walter Savage Landor. FaBoEE

My children tug at my coat and ask. Returning Home. Tu Mu, *Chinese*. SuSp, tr. by John M. Ortinau

My children, when at first I liked the whites. *Arapaho Oral Tradition, Arapaho*. STP *Fr.* Songs of the Arapaho. APN-2 *Fr.* Ghost-Dance Songs. PaTW, tr. by James Mooney

My Chinese uncle, gouty, deaf, half-blinded. Grotesques. Robert Graves. OBCoV

My Choice. *Unknown*. CTV

My Christ, by Thee. (LL) A Thanksgiving to God for His House. Robert Herrick. BeJo; CavPo; FaBoBe; HAP; NOSC; PeECV; PoRA; PoToHe; SeCP; TrCP

My Christmas; Mum's Christmas. Sarah Forsyth. OBCP

My chums will burn their Indian weeds. Smith of Maudlin. George Walter Thornbury. PeVV

My church has but one temple. My Church. "E. O. G." BLPA

My church is filled with snow. Epiphany. Nancy Paddock. LoHo

My City. James Weldon Johnson. NAAAL

My city mine. No more can I. Amir Gilbo'a, *Hebrew*. IP, tr. by Warren Bargad *and* Stanley F. Chyet

My city slept. The Beginning of a Long Poem on Why I Burned the City. Lawrence Benford. TTY

My claw is tired of scribing! An Invocation. Saint Columcille. NOIV

My CLose-Committee. Mildmay Fane. BeJo

My clothing was once of the linsey woolsey fine. Poor Old Horse. *Unknown*. CH

My clumsiest dear, whose hands shipwreck vases. Love Poem. John Frederick Nims. HoPM; inPK-6; SAGP

My clumsy poem on the inn-wall none cared to see. The Poem on the Wall. Po Chü-i, *Chinese*. ChiP; ChiPo, tr. by Arthur Waley

My Cocoon tightens—Colors tease. Emily Dickinson. APN-2; NAAL-1; NAAL-3; PAR

My Coffin Is a Deckchair. Rodney Hall. *Fr.* Black Bagatelles. CBAP

My colored child / hood wuz mostly music. Make/n My Music. Angela Jackson. SeSe

My come unto the general dance. (LL) My Dancing Day. *Unknown*. OxBoLi; PoEL-1

My Comforter. Emily Jane Brontë. VWP

My comforts drop and melt away like snow. The Answer. George Herbert. FaBoVe

My Company. Sir Herbert Read. PoWW

My comrade is in the final agony before death. Yona Degen, *Russian*. TCRP, tr. by Albert C. Todd

My Confessional Sestina. Dana Gioia. RA

My conscience has given me several twitches. To My Cousin Mary, for Mending My Tobacco Pouch. Francis Scott Key. OBAL

My consecrated Vessel hangs at last. Horace. *See* 4.7.

My contact and my pal. (LL) Naturally the Foundation Will Bear Your Expenses. Philip Larkin. FaBoPV; PeLV

My contemporary. He died, not I. To a Poet. Agnes Nemes Nagy, *Hungarian*. CEEP; PoSu, tr. by Bruce Berlind

My cotton shirts float on the line. The Women. Cyrus Cassells. UnSA

My counterpane is soft as silk. A Child's Song of Christmas. Marjorie Lowry Christie Pickthall. BoTP

My Country. Olga Berggolts, *Russian*. TCRP, tr. by Daniel Weissbort

My Country. Elolongue Epanya Yondo, *French*. NegPo, tr. by Ellen Conroy Kennedy

My Country Audit. Mildmay Fane. BeJo; NOSC

My country is not a country. Envoi. Eli W. Mandel. NOBC

My country need not change her gown. Union. Emily Dickinson. FaBoA

My county, 'tis of thee. America. Samuel Francis Smith. AiP; CTV; EBEvV; FaBoBe; PoLF

My country, / t'is of thee / I sing. A Lover's Question. James Baldwin. GLP

My Country, to Thy Shore. Theodore Chickering Williams. AH

My countryman, the poet, wears a Stetson. David Wright. *Fr.* Seven South African Poems. PeSA

My countrymen have now become too base. April 1962. Paul Goodman. VGW

My Cousin Agueda [*or* Agatha]. Ramón López Velarde, *Spanish*. OBVE, tr. by Unknown

My Cousin German came from France. *Unknown*. FaBoCh

My cousin named her baby Rose. Rose. Cill Janeway. IFJA

My Creed. Samuel Ellsworth Kiser. PoToHe

My crown desired, my true love and joy. A Love Letter to Elizabeth Thatcher. Thomas Thatcher. SCAP

My curse be on the day when first I saw. Sonnet: To the Lady Pietra degli Scrovigni. Dante, *Italian*. AWP, tr. by D. G. Rossetti

My cuticles are a mess. Oh honey, by the way. The Motorcyclists. James Tate. NoAM

My dad had done the same. (LL) Epitaph on a Pessimist. Thomas Hardy. FaBoEE; PFE; TRP

My Dad Is a Magician. Leslie Reese.

"They say that all little girls adore their fathers / want to marry." MoLi

My Dad was worried about his brother. Lucilius, *Greek*. GrAn, tr. by Peter Porter

My dad works late in a coffee shop. Laura Whipple. CA

My Daddy has paid the rent. Good Times. Lucille Clifton. AmPA; BPo; ISC; InPS-3; MBE; PoBA; SoSe-8; TAP; TRP; TwCP

My daddy is an engineer. Wanderin'. *Unknown*. AS

My daddy played the market. January 1st. Anne Sexton. HCAP

My daddy rides me piggy-back. Piggy-back. Langston Hughes. TLR

My daddy said, 'My son, my son'. Bad Report—Good Manners. Spike Milligan. NOxBChV

My Daddy, Whenever He Went Some Place. David Huddle. PBCAP

My Dad's Dinner Pail. Edward Harrigan. BLPA

My daily affairs are quite ordinary. Layman P'ang, *Chinese*. EnlH, tr. by Stephen Mitchell

My Daily Creed. *Unknown*. CTV; PWR

My dame hath a lame tame crane. *Unknown*. OxNR

My Damon was the first to wake. Meeting. George Crabbe. OBEV

My Dancing Day. *Unknown*. OxBoLi

("Tomorrow shall be my dancing day.") PoEL-1

My dancing is, in my opinion, good. Of Dancing. Alan Brownjohn. FaBoMo

My Daphne's hair is twisted gold. Daphne. John Lyly. NoSic *Fr.* Midas.

My dark and sultry / love. (LL) The Invention of Comics. Imamu Amiri Baraka. CAPP-1; CRP; GT; LiTM; NAAAL; PBMP; PoBA

My Dark Fathers. Brendan Kennelly. BIrV; CIP-2; PBCIP

My Dark Rosaleen! (LL) Dark Rosaleen. Owen Roe MacWard *and* Hugh O'Donnell, *Irish*. AWP; BIrV; CH; IIP; NOIV; OBEV; OxAEP-2, tr. by James Clarence Mangan

My darkling child the stars have obeyed. George Barker. TwCP *Fr.* To My Son.

My Darling. "Michael Field." CPO

My darling lady readers. The Mystery Corset. André Breton, *French*. PFTM, tr. by Pierre Joris

My darling little Lou how I love you. Guillaume Apollinaire. PFTM, tr. by Jerome Rothenberg *Fr.* Poems for Lou.

My darling, my love. Desmond O'Grady. CIP-2, tr. by Desmond O'Grady *Fr.* In the Greenwood.

My darling, thou wilt never know. On the Death of Emily Jane Brontë. Charlotte Brontë. VWP

My darling, we sat together. Mein Liebchen, wir sassen zusammen. Heinrich Heine, *German*. AWP, tr. by James Thomson

My darling, won't you try this little game? Soap Bubbles. Bùi Khái Nguyễn, *Vietnamese*. AVP, tr. by Huỳnh Sanh Thông

My darling works until she finishes I resist starting. Countryside. Jane Miller. PUP-19

My darling, you know how much I like to see the light on a. The Black Hairs. Heinz Pasman, *German*. RaBo, tr. by Robert Bly

My darlings, do you hear me? Trim the fires! (LL) My Lighthouses. Helen Hunt Jackson. APN-2; ColAP

My darling's features, painted by the light. George Henry Boker. APN-2 *Fr.* Sonnets: A Sequence on Profane Love.

My Darling's on the Deep Blue Sea. *Unknown*. AmFP

My daughter. T. S. Eliot. *See* Marina.

My daughter, age six, drew her first official drawing today. My Daughter's Pundalunda. William Joyce. EC3

My daughter, all is not vanity. The Song to the Wife of His Youth. Nathan Alterman. MHP, tr. by Ruth Finer Mintz *Fr.* The Joy of the Poor.

My Daughter and Apple Pie. Raymond Carver. MoLi

My Daughter at 14: Christmas Dance, 1981. Maria Gillan. IFJA

My daughter, at eleven. Little Girl, My String Bean, My Lovely Woman. Anne Sexton. NYBP

My daughter came home from school one day. The Battle, Over and Over Again. Safiya Henderson-Holmes. UnSA

My daughter cries when we have to talk about money. The Money Cry. Peter Davison. FYAP

My daughter denies she is like me. Breaking Tradition. Janice Mirikitani. NMM-2

My daughter has turned against eggs. Age six. Eggs. Sharon Olds. CrSp

My daughter makes songs from the words. Riding Hood. Betsy Sholl. CrSp

My daughter plays on the floor. Spelling. Margaret Atwood. NALW; NoAM

My daughter practicing her vowels at dawn. Rolling in Clover. Jeffrey Skinner. WeT

My daughter spreads her legs. After Reading *Mickey in the Night Kitchen* for the Third Time Before Bed. Rita Dove. LoL; NMM-2

My Daughter Very Ill. Paul Goodman. MoLi

My daughter / walks in grace. For Miranda. Gregory Corso. MoLi

My daughter wants the car tonight, no. Sins of the Fathers. Mark Vinz. IFJA

My daughter's dear child here I hold on my lap. After the Inscription on a Greek Stele of a Woman Holding Her Grandchild on Her Knees. *Unknown, Greek.* GrAn, *tr. by* Stephen Spender

My daughter's heavier. Light leaves are flying. Song 385. John Berryman. MoLi *Fr.* Dream Songs.

My daughter's pajamas lie on the floor. Pajamas. Sharon Olds. NMM-2

My Daughter's Pundalunda. William Joyce. EC3

My Day. Tennyson. NAEL-2; NOBVV *Fr.* Maud [A Monodrama]. EnVR

My days among the Dead are past. The Scholar. Robert Southey. GTBS-P; LaPo; OBEV; OxAEP-2

My Days are Gliding Swiftly By. David Nelson. AH

My day's delights, my spring[e]time joy[e]s for[e]done. A Poem Entreating of Sorrow. Sir Walter Ralegh. SiPS *Fr.* The Ocean's Love to Cynthia.

My Days Go On. Frances Partridge. LBC

My Days of Love Are Over. Byron. OBNC *Fr.* Canto the First. NAEL-2; OAEL-2; PoE *Fr.* Don Juan.

My days overgrown with coffee blossoms. Joseph Miezan Bognini. PBMAP *Fr.* Ce Dur Appel de l'Espoir (1960).

My dead brother. Nicholas Virgilio. HA

My dead friend's face as well. (LL) Requiem: "Pour out your light, O stars." Ivor Gurney. FaBoEE; FaBoTw

My dead Love came to me, and said. The Apparition. Stephen Phillips. LBC; OBEV

My dead piled up, thick, fragrant, on the fire escape. Autumn Leaves. Marilyn Chin. PoPoPo

My Dear and Only Love. James Graham. *See* I'll Never Love Thee More.

My dear Antenor now give ore. To My Antenor, March 16, 1661/2. Katherine Philips. KTR

My dear Brother, wt courage bear the crosse. A Sonnet sent to Blackness to Mr. John Welsch, by the Lady Culross. Elizabeth Melvill, Lady Culross. KTR

My dear child, first thyself enable. The Boy Serving at Table. John Lydgate. OxBChV

My dear, darkened in sleep turned from the moon. To Judith Asleep. John Ciardi. LiTM

My dear deaf father, how I loved him then. John Betjeman. OxBTC *Fr.* Summoned by Bells.

My dear, do you know. The Babes in the Wood. *Unknown.* OxBChV

My dear, do you remember that country. Remember That Country. Jean Garrigue. VGW

My dear, dumb friend, low lying there. To My Dog "Blanco." Josiah Gilbert Holland. PoLF

My Dear Editor Manchette. Quote Me Wrong Again and I'll Slit the Throat of Your Pet Iguana. David St. John. RACG

"My dear fellow!" said the great poet. Fiction: A Message. Gavin Ewart. OxBC

My dear, I wonder if before the end. To D———, Dead by Her Own Hand. Howard Nemerov. PoA

My dear Mrs. Bloomer. Part of a True Story. Marilyn Hacker. Poetr

My dear, my dear, I know. To a Young Girl. W. B. Yeats. EBEV

My dear, my dearest dust; I come, I come. Lady Catherine Dyer. *See* Epitaph on the Monument of Sir William Dyer at Colmworth, 1641.

My dear Orange brothers, have you heard of the news. The Orange Lily. *Unknown.* NOIV

'My dear son I am well thanks be to God'. Home News. Ahmed Tidjani-Cissé. PBMAP

My Dear Son John's deceas'd ah! gone from hence. A Brief Elegie on My Dear Son John. John Saffin. SCAP

My dear Telemachus, / The Trojan War. Odysseus to Telemachus. Joseph Brodsky, *Russian.* BLT, *tr. by* George L. Kline

My dear! this morning we will take a ride. The Tête à Tête; or, Fashionable Pair: an Eclogue. Ann Murry. ECWP

My dear, / Today a letter from Berlin. A Letter from Berlin. Jon Stallworthy. MoP; OBWP; OxBC

My dear, what you said was one thing. Marge Piercy. MDDM *Fr.* My Mother's Body.

My deare, my dearest dust; I come, I come. (LL) Epitaph on the Monument of Sir William Dyer at Colmworth, 1641. Lady Catherine Dyer. BoLoP; EnLoPo; OxBM

My dearely loved friend how oft have we. Michael Drayton. *See* First Steps Up Parnassus.

My dearest Boy, / Since time begun. To a School-Boy at Eton, Yes and No. Mary Savage. ECWP

My dearest dear, the time draws near. The Lover's Lament. *Unknown.* AS

My dearest dust, could not thy hasty day. Epitaph on the Monument of Sir William Dyer at Colmworth, 1641. Lady Catherine Dyer. BoLoP; EnLoPo; OxBM *Fr.* Sir William Dyer, Knight.

My dearest friend is struck, and I must stern beware. He Loves. David Schirmer, *German.* GePo, *tr. by* George C. Schoolfield

My dearest rival, lest [*or* least] our love. Sir John Suckling. BeJo; CavPo; MeLP

My dearest, to let you or the world know. The Forfeiture. Henry, Bishop of Chichester King. NOSC

My dearly loved friend how oft have we. First Steps Up Parnassus. Michael Drayton. NOBE

My dears, 'tis said in days of old. The Bee, the Ant, and the Sparrow. Nathaniel Cotton. OxBChV

My Death. Carl Zuckmayer, *German.* TrJP, *tr. by* E. B. Ashton

My death was arranged by special plans in Heaven. A New England Bachelor. Richard Eberhart. MoAmPo; NoAM

My deerest Mistrisse, let us live and love. Catullus, *Latin.* OBCVT, *tr. by* William Corkine

My Deery Honey. *Unknown.* PBCV

My Delight and Thy Delight. Robert Bridges. CMoP; NOBE; OBEV; PoEL-5

My demands upon life are quite modest. Limerick. Robert Conquest. PeLi

My departed soul. Having molded clay in the shape of my ailing form. Masaoka Shiki, *Japanese.* MJT, *tr. by* Ueda, Makoto

My desire for revenge, the bitterness. Till Death Do Us Part. Leila Miccolis, *Portuguese.* BoWoP, *tr. by* Willis Barnstone *and* Nelson Cerqueira

My desk, most loyal friend. Desk. Marina Tsvetayeva, *Russian.* FP, *tr. by* Elaine Feinstein *Fr.* Desk.

My desk's at the back of the class. The Marrog. R. C. Scriven. SpW

My Detached Villa. Li Shan-fu. SuSp, *tr. by* Edward H. Schafer

"My deth I love, my lif ich hate." *Unknown.* MiEL

My dew is everywhere. Trumbull Stickney. *Fr.* Pandora's Songs. APN-2 *Fr.* Prometheus Pyrphoros.

My Diamond Stud. Alice Fulton. WWSi

My disaffected gaze falls on the city. Côte de Liesse. Daryl Hine. NoP-4

My Divine Lysi. Sister Juana Inés de la Cruz. CPO

My Dog. John Kendrick Bangs. BLPA; FaBoBe

My Dog. Marchette Chute. ImGa; WHSW

My Dog. Emily Lewis. OTCP

My dog lay dead five days without a grave. The Pardon. Richard Wilbur. FP; MoP; NOBA; NoAM; Poetr

My Dog, Spot. Rodney Bennett. BoTP

My dog went mad and bit my hand. D is for Dog. W. H. Davies. OxBSP

My Doggie. C. Nurton. BoTP

My dog's so furry I've not seen. The Hairy Dog. Herbert Asquith. CTAV; CTV; PeP

My dolour is ane cup. Ressaif My Saul. R. Crombie Saunders. OxBS

My Dolphin, you only guide me by surprise. Dolphin. Robert Lowell. NOBA; NoAM; VCAP

My donkey has a bridle. The Donkey. Rose Fyleman. BoTP

My donkey stops. At Her Grave. Kuthaiyir, *Arabic.* ArPe, *tr. by* Omar S. Pound

My dove, my beautiful one. James Joyce. ChIV-1

My downfall: those pink articulate lips. Dioscorides, *Greek.* EP; GrAn; LoP, *tr. by* Peter Whigham

My dragon's name is Jocelyn. Jocelyn, my Dragon. Colin West. PeP

My Dream. Lew Blockcolski. VoR

My Dream. Christina Rossetti. BrRo; VWP

My dream a drink with Lonnie Johnson we discuss the code. Sonnet. Ted Berrigan. NoAM *Fr.* The Sonnets.

My Dream About the Cows. Lucille Clifton. TRP

My Dream About the Poet. Lucille Clifton. TRP

My dream is the dream of a pond. Gifts. "Shu Ting," *Chinese.* VCWP, *tr. by* Carolyn Kizer

My dream of America. Chinese Hot Pot. Wing Tek Lum. UnSA

My dreams are of a field afar. A. E. Housman. PeVV

My Dreams, My Works Must Wait Till after Hell. Gwendolyn Brooks. NoP-4

My dress is silent when I tread the ground. *Unknown.* NoP-4

My dress of many years is all worn out. Buying a Dress for My Love. Đông Hồ, *Vietnamese.* AVP, tr. by Huỳnh Sanh Thông

My Drinking Song. Richard Dehmel, *German.* AWP, tr. by Ludwig Lewisohn

My driver's license is lapsing and so I appear. The Vision Test. Mona Van Duyn. FFC

My drum, hollowed out thru the thin slit. La Chute. Charles Olson. InPK-6

My dugout canoe goes. Paddling Song. *Unknown, Bantu.* PBA, tr. by Max Exner

My eager waiting heart can bear no more. He Comes Not To-night. Josephine D. Henderson Heard. CBWP-4

My *Ear* thus charm'd, mine *Eye* with Pleasure sees. The Humming Bird. Richard Lewis. APo *Fr.* A Journey from Patapsko to Annapolis.

My earliest flame, to whom I owe. A Letter from a Captain in Country Quarters to his Corinna in Town. Isaac Hawkins Browne. ECEV

My Early Home. John Clare. BoTP; PoLF

My early home was this. (LL) My Early Home. John Clare. BoTP; PoLF

My early Mistress, now my ancient Muse. Preface to *The Progress of Learning.* Sir John Denham. NOSC; OxBSP

My Easter Dove. Henrietta Cordelia Ray. CBWP-3

My een are nae on Calvary. Sorley MacLean, *Gaelic.* FaBoTC, tr. by Douglas Young

My elder, / Born into death like a message into a bottle. To My Brother Hanson. W. S. Merwin. NAAL-2

My elder sister stays by my side. Happy about Being Old. Yüan Mei, *Chinese.* CoBLCP, tr. by Jonathan Chaves

My eldest sister arrived home that morning. Cuba. Paul Muldoon. CIP-2; PNI

My embarrassment at his nakedness. The Pool. Robert Creeley. CoAP

My empire of flamboyans. Areyto. Victor Hernandez Cruz. PmAP

My enemy came nigh. Hate. James Stephens. MoBrPo

My enemy had bidden me as guest. The Compassionate Fool. Norman Cameron. GTBS-P; OxBSP; OxBTC; RB

My entire life / has been spent / in refugee camps. Wired In. Lamont B. Steptoe. UnSA

My Epitaph. H. J. Daniel. FaBoEE

My Epitaph. David Gray. EBVV

My epitaph write on your heart. Love's Epitaph. William Cavendish. OxBSP

My Erotic Double. John Ashbery. LCAP-2; PoE; SAGP; VCAP

My Estate. John Norris. NOSC

My Evening Prayer. Charles H. Gabriel. BLPA; FaBoBe

My eye cried and woke me. The Night. Al-Khansa, *Arabic.* BoWoP, tr. by Willis Barnstone

My eye descending from the Hill, surveys. The Thames from Cooper's Hill. Sir John Denham. OAEL-1; OxAEP-1 *Fr.* Cooper's Hill. BeJo; CABP; PBRV; SeCP

My eye is not on Calvary. Calvary. Sorley MacLean. FaBoTC

My eyelids red and heavy are. A Poor Scholar of the 'Forties. Padraic Colum. NOIV

My eyes already touch the sunny hill. A Walk. Rilke, *German.* RaBo, tr. by Robert Bly

My eyes are dim, my hands are clumsy. Getting on Horseback. Yü Chi, *Chinese.* CoBLCP, tr. by Jonathan Chaves

My eyes are full of rivers and trees tonight. After a Train Journey. May Sarton. GM

My eyes are red, my mouth black. Elf. Sándor Weöres, *Hungarian.* CEEP, tr. by Emery E. George

My eyes are the enemy's eyes. The Enemy's Eyes. Emma Lee Warrior. HATNAP

My eyes are thirsty. Mirabai, *Hindi.* BoWoP, tr. by Willis Barnstone *and* Usha Nilsson

My eyes are white stones. River God's Song. Anne Ridler. NYBP

My eyes catch ruddy necks. Marching. Isaac Rosenberg. NSI; PeFWW

My eyes fly out of the window. Passing through Rajasthan. Umashankar Joshi, *Gujarati.* OMIP, tr. by Niranjan Bhagat *and* Carlo Coppola

My eyes have seen and chosen for me a handsome youth. Meinloh von Sevelingen, *German.* GePo, tr. by J. W. Thomas

My Face. Anthony Euwer. *See* The Face.

My face is grass. Legacy. Maurice Kenny. HATNAP

My face is Mrs. Heyward's. A Poem about Faith. Kathleen Norris. CrSp

My Face Is My Own, I Thought. Tom Raworth. SPE

My face is wet with rain. Walking at Night. Amory Hare. PoLF

My faint spirit was sitting in the light. From the Arabic: An Imitation. Shelley. OBEV

My fair-haired child dancing in the dunes. Poem for Melissa. Nuala Ni Dhomhnaill. BiHa

My Fair Lady. *Unknown.* EnLoPo; PoEL-1
(Under the Leaves Green.) OxBoLi

My fair says, she no spouse but me. Catullus. *See* Carmen 70 ("Lesbia says she'ld rather marry me").

My fairest child, I have no song to give you. A Farewell. Charles Kingsley. BLPA; EBVV; OxBChV
(My fairest child, I have no song to sing thee.) BoTP

My Fairy. "Lewis Carroll." CBNP

My Faith Looks Up to Thee. Ray Palmer. AH

My faithful friend, if you can see. Impossibilities to His Friend. Robert Herrick. OxBSP

My Faithful Mother Tongue. Czeslaw Milosz, *Polish.* VCWP, tr. by Czeslaw Milosz *and* Robert Hass

My falling tears wet the double gates. (LL) Old Poem. *Unknown, Chinese.* AWP, tr. by Arthur Waley; CoBCP, tr. by Burton Watson

My family asleep. Leroy Gorman. HA

My family complains like cackling geese. Borrowing Rice from Ju-hui. Mei Yao Ch'en, *Chinese.* SuSp, tr. by Jonathan Chaves

My family has married me. Song of Sorrow. *Unknown, Chinese.* CoBCP, tr. by Burton Watson

My family tree is mist and darkness. Family History. Irving Feldman. VCAP

My family's all so squalid. Dressing Up. Jackie Kay. CPO

My fancy fled to the South again. (LL) The Daisy. Tennyson. EnLoPo; NOBVV; OBNC; PoEL-5

My Father. Yehuda Amichai, *Hebrew.* IP, tr. by Warren Bargad *and* Stanley F. Chyet

My Father. James Berry. PBCV

My Father. Felix Mnthali. PBMAP

My Father after Work. Gary Gildner. Poetsp

My Father / Against the victories of age. Plaisir d'Amour. Patrick Galvin. BiHa

My Father and God. Linda Gregg. MoLi

My father and mother left me a good living. Han-shan, *Chinese.* CoBCP, tr. by Burton Watson

My father and mother, my brother and sister. The Sightseers. Paul Muldoon. BiHa; CIP-2

My father and mother (what ails 'em?). The Rural Lass. Catherine Jemmat. ECWP; NOEC

My father and my mother never quarrelled. Because. James McAuley. BMAP; CBAP; NOBAu

My Father and the Figtree. Naomi Shihab Nye. UnSA

My father asks me how I stand it all. Parents. Vincent Buckley. CBAP

My father at the dictionary-stand. Supernatural Love. Gjertrud Schnackenberg. DiPo; NoAM; NoP-4; VCAP

My father beat the robins. Exiles. Judy F. Ham. LoHo

My father bequeathed me no wide estates. Heirloom. Abraham Moses Klein. NOBC; TrJP

My father brought that dog home. Bony. Simon J. Ortiz. CDW

My father brought the emigrant bundle. Europe and America. David Ignatow. NNaP; PBMP; UnPo

My father by some strange conjunction had mice for sons. In All the Days of My Childhood. Russell Edson. AmPA

My father came in the darkness. Hyena. *Unknown, Hurutsche.* TTY, tr. by George Economou

My father confessor is strict and holy. Spots in the Sun. Coleridge. Ro *Fr.* Morning Post, no. 10,614.

My father could go down a mountain faster than I. That Dark Other Mountain. Robert Francis. CRP

My father died a month ago. *Unknown.* OxNR

My father died near evening, having spent. The Truth. Frankie Paino. NAmP90

My father died nine months before. Birth of a Son. Sam Hunt. PeNZ

My father died of a heart attack / during an afternoon nap. Upkeep. Miriam Goodman. UnSA

My Father Died This Spring. Joanne Kyger. PoM

My father entered the kingdom of roots. 1933. Philip Levine. LCAP-2

My father, for example. A Visitor. Mary Oliver. MoLi

My father found it after the war—. The House on Buder Street. Gary Gildner. TAP

My father, gasping, in his white calked shoes. The Course. Robert Huff. CoAP

My father had a glass eye. My Father's Eye. Eléni Vakaló, *Modern Greek.* BoWoP, tr. by Kimon Friar

My father had a lot of friendly enemies. Father-Sequence. Luigi Fontanella, *Italian.* NeIt, *tr. by* Michael Palma

My father has forgotten me. Metamorphosis. Louise Glück. MoLi *Fr.* Metamorphosis. MoLi

My father he died, but I can't tell you how. Mother Goose. CBNP; OxNR

My father, he was a mountaineer. The Ballad of William Sycamore. Stephen Vincent Benét. MoAmPo; PoRA; SAGP

My father, his mouth full of nails. Nails. Gary Gildner. PBCAP; TAP

My father, in a 1956 gray suit. Dance of the Letters. Vince Gotera. OpBo

My father in the night commanding No. Louis Simpson. CoAP; CoAmPo; HeIP-4; NOBA; NYBP; NoAM; TAP; TwCP; VGW; WeT

My father in the snowy window, face incandescent. Riding the Empire Builder, 1948. David Wojahn. GM

My father is a hand-/ some guy. A Daddy Poem. William J. Harris. ISC; UnSA

My father is a quiet man. Fruit of the Flower. Countee Cullen. PoLF

My father is a retired magician. Ntozake Shange. MoLi

  ("Love it / bein colored.") (LL) ISC

My father is clearing the first Party shrine. Party Shrine. Thomas McCarthy. BiHa

My father is dead. Song of the Bush-Shrike. *Unknown, Zulu.* PeSA

My father is dead and there is nothing left. Not Saying Much. Linda Gregg. AiP

My father is lying in a green. At Mt. Auburn Cemetery. Diana Der Hovanessian. LoHo

My father is sleeping. His noble face. The Distant Footsteps. César Vallejo, *Spanish. RaBo, tr. by* James Wright *and* John Knoepfle

My father is standing on a railroad platform. Departure. Louise Glück. GM

My Father, it is surely a blue place. Hunchback Girl: She Thinks of Heaven. Gwendolyn Brooks. ChAP *Fr.* A Street in Bronzeville. BPo; BlSi; FaBoWP

My father laughing over the morning paper. Reading Before We Read, Horoscope and Weather. Wyatt Prunty. RA

My father leaves us in the car. Signal Hill. Sharon Doubiago. MoLi

My father left his English home. The Song of the Bounder. Edgar Wallace. PeSAV

My father left me three acres of land. Sing Ivy. *Unknown.* BoTP; OxNR

My father, let no similes eclipse. In Memoriam. Michael Longley. PNI

My father lies black and hushed. The Worker. Richard W. Thomas. PoBA

My father lives by the ocean. Certain People. Richard Jones. NAmP90

My father, looking for trouble, would find it. The Man of the House. David Wagoner. NoAM

My father made a synagogue of a boat. Two Fishermen. Stanley Moss. CoAP

My father moved through dooms of love. E. E. Cummings. CMoP; ColAP; FYAP; HAP; MeMAP; MoP; NAAL-2; NOBA; NoAM; NoP-4; OxBA; TAP; UnPo

My father moves through the South hunting duck. Treetops. Marvin Bell. AmPA

My Father, My Son. John Malcolm Brinnin. NYBP

My father paces the upstairs hall. Spree. Maxine W. Kumin. NoAM

My Father Paints the Summer. Richard Wilbur. NOBA

My father played the melodion. Patrick Kavanagh. PChr; RB *Fr.* A Christmas Childhood. IIP

My father put me in my mother. Where I Came From. Ruth Stone. NAmP90

My father remembered what it was to be small. In the Giant's Castle. Ruth Dallas. PeNZ

My father said I could not do it. The Leaving. Brigit Pegeen Kelly. APAD

My father saw it back in 1910. Halley's Comet. Norman Nicholson. NoP-4

My Father Scything. Sam Hunt. PeNZ

My father sits quietly in his brown Naugahyde chair watching / TV with the remote control. Portrait of Assimilation. "Chrystos." UnSA

My Father Spoke with Swans. Patrick Galvin. BiHa

My father the hawk. Latvian Songs. Johannes Bobrowski, *German.* AF, *tr. by* Matthew Mead

My father, the least happy. The Cage. John Montague. CIP-2; PNI

My Father Today. Sam Hunt. PeNZ

My father travels on the late evening train. Dilip Chitre. OMIP

My father used to say. Silence. Marianne Moore. CMoP; FaBoMo; FaBoWP; InPS-3; NALW; NOBA; TRP

My father was a barber-surgeon. The Worker (We Own Two Houses). Charles Fort. CMAP

My father was a farmer gay. One-and-Twenty. *Unknown.* AmFP

My father was a Frenchman. *Unknown.* OxNR

My father was a sailor. Antonio Machado Ruiz. *Fr.* Spanish Folk Songs. AWP, *tr. by* Havelock Ellis

My father was a servant-boy. The Mixed Marriage. Paul Muldoon. PNI

My father was always out in the garage. Eli W. Mandel. MoCV *Fr.* Minotaur Poems.

My father was four years at their war. Yehuda Amichai. MHP, *tr. by* Ruth Finer Mintz *Fr.* Here We Loved.

My father was one of the first men. Space Settlement. Albert Rowe. SpW

My father was sixty when I was born. My Father Scything. Sam Hunt. PeNZ

My Father Washes His Hands. Fred Chappell. MT

My Father Went to Funerals. Howard Nelson. RaBo

My father! when I saw thee last. To Father. Mary E. Tucker. CBWP-1

My father who found the English landscape tame. Woods. Louis MacNeice. IIP

My father, who works with stone. A Story of How a Wall Stands. Simon J. Ortiz. HATNAP

My father won't talk about the numbers. Tattoo. Gregg Shapiro. UnSA

My father wore it working coal at Shotts. The Miner's Helmet. George MacBeth. OxBTC

My father worked with a horse-plough. Follower. Seamus Heaney. CABP; IIP; PNI

My father, you say. Reply. Reiner Kunze, *German.* CEEP; PoSu, *tr. by* Ewald Osers

My Father's a Still Day. Geoffrey Lehmann. *Fr.* Ross's Poems. CBAP

My Father's Back. Edward Hirsch. VCAP

My father's back. Secret Love. Milton Kessler. UnSA

My Fathers blood revenged shall be. (LL) Johnie Armstrong. *Unknown.* PBRV

My Father's Body. William Matthews. PuP-17

My father's body was a globe of fear. Letters and Other Worlds. Michael Ondaatje. NOBC; NoAM; NoP-4

My father's brother has a farm in the forest. Meditation among Trees. Marbod of Rennes, *Latin.* MLL, *tr. by* Helen Waddell

My Father's Close. *Unknown, French.* AWP, *tr. by* D. G. Rossetti

My Father's Cot. Sir John Collings Squire.

  "I left thee with a courage high." BXAP

My Father's Country. Joyce Lee. NOBAu

My Father's Death. Constance Urdang. PBCAP

My Father's Desk. Kate Daniels. MoLi

My Father's Eye. Eléni Vakaló, *Modern Greek.* BoWoP, *tr. by* Kimon Friar

My Father's Fights. Stuart Dybek. PBCAP

My Father's First Baseball Game. Michael S. Weaver. PBCAP

My father's friend came once to tea. A Recollection. Frances Darwin Cornford. FaBoWP; NTP

My Father's Garden. E. K. Miller. IFJA

My Father's Garden. David Wagoner. DiPo; NIP-4

My Father's Geography. Michael S. Weaver. GT; PBCAP

My father's hands. Jeni Couzyn. PeSAV

My father's heart is on television. Medical Science. Robin Becker. PBCAP

My Father's Heroes. Allison Joseph. SeSe

My Father's House. Calvin Forbes. WeT

My Father's Leaving. Ira Sadoff. AmPA

My father's life is alchemy. Words and Legacy. Cyril Dabydeen. PBCV

My Father's Love Letters [or Loveletters]. Yusef Komunyakaa. ISC; NAmP90; PoPoPo; WeT

My Father's Martial Art. Stephen Shu Ning Liu. InPK-6

My Father's Neckties. Maxine W. Kumin. AFr

My father's photo in his dark strained frame. Icon. Hugh Seidman. BAP-93

My Father's Song. Simon J. Ortiz. HATNAP

My Father's Story. Priscilla Jane Thompson. CBWP-2

My Father's Watch. Thomas Rabbitt. CMAP

My Father's Wedding. Robert Bly. InPS-3; NoAM; RaBo

My father's white uncle became. Todd. Stewart Conn. FaBoTC

My favorite student lately is the one who wrote about feeling clumbsy. The Spell against Spelling. George Starbuck. FYAP

My favourite view of people. Fish Shop Windows. Geoffrey Dutton. NOBAu

My feet are elms, roots in the earth. They Tell Me I Am Lost. Maurice Kenny. HATNAP

My feet have felt the sands. Determination. John Henrik Clarke. PoBA

My feet shall tread no more thy mossy side. To the Wissahiccon. Frances Anne Kemble. APN-1

My feet strike an apex of the apices of the stairs. Infinity. Walt Whitman. *Fr.* Song of Myself. AmPP; MoAmPo; NAAL-3; NOBA; OxBA

My feet taste funny. Why I Didn't Go to Delphi. James Welch. CDW

My feet they are sore, and my limbs they are weary. The Orphan Child. Charlotte Brontë. VWP

My feet two hundred years old. (LL) Montgomery. Sam Cornish. MBE; PoBA; Poetsp

My feet were nourished on her breasts all night. (LL) 'Tis Christmas weather, and a country house. George Meredith. NAEL-2; NOBVV

My female friends, whose tender hearts. Jonathan Swift. NOBL *Fr.* Verses on the Death of Dr. Swift, D.S.P.D.

My fifth housebonde, god his soule blesse! Chaucer. *Fr.* The Wife of Bath's Prologue. FHYEP; NAEL-1; OAEL-1, *ll.* 1–862 *complete Fr.* The Canterbury Tales.

My fiftieth year had come and gone. W. B. Yeats. RaBo *Fr.* Vacillation. NoAM

My fighting days are done. Mnasalcas, *Greek.* GrAn, *tr. by* Edward Lucie-Smith

My Final Agonies. Benjamin Péret, *French.* PFTM, *tr. by* James Laughlin

My fine web sparkles. The Christmas Spider. Michael Richards. Spl

My fingers are antennae. Mary O'Neill. KaS

My first big love was cosmically correct. My Chakabuku Mama. Jewelle Gomez. GLP

My first day in new orleans. A Coltrane Memorial. David Henderson. MoNo

My First Forty Years. Kevin Ireland. PeNZ

My first is in life (not contained within heart). Riddle-Me-Ree. Liz Lochhead. OPOU

My first itch. The Itch. K. Ayyappa Paniker, *Malayalam.* OMIP, *tr. by* K. Ayyappa Paniker

My first love sighed for brooches. Prices. Louis Ginsberg. TrJP

My First Memory, Switzerland, Circa 1947. Joan Dobbie. LoHo

My First Riot: Bronx, NYC. Safiya Henderson-Holmes. UnSA

My first thought was, he lied in every word. Childe Roland to the Dark Tower Came. Robert Browning. EnVR; NAEL-2; NOBVV; NoP-4; OAEL-2; OBNV; PeVV; PoE; PoPoPo

My first vivid memory of you / mamacita. To Jesus Villanueva, with Love. Alma Villanueva. NMM-2; UnSA

My first week in Cambridge a car full of white boys. Boston Year. Elizabeth Alexander. GT

My fixed abode is Glen Bolcain. Suibne Geilt. NOIV

My *Flaccus,* if thou needs wouldest crave. Ad Flaccum. Martial, *Latin.* OBCVT, *tr. by* R. Fletcher

My flesh is at a distance from me. The Virgin. Laura Riding Jackson. ChIV-2

My flowers will not come to an end. Flower Songs. Nezahualcoyotl. PaTW

My flowery and green age was passing away. He Understands the Great Cruelty of Death. Petrarch. OBMV, *tr. by* J. M. Synge *Fr.* Sonnets to Laura.

My Flute. Herbert Krohn. CDa

My foamlesss heart, the bloodleap at my wrist. (LL) Rattler, Alert. Brewster Ghiselin. HAP; WeW-3

My foe outstretched [*or* outstretch'd] beneath the tree. (LL) A Poison Tree. William Blake. AWP; FHYEP; HAP; HoPM; ImPo; NAEL-2; NTP; OxAEP-2; PoEL-4; RB; SCV; SoSe-8; TFi; WeW-3

My folk, now answere me. *Unknown.* MiEL

My folk, what habbe I do thee. *Unknown.* MiEL

My folks could beg or borrow. (LL) Saturday's Child. Countee Cullen. LiTM; NAAAL; PoBA

My food was pallid till I heard it ring. King Midas. Howard Moss. CoAP; PoA; TAP

My footsteps in this street. Here. Octavio Paz, *Spanish.* STV, *tr. by* John Frederick Nims

My forty-year-old father learned to fly. The Hang-Glider's Daughter. Marilyn Hacker. MoLi

My foundling, my fondling, my frolic first-footer. A Blason. Alec Derwent Hope. NOBAu

My four adopted sons in photographs. Shelter. Louise Erdrich. FiLi

My frame of nature is a ruffled sea. The Hurry of the Spirits, in a Fever and Nervous Disorders. Isaac Watts. NOEC

My freehold of thanksgiving. (LL) My Triumph. John Greenleaf Whittier. APN-1; NOBA

My freshmen / settle in. Achilles. Freshmen. Barry Spacks. NYBP

My friend, a man I love as wholly. David St. John. PUP-20

My friend April Fallon tells me. Oh, By the Way. Ed Ochester. PuP-17

My friend from Asia has powers and magic, he plucks a blue leaf from the young blue-gum. Credo. Robinson Jeffers. MoAmPo

My friend, have you heard of the town of Nogood. The Town of Nogood. W. E. Penny. BLPA

My friend, I went to the market and bought the Dark One. It's True I Went to the Market. Mirabai, *Rajasthani.* WPoS, *tr. by* Robert Bly

My friend: / In what language shall we begin our conversation? Brief Letter to Donald Walsh (in memoriam). Angel Cuadra, *Spanish.* AF, *tr. by* Katherine Rodriguez Nieto

My friend is always doing good. Faith and Works. Muriel Spark. OxBSP

My friend is dwelling in the eastern mountain. To Tan Ch'iu. Li Po, *Chinese.* TAL, *tr. by* Robert Payne

(My friend is lodging high in the Eastern Range.) AWP; ChiP, *tr. by* Arthur Waley

My friend, judge not me. Epitaph. *Unknown.* NOSC

My friend must be a Bird. Emily Dickinson. TAP

My friend, my bonny friend, when we are old. The Word. John Masefield. FP

My friend, my friend. The Black Man. Sergey Aleksandrovich Yesenin, *Russian.* TCRP, *tr. by* Geoffrey Thurley

My friend Priapus with myself shall rise? (LL) Quaerè. George Farewell. NOEC; OBCoV

My friend says I was not a good son. Yesterday. W. S. Merwin. FYAP; LCAP-2; RaBo

My friend, speak always once, but listen twice. The Mouth and the Ears. Shem-Tob ben Joseph Palquera, *Hebrew.* TrJP, *tr. by* J. Chotzner

My friend the blue paisley shirt is always assured. The Blue Paisley Shirt. Thomas William Shapcott. BMAP

My Friend the Cuckold. Morris Gilbert Bishop. OBCoV

My Friend the Wind. King D. Kuka. VoR

My friend, this body is His lute. He tightens the strings and plays its songs. Kabir, *Hindi.* EnlH, *tr. by* Robert Bly

My friend wears boots to sleep. Following Her to Sleep. Jeffrey McDaniel. BAP-94

My friend, who was a heroin addict. Certain Choices. Richard Shelton. Poetsp

My friend, you don't understand. Philip Appleman. BXAP

My friend, your face. Who Is My Brother? Pinkie Gordon Lane. BlSi

My Friendly People. Frank Mkalawile Chipasula. HBAPE

My friends. Cacamatzin. PaTW

My Friends. Mikhail Kuz'mich Lukonin, *Russian.* TCRP, *tr. by* Albert C. Todd

My friends & I speak mostly to one another's machine. The Answering Machine. Philip Schultz. NAmP90

My friends are borne to one another. Martin Buber in the Pub. Max Harris. NOBAu

My friends are little lamps to me. Elizabeth Whittemore. PoToHe

My friends are real, though very few. (LL) Money. W. H. Davies. OBEV; OBMV

My friends, / I am amazed. Acceptance Speech. Marvin Bell. AmPA

My friends, I love your fame; I joy to raise. Joel Barlow. *See* The Columbiad.

My friend's knife by my side. On the Gift of a Knife. Muireadhach Albanach O'Dalaigh. NOIV

My friends murmur in my ears. The Bachelor. Sandor Csoori, *Hungarian.* CEEP, *tr. by* Nicholas Kolumban

My friends, my sweet barbarians. A Breakfast for Barbarians. Gwendolyn MacEwen. NOBC

My friends, our race is ostracised. Ajax' Conclusion. Frank Barbour Coffin. AAP

My friend's sweet love came into town. Song to Hymen: 1942. Anthony Richardson. PoWW

My Friends the Pigeons. Richard Katrovas. NAmP90

My frowning students carve. E. S. L. Charles Martin. RA

My funeral-shaft, and marble shapes that dwell. Baucis. Erinna, *Greek.* AWP, *tr. by* Richard Garnett

My future will not copy fair my past. Sonnet. Elizabeth Barrett Browning. EnVR *Fr.* Sonnets from the Portuguese.

My Galley. Petrarch, *Italian.* AEP; GSo; InPS-3; NAEL-1, *tr. by* Sir Thomas Wyatt

(The Galley.) AAS; HAP; OAEL-1; OBVE; SCGP; SiPS; Son; WeW-3, *tr. by* Sir Thomas Wyatt *Fr.* Sonnets to Laura.

My Gang. Jack Kerouac. PoM

My garage is a structure of excessive plainness. Detail. Mary Ursula Bethell. PeNZ

My Garden. Thomas Edward Brown. EBEvV; InPK-6; OBEV; OBGa; PoLF; UV

My Garden. P. R. Hines. UV

My Garden. Norah E. Hussey. BoTP

My Garden, *parody.* J. A. Lindon. InPK-6

My Garden. Janice Appleby Succorsa. HoPM

My garden is a pleasant place. Louise Driscoll. BLPA; FaBoBe

My Garden, My Daylight. Jorie Graham. HCAP; Poetr

My Gartmore friends a blessing on ye. Epistle to Her Friends at Gartmore. Susanna Blamire. ECWP

My Gecko and I. Colin West. PeP

My generous muse, assistance lend. The Favourite Swain. Elizabeth Hands. WoRP

My gentle father. Feliks Skrzynecki. Peter Skrzynecki. CBAP

My gentle friend! I hold no creed so false. Retirement. Henry Timrod. APN-2

My gentle son is performing tricks for me on his bicycle. Visitation Rites. Jack Myers. NAmP90

My Gerbil. John Kitching. PeP

My ghost may land the ghosts of fish. (LL) The Last Chance. Andrew Lang. OxBSn

My Ghostly Father, I me confess. My Gostly Fader, I Me Confesse. Charles, Duc d' Orléans. BoLoP; EnLoPo; MiEL; NOBE

(My Ghostly Fader.) EnVB

("My ghostly fadir, I me confess.") EnVB; GBL

My Gift. Christina Rossetti. PChr *Fr.* A Christmas Carol: "In the bleak mid-winter." ACTP; InPS-3; NOBVV; VWP

("Give Him my heart.") (LL) CTV

My girl is waiting for me. Hitomaro, *Japanese.* OHPJ, tr. by Kenneth Rexroth

My girl, thou gazest much. The Lover to His Lady. Plato, *Greek.* CTC; FaBoEE, NoSic; PFE, tr. by George Turberville

My Girlfriends. Erich Fried, *German.* AF, tr. by Georg Rapp

My girlhood was surrounded by flickering screens. The Grand Tradition of Western Culture. Julia Stein. LoHo

My glad feet shod with the glittering steel. The Skater. Sir Charles G. D. Roberts. NOBC

My glass shall not persuade me I am old. Sonnet 22. Shakespeare. Son *Fr.* Sonnets.

My glittering sky, high, clear, profound. The Lovers. Marya Alexandrovna Zaturenska. MoAmPo

My Gloriana. Bessie. Alvin Aubert. SeSe

My glory, honor, all depend. The Gentleman. Menahem ben Judah Lonzano, *Hebrew.* TrJP, tr. by A. B. Rhine

My Glumdalclitch, come here and sit with me. A Tryst in Brobdingnag. Adrienne Rich. NYBP

My God, a verse is not a crown. The Quidditie [or Quiddity]. George Herbert. GeHe; NOSC; PoEL-2

My God and King! to thee. Anguish. Henry Vaughan. FMP; OxAEP-1

My God, how gracious art thou! I had slipt. The Relapse. Henry Vaughan. ESCV; TrCP

My God, how perfect are thy ways! Jehovah Our Righteousness. William Cowper. NOCV *Fr.* Olney Hymns.

My God, I heard this day. Man. George Herbert. ESCV; FSCP; GeHe; ImPo; NAEL-1; NoP-4; PoEL-2; SeCP

My God, I know that those who plead. Solomon ibn Gabirol. TrJP, tr. by Alice Lucas *Fr.* The Royal Crown. AWP, tr. by Israel Zangwill

My God, I mean my sinful heart. (LL) The Dwelling-Place. Henry Vaughan. GeHe; MeLP; NOSC; PeECV

My God, I Thank Thee. Andrews Norton. AH

My God, if writings may. Obedience. George Herbert. ESCV; GeHe

My God, I'm wounded by my sin. To God: an Anthem, Sung in the Chapel at White-Hall, Before the King. Robert Herrick. ChIV-1

My God in Heaven said to me. Fenton Johnson. NAAAL

My God is just, yes he is. *Unknown, Pashto.* PBWP, tr. by Saduddin Shpoon

My God most glad to look, most prone to hear [or heere], par. by Countess of Pembroke, Mary Sidney Herbert. Psalm 55. Bible, *O.T.* OBVE, *stanzas* 1–4; WPE *Fr.* Psalms.

My God, my God, have mercy on my sin. Ash Wednesday. Christina Rossetti. TrCP

My God, My God, he cried. Eli, Eli. Miriam Kessler. CrSp

My God, My God, Look upon Me. Chad Walsh. *Fr.* The Psalm of Christ. TrCP

My God, my God, what queer corner am I in? In the Deep Museum. Anne Sexton. MoAmPo

My God, prepare me for that hour. Written a Few Hours before the Birth of a Child. Jane Cave. ECWP

My God shall raise me up, I trust. (LL) Verses Made the Night before He Died [or Dyed]. Sir Walter Ralegh. AAS; FaBoEE; HAP; ImPo; NAEL-1; NOBE; NTP; NoSic; OBEV; OxBSP; PeECV; PoRA; RB; SCGP; SiPS; TFi; TRP

My God, sometimes I cannot pray. Unuttered Prayer. Josephine D. Henderson Heard. CBWP-4

My God, the poore expressions of my Love. Perseverance. George Herbert. PBRV

My God, thou that didst dye for me. The Dedication. Henry Vaughan. ESCV

My God! till I receiv'd thy stroke. Ephraim Repenting. William Cowper. ChIV-1 *Fr.* Olney Hymns.

My God, what a dream I had. Us Two. Nina Cassian, *Romanian.* PoSu, tr. by Nina Cassian

My God, when I walk [or walke] in those groves. Religion. Henry Vaughan. ESCV; NOCV; OAEL-1; OxAEP-1; PeECV; TOF

My God, where is that ancient heat towards Thee. Sonnet. George Herbert. ESCV; FSCP; GeHe; NOSC; OAEL-1

My God would give a Sun-shine after raine. (LL) The Shower [or Showre]. Henry Vaughan. ESCV; GeHe; SeCP

My godmother invited my cousin. My Cousin Agueda [or Agatha]. Ramón López Velarde, *Spanish.* OBVE, tr. by Unknown

My gold star mother. Nicholas Virgilio. HA

My Grace Is Sufficient. Josephine D. Henderson Heard. CBWP-4

My gracious Lord, I would thee glory doe. Edward Taylor. SCAP *Fr.* Preparatory Meditations Before My Approach to the Lord's Supper.

My Grandad Lewis. Shed in Space. Gareth Owen. SpW

My Grandfather. Joanne Hotchkiss. CrSp

My grandfather ate squash, ate corn. He ate corn. How to Eat Corn. Dick Bakken. EC2

My grandfather emerges. The Dead Will Not Praise You. David Shapiro. KSG

My grandfather had the right-hand side of his seat inscribed. Exhorting Myself. Ssu-k'ung Shu, *Chinese.* SuSp, tr. by Hellmut Wilhelm

My grandfather placed wood. Mythology. Earle Thompson. HATNAP

My grandfather said to me. Manners. Elizabeth Bishop. NOxBChV; OxBC; RB

My grandfather used to pray. The Wicked Neighbor. "Zelda," *Hebrew.* WPOW, tr. by Hannah Hoffman

My grandfather was an elegant gentleman. David Wright. *Fr.* Seven South African Poems. PeSA

My grandfather's clock was too large for the shelf. Grandfather's Clock. Henry Clay Work. BLPA

My Grandfather's Death. Vicente Aleixandre, *Spanish.* IMW, tr. by Stephen Kessler

My Grandfather's Funeral. James Applewhite. MT

My grandfather's painted grandfather. Cracked Portraits. Agha Shahid Ali. OpBo

My grandma likes to play with God. Grandma. Ann Johnson. CTV

My grandma thinks only of me. Grandmother. Fily-Dabo Sissoko, *French.* NegPo, tr. by Ellen Conroy Kennedy

My Grandmama / dont believe they walked in space. It's All the Same. Thadious M. Davis. BlSi

My Grandmother. Perseus Adams. PeSA

My Grandmother. Elizabeth Jennings. NoP-4

My grandmother, a few days from ninety. Second Childhood. Robin Boody Galguera. IFJA

My Grandmother Green. *Unknown.* AmFP

My grandmother grew tiny grapes and tiger-lilies. Her Garden. Freda Downie. FaBoWP

My grandmother had a small shelf of books. Footbinding. Patricia Beer. NoP-4

My grandmother had bones as delicate. Judith Hemschemeyer. WeT

My grandmother had braids. Keeping Hair. Ramona Wilson. CrSp; VoR

My grandmother / haunted the halls. The Feeding. Toi Derricotte. NMM-2

My grandmother lived on yonder green. My Grandmother Green. *Unknown.* AmFP

My grandmother moves to my mind in context of sorrow. Karl Shapiro. VGW

My grandmother puts cupcakes. The Other World. Vasco [or Vasko] Popa, *Serbian.* CEEP, tr. by Charles Simic

My grandmother / raised me Georgia style. This Is the Poem I Never Meant to Write. Colleen J. McElroy. NMM-2

My grandmother / rakes up chicken shit / mixed with mud / to feed her roses. The Upside Down Basket. Alan Chong Lau. UnSA

My Grandmother said, "Now isn't it queer." Wonders of Nature. *Unknown.* OTCP

My grandmother sent me a new-fashioned three-cornered cambric country-cut handkerchief. *Unknown.* OxNR

My grandmother, she, at the age of eighty-three. Grandmother's Old Armchair. *Unknown.* BLPA

My grandmother turned into an old man. Being Pharaoh. Beckian Fritz Goldberg. BAP-95

My grandmother was a wrinkled little girl. Genealogy. Eléni Vakaló, *Modern Greek.* PBWP, tr. by Paul Merchant

My grandmother was insane. Genesis. K. Satchidanandan, *Malayalam.* OMIP, tr. by K. Satchidanandan

My Grandmother Washes Her Feet. Fred Chappell. MT

My Grandmother Washes Her Vessels. Fred Chappell. MT

My grandmother's. Door. Valerie Worth. CA

My Grandmother's Burial Ground. Elizabeth Cook-Lynn. HATNAP

My Grandmother's Funeral. Thomas Lux. WeW-3

My Grandmother's Ghost. James Wright. Son

My Grandmother's Love Letters. Hart Crane. CMoP; FaBoBe; InPK-6; NOBA; NoAM; NoP-4; Poetr

My grandmothers were strong. Lineage. Margaret Abigail Walker. BlSi; CrSp; NALW; NMM-2; OxWW; PBWP; PoBA

My Grandpa lives in a wonderful house. The Painted Ceiling. Amy Lowell. OBAL

My grandparents lived to a great age in the cold. Cold. Dorothy Roberts. NOBC

My granny used to say that if a shadow. August the First: The Shadow. Patel Speaks. Marjorie Oludhe Macgoye. HBAPE

My great-aunt Elizabeth Fortune. Strawberry Moon. Mary Oliver. InPS-3

My great God, You been a tenderness to me. Black Mother Praying. Owen Dodson. ISC

My great-grandfather hunted elephants. A Ballad of Hunters. C. J. Driver. PeSAV

My great-grandfather spoke to Edmund Burke. The Seven Sages. W. B. Yeats. NOIV

My great-grandmother's native. Heirloom. Cinda Thompson. LoHo

My Great Great Etc. Uncle Patrick Henry. James Tate. CMAP; OBAL

My great wars close. Treaties. A. R. Ammons. HCAP

"My green leaves are more beautiful." Leaves. Frank Asch. NTCP

My Greenhouse. Edwin Morgan. OBGa

My grey-eyed father kept pigs on his farm. The Pigs. Geoffrey Lehmann. CBAP

My grief on the ocean. Unknown, Irish. NOIV, tr. by Thomas Kinsella

My Grief on the Sea. Biddy Cussrooee, Modern Irish. OBEV, tr. by Douglas Hyde

My grief, quoth I, is called Ignorance. Rachel Speght. KTR Fr. A Dream. WPE

My Guardian Angel Stein. Philip Schultz. InPS-3

My gudame wes a gay wif, bot scho wes ryght gend. The Ballad of Kynd Kittok. William Dunbar. OxBoLi; PeLV

My guest! I have not led you thro'. Interlude. Walter Savage Landor. GTBS-P

My hair, Delphic laurel. (LL) 3.30: This Monument Will Outlast (Exegi momumentum aere perennius). Horace. OBCVT, tr. by Ezra Pound

My hair has dried. Self Dirge. Wendy Rose. CDW

My hair has thinned, my teeth have worn away. Nguyễn Bỉnh Khiêm, Vietnamese. AVP, tr. by Huỳnh Sanh Thông

My hair is old. The startle of it! No Abstraction. Genevieve Taggard. NMM-2

My hair is springy like the forest grasses. Black Woman. Naomi Long Madgett. BlSi; GT; ISC; PoBA

My Hairs are hoary, wrinkled is my Face. An Ode of Anacreon. Anacreon, Greek. OBCVT, tr. by Philip Ayres

My hair's tightly plaited. I've Got an Apple Ready. John Walsh. NOxBChV

My Hairt Is Heich Aboif. Unknown. OxBS

My Hairy Dog. Herbert Asquith. See The Hairy Dog.

My half-sister comes to me to be painted. The Sitting. Medbh McGuckian. CABP; PNI

My hand. Comparison of Hands One Day Late Summer El Sobrante. Wendy Rose. HATNAP

My hand is blazing on the cold tumbler. The Glass of Water. Iain Crichton Smith. FaBoTC

My hand is dirty. The Dirty Hand. Carlos Drummond de Andrade, Portuguese. PFTM, tr. by Mark Strand

My hand is lonely for your clasping, dear. You and I. Henry Alford. BLPA; FaBoBe

My hand is steady. Towards the End of a Century. E. A. Markham. NBrP

My hand is weary with [or has a pain from] writing. St. Columcille the Scribe. Saint Columcille, (Latin?). BIrV, tr. by Flann O'Brien

My hand moves out. John Wills. HA

My hand of peace, this wound which does not heal. Philip Schultz. See For My Mother.

My hands are murder-red. Many a plump head. Strawberrying. May Swenson. VCAP

My hands are tender feathers. Calypso's Song to Ulysess. Adrian Mitchell. GBL

My hands are withered. Unknown. NOIV

My hands are wrinkled from the cold. Pale Ant. Elleasc Southerland. GT

My hands creep forward on the hot sand. Sand. Nina Cassian, Romanian. PoSu, tr. by Nina Cassian and Naomi Lazard

My hands did numb to beauty. I Held a Shelley Manuscript. Gregory Corso. BB; PmAP; VGW

My hands have not touched water since your hands,—. Carrier Letter. Hart Crane. BoLoP; GLoP

My hands here, gentle, where her breasts begin. No Continuing City. Michael Longley. PNI

My hands, my fists, my small bells. Oh Yes. William Matthews. AmPA

My hands / Open the curtains of your being. Touch. Octavio Paz, Spanish. EP, tr. by Charles Tomlinson; BoLoP

My hands that guide a needle. Instruction. Hazel Hall. NMM-2

My handsewn leather schoolbag. Forty years. The Schoolbag. Seamus Heaney. BiHa

My Handsome Gilderoy. Unknown. CH

My harbouring arms. (LL) Midsummer, Tobago. Derek Walcott. OPOU; VCWP

My hart is love, for these in it are grounded. (LL) If Love In These Be Founded. Henry Constable. AAS; Son

My Hat. Stevie Smith. BrRo; CBNP

My hated birthday is here, and I must go. Sulpicia, Latin. BoWoP, tr. by Aliki and Willis Barnstone

My hatred. Gwendolyn B. Bennett. See Hatred.

My hazard wouldn't be yours, not ever. Advice. Ruth Stone. CrSp; MDDM; NMM-2

My head and my shoulders, and my book. The Signature of All Things. Kenneth Rexroth. NNaP

My head and shoulders, and my book. The Signature of All Things. Kenneth Rexroth. APSN; BLT; NNaP; TRP

My head felt stabbed. I Would Not Recommend Love. Harold Norse. CLPP

My head is bald, my breath is bad. Late-Flowering Lust. John Betjeman. CMoP; EP

My head is immense. Charles Nokan. PBMAP

My head is unhappy. Poem in Time of Winter. Ray Mathew. NOBAu; OBCoV

My head, my heart, mine Eyes, my life, nay more. A Letter to Her Husband, Absent upon Public[k] Employment. Anne Bradstreet. HAP; HeIP-4; KTR; NAAL-1; NAAL-3; NALW; NoP-4; PEW; PoPoPo; SCAP

My head on moss reclining. A Song. Unknown. NOEC

My head's a dark lantern with shattered panes. A Stylized Donkey. "Sasha Chorny," Russian. TCRP, tr. by Bernard Meares

My Heart. Frank O'Hara. PiM

My heart. Tanka. Tawara Machi, Japanese. MJT, tr. by Makoto Ueda

My heart aches and a drowsy numbness pains. Ode to a Nightingale. Keats. AWP; CABP; ClHu; EBEV; FaBoBe; GEA; GTBS-P; HAP; HeIP-4; ImPo; InPS-3; NAEL-2; NAWM-2; NOBE; NOBRP; NoP-4; OAEL-2; OBEV; OBNC; PFE; PoE; PoEL-4; PoPoPo; PoRA; RB; Ro; SCGP; SoSe-8; TFi; TOF; UnPo

My Heart and I. Elizabeth Barrett Browning. VWP

My heart and my body want to separate. Friedrich von Hausen, German. GePo, tr. by Frederick Goldin

My heart beating, my blood running. Time's Dedication. Delmore Schwartz. VGW

My heart beats to the feet of the first faithful. An Interlude. Robert Duncan. CMoP

My Heart Belongs to Daddy. Cole Porter. OBAL

My heart burns up. Ono no Komachi. See He does not come.

My heart chars. (LL) He does not come. Ono no Komachi, Japanese. WPJ, tr. by Kenneth Rexroth and Ikuko Atsumi

My heart cried like a beaten child. Song Making. Sara Teasdale. SAGP

My heart did heave, and there came forth, O God! Affliction (3). George Herbert. NOSC

My heart doth in the Lord rejoice [or rejoiceth in the Lord], that living Lord of might. Hannah's Song of Thanksgiving. Bible, O.T. TrCP, ad. by Michael Drayton; AWP Fr. First Samuel.

My heart emptied. Saigyo, Japanese. OHMPJ, tr. by Kenneth Rexroth

My heart gives you love. (LL) Dirge for Two Veterans. Walt Whitman. APN-1; BLT; CBCWP; MoAmPo; PoEL-5

My heart grows sick before the wide-spread death. The Grave-Yard. Jones Very. NOBA

My heart has grown rich with the passing of years. The Solitary. Sara Teasdale. MoAmPo

My Heart Has Known its Winter. Arna Bontemps. GT

My heart has made its mind up. Valentine. Wendy Cope. NoP-4

My heart has thank'd thee, Bowles! for those soft strains. To the Rev. [or Reverend] W. L. Bowles. Coleridge. Son Fr. Effusions.

My Heart, How Very Hard It's Grown. Cotton Mather. AH

My heart, I cannot still it. Auspex. James Russell Lowell. PoEL-5; TAP

My heart is a-breaking, dear Tittie. Tam Glen. Robert Burns. AWP; OxBS

My heart is a flag / that is hoisted unnoticed. Heart's Flag. Namjo Kim, Korean. CKP, tr. by Jaihiun Kim

My heart is an oil lamp. A Rapier of Treason. Unknown, Arabic. BoWoP, tr. by Willis Barnstone

My heart is broken (oh my God). Contrition. Ralph Knevet. ChIV-2

My heart is capable of every form. Ibn al-Arabi, *Persian*. TOF, *tr. by* R. A. Nicholson

My heart is empty. All the fountains that should run. The Naked Seed. C. S. Lewis. TrCP

My heart is fallen in despair. The Broken Friendship. Stevie Smith. FP

My Heart Is High Above. Alexander Scott. OBEV

My Heart Is in Merioneth. *Unknown, Welsh.* OBWVE, *tr. by* Richard Llwyd

My Heart Is in the East. Judah Halevi, *Hebrew.* TrJP

My heart is in woe. The Downfall of the Gael. Fearflatha O'Gnive, *Late Middle Irish.* AWP, *tr. by* Sir Samuel Ferguson

My heart is just as heavy. Grief. *Unknown, Welsh.* OBWVE, *tr. by* Aneirin Talfan Davies

My heart is lame with running after yours so fast. Charlotte Mew. BWW; CPO

My heart is lighter than the poll. The New-slain Knight. *Unknown.* ESPB

My Heart Is like a Ship. "E. C." *Fr.* Emaricdulfe. Son

My heart is like a singing bird. A Birthday. Christina Rossetti. AWP; CABP; CH; EBEvV; GLoP; ITG; ImPo; LW; NAEL-2; NALW; NOBE; NOBVV; OAEL-2; OBEV; PEW; PFE; PeVV; PoE; SDW; TFi; TTTS; UV; VWP; WPE

My heart is like one asked to dine. An Unexpected Pleasure. *Unknown.* UV

My heart is like the failing hearth. Song. Letitia Elizabeth Landon. NOBRP *Fr.* The Golden Violet.

My heart is like the sun / drowned in darkness. Akiko Yosano, *Japanese.* WPJ, *tr. by* Kenneth Rexroth *and* Ikuko Atsumi

My heart is not of wax; nor may it one compare. She Boasts of Her Constancy. Johann Rist, *German.* GePo, *tr. by* George C. Schoolfield

My heart is on my fist. The Tomb of the Kings. Anne Hébert. BoWoP, *tr. by* Aliki *and* Willis Barnstone

My heart is set upon a lusty pin. Queen Elizabeth of York. WPE

My heart is very faint and low. The Dying Child. Mary Howitt. VWP

My heart leaps up when I behold. Song to Be Sung by the Father of Infant Female Children. Ogden Nash. MoAmPo

My heart leaps up when I behold. Wordsworth. APAD; BLPA; ChAP; EBEvV; FHYEP; GTBS-P; ImPo; InPK-6; InPS-3; LiLi; NAEL-2; NOBE; NOBRP; NTP; NoP-4; OAEL-2; OBEV; OBNC; OxBSP; PBMP; PiM; PoPoPo; Ro; TFi

("Or let me die!") (LL) CTV

My heart like an upside down flame. Heart. Guillaume Apollinaire. TTTS, *tr. by* Roger Shattuck *Fr.* Heart, Crown, and Mirror.

My heart, like my clothing / is saturated with your fragrance. Kenrei Mon-in Ukyo no Daibu, *Japanese.* WPJ, *tr. by* Kenneth Rexroth *and* Ikuko Atsumi

My heart, my dove, my snail, my sail, my. Song. Cynthia Zarin. NoP-4

My heart, my heart is mournful. Mein Herz, Mein Herz Ist Traurig. Heinrich Heine, *German.* AWP, *tr. by* James Thomson

My heart [*or* harte] of gold[e] as true as steel [*or* stele]. Nonsense Song. *Unknown.* CBNP

My heart still hovering round about you. Epigram. Robert Nugent, Earl Nugent. NOEC

My heart stirs quietly now to think. A Hermit's Song. *Unknown, Irish.* BIrV, *tr. by* James Simmons

My heart, thinking / "How beautiful he is." Lady Otomo no Sakanoé. AWP; PBWP, *tr. by* Arthur Waley *Fr.* Manyo Shu, Part 3 of 4.

My heart throbbed like a boat on the water. Hamlet in Russia, A Soliloquy. Boris Pasternak, *Russian.* FaBoPV, *tr. by* Robert Lowell

My heart was darkened over with grief, and whatever I. Saint Augustine. LBC

My heart was heavy, for its trust had been. Forgiveness. John Greenleaf Whittier. GSo; TrCP

My heart was split, and a flower. *Unknown.* EnlH, *tr. by* Stephen Mitchell *Fr.* The Odes of Solomon.

My heart was your approaching feet. (LL) The Footsteps. Paul Valéry, *French.* FLP; LoP, *tr. by* Alistair Elliot

My heart's fit to break, yet no tear fills my eye. Lady Caroline Lamb. Ro *Fr.* Fugitive Pieces and Reminiscences of Lord Byron with Some Original Poetry, Letters and Recollections of Lady Caroline Lamb, ed. I. Nathan.

My heart's friend, will you tell me who this mischievous youngster is? Dancing-Girl's Song. Kshetrayya, *Telugu.* BoWoP, *tr. by* Tambimuttu *and* R. Appalaswamy

My heart's in the Highlands, my heart is not here. Robert Burns. ChAP

My heart's in the Highlands, wherever I go! (LL) My heart's in the Highlands, my heart is not here. Robert Burns. ChAP

My heart's in the kitchen, my heart is not here. Maria Jane Jewsbury. VWP

My heart's own darling's face. (LL) Es Stehen Unbeweglich. Heinrich Heine, *German.* AWP; TrJP, *tr. by* James Thomson

My heart's so heavy with a hundred things. Sonnet: In Absence from Becchina. Cecco Angiolieri, da Siena, *Italian.* AWP, *tr. by* D. G. Rossetti

My heid did yak yester nicht. The Magryme. William Dunbar. FaBoVe

My help, my hope, my strength shall be. The Law. Abraham ibn Ezra, *Hebrew.* TrJP, *tr. by* Alice Lucas

My helpless paradox—because. (LL) Reading a Medal. Terence Tiller. FaBoTw; GTBS-P

My Heritage. Adah Isaacs Menken. AAP; CBWP-1

My high hand makes fine patterns. Reason. Philippe Jaccottet, *French.* MFP, *tr. by* Martin Sorrell

My highway is unfeatured air. Hymn of the Earth. William Ellery Channing. APN-1

My hill friends will soon be sending poems to call me home. (LL) Written on a Painting Entitled "Misty Yangtze and Folded Hills." Su Tung-p'o, *Chinese.* CoBCP, *tr. by* Burton Watson

My hips are a desk. The Secretary Chant. Marge Piercy. IFJA

My hoary locks I dye with care. Self-Defense. Santob De Carrion, *Spanish.* TrJP, *tr. by* George Ticknor

My Home. Yên Thao, *Vietnamese.* AVP, *tr. by* Huỳnh Sanh Thông

My home? I'm stopping near the town. Stopping Wine. T'ao Ch'ien, *Chinese.* CoBCP, *tr. by* Burton Watson

My home is a house. The Country Child. Irene Thompson. BoTP

My home is the mountain. Akhtar Amiri. WPOW, *tr. by* Fereshte Mahamadi *Fr.* I Am a Woman.

My home over there, my home over there. That Mountain Far Away. *Unknown, Tewa Indian.* PBMP, *tr. by* Herbert Joseph Spinden

My home over there, now I remember it. (LL) That Mountain Far Away. *Unknown, Tewa Indian.* PBMP, *tr. by* Herbert Joseph Spinden; CA

My home was at Cold Mountain from the start. Gary Snyder. EnlH

My home's in Montana, I wear a bandanna. Cowboy's Lament, The Smoky Mountains. *Unknown.* AmFP

My Honey, My Love. Joel Chandler Harris. FaBoBe *Fr.* Uncle Remus and His Friends.

My Honeyed Languor. "Eduard Georgievich Bagritzky," *Russian.* TrJP, *tr. by* Babette Deutsch

My hope, alas, hath me abused. Sir Thomas Wyatt. SiPS

My hope and treasure lies above. (LL) Here Follows Some Verses upon the Burning of Our House [July 10th, 1966. Copied Out of a Loose Paper]. Anne Bradstreet. AiP; BoWoP; ColAP; NAAL-1; NAAL-3; NALW; NOBA; NOSC; NoP-4; OxBA; PEW; Poetr; SCAP; TAP; WPE

My Hope, My Love. *Unknown, Irish.* BIrV, *tr. by* Edward Walsh

My hopes retire; my wishes as before. Walter Savage Landor. GBL; OBNC *Fr.* Ianthe.

My horny feet are cutting through the fog. Satyr. Charles Gullans. PoA

My horse a thing of wings, myself a god. (LL) St. Valentine's Day. Wilfrid Scawen Blunt. GLoP

My horse has wings. The Ride. Lucinda Roy. GT

My horse threads a mountain trail through bamboos just yellowing. Journey to a Village. Wang Yü-ch'eng, *Chinese.* CoBCP, *tr. by* Burton Watson
(My horse threads the mountain path as chrysanthemums begin to yellow.) SuSp, *tr. by* Irving Y. Lo

My horse whose tail is like a trailing black cloud. (LL) The War God's Horse Song. *Unknown, Navajo Indian.* RB, *tr. by* Louis Watchman; TTTS

My horse's feet beside the lake. A Farewell. Matthew Arnold. EnVR *Fr.* Switzerland.

My hour switched on the cameras take. The Voice of America, 1961. James Liddy. CIP-2

My House. Robert Adamson. BMAP; CBAP

My house, I say. But hark to the sunny doves. Robert Louis Stevenson. NOBVV

My house is a boat. Houseboat Mouse. Charles Sullivan. ImGa

My house is at the foot of the green cliff. In an Abandoned Garden. Han-shan, *Chinese.* GaP, *tr. by* Burton Watson

My house is bugged. Mafika Pascal Gwala. PeSAV

My house is granite. George Bruce. OxBS

My house is not quiet, I am not loud. Fish in River: "My house is not quiet, I am not loud." Cynewulf. AnOE, *tr. by* Charles W. Kennedy *Fr.* Riddles (Exeter Book).

My house is poor; those that I love have left me. Winter Night. Po Chü-i, *Chinese.* ChiP, *tr. by* Arthur Waley

My house is red—a little house. A Happy Child. Kate Greenaway. BoTP

My house is simple, lying beside the sea. Antipater of Sidon, *Greek.* InMo, *tr. by* Sam Hamill

My hovering[e] thought[e]s would fly to heaven. Man's Civil[l] War[re]. Robert Southwell. NoSic

My humble Muse sad, and in lonely state. To His Excellency Joseph Dudley. John Saffin. SCAP

My hunger is infinite and my hands always empty. Rade Drainac, *Serbo-Croatian.* HSix, *tr. by* Charles Simic

My hunter of dragonflies. Chiyojo, *Japanese.* WPJ, *tr. by* Kenneth Rexroth *and* Ikuko Atsumi

My husband gives me an A. Marks. Linda Pastan. NIP-4

My husband had a knack of knowing things. The Message. Michael Heffernan. RACG

My husband is the same who took my maidenhead. Silabhattarika. PBWP, *tr. by* Daniel H. H. Ingalls *Fr.* Wanton.

("My husband is the same man who first pierced me.") BoWoP, *tr. by* Willis Barnstone

My husband never desired the official seal of a marquis. Lament of a Soldier's Wife. Kao Ch'i, *Chinese.* SuSp, *tr. by* Irving Y. Lo

My husband, our opened home has broken my heart. The Slighted Wife. Aaron Hodza, *Shona.* PeSAV, *tr. by* George Fortune

My husband says. Alice Walker. MT

"My husband"—women say—. Emily Dickinson. ITG

My Husband's Birthday. Josephine D. Henderson Heard. CBWP-4

My Hut. Eileen Mathias. BoTP

My hut, beside the crystal stream. Wu Chia-chi, *Chinese.* CoBLCP, *tr. by* Jonathan Chaves

My Iambic Pentameter Lines. Robert Crawford. InPK-6

My ice skates on a wall. Cold Lost Marbles. William S. Burroughs. BB

My idleness curdles. Ted Hughes. HAP, *sect.* 5 *Fr.* Skylarks.

My Illness and Other Animals. Maria Jastrzebska. NBrP

My Imperialism. Ryuichi Tamura, *Japanese.* AF; VCWP, *tr. by* Christopher Drake

My Infelice's face, her brow, her eye. A Portrait. Thomas Dekker *and others.* OxAEP-1

My Infundibuliform Hat. Charles Follen Adams. OBAL

My Inmost Hope. Sarah Copia Sullam, *Italian.* TrJP

My intention is to tell of bodies changed. Ovid. NAWM-1, *tr. by* Rolfe Humphries *Fr.* Metamorphoses.

My, it's nice. Tea Party. Mary Rita Hurley. CTV

My joke and me. (LL) Sphinx. Robert Earl Hayden. GT; HCAP

My jolly fop, my Jo—. (LL) The Creditor to His Proud Debtor. George Moses Horton. AAP; NAAAL

My Journal. Adelaide Anne Procter. VWP

My Joy, My Jockey, My Gabriel. George Barker. MoBrPo *Fr.* First Cycle of Love Poems.

My Joy, my Life, my Crown! A True Hymn. George Herbert. GeHe; NOCV

My joys to weep, and now my griefs to sing. (LL) Joseph's Coat. George Herbert. ChIV-1; GeHe; KSG

"My King and Country needed me," to fight. Afterwards. H. B. K. Allpass. NSI

My kingdom for a horse! Kingdom. Leopold Staff, *Polish.* PoSu, *tr. by* Adam Czerniawski

My kingdom, my power, and my glory. (LL) Lord's Prayer. D. H. Lawrence. GI; PeECV

My kite is three feet broad, and six feet long. The Kite. Adelaide O'Keeffe. NOxBChV; OxBChV

My Kitten. Mother Goose. ReMoGo

My kitten walks on velvet feet. Night. Lois Weakley McKay. CTV

My ladies haire is threeds [*or* threads] of heaten gold. Bartholomew Griffin. AAS *Fr.* Fidessa, More Chaste than Kind[e].

My lady ain't no lady. Patricia Parker. CPO

My Lady Carenza of the lovely body. *Unknown, Provençal.* BoWoP, *tr. by* Willis Barnstone

My lady carries love within her eyes. Dante. AWP *Fr.* La Vita Nuova.

My Lady Carries Stones. Nick Piombino. FTOS

My lady / fair with / soft. A Token. Robert Creeley. VGW

My lady has a lovely rite. "Michael Field." CPO

My Lady Is a Pretty One. *Unknown.* OxBoLi

My lady looks so gentle and so pure. Dante. AWP *Fr.* La Vita Nuova.

My Lady mine, I send. Canzonetta: Of His Lady, and of His Making Her Likeness. Jacopo da Lentino, *Italian.* AWP, *tr. by* D. G. Rossetti

My lady pleases me and I please her. Robert Bridges. Son *Fr.* The Growth of Love.

My Lady Spring. *Unknown.* BoTP

My lady unto Madam makes her bow. George Meredith. NOBVV *Fr.* Modern Love.

My lady walks her morning round. The Henchman. John Greenleaf Whittier. OBEV

My lady woke upon a morning fair. On His Lady's Waking. Pierre de Ronsard, *French.* AWP, *tr. by* Andrew Lang

My Lady's Bath. John Barlas. ADE

My Lady's face it is they worship there. Sonetto XXXV: To Guido Orlando. Guido Cavalcanti, *Italian.* CTC, *tr. by* Ezra Pound

My Lady's Grave. Emily Jane Brontë. *See* Song: "The Linnet in the rocky dells."

My lady's presence makes the roses red. Of his Mistress, upon Occasion of her Walking in a Garden. Henry Constable. NIP-4; OBGa *Fr.* Diana.

My Lady's Tears. *Unknown.* EBEV; NOBE; OBEV

My Lai / Remuera / Ponsonby. David Mitchell. PeNZ

My lamp and life, both shall in Thee abide. (LL) The Morning-Watch. Henry Vaughan. ESCV; FMP; GeHe; NOSC; NTP; PeECV

My land is bare of chattering folk. Sanctuary. Dorothy Parker. NBLV

My land, my love, sleep well. (LL) Nightsong: City. Dennis Brutus. HBAPE; PBMAP

My lank limp lily, my long lithe lily. A Maudle-in Ballad. *Unknown.* BXAP

My Last Afternoon with Uncle Devereux Winslow. Robert Lowell. NAAL-2; NoP-4; VGW

My Last Dance. Julia Ward Howe. APN-1

My last defense / Is the present tense. Old Mary. Gwendolyn Brooks. PFE

My Last Duchess [Ferrara]. Robert Browning. AWP; ClHu; EBNV; EBVV; EBVVPR; EnVR; FHYEP; FaBoPV; GTBS-P; HAP; HeIP-4; HoPM; ImPo; InPK-6; InPS-3; NAEL-2; NIP-4; NOBE; NOBVV; OAEL-2; OBNC; PBMP; PeVV; PoE; PoEL-5; PoLF; Poetr; SCGP; SCV; SoSe-8; TFi; TRP

(My Last Duchess.) CABP; NoP-4; OxBoV; PFE; PoPoPo; SAGP

My Latest Sun Is Sinking Fast. Jefferson Haskell. AH

My leafing of myself is like the casting of one's own fortune. Speeches in the Interior. Juhan Viiding, *Estonian.* CEEP, *tr. by* Ivar Ivask

My leafless maple tree, your icy coating. Sergey Aleksandrovich Yesenin, *Russian.* TCRP, *tr. by* Daniel Weissbort

My lefe is faren in a lond. Separated Lovers. *Unknown.* OAEL-1

My left eye is blind and jogs like. Sketch for a Job Application Blank. James Harrison. AmPA; MoP

My left hand's like after a vow. It hurts. I'm trying to dream again. Amir Gilbo'a, *Hebrew.* IP, *tr. by* Warren Bargad *and* Stanley F. Chyet

My Legs Señor. William S. Burroughs. BB

My legs swollen from pressing pedals. I'm A Worker. Jayne Cortez. NBV

My lemmon she shal be. (LL) The Hawthorn. *Unknown.* EnVB; MiEL

My *Lesbia* and I did kiss. Catullus. *See* Carmen 5 ("My sweetest Lesbia, let us live and love").

My Lesbia, Caelius, that same Lesbia. Carmen 58. Catullus, *Latin.* OBCVT, *tr. by* Clucas, Humphrey *Fr.* Carmina.

My less erotic god condemned. The Snake in the Garden Considers Daphne. William Wadsworth. BAP-94

My Lessons in the Jail. Miriam Waddington. MoCV

My letters! all dead paper, mute and white. Sonnet. Elizabeth Barrett Browning. HAP; OxAEP-2 *Fr.* Sonnets from the Portuguese.

My Lief Is Faren in Londe. *Unknown.* NAEL-1

My Life. Lyn Hejinian.

"Moment yellow, just as four years later when, A." PmAP

"Tree rows in orchards are capable of patterns. What, The." FTOS

My Life. Mark Strand. NoAM

My life closed twice before its close—. Parting. Emily Dickinson. APAD; APN-2; AmPP; BoLoP; BoWoP; ColAP; EBEvV; GBL; GLoP; HeIP-4; ImGa; LW; MeMAP; MoAmPo; MoP; NAAL-1; NAAL-3; NIP-4; NOBA; NoAM; OxBA; OxBSP; PAR; PFE; Poetr; SAGP; SAmP; SCV; TFi

My Life had stood—a [Loaded Gun—]. Emily Dickinson. APN-2; AmPP; HAP; HeIP-4; InPK-6; NAAL-1; NAAL-3; NALW; NAWM-2; NCAP; NIP-4; NoP-4; OxWW; PAR; PoPoPo; Poetr; SAmP; TRP; WPOW; WeW-3

(Fascicle 34 Poem 9.) PFTM

My life had taken the form of a small square. The Small Square. Sophia De Mello Breyner, *Portuguese.* VCWP, *tr. by* Ruth Fainlight

(My life had taken the shape of the small square.) WPOW, *tr. by* Alexis Levitin

My life has been the poem I would have writ. Henry David Thoreau. APN-1; NCAP

("But could not both live and utter it.") (LL) PAR

My life has crept so long on a broken wing. Tennyson. OAEL-2; OBWP *Fr.* Maud [A Monodrama]. EnVR

My Life Is a———. Frederick Locker-Lampson. OBCoV

My Life Is a Bowl. May Riley Smith. BLPA

My life is bitter with thy love; thine eyes. Anactoria. Swinburne. RACG

"My life is done, yet all remains." Robert the Bruce. Edwin Muir. OxBS

My life is engraved on my poems. Of Myself. Leah Goldberg, *Hebrew.* BoWoP, *tr. by* Ramah Commanday

My life is like a music-hall. Prologue: In the Stalls. Arthur Symons. ADE

My life is like the summer rose. The Lament of the Captive. Richard Henry Wilde. APN-1; ColAP

My life is measur'd by this glass[e], this glass[e].   On an Hour[e]-Glass[e]. John Hall. MeLP

My Life, my Strength, my Joy, my All. (LL) A Hymn to My God in a Night of My Late Sickness[e]. Sir Henry Wotton. MeLP; NOSC

My life, the quality of which. Etheridge Knight. NNaP

My life—to Discontent a prey. Rhymes (?). Henry Sambrooke Leigh. NOBL

My life was never so precious. Inscription for the Tank. James Wright. TwCP

My life, your light green eyes. Last Words. James Merrill. TAP

My lifeless eye and your quickening hand. Wiiralt Drawing in Chartres. Aleksis Rannit, *Estonian*. CEEP, *tr. by* Emery George

My light will tip tankards of fire in the sky. A Constant Labor. James W. Thompson. BPo

My Lighthouses. Helen Hunt Jackson. APN-2; ColAP

My lips are sweet, inspired with Stella's kiss. (LL) Sonnet 74: "I never drank of Aganippe well." Sir Philip Sidney. NAEL-1; NoSic; Son

My lips from this day forgot how to smile. Auguste Lacaussade. TTY *Fr.* Salaziennes, Les.

My lips (the inconstancy of man!). Fragment. Rupert Brooke. NSI

My little baby sleeps, the little birds sleep. Lullaby. *Unknown, Greek.* GrIP, *tr. by* Philip P. Argenti *and* H.N. Rose

My little bagpipe-Muse, Musette. The Grave of Marmousette. Antoine Girard *and* Sieur de Saint-Amant, *French.* FLP, *tr. by* Alistair Elliot

My little Ben, whilst thou art young. To His Son Bennet. John Hoskyns. FaBoEE

My Little Bird. Of the Child with the Bird on the Bush. John Bunyan. OxBChV

My little bird, far away in a foreign land, sad and with heavy heart. Farewell Folk Song. *Unknown, Greek.* GrIP, *tr. by* Loring N.Danforth

My little boat emerges at Heng-t'ang. Late Spring—Traveling through the Mountains. Chu Yün-ming, *Chinese.* CoBLCP, *tr. by* Jonathan Chaves

My little boy Kun-shih. Poem for My Little Boy. Li Shang-yin, *Chinese.* CoBCP, *tr. by* Burton Watson

My little breath, under the willows by the water-side we used to sit. A Lover's Lament *or* The Willows by the Water Side. *Unknown, Tewa Indian.* AWP, *tr. by* H. J. Spinden

My little cousin, if you'll be. To My Youngest Kinsman, R. L. Abraham Chear. OxBChV

My little cup, go now and taste. Leontius Scholasticus, *Greek.* InMo, *tr. by* Sam Hamill

My little darling looked so pale today. My Daughter Very Ill. Paul Goodman. MoLi

My little dears, who learn to read, pray early learn to shun. Cautionary Verses to Youth of Both Sexes. Theodore Hook. OxBChV

My Little Dog. Pearl Forbes MacEwen. BoTP

My Little Dreams. Georgia Douglas Johnson. BlSi; NAAAL

My little friend Marie has died. Her Toys. Théophile Gautier, *French.* FLP, *tr. by* Alistair Elliot

My Little House. J. M. Westrup. BoTP

My little island girl. Song by Klipstein and Krumpacker. T. S. Eliot. *Fr.* Two Songs from *Sweeny Agonistes.* UnPo *Fr.* Sweeney Agonistes.

My Little Lize. James Martinez. PBCV

My little lord, methinks 'tis strange. A Prognostication on Will Laud, Late Archbishop of Canterbury. *Unknown.* OxBoLi

My Little Love Lies on the Ground. Larin Paraske, *Finnish.* PBWP, *tr. by* Jaakko A. Ahokas

My Little Maid. *Unknown.* ReMoGo

My little old man and I fell out. The Quarrle. Mother Goose. OxNR; ReMoGo

My little pretty patch of wilderness. Touching Heartsease. Janet Sutherland. NBrP

My little scholar, to thy book inclined. A Schoolmaster's Precepts. John Penkethman. OxBChV

'My Little Sister'. Abba Kovner, *Hebrew.* Far, Far a City Lies. HP, *tr. by* Shirley Kaufman

My little son enters. Transformations. Tadeusz Rózewicz, *Polish.* ChAP, *tr. by* Czeslaw Milosz

My little son, I have cast you out. Choosing a Name. Anne Ridler. NOBE

My little son, when you could command marvels. Geoffrey Hill. NoAM *Fr.* Funeral Music.

My little son, who looked from thoughtful eyes. The Toys. Coventry Patmore. EBEV; EBVV; NOBVV; OBEV; OxAEP-2; PoToHe; SoSe-8 *Fr.* The Unknown Eros.

My little stone. Letters [*or* Notes] Found near a Suicide. Frank Horne. PoBA

My little wandring sportful Soule. Emperor Hadrian, *Latin.* OBCVT, *tr. by* John Donne

My lizard, my lively writher. Wish for a Young Wife. Theodore Roethke. MoP; NAAL-2; NoAM; NoP-4; OxBSP; TAP

My locker, green steel. Game Resumed. Richmond Lattimore. NYBP

My long poem, the 'Eternal Grief,' is a beautiful and moving work. The Fifteenth Volume. Po Chü-i, *Chinese.* ChiP, *tr. by* Arthur Waley

My long scythe whispered and left the hay to make. (LL) Mowing. Robert Frost. CMoP; ColAP; HoPM; NAAL-2; NOBA; OxBA; TRP; VGW

My long two-pointed ladder's sticking through a tree. After Apple-Picking. Robert Frost. AmPP; CMoP; InPS-3; MeMAP; MoAmPo; MoP; NAAL-2; NOBA; NTP; NoAM; OxBA; PoE; Poetr; SAGP; SAmP; SoSe-8; TAP; TFi; TRP; UnPo

My longing for the past deeper than words. (LL) Matching a Poem by Secretary Kuo. T'ao Ch'ien, *Chinese.* CoBCP, *tr. by* Burton Watson

My longing for your waxen hands. Antico Inverno. Salvatore Quasimodo, *Italian.* NNPT, *tr. by* W. C. Fitzgerald

My Lord and King. Tennyson. *Fr.* In Memoriam A. H. H.

My Lord Archbishop, what a scold you are. To Archbishop Lang. *Unknown.* OBCoV

My lord, as I was sewing in my closet. Shakespeare. OxAEP-1 *Fr.* Hamlet. NAWM-1

My Lord, fallen, sin-stained. Sticheron for Matins, Wednesday of Holy Week. Kassia, *Greek.* WPOW, *tr. by* Patrick Diehl

My lord has great shoulders. A Woman in Love with a Captive King. Nakkannaiyar, *Tamil.* PLW, *tr. by* A. K. Ramanujan

My lord hath called for my sonne. Wretten by Me att the Same Tyme; on the Death of My 4th, & Only Child, Robert Payler. Mary Carey. KTR

My lord, I was accustomed to swill about the sky. The Dove Apologizes to His God for Being Caught by a Cat. Anthony Eaton. PeSA

My Lord / if I worship Thee from fear of Hell. Rabi'a al-Adawiyya, *Arabic.* WPOW, *tr. by* Margaret Smith, *ad. by* Deirdre Lashgari

My lord is all a-glow. My Lord Summons Me. *Unknown, Chinese.* ChiP, *tr. by* Arthur Waley

My lord is full of delight. *Unknown, Chinese.* TAL, *tr. by* Robert Payne

My Lord, my life, can envy ever bee. Edward Taylor. PoEL-3 *Fr.* Preparatory Meditations Before My Approach to the Lord's Supper.

My Lord recalls Ferrara? How walls. Nikolaus Mardruz to his Master Ferdinand, Count of Tyrol, 1565. Richard Howard. NoP-4

My lord said to my lady. Lamkin. *Unknown.* ESPB

My Lord Summons Me. *Unknown, Chinese.* OxBM

(Wedding Song.) ChiP, *tr. by* Arthur Waley

My Lord, th' Indictment do's not run. Martial, *Latin.* OBCVT, *tr. by* Jabez Hughes

My Lord Tomnoddy's the son of an Earl. Robert Barnabas Brough. PeLV

My Lord, what a mornin' [*or* morning when de stars begin to fall]. *Unknown.* APN-2; NoP-4

My Lord, What a Morning. Waring Cuney. TTY

My Lord's Gone to Service. *Unknown, Chinese.* CoBCP, *tr. by* Burton Watson

My Lost Youth. Henry Wadsworth Longfellow. APN-1; AWP; AmPP; FaBoBe; FaPoR; ImGa; MeMAP; NAAL-1; NAAL-3; NOBA; OBEV; OxBA; PAR; PoEL-5; PoLF; PoRA; TAP; TFi

My loud machine for making hay. An Old Field Mowed. William Meredith. NYBP

My lov'd [*or* loved], my honor'd [*or* honored], much respected friend. The Cotter's Saturday Night [*or* ascribed to Robert Aiken] [*or* R. A.], Esq.]. Robert Burns. FaBoBe; NOBRP; PoLF

My Love. "Sasha Chorny," *Russian.* TCRP, *tr. by* Bernard Meares

My Love. Bartholomew Griffin. *See* Faire Is My Love.

My Love. James Russell Lowell. FaBoBe

My Love. *Unknown.* ReMoGo

My Love? alas! I must not call you Mine. To J.G. on the News of His Marriage. "Ephelia." LW

My love and I for kisses played [*or* play'd]. Kisses. William Strode. FaBoEE; NOSC

My love came back to me. All Souls' Night. Frances Darwin Cornford. EnLoPo; LBC; OxBSP; OxBTC

My Love comes behind me. Old Love and New Love. Naomi Mitchison. WPN

My Love Eats an Apple. Ralph Gustafson. MoCV

My love for him shall be. *Unknown.* *Fr.* Medieval Norman Song. AWP, *tr. by* John Addington Symonds

My Love For You. *Unknown.* Spl

"My love for you has faded"—thus the Bad. Versions of Love. Roy Fuller. CBLP; LiTM

My love forever! *Unknown.* BIrV; PBWP, *tr. by* Eilis Dillon *Fr.* The Lament for Arthur O'Leary.

"My love has built a bonny ship, and set her on the sea." The Lowlands o' [*or* of] Holland. *Unknown.* AmFP; CH; OxBB

My love has gone down to his garden. Bible, *O.T.* BoWoP, *tr. by* Willis Barnstone *Fr.* The Song of Songs. AWP

My love has left me has gone from me. Souvenirs. Dudley Randall. BPo

My love he built me a bonnie bower. The Lament of the Border Widow. *Unknown.* CH; OxBB

My love, how could your heart consider. Motet. *Unknown, Old French.* PBWP, *tr. by* Carol Cosman

My love hurts me because you cannot know. Lady Otomo no Sakanoé, *Japanese.* WPJ, *tr. by* Kenneth Rexroth *and* Ikuko Atsumi

My Love I Gave to you for Hate. *Unknown, Irish.* BIrV, *tr. by* George Hay

My love I give to you a threefold thing. Branwell's Sestina. James Reaney. MoCV *Fr.* A Suit of Nettles.

My Love in her attire doth show her wit. Madrigal. *Unknown.* BoLoP; GTBS-P; HeIP; HeIP-4; ImPo; NAEL-1; NIP-4; NOBE; OBEV; OxBSP; TFi

My love is a lotus blossom. Love Song. *Unknown, Egyptian.* TTY, *tr. by* J. E. Manchip White

My love is as a fever [*or* feaver],k longing still. Sonnet 147. Shakespeare. EBEV; HoPM; NAEL-1; OxAEP-1; PoEL-1 *Fr.* Sonnets.

My love is falle upon a may. *Unknown.* MiEL

My love is in my house. Mirabai, *Hindi.* BoWoP, *tr. by* Willis Barnstone *and* Usha Nilsson

My Love is Like a Myrtle. Moses ibn Ezra, *Hebrew.* TrJP, *tr. by* Solomon Solis-Cohen

My love is like a red red rose. Robert Burns. *See* A Red, Red Rose.

My love is like Mies van der Rohe's. Dea ex Machina. John Updike. UV

My Love / I Like the grasses. Ono no Yoshiki, *Japanese.* AWP; TAL, *tr. by* Arthur Waley *Fr.* Kokin Shu.

My love is like to ice, and I to fire. Sonnet 30. Edmund Spenser. APAD; ImPo *Fr.* Amoretti. AAS

My love is living. South of the Great Sea. *Unknown, Chinese.* ChiP, *tr. by* Arthur Waley

My love is no short year's sentence. Love. *Unknown, Irish.* BIrV, *tr. by* John Montague

My love is o' comely height, an' straïght. White an' Blue. William Barnes. GBL; GTBS-P

My Love is of a birth as rare. The Definition Of Love. Andrew Marvell. BoLoP; CBLP; EBEV; ESCV; FHYEP; FMP; FSCP; GBL; GLoP; GeHe; HoPM; ImPo; InPS-3; LoP; MeLP; NAEL-1; NOBE; NOSC; NoP-4; OAEL-1; OBEV; PBRV; PoEL-2; SCGP; SeCP; TFi; UnPo

My Love is Past. Thomas Watson. NoSic

My love is strengthen'd, though more weak in seeming. Sonnet 102. Shakespeare. AWP; OBEV *Fr.* Sonnets.

My love is tasting the fragrance. *Unknown, Pashto.* PBWP, *tr. by* Saduddin Shpoon

My love is the maid ov all maidens. In the Spring. William Barnes. GBL

My love is white and ruddy. Bible, *O.T.* BoWoP, *tr. by* Willis Barnstone *Fr.* The Song of Songs. AWP

  ("I am come into my garden, my sister, my spouse: I have gathered my.") APAD

  ("Is my friend, O daughters of Jerusalem.") (LL) APAD

My Love Is Young. Earle Birney. NOBC

My love lies in the gates of foam. The Churchyard on the Sands. John Warren. CH; GBL; OBNC

My love lies underground. Hymn to Priapus. D. H. Lawrence. CMoP; OBMV; PoE; SCGP

My love looks like a girl to-night. The Bride. D. H. Lawrence. NoAM; OxBTC

My love, my love, if you could come once more. If You Could Come. Katharine Lee Bates. CPO

My love of you was life and not a breath. (LL) From Monna Innominata. Christina Rossetti. CABP; LoP; OBNC

My love on Wednesday letting fall her body. In Crisis. Lawrence Durrell. LiTM

My love, pills in her purse. Figures of the Human. David Ignatow. WeT

My love sent me a chicken without e'er a bone. *Unknown.* OxNR

My love shall in my verse live young. (LL) Sonnet 19. Shakespeare. AWP; EBEV; HeIP-4; ImPo; NAEL-1; NoSic; OAEL-1; OxAEP-1; PBRV; PoE; PoEL-2; SCGP

My love she is a gentlewoman. Auld Matrons. *Unknown.* ESPB

My Love She Passed Me By. *Unknown.* AmFP

My Love-Song. Else Lasker-Schüler, *German.* TrJP, *tr. by* Jethro Bithell

My love, this is the bitterest, that thou. Any Wife to Any Husband. Robert Browning. OBNC; RACG

My love / thy hair is one kingdom. E. E. Cummings. LiTM; VGW

My love took scorn my service to retain. Sir Thomas Wyatt. SiPS

My Love Was Light. Tennessee Williams. PoA

My Love When This Is Past. Stephany Fuller. BPo

My love whose bangles. What He Said. Ammuvanar, *Tamil.* PLW, *tr. by* A. K. Ramanujan

My love will come. Yevtushenko, *Russian.* TCRP, *tr. by* Albert C. Todd

My loved one is unique, without a peer. Love Song. *Unknown, Egyptian.* TTY, *tr. by* J. E. Manchip White

My lovely friends. Sappho, *Greek.* FP, *tr. by* Mary Barnard

My lover capable of terrible lies. Kaccipettu Nannakaiyar, *Tamil.* BoWoP; PBWP; WPOW, *tr. by* A. K. Ramanujan

My lover will soon be here. *Unknown, Chinese.* OHMPC, *tr. by* Kenneth Rexroth

My lover's a cowboy, wild broncos he breaks. Bucking Bronco. *Unknown.* AmFP

My lovers come, not from the floating classes. A Thousand and Three. Paul Verlaine, *French.* EP, *tr. by* Alistair Elliot

My love's eyes are red as the sargasso. The Talking Fish. Ruth Stone. BoWoP

My Love's Guardian Angel. William Barnes. GBL; PoEL-4

My love's manners in bed. The Way. Robert Creeley. APAD; BoLoP; LiLi; LiTM; NeAP

My Lulu. *Unknown.* AS

My lute, awake! Perform [the] last. The Lover Complaineth the Unkindness of His Love. Sir Thomas Wyatt. AAS; BoLoP; EBEV; GBL; HAP; InPS-3; NAEL-1; NOBE; NoP-4; NoSic; OAEL-1; OBEV; PoEL-1; SCGP; SiPS; TFi

My lute, be as thou wast [*or* wert] when thou didst grow. To His Lute. William Drummond, of Hawthornden. GSo; GTBS-P; NOSC; SCGP; Son

"My lute, be as thou wert when thou didst grow." William Drummond, of Hawthornden. *See* To His Lute.

My lute be still for I have done. (LL) The Lover Complaineth the Unkindness of His Love. Sir Thomas Wyatt. AAS; BoLoP; EBEV; GBL; HAP; InPS-3; NAEL-1; NOBE; NoP-4; NoSic; OAEL-1; OBEV; PBRV; PoEL-1; SCGP; SiPS; TFi

"My luve she lives in Lincolnshire." Alison and Willie. *Unknown.* ESPB

My Luve's in Germany. *Unknown.* CH

My lyfe shall everlastingly bee lengthened still by fame. (LL) Conclusion. Ovid, *Latin.* OBCVT; OBVE, *tr. by* Arthur Golding

My LYRE! oh, let thy soothing power. To My Lyre. Eliza Cook. VWP

My madda cut our hair so short. Yarn Wig. Lois-Ann Yamanaka. PUP-19

My madness is dear to me. Mad Song. Denise Levertov. TAP

My Madonna. Robert W. Service. BLPA

My maid Mary, / She minds the dairy. Mother Goose. OxNR; ReMoGo

My Maker shunneth me. Spiritual Isolation. Isaac Rosenberg. TrJP

My Mall, I mark that when you mean to prove me. The Author to His Wife, of a Woman's Eloquence. Sir John Harington. BoLoP; OxBM

My Mama moved among the days. Lucille Clifton. BlSi; PoBA

My Mamma is a mean old sing. Insulted. Priscilla Jane Thompson. CBWP-2

My mamma is dead and she's buried. My Darling's on the Deep Blue Sea. *Unknown.* AmFP

My Mammogram. J. D. McClatchy. BAP-95

My mammy she told me to open the door. Old Gray Beard a-Shaking. *Unknown.* AmFP

My mammy's in the cold, cold ground. Po' Boy. *Unknown.* AS

My man don't love me. Fine and Mellow. Billie Holiday. NAAAL

My man is a bone ringèd with weed. Lament. Brenda Chamberlain. WPE; WPOW

My man is a bone ringèd with weed. (LL) Lament: "My man is a bone ringèd with weed." Brenda Chamberlain. WPE; WPOW

My man loved me so much. So Long. Jayne Cortez. BoWoP; LW

My man, now you've come back without one arm. Folk Songs For Today. Nguyễn Tất Nhiên, *Vietnamese.* AVP, *tr. by* Huỳnh Sanh Thông

My Man Pa Replies. Li Ho, *Chinese.* CoBCP, *tr. by* Burton Watson

My man, Willard Franklin 'The Bunny' Goodjarrah. The Story of Frankie. . . My Man. Archie Weller. BMAP

My Many-Coated Man. Laurie Lee. NYBP

My Martial owns a garden, famed to please. De Hortis Julii Martialis. Martial, *Latin.* GaP; OBGa, *tr. by* Robert Louis Stevenson

My Mary. John Clare. NOBRP

My Mary! William Cowper. *See* To Mary.

My Maryland. James Ryder Randall. CBCWP; FaBoBe

  (Maryland.) APN-2

My master hath a garden, full-filled with divers flowers. *Unknown.* CH

My Masters. Sandor Csoori, *Hungarian.* VCWP, *tr. by* Len Roberts

My masters all, *Good day to you.* (LL) The Bellman. Robert Herrick. CH; CaPo

My masters twain made me a bed. Said the Canoe. Isabella Valancy Crawford. NOBC

My meal finished, one short nap. After Eating. Po Chü-i, *Chinese.* CoBCP, *tr. by* Burton Watson

My meaning passes like wild nightbirds. Credo. Brewster Ghiselin. PoA

My Memory immortal grew. (LL) Lines Written beneath a Picture. Byron. OxBSP; Ro

My men go wearily. Sir Herbert Read. PoFWW

My microscopic cushion shows its claws. (LL) The Microscope in Winter. Sandra McPherson. LCAP-2; VCAP

"My milk-white doo," said the young man. The Young Man and the Young Nun. Albert D. Mackie. OxBS

My mill grinds pepper and spice. *Unknown.* OxNR

My mind i th' mines of rich Philosophy. On My Lord Bacon. John Danforth. SCAP

My mind is a lake. Tongmyong Kim, *Korean.* CKP, *tr. by* Jaihiun Kim

My mind is intact, but the shapes. Riddle in the Garden. Robert Penn Warren. NoAM

My mind is sad and weary thinking how. Odell. James Stephens. MoBrPo

My mind is stuffed with tablecloths. Poland / 1931 "The Wedding." Jerome Rothenberg. FTOS; PoM

My mind is worn out, my features grown sharp and gaunt. Sitting at Night with My Nephew Who Has Just Come from Afar. Su Tung-p'o, *Chinese.* TAL, *tr. by* Robert Payne

My mind lets go a thousand things. Memory. Thomas Bailey Aldrich. CTV; PoLF

My mind shattered. Tanka. Kanoko Okamoto, *Japanese.* MJT, *tr. by* Makoto Ueda

My mind shrugs off his threadbare winter poems. Time Out. Donald Finkel. HoPM

My mind takes a leap. Cor Van den Heuvel. HA

My mind [or minde *or* mynde] to me a kingdom [or kyngdome] is. Sir Edward Dyer, *Unknown, wr. at. to.* EBEvV; FaBoBe; ImPo; NAEL-1; NOBE; NoSic; PoEL-1; SCGP

My mind to me mangles iron. An error is mirror to the truth. Stephen Rodefer. PmAP *Fr.* Plane Debris.

My mind was heavy and my luck was dark. Richard Eberhart. *Fr.* Brotherhood of Men. PoWW

My mind was once the true survey. The Mower's Song. Andrew Marvell. CBLP; ESCV; FMP; NAEL-1; NOSC; PoEL-2; SeCP

My mirror is always a little taller than I am. Mirror. Chimako Tada, *Japanese.* BoWoP; WPJ, *tr. by* Kenneth Rexroth *and* Ikuko Atsumi

My mistress' eyes are nothing like the sun;. Sonnet 130. Shakespeare. AEP; AWP; BoLoP; CABP; EBEV; GLoP; HAP; HeIP-4; HoPM; ImPo; InPK-6; InPS-3; NAEL-1; NIP-4; NoSic; OAEL-1; OxAEP-1; PBMP; PFE; PoE; PoPoPo; Poetr; SoSe-8; Son; TFi; WeW-3 *Fr.* Sonnets.

My mistress frowns when she should play. Madrigal. John Hilton. CH; OxBoLi

My mistress is as fair as fine. Madrigal. Thomas Ravenscroft. CH; OxBoLi

My mistress loves no woodcocks. *Unknown.* NOSC; OBCoV

My Mistresse sayes she'll marry none but me. Catullus. *See* Carmen 70 ("Lesbia says she'ld rather marry me").

My misunderstandings: for years I thought "muso bello" meant "Bell Muse," I thought it was a kind of. Taking a Walk with You. Kenneth Koch. CAPP-1

My moccasins are black obsidian. The Song of the Black Bear. *Unknown, Navajo.* RaBo

My Mocking Bird. Josephine D. Henderson Heard. CBWP-4

My most distinguished guest and learnèd friend. Edna St. Vincent Millay. VGW

My most respected / comrades of posterity! At the Top of My Voice. Vladimir Mayakovsky, *Russian.* AF, *tr. by* George Reavey; TRCP, *tr. by* Max Hayward and George Reavey.

My Mother. Francis Ledwidge. TIRV

My Mother. Claude McKay. GT; NAAAL

My mother. Mother. P. Lankesh, *Kannada.* OMIP, *tr. by* A. K. Ramanujan

My Mother? (LL) My Mother. Ann Taylor. BLPA; OxBChV

My mother. My Mother's Friend. Lily Brett. HP

My Mother. William Bell Scott. GSo

My Mother. Ann Taylor. BLPA; OxBChV

My Mother. John Wieners. BB; GLP; PmAP

My mother always said. My Mother's Homeland. Belkis Cuza Malé, *Spanish.* LoHo, *tr. by* Pamela Carmell

My mother always said. Sappho, *Greek.* BoWoP, *tr. by* Willis Barnstone

My mother and father are two wounds, hanging. Two Blue Swans. Elizabeth Kirschner. CMAP

My mother and your mother. *Unknown.* OxNR

My mother asks me if I like my sandwich. A Geography of Lunch. Mary Jo Schimelpfenig. IFJA

My mother bids me bind my hair. A Pastoral Song. Anne Hunter. ECWP

My mother bore me. Foolish Child. *Unknown, Akan.* PBA, *tr. by* J. B. Danquah

My mother bore me in the heat of summer. On Approaching My Birthday. Vassar Miller. NMM-2

My mother bore me in the southern wild. The Little Black Boy. William Blake. AWP; CABP; CH; ChAP; FHYEP; HeIP-4; NAEL-2; NAWM-2; NOBRP; NOEC; NoP-4; OAEL-2; OBEV; OBNC; OxBChV; PeECV; PoE; PoEL-4; PoPoPo; Ro; SCGP; TFi *Fr.* Songs of Innocence.

My mother called all street vendors. Good Cheer. John Skoyles. CMAP

My mother called me to her deathbed side, these words she said to me. Coon Can (Poor Boy). *Unknown.* AS

My mother crawled with the rest. The Alphabet by the Pool on a Sunday Afternoon. Lusia Slomkowska. LoHo

My mother drives the goat. Pictures. Sarah Kirsch, *German.* AF, *tr. by* Wayne Kvam

My mother, from the first, I was your son. My Mother's Son. Trần Huiền Ân, *Vietnamese.* AVP, *tr. by* Huỳnh Sanh Thông

My mother gave me a bitter tongue. Rhyme of My Inheritance. Joan Larkin. GLP

My mother groaned! [or groan'd!, or groand!] my father wept. Infant Sorrow. William Blake. EBEvV; FHYEP; InPS-3; NAEL-2; OBNC; OxAEP-2; OxBM; OxBSP; PoEL-4; RB *Fr.* Songs of Experience.

My mother grumbles. A Bard's Family. Peruncittiranar, *Tamil.* PLW, *tr. by* A. K. Ramanujan

My mother had two faces and a frying pot. From the House of Yemanjá. Audre Lorde. NALW; NoAM; NoP-4

My mother—half-deaf. The Hearing Aid. Richard Jones. NAmP90

My mother has died, but I visit her weekly. Adeline Naiman. MDDM *Fr.* Jennie Lubell Is In a Nursing Home in Provincetown.

My mother hates the sea. Sea Chanty. Gregory Corso. BB

My mother held me by my hand. A Dead Child Speaks. Nelly Sachs, *German.* HP; PoSu, *tr. by* Ruth *and* Matthew Mead

My Mother, If She Had Won Free Dance Lessons. Cornelius Eady. FiLi; ISC

My Mother in Old Age. Eric Ormsby. NIP-4

My Mother is a God Fearing Woman. Cornelius Eady. ISC

My mother is a poem I'll never be able to write. Sharon Doubiago. MDDM *Fr.* Mother.

My mother is a / red / woman. Natural High. Jean Binta Breeze. HCP

My mother is here. Toy Factory. Charles Simic. AF

My mother kisses me goodnight for the thousandth time. A Raincoat. Michael Burkard. FiLi

My mother left me at the foot of the fence. The Abandoned. Nathan Alterman, *Hebrew.* MHP, *tr. by* Ruth Finer Mintz

My mother lies spread-eagle upon the bed. In My Mother's Room. Colleen J. McElroy. GT; NMM-2

My Mother, Life. John Godfrey. FTOS

My mother lives in a house. My House. Robert Adamson. BMAP; CBAP

My mother loved me in my green prom dress. Fitting Room. Lois Marie Harrod. IFJA

My mother married when she was fifteen. Two Facts. David Huddle. IFJA

My mother near her death. For Margaret. Stanley Moss. FiLi; IMW

My mother never forgave my father. The Portrait. Stanley Kunitz. FiLi; IMW; LoL; Poetsp; RaBo

My mother never learned to swim, so we did. Red Cross Lessons at City Park Pool. Melody Lacina. IFJA

My mother never taught me sweeping.. . . . How I Learned to Sweep. Julia Alvarez. FFC; RA

My mother of the blue / Anglo-Saxon eyes. The Eyes, the Blood. David Meltzer. PoM

My Mother on an Evening in Late Summer. Mark Strand. FYAP

My Mother Once Told Me. Yehuda Amichai, *Hebrew.* NYBP, *tr. by* Assia Gutmann

My mother peers. 1973. Reuben Jackson. GT

My mother phoning from far off. Breathing Exercises. Leonard Nathan. PBCAP

My Mother Pieced Quilts. Teresa Palma Acosta. MDDM; WPOW

My mother—preferring the strange to the tame. The Intruder. Carolyn Kizer. BoWoP; InPK-6

My mother said. Against Idleness. *Unknown.* ACTP

My mother said, / [that] I never should. Gypsies in the Wood. *Unknown.* BoTP; OTCP; OxBoLi; OxNR

My mother said, "If just once more." Mother's Nerves. X. J. Kennedy. ChAP

My mother saw the green tree toad. Lorine Niedecker. VGW

My mother sent us to the school. The Shoemakker. *Unknown.* FaBoVe

My Mother Shoots the Breeze. Fred Chappell. MT

My mother sliced the south for us. Lullaby for Ann-Lucian. Calvin Forbes. NBV; PoBA

My Mother Spinning. Peter Olds. PeNZ

My mother talked of breakfast or laundry. Michele Murray. MDDM *Fr.* Poem of Two.

My mother tells me she dreamed. Soloing. Philip Levine. FiLi

My mother, the sage of Aliceville, Alabama. Annie Pearl Smith Discovers Moonlight. Patricia Smith. GT

My mother took care of my father's shirts. Tracing Back. Jane Mayhall. IFJA

My mother took me because she couldn't. Madre Sofía. Alberto A. Ríos. NAmP90; NoAM

My mother took us, when we went walking. The Dell. Gavin Ewart. OxBC

My mother twice in her life on worn feet. Frederick Douglass. Sam Cornish. PoBA

My mother used to work for me. Patches. Thomas Russell Shelton. PWR

My mother wants to know. Brown Circle. Louise Glück. NAmP90; NMM-2

My mother was a cotton flower. The Song of a Cotton Yarn. Ho Chi Minh, Vietnamese. AVP, tr. by Huỳnh Sanh Thông

My mother was a Florentine. Elizabeth Barrett Browning. NALW Fr. Aurora Leigh. VWP

My mother was a romantic girl. Papa Love Baby. Stevie Smith. NALW

My mother was an ill woman. The Death of Lord Warriston. Unknown. OxBB

My mother was not impressed with her beauty. Christmas Eve: My Mother Dressing. Toi Derricotte. NAmP90

My mother was some witch or slut. Sans Culotte. Pavel Grigoryevich Antokolsky, Russian. TCRP, tr. by Bernard Meares

My mother wept loudly. Austin Clarke. CIP-2 Fr. Tiresias.

My mother, when young, scrubbed laundry in a tub. In an Iridescent Time. Ruth Stone. MoAmPo; NALW; NMM-2; OxWW

My Mother, Who Came from China, Where She Never Saw Snow. Laureen Mar. CrSp; WPOW

My mother, who has a hide. The Hide of My Mother. Edward Dorn. NeAP

My mother who loses a piece. Now It Is Broccoli. Jeff Tagami. EC2

My Mother! With the angels now. Mrs. Louise B. Weston. Mary Weston Fordham. CBWP-2

My mother would be a falconress. Robert Duncan. FTOS; GLP; PoM; Poetr; RaBo

My mother would drift away. (LL) The Great Blue Heron. Carolyn Kizer. CoAP; IMW; WPE

My mother's an expert at one thing. Lullaby. Louise Glück. NAmP90

My Mother's Blue Vase. Jeannette Doob. IFJA

My Mother's Body. Marge Piercy.
    "In sleep the other night I met you, seventeen." MDDM
    "My dear, what you said was one thing." MDDM

My Mother's Body, My Professor, My Bower. Jean Valentine. NMM-2

My mother's brother hauled me to the big-boys' club. Fall In. Lincoln Kirstein. MoP

My Mother's Burying. Sean O Riordain, Irish. TIRV, tr. by Valentine Iremonger

My mother's Council house is occupied. Ornaments. Frank Ormsby. CIP-2

My Mother's Death. Judith Hemschemeyer. MDDM

My Mother's Face Never Moved. Anne C. Bromley. CMAP

My Mother's Feet. Stanley Plumly. FiLi

My Mother's Friend. Lily Brett. HP

My Mother's Garden. Alice E. Allen. BLPA; FaBoBe

My mother's hair is a maze I cannot read. Against Simple Reading. Meredith Stricker. LoHo

My Mother's Hands. Unknown. PFE

My Mother's Homeland. Belkis Cuza Malé, Spanish. LoHo, tr. by Pamela Carmell

My mother's insomnia over at last. The Chain. Maxine W. Kumin. NMM-2

My mother's lamp once out. Scenes of Childhood. James Merrill. CoAP

My Mother's Lips. C. K. Williams. FiLi

My mother's maids [or maydes] when they did sew [or sowe] and spin [or spynne]. Sir Thomas Wyatt. AAS; NoSic; SiPS Fr. Satires.

My mother's mother died. From My Mother's Home. Leah Goldberg, Hebrew. PBWP, tr. by Robert Alter Fr. My Mother's House.

My Mother's Novel. Marge Piercy.
    "I am my mother's daughter." MDDM

My mother's old leather handbag. Handbag. Ruth Fainlight. OPOU

My mother's phantom hovers here. Behind Bars, Sel. Fadwa Tuqan, Arabic. AF, tr. by Hatem Hussaini

My mother's playing cards with my aunt. Widows. Louise Glück. NAmP90

My Mother's Prayer. T. C. O'Kane. BLPA; FaBoBe

My Mother's Sabbath Days. Irena Klepfisz. NMM-2

My Mother's Sister. C. Day Lewis. OxBTC

My Mother's Son. Trần Hiền Ân, Vietnamese. AVP, tr. by Huỳnh Sanh Thông

My Mother's Suitors. Liz Lochhead. FaBoTC

My Mother's Voice. Mary E. Tucker. CBWP-1

My mother's voice is at my throat. Bluebird. Joyce Peseroff. CMAP

My Mother's Young Sister. Roy McFadden. PNI

My mountains, God has company in heaven. In High Places. Harriet Monroe. PoA

My mouth doth water, and my breast doth swell. Sonnet 37. Sir Philip Sidney. NAEL-1; Son Fr. Astrophil and Stella. AAS; SiPS

My mouth hovers across your breasts. Adrienne Rich. LW Fr. Contradictions: Tracking Poems.

My mouth,steer our lost bodies carefully downward. (LL) Who's most afraid of death?thou. E. E. Cummings. CMoP; PoE; VGW

My movable empire between Athens and Megara. Damastes (Also Known As Procrustes) Speaks. Zbigniew Herbert, Polish. PoSu, tr. by John Carpenter and Bogdana Carpenter

My muse bad[e], Bedford write, and that was she. (LL) On Lucy Countess[e] of Bedford. Ben Jonson. BeJo; NOSC; SeCP

My Muse had slept, and none had known my mind. (LL) Beauty, Time and Love. Samuel Daniel. AAS; GSo; HoPM; NOBE; OBEV

My muse in meads has spent her many hours. To Mistress Katherine Bradshaw, the Lovely, That Crowned Him with Laurel. Robert Herrick. CaPo

My muse is in the sulks to-day. Knitting. Mary E. Tucker. CBWP-1

My Muse may well grudge at my heav'nly joy. Sonnet 70. Sir Philip Sidney. Fr. Astrophil and Stella. AAS; SiPS

My Muse sits forlorn. Stevie Smith. BWW

My Muse, though airy, glides softly along. The Song of the Pen. Judah Al-Harizi, Hebrew. TrJP, tr. by J. Chotzner

My Muse will now by chymistry draw forth. To the Learned and Reverend Mr. Cotton Mather, on His Excellent Magnalia. Grindall Rawson. SCAP

My Naked Aunt. Archibald MacLeish. MeMAP

My naked simple life was I. My Spirit. Thomas Traherne. GeHe

My Name. Daniel Berrigan. AF

My Name and I. Robert Graves. NYBP; NoAM

My Name Is Afrika. Keorapetse Kgositsile. PoBA

My name is David Lowston, I did seal, I did seal. David Lowston. Unknown. PeNZ

My name is dreidfu. Did it garr ye snirk? Merulius Lacrymans. Robert Garioch. FaBoTC

My name is easy to pronounce, isn't it? Her story. E. A. Markham. HCP

My name is Edgar Poe and I was born. On the Edge. Philip Levine. CoAP; TAP

My name is Edward Hollander, as you may understand. The Flying Cloud. Unknown. AmFP

My name is Eteocles. The sea seduced me from my farm. Isidorus, Greek. GrAn, tr. by Edwin Morgan

My name is Fermin. Tobera. Jeff Tagami. OpBo

My name is Frank Taylor, a bachelor I am. Starving to Death on a Government Claim. Unknown. AmFP; OBAL

My name is George Nathaniel Curzon. On the Hon. George Nathaniel Curzon, Commoner of Balliol. John William Mackail and Cecil Arthur Spring-Rice. FaBoEE; NOBL; OBCoV; PeLV Fr. Balliol Rhymes.

My name is "I am living." I Have Bowed before the Sun. Anna Walters. WPOW

My name is James A. Wright, and I was born. At the Executed Murderer's Grave. James Wright. HCAP; VCAP

My name is Jesus, I am Mary's son. D. H. Lawrence. PeECV

My name is John J. Curtis. John J. Curtis. Joseph Gallagher. AmFP

My name is Johnson. Madam's Past History. Langston Hughes. MoP; NoAM; SAmP

My name is Judith meaning. Judy Grahn. NMM-2 Fr. Confrontations with the Devil in the Form of Love.

My name is O'Kelly, I've heard the Revelly. Shillin' a Day. Rudyard Kipling. NoAM

My name is Parrot, a bird [or byrd] of Paradise. John Skelton. OBCoV Fr. Parrot's Soliloquy. NoSic; OxBoLi; PoEL-1 Fr. Speak [or Speke], Parrot.

My name is Peter Emily. Peter Amberley. John Calhoun. AmFP

My name is Saartjie Baartman and I come from Kat Rivier. Hottentot Venus. Stephen Gray. PeSAV

My name is Samuel Hall, Samuel Hall. Sam Hall. Unknown. AmFP

My name is Sanford Barney, and I came from Little Rock town. Sanford Barney. Unknown. AmFP

My name is Sluggery-wuggery. Pauline Clarke. FuFo

My name is Solomon Levi. An Old Cracked Tune. Stanley Kunitz. LoL

My name is Stanford Barnes, I come from Nobleville town. The State of Arkansas. Unknown. APN-2

My name is Tom Bone. Tom Bone. Charles Causley. FuFo

My name it is [or is] Joe Bowers, I have [or I've got] a brother Ike. Joe Bowers. *Unknown.* AmFP

My name—my country—what are they to thee? Epitaph, An: "My name—my country—what are they to thee." Paulus Silentiarius, *Greek.* AWP, *tr. by William Cowper*

My name, my speech, my self I had forgot. Shock. Rudyard Kipling. *Fr.* Epitaphs of the War [1914–1918]. OBWP

My Name shall mount upon Eternitie. (LL) Whilst thus my pen strives to eternize thee. Michael Drayton. AAS; Son

My name was Pnytagoras; I died by drowning. Argentarius, *Greek.* GrAn, *tr. by Fleur Adcock*

My name was—(Well—what signifies?)—my nation. An Epitaph to Let. Paul The Silentiary, *Greek.* OBCVT, *tr. by Leigh Hunt*

My name's Philip Marlowe, the chivalrous shamus. Raymond Chandler: The Big Sleep. Basil Ransome-Davies. OBCoV

My name's Polly Parker I come o'er. The Collier Lass. Frankie Armstrong. BrRo

My native clay. Growing in Grace. Jack R. Clemo. NOCV

My Native Land. Sir Walter Scott. *See* Caledonia.

My native land is up there. At Gold Hill Monastery. Su Tung-p'o, *Chinese.* OHPC, *tr. by Kenneth Rexroth*

My Native Land, thy Puritanic stock. "Orpheus C. Kerr." *Fr.* The Rejected "National Hymns." OBAL

My nature singing in me is your nature singing. Singing & Doubling Together. A. R. Ammons. NAAL-2; NoAM

My necktie, my gloves. Charlie's Sad Date. Rafael Alberti, *Spanish.* CBNP, *tr. by Mark Strand*

My Neighbor. Roque Dalton, *Spanish.* AF, *tr. by Richard Schaaf*

My neighbor, a scientist and art-collector, telephones me in a. The Burning of Paper instead of Children. Adrienne Rich. LCAP-2; NAAL-2; VCAP

My neighbor brings me bottom fish. My Garden, My Daylight. Jorie Graham. HCAP; Poetr

My neighbor Hunks's house and mine. Near Neighbors. Martial, *Latin.* AWP, *tr. by Swift*

My Neighbor in the Mirror. Louise Glück. Son

My neighbor runs to me with. In the Country. Lu Yu, *Chinese.* OHMPC, *tr. by Kenneth Rexroth*

My neighbor to the East has. Rain in the Aspens. Su Tung-p'o, *Chinese.* OHPC, *tr. by Kenneth Rexroth*

My Neighbor to the South, the Office Clerk Hsiao, Came in the Evening to Say Good-bye. Harry Mathews, *Chinese.* CoBCP, *tr. by Burton Watson*

My Neighborhood. Stuart Dybek. PBCAP

My neighbor's child cries in the middle of the night. Kung Tzu-chen, *Chinese.* SuSp, *tr. by Wu-chi Liu*

My neighbors on the right. Next Door. Mei Yao Ch'en, *Chinese.* OHPC, *tr. by Kenneth Rexroth*

My Neighbor's Reply. *Unknown.* PoToHe

My neighbor's rooster hops the stick i throw. Marlene Mountain. HA

My Neighbor's Roses. Abraham L. Gruber. BLPA; PoToHe

My neighbor's son, learning piano. Justice without Passion. Jane Hirshfield. WeT

My neighbor's willow sways its frail. The Willow. Tu Fu, *Chinese.* OHPC, *tr. by Kenneth Rexroth*

My neighbour, Mrs Fanshaw, is portly-plump and gay. Stately as a Galleon. Joyce Grenfell. OxVerse

My nephew, who is six years old, is called 'Tortoise'. Children. Po Chü-i, *Chinese.* ChiP, *tr. by Arthur Waley*

My nest of mercies in the rude, red tree. (LL) Let the tale's sailor from a Christian voyage. Dylan Thomas. CMoP; FaBoMo; OAEL-2

My net / Is heavy with weed. The Disappointed Shrimper. P. A. Ropes. BoTP

My new-cut ashlar takes the light. A Dedication. Rudyard Kipling. PoEL-5 *Fr.* Life's Handicap.

My New Garden Field. *Unknown.* AmFP

My new Province is a land of bamboo-groves. Eating Bamboo-Shoots. Po Chü-i, *Chinese.* ChiP; OBVE, *tr. by Arthur Waley*

My New Rabbit. Elizabeth Gould. BoTP; OTCP

My New Umbrella. M. M. Hutchinson. BoTP

My newly rented home commands a view of the temple hall. A Solitary Falcon above the Buddha Hall of the Monastery of universal Purity. Mei Yao Ch'en, *Chinese.* SuSp, *tr. by Jonathan Chaves*

My Newts. Clarissa Hinsley. PeP

My niece past marriageable age. Labyrinth. Yojong Kim, *Korean.* CKP, *tr. by Jaihiun Kim*

My Night with Philip Larkin. Rachel Loden. BAP-95

My Nightingale. Boris Petrovich Kornilov, *Russian.* TCRP, *tr. by Bernard Meares*

My noble, lovely, little Peggy. A Letter to the Honourable Lady Miss Margaret Cavendish Holles-Harley. Matthew Prior. NOBE; NOEC; NoAM; OBEV; OxBC; OxBChV; OxBSP

My normal dwelling is the lungs of swine. Autobiography of a Lungworm. Roy Fuller. MoP; NoAM; OxBC

My northern pines are good enough for me. Boston. Edwin Arlington Robinson. APN-2

My nose cuts the air. Life-Saving Medal. Philippe Soupault. PFTM

My nosegays are for Captives. Emily Dickinson. NCAP

My November Guest. Robert Frost. OxBA; PoLF

My obnoxious brother Bobby. Colin West. PeP

My Observation at Sea. Mildmay Fane. BeJo

My obsession. (LL) Documentary. Claribel Alegría, *Spanish.* LoL; VCWP, *tr. by D. J. Flakoll*

My old cat [is dead]. Hal Summers. KaS; OxBTC

My old companion! and my friend! To My Worthy Friend, Mr. James Bayley. Nicholas Noyes. SCAP

My old desire to live in the Southern Village. Moving House. Ch'ien T'ao, *Chinese.* ChiP, *tr. by Arthur Waley*

My Old Dutch. Albert Chevalier. LBC

My old flame, my wife! The Old Flame. Robert Lowell. BoLoP; CBLP; NOBA; NoAM

My old friend, going west, bids farewell at Yellow Crane Terrace. Seeing Meng Hao-jan Off to Kuang-ling. Li Po, *Chinese.* SuSp, *tr. by Paul W. Kroll*

My old friend prepares chicken and millet. Stopping at a Friend's Farm. Meng Hao Jan, *Chinese.* SuSp, *tr. by Daniel Bryant*

My old friend takes leave of the west at Yellow Crane Tower. At Yellow Crane Tower Taking Leave of Meng Hao-jan. Li Po, *Chinese.* CoBCP, *tr. by Burton Watson*

My Old Hammah. *Unknown.* AS

My old home is there on the southern mountain. (LL) Poem without a Category ("Sun and moon refuse to slow their pace"). T'ao Ch'ien, *Chinese.* CoBCP, *tr. by Burton Watson*

My Old Kentucky Home[, Good Night!]. Stephen Collins Foster. APN-2; FaBoBe; PoLF

(My Old Kentucky Home.) FaBoA

("Then my old kentucky home, good night.") (LL) FaBoA

My old lady died. Kitchen Door Blues. Tennessee Williams. OBAL

My Old Man. Charles Bukowski. PmAP

My old man's a white old man. Cross. Langston Hughes. ColAP; GT; LiTM; NoP-4; PoBA; PoLF; SAmP; SoSe-8; TAP

My old [or ole] Mistiss promise me. Promises of Freedom. *Unknown.* BPo; CrDW; NAAAL

My old mule. Me and the Mule. Langston Hughes. PoPoPo

My Old Palette. Christopher Pearse Cranch. APN-1

My Old Straw Hat. Eliza Cook. BrRo

My old time daddy. Lover's Return. Langston Hughes. SAmP

My oldest friend looks for me. Three Small Songs for the Muse. Kathleen Norris. CrSp

My ole man took me to the fulton fish market. Knees of a Natural Man. Henry Dumas. GT

My once dear love; hapless that I no more. The Surrender. Henry, Bishop of Chichester King. BoLoP; CBLP; EBEV; NOSC

My only love was dead. (LL) In the Mile End Road. Amy Levy. PEW; RACG

My only son, more God's than mine. Jesus and His Mother. Thom Gunn. OxBC

My Orcha'd in Linden Lea. William Barnes. EBVV; FaBoVe; NOBVV

My *outside Woman*, and your *inside Man*. (LL) The Change. Abraham Cowley. CBLP; MeLP; SeCP

My own Araminta, say 'No!'. (LL) A Letter of Advice. Winthrop Mackworth Praed. NOBL; OxBoLi; PeLV

My Own Cáilin Donn. George Sigerson. FaBoBe

My own dark head (my own, my own). *Unknown, Irish.* NOIV, *tr. by Thomas Kinsella*

My own dim life should teach me this. Tennyson. EnVR; FHYEP; OAEL-2 *Fr.* In Memoriam A. H. H.

My Own Epitaph. Mary Chandler. ECWP

My Own Epitaph. John Gay. CABP; FaBoEE; LiLi; NIP-4; NOEC; PeLV

My own flesh and blood--. Antigone. Sophocles, *Greek.* NAWM-1, *tr. by Robert Fagles*

My own forever, my mother. The Teacher I Wanted to Be. Ingrid Wendt. IFJA

My Own Hallelujahs. Zack Gilbert. PoBA

My own heart let me have. More pity on. Sonnet 2. Nell Altizer. FFC *Fr.* Love Letters to Her Who Lives [Alas!] Away.

My own heart let me more have pity on; let. Gerard Manley Hopkins. APAD; EnVR; FaBoMo; InPS-3; LiTM; MoBrPo; NOBVV; NoP-4; TOF

My own in a foreign land. The Jewish Conscript. Florence Kiper Frank. TrJP

My Ox Duke. John Dyer. NOEC

My Packard Bell was set up in the vacant lot near the stump. The Campaign. Josephine Miles. WPE

My pain[e], still smothered [or smother'd] in my grievèd bre[a]st. Sonnet 6. Mary Sidney Wroth, Countess of Montgomery. NOSC *Fr.* Pamphilia to Amphilanthus.

My palace builded is, and lo now here I lie. (LL) A Rueful Lamentation on the Death of Queen Elizabeth. Sir Thomas More. AAS; NoSic

My papa knows you, and he says you're a man who makes reading for / books. Miss Edith's Modest Request. Bret Harte. NOxBChV

My Papa's Waltz. Theodore Roethke. CMoP; ChAP; ClHu; ColAP; HAP; HCAP; HeIP-4; HoPM; InPK-6; InPS-3; LCAP-2; LiTM; MoP; NAAL-2; NBLV; NIP-4; NOBA; NOxBChV; NTP; NoAM; NoP-4; PBMP; PoE; PoPoPo; Poetr; RaBo; SAGP; TAP; TFi; TRP; VGW

My Parents En Route. David Ferry. WeT

My parents felt those rumblings. The Hongo Store 29 Miles Volcano Hilo, Hawaii. Garrett Kaoru Hongo. PoPoPo; WeT

My parents kept me from children who were rough. Rough. Stephen Spender. PBMP

My parents raised me tenderly. The Girl I Left behind Me. *Unknown.* AmFP

My parents were fish. Digging in the Streets of Gold. Barry Seiler. UnSA

My Paris is a land where twilight days. Paris. Arthur Symons. NOBVV

My Party. Queenie Scott-Hopper. BoTP

My passion is as mustard strong. A New Song of New Similies . John Gay. CBNP; NOBL

My passion is like turbulence at the head of waters. *Unknown, Arabic.* BoWoP, tr. by Willis Barnstone

My Past. Dennis Cooper. GLP

My "Patch of Blue." Mary Newland Carson. BLPA

My patent pardouns ye may see. Sir David Lindsay. OBSV *Fr.* Ane Satire [or Satyre] of the Three [or Thrie] Estaitis.

My paths out of sand, the heavens. The Lithuanian Well. Johannes Bobrowski, *German.* CEEP, tr. by Juliette Victor-Rood

My Peggy is a young thing. The Wawking of the Fauld. Allan Ramsay. OBEV; OxBS; SCGP *Fr.* The Gentle Shepherd.

My pen, take pain a little space. Sir Thomas Wyatt. SCGP; SiPS

My pensioners who daily. Pensioners. Winifred M. Letts. BoTP

My pensive Public, wherefore look you sad? Playhouse Musings. James Smith. OxAEP-2

My pensive Sara! thy soft cheek reclin'd. The Eolian Harp. Coleridge. FHYEP; NAEL-2; NOBRP; OAEL-2 *Fr.* Effusions.

My People. Langston Hughes. MBE; NOxBChV

My People. Else Lasker-Schüler, *German.* WPOW, tr. by Michael Hamburger

My People Are Destroyed for Lack of Knowledge. Jones Very. ChIV-1

My people have married me. Lament of Hsi-chün. Hsi-chün, *Chinese.* BoWoP; ChiP, tr. by Arthur Waley

My people? Who are they? Who Are My People? Rosa Zagnoni Marinoni. BLPA; PoToHe

My perennial nest. (LL) Her breast is fit for pearls. Emily Dickinson. CPO; HeIP-4

My period had come for Prayer. Emily Dickinson. APN-2

My periods have changed. It is years. Tampons. Ellen Bass. NMM-2

My Pet Goldfish. Edward Williams. PeP

My Pet Hare. William Cowper. APo; FP *Fr.* The Task.

My Pet Koala. *Unknown.* PeP

My Phillis hath the morning sun. Phillis 1. Thomas Lodge. OBEV *Fr.* Phyllis.

My Photograph. Vadim Konstantinovich Strelchenko, *Russian.* TCRP, tr. by Lubov Yakovleva

My photograph already looks historic. The Middle of a War. Roy Fuller. OBWP; PoWW

My Picture. Abraham Cowley. CBLP

My Picture-Gallery. Walt Whitman. NAAL-1; NAAL-3

My Picture Left in Scotland. Ben Jonson. BeJo; CBLP; FMP; NAEL-1; PBRV; PoEL-2; SeCP

My pictures blacken in their frames. Death of the Day. Walter Savage Landor. NoP-4

My "place of clear water." Anahorish. Seamus Heaney. PBCIP

My plaid awa, my plaid awa. Lady Isabel and the Elf-Knight [or The Elfin Knight]. *Unknown.* CH

My Plan. Marchette Chute. WHSW

My plants are whispering to one another. Consolations After an Affair. James Tate. WeT

My plate's empty. (LL) One, two, / Buckle my shoe. Mother Goose. BoTP; LB; OxNR; ReMoGo

My Playmate. Mary I. Osborn. BoTP; OTCP

My Playmate. John Greenleaf Whittier. APN-1; NOBA

My Poem. Nikki Giovanni. BPo; NBV; PoBA

My poem is a bridge, silent, lonely;. Huang Guobin, *Chinese.* ChiPo, tr. by Mok Wing-yin *and* Huang Guobin

My poem would eat nothing. The Poem You Asked For. Larry Levis. AmPA; PBCAP

My poem's in the oven where it. Kris Hemensley. BMAP *Fr.* A Mile from Poetry.

My poet, thou canst touch on all the notes. Sonnet. Elizabeth Barrett Browning. BrRo *Fr.* Sonnets from the Portuguese.

My poetry, an imperfect metaphor of life! (LL) On Being a Poet in Sierra Leone. Syl Cheney-Coker. HBAPE; PBMAP

My poetry is exacting a confession. Manifesto on Ars Poetica. Frank Mkalawile Chipasula. HBAPE

My poetry is no poetry, no. Nguyễn Chí Thiện, *Vietnamese.* AVP, tr. by Huỳnh Sanh Thông

My Poker Girl. Tom Masson. OBAL

My poor body is alas unworthy. Ch'in Chia's Wife's Reply. *Unknown, Chinese.* BoWoP; ChiP, tr. by Arthur Waley

My poor expecting Heart beats for thy Breast. To My Heavenly Charmer. Martha Sansom. LW

My Portion is Defeat—today. Emily Dickinson. APN-2; OBWP

My Portrait. Moyshe-Leyb Halpern, *Yiddish.* TrJP, tr. by Joseph Leftwich

My prayer is that I have friends. Patrick O'Connor. TIRV

My Prayers are heard, O Lyce, now. Horat. Carm. lib. 4. Ode 13. Horace, *Latin.* OBCVT, tr. by William Cartwright

My precious life I spent considering. Take the Crust. Sadi. AWP, tr. by L. Cranmer-Byng *Fr.* The Gulistan.

My Pretty [Little] Pink. *Unknown.* AS; AmFP
("My pretty little pink, I once did think.") ACTP

My Pretty Rose-Tree. William Blake. BoLoP; FHYEP; NAEL-2; NOBRP *Fr.* Songs of Experience.
("Flower was offered to me, A.") Ro

My prime of youth is but a frost of cares. Tichborne's Elegy. Chidiock Tichborne. EBEV; GEA; HAP; HeIP-4; InPK-6; InPS-3; NOBE; NoP-4; NoSic; OAEL-1; PoPoPo; RB; SCGP; SCV; TFi; WeW-3

My puberty tree swayed big, saw-edged leaves. The Puberty Tree. D. M. Thomas. TOF

My pulses rushed, and, quick, to saddle! The Meeting, the Departure. Goethe, *German.* STV, tr. by John Frederick Nims

My purpose is to tell my own true tale. The Seafarer. *Unknown.* EBEV, tr. by John Wain

My purpose was purely corrective. Limerick. Leslie Johnson. PeLi

My Purse. *Unknown.* EBEV

My Queen her sceptre did lay down. Regina. Mary Elizabeth Coleridge. NALW

My quiet kin, must I affront you. Preliminary to Classroom Lecture. Josephine Miles. MoP; NoAM

My quiet prison guards, much tried. My beloved. Pictures of the Jews. Haim Guri, *Hebrew.* MHP, tr. by Ruth Finer Mintz

My quietness has a man in it, he is transparent. In Memory of My Feelings. Frank O'Hara. APSN; ColAP; NAAL-2; NeAP; PoM

My quill is charged with fire. Song of Hate. Jacob ben David Frances, *Hebrew.* TrJP, tr. by A. B. Rhine

My Ratclif [or Ratcliffe], when the rethlesse [or retchless or rechless] youth offendes. Exhortation to Learn of Others' Trouble. Henry Howard, Earl of Surrey. AAS; FaBoEE; SiPS

My ravist spreit in that desart terribill. Nightmare. Gawin Douglas. PoEL-1 *Fr.* The Palace [or Palice] of Honor [or Honour].

My reckless race is run, green youth and pride be past. A Gloze Upon This Text, *Dominus iis opus habet.* George Gascoigne. ChIV-2

My red engine goes chuff-chuff-choo! chuff-chuff-choo! My Toys. Lilian McCrea. BoTP

My reflection. Ray A. Young Bear. STP

My relatives are dead. As for my friends. Silence. René Maran, *French.* NegPo, tr. by Ellen Conroy Kennedy

My rent His Son should pay if I believed. (LL) My Country Audit. Mildmay Fane. BeJo; NOSC

My report is not of schools. Return from Luluabourg. Michael Jackson. PeNZ

My reproach is like the mottled bamboo. Complaint of a Neglected Wife. Meng Chiao, *Chinese.* PLT, tr. by A. C. Graham

My research. Tanka. Shaku Chōkū, *Japanese.* MJT, tr. by Makoto Ueda

My Rich Uncle, Whom I Only Met Three Times. Marge Piercy. UnSA

My rifle cocked, in savage calm. The Hunter's Song at Nightfall. Goethe, *German.* STV, tr. by John Frederick Nims

My Right Hand Don't Leave Me No More. Carter Revard. HATNAP

My Ringless Fingers on the Steering Wheel Tell the Story. Laura Boss. UnSA

My Rival. Rudyard Kipling. OxBTC

My robe is wet with tears, remembering. (LL) Facing Wine with Memories of Lord Ho. Li Po, *Chinese*. CoBCP, *tr. by* Burton Watson (b. 1925)

My Rocking Chair. Doris I. Bateman. CTV

My room. Masaoka Shiki, *Japanese*. MJT, *tr. by* Ueda, Makoto

My room in Florence was the color of air. Above the Arno. May Swenson. NYBP

My room is blue, the carpet's blue. The Blue Room. Richard Edwards. Spl

My room is so small. Leah Goldberg. BoWoP, *tr. by* Ramah Commanday *Fr.* Nameless Journey.

My room's a square and candle-lighted boat. The Country Bedroom. Frances Darwin Cornford. MoBrPo

My room's bigger than a coffin. On Saint-Urbain Street. Milton Acorn. NOBC

My Russia, mine! Yury Mikhailovich Kublanovsky, *Russian*. TCRP, *tr. by* Albert C. Todd *and* Yevgeny Yevtushenko

My Sad Captains. Thom Gunn. CMoP; FaBoMo; LiTM; NAEL-2; NoAM; NoP-4; PoPoPo

My sad heart slobbers at the poop. The Stolen Heart. Rimbaud, *French*. NNPT, *tr. by* Wallace Fowlie

My Sad Self. Allen Ginsberg. Poetr; UnPo; VCAP

My Sadness Sits around Me. June Jordan. BPo

My Saigon daughter I saw only once. A Black Soldier Remembers. Horace Coleman. CDa

My Samsons. Haim Guri, *Hebrew*. IP, *tr. by* Warren Bargad *and* Stanley F. Chyet

My Savior, hear my prayer. Henry L. Jenner. CTV

My Savior, let me hear Thy voice tonight. I'll Follow Thee. Clara Ann Thompson. CBWP-2

My sculptor husband, when he *was* mine, possessed. The Bride of Quietness. Kelly Cherry. FFC

My Seasonal Body, My Ears. Clarence Major. WeT

My second daughter, I loved her so much! Seeing Flowers I Remember My Late Daughter, Shu. Kao Ch'i, *Chinese*. CoBLCP, *tr. by* Jonathan Chaves

My secrets cry aloud. Open House. Theodore Roethke. NOBA; NoAM

My self to die, and prove mine owne. (LL) The Garden. James Shirley. BeJo; NOSC

(My selves dissolving, old whore petticoats)——— / To Paradise. (LL) Fever 103°. Sylvia Plath. CMoP; FaBoWP; NOBA; NoAM; VCAP; VGW

My serious son! I see thee look. Before a Saint's Picture. Walter Savage Landor. OxBChV

My servant wakes at break of dawn. Rough Ridge. Yüan Mei, *Chinese*. CoBLCP, *tr. by* Jonathan Chaves

My servant wakes me: "Master, it is broad day." Po Chü-i, *Chinese*. ChiP, *tr. by* Arthur Waley

My service thus is growne into disdayne. (LL) In Cipres springes [*or* Cyprus springs] (wheras [*or* whereas]) dame Venus dwelt). Henry Howard, Earl of Surrey. AAS; SiPS

My seven sons came back from Indonesia. Homecoming. Peter Viereck. CoAP

My shack has two rooms; I use one. Robert Bly. *Fr.* Six Winter Privacy Poems. LCAP-2

My Shadow. W. Hodgson Burnett. UV

My Shadow. Robert Louis Stevenson. CTV; ChAP; FaBoBe; OTCP; OxBChV; PWR; UV

("Asleep in bed.") (LL) FPC

My Shadow and I. Phan Bội Châu, *Vietnamese*. AVP, *tr. by* Huỳnh Sanh Thông

My Shadow's Stature. John James Piatt. APN-2

My shag-hair Cyclops, come, lets ply. Vulcan's Song. John Lyly. EBEV; NoSic *Fr.* Sapho and Phao.

My shattred phancy stole away from mee. Edward Taylor. NOSC; SCAP *Fr.* Preparatory Meditations Before My Approach to the Lord's Supper.

My sheep are thoughts, which I both guide and serve, *speech of Dorus.* Sir Philip Sidney. NoSic; SiPS *Fr.* Arcadia.

My Shepherd Is the Living Lord. Thomas Sternhold. AH

My Ship Does Not Need a Helmsman. Alan Chong Lau. OpBo

My Ships. Ella Wheeler Wilcox. PoLF

My shirt is a token and symbol. Shirt. Carl Sandburg. CA

My Shoes. Charles Simic. CoAP; HCAP; VCAP

My shoes are almost dead. Caesar. W. S. Merwin. LCAP-2

My shoes. / I have just taken them off. 17. IV. 71. Paul Blackburn. PoM

My shoulders prick, as though they were half-fledged. (LL) Field-Glasses. Andrew Young. GTBS-P; RB

My shrink told me it was unnatural to be. Invisible History. Walta Borawski. GLP

My silent jailers, well experienced. Who love me. Pictures of Jews. Haim Guri, *Hebrew*. IP, *tr. by* Warren Bargad *and* Stanley F. Chyet

My silk legs give rise to bird calls. The Innate Deception of Unspoiled Beauty. Dara Wier. CMAP

My silks and fine array. Song. William Blake. GBL; OBNC; RACG; SCGP; UnPo

My sin! my sin, my God, these cursed dregs. Edward Taylor. SCAP *Fr.* Preparatory Meditations Before My Approach to the Lord's Supper.

My Singing Aunt. James Reeves. FuFo

My sins in their completeness. Mael Isu O Brolchain. NOIV

My Sister. Abba Kovner, *Hebrew*. TOF, *tr. by* T. Carmi

My Sister. Alfonsina Storni, *Spanish*. BoWoP, *tr. by* Aliki *and* Willis Barnstone

My sister and I used to play this game called Red Hot. Red Hot. Laurie Anderson. OxWW

My sister and I used to tease her. The Apple-Eater. Linda Curtis Meyers. IFJA

My sister Clarissa spits twice if I kiss her. George Barker. FuFo

My sister does not write poems. Wislawa Szymborska. *See* In Praise of My Sister.

My sister doesn't write poems. In Praise of My Sister. Wislawa Szymborska, *Polish*. PoSu, *tr. by* Adam Czerniawski

My sister had a slumber party. Slumber Party. Carson McCullers. CTV

My sister has never fallen. Elizabeth, Listening. Sabina Grogan. PUP-20

My sister in her well-tailored silk blouse hands me. The Photos. Diane Wakoski. NIP-4

My sister Laura's bigger than me. Spike Milligan. NTCP

My sister! my sweet sister! if a name. Epistle to Augusta. Byron. FHYEP

My sister rubs the doll's face in mud. The Kid. Ai. GT; NoAM

My sister singing the Kyrie. Near Burning. Kathleen Peirce. PBCAP

My sister, you are a stranger to this place. God Hasn't Made Room. Mririda n'Ait Attik. PBWP, *tr. by* Daniel Halpern *and* Paula Paley

My Sisters, O My Sisters. May Sarton. NALW

My Sister's Sleep. D. G. Rossetti. EnVR; NAEL-2

My skin is pumiced to a fault. Fado Singer. Wole Soyinka. HBAPE

My skinny horse. The Shrine of General Pien. Chu Yün-ming, *Chinese*. CoBLCP, *tr. by* Jonathan Chaves

My sleep in any city is still. Parents Sleeping. Linda Mizejewski. CMAP

My softness heaves its spinal canopy. Snail. Elisabeth Eybers, *Afrikaans*. PeSA; PeSAV, *tr. by* Elisabeth Eybers

My Son. James D. Hughes. BLPA

My Son. Ruth Stone. WPE

My Son and I. Rosemary Norman. BrRo

My Son and I Go See Horses. Marianne Boruch. WeT

My son and I kiss the same woman goodbye. Lies. Christopher Bursk. CDa

My son, come pierce my soul with a sword. Ballad of the Scarecrow Christ. Elder Olson. ChIV-2

My son, forget not my law; but let thine heart keep my commandments. Bible, *O.T.* CTV *Fr.* The Bible, Proverbs 3:1–4.

My Son, Forsake Your Art. Mahon O'Heffernan, *Irish*. BIrV, *tr. by* Maire Cruise O'Brien

My son has birds in his head. Daedalus. Alastair Reid. NYBP

My son, in whose face there is already a sign. Yehuda Amichai. LiLi

My son invites me to witness with him. Mousemeal. Howard Nemerov. TwCP

My son is five years old and tonight he sang this song to me. A Loud Song, Mother. Isabella Gardner. FiLi

My son, my executioner. Donald Hall. LoL; TRP

"My son my son" the Blakean figure mourns and affirms. Brian Coffey. BiHa *Fr.* Advent.

My son smells of peace when I lean over him. Two Songs of Peace. Yehuda Amichai, *Hebrew*. AF, *tr. by* Assia Gutmann

My son squats in the snow in his blue snowsuit. Illuminations. Louise Glück. NALW

My son tells his aunt. A San Diego Poem. Simon J. Ortiz. CDW

My son was killed while laughing at some jest. I Have a Son. Rudyard Kipling. FaBoEE; PeFWW *Fr.* Epitaphs of the War [1914–1918]. OBWP

My son wears a nappy. My Son and I. Rosemary Norman. BrRo

"My son!" What simple, beautiful words! To My Unborn Son. Cyril Morton Thorne. BLPA

My son, where is your soul? And If the Angel Should Ask. Hayyim Nahman Bialik, *Hebrew*. MHP, *tr. by* Ruth Finer Mintz

My son, you are a sweet bitter shadow. On Your Twenty-First Birthday. Joan Austin Geier. FFC

My son, you loved telling the story of Prince Nata. T'ang Hsien-tsu. CoBLCP, *tr. by* Jonathan Chaves *Fr.* Twenty-two Quatrains on Receiving the Obituary Notice for my Son Shih-Chü.

My Song. King D. Kuka. VoR

My Song. James Ephriam McGirt. AAP

My Song, I fear that thou wilt find but few. Epipsychidion. Shelley.

My Song Is Love Unknown. Samuel Crossman. OxBChV

My Song to the Jewish People. Leib Olitski, *Yiddish.* TrJP, *tr. by* Jacob Sonntag

My song today is the storm-cock's song. The Storm-Cock's Song. "Hugh MacDiarmid." OxBTC

My songs, they say, are poisoned. My Songs Are Poisoned. Heinrich Heine, *German.* AWP, *tr. by* Louis Untermeyer

My Sons. Ron Loewinsohn. NeAP

My son's father is Kiowa-Comanche. Super-Brave. Teresa Whitman. LoHo

My son's house. 2nd Wind. Barbara Howes. FiLi

My Son's One-Year Test: Improvised. Wen Cheng-ming, *Chinese.* "Smiling, we set the testing tray before the hall." CoBLCP, *tr. by* Jonathan Chaves

My sons / sometimes I can. Efficiency Apartment. Gerald William Barrax. PoBA

My sorrow, Donncha, my thousand-cherished. Padraig O Heigeartaigh, *Irish.* NOIV, *tr. by* Thomas Kinsella

My sorrow is so wide. Kings River Canyon. Kenneth Rexroth. *Fr.* Andrée Rexroth. APSN; VGW

My sorrow that I am not by the little dún. The Starling Lake. "Seumas O'Sullivan." AWP

My sorrow, when she's here with me. My November Guest. Robert Frost. OxBA; PoLF

My soul. Walt Whitman. *See* A Noiseless patient spider.

My soul, be not disturbed. Address to My Soul. Elinor Wylie. AWP; LiTM; OxBA

My Soul before Thee Prostrate Lies. C. F. Richter, *German.* AH, *tr. by* John Wesley

My soul, calm sister, towards thy brow, whereon scarce grieves. Sigh. Stéphane Mallarmé, *French.* AWP, *tr. by* Arthur Symons

My soul doth magnify the Lord. The Song of the Virgin Mary. Miles Coverdale. ChIV-2

My soul, dread not the pestilence that hags. Preparations for Victory. Edmund Blunden. PeFWW

My soul enchanted soareth free. (LL) The Rainy Season in California. John Rollin Ridge. APN-2; PAR

My soul from a mother's old Arm-chair. (LL) The Old Arm-Chair. Eliza Cook. BrRo; InPK-6; Poetr; VWP

My soul has grown deep like the rivers. (LL) The Negro Speaks of Rivers. Langston Hughes. AiP; BPo; CrDW; HAP; HCAP; HeIP-4; ISC; NAAAL; NAAL-2; NIP-4; NOBA; NoAM; NoP-4; OBCA; PoBA; Poetr; RaBo; SSLK; TAP; TFi; TTY; WeW-3

My soul[e] I'll [*or* Ile] pour[e] into thee. (LL) The Night-Piece, to Julia. Robert Herrick. BeJo; BoTP; CBLP; CH; CaPo; EBEvV; NAEL-1; NOSC; NoP-4; OAEL-1; OBEV; PoE; PoEL-3; PoRA; SAGP; SCGP; SeCP; TFi

My Soul in the Bundle of Life. *Unknown.* TrJP, *tr. by* E. Margaret Rowley *Fr.* The Dead Sea Scrolls.

My soul is a witness for my Lord. Who'll Be a Witness for My Lord? *Unknown.* CrDW

My soul is awakened, my spirit is soaring. Lines Composed in a Wood on a Windy Day. Anne Brontë. EBVV; SDW; VWP

My soul is enchanted boat. Shelley. FHYEP *Fr.* Prometheus Unbound. NOBRP; OAEL-2

My soul is like the oar that momently. Struggle. Sidney Lanier. OxBA

My soul is the veil of his love. Hafiz, *Persian.* TOF, *tr. by* R. A. Nicholson

My Soul Is Weary of My Life. Bible, *O.T. Fr.* Job. NAWM-1

My soul looked down from a vague height, with Death. The Show. Wilfred Owen. ImPo; LiTM; MoBrPo; NSI; OBWVE; OxBTC; PeFWW

My soul looks over the courtyard. Early in the morning. Jules Supervielle, *French.* MFP, *tr. by* Martin Sorrell

My soul magnifies the Lord. The Magnificat. Bible, *N.T.* BoWoP *Fr.* St. Luke.

My soul, my pleasant soul and witty. Emperor Hadrian, *Latin.* OBCVT, *tr. by* Henry Vaughan

My soul of sunset every human day. Trumbull Stickney. *Fr.* Pandora's Songs. APN-2 *Fr.* Prometheus Pyrphoros.

My soul shall spurn them evermore. (LL) The Holy Office. James Joyce. FaBoTw; NoAM; OxBTC

My soul, sit thou a patient looker-on. Epigram. Francis Quarles. NIP-4; NOBE; OBEV; PoToHe

My soul stands at the window of my room. Nostalgia. Karl Shapiro. CMoP; CoAP; TrJP; TwCP

My soul surcharged with grief now loud complains. Sonnet. Rachel Morpurgo, *Hebrew.* TrJP, *tr. by* Nina Davis Salaman

My Soul, there is a country [*or* countrie]. Peace. Henry Vaughan. AWP; EBEV; ESCV; FMP; FSCP; FaBoCh; GeHe; HAP; NOBE; NOCV; OBEV; OxAEP-1; PoE; SCGP; TFi; TOF; TrCP; WeW-3

My Soul Thirsteth for God. William Cowper. TrCP *Fr.* Olney Hymns.

My soul, thy love is dear: 'twas thought a good. Epigram. Francis Quarles. OAEL-1 *Fr.* Emblems.

My soul. . . , turn we to survey. Oliver Goldsmith. FHYEP *Fr.* The Travel[l]er; or, A Prospect of Society.

My Soul Wanders About. Amir Gilbo'a, *Hebrew.* IP, *tr. by* Chyet, Stanley and Warren Bargad; IP, *tr. by* Warren Bargad *and* Stanley F. Chyet

My Soul, Weigh Not Thy Life. Leonard Swain. AH

My soul, what's lighter than a feather? Wind. Francis Quarles. FaBoEE

My Soul Would Fain Indulge a Hope. Joseph Steward. AH

My soule a world is by Contraccion. William Alabaster. ESCV *Fr.* Divine Meditations.

My Soule is like a Bird; my Flesh, the Cage. Francis Quarles. ESCV *Fr.* Emblems.

My Spanish isn't enough. Elena. Pat Mora. UnSA

My specialty is living said. E. E. Cummings. NOBA

My Spectre around me night & day. William Blake. OAEL-2

My Spirit. Thomas Traherne. GeHe

My spirit and flesh, parting now. At the End. Richard Ryan. PBCIP

My spirit is too weak—mortality. On Seeing the Elgin Marbles. Keats. GSo; ImPo; NAEL-1; NIP-4

My spirit leans in joyousness tow'rd thine. Lines. "Ada." BlSi

My spirit leaps in joyousness tow'rd thine. "Ada." *See* Lines.

My spirit longeth for Thee. John Byrom. OxAEP-1

My spirit loves with thine in peace to dwell. (LL) The Prayer. Jones Very. APN-1; OxBA; PAR; TrCP

My spirit to yours dear brother. To Him That Was Crucified. Walt Whitman. ChIV-2

My spirit will not haunt the mound. Thomas Hardy. FaBoVe; MoBrPo; OBNC

("In backward days.") (LL) OxBSn

My Spirit's Complement. Henrietta Cordelia Ray. AAP; CBWP-3

My spotless love hovers, with purest wings. The Most Unloving One. Samuel Daniel. OBEV *Fr.* To Delia.

My spouse, Chunaychunay. *Unknown, Quechua (Peru).* BoWoP, *tr. by* W. S. Merwin

My Spring Thing. Everett Hoagland. BPo

My Springs. Sidney Lanier. UnPo

My spririt grieves. (LL) Beloved, my glory in thee is not ceased. "Michael Field." VWP

My star, start-gazing?—If only I could be. Aster. Plato, *Greek.* GrAn, *tr. by* Peter Jay

My steadfast love! Eibhlin Dubh O'Connell. NOIV, *tr. by* Thomas Kinsella *Fr.* The Lament for Art O Laoghaire.

My Stearine Candles. James Henry. NOBVV

My stick fingers click with a snicker. Player Piano. John Updike. PFE; Poetr; WeW-3

My stiff-spread arms / Break into sudden gesture. John Gould Fletcher. *Fr.* Irradiations. MoAmPo

My stock has gone down and my tailor has sent. A Companion's Progress. Paul Laurence Dunbar. GT

My stock lies dead, and no increase. Grace. George Herbert. ChIV-1; GeHe

My stocking's where. David McCord. PChr *Fr.* A Christmas Package.

My stomach is of many minds. Stomach. Kathleen Norris. OBAL

My Stone-Age self still scorn. Stubborn. Ruth Fainlight. CMAP

My Story. Carla Harryman. PmAP

My story would have been longer. (LL) Three wise men of Gotham. Mother Goose. CBNP; FaBoBe; OxNR; ReMoGo; Spl

My straw sandal stamping the first print in it. (LL) *Keng-tzu* (1180), First Month, Fifth Day, Dawn. Yang Wan-li, *Chinese.* CoBCP, *tr. by* Burton Watson

My straying thoughts, reduced stay. Song. Anne Collins. WPE

My Students. Lisa Lewis. PUP-19

My Students Catch Me Dancing. Leslie Adrienne Miller. CMAP

My students look at me expectantly. The Mountain. Louise Glück. NoAM

My students, you? What students I must teach! To Some Students Caught Nodding in Class. Nguyễn Khuyến, *Vietnamese.* AVP, *tr. by* Huỳnh Sanh Thông

My suite is just, just lord to my suite hark, *par. by* Sir Philip Sidney. Psalm 17. Bible, *O.T.* OBVE *Fr.* Psalms.

My sun has set, I dwell. Despised and Rejected. Christina Rossetti.

My Sun, / You smile at the granite of Milton. The Street of Named Houses. Robert David Cohen. NYBP

My sunlight came pre-packaged. Nomen. Naomi Long Madgett. BlSi; MoLi

My supermarket is bigger than your supermarket. That's. Supermarket. Peter Meinke. PBCAP

My sweet did sweetly sleep. Stolen Pleasure. William Drummond, of Hawthornden. EnLoPo

My sweet-faced, tattle-tale brother was born blind. The Twins. Mona Van Duyn. VCAP

My Sweet Gazelle! Immanuel di Roma, *Italian.* TrJP

My sweet old etcetera. E. E. Cummings. AmPP; CMoP; HeIP-4; InPS-3; OBAL; OBWP; OxBA; PeFWW

My Sweet Sweeting. *Unknown.* CH

"My sweetest Dorothy," said John. Dorothy's Dower. Phoebe Cary. PAR

My sweetest Elpis. Letter from Ephesos. Rufinus, *Greek.* GrAn, *tr. by* Alan Marshfield

My sweetest Lesbia, let us live and love. Carmen 5. Catullus, *Latin.* AAS; AWP; EBEV; GBL; HAP; HeIP-4; InPS-3; NAEL-1; NoP-4; NoSic; OAEL-1; OBCVT; OBVE; PoE; PoRA; SCGP; TFi; WeW-3, *tr. by* Thomas Campion

My Sweetheart's Dainty Lips. Judah Halevi, *Hebrew.* TrJP, *tr. by* Emma Lazarus

My Sweetie's a Mule in the Mine. *Unknown.* AmFP

My swirling wants. Your frozen lips. A Valediction Forbidding Mourning. Adrienne Rich. NAAL-2; NoAM; NoP-4

My sword I shook. The Sword. Abu Bakr, *Arabic.* TTY, *tr. by* A. J. Arberry

My tailor is against parting. Against Parting. Natan Zach, *Hebrew.* HP; PoSu, *tr. by* Peter Everwine *and* Shulamit Yasny-Starkman

My tale had been longer. Mother Goose. *See* Three wise men of Gotham.

My Talk with an Elegant Man. Kevin Walker. BAP-94

My Task. Maude Louise Ray. PWR

My tea is nearly ready and the sun has left the sky. The Lamplighter. Robert Louis Stevenson. EBVV; OxBChV

My teachers are dead men. I was too young. Autopsy. Arthur Nortje. HBAPE

My tears were Orion's splendor with sextuple suns. Tears. Dame Edith Sitwell. CMoP

My temples throb, my pulses boil. To Minerva. Thomas Hood. NBLV; NOBL; OxBoLi; PeLV

My tender parents brought me here. The Wexford Girl. *Unknown.* AmFP

My Tenth Birthday. Robert Adamson. BMAP

My Thing from Outer Space. James Kirkup. SpW

My Thirty Years. Juan Fransico Manzano, *Spanish.* TTY, *tr. by* Oliver Cobarn *and* Ursula Lehrburger

My thought awaked me with Thy Name. Meditation on Communion with God. Judah Halevi, *Hebrew.* TrJP, *tr. by* Solomon Solis-Cohen

My thought is caught in the eyes of love. Entanglement. Francis Sparshott. MoCV

My thoughts. Bullion. Amy Lowell. CPO

My thoughts are as a garden-plot, that knows. Thy Garden. Don Allen Johnson, *Arabic.* AWP, *tr. by* Dulcie L. Smith

My thoughts are at a banquet; for the deed. The Changeling. Thomas Middleton. FaBoSe

My Thoughts Are Not Your Thoughts. Bible, *O.T.* TrJP *Fr.* Isaiah.

My thoughts are of thee love though thou thinkest not of me. Song—Molly Magee. John Clare. EnVR

My thoughts are winged with hopes. Sir Walter Ralegh. GBL

My thoughts are with a boat. Hitomaro, *Japanese.* TAL, *tr. by* Arthur Waley

My Thoughts Do Harbour. Shakespeare. CTC *Fr.* The Two Gentlemen of Verona.

My thoughts flow in streams around this tower. Liu E. *Fr.* On the Fifteenth Day of the Eighth Month: Watching a Rainstorm from a Tower in Seoul. CoBLCP, *tr. by* Jonathan Chaves

My thoughts hold mortal[l] strife. Madrigal. William Drummond, of Hawthornden. GTBS-P; NOBE; NOSC; OBEV; OxBSP

My thoughts impelled me to the resting place. Elegy. Moses ibn Ezra, *Hebrew.* TrJP, *tr. by* Emma Lazarus

My thoughts, like sailors becalmed in Cape Town harbor. Sailor's Harbor. Henry Reed. MoBrPo

My thoughts, my grief! are without strength. A Poem Written in Time of Trouble by an Irish Priest Who Had Taken Orders in France. *Unknown, Irish.* OBMV, *tr. by* Lady Augusta Gregory

My Thread. Dovid Hofshteyn, *Yiddish.* TrJP, *tr. by* Joseph Leftwich

My three sisters are sitting. Women. Adrienne Rich. NMM-2; TRP

My Three Wives. *Unknown, after* Etienne Pasquier. FaBoEE

My throats / a hungry saxophone. Ohnedaruth. Angela Jackson. SeSe

My tidings for you: the stag bells. Summer Is Gone. *Unknown, Old Irish.* FaBoCh, *tr. by* Kuno Meyer

My time he said was not my own. Private But Sulphurous. Tom Matthews. PNI

My Times Are in Thy Hand. Anna L. Waring. PWR

My time's too short, your highness. It was I. Jean Racine, *French.* EP, *tr. by* Robert Lowell

My Toilette, Patches, all the World, Adieu! (LL) Saturday: The Small-Pox. Lady Mary Wortley Montagu. BWW; ECWP; NOEC; WPE

My tongue paints a path of fire. Eugene B. Redmond. ISC

My tongue-tied Muse in manners holds her still. Sonnet 85. Shakespeare. Son *Fr.* Sonnets.

My Tortoise. Stevie Smith. PeP

My towers at last! Herman Melville. Conrad Potter Aiken. NoAM; TAP

My towers at last! these rovings end. The Return of the Sire de Nesle *A.D. 16.* Herman Melville. NOBA

My townspeople, beyond in the great world. Gulls. William Carlos Williams. OxBA

My Toys. Lilian McCrea. BoTP

My trade takes me frequently into decaying houses. From a Museum Man's Album. John Hewitt. OxBTC

My traveling provisions are short, and won't see me through. Sufi Quatrain. Rabi'a bint Isma'il of Syria, *Arabic.* WPOW, *tr. by* Deirdre Lashgari

My treadmill memory draws from you yet. (LL) Crystals like Blood. "Hugh MacDiarmid." HAP; RB

My Triumph. John Greenleaf Whittier. APN-1; NOBA

My Triumph lasted till the Drums. Emily Dickinson. APN-2; OBWP

My trouble / is that I have the spirit of Gertrude Stein. Diane Wakoski. NALW

My true love breathed her latest breath. The Murderer. Stevie Smith. FaBoWP; OxBSP

My True Love Hath My Heart. Naomi Mitchison. LW

My True Love Hath My Heart. Marcel Proust, *French.* LBC, *tr. by* Charles Kenneth Michael Scott Moncrieff

My true love hath my heart and I have hers. Strugnell's Bargain. Wendy Cope. UV

My True Love Hath My Heart and I Have His. Mary Elizabeth Coleridge. BoLoP

My true love hath my heart and I have his. Patricia Stockbridge. UV

My true love hath my heart and I have his. (LL) The Bargain. Sir Philip Sidney. AWP; BoLoP; CH; EBEvV; FaBoBe; GBL; GTBS-P; NOBE; NoSic; OBEV; OxAEP-1; PoE; PoEL-1; SCGP; SiPS; TFi; UV

My true love makes me happy. Beatrice, Countess de Die, *Provençal.* WPOW, *tr. by* Doris Earnshaw

My Trundle Bed. J. G. Baker. BLPA; FaBoBe

My TV came down with a chill. Willard R. Espy. TLR

My twentieth summer I got a job in Door Locks. Assembler. Debra Allbery. PBCAP

My twin brother swears that at age thirteen. The Old Testament. Philip Levine. PUP-18

My uncle. Tanka. Kitahara Hakushū, *Japanese.* MJT, *tr. by* Makoto Ueda

My uncle, a craftsman of hammers and wood. Willy Lyons. James Wright. HCAP; NNaP; PoE

My Uncle Ben, who's been. Kiph. Walter De la Mare. CBNP

My Uncle Dan's an inventor, you may think. Ted Hughes. FuFo

My Uncle from the realms of Death. Le Revenant. Stevie Smith. OxBSn

My uncle is buried at Sheik Bad'r. Luxury. Yehuda Amichai, *Hebrew.* PoSu, *tr. by* Assia Gutmann

My Uncle Jehoshaphat. Laura Elizabeth Richards. OxBChV

My Uncle Paul of Pimlico. Mervyn Laurence Peake. OTCP

My uncle sleeps in the image of death. Lawrence Durrell. FaBoMo *Fr.* Death of General Uncebunke, The; a Biography in Little.

My uncle was Sabbath crazed. Ichthycide. Joe Rosenblatt. NOBC

My urine smells of smoke. Desert in the Sea. Brian Swann. AmPA

My valiant helper, a small-sized tiger. To Mrs. Professor in Defense of My Cat's Honor and Not Only. Czeslaw Milosz, *Polish.* PC, *tr. by* Robert Hass

My Village Home. Lu Yu, *Chinese.* CoBCP, *tr. by* Burton Watson

My Voice. Oscar Wilde. EBVV

My voice is sweeter than the lute. The Siren. "Violet Fane." VWP

My voice is the measure of my life. The Revolution of the Aged. Njabulo S. Ndebele. PeSAV

My voice is thin I stand in the shower what's that I ask. The Shower. Linda Smukler. GLP

My voice rings down through thousands of years. Sappho's Reply. Rita Mae Brown. OxWW

My voice to thee it self extreamly strayning. Voce mea ad Dominum Psalm 142. Mary Sidney Herbert, Countess of Pembroke. PBRV

My Wage. Jessie Belle Rittenhouse. BLPA; PoToHe

My walls outside must have some flowers. Truly Great. W. H. Davies. OBMV

My wardrobe door will not stay closed these days. The Presence. Medbh McGuckian. PNI

My way is in the sand flowing, *Author's own English vers. of his* "Je suis ce cours de sable qui glisse." Samuel Beckett. NOIV

My way is not thy way, and thine is not mine. D. H. Lawrence. CMoP

My Way's Cloudy. *Unknown.* CrDW

My wealth's a burly spear and brand. Song of Hybrias the Cretan. Hybrias The Cretan, *Greek.* OBCVT, *tr. by* Thomas Campbell

My wearied bark, O let it now be crowned! To Crown[e] It. Robert Herrick. CaPo

My weary eyes shall close like folding flowers in sleep. (LL) The Columbine. Jones Very. ColAP; GSo; PAR

My wee wee man was clean awa'. (LL) The Wee Wee Man. *Unknown.* CH; EBEV; ESPB; FaBoCh; OAEL-1; OxBB

My well-beloved was stripped. Knowing my whim. The Jewels. Charles Baudelaire, *French.* BoLoP; LoP, *tr. by* Roy Campbell

My well-dressed friend. What She Said to Her Girl Friend, after a Tryst at Night (Which Turned Out to Be a Fiasco). Kapilar, *Tamil.* PLW, *tr. by* A. K. Ramanujan

My Wellington boots go. Boots and Shoes. Lilian McCrea. BoTP

My whining lover, what needs all. Against Absence. Sir John Suckling. CaPo; CavPo

My whiskey is / a tough way of life. Drink. William Carlos Williams. OxBA

My white canoe, like the silvery air. The Camp of Souls. Isabella Valancy Crawford. NOBC

My white hair of thirty thousand feet. Li Po. SuSp, *tr. by* Irving Lo *Fr.* Songs of Ch'iu-p'u.

My whole eye was sunset red. Eye and Tooth. Robert Lowell. NAAL-2

My whole family floats out on the lake. Yüan Mei. *Fr.* Moments of Fullfillment—mdash;Writing Down Miscellaneous. CoBLCP, *tr. by* Jonathan Chaves

My whole life has been a chronology of—changes. For Malcolm: After Mecca. Gerald William Barrax. PoBA

My whole life has led me here. Woolworth's. Donald Hall. OBCoV

My Wicked Uncle. Derek Mahon. OxBC

My Wife. Nikolai Ivanovich Glazkov, *Russian.* TCRP, *tr. by* Daniel Weissbort

My wife and children were waiting for ice cream. Jaan Kaplinski, *Estonian.* BLT, *tr. by* Jaan Kaplinski, Sam Hamill (b. 1942) *and* Riina Tamm

My wife and I have asked a crowd of craps. Vers de Société. Philip Larkin. FP; PeLV

My wife and I lived all alone. Ballad of the Despairing Husband. Robert Creeley. NeAP; OBAL; RaBo

My wife and I lived [or live] all alone. Little Brown Jug. Joseph E. Winner. OBAL

My wife broke a dollar tube of perfume. The Problem. Paul Blackburn. NeAP

My wife complains I pray no more. Al-Ifriqi al-Mutayyam, *Arabic.* ArPe, *tr. by* Omar S. Pound

My wife is left-handed. For Hettie. Imamu Amiri Baraka. GT; NOBA; NeAP

My Wife Is My Shirt. Stephen Tropp. InPK-6

My wife sits reading in a garden chair. October. Barry Spacks. PoA

My wife still asleep. Gary Hotham. HA

My wife went away, left me. Katda, *Tlingit Indian.* STP, *tr. by* James Koller

My wife whose hair is a brush fire. Free Union. André Breton, *French.* PFTM; TTTS, *tr. by* David Antin

My wife with eyes that are the equal of water and air and earth and fire. (LL) Free Union. André Breton, *French.* PFTM; TTTS, *tr. by* David Antin

My wife, you claim that French is mere child's play. No, Thank You! Trần Tế Xu'ọng, *Vietnamese.* AVP, *tr. by* Huỳnh Sanh Thông

My window, framed in pear-tree bloom. Villeggiature. Edith Nesbit. LW; NOBVV; OxBSn; PEW

My window looks upon a world grown gray. Midwinter. Margaret E. Bruner. PoToHe

My window opens out into the trees. Solace. Clarissa Scott Delany. PoBA

My window shook all night in Camden Town. Responsibilities. Anthony Cronin. PBCIP

My windows now are giant drops of dew. A Bright Day. W. H. Davies. OBWVE

My Winsome Dear. Robert Fergusson. VGW *Fr.* Leith Races.

My Winter Past. Eldon Grier. NOBC

My wish for my land is that ladies be beautiful. Randolph Stow. NOBAu

My wish for you / that God should make your love. Rabi'a of Balkh, *Farsi.* WPOW, *tr. by* Deirdre Lashgari

My wives do not write. Memory. Michael Hamburger. OxBTC

My woman leaves to visit her brothers. Practicing Death Songs. Adrian C. Louis. PUP-19

My wont is not to write in verse. An Imprisoned Recusant Writes to His Wife. Francis Tregian. NoSic

My Words. William Hathaway. EOEF

My words and thoughts do both express this notion. Our Life Is Hid with Christ in God. George Herbert. ChIV-2; OAEL-1

My words I know do well set forth my mind. Sonnet 44. Sir Philip Sidney. *Fr.* Astrophil and Stella. AAS; SiPS

My world has been laid low, and the wind blows. Quatrain without Sparrows, Helpful Bells or Hope. Thomas McCarthy. PBCIP

My worries: several strands of white hair. Written upon Returning to the Mountains. Ku K'uang, *Chinese.* SuSp, *tr. by* Irving Y. Lo

My worthy [*or* woorthy] Lord, I pray you wonder not. Gascoigne's Woodmanship. George Gascoigne. AAS; CABP; NoSic; PBRV; PoEL-1

My years on earth were short, but long for me. On a Shipmate, Pero Moniz, Dying at Sea. Luis de Camões, *Portuguese.* PeSAV, *tr. by* Roy Campbell

My Yellow Straw Hat. Lessie Jones Little. TLR

My young love said to me, "My brothers won't mind." She Moved through the Fair. Padraic Colum. BIrV; NOIV

My young man's a Cornishman. Charles Causley. NTP

My young mother, her face narrow. Jane Cooper. FaBoWP; MDDM

My younger brother is stronger than me. Igor Shklyarevsky, *Russian.* TCRP, *tr. by* Lubov Yakovleva

Myall in Prison, The. Mary Gilmore. CBAP

Mycilla dyes her locks, 'tis said. On an Old Woman. Lucilius, *Greek.* AWP; PFE, *tr. by* William Cowper

Mye love toke skorne my servise to retaine. Sir Thomas Wyatt. AAS

Myfanwy. John Betjeman. BoLoP

Myn owne John poyntz sins ye delight to know. Sir Thomas Wyatt. PBRV *Fr.* Satires.

  ("Mine own John Poins, since ye delight to know.") NoP-4

  (Of the Courtier's Life.)

  ("Thou shalt be judge how I do spend my time.") (LL) NoP-4

  ("Thou shalt be Judge how I do spend my tyme.") (LL) PBRV

Mynstrelles Songe: "Angelles bee wrogte to bee of neidher kynde." Thomas Chatterton. EnLoPo *Fr.* Aella; a Tragycal Enterlude.

Mynstrelle's Songe ("O! synge untoe mie roundelaie"). Thomas Chatterton. EnLoPo; NOEC; OxAEP-1 *Fr.* Aella; a Tragycal Enterlude.

  (Minstrel's Song.) HAP; SCGP

  (Mynstrelles Songe.) CABP

  ("O! synge untoe mie roundelaie.") CABP

  ("Thos the damfelle epake, and dyed.") (LL) CABP

Myra. Greville Fulke. NOBE; OBEV *Fr.* Caelica.

  ("I with whose colors *Myra* drest her head.") PBRV

  ("*No man can print a kisse, lines may deceive.*") (LL) PBRV

  (To Myra.)

Myriad cicadas seethe and buzz in the setting sun. Summer. Fan Ch'eng-ta. SuSp, *tr. by* Irving Y. Lo *Fr.* Seasonal Poems on Fields and Gardens.

Myriad times, Ptolemy, your father, myriad times. Antipater of Sidon. HePo, *tr. by* Barbara Hughes Fowler *Fr.* Epigrams.

Myriads and myriads plumed their glittering wings. Leaves. Katharine Tynan. BoTP

Myrres vous y. John Skelton. *See* Upon a Dead Man's Head.

Myrtle. John Ashbery. BAP-94

Myrtle bush grew shady, The. Jealousy. Mary Elizabeth Coleridge. CH; EnLoPo; LW; OBNC; WPE

Myrtle for Two. Horace. *See* Simplicity.

Mysel I will cast in. (LL) Lady Maisry ("The Young lords o' the north country"). *Unknown.* ESPB; OxBB

Myself. Walter De la Mare. GaP

Myself. E. A. Guest. BLPA

Myself. Adah Isaacs Menken. CBWP-1

Myself. *Unknown.* PWR

Myself. Walt Whitman. *See* Song of Myself.

Myself am Hang the buccaneer. The Flying Fish. John Gray. NOBVV

Myself and Curtis Dean are seniors together. Double Date. Lincoln Kirstein. PeLV

Myself I saw in the window reflected. (LL) Starting from San Francisco. Lawrence Ferlinghetti. GM

Myself I Sing. George Oppen. FTOS

Myself made otherwise by all his pain. (LL) Baby Villon. Philip Levine. CoAP; WeT

Myself unto myself will give. The Holy Office. James Joyce. FaBoTw; NoAM; OxBTC

Myself When I Am Real. Al Young. PoBA

Myself When Young. Tom Donnelly. BXAP

Myself when young did eagerly frequent. Omar Khayyám. TRP *Fr.* The Rubáiyát of Omar Khayyám [of Naishápúr]. AWP; EBVV; FaBoBe; FaPoR; HAP; NAEL-2; PoEL-5

Myself when young did eagerly frequent. 27. Edward Fitzgerald. CABP

Myselves / The grievers. Ceremony after a Fire Raid. Dylan Thomas. AF; CMoP

Mysteries of Caesar, The. Anthony Hecht. NoP-4

Mysteries of Life. Mary E. Tucker. CBWP-1

Mysteries of Udolpho, The. Ann Radcliffe.
    Rondeau: "Soft as yon silver ray that sleeps." Ro

Mysteries Remain, The. Hilda Doolittle. NOBA; TAP; VGW; WPOW

Mysteries Revealed after Death. John Reynolds. NOEC *Fr.* Death's Vision.

Mysterious Cat, The. Vachel Lindsay. OBCA

Mysterious East. William Cole. OBAL

Mysterious Maps, The. Mark Strand. BAP-94

Mysterious Night! when our first parent knew. To Night. Joseph Blanco White. EBEV; GSo; OBEV; OxAEP-2; Son

Mysterious Nothing! how shall I define. Sonnet to Nothing. Thomas Beck. NOBRP

Mysterious Presence! Source of All. Seth Curtis Beach. AH

Mysterious shapes, with wands of joy and pain. Dreams. Helen Hunt Jackson. APN-2

Mystery, The. Amergin, *Irish.* TIRV, tr. by Douglas Hyde

Mystery, The. Paul Laurence Dunbar. APN-2

Mystery, The. Ralph Hodgson. CH; MoBrPo

Mystery, The. David Wevill. IFJA

Mystery. "Yehoash," *Yiddish.* TrJP, tr. by Marie Syrkin

'Mystery Boy' Looks for Kin in Nashville. Robert Earl Hayden. LCAP-2; NoAM; NoP 4; PoE

Mystery Corset, The. André Breton, *French.* PFTM, tr. by Pierre Joris

Mystery of Emily Dickinson, The. Marvin Bell. CMAP

Mystery of Life, The. John Gambold. NOEC

Mystery of the Caves, The. Michael Waters. CMAP

Mystery of the Charity of Charles Péguy, The. Geoffrey Hill.
    "Dear lords of life, stump-toothed, with ragged breath." DiPo

Mystery Ships, The. Ronald Arthur Hopwood. NSI

Mystery Story. Howard Nemerov. NBLV

Mystery Train: A Sequence. David Wojahn.
    Assassination of John Lennon as Depicted by the Madame Tussaud Wax Museum, Niagara Falls, Ontario, 1987, The. NAmP90; PBCAP
    At Graceland with a Six Year Old, 1985. PBCAP
    Buddy Holly Watching *Rebel Without a Cause*, Lubbock, Texas, 1956. PBCAP
    Colorizing: Turner Broadcasting Enterprises, Computer Graphics Division, Burbank, California, 1987. PBCAP
    Custom Job: Hank Williams, Jr., and the Death Car, 1958. PBCAP
    Fab Four Tour Deutschland: Hamburg, 1961. PBCAP
    Homage: Light from the Hall. PBCAP
    Matins: James Brown and His Famous Flames Tour the South, 1958. NAmP90; PBCAP
    "Mystery Train" Janis Joplin Leaves Port Arthur for Points West, 1964. GM; PBCAP
    Tattoo, Corazon: Ritchie Valens, 1959. PBCAP
    Trashmen Shaking Hands with Hubert Humphrey at the Opening of Apache Plaza Shopping Center, Suburban Minneapolis, August 1963, The. PBCAP
    Woody Guthrie Visited by Bob Dylan: Brooklyn State Hospital, New York, 1961. PBCAP

Mystic. D. H. Lawrence. BLT

Mystic. Sylvia Plath. NYBP

Mystic and Cavalier. Lionel Pigot Johnson. ADE; MoBrPo
    ("To make with you mine home.") (LL) ADE

Mystic Drum, The. Gabriel Okara. TTY

Mystic finishes in time, The. The Insomniacs. Adrienne Rich. NYBP

Mystic in the morning, half asleep, A. Bachelor. William Meredith. NoAM

Mystic Magi, The. Robert Stephen Hawker. OBCP

Mystic River. John Ciardi. NYBP

Mystical strains unheard. A Clymène. Paul Verlaine. AWP, tr. by Arthur Symons

Mysticism, but let us have no words. Conrad Potter Aiken. *Fr.* Time in the Rock [or, Preludes to Definition]. VGW

Mystique. David Ignatow. PFE

Myth, The. Edwin Muir. CMoP

Myth. Muriel Rukeyser. CrSp; FaBoWP; NALW; NNaP

Myth lilies. A smog-edge sky blurs his eyes. Crow's Way. Duane Niatum. CDW

Myth on Mediterranean Beach: Aphrodite as Logos. Robert Penn Warren. HAP

Mythic Fragment. Louise Glück. NMM-2; NoAM

Mythical Journey, The. Edwin Muir. NoAM; OxBS

Mythistorima. George Seferis, *Greek.*
    "And if the soul." GrIP
    "Our country is closed in [enclosed], all mountains." GrIP

Mythological Beast. Howard Nemerov. *Fr.* Epigrams. OBAL

Mythological Sonnets. Roy Fuller.
    "How startling to find the portraits of the gods." Son
    "Suns in a skein, the uncut stones of night." GTBS-P
    There Actually Stood. Son
    Well Now, the Virgin. Son

Mythology. Lawrence Durrell. OxBTC

Mythology. Marilyn Hacker. NoAM

Mythology. Earle Thompson. HATNAP

Mythos of Samuel Huntsman, The. Hyam Plutzik. LiTM

Myths. Guy Butler. PeSA

Myths and Texts. Gary Snyder.
    Burning. NeAP; PoM
    John Muir on Mt. Ritter. NOBA
    Second Shaman Song. NOBA; NeAP; PoM
    Text, The. NAAL-2

Myxomatosis. Philip Larkin. CMoP; MoP; NoAM; PFE

N

N. Hugh Seidman. PoA

N blo Win. Writing through a Text by Chris Mann. John Cage. EOEF

N. N. Tries to Remember the Words of a Prayer. Stanislaw Baranczak, *Polish.* GI, tr. by Kevin Windle

N T. Charles Wesley. ChIV-2

Na Audiart. Ezra Pound. MeMAP

Naaman's Song. Rudyard Kipling. ChIV-1

Naayawa Taawi. Wendy Rose. UnSA

Nabara, The. C. Day Lewis. EBNV; OBNV

Nadar. Richard Howard. GS

Nae man wha loves the lawland tongue. The Makar. William Soutar. FaBoTC; OxBS

Nahum 2.10. Francis Quarles. ChIV-1

Naiad changes / Quick as these. (LL) Gardener Janus Catches a Naiad. Dame Edith Sitwell. MoBrPo; OBGa

Naiad, hid beneath the bank. Dirge. William Johnson Cory. OBNC

Nail, The. Vasco [or Vasko] Popa. PoSu *Fr.* Games. RB, tr. by Anne Pennington

Nailed like the illegible bronze on the futureless future. (LL) Fishnet. Robert Lowell. HCAP; VCAP

Nails. Gary Gildner. PBCAP; TAP

Nailsworth Hill. W. H. Davies. OTCP

Naima. Edward Kamau Brathwaite. HCP

Naive Invocation. David Rivard. NAmP90

Naïve young lady of Bude, A. Limerick. C. Chevallier. PeLi

Naïve young lady of Cork, A. Limerick. Reg Yearley. PeLi

Naked and knowing my heart my love had left on. The Jewels. Charles Baudelaire, *French.* NAWM-2, tr. by David Paul; BoLoP, tr. by Roy Campbell

Naked and the Nude, The. Robert Graves. EP; NYBP; SoSe-8

Naked Ape, The. John Updike. EOEF

Naked as from the earth we came. Submission to Afflictive Providences. Isaac Watts. NOCV

Naked blond head. Peace. Jonetta Barras. ISC

Naked earth is warm with Spring, The. Into Battle. Julian Grenfell. FaPoR; OBEV; OBMV; OBWP; OxBTC; PeFWW; PoFWW

Naked Girl and Mirror. Judith Wright. NALW

Naked Girl Swimming, A. Arthur Rex Dugard Fairburn. PeNZ

Naked, he lies in the blinded room. Soledad. Robert Earl Hayden. MoNo; NAAAL

Naked house, a naked moor, A. The House Beautiful. Robert Louis Stevenson. NOBE

Naked I came, naked I leave the scene. Epitaph for Someone or Other. James Vincent Cunningham. OBAL; PFE; TRP; VGW *Fr.* Five Epigrams.

Naked I came when I began to be. Nudus Redibo. Thomas Flatman. OxBSP

Naked I saw thee. Ideal. Padraic Pearse, *Modern Irish.* AWP, *tr. by* Thomas Macdonagh

Naked I saw thee. Renunciation. Padraic Pearse, *Irish.* NOIV, *tr. by the author*

Naked in Borneo. May Swenson. NYBP

Naked is the earth. Poem. Antonio Machado Ruiz, *Spanish.* AWP, *tr. by* John Dos Passos

Naked Jaina monk, A. Pleasure. A. K. Ramanujan. VCWP

Naked Land, The. Kenneth Patchen. SPE

Naked out of the dark we came. Kenneth Rexroth. FaBoEE

Naked Seed, The. C. S. Lewis. TrCP

Naked she lay, clasped in my longing arms. The Imperfect Enjoyment. John Wilmot, 2d Earl of Rochester. BoLoP; EP

Naked sun—a yellow sun—, A. Omen. Birago Diop, *French.* NegPo, *tr. by* Ellen Conroy Kennedy

Naked to the naked moon. (LL) In Bertram's Garden. Donald Justice. BoLoP; MT; SAGP; VGW

Naked Town, A. Zbigniew Herbert, *Polish.* CEEP, *tr. by* Czesw Milosz

Naked War. Michael Heffernan. BXAP

Naked warmth of you is still, The. Philodemus, *Greek.* GrAn, *tr. by* William Moebius

Naked woman and a dead dwarf, A. Stephen Crane. APN-2

Naked woman, black woman. Black Woman. Léopold Sédar Senghor, *French.* TTY, *tr. by* Anne Atik

Naked you have [*or* you've have] odds enough of any man. (LL) The Damp[e]. Donne. NOSC; SeCP

Nam. Mike Lowery. Poetsp

Namaqualand after Rain. William Plomer. PeSAV

Namby-Pamby. Henry Carey. CBNP; NOEC; OBSV; UV

Namby-Pamby; or, A Panegyric on the New Versification. Henry Carey. NOEC; OBSV

Name. Alan Davies.
"Personality syndrome, The." FTOS

Name, A. Aleksandr Samsonovich Ginger, *Russian.* TCRP, *tr. by* Albert C. Todd

Name Alissa, The. In Which Names. Ilse Aichinger, *German.* AF, *tr. by* Allen H. Chappel

Name all the shadows astride & back from the street. Take the Toys from the Boys. Ulli Freer. NBrP

Name for All, A. Hart Crane. VGW

Name Giveaway. Phillip William George. VoR

Name in block letters *None that signifie.* A Form of Epitaph. Laurence Whistler. GTBS-P

Name is hard, The. On the 25th Anniversary of the Liberation of Auschwitz. Eli W. Mandel. NOBC

Name not to be worn out with the years, A. (LL) Shades of Callimachus, Coan ghosts of Philetas. Ezra Pound. CMoP; HAP; NOBA; OBVE; OxBA

Name of "Gêlert's Grave.," The. (LL) Beth Gêlert; or, The Grave of the Greyhound. William Robert Spencer. BLPA; EBNV; OBNV

Name—of it—is "Autumn," The. Name—of it—is "Autumn," The. Emily Dickinson. InPS-3; NCAP

Name of Jesus, The. John Newton. ECEV; NOEC
"Jesus! my Shepherd, Husband, Friend."

Name of my heroine, simply "Rose." The Tale of a Pony. Bret Harte. OBNV

Name of Our Country, The. Dennis Schmitz. AmPA

Name of the product I tested is "Life," The. A Consumer's Report. Peter Porter. NOBL; NTP; NoP-4

Name of this poem is, The. Cameo No. II. June Jordan. BPo

Name only once. America. Kofi Awoonor. HBAPE

Name Poem. A. J. Seymour. HCP

Name something else. (LL) The Family Is All There Is. Pattiann Rogers. NIP-4; PuP-14

Name, you might think, The. French Horn. Robin Behn. PUP-18

Nameless. Natan Zach, *Hebrew.* IP, *tr. by* Warren Bargad *and* Stanley F. Chyet

Nameless Doon [*or* Dun], The. William Larminie. BIrV

Nameless Epitaph, A. Matthew Arnold. FaBoEE

Nameless Journey. Leah Goldberg, *Hebrew.*
"My room is so small." BoWoP, *tr. by* Ramah Commanday

Nameless One, A. Margaret Avison. HeIP-4; NOBC

Nameless One, The. James Clarence Mangan. BIrV; IIP; NOIV; OBEV

Nameless Ones, The. Conrad Potter Aiken. OxBA

Namelessness. Sangbyong Ch'on, *Korean.* CKP, *tr. by* Jaihiun Kim

Namelessness. David Wevill. IFJA

Names. Gerald Dawe. IIP; PNI

Names. Robert Earl Hayden. GT

Names. Jelaluddin Rumi, *Persian.* RaBo

Names and Order of the Books of the Old Testament, The. Thomas Russell. BLPA
(Books of the Old Testament, The.) ChIV-1

Names change, The. In Light of Time. Heather McHugh. CMAP

Names for everything I touch. The Hollow Thesaurus. Roger McDonald. BMAP; CBAP

Names in Monterchi: To Rachel. James Wright. NNaP

Names like Conger, Bridger, Rollins, Meeker, Berthoud. Mountain Men. Tom Clark. IFJA

Names of Georgian Women, The. Bella Akhatovna Akhmadulina, *Russian.* BoWoP, *tr. by* Stanley Noyes *and* Olga Carlisle

Names of Horses. Donald Hall. AFr; HAP; InPK-6; SoSe-8; TRP

Names of the dead, The. Eric Amann. HA

Names of the Hare, The. *Unknown, Middle English.* RB, *tr. by* Seamus Heaney

Names of the Humble, The. Les A. Murray. CBAP

Names of things, The—sparks! Resigning from a Job in a Defense Industry. Sandra McPherson. LCAP-2

Names will change. Election Time. Lamont B. Steptoe. UnSA

Naming Day, A. Odia Ofeimun. HBAPE; PBMAP

Naming of Cats is a difficult matter. T. S. Eliot. NBLV

Naming Of Parts. Henry Reed. EBEvV; HoPM; ImPo; InPS-3; MoBrPo; NOBE; OxBTC; PoRA; Poetr; RaBo; SoSe-8; TFi; UV; UnPo *Fr.* Lessons of the War. HeIP-4; OBWP
("For to-day we have naming of parts.") (LL) PFE
(Lessons of the War.) NoP-4
("Today we have naming of parts. Yesterday.") APAD; NoP-4; PoPoPo; SAGP

Naming of Private Parts. John Lloyd Williams. BXAP

Naming of the Beasts, The. Francis Sparshott. NOBC

Naming of Things, The. Bahinabai Chaudhari, *Marathi.* OMIP, *tr. by* Philip Engblomb *and* Jayant Karve

Naming Power. Wendy Rose. OxWW

Naming Souls. Uri Zvi Greenberg, *Hebrew.* PeFWW, *tr. by* Jon Silkin *and* Ezra Spicehandler

Naming the Animals. Anthony Hecht. ChIV-1

Naming the Fabrics. Julia Alvarez. FFC

Naming the Shells. Judith C. Root. CMAP

Naming the Unborn. Daniel Halpern. MoLi

Naming's over. Day is done. (LL) Adam's Task. John Hollander. APo; NoP-4

Nancy Dawson was so fine. *Unknown.* ReMoGo

Nancy Hanks. Rosemary Benét *and* Stephen Vincent Benét. NTCP

Nancy Hanks, Mother of Abraham Lincoln. Vachel Lindsay. CMoP

Nancy, the hogs don't know us. Mirror for the Barnyard. Jack Myers. AmPA

Nancy where art thou? Ezra Pound. *See* Canto 80.

Nane of them durst cum neir his Hald. (LL) Johnie Armstrang. *Unknown.* ESPB; IBB; OxBB

Nani. Alberto A. Ríos. SoSe-8; UnSA

Nani Worries about Her Father's Happiness in the Afterlife. Ana Castillo. MoLi

Nano's Song. Ben Jonson. *Fr.* Volpone. NAEL-1

Nansen. Gary Snyder. BB

Nantucket. William Carlos Williams. HAP; InPS-3; OxBA; TAP; TRP; WeW-3

Naomi. Gwendolyn Brooks. NAAL-2

Naomi and Ruth. Bible, *O.T.* TrJP *Fr.* Ruth.

Naomi (Omie) Wise. *Unknown.* AmFP

Napa, California. Ana Castillo. WPOW

Napalm: the word suspended by a thread. Twenty One Times. John Taggart. PT

Nape. Jane Epton Seale. CrSp

Napkin and Stone. Vernon Watkins. NYBP

Naples Again. Arthur Freeman. NYBP

Napoleon. Walter De la Mare. FaBoCh; FaBoTw; NOBE; RB; Spl

Napoleon. Miroslav Holub, *Czech.* PoSu, *tr. by* Káča Poláčková; ChAP, *tr. by* Kaca Polakova

Napoleon after Sedan. Rimbaud. FaBoPV; OBWP, *tr. by* Robert Lowell *Fr.* Eighteen-Seventy.

Napoli Again. Richard Hugo. AF; LCAP-2

Napolo has spoken: Death. The Messengers. Steve Chimombo. HBAPE

Nappy Edges (A Cross Country Sojourn). Ntozake Shange. BlSi; NAAAL

Narcissa. Gwendolyn Brooks. NTCP
("Anything at all.") (LL) CA

Narcissi look up like children, quickly and whitely, The. (LL) Among the Narcissi. Sylvia Plath. FaBoMo; RB; SCV

Narcissism / is an ugly fault. Antonio Machado Ruiz. RaBo, *tr. by* Robert Bly *Fr.* Moral Proverbs and Folk Songs.

Narcissist's eye is blue, fringed with white and covered, The. The Eye. Michael Benedikt. CoAmPo

Narcissus. Gerda Mayer. LW

Narcissus. Paul Valéry, *French.* AWP, *tr. by* Joseph T. Shipley

Narcissus and chrysanthemum. Ch'ien Ch'ien-i. *Fr.* In Lamplight, Watching My Wife Preparing a Flower Arrangement—Playfully Inscribing Four Poems. CoBLCP, *tr. by* Jonathan Chaves

Narcissus and Echo. Fred Chappell. MT

Narcissus in Camden. Helen Gray Cone. BXAP

Narcissus on the grassy Verdure lies. Ovid, *Latin.* OBCVT, *tr. by* Joseph Addison

Narcissus: To Himself. David Galler. PoA

Narcolepsy. Maureen Owen. TTTS

Narrative. Russell Atkins. GT; PoBA

Narrative. Elisabeth Eybers, *Afrikaans.* PeSA; PeSAV, *tr. by the author*

Narrative Hooper and L.D.O. Sestina with a Long Last Line, The. James Whitehead. HoPM

Narrative of the Life and Times of John Coltrane: Played by Himself, A. Michael S. Harper. MoNo; SeSe

Narrative of the Life of Frederick Douglass, an American Slave. Frederick Douglass. Parody, A. NAAL-1; NAAL-3; NAWM-2

Narrator, The. Milo De Angelis, *Italian.* NeIt, *tr. by* Lawrence Venuti

Narrator of folktales was boasting, A. Atomic Fairy Tale. Yury Kuznetsov, *Russian.* TCRP, *tr. by* Anatoly Liberman

NARRATOR: Suddenly someone wakes me. Still half-asleep, I see standing in front. Douglas Messerli. FTOS *Fr.* Along Without: A Fiction in Film for Poetry.

Narrow Fellow in the Grass, A. Emily Dickinson. APo; AmPP; BLT; BoWoP; CMoP; CTAV; ChAP; ClHu; ColAP; HAP; HeIP-4; HoPM; LiTM; MeMAP; NAAL-1; NAAL-3; NALW; NIP-4; NOBA; NTP; NoAM; NoP-4; OBCA; OBxA; PAR; PBMP; PoE; PoEL-5; PoLF; PoPoPo; Poetr; RB; SAmP; SoSe-8; TAP; TFi; TRP; WeW-3

Narrow glade unfolded, such as Spring, A. An Interview near Florence. Samuel Rogers. *Fr.* Italy. OBNC

Narrow Path, The. Norman Pritchard Henry, II. GT

Narrow Path into the Back Country. Diane Di Prima. NMM-2

Narrow Sea, The. Robert Graves. FaBoEE; FaBoMo

Narrow sickle of moon, A. Before Dawn. Alfonsas Nyka-Niliunas, *Lithuanian.* CEEP, *tr. by* Jonas Zdanys

Narrowing of knowledge to one window to a door, A. Elegy for William Soutar. William Montgomerie. OxBS

Narrowing sea embraces it forever, The. The Urumbula Song. *Unknown, Aranda.* CBAP, *tr. by* T. G. H. Strehlow

Narrows of Birth, The. William Everson. PoM

Nasal whine of power whips a new universe. Power. Hart Crane. MoAmPo *Fr.* Cape Hatteras. InPS-3; MoAmPo *Fr.* The Bridge. NAAL-2

Nashoba. Jim Barnes. *Fr.* Four Things Choctaw. HATNAP

Naskeag. Alfred Corn. VCAP

Naso lets none drinke in his glasse but he. A Monsieur Naso, verolè. Martial, *Latin.* OBCVT, *tr. by* Francis Davison

Nasturtium Scanned. Judith Rodriguez. BMAP

Nasty snake once bit a Cappadocian, A. Demodocus, *Greek.* GrAn, *tr. by* Peter Jay

Nasty surprise in a sandwich, A. God, A Poem. James Fenton. DiPo; NoAM; NoP-4; OBCoV

Natal Address to My Child, March 19th 1844, A. Eliza Ogilvy. VWP

Natal Hunters, The. Allen F. Gardiner. PeSAV

Natalya Nikolayevna Goncharov. Don Coles. NOBC

Nathan, no thought today. The Bratzlav Rabbi to His Scribe. Jacob Glatstein, *Yiddish.* TrJP, *tr. by* Jacob Sloan

Nathaniel, born Hathorne, you who set. The Secret. Suzanne Noguere. FFC

Nathaniel Lee to Sir Roger L'Estrange. Nathaniel Lee. FaBoEE

Nation. Charlie Cobb. PoBA

Nation is like our selves, together, The. The Nation Is Like Ouselves. Imamu Amiri Baraka. PmAP

Nation Is Like Ouselves, The. Imamu Amiri Baraka. PmAP

Nation of trees, drab green and desolate grey [*or* gray], A. Australia. Alec Derwent Hope. BMAP; NoAM; NoP-4

Nation Once Again, A. Thomas Osborne Davis. IIP; NOIV

Nation shattered, hills and streams remain, The. Spring Prospect. Tu Fu, *Chinese.* CoBCP, *tr. by* Burton Watson

Nation true to honor's cause, The. On the Great Western Canal of the State of New York. Philip Freneau. APN-1

Nation Wrapped in Stone, A. Roberta Hill Whiteman. BoWoP; CDW

National Anthem. Egbert Martin. PBCV

National Assessment. Connie Deanovich. WWSi

National Bird. N. Pichamurti, *Tamil.* OMIP, *tr. by* Rajagopal Parthasarathy

National Cemetery, Beaufort, South Carolina, The. Josephine D. Henderson Heard. CBWP-4

National Cold Storage Company contains, The. Harvey Shapiro. VGW; WeT

National Federation is a grand and glorious band, The. All We Ask Is Justice. Mrs. Henry Linden. CBWP-4

National Hero, The. Gojko Djogo, *German.* AF, *tr. by* Michael March *and* Dušan Puvaić

National Miner, The. *Unknown.* AmFP

National Painting, The. Joseph Rodman Drake. GS

National Painting [*or* Paintings], The. Fitz-Greene Halleck *and* Joseph Rodman Drake. APN-1 *Fr.* The Croaker Papers.

National Police Headquarters. Nicolás Guillén. PFTM, *tr. by* Vera M. Kutzinski *Fr.* The Daily Daily.

National Trust. Tony Harrison. NAEL-2 *Fr.* The School of Eloquence. NAEL-2; NoAM

National Winter Garden. Hart Crane. EP; InPS-3; LiTM; NAAL-2; OxBA *Fr.* Three Songs. NAAL-2 *Fr.* The Bridge. NAAL-2

Nationality. Mary Gilmore, *Eskimo.* CBAP

Nation's Friend, The. Alfred Islay Walden. AAP

Nations That Long in Darkness Walked. John Barnard. AH

Native, The. W. S. Merwin. PoRA

Native Born. Eve Langley. WPE

Native moments—when you come upon me—ah you are here now. Walt Whitman. MeMAP; OxBA

Native Village. Chiyong Chong, *Korean.* CKP, *tr. by* Jaihiun Kim

Native Water-Carrier (M.E.F.) Rudyard Kipling. *Fr.* Epitaphs of the War [1914–1918]. OBWP

Natives, The. David Mura. CDa; WeW-3

Natives camped on the hatches, who sang through the, The. The Calenture. Randolph Stow. BMAP

Native's Letter. Arthur Nortje. HBAPE; PeSAV

Natives of America, The. Ann Plato. BlSi

Nativité. André Spire, *French.* PC, *tr. by* Stanley Burnshaw

Nativities. U. A. Fanthorpe. NoP-4

Nativity [*or* Nativitie]. Donne. *Fr.* La Corona. ChIV-2; ESCV; Son *Fr.* Holy Sonnets.

Nativity, The. Mary Weston Fordham. CBWP-2

Nativity. Gladys May Casely Hayford. PBA; TTY

Nativity, A. Rudyard Kipling. GI

Nativity, The. C. S. Lewis. ChIV-2; TrCP

Nativity. James Montgomery. NOCV

Nativity. Craig Powell. NOBAu

Nativity Chant, The. Sir Walter Scott. FaBoCh *Fr.* Guy Mannering.

Nativity of Our Lord, The. Christopher Smart. EBEV; HAP; NOBE; PoEL-3; SCGP *Fr.* Hymns and Spiritual Songs for the Fasts and Festivals of the Church of England.

(Nativity of Our Lord and Saviour Jesus Christ, The.) NOCV Christmas Day. OBCP

Nativity of St. John the Baptist, The. Christopher Smart. ChIV-2 *Fr.* Hymns and Spiritual Songs for the Fasts and Festivals of the Church of England.

Nativity Poem. Louise Glück. GI

Natura Naturans. Arthur Hugh Clough. CBLP; EnVR; HAP; NOBVV

Natura Naturans. Kathleen Jessie Raine. NYBP

Natural Child, The. Helen Leigh. ECWP; WoRP

Natural Death. Jessica Hagedorn. WWSi

Natural demeanor warm and soft. Tune: "Rapt with Wine, Loudly Singing; Joy in Spring's Coming." Kuan Yün-shih, *Chinese.* SuSp, *tr. by* Richard John Lynn

Natural High. Jean Binta Breeze. HCP

Natural History. Richard Howard. TAP

Natural History. Karl Kirchwey. WWSi

Natural History. Harold Monro. "Vixen woman, The." OBMV

Natural History, (*diff. vers.*). Mother Goose. OxNR

Natural History. *Unknown.* ACTP

Natural History. Robert Penn Warren. NAAL-2

NATURAL PUSSY. Bitter Herbs. "Alta." NMM-2

Natural Religion. Robert Southey. Ro *Fr.* Joan of Arc.

Natural Selection. Constance Naden. VWP

Natural Selection. Jess Williamson. PC

Natural silence of a tree, The. Fortune. Charles Madge. FaBoMo

Natural Stockade at Bamboo Lake, The. Yang Shih-ch'i. *Fr.* Ten Scenes at the Hsiao Family Stone Ridge. CoBLCP, *tr. by* Jonathan Chaves

Natural Theology, A. James Whitehead. MT

Naturalist's Summer-Evening Walk, The. Gilbert White. NOEC

Naturally. Audre Lorde. BlSi; ISC

Naturally the Foundation Will Bear Your Expenses. Philip Larkin. FaBoPV; PeLV

Nature [1836]. Ralph Waldo Emerson. APN-1; AWP

(Motto to "Nature.") NCAP

Nature [1844]. Ralph Waldo Emerson. APN-1

Nature. Henry Wadsworth Longfellow. FaBoBe; PoLF; TAP

Nature. Edmund Spenser. *See* Dame Nature.

Nature. Walter Stone. NYBP

Nature. Henry David Thoreau. AiP; FaBoBe

Nature. Jones Very. ColAP

Nature. Alfred de Vigny, *French.* AWP, tr. *by* Margaret Jourdain

Nature and Art. Goethe, *German.* STV, tr. *by* John Frederick Nims

Nature and Nature's Laws lay hid in Night. Intended for Sir Isaac Newton. Alexander Pope. ECEV; FaBoEE; InPK-6; PFE; WeW-3

Nature assigns the Sun. Emily Dickinson. FP

Nature Be Damned. Anne Wilkinson. NOBC

Nature centres into balls. Circles. Ralph Waldo Emerson. APN-1

Nature, creations law, is judged [*or* judg'd] by sense. Upon Love Fondly Refused [*or* Refus'd] for Conscience's Sake. Thomas Randolph. BeJo; OAEL-1

Nature had long a treasure made. The Match. Andrew Marvell. EBEV

Nature had made them hide in crevices. New Hampshire, February. Richard Eberhart. LiTM; TwCP

Nature has endowed her with complete charm. T'ang Yin. Fr. On a Painting of a Woman Shown Half-Length. CoBLCP, tr. *by* Jonathan Chaves

Nature has shaped this rock just like a mound. The Funny Grotto. Ho Xuan Huong, *Vietnamese.* AVP, tr. *by* Huỳnh Sanh Thông

Nature herself doth Scotchmen beasts confess. John Cleveland. OBSV *Fr.* The Rebel [*or* Rebell] Scot.

Nature in eternity. (LL) Sistrum. Margaret Fuller. APAD; APN-1; PAR

Nature in her wisdom has formed the human head. Four Heads & How to Do Them. John Forbes. BMAP; CBAP

Nature is rising from the dead. Epigram on the First of April. John Winstanley. NOEC

Nature is so near: the rooks in the college garden. Oxford. W. H. Auden. OxAEP-2

Nature Morte. Joseph Brodsky, *Russian.* TCRP, tr. *by* George L. Kline

Nature Morte. Louis MacNeice. NoAM

Nature most calm is often a crisis. Chesapeake. Gerta Kennedy. NYBP

Nature Notes. Louis MacNeice.

Nature Notes: Dandelions. FP

Nature of Man, The. Charles Hubert Sisson. FaBoTw

Nature of Musical Form, The. William Bronk. PT

Nature one hour appears a thing unsexed. Francis Thompson. OBNC *Fr.* Contemplation.

Nature Poem. Adrian Mitchell. Spl

Nature requires five; custom gives seven. Hours of Sleep. *Unknown.* NBLV

Nature selects the longest way. A Northern Suburb. John Davidson. NOBVV; OBNC

Nature—sometimes sears a Sapling. Emily Dickinson. NAAL-1; NAAL-3

Nature Study. Craig Raine. NoAM

Nature Study, After Dufy. Helen Smith Bevington. NYBP

Nature that day a woman was in weakness. A Storm in Summer. Wilfrid Scawen Blunt. FaBoTw

Nature That Framed Us of Four Elements. Marlowe. PoEL-2 *Fr.* Tamburlaine the Great.

Nature, that washed her hands in milk. Love and Time. Sir Walter Ralegh. SiPS

Nature, that washed her hands in milk. Sir Walter Ralegh. NoP-4

Nature—the Gentlest Mother is. Emily Dickinson. EnlH

Nature thy Muse (like LUCANS) did create. (LL) To the Translator of Lucan [*or* Lucan's Pharsalia, 1614]. Sir Walter Ralegh. PBRV; SiPS

Nature, which is the vast creation's soul. To Mr. Henry Lawes. Katherine Philips. NoP-4; WPE

Nature withheld Cassandra in the skies. Fragment of a Sonnet. Pierre de Ronsard, *French.* AWP; OBVE, tr. *by* Keats

Nature without check with original enery. Walt Whitman. *See* Song of Myself.

Nature's confectioner, the bee. Fuscara, or the Bee Errant. John Cleveland. CBLP

Nature's Cook. Margaret Lucas Cavendish, Duchess of Newcastle. BWW; PBWP; PEW

("Then powdered up with phlegm, and rheum that's salt.") (LL) PEW

("When with salt rheum and phlegm they powdered are.") (LL) PBWP

Nature's decorations glisten. Christmas Day. Christopher Smart. OBCP *Fr.* The Nativity of Our Lord. EBEV; HAP; NOBE; PoEL-3; SCGP *Fr.* Hymns and Spiritual Songs for the Fasts and Festivals of the Church of England.

Nature's Farewell. Felicia Dorothea Hemans. Ro

Nature's first green is gold. Nothing Gold Can Stay. Robert Frost. AmPP; ColAP; MoAmPo; NAAL-2; NOBA; Poetr; SoSe-8; TAP; VGW

Nature's Influence on Man. Mark Akenside. NOEC *Fr.* The Pleasures of Imagination.

(Love of Nature.) NOEC

Nature's lay idiot [*or* Ideot], I taught thee to love. Elegie: "Nature's lay ideot, I taught thee to love." Donne. CBLP; OxAEP-1; PeLV; SeCP *Fr.* Elegies.

Nature's Lineaments. Robert Graves. FaBoTw; RB

Nature's Minor Chords. Henrietta Cordelia Ray. CBWP-3

Nature's Questioning. Thomas Hardy. EnVR; PBMP

Nature's Reply to Mutability. Edmund Spenser. NOBE *Fr.* Wood Of Error. AEP

Nature's Sympathy with the Poet. Sir Walter Scott. *See* The Minstrel Responds to Flattery.

Nature's Travail. *Unknown, Greek.* AWP, tr. *by* Goldwin Smith

Nature's Uplifting. Henrietta Cordelia Ray. CBWP-3

Nature's workings made this gentle place. Yün Shou-p'ing. *Fr.* On the Painting, Mist Over Ten Thousand Mountains by Shih-ku. CoBLCP, tr. *by* Jonathan Chaves

Natzweiler. Rutger Kopland, *Dutch.* VCWP, tr. *by* James Brockway

Naught but tradition remains of the beautiful village of Grand-Pré. (LL) From Evangeline. Henry Wadsworth Longfellow. APN-1; NoP-4; UV

Naught in the world keeps an immortal stay. Juvencus, *Latin.* MLL, tr. *by* Helen Waddell

Naught's a naught. Learn to Count. *Unknown.* NAAAL

Naughty Boy. Robert Creeley. HeIP-4; NOBA; NoAM

Naughty Boy, The. Keats. CTV *Fr.* A Song about Myself.

("And he wondered.") (LL) CTV

("Shoes and he wonder'd.") (LL)

(Song about Myself, A.)

Naughty Nan. Angelina Weld Grimké. CPO

Naughty Paughty Jack-a-Dandy. Namby-Pamby; or, A Panegyric on the New Versification. Henry Carey. NOEC; OBSV

Naughty Preposition, The. Morris Gilbert Bishop. NBLV; NYBP; PeLV

Naulahka, The. Rudyard Kipling.

Lie, The. NOBL

Nausicaa. Homer. *Fr.* Odyssey. NAWM-1, tr. *by* Robert Fitzgerald

Nausicaa. Judita Vaiiunaite. CEEP, tr. *by* Irene Pogoželskyte Suboczewski *Fr.* Four Portraits.

Nautical Ballad, A. Charles Edward Carryl. *See* The Walloping Window-Blind.

Nautilus Island's hermit. Skunk Hour. Robert Lowell. AmPP; CMoP; CoAP; CoAmPo; ColAP; FaBoMo; HAP; HCAP; HeIP-4; InPK-6; InPS-3; LCAP-2; MoAmPo; MoP; NAAL-2; NIP-4; NOBA; NoAM; NoP-4; OxBC; PoE; PoPoPo; Poetr; SAGP; SCV; TAP; TFi; TRP; VCAP

Nauty Pauty Jack-a-Dandy. *Unknown.* OxNR

Nauvoo. Bayard Taylor. OBAL

Naval Base (Part III), The. Jeremy Cronin. AF

Naval Trainees Learn How to Jump Overboard, The. David Wagoner. VCAP

Navidad, St. Nicholas Ave. Alfred Corn. NoP-4

Navigation. Ralph Knevet. NOSC

Navigators, The. Walter James Turner. OBMV

Nay, be content—our door that opens wide. Fall. George Cabot Lodge. APN-2

Nay, but of such an one. *Unknown.* TOF, tr. *by* Sir Edwin Arnold *Fr.* The Bhagavad-Gita.

Nay, Death, thou art a shadow! Even as light. Lux Est Umbra Dei[1]. John Addington Symonds. GSo

Nay, do not dream, designer dark. Death's Valley. Walt Whitman. GS

Nay do not smile: my lips shall rather dwell. One Desiring Me to Read, But Slept It Out, Wakening. George Daniel. OxBSP

Nay, Doll, quoth Roger, now you're caught. Dol and Roger. Laetitia Pilkington. PEW

Nay fie, Platonics, still adoring. Epithalamy. Alexander Brome. NOSC

Nay, he could sail a yacht both nigh and large. The Cabin-Boy. George Villiers. NOSC

Nay, if there's room for poets in this world. Fifth Book. Elizabeth Barrett Browning. PEW

Nay, Ivy, Nay. *Unknown.* CH

Nay, lady, one frown is enough. To Helen in a Huff. Nathaniel Parker Willis. OBAL

Nay, lady, sit; if I but wave this wand. Milton. OxAEP-1 *Fr.* A Mask. OxAEP-1 *Fr.* Comus; a Masque Presented at Ludlow Castle. FHYEP; OAEL-1

Nay mum for that. (LL) Idyll. Theocritus, *Greek.* OBCVT, *tr. by* John Dryden

Nay, nay, my boy—'tis not for me. Horace. *See* Simplicity.

Nay, prethee [*or* prithee] dear, draw nigher. A Loose Saraband. Richard Lovelace. BeJo; CaPo; PoEL-3

Nay, prithee tell me, Love, when I behold. The Transfiguration of Beauty. Michelangelo Buonarroti, *Italian.* AWP, *tr. by* John Addington Symonds

Nay, rush not: time serves: we are going, / Gentlemen. (LL) An Ancient to Ancients. Thomas Hardy. CMoP; GTBS-P; LiTM; OxBTC; SCGP

Nay, tempt me not to love again. Thomas Moore. OBNC *Fr.* Odes to Nea.

Nay, thank me not again for those. Reproof of Thanks. Walter Savage Landor. CBLP

Nay then, farewell, if this be so. To Avisa. Henry Willoby. CBLP *Fr.* Willobie His Avisa.

Nay, Traveller. Lines Left upon a Seat in a Yew-Tree which Stands near the Lake of Esthwaite, on a Desolate Part of the Shore, yet Commanding a Beautiful Prospect. Wordsworth. Ro

Nay, Xanthias, feel unashamed. 2.4: Ad Xanthiam Phoceum ("Ne sit ancillae"). Horace. AWP, *tr. by* Franklin P. Adams *Fr.* Odes.

Nazareth. Rosario Castellanos, *Spanish.* GI, *tr. by* Magda Bogin

Nazi Song. Paul Éluard, *French.* AF, *tr. by* Lloyd Alexander

Nazis. Ira Sadoff. LTA; NAmP90

Ndaaya's Kàsálà. Citèkù Ndaaya, *tr. after French-Luba texts by* Judith Gleason.

"Ndaaya, I, am so poor." PBWP

"Ne crede colori," the Poet erst sang. Prejudice against Colour. Langham Dale. PeSAV

Nę Mę Tangito. Charlotte Mew. VWP

Ne Plus Ultra. Coleridge. OAEL-2

Ne swik thu naver nu [*or* thou never now]! *Unknown. See* Sumer is icumen in.

Ne thence the Irishe Rivers absent were. The Rivers of Ireland. Edmund Spenser. *Fr.* Wood Of Error. AEP

Neaera when I'm there is adamant. James Vincent Cunningham, *after the Latin of* George Buchanan. OBVE

Near. William Stafford. CoAmPo

Near a shady wall a rose once grew. The Rose Still Grows beyond the Wall. A. L. Frink. BLPA

Near a Waterfall at Ryumon. Lady Ise, *Japanese.* BoWoP, *tr. by* Etsuko Terasaki *and* Irma Brandeis

Near an Old Prison. Frances Darwin Cornford. OBMV

Near, and more near, without sight or sound. Anniversaries. May Probyn. VWP

Near Avalon. William Morris. OAEL-2

Near blackened alcoves. Railway Allotments. M. R. Peacocke. OBGa

Near Burning. Kathleen Peirce. PBCAP

Near Cedar on Lake Street, where the used cars live. (LL) The Poet's Final Instructions. John Berryman. Son; VGW

Near Damascus. W. S. Di Piero. ChIV-2

Near Hartington. Roy Fisher. NBrP *Fr.* Wonders of Obligation.

Near Helikon. Trumbull Stickney. *Fr.* Sonnets from Greece. APN-1

Near Hermes. Drew Gardner. PT

Near Lanivet, 1872. Thomas Hardy. AWP; CMoP; NoAM

Near Miss. Nayo-Barbara Watkins. BkSV

Near Moscow living, I, this winter. On Early Trains. Boris Pasternak, *Russian.* TCRP, *tr. by* George Reavey

Near Mourning Ground. Victor D. Questel. HCP

Near mud-tide mangrove swamps, under the drilling sun. Along the Mekong. John Balaban. CDa

Near my bosom. (LL) The Blossom. William Blake. CTAV; FHYEP; Ro

Near Neighbors. Martial, *Latin.* AWP, *tr. by* Swift

Near-neighboured by a blandly boisterous Dean. The Blues at Lord's. Siegfried Sassoon. PeLV

Near Perigord. Ezra Pound. FaBoMo; LiTM

Near Rhydcymerau. Rhydcymerau. David Gwenallt Jones, *Welsh.* OBWVE, *tr. by* Anthony Conran

Near Roscoe and Coldwater. Amy Uyematsu. OpBo

Near Rose's Chop Suey and Jinosuke's grocery. An Argument: On 1942. David Mura. PoPoPo

Near-sighted fellow named Walter, A. Limerick. *Unknown.* PeLi

Near-Sightedness. Edmond Yi-teh Chang. OpBo

Near some fair Town, I'd have a private Seat. No Barren Leaves. John Pomfret. GaP

Near. Strange. Striding the Rue Royale. So I See You Still. Aleksis Rannit, *Estonian.* CEEP, *tr. by* Henry Lymann

Near sun down: 6th street. Lydia Tomkiw. *Fr.* New York Love Song (Part 1—Lower East Side). WWSi

Near the book a notebook. Stars. Oktay Rifat, *Turkish.* PC, *tr. by* Taner Baybars

Near the Border of Insanities. Dannie Abse. PoA

Near the celebrated Lido where the breeze is fresh and free. Longfellow's Visit to Venice. John Betjeman. NOBL; OBCoV

Near the City of Petersburg. The V. N. and C. I. Maggie Pogue Johnson. CBWP-4

Near the curving harbor where pine trees father. Heart's Ease. Paul Hoover. PmAP

Near the Cymmerians, in his dark abode. Ovid. OBVE, *tr. by* Dryden *Fr.* Metamorphoses.

Near the Desert Test Sites. Sherod Santos. WeT

Near the Docks. Dave Jeddie Smith. CMAP

Near the dry river's water-mark we found. A Note Left in Jimmy Leonard's Shack. James Wright. HCAP; NoP-4

Near the East Gate. *Unknown, Chinese.* SuSp, *tr. by* Heng Kuan

Near the end of an extremely important discourse. The Discourse on Peace. Jacques Prévert, *French.* CLPP, *tr. by* Lawrence Ferlinghetti

Near the frayed edges of towns. Lovers in Summer. Vern Rutsala. WeT

Near the headwaters of the longest river. The Banished Gods. Derek Mahon. OxBC

Near the hermitage midnight discovers. In the Mountains. Lucian Blaga, *Romanian.* CEEP, *tr. by* Peter Jay *and* Virgil Nemoianu

Near the mountain's summit, where the bells. The Fox. R. Williams Parry, *Welsh.* OBWVE, *tr. by* Gwyn Williams

Near the Ocean. Robert Lowell. NOBA

Near the rim of Hsi-sai Mountain, white egrets fly. Chang Chih-ho. SuSp, *tr. by* Irving Y. Lo *Fr.* Fisherman's Songs.

Near the salt pans. What Her Girl Friend Said to Him. Centaṉ Kaṇṇaṉār, *Tamil.* PLW, *tr. by* A. K. Ramanujan

Near the School for Handicapped Children. Thomas William Shapcott. CBAP

Near the top a bad turn some dare. Well. Whether There Is Sorrow in the Demons. John Berryman. LiTM

Near the Vipsanian columns where the aqueduct. Martial, *Latin.* OBVE, *tr. by* Peter Porter

Near this spot. Epitaph to a Dog. Byron. BLPA

Near to me as my flesh, my flesh and blood. Allen Tate. PoA *Fr.* Sonnets of the Blood.

("Near to me as perfection in the blood.")

Near to the bank of the river, o'ershadowed by oaks, from whose branches. Henry Wadsworth Longfellow. *Fr.* Part the Second. *Fr.* Evangeline, a Tale of Acadie.

Near[e] to the silver Trent. The Trent. Michael Drayton. OBEV; PoEL-2 *Fr.* The Shepherd's Sirena.

Near Twelve Mile Point. Lance Henson. HATNAP

Neare Enna walles there standes a Lake Pergusa is the name. Ovid. OBVE, *tr. by* Arthur Golding *Fr.* Metamorphoses.

Nearer. Judith Herzberg, *Dutch.* BoWoP, *tr. by* Shirley Kaufman

"Nearer God, Nearer Realite." Joellen Kwiatek. PUP-18

Nearer her they get, The. (LL) What mystery pervades a well! Emily Dickinson. NAAL-1; NAAL-3; NCAP

Nearer Home. Phoebe Cary. PWR

Nearer, My God, to Thee. Sarah Flower Adams. FaBoBe; PoLF

Nearest Dream recedes—unrealized, The. Emily Dickinson. APN-2

Nearing Again the Legendary Isle. C. Day Lewis. FaBoTw; MoBrPo *Fr.* The Magnetic Mountain.

Nearing La Guaira. Derek Walcott. TTY

Nearing the mountain. Foster Jewell. HA

Nearing the Snow-Line. Oliver Wendell Holmes. APN-1

Nearing Winter. Ernest Sandeen. NYBP

Nearly a hundred when she died. Grandmother, a Caribbean Indian, Described by My Father. Yvonne Sapia. UnSA

Nearly a twelvemonth we had laboured to complete our house. Visitation. John Dronsfield. PeSAV

Nearly a Valediction. Marilyn Hacker. NMM-2

Nearly right, The. To the Tune of the Coventry Carol. Stevie Smith. FaBoTw

Nearsighted, The. Elizabeth Macklin. BAP-93

Nearsighted child has taken off her glasses, The. Country Stars. William Meredith. AFr; VCAP

Neat Marlowe, bathed in the Thepian springs. Michael Drayton. EPCY *Fr.* To Henry Reynolds, of Poets and Poesy.

Neath blue-bell or streamer. Song. Edgar Allan Poe. AmPP; OxBA *Fr.* Song: "Young flowers were whispering in melody." NOBA *Fr.* Al Aaraaf. APN-1

'Neath every one a friend. (LL) Sixty-Eighth Birthday. James Russell Lowell. OxBSP; PFE; PoEL-5

Nebamun's Cat. Felicity Bast. PC

Neber min' what's in your cran'um. The Don't-Care Negro. Joseph Cotter, Sr. AAP

Nebraska. Barbara Guest. FTOS

Nebuchadnezzar. Elinor Wylie. ChIV-1; KSG; MoAmPo

Nebuchadnezzar's Dream. Keats. ChIV-1; KSG

Nebuchadnezzar's Kingdom-Come. David Rowbotham. ChIV-1; NOBAu

Necessary Angel, The. Phyllis Janowitz. BAP-94

Necessary Miracle, A. Eda Lou Walton. NYBP

Necessary Story. Dionisio D. Martinez. WWSi

Necessitarian's Epitaph, A. Thomas Hardy. FaBoEE

Necessities of Life. Adrienne Rich. HCAP; NOBA; PoPoPo; Poetr

("TO TELL their tales.") (LL) PoPoPo

Necessity, The. Alice B. Fogel. BAP-93

Necessity. Harry Graham. PeLV *Fr.* Some Ruthless Rhymes.

Necessity. Langston Hughes. APSN; NOBA; RaBo

Necessity, if not choice, I live here too. (LL) Glengormley. Derek Mahon. CIP-2; IIP

Necessity of Falling, The. William Mills. MT

Necessity of Fate, The. Jane Barker. BWW

Nechama. Shirley Kaufman. LCAP-2

Necklace of flame, little dropped hearts. Tattoos. Charles Wright. HCAP

Necklace of human bones. Regalia in Immediate Demand! Philip Whalen. BB

Neckties. Liz Lochhead. OBCoV

Necrological. John Crowe Ransom. FuPo; MeMAP

Necromance. Rae Armantrout. FTOS; PmAP

Necropolis. Karl Shapiro. PoA

Ned. Eleanor Farjeon. OTCP

Ned knew I was short of tobacco one day. Ned's Delicate Way. Henry Lawson. CBAP

Ned Vaughan. Walter De la Mare. FaBoEE

Ned's Delicate Way. Henry Lawson. CBAP

Ned's Psalm of Life for the Negro. Joseph Cotter, Sr.. AAP

Need for Censorship, The. Reiner Kunze, *German.* PoSu, *tr. by* Michael Hamburger

Need for consistency, The. Horace, *Latin.* OBCVT, *tr. by* John Oldham

Need from excess—excess from folly growing. Epigram. Samuel Bishop. NOEC

Need Increasing Itself by Rounds. Kathleen Peirce. PBCAP

Need Is Our Name. Luci Shaw. TrCP

Need of Being Versed in Country Things, The. Robert Frost. NOBA; NoAM; OxBA; SAmP; TRP; UnPo

Need of Loving. Strickland W. Gillilan. BLPA; PoToHe

Need to explore, The. Explorers as Seen by the Natives. Doug Fetherling. NOBC

Need to find a place always returns, The. The Renewal. George MacBeth. FaBoTC

Need to Win, The. Chuang Tzu, *Chinese.* BLT, *tr. by* Thomas Merton

Needed urgently to hear it, God kept a secret. (LL) Questions for Ecclesiastes. Mark Jarman. BAP-93

Needing someone. Discover Me. Opal Palmer Adisa. GT

Needle and thread, A. (LL) Old Mother Twitchett had [*or* has] but one eye. Mother Goose. NTCP; OxNR; ReMoGo

Needle and Thread. Pan Chao, *Chinese.* WPoS; WPOW, *tr. by* Richard Mather *and* Rob Swigart

Needle: For a Friend Who Disappeared, The. Franz Wright. CMAP; NAmP90

Needled by death for change, for simple change. The Vegetable Garden. Wyatt Prunty. OBGa

Needles and pins, needles and pins. Proverb. *Unknown.* FaBoBe; ReMoGo

Needle's Eye, The. *Unknown.* AmFP

Needles of the lofty pine, The. *Unknown, Greek.* GrAn, *tr. by* W. G. Shepherd

Needless Return. Dan Pagis, *Hebrew.* IP, *tr. by* Warren Bargad *and* Stanley F. Chyet

Needless to catalogue heroes. No Man Knows War. Edwin Rolfe. TrJP

Needling / threading nighttime sewing machine. What Were You Patching? Ruth Lisa Schechter. UnSA

Needs. A. R. Ammons. NIP-4; OBAL; PFE

Needy knife-grinder! whither are you going? The Friend of Humanity and the Knife Grinder. George Canning *and* John Hookham Frere. BXAP; NOBRP; NOEC; OBCoV; UV

Needy were lined up by order of famine, The. The Offended. Anne Hébert, *French.* BoWoP, *tr. by* Willis Barnstone

Ne'er fail in old Scotland! (LL) John Barleycorn [a Ballad]. Robert Burns. FaBoCh; RB

Ne'er fash your *thumb* what *gods* decree. Horace, *Latin.* OBCVT, *tr. by* Robert Fergusson

Ne'er to be found again[e]. (LL) To Daffodils [*or* Daffadills]. Robert Herrick. APAD; AWP; AYFP; BeJo; CaPo; EBEvV; FaBoCh; GTBS-P; InPS-3; NOBE; NOSC; NTP; NoP-4; OBEV; OxAEP-1; PoEL-3; PoRA; SCGP; SeCP; TFi; TTTS; UnPo

Negative Love. Donne. FSCP

Negative Passage. Michael Newman. PoA

Negative tree, you are belief. Bound. Theodore Roethke. PoA

Negatives. Charles Wright. PoA

Negev. David Rokeah, *Hebrew.* MHP, *tr. by* Ruth Finer Mintz

Neglected Muse! of this our western clime. James Kirke Paulding. APN-1 *Fr.* The Backwoodsman.

Neglected now the early daisy lies. Spring. Robert Bloomfield. Ro *Fr.* The Farmer's Boy.

Neglectful Edward. Robert Graves. MoBrPo

Neglecting thy derision. (LL) To Fortune. Robert Herrick. CavPo; OxBSP

Negotiation. Alan Brownjohn. PeLV

Negotiations. Ray Catina. CDa

Negotium Perambulans. Peter Redgrove. OBGa

Negritude. James A. Emanuel. BPo

Negro, The. James A. Emanuel. HoPM; InPK-6

Negro Ballot, The. Lizelia Augusta Jenkins Moorer. CBWP-3

Negro Cemetery Next to a White One, A. Howard Nemerov. OxBSP

Negro Dreams. Doughtry Long. PoBA

Negro Has a Chance, The. Maggie Pogue Johnson. CBWP-4

"Negro" Hero. Gwendolyn Brooks. ColAP; RACG

Negro Heroines. Lizelia Augusta Jenkins Moorer. CBWP-3

Negro holds firmly the reins of his four horses, The. The Drayman. Walt Whitman. *Fr.* Song of Myself. AmPP; MoAmPo; NAAL-3; NOBA; OxBA

Negro Love Song, A. Paul Laurence Dunbar. AAP; APAD; APN-2; ColAP; CrDW; NAAAL; SSLK

Negro Mask. Léopold Sédar Senghor, *French.* NegPo, *tr. by* Ellen Conroy Kennedy

Negro Meets to Pray, The. Daniel Webster Davis. AAP

Negro peddler of revolt. Jacques Roumain. NegPo, *tr. by* Ellen Conroy Kennedy *Fr.* Ebony Wood.

Negro Reel. *Unknown.* AS

Negro Schools, The. Lizelia Augusta Jenkins Moorer. CBWP-3

Negro Sermon—Simon Legree, A. Vachel Lindsay. *See* Simon Legree—A Negro Sermon.

Negro Servant. Langston Hughes. VGW

Negro Soldier's Civil War Chant. *Unknown.* BPo

(Black Soldier's Civil War Chant.) TAP

Negro Soldier's Viet Nam Diary, A. Herbert Martin. PoBA

Negro Song, A. *Unknown.* PBCV

Negro Song at Cornwall. *Unknown.* PBCV

Negro Speaks of Rivers, The. Langston Hughes. AiP; BPo; ColAP; CrDW; HAP; HCAP; HeIP-4; ISC; NAAAL; NAAL-2; NIP-4; NOBA; NoAM; NoP-4; OBCA; PoBA; Poetr; RaBo; SSLK; TAP; TFi; TTY; WeW-3

("My soul has grown deep like rivers.") (LL) ColAP

Negro sprouts from the pavement like an asparagus, A. Stumpfoot on 42nd Street. Louis Simpson. NNaP; UnPo; VGW

Negro Tramp. David Diop, *French.* NegPo, *tr. by* Ellen Conroy Kennedy

Negro, / With the trumpet at his lips, The. Trumpet Player. Langston Hughes. NAAL-2; TTY

Negro Woman. Lewis Alexander. PoBA

Negro Woman, A. William Carlos Williams. SAmP

Negroes, labouring, The. Guadalupe, W.I. Nicolás Guillén, *Spanish.* TTY, *tr. by* Anselm Hollo

Negroes, / Sweet and docile. Warning. Langston Hughes. BPo

Negro's Complaint, The. William Cowper. CABP

Negro's Lament, The. John Willis Menard. AAP

Negro's Tragedy, The. Claude McKay. BPo

Neighbor. Langston Hughes. APSN; PFTM

Neighbor of mine in the village, A. A Girl's Garden. Robert Frost. GaP

Neighborhood House, The. Jay Wright. NBV

Neighborhood of my youth. A Trip Through the Mind Jail. Raul Salinas. FaBoA

Neighbors. David Allan Evans. Poetsp

Neighbors. James Tate. LCAP-2

Neighbour mine not long ago there was, A. A Tale for Husbands. Sir Philip Sidney. SiPS *Fr.* Arcadia.

Neighbour sits in his window and plays the flute, The. Music. Amy Lowell. ColAP

Neighbours. Rudyard Kipling. FP

Neither Durst Any Man From That Day Ask Him Any More Questions. Richard Crashaw. ChIV-2

Neither father nor lover. (LL) Elegy for Jane. Theodore Roethke. AmPP; CoAP; ColAP; HAP; HCAP; IMW; InPK-6; InPS-3; LiLi; LiTM; MoAmPo; MoLi; NoP-4; PoE; PoPoPo; Poetr; SAGP; TAP; TFi; TRP; TwCP; WeW-3

Neither Fish Nor Fowl. Nguyễn Hũ'u Chu, Vietnamese. AVP, tr. by Huỳnh Sanh Thông

Neither had said they were going to climb to it. The Source. David Wagoner. VCAP

Neither Here nor There. William Robert Rodgers. ImPo; LiTM; MoBrPo

Neither in idleness consume thy days. Walter Savage Landor. FaBoEE

Neither Logician nor Rhetorician. (LL) Another Song. Anne Collins. KTR

Neither of them was better than the other. From Plane to Plane. Robert Frost. MoAmPo

Neither on horseback nor seated. Walt Whitman at Bear Mountain. Louis Simpson. CoAmPo; LiTM; TRP

Neither our vices nor our virtues. Poetry, a Natural Thing. Robert Duncan. NOBA; NoAM; PmAP; TRP

Neither Out Far Nor In Deep. Robert Frost. AmPP; HAP; MeMAP; MoP; NAAL-2; NOBA; NoAM; NoP-4; OxBoS; PFE; Poetr; TAP; TRP; WeW-3

Neither Poverty nor Riches. Bible, O.T. TrJP Fr. Proverbs.

Neither Shadow of Turning. Jack R. Clemo. NOCV

Neither the actors nor the audience knew what was coming next. Amnesia. David Lehman. EOEF

Neither the paths determine, nor the goal. The Command. Avraham Huss, Hebrew. MHP, tr. by Ruth Finer Mintz

Neither war, nor cyclones, nor earthquakes. Antipater of Thessalonica, Greek. GrAn; PGA, tr. by Kenneth Rexroth

Neither will I put myself forward as others may do. Eternal Masculine. William Rose Benét. AWP; MoAmPo

Nel mezzo dle camino I found myself. Circle Jerk. Andrei Codrescu. PmAP

Nell by night or such a Divel. (LL) Out of an Epigram of Martial. Martial, Latin. OBCVT, tr. by Sir John Denham

Nellie Gives into Blanche. Leslie Simon. FFC

Nellie named her Blanche for white and French. two. Nellie Gives into Blanche. Leslie Simon. FFC

Nellie Rakerfield. Raymond Knister. NOBC Fr. A Row of Stalls.

Nelly Kelly loved baseball games. Take Me Out to the Ball Game. Jack Norworth. OBAL

Nelly kissed me when we met. Rondeau. Leigh Hunt. Ro Fr. Morning Chronicle, 2 436.

Nelly Trim. Sylvia Townsend Warner. MoBrPo

Nelly's Lament for the Pirnhouse Cat. Ellen Johnston. VWP

Nelson, Pitt, Fox. Sir Walter Scott. OBEV Fr. Marmion.

Nemea. Lawrence Durrell. FaBoTw; GTBS-P

Nemesis. Ralph Waldo Emerson. NOBA

Nemunas. Justinas Marcinkeviius, Lithuanian. CEEP, tr. by Irene Pogoželskyte Suboczewski

Neo-Classical Urn, The. Robert Lowell. NAAL-2

Neo-Thomist Poem. Ernest Hemingway. OBAL

Neocolonialism. Felix Mnthali. PeSAV

Neon sign blinked red, A. Something Old, Something New. Carl H. Greene. NBV

Neon sign missing a letter. Pawtucket Postcards. Franz Wright. CMAP

Neon Signs. Langston Hughes. APSN; PFTM

("CASBAH.") (LL) PFTM

("WONDER BAR.") PFTM

Neon stripes tighten my wall. The Zebra Goes Wild Where the Sidewalk Ends. Henry Dumas. GT

Neonbright orange. Robben Island Sequence. Dennis Brutus. HBAPE; VCWP

Nepenthe. George Darley.

Hoopoe. OBNC

Hundred-gated Thebes. NOBE

In Dreamy Swoon. OBNC

O Blest Unfabled Incense Tree. BIrV; FaBoCh; OBEV

(Phoenix, The.) NOBE; OAEL-2

Onward to Far Ida. OBNC

Unicorn, The. OBNC; PoEL-4

Nepenthe. Charlotte Smith. NoP-4

Nephelidia. Swinburne. BXAP; EnVR; HoPM; PeVV Fr. The Heptalogia.

Neptune Goes to the Greeks. Homer. NOSC, tr. by George Chapman Fr. The Iliad.

Neptune—Polka. Dame Edith Sitwell. NOBE

Ne'r may Prophetique Daphne crown my Brow. (LL) The Welcome to Sack. Robert Herrick. BeJo; CaPo; SeCP

Nero commanded; but withdrew his eyes. Cruelties. Robert Herrick. CavPo

Nero wasn't worried at all when he heard. Nero's Deadline. Constantine P. Cavafy, Greek. OxBSn, tr. by Kelly, Edmund and Phillip Sherrard

Nero's Deadline. Constantine P. Cavafy, Greek. OxBSn, tr. by Kelly, Edmund and Phillip Sherrard

Nerve pivots and that space, A. Finite Intuition. Milo De Angelis, Italian. NeIt, tr. by Lawrence Venuti

Nerves. David Huddle. CDa Fr. Tour of Duty. Son
("Training I received did not apply because.")

Nerves. "Sagittarius." OxBTC

Nerves. Arthur Symons. CABP; FaBoTw

Nerves are foolish invisibility induces offers, The. Lateness. David Shapiro. PT

Nerves in stounds o' delight. Man and the Infinite. "Hugh MacDiarmid." FaBoTC Fr. A Drunk Man Looks at the Thistle.

Nervous hose is dribbling on the tar, A. The Roof Garden. Howard Moss. GaP

Nervous Prostration. Anna Wickham. FaBoWP

Nervy with neons, the main drag. At Barstow. Charles Tomlinson. MoP; NoAM; TwCP

Nescience, say th' fiery scent I owe whets crookeder. Catullus. See Carmina, LXXXV.

Nest, The. Andrew Young. Spl

Nest in a Wall, A. Richard Murphy. BiHa; CIP-2

Nesting among Clouds. Yang Chi, Chinese. CoBLCP, tr. by Jonathan Chaves

Nesting of Layer Protocols. Kit Robinson. FTOS

Nestle-down Cottage. Mary Weston Fordham. CBWP-2

Nests in Elms. "Michael Field." VWP

Nests of golden porridge shattered in the silky-oak trees. Equanimity. Les A. Murray. BMAP; NOBAu

Nests well hidden. Secret Places. Irene Thompson. BoTP

Nestus Gurley. Randall Jarrell. HeIP-4; TwCP

Net, The. Fleur Adcock. PeNZ

Net, The. William Robert Rodgers. BoLoP; CIP-2; PNI

Net and the Sword, The. Douglas Le Pan. NOBC

Net-houses, saunas, barns. Jaan Oks. Aleksis Rannit, Estonian. CEEP, tr. by Henry Lymann

Net of Moon, The. Unknown, Pawnee Indian. STP, tr. by Jerome Rothenberg

Net of Place, The. Paul Blackburn. PmAP

Net rests on the water's surface, The. Elena Clementelli. Fr. Etruscan Notebook. PBWP, tr. by Ruth Feldman and Brian Swann

Net to Snare the Moonlight, A. Vachel Lindsay. PoLF

Netheherd. Theocritus, Greek. OBCVT, tr. by Unknown Fr. Idylls.
("Eunica skorned me, when her I would have sweetly kist.") OBCVT, tr. by Unknown
("In cittie, nor on hill, but al the night must sleepe alone.") (LL) OBCVT, tr. by Unknown

Netley Abbey. William Lisle Bowles. Son

Netley Abbey; Midnight. William Sotheby. NOEC

Nets are real, The—heroin (sniffed) clears them. For Artaud. Michael McClure. NeAP

Nettles, The. Thomas Hardy. OxBSP

Nettles in May. Euros Bowen, Welsh. OBWVE, tr. by the author

Network, The. Arthur Sze. AiP; OpBo

Network of the Imaginary Mother, The. Robin Morgan.
("And this is the fragrance, almost forgotten.") CrSp
("As it was in the beginning.") CrSp
("Blessed be my brain.") CrSp
("Little heart, little heart.") CrSp

Neurasthenia. Agnes Mary Frances Robinson. NOBVV

Neutral British Gentleman, The. "Orpheus C. Kerr." Son

Neutral Tones. Thomas Hardy. CABP; CMoP; EBVV; EnVR; HAP; HeIP-4; InPK-6; InPS-3; MoBrPo; MoP; NAEL-2; NOBVV; NoAM; OAEL-2; TFi; UnPo
("And a pond edged with greyish leaves.") (LL) NoP-4

Neutrality. Sidney Keyes. MoBrPo

Neutrality Loathsome. Robert Herrick. ChIV-1
("Abhor, and spew out all neutralities.") (LL) NoP-4

Never. George Reavey. BIrV

Never a careworn wife but shows. Wives in the Sere. Thomas Hardy. NOBE; NOBVV

Never a day, never a day passes. Europe's Prisoners. Sidney Keyes. PoWW

Never a ploughman. Never a one. (LL)   Ha'nacker Mill.   Hilaire Belloc. FaPoR; MoBrPo; OxBTC; RB

Never able to enter.   Farmers.   Kathleen Peirce.   PBCAP

Never afflict yourself to know the cause.   Refrain.   Mary Jo Salter.   EOEF

Never Again.   Jaroslav Seifert, *Czech.*   AF, *tr. by* Ewald Osers

Never Again.   Richard Henry Stoddard.   PWR

Never again, Orpheus.   Antipater of Sidon, *Greek.*   GrAn; OBVE; PGA, *tr. by* Kenneth Rexroth

Never again rising at dawn.   A Cock.   Anyte, *Greek.*   GrAn, *tr. by* Sally Purcell

Never again / When the heat overwhelms us.   Long Hot Summer.   Archibald MacLeish.   AFr

Never Again Would Birds' Song Be The Same.   Robert Frost.   FYAP; HAP; InPK-6; LoP; NIP-4; NoAM; NoP-4; SoSe-8; Son; VGW

Never any more.   In a Year.   CBLP

"Never Apologize; Never Explain."   Philip Whalen.   BB

Never ask me whose. (LL)   Is my team ploughing.   A. E. Housman.   CBLP; CMoP; EBEvV; EBVV; LiTM; MoBrPo; NoAM; NoP-4; OBEV; Poetr; SAGP

Never ask of money spent.   The Hardship of Accounting.   Robert Frost. FaBoCh; OBAL   *Fr.* Ten Mills.

Never be rude.   Tips for Living.   Leandra Garcia.   CTV

Never before without a ring.   My Ringless Fingers on the Steering Wheel Tell the Story.   Laura Boss.   UnSA

Never believe all you hear.   Wolf.   Kenneth Rexroth.   NNaP   *Fr.* A Bestiary.   OBAL

Never, believe me, / Appear the Immortals.   The Visit of the Gods. Coleridge.   OBVE

Never closer the whole rest of our lives. (LL)   When all the others were away at Mass.   Seamus Heaney.   BLT

Never could I think / Our love a worldly commonplace.   Lady Izumi, *Japanese.*   PBWP, *tr. by* Edwin A. Cranston

Never dare to wear an open-hearted face? (LL)   Song of a Dream Visit to T'ien-mu.   Li Po, *Chinese.*   CoBCP, *tr. by* Burton Watson

Never-Dead, The.   Anna Couani.   BMAP

Never forgetting him that kept coming constantly so near. (LL)   The World as Meditation.   Wallace Stevens.   HeIP-4; LCAP-2

Never Give a Bum an Even Break.   James Welch.   NoAM

Never give all the heart, for love.   W. B. Yeats.   BoLoP; CMoP; GLoP

Never have I.   Tanka.   Mori Ōgai, *Japanese.*   MJT, *tr. by* Makoto Ueda

Never have I seen the sky more clear.   Depressed by the Death of the Horse That He Bought from Robert Bly.   Henry Taylor.   BXAP

Never in My Life.   Walter McDonald.   MT

Never let a ghost.   Masked Angel Costume / The Sayings of Mantan Moreland.   Imamu Amiri Baraka.   EC3

Never love unless you can.   Advice to a Girl.   Thomas Campion.   SAGP

Never love with all your heart.   Song in Spite of Myself.   Countee Cullen. ISC

Never May the Fruit Be Plucked.   Edna St. Vincent Millay.   NAAL-2; OxBSP

Never mind now. You have done all that was needful.   Beauty the Lover's Gift.   Winifred Holtby.   WPN

Never mind why—the gods behave with whimsy—but once.   The Monkey. Avianus, *Latin.*   OBCVT, *tr. by* David R. Slavitt

Never more will the wind.   Hilda Doolittle.   CTC   *Fr.* Hymen.

Never, my partridge, O patient heart.   Partridge.   Agathias, *Greek.*   FP; GrAn, *tr. by* Guy Davenport

Never, never may the fruit be plucked from the bough.   Never May the Fruit Be Plucked.   Edna St. Vincent Millay.   NAAL-2; OxBSP

Never, O never! (LL)   Fitz-Eustace's Song.   Sir Walter Scott.   CH; GTBS-P; NOBRP; PoEL-4

Never on this side of the grave again.   A Life's Parallels.   Christina Rossetti.   NAEL-2; PoEL-5

Never Pain to Tell Thy Love.   William Blake.   NAEL-2; OAEL-2 (Love's Secret.)   GLoP

Never Pharaoh's Night.   In the Desert.   Herman Melville.   NCAP

Never presume that in this marble stable.   The Brass Horse.   Drummond Allison.   FaBoTw

Never put anybody down.   Rules to Live By.   Paula Del Giudice.   CTV

Never saw him.   The Negro.   James A. Emanuel.   HoPM; InPK-6

Never Say Fail.   *Unknown.*   PWR

Never say no when I speak to you from afar. . . .   Edouard J. Maunick. *See* Further off is the measured force the word of the sea.

Never Seek to Tell Thy Love.   John Ashbery.   HCAP; InPS-3

Never seek [*or* pain] to tell thy love, *see also* "I told my love I told my love."   Never Pain to Tell Thy Love.   William Blake.   CBLP; EnLoPo; GLoP; InPS-3; NAEL-2; NOBE; OAEL-2; OBNC; PoEL-4; SCGP

Never shall a young man.   For Anne Gregory.   W. B. Yeats.   CMoP; ImPo; LiTM; NAEL-2; OxAEP-2; Poetr

Never shall I forget that night.   Elie Wiesel.   HP

Never show your face again.   Mother Goose.   *See* Rain, rain, go to Spain.

Never since Eden.   Raymond Wilson.   SpW

Never / stop!   Joseph Ceravolo.   *See* Ho Ho Ho Caribou.

Never such innocence again. (LL)   MCMXIV.   Philip Larkin.   EBEV; NAEL-2; NSI; NoAM; NoP-4; OBWP; OxAEP-2

Never Such Love.   Robert Graves.   BoLoP; LoP

Never talk down to a glowworm.   Glowworm.   David McCord.   NTCP

Never Tell.   *Unknown, Welsh.*   OBWVE, *tr. by* Anthony Conran

Never the same.   Moon.   Jean Kenward.   SpW

Never the time and the place.   Robert Browning.   EnLoPo

Never the tramp of foot or horse.   Farewell to Anactoria.   Sappho, *Greek.* AWP, *tr. by* Allen Tate

Never think she loves him wholly.   Appraisal.   Sara Teasdale.   MoAmPo

Never think you fortune can bear the sway.   On Fortune.   Elizabeth I, Queen of England.   PBWP; WPE

Never to be lonely like that.   Face to Face.   Adrienne Rich.   LiTM; NAAL-2; NoAM

Never to Meet Again.   Pyong-hwa Cho, *Korean.*   CKP, *tr. by* Jaihiun Kim

Never to part more. (LL)   Meeting.   Christina Rossetti.   CBLP; GBL; LW

Never to rise again, oh! (LL)   Open the Door to Me, Oh!   Robert Burns. FaBoCh; PoEL-4; SCGP

Never to see ghosts? Then to be.   Ghosts.   Alastair Reid.   NYBP

Never Too Late.   Robert Greene. Palmer's Ode, The.   CTC; NoSic; SCGP

Never Too Late.   John Taggart.   FTOS

Never too many fish in a swift creek.   Jelaluddin Rumi.   RaBo, *tr. by* John Moyne *and* Coleman Barks   *Fr.* Three Quatrains.

Never travel such roads of love.   Hitomaro.   *See* May the men who are born.

Never twice that river.   By the River Eden.   Kathleen Jessie Raine.   NYBP

Never until the mankind making.   A Refusal to Mourn the Death, by Fire, of a Child in London.   Dylan Thomas.   AF; CMoP; EBEV; FaBoMo; GTBS-P; HeIP-4; HoPM; ImPo; LiTM; MoBrPo; MoP; NOBE; NoAM; NoP-4; OAEL-2; OBWVE; OxAEP-2; OxBTC; PoE; PoWW; TFi; TwCP; UnPo

Never wake up in a million years. (LL)   A First Night.   Peter Kane Dufault.   NoP-4

Never was grief like mine. (LL)   The Sacrifice.   George Herbert.   GeHe; PoEL-2

Never weather-beaten sail[e] more willing bent to shore.   O Come Quickly! Thomas Campion.   NOBE; OAEL-1; OBEV; OxAEP-1; OxBSP; PoEL-2

Never will I hear the sweet voice of God.   Yona Wollach.   IP, *tr. by* Warren Bargad *and* Stanley F. Chyet   *Fr.* Poetry (1976).

NEVER YOUR CAPTIVE! (LL)   Blues Note.   Bob Kaufman.   PoBA

NEVER YOUR CAPTIVE! (LL)   How High the Moon.   Lance Jeffers. PoBA; SeSe

Nevermore.   Paul Verlaine, *French.*   FLP; LoP, *tr. by* Alistair Elliot

Nevertheless.   Marianne Moore.   CMoP; MeMAP; NAAL-2; NoP-4; OxBA

Nevertheless I prefer.   Nineteen Sixty Eight.   Petra von Morstein, *German.* BoWoP, *tr. by* Rosemarie Waldrop

Nevertheless you've seen a strawberry.   Marianne Moore.   CMoP; OxBA; SoSe-8

New.   Jennifer Maiden.   BMAP

New Age, The.   Stevie Smith.   NAEL-2

New air has come around us.   Dakota: October, 1822, Hunkpapa Warrior. Rod Taylor.   WeW-3

New Ancient of Days, The.   Herman Melville.   OBAL

New and singular sex?, A. (LL)   Polar Exploration.   Stephen Spender. FaBoMo; NoAM

New Apartment.   Linda Hogan.   HATNAP; UnSA

New Approach Needed.   Kingsley Amis.   NoAM; OxBTC

New Army Education.   *Unknown.*   NSI

New Arrival.   Kenneth Mackenzie.   *See* The Hospital—Retrospections.

New Bamboo in the North Garden at Ch'ang-ku.   Li Ho, *Chinese.*   SuSp, *tr. by* Irving Y. Lo

New Bath Guide, The.   Christopher Anstey. "Hearken, Lady Betty, hearken."   NOEC "This morning, dear mother, as soon as 'twas light."   ECEV

New Birth, The.   Jones Very.   APN-1; NCAP; NOBA; PAR

New-born moon gives little light, The.   To the Tune "New Moon."   Yang Shen, *Chinese.*   CoBLCP, *tr. by* Jonathan Chaves

New Boy's View of Rugger.   Rupert Brooke.   AYFP

New Buildings.   Horace, *Latin.*   OBCVT, *tr. by* James Smith

New Canaans Genius; Epilogus.   Thomas Morton.   SCAP

New Cantata, A.   Clara Reeve.   ECWP

New Canto, A.   Lady Caroline Lamb.   Ro

New Cecilia, The.   Thomas Lovell Beddoes.   OAEL-2 (Legend of St. Gingulph's Relict, The.)   CBNP

New Church Organ, The. Will M. Carleton. PoLF

New cinematic emporium, The. Limerick. *Unknown.* PeLi

New Coasts and Poseidon's Son. Homer. *Fr.* Odyssey. NAWM-1, *tr. by* Robert Fitzgerald

New Colossus, The. Emma Lazarus. APAD; APN-2; AiP; CA; FaBoA; GS; GSo; NoP-4; PAR; PoLF; SAGP; Son; WPE

New-come buckra/ He get sick. *Unknown. Fr.* Songs. PBCV

New Corn. Ch'ien T'ao, *Chinese.* ChiP, *tr. by* Arthur Waley

New Courtly Sonnet of the Lady Greensleeves, A. *Unknown. See* Lady Greensleeves.

New Cup and Saucer, A. Gertrude Stein. TTTS *Fr.* Tender Buttons.

New Dark Ages. Donald Revell. WeT

New Dawn, A. Robert Blair. LBC

New Dawn, The. Mafika Pascal Gwala. PeSAV

New Day, The. Richard Watson Gilder.
   Prelude: "Night was dark, though sometimes a faint star, The." PoLF

New Day. Naomi Long Madgett. BlSi

New Day. Ed Ochester. CMAP

New decade, the teacher cried, A. My Mother's Young Sister. Roy McFadden. PNI

New Delhi, 1974. Vinay Dharwadker. OMIP

New Diary, A. Dannie Abse. NoAM

New Dodo is finished. O! come to my nest, The. (LL) Song by Isbrand. Thomas Lovell Beddoes. NOBVV; OBNC

New Dodo: Isabrand's Song, The. Thomas Lovell Beddoes. CBNP

New doth the sun appear. Change Should Breed Change. William Drummond, of Hawthornden. OBEV

New Duckling, The. Alfred Noyes. BoTP

New Emigration, The. Kay Boyle. WPE

New England. Anne Bradstreet. KTR *Fr.* A Dialogue between Old England and New.

New England. Edwin Arlington Robinson. HeIP-4; MeMAP; MoAmPo; NAAL-2; NOBA; OxBA; PoPoPo; TAP

New England Bachelor, A. Richard Eberhart. MoAmPo; NoAM

New-England Boy's Song About Thanksgiving Day, The. Lydia Maria Child. *See* Thanksgiving Day.

New England Primer, The. *Unknown.*
   John Rogers' Exhortation to His Children. OBCA

New England Wind. Eileen Myles. PmAP

New England's Annoyances. An Old Song, Wrote by One of Our First New-England Planters. *Unknown.* SCAP

New-Englands Crisis. Benjamin Tompson. SCAP

New English Canaan; Prologue. Thomas Morton. SCAP

New Every Morning. "Susan Coolidge." APAD

New every morning. John Keble. FaPoR; NOCV

New every morning is the love. Prime. Donald Davie. *Fr.* Horae Canonicae. CRP

New every morning is the power. Terce. Donald Davie. *Fr.* Horae Canonicae. CRP

New Ezekiel, The. Emma Lazarus. ColAP

New face, strange face, for my unrest. Modes of Pleasure. Thom Gunn. EP

New Faces, The. W. B. Yeats. GTBS-P

New Fashions. George Moses Horton. OBAL

New feet within my garden go—. Emily Dickinson. MeMAP

New follies spring; and now we must be taught. Picturesque; a Fragment. John Aikin. NOEC

New Friends and Old Friends. Joseph Parry. BLPA; PoToHe

New from Ethiopia and the Sudan, The. J. P. Clark Bekederemo. HBAPE

New Guinea. James Philip McAuley. NOCV

New Guinea Time. Louis Johnson. PeNZ

New Hampshire. T. S. Eliot. FaBoCh; GTBS-P; NoAM; WeW-3 *Fr.* Landscapes. RB

New Hampshire. Robert Frost.
   "If I must choose which I would elevate." UV

New Hampshire. Donald Hall. LCAP-2

New Hampshire, February. Richard Eberhart. LiTM; TwCP

New Heart, The. Semyon Isaakovich Kirsanov, *Russian.* CLPP, *tr. by* Anselm Hollo

New Heaven and Earth. D. H. Lawrence. CMoP

New Heaven, New War[re]. Robert Southwell. ChIV-2; ESCV; NOBE; NoP-4

New Holland is a barren place, in it there grows no grain. The Lowlands of Holland. *Unknown.* OxBB

New home at the mouth of Meng-ch'eng, A. Meng-ch'eng Hollow. Wang Wei. *Fr.* Twenty Views of Wang-ch'uan. CoBCP, *tr. by* Burton Watson

New House, The. Edward Thomas. EBEV; MoBrPo; NOBE; OBEV; OBWVE

New hunt / the morning bent, A. Clark Coolidge. APSN *Fr.* At Egypt.

New Incidents in the Life of Shelley. Robert Johnstone.
   "Not from our dreams, not from our daft cadres." PNI

New Indian Medicine. Emma Lee Warrior. HATNAP

New Inn, The. Ben Jonson.
   Vision of Beauty, A. NOSC

New Jail. *Unknown.* AmFP

New Jersey Turnpike. Richard Cumbie. NBLV

New Jerusalem, The. William Blake. *See* Jerusalem.

New Jerusalem, The. Allan M. Laing. UV

New Jewish Hospital at Hamburg, The. Heinrich Heine, *German.* TrJP, *tr. by* Charles Godfrey Leland

"New King Arrives in His Capital by Air. . . ."—Daily Newspaper. John Betjeman. OxBoLi
   (Death of King George V.) NOBE

New Knighthood, The. Rudyard Kipling. UV

New knowledge of reality, A. (LL) Not Ideas about the Thing but the Thing Itself. Wallace Stevens. HAP; HCAP; LCAP-2; MeMAP; SAmP; TAP

New Language, The. Elizabeth Robinson. PT

New laugh, The. Woman Dragged by Welsh Corgis. Joan Retallack. FTOS

New Leaf, A [*or* The]. Helen Field Fischer, *at. to* Kathleen Wheeler. PoToHe

New Life. Joseph E. Kariuki. TTY

New Light, A. William Hawkins. MoCV

New light gives new directions, Fortunes new. George Chapman. NoSic; OAEL-1; PBRV *Fr.* Hero and Leander. AAS

New Lines for Cuscuscaraway and Mirza Murad Ali Beg. Louis Simpson. OBAL

New Litany, Occasioned by an Invitation to a Wedding, A. Elizabeth Thomas. ECWP

New little boy moved in next door, A. Harry Behn. TLR

New London, The. Dryden. FaBoCh *Fr.* Annus Mirabilis.
   (London after the Great Fire, 1666.) NOBE

New Love. Vidyapati, *Sanskrit.* EP, *tr. by* Deben Bhattacharya

New love and the gentle heart are the same thing. Dante. RaBo

New Lullaby, The. Trần Dạ Từ', *Vietnamese.* AVP, *tr. by* Huỳnh Sanh Thông

New Man, The. Jones Very. APN-1; NOBA

New man flies in from Manchester, A. A New Poet Arrives. Gavin Ewart. OxBTC

New Mexican Mountain. Robinson Jeffers. InPS-3; MoP; NoAM; SAGP
   ("That civilization is a transient sickness.") (LL) SAGP

New Mistress, The. A. E. Housman. MoBrPo

New Monthly Magazine, 43 329. Felicia Dorothea Hemans.
   Thoughts During Sickness: II. Sickness Like Night. Ro

New Monthly Magazine, 44 286–8. Letitia Elizabeth Landon.
   Stanzas on the Death of Mrs Hemans. Ro; VWP

New Moon. *Aborigine Oral Tradition. Fr.* Moon-Bone Song [*or* Cycle]. CBAP, *tr. by* R. M. Berndt

New Moon, The. William Gilmore Simms. APN-1

New Moon. Tu Fu, *Chinese.* OHPC, *tr. by* Kenneth Rexroth

New moon hangs like an ivory bugle, The. The Penny Whistle. Edward Thomas. MoBrPo

New moon has come up and the autumn dew is light, A. Song of Autumn Night. Wang Ya, *Chinese.* SuSp, *tr. by* Irving Y. Lo

New Morality. George Canning.
   "From mental mists to purge a nation's eyes." NOEC

New Mother. Sharon Olds. CrSp

New-mown hay smell and wind of the plain made her a woman whose. Population Drifts. Carl Sandburg. OxBA

New Music. Gwen Harwood. CBAP

New Negro Sermon. Jacques Roumain, *French.* NegPo, *tr. by* Ellen Conroy Kennedy

New Night Thoughts on Death; a Parody. William Whitehead. NOEC

New Noah, The. "Adunis," *Arabic.* AF, *tr. by* Abdullah Al-Udhari

New Notebook, The. Maria Banus, *Rumanian.* PBWP, *tr. by* Laura Schiff *and* Dana Beldiman

New Nutcracker Suite, The. Ogden Nash.
   "Little girl marched around her Christmas tree, A." PChr

New Organ, The. Josephine D. Henderson Heard. CBWP-4

New Orleans. Joy Harjo. HATNAP

New peach blossoms are glowing, The. Flying Petals. Hsiao Kang, *Chinese.* OHMPC, *tr. by* Kenneth Rexroth

New Pietà: For the Mothers and Children of Detroit, The. June Jordan. PoBA

New Poem, A. Robert Duncan. NNaP; PoM

(New Poem (for Jack Spicer), A.) FTOS

New Poem, The. Charles Wright. HCAP; WeT

New Poem (for Jack Spicer), A. Robert Duncan. *See* A New Poem.

New Poet Arrives, A. Gavin Ewart. OxBTC

New Presbyter is but old Preist writ[t] large. (LL) On the New Forcers of Conscience Under the Long Parliament. Milton. FaBoPV; NAEL-1; NOSC; Son

New Prince, New Pomp[e]. Robert Southwell. ESCV; NOBE; NOCV; NoSic; TrCP

New Purpose of Hadrian's Army, The. Volker Braun, *German*. CEEP, *tr. by* Edward Mackinnon *and* A. M. Elliott

New Realism, The. John Ashbery.

"There was calm rapture in the way she spoke." WeT

New Realism. Joseph Ceravolo. PmAP

New Reality Is Better Than a New Movie!, A. Imamu Amiri Baraka. NoAM

New Refugee, A. Marisella Veiga. LoHo

New ridge spreads underneath. Volcanoes, offten, A. Wandering Curves. Keith Waldrop. PmAP

New River Head, a Fragment, The. E. Dower. NOEC

New road runs into, The. Directions. William Matthews. AmPA

New Rule, The. Jelaluddin Rumi, *Persian*. RaBo, *tr. by* Robert Bly *and* Coleman Barks

New Saddhus, The. Robert Pinsky. NAmP90

New Sentience, The. Alan Davies. FTOS

New Sermons and Preachings of the Christ of Elqui (1979). Nicanor Parra, *Spanish*.

"Who are my friends / the sick / the weak / the poor in spirit." GI, *tr. by* Sandra Reyes

New Shoes. John Agard. OTCP

New shoes, new shoes. Choosing Shoes. Ffrida Wolfe. ChAP

New Sights. *Unknown*. BoTP

New-slain Knight, The. *Unknown*. ESPB

New Song, A. Seamus Heaney. CABP; CIP-2; FaBoTw

New Song of New Similies, A. John Gay. CBNP; NOBL

New Song of Wood's Halfpence, A. Jonathan Swift. OxBoLi

New Song on the Birth of the Prince of Wales, A. John Harkness. NOBVV

New songs of Praise to CHRIST our KING. (LL) Once More, Our God, Vouchsafe to Shine! Samuel Sewall. AH; SCAP

New Speaker. James Berry. NBrP

New splendour to the dead. (LL) To Stella. Plato, *Greek*. OBCVT, *tr. by* Shelley; EnLoPo; FaBoEE; OBVE, *tr. by* Shelley

New Spoon River, The. Edgar Lee Masters.

Marx the Sign Painter. NoAM; TAP

Unknown Soldiers. NoAM; TAP

New Spring, A. Albert D. Mackie. OxBS

New stirrings converge in the mist. Anti-mnemonic self-vaccination. Joyce Mansour, *French*. MFP, *tr. by* Martin Sorrell

New Storefront. Russell Atkins. GT

New Strain. George Starbuck. TwCP

New Style, The. David O'Bruadair, *Irish*. BIrV, *tr. by* John Montague

New-Style Examinations. Trần Tế Xu'o'ng, *Vietnamese*. AVP, *tr. by* Huỳnh Sanh Thông

New styles of architecture, a change of heart. (LL) Petition. W. H. Auden. CMoP; MeMAP; NAEL-2; Son

New Suit, The. Nidia Sanabria de Romero, *Spanish*. ChAP, *tr. by* Morán, Arnaldo D. Larrosa and Naomi Shihab Nye

New Tarantella. Paul Griffin. UV

New Tenants, The. Edwin Arlington Robinson. NoAM

New Thatched Hall, A. Po Chü-i, *Chinese*. CoBCP, *tr. by* Burton Watson

New thatched hall, five spans by three, A. Po Chü-i, *Chinese*. CoBCP, *tr. by* Burton Watson

New things succeed, as former things grow old. (LL) Ceremonies for Candlemas[se] Eve. Robert Herrick. BeJo; CaPo

New ties, fifteen each, ten. Ties. Raymond Souster. MoCV

New Tiles. Xuân Diệu, *Vietnamese*. AVP, *tr. by* Huỳnh Sanh Thông

New Toy, The. Thomas Hardy. ChAP

New Vestments, The. Edward Lear. NOBVV

New Vicar of Bray, The. Colin Ellis. NOBL

New volcano has erupted, A. Crusoe in England. Elizabeth Bishop. FaBoVe; HCAP; PoPoPo; RACG

New Wife, The. Ng Shao, *Chinese*. OHMPC, *tr. by* Kenneth Rexroth

New Wife, The. Wang Chien. *See* Words of the Newly Wed Wife.

New Windows, *The stewardess gave me—I had just / turned six—a white eyelet sweater. / It was late November, 1968. "This is America," she told me, "cold, not like the West Indies. / One needs a jacket of some kind here."* Claudia Rankine. GT

New Wings for Icarus. Henry Beissel.

"In the one-two domestic goose one-two one-two step." MoCV

New Words. Coleman Barks.

"So it is." CRP

New World, The. Imamu Amiri Baraka. NoAM; NoP-4; PmAP

New World, The. Jones Very. APN-1; PAR

New World. Derek Walcott. OxBC

New World A-Comin'. Edward Kamau Brathwaite. NoP-4 *Fr.* The Arrivants: A New World Trilogy.

New World Symphony, A. Kit Wright. NBLV; PeLV

New Year, The. Bible, *O.T.* CTV

New Year. Naomi Shihab Nye. LoL; MT

New Year, The. Horatio Nelson Powers. PoToHe

New Year. Stephen Spender. AWP

New Year, The. Mark Strand. UnPo *Fr.* Elegy for My Father. HCAP; LCAP-2

New Year, The. *Unknown*. *See* A New Year Carol.

New-year bells are wrangling with the snow, The. (LL) Year's End. Richard Wilbur. CoAP; HeIP-4; LiTM; NAAL-2; NYBP

New Year Carol, A. *Unknown*. BoTP; CH; OxBoLi

(New Year, The.) OBCP

New year, forth looking out of Janus' gate. Sonnet 4. Edmund Spenser. NoSic *Fr.* Amoretti. AAS

New year has dawned and we meet it with gladness, The. New Year's Morning; or, the First Day of the Year. Mrs. Henry Linden. CBWP-4

New Year Letter. W. H. Auden.

"Long time since it seems today, A." FaBoA

"Self-educated WILLIAM BLAKE." EPCY

New Year Letter. Edward Kamau Brathwaite. GT

New Year March: A Declaration, The. Yuly Markovich Daniel, *Russian*. TCRP, *tr. by* David Burg *and* Arthur Boyars

New Year on Dartmoor. Sylvia Plath. FaBoWP

New-Yeares-Gift Sung to King Charles, 1635, A. Ben Jonson. SeCP

New Year's. Charles Reznikoff. VGW

New Year's Blizzard, The. Su Tung-p'o, *Chinese*. CoBCP, *tr. by* Burton Watson

New Year's Day. Robert Lowell. AmPP; CoAmPo; LiTM; TRP

New Year's Day—Following the Rhymes of Inspector Luan-chiang. Pien Kung, *Chinese*. CoBLCP, *tr. by* Jonathan Chaves

New Year's Days. Celia Standish. BoTP

New Year's Eve. John Berryman. LiTM

New Year's Eve. Boethius, *Latin*. MLL, *tr. by* Helen Waddell *Fr.* Consolation of Philosophy, The ("De Consolacione Philosophie").

New Year's Eve. John Davidson.

Imagination. APAD; MoBrPo

New Year's Eve. Thomas Hardy. MoBrPo; NoAM

New Year's Eve. D. H. Lawrence. BoLoP

New Year's Eve. Liu E, *Chinese*. ChiPo; CoBLCP, *tr. by* Jonathan Chaves

New Year's Eve. Su Tung-p'o, *Chinese*. CoBCP, *tr. by* Burton Watson

New Year's Eve. Wen Cheng-ming, *Chinese*. CoBLCP, *tr. by* Jonathan Chaves

New Year's Eve blizzard kept me from leaving, The. Su Tung-p'o, *Chinese*. CoBCP, *tr. by* Burton Watson

New Year's Eve Poem 1965. Peter Levi. OxAEP-2

New Year's Eve—you'd think I could go home early. Su Tung-p'o, *Chinese*. CoBCP, *tr. by* Burton Watson

New years [*or* yeares], expect new gifts: sister, your harp[e]. Ben Jonson. SeCP

New Year's Gift, A. William Cartwright. BeJo; OxAEP-1

New-Year's [*or* New-Yeares] Gift Sent to Sir Simeon Steward, A. Robert Herrick. CaPo

New Year's Morning; or, the First Day of the Year. Mrs. Henry Linden. CBWP-4

New Year's Poem. Margaret Avison. LiTM; NOBC

New Year's Sacrifice: To Lucinda, A. Thomas Carew. CaPo

New Year's [*or* Year] Song. Ted Hughes. OBCP

New Year's temple bells. Tanka. Shaku Chōkū, *Japanese*. MJT, *tr. by* Makoto Ueda

New Year's Wish for a Little Refugee, A. Trần Mộng Tú, *Vietnamese*. AVP, *tr. by* Huỳnh Sanh Thông

New York. "Æ." OBMV

New York. Federico García Lorca, *Spanish*. RaBo, *tr. by* Robert Bly

New York. William Logan. EOEF

New York. Marianne Moore. FaBoA; NAAL-2

("But 'accessibility to experience'.") (LL) FaBoA

New York. Toki Zenmaro, *Japanese*. MJT, *tr. by* Makoto Ueda

New York. 5 A.M. / The sidewalks empty. Ai. *See* The Man with the Saxophone.

New York Airport at Night. Andrey Andreievich Voznesensky, *Russian.* TCRP, *tr. by* William Jay Smith

New York! At first I was confused by your beauty, those tall long-legged golden girls. To New York. Léopold Sédar Senghor, *French.* NegPo, *tr. by* Ellen Conroy Kennedy

New York City. Helen Waddell. MLL

New York City Mira Mira Blues. Gloria Vando. LoHo

New York City 1970. Audre Lorde. NBV

New York City—1935. Gregory Corso. Poetsp

New York Elegy. Yevtushenko, *Russian.* TCRP, *tr. by* John Updike *and* Albert C. Todd

New York Everywhere. Berysh Vaynshteyn, *Yiddish.*
    Mangin Street. CEEP, *tr. by* Benjamin Harshav *and* Barbara Harshav

New York. Five A.M.. The Man with the Saxophone. Ai. SeSe; WWSi

New York has had it, newsmen all proclaim. New York Sonnet. Judith Rodriguez. NOBAu

New York Love Song (Part 1—Lower East Side). Lydia Tomkiw. WWSi

New York Map Company (1). John Yau. WWSi

New York Sonnet. Judith Rodriguez. NOBAu

New York's lovely weather / hurts my forehead. Bean Spasms. Ted Berrigan. PmAP; SPE

New Zealand. James Keir Baxter. NoP-4

Newark. Robert Kelly. MoNo; SeSe
    ("He made it / say itself inside our heads.") (LL) SeSe

Newark Abbey. Thomas Love Peacock. NOBE; OBNC

Newark, for Now (68). Carolyn M. Rodgers. PoBA

Newark Public Library Reading Room, The. Sotère Torregian. NBV

Newberry. *Unknown.* AmFP

Newborn progeny) that punctuality / is not a crime. (LL) Four Quartz Crystal Clocks. Marianne Moore. AmPP; TwCP

Newcombe at the Croydon Gallery. Arthur Nortje. HBAPE

Newcomer's Wife, The. Thomas Hardy. BoLoP; OxBTC

Newdigate Prize Poem 1937, The. Margaret Stanley-Wrench.
    Man in the Moon, The. WPN

Newe enterlued for chyldren to playe named Jacke Jugeler, A. Plautus Titus Maccius, *Latin.*
    From Amphitryon. OBCVT, *tr. by* Nicholas Udall

Newest Banana Plant Leaf, The. Ingrid Wendt. NMM-2

Newgate's Garland. John Gay. ECEV; PeLV

Newletter from My Mother. Michael S. Harper. PoBA

Newly Dead and Newly Born. Eliza Ogilvy. VWP

Newly Discovered "Homeric" Hymn, A. Charles Olson. MoP; NeAP; NoAM; PoM

Newly Pressed Suit, The. Roger McGough. MoP

Newly say dickered my love air my own would marry me all. Catullus. *See* Carmen 70 ("Lesbia says she'ld rather marry me").

Newly shaven, your eyes only slightly bloodshot. Desires. Connie Bensley. FaBoWP

Newlyweds, The. Cloyd Mann Criswell. PoLF

Newlyweds, The. John Updike. OBCoV

News. Louis Dudek. *Fr.* Provincetown. MoCV

News, The. Tuini Ngawai, *Maori.* PeNZ, *tr. by* Kumeroa Ngoingoi Pewhairangi

News. Lorine Niedecker. PFTM

News bulletin from Keith Lampe. Joanne Kyger. BB

News for the Delphic Oracle. W. B. Yeats. CMoP; FaBoMo; LiTM; NoAM

News from a foreign [*or* forein *or* forrein] country came. On News. Thomas Traherne. ESCV; GeHe; NOBE; OBEV *Fr.* The Third Century.

News from a foreign country came. Thomas Traherne. *See* On News.

News from a Pacified Area. James Keir Baxter. OxBC

News from Behind the Seven Hills. Günter Kunert, *German.* CEEP, *tr. by* Michael Hamburger

News from Norwood. Christopher Middleton. FaBoMo

News from the Cabin. May Swenson. NYBP

News from the House. Michael Dennis Browne. NYBP

News, Indeed!—pray do you call it news, The. John Godfrey Saxe. NBLV

News is of camps, outpost, little progress, The. Lecturing on the Theme of Motherhood. Michael S. Harper. FiLi

News Item. Dorothy Parker. NALW; OBAL *Fr.* Some Beautiful Letters.

News of My Mother. Jean-Baptiste Tati-Loutard. PBMAP *Fr.* Poèmes de la Mer (1968).

News of the Occluded Cyclone. Alice Fulton. WeW-3

News of the palace. Lady Ise, *Japanese.* BoWoP, *tr. by* Etsuko Terasaki *and* Irma Brandeis

News of the Phoenix. Arthur James Marshall Smith. MoCV

News of the World II. George Barker. FaBoTw

News of the World III. George Barker. FaBoTw; LiTM

NEWS peels off my arms and legs in a wind that doesn't quite hurt. The, The. What Say. John Godfrey. FTOS

News Report. David Ignatow. TwCP

News Update. John Balaban. AF; CDa

News which might well reach you / before this letter?, The. (LL) Ellen West. Frank Bidart. RACG

Newspaper is a collection of half injustices, A. Stephen Crane. APN-2; AmPP; MeMAP; NAAL-2 *Fr.* War Is Kind.

Newspapers rise high in the air over Maryland. At a March against the Vietnam War. Robert Bly. CDa; SPE

Newsreel. C. Day Lewis. MoBrPo

Newsreel. Adrienne Rich. FaBoWP; HCAP *Fr.* Shooting Script.

Newsvendor with his hut and crutch, The. The Imprisoned. Robert Fitzgerald. TwCP

Next, bidding all draw near on bended knees. Idle Pursuits. Alexander Pope. ECEV, *book* IV, *ll.* 565–604; OBSV *Fr.* Yet, yet a moment, one dim ray of light. NAEL-1; OAEL-1; PoEL-3 *Fr.* The Dunciad.

Next came Bob, but before him I had Phil. Robyn Selman. PUP-19

Next came one / Who mourn'd in earnest, when the Captive Ark. Milton. EBEV *Fr.* Book I. FHYEP; NAEL-1; OAEL-1; OxAEP-1 *Fr.* Paradise Lost.

Next comes the dull disciple of thy school. Byron. EPCY *Fr.* English Bards and Scotch Reviewers.

Next Day. Randall Jarrell. HAP; HCAP; MoP; NAAL-2; NYBP; NoAM; NoP-4; Poetr; VCAP; WeW-3

Next day, the deadlock broke. (LL) What the Moon Saw. Vachel Lindsay. FaBoEE; OxBSP

Next Day the Fog Was Even Worse, The. Yüan Mei, *Chinese.* CoBLCP, *tr. by* Jonathan Chaves

Next day they rambled round the town, and swore. James Bisset. NOEC *Fr.* Ramble of the Gods through Birmingham.

Next died the Lady, who yon Hall possess'd. The Lady of the Manor. George Crabbe. NOBE; OBNC *Fr.* Burials. OAEL-1 *Fr.* The Parish Register.

Next Door. Laini Mataka. ISC

Next Door. Mei Yao Ch'en, *Chinese.* OHPC, *tr. by* Kenneth Rexroth

Next, for October, to some sheltered coign. October. Folgore da San Geminiano. *Fr.* Sonnets of the Months. AWP, *tr. by* D. G. Rossetti

Next Heaven [*or* Heav'n] my vows to thee (O sacred Muse!). Upon the Saying That My Verses Were Made by Another. Anne Killigrew. CABP; KTR; NALW; PEW; WPE

Next him Jack Squire through his own tear-drops sploshes. Roy Campbell. OxBTC *Fr.* The Georgiad.

Next, in a low-browed cave, a little hell. William Thompson. ECEV *Fr.* Sickness.

Next is your lot, fair, to be numbered one. To His Kinswoman, Mrs. Penelope Wheeler. Robert Herrick. CaPo

Next Page. Atmanam, *Tamil.* OMIP, *tr. by* A. K. Ramanujan

Next, Please. Philip Larkin. CABP; MoBrPo

Next Poem, The. Dana Gioia. DiPo; NoP-4

Next shall clean out of my breast it pluck, The. (LL) Alas, madam[e], for stealing [*or* stelying] of a kiss [*or* kysse]. Sir Thomas Wyatt. BoLoP; CBLP

Next Story, The. Pattiann Rogers. NAmP90

Next they leave it leagues behind, The. (LL) Anno 1829. Heinrich Heine, *German.* AWP; OBVE, *tr. by* Charles Stuart Calverley

Next thing, I wake up in a swaying bunk. Journey: the North Coast. Robert Gray. BMAP

Next time 1930 rolls around. (LL) This One's on Me. Phyllis Gotlieb. MoCV; NOBC

Next to my best friend I woke up. Old-fashioned. Dara Wier. NAmP90

Next to my own skin, her pearls. My mistress. Warming Her Pearls. Carol Ann Duffy. NoP-4

Next to of course god america i. E. E. Cummings. AmPP; EBEvV; FaBoA; FaBoPV; InPK-6; LiTM; MeMAP; NAAL-2; NBLV; NoP-4; OBWP; OxBA; PoWW; RaBo; SAGP; TAP; TFi; VGW

Next to the fair ascent our steps we traced. The Triumphs of Nature. Samuel Boyse. OBGa *Fr.* The Triumphs of Nature.

Next to the fresh grave of my beloved grandmother. Ireland 1972. Paul Durcan. PBCIP

Next to the white window. Fifteen. Jan Freeman. OxWW *Fr.* Autumn Sequence.

Next to will / I value reason. Swimming Pool. Maria Teresa Horta, *Portuguese.* PBWP, *tr. by* Suzette Macedo

Next unto God, to whom I owe. To Retiredness. Mildmay Fane, 2d Earl of Westmorland. BeJo; NOSC

Next War, The. Wilfred Owen. Son

Next War, The. Sir Osbert Sitwell. NSI; PoWW

Next, who 'as leave to domineer, The. Alicia D'Anvers. KTR *Fr.* Academia; or The Humours of the University of Oxford.

Next whose fortune 't was a tale to tell, The. Fitz Adam's Story. James Russell Lowell. AmPP

Next Year, in Jerusalem. Shirley Kaufman. UnSA

"Next year, next year," we say. Nora Perry. PoToHe

Next year the grave grass will cover us. Street Corner College. Kenneth Patchen. CLPP; MoAmPo

Next year we are to bring the soldiers home. Homage to a Government. Philip Larkin. EBEV; FaBoPV; NoAM

"Next year you must come again." Liu E. *Fr.* Poems for Yukiko of Tamba. CoBLCP, *tr.* by Jonathan Chaves

Ngaa. . . now then. Paddy Biran's Song. Paddy Biran, *Girramay.* CBAP, *tr.* by R. M. W. Dixon

Ngoh m' sick gong tong hwa. Going Home. Wing Tek Lum. UnSA

Ngoni Burial Song. *Unknown, Zulu.* PeSA

Ngungalari. Archie Weller. RACG

Nguyễn Du, a poet towering over all! To Nguyễn Du. Đằng Phu'o'ng, *Vietnamese.* AVP, *tr.* by Huỳnh Sanh Thông

Ni Tsan Poem Following Rhyme-Words of Wu Chen. Wu Chen, *Chinese.* CoBLCP, *tr.* by Jonathan Chaves

Niagara. Joseph Rodman Drake. APN-1

Niagara Falls. Alan Dugan. PoA

Nialls' cottage had one, The. Hearth Song. John Montague. PNI

Nibble, nibble, little sheep. Sheep. Samuel Hoffenstein. TrJP

Nicander, ooh, your leg's got hairs! Epigram. Alcaeus, *Greek.* GrAn, *tr.* by Tony Harrison

Nice Day for a Lynching. Kenneth Patchen. APAD

Nice Mountain. Gerald Stern. PuP-14

Nice Mrs. Eberle early had been told. La Donna E Perpetuum Mobile. Irwin Edman. NYBP

Nice of you, white. Red. Gerald William Barrax. *Fr.* The Old Gory. NBV

Nice Part of Town, A. Alfred Hayes. NYBP

Nice pot of gold that was mari, A. Limerick. Arthur Shaw. PeLi

Nice Thing About Counting Stars, The. Dwight Okita. UnSA

Nice Valor, The. John Fletcher.

Melancholy. GTBS-P; OBEV

(Song.) PoEL-2

Nicest child I ever knew, The. Charles Augustus Fortescue. Hilaire Belloc. NoAM

Nicest Phantasies Are Shared, The. Brian Coffey. CIP-2

Nicetes begins with gentle declamation. Automedon, *Greek.* GrAn, *tr.* by Frederick Garber

Nichita Stanescu. Brian Turner. PeNZ

Nicholas Ned. Laura Elizabeth Richards. NTCP

Nicholas Nye. Walter De la Mare. BoTP

Nick and the Candlestick. Sylvia Plath. CoAP; FiLi; LCAP-2; NALW; PBWP; Poetr

Nickleplate moon, The. Kansas City West Bottoms. Edward Dahlberg. PoA

Nicky, the word has come to the West Coast. Smoke. Charles Wright. NYBP

Nicodemus. Howard Nemerov. GI

Nicolas Guillen brought me your letter, written. Letter to Miguel Otero Silva, in Caracas. Pablo Neruda, *Spanish.* AF, *tr.* by Robert Bly

Nicole at Thirteen. Gregory Orr. MoLi

Nicole may have been a beauty long ago. Nicarchus of Alexandria, *Greek.* InMo, *tr.* by Sam Hamill

Niconoë has just inched past her prime. Nicarchus of Alexandria, *Greek.* GrAn, *tr.* by Peter Porter

Nico's bedroom talents entice men. *Unknown, Greek.* InMo, *tr.* by Sam Hamill

Nid-nod through shuttered streets at dead of night. The Last Bus. Edmund George Valpy Knox. BXAP

Niddle Noddle. Mother Goose. OxNR

Nietzsche is pietsche. Graffiti. Alice Archer Sewall James. NBLV

Nievie nievie nick nack. *Unknown.* OxNR

Nigeria in the Year 1999. Catherine Obianuju Acholonu. HBAPE

Nigga Section, The. Welton Smith. BPo

Nigger. Sonia Sanchez. BPo

Nigger. Karl Shapiro. OxBA

Nigger and Some Poofters, A. Nigel Roberts. BMAP

Nigger / Can you kill. True Import of Present Dialogue, Black vs, The Negro. Nikki Giovanni. BPo; PoBA

Nigger-Lover is a song, spat out. Song. Cornelius Eady. GT

Nigger Song: An Odyssey. Rita Dove. AmPA

Niggerlips was the high school name / for me. Martín Espada. UnSA

Nigger's Got to Go, De. Daniel Webster Davis. AAP

Nigger's Leap, New England. Judith Wright. NOBAu

Night, The. Al-Khansa, *Arabic.* BoWoP, *tr.* by Willis Barnstone

Night, The. Hilaire Belloc. OBEV

Night. William Rose Benét. MoAmPo

Night. Hayyim Nahman Bialik, *Hebrew.* AWP, *tr.* by Maurice Samuel

Night. William Blake. BoTP; CH; FHYEP; FaBoBe; OBEV; OxBChV; PoLF; Ro *Fr.* Songs of Innocence.

Night. Robert Bly. WeT

Night. Louise Bogan. NoP-4; Poetr; UnPo

Night. Augusta Cooper Bristol. APN-2

Night. Anne Brontë. VWP

Night. Henri De Regnier, *French.* AWP, *tr.* by "Seumas O'Sullivan"

Night. Georgi Djagarov, *Bulgarian.* CEEP, *tr.* by Jascha Kessler and Aleksandar Shurbanov

Night. Peter Everwine. NNaP

Night. Louise Glück. MoLi *Fr.* Metamorphosis. MoLi

Night. Josephine D. Henderson Heard. CBWP-4

Night. Hermann Hesse, *German.* AWP, *tr.* by Ludwig Lewisohn

Night. Robinson Jeffers. AWP; ColAP; MoAmPo; NOBA; OxBA

Night. Etheridge Knight. See Cell Song.

Night, The. Helen Leuty. BoTP

Night. Henry Wadsworth Longfellow. APN-1

Night. Lois Weakley McKay. CTV

Night. Boris Pasternak, *Russian.* TCRP, *tr.* by Edwin Morgan

Night. Ann Radcliffe. NOBRP; WPE

Night. Sir Philip Sidney. SiPS *Fr.* Arcadia.

Night. Wole Soyinka. PBMAP *Fr.* Idanre and Other Poems (1967).

Night, The. James Stephens. BoTP

Night. Sara Teasdale. NOxBChV

Night. Georg Trakl, *German.* PeFWW, *tr.* by David McDuff, Jon Silkin, and R. S. Furness

Night. Tu Fu, *Chinese.* SuSp, *tr.* by Jan W. Walls

Night. *Unknown.* BoTP

Night, The. Henry Vaughan. ChIV-2; EBEV; ESCV; FSCP; GeHe; MeLP; NAEL-1; NOBE; NOCV; NoP-4; OAEL-1; OBEV; OBWVE; OxAEP-1; PoEL-2; SCGP; TFi; TOF

("Might live invisible and dim!") (LL) FSCP; NoP-4

Night. Edward Young. See Night Thoughts.

Night a Sailor Came to Me in a Dream, The. Diane Wakoski. TAP; VGW

Night above the Town. Thomas Lux. SeSe

Night After Bushfire. Judith Wright. BMAP

Night after night from our camp on Sugar Loaf Hill. The Influence of Natural Objects. James Simmons. PNI

Night again. Again the grim sky closes. Night over Birkenau. Tadeusz Borowski, *Polish.* HP, *tr.* by Tadeuszt Pióro

Night along the Mackinac Bridge. Roberta Hill Whiteman. CDW

Night; an Epistle to Robert Lloyd. Charles Churchill.

"Spectators only on this bustling stage." OBSV

Night and a Distant Church. Russell Atkins. PoBA

Night and a starless sky. Shipwreck. Mary Weston Fordham. CBWP-2, *tr.* by Mary Ann Caws

Night, and beneath star-blazoned summer skies. The South. Emma Lazarus. APN-2; ColAP

Night and Day. Michael Drayton. *Fr.* Idea.

("Dear, why should you command me to my rest.") GSo

(Sonnet: "Dear [or Deere], why should you command me to my rest.")

Night and Day. Cole Porter. CBLP

Night and day arrive, and day after day goes by. For My Son Noah, Ten Years Old. Robert Bly. InPS-3; LoL; RaBo

Night and day under the rind of me. Parodies of Cole Porter's "Night and Day." Ring Lardner. OBAL

Night / and in the warm blackness. Upon Your Leaving. Etheridge Knight. NNaP

Night, and its muffled creakings, as the wheels. The Shako. Robert Lowell. Son

Night and mist, what bones you have eaten. Leonidas of Tarentum, *Greek.* GrAn, *tr.* by Peter Levi

Night and Morning. Austin Clarke. CIP-2

Night and Morning. *Unknown, Welsh.* OBWVE, *tr.* by R. S. Thomas

Night and Night's longing. Meleager, *Greek.* GrAn, *tr.* by Peter Whigham

Night, and on all sides only the folding quiet. S. D. R. Sutu, *Sotho.* PeSA; TTY, *tr.* by Dan Kunene and Jack Cope

Night, and one single ridge of narrow path. Robert Browning. EBVVPR *Fr.* Pauline, mine own, bend o'er me—thy soft breast.

Night and Sleep. Coventry Patmore. EBVV

(Shadow of Night, The.) CH

Night, and the down by the sea. Rain on the Down. Arthur Symons. OBNC *Fr.* At Dieppe.

Night, and the heavens beam serene with peace. Solomon ibn Gabirol, *Hebrew.* TrJP, *tr. by* Emma Lazarus

Night and the hood. Prelude. Conrad Kent Rivers. PoBA

Night, / And the yellow pleasure of candlelight. Song of the Rain. Hugh Raymond McCrae. CBAP

Night and we heard heavy and cadenced hoofbeats. The Return. John Peale Bishop. ImPo; OxBA

Night arches England, and the winds are still. Peace. Walter De la Mare. MoBrPo

Night at an Airport. David Ignatow. NNaP

Night at Anchor by Maple Bridge. Chang Chi, *Chinese.* OHMPC, *tr. by* Kenneth Rexroth

Night attendant, a B.U. sophomore, The. Waking in the Blue. Robert Lowell. CoAP; HCAP; MoAmPo; UnPo

Night before Christmas, The. Clement Clarke Moore. *See* A Visit from St Nicholas.

Night Before Good-Bye, The. Mitsuye Yamada. NMM-2

Night Before His Parents' First Trip to Europe His Mother Writes a Letter "To Our Children," The. Michael J. Rosen. BAP-95

Night before Larry was stretched, The. *Unknown.* BIrV; NOBL; NOIV; OxBoLi

Night before my uncle Carter got shot, The. Support Your Local Police Dog. Carter Revard. VoR

Night Before the Soviets, The. Velemir Khlebnikov, *Russian.* "She came and spoke low." TCRP, *tr. by* Gary Kern

Night before they meant to pluck his eyes, The. Among Philistines. R. S. Gwynn. MT; RA

Night before Waterloo, The. Byron. *See* The Eve of Waterloo.

Night begins to gather between her breasts. George Swede. HA

Night Bird. James Dickey. WeT

Night-Blooming Cereus, The. Robert Earl Hayden. NoP-4

Night-Blooming Flowers. Felicia Dorothea Hemans. NOBRP

Night-Blooming Jasmine, The. Audre Lorde. ColAP

Night breaths, short ones. In the Hospital. Laura Jensen. AmPA

Night by nightfall more benighted. Garcia Lorca Murdered in Granada. John Streeter Manifold. CBAP

Night by the Sea, A. Heinrich Heine. AWP, *tr. by* Howard Mumford Jones *Fr.* The North Sea.

Night Café. Gottfried Benn, *German.* PFTM, *tr. by* Michael Hamburger

Night Catch. Heather McHugh. AmPA

Night Chant, The. *Navajo Oral Tradition, Navajo.* ITG, *tr. by* Matthews, Washington and Robert Hass

Night Chant, The. Rimbaud. After Bitahatini. PFTM

Night Chant, The. *Unknown, Navajo.* APN-2, *tr. by* Washington Matthews

Night Chill. Li Shang-yin, *Chinese.* SuSp, *tr. by* Eugene Eoyang *and* Irving Y. Lo

Night City, The. W. S. Graham. FaBoTC

Night Clouds. Amy Lowell. MoAmPo

Night Club. Louis MacNeice. OxBSP *Fr.* Entered in the Minutes.

Night Club. Francis Reginald Scott. NOBC

Night Coach. Phillis Levin. RA

Night comes. Gary Hotham. HA

Night comes and, drowsy with drink, I'm slow to shed my /ornaments, Tune: "Telling of Innermost Feelings." Li Ch'ing-chao, *Chinese.* CoBCP, *tr. by* Burton Watson

Night comes. Day runs for its life into my eyes. Gil Orlovitz. PoA *Fr.* Art of the Sonnet.

Night coming tenderly / Black like me. Langston Hughes. *See* Dream Variation[s].

Night covers the pond with its wing. The Pond. Louise Glück. ColAP

Night / creeps in, The. Myra Cohn Livingston. TLR

Night Cries, Wakari Hospital. Charles Brasch. Winter Anemones. PeNZ

Night Crow. Theodore Roethke. HoPM; InPK-6; OxBSP; VGW

Night crushes you so I look for you, The. No. José Hidalgo, *Spanish.* IMW, *tr. by* Stephen Berg

Night Dances, The. Sylvia Plath. LCAP-2

Night, Death, Mississippi. Robert Earl Hayden. ColAP; LCAP-2; NoP-4; PoPoPo; VCAP; VGW

("Quavering cry. Screech-owl?, A.") ColAP; NoP-4; PoPoPo

Night descended on us with a chill. Tomas Venclova, *Lithuanian.* CEEP, *tr. by* David McDuff

Night Don Juan came to pay his fees, The. Don Juan in Hell. Charles Baudelaire, *French.* AWP, *tr. by* James Elroy Flecker

Night-dreams trace on Memory's wall. Memory. Ralph Waldo Emerson. APN-1 *Fr.* Quatrains.

Night Dust-off. Basil T. Paquet. CDa

Night Fear. Don Receveur. CDa

Night Feeding. Muriel Rukeyser. MDDM; NMM-2; NoP-4; WPE

Night fell, but you never came back. *Unknown. See* They fought south of the walls.

Night Ferry. Mark Doty. NAmP90

Night Flare Drop, Tan Son Nhut. Horace Coleman. CDa

Night Flight. Marion Alexopoulos. NOBAu

Night Flower. Geoffrey Lehmann. NOBAu

Night for menace with weary eyes. (LL) The Trenches. Frederic Manning. NOBAu; NSI; PoWW

Night forked stigmata. Different Horizon. Aimé Césaire, *French.* VCWP, *tr. by* Clayton Eshleman *and* Annette Smith

Night found me so flushed with wine. Tune: "Telling of Innermost Feelings." Li Ch'ing-chao, *Chinese.* SuSp, *tr. by* Eugene Eoyang

Night from a railroad car window. Window. Carl Sandburg. PiM

Night full of talking that hurts, A. Jelaluddin Rumi. RaBo, *tr. by* John Moyne *and* Coleman Barks *Fr.* Three Quatrains.

Night Fun. Judith Viorst. TLR

Night funeral / In Harlem. Langston Hughes. InPS-3; SAGP

Night Game of the Maker of Faces, The. Novica Tadic, *Serbo-Croatian.* HSix, *tr. by* Charles Simic

Night Gives Old Woman the Word. Gail Tremblay. HATNAP

"Night". . . "Good night." (LL) In The Orchard. Muriel Stuart. EBNV; OxBTC

Night Has a Thousand Eyes, The. When Love Is Done. Francis William Bourdillon. APAD; BLPA; BoLoP; CTV; FaBoBe; LBC; OBEV; OxBSP; PFE; PoToHe

Night has come on like a woman sleeping, The. Moon Poems. John Wieners. VGW

Night has entered the town, unheralded. Anno Domini. Lucian Blaga, *Romanian.* CEEP, *tr. by* Peter Jay *and* Virgil Nemoianu

Night has secreted us. Amen. Richard W. Thomas. PoBA

Night he died, earth's images all came, The. Poet. Peter Viereck. HoPM; MoAmPo

Night held me as I crawled and scrambled near. The Turkish Trench Dog. Geoffrey Dearmer. NSI

Night-herding Song[, A]. Harry Stephens. NTP

Night here, a covert. Gary Snyder. *Fr.* Burning. NeAP; PoM *Fr.* Myths and Texts.

Night here, the owners asleep upstairs. Up Late. Arthur Nortje. PBMAP

Night hides our thefts; all faults then pardoned [*or* pardon'd] be. In the Dark None Dainty. Robert Herrick. CaPo; CavPo

Night hung o'er Virginia's forest wild, The. Capt. Smith and Pocahontas. Eloise Bibb. CBWP-4

Night I fell in love with you I lost my watch, The. Perfect Timing. Sarah Maguire. LW

Night, I know you are powerful and artistic. For Bill Hawkins, a Black Militant. William J. Harris. PoBA

Night I lost you, The. The Five Stages of Grief. Linda Pastan. IMW

Night I seldom remember, A. Obeah Night. Jean Rhys. PBCV

Night II (Enion's Lament). William Blake. PoE *Fr.* Vala; or The Four Zoas.

(Enion's Lamentation.) Ro

Night in a Village, A. Ivan Savvich Nikitin, *Russian.* AWP, *tr. by* P. E. Matheson

Night in June, A. Wordsworth. BoTP

Night in Nigeria. Ellease Southerland. GT

Night in Odessa, A. Louis Simpson. NNaP

Night in soft slumbers rolled gently away, The. Miss F[——]ny M[——]t[——]ly to Miss P[——]ly B[——]s. Fanny [*or* Frances] Macartney Greville. ECWP

Night in the bloodstained snow: the wind is chill. Hialmar Speaks to the Raven. Charles Marie René Leconte de Lisle, *French.* AWP, *tr. by* James Elroy Flecker

Night in the Forest. Galway Kinnell. TAP

Night in the House by the River. Tu Fu, *Chinese.* OHPC, *tr. by* Kenneth Rexroth

Night in the Royal Ontario Museum, A. Margaret Atwood. PBWP

Night in the Trench, A. Velemir Khlebnikov, *Russian.* "Clan of stony desert women, A." TCRP, *tr. by* Gary Kern

Night in the Villa by the River. Tu Fu, *Chinese.* TAL, *tr. by* Robert Payne

Night in the Village. Christoph Eisenhuth, *German.* CEEP, *tr. by* Allen H. Chappel

Night is a furrow, a queasy, insistent wound, The. Nightletter. Charles Wright. PoA

Night is beautiful, The. My People. Langston Hughes. MBE; NOxBChV

Night is black swan wholly adrift. Hotel in Paris. Dennis Trudell. PoA

Night is calm, the cygnet's down, The. On a Calm Summer's Night. John Nicholson. EnLoPo

Night is cold and frosty, The. A Winter Night. Priscilla Jane Thompson. CBWP-2

Night is cold on the Great Bog, The. *Unknown. Fr.* Toward Winter. NOIV

Night is come, but not too soon, The. The Little Moon. Henry Wadsworth Longfellow. BoTP

Night is come. The land is wrapt in sleep, The. (LL) Storm is over, the land hushes to rest, The. Robert Bridges. GTBS-P; LiTM; OBMV

Night is dark, The. Yury Timofeievich Galanskov, *Russian.* TCRP, *tr. by* Albert C. Todd

Night is dark, the wind has dashed, The. Midnight Prayer. Hayyim Nahman Bialik, *Hebrew.* TrJP, *tr. by* Helena Frank

Night is darkening round me, The. Spellbound. Emily Jane Brontë. NOBE; NOBVV; OBNC; PoEL-5; VWP

Night is dewy as a maiden's mouth, The. A Summer's Night. Paul Laurence Dunbar. APN-2; NoP-4

Night is divided. And behind us. Stone and Ashes. Husein Tahmisic, *Serbian.* CEEP, *tr. by* Ewald Osers

Night is freezing fast, The. Winter. A. E. Housman. CMoP; LBC; LiTM; OxBSP; PFE

Night is full of storm clouds, The. Freezing Night. T'ao Hung Ching, *Chinese.* OHMPC, *tr. by* Kenneth Rexroth

Night is long, she cannot sleep, The. Song of Tzu-yeh. *Unknown, Chinese.* SuSp, *tr. by* Ronald C. Miao

Night is my sister, and how deep in love. Edna St. Vincent Millay. HAP; SAGP

Night Is Near [*or* Neir] Gone, The. Alexander Montgomerie. OBEV; OxBS (Hey! Now the Day Dawns.) CH

Night is neir gone, The. (LL) The Night Is Near [*or* Neir] Gone. Alexander Montgomerie. CH; OBEV; OxBS

Night is o'er England, and the winds are still. Peace. Walter De la Mare. MoBrPo

Night is on the downland, on the lonely moorland. Night on the Downland. John Masefield. LiTM; MoBrPo *Fr.* Lollingdon Downs.

Night is still. The unfailing surf, The. Miramar Beach. James Vincent Cunningham. PoA *Fr.* To What Strangers, What Welcome. NoAM

Night is tranquil, the wind-blown curtain, The. Spring Night. Chang Yü. *Fr.* Twelve Miscellaneous Poems on the Fang Garden. CoBLCP, *tr. by* Jonathan Chaves

Night it was, dear, when we kissed. Betrayal. *Unknown, Greek.* GrIP, *tr. by* Philip Sherrard

Night it was horribly dark, The. Measles in the Ark. "Susan Coolidge." OxBChV

Night John Henry is born an ax, The. The Birth of John Henry. Melvin Beaunearus Tolson. BPo; NAAAL; TTY *Fr.* Harlem Gallery.

Night Journey. Theodore Roethke. GM; KaS; NYBP; SAGP

Night Journey of a River, The. William Cullen Bryant. APN-1

Night knows nothing of the chants of night, The. Re-statement of Romance. Wallace Stevens. ITG

Night Las Vegas caught fire, The. The Case. Hoffman Reynolds Hays. SPE

Night Letter. Stanley Kunitz. AF

Night licks the backyard with its reptile tongue. Clockface. Rhyll McMaster. BMAP

Night lies blue and white, The. Minor Key. Judah Leib Teller, *Yiddish.* CEEP, *tr. by* Gabriel Preil *and* Howard Schwartz

Night-life. Letters, journals, bourbon. Origins and History of Consciousness. Adrienne Rich. NIP-4; Poetr

Night Light. Nancy Willard. LCAP-2

Night, lighter than day! Night, more than brilliant night. On the Birth of Jesus. Andreas Gryphius, *German.* GePo, *tr. by* George C. Schoolfield

Night! loathed [*or* loathèd] jailor of the locked-up [*or* lock'd up] sun. Richard Lovelace. CaPo

Night long and wintry / the Pleiades half set. Asclepiades, *Greek.* GrAn, *tr. by* Alan Marshfield

Night Mail, The. W. H. Auden. OxBTC

Night Mail North, The. Henry Cholmondeley-Pennell. EBVV

Night makes no difference 'twixt the Priest and Clerk. No Difference in the Dark [*or* i'th'dark]. Robert Herrick. CaPo

Night-March, The. Herman Melville. NCAP

Night Mirror, The. John Hollander. NYBP; VCAP

Night Music. Linda Gregg. BLT

Night-Music. Philip Larkin. InPS-3

Night-Music. Muriel Rukeyser. PoA
    Time Exposures. PoA

Night music slanted. Cell Song. Etheridge Knight. NNaP; PoBA

Night Nurse Goes Her Round, The. John Gray. OBNC

Night of Battle. Yvor Winters. PoA

Night of Death, The. Frances Ellen Watkins Harper. PWR

Night of gentle thunder fells a thousand catkins, A. Spring Rain. Ch'in Kuan, *Chinese.* SuSp, *tr. by* Stephen West

Night of iron wheels and rain, A. The Red Flag. Michael Jackson. PeNZ

Night of love, A. The Second Madrigal. Anna Swirszczynska, *Polish.* BLT, *tr. by* Czeslaw Milosz *and* Leonard Nathan

Night of love was pure, The. The First Madrigal. Anna Swirszczynska, *Polish.* CEEP, *tr. by* Magnus J. Krynski *and* Robert A. Maguire

Night of My Blood (1971). Kofi Awoonor.
    At the Gates. PBMAP; VCWP

Night of our parting in the red tower is enough for sorrow, The. Tune: "Deva-like Barbarian." Wei Chuang, *Chinese.* SuSp, *tr. by* Lois M. Fusek

Night of rain on the autumn river, A. Tsung Ch'en. *Fr.* Miscellaneous Words on the Lake. CoBLCP, *tr. by* Jonathan Chaves

Night of Sine. Léopold Sédar Senghor, *French.* NegPo, *tr. by* Ellen Conroy Kennedy; PBA; PBMAP
    ("Woman, rest your balsam hands upon my brow.") NegPo, *tr. by* Ellen Conroy Kennedy

Night of Souls. Ann Stanford. WPE

Night of Spring. Thomas Westwood. BoTP

Night of the eclipse we're parallel, The. Total Eclipse. Michael J. Rosen. DiPo

Night of the Fifteenth, Second Month. Yüan Mei, *Chinese.* CoBLCP, *tr. by* Jonathan Chaves

Night of the First Full Moon, The. Li K'ai-hsien, *Chinese.* CoBLCP, *tr. by* Jonathan Chaves

Night of the Fourteenth. Ho Ching-ming, *Chinese.* CoBLCP, *tr. by* Jonathan Chaves

Night of the Seventeenth, The. Li K'ai-hsien, *Chinese.* CoBLCP, *tr. by* Jonathan Chaves

Night of the Shirts, The. W. S. Merwin. VCAP

Night of Trafalgar, The. Thomas Hardy. FaBoCh; MoBrPo; OBMV *Fr.* The Dynasts.
    (Trafalgar.) CH

Night of utter silences, A. Shadows. "Yehoash," *Yiddish.* TrJP, *tr. by* Elias Lieberman

Night on Clinton. Robert Mezey. AmPA

Night on earth and sky. A Terrible Thought. Eliezer Steinbarg, *Yiddish.* TrJP, *tr. by* Joseph Leftwich

Night on the Conroy. Siegfried Sassoon. NSI

Night on the Downland. John Masefield. MoBrPo *Fr.* Lollingdon Downs.

Night on the Great River. Meng Hao Jan, *Chinese.* OHMPC, *tr. by* Kenneth Rexroth

Night on the Kho Bha Dinh. Steve Denning. CDa

Night on the Prairies. Walt Whitman. PaTW

Night opens like an almond. Yvonne Caroutch, *French.* BoWoP, *tr. by* Elene Margot Kolb

Night Operations, Coastal Command RAF. Howard Nemerov. AF

Night Ottawa brought down the budget, The. Spleen. August Kleinzahler. PmAP

Night, our [*or* the] black summer, simplifies her smells. Nights in the Gardens of Port of Spain. Derek Walcott. NAEL-2; NoP-4; OxBC

Night over Birkenau. Tadeusz Borowski, *Polish.* HP, *tr. by* Tadeusz Pióro

Night passd and Enitharmon eer the dawn returnd in bliss. Song of Enitharmon. William Blake. OAEL-2 *Fr.* Vala; or The Four Zoas.

Night Patrol. William Daniel Ehrhart. CDa

Night Patrol. Alan Ross. OxBoS

Night Patrol, The. Arthur Graeme West. NSI; PoFWW

Night-Piece. Léonie Adams. MoAmPo

Night-Piece. Fleur Adcock.
    Before Sleep. PeNZ

Night Piece. "Ern Malley." BMAP

Night Piece. Louise Glück. FiLi

Night-Piece. Frances Horovitz. LW

Night-Piece. John Streeter Manifold. LiTM; MoBrPo

Night-Piece. Raymond R. Patterson. PoBA

Night-Piece, The. Virgil. OAEL-1 *Fr.* The Aeneid [*or* Eneados, *Aeneis*].

Night Piece on Death. Thomas Parnell. NOEC
    "How deep yon azure dyes the sky!" OxAEP-1

Night-Piece; or, Modern Philosophy, A. Christopher Smart. NOEC

Night Piece: the Trojans outside Troy. Homer, *Greek.* OBVE, *tr. by* George Chapman *Fr.* The Iliad.
    ("And all did wilfully expect the silver-throned morne.") (LL) OBCVT, *tr. by* George Chapman
    (Fire-light.) OBCVT, *tr. by* George Chapman

("This speech all Trojans did applaud; who from their traces losde.") OBCVT, *tr. by* George Chapman

Night-Piece, to Julia, The. Robert Herrick. BeJo; CBLP; CH; CaPo; EBEvV; NAEL-1; NOSC; NoP-4; OAEL-1; OBEV; PoE; PoEL-3; PoRA; SAGP; SCGP; SeCP; TFi

(On a Dark Road.) BoTP

Night Prayer, A. Alcuin, *Latin*. MLL, *tr. by* Helen Waddell

Night Prayer. *Unknown, Irish*. TIRV, *tr. by* Douglas Hyde

Night Prayer of Glückel of Hameln, The. Edouard Roditi. CRP

Night-Quarters. Henry Howard Brownell. PAR

Night Raid. Desmond Hawkins. PoWW

Night Rain. J. P. Clark Bekedermo. PBMAP *Fr. A Reed in the Tide.*

Night Rain. Countee Cullen. GT

Night Rain. Karen L. Mitchell. GT

Night Rain: A Wall Collapses—Sent To My Neighbors. Yang Shih-ch'i, *Chinese*. CoBLCP, *tr. by* Jonathan Chaves

Night Rain beneath the City Walls of P'i-chou. Yang Shih-ch'i, *Chinese*. CoBLCP, *tr. by* Jonathan Chaves

Night Rains: to my Wife up North. Li Shang-yin, *Chinese*. PLT, *tr. by* A. C. Graham

Night Ray. Paul Celan, *French*. AF, *tr. by* Michael Hamburger

Night rests like a ball of fur on my tongue. (LL) Adolescence—II. Rita Dove. AmPA; HCAP; ISC; NoAM; PoPoPo; VCAP

Night-Ride, The. Kenneth Slessor. BMAP

Night sank upon the dusky beach, and on the purple sea. Thomas Babington Macaulay, 1st Baron Macaulay. EBEvV; OBNC; PeVV *Fr. The Armada.* FaBoCh; FaPoR

Night saw the crew like pedlars with their packs. Lunar Stanzas. Henry Coggswell Knight. CBNP

Night, say all, was made for rest, The. Upon Visiting His Lady by Moonlight. "A. W." CTC

Night Scenes. Robert Duncan. VGW

Night Scenes of Other Times. Joanna Baillie.

Ghost of Edward. ECWP

Night sea quickens, The. On the shoal or rock. Lighthouses. Dorothy, Duchess of Wellington Wellesley. WPE

Night Serene, The. Luís De León, *Spanish*. TrJP, *tr. by* Thomas Walsh

Night Shift. Sylvia Plath. AFr

Night Shift at the Fruit Cannery. Ilze Mueller. LoHo

Night Shore. Barry O. Higgs. PeSA

Night Singing. W. S. Merwin. PUP-19

Night Sky. Louise Erdrich. HATNAP

Night Sky, The. G. D. Roberts. GSo

Night Sky, The. *Unknown*. BoTP

Night, sleep, death and the stars. (LL) A Clear Midnight. Walt Whitman. HAP; NTP; OxBSP; PAR; SAmP; Spl

Night sleeps, but the chill, The. The Harp of David. Jacob Cohen, *Hebrew*. TrJP, *tr. by* Sholom J. Kahn

Night Snow. Po Chü-i, *Chinese*. CoBCP, *tr. by* Burton Watson

Night snows stars and the earth creaks, The. (LL) The Howling of Wolves. Ted Hughes. APo; OxBTC

Night soaks itself, The. Serenata. Federico García Lorca, *Spanish*. EP, *tr. by* Derek Parker

Night Song at Amalfi. Sara Teasdale. MoAmPo

Night Song for a Child. Charles Williams. OBEV

Night Song for a Woman. Alfred Wellington Purdy. NOBC

Night Song for Two Mystics. Paul Blackburn. NeAP

Night Song of the Personal Shadow. György Petri, *Hungarian*. VCWP, *tr. by* Wilmer, Clive and George Gömöri

Night Sowing. David Campbell. CBAP

Night spreads like purple heather. Earthset. Judith Nicholls. SpW

Night Starvation or The Biter Bit. Carey Blyton. FuFo

Night stirs the trees. By Achmelvich Bridge. Norman MacCaig. OxBS

Night, street, a lamp, a chemist's window. Aleksandr Blok. OBVE, *tr. by* Jon Stallworthy *and* Peter France, *See also* Night, the street, the lamp, the drugstore, The *Fr. Dances of Death.*

Night Sweat. Robert Lowell. NAAL-2; TAP; VGW

Night sweat: my temperature spikes to 102. December 27, 1966. Louis Edward Sissman. DiPo

Night Sweats. Gwen Head. PuP-16

Night Sweats 2. Boyer Rickel. WeT

Night that cuts between you and you, A. People at Night. Denise Levertov. CLPP

Night that has no star lit up by God, The. The New World. Jones Very. APN-1; PAR

Night the Eighth: Camerados. Bayard Taylor. APN-2 *Fr. The Echo Club.*

Night, the rain, who could forget, The? In the Street. John Shaw Neilson. CBAP

Night the Second: All or Nothing. Bayard Taylor. APN-2 *Fr. The Echo Club.*

Night the Sixth: Hadramaut. Bayard Taylor. APN-2 *Fr. The Echo Club.*

Night, the starless[e] night of passion, The. William Alabaster. ESCV *Fr. Divine Meditations. Son*

Night, the street, the lamp, the drugstore, The. Aleksandr Blok. TCRP, *tr. by* Yakov Hornstein, *See also* Night, street, a lamp, a chemist's window *Fr. Dances of Death.*

Night Thought. Gerald Jonas. NYBP

Night Thoughts. Henri Coulette. FYAP

Night Thoughts. Lu Yu, *Chinese*. OHPC, *tr. by* Kenneth Rexroth

Night-Thoughts. Solomon ibn Gabirol, *Hebrew*. TrJP, *tr. by* Emma Lazarus

Night Thoughts. Edward Young.

"Bell strikes *one*: we take no note of time." ECEV

Consolation, The. NOEC

"How poor, how rich, how abject, how august." OAEL-1

Infidel Reclaimed, The. NOEC

Night Thoughts. OxAEP-1

"Where, thy true treasure? Gold says, 'Not in me'." OAEL-1

Night Thoughts aboard a Boat. Tu Fu, *Chinese*. SuSp, *tr. by* James J. Y. Liu *and* Irving Y. Lo

Night Thoughts: Baby & Demon. Gwen Harwood. CBAP

Night Thoughts Concerning a Dream. Daniel Casper von Lohenstein, *German*. GePo, *tr. by* George C. Schoolfield

Night Thoughts in Age. John Hall Wheelock. NYBP

Night Thoughts While Travelling. Tu Fu, *Chinese*. OHPC, *tr. by* Kenneth Rexroth

Night town, strange winds of mystery. Clinton. Sterling Plumpp. BkSV *Fr. Clinton.*

Night Train. Robert Francis. GM

Night Train, The. Trần Gia Thoại, *Vietnamese*. AVP, *tr. by* Huỳnh Sanh Thông

Night train passes, A. Eric Amann. HA

Night Traveller. Ion Cristofor, *Romanian*. CEEP, *tr. by* Brenda Walker *and* Michaela Celea-Leach

Night, two o'clock: moonlight. The train has stopped. Tomas Tranströmer. *See* Track.

Night under shete, A. (LL) The Peasant's Song. *Unknown*. FaBoPV; FaBoVe

Night universe scallop-edged with his faces—, A. Some Metaphysics of Junior Wells. Sandra McPherson. SeSe

Night usually computes itself in stars. News of the Occluded Cyclone. Alice Fulton. WeW-3

Night VIII (The Eternal Man). William Blake. PoE *Fr. Vala; or The Four Zoas.*

Night Vision. Paula Gunn Allen. NMM-2

Night Vision. Lucille Clifton. UnSA

Night Visitor, A. Robert Greene. NoSic

Night Visits. "Chrystos." CPO

Night: Volcano, California. Ellery Akers. CMAP

Night Walk. Max Fatchen. OTCP

Night Walk. Sylvia Plath. NYBP

Night was coming very fast, The. The Hens. Elizabeth Madox Roberts. OBCA

Night was dark, the rain came down, The. Over the Top with Pershing. Zelda Sayre Fitzgerald. AiP

Night was dark, though sometimes a faint star, The. Prelude. Richard Watson Gilder. PoLF *Fr. The New Day.*

Night was faint and sheer, The. A Nocturne for October 31st. Yvor Winters. PoA

Night was gloomy. Through the skies of June, The. A Dream. "Barry Cornwall." Ro *Fr. Dramatic Scenes and Other Poems.*

Night was growing cold, The. *Unknown*. WHSW

Night was growing old, The. In the Night. *Unknown*. FPC; NBLV

Night was stormy and dark, The town was shut up in sleep:, The. The Speculators. William Makepeace Thackeray. OBCoV; OBSV

Night was thick and hazy, The. Robinson Crusoe's Story. Charles Edward Carryl. PoRA *Fr. Davy and the Goblin.*

Night wasn't over / when the moon stood beside my bed. A Prison Daybreak. Faiz Ahmad Faiz, *Arabic*. AF, *tr. by* Agha Shahid Ali

Night Watch of the Trojans before Troy. Homer. *See* Specimen of a Translation of the Iliad in Blank Verse.

Night Watchman of Pont-au-Change, The. Robert Desnos, *French*. AF, *tr. by* Carolyn Forché

Night-watchmen think of dawn and things auroral. Blindman's Buff. Peter Viereck. LiTM; MoAmPo

Night we bailed out Jolene from Riker's Island, The. Amaranth and Moly. Amy Clampitt. WWSi

Night we went to see the Brisbane River, The. Profiles of My Father. Rhyll McMaster. CBAP

Night we were to meet in the hotel, The. Song for the Lost Private. Bruce Weigl. CDa

Night, welcome art thou to my mind destrest. From Pamphilia to Amphilanthus. Mary Sidney, Countess of Montgomery Wroth. NoP-4 *Fr.* Pamphilia to Amphilanthus.

Night, what more do you want? Other Obit. Dean Young. NAmP90

Night when she first gave birth, The. Mary. Bertolt Brecht, *German.* GI, *tr.* by Michael Hamburger *and* Max Hayward

Night Whispers, The. Ken Smith. NBrP

Night Will Never Stay, The. Eleanor Farjeon. BoTP; CH; NTCP; OxBChV

Night Wind, The. Emily Jane Brontë. EBVV; NAEL-2; NALW

Night wind, The. Rags. Judith Thurman. AYFP

Night Wind in Fall. William Robert Moses. WeT

Night winds! Dark mountainous skies. Daniil Leonidovich Andreyev. TCRP, *tr.* by Rose Styron *and* Olga Carlisle *Fr.* The Russian Gods.

Night with a Friend, A. Li Po, *Chinese.* CoBCP, *tr.* by Burton Watson

Night without end. I cannot sleep. *Unknown, Chinese.* OHMPC, *tr.* by Kenneth Rexroth

Night without end. Loneliness. Kenneth Rexroth. APSN *Fr.* The Love Poems of Marichiko.

Night Without Stars, A. Nancy Eimers. BAP-96

Nightfall. Walter Davies, *Welsh.* OBWVE, *tr.* by Anthony Conran

Nightfall. "Michael Field." VWP

Nightfall. Gwen Harwood. BMAP

Nightfall. Alexander L. Posey. APN-2

Nightfall. Charles Hanson Towne. *See* At Nightfall.

Nightfall. Clouds scatter and vanish. The Turning Year. Su Tung-p'o, *Chinese.* OHPC, *tr.* by Kenneth Rexroth

Nightfall. He jumped over the hedge. *Unknown, Chinese.* OHMPC, *tr.* by Kenneth Rexroth

Nightfall. I return from a. Homecoming—Late at Night. Tu Fu, *Chinese.* OHPC, *tr.* by Kenneth Rexroth

Nightfall I sink. Domestic Poem. Eileen Moeller. CrSp

Nightfall, Midwinter, Missouri. Brian Coffey. CIP-2 *Fr.* Missouri Sequence.
("Inside the house is warm.") IIP

Nightfall, that saw the morning-glories float. On the Skeleton of a Hound. James Wright. LiTM

Nightfishing. Gjertrud Schnackenberg. WeW-3

Nighthawks circle / through the midwestern elms. For a Winnebago Brave. Joseph Bruchac. CDW

Nightingale, The. Mark Akenside. *See* To the Evening Star.

Nightingale, The. Richard Barnfield. *See* Philomel.

Nightingale. Christian Carstairs. ECWP

Nightingale, The. John Clare. EBVV

Nightingale, The. Coleridge. FHYEP
(Nightingale; A Conversational Poem, The.) Ro
("No cloud, no relique of the sunken day.")
("Sweet nightingale! Once more, my friends, farewell!") (LL) Ro

Nightingale, The. LaPo

Nightingale, The. Marie de France, *French.* BoWoP, *tr.* by Patricia Terry

Nightingale, The. William Strode, *after the Latin of* Famianus Strada. OBVE

Nightingale, The. Katharine Tynan. BoTP

Nightingale, The. *Unknown. See* One Morning in May [*or* The Nightingale].

Nightingale; A Conversational Poem, The. Coleridge. *See* The Nightingale.

Nightingale and the Glowworm, The. William Cowper. CTV *Fr.* The Nightingale and Glow-Worm.

Nightingale as soone as Aprill bringeth, The. Sir Philip Sidney. OxAEP-1; PBRV; SCGP
("Nightingale, as soon as April bringeth, The.") NoP-4
("Thy thorn without, my thorn my heart invadeth.") (LL) NoP-4
("Thy thorne without, my thorne my heart invadeth.") (LL) PBRV

Nightingale has a lyre of gold, The. The Blackbird. William Ernest Henley. HoPM; MoBrPo *Fr.* Echoes.

Nightingale, in dead of night, The. The Happy Nightingale. *Unknown.* OxBChV

Nightingale near the House, The. Harold Monro. MoBrPo

Nightingale Path, The. So Chong-Ju, *Korean.* CKP, *tr.* by Jaihiun Kim

Nightingale that all day long, A. The Nightingale and the Glowworm. William Cowper. CTV *Fr.* The Nightingale and Glow-Worm.

Nightingale voices of memory, The. Sebastian's Lament, 1943. Sigitas Geda, *Lithuanian.* CEEP, *tr.* by Jonas Zdanys

Nightingale, whose happy noble hart, The. The Steele Glas. George Gascoigne. AAS

Nightingales. Robert Bridges. CMoP; ImPo; LiTM; MoBrPo; NOBE; OAEL-2; OBEV; OBMV; OBNC; SCGP; TFi; UnPo

Nightingales. Mikhail Aleksandrovich Dudin, *Russian.* TCRP, *tr.* by Albert C. Todd

Nightingales in America. Jane Flanders. CrSp; SAGP

Nightingales of Spring, The. *Unknown.* AmFP

Nightingales, the nightingales!, The. (LL) Bianca Among the Nightingales. Elizabeth Barrett Browning. BrRo; GTBS-P

Nightingales' tongues, your majesty? Figgie Hobbin. Charles Causley. NOxBChV; NTP

Nightingales warbled without. In the Garden at Swainston. Tennyson. OBEV; OBNC

Nightletter. Charles Wright. PoA

Nightline: An Interview with the General. Ronald Wallace. PBCAP

Nightly the watchman's rattle startles my sleep. Ch'ien Ch'ien-i. SuSp, *tr.* by Irving Y. Lo *Fr.* Poems Written in Prison.

Nightly tormented by returning doubt. The Struggle. René François Armand Sully-Prudhomme, *French.* AWP, *tr.* by Arthur O'Shaughnessy

Nightmare. Gawin Douglas. PoEL-1 *Fr.* The Palace [*or* Palice] of Honor [*or* Honour].

Nightmare. Rita Dove. GT

Nightmare. James A. Emanuel. BPo

Nightmare. Isabella Gardner. CoAP

Nightmare, [A *or* The]. Sir William Schwenck Gilbert. NOBL; NTP; OBCoV; OxBoLi; PBMP; PeLV; PoRA *Fr.* Iolanthe.
(Chancellor's Nightmare, The.) CBNP

Nightmare, The. Wang Yen-Shou, *Chinese.* ChiP, *tr.* by Arthur Waley

Nightmare Abbey. Thomas Love Peacock.
Song by Mr. Cypress. OAEL-2; OBNC
Three Men of Gotham. FaBoCh; OBEV; OxAEP-2
(Wise Men of Gotham, The.) BXAP; CBNP

Nightmare at Noon. Stephen Vincent Benét. OxBA

Nightmare begins responsibility. (LL) Nightmare Begins Responsibility. Michael S. Harper. GT; HCAP; LCAP-2; LoL; PoPoPo; TAP; VCAP

Nightmare Boogie. Langston Hughes. APSN

Nightmare leaves fatigue. Louis MacNeice. BIrV; CIP-2; PNI *Fr.* Autumn Journal.

Nightmare Number Three. Stephen Vincent Benét. MoAmPo

Nightmare of beasthood, snorting, how to wake. Moly. Thom Gunn. CABP; HAP; MoP; NoAM; Poetr

Nightmare shower room. My tormentor leers, The. Days of 1941 and '44. James Merrill. GLP

Nightmarkets, The. Alan Wearne.
Division of O'Dowd, The. BMAP
Elise. BMAP
Terri. BMAP

Nightpiece. James Joyce. PoA

Nights along the River. Charles Sullivan. AiP

Nights are long and I cannot sleep. *Unknown. See* All night I could not sleep.

Night's bible-black darkness prevails. Limerick. V. R. Ormerod. PeLi

Nights bring you the fever. Prometheus. Jenny Mastoraki, *Modern Greek.* BoWoP, *tr.* by Nikos Germanakos

Night's Delights. Kaspar Stieler, *German.* GePo, *tr.* by Ingrid Wal[ø]e-Engel

Night's drifts, The. A Winter Daybreak above Vence. James Wright. InPS-3; LCAP-2; VCAP

Night's first sweet silence fell, and on my bed. The Malady of Love Is Nerves. Petronius Arbiter, *Latin.* AWP, *tr.* by Howard Mumford Jones

Nights I stay awake without hope. Yannis Papaionnou, *Greek.* GrIP, *tr.* by Gail Holst

Nights in Black Valley. Gerald Mangan. FaBoTC

Nights in Nha Trang. Jan Barry. CDa

Nights in the Gardens of Port of Spain. Derek Walcott. NAEL-2; NoP-4; OxBC

Nights into white stars. Carl Sandburg. *See* Prayers of Steel.

Nights like this: on the cold apple–bough. Amends. Adrienne Rich. BAP-93 *Fr.* Not Somewhere Else, But Here. BAP-93

Nights of 1964–1966: The Old Reliable. Marilyn Hacker. RA; VCAP

Night's still silken. Curtains spread red silk, The. Dimmed Observation. Abba Kovner, *Hebrew.* IP, *tr.* by Warren Bargad *and* Stanley F. Chyet

Nights when I lie. To The Barbarian. Else Lasker-Schüler, *German.* PFTM, *tr.* by Pierre Joris *and* Jerome Rothenberg

Nights, when I was a boy, my dad and I. Short-Wave. Christopher Cokinos. IFJA

Nightscape. Donna Masini. WWSi

Nightsea and violet wave. A Storm of Love. Hilary Corke. NYBP

Nightsong. Frank Mkalawile Chipasula.

Dusk. HBAPE

Nightsong. Louis O. Coxe. FYAP

Nightsong: City. Dennis Brutus. HBAPE; PBMAP

Nighttime. The faithful prison guard. Bedtime Story. Lou Lipsitz. VGW

Nightwalker. Thomas Kinsella.

"Foot of the tower. An angle where the darkness, The." PBCIP

"I must lie down with them all soon and sleep." BIrV

Nightwatcher:/ Fast falls the night unfurling its vile veil. Dusk. Frank Mkalawile Chipasula. HBAPE *Fr.* Nightsong.

Nightwind sings and rustles through the reeds, The. Nocturne in G Minor. Karl Gustav Vollmoeller, *German.* AWP, *tr. by* Ludwig Lewisohn

Nightwood. William Jay Smith. PoA

Nihilism. Lionel Pigot Johnson. ADE

Nihilist as Hero, The. Robert Lowell. VCAP

Nijinsky. Parker Tyler. PoA

Nikarete's face, sweetly moistened. Asclepiades, *Greek.* GrAn, *tr. by* Alan Marshfield

Nikki-Rosa. Nikki Giovanni. BlSi; CrSp; FaBoA; GT; HeIP-4; ISC; MoP; NAAAL; PBMP; PoBA; SSLK; TAP; UnSA

Nikolaus Mardruz to his Master Ferdinand, Count of Tyrol, 1565. Richard Howard. NoP-4

Nile, The. Albert Goldbarth. NAmP90

Nile, The. Leigh Hunt. EBEV; GSo; NOBE; OBNC

Nile the Hermit. *Unknown, Greek.* GrAn, *tr. by* Guy Davenport

Nima, The. Jorge Isaacs, *Spanish.* TrJP, *tr. by* Alice Jane McVan

Nimble cat and lazy maid, A. On Maids and Cats. Henricus Selyns. SCAP

Nimble-fingered / finding all of the stops. Jorie Graham. *See* San Sepolcro.

Nimble sigh, on thy warm wings. To Amoret. Henry Vaughan. EnLoPo

Nimble swan plays in the river pool, The. Presented as a Farewell to Secretary Fu. Pao Chao, *Chinese.* SuSp, *tr. by* Daniel Bryant

Nimbus. Douglas Le Pan. MoCV

Nîmes, August, 1966, and I. The Survivor. Philip Levine. UnSA

Nimium Fortunatus. Robert Bridges. MoBrPo

Nimmers, The. John Byrom. OxAEP-1

Nimphs [*or* Nymph's] Reply to the Sheepheard [*or* Shepherd], The. Sir Walter Ralegh. CTC; ClHu; EBEvV; HAP; HeIP-4; HoPM; ImPo; InPK-6; InPS-3; NAEL-1; NBLV; NIP-4; NOBE; NoP-4; NoSic; PFE; PoE; PoPoPo; Poetr; RACG; RB; SCGP; SiPS; TFi; TRP; WeW-3

(Answer to Marlowe.) OAEL-1

(Her Reply.) BoLoP; OBEV

Nimrod gazed across the plain. The Tower of Babel. Laurance Wieder. ChIV-1

Nina Simone. Lance Jeffers. SeSe

Nine adulteries, 12 liaisons, 64 fornications and something approaching a rape. The Temperaments. Ezra Pound. BoLoP; MeMAP; NOBA; NoAM; OBCoV

Nine birds(rising / through a gold moment)climb. E. E. Cummings. UnPo

Nine days old. (LL) Pease porridge [*or* pudding] hot. Mother Goose. LB; ReMoGo

Nine grenadiers, with bayonets in their guns. The Dream of a Boy Who Lived at Nine Elms. William Brighty Rands. OxBChV

Nine hundred and ninety-nine smiles. 999 Smiles. Atukwei Okai. PBMAP

Nine hundred thousand prisoners of war. To Her of Whom They Dream. Paul Éluard, *French.* AF, *tr. by* Lloyd Alexander

Nine Little Goblins, The. James Whitcomb Riley. NOxBChV; OBCA

Nine Lyric Poets, The. *Unknown, Greek.* GrAn, *tr. by* Peter Jay

Nine miles from here. Miklós Radnóti. *See* Postcard (Found on His body after He Was Killed by the Nazis).

Nine months I waited in the dark beneath. Pro Sua Vita. Robert Penn Warren. MoAmPo

Nine Nectarines and Other Porcelain. Marianne Moore. OxBA

999 Call. Elizabeth Bartlett. FaBoWP

Nine o'Clock. Katharine Pyle. *Fr.* The Wonder Clock. OBCA

9 o'clock. The bells come floating in. The Journey. Franz Wright. LCAP-2

Nine on Happy Reunion. Peyanar, *Tamil.* PLW, *tr. by* A. K. Ramanujan

What He Said ("As the deer begin to hide"). PLW

What He Said ("As wild oxen bellowed"). PLW

What He Said ("Because peacocks moved like you"). PLW

What He Said ("In this time of rain and thunder"). PLW

What He Said ("Red earth, The"). PLW

What her Girl Friend Said ("As the cassias blossom"). PLW

What her girl friend said ("Her eyes"). PLW

("Her eyes lined with kohl.")

What her Girl Friend Said ("Saying to himself"). PLW

What her Girl Friend Said ("Your arms are beautiful again"). PLW

9.1.59: II. Pablo Picasso, *French.* CLPP, *tr. by* Paul Blackburn

9.1.59: VI. Pablo Picasso, *French.* CLPP, *tr. by* Paul Blackburn

Nine Poems for the Unborn Child. Muriel Rukeyser.

They Came to Me and Said, "There Is a Child." Son

Nine Points of the Law. Peter Porter.

"Managed as they say about such men." PeLV

Nine Songs. Ch'u Yüan, *Chinese.* CoBCP, *tr. by* Burton Watson

Lord among the Clouds, The. ChiPo, *tr. by* Burton Watson

Nine swallows sat on a telephone wire. The Swallows. Elizabeth Jane Coatsworth. TLR

Nine Times. James Michie. DiPo

Nine times out of ten. Airs and Graces. Peter Fallon. PBCIP

Nine times the sun his yearly course had run. Elizabeth Thomas. ECWP *Fr.* Jill, A Pindaric Ode.

Nine white chickens come. A Black November Turkey. Richard Wilbur. LCAP-2; NAAL-2

999 Smiles, *(to Guy Warren).* Atukwei Okai. PBMAP

1967, Detroit. My grandfather watches. Time, Temperature. Jim Daniels. LTA

Nineteen. Elizabeth Alexander. GT; PoPoPo

Nineteen. George Bogin. IFJA

19. Edward Fitzgerald. CABP

19. Jay Wright. MoNo

1918-1941. Robert David Fitzgerald. CBAP

(1980). C. S. Giscombe. GT

1980. Abraham Sutskever, *Yiddish.* HP, *tr. by* Cynthia Ozick *Fr.* Poems from a Diary.

1915. Roger McDonald. NOBAu

1915: A Pre-Raphaelite Ending, London. Richard Howard. RACG

Nineteen Fifty-five. Sherod Santos. NAmP90

1951. Frank O'Hara. LCAP-2

1956. Maxine Scates. PBCAP

194. . . . Mikhail Valentinovich Kulchitsky, *Russian.* TCRP, *tr. by* Daniel Weissbort

1945. Sheila Cussons, *Afrikaans.* PeSA, *tr. by* Jack Cope *and* Uys Krige

1945. Sir Herbert Read. OxBTC

1941. Everette Maddox. MT

1947. That winter they talk of. Freeze-Frame. Alison Fell. FaBoTC; NBrP

1943. Sandra McPherson. FaBoWP

1904. Frederick Morgan. WeW-3

MCMXIV. Philip Larkin. EBEV; NAEL-2; NSI; NoAM; NoP-4; OBWP; OxAEP-2

1914. Rupert Brooke.

Dead, The ("These hearts were woven"). CH; PeFWW; PoA; SoSe-8

Peace. OBWP; PoA; PoFWW

Safety. EnLoPo

Soldier, The. APAD; CABP; EBEvV; FaPoR; GSo; HeIP-4; LiTM; MoBrPo; NAEL-2; NOBE; NSI; NoP-4; OBEV; OBWP; OxBTC; PeFWW; PoA; PoFWW; PoLF; PoRA; PoWW; Son; TFi; UV

1914. Max Jacob. PFTM

1914 Box, The. Marcel Duchamp. PFTM

1940. Bertolt Brecht, *German.* HP, *tr. by* Willet, John

Nineteen Hundred and Nineteen. W. B. Yeats.

"Many ingenious lovely things are gone." BIrV; PoE

"Some moralist or mythological poet." PoE

19 January 1944. Salvatore Quasimodo, *Italian.* AF, *tr. by* Jack Bevan

Nineteen Old Poems of the Han. Mei Sheng *and* Fu I, *Chinese.* CoBCP, *tr. by* Burton Watson

"Green green, river bank grasses." ChiPo, *tr. by* Watson, Burton

"We hold a splendid feast today."

(1978, Remembering 1962). C. S. Giscombe. GT

1975. Wayne Koestenbaum. BAP-95

1975. Anne Spencer. NMM-2

1974—The Sounds. Christina Beer. PeNZ

1977: Poem for Mrs. Fannie Lou Hamer. June Jordan. NMM-2

1976 Ford. A shiny lacquered, A. Front Page. Abba Kovner, *Hebrew.* IP, *tr. by* Warren Bargad *and* Stanley F. Chyet

1973. Marilyn Hacker. GLP

1973. Reuben Jackson. GT

1916. R. S. Gwynn. MT

1916 Seen from 1921. Edmund Blunden. NoP-4; PeFWW

Nineteen Sixty Eight. Petra von Morstein, *German.* BoWoP, *tr. by* Rosemarie Waldrop

1966. David Rivard. PBCAP

(1962 at the edge of town). C. S. Giscombe. GT; PUP-19 *Fr.* Look Ahead—Look South.

1935. Stephen Vincent Benét. MoAmPo

1933. Philip Levine. LCAP-2

1938. Ruth Pitter. WPN

1912–1952, Full Cycle. Peter Viereck. OBAL

1925. Edwin Honig. NoAM *Fr.* To Restore a Dead Child.

1929. W. H. Auden. OxAEP-2

1920 Photo. Patricia Dobler. CMAP

1926. Weldon Kees. CoAP

Nineteenth Century and After, The. W. B. Yeats. FaBoEE

19th Idyllium of Theocritus attempted in the Cumberland Dialect, The. Theocritus, *Greek.* OBCVT, *tr. by* Josiah Relph

Ninety. Mary Elizabeth Fullerton. CBAP

Ninety-fifth. Isaac Watts. AmFP

Ninety-Mile, The. Five. One. Laurie Duggan. BMAP *Fr.* The Ash Range.

Ninety-Nine. Elizabeth Godley. NOxBChV

90 North. Randall Jarrell. CoAP; FYAP; MT; NAAL-2; NOBA; NoAM; TAP; VCAP

Ninety percent of the mass of the Universe. Certainty Before Lunch. John Berryman. LCAP-2; OxBC

Ninety summers—and never a platitude. Limerick. Stanley J. Sharpless. PeLi

Nineveh, Tyre. Memphis Blues. Sterling Brown. NAAAL

Ninth Canticle, The. George Wither. ChIV-1

Ninth height of Heaven. Li Po. *See* Viewing the Waterfall at Mount Lu.

9th July, 1932. Mary Ursula Bethell. PeNZ

Ninth of Av. Myra Sklarew. CRP

Ninth of July, The. John Hollander. CoAP

Ninth Secret Poem, The. Guillaume Apollinaire, *French.* APAD, *tr. by* Oliver Bernard

Ninth Song. Sir Philip Sidney. NoSic *Fr.* Astrophil and Stella. AAS; SiPS

Ninth Symphony of Beethoven Understood at Last as a Sexual Message, The. Adrienne Rich. TAP

Ninth Vertical Poetry. Roberto Juarroz, *Spanish.*
"To die, but far away." VCWP, *tr. by* Mary Crow

Niobe. Henrietta Cordelia Ray. CBWP-3

Niobe. *Unknown, Greek.* GrAn, *tr. by* Peter Jay

Niobe is very old now. Bus Ride. Kate Daniels. PBCAP

Niobe lives in the desert, too. Ethiopia. Kate Daniels. PBCAP

Niobe on *Phrygian* sands. The Wish. Anacreon, *Greek.* OBCVT, *tr. by* Thomas Stanley

Niobe on Phrygian sands. The Wish. Thomas Stanley. AWP

Nip in the air today, and autumn, A. August Ends. Leonard Clark. AYFP

Nip in the blossom all our hopes and thee. (LL) The Picture of Little T. C. in a Prospect of Flowers. Andrew Marvell. ESCV; FMP; GeHe; MeLP; NAEL-1; NOBE; NoP-4; OAEL-1; OBEV; OxAEP-1; PoE; SCGP; SeCP; TFi

Nipkow and Cosulich. Suddenly. Louis Simpson. BAP-93

Nipping chill, the frost killed spring. Meng Chiao. SuSp, *tr. by* Stephen Owen *Fr.* Apricots Die Young.

Nipplewhip, The. Michael Benedikt. WeT

Nirvâna. Sidney Lanier. NCAP

Nirvana. Rosamund Marriott Watson. VWP

Nirvana. John Hall Wheelock. MoAmPo

Nisei Picnic: From an Album, A. David Mura. LoL

Nisei: Second Generation Japanese-American. Jim Mitsui. OpBo

—NIVERSITY of *Gottingen.* (LL) Rogero's Song. George Canning, George Ellis, *and* John Hookham Frere. NOEC; OBCoV; PeLV

Nizam the pederast, whose delight in boys. Surprise, Surprise. *Unknown, Arabic.* EP, *tr. by* Derek Parker

'Nkongane. W. C. Scully. PeSAV

"No!" Eliza Cook. PoToHe

No! The Growing. Mongane Wally Serote. PBMAP

No. José Hidalgo, *Spanish.* IMW, *tr. by* Stephen Berg

No. Lady Ki No Washika, *Japanese.* NNPT, *tr. by* Graeme Wilson

No. (LL) Overheard on a Saltmarsh. Harold Monro. BoTP; CH

No Abstraction. Genevieve Taggard. NMM-2

No air, no mist, no man, no beast. Moonscape. Judith Nicholls. SpW

No alien dust covers your tomb. Simonides, *Greek.* GrAn, *tr. by* Peter Jay

No altarpiece includes the painter. J. Kates. GI

No ancestral bones of ours. A Visit to the Village. Michael Smith. PBCIP

No angel has descended here. The Visitation. Jan Owen. NOBAu

No animals will live. Ritual Murder. Aig Higo. PBMAP

No argument, no anger, no remorse. Hedges Freaked With Snow. Robert Graves. OxBTC *Fr.* Three Songs for the Lute.

No Barren Leaves. John Pomfret. GaP

No bars are set too close, no mesh too fine. The Sparrow in the Zoo. Howard Nemerov. MoP; NIP-4 *Fr.* Epigrams. OBAL

No bees, no honey;. *Unknown.* CTV

No belly / no cry. (LL) The Starry Night. Anne Sexton. ColAP; NoAM; PoE; VCAP

No better fate is given than to die in Rome. Aleksandr Semionovich Kushner, *Russian.* TCRP, *tr. by* Paul Graves *and* Carol Ueland

No better lost than any other woman. Canzone. Marilyn Hacker. NoAM

No birth, no death, no time nor sun / In answer. (LL) North Labrador. Hart Crane. CMoP; FaBoMo

No bitterness: our ancestors did it. Ave Caesar. Robinson Jeffers. FaBoPV; MoP; NOBA; NoAM; OxBA; OxBSP

No black and swirling cloak, no faceless grin. Waiting for the Post. Dorothy Auchterlonie. CBAP

No blacker than others in winter, but. Burning Mountain. W. S. Merwin. NYBP

No Blacks, No Irish. Gabriel Gbadamosi.
    Scene 6 The Boat Passage. NBrP

No blooming youth shall ever make me err. Katherine Philips. KTR

No bottom, / Mark four. *Unknown.* AmFP

No bracelet—accept this. Hilda Doolittle. *See* At Baia.

No branch nor the last grass. Fossil. E. D. Blodgett. NOBC

No breath of air to break the wave. The Giaour. Byron. NOBRP

No burning leaf; prithee, let no bird call. (LL) God's World. Edna St. Vincent Millay. CMoP; FaBoBe; MoAmPo; PFE; SAGP; TrCP

No, but lovely in that way. (LL) Part of Plenty. Bernard Spencer. GBL; LiTM

No call upon anyone but the timber drifting in the waves. Lament for the Makers. Jack Spicer. FTOS

No camellia. Akiko Yosano, *Japanese.* PBWP, *tr. by* Geoffrey Bownas *and* Anthony Thwaite

No Categories! Stevie Smith. NoP-4

No Change in Me. *Unknown.* AmFP

No changes of support—only. Last Month. John Ashbery. CAPP-1; CoAP

No charm. Kapitonos, *Greek.* InMo, *tr. by* Sam Hamill

No charm can stay, no medicine can assuage. Walter Savage Landor. FaBoEE

No Child. Padraic Colum. OBMV

No Chinaman nor one of us is he. Poking Fun At a Bonze. Ho Xuan Huong, *Vietnamese.* AVP, *tr. by* Huỳnh Sanh Thông

No city in the spacious universe. London. Daniel Defoe. NOEC *Fr.* Reformation of Manners.

No city primness train'd my feet. Rustic Childhood. William Barnes. OBNC

No classes here! Why, that is idle talk. Ella Wheeler Wilcox. APN-2

No cloud, no relic of the sunken day. The Nightingale. Coleridge. LaPo; Ro *Fr.* The Nightingale. FHYEP

No Cold Approach. *Unknown.* EBEV

No Coming to God without Christ. Robert Herrick. OxBSP

No conozco la palabra to say I sometimes miss you *en español.* Invisible Boundaries. Maureen Hurley. LoHo

No Continuing City. Michael Longley. PNI

No coward soul is mine. Emily Jane Brontë. APAD; BWW; BrRo; CABP; EBEvV; EBVV; EnVR; NALW; NoP-4; OBNC; OxAEP-2; PEW; PoEL-5; PoPoPo; TRP; TrCP; VWP; WPoS

No Coward's Song. James Elroy Flecker. OxBSP

No Credit. Kenneth Fearing. CMoP

No crooked leg, no bleared eye. Written in Her French Psalter. Elizabeth I, Queen of England. PBWP; PEW; WPE

No Dawns. Julianne Perry. PoBA

No day was sad as the day Sakhr. On Her Brother Sakhr. Al-Khansa, *Arabic.* BoWoP, *tr. by* Willis Barnstone

No Delicacies. Ingeborg Bachmann, *Hebrew.* PoSu, *tr. by* Mark Anderson

No Deposit. Earle Thompson. HATNAP

No, dere ain't no use r workin' in de blazin' summertime. When de Sun Shines Hot. James Ephriam McGirt. AAP

No detail here, nothing but you. Unbroken gaze. Glance in White Space. Clark Coolidge. FTOS

No Difference in the Dark [*or* i'th'dark]. Robert Herrick. CaPo

No difference in the gray gulls, sobbing. Return to Seattle: Bastille Day. Carolyne Wright. WWSi

No different, I said, from rat's or chicken's. Not to Be Born. David Sutton. OxBM

No dignity without chromium. Ballad of Faith. William Carlos Williams. OBAL

No doubt he well invented, nobly felt. Hartley Coleridge. EPCY *Fr.* Chaucer.

No doubt I'm spoiled. One's soon accustomed to. Home Thoughts from Home. Alasdair Maclean. FaBoTC

No doubt in the mind of Brébeuf that this was the last. The Martyrdom of Brébeuf and Lalemant, 16 March 1649. Edwin John Pratt. NOBC *Fr.* Brébeuf and His Brethren.

No doubt left. Enough deceiving. James Agee. *Fr.* Lyrics. MoAmPo

No doubt this way is best. No Use. W. D. Snodgrass. BoLoP

No doubt to-morrow I will hide. At Mass. Vachel Lindsay. VGW

No doubts defend? (LL) Time Passing, Beloved. Donald Davie. BoLoP; NoP-4

No dream of mortal joy. Love and Lust. Isaac Rosenberg. TrJP

No dust have I to cover me. An Inscription by the Sea. Edwin Arlington Robinson, *after* Glaucus. AWP; FaBoEE

No dust have I to cover me. An Inscription by the Sea. Glaukos. AWP; FaBoEE *Fr.* Variations of Greek Themes.

No ears could hear then the mutter of the Milky Way. Prophecy. Eileen Duggan. PeNZ

No earthquake. Chapped, a lifting in this field. Dead Center. Chester Kallman. PoA

No Easy Answer. John Lehmann. LBC

No Easy Harbour. Anne Hartigan. CIP-2

No easy thing to bear, the weight of sweetness. The Weight of Sweetness. Li-Young Lee. RaBo

No empty bed blues. 29 Songs. Louis Zukofsky.

No end in sight to the days of my wandering. Written on the Thirtieth Day, Ninth Month, Second Year of the Ta-li Reign [767]. Tu Fu, *Chinese.* SuSp, *tr.* by Irving Y. Lo

No End of No-Story. George Macdonald. NOBVV

No "fan is in his hand" for these. The Threshing Machine. Alice Thompson Meynell. WPE

No festoons, no plaited garlands were draped from the lintel. Cato at his wedding. Lucan, *Latin.* OBCVT, *tr.* by P. F. Widdows

No fields but are his own. (LL) That night when joy began. W. H. Auden. OxBTC; SoSe-8

No first-class war can now be fought. Civil Defense. Kenneth Burke. OBAL

No fish has ever told another of danger. Ausonius. OBCVT, *tr.* by Isbell, Harold *Fr.* The Moselle.

No flowers! / Let's blame the god in charge of flowers. Poem on Drinking Wine with the Degree-Holder Ku. Ch'ien Ch'ien-i, *Chinese.* CoBLCP, *tr.* by Jonathan Chaves

No flowers now to wear at. The Waning of the Harvest Moon. John Wieners. PmAP

No flowers will live in my room. Nikolai Stepanovich Gumilyov, *Russian.* TCRP, *tr.* by Yakov Hornstein

No foot of man. (LL) Silence. Edgar Allan Poe. APN-1; ColAP; MeMAP; NCAP; NOBA; PAR

No foot of man, commend thyself to God! Edgar Allan Poe. *See* Silence.

No, for I'll save it! Seven years since. Apparent Failure. Robert Browning. EBVVPR; NAEL-2; NOBE

No for you, my queyn, will I prepare. The Real Muse. Tom Scott. PoA

No foreign sky protected me. Requiem. "Anna Akhmatova," *Russian.* AF; TCRP, *tr.* by Stanley Kunitz *with* Max Hayward

No form at all—it's impossible to imagine its being. Lyn Hejinian. FTOS *Fr.* Oxota: A Short Russian Novel.

No fortune base, nor frail, shall alter me. (LL) Fortune hath taken away my love. Sir Walter Ralegh. NoSic

No Foundation. John Hollander. OBAL; OBCoV

No Friend Like Music. Daniel Whitehead Hicky. PoToHe

No friendly shade thy shade shall company! (LL) Sapphic Fragment. Thomas Hardy. CTC; OBVE

No Friends of the Heart. Nancy Eimers. WeT

No fruits, no flowers, no leaves, no / birds— / November! (LL) No sun—no moon! Thomas Hood. CTV; PBMP

No Funeral Gloom. Ellen Terry. BLPA

No funeral gloom, my dears, when I am gone. William Allingham. NOBVV

No future hope no fear for evermore. (LL) Cobwebs. Christina Rossetti. CABP; NAEL-2; NALW; VWP

No Ghost Is True. Leslie A. Fiedler. PoA

No, go back into your exile, go back quick. After Wiriyamu Village Massacre by Portuguese. Jack A. Mapanje. AF; PeSAV

No, go back until our anger has simmered. (LL) After Wiriyamu Village Massacre by Portuguese. Jack A. Mapanje. AF; PeSAV

No, Go On. Maura Dooley. LW

No God. Dennis Cooper. PmAP

No god shall crown the board, nor goddess bless the bed. (LL) The Messiah. Virgil. AWP, *tr.* by Dryden; OBVE, *tr.* by Sir John Beaumont

No gorgeous coat has he. My Mocking Bird. Josephine D. Henderson Heard. CBWP-4

No great house is finer. An Ivied Tree-Top. *Unknown.* NOIV

No Great Matter. David Lawson. VGW

No Grudge. Lionel Fogarty. BMAP

No happier state, and know to know no more. (LL) Adam and Eve in the Garden. Milton. ITG, *tr.* by Robert Hass

No haste but good, where wisdome makes the waye. George Gascoigne. AAS; NoSic; Son *Fr.* Gascoigne's Memories.

No hawk hangs over in this air. The Snow Storm. Edna St. Vincent Millay. NAAL-2; PoA

No, He is too quick. We never. Getting Inside the Miracle. Luci Shaw. TrCP

"No!" He Said. Wole Soyinka. HBAPE

No head-ropes or dung. Lament for an Arab Encampment. Abid ibn al-Abras, *Arabic.* ArPe, *tr.* by Omar S. Pound

No Help. Sarah Morgan Bryan Piatt. NCAP

No help I'll call till I'm put in the narrow coffin. Egan O'Rahilly, *Irish.* NOIV, *tr.* by Thomas Kinsella

No hesitation. Mourning Letter, March 29 1963. Edward Dorn. CoAmPo

No Hint of Stain. William Vaughn Moody. *Fr.* An Ode in Time of Hesitation. APN-2; CBCWP; OxBA

"No home, no home," cried an orphan girl. The Orphan Girl. *Unknown.* AS; AmFP

No hope have I to live a deathless name. Poietes Apoietes. Hartley Coleridge. OBNC

No house of stone. The Elements. W. H. Davies. MoBrPo

No hungr[y] hawke poore patridge to devoure. Mr. Thomas Shepeard. Edward Johnson. SCAP

No, I Am Not as Others Are. François Villon, *French.* AWP, *tr.* by Arthur Symons

No, I am not death wishes of sacred rapists, singing on candy. I, Too, Know What I Am Not. Bob Kaufman. GT

No, I am through and you can call in vain. Admonition. Philip Stack. BLPA

No, / I cannot / turn from love. To Turn from Love. Sarah Webster Fabio. BlSi

No! I don't begrudge en his life. The Bachelor. William Barnes. PeVV

No, I don't love you. Anti-Love Poems. Elizabeth Brewster. NOBC

No, I have never found. Places, Loved Ones. Philip Larkin. CMoP

No, I have not been cheated by life. Aleksandr Trifonovich Tvardovsky, *Russian.* TCRP, *tr.* by Cathy Porter

"No, I have tempered haste." The Mount. Léonie Adams. MoAmPo

No—I'll endure ten thousand deaths. Chaste Florimel. Matthew Prior. BoLoP

No, I'll not, carrion, comfort you. Comfort. Sonnet 5. Nell Altizer. FFC

No, I'm not afraid: after a year. Irina Ratushinskaya, *Russian.* APAD, *tr.* by David McDuff

No, I'm not going to. De Souza Prabhu. Eunice De Souza. FaBoVe

No Images. Waring Cuney. ISC; NIP-4; PFE; SAGP; SSLK; TTY

("And dishwater gives back no images.") (LL) SAGP

("Images.") (LL) ISC

No imagination to forestall woe. (LL) Charleston in the Eighteen-Sixties. Adrienne Rich. CoAP; NAAL-2

No, in the New World, happiness is enforced. 'In the New World Happiness is Allowed'. Peter Porter. BMAP

No Interims in History. Norman MacCaig. FaBoTC

No, it does not happen. Snakes. A. K. Ramanujan. NoP-4

No, it isn't so bad being. Later History. David Rivard. NAmP90

No, it was not under a strange sky. Requiem. "Anna Andreyevna Akhmatova." PFTM *Fr.* Requiem 1935-1940. BoWoP, *tr.* by Richard McKane

No, it was only a touch of dysentery, he said. He was doing fine. The Taking of the Koppie. Uys Krige. PeSAV

No it wasn't. Nothingmas Day. Adrian Mitchell. NOxBChV

No. It's an impudent falsehood. Men did not. On a Vulgar Error. C. S. Lewis. OxBTC

No kings be crowned [*or* crown'd], but they some covenants make. (LL) Sonnet 69: "O joy, too high for my low style to show." Sir Philip Sidney. NAEL-1; OxAEP-1

No labor-saving machine. Walt Whitman. APN-1

No lake is so still but that it has its wave. *Unknown, Chinese.* Spl, *tr.* by Arthur Waley

No lame excuses can gloss over. Green Rock, Winthrop Bay. Sylvia Plath. AFr

No less fabulous than the carved marble inner. Leap of Faith. David St. John. NAmP90

No Less than Prisoners. Frederick Thomas Bennett Macartney. CBAP

No, let it stay. It speaks but truth. The First Grey Hair. Mary E. Tucker. CBWP-1

No Letter. Mary E. Tucker. CBWP-1

No light except the stars, but from the cliff. The Sea Birds. Van K. Brock. NYBP

No light to guide but the moon's pallid ray. Contrition. Henry More. NOSC *Fr.* Psychozoia, or, the Life of the Soul.

No lights are burning in the ivory tower. Absence. Vita Sackville-West. WPN

No limbo this week. Or next. Now it turns out. The Limbo Dancer. Josephine Jacobsen. FFC; PuP-16

No, listen, there's this albatross. Limerick. Bill Greenwell. PeLi

No Loathsomnesse in Love. Robert Herrick. BeJo; GBL; PBMP

("She's to be a Paragon.") (LL) PBMP

No Lock against Lechery. Robert Herrick. CaPo

No longer any man needs me. Widow. Dorothy Livesay. IMW

No longer are the forests green. Storms. Steel Usurps the Forests; Silence Dethrones Dialogue. Bible, Apocrypha. HBAPE

No longer, as before, will you wake at dawn and flap. Anyte. HePo, *tr. by* Barbara Hughes Fowler *Fr.* Epigrams.

No longer can I tarry. Isabella Whitney. *See* The Aucthour Maketh Her Wyll and Testament.

No longer, cricket, sitting. Mnasalcas, *Greek.* GrAn, *tr. by* Edward Lucie-Smith

No longer for me is there anything late. All is late. Tomorrow the Past Comes. Ion Caraion, *Romanian.* AF, *tr. by* Marguerite Dorian *and* Elliott B. Urdang

No longer mourn for me when I am dead. Sonnet 71. Shakespeare. AWP; EBEV; GBL; GTBS-P; HAP; HeIP-4; IMW; ImPo; LBC; NAEL-1; NoSic; OxAEP-1; PoRA; SCGP; Son; TFi *Fr.* Sonnets.

No longer shall I exult in the floating seas and arch. Anyte. HePo, *tr. by* Barbara Hughes Fowler *Fr.* Epigrams.

No longer throne of a goddess to whom we pray. Full Moon. Robert Earl Hayden. BPo; GT

No longer to lie reading Strauss's *Life.* Memories of Aunt Maria-Martha. William Zaranka. BXAP

No longer to lie reading *Tess of the d'Urbervilles.* The Lesson. Robert Lowell. CMoP; LCAP-2

No longer truth, though shown in verse, disdain. George Crabbe. OxAEP-1 *Fr.* The Village.

No louder now than falling leaves. (LL) Hillcrest. Edwin Arlington Robinson. MeMAP; OxBA

No love deserves the death it has. Phonemics. Jack Spicer. PmAP

No Love, to Love of Man and Wife. Richard Eedes. ITG

No lovelier city than all of this. Toast. Thomas McCarthy. PBCIP

No lover saith, I love, nor any other. The Paradox. Donne. NOSC

No man can bid a fool or sage. The Power of Thought. Süsskind von Trimberg, *Middle High German.* TrJP

No man can print a kiss: lines may deceive. (LL) Myra. Greville Fulke. GBL; HAP; NOBE; NoSic; OBEV

No man can serve two masters. Bible, *N.T.* OBVE *Fr.* St. Matthew.

No man could have been more unfaithful. The Turkish Carpet. Paul Durcan. CIP-2

No man has seen the third hand. Mystique. David Ignatow. PFE

No man,if men are gods;but if gods must. E. E. Cummings. VGW

No man knows. When A Woman Gets Blue. Norman Jordan. ISC; NBV

No Man Knows War. Edwin Rolfe. TrJP

No man outlives the grief of war. The Permanence of the Young Men. William Soutar. OxBS

No man takes the farm. John Masefield. UV

No man's forever fully satisfied. Nicarchus of Alexandria, *Greek.* InMo, *tr. by* Sam Hamill

No-Man's-Land. "H. d'A. B." NSI

No Man's Land. Gloria Escoffery. PBCV

No man's trust let woman claim. The Roman Earl. *Unknown, Irish.* OBVE, *tr. by* Douglas Hyde

No Man's Wood. W. H. Davies. OBGa

No Marvel Is It. Bernard de Ventadour, *Provençal.* AWP, *tr. by* Harriet Waters Preston

"No, Master, Never!" Joshua McCarter Simpson. AAP

No Matter. Paulus Silentiarius. *See* Epitaph, An: "My name—my country—what are they to thee."

No matter by what hand or trick. (LL) Sonnet: "Of thee, kind boy, I ask no red and white." Sir John Suckling. BeJo; CaPo; CavPo; MeLP; NOSC; NoP-4; OxBoLi; SeCP

No matter how hard I listen, the wind speaks. For Zbigniew Herbert, Summer, 1971, Los Angeles. Larry Levis. CMAP; FYAP

No matter how I concealed them, even the. Tristia. Osip Emilevich Mandelstam. PFTM, *tr. by* Bruce McClelland *Fr.* Tristia.

No matter how I shout—there's no reply. Vladimir Aleksandrovich Smolensky, *Russian.* TCRP, *tr. by* Albert C. Todd

No matter how loudly I call you the sound of your name. Poem for Guatemala. June Jordan. NAAAL

No matter how many times I try I can't stop my father. How Many Times. Marie Howe. MoLi

No matter how much more waiting I'll have to do. Vladimir Mayakovsky. TCRP, *tr. by* Daniel Weissbort *Fr.* Pro Eto.

No matter how small. Smalltown Memorials. Geoff Page. BMAP

No matter what life you lead. Snow White and the Seven Dwarfs. Anne Sexton. HCAP; PoPoPo

No matter where I turn, she is there. Statistic: The Witness. Rita Dove. NAAAL *Fr.* Mother Love.

No matter where it's going. (LL) Travel. Edna St. Vincent Millay. OBCA; PiM

No matter where we go, we always arrive too late. Henrik Nordbrandt, *Danish.* VCWP, *tr. by* Henrik Nordbrandt *and* Alexander Taylor

No matter who you are, you are alive: pass quickly. A Young Dead Woman. José-Maria de Heredia, *Spanish.* FLP; LoP, *tr. by* Alistair Elliot

No matter why, nor whence, nor when she came. The Story of the Ashes and the Flame. Edwin Arlington Robinson. MeMAP

No McTavish. Genealogical Reflection. Ogden Nash. OBAL

No Mean City. Patrick MacDonogh. BIrV; OxBSP

No memory is here of things once done. The Mood of Vichy. Hildebert, *Latin.* MLL, *tr. by* Helen Waddell

No. Merely to have writ. Peruke of Poets. William Zaranka. BXAP

No mo meetings. Listenen to Big Black at S. F. State. Sonia Sanchez. BPo

No money for lunch so I rode an elevator to the top of the ONB. Vision (2). Sherman Alexie. UnSA

No money to bury him. Ballad of the Man Who's Gone. Langston Hughes. SAmP

No monument stands over Babii Yar. Babii Yar. Yevgeny Yevtushenko, *Russian.* HP; TCRP; VCWP, *tr. by* George Reavey

No monuments or landmarks guide the stranger. A Country without a Mythology. Douglas Le Pan. MoCV; NOBC

No moon, no chance to meet. Ono no Komachi, *Japanese.* WPOW, *tr. by* Rob Swigart

No Moon, No Star. Babette Deutsch. NYBP

No more alone sleeping, no more alone waking. Marriage. Mary Elizabeth Coleridge. LW; NALW; PEW; VWP

No more, America, in mournful strain. Phillis Wheatley. WPOW *Fr.* To the Right Honourable William, Earl of Dartmouth. AmPP

No More Anxiety. Vũ Hoàng Chu'o'ng, *Vietnamese.* AVP, *tr. by* Huỳnh Sanh Thông

No more auction block for me. *Unknown.* APN-2; BPo; ISC; NAAAL; RaBo

("Knows dat Cap'n sure is bound to die.") (LL) BkSV

No more ballads in Eynhallow. Books. George Mackay Brown. FaBoTC *Fr.* Runes from a Holy Island.

No more be[e] grieved [*or* greev'd] at that which thou hast done. Sonnet 35. Shakespeare. HeIP-4; ImPo; NAEL-1; NoSic; OxAEP-1; PoE; SCGP; UnPo *Fr.* Sonnets.

No More Beneath the Oppressive Hand. *Unknown.* AH

No more boomerang. Oodgeroo of the tribe Noonuccal. BMAP

No More Booze. *Unknown.* OBAL

(Fireman Save My Child.) AS

No more could reach me than her silence. Jonathan Swift. *See* On His Own Deafness.

No More Crying Out. Giuseppe Ungaretti, *Italian.* PeFWW, *tr. by* Jon Silkin

No more dying. (LL) Ode to Joy. Frank O'Hara. GLP; NeAP; PmAP

No more exercises of style for him. A Younger Poet. Peter Schjeldahl. PoA

No more for sin's dark stain the debt of death to pay. (LL) The Garden. Jones Very. APN-1; OxBA; PAR; TAP

No more I seek, the prize is found. The Harbor. William Ellery Channing. APN-1

No more in any house can I be at peace. A Dream. Charles Williams. OBEV

No more in delightful chase through buoyant seas. On a Dolphin. Anyte, *Greek.* GrAn, *tr. by* John Heath-Stubbs *and* Carol A. Whiteside

No more let Greece her bolder fables tell. On the Famous Voyage. Ben Jonson. BeJo

No More Lewd Lays. Barnabe Barnes. Son *Fr.* A Divine Century of Spiritual Sonnets.

No More Love Poems #1. Ntozake Shange. BlSi *Fr.* For Colored Girls Who Have Considered Suicide When the Rainbow Is Enuf.

No more may fear to die. (LL) A Dirge: "Calm on the bosom of thy God." Felicia Dorothea Hemans. OBEV; WoRP

"No more mistresses," King Edward said. Limerick. Frank Richards. PeLi

No more, my dear, no more these counsels try. Sonnet 64. Sir Philip Sidney. SCGP *Fr.* Astrophil and Stella. AAS; SiPS

No more, my Stella, to the sighing shades. To Stella. Hester Mulso. ECWP

No more ne will I wicked be. *Unknown.* MiEL

No more, no more Jewish townships in Poland. Elegy. Antoni Slonimski, *Polish.* HP, *tr. by* Komen, Isaac

No more--no more--Oh! never more on me. My Days of Love Are Over. Byron. OBNC *Fr.* Canto the First. NAEL-2; OAEL-2; PoE *Fr. Don Juan.*

No more, no more, / We are already pined [pin'd]. Riddle. Alexander Brome. NOSC

No more, O my spirit. Euripides. AWP, *tr. by* Hilda Doolittle *Fr. Hippolytus.*

"No more of I and thou." Hitler Speaks. Helen Waddell. MLL

No more of talk where God or Angel Guest. Higher Argument. Milton. EPCY; NOSC; TOF *Fr.* Book IX. FHYEP; NAEL-1; NAWM-1; OAEL-1 *Fr.* Paradise Lost.

No more of talk where God or angel guest. Milton. *See* Book IX.

No more of your titled acquaintants boast. Robert Burns. FaBoEE

No more—Oh, never more! (LL) A Lament: "O world! O life! O time!" Shelley. GTBS-P; NAEL-2; NOBE; PoRA

No more peck o' corn for me. Many Thousand Gone. *Unknown.* CrDW

No more post-stops on the road. Following the Rhymes of Yang T'ing-ho's Poem, "On the Road Back, Accompanying the Imperial Retinue on a Visit to the Tombs of Former Emperors." Li Tung-yang, *Chinese.* CoBLCP, *tr. by* Jonathan Chaves

No more shall I see. Frithiof's Farewell. Esaias Tegnér. *Fr.* Frithiof's Saga. AWP, *tr. by* Longfellow

No more shall I, since I am driven hence. To Larr [*or* Lar]. Robert Herrick. CaPo

No more shall walls, no more shall walls confine. Hosanna. Thomas Traherne. ChIV-2; PoEL-2

No more [of] talk where God or Angel Guest. Book IX. Milton. FHYEP; NAEL-1; NAWM-1; OAEL-1 *Fr.* Paradise Lost.

No More than Five. Fred Levinson. AmPA

No more the English girls may go. High Germany. Edward Richard Burton Shanks. OBMV

No more the highschool land. Canada: Case History: 1973. Earle Birney. PeLV

No more the scarlet maples flash and burn. December. Christopher Pearse Cranch. APN-1

No more unto my thoughts appear. Sidney Godolphin. BeJo

No more walks in the wood. An Old-Fashioned Song. John Hollander. NoP-4

No more wine? then we'll push back chairs and talk. Bishop Blougram's Apology. Robert Browning. EBVVPR; OBNC; PoEL-5

No more with overflowing light. For a Dead Lady. Edwin Arlington Robinson. CMoP; FYAP; HeIP-4; HoPM; LiTM; MoAmPo; MoP; NOBA; NoAM; OxBA; PoEL-5; PoRA; TFi

No more words! To the field, to arms. Veronica Franco, *Italian.* PBWP, *tr. by* Lynne Lawner

No more work and no more play. Good Night. Ruth Ainsworth. BoTP

No mortal man beneath the sky. Epitaph for George Moore. Thomas Hardy. FaBoEE

No mortal thing enthralled these longing eyes. Celestial Love. Michelangelo Buonarroti, *Italian.* AWP, *tr. by* John Addington Symonds

No mother! No father! Issa. PeP

No mountain and no forest, land nor sea. To Arno of Salzburg. Alcuin, *Latin.* MLL, *tr. by* Helen Waddell

No mountains or ocean, but we had orchards. Produce. Debra Allbery. PBCAP

No Need. Raymond Carver. LBC

No need to scan the skies. John Kitching. SpW

No, never think, my dear, that in my heart I treasure. Aleksandr Sergeyevich Pushkin, *Russian.* EP, *tr. by* Babette Deutsch

No new delights to our desire. Singers to Come. Alice Thompson Meynell. WPE

No New Music. Stanley Crouch. GT; PoBA

No new poems his brush will trace. On Hearing Someone Sing a Poem by Yüan Chên. Po Chü-i, *Chinese.* ChiP, *tr. by* Arthur Waley

No New Thing. Vincent Buckley. CBAP

No News at All. Jack Butler. MT

No news of him. Tanka. Toki Zenmaro, *Japanese.* MJT, *tr. by* Makoto Ueda

No news of navies burnt at seas. A New-Year's [*or* New-Yeares] Gift Sent to Sir Simeon Steward. Robert Herrick. CaPo

No, no, don't, please. Crimes of Passion: The Phone Caller. Terry Stokes. AmPA

No, no, fair heretic[k], it needs must be. Song. Sir John Suckling. BeJo; CaPo *Fr.* Aglaura.

No, no; for my virginity. A True Maid. Matthew Prior. EP; FaBoEE; NAEL-1; NIP-4; NOEC; PeLV

No, no! Go from me. I have left her lately. A Virginal. Ezra Pound. CMoP; ColAP; MeMAP; MoAmPo; NAAL-2; NIP-4; NOBA; OxBA; Poetr; Son; TAP

No, no, go not to Lethe, neither twist. Ode on Melancholy. Keats. CABP; FHYEP; HAP; ImPo; InPK-6; InPS-3; NAEL-2; NAWM-2; NOBE; NoP-4; OAEL-2; OBEV; OBNC; OxAEP-2; PoE; PoEL-4; PoRA; Poetr; Ro; SCGP; TFi

No, no I don't want my heart broken again today. Have a Nice Day. Jack Myers. NAmP90

No, no, it cannot be; for who e'er set. Beauty and Denial. William Cartwright. BeJo

No no, it will not do, it will not be. Post-Referendum. Edwin Morgan. FaBoTC *Fr.* Sonnets from Scotland.

No, no, no, I know I was not important as I moved. Come Dance with Kitty Stobling. Patrick Kavanagh. MoP; NoAM; Poetr

No, no, no, no, I cannot hate my foe. Song. Sir Philip Sidney. SiPS

No, no, no, no, my dear, let be. (LL) Fourth Song. Sir Philip Sidney. GBL; HAP; NAEL-1; NoP-4; NoSic

—No, no, no, she tells me. Why bring it back? An Argument: on 1942. David Mura. LoL

No no: of course they. Testimony. Dan Pagis, *Hebrew.* IP, *tr. by* Warren Bargad *and* Stanley F. Chyet

No, no, poor suffering heart, no change endeavor. One Happy Moment. Dryden. OBEV *Fr.* Cleomenes.

No no: they definitely were. Testimony. Dan Pagis, *Hebrew.* HP; PoSu; HP *tr. by* Stephen Mitchell

No, not earth, nor a stone slab. Glaukos, *Greek.* GrAn, *tr. by* Clive Sansom

No, not tonight. In Teesdale. Andrew Young. OxBSP

No, not under the vault of another sky. Requiem 1935-1940. "Anna Akhmatova," *Russian.* BoWoP, *tr. by* Richard McKane

No, not writers for Heaven's sake. That bunch of slobbers. Brothers and Sisters. Michael Foley. PNI

No occasion to. (LL) You cannot hope. Humbert Wolfe. FaBoEE; OBCoV; OxBTC

No Occupation. George Rostrevor Hamilton. FaBoEE

No octopus-candelabra. Ascension on Fire Island. Henri Cole. PuP-15

No Offence. D. J. Enright. OxBTC

No Offense. Kevin Young. LTA

No One. Lilian Moore. TLR

No one asks. Jorge the Church Janitor Finally Quits. Martín Espada. LTA

No one believes in the calm. Belief. Philip Levine. ColAP

No one can hurt me. They've tried to kill me. Alone. "Anna Akhmatova," *Russian.* BoWoP, *tr. by* Stephen Berg

No one can tell you why. W. D. Snodgrass. *Fr.* Heart's Needle. CAPP-1

No one cares less than I. Edward Thomas. NSI

No one comes here to learn. The School of Pain. Donna Brook. EC2

No one comes to this deserted mountain. The Cliff of the Ancient Tomb. Chang Yü. *Fr.* Seven Poems on Living in the Mountains: Seeing Off. CoBLCP, *tr. by* Jonathan Chaves

No one could have a blacker tail. Othello Jones Dresses for Dinner. Ed Roberson. PoBA

No one discovers anything for you, alone. Deornamentation. Ion Caraion, *Romanian.* CEEP, *tr. by* Marguerite Dorian *and* Elliott B. Urdang

No one ever came out of there. Why? Wassily Kandinsky, *Russian.* TCRP, *tr. by* Albert C. Todd

No one ever walking this our only earth, various, very clouded. He Had a Quality of Growth. Muriel Rukeyser. NNaP

No one goes there now. The Tune of Seven Towers. William Morris. EnVR

No one has ever loved but you and I. (LL) The Ragged Wood. W. B. Yeats. CBLP; GBL

No one has sung "Let the world know!" Antiphonal Hymn in Praise of Inanna. Enheduanna, *Sumerian.* BoWoP, *ad. by* Aliki *and* Willis Barnstone

No one has yet looked at. (LL) Beach Glass. Amy Clampitt. FaBoWP; NoAM; NoP-4; VCAP

No One Heard Him Call. Dorothy Aldis. TLR

No one in the garden. Laughter. Olive Enoch. BoTP

No one invited me. Tune: "Magnolia Blossoms, Abbreviated." Chu Tun-ju, *Chinese.* SuSP, *tr. by* James J. Y. Liu

No one is too small to be able to help. *Unknown.* CTV

No one is "Woman" to another. Mother II. Marilyn Hacker. NMM-2

No one kneads us again out of earth and clay. Psalm. Paul Celan, *German.* PoSu, *tr. by* John Felstiner

No one knew the secret of my flutes. Something Whispered in the *Shakuhachi.* Garrett Kaoru Hongo. InPS-3

No one knows how old this tree is, standing before the mountain. Song of the Old Oak. Chang Yü, *Chinese*. CoBLCP, *tr. by* Jonathan Chaves

No one knows the way out of his mother. String. Dennis Schmitz. LCAP-2

No one knows what you mean. (LL) Nails. Gary Gildner. PBCAP; TAP

No one knows where the undertaker lives. The Owl In Daytime. Thylias Moss. GT

No one knows why he came, or why he turned away, and did not climb the hill. (LL) Snowbanks North of the House. Robert Bly. AiP; LCAP-2; RaBo

No one lives past a hundred. Wang Fan-chih, *Chinese*. SuSp, *tr. by* Eugene Eoyang

No one molds us again out of earth and clay. Paul Celan. *See* Psalm: "No one kneads us again out of earth and clay."

No one needs to ask. Reinmar der Alte, *German*. GePo, *tr. by* Frederick Goldin

No one, not even Cambridge, was to blame. A. E. Housman. W. H. Auden. OxAEP-2

No one, not even God, can put back a leaf on to a tree. Fatality. D. H. Lawrence. PeECV

No One Remembers Abandoning the Village of White Fir. Duane Niatum. CDW

No One So Much as You. Edward Thomas. GBL; LoP

No one spoke. Ōshima Ryōta, *Japanese*. OHPJ; TTTS, *tr. by* Kenneth Rexroth

No one understands the Windigo, his voice like. Windigo. Paulette Jiles. NOBC

No one waits down below, as when we were young. Anatoly Sergeievich Shteiger, *Russian*. TCRP, *tr. by* Bradley Jordan

No one walks when the guardian drum sounds. Thinking of My Brothers on a Moonlit Night. Tu Fu, *Chinese*. TAL, *tr. by* Robert Payne

No one wanted to dance with us. Junior High Dance. Allison Joseph. UnSA

No one wants to hear about the war. Nam. Mike Lowery. Poetsp

No one will write poetry anymore. Matija Beckovic, *Serbo-Croatian*. HSix, *tr. by* Charles Simic

No one's dancing here tonight. The Dance. Daniel Halpern. ChAP

No one's fated or doomed to love anyone. Adrienne Rich. *Fr.* Twenty-one Love Poems. GLP

No one's going to read. A Dance for Militant Dilettantes. Al Young. NBV; PoBA

No Ordinary Sun. Hone Tuwhare. PeNZ

No ornaments but the double bed and open. The Outer Banks. Emily Grosholz. RA

No Other Choice. Tobias Hume. EBEV; GBL; NOBE

No other name but thine. (LL) Praise for the Fountain Opened. William Cowper. ChIV-1; InPK-6

No other sign from the water. (LL) Mythic Fragment. Louise Glück. NMM-2; NoAM

No part left out. (LL) Watching the moon. Lady Izumi, *Japanese*. EnlH; WPoS, *tr. by* Jane Hirshfield *and* Mariko Aratani

No Passenger was known to flee. Emily Dickinson. SAmP

No pavement chalks the plain with memories. Beginning the Year at Rosebud, S. D. Roberta Hill Whiteman. CDW

No peace or quiet in the countryside. Farewell of an Old Man. Tu Fu, *Chinese*. SuSp, *tr. by* Michael E. Workman

No Picture. Lutz Rathenow, *German*. CEEP, *tr. by* Boria Sax

No place, indeed, should murder sanctuarize. Shakespeare. *Fr.* Hamlet. NAWM-1

No Place Like Home. Llawdden, *Welsh*. OBWVE, *tr. by* Gwyn Jones

No place seemed farther than your death. And I Am Old to Know. Pauline Hanson. TAP

No Platonic [*or* Platonique] Love. William Cartwright. BeJo; GBL; ImPo; NOSC; OAEL-1; PoEL-2

(No Platonic Love.) EP

("They only find a Med'cine for the Itch.") (LL) EP; GEA

No, please don't. On Thinking of Photographing My Fantasies. Nellie Wong. OpBo

No poem you send. Buson, *Japanese*. TAL, *tr. by* Harold G. Henderson

No poetry before ours. Correction of proofs + desires in speed. Filippo Tommaso Marinetti. PFTM, *tr. by* Richard J. Pioli *Fr.* Zang Tumb Tuuum.

No poet's calling were we granted. Old Derzhavin. "David Samuilovich Samoylov," *Russian*. TCRP, *tr. by* Lubov Yakovleva

No point now my friend in telling. Heemi. Hone Tuwhare. PeNZ

No point / waking / troubling you / with telegrams. Vladimir Mayakovsky. *See* Mayakovsky's Suicide Note.

No poisoned image yours against the sky. A Hemlock at Sunset. Alec Brock Stevenson. FuPo

No porter guards the passage of your door. Dryden. EBEV *Fr.* To My Honoured [*or* Honour'd] Kinsman, John Driden [of Chesterton in the County of Huntingdon, Esquire].

No Portuguese Lady is Nautical. Limerick. Sydney Hoffman. PeLi

No Possum, No Sop, No Taters. Wallace Stevens. HCAP; MeMAP; OxBA; TAP; VGW

No praying allowed, no sneezing. Warnings. Nicanor Parra, *Spanish*. AF, *tr. by* Miller Williams

No primal star is half so bright. (LL) Perspective. Coventry Patmore. FaBoEE; GBL

No private grudge they need, no personal spite. Modern Critics. Coleridge. FaBoEE

No promise then: / delivered / palpable / ours. Adrienne Rich. *See* Snapshots of a Daughter-in-Law.

No, Quetzalcoatl, don't come back. Pentti Saarikoski. VCWP, *tr. by* Herbert Lomas *Fr.* Invitation to the Dance.

No Rack can torture me. Emily Dickinson. MeMAP; NALW

No rain, and yet my saddle is damp. Fog at Liang-hsiang. Yüan Mei, *Chinese*. CoBLCP, *tr. by* Jonathan Chaves

No Rembrandt's mother's face. Relative. Alastair Fowler. FaBoTC

No Remedy. Drummond Allison. OxBTC

No rest! No rest on this bleak earth for me. Crazed. Mary E. Tucker. CBWP-1; RACG

No resurrection in the minds of men. (LL) Sonnet: "It is not death, that sometime in a sigh." Thomas Hood. GSo; OBNC

No rice—In that hour. Basho, *Japanese*. TAL, *tr. by* Harold G. Henderson

No riches from his scanty store. A Song. Helen Maria Williams. WoRP

No Road. Philip Larkin. CBLP; EBEV; MoBrPo; OxAEP-2

No robe, no sleeves, my hair uncombed. Chu Yün-ming. *Fr.* Improvisations. CoBLCP, *tr. by* Jonathan Chaves

No rooftops to rest on. Madison Square. A. Glanz-Leyeles, *Yiddish*. CEEP, *tr. by* Keith Bosley

No room for fear. Langston Hughes. *See* Subway Rush Hour.

No room for mourning: he's gone out. Wordsworth. Sidney Keyes. OxBTC

No room in the inn, of course. What the Donkey Saw. U. A. Fanthorpe. OBCP

No rooster wakes them. A donkey brays. In the Madison Zoo. Roberta Hill Whiteman. CDW

No round-shouldered pitchers here[, no stewards]. Cana Revisited. Seamus Heaney. FaBoMo; GI

No runner clears the final fence. The Unfinished Race. Norman Cameron. OxBS

"No," said Charles Peace. Edmund Clerihew Bentley. NOBL *Fr.* Clerihews.

No scar. Tanka. Maekawa Samio, *Japanese*. MJT, *tr. by* Makoto Ueda

No Second Troy. W. B. Yeats. CMoP; EnLoPo; GTBS-P; MoP; NAEL-2; NOBE; NoAM; OAEL-2; OxAEP-2; OxBTC; PoEL-5; TFi; WeW-3

No Sects in Heaven. Elizabeth Hannah Jocelyn Cleaveland. BLPA

No, señora rodriguez. Ancestral Messengers/Composition 13. Ntozake Shange. GT

No sheet of sound enshroud. John Coltrane Arrived with an Egyptian Lady. Nathaniel Mackey. MoNo; PT

No, she's brushing a boy's hair. (LL) Facing It. Yusef Komunyakaa. NAAAL; PoPoPo

No Shoes No Shirt No Service. Gary Snyder. BB

No Shop Does the Bird Use. Elizabeth Jane Coatsworth. OBCA

No sickness worse than secret love. *Unknown*. NOIV

No sign is made while empires pass. Continuity. "Æ." MoBrPo

No Sign of Blood. Faiz Ahmad Faiz, *Arabic*. AF, *tr. by* Naomi Lazard

No Simple Explanations. Jayne Cortez. GT

No single hour can stand for naught. John Clare. OBNC

No Single Thing Abides. Lucretius, *Latin*. AWP, *tr. by* W. H. Mallock *Fr.* De Rerum Natura (On the Nature of Things).

No, Sir, No. *Unknown*. AmFP

"No, sir," said General Sherman. Edmund Clerihew Bentley. NOBL; OBCoV *Fr.* Clerihews.

No situation presents itself. Every Time We Say Goodbye. James Cushing. SeSe

No sleep for twelve days. What Happened to a Young man in a Place Where He Turned to Water. *Unknown, Apache Indian*. STP, *tr. by* Anselm Hollo

No sleep. The sultriness pervades the air. The House-Top. Herman Melville. APN-2; CBCWP; NAAL-1; NAAL-3; NCAP; NOBA

No sleep tonight. Summary. Sonia Sanchez. BPo

No So. Not So. Anne Sexton. CrSp

No sooner come [*or* came] but gone, and fallen [*or* fall'n] asleep. On My Dear Grandchild Simon Bradstreet, [Who Died on 16TH November,

1669, Being But A Month And One Day Old]. Anne Bradstreet. ColAP; KTR; NAAL-1; NAAL-3; SCAP

No sooner did the Cymbrians overcommer. The Antidoted Fanfreluches: or, a Galimatia of Extravagant Conceits Found in an Ancient Monument. François Rabelais, *French.* CBNP, *tr. by* Sir Thomas Urquhart

No sound is dissonant which tells of Life. (LL) This Lime-Tree Bower My Prison. Coleridge. FHYEP; FP; HeIP-4; NAEL-2; OBGa; OxAEP-2; PoE; PoEL-4; Ro; TOF

No sound of any storm that shakes. Hillcrest. Edwin Arlington Robinson. MeMAP; OxBA

No Speech from the Scaffold. Thom Gunn. OxBTC

No speed of wind or water rushing by. The Master Speed. Robert Frost. ITG

No spot of earth where men have so fiercely for ages of time. Antrim. Robinson Jeffers. BlrV; IIP; NOBA; SAGP; VGW

No spring, nor summer beauty hath such grace. The Autumnal[l]. Donne. FSCP; InPS-3; NOSC; PoEL-2 *Fr.* Elegies.

No square poet's job. (LL) Haiku: "Eastern guard tower." Etheridge Knight. BPo; MoP; TAP

No stab thy soul[e] can kill. (LL) The Lie. Sir Walter Ralegh. AAS; CTC; EBEV; FaBoPV; GEA; HAP; ImPo; NAEL-1; NOBE; NoSic; PBRV; PoEL-2; RB; SCGP; SCV; SiPS; TFi

No Stars Her Eyes. Thomas Lodge. Son *Fr.* Phyllis.

No Stewart art thou, Galloway. On Lord Galloway. Robert Burns. FaBoEE

No Stewart art thou, Galloway. On Lord Galloway. Robert Burns. FaBoEE *Fr.* Epigrams on Lord Galloway.

No stir in the air, no stir in the sea. The Inchcape Rock. Robert Southey. EBEvV; EBNV; FaBoBe; OBNV; OBSP; OxAEP-2

No strength of Nature can suffice. Love Constraining to Obedience. William Cowper. NOCV *Fr.* Olney Hymns.

No sun—no moon! Thomas Hood. AYFP; CTV; OBCoV, PMDP

No sunrise here three layers of green. Illumination. D. F. Brown. CDa

No surely, now it cannot be pride. (LL) She came to the village church. Tennyson. EBVV; NAEL-2

No Swan So Fine. Marianne Moore. MeMAP; NALW; NoP-4; OxBA; PoA; UnPo

No task could be easier. Planting Bulbs. Marge Piercy. *Fr.* Six Underrated Pleasures. EC2

No, Thank You! Trần Tế Xu'o'ng, *Vietnamese.* AVP, *tr. by* Huỳnh Sanh Thông

No, Thank You, John. Christina Rossetti. NAEL-2

No Thanks, No. 70. E. E. Cummings. PFTM

No, the Christian faith, as at any rate I understood it. Claude to Eustace. Arthur Hugh Clough. EnVR *Fr.* Amours de Voyage. NOBVV

No, the human heart. Ki no Tsurayuki, *Japanese.* OHPJ, *tr. by* Kenneth Rexroth

No, the serpent did not. Theology. Ted Hughes. FaBoMo; NAEL-2; NoAM; NoP-4

No Theory. David Ignatow. NNaP; RaBo

No thing / no-thing. Cathexis. Frederick Bryant, Jr. NBV; PoBA

No this isn't a road intersected by enemy lines or foreign tongues or silence. Piyyut for the New Year. Haim Guri, *Hebrew.* IP, *tr. by* Warren Bargad *and* Stanley F. Chyet

No Thoroughfare. Ruth Holmes. BoTP

No! those days are gone away. Robin Hood. Keats. AWP; SCGP

No, thou hast never griev'd but I griev'd too. Walter Savage Landor. GBL

No; thou'rt a fool, I'll swear, if e'er thou grant. Against Fruition. Abraham Cowley. BeJo; NOSC *Fr.* The Mistress.

No thunder blasts Jove's plant, nor can. Occasioned by Seeing a Walk of Bay Trees. Mildmay Fane, 2d Earl of Westmorland. BeJo; NOSC; OxBSP

No thyng is to man so dere. Praise of Women. Robert Mannyng. OBEV

No time ago / or else a life. E. E. Cummings. OxBSP

No Time for Lamentation Now. Milton. *Fr.* Samson Agonistes. FHYEP; OAEL-1; PoEL-3

No time, no room, no thought, or writing can. Sonnet 101. Mary Sidney, Countess of Montgomery Wroth. PEW *Fr.* Pamphilia to Amphilanthus.

No time, no time / and with so many in line to be. The Suburb. Anne Stevenson. NMM-2; WeT

No, Time, thou shalt not boast that I do change. Sonnet 123. Shakespeare. OxAEP-1; Son *Fr.* Sonnets.

No touch, but forever and ever this. (LL) At Baia. Hilda Doolittle. ColAP; NAAL-2; NOBA

No trellises [*or* trellisses], no vines. Iron Landscapes (and the Statue of Liberty). Thom Gunn. FaBoA; FaBoPV

No tricks / nothing doing. Tune: "Greeting the Immortal Guest." Yün-k'an Tzu, *Chinese.* SuSp, *tr. by* Jerome P. Seaton

No Use. W. D. Snodgrass. BoLoP

No use in my going. Blue Monday. Langston Hughes. SAmP

No use, no use, now, begging Recognize! Amnesiac. Sylvia Plath. NYBP

No use waiting for it to stop. Apples. Shirley Kaufman. CrSp; MDDM; NMM-2

No village dames and maidens now are seen. Cottage Pictures. Samuel Jackson Pratt. OBGa *Fr.* Cottage Pictures.

No walls confine! Can nothing hold my mind? Insatiableness. Thomas Traherne. NOSC

No wars allowed now for the true faith. Nuts and Raisins. Carl Dennis. CMAP

No water is still, on top. The Movement of Fish. James Dickey. NYBP; VGW

No water so still as the / dead fountains of Versailles. No swan. No Swan So Fine. Marianne Moore. MeMAP; NALW; NoP-4; OxBA; PoA; UnPo

No waters breed or break. (LL) Next, Please. Philip Larkin. CABP; MoBrPo

No way too long--no path too steep. Stefan George. AWP, *tr. by* Daisy Broicher *Fr.* Jahr der Seele, Das.

No, we don't accomplish our love in a single year. Rilke. ITG, *tr. by* Stephen Mitchell *Fr.* The Third Duino Elegy.

No, we will not make vows to the ever-winning goddess. What She Said to Her Girl Friend. Korran, *Tamil.* PLW, *tr. by* A. K. Ramanujan

No weather is ill. *Unknown.* FaBoVe

No, we'll be wits, and then men must be fools. (LL) The Emulation. Sarah Fyge Egerton. CABP; PEW

No West Indians that I could see at my grandfather's funeral. (1962 At the Edge of Town). C. S. Giscombe. GT; PUP-19 *Fr.* Look Ahead—Look South.

No whimsy of the purse is here. Inscription for the Moss-Hut at Dove Cottage. Wordsworth. OBGa

No winter shall abate the spring's [*or* springs] increase [*or* encrease]. (LL) Love's Growth. Donne. ESCV; NOSC; NoP-4; PBRV

No woman's pleasure did I feel. Evidence at the Witch Trials. James Keir Baxter. OxBC

No women wear under. Penthouse Playboy. Lyn Lifshin. DeD

No wonder I slipped, being soaked. Dionysius Sophistes, *Greek.* GrAn, *tr. by* Barriss Mills

No wonder if he wish he ne'er had learned to eat. (LL) The Two Boys. Mary Lamb. Ro

No Word. Tu Fu, *Chinese.* SuSp, *tr. by* Eugene Eoyang

No words, no tears can mend. (LL) Father and Child. Gwen Harwood. CBAP; WPE

No, worldling, no, 'tis not thy gold. The Second Rapture. Thomas Carew. CaPo

No worst, there is none. Pitched past pitch of grief. Sonnet. Gerard Manley Hopkins. APAD; CMoP; EBVV; EnVR; FaBoMo; GSo; GTBS-P; HeIP-4; InPS-3; LiTM; MoBrPo; MoP; NAEL-2; NOBE; NOBVV; NoAM; NoP-4; OAEL-2; OBNC; OxAEP-2; PeVV; PoE; PoEL-5; PoPoPo; Poetr; TFi

No' yirdit thaim. (LL) The Eemis-Stane. "Hugh MacDiarmid." FaBoTC; NAEL-2

No, you never will bind him. God (3). Marina Tsvetayeva, *Russian.* WPoS, *tr. by* Paul Graves

Noah. Wayne Brown. PBCV

Noah. Gerda Mayer. OTCP

Noah. *Unknown.*

"I thank the, Lord so dere, that wold vowchsayf." PoE

Noah an' Jonah an' Cap'n John Smith. Don Marquis. PoLF

Noah was an Admiral. James Reeves. OTCP

Noah's Ark. Roger McGough. OBSP

Noah's Ark. Marguerite Young. WPE

Noah's Flood. Caedmon. AnOE, *tr. by* C. W. Kennedy *Fr.* Genesis.

Noah's Flood. Michael Drayton.

"By this the sun had sucked up the vast deep." NOSC

"Eternall and all-working God, which wast." PoEL-2

"Hundred years the Ark in the building was, A." ChIV-1

Noah's Prayer. Carmen Bernos de Gasztold, *French.* TrCP, *tr. by* Rumer Godden

Noah's Raven. W. S. Merwin. ChIV-1; HCAP

Nobility. Oumar Ba. PBMAP

Noble ambition spans the four seas, A. T'ao Ch'ien, *Chinese.* SuSp, *tr. by* Eugene Eoyang

Noble Balm, The. Ben Jonson. *See* Ode, An: "High-spirited friend, / I send not balms, nor corsives to your wounds."

Noble Fisherman; or, Robin Hood's Preferment, The. *Unknown.* ESPB

Noble hart, that harbours vertuous [*or* virtuous] thought, The. The Fight of the Red Cross Knight and the Heathen Sansjoy. Edmund Spenser. FHYEP; NoSic *Fr.* Wood Of Error. AEP

Noble horse with courage in his eye, The. Aristocrats. Keith Douglas. FaBoMo; NAEL-2; NoAM; NoP-4; OBWP

Noble King of Brentford, The. The King of Brentford's Testament, *abr.* William Makepeace Thackeray. OBNV

Noble Mayde, still standing, all this vewd, The. Edmund Spenser. PoEL-1 *Fr.* The Mask of Cupid. *Fr.* Wood Of Error. AEP

Noble Nature, The. Ben Jonson. GTBS-P *Fr.* To the Immortal[l] Memory [*or* Memorie] and Friendship of That Noble Pair[e], Sir Lucius Cary and Sir H. [*or* Henry] Morison. BeJo; NAEL-1; NOBE; NOSC; OAEL-1; PoEL-2; SeCP

   (Part of an Ode, A.) OBEV

Noble range it was, of many a rood, A. The Story of Rimini. Leigh Hunt. OBGa

Noble Ritter Hugo, Der. Ballad by Hans Breitmann. Charles Godfrey Leland. BXAP; NOBL

Noble Scholar Playing the Lute, A. Yang Chi, *Chinese.* CoBLCP, *tr. by* Jonathan Chaves

Noble Sidney with this last arose, The. Michael Drayton. EPCY *Fr.* To Henry Reynolds, of Poets and Poesy.

Noble Sisters. Christina Rossetti. VWP

Noble Six Hundred! (LL) The Charge of the Light Brigade. Tennyson. APAD; BLPA; CABP; ChAP; EBEvV; EnVR; FHYEP; FaBoBe; FaPoR; HoPM; NAEL-2; NOBVV; NoP-4; OBWP; OxAEP-2; PBMP; PeVV; TFi; UV

Nobler funeral pyre!, A. (LL) John Maynard. Horatio Alger Jr. BLPA; FaBoBe

Nobles and heralds, by your leave. On Himself. Matthew Prior. FaBoEE; OBCoV

Noblesse oblige. Josephine Miles. *See* Belief.

Noblesse Oblige. Celeste Turner Wright. Poetsp

Noblest bodies are but gilded clay. Samuel Harding. NOSC

Noblest Charis, you that are. His Discourse with Cupid. Ben Jonson. *Fr.* A Celebration of Charis in Ten Lyric[k] Pieces [*or* Peeces]. BeJo; OxAEP-1; SeCP

Noblest of men, woo't die? Shakespeare. IMW, *act* V, *scene* 1; OxAEP-1, *sect.* IV, xiii *Fr.* Antony and Cleopatra.

Nobly Born, The. Frances Ellen Watkins Harper. PWR

Nobly, nobly Cape Saint Vincent to the North-west died away. Home-Thoughts, from the Sea. Robert Browning. EBEvV; NAEL-2; SCGP

Nobody. Novica Tadic, *Serbo-Croatian.* HSix; VCWP, *tr. by* Charles Simic

Nobody asked you, sir, she said. (LL) The Milk Maid. Mother Goose. LB; OxNR; ReMoGo

Nobody but Lester let Lester leap. Lester Leaps In. Al Young. MoNo; SeSe

Nobody comes up from the sea as late as this. You Will Know When You Get There. Allen Curnow. NoP-4; PeNZ

Nobody does any waiting. 27th Dance—Walking—22 March 1964. Jackson Mac Low. FTOS

Nobody doubts / that it is snowing now. Taking a Look. David Shapiro. PT

Nobody else can have as much fun as. The Twenty Grand (Saturday Night on the Block). Naomi Long Madgett. NBV

Nobody else living knows that song as well as I do. Gerald Stern. CMAP

Nobody even dared look. (LL) Crucifixion. "Anna Andreyevna Akhmatova." IMW

Nobody had what he had. Hannibal. Eugen Jebeleanu, *Romanian.* CEEP, *tr. by* Donald Eulert *and* Stefan Avadanei

Nobody heard him, the dead man. Not Waving But Drowning. Stevie Smith. APAD; CABP; FaBoWP; GTBS-P; HAP; HeIP-4; MoP; NAEL-2; NALW; NOBE; NoAM; NoP-4; OAEL-2; OxAEP-2; OxBTC; PoE; PoPoPo; Poetr; TFi; UV; WeW-3

Nobody I know would like to be buried. Thanksgiving for a Habitat. W. H. Auden. NYBP

Nobody in the lane, and nothing, nothing but blackberries. Blackberrying. Sylvia Plath. HAP; HCAP; NAAL-2; NOBA; NYBP; NoAM; PoPoPo

Nobody in the widow's household. Passing Through. Stanley Kunitz. LoL

Nobody is dead yet and won't be. Right. A Local Contractor Flees His Winter Trouble and Saves Some Lives in a Knoxville Motel Room. James Whitehead. MT

Nobody is ever missing. (LL) There sat down, once, a thing on Henry's heart. John Berryman. CAPP-1; HAP; HCAP; NoP-4; PoE; VCAP

Nobody is going to slap him around. (LL) Hedgehog. Chu Chen Po, *Chinese.* OHMPC; PiM, *tr. by* Kenneth Rexroth

Nobody knew his name. El Heroe. Sylvia Townsend Warner. WPN

Nobody knew when it would start again. Schizophrenic. Patricia K. Page. HeIP-4

Nobody knocks at my door. Nobody comes to hit me. Invocation. Maria Elena Cruz Varela, *Spanish.* VCWP, *tr. by* Mairym Cruz-Bernal *and* Deborah Digges

Nobody Knows but Mother. Mary Morrison. BLPA

Nobody Knows de Trouble I've Seen. *Unknown.* AH

Nobody knows the other side. 127th Chorus. Jack Kerouac. NeAP; PmAP *Fr.* Mexico City Blues.

Nobody Knows the Trouble I've Had. *Unknown.* APAD; APN-2

Nobody knows the world but me. Professor Noctutus. George Macdonald. NOBVV

Nobody knows what I feel about Freddy. Freddy. Stevie Smith. LW

Nobody knows what love is anymore. For a Masseuse and Prostitute. Kenneth Rexroth. NNaP

Nobody knows what's growing in Bridget. The Bulge. George Johnston. MoCV

Nobody lives in the cottage now. Fairy Feet. Phyllis L. Garlick. BoTP

Nobody loses all the time. E. E. Cummings. CMoP; LiTM; NAAL-2; NBLV; NOBA; RB; TwCP

Nobody loves me. Shel Silverstein. OTCP

Nobody loves you Chloe, you sly minx. To His Coy Mistress. Edward Bird. BXAP

Nobody mentioned war. Malcolm. Lucille Clifton. NAAAL

Nobody noogers the shaff of a sloo. On a Flimmering Floom You Shall Ride. Carl Sandburg. OBAL

Nobody on earth has a book of matches. Race of the Kingfishers. Ray A. Young Bear. HATNAP

Nobody painted Mrs. Aherne's store. Dakota: Five Times Six. Joseph Hansen. NYBP

Nobody planted roses, he recalls. Summertime and the Living. Robert Earl Hayden. PoBA; TwCP

Nobody put their hand out. All Clear. Roger Woddis. PeLV

Nobody read him, the poor sod. Not Wavell but Browning. Gavin Ewart. UV

Nobody Riding the Roads Today. June Jordan. BPo; NoAM

Nobody said Apples for nearly a minute. Political Intelligence. Arthur James Marshall Smith. SPE

Nobody stays here long. Not in the Guide-Books. Elizabeth Jennings. LiTM

Nobody stuffs the world in at your eyes. Snow. Margaret Avison. NOBC

Nobody talks earth's language. Kalju Lepik, *Estonian.* CEEP, *tr. by* Ivar Ivask

Nobody Thinks Hard Enough for Poetry. Kelvin Corcoran. NBrP

Nobody wanted this infant born. Burial. Mark Van Doren. MoBS

Nobody will open the door for you. Blanca Varela, *Spanish.* BoWoP, *tr. by* Willis Barnstone

Nobody with me. Tanka. Masaoka Shiki, *Japanese.* MJT, *tr. by* Ueda, Makoto

Nobody's Chasing Me. Cole Porter. CBLP

Nobody's newspaper tells what the Costa Ricans did. Naomi Shihab Nye. EC2

Noces. Marilyn Hacker. DeD *Fr.* Love, Death and the Changing of the Seasons.

Nochebuena. Rosario Caicedo. LoHo

Nocht o' Mortal Sicht. Bessie J. B. Macarthur. OxBS

Noctambule. George Johnston. MoCV

Nocturn at the Institute. David McElroy. Poetsp

Nocturnal. Sally Ball. BAP-95

Nocturnal Heart. Anne-Maric Kegels, *French.* BoWoP, *tr. by* W. S. Merwin

Nocturnal honey that glides down from the flanks, The. White on White. Maria Luisa Spaziani, *Italian.* NeIt, *tr. by* Beverly Allen

Nocturnal Journey. Ory Bernstein, *Hebrew.* IP, *tr. by* Warren Bargad *and* Stanley F. Chyet

Nocturnal Landscape. Malcolm Cowley. PoA

Nocturnal Landscape. Anton Schnack, *German.* PeFWW, *tr. by* Christopher Middleton

Nocturnal, my panther, has eyes that spark, The. Lullaby. Tuvia Rivner, *Hebrew.* MHP, *tr. by* Ruth Finer Mintz

Nocturnal Reverie, A. Anne Finch, Countess of Winchilsea. BWW; EBEV; ECEV; ECWP; GEA; NAEL-1; NALW; NOEC; NoP-4; OxAEP-1; PBWP; PoE; PoEL-3; Poetr; WPE

   ("Or pleasures, seldom reach'd, pursu'd.") (LL) CABP

Nocturnal Sketch, A. Thomas Hood. PeLV

Nocturnal Sounds. Kattie M. Cumbo. BlSi

Nocturnal[l] upon Saint Lucy's [*or* S. Lucies] Day, Being the Shortest Day, A. Donne. CABP; EBEV; ESCV; FHYEP; GBL; MeLP; NAEL-1; NOBE; NoP-4; NOSC; OAEL-1; OxAEP-1; PBRV; PoE; PoEL-2; SCGP; SeCP; TFi

Nocturnal Visits. Claribel Alegría, *Spanish.* VCWP, *tr. by* D. J. Flakoll

Nocturnal water, primaeval silences. Useless Day. Rosario Castellanos. WPOW, *tr. by* Maureen Ahern

Nocturne. Eavan Boland. NBrP

Nocturne. Robert Silliman Hillyer. FYAP, *tr. by* John Moyne *and* Coleman Barks

Nocturne. James McAuley. BMAP

Nocturne: "Be thou at peace this night." Edward Davison. CH

Nocturne: "Listening for the sound." Pinkie Gordon Lane. BlSi

Nocturne: "Moon has gone to her rest, The." Wilfrid Scawen Blunt. OBMV

Nocturne: "Red flame flowers bloom and die, The." Crosbie Garstin. CH

Nocturne: "Wildness of haggard flights." Roussan Camille, *French*. TTY, *tr. by* Seth L. Wolitz

Nocturne at Bethesda. Arna Bontemps. ChIV-2; NAAAL

Nocturne at Danieli's, A. Sir Owen Seaman. UV

Nocturne by Ben Shahn. Ronald Stuart Thomas. OxAEP-2

Nocturne for October 31st, A. Yvor Winters. PoA

Nocturne in a Deserted Brickyard. Carl Sandburg. MoAmPo

Nocturne in G Minor. Karl Gustav Vollmoeller, *German*. AWP, *tr. by* Ludwig Lewisohn

Nocturne in the Women's Prison. Maria Beneyto, *Spanish*. WPOW, *tr. by* Catherine Rodriguez-Nieto

Nocturne Militaire. Thomas McGrath. AF

Nocturne of the Self-evident Presence. Thomas MacGreevy. BIrV; CIP-2

Nocturne of the Wharves. Arna Bontemps. BPo; ColAP; GT

Nocturne Varial. Lewis Alexander. PoBA

Nod. Walter De la Mare. BoTP; MoBrPo; OxBTC

Nodding and beckoning across, observed of Attaché and Guardsman. Arthur Hugh Clough. FaBoPV *Fr.* Bothie of Tober-na-Vuolich, The.

Nodding, its great head rattling like a gourd. Original Sin. Robert Penn Warren. FuPo; HoPM; LiTM; NOCV; TAP

Nodding Off. Kao Ch'i, *Chinese*. CoBLCP, *tr. by* Jonathan Chaves

Noe more unto my thoughts appeare. Song. Sidney Godolphin. MeLP

Noël. Hilaire Belloc. UV

Noel; Christmas Eve, 1913. Robert Bridges. NOCV; OBCP; PoEL-5

Noel, noel, noel, / Noel, noel, noel! Out of Your Sleep Arise and Wake. *Unknown*. NoP-4

Noel of the marvelous night. To Noel. Gabriela Mistral, *Spanish*. PChr, *tr. by* Doris Dana

Noise began in my belly, The. For Carlos Charles Bucillio. Alice Sadongei. HATNAP

Noise dies down. I have appeared, The. Hamlet. Boris Pasternak, *Russian*. TCRP, *tr. by* Yakov Hornstein

Noise Grimaced. Larry Eigner. NeAP

Noise of death is in this desolate bar, The. The Drunkards. Malcolm Lowry. NYBP

Noise of hammers once I heard. The Hammers. Ralph Hodgson. MoBrPo; NOBE; OxBTC

Noise of the Village, The. *Unknown, Chippewa*. OBVE, *tr. by* Frances Densmore

Noise of water teased his literal ear[s], The. Persistent Explorer. John Crowe Ransom. OxBA

Noise outside. Spring. Pinkie Gordon Lane. GT

Noise That Time Makes, The. Merrill Moore. MoAmPo
   ("Noise Time makes in passing by, The.") FuPo

Noiseless patient spider, A. Walt Whitman. APN-1; AWP; AmPP; CTAV; HAP; HeIP-4; ImPo; InPK-6; InPS-3; MoAmPo; NAAL-1; NAAL-3; NCAP; NOBA; NTP; OxBA; OxBSP; PBMP; PFE; PoE; PoPoPo; Poetr; SAmP; SCV; TAP; TFi
   ("My soul.") (LL) APo
   ("Soul.") (LL) GEA
   ("Till the gossamer thread you fling catch somewhere, O my soul.") (LL) BLT; ColAP; NoP-4; PAR

Noiselessly. Tanka. Yosano Tekkan, *Japanese*. MJT, *tr. by* Makoto Ueda

Noiselessly, the mountain stream. A Sketch of Mount Chung. Wang An-shih, *Chinese*. SuSp, *tr. by* Jan W. Walls

Noises at night never struck us at all. Reading Milosz. Lev Vladimir Loseff, *Russian*. TCRP, *tr. by* G. S. Smith

Noises in the Night. Lilian McCrea. BoTP

Noises of the harbour die, the smoke is petrified, The. The Statue. John Fuller. NOBE

Noisy politicians confuse the world. Rhyming with a Friend. Yü Hsüan-chi. BoWoP, *tr. by* Geoffrey Waters

Noisy urchins scampered round, The. Much Distressed. *Unknown*. CBAP

Nokes went, he thought, to Styles's wife to bed. A Case to the Civilians. *Unknown*. FaBoEE

Noli Me Tangere. Jan Polkowski, *Polish*. AF, *tr. by* Michael March *and* Jaroslaw Anders

Nomad, A. Jean Daive, *French*. MFP, *tr. by* Martin Sorrell

Nomad Exquisite. Wallace Stevens. ColAP

Nomen. Naomi Long Madgett. BlSi; MoLi

Nomenclaturik. Harry Hearson. OBCoV

Nominalist and Realist. Ralph Waldo Emerson. APN-1

Nomine Domini / Theotocopoulos. High Renaissance. George Starbuck. NBLV; OBAL

Non Amo Te. Thomas Brown. *See* Doctor Fell.

Non Dolet. Oliver St. John Gogarty. OBMV

Non ego hoc ferrem calida juventâ. At Thirty Years. Byron. *Fr.* Canto the First. NAEL-2; OAEL-2; PoE *Fr.* Don Juan.

Non-gae. Yongno Pyon, *Korean*. CKP, *tr. by* Jaihiun Kim

Non Nobis. Henry Cust. OBEV

Non Omnis Moriar. Allen Tate. FuPo

Non Piangere, Liù. Peter Porter. CBLP; OxBC

Non Que Je Veuille Ôter la Liberté. Pernette De Guillet, *French*. WPOW, *tr. by* Raymond Oliver

Non-sense. *Unknown*. CBNP

Non Sequitor [*or* Sequitur], A. Richard Corbet. CBNP

Non Sum Qualis Eram Bonae sub Regno Cynara[e]. Ernest Christopher Dowson. ADE; APAD; AWP; BLPA; BoLoP; CABP; CBLP; ClHu; EBVV; EnLoPo; FaBoBe; GBL; GLoP; GTBS-P; HAP; HeIP-4; ImPo; MoBrPo; NOBE; NoP-4; OAEL-2; OBEV; OBMV; OBNC; PeVV; PoRA; SAGP; TFi; UnPo

Non Ti Fidar. Louis Zukofsky. VGW

Non ti scordar di me! (LL) Aux Italiens. "Owen Meredith." BLPA; FaBoBe

Nona poured oil on the water and saw the eye. The Evil Eye. John Ciardi. MoBS

Nondescript express in from the South, A. Gare du Midi. W. H. Auden. OxBSP

None. Josephine Miles. VGW

None alive will pity me. (LL) Philomel. Richard Barnfield. AWP; CH; GBL; GTBS-P; NOBE; OBEV

None but a Muse in love, can tell. On Fruition. Sir Charles Sedley. NOSC

None but my Lely [*or* Lilly] ever drew a mind[e]. (LL) To My Worthy Friend Mr. Peter Lely [*or* Lilly]. Richard Lovelace. CaPo, NOSC

None but Zion's children know. (LL) Glorious Things of Thee Are Spoken. John Newton. NOCV; NOEC

None can experience stint. Emily Dickinson. NCAP

None could better our sex limousine. Limerick. *Unknown*. PeLi

None could ever say that she. Catullus. *See* Carmen 75 ("Reason blinded by sin, Lesbia").

None ever was in love with me but grief. "My True Love Hath My Heart and I Have His." Mary Elizabeth Coleridge. BoLoP

None from thy laws are free. Boethius. OBCVT, *tr. by* J. T. [Michael Walpole] *Fr.* The Consolation of Philosophy.

None Is Happy. Hartmann von Aue, *German*. AWP, *tr. by* Jethro Bithell

None is like Jeshurun's God! Charles Wesley. NoP-4

None is, slight things do lightly please. (LL) His Grange, or Private Wealth. Robert Herrick. BeJo; CaPo; CavPo

None is the same as another. Iain Crichton Smith. NTP

None of it true; for Christ's sake, spill the ink. "Robin Hyde." PeNZ *Fr.* The Houses.

None of the other birds seem to like it. Stevie Smith. BWW

None of them come! (LL) Sir Beelzebub. Dame Edith Sitwell. BoWoP; FaBoMo; FaBoWP; HoPM; MoBrPo; NALW; OBCoV; OxBTC

None of this makes any sense. The Ghost-Who-Walks. Colleen J. McElroy. GT

None of us remembers these, the days. Summer 1983. Mary Jo Salter. RA

None of your business. (LL) Jesus Dies. Anne Sexton. CrSp; RACG

None other fame mine unambitious muse. Samuel Daniel. AAS *Fr.* To Delia.

None said anything startling from the rest. Lunchtime. David Ignatow. IFJA

None shall gainsay me. I will lie on the floor. Gloriana Dying. Sylvia Townsend Warner. FaBoWP

None with swift feet. (LL) Dance Figure. Ezra Pound. HeIP-4; MoAmPo

None'll come, and then a lot'll. (LL) On Tomato Ketchup. *Unknown*. NBLV; Spl

Nones. Donald Davie. *Fr.* Horae Canonicae. CRP

Nonflying Weather. Robert Ivanovich Rozhdestvensky, *Russian*. TCRP, *tr. by* Albert C. Todd

Nonpareil. Matthew Prior. EnLoPo

Nonplussed. Ken Bolton. BMAP

Nonsense [*or* Nonsence]. Richard Corbet. CBNP; FaBoVe

Nonsense. Thomas Moore. FaBoEE

Nonsense. *Unknown*. EBEV

Nonsense Rhyme, A. James Whitcomb Riley. NOxBChV

Nonsense Rhyme. Elinor Wylie. PBMP

Nonsense Song, A. Stephen Vincent Benét. OBAL
   (Sad Song, A.) NOxBChV

Nonsense Song. *Unknown*. CBNP

Nonsense term. To walk, A. Space Walk. Raymond Wilson. SpW

Nonsense Verses. Charles Lamb. CBNP; OBCoV

Nook. George Barlow. GT

Noon. John Clare. OxAEP-2

Noon. "Michael Field." NOBVV

Noon. Robinson Jeffers. MoAmPo

Noon. Robert Malise Bowyer Nichols. PoFWW

Noon. Perry Oldham. CDa

Noon heat in the yard, The. Hen Woman. Thomas Kinsella. CIP-2; PBCIP

Noon in the intermountain plain. Headwaters. N. Scott Momaday. NoP-4

Noon is beautiful, The: the perfect wheel. Elegy. Yvor Winters. VGW

Noon of the Sunbather. Marge Piercy. NMM-2

Noon on the mountain! Walt Whitman. Emanuel Carnevali. PoA

Noon Point. Clark Coolidge. PmAP

Noon sun beats down the leaf; the noon. Grapes Making. Léonie Adams. FYAP; UnPo

Noon. The luminous tide. Ballydavid Pier. Thomas Kinsella. BIrV

Noon Walk on the Asylum Lawn. Anne Sexton. OBGa

Noonday Axeman. Les A. Murray. NoP-4

Noonday in Immaturity. Jean-Baptiste Tati-Loutard. PBMAP *Fr.* Les Racines Congolaises (1968).

Noonday Thought. Henrietta Cordelia Ray. *Fr.* A Group of Musings. CBWP-3

Noonlight is sudden full of the spirits. The Storm. Robert Wallace. NYBP

Noon's Dream-Song. Eugene Lee-Hamilton. NOBVV

Noontide. Henrietta Cordelia Ray. *Fr.* Idyl. CBWP-3

Nooo!/ me nah call him. Wasting Time. Opal Palmer. FaBoVe

Nor a thorn nor a threat stain her beauty bright. (LL) The Lily. William Blake. FHYEP; NOBRP; Ro

Nor all that glisters, gold[!]. (LL) Ode on the Death of a Favourite [or Favorite] Cat, Drowned in a Tub [or Bowl] of Gold Fishes. Thomas Gray. ClHu; EBEV; EBEvV; EBNV; ECEV; FHYEP; FaBoBe; GTBS-P; HoPM; InPS-3; NAEL-1; NBLV; NOBE; NOBL; NOEC; OAEL-1; OBCoV; OxAEP-1; PBMP; PeLV; PoE; PoEL-3; PoLF; PoRA; TFi

Nor antlers through the thickness of his curls. (LL) Arms and the Boy. Wilfred Owen. CMoP; HAP; ImPo; LiTM; MoBrPo; OAEL-1; OAEL-2; OxBSP; PBMP; PFE; PoE; Poetr; SAGP; WeW-3

Nor any bird of the air. (LL) The Deserted House. Mary Elizabeth Coleridge. BoTP; CH

Nor any knows, save the bright watching moon. (LL) Losing a Slave-Girl. Po Chü-i, *Chinese*. ChiP, *tr. by* Arthur Waley

Nor beauty's want my first good will remove. (LL) To His Friend. George Turberville. AEP; CTC

Nor, by God, shall we neglect. Diogenes Laertius, *Greek*. GrAn, *tr. by* Robin Skelton

Nor came the Rivals equal to the Field. Pompey compared with Caesar. Lucan, *Latin*. OBCVT, *tr. by* Nicholas Rowe

Nor can I fall more low, mounting no higher. (LL) Song: "I feed a flame within, which so torments me." Dryden. AWP; OBEV

Nor can I for my soul delight. Soame Jenyns. ECEV *Fr.* An Epistle Written in the Country to the Right Honourable the Lord Lovelace.

Nor dare we think on what we are. (LL) Stanzas for Music. Byron. NAEL-2; OxBSP

Nor desist, their ray how marring o my own, see if—who cares. Catullus. *See* Carmen 75 ("Reason blinded by sin, Lesbia").

Nor did the peach complain. (LL) The Blue-Fly. Robert Graves. APo; CMoP; NAEL-2; NYBP; NoAM; PFE

Nor do these gentle creatures wrong. (LL) Kindness to Animals. *Unknown.* BoTP; WHSW

Nor do we see the knapsack on our back's the ghost. Catullus. *See* To Varus.

Nor dread nor hope attend. Death. W. B. Yeats. OxAEP-2; OxBSP

Nor ever chast, except you ravish mee. (LL) "Batter my heart, three-person'd God; for you." Donne. PBRV

Nor ever did a wise one. (LL) Impromptu on Charles II. John Wilmot. FaBoEE; NBLV; NOBL; NTP; OBSV; OxAEP-1; PeLV

Nor exults he nor complains he; silent bears whate'er befalls him. Ever Watchful. Ta' Abbata Sharra, *Arabic*. AWP, *tr. by* W. G. Palgrave

Nor fear the God whom priests and kings have made. (LL) To the Poor. Anna Laetitia Barbauld. ECWP; NoP-4

Nor fear thy latest day, nor wish therefore. (LL) Things that make the happier life, are these, The. Ben Jonson, *ad. fr. the Latin of Martial*. FaBoEE; OBVE

Nor feare, or wish your dying day. (LL) Country Life, A: To His Brother, Master Thomas Herrick. Robert Herrick. CaPo; SeCP

Nor feel the heart-break in the heart of things? (LL) Lament: "We who are left, how shall we look again." Wilfrid Wilson Gibson. NSI; OxBTC

Nor for the crabbed state-creed, wayward wight. James Hogg. EPCY *Fr.* To The Right Honourable Lord Byron.

Nor go when dust is gone to dust. (LL) Remain, Ah Not in Youth Alone. Walter Savage Landor. HAP; OBNC

Nor God, nor man, the image thou dost see. Hildebert, *Latin*. MLL, *tr. by* Helen Waddell

Nor had that sweet fa-laing. (LL) Since Bonny-Boots Was Dead. *Unknown.* OxBoLi; PoEL-2

Nor Hammond's love nor Shenstone's was sincere. Elegy. John, Lord Dreghorn Maclaurin. NOEC

Nor has my father nor his father / nor any grandmothers. I Have Not Signed a Treaty with the United States Government. "Chrystos." UnSA

Nor I, him. Frances Darwin Cornford. *See* All Souls' Night.

Nor *Jove* gets the command of me. Homer. *See* Priam and Achilles.

Nor know, for longing, that which I should do. (LL) Autumn Idleness. D. G. Rossetti. GBL; OAEL-2

Nor knows he makes the shadow, he pursues! (LL) Constancy to an Ideal Object. Coleridge. NAEL-2; NOBRP

Nor lingered Paris in the lofty house. Homer. OBVE, *tr. by* Tennyson *Fr.* The Iliad.

Nor long the Trench or lofty Walls oppose. The Destruction of the Grecian Fort. Homer. OBVE, *tr. by* Alexander Pope *Fr.* The Iliad.

Nor my titanic tears, the seas, be dried. (LL) The End. Wilfred Owen. CH; ChIV-1

Nor oils of balmy scent produce. On Pallas Bathing, from a Hymn of Callimachus. Callimachus, *Greek*. OBCVT, *tr. by* William Cowper

Nor Pirate, though a Prince he be. (LL) Upon Kind[e] and True Love. Aurelian Townshend. MeLP; NOSC

Nor poverty the mind appall. (LL) Holy Thursday [II.] ("Is this a holy thing to see"). William Blake. FHYEP; InPS-3; NAEL-2; NOBRP; NOEC; NOxBChV; NoP-4; OAEL-2

Nor practising virtue nor committing crime. Epitaph. Geoffrey Taylor. FaBoEE

Nor second he, that rode sublime. Thomas Gray. EPCY *Fr.* The Progress of Poesy. AWP; GTBS-P; NOEC; OBEV

Nor seek contingent patient touch to illumine clear air. Catullus. *See* Carmen 64 ("In old days / driving through soft waters").

Nor seeke him soe giv'n to flying. (LL) Song: "Love a child is ever criing [or crying]." Mary Sidney Wroth. KTR; NOSC

Nor shall you for your fields neglect your stock. Young Stock. Vita Sackville-West. OxBTC

Nor, Shenstone, thou / Shalt withou thy meed, thou son of peace! William Mason. EPCY *Fr.* The English Garden.

Nor skin nor hide nor fleece. Lethe. Hilda Doolittle. CMoP; FaBoWP; LiTM; MoAmPo; PoRA; VGW

"Nor sought in me much more than thou couldst find." (LL) Epitaph: "I never cared for Life: Life cared for me." Thomas Hardy. FaBoEE; LiLi

Nor strange it is, to us who walk in bonds. Frederick Goddard Tuckerman. APN-2 *Fr.* Sonnets.

Nor success make proud. (LL) Rock and Hawk. Robinson Jeffers. ColAP; NOBA; NoAM; OxBA; PaTW; Poetr

Nor the full moon more quick to chill. (LL) Voices from the Other World. James Merrill. TwCP; VCAP

Nor the lion's growl. (LL) The Little Girl Found. William Blake. FHYEP; NOBRP; Ro

Nor the songs. (LL) And Pergamos, / City of the Phrygians. Euripides. AWP; OBVE, *tr. by* Hilda Doolittle

Nor think, in nature's state they blindly trod. Alexander Pope. OAEL-1 *Fr.* An Essay on Man.

Nor thirteen pence a day. (LL) Grenadier. A. E. Housman. OBMV; OBWP

Nor thou nor other songs shall unremembered be. (LL) Hymn to Earth the Mother of All. *Unknown.* AWP

Nor truth nor good did they know. Gloss. Padraic Fiacc. CIP-2; PNI

Nor used this complaint, nor have thought the day to be so long. (LL) Constant Penelope sends to thee, careless Ulysses. Ovid, *Latin*. EnLoPo; GBL; NAEL-1; NoSic; OAEL-1

Nor vain with careless heart. (LL) Vain and Careless. Robert Graves. NOxBChV; NTP

Nor what God blessed once, prove accurst [or accursed]. (LL) Apparent Failure. Robert Browning. EBVVPR; NAEL-2; NOBE

Nor will ingenious women, free from pride. Lucretius. KTR, *tr. by* Lucy Hutchinson. *Fr.* De Rerum Natura (On the Nature of Things).

Nor will the search be hard or long. Epistle to the President of the Scottish Society of Antiquaries: On Being Chosen a Correspondent Member. Alexander Geddes. OxBS

Nor yet do I, your knowing lover. Portrait. John Lyle Donaghy. BIrV

Norfolk sprang [or sprung] thee, Lambeth holds thee dead. Epitaph on Thomas Clere. Henry Howard, Earl of Surrey. AAS; NoP-4; NoSic; OBWP; PBRV; SiPS

Norma. Sonia Sanchez. UnSA

Norman conquest all historians fix, The. The English Succession. *Unknown.* OxBChV

Norse Lullaby. Eugene Field. BoTP

North, The. Ai Ch'ing, *Chinese.* ChiPo, *tr. by* Cyril Birch

North. Seamus Heaney. InPS-3

North, The. Barry McKinnon. NOBC

North, The. Stephen Spender. *See* Polar Exploration.

North. Tony Towle. PmAP

North American Death Song. Anne Hunter. ECWP

North American Haiku. Gavin Ewart. APAD

North American Sequence. Theodore Roethke.

  Far Field, The. ColAP; NAAL-2; NoAM

  Journey to the Interior. DiPo

  Long Waters, The. NYBP

  Meditation at Oyster River. CMoP; MoAmPo; NYBP

  ("Shining, A.") (LL) PaTW

  Rose, The. NOBA; NYBP; TRP

North American Time. Adrienne Rich.

  "Suppose you want to write." LoL

North and South. Claude McKay. AmPP

North Corridor. Michael Collier. GM

North Country. Kenneth Slessor. CBAP

North-country maid up to London had stray'd, A. The Oak and the Ash. *Unknown.* FaBoCh

North Dakota, North Light. N. Scott Momaday. HATNAP

North-east wind did briskly blow, The. Bryan and Pereene. James Grainger. ECEV

North Express. Joyce Mansour, *French.* WPOW, *tr. by the author*

North Haven. Elizabeth Bishop. HCAP

North Labrador. Hart Crane. CMoP; FaBoMo

North of my grandfather's house. Lance Henson. HATNAP

North of my lodge, south of my lodge, spring rivers all. A Guest Arrives. Tu Fu, *Chinese.* CoBCP, *tr. by* Burton Watson

North of our science, east of the hashish dream. The Inglorious Milton. Francis Letters. NOBAu

North of Santa Monica. Carter Revard. VoR

North of the great lake of K'un-ming. Han Yü. PLT, *tr. by* A. C. Graham *Fr.* The South Mountains.

North Philadelphia, Trenton, and New York. Richmond Lattimore. NYBP

North Pole Story, A. Menella Bute Smedley. OxBChV

North Sea. Jeffery Day. NSI; PoWW

North Sea, The. Heinrich Heine, *German.*

  Epilogue: "Like the stalks of wheat in the fields." TrJP, *tr. by* Emma Lazarus

  (Epilog: "Like the ears of wheat in a wheat-field growing.") AWP, *tr. by* Louis Untermeyer

  Evening Twilight. AWP, *tr. by* John Todhunter

  Night by the Sea, A. AWP, *tr. by* Howard Mumford Jones

North Sea off Carnoustie. Anne Stevenson. OxBoS

North Ship, The. Philip Larkin. RB

North Star, The. John Morris-Jones, *Welsh.* OBWVE, *tr. by* Anthony Conran

North: the watered-down sun. The Ideal. T. R. Hummer. LTA

North to Milwaukee. Gerald Vizenor. VoR

North Wales girl was once my passion, A. Two-Faced Too. *Unknown, Welsh.* OBWVE, *tr. by* Glyn Jones

North we climb the T'ai-hang Mountains. Song on Enduring the Cold. Ts'ao Ts'ao, *Chinese.* CoBCP, *tr. by* Burton Watson

North Wind, The. Dorothy Graddon. BoTP

North. . . Wind. . . ???. . . again! (LL) The Moon's the North Wind's cooky. Vachel Lindsay. NOxBChV

North wind blows, cracking the earth, The. The New Year's Eve. Liu E, *Chinese.* ChiPo; CoBLCP, *tr. by* Jonathan Chaves

North wind doth blow, The. Mother Goose. OxNR; ReMoGo

North wind heard is heard always, A. Reverberation. Maurice Kenny. HATNAP

North Wind sighed, The. Ice. Walter De la Mare. AYFP; OTCP

North wind whirls low. Song of the White Snow: Saying Farewell to Supervisor Wu Returning to the Capital. Ts'en Shen, *Chinese.* SuSp, *tr. by* C. H. Wang

Northboun.' Lucy Ariel Williams Holloway. BlSi

Northeast wind was the wind off the lake, The. Weather. Archibald MacLeish. MoAmPo

Northern breath, that freezes floods, he binds, The. Ovid. OBVE, *tr. by* Dryden *Fr.* Metamorphoses.

Northern Cobbler, The. Tennyson. EBEV

Northern Cold, The. Li Ho, *Chinese.* PLT, *tr. by* A. C. Graham

Northern Farmer: New Style. Tennyson. EnVR; NAEL-2; OBCoV; OxAEP-2; PeVV

Northern Farmer: Old Style. Tennyson. EnVR

Northern har, A. *Unknown.* FaBoVe

Northern Ireland: Two Comments. Seamus Deane. CIP-2

Northern landscape, / Thousand miles around covered by ice. Tune: "Spring in Ch'in's Garden." Mao Tse-tung, *Chinese.* SuSp, *tr. by* Eugene Eoyang

Northern light should have been veiled like Venus, with, A. This Poem Should Have Etc. Yona Wallach, *Hebrew.* IP, *tr. by* Warren Bargad *and* Stanley F. Chyet

Northern pair, we waive the name, A. The Power of Innocence. "C. G. H." NOEC

Northern Pike. James Wright. NAAL-2

Northern Romance. Haim Guri, *Hebrew.* IP, *tr. by* Warren Bargad *and* Stanley F. Chyet

Northern Spring, A. Frank Ormsby.

  Apples, Normandy, 1944. PNI

  Soldier Bathing. PNI

  "Some of us stayed forever, under the lough." CIP-2

Northern Suburb, A. John Davidson. NOBVV; OBNC

Northern Vigil, A. Bliss Carman. OBEV

Northern Wind / sweeping down from the Sahara. Exile in Nigeria. Ezekiel Mphahlele. PBA

Northhanger Ridge. Charles Wright. HCAP

Northland in Cold, The. Li Ho, *Chinese.* CoBCP, *tr. by* Burton Watson

Northumberland Betray[e]d by Douglas [*or* Dowglas]. *Unknown.* ESPB; OxBB

Northward bound / the ice mumbled. Drumlin Prayer. Tom MacIntyre. CIP-2

Northwest Airlines. Fred Chappell. HoPM

Northwest the tall tower stands. Mei Sheng *and* Fu I. *Fr.* Nineteen Old Poems of the Han. CoBCP, *tr. by* Burton Watson

Northwestern Mathematics. Tony Esolen. BAP-94

Northwind fallen, in the newstarrèd night, The. The Hesperides. Tennyson. OAEL-2

Nortumblum callimuquash omysteliton quashte burashte. Epitaph in the Utopian Tongue. John Taylor. CBNP

Nosce Teipsum. Sir John Davies. NoSic

  Affliction. NOBE

  Dedication II: "Strongest and the noblest argument, The." SiPS

  Man.

    "I know my soul hath power to know all things." OBEV

  Soul and the Body, The. CTC; NOBE

  (In What Manner the Soule Is United to the Body.) PoEL-2

Nose. Ambrose Bierce. APN-2; OBAL *Fr.* The Devil's Dictionary.

Nose, nose, jolly red nose. Francis Beaumont *and* John Fletcher. FaBoCh; OxNR *Fr.* The Knight of the Burning Pestle.

Nose only above water. Sandra: At the Beaver Trap. Michael S. Harper. NoAM

Nose, the Grand Canyon, and the Sixties, The. Arthur Vogelsang. BAP-95

Nose went away by itself, The. Iain Crichton Smith. OBSP; RB

Nosegay. Elizabeth Jane Coatsworth. OBCA

Nosegay, A. John Reynolds. OBEV

Nosobame, The. Christian Morgenstern. CBNP

Nostalgia. Christopher Buckley. SeSe

Nostalgia. Walter De la Mare. LiTM

Nostalgia. D. H. Lawrence. PoA

Nostalgia. Louis MacNeice. OxAEP-2

Nostalgia. Bin Ramke. MT

Nostalgia. Vita Sackville-West. WPN

Nostalgia. Karl Shapiro. CMoP; CoAP; TrJP; TwCP

Nostalgia and Complaint of the Grandparents. Donald Justice. LCAP-2; NoAM

Nostalgia for Titian. Ivan Krustev, *Bulgarian.* CEEP, *tr. by* Belin Tonchev

Nostalgic song for my beloved. Adolf Wolfli, *German.* PFTM, *tr. by* Aaron H. Esman

Nostalgic Urge. Chiyong Chong, *Korean.* CKP, *tr. by* Jaihiun Kim

Noster was a ship of swank, The. E. E. Cummings. OBCoV

Nostoi. Rodolfo Di Biasio, *Italian.* NeIt, *tr. by* Stephen Sartarelli

Not. The Mona Lisa Tea Towel. Nigel Roberts. BMAP

Not a breath of air. Marjory Bates Pratt. HA

Not a Cage. Joan Retallack. FTOS

Not a cage but an organ. Elevator Man, 1949. Rita Dove. LoL; NAmP90

Not a day goes by without someone borrowing books from me. Li K'ai-hsien. CoBLCP, *tr. by* Jonathan Chaves *Fr.* Early Summer: At the Riverside, Seeing Off Li Chiu-ho as He Returns to Yeh with the Books I Lent Him.

Not a drum was heard, not a funeral note. The Burial of Sir John Moore after [*or* at] Corunna. Charles Wolfe. EBEvV; FaPoR; GTBS-P; NOBE; NOBRP; NTP; OBEV; OBWP; OxAEP-2; PWR; PoRA; TFi; UV

Not a Herod's oath that cannot change. (LL) The Mind Is an Enchanting Thing. Marianne Moore. CMoP; HeIP-4; InPK-6; MeMAP; MoAmPo; NAAL-2; NoP-4; OxBA; PoE; WPOW

Not a line of her writing have I. Thoughts of Phena. Thomas Hardy. EBVV; NOBVV; NoP-4; OxBTC

Not a Man and Yet a Man. Albery Allson Whitman.
  End of the Whole Matter, The. AAP
  Flight of Leeona. AAP
  In the House of the Aylors. AAP
  Old Sac Village, The. AAP
  Runaway, The. AAP
  Saville in Trouble. AAP

Not a picturing. Unclosing landscape. "Claude Monet sur son lit do mort." Michael White. BAP-94

Not a red rose or a satin heart. Valentine. Carol Ann Duffy. APAD

Not a roof but a field of stars. (LL) Rent. Jane Cooper. FYAP; TAP

Not a *sous* had he got,—not a guinea or note. "Thomas Ingoldsby." UV

Not a thing could I see. Frustrated. May Probyn. VWP

Not a thing on the river McCluskey did fear. The Little Brown Bulls. *Unknown.* AmFP

Not a tree but the tree. There Is Only One of Everything. Margaret Atwood. NOBC

Not a twig or a leaf on the old tree. A Withered Tree. Han Yü, *Chinese.* PLT, *tr. by* A. C. Graham

Not a Very Cheerful Song, I'm Afraid. Adrian Mitchell. OTCP

Not a word, not a word, not a word. (LL) Crucifixion. *Unknown.* BPo; TAP

Not a word, or to the knowing. Ecstatic Longing. Goethe, *German.* STV, *tr. by* John Frederick Nims

Not a word to each other; we kept the great pace. Robert Browning. Poetr *Fr.* How They Brought the Good News from Ghent to Aix. EBEvV; EBNV; FHYEP; FaBoBe; FaPoR; HoPM; NAEL-2; OBSP; PeVV; UV

Not Adlestrop. Dannie Abse. NoAM

Not all of them were human. The Village Tudda. Kenneth Patchen. VGW

Not all of us were warm, not all of us. Spring. James Still. MT

Not all pale Hecate's direful charms. Lines Occasioned by the Burning of Some Letters. Sarah Dixon. ECWP; NOEC

Not all these legends, I suppose. Popular Mythologies. Vernon Scannell. OBCoV

Not all thy flushing suns are set. An Ode to Master Endymion Porter, upon His Brother's Death. Robert Herrick. CaPo

Not Allowed to Make a Movie in This Country. David Avidan. *Fr.* Traveling in the City. IP, *tr. by* Warren Bargad *and* Stanley F. Chyet

Not Alone for Mighty Empire. William Pierson Merrill. AH

Not always give a melting kiss. Johannes Secundus. OBVE, *tr. by* Thomas Stanley *Fr.* Basia.

Not always as the whirlwind's rush. The Call of the Christian. John Greenleaf Whittier. NOCV

Not an editorial-writer, bereaved with bartlett. Portrait of the Poet as Landscape. Abraham Moses Klein. NOBC; NoAM

Not and tries less once tries tries AH, GOD—. (LL) Falling. James Dickey. LCAP-2; MT; NYBP; NoAM

Not any higher stands the Grave. Emily Dickinson. SAmP

Not as all other women are. My Love. James Russell Lowell. FaBoBe

Not as Black Douglas, bannered, trumpeted. Two Wise Generals. Ted Hughes. MoBS

Not as height rises into lightness. Breadth. Circle. Desert. Monarch. Month. Wisdom. John Hollander. PoA

Not, as it used to be, round. The Poison. Hans Magnus Enzensberger, *German.* VCWP, *tr. by* Hans Magnus Enzensberger and Michael Hamburger

Not as she is, but as she fills his dream. (LL) In An Artist's Studio. Christina Rossetti. NAEL-2; NALW; NoP-4; PEW; Poetr; VWP

Not as the thirsty soyle desires soft showres. Francis Quarles. ESCV *Fr.* Emblems.

Not as we are but as we must appear. Geoffrey Hill. NoAM *Fr.* Funeral Music.

Not as when some great Captain falls. Abraham Lincoln. Richard Henry Stoddard. FaBoBe

Not as Wont. Joseph Skipsey. NOBVV

Not at [the] first sight, nor with a dribbed shot. Sonnet 2. Sir Philip Sidney. NAEL-1; OAEL-1 *Fr.* Astrophil and Stella. AAS; SiPS

Not at Home. Robert Graves. CABP

Not at Home to Callers. Emily Dickinson. NOxBChV

Not at midnight, not at morning, O sweet city. Caryatid. Léonie Adams. LiTM

Not at the full moon will she pick those flowers. Her Garden. Elizabeth Jennings. GaP

Not because of his eyes. The Turtle. William Carlos Williams. RaBo; SAmP

Not because of victories. Te Deum. Charles Reznikoff. ChIV-1; TrJP

Not because of you, not because of me, just that. Natalya Gorbanevskaya, *Russian.* BoWoP, *tr. by* Daniel Weissbort

Not because you suck / off a sugar-cane. Distaste. Ammianus, *Greek.* GrAn, *tr. by* Peter Jay

Not being Breedlove, whose immortal skid. To Dorothy on Her Exclusion from the *Guinness Book of World Records.* X. J. Kennedy. Poetsp

Not Being Oedipus. John Heath-Stubbs. OxBC

Not but they die, the teasers and the dreams. The Teasers. William Empson. OxBTC

Not by Amphialus. (LL) Sonnet: "O[h]! for some honest lover's ghost." Sir John Suckling. BXAP; BeJo; BoLoP; CaPo; MeLP; NOBE; OBEV; PoEL-3; SeCP

Not by Bread Alone. *Unknown, Greek.* PoLF, *tr. by* James Terry White

Not by hammering the furious word. Harlem Riot, 1943. Pauli Murray. PoBA

Not by lost killers stranded. The Biggest Killing. Edward Dorn. VGW

Not by the city bells that chime the hours. A Summer Day. Florence Harrison. BoTP

Not by the railing tongues of angry men. Slavery. Jones Very. NCAP

Not by wayout hairdos, bulbous Afro blowouts and certainly. Only in This Way. Margaret Goss Burroughs. BlSi

Not Caesar's deeds, nor all his honours won. To Clement Edmonds, on His *Caesar's Commentaries* Observed, and Translated. Ben Jonson. NOSC

Not caring to observe the Wind. Of Loving at First Sight. Edmund Waller. NOSC; SeCP

Not, Celia, that I juster am. To Celia. Sir Charles Sedley. AWP; GTBS-P; NOBE; OBEV

Not comin' back tonight, matey. Matey. Patrick MacGill. NSI; PoWW

Not daylight and not the dark. The Suicide. Edith Jay Scovell. WPN

Not Dead, but Sleeping. Clara Ann Thompson. CBWP-2

Not die of famine, amid dreams of gold. (LL) The Fishermen. Theocritus. AWP; OBVE, *tr. by* Charles Stuart Calverley

Not direction—"every step and arrival." (LL) Overland to the Islands. Denise Levertov. PmAP; UnPo

Not distant far from thence a murmuring sound. Milton. OBCVT *Fr.* Paradise Lost.

Not easy to state the change you made. Love Letter. Sylvia Plath. LW; NOBA

Not enough. Field Trip. Kevin Young. GT

Not even. Albert Speer. W. D. Snodgrass. NoAM

Not even an hour. (LL) Sent from the Capital to Her Elder Daughter. Lady Otomo no Sakanoé, *Japanese.* BoWoP; MDDM; WPOW, *tr. by* Geoffrey Bownas *and* Anthony Thwaite

Not even death could make these men alike. Cemetery in Punta Arenas. Enrique Lihn, *Spanish.* VCWP, *tr. by* David Unger

Not even dried-up leaves. Thesis, Antithesis and Nostalgia. Alan Dugan. AFr

Not even for a moment. He knew, for one thing, what he was. Leda. Mona Van Duyn. NMM-2

Not even Goldie could have told. One Summer. C. D. Wright. CMAP

Not even I—would undo me so! (LL) The Going. Thomas Hardy. CBLP; EBEV; LoP; NOBE; OxAEP-2; SCGP; UnPo

Not even in a dream. The Victims of the Little Box. Vasco Popa, *Serbo-Croatian.* CEEP; HSix, *tr. by* Charles Simic

Not even in death can I. Archias of Byzantium, *Greek.* GrAn, *tr. by* Clive Sansom

Not even in dreams / Can I meet him anymore. Lady Ise, *Japanese.* WPOW, *tr. by* Donald Keene

Not Even Mythology. Yannis Ritsos, *Greek.* AF, *tr. by* Edmund Keeley

Not even sleep (though I'm ashamed of that too). Twice Removed. Ralph Angel. PUP-19

Not even the cops who can do anything could do this. Laundry. Bruce Smith. Son

Not Every Day Fit for Verse. Robert Herrick. BeJo; PoRA

Not every man has gentians in his house. Bavarian Gentians. D. H. Lawrence. CABP; CMoP; FaBoCh; FaBoMo; GTBS-P; HAP; ImPo; InPK-6; InPS-3; MoP; NAEL-2; NOBE; NoAM; NoP-4; OAEL-2; PoE; PoPoPo; Poetr; TFi; TRP; TTTS

Not every man knows what he shall sing at the end. The End. Mark Strand. TRP

Not far beyond the town wild flowers grow. Sanctuary. Clifford Dyment. PoA

Not far from these *Phœnician Dido* stood. Dido in the Elysian Fields. Virgil, *Latin*. OBCVT, *tr. by* John Dryden *Fr.* The Aeneid.

Not Flesh of Brass. Bible, *O.T.* TrJP *Fr.* Job. NAWM-1

Not for all of beauty. Commentary Applied to Spiritual Things. Saint John of the Cross, *Spanish*. TOF, *tr. by* K. Kavanaugh *and* O. Rodrigues

Not for me! (LL) Bat. D. H. Lawrence. APo; GTBS-P; HAP; OAEL-1; OAEL-2

Not for that city of the level sun. Charlotte Mew. ChIV-2; MoBrPo; VWP

Not for the glory on their heads. On Wordsworth's Cottage, near Grasmere Lake. Letitia Elizabeth Landon. Ro *Fr.* The Zenana, and Minor Poems of L.E.L.

Not for the promise of the laboured field. Ode to the Poppy. Henrietta O'Neill. ECWP; WPE

Not for these lovely blooms that prank your chambers did I come. Indeed. Rendezvous. Edna St. Vincent Millay. NALW

Not for us alone did the god, Nicias. Hylas. Theocritus, *Greek*. HePo, *tr. by* Barbara Hughes Fowler *Fr.* Idylls.

Not Fortune's worshipper, nor Fashion's fool. Apologia pro Vita Sua. Alexander Pope. NOBE *Fr.* Epistle to Dr. Arbuthnot. FHYEP; InPS-3; NoP-4; OAEL-1; OxAEP-1; PoE; PoEL-3; TFi

Not free from faults, nor yet too vain to mend. (LL) An Essay on Criticism. Alexander Pope. NAEL-1; PoEL-3; TFi

Not from cupped hands. It isn't the same at all. (LL) Aubade: "It's all the same to morning what it dawns on." Nuala Ni Dhomhnaill, *Irish*. BiHa; PBCIP, *tr. by* Michael Longley

Not from old age our death will come. Semyon Petrovich Gudzenko, *Russian*. TCRP, *tr. by* Vera Rich

Not from our dreams, not from our daft cadres. Robert Johnstone. PNI *Fr.* New Incidents in the Life of Shelley.

Not from successful love alone. Halcyon Days. Walt Whitman. OxBA

Not from that / could you get it. The City. Robert Creeley. LCAP-2

Not from the stars do I my judgement pluck. Sonnet 14. Shakespeare Son *Fr.* Sonnets.

Not from the unmapped valleys of darkness, nor. Hall of Ocean Life. John Hollander. PoA

Not from Titania's Court do I. Hob Gobbling's Song. James Russell Lowell. OBCA

Not furred nor wet, the pointing words yet make. Beaver Pond. Anne Marriott. NOBC

Not glad, like those that have new hopes, or suits. To the Same [Robert, Earl of Salisbury] [Upon the Accension of the Treasurership to Him]. Ben Jonson. NOSC

Not greatly moved with awe am I. The Two Deserts. Coventry Patmore. PFE

Not guns, not thunder, but a flutter of clouded drums. Fireworks. Babette Deutsch. NYBP; Poetr

Not happy with what he has. What Her Girl Friend Said to Her. Pālaipāṭiya Peruṅkaṭuṅkō, *Tamil*. PLW, *tr. by* A. K. Ramanujan

Not he who holds the sceptre high atop the eagle's throne. Why the Resurrection Was Revealed to Women. Catharina Regina von Greiffenberg, *German*. PBWP, *tr. by* Michael Hamburger

Not heat flames up and consumes. Walt Whitman. APN-1

Not heaving from my ribb'd breast only. Walt Whitman. APN-1

Not hell but a street, not. 209 Canal. Richard Howard. TAP

Not Here. Edmund Wilson. PoA

Not Hers who brings it nightly to my Ear. (LL) Higher Argument. Milton. EPCY; NOSC; TOF

Not his clothes, but their chimerical creases. In This His Suit. Mark Cox. NAmP90

Not honey, / not the plunder of the bee. Fragment 113. Hilda Doolittle. NAAL-2

Not—"How did he die?" But—"How did he live?" The Measure of a Man. *Unknown.* PoLF

Not I. Robert Louis Stevenson. NOBL

Not I, not I, but the wind that blows through me! The Song of a Man Who Has Come Through. D. H. Lawrence. APAD; CMoP; FaBoMo; GTBS-P; InPS-3; LiTM; OxBTC; PeFWW; PoF; RaBo; TRP

Not, I/ said pushing. Uncertain Steps. Richard Caddel. NBrP

Not Ideas about the Thing but the Thing Itself. Wallace Stevens. HAP; HCAP; LCAP-2; MeMAP; SAmP; TAP

Not idly hast thou builded on a rock. To Peter, Bishop of Poitiers, Who Withstood William of Aquitaine and Died in Exile. Hildebert, *Latin*. MLL, *tr. by* Helen Waddell

Not if men's tongues and angels' all in one. Shakespeare. Swinburne. EPCY

Not, I'll not, carrion comfort, Despair, not feast on thee. Carrion Comfort. Gerard Manley Hopkins. CABP; CMoP; EnVR; GSo; HeIP-4; NAEL-2; NoAM; NoP-4; OAEL-2; OBNC; PoE; PoEL-5; Son; TFi; TOF

Not in a silver casket cool with pearls. Edna St. Vincent Millay. CMoP; VGW

Not in anger does the sea. Looking at the Sea. Pamela Kircher. BAP-93

Not in envy, ire, or grief. A Farewell to the Muse. Maria Jane Jewsbury. VWP

Not in my saddle, but above it. Indian Summer: Montana, 1956. W. M. Ransom. CDW

Not in our time, O Lord. Hilda Doolittle. NOBA *Fr.* Tribute to the Angels.

Not in rich furniture, or fine array. The H[oly] Communion. George Herbert. ChIV-1; ESCV

Not in sleep I saw it, but in daylight. Kindly Vision. Otto Julius Bierbaum, *German*. AWP, *tr. by* Jethro Bithell

Not in the city, Philoterus. Nicaenetus, *Greek*. GrAn, *tr. by* Peter Whigham

Not in the crises of events. The Spirit's Epochs. Coventry Patmore. EBEV; GBL; OxBSP *Fr.* The Angel in the House.

Not in the days of Adam and Eve, but when Adam. In the Days of Prismatic Color. Marianne Moore. MeMAP

Not in the Guide-Books. Elizabeth Jennings. LiTM

Not in the poet is the poem or. George Barker. OxAEP-2; OxBSP

Not in the sky. The Lost Pleiad. William Gilmore Simms. APN-1

Not in the street and not in the square. Sequel to 'A Reminiscence,' The. Amy Levy. VWP

Not in the world of light alone. The Living Temple. Oliver Wendell Holmes. APN-1 *Fr.* The Autocrat of the Breakfast Table.

Not in those climes where I have late been straying. Dedication: To Ianthe. Byron. OBNC *Fr.* Childe Harold's Pilgrimage.

Not in thy body is thy life at all. Life-in-Love. D. G. Rossetti. HAP *Fr.* The House of Life.

Not incorrectly. Precautions. Eugenio Montale, *Italian*. PiM, *tr. by* Jonathan Galassi

Not just folklore, or. Fast Ball. Jonathan Williams. NeAP

Not just the temples, lifting. Waiting for the Fire. Philip Appleman. CDa

Not Just Yet. Carter Revard. VoR

Not Knowing. Gary Soto. NoP-4

Not knowing in what season this again. Parting: 1940. John Frederick Nims. PoA

Not knowing where he was or how he got there. A Bewilderment at the Entrance of the Fat Boy into Eden. Daryl Hine. NOBC

Not less because in purple I descended. Tea at the Palaz of Hoon. Wallace Stevens. FaBoMo; PoA

Not less nor more, but even that word alone. (LL) The One Hope. D. G. Rossetti. GSo; NAEL-2; OAEL-2

Not less nor more than five and forty years ago. In Heytesbury Wood. Siegfried Sassoon. OBGa

Not like the brazen giant of Greek fame. The New Colossus. Emma Lazarus. APAD; APN-2; AiP; CA; FaBoA; GS; GSo; NoP-4; PAR; PoLF; SAGP; Son; WPE

Not like the white filmstars, all rib. Indian Movie, New Jersey. Chitra Divakaruni. UnSA

Not like we used to with pipes. Bubbles. George Garrett. MT

Not long ago a man was smoking on a balcony. Birth of the Cool. Charles David Wright. MT

Not long ago I hied me apace. Charles D'Orleans. EnVB

Not long ago I met a clerk. *Unknown, Middle English*. OxBoV, *tr. by* Brian Stone

Not long this transport held its place. The Third Voice. "Lewis Carroll." *Fr.* The Three Voices. BXAP

Not lorst, but gorn before!' (LL) Dahn the Plug'ole. *Unknown*. RB, *tr. by* Robert Bly; NOxBChV

Not Love Perhaps. Arthur Seymour John Tessimond. APAD

Not-loving. Sylvia Kantaris. LW

Not magnitude, not lavishness. Greek Architecture. Melville. NoP-4

Not Marble nor the Gilded Monuments. Archibald MacLeish. BoLoP; CMoP; IIoPM; McMAP; PoRA; TwCP

Not marble, nor the gilded monuments. Sonnet 55. Shakespeare. AEP; AWP; CABP; CTC; EPCY; GSo; HeIP-4; ImPo; LoP; NAEL-1; NIP-4; NOBE; NoP-4; NoSic; OAEL-1; OxAEP-1; PoE; PoEL-2; PoRA; Poetr; SAGP; SCGP; Son *Fr.* Sonnets.

Not marching in the fields of Trasimene. Doctor Faustus. Marlowe. NAEL-1; OAEL-1

Not Martha nor Diana—only a woman. On Vermeer's "Young Woman with a Water Jug" (1658) in the Metropolitan Museum. Helen Pinkerton. FFC

Not met and marred with the year's whole turn of grief. James Agee. *Fr.* Lyrics. MoAmPo

Not Mine. Julia Caroline Ripley Dorr. PWR

Not mine. I-Thou, cat, I-Thou. (LL) The Cat as Cat. Denise Levertov. NOBA; PC

Not mine own fears nor the prophetic soul. Sonnet 107. Shakespeare. AWP; CTC; EBEV; HAP; ImPo; NAEL-1; NoSic; OAEL-1; OxAEP-1; SCGP *Fr.* Sonnets.

Not more of light I ask, O God. Understanding. *Unknown.* PoToHe

Not much longer now. Lament in Spring. "Jan Struther." WPN

Not much more than being. Louis Zukofsky. PoE *Fr.* 29 Poems.

Not Much Talking. *Unknown.* PWR

Not my best side, I'm afraid. U. A. Fanthorpe. FaBoWP

Not my hands but green across you now. The Lady in Kicking Horse Reservoir. Richard Hugo. CoAP; LCAP-2; NAAL-2; NoAM; NoP-4; VCAP

Not of All My Eyes See. Gerard Manley Hopkins. OxBSP

Not, of course, the monster hunched downtown. Dome Poem. Dave Jeddie Smith. PoA

Not of father nor of mother. The Song of Blodeuwedd. Robert Graves. NoP-4

Not of Gennesareth, but Thames! (LL) In No Strange Land. Francis Thompson. FaPoR; GTBS-P; HAP; MoBrPo; NOBE; NOCV; OBEV; TrCP

Not of itself but thee! (LL) To Celia. Ben Jonson. APAD; AWP; BeJo; BoLoP; CBLP; ClHu; EBEvV; EnLoPo; FaBoBe; GBL; GLoP; GTBS-P; ImPo; InPK-6; NAEL-1; NOBE; NOSC; NoP-4; OAEL-1; OBEV; OBVE; OxAEP-1; PoE; PoEL-2; PoLF; SAGP; SCGP; SeCP; SoSe-8; TFi; UV

Not of Itself but Thee. *Unknown, Greek.* AWP, *tr. by* Richard Garnett; GrAN, *tr. by* Dudley Fitts

Not of ourselves are we free. Heritage. Mary Gilmore. CBAP

Not of the princes and prelates with periwigged charioteers. A Consecration. John Masefield. MoBrPo

Not often *con brio,* but *andante, andante.* Stanley Matthews. Alan Ross. OxBTC

Not on our golden fortunes builded high. The Forgotten Man. Edwin Markham. PoLF

Not one of them has seen! John Godfrey Saxe. *See* The Blind Men and the Elephant.

Not one poem about an animal, she said. Florida. Dannie Abse. OxBC

Not one whisper. Momcilo Nastasijevic. HSix, *sect.* 1, *tr. by* Charles Simic *Fr.* Deaf Things.

Not Only around Our Infancy. James Russell Lowell. ImPo *Fr.* The Vision of Sir Launfal.

Not only doesn't the Ohio. Elegy. Gregory Orr. WeT

Not only how far away, but the way that you say it. Judging Distances. Henry Reed. BoLoP; GTBS-P; NIP-4; NOBE; NoP-4; PoWW; Poetr *Fr.* Lessons of the War. HeIP-4; OBWP

Not only that / But peace regenerates man. Peace. Bacchylides. GrIP, *tr. by* Robert Fagles *Fr.* Paean.

Not only when you go to bed / And sleep. (LL) Knoxville, Tennessee. Nikki Giovanni. BPo; BlSi; MBE; PoBA

Not Only Where God's Free Winds Blow. Shepherd Knapp. AH

Not only with my sense of shame. Tennyson. FaBoEE

Not oriental Indus' crystal streams. Lady Cicely Wemyss. James I, King of England. NOSC

Not ours the fighter's glow. Mine-Sweeping Trawlers. E. Hilton Young. NSI

Not over-kind nor over-quick in study. Edna St. Vincent Millay. *Fr.* Sonnets from an Ungrafted Tree. NALW

Not palaces, an era's crown. Stephen Spender. CMoP; FaBoMo; LiTM; MoBrPo; NoAM

Not pale, as one in sleep or holier death. On A Picture. John Gray. ADE

Not pall, but shadows. My Words. William Hathaway. EOEF

Not Pallas, not ev'n Spleen it self could blame. Ovid. OBVE, *tr. by* John Gay. *Fr.* Metamorphoses.

Not picnics or pageants or the improbable. Terror. Robert Penn Warren. PoA

Not power nor the casual [*or* storied] hand of God. Allen Tate. PoA *Fr.* Sonnets of the Blood.

Not public like mountains' but private like companions.' (LL) On a Painting by Patient B of the Independence State Hospital for the Insane. Donald Justice. CoAP; CoAmPo; NoAM; WeT

Not realizing. Six Feet Under. Janet Campbell Hale. VoR

Not really hate, or some demento girl-boy thing. Burning the Dolls. Richard Peabody. IFJA

Not "Revelation" 'tis, that waits. Emily Dickinson. EnlH

Not Rice, Not Water. Mocikiranar, *Tamil.* PLW, *tr. by* A. K. Ramanujan

Not rose of death. Rose in the Afternoon. Jenny Joseph. BrRo

Not Saying Much. Linda Gregg. AiP

Not seeing. Anita Virgil. HA

Not Seeing Is Believing. Paul Petrie. TAP

Not Sense. Gail Tremblay. WeW-3

Not serious about drugs. Angel. John Forbes. NOBAu

Not she with traitorous kiss her Saviour stung. Woman. Eaton Stannard Barrett. TIRV

Not, Silence, for thine idleness I raise. To Silence. Alice Thompson Meynell. VWP

Not Singing. Kate Daniels. PBCAP

Not slowly wrought, nor treasured for their form. Snowflakes. Howard Nemerov. HCAP

Not-so-good Earth, The. Bruce Dawe. CBAP

Not so with me as with the little page. Ausiàs March, *Catalan.* STV, *tr. by* John Frederick Nims

Not sobered up from my muddy Kao-yang drunk. Yang Shih-ch'i. CoBLCP, *tr. by* Jonathan Chaves *Fr.* Hsi-li Echoed My Poems, and I Respond to Him, Using the Same Rhymes—Also Sent to Tsung-lien.

Not solely that the Future she destroys. George Meredith. GBL *Fr.* Modern Love.

Not Somewhere Else, But Here. Adrienne Rich. BAP-93
  Amends.
  Miracle Ice Cream.
  To the Days. LoL
  What Kind of Times Are These. LoL

Not soon shall I forget—a sheet. Farewell. Katharine Tynan. CH

Not speaking. Alexis Rotella. HA

Not strangeness, but strange likeness. Obstinate. Geoffrey Hill. HAP; NoAM *Fr.* Mercian Hymns.

Not Such Your Burden. Agathias, *Greek.* AWP, *tr. by* William M. Hardinge

Not that by this disdain. The Repulse. Thomas Stanley. BeJo; MeLP

Not That Far. May Miller. BlSi

Not that he promised not to windowshop. One Man's Wife. Philip Booth. VGW

Not that her blooms are marked with beauty's hue. To Mr. Gray. Thomas Warton, the Younger. EPCY; Son

Not that I cared about the other women. Colder. Erica Jong. LW

Not that I wish to take the liberty. Non Que Je Veuille Ôter la Liberté. Pernette De Guillet, *French.* WPOW, *tr. by* Raymond Oliver

Not that in colour it was like thy hair. The Bracelet. Donne. NoSic

Not that it always transpired. Limerick. Cyril Ray. PeLi

Not that the earth is changing, O my God! On Refusal of Aid between Nations. D. G. Rossetti. EBEV; OxAEP-2; SCGP

Not that the Pines were darker there. The Long Voyage. Malcolm Cowley. SoSe-8

Not that the tree in my garden does not bloom. Harp Song. Lu Yu, *Chinese.* CoBCP, *tr. by* Burton Watson

Not that they die but that they die like sheep. (LL) The Leaden-eyed. Vachel Lindsay. CMoP; FaBoEE; ImPo; OxBSP; PBMP; PoE; RB

Not that we are weary. In the Trenches. Richard Aldington. PeFWW

Not the attendance of stones. Black Maps. Mark Strand. PoA

Not the beautiful youth with features of bloom & brightness. Beauty. Walt Whitman. WeW-3

Not the dead today shall praise you, God! Of Those Who Go, Not to Return. Benyamin Galai, *Hebrew.* MHP, *tr. by* Ruth Finer Mintz

Not the dumb earth, wherein they set their graves. (LL) Cassandra. Louise Bogan. HAP; MoAmPo; NALW; PBWP; VGW

Not the End of the World. Michael Ryan. NAmP90

Not the living but the dead. Requiem. Zhao Zhenkai, *Chinese.* ChiPo, *tr. by* McDougall, Bonnie S. and Chen Maiping

Not the numbers but the sound. Death March. Charles Fishman. CDa

Not the poor singer of an empty day. (LL) An Apology. William Morris. AWP; EBVV; EnVR; NAEL-2; NoP-4; OAEL-2; OBNC

Not the sea-wave so bellows abroad when it bursts upon shingle. Clash in Arms of the Achaians and Trojans. Homer, *Greek.* OBCVT, *tr. by* George Meredith *Fr.* The Iliad.

Not the sharp torture of the critic's pen. To an Author who Loved Truth More than Fame. Bessie Rayner Parkes. VWP

Not the shouted poetry. Monkey's Pride. John Forbes. BMAP

Not the songs that nobly tell. Stanzas on the Psalms. Thomas Warton, the Elder. ChIV-1

Not the symbol but the scene this pavement leads. George Oppen. APSN *Fr.* Route.

Not the wild olive, not the fatal stones. Euphorion, *Greek.* GrAN, *tr. by* Alistair Elliot

Not the womb yields the babe in its time more surely than I shall be / yielded from you in my time. Walt Whitman. *See* The Sleepers.

Not them, O no, but you in them I love. (LL) Sonnet 91: "Stella, while now by honour's cruel might." Sir Philip Sidney. NAEL-1; PoE

Not There. Tess Gallagher. NIP-4

Not these cut heads posed in a breathless room. Flower Poem. Alec Derwent Hope. BMAP

Not they who died. The Clan MacLean. Sorley MacLean. FaBoTC

Not they who soar, but they who plod. Paul Laurence Dunbar. NAAAL

Not Thinking of America. Judith Kroll. AmPA

Not Thinking of Himself. Jack Myers. NAmP90

Not this. / What then? Ron Silliman. PmAP *Fr.* Tjanting.
    ("Dig in. Wicker throne. Scratch that. Keep moving. Dressd to kill. Burgundy jumpsuit.") (LL) FTOS
    ("Not this.") FTOS

Not this with Cataracts and Creeks. (LL) The Waterfall [*or* Water-Fall]. Henry Vaughan. ESCV; FMP; FSCP; GeHe; MeLP; NAEL-1; NOBE; NOCV; NOSC; NoP-4; OBWVE; OxAEP-1; PBRV; PoEL-2

Not thither, Caesar, yet. Cornelia's Defiance. Katherine Philips. NOSC *Fr.* Corneille's Pompey.

Not those patient men who knocked and were unheeded. 1918-1941. Robert David Fitzgerald. CBAP

Not Thou but I. Philip Bourke Marston. BLPA

Not three years since—and now he asks my name! The Model. May Probyn. VWP

Not to Be Born. David Sutton. OxBM

Not to be born, or being born, to die? (LL) Life. Francis Bacon. GTBS-P; NoSic; OxAEP-1; PFE

Not to be bound with ore-nice *Pedantry.* (LL) The Claspe. Margaret Lucas Cavendish, Duchess of Newcastle. BWW; PBRV

Not to believe the phoebes wept. (LL) The Need of Being Versed in Country Things. Robert Frost. NOBA; NoAM; OxBA; SAmP; TRP; UnPo

Not to Choose. Alan Dugan. AFr

Not to do but work. The Sum of Life. Ben King. CTC

Not to Forget Miss Dickinson. Marshall Schacht. LiTM

Not to Keep. Robert Frost. CMoP; OxBA; Poetr

Not to know vice at all, and keep[e] true state. Epode. Ben Jonson. BeJo; SeCP

Not to lose the feel of the mountains. The Double-headed Snake. John Newlove. MoCV

Not To Love. Robert Herrick. CaPo

Not to meddle with my toys. (LL) Looking Forward. Robert Louis Stevenson. ACTP; NBLV; OxBChV

Not to reduce the thing to nothing. George Oppen. APSN *Fr.* Route.

Not to say what everyone else was saying. Different. Clere Parsons. APAD; FaBoTw

Not to sigh and to be tender. Aphra Behn. BoWoP

Not to the butcher did he pass. The Old Ox. George Rostrevor Hamilton, *after the Greek of* Addaios of Makedon. FaBoEE

Not to the mother of solitude will I give myself. A Busy Man Speaks. Robert Bly. CoAmPo

Not to Us, Not unto Us, Lord. *Unknown.* AH

Not too far north from where I write set dawn. Hint for the Incomplete Angler. Kendrick Smithyman. PeNZ

(Not too far past) may to their wits be brought. (LL) As other men, so I myself do muse. Michael Drayton. NOSC; NoSic; Son

Not Translation, Not Poetry. Daryl Ngee Chinn. LTA

Not turn out like ha rum-sucker chamar dadee. (LL) Coolie Mother. David Dabydeen. HCP; NBrP

Not twice a twelvemonth [*or* twelve-month] you appear in Print. Epilogue to the Satires, in Two Dialogues. Alexander Pope. OAEL-1

Not Ulysses, no, nor any other man. Sonnet 1. Louise Labé, *Italian.* BoWoP, *tr. by* Willis Barnstone

Not Understood. Thomas Bracken. BLPA

Not unlike a fish. Tanka. Yosano Tekkan, *Japanese.* MJT, *tr. by* Makoto Ueda

Not unto us, O Lord. Non Nobis. Henry Cust. LBC; OBEV

Not unto us, O Lord, not unto us. Bible, *O.T. See* Psalm 115.

Not upon earth, as you suppose. "Tu Non Se' in Terra, Si Come Tu Credi." Kathleen Jessie Raine. WPE

Not us, I say, not us. Psalm 115. Bible, *O.T.* NOCV *Fr.* Psalms.

Not very long ago. The Orange Poem. George MacBeth. OBCoV

Not waking, in my dreams, my dreams. Infidelity. Olga Fiodorovna Berggolts, *Russian.* BoWoP; IMW, *tr. by* Daniel Weissbort

Not Wavell but Browning. Gavin Ewart. UV

Not Waving But Drowning. Stevie Smith. APAD; CABP; FaBoWP; GTBS-P; HAP; HeIP-4; MoP; NAEL-2; NALW; NOBE; NoAM; NOBV; OAEL-2; OxAEP-2; OxBTC; PoE; PoPoPo; Poetr; TFi; UV; WeW-3

Not weaned yet, without comprehension loving. Love's Immaturity. Edith Jay Scovell. GBL

Not wept for and not buried *in this tomb.* Philip at Kynoskephalai. Alcaeus, *Greek.* GrAn, *tr. by* Alistair Elliot

Not what you seem, but always what you see. (LL) In the great world—which, being interpreted. Byron. OxBoLi; PeLV

Not when leaves are brown and sere. When I Would Die. Josephine D. Henderson Heard. CBWP-4

Not when you glittered, royally attended. For the Ghost of Elinor Wylie. Winifred Holtby. WPN

NOT, where the stairway turns in the dark. Jennie McGrew. Edgar Lee Masters. RACG

Not while, but long after he had told me. Each Bird Walking. Tess Gallagher. CrSp; FaBoWP; FiLi; NAmP90

Not wholly in the busy world, nor quite. Suburban Garden. Tennyson. GaP

Not wide but a wing. The Table. Ray DiPalma. FTOS

Not willing to exert the mind enough even to sense the quality of the. Late at Night. Vern Rutsala. WeT

Not winds to voyagers at sea. The Resurrection. Abraham Cowley. ChIV-2

Not with a bang but a whimper. (LL) The Hollow Men. T. S. Eliot. ImPo; InPS-3; LiTM; MoAmPo; NAAL-2; OAEL-2; OBMV; PBMP

Not with impunity the youth enters, light in hand. The Cave of Words. Vladimir Holan, *German.* CEEP, *tr. by* Bronislava Volek *and* Andrew Durkin

Not with libations, but with shouts and laughter. Edna St. Vincent Millay. MeMAP

Not with more glories, in th'ethereal plain. The Voyage on the Thames. Alexander Pope. EBEV; EBNV; ECEV; NOBE; NOEC; OxAEP-1 *Fr.* The Rape of the Lock[, an Heroi-Comical Poem]. FHYEP; HAP; ImPo; OAEL-1; OBNV; PeLV; PoEL-3

Not with snow only, east of Buchenwald. (LL) A Letter from Berlin. Jon Stallworthy. MoP; OBWP; OxBC

Not without hope we suffer and we mourn. (LL) Elegiac Stanzas Suggested by a Picture of Peele Castle, in a Storm [Painted by Sir George Beaumont]. Wordsworth. GS; GTBS-P; NAEL-2; NOBRP; NoP-4; OAEL-2; OBNC; PoE; Ro

Not wooing, no longer shall wooing, voice that has outgrown it. Rilke. EnlH, *tr. by* Stephen Mitchell *Fr.* Duino Elegies.

Not Wordsworth's genius, Pestalozzi's love. Sonnet 14. Amos Bronson Alcott. APN-1

Not Working. Henry Taylor. Poetr

Not working, not breathing. Autumn. Bella Akhatovna Akhmadulina, *Russian.* BoWoP, *tr. by* Barbara Einzig

Not writ in water[,] nor in mist. For John Keats, Apostle of Beauty. Countee Cullen. *Fr.* Four Epitaphs. PoBA

Not wrongly moved by this dismaying scene. Sonnet. William Empson. LiTM

Not Yet. William Cullen Bryant. NCAP

Not yet. James Wright. *See* Small Frogs Killed on the Highway.

Not yet dead, not yet alone. Osip Emilevich Mandelstam, *Russian.* OBVE, *tr. by* James Greene

Not yet in sight. 'Twere well to step aside. At the Polo-Ground. Sir Samuel Ferguson. NOIV

Not yet, not yet. The Tree. Joel Sloman. VGW

"Not yet. Not yet," between the lines. Boy Reading. John Holmes. ImGa

"Not yet, not yet; steady, steady!" Bunker Hill. George Henry Calvert. FaBoBe

Not yet will those measureless fields be green again. The Cenotaph. Charlotte Mew. OxAEP-2; WPE

Not you, lean quarterlies and swarthy periodicals. To the Film Industry in Crisis. Frank O'Hara. CAPP-1; NOBA; OBAL

Not young and not renewable, but man. (LL) Mirror in February. Thomas Kinsella. CIP-2; GTBS-P; NoAM

Not your winged lust but his must now change suit. William Empson. UV *Fr.* The Death of the King's Canary.

Nota: man is the intelligence of his soil. The Comedian as the Letter C. Wallace Stevens. OxBA

Notable Dinner, A. Lizelia Augusta Jenkins Moorer. CBWP-3

Notation in Gold. Ljubomir Simovic, *Serbo-Croatian.* HSix, *tr. by* Charles Simic

Note, The. Melvin B. Tolson. GT

Note. Dimitris Tsaloumas. BMAP

Note. Meir Wieseltier, *Hebrew.* IP, *tr. by* Warren Bargad *and* Stanley F. Chyet

Note 25. Hyon-jong Chong, *Korean.* CKP, *tr. by* Jaihiun Kim

Note Delivered by a Female Impersonator. Heather McHugh. AmPA; RACG

Note I Left for Gerald Stern in an Office I Borrowed, and He Would Next, at a Summer Writers' Conference. William Matthews. PUP-18

Note is sad, yet musick for a king, The. (LL) Sion. George Herbert. ChIV-1; ESCV

Note Left in Jimmy Leonard's Shack, A. James Wright. HCAP; NoP-4

Note nothing of why or how, enquire. Instructions From England 1936. Valentine Ackland. WPN

Note of Thanks, A. Wyatt Prunty. RA

Note old chestnut tie in foreground. The Tie. William Heyen. GM

Note on a Shop in the Muceque. Geraldo Bessa Victor, *Portuguese*. PeSAV, *tr. by* Donald Burness

Note on Local Flora. William Empson. EBEV; FaBoMo; OxAEP-2

Note on My Son's Face, A. Toi Derricotte. FiLi; ISC

Note on Propertius I.5. Fleur Adcock. BoLoP; EP; PeNZ

Note on the L and N. Richmond Lattimore. GM

Note on the Latin Gerunds, A. Richard Porson. FaBoEE

Note on Wyatt, A. Kingsley Amis. WeW-3

Note that the fire. The Fire Poem. Theodore Enslin. CRP

Note: The Sea Grinds Things Up. Alan Dugan. AFr

Note the stump, a peach tree. We had to cut it down. Places and Ways to Live. Richard Hugo. NIP-4

Note this survivor, bearing the mark of the violator. Swedenborg's Skull. Vernon Watkins. FaBoTw

Note to Olga (1966), A. Denise Levertov. CAPP-1; NALW

Note to the Ophthalmologist. Dolores Kendrick. FFC

Note to Tony Towle (After WS), A. Charles North. FTOS; PmAP

Note to Wang Wei. John Berryman. NYBP

Notebook of a Return to the Native Land. Aimé Césaire, *French*. "Islands scars of the water." PFTM, *tr. by* Clayton Eshleman *and* Annette Smith

Notebook, Two. Edmond Jabès, *French*. AF, *tr. by* Rosemarie Waldrop

Noted in The New York Times. Maxine W. Kumin. AFr

Noted outside the window: a fly, the sun on his back. Cold Fly. Yang Wan-li, *Chinese*. CoBCP, *tr. by* Burton Watson

Notes. A Friend. Paul Klee, *German*. PFTM, *tr. by* Anselm Hollo

Notes after Blacking Out. Gregory Corso. NeAP

Notes for a History of Poetry. David Daiches. PoA

Notes for a Lecture. David Ignatow. NNaP

Notes for a Movie Script. M. Carl Holman. PoBA

Notes for a Poem on Being Asian American. Dwight Okita. UnSA

Notes for a Revised Sonnet. "Edward Pygge." BXAP *Fr.* Robert Lowell's Notebook.

Notes for a Southern Road Map. Phyllis McGinley. NBLV

Notes for Echo Lake 2. Michael Palmer. PT

Notes for Echo Lake 3. Michael Palmer. PmAP

Notes for My Son. Alex Comfort. LiTM; MoBrPo *Fr.* The Song of Lazarus.

Notes for the Chart in 306. Ogden Nash. NYBP

Notes for the Legend of Salad Woman. Michael Ondaatje. NoAM

Notes for the Park Keeper. Peter Bland. OBGa

Notes From a Chinese Love Manual. Sarah Gorham.
White Tiger Leaps, The. FFC

Notes From a Youngest Daughter. Betsy Sholl.
"This old woman." MDDM

Notes from an Analyst's Couch. Anita Endrezze-Danielson. CDW

Notes from the Childhood and the Girlhood. Gwendolyn Brooks. LCAP-2
Ballad of Late Annie, The. ColAP
"Do not be afraid of no." ColAP
Old Relative. ColAP
Parents: People Like Our Marriage Maxie and Andrew, The. ColAP
"Pygmies Are Pygmies Still, Though Percht on Alps." ColAP
Sunday Chicken. ColAP
Throwing Out the Flowers. ColAP

Notes from the Delivery Room. Linda Pastan. NMM-2

Notes from the house of the dead. Aleksandr Soprovsky. TCRP, *tr. by* Vladimir Lunis *and* Albert C. Todd *Fr.* Two Poems.

Notes Made in the Piazza San Marco. May Swenson. CoAP

Notes on a Life to Be Lived. Robert Penn Warren. NYBP

Notes on a Visit to Le Tuc d'Audoubert. Clayton Eshleman. PmAP

Notes on My Contemporaries. Michael Hartnett.
Person as Dreamer: We Talk about the Future, The. PBCIP

Notes on My Father. Katerina Anghelaki-Rooke.
"Old man moved into his night, The." PBWP

Notes on Sound, Speech, Speech-Crystals and the Celestial Echo. Gustaf Sobin. PT

Notes on the Art of Memory. Diane Di Prima. SeSe

Notes on the Broadway Theatre. Langston Hughes. SSLK

Notes on the Impossible. Leonid Lavrov, *Russian*.
"Farewell, I say, farewell to the incomplete." TCRP, *tr. by* Lubov Yakovleva

Notes on the Peanut. June Jordan. NoAM

Notes to my Daughters. Shirley Kaufman. NMM-2

Notes to the Reader. Robert Bringhurst. NOBC

Notes toward a Supreme Fiction. Wallace Stevens.
Epilogue: "Soldier, there is a war between the mind." ColAP
To Henry Church. ColAP

Notes towards a Poem That Can Never Be Written. Margaret Atwood. NOBC

Notes Written in Obory. Aleksander Wat, *Polish*.
"X was asked." CBNP

Nothing. Julia De Burgos. BoWoP, *tr. by* Aliki *and* Willis Barnstone

Nothing. James Fenton. APAD

Nothing. Tom Raworth. NBrP

Nothing. Charles Simic. NNaP

Nothing. Burns Singer. OxBS

Nothing. Tanka. Toki Zenmaro, *Japanese*. MJT, *tr. by* Makoto Ueda

Nothing about the emptied family. (LL) Eviction. Lucille Clifton. InPS-3; NTCP

Nothing about the first abandonment. Belongings. Catherine Davis. FFC

Nothing ades to Loves fond fire. Song. Elizabeth Wilmot, Countess of Rochester. KTR; LW

Nothing, and is nowhere, and is endless. (LL) High Windows. Philip Larkin. FaBoMo; NAEL-2; NoAM; PoPoPo

Nothing and Something. Frances Ellen Watkins Harper. PWR

Nothing at All. Ivor Armstrong Richards. CRP

Nothing but a hovel now. The Ruin. Dafydd ap Gwilym, *Welsh*. OBWVE, *tr. by* Rolfe Humphries

Nothing but a little bit of flesh on her—. Fearless One. Genrik Veniaminovich Sapgir, *Russian*. TCRP, *tr. by* Albert C. Todd

Nothing but a man. Nadia Tuéni, *French*. BoWoP, *tr. by* Willis Barnstone

Nothing but a plain black boy. (LL) Of De Witt Williams on His Way to Lincoln Cemetery. Gwendolyn Brooks. NOBA; NoAM

Nothing but anniversaries, anniversaries. . . . Konstantin Konstantinovich Sluchevsky, *Russian*. TCRP, *tr. by* Albert C. Todd

Nothing but Death. Pablo Neruda, *Spanish*. SPE, *tr. by* Robert Bly
(Only Death.) PFTM, *tr. by* Clayton Eshleman
("There are lonely cemeteries.") PFTM, *tr. by* Clayton Eshleman
("Where death is waiting, dressed as an admiral.") (LL) PFTM, *tr. by* Clayton Eshleman

Nothing but laughter, nothing. Glycon, *Greek*. PGA, *tr. by* Kenneth Rexroth

Nothing but no and I, and I and no. Michael Drayton. GBL; PoEL-2 *Fr.* Idea.

Nothing can be done about the rain in your meal. The Same Corpse. Kojo Laing. HBAPE

Nothing can console me. You may bring silk. Demeter Mourning. Rita Dove. NAAAL *Fr.* Mother Love.

Nothing could make me sooner to confess[e]. The Second Anniversary [*or* Anniversarie]. Donne. ESCV; SeCP *Fr.* Of the Progres[se] of the Soule; the Second Anniversarie.

Nothing Could Take Away the Bear-King's Image. Ray A. Young Bear. HATNAP

Nothing delights me as I sit. Somewhere East of Suez. H. W. Berry. NSI

Nothing derivative here. The Litrajure of Everyday Life. Michael C. Blumenthal. NoAM

Nothing Elegant. Gertrude Stein. PBWP *Fr.* Tender Buttons.

Nothing for a dirty man. All That Is Lovely in Men. Robert Creeley. RaBo

Nothing for sale in / Stupidity Street. (LL) Stupidity Street. Ralph Hodgson. CH; LiTM; MoBrPo; OxBTC

Nothing For Tears. Milton. *Fr.* Samson Agonistes. FHYEP; OAEL-1; PoEL-3

Nothing from a straight line swerves. Samuel Hoffenstein. *Fr.* Songs about Life and Brighter Things Yet. NBLV

Nothing Gold Can Stay. Robert Frost. AmPP; ColAP; MoAmPo; NAAL-2; NOBA; Poetr; SoSe-8; TAP; VGW

Nothing grows in vain. Use plants to heal. Creed of Mr. Nicholas Culpeper. Patricia Beer. OxBC

Nothing Happened. Belle Waring. PBCAP

Nothing human is alien to me. Human Qualities. Dahlia Ravikovitch, *Hebrew*. IP, *tr. by* Warren Bargad *and* Stanley F. Chyet

Nothing in Heaven Functions as It Ought. X. J. Kennedy. Son

Nothing in my body escapes me. Song of a Prisoner. Jack Spicer. APSN

Nothing in our lives to stop us. Following the Rhymes of Kao Chi-ti's Poem: "We Had Planned to Travel to Cloud Cliff But Couldn't Because of Rain." Hsü Pen, *Chinese*. CoBLCP, *tr. by* Jonathan Chaves

Nothing in that drawer. Ron Padgett. PmAP

Nothing in the air to call me here—. What You Find in the Woods. James Longenbach. BAP-95

Nothing in this bright region melts or shifts. From the Highest Camp. Thom Gunn. Son; TwCP

Nothing Is. Sun-Ra. PoBA

Nothing is better, I well think. The Leper. Swinburne. GBL; NOBVV

Nothing is certain, only the certain spring. (LL) Now is the time for the burning of the leaves. Laurence Binyon. GTBS-P; NOBE; OxBTC

Nothing Is Enough. Laurence Binyon. MoBrPo

Nothing is here for tears, nothing to wail. Nothing For Tears. Milton. *Fr.* Samson Agonistes. FHYEP; OAEL-1; PoEL-3

Nothing is left. Nothing can be recognized. Marina. Nichita Stanescu, *Romanian.* CEEP, *tr. by* Mariana Carpinisan *and* Mark Irwin

Nothing Is Lost. Anne Ridler. WPE

Nothing is new: we walk where others went. Nothing New. Robert Herrick. CaPo

Nothing is plumb, level or square. Love Song: I and Thou. Alan Dugan. HoPM; InPK-6; MoP; NoAM

Nothing is quite alien or quite recognizable at this speed. Barbie's Ferrari. Lynne McMahon. NAmP90

Nothing is quite so quiet and clean. Snow in Town. Rickman Mark. BoTP

Nothing is real. The world has lost its edges. Scarcely Spring. Louis Untermeyer. AYFP

Nothing is sacred now but Villany. (LL) The Triumph of Vice. Alexander Pope. NOBE; OBSV

Nothing is so beautiful as Spring—. Spring. Gerard Manley Hopkins. APAD; EBVV; GSo; HAP; LiTM; MoBrPo; NAEL-2; NOBE; NOBVV; NoAM; OAEL-2; OBMV; OBNC; RB; TFi; TrCP

Nothing is sweeter than love[, all other blessings]. Nossis, *Greek.* GrAn, *tr. by* Peter Jay; PGA, *tr. by* Kenneth Rexroth

Nothing / Is worse for a city than an absolute ruler. Euripides. GrIP, *tr. by* Frank Jones *Fr.* The Suppliant Women.

Nothing like her ever came his way before. Semi-Skilled Lover. Maureen Duffy. LW

Nothing, like something, happens anywhere. (LL) I Remember, I Remember. Philip Larkin. NOBL; NTP

Nothing like that road runs from me. A Cabin in Minnesota. Marvin Bell. HoPM

Nothing lives long. The Death Song of White Antelope. *Cheyenne Oral Tradition, Cheyenne.* PaTW, *tr. by* George Bird Grinnell

Nothing move thee. Poem. Saint Theresa, of Avila, *Spanish.* CRP, *tr. by* Yvor Winters

Nothing moves. Lying Down. Kate Daniels. FiLi

"Nothing much here!" they say. With careless glance. Auction Sale— Household Furnishings. Adele DeLeeuw. PoToHe

Nothing nastier than a white person! The Great Palaces of Versailles. Rita Dove. NMM-2; NoAM

Nothing New. Robert Herrick. CaPo

Nothing New. Ella Wheeler Wilcox. APN-2

Nothing, not even fear of punishment. Young Girls. Patricia K. Page. SAGP

Nothing. Not even you, Dave, speak. Driving Home. Peter Kane Dufault. PFE

Nothing, nothing, nothing. For Josef Herman. Burns Singer. FaBoTC

Nothing now to mark the spot. Epilogue. Rachel Lyman Field. OBCA *Fr.* A Circus Garland.

Nothing of it? (LL) Fury of Overshoes. Anne Sexton. LCAP-2; NIP-4

Nothing out of which to create a new, A. None. Josephine Miles. VGW

Nothing pleases me anymore. No Delicacies. Ingeborg Bachmann, *Hebrew.* PoSu, *tr. by* Mark Anderson

Nothing Sacred. Roger Woddis. NOBL

Nothing so far but moonlight. Laura Riding Jackson. ColAP

Nothing so sharply reminds a man he is mortal. Departure in the Dark. C. Day Lewis. TwCP

Nothing so true as what you once let fall. Epistle [II,] to a Lady[: Of the Characters of Women]. Alexander Pope. NAEL-1; NOEC; OAEL-1; OxBoLi

Nothing so true as what you once let fall. To a Lady. Alexander Pope. OxBoLi *Fr.* Epistle [II,] to a Lady[: Of the Characters of Women]. CABP; NAEL-1; NOEC; OAEL-1

Nothing So Wise. Jeanne Lohmann. CrSp

Nothing / substance utters or time. The Word. Basil Bunting. PoA

Nothing takes its place. (LL) Poem: Alte Zachen. Abba Kovner, *Hebrew.* IP, *tr. by* Warren Bargad *and* Stanley F. Chyet

Nothing that is not there and the nothing that is. (LL) The Snow Man. Wallace Stevens. AFr; CMoP; ColAP; EnlH; HAP; HCAP; HeIP-4; NAAL-2; NoAM; NoP-4; PoE; PoPoPo; Poetr; SoSe-8; TRP; WeW-3

Nothing that is said or done. At First. Charles Hubert Sisson. OxBC

Nothing: the nothing for which there's no reward. (LL) Thinking of the Lost World. Randall Jarrell. NOBA; NoAM

Nothing there? nothing up the sky alive. John Berryman. BoLoP *Fr.* Sonnets to Chris.

Nothing! thou elder brother ev'n [*or* even] to shade. Upon Nothing. John Wilmot, 2d Earl of Rochester. NOSC; OBCoV; OBSV; OxAEP-1; PoEL-3

Nothing to be done? Tanka. Saitō Mokichi, *Japanese.* MJT, *tr. by* Makoto Ueda

Nothing to be Said. Philip Larkin. OxBTC

Nothing to be said about it, and everything. Dying. Robert Pinsky. HCAP; VCAP

Nothing to bury but dead. (LL) The Pessimist. Ben King. BLPA; CTC; NBLV; OBAL

Nothing to Do. James Ephriam McGirt. AAP

Nothing to do but work. The Pessimist. Ben King. BLPA; CTC; FuFo; NBLV; OBAL

Nothing to Fear. Kingsley Amis. EP; OxBC; OxBoV

Nothing to Wear. William Allen Butler. OBAL; PoLF

Nothing [*or* Nothin'] very bad hapen to me lately. Henry's Confession. John Berryman. LCAP-2; MoP; NAAL-2; NoAM; PoE; TwCP; VCAP *Fr.* Dream Songs.

Nothing was said until the house grew dark. A Short History of the Vietnam War Years. Dick Allen. BAP-94

Nothing Will Die. Tennyson. PBMP

Nothing will fill the salt caves our youth wore. Alone. Edith Jay Scovell. GBL

Nothing will keep. Personal Letter No. 3. Sonia Sanchez. SSLK

Nothing would sleep in that cellar, dank as a ditch. Root Cellar. Theodore Roethke. AmPP; ColAP; HeIP-4; InPK-6; NoP-4; PFE; SAGP; VCAP

Nothing you could know, or name, or say. Peppergrass. Stanley Plumly. LCAP-2

Nothingmas Day. Adrian Mitchell. NOxBChV

Nothingness. Xuân Diệu, *Vietnamese.* AVP, *tr. by* Huỳnh Sanh Thông

Nothingness, for the, The. Paul Celan, *German.* PoSu, *tr. by* John Felstiner

Nothing's going to become of anyone. Play. A. R. Ammons. PoA

Nothing's sadder than my sister's grave. Mount Ararat. Louise Glück. ColAP

Nothing's so dainty sweet as lovely melancholy. (LL) Melancholy. John Fletcher. GTBS-P; OBEV; PoEL-2

Notice. Steve Kowit. BLT

Notice. Robert Lowell. NoAM

Notice how he has numbered the blue veins. Mr. Mine. Anne Sexton. AFr

Notice the convulsed orange inch of moon. E. E. Cummings. VGW

Notice the oak, the high. Baii. Jim Barnes. *Fr.* Four Things Choctaw. HATNAP

Notice What This Poem Is Not Doing. William Stafford. LCAP-2

Noticing from what they talk about, and how they stand, or walk. Remembering Lunch. Douglas Dunn. OxBC

Notify someone of authority. If You See This Man. Thomas Lux. AmPA

Notions of freedom are tied up with drink. We Sit Unhackled Drunk and Mad to Edit. Malcolm Lowry. *Fr.* The Drunkards. NYBP

Notorious Glutton, The. Ann Taylor. OxBChV

Notre Dame. Osip Emilevich Mandelstam, *Russian.* OBVE, *tr. by* James Greene

Notre Dame, Sainte Chapelle, Sacré Coeur by foot—. Debora Greger. NoP-4 *Fr.* Lives of the Saints.

Nottamun Town. *Unknown.* CBNP; OxBoLi

Nottingham Fair. *Unknown.* AmFP

Nou goth sonne under wode. *Unknown. See* Now Goeth Sun under Wood.

Nought is on earth more sacred or divine. Edmund Spenser. OAEL-1 *Fr.* Wood Of Error. AEP

Nought is there under heav'ns wide hollownesse. Edmund Spenser. FHYEP *Fr.* Wood Of Error. AEP

Nought loves another as itself. A Little Boy Lost. William Blake. FHYEP; PeECV; Ro *Fr.* Songs of Experience.

Nought may endure but Mutability. (LL) Mutability. Shelley. NAEL-2; OBNC

Nought vnder heauen so strongly doth allure. Edmund Spenser. NoSic *Fr.* Wood Of Error. AEP

Nova. Robinson Jeffers. CMoP; HAP

Novas. Van K. Brock. MT

Novel of High Life, A. Thomas Haynes Bayly. OxAEP-2

Novelettes. Louis MacNeice.
    Gardener, The. IIP
    Les Sylphides. BoLoP

Novelist, The. W. H. Auden. MeMAP

Novelist, flushed with success, A. Limerick. Thomas Thorneley. PeLi

Novelist of the Absurd, A. Limerick. Ogden Nash. PeLi

Novel's end. Rod Willmot. HA

Novelty Shop, The. Duane Niatum. CDW

Novelty today, tomorrow a ruin from the past, buried and, A. I Speak of the City. Octavio Paz, *Spanish.* VCWP, *tr. by* Eliot Weinberger

November. Margaret Atwood. NOBC

November. Robert Bridges. OBNC; PoEL-5

November. William Cullen Bryant. APN-1; GSo; Son

November. Alice Cary. AYFP; OBCA

November. John Clare. AYFP

November. Hartley Coleridge. LaPo; OBNC *Fr.* Sonnets to the Seasons.

November. Frederick William Harvey. OxBTC

November. William Dean Howells. APN-2; GaP

November. Ted Hughes. CMoP; GTBS-P

November. John Keble. OBEV; OBNC *Fr.* Forest Leaves in Autumn.

November. William Morris. EnVR *Fr.* The Earthly Paradise.

November. Henrietta Cordelia Ray. CBWP-3

November. Folgore da San Geminiano. *Fr.* Sonnets of the Months. AWP, *tr. by* D. G. Rossetti

November. Edmund Spenser. PoEL-1 *Fr.* The Shepheardes [*or* Shepeards *or* Shepherd's] Calender.

November. Frederick Goddard Tuckerman. NOBA

November 1936. Paul Éluard, *French.* AF, *tr. by* Gilbert Bowen

November and Aunt Jemima. Thylias Moss. TRP

November Blue. Alice Thompson Meynell. MoBrPo

November Calf. Jane Kenyon. InPS-3

November chill blaws loud wi' angry sugh. Robert Burns. *Fr.* The Cotter's Saturday Night. FaBoBe; NOBRP; PoLF

November Cotton Flower. Jean Toomer. ColAP; MoP; NoAM; UnPo

November, 1806. Wordsworth. OBWP

November evening. Cor Van den Heuvel. HA

November evening. John Wills. HA

November Harvest. Anita Endrezze-Danielson. HATNAP

November in Boston. Thomas McCarthy. BiHa

November is a spinner. Margaret Rose. BoTP

November Landscape, A. Sarah Helen Whitman. ColAP

November light spreads a sheet. Small Differences. Judith C. Root. CMAP

November Night. Adelaide Crapsey. FPC; Spl

November 1956. Evan Jones. PBCV

November Poppies. Hilary Corke. NYBP

November '73. Dan Pagis, *Hebrew.* IP, *tr. by* Warren Bargad *and* Stanley F. Chyet

November '63: eight months in London. Immigrant. Fleur Adcock. OPOU

November Song. Mark Vinz. Poetsp

November Sunday Morning. Alvin Feinman. CoAP

November Surf. Robinson Jeffers. NAAL-2; OxBA

November through a Giant Copper Beech. Edwin Honig. NYBP; NoAM

November Twenty-sixth Nineteen Hundred and Sixty-three. Wendell Berry. LiTM

Novice, A. Dollie Radford. SDW

Novice was sitting on a cornice, A. Illustration. John Ashbery. NAAL-2

Novice when I came beneath thy gaze, A. Stanzas Concerning Love. Stefan George, *German.* AWP, *tr. by* Ludwig Lewisohn

Now. Sarah Knowles Bolton. PWR

Now. Robert Browning. CBLP; EP

Now. Christopher Gilbert. GT

Now. William Stafford. NNaP

Now. *Unknown.* PWR

Now, after a party with the consul and our best friend. Summer, 1970. Daniel Halpern. AmPA

Now after David had lived seventy years. The Death of David. Hayyim Nahman Bialik, *Hebrew.* TrJP, *tr. by* Herbert Danby, *ad. by* Sholom J. Kahn

Now after the sabbath. Matthew 28:1–6; Now after the sabbath. Bible, N.T. GI, *tr. by* Czeslaw Milosz *Fr.* St. Matthew.

Now Ain't That Love? Carolyn M. Rodgers. BPo

Now air is air and thing is thing: no bliss. E. E. Cummings. PBMP

Now al is done; bring home the bride againe. Edmund Spenser. *Fr.* Epithalamion: "Ye learned sisters which have oftentimes." AAS; BoLoP; CABP; FHYEP; InPS-3; NOBE; NoP-4; NoSic; OAEL-1; OBEV; OxAEP-1; PBRV; PoEL-1; PoPoPo

Now, alas, it is too late. Samuel Hoffenstein. OBCoV *Fr.* Songs of Fairly Utter Despair.

Now all aloud the wind and rain. The Watercress Seller. Thomas Miller. OxBChV

Now all day long the man who is not dead. Mother and Son. Allen Tate. MoAmPo

Now all of change. Sir Thomas Wyatt. SiPS

Now all our hurries that hung up on hooks. War-Time. William Robert Rodgers. OxBSP

Now all that sound of laughter, sound of singing. Rosalía de Castro, *Galician.* BoWoP; STV, *tr. by* John Frederick Nims

Now all the dogs with folded paws. Suburban Song. Elizabeth Riddell. CBAP; NOBAu

Now all the lights of Dublin. The Lights of Dublin. Patrick O'Connor. TIRV

Now all the peacefull regents of the night. George Chapman. PoEL-2 *Fr.* Bussy d'Ambois.

Now all the truth is out. To a Friend Whose Work Has Come to Nothing. W. B. Yeats. AWP; InPK-6; LiTM; MoBrPo; OAEL-2; OBMV; OxAEP-2; PoA

Now all the world she knew is dead. House of Rest. John Betjeman. LBC; OxAEP-2

Now all these lies he made appear so truthful. Penelope weeps. Homer. OBCVT, *tr. by* Robert Fitzgerald *Fr.* The Odyssey.

Now am I haunted by that taste! that sound! (LL) Love Dies. George Meredith. BoLoP; EnVR; NOBVV

Now an angel of the Lord appeared to. The Celestial Fire. Yannai, *Hebrew.* NNPT, *tr. by* T. Carmi

Now and Afterwards. Dinah Maria Mulock Craik. PoLF

Now and again dipping their long oval leaves in the water. (LL) Betrothed. Louise Bogan. CrSp; NMM-2

Now and for ever, my hail and my farewell. Catullus. *See* On the Burial of His Brother.

Now and then. Tears. Hyonsung Kim, *Korean.* CKP, *tr. by* Jaihiun Kim

Now and then there will arise. Song. *Unknown, Chippewa Indian.* OBVE, *tr. by* Frances Densmore

Now another day is breaking. Morning Prayer. Ogden Nash. OxBChV

Now, Antonius, in a smiling age. De M. Antonio. Martial, *Latin.* OBCVT, *tr. by* Robert Louis Stevenson

Now *Ardea* was besieg'd, the Town was strong. The Story of Lucretia out of Ovid de Fastis. / Book II. Ovid. OBCVT, *tr. by* Thomas Creech *Fr.* Fasti (Roman Feast-Days).

Now are our prayers divided, now. At the "Ye That Do Truly." Charles Williams. NOCV

Now Arethusa from her snow couches arises. Shelley's "Arethusa" Set to New Measures. Robert Duncan. CMoP

Now as at all times I can see in the mind's eye. The Magi. W. B. Yeats. CMoP; ChIV-2; GI; HAP; InPK-6; NoAM; OAEL-2; OxAEP-2; PChr; PoA; PoE; TRP; TrCP

Now as I was young and easy under the apple boughs. Fern Hill. Dylan Thomas. CABP; CMoP; ChAP; ClHu; GEA; GTBS-P; HAP; HeIP-4; ImPo; InPK-6; InPS-3; LiTM; MoBrPo; MoP; NAEL-2; NIP-4; NOBE; NTP; NoAM; NoP-4; OAEL-2; OBWVE; OxBTC; PoE; PoLF; PoPoPo; PoRA; Poetr; SAGP; SoSe-8; TFi; TRP; TwCP

Now as I watch the progress of the plague. The Missing. Thom Gunn. NoP-4

Now as Medea walks, dark echoes fill. Gaius Valerius Flaccus. OBCVT, *tr. by* Frederic Raphael *and* Kenneth McLeish *Fr.* The Argonautica.

Now as the train bears west. Night Journey. Theodore Roethke. GM; KaS; NYBP; SAGP

Now as Then. Anne Ridler. WPN

Now as they went on their way. Luke 10:38–42; Now as they went on their way. Bible, N.T. GI, *tr. by* Anna Kamienska *Fr.* St. Luke.

Now as we cross this white page together. The Escape. William Stafford. NNaP

Now at last I've come to touch. The Absolute Solitude. Hyonsung Kim, *Korean.* CKP, *tr. by* Jaihiun Kim

Now, at the time that was before agreed. Edmund Spenser. OAEL-1 *Fr.* Wood Of Error. AEP

Now at the turn of the year this coil of clay. The Mad Potter. John Hollander. ColAP; VCAP

Now austere lips are laid. The Hard Lovers. George Dillon. PoA

Now banished art, but yet alas how shall? (LL) Sonnet 72: "Desire, though thou my old companion art." Sir Philip Sidney. NAEL-1

Now be for ever still. To Himself. Giacomo Leopardi, *Italian.* NNPT, *tr. by* John Heath-Stubbs

Now Be the Gospel Banner. Thomas Hastings. AH

Now beginneth Glutton [*or* biginneth Glotoun] for to go to shrift[e]. The Glutton [*or* Glutton in the Tavern.] William Langland. PoE *Fr.* The Vision of Piers Plowman.

Now Behold the Saviour Pleading. John Leland. AH

Now being arrived at his Colledge. Alicia D'Anvers. KTR *Fr.* Academia; or The Humours of the University of Oxford.

Now, being invisible, I walk without mantilla. The Souls of Women at Night. Wallace Stevens. CMoP

Now Bekotsidi, that am I. For them I make. The Song of Bekotsidi. *Unknown, Navajo.* OBVE, *tr. by* Washington Matthews

Now bernes, buirdes, bolde and blithe. *Unknown.* MiEL

Now Blue October. Robert Nathan. FYAP

Now bold Robin Hood to the north would go. Robin Hood and the Scotchman. *Unknown.* ESPB

Now, bride and bridegroom, help to sing. Ben Jonson, *English.* ITG, *tr. by* Robert Hass

Now, brighter than the host that all night long. Daybreak. Richard Henry Dana. APN-1

Now, brother, time being money, I say farewell. Catullus. *See* On the Burial of His Brother.

Now burley's curing in the high-tiered barn. Squirrel Stand. Jim Wayne Miller. MT

Now burst above the city's cold twilight. Six o'Clock. Trumbull Stickney. APN-2; OxBA

Now, by one year, time and our frailty have. Elegy on D. D. Sidney Godolphin. BeJo

Now calumnies arise, and black reproach. Mary Latter. ECWP *Fr.* Soliloquies on Temporal Indigence.

Now Came Still Evening On. Milton. *Fr.* Book IV. OAEL-1 *Fr.* Paradise Lost.

Now came still Ev'ning [*or* evening *or* Eevning] on, and Twilight gray [*or* grey]. Evening in Paradise. Milton. NOBE, *ll.* 598–656; PeECV, *ll.* 598–688 *Fr.* Book IV. OAEL-1 *Fr.* Paradise Lost.

Now can you see the monument? It is of wood. The Monument. Elizabeth Bishop. HCAP; NOBA; NoAM; Poetr; TRP

Now chaos has pitched a tent. Revival. George Garrett. MT

Now children may. May. John Updike. AYFP; NOxBChV; OBCA *Fr.* A Child's Calendar.

Now Christmas is come. *Unknown.* PChr

Now Civill Warres a second Age consume. Horace. OBCVT, *tr. by* Sir Richard Fanshawe *Fr.* To the People of Rome, Commiserating the Common-Wealth, in respect of the Civil Warres.

Now close at hand. Hector's flight. Homer. OBCVT, *tr. by* Robert Fitzgerald *Fr.* The Iliad.

Now close your eyes. Wedding Reception. Melinda Goodman. GLP

Now coldness comes sifting down, layer after layer. Flute Notes from a Reedy Pond. Sylvia Plath. FaBoMo

Now comes the evening of the mind. The Evening of the Mind. Donald Justice. VCAP

Now comes the good rain farmers pray for(and). E. E. Cummings. NoAM

Now comes the happy morning long desired. The Village Fair. James Hurdis. ECEV *Fr.* The Village Curate.

Now cometh alle ye that ben ibroght. Huc omnes pariter. Boethius. OBMV, *tr. by* John Walton *Fr.* Consolation of Philosophy, The ("De Consolacione Philosophie").

Now corn pushes past the foam. Ode to a Dead Dodge. David McElroy. AmPA

Now Cunningham, who rhymed by fits and starts. Terse Elegy for J.V. Cunningham. X. J. Kennedy. DiPo

Now Curll his shop from rubbish drains. Jonathan Swift. PeLV *Fr.* Verses on the Death of Dr. Swift, D.S.P.D.

Now Cynthia shone serene, and ev'ry star. The Daventry Wonder. "Agricola." NOEC

Now daisies pied, and violets blue. Shakespeare. *See* Spring.

Now, damn you, you're stiff, uptight—. Private Poem. Strato, *Greek.* GrAn, *tr. by* Teddy Hogge

Now dare I speake, soo mote I thee. From Amphitryon. Plautus Titus Maccius. OBCVT, *tr. by* Nicholas Udall *Fr.* A Newe enterlued for chyldren to playe named Jacke Jugeler.

Now day and night sit balanced. Spring Equinox. Peter Blue Cloud. ChAP *Fr.* Within the Seasons. HATNAP

Now did you mark a falcon. Noble Sisters. Christina Rossetti. VWP

Now do our eyes behold. Lament for the Two Brothers Slain by Each Other's Hand. Aeschylus, *Greek.* OBCVT, *tr. by* Alfred Edward Housman *Fr.* The Seven against Thebes.

Now, do you doubt that your Bird was true? (LL) Split the Lark—and you'll find the Music. Emily Dickinson. APN-2; ChIV-2; NoP-4

Now does our world descend. E. E. Cummings. NYBP

Now, does she still want to live? Babouchka. Sophie Slingeland. LoHo

Now Dreary Dawns the Eastern Light. A. E. Housman. CMoP

Now each creature joys the other. Ode. Samuel Daniel. NoSic

Now, earth, take to thy cold embrace. Prudentius. OBCVT, *tr. by* Simon Patrick *Fr.* A Funeral Hymn upon the Obsequies of a Friend.

Now Endymion dedicates / his cold bed's failure to the moon. Isidorus, *Greek.* GrAn, *tr. by* Robin Skelton

Now Energy's bound to diminish. Ether Insatiable. May Kendall. CABP

Now entertain conjecture of a time. Before Agincourt. Shakespeare. EBEV; OxAEP-1; RB *Fr.* King Henry V.

Now, Epicure. The Alchemist. Ben Jonson. FaBoSe

Now ere sweet summer bids its long adieu. Summer. Robert Bloomfield. Ro

Now especially, each flower moves. Variation on the Gothic Spiral. W. S. Merwin. PoA

Now Evening Puts Amen to Day. Paul Horgan. AH

Now every man at my request. *Unknown.* OBCP

Now every thing that shadowy thought. In Festubert. Edmund Blunden. OBMV

Now Ev'ning fades! her pensive step retires. Night. Ann Radcliffe. NOBRP; WPE

Now Fade the Rose and Lily-Flower. *Unknown, Middle English.* NOCV, *tr. by* Brian Stone

Now fades the last long streak of snow. And buds and blossoms like the rest. Tennyson. EBVV; FHYEP; GTBS-P; NOBE; OBNC *Fr.* In Memoriam A. H. H.

Now faintly the falling sun. Chengtu. Tu Fu, *Chinese.* TAL, *tr. by* Robert Payne

Now, Fanny, 'tis too bad, you teazèn maïd! A Bit o' Sly Coorten. William Barnes. PeLV

Now, Faustus, what wouldst thou have me do? Marlowe. OxBSn *Fr.* Doctor Faustus.

Now ferkes to the firthe thees fresche men of armes. Sir Gawain Encounters Sir Priamus. *Unknown.* PoEL-1 *Fr.* Morte Arthur.

Now, fie on foolish love! It not befits. Fie on Love. James Shirley. OxBSP

Now fie upon that everlasting life, I dye! Valiant Love. Richard Lovelace. SeCP

Now *Fight Cancer* is there. (LL) Sunny Prestatyn. Philip Larkin. NoAM; OBCoV

Now first, as I shut the door. The New House. Edward Thomas. EBEV; MoBrPo; NOBE; OBEV; OBWVE

Now first of all he means the night. A Song for the Middle of the Night. James Wright. WeW-3

Now for a little I have fed on loneliness. Fruit of Loneliness. May Sarton. PoA

Now for I see the fields in flower. From the Provençal of William of Poitiers. William of Aquitaine, *Provençal.* MLL, *tr. by* Helen Waddell

Now for that slawnders sake. *Unknown.* PBRV *Fr.* Jack of the North.

Now for the first time on the night of your death. An Elegy for Ernest Hemingway. Thomas Merton. BLT

Now for the long years when I could not love you. In Recompense. Eda Lou Walton. LW

Now for the people in thee left. Isabella Whitney. BWW *Fr.* The Manner of Her Will and What She Left to London and to All Those in It, at Her Departing. NoSic

Now for the spirit of the people. Here. W. H. Auden. FaBoPV *Fr.* Letter to Lord Byron.

Now from each van. War Poetry. John Philips. NOEC *Fr.* Blenheim.

Now from Labor and from Care. Thomas Hastings. AH

Now from Leander's place she rose, and found. George Chapman. EBEV *Fr.* Hero and Leander. AAS

Now from the marshlands under the mist-mountains. The Coming of Grendel. *Unknown.* OPOU, *tr. by* Gerald Benson *Fr.* Beowulf. ASW, *tr. by* Kevin Crossley-Holland; OAEL-1, *tr. by* Charles W. Kennedy

Now from the sixth hour there was darkness over all the land. Matthew 27:45–56; Now from the sixth hour there was darkness. Ted Hughes. GI *Fr.* St. Matthew.

Now Front to Front the hostile Armies stand. Paris and Menelaus. Homer. OBVE, *tr. by* Alexander Pope *Fr.* The Iliad.

Now gently winding up the fair ascent. Homer. OBVE, *tr. by* Pope *Fr.* The Odyssey. NAWM-1, *tr. by* Robert Fitzgerald

Now, George the third rules not alone. On the Conflagrations at Washington. Philip Freneau. APN-1

Now get thee back, retreat, depart, O Serpent. He Overcometh the Serpent of Evil in the Name of Ra. *Unknown.* AWP *Fr.* Book of the Dead.

Now Gilderoy was a bonny boy, and he would not the ribbons wear. My Handsome Gilderoy. *Unknown.* CH

Now ginnes this goodly frame of temperaunce. The Bower of Bliss. Edmund Spenser. PoEL-1 *Fr.* Wood Of Error. AEP

Now, God be thanked Who has matched us with His hour. Peace. Rupert Brooke. OBWP; PoA; PoFWW *Fr.* 1914

Now God is truly naught, and if He aught may be. God Is Nothing Physical. "Angelus Silesius." GePo, *tr. by* George C. Schoolfield *Fr.* The Cherubical Wanderer.

Now God preserve, as you well do deserve. The Masque of Christmas. Ben Jonson. OxBoLi

Now God Stand Up for Bastards. Brian Merriman. BIrV, *tr. by* Arland Ussher *Fr.* The Midnight Court. NOIV, *tr. by* Thomas Kinsella

Now Goeth Sun under Wood. *Unknown.* MiEL; NAEL-1

("Me reweth, Marie, thi sone and the.") (LL) NoP-4

("Nou goth sonne under wode.") NoP-4

Now goodnight. (LL) Good Night. Eleanor Farjeon. NOxBChV; NTP; OTCP

Now gowans sprout, an' lavrocks sing. Ode to Mr. F— [or Mr. Forbes]. Allan Ramsay, after Horace. NOEC; OBVE

Now graceful truce suspends the burning war. Joel Barlow. APN-1 Fr. The Columbiad.

Now grapes are plush upon the vines. Contrary Theses (I). Wallace Stevens. OxBA; SAmP

Now grimy April comes again. For City Spring. Stephen Vincent Benét. BXAP; NBLV

Now had night measured with her shadowy cone. Then when I Am Thy Captive, Talk of Chains. Milton. Fr. Book IV. OAEL-1 Fr. Paradise Lost.

Now had the loophole of that dungeon, still. Ugolino. Dante. Fr. Inferno. NAWM-1, tr. by John Ciardi Fr. Divina Commedia.

Now had the seasons returned, when the nights grow colder and longer. Henry Wadsworth Longfellow. Fr. Part the First. Fr. Evangeline, a Tale of Acadie.

Now hand in hand, you little maidens, walk. Spring. André Spire, French. AWP, tr. by Jethro Bithell

Now hands to seedsheet, boys! The Sower's Song. Thomas Carlyle. SCGP

Now hardly here and there a[n] hackney-coach. A Description of the Morning. Jonathan Swift. EBEV; ECEV; HAP; HeIP-4; InPS-3; NOBE; NOEC; NoP-4; OAEL-1; OxAEP-1; PFE; PoPoPo; Poetr; SoSe-8; TFi

Now has ended the battle of Saul. Saul. Nathan Alterman, Hebrew. TrJP, tr. by Dov Vardi

Now haste, my Muse, pursue thy destined way. Soame Jenyns. ECEV Fr. The Art of Dancing.

Now hath my life across a stormy sea. On the Brink of Death. Michelangelo Buonarroti, Italian. AWP, tr. by John Addington Symonds

Now haud your tongue, baith wife and carle. Red Harlaw. Sir Walter Scott. OxBB Fr. The Antiquary.

Now have I brought a woork to end which neither Joves fierce [or feerce] wrath. Conclusion. Ovid, Latin. OBVE, tr. by Arthur Golding Fr. Metamorphoses.

Now having leisure, and a happy wind. John Fletcher and others. GBL Fr. The Maid in the Mill.

Now hawk, wind's jockey, sitting tight. Kite. John Robert Lee. PBCV

Now he comes! will he come? alas, no, no! (LL) Complaint of the Absence of Her Lover Being upon the Sea. Henry Howard, Earl of Surrey. AAS; EBEV; GBL; NOBE; NoSic; OBEV; SCGP; SiPS

Now he is gone and we had not understood one another. The Year's Ending. St. J. Page Yako, Xhosa. PeSA, tr. by C. M. Mcanyangwa and Jack Cope

Now, he recalls the lamentable wail. John Pierpont. APN-1 Fr. Airs of Palestine.

Now heaven be thanked. I am out of love again! Freedom. "Jan Struther." LW

Now Heaven conduct thee with a parent's love! (LL) To Mr. S. T. Coleridge. Anna Laetitia Barbauld. CABP; ECWP; NOBRP; NOEC; NoP-4; Ro; WoRP

Now Help Us, Lord. Unknown. AH, ad. by Charles E. Ives

Now here is a typical children's story. The Leaf Pile. Alicia Ostriker. FiLi

Now high and low, where leaves renew. Autet e bas. Arnaut Daniel, Provençal. CTC, tr. by Ezra Pound

Now his nose's bridge is broken, one eye. On Hurricane Jackson. Alan Dugan. CoAP; TRP

Now holde [or hoold] your[e] pees, my tale I wol beginne [or biginne, or bigynne]. (LL) The Pardoner's Prologue. Chaucer. FHYEP; NAEL-1; OAEL-1; PoE

Now hollow fires burn out to black. A. E. Housman. NOBVV

Now homing tradesmen scatter through the streets. Place Pigalle. Richard Wilbur. HeIP-4

Now I am dry bones and my face a stony skull staring in yellow surprise at the /sun. . . . (LL) Between the World and Me. Richard Wright. ISC; LiTM; MoP; PoBA

Now I am glad to be one whom people ignore. At a Reception. Karen Gershon. LW

Now I am going / to rape you. The Thing Itself. Alice Walker. NMM-2

Now I am slow and placid, fond of sun. With Child. Genevieve Taggard. MoAmPo; NMM-2

Now I become myself. It's taken. May Sarton. CrSp

Now I believe tradition, which doth call. Upon the Author. By a Known Friend. Benjamin Woodbridge. SCAP

Now I can tell you. Hearing the shrill leaves. The Thrasher in the Willow by the Lake. Robert Pack. ColAP

Now I do believe that he has died. B. W. Vilakazi, Zulu. PeSAV, tr. by Cherie Maclean

Now I find myself dried. Psalm 2. Mahmoud Darwish, Arabic. AF, tr. by Denys Johnson-Davies

Now I go down here and bring up a moon. Auctioneer. Carl Sandburg. NOxBChV

Now I have come to reason. C. Day Lewis. CMoP

Now I have forgotten how to breathe and cry. To My Daughter. Vadim Leonidovich Andreyev, Russian. TCRP, tr. by Belinda Brindle

Now I have found thee, I will ever more. William Alabaster. ESCV Fr. Divine Meditations. Son

Now I have found thee I will evermore. Upon the Crucifix. William Alabaster. NoSic; PoEL-2

Now I have known, O Lord. Al-Junaid. TOF, tr. by A. J. Arberry

Now I Have Nothing. Stella Benson. LW; OxBTC

Now I hear it, my friends, of the Metai, who are sitting about me. Song for the Metai, or for Medicine Hunting. Unknown. Fr. Music and Poetry of the Indians. APN-2, tr. by John Tanner

Now I invest the world. What is Beautiful. Jay Wright. GT

Now I knew I lost her. Emily Dickinson. CPO

Now I lay me down to sleep. Compline. Donald Davie. Fr. Horae Canonicae. CRP

Now I lay me down to sleep. An Evening Prayer. Unknown. CTV

"Now I Lay Me Down to Sleep." Eugene Henry Pullen. FaBoBe

Now I Lay Me Down to Take My Sleep. Unknown. OxNR

Now I may wither into the truth. (LL) The Coming of Wisdom with Time. W. B. Yeats. FaBoEE; SoSe-8

Now I must betray myself. Prothalamion. Delmore Schwartz. OxBA

Now I out walking. Away! Robert Frost. NOBA

Now I pray the man who may love this lay. Cynewulf. AnOE, tr. by Charles W. Kennedy Fr. Fates of the Apostles.

Now I remember: in our town the druggist. Serving with Gideon. William Stafford. LCAP-2

Now I say in structuring the simple slips a seems. An Essay on Concrete. Douglas Messerli. FTOS

Now I see its whiteness. The Dead Butterfly. Denise Levertov. NoP-4

Now I see lotus-pickers singing the lotus-pickers' song. Tune: "Pomegranate Blossoms." Kuan Yün-shih. SuSp, tr. by Richard John Lynn Fr. Medley of Southern and Northern Tunes—Scenic Tour of West Lake.

Now I shall ask you to imagine how. Achilles sets out. Homer. OBCVT, tr. by Christopher Logue Fr. The Iliad.

Now I walk with you through the ruins of the city. Some Walks with You. John Hollander. NoAM

Now I wear my named pants. Glose. Michael Malinowitz. EOEF

Now I will abandon the route of my life. Mr. Wakeville on Interstate 90. Donald Hall. AFr

Now I will ask for one true word beyond. Grandfather and Grandmother in Love. David Mura. TRP

Now I will do nothing but listen. Walt Whitman. HoPM; SAmP Fr. Song of Myself. AmPP; MoAmPo; NAAL-3; NOBA; OxBA

Now I will fashion the tale of a fish. The Whale. Unknown. AnOE; APo, tr. by Charles William Kennedy Fr. Physiologus.

Now I will make fat puddings. Advent. Anne Hartigan. CIP-2

Now I Will Only Believe. B. W. Vilakazi. PeSAV

Now I will sing about a kind of fish. Unknown. See The Whale.

Now ice-covered. Geraldine Clinton Little. HA

Now ich see blostme springe. Of Jesu Christ I Sing. Unknown. PoE

Now if ever it is time to cleanse Helicon. Ezra Pound. VGW Fr. Homage to Sextus Propertius.

Now, if I could, its whirling vacuum. (LL) Elegy for My Father. Howard Moss. CoAP; LiTM

Now if the dull and thankless heart declare. Malediction Upon Myself. Elinor Wylie. ColAP

Now if thou hast one dram of Grace. Carmina, LV. Catullus. OBVE, tr. by Nahum Tate Fr. Carmina.

Now in a thought, now in a shadowed word. L'Envoi. Edwin Arlington Robinson. TrCP

Now in an hour you have me, tight, and loose me. The Fool. Kenneth Mackenzie. BMAP

Now in midsummer come and all fools slaughtered. Credences of Summer. Wallace Stevens. MeMAP

Now in my / heart I / see clearly. Sappho, Greek. BoWoP, tr. by Willis Barnstone

Now in my Samarkand of blue enamels. Journey in the Orient. Maria Luisa Spaziani, Italian. BoWoP, tr. by Ruth Feldman

Now in the Boat defenceless Pompey sate. Pompey's death and apotheosis. Lucan, Latin. OBCVT, tr. by Nicholas Rowe

Now in the dawn before it dies, the eagle swings. The Story of a Well-made Shield. N. Scott Momaday. CDW; HATNAP

Now in the palace gardens warm with age. Eride, V. Trumbull Stickney. APN-2 Fr. Eride.

Now in the patron's mansion see the wight. Richard Savage. OBSV Fr. The Progress of a Divine.

Now in the people. Hildegard von Bingen, Latin. CrSp

Now, in the storm before the calm. Yehuda Amichai, *Hebrew*. IP, *tr. by* Warren Bargad *and* Stanley F. Chyet

Now in the suburbs and the falling light. Father and Son. Stanley Kunitz. AF, *tr. by* Jack Bevan; MoP; Poetr; TwCP

Now in the third voice. W. S. Graham. *Fr.* The Dark Dialogues. OxBS

Now in this mirthfull tyme of May. Four May Poems, II. *Unknown.* OxBS

Now in this while gan Daedalus a wearinesse to take. Daedalus. Ovid. CTC; OBVE, *tr. by* Arthur Golding *Fr.* Metamorphoses.

Now in thy dazzling half-oped eye. A Mother to Her Waking Infant. Joanna Baillie. ECWP; NOEC; NoP-4; WoRP

Now incense fills the air. After Yeats. Allen Ginsberg. FTOS; PFE

Now, innocent, within the deep. M., Singing. Louise Bogan. ColAP; NoAM

Now is a bursting in me. Argent Solipsism. Howard Blake. PoA

Now is a ship / which captain am. E. E. Cummings. Spl

Now is it most like as if on ocean. The Voyage of Life. Cynewulf. AnOE *Fr.* Christ 2.

Now is it? You'll remember Mercury. (LL) The First Men on Mercury. Edwin Morgan. CBNP; PeLV; SpW

Now is my father. Poem for My Father's Ghost. Mary Oliver. InPS-3

Now is the globe shrunk tight. Snowdrop. Ted Hughes. FaBoMo

Now is the hour when, swinging in the breeze. Harmonie du Soir. Charles Baudelaire, *French*. AWP, *tr. by* Lord Alfred Douglas

Now is the month of maying. *Unknown.* EBEV; NoSic ("Shall we play barley-break?") (LL) LiLi

Now is the time. Hisako Fukui, *Japanese*. WPJ, *tr. by* Kenneth Rexroth *and* Ikuko Atsumi

Now is the time for mirth. To Live Merrily, and To Trust to Good Verses. Robert Herrick. AWP; BeJo; CaPo; CavPo; NOSC; SeCP

Now is the time for the burning of the leaves. Laurence Binyon. GTBS-P; NOBE; OxBTC *Fr.* The Burning of the Leaves.

Now is the time, when all the lights wax dim. To Anthea. Robert Herrick. PoEL-3

Now is the time when the great urban heart. City Christmas. Phyllis McGinley. OBCoV

Now is the winter of our discontent. Hate the Idle Pleasures. Shakespeare. EBEvV; PoE *Fr.* King Richard III.

Now is the winter of our discontent. Shakespeare. OxBoV *Fr.* King Richard III.

Now is the world withdrawn all. Carol. Howard Nemerov. TrCP

Now is this love already forth to come. Edmund Spenser. ITG, *tr. by* Robert Hass *Fr.* Epithalamion.

Now is when we love to sit before mirrors. This Couple. C. D. Wright. CMAP

Now Israel May Say, and That Truly. William Whittingham. AH

Now issued from the Ships the warrior Train. Achilles sets out. Homer. OBCVT, *tr. by* Alexander Pope *Fr.* The Iliad.

Now it belongs not to my care. Richard Baxter. NOSC

Now it grows dark. Hymn to Night. Melville Cane. MoAmPo

Now it is almost night, from the bronzey soft sky. Storm in the Black Forest. D. H. Lawrence. FaBoVe

Now it is autumn and the falling fruit. The Ship of Death. D. H. Lawrence. CMoP; FaBoTw; GTBS-P; MoBrPo; MoP; NAEL-2; NoAM; NoP-4; OAEL-2; OxAEP-2

Now It Is Broccoli. Jeff Tagami. EC2

Now it is fifteen years you have lain in the meadow. Lines for an Interment. Archibald MacLeish. CMoP; NOBA

Now it is midsummer and the long sun shines. For Hokey and Henrietta. Norman Nicholson. NoP-4

Now it is only hours before you wake. Letter to My Daughter at the End of Her Second Year. Donald Finkel. CoAP

Now it is September and the web is woven. The Dwarf. Wallace Stevens. MeMAP

Now it is winter and the fallen snow. Los Mineros. Edward Dorn. PoM

Now it was that the Morrigan settled in bird shape. The Morrigan. *Unknown, Irish*. BIrV, *tr. by* Thomas Kinsella

Now it's eight o'clock. (LL) Willie Winkie. William Miller. LB; OxBChV; ReMoGo

Now it's in all the novels, what's pornography to do? Peter Porter. OBCoV *Fr.* The Sanitized Sonnets.

Now it's styrofoam pellets. White Trash. Jim Hall. MT

Now Jesus had not yet come to the village. John 11:30–44; Now Jesus had not yet come to the village. Bible, N.T. GI, *tr. by* Rainer Maria Rilke *Fr.* St. John.

Now Jesus stood before the governor. Matthew 27:11–24; Now Jesus stood before. Bible, N.T. GI, *tr. by* René Daumal *Fr.* St. Matthew.

Now Johnson would go up to join the [great] simulacra of men. Up Rising. Robert Duncan. APSN; NNaP *Fr.* Passages.

Now, Joy is born of parents poor. Joy and Pleasure. W. H. Davies. OBMV

Now kept it flat, and raked the walks and shrubs. (LL) His heart was in his garden; but his brain. Frederick Goddard Tuckerman. APN-2; NoP-4

Now kiss me, lovely Ganimede, for see. Jupiter and Ganimede. Thomas Heywood. FaBoSe

Now, ladies, if you'll listen, a story I'll relate. Pearl Bryan. *Unknown.* AmFP

Now leave the check-reins slack. To the Man after the Harrow. Patrick Kavanagh. CIP-2; GTBS-P

Now let forever the phlox and the rose be tended. The Hardy Garden. Edna St. Vincent Millay. GaP

Now let my habitude be where the vine. Descending Chestnut Ridge. Donald Davidson. FuPo *Fr.* Hermitage.

Now let no charitable hope. Let No Charitable Hope. Elinor Wylie. ColAP; LiLi; LiTM; MoAmPo; NAAL-2; NALW; NMM-2; OxBA; OxBSP; PiM; VGW

Now Let Our Hearts Their Glory Wake. Elizabeth Scott. AH

Now let the cycle sweep us here and there. Hilda Doolittle. VGW *Fr.* Sigil.

Now let the legless boy show the great lady. In the Children's Hospital. "Hugh MacDiarmid." NAEL-2

Now Liddesdale [*or* Liddesdale] has ridden a raid. Jock o' the Side. *Unknown.* ESPB; IBB; OxBB

Now Liddesdale [*or* Liddesdale] has lain long [*or* layen lang] in. Dick o' the Cow. *Unknown.* ESPB; IBB; OxBB

Now light the candles; one; two; there's a moth;. Repression of War Experience. Siegfried Sassoon. AF; CMoP; NSI; NoAM; PeFWW; PoE

Now lighted windows climb the dark. Manhattan Lullaby. Rachel Lyman Field. TLR

Now list and lithe, you gentlemen. Northumberland Betray[e]d by Douglas [*or* Dowglas]. *Unknown.* ESPB; OxBB

Now list you, lithe you, gentlemen. Robin Hood and Queen Katherine. *Unknown.* ESPB

Now listen I am speaking to you through the miracle of rice through steelwool through Japanese microphones. Election Speech for the Presidency of the United States of Chinamerica. David Avidan, *Hebrew*. IP, *tr. by* Warren Bargad *and* Stanley F. Chyet

Now, listen. / I want you new girls, every morning. To the Virgins, to Make the Most of Time. Gavin Ewart. OBCoV

Now listen! / If the stars shine. Vladimir Mayakovsky, *Russian*. TCRP, *tr. by* Bernard Meares

Now listen to boasting which leaves the heart dazed. Al-Samau'al ibn Adiya. TrJP, *tr. by* Hartwig Hirschfeld *Fr.* Are We Not the People.

Now London have I [for the sake]. Isabella Whitney. BWW *Fr.* The Manner of Her Will and What She Left to London and to All Those in It, at Her Departing. NoSic

Now look, you see, it's this way like. The Road to Hogan's Gap. Andrew Barton Paterson. CBAP

Now Lord, or never, they'l[l] believe [*or* beleeve] on Thee. On the Miracle of Loaves. Richard Crashaw. OxBSP

Now lufferis cummis with larges lowd. The Petition of the Gray Horse, Auld Dunbar. William Dunbar. OxBS

Now, Mamma, *couldn't* you? (LL) A Lesson for Mamma. Sydney Dayre. OBCA; OxBChV

Now manhood and garbroyls I chaunt, and martial horror. Virgil. BIrV; OBVE, *tr. by* Richard Stanyhurst *Fr.* The Aeneid [*or* Eneados, Aeneis].

Now may we turn aside and dry our tears. Inis Fal. Egan O'Rahilly, *Irish*. BIrV; OBMV, *tr. by* James Stephens

Now milkmaids' pails are deckt with flowers. Stool Ball. *Unknown.* CH

Now, miners, if you'll listen, I'll tell you quite a tale. Coming around the Horn. John A. Stone. AmFP

Now mirk December's dowie face. The Daft Days. Robert Fergusson. CABP; NOEC; OxAEP-1

Now more and more on my concern with the lifted waves of genius gaining. On the Ocean Floor. "Hugh MacDiarmid." FaBoMo; HAP

Now morning from her orient chamber came. To Hope. Keats. LaPo *Fr.* Imitation of Spenser.

Now Muse assist me, aptly to describe. Alec Derwent Hope. BXAP *Fr.* Dunciad Minor.

Now must all satisfaction. Certain Mercies. Robert Graves. GTBS-P

Now must I le[a]rn[e] to live [*or* lyve] at rest. Sir Thomas Wyatt. AAS; SiPS

Now must I mend my manners. Marbod of Rennes, *Latin*. MLL, *tr. by* Helen Waddell

Now must I these three praise. Friends. W. B. Yeats. FP; IIP; MoP; NoAM

Now my charms are all o'erthrown. Epilogue. Shakespeare. CTC *Fr.* The Tempest. OAEL-1

Now my charms are all o'erthrown. Shakespeare. *Fr.* The Tempest. OAEL-1

Now my fair'st friend. Some Flowers o' the Spring. Shakespeare. *Fr.* The Flowers of Perdita. *Fr.* The Winter's Tale.

Now my heart turns to and fro. Hatshepsut. WPOW, *tr. by* Mariam Lichtheim *Fr.* Obelisk Inscriptions.

Now my kinching-cove is gone. The Rum Mort's Praise of Her Faithless Maunder. *Unknown.* CBNP

Now my life has gained some meaning. Walther von der Vogelweide, *German.* GePo, *tr. by* J. W. Thomas

Now my old bawd is dead? (LL) John Kinsella's Lament for Mrs. Mary Moore. W. B. Yeats. CMoP; LiTM; OAEL-2; RB

Now, my son, is life for you. Wishes for My Son. Thomas Macdonagh. TIRV

Now, My Usefullness Over. Edwin Honig. NoAM

Now neghes the New Yere and the night passes. *Unknown.* EnVB *Fr.* Sir Gawain and the Green Knight. OAEL-1, *tr. by* Brian Stone

Now new old first day jump. (LL) The Fire. Robert Duncan. APSN; VGW

Now new-vamped silks the mercer's window shows. A Description of Spring in London. *Unknown.* NOEC

Now nobly tow'ring o'er the rest appears. The Battle in the balance. *Unknown.* OBCVT, *tr. by* Thomas Parnell *Fr.* Batrachomyomachia (The Battle of the Frogs and Mice).

Now, not a tear begun. A Woman Mourned by Daughters. Adrienne Rich. IMW; Poetr

Now, now's the time so soft by Truth. An Epithalamy to Sir Thomas Southwell and His Lady. Robert Herrick. CaPo

Now o'er the one half-world. Shakespeare. OxAEP-1 *Fr.* Macbeth.

Now o'er the sea from her old love comes she. I, 13. Elegy: Ad Auroram, ne properet. Ovid. FMP, *tr. by* Marlowe *Fr.* Elegies.

Now of that vision I, bereaven. Francis Thompson. MoBrPo *Fr.* Grace of the Way.

Now of wemen this I say for me. In Praise of Women. William Dunbar. CABP; NoP-4

Now on the first day of Unleavened Bread the disciples came to Jesus. Matthew 26:17–29. Bible, N.T. GI, *tr. by* Rainer Maria Rilke *Fr.* St. Matthew.

Now, on the moors where the guns bring down. The Guns. William Soutar. FaBoTC

Now on their coasts our conquering navy rides. Dryden. OxAEP-1 *Fr.* Annus Mirabilis.

Now once again the gloomy scene explore. The Pauper's Funeral. George Crabbe. OBNC *Fr.* The Village.

Now one in verse makes many more in prose. Alexander Pope. *See* 'Tis hard to say, if greater want of skill.

Now or Never. "Astra." BrRo

Now or Never. Judith Moffett. Son

Now ore the sea from her old Love comes she. Marlowe. PBRV *Fr.* Ovids Elegies Book 1.

Now, Parrot, my sweet bird, speak our yet once again. John Skelton. NoSic *Fr.* Speak [*or* Speke], Parrot.

Now Phillipa Is Gone. Anne Ridler. FaBoTw

Now piece by piece we slip away. Sergey Aleksandrovich Yesenin, *Russian.* TCRP, *tr. by* Geoffrey Thurley

Now pines lift. Carolyn Forché. *See* Burning the Tomato Worms.

Now Poem. For Us. Sonia Sanchez. PoBA

Now polish the crucible. Hilda Doolittle. NALW *Fr.* Tribute to the Angels.

Now ponder well, you parents dear. The Babes in the Wood. *Unknown.* EnSB; OBNV; OxAEP-1

Now Pontius Pilate is to judge the cause. Emilia Lanier. NALW; NOSC *Fr.* Salve Deus Rex Judaeorum.

"Now pray, where are you going, child?" [said Meet-on-the-Road]. Meet-on-the-Road. *Unknown.* OBSP; OTCP; TTTS

Now precedent songs, farewell—by every name farewell. Walt Whitman. NAAL-3

Now quenched each midnight window is. Now unimpeded. The Single Woman. Frances Darwin Cornford. WPN

"Now rede me, dear mither, a sonsy rede." The Mer-Man, and Marstig's Daughter. *Unknown, Danish.* AWP, *tr. by* Robert Jamieson

Now rest for evermore, my weary heart! A Sè Stesso. Giacomo Leopardi, *Italian.* AWP, *tr. by* Lorna De' Lucchi

Now rising shades a solemn scene display. Apollonius Rhodius. OBCVT, *tr. by* Francis Fawkes *Fr.* Argonautica.

Now Robin Hood, Will Scadlock and Little John. Robin Hood and the Prince of Aragon. *Unknown.* ESPB

Now rock the boat to a fare-thee-well. Rite of Passage. Audre Lorde. PoBA

Now, rocking horse! rocking horse! where shall we go? Through Nurseryland. *Unknown.* BoTP; OTCP

Now, said the cook, I will teach you. How to Stuff a Pepper. Nancy Willard. CrSp

Now seals the fair creation from my sight. (LL) To S. M., a Young African Painter, on Seeing His Works. Phillis Wheatley. BlSi; ColAP; NAAAL; NAAL-1; NAAL-3; NoP-4

Now secretness dies of the open. For the Nightly Ascent of the Hunter Orion over a Forest Clearing. James Dickey. TwCP

Now, Serena, be not coy. To His Love When He Had Obtained Her. Sir Walter Ralegh. NoSic

Now shal y tellen to ye, y wis. The Lay of the Ettercap. John Leyden. BXAP

Now shall I make my soul. W. B. Yeats. *Fr.* The Tower. CMoP; LiTM; NoAM; PoE; SCGP

Now shall I unseal myself to yourself alone. The Husband's Message. *Unknown, Anglo-Saxon.* EEP, *tr. by* Michael Alexander

Now shall I walk. The Best Friend. W. H. Davies. OBMV

Now shall the praises of the Lord be sung. The First Song of Moses. George Wither. ChIV-1

Now shall we see, that nature hath no end. George Chapman. PoEL-2 *Fr.* Bussy d'Ambois.

Now she burn[e]s as well as I. Song: To Her Again[e], She Burning in a Fe[a]ver. Thomas Carew. SeCP

Now She Is like the White Tree-Rose. C. Day Lewis. CMoP; FaBoTw; MoBrPo *Fr.* From Feathers to Iron.

Now she is unadorned. Milo De Angelis, *Italian.* NeIt, *tr. by* Lawrence Venuti

Now she's dead, I'll draw the line. (LL) Oh, My Darling Clementine. Percy Montross. AmFP; FaBoBe; OBAL

Now she's ninety I walk through the local park. A Winter Visit. Dannie Abse. NoAM

Now shout into my dream. These trumpets snored. Farewell in a Dream. Stephen Spender. MoBrPo

Now show thy joy, frolic in Angels' sight. Leviathan. Jay Macpherson. MoCV

Now side by side, with like unweary'd care. Ajax and his Brother. Homer. OBVE, *tr. by* Alexander Pope *Fr.* The Iliad.

Now since Sophia have a-crossed the sea. (LL) Young Beichan. *Unknown.* AmFP; EnSB

Now since the members of the world we view. Lucretius. OBVE, *tr. by* Thomas Creech *Fr.* De Rerum Natura (On the Nature of Things).

Now sing we, as we were wont. John Skelton. SCGP

Now sinks another day to rest. The Bull. Vita Sackville-West. WPE

Now sits the autumn cricket in the grass. Autumn. Edna St. Vincent Millay. LBC

Now sitting, I think, 'twixt thee and me! (LL) Jock o' the Side. *Unknown.* ESPB; IBB; OxBB

Now skrinketh rose and lilie-flour. *Unknown.* MiEL

Now sleep, bind fast the flood of air. Bridal Song. George Chapman. OxBSP *Fr.* The Masque of the Middle Temple and Lincoln's Inn.

Now sleep mountain-top and chasm. The Creatures Rest. Alkman, *Greek.* APo, *tr. by* John Hollander

Now Sleep My Little Child So Dear. Casper Kriebel, *German.* AH, *tr. by* Sheema Z. Buehne

Now Snow Descends. Jean Garrigue. WPE

Now so beautiful. Parting. Hanmo Chong, *Korean.* CKP, *tr. by* Jaihiun Kim

Now so high. The Swing. Mary I. Osborn. BoTP

Now so many people that are living. Thank You: A Poem in Seventeen Parts. *Unknown, Seneca Indian.* STP, *tr. by* Richard Johnny John *and* Jerome Rothenberg

Now some may drink old vintage wine. Early Morning Meadow Song. Charles Dalmon. CH

Now spears lift them by their ribs. Dog Sacrifice at Lake Ronkonkoma. William Heyen. AmPA

Now Spring returning beckons the little boats. Priapos of the Harbor. Antipater of Sidon, *Greek.* GrAn, *tr. by* Dudley Fitts

Now springes, *etc.* (LL) Now Springs the Spray. *Unknown.* MiEL; OAEL-1; PoE

Now springes the spray. Now Springs the Spray. *Unknown.* MiEL; OAEL-1; PoE

Now Springs the Spray. *Unknown.* MiEL; OAEL-1; PoE

Now stamp the Lord's Prayer on a grain of rice. Dylan Thomas. FaBoMo *Fr.* A Sequence of Sonnets.

Now stands our love on that still verge of day. James Agee. *Fr.* Sonnets. MoAmPo

Now stern Æneas waves his weighty Spear. End. Virgil, *Latin.* OBCVT, *tr. by* John Dryden

Now stoops the sun, and dies day's cheerful light. The Gauls Sacrifice. Charles Montague Doughty. FaBoTw *Fr.* The Dawn in Britain.

Now stop you noses, Readers, all and come. Og [and Doeg]. John Dryden *and* Nahum Tate. AWP *Fr.* Absalom and Achitophel, Pt. II.

Now strike your sailes, ye jolly mariners. Edmund Spenser. *Fr.* Wood Of Error. AEP

Now, suddenly, the table rocks, a bell. Séance. William Abrahams. NYBP

Now sulkies come haunting softwheeled down the. The Ghost at Anlaby. Randolph Stow. NOBAu

Now sunk the sun, now twilight sunk, and night. A Rhapsody, Written at the Lakes in Westmorland. John Brown. NOEC

Now supposing the French or the Neopolitan soldier. Claude to Eustace. Arthur Hugh Clough. PeLV *Fr.* Amours de Voyage. NOBVV

Now swarthy Summer, by rude health embrowned. Summer Images. John Clare. OBNC

Now take my word for jewel in the open light. Audre Lorde. *See* Coal.

Now take your fill of love and glee. A Double Ballad of Good Counsel. François Villon, *French.* AWP, *tr. by* Swinburne

Now tell me, my merry woodman. The Estray. Forceythe Willson. APN-2

Now tell me where my easy rider gone. Easy Rider Blues. Blind Lemon Jefferson. GM

Now thank we all our God. Martin Rinckhart, *German.* GePo

Now that all your distance surrounds me. Distance. Andrea Zanzotto, *Italian.* VCWP, *tr. by* Ruth Feldman *and* Brian Swann

Now that black ground and bushes. Winter Sketches. Charles Reznikoff. PoA

Now that Fate is dead and gone. Song. Dame Edith Sitwell. MoBrPo

Now that he's free, relatively, often he shuffles. The Holiday. Hans Magnus Enzensberger, *German.* VCWP, *tr. by* Hans Magnus Enzensberger *and* Michael Hamburger

Now that high, oft-affronted bosom heaves. To the Lady Portrayed by Margaret Dumont. John Hollander. OBAL, PoA

Now that his name has turned to elegy. Photo of My Father in a Snowbound Train. David Wojahn. GM

Now that I am fifty-six. Rondel. Muriel Rukeyser. NoP-4

Now That I Am Forever with Child. Audre Lorde. CrSp; NAAAL; NALW; PoBA; Poetr

Now That I Am Never Alone. Tess Gallagher. NAmP90

Now that I have your face by heart, I look. Song for the Last Act. Louise Bogan. NYBP; NoP-4; UnPo; WPE

Now that I have your hand, let me persuade you. One Last Word. John Glassco. NOBC

Now that I have your heart by heart, I see. (LL) Song for the Last Act. Louise Bogan. NYBP; NoP-4; UnPo; WPE

Now that I know. Knowledge. Louise Bogan. PoA

Now that I, tying thy glass mask tightly. Laboratory, The [Ancien Régime]. Robert Browning. EnVR; NAEL-2; OBEV

Now that I've been married for almost four weeks, Mama. Daughter's Difficulties as a Wife, A: Mrs. Reuben Chandler to Her Mother in New Orleans. Anne Stevenson. OxBM

Now that I've nearly done my days. The Things That Matter. Edith Nesbit. OxBTC; VWP

Now that I've wasted. My Alba. Allen Ginsberg. CLPP; NOBA

Now that my seagoing self-possession wavers. Autobiography. Charles Causley. LiTM; Son

Now that night is creeping. Evensong. C. S. Lewis. TIRV; TrCP

Now that of absence the most irksome night. Sonnet 89. Sir Philip Sidney. NAEL-1 *Fr.* Astrophil and Stella. AAS; SiPS

Now that peasantry is in vogue. Coolie Odyssey. David Dabydeen. NBrP

"Now that poor, wayward Jane is big with child." Repentance. Louis Untermeyer. NBLV

Now that the April of your youth adorns. Edward Herbert, 1st Baron Herbert of Cherbury. OxAEP-1

Now that the barbarians have got as far as Picra. Translation. Roy Fuller. NOBE; OxBTC

Now that the day is done. Centaur Song. Hilda Doolittle. VGW

Now that the hearth [or harth] is crowned [or crown'd] with smiling fire. Ode. To Sir William Sydney, on His Birthday. Ben Jonson. BeJo

Now that the men have gone off to the choleric wars. The Stay Behind. Andrew Elliott. PNI

Now that the midd day heate doth scorch my shame. William Alabaster. ESCV *Fr.* Divine Meditations. Son

Now that the others are gone, all of them, forever. Tomorrow. Kenneth Fearing. CMoP

Now, that the public sorrow doth subside. To the Pious Memory of C. W. Esquire. Henry Vaughan. PeECV

Now that the red glare of thy fall is blown. Francis Thompson. OBNC *Fr.* Ode to the Setting Sun.

Now that the sky and earth and wind are still. Petrarch. ItIP

Now that the time has come wherein. Advice from Poor Robin's Almanack. *Unknown.* OBCP

Now that the time seems all mine. Patrizia Cavalli, *Italian.* VCWP, *tr. by* Judith Baumel

Now that the triumphant march has entered the last street corners. Come Thunder. Christopher Okigbo. PBMAP; VCWP

Now that the Village-Reverence doth lye [*or* lie] hid. A New Year's Gift. William Cartwright. OxAEP-1

Now that the war is over. A Downed Black Pilot Learns How to Fly. Horace Coleman. CDa

Now that the Winter's gone, the earth hath lost. The Spring. Thomas Carew. BeJo; CaPo; CavPo; NoP-4; PBRV; PoE; PoEL-3

Now that the world is all in a maze. The Unconcerned. Thomas Flatman. FaBoCh; NOSC

Now that the young buds are tipped with a falling sun. Early Spring. Sidney Keyes. MoBrPo

Now that these wings to speed my wish ascend. The Philosophic Flight. Giordano Bruno, *Italian.* AWP, *tr. by* John Addington Symonds

Now that they've got it settled whose I be. The Pauper Witch of Grafton. Robert Frost. *Fr.* Two Witches. CMoP

Now that time seems all mine. Patrizia Cavalli, *Italian.* NeIt; VCWP, *tr. by* Judith Baumel

Now that we are on our own I can explain this secret stave. *Unknown. See* The Husband's Message.

Now that we move and we breathe apart. You Have to Strike Back. Kate Lilley. BMAP

Now that we're almost settled in our house. In Memory of Major Robert Gregory. W. B. Yeats. EBEV; OAEL-2; SCGP

Now that we're alone we can talk prince man to man. Elegy of Fortinbras. Zbigniew Herbert, *Polish.* CEEP; FaBoPV; PoSu, *tr. by* Czeslaw Milosz; VCWP; BLT, *tr. by* Czeslaw Milosz *and* Peter Dale Scott

Now that we've come to the end. The Avenue. Paul Muldoon. PBCIP

Now that we've done our best and worst, and parted. The Busy Heart. Rupert Brooke. MoBrPo

Now that you have gone. Except. Wendell Berry. EC2

Now that your ship is ready, Susan, that hoop skirt sailing. Museum Piece. Angela Sorby. BAP-95

Now that your sons are dust. (LL) Father of Women, A [Ad Sororem E. B.]. Alice Thompson Meynell. VWP

Now the bat circles on the breeze of eve. Sonnet. Ann Radcliffe. WPE

Now the birds. Outside My Cabin. Wayne Dodd. CMAP

Now the birds begin to crow. It is time for them to crow. Blues for the Lonely. Jeremy Robson. SeSe

Now the birth of Jesus Christ took place in this way. Matthew 1:18–25; Now the birth of Jesus Christ took place. Bible, N.T. GI, *tr. by* philip Appleman *Fr.* St. Matthew.

Now the bitter pangs of hope deferred. The Mail Has Come. Mary E. Tucker. CBWP-1

Now the bright crocus flames, and now. In the Spring. Meleager, *Greek.* AWP, *tr. by* Andrew Lang

Now the bright morning Star, Dayes [*or* day's] harbinger. Song: on [*or* of] May Morning. Milton. CH; PBRV

Now the crops grow green and the fields flourish with life. Request for Meat and Drink. Sedulius Scottus, *Latin.* NOIV

Now the crossing, now the crossing! The Crossing. Aleksandr Trifonovich Tvardovsky. TCRP, *tr. by* April FitzLyon *Fr.* Vasily Tyorkin.

Now the day is over. Hymn. Sabine Baring-Gould. OxBChV; WHSW

Now the declining fulgent orb of day. Sir John Collings Squire. BXAP *Fr.* Doris and Philemon.

Now the declining sun 'gan downwards bend. The Nightingale. William Strode, *after the Latin of* Famianus Strada. OBVE

Now the dreary winter's over. Spring Song. Nahum, *Hebrew.* TrJP, *tr. by* Emma Lazarus

Now the eleven disciples went to Galilee. Matthew 28:16–20; Now the eleven disciples went to Galilee. Bible, N.T. GI, *tr. by* W. B. Yeats *Fr.* St. Matthew.

Now the eyes of my eyes are opened. (LL) I thank You God for most this amazing. E. E. Cummings. APAD; MeMAP; NTP; TAP; TrCP

Now the fingers and toes are formed. Magnificat. Chana Bloch. CrSp

Now the fireflies of our youth. Kenneth Rexroth. APSN *Fr.* The Love Poems of Marichiko.

Now the golden morn aloft. Thomas Gray. GTBS-P; NOEC *Fr.* Ode on the Pleasure Arising from Vicissitude.

Now the green plane-tree hides the lovers, hides the lovers'/ rites. Thallus, *Greek.* GrAn, *tr. by* Edwin Morgan

Now the hard margin bears us on, while steam. Dante. *Fr.* Inferno. NAWM-1, *tr. by* John Ciardi *Fr.* Divina Commedia.

Now the heart sings with all its thousand voices. The Gateway. Alec Derwent Hope. BoLoP

Now the Holy Lamp of Love. Patrick MacDonogh. BIrV

Now the Hungry Lion Roars. The Fairy Blessing. Shakespeare. CH; CTC; OxBoLi *Fr.* A Midsummer Night's Dream.

Now the ice lays its smooth claws on the sill. Scotland's Winter. Edwin Muir. OxBS; OxBTC

Now the idea is to aim a camera on one tree from morning until. Absolutely. David Ignatow. BAP-93

Now the Laborer's Task Is O'er. John Lodge Ellerton. BLPA

Now the last day of many days. To Jane: The Recollection. Shelley. GTBS-P; OBNC

Now the late fruits are in. For a Wine Festival. Vernon Watkins. OxBTC

Now the Leaves Are Falling Fast. W. H. Auden. CMoP

Now the leaves are still. O. Mabson Southard. HA

Now the light o' the west is a-turn'd to gloom. Evenen in the Village. William Barnes. EBVV

Now the little green blackbird liked a mouse. Because It's Good to Keep Things Straight. Kenneth Patchen. CBNP

Now the long blade of the sun, lying. Thebes of the Seven Gates. Sophocles. *Fr.* Antigone. NAWM-1, *tr. by* Robert Fagles.

Now the lotuses in the imperial lake. Wang Ch'ing-hui, *Chinese.* BoWoP, *tr. by* Kenneth Rexroth *and* Ling Chung

Now the lusty spring is seen. Love's Emblems. John Fletcher. BoLoP; NOBE; NOSC *Fr.* The Tragedy of Valentinian.

Now the moisty wood discloses. Spring Morning. Frances Darwin Cornford. BoTP

Now the moon is. Sinking Rising. Dahlia Ravikovitch, *Hebrew.* IP, *tr. by* Warren Bargad *and* Stanley F. Chyet

Now the narrowing track. The Look. Elizabeth Daryush. PoA

Now the New Moon is hanging, having cast away his bone. New Moon. *Aborigine Oral Tradition. Fr.* Moon-Bone Song [*or* Cycle]. CBAP, *tr. by* R. M. Berndt

Now the People Have the Light. Charles G. Ballard. VoR

Now the pines lift. Burning the Tomato Worms. Carolyn Forché. AmPA

Now the pumpkin is ripe. A Letter to a Son. Charles Mungoshi. PeSAV

Now the rain is falling, freshly, in the intervals between sunlight. Spring Rain. Robert Hass. PaTW

Now! The Red Tobacco has come to strike your soul. *Unknown.* STP *Fr.* Run toward the Nightland.

Now the rich cherry, whose sleek wood. Country Summer. Léonie Adams. LiTM; MoAmPo

Now the river is rich, but her voice is low. The River in March. Ted Hughes. OxBC

Now the seasons are closing their files. Year's End. Ted Kooser. PBCAP

Now the serpent was more subtil than any beast of the field. Bible, *O.T.* OxBoV *Fr.* Genesis.

Now the shiades o' the elems da stratch muore an muore. Evening, and Maidens. William Barnes. OBEV

Now the spade. Rod Willmot. HA

Now the summer is grown old. Autumn. Charlotte Zolotow. AYFP

Now the sun's gane out o' sight. Up in the Air. Allan Ramsay. NOEC

Now the swing is still. Nicholas Virgilio. HA; KaS

Now the thing the Negro has GOT to do—. View from the Corner. Samuel Allen. SSLK

Now the thinkers our old ones remember. Dance of the Rain Gods. *Unknown, Cora Indian.* STP, *tr. by* Anselm Hollo

Now the trouble with SETting down a: written calypso. Calypsomania. Anthony Brode. PeLV

Now the twin-light of my eyes. Bible, *O.T. See* Psalm 121.

Now the waves murmur. Torquato Tasso. ItIP

Now the white violet blooms and narcissus that loves. Meleager. HePo, *tr. by* Barbara Hughes Fowler *Fr.* I'll Twine White Violets. NIP-4, *tr. by* Goldwin Smith

Now the winds are all composure. St. Philip and St. James. Christopher Smart. NOCV; NOEC *Fr.* Hymns and Spiritual Songs for the Fasts and Festivals of the Church of England.

Now Thebes stood in good estate, now Cadmus might thou say. Acteon. Ovid. CTC, *tr. by* Arthur Golding *Fr.* Metamorphoses.

Now then, take your seats! for Glasgow and the North. The Night Mail North. Henry Cholmondeley-Pennell. EBVV

Now then, what are you up to, Dai? Langwell. Kingsley Amis. NOBL; OxBC *Fr.* The Evans Country.

Now there are gold reflections on the water. In Time of Gold. Hilda Doolittle. PoA

Now there are no bonds except the flesh; listen. Manzini; Escape Artist. Gwendolyn MacEwen. NOBC

Now there comes / The Christmas rose. New Year's [*or* Year] Song. Ted Hughes. OBCP

Now there is none of the living who can remember. Epitaph for a Concord Boy. Stanley Young. ChAP

Now there was a man of the Pharisees, named Nicode'mus. John 3:1–15; Now there was a man. Bible, N.T. GI, *tr. by* Howard Nemerov *Fr.* St. John.

Now there's many fool things a woman will do. Gold Tooth Blues. Tennessee Williams. OBAL

Now they are trying to make you. For W C W. Harvey Shapiro. WeT

Now they have two cars to clean. Do It Yrself. Larry Eigner. NeAP; PoM

Now they're pillaging the last coast. The Vandals. Jenny Mastoraki, *Modern Greek.* BoWoP, *tr. by* Nikos Germanakos

Now thin mists temper the slow-ripening beams. The Garden in September. Robert Bridges. GaP; OBGa

Now this bloody war is over. Song. George Barker. PeLV

Now this is my first counsel. Counsels of Sigrdrifa. *Unknown.* AWP; OBVE *Fr.* The Elder Edda.

Now this particular girl. Spinster. Sylvia Plath. FaBoWP; LW; SoSe-8

Now this is my first counsel. Counsels of Sigrdrifa. *Unknown.* AWP; OBVE *Fr.* The Elder Edda.

Now thou art dead, no eye shall ever see. Upon His Spaniel[l] Tracie [*or* Tracy]. Robert Herrick. BeJo

Now thou hast lov'd [*or* loved] me one whole day. Woman's Constancy. Donne. ESCV; FMP; FSCP; NBLV; NOSC; NoP-4; SAGP

Now through Night's Caressing Grip. W. H. Auden. PoRA

Now through the ocean in great haste they plunder. Luis de Camões. *Fr.* The Lusiads. OBVE, *tr. by* Sir Richard Fanshawe

Now Time's Andromeda on this rock rude. Andromeda. Gerard Manley Hopkins. EBEV; FaBoMo; OxAEP-2; SCGP

Now to a softer theme descends my muse. On Richmond Park. Stephen Duck. OBGa *Fr.* On Richmond Park.

Now to Aurora, borne by dappled steeds. Walter Savage Landor. NOBRP *Fr.* Gebir.

Now to be clean he must abandon himself. The Swan Bathing. Ruth Pitter. MoBrPo

Now to depart from all this complication. The Departure of the Prodigal Son. Rilke, *German.* GI, *tr. by* David Curzon, Lori Seibel *and* Will Alexander Washburn

Now to dispose the dead, the care remains. Execution of the faithless maids. Homer, *Greek.* OBCVT, *tr. by* Alexander Pope; OBVE, *tr. by* Pope *Fr.* Odyssey. NAWM-1, *tr. by* Robert Fitzgerald

Now to Great Britain we must make our way. Of England, and of Its Marvels. Fazio degli Uberti, *Italian.* AWP, *tr. by* D. G. Rossetti

Now to meet only in dreams. Yakamochi, *Japanese.* OHPJ, *tr. by* Kenneth Rexroth

Now, to tense stillness as the door is slammed. Their Thoughts Cling to Everything They See on the Way. Allen Afterman. NOBAu

Now to th'ascent of that steep savage hill. Satan Journeys to the Garden of Eden. Milton. *Fr.* Book IV. OAEL-1 *Fr.* Paradise Lost.

Now to you my Country wench I'le bringe. The 4th Sheppard Speakes This. Lady Jane Cavendish. KTR *Fr.* A Pastorall.

Now toils the Heroe; trees on trees o'erthrown. Homer. OBVE, *tr. by* Pope *Fr.* Odyssey. NAWM-1, *tr. by* Robert Fitzgerald

Now touch the air softly. A Pavane for the Nursery. William Jay Smith. ITG; MoAmPo

Now tow'rd the Hunter's gloomy sides we came. The Hospital Prison Ship. Philip Freneau. AmPP *Fr.* The British Prison Ship.

Now trouble comes between the forest's selves. Russian New Year. Bill Berkson. PmAP

Now twenty springs had clothed the park with green. The Toilette. John Gay. ECEV

Now upon sale, a bankrupt island. John Byrom. *Fr.* Four Epigrams on the Naturalization Bill. NOBL

Now upon this piteous year. The Stranger. Jean Garrigue. LiTM; NOBA; TwCP

Now van to van the foremost squadrons meet. Dryden. OBWP *Fr.* Annus Mirabilis.

Now Voyager / how do you see—. Elegy for Jack Moffat. Charlotte Painter. IMW

Now—wagon full of thunder. Wagon Full of Thunder. Louis Oliver. HATNAP

Now war and vengeance claim. The Death of Sohráb. Firdausi. TAL, *tr. by* James Atkinson *Fr.* The Shahnamah.

Now war is all the world about. Ode on His Majesty's Proclamation. Sir Richard Fanshawe. NOBE *Fr.* Il Pastor Fido.

Now was there made fast by the touris wall. James I, King of Scotland. *See* The King is Quair.

Now was there maid fast by the towris wall. The King is Quair. James I, King of Scotland. EBEV *Fr.* The Kingis Quair.

Now watch this autumn that arrives. Song at the Beginning of Autumn. Elizabeth Jennings. OxBTC

Now we are back to normal, now the mind is. Louis MacNeice. CMoP; OxAEP-2 *Fr.* Autumn Journal.

Now we are left out. Funeral Song. *Unknown, Sotho.* PeSA, *tr. by* Dan Kunene *and* Jack Cope

Now we enter a strange world, where the Hessian Christmas. After the Industrial Revolution, All Things Happen at Once. Robert Bly. CoAP; CoAmPo

Now we flourish / as others have / before. *Unknown, Greek.* GrAn, *tr. by* Peter Jay

Now we have always with us these men—these men! Memo. Hildegarde Flanner. NYBP

Now we have buried the face we never knew. Easter, 1968. May Sarton. CrSp

Now we have heard stories of high valor. *Unknown, Armenian.* CABP, *tr. by* Ruth P. M. Lehmann

Now we must get up quickly. Two Lines from the Brothers Grimm. Gregory Orr. AmPA

Now we must praise the Guardian of Heaven. Cædmon's Hymn. Caedmon, *Anglo-Saxon.* ASW, *tr. by* Kevin Crossley-Holland

Now weary labourers perceivem well pleased. Evening. Joanna Baillie. ECWP *Fr.* A Summer Day.

Now welcom[e], Somer [*or* Summer] with thy sunne soft. Roundel. Chaucer. CTC; EnLoPo; HAP; OAEL-1; OPOU; OxBSP *Fr.* The Parlement of Foules.

Now we'll never, etc. (LL) Sheath and Knife. *Unknown.* CH; ESPB

Now we're met, my brethren Benchers. The Humours of the King's Bench Prison, a Ballad. Leonard Howard. NOEC

Now we're stuck there. Heaving the Lead Line. *Unknown.* AmFP

Now westward Sol had spent the richest beam[e]s. Music[k]'s Duel[l]. Richard Crashaw. GeHe; OAEL-1; SeCP

Now we've made a child. And What About the Children. Audre Lorde. PoBA

Now what do you think. *Unknown.* OxNR

Now what do you think of that! (LL) Catkin. *Unknown.* ACTP; CTV

Now what in the world shall we dioux. The Sioux. Eugene Field. GoJo-1

Now what my mother told me one day as we sat at dinner / together. Walt Whitman. BLT *Fr.* "Sleepers," The.

Now what will we do for timber. Cill Chais. *Unknown, Irish.* NOIV, *tr. by* Thomas Kinsella

Now what you Get, but what you. Of Giving. Arthur Guiterman. CTV

Now what's here a Hee cave, as was a Shee. The 3d Sheppard Speakes This to the Rest. Lady Jane Cavendish. KTR *Fr.* A Pastorall.

Now, when he and I meet, after all these years. Bitch. Carolyn Kizer. NMM-2

Now when I have thrust my body. To Forget Me. Theodore Weiss. CoAP

Now when I walk around at lunchtime. Personal Poem. Frank O'Hara. CAPP-1; CLPP; PmAP

Now when Jesus was born in Bethlehem of Judea in the days of Herod the king. Matthew 2:1–12. Now when Jesus was born. Bible, N.T. GI, *tr. by* T. S. Eliot *Fr.* St. Matthew.

Now when the solemn Rites of Pray'r were past. The Sacrifice to Apollo. Homer. OBVE, *tr. by* Dryden *Fr.* The Iliad.

Now when thy folke are fed and clad. Isabella Whitney. BWW *Fr.* The Manner of Her Will and What She Left to London and to All Those in It, at Her Departing. NoSic

Now, when twelve days compleat had run their Race. Thetis Asks Jove to Revenge Her Son Achilles. Homer, *Greek.* OBVE, *tr. by* Dryden *Fr.* The Iliad.

Now where's a song for our small dear. The Unwritten Song. Ford Madox Ford. BoTP

Now, whether it were by peculiar grace. Wordsworth. UV *Fr.* Resolution and Independence. EBEV; FHYEP; HAP; InPS-3; NOBE; NOBRP; NOCV; NoP-4; OAEL-2; OBNC; OxAEP-2; PoEL-4; Ro; TFi

Now which is wrong or right? Too glib we talk. Falkland at Newbury, 1643. Hugh Conway. EBVV

Now, while amid those dainty downs and dales. To His Pandora, from England. Alexander Craig. Son

Now, while the birds thus sing a joyous song. Wordsworth. *Fr.* Ode: Intimations of Immortality [from Recollections of Early Childhood]. AWP; FHYEP; HAP; HeIP-4; NOBE; NOBRP; OAEL-2; OBEV; OBNC, PBMP; PoE; PoEL-4

Now, while thou hast the wondrous power of word. The Gift of Speech. Sadi. AWP, *tr. by* L. Cranmer-Byng *Fr.* The Gulistan.

Now Whitehall's in the grave. A Mock Song. Richard Lovelace. BeJo; CaPo

Now who could take you off to tiny life. The Independent Man. Gwendolyn Brooks. *Fr.* A Street in Bronzeville. BPo; BlSi; FaBoWP

Now who is he on earth that lives. *Unknown. Fr.* Medieval Norman Song. AWP, *tr. by* John Addington Symonds

Now whyle Hippomenes/ Debates theis things. Ovid. OBVE, *tr. by* Arthur Golding *Fr.* Metamorphoses.

Now will I a lover be. The Combat. Thomas Stanley. AWP

Now will I open unto thee—whose heart. *Unknown.* TAL, *tr. by* Sir Edward Arnold *Fr.* The Bhagavad-Gita.

Now will you stand for me, in this cool light. Love in the Museum. Adrienne Rich. NYBP

Now wind torments the field. February: Thinking of Flowers. Jane Kenyon. LoL

Now winedrinkers, this way to an airy shrine. A Musical Wine-Jar. Hedylos, *Greek.* GrAn, *tr. by* William Moebius

Now winter downs the dying of the year. Year's End. Richard Wilbur. CoAP; HeIP-4; LiTM; NAAL-2; NYBP

Now winter nights enlarge. Thomas Campion. AAS; EBEV; NOSC; NTP; NoP-4; OxAEP-1; PBRV

Now Winter's winds are banished from the sky. Spring. Meleager, *Greek.* AWP, *tr. by* William M. Hardinge

Now / with your head thrown back. I Tell of Another Young Death. César Tiempo, *Spanish.* TrJP, *tr. by* Donald Devenish Walsh

Now, with your palms on the blades of my shoulders. Dead Still. Andrey Andreievich Voznesensky, *Russian.* BoLoP; LoP, *tr. by* Richard Wilbur

Now wol I seye my tale, if ye wol heere. Chaucer. *See* The Wife of Bath's Prologue.

Now wolde I fayne sum merthis [*or* faine some merthes] mak[e]. Song for My Lady. A. Godwin. CH; MiEL; OxBoLi

Now would to God swift ships had ne'er been made! Sopolis. Callimachus, *Greek.* AWP, *tr. by* William M. Hardinge

Now wretched *Oedipus,* depriv'd of Sight. Publius Papinius Statius. OBCVT, *tr. by* Alexander Pope *Fr.* The Thebaid.

Now, wrought the charm, with potent sway. Stealing the Golden Fleece. Apollonius Rhodius, *Greek.* OBCVT, *tr. by* William Preston

Now, yield thee, or by Him who made. Sir Walter Scott. OxBS *Fr.* The Lady of the Lake.

Now, yields you, with some sighs, our explanation. (LL) To R. B. Gerard Manley Hopkins. CMoP; EPCY; EnVR; GTBS-P; OAEL-2; OxAEP-2

Now you are dead. (LL) Lines for an Interment. Archibald MacLeish. CMoP; NOBA

Now you are going, what can I do but wish you. The Poet's Farewell to His Teeth. William Dickey. PoA

Now you are standing face to face with the clear light. Prayer for the Little Daughter between Death and Burial. Diana Scott. BrRo

Now you can see him, exactly as he came. Herakles. Parrhasios, *Greek.* GrAn, *tr. by* Peter Jay

Now you come again. Happiness of 6 A.M. Harvey Shapiro. NYBP

Now, you great stanza, you heroic mould. Single Sonnet. Louise Bogan. Son

Now You Have Burned. John Thompson. NOBC

Now you have come. The Foot-Washing. A. R. Ammons. ChIV-2

Now you have freely given me leave to love. To a Lady That Desired I Would Love Her. Thomas Carew. BeJo; CBLP; CaPo; CavPo; MeLP; SCGP

Now you have stabbed her good. Kreutzer Sonata. Ted Hughes. FaBoMo

Now you lie—a grape-offering. Moiro, *Greek.* GrAn, *tr. by* Fleur Adcock

Now you love me. Divorce Song. *Unknown, Tsimshian Indian.* STP, *tr. by* Carl Cary

"Now you must die," the young one said. The Rite. Dudley Randall. HoPM

Now you take ol Rufus. He beat drums. For Freckle-Faced Gerald. Etheridge Knight. BPo

Now you think that is right, sah? Talk the truth. The Carpenter's Complaint. Edward Baugh. HCP; OBCoV; PBCV

Now you will feel no rain. *Apache Oral Tradition, Apache.* ITG, *tr. by Unknown*

Now You're Content. André Spire, *French.* TrJP, *tr. by* Stanley Burnshaw

Now you've learned not to let your eyes. Battle Lines. John C. Schafer. CDa

Nowadays the mess is everywhere. The Survivors. Daryl Hine. TwCP

Nowhere else but on the mouth. How He Should Like to Be Kissed. Paul Fleming, *German.* GePo, *tr. by* Harold B. Segel

Nowhere else does screened porch wire. Marriage Portrait. James Applewhite. MT

Nowhere, not among the warriors at their festival. Atimantiyar, *Tamil.* WPOW, *tr. by* A. K. Ramanujan

Nowhere, nowhere is there any trace of blood. No Sign of Blood. Faiz Ahmad Faiz, *Arabic.* AF, *tr. by* Naomi Lazard

Nowhere on the leaves. Tanka. Shaku Chōkū, *Japanese.* MJT, *tr. by* Makoto Ueda

Nowhere Water, The. Mark Rudman. FiLi

Now's the time for mirth and play. For Saturday. Christopher Smart. FaBoCh; NOEC; NOxBChV; OxBChV *Fr.* Hymns for the Amusement of Children.

Nox Nocti Indicat Scientiam. William Habington. BeJo; MeLP; NOBE; OBEV; SCGP *Fr.* Castara.

Nox was lit by lux of Luna, The. Carmen Possum. *Unknown.* BLPA; NBLV

Nozizwe. Raymond Mazisi Kunene, *Zulu.* PeSAV, *tr. by the author*

Ntabuu / Ntabuu Selina and. The Sisters. Alexis De Veaux. GLP

Nu-numma-kwiten formerly sang. The Song of Nu-Numma-Kwiten. *Unknown, Bushman.* PeSA

Nu-plastik Fanfare Red. Judith Rodriguez. BMAP

Nu thu, unsely body, upon bere list. *Unknown.* MiEL

Nuances of a Theme by Williams. Wallace Stevens. CMoP

Nub. Chris Wallace-Crabbe. BMAP

Nuchal, a Fragment. Thomas Kinsella. PBCIP

Nuclear ecstasy on the picket line. Cheap Replicas of the Eiffel Tower. Elton Glaser. PBCAP

Nuclear Umbrella. Herberto Padilla, *Spanish.* AF, *tr. by Alastair Reid*

Nude Descending a Staircase. X. J. Kennedy. APAD; CoAmPo; HoPM; NIP-4; OxBSP; PoA; SAGP

Nude in a Fountain. Norman MacCaig. OxBS

Nude Study. Yusef Komunyakaa. BAP-96

Nude Swim, The. Anne Sexton. WPE

Nudes—stark and glistening. Louse Hunting. Isaac Rosenberg. EBEV; NAEL-2; NSI; NoAM; NoP-4; OxAEP-2; OxBTC; PeFWW

Nudities. André Spire, *French.* AWP, *tr. by Jethro Bithell;* TrJP, *tr. by Stanley Burnshaw*

Nudo de Claridad. Miguel Algarin. PmAP

Nudus Redibo. Thomas Flatman. OxBSP

Nuit Blanche: North End. Conrad Potter Aiken. OxBA

Nulla Fides. Patrick Carey. SCGP

Nullarbor. William Hart-Smith. BMAP

Number Four. Doughtry Long. PoBA

Number of positions to take with respect to the present, A. The Form of Chiasmus; The Chiasmus of Forms. Michael Davidson. PmAP

Number One / I slouch in bed. Two Hangovers. James Wright. LCAP-2

Number one is a good clean number, The. The Million. Peter Redgrove. OxBC

Number seems more honest than the poem, The. Poem at Forty. Chung-hee Moon, *Korean.* CKP, *tr. by Jaihiun Kim*

#2, Shoes. Elizabeth Cohen. WWSi

Number, Weight, and Measure. Abraham Cowley. NOSC *Fr. Davideis.*

Numberless wonders / terrible wonders walk the world but none the match for man—. Sophocles. GrIP *Fr. Antigone.* NAWM-1, *tr. by Robert Fagles*

Numbers. Bible, *O.T. See also* Bible, Numbers.

  Balaam's Blessing. OBVE, *tr. by William Tyndale*

  Benediction. OBVE, *tr. by William Tyndale*

  (Blessing of the Priests.) TrJP

  Song of the Well. TrJP

Numbers in ass, The. Strato, *Greek.* GrAn, *tr. by Thomas Meyer*

Numbers, Letters. Imamu Amiri Baraka. BPo; NOBA

Numbly dont get there. (LL) 113th Chorus. Jack Kerouac. NeAP; PmAP

Numeri XIII. John Hall. ChIV-1

Numerology. Jerome Rothenberg. FTOS

Numerous Celts. Sir John Collings Squire. BXAP

Numerous host of dreaming saints succeed, A. Zimri: The Duke of Buckingham. Dryden. AWP; NOBE; OBSV *Fr. Absalom and Achitophel, Pt. I.* EBEvV; FHYEP; FaBoPV; HAP; NOSC; OAEL-1; PoE

Nun, The. Edward Moore. ECEV

Nun in Ninh Hoa, A. Jan Barry. CDa

Nunc Dimittis. John Cowper Powys. LBC

Nunc est bibendum, Cleopatra's Death. Horace, *Latin.* OBCVT, *tr. by Robert Lowell*

Nunc est bibendum, nunc pede liberum. Nunc est bibendum, Cleopatra's Death. Horace, *Latin.* OBCVT, *tr. by Robert Lowell*

Nunc Viridant Segetes. Sedulius Scottus, *Medieval Latin.* BIrV; NAWM-1, *tr. by Helen Waddell*

Nungesser und Coli Sind Verreckt. Benjamin Péret, *French.* AF, *tr. by Keith Hollaman*

Nunnery, The. Anna Williams. ECWP

Nuns at Eve. John Malcolm Brinnin. TwCP

Nun's Dance, The. Chi-hun Cho, *Korean.* CKP, *tr. by Jaihiun Kim*

Nuns fret not at their convent's narrow room;. Wordsworth. EBEV; GSo; NIP-4; NoP-4; OBEV; Poetr; Son

Nuns Go Walking. Aldo Palazzeschi, *Italian.* PFTM, *tr. by Jerome Rothenberg*

Nuns, his nieces, bring the priest in the next. A Far Cry after a Close Call. Richard Howard. NYBP; UnPo

Nuns in the Wind. Muriel Rukeyser. NNaP

Nuns of Childhood: Two Views, The. Maxine W. Kumin. FFC

Nuns of the Perpetual Adoration. Ernest Christopher Dowson. ADE

Nun's Priest's Prologue, The, *see* Prologue of the Nun's Priest's Tale, The. Chaucer. FHYEP *Fr. The Canterbury Tales.*

  (Prologue of the Nun's Priest's Tale, The.) OAEL-1

  ("This precious priest, this goodly man, Sir John.") (LL) NAWM-1

Nun's Priest's Tale, The. Chaucer. FHYEP; OAEL-1 *Fr. The Canterbury Tales.*

  ("And bring us to your holy bliss! Amen.") (LL) NAWM-1

  ("Poore widwe [*or* widow], somdeel [*or* somedeal] stape in age, A.") NAEL-1

  There liv'd, as Authors tell, in Days of Yore. OBVE

Nuptial Dialogues. Edward Ward.

  Dialogue between a Squeamish Cotting Mechanic and His Sluttish Wife, in the Kitchen. NOEC

Nuptial Eve, A. Sydney Thompson Dobell. OBNC

  Ballad of Keith of Ravelston, The. OBEV

  (Keith of Ravelston.) CH

Nuptial Sleep. D. G. Rossetti. EBVV; EnVR; NAEL-2; NOBVV *Fr. The House of Life.*

Nuptial Song. John Byrne Leicester Warren, 3d Baron De Tabley. GTBS-P; PeVV

  ("Dawn enters; my Love wakes; here is day.") (LL) RACG

Nuptial Song of Julia and Manlius, The. Catullus, *Latin.*

  O divine Urania's son. OBCVT, *tr. by Leigh Hunt*

Nuptiall Song, or Epithalamie, on Sir Clipseby Crew and His Lady, A. Robert Herrick. BeJo; CBLP; CaPo; PoEL-3; SeCP

Nuptials of Attila, The. George Meredith.

  Flat as to an eagle's eye. PeVV

  Square along the couch, and stark. PeVV

Nuremberg. Henry Wadsworth Longfellow. AmPP

Nuremberg. Kenneth Slessor. BMAP

Nurse. Frances Darwin Cornford. WPN

Nurse, The. G. M. Mitchell. NSI

Nurse believed the sick man slept, The. Charlotte Brontë. NOBVV

Nurse carried him up the stair, The. At Thomas Hardy's Birthplace, 1953. James Wright. CoAmPo; WeT

Nurse-life Wheat within his greene huske growing, The. Sonnet: "Nurse-life wheat within his green husk growing, The." Greville Fulke. AAS; PBRV *Fr. Caelica.*

Nursery, The. Laurel Trivelpiece. BAP-95

Nursery boast, The. On Seeing My Birthplace from a Jet Aircraft. John Pudney. NYBP

Nursery Rhyme. Kenneth Burke. OBAL

Nursery Rhyme. Gavin Ewart. UV

Nursery Rhyme. Lorine Niedecker. NMM-2

Nursery Rhyme. Kit Robinson. FTOS

Nursery Rhyme. May Sarton. NOxBChV

Nursery Rhyme of Innocence and Experience. Charles Causley. NOxBChV; NTP

Nursery Song. Anna Wickham. NOxBChV

Nursery Vignette. Edmund Wilson. OBCoV *Fr. Easy Exercises in the Use of Difficult Words.*

Nurses, The. Rudyard Kipling. NoAM *Fr. Land and Sea Tales.*

Nurse's Dole in the Medea, The. Byron. OBVE

Nurse's Lament, The. Mary Elizabeth Coleridge. NOBVV; OxBSP

Nurse's Song. *Unknown. See* Lullaby: "Sleep, baby, sleep."

Nurse's Song ("When the voices of children are heard on the green / And laughing is heard on the hill"). William Blake. AWP; CH; FHYEP; FaBoBe; NAEL-2; OxBChV; PeLV; RACG; SCGP *Fr. Songs of Innocence.*

  ("And all the hills echoed.") (LL) RACG

  ("When the voices of children are heard on the green.") RACG

Nurse's Song ("When the voices of children are heard on the green / And whisperings [*or* whisprings] are in the dale"). William Blake. FHYEP *Fr. Songs of Experience.*

Nursing: Mother. Marie Ponsot.

  Tranquilized, she speaks or does not speak. MDDM

Nursing the tough skins of figs. (LL) This Life. Rita Dove. AmPA; GT

Nursing your nerves / to rest, I've roused my own; well. The Afterwake. Adrienne Rich. NOBA

Nut-brown Maid, The. *Unknown.* NoSic; OBEV

Nut Tree, A. Mother Goose. TTTS

  ("And all for the sake of my little nut-tree.") (LL) LB

Nutcrackers and the Sugar-Tongs, The. Edward Lear. PoLF

Nutcrackers sate by a plate on the table, The. The Nutcrackers and the Sugar-Tongs. Edward Lear. PoLF

Nuts and Raisins. Carl Dennis. CMAP

Nuts in May. Louis MacNeice. MoBrPo

Nutting. Wordsworth. NAEL-2; NOBRP; OAEL-2; Poetr; RB

Nux (The Walnut Tree). Ovid. OBCVT, *tr. by* R. Hatton. *Fr.* Ovids Walnut-Tree transplanted.

NW5 and N6. John Betjeman. SCV

Nwinnng buht nawuNNN baheegwinnng. (LL) The 12th Horse Song of Frank Mitchell (Blue). Frank Mitchell, *Navajo Indian*. APSN; STP, *tr. by* Jerome Rothenberg

Nyanu was appointed. Early Losses: a Requiem. Alice Walker. BlSi

Nymph and Her Fawn, The. Andrew Marvell. CTAV; FaBoCh *Fr.* The Nymph Complaining for the Death of Her Faun [*or* Fawn]. CH; ESCV; GeHe; HeIP-4; NAEL-1; OAEL-1; PoEL-2; RAGG; SeCP

(Girl and Her Fawn, The.) BoTP

Nymph and shepherd raise electric tridents. Chances "R." Allen Ginsberg. HCAP

Nymph Complaining for the Death of Her Faun [*or* Fawn], The. Andrew Marvell. CH; ESCV; GeHe; HeIP-4; NAEL-1; OAEL-1; PoEL-2; RAGG; SeCP

Nymph and Her Fawn, The. CTAV; FaBoCh

(Girl and Her Fawn, The.) BoTP

Nymph died more quick, and the shepherd more slow, The. (LL) Whil'st Alexis Lay Prest [*or* Press'd]. Dryden. BoLoP; PeLV

Nymph Fanarett, supposed to be. A Penance. Francis Daniel Pastorius. NOSC

Nymph I come once more awooing. Ay or Nay? Ralph Schomberg. *Fr.* The Judgment of Paris. TrJP

Nymph in vain bestows her pains, The. A Song. Anne Finch, Countess of Winchilsea. OxBSP

Nymph, nymph, what are your beads? Overheard on a Saltmarsh. Harold Monro. BoTP; CH; NOxBChV

Nymph of the garden where all beauties be. Sonnet 82. Sir Philip Sidney. PoE *Fr.* Astrophil and Stella. AAS; SiPS

Nymph turnd home, The. He fell to felling downe. Homer. OBVE, *tr. by* George Chapman *Fr.* Odyssey. NAWM-1, *tr. by* Robert Fitzgerald

Nymphs, The. Leigh Hunt.
There are the fair-limbed nymphs o' the woods. OBNC

Nymphs and Graces Dancing, The. Edmund Spenser. *Fr.* Wood Of Error. AEP

Nymphs of the surface, whom Hermokreon gave. Hermocreon, *Greek*. GrAn, *tr. by* Alistair Elliot

Nymphs of water, daughters of Doros. Leonidas of Tarentum, *Greek*. GrAn, *tr. by* Peter Levi

Nymph's Passion, A. Ben Jonson. BeJo

(Nymph's Secret, A.) OBEV

Nymph's Reply to the Shepherd, The. Sir Walter Alexander Raleigh. SAGP

Nymph's Secret, A. Ben Jonson. *See* A Nymph's Passion.

Nymph's Song to Hylas, The. William Morris. *See* A Garden By The Sea.

Nyooz. belt up. (LL) This is thi. Tom Leonard. FaBoTC; NBrP

O

Ö. Rita Dove. HCAP; WeW-3

O. Ode to a Goldfish. Gyles Brandreth. PeP

O a year from tomorrow I left my own people. Clonmel Jail. *Unknown, Irish*. BIrV, *tr. by* Valentin Iremonger

O Abishag, my little serving-maid. Abishag. André Spire, *French*. TrJP, *tr. by* Emanuel Eisenberg

O absent presence, Stella is not here. Sonnet 106. Sir Philip Sidney. *Fr.* Astrophil and Stella. AAS; SiPS

O ah drove three mules foh Gawge McVane. Mule Skinner's Song. *Unknown*. AS

O Alison Gross, that lives in yon tower [*or* tow'r]. Alison [*or* Allison] Gross. *Unknown*. CH; ESPB; FaBoCh; OxBB

O All Down within the Pretty Meadow. Kenneth Patchen. HAP; WeW-3

O all the problems other people face. Alcoholic. John Berryman. NOCV

O all ye fair ladics with your colours and your graces. The Revenant. Walter De la Mare. GBL

O[h] *all ye*, who pass[e] by, whose eyes and mind[e]. The Sacrifice. George Herbert. GeHe; PoEL-2

O all you host of heaven! O earth! What else? Shakespeare. *Fr.* Hamlet. NAWM-1

O all you lands, the treasures of your joy. Psalm 100. Mary Sidney Herbert, Countess of Pembroke. CABP

O all you little blackey tops. Scaring Crows. *Unknown*. BoTP; OxNR

O all your ages at the mercy of my loves. John Berryman. NOBA *Fr.* Homage to Mistress Bradstreet.

—O Alma Magna Mater, deathless the living death of pride. (LL) Sonnet on Famous and Familiar Sonnets and Experiences. Delmore Schwartz. Son; TRP

O amiable prospect! New Lines for Cuscuscaraway and Mirza Murad Ali Beg. Louis Simpson. OBAL

O an old King in a story. After W. B. Yeats. G. K. Chesterton. NOBL

O! And I forsooth in love! Shakespeare. OBCoV *Fr.* Love's Labour's Lost.

O anti-verdurous phallic were't not for your pouring height. Ode to Coit Tower. Gregory Corso. CLPP

O antique city on St. Lawrence shore. Quebec. Henrietta Cordelia Ray. CBWP-3

O! Are Ye Sleepin, Maggie? Robert Tannahill. OxBS

O Art, high gift of Heaven! how oft defamed. Art. Washington Allston. APN-1

O Artemis and your virgin girls. Telesilla, *Greek*. BoWoP, *tr. by* Willis Barnstone

O Atthis. Ezra Pound. PoA

O Attic shape! Fair attitude! with brede. Keats. GrIP *Fr.* Ode on a Grecian Urn. AWP; CABP; ChAP; ClHu; EBEV; FaBoBe; HAP; HeIP-4; HoPM; ImPo; InPS-3; NAEL-2; NAWM-2; NIP-4; NOBE; NOBRP; NoP-4; OAEL-2; OBEV; OBNC; PBMP; PFE; PoE; PoEL-4; PoPoPo; Ro; SCGP; TFi; TOF; UnPo

O Autumn, laden with fruit, and stained. To Autumn. William Blake. NAEL-2

O baby, where you been so long? Lord, Lord, Lord, Lord. Levee Moan. *Unknown*. AS

O Bacchus, what a world of toil, both now. The Cyclops. Euripides, *Greek*. OBCVT, *tr. by* J. P. Sullivan

O barbarous Corsica, locked in by crags. Seneca, *Latin*. OBCVT, *tr. by* J. P. Sullivan

O bards! weak heritors of passion and of pain! Miserimus. Adah Isaacs Menken. CBWP-3

O, be my friend, and teach me to be thine! (LL) Forbearance. Ralph Waldo Emerson. MeMAP; TAP

O, Be Not Too Hasty, My Dearest. "Orpheus C. Kerr." OBAL

O be swift. The Helmsman. Hilda Doolittle. CMoP; OxBA

O! bear me witness, night. Shakespeare. OxAEP-1 *Fr.* Antony and Cleopatra.

O beautiful. A Boat. Richard Brautigan. KaS

O beautiful for spacious skies. America the Beautiful. Katharine Lee Bates. APN-2; BLPA; CTV; EBEvV; FaBoA; FaBoBe; TAP

O Beautiful, My Country. Frederick Lucian Hosmer. AH

O beech, unbind your yellow leaf, for deep. Ghostly Tree. Léonie Adams. MoAmPo

O benign Jesu, my sovereign Lord and King. John Skelton. SCGP *Fr.* To the Second Person.

O Bessie Bell and Mary Gray. Bessy [*or* Bessie] Bell and Mary Gray. *Unknown*. ESPB; OxBB

O Billie, billie, bonny billie. The Battle of Bothwell Bridge. *Unknown*. OxBB

O Bird, So Lovely. Louis Golding. TrJP

O bird that flies about. Bird. Hanmo Chong, *Korean*. CKP, *tr. by* Jaihiun Kim

O bird's singing! Takajo Mitsuhashi, *Japanese*. WPJ, *tr. by* Kenneth Rexroth *and* Ikuko Atsumi

O Black and unknown bards of long ago. James Weldon Johnson. BPo; ColAP; CrDW; HeIP-4; NAAAL; PoBA; TTY; UnPo

O black winter of savage death. On a Young Wife. Julianus of Egypt, *Greek*. GrAn, *tr. by* Willis Barnstone

O Blackbird, what a boy you are! Vespers. Thomas Edward Brown. BoTP

O blazing Sun, how happy you are then. Sonnet 22. Louise Labé, *French*. BoWoP, *tr. by* Willis Barnstone

O blessed body [*or* bodie]! Whither art thou thrown? Sepulchre. George Herbert. ESCV; MiEL

O blessed breeding sun! draw from the earth. Shakespeare. OxAEP-1 *Fr.* Timon of Athens.

O blessed letters, that combine in one. Samuel Daniel EPCY *Fr.* Musophilus; or, Defence of All Learning.

O Blessed man, that in th'advice. Psalm 1. *Unknown*. SCAP *Fr.* The Bay Psalm Book.

O blessed Solitude. (LL) A Woman Alone. Denise Levertov. NMM-2

O Blest Estate, Blest from Above. George Sandys. AH

O Blest Unfabled Incense Tree. George Darley. BIrV; FaBoCh; NOBE; OAEL-2; OBEV *Fr.* Nepenthe.

(Phoenix, The.) NOBE; OAEL-2

O blisful light, of which the beames clere. Wooing of Criseide, The, III. Chaucer. PoEL-1 *Fr.* Troilus and Criseyde [*or* Criseide]. EnVB

O blithe New-comer! I have heard. To the Cuckoo. Wordsworth. BoTP; EBEvV; GTBS-P; NOBRP; PoLF; UV

O blonde thing! (LL) Sylvia's Death. Anne Sexton. LCAP-2; NAAL-2; NALW

O blush not so! O blush not so! Sharing Eve's Apple. Keats. ChIV-1; NBLV; PeLV

O-Bon: Dance for the Dead. Garrett Kaoru Hongo. LoL

O Bonny Baby Livingston. Bonny Baby Livingston. *Unknown.* ESPB

O bonny, bonny sang the bird. The Unquiet Grave. *Unknown.* EnSB

O, born in luckless hour, with every muse. To the Editor of Mr. Pope's Works. Thomas Edwards. Son

O Boston, though thou now art grown. Of Boston in New England. William Bradford. SCAP

O boy cutting grass. Hitomaro. AWP, *tr.* by Arthur Waley *Fr.* Manyo Shu, Part 3 of 4.

O boys, O strong of heart in vain. Virgil. MLL, *tr.* by Helen Waddell *Fr.* The Aeneid [*or* Eneados, *Aeneis*].

O, bretheren, my way, my way's cloudy, my way. My Way's Cloudy. *Unknown.* CrDW

O brightness / of peony's buds. Tatsuko Hoshino, *Japanese.* WPJ, *tr.* by Kenneth Rexroth *and* Ikuko Atsumi

O brothers mine, to-day we stand. Fifty Years. James Weldon Johnson. NAAAL

O brothers, why do you talk. Mahadevi, *Kannada.* WPOW, *tr.* by A. K. Ramanujan

O Bury Me Beneath the Willow. *Unknown.* AS

"O [*or* Oh] bury me not on the lone prairie." Bury Me Not on the Lone Prairie. *Unknown.* AS; FaBoBe

O but there is wisdom. Consolation. W. B. Yeats. OxBSP

O but we talked at large before. Sixteen Dead Men. W. B. Yeats. FaBoPV; OBWP

O by the by / has anybody seen. E. E. Cummings. OxBA

O Caesar, we who are about to die. Morituri Salutamus. Henry Wadsworth Longfellow.

O Caledonia! Sir Walter Scott. *Fr.* Caledonia. FaPoR; NOBE; OBEV; OBNC; OxAEP-2; PBMP; Ro *Fr.* The Lay of the Last Minstrel.

O cam ye in by the House o Rodes. John Thomson and the Turk. *Unknown.* ESPB

O camp of flowers, with poplars girdled round. Memory. Erik Johann Stagnelius, *Swedish.* AWP, *tr.* by Sir Edmund Gosse

O Captain! my Captain! our fearful trip is done. Walt Whitman. APAD; APN-1; CBCWP; ChAP; EBEvV; FaBoBe; FaBoCh; FaPoR; ImPo; InPK-6; MeMAP; MoAmPo; OBCA; PBMP; PoLF; SAGP; SAmP; TAP; TFi *Fr.* Memories of President Lincoln.

O Carib Isle! Hart Crane. NoAM; PFTM; PoA; VGW

O Cat of Carlishkind. John Skelton. *Fr.* Phyllyp Sparowe [*or* Philip Sparrow]. AAS; PoEL-1

O chansons foregoing. Epilogue. Ezra Pound. OxBA

O Chatterton, how very sad thy fate! To Chatterton. Keats. EPCY

O Cheese. Donald Hall. DiPo

O Child, Do Not Fear the Dark and Sleep's Dark Possession. Delmore Schwartz. NOxBChV

O Child of Lowly Manger Birth. Ferdinand Q. Blanchard. AH

O child, when you go down to sleep and sleep's secession. O Child, Do Not Fear the Dark and Sleep's Dark Possession. Delmore Schwartz. NOxBChV

O Children, Would You Cherish? Christopher Dock, *German.* AH, *tr.* by Samuel W. Pennypacker

O child's tremble. Forming Child Poems. Simon J. Ortiz. CDW

O chillen, run, Cunjah man. Cunjah Man, De. James Edwin Campbell. AAP

O Christ of Bethlehem. H. Glenn Lanier. AH

O Christ, receive these souls in thy Mother's house. Hibernicus Exul, *Latin.* MLL, *tr.* by Helen Waddell

O Christ, who in Gethsemane. Prayer. Henrietta Cordelia Ray. CBWP-3

O Christmas Night. Henricus Selyns, *Dutch.* AH, *tr.* by Howard Murphy, (*sts.* 1, 2, 4, 6)

O city metropole, isle riverain! Montreal. Abraham Moses Klein. MoCV

O city of the world, with sacred splendor blest. Longing for Jerusalem. Judah Halevi, *Hebrew.* TrJP, *tr.* by Emma Lazarus

O clemens! O pia! O dolcis! / Maria! (LL) For Eleanor and Bill Monahan. William Carlos Williams. CRP; VGW

O, close your pale legs! Valery Yakovlevich Bryusov, *Russian.* TCRP, *tr.* by Simon Franklin

O cloud that wants to be the sky's arrow. Rosario Castellanos, *Spanish.* BoWoP, *tr.* by Willis Barnstone

O Columbia, the gem of the ocean. Columbia, the Gem of the Ocean. *Unknown, at. to* Thomas à Becket. CTV; FaBoBe

O, come erlong, come erlong. Mobile-Buck. James Edwin Campbell. AAP

O, come, let us sing unto the Lord. Psalm 95. Bible, *O.T.* AWP *Fr.* Psalms.

O Come Quickly! Thomas Campion. NOBE; OAEL-1; OBEV; OxAEP-1; OxBSP; PoEL-2

O come, soft rest of cares, come Night. Bridal Song. George Chapman. NOBE; OBEV *Fr.* Hero and Leander. AAS

O come to me in my dreams love! Lines to————. Mary Weston Fordham. CBWP-2

O come to me, my brother Green, for I am shot and bleeding. Brother Green. *Unknown.* AmFP

O come with me, thus ran the song. Emily Jane Brontë. NOBVV

O come you pious youth! adore. Jupiter Hammon. AmPP *Fr.* An Address to Miss Phillis Wheatley.

O commemorate me where there is water. Lines Written on a Seat on the Grand Canal, Dublin. Patrick Kavanagh. BIrV; CMoP; InPS-3; NOIV

O comrades, come gather and join in my ditty. The *Cumberland's* Crew. *Unknown.* AmFP

O Constellations of the early night. The Constellations. William Cullen Bryant. APN-1

"O Cormac, grandson of Conn," said Carbery. *Unknown.* BIrV, *tr.* by Kuno Meyer *Fr.* The Instructions of King Cormac.

O could I be as I have been. John Clare. Ro

O Could I Find from Day to Day. Benjamin Cleavland. AH

O could I flow like thee, and make thy stream. Sir John Denham. EPCY *Fr.* Cooper's Hill. CABP

"O could I love!" and stops, God writeth, "Loved." (LL) A True Hymn. George Herbert. GeHe; NOCV

O! could my sweet plaint lull to rest. Nightingale. Christian Carstairs. ECWP

O country people, you of the hill farms. John Hewitt. IIP

O courteous Christkind guest, most gracious host. To a Crucifix. Anna Wickham. MoBrPo

O cricket, from your cheery cry. Basho, *Japanese.* AWP, *tr.* by Curtis Hidden Page

O crimson blood. Hildegard von Bingen, *Latin.* WPOW, *tr.* by Patrick Diehl

O crownless soul of Ishmael! Hemlock in the Furrows. Adah Isaacs Menken. CBWP-1

O cruel Death, give three things back. Three Things. W. B. Yeats. OBMV

O cruel Love! on thee I lay. Sapho's Song. John Lyly. NoSic *Fr.* Sapho and Phao.

O Cuckoo. *Unknown.* AWP, *tr.* by Arthur Waley *Fr.* Kokin Shu.

O Cuckoo! shall I call thee Bird. Examination Question. *Unknown.* OBCoV

O Cuckoo! shall I call thee Bird. F. H. Townsend. UV

O cuckoo that sang to us and art fled. Lament for the Cuckoo. Alcuin, *Latin.* NAWM-1, *tr.* by Helen Waddell

O Cupid! Monarch over Kings. John Lyly. CBLP *Fr.* Mother Bombie.

O, cut the sweet apple and share it! (LL) Sharing Eve's Apple. Keats. ChIV-1; NBLV; PeLV

O Daedalus, Fly Away Home. Robert Earl Hayden. HAP; NAAAL; PoBA

O Dandelion. *Unknown.* BoTP

O David, highest in the list. Christopher Smart. NOEC *Fr.* A Song to David. ImPo; NAEL-1; NOBE; OAEL-1; OBWVE; PoE; PoEL-3

O David, if I had. That Harp You Play So Well. Marianne Moore. MoAmPo; PoA

O Day! he cannot die. A Death Scene. Emily Jane Brontë. OxAEP-2

O Day most calm, most bright. Sunday. George Herbert. GeHe; PeECV; TrCP

O Day of God, Draw Nigh. Robert Balgarnie Young Scott. AH

O Day of Light and Gladness. Frederick Lucian Hosmer. AH

O days and hours, your work is this. Tennyson. PeECV *Fr.* In Memoriam A. H. H.

O' de wurl' ain't flat! Northboun'. Lucy Ariel Williams Holloway. BlSi

O dea certe! (LL) Aprill. Edmund Spenser. NAEL-1; OBEV; PoEL-1

O dear! How disgusting is life! Edward Lear. NOxBChV

O dear! I cannot choose but write. Eve. Oliver Herford. OBAL

O dear life, when shall it be. Tenth Song. Sir Philip Sidney. *Fr.* Astrophil and Stella. AAS; SiPS

O, Dear! What Can the Matter Be? *Unknown.* CBLP; CH; OxNR

O dearest, canst thou tell me why. Warum sind denn die Rosen so blass. Heinrich Heine, *German.* AWP, *tr.* by Richard Garnett

O Dearest Dread, most glorious King. A Prayer unto Christ the Judge of the World. Michael Wigglesworth. SCAP

O dearest life! joy's sweet! O sweetest love! (LL) And Is It Night? Are they thine eyes that shine? *Unknown.* CBLP; GBL

O, dearlie they deed. El Alamein. Sydney Goodsir Smith. FaBoTC *Fr.* Armageddon in Albyn.

O dearly-bought revenge, yet glorious! Heroic Vengeance. Milton. *Fr.* Samson Agonistes. FHYEP; OAEL-1; PoEL-3

O Death. Bible, Apocrypha. TrJP *Fr.* Ecclesiasticus.

O death, rock me asleep. George Boleyn. SCGP; WPE

O death, thy certainty is such. Henry Luttrell. FaBoEE

O Death! where is thy Sting? (LL) The Dying Christian to His Soul. Alexander Pope, *par. fr. the Latin of* Emperor Hadrian. AWP; ChIV-2; ImPo; OBEV

O Death! Why dost thou steal the great. In Memoriam Frederick Douglass. Eloise Bibb. CBWP-4

O deep, creating Light. Eagle Song. Gordon Bottomley. MoBrPo *Fr.* Suilven and the Eagle.

O Deep of Heaven, 'tis thou alone art boundless. The Night Sky. G. D. Roberts. GSo

O Deep River, O Dark Stream. Deep River. Eugène Marais, *Afrikaans.* PeSAV, *tr. by* Hugh Finn

O depth sufficient to desire. Adam's Song to Heaven. Edgar Bowers. CoAmPo

O Did you ever hear of the brave Earl Brand. Earl Brand. *Unknown.* OxBB

O, dim, forsaken mirror! The Mirror in the Deserted Hall. Felicia Dorothea Hemans. NOBRP

O dinna ye spy yon castel braw. The Stown Bairn. Lewis Spence. FaBoTC

O Dirty Bird Yr Gizzard's Too Big & Full of Sand. James Koller. PoM

O distant, distant; deep unapproachable; receive always. The Distant. Yannis Ritsos, *Greek.* VCWP, *tr. by* Edmund Keeley

O divine star of heaven. John Fletcher. GBL *Fr.* The Mad Lover.

O divine Urania's son. Catullus. OBCVT, *tr. by* Leigh Hunt *Fr.* The Nuptial Song of Julia and Manlius.

O do, Lord, remember me! Lord, Remember Me! *Unknown.* APN-2

O do not grieve, Dear Heart, nor shed a tear. Margaret Lucas Cavendish, Duchess of Newcastle. EnLoPo

O do not use me / After my sin[ne]s! look not on my desert. Sighs and Groans [*or* Grones]. George Herbert. PoEL-2

O do you in fedora or trenchcoat bear record. Fragmented Address to the FBI. Diane Di Prima. BB

O Donal[l] Oge, if you go across the sea. Donal[l] Oge [*or* Og]: Grief of a Girl's Heart. *Unknown, Modern Irish.* GBL; PBWP; RB, *tr. by* Lady Augusta Gregory

O Donald! ye are just the man. Susanna Blamire. LW

O don't, don't ever ask me for alms. Death and the Plowman. Sidney Keyes. OxBTC

O! don't you wish that you were me? (LL) Foreign Children. Robert Louis Stevenson. BoTP; GoJo-1

O down in the orchard. Apple Harvest. Helen Leuty. BoTP

O dream from the blackness. Sappho, *Greek.* BoWoP, *tr. by* Willis Barnstone

O Dream, where art thou now? Emily Jane Brontë. NOBVV

O Dreams, O Destinations. C. Day Lewis.
    "To travel like a bird, lightly to view." GTBS-P

O dull cold northern sky. Robert Louis Stevenson. EBVV

O Earl Rothes, an thou wert mine. Earl Rothes. *Unknown.* ESPB

O early one morning I walked out like Agag. The Streets of Laredo. Louis MacNeice. MoBS; OBWP

O Earnest Be. *Unknown.* AH

O Earth, adore creative power. Creation. Mary Weston Fordham. CBWP-2

O Earth! Earth! Earth heare my voice, and be. To his Paternall Countrey. Ovid, *Latin.* OBCVT, *tr. by* Robert Herrick

O Earth, lie heavily upon her eyes. Rest. Christina Rossetti. GSo; NOBE; OAEL-2; OBEV; OBNC

O Earth, Turn! George Johnston. MoCV

O Earth, unhappy planet born to die. Edna St. Vincent Millay. HeIP-4 *Fr.* Epitaph for the Race of Man.

O elephants, elephants all! Elephants. Tô Hū'u, *Vietnamese.* AVP, *tr. by* Huỳnh Sanh Thông

O eloquent and caustic sage. Frederick Douglass. Joseph Cotter, Sr.. AAP

O England, Country of My Heart's Desire. Edward Verrall Lucas. BoTP

O English Food! How I adore looking forward. An Ode to English Food. George MacBeth. FaBoTC

O Englishwoman on the Pincian. Thomas Edward Brown. NOBVV; OBNC *Fr.* Roman Women.

O Eros of the mountains, of the earth. Eros. Michael Field. VWP

O Eros, silently smiling one, hear me. Hymn to Eros. Denise Levertov. LW

O eternal grass. On the Meadow. Katri Vala, *Finnish.* PBWP, *tr. by* Jaakko A. Ahokas

O Eternal, in thy majesty ride. Jewish Arabic Liturgies. *Unknown, Arabic.* TrJP, *tr. by* Hartwig Hirschfeld

O, ever dear! thy precious, vital powers. Sonnet 31. Anna Seward. CPO

O everie living warldly wight. Of Gods Omnipotencie. Alexander Hume. NOCV

O everlasting Kingdom of the Scepter. He Maketh Himself One with the Only God, Whose Limbs Are the Many Gods. *Unknown.* AWP *Fr.* Book of the Dead.

O evil Angel, set me free! (LL) A Clever Woman. Mary Elizabeth Coleridge. BrRo; VWP

O excellent sovereigne, most semely to see. *Unknown.* MiEL

O eye, weep for a rider. Rain to the Tribe. Al-Khansa, *Arabic.* BoWoP, *tr. by* Willis Barnstone *and* Tony Nawfal

O eyes clear with beauty, O tender gaze. Sonnet 11. Louise Labé, *French.* BoWoP, *tr. by* Willis Barnstone

O eyes, which do the spheres of beauty move. Sonnet 42. Sir Philip Sidney. *Fr.* Astrophil and Stella. AAS; SiPS

O fair is our Lord's own city. Fair is Our Lord's Own City. *Unknown, Irish.* TIRV, *tr. by* Coslett Quin

O fair! O sweet! when I do look on thee. Song. Sir Philip Sidney. ITG; SiPS

O faithless world, and thy more faithless part. A Poem Written by Sir Henry Wotton, in His Youth. Sir Henry Wotton. NoSic

O, Falmouth is a fine town with ships in the bay. Home. William Ernest Henley. MoBrPo; PoLF

O false and treacherous Probability. Sonnet: "O false and treacherous Probability." Greville Fulke. AAS *Fr.* Caelica.

O famished Prodigal, in vain. Echo. John Banister Tabb. APN-2

O far withdrawn into the lonely West. To K. H. Thomas Edward Brown. OBNC

O fare you well, my darling. Ten Thousand Miles. *Unknown.* AmFP

O! farewell, my country—my kindred—my lover. The Exile of Erin. *Unknown.* NOBAu

O farther, farther, farther sail! (LL) Passage to India. Walt Whitman. APN-1; AmPP; NAAL-1; NCAP; PoEL-5

O fast her amber blood doth flow. O Blest Unfabled Incense Tree. George Darley. OBEV *Fr.* Nepenthe.

O fate, O fault, O curse, child of my bliss. Sonnet 93. Sir Philip Sidney. *Fr.* Astrophil and Stella. AAS; SiPS

O father, frendes, my countrey eke, and Priams house farewell. Ennius, Quintus. OBCVT, *tr. by* John Dolman *Fr.* Andromache Captive.

O Father, give the spirit power to climb. Boethius, *Latin.* MLL, *tr. by* Helen Waddell *Fr.* Consolation of Philosophy, The ("De Consolacione Philosophie").

"O Father, I acknowledge, " Job replied. George Sandys. ChIV-1 *Fr.* A Paraphrase Upon Job.

O Father of all lights, to thee, *par. by* Countess of Pembroke, Mary Sidney Herbert. Bible, *O.T. See* Psalm 139.

O fearfull, frowning nemesis. Samuel Daniel. PoEL-2 *Fr.* Cleopatra.

O first created and creating source. Ode to the Sea. Howard Baker. OxBA

O Flame of Living Love. Saint John of the Cross, *Spanish.* AWP, *tr. by* Arthur Symons

O flower fawn. Five Flower World Variations. *Unknown, Yaqui Indian.* STP, *tr. by* Jerome Rothenberg

O flower garment!/ when I take it off. Hisajo Sugita, *Japanese.* WPJ, *tr. by* Kenneth Rexroth *and* Ikuko Atsumi

O flowers of Mekhmekh, give us peace! *Unknown, Egyptian hieroglyphics.* BoWoP, *tr. by* Ezra Pound *and* Noel Stock

O fly away home fly away. (LL) O Daedalus, Fly Away Home. Robert Earl Hayden. HAP; NAAAL; PoBA

O fond, but fickle and untrue. Walter Savage Landor. CBLP; GBL

O foolish tears, go back! In Vain. Adah Isaacs Menken. CBWP-1

O foolish wisdom sought in books! Longing. Ina Coolbrith. PaTW

O foolishnes of men! that lend their ears. Comus's Praise of Nature. Milton. PoEL-3 *Fr.* Comus; a Masque Presented at Ludlow Castle. FHYEP; OAEL-1

O foot, O leg, O thighs for which I rightly died. Philodemus. HePo, *tr. by* Barbara Hughes Fowler *Fr.* Epigrams.

O for a Booke. *Unknown.* CH

O! [*or* Oh] for a bowl of fat canary. A Serving Men's Song. John Lyly. NOBE; NoSic *Fr.* Alexander and Campaspe.

O for a ferryman to steer my yearning. Home-Sickness. Hedwig Lachmann, *German.* TrJP, *tr. by* Jethro Bithell

O for a muse of fire, a sack of dough. Sonnet with a Different Letter at the End of Every Line. George Starbuck. OBAL

O for a Muse of fire, that would ascend. A Muse of Fire. Shakespeare. OxAEP-1; SCV *Fr.* King Henry V.

O for a rope of Onions from Saint Omers. John Taylor. CBNP *Fr.* Odcomb's Complaint.

O for a sculptor's hand. Balaam. John Keble. OBNC

O for a toe, such as the funeral pyre. Sir Thomas Browne. FaBoEE

O for doors to be open and an invite with gilded edges. Song of the Beggars. W. H. Auden. PeLV *Fr.* Twelve Songs.

O, for my sake do you with Fortune chide. Sonnet 111. Shakespeare. OxAEP-1 *Fr.* Sonnets.

O for our upland meads. Shepherd and Shepherdess. Thomas Hennell. FaBoTw

O[h]! for some honest lover's ghost. Sonnet. Sir John Suckling. BXAP; BeJo; BoLoP; CaPo; MeLP; NOBE; OBEV; PoEL-3; SeCP

O for ten years, that I may overwhelm. Keats. NAEL-2; OAEL-2 *Fr.* Sleep and Poetry.

O, for that warning voice, which he who saw. Book IV. Milton. OAEL-1 *Fr.* Paradise Lost.

O for that warning voice which he who saw. The Prospect of Eden. Milton. OxAEP-1, *ll.* 1–535; NAEL-1; PoEL-3, *ll.* 1–775 *Fr.* Book IV. OAEL-1 *Fr.* Paradise Lost.

O for the Happy Hour. George Washington Bethune. AH

O for the time when I shall sleep. Emily Jane Brontë. *Fr.* The Philosopher. BWW

O for the Wings of a Dove. Euripides. AWP, *tr. by* Gilbert Murray *Fr.* Hippolytus.

O for wings. The Chorus sing of escape. Euripides, *Greek.* OBCVT, *tr. by* Hilda Doolittle *Fr.* Hippolytus.

O Fortune. *Unknown, Latin.* MLL, *tr. by* Helen Waddell *Fr.* Carmina Burana.

O fountain of Bandusia. 3.13: To the Fountain[s] of Bandusia ("O fons Bandusiae"). Horace. AWP, *tr. by* Eugene Field *Fr.* Odes.

O Frail Adam. Epitaph for Mr. Moses Levy. *Unknown.* TrJP

O frail flower. Alcaeus, *Greek.* InMo, *tr. by* Sam Hamill

O Frame the strains anew. Bible, *O.T. See* Psalm 98.

O free at last. (LL) I Thank God I'm Free at Las'. *Unknown.* APN-2

O Freedom! Freedom! O! how oft. Charles Lewis Reason. AAP *Fr.* Freedom.

O Freedom! / O Freedom! *Unknown.* CrDW

O Friend! I know not which way I must look. Written in London, September, 1802. Wordsworth. FaBoPV; GTBS-P; OBEV

O friend, understand: the body. Mirabai, *Indian.* WPoS, *tr. by* Jane Hirshfield

O friends, I am mad. Mirabai, *Rajasthani.* WPoS, *tr. by* Jane Hirshfield

O friends on this Path. Mirabai, *Indian.* WPoS, *tr. by* Jane Hirshfield

O friends! who have accompanied thus far. Walter Savage Landor. GBL

O friends! with whom my feet have trod. The Eternal Goodness. John Greenleaf Whittier.

O Friendship! Friendship! the shell of Aphrodite. Walter Savage Landor. GBL

O, from [*or* O! From] what power hast thou this powerful might. Sonnet 150. Shakespeare. OxAEP-1; SCGP *Fr.* Sonnets.

O furrowed plaintive face. The Hurrier. Harold Monro. MoBrPo

O Future bards. A Prophecy. Allen Ginsberg. TAP

O gallant brothers of the generous South. Henry Peterson. FaBoBe *Fr.* Ode for Decoration Day.

O generation of the thoroughly smug / and thoroughly uncomfortable. Salutation. Ezra Pound. HeIP-4; MeMAP; MoAmPo; NOBA; OxBA; TAP; VGW

O gentle, gentle land. Night Sowing. David Campbell. CBAP

O[h,] gentle Love, do not forsake the guide. Upon Some Alterations in My Mistress, after My Departure into France. Thomas Carew. CaPo

O Gentle Ships. Meleager, *Greek.* AWP, *tr. by* Andrew Lang

O gentle Sleep, come, wave thine opiate wing. On Dreams, October 15, 1782. Sir Samuel Egerton Brydges. Son

O gentle Sleep! do they belong to thee. To Sleep. Wordsworth. Son

O gin my love were yon red rose. Robert Burns. *Fr.* O were my Love yon Lilac[k] fair. GBL; GBRV

O give thanks unto the Lord; for he is good: because his mercy endureth for ever. Psalm 118. Bible, *O.T.* TrJP *Fr.* Psalms.

O give thanks unto the Lord, for he is good: for his mercy endureth for ever. Psalm 107. Bible, *O.T.* OxBoS *Fr.* Psalms.

O give thanks unto the Lord; for he is good [*or* gracious]: for his mercy endureth for ever. Psalm 136. Bible, *O.T.* AWP *Fr.* Psalms.

O Give yee thanks unto the Lord. Psalm 107. *Unknown.* SCAP *Fr.* The Bay Psalm Book.

O Glorious Childbearer. Joseph Campbell. TIRV

O Glorious Christ of God; I live. Cotton Mather. SCAP

O glorious Eie, thou miracle of Sight. Aristophanes. OBCVT, *tr. by* Oldisworth, Nicholas *Fr.* The Ecclesiazusae.

O God, above the Drifting Years. John Wright Buckham. AH

O God, Accept the Sacred Hour. Samuel Gilman. AH

O God, and his good angels! whither, whither. Ben Jonson. FaBoSe *Fr.* Volpone.

O God, for as much as without Thee. Ronald Arbuthnott Knox. PeLi ("It knows nothing whatever about Thee.") (LL) OBCoV

O God, Great Father, Lord, and King. E. Embree Hoss. AH

O God, I Cried, No Dark Disguise. Edna St. Vincent Millay. AH

O God, in the dream the terrible horse began. The Dream. Louise Bogan. InPK-6; LiTM; MoAmPo; NALW; NoAM

O God, in Whom the Flow of Days. Donald Campbell Babcock. AH

O God, in whom we half believe. Offertorium. C. Day Lewis. TIRV *Fr.* Requiem for the Living.

O God, in Whose Great Purpose. James G. Gilkey. AH

O God, keep not Thou silence. Psalm 83. Bible, *O.T.* TrJP *Fr.* Psalms.

O God! Look, you gave us a vessel made. The Body. Huy Cận, *Vietnamese.* AVP, *tr. by* Huỳnh Sanh Thông

O God, my dream! I dreamed that you were dead; On the Threshold. Amy Levy. LW; NOBVV; SDW

O God! O Montreal! Samuel Butler. OBSV; OxBoLi; PeLV

O God, O Venus, O Mercury, patron of thieves. The Lake Isle. Ezra Pound. OBCoV; OxBSP; PoA

O God of Hosts, thine Ear incline. Hymn. *Unknown.* NOBRP

O God of love unbounded! Lord supreme! Prayer to God. "Placido," *Spanish.* TTY, *tr. by* Raoul Abdul

O God of Mercy. God of Mercy. Kadya Molodovsky, *Yiddish.* WPOW, *tr. by* Irving Howe

O God of My Salvation, Hear. Joel Barlow. AH

O god of spring forgive me. Pete Winslow. CLPP

O God of Stars and Distant Space. John Franzen. AH

O God of Youth. Bates G. Burt. AH

O God, Our Help in Ages Past. Isaac Watts. FaPoR; NOCV

O God, our loving Father, help us. A Christmas Prayer. Robert Louis Stevenson. TrCP

O God, Send Men. Elizabeth Burrowes. AH

O God that art the only hope of the world. Prayer of the Venerable Bede. The Venerable Bede, *Latin.* MLL, *tr. by* Helen Waddell

O God, the heathen are come into thine inheritance. The Heathen Are Come into Thine Inheritance. Bible, *O.T.* TrJP *Fr.* Psalms.

O God, the Rock of Ages. Edward Henry, Bishop of Exeter Bickersteth. BLPA

O God, the soules pure fi'ry Spring. Prudentius. OBCVT, *tr. by* Sir John Beaumont *Fr.* A Funerall Hymne out of Prudentius.

O God, though Countless Worlds of Light. James D. Knowles. AH

O God thy Judgments unto sinfull eye. On the Death of My Deare Sister the Countesse of Bridgewater. Lady Jane Cavendish *and* Lady Elizabeth Brackley. KTR

O God, when You send for me, let it be. Prayer to Go to Paradise with the Asses. Francis Jammes, *French.* AWP, *tr. by* Jethro Bithell

O God, who made me. The Prayer of the Donkey. Carmen Bernos de Gasztold. PChr

O God Whose Presence Glows in All. Nathaniel Langdon Frothingham. AH

O God! whose thunder shakes the sky. Resignation. Thomas Chatterton. TrCP

O God, why hast thou thus / Repuls'd, and scatter'd us? Psalm 74. Bible, *O.T.* NOCV *Fr.* Psalms.

O[h] Goddess! hear these tuneless numbers, wrung. Ode to Psyche. Keats. FHYEP; InPS-3; NAEL-2; NOBE; NOBRP; NoP-4; OAEL-2; OBEV; OBNC; OxAEP-2; PoE; PoEL-4; Ro; TFi; TOF

O! Gods! how very wretched am I grown! Agamemnon struggles to avert the sacrifice of his daughter Iphigeneia]. Euripides, *Greek.* OBCVT, *tr. by* Charles Gildon

O golden child the world will kill and eat. (LL) Mary's Song. Sylvia Plath. ChIV-2; FaBoMo; FaBoWP

O Golden Fleece ("O Golden Fleece she is where she lies tonight"). George Barker. LiTM; MoBrPo *Fr.* Secular Elegies.

(Secular Elegy V.) EP

O[h] golden-tongued Romance with serene lute! On Sitting Down to Read "King Lear" Once Again. Keats. CABP; EBEV; EPCY; GSo; NAEL-2; NoP-4; PoPoPo; Ro

O golden yellows and browns and still resistant greens. Annul. Simon Pettet. PT

O Goldfish! Robert Fisher. PeP

O Gongyla, my darling rose. Sappho, *Greek.* BoWoP, *tr. by* Willis Barnstone

O good Lord Judge, and sweet Lord. *Unknown. See* The Maid Freed from the Gallows.

"O good Lord Judge, and sweet Lord Judge." The Maid Freed from the Gallows. *Unknown.* AWP; ESPB

O! good my lord, tax not so bad a voice. Shakespeare. OxAEP-1 *Fr.* Much Ado About Nothing.

O good painter, tell me true. An Order for a Picture. Alice Cary. BLPA

O good sun. Song for Fine Weather. *Unknown, Haida.* AWP, *tr. by* Constance Lindsay Skinner *Fr.* Three Songs from the Haida.

O goodly golden chaine, werewith yfere. Edmund Spenser. FHYEP *Fr.* Wood Of Error. AEP

O Goodly Hand. Sir Thomas Wyatt. SiPS

O Gracious Father of Mankind. Henry Hallam Tweedy. AH

O gracious God, how far have we. Dryden. EPCY *Fr.* To the Pious Memory of the Accomplished Young Lady, Mrs. Anne Killigrew.

O gracious gods, take compassion. John Marston. OAEL-1 *Fr.* The Metamorphosis of Pygmalion's Image.

O Gracious Jesus, Blessed Lord! Andrew Fowler. AH

O Grammer rules, ô now your virtues show. Sonnet 63. Sir Philip Sidney. NoP-4 *Fr.* Astrophil and Stella. AAS; SiPS

O grandest of the Angels, and most wise. Litany to Satan. Charles Baudelaire, *French.* AWP, *tr. by* James Elroy Flecker.

O grant me darkness! Let no gleam. 'But in that Sleep of Death what Dreams may Come?'. Mary Elizabeth Coleridge. VWP

O grant that like to Peter I. Keats. CBNP; ChIV-2 *Fr.* Three Undated Fragments.

O grasses wet with dew, yellow fallen leaves. A Glimpse. Frances Darwin Cornford. OBMV

O graunt that of my love at last I may not misse! (LL) Address to Venus. Lucretius. OBCVT, *tr. by* Edmund Spenser; AWP, *tr. by* Spenser

O Great Mary. Litany to Our Lady. *Unknown, Irish.* TIRV, *tr. by* Eugene O'Curry

O Great Queen Whom I idolize. Limerick. Jeffery Littman. PeLi

O great tone-master! low thy massive head. Beethoven. Henrietta Cordelia Ray. CBWP-3

O green, beneath which all of them shall drown! (LL) Fresh Air. Kenneth Koch. CAPP-1; NNaP; NeAP

O' gude Braid Claith. (LL) Braid Claith. Robert Fergusson. NOEC; OxBS

O guide my judgment and my taste. Taste. Christopher Smart. ChIV-1; NOCV *Fr.* Hymns for the Amusement of Children.

O had I known that it ends like this. Boris Pasternak, *Russian.* TCRP, *tr. by* Edwin Morgan

O had truth power the guiltless could not fall. His Petition to Queen Anne of Denmark (1618). Sir Walter Ralegh. SiPS

O Hand of Fire / gatherest. (LL) The Tunnel. Hart Crane. CMoP; MoAmPo; OxBA

O handsome chestnut eyes, evasive gaze. Sonnet 2. Louise Labé, *French.* BoWoP, *tr. by* Willis Barnstone

O happy [or happie] dames, that may embrace. Complaint of the Absence of Her Lover Being upon the Sea. Henry Howard, Earl of Surrey. AAS; EBEV; GBL; NOBE; NoSic; OBEV; SCGP; SiPS

O happy hour. *Unknown, Latin.* MLL, *tr. by* Helen Waddell *Fr.* Carmina Burana.

O happy hour, and happier hours. Tennyson. EnVR *Fr.* O true and tried, so well and long. OAEL-1 *Fr.* In Memoriam A. H. H.

O Happy people, where good princes reign. The Tower of Babel. Joshua Sylvester. NoSic *Fr.* The Divine Weeks and Works of Guillaume de Saluste Sieur Du Bartas.

O happy Thames, that didst my Stella bear. Sonnet 103. Sir Philip Sidney. OxAEP-1 *Fr.* Astrophil and Stella. AAS; SiPS

O happy Tithon! if thou know'st thy harp. Sir William Alexander, Earl of Stirling. OBEV *Fr.* Aurora.

O Hark to the Herald. Eleazar ben Kalir, *Hebrew.* TrJP, *tr. by* Israel Zangwill

O Harry Heine, curses be. Translator to Translated. Ezra Pound. FaBoEE

O, Harry! thou hast robb'd me of my youth. Shakespeare. OxAEP-1 *Fr.* King Henry IV, Pt. I. NAEL-1

O, have ye been in love, me boys. I Met Her in the Garden Where the Praties Grow. *Unknown.* AS

O have ye na heard o' the fause Sakelde? Kinmont Willie. *Unknown.* ESPB; IBB; OxBB

O Have You Caught the Tiger? A. E. Housman. BXAP

O, have you seen the leper healed. The Healing of the Leper. Vernon Watkins. FaBoTw

O have you seen the Stratton flood. Stratton Water. D. G. Rossetti. OxBB

O he is a rest that requires. Anna Trapnell. PBRV *Fr.* The Cry of a Stone.

O, he who flashed above the moon afar. "Georgy Avdeievich Rayevsky," *Russian.* TCRP, *tr. by* Albert C. Todd

O Hear My Prayer, Lord. John Craig. AH

O heard ye never of Wat o' the Cleuch? Walsinghame's Song. James Hogg. BXAP

O heard ye of a silly Harper. The Lochmaben Harper. *Unknown.* OxBB

O heard ye of Sir James the Rose. Sir James the Rose. *Unknown.* ESPB

O hearken and hear, and I will you tell. Friar in the Well. *Unknown.* ESPB

O heart green acre sown with salt. An Upward Look. James Merrill. PoPoPo

O heart, small urn. Hilda Doolittle. *Fr.* The Walls Do Not Fall. NAAL-2

O heart / sorrowing. A Young Warrior. Ponmutiyar, *Tamil.* PLW, *tr. by* A. K. Ramanujan

O Heart! the equal poise of love's both parts. Richard Crashaw. GeHe *Fr.* The Flaming Heart. CABP; NAEL-1; OAEL-1; PoEL-2

O Heaven Indulge. Stephen Tilden. AH

O heavenly color, London town. November Blue. Alice Thompson Meynell. MoBrPo

O Heavens! O Earth! heer I must pause a space. Sir William Mure. PBRV *Fr.* The Cry of Blood, and of a Broken Covenant.

O heavy day! oh day of woe! The Lament of Toby the Learned Pig. Thomas Hood. CBNP

O Heavy Step of Slow Monotony. Ernst Toller, *German.* TrJP, *tr. by* Ashley Dukes

O Hector, thou wert rooted in my heart. Helen's Lamentation. Homer. OBVE, *tr. by* Congreve *Fr.* The Iliad.

O Heitsi-Eibib. Hunter's Prayer. *Unknown, Hottentot.* PeSA

O[h] Hell, what do mine eyes. Milton by Firelight. Gary Snyder. BB; CoAP; CoAmPo; InPS-3; NAAL-2; SAGP

O Hell! what do mine eyes with grief behold! Satan Beholds Adam and Eve in Eden. Milton. *Fr.* Book IV. OAEL-1 *Fr.* Paradise Lost.

O helpless few in my country. The Rest. Ezra Pound. AmPP; MeMAP; MoAmPo; NOBA; NoAM; OxBA; PoA *Fr.* Lustra.

O here it is! And there it is! Mervyn Laurence Peake. NOxBChV

O hermitage well found. The Young Pilgrim Finds Refuge with the Goatherds. Luis de Góngora y Argote. *Fr.* The First Solitude. OBVE, *tr. by* Edward Meryon Wilson

O Hero. Eve Shelnutt. CMAP

O Hesperus! thou bringest all good things. Hesperus the Bringer. Byron. AWP *Fr.* Canto the Third. *Fr.* Don Juan.

O hideous little beat, the size of snot. The Fly. Karl Shapiro. LiTM; MoP; NoAM; PBMP; PFE; SoSe-8

O, hits time fur de plantin' ur de co'n. Song of the Corn. James Edwin Campbell. AAP

O Holy City Seen of John. Walter Russell Bowie. AH

O Holy Ghost. Stephen Langton, *Latin.* MLL, *tr. by* Helen Waddell

O Holy Ghost, O faithful Paraclete. For Whitsuntide. Hildebert, *Latin.* MLL, *tr. by* Helen Waddell

O Holy Ghost, whose temple I. The Holy Ghost. Donne. NOCV *Fr.* The Litanie. PoEL-2

O Holy, Holy, Holy, Lord. James Wallis Eastburn. AH

O holy Jerusalem, Vision of peace. *Unknown. Fr.* Christ 1. AnOE, *tr. by* Charles W. Kennedy

O Holy Mother, thou who still dost send. At the Tomb of Rachel. "Yehoash," *Yiddish.* TrJP, *tr. by* Isidore Goldstick

O holy talk show host. The Wish Foundation. Carol Muske. PBCAP

O holy virgin! clad in purest white. To Morning. William Blake. OxAEP-2

O Holy Water. Margot Ruddock. OBMV

O / Holy / Wood. Sister Mary Madeleva. CRP

O! Honour! Honour! Honour! Oh! the Gain! God's Selecting Love in the Decree. Edward Taylor. PoEL-3 *Fr.* God's Determinations [touching his Elect].

O horrible enchantment, that him so did blend. Edmund Spenser. *See* In the Bower of Bliss.

O how canst thou renounce the boundless store. The Youth of a Poet. James Beattie. NOEC *Fr.* The Minstrel.

O, how I faint when I of you do write. Sonnet 80. Shakespeare. OxAEP-1 *Fr.* Sonnets.

O how much I would like—. Osip Emilevich Mandelstam, *Russian.* PFTM, *tr. by* James Greene

O[h], how much more doth beauty beauteous seem. Sonnet 54. Shakespeare. AWP; OBEV; PoE; SCGP *Fr.* Sonnets.

O how my mind. Confusion. Christopher Hervey. BXAP; UV

O! How shall I picture, in delicate strain. Miss Emily Brittle Sails for India. Sir George Dallas. NOEC *Fr.* India Guide, The; or, Journal of a Voyage to the East Indies in 1780.

O, how sick and weary I. In a Myrtle [or Mirtle] Shade. William Blake. ChIV-1

—O how that glittering taketh me! (LL) Upon Julia's Clothes. Robert Herrick. APAD; AWP; BLPA; BeJo; CABP; CaPo; CavPo; ClHu; EBEV; EBEvV; EnLoPo; GBL; GLoP; GTBS-P; HAP; HeIP-4; HoPM; ImPo; InPS-3; NAEL-1; NBLV; NIP-4; NOBE; NOSC; NoP-4; OAEL-1; OBEV; OxAEP-1; OxBSP; PFE; PeLV; PoE; PoEL-3; PoPoPo; Poetr; SCGP; SeCP; TFi; TRP; TTTS; UV; WeW-3

O how the pleasant airs of true love be. Sonnet 78. Sir Philip Sidney. *Fr.* Astrophil and Stella. AAS; SiPS

O how unlike the scene my fancy forms. Against Formal Gardens. William Mason. GaP

O howls of crystal, milky souvenirs, desire piercing it's own. Cold Cash. Stephen Berg. BAP-93

O hundred-towered Prague. City With Towers. Vítězslau Nezval, *Czech.* PFTM, *tr. by* Jerome Rothenberg *and* Frantiseak Deak

O, hungry heart. Heart-Hungry. Josephine D. Henderson Heard. CBWP-4

O hurry where by water among the trees. The Ragged Wood. W. B. Yeats. CBLP; GBL

O, hush thee, my babie [*or* baby], thy sire was a knight. Lullaby of an Infant Chief. Sir Walter Scott. OxBChV

O! hush thee, my darling, sleep soundly my son. Lullaby. *Unknown, Yiddish.* TrJP, *tr.* by Alice Lucas

O! I do love thee, meek Simplicity! To Simplicity. Coleridge. *Fr.* Sonnets Attempted in the Manner of Contemporary Writers. Son

O I forbid you, maidens a' [*or* all]. Tam Lin. *Unknown.* ESPB; NOBE; OBEV; OBNV; OxBB; OxBS

O I had a future. I Had a Future. Patrick Kavanagh. BIrV; NoAM

O I had been to sunny Spain. On First Looking into Chapman's Homer. T. Griffiths. BXAP

O, I hae come from far away. The Witch's Ballad. William Bell Scott. CH; NOBVV; OBEV; PeVV; RACG

O I hae tint my rosy cheek. *Unknown.* FaBoVe

O, I remember you. The Removal of Our Village, KwaBhanya. Mbuyiseni Oswald Mtshali, *Zulu.* PeSAV, *tr.* by the author

O I say now these are the soul! (LL) Leaves of Grass (1855). Walt Whitman. CTC

O, I wad like to ken—to the beggar-wife says I. The Spaewife. Robert Louis Stevenson. OxBS

O I went into the stable. Our Goodman. *Unknown.* AmFP; ESPB

O I will sing to you a sang. The Clerk's Twa Sons o Owsenford. *Unknown.* ESPB

O, I yearn to go back to the Cam! Limerick. E. O. Parrott. PeLi

O I'm a jolly old cowboy. *Unknown.* CA

O I'm off to Hullaboola where the climate's never cooler. Folk Song. Bruce Beaver. OBCoV

O Immaculate Virgin. Conversation of a Private and the Virgin. Nikolai Ivanovich Glazkov, *Russian.* TCRP, *tr.* by Daniel Weissbort

O, insatiable monster! Could'st thou not. Requiem. Mary Weston Fordham. CBWP-2

O interminable desires, O futile hope. Sonnet 3. Louise Labé, *French.* BoWoP, *tr.* by Willis Barnstone

O Isis, Mother of God, to thee I pray! Prayer to Isis. Christina Walsh. BrRo

O islets green, Nature's immortal gems. Hymn to the Thousand Islands. Henrietta Cordelia Ray. CBWP-3

O it fell out upon a day. The Laird o Drum. *Unknown.* ESPB

O, it is hard to work for God. The Right Must Win. Frederick William Faber. PWR

O Italy, I see the lonely towers. To Italy. Giacomo Leopardi, *Italian.* AWP, *tr.* by Romilda Rendel

O it's best to be a total boor. David O'Bruadair, *Irish.* NOIV, *tr.* by Thomas Kinsella

O it's up in the Highlands, and along the sweet Tay. Bonnie James Campbell. *Unknown.* ESPB

O-JAZZ-O War Memoir: Jazz, Don't Listen To It At Your Own Risk. Bob Kaufman. *See* War Memoir: Jazz, Don't Listen to It at Your Own Risk.

O Jean, my Jean, when the bell ca's the congregation. Tam i' the Kirk. Violet Jacob. GBL

O Jehovah our Lord, how wondrous great, *par.* by Milton. Bible, *O.T. See* Psalm 8.

O Jellon Grame sat in Silver Wood. Jellon Grame. *Unknown.* EBEV; ESPB; OxBB

O Jenny dear, lay by your pride. Susanna Blamire. ECWP

O Jenny, don't sobby! vor I shall be true. A Zong. William Barnes. BoLoP

O Jesus Christ, True Light of God. John F. Ernst. AH

O Jesus, drink of me. (LL) A Better Resurrection. Christina Rossetti. NOBVV; VWP

O Jesus, My Savior, I Know Thou Art Mine. Caleb J. Taylor. AH

O John "Doctor" Donne, O John "Doctor" Donne. Death Again. T. Hope. BXAP

O Johney was as brave a knight. Johnie Scot. *Unknown.* ESPB

O, Jordan bank was a great old bank! One More River. *Unknown.* APN-2

O joy of creation / To be! What the Bullet Sang. Bret Harte. APAD; APN-2; OBEV

O joy! that in our embers. Wordsworth. *Fr.* Ode: Intimations of Immortality [from Recollections of Early Childhood]. AWP; FHYEP; HAP; HeIP-4; NOBE; NOBRP; OAEL-2; OBEV; OBNC; PBMP; PoE; PoEL-4

O joy, too high for my low style to show. Sonnet 69. Sir Philip Sidney. NAEL-1; OxAEP-1 *Fr.* Astrophil and Stella. AAS; SiPS

O keen pellucid air! nothing can lurk. A Brilliant Day. Charles Tennyson Turner. NOBVV

O Keeper of the Sacred Key. In State. Forceythe Willson. APN-2

O Keeper of the Sacred Key. Forceythe Willson. *Fr.* In State. APN-2

O Kentucky! my parents were driving. A Poem of the Forty-eight States. Kenneth Koch. NNaP; OBAL

O King, give Angilbert thy rest. Epitaph. Angilbert, *Latin.* MLL, *tr.* by Helen Waddell

O King, I know you gave me poison. Mirabai, *Medieval Hindi.* PBWP; WPOW, *tr.* by Usha Nilsson

O[h] King of grief! (a title strange, yet true). The Thanksgiving. George Herbert. ESCV; GeHe

O King of Saints, We Give Thee Praise and Glory. Mary A. Thomson. AH

O King of terrors. To Death. Anne Finch, Countess of Winchilsea. NoP-4

O King of the Friday. *Unknown, Irish.* BIrV, *tr.* by Douglas Hyde

O kiss, which dost those ruddy gems impart. Sonnet 81. Sir Philip Sidney. NAEL-1; Son *Fr.* Astrophil and Stella. AAS; SiPS

O knit me, that am crumbled dust! the heape. Distraction. Henry Vaughan. GeHe; SeCP

O Lady amorous, / Merciless lady. Canzonetta: A Bitter Song to His Lady. Pier Moronelli da Fiorenza, *Italian.* AWP; OBVE, *tr.* by D. G. Rossetti

O, Lady, awake! The azure moon. Aubade. *Unknown.* PFE

O lady full of guile. Geoffrey Keating, *Irish.* NOIV, *tr.* by Thomas Kinsella

O Lady Moon, your horns point toward the east. Christina Rossetti. OxBChV

O lady of all truths bright light going forth. Enheduanna. WPOW, *tr.* by Anne Draffkorn Kilmer *Fr.* Inanna Exalted.

O, Lady, rock never your young son young. Young Hunting. *Unknown.* ESPB; OxBB

O Lamb Give Me My Salt. *Unknown, Ibo.* PBA, *tr.* by Dennis C. Osadebay

O lapwing, thou fliest around the heath. William Blake. FaBoEE

O laugh it out, you laughsters! Incantation by Laughter. Velemir Khlebnikov, *Russian.* CBNP, *tr.* by Gary Kern

O, Lay Thy Hand in Mine, Dear! Gerald Massey. EBVV

O leafy yellowness you create for me. October. Patrick Kavanagh. CIP-2; GTBS-P

O leave me easy, leave me alone. (LL) The Libertine. Louis MacNeice. MoP; NoAM

O Leerie, see a little child and nod to him to-night! (LL) The Lamplighter. Robert Louis Stevenson. EBVV; OxBChV

O! Lest the world should task you to recite. Sonnet 72. Shakespeare. OxAEP-1 *Fr.* Sonnets.

O let me be in loving nice. Punctilio. Mary Elizabeth Coleridge. OBEV

O let me soar on steadfast wing. Prayer. Dennis Brutus. AF

O, let not e'er this quarrel be averred! *Unknown.* OBCVT, *tr.* by Shelley *Fr.* Hymn to Hermes.

O let the solid ground. My Day. Tennyson. NAEL-2; NOBVV *Fr.* Maud [A Monodrama]. EnVR

O Liberty, God-gifted. To the Bartholdi Statue. Ambrose Bierce. APN-2

O Life I Love and Cherish Like My Wife! Việt Phu'o'ng, *Vietnamese.* AVP, *tr.* by Huỳnh Sanh Thông

O, Life of Dreams! O, Dreams of Life! Timothy Thomas Fortune. AAP *Fr.* Dreams of Life.

O Life That Maketh All Things New. Samuel Longfellow. AH

O Life, who art thou that with scarcely scanned. Life Plastic. "Michael Field." VWP

O Light, 'tis I, who from death's other shores. Helen. Paul Valéry, *French.* OBVE, *tr.* by Robert Lowell

O lips full of lust and of laughter. Swinburne. UV *Fr.* Dolores.

O, listen for a moment, lads, and hear me tell my tale. Jim Jones. *Unknown.* CBAP

O listen, gude peopell, to my tale. The Laird o' Logie. *Unknown.* CH; ESPB

O [*or* Oh] listen, listen, ladies gay! Rosabelle. Sir Walter Scott. GTBS-P *Fr.* The Lay of the Last Minstrel.

O little broken doll, dropped in the well. The Broken Doll. Nuala Ni Dhomhnaill, *Irish.* BiHa, *tr.* by John Montague

"O little cloud," the virgin said, "I charge thee tell to me." William Blake. *Fr.* The Book of Thel. NAEL-2; OAEL-2; OBNC; PoE; PoEL-4

O little friend, your nose is ready; you sniff. Dog. Harold Monro. MoBrPo

O little Land of lapping seas. The Promised Land. Jessie E. Sampter. TrJP

O little mouse, so frightened of each sound. O Pity Our Small Size. Benjamin Rosenbaum. TrJP

O little town of Bethlehem. Phillips Brooks. AH; APN-2

O littleblood, hiding from the mountains in the mountains. Littleblood. Ted Hughes. *Fr.* Crow. PoE

O living always, always dying! Walt Whitman. NOBA

O living will that shalt endure. The Prayer. Tennyson. EBVV; EBVVPR; FaBoBe; OAEL-2 *Fr.* In Memoriam A. H. H.

O loathsome rodent with your endless squeaking. To the Rats. Edward John Langford Garston. NSI

O lonely workman, standing there. In the Moonlight. Thomas Hardy. NoAM *Fr.* Satires of Circumstance in Fifteen Glimpses.

O lonesome sea-gull, floating far. Sea-Birds. Elizabeth Akers Allen. FaBoBe

O, long their coupled joys maintain! Sir Philip Sidney. *See* Long Their Coupled Joys Maintain.

O, look at the moon. *Unknown.* CTV

O look not, lady, with disdain! The Tooth. Rebekah Carmichael. ECWP

O Lord, Almighty God. *Unknown.* AH

O Lord, Bow Down Thine Ear. Thomas Prince. AH

O Lord, How Lovely Is the Place. *Unknown.* AH, *ad. by* Francis Hopkinson

O Lord, how manifold are thy works! / In wisdom hast thou made them all. Bible, *O.T. See* Psalm 104.

O Lord, I been a-working. Trifling Women. *Unknown.* AmFP

O lord, I dred, and that I did not dred. Psalm 6. Bible, *O.T.* OBVE *Fr.* Psalms.

O Lord I shall be whole in deed. Jeremie 17. Bible, Apocrypha. ChIV-1

O, Lord/ If in life eternal. "Ping Hsin." WPOW *Fr.* Spring Waters.

O Lord in me there lieth nought. O Lord, Thou Hast Searched and Known Me. Mary Sidney Herbert, Countess of Pembroke. KSG; PEW

O Lord, in me there lieth nought, *par. by* Countess of Pembroke, Mary Sidney Herbert. Psalm 139. Bible, *O.T.* OBVE, *stanzas 7–10;* NOCV; NoSic; WPE *Fr.* Psalms.

O Lord, it was all night. Sun. James Dickey. CAPP-1

O Lord my sinne doth over-charge my brest. Sinnes Heavie Loade. Robert Southwell. ESCV

O Lord, my strength and my redemer, *ad. by* Miles Coverdale. Bible, *O.T. See* Psalm 19.

O Lord of Life. Washington Gladden. AH

O Lord of Light! A Mystic Sage Returns to Realms of Eternity! Askia Muhammad Touré. SeSe

O Lord, our God, Thy mighty hand. Peace Hymn of the Republic. Henry Van Dyke. AH

O Lord our God, how excellent is thy name in all the earth! (LL) Psalm 8. Bible, *O.T.* AWP; NAWM-1; PBMP; TrJP *Fr.* Psalms.

O Lord, rebuke me not in thine anger. Bible, *O.T. See* Psalm 6.

O Lord, Save We Beseech Thee. *Unknown.* TrJP

O Lord, sir, let me live, or let me see my death! Shakespeare. OxAEP-1 *Fr.* All's Well That Ends Well.

O Lord, spare him the Call. Salvation. George Ella Lyon. CrSp

O Lord, That Art My God and King. John Craig. AH

O Lord, that rul'st the human heart, *par. by* Christopher Smart. Bible, *O.T. See* Psalm 19.

O Lord, Thou Hast Been to the Land. *Unknown.* AH

O Lord, Thou Hast Enticed Me. Bible, *O.T.* TrJP *Fr.* Jeremiah.

O Lord, Thou Hast Searched and Known Me. Mary Sidney Herbert, Countess of Pembroke. KSG

(Psalm 139: Domine, Probasti.) PEW

O Lord, thou hast searched me, and known me. Bible, *O.T. See* Psalm 139.

O Lord thou seest my wrongs abound. Ode XV. Thomas Stanley. ChIV-1

O Lord, Turn Not Away Thy Face. John Marckant. AH

O Lord two things I thee require. Proverb, XXX. John Hall. ChIV-1

O Lord, we come this morning. Listen, Lord—[a Prayer]. James Weldon Johnson. BPo

O Lord, you know my inmost hope and thought. My Inmost Hope. Sarah Copia Sullam, *Italian.* TrJP

O Loss of sight, of thee I most complain. The Blindness of Samson. Milton. ImPo *Fr.* Samson Agonistes. FHYEP; OAEL-1; PoEL-3

O lost moon sisters. Diane Di Prima. *See* Ave.

O lost moon sisters / crescent in hair. Ave. Diane Di Prima. BB *Fr.* Loba.

O love, be fed with apples while you may. Sick Love. Robert Graves BoLoP; CMoP; EBEV; FaBoMo; GTBS-P; HAP; NOBE; OAEL-2; OxAEP-2

O Love Divine, That Stooped to Share. Oliver Wendell Holmes. AH *Fr.* The Professor at the Breakfast Table.

O! Love! how cold, and slow to take my part! Ovid. OBCVT, *tr. by* John Wilmot, 2d Earl of Rochester *Fr.* To Love.

O Love, how thou art tired out with rhyme! Of the Theme of Love. Margaret Lucas Cavendish, Duchess of Newcastle. OxBSP; PEW

O love, I never, never thought. Cancion. Juan II, of Castile, *Spanish.* AWP, *tr. by* George Ticknor

O Love in Me. Robert Graves. *See* Sick Love.

O, love, in your sweet name enough. Anne Finch. FaBoTw *Fr.* Essay on Marriage.

O Love, Love, Love! O withering might! Fatima. Tennyson. GBL; UnPo

O Love, my love, and perfect bliss! *Unknown. Fr.* Medieval Norman Song. AWP, *tr. by* John Addington Symonds

O Love, O thou that, for my fealty. Sonnet: To Love, In Great Bitterness. Cino da Pistoia, *Italian.* AWP, *tr. by* D. G. Rossetti

O Love That Lights the Eastern Sky. Louis FitzGerald Benson. AH

O Love! that stronger art than wine. Aphra Behn. *See* Song: "Oh! Love, that stronger art than wine."

O love, the interest itself in thoughtless heaven. Prologue. W. H. Auden. EBEV; FaBoMo

O love, turn from the unchanging sea, and gaze. October. William Morris. EnVR; OBNC *Fr.* The Earthly Paradise.

O Love! what art thou, Love? the ace of hearts. Love. Thomas Hood. CBLP

O love, what hours were thine and mine. The Daisy. Tennyson. EnLoPo; NOBVV; OBNC; PoEL-5

"O love, / where are you / leading / me now?" (LL) Kore. Robert Creeley. InPS-3; RaBo

O Love, who all this while hast urged me on. Canzone: To Love and to His Lady. Guido Delle Colonne, *Italian.* AWP, *tr. by* D. G. Rossetti

O Love, whose patient pilgrim feet. The Golden Wedding. David Gray. FaBoBe

O, loveliest throat of all sweet throats. Edna St. Vincent Millay. OxBA *Fr.* Memorial to D. C.

O lovely age of gold! Pastoral[I], A: "Oh [*or* O] happy golden age." Torquato Tasso. AWP; OBVE, *tr. by* Leigh Hunt; OAEL-1; PoEL-2, *tr. by* Samuel Daniel *Fr.* Aminta.

O lovely April, rich and bright. Song. Gustave Kahn, *French.* TrJP, *tr. by* Ludwig Lewisohn

O lovely maiden, thou hast drawn my heart. The Unhappy Lover. Judah Al-Harizi, *Hebrew.* TrJP, *tr. by* J. Chotzner

O lovely O most charming pug. Sonnet, A: "O lovely O most charming pug." Marjory Fleming. NBLV

O lovely thing. Psalm 92: Bonum Est Confiteri. Mary Sidney Herbert, Countess of Pembroke. PEW

O [*or* Oh] lovers' eyes are sharp to see. The Maid of Neidpath. Sir Walter Scott. GTBS-P

O luely, luely can she in. The Tryst [*or* Trysting Place]. William Soutar. BoLoP; EBEV; FaBoTC; OxBS

O Lusty May, with Flora queen! Lusty May. *Unknown.* OBEV; OxBS

O luxury! Thou curst by Heaven's decree. Oliver Goldsmith. BIrV *Fr.* The Deserted Village. NOEC; OAEL-1; PoEL-3

O Lyric Love. Winfield Townley Scott. VGW

O madam, I will give to you the keys of Canterbury. The Keys of Canterbury. *Unknown.* AmFP

O magnificent and many. *Unknown, Chinese.* SuSp, *tr. by* C. H. Wang

O maister deere and fader reverent! Thomas Hoccleve. EBEV *Fr.* De Regimine Principum.

O Maistres Myn. *Unknown.* OxBS

O make me a mask and a wall to shut from your spies. Dylan Thomas. PoA

O Maker of the starry world. Boethius, *Latin.* MLL, *tr. by* Helen Waddell *Fr.* Consolation of Philosophy, The ("De Consolacione Philosophie").

O man of the seashore. What Her Girl Friend Said to Him When He Wanted to Come by Day. Ammuvanar, *Tamil.* PLW, *tr. by* A. K. Ramanujan

O! Mankinde. See! Here, My Heart. *Unknown.* NoP-4

O, Mare Atlanticum. The Sleep of My Lions. Douglas Livingstone. PeSAV

O Margie, Marge, dear Margaret. Oswald von Wolkenstein, *German.* GePo, *tr. by* J. W. Thomas

O [*or* Oh] Mary, at the window be. Mary Morison. Robert Burns. AWP; GTBS-P; OBEV; OxBS

"O Mary, go and call the cattle home." Charles Kingsley. *See* The Sands of Dee.

O [*or* Oh] Mary, go and call the cattle home. The Sands of Dee. Charles Kingsley. CH; EBEvV; EBVV; FaPoR; OxAEP-2 *Fr.* Alton Locke.

O Mary Hamilton to the kirk is gane. Mary Hamilton. *Unknown.* NOBE; OxBB

O Mary Mary lying on the wheel. Visitor's Parking. Anne Szumigalski. NOBC

O Mary sing thy songs to me. Song. John Clare. CBLP

O master dear, and father reverent! An Admirer's Lament of Chaucer. Thomas Hoccleve. EPCY *Fr.* Regiment of Princes.

O Master, Let Me Walk with Thee. Washington Gladden. AH; PWR

O Master Masons. Ernst Toller, *German.* TrJP, *tr. by* Ashley Dukes

O Master of the heart, whose magic skill. To the Author of Clarissa. Thomas Edwards. Son

O Master-Workman of the Race. Jay Thomas Stocking. AH

O [*or* Oh] may I join the choir invisible. The Choir Invisible. "George Eliot." EBVV; OBNC

O may I with myself agree. John Dyer. *Fr.* Grongar Hill. CABP; NOEC; NoP-4; OxAEP-1; PoEL-3

O May she comes, and May she goes. The Bonny Hind. *Unknown.* ESPB; OxBB

O me, oh my, oh you. Does the Spearmint Lose Its Flavor on the Bedpost Overnight? Billy Rose. OBAL

O[h] me[e], the time is [or has] come to part. Song. Mary Sidney, Countess of Montgomery Wroth. NOSC *Fr.* Pamphilia to Amphilanthus.

O me! what eyes hath Love put in my head. Blind Love. Shakespeare. GTBS-P *Fr.* Sonnets.

O 'Melia, my dear, this does everything crown! The Ruined Maid. Thomas Hardy. BoLoP; CMoP; FaBoVe; HeIP-4; NAEL-2; NBLV; NOBL; OxBTC; PeLV; PeVV; SCV; TFi; TRP

O Meliwa, I come, a messenger of the Beautiful Ones. "Advice" to a Young Poet. Raymond Mazisi Kunene, *Zulu.* PeSAV, *tr. by the author*

O memory! that which I gave thee. Flight. Charles Stuart Calverley. OBCoV

O Memory, Thou Fond Deceiver'. Oliver Goldsmith. OxBSP *Fr.* The Captivity.

(Memory.) OBEV

O men from the fields! A Cradle Song. Padraic Colum. TIRV

O men, walk on the hills. Poem. Maxwell Bodenheim. TrJP

O merciful God, hear this our request. A Prayer to Be Said When Thou Goest to Bed. Francis Seager. OxBChV

O Merlin in your crystal cave. Merlin. Edwin Muir. FaBoTw; OxBS; RB

O! mestress, why. *Unknown.* MiEL

O Michael, servant of the eternal King. Dedication to St. Michael. Alcuin, *Latin.* MLL, *tr. by* Helen Waddell

O mickle yeuks the keckle doup. Justice to Scotland. *Unknown.* NBLV

O might some verse with happiest skill persuade. William Collins. EPCY *Fr.* Epistle, An, Addressed to Sir Thomas Hanmer, on His Edition of Shakespeares Works.

O might those sigh[e]s and tear[e]s return[e] again[e]. Donne. *Fr.* Holy Sonnets. ESCV *Fr.* Holy Sonnets.

O mighty Cæsar! dost thou lie so low? Shakespeare. OxAEP-1 *Fr.* Julius Caesar.

O mighty-mouthed [or mouth'd] inventor of harmonies. Milton [Alcaics]. Tennyson. EPCY; PeECV

O Mighty Nothing! unto thee. And He Answered Them Nothing. Richard Crashaw. ChIV-2

O mightye Muse. George Puttenham. PBRV *Fr.* Partheniades.

O mild Christ. Ellen Bryant Voigt. CrSp *Fr.* Feast Day.

O mine own sweet heart. Simon and Susan. *Unknown.* OxBoLi

O miraculous blown country. The Mental Traveller's Landfall. Chris Wallace-Crabbe. BMAP

O miserable sorrow withouten cure! Sir Thomas Wyatt. SiPS

O miss, I'll give you a paper of pins. *Unknown. See* Paper of Pins.

O mistress mine, till you I me commend. O Maistres Myn. *Unknown.* OxBS

O mistress mine, where are you roaming? Shakespeare. *See* Oh [or O] Mistress Mine.

O money is the meat in the cocoanut. Money. *Unknown.* AS

O months of joy, why hurry so? Slow down. Revolutionary Youth. Hồ Văn Hảo, *Vietnamese.* AVP, *tr. by* Huỳnh Sanh Thông

O months of blossoming, months of transfigurations. The Lilacs and the Roses. Louis Aragon, *French.* NNPT; OBWP, *tr. by* Louis MacNeice

O Moon, Mr. Moon. Mr. Moon. Bliss Carman. FPC

O more, and more! this was so well. Song. Ben Jonson. *Fr.* Pleasure Reconciled to Virtue. NAEL-1; OAEL-1

O Mors! Quam Amara Est Memoria Tua Homini Pacem Habenti In Substantiis Suis. Ernest Christopher Dowson. ADE; OBMV

("Lest I fail!") (LL) ADE

O mortal folk you may behold and see. The Epitaph of Graunde [or La Graunde] Amoure. Stephen Hawes. EBEV; FaBoEE; NoSic; OBEV *Fr.* The Pastime of Pleasure. OBGa

O mortal man, that lives by bread. Julius Caesar Ibbetson. FaBoEE

O Mother-heart! when fast the arrows flew. Niobe. Henrietta Cordelia Ray. CBWP-3

O mother, lay your hand on my brow! The Sick Child. Robert Louis Stevenson. CH

O mother, open the window wide. At Last. Elizabeth Siddal. VWP

O Mother Race! to thee I bring. Ode to Ethiopia. Paul Laurence Dunbar. NAAAL

O mother / what have I left out. IV. Allen Ginsberg. BB; CLPP *Fr.* Kaddish.

O [or Oh] my aged uncle Arly! Incidents in the Life of My Uncle Arly. Edward Lear. CBNP; OAEL-2; OBCoV; OxBoLi

O my body! I dare not desert the likes of you in other men and women, nor the likes of the parts of you. Walt Whitman. *Fr.* Leaves of Grass (1855). APN-1

O my bright star. Star. Pavel Davydovich Kogan, *Russian.* TCRP, *tr. by* Albert C. Todd

O my chief good. Good Friday. George Herbert. GeHe

O my chief good! The Passion. Henry Vaughan. ESCV

O my coy darling, still. Ode to a Dressmaker's Dummy. Donald Justice. NoAM

O [or Oh] my dark Rosaleen. Dark Rosaleen. Owen Roe MacWard *and* Hugh O'Donnell, *Irish.* AWP; BIrV; CH; IIP; NOIV; OBEV; OxAEP-2, *tr. by* James Clarence Mangan

O my dear father! Restoration, hang. Shakespeare. OxAEP-1 *Fr.* King Lear.

O my dearest [or deerest], I shall grieve thee. The Complement. Thomas Carew. CBLP

O my deir hert, young Jesus sweit. Balulalow. John James *and* Robert Wedderburn. OBEV

O my fair warrior! Shakespeare. OxAEP-1 *Fr.* Othello.

O my friends. Mirabai, *Rajasthani.* EnlH, *tr. by* Jane Hirshfield

'O, My Heart Is Woe'. *Unknown.* ChIV-2

O my Heart, my Mother, my Heart, my Mother. He Approacheth the Hall of Judgment. *Unknown.* AWP *Fr.* Book of the Dead.

O my heart's heart, and you who are to me. Christina Rossetti. *Fr.* Monna Innominata. BWW

O My Honey, Take Me Back. *Unknown.* AS

O my hornbill husband, you have a bad smell. Lament for a Husband. *Unknown, Papuan.* BoWoP, *tr. by* Don Laycock

O my Hornby and my Barlow long ago! (LL) At Lord's. Francis Thompson. EBVV; OPOU; OxBSP; PeLV

O my husband. . . / cut off from life so young! You leave me a widow. Homer. GrIP, *tr. by* Robert Fagles *Fr.* Priam and Achilles. NOSC; OBCVT, *tr. by* George Chapman *Fr.* The Iliad.

O My Invisible Estate. Bruce Smith. Son

"O my Joseph, Jacob's son." *Unknown.* ASW, *tr. by* Kevin Crossley-Holland *Fr.* Christ 1. AnOE, *tr. by* Charles W. Kennedy

O my lady, the Anunna, the great gods. Inanna and the Anunna. Enheduanna, *Sumerian.* BoWoP, *ad. by* Aliki *and* Willis Barnstone

O my land! O my love! Lament for Banba. Egan O'Rahilly. AWP, *tr. by* James Clarence Mangan

O my Lord. Rabi'a al-Adawiyya, *Persian.* WPoS, *tr. by* Jane Hirshfield

O my Lord, if I worship you from fear of Hell. Rabi'a al-Adawiyya, *Arabic.* BoWoP, *tr. by* Willis Barnstone

O my Lord, the stars glitter and eyes of men are closed. Rabi'a al-Adawiyya. BoWoP, *tr. by* Willis Barnstone.

O my lost husband! let me ever mourn. Andromache's Lamentation. Homer. OBVE, *tr. by* Congreve *Fr.* The Iliad.

O my love is like a red, red rose. Robert Burns. *See* A Red, Red Rose.

O my love, my wife! Shakespeare. OxAEP-1 *Fr.* Romeo and Juliet.

O my love / The pretty towns. Kenneth Patchen. VGW

O my lover, blind me. The Tired Woman. Anna Wickham. MoBrPo

O my Lucasia, let us speak our love. To My Lucasia, in Defence of Declared Friendship. Katherine Philips. MeLP

O[h] my luve's [or luve is or love is] like a red, red rose. A Red, Red Rose. Robert Burns. AWP; BoLoP; CBLP; FaBoBe; GBL; GTBS-P; HAP; HeIP-4; HoPM; ImPo; InPK-6; NAEL-2; NIP-4; NOBE; NOBRP; NOEC; NTP; OAEL-1; OBEV; OxAEP-2; OxBS; PoEL-4; PoLF; Poetr; SCGP; TFi; UV

O my mother. Nelly Sachs, *German.* MDDM, *tr. by* Ruth *and* Matthew Mead

O My Mother Isle! Coleridge. *Fr.* Fears in Solitude. FHYEP; OBWP

O my much praised but-not-altogether-satisfactory lady. (LL) The Bathtub [or Bath Tub]. Ezra Pound. PFE

O! my offense is rank, it smells to heaven. Shakespeare. OxAEP-1 *Fr.* Hamlet. NAWM-1

O my people, O my people, how to love you delicately? (LL) Song at the African Middle Class. Molara Ogundipe-Leslie. HBAPE; PBMAP

O My Poor Darling. Wilfred Watson. EnLoPo

O my pretty pink frock. The Pink Frock. Thomas Hardy. OxBSP

O my seven-stringed board. Drawer. Zbigniew Herbert, *Polish.* VCWP, *tr. by* Miosz, Czeslaw *and* Peter Dale Scott

O my son, farewell! Song for a Fallen Warrior. *Unknown, Blackfeet Native American.* APN-2, *tr. by* John Mason Browne

O My songs. Coda. Ezra Pound. NOBA; SAGP

O, my strong-minded sisters, aspiring to vote. Advice Gratis to Certain Women. Phoebe Cary. APN-2; PAR

O My Swallows! Ernst Toller, *German.* TrJP, *tr. by* Ashley Dukes

O my thoughts' sweet food, my only owner. Lady My Treasure. Sir Philip Sidney. GBL

O Mzingeli son of the illustrious clans. Elegy. Raymond Mazisi Kunene. PBMAP

O native Britain! O my Mother Isle! O My Mother Isle! Coleridge. *Fr.* Fears in Solitude. FHYEP; OBWP

O Nature! I do not aspire. Nature. Henry David Thoreau. AiP; FaBoBe

O Nature, thou to me was cruel. An Address to Nature on its Cruelty. Ellen Johnston. VWP

O Nectar! O Delicious Stream! Love. Thomas Traherne. GeHe

O Ness, let all men stand. The Song of Childbirth. *Unknown, Irish.* TIRV, *tr. by* Eleanor Hull

O [*or* Oh], never say that I was false of heart. Sonnet 109. Shakespeare. GTBS-P; NOBE; OBEV; OxAEP-1 *Fr.* Sonnets.

O New England, thou canst not boast. A Word to New England. William Bradford. SCAP

O NICIAS, there is no other remedy for love. Theocritus, *Greek.* NoSic ("O Nicias, there is no other remedie for love.") OBCVT, *tr. by Unknown* ("Which mighty Venus gave, and in his liver strucke the dart.") (LL) OBCVT, *tr. by Unknown*

O Night and Dark. Hymn for Morning. Prudentius, *Latin.* MLL, *tr. by* Helen Waddell

O night betrayed by darkness not its own. (LL) Night, Death, Mississippi. Robert Earl Hayden. ColAP; LCAP-2; NoP-4; PoPoPo; VCAP; VGW

O night cold without your nearness. Love. Elolongue Epanya Yondo, *French.* NegPo, *tr. by* Ellen Conroy Kennedy

O Night! dark Night! wrapped round with Stygian gloom! New Night Thoughts on Death; a Parody. William Whitehead. NOEC

O night, the ease of care, the pledge of pleasure. Night. Sir Philip Sidney. SiPS *Fr.* Arcadia.

O nightingale of woodland gay. *Unknown. Fr.* Medieval Norman Song. AWP, *tr. by* John Addington Symonds

O Nightingale, that on yon bloomy Spray. Milton. SCGP

O, No, John [*or* The One Answer]. *Unknown.* PeLV

O none but gods have power their love to hide. Marlowe. OxAEP-1 *Fr.* Hero and Leander. AAS

O nothing but the cold cry of the snow. (LL) In Memory of Kathleen. Kenneth Patchen. IMW; MoAmPo

O! nothing earthly save the ray. Al Aaraaf. Edgar Allan Poe. APN-1

O nothing in this corporal earth of man. All's Vast. Francis Thompson. GTBS-P; MoBrPo; OBMV; Son *Fr.* The Heart.

O now the drenched land wakes. Kenneth Patchen. CLPP; PoA

O now you come in rut. To Frighten a Storm. Gladys Cardiff. CDW

O nymph, compar'd with whose young bloom. To Lady Anne Fitzpatrick, When about Five Years Old, with a Present of Shells, 1772. Horace Walpole, 4th Earl of Orford. NOEC

O Nymphs, did Daphnis, passing by. Pan and the Nymphs. Glaukos, *Greek.* GrAn, *tr. by* Dudley Fitts

O nymphs that haunt the old Sicilian stream. Lament for Damon. John Milton, *Latin.* MLL, *tr. by* Helen Waddell

O-o-o-oh, lil' man. Chahcoal Man. *Unknown.* AS

O, one I need to love me. Friends—With a Difference. Mary Elizabeth Coleridge. VWP

O only Source of all our light and life. Qui Laborat, Orat. Arthur Hugh Clough. EnVR

O, Open the Door to Me, O! Robert Burns. *See* Open the Door to Me, Oh!

O, Opportunity, thy guilt is great. Opportunity. Shakespeare. NOBE; PoEL-2 *Fr.* The Rape of Lucrece.

O Osbert father Osbert. To Osbert Sitwell. Cyril Connolly. OBCoV

O our Mother the Earth, O our Father the Sky. Song of the Sky Loom. *Tewa Oral Tradition, Tewa.* PaTW, *tr. by* Herbert J. Spinden

O over / the thorn. Paul Celan. *See* Psalm: "No one kneads us again out of earth and clay."

O [*or* Oh] Paddy, dear, and [*or* an'] did you hear the news that's going [*or* goin'] 'round? The Wearing of [*or* Wearin' o'] the Green. *Unknown.* AWP; FaPoR; IIP; OxBoLi

O Painter of the fruits and flowers. Garden. John Greenleaf Whittier. OBGa

O Paleys [*or* palace], whylom [*or* whilom] croune [*or* crown] of houses all[e]. The Complaint of Troilus. Chaucer. NOBE; OBEV *Fr.* Troilus and Criseyde [*or* Criseide]. EnVB

O Parcy Reed has Crozer ta'en. Parcy Reed. *Unknown.* OxBB

O, pardon me, thou bleeding piece of earth. Shakespeare. EBEvV; OxAEP-1 *Fr.* Julius Caesar.

O Passenger, pray list and catch. The Levelled Churchyard. Thomas Hardy. NOBL

O patient shore, that canst not go to meet. Tides. Helen Hunt Jackson. LW

O Patrick, hail, who once the wand'ring race. Saint Patrick. Sir Shane Leslie. TIRV

O Peace, O Dove, O shape of the Holy Ghost. To Peace. Richard Watson Dixon. OxAEP-2

O peerless marble marvel! what of grace. The Venus of Milo. Henrietta Cordelia Ray. CBWP-3

O people who live in the world. Andal, *Tamil.* BoWoP, *tr. by* Willis Barnstone

O perfite light, quhilk schaid away. Of the Day Estivall. Alexander Hume. NOCV; OxBS

O Peter, O Apostle, hast thou seen my bright love. The Keening of Mary. *Unknown, Irish.* TIRV, *tr. by* Padraic Pearse

O pine-tree standing. Hakutsu, *Japanese.* AWP; TAL, *tr. by* Arthur Waley *Fr.* Manyo Shu, Part 3 of 4.

O Pioneers! John Peale Bishop. VGW

O Pity Our Small Size. Benjamin Rosenbaum. TrJP

O Pleasing Thoughts. Thomas Lodge. Son *Fr.* Phyllis.

O, po' sinner, O, now is yo' time. What Yo' Gwine to [*or* t'] Do When Yo' [*or* de] Lamp Burn Down? *Unknown.* APN-2; BPo

O Poesy! for thee I hold my pen. Keats. FHYEP *Fr.* Sleep and Poetry.

O poet gifted with the sight divine! Milton. Henrietta Cordelia Ray. BlSi; CBWP-3

O poet rare and old! Astræa. John Greenleaf Whittier. APN-1

O poet strutting from the sandbagged portal. As One Non-Combatant to Another. George Orwell. OxBTC

O Polly, you might have toy'd and kist. John Gay. EnLoPo *Fr.* The Beggar's Opera. OAEL-1

O Polyphemus, while your flocks you keep. Theocritus. OBCVT, *tr. by* Francis Fawkes *Fr.* The Herdsmen.

O poor Catullus, stupid long enough! Catullus. *See* Carmen 8 ("Break off / fallen Catullus").

O poor me! / Who am going out to fight the enemy. The Song of the Lenape Warriors Going against the Enemy. *Unknown, Delaware Native American.* APN-2, *tr. by* John Heckewelder

O Powers Celestial, with what sophistry. Barnabe Barnes. EnLoPo *Fr.* Parthenophil and Parthenophe.

O pr / gress verily thou art m. E. E. Cummings. UV

O pray! Example take too, and have care. (LL) After the Pleasure Party. Herman Melville. APN-2; NAAL-1; NAAL-3; NCAP; PAR; PoEL-5

O precious codex [*or* code], volume, tome. To a Thesaurus. Franklin Pierce Adams. NBLV

O quick quick quick, quick hear the song-sparrow. Cape Ann. T. S. Eliot. NAEL-2; NoAM *Fr.* Landscapes. RB

O quondam pre-and-post-bellum. The Bitch-Kitty. Jonathan Williams. PoM

O Rab an' Dave an' rantin' Jim. Jock, to the First Army. Violet Jacob. NSI

O radiance, into which I go on dying. . . . (LL) Monet: 'Les Nymphéas'. W. D. Snodgrass. CoAP; CoAmPo

O radiant luminary of light interminable. A Prayer to the Father of [*or* in] Heaven. John Skelton. HoPM

O raging seas, and mighty Neptune's reign! Coming Homeward out of Spain. Barnabe Googe. NoSic

Virginia. Hart Crane. *Fr.* Three Songs. NAAL-2 *Fr.* The Bridge. NAAL-2

O rain, depart with blessings. Song of the Dew. *Unknown, Hebrew.* TrJP, *tr. by* Solomon Solis-Cohen

O! raise the woefull Pillalu. An Irish Lamentation. Goethe, *German.* AWP, *tr. by* James Clarence Mangan

O [*or* Oh] rare Harry Parry. Harry Parry. *Unknown.* OxNR

O rare Narcissus! sunny-haired! Echo's Complaint. Henrietta Cordelia Ray. CBWP-3

O Realm Bejewelled. Forugh Farrokhzad, *Farsi.* WPOW, *tr. by* Jascha Kessler *and* Amin Banani

O, red-hot pepper pod. Hymn to the Pepper. Novella Nikolaevna Matveyeva, *Russian.* TCRP, *tr. by* Deming Brown

O, rest ye, brother mariners, we will not wander more. (LL) The Lotus-Eaters. Tennyson. EBEvV; EBVVPR; EnVR; FHYEP; NAEL-2; NoP-4; OAEL-2; PoEL-5; SCGP

O restless, caressing eyes. *Unknown, Greek.* PGA, *tr. by* Kenneth Rexroth

O Restless Heart, Be Still! Henrietta Cordelia Ray. CBWP-3

O Ride On, Jesus. *Unknown.* AH

O Risen Lord upon the Throne. Louis FitzGerald Benson. AH

O river, green and still. Boy in Ice. Laurie Lee. NYBP

O road in dizzy moonlight bleak and blue. La Quinque Rue. Edmund Blunden. PeFWW

O rocking boat, rocking boat poised on the wave. Boat Song. Henrietta Cordelia Ray. CBWP-3

O Roger, Mackerel, Riley, Ned, Nellie, Chester, Lady Ghost. (LL) Names of Horses. Donald Hall. AFr; HAP; InPK-6; SoSe-8; TRP

O Rose the Red and White Lil[l]y. Rose the Red and White Lil[l]y. *Unknown.* ESPB; OxBB

O Rose, thou art sick[!]. The Sick Rose. William Blake. AWP; BoLoP; ClHu; EBEvV; EnLoPo; FHYEP; HAP; HeIP-4; InPK-6; InPS-3; NAEL-2; NAWM-2; NIP-4; NOBE; NOBRP; NOEC; OAEL-2; OBNC; OPOU; OxAEP-2; OxBSP; PoE; PoEL-4; Poetr; RB; SCGP; SoSe-8; TFi; TRP; WeW-3 *Fr.* Songs of Experience.

O Ross, thou wale of hearty cocks. To Mr. Alexander Ross. James Beattie. OxBS

O rosy red, O torrent splendour. Come On, My Lucky Lads. Edmund Blunden. PeFWW

O Rourk's noble fare. The Description of an Irish Feast. Hugh MacGowran, *Irish*. NOIV; OBCoV, *tr. by* Jonathan Swift

O rows and rows of mounds for the dead! War Poems 7. Sang Ku, *Korean*. CKP, *tr. by* Jaihiun Kim

O ruddier than the cherry! Air. John Gay. CBLP; EBEvV; NAEL-1; NOBE; NOEC *Fr.* Acis and Galatea.

O ruined father dead, long sweetly rotten. For the Word Is Flesh. Stanley Kunitz. VGW

O sacred head, now wounded. Paul Gerhardt, *German*. GePo

O sacred poesie, thou spirit of artes. Ben Jonson. PoEL-2 *Fr.* The Poetaster.

O sage of the stage, Shaw of Shaws! Limerick. Harold Ellis. PeLi

O sailing stars! Star Song. Henrietta Cordelia Ray. CBWP-3

O sailor, come ashore. Christina Rossetti. BoTP *Fr.* Sing-Song.

O sailor, come ashore, / What have you brought for me? Christina Rossetti. BoTP

O salty sea, how much of your salt. The Portuguese Sea. Fernando Pessoa. PeSAV

O save thy children blue Ontario! John Neal. APN-1 *Fr.* The Battle of Niagara.

O Saviour of a World Undone. Leonard Withington. AH

"O saw ye my father? or saw ye my mother?" The Grey Cock, or, Saw You My Father? *Unknown*. ESPB

O saw ye not fair Ines? Fair Ines. Thomas Hood. OBEV

O, Saw Ye the Lass. Richard Ryan. FaBoBe

O say can u see. On Watching a World Series Game. Sonia Sanchez. NBV

O say, can you see, by the dawn's. Francis Scott Key. *See* The Star-Spangled Banner.

O say, have you seen at the Willows so green. The Ballad of the Emeu. Bret Harte. NBLV

O say what is that thing call'd Light. The Blind Boy. Colley Cibber. GTBS-P; NOEC; OxBChV

O sea, break as you pour down from heaven. The Youthful Sea. Tujin Park, *Korean*. CKP, *tr. by* Jaihiun Kim

O sea goddess Nuliajuk. Magic Words for Hunting Seal. *Unknown, Eskimo*. STP, *tr. by* Edward Field

O sea-gulls that are crying. *Unknown, Japanese*. TAL, *tr. by* Arthur Waley

O Sea, take all, since thou hast taken him. Henry I to the Sea. Eugene Lee-Hamilton. PeVV

O see how narrow are our days. Prayer of the Maidens to Mary. Rilke, *German*. AWP, *tr. by* Jethro Bithell

O seeded grass, you army of little men. John Gould Fletcher. *Fr.* Irradiations. MoAmPo

O, Seeger, the might you tied the cabbie. Quarry/Rock. Paul Mariah. GLP

O! seize again thy golden quill. To Della Crusca. The Pen. Hannah Cowley. NOBRP

O! sely anker, that in thy celle. Go, Sad Complaint. Charles, Duc d' Orléans. EnVB

O Shadow, in thy fleeting form I see. The Shadow. John Banister Tabb. APN-2

O Shannadore, I love your daughter. The Wide Mizzoura. *Unknown*. AS

O she looked out of the window. The Two Magicians. *Unknown*. OAEL-1; OxBoLi

O[h], she walked unaware of her own increasing beauty. She Walked Unaware. Patrick MacDonogh. BoLoP; FaBoTw

O she was full of loving fuss. One of the Principal Causes of War. "Hugh MacDiarmid." OxBSP

O shield me from his rage, celestial Powers! Esther Johnson. *See* Jealousy.

O shining and wreathed in violets, city of singing. Athens. Pindar, *Greek*. OBCVT, *tr. by* Richmond Lattimore

O Ship of State. Henry Wadsworth Longfellow. *See* The Ship of State.

O short shrift's the best shrift to give to this *Festschrift*! Unlikely Obbligato of Andersonstown. Kit Wright. OBCoV

O! should all Potentates whose higher birth. William Browne. PBRV *Fr.* Britannia's Pastorals Book 2.

O silent wood, I enter thee. A Silent Wood. Elizabeth Siddal. NOBVV

O silver splendor, marvelous! A Vision of Moonlight. Henrietta Cordelia Ray. CBWP-3

O [*or* Oh] silver-throated swan. The Dying Swan. Thomas Sturge Moore. OBMV

O, silver tree! Langston Hughes. *See* Jazzonia.

O Simplicitas. Madeleine L'Engle. OBCP; PChr *Fr.* Three Songs of Mary.

O Sing to Me of Heaven. Mary Stanley Bunce Dana. AH

O sing unto the Lord a new song; for he hath done marvellous [*or* marvelous] things. Psalm 98. Bible, *O.T.* TrJP *Fr.* Psalms.

O! sing ye a dirge for the loved and the lost. Tribute to a Lost Steamer. Mary Weston Fordham. CBWP-2

O singer of Persephone! Theocritus. Oscar Wilde. NOBE

O Sion, Haste, Thy Mission High Fulfilling. Mary A. Thomson. AH

O sister of wealth. Andal. WPoS *Fr.* The Tiruppavai.

O sister, / where do you pitch your tent? Nelly Sachs, *German*. AF, *tr. by* Matthew Mead *and* Ruth Mead

O skull, a human creature owned you once! The Human Skull. Chế Lan Viên, *Vietnamese*. AVP, *tr. by* Huỳnh Sanh Thông

O sky & earth! How ye are linked together. Lago Maggiore. Thomas Cole. APN-1

O sleep, my babe, hear not the rippling wave. Sara Coleridge. OBNC *Fr.* Phantasmion.

O Sleep, O tranquil son of noiseless Night. To Sleep. Giovanni Della Casa, *Italian*. AWP, *tr. by* John Addington Symonds

O sleepy city of reeling wheelchairs. The Wheelchair Butterfly. James Tate. LCAP-2; NoAM

O small and squat. Songs of the Fruits and Sweets of Childhood. Lorna Goodison. VCWP

O smooth flatterers, go over sea. Reflection and Advice. Ezra Pound. OBSV

O [*or* Oh] snatch'd away in beauty's bloom! Elegy. Byron. GTBS-P

O snowflake clouds, O feath'ry clouds. Cloud Song. Henrietta Cordelia Ray. CBWP-3

O so white, O so soft, O so sweet is she! (LL) So White, So Soft, So Sweet. Ben Jonson. APAD; OBEV

O soft embalmer of the still midnight! To Sleep. Keats. EBEvV; LaPo; NAEL-2; NIP-4; OBEV; PoEL-4; Son

"O soldier, O soldier, won't you marry me now." Soldier, Won't You Marry Me? *Unknown*. AmFP; OxBoLi; PeLV

O soldiers, soldiers, get ye back, I pray! Saved. Adah Isaacs Menken. CBWP-1

O solo mio, hot diggety, nix 'I wather think I can'. Poem. Frank O'Hara. TTTS

O! Solomon! let us try again. (LL) Solomon and the Witch. W. B. Yeats. ChIV-1; NoAM

O sometimes in the street, or in the Paris Metro. Remembrance. Antoni Slonimski, *Polish*. TrJP, *tr. by* Frances Notley

O Son of God, it would be sweet. Saint Columcille. NOIV

O Son[ne] of God, who seeing two things. The Son. Donne. NOCV *Fr.* The Litanie. PoEL-2

O son of man, by lying tongues adored. On the Russian Persecution of the Jews. Swinburne. Son

O Son of Man, Thou Madest Known. Milton S. Littlefield. AH

O son of man, when thou findest wine. Five Arabic Verses in Praise of Wine. *Unknown, Arabic*. TrJP, *tr. by* Hartwig Hirschfeld

O son of mine, when dusk shall find thee bending. From Generation to Generation. Sir Henry John Newbolt. FaBoTw

O Son of the living God. Manchán's Prayer. Saint Manchán. NOIV

O song as yet unsung! A Song as Yet Unsung. "Yehoash," *Yiddish*. TrJP, *tr. by* Isidore Goldstick

O! sop of sorrow, sonkin into cair. Cresseid's Complaint against Fortune. Robert Henryson. *Fr.* The Testament of Cresseid. OxBS

O Sorrow, cruel fellowship. Tennyson. EBVVPR; EnVR; HAP; OAEL-2 *Fr.* In Memoriam A. H. H.

O sorrow! He is one who jumps. Springbok. *Unknown, Hottentot*. PeSA

O Sorrow,/ Why dost borrow. Song of the Indian Maid. Keats. CH; NOBE; OBEV *Fr.* Endymion: Poetic Romance.

O soul, canst thou not understand. Aridity. "Michael Field." OBMV

O soul, why shouldst thou downcast be? Hope Thou in God. Josephine D. Henderson Heard. CBWP-4

O Soul, with Storms Beset. Solomon ibn Gabirol, *Hebrew*. TrJP, *tr. by* Alice Lucas

O sovereign power of love! O grief! O balm! Keats. OBNC *Fr.* Endymion: Poetic Romance.

O spare a tear for poor Tom Hood. Elegy on Thomas Hood. Martin Fagg. BXAP; NOBL; UV

O spirit of the days gone bye. January. John Clare. Ro *Fr.* The Shepherd's Calendar.

O Spring, thou youthful beauty of the year. Spring. Giovanni Battista Guarini, *Italian*. AWP, *tr. by* Leigh Hunt

O St. James Road. Swath. Federico García Lorca. PFTM

O stagnant east-wind, palsied mare. A Room on a Garden. Wallace Stevens. NoP-4; OBGa

O Star (the fairest one in sight). Choose Something like a Star. Robert Frost. MoAmPo

O starry Temple of unvalted space. William Alabaster. ESCV *Fr.* Divine Meditations. Son

O! start a revolution, somebody! D. H. Lawrence. FaBoEE

O stay that covetous hand! First turn all eye. Upon the Curtain[e] of Lucasta's Picture [It Was Thus Wrought]. Richard Lovelace. CaPo

O stiffly shapen houses that change not. Suburbs on a Hazy Day. D. H. Lawrence. OBMV

O still small voice of calm. (LL) Dear Lord and Father of Mankind. John Greenleaf Whittier. AH; NOCV

O still their Tongues till morning comes! (LL) Resentments Composed because of the Clamor of Town Topers Outside My Apartment. Sarah Kemble Knight. AiP; SCAP

O stony grey soil of Monaghan. Stony Grey Soil. Patrick Kavanagh. CIP-2

O stormy, stormy world. Happiness Makes Up in Height for What It Lacks in Length. Robert Frost. MoAmPo; SoSe-8

O Strength and Stay upholding all creation. Saint Ambrose, *Latin*. OBCVT, *tr. by* Ellerton, John and Fenton John Anthony Hort

Ô[h] strive not[t] still to heap[e] disdain[e] on me[e]. Sonnet 6. Mary Sidney, Countess of Montgomery Wroth. NOSC *Fr.* Pamphilia to Amphilanthus.

O study Nature! and with thought profound. The Rise and Progress of the Present Taste in Planning Parks, Pleasure Grounds, Gardens, etc. *Unknown.* OBGa *Fr.* The Rise and Progress of the Present Taste in Planning Parks, Pleasure Grounds, Gardens, etc.

O subtle, musky, slumbrous clime! To the South. Maurice Thompson. CBCWP

O such a commotion under the ground. Flower Chorus. Ralph Waldo Emerson. BoTP

O Suen, the usurper Lugalanne means nothing to me! Appeal to the Moongod Nanna-Suen to Throw Out Lugalanne. Enheduanna, *Sumerian.* BoWoP, *tr. by* Aliki *and* Willis Barnstone

O suitably-attired-in-leather-boots. Fragment of a Greek Tragedy. A. E. Housman. NOBL; PeLV

O sun, and moonlight shining in the woods. Carmen Saeculare. Charles Hubert Sisson, *after the Latin of* Horace. OBVE

O sun, be his protection. Branwen's Starling. R. Williams Parry, *Welsh.* OBWVE, *tr. by* Gwyn Jones

O sun, great Oriental, my proud mind's golden cap. Nikos Kazantzakis. GrIP, *tr. by* Kimon Friar *Fr.* The Odyssey: A Modern Sequel.

O Sun! O age-old labor mixed with ocean. Edouard Glissant. NegPo, *tr. by* Ellen Conroy Kennedy *Fr.* The Indies.

O sundew, not remembering her. (LL) The Sundew. Swinburne. OBNC; PeVV

O suns [*or* sun] and skies and clouds of June. October's Bright Blue Weather. Helen Hunt Jackson. BLPA; FaBoBe

O supercilious delicious Rhodope. Irenaeus Referendarius, *Greek.* GrAn, *tr. by* Andrew Miller

"O Swallow, Swallow, flying, flying south". Tennyson. SCGP

O, sweep of stars over Harlem streets. Stars. Langston Hughes. GLP

O sweet and bitter monuments of pain. Upon the Ensigns of Christ's Crucifying. William Alabaster. NoSic

O sweet are tropic lands for waking dreams. North and South. Claude McKay. AmPP

O sweet dead artist and seer, O tender prophetic priest. The Separated East. Ernest Francisco Fenollosa. APN-2 *Fr.* East and West.

O sweet delight, O more than human[e] bliss[e]. Song. Thomas Campion. CBLP

O sweet everlasting Voices be still. The Everlasting Voices. W. B. Yeats. AWP

O sweet frustrations, I shall be back for more. (LL) A Voice from under the Table. Richard Wilbur. AmPP; HAP; NOBA

O sweet, sad, singing river. Song. Henrietta Cordelia Ray. CBWP-3

O sweet spontaneous. E. E. Cummings. APAD; MoP; NAAL-2; NoAM; Poetr; RaBo

O sweet woods, the delight of solitariness! Solitariness. Sir Philip Sidney. NoSic; PoEL-1; SCGP; SiPS *Fr.* Arcadia.

O[h] sweet woods, the delight of solitariness! Sweetly Empty Woods. Sir Philip Sidney. *Fr.* Solitariness. SCGP; SiPS *Fr.* Arcadia.

O sweete and bitter monuments of paine. Upon the Ensignes of Christes Crucifying. William Alabaster. ESCV *Fr.* Divine Meditations. Son

O SWEETEST WATER O GLORIOUS / WHEELING / BIRD. (LL) Song of the Turkey Buzzard. Lew Welch. BB

O swiftly, re-light the flame. Hilda Doolittle. NALW *Fr.* Tribute to the Angels.

O, Swimmers, this is the dream. Prayer to the Sockeye Salmon. *Kwakiutl Oral Tradition, Kwakiutl.* PaTW, *tr. by* Franz Boas

O Swine that takest away our sins / That takest away. Anthony Hecht. *See* Pig.

O sylvan priest of nature! rightly thou. A Thought at Walden. Henrietta Cordelia Ray. CBWP-3

O Sylvan prophet, whose eternal fame. Hymn for St. John's Eve. *Unknown, Latin.* AWP, *tr. by* Dryden

O Sylvia, Sylvia. Sylvia's Death. Anne Sexton. LCAP-2; NAAL-2; NALW

O! synge untoe mie roundelaie. Thomas Chatterton. *See* Mynstrelle's Songe ("O! synge untoe mie roundelaie").

O Syrian dancing-girl with the filleted hair. Copa: The Barmaid. Virgil, *Latin.* NNPT, *tr. by* Jack Lindsay

O-ta-pa! / I am creeping on your track. The Approaching Dance. *Unknown.* APN-2 *Fr.* War Dance. APN-2, *tr. by* George Catlin

O-ta-pa! / Why run you from us when you. Eh-Ros-ka, the Warrior's Dance. *Unknown.* APN-2 *Fr.* War Dance. APN-2, *tr. by* George Catlin

O take me to the sullen flats. From the Righteous Man Even the Wild Beasts Run Away. David Bromwich. PoA

O tan-faced prairie-boy. Walt Whitman. EP

O Taste and See. Denise Levertov. ChIV-1; CrSp; NoP-4; PBWP; PoPoPo; TAP

    ("And plucking / the fruit.") (LL) NoP-4

    ("Fruit, The.") (LL) PoPoPo

    ("World is, The.") NoP-4; PoPoPo

O tears, no tears, but rain from beauty's skies. Sonnet 100. Sir Philip Sidney. Son *Fr.* Astrophil and Stella. AAS; SiPS

O tell me, pretty river! The River. *Unknown.* PWR

O tell me whence that joy doth spring. The Queer. Henry Vaughan. PoEL-2

O tender-heartedness right bitter grown. Fragmenti. Ezra Pound. PoA

O Tender under Her Right Breast. George Barker. MoBrPo *Fr.* Second Cycle of Love Poems.

O terrible is the highest thing. Kenneth Patchen. VGW

O Thalassa! Thalassa! Where, where. The Singers. George Bruce. OxBS

O that great Sabbaoth God graunt me that Sabaoths sight! (LL) Mutability. Edmund Spenser. PoEL-1

O that I could a sin once see! Sin. George Herbert. OxBSP

O, That I Had Some Secret Place. *Unknown.* AmFP

O that it were possible we might. John Webster. IMW *Fr.* The Duchess of Malfi. NAEL-1

"O that mastering tune!" And up in the bed. In the Nuptial Chamber. Thomas Hardy. InPK-6 *Fr.* Satires of Circumstance in Fifteen Glimpses.

O that mine eyes might closed be. A Prayer. Thomas Elwood. PWR

O that our dreamings all, of sleep or wake. Keats. OAEL-2 *Fr.* To J. H. Reynolds, Esq.

O, that the Holy Angels would indite. The Quarto Centennial. Josephine D. Henderson Heard. CBWP-4

O that the rain would come—the rain in big battalions. Precursors. Louis MacNeice. OxBSP

O, that the years had language! time would / tell. Judith. Eloise Bibb. CBWP-4

O! that this too too solid flesh would melt. Frailty, Thy Name is Woman. Shakespeare. OxAEP-1; SCV *Fr.* Hamlet. NAWM-1

O[h] that 'twere possible. If Only. Tennyson. BoLoP; CBLP; IMW; NAEL-2; NOBE; NOBVV; OAEL-2; OBEV; PoE *Fr.* Maud [A Monodrama]. EnVR

O! that we now had here. Before Agincourt. Shakespeare. OxAEP-1 *Fr.* King Henry V.

O that yon river micht nae mair. Great Tay of the Waves. Lewis Spence. FaBoTC

O the beautiful garment. The Flowering of the Rod. Hilda Doolittle.

O the breasts of youth. The Caryatids. Andreas Embiricos, *Greek.* GrIP, *tr. by* Kimon Friar

O the Chimneys. Nelly Sachs, *German.* HP, *tr. by* Michael Hamburger; AF, *tr. by* Michael Roloff

O! / The constellation glitters. Stars abound. Passages 37. Robert Duncan. FTOS

O the cuckoo she's a pretty bird. The Cuckoo. *Unknown.* RB

O the days gone by! O the days gone by! The Days Gone By. James Whitcomb Riley. APN-2; OBCA

O the days of the Messiah are at hand, are at hand! Ballad of the Days of the Messiah. Abraham Moses Klein. TrJP

O the evening's for the fair, bonny lassie O! Bonny Lassie O! John Clare. CH

O [*or* Oh] the French are on the sea. The Shan Van Vocht. *Unknown.* FaBoPV; OxBoLi

O the goose and the gander walk'd over the green. The Goose and the Gander. *Unknown.* RB

O, the grand old Duke of York. *Unknown. See* The Grand old Duke of York.

O the Harbour of Fowey. The Harbour of Fowey. Sir Arthur Thomas Quiller-Couch. OBCoV

O the hog-eye men are all the go. The Hog-Eye Man. *Unknown.* AS

O the hurt, the hurt, and the hurt of love! The Hurt of Love. George Macdonald. TrCP

O the little rusty dusty miller. *Unknown.* OxNR

O, the lovely rivers and lakes of Maine! The Lovely Rivers and Lakes of Maine. George B. Wallis. BLPA

O the month of May, the merry month of May. May. Thomas Dekker *and others.* NoSic *Fr.* The Shoemaker's Holiday.

O the night of the weeping children! Nelly Sachs, *German.* HP, *tr. by* Michael Hamburger

O the opal and the sapphire of that wandering western sea. Beeny Cliff. Thomas Hardy. CABP; OBNC; OxAEP-2; RB

O the Ploughboy was a-ploughing. The Simple Ploughboy. *Unknown.* FaBoCh

O The Raggedy Man! He works fer Pa. The Raggedy Man. James Whitcomb Riley. FPC; OBCA; OxBChV

O, the rain, the weary, dreary rain. Twenty Golden Years Ago. James Clarence Mangan. NOBVV

O the sad day! The Sad Day. Thomas Flatman. OBEV

O, the Temeraire no more! (LL) The *Temeraire.* Herman Melville. APN-2; GS; NCAP

O the treacherous Scots revengd hee'd be. (LL) Johnie Armstrong. *Unknown.* ESPB; HoPM

O the warm, sweet, mellow summer noon. The Favorite Flower. Celia Laighton Thaxter. AiP

O, there are times / When all this fret. Daily Trials. Oliver Wendell Holmes. PoEL-5

O, there be many things. Many Things. Oliver Wendell Holmes. PoToHe

O there is blessing in this gentle breeze. Wordsworth. OAEL-2 *Fr.* Introduction—Childhood and School-Time. FHYEP *Fr.* The Prelude; Growth of a Poet's Mind [1850 vers.]

O [*or* Oh] there was a woman, and she was a widow. Flowers in the Valley. *Unknown.* OxBoLi

O [*or* Oh] there was an old soldier and he had a wooden leg. There Was an Old Soldier. *Unknown.* AS

O these wakeful[l] wounds of thine! On the Wounds of Our Crucified Lord. Richard Crashaw. NAEL-1

O, / these wild trees. Hymn for Lanie Poo. Imamu Amiri Baraka. BB

O they took my blessed Lawd. He Never Said a Mumblin' Word. *Unknown.* APN-2

O this weather! this weather! A Hot Day In Sydney. *Unknown.* NOBAu

O thou afflicted, drunken not with wine! Dirge for the Ninth of Ab. *Unknown, Hebrew.* TrJP, *tr. by* Nina Davis Salaman

O thou all-eloquent, whose mighty mind. Man's Going Hence. Samuel Rogers. OBNC *Fr.* Human Life.

O, Thou, beloved of my twenty seven senses. Anna Blossom Has Wheels. Kurt Schwitters, *German.* PFTM, *tr. by* Kurt Schwitters

O thou bright jewel in my aim I strive. On Virtue. Phillis Wheatley. TAP

O thou, by Nature taught. Ode to Simplicity. William Collins. NOBE; OBEV; OxAEP-1

O Thou Eternal Victim Slain. Charles Wesley. NOCV

O thou Great Mantle which envelops us. Great Hymn. Ntsikana Gaba, *Xhosa.* PeSAV, *tr. by* Thomas Pringle

O thou great Wrong, that, through the slow-paced years. The Death of Slavery. William Cullen Bryant. CBCWP

O thou Moor of Morería. Abenamar, Abenamar. *Unknown, Spanish.* AWP, *tr. by* Robert Southey

O thou Most High, who rulest all. Upon My Dear and Loving Husband His Going into England. Anne Bradstreet. AH

O, thou, my lovely boy, who in thy power. Sonnet 126. Shakespeare. HeIP-4; NAEL-1 *Fr.* Sonnets.

O Thou my soule, Jehovah blesse. Psalm 103. *Unknown.* SCAP *Fr.* The Bay Psalm Book.

O thou newcomer who seek'st Rome in Rome. Rome. Joachim Du Bellay, *French.* AWP, *tr. by* Ezra Pound

O thou that after toil and storm. Tennyson. PeECV *Fr.* In Memoriam A. H. H.

O thou, that art my *Light,* my *Life,* my *Way.* (LL) Wherefore Hidest Thou Thy Face, and Holdest Me for Thine Enemie [*or* Enemie]? Francis Quarles. MeLP; NOSC; OxAEP-1

O Thou, that dost cover the heavens. Song of the Wind and the Rain. Solomon ibn Gabirol, *Hebrew.* TrJP, *tr. by* Solomon Solis-Cohen

O thou that from thy mansion. For My Funeral. A. E. Housman. CMoP

O thou that held'st the blessed Veda dry. Hymn to Vishnu. Jayadeva. AWP, *tr. by* Sir Edwin Arnold *Fr.* The Gita Govinda.

O Thou that in the heavens does dwell! Holy Willie's Prayer. Robert Burns. CABP; EBEV; InPS-3; NOBRP; NOEC; OAEL-1; OBCoV; OBSV; OxBS; OxBoLi; PoE; PoEL-4; TFi

O thou that lovest a pure, and whitend soul! Dressing. Henry Vaughan. ESCV

O thou that often hast within thine eyes. Sonnet: He Speaks of a Third Love of His. Guido Cavalcanti, *Italian.* AWP, *tr. by* D. G. Rossetti

O thou, that sit'st upon a throne. Christopher Smart. EBEV; OxAEP-1 *Fr.* A Song to David. ImPo; NAEL-1; NOBE; OAEL-1; OBWVE; PoE; PoEL-3

("Frantic throes of Saul, The.") (LL) EBEV

O Thou, that sit'st upon a throne. A Song to David. Christopher Smart. ImPo; NAEL-1; NOBE; OAEL-1; OBWVE; PoE; PoEL-3

O thou that sleep'st like pig in straw. Sir William Davenant. NOSC

O[h] thou that swing'st [*or* swingest] upon the waving hair[e] [*or* ear *or* eare]. The Grasshopper. Richard Lovelace. BeJo; CaPo; EBEV; FaBoPV; MeLP; NAEL-1; NOBE; NOSC; OAEL-1; OBEV; OxAEP-1; SCGP; TFi

O thou that with surpassing Glory crowned. Satan's Soliloquy. Milton. *Fr.* Book IV. OAEL-1 *Fr.* Paradise Lost.

O Thou! the first fruits of the dead. Burial. Henry Vaughan. GeHe

O, Thou, the first, the greatest friend. The *First Six Verses* of the Ninetieth Psalm. Robert Burns. ChIV-1

O thou, the wonder of all day[e]s! The Dirge of Jephthah's Daughter. Robert Herrick. ChIV-1

O thou undaunted daughter of desires! Upon the Book and Picture of the Seraphical Saint Teresa. Richard Crashaw. HAP; NOBE; OBEV *Fr.* The Flaming Heart. CABP; NAEL-1; OAEL-1; PoEL-2

O, Thou, wha in the heavens dost dwell. Robert Burns. *See* Holy Willie's Prayer.

O thou! whatever title suit thee. Address to the Deil. Robert Burns. NOEC; OAEL-1; OxBS; PoEL-4

O thou who camest from above. Inextinguishable Blaze. Charles Wesley. NOEC

O thou who didst furnish. Hymn to Moloch. Ralph Hodgson. OxBTC

O Thou, Who Didst Ordain the Word. Edwin Hubbell Chapin. AH

O thou! / Who from *"a wilderness of Suns."* Ode to Della Crusca. Hannah Cowley. NOBRP

O thou, who lately closed my eyes. A Morning Hymn. Christopher Smart. OxBChV

O Thou, who man of baser earth didst make. Omar Khayyám. *Fr.* The Rubáiyát of Omar Khayyám [of Naishápúr]. AWP; EBVV; FaBoBe; FaPoR; HAP; NAEL-2; PoEL-5

O thou who never harbored fear. Sonnet. Eloise Bibb. CBWP-4

O thou, who plumed with strong desire. The Two Spirits[: An Allegory]. Shelley. CH; OAEL-2

O Thou who speedest Time's advancing wing. He Asketh Absolution of God. *Unknown.* AWP *Fr.* Book of the Dead.

O thou who standest 'mid the bards of old. On Kean's Hamlet. Washington Allston. APN-1

O, thou, whose eyes were closed in death's pale night. Epitaph on a Child Killed by Procured Abortion. *Unknown.* NOEC

O thou whose face hath felt the Winter's wind. What the Thrush Said. Keats. EBEV

O thou! whose fancies from afar are brought. To H. C.[, Six Years Old]. Wordsworth. PoEL-4

O Thou Whose Feet Have Climbed Life's Hill. Louis FitzGerald Benson. AH

O Thou Whose Gracious Presence Shone. Marion Franklin Ham. AH

O thou, whose mighty palace roof doth hang. Hymn to Pan. Keats. PoEL-4 *Fr.* Endymion: Poetic Romance.

O Thou Whose Own Vast Temple Stands. William Cullen Bryant. AH

O thou whose pow'r o'er moving worlds presides. Boethius. OBVE, *tr. by* Samuel Johnson *Fr.* Consolation of Philosophy, The ("De Consolacione Philosophie").

O Thou! Whose Presence Went Before. John Greenleaf Whittier. AH

O Thou whose reason guides the universe. Boethius, *Latin.* MLL, *tr. by* Helen Waddell *Fr.* Consolation of Philosophy, The ("De Consolacione Philosophie").

O thou wild Fancy, check thy wing! No more. Coleridge. *See* Written in Early Youth, the Time an Autumnal Evening.

O thou, with dewy locks, who lookest down. To Spring. William Blake. BoTP; NAEL-2; NOEC; OAEL-2; OBEV; PoEL-4; PoLF; SCGP

O thought I! Dorothy Wordsworth. NTP

O thow archbishop and metropolitan. *Unknown.* NOIV *Fr.* A Letter Sent by the Mayor and Inhabitants of the Citie of Waterford.

O thrilling voice of Zeus. Oedipus Rex. Sophocles. *Fr.* Oedipus the King [*or* Oedipus Rex]. NAWM-1, *tr. by* Robert Fagles

O thy bright eyes must answer now. Emily Jane Brontë. BrRo; PEW; VWP ("Oh, thy bright eyes must answer now.") PoEL-5

O Tim, my own Tim I must call 'ee—I will! Thomas Hardy. FaBoVe *Fr.* The Bride-Night Fire.

O Time the fatal wrack of mortal things. Contemplations. Anne Bradstreet. PBWP; WPOW *Fr.* Contemplations. AmPP; NAAL-3; PoEL-3; SCAP; WPE

O Time, whence comes the Mother's moody look amid her labours. The Lacking Sense. Thomas Hardy. CMoP; PoEL-5

O Time! who know'st a lenient hand to lay. Time and Grief. William Lisle Bowles. GSo; LBC; OBEV

O Times most bad. Upon the Troublesome Times. Robert Herrick. CaPo; CavPo

O To Be A Dragon. Marianne Moore. CTC; ChIV-1; KSG; NALW; NMM-2

O to be blind! The Blind Man at the Fair. Joseph Campbell. AWP

O to be in England. Robert Browning. *See* Home-Thoughts, From Abroad.

O to be in the news again—now as fashion runs. Robert Adamson. BMAP *Fr.* Sonnets to be Written from Prison.

O to break loose, like the chinook. Waking Early Sunday Morning. Robert Lowell. FaBoMo; HCAP; NOBA; OxBC; VCAP

O [*or* Oh], to have a little house! The Old Woman of the Roads. Padraic Colum. BoTP; CH; FYAP; FaBoBe; MoBrPo; NOIV; OBEV; PoRA; TIRV

O to scuttle from the battle and to settle on an atoll far from brutal mortal neath a wattle portal! Justin Richardson. UV

O Trade! O Trade! would thou wert dead! The Symphony. Sidney Lanier. AmPP

O tragic hours when lovers leave each other! Partings. Charles Guérin, *French.* AWP, *tr. by* Jethro Bithell

O treacherous scent, O thorny sight. Another for the Briar Rose. William Morris. NOBVV

O trees, to whom the darkness is a child. Advice to a Forest. Maxwell Bodenheim. TrJP

O tremble, all ye earthly princes. The Revolutionaries. Richard Percival Lister. NOBL

"O Troy Muir, my lily-flower." The Queen of Scotland. *Unknown.* ESPB

O true and tried, so well and long. Tennyson. OAEL-2 *Fr.* In Memoriam
  A H H

  "O happy hour, and happier hours." EnVR

O tuou whom Poetry [*or* Poesy] abhors. On Elphinston's Translation of Martial. Robert Burns. FaBoEE

O [*or* Oh] turn away those cruel eyes. The Relapse. Thomas Stanley. BeJo; NOSC; OBEV

O Turn Ye, O Turn Ye. Josiah Hopkins. AH

O 'twas on a bright mornin' in summer. Who's the Pretty Girl Milkin' the Cow? *Unknown.* AS

O Tweed! a stranger, that with wandering feet. The Tweed Visited. William Lisle Bowles. Son

O two-horned moon, you love the parties that last all night. Philodemus. HePo, *tr. by* Barbara Hughes Fowler *Fr.* Epigrams.

O-U-G-H. Charles Battell Loomis. NBLV

O uncreated Lord of all creation. Prayer to God the Father. Marbod of Rennes, *Latin.* MLL, *tr. by* Helen Waddell

O universal Mother, who dost keep. Hymn to Earth the Mother of All. *Unknown.* AWP, *Fr.* Homeric Hymns.

O universal Mother, who dost keep. Hymn to the Earth. *Unknown, Latin.* OBCVT, *tr. by* Shelley

O unspeakable passionate love. . . . (LL) I am the poet of the Body and I am the poet of the Soul. Walt Whitman. ColAP; WeW-3

O Urizen! Creator of men! mistaken Demon of heaven! Take Thy Bliss, O Man. William Blake. *Fr.* Visions of the Daughters of Albion. CABP; OAEL-2; Ro

O *Venus,* Beauty of the Skies. An Hymn to Venus. Sappho, *Greek.* OBCVT, *tr. by* Ambrose Philips

O, very gloomy is the House of Woe. Thomas Hood. *Fr.* The Haunted House. EBEV

O Virtuous Light. Elinor Wylie. MoAmPo

O Visionary who adjust your lens. The Higher Empiricism. Francis C. Golffing. PoA

O wad this braw hie-heapit toun. The Prows O' Reekie. Lewis Spence. FaBoTC; OxBS

O wall-flower! or ever thy bright leaves fade. The Wall-Flower. Henrik Arnold Thaulov Wergeland, *Norwegian.* AWP, *tr. by* Sir Edmund Gosse

"O waly, waly, my gay goss-hawk." The Gay Goshawk [*or* Goss-Hawk]. Anna Gordon Brown. ESPB; OxBB; WPE

O[h] waly, waly, up the burn [*or* yon] bank. Waly, Waly [Love Be Bonny]. *Unknown.* ESPB; EnLoPo; EnSB; GTBS-P; HAP; NOSC; OBEV; OxBB; OxBS; TFi

O waly waly waly waly. The Holloe Menn. Harrison Everard. BXAP

O warm, enthusiastic maid. Joseph Warton. NOEC *Fr.* Ode to Fancy.

O wastfull riot, never well content. Lucan. OBVE, *tr. by* Sir Walter Ralegh *Fr.* Pharsalia.

O Wave God who broke through me today. Burning Island. Gary Snyder. APSN; VCAP

O! we know not we know not, what future joys. There's a Silvery Lining to Every Cloud. Matilda Caroline Edwards. PWR

O, we loved long and happily, God knows! The Custom of the World. Louis Simpson. BoLoP

"O we were sisters seven, Maisry." Fair Mary of Wallington. *Unknown.* ESPB; OxBB

O we were sisters, sisters seven. Earl Crawford. *Unknown.* ESPB

O[h] wearisome condition of humanity. Chorus Sacerdotum. Greville Fulke. HAP; NAEL-1; NOBE; NoSic; OAEL-1; OxAEP-1; PoEL-1 *Fr.* Mustapha.

O wearisome condition of humanity! Greville Fulke. *See* Chorus Sacerdotum.

O weary Champion of the Cross, lie still. Cardinal Newman. Christina Rossetti. NAEL-2

O weary pilgrims, chanting your woe. Robert Bridges. MoBrPo *Fr.* The Growth of Love.

O well for him whose will is strong! Horace. OBCVT, *tr. by* Alfred Tennyson, 1st Baron Tennyson *Fr.* Will.

O wen, wen, O little wennikins. A Charm. *Unknown, Anglo-Saxon.* RB, *tr. by* Richard Hammer

O Wendy, Arthur. Maurice Kenny. HATNAP

O were my Love yon Lilac[k] fair. Robert Burns. GBL; OBEV

O [*or* Oh] wert thou in the cauld blast. Robert Burns. EBEV; FaBoVe; HAP; NOBE; NoP-4; OxAEP-2; OxBS; PoPoPo; SCGP

O western wind when wilt thou blow. *Unknown.* APAD; ImPo

O wha my babie-clouts will buy? The Rantin' Dog, the Daddie o't. Robert Burns. FaBoVe; OxBoLi; PeLV

"O wha will bake my bridal bread." Fair Annie. *Unknown.* ESPB

"O wha will shoe my bonny foot?" Fair Isabell of Rochroyall. *Unknown.* OxBB

"O wha will shoe my fair foot?" The Lass of Roch Royal. *Unknown.* AmFP; ESPB

O wha would [*or* wou'd] wish the win to blaw. Brown Adam. *Unknown.* ESPB; OxBB

"O whare are ye gaun?" [*or* "O where are you going?"]. The False Knight upon [*or* on] the Road. *Unknown.* AmFP; CH; ESPB; EnSB; FaBoCh; OxBS; OxBoLi

"O whare hae ye been a' day, Lord Donald, my son?" Lord Randal. *Unknown.* ESPB

"O [*or* Oh] whare hae ye been a' day, my bonnie wee croodlin dow?" Lord Randal. *Unknown.* ESPB; EnSB

O whare hae ye been, my dearest dear. The Carpenter's Wife. *Unknown.* OAEL-1; OxBB

"O whare hae ye been, Peggy?" Young Peggy. *Unknown.* ESPB

O wha's the bride that carries the bunch. "Hugh MacDiarmid." FaBoTC; GTBS-P; RaBo

O[h] what a cunning guest. Confession. George Herbert. ESCV

O what a happy soul am I! Blind but Happy. Fanny Crosby. CTV

O, what a noble mind is here o'erthrown! Shakespeare. *Fr.* Hamlet. NAWM-1

O what a physical effect it has on me. In Love with You. Kenneth Koch. CAPP-1

O what a strange parcel of creatures are we. On an Unsociable Family. Elizabeth Hands. ECWP; WoRP

O what a tangled web we weave. A Word of Encouragement. J. R. Pope. NBLV; NOBL

O what a weary while it is to stand. Eternity. James Whitcomb Riley. GSo

O what an endelesse worke have I in hand. Edmund Spenser. *Fr.* Wood Of Error. AEP

O, what can ail thee, knight at arms. Answer to a Kind Enquiry. Mary Holtby. UV

O [*or* Oh *or* Ah], what can ail thee, knight-at-arms [*or* wretched wight]. La Belle Dame Sans Merci. Keats. AWP; BLPA; CH; ClHu; EBEV; FHYEP; FaBoBe; FaBoCh; GTBS-P; HAP; HeIP-4; ImPo; InPS-3; NAEL-2; NAWM-2; NOBE; NOBRP; NTP; OAEL-2; OBEV; OBNC; OBSP; OxAEP-2; PBMP; PoE; PoEL-4; PoRA; Poetr; RB; SCGP; SCV; SoSe-8; TFi; TRP; UV; UnPo

O, what can be the matter with thee, Knight-at-arms. La Belle Dame sans Merci. T. Griffiths. BXAP

O what could be more nice. Light Listened. Theodore Roethke. EP; MoAmPo

O what harper could worthily harp it. The Schoolmaster Abroad with His Son. Charles Stuart Calverley. NOBL; PeLV

O what is that sound [which so thrills the ear]. Ballad. W. H. Auden. CMoP; FaBoPV; MeMAP; MoBrPo; PoE

O what tears in eyes now. Marina Tsvetayeva, *Russian.* TCRP, *tr. by* Elaine Feinstein *Fr.* March.

("They took quickly, they took hugely.") AF, *tr. by* Elaine Feinstein

O what their joy and their glory must be. Hymn for the Close of the Week. Peter Abelard, *Latin.* TrCP

O what transparent waves, what a tranquil sea. Vittoria da, Marchesa di Pescara Colonna, *Italian*. PBWP, *tr.* by Lynne Lawner

O what will a' the lads do. When Maggy Gangs Away. James Hogg. CABP

O what's the blood that's [*or* 'at's] on your sword. Son David. *Unknown*. OxBB; OxBS

O what's the weather in a Beard? Dinky. Theodore Roethke. OBAL; OBCA

O [*or* Oh] when our clergy at the dreadful day. On Those That Deserve It. Francis Quarles. NOCV; NOSC

O when, through ev'ry province, shall be raised. The Happy Workhouse and the Good Effects of Industry. John Dyer. NOEC *Fr.* The Fleece.

O when will they let them love. 1938. Ruth Pitter. WPN

O when you were little, you were really big. Duet. Theodore Roethke. OBCoV

O where are Mina Bell's cows who gave no milk. Mina Bell's Cows. Wesley McNair. TRP

O where are they now, your harridan nuns. The Nuns of Childhood: Two Views. Maxine W. Kumin. FFC

"O where are you going?" said reader to rider. Epilogue: " 'O where are you going?' said reader to rider." W. H. Auden. CMoP; FaBoCh; LiTM; MeMAP; NOBE; NoAM; OAEL-2; PFE; UV *Fr.* Five Songs.

O [*or* Oh] where are you going? says [*or* said] Milder to Malder. The Cutty Wren. *Unknown*. OxBoLi; UV

O where ha' you been, Lord Randal, my son? *Unknown. See* Lord Randal[1].

O where have you been all day. In the Woods. Dorothy Baker. BoTP

O[h] where have [*or* ha *or* hae] you [*or* ye] been, Lord Randal [*or* Rendal *or* Randall] my son? Lord Randal[1]. *Unknown*. AWP; AmFP; EBEV; EBEvV; EBNV; ESPB; HAP; HeIP-4; HoPM; ImPo; NTP; OAEL-1; OxBB; OxBS; Poetr; SCGP; TFi; TRP; WeW-3

"O where [*or* whare] have you [*or* hae ye] been, my dear, dear [*or* dearest dear *or* long, long] love." The Demon Lover. *Unknown*. AS; AmFP; ESPB; EnSB; HAP; OAEL-1; OxBB; PBMP; SCGP; TFi; UnPo; WeW-3

O, where were we before time was. Max Dunn. NOBAu

O where were ye, my milk-white steed. The Broomfield Hill. *Unknown*. CH

O, where, where are the winter grounds of angels. The Angels. Marguerite Young. WPE

O while within a Jewish breast. Hatikvah—a Song of Hope. Naphtali Herz Imber, *Hebrew*. TrJP, *tr.* by Henry Snowman

O whisper, O my soul! The afternoon. The Tired Worker. Claude McKay. BPo

O whistle, and I'll come to you [*or* ye], my lad. Whistle, and I'll Come to You, My Lad. Robert Burns. CBLP; OxAEP-2; OxBoLi

O whitewashed chapel. Greece. Gunnar Ekelof. BLT

O Whither will you lead the Fair. The Countess of Anglesey lead Captive by the Rebels, at the Disforresting of Pewsam. Sir William Davenant. PBRV

O who can ever praise enough. Poem. W. H. Auden. PoA

O who rides by night thro' the woodland so wild? The Erl-King. Goethe, *German*. AWP; OBVE; OxBSn, *tr.* by Sir Walter Scott

O [*or* Oh], who shall from this dungeon raise. A Dialogue between the Soul and [the] Body. Andrew Marvell. ESCV; GeHe; HAP; InPS-3; MeLP; NAEL-1; OAEL-1; OxAEP-1; PoEL-2; SeCP; SoSe-8; TFi

O, who will drive the chariot when she comes? She'll Be Comin' Round the Mountain. *Unknown*. AS

"O who will shoe my fair foot." Fair Annie of Lochyran. *Unknown*. AS

"O who will shoe my little feet." The Lass of Roch Royal. *Unknown*. AmFP

O who will shoe your pretty little foot. Who Will Shoe Your Pretty Little Foot? *Unknown*. AS

O who will show me those delights on high? Heaven. George Herbert. ESCV; GeHe; SeCP; TTTS; TrCP

O who will walk a mile with me. A Mile with Me. Henry Van Dyke. BLPA

O who would not sleep with the brave? (LL) Lancer. A. E. Housman. MoBrPo; OBWP

O why do you walk through the fields in gloves. To a Fat Lady Seen from the Train. Frances Darwin Cornford. APAD; BLPA; EBEvV; FaBoWP; MoBrPo; OBMV; UV; WeW-3

O! why should heavenly God to men have such regard? (LL) Guardian Angels. Edmund Spenser. NOCV; NoSic; OAEL-1

O, why should Nature niggardly restraine! Michael Drayton. PBRV *Fr.* Idea.

O, why should we the dead deplore. African Dirge. M. J. Chapman. PBCV

O wife, wife, wife! As if the sacred name. The Last Giustiniani. Edith Wharton. APN-2

O wild-reäven west winds, as you do roar on. Jenny out from Hwome. William Barnes. SCGP

O wild West Wind, thou breath of Autumn's being. Ode to the West Wind. Shelley. AWP; CABP; CH; ClHu; EBEV; FHYEP; FaBoBe; GTBS-P; HAP; HeIP-4; ImPo; InPS-3; LaPo; NAEL-2; NAWM-2; NIP-4; NOBE; NOBRP; NoP-4; OAEL-2; OBEV; OBNC; OxAEP-2; PBMP; PFE; PeECV; PoE; PoEL-4; PoLF; PoPoPo; PoRA; Poetr; SCGP; TFi; TRP; WeW-3

O Willie brew'd a peck o' maut. Willie Brew'd [*or* Brewed] a Peck o' Maut. Robert Burns. AWP; OxBS

O Willie's large o' limb and lith. The Birth of Robin Hood. *Unknown*. ESPB; OAEL-1; OxBB

O Willy was as brave a lord. Willie o Douglas Dale. *Unknown*. ESPB

O wind, rend open the heat. Heat. Hilda Doolittle. CMoP; HeIP-4; InPK-6; MoAmPo; OxBA; PiM; TAP; TRP; UnPo *Fr.* The Garden. NoAM

O wind, that sings so loud a song! (LL) The Wind. Robert Louis Stevenson. BoTP; CTV

O Wind, thou hast thy kingdom in the trees. "Michael Field." VWP

O Winter Aphrodite! O acute. To the Winter Aphrodite. "Michael Field." VWP

O winter wind, lat grievin be. Villanelle. Margaret Winefride Simpson. OxBS

O, winter, your gesture. Winter. Bella Akhatovna Akhmadulina, *Russian*. BoWoP, *tr.* by Barbara Einzig

O Winter's a beautiful time of the year. Winter. Enid Blyton. BoTP

O wistful eyes that haunt the gloom of sleep. Unborn. John Le Gay Brereton. NOBAu

O withering seas. George Oppen. NNaP *Fr.* Some San Francisco Poems.

O woe, woe, / People are born and die. Mr. Housman's Message. Ezra Pound. FaBoEE

O Woman of Three Cows, agra [*or* agragh] [;don't let your tongue thus rattle!]. The Woman of Three Cows. *Unknown*, *Irish*. NOIV; OBCoV, *tr.* by James Clarence Mangan

O Woman, Shapely as the Swan. *Unknown*, *Irish*. BIrV, *tr.* by Padraic Colum; CTC

(I Shall Not Die for Thee.) IIP, *tr.* by Douglas Hyde

O wonder!/ How many goodly creatures are there here! Brave New World. Shakespeare. *Fr.* The Tempest. OAEL-1

O wonderful nonsense of lotions of Lucky Tiger. Haircut. Karl Shapiro. TwCP

O, wondrous depth to which my soul is stirr'd. Music. Josephine D. Henderson Heard. CBWP-4

O wondrous thing it is. Excitation. Lorenzo Thomas. FTOS

"O words are lightly spoken." The Rose Tree. W. B. Yeats. CMoP; FaBoPV; OBMV

O world, I cannot hold thee close enough! God's World. Edna St. Vincent Millay. CMoP; FaBoBe; MoAmPo; PFE; SAGP; TrCP

O world invisible, we view thee. In No Strange Land. Francis Thompson. FaPoR; GTBS-P; HAP; MoBrPo; NOBE; NOCV; OBEV; TrCP

O world! O life! O time! A Lament. Shelley. GTBS-P; NAEL-2; NOBE; PoRA

O world, thou choosest not the better part! Sonnet III. George Santayana. APN-2 *Fr.* Sonnets.

O would I were where I would be! Suspiria. *Unknown*. OBEV

O wretch! hath madness cured thy dire despair? On Seeing an Officer's Widow Distracted. Mary Barber. ECWP; NOEC

O wretched offspring! O unhappy state. Death the Consequence of the Fall. Dryden. *Fr.* The State of Innocence. NOCV

O ye, all ye that walk in Willowwood. Willowwood ("O ye, all ye that walk in Willowwood"). D. G. Rossetti. NAEL-2; OAEL-2 *Fr.* The House of Life.

O ye dead Poets, who are living still. The Poets. Henry Wadsworth Longfellow. GSo

O ye that put your trust and confidence. A Rueful Lamentation on the Death of Queen Elizabeth. Sir Thomas More. AAS; NoSic

O Ye That Would Swallow the Needy. Bible, *O.T.* TrJP *Fr.* Amos.

O Ye Tongues. Anne Sexton. NALW

Third Psalm. NALW

O [*or* A *or* Oh] ye wha are sae guid yoursel. Address to the Unco Guid, or the Rigidly Righteous. Robert Burns. ChIV-1; NOBE; NOCV; OxBS

O ye wretched Scots. John Skelton. OBSV *Fr.* How the Doughty Duke of Albany like a Coward Knight Ran Away Shamefully.

O Year, grow slowly. Exquisite, holy. Slow Spring. Katharine Tynan. BoTP

O Years! and Age! Farewell. Eternity. Robert Herrick. CavPo

O yee, whome lorde of lande and waters wyde. Seneca. OBVE, *tr.* by Jasper Heywood *Fr.* Thyestes.

O' yes. Lamont B. Steptoe. ISC

O Yes? Do they come on horses. So Mexicans Are Taking Jobs from Americans. Jimmy Santiago Baca. LTA; UnSA

O yes, I love you, book of my confessions. Water under the Earth. Robert Bly. NNaP

O yes, the Chinese Garden! Do you remember. The Chinese Garden. Horace Gregory. OBGa

O yes, we've seen / your girl friend, / haven't we? Six Said by the Concubines to Him. Ammuvanar, *Tamil*. PLW, *tr. by* A. K. Ramanujan

O yes—you understand, I say. Hilda Doolittle. NALW *Fr.* Tribute to the Angels.

O yesterday the cutting edge drank thirstily and deep. To-morrow. John Masefield. MoBrPo

O[h] yet we trust that somehow good. 54. Tennyson. EBVV; EBVVPR; EnVR; FHYEP; ImPo; OAEL-2; OBNC; PeECV *Fr.* In Memoriam A. H. H.

O Yonge fresshe folks, he or she. The Love Unfeigned. Chaucer. OBEV

O You among Women. Frederick Robert Higgins. BIrV

O you chorus of indolent reviewers. Hendecasyllabics. Tennyson. EBEV; NOBL; PeLV

O you in that little bark. Michael Palmer. PT

O you lovers that are so gentle, step occasionally. The Sonnets to Orpheus. Rilke, *German*. RaBo, *tr. by* Robert Bly *Fr.* Sonnets to Orpheus.

O, you plant the pain in my heart with your wistful eyes. An Irish Love Song. John Todhunter. IIP

O you so long dead. To My Brother: Killed: Hammont Wood: October, 1918. Louise Bogan. AiP; NYBP

O you tender ones, walk now and then. Rilke. *See* The Sonnets to Orpheus.

O you that hear this voice. Sixth Song. Sir Philip Sidney. *Fr.* Astrophil and Stella. AAS; SiPS

O you, / Who came upon me once. Carrefour. Amy Lowell. BoWoP; LW

O you who guard over. Andal. WPoS *Fr.* The Tiruppavai.

O you whom I often and silently come where you are that I may be with you. Walt Whitman. APN-1

O you would clothe me in silken frocks. The Wild Goat. Claude McKay. RACG

O you, you wear flowers of gold. What She Said to Her Girl Friend. Kapilar, *Tamil*. PLW, *tr. by* A. K. Ramanujan

O, Young Lochinvar is come out of the west. Sir Walter Scott. *See* Lochinvar.

O young Mariner. Merlin and the Gleam. Tennyson. FHYEP; NTP; OAEL-2

O younge [*or* yonge] fres[s]he folkes, he or she. Love Unfeigned. Chaucer. NOBE; OBEV *Fr.* Troilus and Criseyde [*or* Criseide]. EnVB

O youngest, best-loved daughter of Hsieh. An Elegy. Yüan Chên, *Chinese*. NNPT, *tr. by* Witter Bynner

"O your hair," he said. What She Said. Kapilar, *Tamil*. PLW, *tr. by* A. K. Ramanujan

O, you're braw wi' your pearls and your diamonds. Lassie, What Mair Wad You Hae? Heinrich Heine, *German into Scottish*. OxBS, *tr. by* Alexander Gray

O zummer clote! when the brook's a-glidèn [*or* a-sliden]. The Clote (Water-Lily). William Barnes. FaBoVe; PoEL-4

O' zummer night, as day did gleam. The Lost Little Sister. William Barnes. PoEL-4

Oaf. Song of a Young Girl. Flavien Ranaivo. PBMAP

Oak, The. Tennyson. CTV

Oak and the Ash, The. *Unknown*. FaBoCh

Oak and the Olive, The. George Barker. FaBoMo

Oak inns creak in their joints as light declines, The. Derek Walcott. NoAM *Fr.* Midsummer.

Oak is called the king of trees, The. Trees. Sara Coleridge. ACTP; BoTP; FPC; OxBChV

Oak toad and the red-spotted toad love their love. The Power of Toads. Pattiann Rogers. NAmP90

Oakland. Robert Grenier.

"Open the door Oakland." FTOS

Oakland Blues. Ishmael Reed. NAAAL

Oaks and Squirrels. Anne Porter. ChIV-1

Oaks are stricken by a serious illness, The. More than Suspect. André Breton, *French*. AF, *tr. by* Mary Ann Caws *and* Jean-Pierre Cauvin

Oaks, how subtle and marine, The. Bearded Oaks. Robert Penn Warren. ColAP; FuPo; LiTM; MoAmPo; MoP; NAAL-2; NOBA; NoAM; NoP-4; PoA; PoE; TAP; TwCP

Oaks shone / gaunt gold, The. Lightning. Mary Oliver. Poetr

Oars fell from our hands, The. The Island. George Woodcock. MoCV

Oasis, An. Agnes Mary Frances Robinson. VWP

Oasis, light incarnate. (LL) "A World Without Objects Is a Sensible Emptiness." Richard Wilbur. CoAmPo; LiTM; MoAmPo; MoP; NAAL-2; NOBA; NoAM; PoA

Oasis Motel, The. William Olsen. NAmP90

Oaten Pipe. Ha'un Han, *Korean*. CKP, *tr. by* Jaihiun Kim

Oath, The. Allen Tate. FaBoMo; LiTM; OxBA; VGW

Oath of Friendship. *Unknown, Chinese*. TTTS, *tr. by* Arthur Waley

Oath of the Canting Crew, The. *Unknown*. CBNP

Oaths. Thomas Brown. FaBoEE; OBCoV

Oaths of Friendship. *Unknown*. ChiP; FP, *tr. by* Arthur Waley *Fr.* The Book of Songs.

Oatmeal was in their blood and in their names. The Gathering. Edwin John Pratt. MoCV *Fr.* Towards the Last Spike.

Ob all de subjects I kin read. Men Folks ob Today, De. Maggie Pogue Johnson. CBWP-4

Oban in autumn, and reflective Mull. Oban 1955–82. Iain Crichton Smith. FaBoTC *Fr.* A Life.

Obeah Night. Jean Rhys. PBCV

Obedience. George Herbert. ESCV; GeHe

Obedience of the Corpse. C. D. Wright. LCAP-2; MT

Obedient, The. Rudyard Kipling. *Fr.* Epitaphs of the War [1914–1918]. OBWP

Obelisk Inscriptions. Hatshepsut, *Egyptian*.

"Now my heart turns to and fro." WPOW, *tr. by* Mariam Lichtheim

Ober de mountains, slick as an eel. Boatman's Dance. Daniel Decatur Emmett. APN-1

Obermann Once More. Matthew Arnold. PoEL-5

Oberon and Titania to the Fairy Train. Shakespeare. *See* Through the House.

Oberon, the Fairy Prince. Ben Jonson.

Catch, A. CBNP

(Buzz and Hum.) OxNR

Oberon's Feast. Robert Herrick. BeJo; CaPo; NOSC

Oberon's Palace. Robert Herrick. CaPo

Obese man with a goiter, The. The Flood. Dara Wier. NAmP90

Obit. Robert Lowell. HCAP; VCAP

Obit on Parnassus. F. Scott Fitzgerald. NBLV; NYBP

Obiter Dicta. Hilaire Belloc. OBCoV

Obituary. Conrad Potter Aiken. OBAL

Obituary. Steve Chimombo. HBAPE

Obituary. Kenneth Fearing. VGW

Object among dreams, you sit here with your shoes off, An. A Girl in a Library. Randall Jarrell. NAAL-2; NOBA; NoAM

Objection to Being Stepped On, The. Robert Frost. NBLV; OBCoV

Objects in Mirror are Closer Than They Appear. Jeffrey Skinner. PBCAP

Objects of Immortality, The. Pattiann Rogers. WeT

Objets D'Art. Cynthia MacDonald. NMM-2

Oblique cloud of purple smoke, An. Woman Walking. William Carlos Williams. ColAP

Oblique light on the trite, on brick and tile. Courtyards in Delft. Derek Mahon. CIP-2; PBCIP; PNI

Oblique Rain. Fernando Pessoa, *Portuguese*.

Poem 2: "Inside, the church lights up today's rain." PFTM, *tr. by* Edwin Honig *and* Susan M. Brown

Obliterate / mythology as you unwind. The Cavern. Charles Tomlinson. CMoP

Oblivion. Jessie Redmond Fauset, *fr. the French of* Massillon Coicou. NegPo

Oblivion. Ellis Ayitey Komey. PBA; PBMAP

Oblivion! is it not one name of death? John Barlas. ADE

Oblivion! Skin. Nelly Sachs, *German*. PBWP, *tr. by* Michael Roloff

Oboe. Laurence McKinney. NBLV

Obon: Festival of the Dead. Mitsuye Yamada. LoHo

O'Bruadair. David O'Bruadair, *Irish*. BIrV, *tr. by* James Stephens

Obscene Caller, The. Philip Dacey. AmPA

Obscure, The. Norman Dubie. NoAM

Obscure and little seen my way. Charlotte Brontë. VWP

Obscure Night of the Soul, The. Saint John of the Cross. AWP; OBMV, *tr. by* Arthur Symons. *See* The Dark Night

Obscurely yet most surely called to praise. Praise in Summer. Richard Wilbur. NoP-4

Obscurest night involved [*or* involv'd] the sky. The Castaway. William Cowper. NAEL-1; NOBE; NOBRP; NOEC; OAEL-1; OxBoS; PoE; PoEL-3; TRP

Obscurity has its tale to tell. Focus. Adrienne Rich. FaBoWP

Obscurity of Woman's Worth. Caroline Elizabeth Norton. VWP

Obsequies of Stuart. John Randolph Thompson. CBCWP

Obsequy for Dylan Thomas. James Keir Baxter. PeLV

Observant of the way she told. Tact. Edwin Arlington Robinson. NoAM

Observation ("Virgin-Mother stood at distance (there), The"). Robert Herrick. ChIV-2

Observation Car. Alec Derwent Hope. MoP; NoAM
("But something went wrong with the plan: I am still on the /train train.") (LL) BMAP; GEA

Observation Car and Cigar. William Stafford. LCAP-2

Observation of a Bee. Leah Goldberg, *Hebrew*. WPOW, *tr. by* Stephen Mitchell

Observations. Hilaire Kirkland. PeNZ

Observations in a Cornish Teashop. Kenneth Rexroth. OBAL

Observations in the Art of English Poesie. Thomas Campion.
Elegye, An: "Constant to none, but ever false to me." AAS
"Follow, follow[e] / Though with mischiefe." EnLoPo
Laura. NOBE; OBEV
("Ever perfect, ever in them- / Selves eternal.") (LL) CABP
("Ever perfet, ever in them- / selves eternall.") (LL) PBRV
(Rose-cheeked Laura.) NoP-4
("Rose-cheekt *Lawra* come.") AAS; PBRV
("Selves eternall.") (LL) NoP-4
"Raving warre, begot / In the thirstye sands." AAS

Observations of the Life of Epictetus. Elizabeth Tipper. KTR *Fr.* Pilgrim's Viaticum; or, The Destitute, But Not Forlorn.

Observe how Eros works his magic spells. Vizentzos Cornaros. GrIP, *tr. by* Theodore P. Stephanides *Fr.* Erotocritos.

Observe how he negotiates his way. Swimmer. Robert Francis. WeW-3

Observe. Ridged, raised, tactile, the horror. The Scream. Donald Hall. GS

Observe the weary birds ere night be done. Orinda to Lucasia. Katherine Philips. NOSC

Observe the young and tender frond. Conversation in the Bush. Arthur Rex Dugard Fairburn. PeNZ *Fr.* Album Leaves.

Observe what Characters your persons fit. The Need for consistency. Horace, *Latin*. OBCVT, *tr. by* John Oldham

Observed Observer, The. Alan Gould. BMAP

Obsessed by betrayal. Palm Leaf of Mary Magdalene. Cheryl Clarke. GLP

Obsession. Léon Damas, *French*. NegPo, *tr. by* Ellen Conroy Kennedy

Obsession is the mania dawn breaks blush. Weathered Ides Grant Young Flesh. Steve Ellis. PT

Obsessions. Denise Levertov. LiTM

Obsessive Combination of Ontological Inscape, Trickery and Love, An. Anne Sexton. PiM

Obvious, The. Anna Couani. BMAP

Occam's Razor Starts in Massachusetts. "Edward Pygge." BXAP

Occasion and expediency determines the form, The. (LL) The Past Is the Present. Marianne Moore. MeMAP; NAAL-2

Occasional Poem ("Ancient annals strewn left and right"). Han Yü, *Chinese*. SuSp, *tr. by* Charles Hartman

Occasional Poem. A. E. Housman. NOBL; PeLV

Occasional Poem, A. Lu Yu, *Chinese*. SuSp, *tr. by* Chiang Yee

Occasional Poem, An. Ssu-k'ung Shu, *Chinese*. SuSp, *tr. by* Irving Y. Lo

Occasional Verse. Wang Ts'an, *Chinese*. SuSp, *tr. by* Ronald C. Miao

Occasional Verses. Marilyn Hacker. Son

Occasioned by Seeing a Walk of Bay Trees. Mildmay Fane, 2d Earl of Westmorland. BeJo; NOSC; OxBSP

Occasionial Poem: Upon Seeing Lotuses Bloom in a Vase. Wang Shih-chieng, *Chinese*. SuSp, *tr. by* Richard John Lynn

Occupation: Housewife. Phyllis McGinley. WPE *Fr.* I Know a Village.

Occupations of Hell. Milton. NOSC *Fr.* Book II. FHYEP; NAEL-1; OxAEP-1 *Fr.* Paradise Lost.

Occurrences, The. George Oppen. FTOS

Ocean, The. Byron. PoEL-4 *Fr.* Childe Harold's Pilgrimage.
(By the Deep Sea.) OBNC
"And I have loved thee, Ocean! and my joy." OxBoS
Sea, The. FaBoBe; ImPo
(Ocean, The.) TFi
"Thou glorious mirror, where the Almighty's form." OxBoS
To the Ocean.

Ocean, The. Christopher Pearse Cranch. PAR

Ocean, The. Louis Dudek. *Fr.* Provincetown. MoCV

Ocean, The. Moschus, *Greek*. AWP; OBVE, *tr. by* Shelley
(Translated from the Greek of Moschus.) OBCVT, *tr. by* Shelley

Ocean, The. Tanka. Kondō Yoshimi, *Japanese*. MJT, *tr. by* Makoto Ueda

Ocean air is heavy in autumn, The. Climbing to the Top of the City Walls at Kan-yü. Wang T'ing-hsiang, *Chinese*. CoBLCP, *tr. by* Jonathan Chaves

Ocean has its silent caves, The. Nathaniel Hawthorne. APN-1; PAR

Ocean has not been so quiet for a long while, The. Evening Ebb. Robinson Jeffers. NoAM

Ocean, its waves tumbling me. Blue. Sally Croft. DeD

Ocean Musing, An. Henrietta Cordelia Ray. CBWP-3

Ocean of Light. Phineas Fletcher. NOSC
("Seek on his cross: there, then, thus Love stands nail'd with love.") (LL) PBRV
("Vast Ocean of light, whose rayes surround.") PBRV

Ocean of the Streams of Story. Primus St. John. GT

Ocean Spirit. Song for Smooth Waters. Haida. CA

Ocean tides curl in anger, swift winds rage. Inscribed on a Painting of Dragons by Ch'en So-weng. Hsieh Chin, *Chinese*. CoBLCP, *tr. by* Jonathan Chaves

Ocean too has winter-views serene, The. Winter Views Serene. George Crabbe. OBNC *Fr.* The Borough.

Ocean's Love to Cynthia, The. Sir Walter Ralegh.
(Ocean to Cynthia, The.) NoSic
("Sufficeth it to yow my joyes interred.") PBRV
Ocean's Love to Cynthia, The. SiPS
(Ocean to Cynthia, The.) NoSic
("Sufficeth it to yow my joyes interred.") PBRV
Poem Entreating of Sorrow, A. SiPS

Och hey! for the splendour of tartans! The Return. Pittendrigh Macgillivray. OxBS

Och hon for somebody! Somebody. *Unknown*. OxBS

Och, Johnny, I hardly knew ye.' (LL) Johnny, I Hardly Knew Ye. *Unknown*. BIrV; IIP; OxBoLi

Oche Iron. Peter Blue Cloud. HATNAP

Ock Gurney and old Pete were there. John Masefield. CMoP *Fr.* Reynard the Fox.

"O'clock." Fanny Howe.
"Set golden butter out in a dish." FTOS

Octaves. Edwin Arlington Robinson.
Octaves. NCAP

Octet Before Winter. Claire Malroux, *French*. VCWP, *tr. by* Marilyn Hacker

October. William Cullen Bryant. APN-1

October. Mary Weston Fordham. CBWP-2

October. Paul Hamilton Hayne. APN-2

October. Helen Hunt Jackson. APN-2

October. Patrick Kavanagh. CIP-2; GTBS-P

October. Denise Levertov. TRP

October. Audre Lorde.
"Seboulisa, mother of power." CrSp

October. William Morris. EnVR; OBNC *Fr.* The Earthly Paradise.

October. Vladimir Ivanovich Narbut, *Russian*. TCRP, *tr. by* Lubov Yakovleva

October. Greg Pape. AmPA

October. Aleksandr Sergeyevich Pushkin, *Russian*. FP, *tr. by* D. M. Thomas

October. Henrietta Cordelia Ray. CBWP-3

October. Christina Rossetti. BoTP

October. Folgore da San Geminiano. *Fr.* Sonnets of the Months. AWP, *tr. by* D. G. Rossetti

October. Clive Sansom. AYFP

October. Barry Spacks. PoA

October. Edmund Spenser. NAEL-1; OAEL-1 *Fr.* The Shepheardes [*or* Shepeards *or* Shepherd's] Calender.

October. Edward Thomas. CABP; NoAM

October. S. W. Whitman. BoTP

October. Charles Wright. MT

October 23, 1983. June Jordan. SeSe

October: and the fires go out along the coast. Rodney Hall. *Fr.* Black Bagatelles. CBAP

October at last has come! The thicket has shaken. Autumn. Aleksandr Sergeyevich Pushkin, *Russian*. AWP, *tr. by* Max Eastman

October Elegy. Margaret Gibson. FYAP

October Garden, An. Christina Rossetti. GaP; OBGa

October gave a party. October's Party. George Cooper. BoTP; PoLF

October in the Country: [1983]. James Simmons. BiHa; CIP-2

October is a piper. Autumn Song. Margaret Rose. BoTP

October Is Here. Mrs. Henry Linden. CBWP-4

October, Isle of Skye. Carter Revard. NoP-4

October its brilliance. In October. Claire Malroux, *French*. VCWP, *tr. by* Marilyn Hacker

October Journey. Margaret Walker Alexander. GT

October Journey. Margaret Abigail Walker. PoBA

October Morning, An. Jayanta Mahapatra. OMIP

October 1. Karl Shapiro. MoAmPo; PoA

October Poem. Tamura Ryuichi, *Japanese*. AF, *tr. by* Christopher Drake

October Redbreast, The.   Alice Thompson Meynell.   MoBrPo

October robin kept, An.   Ted Hughes.   NOxBChV; NTP

October 16[: The Raid].   Langston Hughes.   PoBA

October. They decide it is time to move.   Sestina for the House.   Ronald Wallace.   PBCAP

October Tuesday.   Russell Hoban.   AYFP

October Tune.   Joseph Brodsky, *Russian*.   VCWP, *tr. by the author*

October turned my maple's leaves to gold.   Thomas Bailey Aldrich.   AYFP; FPC

October wind, An.   Zaro Weil.   AYFP

October's Bright Blue Weather.   Helen Hunt Jackson.   BLPA; FaBoBe

October's bright blue weather. (LL)   October's Bright Blue Weather.   Helen Hunt Jackson.   BLPA; FaBoBe

October's gold is dim—the forests rot.   Sonnet.   David Gray.   OxAEP-2

October's Party.   George Cooper.   BoTP; PoLF

Octopus.   Arthur Clement Hilton.   BXAP; UV

Octopus, The.   James Merrill.   APo; CoAP

Octopus, The.   Ogden Nash.   CTV; RB

Octopus, The.   Stevie Smith.   WPN

Octopus in hot sauce.   Just the Two of Us.   Kate Jennings.   BMAP

Octoroon, The.   Albery Allson Whitman.

   "Before the world, I hold that none of these."   AAP

   "But, 'if a man die, shall he live again?'."   AAP

   "If it be shame to love a pretty woman."   AAP

   "Let scoffers mock, let unbelief deny."   AAP

   "Mind knows no death. Life is the 'first and last.'"   AAP

   "These creatures of the languid Orient."   AAP

   "When genial Spring first bears the mating thrush."   AAP

Odcomb's Complaint.   John Taylor.

   "O for a rope of Onions from Saint Omers."   CBNP

   Sonnet in Praise of Mr. Thomas the Deceased.   CBNP

Odd day, An. For the first time in years.   The View from a Cab.   Henry Taylor.   NBLV

Odd, friendless boy raised by four aunts, The.   Thumb.   Philip Dacey.   KaS

Odd rot it what a shame it is.   To Miss B.   John Clare.   NOBVV

Odd silence / Falls as we enter, An.   Dreams of Water.   Donald Justice.   LCAP-2; NYBP

Odd way you comb your hair, The.   Lady in a Distant Face.   James Welch.   AmPA

Odd, *You* should fear the touch.   Ne Me Tangito.   Charlotte Mew.   VWP

Oddly shaped.   Tanka.   Shaku Chōkū, *Japanese*.   MJT, *tr. by Makoto Ueda*

Ode: "Ah poor Olinda never boast."   Elizabeth Taylor.   KTR

Ode: "At her fair hands how have I grace entreated."   Walter Davison.   BoLoP

Ode: "Bards of passion and of mirth."   Keats.   FHYEP; OBEV; OxAEP-2

   (Ode on the Poets.)   GTBS-P

Ode, An: "High-spirited friend, / I send not balms, nor corsives to your wound."   Ben Jonson.   BeJo

   (Noble Balm, The.)   OBEV

Ode: "How are thy servants blest, O Lord!"   Joseph Addison.   OxBoS

   (Hymn.)   OxAEP-1

Ode: "I hate that drum's discordant sound."   John Scott of Amwell.   NIP-4; NOEC; OxAEP-1

   (Ode: Against War.)   ECEV

Ode: "I sing a song of sixpence, and of rye."   Anthony C. Deane.   NOBL

Ode: "Idea of justice may be precious, An."   Frank O'Hara.   NeAP

Ode, An: "Merchant, to secure his treasure, The."   Matthew Prior.   AWP; EnLoPo; NOEC; PoRA

   ("Remarked how ill we all dissembled.") (LL)   GLoP; NoP-4

   (Song.)   OBEV

Ode: "Mistah Berrybones, you daid?"   William Zaranka.   BXAP

Ode: "Now each creature joys the other."   Samuel Daniel.   NoSic

Ode: "Sleep sweetly in your humble graves."   Henry Timrod.   CBCWP; NOBA; OxBA; TAP

   ("By mourning beauty crowned!") (LL)   ColAP; PAR

   (Lines.)   APN-2; PAR

Ode: "Spacious firmament on high, The."   Joseph Addison.   BLPA; ChIV-1; ECEV; FaBoBe; FaPoR; NOCV; NOEC; PoEL-3; TOF

Ode: "That I have often been in love, deep love."   "Peter Pindar."   NOEC

Ode: "They journeyed, / When the darkness of night."   Ibn al-Arabi, *Arabic*.   AWP, *tr. by R. A. Nicholson*

Ode: "Trees have their doubts but we have ours."   Paul Evans.   NBrP

Ode: "Until thine hands clasp girdlewise the waist of the Belov'd."   Sadi, *Persian*.   AWP, *tr. by R. A. Nicholson*

Ode: "We are the music-makers."   Arthur William Edgar O'Shaughnessy.   FaPoR; IIP; OBEV

   ("And a singer who sings no more.") (LL)   CABP

(Ode (We Are The Music Makers).)   APAD

Ode: "Weep, ah weep love's losing, love's with its dwelling place."   Imr el Kais, *Arabic*.   AWP; TAL, *tr. by Lady Anne Blunt and Wilfrid Scawen Blunt   Fr.* The Mu'allaqat.

Ode: "Who can support the anguish of love?"   Ibn al-Arabi, *Arabic*.   AWP, *tr. by R. A. Nicholson*

Ode: "Why will they never sleep."   John Peale Bishop.   LiTM

Ode.   Elizabeth Alexander.   GT; PoPoPo

Ode.   Horace.   LoP, *tr. by Abraham Cowley   Fr.* Odes.

Ode.   Hugh Maxton.   PBCIP

Ode.   Philip Schultz.   NAmP90

Ode.   Ralph Waldo Emerson.   *See* Ode, Inscribed to W. H. Channing.

Ode.   Richard Lovelace.   *See* To Lucasta: The Rose.

Ode.   Thomas Gray.   *See* Ode on the Death of a Favourite [*or* Favorite] Cat, Drowned in a Tub [*or* Bowl] of Gold Fishes.

Ode.   William Collins.   *See* Ode Written in the Beginning of the Year 1746.

Ode.   Wordsworth.   *See* Ode: Intimations of Immortality [from Recollections of Early Childhood].

Ode 3: "Of late, what time the Bear turned round."   Anacreon, *Greek.   Fr.* Odes.

   ("Of late, what time the Beare turn'd round.")   OBCVT, *tr. by Anomos*

   ("Your heart may hap to feele the paine.") (LL)   OBCVT, *tr. by Anomos*

Ode V: "Of thee the Northman by his beachèd galley."   George Santayana.   APN-2

Ode 44: "Last night, as half asleep I dreaming lay."   Hafiz, *Persian*.   EP, *tr.*

Ode 46: "See—the young, the rosy Spring."   Anacreon, *Greek*.   OBCVT, *tr. by Thomas Moore*

Ode 51: "Fly not thus my brow of snow."   Anacreon, *Greek*.   OBCVT, *tr. by Thomas Moore*

Ode 105.   Hafiz, *Persian*.   EP, *tr. by Richard Le Gallienne*

Ode 147: "Beauty alone will not account for her."   Hafiz, *Persian*.   EP, *tr. by Richard Le Gallienne*

Ode 173: "All the long night we talked of your long hair."   Hafiz, *Persian*.   EP, *tr. by Richard Le Gallienne by Richard Le Gallienne*

Ode 487: "With last night's wine still singing in my head."   Hafiz, *Persian*.   EP, *tr. by Richard Le Gallienne*

Ode against St. Cecilia's Day.   George Barker.   PoA

Ode: Against War.   John Scott of Amwell.   *See* Ode: "I hate that drum's discordant sound."

Ode and Elegy and Sonnet. (LL)   Lines on Thomas Warton's Poems.   Samuel Johnson.   EPCY; FaBoEE; SCGP

Ode: Autumn.   Thomas Hood.   OAEL-2; OBNC; PoEL-4; Ro; UnPo

   (Autumn.)   ImPo; OBEV; OxAEP-2

Ode Composed in Sleep, An.   Judith Madan.   ECWP

Ode for a Social Meeting.   Oliver Wendell Holmes.   OBAL

Ode for Ben Jonson, An.   Robert Herrick.   AWP; BeJo; EPCY; SCGP; SeCP

   (Ode for Him, An.)   CaPo; NOSC

Ode for Decoration Day.   Henry Peterson.

   "O gallant brothers of the generous South."   FaBoBe

Ode for Him, An.   Robert Herrick.   *See* An Ode for Ben Jonson.

Ode for Soft Voice.   Michael McClure.   NeAP

Ode for the American Dead in Asia.   Thomas McGrath.   AiP; RaBo

   (Ode for the American Dead in Korea.)   VGW

Ode for the Burial of a Citizen.   John Ciardi.   LiTM

Ode for the Dancing Khlysty.   Yury Ivask, *Russian*.   TCRP, *tr. by Burton Raffel and Alla Burago*

Ode for the New Year, An.   John Gay.   OxBoLi

Ode for Three Koras and Balaphong.   Léopold Sédar Senghor, *French*.

   "After this day's hope—see how the Somme, the Seine, and the wild Slav."   NegPo, *tr. by Ellen Conroy Kennedy*

Ode for Walt Whitman.   Federico García Lorca, *Spanish*.   PFTM, *tr. by Jack Spicer*

Ode: Hastening His Friend into the Country.   Eldred Revett.   NOSC

Ode I.   Erich Arendt, *German*.   CEEP, *tr. by David Scrase*

Ode in Honour.   Francis Scarfe.   SPF

Ode in May.   Sir William Watson.   OBEV

Ode in Time of Hesitation, An.   William Vaughn Moody.   APN-2; CBCWP; OxBA

Ode, Inscribed to W. H. Channing.   Ralph Waldo Emerson.   APN-1; AmPP; HAP; MeMAP; NAAL-1; NAAL-3; NOBA; OxBA; PAR; TAP

   (Ode.)   ColAP; NCAP; NoP-4

Ode: Intimations of Immortality [from Recollections of Early Childhood].   Wordsworth.   AWP; FHYEP; HAP; HeIP-4; NOBE; NOBRP; NoP-4; OAEL-2; OBEV; OBNC; PBMP; PoE; PoEL-4

   (Ode.)   PoPoPo; Ro

   "There was a time when meadow, grove and stream."   ImPo; NAEL-2; PBMP; SCGP; TFi; TOF; TRP

Ode Occasioned by the Death of Mr. Thomson. William Collins. EPCY; NOEC; PoE

(Ode on the Death of [Mr.] Thomson.) NAEL-1

Ode of Anacreon, An. Anacreon, *Greek.* OBCVT, *tr. by* Philip Ayres

Ode of Anacreon, Paraphras'd / The Cup, An. Anacreon, *Greek.* OBCVT, *tr. by* John Oldham

Ode of Horace, not exactly copyed, but rudely imitated, An. Horace.

"Hence, ye Profane; I hate ye all." OBCVT, *tr. by* Abraham Cowley

Ode: Of Wit. Abraham Cowley. BeJo; MeLP; NAEL-1; NOSC; OAEL-1; SeCP

(Poetic wit.) EPCY

Ode on a Distant Prospect of Clapham Academy. Thomas Hood. BXAP

Ode on a Distant Prospect of Eton College. Thomas Gray. GTBS-P; ImPo; NAEL-1; NOBE; NOEC; NoP-4; OAEL-1; OxAEP; PoE; PoEL-3; SCGP

Ode on a Grecian Urn. Keats. AWP; ClHu; EBEV; FaBoBe; HAP; HeIP-4; HoPM; ImPo; InPS-3; NAEL-2; NAWM-2; NIP-4; NOBE; NOBRP; NoP-4; OAEL-2; OBEV; OBNC; PBMP; PFE; PoE; PoEL-4; PoPoPo; Ro; SCGP; TFi; TOF; UnPo

"O Attic shape! Fair attitude! with brede." GrIP

("Thou still unravish'd bride of quietness.") CABP; ChAP; PFE

Ode on a Grecian Urn. Edward Abbott Parry. BXAP

Ode on a Grecian Urn Summarized. Desmond Skirrow. NIP-4; NOBL

Ode on [or to] a Jar of Pickles. Bayard Taylor. BXAP

Ode on a Storm. *Unknown.* OxBoS

Ode on Celestial Music. Brian Patten. OxBTC

Ode: On First Looking into Chapman's Homer. Keats. *See* On First Looking into Chapman's Homer.

Ode on Gas, An. *Unknown.* OBAL

Ode on His Majesty's Proclamation. Sir Richard Fanshawe. NOBE *Fr.* Il Pastor Fido.

Ode on Indolence. Keats. NAEL-2; OBNC; Ro

Ode on Lord Macartney's Embassy to China. William Shepherd. NOEC

Ode on Melancholy. Keats. CABP; FHYEP; HAP; ImPo; InPK-6; InPS-3; NAEL-2; NAWM-2; NOBE; NoP-4; OAEL-2; OBEV; OBNC; OxAEP-2; PoE; PoEL-4; PoRA; Poetr; Ro; SCGP; TFi

Ode on Reincarnation. Ernest Francisco Fenollosa.

"Here let me sit, in this empty, cool, terraced hall." APN-2

"I remember an ancient Chinese picture kept over there in Daitokuji." APN-2

Ode on Solitude. Alexander Pope. AWP; EBEvV; FHYEP; HeIP-4; NAEL-1; NOSC; PoRA; SCGP

(Quiet Life, The.) GTBS-P; PoToHe

Ode on Solitude. Alexander Pope. GEA

Ode on the Death of a Favourite [*or* Favorite] Cat, Drowned in a Tub [*or* Bowl] of Gold Fishes. Thomas Gray. ClHu; EBEV; ECEV; FHYEP; FaBoBe; HoPM; NAEL-1; NBLV; NOBE; NOBL; NOEC; OAEL-1; OBCoV; PBMP; PeLV; PoE; PoEL-3; TFi

("Favorite has no friend!, A.") (LL) PBMP

("Nor all that glisters gold.") (LL) APo; NoP-4; PC; PFE

(Ode.) NoP-4; PC; PFE

(On a Favorite Cat Drowned in a Tub of Gold Fishes.) EBEvV; EBNV; GTBS-P; OxAEP-1

Ode on the Death of Haig's Horse. Douglas Garman.

"Bury the Great Horse." UV

Ode on the Death of the Duke of Wellington. Tennyson.

"Bury the Great Duke." EBVVPR; UV

("Our loyal passion for our temperate kings.") (LL) UV

Ode on the Death of [Mr.] Thomson. William Collins. *See* Ode Occasioned by the Death of Mr. Thomson.

Ode on the Morning of Christ's Nativity. Milton. *See* On the Morning of Christ's Nativity.

Ode on the Passion. Thomas, the Elder Warton. ChIV-2

Ode on the Pleasure Arising from Vicissitude. Thomas Gray.

"Now the golden morn aloft." GTBS-P; NOEC

Ode on the Poetical Character. William Collins. NAEL-1; NOEC; NoP-4; OAEL-1; PoE; PoEL-3

("Or curtained close such scene from every future view.") (LL) NoP-4

"High on some cliff, to heaven up-piled." EPCY

Ode on the Poets. Keats. *See* Ode: "Bards of passion and of mirth."

Ode on the Popular Superstitions of the Highlands of Scotland, An. William Collins. NOEC; OAEL-1; OxAEP-1

"In scenes like these, which, daring to depart." EPCY

Stormy Hebrides, The. NOBE

Ode on the Revolution. Vladimir Mayakovsky, *Russian.* TCRP, *tr. by* Daniel Weissbort

Ode on the Spring. Thomas Gray. GTBS-P; NOEC

Ode on the Twentieth Century. Henrietta Cordelia Ray. CBWP-3

Ode on the Whole Duty Of Parents. Frances Darwin Cornford. WPN

Ode on Zero. Phoebe Pettingell. PoA

Ode Recited at the Harvard Commemoration (July 21, 1865). James Russell Lowell. APN-1; CBCWP; NOBA; OBWP

"I praise him not." AiP

Ode: Rule, Brittania! James Thomson *and* David Mallet. *See* Rule, Britannia!

Ode: Salute to the French Negro Poets. Frank O'Hara. GLP; NNaP; NeAP; PoM

Ode: The Dying Christian to His Soul. Alexander Pope. *See* The Dying Christian to His Soul.

Ode: The Spirit Wooed. Richard Watson Dixon. OBNC

Ode to a Butterfly. Thomas Wentworth Higginson. FaBoBe

Ode to a Country Childhood. Olafs Stumbrs, *Latvian.* CEEP, *tr. by* Olafs Stumbrs

Ode to a Country Hoyden. "Peter Pindar." NOEC

Ode to a Dead Dodge. David McElroy. AmPA

Ode to a Dressmaker's Dummy. Donald Justice. NoAM

Ode to a Goldfish. Gyles Brandreth. PeP

Ode to a Jacobin. *Unknown.* UV

Ode to a Lost Cargo in a Ship Called Save. José Craveirinha, *Portuguese.* PeSAV, *tr. by* Chris Searle

Ode to a Model. Vladimir Nabokov. OBAL

Ode to a Nightingale. Keats. AWP; CABP; ClHu; EBEV; FaBoBe; GEA; GTBS-P; HAP; HeIP-4; ImPo; InPS-3; NAEL-2; NAWM-2; NOBE; NOBRP; NoP-4; OAEL-2; OBEV; OBNC; PFE; PoE; PoEL-4; PoPoPo; PoRA; RB; Ro; SCGP; SoSe-8; TFi; TOF; UnPo

Ode to a Nightingale. Roy Kelly. BXAP

Ode to a Pig while His Nose Was Being Bored. Robert Southey. NOBL

Ode to a Skylark. Shelley. *See* To a Skylark.

Ode to Africa. Bernard Dadié, *French.* NegPo, *tr. by* Ellen Conroy Kennedy

Ode to All Flowers. Nguyễn Công Trứ, *Vietnamese.* AVP, *tr. by* Huỳnh Sanh Thông

Ode to Anactoria. Sappho, *Greek.* AWP, *tr. by* William Ellery Leonard

Ode to Aphrodite. Sappho, *Greek.* AWP, *tr. by* William Ellery Leonard

Ode to Autumn. Keats. *See* To Autumn.

Ode to Beauty. Ralph Waldo Emerson. AmPP

"Who gave thee, O Beauty." PoEL-4

Ode to Chicago. Elaine Equi. WWSi

Ode to Coit Tower. Gregory Corso. CLPP

Ode to Death. Charlotte Smith. NoP-4

Ode to Della Crusca. Hannah Cowley. NOBRP

Ode to Duty. Wordsworth. AWP; FHYEP; GTBS-P; ImPo; NAEL-2; NOBRP; OAEL-2; OBEV

Ode to English Food, An. George MacBeth. FaBoTC

Ode to Ethiopia. Paul Laurence Dunbar. NAAAL

Ode to Evening. William Collins. AWP; CABP; EBEV; ECEV; FaBoBe; GTBS-P; HAP; ImPo; NAEL-1; NOBE; NOEC; NoP-4; OAEL-1; OBEV; OxAEP-1; PoE; PoEL-3; SCGP; TFi

("And love thy favorite name!") (LL) GTBS-P

(To Evening.) GTBS-P

Ode to Evening. Joseph Warton. OxAEP-1

Ode to Fallen Leaves. Toksu Moon, *Korean.* CKP, *tr. by* Jaihiun Kim

Ode to Fancy. Joseph Warton.

"O warm, enthusiastic maid." NOEC

Ode to Fear. William Collins. NOEC; SCGP

Ode To Himself, An. Ben Jonson. BeJo; CABP

(Ode. To himselfe, An.) HAP; NOBE; NOSC; NoP-4; OxAEP-1; PBRV; PoEL-2; SCGP; SeCP

("Safe from the wolve's black jaw, and the dull ass's hoof.") (LL) NoP-4; PBRV

Ode to Himself. Ben Jonson. BeJo; NAEL-1; OAEL-1; SeCP

(On *The New Inn*: Ode, To Himself.) EPCY

Ode. To himselfe, An. Ben Jonson. *See* An Ode To Himself.

Ode to Jackson Pollock. Michael McClure. PmAP

Ode to Joy. Frank O'Hara. GLP; NeAP; PmAP

Ode to Language. Robert Kelly. SeSe

Ode to Liberty, *tr. fr. the Greek of* Dionysios Solomos. Rudyard Kipling. GrIP

Ode to Liberty. Shelley.

"Athens rose: a city such as vision." GrIP

Ode to Lovers. Sir John Suckling. UV

Ode to Master Endymion Porter, upon His Brother's Death, An. Robert Herrick. CaPo

Ode to Memory. William Mason.

"Rise, hallowed Milton! rise, and say." EPCY

Ode to Merciful Bodhisattva. Hijin Park, *Korean.* CKP, *tr.* by Jaihiun Kim

Ode to Michael Goldberg's Birth and Other Births. Frank O'Hara. NeAP

Ode to Miss Hoyland. Thomas Chatterton. BXAP

Ode: To Miss Margaret Pulteney. Ambrose Philips. OxAEP-1; Poetr; UV

Ode to Moderation. Annabella Plumptre.
 "To thee, whose cautious step and specious air." ECWP; NOEC

Ode to Mr. Anthony Stafford to Hasten Him into the Country, An. Thomas Randolph. BeJo; NOSC

Ode to Mr. [or Master] Anthony Stafford to Hasten Him into the Country, An. Thomas Randolph. NOBE; OBEV

Ode to Mr. F— [or Mr. Forbes]. Allan Ramsay, *after* Horace. NOEC; OBVE

Ode to Mr. Hobbes. Abraham Cowley. *See* To Mr. Hobbes [or Hobs].

Ode to My Car. Gig Ryan. BMAP

Ode to My Daugther's Plimsolls and the Mess in Her Room. Caroline Halliday. NBrP

Ode: To My Pupils. W. H. Auden. MoBrPo

Ode to My Socks. Pablo Neruda, *Spanish.* RaBo; TRP, *tr.* by Robert Bly

Ode to My Soul. Lord Alfred Bruce Douglas. ADE

Ode to Peace. Mary Weston Fordham. CBWP-2

Ode to Pornography. Jack Anderson. PoA

Ode to Psyche. Keats. FHYEP; InPS-3; NAEL-2; NOBE; NOBRP; NoP-4; OAEL-2; OBEV; OBNC; OxAEP-2; PoE; PoEL-4; Ro; TFi; TOF

Ode to Rhys ap Maredudd of Tywyn. Dafydd Nanmor, *Welsh.* OBWVE, *tr.* by H. Idris Bell

Ode to Santorini. Odysseus Elytis, *Greek.* GrIP, *tr.* by Edmund Keeley and Philip Sherrard

Ode to Sappho. Elizabeth Oakes Smith. ColAP

Ode to Simplicity. William Collins. NOBE; OBEV; OxAEP-1

Ode. To Sir William Sydney, on His Birthday. Ben Jonson. BeJo

Ode to Society, An. Hester Lynch Salusbury Thrale [*later* Mrs. Piozzi]. ECWP

Ode to Spring. Anna Laetitia Barbauld. OxAEP-1

Ode to Stephen Dowling Bots, Dec'd. "Mark Twain." *See* Emmeline Grangerford's "Ode to Stephen Dowling Bots, Dec'd."

Ode to Suburbia. Eavan Boland. PBCIP

Ode to Swansea. Vernon Watkins. OBWVE

Ode to Tanaquil Leclercq: "Smiling through my own memories of painful excitement your wide eyes." Frank O'Hara. FTOS

Ode to Tennis. Paul Evans. NBrP

Ode to Terminus. W. H. Auden. HAP

Ode to the Betel Palm. *Unknown, Vietnamese.* AVP, *tr.* by Huỳnh Sanh Thông

Ode to the Candle. Phan chu Trinh, *Vietnamese.* AVP, *tr.* by Huỳnh Sanh Thông

Ode to the Cat. Pablo Neruda, *Spanish.* VCWP, *tr.* by John Hollander

Ode to the Cat. Pablo Neruda. PiM, *tr.* by Ken Krabbenhoft *Fr.* Ode to the Cat.

Ode to the Confederate Dead. Allen Tate. AiP; CBCWP; ColAP; FaBoMo; FuPo; HeIP-4; LiTM; MoAmPo; MoP; NAAL-2; NOBA; NoAM; NoP-4; OBWP; OxBA; TAP; TFi; UnPo

Ode: To the Cuckoo. Michael Bruce. *See* To the Cuckoo.

Ode to the Diencephalon. W. H. Auden. OxAEP-2

Ode to the End of Summer. Phyllis McGinley. NBLV

Ode to the Fan. Ho Xuan Huong, *Vietnamese.* AVP, *tr.* by Huỳnh Sanh Thông

Ode to the German Drama. *Unknown.* NOEC

Ode to the Human Heart. Edward Laman Blanchard. NOBL

Ode to the Maguire. Eochadh O'Hussey. *See* O'Hussey's Ode to the Maguire.

Ode to the Medieval Poets. W. H. Auden. PoA

Ode to the Northeast Wind. Charles Kingsley. FaPoR; OxAEP-2

Ode to the Pious Memory of the Accomplished Young Lady, Mrs. Anne Killigrew. Dryden. *See* To the Pious Memory of the Accomplished [or Accomplisht] Young Lady, Mrs. Anne Killigrew, [Excellent in the Two Sister Arts of Poesie and Painting]

Ode to the Poppy. Henrietta O'Neill. ECWP; WPE

Ode to the Sea. Howard Baker. OxBA

Ode to the Setting Sun. Francis Thompson.
 "Now that the red glare of thy fall is blown." OBNC
 Sun, The. MoBrPo

Ode to the Sewing Needle. *Unknown, Vietnamese.* AVP, *tr.* by Huỳnh Sanh Thông

Ode to the Sun. Eloise Bibb. CBWP-4

Ode to the Toad. *Unknown, Vietnamese.* AVP, *tr.* by Huỳnh Sanh Thông

Ode to the Watermelon. Pablo Neruda, *Spanish.* SPE, *tr.* by Robert Bly

Ode to the Watermelon. *Unknown, Vietnamese.* AVP, *tr.* by Huỳnh Sanh Thông

Ode to the West Wind. Shelley. AWP; CH; ClHu; EBEV; FHYEP; FaBoBe; GTBS-P; HAP; HeIP-4; ImPo; InPS-3; NAEL-2; NAWM-2; NIP-4; NOBE; NOBRP; NoP-4; OAEL-2; OBEV; OBNC; OxAEP-2; PBMP; PFE; PeECV; PoE; PoEL-4; PoLF; PoPoPo; PoRA; Poetr; Ro; SCGP; TFi; TRP; WeW-3
 ("Destroyer and Preserver; hear, O hear!") (LL) LaPo
 ("Destroyer and preserver; hear, oh, hear!") (LL) CABP
 ("Oh wild west wind, thou breath of autumn's being.") Ro

Ode to Tomatoes. Francisco Alarcon. IFJA

Ode to Tranquillity. Coleridge. LaPo

Ode to Truth. Mary Whateley. ECWP

Ode to Winter. Thomas Campbell. GTBS-P

Ode to Wisdom. Elizabeth Carter. CABP; ECWP
 ("Is vanity and woe.") (LL) CABP

Ode to Zion. Judah Halevi, *Hebrew.* TrJP, *tr.* by Nina Davis Salaman

Ode, upon a Question Moved, Whether Love Should Continue Forever? An. Edward Herbert, 1st Baron Herbert of Cherbury. MeLP; NOBE; OxAEP-1; SeCP

Ode upon Doctor Harvey. Abraham Cowley. PoEL-2
 "Coy Nature (which remain'd, though aged grown)."

Ode, upon Occasion of His Majesties Proclamation in the Year 1630, An. Sir Richard Fanshawe. *See* On His Majesty's Proclamation.

Ode (We Are The Music Makers). Arthur William Edgar O'Shaughnessy. *See* Ode: "We are the music-makers."

Ode, which Was Prefixed to a Little Prayer-Book Givin to a Young Gentlewoman, An. Richard Crashaw. ESCV

Ode: Written After Reading Some Modern Love-Verses. John Scott of Amwell. ECEV

Ode Written in the Beginning of the Year 1746. William Collins. AWP; HAP; NAEL-1; NOEC; NoP-4; OxBSP; PoE; PoEL-3
 (Ode.) SCGP

Ode Written in the Peak[e], An. Michael Drayton. NOSC

Ode XV. Thomas Stanley. ChIV-1

Odell. James Stephens. MoBrPo

Odes. Anacreon.
 Ode 3: "Of late, what time the Bear turned round." OBCVT, *tr.* by Anomos

Odes. Hafiz, *Persian.*
 "Comrades, the morning breaks, the sun is up." AWP, *tr.* by Richard Le Gallienne
 "Days of spring are here, The! the eglantine." AWP, *tr.* by Gertrude Lowthian Bell
 "Flower-tinted cheek, the flowery close, A." TAL, *tr.* by Gertrude Lowthian Bell
 "From Canaan Joseph shall return, whose face." TAL, *tr.* by Gertrude Lowthian Bell
 "Grievous folly shames my sixtieth year, A." AWP, *tr.* by Richard Le Gallienne
 "I cease not from desire till my desire." AWP; TAL, *tr.* by Gertrude Lowthian Bell
 "I have borne the anguish of love, which ask me not to describe." AWP, *tr.* by John Hindley
 "I said to heaven that glowed above." AWP, *tr.* by Ralph Waldo Emerson
 "If my darling should depart."
 "Jewel of the secret treasury, The." AWP, *tr.* by Gertrude Lowthian Bell
 "Lady that hast my heart within thy hand." AWP, *tr.* by Gertrude Lowthian Bell
 "Mirth, Spring, to linger in a garden fair." TAL, *tr.* by Gertrude Lowthian Bell
 "Oft have I said, I say it once more." AWP, *tr.* by Ralph Waldo Emerson
 "Rose has flushed red, the bud has burst, The." TAL, *tr.* by Gertrude Lowthian Bell
 "Rose is not the rose unless thou see, The." AWP, *tr.* by Richard Le Gallienne
 "Saki, for God's love, come and fill my glass." AWP, *tr.* by Richard Le Gallienne
 "What is wrought in the forge of the living and life." TAL, *tr.* by Gertrude Lowthian Bell
 "Where is my ruined life, and where the fame." AWP; TAL, *tr.* by Gertrude Lowthian Bell
 "Wind from the east, oh Lapwing of the day." AWP; TAL, *tr.* by Gertrude Lowthian Bell

Odes. Horace, *Latin.*
 1.3: To the Ship on Which Virgil Sailed to Athens ("Sic te diva potens Cyri"). AWP, *tr.* by John Dryden
 1.5. EBEV; EnLoPo; OBVE; PoEL-3, *tr.* by Milton
 (Fifth Ode of Horace, The.) EBEV; EnLoPo; PoEL-3, *tr.* by Milton
 ("Pyrrha, what slender well-shap'd beau.") OBVE, *tr.* by Anthony Horneck

("Tell me, Pyrrha, what fine youth.") OAEL-1, *tr.* by William Browne

(To Pyrrha.) AWP, *tr.* by Milton

("What stripling now thee discomposes.") OBVE, *tr.* by Sir Richard Fanshawe

1.8. OBVE, *tr.* by Sir Richard Fanshawe

1.9. OBVE, *tr.* by Dryden; STV, *tr.* by John Frederick Nims

(To Thaliarchus ("Thou seest the hills").) OBVE, *tr.* by Sir Richard Fanshawe

("You see how, white with snows to the north of us.") STV, *tr.* by John Frederick Nims

1.11. STV, *tr.* by John Frederick Nims

(Ad Leuconoen.) AWP, *tr.* by F. P. Adams

("Don't ask—knowing's taboo—what's in the cards, darling, for you, for me.") STV, *tr.* by John Frederick Nims

1.14: Ship of State, The ("O navis, referent"). AWP, *tr.* by William Ewart Gladstone

1.21: To Apollo and Diana ("Dianam tenerae dicite virgines"). OBVE, *tr.* by Branwell Brontë

(Invocation: "Maidens young and virgins tender.") AWP, *tr.* by Louis Untermeyer

1.22. OBVE, *tr.* by the Earl of Roscommon

("Man in righteousness arrayed, The.") AWP, *tr.* by John Quincy Adams

(To Sally.) AWP, *tr.* by John Quincy Adams

1.23: To Chloë ("Vitas hinnuleo"). AWP; OBVE

1.25: Ribald Romeos Less and Less Berattle ("Parcius iunctas quatiunt fenestras"). BoLoP, *tr.* by James Michie; STV, *tr.* by John Frederick Nims

("As a gift to the east wind, winter's friend.") (LL) LoP

("Bloods and bucks of this lewd town, The.") OBVE, *tr.* by the Young Gentlemen of Mr. Rule's Academy at Islington

("Figure the hell with.") (LL) OBCVT, *tr.* by John Frederick Nims

(To Lydia.) OBVE, *tr.* by Philip Francis

1.31. CTC, *tr.* by Ezra Pound

1.33: Albi, Ne Doleas. AWP, *tr.* by Austin Dobson

2.4: Ad Xanthiam Phoceum ("Ne sit ancillae"). AWP, *tr.* by Franklin P. Adams

2.7. OBWP, *tr.* by James Michie

2.8. STV, *tr.* by John Frederick Nims

2.10. OBVE, *tr.* by William Cowper

("Of thy lyfe [*or* life], Thomas, this compass well mark.") OBVE, *tr.* by Henry Howard, Earl of Surrey

(To Licinius.) AWP, *tr.* by William Cowper

2.11: To an Ambitious Friend ("Quid bellicosus"). AWP, *tr.* by Matthew Arnold

2.18. OBVE, *tr.* by Christopher Smart

2: Moderation. PoToHe, *tr.* by William Cowper

3.1. OBVE, *tr.* by Gerard Manley Hopkins

("Hence ye prophane; I hate ye all.") OBVE, *tr.* by Abraham Cowley, (2 *sts.*)

(Profane, The.) AWP, *tr.* by Abraham Cowley

3.2. OBWP, *tr.* by James Michie

("Let the hardened by a sharp soldier's life.")

3.5: Carthaginian Peace, The. MLL, *tr.* by Helen Waddell

3.7. OBVE, *tr.* by George Stepney

3.9: Dialogue between Horace and Lydia, A ("Donec gratus eram"). OBVE, *tr.* by Robert Herrick

("Franklin P. Adams.") (LL) NBLV

(Reconciliation: A Modern Version, The.) NBLV, *tr.* by Franklin P. Adams

("What time I was your one best bet.") NBLV, *tr.* by Franklin P. Adams

3.10: Extremum Tanain. AWP, *tr.* by Austin Dobson

3.13: To the Fountain[s] of Bandusia ("O fons Bandusiae"). AWP, *tr.* by Eugene Field

3.22: Pine Tree for Diana, The ("Montium custos nemorumque"). AWP, *tr.* by Louis Untermeyer

3.23: To Phidyle ("Caelo supinas si tuleris"). AWP, *tr.* by Austin Dobson

3.28: Holiday ("Festo quid potius die"). AWP, *tr.* by Louis Untermeyer

3.30: This Monument Will Outlast (Exegi momumentum aere perennis). CTC, *tr.* by Ezra Pound

("This monument will outlast metal and I made it.") OBCVT, *tr.* by Ezra Pound

4.2: Praise of Pindar, The ("Pindarum quisquis studet aemulari"). OAEL-1, *tr.* by Abraham Cowley

4.7. NAEL-1; OBVE, *tr.* by Samuel Johnson

(Diffugere Nives.) OBVE, *tr.* by Alfred Edward Housman

("My consecrated Vessel hangs at last.") (LL) EP, *tr.* by Duncombe, James

("To whom now Pyrrha, art thou kind?") EP, *tr.* by Duncombe, James

4.9. EPCY

(Immortality of Verse, The.) AWP

4.13: Revenge ("Audivere, Lyce"). AWP, *tr.* by Louis Untermeyer

Ode. LoP, *tr.* by Abraham Cowley

Spring. OBCVT, *tr.* by Robert Lowell

To Aristius Fuscus. OBVE

To Maecenas. AWP; OBVE, *tr.* by John Dryden

("In time to come, if such a crime should be.") AWP; OBVE, *tr.* by Dryden

To Venus. AWP; OBVE

(IV, 1. To Venus.) OBVE

Odes. Tibullus, *Latin.*

Elegies 1.iv: "Far from the tender Tribe of Boys remove." EP, *tr.* by Dart, John

("He'll struggle, but at length comply with ease.") (LL) OBCVT, *tr.* by Dart, John

Odes and Days. Bruce Beaver.

Day 20. BMAP

Odes of Solomon, The. *Unknown, Greek.*

"My heart was split, and a flower." EnlH, *tr.* by Stephen Mitchell

Odes Sung in Commemoration of the Marine Society. Anne Penny.

Sung at Table by the Same Choir. ECWP

Sung by a Choir of Boys Marching Round the Room. ECWP

Odes to Nea. Thomas Moore.

"I pray you, let us roam no more." OBNC

"Nay, tempt me not to love again." OBNC

Odor has remained among the sugarcane, An. The Dictators. Pablo Neruda, *Spanish.* AF, *tr.* by Robert Bly

Odorous shade lingers the fair day's ghost, An. Night. Henri De Regnier, *French.* AWP, *tr.* by "Seumas O'Sullivan"

Odour from the flower is gone, The. On a Faded Violet. Shelley. PFE

Odour I bequeath, The. (LL) Unprofitablenes. Henry Vaughan. ESCV; FMP; GeHe; NOSC

Odour. 2. Cor. 2, The. George Herbert. ChIV-2; ESCV

O'Driscoll drove with a song. The Host of the Air. W. B. Yeats. CH

Odysseus. Padraic Fallon. CIP-2

Odysseus. Haim Guri, *Hebrew.* MHP, *tr.* by Ruth Finer Mintz

Odysseus. W. S. Merwin. NOBA; NoP-4

Odysseus heard the sirens; they were singing. The Sirens. John Streeter Manifold. LiTM; MoBrPo; Son

Odysseus to Telemachus. Joseph Brodsky, *Russian.* BLT, *tr.* by Kline, George L.

Odysseus under wet snapping sheets. Christian Karlson Stead. PeNZ *Fr.* Quesada.

Odyssey. Homer, *Greek.* NAWM-1, *tr.* by Robert Fitzgerald

Alkinoos' Garden. GrIP, *tr.* by Robert Fitzgerald

"And now the Queene of women had intent." OBVE, *tr.* by George Chapman

Butchers, The. OBCVT, *tr.* by Michael Longley

"Cave we found, but vacant all within, The." OBVE, *tr.* by Pope

Circe. OBCVT, *tr.* by Alexander Pope

Cyclops and No-Man. OBCVT, *tr.* by George Chapman

Demodocus sings the fall of Troy. OBCVT, *tr.* by George Chapman

Demodocus sings the fall of Troy. OBCVT, *tr.* by Robert Fitzgerald

Downe to the king's most bright-kept baths they went. CTC, *tr.* by George Chapman

Execution of the faithless maids. OBCVT, *tr.* by Alexander Pope

"First to the Corse the weeping Consort flew." OBCVT, *tr.* by Alexander Pope

"For my part, I'le not meddle with the cause." CTC, *tr.* by George Chapman

"From her bed's high and odoriferous roome." CTC, *tr.* by George Chapman

Gardens of Alcinous, The. GaP; OAEL-1; OBVE, *tr.* by Alexander Pope

Gardens of Alcinous, The. OAEL-1; OBVE, *tr.* by George Chapman

"God who mounts the winged winds, The." OBVE, *tr.* by Pope

"He ended, nor the Argicide refus'd." OBVE, *tr.* by William Cowper

"Here open'd Hell, all Hell I here implor'd." OxBSn

"Just then, forgetful of the strict command." OBVE, *tr.* by William Cowper

Landfall. OBCVT, *tr.* by George Chapman

Mars and Venus. OBCVT, *tr.* by William Broome

"Mighty wave rush'd o'er him as he spoke, A." OBVE, *tr.* by Pope

"Now gently winding up the fair ascent." OBVE, *tr.* by Pope

"Now toils the Heroe; trees on trees o'erthrown." OBVE, *tr.* by Pope

"Nymph turnd home, The. He fell to felling downe." OBVE, *tr. by* George Chapman

Penelope hesitates. OBCVT, *tr. by* Robert Fitzgerald

Penelope weeps. OBCVT, *tr. by* Robert Fitzgerald

"She thus; when I had great desire to prove." OBVE, *tr. by* George Chapman

Suitors watch Ulysses string the bow, The. OBCVT, *tr. by* Alexander Pope

("Pierc'd thro' and thro', the solid gate resounds.") (LL) OBCVT, *tr. by* Alexander Pope

"There grew two olives, closest of the grove." OBVE, *tr. by* Pope

"This spoke, a huge wave tooke him by the head." OBVE, *tr. by* George Chapman

"Thus charg'd he; nor Argicides denied." OBVE, *tr. by* George Chapman

"Thus, many tales *Ulysses* told his wife." OBCVT, *tr. by* George Chapman

"Trembling the spectres glide, and plaintive vent." OBVE, *tr. by* Pope

"Twelve herds of oxen, no less flockes of sheepe." CTC, *tr. by* George Chapman

Ulysses Insults over the Cyclops. NOSC, *tr. by* George Chapman

Ulysses Invokes the Dead. NOSC, *tr. by* George Chapman

Ulysses Leaves the Nymph Calypso.

"Great wave drove at him with toppling crest, A." GrIP, *tr. by* Robert Fitzgerald

Ulysses Reunited with Penelope. NOSC, *sect.* XXIV

"Where neither King nor shepheard want comes neare." CTC, *tr. by* George Chapman

"While thus he thought, a monst'rous wave up-bore." OBVE, *tr. by* Pope

"With many a weary step, and many a groan." UV

"Youth there was, Elpenor was he nam'd, A." OBVE, *tr. by* Pope

Odyssey, The. Andrew Lang. OBEV; OBNC; PoLF; PoRA

Odyssey. Alexander Pope, *Greek.*

Gardens of Alcinous, The. OBGa, *tr. by* Alexander Pope

Odyssey, The. Sipho Sepamla. AF

Odyssey: A Modern Sequel, The. Nikos Kazantzakis, *Greek.*

"O sun, great Oriental, my proud mind's golden cap." GrIP, *tr. by* Kimon Friar

Odyssey of Big Boy. Sterling Brown. NAAAL

Odyssey or "On Absence," The. Chimako Tada, *Japanese.* VCWP, *tr. by* Naoshi Koriyama *and* Edward Lueders

Oeconomy of Love; a Poetical Essay, The. John Armstrong.

Advice to Lovers. NOEC

Oedipus. Thomas Blackburn. FaBoTw

Oedipus. Dryden.

"When Athens all the Graecian state did guide." NOSC

Oedipus. Josephine Miles. SoSe-8; WPE

Oedipus. Edwin Muir. CMoP

Oedipus. Seneca, *Latin.*

"Fate is the master of everything it is vain to fight against fate." OBCVT, *tr. by* Ted Hughes

Oedipus at Colonus. Sophocles, *Ancient Greek.*

Chorus: "What man is he that yearneth." AWP

(Chorus reflect on Oedipus' fate, The.) OBCVT, *tr. by* Alfred Edward Housman

Colonus' Praise. OBVE, *tr. by* W. B. Yeats; OBCVT, *tr. by* W. B. Yeats

"Endure what life God gives and ask no longer span." OBMV, *tr. by* W. B. Yeats

Oedipus said to the Sphinx. Limerick. Victor Gray. PeLi

Oedipus the King [*or* Oedipus Rex]. Sophocles, *Ancient Greek.* NAWM-1, *tr. by* Robert Fagles

Chorus: "Oh, may my constant feet not fail."

Oedipus Tyrannus. Sophocles, *Greek.*

"What is God singing in his profound." OBCVT, *tr. by* Fitts, Dudley (1903-68) and Robert Fitzgerald

Oenone and Paris. George Peele. *See* Fair and Fair.

O'er a small suburban borough. The Domineering Eagle and the Inventive Bratling. Guy Wetmore Carryl. OBAL

O'er all miracles preceding / His inestimable death. (LL) St. Philip and St. James. Christopher Smart. NOCV; NOEC

O'er all the hill-tops. The Second Poem the Night-Walker Wrote. Goethe. AWP *Fr.* Wanderer's Night-Songs.

O'er Continent and Ocean. John Haynes Holmes. AH

O'er countless shapes yet seem to gaze on One. (LL) On the Group of the Three Angels Before the Tent of Abraham, by Raffaelle, in the Vatican. Washington Allston. APN-1; GS

O'er English dust. A broken heart lies here. (LL) A Jacobite's Epitaph. Thomas Babington Macaulay, 1st Baron Macaulay. EBEV; FaPoR; NOBE; NOBVV; OBEV; OBNC; OxAEP-2

O'er me, alas! thou dost to much prevail. The Power of Spleen. Anne Finch, Countess of Winchilsea. ECWP *Fr.* The Spleen, a Pindaric Poem.

O'er the glad waters of the dark blue sea. The Corsair. Byron.

O'er the land of the free, and the home of the brave. (LL) The Star-Spangled Banner. Francis Scott Key. APN-1; AiP; BLPA; CTV; EBEvV; FaBoBe; NoP-4; TAP; UV

O'er the men of Ethiopia she would pour her cornucopia. Husband and Heathen. Sam Walter Foss. OBAL

O'er the Muir Amang the Heather. Jean Glover. RACG

O'er the round throat her little head. Harebell and Pansy. Laurence Binyon. CABP

O'er the rugged mountain's brow. Calculating Clara. Harry Graham. PeLV *Fr.* Some Ruthless Rhymes.

O'er the snow, through the air, to the mountain. Alpine Spirit's Song. Thomas Lovell Beddoes. OBNC

O'er the warm kettles, and the savoury streams. In the Kitchen. Mary Leapor. ECWP *Fr.* Crumble Hall.

O'er the Water to Charlie. Robert Burns. FaBoCh

O'er the Wild Gannet's Bath. George Darley. PoEL-4 *Fr.* Ethelstan.

O'er this wide extended country. To the White People of America. Joshua McCarter Simpson. AAP

O'er Waiting Harp-Strings of the Mind. Mary Baker Eddy. AH

O'erlooking a superior spectre— / Or More. (LL) One need not be a Chamber—to be Haunted. Emily Dickinson. APN-2; NALW

O'erwhelm'd with sorrow, and sustaining long. Verses Intended to Have Been Prefixed to the Novel of Emmeline, but Then Suppressed. Charlotte Smith. BWW

Of. Debora Greger. EOEF

Of:/ my crow / Pluto. To Victor Hugo of My Crow Pluto. Marianne Moore. CBNP

Of a cake in the throes of love. (LL) The Frivolous Cake. Mervyn Laurence Peake. CBNP, PeLV

Of a child in Brooklyn. (LL) The Locket. John Montague. BiHa; PBCIP

Of a Country Life. James Thomson.

"How sweet and innocent are country sports." UV

Of a covetous Niggard, and a needie Mouse. Lucilius, *Greek.* OBCVT, *tr. by* George Turberville

Of a dark dial in a sunless place. (LL) The Sea of Death. Thomas Hood. OBNC; PoEL-4

Of a day I had rued. (LL) Dust of Snow. Robert Frost. CMoP; ChAP; OxBA; OxBSP; PFE; SAmP; SoSe-8; TAP; UnPo; WeW-3

Of a Fair Lady Playing with a Snake. Edmund Waller. *See* To a Fair Lady Playing with a Snake.

Of a fallen sparrow, the prairie dog first softens. Gnawing the Breast. Sandra McPherson. LCAP-2

Of a Good Prince and an Evil. Timothy Kendall. NoSic

Of a horse shoe nail. (LL) For want of a nail[, the shoe was lost]. Mother Goose. FaBoBe; OxNR; ReMoGo

Of a hungry devil. (LL) I dreamed I held / A sword against my flesh. Kasa no Iratsume, *Japanese.* BoWoP; WPOW, *tr. by* Kenneth Rexroth

Of a Husbandman. Joshua Sylvester. NOSC

Of a lady fair to see. Lines to Mrs. M. C. Turner. Eloise Bibb. CBWP-4

Of a Lady That Refused to Dance with Him. Henry Howard. SiPS

Of a leg, or a head, or an arm. (LL) The African Lion. A. E. Housman. CBNP; NOxBChV

Of a little love. (LL) At a Window. Carl Sandburg. FaBoBe; PoToHe

Of a little take a little. *Unknown.* OxNR

Of a love or a season? (LL) Reluctance. Robert Frost. CMoP; MoAmPo; NOBA; OxBA; SAGP

Of a mon Matheu thoghte. *Unknown.* MiEL

Of a pendulum's mildness, with her feet up. A Timepiece. James Merrill. HoPM

Of a Rose, a Lovely Rose. *Unknown.* OBEV

Of a sudden, the great prima donna. Limerick. *Unknown.* PeLi

Of a tall stature and of sable hue. Charles II. *Unknown.* FaBoEE

Of a' the airts the wind can blaw. Robert Burns. AWP; GLoP; NoP-4; OBEV; OxBS

("As my sweet lovely Jean!") (LL) GTBS-P

Of a' the maids o' fair Scotland. Young Benjie. *Unknown.* ESPB; OxBB

Of a Zealous Lady. Sir John Harington, *after the Latin of* Martial. FaBoEE

Of about one year and a half. (LL) Judging Distances. Henry Reed. BoLoP; GTBS-P; NIP-4; NOBE; NoP-4; PoWW; Poetr

Of Adam's first wife, Lilith, it is told. Body's Beauty. D. G. Rossetti. OAEL-2; PoEL-5; Son *Fr.* The House of Life.

Of aid from them—She was the Universe. (LL) Darkness. Byron. CABP; GEA; NAEL-2; OAEL-2; PoE; PoEL-4; Ro

Of al this world ne give ich a pese! (LL) All Too Late. *Unknown.* EBEV; OAEL-1

Of all are living, or have been. (LL) Queens. John Millington Synge. GBL; MoBrPo; OBMV; PeVV

Of all creatures women be best. What Women Are Not. *Unknown.* MiEL

Of all despondencies, death-despair must be the worst. Enrique Lihn, *Spanish.* VCWP, tr. by Alastair Reid

Of all five norms observed from first to last. King and Subjects. *Unknown, Vietnamese.* AVP, tr. by Huỳnh Sanh Thông

Of all garments. Dhu'l-Rumma, *Arabic.* ArPe, tr. by Omar S. Pound

Of all God's jokes none is bluer. Limerick. A. Cinna. PeLi

Of all God's mercies, is my posy [or posie] still. (LL) The Posy [or Posie]. George Herbert. ChIV-1; NOSC

Of all its music! (LL) The Nightingale. Coleridge. LaPo

Of All My Loves. Abba Kovner, *Hebrew.* IP, tr. by Warren Bargad *and* Stanley F. Chyet

Of all sad words of tongue or pen. The Saddest Words. John Greenleaf Whittier. ImPo *Fr.* Maud Muller on a summer's day. APN-1; FaBoBe; PoLF; TAP

Of all sins of the flesh, that reprobate. Hangover Mass. X. J. Kennedy. DiPo

Of all that God has shown me. Mechthild von Magdeburg, *German.* EnlH; WPoS, tr. by Jane Hirshfield

Of all that Orient lands can vaunt. The Haschish. John Greenleaf Whittier. APN-1; NCAP; OBAL

Of all that shines below. (LL) The Sun-Flower. Dora Greenwell. PEW; VWP

Of all the animals, my heart belongs to the camel. Camel. Boris Alekseievich Chichibabin, *Russian.* TCRP, tr. by Albert C. Todd

Of all the birds I know, few can. The Toucan. Pyke Johnson, Jr. NTCP

Of All the Birds That I Do Know. George Gascoigne. CH *Fr.* The Praise of Philip Sparrow.

Of all the birds that sing and fly. Samuel Hoffenstein. *Fr.* Songs about Life and Brighter Things Yet. NBLV

Of all the brave captains that ever were seen. Sir Dilberry Diddle, Captain of Militia. *Unknown.* NOEC

Of all the causes which conspire to blind. Alexander Pope. OxAEP-1 *Fr.* An Essay on Criticism. NAEL-1; NoP-4; PoEL-3; TFi

Of all the cities in Romanian lands. Disdain Punished. Dryden. EBNV; NOSC *Fr.* Theodore and Honoria, From [Fables Ancient and Modern from] Boccace.

Of all the creatures, in the world, that be. John Oldham. OBVE *Fr.* Satires.

Of all the famous Hangchou sights. Yüan Mei. *Fr.* Five Poems on Returning to Hangchou. CoBLCP, tr. by Jonathan Chaves

Of all the flowers rising now. Maritae Suae. William Philpot. OBEV

Of all the girls that are so smart. Sally in Our Alley. Henry Carey. AWP; BoLoP; FaBoBe; GLoP; GTBS-P; NOBE; NOEC; OBEV; OxAEP-1

Of all the huntresses. Patrizia Cavalli, *Italian.* NeIt, tr. by Robert McCracken

Of all the kings that ever here did reign. Sonnet 75. Sir Philip Sidney. NoSic *Fr.* Astrophil and Stella. AAS; SiPS

Of all the lives I cannot live. Dickinson. Annie Finch (b. 1956). FFC

Of all the people who went into the snowy mountains. Discovery. Gu Cheng, *Chinese.* VCWP, tr. by Eva Hung

Of all the plants, bamboo is the most difficult to paint. Painting Bamboo, a Song. Po Chü-i, *Chinese.* SuSp, tr. by Irving Lo

Of all the pleasant ways. Driving in the Park. *Unknown.* OxBoLi; PeLV

Of all the race of animals, alone. Of Bees. Virgil. APo, tr. by John Dryden *Fr.* The Georgics.

Of all the rides since the birth of time. Skipper Ireson's Ride. John Greenleaf Whittier. APN-1; NCAP; NOBA; OBAL; OBCA; OxBA; PoLF

Of all the sayings in this world. *Unknown.* OxNR

Of all the seas that's coming. *Unknown.* EBEV

Of all the ships upon the blue. Captain Reece. Sir William Schwenck Gilbert. OBCoV

Of all the Souls that stand create—. Emily Dickinson. AmPP; ITG; NAAL-1; NAAL-3; PAR

Of all the Sounds despatched abroad. Emily Dickinson. APN-2

Of all the Splendor. Ory Bernstein, *Hebrew.* IP, tr. by Warren Bargad *and* Stanley F. Chyet

Of all the tales of human struggle, hear this one from Tennessee. Bryan's Last Battle. *Unknown.* AmFP

Of all the thoughts of God that are. The Sleep. Elizabeth Barrett Browning. ChIV-1; OxAEP-2

Of all the times when not to speak is best. Three Silences. Rachel Hadas. RA

Of all the torments, all the cares. Rivals. William Walsh *and* Sir George Etherege. OBEV

Of all the Trees that in the Garden grew. Alice Sutcliffe. KTR *Fr.* Meditations of Man's Mortalitie; or, A Way to True Blessedness.

Of all the wild deeds upon murder's black list. Verses on Daniel Good. *Unknown.* OxBB

Of all the world's enjoyments. The Fisherman's Song. Thomas D'Urfey. NOSC

Of all thes kene conquerours to carpe it were kynde. The Tournament of Tottenham. *Unknown.* OxBoLi

Of All Things for You to Go Away Mad. Joanne Kyger. PoM

Of all things which are living and can form a judgment. Euripides. GrIP, tr. by Rew Warner *Fr.* Medea. NAWM-1; OxBM

Of Althea and Flaxie. Cheryl Clarke. GLP

Of an Heroical Answer of a Great Roman Lady to Her Husband. Sir John Harington. BoLoP; OxBM

Of an old king in a story. Old King Cole ("Of an old king in a story"). G. K. Chesterton. BXAP *Fr.* Variations on an Air Composed on Having to Appear in a Pageant as Old King Cole. NOBL

Of an old King in a story. Variations on an Air: After W. B. Yeats. G. K. Chesterton. BXAP; NOBL

Of an unvisited garden in Mexico. (LL) Dream Record: June 8 1955. Allen Ginsberg. CoAmPo; NOBA

Of Anantanarayanan— / M. Anantanarayanan. (LL) I Missed His Book, but I Read His Name. John Updike. OBAL

Of Angels and of Angel-men the King. (LL) A Hymn for Christmas Day. John Byrom. ECEV; NOCV; PoEL-3

Of angels to the perfect shape of man. (LL) To —. With the Following Poem. Tennyson. EnVR; NOBRP

Of animals' houses / Two sorts are found. Animals' Houses. James Reeves. OTCP

Of apparitions, he (Johnson) observed, A total disbelief. Do They Return? Samuel Johnson. LBC

Of ashes the lifeless land. Lost Bay. Erich Arendt, *German.* CEEP, tr. by David Scrase

Of asphodel, that greeny flower. William Carlos Williams. CMoP *Fr.* Asphodel, That Greeny Flower.

Of attractions the Sabines ain't stinted. Limerick. D. W. Barker. PeLi

Of August strikes like a hawk the crouching hare. (LL) Emblems. Allen Tate. AWP; VGW

Of Autumn. Veronica Porumbacu, *Rumanian.* BoWoP, tr. by Willis Barnstone *and* Matei Calinescu

Of Bacchus let me tell a sparkling story. Bacchus, or the Pirates. *Unknown, Latin.* OBCVT, tr. by Leigh Hunt

Of banks and stones and every blooming thing. (LL) Inniskeen Road: July Evening. Patrick Kavanagh. CIP-2; MoP; NoAM; Poetr

Of beads and receipts and dolls and clothes, tobacco crumbs, / vases and fringes. Gwendolyn Brooks. *See* The Bean Eaters.

Of beasts am I, of men was he most brave. The Lion over the Tomb of Leonidas. *Unknown, Greek.* AWP, tr. by Walter Leaf

Of Beauty. Sir Richard Fanshawe. BoLoP *Fr.* Il Pastor Fido. (Beauty.) GBL

Of Bees. Virgil. APo, tr. by John Dryden *Fr.* The Georgics.

Of Being Numerous. George Oppen.
"It is difficult now to speak of poetry." NNaP

Of bells comprehended through incense. (LL) My love / thy hair is one kingdom. E. E. Cummings. LiTM; VGW

Of Bison Men. James Fenton. PeLV *Fr.* Wild Life Studies.

Of black silent waters weep. (LL) Thrushes. Ted Hughes. FaBoMo; TRP

Of blackberry-eating in late September. (LL) Blackberry Eating. Galway Kinnell. InPK-6; NIP-4; PiM; SoSe-8

Of Boston in New England. William Bradford. SCAP

Of Breakfast, then of walking to the pond. Good Appetite. Mark Van Doren. OxBSP; Spl

Of bricks. . . Who built it? Like some crazy balloon. Our Youth. John Ashbery. CoAmPo; VGW; WeT

Of bright cities / and citrus. Florida. Carl Rakosi. TAP

Of Bronze—and Blaze. Emily Dickinson. APN-2; NCAP; PAR

Of cannons. Jacques Prévert. *See* Pater Noster.

Of Caution. Francesco da Barberini, *Italian.* AWP, tr. by D. G. Rossetti

Of Certain Irish Fairies. Arthur Guiterman. PoLF

Of Change of Opinions. Victor Gustave Plarr. NOBVV

Of Choice. William Meredith. VCAP *Fr.* Consequences.

Of Christ's Nativity. William Dunbar. EnVB
(Unto Us a Child is Born.) ChIV-2

Of coiled mist, he sighed for lost freedom. (LL) Mount Eagle. John Montague. BiHa; IIP

Of Colours and Shadows. Ahmed Tidjani-Cissé. PBMAP

Of comfort no man speak! Let's Talk of Graves. Shakespeare. FaBoBe *Fr.* King Richard II.

Of Common Devotion. Francis Quarles. OxBSP

Of composts shall the Muse descend to sing. Compost. James Grainger. NOEC *Fr.* The Sugar Cane.

Of Constance holy legends tell. The Nun. Edward Moore. ECEV

Of cord and cassia-wood is the lute compounded;. The Old Lute. Po Chü-i, *Chinese*. ChiP, *tr. by* Arthur Waley

Of course each shrub and rodent has a name, sometimes more than one. Against the Literal. Janet Holmes. BAP-95

Of course he is right, otherwise he would. The Thing Is to Not Let Go of the Vine. Ron Koertge. EC2

Of course, I don't know very much. Aunt Chloe's Politics. Frances Ellen Watkins Harper. NAAAL; NALW

Of Course—I prayed. Emily Dickinson. APN-2; BoWoP; MoAmPo

Of course I tried to tell him. Poets Hitchhiking on the Highway. Gregory Corso. BB; NeAP; PoM

Of course, she's only a digestive tube, like all of us. A Dialogue between the Head and Heart. Gavin Ewart. CBLP

Of course, the entire effort is to put my [*or* one] self. Thoughts During an Air Raid. Stephen Spender. MoBrPo

Of course, the familiar rustling of programs. Peripeteia. Anthony Hecht. VCAP

Of course they had servants, dressed for dinner. Goethe and Brentano. Andrew Taylor. BMAP *Fr.* Travelling to Gleis-Binario.

Of course, wait. (LL) Dinner Guest: Me. Langston Hughes. LTA; SSLK

Of course, we have Guide Dogs For The Blind. Who Likes the Idea of Guide Cats? Gavin Ewart. NOxBChV

Of course, we would wish them angelic lookouts. Irving Feldman. VCAP *Fr.* All of Us Here.

Of course when someone leaves you forever. Back. Angela McCabe. AmPA

Of course Zimmer was late for the gig. The Duke Ellington Dream. Paul Zimmer. PBCAP

Of Courtesy. Arthur Guiterman. Spl

"Of Dame Wiggins of Lee." (LL) Dame Wiggins of Lee. *Unknown*. FaBoBe; OxBChV

Of Dancing. Alan Brownjohn. FaBoMo

Of Dandelions & Tourists. Joe Rosenblatt. NOBC

Of dark habits, / keeping their difficult balance. (LL) Love Calls Us to the Things of This World. Richard Wilbur. AmPP; CMoP; HAP; HeIP-4; InPS-3; MoAmPo; NIP-4; NoAM; PoE; PoRA; Poetr; TAP; TFi; UnPo; VCAP; VGW

Of darkness in the sea. (LL) The Friendship. Toi Derricotte. IFJA; PBCAP

Of De Witt Williams on His Way to Lincoln Cemetery. Gwendolyn Brooks. NOBA; NoAM *Fr.* A Street in Bronzeville. BPo; BlSi; FaBoWP

Of Death, of Life, those inwound notes are mine. (LL) A Ballad of Past Meridian. George Meredith. OAEL-2; PeVV

Of Difference Does It Make. Tom Paulin. BiHa

Of diverse monsters I have sometimes read. Strange Monsters. Rowland Watkyns. FaBoEE

Of driving the nail in, these also lasted. (LL) Mighty Forms. Brenda Hillman. PuP-16; WeT

Of Dronkennesse. Antimedon, *Greek*. OBCVT, *tr. by* George Turberville

Of Drunkenness. George Turberville. NBLV

Of dust the primal Adam came. Kosmos. Julia Ward Howe. ColAP

Of dying. (LL) I Give You Back. Joy Harjo. LoL

Of Dying Beauty. Louis Zukofsky. PoA

Of dying is love. (LL) Little Sleep's-Head Sprouting Hair in the Moonlight. Galway Kinnell. InPS-3; LCAP-2

Of each bruised and heart-/ Shaped petal. (LL) The Wild Dog Rose. John Montague. BIrV; CIP-2; PBCIP; PoE

Of eager and extravagant anger. (LL) The Lovers. William Robert Rodgers. BIrV; OxBSP; PNI

Of Earthly Love. Susanna Valentine Mitchell. LW

Of Edenhall the youthful lord. The Luck of Edenhall. Ludwig Uhland, *German*. AWP, *tr. by* Longfellow

(Of elephop and telephong!) (LL) Eletelephony. Laura Elizabeth Richards. CTV; ImGa; NBLV; NOxBChV; NTCP; OBCA; OxBChV

Of Elizabeth, frigidly stretched. (LL) This Houre Her Vigill. Valentin Iremonger. CIP-2; NOIV; OxBTC

Of England, and of Its Marvels. Fazio degli Uberti, *Italian*. AWP, *tr. by* D. G. Rossetti

Of English Verse. Edmund Waller. BeJo; CABP; GEA; NAEL-1; NOSC; OAEL-1; PoE; SeCP

("But as long-lived as present love.") (LL) GEA

Of Ethiopia spreading her gorgeous wings. (LL) Summertime and the Living. Robert Earl Hayden. PoBA; TwCP

Of every kinne [*or* everykune] tree, of every kinne [*or* everykune] tree. The Hawthorn. *Unknown*. EnVB; MiEL

Of every vice pursued by those. Gambling. Royall Tyler. TAP

Of fading pleasures in successive flight. (LL) Sonnet VI. To the Torrid Zone. Helen Maria Williams. NOBRP; NoP-4

Of feathered fouls, that fan the buxom air. Fashioned After the Manner of Master Geoffrey Chaucer in His Assembly of Fowls. Thomas, the Elder Warton. ChIV-1

Of feathered fowls, that fan the buxom air. Thomas, the Elder Warton. *See* Fashioned After the Manner of Master Geoffrey Chaucer in His Assembly of Fowls.

Of February, 1918. (LL) In the Waiting Room. Elizabeth Bishop. FaBoWP; HeIP-4; InPS-3; LCAP-2; LiLi; NAAL-2; NALW; NOBA; NoAM; PoE; VCAP

Of festive goodness in back of their hard, or veiled, or shining, / unknowable gaze. (LL) Olga Poems. Denise Levertov. LCAP-2; NNaP

Of few words, Sir, you seem to be. *Unknown*. SiPS

Of Fiammetta Singing. Giovanni Boccaccio. AWP *Fr.* Sonnets.

Of finite hearts that yearn. (LL) Two in the Campagna. Robert Browning. APAD; EBEV; EBVV; EnVR; FHYEP; GTBS-P; NAEL-2; NOBE; NOBVV; NoP-4; OAEL-2; OBNC; OxAEP-2; OxBM; PoE; PoEL-5; SCGP; TFi; TOF

Of Flesh and Spirit. Wang Ping. BAP-93

Of flesh. O star of men! (LL) A Camp in the Prussian Forest. Randall Jarrell. CMoP; HP; MoAmPo; OBWP; OxBC; PoWW

Of Forced Sightes and Trusty Ferefulness. Jorie Graham. PoPoPo

Of Frankfurt—1945. (LL) Frankfurt. János Pilinszky, *Hungarian*. PoSu, *tr. by* Janos Csokits *and* Ted Hughes

Of Friendship. Charles Stuart Calverley. FP

Of Gardens. Rene Rapin, *French*. OBGa, *tr. by* John Evelyn, the Younger

Of Gardens. OBGa, *tr. by* John, the Younger Evelyn

Of gasoline and desert air. (LL) At Barstow. Charles Tomlinson. MoP; NoAM; TwCP

Of genius here at home. Once the Sole Province. Douglas Crase. EOEF

Of George and Caroline! (LL) A Lilliputian Ode on Their Majesties' Accession. Henry Carey. FaBoVe; NOEC; OBCoV

Of Giving. Arthur Guiterman. CTV

Of God we ask one favor. Emily Dickinson. MeMAP

Of Gods Omnipotencie. Alexander Hume. NOCV

Of gold or gowns my mother had not much. She Would Have Roses. Nicholas Lloyd Ingraham. PWR

Of gold then but now locked in brass. Epitaph: Chryseomallus the Mime. Paulus Silentiarius, *Greek*. GrAn, *tr. by* Andrew Miller

Of Gravity & Angels. Jane Hirshfield. DeD

Of Green Steps and Laundry. Ralph Gustafson. NoP-4

Of Grief. May Sarton. MDDM

"I did not weep my father." MDDM

Of hacked, beheaded coconuts towards home. (LL) Nights in the Gardens of Port of Spain. Derek Walcott. NAEL-2; NoP-4; OxBC

Of happiness, haply hysterics. Is. (LL) The Rites for Cousin Vit. Gwendolyn Brooks. BPo; HAP; NAAAL; NoP-4; WPE; WeW-3

Of Heaven, and hope to have it after all. (LL) The Argument of His Book. Robert Herrick. AWP; BeJo; CaPo; CavPo; EBEV; HAP; ImPo; NAEL-1; NOSC; NoP-4; OAEL-1; OxAEP-1; PeECV; PoE; PoEL-3; PoPoPo; PoRA; SeCP; TFi; TTTS

Of heaven, and, waking in the darkness, screams. (LL) Nerves. Arthur Symons. CABP; FaBoTw

Of Heaven Considered as a Tomb. Wallace Stevens. PoA

Of Heaven or Hell I have no power to sing. An Apology. William Morris. AWP; EBVV; EnVR; NAEL-2; NoP-4; OAEL-2; OBNC *Fr.* The Earthly Paradise.

Of Helen's brothers, one was born to die. Sonnet XLVIII. George Santayana. APN-2 *Fr.* Sonnets.

Of her Jacks, Latin. Jane. Philip Hammial. BMAP

Of her soft armory. (LL) The Catch. Richard Wilbur. DiPo; WeW-3

Of Himself. Meleager, *Greek*. AWP, *tr. by* Richard Garnett

Of hireling wolves whose Gospel[l] is their maw. (LL) To the Lord General[l] Cromwell[, on the Proposals of Certain Ministers at the Committee for the Propagation of the Gospel *or* May 1652]. Milton. FaBoPV; GSo, IIP; NAEL-1; NOSC; NoP-4; PBRV; PoPoPo; SCGP; Son

Of His Dear Son, Gervase. Sir John Beaumont. OBEV *Fr.* Of My Dear Son, Gervase Beaumont. NOBE

Of His Death. Meleager, *Greek*. AWP, *tr. by* Andrew Lang

Of his glory. *So farewell.* (LL) Upon Ben Jo[h]nson. Robert Herrick. BeJo; CaPo; FaBoEE; NoP-4

Of His Lady in Heaven, *sonnet*. Jacopo da Lentino, *Italian*. AWP, *tr. by* D. G. Rossetti

Of His Lady's Old Age. Pierre de Ronsard, *French*. AWP; CTC, *tr. by* Andrew Lang

Of His Last Sight of Fiammetta. Giovanni Boccaccio. AWP *Fr.* Sonnets.

Of His Life. Wayne Dodd. BLT

Of his long marvellous letters but kept none. (LL) Who's Who. W. H. Auden. MeMAP; MoBrPo; MoP; NoAM; Son

Of his Mistress, upon Occasion of her Walking in a Garden. Henry Constable. OBGa *Fr.* Diana.

Of History More Like Myth. Jean Garrigue. NYBP

Of honest Theft. To my good friend Master Samuel Daniel. Sir John Harington. PBRV

Of horrors that happen so? (LL) The Apparition. Herman Melville. APN-2; NCAP

Of horses and horses of the sea, white horses. (LL) Colonus' Praise. Sophocles. OBVE; OBCVT, *tr. by* W. B. Yeats

Of how her end shall be. (LL) November. Robert Bridges. OBNC; PoEL-5

Of how small estimation is EXORBITANT WEALTH in the sight of GOD, by bestowing it on the most UNWORTHY of ALL MORTALS. (LL) Epitaph on Colonel Francis Chartres. John Arbuthnot. FaBoEE; OBSV

Of Human Knowledge. Sir John Davies.
 "Why did my parents send me to the schools." ChIV-1

Of idleness are still left to live. (LL) The Temple. Po Chü-i, *Chinese.* ChiP, *tr. by* Arthur Waley

Of imagery. I love you, I'd like to go. (LL) You (III). Tom Clark. PmAP; SPE

Of interest to John Calvin and Thomas Aquinas. Why God Permits Evil: For Answers to This Question of Interest to Many Write Bible Answers Dept. E-7. Miller Williams. MT

Of it / Themselves. Alice Walker. *See* Women.

Of Itzig and His Dog. Dannie Abse. EC2

Of Jesu Christ I Sing. *Unknown.* PoE

Of John Bunyan's Life. John James. SCAP

Of John Cabanis' wrath and of the strife. The Spooniad. Edgar Lee Masters. OBAL *Fr.* Spoon River Anthology.

Of joy that's left behind us. (LL) The Journey Onwards. Thomas Moore. GTBS-P; OxAEP-2

Of Kate's Baldness. John, of Hereford Davies. FaBoEE

Of Lalage and Barbara. (LL) The Private Dining Room. Ogden Nash. NYBP; OBCoV; PFE

Of Late. George Starbuck. VGW

Of late from time to time there's risen. Amir Gilbo'a, *Hebrew.* IP, *tr. by* Warren Bargad *and* Stanley F. Chyet

Of late / thin little Vanya. Smells. Yelena Sergeievna, Countess de Carli Shchapova, *Russian.* TCRP, *tr. by* Bradley Jordan

Of late, what time the Bear turned round. Ode 3. Anacreon, *Greek.* NoSic *Fr.* Odes.

Of late, what time the Beare turn'd round. Anacreon. *See* Ode 3: "Of late, what time the Bear turned round."

Of lead and emerald. A Note to Olga (1966). Denise Levertov. CAPP-1; NALW

Of leaves and lamps and the city street mingled before me. (LL) Brooding Grief. D. H. Lawrence. CMoP; IMW; PoE

Of Lentren in the first morning. All Erdly Joy Returns in Pane. William Dunbar. EnVB

Of Liberty, Reforms and Rights I sing. Instructions, Supposed to Be Written in Paris, for the Mob in England. Mary Alcock. ECWP

Of life, of a cloud, of height. (LL) The Call of the Lake. Andrey Andreievich Voznesensky, *Russian.* TCRP; VCWP, *tr. by* Stanley Kunitz

Of like importance is the posture too. The Posture. Lucretius, *Latin.* EP, *tr. by* John Dryden

Of little use the man you may suppose. Alexander Pope. EBEV *Fr.* The First Epistle of the Second Book of Horace Imitated.

Of lost connections. (LL) Memories of West Street and Lepke. Robert Lowell. AF; AmPP; CMoP; InPS-3; NAAL-2; NOBA; NoAM; PoE; SAGP; VCAP

Of Love. Kahlil Gibran. PoLF *Fr.* The Prophet.

Of Love. William Meredith. VCAP *Fr.* Consequences.

Of love he sang, full hearted one. A Forced Music. Robert Graves. MoBrPo

Of love's austere and lonely offices? (LL) Those Winter Sundays. Robert Earl Hayden. APAD; ChAP; ColAP; GEA; HAP; HCAP; ISC; InPK-6; LCAP-2; MoP; NIP-4; NoAM; NoP-4; PiM; PoBA; PoPoPo; Poetr; RaBo; SAGP; SSLK; SoSe-8; TFi; UnPo; WeW-3

Of loves perfection perfectly to speake. Edmund Spenser. OAEL-1 *Fr.* Colin Clout's Come Home Again.

Of Loving at First Sight. Edmund Waller. NOSC; SeCP

Of man's Divinity alive in stone. (LL) St. Isaac's Church, Petrograd. Claude McKay. NAAAL

Of Man's [*or* Mans] First Disobedience, and the Fruit. Book I. Milton. FHYEP; NAEL-1; OAEL-1; OxAEP-1 *Fr.* Paradise Lost.

Of Man's First Disobedience, and the Fruit. Invocation. Milton. EBEvV; EPCY; NAWM-1; NOSC; PeECV; PoE; PoEL-3; SCV; TOF, *ll.* 1–26;

EBEV, *ll.* 1–270; NIP-4, *ll.* 1–49 *Fr.* Book I. FHYEP; NAEL-1; OAEL-1; OxAEP-1 *Fr.* Paradise Lost.

Of many things adulterate. Epitaph. Tristan Corbière, *French.* AWP, *tr. by* Joseph T. Shipley

Of Many Worlds in This World. Margaret Lucas Cavendish. NOSC

Of Mars Hill, Maine. Wesley McNair. *See* House in Spring.

Of Mary. Sister Mary Madeleva.
 Dumb Oxen. CRP

Of May. Alexander Scott. OxBS

Of meat. To stay alive this way, it's hard. (LL) Surviving. James Welch. CDW; HATNAP

Of mercy by a gracious God. (LL) To Retiredness. Mildmay Fane, 2d Earl of Westmorland. BeJo; NOSC

Of Mere Being. Wallace Stevens. HCAP; NoP-4

Of Merlin and his skill what Region doth not heare? Poly-Olbion. Michael Drayton. OxBSn

Of mighty love the wings for this me give. (LL) In Spayn. Sir Thomas Wyatt. AAS; NoSic; OPOU; SCGP

Of Miles Davis. William Ford. SeSe

Of-millions-of sea. (LL) Boat Poem. Bernard Spencer. FaBoTw; OxBTC

Of modern Manners let me sing. Modern Manners. Mary Alcock. ECWP

Of Modern Poetry. Wallace Stevens. ColAP; MoP; NAAL-2; NoAM; OxBA; Poetr; TAP

Of Modesty. Mary Mollineux.
 "Thus Modesty, and Spotless Innocence." KTR

Of Mohenjo Daro at Oxford. Keki N. Daruwalla. OMIP

Of Money. Barnabe Googe. GEA; NBLV; NoSic; SoSe-8

Of Mortmain. Herman Melville. APN-2 *Fr.* Clarel: A Poem and Pilgrimage in the Holy Land.

Of Moulds and Mushrooms. Ruthven Todd. FaBoTC

Of music, joy, life and eternity. (LL) Change. Donne. CBLP; EBEV

Of My Dear Son [*or* Deare Sonne], Gervase Beaumont. Sir John Beaumont. NOBE
 (Of My Dear Son Gervaise.) IMW
 Of His Dear Son, Gervase. OBEV

Of my drowsy mouth. (LL) Breasts. Charles Simic. NNaP; RaBo

Of my flesh and blood, only one remains. Yüan Mei. *Fr.* Five Poems on Returning to Hangchou. CoBLCP, *tr. by* Jonathan Chaves

Of my fond heart, hath made me poor. (LL) A Complaint. Wordsworth. NOBE; PoEL-4; RaBo

Of my great grief the great excess. (LL) Farewell, all my welfare. Sir Thomas Wyatt. GBL; SiPS

Of my husband I do not ask much. Limerick. *Unknown.* PeLi

Of My Lady Isabella Playing on the Lute. Edmund Waller. HAP
 (On My Lady Isabella Playing on the Lute.) SeCP

Of my shoulder and quickly, too quickly, I am gone? (LL) Angel Surrounded by Paysans. Wallace Stevens. HCAP; LCAP-2

Of myghty love the winges for this me gyve. Sir Thomas Wyatt. *See* In Spayn.

Of Myself. Leah Goldberg, *Hebrew.* BoWoP, *tr. by* Ramah Commanday

Of Nature's Chain how regular the Links! The Great Chain of Being. Oppian, *Greek.* OBCVT, *tr. by* William Diaper

Of nearness to her sundered Things. Emily Dickinson. OxBSn; PoE

Of Necco Wafers, Nibs, and Juju Beads. (LL) Ex-Basketball Player. John Updike. InPK-6; NYBP; TRP

Of Nelson and the North. Battle of the Baltic. Thomas Campbell. FaPoR; GTBS-P; OBEV

Of Neptune's empire [*or* Empyre] let us sing. A Hymn in Praise of Neptune. Thomas Campion. NOBE; OBEV

Of nights / some bear. Ojars Vacietis, *Latvian.* CEEP, *tr. by* Inara Cedrins

Of no removes! (LL) Fine knacks for ladies, cheap, choice, brave and new! *Unknown.* CH; EBEV; HAP; NoP-4; NoSic; OAEL-1

Of nothing, nothing, nothing—nothing at all. (LL) The End of the World. Archibald MacLeish. CMoP; GSo; HoPM; ImPo; InPK-6; LiTM; MeMAP; MoAmPo; NOBA; NoAM; OBAL; OxBA; PBMP; PFE; SAGP; Son; TAP; TFi; VGW

Of now done darkness I wretch lay wrestling with (my God!) my God. (LL) Carrion Comfort. Gerard Manley Hopkins. CABP; NoP-4

Of Objects Considered as Fortresses in a Baleful Place. Hyam Plutzik. VGW

Of old and now, the world has tales to tell. Catfish and Toad. *Unknown, Vietnamese.* AVP, *tr. by* Huỳnh Sanh Thông

Of old when folk lay sick and sorely tried. On Hygiene. Hilaire Belloc. MoBrPo

Of old when Nature, in her verve defiant. The Giantess. Charles Baudelaire, *French.* OBVE, *tr. by* Roy Campbell

Of old when Nature, in her verve defiant. The Giantess. Charles Baudelaire, *French.* OBVE, *tr. by* Roy Campbell

Of old, when Scarron his companions invited. Poem. Oliver Goldsmith. NOIV; OxBoLi *Fr.* Retaliation. OxBoLi

Of One Dead. Tennyson. ImPo *Fr.* In Memoriam A. H. H.

Of One That Died of the Wind-Colic. *Unknown.* CBNP

Of One That Had a Great Nose. George Turberville, *after the Greek of Trajan.* FaBoEE

Of one that longs for love in vain. (LL) The Wife's Lament. *Unknown.* AnOE, *tr. by* Charles W. Kennedy; BoLoP, *tr. by* Michael Alexander

Of one that longs for love in vain. (LL) Wife's Lament. *Unknown, Anglo-Saxon.* PBWP; PoE, *tr. by* Kemp Malone

Of one who grew up at Gallipoli. War Story. Jon Stallworthy. OxBC

Of one who was much to me. A Burial. Sydney Tremayne. FaBoTC

Of other days around me. (LL) Oft in the stilly night. Thomas Moore. APAD; EBEvV; FaBoBe; GTBS-P; IMW; LBC; NOBE; OBEV; OBNC; PoEL-4; SCGP

Of our desires the farder [*or* farther] down to slide. (LL) Sonnet 35: "False [*or* Faulce] hope which feeds but[t] to destroy, and spill." Mary Sidney Wroth, Countess of Montgomery. KTR; NAEL-1

Of our own enslavements. But Bird *was* a junkie! (LL) Historiography. Lorenzo Thomas. MoNo; SeSe

Of our return / At the end. (LL) Good Night, Willie Lee, I'll See You in the Morning. Alice Walker. CrSp; IMW; NAAAL; WeW-3

Of Oxfordshire and Gloucestershire. (LL) Adlestrop. Edward Thomas. APAD; AYFP; CH; EBEvV; HAP; NAEL-2; NOBE; NoP-4; OBEV; OxBTC; UV

Of pale cold light that was alive. (LL) The Signature of All Things. Kenneth Rexroth. APSN; NNaP; TRP

Of Paul and Silas it is said. Emily Dickinson. ChIV-2

Of peace on earth, good-will to men. (LL) Christmas Bells. Henry Wadsworth Longfellow. CTV

Of people running down the street. A Picture. Howard Nemerov. OxBC

Of person rare, strong limbs, and manly shape. A Sonnet Written upon My Lord Admiral Seymour. John Harington. NoSic

Of Phyllis. William Drummond, of Hawthornden. CBLP

Of Poor B.B. Bertolt Brecht, *German.* RB, *tr. by* Michael Hamburger

Of Power, Money, Cheese, Real Estate, Conboberation, Hoohah. Mac Wellman. FTOS *Fr.* Terminal Hip.

Of Promises and Prophecy. Steve Chimombo. HBAPE

Of quality and fabric more divine. (LL) Conclusion: "In one of those excursions (may they ne'er)." Wordsworth. OAEL-2; OBNC

Of Rain and Air. Wayne Dodd. BLT

Of red berries. Will he wake? (LL) Scenes from the Life of the Peppertrees. Denise Levertov. LiTM; NeAP; NoP-4; PoM

Of remembrance, whispers out of time. (LL) Self-Portrait in a Convex Mirror. John Ashbery. HCAP; NAAL-2

Of repentance for the false day that's fled. (LL) White Christmas. William Robert Rodgers. LiTM; MoBrPo

Of Robert Frost. Gwendolyn Brooks. MoP; NOBA; NoAM
("Some specialness within.") (LL) ColAP

Of Rome. Herman Melville. OxBA *Fr.* Clarel: A Poem and Pilgrimage in the Holy Land.

Of room to lodge th' inhabitant. (LL) Another [Epitaph on the Lady Mary Villiers] ("The Purest soul that e'er was sent"). Thomas Carew. BeJo; CaPo; CavPo

Of Roses and Hyacinths. Rene Rapin, *Latin.* GaP, *tr. by* John Evelyn

Of roses thrown on marble stairs. (LL) The Gift of God. Edwin Arlington Robinson. MoAmPo; OxBA

Of Royal Issue. Brigit Pegeen Kelly. PUP-20

Of Saint Theresa in her wild lament. (LL) The Groundhog. Richard Eberhart. CMoP; FaBoMo; ImPo; LiTM; MoAmPo; MoP; NoAM; RaBo; TAP; TFi; TRP; UnPo

Of Sarah Byng the tale is told. Hilaire Belloc. *See* Sarah Byng Who Could Not Read and Was Tossed into a Thorny Hedge by a Bull. A Cautionary Tale.

Of Scolding Wives and the Third Day Ague. Henricus Selyns. AiP; SCAP

Of sea-birds on the shore. (LL) The Storm. Walter De la Mare. NOxBChV; NoP

Of service which thou renderest. (LL) Reward of Service. Elizabeth Barrett Browning. BLPA; FaBoBe

Of simple choice they are the villagers; their clothes come. Adrienne Rich. HCAP *Fr.* Shooting Script.

Of simple tastes and mind content! (LL) Contentment. Oliver Wendell Holmes. APN-1; AmPP; OxBA; PWR

Of Sir Fraúncis Walsingham Sir Phillipp Sydney, and Sir Christopher Hatton, Lord Chancelor. *Unknown.* PBRV

Of some child scrabbling in the dark. (LL) Adam's Footprint. Vassar Miller. MT; WeT

Of Spenser's Faery Queen. Sir Walter Ralegh. *See* A Vision upon This Concei[p]t of the Faerie [*or* Faery] Queen[e].

Of spinach and gammon. The Right Heart in the Wrong Place. James Joyce. FaBoPV

Of Spring water—thirty or forty miles. How I Sailed on the Lake till I Came to the Eastern Stream. Lu Yu, *Chinese.* ChiP, *tr. by* Arthur Waley

Of St Stephen. Francis Quarles. NOSC

Of Stars. Margaret Lucas Cavendish, Duchess of Newcastle. NOSC

Of such a wit the world should have no more. (LL) An Ode for Ben Jonson. Robert Herrick. AWP; BeJo; CaPo; EPCY; FP; NOSC; SCGP; SeCP

Of such an intense azure. The Blue City. Alfred Wellington Purdy. NoP-4

Of Suicide. John Berryman. NoAM

Of sun! Langston Hughes. *See* As I Grew Older.

Of sundry kirks and tabernacles in that country. (LL) Settlers. Tom Paulin. IIP; PNI

Of surgery, and remedies for wounds. (LL) At last, by chance and guardian fancy led. Philip Freneau. NAAL-1; NAAL-3

Of Taste; an Essay. James Cawthorn.
Englishman at the Table, The. ECEV

Of that I leave them till. Isabella Whitney. *See* The Aucthour Maketh Her Wyll and Testament.

Of that late death took all my heart for speech. (LL) In Memory of Major Robert Gregory. W. B. Yeats. EBEV; OAEL-2; SCGP

Of that medusa strange. The Statue of Medusa. William Drummond of Hawthornden. GS

Of that mysterious race. (LL) Poem: "At night Chinamen jump." Frank O'Hara. CBNP; NOBA; NoAM; PmAP

Of that old fox; a sheep-dog bounding at his stirrup. Randall Jarrell. *See* The Knight, Death, and the Devil.

Of that short Roll of friends writ in my heart. To Mr I. L. Donne. FP

Of that table in the café. Cafe. Czeslaw Milosz, *Polish.* PoSu, *tr. by* Jan Darowski

Of that which once was great, is [*or* has] passed [*or* pass'd] away. (LL) On the Extinction of the Venetian Republic. Wordsworth. GTBS-P; NOBE; OBEV; OBNC

Of the Aegean. Odysseus Elytis. GrIP, *tr. by* Kimon Friar *Fr.* Orientations.

Of the Animal Spirits. Margaret Lucas Cavendish, Duchess of Newcastle. PEW

Of the Azazmeh Too. Haim Guri, *Hebrew.* IP, *tr. by* Warren Bargad *and* Stanley F. Chyet

Of the beauty of kindness I speak. Kindness. Thomas Sturge Moore. OBMV

Of the bee's [*or* bees] honey and her sting. (LL) Upon a Mole in Celia's Bosom. Thomas Carew. CBLP; CaPo

Of the birds that fly in the farthest sea. John Gray. OBNC *Fr.* The Flying Fish.

Of the Birth and Bringing Up of Desire. Edward De Vere, 17th Earl of Oxford. FaBoEE; NoSic; SCGP

Of the Blessed Sacrament of the Altar [*or* Aulter]. Robert Southwell. OBEV

Of the Boy and Butterfly. John Bunyan. OxBChV

Of the brave! (LL) Battle of the Baltic. Thomas Campbell. FaPoR; GTBS-P; OBEV

Of the broad road that stretches and the roadside fire. (LL) The Song of a Traveller. Robert Louis Stevenson. BoTP; EBVV; ITG; MoBrPo; OBEV

Of the Child with the Bird on the Bush. John Bunyan. OxBChV

Of the Colossal substance / Of Immortality. (LL) Soul's Superior instants, The. Emily Dickinson. APN-2; EnlH

Of the Courtier's Life. Sir Thomas Wyatt. *See* Myn owne John poyntz sius ye delight to know.

Of the Creator. And he waits for the world to begin. (LL) Leviathan. W. S. Merwin. APo; ChIV-1; MoP; NOBA; NoAM

Of the dark past. Ecce Puer. James Joyce. BIrV; ChIV-2; EBEV; IMW; MoP; NoAM; TrCP

Of the Day Estivall. Alexander Hume. NOCV; OxBS
Midsummer Day in France.

Of the Elmira Wood. Her Apron through the Trees. Roger Weingarten. AmPA

Of the eyes of my Annie. (LL) For Annie. Edgar Allan Poe. APN-1; AmPP; MeMAP; NOBA; OBEV; OxBA

Of the far sea, / Tho' far off it be. (LL) Spring Quiet. Christina Rossetti. BoTP; CH; GTBS-P; InPS-3; PoE; PoEL-5; WPE

Of the far Waterfall like Doom. (LL) Tarantella. Hilaire Belloc. APAD; CH; EBEvV; FaBoCh; MoBrPo; OBMV; RB; UV

Of the fathoms of set eyes. (LL) The Fire at Alexandria. Theodore Weiss. NoAM; PoA; SAmP; TAP

Of the first Paradice there's nothing found. On St. James's Park, as Lately Improved by His Majesty. Edmund Waller. BeJo; NOSC

Of the first *yes* that comes from lips you love! (LL) Nevermore. Paul Verlaine, *French.* FLP; LoP, *tr. by* Alistair Elliot

Of the forest bees? (LL) Carrefour. Amy Lowell. LW

Of the four louts who threw him off the dock. A Finished Man. Richard Wilbur. AFr

Of the French Kings Nativity. Benjamin Harris. SCAP

Of the Gentle Heart, *canzone.* Guido Guinicelli, *Italian.* AWP; CTC; OBVE, *tr. by* D. G. Rossetti

Of the Going Down of the Sun. John Bunyan. CH

Of the Great and Famous. . . Sir Francis Drake, and of My Little-Little Selfe. Robert Hayman. CH; FaBoCh

Of the great moon. (LL) The Letter. Amy Lowell. CPO; NALW

Of the ills we daily see. The Social Life. Lizelia Augusta Jenkins Moorer. CBWP-3

Of the Lady Pietra degli Scrovigni, *Sestina I.* Dante, *Italian.* AWP; OAEL-2; OBVE, *tr. by* D. G. Rossetti

Of the lapsing, unsoilable, Whispering sea. (LL) Ringsend. Oliver St. John Gogarty. OBMV; OxBTC

Of The Last Verses in the Book. Edmund Waller. BeJo; EBEV; HAP; NOSC; NoP-4; PeECV; PoPoPo; SCGP; SeCP

Old Age. NOBE; OBEV

Of the look of a room on returning thence. (LL) The Walk. Thomas Hardy. CMoP; NAEL-2; PoE; PoEL-5

Of the Loss of Time. John Hoskyns. FaBoEE

Of the loud languorous nightingale. (LL) Fantoches. Paul Verlaine. AWP; OBMV, *tr. by* Arthur Symons

Of the mad locomotive riverbank sunset Frisco hilly tincan / evening sitdown vision. Allen Ginsberg. *See* Sunflower Sutra.

Of the Manner of Addressing Clouds. Wallace Stevens. PoA

Of the many known and proven. Curing Homosexuality. Jim Everhard. GLP

Of the many men whom I am, whom we are. We Are Many. Pablo Neruda, *Spanish.* VCWP, *tr. by* Alastair Reid

Of the Marriage of the Dwarfs. Edmund Waller. CBLP

Of the meane and sure estate. Seneca. *See* Senec. Traged. ex Thyeste Chor. 2.

Of the million or two, more or less. Instans Tyrannus. Robert Browning. EBEV

Of the moon. They can't see / Not yet. (LL) Small Frogs Killed on the Highway. James Wright. HCAP; NNaP; NoAM

Of the night. (LL) Poem at Thirty. Sonia Sanchez. BPo; BlSi; NAAAL; NMM-2; NTP; PoBA

Of the no need. Hilda Doolittle. NALW *Fr.* Tribute to the Angels.

Of the not born, yet buried, here's the tomb. (LL) To Fine Lady Would-Be. Ben Jonson. FaBoEE; NOSC; NoP-4; OxBSP

Of the old Egyptian boys. (LL) Travel. Robert Louis Stevenson. CTV; FaBoCh; OTCP

Of the old house, only a few crumbled. The House That Was. Laurence Binyon. MoBrPo

Of the petrel and the porpoise. In the end is my beginning. (LL) East Coker. T. S. Eliot. HAP; VGW

Of the planet of which they were part. (LL) The Planet on the Table. Wallace Stevens. HAP; HCAP; PoPoPo; SAmP

Of the primeval Priests assum'd power. The Book of Urizen [*or* First Book of Urizen]. William Blake. NOBRP

Of the Progres[se] of the Soule; the Second Anniversarie, *sels.* Donne.

Second Anniversary [*or* Anniversarie], The. ESCV; SeCP

("We see in authors, too stiff to recant.") NOSC, *ll.* 281–300

"We now lament not, but congratulate." NOSC

Of the Pythagorean Philosophy. Ovid, *Latin.* OBVE, *tr. by* Dryden *Fr.* Metamorphoses.

"This let me further add, that nature knows." OBVE

"Time was, when we were sow'd, and just began." OBCVT, *tr. by* John Dryden

Of the Realme of Scotland. Sir David Lindsay. OxBS *Fr.* The Dreme.

Of the Reed That the Jews Set in Our Saviour's Hand. William Alabaster. NoSic

Of the Resurrection. Miles Coverdale. ChIV-2

Of the Resurrection of Christ. William Dunbar. *See* On the Resurrection of Christ.

Of the Resurrection of the Body. Marbod of Rennes, *Latin.* MLL, *tr. by* Helen Waddell

Of the rumpling of my Gown a. (LL) The Baffled Knight. *Unknown.* ESPB; OxBB

Of the Scythians. Katha Pollitt. DiPo; InPS-3

Of the snow, and the new year. (LL) New Year's Poem. Margaret Avison. LiTM; NOBC

Of the sound of jade tinkling on your bridle-straps. (LL) To Li Chien. Po Chü-i, *Chinese.* ChiP, *tr. by* Arthur Waley

Of the summer moor. (LL) Unknown love/ Is as bitter a thing. Lady Otomo no Sakanoé. AWP; PBWP, *tr. by* Arthur Waley; BoWoP, *tr. by* Willis Barnstone

Of the swaddies. Seven Good Germans. Hamish Henderson. FaBoTC

Of the terrible doubt of appearances. Walt Whitman. APN-1

Of the Theme of Love. Margaret Lucas Cavendish. OxBSP

(Of the Theam of Love.) PEW

Of the three Wise Men. Carol of the Brown King. Langston Hughes. PChr

Of the toy's purchase with the length of life. (LL) Blight. Ralph Waldo Emerson. APN-1; NCAP; NOBA

Of the two kinds of wing-shaped rings on his desk. The Ring. Ikuko Atsumi, *Japanese.* WPJ, *tr. by* Kenneth Rexroth *and* Ikuko Atsumi

Of the unended in the speed of. Anne-Marie Albiach. PBWP, *tr. by* Paul Auster *Fr.* État.

Of the unforgivable landscape. (LL) The Mouth of the Hudson. Robert Lowell. AiP; VCAP

Of the unnamed poor. (LL) The Minneapolis Poem. James Wright. FYAP; NoAM; UnPo

Of the very world he made. (LL) The Nativity of Our Lord. Christopher Smart. EBEV; HAP; NOBE; NOCV; NOEC; PoEL-3; SCGP

Of the Wars in Ireland. John Harington. NoSic

Of the war's obscenity. (LL) Fabrication of Ancestors. Alan Dugan. CBCWP; NoAM

Of thee' and thy house, which doth in eating heal. (LL) I am a little world made cunningly. Donne. ChIV-1; NAEL-1; NIP-4; NoP-4; PoE; SeCP; Son

Of thee, kind boy, I ask no red and white. Sonnet. Sir John Suckling. BeJo; CaPo; CavPo; MeLP; NOSC; NoP-4; OxBoLi; SeCP

Of thee the Northman by his beachèd galley. Ode V. George Santayana. APN-2

Of their brilliance Miracle / of. (LL) Exodus. George Oppen. ChIV-1; KSG; MoLi

Of their iniquity. (LL) The Ballad Which Anne Askew[e] Made and Sang When She Was in Newgate. Anne Askew. CABP; NoP-4

Of their kin perpetual, brother, ever out here fare well. Catullus. *See* On the Burial of His Brother.

Of their unthinking Drums. (LL) I dreaded that first Robin, so. Dickinson. APN-2; AmPP; HAP; MeMAP; MoAmPo; NAAL-1; NAAL-3

Of them all—those laboring men who knew my first name. At the Sign-Painter's. Jared Carter. FYAP

Of them and rolled her head away. (LL) The Last Words of My English Grandmother. William Carlos Williams. RB; RaBo; SAmP

Of these houses. San Martino del Carso. Giuseppe Ungaretti, *Italian.* PeFWW, *tr. by* David McDuff *and* Jon Silkin

Of these the false Achitophel was first. Achitophel: The Earl of Shaftsbury. Dryden. AWP; HAP; InPS-3; NOBE; NOSC; PoEL-3 *Fr.* Absalom and Achitophel, Pt. I. EBEvV; FHYEP; FaBoPV; HAP; NOSC; OAEL-1; PoE

Of these two spitefull rocks, the one doth shove. Scylla and Charybdis. Homer. *Fr.* Odyssey. NAWM-1, *tr. by* Robert Fitzgerald

Of th'eternal silence. (LL) Noel; Christmas Eve, 1913. Robert Bridges. NOCV; OBCP; PoEL-5

Of things exactly as they are. (LL) Man bent over his guitar, The. Wallace Stevens. CMoP; NoAM; RaBo

Of things from my heart. (LL) Many red devils ran from my heart. Stephen Crane. MeMAP; TAP

Of things moving back to where they came from. (LL) A Procession at Candlemas. Amy Clampitt. PoPoPo

Of this / all things. The Little Pin: Fragment. George Oppen. FTOS

Of this bad world the loveliest and the best. On a Dead Hostess. Hilaire Belloc. MoBrPo

Of this cloth doll which. Michael Palmer. NoP-4

Of this day's glorious feast and revel. *Unknown.* ChiP, *tr. by* Arthur Waley *Fr.* Seventeen Old Poems.

Of this fair[e] volume which we World do[e] name. The Book. William Drummond, of Hawthornden. CH; ChIV-1; GTBS-P

Of this house I know the backwindow. Eyeglasses. Tom Clark. CoAmPo

Of this world's Theatre in which we stay. Sonnet 54. Edmund Spenser. CABP; NAEL-1; NoP-4; OAEL-1 *Fr.* Amoretti. AAS

Of those by whom I was subdued? (LL) The Trumpet. Ilya Grigoryevich Ehrenburg, *Russian.* TCRP; TrJP, *tr. by* Yakov Hornstein

Of those few fools, who with ill stars are cursed. Prologue. William Congreve. *Fr.* The Way of the World. NAEL-1

Of those rebellions that we start in jest. Fear Test: Integrity of Heroes. James Simmons. CIP-2

Of those, thou woundest with thy Dart! (LL) The Wounded Cupid. Robert Herrick. AWP; OBVE

Of those, thou woundest with thy Dart! (LL) The Wounded Cupid. Song. Anacreon, *Greek.* LoP; OBCVT, *tr. by* Robert Herrick

Of Those Who Go, Not to Return. Benyamin Galai, *Hebrew.* MHP, *tr. by* Ruth Finer Mintz

Of Thought is death, *earlier version.* William Blake. *See* The Fly.

Of three eyes, I would still give two for one. The Third Eye. Jay Macpherson. MoCV

Of Three Friendly Warnings This Is the Second. *Unknown, Seneca Indian.* STP, *tr. by* Jerome Rothenberg *and* Richard Johnny John

Of Three Friendly Warnings This Is the Third. *Unknown, Seneca Indian.* STP, *tr. by* Jerome Rothenberg *and* Richard Johnny John

Of Three Girls and of Their Talk. Giovanni Boccaccio. AWP *Fr.* Sonnets.

Of thy departure, when thou wentest forth, it went out / after thee. (LL) Parting. Judah Halevi, *Hebrew.* AWP; TrJP, *tr. by* Nina Davis Salaman

Of thy life [*or* lyfe], Thomas, this compass[e] well mark. The Golden Mean. Henry Howard, Earl of Surrey, *after* Horace. OBVE; SiPS

Of thy lyfe [*or* life], Thomas, this compass well mark. Horace. *See* Odes 2.10.

Of Time and the Line. Charles Bernstein. FTOS; PmAP

Of too much was our talk, of. Zürich, the Stork Inn. Paul Celan, *French.* HP, *tr. by* Michael Hamburger

Of touch they are, and poor I am their straw. (LL) Sonnet 9: "Queen Virtue's court, which some call Stella's face." Sir Philip Sidney. NAEL-1

Of Treason, *epigram.* Sir John Harington. FaBoEE; InPK-6; NoSic; OBCoV; OxBoLi; PBRV; PFE; SoSe-8

(Epigram IV.v: Of Treason.) NOSC

Of two fair virgins, modest, though admired. On a Nun. Jacopo Vittorelli, *Italian.* AWP, *tr. by* Byron

Of Tyndarus, That Frumped a Gentlewoman. *Unknown, Latin.* BIrV, *tr. by* Richard Stanyhurst

Of under me you so quite new. (LL) I like my body when it is with your. E. E. Cummings. BoLoP; Son; VGW

Of underground streams, what I see is a limestone landscape. (LL) In Praise of Limestone. W. H. Auden. CMoP; FYAP; FaBoPV; HAP; MoP; NAEL-2; NoAM; NoP-4; OAEL-2

Of unsaciable purchasers. Robert Crowley. PBRV

Of us naked women. (LL) In My Mother's Room. Colleen J. McElroy. GT; NMM-2

Of us / not much is known. Degli Sposi. Rika Lesser. FYAP

Of Use. John Heywood. FaBoEE

Of vacant darkness and to cease. (LL) My own dim life should teach me this. Tennyson. EnVR; FHYEP; OAEL-2

Of vast import to the nation. (LL) Pastoral: "When I was younger." William Carlos Williams. AmPP; OxBA; SAmP

Of Verbal Criticism. David Mallet.

"Pride of his own, and wonder of his age." EPCY

Of violets, and my soul's forgotten gleam. (LL) Sonnet: "I had no thought of violets of late." Alice Moore Dunbar-Nelson. BlSi; PoBA; Son

Of virtues I most warmly bless. Gerard Manley Hopkins. FaBoEE *Fr.* Seven Epigrams.

Of Walter White's Father in the Rain. Houston A. Baker, Jr. SeSe

Of water, water, water. (LL) The Lifeguard. James Dickey. NYBP; NoP-4; SoSe-8

Of wealthy lustre was the banquet-room. The Banquet. Keats. *Fr.* Lamia. FHYEP

Of western New York state. As You Came from the Holy Land. John Ashbery. GEA

Of what a quality is courage made. Donagh MacDonagh. CIP-2 *Fr.* Charles Donnelly.

Of what good can Paradise be. Paradise. Immanuel di Roma, *Hebrew.* TrJP, *tr. by* J. Chotzner

Of what I felt for thee. (LL) The Secret. John Clare. GLoP

Of what is past, or passing, or to come. (LL) Sailing To Byzantium. W. B. Yeats. APAD; CABP; CMoP; ClHu; GTBS-P; GrIP; HAP; HeIP-4; HoPM; IIP; ImPo; InPK-6; InPS 3; LiTM; MoBrPo; MoP; NAEL-2; NAWM-2; NIP-4; NOBE; NoAM; NoP-4; OAEL-2; OBMV; OxBTC; PoE; PoPoPo; PoRA; RaBo; SAGP; SCGP; SoSe-8; TFi; TIRV; TOF; UnPo; WeW-3

Of what mould did Nature frame me. The Tinder. Thomas Carew. CaPo

Of What The Music to Me. Clark Coolidge. MoNo

Of what use to me are the nights full of wine. Nina Grachova, *Russian.* TCRP, *tr. by* Nina Kossman

Of which we are too distantly a part. (LL) Less and Less Human, O Savage Spirit. Wallace Stevens. AFr; VGW

Of wilding in his hand. (LL) The Two April Mornings. Wordsworth. EBEV; GTBS-P; NAEL-2

Of windows closing on muslin curtains. Air-Conditioned Air. Debora Greger. WWSi

Of woman and wine, of woods and spring. Inexhaustible. Israel Zangwill. TrJP

Of woods, of plains, of hills and dales. Upon a Rich Country Gentleman. *Unknown.* FaBoEE

Of wool among their flock!. . . . (LL) And if ye stand in doubt. John Skelton. NAEL-1; OAEL-1

Of writing many books there is no end! Elizabeth Barrett Browning. NOBVV *Fr.* Aurora Leigh. VWP

Of your beloved in sleep. (LL) He Hears the Cry of the Sedge. W. B. Yeats. OxBTC; RB

Of your faire eies whereby the light is lost. (LL) Complaint That His Ladie After She Knew of His Love Kept Her Face Alway Hidden from Him. Henry Howard, Earl of Surrey. AAS; PoEL-1; SiPS

Of Your Father's Indiscretions and the Train to California. Lynn Emanuel. MoLi; NAmP90

Of your hand I could say this. Dawn. Jeni Couzyn. NBrP

Of your horses, all knot-free. (LL) Another Charme for Stables. Robert Herrick. BeJo; OxBSn

Of your making, tell them I am. (LL) The Hand. Ronald Stuart Thomas. NOCV; OxBC

Of your misprision and my impotence. (LL) On the Threshold. Amy Levy. LW; SDW

Of your path. (LL) Heat. Hilda Doolittle. CMoP; HeIP-4; InPK-6; MoAmPo; OxBA; PiM; TAP; TRP; UnPo

Of your trouble, Ben, to ease me. Her Man Described by Her Own[e] Dictamen. Ben Jonson. *Fr.* A Celebration of Charis in Ten Lyric[k] Pieces [*or* Peeces]. BeJo; OxAEP-1; SeCP

Of your white hand, they are mine. (LL) On Mr. G. Herberts Booke, The Temple. Richard Crashaw. CABP; EPCY; ESCV; FSCP; GeHe; OxAEP-1

Of Youth He Singeth. Robert Wever. *See* In Youth Is Pleasure.

Ofatedo / seek it out upon the skin of Africa. Edouard J. Maunick. NegPo, *tr. by* Ellen Conroy Kennedy *Fr.* As Far as Yoruba Land.

Ofay-Watcher Looks Back. Mongane Wally Serote. PBMAP

Off again, / thrusting up at scald. Caliban in Blue. Walter McDonald. CDa

Off all the lords in faire Scottland. The Heir of Linne. *Unknown.* ESPB

Off an ancient story Ile tell you anon. King John and the Bishop. *Unknown.* ESPB

Off at dawn to service in the walled and storied palace. Lu Chi. CoBCP, *tr. by* Burton Watson *Fr.* Two Poems Presented to the Gentleman in the Office of Palace Writers Ku Yen-hsien.

Off Brighton Pier. Alan Ross. OBWP

Off Coronel. Austin Threlfall Nankivell. NSI

Off Crane's Neck the sun. The Spirit of Wrath. William Heyen. AmPA

Off Duty. Elizabeth Daryush. WPN

Off Februar the fyiftene nycht. The Dance of the Sevin Deidly Synnis. William Dunbar. MiEL; OxBS; PoE

Off Havana the ocean is green this morning. Havana Birth. Susan Mitchell. NAmP90

Off Highway 106. Cherrylog Road. James Dickey. CoAP; ColAP; HAP; HCAP; InPS-3; MT; NAAL-2; NIP-4; NYBP; Poetr; TwCP; WeW-3

Off in the forest. Found. Goethe, *German.* STV, *tr. by* John Frederick Nims

Off in the twilight hung the low full moon. Full Moon. Sappho, *Greek.* AWP, *tr. by* William Ellery Leonard

Off in the wilderness bare and level. The Temptations of Saint Anthony. Phyllis McGinley. OxBSP

Off our New England coast the sea to-night. The House of Falling Leaves. W. S. Braithwaite. NAAAL

Off-shore, by islands hidden in the blood. I, Maximus of Gloucester, to You. (Off-shore, by islands hidden in the blood). Charles Olson. LiTM; NOBA; NoAM; PmAP; PoM *Fr.* The Maximus Poems.

Off that landspit of stony mouth-plugs. Medusa. Sylvia Plath. CAPP-1; NALW

Off the Aleutian Chain. Linda Bierds. NAmP90

Off the Back of a Lorry. Tom Paulin. PBCIP

Off the coast of Ireland. Seascape. Langston Hughes. GT

Off to hunt ducks. Song of the Duck Hunters. Kao Ch'i, *Chinese.* CoBLCP, *tr. by* Jonathan Chaves

Off to Outer Space Tomorrow Morning. Norman Nicholson. SpW

Off to Patagonia. Theodore Weiss. TAP

Off to Philadelphia in the morning. Dennis Brutus. GT

Off We Go to Market. Gwen A. Smith. BoTP

Off with sleep, love, up from bed. Love in May. Jean Passerat, *French.* AWP, *tr. by* Andrew Lang

Off with you, boy! Pretended prude! Strato, *Greek.* GrAn, *tr. by* Edward Lucie-Smith

Off Womanheid Ane Flour Delice. *Unknown.* OxBS

Offended, The. Anne Hébert, *French.* BoWoP, *tr. by* Willis Barnstone

Offensive, The. Keith Douglas. PoWW

Offer, An. Arthur Guiterman. TrJP

Offer it up plank it down. Ooftish. Samuel Beckett. NoAM

Offer varied attractions to Whistler. (LL) Limerick: "There's a combative artist named Whistler." D. G. Rossetti. FaBoEE; PeLi

Offered to a Man Who Sells Pines. Yü Wu-ling, *Chinese.* SuSp, *tr. by* Edward H. Schafer

Offering. Debra Allbery. PBCAP

Offering, An. Eloise Bibb. CBWP-4

Offering. Thomas McGrath. RaBo

Offering. Sharan Strange. BAP-94; GT

Offering for the Cat, An. Mei Yao Ch'en, *Chinese.* CoBCP; PC, *tr. by* Burton Watson

Offering of the Heart Tapestry from Arras, XV Century, The. Rolfe Humphries. FYAP

Offering: Part One, The. Mary Lee, Lady Chudleigh. WPE

Offering Wine. Yü Wu-ling, *Chinese.* CoBCP, *tr. by* Burton Watson

Offers me plum blossoms for my hair. (LL) Morning. Chu Shu-chen, *Chinese.* BLT; OHPC, *tr. by* Kenneth Rexroth

Offers the boon of Death. (LL) Compensation. Paul Laurence Dunbar. APN-2; BPo

Offertorium. C. Day Lewis. TIRV *Fr.* Requiem for the Living.

Offertory. John F. Deane. TIRV

Office feels like a sealed glass case today, The. What Grandma Knew. Edward Field. Poetsp

Office Friendships. Gavin Ewart. FP; PeLV

Office Party. Phyllis McGinley. OBSV

Office work: a wearisome jumble. Poem without a Category. Liu Cheng, *Chinese.* CoBCP, *tr. by* Burton Watson

Officer at the Rapids, The. Han Yü, *Chinese.* SuSp, *tr. by* Charles Hartman

Officer, I broke your gun. (LL) A Mother Speaks: The Algiers Motel Incident, Detroit. Michael S. Harper. AmPA; BPo; NBV

Officers. Josephine Miles. FaBoWP

Officers' kit and the long low limbers, The. Cookers, The: A Song of the Transport. Sir Alan Patrick Herbert. NSI

Officers' Mess. Gavin Ewart. OxBTC

Official document blows through a forest, An. The Long Picnic. Russell Edson. LCAP-2

Official Piety. John Greenleaf Whittier. NCAP

Officialdom. Nguyễn Công Trứ, *Vietnamese.* AVP, *tr. by* Huỳnh Sanh Thông

Officials checked to make certain we'd. Abundance. John Cage. APSN *Fr.* Diary: How to Improve the World (You Will Only Make Matters Worse)

Offspring. Naomi Long Madgett. CrSp; GT; SoSe-8

Offspring of modern poetry, attend. Morning. *Unknown.* NOEC

Oft am I by the women told. Age. Abraham Cowley. AWP

Oft did I hear our eyes the passage were. Sir John Davies. *Fr.* Sonnets to Philomel. SiPS

Oft has this planet rolled around the sun. Sir Samuel Garth. *Fr.* The Dispensary. OBSV

Oft have I heard my lief[e] Corydon [*or* Coridon] report on a love-day. Hexametra Alexis in Laudem Rosamundi. Robert Greene. GBL; PoEL-2 *Fr.* Greene's Mourning Garment.

Oft have I heard thee mourn the wretched lot. Charles Churchill. OBSV *Fr.* The Prophecy of Famine.

Oft have I mused, but now at length I find. A Farewell. Sir Philip Sidney. GBL; NOBE; SiPS

Oft have I played at cards and dice. The Rantin Laddie. *Unknown.* AmFP

Oft have I said, I say it once more. Hafiz. AWP, *tr. by* Ralph Waldo Emerson *Fr.* Odes.

Oft have I said, the praise of doing well. Matthew Prior. ChIV-1 *Fr.* Pleasure: The Second Book of Solomon on the Vanity of the World.

Oft have I seen at some cathedral door. Divina Commedia. Henry Wadsworth Longfellow. APN-1; HAP; OxBA; TAP

Oft have I seen, ere Time had ploughed my cheek. Decay of Piety. Wordsworth. TrCP

Oft have I seen, when that renewing breath. Resurrection and Immortality. Henry Vaughan. ESCV

Oft have I thrilled at deeds of high emprise. To Madame Curie. Alice Moore Dunbar-Nelson. NMM-2

Oft have you hinted to your brother peer. Epistle to Lord Burlington. Alexander Pope. OBGa *Fr.* Epistle to Lord Burlington.

Oft I had heard of Lucy Gray. Lucy Gray; or, Solitude. Wordsworth. CH; GEA; NAEL-2; NOBRP; OAEL-2; OxAEP-2; OxBChV

Oft I must strive with wind and wave. Anchor: "Oft I must strive with wind and wave." Cynewulf. AnOE, *tr. by* Charles W. Kennedy *Fr.* Riddles (Exeter Book).

Oft in Danger yet alive. To Mrs Thrale [on Her Thirty-fifth Birthday]. Samuel Johnson. FaBoEE

Oft in her Glass the musing Shepherd spies. Ausonius. OBCVT, *tr. by* Alexander Pope *Fr.* Windsor-Forest.

Oft in my thought full busily have I sought. Charles D'Orleans. NoP-4

Oft in the hall I have heard my people. *Unknown.* HeIP-4, *tr. by* Charles W. Kennedy *Fr.* Beowulf. OAEL-1, *tr. by* Charles W. Kennedy

Oft in the lone church-yard at night I've seen. Robert Blair. OxAEP-1 *Fr.* The Grave.

Oft, in the silence of the night. Our Little Ghost. Louisa May Alcott. OBCA

Oft in the Silent Night. Otto Julius Bierbaum, *German.* AWP, *tr. by* Ludwig Lewisohn

Oft in the stilly night. Thomas Moore. APAD; EBEvV; FaBoBe; GTBS-P; IMW; LBC; NOBE; OBEV; OBNC; PoEL-4; SCGP

Oft is the medal faithful to its trust. In a Garden in the Grounds of Coleorton, Leicestershire. Wordsworth. OBGa

Oft it befalls by the grace of God. Fates of Men (Exeter Book). *Unknown, Old English.* AnOE, *tr. by* Charles W. Kennedy

Oft I've implored the gods in vain. A Prayer for Indifference. Fanny [*or* Frances] Macartney Greville. ECWP; NOEC

Oft mighty elephants by little Moors are led. Powerful Servants. Friedrich von Logau, *German.* GePo, *tr. by* George C. Schoolfield

Oft o'er my brain does that strange fancy roll. Composed on a Journey Homeward; the Author Having Received Intelligence of the Birth of a Son. Coleridge. Son

Oft-Repeated Dream, The. Robert Frost. Poetr *Fr.* The Hill Wife. CMoP; HAP; InPS-3; LiTM; NoP-4; RACG

Oft to the Wanderer, weary of exile. The Wanderer. *Unknown, Anglo-Saxon.* AnOE; NAWM-1; OAEL-1, *tr. by* Charles W. Kennedy

Oft when I'm sitting without anything to read. Lines to a World-famous Poet Who Failed to Complete a World-famous Poem; or, Come Clean, Mr. Guest! Ogden Nash. OBAL

Oft when I've seen some lonely mansion stand. The Landscape. Richard Payne Knight. OBGa *Fr.* The Landscape.

Oft when my spirit doth spread her bolder wings. Sonnet 72. Edmund Spenser. Son *Fr.* Amoretti. AAS

Oft with true sighs, oft with uncalled tears. Sonnet 61. Sir Philip Sidney. NAEL-1 *Fr.* Astrophil and Stella. AAS; SiPS

Often a friend will greet me thus. Hartmann von Aue, *German.* GePo, *tr. by* Frederick Goldin

Often after we make love. The Old Man. Penelope Shuttle. LW

Often, / around certain backwaters. Great Blue. Brendan Galvin. AFr

Often, before I came to lie down here, I wept. Fanny Brawne's Letter Put Unopened In Keats's Coffin. Valentine Ackland. WPN

Often beneath the wave, wide from this ledge. At Melville's Tomb. Hart Crane. HAP; MoAmPo; MoP; NAAL-2; NoAM; NoP-4; PoA; TAP; UnPo; VGW

Often, half-way to sleep. In Procession. Robert Graves. TwCP

Often I Am Permitted to Return to a Meadow. Robert Duncan. CMoP; ColAP; NOBA; PmAP

Often I compare my lord to heaven. Gaspara Stampa, *Italian.* PBWP, *tr. by* Lynne Lawner

Often I go to bed as soon after dinner. 4 Often. Jane Kenyon. BAP-93; LoL *Fr.* Having It Out With Melancholy. BAP-93

Often I saw, as on my balcony. Christ Church Meadows, [Oxford]. Donald Hall. NYBP

Often I sit in the sun and brooding over the city, always. Dennis Lee. NOBC *Fr.* Civil Elegies.

Often I think of the beautiful town. My Lost Youth. Henry Wadsworth Longfellow. APN-1; AWP; AmPP; FaBoBe; FaPoR; ImGa; MeMAP; NAAL-1; NAAL-3; NOBA; OBEV; OxBA; PAR; PoEL-5; PoLF; PoRA; TAP; TFi

Often I turn on people / in rather strange & / inexplicable ways. Maxfield Parrish. Eileen Myles. PT

Often in summer, on a tarred bridge plank standing. Wild Bees. James Keir Baxter. NoP-4

Often in the morning the fog is thick over Jersey. A View of Jersey. Edward Field. NeAP

Often, in these blue meadows. Pursuit from Under. James Dickey. HAP

Often, it's a field at dark. Gleanings. Lorna Goodison. HCP

Often I've wished that I'd been born a woman. A Wish. Laurence David Lerner. OxBTC

Often likened. Tanka. Saitō Mokichi, *Japanese.* MJT, *tr. by* Makoto Ueda

Often on this her daughter's tomb did Cleina grieve. Anyte. HePo, *tr. by* Barbara Hughes Fowler *Fr.* Epigrams.

Often rebuked, yet always back returning. Stanzas. Emily Jane Brontë. GEA; NALW; NOBVV; OAEL-2; OBEV; OBNC; PBWP; PEW; SCGP; VWP

Often the start went wrong. Start. Martin Sorescu, *Romanian*. VCWP, *tr. by* Michael Hamburger

Often / there's nothing in its place? Abba Kovner. *See* Poem: Alte Zachen.

Often think of, tenderly, and acquire. (LL) Three Riddles from *The Exeter Book*. Cynewulf. ASW; PeLV, *tr. by* Kevin Crossley-Holland

Often this thought wakens me unawares. Night. Hermann Hesse, *German*. AWP, *tr. by* Ludwig Lewisohn

Often waking / before the sun decreed. Author of *Christine*, The. Richard Howard. CoAP

Often when alone I liken my lord / to the cosmos. Gaspara Stampa, *Italian*. BoWoP, *tr. by* J. Vitiello

Often, when o'er tree and turret. Hic Vir, Hic Est. Charles Stuart Calverley. OxBoLi; PeLV

Often when warring for he wist not what. Thomas Hardy. GSo

Often you walked at night, houselights made. In Sepia. Jon Anderson. PoA

Oftener seen, the more I lust, The. Out of Sight, Out of Mind. Barnabe Googe. InPS-3

Oftentimes, I grew dejected and sobbed. Ch'u Yüan. SuSp, *tr. by* Wu-chi Liu *Fr.* Li Sao.

Ofttimes have I heard you speak of one who commits a. Crime and Punishment. Kahlil Gibran. PoToHe *Fr.* The Prophet.

Og [and Doeg]. John Dryden *and* Nahum Tate. AWP *Fr.* Absalom and Achitophel, Pt. II.

O'Grady lived in Shantytown. O'Grady's Goat. Will S. Hays. PoLF

Ogre does what ogres can, The. August 1968. W. H. Auden. OxBSP

Ogres and Pygmies. Robert Graves. CMoP; FaBoMo; LiTM; MoP; NoAM

Oh. High Flight. John Gillespie Magee Jr. ImGa; PoWW; SAGP

Oh, a capital ship for an ocean trip. Charles Edward Carryl. *See* The Walloping Window-Blind.

Oh, a day in the city-square, there is no such pleasure in life! (LL) Up at a Villa—Down in the City. Robert Browning. FHYEP; GTBS-P; InPS-3; NOBE; PoRA

Oh, a hidden power is in my breast. Song of the Moon. Priscilla Jane Thompson. CBWP-2

Oh a high holiday, on a high holiday. Little Musgrave and Lady Barnard. *Unknown*. AmFP

Oh, a poor aviator lay dying. A Poor Aviator Lay Dying. *Unknown*. NSI

Oh! a private buffoon is a light-hearted loon. The Family Fool. Sir William Schwenck Gilbert. NBLV *Fr.* Yeoman of the Guard.

Oh a shantyman's life is a wearisome [*or* drearisome] life. A Shantyman's Life. *Unknown*. AS; AmFP

Oh, a soldier told me, before he died. The Soldier's Tale. *Unknown*. PeLV

Oh, a wonderful horse is the Fly-Away Horse. The Fly-Away Horse. Eugene Field. CTAV

Oh [*or* O], a wonderful stream is the River Time. The Long Ago. Benjamin Franklin Taylor. BLPA

Oh, about the joy of owning a crab hut at Sung-chiang! Chang Chih-ho. SuSp, *tr. by* Hellmut Wilhelm *Fr.* Fisherman's Songs.

Oh Achilles of the moleskins. To "Chick." Frank Horne. BPo *Fr.* Letters [*or* Notes] Found near a Suicide. PoBA

Oh, Adam was a gardner, and God. The Glory of the Garden. Rudyard Kipling. CTV *Fr.* The Glory of the Garden.

Oh, America / The sun sets in you. The Evening Land. D. H. Lawrence. FaBoA

Oh angels! will ye never sweep the drifts from my door? Drifts That Bar My Door. Adah Isaacs Menken. CBWP-1

Oh, as I went down to Derby Town. The Derby Ram. *Unknown*. AmFP

Oh, Athelstane, the faithful! Athelstane. Priscilla Jane Thompson. CBWP-2

Oh author of my being!—far more dear. To Charles Burney. Frances Burney, Mme D'Arblay. ECWP

Oh, away down South where I was born. Roll the Cotton Down. *Unknown*. AmFP

Oh, baby, baby, baby dear. Song. Edith Nesbit. NOBVV; PEW; VWP

Oh, be but still, you half-part of my breast! Departure Aria. Johann Christian Günther, *German*. GePo, *tr. by* George C. Schoolfield

Oh be thou blest with all that Heav'n can send. To Mrs. M. B. on Her Birth-Day. Alexander Pope. EnLoPo

Oh, big sighs. Windy sighs. And ghostly laughter. (LL) News Update. John Balaban. AF; CDa

Oh, black Persian cat! Mujer. William Carlos Williams. PC; SAmP

Oh! blame not the bard, if he fly to the bowers. Thomas Moore. NOIV

Oh blessed Lord! and wouldst thou die. On the Death of Our Lord. Richard Flecknoe. TIRV

Oh! blest [*or* bless'd] of heav'n [*or* Heaven], whom not the languid songs. Nature's Influence on Man. Mark Akenside. NOEC *Fr.* The Pleasures of Imagination.

Oh, blush not so, oh, blush not so. Song. Keats. APAD; CBLP

Oh Boney was a warrior. Boney. *Unknown*. FaBoVe

Oh Boney's on the sea. The Shan Van Vocht. *Unknown*. OxBoLi

Oh, Bonnie is the little cow. Midnight in Bonnie's Stall. Siddie Joe Johnson. PChr

Oh Book! infinite sweetnesse! let my heart. The H. Scriptures. George Herbert. ChIV-1; ESCV; MiEL

Oh, bow your head, Tom Dooley. Tom Dooley. *Unknown*. AmFP

Oh brew me a potion strong and good! The Elixir. Emma Lazarus. SDW

Oh bright-glancing Silver, who marriage has made. Stroll-Joy. Johann Klaj, *German*. GePo, *tr. by* George C. Schoolfield

Oh, brother, oh, brother, can you play ball. The Two Brothers. *Unknown*. AmFP

Oh bury me not on the lone prairie. (LL) Bury Me Not on the Lone Prairie. *Unknown*. AS; FaBoBe

Oh, but it is dirty! Filling Station. Elizabeth Bishop. FaBoMo; HAP; HCAP; InPK-6; NYBP; NoP-4; VCAP; WeW-3

Oh but It Was Good. Harold Littlebird. VoR

Oh, By the Way. Ed Ochester. PuP-17

Oh, call my brother back to me. The Child's First Grief. Felicia Dorothea Hemans. BLPA; CH

Oh, can we love and live? Pray, let us die. Love's Sun. William Cavendish, Duke of Newcastle. NOSC

Oh, Charlie's sweet and Charlie's neat. Weevily Wheat. *Unknown*. AS; AmFP

Oh children think about the Good times. (LL) Good Times. Lucille Clifton. AmPA; BPo; InPS-3; PoBA; SoSe-8; TAP; TRP; TwCP

Oh come, let us sing unto Jehovah. Bible, *O.T. See* Psalm 95.

Oh, come let us welcome sweet Sabbath the Queen! Welcome, Queen Sabbath. Zalman Schneour, *Hebrew*. TrJP, *tr. by* Harry H. Fein

Oh come, my beloved! from thy winter abode. California Madrigal. Bret Harte. APN-2

Oh, come to me in dreams, my love! Stanzas. Mary Wollstonecraft Shelley. LW

Oh come with me by moonlight, love. A Cherokee Love Song. John Rollin Ridge. APN-2; PaTW

Oh, come with me in my little canoe. Ossian's Serenade. Calder Campbell. BLPA

Oh, come with old Khayyám and leave the Wise. Omar Khayyám. UV *Fr.* The Rubáiyát of Omar Khayyám [of Naishápúr]. AWP; EBVV; FaBoBe; FaPoR; HAP; NAEL-2; PoEL-5

Oh, could I but sing as the minstrels of old! Lines to Emma. Priscilla Jane Thompson. CBWP-2

Oh could I raise the darken'd veil. Nathaniel Hawthorne. APN-1; PAR

Oh country, marvel of the earth! Not Yet. William Cullen Bryant. NCAP

Oh! craven, craven! while my brothers fall. George Henry Boker. APN-2

Oh (cry'd the Goddess) for some pedant Reign! Alexander Pope. *Fr.* Yet, yet a moment, one dim ray of light. NAEL-1; OAEL-1; PoEL-3 *Fr.* The Dunciad.

Oh, Day of Days. LeRoy V. Brant. AH

Oh, de boll weevil am a little black bug. Boll Weevil Song. *Unknown*. AS

Oh, de ole sheep, dey know de road. De Ole Sheep Dey Know de Road. *Unknown*. BPo

Oh, Dear! *Unknown*. ReMoGo

Oh dear, my heart was ready to burst! (LL) As I was going by Charing Cross. *Unknown*. CH; FaBoCh; OxNR

Oh, dear! Oh, me! Oh, my! Song. Gregory Corso. BB

Oh dear what can the matter be? Saturday Night. Victoria Wood. OBCoV

Oh, dear, what can the matter be? / Two old women got up in an apple-tree. The Bunch of Blue Ribbons. *Unknown*. ReMoGo

Oh, dearest grandpa, come and see. The Dead Sister. Caroline Gilman. OBCA

Oh! Death. *Unknown*. AmFP

Oh! Death will find me, long before I tire. Sonnet. Rupert Brooke. MoBrPo; NoP-4; PoRA; SAGP; Son

Oh, Dem Golden Slippers! James A. Bland. APN-2

Oh, dewy [*or* O Dewey] was the morning, upon the first of May. Manila Bay. Eugene Fitch Ware. OBCoV

Oh Dick! You may talk of your writing and reading. Thomas Moore. OBCoV *Fr.* The Fudge Family in Paris.

Oh, did you go to see the show. The Orange Lily. *Unknown*. FaBoPV

Oh! Did you ne'er hear of Kate Kearney? Kate Kearney. Sydney, Lady Morgan Owenson. BLPA; FaBoBe

Oh, do buzz off, you bumptious Sun. Busy Old Fool. Ian Kelso. BXAP

Oh do not die, for I shall hate. A Fever. Donne. OAEL-1

Oh do[e] not wanton with those eyes. A Song. Ben Jonson. CBLP; SeCP

Oh, do you remember sweet Betsey from Pike. Sweet Betsey from Pike. *Unknown, sometimes at. to* John A. Stone ("Old Put"). AS; AmFP; OBAL; OxBoLi

Oh doe not die, says Donne, for I shall hate. Joys Once Shared. C. S. Lewis. LBC

Oh, don't you remember Sweet Betsey from Pike. *Unknown. See* Sweet Betsey from Pike.

Oh! don't you see the turtle-dove. The Turtle-Dove. *Unknown.* OxBoLi

Oh Dreams, Oh Destinations. C. Day Lewis.

    Symbols of Gross Experience. Son

Oh, East is East, and West is West, and never the twain shall meet. The Ballad of East and West. Rudyard Kipling. EBNV; FaBoBe; FaPoR; OBNV

Oh, Eleazar Wheelock was a very pious man. Eleazar Wheelock. Richard Hovey. OBAL

Oh Eliza look at your Uncle Jim! Soldiers' Chorus from Faust. *Unknown.* NOBAu

Oh, England is a pleasant place for them that's rich and high. The Last Buccaneer. Charles Kingsley. EBEvV; EBVV; FaBoBe; PeVV

Oh, England. / Sick in head and sick in heart. England. *Unknown.* FaBoEE; OxBSP

Oh Erica, Not Again! Max Fatchen. FuFo

Oh! Erin my country, my ancestor's home! Song to Erin. Mary Weston Fordham. CBWP-2

Oh, ever skilled to war the form we love! Sonnet to Hope. Helen Maria Williams. ECWP

Oh! ever thus from childhood's hour. Thomas Moore. UV *Fr.* Lalla Rookh.

Oh, everything is far. Lament. Rilke, *German.* TrJP, *tr. by* C. F. MacIntyre

Oh, face to face with trouble. Margaret Elizabeth Munson Sangster. PoToHe

Oh [*or* O] fair[e] sweet face, oh [*or* O] eyes celestial[l] bright. Song. John Fletcher. NOSC; PoEL-2 *Fr.* Women Pleased.

Oh fairest of the rural maids! William Cullen Bryant. APN-1; TAP

Oh, fare you well, my darling. Fare You Well, My Darling. *Unknown.* AmFP

Oh father, answer me. Dialogue. Howard Nemerov. NYBP

Oh, Father! must they part? Frances Ellen Watkins Harper. *See* The Slave Mother.

Oh father, now that I have touched. Wendy Rose. CDW

Oh feet, oh legs, oh thighs / that formed the deathrow. Philodemus, *Greek.* GrAn, *tr. by* William Moebius

Oh flame falling, as shaken, as the stories. The Fire. Robert Creeley. NOBA

Oh, for a book and a shady nook. Open Sesame. *Unknown.* BoTP

Oh, for a bowl of fat Canary. John Lyly. *See* A Serving Men's Song.

Oh! for a closer walk with God. Walking with God. William Cowper. ECEV; NOCV; NOEC; PeECV; PoEL-3; SCGP; TOF *Fr.* Olney Hymns.

Oh, for a drink, to-night. Charmion's Lament. Eloise Bibb. CBWP-4

Oh for a pleasant book to cheat the sway. Winter Fields. John Clare. EnVR

Oh for a poet—for a beacon bright. Sonnet. Edwin Arlington Robinson. APN-2; NCAP; OxBA

Oh! for a thousand tongues to sing. The Farmer's Soliloquy. Robert Charles O'Hara Benjamin. AAP

Oh for boyhood's painless play. John Greenleaf Whittier. AiP *Fr.* The Barefoot Boy. APN-1; FaBoBe; OBAL; OBCA; PoLF

Oh for far-off monkeyland. Monkeyland. Sándor Weöres, *Hungarian.* RB, *tr. by* Edwin Morgan

Oh! for imperial Polydamna's art. Nepenthe. Charlotte Smith. NoP-4

Oh for one hour of youthful joy! The Old Man Dreams. Oliver Wendell Holmes. PoLF

Oh, for the veils of my far away youth. Lost Illusions. Georgia Douglas Johnson. NAAAL

Oh for the wings of a dove. Song. Agnes Mary Frances Robinson. VWP

Oh for words with which. In the Potting Shed. Sir Osbert Sitwell. OBGa

Oh fortune, [how] thy wresting wavering state. Written on a Wall at Woodstock. Elizabeth I, Queen of England. PBWP; WPE

Oh, foully slighted Ethiope maid! The Song. Priscilla Jane Thompson. CBWP-2

Oh friend, we arrived too late. Friedrich Hölderlin. RaBo *Fr.* Bread and Wine.

Oh, gallant was our galley from her carven steering-wheel. The Galley-Slave. Rudyard Kipling. PeVV

Oh, gallant was the first love, and glittering and fine. Pictures in the Smoke. Dorothy Parker. NBLV

Oh, gallantly they fared forth in khaki and in blue. America's Welcome Home. Henry Van Dyke. AiP

Oh [*or* O] Galuppi, Baldassaro, this is very sad to find! A Toccata of Galuppi's. Robert Browning. EBVV; EBVVPR; EnVR; FaBoVe; GTBS-P; HAP; NAEL-2; NOBE; NOBVV; OAEL-2; UV

Oh, Georgie Wedlock is my name. Georgie Wedlock. *Unknown.* AmFP

Oh, get you forth, my son Willy. Marm Grayson's Guests. Mary Eleanor Wilkins Freeman. OBCA

Oh, Gingilee, my aching heart. Gingilee. Moyshe-Leyb Halpern, *Yiddish.* TrJP, *tr. by* Joseph Leftwich

Oh give it Motion—deck it sweet. Emily Dickinson. NCAP

Oh give me a home where the buffalo roam. A Home on the Range. *Unknown, sometimes att. to* Brewster Higley. APN-2; FaBoBe

Oh, Give Me the Hills. *Unknown.* AmFP

Oh, give thanks to Him who made. Give Thanks. *Unknown.* CTV

Oh! give to me of the bright green leaves. I Am Fashion's Toy. Mary E. Tucker. CBWP-1

Oh, Give Us Back the Days of Old! John Mason Neale. NOCV

Oh, give us pleasure in the flowers today. A Prayer in Spring. Robert Frost. AH; TrCP

Oh, go to old Ireland and then you will know. Go to Old Ireland. *Unknown.* AmFP

Oh, God, beneath thy guiding hand. The Pilgrim Fathers. Leonard Bacon. AH

Oh God Forbid. Freddie Greenfield. GLP

Oh God! It's great! Chocolate Milk. Ron Padgett. TTTS

Oh God! my heart is thine. In the Valley. Priscilla Jane Thompson. CBWP-2

Oh God of mercy, oh wild God. (LL) The Dancing. Gerald Stern. LoL; UnSA

(Oh God, she said). Song My. Susan Griffin. NMM-2; WPOW

Oh God, that I were dead! (LL) Mariana. Tennyson. AWP; CBLP; CH; EBVVPR; EnVR; FHYEP; InPS-3; NAEL-2; NOBE; NOBRP; NoP-4; OAEL-2; OBEV; OBNC; OxAEP-2; PeVV; PoE; PoEL-5; Ro; SCGP; TFi; UnPo

Oh God, we're rich. James Welch. *See* Harlem, Montana.

Oh, golden flower opened up. A Poem to the Mother of the Gods. *Unknown, Aztec Indian.* STP, *tr. by* Edward Kissam

Oh golden life, waken! Fortunate night! Johann Klaj, *German.* GePo, *tr. by* George C. Schoolfield

Oh! Golden Rose! Oh. Glittering Lilly White. Edward Taylor. SCAP *Fr.* Preparatory Meditations Before My Approach to the Lord's Supper.

Oh, good gigantic smile o' the brown old earth. Among the Rocks. Robert Browning. OxBSP *Fr.* James Lee's Wife.

Oh! Good, good, good, my Lord. What more love yet. Edward Taylor. NOBA *Fr.* Preparatory Meditations Before My Approach to the Lord's Supper.

Oh! had I now an overcoat. Wish for an Overcoat. Alfred Islay Walden. AAP

"Oh, halt!" cried Virginia, "Enough!" Limerick. Otto Watteau. PeLi

Oh hame cam his guid horse, but never cam he. (LL) Bonnie [*or* Bonny] George [*or* James] Campbell. *Unknown.* AmFP; CH; ESPB; OxBB; OxBoLi; SCGP

Oh, hangman, hangman, slacken your rope. The Sycamore Tree. *Unknown.* AmFP

Oh, hapless sire, distraught with cares. The Yoke. Kalonymos ben Kalonymos. *Fr.* The Touchstone. TrJP, *tr. by* J. Chotzner

Oh happy hero come, oh enter, worthy groom. To Be Read above the Castle-Gate, When His Princely Highness Rode in to His Marriage Bed. Simon Dach, *German.* GePo, *tr. by* George C. Schoolfield

Oh happy I if I had loved never. (LL) The Affectionate Shepherd. Richard Barnfield. CABP; NoSic

Oh happy shades—to me unblest! The Shrubbery. William Cowper. NOBE; OBGa

Oh, hark the dogs are barking, love. The Banks of the Condamine. *Unknown.* NOBAu

Oh, have you heard de lates'. De Ballit of de Boll Weevil. *Unknown.* NOBA

Oh, have you seen the *Tattlesnake.* The Journal of Society. Godfrey Turner. NOBL; PeLV

Oh, he was a handsome trotter, and he couldn't be completer. How We Drove the Trotter. W. T. Goodge. NOBAu

Oh! hear a pensive prisoner's prayer. The Mouse's Petition. Anna Laetitia Barbauld. ECWP; OxBChV

Oh, hear you a horn, mother, behind the hill? The Horn. James Reeves. OTCP

Oh heart rejoice! For I Have Done a Good and Kindly Deed. Franz Werfel, *German.* TrJP, *tr. by* Edith Abercrombie Snow

Oh, her beauty—the tender maid! Its brilliance gives light. Ibn al-Arabi, *Persian.* TOF, *tr. by* R. A. Nicholson

Oh Hesperus! thou bringest all good things. Sappho. OBCVT, *tr. by* Byron *Fr.* Don Juan.

Oh hold me, for I am afraid. (LL) Woman to Man. Judith Wright. BMAP; CBAP; NoP-4; WPE

Oh, how can I live in a torture so wild. Disappointment. Mary E. Tucker. CBWP-1

Oh [or O] how comely it is and how reviving. The Deliverer. Milton. NOBE; NOCV; OBEV; OxAEP-1   Fr. Samson Agonistes. FHYEP; OAEL-1; PoEL-3

Oh! How his printed language, like a dart. Cant. 5.6 & c. Elizabeth Singer. ChIV-1; KTR

Oh, how I love Humanity. The World State. G. K. Chesterton. FP

OH HOW I WANT THEE FAME! Mad Sonnet: Fame. Michael McClure. BB

Oh how I wish that an embargo. The Nurse's Dole in the Medea. Byron. OBVE

Oh, how slowly he goes. Chalk and Soot. Wassily Kandinsky, *Russian*. PFTM, *tr. by* Elizabeth R. Napier

Oh, how the hand the lover ought to prize. Aphra Behn. LW

Oh, how the world has altered since some fifty years ago! Song of the Modern Time. Eliza Cook. VWP

Oh humming all and. Detach, Invading. Ron Padgett. FTOS

Oh! hush Thee, oh! hush Thee, my Baby so small. Cradle Song at Bethlehem. E. J. Falconer. BoTP

Oh hush up. Breakfast. Everette Maddox. MT

Oh! I admit I'm dull and poor. The Claim. Edith Nesbit. NOBVV

Oh I am a cat that likes to. The Galloping Cat. Stevie Smith. BrRo

Oh, I am a Texas cowboy, just off the Texas plains. The Texas Cowboy. *Unknown*. AmFP

Oh I am a Yankee sailor boy. Sailor Boy's Song. *Unknown*. CA

Oh, I am wild—wild! Sale of Souls. Adah Isaacs Menken. CBWP-1

Oh, I can smile for you, and tilt my head. A Certain Lady. Dorothy Parker. NIP-4

Oh I can't decide between my two loves *ei!* Women's Songs. *Unknown*, *Maori*. PeNZ, *tr. by* Margaret Orbell

Oh, I don't want to be a gambler. I Don't Want to Be a Gambler. *Unknown*. AS

Oh I got up and went to work. On a Seven-Day Diary. Alan Dugan. OBAL

Oh, I had a bird and the bird pleased me. The Barnyard. *Unknown*. AmFP

Oh, I had a horse and his name was Bill. The Horse Named Bill. *Unknown*. AS

Oh I have grown so shrivelled and sere. Body of John. Ronald Allison Kells Mason. PeNZ

Oh, I have no illusions as to what. Penelope. James Harrison. NIP-4

Oh, I laugh to hear what grown folk. Mrs. Kriss Kringle. Edith Matilda Thomas. OBCA

Oh! I love to travel far and near throughout my native land. Wizard Oil. *Unknown*. AS

Oh, I never had but one true love. The Unquiet Grave. *Unknown*. AmFP

Oh, I should love to be like one of those. The Youth Dreams. Rilke, *German*. AWP; TrJP, *tr. by* Ludwig Lewisohn

Oh I suppose I should. Le Médecin Malgré Lui. William Carlos Williams. PoA

Oh, I used to sing a song. The Endless Song. Ruth McEnery Stuart. OBAL

Oh! I vu'st know'd o' my true love. Heedless o' My Love. William Barnes. GBL

Oh, I went to California in the spring of seventy-six. Root, Hog, or Die. *Unknown*. AmFP

Oh! I wish I were a tiny brown bird from out the south. Valentine's Day. Charles Kingsley. BoTP

Oh, I Wish I Were Single Again. *Unknown*. AmFP

Oh, I wonder where my lost Johnny's gone. Lost Johnny. *Unknown*. AmFP

Oh, I would have these tongues oracular. At a Symphony. Louise Imogen Guiney. APN-2

Oh, if but a single hour. Permanence in Change. Goethe, *German*. HoPM, *tr. by* John Frederick Nims

Oh! if by any unfortunate chance I should happen to die. The Soldier. J. Y. Watson. BXAP

Oh [or O], if thou knew'st how thou thyself dost harm. To Aurora. Sir William Alexander, Earl of Stirling. GTBS-P; Son   Fr. Aurora.

Oh, ill-starred Ethiopia. Address to Ethiopia. Priscilla Jane Thompson. CBWP-2

Oh, I'm 10 Months Pregnant. Ntozake Shange. GT

Oh, I'm a good old Rebel. The Rebel. Innes Randolph. CBCWP; NBLV; OBAL; OxBoLi

Oh I'm Dirty Dan, the world's dirtiest man. The Dirtiest Man in the World. Shel Silverstein. OBCA

Oh I'm in love with the janitor's boy. The Janitor's Boy. Nathalia Crane. PoLF

Oh, I'm sailing away my own true love. Boots of Spanish Leather. "Bob Dylan." NoP-4

Oh! I'm the New Year. The New Year. *Unknown*. BoTP

Oh in eighteen hundred and forty-one. Poor Paddy Works on the Railway. *Unknown*. AS; GM

Oh, in the fourteenth the faith landed. The Land Is Gone. *Unknown*, *Maori*. PeNZ, *tr. by* Margaret Orbell

Oh, in the merry month of May. Bonny Barbara Allan. *Unknown*. AWP; BoLoP; CH; ESPB; HeIP-4; OxBB

Oh in the Stonegut Sugar Works. Ballad of the Stonegut Sugar Works. James Keir Baxter. PeNZ

Oh, is it, then, Utopian. De Profundis. Dorothy Parker. NAAL-2

Oh, it is done, my love, my death, my life, my prize. To the Superhuman Adelmund, When She Would Undo the Kiss Already Done. Philipp von Zesen, *German*. GePo, *tr. by* George C. Schoolfield

Oh, it's fiddle-de-dum and fiddle-de-dee. The Dancing Bear. Albert Bigelow Paine. OBCA

Oh, it's hard to grow up at the way-station side! A Boatman's Song. Wang Chien, *Chinese*. SuSp, *tr. by* William H. Nienhauser

Oh, It's Nine Years Ago I Was Digging in the Land. *Unknown*. AmFP

Oh, it's twenty gallant gentlemen. The Last Hunt. William Roscoe Thayer. FaBoBe

Oh, I've got no use for the women. I've Got No Use for the Women. *Unknown*. AmFP

Oh [or O] joys [or joyes]! Infinite sweetness! with what flowers [or flowres]. The Morning-Watch. Henry Vaughan. ESCV; FMP; GeHe; NOSC; NTP; PeECV

Oh! kangaroos, sequins, chocolate sodas! Today. Frank O'Hara. TTTS

Oh King of Saints, how great's thy work, say we. Edward Johnson. SCAP

Oh King of stars! Hospitality in Ancient Ireland. *Unknown*, *Irish*. TIRV, *tr. by* Kuno Meyer

Oh king, whose head alone can rule Earth's company. Concerning the King of Sweden. Georg Rudolph Weckherlin, *German*. GePo, *tr. by* George C. Schoolfield

Oh! Ladies and gentlemen, please to draw near. Down, Down Derry Down. *Unknown*. AS

Oh Lana Turner we love you get up. (LL) Poem: "Lana Turner has collapsed!" Frank O'Hara. CLPP; FTOS; PmAP; VGW

Oh last Thursday morning while playing at ball. Willie. *Unknown*. AmFP

Oh Lawd have mussy now upon us. Blessing without Company. *Unknown*. BPo

Oh leaden heeld. Lord, give, forgive I pray. Edward Taylor. SCAP   Fr. Preparatory Meditations Before My Approach to the Lord's Supper.

Oh! leave the Past to bury its own dead. To One Who Would Make a Confession. Wilfrid Scawen Blunt. GSo

Oh let me be alone, far from the eyes and faces. Weariness. Sara Teasdale. SAGP

Oh, let me lay my head tonight upon your breast. I Am Your Wife. *Unknown*. PoToHe

Oh, let me run and hide. Spring Ecstasy. Lizette Woodworth Reese. MoAmPo

Oh! let that day from time be blotted quite. On the Fatal Day January 30, 1648. Thomas Fairfax, Baron Fairfax of Cameron. NOSC

Oh, Let Thy Teachings. Immanuel di Roma. *Fr.* Machberoth. TrJP, *tr. by* J. Chotzner

Oh, let us do so too. (LL) Good-night. James Shirley. BeJo; NOSC

Oh Liberty, my spirit felt thee there! (LL) France. Coleridge. Ro

Oh, life is a glorious cycle of song. Comment. Dorothy Parker. LW; NBLV; NIP-4; OBAL; OBCoV   Fr. Some Beautiful Letters.

Oh, like a tree. The Tree. John Freeman. BoTP

Oh List to My Song! Clara Ann Thompson. CBWP-2

Oh listen while I sing to thee. Mary Wollstonecraft Shelley. Ro

Oh Living Lord, I still will laud thy name. An Other Song of the Faithful, for the Mercies of God. Michael Drayton. ChIV-1

Oh loathsome place! where I. Henry Howard, Earl of Surrey. SiPS

Oh, long, long. The Grass on the Mountain. Mary Austin. PaTW

Oh, long, long / The snow has possessed the mountains. The Grass on the Mountain. *Unknown*, *Paiute Indian*. AWP, *tr. by* Mary Austin

Oh, long narrow home heavy with living. To the Family Home Awaiting Repair. A. J. Seymour. HCP

Oh! Look at the Moon. Eliza Lee Cabot Follen. BoTP

Oh Lord Cozens Hardy. Lord Cozens Hardy. John Betjeman. OxBTC

Oh, Lord! I lift my heart. A Prayer. Priscilla Jane Thompson. CBWP-2

Oh, Lord, we call to you from our apartment. A Gay Psalm from Fort Valley. Louie Crew. GLP

Oh Lord, when all our bones are thrust. Supplication. Edgar Lee Masters. TrCP

Oh lordy, lord, oh lordy, lord. Worried Life Blues. *Unknown*. AmFP

Oh love! no habitant of earth thou art. The Fatal Spell. Byron. CBLP; OBNC *Fr.* Childe Harold's Pilgrimage.

Oh Love! oh Love! whose shafts of fire. Euripides. OBCVT, *tr. by* Thomas Love Peacock *Fr.* Hippolytus.

Oh! love, that stronger art than wine. Song. Aphra Behn. WPE; WPOW *Fr.* The Lucky Chance.

Oh, love this house, and make of it a Home—. For a New Home. Rosa Zagnoni Marinoni. PoToHe

Oh Lovely Fishermaiden. Heinrich Heine, *German.* AWP, *tr. by* Louis Untermeyer

Oh lyre divine, what daring spirit. Thomas Gray. EPCY *Fr.* The Progress of Poesy. AWP; GTBS-P; NOEC; OBEV

Oh, Maika in a maika, there's the smell of summer. Viktor Arkad'evich Urin, *Russian.* TCRP, *tr. by* Lubov Yakovleva

Oh, Mammy, Mammy, now I'm married. Will the Weaver. *Unknown.* AmFP

Oh man, be born of God: for at His Godhead's throne. Only His Son Is With God. "Angelus Silesius." GePo, *tr. by* George C. Schoolfield *Fr.* The Cherubical Wanderer.

Oh, Man can seek the downward glance. Nathaniel Hawthorne. PAR

Oh [*or* O] many a day have I made good ale in the glen. The Outlaw of Loch Lene. *Unknown, Modern Irish.* BIrV; CH; GBL; NTP; OBEV, *tr. by* Jeremiah Joseph Callanan

Oh, Mary and the Baby, sweet Lamb. Mary and the Baby, Sweet Lamb. *Unknown.* AmFP

Oh, Mary, this London's a wonderful sight. The Mountains of Mourne. William Percy French. OBCoV

Oh May, bonnie May is to the Yowe buchts gane. The Laird o' Ochiltree Wa's. *Unknown.* OxBB

Oh me good friend, Mr. Wilberforce, make we free! Song of the King of the Eboes. *Unknown.* PBCV

Oh me / is that the ambulance chasing out of town? Alan Brunton. PeNZ

Oh, meet me tonight in the moonlight. New Jail. *Unknown.* AmFP

Oh men are beaten, beaten, beaten down. The Land Laws. Merimeri Penfold, *Maori,* PeNZ, *tr. by* Margaret Orbell

Oh Menelaus. On Hearing the First Cuckoo. Richard Church. OBMV

Oh, might it die or rest at last! (LL) Chorus: "World's great age begins anew, The." Shelley. NoP-4

Oh, Missouri, she's a mighty river. *Unknown. See* Shenandoah.

Oh [*or* O] mistress mine, where are you roaming? Sweet-and-Twenty. Shakespeare. AWP; BoLoP; CTC; ClHu; GBL; GTBS-P; HAP; ImPo; InPS-3; NAEL-1; NBLV; NOBE; NoSic; OAEL-1; OBEV; OxBSP; OxBoLi; PoE; PoRA; SCGP; TFi *Fr.* Twelfth Night.

Oh, Molly, oh, Molly, I've told you before. Red Whiskey. *Unknown.* AmFP

Oh moon, oh moon! *Unknown, Papuan.* BoWoP, *tr. by* Mari Marase

Oh mother, holiest mother, mother night! To Night, the Mother of Sleep and Death. John Addington Symonds. Son

Oh, mother, I shall be married to Mr. Punchinello. To Mr. Punchinello. *Unknown.* CBNP; OxNR

Oh mother my mouth is full of stars. Song of the Dying Gunner A.A.1. Charles Causley. PoWW

Oh mother of a mighty race. William Cullen Bryant. FaBoBe

Oh Mother, so many times. Mother with Child. Lenore Keeshig-Tobias. FFC

Oh! mourn not for Anacreon dead. On Tom Moore's Translation of Anacreon. Thomas Erskine, 1st Baron Erskine. FaBoEE

Oh Muse! I crave a favor. The Muse's Favor. Priscilla Jane Thompson. AAP; CBWP-2

Oh, Musgrove, he persuaded me. Musgrove. *Unknown.* AmFP

Oh, my belovèd, have you thought of this. Sonnet. Edna St. Vincent Millay. HeIP-4; LW

Oh my black[e] soul[e]! now thou art summoned. Donne. EBEV; FMP; OAEL-1; OxAEP-1; Poetr; Son; TOF *Fr.* Holy Sonnets. ESCV *Fr.* Holy Sonnets.

Oh my boy: Jesus. The Confession Stone. Owen Dodson. TTY

Oh my bride, my bride. (LL) I Remember. Stevie Smith. BoLoP; BoWoP; FaBoWP; InPK-6; OxBC

Oh, My Darling Clementine. Percy Montross. APN-2; FaBoBe; OBAL

("And so I lost my Clementine.") (LL) APN-2

(Clementine.) AmFP; OBAL

("In a cabin, in a canon.") APN-2

Oh, my God is in the whirlwind. Song of the Whirlwind. Fenton Johnson. NAAAL

Oh my God, screamed Mommy, you went and ate the baby. The Snack. L. L. Zeigler. BXAP

Oh, my golden slippers am [*or* are] laid away. Oh, Dem Golden Slippers! James A. Bland. APN-2

Oh, my Lord. My Lord, What a Morning. Waring Cuney. TTY

Oh my love, I will carry. Toward the Greater Romance, Please Place Roses in my Skull (A Tantric Love Song). Daniela Gioseffi. DeD

Oh, my mother's moaning by the river. The Lonely Mother. Fenton Johnson. NAAAL

Oh My Own Little Daughter, Four Years Old. *Unknown.* ECWP

Oh My People I Remember. Wendy Rose. CDW

Oh, my pretty cock, oh, my handsome cock. Cock-A-Doodle-Do. *Unknown.* ReMoGo

Oh Nature! World! Oh Life! Oh Time! Thus Passeth. *Unknown.* PFE

Oh, neighbours! what had I a-do for to marry! Hooly and Fairly. Joanna Baillie. RACG; WoRP

Oh never marry Ishmael! Song for Unbound Hair. Genevieve Taggard. PoRA

Oh never on my youthful ear. My Mother's Voice. Mary E. Tucker. CBWP-1

Oh, never say that you have reached the very end. We Survive! Hirsch Glick, *Yiddish.* TrJP, *tr. by* Ruth Rubin

Oh never weep for love that's dead. Dead Love. Elizabeth Siddal. LW; NOBVV

Oh nimber, nimber Will-o! Chuck Will's Widow Song. *Unknown.* BPo

Oh No. Robert Creeley. HeIP-4; InPK-6

Oh no! He's going to *show* it to me—. The Only Dance There Is. Rebecca Byrkit. BAP-94

Oh, no, Mistress Pussy, you'd bite off our heads! Mother Goose. *See* Six little mice sat down to spin;.

Oh [*or* O], no more, no more, too late. Love's Martyrs. John Ford. GBL; NOBE; NOSC; OxBSP; PoEL-2 *Fr.* The Broken Heart.

Oh, no one can deny. Self's the Man. Philip Larkin. NOBL; PeLV

Oh! no, Poll, no! Since they've a-took. The Common a-Took In. William Barnes. EnVR

Oh, Noa, Noa! William Cole. NBLV

Oh, not more subtly silence strays. To the Beloved. Alice Thompson Meynell. VWP

Oh, not to be in England. Abroad Thoughts. Edward Blishen. NOBL

Oh, Nothing. John Ashbery. NAAL-2

Oh, now I feel as though another sense. On the Group of the Three Angels Before the Tent of Abraham, by Raffaelle, in the Vatican. Washington Allston. APN-1; GS

Oh, now I've come back to you, Mother. The Cripple for Life; or, The Poor Volunteer. *Unknown.* AmFP

Oh oh—ah ah. *Ti-ch'ü* Song Words. *Unknown, Chinese.* CoBCP, *tr. by* Burton Watson

Oh, Oh, you will be sorry for that word! Edna St. Vincent Millay. BoWoP; HeIP-4; NALW; SAGP

Oh, on an early morning I think I shall live forever! Poem in Three Parts. Robert Bly. CoAmPo; NOBA

Oh, once I lived in Cottonwood and owned a little farm. Once I Lived in Cottonwood. *Unknown.* AmFP

Oh, once I was a policeman young and merry (young and merry). A Policeman's Lot. Wendy Cope. FaBoWP

Oh, open the door, some pity to shew. Open the Door to Me, Oh! Robert Burns. FaBoCh; PoEL-4; SCGP

Oh, Paddy dear! and did ye hear the news that's goin' round? The Wearin' o' the Green. *Unknown.* NOIV

Oh, Passage town is of great renown. The Town of Passage. *Unknown.* OxBoLi

Oh pile of white shirts who is coming. The Night of the Shirts. W. S. Merwin. VCAP

Oh, Pillykin Willykin Winky Wee! Punkydoodle and Jollapin. Laura Elizabeth Richards. OBCA

Oh pleasant eventide! Twilight Calm. Christina Rossetti. OBNC

Oh poesy is on the wane. Decay. John Clare. EnVR

Oh, Poet of our Race. Poet of Our Race. Maggie P. Johnson. CBWP-4

Oh! poverty is a weary thing, 'tis full of grief and pain. The Sale of the Pet Lamb. Mary Howitt. CH

Oh praise Him, praise Him, praise without an end or aim. Zealous Admonition to Praise. Catharina Regina von Greiffenberg, *German.* GePo, *tr. by* George C. Schoolfield

Oh, Priest Pangeivi, you let go. Funeral Eva. Koroneu. RaBo

Oh princess of your land, whom Holstein cousin names. To the Great City of Moscow, as He Was Leaving June 25, 1636. Paul Fleming, *German.* GePo, *tr. by* George C. Schoolfield

Oh, pure and sportive little child. To a Little Colored Boy. Priscilla Jane Thompson. CBWP-2

Oh, quietly mad I'd like to be. Ballad. Vladislav Felitsianovich Khodasevich, *Russian.* TCRP, *tr. by* Michael Frayn

Oh, rare Harry Parry. *Unknown. See* Harry Parry.

Oh River, gentle River! gliding on. The Night Journey of a River. William Cullen Bryant. APN-1

Oh, rock-a-by, baby mouse, rock-a-by, so! The Mouse's Lullaby. Palmer Cox. NOxBChV; OBCA; TLR

Oh roses for the flush of youth. Song. Christina Rossetti. GTBS-P; NOBVV

Oh sacred Time! how soon thou'rt gone! Midnight Thought, A [on the Death of Mrs. *E. H.* and Her Little Daughter]. Elizabeth Thomas. KTR; NOSC

Oh, Sally Brown, of New York City. Sally Brown. *Unknown.* AmFP

Oh [*or* O] say, [*or* O! say] can you see, by the dawn's early light. The Star-Spangled Banner. Francis Scott Key. APN-1; AiP; BLPA; EBEvV; FaBoBe; TAP; UV

Oh say not that my heart is cold. Song. Charles Wolfe. OxAEP-2

Oh, say you can hear / On the Watergate tapes. Final Curtain. Roger Woddis. UV

Oh, says the linnet, if I sing. Birds' Lament. John Clare. PoEL-4

Oh! scorn me not as a fameless thing. Song of the Rushlight. Eliza Cook. VWP

Oh see how thick the goldcup flowers. A. E. Housman. MoBrPo

Oh, see my little boat. The Boat. Caroline Gilman. OBCA

Oh send to me an apple that hasn't any kernel. *Unknown, Welsh.* FaBoCh, *tr. by* Gwyn Williams

Oh! she is very old. I lay. Africa. Joaquin Miller. APN-2

Oh, she said. For Elaine de Kooning. Hilda Morley. PmAP

Oh, shield me from his rage, celestial Powers! Jealousy. Esther Johnson. OxBSP

Oh ship! new billows sweep thee out. 1.14: Ship of State, The ("O navis, referent"). Horace. AWP, *tr. by* William Ewart Gladstone *Fr.* Odes.

Oh, show us the way to the next whisky-bar. Alabama Song. Bertolt Brecht. PFTM

Oh, sick I am to see you, will you never let me be? The New Mistress. A. E. Housman. MoBrPo

Oh, silver tree! Jazzonia. Langston Hughes. ColAP

Oh, Sing to God. Jacob Steendam, *Dutch.* AH

Oh! sing unto my roundelay [*or* O! Synge untoe mie roundelaie]. Mynstrelle's Songe ("O! synge untoe mie roundelaie"). Thomas Chatterton. CH; EnLoPo; HAP; ImPo; NOBE; NOEC; OBEV; OxAEP-1; SCGP *Fr.* Aella: a Tragycal Enterlude.

Oh, sister Phoebe, how merry were we. Tom Jones's Plum Tree. *Unknown.* AmFP

Oh, sleep forever in the Latmian cave. Edna St. Vincent Millay. CMoP; GSo; LiTM; MoAmPo; NALW; NoAM; Poetr

Oh! sleep in peace where poppies grow. Reply to "In Flanders Fields." John Mitchell. BLPA

Oh [*or* O], slow to smite and swift to spare. The Death of Lincoln. William Cullen Bryant. CBCWP; NAAL-1; NAAL-3; TAP

Oh, slow up, dogies, quit your roving round. Night-herding Song[, A]. Harry Stephens. NTP

Oh smooth adder/ who with fanged kisses changedst my natural blood. Augusta Davies Webster. BrRo *Fr.* Medea in Athens.

Oh so fickle, oh so vain, oh so false, so false is she! (LL) A Song to a Lute. Sir John Suckling. BeJo; CaPo; EnLoPo

Oh some are fond of red wine, and some are fond of white. Captain Stratton's Fancy. John Masefield. MoBrPo; OBEV

Oh some have killed in angry love. A Rope for Harry Fat. James Keir Baxter. MoBS

Oh, some like trips in luxury ships. Riding on a Railroad Train. Ogden Nash. PiM

Oh! Sovereign of the willing soul. Pindar. OBCVT, *tr. by* Thomas Gray *Fr.* The Progress of Poesy.

Oh spirit land, thou land of dreams! The Land of Dreams. Felicia Dorothea Hemans. Ro *Fr.* Songs of the Affections, with Other Poems.

Oh! Stalin is my darling, my darling, my darling. Stalin Moy Golubchik. "Sagittarius." OBCoV

Oh strong-ridged and deeply hollowed. Smell. William Carlos Williams. MoAmPo; RaBo; SAmP

Oh Sumptuous moment. Emily Dickinson. NAAL-1; NAAL-3

Oh! surely for thee were the gates ajar. Rev. Samuel Weston. Mary Weston Fordham. CBWP-2

Oh! surely 'tis a theme sublime. Dedicated to the Right Rev'd D. A. Payne. Mary Weston Fordham. CBWP-2

Oh! Susanna. Stephen Collins Foster. OBAL
(Susanna.) APN-2

Oh, Sweet Content. W. H. Davies. CH

Oh sweet is the sound o' the dove's clapping wings. John Clare. EnVR

Oh swings: beyond complete immortal now. (LL) Soledad. Robert Earl Hayden. MoNo; NAAAL

Oh [*or* O], talk not to me of a name great in story. Stanzas Written on the Road between Florence and Pisa. Byron. GTBS-P; NAEL-2

Oh, Teddy wants a nine-dollar shawl. I Wish I Was a Mole in the Ground. *Unknown.* AmFP

Oh! tell me not of fatherland. This Is a Fatherland to Me. Joseph Cephas Holly. AAP

Oh, tell me why you make the school. Retrospection. Dunstan Shaw. NOBAu

Oh thank you cowboy with four-wheel drive. For Drum Hadley. Harold Littlebird. VoR

Oh thank you for giving me the chance. Thank You. Kenneth Koch. NeAP; PoM

Oh that horse I see so high. A Gift of Great Value. Robert Creeley. LCAP-2

Oh! that I always breath'd in such an aire. The Experience. Edward Taylor. AmPP *Fr.* Preparatory Meditations Before My Approach to the Lord's Supper.

Oh that I knew how all thy lights combine. The H. Scriptures. George Herbert. ChIV-2; CH

Oh that I was the Bird of Paradise! Edward Taylor. NOCV *Fr.* Preparatory Meditations Before My Approach to the Lord's Supper.

Oh! That I were a poet now in grain! An Elegie upon The Death of the Reverend. . . Mr. Thomas Shepard. Urian Oakes. SCAP

Oh that I were all soul, that I might prove. Upon Platonic Love: To Mistress Cicely Crofts, Maid of Honour. Sir Robert Ayton. NOSC

Oh That I Were in the Wilderness. Bible, *O.T.* TrJP *Fr.* Jeremiah.

Oh that I were / Where I would be. *Unknown.* OxNR

Oh that my lungs could bleat like butter'd pease. Non-sense. *Unknown.* CBNP; NOBL

Oh That my young life were a lasting dream! Dreams. Edgar Allan Poe. NCAP

Oh! that my young life were a lasting dream! Edgar Allan Poe. AmPP; MeMAP; OxBA; Poetr; TAP, *ll.* 1–12 *Fr.* Dreams. NCAP

Oh! that mine head [*or* desart] were my dwelling-place. The Ocean. Byron. OBNC; PoEL-4 *Fr.* Childe Harold's Pilgrimage.

Oh, that they had pity, the men we serve so truly! The Cry of the Animals. Mary Howitt. VWP

Oh that those lips had language! Life has pass'd. William Cowper. *Fr.* On the Receipt of My Mother's Picture out of Norfolk [the Gift of My Cousin Ann Bodham]. NOEC; OxAEP-1
Lines on Receiving His Mother's Picture. CH

Oh the anguish of these secret meetings. Kenneth Rexroth. APSN *Fr.* The Love Poems of Marichiko.

Oh, the bosses' tricks of '76. Two-Cent Coal. *Unknown.* AmFP

Oh, the brave old Duke of York. The Brave Old Duke of York. *Unknown.* OxNR

Oh the charming month of May! Song. Joseph Addison. NOEC

Oh, the comfort—the inexpressible comfort of feeling safe with a person. Friendship. Dinah Maria Mulock Craik. BLPA; PoToHe

Oh the corrugated-iron town. Douglas Stewart. CBAP *Fr.* The Birdsville Track.

Oh the dance of our Sister! The Dance of the Rain. Eugène Marais, *Afrikaans.* PeSA, *tr. by* Jack Cope *and* Uys Krige

Oh, the days when I was young. Richard Brinsley Sheridan. OxAEP-1 *Fr.* The Duenna.

Oh, the Devil in hell they say he was chained. Hell in Texas. *Unknown.* BLPA

Oh! the eastern winds are blowing. The Cornish Emigrant's Song. Robert Stephen Hawker. EBVV

Oh the falling snow! For Snow. Eleanor Farjeon. CH

Oh, the Funniest Thing. *Unknown.* CTV

Oh, the girl that I loved she was handsome. The Man on the Flying Trapeze. *Unknown.* BLPA; OxBoLi

Oh! the Golden Age. The Golden Age. William Browne. NOSC *Fr.* Britannia's Pastorals.

Oh, the gorgeous leaves of autumn! Autumn Leaves. Clara Ann Thompson. CBWP-2

Oh, the hireling sun in a slipshod way. The Field of the Cloth of Gold. Patrick Joseph Hartigan. NOBAu

Oh the Inconstant. N. P. van Wyk Louw, *Afrikaans.* PeSA, *tr. by* Uys Krige *and* Jack Cope

Oh! the king's gane gyte. Cophetua. "Hugh MacDiarmid." OxBS

Oh the maggots marched down Pitt Street. Maggot Song. *Unknown.* NOBAu

Oh the magnificence of hell! Hell. Edith Södergran, *Finnish.* NNPT; PFTM, *tr. by* Stina Katchadourian

Oh the many joys of a harlot's wedding. Hail Wedded Love! Jay Macpherson. MoCV

Oh the north countree is a hard countree. The Ballad of Yukon Jake. Edward E. Paramore Jr. BLPA

Oh, the old gray mare, she ain't what she used to be. Old Gray Mare. *Unknown.* AS

Oh! the old swimmin'-hole! whare the crick so still and deep. The Old Swimmin'-Hole. James Whitcomb Riley. APN-2

Oh, the Pilliwinks lived by the portals of Loo. The Cooky-Nut Trees. Albert Bigelow Paine. OBCA

Oh the rocks and the thimble. Meditations of a Parrot. John Ashbery. TTTS

Oh the rose of keenest thorn! The Iniquity of the Fathers upon the Children. Christina Rossetti. FaBoVe

Oh, the slimy, squirmy, slithery eel! Song of Hate for Eels. Arthur Guiterman. OBAL

Oh! the snow, the beautiful snow. The Beautiful Snow. John Whittaker Watson. BLPA

Oh the streams of lovely Nancy are divided into three parts. The Streams of Lovely Nancy. Unknown. OxBoLi

Oh, the sweet contentment. Coridon's Song. John Chalkhill. NOSC

Oh! the time that is past. Unknown. BoLoP

Oh, the times are hard and the wages low. Across the Western Ocean or Leave Her, Bullies, Leave Her. Unknown. AS

Oh, the train's off the track. The Train Is Off the Track. Unknown. AmFP

Oh, the white sea-gull, the wild sea-gull. The Sea-Gull. Mary Howitt. BoTP; OxBChV

Oh, the wild joys of living! the leaping from rock up to rock. Youth. Robert Browning. BoTP Fr. Saul.

Oh! the world gives little of love or light. Song of the Ugly Maiden. Eliza Cook. VWP

Oh there hasn't been much change. The Grange. Stevie Smith. OBCoV

Oh, there once was a Puffin. There Once Was a Puffin. Florence Page Jaques. CTV; NTCP

Oh! there was a moanish lady. Moanish Lady. Unknown. AS

Oh, there was a youth and a noble youth. The Bailiff's Daughter of Islington. Unknown. AmFP; ESPB; OxBB; OxBoLi

Oh! they found a bit of iron what. They Called Them RAF 2C's. Unknown. NSI

Oh! they're sluts indeed. (LL) They that wash on Monday. Mother Goose. LB

Oh this is the animal that never was. Rilke. TTTS, tr. by Stephen Mitchell Fr. The Unicorn.

Oh, this little light of mine. This Little Light of Mine. Unknown. NAAAL

Oh this man. Magnificat. Michele Roberts. APAD; BrRo; NBrP

Oh those big floppy ears which hated flies. For Polla. Uku Masing, Estonian. CEEP, tr. by Ivar Ivask

Oh! thou dead / And everlasting witness! whose unsinking. Byron. ChIV-1 Fr. Cain: A Mystery.

Oh [or O] thou great Power, in whom I move. A Hymn to My God in a Night of My Late Sickness[e]. Sir Henry Wotton. MeLP; NOSC

Oh, thou immortal bard! Byron. J. Gordon Coogler. OBAL

Oh, thou! in Hellas deemed of heavenly birth. Byron. NAEL-2 Fr. Childe Harold's Pilgrimage.

Oh thou, that dear and happy isle. Andrew Marvell. OxBoLi Fr. Upon Appleton House [To My Lord Fairfax]. FaBoPV; GeHe; SeCP

Oh, thou! whose tender smile most partially. Sonnet Addressed to My Mother. Mary Tighe. NoP-4

Oh, 'tis my delight on a shining night, in the season of the year. (LL) The Lincolnshire Poacher. Unknown. CH; OxBoLi; PeLV

Oh, 'tisn't manly, of course, 'tisn't manly, this method of / wooing;. Arthur Hugh Clough. EBVVPR, canto 2, 14 Fr. Amours de Voyage. NOBVV

Oh to be a bride. The Bride. Bella Akhatovna Akhmadulina, Russian. BoWoP, tr. by Stephan Stepanchev; LiLi, tr. by Stephen Stepanchev

Oh to be at Crowdieknowe. Crowdieknowe. "Hugh MacDiarmid." InPS-3; OxBS

Oh, to be in England. Home-Thoughts, From Abroad. Robert Browning. AWP; BoTP; CABP; ClHu; EBEvV; EBVV; FHYEP; FaBoBe; FaPoR; HeIP-4; ImPo; NAEL-2; NOBE; NOBVV; NoP-4; OBEV; OBNC; PBMP; PoLF; PoRA; TFi; UV

Oh, to be in England. Home Truths from Abroad. Unknown. UV

Oh to be in England now that Winston's out, subsel. Ezra Pound. See Canto 80.

Oh to Be Odd! Ogden Nash. CBNP

Oh to be seventeen years old. Kenneth Koch. Fr. Fresh Air. CAPP-1; NNaP; NeAP

Oh! to have hidden in the undergrowth. King Lot's Envoys. Drummond Allison. OxBSP

Oh, to those who know no better. That Little Lump of Coal. Unknown. AmFP

Oh, to vex me, two contraries meet in one. Donne. ESCV; NOSC; OAEL-1; PoEL-2; Son Fr. Holy Sonnets.

Oh trial! Unknown. FaBoVe

Oh! true was his heart while he breathed. The King of Thulé. Goethe, German. AWP, tr. by James Clarence Mangan

Oh virgin queen of mountain-side and woodland. 3.22: Pine Tree for Diana, The ("Montium custos nemorumque"). Horace. AWP, tr. by Louis Untermeyer Fr. Odes.

Oh! water for me! Bright water for me! The Water-Drinker. Edward Jonson. BXAP

Oh! waves in the sunlight gleaming. Sonnet to My First Born. Mary Weston Fordham. CBWP-2

Oh, way down South where I was born. Roll the Cotton Down. Unknown. AmFP

Oh, we come on the sloop John B. The John B. Sails. Unknown. AS

Oh, weep for Columbia! oh, weep for the time! The Patriot's Lament. Joseph Cephas Holly. AAP

Oh, weep for Mr. and Mrs. Bryan! The Lion. Ogden Nash. TLR; WHSW

Oh! weep for those that wept by Babel's stream. Byron. ChIV-1

Oh! weep not me the changing scene. A Letter to My Love—All Alone, Past 12, in the Dumps. "The Amorous Lady." ECWP

Oh, we'll rally 'round the flag, boys, we'll rally once again. The Battle Cry [or Battle-Cry] of Freedom. George Frederick Root. FaBoBe

Oh well tonight or some other night. Te Kaha. Rachel McAlpine. PeNZ

Oh were I at the moss house, where the birds do increase. The Streams of Bunclody. Unknown. BIrV

Oh! what a cruel wicked thing. Poem for Children, A; or, On Cruelty to the Irrational Creation. Jane Cave. ECWP

Oh, what a dawn of day! A Lovers' Quarrel. Robert Browning. EBVVPR

Oh, what a dreary place this was when first the Mormons found it. St. George. Charlie Walker. AmFP

Oh what a gay, what a rambling life a Settler's leading. Polyglot Medley. Andrew Geddes Bain. PeSAV

Oh, what a kiss. The Modern Mother. Alice Thompson Meynell. VWP

Oh what a pity, Oh! don't you agree. Innocent England. D. H. Lawrence. OBCoV

Oh [or O!] what a plague is Love! Phillida Flouts Me [or The Disdainful Shepherdess]. Unknown. OBEV

Oh, what a tangled web we weave. Sir Walter Scott. CTV Fr. Marmion.

Oh! what a thing is man? Lord, who am I? Meditation 38. Edward Taylor. MeMAP; NAAL-1; NAAL-3; NOBA; OxBA Fr. Preparatory Meditations Before My Approach to the Lord's Supper.

Oh, what a waste of feeling and of thought. Gifts Misused. Letitia Elizabeth Landon. VWP

Oh, what am I but an engine, shod. Nothing New. Ella Wheeler Wilcox. APN-2

Oh, what have you got for dinner, Mrs. Bond? Dilly Dilly. Unknown. OxNR

Oh, what is so merry, so merry, heigh-ho! The Light-hearted Fairy. Unknown. BoTP

Oh! what is that comes gliding in. Sally Simpkin's Lament, [or John Jones's Kit-Cat-astrophe]. Thomas Hood. CABP; CBNP

Oh! What is the matter? Unknown, Greek. PGA, tr. by Kenneth Rexroth

"Oh! what shall I do?" sobbed a tiny mole. Who'll Help a Fairy? Unknown. BoTP

Oh, what was your name in the States? What Was Your Name in the States? Unknown. AS

"Oh, what's that stain on your shirt sleeve?" Edward. Unknown. AmFP

Oh, what's the matter wi' [or with] you, my lass. Jimmy's Enlisted; or, The Recruited Collier. Unknown. EBEV

Oh, when I come to die. Give Me Jesus. Unknown. BPo

Oh when I think of my long-suffering race. Enslaved. Claude McKay. BPo; NAAAL

Oh, when I was in love with you. A. E. Housman. BoLoP; CBLP; GLoP; LoP; MoBrPo; SAGP; TTTS

Oh, when I was single, oh then, oh then! I Wish I Were [or Was] Single Again. Unknown. AS; AmFP

Oh, when I'm in trouble. Do, Lord, Remember Me. Unknown. AmFP

Oh, When Shall I See Jesus? Ecstasy. Unknown. AH

Oh when the early morning at the seaside. East Anglian Bathe. John Betjeman. NoP-4

Oh, when this earthly tenement. "Ada." BISi

Oh, when we going to marry, to marry, to marry. Buffalo Boy. Unknown. AmFP

Oh, Whence Comes the Gladness? Priscilla Jane Thompson. CBWP-2

Oh whence do you come, my dear friend, to me. The Poor Ghost. Christina Rossetti. GBL

Oh, where are you going, my kind old husband. The Best Old Fellow in the World. Unknown. AmFP

Oh, where are you going, my little maiden fair. The Milkmaid. Unknown. AmFP

Oh, where are you going to, my pretty little dear. Dabbling in the Dew. Unknown. CH

Oh where are you going with your love-locks flowing. Amor Mundi. Christina Rossetti. NoP-4; PEW; RACG

Oh, where do you come from. Little Raindrops. Jane Euphemia Browne. BoTP; OxBChV

Oh, where have you been, Billy boy, Billy boy? Billy Boy. *Unknown.* AmFP; BLPA; HoPM

Oh where is the word. The Word. Stevie Smith. WPN

Oh where, oh where has my little dog gone? Where Is He? Mother Goose. OxNR

Oh! wherefore come ye forth, in triumph from the North. The Battle of Naseby. Thomas Babington Macaulay. OxAEP-2

Oh, where's the maid that I can love. One to Love. Alfred Islay Walden. AAP

Oh! where's the slave so lowly. Thomas Moore. NOIV

Oh, whiffaree an' a-whiffo-rye. Honey, Take a Whiff on Me. *Unknown.* OxBoLi

Oh, whisky here, and whisky there. Whisky, Johnny. *Unknown.* AmFP

Oh, who can make a flower? Grace W. Owens. CTV

Oh, who crumbles up the heavens! Song of the Snow. Zalman Schneour, *Hebrew.* MHP, tr. by Ruth Finer Mintz.

Oh, who has not heard of the Wooyeo Ball. The Wooyeo Ball. *Unknown.* NOBAu

Oh who is that young sinner with the handcuffs on his wrists? A. E. Housman. FaBoTw; NOBVV; SoSe-8

Oh! who is there of us that has not felt. November. Frederick Goddard Tuckerman. NOBA

Oh who that ever lived and loved. The Egg. Clarence Day. NBLV

Oh, who will shoe your feet, my love. The Mournful Dove. *Unknown.* AmFP

Oh, who would live, if this be death? (LL) The Geranium. Richard Brinsley Sheridan. BoLoP; EP

Oh, why did God, / Creator wise, that peopled highest Heaven. Adam Speaks. Milton. *Fr.* Book X. FHYEP *Fr.* Paradise Lost.

Oh why did I awake? when shall I sleep again? (LL) Be still, my soul, be still; the arms you bear are brittle. A. E. Housman. MoBrPo; NOBVV; OAEL-2; OBNC; SCGP

Oh, why does the white man follow my path. The Indian Hunter. Eliza Cook. BLPA

Oh, why don't you [*or* I] work like other men do? Hallelujah, I'm a Bum. *Unknown.* AS

Oh why must it matter? (LL) The Colors of Desire. David Mura. LoL; NAmP90

Oh! why should the spirit of mortal be proud? William Knox. BLPA

Oh wide and sad land, alone. N. P. van Wyk Louw, *Afrikaans.* PeSAV, tr. by Adam Small.

Oh! Wilberforce, our star of hope. Golden Jubilee of Wilberforce. Mrs. Henry Linden. CBWP-4

Oh wild west wind, thou breath of autumn's being. Shelley. *See* Ode to the West Wind.

Oh, will you wear red? I'll Wear Me a Cotton Dress. *Unknown.* BPo

"Oh, willow, titwillow, titwillow!" (LL) Ko-Ko's Song. Sir William Schwenck Gilbert. ImPo; NoP-4

Oh witness! to be sure. To My Mother. Frank O'Hara. FiLi

Oh woe is me! Oh misery! (LL) The Thorn. Wordsworth. FaBoSe; Ro

Oh Woman, Blessed Woman! Mrs. Henry Linden. CBWP-4

Oh, women dear, and did ye hear the news that's going round. The Purple, White and Green. L. E. Morgan-Browne. BrRo

Oh wonder! He is making a turmoil on the earth. Song of Nū' LmaL, La' Lasiqoala. *Unknown. Fr.* Dances and Songs of the Winter Ceremonial. APN-2, tr. by Franz Boas.

Oh! wondrous force of sympathy. The Triumvirate. Elizabeth Thomas. ECWP

"Oh [*or* O], World-God, give me Wealth!" the Egyptian cried. Gifts. Emma Lazarus. TrJP

Oh would I could subdue the flesh. Senex. John Betjeman. RB

Oh! would I had my Hours of Life began. The Iron Age. Hesiod, *Greek.* OBCVT, tr. by Thomas Cooke.

Oh, would that I knew, the day my loss is lamented. Al-Samau'al ibn Adiya, *Arabic.* TrJP

Oh would you know why Henry sleeps. Inhuman Henry. A. E. Housman. NBLV

Oh wretched World, but wretched above all. Fidelia Arguing with Her Self on the Difficulty of Finding the True Religion. Jane Barker. KTR

Oh, Ye Censurers. Al-Samau'al ibn Adiya, *Arabic.* TrJP, tr. by Hartwig Hirschfeld

Oh, ye lost ones, ye departed, who have passed that silent shore. Beyond. *Unknown.* PWR

Oh Yes. William Matthews. AmPA

Oh yes, we are so thankful. The Black Army. S. E. K. Mqhayi, *Xhosa.* PeSA, tr. by C. M. Mcanyangwa *and* Jack Cope

Oh yes / We got Mr. President Roosevelt. President Roosevelt. Big Joe Williams. FaBoPV

Oh, you come along, boys, you listen to my tale. The Old Chisholm Trail. *Unknown.* AmFP

"Oh you kid!" / Shouted Id. The Adventures of Id. Morris Gilbert Bishop. OBCoV

Oh, you must answer my questions nine. The Devil's Nine Questions. *Unknown.* AmFP

Oh, you powerful Gods, if I must be. Song. Frances Boothby. KTR *Fr.* The Marcelia; or, Treacherous Friend.

Oh young girls in a classroom. Propaganda Poem: Maybe for Some Young Mamas. Alicia Ostriker. NMM-2

Oh [*or* O], young Lochinvar is come out of the west. Lochinvar. Sir Walter Scott. BoTP; EBEvV; EBNV; FaBoBe; NOBE; NTP; OBNV; OxAEP-2; OxBS; PoRA; TFi *Fr.* Marmion.

Ohakune Fires. Lauris Edmond, *Maori.* PeNZ, tr. by Margaret Orbell

Ohé, long-haired beauty! Distress. Flavien Ranaivo, *French.* NegPo, tr. by Ellen Conroy Kennedy

Ohhh break love with white things. Sacred Chant for the Return of Black Spirit and Power. Imamu Amiri Baraka. NBV

Ohio Is the Iroquois Word for Beautiful. Helen Ruggieri. LoHo

Ohio Valley Swains. James Wright. NNaP

Ohioan Pastoral. James Wright. LCAP-2

Ohnedaruth. Angela Jackson. SeSe

O'Hussey's Ode to the Maguire. Eochadh O'Hussey, *Irish.* CABP; NOIV, tr. by James Clarence Mangan

(Ode to the Maguire.) BIrV

Oil. Hansjörg Mayer. WeW-3

Oil and Blood. W. B. Yeats. OxBSn

Oil brown smog over Denver. Who Runs America? Allen Ginsberg. FaBoA

Oil Slick. Judith Thurman. SSCS

Oil-slick, slack shocks, ancient engine. Apples on Champlain. Richard Kenney. NoP-4

Oileus by his brother's side stood close and would not thence. The Two Ajaxes Compared to Oxen. Homer. ORVE, tr. by George Chapman *Fr.* The Iliad.

Oiseaurie. Margaret Widdemer. BXAP

Oisin, tell me the famous story. W. B. Yeats. *See* The Wanderings of Oisin.

Ojibwa War Songs. *Unknown, Ojibwa Indian.* AWP, tr. by H. H. Schoolcraft

Ojichan was a fisherman/farmer. The Fisherman. Janice Mirikitani. OpBo

Ojistoh. Emily Pauline Johnson. NOBC

OK Corral East Brothers in the Nam. Horace Coleman. CDa

OK, it's imperishable or a world as Will. The Same Old Jazz. Philip Whalen. NeAP

OK Neal / aethereal Spirit. Elegy for Neal Cassady. Allen Ginsberg. CLPP

OK. So she got back the baby. Onesided Dialog. June Jordan. NoAM

Okay "Negroes." June Jordan. BPo

Okay, Prince, we understand the instructions. First Actor to Hamlet. Ivan V. Lalic, *Serbo-Croatian.* HSix, tr. by Charles Simic

Oklahoma Ligno and Lithograph Co, The. Corporate Entity. Archibald MacLeish. OBAL

Okra to greens. Ntozake Shange. MoNo

Different Love Poem / We Need a Change, A. UnSA

Ol' Bunk's Band. William Carlos Williams. NOBA

Ol' Clothes. *Unknown.* PoToHe

Ol' Doc' Hyar. James Edwin Campbell. AAP

Ol' Hannah. Doc Reese. PFTM

Ol' plantation wither. For Consciousness. Mervyn Morris. PBCV

Old, The. Franz Wright. LCAP-2

Old Abram Brown is dead and gone. Abram Brown. *Unknown.* OxNR

Old Adam, The. Denise Levertov. UnPo

Old Adam. *Unknown.* AS

Old Adam, the carrion crow. The Carrion Crow. Thomas Lovell Beddoes. APo; EBEV; NAEL-2; OAEL-2; PoEL-4; TFi *Fr.* Death's Jest Book.

Old Age. Al-Aswad, son of Ya'fur. *Fr.* The Mufaddaliyat. AWP, tr. by Sir Charles Lyall

Old Age. Caroline Clive. VWP

Old Age. Jerzy Harasymowicz, *Polish.* CEEP, tr. by Victor Contoski

Old Age. Bernard Kangro, *Estonian.* CEEP, tr. by Ivar Ivask

Old Age. E. Keary. NOBVV

Old Age. Nguyễn Khuyến, *Vietnamese.* AVP, tr. by Huỳnh Sanh Thông

Old Age. Ou-yang Hsiu, *Chinese.* OHPC, tr. by Kenneth Rexroth

Old Age. Po Chü-i, *Chinese.* ChiP, tr. by Arthur Waley

Old Age. Sir Philip Sidney. SiPS *Fr.* Arcadia.

Old Age. Frederick Tennyson. NOBVV

Old Age. Edmund Waller. NOBE; OBEV *Fr.* Of The Last Verses in the Book. BeJo; EBEV; HAP; NOSC; NoP-4; PeECV; PoPoPo; SCGP; SeCP

Old Age Compensation. James Wright. NNaP

Old Age Gets Up. Ted Hughes. NoAM

Old age has little joy. Fresh Flowers. Wang An-shih, *Chinese*. CoBCP, *tr. by* Burton Watson

Old Age in His Ailing. Herman Melville. TAP

Old age in the towns. War. Miguel Hernández, *Spanish*. RaBo, *tr. by* Hardie St. Martin; AF, *tr. by* St. Martin, Hardie

Old age is. To Waken an Old Lady. William Carlos Williams. HAP; InPK-6; LiLi; SoSe-8; WeW-3

Old age is at our heels, and youth returns no more. Horace. *See* I.9.

"Old age never comes alone"—it brings sighs. John Morris-Jones, *Welsh*. OBWVE, *tr. by* Anthony Conran

Old Age of Michelangelo, The. Frank Templeton Prince. PeSA

Old Age, on tiptoe, lays her jewelled hand. A Minuet on Reaching the Age of Fifty. George Santayana. ImPo

Old age sticks / up Keep. E. E. Cummings. InPS-3

Old album, The. Elizabeth Searle Lamb. HA

Old always gives way and is replaced by the new, and, The. The Threshold Of The New. Lucretius. LBC

Old am I in years and wisdom and. Old I Am. Herman Charles Bosman. PeSA

Old Amusement Park. Marianne Moore. NYBP

Old and abandoned by each venal friend. On Lord Holland's Seat near Margate, Kent. Thomas Gray. NOEC; OAEL-1; OBGa

Old and alone, sit we. The Old Men. Walter De la Mare. MoBrPo

Old and gnarled; wizened faces dreaming of. Grandparents. Sheila Bramfit. OxBM

Old and New ("She went up the mountain to pluck wild herbs"). *Unknown, Chinese*. AWP; ChiP, *tr. by* Arthur Waley

Old and New Year Ditties. Christina Rossetti.
    Passing Away, Saith the World, Passing Away. NoP-4

Old and sick, many strange broodings. Meng Chiao. SuSp, *tr. by* Stephen Owen *Fr.* Autumn Meditations.

Old and sick, you turn away from mirrors, whether. Late Reflections. Babette Deutsch. NYBP

Old and the New, The. Clara Ann Thompson. CBWP-2

Old and young, everyone's asleep. The Cold Lantern. Yang Wan-li, *Chinese*. SuSp, *tr. by* Jonathan Chaves

Old Anguish, The. Chu Shu-chen, *Chinese*. BoWoP; OHPC, *tr. by* Kenneth Rexroth

Old Apple Trees. W. D. Snodgrass. FYAP

Old archaeologist, Throstle, An. Limerick. *Unknown*. PeLi

Old Arm-Chair, The. Eliza Cook. BrRo; InPK-6; Poetr; VWP

Old as I am, for ladies' love unfit. Cymon and Iphigenia. Dryden. EPCY; OBNV

Old astronomer there was, An. A Marvel. Carolyn Wells. OBCA

Old Astronomer to His Pupil, The. Sarah Williams. BLPA

Old Australian Ways. Andrew Barton Paterson. NOBAu

Old Bachelor Brother. Brad Leithauser. NoP-4; RA

Old Banyan Tree, The. Nguyễn Trãi, *Vietnamese*. AVP, *tr. by* Huỳnh Sanh Thông

Old Barbarossa. Sleeping Heroes. Edward Richard Burton Shanks. OBMV

Old battle field, fresh with Spring flowers again. All That Is Left. Basho, *Japanese*. AWP, *tr. by* Curtis Hidden Page

Old Beauty, The. Phyllis McGinley. FaBoEE

Old Black ladies. Weeksville Women. Elouise Loftin. ISC; PoBA

Old Black Men. Georgia Douglas Johnson. NMM-2; PoBA

Old Black Men Say. James A. Emanuel. MBE; PoBA

Old blanket, The. The crumbs of rubbed wool turning up, The. Adrienne Rich. HCAP *Fr.* Shooting Script.

Old Boards. Robert Bly. CAPP-1

Old Boast, The. W. S. Merwin. NOBA

Old Boatman of Death's River, The. R. Williams Parry, *Welsh*. OBWVE, *tr. by* Joseph P. Clancy

Old Bob-white and Chipbird, The. A Few of the Bird-Family. James Whitcomb Riley. NOxBChV

Old Boniface he loved good cheer. *Unknown*. OxNR

Old Books, The. Vernon Scannell. OxBC

Old boy's seventy-three this year, The. A Eulogy on My Own Portrait. Yang Shih-ch'i, *Chinese*. CoBLCP, *tr. by* Jonathan Chaves

Old boys, the cracked boards spread before. Bread. James Dickey. LCAP-2

Old Brass Wagon. *Unknown*. AS

Old brown hen and the old blue sky, The. Continual Conversation with a Silent Man. Wallace Stevens. LiTM

Old Brown Horse, The. W. F. Holmes. BoTP

Old brown thorn-trees break in two high over Cummen Strand, The. Red Hanrahan's Song about Ireland. W. B. Yeats. CMoP; FaBoCh; IIP; NOIV

Old Buildings, The. Pedro Juan Pietri. UnSA

Old Cabin, The. Paul Laurence Dunbar. PoLF

Old Calligrapher, The. Vũ Đình Liên, *Vietnamese*. AVP, *tr. by* Huỳnh Sanh Thông

Old calypsonian sings, The. Politics Kaiso. Roger McTair. PBCV

Old canoe in, The. Sunrise. Jim Tollerud. VoR

Old cans sparkle. Tie slaps at the chin. Poem in March. Iain Crichton Smith. FaBoTC

Old Cat Care. Richard Hughes. OBMV

Old cat whose calm, The. Her Seventeenth Winter. John Leax. CRP

Old Cat's Confessions, An. Christopher Pearse Cranch. APN-1; OBCA

Old Cat's Dying Soliloquy, An. Anna Seward. ECWP; NOEC

Old Chairs to Mend. *Unknown*. *See* Chairs to Mend.

Old Champagne Glass. Eddy Van Vliet, *Dutch*. VCWP, *tr. by* John Van Tiel

Old charcoal seller, An. Po Chü-i, *Chinese*. SuSp, *tr. by* Eugene Eoyang

Old Chaucer, like the morning Star. On Mr. Abraham Cowley, His Death and Burial amongst the Ancient Poets. Sir John Denham. BeJo

Old, childless, husbandless, bereaved, alone. Ruth Pitter. WPN

Old Chisholm Trail, The. *Unknown*. AmFP; FaBoBe

Old Christmas Morning. Roy Helton. MoAmPo

Old chronicler. Iroko. Onwuchekwa Jemie. PBMAP

Old *Chüeh-chü*. *Unknown, Chinese*. CoBCP, *tr. by* Burton Watson

Old Churchyard of Bonchurch, The. Philip Bourke Marston. EBVV; OBNC

Old Circles. Jennifer Rankin. BMAP

Old City, The. Ruth Manning-Sanders. CH

Old Clock on the Stairs, The. Henry Wadsworth Longfellow. PWR

Old cloud passes mourning her daughter. Sunset after Rain. W. S. Merwin. PoA

Old cob swan his cygnets thus addressed, An. Lakeside. Edmund Wilson. OBCoV *Fr.* Easy Exercises in the Use of Difficult Words.

Old Codger of Broome, The. *Unknown*. FuFo

Old colonial house, The. Homeland. Pauline Melville. HCP

Old Complex, The. John Ashbery. FTOS

Old Countryside. Louise Bogan. HAP; WPE

Old Couple, The. F. Pratt Green. OxBTC

Old Couple. Charles Simic. HCAP; PoPoPo

Old cow lags, the. John Wills. HA

Old Cowboy, The. Kao Ch'i, *Chinese*. OHMPC, *tr. by* Kenneth Rexroth

Old Coyote. . . "If he hadn't looked back." Telling About Coyote. Simon J. Ortiz. STP

Old Cracked Tune, An. Stanley Kunitz. LoL

Old Crib, The. Mary E. Tucker. CBWP-1

Old crow of Shang Mountain, you are cruel! Song of the Crow Pecking at My Scarred Donkey. Wang Yü-ch'eng, *Chinese*. SuSp, *tr. by* Jonathan Chaves

Old Crow, upon the tall tree-top. The Crow. Cecil Frances Alexander. CTAV

Old Crow, upon the tall tree-top. The Crow. Mrs. ——— Alexander. BoTP

Old Currawong. Jennifer Rankin. BMAP

Old Danish jester named Yorick, An. Limerick. Ogden Nash. PeLi

Old Dan'l. Leonard Alfred George Strong. MoBrPo

Old daughter, small traveler. Making the Jam without You. Maxine W. Kumin. NALW

Old Davis owned a solid mica mountain. A Fountain, a Bottle, a Donkey's Ears and Some Books. Robert Frost. VGW

Old dears gardening in fur coats. The House Next Door. Douglas Dunn. OxBC

Old Derzhavin. "David Samuilovich Samoylov," *Russian*. TCRP, *tr. by* Lubov Yakovleva

Old Doc. Mark Vinz. Poetsp

Old Doctor Foster. *Unknown*. OxNR

Old dog barks backward without getting up, The. The Span of Life. Robert Frost. HoPM; LiTM; SoSe-8 *Fr.* Ten Mills.

Old dog bends his head listening, The. Robert Bly. Poetr

Old Dog in the Ruins of the Graves at Arles, The. James Wright. NNaP

Old dog used to herd me through the street, The. Turnabout. Linda Pastan. NIP-4

Old dream comes again to me, The. Mir träumte wieder der alte Traum. Heinrich Heine, *German*. AWP, *tr. by* James Thomson

Old Dream Oven, The. Jacinto Jesús Cardona. IFJA

Old dutch woman would spend half a day, The. Gary Snyder. NAAL-2

Old earth, how she sulks. Jacaranda. Roo Borson. NOBC

Old East End worker called Jock, An. Limerick. Victor Gray. NOBL

Old Eben Flood, climbing alone one night. Mr Flood's Party. Edwin Arlington Robinson. AWP; AmPP; CMoP; ClHu; ColAP; EBNV; FP; HAP; HeIP-4; HoPM; LiTM; MeMAP; MoAmPo; MoP; NAAL-2; NIP-

4; NOBA; NoAM; NoP-4; OxBA; PoE; PoRA; Poetr; SoSe-8; TAP; TFi; TRP; UnPo; WeW-3

Old Eddie's face, wrinkled with river lights. The Glory Trumpeter. Derek Walcott. GT; NAEL-2; NoP-4; SeSe

Old Edinburgh. Norman MacCaig. FaBoTC

Old Egyptians hid their wit, The. On Mr. Nash's Picture at Full Length. Jane Brereton. WPE

Old elm that murmured in our chimney top. The Fallen Elm. John Clare. FHYEP; FaBoPV

Old England. Anne Bradstreet. KTR *Fr.* A Dialogue between Old England and New.

Old England has not lost her prayer. Robert Lloyd. ECEV *Fr.* The Poetry Professors.

Old England is eaten by Knaves. Song. Alexander McLachlan. NOBC *Fr.* The Emigrant.

Old English Riddle. (*See also* Book Moth: "A moth ate a word. To me it seemed" *tr.* by Charles W. Kennedy, *and* "Bookmoth: A moth devoured words. When I heard" *tr.* by Kevin Crossley-Holland.) Cynewulf. OPOU, *tr.* by Gerard Benson *Fr.* Riddles (Exeter Book).

Old Familiar Faces, The. Charles Lamb. AWP; BLPA; FP; FaBoBe; FaPoR; GTBS-P; NOBE; NOBRP; OBEV; OxAEP-2; RB; Ro ("Where are they gone, the old familiar faces?") NOBRP

Old Farmer Giles. *Unknown.* OxNR

Old farmer, nearing death, asked, The. Field Day. William Robert Rodgers. BIrV; IIP; PNI

Old Farmer Oats and his son Ned. Song. John Jay Chapman. PoEL-5

Old-fashioned. Dara Wier. NAmP90

Old-Fashioned Garden, An. Cole Porter. OBGa

Old-Fashioned Song, An. John Hollander. NoP-4

Old Father Greybeard. *Unknown.* OxNR

Old father tongue sticking out. Rehearsal. Cyril Dabydeen. PBCV

Old Fellow from Tyre, The. *Unknown.* FuFo

Old field is sad, The. D. J. Enright. AYFP

Old Field Mowed, An. William Meredith. NYBP

Old fish fiddle with their fins and glide, The. Aquarium. George T. Wright. NYBP

Old Fisherman, The. Emily Grosholz. RA

Old fisherman spends his night beneath the western cliffs. Ou-yang Hsiu, *Chinese.* BLT, *tr.* by J. P. Seaton

Old Fisherman with Guitar. George Mackay Brown. FaBoTC; OxBC

Old Fitz, who from your suburb grange. To E. Fitzgerald. Tennyson. FP; NOBVV; PoEL-5

Old Flame, The. Robert Lowell. BoLoP; CBLP; NOBA; NoAM

Old Florist. Theodore Roethke. OxBSP

Old Folk, The. Tove Ditlevsen, *Danish.* PBWP, *tr.* by Nadia Christensen

Old Folks at Home[, The]. Stephen Collins Foster. APN-2; FaBoBe

'Old fool'. (LL) The Greatest Love. Anna Swirszczynska, *Polish.* PoSu, *tr.* by Czeslaw Milosz *and* Leonard Nathan

Old forms are like birdhouses that, The. Poetry. Greg Kuzma. PoA

Old Fortress, The. Elisaveta Bagryana, *Bulgarian.* CEEP, *tr.* by Jascha Kessler *and* Aleksandar Shurbanov

Old Fortunatus. Thomas Dekker *and others.*
  Fortune and Virtue. NoSic
  Priest's Song, A.
    (Song: "Virtue's branches wither, virtue pines.")

Old Forty-five Per Cent. *Unknown.* FaBoEE

Old Freedman, The. Priscilla Jane Thompson. CBWP-2

Old Friend. Dimitris Tsaloumas. BMAP

Old friend, kind friend! lightly down. To My Old Schoolmaster. John Greenleaf Whittier. ColAP; NOBA

Old friend, you. Back from the Word-Processing Course, I Say to My Old Typewriter. Michael C. Blumenthal. NoAM

Old friend, your place is empty now. No more. To Scott. Winifred M. Letts. PoLF

Old Friends. John Betjeman. FP
  ("Sky widens to Cornwall, The. A sense of sea.")
  In Memoriam: A. C., R. J. O., K. S.

Old friends know what I like. T'ao Ch'ien. SuSp, *tr.* by Wu-chi Liu *Fr.* Drinking Wine. CoBCP, *tr.* by Burton Watson

Old friends sigh at long separation. Saying Farewell to Magistrate Ch'en Ta-yu. Lin Hung, *Chinese.* SuSp, *tr.* by Irving Y. Lo

Old Fritz, on this rotating bed. A Flat One. W. D. Snodgrass. LiTM

Old Furniture. Thomas Hardy. OxBTC

Old gardens, a ruined terrace, willow trees new. At Su Terrace Viewing the Past. Li Po, *Chinese.* CoBCP, *tr.* by Burton Watson

Old General Artichoke lay bloated on his bed. The Old Land Dog. John Betjeman. OBCoV

Old gilt vane and spire receive, The. The Late, Last Rook. Ralph Hodgson. MoBrPo

Old Gory, The. Gerald William Barrax. NBV

Old gourmet who's grown somewhat stout, An. Limerick. "Yorick." PeLi

Old Grahame he is to Carlisle gone. Bewick and Graham. *Unknown.* ESPB

Old Gramophone Records. James Kirkup. NYBP

Old Grandpaw Yet. *Unknown.* AmFP

Old Gray Beard a-Shaking. *Unknown.* AmFP

Old Gray Couple, The. Archibald MacLeish. AFr

Old Gray Goose, The. *Unknown.* AmFP

Old Gray Mare. *Unknown.* AS

Old Green River knife had to be scraped, An. Canst Thou Draw Out Leviathan with an Hook. Allen Curnow. PeNZ

Old grey hearse goes rolling by, The. The Hearse Song. *Unknown.* AS; OxBoLi; RB

Old Grimes. Albert Gorton Greene. ReMoGo

Old Guitar, The. John Hollander. DiPo

Old guy put down his beer, The. Do the Dead Know What Time It Is? Kenneth Patchen. HoPM; MoAmPo

Old habits it seems cannot be swept away. Yüan Mei. *Fr.* Miscellaneous Poems on Growing Old. CoBLCP, *tr.* by Jonathan Chaves

Old hare and the chilled frog weep the sky's sheen, The. A Dream of Heaven. Li Ho, *Chinese.* PLT, *tr.* by A. C. Graham

Old harem is quiet and deserted, The. Li Shang-yin, *Chinese.* OHMPC, *tr.* by Kenneth Rexroth

Old Haven. Jean Garrigue. WPE

Old Hogan's goat was feeling fine. *Unknown.* PeP

Old Hokum Buncombe, The. Robert E. Sherwood. NBLV

Old Hound, The. Huỳnh Mẫn Đạt, *Vietnamese.* AVP, *tr.* by Huỳnh Sanh Thông

Old house felt unfriendly, The. The Empty House. Max Williams. CBAP

Old house from my childhood, The. Yüan Mei. *Fr.* In Late Spring of the Year *Keng-hsü* (1790), I Stayed at the Sun Family's Gemstone Mountain Villa at West Lake. Before Leaving, I Wrote These Poems as Mementos. CoBLCP, *tr.* by Jonathan Chaves

Old house with trees and twisting river, An. A Visit to Bridge House. Richard Weber. BIrV

Old Houses. Homer D'Lettuso. PoToHe

Old Houses. Jennie Romano. PoToHe

Old Houses. Melvin B. Tolson. GT

Old Houses of Flanders, The. Ford Madox Ford. CTC

Old houses were scaffolding once. Image. Thomas Ernest Hulme. InPK-6; OxBTC

Old Humpy. *Unknown.* AmFP

Old Hundredth, *metrical vers.* by William Kethe. Bible, *O.T. See* Psalm 100.

Old Husband Suspects Adultery, An. Gavin Ewart. NoAM

Old I Am. Herman Charles Bosman. PeSA

Old I Am. Thomas Stanley, *after the Greek of* Anacreon. AWP

Old Ila, to show his fine delicate taste. On Lord Ila's Improvements, near Hounslow Heath. Philip Dormer Stanhope. OBGa

Old Indian chief, Running B'ar, An. Limerick. Mary Rita Hurley. PeLi

Old Ireland. Walt Whitman. IIP

Old Ironsides. Oliver Wendell Holmes. APAD; APN-1; AiP; BLPA; CTV; EBEvV; FaBoBe; NAAL-1; NAAL-3; NCAP; PAR; PWR; TAP; TFi

Old Ironsides at anchor lay. The Main-Truck; or, A Leap for Life. George Pope Morris. PoLF

Old Jack-o'-lantern lay on the ground, An. Judging by Appearances. Emilie Poulsson. FPC

Old Japan. Tanka. Toki Zenmaro, *Japanese.* MJT, *tr.* by Makoto Ueda

Old Jason, the Argonaut, The. Denis Glover. PeNZ

Old Jockey, The. Frederick Robert Higgins. OBMV; OxBTC

Old Joe. *Unknown.* OxBoLi

Old Joe Clark. *Unknown.* APN-2

Old Joe Jones and his old dog Bones. Laura Elizabeth Richards. TLR

Old Kimball. *Unknown.* AmFP

Old King Cabbage. Richard Kendall Munkittrick. OBCA

Old King Cole. G. K. Chesterton. *See* Variations on an Air: After Robert Browning.

Old King Cole ("Me clairvoyant"). G. K. Chesterton. BXAP; NOBL; UV *Fr.* Variations on an Air Composed on Having to Appear in a Pageant as Old King Cole. NOBL

Old King Cole ("Of an old king in a story"). G. K. Chesterton. BXAP *Fr.* Variations on an Air Composed on Having to Appear in a Pageant as Old King Cole. NOBL

Old King Cole was a merry old soul. Mother Goose. FaBoBe; LB; OTCP; OxNR; ReMoGo

Old Kitchen Clock, The. Ann Hawkshawe. BoTP

Old Knight, The. George Peele. *See* A Farewell to Arms.

Old Ladies. Will Allen Dromgoole. WeW-3

Old Ladies, The. Colin Ellis. OxBTC

Old ladies and tulips, model boats. Kensington Gardens. Muriel Spark. OBGa

Old Lady Across the Hall Has Gone to Live Behind the Door, The. Colette Inez. CMAP

Old lady, I now celebrate. The Little Flower's Disciple. John Montague. CIP-2; TIRV *Fr.* The Leaping Fire.

Old Lady of Harrow, An, *limerick. Unknown.* PeLi

Old Lady of London, The. *Unknown.* AmFP

Old lady Shih, braving acerbity, pokes in her three-foot beak. To Go with Shih K'o's Painting of an Old Man Tasting Vinegar. Huang T'ing-chien, *Chinese.* CoBCP, *tr. by* Burton Watson

Old Lady Sitting in the Dining Room. *Unknown.* AmFP

Old lady writes me in a spidery style, An. A Letter from Brooklyn. Derek Walcott. FP; OxBTC

Old Lady's Lament for Her Youth, The. François Villon, *French.* BoLoP, *tr. by* Robert Lowell

Old Lambro pass'd unseen a private gate. Byron. *Fr.* Canto the Third. *Fr.* Don Juan.

Old Land Dog, The. John Betjeman. OBCoV

Old Leaves from the Chinese Earth. Sadanand Rege, *Marathi.* OMIP, *tr. by* Dilip Chitre

Old Lem. Sterling Brown. BPo; PoBA; TTY

Old Liberia Is Not the Place for Me. Joshua McCarter Simpson. AAP

Old Lie: Dulce et decorum est / Pro patria mori, The. Wilfred Owen. *See* Dulce Et Decorum Est.

Old light & owl-light. 2nd Light Poem: For Diane Wakoski. Jackson MacLow. PoM

Old light smoulders in her eye, An. Pity. Trumbull Stickney. ColAP

Old Lobsterman, The. John Townsend Trowbridge. APN-2

Old Love and New Love. Naomi Mitchison. WPN

Old Love Butchered (Colorado Springs and Huachuca). Lance Jeffers. NBV

Old Loves. Henry Murger, *French.* AWP, *tr. by* Andrew Lang

Old Lute, The. Po Chü-i, *Chinese.* ChiP, *tr. by* Arthur Waley

Old Lutheran Bells at Home, The. Wallace Stevens. NoAM

Old, mad, blind, despised, and dying king,—An. England in 1819. Shelley. FaBoPV; GSo; NAEL-2; NOBE; NoP-4; OAEL-2; OxAEP-2; PBMP; Poetr; PoPoPo; Ro; SAGP; Son; TFi; UnPo

Old Magic. Grace Nichols. PBCV

Old maid, an old maid, An. *Unknown.* OxNR

Old maid early eer I knew, An. William Blake. OxBSP

Old Maids. *Unknown.* AmFP

Old Maid's Soliloquy. Maggie Pogue Johnson. CBWP-4

Old Maid's Song. *Unknown.* AmFP

Old Malediction, An. Anthony Hecht, *after* Horace. NoAM; OBCoV

Old Mama Saturday. Marie Ponsot. BAP-95

Old man, The. Birdfoot's Grampa. Joseph Bruchac. UnSA

Old Man, The. He Was Lucky. Anna Swirszczynska, *Polish.* HP; PoSu, *tr. by* Magnus J. Krynski *and* Robert A. Maguire

Old Man. James Henry. NOBVV

Old Man, The. Penelope Shuttle. LW

Old Man [Travelling], An. Wordsworth. OBWP

   (Old Man Travelling; Animal Tranquillity and Decay, A Sketch.) Ro ("With envy, what the Old Man hardly feels.") (LL) FaBoCh

Old man, a slight smile on his lips, rides a grey deer, The. Song of the Painting of the Long-Life Star. Wang Chiu-ssu, *Chinese.* CoBLCP, *tr. by* Jonathan Chaves

Old Man at the Crossing, The. Leonard Alfred George Strong. OBMV

Old man bending I come among new faces, An. The Wound-Dresser. Walt Whitman. APN-1; AmPP; CBCWP; ColAP; NAAL-1; NOBA; OBWP; TAP

Old man bending I come among new faces, An. The Wound-Dresser. Walt Whitman. NAAL-3

Old man Brown. The Cheerful Chilterns. Frank Sidgwick. BXAP

Old man Chang, sick three years, finally up and died. The Rain Cleared and the Breeze and Sunshine Are Superb as I Stroll Outside the Gate. Lu Yu, *Chinese.* SuSp, *tr. by* Burton Watson

Old man Chih-shan has a head of white hair. Chu Yün-ming. *Fr.* Improvisations. CoBLCP, *tr. by* Jonathan Chaves

Old Man Dreams, The. Oliver Wendell Holmes. PoLF

Old Man from Darjeeling. *Unknown.* NTCP

Old man from Hsin-feng, eighty-eight years old, An. The Old Man of Hsin-feng witih the Broken Arm. Po Chü-i, *Chinese.* SuSp, *tr. by* Eugene Eoyang

Old Man from Peru, An. *Unknown. See* Limerick: "There was an old man of [or from] Peru / Who dreamt [or dreamed] he was eating his shoe."

Old man gets up turns, An. Zeimbekiko. Robin Magowan. SPE

Old man going a lone highway, An. Building the Bridge. Will Allen Dromgoole. PoToHe; WeW-3

Old man in a lodge within a park, An. Chaucer. Henry Wadsworth Longfellow. APN-1; AWP; HeIP-4; MeMAP; NOBA; OBEV; OxBA; PoE; PoRA; Son; TAP; TFi

Old Man in a Moon Loft. T. Glynne Davies, *Welsh.* OBWVE, *tr. by the author*

Old Man in New Country. James Berry. NBrP

Old man in the crystal morning after snow. Poem. Delmore Schwartz. PoA

Old man is gone, The. Epitaph. John Figueroa. HCP

Old man it much concerns you to confute. The Son learns how to beat his father. Aristophanes, *Greek.* OBCVT, *tr. by* Thomas Stanley

Old Man Know-All. *Unknown.* BPo

Old man leaning on a gate, An. From My Window. Mary Elizabeth Coleridge. OBNC

Old man / man black man. Tony Get the Boys. D. L. Graham. PoBA

Old Man Mose. 221st Chorus. Jack Kerouac. NeAP *Fr.* Mexico City Blues.

Old man moved into his night, The. Katerina Anghelaki-Rooke. PBWP *Fr.* Notes on My Father.

Old man mumbling in his dotage, or crying child, unborn? (LL) For Malcolm X. Margaret Abigail Walker. BPo; NAAL; PoBA; Son

Old Man Ocean, how do you pound. Russell Hoban. TLR

Old Man of Hsin-feng witih the Broken Arm, The. Po Chü-i, *Chinese.* SuSp, *tr. by* Eugene Eoyang

Old Man of Nantucket, The. *Unknown.* PeLi

Old Man of Nine Dragon Mountain, The. The Long Handscroll of Bamboo by Wang Meng-tuan. Li Tung-yang, *Chinese.* CoBLCP, *tr. by* Jonathan Chaves

Old man of the mountains loves the mountains, The. Winter. Chang Yü. *Fr.* The Four Seasons in the Mountains. CoBLCP, *tr. by* Jonathan Chaves

Old Man of Verona, The. Claudian, *Latin.* AWP; OBVE, *tr. by* Abraham Cowley

   (Claudian's Old Man of Verona.) OBCVT, *tr. by* Abraham Cowley

Old Man of Verona, The. Claudian, *Latin.* MLL, *tr. by* Helen Waddell

Old Man, or Lad's-Love,—in the name there's nothing. Edward Thomas. LiTM; SCV

Old Man Playing with Children. John Crowe Ransom. MeMAP

Old Man Pondered. John Crowe Ransom. MoAmPo

Old Man Potchikoo. Louise Erdrich. HATNAP

Old man pushing seventy. Written in a Carefree Mood. Lu Yu, *Chinese.* CoBCP, *tr. by* Burton Watson

Old man selling charms in a cranny of the town wall, An. The Pedlar of Spells. Lu Yu, *Chinese.* ChiP, *tr. by* Arthur Waley

Old man sits in wrinkled reverie, An. An Evasion. Douglas Livingstone. PeSA

Old Man Stirs the Fire to a Blaze, An. W. B. Yeats. RB *Fr.* The Wanderings of Oisin.

Old Man Told Me. Lance Henson. VoR

Old Man Travelling; Animal Tranquillity and Decay, A Sketch. Wordsworth. *See* An Old Man [Travelling].

Old man wants to dance, The. January. Cornelius Eady. IFJA

Old man waves to me through iron bars, The. Robyn Selman. PUP-19

Old man, we do not speak of crosses. (LL) Father and Daughter. Sonia Sanchez. FFC; GT

Old man went to meetin', for the day was bright and fair, The. The Preacher's Vacation. *Unknown.* BLPA

Old man who seined. Lorine Niedecker. VGW

Old man with fire in his eyes, An. The King. Anthony Kellman. HCP

Old Man with the Broken Arm, The. Po Chü-i, *Chinese.* ChiP, *tr. by* Arthur Waley

Old Man's Case, The. Martial, *Latin.* OBCVT, *tr. by* Philip Murray

Old Man's Comforts and How He Gained Them, The. Robert Southey. EBEvV; HoPM; OxBChV; UV; UnPo

   (Old Man's Comforts, The.) APAD

Old Man's Complaint, The. *Unknown.* OxBSP

Old man's eagle mind, An. (LL) An Acre of Grass. W. B. Yeats. CMoP; NoAM

Old man's fair-haired consort, whole dewy axle-tree, The. 1.14. Ovid. AWP, *tr. by* Kirby Flower Smith *Fr.* Elegies.

Old Man's Lazy, The. Peter Blue Cloud. HATNAP; LTA

Old Man's Son, An. Russell Edson. LCAP-2

Old Man's Song, about His Wife, The. *Unknown, Eskimo.* STP, *tr. by* Armand Schwerner

Old Man's Tale, The. Brian Merriman. BlrV, *tr. by* David Marcus *Fr.* The Midnight Court. NOIV, *tr. by* Thomas Kinsella

Old Man's Winter Night, An. Robert Frost. AFr; AWP; HAP; MoAmPo; NAAL-2; NoAM; OxBA; VGW

Old Man's Wish, The. Walter Pope. NOSC

Old Mansion. John Crowe Ransom. FuPo; HeIP-4; MeMAP; NOBA; OxBA

Old Maps and New. Norman MacCaig. OxBC

Old Mare, The. Elizabeth Jane Coatsworth. MoAmPo

Old Marlborough Road, The. Henry David Thoreau. PoEL-4

Old-Marrieds, The. Gwendolyn Brooks. PoBA

Old Marse John. *Unknown.* TTY

Old Mary. Gwendolyn Brooks. PFE

Old master always said. "No, Master, Never!" Joshua McCarter Simpson. AAP

Old master yourself now, Auden, An. As You Like It. Theodore Weiss. TAP

Old May Song. *Unknown.* BoTP; CH

Old mayor climbed the belfry tower, The. The High Tide on the Coast of Lincolnshire, 1571. Jean Ingelow. EBVV; OxAEP-2; PEW

Old Meg she was a gipsy [*or* gypsy]. Meg Merrilies [*or* Merrilees]. Keats. BoTP; FHYEP; FaBoCh; OxBChV

Old Memories of Earth. Ronald Allison Kells Mason. PeNZ

Old Men, The. Walter De la Mare. MoBrPo

Old Men, The. Irving Feldman. TwCP

Old Men, The. Alexander Javitz. TrJP

Old Men, The. Rudyard Kipling. OBSV

Old Men. Ogden Nash. InPS-3; RB

Old Men Admiring Themselves in the Water, The. W. B. Yeats. CMoP; FaBoCh; KaS

Old Men and Old Women Going Home on the Street Car. Merrill Moore. MoAmPo

Old men and women, The. July. Sonia Sanchez. GT

Old men are like little boys. Han Yü, *Chinese.* *Fr.* A Pond in a Jardiniere. CoBCP, *tr. by* Burton Watson

Old Men at Pevensey. Rudyard Kipling. NoAM; PoEL-5 *Fr.* Puck of Pook's Hill.

Runes on Weland's Sword, The. NoAM; PoEL-5

Old men in blue: and heavily encumbered. Pihsien Road. "Robin Hyde." WPE

Old Men not staid with Age, Virgins with shame. Claudian. OBCVT, *tr. by* Ben Jonson *Fr.* Sejanus his Fall.

Old Men of Athens, The. Gail Holst-Warhaft. GI

Old men, white-haired, beside the ancestral graves. Basho, *Japanese.* AWP, *tr. by* Curtis Hidden Page

Old Menalcas on a day. The Palmer's Ode. Robert Greene. CTC; NoSic; SCGP *Fr.* Never Too Late.

Old men's wives, The. The Old Men of Athens. Gail Holst-Warhaft. GI

Old Merina Theme. Flavien Ranaivo, *French.* NegPo, *tr. by* Ellen Conroy Kennedy

Old Miner's Refrain, The. *Unknown.* AmFP

Old moder Phoebe how happy you be. Moder Phoebe. *Unknown.* FaBoVe

Old Mog the mechanic, I remember him well. The Ballad of Morgan the Moon. Max Boyce. SpW

Old Moke. Harold Littlebird. VoR

Old Molly Means was a hag and a witch. Molly Means. Margaret Abigail Walker. BlSi; NALW; NMM-2

Old monk perches at the tip of a tree, An. A Wall Painting by Wu Wei. Wang T'ing-hsiang. *Fr.* Miscellaneous Poems on Spirit-Valley Temple. CoBLCP, *tr. by* Jonathan Chaves

Old moon is tarnished, The. Sea Lullaby. Elinor Wylie. PBMP

Old moon my eyes are new moon with human footprint. Poem Rocket. Allen Ginsberg. VGW

Old Morgan. G. D. Roberts. BoTP

Old Mortality. Sir Walter Scott.

Sound, Sound the Clarion. FaBoEE; FaPoR; NOBE; OxAEP-2

(Call, The.) OBEV

Old mortality, these evening doorways into rooms, An. Birthday. Stanley Plumly. NAmP90

Old Mother, The. *Unknown.* PoToHe

Old Mother Duck has hatched a brood. Mother Duck. *Unknown.* BoTP

Old Mother Earth woke up from her sleep. A Spring Song. *Unknown.* PoLF

Old Mother Goose. Mother Goose. BoTP; LB; OxNR; ReMoGo

("Egg of pure gold, An.") (LL) LB

("Flew up to the moon.") (LL) OxNR

Old Mother Hubbard. The Comic Adventures of Old Mother Hubbard and Her Dog. Sarah Catherine Martin. CBNP; FaBoBe; LB; OxBChV; OxNR; ReMoGo

Old Mother Hubbard. *Unknown.* CTAV

Old Mother Niddity Nod. *Unknown.* OxNR

Old Mother Shuttle. *Unknown.* OxNR

Old Mother Twitchett had [*or* has] but one eye. Mother Goose. NTCP; OxNR; ReMoGo

("She left a bit of her tail in a trap.") (LL) LB

Old Mothers. Charles Sarsfield Ross. PoToHe

Old Motif. Aleksandar Ristovic, *Serbo-Croatian.* HSix, *tr. by* Charles Simic

Old mountain man is learning to garden, The. Vegetable Garden. Lu Yu, *Chinese.* CoBCP, *tr. by* Burton Watson

Old Mountain Road. Charles Simic. FYAP

Old Mrs. Jarvis. Elizabeth Fleming. BoTP

Old Mrs. Lazibones. Gerda Mayer. OTCP

Old Mrs Thing-um-e-bob. Charles Causley. FuFo; OTCP

Old Mrs. Tressider / Over at Winches. The Scarf. Ivy O. Eastwick. BoTP

Old Mythologies. John Montague. NoP-4

Old Nelly's Birthday. Ruth Pitter. NALW

Old newspapers nobody's ever got to read again. (LL) Twenty-Year Marriage. Ai. BoWoP; DeD; GT; NoAM

Old Nico brought wreaths to the tomb of Melite. Philip of Thessalonica, *Greek.* GrAn, *tr. by* Edwin Morgan

Old Noah he had an ostrich farm and fowls on the largest scale. Wine and Water. G. K. Chesterton. ChIV-1; MoBrPo *Fr.* The Flying Inn.

Old Noah once he built an ark. Old Noah's Ark. *Unknown.* ImGa

Old Noah, trailing plummets, found. Captain Noah. Frederick Robert Higgins. KSG

Old Noah's Ark. *Unknown.* ImGa

Old Nobility, The, *epigram.* Friedrich von Logau, *German.* GePo, *tr. by* George C. Schoolfield

Old now. Benjamin Banneker Sends His *Almanac* to Thomas Jefferson. Jay Wright. VCAP

Old oak, old timber, sunk and rooted. G. M. B. Donald Davie. OxBC

Old Oak Tree at Hatfield Broadoak, The. Frederick Locker-Lampson. OxAEP-2

Old Oaken Bucket, The, *parody.* *Unknown.* BLPA

Old Oaken Bucket, The. Samuel Woodworth. BLPA; FaBoBe

Old, old house by the side of the sea, An. Katrina on the Porch. Alice Cary. APN-2

Old, old/ To live on, wretched to behold. Owen Gruffydd. OBWVE, *tr. by* Anthony Conran *Fr.* The Men That Once Were.

Old ones go to each other's funerals, The. Burials. Geoffrey Grigson. PoA

Old ones to the side. Psalm. Charles Simic. AmPA; LCAP-2

Old [*or* Ould] Orange Flute, The. *Unknown.* OBCoV; OxBoLi

Old Ox, The. George Rostrevor Hamilton, *after the Greek of* Addaios of Makedon. FaBoEE

Old Paintings on Italian Walls. Kathleen Jessie Raine. NYBP

Old Parson Beanes hunts six days [*or* dayes] of the week. Upon Parson Beanes. Robert Herrick. BeJo

Old Penobscot Indian, The. Flux. Richard Eberhart. Poetsp; VGW

Old People. Michael Davitt, *Irish.* PBCIP, *tr. by* Michael Hartnett

Old people are like birds. City Pigeons. Helen Chasin. WeW-3

Old person of Troy, An. First Limick. Ogden Nash. PeLi

Old Peter Grimes made fishing his employ. Peter Grimes. George Crabbe. EBNV; ECEV; FHYEP; OBNV; PoEL-4; Ro *Fr.* The Borough.

Old Pettigrew. Melvin B. Tolson. GT

Old photographs would have her bookish, sitting. Ma. Paul Muldoon. PNI

Old Picture, An. Howard Nemerov. OxBSP

Old Pilot, The. Donald Hall. LCAP-2

Old Pine, An. Wang An-shih, *Chinese.* SuSp, *tr. by* Jan W. Walls

Old pine trees, their shaggy manes. Pei-mang Cemetery. Yüan Hung-tao, *Chinese.* CoBLCP, *tr. by* Jonathan Chaves

Old Place, The. Blanche Edith Baughan. PeNZ

Old Platthis often thrust away her morning's sleep. Leonidas of Tarentum. HePo, *tr. by* Barbara Hughes Fowler *Fr.* Epigrams.

Old Poem. *Unknown, Chinese.* AWP, *tr. by* Arthur Waley

("I know the new wife can't equal the old!") (LL) CoBCP, *tr. by* Burton Watson

Old Poem. *Unknown, Chinese.* AWP; BoWoP, *tr. by* Arthur Waley

Old poet called Omar cried: "Now," An. Limerick. "J. E. C." PeLi

Old Poet, Poetry's final subject glimmers months ahead. Don't Grow Old. Allen Ginsberg.

Old poets foster'd under friendlier skies. Poets and Their Bibliographies. Tennyson. GSo

Old pond:/ frog-jump-in. Basho, *Japanese.* TAL, *tr. by* Harold G. Henderson

Old pond, / frog jumps in. Basho. EnIH, *tr. by* Michael Katz *Fr.* Seventy-six Hokku.

Old pond— / The sound, An. Basho, *Japanese*. OHPJ, *tr.* by Kenneth Rexroth

Old Postcards. Günter Eich, *German*. AF, *tr.* by Stuart Friebert

Old Priest, The. Vladimir Holan, *Czech*. PoSu, *tr.* by George Theiner

Old priest Peter Gilligan, The. The Ballad of Father Gilligan. W. B. Yeats. EBVV; MoBrPo; PoRA

Old Prison, The. Judith Wright. BMAP

Old professor of zoology, The. The Parrot. James Elroy Flecker. FaBoTw

Old Pro's Lament, The. Paul Petrie. TAP

Old Python Nose with the wind-rolling ears. To a Dead Elephant. Douglas Livingstone. PeSA

Old question. Will not God do right?, The. (LL) The Leper. Swinburne. GBL; NOBVV

Old Quin Queeribus. Nancy Byrd Turner. FuFo

Old Relative. Gwendolyn Brooks. ColAP   *Fr.* Notes from the Childhood and the Girlhood. LCAP-2

Old Rhyme, An. *Unknown*. BoTP

Old ridiculous partner is back again, The. The She Wolf. Muriel Spark. NYBP

Old Roads. Eiléan Ní Chuilleanáin. CIP-2; IIP

Old Robin of Portingale. *Unknown*. ESPB

Old Roger. *Unknown*. OxBoLi

Old Room, The. W. S. Merwin. NYBP

Old rooster crows, The. O. Mabson Southard. HA

Old rude church, with bare, bald tower, is here, The. Wordsworth's Grave. Sir William Watson. OBNC

Old Rugged Cross, The. George Bennard. AH

Old Ruralities: A Regret. Charles Tennyson Turner. EBVV; Son

Old Russian spits up a plum, The. A Man Then Suddenly Stops Moving. Alberto A. Ríos. NoAM

Old Russia's slavery rights. Boiler room. Night. Olga Beshenkovskaya, *Russian*. TCRP, *tr.* by Vera Dunham

Old Rustic Mill, The. George Sands Johnson. PWR

Old Sac Village, The. Albery Allson Whitman. AAP   *Fr.* Not a Man and Yet a Man.

Old Sailor Looking at a Container Ship. Robert Carson. AiP

Old Saint's Prayer, The. Priscilla Jane Thompson. CBWP-2

Old saltman, hair turned white, The. Wu Chia-chi, *Chinese*. CoBLCP, *tr.* by Jonathan Chaves

Old Sam. Stanley Holloway. OBCoV

Old sandpiper contemplates his age, The. Summer's Early End at Hudson's Bay. Hayden Carruth. NYBP

Old-Saxon Fragment. *Unknown*. CBNP; OBCoV

Old Scent of the Plum Tree. Ietaka, *Japanese*. AWP, *tr.* by E. Powys Mathers

Old Section Boss, The. *Unknown*. BPo

Old Shellover. Walter De la Mare. BoTP; OxBChV

Old Shepherd's Prayer. Charlotte Mew. MoBrPo; OxBTC; WPE

Old Ships, The. James Elroy Flecker. CH; MoBrPo; OBMV; PoRA

Old Ships. David Morton. CTV

Old ships are preserved. The Taste. George Oppen. NNaP   *Fr.* Some San Francisco Poems.

Old shoe, an old pot, an old skin, An. Autumn Sequence. Adrienne Rich. VGW

Old Sipsey Valley Road, The. Thomas Rabbitt. MT

Old Sir Simon the king. *Unknown*. OxNR

Old Sister Death bit you off. On the Death of Muriel Rukeyser. Billy Marshall-Stoneking. BMAP

Old Skinflint. Wilfrid Wilson Gibson. OBMV

Old snake, old hole in the corner man. A Dead Weasel. David Helwig. NOBC

Old Snapshot. Ronald G. Everson. MoCV

Old soak from Stoke, An. C. J. Parker. PeLi

Old Soldier. Padraic Colum. OBMV

Old soldier, An. Tanka. Toki Zenmaro, *Japanese*. MJT, *tr.* by Makoto Ueda

Old soldiers true, ah, them all men can trust. A Prophecy. Maurice Thompson. *Fr.* Lincoln's Grave. CBCWP

Old—some eighty, or thereabouts. 'Nkongane. W. C. Scully. PeSAV

Old Song, The. G. K. Chesterton. FaBoTw

Old Song. Edward Fitzgerald. OBEV; OxAEP-2

Old Song. *Unknown*. RaBo

Old Song. Andrey Andreievich Voznesensky, *Russian*. VCWP, *tr.* by Smith, William Jay and Vera Dunham

Old Song, An. "Yehoash," *Yiddish*. AWP, *tr.* by Marie Syrkin

Old Song Ended, An. D. G. Rossetti. BoLoP; EBVV

Old Song of Rejoicing, An. *Unknown, Maori*. PeNZ, *tr.* by Margaret Orbell

Old Song, Wrote by One of Our First New-England Planters, An. *Unknown*. SCAP

Old South Boston Aquarium stands, The. For the Union Dead. Robert Lowell. AmPP; CBCWP; CoAP; ColAP; FYAP; FaBoA; FaBoPV; HAP; HCAP; HeIP-4; InPS-3; LCAP-2; LiTM; MoP; NAAL-2; NOBA; NoAM; NoP-4; OBWP; PoE; PoPoPo; Poetr; SCV; TFi; TRP; TwCP; UnPo; VCAP; WeW-3

Old spider web, An. J. W. Hackett. HA

Old spirit, in and beyond me. Hope. Philip Booth. APAD

Old spoon, An. The Spoon. Charles Simic. NNaP

Old Squire, The. Wilfrid Scawen Blunt. FaPoR; OBEV; SCGP

Old / star / shuts her bleary eyes, The. In a Corner of the Sky. Federico García Lorca. PFTM

Old Stephen. Charles Tennyson Turner. EBVV

Old Stoic, The. Emily Jane Brontë. BWW; FaPoR; NALW; NOBE; OBEV; OBNC; OxAEP-2; PoLF; SDW

Old Stone Cross, The. W. B. Yeats. PBMP

Old Story, The. Argentarius. AWP, *tr.* by E. A. Robinson   *Fr.* Variations of Greek Themes.

Old Story. Lance Henson. VoR

Old Story, The. Louis MacNeice. GBL

Old Story, An. Howard Nemerov.   *Fr.* Epigrams. OBAL

Old Story, An. E. A. Robinson. MoAmPo; OxBSP

Old Summerhouse, The. Walter De la Mare. CMoP; GTBS-P

Old Susan. Walter De la Mare. CMoP; MoBrPo

Old Sussex Road, The. Ian Serraillier. NTCP

Old Sweetheart of Mine, An. James Whitcomb Riley. BLPA

Old Swimmin'-Hole, The. James Whitcomb Riley. APN-2

Old tales were told of Sigemund's daring. The Tale of Sigemund. *Unknown*. AnOE, *tr.* by Charles W. Kennedy   *Fr.* Beowulf. OAEL-1, *tr.* by Charles W. Kennedy; ASW, *tr.* by Kevin Crossley-Holland

Old Talk, or West Indian History. Edward Baugh. HCP

Old Temple, The. Zhao Zhenkai, *Chinese*. ChiPo, *tr.* by Bonnie S. McDougall

Old temple leans against the green hillside, An. Tune: "Stretch of Cloud over Mount Wu, A." Li Hsün, *Chinese*. SuSp, *tr.* by Hellmut Wilhelm

Old Testament, The. Philip Levine. PUP-18

Old Testament Contents. *Unknown*. BLPA

Old-Testament Gospel. William Cowper. ChIV-2; TrCP   *Fr.* Olney Hymns.

Old, the mad, the blind have fairest daughters, The. The Beauty of Job's Daughters. Jay Macpherson. ChIV-1; MoCV; NOBC

Old, their big shoulders humped, The. Stations. Philip Booth. GM

Old Thought for a New Couple, An. E. A. Markham. PBCV

Old-Time Childhood in Kentucky. Robert Penn Warren. AiP

Old Time is lame and halt. Wie langsam kriechet sie dahin. Heinrich Heine, *German*. AWP, *tr.* by Richard Monckton Milnes

Old-Time Religion. *Unknown*. APN-2

Old-Time Sea-Fight, An. Walt Whitman. *See* Battle of the *Bonhomme Richard* and the *Serapis*.

Old Timers. Carl Sandburg. NoAM

Old Times. Daniel Mark Epstein. DiPo

Old towel folding it again autumn evening. Marlene Mountain. HA

Old town lies afar, An. There Is an Old City. Karl Bulcke, *German*. AWP, *tr.* by Ludwig Lewisohn

Old Trip by Dream Train, The. Brendan Galvin. GM

Old Triton Time. Vernon Watkins. OxBSP

Old Trojan Chiefs See Helen, The. Homer. OBVE, *tr.* by Alexander Pope   *Fr.* The Iliad.

Old Tune, An. Gérard de Nerval, *French*. AWP, *tr.* by Andrew Lang

Old two-hearted sadness, old blight. Parents. Robert Wrigley. PuP-17

Old Vicarage, Grantchester, The. Rupert Brooke. EBEvV; MoBrPo; OxBTC; PoRA

Old violence is not too old to beget new values. (LL) The Bloody Sire. Robinson Jeffers. CMoP; ImPo; LiTM; PoA

Old virgin, your airs are proper. To an Elderly Virgin. Mael Isu O Brolchain, *Old Irish*. NOIV, *tr.* by Thomas Kinsella

Old Vow, The. Trần Huiên Ân, *Vietnamese*. AVP, *tr.* by Huỳnh Sanh Thông

Old walls creak. Restoring the Ancestral House. Katerina Te Hei Koko Mataira, *Maori*. PeNZ, *tr.* by Katerina Te Hei Koko Mataira

Old Walt Whitman. Langston Hughes. HeIP-4

Old War-Dreams. Walt Whitman. OxBSP

Old warder of these buried bones. Tennyson. PeECV; PoEL-5   *Fr.* In Memoriam A. H. H.

Old watch: their, The. Vapor Trail Reflected in the Frog Pond. Galway Kinnell. OBWP; VCAP; VGW

Old West, the old time, The. Spanish Johnny. Willa Silbert Cather. AiP; PaTW

Old Whim Horse, The. Edward Dyson. CBAP

Old Whore Becomes a Nun, The. Huỳnh Mẫn Đạt, *Vietnamese*. AVP, *tr. by* Huỳnh Sanh Thông

Old Whorehouse, An. Mary Oliver. CMAP

Old Wife and the Ghost, The. James Reeves. OTCP

Old Wife in High Spirits. "Hugh MacDiarmid." CMoP; OxBTC; PoE

Old wigwam woman sitting beside the fire. And singing. Friend to Birds. Eric Groch, *Czech and Slovak*. CEEP, *tr. by* Eric Groch

Old Witherington. Dudley Randall. NBV; NoAM

("Old Witherington had drunk too much again.") CoAmPo

Old Wives' [*or* Wife's] Tale, The. George Peele.

   Fair Maiden. PoEL-2

   Song: "When as [*or* whenas] the rye [*or* rie] reach to the chin." CBNP; FaBoVe; OxBoLi; PoEL-2

     (Summer Song, A.) GLoP; NOBE; OBEV

     ("When as the rye reach to the chin.") GLoP; NoP-4

   "Spread, table, spread." NoSic

   "Three merry men, and three merry men." NoSic

   Voice [Speaks] from the Well, A. CBNP; FaBoCh; NOBE; OxBoLi

   Voice from the Well [of Life Speaks to the Maiden], The. NOBE; NoSic

     (Song for the Head.) RB

Old Wives' Tales. Constance Urdang. PBCAP

Old wolf, I said. The Case. Karen Volman. BAP-96

Old Woman, The. Joseph Campbell. AWP; MoBrPo; OxBTC; PoToHe

Old Woman, An. David Gwenallt Jones, *Welsh*. OBWVE, *tr. by* H. Idris Bell

Old Woman, The. Beatrix Potter. NTCP

Old Woman, An. Charles Henry Ross. OxBChV

Old Woman. Iain Crichton Smith. FaBoTw; OxBTC

Old woman across the way, The. The Whipping. Robert Earl Hayden. FiLi; PoBA; PoE; SSLK; SoSe-8

Old Woman and the Pedlar, The. Mother Goose. ReMoGo

   ("Lackamercyme, this is none of I!") (LL) LB

Old Woman and the Sandwiches, The. Libby Houston. OBSP

Old Woman Awaiting the Greyhound Bus. Duane Niatum. CDW

Old woman, blue eyed and sun burned. Leah Goldberg. MHP, *tr. by* Ruth Finer Mintz *Fr.* On Blossoming.

Old woman by a window watching the storm, An. The Reading of the Psalm. Robert Francis. AFr

Old Woman from France, The. *Unknown*. ReMoGo

Old woman grabs, An. Jejuri Arun Kolatkar. LiLi

Old woman in me walks patiently to the hospital, An. Revelation. Carole C. Gregory Clemmons. BlSi

Old woman likes to melt her husband. She puts him in a, An. Feeding the Dog. Russell Edson. RaBo

Old woman must stand, The. *Unknown*. OxNR

Old Woman Nature. Gary Snyder. BB; NoAM; RaBo

Old Woman of Beare Regrets Lost Youth, The. *Unknown, Irish*. OBMV, *tr. by* Frank O'Connor

Old Woman of Gloucester, The. *Unknown*. ReMoGo

Old Woman of Harrow. *Unknown*. ReMoGo

Old Woman of Leeds, The. *Unknown*. ReMoGo

Old Woman of Norwich, The. *Unknown*. ACTP

Old Woman of Surrey. Mother Goose. ReMoGo

Old Woman of the Roads, The. Padraic Colum. BoTP; CH; FYAP; FaBoBe; MoBrPo; NOIV; OBEV; PoRA; TIRV

Old Woman. Mother Goose.

   ("And I'll be with you by-and-by.") (LL) ReMoGo

Old woman, old woman, are you fond of carding? *Unknown*. AmFP

Old woman, old woman, / Shall we go a-shearing? Shall We Go A-Shearing? Mother Goose. OxNR; ReMoGo

Old Woman, Outside the Abbey Theater, An. Leonard Alfred George Strong. MoBrPo

Old Woman Remembers, An. Sterling Brown. ISC; PoBA

Old woman sits on a bench before the door and quarrels, The. Fawn's Foster-Mother. Robinson Jeffers. MoP; NOBA; NoAM

Old Woman Speaks of the Moon, An. Ruth Pitter. WPE

Old woman, time and your own. To Grandmother on Her Going. Gail Tremblay. HATNAP

Old woman was struck down by a chance shot, The. 27 July 1830. Georgy Arkadevich Shengeli, *Russian*. TCRP, *tr. by* Daniel Weissbort

Old woman was sweeping her house, and she found, An. *Unknown*. LB

Old woman went to market and bought a pig, An. *Unknown*. OxNR

Old Woman who lived in the Shoe, The. Limerick. Joyce Johnson. PeLi

Old woman's hair, The. Mothers. Punkanuttiraiyar, *Tamil*. PLW, *tr. by* A. K. Ramanujan

Old Woman's Lamentations, An. François Villon, *French*. MoBrPo; OBMV, *tr. by* J. M. Synge

Old woman's shoulders, The. Mothers. Kākkai Pāṭiṇiyār Naccĕḷḷaiyār, *Tamil*. PLW, *tr. by* A. K. Ramanujan

Old Woman's Song, An. Akjartoq, *Eskimo into Danish*. WPOW, *tr. by* Knud Rasmussen; *English vers. by* Tom Lowenstein

Old Women, The. George Mackay Brown. NoP-4; OxBS

Old women all their lives, they're a mixture of whitelime and brine. Women at the Market. Angela Figueroa-Aymerich, *Spanish*. PBWP, *tr. by* Hardie St. Martin

Old Women beside a Church. Keith Wilson. Poetsp

Old Women of Toronto. Miriam Waddington. NOBC

Old women say that men don't know. Becoming a Dad. E. A. Guest. PoLF

Old women watch the soldiers. Robert Bly. *See* The Teeth Mother Naked at Last.

Old wood stands uncut, of long years' space, An. Elegies 3.1. Ovid, *Latin*. CABP, *tr. by* Marlowe *Fr.* Elegies.

Old woodcutter of the sea, The. Song of the Woodcutter of the Sea. Pien Kung, *Chinese*. CoBLCP, *tr. by* Jonathan Chaves

Old wooden house a soft, The. Brass Tacks. Denise Levertov. InPS-3

Old wooden steps to the front door, The. A Time Past. Denise Levertov. NoAM

Old words sing. Song of Words. Konstantin Konstantinovich Vaginov, *Russian*. TCRP, *tr. by* Nina Kossman

Old-World Thicket, An. Christina Rossetti. VWP

Old wound aches and shews its fellow scar, The. (LL) The Scar. John Hewitt. CIP-2; PNI

Old wound in my ass, The. Fabrication of Ancestors. Alan Dugan. CBCWP; NoAM

Old WPA Swimming Pool in Martins Ferry, Ohio, The. James Wright. WeT

Old Year, The. Priscilla Jane Thompson. CBWP-2

Old Year, The. Clarence Thomas Urmy. PoToHe

Old Year's gone away, The. John Clare. AYFP; NOBVV; OBCP

Old yellow stucco, The. Winter Nightfall. Sir John Collings Squire. OxBTC

Old yew, which graspest at the stones. Tennyson. EBVV; EBVVPR; EnVR; GTBS-P; NOBE; OAEL-2; OBNC; PoEL-5; UnPo *Fr.* In Memoriam A. H. H.

Olden Days, The. Joseph Hall. *Fr.* Virgidemiarum.

Older American, The. Cheryl Clarke. GLP

Older, but no wiser than the defect of love. (LL) The New World. Imamu Amiri Baraka. NoAM; NoP-4; PmAP

Older Men. Alfred Corn. GLP

Older, more generous. The Gift. N. Scott Momaday. NoP-4

Older now, I know just how hard the going can be. (LL) Blue Rapids. Lu Yu, *Chinese*. CoBCP, *tr. by* Burton Watson

Older than anything that dies can be. (LL) The Knife. Richard Tillinghast. MT; WeT

Older than the ancient Greeks. Pigeons. Marianne Moore. PoA

Older than this psalm I'm singing right to the end. (LL) Psalm: "Old ones to the side." Charles Simic. AmPA; LCAP-2

Older women were Sunbeams and I guess we, The. Nightingales in America. Jane Flanders. CrSp; SAGP

Older women wise and tell Anna, The. Birth Stone. Lorna Goodison. VCWP

Oldest human fossil, The. Fire. Mark O'Connor. NOBAu

Oldest man in the world wears shoes, The. Passage. Billy Marshall-Stoneking. BMAP; NOBAu

Oldest of us burst into tears and cried, The. Allen Curnow. PeNZ *Fr.* Tomb of an Ancestor.

Oldest Place, The. Thomas Kinsella. PBCIP

Ole Abe (God bless 'is ole soul!). Negro Soldier's Civil War Chant. *Unknown*. BPo; TAP

Ole Aunt Dinah, she's jes lak me. Jack and Dinah Want Freedom. *Unknown*. BPo; NAAAL

Ole Sheep Dey Know de Road, De. *Unknown*. BPo

Oleander: coral. The Garden. Rae Armantrout. FTOS

Oleander on the wall, The. By the Arno. Oscar Wilde. EBVV

Olga Poems. Denise Levertov. LCAP-2; NNaP

   Everything flows. NAAL-2

Oliphaunt. J. R. R. Tolkien. NOxBChV

Olive Garden, The. Rilke, *German*. GI, *tr. by* David Curzon *and* Will Alexander Washburn

Olive garden for the nightingales, The. (LL) Painted Head. John Crowe Ransom. FuPo; LiTM; MeMAP; MoAmPo; NOBA; NoAM; OxBA

Olive in its orchard, The. A. E. Housman. NoAM

Olive journeys. Journey round the World. Ingrid Jonker, *Afrikaans.* PBWP, *tr. by* Jack Cope *and* William Plomer

Olive Tree. Lorenzo Mavilis, *Greek.* GrIP, *tr. by* Rae Dalven

Olive Trees. Bernard Spencer. NoAM

Oliver, according to TuTu. Eating the Elephant Whole. Jonathan Small. HCP

Oliver Twist. Marlene Philip. PBCV
("Oliver Twist can't do this.") NOxBChV

Oliver's singing. Oliver Singing. Israel Zangwill. NSI

Olives and Mountains. Elizabeth Barrett Browning. *Fr. Aurora Leigh.* VWP

Olivia's lewd, but looks devout. Elijah Fenton. ECEV

Olivier Metra's Waltz of Roses. La Mélinite: Moulin-Rouge. Arthur Symons. ADE; PeVV

Olney Hymns. William Cowper.
   Contentment. ChIV-2
   Contrite Heart, The.
   Ephraim Repenting. ChIV-1
   Exhortation to Prayer. NOCV
   House of Prayer, The. ChIV-2
   Hymn 10. ChIV-1
   Jehovah Our Righteousness. NOCV
   Joy and Peace in Believing. NOCV
   Light Shining out of Darkness. CABP; EBEV; ECEV; FHYEP; FaBoCh; ImPo; NOBE; NOCV; NOEC; PWR; PoEL-3; SCGP; TFi; TOF
   (From Olney Hymns.) NoP-4
   Love Constraining to Obedience. NOCV
   Lovest Thou Me? ChIV-2
   My Soul Thirsteth for God. TrCP
   Old-Testament Gospel. ChIV-2; TrCP
   Praise for the Fountain Opened. InPK-6
   (Fountain, The.) ChIV-1
   Sardis. ChIV-2
   Self-Acquaintance. NOCV
   Sower, The. ChIV-2
   Walking with God. ECEV; NOCV; NOEC; PeECV; PoEL-3; SCGP; TOF
   Wisdom. ChIV-1

Olokun. J. P. Clark Bekedermo. PBMAP *Fr. A Reed in the Tide.*

Olympian I. Pindar, *Greek.*
   Water is preeminent and gold, like a fire. OBCVT, *tr. by* Frank J. Nisetich

Olympian Ode for Hiero of Syracuse (Four-Horse Chariot Race). Bacchylides, *Greek.*
   Yet of all that Hellas holds. OBCVT, *tr. by* Robert Fagles

Olympians. Homer. *See* Thetis Asks Jove to Revenge Her Son Achilles.

Olympicus, the welter-weight. Lucilius, *Greek.* GrAn, *tr. by* Peter Porter

Olympikos, with your ugly face. Lucilius, *Greek.* InMo, *tr. by* Sam Hamill

Omagh Post Office Rhyme. *Unknown.* FaBoVe

Omaha. Carl Sandburg. *See* Limited.

Ombre and basset laid aside. A Song on the South Sea. Anne Finch. ECWP; NOEC

Omelet of A MacLeish, The. Edmund Wilson. NYBP

O'Melia, my dear, this does everything crown! Thomas Hardy. *See* The Ruined Maid.

Omen. Birago Diop, *French.* NegPo, *tr. by* Ellen Conroy Kennedy

Omens. Sydney Goodsir Smith. FaBoTC

Omens. *Unknown, Gaelic.* RB, *tr. by* Alexander Carmichael

Omens of the Morning. Faustin Charles. NBrP

Omera. Marjorie Oludhe Macgoye. HBAPE

Omeros. Derek Walcott.
   He yawned and watched the lilac horns of his island. NoP-4

Omit needless words! Preface Shrink Lit: Elements of Style. Maurice Sagoff. NBLV

Omnes gentes plaudite. A Last Drink. *Unknown.* MiEL

Omnes Gentes Plaudite! *Unknown.* OxBSP

Omnia Somnia. Joshua Sylvester. FaBoEE

Omnibus across the bridge, An. Symphony in Yellow. Oscar Wilde. ADE; EBVV; MoBrPo; NOBVV; NoAM; OPOU; OxBSP; PFE

Omnipotent and steadfast God. John Brown's Prayer. Stephen Vincent Benét. CBCWP *Fr. John Brown's Body.*

On a Bank [or Banck] as I Sat [or Sate] a-Fishing; a Description of the Spring. Sir Henry Wotton. NOSC; SeCP
   (May Day, A.) CH

On a Bashful Shepherd. "Ephelia." PEW

On a Bath-House in which Both Men and Women Bathe. Paulus Silentiarius, *Greek.* GrAn, *tr. by* Andrew Miller

On a bed of gravel moving. A Folk Singer of the Thirties. James Dickey. GM

On a Bed of Guernsey Lilies. Christopher Smart. CABP; NOEC; PoPoPo
   ("Ye beauties! O how great the sun.") NOEC

On a Birthday. John Millington Synge. GBL; OBMV

On a Blind Girl. Baha Ad-din Zuhayr, *Arabic.* AWP, *tr. by* E. H. Palmer

On a bone-white dish. (LL) Song: "Afternoon cooking in the fall sun." Robert Hass. LoL

On a Bougainvillaea Vine at the Summer Palace [or in Haiti]. Barbara Howes. MoAmPo; NYBP

On a Box Containing his Own Works. Po Chü-i, *Chinese.* ChiP, *tr. by* Arthur Waley

On a branch covered with jade-green moss. Tune: "Sparse Shadows"—Plum Blossoms. Chiang K'uei, *Chinese.* SuSp, *tr. by* An-yan Tang

On a Bright and Summer's Morning. *Unknown.* AmFP

On a broad plain in a universe of. Matters of Policy. Charles Bernstein. FTOS

On a C.P.R. packet. (LL) Gin the Goodwife Stint. Basil Bunting. CTC; OxBoS

On a Calm Summer's Night. John Nicholson. EnLoPo

On a Carrier Who Died of Drunkenness. Byron. NBLV

On a Cat, Ageing. Sir Alexander Gray. PC

On a Catholic Childhood. Janet Campbell Hale. VoR

On a cat's fur soft as pollen. The Spring is a Cat. Jang-hi Lee, *Korean.* PC, *tr. by* Koh Chang-soo

On a Celtic Mask by Henry Moore. Horace Gregory. PoA

On a Certain Alderman. John Cunningham, *after the Greek of* Simonides. FaBoEE
   (On Alderman W———: The History of His Life.) OBCoV

On a Certain Effeminate Peer. John Winstanley. FaBoEE

On a Certain Lady at Court. Alexander Pope. NOBE; NOEC; OBEV; OxBSP; SAGP

On a Certain Lord Giving Some Thousand Pounds for a House. David Garrick. FaBoEE

On a Child Who Lived One Minute. X. J. Kennedy. HoPM; NYBP; Poetr

On a clear night in Live Oak you can see. Walking Down the Road. Adrienne Rich. NIP-4

On a Clergyman's Horse Biting Him. *Unknown.* FaBoEE; NBLV; OxBoLi
   ("Say, 'All flesh is grass'.") (LL) PFE

On a Cock at Rochester. Sir Charles Sedley. FaBoEE; NOSC; OBCoV

On a cold and frosty morning. *Unknown. See* The Mulberry Bush.

On a Cold Autumn Day. Bonnie Nims. TLR

On a Cold Day I Climbed Tiger Hill With Professor Ho. At the Time, the Local Prefect Had Prohibited Pleasure Excursions and Feasts, But the Mountain Was Quiet and Tranquil, So We Stayed All Day. Mo Shih-lung, *Chinese.* CoBLCP, *tr. by* Jonathan Chaves

On a cold frosty morning in the month of September. Wreck of the Old 97. David Graves George. GM

On a cold night. Solitary. Lance Henson. HATNAP

On a cold night I came through the cold rain. James Vincent Cunningham. HAP; TRP; VCAP

On a cold winter day the snow came down. Proud Little Spruce Fir. Jeannie Kirby. BoTP

On a Columnar Self. Emily Dickinson. APN-2; NoP-4

On a Contentious Companion. John Hoskyns. FaBoEE

On a Crab. P'i Jih-hsiu, *Chinese.* SuSp, *tr. by* William H. Nienhauser

On a Curate's Complaint of Hard Duty. Jonathan Swift. OBCoV; SCGP; TIRV

On a dark and stormy night. The Wreck of the Royal Palm. *Unknown.* AmFP

On a dark night. John F. Deane. BiHa

On a Dark Road. Robert Herrick. *See* The Night-Piece, to Julia.

On a date with a charming young bird. Limerick. *Unknown.* PeLi

On a day. Tanka. Tawara Machi, *Japanese.* MJT, *tr. by* Makoto Ueda

On a day—alack the day! The Blossom. Shakespeare. AEP; GTBS-P; OBEV *Fr. Love's Labour's Lost.*

On a day long and wet we fall upon. Arriving. Daniel Halpern. HoPM

On a day when i would have believed. At Jonestown. Lucille Clifton. NAAAL

On a day when smoke lies down in alleys. Looking Both Ways Before Crossing. John Woods. CoAmPo

On a Dead Child. Robert Bridges. CMoP; EBEV; LiTM; NOBE; NOBVV; NoAM; OBMV; OBNC; OxAEP-2; SCGP

On a Dead Hostess. Hilaire Belloc. MoBrPo

On a dead man's toe. (LL) Latin Night at the Pawnshop. Martín Espada. TRP; WWSi

On a Death's Head. Elizabeth Tollet. ECWP

On a dirt road lies a dead beetle. Seen from Above. Wislawa Szymborska, *Polish.* BLT, *tr. by* Magnus J. Krynski *and* Robert A. Maguire

On a Discovery Made Too Late. Coleridge. GSo; Son *Fr.* Effusions.

On a Distinguished Politician. J. E. Thorold Rogers. FaBoEE

On a Dog of Lord Eglinton's. Robert Burns. OxBSP

On a Dolphin. Anyte, *Greek.* GrAn, *tr. by* John Heath-Stubbs *and* Carol A. Whiteside

On a Drop of Dew. Andrew Marvell. *See see also* Ros.

On a Faded Violet. Shelley. PFE

On a Fair Beggar. Philip Ayres. EnLoPo

On a Fair Lady, Looking in the Glass. Richard Leigh. NOSC

On a Falling Group in the Last Judgement of Michael Angelo, in the Cappella Sistina. Washington Allston. APN-1

On a Favorite Cat Drowned in a Tub of Gold Fishes. Thomas Gray. *See* Ode on the Death of a Favourite [*or* Favorite] Cat, Drowned in a Tub [*or* Bowl] of Gold Fishes.

On a Feast. Francis Quarles. ChIV-2

On a Female Rope-Dancer. *Unknown.* LiLi; NOEC

On a Field Trip at Fredericksburg. Dave Jeddie Smith. HCAP; PoPoPo

On a Fifteenth-Century Flemish Angel. David Ray. CRP

On a Fine Crop of Peas Being Spoiled by a Storm. Henry Jones. OBGa

On a flat road runs the well-train'd runner. The Runner. Walt Whitman. BLT; InPK-6; InPS-3; SAmP

On a Flimmering Floom You Shall Ride. Carl Sandburg. OBAL

On a Fly Drinking out of [*or* from] His Cup. William Oldys. ImPo; OBEV; OxAEP-1

　(Fly, The.) SCGP

On a Forsaken Lark's Nest. Mathilde Blind. VWP

On a Fortification at Boston Begun by Women. Benjamin Tompson. NOSC; SCAP

On a Fowler. Isidorus, *Greek.* AWP, *tr. by* William Cowper

On a Frightful Dream. John Codrington Bampfylde. NOEC

On a General Election. Hilaire Belloc. FaBoEE; NOBE; NOBL; OBSV; OxBTC

　(On a Great Election.) OxBoLi

On a Gentleman Marrying His Cook. Colin Ellis. FaBoEE

On a Gentleman's Complaining to a Lady That He Could Not Eat Meat. *Unknown.* ECWP

On a Gentlewoman that Sung and Played upon a Lute. William Strode. NOSC

On a Gentlewoman Walking in the Snow. William Strode. *See* Chloris in the Snow.

On a Girdle. Edmund Waller. AWP; BeJo; GLoP; GTBS-P; ImPo; InPK-6; NAEL-1; NOSC; NoP-4; OBEV; PoE; PoRA; SCGP; TFi

On a gnarled and naked tree. (LL) Song for a Dark Girl. Langston Hughes. AmPP; NAAAL; NAAL-2; NoP-4; PoBA; SAmP

On a Good Leg and Foot. William Strode. NOSC

On a Government Surveyor. Albert Brodrick. PeSAV

On a Great Election. Hilaire Belloc. *See* On a General Election.

On a green island in the Main Street traffic. Pro Patria. Constance Carrier. AFr; NYBP; WPE

On a Grey-haired Old Lady Knitting at an Orchestral Concert. Suzanne Gardinier. CBAP

On a High House in Byzantium. Paulus Silentiarius, *Greek.* GrAn, *tr. by* Andrew Miller

On a highway over the marshland. Flames and Dangling Wire. Robert Gray. BMAP; NOBAu

On a hill far away. The Old Rugged Cross. George Bennard. AH

On a hill near Petersburg. James Hugo Johnston. Maggie Pogue Johnson. CBWP-4

On a hill there blooms a palm. Hayyim Nahman Bialik. *Fr.* Songs of the People. AWP, *tr. by* Maurice Samuel

On a holy day when sails were blowing southward. The Straying Student. Austin Clarke. BIrV; CIP-2; NOIV

On a Honey Bee [*or* To a Honey Bee]. Philip Freneau. TAP

On a Hopeful Youth. Owen Feltham [*or* Feltham]. NOSC

On a hot summer Sunday. The Cemetery at Academy, California. Philip Levine. NYBP; WeT

On a Hound. Simonides, *Greek.* PGA, *tr. by* Kenneth Rexroth

On a July night, the country's. Introduction to a Poem. Nikolai Ivanovich Glazkov, *Russian.* TCRP, *tr. by* Daniel Weissbort

On *a* Juniper-Tree, Cut Down to Make Busks. Aphra Behn. KTR

On a Lady Indifferent to Poetry. Sappho, *Greek.* STV, *tr. by* John Frederick Nims

On a Lady, Preached into the Colic, by One of Her Lovers. Aaron Hill. ECEV

On a Lady Who P-ssed [*or* P——st] at the Tragedy of Cato. Alexander Pope. OxBSP

On a Lady's Writing. Anna Laetitia Barbauld. PEW

On a Landscape by Myself. Yün Shou-p'ing, *Chinese.* CoBLCP, *tr. by* Jonathan Chaves

On a leaf, a leaf. O. Mabson Southard. HA

On a Line by John Ashbery. James Bertolino. CMAP

On a Line from Valéry. Carolyn Kizer. BAP-95; FFC

On a Little Bird. Martin Donisthorpe Armstrong. CH

On a Little Boy's Endeavouring to Catch a Snake. Thomas Foxton. OxBChV

On a little piece of wood. Mr. and Mrs. Spikky Sparrow. Edward Lear. OxBChV

On a long, long trail, a dark ship. A Ship. Gregor Strnisa, *Slovenian.* CEEP, *tr. by* Vasa D. Mihailovich

On a lorry the centre of a gaping crowd. W. H. Auden. *Fr.* A Happy New Year. OBSV

On a Lover of Books. Geoffrey Grigson. FaBoEE

On a Magazine Sonnet. Russell Hillard Loines. OBAL

On a Maid of Honour Seen by a Scholar in Somerset Garden. Thomas Randolph. OBGa

On a Man Run Over by an Omnibus. Henry Luttrell. FaBoEE

On a man that died for men. (LL) Jim Bludso of the Prairie Belle. John Milton Hay. APN-2; FaBoBe

On a mid-December day. Since. W. H. Auden. CBLP; InPS-3

On a Midsummer Eve. Thomas Hardy. FaBoVe

On a midsummer night, on a night that was eerie with stars. August Night. Sara Teasdale. MoAmPo

On a Miscellany of Poems. John Gay.

　When Pope's harmonious Muse with pleasure roves. EPCY

On a mole-black night when the stars are bright. Andromeda. Judith Nicholls. SpW

On a Monday mornin' it began to rain. Jay Gould's Daughter. *Unknown.* AS

On a Monday morning early as my wandering steps did lead me. The Boys of Mullabaun [*or* Mullaghbawn]. *Unknown.* BIrV

On a Monday morning it began to rain. On the Charlie So Long. *Unknown.* AS

On a Monument to Martí. Walter Adolphe Roberts. PBCV; TTY

On a Moonlit Night, Sent to my Brothers and Sisters. Po Chü-i, *Chinese.* SuSp, *tr. by* Irving Lo

On a morning such as this. Veteran. Lola Ridge. WPE

On a mossy bank reclined. The Stolen Kiss. Robert Dodsley. ECEV

On a mountain of sugar-candy. Arno Holz. PChr, *tr. by* Babette Deutsch *Fr.* Phantasus. AWP, *tr. by* Ludwig Lewisohn

On a needful day. Comfort-Maker. Jerry W. Ward Jr. ISC

On a New Duke. *Unknown.* FaBoEE

On a Night of Snow. Elizabeth Jane Coatsworth. AYFP; MoAmPo; OBCA

On a Night of the Full Moon. Audre Lorde. NALW

　("Delightful.") (LL) CPO

On a Noisy Polemic. Robert Burns. FaBoEE

On a Nomination to the Legion of Honour. *Unknown.* FaBoEE

On a Nook Called Fairyland. Henrietta Cordelia Ray. CBWP-3

On a Note of Triumph. Norman Corwin.

　Man unto His Fellow Man. TrJP

On a Nun. Jacopo Vittorelli, *Italian.* AWP, *tr. by* Byron

On a Painted Woman. Shelley. NBLV

On a Painting "Ancient Trees and Flowing Stream." Yün Shou-p'ing, *Chinese.* CoBLCP, *tr. by* Jonathan Chaves

On a Painting by Hsia Kuei Entitled "Returning in Wind and Snow to a Village Home." Kao Ch'i, *Chinese.* SuSp, *tr. by* Irving Y. Lo

On a Painting by Patient B of the Independence State Hospital for the Insane. Donald Justice. CoAP; CoAmPo; NoAM; WeT

On a Painting by Wang the Clerk of Yen Ling. Su Tung-p'o, *Chinese.* BLT, *tr. by* Kenneth Rexroth

On a Painting of a Knight-Errant. Cheng Hsieh, *Chinese.* CoBLCP, *tr. by* Jonathan Chaves

On a Painting of a Woman Shown Half-Length. T'ang Yin, *Chinese.* CoBLCP, *tr. by* Jonathan Chaves

On a Painting of Ants and Butterflies. Huang T'ing-chien, *Chinese.* SuSp, *tr. by* Michael E. Workman

On a Painting of Mushrooms. Yün Shou-p'ing, *Chinese.* CoBLCP, *tr. by* Jonathan Chaves

On a Painting of the Radiant Emperor's Night Revels by Candlelight. Kao Ch'i, *Chinese.* SuSp, *tr. by* Irving Y. Lo

On a Pair of Garters. Sir John Davies. SiPS

On a Parisian Boulevard. James Kenneth Stephen. NOBL *Fr.* England and America.

On a Pet Grasshopper. Aristodicus of Rhodes, *Greek.* PGA, *tr. by* Kenneth Rexroth

On a Photo of Sgt. Ciardi a Year Later. John Ciardi. AiP

On a Photograph of My Mother at Seventeen. Miller Williams. MT

On a Phrase from Southern Ohio. James Wright. LTA

On A Picture. John Gray. ADE

On a Picture by Michele Da Verona, of Arion as a Boy Riding upon a Dolphin. Anne Ridler. PoA

On a Picture by Poussin Representing Shepherds in Arcadia. John Addington Symonds. FaBoBe

On a Picture of Your House. Douglas G. Jones. NOBC

On a Picture Painted by Herself[, Representing Two Nimphs of Diana's]. Anne Killigrew. KTR; NOSC; PEW

On a piece of our honeymoon. Honeymoon. Barry Goldensohn. NAmP90

On a Piece of Tapestry. George Santayana. APN-2

On a piece of toilet paper. Bladder Song. Leonard Nathan. BLT

On a Piece of Unwrought Pipeclay. John Frederick Bryant. NOEC

On a Pig's Head. Charles Tomlinson. NoAM

On a Poet. Henry Parrot. FaBoEE

On a poet's lips I slept. The Poet's Dream. Shelley. GTBS-P, *ll.* 737–749; EPCY; TOF, *ll.* 737–751 *Fr.* Prometheus Unbound. NOBRP; OAEL-2

On a Political Prisoner. W. B. Yeats. FaBoPV; IIP; OAEL-2; OBMV

On a Portrait of Wordsworth by B. R. Haydon. Elizabeth Barrett Browning. EPCY; HeIP-4

(Sonnet on Mr Haydon's Portrait of Mr Wordsworth.) Ro

On a post. Tanka. Mori Ōgai, *Japanese.* MJT, *tr.* by Makoto Ueda

On a Prize Crucifix by a Student Sculptor. Robert Logan. CAPP-1

On a Puritan. Hilaire Belloc. FaBoEE

On a Puritanicall Lock-Smith. William Camden. FaBoEE

On a Quiet Conscience. Charles I, King of England. CH

On a rainy night, the house is desolate. On Seeing a Firefly in My Room. Yang Chi, *Chinese.* CoBLCP, *tr.* by Jonathan Chaves

On a Raised Beach. "Hugh MacDiarmid." FaBoTC

On a Recent Protest against Social Conditions. David Posner. NYBP

On a Recollected Road. Amir Gilbo'a, *Hebrew.* MHP, *tr.* by Ruth Finer Mintz

On a Replica of the Parthenon. Donald Davidson. FuPo

On a Return from Egypt. Keith Douglas. NoP-4

On a Rhine Steamer. James Kenneth Stephen. FaBoA; NOBL; NOBVV; OBCoV; PeLV *Fr.* England and America.

On a Ring. Asclepiades, *Greek.* GrAn, *tr.* by Alan Marshfield

On a rock, Bishop of Cloyne. Berkeley. Mairtin O Direain. BiHa

On a rock, whose haughty brow. A Pindaric Ode. Thomas Gray. *Fr.* Bard, The [A Pindaric Ode]. GTBS-P; NOBE; NOEC; OAEL-1; OxAEP-1

On A Romantic Lady. Mary Monck. ECWP; NOEC; RACG

On a Rose in December. Ebenezer Elliot. FaBoEE

On a Ruined House in a Romantic Country. Coleridge. *See* The House That Jack Built.

On a Sabbath eve, at dusk on a summer day. A Song of Lies on Sabbath Eve. Yehuda Amichai, *Hebrew.* PoSu, *tr.* by Chana Bloch

On a Saturday afternoon in summer. Under House Arrest. Dennis Brutus. AF

On a Scooter. Desmond A. Greig. PeSA

On a Sea-Storm nigh the Coast. Richard Steere. SCAP

On a Seal. Plato, *Greek.* AWP; FaBoEE, *tr.* by Thomas Stanley

On a Sermon Preach'd Sept. the 6th, 1697 on These Words: You Have Sold Your Selves for Nought. Sarah Fyge Egerton. KTR

On a Seven-Day Diary. Alan Dugan. OBAL

On a Shipmate, Pero Moniz, Dying at Sea. Luis de Camões, *Portuguese.* PeSAV, *tr.* by Roy Campbell

On a sideboard where the sun falls. (LL) A Man in Blue. James Schuyler. FTOS; PmAP

On a Similar Occasion for the Year 1790. William Cowper. NOCV

On a Similar Occasion for the Year 1792. William Cowper. NOCV

On a Small Bath. *Unknown, Greek.* GrAn, *tr.* by Robin Skelton

On a small six-acre farm dwelt John Grist the miller. Under the Drooping Willow Tree. *Unknown.* OxBoLi

On a Snail. Su Shih. SuSp, *tr.* by Irving Y. Lo *Fr.* Two Poems on Insect Painting by Candidate Yin.

On a Soldier Fallen in the Philippines. William Vaughn Moody. NOBA

On a Soldier Killed in the Great War. R. Williams Parry, *Welsh.* OBWVE, *tr.* by H. Idris Bell

On a Spaniel Called Beau Killing a Young Bird. William Cowper. FaBoCh

On a spring morning of young wood, green wood. Burning the Dreams. Muriel Rukeyser. AF

On a squeaking cart, they push the usual stuff. A Removal from Terry Street. Douglas Dunn. FaBoMo; FaBoVe; NoP-4; OxBC

On a Squirrel Crossing the Road in Autumn, in New England. Richard Eberhart. AFr; HeIP-4; LiTM; Poetsp

On a starless night and still. On Being Asked to Write a School Hymn. Charles Causley. OxAEP-2

On a starred [*or* starr'd] night Prince Lucifer uprose. Lucifer in Starlight. George Meredith. AWP; CH; ChIV-1; EBVV; EnVR; HAP; ImPo; InPK-6; NAEL-2; NOBE; NOBVV; OAEL-2; OBEV; OBNC; PBMP; PoE; PoEL-5; SCGP; Son; TFi; UnPo

On a starry night. Tanka. Maekawa Samio, *Japanese.* MJT, *tr.* by Makoto Ueda

On a starry, wintry night. The Christ Child. Mary Weston Fordham. CBWP-2

On a Statue of Pan. *Unknown, Greek.* GrAn, *tr.* by W. G. Shepherd

On a Stingy Beau. John Winstanley. FaBoEE

On a Stone Thrown at a Very Great Man, But Which Missed Him. "Peter Pindar." NBLV

On a stony hill. Yerokastrinos. Karen Chamberlain. APAD

On a summer day in the month of May. The Big Rock Candy Mountains. *Unknown.* FaBoA; NOBA

On a summer night in Odessa. (LL) Dvonya. Louis Simpson. NNaP; NOBA

On a summer's day when the sea [*or* wave] was rippled. The Ship That Never Returned. Henry Clay Work. BLPA

On a summer's day while the waves were rippling, with a quiet and gentle breeze. Henry Clay Work. *See* The Ship That Never Returned.

On a Sunbeam. Thomas Heyrick. NOSC

On a Sundial. Hilaire Belloc. FaBoEE

On a sunny brae alone I lay. A Day Dream. Emily Jane Brontë. NALW

On a thin rope. The Strangled. Antonin Bartusek, *German.* CEEP, *tr.* by Ewald Osers

On a throne of new gold the Son of the Sky. The Emperor. Tu Fu, *Chinese.* AWP, *tr.* by E. Powys Mathers

On a Time the Amorous Silvy. The Wakening. *Unknown.* GBL; OBEV

On A Toad. Su Shih, *Chinese.* SuSp, *tr.* by Irving Y. Lo; APo, *tr.* by Lo, Irving Y. *Fr.* Two Poems on Insect Painting by Candidate Yin.

On a tree by a river a little tom-tit. Ko-Ko's Song. Sir William Schwenck Gilbert. ImPo; NoP-4 *Fr.* The Mikado.

On a Tree Fallen across the Road. Robert Frost. RB

On a tributary of the Amazon. The Lass of Aughrim. Paul Muldoon. NoAM; PBCIP

On a Vase of Gold-Fish. Charles Tennyson Turner. NOBVV

On a verdant summer islet. Burial of a Fairy Queen. Mary E. Tucker. CBWP-1

On a very fine gander. (LL) Old Mother Goose. Mother Goose. ReMoGo

On a very hot Independence Day. Sonnet No. 21. Mark Ameen. GLP

On a Violet in Her Breast. Thomas Stanley. NOSC

On a Virtuous Young Gentlewoman That Died Suddenly. William Cartwright. HAP; OBEV

On a Visit to Ch'ung Chen Taoist Temple. Y'ü Hs'üan-Chi, *Chinese.* ChiPo; PBWP, *tr.* by Kenneth Rexroth *and* Ling Chung

On a Vulgar Error. C. S. Lewis. OxBTC

On a War-worker, 1916. Arundell James Kennedy Esdaile. NSI

On a warm autumn evening, if I shut both eyes. Exotic Scent. Charles Baudelaire, *French.* EP; FLP, *tr.* by Alistair Elliot

On a wet night, laden with books for luggage. The Poet on the Island. Richard Murphy. CIP-2

On a Wet Summer. John Codrington Bampfylde. NOEC

On a Whore. John Hoskyns. FaBoEE

On A Wife. Francis Burdett Money-Coutts. OxBSP

On a winter's night long time ago. Noël. Hilaire Belloc. UV

On a withered branch. Basho, *Japanese.* TAL, *tr.* by Harold G. Henderson

On a Woman. Robert Williams, *Welsh.* OBWVE, *tr.* by H. Idris Bell

On a wooded hillside by a river, a woman pauses. Ukranian Pastorals. Steve Orlen. WeT

On a Worthless Politician. *Unknown, Greek.* GrAn, *tr.* by Peter Jay

On a Young Man and an Old Man. Edward May. OxBSP

On a young pine. Tanka. Masaoka Shiki, *Japanese.* MJT, *tr.* by Ueda, Makoto

On a Young Wife. Julianus of Egypt, *Greek.* GrAn, *tr.* by Willis Barnstone

On Addison. Alexander Pope. *See* Atticus ("Peace to all such! but were there one whose fires").

On Aesthetics, More or Less. Peter Kane Dufault. NYBP

On African Writing. Jack A. Mapanje. HBAPE

On afternoons of drowsy calm. Afternoon Service at Mellstock. Thomas Hardy. PeECV

On Aging. Maya Angelou. LiLi

On Alabama Ave., Paterson, NJ, 1954. Rachel De Vries. UnSA

On Alderman W———: The History of His Life. John Cunningham. *See* On a Certain Alderman.

On Alexis. Plato, *Greek.* AWP, *tr.* by Thomas Stanley

On alien ground, breathing an alien air. Where a Roman Villa Stood, above Freiburg. Mary Elizabeth Coleridge. OBNC

On All Fours. Benjamin Péret, *French.* PFTM, tr. by Charles Simic and Michael Benedikt

On all these living pages of God's book. James Russell Lowell. *See* To the Dandelion.

On an Aberdeen Favourite. *Unknown.* FaBoEE

On an accordion which had seen plenty. The Blind Man. Konstantin Mikhailovich Simonov, *Russian.* TCRP, tr. by Lubov Yakovleva

On an Æolian Harp. George Cabot Lodge. APN-2

On an Air of Rameau. Arthur Symons. OBNC

On an Ancient Tomb East of the Village. Po Chü-i, *Chinese.* TAL, tr. by Robert Payne

On an Anniversary. John Millington Synge. FaBoEE; NOIV; OBMV

On an average afternoon men lay down. A Reminder to the Current President. Christopher Howell. CDa

On an early Sunday in April, a feeble day. An Extract from Addresses to the Academy of Fine Ideas. Wallace Stevens. LiTM

On an East Wind from the Wars. Alan Dugan. AF

On an Engraving by Casserius. Alec Derwent Hope. CBAP

On an Hour[e]-Glass[e]. John Hall. MeLP

On an Indian Tomineois, the Least of Birds. Thomas Heyrick. NOSC

On an Infant. Lucian, *Greek.* OBCVT, tr. by William Cowper

On an Infant Dying as Soon as Born. Charles Lamb. GTBS-P; IMW; OBEV

On an Invitation to the United States. Thomas Hardy. AWP; AiP; FaBoA

On an Inyanga Road. Noel H. Brettell. PeSAV

On an Island. "Ethna Carbery." WPE

On an Island. John Millington Synge. BIrV; FaBoVe; MoBrPo; OxBSP; PeVV

On an island the soft hue of memory. Hugging the Jukebox. Naomi Shihab Nye. NMM-2

On an Old Woman. Lucilius, *Greek.* AWP; PFE, tr. by William Cowper

On an outing with seventeen Czechs. Limerick. *Unknown.* PeLi

On an Unfinished Statue. George Santayana. APN-2

On an Unsociable Family. Elizabeth Hands. ECWP; WoRP

On and on, always on and on. *Unknown.* ChiP, tr. by Arthur Waley *Fr.* Seventeen Old Poems.

On and On for Ever. Li Ho, *Chinese.* PLT, tr. by A. C. Graham

On and on, going on and on. Mei Sheng *and* Fu I. *Fr.* Nineteen Old Poems of the Han. CoBCP, tr. by Burton Watson

On and on, going on and on. *Unknown. See* Going on always on and on.

On and on in the white clouds. Sent to the Taoist of Dragon Mountain, Hsü Fa-leng. Liu Ch'ang-ch'ing, *Chinese.* SuSp, tr. by William H. Nienhauser

On and on we go over steppes. Refugees. Ilya Krichevsky, *Russian.* TCRP, tr. by Albert C. Todd

On Angels. Czeslaw Milosz, *Polish.* AF, tr. by Czeslaw Milosz

On Angels. W. W. Eustace Ross. MoCV

On Another's Sorrow. William Blake. AWP; FHYEP; OxAEP-2; PoEL-4; Ro *Fr.* Songs of Innocence.

On any sheet the least display of mind. (LL) A Considerable Speck. Robert Frost. MoAmPo; OBAL; PBMP; SAmP

On Apples. David Ross. NYBP

On Approaching My Birthday. Vassar Miller. NMM-2

On Archaeanassa. Plato, *Greek.* AWP, tr. by Thomas Stanley

On Arno's bosom, as he calmly flows. John Pierpont. APN-1 *Fr.* Airs of Palestine.

On Arrival. Richard Howard. TAP

On Arthur Hugh Clough. Swinburne. FaBoEE

On Asuka River. *Unknown, Japanese.* OHMPJ, tr. by Kenneth Rexroth

On August nights. Driving By. Robert Wallace. CMAP

On August the Thirteenth. Frances Darwin Cornford. WPN

On Authors and Booksellers [or Publishers]. Alexander Pope. FaBoEE

On Autumn Lake. John Ashbery. LCAP-2

On Balaam, and His Ass. Henry Colman. KSG

On Balaam's Ass. Francis Quarles. ChIV-1

On Ballycastle Beach. Medbh McGuckian. PBCIP

On Barclay's Apology for the Quakers. Matthew Green. NOEC

On beaches washed by seas. What She Said to Her Girl-Friend. Venmanipputi, *Tamil.* PBWP, tr. by A. K. Ramanujan

On Beauty [or Beauety]. James Thomson.
This happy place with all delights abounds. UV

On Becoming a Tiger. Lorna Goodison. GT

On Beer. Emperor Julian, *Greek.* PGA, tr. by Kenneth Rexroth

On Behalf of Some Irishmen Not Followers of Tradition. "Æ." IIP

On Being a Concubine. Ho Xuan Huong, *Vietnamese.* AVP, tr. by Huỳnh Sanh Thông

On Being a Householder. Alan Dugan. NoAM

On Being a Poet in Sierra Leone. Syl Cheney-Coker. HBAPE; PBMAP

On Being a Woman. Dorothy Parker. PoLF

On Being Asked for a Peace Poem. Howard Nemerov. OxBC

On Being Asked for a War Poem. W. B. Yeats. NIP-4; OBWP; OxAEP-2; PoWW

On Being Asked to Write a Poem Against the War in Vietnam. Hayden Carruth. CDa

On Being Asked to Write a Poem for 1979. Jack A. Mapanje. AF; PBMAP

On Being Asked to Write a School Hymn. Charles Causley. OxAEP-2

On Being Assigned as Military Adviser to the Garrison Army. T'ao Ch'ien, *Chinese.* CoBCP, tr. by Burton Watson

On Being Brought from Africa to America. Phillis Wheatley. ColAP; CrDW; FaBoA; ISC; NAAAL; NAAL-1; NAAL-3; NALW; NOBA; NOEC; NoP-4; TAP; TTY; WPE

On Being Cautioned against Walking on an Headland Overlooking the Sea, because It Was Frequented by a Lunatic. Charlotte Smith. ECWP; WoRP

On Being Charged with Writing Incorrectly. "The Amorous Lady." ECWP

On Being Head of the English Department. Pinkie Gordon Lane. BlSi; GT

On Being Kind to Horses. Vladimir Mayakovsky, *Russian.* TCRP, tr. by Bernard Meares

On being Removed from Hsün-yang and Sent to Chung-chou. Po Chü-i, *Chinese.* ChiP, tr. by Arthur Waley

On Being Sixty. Po Chü-i, *Chinese.* AWP; ChiP, tr. by Arthur Waley

On Bellosguardo, when the year was young. To Vernon Lee. Amy Levy. VWP

On Ben Jonson. Sidney Godolphin. BeJo; EPCY

On Ben Jonson. Mildmay Fane. *See* In Obitum Ben. Jons.

On Bertrand Russell's "Portraits from Memory." Donald Davie. FaBoTw

On better days, I bath with Wallace Stevens: dreaming his good. Another Word for Blue. John Engman. NAmP90

On Bishop Burnet's Being Set on Fire in His Closet. Thomas Parnell. ECEV

On Bismillah Khan's Shehnai. Chennavira Kanavi, *Kannada.* OMIP, tr. by A. K. Ramanujan

On black bare trees a stale cream moon. Eau-Forte. Francis Stewart [or "Frank"] Flint. OxBTC

On blood, smoke, rain and the dead. Who Knows Where. Detlev, Freiherr von Liliencron, *German.* AWP, tr. by Ludwig Lewisohn

On Blossoming. Leah Goldberg, *Hebrew.*
How shall we bring our dying heart up. MHP, tr. by Ruth Finer Mintz
Old woman, blue eyed and sun burned. MHP, tr. by Ruth Finer Mintz
Scarlet, warm and heavy in black velvet leaves. MHP, tr. by Ruth Finer Mintz
That death in his windows would rise. MHP, tr. by Ruth Finer Mintz

On blue summer evenings I'll go down the pathways. Sensation. Rimbaud, *French.* TTTS, tr. by Kenneth Koch

On Board a Boat at Chi-ning. Yüan Hung-tao, *Chinese.* CoBLCP, tr. by Jonathan Chaves

On Board Ship: Reading Yüan Chên's Poems. Po Chü-i, *Chinese.* ChiP, tr. by Arthur Waley

On Board Starship *Enterprise. Unknown.* PeLi

On Boetian Roads. Nikos Engonopoulos, *Greek.* GrIP, tr. by Kimon Friar

On Bond the Usurer. *Unknown.* NOSC

On Boston Common a red star. A Winter's Tale. Sylvia Plath. FaBoA

On Botching. John Heywood. FaBoEE

On Burroughs' Work. Allen Ginsberg. NAAL-2; NOBA

On Butler who can think without rage. John Oldham. OBSV *Fr.* A Satire.

On Button the Grave-Maker. *Unknown.* FaBoEE

On Buying a Dog. Edgar Klauber. NTCP

On Buying a Horse. *Unknown.* NBLV; RB

On Catania and Syracuse Swallowed Up by an Earthquake, from the Italian of Filicaja. Anna Seward. Son

On Catullus. Walter Savage Landor. OBEV

On certain fall mornings it is possible to walk Eighteenth. Thumbs Up. Judith Baumel. WWSi

On certain nights as soon as I lie down. The Execution. Vladimir Nabokov, *Russian.* TCRP, tr. by Vladimir Nabokov

On certain nights I hear within the screeching of the horn. Legacies. Léon Laleau. NegPo, tr. by Ellen Conroy Kennedy *Fr.* Black Music.

On Certain Wits. Howard Nemerov. HCAP; OxBC

On Change of Weathers. Francis Quarles. OxBSP

On Chao Ch'ang's Flower Paintings in Wang Po-yang's Collection. Su Shih, *Chinese.*
Hibiscus. SuSp, tr. by Irving Y. Lo
Plum Blossoms. SuSp, tr. by Irving Y. Lo
Sunflower. SuSp, tr. by Irving Y. Lo

On charts they fall like lace. Delos. Lawrence Durrell. GrIP; OxAEP-2

On Chester's fatal tree. (LL) Execution of Alice Holt. *Unknown.* OxBoV

On Children. Kahlil Gibran. OxBM; PoToHe *Fr.* The Prophet.

On Christians, Mercy Will Fall. *Unknown, Welsh.* OBWVE, *tr. by* D. Myrddin Lloyd

On Christmas Day. Robert Boyle. TIRV

On Christmas-Day. Thomas Traherne. PoEL-2

On Christmas Day I weep. Christmas Mourning. Vassar Miller. ChIV-2; MoAmPo

On Christmas day in the morning. (LL) Dame, get up and bake your pies. *Unknown.* BoTP; OxNR

On Christmas Day to My Heart. Clement Paman. NOSC

On Christmas Eve. Tanka. Shaku Chōkū, *Japanese.* MJT, *tr. by* Makoto Ueda

On Christmas Eve I turned the spit. *Unknown.* OxNR

On Christmas Eve my mother read. Christmas Eve. Edna Kingsley Walla. BoTP

On Christmas Eve the little stars. Christmas Eve. Charlotte Druitt Cole. BoTP

On Christmas morn awake did I. He Sports by Himself. Susan Miles. BXAP

On ["Who Wrote Icon Basilike" by Dr.] Christopher Wordsworth, Master of Trinity. Benjamin Hall Kennedy. FaBoEE; OBCoV

On City Streets. Margaret E. Bruner. PoToHe

On Clarastella walking in Her Garden. Robert Heath. NOSC

On Clergymen Preaching Politics. John Byrom. ECEV

On Climbing the Heights on the Ninth Day of the Ninth Moon. Tu Fu, *Chinese.* TAL, *tr. by* Robert Payne

On Climbing the Pagoda of the Temple of Gracious Benevolence with Kao Shih and Hsüeh Chü. Ts'en Shen, *Chinese.* SuSp, *tr. by* Daniel Bryant

On Climbing the Phoenix Tower at Chinling. Li Po, *Chinese.* TAL, *tr. by* Robert Payne

On Clouds. Douglas Livingstone. PeSAV

On cold winter mornings. Winter Morning. Frank Flynn. AYFP; OTCP

On Commonwealth, on Marlborough. Technologies. George Starbuck. NYBP

On Communists. Ebenezer Elliot. NBLV; NOBL (Epigram.) NOBVV

On Consulting "Contemporary Poets of the English Language." Anthony Thwaite. PeLV

On Court-Worm[e]. Ben Jonson. SeCP

On Covering the Bones of Chang Chin, the Hired Man. Liu Tsung-yüan, *Chinese.* SuSp, *tr. by* Jan W. Walls

On Craigie Hill. Stewart Conn. FaBoTC

On Cupid's bow how are my heart-strings bent. Sonnet 19. Sir Philip Sidney. NoSic *Fr.* Astrophil and Stella. AAS; SiPS

On dark nights, when thoughts fly like nightbirds. It Is Important. Gail Tremblay. WeW-3

On days when I go out. My Illness and Other Animals. Maria Jastrzebska. NBrP

On Death. Aleksandr Blok, *Russian.* TCRP, *tr. by* Geoffrey Thurley

On Death. Anne Killigrew. BoWoP; ChIV-1; KTR ("Tell me thou safest end of all our woe.") PEW

On Death. Francis Quarles. PeECV *Fr.* Divine Fancies.

On Death and Love. Janet Campbell Hale. VoR

On Death's domain intent I fix my eyes. To a Gentleman and Lady on the Death of the Lady's Brother and Sister, and a Child of the Name Avis, Aged One Year. Phillis Wheatley. BlSi

On deck. And love's the burning boy. (LL) Casabianca. Elizabeth Bishop. APAD; FaBoWP; OxBSP; PiM

On Dennis. Alexander Pope. FaBoEE

On Dewdrop. Wei Ying-wu, *Chinese.* SuSp, *tr. by* Irving Y. Lo

On Digital Extremities, *limerick.* Frank Gelett Burgess. PeLi

On Dinah. Francis Quarles. ChIV-1

On Diogenes the Cynic. Antiphilus, *Greek.* GrAn, *tr. by* W. S. Merwin

On Discovering a Butterfly. Vladimir Nabokov. NYBP

On Diverse Deviations. Maya Angelou. BlSi

On Don Surly. Ben Jonson. FaBoEE; NAEL-1

On Donne's First Poem. Coleridge. Ro

On Donne's Poetry. Coleridge. EPCY; NAEL-2; OAEL-2; PFE; UV ("Wit's forge and fire-blast, meaning's press and screw.") (LL) PFE

On Door Jambs. Roger Bower. EC2

On Dorinda. Charles Sackville. OxBSP (Song: "Dorinda's sparkling wit, and eyes.") NOSC

On Dorothea Lange's Photograph "Migrant Mother" (1936). Helen Pinkerton. FFC

On Double Creek. James Still. MT

On Dr. Evans Cutting Down a Row of Trees. *Unknown.* FaBoEE

On Dr. Keene, Bishop of Chester. Thomas Gray. FaBoEE

On Dr. Lettsom. *Unknown.* FaBoEE

On Dreams. Jonathan Swift. BIrV

On Dreams, October 15, 1782. Sir Samuel Egerton Brydges. Son

On dull mornings. Mrs. Busk. Sir Osbert Sitwell. OxBTC

On Dullness. Alexander Pope. OxBSP

On Duty. Frederick D'Aguiar. PBCV

On Dwelling. Robert Graves. CMoP; FaBoMo; OxBSP

On ear and ear two noises too old to end. The Sea and the Skylark. Gerard Manley Hopkins. OBMV

On Early Trains. Boris Pasternak, *Russian.* TCRP, *tr. by* George Reavey

On Earth. Forugh Farrokhzad, *Persian.* BoWoP, *tr. by* Girdhard Tikku

On earth but love there is no other pleasure. (LL) Hope, like the hyaena [*or* hyena], coming to be old. Henry Constable. EnLoPo; SCGP; Son

On Earth There Is a Lamb So Small. Nikolaus Ludwig, *German.* AH, *tr. by* Sheema Z. Buehne

On Easter Day. Celia Laighton Thaxter. CTV

On Eastnor Knoll. John Masefield. CH

On Editing Scott Fitzgerald's Papers. Edmund Wilson. NYBP

On Education, December 1789. Elizabeth Bentley. WoRP

On either side the river lie. The Lady of Shalott. Tennyson. EBEvV; EBVVPR; FHYEP; InPS-3; NAEL-2; NOBE; NOBRP; NoP-4; OAEL-2; OBEV; OBNV; OBSP; OxAEP-2; PoE; TFi; TOF

On Eleanor Freeman, Who Died 1650, Aged 21. *Unknown.* OBEV

On Elizabeth Ireland. *Unknown.* FaBoEE

On Elphinston's Translation of Martial. Robert Burns. FaBoEE

On Enclosures. *Unknown. See* Epigram: On Inclosures.

On English Monsieur. Ben Jonson. AEP; NBLV; NoP-4

On Entries Emptiness. Dennis Phillips. FTOS

On Epicurus and Themistokles. Menander, *Greek.* GrAn, *tr. by* Alan Marshfield

On Epiktetos the Stoic. *Unknown, Greek.* GrAn, *tr. by* Peter Jay

On every defeat on every design they've walked with necks outstretched meticulously. On My Words. Abba Kovner, *Hebrew.* IP, *tr. by* Warren Bargad *and* Stanley F. Chyet

On Evolution. John Ciardi. OBAL

On Exodus 3: 14: "I am that I am." Matthew Prior. ChIV-1; NOCV

On Failing the Examination. Meng Chiao, *Chinese.* CoBCP, *tr. by* Burton Watson

On Fairford Windows. William Strode. NOSC

On Falling Asleep by Firelight. William Meredith. ChIV-1; KSG; NYBP; NoAM ("Isaiah said would be the serpent's meat.") (LL) KSG

On Fanny Godwin. Shelley. OBNC

On festal days; or when their work is done. James Grainger. PBCV *Fr.* The Sugar Cane.

On fields oer which the reaper's hand has passed [*or* passd]. Henry David Thoreau. APN-1 ("In subtler webs than finest summer haze.") (LL) PAR

On File. John Kendrick Bangs. PoToHe

On Finding Out that the One You Slept with the Night Before Was Murdered the Next Day. Chuck Ortleb. GLP

On Finding the Truth. Jones Very. TrCP

On First Looking in on Blodgett's Keats's "Chapman's Homer." George Starbuck. OBAL

On First Looking into Chapman's Hesiod. Peter Porter. NOBAu

On First Looking into Chapman's Homer. W. S. Brownlie. BXAP

On First Looking into Chapman's Homer. T. Griffiths. BXAP

On First Looking into Chapman's Homer. Keats. APAD; BLPA; CABP; CH; ClHu; EBEvV; EPCY; FHYEP; FaBoBe; FaBoCh; GSo; GTBS-P; HAP; HeIP-4; HoPM; ImPo; InPK-6; NAWM-2; NIP-4; NOBE; NOBRP; NoP-4; OAEL-2; OBAL; OBEV; OBNC; OPOU; OxAEP-2; PFE; PoE; PoEL-4; PoPoPo; Poetr; Ro; SCGP; SoSe-8; Son; TFi; TRP; UV (Ode: On First Looking into Chapman's Homer.) NAEL-2

On First Looking into Chapman's Homer II. Peter Peterson. BXAP

On First Looking into Krafft-Ebing's *Psychopathosexualis* [*or* Psychopathia Sexualis]. Oliver St. John Gogarty. UV

On First Looking into Loeb's Horace. Lawrence Durrell. FaBoMo; LiTM

On First Returning from Taking the Examinations: Feelings at Cloud-Stop Pavilion. Wen Cheng-ming, *Chinese.* CoBLCP, *tr. by* Jonathan Chaves

On foot I climb Pei-mang Slope. Written on Parting from Mr. Ying. Ts'ao Chih, *Chinese.* CoBCP, *tr. by* Burton Watson

On Foot I Had to Walk Through the Solar Systems. Edith Södergran, *German.* IFJa; WPoS, *tr. by* Stina Katchadourian

On Fortune. Elizabeth I, Queen of England. PBWP; WPE

On four-horse coach, whose luggage pierced the sky. Past and Present. R. E. Egerton Warburton. NOBVV

On Francis Drake. *Unknown.* NOSC; PBRV

On Freedom. James Russell Lowell. ImGa *Fr.* Stanzas on Freedom.

On Freedom and Ambition. Oliver Goldsmith. NOIV *Fr.* The Travel[l]er; or, A Prospect of Society.

On Fridays he'd open a can of Jax. My Father's Love Letters [*or* Loveletters]. Yusef Komunyakaa. ISC; NAmP90; PoPoPo; WeT

On Frosty Days. David Campbell. CBAP

On Fruition. Sir Charles Sedley. NOSC

On Fujiyama / Under the midsummer moon. Akahito, *Japanese.* OHPJ, *tr.* by Kenneth Rexroth

On Galveston Beach. Barbara Howes. MoAmPo

On Gask's deserted ancient hall. The Ghost of Fadon. Joanna Baillie. NOBRP

On gay Anacreon's joy-inspiring line. On the Translation of Anacreon. Horace Walpole. FaBoEE

On Gay Wallpaper. William Carlos Williams. MeMAP; MoAmPo; TAP

On General Paoli and the Corsican Struggle for Liberty. Anna Laetitia Barbauld. ECWP *Fr.* Corsica.

On Genessarett. Josephine D. Henderson Heard. CBWP-4

On Geoffrey Grigson. Cyril Connolly. OBCoV

On George Herbert's "The Temple" Sent to a Gentlewoman. Richard Crashaw. *See* On Mr. G. Herberts Booke, The Temple.

On getting a card. Poem. William Carlos Williams. VGW

On Getting a Natural. Dudley Randall. PoBA

On Giles and Joan. Ben Jonson. NAEL-1; NOBL

On Giving Up Smoking. Lawrence Spooner. NOEC *Fr.* A Looking-Glass for Smokers.

On Glaister's Hill. William Jeffrey.
   Carlyle on Burns. OxBS

On God's Favour. Francis Quarles. PeECV *Fr.* Divine Fancies.

On God's Law. Francis Quarles. ChIV-1

On Gold. Samuel Johnson. *Fr.* The Vanity of Human Wishes [The Tenth Satire of Juvenal Imitated]. EBEV; ECEV; NOEC; OAEL-1; OxAEP-1; PoEL-3; TFi

On golden seas of drink, so the Greek poet said. Alcohol. Louis MacNeice. LiTM

On Grafting. Thomas Randolph. GaP

On Groin. Ben Jonson. NOSC

On Growing Old. John Masefield. CMoP; ImPo; LiTM; MoBrPo; PoLF; PoRA; SAGP

On Growing Up the Darker Berry. Harriet Jacobs. ISC

On Guard. Meir Wieseltier, *Hebrew.* IP, *tr.* by Warren Bargad *and* Stanley F. Chyet

On Gustavus Adolphus, King of Sweden. Sir Thomas Roe. FaBoEE

On Gut. Ben Jonson. NoP-4; PoPoPo

On Harting Down. Thomas Sturge Moore. OxBTC

On Hats and Things. Mcavoy Layne. CDa

On Having Been an Experimental Sacred Cow for Four Years, and a Token African on Faculty. Kofi Awoonor. HBAPE

On Having Piles. Sir Walter Scott. FaBoEE

On Hayley. William Blake.
   ("Do be my enemy—for friendship's sake.") (LL) OxBoV
   ("To forgive enemies H——does pretend.") OxBoV

On Hearing a Lady Praise a Certain Rev. Doctor's Eyes. George Outram. EBVV

On Hearing a Symphony of Beethoven. Edna St. Vincent Millay. LiTM; MoAmPo

On Hearing a Woman Mourn Her Husband. Ho Xuan Huong, *Vietnamese.* AVP, *tr.* by Huỳnh Sanh Thông

On Hearing It Has Been Proclaimed in the Chapterhouse of Ireland That the Friars Make No More Songs or Verses. Pádraigín Haicéad, *Irish.* NOIV, *tr.* by Thomas Kinsella

On Hearing James W. Riley Read. Joseph Cotter, Sr.. AAP

On Hearing of the Intention of a Gentleman to Purchase the Poet's Freedom. George Moses Horton. AAP; APN-1; NAAAL; PAR

On Hearing Prokofieff's Grotesque for Two Bassoons, Concertina and Snare-Drums. Louis Untermeyer. BXAP

On Hearing Someone Sing a Poem by Yüan Chên. Po Chü-i, *Chinese.* ChiP, *tr.* by Arthur Waley

On Hearing that Holders of the *Chin-shih* Degree Are Dealing in Tea. Mei Yao Ch'en, *Chinese.* SuSp, *tr.* by Jonathan Chaves

On Hearing That San-p'ing's Newly Brewed Chrysanthemum Wine Is Ready to Drink—Investigating with a Poem. Pien Kung, *Chinese.* CoBLCP, *tr.* by Jonathan Chaves

On Hearing That the Sea-Barbarians Are About To Attack Hu-chou—Expressing My Feelings to Tzu-yü. Tsung Ch'en, *Chinese.* CoBLCP, *tr.* by Jonathan Chaves

On Hearing That the Students of Our New University Have Joined the Agitation against Immoral Literature. W. B. Yeats. MoP; NoAM

On Hearing That Torture Was Suppressed throughout the Austrian Dominions. John Codrington Bampfylde. Son

On Hearing the Airlines Will Use a Psychological Profile to Catch Potential Skyjackers. Stephen Dunn. AmPA

On Hearing the First Cuckoo. Richard Church. OBMV

On Hearing the Marsh Bird's Water Cry. Duane Niatum. CDW

On Hearing the News of the Japanese Surrender. Liu Ya-tzu, *Chinese.* SuSp, *tr.* by Wu-chi Liu

On Hearing the Rail Cry. Nguyễn Khuyến, *Vietnamese.* AVP, *tr.* by Huỳnh Sanh Thông

On Heaven. Ford Madox Ford. CTC

On Hellespont, guilty of true love's blood. Marlowe. NoSic; OAEL-1; PoE; PoEL-2 *Fr.* Hero and Leander. AAS

On her arms. (LL) A Dream of Glass Bangles. Agha Shahid Ali. OpBo; WeT

On her beautiful face there are smiles of grace. A Pretty Girl. J. Gordon Coogler. OBAL

On Her Blindness. Priscilla Pointon. ECWP *Fr.* To the Critics.

On Her Brother. Al-Khansa, *Arabic.* BoWoP, *tr.* by Willis Barnstone

On Her Brother Sakhr. Al-Khansa, *Arabic.* BoWoP, *tr.* by Willis Barnstone

On her chest. (LL) Motherhood. May Swenson. NoP-4

(On Her Decision to Stop Wearing Clothes). Mahadevi, *Kannada.* WPoS, *tr.* by Jane Hirshfield

On her good name. (LL) Her Eyes. John Crowe Ransom. LiTM; MeMAP; OBAL

On her head. (LL) Eight Sandbars on the Takano River. Gary Snyder. NOBA; VGW

On Her Loving Two Equally. Aphra Behn. NALW; NIP-4

On her most lonely mysteries. W. B. Yeats. *See* He Remembers Forgotten Beauty.

On Her Own Birthday. Judith Madan. ECWP

On her side, reclining on her elbow So-and-So Reclining on Her Couch. Wallace Stevens. AmPP; LiTM; NOBA

On her soft lap he sat, and caught the sounds. (LL) Ye green-robed Dryads, oft at dusky eve. Joseph Warton. ECEV, *ll.* 1–15; NOEC

On her 36th birthday, Thomas had shown her. Wingfoot Lake. Rita Dove. PoPoPo

On Her Vanity. Wilfrid Scawen Blunt. GSo

On Her Way. Gertrude Stein. PFTM

On her white breast a sparkling cross she wore. Alexander Pope. *Fr.* The Rape of the Lock[, an Heroi-Comical Poem]. FHYEP; HAP; ImPo; OAEL-1; OBNV; PeLV; PoEL-3

On high, the moon must wax and wane by turns. A Farewell Song. Huỳnh Thúc Kháng, *Vietnamese.* AVP, *tr.* by Huỳnh Sanh Thông

On him the unpetitioned heavens descend. A Counsel of Moderation. Francis Thompson. MoBrPo

On him was her soft dead body. The Body. Yona Wallach, *Hebrew.* IP, *tr.* by Warren Bargad *and* Stanley F. Chyet

On Himself. Callimachus, *Greek.* GrAn, *tr.* by Peter Jay

On Himself. Cyril Connolly. OBCoV

On Himself. Robert Herrick. BeJo

On Himself. Robert Herrick. *See* On Himselfe ("I fear no earthly powers").

On Himself. Robert Herrick. *See* On Himselfe ("I will no longer kiss").

On Himself. Walter Savage Landor. FaBoEE

On Himself. James Russell Lowell. *See* Lowell.

On Himself. William Oldys. FaBoEE

On Himself. Matthew Prior. FaBoEE
   (Epitaph on Himself.) OBCoV

On Himself, limerick. D. G. Rossetti. FaBoEE

On Himself. David Wright. OPOU

On Himself, upon Hearing What Was His Sentence. James Graham, Marquess of Montrose. *See* His Metrical Prayer.

On Himself[e] ("I fear[e] no earthly powers"). Robert Herrick. CaPo; CavPo; PFE

On Himself[e] ("I will no longer kiss"). Robert Herrick. CaPo; CavPo

On Himselfe ("I'll [*or* Il'e] write no more of Love; but now repent"). Robert Herrick. CaPo

On Himselfe ("Let me not live, if I not love"). Robert Herrick. CaPo

On Himselfe ("Weepe for the dead, for they have lost this light"). Robert Herrick. FaBoEE; NOSC

On his airy perch among the branches. The Fox and the Crow. Jean de La Fontaine, *French.* NAWM-2; OBVE, *tr.* by Marianne Moore

On his Baldness. Po Chü-i, *Chinese.* ChiP, *tr.* by Arthur Waley

On His Being Arrived to the Age of Twenty-Three. Milton. *See* Sonnet: "How soon hath Time the suttle [*or* subtle] theef [*or* thief] of youth."

On His Blindness. Milton. AWP; GSo; HAP; HeIP-4; ImPo; InPK-6; NAEL-1; NOBE; OBEV; PBMP; PFE; PoE; PoEL-3; PoLF; PoRA; Poetr; SoSe-8; TFi; TRP; WeW-3
   (Sonnet: When I Consider.) ChIV-2

On His Books, *epigram.* Hilaire Belloc. FaBoEE; MoBrPo; NBLV; OxBoLi; WeW-3

On his death-bed poor Lubin lies. A Reasonable Affliction. Matthew Prior. NBLV; NOEC

On his deathbed lies our Tsar, Christian Orthodox Tsar! The Death of Ivan. "David Samuilovich Samoylov," *Russian.* TCRP, *tr.* by Lubov Yakovleva

On His Deceased Wife. Milton. CBLP; GLoP; GSo; ImPo; OBEV; OxBM; PoE; SAGP; SCV; TFi

(Dream, A.) LBC

(Sonnet.) EBEV; NOSC; OAEL-1

On his first visit to Puerto Rico. Coca-Cola and Coco Frio. Martín Espada. UnSA

On his free weekends he took. The Military-Industrial Complex. Robley Wilson, Jr. PBCAP

On His Friend Megistias, Who Died at Thermopylai. Simonides, *Greek.* GrAn, *tr.* by Peter Jay

On His Garden Book. Francis Daniel Pastorius. SCAP

On his knees, his back to us: the pale honeydew melons of his. Pornography. Lloyd Schwartz. BAP-94

On his knees with that pickaxe. Gold on Mule. Thomas Lux. CMAP

On His Lady's Waking. Pierre de Ronsard, *French.* AWP, *tr.* by Andrew Lang

On his last swing around. Field Work. Doug Cockrell. Poetsp

On His Mistress [*or* Mistris]. Donne. BoLoP; CBLP; EBEV; ESCV; NAEL-1; NoSic; PoEL-2 *Fr.* Elegies.

("By our first strange and fatal interview.") CABP; FSCP

(Elegy on His Mistress.) GBL; MeLP; SCGP

(On His Mistress.) CABP; FSCP

On His Mistress. Henry Noel *and* William Strode. PoEL-2

On His Mistress Drown'd. Thomas Spratt. EnLoPo

On His Mistress Going from Home [Song]. *Unknown.* NOSC

On His Mistress Looking in a Glass. Thomas Carew. CaPo

On His Mistress [*or* Mistris], the Queen of Bohemia. Sir Henry Wotton. CBLP; EnLoPo; GBL; HAP; MeLP; NOSC; SCGP; SeCP; TFi

(Elizabeth of Bohemia.) BoLoP; FaBoCh; GLoP; GTBS-P; NOBE; OBEV

("Th'eclipse and glory of her kind?") (LL) GLoP

On His Own Deafness. Jonathan Swift. BIrV

("Deaf, giddy, odious to my friends.")

("No more could reach me than her silence.") (LL) FaBoEE

On His Own Poetry. Charles Churchill. NOEC *Fr.* The Prophecy of Famine.

On His Queerness. Christopher Isherwood. OxBTC

On His Royal Blindness Paramount Chief Kwangala. Jack A. Mapanje. AF

On His Seventy-Fifth Birthday. Walter Savage Landor. AWP; EBEV; NTP; OAEL-2; OxAEP-2; PBMP; SCGP *Fr.* The Last Fruit Off an Old Tree.

(Dying Speech of an Old Philosopher.) FaBoEE; GTBS-P; NOBVV; NoP-4

(End, The.)

On His Thirty-Third Birthday. Ch'ang Kuo Fan, *Chinese.* OHMPC, *tr.* by Kenneth Rexroth

On his way to the open hearth where white-hot steel. My Father's Garden. David Wagoner. DiPo; NIP-4

On His Writing Verses. John Hawthorn. NOEC

On Honour. Bernard Mandeville. NOEC

On Hope. Richard Crashaw. *See* Against Hope.

On horseback, I am crossing the river. Crossing the River. Yang Shih-ch'i, *Chinese.* CoBLCP, *tr.* by Jonathan Chaves

On Hot Days. James Reiss. AmPA

On hot summer mornings my aunt set glasses. Water. Leslie Norris. OBWVE

On How the Cobler. *Unknown.* SCAP

On "How to Make Bee-keeping Pay." (LL) Opportunity. Harry Graham. OBCoV; PeLV

On humming rubber along this white concrete. Driving in Oklahoma. Carter Revard. HATNAP; VoR

On Hurricane Jackson. Alan Dugan. CoAP; TRP

On Hygiene. Hilaire Belloc. MoBrPo

On Imagination. Phillis Wheatley. AmPP; BlSi; CrDW; NAAAL; OxWW

On imagine les anges. Guillaume Apollinaire, *French.* PiM, *tr.* by Kenneth Koch

On Imitation. Coleridge. OxBSP

On Induction of the Hand. Clark Coolidge. PmAM

On Inhabiting an Orange. Josephine Miles. NoAM; PoA

On Installing an American Kitchen in Lower Austria. W. H. Auden. NYBP *Fr.* Thanksgiving for a Habitat.

On Its Way. May Swenson. SoSe-8; WPE

On its way I see. Kathleen Jessie Raine. NALW

On J. M. S. Gent. Alexander Pope. FaBoEE

On J. W. Ward. Samuel Rogers. FaBoEE

On Jacob Tonson, His Publisher. Dryden. FaBoEE; OBSV

On Jacob's Purchase. Francis Quarles. ChIV-1

On Jam. Hilaire Belloc. NBLV

On Jealousy. Esther Johnson. *See* Jealousy.

On Jocky Bell. *Unknown.* FaBoEE

On John Donne's Book of Poems. John Marriot. CH

On John So. *Unknown.* FaBoEE

On Jordan's Bank. Byron. ChIV-1

On Jordan's stormy banks I stand. The Promised Land. Samuel Stennett. AmFP

On Judas Iscariot. Francis Quarles. FaBoEE

On Judgement Day. Sipho Sepamla. PBMAP

On July 5 the Associated Press gave the news to the world. Harangue on the Death of Hayyim Nahman Bialik. César Tiempo, *Spanish.* TrJP, *tr.* by Donald Devenish Walsh

On Kean's Hamlet. Washington Allston. APN-1

On Keats. Shelley. FaBoEE

On Keats, 18 January, 1948 (Eve of St Agnes). Christina Rossetti. EPCY

On King Arthur's Round Table, at Winchester. Thomas Warton, the Younger. Son

On King Richard the Third, Who Lies Buried under Leicester Bridge. Sir John Suckling. CaPo

On Knighthood. Folgore da San Geminiano, *Italian.* AWP, *tr.* by John Addington Symonds

On Knowing the Difference Between Prejudice, Discrimination, and Oppression. Tom Leonard. NBrP

On Komochi Mountain. *Unknown, Japanese.* OHMPJ, *tr.* by Kenneth Rexroth

On Kriton the Miser. Lucilius, *Greek.* GrAn, *tr.* by Dudley Fitts

On Lady A———. Nicolas Bentley. PBLV

On Lady Anne Hamilton. Richard Brinsley Sheridan. FaBoEE; OBCoV

On Lady Poltagrue, A Public Peril. Hilaire Belloc. MoBrPo; OBCoV; OxBoV

On Lake Pend Oreille. Richard Shelton. NYBP

On land and sea I strove with anxious care. Bombed in London. Rudyard Kipling. *Fr.* Epitaphs of the War [1914–1918]. OBWP

On Late-acquired Wealth *or* Riches. *Unknown, Greek.* OBVE, *tr.* by William Cowper

(Riches.) AWP

On Lazarus Raised From Death. Henry Colman. ChIV-2

On Leander's Swimming over the Hellespont to Hero. Thomas Warton, the Younger, *after* Martial. FaBoEE

On Leaping over the Moon. Thomas Traherne. GeHe; ImPo; NAEL-1

On Learning. Elizabeth Teft. ECWP

On Learning to Adjust to Things. John Ciardi. KaS; OBCA

On Leave. John Buchan. NSI

On leave, I sat on marsh grass, watched. A Soldier on the Marsh. Andrew Hudgins. CBCWP

On Leaving. Gertrudis Gomez de Avellaneda, *Spanish.* PBWP, *tr.* by Frederick Sweet

On Leaving Baltimore. Duane Niatum. CDW

On Leaving Cuba, Her Native Land. Gertrudis Gomez de Avellaneda, *Spanish.* WPOW, *tr.* by Catherine Rodriguez-Nieto

On Leaving the Artists' Colony. Bruce Bawer. RA

On Leaving the Footpath. John James. NBrP

On Leslie Moore. *Unknown.* CTV

On Liberty and Slavery. George Moses Horton. AAP; APN-1; PAR

On Lien-ch'ang Palace. Yüan Chen, *Chinese.* SuSp, *tr.* by Angela Jung Palandri

On Lieutenant Shift. Ben Jonson. OBSV

On life and extinction with sea wind changes. Open-Eyed Angel. David Rokeah, *Hebrew.* MHP, *tr.* by Ruth Finer Mintz

On light's reflected word. (LL) The Heron. Vernon Watkins. GTBS-P; TwCP; UnPo

On Linden, when the sun was low. Hohenlinden. Thomas Campbell. CABP; CH; FaBoCh; FaPoR; GTBS-P; NOBE; NOBRP; OBNC; OBWP; TFi

On Listening to the Spirituals. Lance Jeffers. PoBA; SSLK

On little rented chairs with gilded backs. (LL) Evening Musicale. Phyllis McGinley. OBAL; OBCoV; Son

On Loch Leven. Christian Carstairs. ECWP

On Lolham Brigs in wild and lonely mood. The Flood. John Clare. RB

On London fell a clearer light. Summer in England, 1914. Alice Thompson Meynell. BrRo; SoSe-8; WPE

On longer evenings. Coming. Philip Larkin. MoBrPo; OxBTC

On Looking into E. V. Rieu's Homer. Patrick Kavanagh. NOIV

On Looking Up by Chance at the Constellations. Robert Frost. CMoP; MeMAP

On Lookout Mountain. Robert Earl Hayden. PoE

On Lord Cobham's Garden. Nathaniel Cotton. OBGa

On Lord Galloway. Robert Burns. FaBoEE *Fr.* Epigrams on Lord Galloway.

On Lord Holland's Seat near Margate, Kent. Thomas Gray. NOEC; OAEL-1; OBGa

On Lord Ila's Improvements, near Hounslow Heath. Philip Dormer Stanhope. OBGa

On Lot's Wife Turned to Salt. Agathias, *Greek.* GrAn, *tr. by* Dudley Fitts

On love was written. The Phoenix Reborn from Its Ashes. Louis Aragon, *French.* CBNP

On love's worst ugly day. First Meditation. Theodore Roethke. LCAP-2; NOBA *Fr.* Meditations of an Old Woman.

On Loving Once and Loving Often. Elizabeth Tollet. LW

On Lucretia Borgia's Hair. Walter Savage Landor. *See* On Seeing a Hair of Lucretia Borgia.

On Lucy Countess[e] of Bedford. Ben Jonson. BeJo; NOSC; SeCP

On Lydia Distracted. Philip Ayres. EnLoPo; Son

On M. Butterfly. Wing Tek Lum. IFJA

On Mackintosh. Charles Lamb. Ro *Fr.* Letter from Charles Lamb to Thomas Manning, 22 August 1801.

On Maguire's Winter Campaign. Eochaidh Ó Heóghusa. PBRV

On Maids and Cats. Henricus Selyns. SCAP

On Mammon. Herman Melville. OxBA *Fr.* Clarel: A Poem and Pilgrimage in the Holy Land.

On Man. Walter Savage Landor. OBNC

On Man. John Wilmot. *Fr.* A Satire [*or* Satyre] against [Reason and] Mankind. NOSC; OAEL-1; OBSV; PoEL-3; SCV

On Man, on Nature, and on Human Life *identical to lines 754–860 of* The Recluse; Home at Grasmere. Wordsworth. FHYEP; PoE *Fr.* The Excursion.

On Man, on Nature, and on Human Life, *identical to* Prospectus *from* The Excursion. Wordsworth and His Music. Wordsworth. EPCY; OAEL-2 *Fr.* The Recluse; Home at Grasmere.

On Margaret Ratcliffe. Ben Jonson. SeCP

On Marriage. Richard Crashaw. FaBoEE

On Marriage. Thomas Flatman. NOBL; PeLV

(Bachelor's Song, The.) EnLoPo

On Mary Magdalene. Richard Crashaw. FMP

On Mary Magdalene. William Drummond, of Hawthornden. OAEL-1

On May Day, the girls of Penzance. Limerick. *Unknown.* PeLi

On May-day, when the lark began to rise. *Unknown.* NoSic *Fr.* The Court of Love.

On Mayday we dance. *Unknown.* BoTP

On Meditation. Robert Bly. *Fr.* Six Winter Privacy Poems. LCAP-2

On Meeting a Gentlewoman in the Dark. *Unknown.* FaBoEE

On Meeting——, Esq., in St. James's Park. *Unknown.* ECWP

On Melancholy. *Unknown.* NOSC

On Mercenary and Unjust Bailiffs. Henricus Selyns. SCAP

On Michael Angelo. Washington Allston. APN-1

On Mike O'Day. *Unknown.* FaBoEE

On miserable Nearchos' bones lie lightly, earth. Last Lines. X. J. Kennedy. OBAL

On Miss Eleanor Ambrose, a Celebrated Beauty in Dublin. Philip Dormer Stanhope. FaBoEE

On Mr. G. Herberts Booke, The Temple. Richard Crashaw. EPCY; ESCV; GeHe

(On George Herbert's "The Temple" Sent to a Gentlewoman.) OxAEP-1
(On Mr. George Herbert's Book, The Temple.) CABP

On Mr Milton's "Paradise Lost." Andrew Marvell. CABP; EPCY; NOSC

("In Number, Weight, and Measure, needs not *Rhime*.") (LL) FSCP

On Mr. Pitt's [*or* Pit's] Hair-Powder Tax. Robert Burns. FaBoEE

On misty waters, vast and vague. Hearing a Flute at Broken Bridge. Yün Shou-p'ing, *Chinese.* CoBLCP, *tr. by* Jonathan Chaves

On Monday man gave God. Adam and God. Anne Wilkinson. MoCV

On Monsieur's Departure. Elizabeth I, Queen of England. CABP; NAEL-1; NALW; WPE

("Or die and so forget what love e'er meant.") (LL) LW; PEW

On moon-washed apples of wonder. (LL) Moonlit Apples. John Drinkwater. BoTP; EBEvV; OBMV; OxBTC; PoRA

On moonlight bushes. Nightingales. Coleridge. *Fr.* The Nightingale. FHYEP

On moonlit heath and lonesome bank. A. E. Housman. CMoP; SCGP

On moors where people get lost and die of air. Water. Ted Hughes. OxBSP

On Mortality. Henry Colman. ChIV-1

On Motel Walls. David Wagoner. DiPo

On Mother's Day. Aileen Fisher. NTCP

On Mother's Day. Grace Paley. NMM-2

On Mount Ching. Meng Chiao, *Chinese.* PLT, *tr. by* A. C. Graham

On Mr. Abraham Cowley, His Death and Burial amongst the Ancient Poets. Sir John Denham. BeJo

His English stream so pure did flow. EPCY

On Mr. Dryden, Renegade. Aphra Behn. FaBoVe

On Mr. Edward Howard, upon His British Princes. Charles Sackville. OBSV

On Mr. George Herbert's Book, The Temple. Richard Crashaw. *See* On Mr. G. Herberts Booke, The Temple.

On Mr. Hobbs, and His Writings. John Sheffield. PoEL-3

On Mr. Nash's Picture at Full Length. Jane Brereton. WPE

On Mr. Nash's Present of His Own Picture at Full Length. Philip Dormer Stanhope. NOEC

On Mr. Paine's Rights of Man. Philip Freneau. NAAL-1; NAAL-3

("Thus briefly sketched the sacred RIGHTS OF MAN.") ColAP
(To a Republican.) AmPP

On Mr. Pricke. *Unknown.* FaBoEE

On Mr. Rice the Manciple of Christ Church in Oxford. Richard Corbet. NOSC

On Mr. Shirley's Poems. Thomas Stanley. BeJo

On Mrs. Montagu. Ann Yearsley. ECWP

On Mumonkan. Toki Zenmaro, *Japanese.* MJT, *tr. by* Makoto Ueda

On Mundane Acquaintances. Hilaire Belloc. FaBoEE; OBCoV; OxBTC

On My Bed I Sought Him. Bible, *O.T.* BoWoP, *tr. by* Willis Barnstone; TrJP *Fr.* Song of Songs. AWP

("In my bed at night.") BoWoP, *tr. by* Willis Barnstone

On My Birthday. Yehuda Amichai, *Hebrew.* MHP, *tr. by* Ruth Finer Mintz

On My Birthday, July 21. Matthew Prior. OBEV

On My Birthday—Sick. Li K'ai-hsien, *Chinese.* CoDLCP, *tr. by* Jonathan Chaves

On My Boy Henry. Lady Jane Cavendish *and* Lady Elizabeth Brackley. KTR

On My Child's Death. Joseph, Freiherr von Eichendorff, *German.* IMW, *tr. by* W. D. Snodgrass

On My Dear Grandchild Simon Bradstreet, [Who Died on 16TH November, 1669, Being But A Month And One Day Old]. Anne Bradstreet. ColAP; KTR; NAAL-1; NAAL-3; SCAP

On my desk, a set of labels. City Gent. Craig Raine. NoAM

On my desk is a small bottle. Jasmine. E. Ethelbert Miller. GT

On my dry palate's roof to rest, / A withered leaf, an ideal guest. Bible, *O.T. See* Psalm 137.

On My First Daughter. Ben Jonson. BeJo; EBEV; FaBoEE; HoPM; InPS-3; NAEL-1; NOBE; NOSC; NoP-4; PFE; PoE; SeCP

On My First Son [*or* Sonne]. Ben Jonson. AWP; BeJo; CABP; ClHu; EBEV; FaBoEE; HAP; HoPM; IMW; InPK-6; InPS-3; NAEL-1; NIP-4; NoP-4; NOSC; OAEL-1; OxBSP; PBMP; PBRV; PFE; PoE; PoEL-2; Poetr; PoPoPo; RB; RaBo; SCGP; SeCP; TFi; TRP; WeW-3

On my fourteenth birthday. Curtis Fuller. Rick Madigan. SeSe

On My Fourteenth Wedding Anniversary I Ride on Trains. Cornelia Veenendaal. GM

On My Joyful Departure from the Same City. Coleridge. NBLV

On my knees to cry, *Who the hell are you, kid?.* (LL) The Roundhouse Voices. Dave Jeddie Smith. ColAP; GM; MT; NoAM; VCAP

On My Lady Isabella Playing on the Lute. Edmund Waller. *See* Of My Lady Isabella Playing on the Lute.

On my land grew a green tree. The Possessor. Arthur Rex Dugard Fairburn. PeNZ *Fr.* Album Leaves.

On My Late Dear Wife. Jonathan Richardson. NOEC

On My Leaving London, June the 29. Sarah Fyge Egerton. KTR

On my little guitar. On My Old Ramkiekie. C. Louis Leipoldt, *Afrikaans.* PeSA, *tr. by* Anthony Delius

On my little magic whistle I will play to you all day. The Magic Whistle. Margaret Rose. BoTP

On my livingroom wall hangs a Navajo rug. Storm Pattern. Greg Pape. PBCAP

On My Lord Bacon. John Danforth. SCAP

On my Northwest coast in the midst of the night a fisherman's group stands watching. The Torch. Walt Whitman. SAmP

On my old battledress tonight, my sweet. (LL) Goodbye. Alun Lewis. BoLoP; NAEL-2; NoP-4; OBWP; OxBM; OxBTC; PoWW

On My Old Ramkiekie. C. Louis Leipoldt, *Afrikaans.* PeSA, *tr. by* Anthony Delius

On My Own. Philip Levine. FYAP

On my return. L. A. Davidson. HA

On my right hand I'll seat one of my loves. Denis Gennad'evich Novikov, *Russian.* TCRP, *tr. by* Bradley Jordan

On my school notebooks. Paul Éluard. TTTS *Fr.* Liberty.

On My Sorrowful Life. Moses ibn Ezra, *Hebrew.* TrJP, *tr. by* Solomon Solis-Cohen

On My Thirty-third Birthday. Byron. FaBoEE

On my wall hangs a Japanese carving. The Mask of Evil. Bertolt Brecht, *German.* PoSu, *tr. by* H. R. Hayes

On my way home from school. The Testing-Tree. Stanley Kunitz. FYAP; UnPo

On my way to Mass. The Lass from Bally-na-Lee. Anthony Raftery, *Irish.* BlrV, *tr. by* Desmond O'Grady

On My Wedding Day. Sarah Fyge Egerton. KTR

On my winter walk. Hugo Majer. Spl

On My Words. Abba Kovner, *Hebrew.* IP, *tr. by* Warren Bargad *and* Stanley F. Chyet

On Myself. Edith Bone. FaBoEE

On Myself. Anne Finch. NoP-4; OxBSP

On National Vanity. J. E. Clare McFarlane. PBCV

On Naucratius, Brother of St. Basil. Saint Gregory of Nazianzus, *Greek.* GrAn, *tr. by* Robin Skelton

On Neal's Ashes. Allen Ginsberg. PmAP; PoM

("Asshole anneal'd to silken skin / all ashes, all ashes again.") (LL) BB

On New Year's Day in the morning. (LL) I saw three ships come sailing by. Mother Goose. LB; OxNR

On New Year's Day of the Year Kuei-ssu (1533), Releasing Live Creatures. Wang T'ing-hsiang, *Chinese.* CoBLCP, *tr. by* Jonathan Chaves

On New Year's Eve of the Year Hsin-wei (1751), Drinking Alone and Sadly Chanting Poems, I Remembered My Aged Wife Who Is Living at Twisting River. Chin Nung, *Chinese.*

Traveler, I've been through a thousand changes, A. CoBLCP, *tr. by* Jonathan Chaves

On News. Thomas Traherne. ESCV; FMP; GeHe *Fr.* The Third Century.

("News from a foreign country came.") FMP

On nights like this, when bayou and lagoon. Orgie. Madison Cawein. APN-2

On nights when hail / falls noisily. Lady Izumi, *Japanese.* BoWoP, *tr. by* Willis Barnstone

On no work of words now for three lean months in the bloody. Dylan Thomas. OxBSP

On Noman, a Guest. Hilaire Belloc. FaBoEE

On Non-dependence of Mind. Dogen. EnlH

On Not Being Milton. Tony Harrison. CABP; FaBoPV; NoP-4 *Fr.* The School of Eloquence. NAEL-2; NoAM

On Not Being Your Lover. Medbh McGuckian. PBCIP; PNI

On Observing a Large Red-Streak Apple. Philip Freneau. NAAL-1; NAAL-3

("Sad memento of the past, A.") (LL) ColAP

On occasion. Tanka. Maekawa Samio, *Japanese.* MJT, *tr. by* Makoto Ueda

On ochre walls in ice-formed caves shaggy Neanderthals. To My Son Parker, Asleep in the Next Room. Bob Kaufman. PoBA; TwCP; VGW

On Oliver Goldsmith. David Garrick. FaBoEE

On, on, on. The Dirigible. Chris Wallace-Crabbe. CBAP

On, on the vessel steals. On the Rhine. Charles Stuart Calverley. PeLV

On, on to the darkest continent. Dedicated to Dr. W. H. Sheppard. Maggie Pogue Johnson. CBWP-4

On One Condition. Charles Madge. SPE

On One Dying in a Convent. Stephen Lucius Gwynn. TIRV

On one fix'd point all nature moves. On the Uniformity and Perfection of Nature. Philip Freneau. AmPP

On one of those days with the Legion. A Day with the Foreign Legion. Reed Whittemore. CoAP; CoAmPo; LiTM

On one side of the world. At Half Past Three in the Afternoon. Jon Stallworthy. EOEF

On one summer's day, sun was shining fine. Bill Bailey, Won't You Please Come Home. Hughie Cannon. OBAL

On One That Lived Ingloriously. John Hoskyns, *after the Greek of* Simonides. FaBoEE

On One Who Died Discovering Her Kindness. John Sheffield. OBEV

On Opening an Old House. Tymoteusz Karpowicz, *Polish.* CEEP, *tr. by* Zak, Ewa

On Originality. Bill Manhire. PeNZ

On Ornament. Yunsuk Hong, *Korean.* CKP, *tr. by* Jaihiun Kim

On other cloudy afternoons. The Double. Irving Feldman. NYBP

On other fields and other scenes the morn. Burnt Lands. G. D. Roberts. GSo

On Our Crucified Lord, Naked and Bloody. Richard Crashaw. HoPM; OAEL-1; OxBSP; TrCP

(Upon the Body of Our Blessed Lord, Naked and Bloody.) NOSC; SeCP

On our meat and on us all. (LL) Grace for a Child. Robert Herrick. AWP; BeJo; BoTP; CTV; FaBoCh; InPS-3; NAEL-1; NOSC; NTP; OBEV; OxAEP-1; OxBChV; PFE; PoE; SCGP; TFi

On our Pharsalian Plaines, comprizing space. Seaconk Plain Engagement. Benjamin Thompson. SCAP

On Our Saviour's Passion. Francis Quarles. PeECV *Fr.* Divine Fancies.

On Oxford. Keats. SCGP

(Lines Rhymed in a Letter from Oxford.) OBCoV

(On Oxford. A Parody.) OxAEP-2

On Pallas Bathing, from a Hymn of Callimachus. Callimachus, *Greek.* OBCVT, *tr. by* William Cowper

On Parade. Fragano Ledgister. PBCV

On parent knees, a naked new-born child. Epigram. Sir William Jones, *after the Sanskrit of* Kalidasa. FaBoEE; OBEV; OxBSP

On Parting. Edward Coote Pinkney. APN-1

On Parting with a Friend. Mary Weston Fordham. CBWP-2

On Parting with Moses ibn Ezra. Judah Halevi, *Hebrew.* TrJP, *tr. by* Solomon Solis-Cohen

On Passing Over a Dreary Tract of Country, and Near the Ruins of a Deserted Chapel, During a Tempest. Charlotte Smith. BoWoP; WPE *Fr.* Montalbert.

On Passing the New Menin Gate. Siegfried Sassoon. NAEL-2; NoAM; NoP-4; OBMV; PoWW; Son

On, Pegasus! Why, whither turn ye? A Survey of the Amphitheatre. Moses Browne. NOEC

On Peter Robinson. Francis Jeffrey. FaBoEE; NBLV

(Epitaph on Peter Robinson.) OxBoLi

On Philiphaugh a fray began. The Battle of Philiphaugh. *Unknown.* ESPB

On Picking Flowers. Ho Xuan Huong, *Vietnamese.* AVP, *tr. by* Huỳnh Sanh Thông

On Platonic Love. Samuel Boyse. ECEV

On Plato's Grave. *Unknown, Greek.* GrAn, *tr. by* William J. Philbin

On Playwright ("Playwright convict of public wrongs to men"). Ben Jonson. NoP-4

On Plaza Garibaldi. Nellie Wong. OpBo

On Poet-Ape. Ben Jonson. Son

On Poetry. Yüan Hao-wen, *Chinese.*

Croaking frog in a well sees the sky from end to end, A. SuSp, *tr. by* Irving Y. Lo

Fade the kingfisher blue, trim the red, blend the colors. SuSp, *tr. by* Irving Y. Lo

Poet's heart is wrenched and wrenched again until his head turns white, A. SuSp, *tr. by* Irving Y. Lo

On Poetry: a Rhapsody. Jonathan Swift.

All human race would fain be wits. HAP; OBSV; PoEL-3

On Poets. Alexander Pope. FaBoEE

On polar and on southern seas. Nikolai Stepanovich Gumilyov. TCRP, *tr. by* Simon Franklin *Fr.* Captains.

On Ponkawtasset, since, we took our way. Henry David Thoreau. NCAP

On Portents. Robert Graves. FaBoMo

On Poulo Condore. Trần Cao Vân, *Vietnamese.* AVP, *tr. by* Huỳnh Sanh Thông

On Primrose Hill in the early spring. Primrose Hill. Rose Fyleman. BoTP

On Prince Frederick. *Unknown.* FaBoEE; NOBL; NTP

(Epitaph on Prince Frederick.) OxBoLi

On Proclus's Great Nose. *Unknown.* PFE

On Professor Cou´e. Charles Cuthbert Inge. OBCoV

On Professor Drennan's Verse. Roy Campbell. GTBS-P

On Pruning. William Cowper. GaP

On Pym. William Drummond. NOSC

On quarry walls the spleenwort spreads. Rockferns. Norman Nicholson. MoBrPo

On Queen Caroline. *Unknown.* FaBoEE

(Queen Caroline.) OBCoV

On Rachmaninoff's Birthday. Frank O'Hara. CAPP-1; PoM

On Ragged Mountain birches twist from rifts in granite. Granite and Grass. Donald Hall. DiPo

On rainy Monday nights of an eternal November. (LL) Classic Ballroom Dances. Charles Simic. LCAP-2; WeW-3

On random wires the rows of summer swallows. Late Autumn. May Sarton. CrSp

On Reading a Love Poem. Kedarnath Singh, *Hindi.* OMIP, *tr. by* Vinay Dharwadker

On Reading Aloud My Early Poems. John Williams. WeW-3

On Reading an Archeological Article. Molara Ogundipe-Leslie. HBAPE

On Reading Dr. Young's Satires. Jonathan Swift. EPCY

On Reading "God." G. K. Chesterton. OBCoV

On Reading Poems to a Senior Class at South High. David Chapman Berry. SoSe-8

On Reading the Buddha's Scriptures. Nguyễn Bỉnh Khiêm, *Vietnamese.* AVP, *tr. by* Huỳnh Sanh Thông.

On Reading the Life of Haroun Er Reshid. Madison Cawein. APN-2

On Reading Wordsworth's Lines on Peele Castle. Mary Wollstonecraft Shelley. Ro

On Receiving a Crown of Ivy from the Same. Leigh Hunt. Son

On Receiving My Letter of Termination. Yüan Hung-tao, *Chinese.* CoBLCP, *tr. by* Jonathan Chaves

On Receiving News of the War. Isaac Rosenberg. MoBrPo; NSI; OBWP; OxAEP-2; PeFWW; PeSAV; PoWW

On Reconnaissance. Mikhail Arkadyevich Svetlov, *Russian.* TCRP, *tr. by* Daniel Weissbort

On Recrossing the Rocky Mountains after Many Years. John Charles Frémont. AiP

On Red Square, on the chopping block. Yury Pavlovich Odarchenko, *Russian.* TCRP, *tr. by* Nina Kossman and Albert C. Todd

On reflection, it all came down to nylon. The Woman Underneath. Robert Maitre. EP

On Refusal of Aid between Nations. D. G. Rossetti. EBEV; OxAEP-2; SCGP

On Rembrant; Occasioned by His Picture of Jacob's Dream. Washington Allston. APN-1

On Returning. Brigitte Frase. LoHo

On Returning to Detroit. Carolyn Forché. GM

On Returning to My Garden and Field. T'ao Ch'ien, *Chinese.*
   I plant beans at the foot of the southern hill. SuSp, *tr. by* Wu-chi Liu
   When I was young, I did not fit into the common mold. SuSp, *tr. by* Wu-chi Liu

On Returning to Sung Mountain. Wang Wei, *Chinese.* SuSp, *tr. by* Paul W. Kroll

On Revisiting Cintra after the Death of Catarina. Luis de Camoês, *Spanish.* AWP, *tr. by* Richard Garnett

On Rhyme. Robert Lloyd.
   Some, Milton-mad (an affectation). EPCY

On Richmond Park. Stephen Duck. OBGa

On Riding to See Dean Swift in the Mist of the Morning. Alexander Pope *and* Thomas Parnell. FaBoEE
   (Visiting Dr Swift.) OBCoV

On roads beyond the camp the Khamsin struck me. Yitzhak Lamdan. MHP, *tr. by* Ruth Finer Mintz   *Fr.* In the Khamsin.

On roads I've trodden, everywhere. New Tiles. Xuân Diệu, *Vietnamese.* AVP, *tr. by* Huỳnh Sanh Thông

On Robert Buchanan, Who Attacked Him under the Pseudonym of "Thomas Maitland." D. G. Rossetti. FaBoEE

On rocky Chios. . . . Chios. Ioanna Tsatsos, *Greek.* GrIP, *tr. by* Jean Demos

On Rodin's "L'Illusion, Sœur d'Icare." Trumbull Stickney. APN-2

On Roman Feet my stumbling Muse declines. An Elegiack Verse on Mr. Elijah Corlet. Nehemiah Walter. SCAP

On Roofs of Terry Street. Douglas Dunn. OxBTC

On Rosania's Apostasy, and Lucasia's Friendship. Katherine Philips. KTR

On Rÿneveld, an Unpopular Dutch judge. *Unknown.* FaBoEE

On S. John the Baptist. Thomas Stanley. ChIV-2

On sacks of cement they eat bread and watermelons. Cathedral Stones. Ion Gheorghe, *Romanian.* CEEP, *tr. by* Donald Eulert *and* Stefan Avadanei

On Saint-Urbain Street. Milton Acorn. NOBC

On Sanazar's being honoured with six hundred Duckets by the Clarissimi of Venice, for composing an Elegiack Hexastick of The City. A Satyre. Richard Lovelace. PBRV

On Sandro's Flora. Trumbull Stickney. APN-2

On Saturday night shall be [all] my care. Saturday, Sunday. Mother Goose. OxNR; ReMoGo

On Saturday sailed from Bremen. Gerard Manley Hopkins. *Fr.* The Wreck of the Deutschland. CMoP; EnVR; FaBoMo; ImPo; LiTM; NOBE; NoAM; OBNC; OxAEP 2; PeECV; PoEL-5

On Saturday with joy Bill dubs his half. The Linen Weaver. *Unknown.* NOEC

On Saturn the sexes are three. Limerick. *Unknown.* PeLi

On Saul and David. Francis Quarles. ChIV-1

On Scafell Pike. Ted Walker. NYBP

On Scott's Poem "The Field of Waterloo." Thomas Erskine. NBLV

On sea and land alike. Poseidippus, *Greek.* GrAn, *tr. by* Edward Lucie-Smith

On Sebastian. Sebastian. Yona Wollach, *Hebrew.* IP, *tr. by* Warren Bargad *and* Stanley F. Chyet

On Seein an Aik-Tree Sprent Wi Galls. Robert Garioch. OxBS

On Seeing a Bird-Catcher. Eliza Cook. VWP

On Seeing a Firefly in My Room. Yang Chi, *Chinese.* CoBLCP, *tr. by* Jonathan Chaves

On Seeing a Hair of Lucretia Borgia. Walter Savage Landor. HAP; WeW-3
   (On Lucretia Borgia's Hair.) SCGP

On Seeing a Little Child Spin a Coin of Alexander the Great. Charles Tennyson Turner. NOBVV

On Seeing a Painting of Plants and Insects by Chü-ning. Mei Yao Ch'en, *Chinese.* SuSp, *tr. by* Jonathan Chaves

On Seeing a Piece of Our Artillery Brought into Action. Wilfred Owen. GSo

On Seeing a Poet of the First World War on the Station at Abbeville. Charles Causley. LiTM

On Seeing a Tapestry Chair-Bottom Beautifully Worked by His Daughter for Mrs Holroyd. Richard Owen Cambridge. ECEV

On Seeing an Officer's Widow Distracted. Mary Barber. ECWP; NOEC

On Seeing an Old Poet in the Café Royal. John Betjeman. UV

On Seeing Francis Jeffrey Riding on a Donkey. Sydney Smith. FaBoEE

On Seeing My Birthplace from a Jet Aircraft. John Pudney. NYBP

On Seeing the Elgin Marbles. Keats. GSo; ImPo; NAEL-2; NIP-4

On Seeing the Field Being Singed. Lady Ise, *Japanese.* BoWoP, *tr. by* Etsuko Terasaki *and* Irma Brandeis

On Seeing the Picture of Æolus by Pelegrino Tibalbi, in the Institute at Bologna. Washington Allston. APN-1

On Seeing Two Brown Boys in a Catholic Church. Frank Horne. PoBA; TTY

On Seeming to Presume. Lawrence Durrell. LiTM

On Shakespeare and Voltaire. Thomas Holcroft. NOEC

On Shakespeare Critics. Alec Derwent Hope. OxBC   *Fr.* Dunciad Minor.

On Shakespear[e]. Milton. EPCY; MeLP; NAEL-1; NOSC; PoE; PoRA; SCGP
   (Epitaph on the Admirable Dramatic Poet, W. Shakespeare, An.) FaBoEE

On shallow straw, in shadeless glass. Take One Home for the Kiddies. Philip Larkin. OxBTC; PeP

On Shiloh's dark and bloody ground. The Drummer Boy of Shiloh. *Unknown.* AmFP

On shining heights where Thought with stately tread. Emerson. Henrietta Cordelia Ray. CBWP-3

On Shooting a Swallow in Early Youth. Charles Tennyson Turner. NOBVV

On Shooting Particles beyond the World. Richard Eberhart. LiTM

On Sight of a Gentlewoman's Face in the Water. Thomas Carew. CaPo

On Sir G. B. his defeat. Alexander Brome. PBRV

On Sir Henry Ferrett, M.P. John Bingham Morton. OBCoV Sarcastic Manner, My Books Would Make Me ; an Ode.

On Sir J—— S—— Saying in a Sarcastic Manner, My Books Would Make Me Mad[; an Ode.] Elizabeth Thomas. CABP; ECWP

On Sir John Calf. *Unknown.* FaBoEE

On Sir John Hill, M. D., Playwright. David Garrick. FaBoEE; NBLV

On Sir John Vanbrugh [Architect]. Abel Evans. FaBoEE

On Sir Joshua Reynolds. William Blake. OxBoV

On Sir Nathaniel Wraxall the Historian. George Colman, the Younger. FaBoEE

On Sir Robert Cotton the Antiquary. Thomas Randolph. NOSC

On Sir Walter Rawleigh at His Execution. *Unknown.* NOSC

On Sitting Down to Read "King Lear" Once Again. Keats. CABP; EBEV; EPCY; GSo; NAEL-2; NoP-4; PoPoPo; Ro

On Sitting Down to Write, I Decide Instead to Go to Fred Herko's Concert. Diane Di Prima. PmAP

On Slavery. Thomas Campbell. Ro   *Fr.* The Pleasures of Hope.

On Slieve Gullion 'men and mountain meet'. Michael Longley. BiHa

On small donkeys they bring in suns. Melons. Moshe Yungman, *Yiddish.* CEEP, *tr. by* Gabriel Preil *and* Howard Schwartz

On Snow. Li K'ai-hsien, *Chinese.*
   Jade trees from the rear courtyard of the empire of Ch'en. CoBLCP, *tr. by* Jonathan Chaves

On Snuff-Taking. Elizabeth Teft. ECWP

On Solitude. Abraham Cowley. OxAEP-1
   (Solitude.) NOSC

On some island I long to be. Saint Columcille, *Irish.* BIrV, *tr. by* John Montague

On some other planet. John Rice. SpW

On some red day in a burst of fists on a new horizon! (LL) I Have Seen Black Hands. Richard Wright. AF

On Some Shells Found Inland. Trumbull Stickney. APN-2; Son

On Some South African Novelists. Roy Campbell. FaBoEE; GTBS-P; InPK-6; MoBrPo; NOBL; OBCoV; OxAEP-2; OxBTC; PeLV

On some Vermont road. Mating the Goats. Aliki Barnstone. BoWoP

On Something, That Walks [or Walkes] Somewhere. Ben Jonson. BeJo; NAEL-1; OxBSP; PoE; SCGP; SeCP

On Sound. Wei Ying-wu, *Chinese.* SuSp, *tr.* by Irving Y. Lo

On Spies. Ben Jonson. BeJo; FaBoVe; NoP-4; OxBSP

On Springfield Mountain there did dwell. Springfield Mountain. *Unknown.* AmFP

On St. James's Park, as Lately Improved by His Majesty. Edmund Waller. BeJo; NOSC

   ("OF the first Paradise there's nothing found.") OBGa

On St. Martin's evening green. Nuns at Eve. John Malcolm Brinnin. TwCP

On starry heights. The Conflict of Convictions. Herman Melville. APN-2; CBCWP; NOBA

On Stella's Birthday, 1718/1719. Jonathan Swift. IIP; InPK-6; NIP-4; NOIV; OAEL-1

   (Stella's Birthday; Written in the Year 1718[/9].) CBLP; EnLoPo

On steps of jade. Jade Stairs Resentment. Li Po, *Chinese.* ChiPo, *tr.* by Greg Whincup

On Stopping Late in the Afternoon for Steamed Dumplings. Toi Derricotte. InPS-3

On street corners east and west. The Girl from Flower Mountain. Han Yü, *Chinese.* SuSp, *tr.* by Charles Hartman

On Stripping Bark from Myself. Alice Walker. NAAAL

On Sturminster Foot-Bridge. Thomas Hardy. OxBSP

On such a day as this. Soundings. Paula Gunn Allen. HATNAP

On such a morning as this. In Memory of Basil, Marquess of Dufferin and Ava. John Betjeman. OBWP

On Summer. George Moses Horton. AAP

On summer evenings blue, pricked by the wheat. Sensation. Rimbaud, *French.* AWP, *tr.* by Jethro Bithell

On Sunday Afternoons. Sunday Afternoons. Anthony Thwaite. OxBTC

On Sunday afternoons in mango season. Mango. John Robert Lee. HCP

On Sunday morning, then he comes. Mr. Wells. Elizabeth Madox Roberts. KaS

On Sunday morning well I knew. *Unknown. Fr.* Popular Songs of Tuscany. AWP, *tr.* by John Addington Symonds

On Sunday the hawk fell on Bigging. The Hawk. George Mackay Brown. NoP-4; RB

On Sunday we buried the icons. Great Serbian Migration 1690. Milorad Pavic, *Serbo-Croatian.* HSix, *tr.* by Charles Simic

On sunnier days a new coat of arms made the ocean high. Boats. Bernadette Mayer. FTOS

On sunny days there in the shade. Three Poems. Bhartrihari, *Sanskrit.* EP, *tr.* by John Brough

On sunny summer Sunday afternoons in Harlem. Passing. Langston Hughes. APSN; SAmP

On Sweet Killen Hill. Tom MacIntyre. CIP-2

   (Sweet Killen Hill.) PBCIP

On Sympathisers with the American Revolution. Charles Wesley. NOCV

On tape and late at night. Late Night Radio. Geoff Page. BMAP

On Tara's hill the daylight dies. The Paschal Fire. Denis Florence MacCarthy. TIRV

On taut air—bells; lifted, adoring eyes. Immolation. Robert Farren. TIRV

On Teaching the Young. Yvor Winters. NOBA; NoAM

On Thanksgiving Day, I'll say a little. A Thanksgiving Prayer. Kristy Woodward. CTV

On that big estate there is no rain. Monangamba. Antonio Jacinto, *Portuguese.* TTY, *tr.* by Alan Ryder

On that day there was a holiday on earth. Remembrance of Yalta. Bella Akhatovna Akhmadulina, *Russian.* TCRP, *tr.* by Albert C. Todd

On that day when I brought wine to Red Bridge. Occasional Poem: Upon Seeing Lotuses Bloom in a Vase. Wang Shih-chieng, *Chinese.* SuSp, *tr.* by Richard John Lynn

On that great, that awful day. Dies IRÆ. Thomas Babington Macaulay. ChIV-2

On that last night before we went. Tennyson. OAEL-2; PoEL-5 *Fr.* In Memoriam A. H. H.

On that sweet form of thine. (LL) The Comet at Yell'ham. Thomas Hardy. CMoP; GBL

On the 3. of September, 1651. Katherine Philips. PBRV

On the 31st day of August in the year 1914. The Little Car. Guillaume Apollinaire, *French.* AF, *tr.* by Oliver Bernard

On the Adequacy of Landscape. Wallace Stevens. SAmP

On the advice of Praxilla. Aristophanes, *Greek.* InMo, *tr.* by Sam Hamill

On the Amtrak from Boston to New York City. Sherman Alexie. PoPoPo

On the Anniversary Of Your Death. Karen L. Mitchell. GT

On the Antiquity of Microbes. Strickland W. Gillilan. NBLV

On the Aphorism "L'Amitié est l'Amour sans Ailes." Charlotte Smith. CABP; PEW

On the Apparition of Oneself. William Burford. PoA

On the Appeal from the Race of Sheba: II. Léopold Sédar Senghor, *French.* TTY, *tr.* by John Reed *and* Clive Wake

On the apple. Raymond Roseliep. HA

On the Army of Spartans, Who Died at Thermopylae. Simonides. FaBoEE

On the Assumption. Richard Crashaw. ESCV

On the Astrologer and Almanac Maker, John Partridge. Jonathan Swift. FaBoEE

On the Asylum Road. Charlotte Mew. MoBrPo; VWP

On the Athenians Who Died at the Hellespont, 440–39 B.C. *Unknown, Greek.* GrAn, *tr.* by Peter Jay

On the Author's Husband Desiring Her to Write Some Verses. Mary Whateley. ECWP

On the avenue the faces change each day. Hope. F. D. Reeve. PoA

On the Babel-Builders. Francis Quarles. ChIV-1

On the Back of a Photograph. János Pilinszky, *Hungarian.* NNPT; PoSu, *tr.* by Peter Jay

On the back trails, in sun glasses. Kenyatta Listening to Mozart. Imamu Amiri Baraka. PmAP

On the Balcony. D. H. Lawrence. GBL

   (Illicit.) PoA

On the balcony of the tower. Exile in Japan. Su Man-shu, *Chinese.* BLT, *tr.* by Kenneth Rexroth

On the Banisters. Margaret E. Gibbs. BoTP

On the bank of Lake Rouge a chestnut steed treads proudly. Su Man-shu. SuSp, *tr.* by Wu-chi Liu *Fr.* Poems Written during My Sojourn in Japan.

On the bank of the river. A Sunbather in Late October. Arthur Gregor. PFE

On the Banks of Salee. *Unknown.* AmFP

On the Banks of the Duero. Antonio Machado Ruiz, *Spanish.* STV, *tr.* by John Frederick Nims

On the Banks of the Little Eau Pleine. *Unknown.* AmFP

On the banks of the Potomac there's an army so grand. The Red, White and Red. *Unknown.* AmFP

On the Baptized Ethiopian. Richard Crashaw. ChIV-2; FaBoEE; NoP-4

On the bare mountain. Distant View. Uys Krige, *Afrikaans.* PeSA, *tr.* by Uys Krige *and* Jack Cope

On the bare veld where nothing ever grows. A Veld Eclogue: The Pioneers. Roy Campbell. OBSV

On the Bath of Pallas. Callimachus. HePo, *tr.* by Barbara Hughes Fowler *Fr.* Hymns.

On the Bay. Richard Watson Gilder. APN-2

On The Beach. John Corben. Spl

On the Beach at Fontana. James Joyce. MoBrPo; OBMV; PoA; RB; RaBo

On the beach at night. Walt Whitman. APN-1; AWP; AmPP; MoAmPo; NOBA; NoP-4; OxBA; SAmP

On the beach at night alone. Walt Whitman. APN-1; TAP

"On the beach," said John sadly, "there's such." Limerick. Isaac Asimov. PeLi

On the beach where we had been idly. Gracious Goodness. Marge Piercy. Poetsp

On the bench I wait. Kenneth Yasuda. HA

On the Benefactions in the Late Frost. Alexander Pope. NOEC; OxBSP

On the beryl-rimmed rebecs of Ruby. Lily Adair. Thomas Holley Chivers. APN-1; OBAL

On the Bible. Thomas Traherne. ChIV-1

On the Bible. *Unknown.* NOSC

On the Birth of His Son. Su Tung-p'o, *Chinese.* AWP; OBVE, *tr.* by Arthur Waley

On the Birth of Jesus. Andreas Gryphius, *German.* GePo, *tr.* by George C. Schoolfield

On the birth of my son. Toki Zenmaro, *Japanese.* MJT, *tr.* by Makoto Ueda

On the Birth of My Son, Malcolm Coltrane. Julius Lester. PoBA

On the black tarmac playground dark. Deaf-and-Dumb School. Anthony Delius. PeSA

On the blank stones of the landing. (LL) The Colossus. Sylvia Plath. AFr; FaBoWP; HCAP; LiTM; NALW; NOBA; NoAM; NoP-4; Poetr; TAP; VCAP

On the Bleeding Wounds of Our Crucified Lord. Richard Crashaw. *See* Upon the Bleeding Crucifix.

On the Blessed Virgins Bashfulnesse. Richard Crashaw. HAP; OxBSP

On the bloody field of Monmouth. Captain Molly. William Collins. ImGa

On the bog road the blackthorn flowers, the turf-stacks. Anthony Cronin. BIrV *Fr.* R.M.S. *Titanic.*

On the bonnie banks o' Fordie. (LL) Babylon; or, The Bonnie Banks o' Fordie. *Unknown.* AmFP; ESPB; OxBB

On the Book. Czeslaw Milosz, *Polish.* CEEP, *tr.* by John Carpenter *and* Bogdana Carpenter

On the Border, First Series. Tu Fu, *Chinese*. CoBCP, *tr. by* Burton Watson

We recruits have our commanders to send us off. CoBCP, *tr. by* Watson, Burton

On the bottom of the sky. Burning Shewolf. Vasco [*or* Vasko] Popa, *Serbo-Croatian*. HSix; VCWP, *tr. by* Charles Simic

On the bridges / And along the banks. Kenneth Rexroth. APSN *Fr.* The Love Poems of Marichiko.

On the Bright Side. Carter Revard. VoR

On the Brink of Death. Michelangelo Buonarroti, *Italian*. AWP, *tr. by* John Addington Symonds

On the broad River Huai, dotted with islets, a village suddenly appears. A Little Village. Mei Yao Ch'en, *Chinese*. SuSp, *tr. by* Jonathan Chaves

On the Building of a New Church. *Unknown*. FaBoEE

On the Burial of His Brother. Catullus, *Latin*. AWP; IMW, *tr. by* Aubrey Beardsley *Fr.* Carmina.

(Carmen 101.) IMW

("Echoing for ever, brother, through a brother's tears. / —'Hail & Farewell'.") (LL) IMW

(Hail and Farewell.) LBC

("Journeying over many seas and through many countries.") IMW

On the Bus. Mitsuye Yamada. *Fr.* Camp Notes. WPOW

On the Butterflies. T'ang Yin, *Chinese*. CoBLCP, *tr. by* Jonathan Chaves

On the cabin-roof I lie. The Strenuous Life. Henry Sidgwick. OBCoV

On the Candidates for the Laurel. Alexander Pope. FaBoEE

On the Card[e]s, and Dice. Sir Walter Ralegh. ChIV-2; RB

(Prognostication upon Cards and Dice, A.) SiPS

On the Carpet, Staring at Myself. Slavko Mihalic. PoSu, *tr. by* Peter Kastmiler

On the Castle of Chillon. Byron. *See* Sonnet on Chillon.

On the ceiling. Gary Hotham. HA

On the chalk cliff edge struggles the final field. The Marginal Field. Stephen Spender. PoA

On the Charlie So Long. *Unknown*. AS

On the chest of a barmaid in Sale. Limerick. *Unknown*. PeLi

On the child crying for the bird of the snow. (LL) Snow. Edward Thomas. FaBoTw; NTP; OPOU; PFE

On the Christmaswhite plains of the floured and flowering kitchen table. The Bread of this World; Praises III. Thomas McGrath. RaBo

On the Circuit. W. H. Auden. FaBoA; NOBL; OxBTC

On the Circumsision: New Year's Day. Luke Wadding. NOIV

On the Civilization of the Western Aboriginal Country. Philip Freneau. APN-1; PaTW

On the clay of the Greeks lowly gleaming. Triplets for Beautiful Mistra. Nikos Karouzos, *Greek*. GrIP, *tr. by* Philip Sherrard

On the clearest night of the earliest spring of my life. Spring Comes to Mid-Ohio in a Holy Shower of Stars. Terry Hummer. NAmP90

On the Clerk of a Country Parish. William Shenstone. FaBoEE

On the Closing of Millom Ironworks. Norman Nicholson. FaBoTw

On the cloudy water. Tanka. Tsukamoto Kunio, *Japanese*. MJT, *tr. by* Makoto Ueda

On the Coast of Coromandel. The Courtship of the Yonghy-Bonghy-Bo. Edward Lear. EnLoPo; OAEL-2; OxBM

On the Coast of Coromandel. Sir Osbert Sitwell. MoBrPo

On the Cold Food Festival, Entertaining at the Southern Estate—the Guests Were Li Chiu-ho, Wang Tung-kao, Li Hu-ch'uan, Huang K'ung-ts'un, Li Lung-t'ang, and Hu Hu-shan. Li K'ai-hsien, *Chinese*. CoBLCP, *tr. by* Jonathan Chaves

On the Collar of Mrs. Dingley's Lap-Dog. Jonathan Swift. FaBoEE

On the Completion of the Pacific Telegraph. Jones Very. TAP

On the Concert. Trumbull Stickney. APN-2

On the Concord River. Henrietta Cordelia Ray. CBWP-3

On the Conflagrations at Washington. Philip Freneau. APN-1

On the Congo. Harry Edmund Martinson, *Swedish*. RB, *tr. by* Robert Bly

On the Coosawattee. James Dickey.

By Canoe through the Fir Forest. NYBP

On the Corner. Kit Robinson. FTOS

On the corner—116th and Lenox. Harlem Freeze Frame. Lebert Bethune. GT; PoBA

On the Countess Dowager of Pembroke. William Browne. AWP; HAP; NoP-4; OAEL-1; PoEL-2; PoRA; TFi

(Epitaph on the Countess[e] Dowager of Pembroke.) FaBoEE; NOBE; OBEV; SCGP

On the craggy mountain-top the mist. Majuba Hill. Roy Macnab. PeSA

On the crooked arm of Columbus, on his cloak. Pigeons. Alastair Reid. NYBP; TwCP

On the Cross ("Adore the lifted standard of the Cross"). Alcuin, *Latin*. MLL, *tr. by* Helen Waddell

On the Cross ("Here, dying for the world, the world's life hung"). Alcuin, *Latin*. MLL, *tr. by* Helen Waddell

On the Cross. Anna Kamienska, *Polish*. GI, *tr. by* David Curzon and Grazyna Drabik

On the crowded subway. Bicentennial Anti-Poem for Italian-American Women. Daniela Gioseffi. UnSA

On the Cuckoo. Francis Quarles. NTP

On the Curve-Edge. Abbie Huston Evans. NYBP

On the dark distant flurry. (LL) Angle of Geese. N. Scott Momaday. CDW; HATNAP

On the dark lake below, the fishermen's bells. Recollection of Bellagio. William Meredith. Poetr

On the Dark, Still, Dry, Warm Weather Occasionally Happening in the Winter Months. Gilbert White. NOEC

On the darkening Green. (LL) The Echoing [*or* Ecchoing] Green. William Blake. BoTP; CH; FHYEP; NAEL-2; NTP; OxAEP-2; PoE; Ro; UnPo

On the day I was born, many visitors came to see me. On My Birthday—Sick. Li K'ai-hsien, *Chinese*. CoBLCP, *tr. by* Jonathan Chaves

On the Day of Atonement. Yehuda Amichai, *Hebrew*. TOF, *tr. by* T. Carmi

On the Day of Cold Food. Spring Sun. Chu Hsi, *Chinese*. OHPC, *tr. by* Kenneth Rexroth

On the day of the explosion. The Explosion. Philip Larkin. EBEV; FaBoMo; HAP; NAEL-2; NoAM; NoP-4; OxAEP-2; OxBC; PeECV; RB; SCV; WeW-3

On the day of the festival Uncle leads our. Obon: Festival of the Dead. Mitsuye Yamada. LoHo

On the Day of the Mid-Autumn Festival of the Year Ping-yin (1686), Together with Chang Han-chan, Ching-fan, and Ching-t'ien, I Saw the Kuei Blossoms at the Northern Garden of Jade Peak. Yün Shou-p'ing, *Chinese*.

In a hidden spot on the northern mountain. CoBLCP, *tr. by* Jonathan Chaves

On the Day of Washing the Buddha in the Year Ting-wei (1607), I Dreamed That My Late Son Shih-ch'ü Was Holding a Book, and Appeared To Be Quite Happy. He Said That He Had Earned His Chin-shih Degree in the Underworld. After We Sighed and Laughed Together for a Long Time, I Woke Up and Wrote This Poem. T'ang Hsien-tsu, *Chinese*. CoBLCP, *tr. by* Jonathan Chaves

On the day that Tiadatha. Trenches. Owen Rutter. NSI *Fr.* The Song of Tiadatha.

On the day the sienna-skinned man. Russia, 1927. Ai. NoAM

On the day when the Savoy. Projection. Langston Hughes. MoNo; PFTM

On the dead oak tree bough. (LL) The Gallows. Edward Thomas. GEA; InPS-3; MoBrPo; MoP; NoAM; SCGP; UnPo

On the Death of a German Philosopher. Stevie Smith. OBCoV

On the Death of a Lady's Owl. Moses Mendes. TrJP

On the Death of a Late Famous General. Jonathan Swift. *See* A Satirical Elegy on the Death of a Late Famous General.

On the Death of a Mad Dog. Oliver Goldsmith. *See* An Elegy on the Death of a Mad Dog.

On the Death of a New Born Child. Mei Yao Ch'en, *Chinese*. OHPC, *tr. by* Kenneth Rexroth

On the Death of a Nightingale. Thomas Randolph. BeJo

On the Death of a Particular Friend. James Thomson. OBEV; SCGP *Fr.* On the Death of Mr. William Aikman the Painter.

On the Death of a Pious Lady. Olof Wexionius, *Swedish*. AWP, *tr. by* Sir Edmund Gosse

On the Death of a Young and Favorite Slave. Martial, *Latin*. AWP, *tr. by* Goldwin Smith

On the Death of an Emperor Penguin in Regent's Park, London. David Wright. NYBP

On the Death of an Infant of Five Days Old. Elizabeth Boyd. ECWP

("And the shock'd father tear for tear return.") (LL) CABP

(On the Death of an Infant of Five Days Old, being a Beautiful but Abortive Birth.) CABP

On the Death of Anne Brontë. Charlotte Brontë. IMW; VWP; WPE

On the Death of Catarina de Attayda. Luis de Camões, *Spanish*. AWP, *tr. by* R. F. Burton

On the Death of Cleopatra-Selene. Crinagoras, *Greek*. GrAn, *tr. by* Alistair Elliot

On the Death of Countess Luise Schwerin. Rilke, *German*. FP, *tr. by* J. B. Leishman

On the Death of Dean Swift. Jonathan Swift. OxAEP-1 *Fr.* Verses on the Death of Dr. Swift, D.S.P.D.

On the Death of Donne. Thomas Carew. NOBE *Fr.* An Elegie upon the Death of the Deane of Pauls, Dr. Donne. MeLP; PBRV; SeCP

On the Death of Dr [*or* Mr] Robert Levet [a Practiser in Physic]. Samuel Johnson. ChIV-2; EBEV; InPS-3; NAEL-1; NOBE; NOEC; NoP-4;

OAEL-1; OBEV; OxAEP-1; PFE; PeECV; PoE; PoEL-3; SCGP; SCV; TFi

On the Death of Echo, A Favourite Beagle. Hartley Coleridge. APo

On the Death of Emily Jane Brontë. Charlotte Brontë. VWP

On the Death of Friends in Childhood. Donald Justice. CoAmPo; ColAP; InPK-6; LCAP-2

On the Death of Henry the Lion. Hildebert, *Latin*. MLL, *tr. by* Helen Waddell

On the Death of Her Body. James Keir Baxter. PeNZ

On the Death of His Baby Son. Su Tung-p'o, *Chinese*. OHPC, *tr. by* Kenneth Rexroth

On the Death of his Father. Wei Wên-Ti, *Chinese*. ChiP, *tr. by* Arthur Waley

On the Death of His Son. Charles Wesley. NOCV

On the Death of His Son Vincent. Leigh Hunt. NOBVV

On the Death of His Wife. Mei Yao Ch'en, *Chinese*. OHPC, *tr. by* Kenneth Rexroth; OxBM

On the Death of His Wife. Muireadhach Albanach O'Dalaigh, *Irish*. BIrV; CIP-2, *tr. by* Frank O'Connor

On the Death of Joseph Rodman Drake. Fitz-Greene Halleck. APN-1; BLPA; PoEL-4

On the Death of Karl Barth. Jack R. Clemo. NOCV

On the Death of Lisa Lyman. Della Burt. BlSi

On the Death of Lord Tennyson. Andrew Lang. EPCY

On the Death of Ludwig Erhard. Hal Colebatch. NOBAu

On the Death of Mistress Mary Prideaux. William Strode. NOSC

On the Death of Mr. Crashaw. Abraham Cowley. BeJo; EPCY; MeLP; SeCP

On the Death of Mr. Persall's Little Daughter, in the Beginning of the Spring, at Amsterdam. *Unknown*. NOSC

On the Death of Mr. Pope. *Unknown*. NOEC

On the Death of Mr. Richard West. Thomas Gray. *See* Sonnet [on the Death of Mr. Richard West].

On the Death of Mr. William Aikman the Painter. James Thomson. On the Death of a Particular Friend. OBEV; SCGP

On the Death of Mr William Hervey. Abraham Cowley. FP *Fr*. On the Death of Mr. William Hervey [*or* Harvey]. EBEV; OBEV; SeCP

It was a dismal and a fearful night. BeJo; NOBE; OxAEP-1

On the Death of Mrs. Bowes. Lady Mary Wortley Montagu. BoWoP; LW

On the Death of Mrs. Rowe. Elizabeth Carter. ECWV

On the Death of Muriel Rukeyser. Billy Marshall-Stoneking. BMAP

On the Death of My Deare Sister the Countesse of Bridgewater. Lady Jane Cavendish *and* Lady Elizabeth Brackley. KTR

On the Death of My First and Dearest Childe, Hector Philipps. Katherine Philips. KTR

(Orinda upon little Hector Philips.) PBRV

("Twice forty months of Wedlock I did stay.") PBRV

On the Death of Old Bennet the News-Crier. *Unknown*. NOEC

On the Death of Our Lord. Richard Flecknoe. TIRV

On the Death of Ronald Ryan. Bruce Dawe. BMAP

On the Death of Sir Philip Sidney. Henry Constable. OBEV

(To Sir Philip Sidney's Soul.) NoSic

On the Death of Squire Christopher. John Wigson. OxBSP

On the Death of Sylvia Plath. Judith Herzberg, *Dutch*. WPOW, *tr. by* Manfred Wolf

On the Death of the Emperor Temmu. Empress Jito, *Japanese*. WPJ, *tr. by* Kenneth Rexroth *and* Ikuko Atsumi

On the Death of the Ferryman, Glaucus. Antiphilus, *Greek*. GrAn, *tr. by* W. S. Merwin

On the Death of the Giraffe. Thomas Hood. FaBoEE

On the Death of the Great Chef Alexis Soyer. *Unknown*. FaBoEE

On the Death of the Late Earl of Rochester. Aphra Behn. NoP-4

On the Death of the Lord Treasurer. *Unknown*. FaBoEE

On the Death of the Queen of Bohemia. Katherine Philips. KTR

On the Death of the Rev. Dr. Kippis. Helen Maria Williams. ECWP

On the Death of the Rev. Mr. George Whitefield, 1770. Phillis Wheatley. ColAP; NAAAL; NAAL-1; NAAL-3

On the Death of William Edward Burghardt Du Bois by African Moonlight and Forgotten Shores. Conrad Kent Rivers. PoBA

On the Debt My Mother Owed to Sears Roebuck. Edward Dorn. CoAmPo; TRP

On the Decease of the Religious and Honourable Jno Haynes Esqr. John James. SCAP

On the Deception of Appearances. Sadi. AWP, *tr. by* L. Cranmer-Byng *Fr*. The Gulistan.

On the deck of Patrick Lynch's boat I sat in woeful plight. The County of Mayo. Thomas Flavell, *Irish*. BIrV; IIP; OBEV, *tr. by* George Fox

On the Departure of Sir Walter Scott from Abbotsford, for Naples. Wordsworth. EBEV

On the Departure of the Nightingale. Charlotte Smith. WoRP

On the Departure Platform. Thomas Hardy. CBLP; NOBE; OBNC; OxBTC

On the Deputy of Ireland's Child. Sir John Davies. FaBoEE

On the Desert. Stephen Crane. LiTM *Fr*. War Is Kind.

On the Detraction Which Followed upon My Writing Certain Treatises. Milton. FaBoPV; PoE

(On the Same.) Son

On the Discoveries of Captain Lewis. Joel Barlow. AmPP

On the Doctors' Telling Him that till He Left off Making Verses He Was Not Fit to be Discharged. James Carkesse. NOSC

On the Duke of Buckingham. Dryden. *See* Zimri: "Some of their chiefs were princes of the land."

On the Duke of Buckingham. James Shirley. FaBoEE

On the Duke of Buckingham, Slain by Felton, the 23rd August, 1628. Owen Felltham [*or* Feltham]. NOSC

On the Earl of Leicester. *Unknown*. FaBoEE

On the Eastern horizon. Hitomaro, *Japanese*. OHMPJ, *tr. by* Kenneth Rexroth

On the eastern seacoast lives a sick man. Inscribed on a Painting by Myself. Ni Tsan, *Chinese*. CoBLCP, *tr. by* Jonathan Chaves

On the Eclipse of the Moon of October 1865. Charles Tennyson Turner. OBNC

On the Edge. Philip Levine. CoAP; TAP

On the eighth day, the rain stopped before dusk. The Loon's Egg. Peter Dale Scott. MoCV

On the electrified ocean. An Evening Scene. Zhao Zhenkai, *Chinese*. VCWP, *tr. by* McDougall, Bonnie S. and Chen Maiping

On the embankment he washes himself. Troop Train. Aleksandr Petrovich Mezhirov, *Russian*. TCRP, *tr. by* Deming Brown

On the Emigration to America [and Peopling the Western Country]. Philip Freneau. ColAP; NAAL-1; NAAL-3; TAP

On The Empress's Mind. John Ashbery. RACG

On the Entrance of the Castle Bridge. Simon Dach, *German*. GePo, *tr. by* George C. Schoolfield

On the envelope, her lone instruction. The Night Before His Parents' First Trip to Europe His Mother Writes a Letter "To Our Children." Michael J. Rosen. BAP-95

On the Erection of Shakespeare's Statue in Westminster Abbey. Alexander Pope. FaBoEE

On the Erie Canal, it was. The Aged Pilot Man. "Mark Twain." OBAL

On the Escalator. Adam Zagajewski, *Polish*. CEEP, *tr. by* Gorczynski, Renata

On the esplanade. The Edge of the War (1939–). William Montgomerie. FaBoTC

On the eve of death. Masaoka Shiki, *Japanese*. OHMPJ, *tr. by* Kenneth Rexroth

On the Eve of Our Mutually Assured Destruction. C. D. Wright. LCAP-2

On the Eve of the Plebiscite. Kenneth Rexroth. NNaP

On the Expected General Rising of the French Nation [in 1792]. Anna Laetitia Barbauld. CABP; ECWP

On the Extinction of the Venetian Republic. Wordsworth. GTBS-P; NOBE; OBEV; OBNC

On the face. George Swede. HA

On the fair green hills of Rio. The Burglar of Babylon. Elizabeth Bishop. InPS-3; NYBP; RB

On the Famous Voyage. Ben Jonson. BeJo

"By this time had they reached the Stygian pool." NOSC

On the far edge of a plain. The Watcher. John Peck. AmPA

On the Far Edge of Kilmer. Gerald Stern. LoL

On the far side. A Late Spring: Eastport. Philip Booth. Poetsp

On the far side of the water, high on a sand bar. Arkansas Traveller. Charles Wright. MT

On the Farm. Ronald Stuart Thomas. NoP-4; OxBTC

On the farm it never mattered. The Assistance. Paul Blackburn. NeAP; PoM

On the Farther Wall, Marc Chagall. Phyllis McGinley. OBSV *Fr*. Spectator's Guide to Contemporary Art.

On the Fatal Day January 30, 1648. Thomas Fairfax, Baron Fairfax of Cameron. NOSC

On the Ferry, Toward Patras. Emily Grosholz. RA

On the fibula of Sir——— or Sir———. (LL) The Wishbone. Paul Muldoon. CIP-2; PBCIP

On the Fifteenth Day of the Eighth Month: Watching a Rainstorm from a Tower in Seoul. Liu E, *Chinese*. CoBLCP, *tr. by* Jonathan Chaves

On the Fifteenth Day of the Ninth Month of the Year Kuei-mao of the Chih-cheng Period (Oct. 22, 1363), I Painted This to Send to the Summoned

Scholar, Sheng-po, and Inscribed This Poem on It. Ni Tsan, *Chinese*. CoBLCP, *tr. by* Jonathan Chaves

On the Fifteenth Day of the Seventh Month I Came Home Late from the City. Shen Chou, *Chinese*. CoBLCP, *tr. by* Jonathan Chaves

On the Fifth Anniversary of My Father's Death. Carolyn Lau. MoLi

On the fifth day after the rise of Spring. Parting from the Winter Stove. Po Chü-i, *Chinese*. ChiP, *tr. by* Arthur Waley

On the Fine Arts Garden, Cleveland. Russell Atkins. PoBA

On the first cool day in half a year. Sky. Richard Katrovas. LTA

On the first day / malcolm. The Easter Bunny Blues or All I Want for Xmas Is the Loop. Ebon Dooley. PoBA

On the first day of Christmas. *Unknown. See* The Twelve Days of Christmas.

On the first day of Philosophy 148, a small girl walked in. Nineteen. George Bogin. IFJA

On the first day of school the teacher asked me. How a Girl Got Her Chinese Name. Nellie Wong. WPOW

On the first day of spring. Virginia Brady Young. HA

On the first hour of my first day. The Beginner. Rudyard Kipling. FaBoTw *Fr.* Epitaphs of War [1914–1918]. OBWP

On the first of March. The Rooks. *Unknown.* OxNR

On the first of May. Mountain Greenery. Lorenz Hart. OBAL

On the first of the Feast of Feasts. Epilogue. Robert Browning. ChIV-2

On the first of Tishre I was walking the field in the evening breeze. Tashlich. Abba Kovner, *Hebrew.* IP, *tr. by* Warren Bargad *and* Stanley F. Chyet.

On the first page of my dreambook. Empire of Dreams. Charles Simic. BLT; LCAP-2; VCAP

On the fleet streams, the Sun, that late arose. Anna Seward. WoRP *Fr.* Sonnets.

On the Flesh of Christ. John William Corrington. MT

On the Flightiness of Thought. *Unknown, Irish.* TIRV, *tr. by* Brendan Kennelly

On the flood is of Babiloyne there we saten. Bible, *O.T. See* Psalm 137.

On the floor of the universe. Phew. Roger McGough. SpW

On the Fly-Leaf of Pound's Cantos. Basil Bunting. FaBoTw; NoAM; OxBTC

On the Following Work and Its Author. Jonathan Mitchell. SCAP

On the forgotten si- / ding. Tank Town. John Atherton. NYBP

On the Founding of Liberia. Melvin Beaunearus Tolson. UnPo *Fr.* Libretto for the Republic of Liberia.

On the Fragile Labyrinth. José Emilio Pacheco, *Spanish.* STV, *tr. by* John Frederick Nims

On the Frequent Review of the Troops. "M." NOEC

On the Frontier. Li Ho, *Chinese.* PLT, *tr. by* A. C. Graham

On the Fruit-Providing Autumn Season. Catharina Regina von Greiffenberg, *German.* WPoS, *tr. by* Michael Hamburger

On the Funeral of a Rich Miser. *Unknown.* PFE

On the Gift of a Knife. Muireadhach Albanach O'Dalaigh. NOIV

On the Gold Mines. B. W. Vilakazi. *See* In the Gold Mines.

On the Gospel. Francis Quarles. ChIV-2

On the Göta Canal, 1986. Joan Swift. PuP-14

On the Grasshopper. Anacreon, *Greek.* OBCVT, *tr. by* John Addison

On the Grasshopper and [the] Cricket. Keats. BoTP; FHYEP; FaBoBe; ImPo; NIP-4; OAEL-2; OxAEP-2; Poetr; Son; TTTS

(Grasshopper and Cricket, The.) APo

On the grassy banks / Lambkins at their pranks. Lambs at Play. Christina Rossetti. BoTP

On the gray sidewalks of America. (LL) Katori Maru, October 1920. Jim Mitsui. OpBo

On the Great Fog in London, December 1762. James Eyre Weeks. NOEC

On the Great Frost (1634). William Cartwright. NOSC

On the Great Western Canal of the State of New York. Philip Freneau. APN-1

On the green banks of Shannon, when Sheelah was nigh. The Irish Harper and His Dog. Thomas Campbell. CH

On the green sheep-track, up the heathy hill. Coleridge. OBNC *Fr.* Fears in Solitude. FHYEP; OBWP

On the grey sand beside the shallow stream. Ego Dominus Tuus. W. B. Yeats. CMoP; EPCY

On the ground are my sketches of the contours. The Painter in the Lion Cage. Betti Alver, *Estonian.* BoWoP, *tr. by* Willis Barnstone *and* Felix Oinas

On the ground floor of the sinking apartment house. Fragments of Ten Poems. Gábor Görgey, *Hungarian.* CEEP, *tr. by* Jascha Kessler

On the ground there was a tree. The Tree in the Wood. *Unknown.* AmFP

On the Group of the Three Angels Before the Tent of Abraham, by Raffaelle, in the Vatican. Washington Allston. APN-1; GS

On the Hall at Stowey. Charles Tomlinson. PoE

On the Hall of Precious Virtue. Yang Shih-ch'i, *Chinese.* CoBLCP, *tr. by* Jonathan Chaves

On the hall stand hangs a fur coat. Yevgeny Mikhailovich Vinokurov, *Russian.* TCRP, *tr. by* Daniel Weissbort

On the Happy Corydon and Phyllis. Sir Charles Sedley. BoLoP

On the headland's grassed and sheltered side. Storm. Judith Wright. WPE

On the Heart's Beginning to Cloud the Mind. Robert Frost. CMoP; GM

On the Heights. Walter Savage Landor. FaBoEE

On the high hill pastures. Wild Thyme. Joyce Sambrook. BoTP

On the highway. Está Muy Caliente. George Bowering. MoCV

On the hill tops I visit the snares. Love Song. *Unknown, Maori.* PeNZ, *tr. by* Margaret Orbell

On the hill's top we stood. Distances. Jeremy Kingston. NYBP

On the hillside. Bilberries. Gerda Mayer. Spl

On the Historians Freeman and Stubbs. J. E. Thorold Rogers. FaBoEE

(Two Historians.) OBCoV

On the holy day of your going out to war. Mohodahi, *Sanskrit.* BoWoP, *tr. by* Willis Barnstone

On the Holy Scriptures. Francis Quarles. ChIV-2

On the Hon. George Nathaniel Curzon, Commoner of Balliol. John William Mackail *and* Cecil Arthur Spring-Rice. OBCoV *Fr.* Balliol Rhymes.

On the horizon, the peaks assembled. Stephen Crane. MeMAP

On the humps of the low river hills. . . go to it, O jazzmen. Carl Sandburg. *See* Jazz Fantasia.

On the Ice Islands Seen Floating in the German Ocean. William Cowper. OAEL-1

On the idle hill of summer. A. E. Housman. MoBrPo; NOBE; OAEL-2; OBNC; OBWP

On the Ile de Gorée, M. Diop elegant. Double Take at Relais de L'Espadon. Thadious M. Davis. BlSi

On the Imprint of the First English Edition of "The Works of Max Beerbohm." Max Beerbohm. InPK-6; OBCoV

On the Inclusion of Miniature Dinosaurs in Breakfast Cereal Boxes. John Updike. OBCoV

On the Inconstancy of Women. Catullus. *See* Carmen 70 ("Lesbia says she'ld rather marry me").

On the Ineffable Inspiration of the Holy Spirit. Catharina Regina von Greiffenberg, *German.* PBWP; WPoS, *tr. by* Michael Hamburger

On the Infrequency of Celia's Letters. William Hammond. CBLP

On the inner walls. (LL) Stone. Charles Simic. ChAP; InPS-3

On the Inscription Over the Head of Christ on the Cross. Henry Colman. ChIV-2

On the Irish Club. Jonathan Swift. OBSV

On the Island. Dennis Brutus. AF

On the Island. Lawrence Raab. CMAP

On the Island. Louis Edward Sissman. NYBP

On the Island of the Spirits of the Dead. The Two Sisters. *Aborigine Oral Tradition.* NOBAu, *tr. by* Manoowa

On the Islands. Aleksandr Blok, *Russian.* TCRP, *tr. by* Geoffrey Thurley

On the Islands of All Winds. Aimé Césaire, *French.* VCWP, *tr. by* Clayton Eshleman *and* Annette Smith

On the Isle of Man shore, I carelessly wandered. The Isle of Man Shore. *Unknown.* AmFP

On the jewelweed. Larry Gates. HA

On the Jubilee of Queen Victoria. Tennyson. UnPo

On the Killing at Lindisfarne. Alcuin, *Latin.* MLL, *tr. by* Helen Waddell

On the kitchen table, under. Primer. Chana Bloch. IFJA

On the kitchen wall a flash. The World Outside. Denise Levertov. CoAmPo; TRP

On the Lady Arabella. Richard Corbet. NOSC

On the Lake. Vita Sackville-West. OBMV

On the Lake Poets. Charles Townsend. FaBoEE

On the lake, the autumn wind blows blue ripples. As I Looked at a Lake, My Thoughts Turned to a Certain Friend. Chu Yün-ming, *Chinese.* CoBLCP, *tr. by* Jonathan Chaves

On the Lakes of Ponchartrain. *Unknown.* AmFP

On the Lamented Death of Mrs. Throckmorton's Bullfinch. William Cowper. NOEC

On the landscape, to make of us what we could. (LL) Street Musicians. John Ashbery. HCAP; PoPoPo

On the last day of the year we have so much to be thankful for. The Last Day of the Year; or, New Year's Eve. Mrs. Henry Linden. CBWP-4

On the last year's trip I enjoyed this place. On the Road through Chang-te. Sun Yün-feng, *Chinese.* BoWoP; WPOW, *tr. by* Kenneth Rexroth *and* Ling Chung

On the Late Improvements at Nuneham, the Seat of the Earl of Harcourt. William Whitehead. OBGa

On the Late Massacre [or Massacher] in Piedmont [or Piemont]. Milton. AWP; GTBS-P; HAP; HeIP-4; NAEL-1; NOBE; OBWP; PoEL-3; Poetr; SCGP; Son; TFi; TRP; UnPo; WeW-3

("Early may fly the Babylonian woe.") (LL) CABP; GSo; NoP-4; PFE; PoPoPo

(Sonnet: On the Late Massacre in Piedmont.) NOCV

On the lawn at the villa. Louis Simpson. CoAP; OBAL; OxBC; WeT

On the lawn, beside the red house. The Weeds. Gregory Orr. WeT

On the Legends of a Dancer. Jean Garrigue. NMM-2

On the length and the breadth of the marvellous marshes of Glynn. (LL) The Marshes of Glynn. Sidney Lanier. AmPP; ImPo; NOBA; OxBA

On the Life of Man. Francis Quarles. ChIV-2; PeECV Fr. Divine Fancies.

On the Life of Man. Sir Walter Ralegh. NAEL-1

On the lips a taste of tolling we are blind. (Poem) (Chicago) (The Were-Age). Bill Knott. SPE

On the long shore, lit by the moon. The Goose Fish. Howard Nemerov. CMoP; HeIP-4; LiTM; NIP-4; NoAM; NoP-4; PoE; Poetr

On the Lord Gen[eral] Fairfax at the Siege of Colchester. Milton. NOSC

On the Loss of the Royal George. William Cowper. EBEV; NOBE

(Loss of the Royal George.) GTBS-P; OxAEP-1

("Shall plough the wave no more.") (LL) GTBS-P

On the Luxembourg Gallery. Washington Allston. APN-1

On the mantelpiece. Studio Poem. Cilla McQueen. PeNZ

On the many-leafed bedscreens, gold flickers and fades. Tune: "Deva-like Barbarian." Wen T'ing-yün, Chinese. CoBCP, tr. by Burton Watson

On the Marginal Way. Richard Wilbur. CAPP-1; CoAP; NOBA

On the Marriage at Cana. Rilke, German. GI, tr. by David Curzon and Will Alexander Washburn

On the Marriage of a Virgin. Dylan Thomas. EnLoPo; OxBM

On the Marriage of T. K. and C. C.: The Morning Stormy. Thomas Carew. BoLoP

On the marriage platform made of gold. Parancoti Munivar. ITG, tr. by William P. Harman Fr. The Sacred Marriage of Shiva and Parvati.

On the Masquerades. Christopher Pitt. ECEV; NOEC

On the Meadow. "Katri Vala," Finnish. PBWP, tr. by Jaakko A. Ahokas

On the Medusa of Leonardo da Vinci in the Florentine Gallery. Shelley. GS

On the Meetings of the Scotch Covenanters. Unknown. FaBoEE

On the Memorial building's. Under Cancer. John Hollander. CoAP

On the Memory of Mr. Edward King, Drowned in the Irish Seas. John Cleveland. OAEL-1; SeCP

(Upon the Death of Mr. King Drowned in the Irish Seas.) HAP

On the merry-go-round. Alan Pizzarelli. HA

On the Merry, Merry-Go-Round. Dorothy McGrath Martin. CTV

On the metro the man across. Here's Looking at You Francis Bacon. Joan Retallack. FTOS

On the mid stairs, between the light and dark. King Mark, Tristram, and Palamede. Swinburne. EBNV Fr. Tristram of Lyonesse.

On the Miracle of Loaves. Richard Crashaw. OxBSP

On the Miracle of Multiplied [or Multiplyed] Loaves. Richard Crashaw. OxBSP

On the Mississippi. Hamlin Garland. APN-2

On the moor of Kasuga. Hitomaro. AWP, tr. by Arthur Waley Fr. Manyo Shu, Part 3 of 4.

On the Morning of Christ's Nativity. Milton. MeLP; NOCV; PoEL-3; SCGP

("Bright-harnessed angels sit in order serviceable.") (LL) NoP-4

("Bright-harnest Angels sit in order serviceable.") (LL) PBRV

(Ode on the Morning of Christ's Nativity.) GTBS-P; ImPo

(Hymn on the Morning of Christ's Nativity [or On the Morning of Christ's Nativity].) NAEL-1; NOBE; OBEV

But peaceful was the night. FaBoCh

Oracles are dumm, The. GrIP

Magi, The.

This is the month, and this the happy morn. FaBoCh

On the Morning of Christ's Nativity. Prudentius, Latin.

Oracles are dumm, The. OBCVT, tr. by John Milton

On the morning of the crowning we chorused our. Geoffrey Hill. HAP Fr. Mercian Hymns.

On the Morning of the Third Night above Nisqually. W. M. Ransom. CDW

On the Motor Bus. Alfred Denis Godley. See Motor Bus.

On the Mountain. John Haines. BLT

On the Mountain. Neidhart von Reuental, German. AWP, tr. by Jethro Bithell

On the Mountain. Ruth Stone. BoWoP

On the mountain, Epicydes the hunter seeks. Callimachus. HePo Fr. Epigrams.

On the Mountain of Boiled Rice I met Tu Fu. To Tu Fu. Li Po, Chinese. TAL, tr. by Robert Payne

On the mountain, old trees, still green in autumn. Inscribed on a Painting. T'ang Yin, Chinese. CoBLCP, tr. by Jonathan Chaves

On the mountain peak, called "Going-to-the-Sun." The Apple-Barrel of Johnny Appleseed. Vachel Lindsay. OxBA

On the Mountain: Question and Answer. Li Po, Chinese. ChiPo, tr. by C. H. Kwock and Vincent McHugh

On the mountain slope. Gerard John Conforti. HA

On the Move. Thom Gunn. CMoP; HAP; LiTM; NoP-4; OAEL-2; OxAEP-2; OxBTC; PoE; TRP; TwCP

On the Name of Jesus. Richard Crashaw. ESCV

("And break before thee.") (LL) FSCP

(To the Name Above Every Name, the Name of Iesvs a Hymn.) FSCP

On the Nature of Food. Alberta Turner. LCAP-2

On the Nature of the Iconic. Gustaf Sobin. PT

On the navel of the Boer's domain. Lesotho. Bennett Makalo Khaketla, Sotho. PeSA, tr. by Dan Kunene and Jack Cope

On the New Forcers of Conscience Under the Long Parliament. Milton. FaBoPV; NAEL-1; NOSC; PBRV; Son

("New Presbyter is but Old Priest writ Large.") (LL) PBRV

On The New Inn: Ode, To Himself. Ben Jonson. See Ode to Himself.

On the new sand. What Her Girl Friend Said, the Lover within Earshot, behind a Fence. Ulloccanar, Tamil. PLW, tr. by A. K. Ramanujan

On the Night. Ivor Gurney. OxBSP

On the Night in Question. Patricia Goedicke. TAP

On the night of the Belgian surrender the moon rose. The Moon and the Night and the Men. John Berryman. CoAP; GEA; VCAP; VGW

On the Night of the Fifteenth Day of the First Month I Go Out and Return. Mei Yao Ch'en, Chinese. SuSp, tr. by Jonathan Chaves

On the Night of the Sixteenth of the Eighth Month: Watching the Moon from the Deck of the Ship, Aimo-maru in the Black Water Sea. Liu E, Chinese. CoBLCP, tr. by Jonathan Chaves

On the night road from El Rama the cows. Second Poem from Nicaragua Libre: War Zone. June Jordan. NoAM

On the ninth of November by the dawning of the day. Farewell to Kingsbridge. Unknown. ECEV

On the North Shore a reptile lay asleep. The Precambrian [or Pre-Cambrian] Shield. Edwin John Pratt. MoCV; NOBC Fr. Towards the Last Spike.

On the Numerous Accesse of the English to Waite upon the King in Holland. Katherine Philips. KTR

(On the Numerous Access of the English to Wait upon the King in Flanders.) NOSC

On the occasion of becoming an echo. Anselm Hollo. PT

On the Occurrence of a Spell of Arctic Weather in May, 1858. Paul Hamilton Hayne. APN-2

On the Ocean Floor. "Hugh MacDiarmid." FaBoMo; HAP

On the ocean floor as the foraminifera die. (LL) On the Ocean Floor. "Hugh MacDiarmid." FaBoMo; HAP

On the ocean that hollows the rocks where ye dwell. Hy-Brasail—the Isle of the Blest. Gerald Griffin. BLPA

On the old bicycle the plumber brought me. One for the Road. Nancy Willard. LiLi

On the old scarecrow. Lorraine Ellis Harr. HA

On the one-ton temple bell. Buson, Japanese. InPK-6

On the open side, look out. Roy Fisher. NBrP

On the Oregon Coast. Galway Kinnell. NoAM

On the Origin of Evil. John Byrom. NOEC

On the Origin of the Contrary. Miroslav Holub, Czech. VCWP, tr. by Stuart Friebert and Dana Hábová

On the Other Side. Czeslaw Milosz, Polish. PoSu, tr. by Jan Darowski

On the other side. Ohioan Pastoral. James Wright. LCAP-2

On the other side of the world I heard. Elegy for a Schoolmate. Vincent O'Sullivan. PeNZ

On the outside, in shape. Human Nature. Phan Bội Châu, Vietnamese. AVP, tr. by Huỳnh Sanh Thông

On the outskirts, dumplings of mud. Wang Fan-chih, Chinese. SuSp, tr. by Eugene Eoyang

On the Oxford Book of Victorian Verse. "Hugh MacDiarmid." MoBrPo

On the padlock. Penny Harter. HA

On the Pains of Translating Miklós Radnóti. Frederick Turner. RA

On the Painter Val Prinsep. D. G. Rossetti. FaBoEE

("There is a creator called God.") OBCoV

On the Painting "Joys of Village Life." Yün Shou-p'ing, Chinese.

For a hundred miles the west wind carries the fragrance of millet. CoBLCP, tr. by Jonathan Chaves

On the Painting, Mist Over Ten Thousand Mountains by Shih-ku. Yün Shou-p'ing, Chinese. CoBLCP, tr. by Jonathan Chaves

On the Painting of the Sistine Chapel. Michelangelo Buonarroti. *See* To Giovanni da Pistoia When the Author Was Painting the Vault of the Sistine Chapel, 1509.

On the path. Under the Maud Moon. Galway Kinnell. NNaP

On the path, / by this wet site. Under the Maud Moon. Galway Kinnell. NNaP

On the path winding. The Path among the Stones. Galway Kinnell. NNaP; NOBA

On the pathway mica glints. Water and Worship: An Open-Air Service on the Gatineau River. Margaret Avison. HAP

On the pavement a blind man walks. The Blind Man. Ksenya Nekrasova, *Russian.* TCRP, tr. by Vera Rich

On the pennants of blue are bold characters. Reviewing the Troops at Kuei-lin with Military Inspectors Chiang And Chang. Yang Chi, *Chinese.* CoBLCP, tr. by Jonathan Chaves

On the Phoenix. Jean Adams. ECWP

On the phonograph, the voice. Reunion. Carolyn Forché. NoAM

On the Photograph "Yarn Mill," by Lewis W. Hine. David Ray. WeT

On the Picture of a Child. Henrietta Cordelia Ray. CBWP-3

On the Pilgrims' Road. Andrew Young. FaBoTC

On the Pilgrim's Way in Kent, as It Leads to the Coldrum Stones. "Asphodel." BrRo

On the plain that town flat like an iron sheet. A Naked Town. Zbigniew Herbert, *Polish.* CEEP, tr. by Czesw Miosz

On the Ploughman [or Plough-Man]. Francis Quarles. NOSC

On the Poet, Arthur O'Shaughnessy—. D. G. Rossetti. OBCoV

On the Portrait of a Girl. Erinna, *Greek.* GrAn, tr. by Lenore Mayhew

On the Portrait of a Woman About to Be Hanged. Thomas Hardy. CMoP

On the Prince's Death, to the King. Sir Robert Ayton. NOSC

On the Problem of Choosing a Wife. Phocylides, *Greek.* OBCVT, tr. by Willis Barnstone

On the Prospect from Westminster Bridge. Elizabeth Tollet. ECWP

On the Prospect of Peace. Thomas Tickell.
Ah! curst Ambition, to thy lures we owe. ECEV

On the Prospect of Planting Arts and Learning in America. George Berkeley. AiP; ImPo; NOEC
(Verses on the Prospect of Planting Arts and Learning in America.) FaBoA

On the prow. The Landing. Daniel Halpern. AmPA

On the quays of Papeete, the dawdling white-ducked colonists. Gauguin. Derek Walcott. NoAM *Fr.* Midsummer.

On the Queen's Return from the Low Countries. William Cartwright. OBEV

On the Question of Fans/ The Slave Quarters Are Never Air Conditioned. Hattie Gossett. EC2

On the Railway. Aleksandr Blok, *Russian.* TCRP, tr. by Geoffrey Thurley

On the Railway Platform. Randall Jarrell. GM

On the rank harvest of betrayal they feed. The Rank Harvest of Betrayal. Wilma Stockenström, *Afrikaans.* PeSAV, tr. by Rosa Keet

On the rapids of the St. Lawrence. Henrietta Cordelia Ray. CBWP-3

On the Receipt of My Mother's Picture out of Norfolk [the Gift of My Cousin Ann Bodham]. William Cowper. NOEC; OxAEP-1
(Lines on Receiving His Mother's Picture.) CH

On the Reed of Our Lord's Passion. William Alabaster. PoEL-2

On the reef of Norman's Woe! (LL) The Wreck of the *Hesperus.* Henry Wadsworth Longfellow. APN-1; BLPA; CTV; EBEvV; EBNV; FaBoBe; OBCA; OBNV; PAR

On the Religion of Nature. Philip Freneau. AmPP; NAAL-1; NAAL-3

On the Relinquishment of a Title. Geoffrey Grigson. FaBoEE

On the Resurrection of Christ. William Dunbar. ChIV-2; NOCV; OxBS; PoEL-1
(Of the Resurrection of Christ.) EnVB

On the Reverend Jonathan Doe. *Unknown.* FaBoEE

On the Rhine. Charles Stuart Calverley. PeLV

On the River. Ku K'uang, *Chinese.* SuSp, tr. by Irving Y. Lo

On the River. Tu Fu, *Chinese.* CoBCP, tr. by Burton Watson

On the River. Yü Hsüan-chi, *Chinese.* SuSp, tr. by Jan W. Walls

On the river, every day these heavy rains. Li Po, *Chinese.* CoBCP, tr. by Burton Watson

On the River of Perfumes. The Song on the River of Perfumes. Tô Hū'u, *Vietnamese.* AVP, tr. by Huỳnh Sanh Thông

On the river, the spring tides are calm. Inscribed on an Album Leaf Painted by Dr. Lin. Pien Kung, *Chinese.* CoBLCP, tr. by Jonathan Chaves

On the Road. Seamus Heaney. TOF *Fr.* Sweeney Redivivus.

On the Road. William Kloefkorn. EC2

On the Road. The Prodigal Son. Leah Goldberg, *Hebrew.* GI, tr. by Robert Friend

On the road. Tanka. Toki Zenmaro, *Japanese.* MJT, tr. by Makoto Ueda

On the Road. Tu Mu, *Chinese.* PLT, tr. by A. C. Graham

On the Road at Night There Stands the Man. Dahlia Ravikovitch, *Hebrew.* WPOW, tr. by Chana Bloch

On the Road through Chang-te. Sun Yün-feng, *Chinese.* BoWoP; WPOW, tr. by Kenneth Rexroth and Ling Chung

On the road through the clouds. Den Sute-Jo, *Japanese.* WPJ, tr. by Kenneth Rexroth and Ikuko Atsumi

On the Road Through the Wu-i Mountains—Making Fun of Chia-tse for Falling Off His Horse. Hsü Wei, *Chinese.* CoBLCP, tr. by Jonathan Chaves

On the Road to California; or, The Buffalo Bullfight. *Unknown.* AmFP

On the road to Ch'ang-an my horse goes slowly. Tune: "Wanderings of a Youth." Liu Yung, *Chinese.* SuSp, tr. by Jerome P. Seaton

On the road to Damascus, Maryland. Enid Dame. UnSA

On the Road to Hsin-ch'eng. Su Tung-p'o, *Chinese.* CoBCP, tr. by Burton Watson

On the Road to Pyongyang—An Improvisation. Liu E, *Chinese.* CoBLCP, tr. by Jonathan Chaves

On the Road to San Romano. André Breton, *French.* PFTM, tr. by Simic, Charles and Michael Benedikt

On the road to the bay was a lake of rushes. The Bay. James Keir Baxter. PeNZ

On the Road to the Sea. Charlotte Mew. BrRo; CPO; FaBoWP

On the Road to Western Hill. Ch'ien Ch'ien-i, *Chinese.* SuSp, tr. by Irving Y. Lo

On the roads at night I saw the glitter of eyes. Eyes of Night-Time. Muriel Rukeyser. BoWoP

On the roadside. Tanka. Ishikawa Takuboku, *Japanese.* MJT, tr. by Makoto Ueda

On the rocky grassy slope of this hill, Topsy and I. On the Slope of this Hill. Shamsher Bahadur Singh, *Hindi.* OMIP, tr. by Vinay Dharwadker

On the Rouge. Raymond Souster. NOBC

On the rough diamond. Sign for My Father, Who Stressed the Bunt. David Bottoms. MT

On the Russian Persecution of the Jews. Swinburne. Son

On the rusting fender of the old. Buick. Marianne Boruch. WeT

On the salt water streets. Venice Recalled. Bruce Boyd. NeAP

On the Same. Roy Campbell. OBCoV; OxBTC

On the Same. Milton. *See* On the Detraction Which Followed upon My Writing Certain Treatises.

On the Same Nobleman. Robert Burns. *See* On Lord Galloway.

On the Same Picture. Walt Whitman. GS

On the Same [Death of My Dear Brother, Mr. H.S., Drowned]: The Boat. William Hammond. NOSC

On the sands is seen the sun rising. Composed at Sunset at the Dunes of Ho-yen. Ts'en Shen, *Chinese.* SuSp, tr. by Ronald C. Miao

On the sandy beach. Tanka. Maekawa Samio, *Japanese.* MJT, tr. by Makoto Ueda

On the school platform, draping the folding seats. Political Meeting. Abraham Moses Klein. MoCV

On the Sea. Keats. NoP-4; OAEL-2
(Sea, The.) OxBoS

On the sea and at the Hogue, sixteen hundred ninety-two. Hervé Riel. Robert Browning. FaBoBe

On the sea-floor a stone bell, tolling. The August Sleepwalker. Zhao Zhenkai, *Chinese.* VCWP, tr. by Donald Finkel

On the sea of motherhood and death you voyaged, waif / of eternity. The Death. Hayden Carruth. FiLi *Fr.* Mother.

On the Second Day of the Fifth Month—Written after Drink. Liu Ya-tzu, *Chinese.* SuSp, tr. by Wu-chi Liu

On the second of October, a Monday at noon. Walter Lesly. *Unknown.* ESPB

On the secret map the assassins. Rivers and Mountains. John Ashbery. CoAP; FTOS; NOBA; NoAM; NoP-4; TRP

On the Setting Up of Mr. Butler's Monument in Westminster Abbey. Samuel Wesley. NBLV; NOEC; OxBSP

On the seventh day. Love Affair 36. Jennifer Rankin. BMAP

On the Seventh day of the Seventh month, in the. The Everlasting Sorrow. Po Chü-i. ChiPo, tr. by Witter Bynner

On the sheep-cropped summit, under hot sun. Cat and Mouse. Ted Hughes. OxBSP

On the shimmering, mingled throngs of the poor. (LL) The Underworld. Garrett Kaoru Hongo. NAmP90; WWSi

On the shingle. Hitomaro, *Japanese.* OHPJ, tr. by Kenneth Rexroth

On the shore fish toss in the stretched nets of Simon, James, and John. Abundant Catch (Luke 5:4–10). Czeslaw Milosz, *Polish.* GI, tr. by Czeslaw Milosz and Lillian Vallee

On the shore of Nawa. Hioki no Ko-okima. AWP, tr. by Arthur Waley *Fr.* Manyo Shu, Part 3 of 4.

On the Sicilian strand a hare well wrought. Ausonius, *Latin*. OBVE, *tr. by* Richard Lovelace

On the sightless seas of ether. Mikhail Yuryevich Lermontov. AWP, *tr. by* Babette Deutsch *and* Avrahm Yarmolinsky *Fr.* The Daemon.

On the Siu Cheng Road. Su Tung-p'o, *Chinese*. OHPC, *tr. by* Kenneth Rexroth

On the Sixteenth Day I Visit the Temple Again. Pien Kung, *Chinese*. CoBLCP, *tr. by* Jonathan Chaves

On the sixteenth day of September, nineteen twenty-eight. The West Palm Beach Storm. *Unknown*. AmFP

On the sixth day we came. (LL) The Animals. Edwin Muir. CMoP; CRP; ChIV-1; EBEV; HeIP-4; KSG; MoBrPo

On the Skeleton of a Hound. James Wright. LiTM

On the Slope of the Desolate River. Rabindranath Tagore. OBMV *Fr.* Gitanjali.

On the Slope of this Hill. Shamsher Bahadur Singh, *Hindi*. OMIP, *tr. by* Vinay Dharwadker

On the slopes of the mountain. Clear Bright. Huang T'ing-chien, *Chinese*. OHMPC, *tr. by* Kenneth Rexroth

On the smooth brow and clustering hair. Walter Savage Landor. GBL

On the snow. Tanka. Tsukamoto Kunio, *Japanese*. MJT, *tr. by* Makoto Ueda

On the Snuff of a Candle. Sir Walter Ralegh. FaBoEE; SiPS

On the Sonnet. Keats. NIP-4; NoP-4; OAEL-2

On the South Coast of Cornwall. John Gray. NOBVV

On the South Downs. Sara Teasdale. MoAmPo

On the southwest side of Capri. The Nude Swim. Anne Sexton. WPE

On the Spartan Dead at Thermopylae. Simonides. *See* For the Spartan Dead at Thermopylai (480 B.C.).

On the Spirit Adulterated by the Flesh. Thomas Warton, the Elder. ChIV-1

On the Spirit of the Heart as Moon-Disk. Kojijū, *Japanese*. WPoS, *tr. by* Edwin A. Cranston

On the spring river, you depart. Tsung Ch'en. CoBLCP, *tr. by* Jonathan Chaves *Fr.* Song of Chiang-nan.

On the Spur of the Moment. Tu Fu, *Chinese*. CoBCP, *tr. by* Burton Watson

On the stage I stumbled. Indian Blood. Mary TallMountain. LoL; UnSA

On the stage, mirrored many times. The Stripper. Anita Endrezze-Danielson. CDW

On the stairway fragrance assails the bosom. A Spring Song of Tzu-yeh. Hsiao Yen, *Chinese*. SuSp, *tr. by* Jan W. Walls

On the stars below in Frederick town! John Greenleaf Whittier. *See* Barbara Frietchie.

On the Statue of an Angel, by Bienaimé, in the Possession of J.S. Copley Greene, Esq. Washington Allston. APN-1

On the Statue of Epaminondas in Thebes. *Unknown, Greek*. GrAn, *tr. by* Peter Levi

On the steps of the Pentagon I tucked my skull. Revised Notes for a Sonnet. "Edward Pygge." BXAP *Fr.* Robert Lowell's Notebook. OBCoV

On the stiff twig up there. Black Rook in Rainy Weather. Sylvia Plath. LiTM; NAAL-2; NoP-4; Poetr

On the stone terrace, underneath the shade. The Summer Landscape; or, The Dragon's Teeth. Rolfe Humphries. NYBP

On the Strange Apparitions at Christ's Death. Henry Colman. ChIV-2

On the Street. Constantine P. Cavafy, *Greek*. BoLoP, *tr. by* Rae Dalven

On the Street of Lo-yang. Meng Hao Jan, *Chinese*. SuSp, *tr. by* Paul W. Kroll

On the street / Slung on his shoulder is a handle half way across. The Shovel Man. Carl Sandburg. HAP

On the street, the sun. Bent. Martin Carter. HCP; PBCV

On the subject of nude bodies, my father asked. Send Pictures, You Said. . . . Laurie Duesing. DeD

On the Subject of Waves. Eldon Grier. MoCV

On the suburban street, guarded by patient trees. I Did Not Know the Truth of Growing Trees. Delmore Schwartz. LiTM

On The Subway. Sharon Olds. LTA

On the Suicide of a Friend. Reed Whittemore. CoAmPo

On the Suicide of Young Writers. Wilma Stockenström, *Afrikaans*. PeSAV, *tr. by* Stephen Gray

On the summer road that ran by our front porch. Lizards and Snakes. Anthony Hecht. FaBoMo; TwCP

On the Sun Coming Out in the Afternoon. Henry David Thoreau. OxBSP; PoEL-4

On the Swag. Ronald Allison Kells Mason. PeNZ

On the Sweet Comfort Brought by Grace. Catharina Regina von Greiffenberg, *German*.
"I look." WPoS, *tr. by* Hirshfield, Jane and Samuel Michael Halevi

On the Symbolic Consideration of Hands and the Significance of Death. Miller Williams. InPK-6

On the table, a book of glass. A Book of Glass. David Shapiro. PT; PmAP

On the table—white dishes, bread and yellow apples. Museum Street. Judita Vaiiunaite, *Lithuanian*. CEEP, *tr. by* Jonas Zdanys

On the Tack. Thomas Hearne. ECEV

On the tall hill. What She Said to Her Girl Friend. Paranar, *Tamil*. PLW, *tr. by* A. K. Ramanujan

On the Telescopic Moon. John Swanwick Drennan. BIrV

On the television screen. Galway Kinnell. *Fr.* The Dead Shall Be Raised Incorruptible. NOBA; PoE

On the temple bell. Spring Scene. Buson, *Japanese*. TTTS, *tr. by* Kenneth Koch *and* Harold Henderson

On the temple porch of Syrian Astarte. To Astarte. *Unknown, Greek*. GrAn, *tr. by* Guy Davenport

On the tenth day of December. Musselburgh Field. *Unknown*. ESPB

On the Tercentenary of Milton's Death. Gavin Ewart. OxBC

On the Thessalians Who Fought at Marathon. Aeschylus, *Greek*. GrAn, *tr. by* Edwin Morgan

On the third day of the third month, in fresh weather. The Elegant Women. Tu Fu, *Chinese*. SuSp, *tr. by* Mark Perlberg

On the third day rose Arp. Resurrection of Arp. Arthur James Marshall Smith. MoCV; NOBC

On the third day she went down to the kitchen. Wang Chien. *See* Words of the Newly Wed Wife.

On the third day there was a marriage at Cana in Galilee. John 2:1–12; On the third day there was a marriage. Rilke. GI *Fr.* St. John.

On the third finger of my left hand. Ceremony. William Stafford. LCAP-2

On the third planet too, life is found. Excerpt from a Report to the Galactic Council. Robert Conquest. OxBC

On the Thirteenth Day of Christmas. Charles Causley. OBCP

On the Thirteenth Day of the Eleventh Month I Went to the Granary for the First Time since My Illness. Mei Yao Ch'en, *Chinese*. SuSp, *tr. by* Jonathan Chaves

On the Three Children in the Fiery Furnace. Henry Colman. ChIV-1

On the Threshold. Karl Kraus, *German*. TrJP, *tr. by* Albert Bloch

On the Threshold. Amy Levy. LW; NOBVV; SDW

On the Threshold. *Unknown*. BLPA

On the threshold of heaven, the figures in the street. To an Old Philosopher in Rome. Wallace Stevens. ColAP; EnlH; MeMAP; MoP; NOBA; NoAM; Poetr

On the tidal mud, just before sunset. Daybreak. Galway Kinnell. BLT; ChAP

On the Tomb of Orpheus. Damagetus, *Greek*. GrAn, *tr. by* John Heath-Stubbs *and* Carol A. Whiteside

On the Tombs in Westminster Abbey. Francis Beaumont. CH; GTBS-P; OxAEP-1
(Lines on the Tombs in Westminster.) FaPoR; NOBE; OBEV; SCGP

On the top fence-rail. O. Mabson Southard. HA

On the top of the Crumpetty Tree. The Quangle Wangle's Hat. Edward Lear. CBNP; EBEV; FPC; PeVV

On the Tower. Annette von Droste-Hülshoff, *German*. PBWP; WPOW, *tr. by* James Edward Tobin

On the Tower of Gathering Remoteness. Su Tung-p'o, *Chinese*. TAL, *tr. by* Robert Payne

On the Town's Honest Man. Ben Jonson. NOSC

On the train. Going Uptown to Visit Miriam. Victor Hernandez Cruz. LoL

On the Translation of Anacreon. Horace Walpole. FaBoEE

On the Treasury of the True Dharma Eye. Dogen. EnlH

On the trunk of a haunted tree. (LL) The Haunted Oak. Paul Laurence Dunbar. AAP; ColAP; NAAAL; UnPo

On the Turning Up of Unidentified Black Female Corpses. Toi Derricotte. NAmP90; NMM-2

On the twelfth floor. Martin Burke. HA

On the twentieth, at a certain moment. Christmas 1956. György Petri, *Hungarian*. VCWP, *tr. by* Wilmer, Clive and George Gömöri

On the Twentieth Day. Ni Tsan, *Chinese*. CoBLCP, *tr. by* Jonathan Chaves

On the 25th Anniversary of the Liberation of Auschwitz. Eli W. Mandel. NOBC

On the Twenty-fifth of July. David Cornel DeJong. NYBP

On the Twenty-First Day of the Fifth Month, I Reached Home. Yüan Mei, *Chinese*. CoBLCP, *tr. by* Jonathan Chaves

On the Twenty-fourth: Improvisations. Liu E, *Chinese*. CoBLCP, *tr. by* Jonathan Chaves

On the Twenty-fourth of the Third Month, in the Year Ting-wei Sailed across Lake T'ai from Behind the Mountain. Wu Wei-yeh, *Chinese*. SuSp, *tr. by* Chang Yin-nan *and* Lewis C. Walmsley

On the 21st March 1960. I Remember Sharpeville. Sipho Sepamla. AF

On the Two Great Floods. Francis Quarles. ChIV-1

On the Uniformity and Perfection of Nature. Philip Freneau. AmPP

On the Union. Ben Jonson. PBRV

On the University Carrier Who Sick'n'd [or Sickened] in the Time of His Vacancy [, Being Forbid to go to London, by Reason of the Plague]. Milton. EBEV; FaBoCh; FaBoEE; NOSC; OxAEP-1

On the Unusual Cold and Rainy [or Rainie] Weather in the Summer, 1648. Robert Heath. NOSC

On the up-platform at Morpeth station. The Complaint of the Morpethshire Farmer. Basil Bunting. CTC

On the Use of Jayshus. Oliver St. John Gogarty. FaBoEE

On the Use of New and Old Words in Poetry. Anna Seward. Son

On the Vanity of Earthly Greatness. Arthur Guiterman. APAD; BXAP; HeIP-4; HoPM; OBCA; TrJP

On the Village Green. William Somervile. ECEV Fr. Hobbinol.

On the Wall. Immanuel di Roma, Hebrew. TrJP, tr. by Solomon Solis-Cohen

On the wall by the bathtub there clings. Things Grow Up out of the Dark. Joan Dobbie. LoHo

On the Wall of a KZ-Lager. János Pilinszky, Hungarian. AF; PoSu, tr. by Janos Csokits and Ted Hughes; HP, tr. by Ted Hughes

On the wan sea-strand. Evening Twilight. Heinrich Heine. AWP, tr. by John Todhunter Fr. The North Sea.

On the warm July river. Inner Tube. Michael Ondaatje. NoAM

On the water. Tanka. Tsukamoto Kunio, Japanese. MJT, tr. by Makoto Ueda

On the Water of Our Lord's Baptism[e]. Richard Crashaw. GeHe

On the Waterfront. Michael Foley. PNI

On the Watergate Women. Robin Morgan. GLP

On the Way. Peter Huchel, German. CEEP, tr. by Michael Hamburger

On the way and be their best. (LL) A Prayer: "Teach me, Father, how to go." Edwin Markham. CTV

On the way down. The Way Down. Philip Levine. NOBA

On the Way Home. Chế Lan Viên, Vietnamese. AVP, tr by Huỳnh Sanh Thông

On the way home. Tanka. Miya Shūji, Japanese. MJT, tr. by Makoto Ueda

On the way to God the difficulties. Lal Ded, Kashmiri. WPoS, tr. by Coleman Barks

On the Way to Hangchow: Anchored on the River at Night. Po Chü-i, Chinese. ChiP, tr. by Arthur Waley

On the Way to Huang-ch'i River. Wang Shih-chieng, Chinese. SuSp, tr. by Richard John Lynn

On the Way to Kew. William Ernest Henley. MoBrPo Fr. Echoes.

On the Way to Mind. Milo De Angelis, Italian. NeIt, tr. by Lawrence Venuti

On the Way to Pa-ling. Yüan Mei, Chinese. CoBLCP, tr. by Jonathan Chaves

On the way to the evening reading. The Shrine and the Burning Wheel. Mark Jarman. NAmP90

On the Way to the Mission. Duncan Campbell Scott. NOBC

On the way up from Sheet I met some children. To Edward Thomas. Alun Lewis. PoWW

On the Welsh Language. Katherine Philips. NOSC

("If honor to an ancient name be due.") NoP-4

("Least her own captive else should her subdue.") (LL) CABP

(On the Welch Language.) NoP-4

On the Welsh Marches. Walter Stone. NYBP

On the western hills the sun sets, the eastern hills darken. A Piece for Magic Strings. Li Ho, Chinese. PLT, tr. by A. C. Graham

On the wet sand the queen emerged from forest. Theseus: A Trilogy. Yvor Winters. NOBA

On the white throat of the useless passion. Ad Finem. Ella Wheeler Wilcox. BLPA

On the whole, we conclude the Romans won't do it, and I shan't. (LL) Dulce it is, and decorum, no doubt, for the country to fall, to. Arthur Hugh Clough. EBVV; EnVR; FaBoPV; OxAEP-2

On the wide heath at evening overtaken. Edna St. Vincent Millay. CMoP; WPE

On the wide level of a mountain's head. Time, Real and Imaginary. Coleridge. NOBE; OBEV; OxBSP; PBMP

On the wind, a drifting echo. Christmas Night. Lawrence Sail. OBCP

On the wind of January. The Wind of January. Christina Rossetti. BoTP Fr. A Year's Windfalls.

On the windows, the dirty film. The Finder. Robin Blaser. FTOS

On the Wing. Christina Rossetti. VWP

On the wings of the buck and wing. (LL) Buckdancer's Choice. James Dickey. HeIP-4; NOBA; NYBP; NoAM; NoP-4; WeT

On the Wings of the Morning. Jeffery Day. NSI

On the World. Francis Quarles. HAP

On the Wounds of Our Crucified Lord. Richard Crashaw. NAEL-1

On the Yangtze. Wang An-shih, Chinese. SuSp, tr. by Jan W. Walls

On the Yard. Etheridge Knight. RaBo

On the Yellow Footprints. Mcavoy Layne. CDa

On thee thou must take a long journey. Unknown. Fr. Everyman. NAEL-1; NAWM-1; OAEL-1; PoEL-1

On Theodoros. Simonides, Greek. GrAn

On these ancient discs, smooth-backed, severe. Old Gramophone Records. James Kirkup. NYBP

On these white cliffs, that calm above the flood. Dover Cliffs. William Lisle Bowles. OxAEP-1

On Things Seen. Tsung Ch'en, Chinese.

Rebels' cavalry are everywhere, The. CoBLCP, tr. by Jonathan Chaves

On Thinking of Photographing My Fantasies. Nellie Wong. OpBo

On this bald hill the new year hones its edge. Parliament Hill Fields. Sylvia Plath. HCAP; NALW

On this bus to oblivion i bleed in the seat. Today I Am a Homicide in the North of the City. Wanda Coleman. NAAAL

On this cold. Marlene Mountain. HA

On This Day. M. B. Goffstein. NTCP

On This Day I Complete My Fortieth Year. Peter Porter. BMAP

On This Day I Complete My Thirty-sixth Year. Byron. FHYEP; OAEL-2; OBWP; PoE

("And take thy rest.") (LL) NoP-4; Ro

(Messalonghi. January 22, 1824. On This Day I Complete My Thirty-sixth Year.) NOBRP

("'Tis time this heart should be unmoved.") NoP-4; Ro

On this day man's disgust is known. On Shooting Particles beyond the World. Richard Eberhart. LiTM

On this day of my birth, I see no visitors. The Evening of My Birthday. Yang Shih-ch'i, Chinese. CoBLCP, tr. by Jonathan Chaves

On this day, the sun. Hiroshima. "Agyeya," Hindi. OMIP, tr. by Agyeya and Leonard Nathan

On this day they break bread. Leah Goldberg, Hebrew. MHP, tr. by Ruth Finer Mintz

On this day when you have needed to sleep forever. Healing Animal. Joy Harjo. SeSe

On this feast day, oh, cursèd day and hour! Love at First Sight. Marlowe. NOBE Fr. Hero and Leander. AAS

On this ground I may look for rest. My Detacted Villa. Li Shan-fu. SuSp, tr. by Edward H. Schafer

On this her daughter's tomb. Anyte, Greek. GrAn, tr. by Sally Purcell

On this high hill in a year's turning. (LL) Poem in October. Dylan Thomas. EBEvV; ImPo; NAEL-2; NoAM; OxAEP-2; PoA; PoRA; RB; SoSe-8; UV

On this hotel, their rumpled royalties. The West Forties: Morning, Noon, and Night. Louis Edward Sissman. CoAP; NYBP

On This Island. W. H. Auden. CMoP; NAEL-2; PoE

On this lone Isle, whose rugged rocks affright. Sonnet: "Suppos'd to Be Written at Lemnos." Thomas Russell. NOBRP; NOEC

On this map white. A state thick as a fist. A Map of Montana in Italy. Richard Hugo. LCAP-2

On this primeval strip of western land. Destroyers. Sir Henry Head. NSI

On this resemblance, where we find. On a Death's Head. Elizabeth Tollet. ECWP

On this road / no one will follow me. Basho, Japanese. OHPJ, tr. by Kenneth Rexroth

On this side, and on that, men see their friends. All Impelled Onward Alike. Robert Blair. OxAEP-1 Fr. The Grave.

On this small island that undoes us daily, gently. Blue Guide. Stephen Yenser. BAP-95

On this summer night. Chikako, Japanese. WPoS, tr. by Edwin A. Cranston

On this tiny planet. Tune: "Full River Red"—A Reply to Kuo Mo-jo. Mao Tse-tung, Chinese. SuSp, tr. by Eugene Eoyang

On this tree thrown up. Spindrift. Galway Kinnell. NYBP

On this whole earth who can compare with him? Poor and Happy. Trần Tế Xu'o'ng, Vietnamese. AVP, tr. by Huỳnh Sanh Thông

On this winter night. Lady Izumi, Japanese. BoWoP, tr. by Willis Barnstone

On those black plowed fields. Descending. Ioan Alexandru, Romanian. CEEP, tr. by Donald Eulert and Stefan Avadanei

On Those That Deserve It. Francis Quarles. NOCV; NOSC

On Those That Hated "The Playboy of the Western World" 1907. W. B. Yeats. NOIV

On three crosses of a tree. A Charm Rhyme. Unknown. FaBoVe

On three sides / the sea's. On a High House in Byzantium. Paulus Silentiarius, Greek. GrAn, tr. by Andrew Miller

On thrones from China to Peru. A Model for the Laureate. W. B. Yeats. CMoP

On through it into the future, into the night. (LL) Six Years Later. Joseph Brodsky, *Russian.* TCRP; VCWP, *tr.* by Richard Wilbur

On thy fair bosom, silver lake. To Senaca Lake. James Gates Percival. BoTP

On thy stars below in Frederick town! (LL) Barbara Frietchie. John Greenleaf Whittier. APN-1; AiP; BoTP; CBCWP; CTC; ColAP; EBNV; FaBoBe; FaPoR; NCAP; NOBA; OBAL; OBCA; PAR; PoLF; TFi

On thy stupendous summit, rock sublime! Beachy Head. Charlotte Smith. NOBRP; NoP-4

On thy verdant Throne elate. On the Grasshopper. Anacreon, *Greek.* OBCVT, *tr.* by John Addison

On Time. Richard Hughes. MoBrPo

On Time. Milton. ImPo; OBEV; SCGP

On, to the City of God. (LL) Rugby Chapel. Matthew Arnold. EBVVPR; EnVR; PeECV; PoEL-5

On to the Morgue. *Unknown.* AS

On Tobacco. Charles Cotton. OBSV

On Tom Holland and Nell Cotton. *Unknown.* FaBoEE

On Tom Moore's Translation of Anacreon. Thomas Erskine. FaBoEE

On Tom-o-Combe. *Unknown.* FaBoEE

On Tom Onslow, Earl of Onslow. *Unknown.* FaBoEE

On Tomato Ketchup. *Unknown.* NBLV

(Tomato Ketchup.) Spl

On top of all earthly torments. Vain Attempt. Günter Kunert, *German.* CEEP, *tr.* by Michael Hamburger

On Top of Old Smoky. *Unknown.* KaS

On top of the Crumpetty Tree. The Quangle Wangle's Hat. Edward Lear. OTCP

On Track. Kathleene West. FFC

On Trading Time for Life by Work. Alan Dugan. AFr

On Trash. Vladimir Mayakovsky, *Russian.* TCRP, *tr.* by Daniel Weissbort

On tree-topped hill, on tufted green. Tree-topped Hill. *Unknown.* NOEC

On Trees. Alan Dugan. NoAM

On Trying to Imagine the Kiwi Pregnant. Clarence Major. GT

On Tuesday morn at half-past six o'clock. James Rigg. James Hogg. BXAP

On TV. (LL) May. John Updike. AYFP

On Twisting River Is the Old Home of My Father. Now That My Illness Has Eased Up, I Have Written These Six Poems About the Place. Chin Nung, *Chinese.*

I remember when he took me on a trip to this place. CoBLCP, *tr.* by Jonathan Chaves

On Two Brothers. Simonides, *Greek.* AWP, *tr.* by W. H. D. Rouse

On Two Monopolists. John Byrom. FaBoEE

On Venus, time passes slowly because. Here. Marvin Bell. AmPA

On Vermeer's "Young Woman with a Water Jug" (1658) in the Metropolitan Museum. Helen Pinkerton. FFC

On Viewing Her Sleeping Infant. Maria Frances Cecelia Cowper. ECWP

On Viewing Herself in a Glass. Elizabeth Teft. ECWP

On village green, whose smooth and well-worn sod. A Disappointment. Joanna Baillie. NOEC; WoRP

On vinegar and sour fish sauce Rome's legions stemmed avalanches. The Drugs of War. Les A. Murray. BMAP

On Virtue. Phillis Wheatley. TAP

On Visiting My Son, Port Angeles, Washington. Duane Niatum. CDW

On Visiting the Graves of Hawthorne and Thoreau. Jones Very. TAP

On Vuk Karadzic Street. Steel-Rod Benders. Miroslav Valek, *German.* CEEP, *tr.* by Ewald Osers

On Wakening. Philip Larkin. LBC

On Waking after Dreaming of Raoul. Lynn Emanuel. NAmP90

On wan dark night on Lac St. Pierre. The Wreck of the *Julie Plante.* William Henry Drummond. BLPA; FaBoBe

On washday in the good old bad old days. Washday Battles. Geoffrey Summerfield. NOxBChV

On Watching a Caterpillar Become a Butterfly. Clarence Major. NAAAL

On Watching a World Series Game. Sonia Sanchez. NBV

On Watching Politicians Perform at Martin Luther King's Funeral. Etheridge Knight. NNaP

On Water. Charles Tomlinson. OxBoS

On water the Man-Fisher walks. (LL) The Drunken Fisherman. Robert Lowell. AmPP; CMoP; ChIV-2; ImPo; LiTM; NOBA; OxBA; VGW

On Waterloo's ensanguined plain. On Scott's Poem "The Field of Waterloo." Thomas Erskine. NBLV

On Wednesday night. Wednesday Night Prayer Meeting. Jay Wright. ISC; PoBA

On Wenlock Edge the wood's in trouble. A. E. Housman. APAD; GTBS-P; MoBrPo; NAEL-2; NOBE; NoP-4; OBNC; OxAEP-2; OxBTC; PoEL-5; PoRA; RB; SCGP; TFi

On western hills the sun dies, eastern hills are dusking. Song of the Sacred Strings. Li Ho, *Chinese.* CoBCP, *tr.* by Burton Watson

On Westwall Downes [or On Westwell Downs]. William Strode. NOSC; PoEL-2

On what a brave and curious whim. Clocks. Louis Ginsberg. TrJP

On what foundation stands the warrior's pride. Charles XII of Sweden. Samuel Johnson. NOBE; OBWP *Fr.* The Vanity of Human Wishes [The Tenth Satire of Juvenal Imitated]. EBEV; ECEV; NOEC; OAEL-1; OxAEP-1; PoEL-3; TFi

On what they hunger to become. (LL) Boat People. Yusef Komunyakaa. CDa; PoPoPo

On which God moves, and treads beneath his feet the All! (LL) Sonnet: "The Starry flower, the flower-like stars that fade." Frederick Goddard Tuckerman. APN-2

On Whitsunday morning. Dunt Dunt Dunt Pittie Pattie. *Unknown.* FaBoVe

On William Prynne. Samuel Butler. FaBoEE

On William Wilson, Tailor. *Unknown.* FaBoEE

On windy days. Clothes on the Washing Line. Frank Flynn. OTCP

On windy days the mill. The Unfortunate Miller. Alfred Edgar Coppard. FaBoTw

On Winter. Mary Leapor. PEW

On winter nights. The Car Cemetery. Ciaran Carson. CIP-2

On winter nights, when my grandmother. Nijole Miliauskaite, *Lithuanian.* VCWP, *tr.* by Jonas Zdanys

On Wishes. Mahmoud Darwish, *Arabic.* VCWP, *tr.* by Denys Johnson-Davies

On Witch Moutain the fireflies flit in the autumn night. Upon Seeing the Fireflies. Tu Fu, *Chinese.* SuSp, *tr.* by Wu-Chi Liu

On Wodin's day, sixth of December, thirty-nine. *In re* Solomon Warshawer. Abraham Moses Klein. MoCV

On Woman. W. B. Yeats. CMoP; ChIV-1

On Women ("Britannia's daughters"). Edward Young. ECEV *Fr.* Satires. ECEV

On Women ("Lavinia is polite"). Edward Young. ECEV *Fr.* Satires. ECEV

On wool-soft feet he peeps and creeps. Santa Claus. Walter De la Mare. PChr

On Words and Concepts and Things. Paul Ramsey. CRP

On Wordsworth's Cottage, near Grasmere Lake. Letitia Elizabeth Landon. Ro *Fr.* The Zenana, and Minor Poems of L.E.L.

On Work. Kahlil Gibran. PoToHe *Fr.* The Prophet.

On Worldly Prelates. Charles Wesley. ChIV-2

On Yes Tor. Sir Edmund William Gosse. CH

On yon hill's top which this sweet plain commands. Invites His Nymph to His Cottage. Philip Ayres. EnLoPo

On yonder hill there stands a creature. O, No, John [or The One Answer]. *Unknown.* PeLV

On yonder oak, upon its lordliest height. Mistletoe. Mary E. Tucker. CBWP-1

On your bare rocks, O barren moors. The Barren Moors. William Ellery Channing. APN-1

On your dazzling throne, Aphrodite. Sappho, *Greek.* BoWoP, *tr.* by Willis Barnstone

On Your Own. Tess Gallagher. NMM-2

On your piano aa plaster Beethoven stands. Picture Postcard from Our Youth. Dan Pagis, *Hebrew.* VCWP, *tr.* by Stephen Mitchell

On your slender body. For the Courtesan Ch'ing Lin. Wu Tsao, *Chinese.* BoWoP; WPOW, *tr.* by Kenneth Rexroth *and* Ling Chung

On your throne, a marvel of art, immortal. Sappho, *Greek.* STV, *tr.* by John Frederick Nims

On Your Twenty-First Birthday. Joan Austin Geier. FFC

On Zaccheus [or Zacheus]. Francis Quarles. HAP; NOSC; OxBSP

On Zion and on Lebanon. Henry Ustic Onderdonk. AH

Once. Eric N. Batterham. CH

Once. Alice Walker. BlSi

I/ never liked/ white folks. PoBA

It is true--/ I've always loved. PoBA

Once a boy beheld a bright. The Rose. Goethe, *German.* AWP, *tr.* by James Clarence Mangan

Once a day the rocks, with little warning. Naskeag. Alfred Corn. VCAP

Once a dream did weave a shade. A Dream. William Blake. CH; FHYEP; NOBRP; Ro *Fr.* Songs of Innocence.

Once a forest painted upon. Winter. Helen G. Quigless. BkSV *Fr.* Childhood Scenes in Four Seasons.

Once a jolly swagman camped by a billabong. Waltzing Matilda. Andrew Barton Paterson. CBAP

Once a Kansas zephyr strayed. Zephyr. Eugene Fitch Ware. PoLF

Once, a lady of the O Moores. Parthenogenesis. Nuala Ni Dhomhnaill, *Irish.* CIP-2, *tr.* by Michael Hartnett

Once a little boy, Jack, was, oh! ever so good. The Sad Story of a Little Boy That Cried. *Unknown.* OBSP

Once a little boy was dreaming. Parables, I. Antonio Machado Ruiz, *Spanish.* STV, *tr. by* John Frederick Nims

Once a little girl received a present. The Bear. Vladimir Aleksandrovich Lugovskoy, *Russian.* TCRP, *tr. by* Gordon McVay

Once a long time ago, you remember. Phillip Lopate. IFJA

Once a man is born he has to die. All Intents. Larry Eigner. VGW

Once a man jumped out of a streetcar, but so clumsily that he fell under an automobile. An Event on the Street. Daniil Kharms. AF

Once a mouse, a frog, and a little red hen. The Mouse, The Frog and The Little Red Hen. *Unknown.* BoTP

Once a pallid vestal. The Vestal. Nathalia Crane. TrJP

Once a raven from Pluto's dark shore. The True Facts of the Case. Anthony Euwer. OBAL; PeLi

Once a snowflake fell. Winter Poem. Nikki Giovanni. MBE; PiM

Once a time is how the baby asks for a story. The Height of the Season. Maxine W. Kumin. FFC

Once Again. Liz Sohappy Bahe. CDW

Once again. György Petri, *Hungarian.* CEEP, *tr. by* Robert Austerlitz

Once again a spring has come around. A Natural Theology. James Whitehead. MT

Once again, my luggage packed, I'm returning to Wu. Mooring in the Rain at Sung-ling. Chin Nung, *Chinese.* CoBLCP, *tr. by* Jonathan Chaves

Once again, once again. Velemir Khlebnikov, *Russian.* TCRP, *tr. by* Gary Kern

Once again over your chipped cups brimming with tea. (LL) Poem to My Grandmother in Her Death. Michele Murray. CrSp; IMW

Once Again the Mind. Faiz Ahmad Faiz, *Arabic.* AF, *tr. by* Naomi Lazard

Once again the pine-tree sung. Ralph Waldo Emerson. APN-1 *Fr.* Woodnotes II ("As sunbeams stream through liberal space"). NOBA

Once again the scurry of feet[]those myriads. The Face of the Waters. Robert David Fitzgerald. CBAP

Once again to see West Lake! Yüan Mei. *Fr.* In Late Spring of the Year Keng-hsü (1790), I Stayed at the Sun Family's Gemstone Mountain Villa at West Lake. Before Leaving, I Wrote These Poems as Mementos. CoBLCP, *tr. by* Jonathan Chaves

Once alien here my fathers built their house. John Hewitt. CABP; CIP-2; PNI

Once Allen Ginsberg stopped to pee at a bookstore in New Jersey. Allen Ginsberg. Toi Derricotte. PBCAP

Once, among the transports, was one with children—two freight. Children. Charles Reznikoff. FTOS

Once an ex-con told me. The Rape Poem. Tommi Avicolli. GLP

Once, and but once found in thy company. The Perfume. Donne. ESCV; FSCP; NoSic; SeCP *Fr.* Elegies.

Once and for all I will lie down here like a dead man. The Faces I Love. Gerald Stern. LoL

Once and Upon. Madeline Gleason. NeAP

Once, as a child, I ate raspberries. And forgot. Raspberries. Laurence David Lerner. EBEV

Once as a child I loved to hop. Adam's Footprint. Vassar Miller. MT; WeT

Once as I in my study sat and saw. The Hourglass. Joseph Beaumont. NOSC

Once, as in the darkness I lay asleep by night. The Nightmare. Wang Yen-Shou, *Chinese.* ChiP, *tr. by* Arthur Waley

Once as it was morning and I was in the field. Poppies. Zalman Schneour, *Hebrew.* MHP, *tr. by* Ruth Finer Mintz

Once [or Ons], as methought, Fortune me kissed [or kist or kyst]. The Lover Rejoiceth the Enjoying of His Love. Sir Thomas Wyatt. AAS; BoLoP; SiPS

Once, as old Lord Gorbals motored. Lord Gorbals. Harry Graham. PeLV

Once as we were sitting by. Spring 1942. Roy Fuller. LiTM; OxBTC

Once at a merry wedding feast. St. George Tucker. NBLV *Fr.* The Cynic. OBAL

Once at Swanage. Thomas Hardy. CBLP

Once before I loved this quiet place. Returning to Lotus Village. Kao Ch'i, *Chinese.* CoBLCP, *tr. by* Jonathan Chaves

Once between us the Atlantic. Sundered. Israel Zangwill. TrJP

Once—but no matter when. A Chronicle. *Unknown.* CBNP; OBSP

Once by the Pacific. Robert Frost. CMoP; GSo; HAP; HeIP-4; LiTM; MeMAP; MoAmPo; NAAL-2; NOBA; PFE; Son; TRP; VGW; WeW-3

Once Cypris sent to Europa a sweet dream. Europa. Moschus, *Greek.* HePo, *tr. by* Barbara Hughes Fowler

Once Delpho read—sage Delpho, learned and wise. The Patrons of My Early Song. Mary Leapor. ECWP *Fr.* Epistle to Artemisia.

Once did my Philomel reflect on me. Sir John Davies. *Fr.* Sonnets to Philomel. SiPS

Once Did My Thoughts. *Unknown.* EBEV

Once did She hold the gorgeous east in fee. On the Extinction of the Venetian Republic. Wordsworth. GTBS-P; NOBE; OBEV; OBNC

Once down on my knees to growing plants. A Mood Apart. Robert Frost. OxBSP

Once, Driving West of Billings, Montana. Susan Mitchell. WeT

Once drunk, my delight knows no limits. Written When Drunk. Chang Yüeh, *Chinese.* CoBCP, *tr. by* Burton Watson

Once, far over the breakers. Akiko Yosano, *Japanese.* OHMPJ, *tr. by* Kenneth Rexroth

Once, for a dare. After the Deluge. Wole Soyinka. HBAPE

Once, grave Laodicean profiteer. Lourenço Marques. Charles Eglington. PeSA; PeSAV

Once he puts out the light. The Hermit Has a Visitor. Maxine W. Kumin. BoWoP

Once he will miss, twice he will miss. Death ("Once he will miss, twice he will miss"). *Unknown.* AWP *Fr.* The Thousand and One Nights.

Once I am sure there's nothing going on. Church Going. Philip Larkin. CABP; CMoP; GTBS-P; HeIP-4; LiTM; MoBrPo; MoP; NAEL-2; NIP-4; NoAM; NoP-4; OAEL-2; Poetr; SCV; SoSe-8; TFi; TwCP; UnPo

Once / I believed in exclamation marks. Playing for Keeps. Thomas Erwin, *German.* CEEP, *tr. by* A. Leslie Willson

Once I belonged to Achaimenides. A Field. *Unknown, Greek.* GrAn, *tr. by* Peter Jay

Once I came across / some beardless doctors. Strato, *Greek.* GrAn, *tr. by* Thomas Meyer

Once I courted a fair beauty bride. The Fair Beauty Bride. *Unknown.* AmFP

Once I cried for new songs to sing. I Sing No New Songs. Frank Marshall Davis. PoBA

Once I entered. Like Ana. Nina Cassian, *Romanian.* PoSu, *tr. by* Nina Cassian

Once I followed horses. Thistledown. Denis Glover. PeNZ *Fr.* Sings Harry.

Once I goosestepped across the square. Résumé. Bei Dao, *Chinese.* AF, *tr. by* Bonnie S. McDougall

Once I had a gerbil. My Gerbil. John Kitching. PeP

Once I had a taste. Remembrance of Strange Hospitality. Yelena Shwarts, *Russian.* VCWP, *tr. by* Michael Molnar

Once I heard an old bachelor say. The Bachelor's Complaint. *Unknown.* AmFP

Once I heard him play. At the Half-Note Café. Ira Sadoff. NAmP90

Once, I knew a fine song. Scaped. Stephen Crane. APN-2 *Fr.* The Black Riders [and Other Lines].

Once I lay down with Hermione. Asclepiades, *Greek.* InMo, *tr. by* Sam Hamill

Once I learnt in wilful hour. On A Wife. Francis Burdett Money-Coutts. OxBSP

Once I liked pablum. Siv Widerberg, *Swedish.* NTCP, *tr. by* Verne Moberg

Once I lived in capitals. Italic. Roger McGough. OBCoV

Once I Lived in Cottonwood. *Unknown.* AmFP

Once I lived with my brothers, images. The Centaur Overheard. Edgar Bowers. CoAmPo

Once I loved a spider. The Spider and the Ghost of the Fly. Vachel Lindsay. VGW

Once I pass'd through a populous city imprinting my brain. Walt Whitman. AmPP; GLoP; NAAL-1; NAAL-3; OxBA; RaBo; SAmP

Once I read a story. The Story. Dan Pagis, *Hebrew.* PoSu, *tr. by* Stephen Mitchell

Once I saw a Devil in a flame of fire. A Memorable Fancy. William Blake. *Fr.* The Marriage of Heaven and Hell. NAEL-2; NOBRP; OAEL-2

Once I saw a little bird [going hop, hop, hop]. The Little Bird. Mother Goose. BoTP; CTV; OxNR; ReMoGo

Once I seen a human ruin. Safety-Clutch. Ambrose Bierce. APN-2; OBAL *Fr.* The Devil's Dictionary.

Once I shone afar like a. Kenneth Rexroth. APSN *Fr.* The Love Poems of Marichiko.

Once I tried to be Anglo, played up. Alloy. Robin Boody Galguera. IFJA

Once I was a boy and I sat in a meadow with flowers in it. Time Passes. Richard Percival Lister. NYBP

Once I was a cow, a horse. Wang An-shih. CoBCP, *tr. by* Burton Watson *Fr.* Twenty Poems in Imitation of Han-shan and Shih-te.

Once I was a lizard. A Look in the Past. Jared Angira. PBMAP

Once I was a monarch's daughter. *Unknown.* CH

Once I was a young horse all in my youthful prime. Poor Old Horse. *Unknown.* NTP

Once I was good like the Virgin Mary and the Minister's wife. The Scarlet Woman. Fenton Johnson. NAAAL; PoBA; RACG

Once I was happy, but now I'm forlorn. The Man on the Flying Trapeze. George Leybourne. BLPA; FaBoBe

Once I was in love. Who's been exempted? Philodemus, *Greek*. GrAn, *tr. by* William Moebius

Once I was jealous of lovers. Now I am. The Valley. Stanley Moss. NYBP

Once I was reading Hesiod. Argentarius, *Greek*. GrAn, *tr. by* Alistair Elliot

Once I wished I might rehearse. Freedom. Ralph Waldo Emerson. APN-1

Once, if I remember well, my life was a feast where all hearts opened and all wines flowed. A Season in Hell. Rimbaud *and* Paul Verlaine (1844–96), *French*.

Once in a dream (for once I dreamed of you). On the Wing. Christine Rossetti. VWP

Once in a dream I saw a snake. Snake. Paresh Chandra Raut, *Oriya*. OMIP, *tr. by* Jayanta Mahapatra

Once, in a foreign country, I was suddenly ill. The Widening Spell of the Leaves. Larry Levis. NAmP90; PBCAP

Once in a hundred years the lemmings come. The Lemmings. John Masefield. CMoP

Once in a Lifetime, Snow. Les A. Murray. CBAP; NoP-4

Once in a saintly passion. James Thomson. NOBVV; PFE

Once in a While a Protest Poem. David B. Axelrod. InPK-6

Once in a while in the sounds of wind and voices. White Beach. Reginald Gibbons. BAP-96

Once in a while somebody fights for breath. Vanishing Lung Syndrome. Miroslav Holub, *Czech*. VCWP, *tr. by* David Young *and* Dana Hábová

Once in a while / we'd find a patch. The Children. William Carlos Williams. SAmP

Once in a while when I lean my head back to stare at the sky. Looking for Him. Patty Turner. IFJA

Once in Canandaigua, hitchhiking from Ann Arbor. Faces. John Ciardi. WeW-3

Once, in [a] finesse of fiddles found I ecstasy. The Embankment (The Fantasia of a Fallen Gentleman on a Cold, Bitter Night). Thomas Ernest Hulme. EBEV; FaBoMo; GTBS-P; OPOU; OxBSP; OxBTC

Once, in finesse of fiddles found I ecstasy. Thomas Ernest Hulme. *See* The Embankment (The Fantasia of a Fallen Gentleman on a Cold, Bitter Night).

Once in Mexico an old man was. Visions. William Stafford. NoAM

Once, in my early thirties, I saw. Once There Was Light. Jane Kenyon. LoL *Fr.* Having It Out With Melancholy. BAP-93

Once in our lives, / Let us drink to our wives. *Unknown*. FaBoEE

Once in Persia reigned a King. Even This Shall Pass Away. Theodore Tilton. BLPA

Once in Royal David's City. Cecil Frances Alexander. OxBChV

Once in the dark of night. The Dark Night. Saint John of the Cross, *Spanish*. AWP; OBMV, *tr. by* Arthur Symons; STV; WeW-3, *tr. by* John Frederick Nims

Once in the dear dead days beyond recall. Love's Old Sweet Song. G. Clifton Bingham. FaBoBe

Once, in the Giant's Ring, I closed my eyes. Home. Frank Ormsby. PBCIP; PNI

Once, / in the pearly once-upon-a-time. Carmen, or the Made-Up Girl. Lyubomir Levchev, *Bulgarian*. CEEP, *tr. by* Jascha Kessler *and* Aleksandar Shurbanov

Once in the Phoenix tower the phoenix made her nest. On Climbing the Phoenix Tower at Chinling. Li Po, *Chinese*. TAL, *tr. by* Robert Payne

Once in the universe ripened. God's Family. Sigitas Geda, *Lithuanian*. CEEP, *tr. by* Jonas Zdanys

Once in the winter. The Forsaken. Duncan Campbell Scott. NOBC

Once it had gorged itself. On a Pig's Head. Charles Tomlinson. NoAM

Once it smiled a silent dell. The Valley of Unrest. Edgar Allan Poe. APN-1; AmPP; NAAL-1; NAAL-3; PAR; PoEL-4

Once it was cards on the table. In Memory of Elizabeth Kearney, Blasket-Islander. Michael Davitt, *Irish*. BiHa, *tr. by the author*

Once, long ago. (LL) Brooms. Charles Simic. AmPA; NNaP

Once, long ago, a friend gave me a book. The Gift. Margaret E. Bruner. PoToHe

Once, long ago, set close beside a wood, *mod. vers. by* Frank Ernest Hill. Chaucer. *See* The Nun's Priest's Tale.

Once looked Gudrun. Gudrun Laments over Sigurd. *Unknown*. OBVE *Fr.* The First Lay of Gudrun. AWP, *tr. by* William Morris *and* Eirikr Magnusson *Fr.* The Elder Edda.

Once loving is a gen'ral Fashion. On Loving Once and Loving Often. Elizabeth Tollet. LW

Once More. Forugh Farrokhzad. BoWoP, *tr. by* Jascha Kessler *and* Amin Banani

Once More a-Lumbering Go. *Unknown*. AmFP

Once more around should do it, the man confided. Flight of the Roller Coaster. Raymond Souster. NOBC

Once more beneath my thumb the globe turns. Childhood. Donald Justice. LCAP-2

Once more by the brook the alder leaves. Hayden Carruth. NNaP

Once more, Cesario. Shakespeare. SCV *Fr.* Twelfth Night.

Once More Fields and Gardens. T'ao Ch'ien, *Chinese*. AWP, *tr. by* Amy Lowell *and* Florence Ayscough

Once More Following the Rhymes of Pin-lao's Poem "Getting Up After Illness." Huang T'ing-chien, *Chinese*. CoBCP, *tr. by* Burton Watson

Once more he sees his companions' faces. The Survivor. Primo Levi, *Hebrew*. HP, *tr. by* Ruth Feldman *and* Brian Swann

Once more I came to Sarum Close. The Cathedral Close. Coventry Patmore. EBVV *Fr.* The Angel in the House.

Once more I come to the white page of art. The Cost of Seriousness. Peter Porter. NoAM

Once more I move among you, dear familiar places. Amagansett Beach Revisited. John Hall Wheelock. NYBP

Once more I visited the place. Female's Lamentations, The; or, The Village in Mourning. Hannah Wallis. ECWP

Once more I walk the round of Hisar's stronghold. The Old Fortress. Elisaveta Bagryana, *Bulgarian*. CEEP, *tr. by* Jascha Kessler *and* Aleksandar Shurbanov

Once more, listening to the wind and rain. The Return. Arna Bontemps. GT; PoBA

Once More, O Lord. George Washington Doane. AH

Once More, Our God, Vouchsafe to Shine! Samuel Sewall. AH; SCAP

Once more the changed year's turning wheel returns. Barren Spring. D. G. Rossetti. EBVV; IMW; NoP-4; OAEL-2; OBNC; PoEL-5 *Fr.* The House of Life.

Once more the cuckoo's call I hear. Spring. Aubrey Thomas De Vere. OBNC *Fr.* A Year of Sorrow.

Once more the leaves. Seattle, Autumn, 1933. Alfred Encarnacion. OpBo

Once more the storm is howling, and half hid. A Prayer for My Daughter. W. B. Yeats. CMoP; HAP; LiTM; MoP; NAEL-2; NoAM; NoP-4; OxBTC; PFE; PoA; PoLF; PoRA; RaBo; TFi

Once more unto the breach, dear friends, once more. Henry V at the Siege of Harfleur. Shakespeare. EBEvV; OxAEP-1 *Fr.* King Henry V.

Once more unto the breach, dear friends, / once more. Shakespeare. SAGP *Fr.* King Henry V.

Once more upon the waters! yet once more! Byron. FHYEP *Fr.* Childe Harold's Pilgrimage.

Once Mr. Daddy Long-legs. The Daddy Long-legs and the Fly. Edward Lear. CBNP

Once Musing as I Sat. The Fly. Barnabe Googe. CH

Once, my braids swung heavy as ropes. The Butcher's Wife. Louise Erdrich. HATNAP; NoP-4

Once, my father got invited. The Age of Reason. Michael Van Walleghen. NAmP90

Once my parents were older. Chiyojo, *Japanese*. BoWoP, *tr. by* David Ray

Once noble custom was: by blood on battleground. The Old Nobility. Friedrich von Logau, *German*. GePo, *tr. by* George C. Schoolfield

Once older than me, now certainly younger. A Portrait by Bronzino. Maura Stanton. NAmP90

Once on a charger there was laid. Salome. Charles Lamb. ChIV-2

Once on a morning of sweet recreation. The Blackbird. *Unknown*. NOIV

Once on a time, a monarch, tired with whooping. The Apple Dumplings and a King. "Peter Pindar." OBSV

Once on a time a thousand different men. James Henry. NOBVV

Once on a time did Eucritus and I. Harvest-Home. Theocritus. AWP, *tr. by* Charles Stuart Calverley *Fr.* Idylls.

Once on a Time, fatigu'd and out of Breath. The Cause of War. *Unknown*. OBCVT, *tr. by* Thomas Parnell *Fr.* Batrachomyomachia (The Battle of the Frogs and Mice).

Once on a time I used to be. Harlot's Catch. Robert Malise Bowyer Nichols. FaBoTw

Once on a time, it came to pass. The Fable of the Piece of Glass and the Piece of Ice. John Hookham Frere. OxBChV

Once on a time (so runs the Fable). Horace. OBCVT, *tr. by* Alexander Pope and Jonathan Swift *Fr.* An Imitation of the Sixth Satire of the Second Book of Horace.

Once on a time, some centuries ago. Monk of Casal-Maggiore, The (The Sicilian's Tale). Henry Wadsworth Longfellow. AmPP; OxBA *Fr.* Tales of a Wayside Inn.

Once on a time there was a pool. Rev. Homer Wilbur's "Festina Lente." James Russell Lowell. OBAL *Fr.* The Biglow Papers.

Once on the mountain's balmy lap reclined. James Montgomery. NOBRP *Fr.* The Brahmin.

Once, once, in Washington. Patriotic Tour and Postulate of Joy. Robert Penn Warren. AiP; NYBP

Once. . . once upon a time. Martha. Walter De la Mare. MoBrPo

Once only the barbarian lyre calls. (LL) The Scythians. Aleksandr Blok, *Russian*. AWP, *tr.* by Babette Deutsch *and* Avrahm Yarmolinsky

Once or twice he eyed me oddly. Once. Temptations of St. Antony by His Housekeeper. Elizabeth Smither. PeNZ

Once-over, The. Paul Blackburn. NeAP; PoM

Once over, the heart-rending war. At Toriwon. Chi-hun Cho, *Korean*. CKP, *tr.* by Jaihiun Kim

Once, playing cricket, beneath a toast-dry hill. Curriculum Vitae. Robert Gray. NOBAu

Once riding in Old Baltimore. Incident. Countee Cullen. BPo; ChAP; KaS; NAAAL; NAAL-2; NOxBChV; NTCP; NoAM; NoP-4; OBCA; PFE; PoBA; PoPoPo; Poetr; SSLK; VGW

Once she was the reason for his festivals. What Her Girl Friend Said, When the Woman Was About to Take Back Her Unfaithful Husband. Orampokiyar, *Tamil*. PLW, *tr.* by A. K. Ramanujan

Once, so long ago. For Paddy Mac. Padraic Fallon. CIP-2; IIP

Once some people were visiting Chekhov. Chocolates. Louis Simpson. InPS-3; OBCoV; OxBC

Once someone loved this piece of junk. The Garage Sale as a Spiritual Exercise. Thomas M. Disch. GI

Once, taking a train into Chicago. Freight Cars. Stephen Dobyns. GM

Once the Days. Denis Glover. PeNZ *Fr.* Sings Harry.

Once, the mighty waves of ocean. The Precious Pearl. Priscilla Jane Thompson. CBWP-2

Once the nation's chief was honored by the company of one. A Notable Dinner. Lizelia Augusta Jenkins Moorer. CBWP-3

Once the realization is accepted that even between the closest people. Rilke. ITG, *tr.* by Stephen Mitchell *Fr.* Letters.

Once the Sole Province. Douglas Crase. EOEF

Once the wind. Shake Keane. AYFP

Once the world was waiting for a song. The History of Poetry. Peter Cooley. NAmP90

Once there lived a little man. *Unknown*. BoTP

Once there was. From an ass to an analyst and back. Joyce Mansour, *French*. MFP, *tr.* by Martin Sorrell

Once there was a bridegroom named Mr. Ormantude whose intentions were hard to disparage. The Strange Case of Mr. Ormantude's Bride. Ogden Nash. OxBM

Once there was a fence here. Former Barn Lot. Mark Van Doren. MoAmPo

Once there was a little boy. Switch on the Night. Ray Bradbury. OBSP

Once there was a little boy whose name was Robert Reese. An Overworked Elocutionist. Carolyn Wells. BLPA

Once there was a little Kitty. Kitty. Elizabeth Payson Prentiss. BoTP

Once there was a man named Mr. Artesian and his activity was tremendous. Mr. Artesian's Conscientiousness. Ogden Nash. NBLV

Once there was a shock. After a Death. Tomas Tranströmer, *Swedish*. VCWP, *tr.* by Robert Bly

Once there was a snowman. The Snowman. *Unknown*. OTCP

Once there was a woman went out to pick beans. The Hairy Toe. *Unknown*. OBSP

Once there was an elephant. Eletelephony. Laura Elizabeth Richards. CTV; ImGa; NBLV; NOxBChV; NTCP; OBCA; OxBChV

Once There Was Light. Jane Kenyon. *Fr.* Having It Out With Melancholy. BAP-93

("'Ones drown!' After that, I wept for days.") (LL) LoL

Once there were peasant pots and a dry brown hare. Joan Miró. Ruthven Todd. SPE

Once there were 3 little Indian girls. Charité Espérance et Foi. Earle Birney. OxBC

Once there were three stones sitting in a patch of soft. The Death of Potchikoo. Louise Erdrich. *Fr.* Old Man Potchikoo. HATNAP

Once they were sticks and stones. Names. Robert Earl Hayden. GT

Once this soft turf, this rivulet's sands. The Battle-Field. William Cullen Bryant. PoLF

Once to every man and nation comes the moment to decide. James Russell Lowell. APN-1; FaPoR *Fr.* The Present Crisis.

("They enslave their children's children who make compromise with sin.") (LL) APN-1

Once to life I said, yes! To Life I Said Yes. Chaim Grade, *Yiddish*. TrJP, *tr.* by Joseph Leftwich

Once to the verge of yon steep barrier came. The Recluse; Home at Grasmere. Wordsworth.

Once told us where. (LL) Landscape Beyond Warsaw. Peter Huchel, *German*. AF, *tr.* by Daniel S. Simko; PoSu, *tr.* by Michael Hamburger

Once, twice, thrice / I give thee warning. *Unknown*. OxNR

Once up u hurl a stone. Mike 65. Lennox Raphael. PoBA

Once upon a colony. Can. Hist. Earle Birney. OxBC

Once upon a midnight dreary, eerie, scary. Ravin's of Piute Poet Poe. C. L. Edson. BXAP

Once upon a midnight dreary, while I pondered [*or* ponder'd], weak and weary. The Raven. Edgar Allan Poe. APN-1; AmPP; BLPA; CH; EBEvV; EBNV; FaBoBe; FaBoCh; HeIP-4; ImGa; NAAL-1; NAAL-3; NIP-4; NOBA; OBCA; OBNV; OxBA; PWR; PoRA; TAP; TFi; UV

Once upon a time. Chernobyl. Mary Jo Salter. FFC

Once upon a time. Gabriel Okara. PBA

Once upon a time, children. Storytime. Judith Nicholls. OBSP

Once upon a time / I caught a little rhyme. Catch a Little Rhyme. Eve Merriam. OBCA

Once upon a time / I composed a witty rhyme. The Minstrel's Last Lay. John Barth. OBAL

Once upon a time I was. To the Tune "The Fall of a Little Wild Goose." Huang O, *Chinese*. WPOW, *tr.* by Kenneth Rexroth *and* Ling Chung

Once upon a time in California. A Friend of the Family. Louis Simpson. NNaP

Once upon a time, the goddesses settled down. First Merseburg Spell. *Unknown, German*. GePo, *tr.* by Carroll Hightower

Once upon a time there was a girl called Annabell. Annabell and the Witches. Mick Gowar. OBSP

Once upon a time / there was a lonely wolf. Fable. János Pilinszky, *Hungarian*. OBVE; PoSu; RB, *tr.* by Ted Hughes *and* Janos Csokits

Once upon a time there was a number. Forgetful Number. Vasco [*or* Vasko] Popa. HSix, *tr.* by Charles Simic *Fr.* The Yawn of Yawns.

Once upon a time there was a story. The Story of a Story. Vasco [*or* Vasko] Popa, *Serbo-Croatian*. CBNP, *tr.* by Anne Pennington

Once upon a time there was a tale. The Tale About a Tale. Vasco [*or* Vasko] Popa. HSix *Fr.* The Yawn of Yawns.

Once upon a time there was a triangle. A Wise Triangle. Vasco [*or* Vasko] Popa. PoSu, *tr.* by Anne Pennington; CBNP, *tr.* by Anne Pennington *and* Charles Simic *Fr.* The Yawn of Yawns.

Once upon a time there was a yawn. The Yawn of Yawns. Vasco [*or* Vasko] Popa. PoSu, *tr.* by Anne Pennington *Fr.* The Yawn of Yawns.

Once upon a time there was an error. Proud Error. Vasco [*or* Vasko] Popa. HSix, *tr.* by Charles Simic *Fr.* The Yawn of Yawns.

Once upon a time there was an infinity of echoes. Petrified Echoes. Vasco [*or* Vasko] Popa. PoSu, *tr.* by Anne Pennington *Fr.* The Yawn of Yawns.

Once upon a time there was an Italian. Columbus. Ogden Nash. FaBoA; NoP-4

Once upon a time there were three little foxes. The Three Foxes. A. A. Milne. OxBChV

Once, walking home, I passed beneath a tree. The Music of a Tree. Walter James Turner. MoBrPo

Once, walking in the woods. Getting at the Root of the Matter. Henry Taylor. BXAP

Once we dreamed of eagles. Reading Indian Poetry. Ramona Wilson. VoR

Once we had a knocker. Lazy. Lu Yu, *Chinese*. OHMPC, *tr.* by Kenneth Rexroth

Once we knew the world well. Wislawa Szymborska, *Polish*. AF, *tr.* by Grazyna Drabik *and* Sharon Olds

Once we played at love together. Mathilde Blind. LW

Once when by Trent's pellucid streams. Elves and Fairies. John Gilbert Cooper. ECEV *Fr.* The Call of Aristippus.

Once when Grandma moved her hand. A Railroad Happening. Daniil Kharms, *Russian*. CBNP, *tr.* by Vladimir Markov *and* Merrill Sparks

Once, when Heracles was ten months old, Alcmena. Little Heracles. Theocritus, *Greek*. HePo, *tr.* by Barbara Hughes Fowler *Fr.* Idylls.

Once when I read the funnies. Looking. Robert Kelly. FTOS

Once, when I ventured on your deeps, Piranha. (LL) An Old Malediction. Anthony Hecht, *after* Horace. NoAM; OBCoV

Once when I walked into a room. Between Ourselves. Audre Lorde. ISC; WPOW

Once when I was coming from art class they surprised me. Daryl Hine. GLP *Fr.* March.

Once when I was tree. Root Song. Henry Dumas. ISC

Once when I was very scared. A Riddle. Charlotte Zolotow. NTCP

Once, when I was young, Juanito. The Mother's Tale. Ai. FiLi

Once, when I wasn't very big. The Cat and the Pig. Gerard Benson. NOxBChV

Once, when midnight smote the air. On Those That Hated "The Playboy of the Western World" 1907. W. B. Yeats. NOIV

Once when our eyes were clean as noon, our rooms. Cana. Thomas Merton. ChIV-2; TrCP

Once when the moon was out about three quarters. White Clover. Marvin Bell. VCAP

Once when the snow of the year was beginning to fall. The Runaway. Robert Frost. AWP; CH; FaBoCh; MoAmPo; SAmP; TwCP; VGW

Once, when their hearts were wild with joy. On Harting Down. Thomas Sturge Moore. OxBTC

Once when young I lay and listened. To the Tune "The Fair Maid of Yu." Chiang Chieh, *Chinese.* OHMPC, *tr. by* Kenneth Rexroth

Once, with a certain pride, we kept attempts. Spot the Ball. Frank Ormsby. CIP-2; PBCIP; PNI

Once, years after your death, I dreamt. The Dream. Irving Feldman. VCAP

Once you go picking flowers, you've got to climb. On Picking Flowers. Ho Xuan Huong, *Vietnamese.* AVP, *tr. by* Huỳnh Sanh Thông

Once you lose it, it keeps coming back to you, forever. Heaven. David Lehman. PuP-15

Once you were sitting far, too far, from me. Distance. Xuân Diệu, *Vietnamese.* AVP, *tr. by* Huỳnh Sanh Thông

Once your name was Bimbircokak. Dear Husband. Yambo Ouloguem, *French.* NegPo, *tr. by* Ellen Conroy Kennedy

Once You've Been to War. Walter McDonald. CDa

Ondt and the Gracehoper, The. James Joyce. BIrV *Fr.* Finnegans Wake.

One. James Berry. HCP; NOxBChV

One. Federico García Lorca. PFTM

One, The. Patrick Kavanagh. MoBrPo; TIRV

One. Carolyn Kizer. NMM-2 *Fr.* Pro Femina.

One. Carolyn M. Rodgers. BPo

One, The. Bruce Weigl. BAP-94

One. . . / I smelt the weird Atlantic. Finistére. Thomas Kinsella. PBCIP

One A.M. Denise Levertov. CAPP-1

One Acre. Jean Goulbourne. HCP

One after another. Stories and Poems. Susan Griffin. CrSp

One after the other. Granada (1000 A.D.) Abu Ishaq al-Ilbin, *Arabic.* ArPe, *tr. by* Omar S. Pound

One afternoon the last week in April. Axe Handles. Gary Snyder. ColAP; LoL; NoAM; PmAP; PoPoPo; VCAP

One AM. Leroy Gorman. HA

One among the Roses. Edmund Blunden. OBGa

One, and then another, they settled before me like flakes of air. Mining in Killdeer Alley. Dabney Stuart. MT

One-and-Twenty. *Unknown.* AmFP

One Another's Mystery. Edward Herbert, 1st Baron Herbert of Cherbury. LBC

One answer: to refuse! (LL) O what tears in eyes now. Marina Tsvetayeva, *Russian.* AF; TCRP, *tr. by* Elaine Feinstein

One arch of the sky. Love in Labrador. Carl Sandburg. VGW

One arm hooked around the frayed strap. Yellow Light. Garrett Kaoru Hongo. InPS-3; OpBo; WWSi; WeT

One-Armed Man in the Undergrowth, The. Bertolt Brecht, *German.* PoSu, *tr. by* Derek Bowman

One Art. Elizabeth Bishop. APAD; DiPo; HAP; NAAL-2; NALW; NoAM; NoP-4; PoE; PoPoPo; SAGP; SoSe-8; VCAP

One Autumn night, in Sudbury town. Prelude: The Wayside Inn. Henry Wadsworth Longfellow. APN-1 *Fr.* Tales of a Wayside Inn.

One bails out into space. Flight. Barbara Howes. NYBP

One be the nail another the pincers. The nail. Vasco [or Vasko] Popa. PoSu *Fr.* Games. RB, *tr. by* Anne Pennington

One beautiful morning in the month of May all was serene and / quiet. May. Mrs. Henry Linden. CBWP-4

One being led? I don't know, The. Scaffold in Winter. János Pilinszky, *Hungarian.* PoSu, *tr. by* Peter Jay

One biting winter morning. The Spider. Hannah Flagg Gould. OBCA

One black horse standing by the gate. The Farmyard. A. A. Attwood. BoTP

One Blackbird. Harold Monro. BoTP

One bliss for which / There is no match. Taboo to Boot. Ogden Nash. RB

One born to hardship in his place and station. Vidya. PBWP, *tr. by* Daniel H. H. Ingalls *Fr.* Substantiations.

One bough in the land of eternal banishment. Poem No. VII. Sang Yi. PFTM

One boy, Saint Dwyn, my bauble. Lament for Siôn y Glyn. Lewis Glyn Cothi, *Welsh.* OBWVE, *tr. by* Joseph P. Clancy

One breaker crashes. O. Mabson Southard. HA

One butterfly is not enough. We need. Abundance and Satisfaction. Pattiann Rogers. BAP-96

One button undone. George Swede. HA

One by one, as harvesters, all heavy laden. Sacheverell Sitwell. MoBrPo *Fr.* Agamemnon's Tomb. OBMV

One by one, as is human, we may remember. The Miracle. Carl Dennis. CMAP

One by one, the ancient. Next Year, in Jerusalem. Shirley Kaufman. UnSA

One by one they appear in. My Sad Captains. Thom Gunn. CMoP; FaBoMo; LiTM; NAEL-2; NoAM; NoP-4; PoPoPo

One by one to the floor all of her shadows. George Swede. HA

One can do one begins to one can only. Reincarnation (II). James Dickey. CAPP-1

One can glimpse Apollo in the door of each thing. Deeds Done and Suffered by Light. Clayton Eshleman. APSN

One cannot begin it too soon. (LL) Brown Penny. W. B. Yeats. BoLoP; CBLP; CMoP; FaBoCh; GLoP; IIP; LiLi

One cannot live in the same room twice. (LL) Variation on Heraclitus. Louis MacNeice. MoP; NoAM

One cannot possess. Heritage. Augustus Young. CIP-2; IIP

One can't converse with shades. Late in the Night. Eugenio Montale, *Italian.* NNPT, *tr. by* G. Singh

One can't / have it. Coming Right Up. A. R. Ammons. OBCoV

One Certainty, The. Christina Rossetti. OBNC

One Christmas Night in Pontgibaud. After Hilaire Belloc. Max Beerbohm. UV

One-coach Penn Central is bound, The. On My Fourteenth Wedding Anniversary I Ride on Trains. Cornelia Veenendaal. GM

One cold damp night, winds pierced the cliffs. January 1939. Ilya Grigoryevich Ehrenburg, *Russian.* TCRP, *tr. by* Cathy Porter

One comes to language from afar, the ear. A Vulnerary. Jonathan Williams. PoM

One constant in a world of variables. Homo Suburbiensis. Bruce Dawe. BMAP

One could do worse than be a swinger of birches. (LL) Birches. Robert Frost. AFr; AmPP; CMoP; FaBoVe; HeIP-4; ImGa; LiTM; MeMAP; MoAmPo; MoP; NAAL-2; NoAM; NoP-4; OxBA; PoLF; PoPoPo; PoRA; Poetr; RB; SAmP; SoSe-8; TAP; TFi; TRP

One crow in a high wind over Chelsea. October Tuesday. Russell Hoban. AYFP

One Crowded Hour. Thomas Osbert Mordaunt. *See* Sound, Sound the Clarion.

One crown that no one seeks. Emily Dickinson. ChIV-2

One Crucifixion is recorded—only. Emily Dickinson. APN-2

One cunning bosom-sin blows quite away. (LL) Sin (1). George Herbert. GeHe; NoP-4; OxAEP-1

One dark and dusty day. Stackolee. *Unknown.* NAAAL

One dark world is all I am. Born Again. Forugh Farrokhzad, *Persian.* PBWP, *tr. by* Jascha Kessler *and* Amin Banani

One day. Dressed Up. E. Ethelbert Miller. IFJA

One Day, The. Donald Hall. AFr

One Day. Ray Mathew. NOBAu

One Day. Bobbi Sykes. BMAP

One day across the lake where echoes come now. The Animal That Drank Up Sound. William Stafford. VGW

One day as he did raunge the fields abroad. The Vision of the Graces. Edmund Spenser. NoSic *Fr.* Wood Of Error. AEP

One day, as I said before. (LL) By the Fire-Side. Robert Browning. EBVV; OAEL-2

One day, as I travelled the highway alone. The Burdened Ass. John Oxenham. NSI

One day as I unwarily did gaze. Sonnet 16. Edmund Spenser. OAEL-1 *Fr.* Amoretti. AAS

One day as I was a-rambling around. Wild Bill Jones. *Unknown.* AmFP

One day / as I was lying on the lawn. The Gift. Ed Ochester. Poetsp

One day at a Perranporth pet-shop. Charles Causley. PeP

One day he perched on a tree with dew. Migratory Bird. Chenjerai Hove. HBAPE

One day I complained about the periphery. Periphery. A. R. Ammons. NOBA

One day I found a lost dog in the street. Dead Dog. Vernon Scannell. OxBC

One day, I left the city and went back. On the Way Home. Chế Lan Viên, *Vietnamese.* AVP, *tr. by* Huỳnh Sanh Thông

One day I met you. Song of Meeting. Tsung Ch'en, *Chinese.* CoBLCP, *tr. by* Jonathan Chaves

One day I observed a grey hair in my head. The Grey Hair. Judah Halevi, *Hebrew.* TrJP, *tr. by* J. Chotzner

One day I saw. Tanka. Nakajō Fumiko, *Japanese.* MJT, *tr. by* Makoto Ueda

One day I saw Chicago river move. Chicago. Margaret Walker Alexander. GT

One day I thought I'd have some fun. The Tenderfoot. D. J. O'Malley. AS

One day I went and bought a fake fur coat. How I Had to Act. Molly Peacock. FFC; NAmP90

One day I wrote her name upon the strand. Sonnet 75. Edmund Spenser. AWP; BoLoP; CABP; CBLP; EBEV; EPCY; GBL; GEA; GLoP; GSo; HAP; HeIP-4; ImPo; InPS-3; NAEL-1; NoP-4; NoSic; OAEL-1; PBMP; PoE; PoPoPo; Son; TFi; WeW-3 *Fr.* Amoretti. AAS

One day, if I am not to keep on fleeing. Upon the Death of His Brother Giovanni. Ugo Foscolo. ItIP

One day I'll lift the telephone. Elegy for My Father, Who Is Not Dead. Andrew Hudgins. RA

One day in a popular quarter of Kharkov. Images. Valery Larbaud, *French.* BLT, *tr.* by William Jay Smith

One day in March, I ranged a verdant plain. On Meeting——, Esq., in St. James's Park. *Unknown.* ECWP

One day in the bluest of summer weather. Bird Language. Christopher Pearse Cranch. APN-1; PAR

One day in the forest there was somebody. The Stranger. W. S. Merwin. BAP-93

One day in the Library. Further Advantages of Learning. Kenneth Rexroth. TAP

One day it will vanish. The Vanishings. Stephen Dunn. BAP-93

One day / Marilyn marched. Chic Freedom's Reflection. Alice Walker. InPS-3

One day, not here, you will find a hand. Again. Charlotte Mew. MoBrPo

One-day-old baby in Wallabout, A. Limerick. Morris Gilbert Bishop. PeLi

One day on our village in the month of July. Death of an Aircraft. Charles Causley. MoBS

One day one young Creole candio. Criole Candjo. George Washington Cable. APN-2

One day over the course of a week or so. Dream of the Artfairy. Carl Morse. GLP

One day ringing men will be a race gone. The Ringers. John Peck, *Italian.* AmPA, *tr.* by William Arrowsmith

One day some young poet. Jean-Joseph Rabéarivelo, *French,* NegPo, *tr.* by Ellen Conroy Kennedy

One day soon he'll tell her it's time to start packing. Drifters. Bruce Dawe. BMAP; CBAP; NoAM

One day Sun found a new canyon. People of the South Wind. William Stafford. NNaP

One day the Amorous *Lysander,.* The Disappointment. Aphra Behn. CABP; LW; NALW; NOSC; NoP-4; PEW

One day, / the apolitical. Apolitical Intellectuals. Otto René Castillo, *Spanish.* AF, *tr.* by Margaret Randall

One day, the bread knife wasn't a bread knife anymore. Child, Invisible Fire. Marcia Southwick. NAmP90

One day the Chinese Bird of Royalty, Fum. Fum and Hum, the Two Birds of Royalty. Thomas Moore. OBSV

One day the god of fond desire. James Thomson. EnLoPo

One day the letters went to school. The Letters at School. Mary Mapes Dodge. OBCA

One day the Nouns were clustered in the street. Permanently. Kenneth Koch. CoAP; NoP-4; PmAP; PoA; PoM; SAGP

One day the sun was rising high. The Peddler and His Wife. *Unknown.* AmFP

One day they said. Purdah, 1. Imtiaz Dharker. OMIP

One day this summer. The Seacoast at Mera. Takada Toshiko, *Japanese.* WPJ, *tr.* by Kenneth Rexroth *and* Ikuko Atsumi

One day, through the primeval wood. The Calf-Path. Sam Walter Foss. PoLF

One day—'twas on a gentle, autumn noon. Leigh Hunt. NOBRP *Fr.* The Story of Rimini.

One day we notice that the sun. Feeding the Sun. Bill Knott. PBCAP

One day we took our lunches. The Circus Parade. Katharine Pyle. OBCA

One day, when childhood tumbled the spongy tufts. Crane. Joseph Langland. NYBP

One day when Coyote. One for Coyote. *Unknown, Skagit Indian.* STP, *tr.* by Carl Cary

One day when me 'n' Dunbar wuz a-hoein' in de co'n. Me 'n' Dunbar. James David Corrothers. NAAAL

One day when the great *Titanic* was sinking away. Shine and the *Titanic. Unknown.* NAAAL

One day, while in a lonesome grove. Newberry. *Unknown.* AmFP

One day you finally knew. The Journey. Mary Oliver. CrSp

One day / You gonna walk in this house. Seduction. Nikki Giovanni. NMM-2

One day you look at the mirror and it's open. Glass. W. S. Merwin. SPE

One day you will collapse at your desk. Old Age. Bernard Kangro, *Estonian.* CEEP, *tr.* by Ivar Ivask

One dazzling mass of solid snow. Soracte. Horace, *Latin.* OBCVT, *tr.* by Charles Stuart Calverley

One deaf man went to law with. Nicarchus of Alexandria, *Greek.* PGA, *tr.* by Kenneth Rexroth

One Desiring Me to Read, But Slept It Out, Wakening. George Daniel. OxBSP

One died, and the soul was wrenched out. Street Musicians. John Ashbery. HCAP; PoPoPo

One dignity delays for all. Emily Dickinson. MeMAP

One disappearing, The. The Fool. Novica Tadic, *Serbo-Croatian.* HSix, *tr.* by Charles Simic

One document at dawn, submitted to the nine-tiered palace. Written on My Way into Exile. Han Yü, *Chinese.* CoBCP, *tr.* by Burton Watson

1. Don't see him. Don't phone or write a letter. Two Cures for Love. Wendy Cope. OBCoV

One door alone is shut, one chamber still. (LL) Gone. Mary Elizabeth Coleridge. OBEV; OBNC; VWP

One doth not stroke me, nor the other strike. (LL) To Fool or Knave. Ben Jonson. FaBoEE; NoP-4

One dove has its head turned. Girl with Doves. Stephen Gray. PeSA

One dream of passion and of beauty more! Properzia Rossi. Felicia Dorothea Hemans. VWP

One duck stood on my toes. Feeding Ducks. Norman MacCaig. FaBoTC; OxBS

One early spring evening when Celia was fourteen. Joan Chase. DeD *Fr.* During the Reign of the Queen of Persia.

One ends in ignominy because one begins mistakenly. Precious Mettle. Lewis Warsh. PT

One-erum, two-erum. *Unknown.* OxNR

One-ery, Ore-ery, Ickery, Ann. *Unknown.* ImGa *Fr.* Counting-out Rhymes.

One-ery, two-ery, [or ore-ery], ickery, Ann. *Unknown.* OxNR

One-ery, two-ery, tickery, seven. *Unknown.* OxNR

One-ery, two-ery / Ziccary zan. *Unknown.* CBNP

One Evening. Ljubomir Simovic, *Serbo-Croatian.* HSix, *tr.* by Charles Simic

One evening a young lady fair, her estate rode out to see. On the Banks of Salee. *Unknown.* AmFP

One evening as the sun went down [*or* when the sun was low]. The Big Rock Candy Mountains. *Unknown.* AmFP; OBAL; TTTS

One evening bright stars they were shining. The Brooklyn Theater Fire. *Unknown.* AmFP

One evening in another town. Pre-Carnival Party. Mervyn Morris. HCP

One evening in August, the light already failing. Elegy for the Unknown Soldier. Michael O'Loughlin. PBCIP

One evening in November I happened for to stray. Johnny Carroll's Camp. *Unknown.* AmFP

One evening last June as I rambled. On the Banks of the Little Eau Pleine. *Unknown.* AmFP

One evening when a genial air. Nightfall. Gwen Harwood. BMAP

One evening, when the sun was just gone down. On the Death of Old Bennet the News-Crier. *Unknown.* NOEC

One evening when we were lounging in his apartment in a relaxed mood. Rain. Anselm Hollo. PoM

One evening, while the cooler shade she sought. Dryden. PoEL-3 *Fr.* The Hind and the Panther.

One ever hangs where shelled roads part. At a Calvary near the Ancre. Wilfred Owen. ChIV-2; GI

One ewe. Shepherd's Night Count. Jane Yolen. TLR

One eye without a head to wear it. On the Farther Wall, Marc Chagall. Phyllis McGinley. OBSV *Fr.* Spectator's Guide to Contemporary Art.

One Eyed Black Man in Nebraska. Sam Cornish. PoBA

One-Eyed Garlic Seller, A: Many were met, men of discretion. *Unknown.* EEP, *tr.* by Michael Alexander *Fr.* Riddles (Exeter Book).

One-Eyed Seller of Arrows: Creature came shuffling where there sat, A. Cynewulf. ASW, *tr.* by Kevin Crossley-Holland *Fr.* Riddles (Exeter Book).

One face looks out from all his canvas[s]es. In An Artist's Studio. Christina Rossetti. NAEL-2; NALW; Poetr

One failure on. Their Sex Life. A. R. Ammons. OBCoV

One Faith and No Faith. Friedrich von Logau, *German.* GePo, *tr.* by George C. Schoolfield

One fall not far from Ozark, Arkansas. The Narrative Hooper and L.D.O. Sestina with a Long Last Line. James Whitehead. HoPM

One fantee wave. Dame Edith Sitwell. OBMV *Fr.* Gold Coast Customs.

One fatal mistake that is made today is gossip. Gossip. Mrs. Henry Linden. CBWP-4

One feather is a bird. The Voice. Theodore Roethke. EP; VGW

One Final Fling. Kemal Khojandi, *Persian.* ArPe, *tr.* by Omar S. Pound

One finds in every boarding school. "Tropicals." René Maran, *French.* NegPo, *tr.* by Ellen Conroy Kennedy

One Fine Day. E. E. Cummings. GM

One Fine Day. János Pilinszky, *Hungarian.* PoSu, *tr.* by Peter Jay

One fine morning they move in for the pinch. Lurid Confessions. Steve Kowit. EC2

One flake at a time teaches grace, / even to stone. (LL) Montana Eclogue. William Stafford. PaTW

One Flesh. Elizabeth Jennings. FaBoWP; LW; NoP-4; OxAEP-2; OxBTC; PBWP

One flower at a time, please. Bouquets. Robert Francis. ChAP

One flutter of memory, then all becomes. Burning the Letters. Gwendolyn Grew. HoPM

One fly everywhere the heat. Marlene Mountain. HA

One foot in Eden still, I stand. Edwin Muir. CMoP; FaBoTC; GTBS-P; NOBE; NoAM

One Foot in the Door. Anne Elder. CBAP

One for another were designed. (LL) To Amoret, Walking in a Starry Evening. Henry Vaughan. BeJo; FMP

One for Coyote. Unknown, Skagit Indian. STP, tr. by Carl Cary

One for money. Unknown. OxNR

One for sorrow, two for joy. Unknown. OxNR

One for the Anthologies. Gavin Ewart. OBCoV

One for the Road. Nancy Willard. LiLi

One forfeit more from life the current claimed. At the Discharge of Cannon Rise the Drowned. Hubert Witheford. PeNZ

One Friday morn when we set sail. The Mermaid. Unknown. CH; ESPB

One from One Leaves Two. Ogden Nash.
    "I pray the Lord my soul to take." NBLV

1 From the Nursery. Jane Kenyon. See From the Nursery.

One Furrow, The. Ronald Stuart Thomas. HoPM; OxBC

One garland. Divorcing. Denise Levertov. NALW

One Generation Passeth Away. Jones Very. ChIV-1

One Girl. Sappho, Greek. AWP; LoP; OBCVT, tr. by D. G. Rossetti

One Girl at the Boys Party, The. Sharon Olds. InPK-6; SAGP

One girl in a red dress leaves the shopping center with. Suburban Dusk. Bert Meyers. SPE

One good crucifixion and he rose from the dead. Easter. Charles Hubert Sisson. OxBSP

One good thing about music. Trenchtown Rock. Bob Marley. PBCV

One goodness ruleth by its single will. Alcuin, Latin. MLL, tr. by Helen Waddell

One got peace of heart at last, the dark march over. After War. Ivor Gurney. OxBSP

One grandma. Two Grandmas. Stanley H. Barkan. UnSA

One granite ridge. Piute Creek. Gary Snyder. CAPP-1; CoAP; CoAmPo; NAAL-2; NOBA; PaTW

One great truth in life I've found. Those We Love the Best. Ella Wheeler Wilcox. PoToHe

One had a lovely face. Memory. W. B. Yeats. APAD; BIrV; PoE

One half of me was up and dressed. The Gentle Check. Joseph Beaumont. NOSC

One hand is smaller than the other. It. Man with One Small Hand. Patricia K. Page. MoCV

One hand on her hip, one hand. Song of the Andoumboulou. Nathaniel Mackey. NAAAL

One hand, two hands. Nothing more. Sphinxes Inclined to Be. Olga Orozco, Spanish. WPOW, tr. by Leslie Keffer

One Happy Moment. Dryden. OBEV Fr. Cleomenes. (Song.)

One hard cold after another came. Winter 1967. Lenard D. Moore. ISC

One Hard Look. Robert Graves. MoBrPo

One has a feeling it is all coming to an end. The Feeling. William Bronk. VGW

One, he loves; two, he loves. Unknown. ReMoGo

One-headed drum, A. Auvaiyar. See A Poet to a Dancer.

One heifer and one fleecy sheep. Aristeides. Antipater of Sidon, Greek. AWP, tr. by Charles Whibley

One hesitates to bring a child into this world without fixing. "Alta." CrSp Fr. 3 : 6.

One higher-pitched doth set his soaring thought. Joseph Hall. EPCY Fr. Virgidemiarum.

One hole can fit just any number in. Ode to the Fan. Ho Xuan Huong, Vietnamese. AVP, tr. by Huỳnh Sanh Thông

One Home. William Stafford. CoAP; VGW

One Hope, The. D. G. Rossetti. GSo; NAEL-2; OAEL-2 Fr. The House of Life.

One Horse Chay, The. Unknown. OxBoLi

One horse you gave me, The. The Appaloosa. Michael S. Weaver. GT

One hue of our flag is taken. "Orpheus C. Kerr." Fr. The Rejected "National Hymns." OBAL

One hugs me. In the Village of My Forefathers. Vasco [or Vasko] Popa. PoSu, tr. by Anne Pennington Fr. Raw Flesh.

One Hundred and Eighty-Third Chorus. Jack Kerouac. NeAP Fr. Mexico City Blues.

182nd Chorus. Jack Kerouac. NeAP Fr. Mexico City Blues.

One Hundred and Fifty Years. Jack Davis. BMAP

One Hundred and Forty-Ninth Chorus. Jack Kerouac. PmAP Fr. Mexico City Blues.

146th Chorus. Jack Kerouac. NeAP Fr. Mexico City Blues.

179th Chorus. Jack Kerouac. NeAP Fr. Mexico City Blues.

113th Chorus. Jack Kerouac. NeAP; PmAP Fr. Mexico City Blues.

127th Chorus. Jack Kerouac. NeAP; PmAP Fr. Mexico City Blues.

108 Tales of a Po 'Buckra. Will Inman.
    "Dark brother touches me, The." GLP

One hundred feet from off the ground. Long-Suffering of God. Christopher Smart. NOCV Fr. Hymns for the Amusement of Children.

104. "Alta." CrSp

104 Boulevard Saint-Germain. Kenneth Pitchford. NYBP

One Hundred Lines for the Coast. Kojo Laing. HBAPE

110 Year Old House. Ed Ochester. Poetsp

One I love, two I love. Unknown. LB; OxNR

One imagines the lives of the Prince. Winter in Étienburgh. Stephen Parker. NYBP

One in ten, as the lot falls. So be it. Thorns. Haim Gouri, Hebrew. IP, tr. by Warren Bargad and Stanley F. Chyet

One in the boat cried out. The Door. Leonard Alfred George Strong. MoBrPo

One Inch Tall. Shel Silverstein. OBCA

One instant is eternity. Wu-Men, Chinese. EnlH, tr. by Stephen Mitchell

One is always nearer by not keeping still. (LL) On the Move. Thom Gunn. CMoP; HAP; LiTM; NoP-4; OAEL-2; OxAEP-2; OxBTC; PoE; TRP; TwCP

One is enough, she cried. Technicalities for Jack Spicer. Philip Whalen. PoM

One is in the cellar. Maids. Aleksandar Ristovic, Serbo-Croatian. HSix, tr. by Charles Simic

One is not hale until one inhales. On Apples. David Ross. NYBP

"One is reminded of a certain person." Kite Poem. James Merrill. TwCP

One is so seldom struck by lightning. For the Poet Who Said Poets Are Struck by Lightning Only Two or Three Times. Peter Klappert. NBLV

One keeps a secret for me. The Secret. Mary Morison Webster. PeSA

One Kind of Freedom Speaks. Erich Fried, German. AF, tr. by Georg Rapp

One king's daughter said to anither. Sheath and Knife. Unknown. CH; ESPB

One kiss. Tess Gallagher. BAP-93

One knight loves both, and both in thee remain. (LL) To His Friend Master R.L., In Praise of Music and Poetry. Richard Barnfield. AAS; EPCY; Son

One Knows Not What One Is. "Angelus Silesius." GePo, tr. by George C. Schoolfield Fr. The Cherubical Wanderer.

One-l lama, / He's a priest, The. The Lama. Ogden Nash. FaBoCh

One last look at your hills, Lysander. Learning Destiny. Herman Charles Bosman. PeSA

One Last Word. John Glassco. NOBC

One leg in front of the other. Unknown. NTP

One-legged Man, The. Siegfried Sassoon. CMoP

One lesson, Nature, let me learn of [or from] thee. Quiet Work. Matthew Arnold. FaBoBe

One lily scented all the dark. It grew. One Night. Lizette Woodworth Reese. APN-2

One Little Boy. Unknown. NOxBChV

One little dicky-bird. Ten Little Dicky-Birds. A. W. I. Baldwin. BoTP

One little Indian boy making a canoe. Ten Little Indian Boys. M. M. Hutchinson. BoTP

One little mess of whelks, so he may 'scape! (LL) Caliban upon Setebos; or, Natural Theology in the Island. Robert Browning. AWP; EBEV; EnVR; FHYEP; NAEL-2; NOBVV; OAEL-2; OxAEP-2; PeVV

One little noise of life remained—I heard. On the Eclipse of the Moon of October 1865. Charles Tennyson Turner. OBNC

One long jump. Lenrie Peters. PBMAP

One long sigh piled on another. Long Sigh. Lu Yu, Chinese. CoBCP, tr. by Burton Watson

One looks from the train. The Orient Express. Randall Jarrell. CMoP; CoAP; NOBA; PoE

One Lost, The. Isaac Rosenberg. MoBrPo

One lovely summer afternoon when balmy breezes blew. To Clements' Ferry. Josephine D. Henderson Heard. CBWP-4

One low yellow light, the back room a cave. The Place Lost and Gone, the Place Found. Minnie Bruce Pratt. CPO

One man follows a straight path. "Anna Akhmatova," *Russian.* TCRP, *tr. by* Daniel Weissbort

One man shall smile one day and say goodbye. Cambodia. James Fenton. AF

One man / Two times larger than life. Untranslatable Factual Items. E. L. T. Mesens, *French.* CBNP

One man we claim of wrought renown. Stonewall Jackson. Herman Melville. NCAP

One Man's Family. Rosemary Catacalos. IFJA

One Man's Wife. Philip Booth. VGW

One memory I have from childhood. Paradigm of a Hero. Jack Matthews. CMAP

One midnight, deep in starlight still. Bankrupt. Cortlandt W. Sayres. PoLF; PoToHe

One midnight, old D. G. Rossetti. Limerick. Victor Gray. PeLi

One might as well conceive this story in the cirrose. Richard Kenney. EOEF *Fr.* The Encantadas.

One Minute of Night Sky. John Engman. NAmP90

One misty, moisty morning. Mother Goose. BoTP; FaBoBe; LB; OxNR; ReMoGo

One misty moisty morning. *Unknown.* BoTP; ReMoGo

One Modern Poet. Carl Sandburg. OBAL

One moment, and that realm is ours. (LL) The Indian Woman's Death-Song. Felicia Dorothea Hemans. PEW; Ro

One monk, you have dissolved phenomena. At the Mountain of the Mysterious Tomb Visiting Master P'ou. Wu Wei-yeh, *Chinese.* CoBLCP, *tr. by* Jonathan Chaves

One more bruised heart laid bare! one victim more! Louisa Sarah Bevington. VWP

One more day gone, / done, found in / the form of days. Again. Robert Creeley. VCAP

One More Day's Work for Jesus. Anna Bartlett Warner. AII

One more hour to remember, one less sip. Insomnia. Ivan V. Lalic, *Serbo-Croatian.* HSix, *tr. by* Charles Simic

One more little spirit to Heaven has flown. Little Libbie. Julia A. Moore. OBAL

One More New Botched Beginning. Stephen Spender. CMoP; NYBP; NoAM

One more night my blood. O Wendy, Arthur. Maurice Kenny. HATNAP

One more rendezvous. John Gneisenau Neihardt. FYAP *Fr.* The Song of Jed Smith.

One More River. *Unknown.* APN-2

One More Sign. Roberta Hill Whiteman. HATNAP

One More Time. Patricia Goedicke. CMAP

One more unfortunate. The Bridge of Sighs. Thomas Hood. EBEV; FaPoR; GTBS-P; OBEV; OxAEP-2

One morn before me were three figures seen. Ode on Indolence. Keats. NAEL-2; OBNC; Ro

One morn I rose and looked upon the world. The Dawn. *Unknown.* PoToHe

One Morning. Timothy Steele. CRP

One morning as I rambled. The Miner Boy. *Unknown.* AmFP

One morning, as we travelled in the fields. The Riders Held Back. Louis Simpson. CoAmPo

One morning de captain wake. Itanami. *Unknown.* PBCV

One morning ere [*or* before] Titan had thought to stir [*or* thought of stirring] his feet. The Vision. Egan O'Rahilly, *Irish.* FaBoPV, *tr. by* Frank O'Connor; NOIV, *tr. by* Thomas Kinsella

One morning I awoke and found that it had been snowing all. January. William Virgil Davis. IFJA

One morning I call for a sedan-chair man. Yüan Mei. *Fr.* Five Poems on Returning to Hangchou. CoBLCP, *tr. by* Jonathan Chaves

One morning I got up. The Little Bird. *Unknown.* PBA, *tr. by* Rolf Italiaander

One morning I shall find. Maisie. James Merrill. HcIP-4

One Morning in May [*or* The Nightingale]. *Unknown.* AmFP; AS; OxBoLi

One Morning in May; or, The Young Girl Cut Down in Her Prime. *Unknown.* AmFP

One morning in spring. Fife Tune. John Streeter Manifold. CBAP; ImPo; InPS-3; LiTM; NBLV; NOBAu

One Morning, Oh, So Early! Jean Ingelow. OxBChV

One morning old Wilfrid Scawen Blunt. Limerick. Victor Gray. NOBL

One morning, one morning, one morning in May. One Morning in May [*or* The Nightingale]. *Unknown.* AS; AmFP; OxBoLi

One morning, one morning, one morning in Spring. I'll Be Fourteen Next Sunday. *Unknown.* AmFP

One morning the Monarch said: "When." Limerick. D. W. Barker. PeLi

One morning with a 12-gauge my brother shot what he said was a linnet. Linnets. Larry Levis. LCAP-2

One mouse adds up to many mice. Singular Indeed. David McCord. OBCA

One Mr. B, / A joker he. Repartée. Charles Follen Adams. OBAL

One musician is sure. The Harp. Ralph Waldo Emerson. APN-1

One mustn't confuse the day and the night;. Nobility. Oumar Ba. PBMAP

One must completely destroy all logic in Variety Theater performances. Futurism Wants to Transform the Variety Theater into a Theater of Amazement, Record-setting, and Body-madness. Filippo Tommaso Marinetti. PFTM, *tr. by* R. W. Flint *and* Arthur A. Coppotelli *Fr.* The Variety Theater Manifesto.

One must have a mind of winter. The Snow Man. Wallace Stevens. AFr; CMoP; ColAP; EnlH; HAP; HCAP; HeIP-4; NAAL-2; NoAM; NoP-4; PoE; PoPoPo; Poetr; SoSe-8; TRP; WeW-3

One must have breakfasted often on automobile primer. A Note to Tony Towle (After WS). Charles North. FTOS; PmAP

One name, Ianthe, shall not die. (LL) Passed Ruin'd Ilion. Walter Savage Landor. NAEL-2; NOBRP; NoP-4

One narcissus among the ordinary beautiful. Persephone, Falling. Rita Dove. NAmP90

One need not be a Chamber—to be Haunted. Emily Dickinson. APN-2; NALW

One needs a lyric poet in these. Julius Lester. *Fr.* In the Time of Revolution. PoBA

One needs sand from the sea, we have known. Morning Hours. Rossana Ombres. Nelt *Fr.* Excursion to Ravenna of A Young Girl with Her Parents.

One Night. Constantine P. Cavafy, *Greek.* EP; LoP, *tr. by* Rae Dalven

One Night. Lizette Woodworth Reese. APN-2

"One night," a doctor said, "last fall." Body-Snatcher. Ambrose Bierce. APN-2 *Fr.* The Devil's Dictionary.

One night a score of Erris men. Danny. John Millington Synge. PeVV

One night all tired with the weary day. The Gnat. Joseph Beaumont. NOSC

One night as I lay on my bed. Death. *Unknown, Welsh.* OBWVE; RB, *tr. by* Aneirin Talfan Davies

One night, as I was pondering of late. John Oldham. NOSC *Fr.* A Satyr.

One Night at Victoria Beach. Gabriel Okara. PBMAP

One Night Away from Day. John Digby. SPE

One-Night Expensive Hotel. Ronald G. Everson. NOBC

One night from the stern I thought, as I watched. Braemar. Galway Kinnell. PoA

One night he dreamed he was a. The Young Man Who Loved the Girl Who Took Care of Her Aged Father. Greg Kuzma. AmPA

One night he heard heart-breaking sound. Austin Clarke. CIP-2; CMoP *Fr.* Mnemosyne Lay in Dust.

One night, I saw a woman. Unlocking the Doors. Jill Breckenridge. LoHo

One night i' th' yeare [*or* in the year], my dearest Beauties, come. To His Lovely Mistresses. Robert Herrick. CTC; CaPo; SeCP

One night in late October. Judged by the Company One Keeps. *Unknown.* BLPA; NBLV

One night in thunder. My Newts. Clarissa Hinsley. PeP

One night Jake telephoned. 26th Precinct Station. Louis Simpson. EOEF

One night of tempest I arose and went. Night and Morning. *Unknown, Welsh.* OBWVE, *tr. by* R. S. Thomas

One Night Stand. Imamu Amiri Baraka. NeAP

One Night Stand. Kenward Elmslie. FTOS

One night the Brownies reached a mound. The Brownies' Celebration. Palmer Cox. OBCA

One night two hunters, drunk, came in the tent. Saints and Strangers. Andrew Hudgins. RA

One night, when I couldn't sleep. The Trick. John Mole. NOxBChV

One night when I was in the House of Death. Birth. Harold Monro. PoA *Fr.* Strange Meetings.

One night when I went down. The Heap of Rags. W. H. Davies. NSI

One night where there is nothing now but air. A Vacant Lot. Gibbons Ruark. PuP-15

One night, your mother is listening to the walls. How You Get Born. Erica Jong. UnPo

One night's east wind made a thousand trees burst into flower. Tune: "Green Jade Cup"—Lantern Festival. Hsin Ch'i-chi, *Chinese.* SuSp, *tr. by* Irving Y. Lo

One noonday, at my window in the town. Ball's Bluff. Herman Melville. CBCWP; OBWP

One nostril means latin. Queer Things. Emanuel Carnevali. SPE

One, not quite ten. Sisters. Saleem Peeradina. OMIP

One November on a nervous amble. Central Park. Martha Hollander. GaP

One. now another. one. Snow Songs. W. D. Snodgrass. BAP-94

One o'Clock. Katharine Pyle. *Fr.* The Wonder Clock. OBCA

One o'Clock. Philippe Soupault, *French.* AF, *tr. by* Schmidt, Paulette

One o'clock in the letter-box. The Meeting. Muriel Rukeyser. MoAmPo; TrJP

One of her hands one of her cheeks lay under. A Supplement of an Imperfect Copy of Verses of Mr. Will. Shakespeare's, by the Author. Sir John Suckling. CavPo

One of King *Henries* Favorites beganne. A Groome of the Chambers religion in King Henry the eights time. Sir John Harington. PBRV

One of King Henry's favourites began. A Groome of the Chamber's Religion in King Henry the Eighth's Time. John Harington. NoSic

One of Many. Stevie Smith. OxBC

One of midnight's charms is a muted terror—. Conversation at Midnight. "Adelina Efimovna Adalis," *Russian.* TCRP, tr. by Bernard Meares

One of my dogs has brought the foreleg of a deer. A Finding. Ted Kooser. CMAP

One of my earliest memories (remember). To My Father. Stewart Conn. FaBoTC

One of my father; he stands. Photographs. Charles Wright. HoPM

One of our race's great lights has gone out to the world. Paul Laurence Dunbar. Mrs. Henry Linden. CBWP-4

One of our race's greatest needs in this country today. The Y. M. C. A. Mrs. Henry Linden. CBWP-4

One of Our Walks. John Hollander. AFr

One of the Awl Songs. *Unknown.* APN-2, tr. by Washington Matthews *Fr.* The Mountain Chant.

One of the Boys. James Simmons. PNI

One of the clock, and silence deep. One o'Clock. Katharine Pyle. *Fr.* The Wonder Clock. OBCA

One of the criminals who were hanged railed at him. Luke 23:39–43; One of the criminals. Jorge Luis Borges. GI *Fr.* St. Luke.

One of the difficulties is in being. Russian Asylum. Marilyn Bowering. NOBC

One of the Jews. Constantine P. Cavafy, *Greek.* TrJP

One of the Lives. W. S. Merwin. BAP-94

One of the Longest Times. Alice Notley. BAP-96

One of the more intelligent members. For the Fly-Leaf of a School-Book. Norman Cameron. OxBS

One of the most distinguished members of his race. (LL) Mr. Z. M. Carl Holman. PFE

One of the ones that Midas touched. Emily Dickinson. APN-2

One of the Principal Causes of War. "Hugh MacDiarmid." OxBSP

One of the things I've repeated to writing. Advice to Young Writers. Ron Padgett. BAP-93

One of the Years. William Stafford. KaS

One of them said: "One life is much too little." Georgy Adamovich, *Russian.* TCRP, tr. by Yakov Hornstein

"One of them takes himself to be an ox." Tune: "Song of Divination"Using Quotations from *Chuang-tzu.* Hsin Ch'i-chi, *Chinese.* SuSp, tr. by Irving Y. Lo

One of them, taking advantage of the crew's momentary carelessness. Edouard Glissant. NegPo, tr. by Ellen Conroy Kennedy *Fr.* The Indies.

One of these nights about twelve o'clock. The Heavenly Aeroplane. *Unknown.* NOCV

One of those days. I Remember Dexedrine. 1970. Pamela Brown. BMAP

One of us. . . Dark and fair He, dark and fair She, gone / The rest—anon. (LL) The Five Students. Thomas Hardy. CMoP; GTBS-P; PoEL-5

One of us had to be the first to lead. Robyn Selman. PUP-19

One of us said, how odd. Hilda Doolittle. NALW *Fr.* Tribute to the Angels.

One of Us Two. Ella Wheeler Wilcox. PoToHe

One of us / will / be. Devils. Norman Mailer. OBAL

One of you is a major made of cord and catskin. Lent in a Year of War. Thomas Merton. SPE

One of you is lying. (LL) Unfortunate Coincidence. Dorothy Parker. LW; NoP-4; PiM

One old Oxford ox opening oysters. *Unknown.* CBNP

One old winter, and gathered the mouth of Thora / to his mouth. (LL) Old Fisherman with Guitar. George Mackay Brown. FaBoTC; OxBC

One. One. Laurie Duggan. BMAP *Fr.* The Ash Range.

One or More Together. John Godfrey. FTOS

One ought not to have to care. The Hill Wife. Robert Frost. CMoP; HAP; InPS-3; LiTM; NoP-4; RACG

One ought not to have to care. Loneliness. Robert Frost. VGW *Fr.* The Hill Wife. CMoP; HAP; InPS-3; LiTM; NoP-4; RACG

One pale morning in June at four o'clock. Rubber. Rolf Jacobsen, *Norwegian.* BLT, tr. by Roger Greenwald

One pass, one pass, and lo, yet one more pass! The Threefold Pass. Ho Xuan Huong, *Vietnamese.* AVP, tr. by Huỳnh Sanh Thông

One peak, stripped sheer. A Trip to Hua-yang Mountain. Tao-chi, *Chinese.* CoBLCP, tr. by Jonathan Chaves

One Perfect Rose. Dorothy Parker. APAD; LoP; NALW; NBLV; NIP-4; NoP-4; OBAL; OBCoV; Poetr

One person. Issa, *Japanese.* TTTS, tr. by Kenneth Koch and Harold Henderson

One Person. Elinor Wylie.
"In our content, before the autumn came." NAAL-2; NALW
Little Beauty That I Was Allowed, The. Son
Sonnet: "I hereby swear that to uphold your house." NAAL-2; OxBA; Son
(Sonnet from "One Person.") MoAmPo
Sonnet: "Let us leave talking of angelic hosts." OxBA

One person present steps on his pedal of speech. The Talker. Mona Van Duyn. PiM

One petal of a blood-red tulip pressed. Hallucination. Arthur Symons. ADE

One plum blossom blooms. Ransetsu, *Japanese.* OHMPJ, tr. by Kenneth Rexroth

One potato, two potato. *Unknown.* ImGa *Fr.* Counting-out Rhymes.

One Presenting a Rare Book to Madame Hull. John Saffin. SCAP

One quick scratch. Lighting a Fire. X. J. Kennedy. NOxBChV

One rainy night that year we saw our wives. Our Wives. Jonathan Galassi. EOEF

One reason a dog is such a lovable. *Unknown.* CTV

One Reason for Stars. Jack Butler. MT

One Reason I Went to Prison. James Moore. CDa

One remains, the many change and pass, The. Shelley. SCV *Fr.* Adonais; An Elegy on the Death of Keats. EBEV; FHYEP; HoPM; ImPo; NOBRP; OAEL-2; OxAEP-2; PoEL-4; TFi

One remembers hysterical laughter. Land of Cotton. Gilbert Sorrentino. FTOS

One ring of clear chimes through the evening mist. Inscribed on My Little Painting of Plum Blossom and Bamboo. Tao-chi, *Chinese.* CoBLCP, tr. by Jonathan Chaves

One road leads to London. Roadways. John Masefield. BoTP; OTCP

One, round the candytuft. I Spy. Norah E. Hussey. BoTP

One Saturday night as we set sail. The Mermaid. *Unknown.* AmFP

One scene as I bow to pour her coffee:—. Vacation. William Stafford. BLT; Poetsp

One scull in the spring wind, one leaf of a boat. Li Yü, *Chinese.* CoBCP, tr. by Burton Watson

One Season. Tony Hoagland. NAmP90

One seem'd all dark and red--a tract of sand. Tennyson. UnPo *Fr.* The Palace of Art. EnVR; NOBRP

One set on the highway to sing. Li Po, *Chinese.* OxBA, tr. by Ezra Pound

One ship drives east and another drives west. The Winds of Fate. Ella Wheeler Wilcox. BLPA

One ship, one only. A Few Days in the South in February. Eleanor Ross Taylor. CBCWP

One showing the eggs unbroken. (LL) The Explosion. Philip Larkin. EBEV; FaBoMo; HAP; NAEL-2; NoAM; NoP-4; OxAEP-2; OxBC; PeECV; RB; SCV; WeW-3

One shuts one eye. Before Play. Vasco [or Vasko] Popa. *Fr.* Games. RB, tr. by Anne Pennington

One side of his world is always missing. Riding a One-eyed Horse. Henry Taylor. HeIP-4; InPK-6

One Sided Shoot-out. Don L. Lee. BPo; NBV; PoBA

One silent night of late. The Cheat of Cupid; or, The Ungentle Guest. Robert Herrick. AWP; OBVE

One single word of heartfelt kindness. Kindness. Mary E. Tucker. CBWP-1

One sinuous wrist is lifted while it shakes. Portrait of a King's Mistress, Nude. Paul Engle. PFE

One Size Fits All: a Critical Essay. David Lehman. OBCoV

One slit's enough to let adultery [or adultry] in. (LL) Upon Scobble [Epigram]. Robert Herrick. BeJo; CaPo; FaBoEE

One sore thing is the way. Lament. Gibbons Ruark. MT

One sound. Then the hiss and whir. The Garden. Louise Glück. AmPA; HCAP; NAAL-2; VCAP

One spring the circus gave. A Hill of Beans. Rita Dove. WWSi

One star fell and another as we walked. Prelude LVII. Conrad Potter Aiken. MoAmPo *Fr.* Preludes for Memnon; or, Preludes to Attitude.

One star that I loved ere the fields went brown. (LL) A Winter Twilight. Angelina Weld Grimké. NAAAL; PoBA

One step twix't me and death, (twas Davids speech). Roger Williams. SCAP

One stone. Inventory. Jacques Prévert, *French.* STV, tr. by John Frederick Nims

One stone sufficeth (lo what death can do). On a Whore. John Hoskyns. FaBoEE

One stood on my path who seemed. Shelley. LaPo *Fr.* Epipsichidion.

One stood still, looking stupid. The other. The Willets. May Swenson. WPE

One stop past her destination. (LL) For Sale. Robert Lowell. AFr; CoAmPo

One stormy morn I chanced to meet. A Kiss in the Rain. Samuel Minturn Peck. OBAL

One student (white). Images. Naomi Long Madgett. LTA

One Summer. C. D. Wright. CMAP

One summer day. An Old-Fashioned Garden. Cole Porter. OBGa

One summer evening (led by her) I found. Lines. Wordsworth. *Fr.* Introduction—Childhood and School-Time. FHYEP *Fr.* The Prelude; Growth of a Poet's Mind [1850 vers.]

One summer he stole the jade buttons. Of Your Father's Indiscretions and the Train to California. Lynn Emanuel. MoLi; NAmP90

One summer, high in Wyoming. Before the Storm. Kenneth O. Hanson. CoAP

One summer I stayed. The Two Families. Joyce L. Brisley. BoTP

One Sunday morning as I went walking, by Brisbane waters I chanced to stray. Moreton Bay. *Unknown.* CBAP

One Sunday morning soft and fine. Brigadier. Arthur James Marshall Smith. MoCV

One surely tires eventually of the frequent references—the gossip. Reading the Unpublished Manuscripts of Louis MacNeice at Kinsale Harbour. Desmond O'Grady. PBCIP

One sweetly solemn thought. Nearer Home. Phoebe Cary. AH; PWR

One Talent, The. William Cutler. PWR

One That Died, The. William Daniel Ehrhart. CDa

One that is ever kind said yesterday. The Folly Of Being Comforted. W. B. Yeats. GBL; HeIP-4; LoP; NAEL-2; PFE

One, they're spooking, two, they're opening letters. The Un-American Women. John Tranter. BMAP

One Thing at a Time. M. A. Stodart. PoToHe

One thing at a time. *Unknown.* OxNR

One thing does not exist: Oblivion. Everness. Jorge Luis Borges, *Spanish.* APAD, *tr. by* Richard Wilbur.

One thing has a shelving bank. A Drumlin Woodchuck. Robert Frost. NOBA; NoAM

One thing in all things have I seen. The Secret. "Æ." MoBrPo

One thing is sure. The Pulse. Mark Van Doren. MoAmPo

One Thing That Can Save America, The. John Ashbery. AiP; FaBoA; NOBA; NoAM; PmAP

One thing that literature would be greatly the better for. Very like a Whale. Ogden Nash. HAP; InPK-6; InPS-3; PoLF

One thing you know is money—not much else. To a Piggy Bank. Tôn Thất Diệm, *Vietnamese.* AVP, *tr. by* Huỳnh Sanh Thông.

One thing you left with us, Jack Johnson. Strange Legacies. Sterling Brown. PoBA; TTY

One thinks of *one* as a pronoun employed principally. John Heath-Stubbs. OBCoV

One thought the recurring "image" in the poet's song. Handbook of Versification. Gilbert Sorrentino. PoA

One thousand and one naked ladies. Salon d'Automne. Stevie Smith. WPN

1001 Nights. Ronald Wallace. EC2

One thousand eight hundred and twenty-four. The Greenland Whale Fishery. *Unknown.* AmFP

One Thousand Fearful Words for Fidel Castro. Lawrence Ferlinghetti. VGW

One Thousand Nine Hundred and Sixty-Eight Winters. Jaci Earley. MBE; PFE

One thousand saxophones infiltrate the city. Battle Report. Bob Kaufman. ISC; MoNo; TTY

One Thousand Seven Hundred and Thirty Eight. A Dialogue Something like Horace. Persius, *Latin.*

"But *Horace,* Sir, was delicate, was nice." OBCVT, *tr. by* Alexander Pope

One Time. Douglas Livingstone. NoP-4; PeSA

One time at Springfield. (LL) The Hill. Edgar Lee Masters. CMoP; ColAP; FYAP; LiTM; NOBA; NoAM; OxBA; TAP

One time / Columbus said this island and the seas. Time of Turtles. Grace Perry. NOBAu

One Time Henry Dreamed the Number. Doughtry Long. BPo; PoBA

One time I wanted two moons. Jacob Nibenegenesabe. STP, *tr. by* Howard Norman *Fr.* The Wishing Bone Cycle.

One time in Alexandria, in wicked Alexandria. Thaïs. Newman Levy. PeLV

One time in the middle of "Goin' Down Slow." Stereo Time with Booker Little. Rick Madigan. SeSe

One time, to a coast of light. (LL) Flames and Dangling Wire. Robert Gray. BMAP; NOBAu

One to Love. Alfred Islay Walden. AAP

One to make ready. *Unknown.* LB; OxNR

One to Nothing. Carolyn Kizer. OBAL

One to Ten. Mother Goose. ReMoGo

One to Ten. *Unknown.* ReMoGo

One Too Many Mornings. David Rivard. PBCAP

One Tourist's Cologne. Hal Colebatch. NOBAu

One Train May Hide Another. Kenneth Koch. BAP-94

One truth is clear, WHATEVER IS, IS RIGHT. (LL) Awake, my St. John! leave all meaner things. Alexander Pope. NAEL-1; PoEL-3

One Tuesday in Summer. James McAuley. BMAP

One, Two. Mervyn Morris. PBCV

One, two, and three. Leaves. Countee Cullen. GT

One, two, Buckle my shoe. The Late Mother. Cynthia MacDonald. Poetsp

One, two, / Buckle my shoe. Mother Goose. BoTP; LB; OxNR; ReMoGo

One, two, buckle my shoe. *Unknown.* ACTP

One, Two, Three. Henry Cuyler Bunner. PoLF

One, Two, Three. Michael Rosen. OTCP

One—Two—Three. Hannah Senesh, *Hungarian.* WPOW, *tr. by* Peter Hay

One, two, three. Toward the Corner. Laura Riding Jackson. NOxBChV

1, 2, 3, 4, 5! / I caught a hare alive. One to Ten. Mother Goose. ReMoGo

One, two, three, four, five / Once I caught a fish alive. *Unknown.* LB; OxNR

("Little one upon the right, The.") (LL) ReMoGo

("One, two, three, four, five!") ACTP

One two three four five six seven eight nine and ten. Kneeling. Gertrude Stein. PFTM

One, two, three, four, / Mary at the cottage door. Mother Goose. LB; OxNR

One, Two, Three—Gough! Eve Merriam. NTCP

One, two, three, / I love coffee. *Unknown.* OxNR

1-2-3 was the number he played but today the number came 3-2-1. Dirge. Kenneth Fearing. HoPM; NIP-4; PoRA; RB; TrJP

One, two, tree / All de same. *Unknown.* Fr. Songs. PBCV

One, two, whatever you do. *Unknown.* CTV; OxNR

One ugly trick has often spoiled. Meddlesome Matty. Ann Taylor. OxBChV

One unkind word in the early morn. The Boomerang. Carrie May Nichols. PoToHe

One-Upmanship. Miriam Chaikin. NTCP

One used and butchered me: another spied. Raped and Revenged. Rudyard Kipling. *Fr.* Epitaphs of the War [1914–1918]. OBWP

One Voter out of Sixteen. Robert Penn Warren. *Fr.* Fall Comes in Back-Country Vermont. NYBP; VGW

One wading a Fall meadow finds on all sides. The Beautiful Changes. Richard Wilbur. CMoP; CoAP; HCAP; InPS-3; PoE

One wants a Teller in a time like this. Gwendolyn Brooks. WPE *Fr.* The Womanhood.

One was fifteen years old, the other sixteen, The. Pensionnaires. Paul Verlaine, *French.* EP, *tr. by* François Pirou

One was kicked in the stomach. Gangrene. Philip Levine. VGW

ONE WAS MORE WISE THAN THE OTHER. (LL) MAN FEARED THAT HE MIGHT FIND AN ASSASSIN, A. Stephen Crane. APN-2; MeMAP; NAAL-2; NoP-4

One watch had passed, and still sweet slumber shed. The Birth of Sohráb. Firdausi. TAL, *tr. by* James Atkinson *Fr.* The Shahnamah.

One-Way Conversation About Radio City Music Hall, A. Miroslav Holub, *German.* CEEP, *tr. by* Simko, Daniel

One Way of Looking at It. Arthur Joseph Munby. NOBVV

One-Way Song. Percy Wyndham Lewis.

"I would set all things whatsoever front to back." CTC

One way there was of muting in the mind. Edna St. Vincent Millay. *Fr.* Sonnets from an Ungrafted Tree. NALW

One We Knew. Thomas Hardy. NAEL-2

One went off to be. Headlands. Jack Hirschman. CLPP

One went spinning down the plughole. Yesterday the House was Full of Flies. Geoffrey Summerfield. OTCP

One wept whose only child was dead. Maternity. Alice Thompson Meynell. OxBSP; PEW; SDW; VWP

1. While the strategies in rush-hour traffic I mention to my husband. Kolohe or Communication. Carolyn Lei-Lanilau. BAP-96

One whistle, a short husky breath. Not There. Tess Gallagher. NIP-4

One white ear up. The White Rabbit. John Walsh. PeP

One white foot, try him. On Buying a Horse. *Unknown.* NBLV; RB

One who could repeat the Summer day, The. Emily Dickinson. NCAP

One who gave the warning with his wings, The. Exile. Karl Shapiro. CRP *Fr.* Adam and Eve.

One who has loved the hills and died, a man. Pony Rock. Archibald MacLeish. MeMAP

One who has pulled his oar in a start of storm, The. Simile. Agnes Nemes Nagy, *Hungarian.* PoSu, *tr. by* Frederic Will

One Who Is at Home, The. Franciso Albanez, *Spanish.* RaBo, *tr. by* Robert Bly

One who is not, we see: but one, whom we see not, is. The Higher Pantheism in a Nutshell. Swinburne. BXAP; CABP; CBNP; EnVR; PeVV *Fr.* The Heptalogia.

One who sees corn and is glad. Chicken. *Unknown. Fr.* Hunter Poems of the Yoruba. RB, *tr. by* Ulli Beier

One Who Struggles, The. Ernst Toller, *German.* TrJP, *tr. by* E. Ellis Roberts

One Who Watches. Siegfried Sassoon. TrJP

One who writes us is now doing four plays a year, The. Paavo Haavikko. VCWP, *tr. by* Herbert Lomas *Fr.* The Short Year.

One whom I knew, a student and a poet. Epitaph. Alex Comfort. MoBrPo

One whose love will never end. Accompanying a Gift. Lizelia Augusta Jenkins Moorer. CBWP-3

One whose majestic presence ever here. In Memoriam Frederick Douglass. Henrietta Cordelia Ray. CBWP-3

One Whose Reproach I Cannot Evade, The. George Hitchcock. SPE

One Wife for One Man. Frank Aig-Imoukhuede. PBA; PBMAP

    ("I done try go church, I done go for court.") PBMAP

One wife gets quilts, the other wife must freeze. On Being a Concubine. Ho Xuan Huong, *Vietnamese.* AVP, *tr. by* Huỳnh Sanh Thông

One winter morning as a child. A Vision of the Garden. James Merrill. GaP

One winter night, at half-past nine. "Lewis Carroll." *See* Phantasmagoria.

One winter night in August. X. J. Kennedy. OBCA; OBSP

One wintry night, at half-past nine. Phantasmagoria. "Lewis Carroll." OxBSn *Fr.* Phantasmagoria.

One with eyes the fairest. Love Song. Euripides. AWP *Fr.* The Cyclops.

'One with this world'. *Unknown, Yokuts.* FaBoA, *tr. by* A. L. Kroeber

One without looks in to-night [*or* tonight]. The Fallow Deer at the Lonely House. Thomas Hardy. AWP; CH; CMoP; OxBSP; RB; TTTS

One word is too often profaned. To———. Shelley. BoLoP; CBLP; EBEvV; GLoP; GTBS-P; ImPo; NOBE; OBEV; OBNC; OxAEP-2; PoLF; TFi

One Word More. Robert Browning. EnVR; PoEL-5

    "I shall never, in the years remaining." EPCY

One word, no more, to say. (LL) Merops. Ralph Waldo Emerson. APN-1; OxBA

One word two vowels one active situation at a time. Never Too Late. John Taggart. FTOS

One would be in less danger. Family Court. Ogden Nash. PeLV

One would continue to contend with one's ideas. (LL) The Glass of Water. Wallace Stevens. MeMAP; MoAmPo; OxBA; TAP

One would never assume, from the toy bulldogs taking the air. A Nice Part of Town. Alfred Hayes. NYBP

One would never suspect there were so many vices. The Destruction of Sodom. Daryl Hine. ChIV-1

One writes, that "Other friends remain." Tennyson. EnVR; PoEL-5 *Fr.* In Memoriam A. H. H.

One Writing against His Prick. *Unknown.* NOSC

One X. E. E. Cummings. FaBoMo

One xxxvii. Laurie Duggan. BMAP *Fr.* The Epigrams of Martial.

1. Ye have been fresh and green. Robert Herrick. *See* To Meadows [*or* Meddowes].

One Year. N. M. Bodecker. TLR

One Year Ago. Adah Isaacs Menken. CBWP-1

One year the town Republicans. Alderman. Marilyn Nelson Waniek. LTA

One year there were too many / frogs. Calendar. Cecil Bodker, *Danish.* BoWoP, *tr. by* Nadia Christensen *and* Alexander Taylor

One Year to Live. Mary Davis Reed. PoToHe

1. You cannot bring about prosper-. Ten Rules of Conduct for Individuals and Nations. Abraham Lincoln. CTV

Onely the Reverend Grave and Godly Mr. Buckly Remaines. Edward Johnson. SCAP

Oneness of the Philosopher with Nature, The. G. K. Chesterton. CBNP

One's Correspondence. Connie Bensley. OBCoV

"Ones drown!" After that, I wept for days. Jane Kenyon. *See* Once There Was Light.

One's grand flights, one's Sunday baths. The Sense of the Sleight-of-Hand Man. Wallace Stevens. HAP; ImPo; LiTM; MoAmPo; NOBA; NoAM; PoA; TwCP; WeW-3

One's none. Little Hundred. *Unknown.* OxNR

One's own body from its instant and heat. (LL) Six Young Men. Ted Hughes. NSI; OBWP; PoWW

One's-Self I sing, a simple separate person. Walt Whitman. ColAP; FaBoPV; NOBA; OxBA; SAGP

"Ones sink!" After that I wept for days. (LL) Once There Was Light. Jane Kenyon. BAP-93

Ones you fear most of all: ask where you were, The. (LL) For the Record. Adrienne Rich. NIP-4; VCAP

Oneself a living armoury? (LL) The Dead Crab. Andrew Young. FaBoTw; RB

Oneself Miss Grant. Miss Grant. Freda Downie. FaBoWP

Onesided Dialog. June Jordan. NoAM

Onesided, stripped of its ghosts. Eccles Street, Bloomsday, 1982. Harry Clifton. PBCIP

Ongoing Story, The. John Ashbery. HCAP

Onion, The. Margaret Gibson. MT

Onion. Katha Pollitt. RaBo

Onion. Wislawa Szymborska, *Polish.* PoSu, *tr. by* Grazyna Drabik *and* Sharon Olds

Onion, The. John Thompson. NOBC

Onion Bucket. Lorenzo Thomas. GT; PoBA

Onion: I'm the world's wonder, for I make women happy. *Unknown.* EEP, *tr. by* Michael Alexander *Fr.* Riddles (Exeter Book).

Onion is frost, An. Lullaby of the Onion. Miguel Hernández, *Spanish.* AF, *tr. by* Robert Bly

Onion lies peeled and white on the cold stove, The. Seven Skins. Sarah Kirsch, *German.* CEEP, *tr. by* Tanaquil Taubes

Onion, Memory, The. Craig Raine. NAEL-2; NoAM; NoP-4

Onion Woman, The. Ted Kooser. IFJA

Onions. Jonathan Swift. *See* Onyons.

Only a Blush. Mary E. Tucker. CBWP-1

Only a cottage border. Changes. May Probyn. VWP

Only a few will really understand. One Sided Shoot-out. Don L. Lee. BPo; NBV; PoBA

Only a fool would eat his heart out so. Ballad of the Bushman. Eileen Duggan. PeNZ

Only a fool would fail. God's Praises. *Unknown, Irish.* TIRV, *tr. by* Brendan Kennelly

Only a gentle swish. Belize Suite. Velma Pollard. HCP

Only a gentle swish. Sea Wall. Velma Pollard. HCP *Fr.* Belize Suite. HCP

Only a knee, no more. (LL) The Knee. Christian Morgenstern, *German.* CBNP; RB, *tr. by* W. D. Snodgrass *and* Lore Segal

Only a Little Thing. M. P. Handy. PoToHe

Only [*or* Onely] a little more. His Poetry His Pillar. Robert Herrick. BeJo; CaPo; NOSC; SeCP

Only a little shall we speak of thee. Mary Elizabeth Coleridge. VWP

Only a man harrowing clods. In Time of "The Breaking of Nations." Thomas Hardy. BoLoP; CMoP; ChIV-1; EBEV; EBEvV; HAP; LiTM; MoBrPo; MoP; NAEL-2; NOBE; NoAM; NoP-4; OAEL-2; OBEV; OBWP; OPOU; OxAEP-2; PoWW; Poetr; RB; TFi; WeW-3

Only a Miner. *Unknown.* AmFP

Only a part of me shall triumph in this. Boult to Marina. "Ern Malley." BMAP

Only a passing thought. (LL) Only a Thought. Charles MacKay. PFE; Poetr

Only a Pin. Isaac Hinton Brown. PWR

Only a Thought. Charles MacKay. PFE; Poetr

Only Alice. Josephine Jacobsen. FFC

Only awake to Universal Mind. One Hundred and Eighty-Third Chorus. Jack Kerouac. NeAP *Fr.* Mexico City Blues.

Only Bar in Dixon, The. James Welch. AmPA

Only brooms / Know the devil. Brooms. Charles Simic. AmPA; NNaP

Only calm here is the trees, waiting, The. A Girl Named Spring. Betsy Sholl. PBCAP

Only calmness will reassure. Honey. Robert Morgan. BLT

Only casually invited, and that several months ago. (LL) Poem: "The Eager note on my door said 'Call me'." Frank O'Hara. NOBA; NoAM; PmAP; Poetr; SPE

Only consonants and vowels. (LL) Survey of Literature. John Crowe Ransom. FaBoCh; MeMAP; NBLV; OBAL; TAP; TwCP; VGW

Only content and we are here, / My baby dear. (LL) Song: "Oh, baby, baby, baby dear." Edith Nesbit. PEW

Only cry for you a little. (LL) An Offering for the Cat. Mei Yao Ch'en, *Chinese.* PC, *tr. by* Burton Watson

Only Dance There Is, The. Rebecca Byrkit. BAP-94

Only Daughter, The. Laura Riding Jackson. FuPo

Only Death. Pablo Neruda. *See* Nothing but Death.

Only deposed kings can know. (LL) A Deposition from Love. Thomas Carew. BeJo; CaPo; CavPo; MeLP

Only depression if I stay at home. On the Night of the Fifteenth Day of the First Month I Go Out and Return. Mei Yao Ch'en, *Chinese.* SuSp, *tr. by* Jonathan Chaves

Only emperor is the emperor of ice-cream, The. (LL) The Emperor of Ice-Cream. Wallace Stevens. AmPP; CBNP; CMoP; FaBoMo; HAP; HCAP; HeIP-4; InPK-6; MeMAP; MoP; NAAL-2; NAWM-2; NIP-4; NOBA; NoAM; NoP-4; OxBA; PoE; PoPoPo; Poetr; SAGP; TAP; TFi; TRP; WeW-3

Only evidence remaining from his existence was his coat, The. Underneath Oblivion. Yannis Ritsos, *Greek.* AF, *tr. by* Minas Savas

Only from Afar. Ory Bernstein, *Hebrew.* IP, *tr. by* Warren Bargad *and* Stanley F. Chyet

Only God is never satisfied. (LL) The Good Shepherd: Atlanta, 1981. Ai. RACG; WWSi

Only head in the sky, The. Giraffe. Stanley Plumly. AmPA; ChAP

Only he's on a par with our times. About a Hat. Alexander Ilyich Bezymensky, *Russian.* TCRP, *tr. by* Daniel Weissbort

Only His Son Is With God. "Angelus Silesius." GePo, *tr. by* George C. Schoolfield *Fr.* The Cherubical Wanderer.

Only I laugh. Alexis Rotella. HA

Only. I would like to to be that unnoticed / & that necessary. (LL) Variation on the Word *Sleep.* Margaret Atwood. DeD; NOBC

Only in Creve Coeur. In Creve Coeur, Missouri. Rosanna Warren. PoPoPo

Only in This Way. Margaret Goss Burroughs. BlSi

Only Jealousy of Emer, The. *Unknown, Irish.* BIrV, *tr. by* John Montague

Only joy, now here you are. Fourth Song. Sir Philip Sidney. GBL; HAP; NAEL-1; NoP-4; NoSic *Fr.* Astrophil and Stella. AAS; SiPS

Only kid, An! an only kid. Had Gadyaa Kid, a Kid. *Unknown, Hebrew.* TrJP

Only last week, walking the hushed fields. Father and Son. Frederick Robert Higgins. BIrV; LBC; OBMV

Only lasting part of me, The. (LL) To Violet [with Prewar Poems]. Basil Bunting. FaBoMo; PoA

Only legend I have ever loved is, The. The Pomegranate. Eavan Boland. CABP; NoP-4

Only let it form within his hands once more—. The Brandy Glass. Louis MacNeice. GEA

Only letting in the cat. Penny Harter. HA

Only major city, one would hope, The. U-24 Anchors off New Orleans. Turner Cassity. MT

Only monarch all obey, The. (LL) Written for My Son, and Spoken by Him at His First Putting on Breeches. Mary Barber. CABP; ECEV; ECWP; NOEC

Only My Opinion. Monica Shannon. CTV

Only News I know, The. Emily Dickinson. APN-2; NOCV

Only now that my hair is gray. Anacreon, *Greek.* InMo, *tr. by* Sam Hamill

Only, of course, they can't sustain the part. (LL) Fireflies in the Garden. Robert Frost. OxBSP; SAmP

Only of myself I knew how to tell. "Rachel," *Hebrew.* MHP, *tr. by* Ruth Finer Mintz

Only on the rarest occasions, when the blue air. The Mountain. W. S. Merwin. VGW

Only once more and not again—the larches. In Ampezzo. Trumbull Stickney. APN-2

Only One, The. Elisaveta Bagryana, *Bulgarian.* CEEP, *tr. by* Jascha Kessler *and* Aleksandar Shurbanov

Only one drifter down in the patrol! A Minesweeper Sunk. Edward Davison. NSI

Only one final trick remains—. Sergey Aleksandrovich Yesenin, *Russian.* TCRP, *tr. by* Geoffrey Thurley

Only one guy and. Issa, *Japanese.* InPK-6, *tr. by* Cid Corman

Only one kiss. Good-bye, my dear. (LL) Jenny. D. G. Rossetti. EnVR; PoEL-5

Only One Mother. George Cooper. CTV; FPC

(Our Mother.) BoTP

Only one of me. One. James Berry. HCP; NOxBChV

Only One Way. Ella Wheeler Wilcox. PWR

Only passages of a poetry, no more. No matter how many times the cards are handled. Structure of Rime XXIII. Robert Duncan. FTOS

Only possible utilisation of electricity "in the arts," The. Electricity Breadthwise. Marcel Duchamp. PFTM

Only record of our great affection, The. A Gravestone at Corinth. *Unknown, Greek.* GrAn, *tr. by* Peter Jay

Only relics left are those long, The. Monuments for a Friendly Girl at a Tenth Grade Party. William Stafford. NoAM

Only response, The. Poem. Bill Knott. InPK-6

Only ribbon round it. (LL) Lucy Locket lost her pocket. Mother Goose. LB; OxBoLi; OxNR; ReMoGo

Only rule is enjoy yourself, The. *Unknown, Greek.* GrAn, *tr. by* Peter Porter

Only safe, The. *Unknown.* CTV

Only serpents change their outward skin. Memory. Nikolai Stepanovich Gumilyov, *Russian.* TCRP, *tr. by* Yakov Hornstein

Only Seven. Henry Sambrooke Leigh. BXAP

Only Son, An. Rudyard Kipling. *Fr.* Epitaphs of the War [1914–1918]. OBWP

Only teaching on Tuesdays, book-worming. Memories of West Street and Lepke. Robert Lowell. AF; AmPP; CMoP; CoAmPo; InPS-3; NAAL-2; NOBA; NoAM; PoE; SAGP; VCAP

Only tell her that I love. John, Baron Cutts Cutts. SAGP

Only temple He delights to fill, The. (LL) Enoch. Jones Very. ChIV-1; HAP

Only the casket left, the jewel gone. Charles Sumner. Charlotte L. Forten Grimke. AAP

Only the clouds were new. The Beast with Two Backs. Andrew Taylor. NOBAu

Only the compass, keeping hope alive. Logbook of a Lost Caravan. Gyula Illyés, *Hungarian.* PFTM, *tr. by* William Jay Smith

Only the Dead. Reed Whittemore. NYBP

Only the deep well. I Break the Sky. Owen Dodson. PoBA

Only the dim-witted say it's evening. What She Said. Milaipperun Kantan, *Tamil.* PLW, *tr. by* A. K. Ramanujan

Only the feathers floating around the hat. Icarus. Edward Field. PFE

Only the foreground's green. Love Overgrows a Rock. Eric Roach. PBCV

Only the grace from simple stone! (LL) Elegy before Death. Edna St. Vincent Millay. CMoP; LiTM; MeMAP

Only / the gray wind. Something for Supper. Carroll Arnett. VoR

Only the green. Tanka. Tawara Machi, *Japanese.* MJT, *tr. by* Makoto Ueda

Only the human being, absolved from kissing and strife. Death Is Not Evil, Evil Is Mechanical. D. H. Lawrence. PBMP

Only the illegitimate are beautiful. Thesis. Edward Dorn. NOBA

Only the lion and the cock. After Galen. Oliver St. John Gogarty. FaBoEE; OBMV; PoRA

Only the Mists are Real. Uku Masing, *Estonian.* CEEP, *tr. by* Ivar Ivask

Only the Polished Skeleton. Countee Cullen. VGW

Only the present instant remembers. Song. Nichita Stanescu, *Romanian.* CEEP, *tr. by* Irina Livezeanu

Only the sand, only the sand. El Alamein Revisited. Roy Macnab. PeSA

Only the short, broad, splayed feet. Young Shepherd Bathing His Feet. Peter Clarke. PBA

Only the tenacious. Above the Tree Line. Kathy Mangan. PuP-15

Only the thief was there, no one else. What She Said. Kapilar, *Tamil.* PLW, *tr. by* A. K. Ramanujan

Only the truly bourgeois. Qantas Bags. Laurie Duggan. BMAP

Only the waning morning moon / visits my garden. Ise Tayu, *Japanese.* WPJ, *tr. by* Kenneth Rexroth *and* Ikuko Atsumi

Only the wholesomest foods you eat. Samuel Hoffenstein. TrJP *Fr.* Poems in Praise of Practically Nothing.

Only the wind sings. Mary Celeste. Judith Nicholls. OBSP

Only then and not before. S.O.S. Léon Damas, *French.* PFTM, *tr. by* Norman R. Shapiro

Only these black translucent wings. Murmur. Esther Iverem. GT

"Only they know who is them." Them. Maureen Owen. BAP-94

Only thing I have of Jane MacNaughton, The. The Leap. James Dickey. NIP-4; Poetr; WeT

Only thing that can be relied on, The. The Snow on Saddle Mountain. Miyazawa Kenji, *Japanese.* ColAP; NOBA; NoAM, *tr. by* Gary Snyder

Only think, dearest Louisa, what fearful scenes we have witnessed! Arthur Hugh Clough. EDVV *Fr.* Amours de Voyage. NORVV

Only this evening I saw again low in the sky. Martial Cadenza. Wallace Stevens. AFr; MeMAP; OxBA; VGW

Only this table by the draughty window. Autumn Supper. Dimitris Tsaloumas. BMAP

Only Thy Dust. Don Marquis. PoLF

Only to fail again! (LL) I never hear the word "escape." Emily Dickinson. CMoP; NCAP; NOBA; SAmP

Only to have a grief. Peeling Onions. Adrienne Rich. BoWoP; HCAP; TAP

Only to say, Here I am in person. (LL) Stumpfoot on 42nd Street. Louis Simpson. NNaP; UnPo; VGW

Only Tourist in Havana Turns His Thoughts Homeward, The. Leonard Cohen. MoCV

On[e]ly true in shreds and stuff[e]. (LL) Upon Some Women. Robert Herrick. BeJo; CaPo

Only true likeness of myself, The. (LL) My Shoes. Charles Simic. CoAP; HCAP; VCAP

Only truth you know now is your hunger, The. The Disorder. Marilyn Chin. LoL

Only until this cigarette is ended. Edna St. Vincent Millay. HeIP-4

Only voice they will obey, The. (LL) The Gray Folk. Edith Nesbit. PEW

Only Waiting. Frances Laughton Mace. BLPA

Only way to be quiet, The. Poetry. Frank O'Hara. HCAP

Only way to have a friend, The. *Unknown.* PoToHe

Only we, blasting your three years of war. Manifesto of the Presidents of the Terrestrial Globe. Velemir Khlebnikov, *Russian.* TCRP, tr. by Gary Kern

Only, we die in earnest— that's no jest. (LL) On the Life of Man. Sir Walter Ralegh. EBEV; FaBoEE; NAEL-1; NOBE; NoSic; OxBSP; SCGP; SiPS; SoSe-8

Only what is heroic and courageous moves our blood. The Flowers of Politics, II. Michael McClure. NeAP

Only when. Tanka. Tsukamoto Kunio, *Japanese.* MJT, tr. by Makoto Ueda

Only when I hear the knock. My Students Catch Me Dancing. Leslie Adrienne Miller. CMAP

Only when my heart freezes. Alden Nowlan. RaBo

Only winds and rivers, / Life and death. (LL) In the highlands, in the country places. Robert Louis Stevenson. FaBoCh; OBEV; OxBS; SCGP

Only Years. Kenneth Rexroth. TAP

Onset, The. Robert Frost. CMoP; MoAmPo; OxBA; PBMP; PFE

Onto the hallowit steid bryng in, thai cry. The Wooden Horse Is Brought into Troy. Virgil. OBVE, tr. by Gawin Douglas *Fr.* The Aeneid [*or* Eneados, *Aeneis*].

Onto the ocean. Catapulting a Stone. Sokch'o Shin, *Korean.* CKP, tr. by Jaihiun Kim

Ontogeny. Jarold Ramsey. NIP-4

Onus of Mercy, The. Yehuda Amichai, *Hebrew.* IP, tr. by Warren Bargad *and* Stanley F. Chyet

Onward, Christian Soldiers. Sabine Baring-Gould. FaBoBe; FaPoR

Onward flies the rushing train. The Engine Driver. "G. S. O." BoTP

Onward led the road again. Hell Gate. A. E. Housman. NoAM; SCGP; UnPo

Onward, Onward, Men of Heaven. Lydia Huntley Sigourney. AH

Onward to Far Ida. George Darley. OBNC *Fr.* Nepenthe.

Onyons. Jonathan Swift. BIrV *Fr.* Verses Made for the Women Who Cry Apples, etc.

Ooftish. Samuel Beckett. NoAM

Oom Gert's Story. C. Louis Leipoldt, *Afrikaans.* PeSAV, tr. by C. J. D. Harvey

Oor best-lo'ed makar has but late grown cauld. Carlyle on Burns. William Jeffrey. OxBS *Fr.* On Glaister's Hill.

Opal. Amy Lowell. NALW

Opal heart of afternoon, The. The Bracelet of Grass. William Vaughn Moody. APN-2

Ope, aged Atlas, open then thy lap. Song. Ben Jonson. *Fr.* Pleasure Reconciled to Virtue. NAEL-1; OAEL-1

Open. Larry Eigner. NeAP

Open Air Where. Larry Eigner. PmAP

Open and Closed Space. Tomas Tranströmer, *Swedish.* SPE, tr. by Robert Bly

Open area outdoors, preferably the courtyard of a church or other religious structure, An. Realtheater Piece Two. Jerome Rothenberg. FTOS

Open as experience, this day, this. Tomarata. Kendrick Smithyman. PeNZ

Open Country. Richard Hugo. LCAP-2

Open Door, The. Elizabeth Jane Coatsworth. TLR

Open Door. Vesna Parun, *Croatian.* CEEP, tr. by Peter Kastmiler

Open Door, The. *Unknown, Irish.* IIP, tr. by Frank O'Connor

Open-Eyed Angel. David Rokeah, *Hebrew.* MHP, tr. by Ruth Finer Mintz

Open House. Theodore Roethke. NOBA; NoAM

Open it. The First Book. Rita Dove. LoL

Open Letter from a Constant Reader. Mona Van Duyn. PoA

Open little box. The Prisoners of the Little Box. Vasco [*or* Vasko] Popa, *Serbo-Croatian.* HSix, tr. by Charles Simic

Open mouth open through. Ted Greenwald. FTOS *Fr.* Word of Mouth.

Open-mouthed quail, The. Something or Other. Ron Padgett. FTOS

Open one's hand. Curriculum vitae. Marie-Claire Bancquart, *French.* MFP, tr. by Martin Sorrell

Open? Open. Shut? Shut. (LL) Cardinal Ideograms. May Swenson. NoP-4

Open Rebuke (Concealed Love). Tom Mandel. BAP-93

Open Sea, The. William Meredith. CoAP; TAP; UnPo

Open Secret. Denise Levertov. PaTW

Open Secrets. Gwendolyn MacEwen. LW

Open Sesame. *Unknown.* BoTP

Open sesame. Venus. Federico García Lorca. PFTM

Open the book of tales you knew by heart. Living Memory. Adrienne Rich. TRP

Open the door Oakland. Robert Grenier. FTOS *Fr.* Oakland.

Open the Door to Me, Oh! Robert Burns. PoEL-4; SCGP

(O, Open the Door to Me, O!) FaBoCh

Open the door, who's there within? *Unknown.* GBL

"Open the gates." The Bonny Earl of Murray. *Unknown.* ESPB

Open the Gates. *Unknown, Hebrew.* TrJP, tr. by Israel Zangwill

Open the window on the high. Earth Tremor in Lugano. James Kirkup. NYBP

Open this evening like a letter. Love in July. Ivan V. Lalic, *Serbo-Croatian.* HSix, tr. by Charles Simic

Open Thy Doors, O Lebanon. Bible, *O.T.* AWP *Fr.* Zechariah.

Open thy gates. To Heaven. Robert Herrick. ChIV-2

Open, Time, and let him pass. Louise Imogen Guiney. APN-2

Open to Me! He Commandeth a Fair Wind. *Unknown.* AWP *Fr.* Book of the Dead.

Open up, gate. H. Leyvik, *Yiddish.* CEEP, tr. by Benjamin Harshav *and* Barbara Harshav

Open Window. Janet Hamill. DeD

Open Windows. Marilyn Hacker. Poetr

Open Windows. Sara Teasdale. ColAP

Open your eyes and stare. Haka: Hinemotu. Te Aomuhurangi te Maaka. PeNZ

Open your eyes that you may see. Emma Bridge Whisenand. PoToHe

Open your front door baby black dark come home for good. (LL) Blues for Franks Wooten. Tom Weatherly. GT; NBV

Open your palms. Request. Jared Angira. PBMAP

Opened, clear as a child's geography. The Summer Countries. Henry Rago. VGW

Opener. Chris Wallace-Crabbe. BMAP *Fr.* The Bits and Pieces.

Opening a vein he called my radial. 40 Days and 40 Nights. Henri Cole. PoPoPo

Opening his. Alexis Rotella. HA

Opening in a good firm for a former cat. (LL) The Lonely Man. Randall Jarrell. FP; OxBC

Opening Le Ba Khon's Dictionary. John Balaban. CDa

Opening of a Door, The. (LL) Suspense. Emily Dickinson. AWP; MoAmPo; OxBA; WPE

Opening of the Indian and Colonial Exhibition by the Queen. Tennyson. EBVVPR

Opening Service, An. Clara Ann Thompson. CBWP-2

Opening the Book. Kim R. Stafford. CMAP

Opening the mailbox. Alan Pizzarelli. HA

Openly send word to Algol and Procyon. (LL) For Heather, Entering Kindergarten. Roberta Hill Whiteman. HATNAP; NoAM

Openly, yes, / with the naturalness. Black Earth. Marianne Moore. FaBoMo

Opens blue and cool on a hot morning. (LL) Pleasures. Denise Levertov. NOBA; NeAP; NoAM; PoE; Poetr

Opera Actors. Phan chu Trinh, *Vietnamese.* AVP, tr. by Huỳnh Sanh Thông

Opera! All that cardboard. Romare Bearden Retrospective at the Brooklyn Museum. Cornelius Eady. WWSi

Opera Teacher neemed Enna, An. Moss Rich. PeLi

Operation, The. W. D. Snodgrass. InPK-6; TAP

Operation Memory. David Lehman. NAmP90

Operative No. 174 Resigns. Kenneth Fearing. NYBP

Ophelia's Song. Shakespeare. EBEV; EBEvV; EnLoPo; NoSic; PoRA; SCGP *Fr.* Hamlet. NAWM-1

(O's Song: ("How should I your true love know").) GBL

Ophra. Judah Halevi, *Hebrew.* TrJP, tr. by Nina Davis Salaman

Opiate Phobia. Joseph Donahue. PT

Opinion is a flitting thing. Emily Dickinson. SAmP

Opinion is not worth a rush. Michael Robartes and the Dancer. W. B. Yeats. OAEL-2

Opinions of the New Student. Regino Pedroso, *Spanish.* TTY, tr. by Langston Hughes

Opium. Thế Lũ', *Vietnamese.* AVP, tr. by Huỳnh Sanh Thông

Opium-Eater, The. Mary E. Tucker. CBWP-1

Opium Fantasy, An. Maria White Lowell. APN-2; InPK-6

Opium Poppy, The. Song-yong Park, *Korean.* CKP, tr. by Jaihiun Kim

Opoponax. Theodore Wratislaw. ADE

Oppenheim's Cup and Saucer. Carol Ann Duffy. LW

Opportunity. Harry Graham. OBCoV; PeLV

Opportunity. John James Ingalls. PoLF

Opportunity. Niccolò Machiavelli, *Italian.* AWP, tr. by James Elroy Flecker

Opportunity. Walter Malone. BLPA; FaBoBe; PWR

Opportunity. Shakespeare. PoEL-2 *Fr.* The Rape of Lucrece. (Outcry upon Opportunity, An.) NOBE

Opportunity. Edward Rowland Sill. APN-2; BLPA; PFE (Broken Sword, The.) PoToHe

Opposite House, The. Robert Lowell. CMoP

Opposite of Green, The. Alvin Aubert. ISC

Opposite to Melancholy. William Strode. NOSC

Opposition. Kaneko Mitsuharu, *Japanese.* NNPT, *tr. by* Geoffrey Bownas *and* Anthony Thwaite.

Opposition Is True Friendship. William Blake. *Fr.* The Marriage of Heaven and Hell. NAEL-2; NOBRP; OAEL-2

Oppressed the soul with misery, grief, and fear. George Crabbe. *See* Peter Grimes.

Oppression. Jimmy Santiago Baca. AF

Optical Prodigal, The. Russell Edson. PmAP

Optics. Alan Sillitoe. SpW

Optimism. Ella Wheeler Wilcox. BLPA; FaBoBE; PWR

Optimism, / trust, / fearless. Scum & Slime. John Giorno. PmAP

Optimist fell ten stories, The. *Unknown.* BLPA ("Optimist fell ten storeys, The.") FuFo

Optimist / "Somebody Said That It Couldn't Be Done." *Unknown.* FuFo

Options. James Seay. WeT

Opulence. Jorie Graham. NoP-4

Opulent oracle—it's a terrible thing! It's a Terrible Thing! Everett Hoagland. BPo

Opus III. Rade Drainac, *Serbo-Croatian.* "Dreams worn out like small coins taken out of circulation." HSix, *tr. by* Charles Simic

Opus Nil. Hans Arp, *German.* CBNP, *tr. by* Michael Hamburger

Opusculum paedagogum. Study of Two Pears. Wallace Stevens. BLT; InPS-3; NAAL-2; NoAM; OxBA

Or a kick on the arse. (LL) The Description of an Irish Feast. Hugh MacGowran, *Irish.* NOIV; OBCoV, *tr. by* Jonathan Swift

Or a piper coming from far away? Isaac Rosenberg. *See* Dead Man's Dump.

Or a Play. Leslie Scalapino. FTOS

Or a young hart upon the mountains of Bether. Bible, *O.T. See* I am the rose of Sharon, and the lily of the valleys.

Or an old man upon a winter's night. (LL) On Being Asked for a War Poem. W. B. Yeats. NIP-4; OBWP; OxAEP-2; PoWW

Or any mortals under happier law? Catullus. *See* Carmen 45 ("Phyllis Corydon clutched to him").

Or any other reason why. (LL) A Catch. Henry Aldrich. FaBoEE; NOSC; OxBSP; PFE

Or as in jewelry shops, do gems. (LL) Prologue: "Lord, can a crumb of dust the earth outweigh." Edward Taylor. NAAL-1; NAAL-3

Or better, be with me— / Yours, Fly. (LL) Letter to Bee. Emily Dickinson. SAmP; TLR; TTTS

Or cease to wonder that she so declines. Catullus. *See* Carmen 69 ("That no fair woman will, wonder not why").

Or come again. My Ben! Robert Herrick. BeJo

—Or, conversely, hungers. Beethoven, Opus 111. Amy Clampitt. NIP-4; NoP-4

Or curtained close such scene from ev'ry future view. (LL) Ode on the Poetical Character. William Collins. NAEL-1; NOEC; OAEL-1; PoE; PoEL-3

Or dead in the Mississippi mud. (LL) A Poem for Myself (Or Blues for a Mississippi Black Boy). Etheridge Knight. AF; BkSV; PoPoPo

Or did I really fall out of love with my country?—. "Naum Korzhavin," *Russian.* TCRP, *tr. by* Albert C. Todd

Or die and so forget what love ere meant. (LL) On Monsieur's Departure. Elizabeth I, Queen of England. CABP; NAEL-1; NALW; WPE

Or does it explode?. (LL) Harlem. Langston Hughes. APSN; AiP; AmPP; CrDW; GLP; GT; HCAP; HeIP-4; InPK-6; InPS-3; LiTM; MBE; NAAAL; NIP-4; NoP-4; PBMP; PoBA; Poetr; RaBo; SAmP; SoSe-8

Or dressed up in blue. (LL) One. James Berry. HCP; NOxBChV

Or dying, there at least may die. (LL) Happy lover who has come, A. Tennyson. EBVVPR; EnVR

Or ele he would forgo his mortal nature. (LL) The Human Seasons. Keats. GTBS-P

Or else quite extinguish mine. (LL) A Prayer to the Wind. Thomas Carew. BeJo; CavPo

Or else, there's no wife in the case. The Spoils of Youth. Robert Browning. *Fr.* A Likeness. CTC

Or else this very moment dies—. (LL) Strephon to Celia. Mary Leapor. ECWP; RACG

Or else you break a faithful heart. (LL) To a Lady on Her Passion for Old China. John Gay. ImPo; SCGP

Or exercise their Spight in Human Woe? (LL) Invocation. Virgil, *Latin.* OBCVT; OBVE, *tr. by* John Dryden

Or from what spring doth your opinion rise. Sir John Davies. *Fr.* Orchestra; or, A Poem[e] of Da[u]ncing. NoSic; SiPS

Or gathers seaward, ebbing out of mind. (LL) The Slow Pacific Swell. Yvor Winters. ColAP; NOBA

Or give sigh for sigh. Thomas Moore. *See* 'Tis the Last Rose of Summer.

Or give the mittee will, or give the gode man power. (LL) An Excelente Balade of Charitie. Thomas Chatterton. EBEV; NOEC; OxAEP-1

Or glittering starlight without thee is sweet. (LL) Eve to Adam. Milton. GBL; UV

Or hawk of the tower. (LL) To Mistress [*or* Maystres] Margaret Hussey. John Skelton. AAS; EBEV; EnLoPo; FaBoCh; HoPM; InPS-3; NAEL-1; NBLV; NOBE; NTP; NoP-4; NoSic; OAEL-1; OBEV; PeLV; PoE; PoEL-1; PoRA; SCGP; SCV; TFi

Or he relieves them cheaply with a tear. (LL) Sensibility: A Poetical Epistle to the Hon. Mrs Boscawen. Hannah More. ECWP; Ro

Or hear old Triton blow his wreathèd horn. (LL) Sonnet: "The World is too much with us; late and soon." Wordsworth. APAD; AWP; CABP; ClHu; EBEvV; FHYEP; FaPoR; GSo; GTBS-P; HAP; HeIP-4; HoPM; ImPo; InPK-6; InPS-3; NAEL-2; NAWM-2; NOBE; NOBRP; NoP-4; OAEL-2; OBEV; OBNC; PBMP; PFE; PWR; PoE; PoEL-4; PoLF; PoPoPo; PoRA; Poetr; RaBo; Ro; SAGP; SCGP; SoSe-8; Son; TFi; TRP; WeW-3

Or help to half-a-crown. (LL) The Man He Killed. Thomas Hardy. CMoP; ChAP; HAP; HeIP-4; LiTM; MoBrPo; NIP-4; OBWP; PBMP; Poetr; RB; TFi; WeW-3

Or her kisses where a serpent hides. (LL) Returning, We Hear the Larks. Isaac Rosenberg. FaBoMo; NAEL-2; NSI; NoAM; OAEL-2; OBWP; PeFWW; PoWW

Or hope relief. (LL) Elegy over a Tomb. Edward Herbert, 1st Baron Herbert of Cherbury. MeLP; NOBE; OBEV; OBWVE; PoEL-2

Or how belovèd above all else that dies. (LL) And you as well must die, belovèd dust. Edna St. Vincent Millay. MeMAP; PoLF; PoRA; TAP

Or if her a sinner. (LL) Song: "Pious Selinda goes to prayers." William Congreve. BoLoP; ECEV; GLoP; NBLV; NOBE; NOEC; OxBSP

Or I shall live your epitaph to make. Sonnet 81. Shakespeare. OxAEP-1 *Fr.* Sonnets.

Or I suppose I can. (LL) Self's the Man. Philip Larkin. NOBL; PeLV

Or I wouldn't be here. (LL) Birdie McReynolds. Samuel Hoffenstein. BXAP; NBLV

Or if I sing one cheerful air / Till thy deliverance is my song. Bible, *O.T. See* Psalm 137.

Or if thou dar'st to climb the highest trees. The Affectionate Shepherd. Richard Barnfield. OBGa *Fr.* The Affectionate Shepherd.

Or in the running stream. Catullus. *See* Carmen 70 ("Lesbia says she'ld rather marry me").

Or innocently seems to graze. Andrew Marvell. *See* To My Lord Fairfax.

Or is it a great tide that covers the rock-pool. Hilda Doolittle. WPoS *Fr.* Sagesse.

Or is it a shadow? (LL) Tenebris. Angelina Weld Grimké. NAAAL

Or it goes to the backyard and stands like an old horse cold in the pasture. (LL) Original Sin. Robert Penn Warren. HoPM; LiTM; NOCV; TAP

Or its advantage—Blue. (LL) I watched the Moon around the House. Emily Dickinson. APN-2; NCAP

Or just some human sleep. (LL) After Apple-Picking. Robert Frost. AmPP; CMoP; InPS-3; MeMAP; MoAmPo; MoP; NAAL-2; NOBA; NTP; NoAM; OxBA; PoE; Poetr; SAGP; SAmP; SoSe-8; TAP; TFi; TRP; UnPo

Or known what death could do. (LL) Carentan O Carentan. Louis Simpson. CoAP; MoBS; NOBA; OBWP; PoE; RB; WeT

Or let me die!—. (LL) Anguish. Henry Vaughan. FMP; OxAEP-1

Or let me die! (LL) My heart leaps up when I behold. Wordsworth. CIV

Or looked [*or* lookt] I back unto the times hence flown. To M. Denham, on His Prospective Poem. Robert Herrick. BeJo

Or love, either. (LL) Spinster. Sylvia Plath. FaBoWP; LW; SoSe-8

Or love me [*or* mee] less [*or* lesse], or love me [*or* mee] more. Song: "Or love me less, or love me more." Sidney Godolphin. BeJo; NOSC

Or many things adulterate. Epitaph. Tristan Corbière, *French.* AWP, *tr. by* Joseph T. Shipley

"Or maybe I will stay a child." (LL) The Question. Karla Kuskin. NTCP; PiM

Or maybe this / is the sacred. Michael Palmer. PT

Or Mists—the Apennine. (LL) Thought beneath so slight a film, The. Emily Dickinson. AmPP; OxBA

Or music [*or* musique] be but[t] [*or* music be but] in sweet thoughts of love? (LL) Sonnet 23: "When every one to pleasing pastime hies." Mary Sidney, Countess of Montgomery Wroth. WPE

Or night beasts in a winter field. (LL) Rain—Birdoswald. Frances Horovitz. APAD; NBrP

Or Noon—in Mazarin? (LL) I found the words to every thought. Emily Dickinson. APN-2; AmPP

Or not untrue and not unkind. (LL) Talking in bed ought to be easiest. Philip Larkin. LoP; NoP-4; PoPoPo

Or nothing. William Carlos Williams. *See* Queen-Anne's-Lace.

Or of his hope / that heat would be arrested on its shore. (LL) Heat. Kenneth Mackenzie. BMAP

Or once measure to move, but as they move in thee. (LL) I Am My Beloved's, and His Desire Is towards Me. Francis Quarles. EBEV; NOCV; OAEL-1; OxAEP-1

Or ought I do but Salem sing. Bible, *O.T. See* Psalm 137.

Or out of time will correct this. (LL) The Country Clergy. Ronald Stuart Thomas. GTBS-P; OxBTC; PeECV

Or pleasures, seldom reach'd, pursu'd. Anne Finch, Countess of Winchilsea. *See* A Nocturnal Reverie.

Or pleasures, seldom reached, again pursued. (LL) A Nocturnal Reverie. Anne Finch, Countess of Winchilsea. BWW; EBEV; ECEV; ECWP; NAEL-1; NALW; NOEC; NoP-4; OxAEP-1; PBWP; PoE; PoEL-3; Poetr; WPE

Or rather the sacred fish with the golden faces. Callimachus. HePo, *tr. by* Barbara Hughes Fowler *Fr.* Galataea.

Or scorn[e], or pity [*or* pittie] on me take. The Dream[e]. Ben Jonson. BeJo; CBLP; NOBE; NOSC; PoEL-2

Or see the raincoats pass. (LL) Lobsters in the Window. W. D. Snodgrass. NYBP; TAP; TRP

Or send it backe to me. (LL) The Cryer. Michael Drayton. NOSC; PoEL-2; SCGP

Or so very little longer! (LL) The Lost Mistress. Robert Browning. BoLoP; LoP; NOBE; OBEV; OBNC; SAGP

Or something very like Him. (LL) Dipsychus. Arthur Hugh Clough. CABP; NAEL-2; NOBE; NOBVV; NoP-4

Or Southey or Barrow! (LL) Keats. Byron. FaBoEE; UV

Or take a day or two, my days are numbered. (LL) An Unborn Child. Derek Mahon. CABP; PNI

Or that of my Alexis, I am lost. (LL) On Her Loving Two Equally. Aphra Behn. NALW; NIP-4

Or the best of our pleasures may turn into pain. (LL) The Mouse and the Cake. Eliza Cook. ACTP; VWP

Or the *Chaplain*, (for 'tis his *Trade*) as in Duty bound, shall ever *Pray*. (LL) To Their Excellencies the Lords Justices of Ireland, the Humble Petition of Frances Harris, Who Must Starve, and Die a Maid if It Miscarries. Jonathan Swift. NOEC; PoEL-3

Or the day's vanity, the night's remorse. (LL) The Choice. W. B. Yeats. CMoP; NoAM; OxBSP; OxBTC

Or the Earl—an Earl? (LL) Did the Harebell loose her girdle. Emily Dickinson. FaBoVe; NCAP

Or the fox from his lair in the morning. (LL) John Peel. John Woodcock Graves. CH; OxBoLi

Or the image-kingdom's idol of the past generation. Saul Tchernichowsky. MHP, *tr. by* Ruth Finer Mintz *Fr.* To the Sun.

Or the light, or the. The Firmament Doth Shake. Ken Edwards. NBrP

Or the old grasshopper molasses-mouthed. (LL) Thin little leaves of wood fern, ribbed and toothed. Frederick Goddard Tuckerman. APN-2; TAP

Or the price of grass-seed? (LL) The Other Side. Seamus Heaney. CIP-2; PNI

Or the prophetic sibballance of song. (LL) The Mad Potter. John Hollander. ColAP; VCAP

Or the rest will be wanting one too! (LL) Limerick: "An Epicure, Dining at Crewe." *Unknown.* NBLV; NTCP; PeLi

Or the "sculpture" of rhyme. (LL) Age demanded an image, The. Ezra Pound. HAP; MoAmPo; VGW

Or the songs of the butterflies be. (LL) Eutopia. Francis Turner Palgrave. OBGa

Or the tears of a girl remembering her dread. (LL) Vaunting Oak. John Crowe Ransom. OxBA; VGW

Or the unimaginable touch of Time. (LL) Mutability. Wordsworth. EBEV; HeIP-4; InPK-6; LaPo; NOBE; NoP-4; OAEL-2; OBEV; PoEL-4

Or they had none there. (LL) Fair Margaret and Sweet William. *Unknown.* ESPB; OxBB

Or Think We've Met subhuman rights Before. (LL) Salesman is an it that stinks excuse, A. E. E. Cummings. NoAM; OxBA; Poetr

Or this doll of death, hideous, we treasure. The Doll. Peyton Houston. *Fr.* Sonnet Variations. Son

Or till blossomed stalks cannot weave a spell. (LL) Spraying the Potatoes. Patrick Kavanagh. BIrV; CABP; IIP

Or to seal up the sun. (LL) To Daisies, Not to Shut So Soon[e]. Robert Herrick. BeJo; CH; CaPo; GBL; OBEV; OxBSP

Or to the play goes but some purse to nip. (LL) Sir Revel. Samuel Rowlands. NoSic; OBCoV

Or too much weight to fly. (LL) Too happy Time dissolves itself. Emily Dickinson. APN-2; NOBA

Or took in vain the same. (LL) Thus everyone before the throne. Michael Wigglesworth. NAAL-3

"Or Venus with her ecstasy." (LL) In a meadow/ Beside the chapel three boys were playing football. Patrick Kavanagh. CIP-2; PoE

Or view the Lord of the unerring bow. Canto 4. Byron. GS *Fr.* Childe Harold's Pilgrimage.

Or was myself—too small? (LL) I took my Power in my Hand. Emily Dickinson. ChIV-1; SAmP

Or what death I should dee. (LL) Mary Hamilton. *Unknown.* NOBE; OxBB

Or what is closer to the truth. When I Buy Pictures. Marianne Moore. ColAP; OxBA

Or where is man soe uncontroul'd a lord? (LL) Verses Written by Mrs. Hutchinson. Lucy Hutchinson. KTR; NOSC

Or whether we shall victorious, or utterly quell'd and / defeated. (LL) As I lay with my head in your lap camerado. Walt Whitman. NCAP

Or which at least I need not mention yet. (LL) Young Juan wandered by the glassy brooks. Byron. OBCoV

Or whistling, I am not a little boy. (LL) The Ball Poem. John Berryman. ChAP; CoAP; MoAmPo; NOBA; NoAM; Poetr

Or who in Moscow, toward the Czar. Assassins. Robert Browning. OxBoV *Fr.* Waring.

Or withoute quiete to have huge labour. (LL) Inordinate Love. *Unknown.* EBEV; MiEL; OxBSP

Or yield or die's the word, what could he mean. Ignotum per Ignotius, or a Furious Hodge-Podge of Nonsense; a Pindaric. *Unknown.* CBNP; NOEC

Or you may guess. (LL) Winter: My Secret. Christina Rossetti. BrRo; NAEL-2; NOBVV; VWP

Oracle Night. Michael Brownstein.

"Oracle night / the porch is frozen." FTOS

Oracle of the Drawned, The. Douglas Oliver. NBrP

Oracles, The. A. E. Housman. HAP

Oracles are dumm, The. Milton. GrIP *Fr.* Hymn on the Morning of Christ's Nativity [*or* On the Morning of Christ's Nativity]. NAEL-1; NOBE; OBEV *Fr.* On the Morning of Christ's Nativity. MeLP; NOCV; NoP-4; PBRV; PoEL-3; SCGP

Oracles are dumm, The. Prudentius. OBCVT, *tr. by* John Milton *Fr.* On the Morning of Christ's Nativity.

Oradour-sur-Glane. Silence. Lucia Cordell Getsi. LoHo

Oral Messages. Lawrence Ferlinghetti.

"I am waiting for my case to come up." AiP; PmAP

Oral Tradition, The. Eavan Boland. NBrP; PBCIP

Orange. Barbara Ferland. PBCV

Orange, The. Matthew Prior. PeLV

Orange air grows fetid with smoke, The. The uneasy dark. Five Songs. Alan Ross. FaBoCh; LiTM

Orange and purple, shot with white and mauve. Orchids. Theodore Wratislaw. ADE

Orange Buds by Mail from Florida. Walt Whitman. NAAL-1; NAAL-3

Orange butterfly trying to drink the tears, An. Buchenwald. Bin Ramke. WeT

Orange Chiffon. Jayne Cortez. BlSi

Orange in the middle of a table. Against Still Life. Margaret Atwood. MoCV

Orange Jews. Ted Berrigan *and* Ron Padgett. SPE

Orange leaves are gone. Lady Izumi, *Japanese.* BoWoP, *tr. by* Willis Barnstone

Orange Lily, The. *Unknown.* FaBoPV; NOIV

Orange line splits the sky, An. The Flint Hills. Lew Blockcolski. VoR

Orange March. Richard Murphy. NOIV *Fr.* The Battle of Aughrim.

Orange on its way. On Its Way. May Swenson. SoSe-8; WPE

Orange on the table, An. Alicante. Jacques Prévert, *French.* BoLoP, *tr. by* Lawrence Ferlinghetti

Orange Poem, The. George MacBeth. OBCoV

Orange rivers and red dogs of Paul Gauguin, The. Slag. Charles David Wright. MT

Orange Tree, The. John Shaw Neilson. CBAP

Orange tree, The. Lady Otomo no Sakanoé, *Japanese.* WPJ, *tr. by* Kenneth Rexroth *and* Ikuko Atsumi

Orange tree, in various light, The. In a Green Night. Derek Walcott. PFE

Orange With the Rind Still Green, An. Xuân Diệu, *Vietnamese.* AVP, *tr. by* Huỳnh Sanh Thông

Oranges, The. Abu Dharr, *Arabic.* TTY, *tr. by* A. J. Arberry

Oranges. Fruit. Kenward Elmslie. FTOS

Oranges. Gary Soto. NoAM; WeW-3

Oranges and lemons, say the bells of St. Clement's. *Unknown.* ACTP

Oranges Returned, The. Gilbert Sorrentino. FTOS

Orara. Henry Clarence Kendall. CBAP

Oration on Death, An. Manoah Bodman.
  "What rich profusion here." APN-1

Orator. Ralph Waldo Emerson. OxBA *Fr.* Quatrains.

Orator Flaccus can commit solecisms. Lucilius, *Greek.* GrAn, *tr. by* Peter Porter

Orator Prigg. William Blake. OBSV

Orator's Epitaph, The. Henry Peter Brougham, 1st Baron Brougham and Vaux. NBLV

Orbit. Gig Ryan. BMAP

Orbit I describe in my environment, The. Orbits. Nina Cassian, *Romanian.* PoSu, *tr. by* Naomi Lazard

Orbiting, the sun itself has a sun. The Great Dark. Martin Carter. PBCV

Orbits. Nina Cassian, *Romanian.* PoSu, *tr. by* Naomi Lazard

Orchard. Hilda Doolittle. CMoP; LiTM; MoAmPo; OxBA

Orchard and the Heath, The. George Meredith. OBNC

Orchard at Avignon, An. Agnes Mary Frances Robinson. NOBVV

Orchard dying, The. Mary Kinzie. FFC

Orchard-Pit, The. D. G. Rossetti. EnLoPo; GLoP; NAEL-2; OAEL-2; PeVV; PoEL-5; SCV

Orchards in July. Zbigniew Machej, *Polish.* BLT, *tr. by* Czeslaw Milosz *and* Robert Hass

Orchestra, The. William Carlos Williams. HAP

Orchestra; or, A Poem[e] of Da[u]ncing. Sir John Davies. NoSic; SiPS
  Dedications, I: To His Very Friend, Master Richard Martin. SiPS
  Dedications, II: To the Prince. SiPS
  Praise of Dancing, The. NOBE
  "Sole heir of virtue, and of beauty both." NAEL-1
  "What eye doth see the heaven but doth admire." PeECV

Orchestra tunes up, each instrument, The. Meditation. Anthony Hecht. EOEF

Orchid House, The. Medbh McGuckian. CABP

Orchid-lipped, loose-jointed, purplish, indolent flowers. Himalayan Balsam. Anne Stevenson. FaBoWP; OxAEP-2

Orchids. Theodore Roethke. CMoP; ColAP; TRP

Orchids. Theodore Wratislaw. ADE

Orchids grow through spring and summer. Ch'en Tzu-ang. SuSp, *tr. by* William H. Nienhauser *Fr.* Impressions of Things Encountered.

Ordained I was a beggar. The File-Hewer's Lamentation. Joseph Mather. FaBoPV; NOEC

Ordeal, The. Olga Fiodorovna Berggolts, *Russian.* TCRP, *tr. by* Daniel Weissbort

Ordeal. Nina Cassian, *Rumanian.* PBWP, *tr. by* Michael Impey *and* Brian Swann

Order for a Picture, An. Alice Cary. BLPA

Order is a lovely thing. The Monk in the Kitchen. Anna Hempstead Branch. MoAmPo

Order of the Dead, The. J. P. Clark Bekederemo. HBAPE

Order the ground? Versions. Robert Kelly. *Fr.* The Book of Persephone. PoM

Ordering my tombstone. Raymond Roseliep. HA

Ordinance on Arrival. Naomi Lazard. BLT

Ordinances of Jehovah are true, and righteous altogether, The, *vv. 7–9 of sl. diff. vers.* Bible, *O.T. See* Psalm 19.

Ordinary Evening in Cleveland, An. Lewis Turco. NYBP

Ordinary Morning, An. Philip Levine. WWSi

Ordinary Women, The. Wallace Stevens. OxBA

O're [*or* O'er] the smooth enamel'd [*or* enameled *or* enamelled] green. Song. Milton. OBEV; OxBSP *Fr.* Arcades.

Oread. Hilda Doolittle. AWP; CMoP; ColAP; HeIP-4; InPS-3; MoAmPo; MoP; NAAL-2; NALW; NOBA; NoAM; OxBA; PoPoPo; Poetr; TAP

Oregon. Bob Kaufman. GT

Oregon Message, An. William Stafford. CoAP

Orf. Ted Hughes. NoAM

Orfeo. Jack Spicer. APSN

Organist, The. George W. Stevens. BLPA

Orgasm completely, The. Sonnet. Tom Clark. CoAP

Orgie. Madison Cawein. APN-2

Orgy. Norman MacCaig. OxBC

Orgy (That Is, Vegetable Market, at Sarno). Gina Labriola, *Italian.* WPOW, *tr. by* Edgar Pauk

Orgy was held on the lawn, The. Limerick. *Unknown.* PeLi

Orient Express, The. Randall Jarrell. CMoP; CoAP; NOBA; PoE

Oriental Apologue, An. James Russell Lowell. PoEL-5

Oriental Ballerina, The. Rita Dove. NAAAL

Oriental histories relate, The. John 1:14 (1964). Jorge Luis Borges, *Spanish.* GI, *tr. by* David Curzon *and* Sarah Recalde

Orientations. Odysseus Elytis, *Greek.*
  Of the Aegean. GrIP, *tr. by* Kimon Friar

Oriflamme. Jessie Redmond Fauset. BlSi; PoBA

Origami. Abdur-Rahman Slade Hopkinson. HCP

Origin. "Eduard Georgievich Bagritzky," *Russian.* TCRP, *tr. by* Vera Dunham

Origin-Legend of the Chou Tribe. *Unknown, Chinese.* ChiP, *tr. by* Arthur Waley

Origin of Baseball, The. Kenneth Patchen. CLPP

Origin of Didactic Poetry, The. James Russell Lowell. PoEL-5

Origin of Landscape or the End of Mercy, The. Odysseus Elytis, *Greek.* VCWP, *tr. by* Edmund Keeley *and* Philip Sherrard

Origin of Man, I, The. Jones Very. APN-1
  ("But find while here we dwell our heavenly home.") (LL) PAR
  (Origin of Man, The.) PAR

Origin of the Skagit Indians, The. Lucy Williams, *Skagit Indian.* STP, *tr. by* Carl Cary

Origin of the Snake, The. *Unknown.* NOxBChV

Original Epitaph on a Drunkard. Royall Tyler. OBAL

Original Mind. Nancy Paddock. LoHo

Original. / Ragged-round. Malcolm X. Gwendolyn Brooks. PoBA; TTY

Original Sequence. Philip Booth. ChIV-1; KSG

Original Sin. Robinson Jeffers. MoAmPo

Original Sin. Alexander Kinnan Laing. NYBP

Original Sin. Robert Penn Warren. FuPo; HoPM; LiTM; NOCV; TAP
  ("Pasture, The.") FuPo

Original Strawberry. Nancy Willard. LCAP-2

Origins. Vincent Buckley. BMAP

Origins. Keorapetse Kgositsile. PoBA

Origins. Eric Ormsby. NoP-4

Origins. Carl Rakosi. FTOS

Origins and History of Consciousness. Adrienne Rich. NIP-4; Poetr

Oriki Erinle. *Unknown, Yoruba.* PBA; TTY, *tr. by* Ulli Beier

ORINDA *and* ROSANIA. (LL) To Mrs M. A. at Parting. Katherine Philips. CPO; FP

Orinda, and the Fair Astrea gone. To the Author of Agnes de Castro. Delariviere Manley. KTR

Orinda to Lucasia. Katherine Philips. NOSC

Orinda upon little Hector Philips. Katherine Philips. *See* On the Death of My First and Dearest Childe, Hector Philipps.

Oriole, a charred and singing coal, The. Amherst. Amy Clampitt. NMM-2

Oriole at Dawn, An. Li Meng-yang, *Chinese.* CoBLCP, *tr. by* Jonathan Chaves

Oriole sings in the greening grove, The. Summer in the South. Paul Laurence Dunbar. GT

Oriole songs hold me to look at the mountains even longer, The. Describing My Feelings While Living in Retirement by the Riverside: Seven Poems to the Tune "Ch'ing-p'ing-yüeh." Yang Chi, *Chinese.* CoBLCP, *tr. by* Jonathan Chaves

Oriole's swinging nest! Robert Lowell. *See* Fall 1961.

Orioles warble / And flowers dance. Tune: "Telling of Innermost Feelings." Wen T'ing-yün, *Chinese.* SuSp, *tr. by* William R. Schultz

Orion. Adrienne Rich. MoP; NAAL-2; NIP-4; NoAM; NoP-4; Poetr; WPE

Orion. Charles Tennyson Turner. GSo

Orisha. Jayne Cortez. BlSi

Orlando Commercial, The. George MacBeth. NOBL; PeLV

Orlando Furioso. Ludovico Ariosto, *Italian.*
  "Alcyna met them at the outer gate." OBVE, *tr. by* Sir John Harington
  "Blessed angell not a word replies, The." OBVE, *tr. by* Sir John Harington
  "Go soule, go sweetest soule for ever blest." OBVE, *tr. by* Sir John Harington
  Medoro's Inscription Book XXIII. NOBRP, *tr. by* William Parsons
  "Soon after, he a crystal stream espying." NoSic, *tr. by* Sir John Harington
  "Thus much he prayed, and thence away he went." NoSic, *tr. by* Sir John Harington

Orlando's Madness. Ludovico Ariosto. ItIP *Fr.* Canto XXIII.

Orlando's Rhymes. Shakespeare. CTC *Fr.* As You Like It.

Ormerod was deeply troubled. Distractions and the Human Crowd. Stevie Smith. OxBC

Ormsby Slatter. Mr. Slatter. N. M. Bodecker. TLR

Ornamental bung, An. Gargoyle. Robert B. Shaw. CRP

Ornamental Syllable. Geoffrey O'Brien. PT

Ornaments. Frank Ormsby. CIP-2

Ornithology. Lynda Hull. SeSe

Ornithology. Laini Mataka. ISC

Ornithomorphous monsters. The Usurers. Nicolás Guillén, *Spanish.* PFTM, *tr. by* Robert Marquez

Orotava Road, The. Basil Bunting. NoAM

O'Rourke's Feast. Hugh MacGowran, *Irish.* BIrV, *tr. by* Charles Wilson; OBVE, *tr. by* Swift

Orphan, The. *Unknown, Chinese.* ChiP; PoA, *tr. by* Arthur Waley

Orphan beat of my heart, The. "Ping Hsin," *Chinese.* BoWoP, *tr. by* Kenneth Rexroth *and* Ling Chung

Orphan Born. Robert Jones Burdette. OBAL

Orphan Child, The. Charlotte Brontë. VWP

Orphan Girl, An. Mrs. Henry Linden. CBWP-4

Orphan Girl, The. *Unknown.* AS; AmFP

Orphanage in the rain. Promises of Leniency and Forgiveness. Charles Simic. LCAP-2

Orphans. Tố Hữu, *Vietnamese.* AVP, *tr. by* Huỳnh Sanh Thông

Orphan's Song, The. Sydney Thompson Dobell. CH; OBNC

Orpheus. John Kinsella. BMAP

Orpheus. Elizabeth Madox Roberts. MoAmPo

Orpheus. Yvor Winters. NOBA; VGW

Orpheus and Eurydice. Robert Browning. *See* Eurydice to Orpheus.

Orpheus and Eurydice. Jorie Graham. VCAP

Orpheus and Eurydice. Geoffrey Hill. TRP

Orpheus and Eurydice. Jean Valentine. FaBoWP; LCAP-2

Orpheus and Eurydice. Virgil. OBCVT, *tr. by* C. Day Lewis

Orpheus, dying, not all Music died. Leontius Scholasticus, *Greek.* GrAn, *tr. by* Peter Whigham

Orpheus he went (as poets tell). Robert Herrick. CaPo

Orpheus I am, come from the deeps below. John Fletcher. GBL *Fr.* The Mad Lover.

Orpheus in the Underworld. David Gascoyne. FaBoTw

Orpheus liked the glad personal quality. Syringa. John Ashbery. APSN; HCAP; NoAM; VCAP

Orpheus to Beasts. Richard Lovelace. CaPo

Orpheus to Woods. Richard Lovelace. CaPo

Orpheus, we learn from Ovid and Lempriere. The Power of song. Horace. OBCVT, *tr. by* Byron *Fr.* Hints from Horace.

Orpheus with his lute made trees. Music. John Fletcher *and* Shakespeare. FaBoCh; NOBE; NOSC; OBEV; PoEL-2 *Fr.* King Henry VIII.

Orphic Hymns, The. *Unknown, Greek.*
  To the Sun. GrIP, *tr. by* Apostolos N. Athanassakis

Orthodox, Orthodox, wha [*or* who] believe in John Knox. The Kirk's Alarm. Robert Burns. OxBoLi

Orthography. Ambrose Bierce. APN-2; OBAL; PeLi *Fr.* The Devil's Dictionary.

Orthone. Philip Pendleton Cooke. APN-1

Ortho's Epitaph. Theocritus, *Greek.* FaBoEE, *tr. by* Charles Stuart Calverley

Orts. Ted Hughes.
  Buzz in the Window. NoAM

O's Song: ("How should I your true love know"). Shakespeare. *See* Ophelia's Song.

Osawatomie. Carl Sandburg. CMoP; OxBA

Oscar Wilde. Dorothy Parker. NALW *Fr.* A Pig's-Eye View of Literature.

Oscar Wilde. Swinburne. PeVV

Osceola. Walt Whitman. NAAL-1; NAAL-3

Osip Mandelstam. Seamus Deane. BiHa; PBCIP

Ospita. Peter Riley. NBrP

Ossian's Serenade. Calder Campbell. BLPA

Ostella forth of Town: To My Heart. John Tatham. NOSC

Ostiones Y Cangrejos Moros. Ricardo Pau-Llosa. CMAP

'Ostler Joe. George R. Sims. BLPA

Ostrich fern on shore. Robert Spiess. HA

Ostrich is a Silly Bird, The. Mary Eleanor Wilkins Freeman. CTV; OBCA; KaS

Ostriches and Grandmothers! Imamu Amiri Baraka. NeAP

O'Sullivan Rua to Mary Lavell. W. B. Yeats. *See* He Remembers Forgotten Beauty.

Otello. Arrigo Boito, *Italian.*
  Spirit of Evil, The. OxBoV, *tr. by* Andrew Porter

Othello. Shakespeare.
  "Her father lov'd me; oft invited me." EBEV; OxAEP-1; SCV
  "I had been happy, if the general camp." OxBM
  "I will in Cassio's lodging lose this napkin." OxAEP-1
  "O my fair warrior!" OxAEP-1
  "That Cassio loves her, I do well believe it." OxBoV

Othello Jones Dresses for Dinner. Ed Roberson. PoBA

Othello loved Desdemona. Limerick. A. Cinna. PeLi

Other, The. Ruth Fainlight. BrRo

Other. Lance Henson. VoR

Other bright days of action have seemed great. John Masefield. OxBTC *Fr.* Biography.

Other burial places console more. Catacomb Suburb. Alastair Fowler. FaBoTC

Other country, is it anticipated or half- / remembered? The. In Your Mind. Carol Ann Duffy. FaBoTC

Other day I was loving a sweet little fruitpie-and-cream, The. Lines. Gavin Ewart. SPE

Other day, when I looked at a tree, The. Roots. Louis Ginsberg. TrJP

Other Fabrics, Other Mores! Anna Maria Lenngren, *Swedish.* PBWP, *tr. by* Nadia Christensen *and* Marianne Tiblin

Other Forms of Slaughter. Catherine Obianuju Acholonu. HBAPE

Other great eye / closed, The. (LL) Käthe Kollwitz. Muriel Rukeyser. NALW

Other Life, the. Nina Cassian, *Romanian.* PoSu, *tr. by* Cristian Andrei *and* Daniel Weissbort

Other Little Tune, T'. Mother Goose. ReMoGo

Other Lives of the Romantics. Jane Flanders. PBCAP

Other lives, their jostle. Transfigurations. Joseph Donahue. PT

Other loves I have known. Proof. Bessie Calhoun Bird. BlSi

Other men are thorn. Mahadevi, *Kannada.* BoWoP, *tr. by* A. K. Ramanujan

Other night the moon, which had grown hungry, The. The Failings. Paul Zimmer. CMAP

Other Obit. Dean Young. NAmP90

Other oxen have long curly horns. The Old Cowboy. Kao Ch'i, *Chinese.* OHMPC, *tr. by* Kenneth Rexroth

Other patients are ill otherwise, and do. The Mad. Robert Pinsky. NoAM *Fr.* Essay on Psychiatrists.

Other People's Glasshouses. Ruth Pitter. OBGa

Other props are gone, The. Je T'Adore. Thomas Kinsella. MoP; NoAM

Other remains / passive today, The. (LL) Classic Scene. William Carlos Williams. NAAL-2; OxBA

Other Side, The. Roy Fuller. OxBC

Other Side, The. Natalie Hardwick. IIP

Other Side, The. Seamus Heaney. CIP-2; PNI

Other Side, The. Meredith Stricker. LoHo

Other Side of a Mirror, The. Mary Elizabeth Coleridge. BoWoP; NALW; PEW; SDW; VWP

  ("That heard me whisper, 'I am she!'.") (LL) PEW

Other Side of the River, The. Charles Wright. MT; VCAP

Other Side of the Valley, The. *Unknown, Chinese.* ChiP, *tr. by* Arthur Waley

Other Side of the Valley, The. *Unknown, Chinese.* CoBCP, *tr. by* Burton Watson

Other Song of the Faithful, for the Mercies of God, An. Michael Drayton. ChIV-1

Other stones the era tell. Inscription. William Cowper. OBGa

Other Syllabus, The. Chenjerai Hove. HBAPE

Other the Wings, The. Donald Revell. CMAP

Other to the Altars God, The. (LL) Two Went Up into the Temple To Pray. Richard Crashaw. ChIV-2; HAP

Other Tradition, The. John Ashbery. FTOS; PmAP

Other Voice, The. Tom Paulin. PNI

Other way Satan went down, Th'. Milton. NAEL-1 *Fr.* Book X. FHYEP *Fr.* Paradise Lost.

Other wings flew into the stone. (LL) Red Lilies. Barbara Guest. FTOS; PmAP; PoM

Other Woman, The. Marion Lomax. LW

Other World, The. Vasco [*or* Vasko] Popa, *Serbian.* CEEP, *tr. by* Charles Simic

Other World, The. *Unknown, Egyptian.* OxBSn, *tr. by* Robert Silliman Hillyer; AWP *Fr.* Book of the Dead.

Others. James Reeves. Spl

Others abide our question. Thou art free. Shakespeare. Matthew Arnold. EBVVPR; EPCY; FHYEP; GSo; HeIP-4; NoP-4; OBEV; OxAEP-2; PoPoPo; SCGP; Son

Others again here lived in my days. Chapman the Translator. Michael Drayton. EPCY *Fr.* To Henry Reynolds, of Poets and Poesy.

Others are even worse off. (LL) New Year's Eve. Liu E, *Chinese.* ChiPo; CoBLCP, *tr. by* Jonathan Chaves

Others argue, and not a few. Michael Wigglesworth. NAAL-3 *Fr.* The Day of Doom. NAAL-1; SCAP

Others because you did not keep. A Deep-sworn Vow. W. B. Yeats. CMoP; OAEL-2; PoE; UnPo

Others have pleasantness and praise. Love's Votary. George Augustus Simcox. NOBVV

Others Hunters in the North the Cree, The. Jerome Rothenberg. PoM

Others, I am not the first. A. E. Housman. CMoP; MoBrPo; NOBVV; OxBTC; PoE

Others made the decisions, others spoke on their behalf. They. The Missing. Yannis Ritsos, *Greek*. AF, *tr. by* Edmund Keeley

Others, many others, must have known. Leaving Buffalo. Charles Martin. PoA

Others may breathing Mettals softer grave. Virgil. OBCVT, *tr. by* Sir Richard Fanshawe *Fr.* The Civill Warres of Rome, Discours'd to his Royall Highness, Prince Charles.

Others may forget you, but not I. Empress Yamato-himé, *Japanese*. OHPJ, *tr. by* Kenneth Rexroth

Others see a rush, a carnival, a million. Some People. A. K. Ramanujan. VCWP

Others taunt me with having knelt at well-curbs. For Once, Then, Something. Robert Frost. GEA; NOBA; NoAM

Others trap in the snarl of frenzy. (LL) Attis. Catullus. OBVE, *tr. by* Peter Whigham

Otherwise. Jane Kenyon. LoL

Otherwise kill me. Louis MacNeice. *See* Prayer Before Birth.

Otranto. Barbara Guest. FTOS

Ottava Rima would, I know, be proper. W. H. Auden. NOBL *Fr.* Letter to Lord Byron.

Ottave. Osip Emilevich Mandelstam, *Russian*.
 "Both Schubert on the waters and Mozart in the din of birds." TCRP, *tr. by* Bernard Meares
 "Tell me, draftsman of the desert." TCRP, *tr. by* Bernard Meares

Otter, The. Seamus Heaney. NoAM; PNI

Otter, An. Ted Hughes. CMoP; MoP; NoAM

Otter is known, The. Lutra, the Fisher. James McMichael. AmPA

Otter, Redewetter. Colin Simms. NBrP

Otto. Gwendolyn Brooks. PChr

Ought is a Sunday soreness. *Meditation Upon* Ought. Alberta Turner. CMAP

Ought odd mere horror design, you cur, *phew* you hint! Catullus. *See* Carmen 69 ("That no fair woman will, wonder not why").

Ought to be told to come and take him in. (LL) The Runaway. Robert Frost. AWP; CH; FaBoCh; MoAmPo; SAmP; TwCP; VGW

Oui Papa. Delano Abdul Malik de Coteau. PBCV

Our age bereft of nobility. A Poem for Painters. John Wieners. BB; NeAP; PoM

Our Ashes. Horst Bienek, *German*. AF, *tr. by* Matthew Mead

Our Asian war is over; others have begun. In Celebration of Spring. John Balaban. CDa

Our author by experience finds it true. Prologue. Dryden. OxBoLi *Fr.* Aureng-Zebe.

Our Backs Are to the Cypress. Leah Goldberg, *Hebrew*. BoWoP, *tr. by* Ramah Commanday

Our bark was out—far, far from land. The Sailor's Grave. Eliza Cook. BLPA

Our beauty is to us that which to men. Sir Richard Fanshawe. OBVE *Fr.* Il Pastor Fido.

Our bedroom ceiling the wide open sky. (LL) A Chinese Banquet. Kitty Tsui. CPO

Our best singers. The Blues (in Two Parts). Val Ferdinand. NBV

Our Bias. W. H. Auden. MoP; OxAEP-2; Poetr
 ("Hour-glass whispers to the lion's paw, The.") OxAEP-2

Our Bird Aegis. Ray A. Young Bear. BAP-96

Our birth is but a sleep and a forgetting. Intimations of Immortality. Wordsworth. *Fr.* Ode: Intimations of Immortality [from Recollections of Early Childhood]. AWP; FHYEP; HAP; HeIP-4; NOBE; NOBRP; OAEL-2; OBEV; OBNC; PBMP; PoE; PoEL-4

Our blue boat drifts. Birdwatching at Fan Lake. Anita Endrezze-Danielson. HATNAP

Our boat touches the bank. Thomas A. Clark. NBrP *Fr.* Sixteen Sonnets.

Our Bog is dood, our Bog is dood. Stevie Smith. CBNP; NAEL-2; NBLV; PoE; WeW-3

Our Bondage It Shall End. Peter Cartwright. AH

Our brains ache, in the merciless iced east winds that knive us. . . . Exposure. Wilfred Owen. AF; FaBoMo; InPS-3; NoAM; OBWP; PeFWW; PoFWW; PoWW; RB

Our brigade's / On the Diyovka-Sukhachovka. Judge Gorba. "Mikhail Semionovich Golodny," *Russian*. TCRP, *tr. by* Simon Franklin

Our broadcast day is over, I've unplugged. Archaic Torso of My Uncle Phil. Mark Cox. NAmP90

Our brown canal was endless to my thought. "George Eliot." NOBVV *Fr.* Brother and Sister. NALW

Our bugles sang truce, for the night-cloud had lowered [*or* lower'd]. The Soldier's Dream. Thomas Campbell. FaPoR; GTBS-P; OxAEP-2

Our candles, lit, re-lit, have gone down now. Twelfth Night. Peter Scupham. OBCP

Our Canterburye's great Cathedrall Bell. Upon Arch-bishop Laud, Prisoner in the Tower. 1641. *Unknown*. PBRV

Our captain stood upon the deck, a spyglass in his hand. Captain Bunker. *Unknown*. AmFP

Our Caribbean / a bandolier. Our Home. Jan Carew. PBCV

Our caves do not go Boom! and make one nervy. Sterkfontein. Ruth Miller. PeSA; PeSAV

Our cherished dualism gone? Journal to Stella. Morton Dauwen Zabel. PoA

Our children have eaten supper. Nightfall, Midwinter, Missouri. Brian Coffey. CIP-2 *Fr.* Missouri Sequence.

Our Christian savages expect. He Shook off the Beast. Charles Wesley. ChIV-2

Our Christmas pudding was made in November. Pudding Charms. Charlotte Druitt Cole. BoTP

Our city declines, the world is still bleak. Beginnings. Peter Sirr. PBCIP

Our City rulers pass in grand array. Mary E. Tucker. *Fr.* Loew's Bridge: A Broadway Idyl. CBWP-1

Our Club Work. Mrs. Henry Linden. CBWP-4

Our collective wastebin. In the Outhouse. Mitsuye Yamada. *Fr.* Camp Notes. WPOW

Our complex love, our mourning without end. (LL) All Souls. May Sarton. CrSp; IMW

"Our couch shall be roses all spangled with dew." A Sensible Girl's Reply to Moore's. Walter Savage Landor. FaBoEE

Our country, in fenced areas, in cool shady streets. (LL) The One Thing That Can Save America. John Ashbery. AiP; FaBoA; NOBA; NoAM; PmAP

Our country is closed in [enclosed], all mountains. George Seferis. GrIP *Fr.* Mythistorima

Our Course. Theognis, *Greek*. OBCVT, *tr. by* Willis Barnstone

Our cup of joy was overfilled. A Dialogue. Lizelia Augusta Jenkins Moorer. CBWP-3

Our Daily Bread. César Vallejo, *Spanish*. GI, *tr. by* James Wright

Our darling's now completely frappé! (LL) L'Enfant Glacé. Harry Graham. CBNP; NBLV; OBCoV; PeLV

Our day was composed of resemblances, take. Sail Away. Robert Adamson. CBAP

Our days, alas! our mortal days. The Shortness and Misery of Life. Isaac Watts. NOCV

Our days were a joy, and our paths through flowers. (LL) After A Journey. Thomas Hardy. CBLP; CMoP; EBEV; EnLoPo; GBL; GTBS-P; LoP; OBNC; OxAEP-2; OxBSn; OxBTC; PoE; PoEL-5

Our Dean of Something thought it would be good. The Classroom at the Mall. R. S. Gwynn. RA

Our Dear Friend Charles. Collaboration: Letter to Charlie Chaplin. Peter Orlovsky. CLPP

Our diaries squatted, toad-like [*or* toadlike]. Nostalgia and Complaint of the Grandparents. Donald Justice. LCAP-2; NoAM

Our Dog Chasing Swifts. U. A. Fanthorpe. Spl

Our dog Fred. The Diners in the Kitchen. James Whitcomb Riley. CTAV; OBAL

Our doom is in our being. We began. James Agee. *Fr.* Sonnets. MoAmPo

Our Dreams. Amir Gilbo'a, *Hebrew*. IP, *tr. by* Warren Bargad *and* Stanley F. Chyet

Our drift-wood fire burns drowsily. The Florida Beach. Constance Fenimore Woolson. APN-2

Our dropping Autumn morning clears apace. Sordello. Robert Browning. OBGa *Fr.* Sordello.

Our Dust. C. D. Wright. NAmP90

Our ears were stunned with noisy drum. To Laura, on the French Fleet Parading before Plymouth. Ann Thomas. ECWP

Our earth in 1969. Doggerel by a Senior Citizen. W. H. Auden. NBLV; NOBL

Our Earth Will Not Die. Niyi Osundare. HBAPE

Our eldest son is like Ishmael, Jacob is like you. Isreal I. Charles Reznikoff. ChIV-1

Our end is Life. Put out to sea. (LL) Thalassa. Louis MacNeice. BIrV; FaBoMo; NOBE

Our England is a garden that is full of stately views. The Glory of the Garden. Rudyard Kipling. OBGa

Our English gamesters scorne to stake. Roger Williams. SCAP

Our epoch takes a voluptuous satisfaction. Hypocrite Auteur. Archibald MacLeish. AmPP

Our Ernest. "Elmo." PWR

Our existence would be that much grimmer ex-. Limerick. Robert Conquest. PeLi

Our eyes have viewed the burnished vineyards where. Letter to a Friend. Robert Penn Warren. MoAmPo

Our faces are the. Poem No. 1. Carolyn M. Rodgers. ISC

"Our Fadder, Which are in Heaben!" He Paid Me Seven. *Unknown.* BPo

Our fairest garland, made of Beauty's flowers. Contention between Four Maids Concerning That Which Addeth Most Perfection to That Sex. Sir John Davies. SiPS

Our faith to regulate. (LL) The Last Night that She lived. Emily Dickinson. ColAP

Our family tree is in the sear. Joseph Cephas Holly. AAP

Our famous Harvey hath made good. The Circulation. Thomas Washbourne. NOCV

Our fancies are but joys all unexprest. A Fragment. Henrietta Cordelia Ray. CBWP-3

Our fate was settled centuries ago. The Dance Half Done. Mary Ann Larkin. IIP

Our Father. Eliza Cook. VWP

Our Father. James Schuyler. ChIV-2

Our Father, by Whose Name. F. Bland Tucker. AH

Our Father, God. Adoniram Judson. AH

Our Father, grant us to lie down in peace. Evening Prayer. *Unknown, Hebrew.* TrJP, *tr. by* Solomon Solis-Cohen

Our Father in Heaven. Sarah Josepha Buell Hale. AH

Our father is three months dead. Woodcutting on Lost Mountain. Tess Gallagher. PaTW

Our Father, Our King. *Unknown.* TrJP

Our Father which art in heaven. Lord's Prayer. Nicanor Parra, *Spanish.* GI, *tr. by* Miller Williams

Our Father which art in heaven. The Lord's Prayer. *Unknown.* CTV *Fr.* The Bible, Matthew 6:9–13.

Our Father which [*or* who] art in heaven. Prayer of-Lord. Bible, *N.T.* PoLF *Fr.* St. Matthew.

Our Father! While Our Hearts Unlearn. Oliver Wendell Holmes. AH

Our Father who art in heaven. Pater Noster. Jacques Prévert, *French.* CLPP; NNPT, *tr. by* Lawrence Ferlinghetti

Our Father who art in heaven, I am drunk. Praying Drunk. Andrew Hudgins. RA

Our father, who art speechless. N. N. Tries to Remember the Words of a Prayer. Stanislaw Baranczak, *Polish.* GI, *tr. by* Kevin Windle

Our father works in us. Father of Women, A [Ad Sororem E. B.] Alice Thompson Meynell. BrRo; NALW; VWP; WPE

Our Fathers. Eighth, Apocrypha. TrJP *Fr.* Ecclesiasticus.

Our fathers all were poor. The Fathers. Edwin Muir. OxBS

Our Fathers' God. Benjamin Copeland. AH

Our fathers took oaths as of old they took wives. Oaths. Thomas Brown. FaBoEE; OBCoV

Our fathers were saved from the deaths. Babylon: 539 B.C.E. Charles Reznikoff. ChIV-1

Our fathers wrung their bread from stocks and stones. Children of Light. Robert Lowell. CMoP; NAAL-2; OxBA

Our Fear. Zbigniew Herbert, *Polish.* VCWP, *tr. by* Czeslaw Milosz and Peter Dale Scott

Our feet meet the earth in this place. Marble Floor. Karol Wojtyla. CRP

Our first ancestor (Abram) alone received his religion from Heaven. Therefore We Preserve Life. Shen Ch'üan, *Chinese.* TrJP, *tr. by* William C. White

Our Flag. *Unknown.* CA

Our Flag Was Still There. Richard Tillinghast. WeT

Our flesh that was a battle-ground. The Litany of the Dark People. Countee Cullen. ChIV-2

Our folk thin / Lamentably. Sylvia Plath. *See* Frog Autumn.

Our foot's in the door. (LL) Mushrooms. Sylvia Plath. FaBoWP; PBMP; PFE; RB; WPOW

Our friend there—he's a little queer. Of Mortmain. Herman Melville. APN-2 *Fr.* Clarel: A Poem and Pilgrimage in the Holy Land.

Our friend would board the *Thu'o'ng-Tín* and go home. Cao Tần, *Vietnamese.* AVP, *tr. by* Huỳnh Sanh Thông

Our friends go with us as we go. Non Dolet. Oliver St. John Gogarty. OBMV

Our friendship, Robert, firm through twenty years. A Letter to Robert Frost. Robert Silliman Hillyer. MoAmPo

Our Gardener here, James Phillips see. Philip Yorke. OBGa

Our garden's very near the trains. Trains. Hope Shepherd. BoTP

Our geodesic dome-shaped lodge. The Personification of a Name. Ray A. Young Bear. HATNAP

Our God and God of our fathers. Prayer for Dew. Eleazar ben Kalir, *Hebrew.* TrJP, *tr. by* Israel Zangwill

Our God and soldiers we alike adore. Of Common Devotion. Francis Quarles. FaBoEE; OxBSP

Our God, for evermore. (LL) The Abiding Love. John White Chadwick. BLPA; FaBoBe

Our God is marching on. Julia Ward Howe. *See* The Battle Hymn [*or* Battle-Hymn] of the Republic.

Our God, our help in ages past. Man Frail, and God Eternal. Isaac Watts. ECEV; NoP-4; OBVE; PWR; TOF

Our God's forgotten, and our soldiers slighted. (LL) Of Common Devotion. Francis Quarles. FaBoEE; OxBSP

Our golden age was then, when lamp and rug. Family Prime. Mark Van Doren. VGW

Our Goodman. *Unknown.* AmFP; ESPB

(Four Nights' Drunk, The.) OBAL

Our guest's wound went unnoticed. Callimachus, *Greek.* GrAn, *tr. by* Peter Jay

Our guns are a league behind us, our target a mile below. Eyes in the Air. Gilbert Frankau. NSI

Our guttural muse. Traditions. Seamus Heaney. FaBoMo

Our hamster's life. Kit Wright. OTCP; PeP

("Watching me / do it.") (LL) PeP

Our hands are hanging, our hearts are numb. (LL) Dappled sky, a world of meadows, A. Jean Ingelow. OBNC; PEW

Our hands have met, but not our hearts;. To a False Friend. Thomas Hood. FP

Our Hands in the Garden. Anne Hébert, *French.* BoWoP, *tr. by* A. Poulin, Jr.

Our haughty life is crowned with darkness. London, from Hampstead Heath. Wordsworth. *Fr.* Extempore Effusion upon the Death of James Hogg. EBEV; NOBE; OAEL-2; SCV

Our heads on fire. (LL) Paper Matches. Paulette Jiles. IFJA; NIP-4; NOBC

Our headteacher has a golden. Goldfish. Barrie Wade. OTCP

Our hearths are gone out, and our hearts are broken. The Raven Days. Sidney Lanier. APN-2; OxBA

Our hearts and lips together. (LL) The Blackbird. William Ernest Henley. HoPM; MoBrPo

Our Hearts Are Ancient Citadels. Vũ Đình Liên, *Vietnamese.* AVP, *tr. by* Huỳnh Sanh Thông

Our hearts are filled with pride to-day. Welcome to Hon. Frederick Douglass. Josephine D. Henderson Heard. CBWP-4

Our hearts beat prouder for the blood we inherit. (LL) Memorial Wreath. Dudley Randall. CBCWP; PoBA

Our hearts' charity's hearth's fire, our thoughts' chivalry's throng's Lórd. (LL) The Wreck of the Deutschland. Gerard Manley Hopkins. CMoP; EnVR; FaBoMo; ImPo; LiTM; NOBE; NoAM; OBNC; OxAEP-2; PeECV; PoEL-5

Our hearts still listen for the landward bells. (LL) An Irishman in Coventry. John Hewitt. BIrV; CIP-2; IIP; PNI

Our heritage the sea. (LL) A Sea-Song. Allan Cunningham. BoTP; FaBoBe; FaPoR; GTBS-P; OxAEP-2

Our Heroes. Phoebe Cary. BLPA

Our Hindi is a widower's new wife. Raghuvir Sahay, *Hindi.* OMIP, *tr. by* Vinay Dharwadker

Our hired man is the kindest man. The Hired Man's Way. John Kendrick Bangs. OBCA

Our Home. Jan Carew. PBCV

Our home, and all we know. (LL) A Prayer for a Little Home. Florence Bone. BLPA; FaBoBe

Our homes are eaten out by time. The Town Betrayed. Edwin Muir. CMoP; FaBoTC

Our horse fell down the well around behind the stable. Good-By Liza Jane. *Unknown.* AS

Our horses whinnied to each other at parting. (LL) Taking Leave of a Friend. Li Po, *Chinese.* FP, *tr. by* Innes Herdan

Our house had filled with moths. The Moths. Michael Jackson. PeNZ

Our Houses. Linda Hogan. CrSp

Our hunting fathers told the story. W. H. Auden. FaBoMo; MoP; NoAM

Our hut puffs streaks of hope. Country Life. Chenjerai Hove. HBAPE

Our improbable support, erected. The Foot. Alice Jones. BAP-94

Our Island Home. Charles Timothy Brooks. APN-1

Our isle is oyster-gray. Fish and Corn. George Mackay Brown. FaBoTC *Fr.* Runes from a Holy Island.

Our Jatti, palace wrestler of Mysore. At Forty. A. K. Ramanujan. VCWP

Our jeep crawls to your village. The Election. Sitakant Mahapatra, *Oriya.* OMIP, *tr. by* Sitakant Mahapatra

Our journey had advanced. Emily Dickinson. APN-2; LiTM; NOCV; PAR; PoEL-5; SoSe-8

Our joy, a rampart to the mind. (LL) The Passing Strange. John Masefield. MoBrPo; OBEV

Our kin are here. / Were here. (LL) Forgiveness Dream. Jean Valentine. NMM-2

Our Kind Creator. Solomon Howe. AH

Our king has wrote a lang letter. Lord Derwentwater. *Unknown.* ESPB

Our king he has a secret to tell. The Bonny Lass of Anglesey. *Unknown.* ESPB

Our king he kept a false steward. Sir Aldingar. *Unknown.* ESPB; OxBB

Our king lay at Westminster. Hugh Spencer's Feats in France. *Unknown.* ESPB

Our King returned, and banished peace restored. George, Baron Lansdowne Granville. EPCY

Our[e] king[e] went forth to Normandy. The Agincourt Carol. *Unknown.* EBEV; OAEL-1

Our King went up upon a hill high. Henry before Agincourt: October 25, 1415. John Lydgate. CH

Our kisses / Rhodope. Paulus Silentiarius, *Greek.* LoP, *tr. by* Andrew Miller

Our kisses / Rhodope / let us steal. Paulus Silentiarius, *Greek.* GrAn, *tr. by* Andrew Miller

Our knowledge is historical, flowing, and flown. (LL) At the Fishhouses. Elizabeth Bishop. CoAP; FaBoWP; GEA; HAP; HCAP; LCAP-2; LiTM; NAAL-2; NALW; NYBP; PoPoPo; PoRA; Poetr; VCAP

Our Lady. Mary Elizabeth Coleridge. OBEV; OBMV; WPE

Our Lady. John Godfrey. PmAP

Our Lady Moon still hidden. Memory. Federico García Lorca. PFTM

Our Lady of Ardboe. Paul Muldoon. BiHa; PBCIP

Our Lady of the Laundromat. Belle Waring. PBCAP

Our Lady's Song. *Unknown.* OBEV

Our Land. Yannis Ritsos, *Greek.* GrIP, *tr. by* Edmund Keeley

Our Land, Our Home. Trần Tuấn Khải, *Vietnamese.* AVP, *tr. by* Huỳnh Sanh Thông

Our landmark is the island, complex thing. Lewis 1928–45. Iain Crichton Smith. FaBoTC *Fr.* A Life.

Our last bridge. Marina Ivanovna Tsvetayeva. *Fr.* The Daughter of Jairus. BoWoP, *tr. by* Paul Schmidt

Our last free summer we mooned about at odd hours. Chrysalides. Thomas Kinsella. BIrV

Our left and right show red and green: mute phonics. Flying Friendly Skies. Turner Cassity. MT

Our Life. Mbella Sonne Dipoko. PBMAP

Our life—impossible to ignore. (LL) Indian Singing in 20th Century America. Gail Tremblay. LTA

Our life in the world is only a great dream. Awakening from Drunkenness on a Spring Day. Li Po, *Chinese.* TAL, *tr. by* Robert Payne

Our life is changed; their coming our beginning. (LL) The Horses ("Barely a twelvemonth after"). Edwin Muir. CABP; CMoP; FaBoTC; GEA; HAP; HeIP-4; MoBrPo; MoP; NOBE; NoAM; OAEL-2; OxBTC; PoE; Poetr; RB; TRP; WeW-3

Our Life Is Hid with Christ in God. George Herbert. OAEL-1
(Colossians 3:3.) ChIV-2

Our life is like a forest, where the sun. Charles Sangster. NOBC *Fr.* Sonnets Written in the Orillia Woods.

Our life is not life, save in the fleeting. Responding Voice. Francisco A. de Icaza, *Spanish.* PBMP, *tr. by* Samuel Beckett

Our life-sick hearts and turn them into dust. (LL) A Last Word. Ernest Christopher Dowson. ADE; GSo

Our life's the model of a winter's day. On the Life of Man. Francis Quarles. PeECV *Fr.* Divine Fancies.

Our Limitations. Oliver Wendell Holmes. NCAP

Our Lips and Ears. *Unknown.* BLPA

Our little Death from which we daily. Sleep is a Deep and Many Voiced Flood. Robert Duncan. CLPP

Our little fleet in July first. The Armada, 1588. John Wilson. OxBChV

Our Little Ghost. Louisa May Alcott. OBCA

Our little sister is worried. *Unknown, Chinese.* OHMPC, *tr. by* Kenneth Rexroth

Our little tantrum, flushed and misery-hollow. Rebeca in a Mirror. Judith Rodriguez. CBAP

Our lives again. (LL) The Goldfish Wife. Sandra Hochman. NYBP; UnPo

Our lives are Swiss. Emily Dickinson. APN-2; NOBA; TAP

Our lives float on quiet waters. Quiet Waters. Blanche Shoemaker Wagstaff. BLPA

Our lives no longer feel ground under them. The Stalin Epigram. Osip Emilevich Mandelstam, *Russian.* AF; FaBoPV; NNPT, *tr. by* W. S. Merwin *and* Clarence Brown

Our lords are to the mountains gane. Hughie Graham. Robert Burns. OxBB

Our Love Hath No Decay. Donne. LBC

Our love is infinite. *Unknown, Japanese.* OHMPJ, *tr. by* Kenneth Rexroth

Our love is like Byzantium. Henrik Nordbrandt, *Danish.* VCWP, *tr. by* Nordbrandt, Henrik and Alexander Taylor

"Our love shall live, and later life renew." (LL) Sonnet 75: "One day I wrote her name upon the strand." Edmund Spenser. AWP; BoLoP; CABP; CBLP; EBEV; EPCY; GBL; GEA; GLoP; GSo; HAP; HeIP-4; ImPo; InPS-3; NAEL-1; NoP-4; NoSic; OAEL-1; PBMP; PoE; PoPoPo; Son; TFi; WeW-3

Our love was conceived in silence and must live silently. At the Dark Hour. Paul Dehn. BoLoP

Our love was pure. Song of Snow-white Heads. Chuo Wen-chün. BoWoP; ChiP, *tr. by* Arthur Waley

Our love which had a thousand leaves. (LL) Winter. Sheila Wingfield. LW

Our love will not come back on fortune's wheel. Obit. Robert Lowell. HCAP; VCAP

Our loyal passion for our temperate kings. Tennyson. *See* Bury the Great Duke.

Our man of the seashore. What Her Girl Friend Said on Her Wedding Day. Ammuvanar, *Tamil.* PLW, *tr. by* A. K. Ramanujan

Our March. Vladimir Mayakovsky, *Russian.* AWP, *tr. by* Babette Deutsch *and* Avrahm Yarmolinsky

Our morning hymne this is, and song at evening. (LL) Double Sestine [*or* Sestina]. Sir Philip Sidney. PBRV

Our Mother. George Cooper. *See* Only One Mother.

Our mother. Incidence. Rae Armantrout. FTOS

Our mother bade us keep the trodden ways. "George Eliot." *Fr.* Brother and Sister. NALW

Our Mother Eve, who tasted of the Tree. Aemilia Bassano Lanyer. PBRV *Fr.* Salve Deus Rex Judæorum.

Our mother was the pussy-cat, our father was the owl. Edward Lear. OBCoV

Our mother, while she turned her wheel. Mother. John Greenleaf Whittier *Fr.* Snow-Bound [*or* Snow-Bound; a Winter Idyl]. APN-1; AiP; AmPP; NAAL-3; NOBA; OxBA; TAP; TFi

Our mothers, / when asked. Feminism. Carolyn M. Rodgers. NMM-2

Our mothers wrung hell and hardtack from row. American Sonnet (10). Wanda Coleman. NAAAL

Our moulting days are in the twilight stage. Garnishing the Aviary. Margaret Danner. BPo *Fr.* Far from Africa: Four Poems. PoBA

Our names do not appear. (LL) Diving into the Wreck. Adrienne Rich. ColAP; HCAP; HeIP-4; inPK-6; InPS-3; MoP; NAAL-2; NALW; NIP-2; NOBA; NoAM; NoP-4; OxWW; PoPoPo; Poetr

Our natural tongue is rude. John Skelton. EPCY *Fr.* Phyllyp Sparowe [*or* Philip Sparrow]. AAS; PoEL-1

Our Naughty Time. Friedrich von Logau, *German.* GePo, *tr. by* George C. Schoolfield

Our neighbor Laura Foley used to love. Take Care. Heather McHugh. WeT

Our new clothes fool no one. Yom Kippur. Chana Bloch. CrSp

Our Noble Booker T. Washington. Mrs. Henry Linden. CBWP-4

Our novels get longa and longa. Limerick. H. G. Wells. PeLi

Our Number. Martin Carter. PBCV

Our nuns come out to shop in the afternoon. Intercessors. Austin Clarke. CMoP

Our old cat has kittens three—. Choosing Their Names. Thomas Hood. ACTP; NOxBChV; PeP

Our oneness is the wrestlers', fierce and close. Wrestling. Louisa Sarah Bevington. LW; PEW

Our Own. Margaret Elizabeth Munson Sangster. BLPA; PoToHe

Our own calm journey on for human sake. (LL) The Nile. Leigh Hunt. EBEV; GSo; NOBE; OBNC

Our own shadows disappear as the feet of thousand. Poem for South AFrican Women. June Jordan. MDDM

Our padre is an old sky pilot. John Betjeman. PeLV

Our Paris part of Belfast has. Intimate Letter 1973. Padraic Fiacc. PNI

Our park empty. Three O'Clock Love Song. Michael S. Harper. GT

Our parodies are ended. These our authors. Horace Twiss. UV

Our party scattered at yellow dusk and I came home to bed. After Getting Drunk, Becoming Sober in the Night. Po Chü-i, *Chinese.* ChiP; BLT, *tr. by* Arthur Waley

Our passions are most like to floods and stream[e]s. Sir Walter Ralegh to the Queen. Sir Walter Ralegh. NoSic; SiPS

Our pastures are bitten and bare. Joseph Gordon MacLeod. *Fr.* Men of the Rocks. OxBS

Our path emerges for a while, then closes / Within a dream. (LL) Vitae Summa Brevis Spem Nos Vetat Incohare Longam. Ernest Christopher Dowson. CABP

Our people know high heaven's bliss on earth. Paradise. Lu'u Văn Vong, *Vietnamese.* AVP, *tr. by* Huỳnh Sanh Thông

Our perverse old *pisatel'* Vladimir. Something for My Russian Friends. Edmund Wilson. OBAL

Our Photograph[s]. Frederick Locker-Lampson. NBLV; NOBL; PeLV

Our Poet tells me I am very pretty. Epilogue. Delariviere Manley. KTR *Fr.* The Royal Mischeif.

Our Pope, they say, once entertained the whim. George Crabbe. EPCY *Fr.* The Patron.

Our portion of fire. The Manichaeans. Gary Snyder. VGW

Our Presidents. *Unknown.* BLPA

Our prize fish is done! Hedylos, *Greek.* GrAn, *tr.* by William Moebius

Our quin's seek, an very seek. Queen Eleanor's Confession. *Unknown.* ESPB

Our regimental stallion. The Stallion. "Mikhail Semionovich Golodny," *Russian.* TCRP, *tr.* by Simon Franklin

Our revels now are ended. These our actors. Epilogue. Shakespeare. ImPo; RB; SAGP; UV *Fr.* The Tempest. OAEL-1

Our Revolutions Must Be Different. Marina Ama Omowale Maxwell. HCP

Our Richard Allen in his early youth. Rt. Rev. Richard Allen. Josephine D. Henderson Heard. CBWP-4

Our roads are ridden. For Sammy Younge. Charlie Cobb. PoBA

Our Rock with loving care. Grace after Meals. *Unknown, Hebrew.* TrJP, *tr.* by Alice Lucas

Our roofs are adjacent. Love Song. *Unknown, Turkish.* BoWoP, *tr.* by Reza Baraheni *and* Zahra-Soltan Shokoohtaezeh

Our Room. Molly Peacock. IFJA; NMM-2

Our ruins run back to memory. Cavafy in Redondo. Mark Jarman. CMAP

Our rural Ancestors, with little blest. Horace. OBCVT, *tr.* by Alexander Pope *Fr.* The First Epistle of the Second Book of Horace, Imitated.

Our sacred earth in our day is our curse. (LL) The Dead in Europe. Robert Lowell. LiTM; OxBA; OxBC

Our sacred Muse, of Israel's Singer sings. Michael Drayton. ChIV-1 *Fr.* David and Goliath.

"Our saints are poets, Milton and Blake." Encounter. Denis Devlin. BIrV

Our sardine fishermen work at night in the dark of the moon; daylight or moonlight. The Purse-Seine. Robinson Jeffers. CMoP; HAP; NOBA; NoAM; OxBA; PaTW; Poetr; WeW-3

Our Savior Christ tracing the bordering hills. Thomas Deloney. ChIV-2 *Fr.* The Destruction of Jerusalem.

Our Saviour / (Paterne of true holinesse). Ensamples of Our Savior. Robert Southwell. PoEL-2

Our Saviour's Golden Rule. Isaac Watts. OxBChV ("Be thou to others kind and true.") NOxBChV

Our Scholar travels yet the loved hill-side. (LL) Thyrsis. Matthew Arnold. EnVR; FHYEP; NAEL-2; NOBE; OBEV; OBNC

Our School Now Closes Out. Edmund Dumas. AH

Our selues become our own best SACRIFICE. Richard Crashaw. *See* In the Holy Nativity of Our Lord God.

Our senses, without reason, are naught worth. Owen's Bracelet. Robert Hayman. NOSC *Fr.* Owen's Epigrams.

Our shells clacked on the plates. Oysters. Seamus Heaney. UV

Our Ship She Lies in Harbour. *Unknown.* NTP

Our ship, the Sea Smithy, swerved out of the tradewinds. On the Congo. Harry Edmund Martinson, *Swedish.* RB, *tr.* by Robert Bly

Our signatures on the contract, as though we were the authors of this story. (LL) Film Noir: Train Trip Out. Lynn Emanuel. BAP-95; PUP-20

Our single purpose was to walk through snow. Polar Exploration. Stephen Spender. FaBoMo; NoAM

Our skin, strenuously tutored to appreciate the vernacular. Skin. Marjorie Welish. PmAP

Our Smoke Has Gone Four Ways. Lance Henson. CDW

Our Solar System. Eric Finney. SpW

Our song the same. (LL) Bulosan Listens to a Recording of Robert Johnson. Alfred Encarnacion. LTA; OpBo

Our song together. (LL) Eadwacer. *Unknown, Anglo-Saxon.* CIP-2, *ad.* by Richard Ryan; PBWP, *tr.* by Kemp Malone; BoWoP, *tr.* by Willis Barnstone *and* Elene Kolb; WPE

Our speech slurs now. Nook. George Barlow. GT

Our States, O Lord. John Mycall. AH

Our storm[e] is past, and that storm[e]'s tyrannous rage. The Calm[e]. Donne. NoSic; OxBoS

Our story isn't a file of photographs. For an Album. Adrienne Rich. VCAP

Our street is known as the street of widows. Bruce Beaver. *Fr.* Letters to Live Poets. CBAP

Our suffering would be unbearable if we couldn't regard it as a. Letter to Youki. Robert Desnos, *French.* AF, *tr.* by Carolyn Forché

Our Sun. George Seferis, *Greek.* AF, *tr.* by Edmund Keeley *and* Philip Sherrard

Our Task. Henrietta Cordelia Ray. CBWP-3

Our Tense and Wintry Minds. Hayden Carruth. AH

Our Town. Cole Swenson. WWSi

Our tropic fruits, nurs'd 'neath a torrid sky. *Unknown.* PBCV *Fr.* A Poetical Epistle, from the Island of Jamaica, to.

Our two soules therefore, which are one. Donne. UV *Fr.* A Valediction: Forbidding Mourning.

Our Two Worthies. John Crowe Ransom. OBAL

Our view of sky, jungle, and fields constricts. The Insert. R. L. Barth. CDa; InPK-6

Our Village—by a Villager. Thomas Hood. FaBoVe; OBSV

Our village pond named Mother Ganga. A Pond Named Ganga. Chandrashekhar Kambar, *Kannada.* OMIP, *tr.* by A. K. Ramanujan

Our Village, that's to say not Miss Mitford's. Our Village—by a Villager. Thomas Hood. FaBoVe; OBSV; PoEL-4

Our vision is our voice. An Anthem. Sonia Sanchez. UnSA

Our voices poured out through. The House Made of Rain. Naomi Shihab Nye. NAmP90

Our voices waved upwards into a tide / that wrapped itself around the island. Island within Island. Henry Dumas. GT

Our wandering eyes are sated with the dancer's skill. The Cock-fight. Ts'ao Chih, *Chinese.* ChiP, *tr.* by Arthur Waley

Our way of life. It's a Woman's World. Eavan Boland. CIP-2

Our Wives. Jonathan Galassi. EOEF

Our Wonderful World. Jessie Orton Jones. CTV *Fr.* (XXI from Secrets).

Our World Is Less Full Now That Mr. Fuller Is Gone. Kalamu ya Salaam. ISC

Our world is very little in the sky. Measurements. Louisa Sarah Bevington. VWP

Our Youth. John Ashbery. CoAmPo; VGW; WeT

Our youth was gay but rough. One of the Boys. James Simmons. PNI

Our youth was happy: why repine. Walter Savage Landor. FaBoEE

Oure Ho[o]ste gan to swere as he were wood. Introduction to the Pardoner's Prologue and Tale. Chaucer. FHYEP; NAEL-1; OAEL-1; PoE *Fr.* The Canterbury Tales.

Ours. Adrienne Rich. *See* Snapshots of a Daughter-in-Law.

Ours are the streets where Bess first met her / cancer. Bess. William Stafford. NNaP

Ours is the ancient story. For Daughters of Magdalen. Countee Cullen. ChIV-2

Ours yet not ours, being set apart. For Friends Only. W. H. Auden. FP *Fr.* Thanksgiving for a Habitat.

Ourselves become our own best sacrifice! (LL) In the Holy Nativity of Our Lord God. Richard Crashaw. ESCV; GeHe; HAP; MeLP; PoEL-2

Ourselves to end ourselves. (LL) Eros, thou yet behold'st me? Shakespeare. EBEV; OxAEP-1

Ourselves we do inter with sweet derision. Emily Dickinson. APN-2; FaBoEE

Ourselves were wed one summer—dear. Emily Dickinson. CPO

Ousel cock, so black of hue, The. Shakespeare. NoSic *Fr.* A Midsummer Night's Dream.

Out and Back on the Fifteenth Night of the First Month. Mei Yao Ch'en, *Chinese.* CoBCP, *tr.* by Burton Watson

Out at the edge of town. The Frozen Man. Kit Wright. AYFP

Out back, Lotte's feeding pillow cases. Typing the Letters. John A. Scott. BMAP

Out beyond ideas of wrongdoing and rightdoing. Jelaluddin Rumi, *Persian.* BLT; EnlH, *tr.* by Coleman Barks *and* John Moyne

Out Early One Morning, I Met an Old Acquaintance. Shen Yüeh, *Chinese.* CoBCP, *tr.* by Burton Watson

Out Early One Morning, I Met an Old Acquaintance. Wang Seng-ta, *Chinese.* CoBCP, *tr.* by Burton Watson

Out Fishin'. E. A. Guest. PoLF

Out Fishing. Barbara Howes. WPE

Out for a walk, after a week in bed. An Urban Convalescence. James Merrill. CoAP; ColAP; NOBA

Out from Jerusalem / The king rode with his great. King Solomon and the Ants. John Greenleaf Whittier. ChIV-1

Out goes the rat. *Unknown.* ImGa *Fr.* Counting-out Rhymes.

Out here, dwarfed by mountains and a sky of fires. Mark Strand. BAP-93 *Fr.* Dark Harbor.

Out here in Ringoes. Rural Recreation. Lillian Morrison. KaS

Out here in the fields, few social affairs. Returning to My Home in the Country. T'ao Ch'ien, *Chinese.* CoBCP, *tr.* by Burton Watson

Out here on Cottage Grove it matters. The galloping. Pyrography. John Ashbery. PoM; VCAP

Out here there are no hearthstones. Sleep in the Mojave Desert. Sylvia Plath. AiP

Out here, where any rambling bed—of sea-. The Reach. Carl Phillips. GT

Out here where the crows turn around. Country Wisdoms. Maggie Anderson. PBCAP

Out in a world of death, far to the northward lying. The Winter Lakes. Wilfred Campbell. NOBC

Out in the blustering darkness, on the deck. Night on the Conroy. Siegfried Sassoon. NSI

Out in the bushlands a creeper grows. Songs of Courtship. *Unknown, Chinese.* ChiP, *tr. by* Arthur Waley

Out in the Cold. George Starbuck. NYBP

Out in the dark over the snow. Edward Thomas. CH; GTBS-P; LiTM; MoBrPo; NOBE; OBWVE; RB

Out in the Desert. Josephine D. Henderson Heard. CBWP-4

Out in the elegy country, summer evenings. Blue Suburban. Howard Nemerov. ColAP

Out in the garden. The Blackbird. Phyllis Drayson. BoTP

Out in the garden. Bubbles. L. Nicholson. BoTP

Out in the garden. The Pigeons. Rodney Bennett. BoTP

Out in the garden, sunny and still. Freedom. Joan Agnew. BoTP

Out in the late amber afternoon. In Shadow. Hart Crane. NOBA

Out in the marsh reeds. Ki no Tsurayuki, *Japanese.* OHPJ, *tr. by* Kenneth Rexroth

Out in the northeast banks of thunderous. Xenophilia. Mary Kinzie. CMAP

Out in the Open. Aleksandar Ristovic, *Serbo-Croatian.* HSix, *tr. by* Charles Simic

Out in the rain a world is growing green. Easter Monday. Christina Rossetti. NOCV

Out in the silent Rockies. The Outcast. P. G. Wodehouse. UV

Out in the sky the great dark clouds are massing. Ships That Pass in the Night. Paul Laurence Dunbar. ColAP

Out in the Snow, Spending the Night at the New Stockade, Extremely Depressed. Huang T'ing-chien, *Chinese.* SuSp, *tr. by* Michael E. Workman

Out in the street. (What Did I Do to Be So) Black and Blue? Thomas ("Fats") Waller, Andy Razaf *and* Harry Brooks. NAAAL

Out in the yellow meadows, where the bee. George Meredith. GBL *Fr.* Modern Love.

Out in this desert we are testing bombs. Trying to Talk with a Man. Adrienne Rich. HCAP

Out into the rain. (LL) For a Broken Needle. Hazel Hall. NMM-2; PaTW

Out-island once, on a south slope. Deer Isle. Philip Booth. VGW

Out it fell! (LL) The Squirrel. *Unknown.* BoTP; OxNR

Out it spake Lizee Linzee. Lizie Lindsay. *Unknown.* ESPB

Out, John! out, John! what are you about, John? Thomas Haynes Bayly. OBCoV

Out of a fired ship, which, by no way. A Burnt Ship. Donne. EBEV; InPK-6; OBWP

Out of a gothic North, the pallid children. Good-Bye to the Mezzogiorno. W. H. Auden. OxBTC

Out of a hat. Out of Our Hands. Cathy Song. UnSA

Out of a War of Wits. Dylan Thomas. PoA

Out of adult hearing. A Picture of Okinawa. Dennis Schmitz. LCAP-2

Out of an Epigram of Martial. Martial, *Latin.* OBCVT, *tr. by* Sir John Denham

Out of brightness, a brightness out of brightness. The Waltz. Hilary Corke. NYBP

Out of burlap sacks, out of bearing butter. They Feed They Lion. Philip Levine. LCAP-2; MoP; NNaP; NOBA; NoAM; NoP-4; VCAP

Out of Chaos Out of Order Out. Michele Roberts. BrRo

Out of Control; the Quarry. Christopher Dewdney. NOBC

Out of Doors. E. North. BoTP

Out of French. Sir Charles Sedley. FaBoEE

Out of friendship and a slow retreat of the blood. Ascending Red Cedar Moon. Duane Niatum. CDW

Out of gas south. Autumn. Philip Levine. NNaP

Out of heaven on your bugles blown! (LL) England, My England. William Ernest Henley. MoBrPo; OBEV; PoLF

Out of Hellas if you please, Aristarchean pedants. Herodicus, *Greek.* GrAn, *tr. by* Peter Jay

Out of her house she crept. Miss Euphemia. John Crowe Ransom. CMoP

Out of her own body she pushed. Grandmother. Paula Gunn Allen. MDDM

Out of her womb of pain my mother spat me. Story Books on a Kitchen Table. Audre Lorde. GT; MDDM *Fr.* Story Books on a Kitchen Table.

Out of his cottage to the sun. Old Dan'l. Leonard Alfred George Strong. MoBrPo

Out of Horace. James Wright. NOSC

Out of it all but this remains. Dead Cities. Madison Cawein. APN-2

Out of it steps our future, through this door. The Door. W. H. Auden. Son *Fr.* The Quest.

Out of Luck. Abraham ibn Ezra, *Hebrew.* TrJP, *tr. by* Solomon Solis-Cohen

Out of me unworthy and unknown. Anne Rutledge. Edgar Lee Masters. CBCWP; CMoP; HAP; ImPo; LiTM; MoAmPo; MoP; NOBA; NoAM; OxBA; TFi *Fr.* Spoon River Anthology.

Out of midsummer's blazing most not night. E. E. Cummings. NoAM

Out of my clothes, I ran past the boathouse. Under the Boathouse. David Bottoms. MT

Out of my flesh that hungers. On a Night of the Full Moon. Audre Lorde. CPO; NALW

Out of my heart, one day, I wrote a song. Misapprehension. Paul Laurence Dunbar. BPo

Out of my mother's womb. Job. I. John Hall. ChIV-1

Out of my own great woe. Proem. Heinrich Heine, *German.* AWP, *tr. by* Elizabeth Barrett Browning

Out of my window high as aerie. Russia 1914/Bolinas 1988. Gail Shafarman. LoHo

Out of my window I could see. Blossoms. Frank Dempster Sherman. OBCA

Out of my window late at night I gape. In the Night. Elizabeth Jennings. NYBP

Out of one golden breath. Love-Song. Else Lasker-Schüler, *German.* TrJP, *tr. by* Jethro Bithell

Out of our daylight into death you burn. Paper Anarchist Addresses the Shade of Nancy Ling Perry. George Woodcock. NOBC

Out of Our Hands. Cathy Song. UnSA

Out of Our Shame. Norman Rosten. TrJP

Out of Petronius. Petronius Arbiter, *Latin.* OBCVT, *tr. by* Richard Crashaw

Out of Sight, Out of Mind. Barnabe Googe. InPS-3

Out of sight they spend whole summers. Conkers. Barrie Wade. AYFP

Out of the blackthorn hedges. Love Song. Ivor Gurney. EnLoPo

Out-of-the-Body Travel. Stanley Plumly. AmPA; LCAP-2

Out of the bosom of the Air. Snow-Flakes. Henry Wadsworth Longfellow. APN-1; BoTP; CA; GEA; NCAP; NOBA; NoP-4; PoEL-5; SAGP; TAP; UnPo

Out of the church she followed [*or* follow'd] them. Maude Clare. Christina Rossetti. EBVV

Out of the clover and blue-eyed grass. Driving Home the Cows. Kate Putnam Osgood. CBCWP

Out of the complicated house, come I. The Hills. Frances Darwin Cornford. MoBrPo

Out of the corpse-warm vestibule of heaven steps the sun. Ingeborg Bachmann, *German.* BoWoP, *tr. by* Janice Orion

Out of the cradle endlessly rocking. Walt Whitman. APN-1; AWP; AmPP; ColAP; HAP; HeIP-4; ImPo; MeMAP; MoAmPo; NAAL-1; NAAL-3; NAWM-2; NCAP; NOBA; NoP-4; OxBA; PoE; PoEL-5; SAmP; TAP; TRP

   ("Sea whisper'd me, The.") (LL) ColAP; NCAP; NoP-4; PAR

Out of the crowd, I have seen you travelling south of Pardoo. The Witch Doctor's Magic Flight. Smiler Narautjarri. NOBAu, *tr. by* Georg von Brandenstein

Out of the dark. The Open Door. Elizabeth Jane Coatsworth. TLR

Out of the dark cup. From the Telephone. Florence Ripley Mastin. LW

Out of the dark raw earth. Alabama. Julia Fields. PoBA

Out of the Darkness. Frankie Armstrong. BrRo

Out of the Darkness. Gertrud Kolmar, *German.* WPOW, *tr. by* Michael Hamburger

Out of the darkness / on a dark path. Lady Izumi, *Japanese.* WPJ, *tr. by* Kenneth Rexroth *and* Ikuko Atsumi

Out of the dead, cold ashes, / Life again. (LL) Evolution. John Banister Tabb. APN-2

Out of the Deep. Clara Ann Thompson. CBWP-2

Out of the deep [*or* depths] have I called [*or* cried unto] thee, O Lord. Psalm 130. Bible, *O.T.* OBVE; TrJP *Fr.* Psalms.

Out of the depths of a heart of love. A Valentine. Priscilla Jane Thompson. CBWP-2

Out of the dusk a shadow. Evolution. John Banister Tabb. APAD; APN-2

Out of the earth. I Sing for the Animals. *Teton Sioux Oral Tradition, Teton Sioux Indian.* TTTS

Out of the earth beneath the water. The Mud Turtle. Howard Nemerov. NYBP

Out of the earth, out of the air, out of the water. Rapparees. Richard Murphy. BIrV; NOIV; PBCIP *Fr.* The Battle of Aughrim.

Out of the earth to rest or range. The Passing Strange. John Masefield. MoBrPo; OBEV

Out of the east window a storm. Wednesday of Holy Week, 1940. Kenneth Rexroth. ChIV-1

Out of the factory chimney tall. Smoke Animals. Rowena Bastin Bennett. CA

Out of the fields I see them pass. Youth's Own. John Galsworthy. NSI

Out of the focal and foremost fire. Little Giffen. Francis Orrery Ticknor. CBCWP

Out of the fog. The Fog Dream. Sandra M. Gilbert. PoA

Out of the Frying Pan into the Fire. James Henry. NOBVV

Out of the furnace. Space Shot. Gareth Owen. SpW

Out of the garden comes the tree. Because Thou Did'st Give. Harry Morris. CRP

Out of the ghetto streets where a Jewboy. Autobiographical. Abraham Moses Klein. MoCV; NoAM

Out of the golden remote wild west where the sea without shore is. Hesperia. Swinburne. OBNC

Out of the grey air grew snow and more snow. Snow. William Robert Rodgers. LiTM

Out of the hills of Habersham. Song of the Chattahoochee. Sidney Lanier. APN-2; ColAP; FaBoBe

Out of the Hitherwhere. James Whitcomb Riley. BLPA

Out of the Hurly-Burly. "Max Adeler." OBAL

Out of the Identical. Gustaf Sobin. PmAP

Out of the Italain. Giovanni Battista Marino, *Italian*. OBVE, *tr. by* Richard Crashaw

Out of the lamplight. Mice in the Hay. Leslie Norris. NOxBChV; OBCP; PChr

Out of the Land of Heaven. Leonard Cohen. MoCV

Out of the life lived, out of the love spent. (LL) An Urban Convalescence. James Merrill. CoAP; ColAP; NAAL-2; NOBA

Out of the light that dazzles me. My Captain. Dorothea Day. BLPA

Out of the lofty cavern wandering. *Unknown.* OBCVT, *tr. by* Shelley *Fr.* Hymn to Hermes.

Out of the midnight sky a great dawn broke. The Shepherd Speaks. John Erskine. TrCP

Out of the mud two strangers came. Two Tramps in Mud Time. Robert Frost. CMoP; ImPo; LiTM; MeMAP; MoAmPo; MoP; NAAL-2; NoAM; SAmP

Out of the Night. Emily Jane Pfeiffer.
    "So the river—yes, the river; I have come to that at last." VWP

Out of the night that covers me. Invictus. William Ernest Henley. APAD; BLPA; CABP; EBEvV; FaBoBe; FaPoR; HoPM; ImPo; MoBrPo; NOBE; OBEV; OBMV; OBNC; PFE; SAGP *Fr.* Echoes.

Out of the part of the earth. Unchained Melody. Gillian Conoley. CMAP

Out of the Past there has come a Face. A Face from the Past. Menella Bute Smedley. VWP

Out of the patched-glass window of boarded shacks. War Poems 1. Sang Ku, *Korean*. ColAP, *tr. by* Jaihiun Kim

Out of the shade. Tanka. Miya Shūji, *Japanese*. MJT, *tr. by* Makoto Ueda

Out of the shadow, I am come in to you whole a black holy man. Study Peace. Imamu Amiri Baraka. APSN; PoBA

Out of the smoke of men's wrath. The Face (Guillemont). Frederic Manning. NSI

Out of the table endlessly rocking. Just Friends. Robert Creeley. NeAP

Out of the tomb, we bring Badroulbadour. The Worms at Heaven's Gate. Wallace Stevens. NoAM

Out of the Wailing. Stephen Caldwell Wright. ISC

Out of the Whirlwind. Bible, *O.T.* AWP *Fr.* Moreover the Lord answered Job, and said. *Fr.* Job. NAWM-1; OBVE

Out of the window a sea of green trees. Open Windows. Sara Teasdale. ColAP

Out of the wind's and the rain's way. (LL) The Old Woman of the Roads. Padraic Colum. BoTP; CH; FYAP; FaBoBe; MoBrPo; NOIV; OBEV; PoRA; TIRV

Out of the wine-pot cry'd the fly. The Fly. Philip Ayres, *after the Spanish of* Quevedo. OBVE

Out of the wood of thoughts that grows by night. Cock-Crow. Edward Thomas. GTBS-P; MoBrPo; NTP; OxBSP; RB

Out of these depths. De Profundis. David Gascoyne. PoWW

Out of these thin, thin cups I drink pale tea. Bone China. Richard Percival Lister. NYBP

Out of this seemliness, this solid order. On August the Thirteenth. Frances Darwin Cornford. WPN

Out of this ugliness may come. Glasgow Street. William Montgomerie. OxBS

Out of those wild, in- / visible circuits, a. Irises. Gustaf Sobin. APSN

Out of Time. Kenneth Slessor.
    "Leaning against the golden undertow." CBAP

Out of Tune. William Ernest Henley. MoBrPo

Out of what calms and pools the cool shell grows. The Atoll in the Mind. Alex Comfort. LiTM

Out of Work, Out of Touch, Out of Sorts. Catherine Davis. FFC

Out of your head the sky is taken. Monotones. B. P. Nichol. FTOS

Out of Your Sleep Arise and Wake. *Unknown.* NoP-4

Out of your whole life give but a moment! Now. Robert Browning. CBLP; EP

Out on a limb and frantically sawing. Martyrdom of Two Pagans. Philip Whalen. NeAP

Out on the board the old shearer stands. Click Go the Shears. *Unknown.* NOBAu

Out on the high "bird islands," Ciboux and Hertford. Cape Breton. Elizabeth Bishop. InPS-3

Out on the ocean, great wide ocean. Great *Titanic*. *Unknown.* AmFP

Out on the wastes of the Never Never. Where the Dead Men Lie. Barcroft Henry Boake. CBAP

Out on the windy hill. The Shepherd's Dog. Leslie Norris. OBCP

"Out, Out—." Robert Frost. ColAP; HAP; HeIP-4; NAAL-2; OxBA; PFE; Poetr; RB; SoSe-8; TRP; UnPo; VGW

Out, Out, Brief Candle! Shakespeare. *See* Tomorrow, and Tomorrow, and Tomorrow.

Out past the window two trees in splendor. Sentiments at Autumn. Han Yü, *Chinese*. SuSp, *tr. by* Charles Hartman

Out scouting for sound counsels? How to prosper? Ausiàs March, *Catalan*. STV, *tr. by* John Frederick Nims

Out that black hole of bush. Third World Snapshots. John Robert Lee. PBCV

Out the southern gate at sundown. *Unknown.* CoBCP, *tr. by* Burton Watson *Fr.* Tzu Yeh Songs.

Out the window, Colombia, out the window. Sharon Doubiago. PBCAP *Fr.* South America Mi Hija.

Out There. Breyten Breytenbach, *Afrikaans*. VCWP

Out there, beyond the boundary fence, beyond. The Singing Bones. Randolph Stow. BMAP; CBAP

Out There Somewhere. Henry Herbert Knibbs. BLPA

Out there, we've walked quite friendly up to Death. The Next War. Wilfred Owen. Son

Out there, with little else to do. Robben Island. Robert Dederick. PeSA

Out, thou silly moon-struck elf. The Idiot-Born. Eliza Cook. VWP

Out through the fields and the woods. Reluctance. Robert Frost. CMoP; MoAmPo; NOBA; OxBA; SAGP

Out, traitor absence: dar'st thou counsel me. Sonnet 88. Sir Philip Sidney. *Fr.* Astrophil and Stella. AAS; SiPS

Out upon it! I have loved [*or* lov'd]. Constant Lover, A [*or* The]. Sir John Suckling. BeJo; CBLP; EBEvV; ImPo; NBLV; NOSC; OxAEP-1; PBMP; PeLV; PoE *Fr.* A Poem with the Answer.

Out, upon the deep old ocean. On Genessarett. Josephine D. Henderson Heard. CBWP-4

Out upon you California. Pennsylvania Places. Thomas Augustin Daly. OBAL

Out walking in July. Released on Parole. James McAuley. BMAP

Out walking in the frozen swamp one gray [*or* grey] day. The Wood-Pile. Robert Frost. InPK-6; NAAL-2; NoAM; SAmP; VGW

Out walking ties left over from a track. Cross Ties. X. J. Kennedy. HoPM

Out West. Gary Snyder. NNaP

Out where the hand-clasp's a little stronger. Out Where the West Begins. Arthur Chapman. AiP; BLPA; FaBoBe

Out where yr going. Robert Creeley. *See* I Know a Man.

Out with a Gun. Vita Sackville-West. WPN

Out with my dog at dawn—we couldn't sleep—. Two Ember Days in Alabama. Andrew Hudgins. RA

Outbound, your bark awaits you. Were I one. Godspeed. John Greenleaf Whittier. GSo; Son

Outbreak. Bill Anderson. VGW

Outcast[, The]. "Æ." OxBSP

Outcast, The. Josephine D. Henderson Heard. CBWP-4

Outcast. Claude McKay. NAAAL; PoBA

Outcast, The. James Stephens. MoBrPo

Outcast. Alice Walker. NAAAL

Outcast, The. P. G. Wodehouse. UV

Outcrop stone is miserly. Still-Life. Ted Hughes. NYBP

Outcry upon Opportunity, An. Shakespeare. *See* Opportunity.

Outer Banks, The. Emily Grosholz. RA

Outer—from the Inner, The. Emily Dickinson. APN-2

Outer Layers of Nervousness, The. Alan Davies. FTOS

Outer provinces are never secure, The. Peace with Honor. Philip Appleman. CDa

Outfangthief is Damgudthyng. (LL) Beoleopard; or, The Witan's Whail. *Unknown.* CBNP; OBCoV

Outgoing Sabbath. *Unknown, Yiddish.* TrJP, *tr. by* Joseph Leftwich

Outhouse. Aleksandar Ristovic, *Serbo-Croatian*. HSix, *tr.* by Charles Simic

Outing, The. Marina Kudimova, *Russian*. TCRP, *tr.* by Albert C. Todd

Outlanders, The. Andrew Glaze. NYBP

Outlanders, The. William Morris. EBVV *Fr.* The Earthly Paradise. (Minstrels and Maids.)

Outlandish idol, brown as night, who overpower. She Is Not Satisfied. Charles Baudelaire, *French*. EP; FLP, *tr.* by Alistair Elliot

Outlaw, The. Seamus Heaney. MoP; OxBC

Outlaw Murray, The. *Unknown*. ESPB; OxBB

Outlaw of Loch Lene, The. *Unknown, Modern Irish*. BIrV; CH; GBL; NTP; OBEV, *tr.* by Jeremiah Joseph Callanan

Outlaw's Song, The. Joanna Baillie. OBEV

Outlines. Audre Lorde. GLP

Outlook wasn't brilliant for the Mudville nine that day, The. Casey at the Bat. Ernest Lawrence Thayer. APN-2; AiP; BLPA; FaBoA; FaBoBe; OBAL; OBCA; OBCoV; PoRA

Outpacing bargain, vocable and prayer. (LL) Capped arbiter of beauty in this street. Hart Crane. FaBoMo; ImPo; LiTM

Outrage. Lucille Iverson. CrSp

Outroars a dead lion. (LL) Koheleth. Louis Untermeyer. ChIV-1; TrJP

Outside. Hugh Chesterman. AYFP; BoTP

Outside, a delicate arch. The Curse. John Hollander. UnPo

Outside, affectionate eyes. Ursula. David Ray. VGW

Outside Bristol Rovers Football Ground. The Ballad of Billy Rose. Leslie Norris. MoBS

Outside Fargo, North Dakota. James Wright. GM; LCAP-2; NNaP; WeT

Outside gnarled rough black. Vegetable Love. Marge Piercy. DeD

Outside, in fact, there wasn't any change. Patrizia Cavalli, *Italian*. NeIt, *tr.* by Judith Baumel

Outside in front of the gate. Brief Reflection on Charlemagne. Miroslav Holub, *German*. CEEP, *tr.* by Stuart Friebert *and* Dana Hábová

Outside, in the arin, on the edge of evening. Dick and Colin at the Salmon Nets. Naomi Mitchison. WPN

Outside is the untreed, tearless light. The Mirror. Mark Jarman. CMAP

Outside it is cold. Inside. Winter for an Untenable Situation. Alan Dugan. PFE

Outside My Cabin. Wayne Dodd. CMAP

Outside/ outside myself/ there is a world. Sunday in the Park. William Carlos Williams. NAAL-2; NoAM *Fr.* Paterson.

Outside Pisa. Chitra Divakaruni. OpBo

Outside somewhere, beneath an atmosphere. Allegory. Rafael Campo. RA

Outside that bulbous Babylon. English Beach Memory: Mr. Thuddock. Sir Osbert Sitwell. NYBP

Outside the Bureau all the trams and trains. Laid Off. Francis Webb. BMAP

Outside the cats are wailing. Leah Goldberg. PBWP, *tr.* by Robert Alter *Fr.* The Symposium.

Outside the children play like flames. The Fever. Rosemary Dobson. FaBoWP

Outside the city, desolate, an ancient terrace. The Flower-Rain Terrace. Tao-chi, *Chinese*. CoBLCP, *tr.* by Jonathan Chaves

Outside the courtroom. Sharpeville Inquiry. Anne Welsh. PeSA

Outside the Depot. Betsy Sholl. LTA

Outside the door! (LL) Spring Morning. D. H. Lawrence. CMoP; MoBrPo

Outside, the freezing desert night. Jelaluddin Rumi, *Persian*. EnIH, *tr.* by Coleman Barks *and* John Moyne

Outside the Furnace. Aziz Qaisi, *Urdu*. OMIP, *tr.* by Baidar Bakht *and* Leslie Lavigne

Outside the great clanging cathedrals of rust and smoke. A Poem Written under an Archway in a Discontinued Railroad Station, Fargo, North Dakota. James Wright. GM

Outside the Holy City. James G. Gilkey. AH

Outside the hotel window, unenlightened pigeons. The Jain Bird Hospital in Delhi. William Meredith. VCAP

Outside, the last kids holler. Leaving the Motel. W. D. Snodgrass. NIP-4

Outside the Line. Dan Pagis, *Hebrew*. IP, *tr.* by Warren Bargad *and* Stanley F. Chyet

Outside, the music is steeped. In the Evening. "Anna Akhmatova," *Russian*. TCRP, *tr.* by Daniel Weissbort

Outside the office of the principal. (LL) Zimmer in Grade School. Paul Zimmer. KaS; PBCAP

Outside the pub. Chuck Brickley. HA

Outside, the rain, pinafore of gray water, dresses the town. Child Beater. Ai. BoWoP

Outside the screen rain drips and splashes. Tune: "Ripples Sifting Sand: A Song." Li Yü, *Chinese*. SuSp, *tr.* by Daniel Bryant

Outside the second grade room. The Girl Who Loved the Sky. Anita Endrezze-Danielson. HATNAP

Outside the Supermarket. Roy Fuller. OxBC

Outside the Terrace of Yellow Cranes. Mooring at Hsia-k'ou at Night. Li Meng-yang, *Chinese*. CoBLCP, *tr.* by Jonathan Chaves

Outside the tower, the east wind's early to arrive. To the Tune "Chao-chün's Sorrow." Yang Shen, *Chinese*. CoBLCP, *tr.* by Jonathan Chaves

Outside the town I've built this little place. Garden Living. Wu Wei-yeh, *Chinese*. CoBLCP, *tr.* by Jonathan Chaves

Outside the whistled gang-call, Twelfth Street Rag. Me Tarzan. Tony Harrison. *Fr.* The School of Eloquence. NAEL-2; NoAM

Outside the world was full, plural. The Christmas Tree. Patricia Beer. OBCP

Outside where the storm goes cracked. Caption for a Miniature. Joanne Kyger. BB

Outside your temple wall. To the Unnamed Buddhist Nun Who Burned Herself to Death on the Night of June 3, 1966. Diane Di Prima. BB

Outside your window venerable with light. A Refugee. Lilian Bowes-Lyon. WPN

Outsider, The. Syl Cheney-Coker. HBAPE

Outsider Art. Kay Ryan. BAP-95

Outskirts. Tomas Tranströmer, *Swedish*. BLT, *tr.* by Robert Bly

Outskirts, Afternoon. Judit Tóth, *Hungarian*. CEEP, *tr.* by Emery E. George

Outspoken buttocks in pink beads. National Winter Garden. Hart Crane. EP; InPS-3; LiTM; NAAL-2; OxBA *Fr.* Three Songs. NAAL-2 *Fr.* The Bridge. NAAL-2

Outward. Louis Simpson. NYBP

Outward Bound. James Simmons. CIP-2

Outward Man Accused, The. Edward Taylor. MeMAP

Outwitted. Edwin Markham. BLPA; MoAmPo; PoToHe

Ouzo Unclouded. Robert Graves. GrIP

Ov all the meäds wi shoals an' pools. Leeburn Mill. William Barnes. EnVR

Ovals of opal on dislustred seas. Memoriter. Charles Spear. PeNZ

Oven Bird, The. Robert Frost. APo; AWP; AmPP; GSo; HeIP-4; MeMAP; MoP; NAAL-2; NOBA; NoAM; NoP-4; OxBA; PoE; Son; TAP

Oven Loves the TV Set, The. Heather McHugh. CrSp

Over a bloomy land, untrod. In Dreamy Swoon. George Darley. OBNC *Fr.* Nepenthe.

Over a dark and quiet empire. Two Poems. Andrey Andreievich Voznesensky, *Russian*. VCWP, *tr.* by William Jay Smith and Patricia Blake

Over a new horizon glows the dawn. Verses for the End of an Era. T. P., *Vietnamese*. AVP, *tr.* by Huỳnh Sanh Thông

Over a sea with death acquainted, yet forever chaste. (LL) Ragged Island. Edna St. Vincent Millay. ColAP; NAAL-2; NoP-4

Over a slow-dying fire. Lachesis. Victor James Daley. CBAP

Over a wild and stormy sea. Mother Shipton's Prophecies. Charles Hindley. BLPA

Over All. Thomas Rabbitt. PUP-19

Over-all picture, The. William Carlos Williams. *See* The Hunters in the Snow.

Over-all picture is winter, The. The Hunters in the Snow. William Carlos Williams. LCAP-2 *Fr.* Pictures from Brueghel.

Over all the hills now. Song of the Traveler at Evening. Goethe, *German*. STV, *tr.* by John Frederick Nims

Over an ash-fawn beach fronting a sea which keeps. Fiascherino. Charles Tomlinson. NoAM

Over and back. At Ithaca. Hilda Doolittle. ColAP; VGW

Over and over. Anita Virgil. HA

Over and over again. (LL) Love Poem. Audre Lorde. CPO; GLP; NoAM

Over and over again I order my students. The Widow Teaches Poetry Writing. Nell Altizer. IMW

Over and over again the papers print. Once in a While a Protest Poem. David B. Axelrod. InPK-6

Over and over again to people. The Limits of Submission. Faarah Nuur, *Somali*. TTY, *tr.* by B. W. Andrzejewski *and* I. M. Lewis

Over and Over Stitch. Joric Graham. HCAP; VCAP

Over and over, when the wayside dust had grayed us. To Be Said at the Seder. Karl Wolfskehl, *German*. TrJP, *tr.* by Carol North Valhope *and* Ernst Morowitz

Over back where they speak of life as staying. The Investment. Robert Frost. CMoP; OxBA

Over Bright Summer Seas. Robert Silliman Hillyer. NYBP

Over come—O bitter sweetness. Sophocles. OBCVT, *tr.* by W. B. Yeats *Fr.* 'Antigone,' The.

Over deep cushions, drenched with drowsy scents. Damned Women. Charles Baudelaire, *French*. BoLoP, *tr.* by Roy Campbell

Over dried grass. David Lloyd. HA

Over every elm, the. You Too Lie down. Dennis Lee. TLR

Over Fayetteville, Arkansas. The Arkansas Testament. Derek Walcott. CBCWP

Over fishes, over stars. Smugglers. "Eduard Georgievich Bagritzky," *Russian.* TCRP, *tr. by* Vera Dunham

Over-Heart, The. John Greenleaf Whittier. ChIV-2; NOCV

Over here in England I'm helpin' wi' the hay. Corrymeela. "Moira O'Neill." AWP

Over his keys the musing organist. Prelude to Part the First. James Russell Lowell. APN-1 *Fr.* The Vision of Sir Launfal.

Over misted blue hills and distant water. To Judge Han Ch'o at Yang-chou. Tu Mu, *Chinese.* PLT, *tr. by* A. C. Graham

Over Mtskheta falls a star. In Memory of Titian Tabidze. Yunna Petrovna Moritz, *Russian.* TCRP, *tr. by* J. R. Rowland

Over my. Tanka. Miya Shūji, *Japanese.* MJT, *tr. by* Makoto Ueda

Over my district north to south, when will my days in office end? Out in the Snow, Spending the Night at the New Stockade, Extremely Depressed. Huang T'ing-chien, *Chinese.* SuSp, *tr. by* Michael E. Workman

Over my head. Freedom in the Air. *Unknown.* NAAAL

Over my head, I see the bronze butterfly. Lying in a Hammock at William Duffy's Farm in Pine Island, Minnesota. James Wright. CoAmPo; ColAP; HAP; HCAP; HoPM; NOBA; Poetr; SAGP; TRP; VCAP; WeT

Over my head the woodland wall. The Scribe. *Unknown, Irish.* TIRV, *tr. by* Robin Flower

Over my shoulder in Danbury, Connecticut, as I drove. The Wonder. Thylias Moss. ChAP

Over North Mountain. On the Death of the Emperor Temmu. Empress Jito, *Japanese.* WPJ, *tr. by* Kenneth Rexroth *and* Ikuko Atsumi

Over northeast mountains. Voyeur's Dream. Barney Bush. HATNAP

Over, o[h] over / the thorn. (LL) Psalm: "No one kneads us again out of earth and clay." Paul Celan, *German.* PoSu, *tr. by* John Felstiner; OBVE, *tr. by* Michael Hamburger, *sl. diff. vers.*

Over obscured by their long hair they seem / to be mourning. (LL) Moving over the hills, crossing the irrigation. George Oppen. APSN; NNaP

Over oceans sped he, Attis, in the speediest of ships. Catullus. *See* Attis.

Over our heads the missiles ran. Loss of an Oil Tanker. Charles Causley. OxBC

Over our naked guilt. (LL) The Net. William Robert Rodgers. BoLoP; CIP-2; PNI

Over, Over. Thomas Love Peacock. OxAEP-2 *Fr.* Maid Marian.

Over Puerto Rican agony lawyers'screams in slums. (LL) A Vow. Allen Ginsberg. OBWP

Over rips and tears and / thin places. (LL) A Nameless One. Margaret Avison. HeIP-4; NOBC

Over rock and wrinkled ground. Beagles. William Robert Rodgers. FaBoTw

Over sheer banks a menacing wind moves. Night. Tu Fu, *Chinese.* SuSp, *tr. by* Jan W. Walls

Over Sir John's Hill. Dylan Thomas. TOF

Over sky and land and down under the sea. Pervigilium Veneris. OBCVT, *tr. by* Allen Tate *Fr.* The Vigil of Venus.

Over that morn hung heaviness, until. Seascape. Francis Brett Young. OxBTC

Over the Arafura sea, the China sea. For John Chappell. Gary Snyder. NNaP

Over the ball of it. Pisgah-Sights. I. Robert Browning. ChIV-1

Over the black mountain, across the black bay, into the / black night and beyond. Encounter. Uys Krige, *Afrikaans.* PeSA, *tr. by the author*

Over the bleak and barren snow. Tony O! Colin Francis. CH

Over the clean sea-beach. (LL) Men of valor, The. Akahito, *Japanese.* AWP; TAL, *tr. by* Arthur Waley

Over the cobbles, in a lost Spring. (LL) Andrée Rexroth. Kenneth Rexroth. APSN; VGW

Over the corpse of Achilles. (LL) Justice. Agathias, *Greek.* GrAn; PC, *tr. by* Peter Whigham

Over the cradle the mother hung. Where Shall the Baby's Dimple Be. Josiah Gilbert Holland. BLPA

Over the dark water. A Kayak Song. Lucy Diamond. BoTP

Over the downs there were birds flying. On the South Downs. Sara Teasdale. MoAmPo

Over the earth I come. Soldier's Song. *Unknown, Sioux Native American.* APN-2, *tr. by* Stephen Return Riggs

Over the Edge. Fleur Adcock. PeNZ

Over the edge of the purple down. The City of Sleep. Rudyard Kipling. NTP

Over the fence. Emily Dickinson. FaBoVe

Over the Fields. Adeline White. BoTP

Over the flat slope of St Eloi. Trenches: St Eloi. Thomas Ernest Hulme. PeFWW

Over, the four long years! And now there rings. Oxford. Lionel Pigot Johnson. OBNC

Over the garden wall. Eleanor Farjeon. ChAP

Over the half-finished houses. The Roofwalker. Adrienne Rich. CoAP; NAAL-2; SAGP

Over the heather the wet wind blows. Roman Wall Blues. W. H. Auden. NTP *Fr.* Twelve Songs.

Over the hill and over the dale. Dawlish Fair. Keats. NTP; PeLV

Over the hill came horsemen, horsemen whistling. A Stared Story. William Stafford. Son

Over the hill I have watched the dawning. Dawning. Richard Watson Dixon. NOBVV

Over the Hill to the Poor-House. Will M. Carleton. BLPA

"Over the hills and far away. (LL) The Gypsy. Edward Thomas. NoAM; NoP-4

Over the Hills and far away. (LL) Song: "Were I laid on Greenland's coast." John Gay. EBEvV, *sect.* I, *pt.* i; CBLP; EnLoPo; NAEL-1; NOBE; NOEC; OxBoLi; PeLV; PoEL-3

Over the hills the loose clouds rambled. The Subjection of Women. Austin Clarke. CIP-2

Over the hills / Where the edge of the light. The Witches' Ride. Karla Kuskin. NOxBChV; TLR

Over the land freckled with snow half-thawed. Thaw. Edward Thomas. EBEV; FaBoTw; GTBS-P; MoBrPo; NTP; OxAEP-2; OxBSP; OxBTC; Spl

Over the last century. Song of Lin Liang's Painting "Two Horned Falcons." Li Meng-yang, *Chinese.* CoBLCP, *tr. by* Jonathan Chaves

Over the lids of thine eye. Images. Richard Schaukal, *German.* AWP, *tr. by* Ludwig Lewisohn

Over the low, barnacled, elephant-colored rocks. Meditation at Oyster River. Theodore Roethke. CMoP; MoAmPo; NYBP; PaTW *Fr.* North American Sequence.

Over the low, barnacled, elephant-colored rocks. Meditation at Oyster River. Theodore Roethke. CMoP; MoAmPo; NYBP

Over the monstrous shambling sea. Marsh Song—At Sunset. Sidney Lanier. NOBA *Fr.* Hymns of the Marshes. APN-2

Over the monstrous shambling sea. Marsh Song—at Sunset. Sidney Lanier. NOBA

Over the month of June the rain is falling. The Rain is Falling. Homero Aridjis, *Spanish.* STV, *tr. by* John Frederick Nims

Over the mountains / And over the waves. Love Will Find Out the Way. *Unknown.* FaBoCh; GBL; GTBS-P; OBEV

Over the Neva. Wilgelm Aleksandrovich Zorgenfrey, *Russian.* TCRP, *tr. by* Sophie Lund

Over the northern pass, dark clouds spread gloom. Our Land, Our Home. Trần Tuấn Khải, *Vietnamese.* AVP, *tr. by* Huỳnh Sanh Thông

Over the old honeymoon cottage. Akiko Yosano, *Japanese.* OHMPJ, *tr. by* Kenneth Rexroth

Over the Pass. Julie Convisser. IFJA

Over the plum snow, the train's blond smoke. On Returning to Detroit. Carolyn Forché. GM

Over the quarry the children went rambling. The Fossil Raindrops. Harriet Prescott Spofford. OBCA

Over the rainy day mountain. Wishes. Patty L. Harjo. VoR

Over the reeds the. *Unknown, Japanese.* OHMPJ, *tr. by* Kenneth Rexroth

Over the right / triangle formed. The Slogan. Paul Blackburn. PoM

Over the rim of the glass. The Ghost in the Martini. Anthony Hecht. DiPo; NoP-4; OxBC

Over the river and through the wood. Thanksgiving Day. Lydia Maria Child. APN-1; ColAP; FPC; ImGa; NTCP; OBCA; WHSW

Over the roof-tops race the shadows of clouds. John Gould Fletcher. *Fr.* Irradiations. MoAmPo

Over the Roofs. Sara Teasdale. ColAP

Over the roofs and cranes, blistered cupola and hungry smokestack. Louis MacNeice. LiTM *Fr.* The Kingdom.

Over the sea our galleys went. The Wanderers. Robert Browning. OBEV *Fr.* Paracelsus.

Over the shoes in pebbles I sit here. In the Park. Iain Crichton Smith. FaBoTC *Fr.* By the Sea.

Over the soughing of the sombre wind. A Summer Poem. Jayanta Mahapatra. VCWP

Over the Spring fields. Yakamochi, *Japanese.* OHMPJ, *tr. by* Kenneth Rexroth *Fr.* Manyo Shu, Part 3 of 4.

Over the stones still rattling, up Pall Mall. Byron. NOBL *Fr.* Canto the Eleventh. NOBRP *Fr.* Don Juan.

Over the stretch of the seas. (LL) The Seafarer. *Unknown, Anglo-Saxon.* AnOE, *tr. by* Charles W. Kennedy; EBEV, *tr. by* John Wain; PoE, *tr. by* Kemp Malone; OxBoS, *tr. by* Kevin Crossley-Holland; OBVE, *tr. by* Michael Alexander

Over! the sweet summer closes. Prologue. Tennyson. GBL *Fr.* Becket.

Over the tender, bow'd locks of the corn. (LL) Summer Dawn. William Morris. GSo; NOBE; NOBVV; OAEL-2; OBEV; OBNC; OxAEP-2

Over the top! The wire's thin here, unbarbed. The Night Patrol. Arthur Graeme West. NSI; PoFWW

Over the Top with Pershing. Zelda Sayre Fitzgerald. AiP

Over the utmost hill at length I sped. Shelley. OBWP Fr. The Revolt of Islam.

Over the vast field of mustard flowers. Buson, *Japanese.* OHPJ, *tr. by* Kenneth Rexroth

Over the vast summer hills. The Echoes. Raymond Mazisi Kunene. PBMAP

Over the Wall: Berlin, May 1975. Charles Hubert Sisson. OxBC

Over the warts on the bumpy. Sadie's Playhouse. Margaret Danner. PoBA

Over the water and over the lea [*or* sea]. *Unknown.* OxNR; ReMoGo

Over the water / and under the water. A Ship's Nail. *Unknown.* ReMoGo

Over the years, horses have changed to Land-Rovers. I To my Brothers. Judith Wright. BMAP Fr. For a Pastoral Family.

Over their edge of earth. The Little Clan. Frederick Robert Higgins. OBMV

Over There. George M. Cohan. FaBoA

Over there?/ Where?. (LL) Café: 3 A.M. Langston Hughes. GLP; HCAP

Over there are faith, life, virtue in the sun. (LL) Report on Experience. Edmund Blunden. FaBoTw; GTBS-P; NOBE; OBMV; OBWP; PeFWW

Over these blunted, these tormented hills. Kanheri Caves. Dom Moraes. NoP-4

Over this battered track. Express Train. Karl Kraus, *German.* TrJP, *tr. by* Albert Bloch

Over this the foresayd lay. John Skelton. PBRV Fr. Collyn Clout.

Over thresholds of welcome dream with wet and moonlit skin. (LL) Elegy for Drowned Children. Bruce Dawe. BMAP; NOBAu

Over to your place. (LL) The Poem You Asked For. Larry Levis. AmPA; PBCAP

Over 2000 Illustrations and a Complete Concordance. Elizabeth Bishop. HCAP; LCAP-2; NAAL-2; NoAM; VCAP

Over us stands the broad electric face. Terminal. Karl Shapiro. GM

Over which Christ wept. (LL) I Have Been Through the Gates. Charlotte Mew. SAGP

Over worn-out hands—oh! beautiful sleep! (LL) Beautiful Things. Ellen Palmer Allerton. BLPA; PWR

Over your body the clouds go. Gulliver. Sylvia Plath. NOBA

Over your head to sleep I bow. (LL) In a Gondola. Robert Browning. APAD; BoLoP; GBL; OBEV

Overcome by the magic of his own charms. Su Tung-p'o. *See* Rhyming with Tzu-yu's "Treading the Green."

Overdose of beautiful words, An. 12th Raga: For John Wieners. David Meltzer. *Fr.* Ragas. NeAP

Overdue Balance Sheet. Thérèse Plantier, *French.* BoWoP, *tr. by* Maxine W. Kumin *and* Judith Kumin

Overgrown roads around here refract water-and-mirror mirages, The. Island Celebration. Kenward Elmslie. FTOS

Overhead at night, above the planet. Désamère. Alice Notley. PT

Overhead, the match burns out. Disregard. Ai. NoAM

Overhead the skull-hill rises. Galway Kinnell. *Fr.* Ruins under the Stars. LCAP-2

Overheard. Denise Levertov. PoM

Overheard / a brother saying. July 27. Norman Jordan. NBV

Overheard in an Orchard. Elizabeth Cheney. CTV

Overheard on a Saltmarsh. Harold Monro. BoTP; CH; NOxBChV

("Give them me. Give them. / No.") (LL) NOxBChV

Overheard over S. E. Asia. Denise Levertov. BoWoP

Overjoyed at Soviet Russia's Entry into the War. Liu Ya-tzu, *Chinese.* SuSp, *tr. by* Wu-chi Liu

Overland to the Islands. Denise Levertov. CoAmPo; PmAP; UnPo

("Not direction—'every step an arrival'.") (LL) CoAmPo

Overlander, The. *Unknown.* NOBAu

Overlooking the Desert. Tu Fu, *Chinese.* OHPC, *tr. by* Kenneth Rexroth

Overlooking the water, a desolate city. Sha-ch'eng, "Sand City." Yang Shih-ch'i, *Chinese.* CoBLCP, *tr. by* Jonathan Chaves

Overnight. Valentine Ackland. WPN

Overnight clouds begin to scatter. Inscribed on the Painting "Spring Dawn at Peach Blossom Spring" by Scholar Shang Te-fu. Chao Meng-fu, *Chinese.* CoBLCP, *tr. by* Jonathan Chaves

Overnight Guest. Ramona Wilson. VoR

Overnight, very / Whitely, discreetly. Mushrooms. Sylvia Plath. FaBoWP; PBMP; RB; WPOW

Overripe Fruit. Kasmuneh, *Arabic.* TrJP

Overruled. John Greenleaf Whittier. NCAP

Overtaken. Michael McClintock. HA

Overtaken by time. Tanka. Sasaki Yukitsuna, *Japanese.* MJT, *tr. by* Makoto Ueda

Overtired branches are fragile. Fazil Abdulovich Iskander, *Russian.* TCRP, *tr. by* Albert C. Todd

Overture. Christopher Okigbo. PBMAP *Fr.* Heavensgate (1961).

Overture for Bubble-Gum and Flute. Alistair Paterson. PeNZ

Overture to a Dance of Locomotives. William Carlos Williams. GM

Overture to Strangers. Phyllis Haring. PeSA

Overtures to Death. C. Day Lewis.

"For us, born into a still." CMoP

Overturned Lake, The. Charles Henri Ford. SPE

Overwhelmed by mist. By mist. O. Mabson Southard. HA

Overworked Elocutionist, An. Carolyn Wells. BLPA

Ovid in the Third Reich. Geoffrey Hill. CABP; FaBoMo; HP; NoAM

Ovid is the surest guide. Written in an Ovid. Matthew Prior. FaBoEE; OBCoV

Ovid, Meet a Metamorphodite. Jonathan Williams. PoM

Ovid on the Dacian Coast. Dunstan Thompson. NYBP

Ovid Twice Exiled. Jerzy Ficowski, *Polish.* PoSu, *tr. by* Frank J. Corliss, Jr., *and* Grazyna Sandel

Ovid would never have guessed how far. Brueghel in Naples. Dannie Abse. NIP-4

Ovid's Banquet of Sense. George Chapman.

Ear's Delight, The. NoSic

Ovids Elegies Book 1. Marlowe.

"Now ore the sea from her old Love comes she." PBRV

Ovid's Metamorphoses Book 6. Arthur Golding.

". . . This Damsell was not famous for the place." PBRV

Ovids Walnut-Tree transplanted. Ovid, *Latin.*

Nux (The Walnut Tree). OBCVT, *tr. by* R. Hatton

Oviparous Tailor, The. Thomas Lovell Beddoes. CBNP

Ovulation. Lily Pond. DeD

Ow much poun fi di yellow yam? Longsight Market. Valerie Bloom. NBrP

Ow! ow! ow! ow! The Spirit of Evil. Goethe. OxBoV, *tr. by* Bayard Taylor *Fr.* Faust.

Owdham Footbo'. Ammon Wrigley. FaBoVe

Owed to New York. Byron Rufus Newton. BLPA; NBLV

Owen Tudor to Queen Katherine. Michael Drayton. NoSic *Fr.* England's Heroical Epistles.

Owens. Biographia Literaria. Joan Retallack. FTOS

Owen's Epigrams. Robert Hayman.

Owen's Bracelet. NOSC

Saturn's Three Sons. NOSC

Owen's praise demands my song. The Triumphs of Owen. Thomas Gray. PoEL-3

Ower t'ills o Bingley. Blake Morrison. FaBoVe *Fr.* The Ballad of the Yorkshire Ripper.

Owl, The. Edward Davison. PoA

Owl, The. Walter De la Mare. OxBSP

Owl. Peter Kane Dufault. NYBP

Owl, The. Tennyson. ACTP; BoTP; CTAV; FaBoCh

Owl, The. Edward Thomas. AF; APo; ChAP; EBEV; FaBoTw; GTBS-P; MoP; NAEL-2; NIP-4; NOBE; NoAM; NoP-4; OAEL-2; OBWVE; OxAEP-2; PeFWW; PoE; Poetr; RB; SCGP; TFi; TRP; UnPo

Owl. Ted Walker. NOxBChV

Owl, The. Robert Penn Warren. MoAmPo

Owl and the astronaut sailed through space, The. Gareth Owen. SpW

Owl and the Eel and the Warming-Pan, The. Laura Elizabeth Richards. OBCA

Owl and the Fox, The. *Unknown.* BLPA

(Owl and the Pussy-Cat, The). Edward Lear. CTV

((Owl and the Pussy-Cat, The).) CTV

("Owl and the Pussycat went to sea, The.") ChAP

(Owl and the Pussy-Cat, The). Edward Lear. *See* (Owl and the Pussy-Cat, The).

Owl and the Pussy-Cat went to sea, The. (Owl and the Pussy-Cat, The). Edward Lear. APAD; BoTP; CABP; CBNP; EBEvV; FPC; FaBoBe; FaBoCh; GEA; GTBS-P; ITG; NBLV; NOBE; NOxBChV; NTCP; NTP; NoP-4; OBCoV; OBSP; OTCP; OxBChV; OxBM; OxBoLi; PC; PeLV; PoLF; PoRA; TFi; TLR; TTTS

Owl,— / Au / The owl, The. Song of the Owl. *Unknown, Ojibwa Native American, from tr. by* Henry Rowe Schoolcraft. APN-2, *tr. by* Henry Wadsworth Longfellow

Owl-Critic, The. James Thomas Fields. BLPA; OBAL

Owl expires, The! Death gave the dreadful word. On the Death of a Lady's Owl. Moses Mendes. TrJP

Owl In Daytime, The. Thylias Moss. GT

Owl in the Oak, The. *Unknown.* OxNR

Owl in the Sarcophagus, The. Wallace Stevens. FaBoMo

Owl Is an Only Bird of Poetry, An. Robert Duncan. NeAP; PoM

Owl of the Greenwood. Patricia Hubbell. OTCP

Owl shall stoop from his turret, the rat cry out. (LL) Watercolor of Grantchester Meadows. Sylvia Plath. LCAP-2; NYBP

Owl shriek'd at thy birth, an evil sign, The. Shakespeare. OxAEP-1 *Fr.* King Henry VI, Pt. III.

Owl / Who? Owl of the Greenwood. Patricia Hubbell. OTCP

Owl / whose home was in the hemlock, The. *Unknown, Seneca Indian.* STP, *tr. by* Jerome Rothenberg *and* Richard Johnny John

Owl winks in the shadows, An. Mother Earth: Her Whales. Gary Snyder. LCAP-2

Owl Woman's Death Song. *Unknown, Papago.* BoWoP, *tr. by* Ruth Underhill

Owl Writes a Detective Story, The. Gavin Ewart. OBCoV

Owls. Charles Baudelaire, *French.* APo, *tr. by* Richard Howard

Owls. Louise Erdrich. TRP

Owls. Bob Merkel. CTV

Owls. W. D. Snodgrass. Poetsp

Owls have feathers lined with down, The. The Hedgehog and His Coat. Elizabeth Fleming. BoTP

Owls mimic human speech. Meng Chiao. SuSp, *tr. by* Stephen Owen *Fr.* Laments of the Gorges.

Owls roost like gray lamps up there, The. Brobdingnag. Adrien Stoutenburg. NYBP

Own. (LL) Offspring. Naomi Long Madgett. GT

Owned her father all the fact'ries. The Pariah. James Edwin Campbell. AAP

Owner of My Face, The. Rodney Hall. CBAP

Owners of the Little Box, The. Vasco [*or* Vasko] Popa, *Serbo-Croatian.* HSix, *tr. by* Charles Simic

Ownership. Lizette Woodworth Reese. MoAmPo

Ox, The. Russell Edson. RaBo

Ox, The. Mary Morison Webster. PeSA

Ox-Bow. Donald Davie. DiPo

Ox Cart Man. Donald Hall. FYAP; InPS-3; LCAP-2; LoL

Ox of my childhood, steaming. Far Away and Long Ago. "Rubén Dario," *Spanish.* PFTM, *tr. by* Denise Levertov

Ox-Soldier, The. Oumar Ba. PBMAP

Ox-Tamer, The. Walt Whitman. RB

Oxaitoq's Song. *Unknown, Eskimo.* APN-2, *tr. by* Franz Boas

Oxen, The. Thomas Hardy. APo; BoTP; CABP; CMoP; ChAP; EBEV; HAP; InPK-6; LiTM; MoBrPo; MoP; NOBE; NTP; NoAM; OAEL-2; OBCP; OxAEP-2; OxBTC; PChr; PeECV; Poetr; RB; SoSe-8; TFi; TOF; TRP; WeW-3

Oxen: Ploughing at Fiesole. Charles Tomlinson. OxBTC

Oxen that rattle the yoke and chain or halt in the leafy shade. Walt Whitman. *Fr.* The Drayman. *Fr.* Song of Myself. AmPP; MoAmPo; NAAL-3; NOBA; OxBA

Oxford. W. H. Auden. OxAEP-2

Oxford. Edward Dorn.

    Comforted by Limestone. NOBA

Oxford. Lionel Pigot Johnson. OBNC

Oxford Canal. James Elroy Flecker. OxBTC

Oxford Girl; or, Expert Town, The. *Unknown.* AmFP

Oxford Hysteria of English Poetry, The. Adrian Mitchell. PeLV

Oxford, since late I left thy peaceful shore. To Oxford. Thomas Russell. Son

Oxhead Temple. Ssu-k'ung Shu, *Chinese.* SuSp, *tr. by* Hellmut Wilhelm

Oxhide: While my ghost lives I go on feet. *Unknown.* EEP, *tr. by* Michael Alexander *Fr.* Riddles (Exeter Book).

Oxota: A Short Russian Novel. Lyn Hejinian.

    "No form at all—it's impossible to imagine its being." FTOS

Oxygen. Joan Swift. NYBP

Oye Mundo/Sometimes. Jesús Papoleto Meléndez. UnSA

Oye, oyeye. Battle Songs of the King Tshaka. *Unknown, Zulu.* PeSA

Oyster, The. Sir Walter Scott. FaBoCh; NTP *Fr.* The Antiquary.

Oyster-Crabs. Carolyn Wells. BXAP

Oyster: Deep sea suckled me, the waves sounded over me. Cynewulf. ASW, *tr. by* Kevin Crossley-Holland *Fr.* Riddles (Exeter Book).

Oyster-Eaters, The. John Blight. NOBAu

Oyster that went to bed x-million years ago, An. Goodnight. John Ciardi. OBAL

Oyster, the size of an average pebble, is of more rugged appearance, The. Francis Ponge, *French.* PFTM, *tr. by* Cid Corman

Oystercatchers. Christopher Middleton. FaBoTw

Oystering. Richard Howard. NoAM

Oysters. Seamus Heaney. UV

Ozymandias [of Egypt]. Shelley. APAD; AWP; CABP; CH; ChAP; ClHu; FaBoBe; FaBoCh; FaPoR; GSo; GTBS-P; HAP; HeIP-4; HoPM; ImPo; InPK-6; InPS-3; NAEL-2; NIP-4; NOBE; NoP-4; OAEL-2; OBNC; OPOU; PFE; PoE; PoLF; PoPoPo; PoRA; RB; Ro; SCGP; SCV; SoSe-8; Son; TFi; UV

("Lone and level sands stretch far away, The.") (LL) Ro

Ozymandias II. Howard Nemerov. Son

Ozymandias Revisited. Morris Gilbert Bishop. BXAP; NBLV; UV

P

P.C. Plod versus the Dale St. Dog Strangler. Roger McGough. MoP; OBSP

P. M. T. Dorothy Porter. BMAP

P.O.E. Lincoln Kirstein. PoWW

P.O.W.s. R. L. Barth. CDa

Pa, Pa, Build Me a Boat. *Unknown.* AmFP

Pachycephalosaurus. Richard Armour. ChAP

Pacific Epitaphs. Dudley Randall. MoP

Pacific Sonnets. George Barker.

    "And now there is nothing left to celebrate." LiTM

    "At midday they looked up and saw their death." ImPo; LiTM

    "From thorax of storms the voices of verbs." ImPo; LiTM

    Memorial for Two Young Seamen. ImPo

Pacifist, The. Hilaire Belloc. OBCoV

Pacifists. George Woodcock. NOBC

Pacing. Raymond Roseliep. HA

Pacing toward what I know. (LL) The Farm on the Great Plains. William Stafford. HAP; VGW

Pacing with bag-pipe in a bosky square. Caledonia. Anthony Powell. NOBL

Pack, The. Frank Prewett. HATNAP

Pack, clouds, away; and welcome, day[!]. Matin Song. Thomas Heywood. BoTP; CH; GBL; GTBS-P; OBEV *Fr.* The Rape of Lucrece.

Pack on our own back / that we don't see, The. Catullus. *See* To Varus.

Package for Another World. Jemal Sharah. NOBAu

Packages under her arm. Line. Cole Swenson. WWSi

Packed in my mind lie all the clothes. The Inward Morning. Henry David Thoreau. AmPP; PAR

Packed with woodpeckers, my head knocks. Raking Leaves. Robert Pack. NYBP

Packington's Pound. John Gay. *Fr.* The Beggar's Opera. OAEL-1

Pact. Kenneth Fearing. CMoP

Pact, A. Ezra Pound. AmPP; ColAP; MeMAP; MoP; NAAL-2; NOBA; NoAM; OxBA; TAP

Pact, The. P. S. Rege, *Marathi.* OMIP, *tr. by* Vinay Dharwadker

Pact that we made was the ordinary pact, The. From a Survivor. Adrienne Rich. LoL; NALW

Paddies lean against each other. Songbu Yi, *Korean.* CKP, *tr. by* Jaihiun Kim

Padding down the street, the. No Shoes No Shirt No Service. Gary Snyder. BB

Paddling Pool, The. E. M. Adams. BoTP

Paddling Song. *Unknown, Bantu.* PBA, *tr. by* Max Exner

Paddock's a lonely space to stay inside, The. The Gate's Open. John Blight. CBAP

Paddy Biran's Song. Paddy Biran, *Girramay.* CBAP, *tr. by* R. M. W. Dixon

Paddy, Get Back. *Unknown.* AmFP

Paddy, I have but stol'n your living. Ebenezer Elliot. FaBoEE

Padraic O'Conaire—Gaelic Storyteller. Frederick Robert Higgins. OBMV

Padraic's Point. Gabriel Gbadamosi. NBrP

Padre, The. Frank Ormsby. BiHa

Paean. Bacchylides, *Greek.*

    Peace. GrIP, *tr. by* Robert Fagles

Pæan of Bacchylides, On Peace, The. Bacchylides, *Greek.* OBCVT, *tr. by* Philip Ayres

Paean to Eve's Apple. James Liddy. CIP-2

Paean to Place. Lorine Niedecker. APSN; FTOS

    ("Fish / fowl.") FTOS

Pagan Isms, The. Claude McKay. BPo

Pagan's myths through marble lips are spoken, The. Worship. John Greenleaf Whittier. ChIV-2; NOCV

Pagans wild confesse the bonds, The. Roger Williams. SCAP

Page. Sandra McPherson. PoA

Page dramatically estranged, nor lacking, A. Casting Sequences. Marjorie Welish. FTOS

Page from a Diary. Desmond O'Grady. NoAM

Page from the New Diary, A. Nida Fazli, *Urdu*. OMIP, *tr. by* Baidar Bakht *and* Leslie Lavigne

Page is being beaten, A. Let's Say. Bob Perelman. PmAP

Page is printed, The. (LL) The Thought-Fox. Ted Hughes. FaBoMo; HeIP-4; InPS-3; MoP; NTP; NYBP; NoAM; NoP-4; Poetr; SCV

Page of Shelley, A. Rod Willmot. HA

Page opens to snow on a field: boot-holed month, black hour, The. Elegy. Carolyn Forché. LoL

Pageant of the Seasons and the Months, The. Edmund Spenser. OxAEP-1 *Fr.* Wood Of Error. AEP

Pageant Verses. Sir Thomas More. AAS

Pages of an Album. Dan Pagis, *Hebrew*. IP, *tr. by* Warren Bargad *and* Stanley F. Chyet

Pages of history open, The. Elegy. Sandra M. Gilbert. PoA

Pages of the album, The. Sonatina in Yellow. Donald Justice. ColAP; LCAP-2

Pages' Song, The. Shakespeare. *See* Song: "It was a lover and his lass."

Pagget, a schoolboy, got a sword, and then. Upon Pagget. Robert Herrick. CaPo; FaBoCh

Pagoda of Master Chih, The. Wang T'ing-hsiang. *Fr.* Miscellaneous Poems on Spirit-Valley Temple. CoBLCP, *tr. by* Jonathan Chaves

"Paid by my lord, one portrait, Lady Anne." Child with a Cockatoo. Rosemary Dobson. CBAP

Paid homage to them of unevent. (LL) A Love Story. Robert Graves. CMoP; FaBoTw; NAEL-2

Paid on Both Sides. W. H. Auden.

    Walking Tour, The. CMoP

    (Chorus: "To throw away the key and walk away.") MoBrPo

Pain. "Æ." MoBrPo

Pain. Mbella Sonne Dipoko. PBMAP

Pain. Elsie Robinson. PoToHe

Pain. Edith Södergran, *Swedish*. PBWP, *tr. by* Jaakko A. Ahokas; WPOW, *tr. by* Samuel Charters

Pain. Alfonsina Storni, *Spanish*. WPOW, *tr. by* Merrilee Antrim

Pain and labor of oppression gave the Western world its birth. The Pharaohs of Today. Lizelia Augusta Jenkins Moorer. CBWP-3

Pain—expands the Time. Emily Dickinson. APN-2

Pain for a Daughter. Anne Sexton. Poetr

Pain—has an Element of Blank. Emily Dickinson. APN-2; ColAP; HeIP-4; LiTM; MoAmPo; NAAL-1; NAAL-3; PAR

Pain—I'm pro it. First Chance Twice. Fanny Howe. FTOS

Pain is a blacksmith. Blacksmith Pain. Otto Julius Bierbaum, *German*. AWP, *tr. by* Jethro Bithell

Pain is something useless. A Private View. Dahlia Ravikovitch, *Hebrew*. IP, *tr. by* Warren Bargad *and* Stanley F. Chyet

Pain of loving you, The. A Young Wife. D. H. Lawrence. MoBrPo; PBMP

Pain penetrates. Sappho, *Greek*. OBCVT, *tr. by* Mary Barnard

Pain / so it turned black. Momcilo Nastasijevic, HSix, *sect.* 10, *tr. by* Charles Simic *Fr.* Deaf Things.

Pain was pulled down over his eyes like a fool's hat. A God. Ted Hughes. GI

Pain we have to suffer seems so broad, The. Belief. Ella Wheeler Wilcox. PWR

"Pain, who made thee?" thus I said once. James Henry. NOBVV

Painful husbandman with sweaty brows, The. The Husbandman. George Wither. NOSC *Fr.* A Collection of Emblemes, Ancient and Moderne.

Pains flip me around, The. Conception. Joseph Ceravolo. FTOS

Pains of insecurity surround me. Back Again, Home. Haki R. Madhubuti. BPo; NAAAL

Pains of Sleep, The. Coleridge. FHYEP; NAEL-2; ONBC; Ro

Paint Castlemaine in colours that will hold. Andrew Marvell. OBSV *Fr.* The Last Instructions to a Painter.

Paint-flaken, it is paint-flaken. March, Upstate. William Bronk. NYBP

Paint last the King, and a dead shade of night. Charles II. Andrew Marvell. OBSV *Fr.* The Last Instructions to a Painter.

Paint me a cavernous waste shore. Sweeney Erect. T. S. Eliot. OxBTC; VGW

Painted Ceiling, The. Amy Lowell. OBAL

Painted Cup, The. William Cullen Bryant. APN-1

Painted Cup, The. Michael Palmer. FTOS

Painted Head. John Crowe Ransom. FuPo; LiTM; MeMAP; NOBA; NoAM; OxBA

    (Painting: A Head.) MoAmPo

Painted Lady, The. Margaret Danner. BPo

Painted with fancies of malignant power! (LL) Trembling I write my dream, and recollect. Philip Freneau. NAAL-1; NAAL-3

Painter, The. John Ashbery. HCAP; NOBA; NoP-4; PoE; PoPoPo

Painter, A. Thomas Cole. APN-1

Painter. Zbigniew Herbert, *Polish*. AF, *tr. by* John Carpenter *and* Bogdana Carpenter

Painter and poet, runner and disk-thrower. One of the Jews. Constantine P. Cavafy, *Greek*. TrJP

Painter, by unmatch'd desert. The Picture. Anacreon, *Greek*. AWP; GrIP, *tr. by* Thomas Stanley

Painter, encumbered with cash, A. Limerick. Thomas Thorneley. PeLi

Painter in the Lion Cage, The. Betti Alver, *Estonian*. BoWoP, *tr. by* Willis Barnstone *and* Felix Oinas

Painter of Dante's awful ferry-ride, The. The Poem. Babette Deutsch. PoA

Painter Paints, The. Natan Zach, *Hebrew*. IP, *tr. by* Warren Bargad *and* Stanley F. Chyet

Painters, The. Judith Hemschemeyer. Poetsp

Painter's Daughter, The. Carol Muske. MoLi

Painting ("Jade cave, ten thousand flowering peach trees, A"). Chang Yü, *Chinese*. CoBLCP, *tr. by* Jonathan Chaves

Painting: A Head. John Crowe Ransom. MoAmPo *See* Painted Head.

Painting a picture of the same shrimp boat. Discovering Your Subject. Pattiann Rogers. MT

Painting a Picture, The Tranquil Boat—Sent to Ko Ju-ching. Wen Cheng-ming, *Chinese*. CoBLCP, *tr. by* Jonathan Chaves

Painting Bamboo, a Song. Po Chü-i, *Chinese*. SuSp, *tr. by* Irving Lo

Painting Drunken Twilight. George Barlow. GT

Painting / (Frida Kahlo). Elizabeth Alexander. GT

Painting Her Nails. Yang Wei-chen, *Chinese*. CoBLCP, *tr. by* Jonathan Chaves

Painting in the Style of Secretary Kao, A. Yün Shou-p'ing, *Chinese*. CoBLCP, *tr. by* Jonathan Chaves

Painting, "Mist and Rain on the Spring River," by Hsiao Chao, The. Tai Piao-yüan, *Chinese*. CoBLCP, *tr. by* Jonathan Chaves

Painting Mount Taranaki. David Eggleton. PeNZ

Painting my age with beauty of thy days. (LL) Sonnet 62. Shakespeare. EBEV; OxAEP-1; PoEL-2

Painting of Bamboo by Ni Yün-lin, A. Yang Chi, *Chinese*. CoBLCP, *tr. by* Jonathan Chaves

Painting of Chrysanthemums in the Boneless Style of Hsü Ch'ung-ssu, A. Yün Shou-p'ing, *Chinese*. CoBLCP, *tr. by* Jonathan Chaves

Painting of My Father. Padraic Fallon. NOIV

Painting of One Hundred Wild Geese, A. Tai Piao-yüan, *Chinese*. CoBLCP, *tr. by* Jonathan Chaves

Painting of Peach Blossom Spring, A. Shen Chou, *Chinese*. CoBLCP, *tr. by* Jonathan Chaves

Painting of People Strolling through a Pine Forest, A. Hsü Wei, *Chinese*. CoBLCP, *tr. by* Jonathan Chaves

Painting of the Butterfly Dream by the Master Artist Li Tsai, A. Chu Yün-ming, *Chinese*. ChiPo; CoBLCP, *tr. by* Jonathan Chaves

Painting of Water Buffaloes, A. Yang Shih-ch'i, *Chinese*.

    "Herdboy returns, none too early, The." CoBLCP, *tr. by* Jonathan Chaves

Painting of Yams, A. Yün Shou-p'ing, *Chinese*. CoBLCP, *tr. by* Jonathan Chaves

Painting ("Slowly I walk the gully path, alone"). Chang Yü. *Fr.* Twelve Miscellaneous Poems on the Fang Garden. CoBLCP, *tr. by* Jonathan Chaves

Painting "Solitary Fisherman by a Spring River" The. Ni Tsan, *Chinese*. CoBLCP, *tr. by* Jonathan Chaves

Painting the Eaves. Tony Towle. PmAP

Painting the Gate. May Swenson. TLR; WeW-3

Painting with a knife the Invader. Iain Sinclair. NBrP

Painting would have been the best way to get things over, A. In Memoriam. Martin Johnston. BMAP; NOBAu

Paintings. Chang Yü, *Chinese*. CoBLCP, *tr. by* Jonathan Chaves

Paintings. Pien Kung, *Chinese*. CoBLCP, *tr. by* Jonathan Chaves

Paintings of Fishermen. Wu Chen, *Chinese*. CoBLCP, *tr. by* Jonathan Chaves

Paintings of Ladies Engaged in Four Springtime Occupations. Yang Chi, *Chinese*.

    Springtime Embroidery. CoBLCP, *tr. by* Jonathan Chaves

Paintings of Various Subjects by Fang Jih-sheng: Baby Chicks Following Their Mother. Pien Kung, *Chinese*. CoBLCP, *tr. by* Jonathan Chaves

Paintings on My Wall Have Been Damaged by the Weather, The. T'ang Hsien-tsu, *Chinese*. CoBLCP, *tr. by* Jonathan Chaves

Paintings with stiff. Primitives. Dudley Randall. BPo; NBV

Painture [*or* Peinture]. Richard Lovelace. CaPo

Pair of blackbirds, A. In Modern Dress. Craig Raine. NoAM

Pair of brothers love me, A. Strato, *Greek*. GrAn, *tr. by* Teddy Hogge

Pair of Glasses, A. Savithri Rajeevan, *Malayalam*. OMIP, *tr. by* K. Ayyappa Paniker *and* Arlene Zide

Pair of golden orioles, A. Far Up the River. Tu Fu, *Chinese.* OHPC, *tr. by* Kenneth Rexroth

Pair of green-painted eyebrows, A. Wang Chien. SuSp, *tr. by* William H. Nienhauser *Fr.* Palace Poems.

Pair of Shoes, A. Theodore Weiss. NoAM

Pair of soft, black eyes, A. A Home Greeting. Priscilla Jane Thompson. CBWP-2

Pair of strange new birds in the maple tree, A. "Never Apologize; Never Explain." Philip Whalen. BB

Pair-Royal of Coxcombs, The. "Ephelia."

    Prologue: "Gallants, / If, as you say, you Love Varietie." KTR

Paired Lives. William Robert Rodgers. CIP-2; IIP

Paisleys squirm with spermatozoa. Neckties. Liz Lochhead. OBCoV

Paiute Ponies. Jim Barnes. CDW

Pajamas. Sharon Olds. NMM-2

Pajaro the men thigh deep in mud. Song of Pajaro. Jeff Tagami. OpBo

Pal, in the Pals of Death Club. This Is a Poem for the Fathers and for Michael Ryan. Thomas Lux. AmPA

Palabras Grandiosas. Bayard Taylor. OBAL

Palace, The. Charles Stuart Calverley. EBVV

Palace at dusk, the pearl blind is lowered. Jade Steps Plaint. Hsieh T'iao, *Chinese,* SuSp, *tr. by* Ronald C. Miao

Palace-Burner, The. Sarah Morgan Bryan Piatt. NCAP

Palace Cook's Tale. Joan Aiken. NOxBChV

Palace girls up early. Wang Chien. SuSp, *tr. by* William H. Nienhauser *Fr.* Palace Poems.

Palace great is builded rich and round. Torquato Tasso. NoSic, *tr. by* Edward Fairfax *Fr.* Godfrey of Bulloigne; or, The Recoverie of Jerusalem.

Palace of Art, The. Tennyson. EnVR; NOBRP

    "One seem'd all dark and red--a tract of sand." UnPo

Palace [*or* Palice] of Honor [*or* Honour], The. Gawin Douglas.

    Nightmare. PoEL-1

Palace of humbug, The. "Lewis Carroll." CBNP

Palace of Pleasant Regard, The. The Lady of the Assembly. WPE *Fr.* The Assembly of Ladies.

Palace of Prince Ma—Now It Is a Buddhist Temple, The. Yang Shih-ch'i. *Fr.* Three Poems on Ch'ang-sha. CoBLCP, *tr. by* Jonathan Chaves

Palace of Rocks, The. Yüan Chieh, *Chinese.* SuSp, *tr. by* William H. Nienhauser

Palace of the Gnomes. Maria Gowen Brooks. APN-1 *Fr.* Zophiël [or, the Bride of Seven].

Palace Poem. Chu Ch'ing-yü, *Chinese.* SuSp, *tr. by* Irving Y. Lo

Palace Poem. Wang Ya, *Chinese.* SuSp, *tr. by* Irving Y. Lo

Palace Poems. Wang Chien, *Chinese.*

    "At home I loved to wear old clothes." SuSp, *tr. by* William H. Nienhauser

    "Early autumn, white rabbits." SuSp, *tr. by* William H. Nienhauser

    "Her silken gown rustles." SuSp, *tr. by* William H. Nienhauser

    "Long the flimsy skirts." SuSp, *tr. by* William H. Nienhauser

    "Pair of green-painted eyebrows, A." SuSp, *tr. by* William H. Nienhauser

    "Palace girls up early." SuSp, *tr. by* William H. Nienhauser

    "Red lantern calls the spring clouds from my sleep, A." SuSp, *tr. by* William H. Nienhauser

    "Spring breeze blows the rain, A." SuSp, *tr. by* William H. Nienhauser

    "Wanting to welcome the emperor." SuSp, *tr. by* William H. Nienhauser

Palace Song. Wang Chien, *Chinese.* CoBCP, *tr. by* Burton Watson

Palace with revolving doors was mine, The. Atameros. John Beevers. SPE

Palais des Arts. Louise Glück. VCAP

Palanquin, The. Charles Marie René Leconte de Lisle, *French.* FLP; LoP, *tr. by* Alistair Elliot

Palaver is finished, The. (LL) Cape Ann. T. S. Eliot. NAEL-2; NoAM

Palaver is silly. (LL) Air: Sentir avec Ardeur. Marie-Françoise-Catherine de, Marquise de Boufflers Beauveau, *French.* CTC; WPOW, *tr. by* Ezra Pound

Pale amber sunlight falls across. Autumnal. Ernest Christopher Dowson. EBVV; OBNC

Pale Ant. Elleasse Southerland. GT

Pale beech and pine-tree blue. In a Wood. Thomas Hardy. OBNC

Pale blossoms, each balanced on a single jointed stem. Carnations. Theodore Roethke. BLT

Pale Blue Casket, The. Oliver Pitcher. PoBA; TTY

Pale brows, still hands and dim hair. The Lover Mourns for the Loss of Love. W. B. Yeats. WeW-3

Pale clouds, away! and welcome, day! Thomas Heywood. *See* Matin Song.

Pale darts still quivering, crocuses. Poem at Equinox. Hilary Corke. NYBP

Pale dawn moon, A. Lorraine Ellis Harr. HA

Pale, drooping girl and the swaggering soldier, The. Just an Old Sweet Song. Donagh MacDonagh. CIP-2

Pale Ebenezer thought it wrong to fight. The Pacifist. Hilaire Belloc. OBCoV

Pale gaslight hangs in the empty sky, The. Gaslight. Kwanggun Kim, *Korean.* CKP, *tr. by* Jaihiun Kim

Pale gold of the walls, gold. Gold. Donald Hall. CoAmPo; SAGP

Pale grey, her guns hooded, decks clear of all impediment. H. M. S. *Hero.* Michael Roberts. OxBTC

Pale hands I love beside the Shalimar. Kashmiri Song. "Laurence Hope." BLPA; FaBoBe

Pale Heinrich he came sauntering by. The Window-Glance. Heinrich Heine, *German.* AWP, *tr. by* John Todhunter

Pale nuns of St. Joseph are here, The. Island of the Three Marias. Alberto A. Ríos. NoAM

Pale ocean rock! that, like a phantom shape. Rockall. E. Sargent. APN-1

Pale ravener of horrible meat. (LL) The Maldive Shark. Herman Melville. APN-2; APo; AmPP; ColAP; GEA; NAAL-1; NAAL-3; NCAP; NOBA; NoP-4; OxBA; PAR; PFE; PoE; PoEL-5; RB; TAP

Pale, struggling blossoms of mankind. Our Father. Eliza Cook. VWP

Pale water carriers in the land's dawn / Before the fall. (LL) After the Fall. Gloria Escoffery. HCP; PBCV

Pale water flowers. Coralie. Frederick Goddard Tuckerman. NCAP

Paleness of hunger, The. The Mutineer's Ballad. Peter Kocan. NOBAu

Palette of Grief. Leonid Gubanov, *Russian.* TCRP, *tr. by* Bradley Jordan

Palimpsest, A. "Michael Field." VWP

Palindrome. Lisel Mueller. WeW-3

Palinode, A. Edmund Bolton. NoSic; PoEL-2

Palinode. "Ern Malley." BMAP

Palinode. Oliver St. John Gogarty. OBMV

Palinode, A. Robert Greene. *Fr.* Greene's Groatsworth of Wit.

Palinodia. Winthrop Mackworth Praed. CBLP

Palladium. Matthew Arnold. GTBS-P; OAEL-2; OBNC

Pallas and / golden-shoed Hera. Rufinus, *Greek.* GrAn, *tr. by* Alan Marshfield

Pallid and moonlike in the smog. A Man Can Complain, Can't He? Ogden Nash. NBLV

Pallid Cuckoo. David Campbell. CBAP

Pallid cuckoo, The. Late Winter. James McAuley. BMAP

Pallid, mis-shapen he stands. The World's grimed thumb. In the Dock. Walter De la Mare. LiTM

Pallid young man with an ardent expression. To a Young Poet. Valery Yakovlevich Bryusov, *Russian.* TCRP, *tr. by* April FitzLyon

Pallor. Agnes Mary Frances Robinson. NOBVV; VWP

Palm, The. Roy Campbell. MoBrPo

Palm at the end of the mind, The. Of Mere Being. Wallace Stevens. HCAP; NoP-4

Palm Leaf of Mary Magdalene. Cheryl Clarke. GLP

Palm of the hand, A. Fumi Saito. *See* Tanka: "Palm of the hand, The, / is not aware of dying."

Palm of the hand, The, / is not aware of dying. Tanka. Fumi Saito, *Japanese.* BoWoP, *tr. by* Edith Marcombe Shiffert *and* Yuki Sawa

Palm Reader, The. Nicholas Christopher. NoP-4

Palm Sunday. Theodore Wratislaw. ADE

Palm Sunday: Naples. Arthur Symons. PeVV

Palm the head just so. Then. How It's Done. Alvin Aubert. MT

Palm Tree, The. Abd-ar-Rahman I, *Arabic.* AWP, *tr. by* J. B. Trend

Palm-tree, The. Henry Vaughan. ESCV

Palm-Tree, The. John Greenleaf Whittier. NCAP

Palm trees against the sky. A Small War. Ory Bernstein. *Fr.* Poems from Mexico. IP, *tr. by* Warren Bargad *and* Stanley F. Chyet

Palmer's Ode, The. Robert Greene. CTC; SCGP *Fr.* Never Too Late.

    (Palmer, The.) NoSic

Palms, The. David Knight. MoCV

Palms and Myrtles. Eleazar ben Kalir, *Hebrew.* TrJP, *tr. by* Alice Lucas

Palmstroem in Animal Costume. Christian Morgenstern, *German.* CBNP, *tr. by* Hugh Haughton

Palmstroem loves to ape the animals. Palmstroem in Animal Costume. Christian Morgenstern, *German.* CBNP, *tr. by* Hugh Haughton

Palo Alto. Robert Hass. PaTW

Palpitating snake, A. Keats. OxBSn

Palsy shakes my pen, while I intend, A. To His Honored Friend Thomas Stanley Esquire, Upon His Elegant Poems. James Shirley. BeJo

Paltry Nude Starts on a Spring Voyage, The. Wallace Stevens. HCAP

Pampered Philainion stabbed me, The. Asclepiades, *Greek.* GrAn, *tr. by* Alan Marshfield

Pampered steed, of swiftness proud. The. The Horse and the Mule. John Huddlestone Wynne. OxBChV

Pamphilia to Amphilanthus, *sometimes appended to* Urania. Mary Sidney Wroth.

From Pamphilia to Amphilanthus. NoP-4

Song: "I, that ame of all most crost." KTR

Song: "Love a child is ever criing [*or* crying]." KTR; LW; NOSC; NoP-4

("Nor seek him so given to flying.") (LL) LW; NoP-4

Song: "O[h] me[e], the time is [*or* has] come to part." NOSC

Song 2: "All night I weep[e], all day I cry, Ay me[e]." NOSC

Sonnet 1: "When night's [*or* nights] black mantle could most darkness prove." CABP; Son

("Yet since, (O me!), a lover have I been.") (LL) CABP

Sonnet 2: "Late in the Forest I did Cupid See." KTR

("Burning my heart who had him kindly warmed.") (LL) LW

(Cupid Lost.) LW

Sonnet 6: "My pain[e], still smothered [*or* smother'd] in my grievèd bre[a]st." NOSC

(Sonnet 68.) PEW

("Yet faith still cries, Love will not falsify.") (LL) PEW

Sonnet 6: "Ô[h] strive not[t] still to heap[e] disdain[e] on me[e]." NOSC

Sonnet 7: "Love leave to urge, thou know'st thou hast the hand." Son

Sonnet 9: "Led by the powre of griefe, to waylings brought." PEW

Sonnet 9: "Be[e] you all pleased [*or* pleas'd]? your pleasures grieve not[t] me[e]." BWW; NOSC

Sonnet 14: "Am I thus conquered [*or* conquer'd]? have I lost the powers." CABP; NAEL-1; NOSC

("I love, and must; so farewell liberty.") (LL) CABP

Sonnet 19: "Come darkest night, be[e]coming sorrow best." NOSC

Sonnet 22: "Like to the Indians, scorched with the sun[ne]." NOSC

Sonnet 23: "When every one to pleasing pastime hies." WPE

("Or musique bee butt in deere thoughts of love?") (LL) PBRV

Sonnet 24: "When last I saw thee, I did not[t] thee see." PEW

Sonnet 26: "Deare cherish this, and with it[t] my soules with." BWW

Sonnet 27: "Fie [*or* Fy] tedious Hope, why do[e] you still rebel[l]?" NOSC

Sonnet 28: "Griefe, killing griefe: have nott my torments binn." KTR

Sonnet 29: "Fly hence O! joy noe longer heere abide." KTR

Sonnet 30: "You blessed shades, which give mee silent rest." KTR

Sonnet 31: "After long trouble in a taedious way." KTR

Sonnet 32: "How fast thou fliest, O Time, on loves swift wings." NOSC

Sonnet 35: "False [*or* Faulce] hope which feeds but[t] to destroy, and spill." KTR; NAEL-1

("Of our desires, the farther down to slide.") (LL) PEW

(Sonnet 40.) PEW

Sonnet 39: "Take heed mine eyes, how you your lookes doe cast." PEW

Sonnet 42: "If ever love had force in huma[i]ne brest?" BWW

Sonnet 48: "How like a fire doth love increase in me[e]." NOSC

Sonnet 101: "No time, noe roome, noe thought, or writing can." PEW

Pan and the Cherries. Paul Fort, *French.* AWP, *tr. by* Jethro Bithell

Pan and the Nymphs. Glaukos, *Greek.* GrAn, *tr. by* Dudley Fitts

Pan as the Son of Penelope. Joanne Kyger. BB

Pan Asks about Daphnis. Diodorus Zonas, *Greek.* GrAn, *tr. by* Alistair Elliot

Pan came out of the woods one day. Pan with Us. Robert Frost. OxBA

Pan Cogito on Virtue. Zbigniew Herbert, *Polish.* PoSu, *tr. by* Adam Czerniawski

Pan Cogito's Thoughts on Hell. Zbigniew Herbert, *Polish.* FaBoPV, *tr. by* Adam Czerniawski

Pan, Echo, and the Satyr. Moschus, *Greek.* OBVE, *tr. by* Shelley

Pan in Battle. *Unknown.* PeNZ

Pan loved his neighbour Echo—but that child. Pan, Echo, and the Satyr. Moschus, *Greek.* OBVE, *tr. by* Shelley

Pan Piping. Plato, *Greek.* FaBoEE, *tr. by* Thomas Stanley

Pan Recipe. John Agard. HCP; PBCV

Pan with Us. Robert Frost. OxBA

Pancake, The. Christina Rossetti. *See* Mix a Pancake.

Pancake Collector, The. Jack Prelutsky. OBCA

Pancake Day. Mother Goose. ReMoGo

Pancakes for the Queen of Babylon. Peter Levi.

"City built in darkness and cold air, A." CRP

Panchatantra, The. *Unknown, Sanskrit.* AWP, *tr. by* Arthur Ryder

Panda has a sixth digit we call, The. Theories of Illusion. Maureen Seaton. PUP-20

Pandora and the Moon. Merrill Moore. MoAmPo

Pandora Speaks. William Vaughn Moody. *Fr.* The Fire-Bringer.

Pandora's Songs. Trumbull Stickney. APN-2 *Fr.* Prometheus Pyrphoros.

Pandosto. Robert Greene.

Fawnia. OBEV

(In Praise of His Loving and Best-beloved Fawnia.) PoEL-2

Panegyric to Sir Lewis Pemberton, A. Robert Herrick. CaPo

Panes of light cracking. A Wet Night. Richard Ryan. CIP-2

Pang of the long century of rains, The. The Lament of Edward Blastock. Dame Edith Sitwell. OBMV

Pangloss's Song: A Comic-Opera Lyric. Richard Wilbur. MoP; NBLV; NoAM

Pangolin, The. Marianne Moore. HAP; NOBA; NoAM; PBWP; Poetr

Pangur Bán. *Unknown, Gaelic.* FaBoCh; NOIV; RB, *tr. by* Robin Flower

Panic. Archibald MacLeish. MoAmPo

Panic Grass. Charles Upton.

"When I was very young." CLPP

Panic in your face, you write questions. My Daughter at 14: Christmas Dance, 1981. Maria Gillan. IFJA

Panmongolism! The word's barbaric. Vladimir Sergeievich Solovyov, *Russian.* TCRP, *tr. by* April FitzLyon

Pannyra of the Golden Heel. Albert Samain, *French.* AWP, *tr. by* James Elroy Flecker

Panope. Dame Edith Sitwell. MoBrPo

Panopticon. Steve McCaffery.

"Homines qouque si taceant, vocem invenient libri." FTOS

Pans at Carnival. Henry Beissel. PBCV

Pan's Song. John Lyly. OxAEP-1 *Fr.* Midas.

(Syrinx.) CBLP

Pan's/ spring rain. Symphony No. 3, in D Minor. Jonathan Williams. VGW *Fr.* Mahler.

Pan's Syrinx was a girl[e] indeed. Pan's Song. John Lyly. CBLP; NoSic; OxAEP-1; SCGP *Fr.* Midas.

Pansy who lived in Khartoum, A. Limerick. *Unknown.* PeLi

Pantheist's Song of Immortality, The. Constance Naden. VWP

Panther. Sam Cornish. PoBA

Panther. The. Rilke, *German.* PFE, *tr. by* Peter J. Seng; APo; PiM, *tr. by* Stephen Mitchell

("And ceases, in his heart, to be.") (LL) PFE, *tr. by* Peter J. Seng

("His vision from the passing by of bars.") PFE, *tr. by* Peter J. Seng

Panther, The. *Unknown, Anglo-Saxon.* ASW, *tr. by* Kevin Crossley-Holland

Panther and Peacock. Gwen Harwood. CBAP

Panther is like a leopard, The. Ogden Nash. OBAL; OBCA

Panther, knowing that his spotted hide, The. Sonnet 53. Edmund Spenser. *Fr.* Amoretti. AAS

Panther lies next to Wharncliffe. Appalachian Front. Robert Lewis Weeks. NYBP

Panther Man. James A. Emanuel. BPo; NBV

Panties on the clothesline lingering mist. George Swede. HA

Pantomime. Paul Verlaine, *French.* AWP, *tr. by* Arthur Symons

Pantry Ghosts, The. Frederic Richardson. FPC

Pants. Lisa Vice. GLP

Pants blown off his seat, The. (LL) Jubilation T. Cornpone. Johnny Mercer. OBAL; OBCoV

Papa above! Emily Dickinson. AmPP

Papa called her Pearl when he came home. Taking in Wash. Rita Dove. MoLi

Papa drank and ate. Ironing. Nellie Wong. FFC

Papa John. Jorge de Lima, *Portuguese.* TTY, *tr. by* John Nist

Papa Love Baby. Stevie Smith. NALW

Papa's Letter. *Unknown.* WeW-3

Paper Anarchist Addresses the Shade of Nancy Ling Perry. George Woodcock. NOBC

Paper Anniversary. Muriel Rukeyser. NoAM

Paper Clip, Historian, Coathanger. Frank Murphy. EC3

Paper come out—done strewed de news. Scottsboro. *Unknown.* APAD; InPK-6

Paper gardens are perhaps richer in memories than, The. The Accessories shop. Pierre McOrlan, *French.* MFP, *tr. by* Martin Sorrell

Paper is neither kind nor cruel. Paperweight. Audre Lorde. Poetr

Paper Kite, The. Samuel Bowden.

"Kite, completed thus, is borne along, The." NOEC

Paper Matches. Paulette Jiles. IFJA; NIP-4; NOBC

Paper Memorial Stone. Sang Yi, *Korean.* PFTM, *tr. by* Walter Lew

Paper Nautilus, The. Marianne Moore. FaBoWP; NALW; VGW

Paper of Pins. *Unknown.* AmFP

("O miss, I'll give you a paper of pins.") TLR

Paper on Humor. Andrei Codrescu. PmAP

Paper Soldier. Bulat Shalvovich Okudzhava, *Russian.* TCRP, *tr. by* Albert C. Todd

Paper tigers roar at noon, The. Tiger. Alec Derwent Hope, *Russian.* OxBC; RB

Papermill Graveyard. Ben Belitt. NYBP
Papers have been sold. In them it's all made clear, The. German Borisovich Plisetsky, *Russian*. TCRP, *tr. by* Lubov Yakovleva
Papers in order; your face. The Journey. Maxine W. Kumin. MDDM
Paperweight. Audre Lorde. Poetr
Paperweight, The. Gjertrud Schnackenberg. VCAP
Paphnutius. Hroswitha von Gandersheim, *Latin*.
  "I bring you a goat." WPOW, *tr. by* Patrick Diehl
Paphos. Lawrence Durrell. NYBP
Pap's got his patent right, and rich as all creation. Back to Griggsby's Station. James Whitcomb Riley. BLPA
Papyrus. Ezra Pound. PFTM
Par avion. Aerogrammes. Russell Leong. OpBo
Para un Revolucionario. Lorna Dee Cervantes. Poetr
Parable, A. Ch'en Tzu-lung, *Chinese*. SuSp, *tr. by* Irving Y. Lo
Parable, A. Li K'ai-hsien, *Chinese*. CoBLCP, *tr. by* Jonathan Chaves
Parable. Bob Orr. PeNZ
Parable, A. Gregory Orr. WeT
Parable. Richard Wilbur. OxBSP
Parable of the Blind, The. William Carlos Williams. LCAP-2; SAmP *Fr.* Pictures from Brueghel.
  ("Follows the others stick in / hand triumphant to disaster.") (LL) GI
  ("In a red winter hat blue.") GI
  ("Pictures from Brueghel.") GI
Parable of the Four-Poster. Erica Jong. LW
Parable of the Good Seed, The. Bible, *N.T.* InPK-6 *Fr.* St. Matthew.
Parable of the Old Man and the Young, The. Wilfred Owen. ChIV-1
  (Parable of the Old Men and the Young, The.) PoFWW
Parable of the Sower, The. Stephen Mitchell. GI
Parables, I. Antonio Machado Ruiz, *Spanish*. STV, *tr. by* John Frederick Nims
Parabola. Alec Derwent Hope. NOBAu; PoA
Parabolas of grief, the hills are never. In Africa. Roy Fuller. PoWW
Paracelsus. Robert Browning.
  Song: "Heap cassia, sandal-buds and stripes." OBEV
  Thus the Mayne Glideth. OBEV
  Wanderers, The. OBEV
Paracelsus. Diane Di Prima. PT
Parachute Men say. Lenrie Peters. PBMAP
Parachutes, My Love, Could Carry Us Higher. Barbara Guest. NeAP
Parachuting Thoor Ballylee. William Zaranka. BXAP
Parachutist, The. Jon Anderson. AmPA; NYBP
Parachutist. Dylan Thomas.
  "I shall never forget his blue eye." UV
Parachutist's Wife, The. Sandra M. Gilbert. LoHo
Parade. Rachel Lyman Field. OBCA *Fr.* A Circus Garland.
Parade. Langston Hughes. PFTM
Parade, A. Perunkunrūr Kilr, *Tamil*. PLW, *tr. by* A. K. Ramanujan
Parade's End. Barbara Guest. PoM
Paradice on earth is found, A. Michael Prayton. PBRV *Fr.* The Muses Elizium.
Paradigm. Babette Deutsch. TrJP
Paradigm, The. Allen Tate. NOBA
Paradigm of a Hero. Jack Matthews. CMAP
Paradigms of Fire. Brian Swann. AmPA
Paradise ("Another side, umbrageous Grots and Caves"). Milton. *Fr.* Book IV. OAEL-1 *Fr.* Paradise Lost.
Paradise. Brian Chan. HCP
Paradise. Peter Damian, *Latin*. MLL, *tr. by* Helen Waddell
Paradise. Louise Glück. NAmP90
Paradise. George Herbert. GaP; GeHe; ImPo; NOSC; OAEL-1; SeCP
Paradise ("His fair large front and eye sublime declared"). Milton. *Fr.* Book IV. OAEL-1 *Fr.* Paradise Lost.
Paradise. Immanuel di Roma, *Hebrew*. TrJP, *tr. by* J. Chotzner
Paradise ("In narrow room nature's whole wealth, yea more"). Milton. NOSC *Fr.* Book IV. OAEL-1 *Fr.* Paradise Lost.
Paradise. Lu'u Văn Vong, *Vietnamese*. AVP, *tr. by* Huỳnh Sanh Thông
Paradise. Elizabeth Nancy Sargent. NYBP
Paradise. Ron Silliman.
  "Sentence in the evening. Today the boxscores are green. Tonight, A." PmAP
Paradise and Hell. Võ Liêm So'n, *Vietnamese*. AVP, *tr. by* Huỳnh Sanh Thông
Paradise I planted see / On open Calvary, A. Joseph Beaumont. *See* The Garden's quit with me: as yesterday.
Paradise Illustrated. D. J. Enright.
  "Days of Adam were 930 years, The." OBCoV

  "'Rich soil,' remarked the Landlord." OBCoV
  "Why didn't we think of clothes before?" OBCoV
Paradise Lost. Milton.
  "Behold alone / The Woman, opportune to all attempts." OxBoV
  Book I. FHYEP; NAEL-1; OAEL-1; OxAEP-1
    Council of Satan, The. PoEL-3
    "If thou beest he; but O how fall'n! how chang'd." SCV
    Immortal Hate. NOBE
    Invocation. NOSC; PoEL-3, *ll.* 1–26
    (Induction, The.) PoE, *ll.* 1–26
    Mulciber. NOSC
    "Next came one / Who mourn'd in earnest, when the Captive Ark." EBEV
    Satan's Summons. NOSC
  Book II. FHYEP; NAEL-1; OxAEP-1
    Hell ("At once with him they rose").
    "High on a throne of royal state, which far." OAEL-1, *ll.* 1–309; NIP-4, *ll.* 1–42
    Occupations of Hell. NOSC
    Satan's Journey. NOSC
    Sin and Death. OBNV, *ll.* 629–889
    "Stygian council thus dissolved; and forth, The." OAEL-1
    "Thus Belial with words clothed in reason's garb." FaBoPV
    "Thus saying, from her side the fatal Key." EBEV
  Book IV. OAEL-1
    Eden. GaP
    (Paradise Lost.) OBGa
    ("Southward through Eden went a river large.") GaP
    Evening in Paradise. NOBE, *ll.* 598–656
    "Fiend / Saw undelighted all delight, all kind, The." FaBoPV
    "Into thir inmost bower." TOF, *ll.* 738–775
    "Me miserable! which way shall I fly." PoE
    Paradise ("In narrow room nature's whole wealth, yea more"). NOSC
    Prospect of Eden, The. PoEL-3, *ll.* 1–775
    "Thus talking hand in hand alone they pass'd." EBEV
  Tenants of Paradise. APo
    "Two of far nobler shape erect and tall." PeECV, *ll.* 288–299
    Unfallen Love. NOSC
    "While thus he spake, th'Angelic Squadron bright." SCV
  Book IX. FHYEP; NAEL-1; NAWM-1; OAEL-1
    ("And of their vain contèst appeared no end.") (LL) NoP-4
    ("No more of talk where God or angel guest.") NoP-4
    Adam and Eve in the Garden. ITG, *tr. by* Robert Hass
    ("Both turned, and under open sky adored.") ITG, *tr. by* Robert Hass
    "As when of old some orator renowed." ChIV-1
    Fall, The. PoEL-3
    "Her long with ardent look his Eye pursu'd." UnPo
    Higher Argument. NOSC
    "How shall I behold the face." TOF
    Temptation of Eve, The. EBNV
    Tempter Disarmed, The. NOSC
    Uncloistered Virtue. NOSC
    "What words have passed thy lips, Adam severe." TrCP
  Book X. FHYEP
    "Be it so, for I submit; his doom is fair." NAWM-1
    "Other way Satan went down, Th'." NAEL-1
    "Such was thir song." PeECV
    "Thus Adam himself lamented loud." OAEL-1
    "Thus began / Outrage from lifeless things; but Discord first." NAEL-1
    Eve tempts Adam. FaBoSe
    "Not distant far from thence a murmuring sound." OBCVT
    Satan tempts Eve. FaBoSe
    "With these came they who, from the bord'ring flood." OxBSn
Paradise Lost as a Haiku. Stanley J. Sharpless. BXAP; OBCoV
Paradise Lost, Book IV, lines 639—654. Leslie Johnson. UV
Paradise Lost, Book V: An Epitome. Anthony Hecht. NBLV
Paradise on earth is found, A. The Description of Elizium. Michael Drayton. OAEL-1 *Fr.* Muses' Elysium [*or* Elizium].
Paradise on earth— that's the city of Suchou! The Scene at Heaven Gate. T'ang Yin, *Chinese*. CoBLCP, *tr. by* Jonathan Chaves
Paradise Re-entered. D. H. Lawrence. ChIV-2
Paradise Regain'd. Martial, *Latin*.
  "Thence to the gates cast round thine eye, and see." OBCVT, *tr. by* John Milton
Paradise reserved for me, A. (LL) Meditations on the Sepulchre in the Garden. Philip Doddridge. NOCV; NOEC; OBGa

Paradise Saved. Alec Derwent Hope. OxBC

Paradox, The. Donne. NOSC

Paradox, The. Paul Laurence Dunbar. AAP; PoBA

Paradox, The. Francesca Yetunde Pereira. PBA

Paradox, A. Aurelian Townshend. SeCP

Paradox. Anna Wickham. LW

Paradox of Time, The. Pierre de Ronsard, *French.* AWP, tr. by Austin Dobson

Paradoxes and Oxymorons. John Ashbery. FTOS; HeIP-4; NoAM; PmAP; PoPoPo; Poetr; SAGP

Paragon of Animals, The. Alexander Pope. *Fr.* An Essay on Man. *See* Know Thyself.

Paraguay. Carl Rakosi. FTOS

Parallax. Maxwell Anderson. NYBP

Paralytic. Sylvia Plath. FaBoWP

Paranoia. Michael Dennis Browne. AmPA

Paranoia in Crete. Gregory Corso. NeAP

Paraphras'd from Anacreon. Anacreon, *Greek.* OBCVT, tr. by Charles Cotton

Paraphrase. ad. fr. the Bible, Proverbs, 6, 6. Samuel Johnson. ChIV-1; KSG
("Shall spring to seize thee, like an ambushed foe.") (LL) KSG

Paraphrase. János Pilinszky, *Hungarian.* CEEP, tr. by Emery E. George

Paraphrase from the French, A. Matthew Prior. OxBoLi; PeLV

Paraphrase of Part of the Book of Ecclesiates, A. Henry Howard.
"I, Solomon, David's son, King of Jerusalem." ChIV-1
"When I bethought me well, under the restless sun." ChIV-1
"When that repentant tears hath cleansed clear from ill." ChIV-1

Paraphrase of the Latter part of the Sixth Chapter of St. Matthew, A. James Thomson. ChIV-2

Paraphrase on Leviticus Chapter XI, After the Manner of Master Geoffrey Chaucer in His Assembly of Fowls, A. Thomas Warton, the Elder. *See* Fashioned After the Manner of Master Geoffrey Chaucer in His Assembly of Fowls.

Paraphrase on the Canticles, A. Elizabeth Singer Rowe.
Chapter II. PEW

Paraphrase on the last speech of Dido in Virgil's Æneas, A. Virgil, *Latin.*
"Mounting the Pile she unsheaths the Trojan sword." OBCVT, tr. by Anne Wharton

Paraphrase Upon Job, A. George Sandys.
"Again when all the radiant sons of light." NOSC
"O Father, I acknowledge, ' Job replied." ChIV-1

Paraphrase Upon Part of the CXXXIX Psalm, A. Thomas Stanley. ChIV-1

Paraphrases. Roy Fisher. PeLV

Parapoetics. Eugene B. Redmond. NBV

Parcæ, The; or, Three Dainty Destinies: The Armilet. Robert Herrick. CaPo

Parchment and paper left clean. The Making of Color. Hugh Seidman. AmPA

Parcy Reed. *Unknown.* OxBB

Pardon. Jane Kenyon. BAP-93 *Fr.* Having It Out With Melancholy. BAP-93
("To my desk, books, and chair.") (LL) LoL

Pardon, The. Richard Wilbur. FP; MoP; NOBA; NoAM; Poetr

Pardon, goddess of the night. Shakespeare. NoSic *Fr.* Much Ado about Nothing.

Pardon mine ears; both I and they do pray. Sonnet 51. Sir Philip Sidney. *Fr.* Astrophil and Stella. AAS; SiPS

Pardon, old fathers, if you still remain. W. B. Yeats. PoEL-5

Pardon sweete flower of matchless Poetrie. The Choise of valentines. Thomas Nashe. PBRV

Pardon / the lag / In writing you. Letter To America. Francisco Alarcon. LTA

Pardon, ye glowing ears; need will it out. Joseph Hall. NoSic *Fr.* Virgidemiarum.

Pardoned in heaven, the first by the throne! (LL) The Lost Leader. Robert Browning. EBEvV; EnVR, FIIYEP; FaBoPV; NAEL-2; PRMP; PWR; SCGP

Pardoner's Prologue, The. Chaucer. FHYEP; NAEL-1; OAEL-1; PoE *Fr.* The Canterbury Tales.
("'In churches,' said the Pardoner, "when I preach."") NAWM-1
("While preaching. Now be still, and I'll begin.") (LL) NAWM-1

Pardoner's Tale, The. Chaucer. FHYEP; NAEL-1; OAEL-1; PoE *Fr.* The Canterbury Tales.
("And so they kissed, and rode along their way.") (LL) NAWM-1
("There was a company of young folk living.") NAWM-1
"But, sires, o word forgat I in my tale." EBEV
Death and the Three Revellers. OBNV
"It's of three rioters I have to tell." SCV
Three Rioters, The. EBNV

Pardons him for writing well. W. H. Auden. *See* In Memory of W. B. Yeats.

Paregoric Babies. Jim Carroll. PmAP

Parent. Josephine Miles. NALW

Parent, The. Ogden Nash. LiLi; Spl

Parent to Children. Robert Graves. OxAEP-2

Parentage. Alice Thompson Meynell. NALW; PeVV; VWP

Parental Critic, The. Keith Preston. NBLV

Parental Ode to My Son, Aged Three Years and Five Months, A. Thomas Hood. OBCoV; PoLF

Parental Recollections. Mary Lamb. OxBSP

Parents. Vincent Buckley. CBAP

Parents. William Meredith. AFr; FYAP

Parents. Hilda Morley. PmAP

Parents. Robert Wrigley. PuP-17

Parents are sinful now, for they must whisper. Marriage. Austin Clarke. BIrV; GTBS-P

Parents: People Like Our Marriage Maxie and Andrew, The. Gwendolyn Brooks. ColAP *Fr.* Notes from the Childhood and the Girlhood. LCAP-2

Parents Sleeping. Linda Mizejewski. CMAP

Parents take their children into the deepest Oregon forests. Anger Against Children. Robert Bly. LoL

Parfum Exotique. Charles Baudelaire, *French.* AWP, tr. by Arthur Symons

Pāri! Pāri! they cry. Kapilar, *Tamil.* PLW, tr. by A. K. Ramanujan

Pariah, The. James Edwin Campbell. AAP

Parihaka. W. H. Oliver. PeNZ

Paring the Apple. Charles Tomlinson. CMoP; OxBTC; PoE; TRP

Paris. Ingeborg Bachmann, *German.* VCWP, tr. by Mark Anderson

Paris. Gregory Corso. VGW

Paris. Gertrud Kolmar, *German.* PBWP, tr. by David Kipp

Paris. Arthur Symons. NOBVV

Paris and Helen. Judy Grahn. CrSp

Paris and Menelaus. Homer. OBVE, tr. by Alexander Pope *Fr.* The Iliad.

Pāri's Green Land, Remembered. Kapilar, *Tamil.* PLW, tr. by A. K. Ramanujan

Pāri's Hill Is Partial to Dancers. Kapilar, *Tamil.* PLW, tr. by A. K. Ramanujan

Paris in the Snow. Léopold Sédar Senghor, *French.* PBA, tr. by Ulli Beier

Paris 1912. *Unknown.* NBrP

Pāri's Parampu hill. His Hill. Kapilar, *Tamil.* PLW, tr. by A. K. Ramanujan

Paris Visitation. Michael Brownstein. FTOS

Parish Poor-Officers, The. Edward Ward. NOEC *Fr.* Journey to Hell, A; or, A Visit Paid to the Devil.

Parish priest, The. The Preacher's Mistake. William Croswell Doane. BLPA; PoToHe

Parish-priest was of the pilgrim train, A. The Character of a Good Parson. Dryden. NOCV

Parish Register, The. George Crabbe.
Burials. OAEL-1
Ancient Virgin, An. OBNC
Lady of the Manor, The. NOBE; OBNC
"Lo! now with red rent cloak and bonnet black." EBEV
"Year revolves, and I explore, The." EPCY

Parish Work-House, The. George Crabbe. *See* The Poor-House.

Park. David Ignatow. Poetsp

Park in Milan, The. William Jay Smith. CoAP

Park is filled with night and fog, The. Spring Night. Sara Teasdale. FaBoBe; MoAmPo

Park Poem. Paul Blackburn. PmAP

Park, the heart, you see at town's center is soft, The. Last Look at La Plata, Missouri. Jim Barnes. CDW

Park where the small deer feed, The. Canto the Tenth. Iván Argüelles. PT *Fr.* That Goddess.

Parked in the fields. The Forms of Love. George Oppen. NNaP

Parker's Mood. Clarence Beeks. NAAAL

Parklands, The. Stevie Smith. MoBS

Parks, The. Rilke, *German.*
"Gently gripped by the." GaP, tr. by Snow, Edward

Parks and Ponds. Ralph Waldo Emerson. PoEL-4

Park's beautiful, The. On the Fine Arts Garden, Cleveland. Russell Atkins. PoBA

Parlement of Foules, The, *see also* Parliament of Fowls, The. Chaucer.
Roundel: "Now welcom[e], Somer [or Summer] with thy sunne soft." CTC; OAEL-1; OPOU; OxBSP
(Foules Rondel.)

(Qui Bien Aime a Tard Oublie.) EnLoPo

Parley of Beasts. "Hugh MacDiarmid." ChIV-1; MoBrPo; MoP; NoAM; OBMV

Parliament Hill Fields. John Betjeman. FaBoTw; NOBE

Parliament Hill Fields. Sylvia Plath. HCAP; NALW

Parliament of Fowls, The. Chaucer. OBGa

Parliament Soldiers, The. *Unknown.* OxNR

Parnell came down the road, he said to a cheering man. W. B. Yeats. CMoP

Paroakial. Tom Leonard. FaBoTC

Parodies of Cole Porter's "Night and Day." Ring Lardner. OBAL

Parody, A. Frederick Douglass. NAAL-1; NAAL-3; NAWM-2 *Fr.* Narrative of the Life of Frederick Douglass, an American Slave.

Parody. Martha Paley Francescato, *Spanish.* BoWoP, *tr. by* Willis Barnstone

Parody [*or* Parodie], A. George Herbert. ESCV

Parody of a Lover. Li Ch'ung, *Chinese.* EP, *tr. by* Anne Birrell

Parody of Bishop Percy. Samuel Johnson. *See* Ballad: "I therefore pray thee, Renny dear."

Parody on "A Psalm of Life," A. Oliver Wendell Holmes. BLPA

Paros. A day mild as morning's milk. Robin Magowan. SPE

Parret, The. Martial, *Latin.* OBCVT, *tr. by* Timothy Kendall

Parrot, The. Oleg Grigorevich Chukhontsev, *Russian.* TCRP, *tr. by* Simon Franklin

Parrot, The. James Elroy Flecker. FaBoTw

Parrot, The. Wilfrid Wilson Gibson. OBMV

Parrot. Po Chü-i, *Chinese.* SuSp, *tr. by* Irving Y. Lo

Parrot, The. John Skelton. *See* Parrot's Soliloquy.

Parrot, The. *Unknown.* CTAV

Parrot Cry, The. "Hugh MacDiarmid." OxBS

Parrot Fish, The. James Merrill. NOBA

Parrot, if I had your wings. The Boy and the Parrot. John Hookham Frere. CTAV; OxBChV

Parrot / Is eating a carrot, The. Who Killed Lawless Lean? Stevie Smith. CBNP

Parrots, The. Wilfrid Wilson Gibson. CH

Parrots dwell in the west country. Han-shan, *Chinese.* SuSp, *tr. by* Edward H. Schafer

Parrot's Soliloquy. John Skelton. PoEL-1 *Fr.* Speak [*or* Speke], Parrot. "My name is Parrot, a bird of Paradise." OBCoV

Parrot's voice snaps out, The. "Psittachus Eois Imitatrix Ales ab Indis." Sacheverell Sitwell. MoBrPo

Parry, of all my friends the best. The Invitation. Goronwy Owen, *Welsh.* OBWVE, *tr. by* George Borrow

Parsifal Imitated from the French of Paul Verlaine. John Gray. ADE

Parsley. Rita Dove. CMAP; HCAP; LoL; NAAAL; NoAM; NoP-4; PoPoPo; VCAP

Parsnip, children, I repeat, The. Ogden Nash. ChAP

Parsnips, those rabbis, The. In the Root Cellar. Maxine W. Kumin. FaBoWP

Parson of a country town was he, The, *mod. vers. by* H.C. Leonard. Chaucer. *See* The Good Parson.

Parson, these things in thy possessing. The Happy Life of a Country Parson. Alexander Pope. BXAP; UV

Parson's Case, The. Jonathan Swift. "Thy curate's place, thy fruitful wife." UV

Parson's Looks, The. Robert Burns. OxBoLi

Parson's Pleasure. Barry O. Higgs. PeSA

Part eye, part tear, unwilling to recognize us. (LL) Stone Canyon Nocturne. Charles Wright. ColAP; HCAP; LCAP-2; VCAP; WeT

Part for the Whole. Robert Francis. PoA

Part I. Elizabeth Barrett Browning. PEW *Fr.* Casa Guidi Windows.

Part II. Elizabeth Barrett Browning. PEW

Part of a Bird. Nina Cassian, *Romanian.* PoSu, *tr. by* Andrea Deletant *and* Brenda Walker

Part of a Chorus in Seneca's Tragedy of Thyestes. Seneca, *Latin.* "'Tis not wealth that makes a king." OBCVT, *tr. by* Leigh Hunt

Part of a Letter. Richard Wilbur. CMoP

Part of a Letter to the Codignola Boy. Pier Paolo Pasolini, *Italian.* VCWP, *tr. by* David Stivender *and* J. D. McClatchy (b. 1945)

Part of a Novel. Gyula Illyés, *Hungarian.* CEEP, *tr. by* Emery E. George

Part of a Poem, Part of a Play. Marianne Moore.
  Hero, The. CMoP; NOBA; OxBA; PoA
  Steeple-Jack, The. BoWoP; CMoP; FaBoMo; FaBoWP; HAP; InPS-3; NOBA; NoAM; OxBA; PBWP; Poetr; WPE
  ("Stands for hope.") (LL) ColAP; PoPoPo
  ("Which on a steeple / stands for hope.") (LL) NoP-4

Part of a True Story. Marilyn Hacker. Poetr

Part of an Ode, A. Ben Jonson. OBEV *Fr.* To the Immortal[l] Memory [*or* Memorie] and Friendship of That Noble Pair[e], Sir Lucius Cary and Sir H. [*or* Henry] Morison. BeJo; NAEL-1; NOBE; NOSC; OAEL-1; PoEL-2; SeCP

(Part of an Ode, A.) OBEV

Part of Eve's Discussion. Marie Howe. NAmP90

Part of him is on my side, A. (LL) Two in Bed. Abram Bunn Ross. CTV; NTCP

Part of Juvenal's Sixth Satire, Modernized in Burlesque Verse. Juvenal, *Latin.* "But say you, if each private Family." OBCVT, *tr. by* Henry Fielding

Part of my charm. Look for You Yesterday, Here You Come Today. Imamu Amiri Baraka. SSLK

Part of Ocean / again, A. (LL) The Phantom Light of All Our Day. Nathaniel Mackey. GT

Part of our nation of our fanatic sun. (LL) The Soul and Body of John Brown. Muriel Rukeyser. CBCWP; MoAmPo

Part of Plenty. Bernard Spencer. GBL; LiTM

Part of the Forest. George Oppen. FTOS

Part of the Lay of Sigrdrifa. *Unknown. See* Counsels of Sigrdrifa.

Part of the Seventh Epistle of the First Book of Horace Imitated: And Address'd to a Noble Peer. Horace. OBCVT, *tr. by* Jonathan Swift *Fr.* The Epistles.

Part of the work[e] remains [*or* remaines]; one part is past. The End of His Work. Robert Herrick. CaPo

Part One. Tristan Tzara. PFTM, *tr. by* Jerome Rothenberg *Fr.* The Approximate Man.

Part otter, part snake, part bird the bird Anhinga. Waterbird. May Swenson. NoP-4

Part, Provence, he loved so well. (LL) To Ford Madox Ford in Heaven. William Carlos Williams. AmPP; ColAP; NOBA

Part-Sequence for Change, A. Robert Duncan. VGW

Part where General Matthei leaves his office, The. General Matthei Drives Home through Santiago. Stephen Dobyns. CMAP

Parta Quies. A. E. Housman. NOBE

Parted. Alice Thompson Meynell. PeVV

Parted. Clara Ann Thompson. CBWP-2

Parted by death, we swallow remorse. Tu Fu. SuSp, *tr. by* Eugene Eoyang *Fr.* Dreaming of Li Po.

Parted me leaf and leaf, divided me, eyelid and eyelid of slumber. (LL) Moonrise. Gerard Manley Hopkins. EnVR; MoBrPo; NOBVV; RB

Parted Souls. Edward Herbert, 1st Baron Herbert of Cherbury. SeCP

Parterre, The. E. Harriet Palmer. NOBL; PeLV

Partheniades. George Puttenham.
  "O mightye Muse." PBRV

Parthenogenesis. Nuala Ni Dhomhnaill, *Irish.* CIP-2, *tr. by* Michael Hartnett

Parthenon, The. Herman Melville. NCAP

Parthenophil and Parthenophe. Barnabe Barnes.
  "Lovely Maya, Hermes' mother." NoSic
  Mistress, Behold, in This True-Speaking Glass. Son
  "O Powers Celestial, with what sophistry." EnLoPo
  "Soft, lovely, rose-like lips, conjoined with mine." EnLoPo
  "Then first with locks dishevelled and bare." NoSic
  "Why do I draw this coole releeving ayer." PBRV
  Would I were Changed. AAS
  Write! Write! Help! Help! Son

Partholan went out one day. The First Lawcase. *Unknown, Irish.* BIrV, *tr. by* John Montague

Partial Accounts. William Meredith. GLP

Partial Comfort. Dorothy Parker. OBAL

Partial Luetic History of an Individual at Risk. J. M. Regan. GLP

Partial Muse, has from my earliest hours, The. Charlotte Smith. BWW

Partial Resemblance. Denise Levertov. CoAP

Parting. A. R. Ammons. NoAM

Parting. Matthew Arnold. EnVR *Fr.* Switzerland.

Parting, The. Sara Berkeley. PBCIP

Parting. Hanmo Chong, *Korean.* CKP, *tr. by* Jaihiun Kim

Parting. Emily Dickinson. SAGP

Parting, The. Michael Drayton. GLoP; OBEV; SCV *Fr.* Idea.
  (Love's Farewell.) GTBS-P
  (Parting, The.) GLoP; OBEV; SCV
  ("Since ther's no helpe, Come let us kisse and part.") GEA

Parting. Judah Halevi, *Hebrew.* AWP; TrJP, *tr. by* Nina Davis Salaman

Parting, The. Josephine D. Henderson Heard. CBWP-4

Parting. Jure Kastelan, *Croatian.* CEEP, *tr. by* Peter Kastmiler

Parting. Coventry Patmore. PoToHe

Parting, *fr.* A Woman Young and Old. W. B. Yeats. FaBoTw

Parting, a thousand cups won't wash away the sorrow. To Tzu-an. Yü Hsüan-chi. BoWoP, *tr. by* Geoffrey Waters

Parting as Descent. John Berryman. MoAmPo

Parting at Morning. Robert Browning. AWP; CABP; EBEvV; EnVR; FHYEP; HeIP-4; ImPo; InPS-3; NAEL-2; NOBE; OBEV; OBNC; OxBSP; PFE; SAGP; SCGP; SoSe-8; TFi; UnPo

Parting at Morning. Dietmar von Aist [*or* Eist], *German*. AWP, *tr. by* Frank C. Nicholson

Parting from Liu Nan-chou. Hsieh Chin, *Chinese*.
   "Wait until I too hang up my carriage." CoBLCP, *tr. by* Jonathan Chaves

Parting from Su Wu. Li Ling, *Chinese*. ChiP, *tr. by* Arthur Waley

Parting from the Courtier Sung. Yin Shih, *Chinese*. CoBCP, *tr. by* Burton Watson

Parting from the dead, I've stifled my sobs. Dreaming of Li Po. Tu Fu, *Chinese*. CoBCP, *tr. by* Burton Watson

Parting from the Winter Stove. Po Chü-i, *Chinese*. ChiP, *tr. by* Arthur Waley

Parting from Wang Wei. Meng Hao Jan, *Chinese*. SuSp, *tr. by* Daniel Bryant

Parting Gift. Elinor Wylie. OxBA

Parting Hymn, A. Charlotte Forten. BlSi; NAAAL

Parting Hymn We Sing, A. Aaron R. Wolfe. AH

Parting in Wartime. Frances Darwin Cornford. APAD; FaBoWP; NIP-4

Parting Is Hard. *Unknown, Chinese*. BoWoP, *tr. by* Geoffrey Waters

Parting Kiss, The. Josephine D. Henderson Heard. CBWP-4

Parting Lovers, The. Mrs. Henry Linden. CBWP-4

Parting: 1940. John Frederick Nims. PoA

Parting of the Red Sea, The. *Unknown*. AnOE, *tr. by* Charles W. Kennedy *Fr.* Exodus.

Parting of Venus and Old Age, The. John Gower. PoEL-1 *Fr.* Confessio Amantis.

Parting Roundel. Jemal Sharah. NOBAu

Parting Song, A. Felicia Dorothea Hemans. VWP

Parting sorrow shattered / Beyond the gauze window. Tune: "Full River Red." Hsin Ch'i-chi, *Chinese*. SuSp, *tr. by* Irving Y. Lo

Parting with Lucasia; a Song. Katherine Philips. CBLP

Parting, without a Sequel. John Crowe Ransom. MeMAP; MoAmPo; NoP-4; OxBA; PFE; SoSe-8

Partings. Charles Guérin, *French*. AWP, *tr. by* Jethro Bithell

Partings. Maria Jane Jewsbury. OxBChV

Partition's people stitched. Sea Breeze, Bombay. Adil Jussawalla. OMIP

Partner, The. Theodore Roethke. EP

Partner in thy destiny! (LL) To an Infant Expiring the Second Day of Its Birth. Mehetabel Wright. ECWP; NOEC

Partridge. Agathias, *Greek*. FP; GrAn, *tr. by* Guy Davenport

Partridge in a pear tree, A. (LL) The Twelve Days of Christmas. *Unknown*. AmFP; LB; OxBoLi; OxNR; PChr

Partridges. John Masefield. OxBTC

Party, The. Margaret Avison. PoA

Party. Cynthia Huntington. NAmP90

Party, The. Antigone Kefala. BMAP

Party, The. William Robert Rodgers. BIrV; PNI

Party. Eddy Van Vliet, *Flemish*. VCWP, *tr. by* John Van Tiel

Party, The. Reed Whittemore. CoAP
   ("With wild surmise.") (LL) CoAmPo

Party at Hydra. Irving Layton. HeIP-4

Party Favour. Daniel David Moses. HATNAP

Party for your Right to Fight. Public Enemy. ISC

Party holds you down and you lie still, The. Nguyễn Chí Thiện. VCWP, *tr. by* Huỳnh Sanh Thông *Fr.* Sundry Notes.

Party left me in the wilds, The. Nguyễn Chí Thiện, *Vietnamese*. AVP, *tr. by* Huỳnh Sanh Thông

Party Piece. Brian Patten. BoLoP; FaBoSe

Party Shrine. Thomas McCarthy. BiHa

Party Song, A. *Unknown*. BuTP

Party to which Wolves are Invited, The. Thylias Moss. NMM-2

Partying by a river near Ellwood City, Pennsylvania. Coming Home in March. Harold Littlebird. VoR

Parvenant. Arthur Hugh Clough. OBCoV *Fr.* Spectator ab Extra. OBCoV; OxBoLi; PeLV; PeVV

Pas de Deux for Lovers. Michael Dransfield. CBAP

Paschal Fire, The. Denis Florence MacCarthy. TIRV

Pass. Edmund Vance Cooke. PWR

Pass away so easily. (LL) Mists rise over, The. Akahito, *Japanese*. OHPJ, *tr. by* Kenneth Rexroth

Pass, Crow. (LL) Examination at the Womb-Door. Ted Hughes. NAEL-2; NoP-4; OxBC

Pass forth, my wonted cries. Sir Thomas Wyatt. SiPS

Pass It On. Henry Burton. PWR

Pass it on, II. Rachel Hadas. NMM-2

Pass me the sweet earthenware jug. Zonas, *Greek*. PGA, *tr. by* Kenneth Rexroth

Pass not, but wonder, and amazed stand. Upon the Much Lamented Death of the Right Honourable, the Lady Elizabeth Langham. Bathsua Pell Makin. KTR

Pass of Death, The. George Darley. NOBRP

Pass Office Song. *Unknown, Afrikaans*. PBA; TTY, *tr. by* Peggy Rutherford

Pass over this as well. Games. Ory Bernstein, *Hebrew*. IP, *tr. by* Warren Bargad *and* Stanley F. Chyet

Pass[e] rascal deer [*or* Rascall Deare], strike me the largest doe. (LL) La Bella Bona-Roba. Richard Lovelace. BeJo; CBLP; CaPo; EBEV; NOSC; OAEL-1; PoEL-3; SeCP

Pass the tambourine, let me bash out praises. The Way We Live. Kathleen Jamie. APAD; FaBoTC

Pass to thy Rendezvous of Light. Emily Dickinson. NAWM-2

Pass we the ills, which each man feels or dreads. Matthew Prior. NOEC; PoEL-3 *Fr.* Solomon on the Vanity of the World.

Passage, The. "Adunis," *Arabic*. VCWP, *tr. by* Samuel Hazo

Passage. Elizabeth Alexander. ISC

Passage. Hart Crane. CMoP; NOBA; PoE

Passage. Billy Marshall-Stoneking. BMAP; NOBAu

Passage of a Year, The. *Unknown*. PoEL-1 *Fr.* Sir Gawain and the Green Knight. OAEL-1, *tr. by* Brian Stone

Passage of the Mountain of St. Gothard, The. Georgiana Cavendish, Duchess of Devonshire. ECWP

Passage Over Water. Robert Duncan. NOBA; NoAM
   ("And within the indestructible night I am alone.") (LL) ColAP

Passage to India. Walt Whitman. APN-1; AmPP; NAAL-1; NCAP; PoEL-5

Passages. Robert Duncan.
   At the Loom. VGW
   Envoy: "Good Night, at last." VGW
   Feast, The. APSN
   Fire, The. APSN; VGW
   Moon, The. APSN, *sect.* 5
   Transgressing the Real. APSN
   Tribal Memories. APSN; NOBA
   Up Rising. APSN; NNaP

Passages. Larry Eigner. NeAP

Passages. Mark Vinz. IFJA

Passages 37. Robert Duncan. FTOS

Passed Ruin'd Ilion. Walter Savage Landor. AWP; SCGP *Fr.* Ianthe. (Ianthe) PoEL-4
   ("One name, Ianthe, shall not die.") (LL) NAEL-2; NOBRP; NoP-4
   ("Past ruin'd Ilion Helen lives.") GLoP
   (Verse: "Past ruin'd Ilion.") OBEV

Passenger Pigeons. Robert Morgan. MT

Passenger Shanty. W. H. Auden. OBCoV

Passengers, The. David Antin. NYBP

Passengers afloat on many thousand feet. Night Flight. Marion Alexopoulos. NOBAu

Passer-by, A. Robert Bridges. CMoP; EBEvV; ImPo; LiTM; MoBrPo; OAEL-2; OBEV; OBNC; OxBTC; SCGP

Passer-by, don't blame this memorial. Carphyllides, *Greek*. GrAn, *tr. by* Alistair Elliot

Passer Mortuus Est. Edna St. Vincent Millay. CMoP; FaBoWP; MoAmPo; OxBA

Passes are blocked by snow, The. Persia. Vita Sackville-West. WPE

Passing. Langston Hughes. APSN; SAmP

Passing. Carl Phillips. PoPoPo

Passing a dull red college-block. A Walk in Würzburg. William Plomer. NYBP

Passing a Ruined Palace. Wen T'ing-yün, *Chinese*. OHMPC, *tr. by* Kenneth Rexroth

Passing across the billowy sea. *Unknown*. *Fr.* Popular Songs of Tuscany. AWP, *tr. by* John Addington Symonds

Passing and Glassing. Christina Rossetti. OBNC

Passing away, saith the World, passing away. Passing Away, Saith the World, Passing Away. Christina Rossetti. NoP-4; OAEL-2; OBNC; WPE *Fr.* Old and New Year Ditties.

Passing between the stumbling generations. The Wandering Jew Comes to the Wall. Edmond Fleg. *Fr.* The Wall of Weeping. TrJP, *tr. by* Humbert Wolfe

Passing by a Mountain Village: Evening. Chia Tao, *Chinese.* SuSp, *tr. by* Stephen Owen

Passing by Huai-yin I Have Feelings. Wu Wei-yeh, *Chinese.* CoBLCP, *tr. by* Jonathan Chaves

Passing by Kamata. Su Man-shu, *Chinese.* SuSp, *tr. by* Wu-chi Liu

Passing By the Battlefield at Feng-k'ou. Kao Ch'i, *Chinese.* CoBLCP, *tr. by* Jonathan Chaves

Passing by the Hot Springs at Hua-ch'ing Palace. Yüan Hung-tao, *Chinese.*
   "Eastern mountains/ and western mountains." CoBLCP, *tr. by* Jonathan Chaves

Passing By Waterwheel Bay. Yang Wan-li, *Chinese.* SuSp, *tr. by* Jonathan Chaves

Passing Chao-ling Again. Tu Fu, *Chinese.* CoBCP, *tr. by* Burton Watson

Passing Ch'ien-hsi as Military Adviser in the Third Month of the Year Yi-ssu. T'ao Ch'ien, *Chinese.* SuSp, *tr. by* Eugene Eoyang

Passing clouds only a stand of aspens is in light. Matsuo Allard. HA

Passing Hung-fu Monastery with Yüan-ming: Inscribed in Jest. Huang T'ing-chien, *Chinese.* SuSp, *tr. by* Michael E. Workman

Passing into Storm. Patrick Lane. NOBC

Passing like a Strauss waltz. The Hoofer. A. K. Redwing. VoR

Passing of a dream, The. Stanzas. John Clare. NOBVV

Passing of Arthur, The. Layamon. PoE *Fr.* The Brut.

Passing of Arthur, The. Sir John Collings Squire. BXAP

Passing of Arthur, The. Tennyson. FHYEP; NAEL-2; OBNC *Fr.* Idylls of the King.
   "And answer made King Arthur, breathing hard." PeECV, *ll.* 330–440; EBEV
   ("Before the eyes of ladies and of kings.") (LL) EBEV
   "Then rose the King and moved his host by night." PeVV

Passing of King Arthur, The. Tennyson. APAD *Fr.* Morte d'Arthur. EBNV; EBVVPR; FaBoBe; NIP-4; NOBVV; OAEL-2; OBNV; OxAEP-2; PoEL-5 *Fr.* Morte d'Arthur. EnVR

Passing of Sorrow, The. Mary Jane Moffat. IMW

Passing of Tennyson, The. Ernest Christopher Dowson. EPCY

Passing of the Forest, The. William Pember Reeves. PeNZ

Passing of the Old Year. Mary Weston Fordham. CBWP-2

Passing of the Poets, The. Fearflatha O'Gnive. NOIV

Passing of the Shee, The. John Millington Synge. BIrV; FaBoEE

Passing Show, The. Ambrose Bierce. APN-2

Passing Strange, The. John Masefield. MoBrPo; OBEV

Passing stranger! you do not know how longingly I look upon you. To a Stranger. Walt Whitman. APN-1; NOBA; SAmP

Passing the American graveyard, for my birthday. Poem for My Twentieth Birthday. Kenneth Koch. PoA

Passing the Graveyard. Andrew Young. FaBoTC

Passing the great plane tree in the square. The Beginning of the End. Jon Stallworthy. OxBC

Passing the Night on a River in Chien-te. Meng Hao Jan, *Chinese.* SuSp, *tr. by* Paul W. Kroll

Passing this tomb with no smile on his face. Thermopylai. Hegemon, *Greek.* GrAn, *tr. by* Peter Jay

Passing Through. Stanley Kunitz. LoL

Passing Through. Patrick Williams. PNI

Passing Through Doorways. Frank Kuppner. FaBoTC

Passing Through Experiences. Robert Adamson. BMAP

Passing through huddled and ugly walls. The Harbor. Carl Sandburg. ColAP; TAP

Passing through My Shih-ning Estate. Hsieh Ling-yün, *Chinese.* SuSp, *tr. by* Francis Westbrook

Passing through Rajasthan. Umashankar Joshi, *Gujarati.* OMIP, *tr. by* Niranjan Bhagat *and* Carlo Coppola

Passing T'ien-mên Street in Ch'ang-an and Seeing a Distant View of Chung-nan Mountains. Po Chü-i, *Chinese.* ChiP, *tr. by* Arthur Waley

Passing Visit to Helen. D. H. Lawrence. CMoP

Passing White Banks Pavilion. Hsieh Ling-yün, *Chinese.* SuSp, *tr. by* Francis Westbrook

Passion. Penelope Shuttle. LW

Passion, The. Henry Vaughan. ESCV

Passion and Exaltation of Christ, The. Isaac Watts. NOCV

Passion, and then the anguish. And with whom. Reconciliation. Goethe. *Fr.* Trilogy of Passion. STV, *tr. by* John Frederick Nims

Passion and Woe in Marriage: A Ukrainian Love Story, The. Peter Oresick. IFJA

Passion at the Chat 'n Chew Diner. Karen Zealand. CMAP

Passion Drinker, The. Anita Endrezze-Danielson. VoR

Passion Flower. Christopher Okigbo. PBMAP *Fr.* Heavensgate (1961).

Passion of Dido for Aeneas, The. Virgil, *Latin.*

"He many waies his labouring thoughts revolves." OBCVT, *tr. by* Sir John Denham

Passion of her white December?, The. (LL) Ice. Stephen Spender. FaBoMo; GTBS-P

Passion of Jesus Considered as an Uphill Race, The. Alfred Jarry, *French.* PFTM, *tr. by* Gary Fletcher

Passion of M'Phail, The. Horace Gregory.
   They Were All like Geniuses. NYBP
   This Is the Place to Wait. MoAmPo

Passion of Our Lord painted by an anonymous hand from the Circle of Rhenish Masters, The. Zbigniew Herbert, *Polish.* GI, *tr. by* Adam Czerniawski

Passion of Ravensbrück. János Pilinszky, *Hungarian.* AF; GI; PoSu, *tr. by* Janos Csokits *and* Ted Hughes; HP, *tr. by* Ted Hughes

Passion Shaved beneath the Grain-Silo. Peter Finch. NBrP

Passion too deep seems like none. Tu Mu. PLT, *tr. by* A. C. Graham *Fr.* Farewell Poem.

Passionate angels serenaded today in Jerusalem. Passover in Jerusalem. Avigdor Hame'iri, *Hebrew.* MHP, *tr. by* Ruth Finer Mintz

Passionate beyond the will. (LL) The Alchemist. Louise Bogan. AWP; MoAmPo

Passionate love is temporary. Landscape with Leaves and Figure. Olga Broumas. BoWoP

Passionate Man['] Pilgrimage, The. Sir Walter Ralegh. AAS; ChIV-2; EBEvV; NOBE; NoSic; OBEV; PeECV; PoE; PoEL-2; PoRA; RB; SCGP; TFi
   ("And thus I'll take my pilgrimage.") (LL) PiM
   ("Give me my scallop-shell of quiet.") NoP-4; PiM
   (His Pilgrimage.) OBEV

Passionate Man's Song, The. John Fletcher. *See* Melancholy.

Passionate pages of his earlier years, The. Thomas Hardy. EPCY *Fr.* Singer Asleep, A (Algernon Charles Swinburne).

Passionate Pilgrim, The. Various authors.
   Madrigal, A: "Crabbed age and youth cannot live together." GTBS-P; InPS-3
   Philomel. CH; NOBE; OBEV
   (Nightingale, The.) AWP; GTBS-P

Passionate Professor, The. Bert Leston Taylor. NBLV

Passionate Profiteer to His Love, The, *par. of* Passionate Shepherd to His Love, The *by* Marlowe. "Sagittarius." OBCoV

Passionate Shepherd, The. Nicholas Breton.
   Merry Country Lad, The. NoSic

Passionate Shepherd [*or* Sheepheard] To His Love, The. Marlowe. AAS; AEP; APAD; AWP; BoLoP; CABP; CBLP; CTC; ClHu; EBEvV; FaBoBe; GEA; GLoP; GTBS-P; HAP; HeIP-4; HoPM; ImPo; InPK-6; InPS-3; NAEL-1; NBLV; NIP-4; NOBE; NoP-4; NoSic; OAEL-1; OBEV; OxAEP-1; PBMP; PBRV; PFE; PoE; PoLF; PoPoPo; PoRA; Poetr; RB; SAGP; SCV; TFi; TRP; TTTS; WeW-3

Passionate Shepherd to His Love, The. Delmore Schwartz. PFE; SCGP

Passionate Summer's dead! the sky's a-glow, The. October. Paul Hamilton Hayne. APN-2

Passionate Sword, The. Jean Starr Untermeyer. TrJP

Passionately joined to all things visible. Invisible Work. Margaret Gibson. MT

Passions; an Ode for [*or* to] Music, The. William Collins. GTBS-P

Passion's excess for thee we need no fear. Sidney Godolphin. EPCY *Fr.* Elegy on Donne.

Passive Participle's Petition, The. John Byrom. ECEV

Passive Resistance. Enid Shomer. BAP-96

Passive sea of white foam, A. Poetic Reflections Enroute To, and During, The Funeral and Burial of Henry Dumas, Poet. E. B. Redmond. ISC

Passive, your glove allows me to enter. Search. Jane Draycott. LBC

Passover. Linda Pastan. NMM-2

Passover in Jerusalem. Avigdor Hame'iri, *Hebrew.* MHP, *tr. by* Ruth Finer Mintz

Passover: the Injections. William Heyen. HP

Passport check. George Swede. HA

Past, The. Kwesi Brew. *See* The Search.

Past, The. Ralph Waldo Emerson. FaBoCh; MeMAP; PoEL-4; TAP

Past, The. Mary Weston Fordham. CBWP-2

Past. Pablo Neruda, *Spanish.* VCWP, *tr. by* Alastair Reid

Past a cow and past a cottage. The Murder on the Downs. William Plomer. OxBoV

Past, a glacier, gripped the mountain wall, The. Full Moon at Tierz; before the Storming of Huesca. John Cornford. OBWP

Past all accident. (LL) The Ivy Crown. William Carlos Williams. NAAL-2; NoAM

Past and Present. R. E. Egerton Warburton. NOBVV

Past and present wilt—I have fill'd them, emptied them, The. Walt Whitman. ColAP *Fr.* Song of Myself.

("Past and present wilt.. . . I have filled them and emptied them, The.") PAR

Past bush paths tarred by tireless treading. Excursion. Niyi Osundare. HBAPE

Past exchanges have left orbits of rain around my face. An Apology. Diane Wakoski. TAP

Past factory workshops, empty. Marina Ivanovna Tsvetayeva. *Fr.* The Daughter of Jairus. BoWoP, *tr. by* Paul Schmidt

Past fifty and cloyed at last. Philetas, *Greek.* GrAn; PGA, *tr. by* Kenneth Rexroth

Past hovering as it revisits the light, The. (LL) It Rains ("It rains, and nothing stirs within the fence"). Edward Thomas. OxBTC; PoE

Past hurts, George, but sing and be merry, The. Old Song. Andrey Andreievich Voznesensky, *Russian.* VCWP, *tr. by* Smith, William Jay and Vera Dunham

Past / Is but the cinders, The. The Search. Kwesi Brew. PBA

Past Is Dark with Sin and Shame, The. Thomas Wentworth Higginson. AH

Past is past, and if one. Salute. James Schuyler. FYAP; NeAP

Past Is the Present, The. Marianne Moore. MeMAP; NAAL-2

Past one o'clock. You must have gone to bed. Vladimir Mayakovsky, *Russian.* AF, *tr. by* George Reavey

Past paths where on their appointed occasions men climb, / and pass. Robert Penn Warren. *See* Colder Fire.

Past ploughed and fallow, at the top. Glenarm. John Lyle Donaghy. AWP; NOBE; PoEL-4

Past ruin'd [*or* ruined] Ilion Helen lives. Passed Ruin'd Ilion. Walter Savage Landor. AWP; CTC; EnLoPo; GBL; HAP; NAEL-2; NOBE; NOBRP; OBEV; OBNC; PoEL-4; PoRA; SCGP; TFi; WeW-3 *Fr.* Ianthe.

Past second cock-crow yacht masts in the harbor go slowly white. Masts at Dawn. Robert Penn Warren. NAAL-2; NoP-4; VCAP

Past seven o'clock: time to be gone. Moonset. Sir Henry John Newbolt. EBVV

Past the abandoned quarry. Stanley Kunitz. *Fr.* The Testing-Tree. FYAP; UnPo

Past the angular maguey fields, a ride on the optic nerve. Into Mexico. Mona Van Duyn. VCAP

Past the hens. Tanka. Saitō Mokichi, *Japanese.* MJT, *tr. by* Makoto Ueda

Past the house where he was got. Austin Clarke. CMoP; PoE *Fr.* Mnemosyne Lay in Dust.

Past the school and down. Directions to the Nomad. James Welch. CDW

Past Thinking of Solomon. Francis Thompson. ChIV-1

Past towns, states, deserts, hills, and rivers borne. Catullus. *See* On the Burial of His Brother.

Pasted to stars already. . . . Gwendolyn Brooks. *See* Strong Men, riding horses. In the West.

Pastel: Masks and Faces. Arthur Symons. NOBVV

Pastiche. Elinor Wylie. NALW

Pastime of Pleasure, The. Stephen Hawes. OBGa

Dame Music. PoEL-1

Epitaph of Graunde [*or* La Graunde] Amoure, The. EBEV; FaBoEE; NoSic; OBEV

Seven Deadly Sins, The. PoEL-1

Time and Eternity. PoEL-1

True Knight [*or* True Knighthood], The. OBEV

Pastime with good company. Henry VIII, King of England. CTC; EBEV; NoSic

Pastor M'Gadi's startling blackness. Halo. Ralph Nixon Currey. PeSA

Pastoral: "Afternoon wears on, The." David Wright. NYBP

Pastoral: "Annette came through the meadows." Henrietta Cordelia Ray. CBWP-3

Pastoral: "Death. / The death of a million." Ron Loewinsohn. NeAP

Pastoral: "Dominic Francis Xavier Brotherton-Chancery." Gavin Ewart. OxBC

Pastoral. Rita Dove. NAAAL

Pastoral: "Dove walks with sticky feet, The." Kenneth Patchen. CLPP

Pastoral, A: "From thence into the open fields he fled," *sels.* Edmund Spenser. *Fr.* Wood Of Error. AEP

Pastoral: "I came to a field." Charles Simic. NNaP

Pastoral: "It all happened so fast. Fenya was in the straight chair." Norman Dubie. AmPA

Pastoral: "Little sparrows, The." William Carlos Williams. SAmP; TwCP

Pastoral: "Lumpish trollop, The !'." Wyndham Lewis. UV

Pastoral[l], A: "Oh [*or* O] happy golden age." Torquato Tasso. OAEL-1; PoEL-2, *tr. by* Samuel Daniel *Fr.* Aminta.

(Golden Age, The.) AWP, *tr. by* Leigh Hunt

Pastoral: "Slopes of the sun and vine, and thou dark stream." George Cabot Lodge. APN-2

Pastoral: "So soft in the hemlock wood." Robert Silliman Hillyer. MoAmPo

Pastoral, A: "There went out in the dawning light." *Unknown, Latin.* AWP, *tr. by* John Addington Symonds

Pastoral: "This field has buried men; is browed." Lilian Bowes-Lyon. WPN

Pastoral: "This is a place of ease." Marion Strobel. PoA

Pastoral: "Today in Peru, this first day of summer." Lawrence Raab. AmPA

Pastoral: "When I was younger." William Carlos Williams. AmPP; OxBA; SAmP

Pastoral Ballad by John Bull, A. Thomas Moore. BIrV; OBSV

Pastoral[l] Dialogue, A. Thomas Carew. CaPo; GBL; SeCP

Pastoral Dialogue. Anne Killigrew. LW

Pastoral Dialogue between Two Shepherdesses, A. Anne Finch, Countess of Winchilsea. ECWP

Pastoral Eclogue upon the Death of Sir Philip Sidney Knight, A. Lodowick Bryskett. NoSic

Pastoral Elegy, A. Tibullus, *Latin.* AWP, *tr. by* Sir Charles Abraham Elton

Pastoral[l] Hymn[e], A. John Hall. MeLP

Pastoral; in the Modern Style, A. "Worcester." NOEC

Pastoral Muses once were scattered, The. Artemidorus, *Greek.* GrAn, *tr. by* Anthony Holden

Pastoral on the King's Death, The; [Written in 1648]. Alexander Brome. NOSC

Pastoral Poesy. John Clare. OAEL-2

(Pastoral Poetry.) FHYEP

Pastoral Song, A. Anne Hunter. ECWP

Pastorall, A. Lady Jane Cavendish.

Antemasque, The: Witches the Nomber Beinge Five. KTR

4th Sheppard Speakes This, The. KTR

Songs Anthòme. KTR

3d Sheppard Speakes This to the Rest, The. KTR

3 Sad Sheppards Sings This in Parts, The. KTR

2 Antemasque, The: Two Countrye Wives, the Songe. KTR

Pasture, The. Robert Frost. CMoP; MoAmPo; NAAL-2; NOBA; NOxBChV; OxBA; PoE; SAGP; SAmP; TLR; TRP; TTTS; WHSW

Pasture, The. Robert Penn Warren. *See* Original Sin.

Pasture, stone wall, and steeple. Question in a Field. Louise Bogan. NYBP

Pat-a-cake, pat-a-cake, baker's man. Mother Goose. LB; OxNR; ReMoGo

Pat Cloherty's Version of *The Maisie.* Richard Murphy. RB

Pat on the head, A. To an Angel in the House. John Sparrow. OBCoV

Pat your foot. Leadbelly Gives an Autograph. Imamu Amiri Baraka. PmAP

Patapan. Bernard De la Monnoye, *French.* PChr

Patch of Old Snow, A. Robert Frost. CMoP; OxBSP; WeW-3

Patch-Shaneen. John Millington Synge. FaBoVe

Patches. Thomas Russell Shelton. PWR

Patches of it. The Luminous. Barbara Guest. PoM

Patches of Sky. Debora Greger. ImGa

Patches of snow. Robert Spiess. HA

Patchwork Quilt, The. Elizabeth Fleming. BoTP

Pater and *Ave* for my peace. (LL) Posthumous Coquetry. Théophile Gautier, *French.* AWP; PeVV, *tr. by* Arthur Symons

Pater Filio. Robert Bridges. CMoP; OBEV

Pater Noster. Jacques Prévert, *French.* CLPP; NNPT, *tr. by* Lawrence Ferlinghetti

("Of cannons.") (LL) NNPT, *tr. by* Lawrence Ferlinghetti

Pater's Bathe. Edward Abbott Parry. OxBChV

Paterson. William Carlos Williams. PFTM

"Beautiful thing/ I saw you." CMoP

Delineaments of the Giants, The. MeMAP; NoAM; TAP

"Edward/ Paterson has grown older." NoAM

Episode 17. OxBA

"I remember." MeMAP

Preface: "Rigor of beauty is the quest. But how will you find beauty when it is locked." NoAM

Preface: "To make a start." CMoP; NOBA; NoAM

"Sun, The." MeMAP

Sunday in the Park. NAAL-2

"There is a woman in our town." CMoP; PoE

"Thought clambers up."

"Two halfgrown girls hailing hallowed Easter." MeMAP

"What / irritation of offensively red brick is this." MeMAP

Paterson: The Falls. William Carlos Williams. ColAP

Path, The. "Valery Frantsevich Pereleshin," *Russian.* TCRP, *tr. by* Albert C. Todd

Path among the Stones, The. Galway Kinnell. NNaP; NOBA

Path by which we twain did go, The. Tennyson. EBVV; PeECV; SCV *Fr.* In Memoriam A. H. H.

Path crossed green closes and went down the lane, The. We Passed by Green Closes. John Clare. EnVR

Path from the field ends in a flowering village, A. May. Yongnang Kim, *Korean.* CKP, *tr. by* Jaihiun Kim

Path Is Long, The. Nikolai Ivanovich Glazkov, *Russian.* TCRP, *tr. by* Daniel Weissbort

Path-let. . . leaving home, leading out. Footpath. Stella Ngatho. WPOW

Path of glory leads but to the grave, The. Nicarchus of Alexandria, *Greek.* GrAn, *tr. by* Peter Porter

Path of Wisdom, The. Bible, Apocrypha. TrJP *Fr.* Baruch.

Path that Leads to Nowhere, The. Corinne Roosevelt Robinson. BLPA

Path to Han-shan's place is laughable, The. Cold Mountain Poems. Han-shan, *Chinese.* BB; ChiPo, *tr. by* Gary Snyder

Path up the mountain is hard, The. Amongst the Cliffs. Han Yü, *Chinese.* OHMPC, *tr. by* Kenneth Rexroth

Pathology of Colours. Dannie Abse. NIP-4; NoAM

Pathos. Kwangsop Kim, *Korean.* CKP, *tr. by* Jaihiun Kim

Pathos of the result. (LL) Eagle Valor, Chicken Mind. Robinson Jeffers. OxBA; OxBSP

Paths, The. Richard Caddel. NBrP

Paths. Josephine Miles. *See* Fields of Learning.

Pathway of light! o'er thy empurpled zone. Sonnet VI. To the Torrid Zone. Helen Maria Williams. NOBRP; NoP-4

Patience. Elaine Feinstein. BrRo; FaBoWP

Patience. Sir William Schwenck Gilbert.

    Bunthorne's Song. CABP; EBVV; OAEL-2

    (Aesthete, The.) EBVV

    If You're Anxious for to Shine in the High Aesthetic Line. NAEL-2; NBLV

Patience. *Unknown.*

    "Hit betidde somtime in the termes of Judé." EnVB

Patience! coy singers of the Delphic wood. To Poets. Walter Savage Landor. FaBoEE

Patience, for I have wrong. Sir Thomas Wyatt. SiPS

Patience for my device. Sir Thomas Wyatt. SiPS

Patience, hard thing! the hard thing but to pray. Sonnet. Gerard Manley Hopkins. EnVR; NOBVV; OBNC; Son

Patience is a virtue. *Unknown.* CTV; OxNR

Patience of all my smart. Sir Thomas Wyatt. SiPS

Patience of the lambs was exhausted, The. Sacred Wrath. Vahan Tekeyan, *Armenian.* GI, *tr. by* Diana Der Hovanessian *and* Marsbed Margossian

Patience. . . patience. Frank Horne. BPo

Patience though I have not. Sir Thomas Wyatt. NoP-4; SiPS

Patience with the Living. Margaret Elizabeth Munson Sangster. PoToHe

Patient. Lynn Emanuel. CMAP

Patient, The. Nicholas Moore. SPE

Patient Joe; or, The Newcastle Collier. Hannah More. ECWP; WoRP

Patient Painstaking. Spendthrifts. Lotte Moos. NBrP

Patient Pan, The. Ralph Waldo Emerson. APN-1

Patient: Rockland County Sanitarium, The. Calvin C. Hernton. PoBA

Patmos. Friedrich Hölderlin, *German.* GrIP; OBVE, *tr. by* David Gascoyne

Patriarch. Robert Burns. ChIV-1

Patriarch in black takes, The. Chana Bloch. CrSp *Fr.* The Sacrifice.

Patriarch wrestled with the angel long, The. Jacob Wrestling with the Angel. Jones Very. ChIV-1

Patriarchal poetry their origin their history their origin. Gertrude Stein. NMM-2 *Fr.* Patriarchal Poetry.

Patriarchs, The. Donne. *Fr.* The Litanie. PoEL-2

Patricians, The. Douglas Dunn. OxBC

Patrick, you chatter too loud. The Praise of Fionn. *Unknown, Irish.* TIRV, *tr. by* Frank O'Connor

Patriot. Cyril Dabydeen. HCP

Patriot, The. Nissim Ezekiel. FaBoVe

Patriot, The. Sir Walter Scott. *See* Caledonia.

Patriot living at Ewell, A. Limerick. Langford Reed. PeLi

Patriot, The [An Old Story]. Robert Browning. FHYEP; PBMP

Patriotic Ode on the Fourteenth Anniversary of the Persecution of Charlie Chaplin. Bob Kaufman. PoBA

Patriotic Poem. Diane Wakoski. VGW

Patriotic Reflections. Yehuda Amichai, *Hebrew.* IP, *tr. by* Warren Bargad *and* Stanley F. Chyet

Patriotic Songs. Yehuda Amichai, *Hebrew.*

    "Even my loves are measured by wars." PoSu, *tr. by* Yehuda Amichai *and* Ted Hughes

"I have nothing to say about the war." IP, *tr. by* Warren Bargad and Stanley Chyet; PoSu, *tr. by* Yehuda Amichai *and* Ted Hughes

    ("And all of Jerusalem is the explanation for his death.") (LL) IP, *tr. by* Warren Bargad and Stanley Chyet

"Let the memorial hill remember, instead of me." PoSu, *tr. by* Yehuda Amichai *and* Ted Hughes

"Town I was born in was destroyed by shells, The." PoSu, *tr. by* Yehuda Amichai *and* Ted Hughes

"War broke out in autumn at the empty border, The." PoSu, *tr. by* Yehuda Amichai *and* Ted Hughes

Patriotic Tour and Postulate of Joy. Robert Penn Warren. AiP; NYBP

Patriotic turns to face, The. A Question of Covenants. Gerald Dawe. PNI

Patriotism. Sir Walter Scott. *See* Caledonia.

Patriotism of a pair of thieves, The. (LL) The Murder of William Remington. Howard Nemerov. CMoP; CoAP

Patriot's Day. Steve Hassett. CDa

Patriot's Lament, The. Joseph Cephas Holly. AAP

Patriot's Progress, The. Horace Twiss. UV

Patriots! who sell their country for a place! Mary Jones. *See* An Epistle to Lady Bowyer.

Patrizia doesn't want to. Talking to Patrizia. Kenneth Koch. BAP-93

Patroclus Spears Thestor. Homer. OBVE, *tr. by* William Cowper *Fr.* The Iliad.

Patroclus's Request to Achilles for his Arms. Imitated from the Beginning of the Sixteenth Iliad of Homer. Homer. OBCVT, *tr. by* Thomas Yalden *Fr.* The Iliad.

Patrolling Barnegat. Walt Whitman. APN-1; OxBoS

Patrols. D. F. Brown. CDa

Patron, The. George Crabbe.

    "Our Pope, they say, once entertained the whim." EPCY

Patron of all those who do good by stealth. December: Prayer to St. Nicholas. John Heath-Stubbs. OBCP

Patron of Flawless Serpent Beauty. Friederike Mayröcker, *German.* WPOW, *tr. by* Michael Hamburger

Patrons of My Early Song, The. Mary Leapor. ECWP *Fr.* Epistle to Artemisia.

Patter of rain, A. O. Mabson Southard. HA

Patter of the Shingle, The. *Unknown.* BLPA

Pattern and mirror of the acts of earth, The. (LL) To Christ Our Lord. Galway Kinnell. HeIP-4; TwCP

Pattern [*or* patterne] of your love!, A. (LL) The Canonization. Donne. CABP; CBLP; ESCV; EnLoPo; FHYEP; FMP; FSCP; FaBoVe; GLoP; HAP; NAEL-1; NAWM-1; NIP-4; NOBE; NOSC; NoP-4; OAEL-1; PBRV; PoE; PoEL-2; PoPoPo; SCGP; SeCP; SoSe-8; TFi; TRP; UnPo

Patterned Lute, The. Li Shang-yin, *Chinese.* PLT, *tr. by* A. C. Graham

Patterns. Amy Lowell. AWP; BoWoP; MoAmPo; NoP-4; OxBA; PBMP; WHSW

Patterns. Roberta Hill Whiteman. HATNAP

Patterns of old green-gold trees. Autumn. Douglas Ridley Beeton. PeSA

Patty-cake, patty-cake / Marcus Antonius. Tact. Paul Pascal. WeW-3

Patty: "Hi, Mom! I'm home!" / *Cathy:* From the beginning, I. Double Trouble. David Trinidad. PmAP

Patty-Poem. Nick Kenny. PoToHe

Paudeen. W. B. Yeats. HAP; OxBSP; PoEL-5

Paul and Silas, bound in jail. All Night Long. *Unknown.* AS

Paul and Silas bound in jail. Keep Your Eyes on the Prize. *Unknown.* CrDW

Paul Bert stands tall—a statue in the park. Wrecking the Statue of Paul Bert. Thiên Thê, *Vietnamese.* AVP, *tr. by* Huỳnh Sanh Thông

Paul comes from Toronto on Sunday. I Am Not a Conspiracy Everything Is Not Paranoid. Susan Musgrave. NoAM

Paul Faber, Surgeon. George Macdonald.

    That Holy Thing. OBEV

Paul Jones's Victory. *Unknown.* AmFP

Paul Klee. Ruthven Todd. SPE

Paul Laurence Dunbar. James David Corrothers. NAAAL

Paul Laurence Dunbar, *for Herbert Martin.* Robert Earl Hayden. GT; NoP-4

Paul Laurence Dunbar. Mrs. Henry Linden. CBWP-4

Paul Revere's Ride (The Landlord's Tale). Henry Wadsworth Longfellow. AiP; BLPA; EBEvV; EBNV; FaBoBe; FaBoTw; FaPoR; ImGa; OBAL; OBCA; OBNV; PWR; TFi *Fr.* Tales of a Wayside Inn.

    ("And the midnight message of Paul Revere.") (LL) ChAP; ColAP; NOxBChV; SAGP

    (Paul Revere's Ride.) CTV; ChAP; ColAP; NOxBChV; SAGP

    ("So through the night rode Paul Revere.") CA

Paul Robeson. Gwendolyn Brooks. PoBA

Paul the First. Pavel Grigoryevich Antokolsky, *Russian.* TCRP, *tr. by* Bernard Meares

Paula Becker to Clara Westhoff. Adrienne Rich. NAAL-2; VCAP

Pauline, mine own, bend o'er me—thy soft breast. Robert Browning.

"Night, and one single ridge of narrow path." EBVVPR

"Sun-treader, life and light be thine for ever!" EPCY

"Thou wilt remember. Thou art not more dear." OAEL-2

Paul's clock struck twelve, 'twas time to go to bed. The Midnight Ramble. Charles Woodward. NOEC

Paul's *niemandsrose*. 18:VI:82. David Meltzer. MoNo

Paul's Wife. Robert Frost. EBNV

Pauper, A. Allen Tate. LiTM

Pauper Witch of Grafton, The. Robert Frost. *Fr.* Two Witches. CMoP

Pauper Woodland. Ronald G. Everson. NOBC

Pauper's Funeral, The. George Crabbe. OBNC *Fr.* The Village.

Pause. Mary Ursula Bethell. PeNZ

Pause. Witter Bynner. IMW

Pause. Octavio Paz, *Spanish*. STV, tr. by John Frederick Nims

Pause, A. Christina Rossetti. VWP

Pause for Breath, A. Ted Hughes. NYBP *Fr.* Root, Stem, Leaf.

Pause of Joe, The. Imamu Amiri Baraka. FTOS

Pause of Thought, A. Christina Rossetti. NOBE; OBNC *Fr.* Three Stages.

Pause over half-known faces. All their eyes are ice, / But nothing happens. Wilfred Owen. *See* Exposure.

Pausing. Elizabeth Searle Lamb. HA

Pausing at the edge of the wood. Cassandra and Friend. Norman Henry, II Pritchard. GT

Pavane for the Nursery, A. William Jay Smith. MoAmPo

Pavement slippery, people sneezing. January, 1795. Mary Robinson. ECWP; WoRP

Pavements lined. Death of a Chief. Khadambi Asalache. PBMAP

Pavilion for Listening to Fragrance, The. Chang Yü, *Chinese*. CoDLCP, tr. by Jonathan Chaves

Pavilions of dance, terraces of song. Ch'ien Ch'ien-i. CoBLCP, tr. by Jonathan Chaves *Fr.* In Spring of the Year *Ping-shen*.

Pavilion-Where-the-Crane-Came, The. Chao Meng-fu, *Chinese*. CoBLCP, tr. by Jonathan Chaves

Pavlov. Naomi Long Madgett. BPo

Pavlov's Dog. Michael Pettit. NAmP90

Pawiak 1943. Jerzy Ficowski, *Polish*. PoSu, tr. by Frank J. Corliss, Jr., *and* Grazyna Sandel

Pawing us who dealt them war and madness. (LL) Mental Cases. Wilfred Owen. CMoP; FaBoMo; NoAM; PeFWW

Pawky auld carle cam[e] ower [*or* owre *or* o'er] the lea [*or* lee], The. The Gaberlunzie Man. *Unknown*. EnSB; OxBB; OxBS

Pawnee War-Song. *Unknown, Pawnee Native American*. APN-2, tr. by Daniel Garrison Brinton

Pawntickets. John C. Ryan. IIP

Pawtucket Postcards. Franz Wright. CMAP

Pax. D. H. Lawrence. EnIH; PeECV; TrCP

"Pax vobis," quod the fox. *Unknown*. MiEL

Pay Cash Only. James Sherry. FTOS

Pay close attention: the world that appears now. A Lesson in Observation. Dan Pagis, *Hebrew*. AF, tr. by Stephen Mitchell

Pay Day at Coal Creek. *Unknown*. AmFP

Pay-off. Kenneth Fearing. CMoP

Pay Your Debts. Mrs. Henry Linden. CBWP-4

Paying a Sick-call to Yao Ts'un-tao in the Rain. Shen Chou, *Chinese*. CoBLCP, tr. by Jonathan Chaves

Paying a Visit to Monk Yung's Cloister. Meng Hao Jan, *Chinese*. SuSp, tr. by Joseph J. Lee

Paying Calls. Thomas Hardy. FP

Paynter if he shoulde adjoyne, A. Horace. OBCVT, tr. by Thomas Drant *Fr.* The Art of Poetry.

Payre: a metrical tag. A Throwing Out at / of (Com)pare (Dis)pair. Tina Darragh. FTOS

Paysage Choisi. Francis Sparshott. MoCV

Paysage Moralisé. W. H. Auden. OAEL-2; UnPo

Paysagesque. Norman Henry, II Pritchard. GT

PBS. Robert Mazzocco. WWSi

P.C., X, 36. Max Beerbohm. *See* Police Station Ditties.

Pcheek pcheek pcheek pcheek pcheek. Galway Kinnell. LiTM *Fr.* The Avenue Bearing the Initial of Christ into the New World.

Pea-Fields, The. Sir Charles G. D. Roberts. NOBC *Fr.* Songs of the Common Day.

Peace. Bacchylides. GrIP, tr. by Robert Fagles *Fr.* Paean.

Peace. Jonetta Barras. ISC

Peace. Bhartrihari, *Sanskrit*. AWP, tr. by Paul Elmer More

Peace. Rupert Brooke. OBWP; PoA; PoFWW *Fr.* 1914.

Peace. Charles Stuart Calverley. EBVV

(Peace: A Study.) NOBVV

Peace. Walter De la Mare. MoBrPo

Peace. Irwin Edman. TrJP

Peace. George Herbert. AWP; ESCV; GeHe; NOCV; NOSC

Peace. Gerard Manley Hopkins. GTBS-P; OxBSP; TrCP

Peace. Langston Hughes. BPo

Peace. Patrick Kavanagh. IIP

Peace. Tibullus, *Latin*. BiHa; CIP-2; OBCVT; PBCIP; PNI, tr. by Michael Longley

Peace. Leslie Ullman. IFJA

Peace. Henry Vaughan. AWP; EBEV; ESCV; FMP; FSCP; FaBoCh; GeHe; HAP; NOBE; NOCV; OBEV; OxAEP-1; PoE; SCGP; TFi; TOF; TrCP; WeW-3

Peace #3. Alma Villanueva. FFC

Peace: A Study. Charles Stuart Calverley. *See* Peace.

Peace: A Wedding Song, The. Aristophanes, *Greek*. ITG, tr. by Robert Hass

Peace and goodwill, to all mankind. Tennyson. *See* The Time draws near the birth of Christ.

Peace and Love. Ella Wheeler Wilcox. PWR

Peace and Mercy and Jonathan. First Thanksgiving of All. Nancy Byrd Turner. ChAP

Peace, and this Cot, and Thee, heart-honor'd [*or* heart-honored] Maid! (LL) The Eolian Harp. Coleridge. FHYEP; NAEL-2; NOBRP; OAEL-2

Peace at the Goal. Ella Wheeler Wilcox. PWR

Peace, Be at Peace, O Thou My Heaviness. Charles Baudelaire, *French*. InPK-6, tr. by Lord Alfred Douglas

Peace Be Still. *Unknown*. NAAAL

Peace be unto you, / Ye ministering angels. Shalom Aleichem. *Unknown, Hebrew*. TrJP

Peace be with you, gentle scrivener. Sholom Aleichem. Elias Lieberman. TrJP

Peace; come away: the song of woe. Tennyson. EBVV; EBVVPR; EnVR; FHYEP; IMW *Fr.* In Memoriam A. H. H.

Peace Delegate. Douglas Livingstone. PeSA

Peace Discovers the Poet. George Chapman. NOSC *Fr.* Euthymiae Raptus; or, The Teares of Peace.

Peace, Horror. Miklós Radnóti, *Hungarian*. AF, tr. by Emery E. George

Peace Hymn of the Republic. Henry Van Dyke. AH

Peace in the sober house of Jonas dwelt. Jonas Kindred's Household. George Crabbe. OBNC *Fr.* Tales.

Peace in the Welsh Hills. Vernon Watkins. GTBS-P; OxBTC

Peace in the World. John Galsworthy. PoLF

Peace in thy hands / Peace in thine eyes. The Ghost. Walter De la Mare. CMoP; EnLoPo; LiTM; MoBrPo; NOBE; OAEL-2; OxBTC

Peace is declared, an' I return. The Return. Rudyard Kipling. MoBrPo

Peace is made with a warlike man. *Unknown, Irish*. BIrV, tr. by John Montague

Peace Is the Mind's Old Wilderness. John Holmes. AH

Peace! / It's truly / wonderful! (LL) Projection. Langston Hughes. MoNo; PFTM

Peace Maketh Plenty. *Unknown*. OxBSP

Peace, my heart's blab! Be ever dumb. Silence: A Sonnet. Henry, Bishop of Chichester King. NOSC

Peace of Death, The. George Chapman. NOSC *Fr.* Euthymiae Raptus; or, The Teares of Peace.

Peace of great doors be for you, The. For You. Carl Sandburg. MoAmPo

Peace of Wild Things, The. Wendell Berry. MT; SAGP; VGW

Peace-Offering, The. Thomas Hardy. OxBSP

Peace on Earth. Bacchylides, *Greek*. AWP, tr. by John Addington Symonds

Peace on Earth. Michael S. Harper. MoNo

Peace on New England, on the shingled white houses, on golden. Jehu. Louis MacNeice. LiTM

Peace! Peace! Đỗ Tấn Xuân, *Vietnamese*. AVP, tr. by Huỳnh Sanh Thông

Peace! Peace! God of our fathers grant us Peace! A Prayer for Peace. Severn Teackle Wallis. CBCWP

Peace, peace! he is not dead, he doth not sleep. An Elegy on the Death of Keats. Shelley. NOBE; OBNC *Fr.* Adonais; An Elegy on the Death of Keats. EBEV; FHYEP; HoPM; ImPo; NOBRP; OAEL-2; OxAEP-2; PoEL-4; TFi

Peace, peace, my friend; these subjects fly. George Crabbe. PoEL-4 *Fr.* Sir Eustace Grey.

Peace, peace, my hony [*or* honey], do not cry. Christ's Reply. Edward Taylor. NAAL-1; NAAL-3; PoEL-3 *Fr.* God's Determinations [touching his Elect].

Peace Pillar. Otto Orban, *Hungarian*. CEEP, tr. by Emery E. George

Peace Poem. Velacan Maturai, *Tamil*. PLW, tr. by A. K. Ramanujan

Peace prat[t]ler, do not lour [or lowre]. Conscience. George Herbert. ESCV

Peace Project (5). Eric Mottram. NBrP

Peace, Shepherd, peace! What boots it singing on? Genius Loci. Margaret Louisa Woods. OBEV

Peace that hallows rudest ways. (LL) Forerunners. Ralph Waldo Emerson. APN-1; OBEV; OxBA

Peace the End of the Good Man. Robert Blair. OxAEP-1 *Fr.* The Grave.

Peace, the wild valley streaked with torrents. The Straw. Robert Graves. OxBTC

Peace-Time. Mervyn Morris. PBCV

Peace to all such! but were there one whose fires. Atticus. Alexander Pope. AWP; InPK-6; NOBE; TRP *Fr.* Epistle to Dr. Arbuthnot. FHYEP; InPS-3; NoP-4; OAEL-1; OxAEP-1; PoE; PoEL-3; TFi

Peace to each swain, who rural rapture owns. London Rurality. George Coleman, the Younger. OBGa *Fr.* London Rurality.

Peace to Lord Hamlet, I have never heard. Grave Doubts. Patricia Beer. NoP-4

Peace to Swift's faults! his wit hath made them pass. Byron. EPCY *Fr.* Hints from Horace.

Peace to the odalisque, the facile slave. Emily Jane Pfeiffer. VWP

Peace to these little broken leaves. Leaves. W. H. Davies. MoBrPo

"Peace upon earth!" was said. We sing it. Christmas: 1924. Thomas Hardy. FaBoEE; OBCP

Peace Walk. William Stafford. Poetsp

Peace, war, religion. This Tokyo. Gary Snyder. CAPP-1; NeAP

Peace! where art thou to be found? Enquiry after Peace. A Fragment. Anne Finch, Countess of Winchilsea. ECWP; PoE

Peace with Honor. Philip Appleman. CDa

Peace, you ungracious clamours! peace, rude sounds! Shakespeare. OxAEP-1 *Fr.* Troilus and Cressida.

Peaceable Kingdom, The. Marge Piercy. TwCP

Peaceful and young, Herculean silence bore. The Peace of Death. George Chapman. NOSC *Fr.* Euthymiae Raptus; or, The Teares of Peace.

Peaceful our valley, fair and green. A Cottage in Grasmere Vale. Dorothy Wordsworth. NALW; PEW; Ro

Peaceful Shepherd, The. Robert Frost. MoAmPo

Peaceful Step, A. Gane Todorovski, *Macedonian.* CEEP, *tr. by* Dragan Milivojevic

Peacefully. Tanka. Masaoka Shiki, *Japanese.* MJT, *tr. by* Ueda, Makoto

Peacefully upon its plantlike stem. (LL) Flowers by the Sea. William Carlos Williams. CMoP; MoAmPo; NoAM; RB; TAP

Peach. Rose Rauter. KaS

Peach and plum blossoms, speechless, keep swaying in the wind. Huang T'ing-chien. SuSp, *tr. by* Michael E. Workman *Fr.* In My Study in Monastery, Rising after a Nap.

Peach Tree Young and Fresh. *Unknown, Chinese.* CoBCP, *tr. by* Burton Watson

Peachblossom is redded because rain fell overnight, The. Morning. Wang Wei, *Chinese.* TAL, *tr. by* Robert Payne

Peaches. Siv Cedering Fox. PBCAP

Peaches. Donald Hall. NoP-4

Peaches and Cream. Mudrooroo. BMAP

Peaches are drying up all around. La Sequia. Alberto A. Ríos. IFJA

Peachstone. Dannie Abse. OxBC; WeW-3

Peachum's Morning Hymn. Bertolt Brecht. OxBoV, *tr. by* Ralph Manheim *and* John Willett *Fr.* The Threepenny Opera.

Peacock. D. H. Lawrence. TTTS

Peacock "At Home," The. Catherine Ann Dorset. OxBChV

"Peacock colored tears and rotten oranges." Midnight on Front Street. Roberta Hill Whiteman. CDW

Peacock drags its tail with its long golden threads, The. Tune: "Eight-beat Barbarian Tune." Sun Kuang-hsien, *Chinese.* SuSp, *tr. by* Hellmut Wilhelm

Peacock flew, far off to the south-east; A. Lu Yün, *Chinese.* ChiP, *tr. by* Arthur Waley

Peacock Poems, The. Sherley Anne Williams.
"I never thought to see us." MDDM

Peacock Poems: 1, The. Sherley Anne Williams. NAAAL

Peacocks. Walter Adolphe Roberts. PBCV

Peacocks: A Mood. Olive Custance. ADE

Peacock's Feather, A. Seamus Heaney. DiPo

Pealing again, prolonged the roar. (LL) In Romney Marsh. John Davidson. EBVV; OxBTC

Peanut sat on a railroad track, A. *Unknown.* TLR

Pear blossoms are pure, The. Spring. Su Tung-p'o, *Chinese.* OHPC, *tr. by* Kenneth Rexroth

Pear Tree. Hilda Doolittle. BoWoP; CMoP; ColAP; MoAmPo; NOBA; PoE; UnPo

Pear-Tree, The. Iwan Goll, *German.* TrJP, *tr. by* Babette Deutsch *and* Avrahm Yarmolinsky

Pear Tree, The. Edna St. Vincent Millay. MoAmPo

Pear-Tree, The. *Unknown.* AWP, *tr. by* Allen Upward *Fr.* Shi King.

Pear tree that last year, The. Shimmer. James Schuyler. VCAP

Pearl. [Matt. 13:45], The. George Herbert. ChIV-2; EBEV; ESCV; FHYEP; FSCP; GeHe; HAP; NOCV; NOSC; OAEL-1; PoEL-2; SeCP

Pearl. *Unknown.*
"Dubbement dere of down and dales, The." EnVB
"Perle, plesaunte to prynces paye." EBEV, *stanzas* 1–5
("Perle plesaunte to prynces paye Pearl, the precious prize of a king.") NoP-4

Pearl Avenue runs past the high-school lot. Ex-Basketball Player. John Updike. InPK-6; NYBP; TRP

Pearl Bryan. *Unknown.* AmFP

Pearl-hen counts; one, two, three, four, The. Christian Morgenstern, *German.* CBNP, *tr. by* Hugh Haughton

Pearl of the sea! Star of the West! On Leaving Cuba, Her Native Land. Gertrudis Gomez de Avellaneda, *Spanish.* WPOW, *tr. by* Catherine Rodriguez-Nieto

Pearl pellets, resplendent young dandies. On the Street of Lo-yang. Meng Hao Jan, *Chinese.* SuSp, *tr. by* Paul W. Kroll

Pearl Perch. John Blight. CBAP

Pearl-teardrops roll and gather. Huang E, *Chinese.* CoBLCP, *tr. by* Jonathan Chaves

Pearle's Poem. Primus St. John. GT

Pearlmother dawn. It is fairly true. Abhorring a Vacuum. Chris Wallace-Crabbe. BMAP

Pearls. Alan Gould. NOBAu

Pearls. Léopold Sédar Senghor, *French.* VCWP, *tr. by* Melvin Dixon

Peasant. W. S. Merwin. NYBP

Peasant, A. Ronald Stuart Thomas. OBWVE

Peasant, The. Leonard Wolf. NYBP

Peasant and the Sheep, The. Ivan Andreevich Kriloff, *Russian.* AWP, *tr. by* C. Fillingham Coxwell

Peasant Declares His Love, The. Emile Roumer, *French.* NegPo; TTY, *tr. by* John Peale Bishop

Peasant haled a sheep to court, A. The Peasant and the Sheep. Ivan Andreevich Kriloff, *Russian.* AWP, *tr. by* C. Fillingham Coxwell

Peasant once unthinkingly, A. The Monk and the Peasant. Margaret E. Bruner. PoToHe

Peasant oppressed by sorrow and misery, A. Song of a Farmer. P'i Jih-hsiu, *Chinese.* SuSp, *tr. by* William H. Nienhauser

Peasant Poet, The. John Clare. FHYEP; OAEL-2; OBNC

Peasant Woman, A. Frances Darwin Cornford. WPN

Peasants, The. Alun Lewis. LiTM; PoWW

Peasants at Work. James Hurdis. ECEV *Fr.* The Favourite Village.

Peasant's shack beside the, A. Country Cottage. Tu Fu, *Chinese.* OHPC, *tr. by* Kenneth Rexroth

Peasant's Song, The. *Unknown.* FaBoPV

Peasants watch them die, The. (LL) The Peasants. Alun Lewis. LiTM; PoWW

Pease porridge [or pudding] hot. Mother Goose. LB; ReMoGo
("Spell me that in four letters.") (LL) OxNR

Pebble, The. Elinor Wylie. ChIV-1; MoAmPo

Pebble falls, A. John Wills. HA

Pebbles. Edith King. BoTP

Pebbles. Herman Melville. NCAP

Pebbles are beneath, but we stand softly. Sea-Marge. Ivor Gurney. NTP

Pebbles skipping off the window woke me. Dawn Raid on an Orchard. Tom Pickard. NBrP

Pecan, The Toucan, The. Robert Williams Wood. NBLV

Peculiar Christmas, A. Roy Fuller. AYFP

Pedalling between lectures, spokes throwing off. Cricket at Oxford. Alan Ross. PeLV

Pedalling Man, The. Russell Hoban. NOxBChV

Peddler and His Wife, The. *Unknown.* AmFP

Peddler's Village. Gerald Stern. CMAP

Pedestal ashtray next to the son who hadn't seen, A. Father Hunger and Son. Roger Weingarten. NAmP90

Pedestrian Woman, The. Robin Morgan. CrSp

Pediatrics. Carol Muske. PBCAP

Pedigree of Honey, The, vers. 1. Emily Dickinson. MoP; NOBA

Pedigree of Honey, The, vers. 2. Emily Dickinson. MoP; SAmP

Pedlar. Confucius. CTC; OBVE, *tr. by* Ezra Pound *Fr.* Wei Wind.

Pedlar, The. Charlotte Mew. NOxBChV

Pedlar I am, that take great care, A. A Pedlar of Small-Wares. Sir John Suckling. CaPo

Pedlar Jim. Florence Hoare. BoTP

Pedlar of Small-Wares, A. Sir John Suckling. CaPo

Pedlar of Spells, The. Lu Yu, *Chinese*. ChiP, *tr. by* Arthur Waley

Pedlar's Caravan, The. William Brighty Rands. BoTP; OxBChV

Pedlar's Song, The. Shakespeare. NBLV; OxBoLi; PeLV *Fr.* The Winter's Tale.

　(Autolycus's Song ("When daffodils begin to peer").) NOBE; OAEL-1

　(Song: "When daffodils begin to peer.") PoEL-2

Pedlar's Song, The. Shakespeare. *See* Autolycus as Peddler.

Pedra. John William Burgon. BLPA

Pee as in pulchritude, The. Poetry. Tom Leonard. FaBoTC

Pee Wee Coach, The. Walter McDonald. IFJA

Peekaboo, I Almost See You. Ogden Nash. EBEvV; PeLV; PoLF

Peeking in through. Praxilla, *Greek*. InMo, *tr. by* Sam Hamill

Peeling an apple somewhere far away. (LL) A Primer of the Daily Round. Howard Nemerov. NYBP; NoP-4; WeW-3

Peeling Onions. Adrienne Rich. BoWoP; HCAP; TAP

Peeling Pippins. Mary TallMountain. HATNAP

Peepin' through the knothole. Go Get the Axe. *Unknown*. AS

Peer of the gods is that man, who. Sappho, *Greek*. OBCVT; OBVE, *tr. by* William Carlos Williams

Peer of the golden gods is he to Sappho. Ode to Anactoria. Sappho, *Greek*. AWP, *tr. by* William Ellery Leonard

Peering into the depths of the stream. T'ao Ch'ien. SuSp, *tr. by* Eugene Eoyang *Fr.* The Seasons Come and Go.

Peering out. Michael McClintock. HA

Peers who died, or orbs. Catullus. *See* Sappho.

Pees maketh plente. *Unknown*. MiEL

Peeter a Whitfeild he hath slaine. Jock o' the Side. *Unknown*. ESPB

Pegasus. Varlam Tikhonovich Shalamov, *Russian*. TCRP, *tr. by* Bradley Jordan

Pegasus Lost. Elinor Wylie. MoAmPo

Peggy. Allan Ramsay. *See* The Wawking of the Fauld.

Peggy Browne. Turlough Carolan, *Irish*. BIrV, *tr. by* Austin Clarke

Pei-mang Cemetery. Yüan Hung-tao, *Chinese*. CoBLCP, *tr. by* Jonathan Chaves

Pekinese / Adore their ease, The. Edward Verrall Lucas. CTAV

Pelican, The. Greg Kuzma. AmPA

Pelican Chorus, The. Edward Lear. CTAV; OBSP

Pelicans. Robinson Jeffers. MoAmPo

Pelicans. Judith Wright. BMAP

Pelicans in the Wilderness (A Grave near Halfa). Rudyard Kipling. PeFWW *Fr.* Epitaphs of the War [1914–1918]. OBWP

Pelleas and Ettarre. Tennyson. NAEL-2 *Fr.* Idylls of the King.

　"Rose, but one, none other rose had I, A." PoEL-5

Pen, The. Mary Weston Fordham. CBWP-2

Pen and four fingers: I watched four fair creatures. Cynewulf. ASW, *tr. by* Kevin Crossley-Holland *Fr.* Riddles (Exeter Book).

Pen-guin. The Sword-fish, The. Robert Williams Wood. NBLV

Pen is an index finger, The. Castration of the Pen. Erica Jong. NALW

Pen slides, The. Valerio Magrelli, *Italian*. NeIt, *tr. by* Dana Gioia

Pen Vine and Scroll. John Taggart. FTOS

Penal Law. Austin Clarke. BoLoP; GTBS-P; NOIV

Penal Servitude for Mrs. Maybrick. *Unknown*. OxBoLi

Penalty of Virtue, The. *Unknown*. *Fr.* The Panchatantra. AWP, *tr. by* Arthur Ryder

Penance, A. Francis Daniel Pastorius. NOSC

Penance for killing mountain goat is pain, The. Trespasses. Paul Zarzyski. PaTW

Pencilled by the Rain. Peter Hooper. PeNZ

Pencil's Sleep, The. Tymoteusz Karpowicz, *Polish*. PoSu, *tr. by* Andrzej Busza *and* Bogdan Czaykowski

Pendulum, The. Michael Cuddihy. CMAP

Pendydd. Kingsley Amis. NOBL *Fr.* The Evans Country.

Penelope. James Harrison. NIP-4

Penelope. Monique Laederach, *French*. BoWoP, *tr. by* Charles Guenther

Penelope. Judita Vaiiunaite, *Lithuanian*. CEEP, *tr. by* Irene Pogoželskyte Suboczewski

Penelope as a *garçon manqué*. Mythology. Marilyn Hacker. NoAM

Penelope for her *Ulisses* sake. Edmund Spenser. NoP-4; PBRV

Penelope hesitates. Homer. OBCVT, *tr. by* Robert Fitzgerald *Fr.* The Odyssey.

Penelope pulls home. Kiltartan Legend. Padraic Fallon. NOIV

Penelope to Ulysses. Anne Wharton.

　"Penelope this slow Epistle sends." KTR

Penelope weeps. Homer. OBCVT, *tr. by* Robert Fitzgerald *Fr.* The Odyssey.

Penelope, who really cried. (LL) An Ancient Gesture. Edna St. Vincent Millay. NALW; NMM-2

Penelope's Despair. Yannis Ritsos, *Greek*. GrIP; VCWP, *tr. by* Edmund Keeley

Penetration. "Michael Field." VWP

Penguin hailed me at the door, A. Penguins in the Home. Helen Smith Bevington. OBAL

Penguin on the Beach. Ruth Miller. PeSA

Penguins. Artur Miedzyrzecki, *Polish*. PoSu, *tr. by* Artur Miedzyrzecki *and* John Batki

Penguins in the Home. Helen Smith Bevington. OBAL

Peninsula, The. Seamus Heaney. IIP

Peninsular arm, Sirmio, insular arm, well. Catullus. *See* Carmen 31 ("Apple of islands, Sirmio, & bright peninsulas, set").

Penitent Considers Another Coming of Mary, A. Gwendolyn Brooks. NoAM; PChr

Penitential Cries of Jupiter Hammond, The. Gary Smith. GT

Penitential Psalms. Sir Thomas Wyatt.

　Prologue: "Love, to give law unto his subject hearts." ChIV-1

Penn Central Station at Beacon, N.Y, The. Ed Ochester. GM

Penniless Indian fakirs and their camels, The. Avarice. Anthony Hecht. OxBSP

Penniless Lovers. Eugenio de Andrade, *Portuguese*. VCWP, *tr. by* Alexis Levitin

Pennsylvania Deutsch. Christopher Darlington Morley. NBLV

Pennsylvania Places. Thomas Augustin Daly. OBAL

Pennsylvania spiders. Morning Harvest. Gerald Stern. LCAP-2

Pennsylvania Station in New York, The. Langston Hughes. GM

Pennsylvania Winter Indian 1974. Harold Littlebird. VoR

Penny. *Unknown*. EnVB; FaBoVe; MiEL

Penny and penny. *Unknown*. OxNR

Penny for a ball of thread, A. Pop Goes the Weasel. *Unknown*. CIV

Penny for you, philosophers of eternity, A. Uri Zvi Greenberg, *Hebrew*. MHP, *tr. by* Ruth Finer Mintz

Penny lost in the lak, The. *Unknown*. OxBS *Fr.* Colkelbie Sow.

Penny Toys. John Mole.

　"Musical monkey is dressed like a flunkey, The." OBCoV

　Song of the Hat-Raising Doll. OBCoV

Penny Trumpet. Raphael Rudnik. NYBP

Penny Whistle, The. Edward Thomas. MoBrPo

Penny Wish, A. Irene Thompson. BoTP

Pennycandystore beyond the El, The. Lawrence Ferlinghetti. HeIP-4; PoM; TAP

Penological Study: Southern Exposure. Robert Penn Warren.

　Wet Hair: If Now His Mother Should Come. NoAM

Pensioners. Winifred M. Letts. BoTP

Pensionnaires. Paul Verlaine, *French*. EP, *tr. by* François Pirou

Pensive at eve on the hard world I mus'd [*or* mused]. Coleridge. *Fr.* Sonnets Attempted in the Manner of Contemporary Writers. Son

Pensive Eliza lately sate. The Triple League to Mrs Susan Dove. Elizabeth Thomas. KTR

Pensive gnu, the staid aardvark, The. For An Amorous Lady. Theodore Roethke. LoP; NBLV

Pensive here I sat. Milton. *Fr.* Book II. FHYEP; NAEL-1; OxAEP-1 *Fr.* Paradise Lost.

Pensive on her dead gazing I heard the Mother of All. Walt Whitman. RB

Pensive they sit, and roll their languid eyes. Keats. CBNP

Pentagon Exorcism. Allen Ginsberg. BB

Pentagonia. G. E. Bates. NYBP

Pentecost Castle, The. Geoffrey Hill. HAP

　"And you my spent heart's treasure." HAP

　"Down in the orchard." HAP

　"I shall go down." HAP

　"Splendidly-shining darkness." HAP

　"They slew by night." HAP

Pentelogia. Francis Quarles.

　"Can he be fair that withers at a blast." PeECV

　"What is the *World*? A great *Exchange* of ware." PBRV

Penthouse Playboy. Lyn Lifshin. DeD

Penus envy, they call it. "Alta." NMM-2

Peonage System, The. Lizelia Augusta Jenkins Moorer. CBWP-3

Peonies. Li Shang-yin, *Chinese*. PLT, *tr. by* A. C. Graham

Peonies at Dusk. Jane Kenyon. LoL

Peonies below the stairs, The. Yüan Mei. *Fr.* In Late Spring of the Year Keng-hsü (1790), I Stayed at the Sun Family's Gemstone Mountain Villa at West Lake. Before Leaving, I Wrote These Poems as Mementos. CoBLCP, *tr. by* Jonathan Chaves

Peony Afternoon. So Chong-Ju, *Korean*. VCWP, *tr. by* David R. McCann

Peony in her hair, The. Tanka. Akiko Yosano, *Japanese*. MJT, *tr. by* Ueda, Makoto

People. Hans Arp, *German*. PFTM, *tr. by* Rosemarie Waldrop

People, The. Robert Creeley. VGW

People, The. Elizabeth Madox Roberts. NOxBChV

People. Jean Toomer. GT

People, The. W. B. Yeats. CMoP

People all say the southland's better. Tune: Deva-like Barbarian. Wei Chuang, *Chinese*. CoBCP, *tr. by* Burton Watson

People all say the southland's better. Wen T'ing-yün, *Chinese*. CoBCP, *tr. by* Burton Watson

People all talk about serving the King of Emptiness. Sent to the Ch'an Master Wu-hsiang. Lo Yin, *Chinese*. SuSp, *tr. by* Geoffrey R. Waters

People along the sand, The. Neither Out Far Nor In Deep. Robert Frost. AmPP; HAP; MeMAP; MoP; NAAL-2; NOBA; NoAM; NoP-4; OxBoS; PFE; Poetr; TAP; TRP; WeW-3

People always find you. Disappearing. David Clewell. IFJA

People always say to me. The Question. Karla Kuskin. NTCP; PiM

People and things crowd in. Nature Morte. Joseph Brodsky, *Russian*. TCRP, *tr. by* George L. Kline

People are eating dinner in that country north of Legge's Lake, The. Les A. Murray. BMAP *Fr.* The Buluhdelah—Taree Holiday Song Cycle.

People are making a camp of branches in that country at Arnhem Bay, The. Song Cycle of the Moon-Bone. *Unknown, Aborigine*. NOBAu, *tr. by* Ronald M. Berndt

People are of two kinds, and he. Tribute on the Passing of a Very Real Person. *Unknown*. PoToHe

People are on the one side understandable. Dmitry Aleksandrovich Prigov, *Russian*. TCRP, *tr. by* Albert C. Todd

People are putting up storm windows now. Storm Windows. Howard Nemerov. CoAmPo; InPK-6; VCAP

People are saying that I am your enemy, The. To Julia de Burgos. Julia De Burgos, *Spanish*. BoWoP; PBWP, *tr. by* Grace Schulman

People at Night *(Derived from Rilke)*. Denise Levertov. CLPP

People chained to aurora, A. Civilization and Its Discontents. John Ashbery. CAPP-1; LCAP-2; TwCP

People come from all over to consult me, bringing their limbs. Margaret Atwood. NALW *Fr.* Circe / Mud Poems.

People die from loneliness. One. Carolyn M. Rodgers. BPo

People do gossip. Sappho, *Greek*. PBWP, *tr. by* Mary Barnard

People expect old men to die. Old Men. Ogden Nash. InPS-3; RB

People getting divorced. Lawrence Ferlinghetti. NoAM

People going straight up to heaven. Amazing Grace. Anselm Hollo. PoM

People Hide Their Love. Emperor Wu of Han, *Chinese*. ChiP, *tr. by* Arthur Waley

People I love the best, The. To Be of Use. Marge Piercy. CrSp

People in My Family. Grace Paley. EC3

People in These Houses. Jack Matthews. CMAP

People is a beast of muddy brain, The. Tommaso Campanella, *Italian*. AWP, *tr. by* John Addington Symonds

People keep tellin me to put my feet on the ground. Advice. Ntozake Shange. NMM-2

People Like Us. William Matthews. APAD

People live forever in Jacksonville and St. Petersburg and Tampa. Come On In, the Senility Is Fine. Ogden Nash. AiP

People lived there. Now we live there. (LL) Lynching and Burning. Primus St. John. ISC

People love each other and the light. Of Love. William Meredith. VCAP *Fr.* Consequences.

People, / male and female. Mahadevi, *Kannada*. BoWoP, *tr. by* A. K. Ramanujan

People need poetry, The. Osip Mandelstam. Seamus Deane. BiHa; PBCIP

People, No, The. Vicki Raymond. NOBAu

People of the islands want a different poem, The. A Different Poem. Onésima Silveira. PBMAP

People of the South Wind. William Stafford. NNaP

People of Unrest. Margaret Walker Alexander. GT

People on Wayward Journeys. Ofelia Zepeda. PaTW

People one, and one supplies the King, The. (LL) The Gardens of Alcinous. Homer, *Greek*. GaP; OAEL-1; OBVE, *tr. by* Alexander Pope

People—people of my kind, my own, The. To the Lacedemonians. Allen Tate. NAAL-2; NoAM

People say the sun is in heaven. Hsieh Chin. *Fr.* What Does the Little Boy Love? CoBLCP, *tr. by* Jonathan Chaves

People say they have a hard time. For de Lawd. Lucille Clifton. IMW; MBE; PoBA; TAP; TwCP

People the Churches love best, The. Limerick. Patrick Braybrook. PeLi

People vs. the People, The. Kenneth Fearing. MoAmPo

People walk upon their heads, The. Topsy-turvy Land. H. E. Wilkinson. BoTP

People were bathing and posturing themselves on the beach. The Gods! The Gods! D. H. Lawrence. CMoP

People were those who. *Unknown*. *See* The Broken String.

People? What do I care about people? Georgy Vladimirovich Ivanov, *Russian*. TCRP, *tr. by* Daniel Weissbort

People who buy flowers in Ch'ang-an. Song of Selling Flowers. Tsung Ch'en, *Chinese*. CoBLCP, *tr. by* Jonathan Chaves

People who come out of nowhere to try to put into words any part of what. All Writing Is Garbage. Antonin Artaud, *French*. PFTM, *tr. by* Helen Weaver

People who have no children can be hard. Gwendolyn Brooks. *Fr.* The Children of the Poor. WPE, *sect.* I, *pt.* 1-2; PoA, *sect.* I, *pt.* 1-3; NAAL *Fr.* The Womanhood.

People Who Must. Carl Sandburg. CA

People who want to live beside the ocean are fundamentalists. Lakes. David Donnell. NoAM

People will live on, The. The People, Yes. Carl Sandburg. MoAmPo; NOBA; NoAM; OxBA; SAGP

"Englishman in the old days, An." FYAP

"From the four corners of the earth." CMoP

"They have yarns / Of a skyscraper so tall they had to put hinges." MoAmPo

"What the people learn out of lifting and hauling and waiting and losing." OBAL

"Who shall speak for the people?" OxBA

"Why did the children." OBAL; PBMP

"Why repeat? I heard you the first time." OBAL

People's fury cannot move, The. Horace, *Latin*. OBCVT, *tr. by* Alfred Tennyson, 1st Baron Tennyson

Peoples House. Nikolai Alekseievich Zabolotsky, *Russian*. TCRP, *tr. by* Daniel Weissbort

People's Literary, De. Maggie Pogue Johnson. CBWP-4

People's welfare is his first concern, The. A King's Portrait. King Lê Thánh–tông, *Vietnamese*. AVP, *tr. by* Huỳnh Sanh Thông

Pepper in ashes, cassia branches broken, the good man grows old, The. Sending Off O.E. Who Brought an Orchid Home to Japan. "Lu Hsün," *Chinese*. SuSp, *tr. by* William R. Schultz

Peppergrass. Stanley Plumly. LCAP-2

Peppertrees, the peppertrees, The! Scenes from the Life of the Peppertrees. Denise Levertov. LiTM; NeAP; PoM

Peppery Man was cross and thin, The. Arthur Macy. FPC

Per Iter Tenebricosum. Oliver St. John Gogarty. OBMV

Peradventure of old, some bard in Ionian Islands. Henry Wadsworth Longfellow. APN-1 *Fr.* Elegiac Verse.

Perambulator Poem. David McCord. *Fr.* Perambulator Poems, I-VII.

Perambulator Poems, I-VII. David McCord.

   Perambulator Poem.

Perceived she stirred, but did not see. (LL) Seeing Her Dancing. Robert Heath. NOSC; OxBSP

Perception of an object costs. Emily Dickinson. APN-2; NOBA

Perchance in days to come. Strange Love. Moses ibn Ezra, *Hebrew*. TrJP, *tr. by* Solomon Solis-Cohen

Perchance that I might learn what pity is. A Prayer for Purification. Michelangelo Buonarroti, *Italian*. AWP, *tr. by* John Addington Symonds

Perchance, the friend who cheered thy early years. Judge Not. Josephine D. Henderson Heard. CBWP-4

Perched in a tower of this ancestral Wall. At the Great Wall of China. Edmund Blunden. GTBS-P

Perching bolt upright. O. Mabson Southard. HA

Percussion, salt and honey. Sappho, *Greek*. OBCVT, *tr. by* Guy Davenport

Percussive, furious, this wind. Mistral. Barbara Howes. NYBP

Shelley: Inscription for the Couch, Still Preserved, on which He Passed the Last Night of His Life. D. G. Rossetti. EPCY

Perdam Sapientiam Sapientium. William Habington. ChIV-2

Perdita. Louis MacNeice. PoA

Perdy [*or* Perdie *or* Perdye], I said[e] it [*or* yt] not. Sir Thomas Wyatt. PoEL-1; SiPS

Père Lalement. Marjorie Lowry Christie Pickthall. NOBC

Peregrine White and Virginia Dare. Rosemary Benét *and* Stephen Vincent Benét. OBCA

Peregrine's Sunday Song. Elinor Wylie. NYBP

Perennial tears descend in gems. (LL) The Valley of Unrest. Edgar Allan Poe. APN-1; AmPP; NAAL-1; NAAL-3; PAR; PoEL-4

Perfect. "Hugh MacDiarmid." NoP-4; RB

Perfect Bliss and Sole Felicity. Marlowe. *See* Nature That Framed Us of Four Elements.

Perfect breakfast, all must own, The. Breakfast. Harry Graham. EBNV

Perfect Child, The. Adrian Porter. NBLV

Perfect Disc of the Moon, The. Richard Kenney. Son

Perfect Gift, The. Edmund Vance Cooke. PChr

Perfect Husband, The. Ogden Nash. Poetr

Perfect is the word I can never hear. Rhymes. Charles Tomlinson. DiPo

Perfect little body, without fault or stain on thee. On a Dead Child. Robert Bridges. CMoP; EBEV; LiTM; NOBE; NOBVV; NoAM; OBMV; OBNC; OxAEP-2; SCGP

Perfect Orchestra, The. Henrietta Cordelia Ray. CBWP-3

Perfect Reactionary, The. Hughes Mearns. NTCP

Perfect Timing. Sarah Maguire. LW

Perfection, if't hath ever been attayned. In the Due Honor of the Author Master Robert Norton. John Smith. SCAP

Perfection, of a kind, was what he was after. Epitaph on a Tyrant. W. H. Auden. AF; HeIP-4; MeMAP; NoAM; OxBSP; OxBoV; RB

Perfection of Dentistry, The. Marvin Bell. AmPA; CoAP

Perfectly beautiful, perfectly ignorant of it. (LL) Piazza di Spagna, Early Morning. Richard Wilbur. InPS-3; NoP-4; OxBSP; PFE; SAGP; VGW

Perfectly happy now, he looked at his estate. Voltaire at Ferney. W. H. Auden. LiTM; PoA

Perfecto Flores. Jimmy Santiago Baca. TRP

Perfervid Roc, sitting on candle light, The. The Roc. Richard Eberhart. CMoP

Perfidia. David Lehman. NAmP90

Perfidious, The. Walter Savage Landor. CBLP

Performance, The. James Dickey. CoAP; CoAmPo; LiTM; MoP; PoE; SAGP; WeT

Performance at Hog Theater, A. Russell Edson. AmPA; PmAP

Performances. Nina Cassian, *Romanian*. IFJA, *tr. by* Brenda Walker

Performances, assortments, résumés. The Tunnel. Hart Crane. CMoP; MoAmPo; OxBA *Fr.* The Bridge. NAAL-2

Performing Seal, The. Rachel Lyman Field. OBCA *Fr.* A Circus Garland.

Perfume, The. Donne. ESCV; FSCP; NoSic; SeCP *Fr.* Elegies.

Perfume, The. Robert Herrick. CaPo

Perfume blows from the kingfisher. Song of Liang Chou. Ou-yang Hsiu, *Chinese*. OHPC, *tr. by* Kenneth Rexroth

Perfume / of flowers! A haw, The. Charles Olson. RaBo

Perfume of the ginger-flowers, The. Ginger-flowers. Kenneth Mackenzie. BMAP

Perfume of the red water lilies, The. To the Tune, "Plum Blossoms Fall and Scatter." Li Ch'ing-chao, *Chinese*. OHPC, *tr. by* Kenneth Rexroth

Perfume sweet I send you. Not of Itself, But Thee. *Unknown, Greek.* GrAn, *tr. by* Dudley Fitts

Perfume! That lingerest round the throat. Frangipani. Theodore Wratislaw. ADE

Perhaps. Sydney Thompson Dobell. NOBVV

Perhaps. Homer. *See* Apollo Defeats Patroclus.

Perhaps because you are the image. To Evening. Ugo Foscolo. ItIP

Perhaps biography is the flat map. Biography. Maura Stanton. CMAP

Perhaps he does. . . O Lord, that House in Stratford! (LL) Ben Jonson Entertains a Man from Stratford. Edwin Arlington Robinson. AmPP; MoAmPo

Perhaps he will fall. (LL) Wilderness Gothic. Alfred Wellington Purdy. HeIP-4; MoCV; NOBC; NoP-4

Perhaps I always knew what they were saying. The Prophets. W. H. Auden. CBLP

Perhaps I may allow, the Dean. Jonathan Swift. EPCY; NOBE; PeLV *Fr.* Verses on the Death of Dr. Swift, D.S.P.D.

Perhaps if she stood for an hour like that. Woman at Lit Window. Eamon Grennan. BLT

Perhaps, if you / Are very good. Hob the Elf. Norman M. Johnson. BoTP

Perhaps it is to avoid some great sadness. Sleeping on the Wing. Frank O'Hara. InPS-3; NAAL-2

Perhaps It's as You Say. Peter Everwine. NNaP

Perhaps I've got to write better longer thinking of it. On Induction of the Hand. Clark Coolidge. PmAP

Perhaps, long hence, when I have passed away. Thomas Hardy. *Fr.* She, to Him. EnVR

Perhaps my mother murdered me. (LL) The Inquest. W. H. Davies. GTBS-P; NOBE; OxBTC; RB

Perhaps on a sunday. Day Song. Lance Henson. HATNAP

Perhaps one day I shall let myself. Open Secret. Denise Levertov. PaTW

Perhaps our cares. "Shu Ting," *Chinese.* ChiPo, *tr. by* W. J. F. Jenner

Perhaps she said, lively at first but once. Farmer Goes Beserk. Anne Elder. CBAP

Perhaps the Socrates he had never read. Why Hast Thou Forsaken Me? Chad Walsh. *Fr.* The Psalm of Christ. TrCP

Perhaps the World Ends Here. Joy Harjo. PaTW

Perhaps these thoughts of ours. "Shu Ting," *Chinese.* BLT, *tr. by* Carolyn Kizer

Perhaps / This is the way. Antigone I. Herbert Martin. PoBA

Perhaps this valley too leads into the head of long-ago days. Grand Abacus. John Ashbery. PoA; SPE

Perhaps you expected a face that was free from tears. Narcissus. Paul Valéry, *French.* AWP, *tr. by* Joseph T. Shipley

Perhaps / You will remember / John Brown. October 16[: The Raid]. Langston Hughes. PoBA

Pericles. Shakespeare.

"Terrible child-bed hast thou had, my dear, A." EBEV; OxAEP-1

Pericles and Aspasia. Walter Savage Landor.

Behold, O Aspasia! I Send You Verses. OBNC; SCGP

Corinna, from Athens, to Tanagra. OBEV

(Corinna to Tanagra.) OBNC

Death of Artemidora, The. OBNC

Dirce. AWP; CTC; EBEV; FaBoEE; GBL; HAP; NOBE; NoP-4; OAEL-2; OBEV; OBNC; OxAEP-2; OxBSP; PoEL-4; PoRA; SCGP; TFi; WeW-3

Perigord pres del muralh, A. Bertrans de Born, *Provençal.* CTC, *tr. by* Ezra Pound

Perimedes [*or* Perimedes, the Blacksmith]. Robert Greene.

Phillis and Coridon. NoSic

(Coridon and Phillis.)

Peripatetic Letter to Isabella Fey, A. David Wright.

"This was as far as I had got." PeSAV

Peripeteia. Anthony Hecht. VCAP

Periphery. A. R. Ammons. NOBA

Periphery. Ruth Stone. NALW

Perirrhanterium. George Herbert. ESCV

Peri's Lament for Hinda, The. Thomas Moore. OBNC *Fr.* Lalla Rookh.

Perish th' illiberal thought which would debase. Hannah More. ECWP *Fr.* Slavery, a Poem.

Perish'd all on the coast of Spain. (LL) The Carpenter's Wife ("O whare hae ye been, my dearest dear"). *Unknown.* OAEL-1; OxBB

Perishing Bird, The. Douglas G. Jones. MoCV

Periwig, A. Rowland Watkyns. NOSC

Perk up, bend down—you toil and don't complain. To a Watering Scoop. Bùi Du'o'ng Lịch, *Chinese.* AVP, *tr. by* Huỳnh Sanh Thông

Perle, plesaunte to prynces paye. *Unknown.* EBEV, *stanzas* 1–5 *Fr.* Pearl. ("Perle plesaunte to prynces paye Pearl, the precious prize of a king.") NoP-4

Permanence in Change. Goethe. HoPM; STV, *tr. by* John Frederick Nims

Permanence of the Young Men, The. William Soutar. OxBS

Permanent occasion, A. Winter Garden. Donald Britton. EOEF

Permanent Tourists, The. Patricia K. Page. LiTM; NOBC

Permanent Wave. Andrew Crozier. NBrP

Permanently. Kenneth Koch. CoAP; NoP-4; PmAP; PoA; PoM; SAGP

Permanently, seriously / Without thought. (LL) At the Ball Game. William Carlos Williams. CMoP; MoP; NOBA; NoAM; OxBA; PoE

Permissive Entry: A Sermon on Fame. Lawrence Goldstein. BAP-95

Permit me here a simple brief aside. To Calliope. Robert Graves. CMoP

Permit Me Voyage. James Agee. MoAmPo

Permit me voyage, love, into your hands. (LL) Infinite consanguinity it bears. Hart Crane. ColAP; OxBA

Permit Us, Lord, to Consecrate. Joseph Green. AH

Permitted to assist you, let me see. St. Valentine. Marianne Moore. NYBP

Pernicious enemy. Ben Jonson. *See* An Epistle to Master John Selden.

Peroration, Concerning Genius. Robert Pinsky. NoAM *Fr.* Essay on Psychiatrists.

Perpetual[l] blush to thine, A. (LL) Song: Good Counsel to a Young Maid. Thomas Carew. CaPo; CavPo

Perpetuum Immobile. Bruce Dawe. CBAP

Perplexity: A Poem. Elizabeth Hands. WoRP

Perse owt of[f] Northombarlande, The. Chevy Chase. *Unknown.* EnSB; EnVB; OxBB

Persephone. Robert Duncan. NOBA

Persephone. Michael Longley. PBCIP

Persephone Abducted. Rita Dove. NAAAL *Fr.* Mother Love.

Persephone and Dis, Dis, have mercy upon her. Ezra Pound. MeMAP *Fr.* Homage to Sextus Propertius.

Persephone, Falling. Rita Dove. NAmP90

Persephone is the woman buried. Robert Kelly. *Fr.* The Book of Persephone. PoM

Persephone That Is to Say Double Issue. René Daumal, *French.* PFTM, *tr. by* Pierre Joris

Persephone Underground. Rita Dove. FFC; NAmP90

Perseus. Robert Earl Hayden. NoAM

Perseus. Louis MacNeice. LiTM

Perseverance. George Herbert. PBRV

Perseverance. Martin Sorescu, *Romanian*. VCWP, *tr. by* Enright, D. J. and Joana Russell-Gebbett

Persia. Vita Sackville-West. WPE

Persian, The. Stevie Smith. FaBoWP

Persian flummery. Horace. *See* Simplicity.

Persian Miniature. William Jay Smith. CoAP

Persian Parables. Aleksander Wat, *Polish*.
   "By a great, swift water." AF, *tr. by* Czeslaw Milosz and Leonard Nathan

Persian pomps, boy, ever I renounce them. Horace. *See* Simplicity.

Persian Song of Hafiz, A. Hafiz, *Persian*. AWP, *tr. by* Sir William Jones

Persian Version, The. Robert Graves. CMoP; LiTM; MoP; NOBL; NoAM; NoP-4; OBWP; WeW-3

Persicos Odi: Pocket Version. Horace. *See* Simplicity.

Persimmons. Li-Young Lee. NIP-4; NoP-4

Persimmons. Virginia Brady Young. HA

Persistence of Nature in Our Lives, The. Andrew Hudgins. DiPo; WeW-3

Persistence of Song, The. Howard Moss. NoP-4

Persistent Explorer. John Crowe Ransom. OxBA

Person, The. Lyn Hejinian.
   "Solitude flared out, The." FTOS

Person as Dreamer: We Talk about the Future, The. Michael Hartnett. PBCIP *Fr.* Notes on My Contemporaries.

Person from Porlock, A. Ronald Stuart Thomas. TOF

Person is very self-conscious about his head, A. Thoughts on One's Head. William Meredith. HAP; VCAP

Person She Is, The. James McMichael.
   "I know I'll lose her." BAP-93

Person sleeping under the chair, The. Chair. Hagiwara Sakutaro, *Japanese*. PFTM, *tr. by* Hiroaki Sato

Personae Separatae. Eugenio Montale, *Italian*. AF, *tr. by* William Arrowsmith

Personal. Langston Hughes. NOBA; NTP

Personal. Samuel Yellen. NYBP

Personal beauty is then first charming and itself when it dissatisfies us. Ralph Waldo Emerson. ITG *Fr.* Love.

Personal Column. Tom Paulin. PNI

Personal Letter No. 3. Sonia Sanchez. SSLK

Personal Poem. Frank O'Hara. CAPP-1; CLPP; PmAP

Personal Poem #9, *sl. diff.* Ted Berrigan. *Fr.* The Sonnets.

Personal Talk. Wordsworth. NOBE

Personality. Agnes Mary Frances Robinson. VWP

Personality syndrome, The. Alan Davies. FTOS *Fr.* Name.

Personification of a Name, The. Ray A. Young Bear. HATNAP

Persons, people, and the years. Velemir Khlebnikov, *Russian*. TCRP, *tr. by* Gary Kern

Person's Tale, The. U. A. Fanthorpe. NoP-4

Persons Unknown. Aidan Carl Mathews. BiHa

Perspective. Constance Carrier. AFr

Perspective. Coventry Patmore. FaBoEE; GBL *Fr.* The Angel in the House.

Perspective Lovesong. "Ern Malley." BMAP

Perspective never withers from their eyes. Quaker Hill. Hart Crane. LiTM *Fr.* The Bridge. NAAL-2

Perspective of Co-ordination. Arthur Davison Ficke. PoA

Perspectives on the Second World War. Irena Klepfisz. NMM-2

Persuade our Feathers Home. (LL) 'Tis not that Dying hurts us so. Emily Dickinson. APN-2; BoWoP

Persuasions to Enjoy. Thomas Carew. BeJo; NOBE; OBEV
   (Song: Persuasions to Enjoy.) CaPo; NAEL-1; NOSC; SeCP

Peru Eye, the Heart of the Lamp. Clark Coolidge. APSN

Perugia. Art Lange. PmAP

Peruke of Poets. William Zaranka. BXAP

Peruked and stately for the final act. (LL) Alceste in the Wilderness. Anthony Hecht. CoAmPo

Perverse habit of cat goddesses, A. Cat Goddesses. Robert Graves. NYBP; OxBSP; PC

Perversion, A. Christopher Reid. OBCoV

Perversion interests me. Note Delivered by a Female Impersonator. Heather McHugh. AmPA; RACG

Pervigilium Veneris. Suzanne Noguere. PoA

Pesach Has Come to the Ghetto Again. Binem Heller, *Yiddish*. TrJP, *tr. by* Max Rosenfeld

Pesci Misti. Leonard Aaronson. FaBoTw

Pessimist, The. Ben King. BLPA; NBLV; OBAL
   ("Can ever withstand these woes.") (LL) FuFo

Pessimist's a cheerless man, The. *Unknown*. PoToHe

Pessimist's Vision, The. Constance Naden. VWP

Pestel, the Poet, and Anna. "David Samuilovich Samoylov," *Russian*. TCRP, *tr. by* Lubov Yakovleva

Pet Deer, The. James Tate. SPE

Pet Lamb, The; A Pastoral. Wordsworth. OxBChV

Pet-name, a common name. Best-selling brand, curt, A. Geoffrey Hill. NoAM *Fr.* Mercian Hymns.

Pet Panther. A. R. Ammons. NoP-4

Pet Shop. Louis MacNeice. PeP

Pet was never mourned as you. Last Words To a Dumb Friend. Thomas Hardy. APo; FP; PC

Petals. Amy Lowell. SDW

Petals fall from Heliodora's image, The. Meleager, *Greek*. GrAn, *tr. by* Peter Whigham

Petals fall in the fountain, The. Ts'ai Chi'h. Ezra Pound. NoP-4

Petals fell white and remorseless as. Garden. Rosanna Warren. GaP

Petals from the trees. Spring in the City. Ruth Fainlight. CMAP

Petals on a wet, black bough. (LL) In A Station of the Metro. Ezra Pound. AmPP; ChAP; ColAP; HAP; HeIP-4; InPK-6; MeMAP; MoAmPo; MoP; NAAL-2; NIP-4; NOBA; NoAM; NoP-4; OxBA; PFE; PoE; PoPoPo; Poetr; TAP; TFi; UnPo; VGW; WeW-3

Petals red and purple turn to mud, and mud to dust. Fallen Blossoms. Yang Wan-li, *Chinese*. SuSp, *tr. by* Sherwin S. S. Fu

Petals step their fragrance off the shelf. In a Hot Country. Wendy Mulford. NBrP

Pete at the Zoo. Gwendolyn Brooks. TLR

Pete Peterson, before this bit, a professional entertainer. Vaudeville. Lincoln Kirstein. MoP

Pete Rousecastle the sailor's son. Rousecastle. David Wright. MoBS

Peter. Marianne Moore. CMoP; NAAL-2; OxBA
   ("Strong and Slippery.") NoP-4

Peter Amberley. John Calhoun. AmFP

Peter and Aleksey. Yaroslav Vasilevich Smelyakov, *Russian*. TCRP, *tr. by* Simon Franklin *and* Albert C. Todd

Peter and John. Elinor Wylie. MoAmPo; MoBS

Peter and Michael were two little menikin. *Unknown*. BoTP

Peter Bell. John Hamilton Reynolds. OBNC

Peter Bell the Third. Shelley.
   "All things that Peter saw and felt." EPCY
   "Devil, I safely can aver, The." OxBoV
   "Devil now knew his proper cue, The." OBSV
   "He was a might poet—and." EPCY
   "Hell is a city much like London." OBSV; OxBSn

Peter broke the ragged branch to push his nostrils closer. West Paddocks. Arthur Davies. NOBAu

Peter Grimes. George Crabbe. EBNV; ECEV; FHYEP; OBNV; PoEL-4; Ro *Fr.* The Borough.
   ("'Again they come!' and muttered as he died.") (LL) Ro
   "Priest attending, found he spoke at times, The." PoE
   "Thus by himself compelled to live each day." NOBE; OBNC

Peter had experienced the tight, nauseous desire. The Wickedness of Peter Shannon. Alden Nowlan. MoCV

Peter hath lost his purse, but will conceal it. *Unknown*. PFE

Peter, o Peter, time has run out. Peter and Aleksey. Yaroslav Vasilevich Smelyakov, *Russian*. TCRP, *tr. by* Simon Franklin *and* Albert C. Todd

Peter-penny, The. Robert Herrick. CaPo

Peter, Peter, pumpkin eater. The Pumpkin-Eater. Mother Goose. LB; OxNR; ReMoGo

Peter Piper picked a peck of pickled pepper[s]. Mother Goose. FaBoBe; LB; OTCP; OxNR; ReMoGo

Peter Quince at the Clavier. Wallace Stevens. AmPP; CMoP; HeIP-4; InPK-6; InPS-3; LiTM; MeMAP; MoAmPo; NAWM-2; NOBA; NoAM; NoP-4; OxBA; PoE; SAmP; TAP; TFi; TwCP

Peter Rabbit. Sandra McPherson. LCAP-2

Peter sleep-walks. Michael Dennis Browne. NYBP

Peter the Great, first Bolshevik. Maksimilian Aleksandrovich Voloshin. TCRP, *tr. by* Bernard Meares *Fr.* Russia.

Peter White will ne'er go right. Mother Goose. OxBoLi; OxNR

Peterhead in May. Burns Singer. FaBoTC; OxBS

Peter's not friendly. He gives me sideways looks. Dream Song 55. John Berryman. CAPP-1; ChIV-2 *Fr.* Dream Songs.

Petersburg. Innokenty Fiodorovich Annensky, *Russian*. TCRP, *tr. by* Lubov Yakovleva *with* Daniel Weissbort

Petersburg Strophes. Osip Emilevich Mandelstam, *Russian*. TCRP, *tr. by* Bernard Meares

Petit Guignol. Philip Hammial. BMAP

Petit Testament. "Ern Malley." BMAP

Petit, the Poet. Edgar Lee Masters. CMoP; ColAP; MoAmPo; NOBA; NoAM; OxBA; TAP   *Fr.* Spoon River Anthology.

Petition. W. H. Auden. CMoP; MeMAP; NAEL-2; Son

Petition, The. Thomas Beedome. NOSC

Petition, A. Frances Anne Kemble. LW

Petition. Ronald Stuart Thomas. FaBoMo

Petition for an Absolute Retreat, The. Anne Finch, Countess of Winchilsea. PoEL-3; WPE

   "Give me, O indulgent fate!" ECWP; NOSC

Petition for Reconciliation. Cynddelw Brydydd Mawr, *Welsh.* OBWVE, *tr.* by Joseph P. Clancy

Petition from the Chain Gang at Newcastle to Captain Furlong the Superintendent, A. Francis MacNamara. NOBAu

Petition of the Gray Horse, Auld Dunbar, The. William Dunbar. OxBS

Petition of the Orangemen of Ireland, The. Thomas Moore. NOIV

Petitioners are full of prayers. The Lament of Swordy Well. John Clare. FaBoVe

Petra. John William Burgon.

   "Match me such marvel save in Eastern clime." UV

Petrarch. Giosuè Carducci, *Italian.* AWP, *tr.* by William Dudley Foulke

Petrarch. Nicholas Kilmer.

   "In my first gentle days." PeECV

Petrifaction toward the core, the geode's rigor? (LL) Medusa. Amy Clampitt. NMM-2; VCAP

Petrified Echoes. Vasco [or Vasko] Popa. PoSu, *tr.* by Anne Pennington   *Fr.* The Yawn of Yawns.

Petroglyph. Joy Harjo. NAmP90

Petropolis. Osip Emilevich Mandelstam, *Russian.* PeFWW, *tr.* by David McDuff

Petrushka's valentine pivots on its pin. (LL) The Wine Menagerie. Hart Crane. NOBA; NoAM; OxBA; VGW

Pets are the Hobby of my Brother Bert. My Brother Bert. Ted Hughes. ChAP; FuFo

Petticoat, A. Gertrude Stein. TTTS   *Fr.* Tender Buttons.

Pettiness, A. D. H. Lawrence. *See* A Snake came to my water-trough.

Pettiness, A. (LL) Snake came to my water-trough, A. D. H. Lawrence. CABP; ChAP; NoP-4

Pettitoes are little feet, The. *Unknown.* OxNR

Petty sneaking Knave I knew, A. Mr. Cromek [or On Cromek]. William Blake. FaBoEE; PeLV

Petulance is purple. Spectrum. Mari E. Evans. BPo

Peveril of the Peak. Sir Walter Scott.

   "Speak not of niceness, when there's chance of wreck." FaBoEE

Pewits Nest. John Clare. FaBoVe

Peyote Poem. Michael McClure. PoM

   "Clear—the senses bright—sitting in the black chair—Rocker." BB; NeAP

Peyote Vision. Lew Blockcolski. VoR

Phaedra. Osip Emilevich Mandelstam, *Russian.* OBVE, *tr.* by James Greene

Phaedra. Jean Racine, *French.* NAWM-2, *tr.* by Kenneth Muir

Phaedria's Island: The Faerie Queene II.vi. 12–17. Edmund Spenser. *See* The Legend of the Knight of the Red Crosse, or of Holinesse.

Phaenomena. Aratus, *Greek.*

   "Beneath both the feet of Boötes you may see." HePo, *tr.* by Barbara Hughes Fowler

   Proem: "From Zeus let us begin, him we mortals never." HePo, *tr.* by Barbara Hughes Fowler

   Weather Signs. HePo, *tr.* by Barbara Hughes Fowler

Phallic Root. Kazuko Shiraishi. WPOW

Phallus. Kazuko Shiraishi. BoWoP, *tr.* by Ikuko Atsumi

Phantasia for Elvira Shatayev. Adrienne Rich. NALW

Phantasies. Emma Lazarus.

   Evening. APN-2

Phantasmagoria. "Lewis Carroll." OxBSn

Phantasmatikon. Stephen Sartarelli. PT

Phantasmion. Sara Coleridge.

   "O sleep, my babe, hear not the rippling wave." OBNC

Phantasus. Arno Holz, *German.* AWP, *tr.* by Ludwig Lewisohn

   "On a mountain of sugar-candy." PChr, *tr.* by Babette Deutsch

Phantom. *Unknown, sometimes at. to.* Samuel Taylor Coleridge, NAEL-2; OAEL-2; OxBSP; PoEL-4

Phantom Anthems. Robert Grenier.

   Easter Roses. FTOS

Phantom appears, A. Tanka. Shaku Chōkū, *Japanese.* MJT, *tr.* by Makoto Ueda

Phantom Bark, The. Hart Crane. CMoP

Phantom Horsewoman, The. Thomas Hardy. CMoP; NOBE; PoEL-5

Phantom Light of All Our Day, The. Nathaniel Mackey. GT

   ("Earth / a part of Ocean / again, The.") (LL) PT

Phantom of Clouds, A. Guillaume Apollinaire, *French.* PFTM, *tr.* by Ron Padgett

Phantom Pain. Maxine Chernoff. EOEF

Phantom streams were in the distance—mocking lights of lake and pool. Christmas Creek. Henry Clarence Kendall. CBAP

Phantom-Wooer, The. Thomas Lovell Beddoes. NAEL-2; OxBSn; Ro

Pharaoh. Jane Kenyon. LoL

Pharaohs of Today, The. Lizelia Augusta Jenkins Moorer. CBWP-3

Pharao's Daughter. Michael Moran. BIrV; ChIV-1

Pharisee murmurs when the woman weeps, conscious of guilt, The. Sequaire. Godeschalk, *Latin.* CTC, *tr.* by Ezra Pound

Pharmaceutical wonders are at work. Credo. Jane Kenyon. BAP-93   *Fr.* Having It Out With Melancholy. BAP-93

Pharoah's Army Got Drownded. *Unknown.* AS

Pharonnida. William Chamberlayne.

   Bad Landlord, The. NOSC

Pharsalia. Lucan, *Latin.*

   "All great things crush themselves; such end the gods." NoSic, *tr.* by Marlowe

   "O wastfull riot, never well content." OBVE, *tr.* by Sir Walter Ralegh

   "Thee Pompey thy past deeds by turns infest." OBVE, *tr.* by Nicholas Rowe

   "When Caesar saw his army prone to war." NoSic, *tr.* by Marlowe

Phases of Darkness, The. Paul Petrie. TAP

Phases of the Moon. Robert Browning. *Fr.* One Word More. EnVR; PoEL-5

Pheasant. Sylvia Plath. RB

Pheasant of the mountain, The. Hitomaro, *Japanese.* OHPJ, *tr.* by Kenneth Rexroth

Phebus fonde first the craft of medecine. *Unknown.* MiEL

Phenomena. Robinson Jeffers. NOBA; OxBA

Phenomenal Survivals of Death in Nantucket. Louise Glück. AmPA

Phenomenal Woman. Maya Angelou. ISC

Phenomenology of Anger, The. Adrienne Rich. PoE

Phenomenology of Stones, The. Thomas McCarthy. PBCIP

Phenomenon, The. Karl Shapiro. CMoP; NYBP

Pheobus, arise! / And paint the sable skies. Invocation. William Drummond, of Hawthornden. GTBS-P; OBEV

Phew. Roger McGough. SpW

Phido the miser's crying. Nicarchus of Alexandria, *Greek.* GrAn, *tr.* by Peter Porter

Philadelphia is a handsome town. Philadelphia. *Unknown.* AmFP

Philaenion is small and swart, but her hair curls darker. Philodemus. HePo, *tr.* by Barbara Hughes Fowler   *Fr.* Epigrams.

Philainion is short and. Philodemus, *Greek.* PGA, *tr.* by Kenneth Rexroth

Philanderer, The. Moses Mendes. *Fr.* The Chaplet. TrJP

Philanthropist and the Jelly-fish, The. May Kendall. VWP

Philatelic Lessons: The German Collection. Lawrence P. Spingarn. NYBP

Philemon and Baucis. Ovid. CTC, *tr.* by Arthur Golding   *Fr.* Metamorphoses.

   Heaven's power is infinite; earth, air, and sea. OAEL-1, *tr.* by Dryden

   Then Lelex rose, an old experienced man. AWP; OBVE, *tr.* by Dryden

Philip and Mildred. Adelaide Anne Procter. VWP

Philip at Kynoskephalai. Alcaeus, *Greek.* GrAn, *tr.* by Alistair Elliot

Philip of Macedon. Alcaeus, *Greek.* GrAn, *tr.* by Alistair Elliot

Philip Sparrow. John Skelton. NOBE; OAEL-1; PeLV; PoEL-1

   ("Farewell, for evermore!") (LL) OBCoV

   (Phyllyp Sparowe.) AAS; OxBoLi

Philip V of Macedon. Alcaeus, *Greek.* GrAn, *tr.* by Alistair Elliot

Philip van Artevelde. Sir Henry Taylor.

   Elena's Song. OBEV; RACG

Philip Whalen's Hat. Joanne Kyger. BB

Philippians 1.23. Francis Quarles. ChIV-2 *See also* Bible, Philippians.

Philistion of Nikaia lies here, whose laughter. Epitaph of a Nicene Actor. *Unknown, Greek.* GrAn, *tr.* by Dudley Fitts

Philistion's a hard bitch:/ in her book 'penniless lover'. Maccius, *Greek.* GrAn, *tr.* by W. G. Shepherd

Phillida and Coridon. Nicholas Breton. OBEV; TTTS   *Fr.* The Honourable Entertainment Given to the Queen's Majesty in Progress at Elvetham, 1591.

   (Ploughman's Song, The.) NOBE

Phillida Flouts Me [or The Disdainful Shepherdess]. *Unknown.* OBEV

Phillip Sparow. John Skelton. NoP-4   *Fr.* Phillip Sparow.

Phillips, whose touch harmonious could remove. An Epitaph upon the Celebrated Claudy Phillips, Musician, Who Died Very Poor. Samuel Johnson. NOEC; OxAEP-1

Phillis and Coridon. Robert Greene. NoSic *Fr.* Perimedes [*or* Perimedes, the Blacksmith].

Phillis is my only joy. Song. Sir Charles Sedley. EnLoPo

Phillis kept sheep along the western plains. Phillis and Coridon. Robert Greene. NoSic *Fr.* Perimedes [*or* Perimedes, the Blacksmith].

Phillis 1. Thomas Lodge. OBEV *Fr.* Phyllis.

Phillis, shou'd we delay. To Phillis. Edmund Waller. SeCP

Phillis 2. Thomas Lodge. OBEV *Fr.* Phyllis.

(Fidelity.)

("Love guards the roses of thy lips.") AEP

Phillis's Age. Matthew Prior. EnLoPo

(Phyllis's Age.) FaBoEE

Phillis's Resolution. William Walsh. OxBSP

Philo the gentleman, the fortune teller. Sir John Davies. NoSic *Fr.* Epigrams.

Philocles. Leonidas of Tarentum, *Greek.* AWP, *tr. by* F. A. Wright

Philoctetes. John Byrne Leicester Warren. NOBVV

Philokles offers his bouncing. Leonidas, *Greek.* GrAn; PGA, *tr. by* Kenneth Rexroth

Philomel. Richard Barnfield. CH; NOBE; OBEV *Fr.* The Affectionate Shepherd. *Also appears as a section in* The Passionate Pilgrim.

(Nightingale, The.) GTBS-P

Philomela. Matthew Arnold. EBVVPR; FHYEP; OAEL-2; OBEV; UnPo

Philomela. John Crowe Ransom. CMoP; FuPo; NAAL-2; NOBA; NoAM; OBAL; OBSV; OxBA

Philomena Andronico. William Carlos Williams. FaBoMo

Philosopher, The. Emily Jane Brontë. BWW

Philosopher, The. Syl Cheney-Coker. PBMAP *Fr.* The Blood in the Desert's Eyes.

Philosopher, A. Sam Walter Foss. OBAL

Philosopher, The. Edna St. Vincent Millay. CMoP

Philosopher. John Frederick Nims. PFE

Philosopher, The. Sara Teasdale. PoToHe

Philosopher and the Birds, The. Richard Murphy. CIP-2

Philosopher and the Lover; To a Mistress Dying, The. Sir William Davenant. *See* Lover and Philosopher.

Philosopher Berkeley once said, The. Limerick. P. W. R. Foot. PeLi

Philosopher, impatient for the black, The. Conversations on the Plurality of Worlds. Molly Bendall. PUP-20

Philosopher to His Mistress, The. Robert Bridges. LiTM; PoEL-5

Philosophers have measured [*or* measur'd] mountains. The Agony [*or* Agonie]. George Herbert. ESCV; GeHe

Philosophers: Lao-Tzu, The. Po Chü-i, *Chinese.* BLT, *tr. by* Arthur Waley

Philosophic Flight, The. Giordano Bruno, *Italian.* AWP, *tr. by* John Addington Symonds

Philosophy. John Kendrick Bangs. PoToHe

Philosophy. Ray Catina. CDa

Philosophy. Paul Laurence Dunbar. BPo; NAAAL

Philosophy of white blood cells, The. Immanuel Kant. Miroslav Holub, *Czech.* VCWP, *tr. by* David Young *and* Dana Hábová

Philosophy, the great and only heir. Abraham Cowley. BeJo *Fr.* To the Royal Society.

Phineas dwelled midst lives of many pieces. Phineas Within and Without. Paul Zimmer. VGW

Phineas Within and Without. Paul Zimmer. VGW

Phlebas the Phoenician, a fortnight dead. Death by Water. T. S. Eliot. OBVE *Fr.* The Waste Land. AmPP; CMoP; FaBoMo; HAP; LiTM; MoAmPo; MoP; NAAL-2; NAEL-2; NAWM-2; NOBA; NOBE; NoAM; NoP-4; OAEL-2; OxAEP-2; OxBA; OxBTC; PoE; TAP; TFi; UnPo

Phlegmatic winter on a bed of snow. Born in Winter. Francis Quarles. NOSC

Phlox Diffusa: A Poem for My Fiftieth Birthday. Sandra McPherson. PUP-20

Phobiphilia. Robin Morgan. EC2

Phoebe in a Rosebush. Clyde Watson. NTCP

Phoebe sate,/ Sweet she sate. Montanus' Sonnet. Thomas Lodge. PoEL-2 *Fr.* Rosalynde; or Euphues' Golden Legacy.

Phoebe's cry, A. Anita Virgil. HA

Phoebus, accept this dinner that I bring you. Automedon, *Greek.* GrAn, *tr. by* Frederick Garber

Phœbus Apollo, from Olympus driven. The Photograph. Christopher Pearse Cranch. APN-1 *Fr.* Seven Wonders of the World.

Phoebus farewell, a sweeter saint I serve, *speech of Basilius.* A Sweeter Saint I Serve. Sir Philip Sidney. SiPS *Fr.* Arcadia.

Phœbus, the goddess variant and changeable. Christine de Pisan. PBWP, *tr. by* Joan Keefe *Fr.* The Epistle of Othea to Hector (A Lytil Bibell of Knyghthod).

Phoebus was a herdsman. Antipater of Thessalonica, *Greek.* GrAn, *tr. by* Alistair Elliot

Phoebus was judge between Jove, Mars, and Love. Sonnet 13. Sir Philip Sidney. *Fr.* Astrophil and Stella. AAS; SiPS

Phoebus with Admetus. George Meredith. NOBE; OBEV

Phoenician Women, The. Euripides, *Greek.*

Daughter, I must commend thy noble heart. OBCVT, *tr. by* George Gascoigne

Phoenix, The. Arthur Christopher Benson. OBEV

Phoenix, The. George Darley. *See* O Blest Unfabled Incense Tree.

Phoenix, The. *Unknown, Anglo-Saxon.*

I have heard that far from here. ASW, *tr. by* Kevin Crossley-Holland

Lo! I have learned of the loveliest of lands. AnOE; OAEL-1, *tr. by* Charles W. Kennedy

When the wind is asleep and the weather set fair. ASW, *tr. by* Kevin Crossley-Holland

Phoenix and the Turtle, The. Shakespeare. ImPo; NOBE; NoP-4; NoSic; OAEL-1; OBEV; OxAEP-1; PeECV; PoEL-2; SCGP

("As chorus to their tragic scene.") (LL) CABP

(Phoenix and Turtle, The.) CABP; PBRV

Phoenix, bird of terrible pride. Sir Herbert Read. FaBoTw *Fr.* Mutations of the Phoenix.

Phoenix birds once frolicked on Phoenix Terrace, The. Climbing Phoenix Terrace at Chin-ling. Li Po, *Chinese.* SuSp, *tr. by* Joseph J. Lee

Phoenix comes of flame and dust, The. Howard Nemerov. LiTM

Phoenix Hairpins. Lu Yu, *Chinese.* OHPC, *tr. by* Kenneth Rexroth

Phoenix on the hot sirocco's breath. Epilogue. Herbert B. Mallalieu. PoA

Phœnix pleads with Achilles. Homer. OBCVT, *tr. by* Edward, Earl of Derby *Fr.* The Iliad.

Phoenix Reborn from Its Ashes, The. Louis Aragon, *French.* CBNP

Phoenix tail on scented silk, flimsy layer on layer. Li Shang-yin, *Chinese.* PLT, *tr. by* A. C. Graham

Phol and Wotan rode through the forest. Second Merseburg Spell. *Unknown, German.* GePo, *tr. by* Carroll Hightower

Phone call. Alexis Rotella. HA

Phone Call to Rutherford. Paul Blackburn. PoM

Phone duet over the radio, A. The Louisiana Weekly #4. David Henderson. PoBA

Phone for the fish-knives, Norman. How to Get On in Society. John Betjeman. NOBL; OBSV; OxBTC; UV

Phonemics. Jack Spicer. PmAP

Phonic. Gail Mazur. NAmP90

'Phoning. Peter Sirr. BiHa

Phosphorescence. Tanka. Miyazawa Kenji, *Japanese.* MJT, *tr. by* Makoto Ueda

Photo at the Bridge. Dan Pagis, *Hebrew.* IP, *tr. by* Warren Bargad *and* Stanley F. Chyet

Photo in the Locket. Jackie Kay. CPO

Photo of Miners, A. Brendan Galvin. AFr

Photo of My Father in a Snowbound Train. David Wojahn. GM

Photo of someone else's childhood, A. The Old Adam. Denise Levertov. UnPo

Photo shows me, The. The Other Hunters in the North the Cree. Jerome Rothenberg. PoM

Photo That Watches, The. Carlota Caulfield, *Spanish.* LoHo, *tr. by* Carol Maier

Photograph, The. Christopher Pearse Cranch. APN-1 *Fr.* Seven Wonders of the World.

Photograph. Quandra Prettyman. PoBA

Photograph & Story in The Press: The Mother Whose Children Burned to Death. Adora Phillips. CMAP

Photograph in a Stockholm Newspaper for March 13, 1910. Don Coles. NOBC

Photograph of a Child, Japanese-American Evacuation, Bainbridge Island, Washington, March 30, 1942. Jim Mitsui. OpBo

Photograph of Haymaker, 1890. Molly Holden. OxBTC

Photograph of Myself, The. Jon Anderson. AmPA

Photographs. Charles Wright. HoPM

Photographs: A Vision of Massacre. Michael S. Harper. PoBA

Photographs from a Book: Six Poems. David Ferry. FaBoA

Photographs of Pioneer Women. Ruth Dallas. PeNZ

Photos, The. Diane Wakoski. NIP-4

Photos of a Salt Mine. Patricia K. Page. NIP-4; NOBC; NoAM

Photosensitive / aesthetes. Roots. Tadeusz Rózewicz, *Polish.* CEEP, *tr. by* Victor Contoski

Phraseology. Jayne Cortez. BISi

Phryne. Donne. FaBoEE

Phyllida and Corydon. Nicholas Breton. *See* Phillida and Coridon.

Phyllidula. Ezra Pound. FaBoTw

Phyllis. Thomas Lodge.

Devoide of reason, thrale to foolish ire. AAS

I Hope and Fear. Son

I would in rich and golden coloured raine. AAS

Love Guards [or Guides] the roses of Thy Lips. AEP; NoSic; OBEV; Son

No Stars Her Eyes. Son

O Pleasing Thoughts. Son

Phillis 1. OBEV

Phillis 2. OBEV

(Fidelity.)

Phyllis. Thomas Randolph. BoLoP

Phyllis [or Phillis] [or Progress of Love, The]. Jonathan Swift. EBNV; OAEL-1; OBCoV; OBSV; PoE; PoEL-3

Phyllis Corydon clutched to him. Carmen 45. Catullus, *Latin.* OBVE, *tr. by* Abraham Cowley; BoLoP *Fr.* Carmina.

Phyllis, loving Demophoon. Cometas, *Greek.* InMo, *tr. by* Sam Hamill

Phyllis! why should we delay. To Phyllis. Edmund Waller. BeJo

Phyllis's Age. Matthew Prior. *See* Phillis's Age.

Phyllyp Sparowe [or Philip Sparrow]. John Skelton. AAS; PoEL-1

It had a velvet cap. FP

Our natural tongue is rude. EPCY

"Pla ce bo! Who is there, who?" AAS; CBNP; NOBE; NoSic; OAEL-1; OxBoLi

Sparrow's Dirge, The. FaBoCh

Yet one thing is behind. EPCY

Physical Comparison With Professors And Others. Robert Pinsky. NoP-4

Physical-education slides. Hullo, Inside. Max Fatchen. NOxBChV

Physical Universe. Louis Simpson. InPS-3

Physician of eminence, some years ago, A. The Lady and the Doctor. Helen Leigh. WoRP

Physicians' Fortune, The, *epigram.* Friedrich von Logau, *German.* GePo, *tr. by* George C. Schoolfield

Physics One. Marie Harris. EC3

Physiologus. *Unknown, Anglo-Saxon.*

Whale, The. AnOE; APo, *tr. by* Charles Kennedy; EBEV, *tr. by* Gavin Bone

("Now I will sing about a kind of fish.") ASW, *tr. by* Kevin Crossley-Holland

π deserves our full admiration. Wislawa Szymborska, *Polish.* PoSu, *tr. by* Adam Czerniawski

P'i-p'a begins the dance, midst changing new sounds, The. Wang Ch'ang-ling. SuSp, *tr. by* Ronald C. Miao *Fr.* Following the Army on Campaign.

Piano, The. Pong-gon Chon, *Korean.* CKP, *tr. by* Jaihiun Kim

Piano, The. Frank Daley. NOBC

Piano. D. H. Lawrence. APAD; CABP; CMoP; GTBS-P; HAP; HeIP-4; InPK-6; MoBRPo; MoP; NAEL-2; NOBE; NoAM; NoP-4; OAEL-2; OPOU; OxBSP; PoE; Poetr; RB; SCGP; TFi; TRP; UnPo; WeW-3

("For the past.") (LL) SAGP

("I weep like a child for / the past.") (LL) GEA

Piano, A. Gertrude Stein. PBWP *Fr.* Tender Buttons.

Piano and Drums. Gabriel Okara. NIP-4; PBA; TTY

Piano di Sorrento. Robert Browning. *Fr.* The Englishman in Italy. PoEL-5

Piano hums, The. Effendi. Michael S. Harper. PoBA

Piano keys sit stiff and stark, sterile, The. Echoes. Naomi Long Madgett. SeSe

Piano Man / my roots are african. Keith Jarrett—Rainmaker. Lorna Goodison. HCP

Piano Pieces. Thomas William Shapcott. CBAP

Piano Practice. Howard Moss. NYBP

Piano practice. Raymond Roseliep. HA

Piano, trembling, makes the lips grow dry, The. Boris Pasternak, *Russian.* TCRP, *tr. by* Yakov Hornstein

Piano-Tuner, The. Valerie Gillies. FaBoTC

Piano tuner spoke to me, that tenderest, The. Pyrargyrite Metal, 9. Cecília Meireles, *Portuguese.* PBWP, *tr. by* James Merrill

Piano Tuner's Wife, The. Karl Shapiro. NoAM

Piarco. Eric Roach. PBCV

Piazza di Spagna, Early Morning. Richard Wilbur. InPS-3; NoP-4; OxBSP; PFE; SAGP; VGW

Piazza Piece. John Crowe Ransom. BoLoP; ColAP; FuPo; GLoP; HeIP-4; MeMAP; MoAmPo; MoP; NAAL-2; NOBA; NoAM; NoP-4; OxBA; Poetr; Son; TFi; TRP

Piazza Tragedy, A. Eugene Field. NBLV

Piazzas. Barbara Guest. NeAP

Pibroch. Ted Hughes. FaBoMo; OAEL-2

Pibroch of Donuil Dhu. Sir Walter Scott. FaBoCh; FaPoR; GTBS-P; OxBS; PoEL-4

Picasso and Anarchism. Leslie Scalapino. FTOS

Picasso flies into a rage at Braque. Picasso Visits Braque. Harold Norse. CLPP

Picasso Visits Braque. Harold Norse. CLPP

Piccolomini, The. Johann Christoph Friedrich von Schiller, *German.* Thekla's Song. AWP

Pick a Bale of Cotton. *Unknown.* NAAAL

Pick a fern, pick a fern, ferns are high. Ezra Pound, *after the Chinese.* OBVE

Pick-up truck. Marlene Mountain. HA

Picketing Supermarkets. Tom Wayman. NIP-4

Pickety fence, The. David McCord. NTCP

Pickin Em Up and Layin Em Down. Maya Angelou. CBLP; NBLV

Picking at a bone. (LL) Put your finger in Foxy's hole. *Unknown.* LB; OxNR

Picking Pole Beans. Marge Piercy. *Fr.* Six Underrated Pleasures. EC2

Picking Rushes. *Unknown, Chinese.* CoBCP, *tr. by* Burton Watson

Picking Tea: A Ballad. Kao Ch'i, *Chinese.* SuSp, *tr. by* Irving Y. Lo

Pickpockets. John Gay. ECEV *Fr.* Trivia; or, The Art of Walking the Streets of London.

Picnic. Kenward Elmslie. FTOS

Picnic. Hugh Lofting. NOxBChV; OTCP

Picnic, The. John Logan. CoAmPo; TRP

Picnic. Nellie Wong. OpBo

Picnic, an Homage to Civil Rights, The. Michael S. Weaver. ISC

Picnic, an Homage to Civil Rights, The. Michael S. Weaver. LTA; PoPoPo

Picnic-goers beautified themselves, The. The Embarkation for Cythera. David Ferry. GS

Picnic Remembered. Robert Penn Warren. NAAL-2

Picnic: the Liberated. M. Carl Holman. PoBA

Picnics. *Unknown.* BoTP

Pictor Ignotus. Robert Browning. CTC

Picture, the Ode 69; *see also* Anacreon by Wordsworth. Anacreon, *Greek.* AWP; GrIP, *tr. by* Thomas Stanley

Picture, A. "Michael Field." VWP

Picture, A. Dora Greenwell. EBVV

Picture, A. Howard Nemerov. OxBC

Picture, A. Henrietta Cordelia Ray. CBWP-3

Picture and book remain. An Acre of Grass. W. B. Yeats. CMoP; NoAM

Picture Bride. Cathy Song. AiP

Picture has no grammar. It has neither evil nor, A. Shall Gaelic Die? Iain Crichton Smith. FaBoTC

Picture lilacs. For Barbara, who said She Couldn't Visualize Two Women Together. Ellen Bass. NMM-2

Picture of a Fine Gentleman, The. Lady Sophia Burrell. ECWP

Picture of a Japanese Farmer, Woodland, California, May 20, 1942. Jim Mitsui. OpBo

Picture of a Man. Calvin Forbes. ISC

Picture of a Nativity. Geoffrey Hill. NoAM; OxBC

Picture of Dorian Gray, The. Oscar Wilde.

Preface: "Artist is the creator of beautiful things, The." NAEL-2

Picture of Eakins and a couple of other people, A. David Ferry. FaBoA

Picture of J. T. in a Prospect of Stone, The. Charles Tomlinson. NoP-4

Picture of Little J. A. in a Prospect of Flowers, The. John Ashbery. CoAmPo; PmAP

Picture of Little T. C. in a Prospect of Flowers, The. Andrew Marvell. ESCV; FMP; GeHe; MeLP; NAEL-1; NOBE; NoP-4; OAEL-1; OBEV; OxAEP-1; PoE; SCGP; SeCP; TFi

("Nip in the blossome all our hopes and Thee.") (LL) FSCP

Picture of Loot. Alan Sillitoe. OxBTC

Picture of my Mother's Family, A. Wing Tek Lum. OpBo

Picture of Okinawa. A. Dennis Schmitz. LCAP-2

Picture of Sappho, The. Caroline Elizabeth Norton. VWP

Picture of the Body, The. Ben Jonson. NOSC *Fr.* Eupheme.

Picture on the front, The. Picture Postcard. Billy Marshall-Stoneking. BMAP

Picture; or, The Lover's Resolution, The. Coleridge. Ro

Picture-Palaces. Philip Heseltine. *See* Limerick: "The Young things who frequent picture-palaces."

Picture Postcard. Billy Marshall-Stoneking. BMAP

Picture Postcard from Our Youth. Dan Pagis, *Hebrew.* VCWP, *tr. by* Stephen Mitchell

Picture Postcard of a Zoo. Oscar Williams. Son

Picture Postcards. Miklós Radnóti, *Hungarian.* AF, *tr. by* Emery E. George

Picture-Show. Siegfried Sassoon. CMoP; NSI

Picture-Writing. Henry Wadsworth Longfellow. APN-1 *Fr.* The Song of Hiawatha.

Pictures. F. Ann Elliott. BoTP

Pictures. Sarah Kirsch, *German.* AF, *tr. by* Wayne Kvam

Pictures from Brueghel. William Carlos Williams. *See* The Parable of the Blind.

Haymaking. NoAM

Hunters in the Snow, The. LCAP-2

("Over-all picture, The.") GS

Landscape with the Fall of Icarus. LCAP-2; NAAL-2; NoAM

("According to Breughel.") PoPoPo

Parable of the Blind, The. LCAP-2; SAmP

("Follows the others stick in / hand triumphant to disaster.") (LL) GI

("In a red winter hat blue.") GI

("Pictures from Brueghel.") GI

Self-Portrait. LCAP-2

Pictures in the Smoke. Dorothy Parker. NBLV

Pictures of a Gone World. Lawrence Ferlinghetti.

Away above a harborful. BoLoP; PoM

Dada would have liked a day like this. NeAP

Sarolla's women in their picture hats. NeAP; PoM

Pictures of [the] Jews. Haim Guri, *Hebrew.* IP, *tr. by* Warren Bargad *and* Stanley F. Chyet; MHP, *tr. by* Ruth Finer Mintz

Pictures of the Floating World. Miyazawa Kenji, *Japanese.* PFTM, *tr. by* Hiroaki Sato

Picturesque; a Fragment. John Aikin. NOEC

"Picturesque / common lot" the unwarranted light, The. Anniversary Poem. George Oppen. APSN; NNaP *Fr.* Some San Francisco Poems.

Piddle-paddling race of critics, rhizome-fanciers. Antiphanes, *Greek.* GrAn; NNPT, *tr. by* Edwin Morgan

Piece by piece I SEEM. Necessities of Life. Adrienne Rich. HCAP; NOBA; PoPoPo; Poetr

Piece for Magic Strings, A. Li Ho, *Chinese.* PLT, *tr. by* A. C. Graham

Piece of art, a scene, a poem, A. Silence, an Eloquent Applause. Leona Gregory. TrCP

Piece of Black Bread, A. "Eduard Georgievich Bagritzky," *Russian.* TrJP, *tr. by* C. M. Bowra

Piece of burned meat, A. Pardon. Jane Kenyon. BAP-93; LoL *Fr.* Having It Out With Melancholy. BAP-93

Piece of buttered popcorn, A. Alan Pizzarelli. HA

Piece of Earth, A. Douglas Livingstone. PeSAV

Piece of flesh gives off, A. Galway Kinnell. *Fr.* The Dead Shall Be Raised Incorruptible. NOBA; PoE

Piece of green pepper, A. Haiku Ambulance. Richard Brautigan. InPK-6

Piece of straw set adrift, A. Signpost. Toksu Moon, *Korean.* CKP, *tr. by* Jaihiun Kim

Piecemeal the summer dies. Exeunt. Richard Wilbur. HeIP-4; PoLF; Poetsp

Pieces. Duane Niatum. HATNAP

Pieces of a green / bottle. (LL) Between Walls. William Carlos Williams. HoPM; TAP; VGW

Pieces of Snot. *Unknown, Bella Bella Indian.* STP, *tr. by* Franz Boas

Pieces O'six—XXIV. Jackson Mac Low. FTOS

Pied Beauty. Gerard Manley Hopkins. APAD; AWP; CMoP; ClHu; EBEvV; EBVV; EnVR; EnlH; FaBoMo; GTBS-P; HAP; HeIP-4; HoPM; ImPo; InPK-6; InPS-3; LiTM; MoBrPo; MoP; NAEL-2; NOBE; NOBVV; NTP; NoAM; NoP-4; OAEL-2; OBEV; OBMV; OBNC; OxAEP-2; OxBSP; PBMP; PoE; PoPoPo; PoRA; Poetr; RB; RaBo; SCGP; SCV; SoSe-8; TFi; TTTS; UV; WeW-3

("Praise Him.") (LL) CABP; ChAP; SAGP

Pied Beauty. Stanley J. Sharpless. UV

Pied Piper of Hamelin, The. Robert Browning. EBNV; FaBoBe; FaBoCh; NOxBChV; OBNV; OBSP; OxBChV; PeLV

Into the street the Piper stept. BoTP; OxAEP-2

Pien River Blocked by Ice. Tu Mu, *Chinese.* PLT, *tr. by* A. C. Graham

Pier, The. Garrett Kaoru Hongo. OpBo

Pier delle Vigne. Dante. HoPM, *tr. by* John Ciardi *Fr.* Inferno. NAWM-1, *tr. by* John Ciardi *Fr.* Divina Commedia.

Pier-Glass, The. Robert Graves. CMoP; NoAM

Pier: Under Pisces, The. James Merrill. LCAP-2; NoAM

Pierc'd thro' and thro', the solid gate resounds. Homer. *See* The Suitors watch Ulysses string the bow.

Pierced / with moons of dark / Indian blood. (LL) Indian Blood. Mary TallMountain. UnSA

Piercing Chill I Feel, The. Buson, *Japanese.* InPK-6, *tr. by* Harold G. Henderson

Piercing winter frost, and winds, and darkened air, The. (LL) November. William Cullen Bryant. APN-1; GSo; Son

Pierre Falcon. Le Tombeau de Pierre Falcon. James Reaney. MoCV

Pierrot, no sentimental swain. Pantomime. Paul Verlaine, *French.* AWP, *tr. by* Arthur Symons

Piers are pummelled by the waves, The. The Fall of Rome. W. H. Auden. InPS-3; OAEL-2; OxBTC; PFE; UnPo

Pietà. Allen Afterman. NOBAu

Pietá. Ann Hayes. CMAP

Pietà. James Philip McAuley. BMAP; CBAP

Pietà. Rilke, *German.* GI, *tr. by* David Curzon *and* Will Alexander Washburn

Pietà. Wislawa Szymborska, *Polish.* VCWP, *tr. by* Magnus J. Krynski *and* Robert A. Maguire

Pietà's Over—and, now, my dear, droll, husband, The. Paul Durcan. PBCIP

"Pietrofesso," I'd repeat to Mr. Wright, the science teacher in / Junior High. Having the Wrong Name for Mr. Wright. Helen Barolini. UnSA

Pig. Paul Éluard, *French.* TTTS, *tr. by* Kenneth Koch

Pig. Anthony Hecht. APo; OxBC

("O Swine that takest away our sins / That takest away.") (LL) GI

Pig, The. *Unknown.* FaBoEE; OBCoV

Pig and i spring rain. Marlene Mountain. HA

Pig, if I am not mistaken, The. Ogden Nash. RB

Pig Island Letters. James Keir Baxter.

From an old house shaded with macrocarpas. PeNZ

When I was only semen in a gland. PeNZ

Pig lay on a barrow dead, The. View of a Pig. Ted Hughes. LiTM; OxAEP-2; OxBTC; TwCP

Pig stands squarely, The. Transubstantiation. Gary Geddes. NOBC

Pig-Sticking Season, The. Jonathan Small. HCP

Pig swelled in the sun, The. The Pig-Sticking Season. Jonathan Small. HCP

Pig-Tale, The, *incl. in* Pig-Tale, The. "Lewis Carroll." *Fr.* Little Birds are dining. *Fr.* Sylvie and Bruno Concluded.

"Pig'back" she brought me where the lake surrounded. Kineo Mountain. Celeste Turner Wright. Poetsp

Pigeon of My Childhood. Sergey Aleksandrovich Vasilyev, *Russian.* TCRP, *tr. by* Lubov Yakovleva *and* Max Hayward

Pigeon purrs in the wood; the wood has gone, The. Idylls of the King. Geoffrey Hill. NoAM; PoE *Fr.* An Apology for the Revival of Christian Architecture in England.

Pigeon wings shatter the sunlight. Prairie Wind. Debra Nystrom. MoLi

Pigeons, The. Rodney Bennett. BoTP

Pigeons. Bert Meyers. SPE

Pigeons. Marianne Moore. PoA

Pigeons. Alastair Reid. NYBP; TwCP

Pigeons are city folk. Marianne Moore. PoA

Pigeons are cityfolk. Lilian Moore. SSCS

Pigeons are the spiks of Birdland. David Hernandez. UnSA

Pigeons flutter'd fieldward, one and all, The. Gout and Wings. Charles Tennyson Turner. NOBVV

Pigeons on the grass alas. Gertrude Stein. TAP *Fr.* Four Saints in Three Acts.

Pigeon's Story, The. Jeannie Kirby. BoTP

Pigeons that peck at the grass in Trinity Churchyard, The. Trinity Place. Phyllis McGinley. MoAmPo; OxBSP; SoSe-8

Piggish young person from Leeds, A. *Unknown.* KaS

Piggy-back. Langston Hughes. TLR

Piggy-wig found he had four little feet. What Piggy-Wig Found. Enid Blyton. BoTP

Pigmalion, whose hie love-hating minde. John Marston. PBRV *Fr.* The Metamorphosis of Pigmalions Image.

Pigmies and Cranes. Walter Savage Landor. NOBVV

Pigmy Scraper wi' his Fiddle, A. Robert Burns. *Fr.* Love and Libery—A Cantata. NOBRP; NOEC

Pigrush, the poverty grass, The. Weeds. J. D. McClatchy. GaP

Pigs, The. Geoffrey Lehmann. CBAP

Pigs, The. Jane Taylor. CTAV

Pig's-Eye View of Literature, A. Dorothy Parker.

Alfred, Lord Tennyson. NALW

D. G. Rossetti. NALW

George Sand. NALW

Harriet Beecher Stowe. NALW

Lives and Times of John Keats, Shelley, and George Gordon Noel, Lord Byron, The. NALW

Oscar Wilde. NALW

Thomas Carlyle. NALW

Walter Savage Landor. NALW

Pigs for Circe in May, The. Joanne Kyger. PoM

Pig's leg fills the plate, wine overflowing the cups, A. Rejoicing the Spirits. Fan Ch'eng-ta. SuSp, *tr. by* Wu-chi Liu *Fr.* Four Songs in Imitation of Wang Chien.

Pig's Tail, The. Norman Ault. BoTP

Pigsty did not reek, The. The Barn-yard. Sheila Cussons, *Afrikaans.* PeSAV, *tr. by* Johann de Lange

Pigtail. Tadeusz Rózewicz, *Polish.* HP; PoSu, *tr. by* Adam Czerniawski ("Pulled at school / by naughty boys.") (LL) AF, *tr. by* Robert A. Maguire *and* Magnus Jan Krynski

Pigwiggen. Michael Drayton. BoTP

Pihsien Road. "Robin Hyde." WPE

Pike, The. Edmund Blunden. LiTM

Pike Street Bus. Colleen J. McElroy. NAAAL

Pike, three inches long, perfect. Ted Hughes. CMoP; FaBoMo; HAP; HeIP-4; InPS-3; LiTM; NAEL-2; OxBTC; PoE
("That rose slowly towards me, watching.") (LL) NoP-4

Pilate. Donald Davie. GI

Pilate. Mervyn Morris. HCP

Pilate at Fortingall. Edwin Morgan. FaBoTC *Fr.* Sonnets from Scotland.

Pilate Remembers. William E. Brooks. ChIV-2

Pilate's Wife. Nina Kossman. GI

Pilate's Wife's Dream. Charlotte Brontë. VWP

Pile of Feathers. Gerald Stern. LoL

Pile the bodies high at Austerlitz and Waterloo. Grass. Carl Sandburg. AWP; ColAP; MoAmPo; MoP; NAAL-2; NOBA; NoAM; NoP-4; OBWP; OxBA; PeFWW; PoLF; PoPoPo; Poetr; SAGP; TFi

Piled deep below the screening apple-branch. The Orchard-Pit. D. G. Rossetti. EnLoPo; GLoP; NAEL-2; OAEL-2; PeVV; PoEL-5; SCV

Piled on a loading dock where I walked. Desks. Dave Jeddie Smith. HCAP

Piled snow hugs the bramble gates. Traveling Early through a Snowy Valley. Yü Chi, *Chinese.* CoBLCP, *tr. by* Jonathan Chaves

Pilgrim, The. John Bunyan. BoTP *Fr.* The Pilgrim's Progress.
("He'll labour, night and day, / To be a Pilgrim.") (LL) CTV
(Pilgrim Song, The.) NOCV
(Valiant's Song.) NOSC

Pilgrim, The. Emma Catherine Embury. OBCA

Pilgrim, The. Brendan Kennelly. TIRV

Pilgrim, The. Nicanor Parra, *Spanish.* VCWP, *tr. by* W. S. Merwin

Pilgrim, The. W. B. Yeats. RB

Pilgrim Cranes, The. John Byrne Leicester Warren. EBVV

Pilgrim Fathers, The. Leonard Bacon. AH

Pilgrim Fathers, The. Felicia Dorothea Hemans. *See* The Landing of the Pilgrim Fathers [in New England].

Pilgrim Fathers, The. Wordsworth. AiP *Fr.* Ecclesiastical Sonnets.

Pilgrim from the East, The. Gustave Kahn, *French.* TrJP, *tr. by* Jethro Bithell

Pilgrim Song, The. John Bunyan. *See* The Pilgrim.

Pilgrimage. Anna Wickham. WPN

Pilgrimage. Austin Clarke. CIP-2; TIRV

Pilgrimage, The. George Herbert. ESCV; GeHe; NAEL-1; NOSC; PoE

Pilgrimage, The. Henry Vaughan. ChIV-2; ESCV

Pilgrimage along the migratory roads, a voyage to ancestral / sources. Song of the Initiate. Léopold Sédar Senghor, *French.* VCWP, *tr. by* Melvin Dixon

Pilgrimage Song. *Unknown, Pueblo Indian.* WPE, *tr. by* Mary Austin

Pilgrimage to Loango Strand. Jean-Baptiste Tati-Loutard. PBMAP

Pilgrims. Carol J. Pierman. CMAP

Pilgrims. Jean Valentine. LCAP-2; TAP

Pilgrims in Mexico. *Unknown.* OBCP

Pilgrims of the Plains. Joaquin Miller. PaTW

Pilgrim's Problem. C. S. Lewis. TrCP

Pilgrim's Progress, The. John Bunyan.
Pilgrim, The. BoTP
("He'll labour, night and day, / To be a Pilgrim.") (LL) CTV
(Pilgrim Song, The.) NOCV
(Valiant's Song.) NOSC
Shepherd Boy Sings [in the Valley of Humiliation], The. NOBE; OBEV
(Shepherd Boy's Song, The.) BoTP; NTP
What danger is the pilgrim in. EBEV

Pilgrim's Song, The. Bible, *O.T. See* Psalm 121.

Pilgrim's Song, The. John Bunyan. *See* The Pilgrim.

Pilgrim's Viaticum; or, The Destitute, But Not Forlorn. Elizabeth Tipper. Observations of the Life of Epictetus. KTR
Satyr, A. KTR
To a Young Lady That Desired a Verse of My Being Servant One Day and Mistress Another. KTR

Pillar of Fame, The. Robert Herrick. BeJo; CaPo; NIP-4; SeCP
("Firm and well-fixed foundation.") (LL) NoP-4
("Jocund his Muse was; but his Life was chaste.") (LL) CavPo

Pillar of Flame. Barbara Unger. LoHo

Pillar of the Cloud, The. John Henry, Cardinal Newman. ChIV-1

Pillar [*or* Piller] perished [*or* pearisht] is whe[a]rto I le[a]nt, The. Sir Thomas Wyatt, *after the Italian of* Petrarch. AAS; FaBoPV; NoSic; OBVE
("Piller pearisht is whearto I Lent, The.") PBRV
("Till dreadfull death, do ease my dolefull state.") (LL) PBRV

Pillar Towers of Ireland, The. Denis Florence MacCarthy. TIRV

Pillars of Salt. Antonin Brousek, *German.*
"Walls shriek, The." CEEP, *tr. by* Ewald Osers

Piller pearisht is whearto I Lent, The. Sir Thomas Wyatt. *See* The Pillar [*or* Piller] perished [*or* pearisht] is whe[a]rto I le[a]nt.

Pillow, The. Herman Melville. APN-2 *Fr.* Clarel: A Poem and Pilgrimage in the Holy Land.

Pillow that knows all, The. Lady Izumi, *Japanese.* WPJ, *tr. by* Kenneth Rexroth *and* Ikuko Atsumi

Pillowed on your arm / only for the dream of a spring night. Lady Suwo, *Japanese.* WPJ, *tr. by* Kenneth Rexroth *and* Ikuko Atsumi

Pilot, The. Russell Edson. LCAP-2

Pilot, The. Renate Wood. CMAP

Pilot from the Carrier, A. Randall Jarrell. PoWW

Pilots, The. Denise Levertov. InPS-3

Pilots, Man Your Planes. Randall Jarrell. MoAmPo

Pilot's Psalm, The. *Unknown.* NSI; PoWW

Pimpernel. Charlotte Druitt Cole. BoTP

Pin, The. Ann Taylor. OxBChV

Pin has a head, but has no hair, A. Christina Rossetti. CTV; VWP

Pin-swin or spine-swine, The. His Shield. Marianne Moore. LiTM; NALW

Pinch him, pinch him black and blue. John Lyly. NoSic *Fr.* Endimion.

Pinch of Salt, A. Robert Graves. MoBrPo

Pindar. Antipater of Sidon, *Greek.* AWP, *tr. by* John Addington Symonds

Pindar. Plato, *Greek.* GrAn, *tr. by* Peter Jay

Pindar is imitable by none. Ode 4.2: Praise of Pindar, The ("Pindarum quisquis studet aemulari"). Horace. OAEL-1, *tr. by* Abraham Cowley *Fr.* Odes.

Pindar on the Eclipse of the Sun. Pindar, *Greek.* OBCVT, *tr. by* Thomas Love Peacock

Pindaric Ode, A. Thomas Gray. *Fr.* Bard, The [A Pindaric Ode]. GTBS-P; NOBE; NOEC; OAEL-1; OxAEP-1

Pindaric on the Grunting of a Hog, A. Samuel Wesley. NOBL

Pindaric Poem, A. Anne Finch.
Hymn, The: "To the Almighty on his radiant throne." ChIV-1

Pindarick To Mrs. Behn on her Poem on the Coronation, A. *Unknown.* KTR

Pindarick, to the Athenian Society, A. Elizabeth Singer. KTR

Pindarique Ode on the Arrival of His Excellency, A. *Unknown.*
"Sing first the heroe in his goodly ship." PBCV

Pindar's Revenge. Edward Sanders. PoM

Pine, The. Saunders Lewis, *Welsh.* OBWVE, *tr. by* Gwyn Morgan

Pine at Timber-Line, The. Harriet Monroe. PoA

Pine boat a-shift, fr. *the Chinese of the* Confucian Odes. Ezra Pound. APSN; OBVE

"Pine flower's blooming," says. Untitled. So Chong-Ju, *Korean.* VCWP, *tr. by* David R. McCann

Pine Music. Kate Louise Brown. BoTP

Pine needles. Penny Harter. HA

Pine pierces the hills' whiteness, The. Epiphany. Andrea Zanzotto, *Italian.* VCWP, *tr. by* Ruth Feldman *and* Brian Swann

Pine Planters, The. Thomas Hardy. FaBoVe

Pine Sounds. Po Chü-i, *Chinese.* CoBCP, *tr. by* Burton Watson

Pine-tree standeth lonely, A. Ein Fichtenbaum steht einsam. Heinrich Heine, *German.* AWP, *tr. by* James Thomson

Pine Tree Tops. Gary Snyder. NOBA

Pine-trees in the Courtyard, The. Po Chü-i, *Chinese.* ChiP, *tr. by* Arthur Waley

Pines and cedars, a hundred feet of green, clinging to the earth. T'ang Yin. *Fr.* Poems Inscribed on Paintings. CoBLCP, *tr. by* Jonathan Chaves

Pines and the Sea, The. Christopher Pearse Cranch. ColAP; PAR

Pines are capped with snow, The. Inscribed on a Painting. Yü Chi, *Chinese.* CoBLCP, *tr. by* Jonathan Chaves

Pines moan when the wind passes, The. Beach. Sophia De Mello Breyner, *Portuguese.* VCWP, *tr. by* Ruth Fainlight

Pines were dark on Ramoth hill, The. My Playmate. John Greenleaf Whittier. APN-1; NOBA

Pines without peer, The. Kelly Cherry. FFC

Pinetree. Agnes Nemes Nagy, *Hungarian.* CEEP; PoSu, *tr. by* Bruce Berlind

Piney Woods. Malcolm Cowley. NYBP

Pinionjay shits pebbles. *Unknown, Navajo Indian.* STP, *tr. by* Jerome Rothenberg

Pink Almond. Katharine Tynan. BoTP

Pink and a bit soft-bodied, with a somewhat jazzy. Physical Comparison With Professors And Others. Robert Pinsky. NoP-4

Pink and white hands like roses and rice cake! Phoenix Hairpins. Lu Yu, *Chinese.* OHPC, *tr. by* Kenneth Rexroth

Pink clover. During a trip. Masaoka Shiki, *Japanese.* MJT, *tr. by* Makoto Ueda

Pink creamy hands. Tune: "Phoenix Hairpin." Lu Yu, *Chinese.* SuSp, *tr. by* James J. Y. Liu

Pink Dog. Elizabeth Bishop. NALW

Pink eraser rubbed to shreds, A. How We Learned about Friction. Carol J. Pierman. CMAP

Pink Frock, The. Thomas Hardy. OxBSP

Pink Locust, The. William Carlos Williams. SAmP

Pink maniac, A. Ray DiPalma. PmAP

Pink neon lit window full of plaster of parts and resin, The. The Real Indian Leans Against. "Chrystos." UnSA

Pink Slip at Tool & Dye. Dave Jeddie Smith. NoAM

Pink tender hand, The. Tune: Phoenix Hairpin. Lu Yu, *Chinese.* CoBCP, *tr. by* Burton Watson

Piñon Nuts. Dixie Salazar. UnSA

Pins. *Unknown.* ReMoGo

Pins are always plentiful. True Story of the Pins. Alberto A. Ríos. NAmP90

Pins of the slack pin seine, The. Our Number. Martin Carter. PBCV

Pioneer Lane. Michael Dransfield. NOBAu

Pioneer Village. Ruth Silcock. PeLi

Pioneer Woman. Vesta Pierce Crawford. AiP

Pioneers. Charles Badger Clark Jr. FaBoBe

Pioneers. Aileen Fisher *and* Olive Rabe. CA

Pioneers. Ann Harris. CTV

Pioneers! O Pioneers! Walt Whitman. FaBoBe; PaTW

Pious magistrate! sound his praise throughout, A. Official Piety. John Greenleaf Whittier. NCAP

Pious Selinda goes to prayers. Song. William Congreve. BoLoP; ECEV; GLoP; NBLV; NOBE; NOEC; OxBSP

Pious wish to whiteness gone over, A/ Or nothing. (LL) Queen-Anne's-Lace. William Carlos Williams. AmPP; MeMAP; MoAmPo; NAAL-2; NOBA; NoAM; TAP

Pipe, The. German Borisovich Plisetsky, *Russian.* TCRP, *tr. by* Keith Boseley

Pipe and Can, I. Robert Wisdome. *See* A Religious Use of [Taking] Tobacco.

Pipe and Can II. Thomas Bonham. *See* In Praise of Ale.

Pipe of Tobacco, A. Isaac Hawkins Browne.
   "Blest leaf! whose aromatic gales dispense." BXAP; UV
   "Boy! bring an ounce of Freeman's best." BXAP

Piper, The. W. S. Merwin. NAAL-2

Piper, A [*or* The]. "Seumas O'Sullivan." BoTP; CH

Piper and His Cow, The. Mother Goose. ReMoGo

Piper in the streets to-day, A. Piper, A [*or* The]. "Seumas O'Sullivan." BoTP; CH

Piper o' Dundee, The. *Unknown.* OxBS

Pipes in the streets were playing bravely, The. Cha Till Maccruimein (Departure of the 4th Camerons). Ewart Alan Mackintosh. NSI

Piping down the valleys wild. Introduction. William Blake. AWP; ChAP; ClHu; FaBoBe; FaBoCh; HeIP-4; ImPo; InPS-3; NAEL-2; NAWM-2; NOBE; NOBRP; NOEC; NOxBChV; NoP-4; OAEL-2; OBEV; OBNC; OxBChV; PoE; PoEL-4; Ro; SoSe-8; TFi *Fr.* Songs of Innocence.

Piping hot, smoking hot. The Hot Pease Man. Mother Goose. OxNR; ReMoGo

Piping of our slender, peaceful reeds, The. Prologue. Oliver Wendell Holmes. NCAP

Piping of plenty. (LL) To Waken an Old Lady. William Carlos Williams. HAP; InPK-6; LiLi; SoSe-8; WeW-3

Piping Peace. James Shirley. NOBE *Fr.* The Imposture.
   (Song: "You virgins that did late despair.") PoEL-2

Pipling. Theodore Roethke. OBCoV *Fr.* Three Epigrams. NBLV

Pippa Passes. Robert Browning.
   Pippa's Song. BoTP; ImPo; NTCP; OBEV; TrCP; UnPo
   (Song.) EBEvV; FHYEP; TFi

Pippa Passes, But I Can't Get Around This Truck. Margaret Blaker. NBLV

Pippa's Song. Robert Browning. BoTP; ImPo; NTCP; OBEV; TrCP; UnPo *Fr.* Pippa Passes.
   (Song.) EBEvV; FHYEP; TFi

Pique at Parting, A. Sarah Morgan Bryan Piatt. NCAP

Piraeus. Haim Guri, *Hebrew.* IP, *tr. by* Warren Bargad *and* Stanley F. Chyet

Piranesi in L.A. Debora Greger. WWSi

Pirate, The. Sir Walter Scott.
   Song of the Reim-Kennar, The. OAEL-2; OBNC

Pirate Ditty. Robert Louis Stevenson. NOBVV *Fr.* Treasure Island.

Pirate Don Durk of Dowdee, The. Mildred Plew Meigs. ChAP

Pirate Story. Robert Louis Stevenson. ACTP; NOxBChV

Pirates of Penzance, The. Sir William Schwenck Gilbert.
   I Am the Very Model [*or* Pattern] of a Modern Major-General. NBLV; NOBL
   (Modern Major-General, The.) NBLV
   "I am the very pattern of a modern major-gineral." UV
   Policeman's Lot, A [*or* The]. NOBL; PeLV

Pirates' Tea-Party, The. Dorothy Una Ratcliffe. BoTP

Pirithous being over hault or mynde and such a one. Philemon and Baucis. Ovid. CTC, *tr. by* Arthur Golding *Fr.* Metamorphoses.

Pisan Canto 124. Ezra Pound.
   "Enormous tragedy of the dream in the peasant's bent / shoulders, The." AF

Pisces. Ronald Stuart Thomas. CABP; OxBC

Pisgah-Sights. I. Robert Browning. ChIV-1

Pisgah-Sights. II. Robert Browning. ChIV-1

Pismire, a conflagration, a, A. (LL) The Clouds. William Carlos Williams. Poetr; VGW

Pistyll Rhaeadr and Wrexham steeple. The Seven Wonders of North Wales. *Unknown, Welsh.* OBWVE

Pit, The. Theodore Roethke. NAAL-2 *Fr.* The Lost Son. HAP; HCAP; LiTM; VGW

Pit—but Heaven over it, A. Emily Dickinson. APN-2; NCAP

Pit of Cologne, The. Boris Abramovich Slutsky, *Russian.* TCRP, *tr. by* J. R. Rowland

Pit, pat, well-a-day. Mother Goose. OxNR

Pit Ponies, The. Leslie Norris. ChAP

Pit Viper. N. Scott Momaday. CDW; HATNAP

Pit Viper. George Starbuck. NYBP

Pitch-Ball. Yang Chi. CoBLCP, *tr. by* Jonathan Chaves *Fr.* Ten Poems on the Tuan-yang Festival.

Pitch black night gave me two deep black eyes, The. A Generation. Gu Cheng, *Chinese.* VCWP, *tr. by* Sam Hamill

Pitch Pines. Brendan Galvin. AFr

Pitch pines fade, The. The Quiet Fog. Marge Piercy. UnPo

Pitcher. Robert Francis. OxBSP; RaBo; WeW-3

Pitcher, The. Yüan Chen, *Chinese.* AWP; ChiP, *tr. by* Arthur Waley

Pite, that I have sought so yore agoo. The Complaint unto Pity. Chaucer. MiEL

Pithecanthropus erectus. On Evolution. John Ciardi. OBAL

Pitiful dupes of old illusion, lost. Sparrows in a Hillside Drift. James Wright. ColAP

Pitiless heat from heaven pours. The Seasons. Kalidasa, *Sanskrit.* AWP, *tr. by* Arthur W. Ryder

Pitman's Common Sense Arithmetic, 1917. Alan Brownjohn.
   Common Sense. NOxBChV

Pitman's Lovesong, A. *Unknown.* FaBoVe

Pitt-Rivers Museum, Oxford, The. James Fenton. FaBoMo *Fr.* Exempla.

Pitter-patter, hear it raining? Rain. Lilian McCrea. BoTP

Pitty Patty Polt! *Unknown.* BoTP

Pity. William Mills. MT

Pity. Trumbull Stickney. ColAP

Pity beyond all telling, A. The Pity of Love. W. B. Yeats. CMoP; NOBVV; PBMP

Pity for him who suffers from his waste. Suffer the Children. Audre Lorde. PoBA

Pity me not because the light of day. Edna St. Vincent Millay. CMoP; FaBoWP; MeMAP; MoAmPo; OxBA

Pity me not because the light of day. Edna St. Vincent Millay. MeMAP

Pity me on my pilgrimage to Lock Derg! At Saint Patrick's Purgatory. Donnchadh Mor O'Dala, *Irish.* TIRV, *tr. by* Sean O'Faolain

Pity! mourn in plaintive tone. The Death of Lesbia's Bird. Catullus. AWP, *tr. by* Samuel Taylor Coleridge *Fr.* Carmina.

Pity not! The Army gave. Ex-Clerk. Rudyard Kipling. *Fr.* Epitaphs of the War [1914–1918]. OBWP

Pity of It, The. Thomas Hardy. CMoP; LiTM

Pity of Love, The. W. B. Yeats. CMoP; NOBVV; PBMP

Pity of the Leaves, The. Edwin Arlington Robinson. APN-2; MoAmPo

Pity poor lovers who may not do what they please. The Envy of Poor Lovers. Austin Clarke. CIP-2; CMoP

Pity poor Philinos—young. Leonidas of Tarentum, *Greek*. InMo, *tr. by* Sam Hamill

Pity the man who English lacks. Michael Hartnett. CIP-2; PBCIP

Pity the nameless, and the unknown, where. The Nameless Ones. Conrad Potter Aiken. OxBA

Pity the sorrows of a poor old man! The Beggar. Thomas Moss. NOEC

Pity this busy monster,manunkind. E. E. Cummings. AmPP; LiTM; MeMAP; NAAL-2; NOBA; OxBA; TAP

Pity Wasted. Freda C. Bond. WPN

Pity; We Were Such a Good Invention, A. Yehuda Amichai, *Hebrew*. BoLoP; OxBM

Pity would be no more. The Human Abstract. William Blake. FHYEP; NAEL-2; NOBRP; NOEC; OAEL-2; OxAEP-2; PoE; PoEL-4; Ro *Fr.* Songs of Experience.

Pitying the Farmer. Li Shen, *Chinese*. CoBCP, *tr. by* Burton Watson

Piute Creek. Gary Snyder. CAPP-1; CoAP; CoAmPo; NAAL-2; NOBA; PaTW

Piyyut for Rosh Hashana. Haim Guri, *Hebrew*. MHP, *tr. by* Ruth Finer Mintz

Piyyut for the New Year. Haim Guri, *Hebrew*. IP, *tr. by* Warren Bargad *and* Stanley F. Chyet

Pizza Joint in Cranston, A. Craig Weeden. BXAP

Pla ce bo. Phillip Sparow. John Skelton. NoP-4 *Fr.* Phillip Sparow.

Pla ce bo! Who is there, who? John Skelton. AAS; CBNP; NOBE; NoSic; OAEL-1; OxBoLi *Fr.* Phyllyp Sparowe [*or* Philip Sparrow]. AAS; PoEL-1

Place. Robert Creeley. LCAP-2

Place, The. Janet Frame. PeNZ

Place a custard stand in a garden. The Invention of New Jersey. Jack Anderson. EC2

Place at Albert Bay, The. Muriel Rukeyser. PoA

Place eternally to sing. Amen, A. (LL) The Bailey Beareth the Bell Away. *Unknown*. GBL; PoEL-1

Place for No Story, The. Robinson Jeffers. AiP

Place, for the Marshal of the Masque! Charles the First. Shelley.

Place in thy memory, dearest, A. Song. Gerald Griffin. BLPA

Place is called the Golden Cock, The. Lunch at the Coq d'Or. Peter Davison. TwCP

Place is calm, dusty worries clear, The. On the Twentieth Day. Ni Tsan, *Chinese*. CoBLCP, *tr. by* Jonathan Chaves

Place is growing difficult, The. Flails of bramble. The Secret Garden. Thomas Kinsella. TwCP

Place is the focus. What is the language. In Defence of Metaphysics. Charles Tomlinson. MoBrPo

Place Lost and Gone, the Place Found, The. Minnie Bruce Pratt. CPO

Place Me in the Breach. Yehuda Karni, *Hebrew*. TrJP, *tr. by* Sholom J. Kahn

Place-Names of China. Alan Bennett. NOBL; UV

Place no longer exists, The. At Sea. Yona Wallach, *Hebrew*. IP, *tr. by* Warren Bargad *and* Stanley F. Chyet

Place of Backs, The. W. S. Merwin. HoPM

Place of Fire. Johannes Bobrowski, *German*. PoSu, *tr. by* Ruth *and* Matthew Mead; CEEP, *tr. by* Ruth Mead *and* Matthew Mead

Place of O, The. Ray A. Young Bear. VoR

Place of the Damned [*or* Damn'd], The. Jonathan Swift. ChIV-2; FaBoEE; OBSV

Place of the Fian is bare tonight, The. *Unknown*. NOIV

Place of V, The. Ray A. Young Bear. VoR

Place on a Grave. Frank Stanford. MT

Place perpetually on heat, A. (LL) This is Anacreon's grave. Here lie. Antipater of Sidon, *Greek*. OBCVT, *tr. by* Robin Skelton

Place Pigalle. Richard Wilbur. HeIP-4

Place, Places. Melvin Dixon. ISC

Place there is, where proudly raised there stands, A. Samuel Daniel. NoSic *Fr.* The Civil Wars.

Place They Have to Go, The. Ian McDonald. HCP

Place to begin is not your death, The. Judith Sornberger. MDDM

Place was famed for, The. Kris Hemensley. BMAP *Fr.* A Mile from Poetry.

Place we could never enter hides away still, The. Last Visit. Robert Finch. NOBC

Place where a great city stands is not the place of stretch'd wharves, docks, The. Walt Whitman. ImGa *Fr.* Song of the Broad-Axe. CA

Place Where He Arose, The. George Barlow. GT

Place where I spend my days, The. *Unknown, Chinese*. CoBCP, *tr. by* Burton Watson

Place where soon I think to lie, The. Walter Savage Landor. CBLP

Place Where the Rainbow Ends, The. Paul Laurence Dunbar. PWR

Place Where Things Got. Heather McHugh. NAmP90

Place which the flying birds do not reach, A. An Excursion to the Dragon Pool Temple on Chung-nan. Meng Chiao, *Chinese*. PLT, *tr. by* A. C. Graham

Place you never thought to, A. Mad Wolf in Lunar Web, Mad Crow on the Beach. Mac Wellman. FTOS

Pla ce bo / Who is there, who? Philip Sparow. John Skelton. AAS; NOBE; OAEL-1; OBCoV; OxBoLi; PeLV; PoEL-1

Placed. Upon receiving potted peonies for a gift. Masaoka Shiki, *Japanese*. MJT, *tr. by* Makoto Ueda

Placed in the west, Manukau spreads out. Tamaki of a Hundred Lovers. Merimeri Penfold, *Maori*. PeNZ, *tr. by* Margaret Orbell

Placed midst the tempest, whose conflicting waves. On the Death of the Rev. Dr. Kippis. Helen Maria Williams. ECWP

Placed on this isthmus of a middle state. Alexander Pope. WeW-3 *Fr.* An Essay on Man.

Placed out in the afternoon sun. (LL) Meditation for a Pickle Suite. Richard H. W. Dillard. HoPM; MT

Placed these worlds in us. (LL) The Lost Pilot. James Tate. CoAP; NoAM; OBWP; TwCP; UnPo; WeT

Placements I. Clayton Eshleman. PFTM

Places and Ways to Live. Richard Hugo. NIP-4

Places I go, leaning on my bramble cane, The. Inscribed on a Painting. T'ang Yin, *Chinese*. CoBLCP, *tr. by* Jonathan Chaves

Places, Loved Ones. Philip Larkin. CMoP

Placid Man's Epitaph, A. Thomas Hardy. MoBrPo

Placid, rotted harbour has no voice, The. Arrival and Departure. Charles Eglington. PeSA

Placing a $2 Bet for a Man Who Will Never Go to the Horse Races Any More. Diane Wakoski. UnPo

Plague, The. Nikolai Stepanovich Gumilyov, *Russian*. TCRP, *tr. by* Simon Franklin

Plague is Love, a plague, A! but yet. The Little Love-God. Meleager, *Greek*. AWP, *tr. by* Walter Headlam

Plague of Dead Sharks. Alan Dugan. LiTM; NoAM

Plague of Starlings, A. Robert Earl Hayden. NoAM

Plague of Telephones, A. Jim Wayne Miller. IFJA

Plague take all your pedants, say I! Sibrandus Schafnaburgensis. Robert Browning. CTC; EBVV *Fr.* Garden Fancies.

Plague take them, every female! The Girls of Llanbadarn. Dafydd ap Gwilym, *Welsh*. DiPo, *tr. by* Leslie Norris

Plague to thy husband, scandal to thy sex. To Marina. Sarah Fyge Egerton. ECWP

Plain, The. Sándor Weöres, *Hungarian*. BLT, *tr. by* J. Kessler

Plain and purl across the ribs of the world. (LL) Poem Ended by a Death. Fleur Adcock. NoP-4

Plain be the phrase, yet apt the verse. A Utilitarian View of the Monitor's Fight. Herman Melville. APN-2; AmPP; ColAP; NAAL-1; NAAL-3; NCAP; PAR; UnPo

Plain Dealing. Alexander Brome. NOSC

Plain Dealing's Downfall. *Unknown*. OBSV

Plain Fare. Daryl Hine. CoAP

Plain Fools. Alexander Pope. OBSV *Fr.* An Essay on Criticism. NAEL-1; PoEL-3; TFi

Plain Humour, shown with her whole various face. John Oldham. EPCY *Fr.* Upon the Works of Ben Joson.

Plain Language from Truthful James. Bret Harte. APN-2; BLPA; CTC; EBNV; FaBoBe; NOBL; OBAL; OBCoV; PaTW; PeLV; UV

Plain of Adoration, The. *Unknown, Irish*. BIrV, *tr. by* John Montague

Plain of wild grasses, broad and tangled, A. Poem in the Form of a Coffin-Puller's Song. T'ao Ch'ien, *Chinese*. CoBCP, *tr. by* Burton Watson

Plain Sense of Things, The. Wallace Stevens. HCAP; NoAM

Plain Song. Craig Raine. TOF

Plain Song for Comadre, A. Richard Wilbur. NoP-4

Plain Song Talk. Richard Eberhart. PoA

Plain Talk. William Jay Smith. MoAmPo

Plain truth would never serve. Take It from Me. Kenneth O. Hanson. CoAP

Plain verse to start, no tricky stuff. The Poet's Progress. Chris Mann. PeSAV

Plain was grassy, wild and bare, The. The Dying Swan. Tennyson. APo

Plainer Dubliners amaze us, The. On the Use of Jayshus. Oliver St. John Gogarty. FaBoEE

Plainest Narrative, The. William Bronk. APSN

Plainness. Jorge Luis Borges, *Spanish*. NYBP, *tr. by* Norman Thomas Di Giovanni

Plainsmen, The. Charles Badger Clark Jr. PaTW

Plainsong. Carol Ann Duffy. FaBoTC

Plainsong. Gail Hanlon. BAP-96

Plainsong. Vladislav Felitsianovich Khodasevich, *Russian*. TCRP, *tr. by* Michael Frayn

Plaint. Chu Shu-chen, *Chinese*. OHPC, *tr. by* Kenneth Rexroth

Plaint. Ebenezer Elliot. OBEV

Plaint. Charles Henri Ford. SPE

Plaint of Flowers, A. Ernest Sandeen. CRP

Plaint of the Camel, The. Charles Edward Carryl. *See* The Camel's Complaint.

Plaint of the Wife, The. *Unknown, Russian*. AWP, *tr. by* W. R. S. Ralston

Plaintive, A. Tanka. Sasaki Yukitsuna, *Japanese*. MJT, *tr. by* Makoto Ueda

Plainview: 3. N. Scott Momaday. CDW

Plaisir d'Amour. Patrick Galvin. BiHa

Plaiting a dark red love-knot into her long black hair. (LL) The Highwayman. Alfred Noyes. ChAP; EBEvV; EBNV; NOxBChV; NTP; OBNV; OBSP; PoLF; SAGP

Plane Debris. Stephen Rodefer.

   "My mind to me mangles iron. An error is mirror to the truth." PmAP

Plane: Earth, The. Sun-Ra. PoBA

Plane Four. Velemir Khlebnikov. PFTM *Fr.* Zangezi.

Plane Geometer. David McCord. NYBP

Plane tilts in to Nashville, The. The Homecoming Singer. Jay Wright. PoBA; VCAP

Planes flew low over the house, The. These Are Not Brushstrokes. Cyrus Cassells. GT

Planes Landing. Jamie Grant. NOBAu

"Planet doesn't explode of itself, A," said drily. Earth. John Hall Wheelock. LiTM; SoSe-8

"Planet doesn't explode of itself," said drily, A. John Hall Wheelock. *See* Earth ("Planet doesn't explode of itself. . .").

Planet is ours, The: and the blue and the desert spaces. The Jungle. Randolph Stow. *Fr.* Thailand Railway. CBAP

Planet Jupiter, The. Epes Sargent. APN-1

Planet of Descendance, A. William Frederick Stevenson. NOBVV

Planet of Nothing fills the sky, The. The Day You Are Reading This. William Stafford. PoA

Planet on the Table, The. Wallace Stevens. HAP; HCAP; PoPoPo; SAmP

Planetarium. Adrienne Rich. FaBoWP; HCAP; MoP; NAAL-2; NALW; NIP-4; NOBA; NoAM; Poetr; VCAP

Planets. Jean Kenward. SpW

Planets turn in stately dance, The. John Kitching. SpW

Plankton. Ruth Miller. PeSA

Planning the Perfect Evening. Rita Dove. GT *Fr.* A Suite for Augustus.

Plans. Brendan Kennelly. BiHa

Plans. Maxine W. Kumin. TLR

Plans. Dan Pagis, *Hebrew*. IP, *tr. by* Warren Bargad *and* Stanley F. Chyet

Plans for Altering the River. Richard Hugo. FYAP

Plant Poem. Edward Field. IFJA

Plant without moisture sweet, A. Rising in the Morning. Hugh Rhodes. OxBChV

Plantation Proverbs. Joel Chandler Harris. CrDW *Fr.* Uncle Remus: His Songs and His Sayings.

Planted Heel, The. Sir Arthur Thomas Quiller-Couch. EBVV

Planter. Richard Murphy. BIrV *Fr.* The Battle of Aughrim.

Planter's Daughter, The. Austin Clarke. CIP-2; OxBTC

Planticru, The. Robert Rendall. OxBS

Planting. George Wither. NOSC *Fr.* A Collection of Emblemes, Ancient and Moderne.

Planting. Okogbule Wonodi. PBMAP

Planting Bamboos. Po Chü-i, *Chinese*. ChiP, *tr. by* Arthur Waley

Planting Bulbs. Marge Piercy. *Fr.* Six Underrated Pleasures. EC2

Planting Flowers on the Eastern Embankment. Po Chü-i, *Chinese*. ChiP; OBGa, *tr. by* Arthur Waley

Planting Initiation Song. *Unknown, Osage*. WPoS, *tr. by* Francis La Flesche

Planting Onions. Jane Flanders. CrSp

Planting Roses. Phillis Levin. FFC

Plantings. Catalina Cariaga. LoHo

Plants don't talk, people say. Rosalía de Castro, *Spanish*. WPOW, *tr. by* Doris Earnshaw

Plants grow. Old Merina Theme. Flavien Ranaivo, *French*. NegPo, *tr. by* Ellen Conroy Kennedy

Plants shrivelled / earth parched. Judgement Day. Rooplall Monar. HCP

Plashes the Fountain. Paul Celan, *German*. OBVE, *tr. by* Michael Hamburger

Plate 134. By Eakins. 'A cowboy is in the West'. David Ferry. FaBoA

Plate 21. William Blake. *See* Opposition Is True Friendship.

Platinum blonde, Goldilocks, A. Limerick. Fiona Pitt-Kethley. PeLi

Platinum fur and brass revolver shine. Song. Michael McClure. BB

Plato, despair! Meditation on Statistical Method. James Vincent Cunningham. CoAP; VGW

Plato told / him. E. E. Cummings. AmPP; CTC; MoP; NOBA; NoAM; OxBA; PoE

Platonic is a pretty name. Dudley North. NOSC

Platonic Lady, The. John Wilmot, 2d Earl of Rochester. NOSC

Platonic[k] Love. Abraham Cowley. BeJo; NoP-4 *Fr.* The Mistress.

Platonic Love. Edward Herbert, 1st Baron Herbert of Cherbury. NOSC

Platonic love!—a pretty name. On Platonic Love. Samuel Boyse. ECEV

Platonic Subject. Anne Lauterbach. PmAP

Plato's Dog. John A. Scott. BMAP

Plato's Tomb. *Unknown. See* Spirit of Plato.

Platted quite neat to catch applause, with a sliding noose at the end. (LL) Her whole life is an Epigram smack smooth & neatly pend. William Blake. FaBoEE; InPK-6; OAEL-2; PeLV

Platypus, The. *Aborigine Oral Tradition*. NOBAu

Platypus, The. Oliver Herford. PeLV

Plaudite, or End of Life, The. Robert Herrick. CaPo

Play. A. R. Ammons. PoA

Play. Frank Asch. NTCP

Play 1. Identity A Poem. Gertrude Stein. PFTM

Play by me, bathe in me, mother and child. (LL) The River's Song. Charles Kingsley. ACTP; OxBChV

Play I could once; but, gentle friend, you see. To His Friend, on the Untunable Times. Robert Herrick. CaPo

Play is one paragraph, The. A Realistic Bar and Grill. David Shapiro. PmAP

Play it once. Saturday Night. Langston Hughes. MoAmPo

Play No Ball. Gerard Benson. NOxBChV

Play, Phoebus, on thy lute. A Canticle to Apollo. Robert Herrick. CaPo

Play Song. Peter Clarke. PBA

Play switches so fast, The. With So Many Voices. Lyn Lifshin. DeD

Play that thing. Jazz Band in a Parisian Cabaret. Langston Hughes. MoAmPo

Play that thing, you jazz mad fools! Jazz Band. Frank Marshall Davis. SeSe

Play Time. William Blake. *See* Nurse's Song ("When the voices of children are heard on the green / And laughing is heard on the hill").

"Play up! play up! and play the game!" (LL) Vitaï Lampada. Sir Henry John Newbolt. BLPA; EBEvV; FaPoR; NSI; OBWP; UV

"Play vanilla," Lester Young is said. Foo to the Infinite. Clayton Eshleman. MoNo

Playboy. Richard Wilbur. MoP; NOBA; NoAM; SAGP

Playboy of the Demi-World[: 1938], The. William Plomer. OxBTC; UV

Played backwards on his grandson's eyes. (LL) Grandfather. Michael S. Harper. LCAP-2; NAAAL; TAP; VCAP

Played with the brook, all day till twilight. At Clear Brook in Ch'ih-chou. Tu Mu, *Chinese*. PLT, *tr. by* A. C. Graham

Player Piano, The. Randall Jarrell. MT; NAAL-2

Player Piano. John Updike. PFE; Poetr; WeW-3

Player with Railroads and Freight Handler to the Nation. Carl Sandburg. *See* Chicago.

Playful Poem on a Chicken Egg, A. Hsieh Chin, *Chinese*. CoBLCP, *tr. by* Jonathan Chaves

Playground, The. Gregory Harrison. NOxBChV

Playgrounds. Laurence Alma-Tadema. BoTP

Playhouse, The. Joseph Addison. ECEV

Playhouse Key, The. Rachel Lyman Field. BoTP

Playhouse Musings. James Smith. OxAEP-2

Playing at Cards. Belle Randall. CRP

Playing Cards, The. Alexander Pope. *Fr.* The Rape of the Lock[, an Heroi-Comical Poem]. FHYEP; HAP; ImPo; OAEL-1; OBNV; PeLV; PoEL-3

Playing for Keeps. Thomas Erwin, *German*. CEEP, *tr. by* A. Leslie Willson

Playing for Time. Christopher Buckley. SeSe

Playing Monopoly's. It's a Bit Rich. Max Fatchen. OTCP

Playing once with facile. Asclepiades, *Greek*. PGA, *tr. by* Kenneth Rexroth

Playing Pocahontas. Lew Blockcolski. VoR

Playing Solitaire, for Jessica. Thulani Davis. GT

Playing the Game. *Unknown*. PWR

Playing the 7th. 48 Words for a Woman's Dance Song. Jerome Rothenberg. PoM

Playing with Fire. James Simmons. CIP-2

Playing with friends one time. What Her Girl Friend Said to Him (on Her Behalf) When He Came by Daylight. *Unknown, Tamil*. PLW, *tr. by* A. K. Ramanujan

Playing your trumpets. Mosquitoes. Franz Wright. LCAP-2

Plays. Walter Savage Landor. NBLV; OxBSP; OxBoLi; PeLV

Plays itself out a half-inch from my fingers. (LL) The Player Piano. Randall Jarrell. MT; NAAL-2

Playwright convict of public wrongs to men. On Playwright. Ben Jonson. NoP-4

Plea. John Ciardi. OxBSP

Plea for a Captive. W. S. Merwin. NYBP; NoAM

Plea for Mercy, A. Kwesi Brew. PBA; PBMAP

Plea for My Heart's Sake. Naomi Long Madgett. SeSe

Plea for Peace. Frank Prewett. HATNAP

Plea for Tolerance. Margaret E. Bruner. PoToHe

Plea for Trigamy, A. Sir Owen Seaman. NOBL; PeLV

Plea of the Midsummer Fairies, The. Thomas Hood. OBNC

Plea to Boys and Girls, A. Robert Graves. GTBS-P; NAEL-2

Plea to Those Who Matter. James Welch. AmPA

Pleaders, The. Peter Davison. NYBP

Pleasant Changes. Jane Euphemia Browne. OxBChV

Pleasant Comedy of Patient Grissell [or Grissel or Grissill], The. Thomas Dekker and others.

    Cradle Song, A: "Golden slumbers kiss your eyes." OxBChV; SCGP

    Happy Heart, The. GTBS-P; RB; SCGP

        (Sweet Content.) APAD; CH; OBEV

        ("Then hey nonny nonny, hey nonny nonny!") (LL) APAD

Pleasant Delusion of a Sumpteous Citty. Sarah Kemble Knight. SCAP

Pleasant it looked. This Newly Created World. Unknown, Winnebago Indian. AiP

Pleasant Joys of Brotherhood, The. James Simmons. OBCoV; PBCIP

Pleasant land of counterpane, The. (LL) The Land of Counterpane. Robert Louis Stevenson. CTV; ChAP; EBEV; FaBoBe; NBLV; NTCP; OxBChV; PWR; TLR; WHSW

Pleasant Life in Newfoundland, The. Robert Hayman. NOBC

Pleasant place I was at today, A. The Woodland Mass. Dafydd ap Gwllym, Welsh. OBWVE, tr. by Gwyn Williams

Pleasant smell of frying sausages, A. Mixed Feelings. John Ashbery. HAP; WeW-3

Pleasant Sounds. John Clare. NTP

Pleasant the House. Unknown, Irish. BIrV, tr. by John Montague

Pleasant waters of the river Lee, The. (LL) The Bells of Shandon. Francis Sylvester Mahony. CH; IIP; OBEV; OxAEP-2

Pleasant winds brushing the forest grove. Hibiscus. Su Shih. SuSp, tr. by Irving Y. Lo Fr. On Chao Ch'ang's Flower Paintings in Wang Po-yang's Collection.

Pleasantly, of the green wood and the dry. (LL) The Rick of Green Wood. Edward Dorn. NeAP; PmAP; PoM

Pleasantly rose next morn the sun on the village of Grand-Pré. Henry Wadsworth Longfellow. Fr. Part the First. Fr. Evangeline, a Tale of Acadie.

Please be silent, now my country, while I fill the speaker's place. The Negro Schools. Lizelia Augusta Jenkins Moorer. CBWP-3

Please, Chung Tzu. Unknown, Chinese. CoBCP, tr. by Burton Watson

Please come forth. A Midwife's Invocation. Unknown, Nahuatl. WPoS, tr. by Coe, Michael D. and Gordon Whittaker

Please Forward. James Welch. CDW

Please Give This Seat to an Elderly or Disabled Person. Nina Cassian, Romanian. PiM, tr. by Naomi Lazard

Please God, forsake your water and dry bread. To a Nun. John Ormond, after the Welsh. EBEV; FaBoTw; NoP-4

Please keep an eye on my house for a few moments. Vidya, Sanskrit. BoWoP, tr. by Willis Barnstone

Please let my hair grow, mother. Unknown, Pashto. PBWP, tr. by Saduddin Shpoon

Please master can I touch your cheek. Allen Ginsberg. GLP

"Please, Please, Please" on the charts permits. Matins: James Brown and His Famous Flames Tour the South, 1958. David Wojahn. NAmP90; PBCAP Fr. Mystery Train: A Sequence.

Please Say Something. Taeko Tomioka, Japanese. WPOW, tr. by Hiroaki Sato

Please send me money enough for at least three weeks. (LL) Baudelaire. Delmore Schwartz. SAGP

Please, to finish my rhyme. (LL) Ballad of the Despairing Husband. Robert Creeley. NeAP; OBAL; RaBo

Please to Remember. Walter De la Mare. NTP

Please to remember. The Gunpowder Plot. Unknown. OxNR

Please to remember / The fifth of November. Gunpowder Plot Day. Unknown. FaBoPV; LB; OxNR

Please you, draw near.--Louder the music there! Shakespeare. EBEV Fr. King Lear.

Please you, excuse me, good five-o'clock people. Afternoon Tea. Charlotte Mew. NTP

Please your Grace, from out your store. The Beggar to Mab, the Fairy [or Fairie] Queen. Robert Herrick. CaPo

Pleased am I, and more than willing. The Lay of the Honeysuckle. Marie de France, French. WPE, tr. by Robin Johnson

Pleased in his loneliness, he often lies. The Shepherd Boy. John Clare. CABP

Pleasing was his shape. The Temptation of Eve. Milton. EBNV Fr. Book IX. FHYEP; NAEL-1; NAWM-1; OAEL-1 Fr. Paradise Lost.

Pleasure, The. David Ignatow. PFE

Pleasure. A. K. Ramanujan. VCWP

Pleasure and pride are not, as duty knows. A Vulgar Error. J. E. Thorold Rogers. FaBoEE

Pleasure Boat, The. Richard Henry Dana. APN-1

Pleasure Dome, The. Shrikant Verma, Hindi. OMIP, tr. by Vinay Dahrwadker and Aparna Dharwadker

PLEASURE FEARS ME, FOOT ROSE, FOOT BREATH. Michael McClure. BB Fr. Ghost Tantras.

Pleasure It Is. William Cornish. CH; CTC

Pleasure must slip. The Condom Tree. Chase Twichell. NAmP90

Pleasure never is at home. (LL) Fancy. Keats. GTBS-P; OBEV

Pleasure of Imagination, The. Mark Akenside.

    Love of Nature. NOEC

Pleasure of Ruins, The. J. D. McClatchy. PoA

Pleasure Reconciled to Virtue. Ben Jonson. NAEL-1; OAEL-1

    Hymn to Comus. NOSC; SCGP

    (Comus's Song.) OBCoV

Pleasure sweet, excitement without end. Sitting Out New Year With My Wife. Hsü Chün-ch'ien, Chinese. EP, tr. by Anne Birrell

Pleasure: The Second Book of Solomon on the Vanity of the World. Matthew Prior.

    "Oft have I said, the praise of doing well." ChIV-1

Pleasure Thermometer, The. Keats. Ro

Pleasures. Denise Levertov. NOBA; NeAP; NoAM; PoE; Poetr

Pleasures, The. Daniel Alexander Payne.

    "Long hast thou slumber'd, O my sounding Lyre!" AAP

Pleasures among the Fields during the Four Seasons. Li K'ai-hsien, Chinese. CoBLCP, tr. by Jonathan Chaves

Pleasures I took from life, The. The Ghost of a Ghost. Brad Leithauser. RA

Pleasures of friendship are exquisite, The. Stevie Smith. FP

Pleasures of Hope, The. Thomas Campbell.

    On Slavery. Ro

Pleasures of Imagination, The. Mark Akenside.

    Creative Process, The. NOEC

    Nature's Influence on Man. NOEC

    (Love of Nature.) NOEC

    Poet the Chief of Artists, The. EPCY

    Poetic Genius. NOEC

Pleasures of Melancholy, The. Thomas, the Younger Warton.

    "Beneath your ruin'd abbey's moss-grown piles." NOEC; OxAEP-1

    "Tapered choir, at the late hour of prayer, the." ECEV

Pleasures of Merely Circulating, The. Wallace Stevens. OBAL

Pleasures of Retirement, The. Edward Benlowes. NOSC Fr. Theophia.

Pleasures of Shinbashi. Liu E, Chinese. CoBLCP, tr. by Jonathan Chaves

Pleasures of the Imagination. Peter McDonald. PNI

Pleasures of Thinking, The. Thomas, 2d Baron Vaux of Harrowden Vaux. NoSic

Pledge at Spunky Point, The. John Milton Hay. OBAL

Pledge of Allegiance to the Flag. Francis Bellamy. CTV

Pleiades, The. Mary Barnard. NYBP

Pleiades, The. S. E. K. Mqhayi, Xhosa. PeSAV, tr. by Jeff Opland

Pleiades are sinking calm as paint, The. Lesbos. Lawrence Durrell. EBEV

Pleiades disappear, The. Sappho, Greek. InMo, tr. by Sam Hamill

Pleiads now no more are seen, The. Sappho, Greek. OBCVT, tr. by Francis Fawkes

Plenary. Unknown. AmFP

Plenteous place is Ireland for hospitable cheer, A. The Fair Hills of Ireland. Unknown, Modern Irish. OBEV, tr. by Sir Samuel Ferguson

Plenteous ransom [or rannzome] shall come with him [or com with hym], I say, / And shall redeem [or redeme] all our iniquity [or iniquitie]. Bible, O.T. See Psalm 130.

Plentiful light. Electricity of Blossoms. Lorenzo Thomas. FTOS; GT

Plentiful sacrifice and believers in redemption. When the Saints Come Marching In. Audre Lorde. CrSp

Plentiful snow deepens the path to the woods. Snow. Ruth Stone. NYBP

Plenty of Flowers. Two Songs about Flowers & Where I Was Walking. Unknown, Seneca Indian. STP, tr. by Jerome Rothenberg and Johnny John

Plied for thee thy household tasks. (LL) Saadi. Ralph Waldo Emerson. APN-1; MeMAP; OxBA

Plight, The. James W. Thompson. BPo

Plot Against the Giant, The. Wallace Stevens. CMoP; OxBA; RACG; SAmP

("It will undo him.") (LL) RACG

Plot Improbable, Character Unsympathetic. Elder Olson. PFE

Plot the agony of resurrection. Robinson Jeffers. See Antrim.

Plot with Bitterness. Vadim Gabrielevich Shershenevich, Russian. TCRP, tr. by Daniel Weissbort

Plough, The. Richard Henry Horne. OBEV

Plough: I keep my snout to the ground; I burrow. Cynewulf. ASW, tr. by Kevin Crossley-Holland Fr. Riddles (Exeter Book).

Plough, sow and reap. I. Charles Reznikoff. FTOS Fr. Jews in Babylonia.

Ploughboy, The. John Clare. PoEL-4

Ploughed field and the fallow field, The. Generations. Ivor Gurney. NTP

Ploughed parallel as print the stony earth. Lines to My Grandfathers. Tony Harrison. Fr. The School of Eloquence. NAEL-2; NoAM

Ploughing. Clive Sansom. AYFP

Ploughing on Sunday. Wallace Stevens. RB; TTTS

Ploughland has gone to bent, The. Gin the Goodwife Stint. Basil Bunting. CTC; OxBoS

Ploughman, The. Oliver Wendell Holmes. CA

Ploughman. Patrick Kavanagh. TIRV

Ploughman, in Imitation of Milton, The. Samuel Jones. NOEC

Ploughman ploughing a level field. To a Schoolboy. Unknown, Serbian. RB, tr. by Anne Pennington

Ploughman Singing. John Clare. EnVR

Ploughman, whose gnarly hand yet kindly wheeled. The Waving of the Corn. Sidney Lanier. APN-2

Ploughman's Horse, The. Robert Bloomfield. ECEV Fr. Winter.

Ploughman's Song, The. Nicholas Breton. See Phillida and Coridon.

Plovers cry, The. Hitomaro, Japanese. OHMPJ, tr. by Kenneth Rexroth

Plow, Maro, the plains. Unknown, Serbo-Croatian. HSix, tr. by Charles Simic

Plow: "My beak is bent downward, I burrow below." Cynewulf. AnOE Fr. Riddles (Exeter Book).

Plower, The. Padraic Colum. MoBrPo

Plowing: A Memory. Hamlin Garland. ChAP

Plowman. Sidney Keyes. PoRA

Plows keep striking, large stones, their. Harrowing. Douglas Messerli. FTOS

Pluck the Fruit and Taste the Pleasure. Thomas Lodge. OxAEP-1 Fr. Robert, Second Duke of Normandy.

Pluck Wins. Unknown. PWR

Plucke the fruite and tast the pleasure. Pluck the Fruit and Taste the Pleasure. Thomas Lodge. OxAEP-1 Fr. Robert, Second Duke of Normandy.

Plucked, The. Tanka. Miyazawa Kenji, Japanese. MJT, tr. by Makoto Ueda

Plucking feathers. Tanka. Yosano Tekkan, Japanese. MJT, tr. by Makoto Ueda

Plucking Out a Rhythm. Lawson Fusao Inada. AmPA

Plucking The Rushes. Unknown, Chinese. ChiP; LoP, tr. by Arthur Waley; BoLoP; OBVE

Plug. Edmund Vance Cooke. PWR

Plug-hole Man, The. Carey Blyton. FuFo

Plum-blossom, The. Akahito, Japanese. AWP; TAL, tr. by Arthur Waley Fr. Manyo Shu, Part 3 of 4.

Plum Blossoms. Chu Shu-chen. PBWP, tr. by Kenneth Rexroth and Ling Chung

Plum Blossoms. Su Shih. SuSp, tr. by Irving Y. Lo Fr. On Chao Ch'ang's Flower Paintings in Wang Po-yang's Collection.

Plum Blossoms on Solitary Hill. Wang An-shih, Chinese. SuSp, tr. by Jan W. Walls

Plum blossoms will be hard to come by. (LL) Tune: "Pure Serene Music." Li Ch'ing-chao, Chinese. CoBCP, tr. by Burton Watson; SuSp, tr. by Eugene Eoyang

Plum flowers all fallen and gone. Unknown. SuSp, tr. by Michael E. Workman Fr. Spring. SuSp Fr. Tzu-yeh Songs of the Four Seasons.

Plum Pudding, A. Mother Goose. ReMoGo

Plum tree breaks out in bees, The. April. Charles Wright. MT

Plum Tree by the House, The. Oliver St. John Gogarty. OBEV; PoRA

Plum Tree Drops Its Fruit, The. Unknown, Chinese. CoBCP, tr. by Burton Watson

Plumber from Lowater Creek, A. Limerick. Unknown. PeLi

Plumber may be a poet, but a poet is not likely, A. The Difference. Stoddard King. OBAL

Plumbers. Susan Miles. NOxBChV

Plume. Richard Kenney. NoP-4

Plumes of love are black, The! Mad Sonnet 1. Michael McClure. PoM

Plumpuppets, The. Christopher Darlington Morley. ChAP

Plums leave their tartness, weakening my teeth. Early Summer Waking from a Nap. Yang Wan-li, Chinese. SuSp, tr. by Sherwin S. S. Fu

Plunge beneath the still green waters of the Grand Canal. (LL) Lost Fugue for Chet. Lynda Hull. PuP-17; SeSe

Plunges into the heart and is gone. (LL) The Panther. Rilke, German. APo; PiM, tr. by Stephen Mitchell

Plunging and labouring on in a tide of visions. In Front of the Landscape. Thomas Hardy. OBNC

Plunging downward through the slimy water. Death by Drowning. Elizabeth Brewster. NOBC

Plunging limbers over the shattered track, The. Dead Man's Dump. Isaac Rosenberg. FaBoMo; GTBS-P; LiTM; NAEL-2; NSI; NoAM; NoP-4; OBWP; PeFWW; PoFWW; PoWW; TrJP

Plunging towards Phrygia over violent water. Attis. Catullus. OBVE, tr. by Peter Whigham Fr. Carmina.

Pluralist and Old Soldier, The. John Collier. NOEC

Plush juice of, The. For Geraldine. Tony Baker. NBrP

Plutarch. Agathias, Greek. AWP, tr. by Dryden

Plutus. Aristophanes, Greek.

"Good morrow to the morn next to my gold." OBCVT, tr. by Thomas Randolph

Pluvia. Donald Hall. BAP-93

Plying our trades, in hopes of a good drowning. (LL) Marginalia. Richard Wilbur. CMoP; PoA

Po' Boy. Unknown. AS

Po' Boy Blues. Langston Hughes. ColAP; NAAAL

Po' los' boy, bebby, / Evahmo'. (LL) Southern Road. Sterling Brown. BPo; PoBA

Po, po, po, po. Unknown. MiEL

Po, the unrivalled poet. To Li Po on a Spring Day. Tu Fu, Chinese. TAL, tr. by Robert Payne

Pobble Who Has No Toes, The. Edward Lear. CBNP; FaBoCh; OTCP; OxBChV

Pocahontas. William Makepeace Thackeray.

"Wearied arm, and broken sword." AiP

Pock-marked player of the accordion, The. Wedding Party. Donald Hall. LCAP-2

Pocket, it is Poems by Pierre Reverdy. (LL) A Step Away from Them. Frank O'Hara. CoAmPo; HCAP; InPS-3; NAAL-2; VCAP; VGW

Pocket Watch. Novica Tadic, Serbo-Croatian. HSix, tr. by Charles Simic

Pockets of our greatcoats full of barley, The. Requiem for the Croppies. Seamus Heaney. BIrV; CIP-2; FaBoMo; OBWP

Pocomania. Philip Sherlock. PBCV

Pod of the Milkweed. Robert Frost. LiTM

Pods Pop and Grin. James Berry. AYFP

Poe. James Russell Lowell. See Poe and Longfellow.

Poe, a very sick man in Baltimore. The Poets of Hell. Karl Shapiro. NYBP

Poe and Longfellow. James Russell Lowell. AmPP; OxBA Fr. A Fable for Critics. NAAL-1; NAAL-3

(Poe.) TAP

("There comes Poe with his raven, like Barnaby Rudge.") OBCoV; PAR

Poe-'em of Passion, A. Charles Fletcher Lummis. BXAP

Poe In Dust. Haunting Poe's Baltimore. Allen Ginsberg. CLPP

Poem: "About the size of an old-style dollar bill." Elizabeth Bishop. FYAP; HCAP; NoAM; PoPoPo; VCAP

Poem: "After your death." Bill Knott. SPE

Poem: "And when I pay death's duty." Robin Blaser. NeAP

Poem: "As the cat / climbed over." William Carlos Williams. InPS-3; PFE; SoSe-8; TTTS

("Flower pot.") (LL) PC

("Flowerpot.") (LL) ChAP; KaS; NoP-4

("Into the pit of / the empty / flowerpot.") (LL) PoPoPo

Poem: "At night Chinamen jump." Frank O'Hara. CBNP; NOBA; NoAM; PmAP

Poem: "Between rebellion as a private study and the public." Charles Donnelly. CIP-2; IIP

(Last Poem.) BIrV

Poem: "At your light side trees shy." Bill Knott. SPE

Poem: "Country / was back in the hands of the patriots, The." Fred Levinson. AmPA

Poem: "Disturbing to have a person." Barbara Guest. FaBoWP

Poem: "Eager note on my door said 'Call me', The." Frank O'Hara. NOBA; NoAM; PmAP; Poetr; SPE

Poem: "Every morning I forget how it is." Charles Simic. NNaP

Poem: "Figures in the fields against the sky!" Antonio Machado Ruiz, *Spanish.* AWP, *tr. by* John Dos Passos

Poem: "First day of May Jack." Tony Baker. NBrP

Poem: "For years I've heard." Robin Blaser. NeAP

Poem: "Form is the woods: the beast." James Harrison. VGW

Poem: "Frail sound of a tunic trailing, A." Antonio Machado Ruiz, *Spanish.* AWP, *tr. by* John Dos Passos

Poem, A: "Gasp sounded, The." Mongane Wally Serote. PeSAV

Poem: "Geranium, houseleek, laid in oblong beds." John Gray. ADE; NOBVV

Poem: "Hate is only one of many responses." Frank O'Hara. NeAP

Poem: "He watched with all his organs of concern." W. H. Auden. PoA *Fr.* The Quest.

Poem: "Here. Forget." Charles Bernstein. FTOS

Poem: "I cannot tell, not I, why she." Walter Savage Landor. GBL; OAEL-2

Poem: "I do not want only." Colleen Thibaudeau. NOBC

Poem: "I don't know as I get what D.H. Lawrence is driving at." Frank O'Hara. LCAP-2

Poem: "I don't know if I can bear this suddenly." Paul Zweig. WeT

Poem: "I had never heard of the whiteness." David Schloss. PoA

Poem: "I keep feeling all space as my image." Sanders Russell. SPE

Poem: "I lived in the first century of world wars." Muriel Rukeyser. UnPo

Poem: "I loved my friend." Langston Hughes. NTCP

Poem: "I sing th' adventures of mine worthy wights." Thomas Morton. SCAP

Poem: "I walk at dawn across the hollow hills." Ruthven Todd. SPE

Poem, A: "I too have been in love, and my sleepless." Boris Pasternak, *Russian.* TCRP, *tr. by* Albert C. Todd

Poem: "I'm like all lovers, wanting love to be." Lesbia Harford. NOBAu

Poem: "In danger of which." Ray DiPalma. FTOS

Poem: "In its going down, the moon." Robert Hoggra. MoCV

Poem: "In the early evening, as now, a man is bending." Louise Glück. HCAP; Poetr

Poem: "In the earnest path of duty." Charlotte Forten. BlSi

Poem: "In the stump of the old tree, where the heart has rotted out." Hugh Sykes Davies. SPE

Poem: "Instant coffee with slightly sour cream." Frank O'Hara. LiLi

Poem: "It doesn't look like a finger it looks like a feather of broken glass." Hugh Sykes Davies. SPE

Poem: "Khrushchev is coming on the right day!" Frank O'Hara. NeAP; PoM

Poem: "Lana Turner has collapsed!" Frank O'Hara. CLPP; FTOS; PmAP; VGW

Poem: "Little brown boy." Helene Johnson. NAAAL; PoBA

("You are.") (LL) NAAAL

Poem: "Look at me 8th." Sonia Sanchez. PoBA

Poem: "Naked is the earth." Antonio Machado Ruiz, *Spanish.* AWP, *tr. by* John Dos Passos

Poem: "Nothing move thee." Saint, of Avila Theresa, *Spanish.* CRP, *tr. by* Yvor Winters

Poem: "O men, walk on the hills." Maxwell Bodenheim. TrJP

Poem: "O solo mio, hot diggety, nix 'I wather think I can'." Frank O'Hara. TTTS

Poem: "O who can ever praise enough." W. H. Auden. PoA

Poem: "Of old, when Scarron his companions invited." Oliver Goldsmith. NOIV; OxBoLi *Fr.* Retaliation. OxBoLi

Poem: "Old man in the crystal morning after snow." Delmore Schwartz. PoA

Poem: "On getting a card." William Carlos Williams. VGW

Poem: "Only response, The." Bill Knott. InPK-6

Poem, The: "Painter of Dante's awful ferry-ride, The." Babette Deutsch. PoA

Poem: "Puriri moth's wing, A." Jan Kemp. PeNZ

Poem, The: "Rise Oedipus, and if thou canst untold." Thomas Morton. NAAL-3; SCAP

Poem: "Rose fades / and is renewed again, The." William Carlos Williams. Poetr

Poem: "So many pigeons at Columbus." Arthur Gregor. VGW

Poem: "So they begin. With two years gone." Boris Pasternak, *Russian.* TrJP, *tr. by* C. M. Bowra

Poem: "Sometimes I wish that I were Helen-fair." Lesbia Harford. NOBAu

Poem: "There I could never be a boy." Frank O'Hara. NNaP

Poem: "There is a wailing baby under every stone and you walk." Norman McCaig. SPE

Poem: "Thing / To do / Is organize, The." Kenneth Koch. CAPP-1

Poem: "This beauty that I see." James Schuyler. PoA

Poem: "This life like no other." Gregory Orr. AmPA

Poem: "Tiny new emotions, The." Tom Clark. CoAmPo

Poem: "Upended, it crouches on broken limbs." Charles Tomlinson. CMoP

Poem: "Walls of the maelstrom are painted with trees, The." Charles Madge. SPE

Poem: "Water wears away a rock." Sugwon Song, *Korean.* CKP, *tr. by* Jaihiun Kim

Poem: "We think to create festivals." Antonio Machado Ruiz, *Spanish.* AWP, *tr. by* John Dos Passos

Poem: "Were I a king, I could command content." Edward, 17th Earl of Oxford De Vere. FaBoEE; NoSic; OxBSP

("Epigram: 'Were I a king, I could command content'.") FaBoEE; OxBSP

Poem, The: "What ailes Pigmalion? Is it lunacy." Thomas Morton. SCAP

Poem, A: "What is there that we can do or say." Ezekiel Mphahlele. AF

Poem: "When I was still a child." Lesbia Harford. NOBAu

Poem: "While we were walking under the top." John Ashbery. SPE

Poem: "Word is fast asleep, The." Labhshankar Thacker, *Gujarati.* OMIP, *tr. by* Sitanshu Yashashchandra

Poem: "You are ill and so I lead you away." Alfred Wellington Purdy. NOBC

Poem: "You hear that heroic big land music?" Alice Notley. PmAP

Poem: "You send me a letter from far, from across the sea." Valentine Ackland. WPN

Poem: "Your face, / so pale now it is blue." David St. John. AmPA

Poem. Aco Šopov, *Macedonian.* CEEP, *tr. by* Vasa D. Mihailovich

Poem. Calvin C. Hernton. GT

Poem. Donald Justice. *See* Houses.

Poem. Henrikas Nagys, *Lithuanian.* CEEP, *tr. by* Jonas Zdanys

Poem. Jack Kerouac. CLPP

Poem. Jorge Rebelo, *Portuguese.* PBMAP

Poem. Pablo Neruda, *Spanish.* CLPP, *tr. by* Kenneth Rexroth

Poem. Paul Klee, *German.* PFTM, *tr. by* Anselm Hollo

Poem. Simon Armitage. APAD

Poem about a Ball in the Nineteenth Century. William Empson. CBNP

Poem about a Wolf Maybe Two Wolves, A. *Unknown, Seneca Indian.* STP, *tr. by* Jerome Rothenberg *and* Richard Johnny John

Poem about Breasts, A. James Wright. TAP

Poem about Breath. David Wagoner. NoAM

Poem about Faith, A. Kathleen Norris. CrSp

Poem about Fan the Fourth, A. Li K'ai-hsien, *Chinese.* CoBLCP, *tr. by* Jonathan Chaves

Poem about Intelligence for My Brothers and Sisters, A. June Jordan. LTA; UnSA

("'I do guess / that's genius for you'.") (LL) UnSA

Poem about Morning. William Meredith. NYBP

Poem About My Rights. June Jordan. GLP; ISC; NAAAL; NMM-2; NoAM

Poem about People. Robert Pinsky. VCAP

Poem about Poems about Vietnam, A. Jon Stallworthy. NoAM

Poem about the Future. Hans Magnus Enzensberger. PoSu

Poem about Youth and Romanticism, A. "Naum Korzhavin," *Russian.* TCRP, *tr. by* Vladimir Lunis *and* Albert C. Todd

Poem after Apollinaire. Ira Sadoff. AmPA

Poem again, of several parts, each having to do, A. Photographs from a Book: Six Poems. David Ferry. FaBoA *Fr.* Photographs from a Book: Six Poems.

Poem against Catholics. James Fenton *and* John Fuller. OBSV; PeLV

Poem against Rats, A. Fred Levinson. AmPA

Poem Against the British. Robert Bly. CoAmPo

Poem against the Rich. Robert Bly. CAPP-1; NOBA

Poem Against the State (Of Things): 1975. June Jordan. ISC

Poem: Alte Zachen. Abba Kovner, *Hebrew.* IP, *tr. by* Warren Bargad *and* Stanley F. Chyet

("Often / there's nothing in its place?") (LL) AF, *tr. by* Shirley Kaufman

(Potato Pie.) AF, *tr. by* Shirley Kaufman

Poem as Mask, The. Muriel Rukeyser. CrSp; NALW; NMM-2; OxWW

("When I wrote of the women in their dances and wildness, it.") NMM-2; OxWW

Poem ascends, The. (LL) The Jacob's Ladder. Denise Levertov. APSN; AmPP; ChIV-1; KSG; PoM

Poem at Equinox. Hilary Corke. NYBP

Poem at Forty. Chung-hee Moon, *Korean.* CKP, *tr. by* Jaihiun Kim

Poem at Thirty. Sonia Sanchez. BPo; BlSi; NAAAL; NMM-2; NTP; PoBA

Poem at Thirty-nine. Alice Walker. CrSp

Poem before Departure. Jean Burden. WPE

Poem Beginning "The." Louis Zukofsky.

Fifth Movement: Autobiography. PFTM

Poem Beginning with a Line by Cavafy. Derek Mahon. PNI

Poem Beginning with a Line by Pindar, A. Robert Duncan. CoAmPo; NNaP; NeAP; PmAP; PoM; VCAP

Poem by a Perfectly Furious Academician. Shirley Brooks. NOBVV; PeLV

Poem by Garnie Braxton, A. James Wright. LiLi

Poem by John Thorpe, A. Kris Hemensley. BMAP *Fr.* A Mile from Poetry.

Poem by the Bridge at Ten-shin. Li Po, *Chinese.* OBVE, *tr.* by Ezra Pound

Poem by the Charles River. Robin Blaser. NeAP

Poem: "By the road to the contagious hospital." William Carlos Williams. *See* Spring and All.

(Poem) (Chicago) (The Were-Age). Bill Knott. SPE

Poem Circling Hamtramck, Michigan, All Night in Search of You, The. Philip Levine. NNaP

Poem Dedicated to Mrs. Blennerhasset, the Only Female Member of the Limerick Hell Fire Club, A. Daniel Hayes. IIP

Poem Ended by a Death. Fleur Adcock. NoP-4; PeNZ

Poem Entitled the Day and the War, A. James Madison Bell. "Though Tennyson, the poet king." AAP; CBCWP

Poem Entreating of Sorrow, A. Sir Walter Ralegh. SiPS *Fr.* The Ocean's Love to Cynthia.

Poem Expressing My Wife's Response to One I Sent Her, A. Li K'ai-hsien, *Chinese.* CoBLCP, *tr.* by Jonathan Chaves

Poem Films Itself, The. J. S. Harry. BMAP

Poem for a Chorus. Marie Cartier. CrSp

Poem for a Dead Poet. Roger McGough. NTP

Poem for a "Divorced" Daughter. Horace Coleman. ISC

Poem for a Guerrilla Leader. Syl Cheney-Coker. PBMAP

Poem for a Little Boy on the Buddha's Birthday. Diane Wakoski. FiLi

Poem for a Lost Lover. Syl Cheney-Coker. PBMAP

Poem for a Militant. Jorge Rebelo. PBMAP

Poem for a Poet, A. Haki Madhbout. PoBA

Poem for an Anniversary. C. Day Lewis. CABP

Poem for Aretha. Nikki Giovanni. BPo; PoBA

Poem for August—or for My Birthday. Geraldine Monk. NBrP

Poem for Ben Barney. Leslie Marmon Silko. CDW; VoR

Poem for Black Boys. Nikki Giovanni. BPo

Poem for Black Hearts, A. Imamu Amiri Baraka. CAPP-1; NAAAL; PoBA; PoM

Poem for Black Hearts, A. Imamu Amiri Baraka. SSLK

Poem for Black Relocation Centers, A. Etheridge Knight. NNaP *Fr.* Two Poems for Black Relocation Centers. NNaP

Poem for Carroll, Descendant of Chiefs. Lance Henson. VoR

Poem for Children, A; or, On Cruelty to the Irrational Creation. Jane Cave. ECWP

Poem for Christmas, A. C. A. Snodgrass. PoToHe

Poem for Claude. Ray DiPalma. FTOS

Poem for Claude. Ray DiPalma. FTOS

Poem for Deep Thinkers, A. Imamu Amiri Baraka. APSN

Poem for Democrats, A. Imamu Amiri Baraka. CAPP-1

Poem for Diane Wakoski, A. Ray A. Young Bear. CDW

Poem for Easter. Robert Kelly. VGW

Poem for Emily, A. Miller Williams. MT; MoLi; WeW-3

Poem for Etheridge. Sonia Sanchez. BPo

Poem for February First 1975, A. Kay Boyle. NMM-2

Poem for Flora. Nikki Giovanni. BPo; CrSp; PoBA

   ("I want to be / like that.") (LL) MBE

Poem for Friends. Quincy Troupe. PoBA

Poem for Garcia Lorca. George Woodcock. NOBC

Poem for George Helm: Aloha Week 1980. Eric Chock. OpBo

Poem for Guatemala. June Jordan. NAAAL

Poem for Half White College Students. Imamu Amiri Baraka. BPo; CAPP-1; TAP; UnPo

Poem for Integration, A. Alvin Saxon. PoBA

Poem for Jacqueline Hill. *Unknown.* BrRo

Poem for Jan. Joseph Bruchac. CDW

Poem for L. C. Peter Klappert. AmPA

Poem (for Langston Hughes), A. Nikki Giovanni. SSLK

Poem for "Magic", A. Quincy Troupe. ISC

   ("'Magic,' like the sho-nuf spaceman, you am.") (LL) LoL

Poem for Maurice O'Shea, A. Geoffrey Lehmann. NOBAu

Poem for Max Nordau, A. Edwin Arlington Robinson. APN-2

Poem for Melissa. Nuala Ni Dhomhnaill. BiHa

Poem for Men Only. Tony Hoagland. NAmP90

Poem for museum goers, A. John Weiners. BB; NeAP

Poem for My Family: Hazel Griffin and Victor Hernandez Cruz. June Jordan. BPo

Poem for My Father. Toi Derricotte. MoLi; NMM-2

Poem for My Father, A. Sonia Sanchez. BPo

Poem for My Father. Quincy Troupe. AF; LTA

   ("Father, it was honor to be there, in the dugout.") AF

Poem for My Father's Ghost. Mary Oliver. InPS-3

Poem for My Grandmother's Grandmother. Lesléa Newman. LoHo

Poem for My Little Boy. Li Shang-yin, *Chinese.* CoBCP, *tr.* by Burton Watson

Poem for my Most Intelligent 10:30 AM Class/Fall 1985, A. Sonia Sanchez. NMM-2

Poem For My Nephew. Nikki Giovanni. NOxBChV

Poem for My Sons. Minnie Bruce Pratt. FiLi; NMM-2

Poem for My Twentieth Birthday. Kenneth Koch. PoA

Poem for My Wet Nurse, A. Cheng Hsieh, *Chinese.* CoBLCP, *tr.* by Jonathan Chaves

Poem for Myself and Mei: Abortion. Leslie Marmon Silko. VoR

Poem for Myself (Or Blues for a Mississippi Black Boy), A. Etheridge Knight. AF; BkSV; PoPoPo

Poem for Nana. June Jordan. BlSi

Poem for Painters, A. John Weiners. BB; NeAP; PoM

Poem for Players, A. Al Young. LTA

Poem for Positive Thinkers, A. Barbara Mahone. PoBA

Poem for Shane on Her Brother's Birthday. Donald T. Sanders. TTTS

Poem for Sigmund. Lorna Crozier. LW

Poem for Some Black Women. Carolyn M. Rodgers. BlSi

Poem for South AFrican Women. June Jordan. MDDM

Poem for Speculative Hipsters, A. Imamu Amiri Baraka. NOBA; NoAM

Poem for the Birthday of Huey P. Newton. Sotère Torregian. NBV

Poem for the Children. Carolyn Beard Whitlow. FFC

Poem for the Insane, A. John Weiners. NeAP; PmAP; PoM

   ("We ride them / and Tingel-Tangel / in the afternoon.") (LL) BB

Poem for the Meeting of the American Medical Association, A. Oliver Wendell Holmes. PoEL-5

Poem for the Name Mary. Mark Cox. NAmP90

Poem for the Old Man, A. John Weiners. NeAP

Poem for the Sefirot as a Wheel of Light, A. Naftali Bacharach, *Hebrew.* PFTM, *tr.* by Jerome Rothenberg *and* Harris Lenowitz

Poem for the Wife of an Imprisoned Leader. James Berry. NBrP

Poem for the Year Twenty Twenty. Alfred M. Lee. AmPA

Poem for the Young White Man Who Asked Me How I, An Intelligent, Well-Read Person Could Believe in the War Between Races. Lorna Dee Cervantes. PBCAP; PoPoPo; WPOW

   ("But in this country / there is war.") (LL) LTA; NMM-2; UnSA

Poem for Trapped Things, A. John Weiners. BB; GLP; NeAP; PmAP; PoM

Poem for Two Daughters. Ishmael Reed. MoLi

Poem for Unwed Mothers. Nikki Giovanni. OBAL

Poem for vipers, A. John Weiners. NeAP

Poem for William Rummel Serving a Life Sentence in a Texas Prison for Not Fixing an Air Conditioner. Paul Fericano. EC2

Poem for Willie Best, A. Imamu Amiri Baraka. CAPP-1

Poem from the Empire State. June Jordan. BPo

Poem in Defense of Children. Joel Oppenheimer. CDa

Poem in March. Iain Crichton Smith. FaBoTC

Poem in October. Dylan Thomas. EBEvV; ImPo; NAEL-2; NoAM; OxAEP-2; PoA; PoRA; RB; SoSe-8; UV

Poem in Praise of Colum Cille, A. Dallán Forgaill. NOIV

Poem in Praise of My Husband (Taos). Diane Di Prima. BB

Poem in Prose. Archibald MacLeish. MeMAP

Poem in Response to Doom, A. William Hathaway. NAmP90

Poem in Rhyme-Prose Form. Pan Chieh-yû, *Chinese.* CoBCP, *tr.* by Burton Watson

Poem in the Form of a Coffin-Puller's Song ("In the old days I had no wine to drink"). T'ao Ch'ien, *Chinese.* CoBCP, *tr.* by Burton Watson

Poem in the Form of a Coffin-Puller's Song. Miu Hsi, *Chinese.* CoBCP, *tr.* by Burton Watson

Poem in the Form of a Coffin-Puller's Song ("Plain of wild grasses, broad and tangled, A"). T'ao Ch'ien, *Chinese.* CoBCP, *tr.* by Burton Watson

Poem in the Form of a Coffin-Puller's Song ("What has a life must have a death"). T'ao Ch'ien, *Chinese.* CoBCP, *tr.* by Burton Watson

Poem in the Shape of a Saxophone. T. R. Hummer. SeSe

Poem in Three Parts. Robert Bly. CoAmPo; NOBA

Poem in Time of Winter. Ray Mathew. NOBAu; OBCoV

Poem in Which My Legs Are Accepted. Kathleen Fraser. AmPA

Poem in Yellow after Tristan Tzara, A. Jerome Rothenberg. PoM

Poem Inscribed on a Landscape Painting. Chu Yün-ming, *Chinese.*

"Clouds are swept into the sunset—mdash;a sky beyond the sky."
CoBLCP, *tr. by* Jonathan Chaves

Poem Like a Grenade, A. John Haines. SPE

Poem Looking for a Reader, A. Haki R. Madhubuti. ISC

Poem looks at the paper, The. The Creative Process. Amrita Pritam,
Punjabi. OMIP, *tr. by* Amrita Pritam *and* Arlene Zide

Poem makes truth a little more disturbing, The. Hands. Donald Finkel.
CoAP

Poem Making Fun of Chi-ti for His Eye Illness, A. Yang Chi, *Chinese.*
CoBLCP, *tr. by* Jonathan Chaves

Poem may boast bravado, A. Ar(chibald')s Poetica. Alan Ribback. BXAP

Poem: modest, The. After David Samuilow. Lutz Rathenow, *German.*
CEEP, *tr. by* Boria Sax

Poem No. 1. Carolyn M. Rodgers. ISC

Poem No. II. Sang Yi. PFTM *Fr.* Crow's-Eye View.

Poem No. III. Sang Yi. PFTM

Poem No. V. Sang Yi. PFTM

Poem No. VII. Sang Yi. PFTM

Poem No. X. Sang Yi. PFTM

Poem No. XV. Sang Yi, *Korean.* PFTM, *tr. by* Walter Lew

Poem not flowery but bare, A. "David Samuilovich Samoylov," *Russian.*
TCRP, *tr. by* Lubov Yakovleva

Poem Not to Be Read at Your Wedding. Beth Ann Fennelly. BAP-96

Poem No. 286 (On Stalin). Osip Emilevich Mandelstam, *Russian.*
("He glows like a broadchested / Georgian munching a raspberry.") (LL)
PFTM, *tr. by* Burton Raffel *and* Alla Burago

("We live, not feeling the ground under our feet.") PFTM, *tr. by* Burton
Raffel *and* Alla Burago

Poem No. 19 in the Old Manner. Li Po, *Chinese.* CoBCP, *tr. by* Burton
Watson

Poem-Object. André Breton, *French.* PFTM, *tr. by* Michael Benedikt

Poem of Alienation. Antonio Jacinto, *Portuguese.* PeSAV, *tr. by* Michael
Wolfers; PBMAP

Poem of Angela Yvonne Davis. Nikki Giovanni. PoBA

Poem of any Virgin. Jorge de Lima, *Portuguese.* PFTM, *tr. by* Dudley
Poore

Poem of Attrition, A. Etheridge Knight. GT

Poem of Death, A. George MacBeth. HP *Fr.* The Rumanian of Maria
Banus.

Poem of Explanations. Dahlia Ravikovitch, *Hebrew.* BoWoP, *tr. by* Chana
Bloch; IP, *tr. by* Warren Bargad *and* Stanley F. Chyet

Poem of Holy Madness. Ray Bremser.
"Let me lay it to you gently, Mr. Gone!" NeAP

Poem of Humankind, The. Đông Hồ, *Vietnamese.* AVP, *tr. by* Huỳnh Sanh
Thông

Poem of Jacobus Sadoletus on the Statue of Laocoon, The. Jacopo Sadoleto,
Italian. GS, *tr. by* H. S. Wilkinson

Poem of João, The. Noémia da Sousa, *Portuguese.* PeSAV, *tr. by* Margaret
Dickinson

Poem of my Heart, The. Liz Rosenberg. FiLi

Poem of Pathos. Tadeusz Rózewicz, *Polish.* FaBoPV, *tr. by* Adam
Czerniawski

Poem of Prefectural Judge Yang T'ien-jui Righting a Wrong. Chao Meng-fu,
Chinese. CoBLCP, *tr. by* Jonathan Chaves

Poem of remembrance, a gift, a souvenir for you, A. (LL) A Ballad of
Remembrance. Robert Earl Hayden. BPo; PoBA

Poem of Return. Jofre Rocha. PBMAP

Poem of Solitude at Columbia University. Federico García Lorca, *Spanish.*
PBMP, *tr. by* Ben Belitt

Poem of the Conscripted Warrior. "Rui Nogar," *Portuguese.* TTY, *tr. by*
Dorothy Guedes *and* Philippa Rumsey

Poem of the Dawn and the Night. Rodolfo Di Biasio, *Italian.* NeIt, *tr. by*
Stephen Sartarelli

Poem of the End, The. Marina Tsvetayeva, *Russian.* PFTM *Fr.* Poem of
the End.
("This is delirium, / please say this bridge cannot / end / as it ends.")
(LL) PFTM

Poem of the End. Marina Tsvetayeva, *Russian.*
"Blatant as factory buildings." PBWP
"Dense as a horse mane is." PFTM
"I didn't want this, not." OBVE; TCRP
Poem of the End, The. PFTM
("This is delirium, / please say this bridge cannot / end / as it ends.")
(LL) PFTM

"Single post, a point of rusting, A." BrRo

"Slope like a path for, A." PFTM, *tr. by* Elaine Feinstein

"This is how they sharpen knives on a." PFTM

Poem of the Forty-eight States, A. Kenneth Koch. NNaP; OBAL

Poem of the Frost and Snow. Lewis Morris, *Welsh.* OBWVE, *tr. by*
Anthony Conran

Poem of the Future Citizen. José Craveirinha, *Portuguese.* TTY, *tr. by*
Dorothy Guedes *and* Philippa Rumsey

Poem of the mind in the act of finding, The. Of Modern Poetry. Wallace
Stevens. ColAP; MoP; NAAL-2; NoAM; OxBA; Poetr; TAP

Poem of the Universe, The. Charles Weldon. PWR

Poem of the Western Fields. Wu Wei-yeh, *Chinese.* CoBLCP, *tr. by*
Jonathan Chaves

Poem of Two. Michele Murray.
My mother talked of breakfast or laundry. MDDM

Poem of Villeneuve St Georges, A, (*for* M—C). Mbella Sonne Dipoko.
PBMAP

Poem on a Little Pine, A. Hsieh Chin, *Chinese.* CoBLCP, *tr. by* Jonathan
Chaves

Poem on Azure. Anna de Noailles, *French.* WPOW, *tr. by* Betty L.
Schwimmer

Poem on Bread. Vernon Scannell. NOxBChV

Poem on Buddha's Begging Bowl—For Hui-ku, His Holiness Ming, A. Hsü
Pen, *Chinese.* CoBLCP, *tr. by* Jonathan Chaves

Poem on Canada. Patrick Anderson.
Cold Colloquy. NOBC
Coming of the White Man, The. MoCV

Poem on Coal, A. Yü Ch'ien, *Chinese.* SuSp, *tr. by* Wu-chi Liu

Poem on Drinking Wine with the Degree-Holder Ku. Ch'ien Ch'ien-i,
Chinese. CoBLCP, *tr. by* Jonathan Chaves

Poem on Elijahs Translation, A. Benjamin Colman. SCAP

Poem on Falling Leaves. Liu E, *Chinese.* CoBLCP, *tr. by* Jonathan Chaves

Poem on Getting Up Early in the Morning (or Even Late in the Morning),
When One is Old, A. Kay Boyle. NMM-2

Poem on His Death-Bed. Cynddelw Brydydd Mawr, *Welsh.* OBWVE, *tr. by*
Joseph P. Clancy

Poem on His Death-Bed. Meilyr Brydydd, *Welsh.* OBWVE, *tr. by* Joseph
P. Clancy

Poem on Losing One's Teeth. Han Yü, *Chinese.* SuSp, *tr. by* Kenneth O.
Hanson

Poem on Passing by Hsin-k'ai Lake at Kao-yu in Light Rain, A. Yang Chi,
Chinese. CoBLCP, *tr. by* Jonathan Chaves

Poem on the Fugitive Slave Law, A. Elymas Payson Rogers.
"In 'fifty, Congress passed a Bill." CBCWP
"Law! what is law? The wise and sage." AAP

Poem on the Inhumanity of the Slave Trade, A. Ann Yearsley. Ro

Poem on the Supposition of an Advertisement; Appearing in a Morning
Paper, of the Publication of a Volume of Poems, by a Servant-Maid, A.
Elizabeth Hands. ECWP; WoRP

Poem on the Supposition of the Book Having Been Published and Read, A.
Elizabeth Hands. ECWP; WoRP

Poem on the Wall, The. Po Chü-i, *Chinese.* ChiP, *tr. by* Arthur Waley

Poem on the Wandering Immortal. Kuo P'o, *Chinese.* CoBCP, *tr. by*
Burton Watson

Poem 143. Charles Olson. APSN; ColAP *Fr.* The Maximus Poems.

Poem, or Beauty Hurts Mr. Vinal. E. E. Cummings. FaBoA; InPS-3;
MoAmPo; NAAL-2; OBAL; OxBA; PFTM; PeLV; TRP

Poem Out of Childhood. Muriel Rukeyser. NMM-2

Poem Put into My Lady Laiton's Pocket, A. Sir Walter Ralegh. SiPS

Poem Rocket. Allen Ginsberg. VGW

Poem Sacred to the Memory of Sir Isaac Newton, A. Lucretius, *Latin.*
"But who can number up his labours? who." OBCVT, *tr. by* James
Thomson

Poem Seen in a Motel Fan. Alberto Blanco, *Spanish.* CLPP, *tr. by* John
Oliver Simon

Poem should be, as our best ever are, A. The Whole Duty of a Poem.
Arthur Guiterman. PoToHe

Poem should be palpable and mute, A. Ars Poetica. Archibald MacLeish.
APAD; AWP; AmPP; CMoP; ColAP; HAP; HeIP-4; HoPM; InPK-6;
LiTM; MeMAP; MoAmPo; NAAL-2; NIP-4; NOBA; NoP-4; OxBA;
PFE; PoA; PoPoPo; PoRA; Poetr; SAGP; TAP; TFi; WeW-3

Poem should not mean / But be, A. (LL) Ars Poetica. Archibald
MacLeish. AWP; AmPP; CMoP; ColAP; HAP; HeIP-4; HoPM; InPK-6;
LiTM; MeMAP; MoAmPo; NAAL-2; NIP-4; NOBA; OxBA; PFE; PoA;
PoRA; Poetr; TAP; TFi; WeW-3

Poem Some People Will Have to Understand, A. Imamu Amiri Baraka.
BPo; GT; NOBA; RaBo; SAGP

Poem That Took the Place of a Mountain, The. Wallace Stevens. LCAP-2

Poem Then, for Love. Michael Harlow.
Anima Has a Predilection, The. PeNZ

Poem to a Nigger Cop. Bobb Hamilton. TTY

Poem to a Redskin. Wendy Rose. CDW

Poem to Answer the Question: How Old Are Fleas? *Unknown.* Spl

Poem to Be Read and Sung. César Vallejo, *Spanish.* SPE, *tr. by* Robert Bly *and* James Wright

Poem to Be Read at 3 A.M. Donald Justice. HoPM

Poem to Be Recited Every 8 Years While Eating Unleavened Tamales. *Unknown, Aztec Indian.* STP, *tr. by* Anselm Hollo

Poem to Be Said on Hearing the Birds Sing, A. Biddy Crummy, *Irish.* AWP, *tr. by* Douglas Hyde

Poem to Begin the Second Decade of AIDS. Boyer Rickel. WeT

Poem: To Brooklyn Bridge. Hart Crane. *See* To Brooklyn Bridge.

Poem to Complement Other Poems, A. Haki R. Madhubuti. BPo; NAAAL; NBV

Poem to Ease Birth. *Unknown, Aztec Indian.* BoWoP; STP, *tr. by* Anselm Hollo

Poem to Explain Everything about a Certain Day in Vermont, A. Genevieve Taggard. NYBP

Poem to Galway Kinnell, A. Etheridge Knight. NNaP

Poem to Her Daughter. Mwana Kupona Msham, *Swahili.*
　"Daughter, take this amulet." WPOW, *ad. by* Deirdre Lashgari

Poem to His Grace the Duke of Marlborough, A. Joseph Addison. OBWP
　Fr. The Campaign.

Poem to Mary, A. Bláthmac Mac Con Brettan.
　"I call you with honest words." NOIV

Poem to my Daughter. Anne Stevenson. NMM-2

Poem to My Death. Julia De Burgos, *Spanish.* BoWoP, *tr. by* Grace Schulman

Poem to My Grandmother in Her Death. Michele Murray. CrSp; IMW

Poem to My Sister, Ethel Ennis, Who Sang "The Star-spangled Banner" at the Second Inauguration of Richard Milhous Nixon. June Jordan. TAP

Poem to Send to Friends in the Capital, A. Liu Tsung-yüan, *Chinese.* CoBCP, *tr. by* Burton Watson

Poem to Shout in the Ruins. Louis Aragon, *French.* PFTM, *tr. by* Geoffrey Young

Poem to Show the Trouble That Befell Him When He Was at Sea, A. Thomas Prys, *Welsh.* OBWVE, *tr. by* Gwyn Williams

Poem to Some of my Recent Poems. James Tate. NoAM

Poem to the Heart of Jesus, A. Teig Gaelach O'Sullivan, *Irish.* TIRV, *tr. by* Thomas Kinsella

Poem to the Mother of the Gods, A. *Unknown, Aztec Indian.* STP, *tr. by* Edward Kissam

Poem to the Sun ("All the cattle are resting in the fields"). *Ancient Egyptian Oral Tradition.* TTTS, *tr. by* Christopher Wertz

Poem to the Sun ("Boats sail upstream and downstream alike, The"). *Ancient Egyptian Oral Tradition.* TTTS, *tr. by* Christopher Wertz

Poem to the Tune of "Tsui hua yin." Li Ch'ing-chao, *Chinese.* WPOW, *tr. by* Marsha Wagner

Poem to the Tune of "Yi chian mei." Li Ch'ing-chao, *Chinese.* WPOW, *tr. by* Marsha Wagner

Poem to the Tune "Riverbank Willows." Yü Hsüan-chi. BoWoP, *tr. by* Geoffrey Waters

Poem Too Late, A. Natan Zach, *Hebrew.* IP, *tr. by* Warren Bargad *and* Stanley F. Chyet

Poem 2: "Inside, the church lights up today's rain." Fernando Pessoa. PFTM, *tr. by* Edwin Honig *and* Susan M. Brown *Fr.* Oblique Rain.

Poem upon the Caelestial Embassy, A. Richard Steere. SCAP

Poem upon the Triumphant Translation of. . . Mrs. Anne Eliot, A. John Danforth. SCAP

Poem, we're going this way. Pike Street Bus. Colleen J. McElroy. NAAAL

Poem With a Limp. Roger McGough. OBCoV

Poem with a Tilde in the Title, A. Nina Zivancevic, *Serbo-Croatian.* CEEP; HSix, *tr. by* Charles Simic

Poem with Capital Letters, A. Jane Cooper. FaBoWP

Poem with the Answer, A. Sir John Suckling.
　Constant Lover, A [*or* The]. CBLP; GLoP; ImPo; NOSC; OxAEP-1; PBMP; SAGP
　("Out upon it.") GLoP; NoP-4; SAGP

Poem without a Category ("Brave man has ambitions wide as the four seas, The"). T'ao Ch'ien, *Chinese.* CoBCP, *tr. by* Burton Watson

Poem without a Category. Gensei, *Japanese.* EnIH, *tr. by* Burton Watson

Poem without a Category. Liu Cheng, *Chinese.* CoBCP, *tr. by* Burton Watson

Poem without a Category ("Sun and moon refuse to slow their pace"). T'ao Ch'ien, *Chinese.* CoBCP, *tr. by* Burton Watson

Poem without a Title. Charles Simic. NNaP

Poem Written by Sir Henry Wotton, in His Youth, A. Sir Henry Wotton. NoSic

Poem Written During a Dream on the Twenty-Third Day of the Intercalary [Month After The] Fourth [Month]. Ch'ien Ch'ien-i, *Chinese.* CoBLCP, *tr. by* Jonathan Chaves

Poem Written for the Celebration of the Fourth Anniversary of President Lincoln's Emancipation Proclamation, A. James M. Whitfield.
　"From year to year the contest grew." CBCWP

Poem Written in Time of Trouble by an Irish Priest Who Had Taken Orders in France, A. *Unknown, Irish.* OBMV, *tr. by* Lady Augusta Gregory

Poem Written under an Archway in a Discontinued Railroad Station, Fargo, North Dakota, A. James Wright. GM

Poem You Asked For, The. Larry Levis. AmPA; PBCAP

Poema de City *see also* Poema del City 2. Ron Padgett. WWSi

Poema del City 2, *see also* Poema del City. Ron Padgett. WWSi

Poema para los Californios Muertos. Lorna Dee Cervantes. PoPoPo

Poèmes de la Mer (1968). Jean-Baptiste Tati-Loutard.
　News of My Mother. PBMAP

Poemes Negres. Tristan Tzara, *French.*
　Dance of the Greased Women, The. PFTM, *tr. by* Pierre Joris

Poems. Anna Laetitia Barbauld.
　Epistle to William Wilberforce, Esq., on the Rejection of the Bill for Abolishing the Slave Trade. Ro

Poems. Gary Gildner. Poetsp

Poems: "Hasten on your childhood to the hour when white in." Pablo Picasso, *French.* SPE, *tr. by* David Gascoyne

Poems. Barbara Hoole.
　Cumberland Rocks. Ro

Poems: "I think that I shall never read." Thomas M. Disch. UV

Poems. Philip O'Connor. SPE

Poems. Amelia Alderson Opie.
　Stanzas Written under Aeolus' Harp. Ro

Poems. Robert Southey.
　Sailor who had Served in the Slave-Trade, The. Ro

Poems. Helen Maria Williams.
　Sonnet to Twilight. Ro

Poems (1773). Anna Laetitia Barbauld.
　Summer Evening's Meditation, A. Ro

Poems About Prison. Dennis Brutus. PBMAP

Poems after Beirut. Mahmoud Darwish, *Arabic.*

Poems are bullshit unless they are. Black Art. Imamu Amiri Baraka. BPo; CAPP-1; NAAAL

Poems are hard to read. A Major Work. William Meredith. Poetr

Poems are not places. Sterling Plumpp. GT

Poems at the Porthole. Lorine Niedecker. FTOS

Poems: Birmingham 1962–1964. Julia Fields. PoBA

Poems Come to Me in the Night. Alice Sadongei. HATNAP

Poems Composed or Suggested During a Tour, in the Summer of 1833. Wordsworth.
　Inner Vision, The. GTBS-P
　Steamboats, Viaducts and Railways. NAEL-2

Poems for Lou. Guillaume Apollinaire, *French.*
　"My darling little Lou how I love you." PFTM, *tr. by* Jerome Rothenberg

Poems for My Brother Kenneth. Owen Dodson.
　"Sleep late with your dream." PoBA

Poems for My Daughter. Horace Gregory. MoAmPo

Poems for the Game of Silence. *Unknown, Chippewa Indian.* STP, *tr. by* Frances Densmore

Poems for the New. Kathleen Fraser. CrSp

Poems for Yukiko of Tamba. Liu E, *Chinese.* CoBLCP, *tr. by* Jonathan Chaves

Poems from a Diary. Abraham Sutskever, *Yiddish.*
　1980. HP, *tr. by* Cynthia Ozick

Poems from a First Year in Boston. George Starbuck.
　Aspects of Spring in Greater Boston. NYBP

Poems from Mexico. Ory Bernstein, *Hebrew.* IP, *tr. by* Warren Bargad *and* Stanley F. Chyet

Poems from Saint Pelagia Prison. Philippe Soupault, *French.* AF, *tr. by* Schmidt, Paulette

Poems from Subway to Work. Peter Orlovsky. CLPP

Poems from the Margins of Thom Gunn's Moly. Robert Duncan.
　Preface to the Suite: "Childhood, boyhood, young manhood." FTOS

Poems in Depression, at Wei Village. Po Chü-i, *Chinese.* ChiP, *tr. by* Arthur Waley

Poems in Praise of Practically Nothing. Samuel Hoffenstein.
　"Only the wholesomest foods you eat." TrJP
　"You buy some flowers for your table." OBCoV; TrJP
　"You buy yourself a new suit of clothes." OBCoV
　"You hire a cook, but she can't cook yet." OBCoV

Poems in the Greek Anthology Mode. Nissim Ezekiel. "When the female railway clerk." OBCoV

Poems in the palm of the hand, life-lines. Rune. Michael Longley. IIP

Poems Inscribed on Paintings. T'ang Yin, *Chinese*. CoBLCP, *tr. by* Jonathan Chaves

Poems Inscribed on Paintings of Bamboo. Wu Chen, *Chinese*. CoBLCP, *tr. by* Jonathan Chaves

Poems / let's / pretend. (LL) Love U.S.A. Kathleen Spivack. LW

Poems of Alfred Venison, the Poet of Titchfield Street, The. Ezra Pound *and* Noel Stock.

   Charge the the Bread Brigade, The. UV

Poems of Our Climate, The. Wallace Stevens. MeMAP; NoP-4; OxBA; SoSe-8; TwCP

Poems of the Pope, The. Nicanor Parra, *Spanish*. VCWP, *tr. by* Edith Grossman

Poems on Man in His Various Aspects under the American Republic. Cornelius Mathews.

   Journalist, The. APN-1

   Masses, The. APN-1

   Sculptor, The. APN-1

Poems on Several Occasions. Charlotte Bury.

   "False and faithless as thou art." Ro

Poems, Potatoes. Sylvia Plath. AFr

Poems to a Brown Cricket. James Wright. NYBP

Poems to Czechoslovakia, *sl. diff. vers.* Marina Ivanovna Tsvetayeva. *See* March.

Poems We Can Understand. Paul Hoover. EOEF; PmAP

Poems Written Chiefly in Retirement. John Thelwall.

   Lines written at Bridgwater in Somersetshire, on 27 July 1797, during a Long Excursion in Quest of a Peaceful Retreat. Ro

Poems Written during My Sojourn in Japan. Su Man-shu, *Chinese*.

   "On the bank of Lake Rouge a chestnut steed treads proudly." SuSp, *tr. by* Wu-chi Liu

   "She puts on a silken blouse and comes down from the western chamber." SuSp, *tr. by* Wu-chi Liu

   "Shouldn't I pilfer wantonly this famed fragrance of a foreign land?" SuSp, *tr. by* Wu-chi Liu

Poems Written in Close Confinement in the Tower and Newgate upon a Charge of Treason. John Thelwall.

   Stanzas on Hearing for Certainty that we were to be Tried for High Treason. Ro

Poems Written in Prison. Ch'ien Ch'ien-i, *Chinese*.

   "Fishing cove and long lines of fishermen's huts, A." SuSp, *tr. by* Irving Y. Lo

   "Nightly the watchman's rattle startles my sleep." SuSp, *tr. by* Irving Y. Lo

   "Spluttering burnt-out lamp blazes in the dusk." SuSp, *tr. by* Irving Y. Lo

Poet, The. William Cullen Bryant. NAAL-1; NAAL-3; NCAP; TAP

Poet, The. Paul Laurence Dunbar. AAP; BPo; CrDW; NAAAL

Poet. Luchezar Elenkov, *Bulgarian*. CEEP, *tr. by* Jascha Kessler *and* Aleksandar Shurbanov

Poet, The. Padraic Fiacc. CIP-2

Poet, The. "Michael Field." ADE

Poet, A. Thomas Hardy. NoAM

Poet. Sterling Plumpp. BAP-96

Poet, The. Thomas Randolph. OxBSP

Poet. Karl Shapiro. CMoP; LiTM; MoAmPo; NoAM

Poet, The. Arseny Aleksandrovich Tarkovsky, *Russian*. TCRP, *tr. by* Peter Norman

Poet ("To clothe the fiery thought"). Ralph Waldo Emerson. OxBA; OxBSP; Spl *Fr.* Quatrains.

Poet. Peter Viereck. HoPM; MoAmPo

Poet, The. Nikiphoros Vrettakos. GrIP *Fr.* Liturgy Under the Acropolis.

Poet, The. Walt Whitman. MoAmPo *Fr.* By blue Ontario's shore. APN-1

Poet alone in my country, A   On Being a Poet in Sierra Leone. Syl Cheney-Coker. HBAPE; PBMAP

Poet / amidst life's hell implores his fate, The. Iron Nerves. Betti Alver, *Estonian*. CEEP, *tr. by* Ivar Ivask

Poet and Botanist. Constance Naden. VWP

Poet and Critic. Samuel Daniel. *Fr.* Musophilus; or, Defence of All Learning.

Poet and His Book, The. Edna St. Vincent Millay. MoAmPo

Poet and His Patron, The. Edward Moore.

   "Why, Celia, is your spreading waist." ECEV

Poet and his song, The. (LL) Auspex. James Russell Lowell. PoEL-5; TAP

Poet and Saint! to thee alone are given. On the Death of Mr. Crashaw. Abraham Cowley. BeJo; EPCY; MeLP; SeCP

Poet and the Rose, The. John Gay. PeLV *Fr.* Fables.

Poet and the Schizophrenic, The. Andrew Duncan. NBrP

Poet and Tsar. Grigory Mikhailovich Pozhenyan, *Russian*. TCRP, *tr. by* John Glad

Poet and War, The. Albert Ehrenstein, *German*. PeFWW, *tr. by* Christopher Middleton

Poet as King of Gotham, The. Charles Churchill. *Fr.* Gotham. NOEC

Poet at Fifty, The. Laurence David Lerner. PeSA

Poet at Night-Fall, The. Glenway Wescott. PoA

Poet at Seven, The. Donald Justice. MT; WeT; WeW-3

Poet at Twenty, A. Donald Hall. SPE

Poet at Work. Richard Tipping. BMAP

Poet came to our games one day, A. Cerealius, *Greek*. InMo, *tr. by* Sam Hamill

Poet, cast your careful eye. On Seeing a Poet of the First World War on the Station at Abbeville. Charles Causley. LiTM

Poet, conserver of the infinite faces of the living, The. René Char. PFTM, *tr. by* Cid Corman *Fr.* Leaves of Hypnos.

Poet Defended, A. Paul Ramsey. InPK-6

Poet felt the rain, The. Rain. Margiad Evans. OBWVE

Poet first his owne high prayses sings, The. The Argument of the Fourth Booke. Lucretius. KTR, *tr. by* Lucy Hutchinson *Fr.* De Rerum Natura (On the Nature of Things).

Poet from Cheltenham Spa, A. Limerick. Betty Morris. PeLi

Poet has died, A. Alcaeus, *Greek*. InMo, *tr. by* Sam Hamill

Poet hath a realm within, and throne, The. Albery Allson Whitman. AAP *Fr.* Twasinta's Seminoles; Or Rape of Florida.

Poet hath the child's sight in his breast, The. Elizabeth Barrett Browning. EPCY

Poet!—He Hath Put His Heart to School, A. Wordsworth. EPCY

'Poet I am neither born, nor bred," A. Margaret Lucas Cavendish, Duchess of Newcastle. KTR; PFW

Poet! I come to touch thy lance with mine. Wapentake. Henry Wadsworth Longfellow. EPCY

Poet! I like not mealy fruit; give me. Walter Savage Landor. FaBoEE

Poet in his joy, A. (LL) The Peasant Poet. John Clare. FHYEP; OAEL-2; OBNC

Poet in his lone yet genial hour, The. Apologia pro Vita Sua. Coleridge. OxBSP

Poet in Old Age Fishing at Evening, The. Desmond O'Grady. CIP-2

Poet in theory worships the moon, The. Moonlight and Gas. Constance Naden. VWP

Poet in Winter. Edward Lucie-Smith. TwCP

Poet is about to write a poem, The. Poem on Bread. Vernon Scannell. NOxBChV

Poet Is Dead, The. William Everson. NoAM

Poet Is Not a Jukebox, A. Dudley Randall. NoAM

Poet is one who writes verses, A. Who Is a Poet. Tadeusz Różewicz, *Polish*. VCWP, *tr. by* Magnus J. Krynski *and* Robert A. Maguire

Poet is priest. Death to Van Gogh's Ear! Allen Ginsberg. VGW

Poet is the dreamer, The. Loneliness. Al Young. PoBA

Poet Laments the Coming of Old Age, The. Dame Edith Sitwell. NAEL-2; NoAM

Poet, let passion sleep. Art, II. Alfred Noyes. OBEV

Poet Lied, The. Odia Ofeimun. HBAPE

Poet Loves a Mistress, but Not to Marry, The. Robert Herrick. CaPo

Poet of Bray, The. John Heath-Stubbs. NOBL

Poet of Nature, thou hast wept to know. To Wordsworth. Shelley. EPCY; FHYEP; NoP-4; Ro; Son

Poet of Our Race. Maggie Pogue Johnson. CBWP-4

Poet of the dead leaves driven like ghosts. Shelley. Charles Simic. TRP

Poet of the Mountains, The. Thomas McCarthy. CIP-2

Poet of the serene and thoughful lay! Wordsworth. Charlotte L. Forten Grimke. AAP

Poet on the Island, The. Richard Murphy. CIP-2

Poet Recognizing the Echo of the Voice, A. Diane Wakoski. NIP-4

Poet Reflects On Her Solitary Fate, The. Sandra Cisneros. FFC

Poet Shadwell, The. Dryden. *See* The Crown Prince of Dullness.

Poet Speaks from the Visitors' Gallery, A. Archibald MacLeish. NYBP

Poet spilled my gin, The. Tropisms on John Berryman. Gerald Vizenor. VoR

Poet suffers making poems, A. Seeing Off Master Tan. Meng Chiao, *Chinese*. SuSp, *tr. by* Stephen Owen

Poet the Chief of Artists, The. Mark Akenside. EPCY *Fr.* The Pleasures of Imagination.

Poet the Dreamer, The. Norman Jordan. NBV

Poet Thinks, A. Lui Chi, *Chinese*. AWP, *tr. by* E. Powys Mathers

Poet to a Dancer, A. Auvaiyar, *Tamil*. PLW

("One-headed drum, A.") PLW, *tr. by* A. K. Ramanujan
Poet to a Painter, A. Aubrey Thomas De Vere. Son
Poet to Tiger. May Swenson. GLP
  Dream, The. DeD
  Hair, The. DeD
    (Poet to Tiger.) CPO
    ("When you're not looking.") (LL) CPO
  Salt, The. DeD
  Sand, The. DeD
Poet, to whose mighty heart, The. Matthew Arnold. EPCY *Fr.*
  Resignation. FHYEP
Poet told me if I was serious, The. Instruction from Bly. Cynthia
  MacDonald. NMM-2
Poet-Tree. Earle Birney. APAD; OxBC
Poet, Trying to Surprise God, The. Peter Meinke. PBCAP
Poet Turned Lawyer, The. Donne. OBSV *Fr.* Satires.
Poet vs. Parson. Ebenezer Elliot. Son
Poet walked with feet upon the ground, The. Rublyov XVth Century.
  Ksenya Nekrasova, *Russian.* TCRP, *tr. by* Vera Rich
Poet was busted by a topless judge, A. Sermonette. Ishmael Reed. PoBA
Poet went to the Isthmian games, A. Cerealius, *Greek.* GrAn, *tr. by* Peter
  Jay
Poet: What Ever Happened to Luther? Haki R. Madhubuti. UnSA
Poet, whoe'er thou art, God damn thee. John Wilmot. FaBoEE
Poet Wondering What He Is Up To. D. J. Enright. OxBC
Poet, write! / Not of a purpose dark and dire. The Crime of the Ages.
  Augusta Cooper Bristol. APN-2
Poeta Fit, Non Nascitur. "Lewis Carroll." OBSV
Poeta Fui. Julia Budenz. FFC
Poeta Loquitur. Swinburne. OAEL-2
Poetaster, The. Ben Jonson.
  "O sacred poesie, thou spirit of artes." PoEL-2
  "Swell me a bowl with lusty wine." BeJo
  "There is no bountie is to be shew'd to such." PoEL-2
Poetaster, The. Samuel Rowlands. *Fr.* Melancholy Conceit. OxBSP
Poète Manqué. Ernest Sandeen. CRP
Poetess's Bouts-Rimés, The. *Unknown.* NOEC
Poetic Frenzy. Shakespeare. EPCY *Fr.* A Midsummer Night's Dream.
Poetic Genius. Mark Akenside. NOEC *Fr.* The Pleasures of Imagination.
Poetic Reflections Enroute To, and During, The Funeral and Burial of Henry
  Dumas, Poet. Eugene B. Redmond. ISC
Poetic wit. Abraham Cowley. *See* Ode: Of Wit.
Poetical Commandments. Byron. OxBCL; PeLV, *canto 1, stanzas*
  204–206 *Fr.* Canto the First. NAEL-2; OAEL-2; PoE *Fr.* Don Juan.
Poetical Epistle, from the Island of Jamaica, to, A. *Unknown.*
  "Our tropic fruits, nurs'd 'neath a torrid sky." PBCV
Poetical Epistle tae Cullybackey Auld Nummer. Thomas Given. FaBoVe
Poetical Numbers. Alexander Pope. *Fr.* An Essay on Criticism. NAEL-1;
  PoEL-3; TFi
  ("Flies o'er the unbending corn, and skims along the main.") (LL) EPCY;
    FHYEP; Poetr
  ("That, like a wounded snake, drags its slow length along.") (LL) ECEV;
    HAP
Poetical Works of the Late Thomas Little Esq, The. Thomas Moore.
  Love in a Storm. Ro
Poetics. August Kleinzahler. PmAP
Poetics against the Angel of Death. Phyllis Webb. MoCV; NOBC
Poetograd, *fragments.* Nikolai Ivanovich Glazkov, *Russian.* TCRP, *tr. by*
  Daniel Weissbort
Poetresses Hasty Resolution, The. Margaret Lucas Cavendish, Duchess of
  Newcastle. KTR
Poetresses Petition, The. Margaret Lucas Cavendish, Duchess of Newcastle.
  KTR
  ("And for her glory, garlands of fresh bays.") (LL) CABP
  ("Like to a fever's pulse my heart doth beat.") CABP
  (Poetress's Petition, The.) CABP
Poetry. Madison Cawein. APN-2
Poetry. Mary Elizabeth Fullerton. GI; NOBAu
Poetry. Greg Kuzma. PoA
Poetry. Tom Leonard. FaBoTC
Poetry. Marianne Moore. AmPP; BoWoP; CMoP; ColAP; FaBoWP; HAP;
  HeIP-4; ImGa; ImPo; LiTM; MoAmPo; MoP; NAAL-2; NALW; NIP-4;
  NOBA; NoAM; NoP-4; OxBA; PoE; PoPoPo; Poetr; TAP; TFi; UnPo
Poetry. Pablo Neruda, *Spanish.* VCWP, *tr. by* Alastair Reid
Poetry. Frank O'Hara. HCAP
Poetry. Abraham Sutskever, *Yiddish.* CEEP, *tr. by* Ruth Whitman
Poetry. Tanka. Sasaki Yukitsuna, *Japanese.* MJT, *tr. by* Makoto Ueda

Poetry (1976). Yona Wollach, *Hebrew.*
  "Never will I hear the sweet voice of God." IP, *tr. by* Warren Bargad *and*
    Stanley F. Chyet
Poetry, a Natural Thing. Robert Duncan. NOBA; NoAM; PmAP; TRP
Poetry, almost blind like a camera. Imaginary Elegies, I-IV. Jack Spicer.
  NeAP; PmAP
Poetry, almost blind like a camera. Jack Spicer. NeAP *Fr.* Imaginary
  Elegies.
Poetry and I set out to visit. Poetry in a Glass Cube. Aleksandar Petrov,
  Serbian. CEEP, *tr. by* Krinka Vidakovic Petrov *and* Mark Strand
Poetry and Joy. Edward Foster. PT
Poetry and Marriage. Wendell Berry.
  From Poetry and Marriage. ITG
  "Meaning of marriage begins in the giving of words. We cannot join,
    The." ITG
Poetry and the Melancholy Man. Milton. EPCY *Fr.* Il Penseroso. AWP;
  FHYEP; GTBS-P; HAP; HoPM; ImPo; NOSC; NoP-4; OAEL-1; OBEV;
  TFi
Poetry and the Poet. Henry Cuyler Bunner. OBAL
Poetry Calendar, A. Chimako Tada, *Japanese.* VCWP, *tr. by* Naoshi
  Koriyama *and* Edward Lueders
Poetry Concert. Michael S. Harper. TAP
Poetry Editor. Yevgeny Mikhailovich Vinokurov, *Russian.* TCRP, *tr. by*
  Daniel Weissbort
Poetry ends like a rope. (LL) A Book of Music. Jack Spicer. APSN; PoM
Poetry Evening. Liljana Dirjan, *Yugoslav.* CEEP, *tr. by* Ewald Osers
Poetry for Supper. Ronald Stuart Thomas. OxBC
Poetry has opened all my pores. After Reading Nelly Sachs. Linda Pastan.
  NMM-2
Poetry in a Glass Cube. Aleksandar Petrov, *Serbian.* CEEP, *tr. by* Krinka
  Vidakovic Petrov *and* Mark Strand
Poetry in an empty dress. Aleksandar Petrov, *Serbian.* CEEP, *tr. by* Krinka
  Vidakovic Petrov *and* Mark Strand
Poetry in England. Samuel Daniel. EPCY; NoSic *Fr.* Musophilus; or,
  Defence of All Learning.
  (Heavenly Eloquence.) NOBE
Poetry in the Underground Passage. Aleksandar Petrov, *Serbian.* CEEP, *tr.*
  by Krinka Vidakovic Petrov *and* Mark Strand
Poetry Is a Destructive Force. Wallace Stevens. MeMAP; OxBA; RaBo
Poetry is a projection across silence of cadences arranged to break that
  silence. Ten Definitions of Poetry. Carl Sandburg. MoAmPo
Poetry is always seeking something special. To men with. From Hear to
  Air. Douglas Messerli. FTOS
Poetry is an applied science. Parapoetics. Eugene B. Redmond. NBV
Poetry is any page from a sketchbook of outlines of a. Carl Sandburg.
  SAGP
Poetry Is Death Cast Out. Sydney Clouts. PeSA
Poetry is like a swoon, with this difference. The Klupzy Girl. Charles
  Bernstein. PmAP
Poetry is made in bed like love. On the Road to San Romano. André
  Breton, *French.* PFTM, *tr. by* Charles Simic and Michael Benedikt
Poetry is the supreme fiction, madame. A High-Toned Old Christian
  Woman. Wallace Stevens. CMoP; MoP; NAAL-2; NOBA; NoAM;
  Poetr; TAP
Poetry? It's a hobby. What the Chairman Told Tom. Basil Bunting. NoP-
  4; OxBTC
Poetry Jump-Up. John Agard. NOxBChV
Poetry Makes Rhythm in Philosophy. Ishmael Reed. MoNo
Poetry of Departures. Philip Larkin. CMoP; HeIP-4; OxBC; PoE; TwCP
  Ultimatum.
Poetry of earth is never dead, The. On the Grasshopper and [the] Cricket.
  Keats. APo; BoTP; FHYEP; FaBoBe; ImPo; NIP-4; OAEL-2; OxAEP-
  2; Poetr; Son; TTTS
Poetry of Gerard Manley Hopkins, The. Monk Gibbon. TIRV
Poetry Paper. Andrei Codrescu. SPE
Poetry Perpetuates the Poet. Robert Herrick. BeJo; FaBoEE
Poetry Professors, The. Robert Lloyd.
  "Old England has not lost her prayer." ECEV
  "Yet matter must be gravely planned." ECEV
Poetry Reading. Vernon Scannell. NOBL
Poetry Reading. Anna Swirszczynska, *Polish.* BLT, *tr. by* Czeslaw Milosz
  and Leonard Nathan
Poetry rushes into. Poetry in the Underground Passage. Aleksandar Petrov,
  Serbian. CEEP, *tr. by* Krinka Vidakovic Petrov *and* Mark Strand
Poetry Visits an Old Lady. Aleksandar Petrov, *Serbian.* CEEP, *tr. by*
  Krinka Vidakovic Petrov *and* Mark Strand
Poetry wud go out of bizness. (LL) To P. J. (2 Yrs Old Who Sed Write a
  Poem for Me in Portland, Oregon). Sonia Sanchez. MBE; NOxBChV
Poetry's a gift wherein but few excell. Nathaniel Ward. SCAP

Poetry's a tree. Yes, the Secret Mind Whispers. Al Young. PoBA

Poetry's Buried. Meir Wieseltier, *Hebrew.* IP, *tr. by* Warren Bargad *and* Stanley F. Chyet

Poets, The. Aleksandr Blok, *Russian.* TCRP, *tr. by* Geoffrey Thurley

Poets. Gavin Ewart. PeLV

Poets, The. Henry Wadsworth Longfellow. GSo

Poet's age is sad: for why?, The. Prologue. Robert Browning. EnVR; OAEL-2

Poets Agree to Be Quiet by the Swamp, The. David Wagoner. CoAP; VGW

Poets and parents say he cannot die. Yet Another Poem about a Dying Child. Janet Frame. PeNZ

Poets and Their Bibliographies. Tennyson. GSo

Poet's Arbour in the Birchwood, The. Edward Williams, *Welsh.* OBWVE, *tr. by* Kenneth Hurlstone Jackson

Poets are among the first witches. Wearing My Cap Backwards. Cheryl Clarke. NMM-2

Poets are usually pure, rugged. Lament for Lu Yin. Meng Chiao, *Chinese.* SuSp, *tr. by* Stephen Owen

Poet's Calendar, The. Henry Wadsworth Longfellow. APN-1

Poets' Corner. Robert Graves. FaBoEE

Poet's Corner, The. Laura Riding Jackson. FuPo

Poet's Counsel, A ("You come from the line of a Cōḷa King"). Kovur Kilar, *Tamil.* PLW, *tr. by* A. K. Ramanujan

Poet's Counsel, A ("Your enemy is not the kind who wears"). Kovur Kilar, *Tamil.* PLW, *tr. by* A. K. Ramanujan

Poet's Credo. Byron. *See* Poetical Commandments.

Poet's daily chore, The. Lens. Anne Wilkinson. MoCV; NOBC

Poet's Day, The. Richard Weber. CIP-2

Poet's Delay, The. Henry David Thoreau. PAR

Poet's Destiny, The. Lady Jane Francesca Wilde. VWP

Poet's Dream, The. William Dunbar. PoEL-1 *Fr.* The Golden [*or* Goldyn] Targe. OxBS

Poet's Dream, The. Shelley. *Fr.* Prometheus Unbound. NOBRP; OAEL-2 ("Nurslings of Immortality!") (LL) GTBS-P

Poet's eye, in a fine frenzy rolling, The. Poetic Frenzy. Shakespeare. EPCY *Fr.* A Midsummer Night's Dream.

Poet's eye obscenely seeing, The. Lawrence Ferlinghetti. LiTM

Poet's Farewell to His Teeth, The. William Dickey. PoA

Poet's Fate, The. Thomas Hood. FaBoEE

Poet's Final Instructions, The. John Berryman. Son; VGW

Poets for deciduous language., The. (LL) Postscript. Ronald Stuart Thomas. FaBoMo; OxBC

Poets have muddied all the little fountains, The. Abla. Antar. AWP, *tr. by* E. Powys Mathers *Fr.* The Mu'allaqat.

Poets have often noticed. Bakhyt Kenzheyev, *Russian.* TCRP, *tr. by* Albert C. Todd

Poets have their ear to the ground more than most people. Peter De Vries. UV

Poet's heart is wrenched and wrenched again until his head turns white, A. Yüan Hao-wen. SuSp, *tr. by* Irving Y. Lo *Fr.* On Poetry.

Poets Hitchhiking on the Highway. Gregory Corso. BB; NeAP; PoM

Poet's Hope, A. William Ellery Channing. PAR

Poets, I want to follow them all. On Originality. Bill Manhire. PeNZ

Poet's Ideal, The. Henrietta Cordelia Ray. CBWP-3

Poets / in a company. A Dancing Concerning a Form of Women. Robert Duncan. FTOS

Poets light but Lamps, The. Emily Dickinson. APN-2; HeIP-4

Poets loiter all their leisure. The Hour Glass. Edward Quillinan. NOBRP

Poet's Lot, The. Oliver Wendell Holmes. PoEL-5

Poet's Love, A. Letitia Elizabeth Landon. Ro *Fr.* Life and Literary Remains of L.E.L.

Poets Love Nature. John Clare. OAEL-2

Poet's Loves, The. Hywel ab Owain Gwynedd, *Welsh.* OBWVE, *tr. by* Gwyn Williams

Poets make pets of pretty, docile words. Pretty Words. Elinor Wylie. NAAL-2

Poets may boast, as safely vain. Of English Verse. Edmund Waller. BeJo; CABP; GEA; NAEL-1; NOSC; OAEL-1; PoE; SeCP

Poet's Memory Is Counsel, A. Kaḷḷil Attiraiyaṉār, *Tamil.* PLW, *tr. by* A. K. Ramanujan

Poet's Ministrants, The. Henrietta Cordelia Ray. CBWP-3

Poet's Obligation. Pablo Neruda, *Spanish.* VCWP, *tr. by* Alastair Reid

Poets of Hell, The. Karl Shapiro. NYBP

Poets of the midwest, The. Hello There! Harvey Shapiro. WeT

Poets only that can tell, The. (LL) On a Picture Painted by Herself[, Representing Two Nimphs of Diana's]. Anne Killigrew. KTR; NOSC

Poet's Paradise, The. Michael Drayton. *See* The Description of Elizium.

Poet's Prayer, The. *Unknown.* OBSV

Poet's Progress, The. Chris Mann. PeSAV

Poet's Request, The. *Unknown, Irish.* BIrV, *tr. by* John Montague

Poet's Shuffle, The. Calvin Forbes. GT; LTA

Poet's Song, The. Tennyson. EBVV; EPCY

Poet's Tale: The Birds of Killingworth, The. Henry Wadsworth Longfellow. *See* Birds of Killingworth, The (The Poet's Tale).

Poet's Terror at the Bailiffs of Exeter, The. Andrew Brice. NOEC *Fr.* Freedom; a Poem, Written in Time of Recess from the Rapacious Claws of Bailiffs.

Poet's Thought, A. "Barry Cornwall." Ro *Fr.* English Songs.

Poet's Voice, The. William Blake. *See* Introduction.

Poet's Welcome to His Love-Begotten Daughter [the First Instance that Entitled Him to the Venerable Appellation of Father], A. Robert Burns. NOEC; OxBoLi; PoEL-4

Poet's Wish; an Ode, The. Allan Ramsay, *after* Horace. OBVE

Poggio. Lawrence Durrell. OxBTC

Poh! did ever one see such a troublesome bear? Delia Very Angry. *Unknown.* NOEC

Poietes Apoietes. Hartley Coleridge. OBNC

Point, The. John Montague. PNI

Point, greatly enlarged, The. Thomas Kinsella. BiHa *Fr.* A Technical Supplement.

Point Grey. Daryl Hine. NOBC

Point, I imagine, is, The. Evan Jones. NOBAu

Point is not the point—, The. David Bromige. FTOS

Point no scornful finger at Yoruba Land. Edouard J. Maunick. NegPo, *tr. by* Ellen Conroy Kennedy *Fr.* As Far as Yoruba Land.

Point of hill. Stairway to Heaven. Robert Creeley. FTOS

Point of No Return. Robert Graves. BIrV

Point Shirley. Sylvia Plath. NIP-4; Poetr

Point your nose to the sun. Trajan, *Greek.* GrAn, *tr. by* Peter Jay

Pointed houses lean so you would swear, The. Amsterdam. Francis Jammes, *French.* AWP, *tr. by* Jethro Bithell

Pointed star, which on a steeple / Stands for hope. (LL) The Steeple-Jack. Marianne Moore. BoWP; CMoP; FaBoWP; HAP; InPS-3; NOBA; NoAM; OxBA; PBWP; Poetr; WPE

Poise of my hands reminded me of yours. (LL) Villanelle. William Empson. CBLP; CMoP; EnLoPo; LoP; MoP; NoAM; OAEL-2; PoE; TRP; UV

Poised between going on and back, pulled. The Base Stealer. Robert Francis. NTCP

Poison, The. Hans Magnus Enzensberger, *German.* VCWP, *tr. by* Hans Magnus Enzensberger *and* Michael Hamburger

Poison flower that in my garden grew, The. Mary Elizabeth Coleridge. PEW

Poison-maker, The. Ian McDonald. HCP

"Flashing messengers of light and swiftness." HCP

"Travelled miles that day." HCP

Poison mushrooms / want to be picked. Woods. Jerzy Harasymowicz, *Polish.* CEEP, *tr. by* Victor Contoski

Poison Tree, A. William Blake. APAD; AWP; FHYEP; HAP; HoPM; ImPo; NAEL-2; NTP; NoP-4; OxAEP-2; PFE; PoEL-4; RB; Ro; SCV; SoSe-8; TFi; WeW-3 *Fr.* Songs of Experience.

Poke-Pole Fishing. Dennis Schmitz. AmPA

Pokeberries. Ruth Stone. IFJA; NMM-2

Poking Fun At a Bonze. Ho Xuan Huong, *Vietnamese.* AVP, *tr. by* Huỳnh Sanh Thông

Pol Pot. Frederick Seidel. BAP-94

Poland / 1931 "The Wedding." Jerome Rothenberg. PoM

("And begin to crow.") (LL) FTOS

(Poland/1931.) FTOS

Poland works nicely. The Story So Far. John Clarke. UV

Polar Bear never makes his bed, The. William Jay Smith. TLR

Polar Circle, The, for Lauri Nykopp. Lyn Hejinian. BAP-94

Polar Cub. Judith Nicholls. NOxBChV

Polar DEW has just warned that, The. Your Attention Please. Peter Porter. OBWP; OxBTC

Polar Exploration. Stephen Spender. NoAM

(North, The.) FaBoMo

Polarities. Kenneth Slessor. CBAP

Pole Star, The. Coslett Coslett, *Welsh.* OBWVE, *tr. by* Kenneth Hurlstone Jackson

Pole Star for This Year. Archibald MacLeish. MeMAP; OxBA

Poles are flying where the two eyes set, The. Discoveries. Vernon Watkins. ImPo; LiTM

Poles rode out from Warsaw against the German, The. The Abnormal Is Not Courage. Jack Gilbert. CoAP

Police are dragging for the bodies, The. Miners. James Wright. CoAmPo

Police / being poisoned, The. A List of the Delusions of the Insane / What They Are Afraid Of. David Antin. APSN

Police Inquiry, The. Christian Morgenstern, *German.* CBNP, *tr. by* Max Knight

Police Station Ditties. Max Beerbohm. NOBL

(P.C., X, 36.) UV

Policeman buys shoes slow and careful, The. Psalm of Those Who Go Forth before Daylight. Carl Sandburg. OxBA

Policeman Cleared in Jaywalking Case. Claire Harris. PBCV

Policeman from Nottingham Junction, A. Limerick. *Unknown.* PeLi

Policeman / is a pig, A. Definition for Blk/Children. Sonia Sanchez. PoBA

Policeman walks with heavy tread, The. Action Rhyme. E. H. Adams. BoTP

Policeman's Lot, A. Wendy Cope. FaBoWP

Policeman's Lot, A [*or* The]. Sir William Schwenck Gilbert. NOBL; PeLV *Fr.* The Pirates of Penzance.

Polis poutre catalane. Luis d'Antin Van Rooten. OBCoV *Fr.* Mots d'Heures: Gousses, Rames.

Polish Eagle, The. Kornel Ujejski, *Polish.* MLL, *tr. by* Helen Waddell

Polish Knot, The. Tomasz Jastrun, *Polish.* AF, *tr. by* Michael March *and* Jaroslaw Anders

Politeness. Una Marson. PBCV

Politeness is to do and say. F. E. Elwell. CTV

Political. Rita Dove. FFC

Political Activist Living Alone. Pat Arrowsmith. BrRo

Political House that Jack Built, The. William Hone. NOBRP

"This is THE MAN—all shaven and shorn." OBCoV

Political Intelligence. Arthur James Marshall Smith. SPE

Political Meeting. Abraham Moses Klein. MoCV

Political Orlando, The. George MacBeth. NOBL

Political Poem. Imamu Amiri Baraka. AF; CoAP; MoP; NAAL-2; NoAM; PmAP

Political Relations. Audre Lorde. GLP

"Political women," thought Yeats. Limerick. R. K. R. Thornton. PeLi

Politician is an arse upon, A. E. E. Cummings. FaBoEE; InPK-6; NBLV; OBAL

Politician's elephantine conk's, The. Maurus. Palladas, *Greek.* GrAn, *tr. by* Tony Harrison

Politicians, heart and soul. Poll Star. Felicia Lamport. NBLV

Politico. Carol Ann Duffy. FaBoTC

Politics. Tom Marshall. NOBC

Politics. W. B. Yeats. CBLP; CMoP; HeIP-4; InPS-3; OxBTC; PoE; SAGP; SCV

Politics Kaiso. Roger McTair. PBCV

Politics of Envy. Duncan Forbes. PeLV

Politics of Rich Painters, The. Imamu Amiri Baraka. VGW

Polka. John Fuller. PeLV *Fr.* Fox-Trot.

Polka. Dame Edith Sitwell. CBNP

Poll. Ed Roberson. PoBA

Poll Star. Felicia Lamport. NBLV

Polly; an Opera. John Gay.

Air: "Sportsmen keep hawks, and their quarry they gain, The." NOEC

"Honour plays a bubble's part." PeLV

"Woman's like the flatt'ring ocean." PeLV

Polly and Sukey. Mother Goose. ReMoGo

Polly Be-en Upzides wi' Tom. William Barnes. NOBVV

Polly Perkins. *Unknown.* OBCoV; OxBoLi; PeLV

Polly put the kettle on. Polly and Sukey. Mother Goose. LB; OxNR; ReMoGo

Polly Vaughn. *Unknown.* AmFP

Polo Grounds. Rolfe Humphries. HoPM

Polo season would start early in April, The. Animal Days. Lee Harwood. NBrP

Polonius' Advice to Laertes. Shakespeare. *See* To Thine Own Self Be True.

Polwart on the Green. Allan Ramsay. NOEC

Polyaenus' daughter, Scyllis, came to the wide gates. Diotimus. HePo, *tr. by* Barbara Hughes Fowler *Fr.* Epigrams.

Polychromatic springtime's gay cadenza. Vernal Equinox. Martin Johnston. CBAP

Polydamas, your depth in augry. Hector's Defiance. Homer. NOSC, *tr. by* George Chapman *Fr.* The Iliad.

Polyglot Medley. Andrew Geddes Bain. PeSAV

Polyhymnia. George Peele.

Farewell to Arms, A. NOBE; OBEV; OBWP; OxAEP-1; PoRA

("His golden locks time hath to silver turned.") NoP-4

(Old Knight, The.)

(Sonnet, A: "His golden locks time hath to silver turned.") InPS-3; PoEL-2

Polynesia. Allen Curnow. PeNZ

Poly-Olbion. Michael Drayton.

"Of Merlin and his skill what Region doth not heare?" OxBSn

(Poly-Olbion Song 6.)

"What spirit can lift you up, to that immortall praise." PBRV

(Polyolbion.)

"By thine own named town made famous in thy fall." NOSC

"March strongly forth, my Muse, whilst yet the temperate air." NOSC

"Then Frome (a nobler flood) the Muses doth implore." NOSC

"Where she, of all the plains of Britain that doth bear." NOSC

"With solitude what sorts, that here's not wondrous rife?" NOSC

Polyphemus. Virgil. NoSic, *tr. by* Richard Stanyhurst *Fr.* The Aeneid [*or* Eneados, *Aeneis*].

"Polyphemus, Galatea with apples pelts your flocks." Damoetas and Daphnis. Theocritus, *Greek.* HePo, *tr. by* Barbara Hughes Fowler *Fr.* Idylls.

Polystylistics is when a knight from the Middle Ages. Nina Iskrenko, *Russian.* TCRP, *tr. by* John High

Polytinus? Chases girls to find a mate. Martial's Favourites. Martial, *Latin.* OBCVT, *tr. by* Hill, Brian

Pomade. Aleksei Eliseievich Kruchyonykh. PFTM, *tr. by* Beth Holmgren *and* Jerome Rothenberg

Pomegranate, The. Eavan Boland. CABP; NoP-4

Pomegranate. Louise Glück. NMM-2

Pomegranate grows in the garden front, The. The Forsaken Wife. Ts'ao Chih, *Chinese.* CoBCP, *tr. by* Burton Watson

Pomegranate just splitting, a peach just furry, A. Diodorus Zonas, *Greek.* GrAn; LoP, *tr. by* Alistair Elliot

Pomegranate speaks, The. *Unknown, Egyptian hieroglyphics.* BoWoP, *tr. by* Ezra Pound *and* Noel Stock

Pomme arac. Derek Walcott. FaBoVe *Fr.* Sainte Lucie.

Pomona. William Morris. NOBVV

Pomp of jewels, the vanity of curled tresses, The. Chanson. René Vivien. CPO

Pompeius, best of all my comrades, you and I.

Pompeius, chief of all my friends, with whom. 2.7. Horace. OBWP, *tr. by* James Michie *Fr.* Odes.

Pompey compared with Caesar. Lucan, *Latin.* OBCVT, *tr. by* Nicholas Rowe

Pompey's death and apotheosis. Lucan, *Latin.* OBCVT, *tr. by* Nicholas Rowe

Pomposo (insolent and loud). Charles Churchill. OBSV *Fr.* The Ghost.

Ponce de León: A Morning Walk. Al Young. HoPM

Pond, The. Louise Glück. ColAP

Pond, The. Anthony Thwaite. NYBP

Pond-chestnuts poke through floating chickweed on the green brocade pool. The Pool behind Ch'i-an. Tu Mu, *Chinese.* PLT, *tr. by* A. C. Graham

Pond in a Basin. Tu Mu, *Chinese.* SuSp, *tr. by* Eddie Tsang

Pond in a Bowl, The. Han Yü, *Chinese.* SuSp, *tr. by* Kenneth O. Hanson

Pond in a Jardiniere, A. Han Yü, *Chinese.*

"My ceramic lake in dawn, water settled clear." CoBCP, *tr. by* Burton Watson

"Old men are like little boys." CoBCP, *tr. by* Burton Watson

"Pond shine and sky glow, blue matching blue." CoBCP, *tr. by* Burton Watson

Pond Named Ganga, A. Chandrashekhar Kambar, *Kannada.* OMIP, *tr. by* A. K. Ramanujan

Pond shine and sky glow, blue matching blue. A Pond in a Jardiniere. Han Yü, *Chinese.* CoBCP, *tr. by* Burton Watson

Ponder,darling,these busted statues. E. E. Cummings. CMoP; NIP-4; PoE

Ponder my words, if so that any be. An Request to the Graces. Robert Herrick. NOSC

Ponder the Ruler's Way with utmost care. The Conduct of Kings. (King) Lê Thánh-tông, *Chinese.* AVP, *tr. by* Huỳnh Sanh Thông

Pond'rous projectiles, hurl'd by heavy hands. "Orpheus C. Kerr." *Fr.* The Rejected "National Hymns." OBAL

Pondy Woods. Robert Penn Warren. MoAmPo

Ponnage Pool, The. Helen B. Cruickshank. FaBoTC

Pont y Caniedydd. Alun Llywelyn-Williams, *Welsh.* OBWVE, *tr. by* Joseph R. Clancy

(*Ponticus*) cause thou ne're doth swive. In Ponticum. Martial, *Latin.* OBCVT, *tr. by* R. Fletcher

Pontoon. Kit Robinson. FTOS

Pontoon-Bridge Miracle, The. Vachel Lindsay. MeMAP

Pontoosuce. Herman Melville. APN-2; NCAP; NOBA

Pony, The. Rachel MacAndrew. BoTP

Pony Farm. Laura Jensen. LCAP-2

Pony Rock. Archibald MacLeish. MeMAP

Pooh! Walter De la Mare. HAP; OBCoV; PeLV

Pool. The. Hayyim Nahman Bialik, *Hebrew*. MHP, *tr. by* Ruth Finer Mintz

Pool, The. Robert Creeley. CoAP

Pool, The. Hilda Doolittle. CMoP

Pool, A. Thomas Whitbread. NYBP

Pool behind Ch'i-an, The. Tu Mu, *Chinese*. PLT, *tr. by* A. C. Graham

Pool Players, The. Gwendolyn Brooks. *See* We real cool. We.

Poor, The. Letitia Elizabeth Landon. VWP

Poor, The. John Langhorne. NOEC *Fr.* The Country Justice.

Poor, The. William Langland. PoEL-1 *Fr.* The Vision of Piers Plowman.

Poor. Myra Cohn Livingston. KaS

Poor, The. Emile Verhaeren, *French*. AWP, *tr. by* Ludwig Lewisohn

Poor, The. William Carlos Williams. MoAmPo

Poor Adam and Eve were from Eden turned out. *Unknown*. Spl

Poor and Happy. Trần Tế Xu'o'ng, *Vietnamese*. AVP, *tr. by* Huỳnh Sanh Thông

Poor, and the dazed, and the idiots, The. Hurrying Away from the Earth. Robert Bly. PoA

Poor Aviator Lay Dying, A. *Unknown*. NSI

Poor beggars!—they'll never see 'ome! (LL) The Widow at Windsor. Rudyard Kipling. NAEL-2; NoAM

Poor But Honest. *Unknown*. NBLV; RB
("Ain't it all a bleeding shame.") (LL) OxBoV

Poor Calpurnius, the most Schweikian soldier in the land. Lucilius, *Greek*. GrAn, *tr. by* Peter Porter

Poor Children, The. Victor Hugo, *French*. AWP, *tr. by* Swinburne

Poor Christian Looks at the Ghetto, A. Czeslaw Milosz, *Polish*. PoSu, *tr. by the author*; VCWP, *tr. by* Czeslaw Milosz; HP

Poor chum, dear chum, so here you lie at rest. Monologue in a Rand Hospital. William Elijah Hunter. PeSAV

Poor crawlin' bodies, sair neglectit. John Learmont. NOEC *Fr.* An Address to the Plebeians.

Poor credulous and simple maid! Phyllis. Thomas Randolph. BoLoP

Poor Crow! Mary Mapes Dodge. OBCA

Poor Cupid sits and blows his nails for cold. (LL) Blame Not My Cheekes. Thomas Campion. AAS; SCGP; UnPo

Poor damned Catullus, here's no time for nonsense. Catullus. *See* Carmen 8 ("Break off / fallen Catullus").

Poor *Damon*! Art thou caught? Is't ev'n so? A Letter to a Brother of the Pen in Tribulation. Aphra Behn. KTR

Poor dear dead have been laid out in vain, The. Thomas Hood. FaBoEE

Poor degenerate from the ape, A. First Philosopher's Song. Aldous Leonard Huxley. AWP

Poor devil that I am, being so attacked. Palladas, *Greek*. OBVE, *tr. by* Tony Harrison

Poor Dick! though first thy airs provoke. Dick Hairbrain Learns the Social Graces. John Trumbull. *Fr.* The Progress of Dulness. AmPP

Poor Doctor Blow went out of church. Queen Anne's Musicians. Thomas Hennell. FaBoTw

Poor drunkards, poor drunkards, take warning by me. John Adkins' Farewell. *Unknown*. AmFP

Poor Ellen Smith. *Unknown*. AmFP

Poor Epictetus, born the Slave of Fate. Observations of the Life of Epictetus. Elizabeth Tipper. KTR *Fr.* Pilgrim's Viaticum; or, The Destitute, But Not Forlorn.

Poor Estate, The. Robert Greene. *See* Maesia's Song.

Poor fawn about to die. Image. Anna de Noailles, *French*. PBWP, *tr. by* Carol Cosman

Poor fellow, what is it to you. Verses. Sir Charles Hanbury Williams. OBWVE

Poor French Sailor's Scottish Sweetheart, A. William Johnson Cory. EBVV

Poor George. George III. Robert Lowell. FaBoPV

Poor Ghost, The. Christina Rossetti. GBL

Poor Girl's Meditation, The. *Unknown, Irish*. BIrV; OBMV, *tr. by* Padraic Colum

Poor[e] girl[e]s, neglected. (LL) To Violets. Robert Herrick. CaPo; OBEV; SeCP

Poor Hal caught his death standing under a spout. Fatal Love. Matthew Prior. NBLV

Poor have hands, and feet, and eyes, The. The Poor Man and His Parish Church. Robert Stephen Hawker. EBVV

Poor heart, unsatisfied! Shadow and Sunrise. Henrietta Cordelia Ray. CBWP-3

Poor hill farmer astray in the grass. The Lonely Farmer. Ronald Stuart Thomas. NoP-4

Poor-House, The. George Crabbe. ECEV *Fr.* The Village.

Poor Houses, The. Ed Roberson. GT

Poor, impious Soul! that fixes its high hopes. Aspiration. Adah Isaacs Menken. AAP; CBWP-1; PAR

Poor in my youth, and in life's later scenes. On Late-acquired Wealth *or* Riches. *Unknown, Greek*. OBVE, *tr. by* William Cowper

Poor in spirit on their rosary rounds, The. Lough Derg. Denis Devlin. BIrV; CIP-2

Poor john, who joined in make of wrong. Welcome the Wrath. Stanley Kunitz. VGW

Poor Johnny looked exceeding blue. Thomas Love Peacock. CBNP *Fr.* Sir Proteus, a Satirical Ballad.

Poor Julia's heart was in an awkward state. Byron. NOBRP *Fr.* Canto the First. NAEL-2; OAEL-2; PoE *Fr.* Don Juan.

Poor Kid. William Cole. OBAL

Poor Kitty Popcorn. *Unknown*. AS

Poor lad once and a lad so trim, A. Jean Richepin's Song. Herbert Trench. OBMV

Poor Lazarus. *Unknown*. NAAAL

Poor Lil' Brack Sheep. Ethel M. C. Brazelton. BLPA

Poor little donkey! It's no joke. Palladas, *Greek*. GrAn, *tr. by* Tony Harrison

Poor little Foal of an oppressed Race! To a Young Ass. Coleridge. OxAEP-2 *Fr.* Effusions.

Poor Little Johnny. *Unknown*. AmFP

Poor little, pretty, fluttering thing. Adriani Morientis ad Animam Suam. Emperor Hadrian, *Latin*. OBVE; OxBSP, *tr. by* Matthew Prior

Poor little timid furry man. (LL) The City Mouse and the Garden Mouse. Christina Rossetti. BoTP; FaBoBe; NTCP

Poor Loneliness and lovely Solitude. Little Eclogue. E. Wylie. NMM-2

Poor Lonesome Cowboy. *Unknown*. AS

Poor Lucy Lake was overgrown. Lucy Lake. Newton Mackintosh. BXAP

Poor Man and His Parish Church, The. Robert Stephen Hawker. EBVV

"Poor man, oh, poor man, come tell to me true." The Jolly Thresherman. *Unknown*. AmFP

Poor man's clothes—ragged and easy to get dirty, A. Shih-hou Pointed Out to Me that from Ancient Times There Had Never Been a Poem on the Subject of Lice. Harry Mathews, *Chinese*. CoBCP, *tr. by* Burton Watson

Poor Man's Pig, The. Edmund Blunden. MoBrPo

Poor Man's Province, The. John Wright. NOEC

Poor man's sins are glaring, The. Rich and Poor; or, Saint and Sinner. Thomas Love Peacock. NOBE; NOBL; OBSV; PeLV

Poor Man's Sunday Walk, The. Charles MacKay. EBVV

Poor Matthias. Matthew Arnold. PoEL-5
Matthias. PC

Poor Merry-andrew, in the [*or* a] neuk. Robert Burns. OBCoV *Fr.* Love and Libery—A Cantata. NOBRP; NOEC

Poor moth, I can't help you. I Can't Help You. Ryszard Krynicki, *Polish*. BLT, *tr. by* Stanislaw Baranczak *and* Clare Cavanagh

Poor Mother, The. Edith Jay Scovell. WPN

Poor Mrs. Prior. Gerda Mayer. OTCP

Poor Naomi. *Unknown*. APN-2

Poor nigger you can't get over dat; / Walk over! (LL) Song: "We raise de wheat." *Unknown*. APN-2

Poor of London, The. William Forster. CBAP

Poor of the Borough, The; Peter Grimes. George Crabbe. *See* Peter Grimes.

Poor old bait got sick & died, The. 1841 (II). Jackson MacLow. APSN *Fr.* The Presidents of the United States of America.

Poor Old Horse. *Unknown*. CH; NTP

Poor old Jonathan Bing. Jonathan Bing. Beatrice Curtis Brown. NOxBChV

Poor Old Lady. *Unknown*. OBCA

Poor old lady, set her aside. The Old Mother. *Unknown*. PoToHe

Poor old lady, she swallowed a fly. Pamela Smith. CTV

Poor old lady, she swallowed a fly. *Unknown*. NOxBChV

Poor old man, The. (LL) A Note Left in Jimmy Leonard's Shack. James Wright. HCAP; NoP-4

Poor old Mr. Bidery. Mr. Bidery's Spidery Garden. David McCord. OTCP

Poor old Reuben Ranzo. Reuben Ranzo. *Unknown*. AmFP

Poor old Robinson Crusoe! (LL) Poor old Robinson Crusoe! Mother Goose. BoTP; OxNR; ReMoGo

Poor Ophelia sighed: "I deplore." Limerick. Frank Richards. PeLi

Poor Paddy Works on the Railway. *Unknown*. AS; GM

Poor painter captures, The. Lucianus, *Greek*. InMo, *tr. by* Sam Hamill

Poor painters oft with silly poets join. Cupid. Sir Philip Sidney. SiPS *Fr.* Arcadia.

Poor people in Springfield go to Dayton to be miserable in style, The. Romance of the Poor. Rodney Jones. WWSi

Poor people use snare-nets, The. Song of the Painting "Catching Fish." Li Tung-yang, *Chinese.* CoBLCP, *tr. by* Jonathan Chaves

Poor Ploughman to a Gentleman for Whom He Had Taken a Little Pains, A. George Turberville. NoSic

Poor Poet-Ape, that would be thought our chief. On Poet-Ape. Ben Jonson. Son

Poor Poll. Robert Bridges. EBEV; OxBTC; OxBoLi

Poor restless Dove, I pity thee. The Captive Dove. Anne Brontë. EBVV; VWP

Poor savage, doubting that a river flows. Watching the Dance. James Merrill. NIP-4

Poor Scholar, The. Abraham ibn Chasdai, *Hebrew.* TrJP, *tr. by* J. Chotzner

Poor Scholar of the 'Forties, A. Padraic Colum. NOIV

Poor sheepish plaything. For Sale. Robert Lowell. AFr; CoAmPo

Poor Snail, The. J. M. Westrup. BoTP

Poor Snow. Denise Riley. NBrP

Poor song. The Tape. Myra Cohn Livingston. NTCP

Poor soul, in this thy flesh what dost thou know? The Soules Ignorance in This Life and Knowledge in the Next. Donne. OAEL-1 *Fr.* The Second Anniversary. ESCV; SeCP *Fr.* Of the Progres[se] of the Soule; the Second Anniversarie.

Poor[e] soul[e] sat[e] sighing by a sycamore [*or* sicamore] tree, The. The Green Willow. *Unknown.* EBEvV; SCGP

Poor[e] soul[e], the centre of my sinful earth. Sonnet 146. Shakespeare. AWP; GTBS-P; HAP; HeIP-4; ImPo; InPS-3; NAEL-1; NOBE; NOCV; OAEL-1; OBEV; OxAEP-1; PoE; PoEL-2; SCGP; Son; TFi *Fr.* Sonnets.

Poor tired Tim! It's sad for him. Tired Tim. Walter De la Mare. BoTP; NTCP

Poor Tom. Charles Dibdin. NOEC; OxBoLi

(Tom Bowling.) OxAEP-1

Poor Tom will injure nothing. (LL) Tom o'Bedlam. *Unknown.* CBNP; CH; EBEV; EnSB; FaBoCh; GEA; HAP; ImPo; NOBE; NTP; OAEL-1; OxBoLi; PoEL-2; PoRA; RB; TFi; WeW-3

Poor unfortunate Hottentot, A. Laura Elizabeth Richards. CTV

Poor vaunting earth, gloss'd with uncertain pride. George Alsop. SCAP

"Poor wanderer," said the leaden sky. The Subalterns. Thomas Hardy. CMoP; MoBrPo; MoP; NOBVV; NoAM; OAEL-2; Poetr

Poor Wayfaring Stranger. *Unknown.* AmFP

Poor wearied pilgrim—in this toiling scene! (LL) To the Moon. Charlotte Smith. BWW; Son

Poor weaver, with the hopeless brow. How Different! Ebenezer Elliot. EBEV

Poor who begs with bated breath, The. The Price of Begging. Emmanuel ben David Frances, *Hebrew.* TrJP, *tr. by* A. B. Rhine

Poor Women in a City Church. Seamus Heaney. TIRV

Poor Working Girl, The. *Unknown.* AS

Poore widwe [*or* widow], somdeel [*or* somedeal] stape in age, A. Chaucer. *See* The Nun's Priest's Tale.

Poorer than X. Vladimir Nikolaevich Kornilov, *Russian.* TCRP, *tr. by* Daniel Weissbort

Pop bottles pop-bottles. Song of the Pop-Bottlers. Morris Gilbert Bishop. KaS

Pop Goes the Weasel! W. R. Mardale. OxNR

Pop Goes the Weasel. *Unknown.* CTV

Pop-out eyes belong to Baldwin, The. Of Miles Davis. William Ford. SeSe

Popcorn is greasy, and I forgot to bring a Kleenex, The. The James Bond Movie. May Swenson. FaBoWP

Popcorn man, The. The Popcorn-Popper. Dorothy Walter Baruch. CTV

Popcorn peanuts clams and gum. Bar-Room Matins. Louis MacNeice. NYBP

Popcorn-Popper, The. Dorothy Walter Baruch. CTV

Pope, The. A. E. Housman. OBCoV

Pope Alexander VI. Geoffrey Lehmann. NOBAu

Pope from penance purgatorial, The. James Vincent Cunningham, *after the Latin of* George Buchanan. OBVE

Pope in Ancona, The. Jaroslaw Iwaszkiewicz. CEEP

Pope's Carnations Knew Him. Thom Gunn. OBGa

Popish Plot, The. Dryden. *Fr.* Absalom and Achitophel, Pt. I. EBEvV; FHYEP; FaBoPV; HAP; NOSC; OAEL-1; PoE

Poplar Field, The. William Cowper. CH; FHYEP; HAP; NOBE; NOEC; PoEL-3

("Have a still shorter date, and die sooner than we.") (LL) GTBS-P

Poplar Leaf, The. George Seferis, *Greek.* PFTM, *tr. by* George Economou

Poplars, The. Peter Huchel, *German.* CEEP, *tr. by* Rich Ives

Poplars. Helen Leuty. BoTP

Poplars. Music. Eugenio de Andrade, *Portuguese.* VCWP, *tr. by* Alexis Levitin

Poplars are felled [*or* fell'd], farewell to the shade, The. The Poplar Field. William Cowper. CH; FHYEP; GTBS-P; HAP; NOBE; NOEC; PoEL-3

Poplars are standing there still as death. Southern Mansion. Arna Bontemps. AiP; GT; LiTM; NAAAL; PoBA; TTY

Poplars like grapes. Moment. Tadeusz Różewicz, *Polish.* CEEP, *tr. by* Victor Contoski

Poplar's Shadow, The. May Swenson. NYBP

Popol Vuh, The. *Unknown, Mayan.* STP, *tr. by* Munro Edmonson

Poppa Chicken. Margaret Abigail Walker. NAAAL

Poppa was a sugah daddy. Poppa Chicken. Margaret Abigail Walker. NAAAL

Poppies. P. A. Ropes. BoTP

Poppies. Zalman Schneour, *Hebrew.* MHP, *tr. by* Ruth Finer Mintz

Poppies in bloom. Tanka. Yosano Tekkan, *Japanese.* MJT, *tr. by* Makoto Ueda

Poppies in July. Sylvia Plath. FaBoWP; LCAP-2; RB

Poppies in October. Sylvia Plath. FaBoWP; HCAP; LCAP-2; NoAM

Poppies in the Garden, The. Ffrida Wolfe. BoTP

Poppies of Wickenburg. Sharlot Mabridth Hall. PaTW

Poppies on the Wheat. Helen Hunt Jackson. APN-2; ColAP; PAR; SDW

Poppies send up their, The. Mary Oliver. BAP-93

Poppy, The. Erasmus Darwin. GaP

Poppy, A. Michael McClintock. HA

Poppy, The. Francis Thompson. MoBrPo

Poppy under a young. Necromance. Rae Armantrout. FTOS; PmAP

Pop's tops! Limerick. Bill Greenwell. PeLi

Popular Functionary, A. Charles Dibdin. NOEC

Popular leader, national hero. Finn's Wishes. Desmond O'Grady, *Irish.* CIP-2, *tr. by the author*

Popular Mythologies. Vernon Scannell. OBCoV

Popular Negro Song, A. *Unknown.* PBCV

Popular, popular, unpopular! Tennyson. NOBL

Popular Romance, A. Kevin Ireland. PeNZ

Popular Songs of Tuscany. *Unknown, Italian.* AWP, *tr. by* John Addington Symonds

Popularity. Robert Browning. OAEL-2

Population. Mark Halliday. NAmP90; PUP-18

Population. George Oppen. PoA

Population Drifts. Carl Sandburg. OxBA

Pora, The. W. H. Auden. MeMAP

"Porcelain is personal," he smiles. For His Ring and Watch on the Night Stand. Gladys Cardiff. HATNAP

Porch, The. Philip Pain. SCAP

Porch, The. Ronald Stuart Thomas. NOCV

Porch beats its yellow wings, The. The Wedding. Pavel Nikolaevich Vasilyev. TCRP, *tr. by* David Macduff *Fr.* The Salt Riot.

Porch diminishes the fat men, The. The Fat Men. Cyril Dabydeen. PBCV

Porch sitting hairbraiding. Initiation. Monifa Atungaye Love. ISC

Porchlight coming on again, The. 1926. Weldon Kees. CoAP

Porcupine, The. Galway Kinnell. NOBA

Porirua Friday Night. Sam Hunt. PeNZ

Porkskin Panorama. Marie Annharte Baker. BAP-96

Porné. Chris Tysh.

"In the morning one often feels." DeD

Porno Love. Philip Dacey. CMAP

Pornography. Lloyd Schwartz. BAP-94

Porous. William Carlos Williams. NYBP

Porphyria's Lover. Robert Browning. AWP; CBLP; EnVR; FHYEP; HAP; NAEL-2; OBEV; OxBoV

("Rain set early in to-night, The.") EP

Porpoises. Norman MacCaig. FaBoTC

Porpoises spout amid the waves. Tune: "Song of Shou-yang." Kuan Yün-shih, *Chinese.* SuSp, *tr. by* Richard John Lynn

Porson on German Scholarship. Richard Porson. FaBoEE

Porson's Visit to the Continent. Richard Porson. *See* Epigram on an Academic Visit to the Continent.

Port, The. Bernadette Mayer. FTOS

Port Bou. Stephen Spender. TwCP

Port Bou. Sylvia Townsend Warner. WPN

Port of Holy Peter. John Masefield. OBMV

Port of Many Ships. John Masefield. OBMV

Port of Spain. Derek Walcott. NoAM

Port Phillip Night. Francis Webb. BMAP

Portent, The. Herman Melville. APAD; APN-2; AmPP; CBCWP; ColAP; InPK-6; NAAL-1; NAAL-3; NCAP; NOBA; NoP-4; OBWP; OxBA; PAR; PoE; PoEL-5; TAP

Portent clear as ever be, brilliant crimson, The. Your Poems at Daybreak, the Destruction of Knossos by Afternoon. Steve Ellis. PT

Porter. Langston Hughes. GM

Porter and keepers, when they're civil. His Rule of Behaviour: If You Are Civil, I Am Sober. James Carkesse. NOSC

Porter to th' infernal[l] gate is Sin, The. Sin, Despair, and Lucifer. Phineas Fletcher. NOSC *Fr.* The Locusts, or Appolyonists.

Portion of this yew. Transformations. Thomas Hardy. PFE; RB; TRP

Portland County Jail. *Unknown.* AS

"Portland" Going Out, The. W. S. Merwin. NYBP

Portly he was, in carriage somewhat grand. The Bunch of Larks. Robert Leighton. EBVV

Portly prince, and goodly to the sight, A. Dryden. OBSV *Fr.* The Hind and the Panther.

Portly pusher of waves, wind-slave. (LL) Winter Ocean. John Updike. InPK-6; Poetr

Portly Roman Senator was sipping his Rock and Rye, A. A War Bird's Burlesque. *Unknown.* AS

Portola Valley. Amy Clampitt. EOEF

Portrait. Antoine-Roger Bolamba. PBMAP

Portrait. E. E. Cummings. NIP-4

Portrait, A. Walter De la Mare. NoAM

Portrait, A. Thomas Dekker *and others.* OxAEP-1

Portrait. John Lyle Donaghy. BIrV

Portrait. Kenneth Fearing. MoAmPo

Portrait, A. "Michael Field." VWP

Portrait. Gail Fox. NOBC

Portrait, The. Robert Graves. CMoP; LoP; PRMP

Portrait, A. Keats. BXAP

   (Stanzas on Charles Armitage Brown.) UV

Portrait, The. Stanley Kunitz. FiLi; IMW; Poetsp; RaBo

   ("Still burning.") (LL) LoL

Portrait. Antonio Machado Ruiz, *Spanish.* RaBo; STV, *tr. by* Robert Bly

Portrait. Beverly Acuff Momoi. LoHo

Portrait. Adèle Naudé. PeSA

Portrait. Brenda Marie Osbey. MT

Portrait. Dahlia Ravikovitch, *Hebrew.*

   ("She sits home for days on end.") IP, *tr. by* Warren Bargad *and* Stanley F. Chyet

Portrait. Carolyn M. Rodgers. MBE

Portrait. Yaroslav Vasilevich Smelyakov, *Russian.* TCRP, *tr. by* Simon Franklin

Portrait, A. Stevie Smith. WPN

Portrait. Leopold Staff, *Polish.* PoSu, *tr. by* Adam Czerniawski

Portrait. Judith Wright. OxBSP; SoSe-8

Portrait by a Neighbour. Edna St. Vincent Millay. OBCA

Portrait by Bronzino, A. Maura Stanton. NAmP90

Portrait d'une Femme. Ezra Pound. CMoP; InPS-3; MeMAP; MoAmPo; MoP; NAAL-2; NOBA; NoAM; NoP-4; PFE; Poetr; TAP; TwCP

Portrait from the Infantry. Alan Dugan. AF

Portrait in Black Paint, with a Very Sparing Use of Whitewash. Elinor Wylie. NALW

Portrait in Georgia. Jean Toomer. NAAL-2; NoP-4; PFE

Portrait in the Guards, A. Laurence Whistler. GTBS-P

Portrait is where you, The. Robert Creeley Also Watches. David Chapman Berry. BXAP

Portrait of a Figure near Water. Jane Kenyon. AFr

Portrait of a Gentleman. Ruth Pitter. WPN

Portrait of a Girl. Conrad Potter Aiken. *See* This Is the Shape of the Leaf.

Portrait of a House Detective. Hans Magnus Enzensberger, *German.* HP, *tr. by* Michael Hamburger; PoSu

Portrait of a Jew Old Country Style. Jerome Rothenberg. NNaP

Portrait of a King's Mistress, Nude. Paul Engle. PFE

Portrait of a Lady. T. S. Eliot. TwCP

Portrait of a Lady. Elizabeth Nannestad. PeNZ

Portrait of a Lady. William Carlos Williams. AmPP; CMoP; MoP; NAAL-2; NOBA; NoAM; OxBA

Portrait of a Lady in the Exhibition of the Royal Academy. Winthrop Mackworth Praed. NOBL; PeLV; PoEL-4 *Fr.* Every-Day Characters.

Portrait of a Machine. Louis Untermeyer. MoAmPo

Portrait of a Married Couple. Margaret Scott. NOBAu

Portrait of a Nun. Bobi Jones, *Welsh.* OBWVE, *tr. by* Joseph P. Clancy

Portrait of a Pregnant Woman. Bobi Jones, *Welsh.* OBWVE, *tr. by* Joseph P. Clancy

Portrait of a Stupid Teacher of Rhetoric. *Unknown, Greek.* GrAn, *tr. by* Peter Jay

Portrait of a Woman (and a Man). John Figueroa. PBCV

Portrait of a Young Girl Raped at a Suburban Party. Brian Patten. OxBTC

Portrait of an Engine Driver. Bobi Jones, *Welsh.* OBWVE, *tr. by* Joseph P. Clancy

Portrait of Assimilation. "Chrystos." UnSA

Portrait of Girl with Comic Book. Phyllis McGinley. SAGP

Portrait of Jonah with woman. Marie-Claire Bancquart, *French.* MFP, *tr. by* Martin Sorrell

Portrait of Malcolm X. Etheridge Knight. PoBA

Portrait of My Mother. Ilya L'vovich Selvinsky, *Russian.* TCRP, *tr. by* Daniel Weissbort

Portrait of Myself with Arshile Gorky and Gertrude Stein. Jerome Rothenberg. FTOS

Portrait of Sidrophel. Samuel Butler. PoEL-3 *Fr.* Hudibras.

Portrait of the Artist, A. Mary Leapor. ECWP *Fr.* Mira's Picture, a Pastoral.

Portrait of the Artist as a Prematurely Old Man. Ogden Nash. ImPo; InPS-3; LiTM

Portrait of the Artist as an Old Man. Michael Dransfield. BMAP; CBAP

Portrait of the Artist with Li Po. Charles Wright. ColAP

Portrait of the Autist as a New World Driver. Les A. Murray. CBAP

Portrait of the Boy as Artist. Barbara Howes. MoAmPo

Portrait of the Poet as Landscape. Abraham Moses Klein. NOBC; NoAM

Portrait of the Pornographer. G. W. Jones. BXAP

Portrait of the Self as Nation, 1990–1991, A. Marilyn Chin. PUP-19

Portrait: The Freedom Fighter. George Jonas. NOBC

Portrait with Background. Oliver St. John Gogarty. OBMV

Portraits, The. Anna Maria Lenngren, *Swedish.* WPOW, *tr. by* C. W. Stork

Portraits and Repetition. Gertrude Stein.

   "How do you like what you have." AiP

Portrush. Walking dead streets in the dark. The Archæologist. James Simmons. PBCIP

Portuguese Sea, The. Fernando Pessoa. PeSAV

Posies. Agnes Mary Frances Robinson. VWP

Position. Léon Damas, *French.* NegPo, *tr. by* Ellen Conroy Kennedy

Position is so well-known, The. Inside Diameter. Clarence Major. PmAP

Position is where you. The Window. Robert Creeley. FTOS; NOBA; NoAM; PmAP; TAP; VGW

Position of Praise, The. Brendan Kennelly. BiHa

Positively on my own again, heart broken so long ago I hardly notice. Where the Weather Suits My Clothes. John Godfrey. PmAP

Positives. Jewel C. Latimore. PoBA

Positives for Sterling Plumpp. Don L. Lee. PoBA

Positivists, The. Mortimer Collins. EBVV

Positivists ever talk in s-/Uch an epic style as Dawkins. John William Mackail. FaBoEE *Fr.* Balliol Rhymes.

Possessed shaman with the spear, The. Murukan, the Red One. Nakkiranar, *Tamil.* PLW, *tr. by* A. K. Ramanujan

Possesseth him, and of his sweetnesse takes her fill. Edmund Spenser. *See* The Garden of Adonis.

Possessing what the owners can but own. (LL) A Summer Morning. Richard Wilbur. FaBoMo; NBLV

Possession. Richard Aldington. MoBrPo

Possession. Marie Ponsot. VGW

Possession: A Zuihitsu. Kimiko Hahn. BAP-96

Possession of those things are none of mine. (LL) The Lady A. L., My Asylum [in a Great Extremity]. Richard Lovelace. CaPo; CavPo

Possessions. Ken Smith. SPE

Possessor, The. Arthur Rex Dugard Fairburn. PeNZ *Fr.* Album Leaves.

Possessor. Things. W. S. Merwin. HAP

Possibilities. Sir Richard Blackmore. Poetr

   "In the wide womb of possibility." Poetr

Possibilities. Peter Kane Dufault. NYBP

Possibilities, The. Beckian Fritz Goldberg. NAmP90

Possibilities. Henry Wadsworth Longfellow. MeMAP

Possibility of New Poetry, The. Robert Bly. CoAmPo

Possibility That Has Been Overlooked Is the Future, The. Michael Hartnett. NOIV

Possible Salvation of Continuous Motion, The. Pattiann Rogers. MT

Possibly a child is not damaged immediately. Lackawanna. Galway Kinnell. GM

Possum's a greasy critter, The. Roast Possum. Rita Dove. Poetr

Post-boy drove with fierce career, The. Alice Fell; or, Poverty. Wordsworth. OBNV

Post Card. Guillaume Apollinaire, *French.* AF, *tr. by* Oliver Bernard

Post-Coitum Tristesse: A Sonnet. Brad Leithauser. EOEF; RA

Post-historic herbivore, A. On the Inclusion of Miniature Dinosaurs in Breakfast Cereal Boxes. John Updike. OBCoV

Post-horses galloped through miasmal wilds. Farewell to two envoys from the Yüan court. Tran Minh-tong (King), *Chinese.* AVP, *tr.* by Huỳnh Sanh Thông

Post-Larkin Triste. Mary Karr. PuP-15

Post Mortem. Robinson Jeffers. MoAmPo

Post Mortem. Arthur Joseph Munby. NOBVV

Post-Mortem, A. Siegfried Sassoon. PBMP

Post Mortem. Shakespeare. GTBS-P *Fr.* Sonnets.

Post Mortem as Angels. Barry Goldensohn. NAmP90

Post-Obits and the Poets. Martial, *Latin.* AWP; FaBoEE; OBVE, *tr.* by Byron

Post-obits rarely reach a poet. (LL) Post-Obits and the Poets. Martial, *Latin.* AWP; FaBoEE; OBVE; OBCVT, *tr.* by Byron

Post Operative. Thomas William Shapcott. BMAP

Post-Rail Song. *Unknown.* AS

Post-Recessional. G. K. Chesterton. UV

Post-Referendum. Edwin Morgan. FaBoTC *Fr.* Sonnets from Scotland.

Post-Script: for Gweno. Alun Lewis. BoLoP; GTBS-P

Post Ulixem Scriptum. James Joyce. OBCoV

Postal authorities in New York City were worried about the shipping of. Fire Parcel. Peter Kostakis. MoNo

Postcard. Margaret Atwood. NoAM

Postcard (Found on His body after He Was Killed by the Nazis). Miklós Radnóti, *Hungarian.* RaBo, *tr.* by Steven Polgar, Stephen Berg, *and* S. J. Marks

  ("Nine miles from here.") HP, *tr.* by Polgar, Steven, S. Berg, and S. J. Marks, S. J.

  (Postcards.) HP, *tr.* by Polgar, Steven, S. Berg, and S. J. Marks, S. J.

Postcard from Berlin, A. Derek Mahon. BiHa

Postcard from Mexico, 16.X.1973. Andrew Salkey. PBCV

Postcard from North Antrim, A. Seamus Heaney. PBCIP; PNI

Postcard from the Garden. Marge Piercy. NoAM

Postcard from the Volcano, A. Wallace Stevens. GEA; HAP; HCAP; MeMAP; NoAM; SAmP; WeW-3

Postcard from Trakl. John Yau. OpBo

Postcard to Send to Sumer, A. William Bronk. VGW

Postcards. Miklós Radnóti. *See* Postcard (Found on His body after He Was Killed by the Nazis).

Posted. John Masefield. Son

Poster Girl, The. Carolyn Wells. BXAP

Poster of Our Dazzling Victory at Saarbrucken, A. Rimbaud. FaBoPV; OBWP, *tr.* by Robert Lowell *Fr.* Eighteen-Seventy.

Poster with my picture on it, The. Unwanted. Edward Field. GLP; LiLi; Poetsp

Posterity. Philip Larkin. OxBC

Posterity hath many fates bemoaned. On Sir Robert Cotton the Antiquary. Thomas Randolph. NOSC

Posterity, thy name is Samuel Johnson. A Dream of Judgement. Douglas Dunn. OxBC

Posterity was always a great reader. D. J. Enright. OBCoV

Posthumous. Michael O'Loughlin. PBCIP

Posthumous Coquetry. Théophile Gautier, *French.* AWP; PeVV, *tr.* by Arthur Symons

Posthumous Rehabilitation. Tadeusz Rózewicz, *Polish.* FaBoPV; HP, *tr.* by Adam Czerniawski

Postilion Has Been Struck by Lightning, The. Patricia Beer. OxBC

Posting to Printing. Robert Herrick. PBRV

Postman, The. Christina Rossetti. CTV

Postman, The. Clive Sansom. BoTP

Postman, The. Alice Todd. BoTP

Postman Cheval. André Breton, *French.* SPE, *tr.* by David Gascoyne

Postman comes when I am still in bed, The. A Sick Child. Randall Jarrell. InPK-6; NoP-4; OxBC; VGW

Postman's Bell Is Answered Everywhere, The. Horace Gregory. MoAmPo; NYBP

Postman's Knock. Rodney Bennett. BoTP

Postmaster-General cried: 'Arsehole!', The. Limerick. Victor Gray. PeLi

Postmen like doctors go from house to house. (LL) Aubade: "I work all day, and get half-drunk at night." Philip Larkin. CABP; GEA; NoP-4; SoSe-8; TRP

Postponed Nightmare. Sandor Csoori, *Hungarian.* VCWP, *tr.* by Roberts, Len and László Vértes

Postponement. Thomas Hardy. EnVR

Postscript. R. L. Barth. CDa

Postscript. Henri Coulette. DiPo

Postscript. Ronald Stuart Thomas. FaBoMo; OxBC

Postscript, 1984. John Hewitt. BiHa

Postscript to a Pettiness. Arthur Seymour John Tessimond. OxBSP

Postscript to an Elegy. Gibbons Ruark. MT

Postscript to Orwell's *Animal Farm,* A. Miadesnia. PeLi

Postscript to Verses on the History of France, A. *Unknown.* NOIV

Postscripts 2. Dennis Brutus. HBAPE

Posture, The. Lucretius, *Latin.* EP, *tr.* by John Dryden

Posture of the tree, The. Lovers in Winter. Robert Graves. FaBoEE; NYBP

Posy, A: "Dear love, I am resolved with thee to live." Sir Robert Ayton. NOSC

Posy [*or* Posie], The. George Herbert. ChIV-1; NOSC

Posy Ring, The. Clément Marot, *French.* AWP, *tr.* by Ford Madox Ford

Pot lilac, / pet thorn / *flick* nest. Lottery & Requiem. Maggie O'Sullivan. NBrP

Pot of Tea, A. Robert W. Service. NSI; PoWW

Pot of wine among flowers, A. Drinking Alone in the Moonlight. Li Po, *Chinese.* AWP; ChiPo; *tr.* by Florence Ayscough *and* Amy Lowell

Pot of wine among the flowers, A. Li Po. SuSp, *tr.* by Irving Lo *Fr.* Drinking Alone beneath the Moon.

Pot Roast. Mark Strand. FiLi

Pot Shot. Padraic Fallon. CIP-2

Potato. Jane Kenyon. AFr

Potato clock, a potato clock, A. Roger McGough. OTCP

Potato Harvest, The. Sir Charles G. D. Roberts. NOBC

Potato Peel. *Unknown.* CTAV

Potato Pie. Abba Kovner. *See* Poem: Alte Zachen.

Potato Thief. Pentti Saarikoski, *Finnish.* VCWP, *tr.* by Herbert Lomas

Potato was deep in the dark under ground. The Tryst. John Banister Tabb. OBAL

Potatoes. David Donnell. NIP-4; NOBC

Potatoes of the corner store sing, The. At Kino Viejo, Mexico. Alberto A. Ríos. NoAM

Potchikoo Marries. Louise Erdrich. *Fr.* Old Man Potchikoo. HATNAP

Potflower on the windowsill says to me, The. The Power of Suicide. Muriel Rukeyser. NALW

Potlicker Blues. Calvin Forbes. GT

Potpourri from a Surrey Garden. John Betjeman. CBLP; NOBL

Potted Swan. Paul Dehn.

  "Devil damn thee black, thou cream-faced loon—, The." OBCoV

Potter, The. *Unknown, Geez.* TTY, *tr.* by Halim El-Dabh

Potter, / O potter. An Urn for Burial. *Unknown, Tamil.* PLW, *tr.* by A. K. Ramanujan

Potter of Jaen, The. Ilya Grigoryevich Ehrenburg, *Russian.* TCRP, *tr.* by Cathy Porter

Potter's Song, The. Henry Wadsworth Longfellow. PoEL-5 *Fr.* Kéramos. APN-1

Potter's Wheel, The, *for Jane.* Calvin Forbes. GT

Pound at Spoleto. Lawrence Ferlinghetti. PoM

  ("His voice / went on / and on / through the leaves.") (LL) BB

Pound-note was the best kind of passport, A. The Emigration Trains. Thomas McCarthy. PBCIP

Pounded spice [*or* spise] both tast[e] and s[c]ent doth please, The. At Fotheringay. Robert Southwell. NoSic; PoEL-2

Pour and say again and again and yet again. Meleager. HePo, *tr.* by Barbara Hughes Fowler *Fr.* I'll Twine White Violets. NIP-4, *tr.* by Goldwin Smith

Pour Commencer. Jon Stallworthy. NoAM

Pour for Heliodora Persuasion and pour for Cypris. Meleager. HePo, *tr.* by Barbara Hughes Fowler *Fr.* I'll Twine White Violets. NIP-4, *tr.* by Goldwin Smith

Pour O pour that parting soul in song. Song of the Son. Jean Toomer. CrDW; ISC; NIP-4; PoBA

Pour out the dark wine, Miriamne. Romancero. Lex Banning. NOBAu

Pour out, ye heav'ns, your veangence on his head. (LL) Sad was his countenance, if we can call. Philip Freneau. NAAL-1; NAAL-3

Pour out your light, O stars. Requiem. Ivor Gurney. FaBoEE; FaBoTw

Pour secrecy upon the dying page. (LL) I Held a Shelley Manuscript. Gregory Corso. BB; PmAP; VGW

Pour this wine. Meleager, *Greek.* GrAn, *tr.* by Peter Whigham

Pour Us Wine. Ibn Kolthum. AWP, *tr.* by E. Powys Mathers *Fr.* The Mu'allaqat.

Pouring orange into GRAPE and grape into ORANGE forever. (LL) Ballad of Orange and Grape. Muriel Rukeyser. ChAP; NoAM; NoP-4

Pouring Out My Feelings after Parting from Yüan Chen. Po Chü-i, *Chinese.* CoBCP, *tr.* by Burton Watson

Pouring unto us from the heaven's brink. (LL) Endymion. Keats. APAD; CTV; LaPo

Poussie, poussie, baudrons. *Unknown.* OxNR

Poverty. Theognis, *Greek.* AWP, *tr. by* John Hookham Frere

Poverty. Thomas Traherne. TrCP

Poverty. *Unknown. Fr.* The Panchatantra. AWP, *tr. by* Arthur Ryder

Poverty. Yang Hsiung, *Chinese.* ChiP, *tr. by* Arthur Waley

Poverty, in Imitation of Milton. Samuel Jones. NOEC

Poverty in London. Samuel Johnson. *Fr.* London: A Poem in Imitation of the Third Satire of Juvenal. PoEL-3

Poverty is a mere mask for rags and tatters. Looking at Mt. Mudung. So Chong-Ju, *Korean.* CKP, *tr. by* Jaihiun Kim

Poverty Knock. *Unknown.* FaBoVe

Poverty on the Bank. Mei Yao Ch'en, *Chinese.* SuSp, *tr. by* Jonathan Chaves

Poverty, remorseless spectre. Christmas Eve, South, 1865. Mary E. Tucker. CBWP-1

Poverty? wealth? seek neither. Epigram. Kassia, *Greek.* WPOW, *tr. by* Patrick Diehl

Poverty's the worst savage crime. Alcaeus, *Greek.* InMo, *tr. by* Sam Hamill

Povre Ame Amoureuse. Louise Labé, *French.* AWP, *tr. by* Robert Bridges

Povre widwe [*or* wyde], somde[e]l stape in age, A. The Nun's Priest's Tale. Chaucer. FHYEP; OAEL-1 *Fr.* The Canterbury Tales.

Powder and scent and silence. The young dwarf. Clair de Lune. Anthony Hecht. NYBP

Powder-light let dust lie / On Musa, who had blue eyes. Epitaph in the Borghese Gardens. *Unknown, Greek.* GrAn, *tr. by* Peter Whigham

Powell (Officer Charged with the beating of Rodney King). Lucille Clifton. RACG

Power. Hart Crane. MoAmPo *Fr.* Cape Hatteras. InPS-3; MoAmPo *Fr.* The Bridge. NAAL 2

Power. Ralph Waldo Emerson. *See* Self-Reliance.

Power. Audre Lorde. GLP; NoAM

Power. Adrienne Rich. ColAP; NALW; TAP

Power above powers, O heavenly Eloquence. Poetry in England. Samuel Daniel. EPCY; NOBE; NoSic *Fr.* Musophilus; or, Defence of All Learning.

Power and Light. James Dickey. NAAL-2

Power and Peace. Robert Herrick. CaPo

Power and the Glory, The. Siegfried Sassoon. OBMV

Power Cut. Seamus Deane. PBCIP

Power Equality. Party for your Right to Fight. Public Enemy. ISC

Power Failure. Michael Dennis Browne. AmPA

Power from God claimed, than God Himself to trust. (LL) Satire 3. Donne. EBEV; ESCV; FHYEP; FMP; FSCP; MeLP; NAEL-1; NOBE; NoP-4; NoSic; OAEL-1; OBSV; OxAEP-1; PoE; PoEL-2; SeCP

Power-house, A. Classic Scene. William Carlos Williams. NAAL-2; OxBA

Power in the People, The. Robert Herrick. CaPo

Power is on the earth and in the air, A. Midsummer. William Cullen Bryant. GSo

Power, [*or* pow'r] must it maintain, A. (LL) An Horatian Ode upon Cromwell's Return from Ireland. Andrew Marvell. EBEV; ESCV; GTBS-P; GeHe; HAP; IIP; InPS-3; NOBE; NOSC; OAEL-1; OBEV; OBWP; OxAEP-1; PoEL-2; SCGP; SeCP; TFi

Power of Destiny, The. Mary Whateley. ECWP

Power of Faith, The. Thomas Rabbitt. NAmP90

Power of Fancy, The. Philip Freneau. AmPP

Power of Innocence, The. "C. G. H." NOEC

Power of Interval, The. John Byrne Leicester Warren, 3d Baron De Tabley. NOBVV; OxBSP

Power of Love, The. Bion, *Greek.* OBCVT, *tr. by* Francis Fawkes

Power of Love, The. Charlotte Dacre. NOBRP

Power of Love, The. Dryden. *Fr.* Cymon and Iphigenia. EPCY; OBNV

Power of love over gods them selves, The. Seneca, *Latin.* OBCVT, *tr. by Unknown*

Power of Maples, The. Gerald Stern. APAD

Power of Music, The. Thomas Lisle. NOBL

Power of my blood, your secret. Witches' Blood. Alma Villanueva. NMM-2

Power of My Mother, The. Sharon Olds. MDDM

Power of Numbers, The. Abraham Cowley. *See* Number, Weight, and Measure.

Power of Prayer, The. Samuel Johnson. NOBE *Fr.* The Vanity of Human Wishes [The Tenth Satire of Juvenal Imitated]. EBEV; ECEV; NOEC; OAEL-1; OxAEP-1; PoEL-3; TFi

Power of Prayer, The. Richard Chenevix Trench. PoToHe

Power of raven be thine. Good Wish. *Unknown, Gaelic.* FaBoCh, *tr. by* Alexander Carmichael

Power of Ridicule, The. Robert Bridges. NOBE

Power of Ridicule, The. Alexander Pope. *See* The Art of Satire.

Power of song, The. Horace. OBCVT, *tr. by* Byron *Fr.* Hints from Horace.

Power of Spleen, The. Anne Finch, Countess of Winchilsea. ECWP *Fr.* The Spleen, a Pindaric Poem.

Power of Suicide, The. Muriel Rukeyser. NALW

Power of Taste, The. Zbigniew Herbert, *Polish.* PoSu, *tr. by* John Carpenter *and* Bogdana Carpenter

Power of the Dog, The. Rudyard Kipling. BLPA

Power of Thought, The. Süsskind von Trimberg, *Middle High German.* TrJP

Power of Time, The. Jonathan Swift. FaBoEE

(Shall I Repine.) OxBSP

Power of Toads, The. Pattiann Rogers. NAmP90

Power of Women, THe. Matilda Barbara Betham-Edwards. ECWP

(From Matilda Betham's Notes.) Ro

Power of Words, The. Letitia Elizabeth Landon. VWP

Power returns. We remember, The. III. Healing Song. Etheridge Knight. BkSV *Fr.* Three Songs.

Power ruptures at a thousand holes. George Oppen. *See* Power, The Enchanted World.

Power speaks only out of sleep and blackness, The. Below Loughrigg. Fleur Adcock. PeNZ

Power Station, The. James Merrill. CoAmPo

Power, that gives with liberal hand, The. On the Religion of Nature. Philip Freneau. AmPP; NAAL-1; NAAL-3

Power, the Enchanted World. George Oppen. FTOS

Power Transformer. Ian Wedde. PeNZ *Fr.* Earthly: Sonnets for Carlos.

Powerful Servants, *epigram.* Friedrich von Logau, *German.* GePo, *tr. by* George C. Schoolfield

Powerless emperor, The. The Hard Listener. William Carlos Williams. OxBSP

Powerless I grieve as the clear night passes. (LL) Restless Night. Tu Fu, *Chinese.* ChiPo; CoBCP, *tr. by* Burton Watson

Powerline Incarnation, The. Les A. Murray. CBAP

Powers and principalities—all the gods. Denise Levertov. CrSp *Fr.* Mass for the Day of St. Thomas Didymus.

Powers of Congress. Alice Fulton. NAmP90

Powers of Darkness. Abraham Cowley. NOSC

Powers of the Pen, The. Evan Lloyd.

Helen like the Rose. OBWVE

Powers of Thirteen. John Hollander.

"After the midwinter marriages—the bride of snow." VCAP

"Like some ill-fated butterfly, the literalists." VCAP

"So we came at last to meet, after the lights were out." VCAP

"These two tales I tell of myself and the life I led." VCAP

"What she and I had between us once, America." VCAP

"'Yes, go on! This is plain talk of plainer feelings now,'." VCAP

Powhatan's Daughter. Hart Crane. *Fr.* The Bridge. NAAL-2

Dance, The. LiTM; MoAmPo; OxBA

Harbor Dawn, The. AmPP; CMoP; LiTM; MoAmPo; NOBA; NoAM; OxBA

River, The. AmPP; CMoP; GM; MoAmPo; NOBA; OxBA

Van Winkle. AmPP; MoAmPo

Pow'r, ever envied, yet with ardour sought. The Favourite's fall. Juvenal, *Latin.* OBCVT, *tr. by* Thomas Morris

Pow'r must it *maintain, A. Andrew Marvell. See* An Horatian Ode upon Cromwell's Return from Ireland.

Powwow. Carroll Arnett. LTA

Powwow. W. D. Snodgrass. NYBP; SoSe-8

Powwow Polaroid. Sherman Alexie. UnSA

Powwow remnants. Lew Blockcolski. VoR

Pox of the statesman that's witty, A. The Cabal at Nickey Nackey's. Aphra Behn. NOSC

Pox on't, says Time to Thomas Hearne. *Unknown.* FaBoEE

Practical Concerns. William J. Harris. PoBA

Practical Poems. David Avidan, *Hebrew.* IP, *tr. by* Warren Bargad *and* Stanley F. Chyet

"Practically all you newspaper people." The Clown. Donald Hall. NYBP

Practice of Magical Evocation, The. Diane Di Prima. PmAP; PoM

("What rhythm add to stillness / what applause?") (LL) BB

Practice your scream I said. Dos Geshray (The Scream). Jerome Rothenberg. FTOS

Practicing calligraphy, not noticing night had come. Calligraphy Practice. Ou-yang Hsiu, *Chinese.* CoBCP, *tr. by* Burton Watson

Practicing Death Songs. Adrian C. Louis. PUP-19

Præfatory Poem to the Little Book, Entituled, Christianus per Ignem, A. Nicholas Noyes. SCAP

Prague. Lutz Rathenow, *German.* CEEP, *tr.* by Boria Sax

Prague in the Midday Sun. Vitĕzslav Nezval, *Czech.* AF, *tr.* by Ewald Osers

Prairie, The. Francis Ponge, *French.* AF, *tr.* by Beth Archer

Prairie Fires. Hamlin Garland. OBCA

Prairie-grass dividing, its special odor breathing, The. Walt Whitman. APN-1

("Prairie-grass dividing—its own odor breathing, The.") PaTW

Prairie Graveyard. Anne Marriott. NOBC

Prairie Houses. Barbara Guest. PmAP

Prairie Spring. Willa Silbert Cather. PaTW

Prairie Town. William Stafford. PFE

Prairie Waters by Night. Carl Sandburg. NAAL-2

Prairie Wind. Debra Nystrom. MoLi

Prairies, The. William Cullen Bryant. APN-1; AmPP; ColAP; NAAL-1; NAAL-3; NCAP; NOBA; OxBA; PAR; PaTW; PoEL-4; TAP

Prairies are broad, and the woodlands are wide, The. The Stolen White Girl. John Rollin Ridge. APN-2; PAR; PaTW

Prais[e]d be Diana[']s fair[e] and harmles[s] light. The Shepherd's Praise of Diana. Sir Walter Ralegh. NoSic; SiPS

Praise. Jane Cooper. TAP

Praise. William Matthews. AmPA

Praise. Christopher Smart. OxBChV *Fr.* Hymns for the Amusement of Children.

Praise. Henry Vaughan. ESCV

Praise and Prayer. Sir William Davenant. OBEV *Fr.* Gondibert.

("*Praise*, is devotion fit for mighty Mindes!") PBRV

Praise for an Urn. Hart Crane. AWP; CMoP; HAP; LiTM; MeMAP; MoAmPo; NOBA; NoAM; OxBA; WeW-3

Praise for Mercies Spiritual and Temporal. Isaac Watts. NOEC

Praise for Sick Women. Gary Snyder. NeAP

Praise for the Fountain Opened. William Cowper. InPK-6 *Fr.* Olney Hymns.

(Fountain, The.) ChIV-1

"Praise God" said Spenser, "You live where you choose". The Position of Praise. Brendan Kennelly. BiHa

Praise Hearst, from whom all blessings flow! Doxology. Bert Leston Taylor. OBAL

Praise Him. Gerard Manley Hopkins. *See* Pied Beauty.

Praise him, praise him. / Praise with us the God of grace, *par.* by Henry Francis Lyte. Bible, *O.T.*

Praise him that aye. Laudate Dominum. Mary Sidney Herbert, Countess of Pembroke. ChIV-1

Praise Him Who Makes Us Happy. Mark Van Doren. AH

Praise in Summer. Richard Wilbur. NoP-4

Praise is a quiet and a gracious thing. R. H. Grenville. PoToHe

Praise is devotion fit for mighty minds. Praise and Prayer. Sir William Davenant. OBEV *Fr.* Gondibert.

Praise memory and forgetfulness! Macedonius, *Greek.* GrAn, *tr.* by Barriss Mills

Praise, my soul, the King of heaven, *par.* by Henry Francis Lyte. Bible, *O.T. See* Psalm 103.

Praise, my soul, the King of heaven. Bible, *O.T. See* Psalm 103.

Praise Now Your God. H. P. Brucker. AH

Praise of a Collie. Norman MacCaig. AH

Praise of a Yellow Skin, The, or An Elizabeth in Gold. John Collop. NOSC

Praise, of course, is best: plain speech breeds hate. Meditation. Palladas, *Greek.* GrAn, *tr.* by Dudley Fitts

Praise of Creation. George Moses Horton. AAP

Praise of Dancing, The. Sir John Davies. NOBE *Fr.* Orchestra; or, A Poem[e] of Da[u]ncing. NoSic; SiPS

Praise of Dust, The. G. K. Chesterton. MoBrPo

Praise of Faith, The. John Hall. ChIV-2

Praise of Fionn, The. *Unknown, Irish.* TIRV, *tr.* by Frank O'Connor

Praise of God. *Unknown.* NOIV

Praise of Godly Love Out of 1 John. 4, The. John Hall. ChIV-2

Praise of His Lady, A. John Heywood. OBEV

Praise of Little Women. Juan, Archpriest of Hita Ruiz, *Spanish.* AWP, *tr.* by Longfellow

Praise [or prayse] of meaner wits this work[e] like profit brings, The. Another of the Same. Sir Walter Ralegh *and* George Clifford. SiPS *Fr.* Commendatory Verses to Edmund Spenser's Fairy Queen.

Praise of Neptune's empery, The. (LL) A Hymn in Praise of Neptune. Thomas Campion. NOBE; OBEV

Praise of Philip Sparrow, The. George Gascoigne.

Of All the Birds That I Do Know. CH

Praise of Spenser. William Browne. OxAEP-1

Praise of Waterford, The. *Unknown.*

"God of his goodnes, praysed that he be." NOIV

Praise of Women. Robert Mannyng. OBEV

Praise the Lord. Milton. FaBoCh

Praise the Lord for all the seasons. Mary Anderson. BoTP

Praise the Tortilla, Praise the Menudo, Praise the Chorizo. Ray Gonzales. UnSA

Praise they that will Times past, I joy to see. The Present Time Best Pleaseth. Robert Herrick. CavPo

Praise thy God, O Zion, *sel., vv. 7–9, 12.* Bible, *O.T. See* Psalm 147.

Praise to God for things we see. M. M. Penstone. CTV

Praise to the emptiness that blanks out existence. Existence. Jelaluddin Rumi, *Persian.* EnlH, *tr.* by Coleman Barks *and* John Moyne

Praise to the End! Theodore Roethke. InPS-3

"Mips and ma the mooly moo." CBNP; NBLV; RB

Praise to the Holiest in the height. Chorus of Angels. John Henry, Cardinal Newman. NOBVV; NOCV; PoEL-5 *Fr.* The Dream of Gerontius.

Praise to the Rich. Marina Tsvetayeva, *Russian.* TCRP, *tr.* by Elaine Feinstein *and* Angela Livingstone

Praise (2). George Herbert. ChIV-1; ESCV

Praise we the Lord / of Heaven's kingdom. Caedmon's Hymn. Caedmon, *Anglo-Saxon.* EBEV, *tr.* by Sally Purcell; OAEL-1, *tr.* by Walter Kendrick

Praise ye the Lord. Bible, *O.T.* Psalm 147. CTV

Praise ye the Lord for the avenging of Israel. The Song of Deborah. Bible, *O.T.* AWP; BoWoP; PBWP; TrJP *Fr.* Judges.

Praise ye the Lord, O celebrate his fame. Peleg Folger. AH; ChIV-1

Praise ye the Lord. Praise ye the Lord from the heavens. Bible, *O.T. See* Psalm 148.

Praise you, "All these were lovely"; say, "He loved." (LL) The Great Lover. Rupert Brooke. HoPM; ImPo; LiTM; MoBrPo; PoRA

Praise youth's hot blood if you will, I think that happiness. Age in Prospect. Robinson Jeffers. MoAmPo

Praised be man, he is existing in milk. Two Hundred and Twenty-Eighth Chorus. Jack Kerouac. NeAP; PmAP *Fr.* Mexico City Blues.

Praised be the moon of books! that doth above. In the Reading-Room of the Brtish Museum. Louise Imogen Guiney. APN-2

Praised be the name of the Lord, who created the wine. Five Arabic Verses in Praise of Wine. *Unknown, Arabic.* TrJP, *tr.* by Hartwig Hirschfeld

Praised be the wooden table. Odysseus Elytis. *See* The Axion Esti.

Praised beyond all Enids be. In Morfudd's Arms. Dafydd ap Gwilym, *Welsh.* OBWVE, *tr.* by Rolfe Humphries

Praisers of women in their proud and beautiful poems, The. Not Marble nor the Gilded Monuments. Archibald MacLeish. BoLoP; CMoP; HoPM; MeMAP; PoRA; TwCP

Praises, The. Charles Olson. VGW

Praises of a Country Life, The. Horace, *Latin.* OBVE; SeCP, *tr.* by Ben Jonson *Fr.* Epodes.

("At th'Calends, puts all out againe.") (LL) OBCVT, *tr.* by Ben Jonson

("*Happie* is he, that from all Businesse cleere.") OBCVT, *tr.* by Ben Jonson

Praises of Field-marshal J. C. Smuts, The. Nongejeni Zuma, *Zulu.* PeSAV, *tr.* by Harry C. Lugg

Praises of King George VI. A. Z. Ngani, *Xhosa.* PeSA, *tr.* by Jack Cope

Praises of the Bantu Kings (1–10). Jerome Rothenberg. FTOS

Praises of the Canna, The. *Unknown, Sotho, from French tr.* by Thomas Arbonsset. PeSAV, *tr.* by John Croumbie Brown

Praises of the King Dingana (Vesi). *Unknown, Zulu.* PeSA

Praises of the King Tshaka. *Unknown, Zulu.* PeSA

Praises of the Train. Demetrius Segooa, *Sotho.* PeSA

Praises, Tamalpais. Song of the Turkey Buzzard. Lew Welch. PoM

Praises to Him for aye! (LL) For Deliverance from a Fever. Anne Bradstreet. NAAL-1; NAAL-3; NALW

Praises to those who can wait. Zealots of Yearning. David Rokeah, *Hebrew.* TrJP, *tr.* by I. M. Lask

Praising Thy worth, despite his cruel hand. (LL) Sonnet 60. Shakespeare. CABP; EBEV; GTBS-P; ImPo; NIP-4; NOBE; NoSic; OxAEP-1; PoPoPo; PoRA; SCGP; Son; TFi; UnPo

Praxinoa at home? Gorgo and Praxinoa. Theocritus, *Greek.* HePo, *tr.* by Barbara Hughes Fowler *Fr.* Idylls.

Pray Billy Pitt explain thy rigs. On Mr. Pitt's [*or* Pit's] Hair-Powder Tax. Robert Burns. FaBoEE

Pray but one prayer for me 'twixt thy closed lips. Summer Dawn. William Morris. GSo; NOBE; NOBVV; OAEL-2; OBEV; OBNC; OxAEP-2

Pray for my soul. More things are wrought by prayer. Prayer. Tennyson. *Fr.* The Passing of Arthur. FHYEP; NAEL-2; OBNC *Fr.* Idylls of the King.

Pray for the lovers. Jayne Cortez. ISC

Pray for the soul of Maire Og at dawning of the day! (LL) The Love-Talker. "Ethna Carbery." CH; WPE

Pray for us now and at the hour of our birth. (LL) Animula. T. S. Eliot. CRP; GEA

Pray how did she look? Was she pale, was she wan? On Lady Anne Hamilton. Richard Brinsley Sheridan. FaBoEE; OBCoV

Pray Remember the Poor. Christopher Smart. NOEC *Fr.* Hymns for the Amusement of Children.

Pray steal me not, I'm Mrs. Dingley's. On the Collar of Mrs. Dingley's Lap-Dog. Jonathan Swift. FaBoEE

Pray tell me, sir, whose dog are you? (LL) Epigram Engraved on the Collar of a Dog Given [*or* Which I Gave] to His Royal Highness. Alexander Pope. FaBoEE; ImPo; InPK-6; KaS; NOEC; NTCP; OxBSP; OxBoLi; SoSe-8; TTTS

Pray thee, take care, that tak'st my book[e] in hand. To the Reader. Ben Jonson. BeJo; PoE

Pray to What Earth Does This Sweet Cold Belong. Henry David Thoreau. NCAP; UnPo

Pray, where are the little bluebells gone. About the Fairies. Jean Ingelow. BoTP

Pray where would lamb and lion be. Nature Be Damned. Anne Wilkinson. NOBC

Pray who lies here? why don't you know. Original Epitaph on a Drunkard. Royall Tyler. OBAL

Pray why are you so bare, so bare. The Haunted Oak. Paul Laurence Dunbar. AAP; ColAP; NAAAL; UnPo

Pray why should any man complain. On Sir G. B. his defeat. Alexander Brome. PBRV

Pray without Ceasing. Ophelia Guyon Browning. BLPA

Prayer: "Be thou my vision, O Lord of my heart." *Unknown, Irish.* TIRV, *tr. by* Eleanor Hull

Prayer, A: "Eternal God, our life is but." "Yehoash," *Yiddish.* TrJP, *tr. by* Isidore Goldstick

Prayer: "Fear of death disturbs me constantly, The." Gabrielle de Coignard, *French.* WPOW, *tr. by* Raymond Oliver

Prayer: "Forgive me, you whom they cast in a name." Avraham Shlonsky, *Hebrew.* MHP, *tr. by* Ruth Finer Mintz

Prayer: "God, I need a job because I need money." Alan Dugan. NoAM

Prayer: "God, though [*or* although] this life is but a wraith." Louis Untermeyer. MoAmPo; TrJP

Prayer: "Grant that no Hobgoblins fright me." John Day. Spl

Prayer. Kumch'an Hwang, *Korean.* CKP, *tr. by* Jaihiun Kim

Prayer: "I left Cornell / with half a wit; six mismated socks." Daniel Berrigan. AF

Prayer, A: "I pray Thee O Lord." Julian Tuwim, *Polish.* TrJP, *tr. by* Wanda Dynowska

Prayer: "If I must of my Senses lose." Theodore Roethke. TwCP

Prayer, A: "If I popped in at Downing Street." Max Beerbohm. UV

Prayer: "In the bright bay of your morning, O God." Claire Goll, *German.* TrJP, *tr. by* Babette Deutsch *and* Avrahm Yarmolinsky

Prayer, A: "Let me do my work each day." Max Ehrmann. BLPA; FaBoBe; PoToHe

Prayer: "Let my words." Joseph Bruchac. UnSA

Prayer: "Let us leave our island woods grown dim and blue." "Æ." TIRV

Prayer: "Lord I am not entirely selfish." Gavin Ewart. OxBC

Prayer, A: "Lord, let me live like a Regular Man." Berton Braley. BLPA

Prayer: "Lord, stand up for the Soviets." Nikolai Ivanovich Glazkov, *Russian.* TCRP, *tr. by* Daniel Weissbort

Prayer: "Master, they say that when I seem." C. S. Lewis. TIRV; TrCP

Prayer: "More things are wrought by prayer." Tennyson. *Fr.* Morte d'Arthur. EBNV; EBVVPR; FaBoBe; NIP-4; NOBVV; OAEL 2; OBNV; OxAEP-2; PoEL-5 *Fr.* Morte d'Arthur. EnVR

Prayer: "O Christ, who in Gethsemane." Henrietta Cordelia Ray. CBWP-3

Prayer: "O let me soar on steadfast wing." Dennis Brutus. AF

Prayer, The: "O living will that shalt endure." Tennyson. *Fr.* In Memoriam A. H. H.

Prayer, A: "O that mine eyes might closed be." Thomas Elwood. PWR

Prayer, A: "Oh, Lord! I lift my heart." Priscilla Jane Thompson. CBWP-2

Prayer: "Pray for my soul. More things are wrought by prayer." Tennyson. *Fr.* The Passing of Arthur. FHYEP; NAEL-2; OBNC *Fr.* Idylls of the King.

Prayer, A: "Searcher of souls, you who in heaven abide." Samuel Butler. FaBoEE

Prayer, A: "Teach me, Father, how to go." Edwin Markham. BoTP; CTV

Prayer: "Thy blessing on the boys—for time has come." Haim Guri, *Hebrew.* TrJP, *tr. by* Ruth H. Lask

Prayer: "What do you take." Bill Manhire. PeNZ

Prayer: "You may be right, divinity." Francis Sullivan. CRP

Prayer. Ioan Alexandru, *Romanian.* CEEP, *tr. by* Dan Duescu

Prayer. Lucille Clifton. NAAAL

Prayer. Hartley Coleridge. GSo

Prayer. Carol Ann Duffy. NoP-4

Prayer, The. John Galsworthy. UV

Prayer. Dana Gioia. NoP-4

Prayer. Patricia Jones. WWSi

Prayer. Gabriela Mistral, *Spanish.*
    "Like those jars that women put out to catch the dew of night." WPoS, *tr. by* Langston Hughes

Prayer, A. Oppian, *Greek.* OBCVT, *tr. by* Thomas Stanley

Prayer. Jason Shinder. WWSi

Prayer. Jean Toomer. NAAAL

Prayer, The. Jones Very. APN-1; OxBA; PAR; TrCP

Prayer 20. Catherine of Siena (A. K. A. Saint Catherine), *Italian.*
    "We were enclosed." WPoS, *tr. by* Suzanne, O. P. Noffke

Prayer after World War. Carl Sandburg. VGW

Prayer at Night ("Fountain of light, Light, Source of light"). Alcuin, *Latin.* MLL, *tr. by* Helen Waddell

Prayer at Night ("He lay with quiet heart in the stern asleep"). Alcuin, *Latin.* MLL, *tr. by* Helen Waddell

Prayer Before Birth. Louis MacNeice. EBEvV; FaBoVe; GTBS-P; PBMP; PNI; TIRV; TwCP
    ("Otherwise kill me.") (LL) AF

Prayer before Sleep. Alice Lucas. TrJP

Prayer for a Day's Walk. Grace Noll Crowell. PoToHe

Prayer for a Little Home, A. Florence Bone. BLPA; FaBoBe

Prayer for a Pilot. Cecil Edric Mornington Roberts. CTV

Prayer for a Second Flood. "Hugh MacDiarmid." EBEV

Prayer for a Tenspeed Heart. Barbara Hendryson. CrSp

Prayer for a Thief. Phil DuPlessis, *Afrikaans.* PeSAV, *tr. by the author*

Prayer for a Very New Angel. Violet Alleyn Storey. BLPA

Prayer for Broken Little Families, A. Violet Alleyn Storey. PoToHe

Prayer for Dew. Eleazar ben Kalir, *Hebrew.* TrJP, *tr. by* Israel Zangwill

Prayer for Every Day, A. Mary Carolyn Davies. BLPA; FaBoBe; PoToHe

Prayer for Every Day. *Unknown, Fanti.* PBA, *tr. by* Kweku Martin

Prayer for Faith, A. Margaret Elizabeth Sangster. PoToHe

Prayer for Forgiveness, A. Aengus the Culdee, *Irish.* TIRV, *tr. by* Eoin Neeson

Prayer for Gentleness to All Creatures. John Galsworthy. BoTP

Prayer for Indifference, A. Fanny [*or* Frances] Macartney Greville. ECWP; NOEC
    ("I ask no kind return in love.") LW

Prayer for Love, A. *Unknown.* CTV

Prayer for My Daughter, A. W. B. Yeats. CMoP; HAP; LiTM; MoP; NAEL-2; NoAM; NoP-4; OxBTC; PFE; PoA; PoLF; PoRA; RaBo; TFi

Prayer for My Son. James Applewhite. BLT

Prayer for My Son, A. W. B. Yeats. EBEV; OxAEP-2; RaBo; TIRV

Prayer for Old Age, A. W. B. Yeats. IIP

Prayer for Peace. Léopold Sédar Senghor, *French.*
    "Lord God, forgive white Europe!" TTY, *sect.* II, *tr. by* John Reed *and* Clive Wake
    "Lord Jesus, at the end of this book which I offer you." NegPo, *tr. by* Ellen Conroy Kennedy

Prayer for Peace, A. Severn Teackle Wallis. CBCWP

Prayer for Purification, A. Michelangelo Buonarroti, *Italian.* AWP, *tr. by* John Addington Symonds

Prayer for Redemption. *Unknown.* TrJP

Prayer for Revolutionary Love. Denise Levertov. CrSp

Prayer for Shut-Ins. Ruth Winant Wheeler. PoToHe

Prayer for Strength. Margaret E. Bruner. PoToHe

Prayer for the End of the Century, A. Herberto Padilla, *Spanish.* VCWP, *tr. by* Alastair Reid *and* Andrew Hurley

Prayer for the Great Family. Gary Snyder. HAP; WeW-3

Prayer for the Little City. Sydney Lea. NAmP90

Prayer for the Little Daughter between Death and Burial. Diana Scott. BrRo

Prayer for the Self, A. John Berryman. *Fr.* Eleven Addresses to the Lord. OxBC

Prayer for the Speedy End of Three Great Misfortunes. *Unknown, Irish.* OBMV, *tr. by* Frank O'Connor

Prayer for the Young and Lovely, A. Helen Steiner Rice. CTV

Prayer for This House. Louis Untermeyer. PoLF; PoToHe

Prayer for Those on the Staff. Julian Grenfell. PoFWW

Prayer Found in Chester Cathedral, A. Thomas Henry Basil Webb. *See* An Ancient Prayer.

Prayer (I). George Herbert.
("Land of spices; something understood, The.") (LL) NoP-4; PBRV; PoPoPo
("Prayer the Churches banquet, Angels age.") FSCP; PBRV
Prayer in a Pestilent Time. Anne Ridler. WPN
Prayer in Autumn. Hyonsung Kim, *Korean.* CKP, *tr. by* Jaihiun Kim
Prayer in Darkness, A. G. K. Chesterton. MoBrPo; PoLF
Prayer in Spring, A. Robert Frost. AH; TrCP
Prayer is so simple. *Unknown.* CTV
Prayer is the little implement. Emily Dickinson. APN-2
Prayer: "Matthew, Mark, Luke, and John." *Unknown. See* Before Sleeping.
Prayer of a Pagan Woman. Cothrai Gogan. TIRV
Prayer of a Woman in Charge of Berry Picking in Knights Inlet. *Unknown.* WPoS
Prayer of an Unemployed Man. W. C. Ackerly. PoToHe
Prayer of Any Husband. Mazie V. Caruthers. PoToHe
Prayer of Columbus. Walt Whitman. AmPP
("Batter'd, wreck'd old man, A.") NCAP
"Thou knowest my years entire, my life."
Prayer of First Dancers. *Unknown. Fr.* The Night Chant. APN-2, *tr. by* Washington Matthews
(After Bitahatini.) PFTM
Prayer of Hezekiah, The. George Wither. ChIV-1
Prayer of Jabez, too, should be our prayer, The. Jones Very. ChIV-1
Prayer of-Lord, *Tswana vers.* Bible, *N.T. Fr.* St. Matthew.
("Father our, he-who is at-the-height, name Thy let-it-be.") PeSAV
Prayer of Nehemiah, The. George Wither. ChIV-1
Prayer of St. Francis of Assisi for Peace. Saint Francis of Assisi, *Latin.* PoLF; PoToHe
("It is in dying that we are born to / eternal life.") (LL) CTV
(Simple Prayer, A.) CTV
Prayer of the Arab Physician, The. Monk Gibbon. TIRV
Prayer of the Cat, The. Carmen Bernos de Gasztold, *French.* PC, *tr. by* Rumer Godden
Prayer of the Donkey, The. Carmen Bernos de Gasztold. PChr
Prayer of the Maidens to Mary. Rilke, *German.* AWP, *tr. by* Jethro Bithell
Prayer of the Old Woman. François Villon, *French.* MoBrPo; PeECV, *tr. by* J. M. Synge
Prayer of the Venerable Bede. The Venerable Bede, *Latin.* MLL, *tr. by* Helen Waddell
Prayer on the Threshold of Tomorrow. Vahan Tekeyan, *Armenian.* AF, *tr. by* Hovanessian, Diana Der *and* Marzbed Margossian
Prayer That Will Be Answered, A. Anna Kamienska, *Polish.* BLT, *tr. by* Stanislaw Baranczak *and* Clare Cavanagh
Prayer the Church's banquet, Angels' age. Prayer (I). George Herbert.
EBEV; ESCV; GSo; GeHe; InPS-3; NAEL-1; NOBE; NOSC; NoP-4; OAEL-1; OBWVE; OxAEP-1; PeECV; PoE; PoEL-2; PoPoPo; TFi; TOF
Prayer to Be Said When Thou Goest to Bed, A. Francis Seager. OxBChV
Prayer to Go to Paradise with the Asses. Francis Jammes, *French.* AWP, *tr. by* Jethro Bithell
Prayer to Go to Paradise with the Donkeys, A. Francis Jammes, *French.* RB, *tr. by* Richard Wilbur
Prayer to God. "Placido," *Spanish.* TTY, *tr. by* Raoul Abdul
Prayer to God the Father. Hildebert, *Latin.* MLL, *tr. by* Helen Waddell
Prayer to God the Father. Marbod of Rennes, *Latin.* MLL, *tr. by* Helen Waddell
Prayer to Hermes. Robert Creeley. PoM
Prayer to Isis. Christina Walsh. BrRo
Prayer to Mother Mary. Padraic Pearse. TIRV
Prayer to My Mother. Pier Paolo Pasolini, *Italian.* VCWP, *tr. by* Norman MacAfee *and* Luciano Martinengo
Prayer to my Muse. Vassar Miller. NMM-2
Prayer to Saint Grobianus. Roger McGough. NOxBChV
Prayer to the Black Bear. *Kwakiutl Oral Tradition, Kwakiutl.* PaTW, *tr. by* Franz Boas
Prayer to the Father of [*or* in] Heaven, A. John Skelton. HoPM
Prayer to the God Thot. *Unknown, Egyptian.* TTY, *tr. by* Ulli Beier
Prayer to the Holy Trinity, A. Richard Stanyhurst. PoEL-2
(Prayer to the Trinity [*or* Trinitie], A.) TIRV
Prayer to the Hunting Star, Canopus. *Unknown, Bushman.* PeSA, *tr. by* W. H. I. Bleek *and* Jack Cope
Prayer to the Lord Ramakrishna, A. James Wright. NNaP
Prayer to the Masks. Léopold Sédar Senghor, *French.* NegPo, *tr. by* Ellen Conroy Kennedy
Prayer to the Pacific. Leslie Marmon Silko. CDW; NoP-4; PoPoPo; VoR; WeW-3
Prayer to the Sockeye Salmon. *Kwakiutl Oral Tradition, Kwakiutl.* PaTW, *tr. by* Franz Boas

Prayer to the Sockeye Salmon. *Unknown.* WPoS
Prayer to the Trinity [*or* Trinitie], A. Richard Stanyhurst. *See* A Prayer to the Holy Trinity.
Prayer to the Virgin. Saint Columcille, *Irish.* TIRV, *tr. by* Kuno Meyer *and* John Strachan
Prayer to the Wind, A. Thomas Carew. BeJo; CavPo
Prayer to the Young Moon. *Unknown, Bushman.* PeSA, *tr. by* W. H. I. Bleek *and* Jack Cope
Prayer to Venus. Lucretius. *See* Address to Venus.
Prayer unsaid, and mass unsung. The Sea-Ritual. George Darley. BIrV; CH; OBNC *Fr.* Syren Songs.
Prayer unto Christ the Judge of the World, A. Michael Wigglesworth. SCAP
Prayer upon Cutting down the Sacred Tree. *Unknown, Sioux Native American.* APN-2, *tr. by* John G. Bourke
Prayer yo Hymen. *Unknown.* NOSC
Prayers. Henry Charles Beeching. BoTP; OBEV
Prayers, Dorcas, Fellowship, and Children's Groups! Gwladys Rhys. W. J. Gruffydd, *Welsh.* OBWVE, *tr. by* Myrddin Lloyd
Prayers: I. Kadya Molodowsky, *Yiddish.* WPoS, *tr. by* Kathryn Hellerstein
Prayers of Steel. Carl Sandburg. CMoP; MoAmPo; SSCS; TrCP
("Nights into white stars.") (LL) SAGP
Prayerwheel: 2. David Meltzer. NeAP
Praying. P. J. Kavanagh. OxBSP
Praying and to be married? It was rare. Isaac's Marriage. Henry Vaughan. ChIV-1
Praying Drunk. Andrew Hudgins. RA
Praying mantis doesn't pray, The. Mantis. David McCord. OBAL
Praying mantis with its length of straw, The. The Praying Mantis Visits a Penthouse. Oscar Williams. LiTM
Pre-admonisheth the writer. The Flight of the Bucket. Rudyard Kipling. BXAP
Pre-Carnival Party. Mervyn Morris. HCP
Pre Domina. Jean Lipkin. PeSA
Pre-Raphaelite Notebook, A. Geoffrey Hill. NoAM
Preacher, The. Al-Mahdi, *Arabic.* TTY, *tr. by* A. J. Arberry
Preacher and the Slave, The. Joe Hill. AS
Preacher quoted, and the cranks, The. A Bad Break! W. T. Goodge. NOBAu
Preacher: Ruminates Behind the Sermon, The. Gwendolyn Brooks. NAAAL; PBMP *Fr.* A Street in Bronzeville. BPo; BlSi; FaBoWP
Preacher took from *Solomon's Song*, The. Rose Window. Herman Melville. APN-2
Preacher's Mistake, The. William Croswell Doane. BLPA; PoToHe
Preacher's Vacation, The. *Unknown.* BLPA
Preamble = sardanapalus. Dada Manifesto on Feeble and Bitter Love. Tristan Tzara. PFTM, *tr. by* Barbara Wright
Preamble to the Constitution of the United States. *Unknown.* CTV
Preamble to the Declaration of Independence. Thomas Jefferson. CTV
Preannual Poem. Yona Wollach. IP, *tr. by* Warren Bargad *and* Stanley F. Chyet *Fr.* Two Gardens (1969).
Precambrian [*or* Pre-Cambrian] Shield, The. Edwin John Pratt. MoCV; NOBC *Fr.* Towards the Last Spike.
Precautions. Eugenio Montale, *Italian.* PiM, *tr. by* Jonathan Galassi
Precautions. Martin Sorescu, *Romanian.* VCWP, *tr. by* Muldoon, Paul *and* Joana Russell-Gebbett
Precede me into this elusive country. The Caravan. Gwendolyn MacEwen. MoCV
Precede us, O Lord, with Thy Grace. Limerick. Frank R. McManus. PeLi
Precept of Silence, The. Lionel Pigot Johnson. MoBrPo
Precepts He Gave His Folk. Elijah ben Menahem Hazaken, of LeMans, *Hebrew.* TrJP, *tr. by* Israel Zangwill
Precinct Station, The. Louis Simpson. EOEF
Precincts at day, quiet leisure of spring, The. Written in the Office Precincts. Wang T'ing-hsiang, *Chinese.* CoBLCP, *tr. by* Jonathan Chaves
Preciosa and the Wind. Federico García Lorca, *Spanish.* STV, *tr. by* John Frederick Nims
Precious Child, So Sweetly Sleeping. Anna Hoppe. AH
Precious dry rose-geranium smell, The. Eiléan Ní Chuilleanáin. *Fr.* The Rose-Geranium. CIP-2
Precious Five. W. H. Auden. PeECV
Precious in the light of the early sun the Housatonic. From a Train Window. Edna St. Vincent Millay. GM
Precious Lord, take my hand. Take My Hand, Precious Lord. *Unknown.* NAAAL
Precious Lord, take my hand. Take My Hand, Precious Lord. Thomas A. Dorsey. ISC

Precious Mettle. Lewis Warsh. PT

Precious—moldering pleasure—'tis, A. Emily Dickinson. APN-2

Precious Moments. Carl Sandburg. MoAmPo

Precious night-blooming cereus. Remembering Fannie Lou Hamer. Thadious M. Davis. BlSi

Precious Pearl, The. Priscilla Jane Thompson. CBWP-2

Precious Stones. Christina Rossetti. *See* Flint.

Precipice, The. Judith Wright. BMAP

Precipice. Sang Yi. PFTM, *tr. by* Walter Lew *Fr.* Critical Condition.

Precipitous point—river and lake. Climbing P'iao-miao Peak. Wu Wei-yeh, *Chinese.* CoBLCP, *tr. by* Jonathan Chaves

Precipitous, rising beyond the purple clouds. The Natural Stockade at Bamboo Lane. Yang Shih-ch'i. *Fr.* Ten Scenes at the Hsiao Family Stone Ridge. CoBLCP, *tr. by* Jonathan Chaves

Precise counterpart, The. The Orchestra. William Carlos Williams. HAP

Precisely because I do not have. Daisy Zamora, *Spanish.* LoL, *tr. by* Margaret Randall

Precisely down invisible threads these oak leaves. October Elegy. Margaret Gibson. FYAP

Precisely their necessity. (LL) They might not need me—yet they might. Emily Dickinson. PoToHe; Spl

Precision, The. Yvor Winters. SPE

Precursors. Louis MacNeice. OxBSP

Predestination and Free Will. Dryden. *Fr.* The State of Innocence. NOCV

Predicament: a corner of / a room. Tenant at Number 9. John Blight. CBAP

Predicter of Famine, The. William Carlos Williams. VGW

Prediction, The. Mark Strand. LCAP-2; NoP-4; SPE; VCAP

Preface: "Artist is the creator of beautiful things, The." Oscar Wilde. NAEL-2 *Fr.* The Picture of Dorian Gray.

Preface. William Blake. *See* Jerusalem.

Preface: "I stood watching / I the parade of floats." Ras Michael. HCP

Preface, The: "Infinity, when all things it beheld." Edward Taylor. AmPP; HAP; MeMAP; NAAL-1; NAAL-3; NOBA; NOSC; OxBA; SCAP *Fr.* God's Determinations [touching his Elect].

Preface, *sl. diff. vers.* Edgar Allan Poe. *See* Introduction: "Romance, who loves to nod and sing."

Preface: "Rigor of beauty is the quest. But how will you find beauty when it is locked." William Carlos Williams. NoAM *Fr.* Paterson.

Preface: "Romance, who loves to nod and sing," *sl. diff. vers.* Edgar Allan Poe.
   ("Connivingly my dreaming-book.") (LL) NAAL-1; NAAL-3; NOBA

Preface: "Sonja Henie, the young girl." Theodore Weiss. VGW

Preface: "To make a start." William Carlos Williams. CMoP; NOBA; NoAM *Fr.* Paterson.

Preface or The Drama of Absence in an Eternal Heart. Roger Gilbert-Lecomte, *French.* PFTM, *tr. by* Pierre Joris

Preface Shrink Lit: Elements of Style. Maurice Sagoff. NBLV

Preface to a Twenty Volume Suicide Note. Imamu Amiri Baraka. BB; CAPP-1; CrDW; MoLi; NAAAL; PoBA; PoM; SAGP; TTY

Preface to *Divine Songs and Meditacions*, The. Anne Collins. KTR

Preface to the Memoirs, A. James Merrill. NOBA

Preface to *The Progress of Learning.* Sir John Denham. NOSC; OxBSP

Preface to the Suite: "Childhood, boyhood, young manhood." Robert Duncan. FTOS *Fr.* Poems from the Margins of Thom Gunn's Moly.

Prefatory Epistle, A. Maria Falconar. ECWP

Prefatory Poem, on. . . *Magnalia Christi Americana.* Nicholas Noyes. SCAP

Preference. Langston Hughes. APSN; HCAP; NOBA; SAGP

Preference Declared, The. Horace. *See* Simplicity.

Pregnancy. Sandra McPherson. BoWoP; LoL; NMM-2

Pregnant again. Janice Bostok. HA

Pregnant girl, under sorrow's sign, A. Under Sorrow's Sign. Gofraidh Fionn O'Dalaigh, *Irish.* BIrV, *tr. by* John Montague

Pregnant Woman. Ingrid Jonker, *Afrikaans.* PeSA, *tr. by* Jack Cope *and* Uys Krige

Prehistoric Burials. Siegfried Sassoon. MoBrPo

Prehistoric Camp, A. Andrew Young. FaBoTC

Prehistory. David Avidan, *Hebrew.* IP, *tr. by* Warren Bargad *and* Stanley F. Chyet

Preiching of the Swallow, The. Robert Henryson. EnVB; OxBS

Prejudice. Georgia Douglas Johnson. PoBA

Prejudice. Lizelia Augusta Jenkins Moorer. CBWP-3

Prejudice against Colour. Langham Dale. PeSAV

Prejudice against the Past, The. Wallace Stevens. LiTM

Preliminary Poem. John Heath-Stubbs. OxBC

Preliminary to Classroom Lecture. Josephine Miles. MoP; NoAM

Prelude. Marilyn Chin. LoL

Prelude. René Depestre. NegPo, *tr. by* Ellen Conroy Kennedy *Fr.* Epiphanies of the Voodoo Gods.

Prelude. Federico García Lorca. PFTM

Prelude. Dame Edith Sitwell. WPN

Prelude: "Along the roadside, like the flowers of gold." John Greenleaf Whittier. APN-1; NAAL-1; OxBA; PoEL-4 *Fr.* Among the Hills.
   (Prelude to *Among the Hills.*) NAAL-3

Prelude: "As one, at midnight, wakened by the call." Wilfrid Wilson Gibson. MoBrPo

Prelude: "England! awake! awake! awake!" William Blake. OBNC *Fr.* Jerusalem; The Emanation of the Giant Albion.

Prelude: "Fields from Islington to Marybone, The." William Blake. *See* The Fields from Islington to Marybone.

Prelude: "Here I am again, doubled over, I'm here, pretending I know what I'm doing." Lydia Tomkiw. *Fr.* New York Love Song (Part 1—Lower East Side). WWSi

Prelude: "I am the bird of the wayside." Christine Ama Ata Aidoo. PBWP

Prelude: "Night and the hood." Conrad Kent Rivers. PoBA

Prelude: "Night was dark, though sometimes a faint star, The." Richard Watson Gilder. PoLF *Fr.* The New Day.

Prelude: "Still south I went and west and south again." John Millington Synge. AWP; IIP; MoBrPo; OBMV

Prelude: "This fugitive between the Earth and Sky." Tu Fu, *Chinese.* TAL, *tr. by* Robert Payne

Prelude: "This short straight sword." Ronald Allison Kells Mason. PeNZ

Prelude: "Woman, Woman, let us say these things to each other." Conrad Potter Aiken. NYBP

Prelude; Growth of a Poet's Mind [1850 vers.], The, *see also* The Prelude; Growth of a Poet's Mind [1805 vers.], sels. Wordsworth.
   Conclusion: "In one of those excursions (may they ne'er)." OAEL-2; OBNC
      "In one of those excursions (may they ne'er)." EBEV, book 14, *ll.* 1–119
      "It was a close, warm, breezeless summer night." PoEL-4
   Introduction—Childhood and School-Time. FHYEP
      "Dust as we are, the immortal spirit grows." SCV
      "Ere I had told / Ten birthdays when among the mountain-slopes." TOF
      "Fair seed time had my soul, and I grew up." HAP; PoE; PoEL-4
      ("Did summon us in his delightful round.") (LL) PoEL-4
      ("Work like a sea?") (LL) HAP
      Influence of Natural Objects [in Calling Forth and Strengthening the Imagination in Boyhood and Early Youth]. AWP
      "O there is blessing in this gentle breeze." OAEL-2
      Skating. CH
   School-Time. FHYEP
      "Blest the infant Babe." TOF
      "But who shall parcel out." TOF
      "Those incidental charms which first attached." OAEL-2

Prelude, Spoken to My Work Tools. Aleksey Ivanovich Parshchikov, *Russian.* TCRP, *tr. by* John High

Prelude: The Troops. Siegfried Sassoon. *See* The Troops.

Prelude: The Wayside Inn. Henry Wadsworth Longfellow. APN-1 *Fr.* Tales of a Wayside Inn.

Prelude to a Volume Printed in Raised Letters for the Blind. Oliver Wendell Holmes. APN-1

Prelude to Akwasidae. *Unknown, Twi.* TTY, *tr. by* Halim El-Dabh

Prelude to *Among the Hills.* John Greenleaf Whittier. *See* Prelude: "Along the roadside, like the flowers of gold."

Prelude to *An American Anthology.* Edmund Clarence Stedman. APN-2

Prelude to an Evening, *vers.* A. John Crowe Ransom. MoAmPo; OxBA *Fr.* Sixteen Poems in Eight Pairings.

Prelude to an Evening, *vers.* B. John Crowe Ransom. SPE *Fr.* Sixteen Poems in Eight Pairings.

Prelude to Commencement. Marie De L. Welch. NYBP

Prelude to Memorial Song: 100 Years Later. Phillip William George. VoR

Prelude to Nothing. Sonia Sanchez. GT

Prelude to Part the First. James Russell Lowell. APN-1 *Fr.* The Vision of Sir Launfal.
   (June ("Over his keys the musing organist").)

Prelude to Winter. William Carlos Williams. SAmP

Preludes for Memnon; or, Preludes to Attitude. Conrad Potter Aiken.
   Cloister. MoAmPo
   (Prelude XX.)
   Prelude I: "Winter for a moment takes the mind; the snow." LiTM; OxBA
   Prelude II: "Two coffees in the Español, the last." FYAP; NoAM
   Prelude VI: "This is not you? These phrases are not you?" MoAmPo
   Prelude VII: "Beloved, let us once more praise the rain." UnPo

Prelude XIV: "You went to the verge, you say, and came back safely." FaBoMo; TwCP

Prelude XIX: "Watch long enough, and you will see the leaf." CMoP; OxBA

Prelude XLII: "Keep in the heart the journal nature keeps." CMoP; OxBA

Prelude XXIX: "What shall we do--what shall we think--what shall we say?" FaBoMo

Prelude XXVIII: "Time has come, the clock says time has come, The." OxBA

Prelude XXXIII: "Then came I to the shoreless shore of silence." OxBA

Prelude LII: "Stood, at the closed door." LiTM

Prelude LVI: "Rimbaud and Verlaine, precious pair of poets." FaBoMo; LiTM; NoAM; TwCP

Prelude LVII: "One star fell and another as we walked." MoAmPo

Preludes (I–IV). T. S. Eliot. HeIP-4; OBMV; Poetr; TwCP; UnPo; VGW; WeW-3

Preludes. PFE; SAGP

   ("Gathering fuel in vacant lots.") (LL) SAGP

Prelusive. Herman Melville. AmPP *Fr.* Clarel: A Poem and Pilgrimage in the Holy Land.

Premeditations. Geoff Page. NOBAu

Premises. Gustaf Sobin. PT

Premonition, The. Hyam Plutzik. WeT

'Prentice Boy, The. *Unknown.* AmFP

Prentys whilom dwelled in oure citee, A. The Cook's Tale. Chaucer. BXAP *Fr.* The Canterbury Tales.

Preparation. Thomas Edward Brown. OBEV

Preparation. Amy Lowell. CPO

Preparations. Leslie Marmon Silko. VoR

Preparations. *Unknown.* NOBE; OBEV

   (Guest, The.) TrCP

   ("Yet if his majesty, our sovereign lord.") NoP-4

Preparations for Seder. Michael S. Glaser. UnSA

Preparations for Victory. Edmund Blunden. PeFWW

Preparative, The. Thomas Traherne. ESCV; GeHe; PoEL-2

Preparatives of fate. Herman Melville. *See* The March into Virginia.

Preparatory Meditations Before My Approach to the Lord's Supper. Edward Taylor.

   "All Dull, my Lord, my Spirits flat, and dead." NOSC

   "Am I thy gold? Or purse, Lord, for thy wealth." MeMAP; NOSC; OxBA; TAP

   "Bran, a chaff, a very barley [y]awn, A." ChIV-2; NOSC

   "Deity of Love Incorporate, A." TAP

   "Dull. Dull indeed! What shall it e'er be thus?" ChIV-1

   Experience, The. AmPP

   "Guilty, my Lord, what can I more declare?" ChIV-1, *sect.* XXV, Division II

   "Leaf[e] gold, Lord of thy golden wedge o'erlaid." NAAL-1; NAAL-3

   "Like to the marigold, I blushing close." ChIV-2; SCAP

   Meditation 8 (First Series). ColAP

      ("I kenning through astronomy divine.") ColAP; NoP-4

      (Meditation 8.) NoP-4

   Meditation 26. NAAL-3

   Meditation 38. NAAL-3

   Meditation 42. NAAL-3

   Meditation 150 (Second Series). ColAP

   "Methinks I spy Almighty holding in." HAP

   "My gracious Lord, I would thee glory doe." SCAP

   "My Lord, my life, can envy ever bee." PoEL-3

   "My shattred phancy stole away from mee." NOSC; SCAP

   "My sin! my sin, my God, these cursed dregs." SCAP

   "Oh! Golden Rose! Oh. Glittering Lilly White." SCAP

   "Oh! Good, good, good, my Lord. What more love yet." NOBA

   "Oh leaden heeld. Lord, give, forgive I pray." SCAP

   "Oh that I was the Bird of Paradise!" NOCV

   Prologue: "Lord, can a crumb of dust the earth outweigh." NAAL-1; NAAL-3

      (Prologue.)

   Reflexion, The. ChIV-1, *sect.* IV, (*Division* I); AmPP; OxBA

      ("Enthrone thy rosy-self within mine eyes.") (LL) ColAP

   "Should I with silver tooles delve through the hill." ChIV-2, *sect.* II, lvi; OxBA; SCAP, *sect.* LVI; MeMAP

   "State, a state, oh! dungeon state indeed, A." ChIV-1, *sect.* LXXVII, Division II

   "Stupendious love! all saints astonishment." MeMAP; OxBA

   "Thy grace, dear Lord's my golden wrack I find." SCAP

   "Thy human frame, my glorious Lord, I spy." ChIV-1; MeMAP

"View, all ye eyes above, this sight which flings." NOSC

"What love is this of thine, that cannot be." AmPP; NOCV; PoEL-3; SCAP

"What shall I say, my Lord? With what begin?" ChIV-2; HAP

"When thy bright beams, my Lord, do strike mine eye." NAAL-1; NAAL-3

"Why should my bells, which chime thy praise, when thou." ChIV-2

"Ye angells bright, pluck from your wings a quill." ChIV-2; PoEL-3

Prepare for death. But how can you prepare. Speculation. Howard Nemerov. TAP

Prepare for death, if here at night you roam. Samuel Johnson. OAEL-1; OBCVT *Fr.* London: A Poem in Imitation of the Third Satire of Juvenal. PoEL-3

Prepare, prepare, the iron helm of war. A War Song [to Englishmen]. William Blake. CH

"Prepare to meet the King of Terrors," cried. Epigram. Ebenezer Elliot. NOBVV

Preparedness. Edwin Markham. MoAmPo

Preparing a Curriculum Vitae. Wislawa Szymborska, *Polish.* CEEP, *tr. by* Magnus J. Krynski *and* Robert A. Maguire

Preparing schmaltz for matzoh balls. Preparations for Seder. Michael S. Glaser. UnSA

Preponderance, The. William Meredith. PBMP

Preposterous. Jim Hall. MT

Preposterous is that Government, (and rude). Ill Government. Robert Herrick. CavPo

Prerogative of Lieder, The. Ray DiPalma. FTOS

Presage and caveat not only seem. The Window Sill. Robert Graves. EnLoPo

Presaging. Rilke, *German.* AWP; TrJP, *tr. by* Jessie Lemont

Presbyterian Knight, The. Samuel Butler. NOBE; NOSC *Fr.* Hudibras.

   (Canto I.) CABP

   ("When civil dudgeon first grew high.") CABP; OAEL-1

Presbyterian Knight and Independent Squire, *abr.* Samuel Butler. *See* The Metaphysical Sectarian.

Presbyterian Study. Tom Paulin. PBCIP

Presbyterians, The. Dryden. NOSC *Fr.* The Hind and the Panther.

Prescient, my hands soothing. Walt Whitman in the Civil War Hospitals. David Ignatow. WeT

Prescott, press my Ascot waistcoat. Ascot Waistcoat. David McCord. NBLV; NYBP

Prescription of Painful Ends. Robinson Jeffers. MoAmPo; OxBA

Presence. Philip Booth. AFr

Presence, The. Maxine W. Kumin. WPE

Presence. Denise Levertov. PaTW

Presence, The. Medbh McGuckian. PNI

Presence, The. Dana Naone. CDW

Presence, The. Jones Very. HAP; PAR

Presence among us. Voyage to the Moon. Archibald MacLeish. PBMP

Presence behind words / manifest as someone. Baring the Device. Andrew Joron. PT

Presence of the Dance / The Resolution of the Music, The. Robert Duncan. FTOS

Presence that so strangely rose beside the waters, The. New York City. Helen Waddell. MLL

Presences. Zoé Karélli, *Modern Greek.* PBWP, *tr. by* Kimon Friar

Presences Perfected. Siegfried Sassoon. MoBrPo

Present, Part Three. Sonia Sanchez. NAAAL; UnSA

   ("Maken pilgrimage to herself, walken.") (LL) WPOW

   ("This woman vomiten [*or* vomiting] her.") WPOW

Present Age, The. Arthur Cleveland Coxe. BLPA

Present Age, The. Frances Ellen Watkins Harper. AAP; PWR

Present Crisis, The. James Russell Lowell.

   "Once to every man and nation comes the moment to decide." FaPoR

   ("They enslave their children's children who make compromise with sin.") (LL) APN-1

Present day we cannot spend, The. Isabella Whitney. *Fr.* Sweet Nosegay, A, or Pleasant Posy. WPE

Present from the Emperor's New Concubine, A. Pan Chieh-yû, *Chinese.* BoWoP; OHMPC, *tr. by* Kenneth Rexroth

Present in Abscence. John Hoskyns, *sometimes at. to* Donne.

   ("And so I both enjoy and miss her.") (LL) GTBS-P

   (Present in Abscence.) GTBS-P

Present is a Dangerous Place to Live, The. Keorapetse Kgositsile.

   In the Mourning. PBMAP

   Mirrors, Without Song. PBMAP

Present of Butter, A. Tadhg Dall O'Huiginn, *Irish.* BIrV, *tr. by* the Earl of Longford

Present Perfect, The. Grace Schulman. BAP-95

Present reigned supreme, The. Home Coming. Lenrie Peters. HBAPE; PBMAP

Present Time Best Pleaseth, The. Robert Herrick. CavPo

Present to a Lady, A. *Unknown.* PeLV

Presentation Piece. Marilyn Hacker. AmPA

Presented as a Farewell to Secretary Fu. Pao Chao, *Chinese.* SuSp, *tr. by* Daniel Bryant

Presented to a Lady within the Palace. Chang Yü, *Chinese.* SuSp, *tr. by* Ronald C. Miao

Presented to Liu Ching-wen. Su Tung-p'o, *Chinese.* CoBCP, *tr. by* Burton Watson

Presented to Piao, the Prince of Pai-ma. Ts'ao Chih, *Chinese.* CoBCP, *tr. by* Burton Watson

Presented to Wang Lun. Li Po, *Chinese.* CoBCP, *tr. by* Burton Watson

Presented to Wang Wen-hsi. Ho Ching-ming, *Chinese.* CoBLCP, *tr. by* Jonathan Chaves

Presented to Wei Pa, Gentleman in Retirement. Tu Fu, *Chinese.* CoBCP, *tr. by* Burton Watson

Presentiment—is that long Shadow—on the Lawn. Emily Dickinson. APN-2; HeIP-4; ImPo; OxBA; PFE

Presentiment of life is alive until death, The. Beast Flower. Yelena Shwarts, *Russian.* TCRP, *tr. by* Nina Kossman

Presently at our touch the teacup stirred. Voices from the Other World. James Merrill. TwCP; VCAP

Presently Lyle gets into bed. What the Instant Contains. Jorie Graham. BAP-93

Preservation. William Stafford. CMAP

Preservation of our traditional / et cetera. . . , The. Jack A. Mapanje. *See* The Cheerful Girls at Smiller's Bar.

Preserve for us rebellion, lightning, the illusory agreement, a laugh for. Unbending Prayer. Rene Char, *French.* AF, *tr. by* Mary Ann Caws

Preserve my speech forever for its taste of sadness and smoke. To A. A. A. (Akhmatova). Osip Emilevich Mandelstam, *Russian.* TCRP, *tr. by* Bernard Meares

Preserve that old kettle, so blackened and worn. My Dad's Dinner Pail. Edward Harrigan. BLPA

Preserve thy sighs, unthrifty girl[e]. The Soldier Going to the Field. Sir William Davenant. NOBE; OBWP

Preserves. Jack Butler. MT

Preserves us, not for specialists. (LL) April Inventory. W. D. Snodgrass. CoAP; ColAP; HAP; LiTM; NoAM; NoP-4; Poetr; TAP; TRP; TwCP; VCAP

Preserving. Roy Fuller. CBLP

Preserving, The. Kevin Young. GT

Preserving remnants of a model ship. (LL) The Glass Blower. James Scully. NYBP; TwCP

President has thus disclosed, The. The Door of Hope. Lizelia Augusta Jenkins Moorer. CBWP-3

President Roosevelt. Big Joe Williams. FaBoPV

President Slumming, The. James Tate. OBAL

Presidents, The. Lizelia Augusta Jenkins Moorer. CBWP-3

Presidents of the United States of America, The. Jackson MacLow.

    1789. APSN

    1797. APSN

    1801. APSN

    1809. APSN

    1817. APSN

    1825. APSN

    1829. APSN

    1837. APSN

    1841 (I). APSN

    1841 (II). APSN

    1845. APSN

Press, The. Thomas Phipson. PeSAV

Press ahead, beloved children. Uncle Rube to the Young People. Clara Ann Thompson. CBWP-2

Press-Gang. George Mackay Brown. FaBoTC *Fr.* Runes from a Holy Island.

Press[e] me not to take more pleasure. The Rose. George Herbert. PoEL-2

Press me to your bread-fruit chest. A Cultural Trip. Opal Palmer Adisa. GT

Press of the Spoon River *Clarion* was wrecked, The. Carl Hamblin. Edgar Lee Masters. CMoP; LiTM; OBSV *Fr.* Spoon River Anthology.

Press often for, (nor, than at this time, more). Vox Oppressi, to the Lady Phipps. Richard Henchman. SCAP

Pressed by the moon, mute arbitress of tides. Sonnet Written in the Church-Yard at Middleton in Sussex. Charlotte Smith. ECWP; NALW; NOEC; NoP-4; PEW; WPE; WoRP

Pressing for Tax Payment. Fan Ch'eng-ta. SuSp, *tr. by* Wu-chi Liu *Fr.* Four Songs in Imitation of Wang Chien.

Pressing my breasts. Tanka. Akiko Yosano, *Japanese.* MJT, *tr. by* Ueda, Makoto

Pressing my forehead. Nicholas Virgilio. HA

Pressure. Anne Waldman. PoM

Pressure Drop. Onuora Oku. PBCV

Pressure lamp hisses into the silence, The. African Student. Noel H. Brettell. PeSAV

Pressure of sun on the rockslide. Water. Gary Snyder. LCAP-2

Pressures, The. Imamu Amiri Baraka. BPo

Prest her cold finger closer to her lips. Keats. *Fr.* The Fall of Hyperion. OAEL-1

Prestidigitator makes things disappear, A. The Prestidigitator 1. Al Young. NBV

Prestidigitator 1, The. Al Young. NBV

Prestidigitator 2, The. Al Young. NBV

Presto, pronto! Two boys, two horses. Boy Riding Forward Backward. Robert Francis. LCAP-2

Preston. *Unknown.* FaBoVe

Pretences. Ibn Rashiq, *Arabic.* TTY, *tr. by* A. J. Arberry

Pretext. Stephen Rodefer. PmAP

Prettiest girl, The. Sucking Cider through a Straw. *Unknown.* AS

Prettiest lady that ever I've seen, The. Pretty Lady. Rose Fyleman. BoTP

Pretty. Stevie Smith. NAEL-2; NoAM; NoP-4

    ("All this is pretty, it could not be prettier.") (LL) PoPoPo

Pretty a day, A. E. E. Cummings. CMoP

Pretty Ambition, A. Mary Eleanor Wilkins Freeman. OBCA

Pretty Bonnie, you are quick as a rabbit. Giving Rabbit to My Cat Bonnie. Anne Stevenson. FaBoVe

Pretty cow, go there and dine. (LL) The Cow. Ann Taylor. CTAV

Pretty Fair Maid, A. *Unknown.* AS; AmFP

Pretty game, my girl, A. The Flirt. W. H. Davies. EnLoPo

Pretty Girl, A. J. Gordon Coogler. OBAL

Pretty girls of the fall, The. The Falls. F. D. Reeve. NYBP

Pretty John Watts. Mother Goose. OxNR; ReMoGo

Pretty Lady. Rose Fyleman. BoTP

Pretty Lady Carenza. Tenson. Carenza *and* Iselda, *Provençal.* WPOW, *tr. by* Bridget Connelly *and* Doris Earnshaw

Pretty little crocus, in your cosy bed. Waking Up. *Unknown.* BoTP

Pretty Maid Marion. Ivy O. Eastwick. BoTP

Pretty maid, pretty maid, / Where have you been? Gift for the Queen. *Unknown.* OxNR

Pretty maid she died, she died, in love-bed as she lay, The. Ballade. Paul Fort, *French.* AWP, *tr. by* Frederick York Powell

Pretty matron, The. Clement Hoyt. HA

Pretty Miss Apathy. Pooh! Walter De la Mare. HAP

Pretty party for people, A. And. Robert Creeley. LCAP-2

Pretty Polly. *Unknown.* AS

Pretty Polly. *Unknown. See* The Gosport Tragedy.

Pretty Polly of Topsham. *Unknown.* AmFP

Pretty prating poll. Little Miss and Her Parrot. John Marchant. OxBChV

Pretty red squirrel lives up in a tree, The. The Squirrel. Mary Howitt. BoTP

Pretty Saro. *Unknown.* AmFP

Pretty Saro. *Unknown.* AmFP

Pretty song, this coming spring, A. Miss Betty's Singing-Bird. John Winstanley. NOEC

Pretty soon / when people hear a quiz show expert. Edith Bruck, *Italian.* AF, *tr. by* Ruth Feldman

Pretty Sport. William Habington. NOBE *Fr.* The Queen of Aragon.

Pretty Woman, A. Simon J. Ortiz. CDW

Pretty women wonder where my secret lies. Phenomenal Woman. Maya Angelou. ISC

Pretty Words. Elinor Wylie. NAAL-2

Prevailing winds lied in intent, The. Statuary. John Ashbery. NoAM

Prevalent Poetry, *limerick.* Charles Follen Adams. PeLi

Prevention of Stacy Miller, The. Peter Miller. MoCV

Previous Occupant, The. Agha Shahid Ali. IFJA

Previsioning death in advance, our doom is delayed. Foresight. Lincoln Kirstein. OBWP; PoWW

Prey swooped up, the iron love seat shudders. Up and Down. James Merrill. GLP

Prey to Prey. David Rowbotham. CBAP

Preyful princess pierc'd and prick'd a pretty pleasing pricket, The. Holofernes's Letter. Shakespeare. CBNP *Fr.* Love's Labour's Lost.

Priam and Achilles. Homer, *Greek*. NOSC, *tr. by* George Chapman *Fr.* The Iliad.

   ("Nor *Jove* gets the command of me.") (LL) OBCVT, *tr. by* George Chapman

   "O my husband. . . / cut off from life so young! You leave me a widow." GrIP, *tr. by* Robert Fagles

Priapos of the Harbor. Antipater of Sidon, *Greek*. GrAn, *tr. by* Dudley Fitts

Priapus and the Pool. Conrad Potter Aiken.

   This Is the Shape of the Leaf. CMoP; NOBA; OxBA

   (Portrait of a Girl.) MoAmPo

   "When trout swim down Great Ormond Street." NOBA; NoAM

Priapus seeing Kimon with a stand. Antipater of Thessalonica, *Greek*. GrAn, *tr. by* Alistair Elliot

Priapus the Scarecrow. Antistius Vetus, *Greek*. GrAn, *tr. by* Alistair Elliot

Price, The. John Davidson. EBVV

Price, The. Anne Stevenson. DiPo

Price of Begging, The. Emmanuel ben David Frances, *Hebrew*. TrJP, *tr. by* A. B. Rhine

Price of Disrespect, The. Lizelia Augusta Jenkins Moorer. CBWP-3

Price of Giving Too Much, The. Vanparanar, *Tamil*, *tr. by* A. K. Ramanujan

Price of Wisdom, *sels.* Bible, O.T. *Fr.* Job. NAWM-1

Price seemed reasonable, location, The. Telephone Conversation. Wole Soyinka. NoP-4; PBMAP; TTY

Prices. Louis Ginsberg. TrJP

Prick a maiden nether holly. W. J. Webster. BXAP

Prickle a lamb. Conjuring Roethke. James Tate. OBAL

Pride. Violet Jacob. OxBS

Pride, The. John Newlove. MoCV; NOBC

Pride cannot see itself by mid-day light. Barten Holyday. FaBoEE

Pride got passed at the breakfast table. The Lesson. Kathleen Cain. LoHo

Pride is his pity, artifice his praise. *Unknown*. FaBoEE

Pride, like a goldfish, flashed a sudden fin. (LL) The Lesson. Edward Lucie-Smith. APAD

Pride, Malice, Folly, against Dryden rose. Alexander Pope. EPCY *Fr.* An Essay on Criticism. NAEL-1; PoEL-3; TFi

Pride of a Jew, The. Judah Halevi, *Hebrew*. TrJP, *tr. by* Israel Cohen

Pride of all the village, The. Married to a Soldier. John Clare. SCGP

Pride of Ancestry. Robert Frost. OBAL

Pride of his own, and wonder of his age. David Mallet. EPCY *Fr.* Of Verbal Criticism.

Pride of the peacock is the glory of God, The. William Blake. RaBo *Fr.* Proverbs of Hell. *Fr.* The Marriage of Heaven and Hell. NAEL-2; NOBRP; OAEL-2

Pride of wrights, the joy of smiths abide, The. The Junk Shop. Henri Coulette. NYBP

Pride of Youth. D. G. Rossetti. OBNC *Fr.* The House of Life.

Pride of Youth, The. Sir Walter Scott. *See* Madge Wildfire Sings.

Priest, The. Bob Boldman. HA

PRIEST:. Song for the Festival of Tlaloc, the Rain God. *Nahuatl Oral Tradition*. PaTW

Priest and the Mulberry-Tree, The. Thomas Love Peacock. BoTP; OxAEP-2 *Fr.* Crotchet Castle.

Priest attending, found he spoke at times, The. George Crabbe. PoE *Fr.* Peter Grimes. EBNV; ECEV; FHYEP; OBNV; PoEL-4; Ro *Fr.* The Borough.

Priest Lake. William Stafford. PoA

Priest of Beauty, the Anointed One, The. The Poet's Destiny. Lady Jane Francesca Wilde. VWP

Priest of Felton. *Unknown*. OxNR

Priest of the spruce of the north, send all your people to work for us. A Rain Song of the Shu'-wi Chai'än (Snake Society). *Unknown, Sia Native American*. APN-2, *tr. by* Matilda Coxe Stevenson

Priest, the Levite, the Samaritan, and the man who fell among thieves meet in heaven to talk over old times, The. The Good Samaritan et Al. Stephen Mitchell. GI

Priesthood, The. George Herbert. ESCV

Priestin' of Father John, The. John D. Sheridan. TIRV

Priests, The. Gregor Strnisa, *Slovenian*. CEEP, *tr. by* Michael Scammell

Priest's Chant, The. John Fletcher. *See* Folding the Flocks.

Priests have a problem, The. Hakeldama. Zbigniew Herbert, *Polish*. GI, *tr. by* John Carpenter *and* Bogdana Carpenter

Priests of Apollo, sacred be the room[e]. The Sacrifice to Apollo. Michael Drayton. NOSC

Priest's Song, A. Thomas Dekker *and others*. *Fr.* Old Fortunatus.

Priests, the elders, and the scribes, The. Death and Resurrection. Priscilla Jane Thompson. CBWP-2

Prig offered Pig the first chance at dessert. Manners. Howard Nemerov. NBLV

Prima Donna Poet Replies, A. Lorri Jackson. EC3

Primaleon of Greece. Anthony Munday.

   Beauty Bathing. NOBE; OBEV

   (Colin.) GTBS-P

Primaries, conventions, elections. The Dream of Instant Total Representation. Anselm Hollo. PmAP

Primarily We Miss Ourselves As Children. Gary Gildner. CMAP

Primary Ground, A. Adrienne Rich. NNaP

Primary Lesson: The Second Class Citizens. Sun-Ra. PoBA

Primavera. David Miller. NBrP

Prime. W. H. Auden. CMoP; PoE *Fr.* Horae Canonicae.

Prime. Donald Davie. *Fr.* Horae Canonicae. CRP

Prime. Langston Hughes. PoBA

Primer. Chana Bloch. IFJA

Primer, The. Josephine Jacobsen. NoP-4

Primer for Blacks. Gwendolyn Brooks. ISC

Primer for Schoolchildren, A. Richard Weber. CIP-2

Primer Lesson. Carl Sandburg. MoAmPo

Primer of Plato. Jean Garrigue. NOBA

Primer of the Daily Round, A. Howard Nemerov. NYBP; NoP-4; WeW-3

Priming Is a Negligee, The. Alice Fulton. BAP-94

Primitive, The. Don L. Lee. BPo

Primitive like an Orb, A. Wallace Stevens. NOBA

Primitive Pithecanthropus erectus, The. Heredity. Arthur Guiterman. OBAL; PeLi

Primitive Place. Mildred Weston. FFC

Primitives. Dudley Randall. BPo; NBV

Primitives Knew How Defenseless, The. Karen Zealand. CMAP

Primo Vere. Giosuè Carducci, *Italian*. AWP, *tr. by* John Bailey

Primrose[, Being at Montgomery Castle, upon the Hill, on Which It Is Situate], The. Donne. GBL

Primrose, The. Robert Herrick. CBLP; OBEV

Primrose Hill. Rose Fyleman. BoTP

Primroses; salutations; the miry skull. A Pre-Raphaelite Notebook. Geoffrey Hill. NoAM

Prince, The, . . . *si quid mea carmina possunt, nulla dies umquam memori vos eximet aevo, dum domus Aeneae Capitoli immobile saxum accolet.* . . . Edgar Bowers. CoAmPo

Prince Absalom and Sir Rotherham Redde. Evening. Dame Edith Sitwell. MoBS

Prince Alfrid's Itinerary. *Unknown, Middle Irish.*

   "I found in Munster, unfettered of any." BIrV, *tr. by* James Clarence Mangan

Prince-Archbishop, Father Adelhard. To Adelhard, Archbishop of Canterbury. Alcuin, *Latin*. MLL, *tr. by* Helen Waddell

Prince Arthur. Edmund Spenser. *Fr.* Wood Of Error.

Prince Charles in his Welsh principality. Limerick. Bernard Levin. PeLi

Prince Enters the Forest, The. Henri Cole. DiPo

Prince Foma. Pavel Nikolaevich Vasilyev, *Russian*. TCRP, *tr. by* David Macduff

Prince Hamlet thought Uncle a traitor. Hamlet. Stanley J. Sharpless. BXAP; NBLV; PeLi

Prince Heathen, *vers.* A. *Unknown*. ESPB

Prince Heathen, *vers.* B. *Unknown*. ESPB

Prince Henry the Navigator. Sydney Clouts. PeSA

Prince New Year, welcome to thy throne. To the New Year. Priscilla Jane Thompson. CBWP-2

Prince of Love, The. William Blake. NOBE

Prince of Peace His Banner Spreads, The. Harry Emerson Fosdick. AH

Prince Robert. *Unknown*. AmFP; ESPB; OxBB

Prince Wen Hui's cook. Cutting up an Ox. Chuang Tzu, *Chinese*. EnlH, *tr. by* Thomas Merton

Prince, with Wonder, sees the stately Tow'rs, The. The Building of Carthage. Virgil. OBVE, *tr. by* John Dryden *Fr.* The Aeneid [or Eneados, Aeneis].

Princely Ditty in Praise of the English Rose, A. Thomas Deloney. BoTP

Princely eagle, and the soaring hawke, The. William Wood. SCAP

Princes of Mercia were badger and raven, The. Geoffrey Hill. HAP; NAEL-2; NoAM; PoE *Fr.* Mercian Hymns.

   ("Princes of Mercia were badger and raven. Thrall, The.") NoP-4

   ("Wrists and / knees garnished with impetigo.") (LL) NoP-4

Prince's Progress, The. Christina Rossetti.

   Bride Song. OBEV; WPE

Princess, The. Dame Edith Sitwell. BWW *Fr.* The Sleeping Beauty.

Princess, The. Tennyson. OBGa

"Ask me no more: the moon may draw the sea." CBLP; GBL; ImPo; NAEL-2; OBNC; PoEL-5

Blow, Bugle, Blow. ImPo; NOBE; OBEV; UnPo

  ("And murmuring of innumerable bees.") (LL) GTBS-P

  (Bugle Song, The.) CTV

  ("Dying, dying, dying.") (LL) CTV

  (Songs from The Princess.) NoP-4

  ("Splendour falls on castle walls, The.") ChAP

"Home they brought her warrior dead." OxAEP-2

Lullaby: "Sweet and low, sweet and low." CTV; PoLF

Princess, The. OBGa

We Kiss'd Again with Tears. PoToHe

Princess Elizabeth of Bohemia, as Perdita. Frank O'Hara. PoA

Princess of Scotland, The. Rachel Annand Taylor. FaBoTC

Princess of the nights, be welcome. Night's Delights. Kaspar Stieler, *German*. GePo, *tr. by* Ingrid Waløe-Engel

Princess Parade. Sarah Gorham. FFC

Princess Sabbath. Heinrich Heine, *German*. TrJP, *tr. by* Charles Godfrey Leland

"Princess," said the Frog, "Do not wince." Limerick. Gina Berkeley. PeLi

Princess, you trapped a guileless Mayor. Envoi. G. K. Chesterton. OxBoV

Print tightened beneath candle grease like the drum-head. Near Mourning Ground. Victor D. Questel. HCP

Print, with his hand, his eye, was more than print. Hiroshige. Mark Perlberg. NYBP

Printed Words. Liz Sohappy Bahe. CDW

Printers. Denis Glover. PeNZ

Printer's Error, The. Aaron Fogel. BAP-95

Printer's Error. P. G. Wodehouse. OBCoV

Printing Bibles is Jenny's daily chore. Printing Jenny. Matthew Mitchell. OxBTC

Printing Jenny. Matthew Mitchell. OxBTC

Printing-Press, The. Christopher Pearse Cranch. APN-1 *Fr.* Seven Wonders of the World.

Printing the stones. (LL) The Otter. Seamus Heaney. NoAM; PNI

Priory of St Saviour, Glendalough, The. Donald Davie. OxBC

Prisms. Philip Dacey. Poetsp

Prisms. Laura Riding Jackson. ColAP

Prison. Mahmoud Darwish, *Arabic*. AF, *tr. by* Denys Johnson-Davies

Prison, The. Samuel Hanagid, *Hebrew*. NNPT, *tr. by* T. Carmi

Prison Cell, A. Nguyễn Văn Năng, *Vietnamese*. AVP, *tr. by* Huỳnh Sanh Thông

Prison Daybreak, A. Faiz Ahmad Faiz, *Arabic*. AF, *tr. by* Agha Shahid Ali

Prison Dreams. Trần Minh Tu'ó'c, *Vietnamese*. AVP, *tr. by* Huỳnh Sanh Thông

Prison Evening, A. Faiz Ahmad Faiz, *Urdu*. VCWP, *tr. by* Agha Shahid Ali

Prison gets to be a friend, A. Emily Dickinson. APN-2; NCAP

Prison House, The. Alan Paton. PeSA

Prison-house in which I live, The. Renewal of Strength. Frances Ellen Watkins Harper. PWR

Prison Impromptu. Nguyễn Đình Kiên, *Vietnamese*. AVP, *tr. by* Huỳnh Sanh Thông

Prison Life. Du'o'ng Bá Trạc, *Vietnamese*. AVP, *tr. by* Huỳnh Sanh Thông

Prison looks like houses or usual Youre nothing going in, A. Into Prison. Bill Griffiths. NBrP

Prison Song. Alan Dugan. PoA

Prison Thoughts. Tố Hũ'u, *Vietnamese*. AVP, *tr. by* Huỳnh Sanh Thông

Prisoned in Windsor, He Recounteth His Pleasure There Passed. Henry Howard. NAFL-1 *Fr.* Windsor Castle.

Prisoner, The, *see also* Julian M. and A. G. Rochelle *and* The Visionary. Emily Jane Brontë. NALW; NOBVV; NoP-4

Prisoner, The. Eduard Friedrich Mörike, *German*. CBNP, *tr. by* Christopher Middleton

Prisoner, The. William Plomer. PeSA

Prisoner, The. Po Chü-i, *Chinese*. ChiP, *tr. by* Arthur Waley

Prisoner. Wole Soyinka. PBMAP *Fr.* Idanre and Other Poems (1967).

Prisoner of Camau, The. Henry Hart. BAP-96

Prisoner of Chillon, The. Byron. PoLF

  "Kind of change came in my fate, A." NOBE

  Sonnet on Chillon. GSo; PBMP

  (On the Castle of Chillon.) GTBS-P

Prisoner of Zenda, The. Richard Wilbur. NBLV; OBCoV

Prisoners, The. Alexander Brome.

  "Come a *brimmer* (my bullies) drink whole ones or nothing." PBRV

Prisoners. Randall Jarrell. OxBA

Prisoners. Denise Levertov. NoAM; VCAP

Prisoners, The. Stephen Spender. FaBoMo; MoBrPo

Prisoners, committed to death, The. Hunger. Jerome Rothenberg. APSN

Prisoner's Funeral, A. Nguyễn Ngọc Thuận, *Vietnamese*. AVP, *tr. by* Huỳnh Sanh Thông

Prisoners of the Little Box, The. Vasco [*or* Vasko] Popa, *Serbo-Croatian*. HSix, *tr. by* Charles Simic

Prisons Are Full of Convicts, The. Yang Yi, *Chinese*. SuSp, *tr. by* Jonathan Chaves

Prithee die and set me free. Out of an Epigram of Martial. Martial, *Latin*. OBCVT; OBVE, *tr. by* Sir John Denham

Prithee, fine lady, come under my bush. (LL) Draw a pail of water. *Unknown*. BoTP; FaBoVe; LB; OxNR

Prithee, let no raindrop fall. A. M. Sayers. BXAP

Prithee, say aye or no. The Resolute Courtier. Thomas Shipman. GBL

Private, The. Robert Adamson. BMAP

Private, A. Edward Thomas. GTBS-P; NSI; PeFWW

Private But Sulphurous. Tom Matthews. PNI

Private Conference of Harry Fat, The. James Keir Baxter. PeLV

Private Dining Room, The. Ogden Nash. NYBP; OBCoV; PFE

Private faces in public places. Dedication. W. H. Auden. FaBoEE; PeLV *Fr.* Shorts [1927–1932].

Private First Class Brooks Morgenstein, U. S. M. C. Bryan Alec Floyd. CDa

Private Ian Godwin, U. S. M. C. Bryan Alec Floyd. CDa

Private Jack Smith, U. S. M. C. Bryan Alec Floyd. CDa

Private Judgement Condemned. Dryden. See Confessio Fidei.

Private Letter to Brazil, A. Gloria C. Oden. GT

Private madness has prevailed, A. O Virtuous Light. Elinor Wylie. MoAmPo

Private Means is dead. Stevie Smith. OxBC

Private Meeting Place, A. James Wright. NYBP

Private Occasion in a Public Place, A. David Antin. PmAP

Private of the Buffs; or, The British Soldier in China. Sir Francis Hastings Doyle. OBEV

Private Pain in Time of Trouble. Kathleen Spivack. AmPA

Private Pantomime. Ruth Stone. PoA

Private Poem. Strato, *Greek*. GrAn, *tr. by* Teddy Hogge

Private Sadness. Bob Kaufman. ISC

Private Transport. Adrian Mitchell. FaBoEE

Private View, A. Dahlia Ravikovitch, *Hebrew*. IP, *tr. by* Warren Bargad *and* Stanley F. Chyet

Privets Come into Season at High Tide. Ted Greenwald. FTOS

Privilege of Being. Robert Hass. NAmP90; NIP-4

Privy Counsellors do not sleep in barns. (LL) Lodging with the Old Man of the Stream. Po Chü-i, *Chinese*. BLT; ChiP, *tr. by* Arthur Waley

Privy-Love for My Landlady. George Farewell. NOEC; OBCoV

Prize Cat, The. Edwin John Pratt. MoP

Prize for Good Conduct. Kenneth Allott. OBWP

Prize-giving. Gwen Harwood. CBAP

Prize Riddle on Herself When 24, A. Elizabeth Frances Amherst. ECWP

Prize [which] they do aim at they [do] procure, The. (LL) Upon the [*or* a] Snail. John Bunyan. OxBSP

Prizefighter's Prayer, The. Menotti Vincent Caprani. TIRV

Pro Eto. Vladimir Mayakovsky, *Russian*.

  "No matter how much more waiting I'll have to do." TCRP, *tr. by* Daniel Weissbort

Pro Femina. Carolyn Kizer.

  One. NMM-2

  Three. NMM-2

  Two. FFC

  ("Springing, full-grown, from your own head, Athena?") (LL) NMM-2

Pro nobis Puer natus est. (LL) Of Christ's Nativity. William Dunbar. ChIV-2; EnVB

Pro Patria. Constance Carrier. AFr; NYBP; WPE

Pro Patria. Adah Isaacs Menken. CBWP-1

Pro patria mori. (LL) Dulce Et Decorum Est. Wilfred Owen. CABP; CMoP; FaBoPV; FaBoTw; HeIP-4; HoPM; InPK-6; LiTM; MoBrPo; NAEL-2; NIP-4; NoAM; NoP-4; OAEL-2; OBWP; PFE; PeFWW; PoE; PoFWW; PoPoPo; PoWW; Poetr; RaBo; SAGP; TFi; TRP; UnPo

Pro Patria Mori. Thomas Moore. GTBS-P; HoPM; OxAEP-2

Pro Sua Vita. Robert Penn Warren. MoAmPo

Probability and Birds in the Yard. Russell Atkins. GT

Probability in the yard is this, The. Probability and Birds in the Yard. Russell Atkins. GT

Probably. Keith Preston. NBLV

Probably to relate to the notes on 4-dim'l perspective. Cast Shadows. Marcel Duchamp, *French*. PFTM, *tr. by* Arturo Schwarz

Probatioun Officeres Tale, The. Gerard Benson. BXAP; NBLV

Problem, The. Paul Blackburn. NeAP

Problem, The. Ralph Waldo Emerson. APN-1; AWP; AmPP; MeMAP; NAAL-1; NAAL-3; NOBA; OxBA; PAR; TAP

Problem, The. Natan Zach, *Hebrew.*
   ("Problem, of course, is to form a shape, The.") IP, *tr. by* Warren Bargad *and* Stanley F. Chyet

Problem Child, The. "Hugh MacDiarmid." FaBoTC *Fr.* A Drunk Man Looks at the Thistle.

Problem here is that, The. Sherbet. Cornelius Eady. CMAP; GT; LTA

Problem in History, A. Robert Wallace. CRP

Problem in Social Geometry—the Inverted Square! Ray Durem. PoBA

Problem is not the letter X, The. Malcolm Is 'Bout More Than Wearing a Cap. Michael Warr. UnSA

Problem, of course, is to form a shape, The. Natan Zach. *See* The Problem.

Problems Of Gender. Robert Graves. LoP

Problems With Hurricanes. Victor Hernandez Cruz. PmAP
   ("Sweet things.") (LL) LoL

Procedures for Underground. Margaret Atwood. NALW

Process. John Montague. CIP-2

Process calls for twenty heads to stare, The. Colorizing: Turner Broadcasting Enterprises, Computer Graphics Division, Burbank, California, 1987. David Wojahn. PBCAP *Fr.* Mystery Train: A Sequence.

Process of Conception, The. Claude Quillet. *Fr.* Callipaedia; or, The Art of Getting Beautiful Children.

Process of time worketh such wonder. Sir Thomas Wyatt. SiPS

Processes of generation; deeds of settlement. Geoffrey Hill. NoP-4 *Fr.* Mercian Hymns.

Procession at Candlemas, A. Amy Clampitt. FaBoWP; HCAP; PoPoPo; Poetr

Procession of ghosts shuffles by, The. Carnival at the River. Robert Greacen. PNI

Procession of honest men, A. Selah. Ronald Stuart Thomas. FaBoMo

Procession of the Flowers, The. Sydney Thompson Dobell. *See* A Chanted Calendar.

Processions that lack high stilts have nothing that catches the eye. High Talk. W. B. Yeats. CBNP; FaBoVe; RaBo

Proclaim liberty throughout. Inscription on the Liberty Bell. Bible, *O.T.* CA

Proclaim the Lofty Praise. Sarah Judson. AH

Proclamation, or Paper Bomb, The. F. W. Reitz, *Afrikaans.* PeSAV, *tr. by* F. W. Reitz

Procne. Peter Quennell. LiTM; MoBrPo

Procne, Philomela, and Itylus. Philomela. John Crowe Ransom. CMoP; FuPo; NAAL-2; NOBA; NoAM; OBAL; OBSV; OxBA

Proconsul of Bithynia. To Petronius Arbiter. Oliver St. John Gogarty. OBMV

Procrastination. George Crabbe. NOBRP

Procrastination. Martial, *Latin.* AWP; FaBoEE; OBVE, *tr. by* Abraham Cowley
   ("To morrow you will Live, you always cry.") OBCVT, *tr. by* Abraham Cowley

Procurers. Novella Nikolaevna Matveyeva, *Russian.* TCRP, *tr. by* Deming Brown

Procuress, The. Herodas, *Greek.* HePo, *tr. by* Barbara Hughes Fowler

Procuress to the Lords of Hell. (LL) How many a father have I seen. Tennyson. EBVVPR; EnVR

Prodigal, The. Elizabeth Bishop. ChIV-2; CoAP; LCAP-2; LiTM; NYBP; TwCP
   ("But it took him a long time / finally to make his mind up to go home.") (LL) GI

Prodigal Son, The. Leah Goldberg, *Hebrew.* GI, *tr. by* Robert Friend

Prodigal Son, The. Rudyard Kipling. NoAM *Fr.* Kim.

Prodigal Son, The. Edwin Arlington Robinson. GI; MoAmPo

Prodigal Son is kneeling in the husks, The. Robert Bly. ChIV-2

"Prodigal Son," The. W. S. Merwin. GI

Prodigious Madness of the writing Race! Prologue to Garrick's *Lethe.* Samuel Johnson. OBCoV

Prodigy. Charles Simic. VCAP
   ("Great ones on several boards / at the same time, The.") (LL) AF

Prodike. Rufinus, *Greek.* GrAn, *tr. by* Alan Marshfield

Produce. Debra Allbery. PBCAP

Produce from the colonies. Pierre McOrlan, *French.* MFP, *tr. by* Martin Sorrell

Produce the urn that Hannibal contains. Hannibal ("Produce the urn that Hannibal contains"). Juvenal. OBVE, *tr. by* William Gifford *Fr.* Satires.

Product of peoples on two sides of a narrow sea, The. Lyle Donaghy, Poet, 1902-1949. George Buchanan. PNI

Proem: "From Zeus let us begin, him we mortals never." Aratus. HePo, *tr. by* Barbara Hughes Fowler *Fr.* Phaenomena.

Proem: "I love the old melodious lays." John Greenleaf Whittier. APN-1; OxBA; TAP

Proem: "Lo, thus, as prostrate, 'In the dust I write'." James Thomson. OxBS *Fr.* The City of Dreadful Night. OBNC
   (City, The.) NOBE

Proem: "Out of my own great woe." Heinrich Heine, *German.* AWP, *tr. by* Elizabeth Barrett Browning

Proem: "Sixty years after the fall of Troy." Richard Aldington. PoFWW

Profane, The. Horace. *See* 3.1.

Professional, The. David Ignatow. NNaP

Professionals. Turner Cassity. MT

Professionals, The. Geoffrey Grigson. PoA

Professor at the Breakfast Table, The. Oliver Wendell Holmes.
   Lord of All Being, Throned Afar. AH
   O Love Divine, That Stooped to Share. AH

Professor Burke's symphony, "Colorado Vistas." Cultural Notes. Kenneth Fearing. CMoP; PoE

Professor Eisenbart, asked to attend. Prize-giving. Gwen Harwood. CBAP

Professor Eisenbart, with grim distaste. Panther and Peacock. Gwen Harwood. CBAP

Professor Gratt. Donald Hall. OBAL

Professor Kelleher and the Charles River. Desmond O'Grady. CIP-2; PBCIP

Professor Noctutus. George Macdonald. NOBVV

Professor of Ethical Culture, A. Limerick. *Unknown.* PeLi

Professor Palamedes darts down Westow Street. News from Norwood. Christopher Middleton. FaBoMo

Professor Robinson each summer beats. Don's Holiday. George Rostrevor Hamilton. OBCoV

Professor stood still, tall, thin, with stains, The. Paul Evans. NBrP *Fr.* Two Sonnets.

Professor White / who switched the heads of two chimpanzees. What Happened to Professor White on Leaving the Hat Store. Ewa Lipska, *Polish.* CEEP, *tr. by* Magnus J. Krynski

Professor's Song, A. John Berryman. HeIP-4; MoP; NAAL-2; NOBA; NoAM; OxBC

Profile like the Barrymores. Undead White European Male. Elton Glaser. BAP-95

Profile of Rose. Glyn Jones. OBWVE

Profile on the Pillow, The. Dudley Randall. BPo; PoBA; TAP

Profiles of My Father. Rhyll McMaster. CBAP

Profit and Batten. Villains. Stevie Smith. OxBoV

Profit and Loss: An Elegy upon the Decease of Mrs. Mary Gerrish. John Danforth. SCAP

Profiteer, The. Ezra Pound. NSI

Profiteers. Alexander Pope. ECEV *Fr.* The First Epistle of the First Book of Horace Imitated.

Profiteers. Jessie Pope. NSI

Profound the radiance issuing. Eve. David Gascoyne. GTBS-P

Progeny of Cain, The. Nikolai Stepanovich Gumilyov, *Russian.* TCRP, *tr. by* Simon Franklin

Prognosis. Louis MacNeice. CMoP; NOBE

Prognostication on Will Laud, Late Archbishop of Canterbury, A. *Unknown.* OxBoLi

Prognostication upon Cards and Dice, A. Sir Walter Ralegh. *See* On the Card[e]s, and Dice.

Progress. Matthew Arnold. ChIV-2

Progress. Robert Conquest. OBCoV

Progress. Samuel Hoffenstein. OBCoV

Progress. Alexander Pope. ECEV *Fr.* Windsor-Forest [*or* Windsor Forest].

Progress. Barrett Watten.
   "Isolate *and.*" FTOS
   "Relax, / stand at attention, and." PmAP

Progress. Ella Wheeler Wilcox. BLPA

Progress Alley. Rodney Jones. WWSi

Progress of a Divine, The. Richard Savage.
   "Now in the patron's mansion see the wight." OBSV

Progress of Beauty, The. Jonathan Swift. GEA; PFE

Progress of Dulness, The. John Trumbull. AmPP

Progress of Evening. Walter Savage Landor. OBNC

Progress of Faust, The. Karl Shapiro. NYBP

Progress of Love, The. Robert Dodsley. ECEV

Progress of Man, The. George Canning *and* William Gifford (1756–1826). NOBRP

Progress of Poesy, The. Matthew Arnold. NOBVV

Progress of Poesy, The. Thomas Gray. AWP; GTBS-P; NOEC; OBEV

"Behold, where Dryden's less presumptuous car." EPCY

"Far from the sun and summer gale." EPCY

"In climes beyond the solar road." OxAEP-1

"Nor second he, that rode sublime." EPCY

"Oh lyre divine, what daring spirit." EPCY

Progress of Poesy, The. Pindar, *Greek.*

"Oh! Sovereign of the willing soul." OBCVT, *tr. by* Thomas Gray

Progress of Poetry, The. "Christopher Caudwell." OxBTC

Progress of Poetry, The. Jonathan Swift. NOIV

Progress[e] of the Soul[e], The. Donne.

"It quickened [*or* quicknd] next a toyful[l] ape, and so." PoEL-2

Progressive Man's Indignation, A. Dimitris Tsaloumas. BMAP

Prohibition, The. Donne. GBL; MeLP; NOSC

Project: Flag. Tadeusz Borowski, *Polish.* AF, *tr. by* Larry Rafferty, Meryl Natchez *and* Tadeusz Pioro

Project for Freight Trains, A. David Young. GM

Project of Linear Inquiry, The. Michael Palmer. PmAP

Projected Scenario of a Performance to Be Given Before the UN. Lawson Fusao Inada. FaBoA

Projection. Langston Hughes. MoNo; PFTM

Projection, A. Reed Whittemore. AiP

Prolegomenon to a Theodicy, A. Kenneth Rexroth.

"Bell, The." PFTM

Prolegomena To A Theodicy. PFTM

Proletarian Portrait. William Carlos Williams. BLT; OBAL; SAmP; TAP

Proletarian, unlikely bird, no monarch, A. On the Death of an Emperor Penguin in Regent's Park, London. David Wright. NYBP

Proletariat Speaks, The. Alice Moore Dunbar-Nelson. NMM-2

Prolific and the Devourer, The. W. H. Auden. GI

Prologue. Audre Lorde.

"Time of lamentation and curses is passing, The." Ci3p

Prologue. James Elroy Flecker. *See* The Golden Journey to Samarkand.

Prologue. "Michael Field." CPO

Prologue. Oliver Wendell Holmes. NCAP

Prologue. William Langland. FaBoPV *Fr.* The Vision of Piers Plowman.

Prologue, The. Tongju Yun, *Korean.* CKP, *tr. by* Jaihiun Kim

Prologue: "And the way goes on in the worn earth." Archibald MacLeish. NoAM *Fr.* Conquistador.

Prologue: "As needy gallants in the scriv'ners' hands." Dryden. OBSV *Fr.* Amboyna; or, The Cruelties of the Dutch to the English Merchants.

Prologue: "Criticks, ye are grown so much unkind of late." Mary de la Rivière. KTR *Fr.* The Royal Mischief.

Prologue: "Deceiv'd Deceiver, and Imposter cheated!" Mary Pix. KTR *Fr.* The Deceiver Deceived.

Prologue: "Exult each patriot heart!—this night is shewn." Royall Tyler. NAAL-3 *Fr.* The Contrast.

Prologue: "First Adventurer for her fame I stand, The." Mary de la Rivière. KTR *Fr.* The Lost Lover.

Prologue: "Gallants, / If, as you say, you Love Varietie." "Ephelia." KTR *Fr.* The Pair-Royal of Coxcombs.

Prologue: "He who writ [*or* wrote] this, not without pains and thought." Dryden. PeLV *Fr.* Secret Love; or, The Maiden Queen.

Prologue: "I have come down." Odia Ofeimun. HBAPE

Prologue: "I'll mock those thoughts of yours." Vladimir Mayakovsky. TCRP, *tr. by* Bernard Meares *Fr.* The Cloud in Trousers.

Prologue: "In a summer season, when soft was the sun," *mod. by* J. B. Trapp (B *text*). William Langland. EBVV; OAEL-1 *Fr.* The Vision of Piers Plowman.

(Field Full of Folk, The.) PoE

("In a summer season when the sun was mild.") NAEL-1

Prologue: "Lord, can a crumb of dust the earth outweigh." Edward Taylor. NAAL-1; NAAL-3 *Fr.* Preparatory Meditations Before My Approach to the Lord's Supper.

Prologue: "Love, to give law unto his subject hearts." Sir Thomas Wyatt. ChIV-1 *Fr.* Penitential Psalms.

Prologue: "Mirra Lokhvitskaia's ashes are now entombed." "Igor Severyanin," *Russian.* TCRP, *tr. by* Bernard Meares

Prologue: "Musing upon the restless bisinesse." Thomas Hoccleve. PoEL-1 *Fr.* De Regimine Principum.

Prologue: "O love, the interest itself in thoughtless heaven." W. H. Auden. EBEV; FaBoMo

Prologue: "Of those few fools, who with ill stars are cursed." William Congreve. *Fr.* The Way of the World.

Prologue: "Our author by experience finds it true." Dryden. OxBoLi *Fr.* Aureng-Zebe.

Prologue: "Over! the sweet summer closes." Tennyson. GBL *Fr.* Becket.

Prologue: "Poet's age is sad: for why?, The." Robert Browning. EnVR; OAEL-2

Prologue: The Wanderers. William Morris. EBVV *Fr.* The Earthly Paradise.

(Introduction.) EnVR

Prologue: "These alternate nights and days, these seasons." Archibald MacLeish. MoAmPo

Prologue, The: "In a summer season when the sun was mild," *mod. by* E. T. Donaldson. William Langland. *See* Prologue: "In a summer season, when soft was the sun."

Prologue, The: "To sing of wars, of captain[e]s, and of kings." Anne Bradstreet. BoWoP; NAAL-1; NAAL-3; NALW; NOBA; OxBA; PoE; SCAP; TAP; WPE

("To sing of wars, of captains, and of kings.") NoP-4; PEW

("Will make your glist'ring gold but more to shine.") (LL) PEW

Prologue: "Under the shadow of the gloomy night." Samuel Rowlands. NOSC

Prologue: "We Who with Songs Beguile Your Pilgrimage." James Elroy Flecker. *Fr.* The Golden Journey to Samarkand.

Prologue: Before the Curtain. Arthur Symons. ADE

Prologue from "Legacy." Patricia Parker. GLP

Prologue: In the Stalls. Arthur Symons. ADE

Prologue of Persius, The. Persius, *Latin.* OBCVT, *tr. by* Unknown

Prologue of the Nun's Priest's Tale, The. Chaucer. *See* The Nun's Priest's Prologue.

Prologue on the Old Winchester Playhouse over the Old Butchers' Shambles. Thomas Warton, the Younger. ECEV

Prologue Spoken by Mr[.] Garrick at the Opening of the Theatre in Drury Lane, 1747. Samuel Johnson. EBEV; EPCY; NAEL-1; NOEC; OxAEP-1

("And unresisted Passion storm'd the Breast.") (LL) EPCY

(Prologue Spoken by Mr. Garrick.) NoP-4

("When Learning's triumph o'er her barbarous foes.") NoP-4

"Then, crushed by rules, and weakened as refined." EPCY

"Then Jonson came, instructed from the school." EPCY

Prologue to a Poem. Natan Zach, *Hebrew.* IP, *tr. by* Warren Bargad *and* Stanley F. Chyet

Prologue to [*or* of] Book VII, The. Virgil. OxBS, *tr. by* Gawin Douglas *Fr.* The Aeneid [*or* Eneados, Aeneis].

Prologue to Garrick's *Lethe.* Samuel Johnson. OBCoV

Prologue to Hugh Kelly's *A Word to the Wise.* Samuel Johnson. EBEV; FaPoR; OxAEP-1

Prologue to "Love Triumphant." Dryden. OxBoLi *Fr.* Love Triumphant.

Prologue to Sir Thopas. Chaucer. NAEL-1 *Fr.* The Canterbury Tales. *See* Introduction to the Tale of Sir Thopas, The.

Prologue to the Avowis of Alexander. John Barbour. OxBS *Fr.* The Buik of Alexander.

Prologue to the First Satire. Persius. AWP, *tr. by* Dryden *Fr.* Satires.

Prologue to the Friar's Tale, The. Chaucer. *See* The Friar's Prologue.

Prologue to "The Lakers; a Comic Opera." James Plumptre.

"Where Cumbria's mountains in the north arise." NOEC

Prologue to the Miller's Tale, The. Chaucer. *See* The Miller's Prologue.

Prologue to the Pardoner's Tale, The. Chaucer. *See* The Pardoner's Prologue.

Prologue to the Wife of Bath's Tale, The. Chaucer. *See* The Wife of Bath's Prologue.

Prologues are over. It is a question, now, The. Asides on the Oboe. Wallace Stevens. FaBoMo; MoAmPo

Prolonged Sonnet: In the Last Days of the Emperor Henry VII. Simone dall' Antela, *Italian.* AWP, *tr. by* D. G. Rossetti

Prolonged Sonnet: When the Troops Were Returning from Milan. Niccolò degli Albizzi, *Italian.* AWP; OBVE, *tr. by* D. G. Rossetti

Promachus hangs here. Mnasalcas, *Greek.* GrAn, *tr. by* Edward Lucie-Smith

Promenade. David Ignatow. TrJP

Promenade, The. U Tam'si Tchicaya, *French.* NegPo, *tr. by* Ellen Conroy Kennedy

Promenading their / skirted galleons of sex. The Return to Work. William Carlos Williams. NYBP

Prometheus. Byron. InPS-3; NOBE; OAEL-2; OxAEP-2; Poetr; Ro

Prometheus. Goethe, *German.* AWP, *tr. by* John S. Dwight

Prometheus. Jenny Mastoraki, *Modern Greek.* BoWoP, *tr. by* Nikos Germanakos

Prometheus. Jonathan Swift. FaBoPV

Prometheus at Coney Island. Quentin Rowan. BAP-96

Prometheus Bound. Aeschylus, *Greek.*

"Beseech you, think not I am silent thus." OBCVT, *tr. by* Elizabeth Barrett Browning

"Bright light, swift-winged winds, springs of the rivers, numberless." GrIP, *tr. by* David Grene

Prometheus brought down fire to men. Native Water-Carrier (M.E.F.) Rudyard Kipling. *Fr.* Epitaphs of the War [1914–1918]. OBWP

Prometheus Monarch of Gods and Daemons, and all spirits. Shelley. *See* Prometheus Unbound.

Prometheus Pyrphoros, *sels.* Trumbull Stickney.

Pandora's Songs. APN-2

Prometheus Unbound. Alec Derwent Hope. OxBC

Prometheus Unbound. Shelley. NOBRP

("*Prometheus* Monarch of Gods and Daemons, and all spirits.") Ro

(Prometheus Unbound; A Lyrical Drama in Four Acts.) Ro

"As I have said, I floated to the earth." FHYEP

"Crawling glaciers pierce me with the spears." FHYEP

Hymn to the Spirit of Nature. GTBS-P

"Monarch of Gods and Dæmons, and all Spirits." NAEL-2; OAEL-2

"My soul is enchanted boat." FHYEP

Poet's Dream, The. GTBS-P, *ll.* 737–749

("Nurslings of Immortality!") (LL) GTBS-P

"This is the day, which down the void abysm." FHYEP

"Thou, Earth, calm empire of a happy soul." PeECV

"Thou knowest that toads and snakes and loathly worms." PoE

PROMETHEUS, when first from heaven high. Sir Edward Dyer. NoSic

Promise, The. Toi Derricotte. GT

Promise. Florence Lacey. BoTP

Promise, The. Jewel C. Latimore. BlSi

Promise, The. Jones Very. NCAP

Promise me no promises, / So will I not promise you. Promises like Pie-Crust. Christina Rossetti. NOBVV

Promise of Peace. Robinson Jeffers. LiTM; MoAmPo

Promise to California, A. Walt Whitman. APN-1

Promise to come, my love, but don't you come. Shilly-Shally. Hồ Dzếnh, *Vietnamese.* AVP, *tr. by* Huỳnh Sanh Thông

Promised Garden, The. Theo Dorgan. APAD

Promised Land, The. Jessie E. Sampter. TrJP

Promised Land, The. Samuel Stennett. AmFP

Promised rain, The. Virgil, *Latin.* OBCVT, *tr. by* John Dryden

Promises like Pie-Crust. Christina Rossetti. NOBVV

Promises of Freedom. *Unknown.* BPo

Promises of Freedom. *Unknown.* CrDW; NAAAL

Promises of Leniency and Forgiveness. Charles Simic. LCAP-2

Promises of mother, The. I Hear You. Shirley Kaufman. MDDM

Promises of the World, The. Moses ibn Ezra. *Fr.* The World's Illusion. TrJP, *tr. by* Solomon Solis-Cohen

Promissory Note, The. Bayard Taylor. BXAP

Promontory Moment, The. May Swenson. NYBP

Prompting of my shadow, The. Roberto Juarroz. VCWP, *tr. by* W. S. Merwin *Fr.* Seventh Vertical Poetry.

Prone couple still sleeps, A. First Light. Thomas Kinsella. BIrV; CMoP; PoE

Proof, The. W. H. Auden. OAEL-2 *Fr.* Five Songs.

Proof. Bessie Calhoun Bird. BlSi

Proof. Dharmakirti, *Spanish.* EP, *tr. by* Octavio Paz

Proof. Brendan Kennelly. CIP-2; PBCIP

Proof. Czeslaw Milosz, *Polish.* TOF, *tr. by the author*

Proof, The. Richard Wilbur. CRP; OxBSP

Proofs. Tadeusz Rózewicz, *Polish.* PoSu, *tr. by* Adam Czerniawski

Propaganda Poem: Maybe for Some Young Mamas. Alicia Ostriker. NMM-2

Proper Clay. Mark Van Doren. PoRA

Proper New Ballad Intituled The Faer Yes Farewell [*or* The Fairies' Farewell]: Or God-A-Mercy Will, A. Richard Corbett [*or* Corbet]. PBRV; PeLV

(Fairies' Farewell, The.) SCGP

Proper Pride. D. H. Lawrence. FaBoEE

Proper scale would pat you on the head, The. The Scales. William Empson. CBLP; CMoP; FaBoMo; LiTM

Proper Song, Entitled: Fain Would I Have a Pretty Thing to Give unto My Lady, A. *Unknown.* NoSic

Proper way to eat a fig, in society, The. Figs. D. H. Lawrence. EP; OAEL-2

Proper way to leave a room, The. Leave-Taking. Frank Gelett Burgess. OBCoV

Properties of a Good Greyhound, The. Dame Juliana Berners. RB

Property. Robert Garioch. FaBoTC

Property of Density, The. Sarah Lindsay. EC3

Properzia Rossi. Felicia Dorothea Hemans. VWP

Prophecy, A. William Blake. *Fr.* America; a Prophecy. OAEL-2

Prophecy. Eileen Duggan. PeNZ

Prophecy, A. Allen Ginsberg. TAP

Prophecy, A. Maurice Thompson. *Fr.* Lincoln's Grave. CBCWP

Prophecy. Elinor Wylie. APAD; BoWoP; FaBoWP; NTP; SAGP; VGW

Prophecy of Famine, The. Charles Churchill.

"Oft have I heard thee mourn the wretched lot." OBSV

On His Own Poetry. NOEC

"Two boys, whose birth beyond all question springs." OBSV

Prophecy on Lethe. Stanley Kunitz. PoA

Prophet, The. Kahlil Gibran.

Crime and Punishment. PoToHe

"Love one another, but make not a bond of love." OxBM

Of Love. PoLF

On Children. OxBM; PoToHe

On Work. PoToHe

Prophet Speaks of Love, The. PFE

PROPHET. Omens of the Morning. Faustin Charles. NBrP

Prophet, The. Aleksandr Sergeyevich Pushkin, *Russian.* AWP, *tr. by* Babette Deutsch *and* Avrahm Yarmolinsky; NNPT, *tr. by* Frances Darwin Cornford *and* Esther Poliabowsky Salaman

Prophet, The. Yevgeny Mikhailovich Vinokurov, *Russian.* TCRP, *tr. by* Daniel Weissbort

Prophet, The. "Yehoash," *Yiddish.* TrJP, *tr. by* Isidore Goldstick

Prophet digs with iron hands, The. Transfiguration. Djuna Barnes. SPE

Prophet, Go, Flee! Hayyim Nahman Bialik, *Hebrew.* MHP, *tr. by* Ruth Finer Mintz

Prophet Jeremiah and the Personification of Israel, The. Eleazar ben Kalir, *Hebrew.* TrJP, *tr. by* Nina Davis Salaman

Prophet of dead words defeats himself, The. Edwin Arlington Robinson. *See* Octaves.

Prophet of the body's roving. Walt Whitman. Edwin Honig. TAP

Prophet speaks, The. Saint Malcolm. Jewel C. Latimore. BPo

Prophet Speaks of Love, The. Kahlil Gibran. PFE *Fr.* The Prophet.

Prophet tribe with burning eyes set forth, The. Gypsies on the Move. Charles Baudelaire, *French.* GS, *tr. by Unknown*

Prophetess, The. Dorothy Livesay. MoCV

Prophetess. John Greenleaf Whittier. *Fr.* Snow-Bound [*or* Snow-Bound; a Winter Idyl]. APN-1; AiP; AmPP; NAAL-3; NOBA; OxBA; TAP; TFi

Prophetic Child, The. Geoffrey O'Brien. PT

Prophetic Powers. *Unknown, Ojibwa Native American.* APN-2, *tr. by* Henry Rowe Schoolcraft

Prophetic Soul. Dorothy Parker. LW

Prophets, The. W. H. Auden. CBLP

Prophets, The. Donne. *Fr.* The Litanie. PoEL-2

Prophets, The. Richard Shelton. NYBP

Prophets at street corners, in neat grey suits. Saturday Night. Antigone Kefala. CBAP

Prophets for a New Day. Margaret Abigail Walker. BPo; NAAAL

Prophets Isaiah and Ezekiel dined with me, and, The. A Memorable Fancy. William Blake. *Fr.* The Marriage of Heaven and Hell. NAEL-2; NOBRP; OAEL-2

Prophets, preaching in new stars. The Pontoon-Bridge Miracle. Vachel Lindsay. MeMAP

Prophet's Warning or Shoot to Kill, The. Ebon Dooley. PoBA

Proportion. Amy Lowell. BoWoP

Proportion'd to their sweetness. (LL) The River of Life. Thomas Campbell. GTBS-P; ImPo; OBNC

Propos of the Wet Snow, A. Nikolai Alekseyevich Nekrasov, *Russian.* "When from dark error's subjugation." NAWM-2, *tr. by* Juliet Soskice

Proposal. Kim R. Stafford. IFJA

Proposal, A. *Unknown.* ACTP

Proposition. Nicolás Guillén, *Spanish.* TTY, *tr. by* Langston Hughes

Proposition. Robert Pinsky. HCAP; NoAM *Fr.* Essay on Psychiatrists.

Proposition and Invocation. Homer. NOSC *Fr.* The Iliad.

Proposition II. Keith Waldrop. InPK-6

Propositions. Phyllis Webb. MoCV

Propped against the crowded bar. Naima. Edward Kamau Brathwaite. HCP

Propped boughs are heavy with apples. In the Huon Valley. James Philip McAuley. CBAP

Propped on a cane, I called on my old friend. Visiting an Old Friend. Đinh An, *Vietnamese.* AVP, *tr. by* Huỳnh Sanh Thông

Propped on a stick he viewed the August weald. The One-legged Man. Siegfried Sassoon. CMoP

Propped on pillows, not attending to business. Sick Leave. Po Chü-i, *Chinese.* ChiP, *tr. by* Arthur Waley

Propriety. Chigetsu, *Japanese.* PC, *tr. by* Kenneth Rexroth *and* Ikuko Atsumi

Props assist the House, The. Emily Dickinson. APN-2; WPoS

Proputty, proputty, proputty—canter an' canter awaäy. (LL) Northern Farmer: New Style. Tennyson. EnVR; NAEL-2; OBCoV; OxAEP-2; PeVV

Pros-pectin' round about one day. Joe's Luck. Albert Brodrick. PeSAV

Prosaic miles of streets stretch all round. Seder-Night. Israel Zangwill. TrJP

Prosaics. Boris Abramovich Slutsky, *Russian*. TCRP, *tr. by* J. R. Rowland

Prose. Bernard Welt. EOEF

Prose for Des Esseintes. Donald Davie, *after the French of* Stéphane Mallarmé. OBVE

Prose of the Trans-Siberian and of Little Jeanne of France, The. Blaise Cendrars, *French*.
 "Back then I was still young." PFTM, *tr. by* Ron Padgett

Prose Poem. Humphrey Jennings. SPE

Prose Poems. Liz Rosenberg.
 "Edith B——and her mother on a Sunday afternoon." UnSA

Proserpina in the Hades of your bed. (LL) She Is Not Satisfied. Charles Baudelaire, *French*. EP; FLP, *tr. by* Alistair Elliot

Proserpine. Swinburne. *Fr.* The Garden of Proserpine. AWP; BLPA; FaPoR; HAP; NAEL-2; NOBE; NOBVV; OBNC; PoE; PoEL-5; PoRA; SCV

Proserpine may pull her flowers. Song of the Stygian Naiades. Thomas Lovell Beddoes. OAEL-2

Proserpine's Ragout. Mary Leapor. ECWP

Prospect. Ambrose Bierce. APN-2; OBAL *Fr.* The Devil's Dictionary.

Prospect. Louis MacNeice. IIP

Prospect Beach. Lou Lipsitz. VGW

Prospect Before Us, The. Constance Carrier. AFr

Prospect of Eden, The. Milton. PoEL-3, *ll.* 1–775 *Fr.* Book IV. OAEL-1 *Fr.* Paradise Lost.

Prospect of Heaven Makes Death Easy, A. Isaac Watts. NOCV; NoP-4; PeECV

Prospect of Release. Tom Mandel. PT

Prospect of the Future, The. Mrs. Henry Linden. CBWP-4

Prospect of the Future Glory of America. John Trumbull. AmPP

Prospecting. A. R. Ammons. CoAmPo

Prospecting Dream. *Unknown*. AmFP

Prospective Immigrants Please Note. Adrienne Rich. AiP; PoPoPo; VGW

Prospectors' Little Waltz, The. Aleksandr Arkadevich Galich, *Russian*. TCRP, *tr. by* Gene Sosin

Prospects. John Dyer. GaP *Fr.* Grongar Hill. CABP; NOEC; NoP-4; OxAEP-1; PoEL-3

Prospects. Anthony Hecht. BAP-95

Prospectus and Specimen of an Intended National Work by William and Robert Whistlecraft. Relating to King Arthur and His Round Table. John Hookham Frere.
 "I've often wish'd that I could write a book." NOBRP

Prosper / O / cell. Beam 25, A Bicentennial Hymn. Ronald Johnson. APSN *Fr.* Ark.

Prosperity and decline have no fixed dwelling. T'ao Ch'ien, *Chinese*. *Fr.* Drinking Wine. CoBCP, *tr. by* Burton Watson

Prospero. Shakespeare. *Fr.* The Tempest. OAEL-1

Prosperous Villager, The. Li K'ai-hsien, *Chinese*. CoBLCP, *tr. by* Jonathan Chaves

Prospice. Robert Browning. APAD; FHYEP; ImPo; NAEL-2; PFE; PoLF; PoRA; SAGP; TrCP

Prostitute living in London, A. Limerick. Douglas Catley. PeLi

Prostitutes at Smiller's Bar beside the dusty road, The. The Cheerful Girls at Smiller's Bar. Jack A. Mapanje. HBAPE; PBMAP; PeSAV

Prostrate on the beach of the shadowy bay. Sleeping Youth. Vesna Parun, *Croatian*. CEEP, *tr. by* Peter Kastmiler

Protect Me, My Talisman. Milo De Angelis, *Italian*. NeIt, *tr. by* Lawrence Venuti

Protect us, the poets. Protect us. Reflections Near the House Where Titian Tabidze Lived. Bulat Shalvovich Okudzhava, *Russian*. TCRP, *tr. by* Deming Brown

Protection of a cheap coat suffices, The. Parmenion of Macedon, *Greek*. GrAn, *tr. by* Peter Jay

Protection of Jehovah, The. Bible, *O.T. See* Psalm 23.

Protective Grigri, The. Ted Joans. PoBA

Protective instinct among the Emperor penguins, The. Penguins. Artur Miedzyrzecki, *Polish*. PoSu, *tr. by* Artur Miedzyrzecki *and* John Batki

Protects the lingering dew-drop from the sun. (LL) To a Child [Written in Her Album]. Wordsworth. OxBChV; OxBSP; Spl

Protégés will come. The True Protocol of Poets. Kapilar, *Tamil*. PLW, *tr. by* A. K. Ramanujan

Protest. Countee Cullen. PFE

Protest. Ioanna Tsatsos, *Greek*. GrIP, *tr. by* Jean Demos

Protest, A. Sir Thomas Wyatt. SiPS

Protest in the Sixth Year of Ch'ien Fu, A. Ts'ao Sung, *Chinese*. ChiP, *tr. by* Arthur Waley

Protest Poem. Vernon Scannell. OBCoV

Protestant graveyard was a forbidden place, The. The Weeping Headstones of the Isaac Becketts. Paul Durcan. PBCIP

Prothalamion. Robert Silliman Hillyer.
 "Hills turn hugely in their sleep, The." MoAmPo

Prothalamion. Maxine W. Kumin. NYBP

Prothalamion. Michael Ryan. AmPA

Prothalamion. Delmore Schwartz. OxBA

Prothalamion. Edmund Spenser. AAS; AWP; EBEV; GTBS-P; HAP; NoSic; OBEV; TFi
 ("Sweete Themmes runne softly, till I end my Song.") (LL) NoP-4
 "Calm was the day, and through the trembling air." EBEvV; ImPo; SCGP
 ("Calme was the day, and through the trembling ayre.") NoP-4; OxAEP-1

Prothalamion for an Autumn Wedding. May Sarton. ITG

Prothalamium. Donagh MacDonagh. BIrV

Protocols. Randall Jarrell. LCAP-2; OxBC; VGW

Protocols. Vikram Seth. APAD

Proton Decay. Robert Pack. ColAP

Proud and beaten we've passed the night. Our Dreams. Amir Gilbo'a, *Hebrew*. IP, *tr. by* Warren Bargad *and* Stanley F. Chyet

Proud and beautiful city of Moscow, The. History Lessons. Seamus Deane. BiHa; PBCIP; PNI

Proud as Apollo on his forked hill. Bufo. Alexander Pope. OBSV *Fr.* Epistle to Dr. Arbuthnot. FHYEP; InPS-3; NoP-4; OAEL-1; OxAEP-1; PoE; PoEL-3; TFi

Proud Egyptian [*or* Aegyptian] queen, her Roman guest, The. And She Washed His Feet with Her Tear[e]s, and Wiped Them with the Hairs of Her Head. Sir Edward Sherburne, *after the Italian of* Giambattista Marina. MeLP; NOSC; OxBSP

Proud Error. Vasco [*or* Vasko] Popa. HSix, *tr. by* Charles Simic *Fr.* The Yawn of Yawns.

Proud fountains, wave your plumes. Fountains. Sir Osbert Sitwell. MoBrPo

Proud Frog, The. Phaedrus, *Latin*. OBCVT, *tr. by* Christopher Smart

Proud in Thy Love. *Unknown*. Son Zepheria.

Proud Lady Margaret. *Unknown*. *See* Proud Margret.

Proud Little Spruce Fir. Jeannie Kirby. BoTP

Proud Maisie is in the wood. Madge Wildfire Sings. Sir Walter Scott. CABP; CH; FaBoCh; GEA; GTBS-P; HAP; NAEL-2; NOBE; NOBRP; OAEL-2; OBEV; OBNC; OxBS; PoEL-4; RACG; SCGP; TFi; UnPo *Fr.* The Heart of Midlothian.

Proud, majestic Southern sun, The. The Husband's Return. Priscilla Jane Thompson. CBWP-2

Proud Margret. *Unknown*. OxBB
 (Proud Lady Margaret.) ESPB

Proud music of the storm. Walt Whitman. APN-1

Proud Nimrod first the bloody chase began. Henry Highland Garnet. CrDW

Proud of his well-spread walls, he views his trees. On Pruning. William Cowper. GaP

Proud of my music, let me often make. Stéphane Mallarmé. *Fr.* Après-midi d'un Faune, L'. AWP, *tr. by* Aldous Huxley

Proud of my pride. A Tale Told by a Head. Lois Moyles. NYBP

Proud *Paulus* late my secrecies revealing. Of honest Theft. To my good friend Master Samuel Daniel. Sir John Harington. PBRV

Proud Preston poor people. Preston. *Unknown*. FaBoVe

Proud Songsters. Thomas Hardy. MoP

Proud with success, richly pleased. Alexander Jannai. Constantine P. Cavafy, *Greek*. TrJP, *tr. by* Simon Chasen

Proud word you never spoke, but you will speak. Walter Savage Landor. CBLP; EnLoPo; GBL; GLoP; OBEV *Fr.* Ianthe.

Proudful and barefoot I stride the street. For a Man Who Walked Sideways. Martin Carter. PBCV

Proust's Madeleine. Kenneth Rexroth. NoAM; TRP

Prove It on Me Blues. Gertrude "Ma" Rainey. NAAAL

Proverb. *Unknown*. FaBoBe

Proverb, XXX. John Hall. ChIV-1

Proverbial Advice on Marriage. *Unknown*. NBLV

Proverbios Morales. Santob De Carrion.
 Friend, A. TrJP

Proverbs. Bible, *O.T. See also* Bible, Proverbs.
 Bible, Proverbs 15:1, The. CTV
 Bible, Proverbs 16:32, The. CTV
 Drunkard, The. TrJP
 Fear of the Lord, The. TrJP
 Go to the Ant [Thou Sluggard]. TrJP

Happy Is the Man. TrJP

Legacy, The. TrJP

Neither Poverty nor Riches. TrJP

She of the Impudent Face. TrJP

Virtuous Woman, The. TrJP

Proverbs. Teresa de Jesús, *Spanish.* AF, *tr. by* Maria Proser, Arlene Scully and James Scully

Proverbs. Samuel Ha-Nagid, *Hebrew.* TrJP, *tr. by* Israel Abrahams

Proverbs of Alfred, The. Alfred, King of England. PoE

Proverbs of Hell. William Blake. *Fr.* The Marriage of Heaven and Hell. NAEL-2; NOBRP; OAEL-2

"Pride of the peacock is the glory of God, The." RaBo

Proverbs 6:6. David Curzon. ChIV-1

Provide, Provide. Robert Frost. AmPP; CMoP; ChIV-1; FP; HAP; KSG; MoP; NAAL-2; NOBA; NoAM; NoP-4; PoE; Poetr; TAP; TFi; TwCP; UnPo; WeW-3

Provided / that the occupants of the cemetery keep calm. Terezin, the Graveyard. Bernd Jentzsch, *German.* CEEP, *tr. by* Ewald Osers

Province has set up shrines, The. Parihaka. W. H. Oliver. PeNZ

Province I govern is humble and remote, The. To Li Chien. Po Chü-i, *Chinese.* AWP; ChiP, *tr. by* Arthur Waley

Province of the Saved, The. Emily Dickinson. TRP

Provinces. C. D. Wright. LCAP-2

Provincetown. Louis Dudek. MoCV

Provincetown, Mass. Harvey Shapiro. PoA

Provincia Deserta. Ezra Pound. OxBA

Provincial Adolescence, A. Michael Foley. PNI

Proving to Death that Love is so and so. (LL) Goodby Betty, don't remember me. E. E. Cummings. CMoP; PoE

Provoke my Pen to write in such a strain. (LL) To a Proud Beauty. "Ephelia." KTR; PEW

Prowling wolf, whose shaggy skin, A. The Wolf and the Dog. Jean de La Fontaine, *French.* OBVE, *tr. by* Elizur Wright

Prows O' Reekie, The. Lewis Spence. FaBoTC; OxBS

Prudence. Ralph Waldo Emerson. OBAL

Prudent Simplicity. Goronwy Owen, *Latin.* FaBoEE, *tr. by* William Cowper

Prudish old lady called Muir, A. Limerick. *Unknown.* PeLi

Pruned Tree, The. Howard Moss. NYBP; VCAP

Pruning, The. Adam David Miller. NBV

Pruning in March. Vita Sackville-West. GaP

Pruning Trees. Po Chü-i, *Chinese.* ChiP, *tr. by* Arthur Waley

Pruzzian Elegy. Johannes Bobrowski, *German.* AF, *tr. by* Matthew Mead

Psalm. Tudor Arghezi, *Romanian.* AF, *tr. by* Andrei Bantas *and* Thomas Amherst Perry; CEEP, *tr. by* Peter Jay *and* Virgil Nemoianu

Psalm. Lucian Blaga, *Romanian.* PFTM, *tr. by* Andrei Codrescu

Psalm. Peter Huchel, *German.* AF, *tr. by* Simko, Daniel

Psalm: "Be still with me, as all bells are still!" Ingeborg Bachmann, *German.* VCWP, *tr. by* Mark Anderson

Psalm: "Happy is the man whom Thou hast set apart." "Yehoash," *Yiddish.* TrJP, *tr. by* Isidore Goldstick

Psalm: "In the small beauty of the forest." George Oppen. NNaP

Psalm: "No one kneads us again out of earth and clay." Paul Celan, *German.* PoSu, *tr. by* John Felstiner; HP, *tr. by* Michael Hamburger; OBVE, *tr. by* Michael Hamburger, *sl. diff. vers.*

("No one molds us again out of earth and clay.") OBVE, *tr. by* Michael Hamburger, *sl. diff. vers.*

Psalm: "Old ones to the side." Charles Simic. AmPA; LCAP-2

Psalm: "While Northward the hot sun was sinking o'er the trees." Robert Bridges. FaBoTw

Psalm Ajar. Tadeusz Nowak, *Polish.* CEEP, *tr. by* Leonard Kress

Psalm and Lament. Donald Justice. DiPo

Psalm and Mosaic for a Springtime in Athens. Odysseus Elytis. GrIP, *tr. by* Nanos Valaoritis *Fr.* The Siblings.

Psalm Concerning the Castle. Denise Levertov. TwCP; WPE

Psalm of Battle. *Unknown.* AWP *Fr.* The Thousand and One Nights.

Psalm of Christ, The. Chad Walsh. TrCP

Psalm of David, A. Bible, *O.T. See* Psalm 23.

Psalm of Life, A. Henry Wadsworth Longfellow. APN-1; CTV; EBEvV; FaBoBe; NAAL-1; NoBA; OBCA; PAR; PWR; PoLF; TAP

"Tell me not in mournful numbers." AH

"Psalm of Life" for thee is o'er, The. Longfellow. Henrietta Cordelia Ray. AAP; CBWP-3

Psalm of Love. Tadeusz Norwalk, *Polish.* CEEP, *tr. by* Leonard Kress

Psalm of Marriage. Phoebe Cary. PWR

Psalm of Praise, A. Richard Baxter.

"Ye holy Angels bright." NOCV

Psalm of the Field. Tadeusz Nowak, *Polish.* CEEP, *tr. by* Leonard Kress

Psalm of Those Who Go Forth before Daylight. Carl Sandburg. OxBA

Psalm To Cheer Up. Tadeusz Nowak, *Polish.* CEEP, *tr. by* Leonard Kress

Psalm to the Creatures. Gwilym R. Jones, *Welsh.* OBVVE, *tr. by* Joseph P. Clancy

PsalmIII: "To God: to illuminate all men. Beginning with Skid Road." Allen Ginsberg. CAPP-1; ChIV-1

Psalmodist. Mani Leib, *Yiddish.* CEEP, *tr. by* David G. Roskies *and* Hillel Schwartz

Psalms. Bible, *O.T. See also* Bible, Psalms.

Psalm 1. AWP; EnlH; SCAP

("Everything they do will succeed.") (LL) ITG, *tr. by* Stephen Mitchell

(Happy Is the Man.) TrJP

Psalm 1:1–3 CTV

Psalm 2. NAAL-1; NAAL-3

("Blesst all that in Him trust.") (LL) NAAL-3

Psalm 3. OBVE

Psalm 6. OBVE

Psalm 8. AWP; NAWM-1; OBVE; PBMP

(How Glorious Is Thy Name.) TrJP

Psalm 11. OBVE

Psalm 13. NoSic; OBVE

Psalm 14. TrJP

Psalm 17. OBVE

Psalm 19. AWP; ChIV-1; EnlH; NAWM-1; OBVE; SCAP; TOF

("And there is nothing hid from the / heat thereof.") (LL) CTV

("Heavens declare the glory of, The.") CTV

Psalm 23. AWP; ChIV-1; FaBoBe; NAWM-1; NIP-4; OBCA; OBVE; PoLF; TFi; TrJP

("And I will dwell in the house of the Lord for ever.") (LL) PFE

("And your house will be my home as long as I live.") (LL) TRP

("Life: and I will dwell in the house of the Lord forever.") (LL) SAGP

("Lord is my shepherd, The; / I have everything I need.") TRP

("Lord to me a shepherd is; want therefore shall not I, The.") PFE

("Lord's my shepherd, I'll not want, The.") AH; TRP

(Psalm of David, A.) PFE

Psalm 24. AWP; TrJP

Psalm 29. AWP

Psalm 37: "Fret not thyself because of evildoers." CTV

Psalm 39.

(Lord, Make Me to Know Mine End.) TrJP

Psalm 42. AWP; TrJP

Psalm 46. AWP

Psalm 50. BrRo

Psalm 52. NoSic; OBVE

Psalm 55.

("Give ear to my prayer, O God.") AWP

("Rowzing him up; and nought shall me dismay.") (LL) OBVE, *stanzas* 1–4

("That it, half spun, death may in sunder shear.") (LL) WPE

Psalm 58. NOCV; NoSic

("Do ye indeed speak righteousness, O congregation?") NAEL-1; WPE

Psalm 59. NoSic

Psalm 62. PBWP

Psalm 72. OBVE

Psalm 73. NoSic

Psalm 74. NOCV

Psalm 77. AWP

Psalm 78. OBVE

Psalm 79.

(Heathen Are Come into Thine Inheritance.) TrJP

Psalm 84. TrJP

Psalm 90. AWP

Psalm 91. AWP

Psalm 95. AWP

Psalm 98. TrJP

Psalm 100. ITG, *tr. by* Stephen Mitchell; NOCV

("And his deep love endures forever.") (LL) ITG, *tr. by* Stephen Mitchell

("And his truth endureth to all / generations.") (LL) CTV

(O Be Joyful in the Lord, All Ye Lands.)

Old Hundredth. FaPoR *metrical vers.* by William Kethe

("Sing to the Lord, all creatures!") ITG, *tr. by* Stephen Mitchell

Psalm 102. OBVE

Psalm 103. AWP; NOCV; SCAP

Psalm 104. NAWM-1

("May all selfishness disappear from me, / and may you always shine from my heart.") (LL) EnlH

("Unnamable God, you are fathomless.")　EnlH

Psalm 107.

("Loving kindenes of the Lord / They clearely shall discerne, The.") (LL)　SCAP

("They that go down to the sea in ships.")　OxBoS

Psalm 114.　OBVE

Psalm 115.　NOCV

Psalm 118.　TrJP

Psalm 119.37.　ChIV-1

Psalm 121.　AWP; OBCA

("He will be your constant friend.") (LL)　GePo

("Now the twin-light of my eyes.")　GePo

("Thy going out, and thy income, / the Lord keeps now and aye.") (LL) OBCA

Psalm 126.

(Like unto Them That Dream.)　TrJP

Psalm 127.

("They shall not be put to shame, / When they speak with their enemies in the gate.")　TrJP

Psalm 130.　TrJP

("F[f]rom depth of[f] sin[n] and from a deep [or diepe] despair [or dispaire].")　NoSic; OBVE

("Plenteous ransom [or rannzome] shall come with him [or com with hym], I say, / And shall redeem [or redeme] all our iniquity [or iniquitie].") (LL)　NoSic; OBVE

Psalm 131.　EnlH

("Lord, my heart is not haughty, nor mine eyes lofty.")

Psalm 133.　AWP

("Beholde, how good and joyfull a thinge it is, brethren to dwell to gether in unitye.")　OBVE

("For the Lorde promised hys blessynge, and lyfe for evermore.") (LL) OBVE

Psalm 134.　NoSic

Psalm 136.　AWP

Psalm 137.　AWP; ChIV-1; NAWM-1; TrJP

("All other joys I shall contemn, / Calling to mind Jerusalem.") (LL) OAEL-1

("And without pity heare their dying grones.") (LL)　OBSP

("Blessed shall he be, that taketh thy chyldren, and throweth them agaynst the stones.") (LL)　OBVE

("By the rivers of Babel we sate.")　OAEL-1

("If I forget thee, O Jerusalem, may my right hand forget to play.") (LL)　OAEL-1

("If I make not Jerusalem the beginning of my joy.") (LL)　OAEL-1

("If that I joy before I see / thy full deliverance past.") (LL)　OAEL-1

("Jerusalem be not the ground.") (LL)　OAEL-1

("Mi tunge cleve to my chekis, if I bithenke not on thee.") (LL) OAEL-1

("On my dry palate's roof to rest, / A withered leaf, an ideal guest.") (LL)　OAEL-1

("On the flood is of Babiloyne there we saten.")　OAEL-1

("Or if I sing one cheerful air / Till thy deliverance is my song.") (LL) OAEL-1

("Or ought I do but Salem sing.") (LL)　OAEL-1

("That in the compass of my thoughts can fall.") (LL)　OAEL-1

("Upon the rivers of Babylon, there we sat and wept.") (LL)　OAEL-1

("When on Euphrates' banks we sate.")　OAEL-1

("Whenas we sat in Babylon.") (LL)　OAEL-1

Psalm 139.　OBVE, stanzas 7–10; NOCV

("And see if there be any wicked way in me, and lead me in the way everlasting.") (LL)　NoSic; WPE

("O Lord, thou hast searched me, and known me.")　NoSic; WPE

Psalm 147.

Psalm 148.　ITG, tr. by Stephen Mitchell; OBVE; TrJP

("Feather'd millions form'd for speed.") (LL)　OBVE

("Hallelujah. Praise ye the Lord from the heavens.")　TrJP

("Light that fills heaven and earth, The.") (LL)　ITG, tr. by Stephen Mitchell

Psalms.　Sir Philip Sidney

Psalm 13.　FMP

Psalms of Love.　Peter Baum, German.　AWP, tr. by Jethro Bithell

Psalter of Avram Haktani, The.　Abraham Moses Klein.

Upon the Heavenly Scarp.　PoA

"Psittachus Eois Imitatrix Ales ab Indis."　Sacheverell Sitwell.　MoBrPo

Psss, the beard is a bit too long.　Faces.　David Chapman Berry.　BXAP

Psyche.　Coleridge.　PBMP

Psyche.　Mary Tighe.

("Illumined bright now shines the splendid dome.")　NOBRP

"'Mid the thick covert of that woodland shade."　NOBRP

Psyche, Before the Tribunal of Venus.　Nathaniel Parker Willis.　APN-1

Psyche; or The Legend of Love.　Mary Tighe.　Ro　Fr. Psyche, with Other Poems, 3rd edition.

Psyche, with Other Poems, 3rd edition.　Mary Tighe.

From Psyche.　NoP-4

Psyche; or The Legend of Love.　Ro

Psyche's Dream.　Anne Lauterbach.　EOEF

Psychiatrist.　Peter De Vries.　OBAL

Psychiatrist fellow from Rye, A.　Limerick.　Stephen Cass.　PeLi

Psychic researcher's elation, A.　Limerick.　Cyril Mountjoy.　PeLi

Psychic's globe whirls its winds, The.　Jail, Flames—Jersey, 1971.　Lynda Hull.　PUP-19

Psycho.　Peter Olds.　PeNZ

Psychoanalysis.　Gavin Ewart.　NYBP

Psycholophon.　Frank Gelett Burgess.　CBNP

Psychopathology of Everyday Life, The.　William Matthews.　NIP-4

Psychotropic Squalls, The.　Will Alexander.　PT

Psychozoia, or, the Life of the Soul.　Henry More.

Contrition.　NOSC

Psyllus lies here. Procuring was his trade.　Argentarius, Greek.　GrAn, tr. by Fleur Adcock

P'u—Hua Fei Hua.　Po Chü-i, Chinese.　IMW, tr. by Duncan Mackintosh

P'u-Shen Sheng Man.　Li Ch'ing-chao, Chinese.　IMW, tr. by Duncan Mackintosh

Puberty.　Nina Cassian, Romanian.　CEEP, tr. by Brian Swann and Michael Impey

Puberty Rite Dance Song (Traditional).　Unknown, Apache Indian.　BoWoP, tr. by Willis Barnstone

Puberty Tree, The.　D. M. Thomas.　TOF

Pubescence at 39.　Vickie Sears.　GLP

Public Aid for Niagara Falls.　Morris Gilbert Bishop.　NBLV

Public Beach (Long Island Sound).　Christopher Darlington Morley.　NBLV

Public Dinner, A.　Thomas Hood.　OBCoV

Public Garden, The.　Arthur Hugh Clough.　PeLV　Fr. Dipsychus [and the Spirit].

Public Garden, The.　Robert Lowell.　OBGa; PoRA; TAP

Public house screaming. The Drunk Man.　Unknown, Aborigine.　NOBAu

Public Journal.　Phyllis McGinley.　NBLV

Public Library.　Dannie Abse.　OxBC

Public Mirror, The.　Richard Katrovas.　NAmP90

Public School No. 18: Paterson, New Jersey.　Maria Gillan.　UnSA

Public Schools.　Robert Lloyd.　NOEC　Fr. A Familiar Epistle to J. B. Esq.

Publication—is the Auction.　Emily Dickinson.　APN-2; AmPP; NAAL-1; NAAL-3; NALW; NCAP; NoP-4; PAR

Publisher went off to France, A.　Limerick.　Unknown.　PeLi

Publisher's Party.　Phyllis McGinley.　OBAL

Puck of Pook's Hill.　Rudyard Kipling.

Children's Song, The.

Old Men at Pevensey.　NoAM; PoEL-5

Runes on Weland's Sword, The.　NoAM; PoEL-5

Puck's Song.　FaBoCh; OxBChV

Puckered breasts like Leiberman's.　Grandma in the Shower.　Dale M. Kushner.　UnSA

Puck's Song.　Rudyard Kipling.　FaBoCh; OxBChV　Fr. Puck of Pook's Hill.

"Pudding and pie."　Greedy Jane.　Unknown.　OxBChV

Pudding Charms.　Charlotte Druitt Cole.　BoTP

Puddmuddle jump in and slide! (LL)　Weather.　Eve Merriam.　TLR

Puddmuddle jump in and slide!, A.　Eve Merriam.　See Weather.

Puella Parvula.　Wallace Stevens.　HCAP; LCAP-2

Puer Aeternus.　Kathleen Jessie Raine.　NYBP

Puerta Rica.　Victor Hernandez Cruz.　LoL

Puerto Rico Song.　William Carlos Williams.　NYBP

Pugilist.　Anna Wickham.　WPN

Puk-Wudjies.　Patrick Reginald Chalmers.　BoTP

Pula.　Matsemela Manaka.

Chorus: "Babylon, I did not come to you for the sake of coming."　PeSAV

Chorus: "In the name of the people."　PeSAV

Pull, The.　Sharon Olds.　PuP-17

Pull me down, ladybug.　Ladybug.　Raymond Souster.　MoCV

Pull my daisy.　Allen Ginsberg.　PoM

Pull up the stems, grass doesn't die.　Expressing My Feelings.　Meng Chiao, Chinese.　SuSp, tr. by Stephen Owen

Pulled at school / by naughty boys.　Tadeusz Rózewicz.　See Pigtail.

Pulley, The. George Herbert. AWP; ChIV-1; EBEvV; FHYEP; FMP; GeHe; HAP; HeIP-4; ImPo; InPK-6; InPS-3; NAEL-1; NOBE; NOCV; NOSC; NoP-4; OAEL-1; OBEV; OxAEP-1; PFE; SCGP; SeCP; TFi

(Gifts of God, The.) GTBS-P

("May tosse him to my breast.") (LL) FSCP

Pullin me in off the corner to wash my face an. Black Jam for Dr. Negro. Mari E. Evans. BPo; PoBA

Pulling a Pig's Tail. Dave Jeddie Smith. NAmP90

Pulling the Chain. Simon Rae. UV

Pulling up flax after the blue flowers have fallen. The Linen Industry. Michael Longley. CBLP; CIP-2; NoP-4; PBCIP; PNI

Pulling up in my car, I went into the cottage. After Five Years. Augustus Young. BIrV

Pulmonary tuberculosis. Limerick. L. G. Udall. PeLi

Pulse, The. Mark Van Doren. MoAmPo

Pulse of your revolt stilled, The. My Friendly People. Frank Mkalawile Chipasula. HBAPE

Pulsing stops where time has been, The. The Bed. Thom Gunn. EP

Pult'ney, methinks you blame my breach of word. Epistle to the Right Honourable William Pulteney, Esq. John Gay.

Pumpernickel. Philip Schultz. NAmP90

Pumpkin, The. John Greenleaf Whittier. ImGa

Pumpkin-Eater, The. Mother Goose. ReMoGo

("And there he kept her very well.") (LL) LB

Pumpkins' crooked grins. Harvest Moon. Jan Barry. CDa

Punch and Judy. Rose Fyleman. NOxBChV

'Punch,' said Judy. Punch and Judy. Rose Fyleman. NOxBChV

Punch, the Immortal Liar. Conrad Potter Aiken.

Puppet Dreams, The. MoAmPo

Punctilio. Mary Elizabeth Coleridge. OBEV

Punctual as bad luck. The Family Goldschmitt. Henri Coulette. CoAP

Punctually at Christmas the soft plush. White Christmas. William Robert Rodgers. LiTM; MoBrPo

Punica, The. Silius Italicus, Latin.

("Again she Arms prepares: One Captain may." OBCVT, tr. by Thomas Ross

Punished in the moment of love. Akiko Baba, Japanese. WPJ, tr. by Kenneth Rexroth and Ikuko Atsumi

Punishment. Seamus Heaney. FaBoPV; InPS-3; NAEL-2; NoAM; NoP-4; OxAEP-2; PBCIP; PoPoPo; SAGP

Punishment, The. Susan Bartels Ludvigson. MT

Punishment in Hell. Claudian, Latin. OBCVT, tr. by Jabez Hughes

Punishments. Rafael Alberti, Spanish. AF, tr. by Geoffrey Connell

Punkydoodle and Jollapin. Laura Elizabeth Richards. OBCA

Punting pole stuck in the reeds. Inscribed on a Painting of a Fisherman. T'ang Yin, Chinese. CoBLCP, tr. by Jonathan Chaves

Pupil. Veronica Porumbacu, Romanian. CEEP, tr. by Dorian, Marguerite and Elliott Urdang

Pupil of fever chills and bewilderment, A. Aleksey Petrovich Tsvetkov, Russian. TCRP, tr. by Albert C. Todd

Puppet, The. Chuck Brickley. HA

Puppet Dreams, The. Conrad Potter Aiken. MoAmPo Fr. Punch, the Immortal Liar.

Puppet king, The. Biodrama. Miroslav Holub, Czech. CBNP, tr. by Ewald Osers

Puppet of the Wolf, The. Margaret Atwood. NoAM

Puppets. Patricia K. Page. MoCV

Puppets on stage let people do what they will. Tune: "Partridge Sky"— Puppet Theater. Ku T'ai-ch'ing, Chinese. SuSp, tr. by Irving Y. Lo

Puppets which perform before the curtains, The. Hsü Wei. Fr. Inscribed on Paintings for the People of Hangchow. CoBLCP, tr. by Jonathan Chaves

Puppy and I. A. A. Milne. BoTP

Puppy Luppy, our super sleek black Lab. Wakinyan. Adrian C. Louis. NAmP90

Purcell in many victories of his. Bounty. Josephine Miles. NoAM

Purdah, 1. Imtiaz Dharker. OMIP

Pure air trembles, O pitiless God, The. Noon. Robinson Jeffers. MoAmPo

Pure amnesia of her face, The. August, Los Angeles, Lullaby. Carol Muske. PBCAP

Pure and worthy Mrs. Stowe, The. Harriet Beecher Stowe. Dorothy Parker. NALW Fr. A Pig's-Eye View of Literature.

Pure as a pane of ice. It's a gift. (LL) Love Letter. Sylvia Plath. LW; NOBA

Pure blood domestic, guaranteed. The Prize Cat. Edwin John Pratt. MoP

Pure contralto sings in the organloft, The. Song of Myself. Walt Whitman. FaBoA; TTTS Fr. Song of Myself. AmPP; MoAmPo; NAAL-3; NOBA; OxBA

Pure Death. Robert Graves. AWP; GTBS-P; LBC

Pure Dust. Maria Luisa Spaziani, Italian. NeIt, tr. by Beverly Allen

Pure gold, bright sky about the sun. The Good Man. Unknown, Irish. TIRV, tr. by Robin Flower

Pure Hypothesis, A. May Kendall. VWP

Pure in Heart Shall See God, The. Frances Ellen Watkins Harper. PWR

Pure is the body on the Earth. He Singeth in the Underworld. Unknown. AWP Fr. Book of the Dead.

Pure nothing, in the middle of the day. (LL) Daystar. Rita Dove. LCAP-2; NAAAL; NIP-2; OxWW

Pure poetry of paranoia was his as he emerged, The. The Moment of Truth. David Lehman. WWSi

Pure products of America, The. To Elsie. William Carlos Williams. CMoP; InPS-3; MeMAP; NAAL-2; NOBA; OxBA; PoE; PoPoPo

Pure Simple Love. Aurelian Townshend. SeCP

Pure Spirit of the always-faithful God. Hymn for Pentecost. James Clarence Mangan. TIRV

Pure stream, in whose transparent wave. To Leven Water. Tobias Smollett. OBEV

Pure sun dazzled, The. The Glazier. Stéphane Mallarmé, French. OBVE, tr. by Keith Bosley

Pure? What does it mean? Fever 103°. Sylvia Plath. CMoP; ColAP; FaBoWP; NOBA; NoAM; VCAP; VGW

Pure woman is to man a crown. The Virtuous Wife. Süsskind von Trimberg, Middle High German. TrJP

Purer than purest pure. E. E. Cummings. AH

Purest soul that e'er was sent, The. Another [Epitaph on the Lady Mary Villiers]. Thomas Carew. BeJo; CaPo; CavPo

Purgatory. W. B. Yeats. CMoP

Purge, The. Michael Hartnett.

"Hartnett, the poet, might as well be dead." BiHa, tr. by Gabriel Fitzmaurice

Puriri moth's wing, A. Poem. Jan Kemp. PeNZ

Purist, The. Ogden Nash. KaS; MoAmPo; NBLV; OBCA

Puritan, The. Karl Shapiro. MoAmPo

Puritan Lady, A. Lizette Woodworth Reese. MoAmPo

Puritan Sonnet. Elinor Wylie. See Puritan Sonnet, IV.

Puritan Sonnet, IV. Elinor Wylie. MoAmPo Fr. Wild Peaches. ColAP; FaBoWP; LiTM; LoP; NAAL-2; NALW; OxBA; WPE

(Puritan Sonnet.) SAGP

Puritans. Elaine Equi. PmAP

Purity. Avigdor Hame'iri, Hebrew. MHP, tr. by Ruth Finer Mintz

Purity of the moonlight, The. Unknown, Japanese. OHPJ, tr. by Kenneth Rexroth

Purple. Lullaby "Purple." Eve Merriam. NOxBChV

Purple blot against the dead white door, A. Monsieur Qui Passe. Charlotte Mew. CPO

Purple butterflies / fly at night through my dreams. Akiko Yosano, Japanese. WPJ, tr. by Kenneth Rexroth and Ikuko Atsumi

Purple Clover. Emily Dickinson. MoAmPo

Purple Cow, The. Frank Gelett Burgess. CBNP; CTV; FPC; NBLV; NTCP; OBAL; OBCA; OBCoV; PoLF; TFi; TLR

Purple headland over yonder. Afternoon. Louisa S. Guggenberger. NOBVV

Purple headland over yonder. Afternoon. Louisa Sarah Bevington. PEW

Purple horses with orange manes. Merry-Go-Round. Rachel Lyman Field. CTV

Purple Indians pas de bourrée. Lord Fluting Dreams of America on the Eve of His Departure from Liverpool. Paul Zimmer. VGW

Purple Island, The. Phineas Fletcher.

"With her, her sister went, a warlike maid." NOSC

Purple orphan was alone, The. (LL) Purple William or The Liar's Doom. A. E. Housman. CBNP; NOxBChV

Purple Peach Tree, The. Su Tung-p'o, Chinese. OHPC, tr. by Kenneth Rexroth

Purple Precincts touch Longevity Mountain, The. I Was Received in an Early Audience at Heaven-Gate and Then at Noon I Was Summoned to the Yu-shun Gate. In the Evening I Withdrew, and Improvised This Poem. Yang Shih-ch'i, Chinese. CoBLCP, tr. by Jonathan Chaves

Purple Valleys, The. Madison Cawein. APN-2

Purple, White and Green, The. L. E. Morgan-Browne. BrRo

Purple William or The Liar's Doom. A. E. Housman. CBNP; NOxBChV

Purple, yellow, red and green. Unknown. OxNR

Purpose. Desmond O'Grady. PBCIP

Purpose of Fable-writing, The. Phaedrus, Latin. AWP, tr. by Christopher Smart

"Purr," says the cat. (LL) Dame Trot and her cat. Mother Goose. BoTP; CTAV; OxNR; ReMoGo

Purse-Seine, The. Robinson Jeffers. CMoP; HAP; NOBA; NoAM; OxBA; PaTW; Poetr; WeW-3

   ("Decay, and life's end is death.") (LL) NoP-4

   ("Our sardine fishermen work at night in the dark of the moon.") NoP-4

Pursuing beauty, men descry. Song. Thomas Southerne. NOSC

Pursuit. Hilda Doolittle. WPE

Pursuit. Julian Tuwim, *Polish*. TrJP, *tr.* by Watson Kirkconnell

Pursuit[e], The. Henry Vaughan. GeHe; NOSC; SeCP; TrCP

Pursuit. Robert Penn Warren. FuPo; HAP; MoAmPo; TwCP

Pursuit from Under. James Dickey. HAP

Pursuit of Love. John Webster *and* William Rowley. *See* Art Thou Gone in Haste?

Push about the brisk bowl, 'twill enliven the heart. The Ass. Moses Mendes. *Fr.* The Chaplet. TrJP

Push, push the heavy door. Skeleton House. Laurence Smith. OTCP

Pushan, God of golden day. Pushan, God of Pasture. *Unknown.* AWP *Fr.* Vedic Hymns.

Pushan, God of Pasture, *fr.* Rig Veda. *Unknown.* AWP *Fr.* Vedic Hymns.

Pushing. Christopher Gilbert. LTA; SoSe-8

Pushing. Michael McClintock. HA

Pushing Forty. Alison Fell. FaBoTC

Pushing the seed into the ground. Listening to a White Man Play the Blues. Silvia Curbelo. MoLi

Pushing young man in Patchogue, A. Limerick. Morris Gilbert Bishop. PeLi

Pushkin. "Anna Akhmatova," *Russian.* TCRP, *tr.* by Daniel Weissbort

Puss and the Boots, The. Henry Duff Traill.

   "Put case I circumvent and kill him: good." BXAP

Puss came dancing out of a barn. *Unknown.* OxNR

Pussicat, wussicat, with a white foot. *Unknown.* OxNR

Pussy. *Unknown.* ACTP

Pussy. *Unknown.* PeP

Pussy-Cat and Puppy-Dog. Lilian McCrea. BoTP

Pussy cat ate the dumplings. Pussycat. Mother Goose. OxNR; ReMoGo

Pussy-cat by [or beside] the fire. Mother Goose. *See* By the Fire.

Pussy-cat Mew jumped over a coal. *Unknown.* ReMoGo

Pussy Cat Mole. *Unknown.* OxNR

Pussy cat, Pussy cat. Christina Rossetti. CTV

Pussy-Cat, Pussy-Cat,/ where have you been? Mother Goose. BoTP; FaBoBe; LB; OxNR; ReMoGo

Pussy-cat said: "Mew, mew, mew," and Robin flew away. Mother Goose. *See* Catch.

Pussy cat sits by the fire. *Unknown.* CTAV

Pussy has a whiskered face. Christina Rossetti. CTV

Pussy said Meow, and Robin flew [or jumped] away. (LL) Catch. Mother Goose. BoTP; LB; OxNR

Pussy sits beside the fire. By the Fire. Mother Goose. OxNR; ReMoGo

Pussycat. Mother Goose. OxNR; ReMoGo

Pussycat sits on a chair. Edward Newman Horn. PC

Put a Woman into the Memory Box. Brigitte Frase. LoHo

Put another nickel in. Blue Gene. Lawson Fusao Inada. MoNo

Put aside the papers, your Honor. The Law. Aleksandar Ristovic, *Serbo-Croatian*. HSix, *tr.* by Charles Simic

Put case I circumvent and kill him: good. Henry Duff Traill. BXAP *Fr.* The Puss and the Boots.

Put Down. Léon Damas, *French*. TTY, *tr.* by Seth L. Wolitz

Put down your weapons. Haka: The Blossoming. Pita Sharples, *Maori*. PeNZ, *tr.* by Pita Sharples

Put 'em up solid, they won't come down! Post-Rail Song. *Unknown.* AS

Put Forth, O God, Thy Spirit's Might. Howard Chandler Robbins. AH

Put forth thy leaf, thou lofty plane. Arthur Hugh Clough. EBEV; EnVR

Put forward your best foot! (LL) Respectability. Robert Browning. CBJP; EnLoPo

Put Hannibal i' th' scale. Hannibal ("Put Hannibal i' th' scale"). Juvenal. OBVE, *tr.* by Henry Vaughan *Fr.* Satires.

Put in something else like page bonded to a neutrality my brother. Remembered Sequel. Hannah Weiner. FTOS

Put it on record. Identity Card. Mahmoud Darwish, *Arabic*. VCWP, *tr.* by Denys Johnson-Davies

Put me into the breach with every rolling stone. Yehuda Karni, *Hebrew*. MHP, *tr.* by Ruth Finer Mintz

Put my Black father on the penny. Monument in Black. Vanessa Howard. MBE

Put off an important decision. 7th Light Poem: For John Cage—17 June 1962. Jackson Mac Low. FTOS

Put Off Constricting Day. Mary Stanley. PeNZ

Put off the deference that this sea compels. Beach Talk. Norman MacCaig. PoA

Put off Thy robe of purple, then go on. Good Friday: Rex Tragicus, or, Christ Going to His Cross[e]. Robert Herrick. NOSC

Put on yo' red silk stockings. Red Silk Stockings. Langston Hughes. NAAAL

Put on your silks, and piece by piece. To His Mistresses. Robert Herrick. CaPo

Put out my hand and touched the face of God. (LL) High Flight. John Gillespie Magee Jr. SAGP

Put out the lights and stop the clocks. Madrid—1937. Langston Hughes. AF

Put out to sea, if wine thou wouldest make. Sent from Egypt with a Fair Robe of Tissue to a Sicilian Vinedresser. Thomas Sturge Moore. OBEV

Put soft paws here. (LL) The Hair. May Swenson. DeD

Put the sun a thought below his prime. Afternoon in the Garden. Ethel Louisa Mason Anderson. NOBAu

Put the word to my lips. Put Your Word to My Lips. Rachel Korn, *Yiddish*. CEEP, *tr.* by Seymour Mayne *and* Rivka Augenfeld

Put things in their place. The Sky Is Blue. David Ignatow. IFJA; NNaP

Put this in your notebooks. The Last Class. Ellen Bryant Voigt. CrSp; MT

Put to sleep my mother's curse? (LL) The Welsh Marches. A. E. Housman. FaBoTw; SCGP

Put u red-eye in. Ron Welburn. NBV

Put up a windmill on. Midwest, Midcentury. Sharyn Jeanne Skeeter. ISC

Put up thy gold: go on,—here's gold,—go on. Shakespeare. OxAEP-1 *Fr.* Timon of Athens.

Put your finger in Foxy's hole. *Unknown.* LB; OxNR

Put your hand on my heart, say that you love me as. A Betrothal. Edith Jay Scovell. GBL

Put your head, darling, darling, darling. Dear Black Head. *Unknown, Gaelic*. BIrV, *tr.* by Sir Samuel Ferguson

Put your / self out. Chasm. A. R. Ammons. OBAL

Put Your Word to My Lips. Rachel Korn, *Yiddish*. CEEP, *tr.* by Seymour Mayne *and* Rivka Augenfeld

Putrefaction is the end. Robert Herrick. CavPo; PFE

Putting an End to the War Stories. Larry Moffi. CDa

Putting away wedding gifts. The Quickness of Fear. Beverly Acuff Momoi. LoHo

Putting in a Word. Rosanne Wasserman. BAP-94

Putting in the Seed. Robert Frost. NoAM; OxBA

Putting On My Shoes I Hear the Floor Cry Out beneath Me. Michael Heffernan. BXAP

Putting On Nightgown. *Unknown.* OxNR

Putting out the candles. My Father after Work. Gary Gildner. Poetsp

Putting soup in his mouth with a spoon. (LL) Soup. Carl Sandburg. NOBA; NOBE; OBCA

Putting the World to Bed. Esther W. Buxton. NOxBChV

Putting to Sea. Louise Bogan. LiTM; PoA

Putting up new curtains. Curtains. Ruth Stone. NAmP90

Puva, puva, puva. Lullaby. *Unknown, Hopi*. TTTS, *tr.* by Natalie Curtis

Puzzle faces in the dying elms. 'Mystery Boy' Looks for Kin in Nashville. Robert Earl Hayden. LCAP-2; NoAM; NoP-4; PoE

Puzzled. Carolyn Wells. OBCA

Pygmalion and the Statue. Ovid, *Latin*.

Pygmalion off'ring, first, approach'd the Shrine. OBCVT, *tr.* by John Dryden

Pygmalion off'ring, first, approach'd the Shrine. Ovid. OBCVT, *tr.* by John Dryden *Fr.* Pygmalion and the Statue.

Pygmalion seeing just to spend their times. Ovid. OAEL-1, *tr.* by George Sandys *Fr.* Metamorphoses.

Pygmalion's Statue Comes to Life. Ovid. OAEL-1, *tr.* by Arthur Golding *Fr.* Metamorphoses.

"Pygmies Are Pygmies Still, Though Percht on Alps" (quote *fr.* Edward Young) Gwendolyn Brooks. ColAP *Fr.* Notes from the Childhood and the Girlhood. LCAP-2

Pylon for some incomplete gateway. The Monadnock. John Gould Fletcher. PoA

Pylons, The. Stephen Spender. AWP; NoAM

Pyramid of Khufu, The. Khaled Mattawa. IFJA

Pyramids, The. Nick Piombino. FTOS

Pyramus and Thisbe. Donne. FMP

Pyrargyrite Metal, 9. Cecília Meireles, *Portuguese*. PBWP, *tr.* by James Merrill

Pyrography. John Ashbery. PoM; VCAP

Pyroxenes, The. James Merrill. PuP-16

Pyrrha, what slender well-shap'd beau. Horace. *See* 1.5.

Pyrrha! your smiles are gleams of sun. Walter Savage Landor. CBLP

Pythagoras planned it. Why did the people stare? The Statues. W. B. Yeats. NoAM; OAEL-2; WeW-3

Pythagoric letter, two ways spread, The. Thomas Stanley. NOSC

Pythia. Stefan Aug. Doinas, *Romanian.* CEEP, *tr. by* Stavros Deligiorgis

Python I should not advise, A. Hilaire Belloc. OxBChV; PeP

Pythoness, The. Kathleen Jessie Raine. MoBrPo

Q

Q-Boat, The. H. E. Wilkes. NSI

Q:dwo / we know of anything which can. E. E. Cummings. OBAL

Qantas Bags. Laurie Duggan. BMAP

Qua Cursum Ventus. Arthur Hugh Clough. EBVVPR; OBEV

Quack, quack, quack! Dumpy Ducky. Lucy Larcom. OBCA

Quaco Sam. *Unknown.* FaBoVe

Quaco Sam. *Unknown.* PBCV

Quadratic function, ambitious, A. Limerick. Leo Moser. PeLi

Quadroon mermaids, Afro angels, black saints. A Ballad of Remembrance. Robert Earl Hayden. BPo; NAAAL; PoBA

Quaerè. George Farewell. NOEC; OBCoV

Quail and rabbit hunters with tawny hounds. Hunters in the Snow: Brueghel. Joseph Langland. *LiTM*

Quail in Autumn. William Jay Smith. Poetsp

Quail Sky. Li Ch'ing-chao, *Chinese.* OHPC, *tr. by* Kenneth Rexroth

Quaint Mazes. Geoffrey Hill. NoAM *Fr.* An Apology for the Revival of Christian Architecture in England.

Quake Theory. Sharon Olds. PBCAP

Quaker Graveyard in Nantucket, The. Robert Lowell. CMoP; ColAP; HAP; LiTM; MoP; NAAL-2; NOBA; NoAM; NoP-4; OxBA; OxBoS; PeECV; Poetr; TAP; UnPo; VCAP

Quaker Hill. Hart Crane. LiTM *Fr.* The Bridge. NAAL-2

Quaker's stiffness, with a tradesman's grin, A. A Character. Clara Reeve. ECWP

Quaker's wife got up to bake, The. *Unknown.* OxNR

Quaker's Wooing, The. *Unknown.* AS

Quality, The. Philip Schultz. NAmP90

Quality of mercy is not strained, The. Mercy. Shakespeare. EBEvV; ImPo *Fr.* The Merchant of Venice.

QUALITY OF NIGHT THAT YOU HATE MOST IS ITS BLACK, THE. Three Movements and a Coda. Imamu Amiri Baraka. NAAAL

Quality of Sprawl, The. Les A. Murray. NoP-4

Quality of the dirt, the fealty changing under my foot, The. (LL) Certain things here are quietly American. Derek Walcott. NAEL-2; NoP-4

Quality of these trees, green height; of the sky, shining; of water, The. Shine, Republic. Robinson Jeffers. FaBoPV

Quan ben m'albir e mon ric pensamen. Ezra Pound. *See* Canto 36.

Quand on n'a pas ce que l'on aime, il faut aimer ce que l'on a–. Stevie Smith. FaBoEE

Quangle Wangle's Hat, The. Edward Lear. CBNP; EBEV; FPC; PeVV; OTCP

Quantum. Martin Johnston. CBAP

Quantum Est Quod Desit. Thomas Moore. *See* Did Not.

Quarrel, The. Conrad Potter Aiken. MoAmPo

Quarrel, The. Diane Di Prima. NMM-2

Quarrel, The. Federico García Lorca, *Spanish.* AF, *tr. by* Robert Bly

Quarrel, The. Josephine D. Henderson Heard. CBWP-4

Quarrel. Grace Paley. IFJA

Quarrel of the Six Beasts, The. *Unknown, Vietnamese.* AVP, *tr. by* Huỳnh Sanh Thông

Quarrel of the sparrows in the eaves, The. The Sorrow of Love. W. B. Yeats. MoBrPo; NOBVV; NoAM; OAEL-2; PoEL-5

Quarrel with Fortune, A. Benjamin Colman. SCAP

Quarreling person is none other than a person who had not been quarreling, A. Poem No. III. Sang Yi. PFTM

Quarrelling. Lyall Tao Tschung Yu. FP

Quarrels have long been in vogue among sages. A Song from the Coptic. James Clarence Mangan. NOIV

Quarrelsome Bishop, A. Walter Savage Landor. FaBoEE

Quarries in Syracuse. Louis Golding. TrJP

Quarrle, The. Mother Goose. ReMoGo

Quarry, The. Vassar Miller. WPE

Quarry Pool, The. Denise Levertov. VGW

Quarry/Rock. Paul Mariah. GLP

Quarter century ago, A. Wilberforce. Josephine D. Henderson Heard. CBWP-4

Quarter less four, / Half twain. *Unknown.* AmFP

Quarter of an hour to wait, A. Underground. May Kendall. VWP

Quartermaster of the spring, The. First Rondeau: After a French Poet of the Fourteenth Century. Johann Nikolaus Götz, *German.* GePo, *tr. by* George C. Schoolfield

Quartet. Charles Borkhuis. PT

Quartet. Sherley Anne Williams. WeT

Quartier Libre. Jacques Prévert, *French.* CLPP, *tr. by* Lawrence Ferlinghetti

Quarto Centennial, The. Josephine D. Henderson Heard. CBWP-4

Quartz Pebble, The. Vasco [*or* Vasko] Popa, *Serbo-Croatian.*

Quartz Pebble, The. Vasco [*or* Vasko] Popa. PoSu, *tr. by* Anne Pennington *Fr.* The Quartz Pebble.

  Adventure of the Quartz Pebble, The. PoSu, *tr. by* Anne Pennington (Adventure of the Pebble.) CEEP, *tr. by* Charles Simic

  ("Fed up with the circle.") CEEP, *tr. by* Charles Simic

  ("Hid in its own shadow.") (LL) CEEP, *tr. by* Charles Simic

  Dream of the Quartz Pebble, The. PoSu, *tr. by* Anne Pennington (Dream of the Pebble.) CEEP, *tr. by* Charles Simic

  ("Hand springs out of the earth, A.") CEEP, *tr. by* Charles Simic

Quartz Tractate. Brenda Hillman. WeT

Quasi Quasi. . . as If Repeated. Glenda George. NBrP

Quatrain: "Above the creek dallies a bright moon." Yüan Hao-wen, *Chinese.* SuSp, *tr. by* Irving Y. Lo

Quatrain: "At this remote village, I have no neighbors." Chang Yü, *Chinese.* CoBLCP, *tr. by* Jonathan Chaves

Quatrain: "Before you praise Spring's advent note." Tu Fu, *Chinese.* TAL, *tr. by* Robert Payne

Quatrain: "Beyond the gate the cormorant had gone and not returned." Tu Fu, *Chinese.* SuSp, *tr. by* Jerome P. Seaton

Quatrain: "Birds the more white, against green stream." Tu Fu, *Chinese.* SuSp, *tr. by* Jerome P. Seaton

Quatrain: "I cry:/ but you want comforting." Jelaluddin Rumi, *Persian.* ArPe, *tr. by* Omar S. Pound

Quatrain: "I lounge on the jetty in the fragrance of catalpa." Tu Fu, *Chinese.* SuSp, *tr. by* Jerome Seaton

Quatrain: "Late sun, the stream and the hills; the beauty." Tu Fu, *Chinese.* SuSp, *tr. by* Jerome Seaton

Quatrain: "My bloodstream chokes on gall and spleen." Barend Toerien, *Afrikaans.* PeSA, *tr. by* the author

Quatrain: "Sarmèd, whom they intoxicated from the cup of love." Sarmèd the Yahud, *Persian.* TrJP, *tr. by* David Shea

Quatrain: "This existence has, without the azure sphere, no reality." Sarmèd the Yahud, *Persian.* TrJP, *tr. by* David Shea

Quatrain: "With you away—despair!" Rudaki, *Persian.* ArPe, *tr. by* Omar S. Pound

Quatrain at Chen-chou. Wang Shih-chieng, *Chinese.* CoBLCP, *tr. by* Jonathan Chaves

Quatrain without Sparrows, Helpful Bells or Hope. Thomas McCarthy. PBCIP

Quatrains. Ralph Waldo Emerson.

  Fate. NoP-4

  Fate ("Her planted eye to-day controls"). APN-1

  Gardener. OxBA

  Memory. APN-1

  Orator. OxBA

  Poet ("To clothe the fiery thought"). OxBA; OxBSP; Spl

  Self-Reliance. APN-1

  Suum Cuique ("Wilt thou seal up the avenues of ill?"). APN-1

Quatrains. Salah Jahin, *Arabic.* TTY, *tr. by* Samir M. Zoghby

Quatrains. Omar Khayyám. *Fr.* The Rubáiyát of Omar Khayyám [of Naishápúr]. AWP; EBVV; FaBoBe; FaPoR; HAP; NAEL-2; PoEL-5

Quavering cry. Screech-owl?, A. Robert Earl Hayden. *See* Night, Death, Mississippi.

Quavering cry. Screech-owl? A. Night, Death, Mississippi. Robert Earl Hayden. LCAP-2; VCAP; VGW

Quay recedes, The. Hurrah! Ahead we go! The Colonel's Soliloquy. Thomas Hardy. OBWP

Quebec. Henrietta Cordelia Ray. CBWP-3

Quebec Farmhouse. John Glassco. NOBC

Queen, The. Kenneth Pitchford. NYBP

Queen, The. Paul Zimmer. CMAP

Queen and huntress, chaste and fair. Hymn to Diana. Ben Jonson. AWP; CH; EBEvV; GTBS-P; HAP; InPS-3; NAEL-1; NOBE; NOSC; NoP-4; OAEL-1; OBEV; PoE; PoEL-2; PoRA; SCGP; SeCP; TFi *Fr.* Cynthia's Revels.

Queen Anne's Lace. June Jordan. TAP

Queen-Anne's-Lace. William Carlos Williams. AmPP; MeMAP; MoAmPo; NAAL-2; NOBA; NoAM; TAP

  ("Or nothing.") (LL) NoP-4

  (Queen-Ann's-Lace.) NoP-4

Queen Anne's Musicians. Thomas Hennell. FaBoTw

Queen-Ann's-Lace. William Carlos Williams. *See* Queen-Anne's-Lace.

Queen Bee, The. Mary K. Robinson. BoTP; CTAV

Queen Bess was Harry's daughter. Stand forward partners all! The Looking Glass. Rudyard Kipling. FaBoTw; NTP; OBMV

Queen Caroline. *Unknown. See* On Queen Caroline.

Queen Catharine; or, The Ruines of Love. Catherine Trotter.
Epilogue: "What Epilogues are made, for who can tell." KTR

Queen Catherine. Mary Pix.
"Work on my brain, help every faculty." KTR, *act* I

Queen Eleanor's Confession. *Unknown.* ESPB

Queen is gone a-hunting in the royal wood, The. A-Hunting. Jennie Dunbar. BoTP

Queen is taking a drive today, The. The Queen's Last Ride. Ella Wheeler Wilcox. BLPA

Queen Jane sat at her window one day. *Unknown. See* The King's Dochter Lady Jean.

Queen Jane was [*or* lay] in labor [*or* labour]. The Death of Queen Jane. *Unknown.* AmFP; ESPB

Queen Jeanie, Queen Jeanie, travel'd six weeks and more. *Unknown. See* The Death of Queen Jane.

Queen Katherine to Owen Tudor. Michael Drayton. NoSic *Fr.* England's Heroical Epistles.

Queen Mother to New Queen. Robert Graves. OBSV

Queen Nefertiti. *Unknown.* OTCP; TLR

Queen next morning fried, The. (LL) King Arthur. Mother Goose. LB; NTP; OxNR

Queen of all Queens, oh! Wonder of the loveliness of women. Hymn to the Virgin Mary. Conor O'Riordan, *Irish.* TIRV, *tr. by* Eleanor Hull

Queen of Aragon, The. William Habington.
Pretty Sport. NOBE

Queen of black-earth Egypt, divine Isis. Philip of Thessalonica, *Greek.* GrAn, *tr. by* Edwin Morgan

Queen of Corinth, The. John Fletcher *and others.*
Weep No More. CH; OBEV; OxAEP-1

Queen of Elfan's [*or* Elfland's] Nourice [*or* Nourrice], The. *Unknown.* ESPB
"I heard a cow low, a bonnie cow low." FaBoCh

Queen of fragrance, lovely rose. The Rose-Bud. William Broome. OBEV

Queen of Hearts, The. Christina Rossetti. CBLP; PeVV
("Misled me to my ruin.") (LL) CBLP

Queen of Hearts, The. The Tarts. Mother Goose. FaBoBe; LB; OxNR; ReMoGo

Queen of Hearts, The. *Unknown.* ACTP

Queen of Heaven Mausoleum. Dennis Schmitz. LCAP-2

Queen of Lydia, The. Charles Hubert Sisson. OxBC

Queen of martials, The. The Shield of Achilles. Homer. NOSC, *tr. by* George Chapman *Fr.* The Iliad.

Queen of Paphos, Erycine, The. *Unknown.* GBL

Queen of Scotland, The. *Unknown.* ESPB

Queen of the Blues. Gwendolyn Brooks. NALW; SeSe

Queen of the Ebony Isles. Colleen J. McElroy. NMM-2

Queen of the mountains far and near. Horace. *See* 3.22: Pine Tree for Diana, The ("Montium custos nemorumque").

Queen of the River. Elizabeth Nannestad. PeNZ

Queen of the silver bow!—by thy pale beam. To the Moon. Charlotte Smith. BWW; Son

Queen, Queen Caroline. *Unknown.* TLR

Queen Sabbath. Hayyim Nahman Bialik, *Hebrew.* TrJP, *tr. by* Jessie Sampter

Queen she kept high festival in Windsor's lordly hall, The. The Royal Banquet. William Edmonstoune Aytoun *and* Sir Theodore Martin. OBCoV

Queen she sent to look for me, The. Grenadier. A. E. Housman. OBMV; OBWP

Queen Virtue's court, which some call Stella's face. Sonnet 9. Sir Philip Sidney. NAEL-1 *Fr.* Astrophil and Stella. AAS; SiPS

Queen was beloved by a jester, A. The Cap and Bells. W. B. Yeats. MoBrPo; NoAM

Queen whom sense of Honor cou'd not move, The. Virgil. OBCVT, *tr. by* John Dryden *Fr.* Fame.

Queen Yang-Se-Fu / Has seventy great castles. Yang-Se-Fu. "Yehoash," *Yiddish.* TrJP, *tr. by* Isidore Goldstick

Queene *Vertues* court, which some call *Stellas* face. Sir Philip Sidney. *See* Sonnet 9: "Queen Virtue's court, which some call Stella's face."

Queenie. Mary Weston Fordham. CBWP-2

Queenie was a blonde, and her age stood still. Joseph Moncure March. OBCoV *Fr.* The Wild Party.

Queens, The. Robert Fitzgerald. NYBP

Queens. John Millington Synge. GBL; MoBrPo; OBMV; PeVV

Queen's After-Dinner Speech, The. William Percy French. OBCoV

Queen's Dream, The. *Unknown.* PeVV

Queen's English, The. Tony Harrison. DiPo

Queen's Last Ride, The. Ella Wheeler Wilcox. BLPA

Queen's Marie, The. *Unknown.* OBEV

Queens of Hell had lissome necks to crane, The. The Tall Girl. John Crowe Ransom. Son

Queen's Wake, The. James Hogg.
Kilmeny. OBEV; OxAEP-2
Witch of Fife, The. Ro

Queer, The. Henry Vaughan. PoEL-2

Queer are the ways of a man I know. The Phantom Horsewoman. Thomas Hardy. CMoP; NOBE; PoEL-5

Queer Thing, A. Nancy Keesing. NOBAu

Queer thing about those waters: there are no, A. Across the Bay. Donald Davie. CABP; NoAM

Queer Things. Emanuel Carnevali. SPE

Queer, what a dim dark smudge you have disappeared into! (LL) The Mosquito Knows. D. H. Lawrence. FaBoEE; OxBTC; RB

Quentin Durward. Sir Walter Scott.
Serenade, A: "Ah! County Guy, the hour is nigh." GTBS-P (Song.) CH

Query. Ebon Dooley. PoBA

Query. Michael McTurk. PBCV

Quesada. Christian Karlson Stead.
"All over the plain of the world lovers are being hurt." PeNZ
"Odysseus under wet snapping sheets." PeNZ
"That the balls of the lover are not larger than the balls of the priest." PeNZ

Quest, The. W. H. Auden.
Door, The. Son
Poem: "He watched with all his organs of concern." PoA

Quest, The. Denise Levertov. LW

Quest. Naomi Long Madgett. BPo

Quest, The. Sharon Olds. NAmP90

Quest, The. James Wright. NYBP

Quest of Silence, The. Christopher John Brennan.
"Fire in the heavens, and fire along the hills." CBAP; NOBAu

Quest of the Ideal, The. Henrietta Cordelia Ray. CBWP-3

Quest of the Sancgreall, The. Thomas Westwood.
"Motionless sat the shadow at the helm." PeVV

Quest of the Sangraal, The. Robert Stephen Hawker.
"Land is lonely now, The: Anathema." EBVV

Questing-for-Spring Arbor. Huang Ching-jen, *Chinese.* SuSp, *tr. by* Chang Yin-nan *and* Lewis C. Walmsley

Question, The. Robert Duncan. NeAP

Question, The. Wilfrid Wilson Gibson. NSI

Question, The. Josephine D. Henderson Heard. CBWP-4

Question, The. Tony Hoagland. EC2

Question. Langston Hughes. APSN

Question, The ("I dream'd that, as I wander'd by the way"). Shelley. CH; LaPo; OBEV
(Dream of the Unknown, The.) GTBS-P
("I dreamed [*or* dream'd] that, as I wandered by the way.") LaPo
("That I might there present it!—Oh! To whom?") (LL) LaPo

Question, The. Karla Kuskin. NTCP; PiM

Question, The. Frank Templeton Prince. BoLoP; GTBS-P; PeSA

Question, The. Muriel Rukeyser. WPOW

Question, The. Shelley. CH; OBEV
(Dream of the Unknown, The.) GTBS-P

Question. Edith Södergran, *German.* WPoS, *tr. by* David McDuff

Question. Martin Sorescu, *Rumanian.* CBNP, *tr. by* Michael Hamburger

Question. May Swenson. BLT; LiTM; PFE; SAGP; VGW
("With cloud for shift / how will I hide?") (LL) BLT

Question, A. John Millington Synge. MoBrPo; NOIV; OBMV; OxBTC; SAGP

Question, The ("To ask the hard question is simple"). W. H. Auden. OxAEP-2

Question, The. Frederick Goddard Tuckerman. APN-2; ColAP

Question, A. *Unknown.* NOSC

Question, The. Charles Kenneth Williams. NoP-4

Question Addressed to Liu Shih-chiu, A. Po Chü-i, *Chinese.* CoBCP, *tr. by* Burton Watson

Question and Answer, The. Thomas Beedome. NOSC

Question and Answer. Langston Hughes. BPo

Question and Answer. Kathleen Jessie Raine. MoBrPo

Question Answered, The [or A]. William Blake. FaBoEE; GBL; OxBM *Fr.* Several Questions Answered.

(*From* Several Questions Answered.) ITG

Question in a Field. Louise Bogan. NYBP

Question is: how does one hold an apple, The. The Gesture. George Oppen. NNaP *Fr.* Five Poems about Poetry.

Question keeps reflecting on itself: when marriage comes to nothing, The. The Marriage of True Minds. Edward Foster. PT

Question mark surrounds a human life, The. No More Anxiety. Vũ Hoàng Chu'o'ng, *Vietnamese.* AVP, *tr.* by Huỳnh Sanh Thông

Question me again. (LL) Casualty. Seamus Heaney. FaBoPV; NAEL-2; PBCIP; PoE

Question not, but live and labor. Adam Lindsay Gordon. PoToHe

("Kindness in another's trouble, / Courage in our own.") (LL) CTV

Question of Climate, A. Audre Lorde. NoAM

Question of Covenants, A. Gerald Dawe. PNI

Question of Form and Content, A. Jon Stallworthy. OxBC

Question of Libel, A. Alexander Pope. *Fr.* The First Satire of the Second Book of Horace [Imitated]. OAEL-1

Question of Time, The. William Peskett. PNI

Question the beauty of the earth. Saint Augustine. Joseph Mary Plunkett. TIRV

Question then, to state it first, The. Samuel Butler. NOBL *Fr.* Hudibras.

Question Time. Jack Lindsay. NOBAu

Question Time. Thomas McCarthy. CIP-2

Question to Life. Patrick Kavanagh. MoBrPo

Question to Lisetta, The. Matthew Prior. OBEV

Question was an academic one, The. Tomorrows. James Merrill. OBAL

Questioner Who Sits So Sly, The. W. H. Auden. OxAEP-2

Questioning. Henrietta Cordelia Ray. CBWP-3

Questionnaire. Susan Saxe. GLP

Questionnaire of Sleeplessness. Miodrag Pavlovic, *Serbo-Croatian.* HSix, *tr.* by Charles Simic

Questions, The. Robert Pinsky. ColAP; NAmP90; NoAM

Questions about Poetry since Auschwitz. Tadeusz Rózewicz, *Polish.* AF, *tr.* by Robert A. Maguire *and* Magnus Jan Krynski

Questions and Answers. Diana O'Hehir. IFJA

Questions and Answers (a ballad). James Kirkup. SpW

Questions for Ecclesiastes. Mark Jarman. BAP-93

("God kept / a secret.") (LL) PUP-18

("What if on a foggy night in a beachtown.") PUP-18

Questions My Son Asked Me, Answers I Never Gave Him. Nancy Willard. LCAP-2

Questions of Ethne Alba, The. *Unknown, Irish.* TIRV, *tr.* by James Carney

Questions of Swimming, 1935. Peter Davison. DiPo

Questions of Travel. Elizabeth Bishop. ColAP; NAAL-2; NOBA

Quetzalcoatl Looks Down on Mexico. D. H. Lawrence. PeECV

Quha Is Perfyte. Alexander Scott. OxBS

Quhare haif ye been, ye ill womyne. The Witch of Fife. James Hogg. Ro *Fr.* The Queen's Wake.

Quhen [or Qwhen or When] Alexander [or Alysandyr] our kynge [or King] was dede. The Death of Alexander. *Unknown.* FaBoCh; OxBS

Quhen Flora Had O'erfret the Firth. *Unknown.* OBEV

(Four May Poems.) OxBS

Quhen he wes yung, and cled in grene. Quhy Sowld Nocht Allane Honorit Be? *Unknown.* OxBS

Quhen [or When] Noy[e] had maid his Sacrifyce [or sacrifice]. After the Flood. Sir David Lindsay. ChIV-1; OxBS *Fr.* The Monarche.

Quhen Tayis bank wes blumyt brycht. Tayis Bank. *Unknown.* FaBoVe

Quhen that I had oversene this regioun. Of the Realme of Scotland. Sir David Lindsay. OxBS *Fr.* The Dreme.

Quhen thou art careit to that cuntree. The Sybil. Virgil. OBVE, *tr.* by Gawin Douglas *Fr.* The Aeneid [or Eneados, *Aeneis*].

Quhom I luve, I dar nocht assay'. (LL) Quhen Flora Had O'erfret the Firth. *Unknown.* OBEV; OxBS

Quhy Sowld Nocht Allane Honorit Be? *Unknown.* OxBS

Quhy wylt ye, merchantis of renoun. To the Merchantis of Edinburgh. William Dunbar. OxBS

Qui Bien Aime a Tard Oublie. Chaucer. *See* Roundel: "Now welcom[e], Somer [or Summer] with thy sunne soft."

Qui Laborat, Orat. Arthur Hugh Clough. EnVR

Quia amore langueo. (LL) Quia Amore Langueo. *Unknown.* ImPo; NOBE; NOCV; OBEV; PoEL-1, *tr.* by Helen Gardner

Quia Amore Langueo. *Unknown, Middle English.* NOBE; NOCV; PoEL-1, *tr.* by Helen Gardner

Quia Amore Langueo. *Unknown.* ImPo; NOBE; NOCV; OBEV; PoEL-1, *tr.* by Helen Gardner

Quick! a last poem before I go. On Rachmaninoff's Birthday. Frank O'Hara. CAPP-1; PoM

Quick And Bitter. Yehuda Amichai, *Hebrew.* BoLoP, *tr.* by Assia Gutmann; LoP; VCWP, *tr.* by Gutmann, Assia; IP, *tr.* by Warren Bargad *and* Stanley F. Chyet

("We could have become the quiet.") (LL) IP, *tr.* by Bargad *and* Chyet

Quick climb to the Incense Terrace, A. In the Mountains, Parting from Master Ning as I Return to West Bank. Kao Ch'i, *Chinese.* CoBLCP, *tr.* by Jonathan Chaves

Quick Eats. Charles Simic. PuP-17

Quick-falling dew. Basho, *Japanese.* AWP, *tr.* by Curtis Hidden Page

Quick Gold, Slant Blue, Sharp Scarlet, The. Peyton Houston. *Fr.* Sonnet Variations. Son

Quick hands on spinning ropes. Dead Horse Bay. Robert Adamson. NOBAu

Quick! Hoist the jib and cast us off, my son. Over Bright Summer Seas. Robert Silliman Hillyer. NYBP

Quick in spite I said unkind. Brazen Tongue. William Rose Benét. MoAmPo

Quick in the April hedge. House. Robert Hass. LoL

Quick lunch! quick lunch! the neon cries, and I. Essay on Lunch. Walker Gibson. NYBP

Quick Night / easy warmth. The World Is Full of Remarkable Things. LeRoi Jones *and* Imamu Amiri Baraka. SSLK

Quick on my feet in those Novembers of my loneliness. A Mad Fight Song for William S. Carpenter, 1966. James Wright. NoAM

Quick sparks on the gorse bushes are leaping, The. The Wild Common. D. H. Lawrence. NoAM

Quick-Step. Robert Creeley. VGW

Quick, tender, virginal, and unprofaned! (LL) To the Body. Coventry Patmore. CABP; EnVR; OAEL-2; PoEL-5

Quick, woman, in your net. The Net. William Robert Rodgers. BoLoP; CIP-2; PNI

Quickly, love, be lyrical & let. La, La, La! Thomas M. Disch. NBLV

Quickness. Thomas Stanley. GeHe; MeLP; NOBE; NOCV; NOSC; SeCP

Quickness. Henry Vaughan. FMP

Quickness of Fear, The. Beverly Acuff Momoi. LoHo

Quickness which my God hath kissed, A. (LL) Quickness. Thomas Stanley. GeHe; MeLP; NOBE; NOCV; NOSC; SeCP

Quicksands. William Zaranka. BXAP

Quid gloriaris? Psalm 52. Mary Sidney Herbert. PBRV

Quid, omit, my simple friend. Ode 2.11: To an Ambitious Friend ("Quid bellicosus"). Horace. AWP, *tr.* by Matthew Arnold *Fr.* Odes.

Quid Sit Futurum Cras Fuge Quaerere. Matthew Prior. FaBoEE

Quidditie [or Quiddity], The. George Herbert. GeHe; NOSC; PoEL-2

Quiescent, a Person Sits Heart and Soul. Ring Lardner. OBAL

Quiet. Marjorie Lowry Christie Pickthall. NOBC

Quiet. Brian Swann. AmPA

Quiet after the rain of morning. Trumbull Stickney. ColAP

Quiet afternoon. Anita Virgil. HA

Quiet beyond recall, / Into irrelevance. (LL) To the Holy Spirit. Yvor Winters. MoAmPo; VGW

Quiet courtyard fills with greenery, The. Wen Cheng-ming. CoBLCP, *tr.* by Jonathan Chaves *Fr.* What It's Like Living in My Studio Late in Spring.

Quiet day, A. Marlene Mountain. HA

Quiet Days. Mildred T. Mey. PoToHe

Quiet deepens. You will not persuade, The. Farewell to Van Gogh. Charles Tomlinson. CMoP; GTBS-P; NoP-4; PoE

Quiet-eyed Cattle, The. Leslie Norris. PChr

Quiet Fog, The. Marge Piercy. UnPo

Quiet, fragrant, and relieved. (LL) The Dusk of Horses. James Dickey. ColAP; LiTM; NYBP; WeT

Quiet Glades of Eden, The. Robert Graves. BoLoP; EP

Quiet has a hidden sound. W. S. Braithwaite. NAAAL

Quiet House, The. Charlotte Mew. BrRo; EBEV; NALW

Quiet House in Ch'ang-lo Ward, A. Po Chü-i, *Chinese.* CoBCP, *tr.* by Burton Watson

Quiet Kingdom, The. Carl Busse, *German.* AWP, *tr.* by Ludwig Lewisohn

Quiet Life, The. William Byrd. NoSic

(Herdmen, The.) NOBE

Quiet Life, The. Alexander Pope. *See* Ode on Solitude.

Quiet moon, immaculate of face, The. "William Baylebridge." CBAP *Fr.* Love Redeemed.

Quiet morning, the new year's first day. Small Birds. Leonard Clark. AYFP

Quiet Neighbour, A. John Heywood. NoSic

Quiet night is solemn and still, The. Sent to the Hsiu-ts'ai on His Entry into the Army. Hsi K'ang, *Chinese.* CoBCP, *tr. by* Burton Watson

Quiet Normal Life, A. Wallace Stevens. NAAL-2; NoAM

Quiet now, feel the kindly pressure of darkness. Winter Solstice Poem. Diana Scott. BrRo

Quiet of the Dead, The. Mary Morison Webster. PeSA

Quiet, pilfering, unprotected race, A. (LL) Gipsies: "The Snow falls deep; the forest lies alone." John Clare. CH; NoP-4; PoEL-4

Quiet, quiet / spring clouds float. Flower Shadows. Mo Shih-lung, *Chinese.* CoBLCP, *tr. by* Jonathan Chaves

Quiet room, the flowers, the perfumed calm, The. Schumann's Sonata in A Minor. Celia Laighton Thaxter. AiP

Quiet rustle, A. Rod Willmot. HA

Quiet season of flowering, the courtyard gate is shut. Palace Poem. Chu Ch'ing-yü, *Chinese.* SuSp, *tr. by* Irving Y. Lo

Quiet Sitting. Wang Chiu-ssu, *Chinese.* CoBLCP, *tr. by* Jonathan Chaves

Quiet Soul, A. John Oldham. OBEV

Quiet (Thames' or Don's or Salween's) *waters by, The.* (LL) Whit Monday. Louis MacNeice. ChIV-1; NYBP; OAEL-2; PeECV

Quiet Things. Grace Noll Crowell. PoLF

Quiet upon the terraces. Chairs in Snow. Elwyn Brooks White. ChAP

Quiet valley with no man's footprints, A. Sitting at Night. Om Ui-Gil, *Chinese.* FP, *tr. by* Jong-Gil, Kim

Quiet Waters. Blanche Shoemaker Wagstaff. BLPA

Quiet Work. Matthew Arnold. FaBoBe

Quieter the people are, The. The Signboard. Robert Creeley. CoAmPo

Quietly. Gary Hotham. HA

Quietly and while at rest on the trim grass I have gazed. The Air of June Sings. Edward Dorn. NeAP; PoM

Quietly at our side the dead. The Dead Men. Sophia de Mello Breyner Andresen, *Portuguese.* PBWP, *tr. by* Allan Francovich

Quietly dozing. Eric Amann. HA

Quietly I enter the closet. Communion. P. M. Snider. PoToHe

Quietly shaping. David Lloyd. HA

Quietly shining to the quiet Moon. (LL) Frost at Midnight. Coleridge. CABP; EBEV; FHYEP; HAP; NAEL-2; NOBE; NoP-4; OAEL-2; OBNC; PoE; PoEL-4; Poetr; TFi; TOF

Quietly step onto a land. Kayenta Times Yet Dreaming On. Nia Francisco. HATNAP

Quietly the world lay sleeping. The Birth of Jesus. Josephine D. Henderson Heard. CBWP-4

Quilt in the Bennington College Library, A. Dave Jeddie Smith. NAmP90

Quilt of Rights. Sandra McPherson. LoL

Quilts. Kathleen Peirce. PBCAP

Quilts sing on, The. (LL) My Mother Pieced Quilts. Teresa Palma Acosta. MDDM; WPOW

Quince Preserved through the Winter, Given to a Lady, A. Antiphilus, *Greek.* GrAn, *tr. by* W. S. Merwin

Quincey is absent, absent as you. The Letters of Mina Harker. Dodie Bellamy. PT *Fr.* The Letters of Mina Harker.

Quinn the Eskimo. "Bob Dylan." RaBo

Quinnapoxet. Stanley Kunitz. AFr; LoL

Quinquireme of Nineveh from distant Ophir. Cargoes. John Masefield. CABP; CMoP; EBEvV; FaPoR; InPK-6; LiTM; MoBrPo; NOBE; OBEV; OBMV; PoRA; TFi

Quintana lay in the shallow grave of coral. Karl Shapiro. VGW

Quintia is beautiful, many will tell you: to me. Catullus, *Latin.* OBCVT, *tr. by* Arthur Symons

Quintia is handsome, fair, tall, straight, all these. De Quintia et Lesbia. Catullus, *Latin.* OBCVT, *tr. by* Richard Lovelace *Fr.* Carmina.

Quintina of Crosses, A. Chad Walsh. TrCP

Quip, The. George Herbert. GeHe; NOSC; OxAEP-1; SeCP

Quirky old gent, name of Freud, A. Limerick. Martin Fagg. PeLi

Quis Optimus Reipublicae Status. Sir Thomas More. PBRV

Quite a posh old house was this. Recollections of an Old Spook. Richard Edwards. NOxBChV

Quite Apart from the Holy Ghost. Adrian Mitchell. OBSV

Quite for no reason. I've Been to a Marvelous Party. Noël Coward. NBLV

Quite Forsaken. D. H. Lawrence. SCGP

Quite horfen, fer a lark, coves on a ship. The Helbatrawss. Kingsley Amis. NOBL

Quite is high. Styro. Clark Coolidge. PmAP

Quite, quite. / Oh I agree. Restricted. Eve Merriam. TrJP

Quite rightly, we remained among the living. The Survivors. Adrienne Rich. NYBP

Quite spent with thoughts I left my cell, and lay. Vanity of Spirit. Henry Vaughan. ESCV; GeHe; NOSC; TOF

Quite the Cheese. H. C. Waring. BXAP

Quite unexpectedly as Vasserot. The End of the World. Archibald MacLeish. CMoP; GSo; HoPM; ImPo; InPK-6; LiTM; MeMAP; MoAmPo; NOBA; NoAM; OBAL; OxBA; PBMP; PFE; SAGP; Son; TAP; TFi; VGW

Quits. Matthew Prior. *See* Epigram: "To John I ow'd great obligation."

Quitter, The. *Unknown.* BLPA

Quo life, the warld is mine. The Flyting o' Life and Daith. Hamish Henderson. OxBS

Quo' the wee boy, and still he stude. (LL) The False Knight upon [*or on*] the Road. *Unknown.* AmFP; CH; ESPB; EnSB; FaBoCh; OxBS; OxBoLi

Quod Dunbar to Kennedy. William Dunbar. OxBoLi

Quondam was I in my lady's grace. Sir Thomas Wyatt. GBL; NoSic

Quoof. Paul Muldoon. CBNP; FaBoVe; PBCIP; PNI

Quotations. George Oppen. NNaP

Quote Me Wrong Again and I'll Slit the Throat of Your Pet Iguana. David St. John. RACG

Quoth a cow in the marshes of Glynne. Limerick. Conrad Potter Aiken. PeLi

Quoth Cibber to Pope, tho' in verse you foreclose. Alexander Pope. FaBoEE

Quoth Dick to me, as once at College. The Madman and the Lethargist. Coleridge. CBNP

Quoth Elizabeth prisoner. (LL) Written with a Diamond On Her Window at Woodstock. Elizabeth I, Queen of England. PBWP; PEW; WPE

Quoth he, Miss Mouse, I'm come to thee. Kitty Alone. *Unknown.* CBNP

Quoth he, My faith as adamantine. Samuel Butler. OBSV *Fr.* Hudibras.

Quoth he, to bid me not to love. Samuel Butler. NOBL *Fr.* Hudibras.

Quoth John to Joan. *Unknown.* CH; OxBM

Quoth she, I wish I could prescribe your help. Rachel Speght. *Fr.* A Dream. WPE

Quoth tongue of neither maid nor wife. Elena's Song. Sir Henry Taylor. OBEV; RACG *Fr.* Philip van Artevelde.

R

R.A.F. (Aged Eighteen). Rudyard Kipling. PoWW; LiLi *Fr.* Epitaphs of the War [1914–1918]. OBWP

R. Alcona to J. Brenzaida. Emily Jane Brontë. *See* Remembrance.

R-and-R Centre: An Incident from the Vietnam War. D. J. Enright. OxBC

R.C. Emily Jane Brontë. *Fr.* The Two Children. PoEL-5

R-E-M-O-R-S-E. George Ade. NBLV; OBAL; OBCoV; PeLV

R.M.S. *Titanic.* Anthony Cronin.
  "On the bog road the blackthorn flowers, the turf-stacks." BIrV
  "Trembling with engines, gulping oil, the river." PBCIP

R', n. 1. lo. Lattice at/of (Com)pare (Dis)pair. Tina Darragh. FTOS

R-p-o-p-h-e-s-s-a-g-r. E. E. Cummings. APo; AmPP; PoE; PoPoPo
  (",grasshopper;.") (LL) APo; PoPoPo

R the reviewer, reviewing my book. Hilaire Belloc. NoAM *Fr.* A Moral Alphabet.

Rabbi Ben Ezra. Robert Browning. NAEL-2; OBNC
  "Grow old along with me!" ImPo; PoToHe

Rabbi Ben Levi, on the Sabbath, read. The Legend of Rabbi Ben Levi. Henry Wadsworth Longfellow. NCAP

Rabbi, we Gadarenes / Are not ascetics. Matthew VIII, 28 ff. Richard Wilbur. GI

Rabbi Yom-Tob of Mayence Petitions His God. Abraham Moses Klein. TrJP

Rabbi Yussel Luksh of Chelm. Jacob Glatstein, *Yiddish.* TrJP, *tr. by* Nathan Halper

Rabbi's Song, The. Rudyard Kipling. ChIV-1

Rabbit, The. Nina Cassian, *Romanian.* PoSu, *tr. by* Christopher Hewitt

Rabbit, The. Edith King. BoTP

Rabbit, The. Mary Oliver. CMAP

Rabbit, The. Elizabeth Madox Roberts. OBCA

Rabbit goes soft-foot, pheasant's caught. *Unknown, Chinese.* ChiPo, *tr. by* Ezra Pound

Rabbit Is King of the Ghosts, A. Wallace Stevens. NoAM; PRMP; TTTS

Rabbit Shoeshine. S. K. Kelen. BMAP

Rabble of six arrived at my house, A. A Satire on the O'Haras. Tadhg Dall O'Huiginn. NOIV

Rabble Soldier. *Unknown.* AS

(. . . rabid or dog-dull.) Let me tell you how. A Professor's Song. John Berryman. HeIP-4; MoP; NAAL-2; NOBA; NoAM; OxBC

Rabinal-Achí. *Unknown, Mayan.*

"Cala-Achí! Ha! Aha! Yeha! Ahau! Wow! Achí!" STP, tr. by Nathaniel Tarn

Raccoon wears a black mask, The. Racoon. Kenneth Rexroth. KaS; NNaP Fr. A Bestiary. OBAL

Race. Karen Gershon. HP

Race, The. Nuala Ni Dhomhnaill, Irish. CIP-2; PBCIP, tr. by Michael Hartnett

Race, The. Sharon Olds. MoLi; RaBo

Race and Battle. D. H. Lawrence. ChIV-1

Race is not to the swift, The. Race and Battle. D. H. Lawrence. ChIV-1

Race of the Kingfishers. Ray A. Young Bear. HATNAP

Race on Gathering Bites. Kojo Laing. HBAPE

Race Question, The. Naomi Long Madgett. BPo; LTA

Race Relations. Carolyn Kizer. LTA

Race round the track of the stadium pupil. (LL) The Stenographers. Patricia K. Page. HeIP-4; LiTM; NALW; NoAM

Race to freedom and herself to fame, A. (LL) Harriet Beecher Stowe. Paul Laurence Dunbar. AAP; BPo; PoPoPo

Racehorses assemble at the starting barrier, The. Flemington Racecourse. Kevin Hart. NOBAu

Racer's Widow, The. Louise Glück. AmPA; NYBP

Races will disappear. Nikolai Ivanovich Glazkov, Russian. TCRP, tr. by Daniel Weissbort

Rachel Goes to the Well for Water ("Rachel stands by the mirror and plaits"). Itsik Manger, Yiddish. CEEP, tr. by Ruth Whitman

Racial Memories. Elizabeth Mische John. LoHo

Racing, reckoning fingers flick. Palladas, Greek. GrAn; OBVE, tr. by Tony Harrison

Racist Psychotherapy. Isaac J. Black. NBV

Racists. Charles Kenneth Williams. LTA

Racoon. Kenneth Rexroth. Fr. A Bestiary. OBAL

Raderus. Donne. PeLV

Radiance of that star that leans on me, The. Delay. Elizabeth Jennings. NIP-4; OPOU; OxBTC

Radiant. James Sherry. FTOS

Radiant dog on doublecross, and I. John Godfrey. FTOS

Radiant Ranks of Seraphim. Valery Yakovlevich Bryusov, Russian. AWP, tr. by Babette Deutsch and Avrahm Yarmolinsky

Radiant Silhouette I. John Yau. OpBo

Radiant Silhouette II. John Yau. OpBo

Radiant Silhouette III. John Yau. OpBo

Radiant Silhouette IV. John Yau. OpBo

Radiant Silhouette V. John Yau. OpBo

Radiation Victim. Colin Thiele. NOBAu

Radiator's hissing hot, The. Studio Up Over In Your Ear. Al Young. GT

Radical War Song, A. Thomas Babington Macaulay, 1st Baron Macaulay. OBSV

Radio. Frank O'Hara. PoA

Radio. Barrett Watten. PmAP

Radio broadcast the news—The, The. Lovers in Fall. Yehuda Amichai, Hebrew. IP, tr. by Warren Bargad and Stanley F. Chyet

Radio Cradle-song. Eugène Marais, Afrikaans. PeSAV, tr. by Stephen Gray

Radio grovels from over the fence, A. Sydney. Robert Harris. NOBAu

Radio is teaching my goldfish Jujitsu, The. Heavy Water Blues. Bob Kaufman. NBV

Radio Sky. Norman Dubie. NAmP90

Radio under the Bed, The. Reed Whittemore. NYBP

Radio Yerevan. Diana Der Hovanessian. LoHo

Radish is / the only dish, The. N. M. Bodecker. Spl

Raft drifted, The. John Heath-Stubbs. PeECV Fr. Artorius. EBEV

Raftsmen on their floats. Buson, Japanese. TAL, tr. by Harold G. Henderson

Rag of black plastic, shred of a kite. Goodbye, Goldeneye. May Swenson. NoP-4

Raga of the drum, the drum the drum the drum the drum, the heartbeat. Unanimity Has Been Achieved, Not a Dot Less for Its Accidentalness. Bob Kaufman. NAAAL

Ragas. David Meltzer. NeAP

15th Raga: For Bela Lugosi.

12th Raga: For John Wieners.

Ragdoll. (LL) Christmas Morning I. Carol Freeman. KaS

Ragged and Dirty. Unknown. AmFP

Ragged Island. Edna St. Vincent Millay. ColAP; NAAL-2; NoP-4

Ragged Robin. Elizabeth Godley. BoTP

Ragged Wood, The. W. B. Yeats. CBLP; GBL

Raggedy Man, The. James Whitcomb Riley. FPC; OBCA; OxBChV

Raggedy! Raggedy! Raggedy Man! (LL) The Raggedy Man. James Whitcomb Riley. FPC

Raging Canawl. Unknown. AS

Ragout. William Zaranka. BXAP

Rags. Edmund Vance Cooke. BLPA

Rags. Judith Thurman. AYFP

Rags and tatters. Ragged Robin. Elizabeth Godley. BoTP

Ragwort. Anne Stevenson. OPOU

Rahab. Diane Glancy. CRP

Raid, The. William Everson. MoP; NoAM

Raid of the Reidswire, The. Unknown. IBB

Raid on a Cheyenne Village. Diane Glancy. LoHo

Raider, The. William Robert Rodgers. MoBrPo

Rail and the Bullfrog, The. Tản Đà, Vietnamese. AVP, tr. by Huỳnh Sanh Thông

Railings of iron. "Anna Akhmatova," Russian. TCRP, tr. by Daniel Weissbort

Railroad, The. William Barnes.

"An' while I went 'ithin a train." EnVR

Railroad and a river and a road, A. Low-Level Cross-Country. Howard Nemerov. GM

Railroad Bill, a conjure man. Ishmael Reed. GM; NAAAL

Railroad Bill, Railroad Bill. Unknown. GM

("I'm going to ride old Railroad Bill.") (LL) NAAAL

("Railroad Bill.") AS

Railroad Blues, The. Unknown. AmFP; GM

Railroad bridge's, De. Homesick Blues. Langston Hughes. MoAmPo

Railroad Cars Are Coming, The. Unknown. AS

Railroad Happening, A. Daniil Kharms, Russian. CBNP, tr. by Vladimir Markov and Merrill Sparks

Railroad Man for Me, A. Unknown. CA

Railroad Section Leader's Song. Unknown. GM

Railroad track is miles away, The. Travel. Edna St. Vincent Millay. OBCA; PiM

Railroad yard in San Jose. In Back of the Real. Allen Ginsberg. AmPP; HeIP-4

Railroader for Me, A. Unknown. AmFP

Railroads and Freight Handler to the Nation. (LL) Chicago. Carl Sandburg. AiP; AmPP; CMoP; ColAP; LiTM; MoAmPo; MoP; NAAL-2; NOBA; NoAM; OxBA; PoA; Poetr; TAP; TFi; TRP; UnPo; VGW

Railway Allotments. M. R. Peacocke. OBGa

Railway Children, The. Seamus Heaney. OPOU

Railway Junction, The. Walter De la Mare. OxBTC

Railway runs down the middle of the road, The. Mildmay Grove. Sue May. NBrP

Raiment We Put On, The. Kelly Cherry. FFC

Rain. John Ashbery. FTOS

Rain. Roo Borson. NoP-4

Rain, The. Robert Crawford. FaBoTC

Rain, The. Robert Creeley. CoAP; CoAmPo; ColAP; PmAP; PoE; RaBo; TRP; VGW

Rain, The. W. H. Davies. BoTP; OxBTC

Rain. Emanuel DiPasquale. InPK-6; KaS

Rain, The. Richard Edwards. AYFP

Rain. Margiad Evans. OBWVE

Rain. Lance Henson. VoR

Rain. Anselm Hollo. PoM

Rain. Brian Lee. AYFP

Rain. Vachel Lindsay. CMoP; RaBo

Rain, The. Alasdair Maclean. FaBoTC

Rain. Lilian McCrea. BoTP

Rain. Marlene Mountain. HA

Rain. Paul Murray. BIrV

Rain. Naomi Shihab Nye. NAmP90

Rain. Po Chü-i, Chinese. BLT; ChiP, tr. by Arthur Waley

Rain. Raymond Roseliep. HA

Rain. Gary Soto. NoAM Fr. The Elements of San Joaquin. PBCAP; PaTW; UnSA

Rain. A heavy mane. Marina Ivanovna Tsvetayeva. Fr. The Daughter of Jairus. BoWoP, tr. by Paul Schmidt

Rain after a Vaudeville Show. Stephen Vincent Benét. MoAmPo

Rain, and a flurry of wind shaking the pear's white blossom. Christian Karlson Stead. PeNZ Fr. Twenty-one Sonnets.

Rain and sunlight and the boat between them. Leaving Inishmore. Michael Longley. IIP

Rain and the Tyrants. Jules Supervielle, French. NNPT, tr. by David Gascoyne

Rain and thunder beat down and flooded the streets. Cartagena. Gary Snyder. BB

Rain at Cold-Food Festival. Su Shih, *Chinese.*
 "Since coming to Huang-chou." SuSp, *tr.* by Irving Y. Lo
 "Spring flood is coming up to my door." SuSp, *tr.* by Irving Y. Lo
Rain at Wildwood. May Swenson. NYBP
Rain beats on trees south of the river. Tune: "Mountain Hawthorns." Wang An-shih, *Chinese.* SuSp, *tr.* by James J. Y. Liu
Rain before [*or* Raan afoor] seven. *Unknown.* FaBoBe; FaBoVe; OxNR
Rain—Birdoswald. Frances Horovitz. APAD; NBrP
Rain brings me back, The. Patrizia Cavalli, *Italian.* NeIt, *tr.* by Judith Baumel
Rain by my throw in a. Subtracted Words. P. Inman. FTOS
Rain came. Fog out of the slough and horses. Day after Chasing Porcupines. James Welch. NoAM
Rain Cleared and the Breeze and Sunshine Are Superb as I Stroll Outside the Gate, The. Lu Yu, *Chinese.* SuSp, *tr.* by Burton Watson
Rain comes and goes. The Green Refrain. Avraham Huss, *Hebrew.* MHP, *tr.* by Ruth Finer Mintz
Rain comes down, it comes without our call, The. The Winter Rain. Jones Very. NCAP
Rain comes down on the desert and the next day, The. My Father and God. Linda Gregg. MoLi
Rain comes down through the alders. Seamus Heaney. *Fr.* Exposure. PBCIP; PNI
Rain comes flapping through the yard, The. Gathering Mushrooms. Paul Muldoon. BiHa; CIP-2; NoP-4; PBCIP; PNI
Rain dampens Sung-ling, spring fills with mist. Hsiu-chou. T'ang Hsien-tsu, *Chinese.* CoBLCP, *tr.* by Jonathan Chaves
Rain Ditch. Pinkie Gordon Lane. ISC
Rain Down. Mary Ellen Solt. BoWoP
Rain Downriver. Philip Levine. VCAP
Rain drifts forever in this place. The Falls of Glomach. Andrew Young. OxBS
Rain drips through. South Coast Haiku. Laurie Duggan. BMAP *Fr.* Dogs.
Rain, falling, The. Evening. Helen G. Quigless. BkSV
Rain Falls and Floods. Amir Gilbo'a, *Hebrew.* IP, *tr.* by Warren Bargad *and* Stanley F. Chyet
 ("Rain falls and floods, says the heart.")
Rain falls like knives, The. Derek Walcott. PBCV *Fr.* Another Life.
Rain feels heavy / on the gray sidewalks of America, The. Jim Mitsui. *See* Katori Maru, October 1920.
Rain fell like grass growing, The. Rain at Wildwood. May Swenson. NYBP
Rain Forest. Eric Rolls. NOBAu
Rain Forest. Dave Jeddie Smith. HCAP; MT
Rain, Four Poems. Tu Fu, *Chinese.*
 "Light rain doesn't slick the road." SuSp, *tr.* by William H. Nienhauser
 "This southern rain nourishes the mossy stones." SuSp, *tr.* by William H. Nienhauser
Rain had fallen, the Poet arose, The. The Poet's Song. Tennyson. EBVV; EPCY
Rain has beaded the panes. At the Office Early. Ted Kooser. PBCAP
Rain has passed, The. Birth. Amir Gilbo'a, *Hebrew.* MHP, *tr.* by Ruth Finer Mintz
Rain hushes the surfaces of tin porches, The. (LL) Rain. Emanuel DiPasquale. KaS
Rain in gusts. John Wills. HA
Rain in its new edition of daily menace, The. Cambridge. John James. NBrP
Rain in my ears: impatiently there raps. Robert David Fitzgerald. CBAP *Fr.* Essay on Memory.
Rain in Ohio. Mary Oliver. InPK-6
Rain in Summer. Henry Wadsworth Longfellow. AYFP; BoTP
Rain in the Aspens. Su Tung-p'o, *Chinese.* OHPC, *tr.* by Kenneth Rexroth
Rain in the Pine Wood. Gabriele D'Annunzio. ItIP
Rain is a dangerous thing. Black and Blue. Charles Wright. PuP-17
Rain is due to fall, The. A Poet Thinks. Lui Chi, *Chinese.* AWP, *tr.* by E. Powys Mathers
Rain is Falling, The. Homero Aridjis, *Spanish.* STV, *tr.* by John Frederick Nims
Rain is falling. The Sound of Rain. Yohan Chu, *Korean.* CKP, *tr.* by Jaihiun Kim
Rain is over and gone!, The. (LL) Written in March [While Resting on the Bridge at the Foot of Brother's Water]. Wordsworth. ACTP; BoTP; CTV; ChAP; NAEL-2; NTCP; PBMP; SCGP; UnPo
Rain is pissing down, the. Night Song of the Personal Shadow. György Petri, *Hungarian.* VCWP, *tr.* by Clive Wilmer and George Gömöri
Rain is raining all around, The. Robert Louis Stevenson. CTV; NTCP

RAIN is speaking it pelts, THE / THE POEM is moving by itself. Then and Now. James Laughlin. PmAP
Rain it raineth all around, The. Charles Synge Christopher Bowen, Baron Bowen. NBLV; NTCP
Rain it raineth every day, The. Pennsylvania Deutsch. Christopher Darlington Morley. NBLV
Rain, it streams on stone and hillock, The. A. E. Housman. CMoP
Rain, midnight rain, nothing but the wild rain. Edward Thomas. NAEL-2; NoP-4; OBWP; OxBTC; PeFWW; PoWW
 ("Cannot, the tempest tells me, disappoint.") (LL) NoP-4
Rain mixed with sleet. Rosamond Haas. HA
Rain Moving In. John Ashbery. NoP-4
Rain of London pimples, The. London Rain. Louis MacNeice. NoP-4; Poetr
Rain of Rites, A. Jayanta Mahapatra. PoA
Rain of Stones Is Finished, The. Faiz Ahmad Faiz. EC3
Rain off and on, The. Insomnia. Timothy Geiger. PuP-17
Rain on a Grave. Thomas Hardy. OxAEP-2
Rain on lilac leaves. In the dusk. Taid's Grave. Gillian Clarke. OPOU
Rain on the Down. Arthur Symons. OBNC *Fr.* At Dieppe.
Rain on the far tip of the grove. Scattered Leaves. Lance Henson. VoR
Rain on the green grass. *Unknown.* BoTP; OxNR
Rain on the River. Lu Yu, *Chinese.* OHMPC; OHPC, *tr.* by Kenneth Rexroth
Rain on the West Side Highway. Adrienne Rich. NAAL-2 *Fr.* Twenty-one Love Poems. GLP
Rain, people, rain! The Mocking-Bird's Song. *Unknown, Tigua Native American.* APN-2, *tr.* by Alice C. Fletcher
Rain, rain, go away. *Unknown.* OxNR; ReMoGo
Rain, rain, go to Spain. Mother Goose. FaBoVe; LB; OxNR; ReMoGo
 ("And never, never, never / Come back again.") (LL) LB
 ("Never show your face again.") (LL) OxNR
Rain Rain on the Splintered Girl. Ishmael Reed. PoBA
Rain. Rain that will not end, The. Good Friday. Driving Weekend. Elizabeth Spires. WWSi
Rain rains sair on Duriesdyke, The. Duriesdyke. Swinburne. OxBB
Rain rins doun through Mirry-land toune, The. Hugh of Lincoln. *Unknown.* ESPB; EnSB; OxBB
Rain, said the first, as it falls in Venice. Song Tournament: New Style. Louis Untermeyer. OBAL
Rain set early in to-night, The. Porphyria's Lover. Robert Browning. AWP; CBLP; EnVR; FHYEP; HAP; NAEL-2; OBEV; OxBoV
Rain smell comes with the wind. Love Poem. Leslie Marmon Silko. UnPo; VoR
Rain Song of the Quer'ränna Chai'än, A. *Unknown, Sia.* APN-2, *tr.* by Matilda Coxe Stevenson
 "White floating clouds."
Rain Song of the Shu'-wi Chai'än (Snake Society), A. *Unknown, Sia Native American.* APN-2, *tr.* by Matilda Coxe Stevenson
Rain stopped for one afternoon, The. Easter: Wahiawa, 1959. Cathy Song. OpBo
Rain Storm. Sasenarine Persand. HCP
Rain-sunken roof, grown green and thin. The Barn. Edmund Blunden. MoBrPo
Rain sweeps in as the gale begins to blow. Wet Day. James McAuley. BMAP
Rain That Fell upon the Height, The. Coventry Patmore. *Fr.* The Victories of Love.
Rain, the welcome rain!, The. (LL) Rain in Summer. Henry Wadsworth Longfellow. AYFP; BoTP
Rain thunderstorms over the Potomac, in Georgetown. Rainscapes, Hydrangeas, Roses, and Singing Birds. Richard Eberhart. MoAmPo
Rain to the Tribe. Al-Khansa, *Arabic.* BoWoP, *tr.* by Willis Barnstone *and* Tony Nawfal
Rain Travel. W. S. Merwin. ColAP
Rain tries the one small foot and at length the other. Towards the Land of the Composer. Francis Webb. BMAP
Rain was full of the freshness, The. The Dark and Falling Summer. Delmore Schwartz. ImGa; NYBP
Rain, wind and fire! The secret, bestial peace! (LL) The Card-Players. Philip Larkin. BLT; OxBC
Rain, with a silver flail. Whale. William Rose Benét. MoAmPo
Rain would fall on me, The. Watchful Wakeful. Amir Gilbo'a, *Hebrew.* IP, *tr.* by Warren Bargad *and* Stanley F. Chyet
Rainbow, The. Opal Palmer Adisa. GT
Rainbow, The. Walter De la Mare. CTV; NTP
Rainbow, The. Gerard Manley Hopkins. OxBSP
Rainbow, The. D. H. Lawrence. NTP

Rainbow, The. Coventry Patmore. GTBS-P *Fr.* The Angel in the House.

Rainbow, The. Christina Rossetti. ACTP; OxBChV
  ("Boats sail on the rivers.") ACTP

Rainbow, A. Alexis Rotella. HA

Rainbow, The. Henry Vaughan. GeHe

Rainbow at Night. Antonio Machado Ruiz, *Spanish.* AF; BLT, *tr. by* Robert Bly

Rainbow at night. *Unknown.* FaBoBe

Rainbow comes and goes, The. Wordsworth. *Fr.* Ode: Intimations of Immortality [from Recollections of Early Childhood]. AWP; FHYEP; HAP; HeIP-4; NOBE; NOBRP; OAEL-2; OBEV; OBNC; PBMP; PoE; PoEL-4

Rainbow faded, the animals dispersed, The. Return to Ararat. Martyn Halsall. TrCP

Rainbow Fairies, The. *Unknown.* BoTP

Rainbow is the shape of god's desire, The. Colour-Scheme. Edward Baugh. PBCV

Rainbow i'th'morning. *Unknown.* FaBoVe

Rainbow; or Curious Covenant, The. Robert Herrick. ChIV-1

Rainbow, rainbow. *Unknown.* NTP

Rainbow stands and summer passes under, A. (LL) I heard a river thro' the valley wander. Trumbull Stickney. APN-2; NoP-4

Raincoat, A. Michael Burkard. FiLi

Raindrops fall. To a Man Who is Rob Southland. Nia Francisco. HATNAP

Rainer, / the man who was about to celebrate his 52nd birthday. The Death of Europe. Charles Olson. NeAP

Rainforest. Judith Wright. OPOU

Rainier. Jim Tollerud. VoR

Raining at every window. Cor Van den Heuvel. HA

Rainmakers, The. Robert Kelly. PmAP

Rainpoem. Michael Dransfield. CBAP

Rains. Mateja Matevski, *Greek.*
  "Arrive sluggish, arrive weary horses of space." CEEP, *tr. by* Charles Simic

Rain's all right. The boys who physic. Biography of Southern Rain. Kenneth Patchen. VGW

Rains, already old, The. What She Said. Okkur Macatti, *Tamil.* PBWP, *tr. by* A. K. Ramanujan

Rains have come, the frogs are bursting with joy, The. Frogs. Buddhadeva Bose, *Bengali.* OMIP, *tr. by* Buddhadeva Bose

Rains have come, the winds are shrill, The. The Rainy Season in California. John Rollin Ridge. APN-2; PAR

Rains in season. What He Said to His Charioteer, on His Way Back. Cittalai Cattanar, *Tamil.* PLW, *tr. by* A. K. Ramanujan

Rain's Marriage, The. Marcia Southwick. NAmP90

Rains pass, the mountains' face is washed. Yüan Mei, *Chinese.* CoBLCP, *tr. by* Jonathan Chaves

Rain's pounding away, The. Sándor Weöres, *Hungarian.* BLT, *tr. by* J. Kessler

Rains pour shower upon shower, winds blow by gusts. Flood. *Unknown, Vietnamese.* AVP, *tr. by* Huỳnh Sanh Thông

Rainscapes, Hydrangeas, Roses, and Singing Birds. Richard Eberhart. MoAmPo

Rainstorm Has Dragged On for Ten Days Now, and There Is No Fire in the Kitchen. Moistening My Inkstone and Chewing on My Brush, I've Lived in Isolation Like a Monk—and Completed Eight Quatrains to Express My Feelings, A. T'ang Yin, *Chinese.*
  "Ten days of wind and rain, depressing darkness!" CoBLCP, *tr. by* Jonathan Chaves

Rainstorms that blacken like a headache. Grasmere. Amy Clampitt. PiM *Fr.* Grasmere.

Rainuv; a Romantic Ballad from the Early Basque. Margaret Widdemer. BXAP

Rainy Day, The. Henry Wadsworth Longfellow. AWP; PoLF

Rainy day, A. Anita Virgil. HA

Rainy fields are glazed with ice, The. Etude in Glass. Janina Degutyte, *Lithuanian.* CEEP, *tr. by* M. G. Slavenas

Rainy Mountain Cemetery. N. Scott Momaday. CDW; HATNAP

Rainy Night. Ho Ching-ming, *Chinese.* CoBLCP, *tr. by* Jonathan Chaves

Rainy Night at the Writers' Colony. Josephine Jacobsen. TAP

Rainy Nights. Irene Thompson. AYFP; BoTP

Rainy Pleiads Wester, The. A. E. Housman. BoLoP; CBLP

Rainy Season, The. Linda Hogan. HATNAP; TRP

Rainy Season in California, The. John Rollin Ridge. APN-2; PAR

Rainy skies, misty mountains. Fifty. Kenneth Rexroth. TAP

Rainy Song. Max Eastman. FaBoBe

Rainy Summer, The. Alice Thompson Meynell. AYFP; OxBSP; OxBTC

Rainy summer night. Gustave Keyser. HA

Rainy winter evening. Martin Burke. HA

Raise a "Rucus" To-Night. *Unknown.* BPo; TAP

Raise greater fires in men. (LL) The Lily in a Crystal. Robert Herrick. BeJo; NAEL-1; NOSC; PoEL-3; SCGP; SeCP

Raise him a tombstone of snow. (LL) Last Rites. Christina Rossetti. FaBoVe; OxBChV

Raise it again, man. We still believe what we hear. (LL) The Singer's House. Seamus Heaney. EBEV; IIP

Raise me up, Lord, who am fallen down. Miguel de Guevara, *Spanish.* PBMP, *tr. by* Samuel Beckett

Raise the Cromlech high! The Lament of Maev Leith-Dherg. *Unknown, Middle Irish.* OBWP, *tr. by* Thomas W. H. Rolleston

Raise the shade. E. E. Cummings. VGW

Raises up both hands and shouts three times! (LL) Meeting the Mountains. Gary Snyder. NoAM; TAP

Raisin, The. Donald Hall. TAP

Raisin Pumpernickel. Marge Piercy. DeD

Raising a Humid Flag. Thylias Moss. GT

Raising its radiance to the moon. (LL) Bread. W. S. Merwin. SPE

Raising of Lazarus, The. Lucille Clifton. CrSp

Raising the Flag. Gerald Vizenor. VoR

Raisins are my currency. Lorna Dee Cervantes. NAmP90

Raja, I wish I knew. To Raja Rao. Czeslaw Milosz. TOF

Raka. N. P. van Wyk Louw.
  Coming of Raka, The. PeSAV, *tr. by* Guy Butler

Rake, The. Abu Nuwas, *Arabic.* ArPe, *tr. by* Omar S. Pound

Rakes of Mallow, The. *Unknown.* OBCoV

Raking Leaves. Robert Pack. NYBP

Ralegh's Prizes. Robert Pinsky. DiPo; VCAP

Raleigh Was Right. William Carlos Williams. NIP-4; NoAM; Poetr; RB

Rally Song. Mary Weston Fordham. CBWP-2

Ralph Leech Believes. Ebenezer Elliot. Son *Fr.* The Year of Seeds.

Ralph Roister Doister. Nicholas Udall.
  I Mun Be Married a Sunday. CBLP

Ram, The. Selima Hill. EP; NBrP

Ram came last of all. And Abraham, The. Heritage. Haim Guri. HP

Rama Kam. David Diop, *French.* NegPo, *tr. by* Ellen Conroy Kennedy

Rama says. Two Women Knitting. Mrinal Pande, *Hindi.* OMIP, *tr. by* Mrinal Pande *and* Arlene Zide

Ramble in St. James's Park, A. John Wilmot, 2d Earl of Rochester. PeLV

Ramble of the Gods through Birmingham. James Bisset.
  Next day they rambled round the town, and swore. NOEC

Rambling Sailor, The. Charlotte Mew. PoRA

Rambuncto. Margaret Widdemer. BXAP

Rampaging spectral images. Just Another Gig. Baron James Ashanti. SeSe

Ram's Horn, The. John Hewitt. BIrV; PNI

Ramshackles, archipelagoes, loose constellations. The Unifying Principle. A. R. Ammons. NOBA

Ran cranberry over logan. Make-Up. Geraldine Monk. NBrP

Rana, I know you gave me poison. Mirabai, *Hindi.* BoWoP, *tr. by* Willis Barnstone *and* Usha Nilsson

Rana, why do you treat me as your enemy? Mirabai, *Hindi.* BoWoP, *tr. by* Willis Barnstone *and* Usha Nilsson

Ranch in the Coulee, The. Gwendolen Haste. PaTW *Fr.* Montana Wives.

Randal Groveling works where I work. Song from a Two-Desk Office. Byron Buck. NYBP

Randall, my son, before you came just now. Donald Davidson. FuPo

Random Generation of English Sentences; or, The Revenge of the Poets. William Jay Smith. OBAL

Random Pleasures. Tu Fu, *Chinese.* SuSp, *tr. by* Irving Y. Lo

Random (Re-arrangeable) Study for *Views*. Tony Towle. PmAP

Random Reflections on a Summer Evening. John Hall Wheelock. NYBP

Random talk has blown in. Raisa Blokh, *Russian.* TCRP, *tr. by* Nina Kossman

Random Thoughts Written in Spring. Wang Yü-ch'eng, *Chinese.* SuSp, *tr. by* Irving Y. Lo

Random Verses on Mountain Life. Yüan Hao-wen, *Chinese.*
  "Clustered trees filled with the sounds of autumn." SuSp, *tr. by* Stephen West
  "Winding creek and scattered maple groves, A." SuSp, *tr. by* Stephen West

Randy young girl called Miranda, A. Limerick. Peter Alexander. PeLi

Range-finding. Robert Frost. MoP; NIP-4; NoAM; OBWP; Poetr; RB

Range in the Desert, The. Randall Jarrell. NOBA; PoWW

Range is French and has a mind of its own, The. The Collector's Marginalia. Peter Sirr. PBCIP

Range Rovers carry. Three xlvii. Laurie Duggan. BMAP

Ranges / of clinker heaps. John Maydew or The Allotment. Charles Tomlinson. OBGa

Rank. Lincoln Kirstein. FaBoA; OBWP

Rank Harvest of Betrayal, The. Wilma Stockenström, *Afrikaans.* PeSAV, *tr.* by Rosa Keet

Rank on rank of false right eyes. Options. James Seay. WeT

Rank stench of those bodies haunts me still, The. Siegfried Sassoon. PeFWW

Rank weeds, that every art and care defy. Virgil. OBCVT, *tr.* by George Crabbe *Fr.* The Village.

Ranks of electroplated cubes, dwindling to glitters. Fixed Ideas. Kenneth Slessor. BMAP

Rannoch, by Glencoe. T. S. Eliot. NAEL-2 *Fr.* Landscapes. RB

Ransomed Spirit to Her Home, The. William Bingham Tappan. AH

Rant Block. Michael McClure. SPE

Rantin' Dog, the Daddie o't, The. Robert Burns. FaBoVe; OxBoLi; PeLV

Rantin' dog, the daddie o't, The. (LL) The Rantin' Dog, the Daddie o't. Robert Burns. FaBoVe; OxBoLi; PeLV

Rantin Laddie, The. Robert Burns. ESPB

Rantin Laddie, The. *Unknown.* AmFP

Rantin, Rovin Robin. Robert Burns. OxBS

Rapacious Spain/ Follow'd her hero's triumphs o'er the main. The Lust of Gold. James Montgomery. *Fr.* The West Indies. PBCV

Rape. Jayne Cortez. GT; NMM-2; PmAP

Rape. Joan Larkin. GLP

Rape. Tom Pickard. FaBoTw

Rape of Lucrece, The. Thomas Heywood.

    Matin Song. GLoP; OBEV

    (Good Morrow.) CH

    ("Pale clouds, away! and welcome, day!") ITG

Rape of Lucrece, The. Ovid, *Latin.* OBCVT, *tr.* by John Gower

Rape of Lucrece, The. Shakespeare.

    Before the Rape. NoSic

    "Her lily hand her rosy cheek lies under." EP

    Lucrece's Death. NoSic

    "Mis-shapen Time, copesmate of ugly Night." OAEL-1

    Opportunity. PoEL-2

    (Outcry upon Opportunity, An.) NOBE

Rape of the Lock[, an Heroi-Comical Poem], The, *see also* To Belinda on the Rape of the Lock. Alexander Pope. FHYEP; HAP; ImPo; OAEL-1; OBNV; PeLV; PoEL-3

    "Belinda still her downy Pillow prest." OxBSn

    "But anxious cares the pensive nymph oppressed." EBNV; OxAEP-1

    "But when to mischief mortals bend their will." OxAEP-1

    "For lo! the board with cups and spoons is crown'd." UV

    Hampton Court. OBSV

    "Hither the heroes and the nymphs resort." ECEV

    Rape of the Lock, The. CABP; NoP-4

    ("What dire offense from amorous causes springs.") CABP; NoP-4

    "'Say why are beauties praised and honoured most'." ECEV

    "She said: the pitying audience melt in tears." EBNV, *canto* V, *abr.*

    "Sol through white curtains shot a tim'rous ray." ECEV; EP

    ("And Betty's praised for labours not her own.") (LL) EP

    Toilet, The. NOBE

    Voyage on the Thames, The. NOBE

    "What dire offence from am'rous causes springs." EBNV; NOEC; Poetr

Rape Poem, The. Tommi Avicolli. GLP

Rape Poem. Marge Piercy. Poetsp

Raped and Revenged. Rudyard Kipling. *Fr.* Epitaphs of the War [1914–1918]. OBWP

Raper from Passenack, The. William Carlos Williams. PFE; PoPoPo

    ("—and disgust.") (LL) PoPoPo

Raphael. Henrietta Cordelia Ray. CBWP-3

Raphael. Priscilla Jane Thompson. CBWP-2

Rapid day is gone; her banner swings the night, The. Evening. Andreas Gryphius, *German.* GePo, *tr.* by George C. Schoolfield

Rapid Transit. James Agee. MoAmPo

Rapier, lie there! and there, my hat and feather! The Poetaster. Samuel Rowlands. *Fr.* Melancholy Conceit. OxBSP

Rapier of Treason, A. *Unknown, Arabic.* BoWoP, *tr.* by Willis Barnstone

Rapist, who reeked of cheap booze, A. Limerick. *Unknown.* PeLi

Rapist's Villanelle, The. Thomas M. Disch. RA

Rapparees. Richard Murphy. BIrV; NOIV; PBCIP *Fr.* The Battle of Aughrim.

Rapt. Irene McKinney. PBCAP

Rapt in the visionary theme. Mrs Robinson to the Poet Coleridge. Mary Robinson. Ro

Rapt with the rage of mine own ravisht thought. An Hymne of Heavenly Beautie. Edmund Spenser. PeECV *Fr.* Fowre Hymnes.

Rapture, The. Henry Baker. NOEC

Rapture, A. Thomas Carew. BeJo; CABP; CaPo; NAEL-1; OAEL-1; OxAEP-1; SeCP

    ("Shall the embraces of our bodyes taste.") (LL) PBRV

    ("Should make men atheists, and not women whores.") (LL) CABP

Rapture, The. Adam Cornford.

    "And it came to pass just as they had foretold." CLPP

Rapture. Stefan George, *German.* AWP, *tr.* by Ludwig Lewisohn

Rapture. Ilsong Kwon, *Korean.* CKP, *tr.* by Jaihiun Kim

Rapture. Susan Mitchell. BAP-93

Rapture, The. Thomas Traherne. GeHe; NOSC

Rapunzel. Olga Broumas. CPO

Rapunzel Rapunzel let down your hair. The After-Thought. Stevie Smith. OxBC

Rare are thy cheeks, Susanna, which do show. Upon Mistresse Susanna Southwell, Her Cheeks. Robert Herrick. BeJo

Rare Birds, The. Imamu Amiri Baraka. MoNo

Rare flower, leaf-fringed, or tender yellow gold. Yellow Sunflower of Szechwan. Chang Yü, *Chinese.* SuSp, *tr.* by Irving Y. Lo

Rare medieval Spirit! brooding seer! Dante. Henrietta Cordelia Ray. CBWP-3

Rare temples thou hast seen, I know. The Fairy Temple; or, Oberon's Chapel. Robert Herrick. CaPo

Rare, twice-in-a-lifetime form of sport, A. The Retort Perfect. Justin Richardson. OBCoV

Rare Willie Drowned in Yarrow; or, The Water o Gamrie, *vers.* A. *Unknown.* ESPB

Rare Willy. *Unknown. See* Rare Willie Drowned in Yarrow; or, The Water o Gamrie.

Rarely, rarely, comest thou. Song. Shelley. FHYEP; GTBS-P; LaPo; OBNC

Rascal far gone in treachery, A. Limerick. *Unknown.* PeLi

Raspberries. Laurence David Lerner. EBEV

Raspberry in the Pudding, The. Philip O'Connor. SPE

Rat, The. W. H. Davies. OBWVE; OxBTC

Rat-a-tat-tat, Rat-a-tat-tat. The Postman. Clive Sansom. BoTP

Rat and the Elephant, The. Jean de La Fontaine, *French.* OBVE, *tr.* by Marianne Moore

Rat-fink Baby. Brothers at the Bar. Naomi Long Madgett. NBV

Rat is in the trap, it is in the trap, The. Song of a Rat. Ted Hughes. CMoP

Rat is the concisest Tenant, The. Emily Dickinson. APo

Rat Song. Margaret Atwood. NIP-4 *Fr.* Songs of the Transformed.

Rat too has a skin (to tan), A. Sans Equity and sans Poise. Confucius. *Fr.* Yung Wind. CTC, *tr.* by Ezra Pound

Rat Trap. Mick Gowar. NOxBChV

Rata blooms explode, the bow-legged tomcat, The. James Keir Baxter. PeNZ *Fr.* Autumn Testament.

Ratatouille. Gina Berkeley. PeLi

Ratcatcher's Daughter, The. *Unknown.* OxBoLi

Rath in front of the oak wood, The. *Unknown.* NOIV

"Rather dead than spotted"; and believe it. Then the Ermine. Marianne Moore. PoA

Rather extreme vegetarian, A. Limerick. "Sagittarius." PeLi

Rather notice, mon cher. To a Solitary Disciple. William Carlos Williams. VGW

Rather remote, all of it. Vanished Work. Hans Magnus Enzensberger, *German.* VCWP, *tr.* by Hans Magnus Enzensberger and Michael Hamburger

Rather skinny beauty, you'll find, / is Diocleia, A. Argentarius, *Greek.* GrAn, *tr.* by Fleur Adcock

Rather than attribute, towards the brush with open sea. (LL) A Note to Tony Towle (After WS). Charles North. FtOS; PmAP

Rather than Live in Snuff, will be put out. (LL) On the Snuff of a Candle. Sir Walter Ralegh. FaBoEE; SiPS

Rather than our bodies the sand. Army Beach with Trumpets. Jack Spicer. APSN

Rather than your fine hotels. Sightseers in a Courtyard. Nicolás Guillén, *Spanish.* TTY, *tr.* by Langston Hughes

Ration Card, The. Liz Sohappy Bahe. CDW

Rational Man. Muriel Rukeyser. AF

Rats, The. Georg Trakl, *German.* APo, *tr.* by John Hollander

Rats, bedbugs, blacks. (LL) From Our Album. Lawson Fusao Inada. PaTW

Rats by night such mischief did, The. Fable XXI: The Rat-catcher and Cats. John Gay. OxAEP-1

Rat's Legs, The. Russell Edson. WeT

Rattan bed, paper netting. I wake from morning sleep. Li Ch'ing-chao, *Chinese*. BoWoP, *tr. by* Willis Barnstone *and* Sun Chu-chin

Rattat! Rattat! Postman's Knock. Rodney Bennett. BoTP

Rattle. Peter Blue Cloud. HATNAP

Rattle Bag, The. Dafydd ap Gwilym, *Welsh*. NBLV; RB, *tr. by* Joseph Clancy; NNPT, *tr. by* Joseph P. Clancy

Rattler, Alert. Brewster Ghiselin. HAP; WeW-3

Rattlesnake Country. Robert Penn Warren. NAAL-2; VCAP

Rattlesnakes have begun to come out, The. Snakes. Peter Wild. AmPA

Rattling like dry leaves on a stunted tree. (LL) Song of the Fucked Duck. Marge Piercy. BoWoP

Rattling, like manacles, the chains on the doors, *sl. diff. vers.* Osip Emilevich Mandelstam. See Leningrad.

Rattling little cart and patches of yellow dust at dusk. A Ballad of the Little Cart. Ch'en Tzu-lung, *Chinese*. SuSp, *tr. by* Wu-chi Liu

Rauf Coilyear. *Unknown*.

   "Coilyear, gudlie in feir, tuke him be the hand, The." OxBS

Rav / of Northern White Russia declined, The. Illustrious Ancestors. Denise Levertov. AmPP; MoP; NAAL-2; NOBA; PmAP; VGW

Ravaged Villa, The. Herman Melville. APN-2; CTC; GaP; NOBA; PoEL-5

Raven, The. Coleridge. NOxBChV

Raven, The. Nikolai Ivanovich Glazkov, *Russian*. TCRP, *tr. by* Daniel Weissbort

Raven, The. Nicarchus of Alexandria. AWP; FaBoEE; OBAL *Fr.* Variations of Greek Themes.

Raven, The. Edgar Allan Poe. APN-1; AmPP; BLPA; CH; ChAP; ColAP; EBEvV; EBNV; FaBoBe; FaBoCh; HeIP-4; ImGa; NAAL-1; NAAL-3; NCAP; NIP-4; NOBA; NoP-4; OBCA; OBNV; OxBA; PAR; PWR; PoRA; TAP; TFi; UV

   ("And my soul from out that shadow that lies floating on the floor / Shall be lifted—never more!") (LL) PAR

   ("Once upon a midnight dreary, while I pondered, weak and weary.") ChAP; ColAP; NoP-4

Raven, The. Edwin Arlington Robinson, *after* Nicarchus. AWP; FaBoEE; OBAL

Raven Days, The. Sidney Lanier. APN-2; OxBA

Raven dies, The. (LL) The Raven. Edwin Arlington Robinson, *after* Nicarchus. AWP; FaBoEE; OBAL

Raven eyes blink. Raven is Two-Faced. Robert H. Davis. HATNAP

Raven, gather us to that dark breast. Raven Tells Stories. Robert H. Davis. HATNAP

Raven himself is hoarse, The. Shakespeare. EBEvV *Fr.* Macbeth.

Raven is Two-Faced. Robert H. Davis. HATNAP

Raven/Moon. Anita Endrezze-Danielson. VoR

Raven sat upon a tree, A. The Sycophantic Fox and the Gullible Raven. Guy Wetmore Carryl. BLPA; NBLV; OBCA; PBMP

Raven Tells Stories. Robert H. Davis. HATNAP

Ravenglass Railway Station, *paraphrased*. Norman Nicholson. NYBP

Ravening Coyote comes. Three Songs of Mad Coyote. *Unknown, Nez Percé Indian*. STP, *tr. by* Herbert J. Spinden

Ravens. Ted Hughes. InPS-3

Ravens at Deer Creek. Robert Wrigley. PuP-16

Ravens gnawing/ men's necks. Before the Last Battle. *Unknown*. *Fr.* The Táin. NOIV, *tr. by* Thomas Kinsella

Raven's Monologue. Ivan V. Lalic, *Serbo-Croatian*. HSix, *tr. by* Charles Simic

Ravine on a Cold Evening. Li Ho, *Chinese*. SuSp, *tr. by* Maureen Robertson

Raving warre, begot / In the thirstye sands. Thomas Campion. AAS *Fr.* Observations in the Art of English Poesie.

Ravings. Thomas Hood Jr. BXAP

Ravin's of Piute Poet Poe. C. L. Edson. BXAP

Ravished by all that to the eyes is fair. Michelangelo Buonarroti. *Fr.* Three Poems. AWP, *tr. by* George Santayana

Ravished [*or* Ravisht] in that fair[e] *Via Lactea*. (LL) Upon Julia's Breasts. Robert Herrick. CaPo

Raw Flesh. Vasco [*or* Vasko] Popa, *Serbo-Croatian*.

   Be Seeing You. HP; PoSu, *tr. by* Anne Pennington

   ("After the third evening round.") HP, *tr. by* Anne Pennington

   In the Village of My Forefathers. PoSu, *tr. by* Anne Pennington

   Time Swept Up. PoSu, *tr. by* Anne Pennington

Rawk o' the autumn hangs over the woodlands, The. John Clare. SCGP

Ray. Hayden Carruth. PuP-17

Ray Charles at Mississippi State. Tom Dent. NBV

Ray Charles is a dangerous man ('way cross town), / And I love him. Bob Kaufman. *See* Blues Note.

Ray Charles is the black wind of Kilimanjaro. Blues Note. Bob Kaufman. BB; PoBA

Ray of light slants through the windows, A. Wedding. Nikolai Alekseievich Zabolotsky, *Russian*. TCRP, *tr. by* Daniel Weissbort

Raymond Chandler: The Big Sleep. Basil Ransome-Davies. OBCoV

Raynsford, a knight, fit to have served King Arthur. Sir John Raynsford's Confession. John Harington. NoSic

Ray's third new car in half as many years. Family Reunion. Louise Erdrich. HATNAP; NoAM

Razors pain you. Résumé. Dorothy Parker. HeIP-4; InPK-6; NAAL-2; NALW; NBLV; NoP-4; OBAL; PFE; Poetr; TrJP; UV *Fr.* Some Beautiful Letters.

Razzle Dazzle! Whiskers Meets Polly. Michael Stillman. TLR

Razzle dazzle maggots are summary, The. Easter. Frank O'Hara. SPE

Razzmatazz. Gilbert Sorrentino. FTOS

Re-act for Action ("Re-act to Animals"). Haki Madhubuti. BPo

Re-birth. *Unknown, Bushman*. PeSA, *tr. by* W. H. I. Bleek *and* Jack Cope

Re-encounter. Joaquim Paço D'Arcos, *Portuguese*. PeSAV, *tr. by* Roy Campbell

Re-forming the Crystal. Adrienne Rich. TAP

Re-plyed, extorted, oft transposed, and fleeting. Sea Voyage. William Empson. CMoP

Re-reading Jane. Anne Stevenson. NALW

Re:searches (Fragments, after Anakreon, for Emily Dickinson). Kathleen Fraser. PmAP

Re-statement of Romance. Wallace Stevens. ITG

Re that winter cloak. Slow Giving. Ibn al-Rumi, *Arabic*. ArPe, *tr. by* Omar S. Pound

Re: the question of poems. Memo from the Desk of X. Donald Justice. TwCP

Re-Verse. Diane Ward. FTOS

Reach. Phyllis Janowitz. IFJA

Reach, The. Carl Phillips. GT

Reach back and bring me the firmness of her hand. (LL) Request to a Year. Judith Wright. NoP-4

Reach for arrows of falling light. A man once sang. Falling Moon. Roberta Hill Whiteman. CDW

Reach like you never reached before past Night's somber robes. Tauhid. Askia Muhammad Touré. PoBA

Reach me down my Tycho Brahe, I would know him when we meet. The Old Astronomer to His Pupil. Sarah Williams. BLPA

Reach out their carved, indulgent arms to me! (LL) Helen. Paul Valéry, *French*. LoP, *tr. by* Robert Lowell

Reach, with your whiter hands, to me. To the Water Nymphs, Drinking at the Fountain. Robert Herrick. BeJo; CaPo; NAEL-1

Reaches the Body. Claire Needell.

   "Color, even whiteness, reaches / the body as a name." PT

Reaching. (LL) Surf. Lillian Morrison. KaS

Reaching out into the sea, passing the waves its exhaust smoking. Mission Work-Boat. *Unknown, Aborigine*. NOBAu, *tr. by* Mungayana Nundhirribala

Reaching Yellow River. Roberta Hill Whiteman. HATNAP

Reactionary Poet, The. Ishmael Reed. GT

Read about the Buddhist monk. Dilemma. Patricia Beer. OxBC

Read and committed to the flames, I call. On Not Being Milton. Tony Harrison. CABP; FaBoPV; NoP-4 *Fr.* The School of Eloquence. NAEL-2; NoAM

Read here: / This is the story of Evarra-man. Evarra and His Gods. Rudyard Kipling. MoBrPo

Read it, and give it her to sing. (LL) The Ballad of Villon and Fat Madge. François Villon, *French*. EP, *tr. by* Algernon Charles Swinburne; OBVE, *tr. by* Swinburne

Read it not, noble lords. Shakespeare. OxAEP-1 *Fr.* Coriolanus.

Read me Euripides. The Follies of Adam. Theodore Roethke. ChIV-1

Read Me, Please! Robert Graves. NYBP

Read my riddle, I pray. An Equal. *Unknown*. ReMoGo

"Read out the names!" and Burke sat back. The Fighting Race. Joseph I. C. Clarke. BLPA

Read some lines a poet wrote in the exile of his town. Town. Marie-Claire Bancquart, *French*. MFP, *tr. by* Martin Sorrell

Read—Sweet—how others—strove. Emily Dickinson. AH; NOCV

Read the Bible, it will tell. The Bible. Lizelia Augusta Jenkins Moorer. CBWP-3

Read this Song of Hiawatha! (LL) Introduction: "Should you ask me, whence these stories?" Henry Wadsworth Longfellow. ColAP; MeMAP; NOBA; PoE; Poetr

Read Your Fate. Charles Simic. BAP-94

Read yr / exile. A Poem for a Poet. Haki Madhubuti. PoBA

Readen ov a Head-Stwone. William Barnes. CH

Reader, The. Thomas Merton. CRP

Reader, The. Wallace Stevens. SAmP

Reader, behold! this monster wild. Infant Innocence. A. E. Housman. NOBL

Reader, beneath this turf I lie. Thomas Brown. FaBoEE

Reader! I am no poet: but I grieve! To the Reader. Urian Oakes. SCAP

Reader, I was born and cried. Epitaph on the Fart in the Parliament House. John Hoskyns. FaBoEE

Reader, I would not have thee mistake. His Own Epitaph, When He Was Sick. John Hoskyns. FaBoEE

Reader, listen ere we go. The Book's Creed. Joseph Seamon Cotter, Sr. AAP

Reader my friend, is in the words here, somewhere. The Cheer. William Meredith. AFr

Reader of Poetry, The. Ilya L'vovich Selvinsky, *Russian*. TCRP, *tr. by* Daniel Weissbort

Reader over My Shoulder, The. Robert Graves. NAEL-2

Reader, pass on, nor idly waste [*or* don't waste] your time. In Peterborough Churchyard. Paulus Silentiarius, *Greek*. FaBoEE; NOBL

Reader, stay, / And if I had no more to say. An Epitaph on Master Philip Gray. Ben Jonson. FaBoEE

Reader upon this field of Marble see. Inscription on Monument of Dorothy, Lady Hubert. Anne King. KTR

Reader, when these dumb stones have told. Another [On the Duke of Buckingham]. Thomas Carew. NOSC

Readers and the hearers like my books, The. Critics. Martial, *Latin*. AWP, *tr. by* Sir John Harington

Readers, forgive me. Ten ii. Laurie Duggan. BMAP

Readers of Newspapers. Marina Tsvetayeva, *Russian*. TCRP, *tr. by* Elaine Feinstein *and* Angela Livingstone

Readers of the *Boston Evening Transcript*, The. The *Boston Evening Transcript*. T. S. Eliot. InPK-6

Reader's threaten'd (not in vain) with "sleep," The. Alexander Pope. *See* Essay on Criticism.

Reading. Elizabeth Barrett Browning. *Fr.* Aurora Leigh. VWP

Reading. Joanne Burns. BMAP

Reading, The. Gabriel Gbadamosi. HBAPE

Reading, A. Virginia Hooper. PT

Reading. P'i Jih-hsiu, *Chinese*. SuSp, *tr. by* William H. Nienhauser

Reading. Jean-Joseph Rabéarivelo, *French*. NegPo, *tr. by* Ellen Conroy Kennedy

Reading a life of Alexander the Great, Alexander. Wine. Raymond Carver. BLT

Reading a Medal. Terence Tiller. FaBoTw; GTBS-P

Reading a Story to My Child. Primus St. John. CMAP

Reading Aloud to My Father. Jane Kenyon. BAP-96

Reading, and reading—little is the gain. Suspiria Noctis. Henry Howard Brownell. APN-2

Reading Aquinas. Michael Heffernan. WeW-3

Reading Before We Read, Horoscope and Weather. Wyatt Prunty. RA

Reading, Dreaming, Hiding. Kelly Cherry. FFC

Reading Emerson. Cottonmouths are moving mildly. Lake Drummond Dream. Dave Jeddie Smith. VCAP

Reading Frank O'Hara in a Mexican Rainstorm. Michael McClure. BB

Reading how even the Swiss had thrown the sponge. Beyond the Alps. Robert Lowell. LCAP-2; NOBA

Reading in Li Po. After the Last Dynasty. Stanley Kunitz. TAP

Reading in my palanquin, I fall asleep and dream. Passing By Waterwheel Bay. Yang Wan-li, *Chinese*. SuSp, *tr. by* Jonathan Chaves

Reading in the Autumn. Shen Chou, *Chinese*. ImGa

Reading in the heat of noon. Summer Day. Yüan Mei, *Chinese*. OHMPC, *tr. by* Kenneth Rexroth

Reading in the Night. Roy Fuller. OxBC

Reading Indian Poetry. Ramona Wilson. VoR

Reading Lesson, The. Richard Murphy. PBCIP

Reading Matter. Martin Sorescu, *Rumanian*. CBNP

Reading Milosz. Lev Vladimir Loseff, *Russian*. TCRP, *tr. by* G. S. Smith

Reading Mother, The. Strickland W. Gillilan. BLPA

Reading my Verses, I like't them so well. The Poetresses Hasty Resolution. Margaret Lucas Cavendish, Duchess of Newcastle. KTR

Reading Myself. Robert Lowell. HCAP; NAAL-2; TAP; VCAP

Reading of the Psalm, The. Robert Francis. AFr

Reading *Paradise Lost* in Protestant Ulster 1984. Seamus Deane. BiHa; PBCIP

Reading Pornography in Old Age. Howard Nemerov. NoAM

Reading some Russian novel. White Gloves. William Plomer. PeSAV

Reading the Annals of Emperor Wu of the Han Dynasty. Wu Wei-yeh, *Chinese*. CoBLCP, *tr. by* Jonathan Chaves

Reading the Bible Backwards. Eleanor Wilner. NoP-4

Reading the Book of Hills and Seas. Ch'ien T'ao, *Chinese*. ChiP, *tr. by* Arthur Waley

Reading the Books Our Children Have Written. Dave Jeddie Smith. HCAP

Reading the Brothers Grimm to Jenny. Lisel Mueller. NYBP

Reading *The Classic of Hills and Seas*. T'ao Ch'ien, *Chinese*. CoBCP, *tr. by* Burton Watson

Reading the Collected Works of Li Po and Tu Fu: A Colophon. Po Chü-i, *Chinese*. SuSp, *tr. by* Irving Y. Lo

Reading the Names of the Vietnam War Dead. Thomas McGrath. CDa

Reading the Poems of an Absent Friend. Ou-yang Hsiu, *Chinese*. OHPC, *tr. by* Kenneth Rexroth

Reading the Poetry Collection of Lü Fang-ch'ing. Chang Yü, *Chinese*. CoBLCP, *tr. by* Jonathan Chaves

Reading the Unpublished Manuscripts of Louis MacNeice at Kinsale Harbour. Desmond O'Grady. PBCIP

Reading through your work tonight. Negative Passage. Michael Newman. PoA

Reading Time : 1 Minute 26 Seconds. Muriel Rukeyser. PBWP

Reading Walt Whitman. Calvin Forbes. NBV; PoBA

Reading with the Poets. Stanley Plumly. PuP-17

Reading Yeats I do not think / of Ireland. 26. Lawrence Ferlinghetti. CLPP

Reading your poems I am aware. A Letter to Peter Levi. Elizabeth Jennings. OxAEP-2

Readings. Czeslaw Milosz, *Polish*. GI, *tr. by* Czeslaw Milosz *and* Lillian Vallee

Readings, Forecasts, Personal Guidance. Kenneth Fearing. MoAmPo

Readings of History. Adrienne Rich. CoAmPo

Ready. Margaret Junkin Preston. PWR

Ready They Make Hauberks Sarrazinese. *Unknown*. *Fr.* The Song of Roland. NAWM-1, *tr. by* Frederick Goldin, abr.

Ready to faint when held. The Opium Poppy. Song-yong Park, *Korean*. CKP, *tr. by* Jaihiun Kim

Readymade. John Perreault. SPE

Real danger. gambles. and the edge of death. (LL) What You Should Know to Be a Poet. Gary Snyder. APSN; NNaP; PoM

Real dead. (LL) Sometime during eternity / some guys show up. Lawrence Ferlinghetti. NoP-4

Real duel of Apollo, The. Apollo and Marsyas. Zbigniew Herbert, *Polish*. PoSu, *tr. by* John *and* Bogdana Capenter

Real Estate. David Antin. FTOS

Real Indian Leans Against, The. "Chrystos." UnSA

Real Live. Ted Berrigan. FTOS *Fr.* The Sonnets.

Real Muse, The. Tom Scott. PoA

Real People Loves One Another, The. Rob Penny. MBE; PoBA

Real poems are being written in outports, The. Without Benefit of Tape. Dorothy Livesay. NOBC

Real Thing, The. Ronald Wallace. IFJA

Realarro. Marc Matthews. HCP

Realism. Carla Harryman. PmAP

Realism. Tom Mandel. PmAP

Realist, The. Carl H. Greene. NBV

Realistic Bar and Grill, A. David Shapiro. PmAP

Realistic dreams with a whiff of terror. 29-77-02. Artur Miedzyrzecki, *Polish*. PoSu, *tr. by* Stanislaw Baranczak *and* Clare Cavanagh

Reality. Léon Damas, *French*. NegPo, *tr. by* Ellen Conroy Kennedy

Reality demands. Wislawa Szymborska, *Polish*. VCWP, *tr. by* Stanislaw Baranczak *and* Clare Cavanagh

Reality Is an Activity of the Most August Imagination. Wallace Stevens. NoAM

Reality is not limited to the tactile. The Love of the Flesh. Janet Holmes. BAP-94

Reality of Autumn, The. Duane Niatum. HATNAP

Reality U.S.A. Mark Halliday. NAmP90

Realization. Günter Kunert, *German*. CEEP, *tr. by* Michael Hamburger

Realization of difference comes, The. Diane Wakoski. NMM-2

Realizing the Futility of Life. Po Chü-i, *Chinese*. ChiP, *tr. by* Arthur Waley

Really, it is not the. In This Age of Hard Trying, Nonchalance Is Good and. Marianne Moore. MeMAP

Realm is here of masquing light, A. Light at Equinox. Léonie Adams. ColAP

Realm of Fancy, The. Keats. *See* Fancy.

Realtheater Piece Two. Jerome Rothenberg. FTOS

Reaper, The. Wordsworth. *See* The Solitary Reaper.

Reapers. Mathilde Blind. WPE

Reapers. Jean Toomer. BPo; ColAP; GT; HAP; MoP; NoAM; NoP-4; PoBA; Poetr; SoSe-8; TRP; WeW-3

Rear-Guard, The. Siegfried Sassoon. MoBrPo; NAEL-2; NoAM; OBWP; PoWW; SAGP

Rear their glad nations and reward their toil. (LL) The Columbiad. Joel Barlow. APN-1; NCAP

Rear Vision. William Jay Smith. NYBP

Reared Within the Mountains! Invocation To Dsilyi N'Eyani. *Unknown.* APN-2, *tr. by* Washington Matthews *Fr.* The Mountain Chant.

Rearmament. Robinson Jeffers. OxBA

Rearrange a "Wife's" affection! Emily Dickinson. NALW; PoEL-5

Reason. Charlotte Brontë. VWP

Reason. Philippe Jaccottet, *French.* MFP, *tr. by* Martin Sorrell

Reason. Josephine Miles. InPK-6; NALW; NoAM; PFE; Poetr; TAP

Reason, The. Eric Pankey. GI

Reason and Religion. Dryden. *Fr.* Religio Laici.

Reason blinded by sin, Lesbia. Carmen 75. Catullus. STV, *tr. by* John Frederick Nims; AWP, *tr. by* Walter Savage Landor *Fr.* Carmina.

Reason enough for anything ugly. It balances the beauty in the /world world. (LL) Justice Is Reason Enough. Diane Wakoski. AmPA; NMM-2

Reason for Poetry, The. Nancy Morejón, *Spanish.* WPOW, *tr. by* Anita Whitney

Reason Has Moons. Ralph Hodgson. FaBoCh; MoBrPo; OxBSP

Reason, in faith thou art well served, that still. Sonnet 10. Sir Philip Sidney. NAEL-1 *Fr.* Astrophil and Stella. AAS; SiPS

Reason, Reason is my middle name. (LL) Reason. Josephine Miles. InPK-6; NALW; NoAM; PFE; Poetr; TAP

Reason, tell me thy mind, if here be reason, *speech of Cleophila.* Love and Reason. Sir Philip Sidney. SiPS *Fr.* Arcadia.

Reason we do not learn from history is, The. Ultima Ratio Reagan. Howard Nemerov. AF

Reason we're asked to endure, The. Limerick. Bill Greenwell. PeLi

Reason Why, The. George Clinton Rowe. AAP

Reason why, The. Chris Van Wyk. PeSAV

Reason why i do it, The. The Making of Poems. Lucille Clifton. CrSp

Reason why the Park is closed, The. Deceit in the Park. Patrick Hare. OBGa

Reason with them. Speak softly. Hide your stick. 13 Ways of Eradicating Blackbirds. Mark DeFoe. BXAP

Reasonable Affliction, A. Matthew Prior. NOEC

(Cause and Effect.) NBLV

Reasons. Thomas James. PoA

Reasons for and against Marrying Widows. Henricus Selyns. SCAP

Reasons for Attendance. Philip Larkin. PoPoPo

Reasons for Music. Archibald MacLeish. MeMAP

Rebeca in a Mirror. Judith Rodriguez. CBAP

Rebecca. Vadim Leonidovich Andreyev, *Russian.* TCRP, *tr. by* Olga Carlisle

Rebecca. E. Ethelbert Miller. ISC

Rebecca Cutlet. Bill Berkson. PmAP

Rebecca, sweet-one, little-one. Susan Griffin. MDDM

Rebecca, Who Slammed Doors for Fun and Perished Miserably. Hilaire Belloc. NOBL

Rebecca's Hymn. Sir Walter Scott. *Fr.* Ivanhoe.

Rebecca's maid: a girl come from afar. Jacob and Esau. Else Lasker-Schüler, *German.* BoWoP, *tr. by* Rosemarie Waldrop

Rebel, The. Mari E. Evans. CRP; PoBA; SAGP

("Trouble.") (LL) SAGP

Rebel, A. John Gould Fletcher. MoAmPo

Rebel, The. Rudyard Kipling. *Fr.* Epitaphs of the War [1914–1918]. OBWP

Rebel, The. Innes Randolph. CBCWP; NBLV; OBAL; OxBoLi

("And I don't care a dam.") (LL) CBCWP

Rebel General, The. Chris Wallace-Crabbe. CBAP

Rebel [*or* Rebell] Scot, The. John Cleveland.

"How? 'Providence', and yet a Scottish crew?" NOSC

"Lord! what a goodly thing is want of shirts." OBSV

Nature herself doth Scotchmen beasts confess. OBSV

Rebellion against the North Side. Naomi Shihab Nye. WeW-3

Rebellion lay in his way, and he found it. Shakespeare. *Fr.* King Henry IV, Pt. I. NAEL-1

Rebellion of the Waters, The. George Darley. NOBRP

Rebellion Over, I See Off a Friend Who Is Returning North, The. Ssu-k'ung Shu, *Chinese.* CoBCP, *tr. by* Burton Watson

("World in turmoil—we came south together; A.") CoBCP, *tr. by* Burton Watson

Rebellion shook an ancient dust. April Mortality. Léonie Adams. MoAmPo

Rebellious fools that scorn to bow. The Bracelet. Thomas Stanley. BeJo

Rebels' cavalry are everywhere, The. Tsung Ch'en. CoBLCP, *tr. by* Jonathan Chaves *Fr.* On Things Seen.

Rebel's Progress. Tom Earley. OBWVE

Rebirth. Margaret E. Bruner. PoToHe

Rebirth. Rudyard Kipling. OBNC

Rebirth. Catriona Stamp. BrRo

Rebirth of Venus, The. Mary Jo Salter. FFC; WWSi

Reborn. Kingsley Amis. OxBC

Rebuke by the Bishop of London, A. Limerick. Victor Gray. PeLi

Rebuke Me Not. John Addington Symonds. Son

Rebuke to Robert Southey, A. *Unknown.* ECWP

Rebuked, she turned and ran. Portrait of a Figure near Water. Jane Kenyon. AFr

Rebus Tact. Ray DiPalma. PmAP

Rebuttal of Tung-p'o's Poem on "Bathing the Infant," A. Ch'ien Ch'ien-i, *Chinese.* SuSp, *tr. by* Irving Y. Lo

Recall, The. Rudyard Kipling. PFE

Recall. Reed Whittemore. NYBP

Recall the other names. (LL) Names. Gerald Dawe. IIP; PNI

Recalled. Edwin Arlington Robinson. MeMAP

Recalling Former Travels. Tu Mu, *Chinese.*

"Caught in a storm outside Cloud Gate Abbey." PLT, *tr. by* A. C. Graham

"Li Po put it in a poem, this West-of-the-Waters Abbey." PLT, *tr. by* A. C. Graham

"Whirled ten years beyond all bounds." PLT, *tr. by* A. C. Graham

Recalling the dead. (LL) Picture of a Nativity. Geoffrey Hill. NoAM; OxBC

Recalling the past years, my heart is often bewildered. Tune: "Decorous and Pretty." Kung Tzu-chen, *Chinese.* SuSp, *tr. by* An-yan Tang

Recalling War. Robert Graves. AF; CMoP; LiTM; NoAM; OAEL-2; OBWP; PeFWW; PoWW

Recalling When I Was Drunk. Yüan Chen, *Chinese.* SuSp, *tr. by* Dell R. Hales

Recantation. Minuchihri, *Persian.* ArPe, *tr. by* Omar S. Pound

Receipt for the Vapours. Lady Mary Wortley Montagu. *See* A Receipt to Cure [*or* for] the Vapours.

Receipt for Writing a Novel, A. Mary Alcock. ECWP

Receipt to Cure a Love Fit, A. *Unknown.* NOEC

Receipt to Cure [*or* for] the Vapours, A. Lady Mary Wortley Montagu. ECWP; NOEC; NoP-4

(Receipt for the Vapours.) PBWP; PeLV

Receive, dear friend, the truths I teach. Ode: 2.10. Horace. AWP; OBVE, *tr. by* William Cowper *Fr.* Odes.

Receives its annual reply! (LL) Altered look about the hills, An. Emily Dickinson. OxBA; SoSe-8

Receiving the Stigmata. Rita Dove. NAAAL

Recension Day. Duncan Forbes. APAD

Recent earthquake, A. Lucilius, *Greek.* GrAn, *tr. by* Peter Porter

(Recent Past, The.) C. S. Giscombe. GT

Recently in Sokol. Igor Kholin, *Russian.* TCRP, *tr. by* Albert C. Todd

Reception, The. June Jordan. FaBoWP

Receptionist has shiny fingernails, The. On Trading Time for Life by Work. Alan Dugan. AFr

Receptive, soft, and absolute. . . . . . . (LL) The Sundays of Satin-Legs Smith. Gwendolyn Brooks. NAAAL; Poetr; SeSe

Recessional. Robert Kelly. FTOS

Recessional. Rudyard Kipling. AWP; BLPA; CABP; CTV; EBEvV; FaBoPV; MoBrPo; NOBE; NOBVV; NoAM; NoP-4; OBEV; OBNC; OxAEP-2; PWR; SAGP; SCGP; TFi; UV; UnPo

Recessional. Thomas MacGreevy. CIP-2

Recipe. Bobbi Katz. CTV

Recipe for a Salad. Sydney Goodsir Smith. *See* A Salad.

Recipe for an Ocean in the Absence of the Sea. Richard Howard. TAP

Recipe for Hell-Broth, The. Shakespeare. *See* Thrice the Brinded Cat Hath Mewed.

Recipe for Living. Alfred Grant Walton. PoToHe

Recipe: Pastime for the Unemployed. Tom Pickard. NBrP

Recipes. Julia Randall. NMM-2

Reciprocal love, the only love that should concern us here, is the love that. The 32 Positions of Love. Paul Eluard *and* Andre Breton. PFTM, *tr. by* Marcel Jean *Fr.* The Immaculate Conception.

Reciprocity. John Drinkwater. PoA

Reciprocity. Vassar Miller. MT

Recital. John Updike. OBAL

Recitation. Ellease Southerland. GT

Recitative. Hart Crane. FaBoMo

Recitative. Iwan Goll. PeFWW, tr. by Patrick Bridgwater Fr. Requiem for the Dead of Europe.

Recitative: "Farmer's son is good and mad," The. Ronald McCuaig. NOBAu

Recite the dangers chiselled on this face. Lines for a Tomb. Donald Davidson. FuPo

Recklessly / I cast myself away. Lady Izumi, Japanese. PBWP, tr. by Edwin A. Cranston

Reckoning, The. Theodore Roethke. PoA

Reckoning. Fay Zwicky. NOBAu

"Reclining Figure." Donald Hall. CoAmPo; LCAP-2

("Laid-by.") (LL) CoAmPo

Recluse, The. Herman Melville. APN-2 Fr. Clarel: A Poem and Pilgrimage in the Holy Land.

Recluse; Home at Grasmere, The. Wordsworth.

(Home at Grasmere.)

Wordsworth and His Music. EPCY

Recluses, The. Stuart Z. Perkoff. NeAP

Recogitabo Tibi Omnes Annos Meos. William Habington. ChIV-1

Recognition, The. Denise Levertov. VGW

Recognition of Eve, The. Karl Shapiro. ChIV-1 Fr. Adam and Eve.

Recognitions. David Mura. MoLi

Recognized Futures. Lisa Suhair Majaj. UnSA

Recognized her a block away. (LL) Not this. / What then? Ron Silliman. PmAP

Recollect thou, in thunder. Tallulah. James Matthew Legaré. APN-2

Recollection, A. John Peale Bishop. Son

Recollection, A. Frances Darwin Cornford. FaBoWP; NTP

Recollection, The. Shelley. See To Jane: The Recollection.

Recollection of Bellagio. William Meredith. Poetr

Recollection of the Stone Circle near Keswick, A. Keats. Fr. Hyperion. OAEL-2; Ro

Recollections of an Old Spook. Richard Edwards. NOxBChV

Recollections of "Lalla Rookh." John Townsend Trowbridge. APN-2; OBAL

Recollections of Love. Coleridge. NAEL-2

Recollections of The Arabian Nights. Tennyson. OBGa

Recollections of the Cross. Vladimir Nikolaevich Sokolov, Russian. TCRP, tr. by Albert C. Todd

Recollections of the Sun. A. L. Hendriks. NBrP

Recompensed? Henrietta Cordelia Ray. CBWP-3

Reconcilement, The. Tennyson. See We Kiss'd Again with Tears.

Reconcilement, The. John, Duke of Buckingham and Normandy Sheffield. OBEV

Reconcilement between Jacob Tonson and Mr Congreve. An Imitation of Horace, Book III. Ode IX, The. Horace, Latin. OBCVT, tr. by Nicholas Rowe

Reconciliation. "Æ." OBMV; TrCP

Reconciliation. C. Day Lewis. PoWW; TwCP

Reconciliation. Else Lasker-Schüler, German. PBWP, tr. by Robert Alter

Reconciliation, The. Archibald MacLeish. MoAmPo

Reconciliation. Siegfried Sassoon. NSI

Reconciliation. Walt Whitman. APN-1; HAP; MeMAP; MoAmPo; NAAL-1; NAAL-3; NoP-4; OBWP; OxBA; OxBSP; SAGP; WeW-3

("In the coffin.") (LL) SAGP

Reconciliation: A Modern Version, The. Horace. See Odes 3.9: Dialogue between Horace and Lydia, A ("Donec gratus eram").

Reconnaissance. Arna Bontemps. BPo

"Reconnaissance in force"—just three brief words. Ilya Grigoryevich Ehrenburg, Russian. TCRP, tr. by Cathy Porter

Record is nothing, and the hero great. Sonnet. John Byrne Leicester Warren, 3d Baron De Tabley. EBVV

Record of a Past Affair, A. Li K'ai-hsien, Chinese. CoBLCP, tr. by Jonathan Chaves

Record of My Trip to Mount She, A. Yüan Hung-tao, Chinese. CoBLCP, tr. by Jonathan Chaves

Recorder, tax collector, landlord, friends. Ode for the Burial of a Citizen. John Ciardi. LiTM

Recorders ages hence. Walt Whitman. HeIP-4, MoAmPo; SAmP

Recording a Dream. Yang Shih-ch'i, Chinese. CoBLCP, tr. by Jonathan Chaves

Recording a Weird Happening. Li K'ai-hsien, Chinese. CoBLCP, tr. by Jonathan Chaves

Recording My Happiness. Wang Chiu-ssu, Chinese. CoBLCP, tr. by Jonathan Chaves

Recording My Happiness upon Returning Home. Wen Cheng-ming, Chinese. CoBLCP, tr. by Jonathan Chaves

Records all agree, The. Against Te Rauparaha. Alistair Campbell. PeNZ Fr. Sanctuary of Spirits.

Recovery, The. Edmund Blunden. MoBrPo

Recovery, The. Thomas Traherne. ESCV Fr. The Third Century.

Recreation. Jane Taylor. OBCoV; OxBoLi; PEW; WoRP

Recruit, The. A. E. Housman. FaPoR

Recruiting Drive. Charles Causley. OxBTC

Recruiting Officer of Shih-hao. Tu Fu, Chinese. SuSp, tr. by Irving Y. Lo

Recruiting Serjeant, The. Isaac Bickerstaffe.

"What a charming thing's a battle!" NOEC; OBCoV

Recruiting Song. Michael Foster. UV

Rectitude, and the terrible upstanding member. Washington in Love. John Berryman. LCAP-2

Rectors and parish priests complained to the bishop. William Langland. FaBoPV Fr. The Vision of Piers Plowman, Prologue.

Recuerdo. Edna St. Vincent Millay. ChAP; ImPo; LiTM; MeMAP; NAAL-2; NoAM; OxBA; PiM; PoA; Poetr; TAP

("And the sun rose dripping, a bucketful of gold.") (LL) PiM

Reculver Bay. Vicki Raymond. NOBAu

Recumbent against any mirror, any stardom. Mimetic. Anne Lauterbach. PmAP

Recuperating in Chang Villa. Huang Tsun-hsien, Chinese. SuSp, tr. by Irving Y. Lo

Recurring Opportunity. David Avidan, Hebrew. IP, tr. by Warren Bargad and Stanley F. Chyet

Recursus. Michael Palmer. APSN

Red. Eugene Field. CA

Red-and-green leather-helmeted. TV Room at the Children's Hospice. Michael Ryan. NAmP90

Red and green neon lights, the jazz hysteria. Nuit Blanche: North End. Conrad Potter Aiken. OxBA

Red and the Green, The. Anne Wilkinson. MoCV

Red Ant Way. Unknown, Navajo Indian.

Song: "Red young men under the ground, The." STP, tr. by Jerome Rothenberg

Red as a house burning down. (LL) Of Your Father's Indiscretions and the Train to California. Lynn Emanuel. MoLi; NAmP90

Red as his guide-book grows, moves on, and offers up a prayer for France. (LL) The Three Musicians. Aubrey Beardsley. NOBVV; PeVV

Red as the guardroom lamp. Heartbreak Camp. Roy Campbell. OxBTC

Red band of light stretches across the west, A. San Francisco/New York. August Kleinzahler. WWSi

Red berries wiping rain at the window. Old Circles. Jennifer Rankin. BMAP

Red blossoms of mountain peach crowd the uplands. Bamboo Branch Song. Liu Yu Hsi, Chinese. CoBCP, tr. by Burton Watson

Red Book of Hergest, The. Unknown, Middle Welsh.

Lament for Urien, The. OBMV, tr. by Ernest Rhys

Red Boots On. Kit Wright. PeLV

Red brick [or bricks] in the suburbs, white horse on the wall. Ballad to a Traditional Refrain. Maurice James Craig. BIrV; TIRV

Red brick monastery in, The. The Semblables. William Carlos Williams. FaBoMo; NOBA

Red-bud, the Kentucky tree, The. Christmas at Freelands. James Stephens. TIRV; TrCP

Red cassia flowers. If Hot Flowers Come to the Street. R. Meenakshi, Tamil. OMIP, tr. by Martha Ann Selby

Red Cliff, The. Su Tung-p'o, Chinese. OHPC, tr. by Kenneth Rexroth

Red cliffs arise. And up them service lifts. NW5 and N6. John Betjeman. SCV

Red Cloud's Song. Unknown. APN-2, tr. by Stephen Powers Fr. Sacred Songs of the Konkau.

Red Cockatoo, The. Po Chü-i, Chinese. ChiP, tr. by Arthur Waley

Red cockatoo crests caught on coral-trees. Early Arrival: Sydney. Vivian Smith. NOBAu

Red cold / guffaw of summer. José Juan Tablada, Spanish. PBMP, tr. by Samuel Beckett

Red comb on its head needs no adorning, The. Inscribed on a Painting of a Cock. T'ang Yin, Chinese. SuSp, tr. by Chiang Yee

Red Cotton Night-Cap Country. Robert Browning. EBVVPR

"Accordingly, on weighty business bound." EDVVPR

"And now let pass a week. Once more behold." EBVVPR, sect. III

"'Thus I bestride the railing, leg o'er leg'." EBVVPR, sect. IV

Red Cow Is Dead, The. Elwyn Brooks White. NBLV; NYBP

Red Cross, The. Mộng Tuyết, Vietnamese. AVP, tr. by Huỳnh Sanh Thông

Red Cross Lessons at City Park Pool. Melody Lacina. IFJA

Red Cross telegram, The. Lotte Kramer. HP

Red dawn clouds coming up! the heavens proclaim you. Morning Light Song. Philip Lamantia. NeAP

Red dew on floral chamber, white honeycomb. Boudoir Feelings. Li Shang-yin, *Chinese*. SuSp, *tr. by* Eugene Eoyang *and* Irving Y. Lo

Red Dog, The. Laura Jensen. LCAP-2

Red-Dress Girl. Ann Turner. SSCS

Red Dust. Philip Levine. NNaP; NoAM

Red earth, The. What He Said. Peyanar. PLW *Fr.* Nine on Happy Reunion. PLW, *tr. by* A. K. Ramanujan

Red Embankment. Tu Mu, *Chinese*. SuSp, *tr. by* John M. Ortinau

Red embroidered carpet. Po Chü-i, *Chinese*. SuSp, *tr. by* Wu-Chi Liu

Red eyes of rabbits, The. The Springtime. Denise Levertov. CoAP; CoAmPo

Red Flag, The. Michael Jackson. PeNZ

Red flag is up, The. We Meet in the Lives of Animals. Peter Everwine. NNaP

Red flame flowers bloom and die, The. Nocturne. Crosbie Garstin. CH

Red-flashing lights. Martin Shea. HA

Red flipped out. Anita Virgil. HA

Red Flower. Ann Turner. SSCS

Red flowers. Tanka. Miya Shūji, *Japanese*. MJT, *tr. by* Makoto Ueda

Red fool, my laughing comrade. To a Comrade in Arms. Alun Lewis. FaBoTw; MoBrPo

Red for Santa's fur-lined cloak. All in Red. Eileen Mathias. BoTP

Red fox, the vixen, The. Abnegation. Adrienne Rich. WPE

Red Geranium and Godly Mignonette. D. H. Lawrence. GTBS-P; NoAM

Red Geraniums. Martha Haskell Clark. BLPA

Red globes of light, the liquor-green, The. William Street. Kenneth Slessor. BMAP; CBAP

Red Glow in the Sky, A. Aleksandr Blok, *Russian*. OBVE, *tr. by* Jon Stallworthy *and* Peter France

Red-Gold Rain, The. Sacheverell Sitwell. MoBrPo

Red granite and black diorite, with the blue. The Skeleton of the Future. "Hugh MacDiarmid." MoBrPo; OBMV

Red Guard. Maksimilian Aleksandrovich Voloshin, *Russian*. TCRP, *tr. by* Albert C. Todd

Red-haired Man's Wife, The. James Stephens. MoBrPo

Red Hanrahan's Song about Ireland. W. B. Yeats. CMoP; FaBoCh; IIP; NOIV

Red Harlaw. Sir Walter Scott. OxBB *Fr.* The Antiquary.

Red Hat, The. Rachel Hadas. RA

Red-head swallows swoop and clip the waves in pairs, so light! Crossing the Yangtze in a Strong Wind. Wang Shih-chieng, *Chinese*. CoBLCP, *tr. by* Jonathan Chaves

Red Heart Station. Yang Shih-ch'i, *Chinese*. CoBLCP, *tr. by* Jonathan Chaves

Red Hills of Home. Chenjerai Hove. HBAPE

Red Hot. Laurie Anderson. OxWW

Red in Autumn. Elizabeth Gould. BoTP

Red Indian Corpse. Peter Redgrove. OxBC

Red Iron Ore. *Unknown*. AS

Red is the battlefield. Tipputtolar, *Tamil*. PLW, *tr. by* A. K. Ramanujan

Red is the down which is covering me. Ankotarinya. *Unknown, Aranda*. CBAP, *tr. by* T. G. H. Strehlow

Red Jacket. Fitz-Greene Halleck. APN-1

Red Journeys. Nellie Wong.
    "I dream red dreams, an oasis of fire and light." MDDM

Red lantern calls the spring clouds from my sleep, A. Wang Chien. SuSp, *tr. by* William H. Nienhauser *Fr.* Palace Poems.

Red Leaf, The. Page Sullivan. ImGa

Red Letters. Mekeel McBride. CMAP

Red Light District Nurse, The. John Fuller *and* James Fentonr. OBCoV

Red light is stuck, A. Why We Are Late. Josephine Miles. NALW

Red Lilies. Barbara Guest. FTOS; PmAP; PoM

Red lips are not so red. Greater Love. Wilfred Owen. APAD; CMoP; EnLoPo; FaBoMo; GTBS-P; ImPo; LiTM; MoBrPo; MoP; NoAM; TFi

Red lotus incense fades on / the jewelled curtain. Li Ch'ing-chao, *Chinese*. BoWoP; OHMPC, *tr. by* Kenneth Rexroth

Red-Man, The. Frank Prewett. HATNAP

Red men embraced my body's whiteness. Birch Canoe. Carter Revard. NoP-4

Red Monkey. *Unknown*. *Fr.* Hunter Poems of the Yoruba. RB, *tr. by* Ulli Beier

Red Moon High in the Sky. Husein Tahmisic, *Serbian*. CEEP, *tr. by* Ewald Osers

Red Mullet, The. Robert Penn Warren. APo

Red mullet, rosy in its sleep. Beaulieu. Clarence Major. FTOS

Red oak leaves rustle in the wind. The Leaves of a Dream Are the Leaves of an Onion. Arthur Sze. OpBo

Red o'er the forest glows the setting sun. November. John Keble. OBNC *Fr.* Forest Leaves in Autumn.

Red of the dawn! The Dawn. Tennyson. NAEL-2

Red on sun sky sail. Six Eagles. Thomas Love Peacock. VoR

Red, orange, yellow, green, turquoise, blue, violet. Tune: "Deva-like Barbarian"—Ta-po-ti. Mao Tse-tung, *Chinese*. SuSp, *tr. by* Eugene Eoyang

Red paths that wander through the gray, and cells. With God Conversing. Gene Derwood. ImPo; LiTM

Red Peonies. Wang Wei, *Chinese*. SuSp, *tr. by* Irving Y. Lo

Red pepper pods. Tanka. Saitō Mokichi, *Japanese*. MJT, *tr. by* Makoto Ueda

Red Poppy. Tess Gallagher. NAmP90

Red Poppy, The. Louise Glück. AFr

Red rag. Tanka. Miyazawa Kenji, *Japanese*. MJT, *tr. by* Makoto Ueda

Red, Red Rose, A. Robert Burns. AWP; BoLoP; CBLP; ChAP; GBL; GLoP; HAP; HeIP-4; ImPo; LBC; NAEL-2; NIP-4; NOBE; NOBRP; NOEC; NTP; NoP-4; OAEL-1; OBEV; OxAEP-2; OxBS; PFE; PoEL-4; PoLF; PoPoPo; Poetr; SAGP; SCGP; TFi; UV
    ("My love is like a red red rose.") APAD
    ("O my love is like a red, red rose.") ChAP; SAGP
    ("O my Luve's like a red, red rose.") ITG; LBC; NoP-4; PoPoPo
    (Song.) EBEvV; Ro
    ("Tho' it were ten thousand mile!") (LL) APAD; ChAP; GLoP; LBC; PFE
    ("Though it were ten thousand mile!") (LL) NoP-4; PoPoPo; SAGP
    ("Though 'twere ten thousand mile.") (LL) Ro
    ("While the sands o' life shall run.") (LL) ITG

Red Ridinghood. Nathan Alterman, *Hebrew*. MHP, *tr. by* Ruth Finer Mintz

Red Rising. Edward Kamau Brathwaite. HCP

Red river, red river. Virginia. T. S. Eliot. FaBoA; InPK-6 *Fr.* Landscapes. RB

Red River Valley. *Unknown*. APN-2; AS; FaBoBe
    ("Is the prayer of the Red River girl.") (LL) APN-2

Red Rock Ceremonies. Anita Endrezze-Danielson. CDW; VoR

Red rock wilderness, The. Sidney Keyes. OBWP; PoWW *Fr.* The Wilderness.

Red Rose and a Beggar. Hilda Doolittle. APSN

Red Rose, proud Rose, sad Rose of all my days! To the Rose upon the Rood of Time. W. B. Yeats. ADE; NoAM

Red rose whispers of passion, The. A White Rose. John Boyle O'Reilly. OBEV

Red Roses. Gertrude Stein. TTTS *Fr.* Tender Buttons.

Red roses, in the slender vases burning. Forlorn. William Dean Howells. APN-2

Red round sun, The. Louise Herlin, *French*. MFP, *tr. by* Martin Sorrell

Red rowans in the rain. Ambulance Train. Wilfrid Wilson Gibson. NSI

Red Sea. James Agee. *Fr.* Two Songs on the Economy of Abundance. MoAmPo

Red Shift. Ted Berrigan. PT

Red silk lines the chamber curtains, their tassels fringed with gold. Ravine on a Cold Evening. Li Ho, *Chinese*. SuSp, *tr. by* Maureen Robertson

Red Silk Stockings. Langston Hughes. NAAAL

Red sky at night, A. *Unknown*. ACTP; OBCoV
    ("Red sky at night is the shepherd's delight, A.") LB; OxNR
    ("Red sky in the morning is the shepherd's warning, A.") (LL) LB

Red Slope. Tu Mu, *Chinese*.
    "Milky in the spring grotto stone fattens, sprouts goose-quills." PLT, *tr. by* A. C. Graham

Red spattered on an orchard path. Thats all. Seed. Charles Buckmaster. BMAP

Red stains on the clean white bib. The Butcher's Apron. Diane Wakoski. BAP-96

Red stockings, blue stockings. *Unknown*. OxNR

Red sun fills the sky and the earth, The. Suffering from Heat. Wang Wei, *Chinese*. SuSp, *tr. by* Hugh M. Stimson

Red walls of the old temple emerge from the blur of the blue-green mountain. Lieh Mountain. Wang Shih-chieng, *Chinese*. SuSp, *tr. by* Richard John Lynn

Red Wheelbarrow, The. William Carlos Williams. CMoP; HeIP-4; HoPM; InPK-6; LiTM; MoAmPo; MoP; NAAL-2; NIP-4; NOBA; NoAM; PoE; Poetr; SAmP; SoSe-8; TAP; TFi; TRP; TTTS; UnPo; WeW-3
    ("Chickens.") (LL) BLT; ChAP; NoP-4
    ("So much depends / upon.") ColAP

Red Whiskey. *Unknown*. AmFP

Red, White and Red, The. *Unknown.* AmFP

Red young men under the ground, The. Song. *Unknown.* STP, *tr. by* Jerome Rothenberg *Fr.* Red Ant Way.

Redbreast smoulders in the waste of snow, The. Anthony Rye. Spl

Redbummed Sweeney bolts the gate. Sweeney, Old and Phthisic, among the Hippopotami. David Cummings. BXAP

Redde pro victoria. (LL) The Agincourt Carol. *Unknown.* EBEV; OAEL-1

Rede rose and the lilie-flowr, The. (LL) A Maiden in the Moor [*or* Mor]. *Unknown.* EnVB; MiEL; PoEL-1; PoEL-5

Redeem Time Past. William Drummond, of Hawthornden. OxAEP-1

Redeemed by what he tried to say. (LL) My Father's Love Letters [*or* Loveletters]. Yusef Komunyakaa. ISC; NAmP90; PoPoPo; WeT

Redeemer, The. Siegfried Sassoon. PoFWW

Redemption. George Herbert. CABP; ESCV; FMP; FSCP; GSo; GeHe; HAP; InPK-6; InPS-3; MeLP; NAEL-1; NOBE; NOCV; NOSC; NoP-4; PBRV; PeECV; PoE; PoPoPo; Poetr; SCGP; SCV; SeCP; SoSe-8; TFi; TrCP; WeW-3

Redemption. Pauli Murray. GT

Redemption's problem unto thee well solved. (LL) Milton. Henrietta Cordelia Ray. BlSi; CBWP-3

Redeployment. Howard Nemerov. LiTM; OBWP; PoWW; TrJP

Redesdale and Wise William. *Unknown.* ESPB

Redingote and the Vamoose, The. Richard Kendall Munkittrick. OBCA

Rediscovery. Kofi Awoonor. TTY

Redivivus. Donald Davidson. FuPo

Rednecks. Martín Espada. BAP-96

Redness: Thinking it Through. Garrett Kaoru Hongo. LTA

Redoubt, laugh! what what's homey crackling every room. Catullus. *See* Carmen 31 ("Apple of islands, Sirmio, & bright peninsulas, set").

Redoubted knights, and honorable Dames. Edmund Spenser. *Fr.* Wood Of Error. AEP

Redress: to receive something, get in exchange. Redress: Thinking it Through. Garrett Kaoru Hongo. LTA

Redshanks, The. Julian Bell. OBMV

Reduce the supply while the demand stays constant and the result is. Arrival at Kennedy. David Lehman. WWSi

Redwings. James Wright. NNaP; WeT

Redwoods, The. Louis Simpson. CoAP

Reed, The. Mikhail Yuryevich Lermontov, *Russian.* AWP, *tr. by* J. J. Robbins

Reed had been weeping, The. Kyongnim Shin, *Korean.* CKP, *tr. by* Jaihiun Kim

Reed: I sank roots first of all, stood. Cynewulf. ASW, *tr. by* Kevin Crossley-Holland *Fr.* Riddles (Exeter Book).

Reed in the Tide, A. J. P. Clark Bekederemo.

  Abiku. PBMAP

  Child Asleep, A. PBMAP

  Cry of Birth. PBMAP

  For Granny (from Hospital). PBMAP

  Night Rain. PBMAP

  Olokun. PBMAP

Reeds give, The. Small Song. A. R. Ammons. NoAM

Reeds of Innocence. William Blake. *See* Introduction: "Piping down the valleys wild."

Reeking of unsolved crimes, the cop. Two Hookers. A. K. Redwing. VoR

Reel unrolling towards the river, The. (LL) The Three Fates. Rosemary Dobson. BMAP

Reel World, The. Jim Hall. CMAP

Reeling Silk. Fan Ch'eng-ta. SuSp, *tr. by* Wu-chi Liu *Fr.* Four Songs in Imitation of Wang Chien.

Reever ryves at the gullie, The. Women's Wather. T. S. Law. OxBS

Refined by bile as yellow as a lump of gold. (LL) For George Santayana. Robert Lowell. CMoP; NAAL-2; VGW

Refined Man, The. Rudyard Kipling. FaBoEE; FaBoTw; PeFWW *Fr.* Epitaphs of the War [1914–1918]. OBWP

Refiner's Gold, The. Frances Ellen Watkins Harper. PWR

Refining Fire. Lizelia Augusta Jenkins Moorer. CBWP-3

Reflected in the pensioner's eye. Karoo Town. Robert Dederick. PeSA

Reflecting on the Aging-Process. Robert Peters. BXAP

Reflection. Elisabeth Eybers, *Afrikaans.* PeSAV, *tr. by the author*

Reflection, A. Thomas Hood. FaBoEE

Reflection. Christina Rossetti. VWP

Reflection. Walter James Turner. OBMV

Reflection and Advice. Ezra Pound. OBSV

Reflection by a Mailbox. Stanley Kunitz. TrJP

Reflection from Rochester. William Empson. PoA

Reflection from Sea and Sky. Walter Savage Landor. FaBoEE

Reflection in a Green Arena. Gregory Corso. VGW

Reflection in Red. Onuora Oku. PBCV

Reflection Kiss, one given, The. Some Kisses from *The Kama Sutra.* Hugo Williams. BoLoP

Reflection on Babies. Ogden Nash. NBLV

Reflection on Ingenuity. Ogden Nash. RB

Reflections. George Crabbe.

  Late Wisdom. OBEV

Reflections. Antoinette Deshoulières, *French.* PBWP, *tr. by* Yvor Winters

Reflections. Carl Gardner. PoBA

Reflections. Carole Satyamurti. IFJA

Reflections. Vivian Smith. CBAP

Reflections at Dawn. Phyllis McGinley. NBLV; NOBL

Reflections in a Slum. "Hugh MacDiarmid." FaBoTw

Reflections in the river: trembling spring trees. Yang Chi. *Fr.* Living in a Riverside Village—Miscellaneous Impressions. CoBLCP, *tr. by* Jonathan Chaves

Reflections Near the House Where Titian Tabidze Lived. Bulat Shalvovich Okudzhava, *Russian.* TCRP, *tr. by* Deming Brown

Reflections on a Visit to the Burke Museum, University of Washington, Seattle. Gail Tremblay. HATNAP

Reflections on Growing Older. Quincy Troupe. GT

Reflections on Having Left a Place of Retirement. Coleridge. LaPo; Ro

Reflections on Hillsborough in Memoriam. T. H. Naisby. NOBAu

Reflections on Ice-breaking. Ogden Nash. AiP; ImPo; LiTM; NBLV; NoP-4; OBAL; PeLV

Reflections on Mirrors. Elder Olson. CRP

Reflections, Written on Visiting the Grave of a Venerated Friend. Ann Plato. BlSi

Reflective. A. R. Ammons. HCAP; PiM; VCAP

Reflects little credit on God. (LL) On the Painter Val Prinsep. D. G. Rossetti. FaBoEE; OBCoV

Reflexion, The. Edward Taylor. ChIV-1, *sect.* IV, (*Division* I); AmPP; ColAP; OxBA *Fr.* Preparatory Meditations Before My Approach to the Lord's Supper.

  ("Enthrone thy rosy-self within mine eyes.") (LL) ColAP

Reflexions on suicide, & on my father, possess me. Of Suicide. John Berryman. NoAM

Reflexions on the Seizure of the Suez, and on a Proposal to Line the Banks of That Canal with Billboard Advertisements. Howard Nemerov. NBLV

Reformation. Anne Finch, Countess of Winchilsea. ECWP

Reformation of Manners. Daniel Defoe.

  London. NOEC

  "Search all the Christian climes from pole to pole." OBSV

  "Yet Ostia boasts of her regeneration." OBSV

Reformer to His Father, A. James Simmons. BIrV

Refracted through years, this neon light comes back. Poem in the Shape of a Saxophone. T. R. Hummer. SeSe

Refrain. (LL) No More Booze. *Unknown.* AS; OBAL

Refrain. Mary Jo Salter. EOEF

Refresh my thoughts of Penelope again. Pan as the Son of Penelope. Joanne Kyger. BB

Refreshing rest, ecstatic dream. In the Grass. Annette von Droste-Hülshoff, *German.* PBWP, *tr. by* James Edward Tobin

Refrigerium. John Henry, Cardinal Newman. OBNC

Refuge. Robert Hill Long. BAP-95

Refuge at the One Step Down. Belle Waring. PBCAP; SeSe

Refuge Even Beyond Refuge. Reiner Kunze, *German.* CEEP, *tr. by* Ewald Osers

Refugee, A. Lilian Bowes-Lyon. WPN

Refugee Blues. W. H. Auden. HP; NYBP; OxAEP-2 *Fr.* Ten Songs. (Song.) NYBP

Refugee Ship. Lorna Dee Cervantes. PoPoPo

Refugees. Donald Davidson. FuPo

Refugees, The. Randall Jarrell. MoAmPo

Refugees. Ilya Krichevsky, *Russian.* TCRP, *tr. by* Albert C. Todd

Refugees, The. Edwin Muir. NoAM

Refugees at Cobh. Sean Dunne. BiHa

Refugee's run / across the desert borderlands, The. Mi Vida: Wings of Fright. Martín Espada. AFr

Refusal to Mourn, A. Derek Mahon. PNI

Refusal to Mourn the Death, by Fire, of a Child in London, A. Dylan Thomas. AF; CMoP; EBEV; FaBoMo; GTBS-P; HeIP-4; HoPM; ImPo; LiTM; MoBrPo; MoP; NOBE; NoAM; NoP-4; OAEL-2; OBWVE; OxAEP-2; OxBTC; PoE; PoWW; TFi; TwCP; UnPo

Refuse Man, The. David Ignatow. WeT

Refuse such fruitless toil, and present pleasures choose. Edmund Spenser. *See* The Legend of the Knight of the Red Crosse, or of Holinesse.

Refused admission! Baby, Baby. The Returned Picture. Mary O'Donovan Rossa. IIP

Refuting the "Invitation to Hiding." Wang K'ang-chü, *Chinese*. CoBCP, *tr. by* Burton Watson

Reg wished me to go with him to the field. My Mother. Claude McKay. GT

Regalia in Immediate Demand! Philip Whalen. BB

Regard her well—the austere face. Röntgen Photograph. Elisabeth Eybers, *Afrikaans*. PeSA, *tr. by* Jack Cope, Uys Krige, *and* Ruth Miller

Regard, O reader, how it is with me. Look, in the Labyrinth of Memory. Delmore Schwartz. TrJP

Regard the capture here, O Janus-faced. Recitative. Hart Crane. FaBoMo

Regarding poets. (LL) The True Protocol of Poets. Kapilar, *Tamil*. PLW

Regarding yours, dear Mrs Nightingale. Mrs Nightingale. Martin Fagg. UV

Regarding yours, dear Mrs Worthington. Noël Coward. UV *Fr.* Mrs Worthingtion.

Regement of Princes. Thomas Hoccleve.
 Admirer's Lament of Chaucer, An. EPCY

Regeneration. Walter Savage Landor. Ro *Fr.* Imaginary Conversations.

Regeneration. Henry Vaughan. ChIV-1; ESCV; FMP; GeHe; MeLP; NAEL-1; NoP-4; PoE
 ("*And let me dye before my death!*") (LL) FSCP

Reggae Cat (for Boston Jack). Kendel Hippolyte. HCP

Reggae fi Dada. Linton Kwesi Johnson. NBrP; PBCV

Regina. Mary Elizabeth Coleridge. NALW

Reginald Pugh, The Man Who Came from the Army. Emma Lee Warrior. HATNAP

Region of life and light! The Life of the Blessed. Luís De León, *Spanish*. AWP, *tr. by* Bryant

Regions of Tyre are noted, The. Meleager, *Greek*. GrAn, *tr. by* Peter Whigham

Regrat. William Drummond, of Hawthornden. PoEL-2

Regret. Yuan Chi, *Chinese*. ChiP, *tr. by* Arthur Waley

Regret, a bright meander on the nights. A Botanical Trope. William Meredith. Poetr

Regretful Thoughts. Yü Hsüan-chi, *Chinese*. BoWoP, *tr. by* Geoffrey Waters

Regrets. Joachim Du Bellay, *French*.
 Hereux Qui, comme Ulysse, A Fait un Beau Voyage. AWP, *tr. by* G. K. Chesterton

Regular Bobbsey Twins. / That story. (LL) Cinderella. Anne Sexton. HeIP-4; InPS-3; NAAL-2

Regulation equipment. Joyce Mansour, *French*. MFP, *tr. by* Martin Sorrell

Rehabilitative Report: We Can Still Laugh. Daniel Berrigan. AF

Rehearsal. Cyril Dabydeen. PBCV

Rehearsal, The. Horace Gregory. VGW

Rehearsing for Death. Angelos Sikelianos, *Greek*. GrIP, *tr. by* Edmund Keeley *and* Philip Sherrard

Reid in the Loch Sayis, The. *Unknown*. OxBS

Reification won't get you out of the parking lot. Things. Bob Perelman. PmAP

Reign of Chaos, The. Alexander Pope. EBEV; FaBoPV; SCV *Fr.* Yet, yet a moment, one dim ray of light. NAEL-1; OAEL-1; PoEL-3 *Fr.* The Dunciad.
 (Triumph of Dullness [*or* Dulness], The.) NOBE

Reign of Terror. Jim Hall. CMAP

Reincarnation. Mae Jackson. PoBA

Reincarnation (I) ["Still, passed through the spokes of an old wheel, on and around"]. James Dickey. HoPM

Reincarnation (II). James Dickey. CAPP-1

Reindeer and Engine. Josephine Jacobsen. WPE

Reindeer Report. U. A. Fanthorpe. OBCP

Reivers they stole Fair Annie, The. Fair Annie. *Unknown*. CH

Rejected. Lord Alfred Bruce Douglas. ADE; PeVV

Rejected Lover, The. *Unknown*. AmFP

Rejected Lover, The. *Unknown*. AmFP

Rejected "National Hymns," The. "Orpheus C. Kerr." OBAL

Rejection, the. Sir Robert Ayton. NOSC

Rejoice bather between two waters. Song. Milorad Pavic, *Serbo-Croatian*. HSix, *tr. by* Charles Simic *Fr.* Holy Mass For Relja Krilatica.

Rejoice eleventh finger reckoner of stars. Song. Milorad Pavic, *Serbo-Croatian*. HSix, *tr. by* Charles Simic *Fr.* Holy Mass For Relja Krilatica.

"Rejoice holy bundles, sacred bundles." They Went to the Moon Mother. *Unknown, Zuni Indian*. STP, *tr. by* Barbara Tedlock

Rejoice in God, O ye Tongues; give the glory to the Lord, and the Lamb. Christopher Smart. FaBoVe, *ll.* 1–22 *Fr.* Fragment A. *Fr.* Jubilate Agno.

Rejoice in God that I am gon. Isabella Whitney. BWW *Fr.* The Manner of Her Will and What She Left to London and to All Those in It, at Her Departing. NoSic

Rejoice in the Abyss. Stephen Spender. AF

Rejoice, Let Alleluias Ring. Sister M. Cherubim Schaefer. AH

Rejoice [*or* Rejoyse]! let me dream [*or* dreme] of your felicity [*or* felicitie]. (LL) You that in love find[e] luck[e] and [h]abunda[u]nce. Sir Thomas Wyatt. AAS; SiPS

Rejoice mason of years. Song. Milorad Pavic. HSix *Fr.* Holy Mass For Relja Krilatica.

Rejoice, O Bridegroom! *Unknown, Hebrew*. TrJP, *tr. by* Israel Abrahams

Rejoice, O youth, in the lovely hind. Moses ibn Ezra. TrJP, *tr. by* Solomon Solis-Cohen *Fr.* Wedding Song in honor of R. Solomon ben Matir.

Rejoice singer of songs for the deaf. Song. Milorad Pavic. HSix *Fr.* Holy Mass For Relja Krilatica.

Rejoice you sots, your idol's come again. Upon the King's Return from Flanders, 1695. Henry Hall. NOSC

Rejoice you who sleep with a finger in your ear. Song. Milorad Pavic. HSix *Fr.* Holy Mass For Relja Krilatica.

Rejoicing at the Arrival of Chi'en Hsiung. Po Chü-i, *Chinese*. AWP, *tr. by* Arthur Waley
 (Rejoicing at the Arrival of Ch'ên Hsiung.) ChiP, *tr. by* Arthur Waley

Rejoicing / because we had met again. The Good Dream. Denise Levertov. NNaP

Rejoicing That Attend the Murder of Famous Men, The. Robley Wilson Jr. PBCAP

Rejoicing That the Zen Master Pao Has Arrived from Dragon Mountain. Liu Ch'ang-ch'ing, *Chinese*. CoBCP, *tr. by* Burton Watson

Rejoicing the Spirits. Fan Ch'eng-ta. SuSp, *tr. by* Wu-chi Liu *Fr.* Four Songs in Imitation of Wang Chien.

Rejoinder to a Critic. Donald Davie. CABP; NoP-4

Relapse, The. Thomas Stanley. BeJo; NOSC; OBEV

Relapse, The. Henry Vaughan. ESCV; TrCP

Relations. Orerulavanar, *Tamil*. PLW, *tr. by* A. K. Ramanujan

Relationships. Elizabeth Jennings. FP

Relative. Alastair Fowler. FaBoTC

Relative Thing, A. William Daniel Ehrhart. CDa

Relatives, The. Ed Ochester. CMAP

Relatives are leaning over, staring expectantly, The. "Dreadful Has Already Happened, The." Mark Strand. HCAP; NoAM; VCAP

Relativities. Louis Untermeyer. BXAP

Relax, / stand at attention, and. Barrett Watten. PmAP *Fr.* Progress.

Relaxed Abalone, The. Rosemarie Waldrop. InPK-6

Relaxed, nothing to do. Letting My Feelings Out. Yü Hsüan-chi, *Chinese*. BoWoP, *tr. by* Geoffrey Waters

Relaxing all day in this tropical atmosphere. Foreign Aid. Lionel Kearns. NOBC

Relaxing in the Evening in My Study. Yang Wan-li, *Chinese*. CoBCP, *tr. by* Burton Watson
 (Relaxing in the Evening in My Study, the Wo-chih-chai.) CoBCP, *tr. by* Burton Watson

Relearning the Alphabet. Denise Levertov. NOBA

Release. R. S. Gwynn. RA

Release. D. H. Lawrence. CMoP

Release, The. Adah Isaacs Menken. CBWP-1

Release. Virgil, *Latin*. OBCVT, *tr. by* John Dryden

Released [*or* Releas'd] from the noise of the butcher and baker. Jinny the Just. Matthew Prior. NOBE; NOEC; OBEV; PoEL-3

Released on Parole. James McAuley. BMAP

Released their own three men. (LL) Robin Hood Rescuing Three Squires. *Unknown*. ESPB; NAEL-1

Releasing a Migrant 'Yen' (Wild Goose). Po Chü-i, *Chinese*. ChiP, *tr. by* Arthur Waley

Relent, my dear yet unkind Coelia. William Percy. AAS; Son *Fr.* Coelia.

Relentless, black on white, the cable runs. T-Bar. Patricia K. Page. NOBC; NoAM

Relentless escalators bore us. Risk Management. Alice Fulton. WWSi

Relic, The. Donne. FHYEP; FMP; FSCP; GBL; GEA; HAP; HeIP-4; ImPo; NOBE; NOSC; NoP-4; OAEL-1; PoEL-2; TFi
 (Relique, The.) ESCV; MeLP; PoEL-2; SCGP; SeCP

Relic. Ted Hughes. NAEL-2; NoP-4

Relief. Charles Vildrac, *French*. PeFWW, *tr. by* Christopher Middleton

Relief of Myopia, The. U. A. Fanthorpe. Spl

Relief of putting your fingers on the keyboard, The. Thanking My Mother for Piano Lessons. Diane Wakoski. NMM-2

Relieved, I let the book fall behind a stone. Depressed by a Book of Bad Poetry, I Walk toward an Unused Pasture and Invite the Insects to Join Me. James Wright. CoAmPo

Religio Laici. Dryden.

"But if there be a power too just and strong." NOCV

"Thus man by his own strength to Heaven would soar." NOCV

Religion. Gwendolyn Brooks. OxWW *Fr.* Ulysses.

Religion. Donne. *See* Satire 3.

Religion. Henry Vaughan. ESCV; NOCV; OAEL-1; OxAEP-1; PeECV; TOF

Religion and the Lower Classes. Evan Lloyd. NOEC *Fr.* The Methodist.

Religion Back Home. William Stafford. OBAL

Religion stands on tip-toe in our land. George Herbert. PBRV *Fr.* The Church Militant.

Religion stands, the church blocking the sun. (LL) The Landscape near an Aerodrome. Stephen Spender. LiTM; MoBrPo; NoAM; OxBTC

Religious Musings. Coleridge. Ro *Fr.* Religious Musings.

Religious Use of [Taking] Tobacco, A. Robert Wisdome. OBCoV; SCGP (Pipe and Can, I.) OBEV

Religious wars of Europe have been numbered with the past, The. The Peonage System. Lizelia Augusta Jenkins Moorer. CBWP-3

Relining Shelves. Nellie Wong. NMM-2

Reliquary. Hart Crane. PoA

Relique, The. Donne. *See* The Relic.

Relish honey. If you please. To a Swallow. John Peale Bishop, *after* Euenus, *Greek,* . GrAn; OBVE

Reluctance. Robert Frost. CMoP; MoAmPo; NOBA; OxBA; SAGP

Remain, Ah Not in Youth Alone. Walter Savage Landor. HAP; OBNC *Fr.* Ianthe.

Remain, Rata. Te Puea Herangi, *Maori.* PeNZ, *tr. by* Margaret Orbell

Remain within its sanctuary! (LL) The Sleeping Beauty Samuel Rogers. GTBS-P; OxAEP-2

Remains. Tony Harrison. FaBoVe

Remains, The. Mark Strand. NYBP

Remains of an Indian Village. Alfred Wellington Purdy. NOBC

Remains of blue bog children, The. Blue Bog Children. Roger Weingarten. AmPA

Remark. Charles Spear. PeNZ

Remarkable race are the Persians, A. Limerick. *Unknown.* PeLi

Remarked [*or* remark'd] how ill we all dissembled. (LL) An Ode: "The Merchant, to secure his treasure." Matthew Prior. AWP; EnLoPo; GTBS-P; NOEC; OBEV; PoRA

Rembrandt—Self Portrait. Gregory Corso. BB

Remedia Amoris. Elizabeth Thomas. LW

Remedies for Love, The. Ovid, *Latin.*

"Come then sick youth unto my sacred skill." OBCVT, *tr. by* F. L. Lucas

Remedy Worse than the Disease, The. Matthew Prior. FaBoEE

Remeidis of Luve. *Unknown.* OxBS

Remember. Ion Caraion, *Romanian.* AF, *tr. by* Marguerite Dorian *and* Elliott B. Urdang

Remember a while ago we happened to meet. My Neighbor to the South, the Office Clerk Hsiao, Came in the Evening to Say Good-bye. Mei Yao Ch'en, *Chinese.* CoBCP, *tr. by* Burton Watson

Remember, Alyosha, the roads of Smolensk. Konstantin Mikhailovich Simonov, *Russian.* TCRP, *tr. by* Lubov Yakovleva

Remember Barbara. Barbara. Jacques Prévert, *French.* AF, *tr. by* Harriet Zinnes

Remember Dear Mary. John Clare. WeW-3

Remember, do you remember those solemn words. Thymocles, *Greek.* GrAn, *tr. by* Peter Jay

Remember Euboulos [*or* Eubolus], who lived and died sober? Leonidas of Tarentum, *Greek.* GrAn, *tr. by* Fleur Adcock

Remember Gascoigne's lullaby. George Gascoigne. *See* The Lullaby [*or* Lullabie] of a Lover.

Remember Haiti, Cuba, Vietnam. Andrew Salkey. PBCV

Remember he was poor and country-bred;. Abraham Lincoln. Mildred Plew Meigs. CA

Remember how unimportant. Milkweed. Philip Levine. LCAP-2

Remember how you always bore me! (LL) Villeggiature. Edith Nesbit. LW; OxBSn; PEW

Remember I am a garnet woman. If I Am Too Brown or Too White for You. Wendy Rose. HATNAP

Remember it, although you're far away. *Unknown.* BXAP

Remember last summer when God turned on the heat. The Honeymoon. James Simmons. PNI

"Remember me" implored the Thief! Emily Dickinson. ChIV-2

Remember me this summer. New England Wind. Eileen Myles. PmAP

Remember me when I am dead. Simplify Me When I'm Dead. Keith Douglas. NoAM; OxBTC

Remember me when I am gone away. Christina Rossetti. AWP; BoLoP; CH; ChAP; EBEvV; EnLoPo; GSo; IMW; LBC; LW; LoP; NOBE; NoP-4; OAEL-2; OBEV; OBNC; OxAEP-2; OxBM; PEW; PoLF; PoRA; SAGP; TFi; VWP

Remember me when thou comest into thy Kingdom. The Discourse of the Good Thief. Nicanor Parra, *Spanish.* GI, *tr. by* Miller Williams

Remember not the promises we made. Helene Johnson. NAAAL

Remember now? Do you. Thymocles, *Greek.* PGA, *tr. by* Kenneth Rexroth

Remember now, my Love, what piteous thing. A Carrion. Charles Baudelaire, *French.* AWP, *tr. by* Allen Tate

Remember Now Thy Creator. Bible, *O.T.* AWP; OBVE *Fr.* Ecclesiastes. (Remember Then Thy Creator.) TrJP

Remember our lamp, its frowzy Victorian hat. The Last Installment. Don Bogen. WeT

Remember, Sinful Youth. *Unknown.* AH

Remember Something Like This. Lionel Fogarty. BMAP

Remember still the first, impetuous form. Leda. Lilian Bowes-Lyon. FaBoSe

Remember Suez? Adrian Mitchell. OxBTC

Remember Tam o' Shanter's mare! (LL) Tam o' Shanter. [A Tale]. Robert Burns. CABP; EBNV; ImPo; NAEL-2; NoP-4; OAEL-1; OBNV; OxBS; PeLV; Ro

Remember That Country. Jean Garrigue. VGW

Remember the evening, just at supper. The Bad Mother. Beatrice Hawley. FiLi

Remember that night. *Unknown, Irish.* NOIV, *tr. by* Thomas Kinsella

Remember that raw youth, some years ago? Old Age. Nguyễn Khuyến, *Vietnamese.* AVP, *tr. by* Huỳnh Sanh Thông

Remember that third month, the year Ất-dậu. They Starved, They Starved. Bàng Bá Lâ, *Vietnamese.* AVP, *tr. by* Huỳnh Sanh Thông

Remember the blackness of that flesh. Memento. Stephen Spender. HP

Remember the covenant of our youth. A Dying Wife to Her Husband. Moses ibn Ezra, *Hebrew.* TrJP

Remember the day the sea turned red. Plankton. Ruth Miller. PeSA

Remember the Giver fading off the lip. (LL) A Drink of Water. Seamus Heaney. OxBC; TRP

Remember the loss is her own, if she lose it. (LL) Nonsense Verses. Charles Lamb. CBNP; OBCoV

Remember the Poor. Matilda Caroline Edwards. PWR

Remember the sky that you were born under. Joy Harjo. CrSp; LoL; OxWW

("Remember the sky that you were born under.") NOxBChV

Remember the sun in the autumn, its rays. The Secret Town. Abraham Sutskever, *Yiddish.* TrJP, *tr. by* Jacob Sonntag

Remember the tree, Charlie? The Punishment. Susan Bartels Ludvigson. MT

Remember Thee! Remember Thee! Byron. BoLoP; OxBSP

Remember then this lullaby! (LL) The Lullaby [*or* Lullabie] of a Lover. George Gascoigne. AAS; EBEV; HAP; NAEL-1; NoSic; OBEV; PoEL-1; SCGP

Remember Then Thy Creator. Bible, *O.T.* See Remember Now Thy Creator.

Remember this. Fury. Lucille Clifton. LoL

Remember those X-ray machines in shoe stores. On Hot Days. James Reiss. AmPA

Remember Thy Creator Now. Peter Long. AH

Remember us poor Mayers all. Song of the Mayers [*or* The Mayers' Song]. *Unknown.* CH

Remember when. Among Strangers. William Stafford. NNaP

Remember, when blinde Fortune knits her brow. Horace, *Latin.* OBCVT, *tr. by* Ben Jonson

Remember when you are bemusing. Limerick. Cyril Hughes. PeLi

Remember when you hear them beginning to say Freedom. Notes for My Son. Alex Comfort. LiTM; MoBrPo *Fr.* The Song of Lazarus.

Remember when you love, from that same hour. Pastoral Dialogue. Anne Killigrew. LW

Remember when you were the first one awake, the first. Little Girl Wakes Early. Robert Penn Warren. PoE

Remember, while you are sleeping here, offshore. Evolution. John Blight. CBAP

Remembered. Sterling Plumpp. GT

Remembered Morning. Janet Lewis. SoSe-8; WPE

Remembered Music. James Russell Lowell. APN-1

Remembered Sequel. Hannah Weiner. FTOS

Remembering Althea. William Stafford. NYBP

Remembering an Island. Robin Fulton. FaBoTC

Remembering Aunt Helen. Vassar Miller. WeT

Remembering Brother Bob. William Stafford. IFJA

Remembering Carrigskeewaun. Michael Longley. PBCIP

Remembering Con Markievicz. C. Day Lewis. IIP

Remembering dark trees of home that keep. Pan in Battle. *Unknown.* PeNZ

Remembering Day. Mary Wright Saunders. CTV

Remembering Dresden. Van K. Brock. HP

Remembering Fannie Lou Hamer. Thadious M. Davis. BISi

Remembering Golden Bells. Po Chü-i, *Chinese.* AWP; ChiP, *tr. by* Arthur Waley

Remembering in Oslo the Old Picture of the Magna Carta. Robert Bly. WeT

Remembering Love. Aleksandr Semionovich Kushner, *Russian.* TCRP, *tr. by* Paul Graves *and* Carol Ueland

Remembering Lunch. Douglas Dunn. OxBC

Remembering Mexico, 1969. Barbara Lau. LoHo

Remembering Min Ch'e. Su Tung-p'o, *Chinese.* OHMPC, *tr. by* Kenneth Rexroth

Remembering My Father. Zbigniew Herbert, *Polish.* VCWP, *tr. by* John Carpenter *and* Bogdana Carpenter

Remembering My Late Wife. Chu Yün-ming, *Chinese.* CoBLCP, *tr. by* Jonathan Chaves

Remembering Nat Turner. Sterling Brown. PoBA

Remembering San Zeno. Charles Wright. WeT

Remembering Snow. Ralph Nixon Currey. PeSA

Remembering that war, I'd near believe. Night Operations, Coastal Command RAF. Howard Nemerov. AF

Remembering the Ardèche. Emily Grosholz. RA

Remembering the Children of Auschwitz. Thomas McGrath. EC2

Remembering the descriptions by Wilson. Passenger Pigeons. Robert Morgan. MT

Remembering the Past in the City of the Soaring Dragon. (Lady) Thanh Quan, *Vietnamese.* AVP, *tr. by* Huỳnh Sanh Thông

Remembering the Strait of Belle Isle or. Large Bad Picture. Elizabeth Bishop. NYBP; OxBC

Remembering the 'Thirties. Donald Davie. FaBoPV; NoP-4; OxBTC

Remembering Walls. Robin Fulton. FaBoTC

Remembering what passed. Old Scent of the Plum Tree. Ietaka, *Japanese.* AWP, *tr. by* E. Powys Mathers

Remembering Yeats. Francis Stuart. BiHa

Remembering your face, I see it here. On Dorothea Lange's Photograph "Migrant Mother" (1936). Helen Pinkerton. FFC

Remembers nothing, neither wind nor wake. (LL) Writing. Howard Nemerov. NYBP; VCAP

Remembers our meeting. Her eye moistens. (LL) Riddle: "I'm a strange creature, for I satisfy women." Cynewulf. ASW, *tr. by* Kevin Crossley-Holland

Remembers thou in Æsope of a taill. Alexander Montgomerie. PBRV

Remembrance. Emily Jane Brontë. BoLoP; BoWoP; CABP; CH; EBEV; EnLoPo; GLoP; HAP; IMW; NAEL-2; NOBE; NOBVV; NoP-4; OBNC; OxAEP-2; PBWP; PEW; PoE; PoEL-5; PoPoPo; Poetr; TFi; WPE; WeW-3

  (R. Alcona to J. Brenzaida.) BrRo; CBLP; EBVV; EnVR; NALW

Remembrance. Margaret E. Bruner. PoToHe

Remembrance. Shakespeare. *See* Sonnet 30.

Remembrance. Antoni Slonimski, *Polish.* TrJP, *tr. by* Frances Notley

Remembrance from a Dream in 1963. Tadeusz Rózewicz. *See* Memory of a Dream From the Year 1963.

Remembrance of a Color inside a Forest, A. Ray A. Young Bear. CDW

Remembrance of Beginnings of Things. Leah Goldberg, *Hebrew.* MHP, *tr. by* Ruth Finer Mintz

Remembrance of Collins, Composed upon the Thames near Richmond. Wordsworth. EPCY

Remembrance of Five Loaves. Mikhail Pozdnyayev, *Russian.* TCRP, *tr. by* Vladimir Lunis *and* Albert C. Todd

Remembrance of My Friend Mr. Thomas Morley, A. John, of Hereford Davies. OxBSP; PFE

Remembrance of Strange Hospitality. Yelena Shwarts, *Russian.* VCWP, *tr. by* Michael Molnar

Remembrance of the Founts of Night. Theo Van Doesburg, *Dutch.* PFTM, *tr. by* Jerome Rothenberg

Remembrance of Things Past. Horace Coleman. CDa

Remembrance of Yalta. Bella Akhatovna Akhmadulina, *Russian.* TCRP, *tr. by* Albert C. Todd

Remembrancer of joys long passed away. To a Golden Heart, Worn round His Neck. Goethe, *German.* AWP, *tr. by* Margaret Fuller Ossoli

Rememorised, Maurice Devane. Austin Clarke. CMoP *Fr.* Mnemosyne Lay in Dust.

Remind you, that there was darkness in my heart. Canticle of Darkness. Wilfred Watson. MoCV

Reminder, The. Thomas Hardy. CMoP; ChAP; OBCP

Reminder to the Current President, A. Christopher Howell. CDa

Reminiscence, A. Anne Brontë. SDW; WPE

Reminiscence. Vladimir Holan, *Czech.* PoSu, *tr. by* George Theiner

Reminiscence. Wallace Irwin. NOBL

Reminiscence, A. Amy Levy. VWP

Remittance Man. Judith Wright. NoAM

Remnant Ghosts at Dawn. Oliver La Grone. NBV

Remnants and relics of a thousand years—here in a pit full of dust. The Book-burning Pit. Lo Yin, *Chinese.* SuSp, *tr. by* Edward H. Schafer

Remnants of a rainbow fall to the western bank at dawn, The. A Poem on Passing by Hsin-k'ai Lake at Kao-yu in Light Rain. Yang Chi, *Chinese.* CoBLCP, *tr. by* Jonathan Chaves

Remnants of counterclockwise. If I Blindfold You. Marjorie Welish. FTOS

Remonstrance, A. John Gerrard. NOEC

Remonstrance, A. James Kenneth Stephen. NOBVV

Remonstrance in the Platonic Shade. Flourishing on an Height. Ann Yearsley.

  "These feeble sounds." ECWP

Remonstrance to the King. William Dunbar. OxBS

Remora. James Merrill. APo

Remorse. John Betjeman. MoBrPo; OxBSP

Remorse. Coleridge.

  Invocation, An: "Hear, sweet spirit, hear the spell." CH; PeECV

  (Voice Sings, A.) CH

Remorse. Richmond Lattimore. PoA

Remorse. Shelley. *See* Stanzas—April, 1814.

Remorse Came Slowly. Junko Nishi, *Japanese.* WPJ, *tr. by* Kenneth Rexroth *and* Ikuko Atsumi

Remorse for Time, The. Howard Nemerov. Son

Remorse—is Memory—awake. Emily Dickinson. NAAL-1; NAAL-3; NOBA; NOCV; NoP-4; PAR; SAmP

Remote and ineffectual Don. Lines to a Don. Hilaire Belloc. MoBrPo; OBSV

Remote, unfriended, melancholy, slow. Oliver Goldsmith. BIrV *Fr.* The Travel[l]er; or, A Prospect of Society.

Removal, The. *Unknown, Seminole Indian.* STP, *tr. by* Frances Densmore

Removal from Terry Street, A. Douglas Dunn. FaBoMo; FaBoVe; NoP-4; OxBC

Removal: Last Part. Carroll Arnett. VoR

Removal of Our Village, KwaBhanya, The. Mbuyiseni Oswald Mtshali, *Zulu.* PeSAV, *tr. by the author*

Remove me from this land of slaves. Ireland. Jonathan Swift. FaBoPV

Removed from Europe's feuds, a hateful scene. A Warning to America. Philip Freneau. TAP

Removing the Plate of the Pump on the Hydraulic System of the Backhoe. Gary Snyder. LoL

Renaissance Drunk, A. George Evans. PmAP

Renaissance of wonder, A. (LL) I am waiting for my case to come up. Lawrence Ferlinghetti. AiP; PmAP

Renaming, The. Valerie Sinason. BrRo

Renascence. Edna St. Vincent Millay. ColAP; MoAmPo

  "All I could see from where I stood." MoAmPo

Renaud is such a handsome thing. Renaud the Woman-killer. *Unknown, French.* FLP, *tr. by* Alistair Elliot

Rendez-vous Manqué dans la Rue Racine. John Millington Synge. BIrV

Rendezvous. Mary Scott Fitzgerald. PoToHe

Rendezvous, The. Maxine W. Kumin. NMM-2

Rendezvous. Edna St. Vincent Millay. NALW

  ("And I wish I did not / feel like your mother.") (LL) NMM-2

  ("Not for these lovely blooms that prank your chambers did I come.") NMM-2

Rendezvous, The. Alan Seeger. FaPoR

Rendezvous, The. Bernard Spencer. GTBS-P

Rendezvous with dweeby Philip in the shower. My Night with Philip Larkin. Rachel Loden. BAP-95

Renegade, The. David Diop. PBMAP

Renegade Wants Words, The. James Welch. CDW

Renegade / wish. (LL) Slipped Quadrant. Nathaniel Mackey. FTOS; PT

René's Songs. T. Carmi, *Hebrew.*

  First Song. MHP, *tr. by* Ruth Finer Mintz

  Second Song. MHP, *tr. by* Ruth Finer Mintz

  Third Song. MHP, *tr. by* Ruth Finer Mintz

Renewal. Diane Averill. CMAP

Renewal. Jonathan Johnson. BAP-96

Renewal, The. George MacBeth. FaBoTC

Renewal, A. James Merrill. OxBSP; PiM; SAGP; VCAP

Renewal, The. Theodore Roethke. VGW

Renewal by Her Element. Denis Devlin. CIP-2; IIP

Renewal Notice. Bruce Dawe. BMAP

Renewal of Strength. Frances Ellen Watkins Harper. PWR

Renoir. Rosanna Warren. GS

Renouncement. Alice Thompson Meynell. BoLoP; GSo; LW; MoBrPo; NOBE; OBEV; OBMV; OBNC; PEW; Son; VWP; WPE

   ("I run, I run, I am gather'd to thy heart.") (LL) GLoP

Renouncing of Love, A. Sir Thomas Wyatt. GBL; Son

   ("Me list no longer rotten boughs to climb.") (LL) GSo

   (Sonnet: 'Farewell, Love'.) AEP

Renowned as Black Geordie. Sporting the Plaid. Chris Wallace-Crabbe. NOBAu

Renowned Generations, The. W. B. Yeats. OxBoLi

Rent. Jane Cooper. FYAP; TAP

Rent man knocked, The. Madam and the Rent Man. Langston Hughes. SAmP

Renunciation. Emily Dickinson. MoAmPo

Renunciation, A. Henry King, Bishop of Chichester. OBEV

Renunciation. Padraic Pearse, Irish. NOIV, tr. by the author

Renunciation—is a piercing Virtue. Emily Dickinson. APN-2; NoP-4

Repartée. Charles Follen Adams. OBAL

Repeal of the Missouri Compromise Considered, The. Elymas Payson Rogers.

   "Covetous Nebraskaites, The." AAP

Repeat after me. Aristophanes. OBCVT, tr. by Douglass Parker Fr. Lysistrata

Repeat that, repeat. The Cuckoo. Gerard Manley Hopkins. MoBrPo; NTP; OxBSP; RB; TTTS

Repeating fly, blueback, thumbthick—so gross, A. Harriet. Robert Lowell. NoP-4

Repeating three clear tones. (LL) Morning Song of Senlin. Conrad Potter Aiken. CMoP; ImPo; LiTM; MoAmPo; NoAM; OxBA

Repeats one note. (LL) Xenophanes. Ralph Waldo Emerson. APN-1; NOBA

Repentance. Brendan Behan, Irish. TIRV, tr. by Ulick O'Conner

Repentance. George Chapman. Fr. Hero and Leander. AAS

Repentance. George Alexander Stevens. NOEC

Repentance. Louis Untermeyer. NBLV

Repentance: The Devil's Blossom. Sigitas Geda, Lithuanian. CEEP, tr. by Jonas Zdanys

Repetition. Anthony Rhodes. NSI

Repetition Complex. "Hugh MacDiarmid." FaBoTC Fr. A Drunk Man Looks at the Thistle.

Repetition of Words and Weather. Ruth Stone. BoWoP

Repetitive Heart, The. Delmore Schwartz.

   "All clowns are masked and all personae." OxBA

   For Rhoda. MoAmPo; OxBA

   (Calmly We Walk Through This April's Day.) LiTM

   Heavy Bear, The. ImPo

Reply. Reiner Kunze, German. PoSu, tr. by Ewald Osers

   ("I say: / yes, that's why.") (LL) CEEP, tr. by Ewald Osers

Reply, The. Philip Levine. PoA

Reply, The. Theodore Roethke. NYBP

Reply, A. Unknown. NBLV; NOBL; PeLi

Reply From His Coy Mistress, A. Annie Finch FFC

Reply to a Marriage Proposal. Irihapeti Rangi Te Apakura, Maori. PBWP, tr. by Roger Oppenheim and Allen Curnow

Reply to "In Flanders Fields." John Mitchell. BLPA

Reply to the Committed Intellectual. Francis Sparshott. NOBC

Reply to the Provinces. Galway Kinnell. NYBP

Replycacion, A. John Skelton.

   "Than, if this noble kyng." PBRV

Replying to a Poem by a New Graduate Lamenting the Loss of His Wife. Yü Hsüan-chi, Chinese. SuSp, tr. by Geoffrey R. Waters

Replying to a Poem by Li T'ien-lin. Yang Wan-li, Chinese. SuSp, tr. by Sherwin S. S. Fu

Replying to a Poem by the Monk Ling-yi at the New Spring. Liu Ch'ang-ch'ing, Chinese. SuSp, tr. by William H. Nienhauser

Replying to a Poem from My Cousin Hui-lien. Hsieh Ling-yün, Chinese. CoBCP, tr. by Burton Watson

Replying to Hsi-mei's "Thoughts in Early Autumn." Lu Kuei Meng, Chinese. SuSp, tr. by Robin D. S. Yates

Replying to "On the Occasion of Morning Audience after Snow" Poem by Assistant Secretary Wang of the Board of Sacrifices. Ts'en Shen, Chinese. SuSp, tr. by Daniel Bryant

Report. Hollis Spurgeon Summers. PFE

Report, The. Jon Swan. NYBP

Report Card, The. Richard Barrows. CTV

Report from a Planet. Richmond Lattimore. FYAP

Report from an Unappointed Committee. William Stafford. CDa

Report from Another Country. Charlene Langfur. LoHo

Report from California. Lois Moyles. NYBP

Report from the Besieged City. Zbigniew Herbert, Polish. AF, tr. by John Carpenter and Bogdana Carpenter

Report from the Correspondent They Fired. David McElroy. AmPA

Report from the Skull's Diorama. Yusef Komunyakaa. LTA

Report of Health. John Updike. PBMP

Report on Experience. Edmund Blunden. FaBoTw; GTBS-P; NOBE; OBMV; OBWP; PeFWW

Report on Her Remains. Daniel David Moses. HATNAP

Report on the Protest in Front of the United States Embassy by the Pino Grande Movement, A. Daisy Zamora, Spanish. CLPP, tr. by Barbara Paschke

Report Song [in a Dream], A. Nicholas Breton. GBL; NoSic

   (Wooing in a Dream.) NOBE

Report to Crazy Horse. William Stafford. NoAM

Report to the Mother. Etheridge Knight. FiLi

Reported Missing. John Clifford Bayliss. PoWW

Reporter of the courage of heroes. Antipater of Sidon, Greek. GrAn, tr. by Peter Jay

Reporting Back. Jo McDougall. EC2

Reportless Subjects, to the Quick. Emily Dickinson. NOBA

Reports Come In, The. J. D. Reed. NYBP

Repose. Una Marson. PBCV

Repose. Henrietta Cordelia Ray. CBWP-3

Repose of Rivers. Hart Crane. AWP; CMoP; ColAP; GEA; LiTM; MeMAP; MoAmPo; NOBA; OxBA; PoE

Repose they know in storefronts, The. The Village of the Presents. James McMichael. AmPA

Reposedly. William Carlos Williams. See The Tulip Bed.

Representing nothing on God's earth now. Lines on the Back of a Confederate Note. Samuel Alroy Jonas. BLPA

Repressed Theme. Barbara Cully. BAP-93

Repression. Charles Kenneth Williams. NoP-4

Repression of War Experience. Siegfried Sassoon. AF; CMoP; NSI; NoAM; PeFWW; PoE

Repressive desublimation. Lines. David Bromige. FTOS

Reprieve. Laurie Duesing. DeD

Reprieve, The. Hans Magnus Enzensberger. PoSu Fr. The Sinking of the Titanic.

Reprieve on the Stoop. Belle Waring. PBCAP

Reprisal[1], The. George Herbert. ESCV; GeHe

Reprisals. W. B. Yeats. OBWP; PoWW

Reprise. Ogden Nash. OxBM

Reproach to Dead Poets. Archibald MacLeish. NAAL-2

Reproach to Julia. Robert Graves. FaBoEE

Reproachful eyes' / beauty but the. Wrath to Sadness. Robert Grenier. PmAP

Reproduction of Profiles, The. Rosemarie Waldrop.

   Feverish Propositions. FTOS

Reproof, A. Bible, O.T. See Go to the Ant [Thou Sluggard].

Reproof Deserved; or After the Lecture. John Betjeman. OBCoV

Reproof of Thanks. Walter Savage Landor. CBLP

Reptilian green the wrinkled throat. Sir Gawaine and the Green Knight. Yvor Winters. MoP; NoAM; PoRA; VGW

Republic of the West. On a Rhine Steamer. James Kenneth Stephen. FaBoA; NOBL; NOBVV; OBCoV; PeLV Fr. England and America.

Repudiate the Forge—. (LL) Dare you see a Soul at the White Heat?. Emily Dickinson. APN-2; NALW; WPoS

Repulse, The. Thomas Stanley. BeJo; MeLP

Repulse Bay. Marilyn Chin. OpBo

Repulse to Alcander, The. Sarah Fyge Egerton. CABP; ECWP

   ("What is't you mean, that I am thus approach'd.") CABP

Request. Jared Angira. PBMAP

Request. "Laurence Hope." SAGP

Request. Langston Hughes. PFTM

Request. Tanikawa Shuntaro, Japanese. VCWP, tr. by Harold Wright

Request for Meat and Drink. Sedulius Scottus, Latin. NOIV

Request Number. G. N. Sprod. AAP

Request of a Dying Child. Lydia Huntley Sigourney. OBCA

Request of Alexis, The. Sarah Dixon. LW

Request to a Year. Judith Wright. CBAP; FaBoWP; NALW; NoAM; NoP-4

Request to the Graces, An. Robert Herrick. NOSC

Requiem. "Anna Andreyevna Akhmatova." PFTM *Fr.* Requiem 1935-1940. BoWoP, *tr. by* Richard McKane

Requiem: "He tossed a life preserver to the young castaway in '55." Otto Orban, *Hungarian.* CEEP, *tr. by* Jascha Kessler

Requiem: "No foreign sky protected me." "Anna Akhmatova," *Russian.* AF; TCRP, *tr. by* Stanley Kunitz *with* Max Hayward

Requiem: "Not the living but the dead." Zhao Zhenkai, *Chinese.* ChiPo, *tr. by* Bonnie S. McDougall and Chen Maiping

Requiem: "O, insatiable monster! Could'st thou not." Mary Weston Fordham. CBWP-2

Requiem: "Pour out your light, O stars." Ivor Gurney. FaBoEE; FaBoTw

Requiem: "So. They and I are back from the outside." Carl Bode. IMW

Requiem: "There was a young belle of old Natchez." Ogden Nash. NoP-4

Requiem: "They say 'the lighthouse keeper's world is round'." Sam Hunt. PeNZ

Requiem: "Under the wide and starry sky." Robert Louis Stevenson. APAD; EBvV; EBVV; FaPoR; NBLV; NOBE; NOBVV; NTP; OBEV; OBNC; PoLF; PoRA; SAGP; SCGP; TFi

Requiem: "Will they stop." Kenneth Fearing. CMoP

Requiem aeternam dona eis, Domine! (LL) *Pla ce bo!* Who is there, who? John Skelton. AAS; CBNP; NOBE; NoSic; OAEL-1; OxBoLi

Requiem after Seventeen Years. Dahlia Ravikovitch, *Hebrew.* IP, *tr. by* Warren Bargad *and* Stanley F. Chyet

Requiem!—and for whom?, A. Mozart's Requiem. Felicia Dorothea Hemans. Ro

Requiem for "Bird" Parker, Musician. Gregory Corso. BB

Requiem for Eduard Streltsov. Aleksandr Petrovich Tkachenko, *Russian.* TCRP, *tr. by* Bradley Jordan

Requiem[:] for Soldiers Lost in Ocean Transports, A. Herman Melville. APN-2; PoEL-5

Requiem for Sonora. Richard Shelton. Poetsp

Requiem for the Croppies. Seamus Heaney. BIrV; CIP-2; FaBoMo; OBWP

Requiem for the Dead of Europe. Iwan Goll, *German.*
    Recitative. PeFWW, *tr. by* Patrick Bridgwater

Requiem for the Living. C. Day Lewis.
    Offertorium. TIRV

Requiem for the Plantagenet Kings. Geoffrey Hill. CABP; NAEL-2; NoAM

Requiem 1935-1940. "Anna Akhmatova," *Russian.* BoWoP, *tr. by* Richard McKane
    Crucifixion. GI, *tr. by* Stanley Kunitz and Max Hayward; IMW
    ("Choir of angels glorified the hour, A.") GI, *tr. by* Stanley Kunitz and Max Hayward
    ("Into her secret eyes. Nobody dared.") (LL) GI, *tr. by* Stanley Kunitz and Max Hayward
    Requiem. PFTM

Requiem on Poros. Yannis Ritsos, *Greek.* VCWP, *tr. by* Edmund Keeley

Requiescam. Trumbull Stickney. ColAP

Requiescat. Matthew Arnold. AWP; EBEvV; FHYEP; NOBE; OBEV; PBMP; PoRA

Requiescat. Haim Guri, *Hebrew.* MHP, *tr. by* Ruth Finer Mintz

Requiescat. Oscar Wilde. EBVV; MoBrPo; OBNC; PeVV; SAGP

Required of You This Night. Peter Redgrove. PoE

Requiring something lovely on his arm. Labor Day. Louise Glück. NoAM

Rereading Old Writing. David Ferry. DiPo

Rescue, The. Robert Creeley. CRP; VCAP

Rescue, The. John Logan. CoAP; NYBP

Rescue. Dabney Stuart. NYBP

Rescue the Dead. David Ignatow. VGW; WeT
    ("Rescue the dead.") (LL) CoAmPo

Rescued Year, The. William Stafford. ColAP; LCAP-2

Rescues them at last, as a star absorbs the night. (LL) The Other Tradition. John Ashbery. FTOS; PmAP

Rescuing gate is wide, The. Like a Mourningless Child. Kenneth Patchen. MoAmPo

Research has shown that ballads were produced by all of society. Hotel Lautréamont. John Ashbery. FTOS

Resentment. Richard Aldington. PeFWW

Resentments Composed because of the Clamor of Town Topers Outside My Apartment. Sarah Kemble Knight. AiP; SCAP

Reservation, The. Susan Clements. UnSA

Reservation Love Song. Sherman Alexie. PoPoPo

Reservation Special. Lew Blockcolski. VoR

Reserved. Walter De la Mare. GTBS-P

Residence of the Emperors of Ch'en, The. Yang Wei-chen, *Chinese.* CoBLCP, *tr. by* Jonathan Chaves

Resident doctor said, The. Notice. Robert Lowell. NoAM

Residual Paralysis. Marie Ponsot. NMM-2

Residue. Carlos Drummond de Andrade, *Portuguese.* VCWP, *tr. by* Mark Strand

Residue. Anthony McNeill. PBCV

Residue of Song. Marvin Bell. AmPA

Residues: Thronging the Heart. Gael Turnbull. NBrP

Resign the rhapsody, the dream. To the Muse. Robert Louis Stevenson. EBEV

Resignation. Matthew Arnold. FHYEP

"Poet, to whose mighty heart, The." EPCY

Resignation. Thomas Chatterton. TrCP

Resignation. Santob De Carrion, *Spanish.* TrJP, *tr. by* George Ticknor

Resignation. Po Chü-i, *Chinese.* ChiP, *tr. by* Arthur Waley

Resignation; an Ode to the Journeyman Shoemakers. "Peter Pindar."
    "Sons of Saint Crispin, 'tis in vain!" NOEC

Resigning from a Job in a Defense Industry. Sandra McPherson. LCAP-2

Resistance. Horst Bienek, *German.* AF, *tr. by* Matthew Mead

Resisting, by embracing, nothingness. (LL) In Santa Maria del Popolo. Thom Gunn. CMoP; FaBoMo; GTBS-P; OxBC; PoE

Resisting poetry I am becoming a poem. Moon. Derek Walcott. MoP

Resolute Courtier, The. Thomas Shipman. GBL

Resolute desire that enters, The. Arnaut Daniel, *Italian.* STV, *tr. by* John Frederick Nims

Resolution. W. S. Merwin. NYBP

Resolution and Independence. Wordsworth. EBEV; FHYEP; HAP; InPS-3; NOBE; NOBRP; NOCV; OAEL-2; OBNC; OxAEP-2; PoEL-4; TFi
    ("I'll think of the Leech-gatherer on the lonely moor!") (LL) NoP-4; Ro
    "Now, whether it were by peculiar grace." UV

Resolution in Four Sonnets, of a Poetical Question Put to Me by a Friend, Concerning Four Rural Sisters. Charles Cotton. PoEL-3; Son
    Two Rural Sisters. BoLoP; EnLoPo

Resolution of Dependence. George Barker. FaBoTw; LiTM

Resolutions. Robin Fulton. FaBoTC

Resolve, The. Alexander Brome. NOSC; OBEV

Resolve, The. Mary Lee, Lady Chudleigh. ECWP; WPE

Resolve. Charlotte Perkins Stetson Gilman. PoToHe

Resolve, The. Lady Mary Wortley Montagu. *See* The Lady's Resolve.

Resolve, The. Henry Vaughan. ESCV

Resolve to make the best of life. Beyond the Beaten Way. George Sands Johnson. PWR

Resolved to Love. Henry Constable. Son *Fr.* Diana.

Resort. George Oppen. FTOS

Resound my voice [*or* voyse], ye woods that hear [*or* here] me plain. Sir Thomas Wyatt. AAS; SiPS
    ("But, as rewarded, death for to be my meed.") (LL) AEP
    ("Resound my voice, ye woods that hear me plain.") AEP

Resource and a touch. So ditditdit daah for Bill Tuckett. (LL) Morse. Les A. Murray. NTP; NoP-4

Resources. Milton. *Fr.* Comus; a Masque Presented at Ludlow Castle. FHYEP; OAEL-1

Respect all surfaces. The skater is. In Defense of Superficiality. Elder Olson. NYBP

Respect for Law and Order, A. John Hughes. PNI

Respect the dreams of old men, said the cricket. Song for September. Robert Fitzgerald. VGW

Respect yourself, my brother. Brothers Loving Brothers. Vega. ISC

Respectability. Robert Browning. CBLP; EnLoPo

Respectable Burgher, The. Thomas Hardy. CMoP; ChIV-2; NoAM

Respectable House. Anne Stevenson. NALW

Respectable People. Austin Clarke. CMoP

Respected, Feared, and Somehow Loved. Marjorie Welish. PmAP

Respice Finem. Thomas Proctor. NoSic

Respite, The. Ingeborg Bachmann, *German.* WPOW, *tr. by* Michael Hamburger

Resplendent studs of heaven's frame. *Unknown.* SCAP

Respondez! Respondez! / (The war is completed—the price is paid—the title is settled beyond recall!) Walt Whitman. APN-1; NoAM; PoEL-5

Responding Voice. Francisco A. de Icaza, *Spanish.* PBMP, *tr. by* Samuel Beckett

Responds to love, don't call him or he will come. (LL) Unwanted. Edward Field. GLP; LiLi; Poetsp

Response. Mary Ursula Bethell. FaBoWP; PeNZ

Response to Rimbaud's Later Manner. Thomas Sturge Moore. CABP; OBMV

Response to Wang Ssu-yüan's Poem on the Moon, A. Shen Yüeh, *Chinese.* SuSp, *tr. by* Richard B. Mather

Responses to Montale. Brian Turner. PeNZ

Responsibilities. Anthony Cronin. PBCIP

Responsive to the tune of lawns and trees. Dogs in the Morning Light. Bruce Dawe. NoAM

Responsory, 1948, A. Thomas Merton. VGW

Ressaif My Saul. R. Crombie Saunders. OxBS

Rest. Slave Gorgo Dimoski, *Yugoslav.* CEEP, *tr. by* Ewald Osers

Rest, The. A Palimpsest. "Michael Field." VWP

Rest, The. Ezra Pound. AmPP; MoAMPo; NOBA; NoAM; OxBA *Fr.* Lustra.

Rest. Christina Rossetti. GSo; NOBE; OAEL-2; OBEV; OBNC

Rest. Jacob Isaac Segal, *Yiddish.* CEEP, *tr. by* Seymour Mayne

Rest. *Unknown.* PoToHe

Rest, and be thankful! On the verge. Adam Lindsay Gordon. CBAP *Fr.* Hippodromania; or, Whiffs from the Pipe.

Rest, beauty, stillness: not a waif of cloud. Evening. Emma Lazarus. APN-2 *Fr.* Phantasies.

Rest, Christ! from tireless war. See, it's midsummer. Derek Walcott. TOF *Fr.* Midsummer.

Rest from Loving and Be Living. C. Day Lewis. MoBrPo; OBMV

Rest in Peace. Wilfred John Funk. PoLF

Rest in peace, warriors of Soweto. Elegy for the Dead of Soweto. Thembinkosi Ndlovu, *Zulu.* PeSAV, *tr. by* Chris Mann

Rest is vanity of vanities, The. (LL) Ecclesiastes. G. K. Chesterton. ChIV-1; MoBrPo; OxBSP

Rest lightly O Earth upon this wretched Nearchos. Epitaph of Nearchos. Ammianus, *Greek.* WeW-3, *tr. by* Dudley Fitts

Rest, little guest. After Annunciation. Anna Wickham. MoBrPo

Rest Only in the Grave. James Clarence Mangan. BIrV

Rest, rest, and rest again. (LL) Nod. Walter De la Mare. BoTP; MoBrPo; OxBTC

Rest thee aged pilgrim, now thy toils are o'er. Death of a Grandparent. Mrs. Jennette Bonneau. Mary Weston Fordham. CBWP-2

Rest! This little Fountain runs. For a Fountain. "Barry Cornwall." OBEV

Rest ye in peace, ye Flanders dead. America's Answer. R. W. Lilliard. BLPA

Restaurant. Maxine Hong Kingston. OpBo

Restaurant is empty, The. On Stopping Late in the Afternoon for Steamed Dumplings. Toi Derricotte. InPS-3

Restful place, reviver of my smart, The. Sir Thomas Wyatt. SiPS

Resting. Josephine D. Henderson Heard. CBWP-4

Restless and discontent. Agathias, *Greek.* PGA, *tr. by* Kenneth Rexroth

Restless and discontent / I lie awake all night long. Agathias, *Greek.* GrAn, *tr. by* Kenneth Rexroth

Restless as a Wolf. Moyshe-Leyb Halpern, *Yiddish.* TrJP, *tr. by* Jacob Sloan

Restless he rolls about from whore to whore. John Wilmot, 2d Earl of Rochester. OBSV *Fr.* A Satire on Charles II.

Restless Heart, The. Henry Howard, Earl of Surrey. SiPS

Restless Night. Tu Fu, *Chinese.* ChiPo; CoBCP, *tr. by* Burton Watson

Restless Night in Camp, A. Tu Fu, *Chinese.* OHPC, *tr. by* Kenneth Rexroth

Restless, restless, craving rest. Camoëns. Herman Melville. NCAP

Restless State of a Lover, The. Henry Howard, Earl of Surrey. AAS; SiPS

Restoration. Jeffrey Skinner. PBCAP

Restoration of Enheduanna to Her Former Station, The. Enheduanna, *Sumerian.* BoWoP, *ad. by* Aliki *and* Willis Barnstone

'Restore the lock!' she cries; and all around. The Rape of the Lock. Alexander Pope. OxAEP-1 *Fr.* The Rape of the Lock[, an Heroi-Comical Poem]. FHYEP; HAP; ImPo; OAEL-1; OBNV; PeLV; PoEL-3

Restored by morning light. (LL) 1001 Nights. Ronald Wallace. EC2

Restoring the Ancestral House. Katerina Te Hei Koko Mataira, *Maori.* PeNZ, *tr. by* Katerina Te Hei Koko Mataira

Restrained. (LL) If there be sorrow. Mari E. Evans. SAGP

Restraining reckless middle-age? (LL) On Hearing That the Students of Our New University Have Joined the Agitation against Immoral Literature. W. B. Yeats. MoP; NoAM

Restricted. Eve Merriam. TrJP

Restroom. Chitra Divakaruni. UnSA

Résumé. Bei Dao, *Chinese.* AF, *tr. by* Bonnie S. McDougall

Résumé. Dorothy Parker. HeIP-4; InPK-6; NAAL-2; NALW; NBLV; NoP-4; OBAL; PFE; Poetr; TrJP; UV *Fr.* Some Beautiful Letters.

Resurgam. Adah Isaacs Menken. CBWP-1

Resurgam. Marjorie Lowry Christie Pickthall. TrCP

Resurrection. Margaret Atwood. CrSp

Resurrection. Richard Palmer Blackmur. PoA

Resurrection, The. Abraham Cowley. ChIV-2

Resurrection. Donne. ESCV *Fr.* La Corona. ChIV-2; ESCV; Son *Fr.* Holy Sonnets.

Resurrection. Margiad Evans. OBWVE

Resurrection. Kenneth Fearing. CMoP; PoE

Resurrection. Joy Harjo. HATNAP

Resurrection. Vladimir Holan, *Czech.* PoSu, *tr. by* George Theiner
("After this life here, we're to be awakened one day.") AF, *tr. by* C. G. Hanzlicek *and* Dana Habova
("We'll be at home again.") (LL) AF, *tr. by* C. G. Hanzlicek *and* Dana Habova

Resurrection. Winifred Holtby. WPN

Resurrection. Frank Horne. PoBA

Resurrection. Marie Luise Kaschnitz, *German.* WPOW, *tr. by* Michael Hamburger

Resurrection. Sidney Lanier. PoEL-5

Resurrection, The. W. B. Yeats.
Two Songs from a Play. FaBoTw; HAP; PoE, *sect.* 1; CMoP; ImPo; NOBE; OAEL-2, *sect.* 1-2

Resurrection. Sachiko Yoshihara, *Japanese.* WPJ, *tr. by* Kenneth Rexroth *and* Ikuko Atsumi

Resurrection: An Easter Sequence. William Robert Rodgers.
"It was a lovely night." PNI

Resurrection and Immortality. Henry Vaughan. ESCV

Resurrection, Imperfect. Donne. ChIV-2

Resurrection of Arp. Arthur James Marshall Smith. MoCV; NOBC

Resurrection of the Right Side. Muriel Rukeyser. LCAP-2; NMM-2

Resurrection Song. Thomas Lovell Beddoes. FaBoEE

Resurrections. Benjamin Alire Sáenz. PaTW

Resuscitation Team. U. A. Fanthorpe. FaBoWP

Retaining tears, but there are no more words. (LL) The Return. Arna Bontemps. GI

Retaliation. Margaret E. Bruner. PoToHe

Retaliation. Oliver Goldsmith.
David Garrick. NOEC
Edmund Burke. NOEC
Poem: "Of old, when Scarron his companions invited." NOIV; OxBoLi
Sir Joshua Reynolds. FaBoEE; NOEC; OBCoV

Reticulations creep upon the slack stream's face. On Sturminster Foot-Bridge. Thomas Hardy. OxBSP

Retire, my daughter. Fragment of an English Opera. A. E. Housman. OBCoV

Retired. Iain Crichton Smith. SpW

Retired ballerinas on winter afternoons. Retired Ballerinas, Central Park West. Lawrence Ferlinghetti. NoAM

Retired Civil Servant from Gateley, A. Limerick. Ida Thurtle. PeLi

Retired Farmer. David Allan Evans. Poetsp

Retired general is talking about restraint, The. Nightline: An Interview with the General. Ronald Wallace. PBCAP

Retired Mandarin's Wife Complains, A. U'ng Bình, *Vietnamese.* AVP, *tr. by* Huỳnh Sanh Thông

Retired Official Yüan's High Pavilion, The. Tu Mu, *Chinese.* PLT, *tr. by* A. C. Graham

Retired Pilot to Himself, The. Walter McDonald. CDa

Retired this hour from wondering crowds. Walter Savage Landor. GBL

Retired [*or* Retyrèd] thought[e]s enjoy their own[e] delight[e]s. Look[e] Home. Robert Southwell. ESCV; NOCV; NoSic

Retirement. William Cowper.
"I praise the Frenchman, his remark was shrewd." BLPA

Retirement. Henry Timrod. APN-2

Retirement. Henry Vaughan. ChIV-1; GeHe
(Retirement (I).) NOSC

Retirement of the Elephant, The. Russell Edson. AmPA

Retort Perfect, The. Justin Richardson. OBCoV

Retort to Jesus. D. H. Lawrence. PeECV

Retreat. Wilfrid Wilson Gibson. NSI

Retreat[e], The. Henry Vaughan. AWP; CABP; ClHu; ESCV; FMP; FSCP; GTBS-P; GeHe; HAP; ImPo; InPK-6; InPS-3; MeLP; NAEL-1; NIP-4; NOBE; NOCV; NOSC; NoP-4; OAEL-1; OBEV; OBWVE; PBRV; PeECV; PoE; PoEL-2; PoRA; SCGP; SeCP; TFi; TOF

Retreat of Ita Cagney, The. Michael Hartnett. CIP-2; PBCIP

Retreat of Liu Kuo-pao, The. Chang Yü, *Chinese.* CoBLCP, *tr. by* Jonathan Chaves

Retreat of Sun Ching-hsiang, The. Chang Yü, *Chinese.* CoBLCP, *tr. by* Jonathan Chaves

Retribution. Aleksandr Blok, *Russian.*
"In those far years of inertia." TCRP, *tr. by* Jon Stallworthy *and* Peter France

Retribution. Ilya Grigoryevich Ehrenburg, *Russian.* TCRP, *tr. by* Gordon McVay

Retribution. Friedrich von Logau, *German.* BLPA; PoToHe, *tr. by* Longfellow

Retribution. Lizelia Augusta Jenkins Moorer. CBWP-3

Retrieval System, The. Maxine W. Kumin. FaBoWP; WeW-3

"Retro Me, Sathana." D. G. Rossetti. ChIV-2

Retrospect. Josephine D. Henderson Heard. CBWP-4

Retrospection. Charlotte Brontë.
   "Dream that stole o'er us in the time." PEW

Retrospection. Henrietta Cordelia Ray. CBWP-3

Retrospection. Dunstan Shaw. NOBAu

Return, The. John Peale Bishop. ImPo; OxBA

Return, The. Arna Bontemps. GT; PoBA

Return, The. Alistair Campbell. PeNZ

Return. Seamus Deane. BIrV; IIP; PBCIP; PNI

Return, The. Emily Dickinson. MoAmPo

Return, The ("Doors flapped open in Ulysses' house, The"). Edwin Muir. CMoP

Return, The. Rudyard Kipling. MoBrPo

Return. Jewel C. Latimore. BlSi

Return. John Robert Lee. PBCV

Return, The. George MacBeth. NYBP

Return, The. Pittendrigh Macgillivray. OxBS

Return, The. Edna St. Vincent Millay. MeMAP; MoAmPo; MoP; NoAM; OxBA; Poetr

Return, The. Edwin Muir. *See* The Return of the Greeks.

Return, The. Molly Peacock. RA

Return, The. Ezra Pound. AmPP; CMoP; ColAP; HAP; MoAmPo; MoP; NOBA; NoAM; OxBA; PFTM; PoE; Poetr; RB; TRP; VGW; WeW-3
   ("Slow on the leash, / pallid the leash-men!") (LL) ColAP; PFTM

Return. Yannis Ritsos, *Greek.* GrIP, *tr. by* Edmund Keeley

Return. John Wilmot, 2d Earl of Rochester. *See* Song: "Absent from thee, I languish still."

Return, The. Theodore Roethke. NAAL-2 *Fr.* The Lost Son. HAP; HCAP; LiTM; VGW

Return, The. Tadeusz Różewicz, *Polish.* HP, *tr. by* Adam Czerniawski

Return, The. Laurie Sheck. WWSi

Return, The. Angelos Sikelianos, *Greek.* GrIP, *tr. by* Edmund Keeley *and* Philip Sherrard

Return. Theodore Spencer. PoA

Return, The. Swinburne. OxBoS

Return, The. Thomas Traherne. GeHe

Return, The. Tu Fu, *Chinese.* TAL, *tr. by* Robert Payne

Return. Wordsworth. HAP *Fr.* The River Duddon [A Series of Sonnets].

Return Alpheus, the dread voice is past. Milton. PeECV *Fr.* Lycidas. AWP; CABP; ClHu; EBEV; EBEvV; FHYEP; GTBS-P; HAP; ImPo; InPS-3; NOBE; NOSC; NoP-4; OAEL-1; OBEV; OxAEP-1; PBRV; PFE; PoEL-3; PoPoPo; Poetr; SCGP; TFi; UnPo

Return from Battle. *Unknown, Chinese.* ChiP, *tr. by* Arthur Waley

Return from Luluabourg. Michael Jackson. PeNZ

Return from the Convention. Reiner Kunze, *German.* CEEP, *tr. by* Lori Fisher

Return is not a way of going forward. Roman Poem Number Nine. June Jordan. GT

Return, my heart from wandering afar. Repose. Una Marson. PBCV

Return, my joys, and hither bring. Opposite to Melancholy. William Strode. NOSC

Return of a Popular Statesman. Vincent Buckley. CBAP

Return of an Ikon. Dimitris Tsaloumas. BMAP

Return of Astraea, The. Ben Jonson. NOBE

Return of Persephone, The. Alec Derwent Hope. BMAP

Return of Robinson Jeffers, The. Robert Hass. AmPA

Return of the Dead, The. Samar Attar.
   "And you came back." PBWP

Return of the Goddess [Artemis]. Robert Graves. PoA

Return of the Greeks, The. Edwin Muir. NoP-4; PoE
   (Return, The.) CMoP

Return of the Native. Imamu Amiri Baraka. APSN; BPo; ColAP

Return of the Proconsul, The. Zbigniew Herbert, *Polish.* FaBoPV; PoSu, *tr. by* Czeslaw Milosz; CEEP, *tr. by* Czeslaw Milosz

Return of the Prodigal Son. Léopold Sédar Senghor, *French.*
   "Elephant of Moissel, hear my pious prayer." NegPo, *tr. by* Ellen Conroy Kennedy

Return of the Sire de Nesle A.D. 16, The. Herman Melville. NOBA

Return of the Wolves. Anita Endrezze-Danielson. HATNAP

Return often and take me. Constantine P. Cavafy, *Modern Greek.* EP, *tr. by* Rae Dalven

Return, Return, O Shulammite. Bible, *O.T.* TrJP *Fr.* The Song of Songs. AWP

Return, Sweet Horse, rise. Cortez's Horse. Pat Mora. UnSA

Return to Ararat. Martyn Halsall. TrCP

Return to English Turn. Tom Dent. BkSV

Return to Heaven. Sangbyong Ch'on, *Korean.* CKP, *tr. by* Jaihiun Kim

Return to Hinton. Charles Tomlinson. CMoP

Return to La Plata, Missouri. Jim Barnes. HATNAP

Return to Mankiller Flats, Oklahoma. Mary Crescenzo Simons. LoHo

Return to My Native Land. Aimé Césaire, *French.* NegPo, *tr. by* Emile Snyders
   "I shall not regard my swelled head as a sign of real glory." TTY

Return to nestle here. (LL) Dream-Love. Christina Rossetti. CH; HAP; PoEL-5

Return to Paris. Jules Supervielle, *French.* MFP, *tr. by* Martin Sorrell

Return to Seattle: Bastille Day. Carolyne Wright. WWSi

Return to the Native Land, A. Aimé Césaire, *French.*
   "This flat city shortly after dawn." NegPo, *tr. by* Ellen Conroy Kennedy

Return to the Tree of Time, A. Vesna Parun, *Croatian.* WPOW, *tr. by* Vasa D. Mihailovich *and* Ronald Morgan

Return to Work, The. William Carlos Williams. NYBP

Return we to the dangers of the night. Juvenal. OAEL-1, *tr. by* Dryden *Fr.* Satires.

Returned, a wraith from her defrauded tomb. Transformation Scene. Constance Carrier. FYAP

Returned American. Kathleen Cain. LoHo

Returned from California. Simon J. Ortiz. HATNAP

Returned from college R——gets a wife. The Discontented Student. St. George Tucker. OBAL

Returned Heart, The. Sarah Dixon. ECWP

Returned Picture, The. Mary O'Donovan Rossa. IIP

Returned to Say. William Stafford. CoAmPo

Returning. Linda Pastan. WeW-3

Returning after dark, I thought. Traditional Red. Robert Huff. HoPM

Returning at Night. James Harrison. VGW

Returning by Night to Lu-Men. Meng Hao Jan, *Chinese.* OHMPC, *tr. by* Kenneth Rexroth

Returning Fire. D. F. Brown. CDa

Returning from Abroad. Ōkuma Nobuyuki, *Japanese.* MJT, *tr. by* Makoto Ueda

Returning from court day after day, I pawn my spring clothes. Tu Fu. SuSp, *tr. by* Irving Y. Lo *Fr.* Meandering River.

Returning from Harvest. Vernon Watkins. NYBP

Returning from its daily quest, my Spirit. To Dante [*or* Sonnet: Guido Cavalcanti to Dante]. Guido Cavalcanti, *Italian.* AWP; OBVE, *tr. by* Shelley

Returning from Kuang-ling. Ch'in Kuan, *Chinese.* SuSp, *tr. by* Stephen West

Returning from the Seventy-Two Mountains. Hsü Wei, *Chinese.* CoBLCP, *tr. by* Jonathan Chaves

Returning Home. Tu Mu, *Chinese.* SuSp, *tr. by* John M. Ortinau

Returning Home. Yüan Mei, *Chinese.* CoBLCP, *tr. by* Jonathan Chaves

Returning Home at Dusk from Town, on the Fifteenth of the Seventh Month. Shen Chou, *Chinese.* SuSp, *tr. by* Irving Y. Lo

Returning, I find her just the same. Passing Visit to Helen. D. H. Lawrence. CMoP

Returning Sails at a Distant Shore. Ma Chih-yüan. *Fr.* Three Poems to the tune "Lo-mei Feng." CoBLCP, *tr. by* Jonathan Chaves

Returning Spring. Pauli Murray. GT

Returning to Goleufryn. Vernon Watkins. OBWVE

Returning to Lotus Village. Kao Ch'i, *Chinese.* CoBLCP, *tr. by* Jonathan Chaves

Returning to my grandfather's house, after this exile. Returning to Goleufryn. Vernon Watkins. OBWVE

Returning to My Home in the Country ("Out here in the fields, few social affairs"). T'ao Ch'ien, *Chinese.* CoBCP, *tr. by* Burton Watson

Returning to My Home in the Country ("So long since I've enjoyed the hills and ponds"). T'ao Ch'ien, *Chinese.* CoBCP, *tr. by* Burton Watson

Returning to My Home in the Country. T'ao Ch'ien, *Chinese.* CoBCP, *tr. by* Burton Watson

Returning to My Home in the Country. T'ao Ch'ien, *Chinese.* CoBCP, *tr. by* Burton Watson

Returning to Roots of First Feeling. Robert Duncan. PoA

Returning to Store Bay. Barbara Howes. Poetsp

Returning to the Alluvial Fields. Wu Chia-chi, *Chinese.*

"In the morning they build embankments against floods." CoBLCP, *tr. by* Jonathan Chaves

Returning to the Fields. Ch'ien T'ao, *Chinese*. ChiP, *tr. by* Arthur Waley

Returning to the Port of Authority: A Picaresque. Constance Urdang. PBCAP

Returning to the room: / I notice how. Margaret Atwood. *Fr.* The Circle Game. MoCV

Returning to the Town Where We Used to Live. Susan Musgrave. NOBC

Returning to the valley. Gary Soto. *See* The Elements of San Joaquin.

Returning to Yin-ch'eng Early in the Year *Ting-ch'ou* (1277). Tai Piao-yüan, *Chinese*. CoBLCP, *tr. by* Jonathan Chaves

Returning, We Hear the Larks. Isaac Rosenberg. FaBoMo; NAEL-2; NSI; NoAM; OAEL-2; OBWP; PeFWW; PoWW

Returns into my Breast. (LL) Song: "Strephon has fashion, wit and youth." Elizabeth Taylor. KTR; LW

Reuben Bright. E. A. Robinson. APN-2; MeMAP; MoAmPo; NOBA; Son; TAP

("In with them, and tore down the slaughter-house.") (LL) GSo; NCAP; NoP-4; SAGP

Reuben Ranzo. *Unknown.* AmFP

Reuben, Reuben. Michael S. Harper. LoL; PoE

Reunion. Carolyn Forché. NoAM

Reunion. Judith Herzberg, *Dutch.* BoWoP, *tr. by* Shirley Kaufman

Reunion. E. A. Robinson. NOBA

Reunion with a Ghost. Ai. DeD

Reunited. Sir Gilbert Parker. OBEV

Reunited. Henrietta Cordelia Ray. CBWP-3

Rev. Andrew Brown, over the Hill to Rest. Josephine D. Henderson Heard. CBWP-4

Rev. Homer Wilbur's "Festina Lente." James Russell Lowell. OBAL *Fr.* The Biglow Papers.

Rev. Nicholas Noyes to the Rev. Cotton Mather, The. Nicholas Noyes. SCAP

Rev Owl. Abraham Moses Klein. TrJP

Rev. Samuel Weston. Mary Weston Fordham. CBWP-2

Revealed glory of sexism. Harry Mathews. *See* Histoire.

Reveille. John Godfrey. FTOS

Reveille. A. E. Housman. CABP; CMoP; LiTM; MoBrPo; NoP-4; PFE; PoLF

Reveille. Primo Levi, *Hebrew.* HP, *tr. by* Ruth Feldman *and* Brian Swann

Réveille. Lola Ridge. WPE

Reveille Matin, or Good Morrow to a Friend. Mildmay Fane. NOSC

Revel, The. Bartholomew Dowling. BLPA

Revel pauses and the room is still, The. Pannyra of the Golden Heel. Albert Samain, *French.* AWP, *tr. by* James Elroy Flecker

Revelation. Carole C. Gregory Clemmons. BlSi

Revelation, The. Stanley Crouch. SeSe

Revelation. Robert Frost. ChIV-2

Revelation. Sir Edmund William Gosse. OBEV

Revelation, The. Coventry Patmore. EnLoPo; GBL; GLoP; GTBS-P; HAP; LoP; OBNC; OxBSP *Fr.* The Angel in the House.

Revelation. Robert Penn Warren. NoAM

Revelation, The. William Carlos Williams. SAmP

Revelation and Decline. Georg Trakl, *German.* PFTM, *tr. by* Keith Waldrop

Revelation in the Mother Lode. George Evans. AF; PmAP

Revelation of St John The Divine, The. Bible, *N.T.*

End To Tears, An. LBC

Revelation: The Movie. Elton Glaser. PBCAP

Revelations. David Meltzer. NeAP

Revelations, First Time. Roger Jones. IFJA

Revelations—we've come to the lewd. Limerick. *Unknown.* PeLi

Revenant, The. Walter De la Mare. GBL

Revenge. Slave Gorgo Dimoski, *Yugoslav.* CEEP, *tr. by* Ewald Osers

Revenge. Letitia Elizabeth Landon. NOBRP

Revenge, The. Pierre de Ronsard, *French.* AWP, *tr. by* Thomas Stanley

Revenge, The. Tennyson. EBVV; FaBoCh; FaPoR; PoRA

"At Flores in the Azores Sir Richard Grenville lay." EBEvV; EBNV; OBWP

Revenge. Mary E. Tucker. CBWP-1

Revenge of America, The. Joseph Warton. ECEV

Revenge of Hamish, The. Sidney Lanier. APN-2; EBNV; NCAP; PoEL-5

Revenge of the Hunted. Robert Arthur Douglas Ford. MoCV

Revenge, Timotheus cries, and in that shout. Stevie Smith. WPN

Revenger's Tragedy, The. Cyril Tourneur.

"Madam, your grace so private?" FaBoSe

"Madame, his grace will not be absent long." PoEL-2

Reverberation. Maurice Kenny. HATNAP

Reverend Arbuthnot-Armitage-Brown, The. George Barker. FuFo

Reverend Butler came by. Madam and the Minister. Langston Hughes. NOBA

Reverend Henry Ward Beecher, The. Limerick. Oliver Wendell Holmes. PeLi

Reverend Mr. Higginson, The. Edward Johnson. SCAP

Reverend Mr. Uprightly, The. Limerick. *Unknown.* PeLi

Reverently. Tanka. Maekawa Samio, *Japanese.* MJT, *tr. by* Makoto Ueda

Reverie, A. Joanna Baillie. ECWP; WoRP

Reverie, A. Mary Weston Fordham. CBWP-2

Reverie. Don Marquis. PoLF

Reverie. Henrietta Cordelia Ray. CBWP-3

Reverie at Dawn. Egan O'Rahilly. *See* The Vision.

Reverie of a Mum. Nancy Keesing. CBAP; NOBAu

Reverie of Poor Susan, The. Wordsworth. GTBS-P; OxBoLi

Reverse Order. Steve Benson.

"As sincerely as possible." FTOS

Reverse the flight of Lucifer. The Task. Ruth Pitter. MoBrPo

REVERSED LIGHT. Artistic Copy. Tymoteusz Karpowicz, *Polish.* CEEP, *tr. by* Ewa Zak

Reversion. Barry O. Higgs. PeSA

Reversionary. Stevie Smith. FaBoEE

Review from Staten Island. Gloria C. Oden. GT; PoBA

Reviewing me without undue elation. A Choice of Weapons. Stanley Kunitz. LiTM; VGW

Reviewing Past Lives while Leaf-Burning. Anita Endrezze-Danielson. HATNAP

Reviewing the Troops at Kuei-lin with Military Inspectors Chiang And Chang. Yang Chi, *Chinese.* CoBLCP, *tr. by* Jonathan Chaves

Reviews are gaudy shows—allowed. On the Frequent Review of the Troops. "M." NOEC

Revised Notes for a Sonnet. "Edward Pygge." BXAP *Fr. Robert Lowell's Notebook.* OBCoV

Revision. Linda McCarriston. NMM-2

Revisionism. Joanne Burns. BMAP

Revival. Steve Crow. HATNAP; PiM

Revival. George Garrett. MT

Revival, The. Henry Vaughan. NOCV; PoEL-2

Revival of the Eternal Man. William Blake. Ro

Revo Lyric. Kendel Hippolyte. HCP

Revocation, A. Sir Thomas Wyatt. *See* Farewell: "What should I say."

Revolt of Islam, The. Shelley.

"Over the utmost hill at length I sped." OBWP

Revolution. Junko Nishi, *Japanese.* WPJ, *tr. by* Kenneth Rexroth *and* Ikuko Atsumi

Revolution. Pentti Saarikoski, *Finnish.* EC2, *tr. by* Anselm Hollo

Revolution is conceived, The. Cycle. Bobbi Sykes. BMAP

Revolution Is One Form of Social Change. Audre Lorde. Poetr

Revolution of the Aged, The. Njabulo S. Ndebele. PeSAV

"Revolution," said Mr. Adams, The. Canto 32. Ezra Pound. PFTM

Revolution Will Not Be Televised!, The. Gil Scott-Heron. NAAAL

Revolutionaries, The. Richard Percival Lister. NOBL

Revolutionaries, The. *Unknown.* NOBL

Revolutionary. Michael Smith. HCP

Revolutionary Letter #1. Diane Di Prima. CLPP

Revolutionary Petunias. Alice Walker. BlSi

Revolutionary Poets. Mutabaruka. PBCV

Revolutionary Revolution. George Buchanan. IIP

Revolutionary Youth. Hồ Văn Hảo, *Vietnamese.* AVP, *tr. by* Huỳnh Sanh Thông

Revolutions. Shakespeare. *See* Sonnet 60.

Revolving auger. (LL) Theris, whose hands were cunning. Leonidas, *Greek.* GrAn; PGA, *tr. by* Kenneth Rexroth

Rev'rend Father stood inculcating, The. Luis de Camóes. PeSAV *Fr.* The Lusiads. OBVE, *tr. by* Sir Richard Fanshawe

Rewaking, The. William Carlos Williams. ITG

Reward. Shimon Halkin, *Hebrew.* MHP, *tr. by* Ruth Finer Mintz

Reward of Innocent Love, The. William Habington. FMP *Fr.* Castara.

Reward of Service. Elizabeth Barrett Browning. BLPA; FaBoBe

Rewarded porters opening their smiles, The. On the Railway Platform. Randall Jarrell. GM

Rewards and Fairies. Roger Woddis. UV

Rewrite. E. A. Markham. PBCV

Rex Mundi. David Gascoyne. NoP-4

Rex regum, for whom praise flows freely. Poem on His Death-Bed. Meilyr Brydydd, *Welsh.* OBWVE, *tr. by* Joseph P. Clancy

Rex Whistler—or is it Joe Isuzu?—stretches. Society. Tom Clark. PmAP

Reynard the Fox. John Masefield.

"Fox knew well, that before they tore him, The." OBNV

"Meet was at 'The Cock and Pye,' The." OxBTC

"Ock Gurney and old Pete were there." CMoP

Run to Mourne End Wood, The. EBNV

Rhapsodies. Judy Turner. CTV

Rhapsody. Cynthia Huntington. NAmP90

Rhapsody. Frank O'Hara. NoAM

Rhapsody, A. Henry Vaughan. BeJo; NAEL-1

Rhapsody of Old Men, A. Dimitris Tsaloumas, *Greek.*

"They brought him one morning." CBAP, *tr. by* Margaret Carroll

Rhapsody on a Windy Night. T. S. Eliot. CMoP; HeIP-4; InPS-3; PoE

Rhapsody on Main Street. Patrick Williams. PNI

Rhapsody, Written at the Lakes in Westmorland, A. John Brown. NOEC

Rheia, submissive in love to Kronos. The Great Father Eating His Children. Hesiod. RaBo, *tr. by* Richmond Lattimore *Fr.* Theogony.

Rhetoric Leads to Cliché. Adrian C. Louis. NAmP90

Rhetoric of Langston Hughes, The. Margaret Danner. BlSi

Rhino is a homely beast, The. The Rhinoceros. Ogden Nash. MoAmPo; OBAL

Rhodanthe. Agathias, *Greek.* AWP, *tr. by* Andrew Lang

Rhode Island. William Meredith. NoP-4

Rhodoclea, I send you this wreath which I wove with my own hands. Rufinus Domesticus. HePo *Fr.* Epigrams.

Rhododaphne. Thomas Love Peacock.

"Magic and mystery, spells Circæan." NOBRP

Rhododendron is happy. Its aloof yet sexual, The. It's a Party (1959). Baron Wormser. SeSe

Rhodope. Rufinus, *Greek.* OBCVT, *tr. by* Andrew Lang

Rhodope is so stuck up / because of her beauty. Rufinus, *Greek.* GrAn, *tr. by* Alan Marshfield

Rhodope, Melite and Rhodoklea / contested. Rufinus, *Greek.* GrAn, *tr. by* Alan Marshfield

Rhodora, The [On Being Asked Whence Is the Flower]. Ralph Waldo Emerson. APN-1; AWP; AmPP; GEA; MeMAP; NAAL-1; NAAL-3; NOBA; NoP-4; OxBA; PAR; PWR; PoE; TAP; TFi

Rhodri Theophilus Owen. Ronald Stuart Thomas. OxAEP-2

Rhotruda. Frederick Goddard Tuckerman. NCAP

Rhydcymerau. David Gwenallt Jones, *Welsh.* OBWVE, *tr. by* Anthony Conran

Rhyme. James Laughlin. WeW-3

Rhyme for a Child Viewing a Naked Venus in a Painting [of "The Judgement of Paris"]. Robert Browning. OBCoV

Rhyme for Night. Joan Aiken. TLR

Rhyme for the Child as a Wet Dog. Judith Johnson Sherwin. TAP

Rhyme for Washing Hands, A. Rodney Bennett. BoTP

Rhyme is after, The. For W.C.W. Robert Creeley. FTOS; LCAP-2

Rhyme nor mars, nor makes, The. His Defence Against the Idle Critic. Michael Drayton. NOSC

Rhyme of Dorothy Rose, The. Pauline Frances Camp. FPC

Rhyme of My Inheritance. Joan Larkin. GLP

Rhyme of Sir Christopher, The. Henry Wadsworth Longfellow. NCAP

Rhyme of the Antique Forest. Henrietta Cordelia Ray. CBWP-3

Rhyme of the Dream-Maker Man, A. William Allen White. PoLF

Rhyme of the poet, The. Merlin II. Ralph Waldo Emerson. PAR; PoEL-4 *Fr.* Merlin. APN-1; AmPP; NAAL-1; NAAL-3; NOBA

Rhyme of the Rail[s]. John Godfrey Saxe. PoLF

Rhyme of the Sun-Dial, A. William Bell Scott. NOBVV

Rhyme-Prose on the Desolate City. Pao Chao, *Chinese.* CoBCP, *tr. by* Burton Watson

Rhyme-Prose on the Goddess of the Lo. Ts'ao Chih, *Chinese.* CoBCP, *tr. by* Burton Watson

Rhyme-Prose on the Idle Life. P'an Yüeh, *Chinese.* CoBCP, *tr. by* Burton Watson

Rhyme-Prose on the Owl. Chia Yi, *Chinese.* CoBCP, *tr. by* Burton Watson

Rhyme-Prose on the Sea. Mu Hua, *Chinese.* CoBCP, *tr. by* Burton Watson

Rhyme-Prose on the Snow. Hsieh Hui-lien, *Chinese.* CoBCP, *tr. by* Burton Watson

Rhyme Sheet of Other Lands, A. Hugh Chesterman. BoTP

Rhyme [*or* Rime], the rack of finest wits. A Fit of Rhyme [*or* Rime] against Rhyme [*or* Rime]. Ben Jonson. BeJo; OAEL-1; PoEL-2; SeCP

Rhymed Words Sent to My Eldest Son. Yang Shih-ch'i, *Chinese.* CoBLCP, *tr. by* Jonathan Chaves

Rhymes (?). Henry Sambrooke Leigh. NOBL

Rhymes. Charles Tomlinson. DiPo

Rhymes for a Modern Nursery. Paul Dehn.

"In a cavern, in a canyon." KaS

"Jack and Jill went up the hill/ To fetch some heavy water." ReMoGo

Rhymes on the Road. Thomas Moore.

"And is there then no earthly place." OBSV

Rhymes with Monk. Clark Coolidge. MoNo

Rhyming a Friend's Poem. Yü Hsüan-chi. BoWoP, *tr. by* Geoffrey Waters

Rhyming with a Friend. Yü Hsüan-chi, *Chinese.* BoWoP, *tr. by* Geoffrey Waters

Rhyming with Tzu-yu's "Treading the Green." Su Tung-p'o, *Chinese.* CoBCP, *tr. by* Burton Watson

("Overcome by the magic of his own charms.") (LL) OHPC, *tr. by* Kenneth Rexroth

("Spring wind raises fine dust from the road, The.") OHPC, *tr. by* Kenneth Rexroth

(Walk in the Country, A.) OHPC, *tr. by* Kenneth Rexroth

Rhythm, The. Robert Creeley. LiTM

Rhythm. Yevgeny Mikhailovich Vinokurov, *Russian.* TCRP, *tr. by* Daniel Weissbort

Rhythm and blues. The Blues Today. Mae Jackson. PoBA

Rhythm it is we. Spirits Unchained. Keorapetse Kgositsile. PoBA

Rib Sandwich. William J. Harris. UnSA

Ribald Romeos less and less berattle. 1.25: Ribald Romeos Less and Less Beratttle ("Parcius iunctas quatiunt fenestras"). Horace, *Latin.* OBCVT; STV, *tr. by* John Frederick Nims *Fr.* Odes.

Ribbe ne rele ne spinne ich ne may. *Unknown.* MiEL

Ribbon-Fish, The. Robert Adamson. CBAP

Ribbons of iodine. Kelp. Nora Dauenhauer. HATNAP

Ribh Considers Christian Love Insufficient. W. B. Yeats. RaBo

Ribs and terrors in the whale, The. The Whale. Herman Melville. APN-2; ChIV-1; KSG Moby Dick.

Ribs of leaves lie in the dust, The. The Coming of the Cold. Theodore Roethke. OBCP

Rice. Chemmanam Chacko, *Malayalam.* OMIP, *tr. by* K. Ayyappa Paniker

Rice. Carol Muske. AmPA

Rice Mill, The. Phan Văn Trị, *Vietnamese.* AVP, *tr. by* Huỳnh Sanh Thông

Rice this year ripens so late! Lament of the Farm Wife of Wu. Su Tung-p'o, *Chinese.* CoBCP, *tr. by* Burton Watson

Rice Will Grow Again. Frank A. Cross Jr. CDa

Rich and Poor; or, Saint and Sinner. Thomas Love Peacock. NOBE; NOBL; OBSV; PeLV

Rich blood disturbed my thought. Arrival. John Wain. EBEV

Rich Days. W. H. Davies. BoTP

Rich earth has not pressed down. Epitaph for Mael Mhuru. *Unknown.* NOIV

Rich families ordered everything in crystal, The. Waterford. Medbh McGuckian. BiHa

Rich, flashy, puffy-faced. Cabaret. Sterling Brown. NAAAL

Rich folks 'cided to take a trip, De. De Titanic. *Unknown.* AS

Rich fools there be, whose base and filthy heart. Sonnet 24. Sir Philip Sidney. *Fr.* Astrophil and Stella. AAS; SiPS

Rich in her weeping Country's Spoils *Versailles.* The Wild. Joseph Warton. GaP

Rich in the simple worship of a day. (LL) Fragment of an Ode to Maia Written on May Day, 1818. Keats. OAEL-2; OBEV; PoEL-4

Rich in the waning light she sat. Waiting. John Freeman. CH

Rich Irish Lady, A. *Unknown.* AmFP

Rich Is the Year with Much Millet and Rice. *Unknown, Chinese.* CoBCP, *tr. by* Burton Watson

Rich king of a rainy country, The. The King in May. Michael Dennis Browne. NYBP

Rich *Lazarus!* richer in those gems, thy teares. Upon Lazarus His Teares. Richard Crashaw. GeHe

Rich little circle south. Bruce Andrews. FTOS

Rich look grand, the poor seem cheap and mean, The. Nguyễn Bỉnh Khiêm, *Vietnamese.* AVP, *tr. by* Huỳnh Sanh Thông

Rich man bought a swan and goose, A. The Swan and the Goose. Aesop, *Greek.* AWP, *tr. by* William Ellery Leonard

Rich man has his motorcar, The. Franklin Pierce Adams. NBLV; OBAL

Rich man lay on his velvet couch, The. Mag's Song. *Unknown.* AS

Rich nights in another climate. Emblems. Douglas Dunn. FaBoMo

Rich Old Miser, A. *Unknown.* AmFP

"Rich soil," remarked the Landlord. D. J. Enright. OBCoV *Fr.* Paradise Illustrated.

Rich Statue, double-faced. To the New Yeere [*or* Year]. Michael Drayton. NOSC; PoEL-2

Rich surplus of consciousness rots at the wharves, The. Clouds. Francis Webb. BMAP

Rich tuft of ivy, A. Suibne Geilt. NOIV

Rich, voluptuous languor of dim pain, A. Vanitas Vanitatum. Israel Zangwill. TrJP

Rich Widow, The. *Unknown.* AmFP

Rich Words! HEAV'N, HEAV'N WILL MAKE AMENDS FOR ALL. (LL) Go then, my dove, but now no longer mine. Cotton Mather. AiP; SCAP

Richard Cory. Edwin Arlington Robinson. APAD; APN-2; AmPP; CMoP; ChAP; ColAP; EBEvV; HAP; ImPo; InPK-6; LiTM; MeMAP; MoAmPo; NAAL-2; NCAP; NOBA; NTP; NoP-4; OxBA; PFE; PoLF; PoPoPo; PoRA; Poetr; SAGP; TAP; TFi

Richard Cory. Paul Simon. InPK-6; PFE

Richard Dick upon a stick. *Unknown.* OxNR

Richard II. Shakespeare. OBGa *Fr.* King Richard II.
("Go bind thou up young dangling apricocks.") GaP
"This royal throne of kings, this scepter'd isle." UV
"You may my glories and my state depose." IMW

Richard III. Shakespeare.
"Set down, set down your honourable load." FaBoSe
"Stay, you that bear the corse, and set it down." OxBoV

Richard, may I ask a question? What is an episteme? Richard Howard. *Fr.* Compulsive Qualifications. PoA

Richard Roe wished himself Solomon. Richard Roe and John Doe. Robert Graves. CMoP

Richard, what will it be like when you ask the questions? Richard Howard. *Fr.* Compulsive Qualifications. PoA

Richard's Blues. Richard Cecil. SeSe

Riches. *Unknown. See* On Late-acquired Wealth *or* Riches.

Riches and honours Buckley layes aside. Onely the Reverend Grave and Godly Mr. Buckly Remaines. Edward Johnson. SCAP

Riches I hold in light esteem. The Old Stoic. Emily Jane Brontë. BWW; FaPoR, NALW; NOBE; OBEV; OBNC; OxAEP-2; PoLF; SDW; VWP

Richie Story. *Unknown.* ESPB

Richly painted zither, for no reason, has fifty strings, The. Li Shang-yin, *Chinese.* SuSp, *tr. by* James J. Y. Liu

Richmond. John Updike. CBCWP

Richmond Gardens: A Poem. *Unknown.* OBGa

Richmond Hill. Thomas Maurice.
Chiswick. OBGa

Rick of Green Wood, The. Edward Dorn. NeAP; PmAP; PoM

Rickety chimney suggests, A. Caravan. Michael Longley. CIP-2; PNI

Ricksha man does quite a simple job, The. Phan Văn Hy, *Vietnamese.* AVP, *tr. by* Huỳnh Sanh Thông

Ricksha Man's Impromptu, A. Phan Trọng Quảng, *Vietnamese.* AVP, *tr. by* Huỳnh Sanh Thông

Riddle, The. Georgia Douglas Johnson. PoBA

Riddle, The. "H. E. H." PoToHe

Riddle: "As I went down that yella bank." *Unknown.* FaBoVe

Riddle: "As I went through a guttery gap / I met a wee man with a red cap." *Unknown.* FaBoVe

Riddle: "As I went through yon guttery gap / I met my Uncle Davy." *Unknown.* FaBoVe

Riddle: "Black'm saut'm rough'm glower'm saw." *Unknown.* FaBoVe

Riddle: "Chip chip cherry." *Unknown.* FaBoVe

Riddle: "Cuckoo and the gowk, the." *Unknown.* FaBoVe

Riddle: "From Belsen a crate of gold teeth." William Heyen. HP; SoSe-8

Riddle: "He went to the wood and caught it." *Unknown.* OxNR

Riddle: "Hickamore hackamore." *Unknown.* FaBoVe

Riddle: "High as the sky it flies." *Unknown.* FaBoVe

Riddle: "Highty, tighty, paradighty, clothed [all] in green." *Unknown.* OxNR

Riddle: "Hopper o'ditches, A." *Unknown.* FaBoVe

Riddle: "House full, [a] yard full, [A]." *Unknown.* LB; NTCP

Riddle: "I'm a strange creature, for I satisfy women." Cynewulf. ASW, *tr. by* Kevin Crossley-Holland *Fr.* Riddles (Exeter Book).
(Three Riddles from *The Exeter Book.*) PeLV

Riddle: "Invisible, chimerical." Daryl Hine. NoP-4

Riddle: "It has a head like a cat, feet like a cat." *Unknown.* NTCP

Riddle: "Land was white, The." *Unknown.* FaBoVe; OxNR

Riddle: "Little trotty hetty coat." *Unknown.* FaBoVe

Riddle: "Lives in winter." *Unknown.* NTCP
(Icicles, An.) ReMoGo

Riddle: "Long slick black feller." *Unknown.* FaBoVe

Riddle: "No more, no more, / We are already pined [pin'd]." Alexander Brome. NOSC

Riddle, A: "Once when I was very scared." Charlotte Zolotow. NTCP

Riddle: "Riddlum riddlum ranty pole." *Unknown.* FaBoVe

Riddle: "Round the house and round the house / and there lies a black glove in the window." *Unknown.* FaBoVe

Riddle: "Round the house and round the house / and there lies a white glove in the window." *Unknown.* FaBoVe

Riddle: "Shoemaker makes shoes without leather, A." *Unknown.* OxNR

Riddle: "Stiff standing on the bed." *Unknown.* GBL

Riddle: "Their tongues are knives, their forks are hands and feet." Adrian Mitchell. FaBoEE; GBL; OxBSP

Riddle, A: "There is one that has a head without an eye." Christina Rossetti. OxBChV

Riddle, A: "'Twas in heaven pronounced, and 'twas muttered in hell." Catherine Maria Fanshawe. NOBRP

Riddle, A: "Upon a bed of humble clay." Thomas Parnell. ECEV

Riddle: "White bird featherless / Flew from Paradise." *Unknown.* FaBoVe; OxNR

Riddle: "White sheep, white sheep, on a blue hill." *Unknown.* FaBoVe

Riddle: "Wooden belly iron back." *Unknown.* FaBoVe

Riddle, A: "Yon laddie wi' the gowdan pow." William Soutar. OxBS

Riddle, a riddle / As I suppose, A. A Sieve. Mother Goose. OxNR; ReMoGo

Riddle a riddle as I suppose, A. *Unknown.* FaBoVe

Riddle cum diddle cum dido. Kindness to Animals. Laura Elizabeth Richards. NTCP

Riddle in the Garden. Robert Penn Warren. NoAM

Riddle-Me-Ree. Liz Lochhead. OPOU

Riddle me, riddle me ree. Mother Goose. OxNR

Riddle: Mute Swan. Cynewulf. *See* Wild Swan: "My attire is noiseless when I tread the earth."

Riddle of the World. Alexander Pope. *See* Know Thyself.

Riddle: On a Kiss, A. William Strode. NOSC

Riddle silently sees its image. It spins evening, The. Dusk in the Country. Harry Edmund Martinson, *Swedish.* RB, *tr. by* Robert Bly

Riddle Song, The. *Unknown.* KaS

Riddle: "Two legs sat upon three legs." Mother Goose. NTCP

Riddle we can guess, The. Emily Dickinson. SAmP

Riddles. *Unknown.* NoP-4

Riddles (Exeter Book). *Unknown, Anglo-Saxon; Formerly at. to* Cynewulf.
"Anchor: I must fight with the waves whipped up by the wind." ASW, *tr. by* Kevin Crossley-Holland

Anchor: "Oft I must strive with wind and wave." AnOE, *tr. by* Charles W. Kennedy

"Beam of Wood, A: I am fire-fretted and I flirt with Wind." EEP, *tr. by* Michael Alexander

"Bellows: O wise man, weigh your words." ASW, *tr. by* Kevin Crossley-Holland

"Bible or Prayer-Book: I am the scalp of myself, skinned by my foeman." EEP, *tr. by* Michael Alexander

"Book: Enemy ended my life, deprived me, An." ASW, *tr. by* Kevin Crossley-Holland

Book Moth: "Moth ate a word. To me it seemed, A." AnOE, *tr. by* Charles W. Kennedy
("Bookmoth: A moth devoured words. When I heard.") ASW, *tr. by* Kevin Crossley-Holland

"Bookworm: I heard of a wonder, of words moth-eaten;." EEP, *tr. by* Michael Alexander

"Bread: I'm told a certain object grows." ASW, *tr. by* Kevin Crossley-Holland

"Bullock: I watched a beast of the weaponed sex." EEP, *tr. by* Michael Alexander

"Chalice: I heard a radiant ring, with no tongue." ASW, *tr. by* Kevin Crossley-Holland

"Coat-of-Mail: Dank earth, wondrously cold, The." ASW, *tr. by* Kevin Crossley-Holland

"Coat of Mail: The womb of the wold, wet and cold." EEP, *tr. by* Michael Alexander

"Cock and Hen: I saw two wonderful and weird creatures." EEP, *tr. by* Michael Alexander

"Cock and Hen: I watched a couple of curious creatures." ASW, *tr. by* Kevin Crossley-Holland

"Creation: Enduring the Creator, He who now guides." ASW, *tr. by* Kevin Crossley-Holland

"Cuckoo: Abandoned unborn by my begetters." EEP, *tr. by* Michael Alexander

"Fire: On earth there's a warrior of curious origin." ASW, *tr. by* Kevin Crossley-Holland

Fish in River: "My house is not quiet, I am not loud." AnOE, *tr. by* Charles W. Kennedy

Honey-Mead: "I am valued by men, fetched from afar." AnOE, *tr. by* Charles W. Kennedy

"Horn: I am always at the aetheling's shoulder." EEP, *tr. by* Michael Alexander

"Horn: I'm loved by my lord, and his shoulder." ASW, *tr. by* Kevin Crossley-Holland

Horn: "Time was when I was weapon and warrior." AnOE, *tr. by* Charles W. Kennedy

"House Martins: This wind wafts little creatures." ASW, *tr. by* Kevin Crossley-Holland

"I saw a woman sit alone." EEP, *tr. by* Michael Alexander

"Ice: On the way a miracle: water become bone." ASW, *tr. by* Kevin Crossley-Holland

"Ice: The wave, over the wave, a wierd thing I saw." EEP, *tr. by* Michael Alexander

"Iceberg: Curious, fair creature came floating on the waves, A." ASW, *tr. by* Kevin Crossley-Holland

"Jackdaws or Crows: Their dark bodies, dun-coated." EEP, *tr. by* Michael Alexander

"Jay: I've one mouth but many voices." ASW, *tr. by* Kevin Crossley-Holland

"Key: Swings by his thigh a thing most magical!" EEP, *tr. by* Michael Alexander

"Leather: I travel by foot, trample the ground." ASW, *tr. by* Kevin Crossley-Holland

"Lot and his two daughters and their sons: Man sat sozzled with his two wives, A." ASW, *tr. by* Kevin Crossley-Holland

"Moon and Sun: A curious and wonderful creature I saw." EEP, *tr. by* Michael Alexander

Old English Riddle. OPOU, *tr. by* Gerard Benson

"One-Eyed Garlic Seller, A: Many were met, men of discretion." EEP, *tr. by* Michael Alexander

"One-Eyed Seller of Arrows: Creature came shuffling where there sat, A." ASW, *tr. by* Kevin Crossley-Holland

"Onion: I'm the world's wonder, for I make women happy." EEP, *tr. by* Michael Alexander

"Oxhide: While my ghost lives I go on feet." EEP, *tr. by* Michael Alexander

"Oyster: Deep sea suckled me, the waves sounded over me." ASW, *tr. by* Kevin Crossley-Holland

"Pen and four fingers: I watched four fair creatures." ASW, *tr. by* Kevin Crossley-Holland

"Plough: I keep my snout to the ground; I burrow." ASW, *tr. by* Kevin Crossley-Holland

Plow: "My beak is bent downward, I burrow below." AnOE

"Reed: I sank roots first of all, stood." ASW, *tr. by* Kevin Crossley-Holland

Riddle: "I'm a strange creature, for I satisfy women." ASW, *tr. by* Kevin Crossley-Holland

(Three Riddles from *The Exeter Book*.) PeLV

Riddle: Cuckoo.

"Shepherd's Pipe: The thing is magic, unimaginable." EEP, *tr. by* Michael Alexander

"Shield: I'm by nature solitary, scarred by spear." ASW, *tr. by* Kevin Crossley-Holland

Shield: "Lonely wanderer, wounded with iron, A." AnOE, *tr. by* Charles W. Kennedy

"Siren: I was in one hour an ashen crone." EEP, *tr. by* Michael Alexander

"Soul and Body: I've heard tell of a noble guest." ASW, *tr. by* Kevin Crossley-Holland

"Storm at Sea: Sometimes I plunge through the press of waves." ASW, *tr. by* Kevin Crossley-Holland

"Sun and Moon: I saw a strange creature." ASW, *tr. by* Kevin Crossley-Holland

Swan, The. RB, *tr. by* Geoffrey Grigson

Swan, The: "Silent is my dress when I step across the earth."

"Swan: When it is earth I tread, make tracks upon water." EEP, *tr. by* Michael Alexander

Three Riddles from *The Exeter Book*. ASW; PeLV, *tr. by* Kevin Crossley-Holland

("Churning (or lovemaking): Young man made for the corner, A.") ASW, *tr. by* Kevin Crossley-Holland

"Weathercock: I am puff-breasted, proud-crested." EEP, *tr. by* Michael Alexander

Weathercock, The: "I puff my breast out, my neck swells." RB, *tr. by* Geoffrey Grigson; ASW, *tr. by* Kevin Crossley-Holland

("Weathercock: My breast is puffed up and my neck is swollen.") ASW, *tr. by* Kevin Crossley-Holland

Wild Swan: "My attire is noiseless when I tread the earth." AnOE, *tr. by* Charles W. Kennedy

Wind: "At times I resort, beyond man's discerning." AnOE

Riddles Wisely Expounded, *vers.* A. *Unknown.* ESPB

Riddles Wisely Expounded. *Unknown.* ESPB

(Jennifer Gentle and Rosemary.) OxBoLi

Riddling Knight, The. *Unknown.* FaBoCh; PBMP; PoEL-1

Riddling Letter, A ("Sir, / Pray discruciate what follows: / A long-eared beast, and a field-house for cattle"). Jonathan Swift. CBNP

"Riddling world, A!" one cried. The Two Questions. Alice Thompson Meynell. WPE

Riddlum riddlum ranty pole. Riddle. *Unknown.* FaBoVe

Riddym Ravings (The Mad Woman's Poem). Jean Binta Breeze. NBrP

Ride. Josephine Miles. FaBoWP

Ride, The. Lucinda Roy. GT

Ride a Cock Horse. Barry Pain. BXAP

Ride a cock-horse to Banbury Cross. *Unknown.* ACTP

Ride a cock-horse to Banbury Cross / To buy little Johnny a galloping horse. *Unknown.* OxNR

Ride a cock-horse [*or* a-cock horse] to Banbury Cross, / To see a fine lady upon a white horse. Mother Goose. BoTP; FaBoBe; OxBoLi; OxNR ("She shall have music wherever she goes.") (LL) LB

Ride a cock-horse to Banbury Cross / To see what Tommy can buy. *Unknown.* OxNR

Ride away, ride away / Johnny shall ride. Mother Goose. OxNR; ReMoGo

Ride-by-Nights, The. Walter De la Mare. ChAP

Ride in, kind Saviour! *Unknown.* CrDW

Ride in the swing. Tune: Crimson Lips Adorned. Li Ch'ing-chao, *Chinese.* PBWP, *tr. by* C. H. Kwock *and* Vincent McHugh

Ride our ill weather out. (LL) Lovers in Winter. Robert Graves. FaBoEE; NYBP

Ride, ride together, for ever ride? (LL) The Last Ride Together. Robert Browning. BoLoP; FHYEP; GLoP; NAEL-2; OBEV; PoEL-5; UnPo

Ride, ride together, for ever ride. (LL) The Last Ride Together (from Her Point of View). James Kenneth Stephen. BXAP; UnPo

Ride round the Parapet, The. Friedrich Rückert, *German.* AWP, *tr. by* James Clarence Mangan

Ride upon the Death Chariot. Mbuyiseni Oswald Mtshali. PBMAP

Rider / is fat, The. Horse & Rider. Wey Robinson. BXAP

Rider Victory, The. Edwin Muir. CMoP; LiTM

Riders, The. Ann Stanford. WPE

Riders Held Back, The. Louis Simpson. CoAmPo

Rides. Gene Derwood. LiTM

Ridge, The. John Cowper Powys.
　"Aye! What a thing is the passing of Cronos, the angular-minded." OBWVE

Ridiculous / How the space between three violins. Cantata. Jack Spicer. APSN

Riding. William Allingham. OxBChV

Riding a Boat on Wu-ling Stream. Tao-chi, *Chinese.* CoBLCP, *tr. by* Jonathan Chaves

Riding a Nervous Horse. Vicki Hearne. APo

Riding a One-eyed Horse. Henry Taylor. HeIP-4; InPK-6

Riding Across John Lee's Finger. Stanley Crouch. GT; PoBA

Riding across the town in a dirty carriage. Riding Over Belmore Park. Robert Harris. BMAP

Riding at dawn, riding alone. Gillespie. Sir Henry John Newbolt. PeVV

Riding birds, feeling under our thighs the soft feathers. Earth. Czeslaw Milosz. ITG, *tr. by* Czeslaw Milosz *and* Robert Hass *Fr.* The Garden of Earthly Delights.

Riding by there every day. Dog Hospital. Peter Wild. AmPA

Riding Double. Peter Wild. AmPA

Riding Down from Bangor. Louis Shreve Osborne. BLPA

Riding Hood. Betsy Sholl. CrSp

Riding in a Stranger's Funeral. Robert Wallace. CMAP

Riding Lesson. Henry Taylor. NBLV

Riding on a Railroad Train. Ogden Nash. PiM

Riding on a Streetcar with My Father. Mary Ann Larkin. AiP

Riding Over Belmore Park. Robert Harris. BMAP

Riding the "A." May Swenson. GM; PiM

Riding the black express from heaven to hell. Lucifer in the Train. Adrienne Rich. GM

Riding the blue sapphire mountains. Mahadevi, *Kannada.* BoWoP; PBWP, *tr. by* A. K. Ramanujan

Riding the Empire Builder, 1948. David Wojahn. GM

Riding the North Point Ferry. Wing Tek Lum. OpBo

Riding the Rock Island Through Kansas. Dave Etter. GM

Riding through life. (LL) Poem of Alienation. Antonio Jacinto, *Portuguese.* PeSAV, *tr. by* Michael Wolfers; PBMAP

Riding through Ruwu swamp, about sunrise. Bête Humaine. Francis Brett Young. CH

Riding Together. William Morris. EnVR; NOBE; OAEL-2

Rifacimento. Paul Violi. PmAP

Rifle, The. Tymoteusz Karpowicz, *Polish*. PoSu, *tr. by* Jan Darowski

Rifle-thin, they stand in their angelic armor. Mannequins. Laurie Sheck. PuP-17

Rifled honeycomb, The. Cave. John Montague. CIP-2; IIP *Fr.* The Cave of Night.

Rigadoon, rigadoon, now let him fly. *Unknown.* OxNR

Rigged poker-stiff on her back. All the Dead Dears. Sylvia Plath. CAPP-1

Right after her birth, they crowded in. Anaesthesia. Jean Valentine. TAP

Right Apprehension. Thomas Traherne. PoEL-2

Right Arm, The. Paul Muldoon. NoAM

"Right as a Ribstone Pippin!" But it lied. (LL) The False Heart. Hilaire Belloc. FaBoCh; FaBoEE; MoBrPo; OxBSP

Right as the star [*or* stern] of day began [*or* begouth] to s[c]hine. The Poet's Dream. William Dunbar. PoEL-1 *Fr.* The Golden [*or* Goldyn] Targe. OxBS

Right at the end of night. Philippe Jaccottet, *French*. VCWP, *tr. by* Derek Mahon

Right down the shocked street with a siren-blast. A Fire-Truck. Richard Wilbur. AiP

Right fresshe flowr, whos I ben have and shal. The Sorrow of Troilus. Chaucer. PoEL-1 *Fr.* Troilus and Criseyde [*or* Criseide]. EnVB

Right from the ambiguous start. D-Zug. Julian Croft. NOBAu

Right good is rest. (LL) Lines for a Bed at Kelmscott Manor. William Morris. CH; NTP; OBEV; PoEL-5

Right Hand, The. Robert Herrick. CavPo

Right hand winnows the sand, The. The Invention. Paul Éluard, *French*. NNPT, *tr. by* Samuel Beckett

Right Heart in the Wrong Place, The. James Joyce. FaBoPV

Right here I was nearly killed one night in February. Solitude. Tomas Tranströmer, *Swedish*. RB, *tr. by* Robert Bly

Right here the other night something. E. E. Cummings. NoAM

Right here with the others. (LL) The Language of the Brag. Sharon Olds. NMM-2; PBCAP

Right in the middle. Arizona Zipper. HA

Right in the Trail. Gary Snyder. PmAP

Right inuff / ma language is disgraceful. Tom Leonard. FaBoTC *Fr.* Ghostie Men.

Right Kind of People, The. Edwin Markham. BLPA; PoToHe

Right Meaning, The. César Vallejo, *Spanish*. RaBo, *tr. by* Robert Bly

Right Must Win, The. Frederick William Faber. PWR

Right now, even if a muscular woman wanted. Trying for Fire. Tim Seibles. NAmP90

Right now I am the flower girl. Flowers. Margaret Atwood. NoP-4

Right of Way. Eugene McCarthy. IIP

Right of Way. Barry Sternlieb. GM

Right-of-Way: 1865, A. William Plomer. PeLV

Right On: White America. Sonia Sanchez. ISC; PoBA

Right or ruth. Susan Howe. PmAP *Fr.* Speeches at the Barriers.

Right Thing, The. Theodore Roethke. PeECV

Right under their noses, the green. The Dusk of Horses. James Dickey. ColAP; LiTM; NYBP; WeT

Right Use of Prayer, The. Sir Aubrey De Vere. TIRV

Right waves gather, The. (LL) From the Wave. Thom Gunn. NAEL-2; NoP-4; OxBoS

Right well I w[r]ote most mighty Soueraine [*or* soveraine]. Edmund Spenser. NoSic; OAEL-1 *Fr.* Wood Of Error. AEP

Righteous Anger. James Stephens. *See* A Glass of Beer.

Righteous Man, The. Samuel Butler. OBSV

Rightful retribution. For My Father's Mother Who Has Alzheimer's. M. Eliza Hamilton. IFJA

Rights. Phan Bội Châu, *Vietnamese*. AVP, *tr. by* Huỳnh Sanh Thông

Rights of Way. Thomas Reiter. GM

Rights of Woman, The. Anna Laetitia Barbauld. CABP; ECWP; NOEC; NoP-4; PEW; Ro; WoRP

Rigid Body Sings. James Clerk Maxwell. UV

(In Memory of Edward Wilson.) BXAP

Rigoletto. Newman Levy. OBAL

Rigor of beauty is the quest. But how will you find beauty when it is locked. Preface. William Carlos Williams. NoAM *Fr.* Paterson.

Rilke. Wayne Brown. HCP

Rilke, my river, I know your locked look of a poet. Visions. Kathleen Spivack. AmPA

Rilloby-Rill. Sir Henry John Newbolt. BXAP

Rillons, Rillettes, they taste the same. Richard Wilbur. NYBP; OBCoV

Rimbaud and Verlaine, precious pair of poets. Prelude LVI. Conrad Potter Aiken. FaBoMo; LiTM; NoAM; TwCP *Fr.* Preludes for Memnon; or, Preludes to Attitude.

Rimbaud Having a Bath. Robert Adamson. BMAP

Rime of the Ancient Feminist, The. Stephanie Markman. "They lived out in a women's house." BrRo

Rime of the Ancient Mariner, The. Coleridge. CABP; CH; EBEV; EBNV; FHYEP; FaBoBe; FaBoCh; HAP; HeIP-4; HoPM; ImPo; InPS-3; NOBE; NoP-4; OAEL-2; OBEV; OBNC; OBNV; OxAEP-2; OxBoS; PeECV; PoE; PoEL-4; PoPoPo; SCGP; TFi; TOF

"He prayeth best, who loveth best." CTV

"He prayeth well, who loveth well." BoTP

"I woke, and we were sailing on." OxBSn

"Loud wind never reached the ship, The." OxBSn

"This Hermit good lives in that wood." Poetr

Rime of the Auncient Waggonere, The. William Maginn. BXAP; ClHu

Rime of the Gentle Pacifist, The. "Pontiff." NSI

Rimer quenches his unheeded fires, The. Ambrose Bierce. APN-2 *Fr.* The Devil's Dictionary.

Rimmed in by cypresses, tin water flashed. White Lake. James Applewhite. MT

Rimmed round with grass, / reposedly. (LL) The Tulip Bed. William Carlos Williams. OBGa

Rimrock, Where It Is. Hayden Carruth. NNaP

Rin and rout, rin and rout. The Deevil's Waltz. Sydney Goodsir Smith. FaBoTw

Ring, The. Ikuko Atsumi, *Japanese*. WPJ, *tr. by* Kenneth Rexroth *and* Ikuko Atsumi

Ring, The. Edwin Muir. FaBoTC

Ring, The. Diane Wakoski. PoA

Ring-a-ring o' roses. Mother Goose. LB; OxNR; ReMoGo

Ring-a-ring o'roses. *Unknown.* ACTP

Ring and the Book, The. Robert Browning.

"Beside, up to my marriage, thirteen years." EBVVPR

"Do you see this square old yellow Book, I toss." FaBoVe

"First of the first, / Such I pronounce Pompilia, then as snow." EBVVPR

"From dawn till now that it is growing dusk." EBVVPR

"If I,—instead of threatening, talking big." EBVVPR

"Thanks, Sir, but, should it please the reverend Court." EBVVPR

Ring around a rosey. Squat Down, Josey. *Unknown.* AmFP

Ring in the Christ that is to be. (LL) Ring Out the Old, Ring In the New. Tennyson. EBEvV; EBVV; FHYEP; FaPoR; ImPo; OAEL-2; OxAEP-2; PeECV

Ring into golden bowls. (LL) An Opium Fantasy. Maria White Lowell. APN-2; InPK-6

Ring of, The. Charles Olson. NOBA; VGW

Ring of the moon, starshine, swept away as I watch. Traveler's Thoughts. Tu Hsün-ho, *Chinese*. CoBCP, *tr. by* Burton Watson

Ring Out the Old, Ring In the New. Tennyson. *Fr.* In Memoriam A. H. H.

Ring out the silence I am nourished by. (LL) This is the day His hour of life draws near. Allen Tate. NAAL-2; Son

Ring out, wild bells, to the wild sky. Ring Out the Old, Ring In the New. Tennyson. EBEvV; EBVV; FHYEP; FaPoR; ImPo; OAEL-2; OxAEP-2; PeECV *Fr.* In Memoriam A. H. H.

Ring out your bells [*or* belles], let mourning shows [*or* shewes] be spread. Dirge. Sir Philip Sidney. GBL; NoSic; OxAEP-1; SCGP; SiPS; UnPo

Ring Presented to Julia, A. Robert Herrick. PeLV

Ring ring ring ring ring! / Catholic bells—! (LL) The Catholic Bells. William Carlos Williams. CMoP; NOBA; OxBA; SAmP

Ring so worn as you behold, The. The Marriage Ring. George Crabbe. BoLoP; EnLoPo; LBC; NOBE; OBEV; OBNC; OxBM

Ring the bells, ring! The Dunce. *Unknown.* OxNR

Ring-ting! I wish I were a primrose. Wishing. William Allingham. BoTP; OxBChV

Ringed Plover by a Water's Edge. Norman MacCaig. NoP-4; OxBC

Ringers, The. John Peck, *Italian*. AmPA, *tr. by* William Arrowsmith

Ringing out from our blue heavens. Journey. Breyten Breytenbach, *Afrikaans*. AF, *tr. by* Denis Hirson

Ringing the Bells. Anne Sexton. CAPP-1; HCAP; PoE; SAGP; TAP; VGW

Ringing the rhythmical gladness of June! (LL) Bird Language. Christopher Pearse Cranch. APN-1; PAR

Ringing tire iron, A. Some Good Things to Be Said for the Iron Age. Gary Snyder. HoPM; TTTS

Ringing Words. Mary Kinzie. FFC

Ringless. Diane Wakoski. NALW

Ringlety-jing! A Nonsense Rhyme. James Whitcomb Riley. NOxBChV

Rings on a stump, The. Wood. Novella Nikolaevna Matveyeva, *Russian*. TCRP, *tr. by* Deming Brown

Ringsend. Oliver St. John Gogarty. OBMV; OxBTC

Rinsing the choked mud, keeping the colours new. (LL) In Carrowdore Churchyard. Derek Mahon. CIP-2; NoP-4; PBCIP; PNI

Riot. Gwendolyn Brooks. BPo; CAPP-1; NAAAL; NALW; NBV; PoBA; TAP

Riot, A. Mrs. Henry Linden. CBWP-4

Riot in the lute song's propinquity. Propose to be guided by the. Pieces O'six—XXIV. Jackson Mac Low. FTOS

Riot; or, Half a Loaf Is Better than No Bread, The. Hannah More. NOEC (Riot; or Half a Loaf is Better than No Bread In a Dialogue between Jack Anvil and Tom Hod, The.) PEW

Riots and Rituals. Richard W. Thomas. PoBA

Rioupéroux. James Elroy Flecker. OBEV

Rip up the day I was born. Job Speaks. David Rosenberg. PT

Ripe apples were caught like red fish in the nets. The Great Scarf of Birds. John Updike. NYBP

Ripe, Being Plunged into Fire. Friedrich Hölderlin, *German*. OBVE, *tr. by* James Blair Leishman

Ripe cherries and ripe maidens. Cherries. Zalman Schneour, *Yiddish*. TrJP, *tr. by* Joseph Leftwich

Ripe plums are dropping. *Unknown, Chinese*. TAL, *tr. by* Robert Payne

Ripeness is all; her in her cooling planet. To an Old Lady. William Empson. FaBoTw; GTBS-P; NOBE; NoAM; OxAEP-2

Ripening. Wendell Berry. RaBo

Ripperty! Kye! Ahoo! Henry Lawson. CBAP

Ripples lap the sand on the beach of Parrot Isle. Tune: "Ripples Sifting Sand." Liu Yu Hsi, *Chinese*. SuSp, *tr. by* Daniel Bryant

Ripples on the surface of the water. Gary Snyder. BAP-93

Rippling in the ocean of that darkening room. Woman at the Piano. Marya Alexandrovna Zaturenska. MoAmPo

Riprap. Gary Snyder. HCAP; NAAL-2; NOBA; NeAP; NoAM; PmAP; PoM; PoPoPo; VCAP

Rise and deride this sepulchre of crime. (LL) On Passing the New Menin Gate. Siegfried Sassoon. NAEL-2; NoAM; NoP-4; OBMV; PoWW; Son

Rise and fall like waves. I regret nothing. (LL) Portrait of the Artist as an Old Man. Michael Dransfield. BMAP

Rise and hold up the curved glass. Pour Us Wine. Ibn Kolthum. AWP, *tr. by* E. Powys Mathers *Fr.* The Mu'allaqat.

Rise and Progress of the Present Taste in Planning Parks, Pleasure Grounds, Gardens, etc, The. *Unknown*. OBGa

Rise and Shine. Richmond Lattimore. NYBP; Poetr

Rise, fair sun. Rise. The Sun. Tujin Park, *Korean*. CKP, *tr. by* Jaihiun Kim

Rise from the wrist, o kestrel. Sonnets for the Novachord. "Ern Malley." BMAP

Rise from your bed of langour. Rise from Your Bed of Languor. Stevie Smith. BWW

Rise from your virgin sheets, that be. Epithalamium: To Mistress M. A. Martin Lluellyn [*or* Lluelyn]. NOSC

Rise, hallowed Milton! rise, and say. William Mason. EPCY *Fr.* Ode to Memory.

Rise heart; thy Lord is risen. Sing his praise. Easter. George Herbert. ESCV; FMP; GeHe; NAEL-1; NOSC; PeECV; TrCP

Rise, heir of fresh eternity. Easter Day. Richard Crashaw. FMP

Rise, mighty nation, in thy strength. On the Expected General Rising of the French Nation. Anna Laetitia Barbauld. CABP; ECWP

Rise odors of ploughed field or flowery mead. (LL) Chaucer. Henry Wadsworth Longfellow. APN-1; AWP; HeIP-4; MeMAP; NOBA; OBEV; OxBA; PoE; PoRA; Son; TAP; TFi

Rise Oedipus, and if thou canst unfold. The Poem. Thomas Morton. NAAL-3; SCAP

Rise of capitalism parallels the advance of romanticism, The. Definition of Blue. John Ashbery. NAAL-2

Rise of Shivaji, The. Zulfikar Ghose. MoBS

Rise, rise from sluggishness, fly fast my Deere. Mary Sidney. *Fr.* Urania.

Rise, shining martyrs. With Meaning. John Weiners. BB

Rise to all eternity. (LL) In Temptation. Charles Wesley. NOEC; PoEL-3

Rise, underground sleepers, rise from the grave. Ode against St. Cecilia's Day. George Barker. PoA

Rise and come, immortal Clouds. Aristophanes. GrIP, *ll.* 275–290, *tr. by* Kenneth Mcleish *Fr.* The Clouds.

Rise up, my love, my fair one, and come away. Bible, *O.T. Fr.* The Song of Songs. AWP

Rise up my soul! Ode to My Soul. Lord Alfred Bruce Douglas. ADE

Rise up, O boat, asleep there in the port. Our Hearts Are Ancient Citadels. Vũ Đình Liên, *Vietnamese*. AVP, *tr. by* Huỳnh Sanh Thông

Rise Up, O Men of God. William Pierson Merrill. AH

Rise up, rise up, / And, as the trumpet blowing. The Trumpet. Edward Thomas. MoBrPo

"Rise up, rise up, now, Lord Douglas," she says. Earl Brand (The Douglas Tragedy). *Unknown*. NTP; NoP-4

Rise, Ye Children. Justus Falckner, *German*. AH, *tr. by* Emma Frances Bevan

Rise You Up, My True Love. *Unknown*. AmFP

Risen from rented rooms, old ghosts. A Winter Ode to the Old Men of Lummus Park, Miami, Florida. Donald Justice. WeW-3

Risen in a / welter of waters. The Birth of Venus. Muriel Rukeyser. NALW

Rises at five, just when a late moon. The Insomniac Sleeps Well for Once and. Hayden Carruth. NNaP

Rises toward her day after day, like a terrible fish. (LL) Mirror. Sylvia Plath. FaBoWP; HAP; NIP-4; NYBP

Risest thou thus, dim dawn, again. Tennyson. EBVV; OBNC; PeECV; PoEL-5 *Fr.* In Memoriam A. H. H.

Rising, The. Jayne Cortez. NBV

Rising and falling back and rising. (LL) Delta Traveller. Charles Wright. AmPA; LCAP-2

Rising deluge he descried, The. The Vision of Noah. May Kendall. VWP

Rising Early in the Morning. Chao Yi, *Chinese*. SuSp, *tr. by* Chang Yin-nan *and* Lewis C. Walmsley

Rising from Sleep. Wang Chiu-ssu, *Chinese*. CoBLCP, *tr. by* Jonathan Chaves

Rising Glory of America, The. Hugh Henry Brackenridge *and* Philip Freneau. AiP

Rising in lamplight dying at dawn. Voices Answering Back: The Vampires. Lawrence Raab. AmPA

Rising in the Morning. Hugh Rhodes. OxBChV

Rising in the North, The. *Unknown*. ESPB

Rising in Winter. Hsiao Kang, *Chinese*. OHMPC, *tr. by* Kenneth Rexroth

Rising Late, and Playing with A-ts'ui, Aged Two. Po Chü-i, *Chinese*. ChiP, *tr. by* Arthur Waley

Rising of the Session, The. Robert Fergusson. OxBS

Rising to Meet It. Chana Bloch. CrSp

Rising Village, The. Oliver, the Younger Goldsmith. Lonely Settler, The. NOBC

Rising was as hard as having died. Agnes Nemes Nagy. *See* Lazarus.

Risk, The. Anne Sexton. BoWoP

Risk is moral death each time we act, The. Some Girls. Susanne Doyle. FFC

Risk Management. Alice Fulton. WWSi

Rita's husband gave Rita her walking papers. Kurt Bartsch, *German*. CEEP, *tr. by* Wayne Kvam

Rite, The. Dudley Randall. HoPM

Rite de Passage. Michele Roberts. NBrP

Rite-ing. Ntozake Shange. MoNo

Rite of Passage. Audre Lorde. PoBA

Rite of Spring. Seamus Heaney. OxBC

Rite of Spring!, The. Homard à Igor Stravinsky: Vernacular Variations. Hugh Haughton. CBNP

Rites. Edward Kamau Brathwaite. "Look wha' happen las' week at de Oval!" FaBoVe

Rites deriv'd from ancient days, The. Translations from the *Medea* of Euripides. Euripides. *Fr.* Medea. NAWM-1; OxBM

Rites for Cousin Vit, The. Gwendolyn Brooks. BPo; HAP; NAAAL; NoP-4; WPE; WeW-3 *Fr.* The Womanhood. ("'Forgive these nigguhs that know not what they do'.") (LL) SSLK ("John Cabot—out of Wilma, once a Wycliffe.") SSLK (Riot.) SSLK

Rites of Manhood, The. Alden Nowlan. RaBo

Rites of Participation. Robert Duncan. PFTM

Rites of Passage. Sharon Olds. FiLi

Ritual, The. Edwin John Pratt. MoP

Ritual Girl. Frank Mkalawile Chipasula. HBAPE

Ritual Mouse, A. William Meredith. PBMP

Ritual Murder. Aig Higo. PBMAP

Ritual of Departure. Thomas Kinsella. CIP-2; CMoP

Ritual Three, In England, the slow methodical torture of two children was recorded on tape by the murderers. David Ignatow. CoAmPo

Ritual to Read to Each Other, A. William Stafford. RaBo

Ritualists, The. William Carlos Williams. NYBP

Rituals along the Arkansas. William Mills. MT

Rival, The. Sylvia Plath. LoP

Rival, The. Sylvia Townsend Warner. MoBrPo

Rival Curates, The. Sir William Schwenck Gilbert. PeLV

Rivals, The. James Stephens. BoTP; OBEV; OBMV

Rivals. William Walsh *and* Sir George Etherege. OBEV

Riven Quarry, The. Gloria C. Oden. GT; PoBA

River, The. Sam Cornish. PoBA

River, The. Hart Crane. AmPP; CMoP; GM; MoAmPo; NOBA; OxBA *Fr.* Powhatan's Daughter. *Fr.* The Bridge. NAAL-2

River, The. Đông Hồ, *Vietnamese.* AVP, *tr. by* Huỳnh Sanh Thông

River. Ted Hughes. NAEL-2; NoP-4

River, The. Jacques Prévert, *French.* MFP, *tr. by* Martin Sorrell

River. Dabney Stuart. NYBP

River. Tanikawa Shuntaro, *Japanese.* VCWP, *tr. by* Harold Wright

River, The. *Unknown.* PWR

River, The. John Wills. HA

River, The. Paul Zweig. MoLi

River Afram. Andrew Amankwa Opoku. PBA

River and hills beyond the fog—I peer but can't make them out. *Keng-tzu* (1180), First Month, Fifth Day, Dawn. Yang Wan-li, *Chinese.* CoBCP, *tr. by* Burton Watson

River and Under the River, The. Davis McCombs. BAP-96

River bank—the evening tides have started to ebb. On the Fifteenth Day of the Ninth Month of the Year Kuei-mao of the Chih-cheng Period (Oct. 22, 1363), I Painted This to Send to the Summoned Scholar, Sheng-po, and Inscribed This Poem on It. Ni Tsan, *Chinese.* CoBLCP, *tr. by* Jonathan Chaves

River Bend. Judith Wright. BMAP

River brought down, The. How We Heard the Name. Alan Dugan. CoAP; NoAM; PFE

River Ching flows rapidly, The. Wu Wei-yeh. *Fr.* Country Scene. CoBLCP, *tr. by* Jonathan Chaves

River Compared to an Oratorical Sentence, The. Luis de Góngora y Argote. *Fr.* The First Solitude. OBVE, *tr. by* Edward Meryon Wilson

River Crossing, The. Denis Glover. PeNZ *Fr.* Arawata Bill.

River drowns itself, The. Walk Through the City. Heinz Czechowski, *German.* CEEP, *tr. by* Ewald Osers

River Duddon [A Series of Sonnets], The. Wordsworth.

After-Thought. OBNC

(Valediction to the River Duddon.) NOBE

"Change me, some God, into that breathing rose!" Son

Return. HAP

River flows to the East, The. The Red Cliff. Su Tung-p'o, *Chinese.* OHPC, *tr. by* Kenneth Rexroth

River God, The. Sacheverell Sitwell. MoBrPo

River God, The. Stevie Smith. BrRo; FaBoSe; FaBoTw; FaBoWP; PBWP

River God's Song. Anne Ridler. NYBP

River gulls bob and toss in reed-flower autumn. Song of the Clear River. Huang T'ing-chien, *Chinese.* CoBCP, *tr. by* Burton Watson

River Has No Hair to Hold Onto, The. Ralph Angel. NAmP90

River, I am passing. River Afram. Andrew Amankwa Opoku. PBA

River in Hell (two poems). Miyazawa Kenji, *Japanese.* MJT, *tr. by* Makoto Ueda

River in its abundance, The. Eros at Temple Stream. Denise Levertov. NALW

River in March, The. Ted Hughes. OxBC

River in the Meadows, The. Léonie Adams. MoAmPo

River! into the street! Allen Ginsberg. *See* II.

River is calm, the moon reflected in its waters, The. A Noble Scholar Playing the Lute. Yang Chi, *Chinese.* CoBLCP, *tr. by* Jonathan Chaves

River is famous to the fish, The. Famous. Naomi Shihab Nye. LoL

River is lined with the, The. At Ch'en Ch'u. Wang Shih-chieng, *Chinese.* OHMPC, *tr. by* Kenneth Rexroth

River is rising, *Ngoho*, the river, The. In a Storm. Antoine-Roger Bolamba, *French.* NegPo, *tr. by* Ellen Conroy Kennedy

River is smooth and calm this evening, The. Spring River Flowers Moon Night. Emperor Yang of Sui, *Chinese.* OHMPC, *tr. by* Kenneth Rexroth

River is so much mica, The. The River; North of Guelph. Douglas G. Jones. NOBC

River is within us, the sea is all about us, The. T. S. Eliot. OxBoS *Fr.* The Dry Salvages. AiP; NoP-4; OxBA *Fr.* Four Quartets.

River Izumi, The. Fujiwara no Go-kanesuke, *Japanese.* OHPJ, *tr. by* Kenneth Rexroth

River jordan run red. Emmett Till. Wanda Coleman. NAAAL

River Mang has always been clear—not a trace of mud, The. Recording a Weird Happening. Li K'ai-hsien, *Chinese.* CoBLCP, *tr. by* Jonathan Chaves

River-Mates. Padraic Colum. AWP

River Merchant's Wife, The; a Letter. Li Po, *Chinese.* AWP; AmPP; BoLoP; ClHu; ColAP; FYAP; GEA; GLoP; HAP; HeIP-4; InPK-6; InPS-3; LiLi; LoP; MeMAP; MoAmPo; MoP; NAAL-2; NIP-4; NOBA; NOBE; NoAM; NoP-4; OBMV; OBVE; OxBA; Poetr; PoPoPo; RACG; RB; RaBo; SAGP; TAP; TFi; TRP; TTTS; TwCP; UnPo; WeW-3 *tr. by* Ezra Pound

("And I will come out to meet you.") (LL) NNPT, *tr. by* Ezra Pound

River-mirror mirrors the cold sky, The. Mists Over the River. William Carlos Williams. ColAP

River; North of Guelph, The. Douglas G. Jones. NOBC

River Now, The. Richard Hugo. VCAP

River of autumn water, pale, cold mist, A. Ni Tsan. *Fr.* Two Poems to the Tune "Hsiao-t'iao hung." CoBLCP, *tr. by* Jonathan Chaves

River of Bees, The. W. S. Merwin. HeIP-4; LCAP-2; VCAP

River of Heaven, The. *Unknown.* AWP, *tr. by* Lafcadio Hearn *Fr.* Manyo Shu, Part 3 of 4.

River of Heaven turns in the night and floats the stars round, The. Up in Heaven. Li Ho, *Chinese.* PLT, *tr. by* A. C. Graham

River of Life, The. Thomas Campbell. GTBS-P; ImPo

(Thought Suggested by the New Year, A.) OBNC

River of Rivers in Connecticut, The. Wallace Stevens. FaBoA; HAP; HCAP; NOBA; VGW

River of sudden, The. Waterfall. Gareth Owen. Spl

River Rhyme. William Carlos Williams. PoA

River Road. Stanley Kunitz. MoP; NoAM

River Road Studio. Barbara Guest. PmAP; PoM

River Roads. Carl Sandburg. VGW

River Roses. D. H. Lawrence. CMoP; GBL; OAEL-2

River Run. Elisaveta Bagryana, *Bulgarian.* CEEP, *tr. by* Jascha Kessler *and* Aleksandar Shurbanov

River Scamander Attacks Achilles. Homer. OBVE, *tr. by* Alexander Pope *Fr.* The Iliad.

River Silence, The. Leonid Martynov, *Russian.* TCRP, *tr. by* J. R. Rowland

River slopes, already into the midmonth of spring. On the Spur of the Moment. Tu Fu, *Chinese.* CoBCP, *tr. by* Burton Watson

River Snow. Liu Tsung-yüan, *Chinese.* CoBCP, *tr. by* Burton Watson

River Still To Be Found, A. Lawrence Ferlinghetti. BB

River strangely named, A. River Run. Elisaveta Bagryana, *Bulgarian.* CEEP, *tr. by* Jascha Kessler *and* Aleksandar Shurbanov

River Swelleth More and More, The. Henry David Thoreau. NOBA

River takes the land, and leaves nothing, The. The Slip. Wendell Berry. NOCV

River that flows nowhere, like a sea, The. (LL) The River of Rivers in Connecticut. Wallace Stevens. FaBoA; HAP; HCAP; NOBA; VGW

River That Flows through Our Land, The. Jeremy Cronin. PeSAV

River That Is East, The. Galway Kinnell. Poetr

River that must turn full after I stop dying. "A"-11 River That Must Turn Full After I Stop Dying. Louis Zukofsky. APSN; ColAP; VGW *Fr.* A.

River that rollest by the ancient walls. Stanzas to the Po. Byron. OAEL-2; Ro

River Town Packin House Blues. Quincy Troupe. LoL

River used to store up in its mouth, The. Roy Macnab. PeSA

River wandering down. Robert Creeley. FTOS

River was announcing, The. The River Crossing. Denis Glover. PeNZ *Fr.* Arawata Bill.

River waters ruffled in the west wind. By the River. Wang An-shih, *Chinese.* CoBCP, *tr. by* Burton Watson

River waters shiver in the west wind. On the Yangtze. Wang An-shih, *Chinese.* SuSp, *tr. by* Jan W. Walls

River, why in ceaseless flow. Maiden and River. Mary Fordham. CBWP-2

Riverbank sunset Frisco hilly tincan evening sitdown vision. Allen Ginsberg. *See* Sunflower Sutra.

Riverbank, the long rigs. Broagh. Seamus Heaney. FaBoVe

River[-]God's Song, The. John Fletcher. NOSC *Fr.* The Faithful Shepherdess.

(Song: "Do not fear to put thy feet.") SCGP

Riverman, The. Elizabeth Bishop. NYBP

Riverrun where can you guess? Limerick. *Unknown.* PeLi

Rivers. Thomas Storer. FaBoCh

Rivers, The. Giuseppe Ungaretti, *Italian.* PeFWW, *tr. by* Jon Silkin; PFTM, *tr. by* Allen Mandelbaum

Rivers and Mountains. John Ashbery. CoAP; FTOS; NOBA; NoAM; NoP-4; TRP

("Slowly out into the sun-blackened landscape.") (LL) FTOS; NoP-4

Rivers and winds among the twisted hills. Robert Louis Stevenson.

"As with heaped bees at hiving time." NOBVV

Rivers Come to the Hall of Proteus for the Marriage of the Thames and the Medway, The. Edmund Spenser. *Fr.* Wood Of Error. AEP

River's flow collects and forms a pool, The. Liang Family Pool. Yang Shih-ch'i. *Fr.* Ten Scenes at the Hsiao Family Stone Ridge. CoBLCP, *tr. by* Jonathan Chaves

River's glint and mountain mist were floating in green. Composed on Horseback, Returning from Lakeview Pavilion at Hangchow, Presented to Yü-ju and Lo-tao. Wang An-shih, *Chinese.* SuSp, *tr. by* Jan W. Walls

River's just beyond that hill, The. Tugela River. William Plomer. PeSAV

Rivers level granite mountains. Sulpicius Lupercus Servasius, *Latin*. OBCVT; PGA, *tr. by* Kenneth Rexroth

Rivers of Ireland, The. Edmund Spenser. *Fr.* Wood Of Error. AEP

Rivers of wings surround us and vast tribulation. (LL) Glazounoviana. John Ashbery. LCAP-2; VCAP

Rivers rush into the sea, The. The Song of the Bird. Henry Wadsworth Longfellow. BoTP

River's Song, The. Charles Kingsley. ACTP *Fr.* The Water Babies. (Tide River, The.)

Rivers that flowed divided each from each. Chinese Poems: Arthur Waley. "C. A. Fair." PeSA

Riverside willows sway their green mist, The. To the Retired Scholar Chang. Ni Tsan, *Chinese*. CoBLCP, *tr. by* Jonathan Chaves

Riversongs of Arion, The. Michael Anania. NoAM

Rivulet, The. William Cullen Bryant. APN-1

Rivulet crossing my ground. Tennyson. *Fr.* Maud [A Monodrama]. EnVR

Rivulet-loving wanderer Abraham, The. Abraham. Edwin Muir. ChIV-1

Rizpah. Tennyson. PeVV; PoEL-5; RACG

RMS Lusitania. Richmond Lattimore. PFE

Roach / came struttin, A. John Raven. BPo; HoPM

Road, The. Conrad Potter Aiken. MoAmPo

Road. David Chapman Berry. MT

Road, The. Helene Johnson. BlSi

Road, The. Herbert Morris. DiPo

Road, The. Edwin Muir. CMoP; ImPo; LiTM

Road, The. Nikolay Ogarev, *Russian*. AWP, *tr. by* P. E. Matheson

Road, The. Zalman Schneour, *Yiddish*. TrJP, *tr. by* Joseph Leftwich

Road ahead, The. On the Road. Seamus Heaney. TOF *Fr.* Sweeney Redivivus.

Road at My Door, The. W. B. Yeats. BIrV; NOBE; PoE *Fr.* Meditations in Time of Civil War.

Road at the top of the rise, The. The Middleness of the Road. Robert Frost. NOBA

Road Back, The. Anne Sexton. NYBP

Road beneath the giant original trees, The. Sanctuary. Judith Wright. WPE

Road Block: Sante Fe, New Mexico. Connie Deanovich. WWSi

Road can't be as sad as a shoe is sad, A. Shoe. John Perreault. SPE

Road climbs steeply till it crests above the hills, The. Inner Mongolia—The Grasslands. Sibyl James. LoHo

Road climbs, villages, The. Going. Peter Everwine. NNaP

Road from Xunantunich. Velma Pollard. HCP *Fr.* Belize Suite. HCP

Road he took was virgin territory, The. Theaitetos. Callimachus, *Greek*. GrAn, *tr. by* Peter Jay

Road in Kentucky, A. Robert Earl Hayden. ColAP

Road is wide and the stars are out and the breath of the night is sweet, The. Roofs. Joyce Kilmer. PoLF

Road is Wider Than Long: An Image Diary from the Balkans, July–August 1938, The. Roland Penrose. SPE *Fr.* The Road Is Wider than Long.

Road Map, The. Thom Gunn. CBLP

Road Not Taken, The. Robert Frost. APAD; AiP; AmPP; CMoP; ChAP; EBEvV; FaBoCh; HAP; HeIP-4; ImPo; LiTM; MeMAP; MoAmPo; MoP; NAAL-2; NIP-4; NTP; NoAM; NoP-4; OxBA; PFE; PoLF; PoPoPo; Poetr; SAGP; SAmP; SoSe-8; TAP; TFi; TRP; TwCP

Road of Life, The. William Morris. OBNC *Fr.* The Earthly Paradise.

Road of terror! The Ice of Ladoga. Aleksandr Petrovich Mezhirov, *Russian*. TCRP, *tr. by* Deming Brown

Road of the Dread, The. Lorna Goodison. VCWP

Road runs straight with no turning, the circle, The. Black People: This Is Our Destiny. Imamu Amiri Baraka. CAPP-1

Road Show. Geoff Page. BMAP

Road that I came by mounts eight thousand feet, The. The Waters of Lung-t'ou. HSü Ling, *Chinese*. ChiP, *tr. by* Arthur Waley

Road to Bologna, The. Roy Macnab. PeSA

Road to Eluela, The. Album. Haim Gouri, *Hebrew*. IP, *tr. by* Warren Bargad *and* Stanley F. Chyet

Road to En-dor is easy to tread, The. En-Dor. Rudyard Kipling. OxBSn

Road to Exile Thinking of Vallejo, The. Syl Cheney-Coker. PBMAP

Road to hell is paved with theologians, The. The Ceremon(y)(ies) of Mutability. William Harmon. WeT *Fr.* Legion: Civic Choruses.

Road to Hogan's Gap, The. Andrew Barton Paterson. CBAP

Road to Patmos, The. John Ennis. PBCIP

Road to Shu Is Hard, The. Li Po, *Chinese*. SuSp, *tr. by* Irving Y. Lo

Road to Town, The. H. M. Sarson. BoTP

Road to Vagabondia, The. Dana Burnet. PoLF

Road turned out to be a cul-de-sac, The. Brother and Sisters. Judith Wright. BMAP; FaBoWP

Road turns back, the desolate mountain parts, The. Passing By the Battlefield at Feng-k'ou. Kao Ch'i, *Chinese*. CoBLCP, *tr. by* Jonathan Chaves

Road twisted through tongues of rock, The. The Vowels of Another Language. Thomas M. Disch. PoA

Road unravels as I go, The. Minstrel. Michael Dransfield. BMAP

Road where Ts'ao Chih watched the fighting cocks, The. Spending the Night in the Eastern Park. Shen Yüeh, *Chinese*. SuSp, *tr. by* Richard B. Mather

Roadmap. Harryette Mullen. ISC

Roads. Peter Huchel, *German*. HP; PoSu, *tr. by* Michael Hamburger ("Choked sunset / Of crashing time.") AF, *tr. by* Daniel S. Simko ("Closed their wounds.") (LL) AF, *tr. by* Daniel S. Simko

Roads. Antonio Machado Ruiz, *Spanish*. IMW, *tr. by* Willis Barnstone *Fr.* The Dream Below the Sun.

Roads. Edward Thomas. PeFWW

Roads also have their wistful rest, The. Wilfred Owen. EBEV

Roadside Fountain. Momcilo Nastasijevic, *Serbo-Croatian*. HSix, *tr. by* Charles Simic

Roadside thistle, eager, The. Basho, *Japanese*. AWP, *tr. by* Curtis Hidden Page

Roadways. John Masefield. BoTP; OTCP

Roaming Immortal. Ts'ao Chih, *Chinese*. SuSp, *tr. by* Ronald C. Miao

Roaming through a field of threshed stubble. Ruth. Jacob Glatstein, *Yiddish*. CEEP, *tr. by* Ruth Whitman

Roar of the Sea and the Darkness, The. Malcolm Lowry. "Lighthouse invites the storm and lights it, The." NOBC

Roar of welcome though the welkin, A. The Elk, The Whelk. Robert Williams Wood. NBLV

Roar, raging torrent! and thou, mighty river. Niagara. Joseph Rodman Drake. APN-1

Roaring alongside he takes for granted, The. Sandpiper. Elizabeth Bishop. AFr; AiP; HeIP-4; NYBP; RB; TOF

Roaring Frost, The. Alice Thompson Meynell. EBVV; WPE

Roaring of the wheels has filled my ears, The. A Cry from the Ghetto. Morris Jacob Rosenfeld, *Yiddish*. TrJP, *tr. by* Charles Weber Linn

Roaring waterfall, the. Su Tung-p'o, *Japanese*. EnlH, *tr. by* Stephen Mitchell

"Roast chestnuts, a shilling." Walking against the Wind. Jon Stallworthy. OxBC

Roast Possum. Rita Dove. Poetr

Roasted Sucking Pig. *Unknown*. BXAP

Roasting alive of rabbis, The. In the Absence of Bliss. Maxine W. Kumin. NoAM

Roasting chestnuts. Ishii Rogetsu, *Japanese*. OHMPJ, *tr. by* Kenneth Rexroth

Rob me and maim me! Why, man, take such pains. To One Who Quotes and Detracts. Walter Savage Landor. FaBoEE

Rob Roy. *Unknown*. ESPB

Robben Island. Robert Dederick. PeSA

Robben Island Sequence. Dennis Brutus. HBAPE ("But what a bruised and broken motley lot we were!") (LL) VCWP

Robber, The. "Hugh MacDiarmid." OBVE

Robber, The. Walter James Turner. MoBrPo

Robber Bridegroom, The. Margaret Atwood. LCAP-2

Robber Bridegroom, The. Allen Tate. CBLP

Robber of Kuan-ssu, The. Wang Chiu-ssu, *Chinese*. "Today I am a farmer in the fields." CoBLCP, *tr. by* Jonathan Chaves

Robby, git down wi'tha, wilt tha? Tennyson. FaBoVe *Fr.* The Spinster's Sweet-Arts.

Robe, The. Jones Very. NCAP

Robed Heart, The. Elizabeth Spires. BAP-94

Robene and Makyne. Robert Henryson. *See* Robin [*or* Robene] and Makyne.

Robene sat on gud grene [*or* green] hill. Robert Henryson. *See* Robin [*or* Robene] and Makyne.

Robert. Wendy Rose. HATNAP

Robert Barnes, or [my] fellow fine. Mother Goose. OxNR; ReMoGo

Robert Bly Finds Something in New Jersey. Carol Poster. BXAP

Robert Bly Says Something Too. Henry Taylor. BXAP

Robert Creeley Also Watches. David Chapman Berry. BXAP

Robert Creeley Listens, Too. David Chapman Berry. BXAP

Robert E. Lee. Julia Ward Howe. CBCWP

Robert Frost. Robert Lowell. MoP; NAAL-2; NoAM; Poetr; Son *Fr.* Writers.

Robert Frost. Novella Nikolaevna Matveyeva, *Russian*. TCRP, *tr. by* Deming Brown

Robert Frost's Left-leaning *Trespassers Will Be Shot* Sign. William Zaranka. BXAP

Robert G. Shaw. Henrietta Cordelia Ray. AAP; BlSi; CBWP-3; Son

Robert Gould Shaw. Paul Laurence Dunbar. CBCWP; PoPoPo; Son

Robert Gould Shaw. William Vaughn Moody. *Fr.* An Ode in Time of Hesitation. APN-2; CBCWP; OxBA

Robert Graves. Gavin Ewart. NoAM

Robert Johnson / Carlos Bulosan— / our names so different, / our song the same. Alfred Encarnacion. *See* Bulosan Listens to a Recording of Robert Johnson.

Robert Lowell's Notebook. "Edward Pygge." OBCoV

  Notes for a Revised Sonnet. BXAP

  Notes for a Sonnet. BXAP

  Revised Notes for a Sonnet. BXAP

Robert Mapplethorpe's Photograph of Apollo (1988). Mark Irwin. PUP-19

Robert of Lincoln. William Cullen Bryant. FaBoBe; OBCA

Robert Penn Warren's book. Anthony Lawrence. BMAP

Robert Rowley rolled a round roll round. Mother Goose. OxNR

Robert Sat. Tom Matthews. PNI

Robert, Second Duke of Normandy. Thomas Lodge.
  Pluck the Fruit and Taste the Pleasure. OxAEP-1

Robert the Bruce. Edwin Muir. OxBS

Robert Whitmore. Frank Marshall Davis. BPo; PoBA

Robes loosely flowing and aspect as free. Seeing Her Dancing. Robert Heath. NOSC; OxBSP

Robespierre and Mozart as Stage. Robert Lowell. FaBoMo

Robespierre could live with himself: "The Republic." Robespierre and Mozart as Stage. Robert Lowell. FaBoMo

Robin, The. Laurence Alma-Tadema. BoTP

Robin, The. O. M. Bent. BoTP

Robin, A. Walter De la Mare. CMoP

Robin, The. Jones Very. Son

Robin-a-Bobbin. *Unknown.* ReMoGo

Robin-a-bobin. Mother Goose. OxNR

Robin; a Pastoral Elegy. John Dobson. NOEC

Robin Adair. Lady Caroline Keppel. FaBoBe

Robin and a robin's son, A. *Unknown.* ACTP; OxNR

Robin and Gandelyn. *Unknown. See* Robyn and Gandeleyn.

Robin [*or* Robene] and Makyne. Robert Henryson. MiEL; OBEV; PeLV; PoE; PoEL-1
  ("Robene sat on gud grene [*or* green] hill.") BoLoP

Robin and Richard / Were two pretty men. Mother Goose. OxBoLi; OxNR; ReMoGo

Robin and the Cows, The. William Dean Howells. CTAV

Robin and the red-breast, The. A Warning. *Unknown.* OxNR

Robin and the wren, The. Greed. *Unknown.* OxNR

Robin cries: *rain!*, The. Rain in Ohio. Mary Oliver. InPK-6

Robin dwelt in greenë wood. The Death of Robin Hood. *Unknown.* EnSB

Robin Friend has gone to bed. Bed-Time. Laurence Alma-Tadema. BoTP; CTAV

Robin Goodfellow. *Unknown.* FaBoCh

Robin he's gane to the wast. The Wife Wrapt [*or* Wrapped] in Wether's Skin. *Unknown.* AmFP; ESPB

Robin Hode and the Munkee. *Unknown. See* Robin Hood and the Monk.

Robin Hood. Keats. AWP; SCGP

Robin Hood. Rachel MacAndrew. BoTP

Robin Hood. Phyllis McGinley. OBSV *Fr.* Speaking of Television.

Robin Hood and Allen [*or* Allin] -a-Dale. *Unknown.* ESPB; FaBoBe; OxAEP-1

Robin Hood and Guy of Gisborne. *Unknown.* ESPB

Robin Hood and Little John. *Unknown.* AmFP; ESPB

Robin Hood and Little John. *Unknown.* ReMoGo

Robin Hood and Maid Marian. *Unknown.* ESPB

Robin Hood and Queen Katherine. *Unknown.* ESPB

Robin Hood and the Beggar, I. *Unknown.* ESPB

Robin Hood and the Beggar, II. *Unknown.* ESPB

Robin Hood and the Bishop. *Unknown.* ESPB

Robin Hood and the Bishop of Hereford. *Unknown.* ESPB

Robin Hood and the Butcher. *Unknown.* ESPB

Robin Hood and the Curtal Friar. *Unknown.* ESPB

Robin Hood and the Golden Arrow. *Unknown.* ESPB

Robin Hood and the Grey Friars. Thomas Love Peacock. OxAEP-2 *Fr.* Maid Marian.

Robin Hood and the Monk. *Unknown.* ESPB; OBNV
  (Robin Hode and the Munkee.) EBNV

Robin Hood and the Pedlars. *Unknown.* ESPB

Robin Hood and the Potter. *Unknown.* ESPB

Robin Hood and the Prince of Aragon. *Unknown.* ESPB

Robin Hood and the Ranger. *Unknown.* ESPB

Robin Hood and the Scotchman. *Unknown.* ESPB

Robin Hood and the Shepherd. *Unknown.* ESPB

Robin Hood and the Tanner. *Unknown.* ESPB

Robin Hood and the Three Squires. *Unknown.* EnSB; NAEL-1 *See* Robin Hood Rescuing Three Squires.

Robin Hood and the Tinker. *Unknown.* ESPB

Robin Hood and the Valiant Knight. *Unknown.* ESPB

Robin Hood / Has gone to the wood. *Unknown.* OxNR

Robin Hood he was [*or* hee was] and a tall young man. Robin Hood's Progress to Nottingham. *Unknown.* ESPB

Robin Hood Newly Revived. *Unknown.* ESPB

Robin Hood Rescuing Three Squires. *Unknown.* ESPB
  (Robin Hood and the Three Squires.) EnSB; NAEL-1

Robin Hood Rescuing Will Stutly. *Unknown.* ESPB

Robin Hood, Robin Hood, / Is in the mickle wood. Mother Goose. BoTP; OxNR

Robin Hood, Robin Hood, / Is in the mickle wood! Robin Hood and Little John. *Unknown.* ReMoGo

Robin Hood's Birth, Breeding, Valor, and Marriage. *Unknown.* ESPB

Robin Hood's Chase. *Unknown.* ESPB

Robin Hood's Death. *Unknown.* ESPB

Robin Hood's Delight. *Unknown.* ESPB

Robin Hood's Golden Prize. *Unknown.* ESPB

Robin Hood's Progress to Nottingham. *Unknown.* ESPB

Robin in December, The. Stanley Cook. AYFP

Robin is a Gabriel, The. Emily Dickinson. APo

Robin is a lovely lad. The Dance. Thomas Campion. FaBoCh *Fr.* The Ayres that Were Sung and Played, at *Brougham Castle* in *Westmerland*, in the Kings Entertainment.

Robin listens, A. William J. Higginson. HA

Robin once lunched with Herbert Read at his club. Robert Sheppard. NBrP *Fr.* Letter from the Blackstock Road.

Robin pipeth now, The. (LL) Song: "The Feathers of the willow." Richard Watson Dixon. CH; FaBoCh; GTBS-P; NOBE; OBEV; OBNC; PFE

Robin Redbreast. William Allingham. FaBoBe; OxBChV

Robin Redbreast. Stanley Kunitz. AFr
  ("Unappeasable sky.") (LL) NoP-4

Robin Redbreast in a cage, A. Three Things to Remember. William Blake. OxBoLi *Fr.* Auguries of Innocence. EBEV; FaBoCh; FaPoR; ImPo; OAEL-1; OBNC; OxAEP-2; OxBoLi; PeECV; PoEL-4; TFi

Robin Redbreast's Testament. *Unknown.* NTP

Robin! Robin! call the Springtime. March. Henrietta Cordelia Ray. CBWP-3

Robin sang sweetly. *Unknown.* BoTP

Robin [*or* Robene] sat on gude green [*or* gud grene] hill. Robin [*or* Robene] and Makyne. Robert Henryson. MiEL; OBEV; PeLV; PoE; PoEL-1

Robin sings in the elm; The. The Robin and the Cows. William Dean Howells. CTAV

Robin the Bobbin. Robin-a-Bobbin. *Unknown.* OxNR; ReMoGo

Robinets and Jenny Wrens. *Unknown.* OxNR

Robins sang in England. Robin's Song. Rodney Bennett. BoTP

Robin's Song. Rodney Bennett. BoTP

Robin's Song, The. C. Lovat Fraser. BoTP

Robinson. Weldon Kees. MoP; NYBP

Robinson at cards at the Algonquin; a thin. Aspects of Robinson. Weldon Kees. CoAP; NYBP

Robinson at Home. Weldon Kees. CoAP; NYBP

Robinson Crusoe. Charles Edward Carryl. *See* Robinson Crusoe's Story.

Robinson Crusoe. Soubhagya Mishra, *Oriya.* OMIP, *tr.* by Jayanta Mahapatra

Robinson Crusoe Daniel Defoe. Maurice Sagoff. NBLV

Robinson Crusoe's Story. Charles Edward Carryl. PoRA *Fr.* Davy and the Goblin.

Robot Camera. Robert Johnstone. PNI

Robyn, A / Joly Robyn. Sir Thomas Wyatt. AAS

Robyn and Gandeleyn. *Unknown.* ESPB; OxBB
  (Robin and Gandelyn.) EnSB

Robyn / Joly Robyn, A. Sir Thomas Wyatt. AAS

Robyn lyæth in grene wode bowndyn. (LL) Robyn and Gandeleyn. *Unknown.* ESPB; EnSB; OxBB

Roc, The. Richard Eberhart. CMoP

Rochester Extempore. John Wilmot, 2d Earl of Rochester. ChIV-1

Rochester to the Post Boy. John Wilmot, 2d Earl of Rochester. OxBoV

Rock, The. *Unknown, Welsh.* GBL, *tr.* by Geoffrey Grigson

Rock. Ch'ihwan Yu, *Korean.* CKP, *tr.* by Jaihiun Kim

"Rock-a-by, baby, up in the tree-top!" In the Tree-Top. Lucy Larcom. OBCA

Rock-a-by Lady, The. Eugene Field. BoTP

Rock-a-bye, baby. Mother Goose. *See* Rock-a-bye, baby, thy cradle is green.

Rock-a-bye baby. *Unknown.* ACTP

Rock-a-bye, baby, thy cradle is green. Mother Goose. LB; OxNR; ReMoGo

Rock among Bamboo. Hsü Wei. *Fr.* A Kite. CoBLCP, *tr. by* Jonathan Chaves

Rock and Hawk. Robinson Jeffers. ColAP; NOBA; NoAM; OxBA; PaTW; Poetr

Rock and precipice. Landscape. Octavio Paz, *Spanish.* OBVE, *tr. by* Charles Tomlinson

Rock, Ball, Fiddle. *Unknown.* CBNP; CH; OxBoLi

Rock Bottom. Michael Ondaatje.
  "For you I have slept." NoP-4

Rock Crumbles, The. Else Lasker-Schüler, *German.* WPOW, *tr. by* Michael Hamburger; TrJP, *tr. by* Ralph Manheim

Rock foundation of the fort was dread, The. Blockhouse. Olga Kirsch, *Afrikaans.* PeSA, *tr. by* Jack Cope

Rock grows brittle, The. My People. Else Lasker-Schüler, *German.* WPOW, *tr. by* Michael Hamburger

Rock Island Line, The. *Unknown.* AmFP

Rock-like the souls of men. Men Fade Like Rocks. Walter James Turner. OBMV

Rock Me to Sleep[, Mother]. Elizabeth Akers Allen. APN-2; BLPA; FaBoBe; MDDM; OBCA

Rock 'n' Roll. Lesley Frost. AiP

Rock 'N' Roll Band. Shel Silverstein. ImGa

Rock of ages, cleft for me. A Living and Dying Prayer for the Holiest Believer in the World. Augustus Montague Toplady. ECEV; FaPoR; NOCV; NOEC; SCGP

Rock of Cashel, The. Sir Aubrey De Vere. IIP

Rock of My Salvation. Mordecai ben Isaac, *Hebrew.* TrJP, *tr. by* Solomon Solis-Cohen

Rock Painting. Carroll Arnett. VoR

Rock Painting. Jack Cope. PeSA

Rock Pilgrim. Herbert Edward Palmer. OxBTC

Rock, Rock, Sleep, My Baby. Clyde Watson. NTCP

Rock, Scissors, Paper. Deborah Digges. NAmP90

Rock-shores of the world and the secret waters. (LL) Birds. Robinson Jeffers. InPS-3; VGW

Rock them, rock them, lullaby. (LL) Cradle Song, A: "Golden slumbers kiss your eyes." Thomas Dekker *and others.* NoSic; OxAEP-1; OxBChV; SCGP

Rock Thrown into the Water Does Not Fear the Cold, A. Audre Lorde. NAAL-2

Rockall. Epes Sargent. APN-1

Rocked in the Cradle of the Deep. Emma Hart Willard. FaBoBe; PWR

Rocked on this dreamy and indifferent tide. (LL) The Absinthe-Drinker. Arthur Symons. FaBoTw; NOBVV

Rockefeller the Center. Marie Ponsot. CLPP

Rockes turn to Rivers, Rivers turn to Men. (LL) To Dean-bourn, a Rude River in Devon, by Which Sometimes He Lived. Robert Herrick. BeJo; CaPo; PBRV

Rocket and the car., The. (LL) Window Ledge in the Atom Age. Elwyn Brooks White. NBLV; OBAL

Rocket Attack. Walter McDonald. CDa

Rockets and quasars. John Rice. SpW

Rockets bubble upward and explode, The. 14 July 1956. Laurence David Lerner. PeSA

Rockferns. Norman Nicholson. MoBrPo

Rockin' A Man, Stone Blind. Carolyn Beard Whitlow. FFC

Rocking Chair, The. Abraham Moses Klein. HeIP-4; NoP-4

Rocking Hymn, A. George Wither. OxBChV *Fr.* Hallelujah; or, Britain's Second Remembrancer.

Rockland. Julia Randall. WPE

Rocks. Florence Parry Heide. NTCP

Rocks, The. William Carlos Williams. *See* A Sort of a Song.

Rocks fallout on us. Rocket Attack. Walter McDonald. CDa

Rocks jagged in the morning mist. The Point. John Montague. PNI

Rocks shutting out the sky, the old life done. (LL) The Walking Tour. W. H. Auden. CMoP; MoBrPo

Rocks turn to rivers, rivers turn to men. Robert Herrick. *See* To Dean-bourn, a Rude River in Devon, by Which Sometimes He Lived.

Rocky Acres. Robert Graves. NoAM; UnPo

Rocky Island, The. *Unknown.* AmFP

Rocky Mountains, The. *Unknown.* AmFP

Rod, The. Georgy Obolduyev, *Russian.* TCRP, *tr. by* Vera Dunham

Rod full of wind and moon, A. Tune: "Immortal at the Magpie Bridge." Lu Yu, *Chinese.* SuSp, *tr. by* James J. Y. Liu

Rod of Jesse, The. Bible, *O.T.* AWP; OBVE; TrJP *Fr.* Isaiah.

Roderigh Vich Alpine dhu, ho! ieroe! (LL) Boat Song. Sir Walter Scott. OxAEP-2; PoEL-4

Rodin's "Gates of Hell." Jane Greer. FFC

Rodomontade on His Cruel Mistress, A. John Wilmot, 2d Earl of Rochester. OxBSP

Roe (and my joy to name) th'art now, to go. To William Roe. Ben Jonson. BeJo; OAEL-1

Roe-Deer. Ted Hughes. NOxBChV; NoAM; OxAEP-2

Roethke Plain. John Malcolm Brinnin. TAP

Rogation Day: Portrush. James Simmons. PBCIP

Roger a doleful widower. The Widower's Courtship. Elizabeth Hands. WoRP

Roger and Dolly. Henry Carey. CBNP; NOEC; OxNR
  (Young Roger and Dolly.) ReMoGo

Roger the Dog. Ted Hughes. ChAP; PeP

Rogero's Song. George Canning, George Ellis, *and* John Hookham Frere. NOEC; OBCoV *Fr.* The Rovers.
  (Song of One Eleven Years in Prison.) PeLV

Rogers in Italy. Frank O'Hara. FTOS

Rogue and Jar: 4/27/77. Thulani Davis. MoNo; SeSe

Rogue Hydrant, August. Karl Kirchwey. WWSi

Róisín, have no sorrow for all that has happened you. Little Black Rose. *Unknown, Irish.* NOIV, *tr. by* Thomas Kinsella

Rokeby. Sir Walter Scott.
  Rover's Adieu [*or* Farewell], The. NOBE; OBEV
  (Song.) EnLoPo; OBNC

Rokeby Venus, The. Robert Conquest. GS; MoP

Roland is dead and the ivory broken. Rockefeller the Center. Marie Ponsot. CLPP

Rolfe and the Palm. Herman Melville. NCAP

Roll back, you fabulous animal. Carnal Knowledge. Gwen Harwood. BMAP; CBAP

Roll Call, The. Dan Pagis, *Hebrew.* HP, *tr. by* Stephen Mitchell

Roll-Call In the Concentration Camp. Dan Pagis, *Hebrew.* PoSu, *tr. by* Robert Friend

Roll Call of Mirrors. Ivan V. Lalic, *Serbo-Croatian.* HSix, *tr. by* Charles Simic

Roll forth, my song, like the rushing river. The Nameless One. James Clarence Mangan. BIrV; IIP; NOIV; OBEV

Roll, Jordan, Roll. *Unknown.* APN-2; CrDW

Roll on! / [It rolls on.] Sir William Schwenck Gilbert. *See* To the Terrestrial Globe.

Roll on, sad world! Not Mercury or Mars. Frederick Goddard Tuckerman. APN-2 *Fr.* Sonnets.

Roll on the Ground. *Unknown.* AmFP

Roll on, thou ball, roll on! To the Terrestrial Globe. Sir William Schwenck Gilbert. APAD; NBLV

Roll on, thou deep and dark blue ocean—roll! To the Ocean. Byron. OxBoS; UV *Fr.* The Ocean. PoEL-4 *Fr.* Childe Harold's Pilgrimage.

Roll the Chariot. *Unknown.* AS

Roll the Cotton Down. *Unknown.* AmFP

Rollcall of Bones, The. César Vallejo, *Spanish.* AF, *tr. by* Robert Bly

Rolled in your fragrances, beautiful turning Earth. Sphere. Jules Supervielle, *French.* MFP, *tr. by* Martin Sorrell

Rolled off a side of mountains or. Serpent Country. A. R. Ammons. EOEF

Rolled over on Europe: the sharp dew frozen to stars. Stephen Spender. CMoP

Roller perched upon the wire, The. Driving Cattle to Casas Buenas. Roy Campbell. PeSA

Roller, pitch, and stumps, and all, The. (LL) Brahma. Andrew Lang. BXAP; NOBL; PeLV; UV

Roller Rink. Betty Adcock. MT

Rolling Chinese Wall, The. Roger Woddis. UV

Rolling English Road, The. G. K. Chesterton. FaBoCh; NOBE; NOBL; OBEV; OBMV; OxAEP-2; OxBTC; UV

Rolling from St. Patrick's, The. Burial of An Irish President. Austin Clarke. BIrV

Rolling in Clover. Jeffrey Skinner. WeT

Rolling mountains push toward the city. Lang Mountain Monastery. Yang Yi, *Chinese.* SuSp, *tr. by* Jonathan Chaves

Rolling the Lawn. William Empson. MoBrPo; OBGa

Rolling wheel, that runneth often round, The. 18. Edmund Spenser. CABP *Fr.* Amorette.

Rolly Trudum. *Unknown.* AmFP

Rom. Cap. 8 Ver. 19. Henry Vaughan. ESCV; GeHe; MeLP

Roma. Namatianus, *Latin.* OBCVT, tr. by Ezra Pound

Roma. Rutilius, *Latin.* CTC, tr. by Ezra Pound

Roman Earl, The. *Unknown, Irish.* OBVE, tr. by Douglas Hyde

Roman Elegies. Joseph Brodsky, *Russian.* VCWP, tr. by Joseph Brodsky
Roman Elegies IV. EP

Roman Elegy Ia. Goethe, *German.* EP, tr. by Michael Hamburger

Roman Epithalamion. Catullus, *Latin.* ITG, tr. by Charles Martin and Robert Hass

Roman Evening. Pier Paolo Pasolini, *Italian.* CLPP, tr. by Lawrence Ferlinghetti *and* Francesca Valente

Roman Fountain. Louise Bogan. NoP-4; WPOW

Roman Fountain. Rilke, *German.* GS, tr. by Snow, Edward

Roman had an, A/ artist, a freedman. Too Much. Marianne Moore. CMoP *Fr.* The Jerboa. FYAP; NALW

Roman miniature urchin, A. Seeking an Explanation. Richard Emil Braun. NoAM

Roman Officer Writes, A. Charles Montague Doughty. FaBoTw *Fr.* The Dawn in Britain.

Roman Poem Number Nine. June Jordan. GT

Roman Presents. Martial, *Latin.* OBCP, tr. by James Michie

Roman road runs straight and bare, The. Thomas Hardy. MoBrPo; NOBE

Roman soldiers come riding in full speed. "Sin-Killer" Griffin. AmFP *Fr.* The Man of Calvary.

Roman Stage, The. Lionel Pigot Johnson. NOBVV

Roman Thank-You Letter, A. Martial, *Latin.* OBCP, tr. by James Michie

Roman threw us a road, a road, The. History. G. K. Chesterton. OBSV *Fr.* Songs of Education.

Roman Virgil [*or* Vergil], thou that singest To Virgil [*or* Vergil]. Tennyson. AWP; EBVVPR; GTBS-P; OAEL-2; PoEL-5

Roman Wall Blues. W. H. Auden. NTP *Fr.* Twelve Songs.

Roman was the victor of the world., The. Petronius Arbiter. MLL, tr. by Helen Waddell *Fr.* Satyricon.

Roman Women. Thomas Edward Brown.
"O Englishwoman on the Pincian." NOBVV; OBNC

Romance, A. Chester Kallman. PoA

Romance. "Gabriel Setoun." BoTP

Romance. Gerald Stern. IFJA

Romance. Richard Stull. EOEF

Romance. Walter James Turner. APAD; CH; EBEvV; MoBrPo; NOBAu; NOBE; NOxBChV; NTP; OBMV; PoRA

Romance is a world, tiny and curved, reflected in a spoon. Perilous as a. Marriage. Amy Gerstler. PmAP

Romance of police in their shiny cruisers washes, The. Have a Nice Day. Robert Long. NAmP90

Romance of the Poor. Rodney Jones. WWSi

Romance [*or* Romaunt] of the Rose, The. Guillaume de Lorris *and* Jean de Meun (d. 1305), *French.*
Garden of Amour, The. PoEL-1, tr. by Geoffrey Chaucer
("Garden *or* gardin was, by measuring, The.") OBGa, tr. by Geoffrey Chaucer
("That casten up full good savour.") (LL) OBGa, tr. by Geoffrey Chaucer
"Short space my feet had traversed ere." OAEL-1, tr. by F. S. Ellis

Romance of the Swan's Nest, The. Elizabeth Barrett Browning. VWP

Romance to Night, A. Georg Trakl, *German.* AF, tr. by Simko, Daniel

Romance, who loves to nod and sing. Preface. Edgar Allan Poe. APN-1; AmPP; MeMAP; NAAL-1; NAAL-3; NCAP; NOBA; OxBA; PAR

Romancer, far more coy than that coy sex! Sonnet 19. Amos Bronson Alcott. APN-1

Romancero. Lex Banning. NOBAu

Romania, Romania. Gerald Stern. LCAP-2

Romans Angry about the Inner World. Robert Bly. NOBA

Romans, rheumatic, gouty, came. La Condition Botanique. Anthony Hecht. GaP

Romantic. George Garrett. HoPM

Romantic Movement, The. Philip Lamantia. CLPP

Romare Bearden Retrospective at the Brooklyn Museum. Cornelius Eady. WWSi

Rome. Madison Cawein. APN-2

Rome. James Vincent Cunningham, *after the Latin of* Janus Vitalis Panormitanus. OBVE

Rome. Joachim Du Bellay, *French.* AWP, tr. by Ezra Pound

Rome. Hildebert, *Latin.* MLL, tr. by Helen Waddell

Rome: Building a New Street in the Ancient Quarter. Thomas Hardy. Son

Rome, Conqueror, Conquered. Joshua Sylvester. FaBoEE

Rome disappoints me still; but I shrink and adapt myself to it. Arthur Hugh Clough. EBVV; EBVVPR; OxAEP-2 *Fr.* Amours de Voyage. NOBVV

Rome has a thousand fountains, and in May they sing. Maria Luisa Spaziani, *Italian.* NeIt, tr. by Beverly Allen

Rome, queen of all, your fame will never die. Constantinople (New Rome). *Unknown, Greek.* GrAn, tr. by Peter Jay

Rome Sunday[,] June 1960. John Hewitt. TIRV

Rome will not suit me, Eustace; the priests and soldiers possess / it;. Arthur Hugh Clough. EBVVPR, *canto* 5, 10 *Fr.* Amours de Voyage. NOBVV

Romeo and Juliet. Shakespeare.
"Even or odd, of all days in the year." SCV
"Gallop apace, you fiery-footed steeds [*or* fierie footed steades]." CBLP; EBEvV; GBL
"I dreamt a dream tonight." OxBSn
"If I profane with my unworthiest hand." OxAEP-1; PFE; SoSe-8; Son
"*Juliet:* Good-night, good-night! as sweet repose and rest." ITG
"O my love, my wife!" OxAEP-1

Rome's guns are spiked; and they'll stay so. Of Rome. Herman Melville. OxBA *Fr.* Clarel: A Poem and Pilgrimage in the Holy Land.

Romira, stay. The Call. John Hall. MeLP; NOSC

Romp. Dave Etter. WeW-3

Ron Endaway, shepherd of the hills at Malvern, looked very sheepish. Come Live with Me. Naomi Marks. BXAP

Ron Mason. Hone Tuwhare. PeNZ

Ronald Reagan screamed out in dismay. Limerick. Frank Richards. PeLi

Ronald Wyn. Robert Bagg. TwCP

Rondanini Pieta, The. Hilda Morley. FiLi

Rondeau. Leigh Hunt. CABP

Rondeau. "Nelly kissed me when we met." Leigh Hunt Ro *Fr.* Morning Chronicle, 2 436.

Rondeau: "Soft as yon silver ray that sleeps." Ann Radcliffe. Ro *Fr.* The Mysteries of Udolpho.

Rondeau: "They are bodies left unburied." Cheryl Clarke. FFC

Rondeau after a Transatlantic Telephone Call. Marilyn Hacker. ColAP; NoAM

Rondeau for You. Mário de Andrade, *Portuguese.* TTY, tr. by John Nist

Rondeau: Jenny Kiss'd [*or* Kissed] Me. Leigh Hunt. BLPA; FaBoBe; HoPM; ImPo; InPK-6; NBLV; NOBE; NOBVV; NTCP; OBEV; OxAEP-2; PeLV; PoRA; SCGP

Rondeaux: "Each page a day." Laura Moriarty. PT

Rondel: "Behold the works of William Morris." *Unknown.* BXAP

Rondel: "Beside the idle summer sea." William Ernest Henley. OBNC

Rondel: "Good-by, the tears are in my eyes." François Villon, *French.* AWP, tr. by Andrew Lang

Rondel: "Love, love, what wilt thou with this heart of mine?" Jean Froissart. AWP, tr. by Longfellow

Rondel: "Now that I am fifty-six." Muriel Rukeyser. NoP-4

Rondel: "Strengthen, my Love, this castle of my heart." Charles, Duc d' Orléans, *French.* AWP, tr. by Andrew Lang

Rondel of Luve [*or* Love], A. Alexander Scott. BoLoP; OBEV; OxBS

Rondel of Merciles Beaute, A. Chaucer. *See* Merciless Beauty.

Rondelet: "Say what you please." May Probyn. VWP

Rondelet: "Which way he went?" May Probyn. VWP

Rondo for the Poet's Children. Jean-Joseph Rabéarivelo, *French.* NegPo, tr. by Ellen Conroy Kennedy

Röntgen Photograph. Elisabeth Eybers, *Afrikaans.* PeSA, tr. by Jack Cope, Uys Krige, *and* Ruth Miller

Roof Garden, The. Howard Moss. GaP

Roof Garden. James Schuyler. OBGa

Roof is made of golden-plated tiles, The. Description of Hagia Sophia. Paulus Silentiarius, *Greek.* GrIP, tr. by Richard Stoneman

Roof of the World, The. Michael Dennis Browne. AmPA

Roof-tops, roof-tops, what do you cover? Charles Hanson Towne. BLPA; PoToHe

Roof-Tree. Richard Murphy. BiHa

Roofs. Joyce Kilmer. PoLF

Roofs of cars were crusted thick with frost, The. Citizen. Chris Wallace-Crabbe. CBAP

Roofs over the shops, The. Christmas Eve. Patricia Beer. OBCP

Roof's peak is eye. Sitting Here. Robert Creeley. MoLi

Roofwalker, The. Adrienne Rich. CoAP; NAAL-2; SAGP

Rook[e] he sells feathers, yet he still doth cry. Upon Rook: Epigram. Robert Herrick. CaPo

Rookhope Ryde. *Unknown.* ESPB; IBB

Rookhope stands in a pleasant place. Rookhope Ryde. *Unknown.* ESPB; IBB

Rooks. Charles Hamilton Sorley. MoBrPo; NSI

Rooks, The. *Unknown.* OxNR

Rooks are alive, The. What the Weather Does. *Unknown.* BoTP

Rooks are building on the trees, The. Jane Euphemia Browne. CTAV; OxBChV

Rooks are cawing up and down the trees!, The. Nests in Elms. "Michael Field." VWP

Rooks are raging where great elms were felled. The World of Simon Raven. Peter Porter. PeLV

Rooks love excitement. When I walked in under the rookery. Ted Hughes. NOxBChV

Rook's nest do rock on the tree-top, The. Lullaby. William Barnes. SCGP

Room. The. Conrad Potter Aiken. LiTM; MoAmPo; NOBA

Room. Robert Finch. MoCV

Room, The. De Leon Harrison. PoBA

Room, The. Galway Kinnell. AFr

Room, The. W. S. Merwin. NOBA

Room, The. Lawrence Raab. CMAP

Room, The. William Soutar. EBEV

Room. Ruth Stone. BoWoP

Room 5600. Ernesto Cardenal, *Spanish.* CLPP, *tr. by* Cohen, Jonathan

Room a dying poet took, The. Vladimir Nabokov. NYBP

Room above the Square, The. Stephen Spender. NOBE

Room after room, / I hunt the house through. Love in a Life. Robert Browning. CBLP; EBVVPR; FHYEP; NOBE; NOBVV; OBNC

Room beneath the Rafters, The. Ella Wheeler Wilcox. PWR

Room contains no sound, The. At 3 A.M. Wendy Cope. LW

Room for a Jovial Tinker: Old Brass to Mend. *Unknown.* OxBB

Room for All. Timothy Holmes. PeSAV

Room for Doubt. C. G. Hanzlicek. CMAP

Room in the Villa, A. William Jay Smith. NYBP

Room is already white, The. Trim it in blue. Life in the City: In Memoriam Edward Gibbon. Philip Whalen. PoM

Room is full of gold, The. Jason. Anthony Hecht. ColAP

Room is prepared, the incense burned, The. The Southern Room Over the River. Su Tung-p'o, *Chinese.* OHPC, *tr. by* Kenneth Rexroth

Room itself. The women. The absence of women, The. Dionisio D. Martinez. NoP-4 *Fr.* What the Men Talk About When the Women Leave the Room.

Room must be warmer than, The. How the Invalids Make Love. Susan Feldman. AmPA

Room of My Life, The. Anne Sexton. VCAP

Room on a Garden, A. Wallace Stevens. OBGa

("With rain.") (LL) NoP-4

Room, room, make room for the bouncing belly. Hymn to Comus. Ben Jonson. NOSC; OBCoV; SCGP *Fr.* Pleasure Reconciled to Virtue. NAEL-1; OAEL-1

Room to go to, A. Sue Standing. MDDM *Fr.* Cellar Door. EC2

Room was a / red glow, the. We Dance Like Ella Riffs. Carolyn M. Rodgers. PoBA; SeSe

Room was divided by a curtain, The. The Tailor's Wedding. Louis Simpson. NNaP

Room was poor and squalid, The. One Night. Constantine P. Cavafy, *Greek.* EP; LoP, *tr. by* Rae Dalven

Room was suddenly rich and the great bay-window was, The. Snow. Louis MacNeice. CIP-2; CMoP; FaBoMo; LiTM; MoP; NOBE; NoAM; OPOU; OxAEP-2; OxBSP; OxBTC; PNI

Room with a View, A. Noël Coward. PeLV

Rooms. Charlotte Mew. PBWP

Rooms and days we wandered through, The. Don't Be Afraid, I Am With You. Peter Porter. LBC

Rooster. James Tate. LCAP-2

Rooster crowed with his beak stuck in the sky, The. Landscape. Rade Drainac, *Serbo-Croatian.* HSix, *tr. by* Charles Simic

Rooster crows like someone being sick, The. City Girl in the Country. Elizabeth Smither. PeNZ

Rooster had hardly crowed when Timofey jumped out of the win-, The. The Beginning of a Beautiful Day (A Symphony). Daniil Kharms, *Russian.* AF, *tr. by* George Gibian

Roosters. Elizabeth Bishop. ChIV-2; LiTM; NALW

Roosters Will Crow, The. Cecília Meireles, *Portuguese.* PBWP, *tr. by* John Nist *and* Yolanda Leite

Root Cellar. Theodore Roethke. AmPP; ColAP; HeIP-4; InPK-6; NoP-4; PFE; SAGP; VCAP

Root, Hog, or Die. *Unknown.* AmFP

Root of Our Evil, The. D. H. Lawrence. ChIV-2

Root Song. Henry Dumas. ISC

Root, Stem, Leaf. Ted Hughes.

Pause for Breath, A. NYBP

Rooting in packingcase of. Digdog. Ruth Pitter. WPN

Roots. Seamus Deane. PNI

Roots. Louis Ginsberg. TrJP

Roots. Seymour Mayne. NOBC

Roots. Tadeusz Rózewicz, *Polish.* CEEP, *tr. by* Victor Contoski

Roots. Charlotte Watson Sherman. ISC

Roots and Branches. Robert Duncan. FTOS; VGW

Roots and leaves themselves alone are these. Walt Whitman. APN-1

Roots around your soul and eyes, The. Sweating It Out on Winding Stair Mountain. Jim Barnes. CDW

Roots of Blue Bells. Nia Francisco. HATNAP

Roots of mankind are tangled in my hair, The. Epitaph. Wendy Rose. CDW

Roots of your hair / what, The. Nappy Edges. Ntozake Shange. NAAAL

Rope, The. Tania Van Zyl. PeSA

Rope fiber and candle gout. Tselkov: An Interpretation. Lev Vladimir Loseff, *Russian.* TCRP, *tr. by* Walter Arndt

Rope for Harry Fat, A. James Keir Baxter. MoBS

Rope swings in, The. Red-Dress Girl. Ann Turner. SSCS

Ropero, so sad and so forlorn. El Ropero. Antonio Di Montorio. TrJP

Ropes, pull them tight!, The. Fishermen's Song. *Unknown, Maori.* PeNZ, *tr. by* Margaret Orbell

Ropewalk, The. Henry Wadsworth Longfellow. MeMAP; NCAP

Ropey, lippy, loopy, scribbly. Nasturtium Scanned. Judith Rodriguez. BMAP

Rorate celi desuper. Of Christ's Nativity. William Dunbar. ChIV-2; EnVB

Rosa dances her feet out. Nudo de Claridad. Miguel Algarin. PmAP

Rosa Luxembourg. Eileen Duggan. PeNZ

Rosa Mundi. W. B. Yeats. *See* The Rose of the World.

Rosabelle. Sir Walter Scott. GTBS-P *Fr.* The Lay of the Last Minstrel.

Rosalynde; or Euphues' Golden Legacy. Thomas Lodge.

    Montanus' Sonnet. PoEL-2

    Rosalind's [*or* Rosalynd's] Madrigal[l]. CBLP; NOBE; NoSic; OBEV; PoEL-2

    ("Love in my bosom like a bee.") NoP-4; RACG

    (Rosalind's Madrigal.) NoP-4; RACG

    ("Spare not but play thee!") (LL) APAD; NoP-4; RACG

    Rosaline. GTBS-P; OBEV

    (Rosalind's [*or* Rosalynde's] Description.) OxAEP-1

Rosary, The. Robert Cameron Rogers. FaBoBe

Rosary Beads. Herman Melville. NCAP

Rosciad, The. Charles Churchill.

    Character of a Critic. NOEC

Rose, A. Sir Richard Fanshawe. OBEV; PoEL-2 *Fr.* Il Pastor Fido.

    (Rose of Life, The.) AWP

Rose, The. Goethe, *German.* AWP, *tr. by* James Clarence Mangan

Rose, The. George Herbert. PoEL-2

Rose. Cill Janeway. IFJA

Rose, The. Gabriela Mistral, *Spanish.* WPoS, *tr. by* Langston Hughes

Rose. Kathleen Jessie Raine. WPE

Rose, The. Theodore Roethke. NOBA; NYBP; TRP *Fr.* North American Sequence.

Rose, The. Pierre de Ronsard, *French.* AWP, *tr. by* Andrew Lang

Rose, The. Vita Sackville-West. GaP

Rose, The. Novica Tadic, *Serbo-Croatian.* HSix, *tr. by* Charles Simic

Rose, The. Elizabeth Tollet. ECWP

Rose, The. William Carlos Williams. NOBA

Rose and gold and violet, The. The Afterglow. Henrietta Cordelia Ray. CBWP-3

Rose and grape, pear and bean. *Unknown, Spanish.* BoWoP, *tr. by* Willis Barnstone

Rose and the lily, the moon and the dove, The. Rose, die Lilie, die Taube, die Sonne, Die. Heinrich Heine, *German.* TrJP, *tr. by* "J. F. C."; NAWM-2, *tr. by* P. G. L. Webb; AWP, *tr. by* Richard Garnett

Rose and the Thorn, The. Paul Hamilton Hayne. FaBoBe

Rose and went a-roving, mother. Lass A-Laundering. *Unknown, Spanish.* STV, *tr. by* John Frederick Nims

Rose-apple is in fruit, The. Show Me The Way. *Unknown, Burmese.* LiLi; PBWP, *tr. by* U Win Pe

Rose, as fair as ever saw the North, A. Vision V. William Browne. CH; NOSC; OBEV; PFE *Fr.* Visions.

Rose Aylmer. Walter Landor. AWP; BoLoP; CABP; CH; EnLoPo; GBL; GLoP; HAP; HoPM; NAEL-2; NOBE; NOBRP; NoP-4; OAEL-2; OBEV; OBNC; OxAEP-2; PoEL-4; Poetr; Ro; SCGP; TFi; UnPo; WeW-3

Rose both white and Rede, The. John Skelton. PBRV *Fr.* A Lawde and Prayse Made for Our Sovereigne Lord the Kyng.

Rose-Bud, The. William Broome. OBEV

Rose, but one, none other rose had I, A. Tennyson. PoEL-5 *Fr.* Pelleas and Ettarre. NAEL-2 *Fr.* Idylls of the King.

Rose-cheeked Laura. Thomas Campion. *See* Laura.

Rose-cheeked Laura, come. Laura. Thomas Campion. EnLoPo; InPK-6; InPS-3; NAEL-1; NOBE; NOSC; NoP-4; OAEL-1; OBEV; PoE; PoEL-2; TFi; TRP *Fr.* Observations in the Art of English Poesie.

Rose-cheekt *Lawra* come. Thomas Campion. *See* Laura.

Rose Connoley. *Unknown.* AmFP

Rose, die Lilie, die Taube, die Sonne, Die. Heinrich Heine, *German.* AWP, *tr. by* Richard Garnett

(Love's Resume.) TrJP, *tr. by* "J. F. C."

Rose fades / and is renewed again, The. Poem. William Carlos Williams. Poetr

Rose Family, The. Robert Frost. OBAL; OBCA

Rose Farmer, The. Herman Melville. APN-2

Rose-footed swan from snow, or girl from rose? (LL) The Swans. Dame Edith Sitwell. CMoP; WPE

Rose for a young head, A. The Watcher. James Stephens. MoBrPo; OBEV

Rose Garland Sonnet. Simon Pettet. PT

Rose-Geranium, The. Eiléan Ní Chuilleanáin. CIP-2

Rose gives a tremulous glance, The. Limerick. Anne Norris. PeLi

Rose Growing into the House, The. Gibbons Ruark. InPK-6

Rose, harsh rose. Sea Rose. Hilda Doolittle. FaBoMo; HeIP-4; NoAM; NoP-4; OxWW; TRP

Rose has flushed red, the bud has burst, The. Hafiz. TAL, *tr. by* Gertrude Lowthian Bell *Fr.* Odes.

Rose in her hand, a rose in her breast, A Kyrielle May Probyn. VWP

Rose in October, A. James Whitcomb Riley. OBAL

Rose in the Afternoon. Jenny Joseph. BrRo

Rose in the Garden. *Unknown.* AmFP

Rose is a rose, The. The Rose Family. Robert Frost. OBAL; OBCA

Rose is not the rose unless thou see, The. Hafiz. AWP, *tr. by* Richard Le Gallienne *Fr.* Odes.

Rose is red, the grass is green, The. *Unknown.* OxNR

Rose is red, the rose is white, The. *Unknown.* OxNR

Rose is red, the violet's blue, The. *Unknown.* OxNR

Rose-Leaves. Austin Dobson.

Urceus Exit. OBEV

Rose Leaves, When The Rose is Dead. Shelley.

"Music, when soft voices die." LaPo

Rose Mary. D. G. Rossetti. Poetr

"And lo! on the ground Rose Mary lay." Poetr

Rose might of the winds. Ark 44, The Rod of Aaron. Ronald Johnson. FTOS

Rose of England, The. *Unknown.* ESPB

Rose of Life, The. Sir Richard Fanshawe. *See* A Rose.

Rose of Sharon / I lost in the tortured night, The. For the New Union Dead in Alabama. Edward Dorn. PoM

Rose of that Garland! fairest and sweetest. To the Most Beautiful Lady, the Lady Bridget Manners. Barnabe Barnes. EnLoPo

Rose of the World, The. John Masefield. PoRA

Rose of the World, The. W. B. Yeats. CMoP; MoBrPo; NAEL-2

(Rosa Mundi.) ADE

Rose, Oh Pure Contradiction. Rilke, *German.* TTTS; EnlH, *tr. by* Stephen Mitchell

Rose on My Cake, The. Karla Kuskin. TLR

Rose Red's hair is brown as fur. An Embroidery (I). Denise Levertov. NMM-2

Rose, regarded here by your external eyes, The. "Angelus Silesius." GePo, *tr. by* George C. Schoolfield *Fr.* The Cherubical Wanderer.

Rose Solitude. Jayne Cortez. MoNo

Rose Still Grows beyond the Wall, The. A. L. Frink. BLPA

Rose the Red and White Lil[l]y. *Unknown.* ESPB; OxBB

Rose Thieves, The. Vasco [*or* Vasko] Popa. HSix *Fr.* Games. RB, *tr. by* Anne Pennington

Rose to the living is more than, A. Nixon Waterman. PoToHe

Rose Tree, The. W. B. Yeats. CMoP; FaBoPV; OBMV

Rose was sick and smiling died [*or* di'd], The. The Funeral[l] Rites of the Rose. Robert Herrick. CaPo; NOSC; OBEV

'Rose, were you not extremely sick?'. (LL) A True Maid. Matthew Prior. EP; FaBoEE; NAEL-1; NIP-4; NOEC; PeLV

Rose Window. Herman Melville. APN-2

Rose Wreaths, The. Friedrich Gottlieb Klopstock, *German.* GePo, *tr. by* J. W. Thomas

Rosebud. Jon Anderson. PaTW

Rosebud in the Heather. Goethe, *German.* STV, *tr. by* John Frederick Nims

Rosemary, Rosemary, let down your hair! A Nonsense Song. Stephen Vincent Benét. NOxBChV; OBAL

Rosemary Spray, The. Luis de Góngora y Argote, *Spanish.* AWP, *tr. by* E. Churton

Roses. "George Eliot." BoTP

Roses. Barbara Guest. NoP-4

Roses. Geoffrey Lehmann. BMAP

Roses. Pierre de Ronsard, *French.* AWP, *tr. by* Andrew Lang

Roses and Revolutions. Dudley Randall. BPo; CoAmPo; PoBA; TAP

Roses are already here. Philodemus, *Greek.* PGA, *tr. by* Kenneth Rexroth

Roses are red. *Unknown.* CTV; OxNR

Roses at first were white. How Roses Came Red. Robert Herrick. BeJo; CaPo

Roses every one were red, The. Spleen. John Gray. NOBVV

Roses first came red, The. (LL) How Roses Came Red. Robert Herrick. BeJo; CaPo

Roses hence, or *Lil[l]ies* rather. (LL) Upon the Infant Martyrs. Richard Crashaw. GeHe; OAEL-1

Roses, I think there is salt on you. Lewis 1928–45. Iain Crichton Smith. FaBoTC *Fr.* A Life.

Roses in breathing forth their scent. Celia Singing. Thomas Stanley. BeJo; NOSC

Roses in December. Geoffrey Anketell Studdert-Kennedy. BLPA

Roses (Love's delight) let's join. Anacreon, *Greek.* AWP, *tr. by* Thomas Stanley

Roses of Sa['ladi, The. Marceline Desbordes-Valmore, *French.* BoWoP, *tr. by* Barbara Howes; WPOW, *tr. by* Deirdre Lashgari

Roses Only. Marianne Moore. LiTM

Roses Red. Arno Holz, *German.* AWP, *tr. by* Jethro Bithell

Roses red upon my neighbor's vine, The. My Neighbor's Roses. Abraham L. Gruber. BLPA; PoToHe

Roses Rising. René Vivien. CPO

Roses, rose-red and white, and green. Alleluya. "Rubén Dario," *Spanish.* TTY, *tr. by* Lysander Kemp

Roses, roses, roses. June. Henrietta Cordelia Ray. CBWP-3

Roses, their sharp spines being gone. A Bridal Song. John Fletcher *and* Shakespeare. NOBE; NOSC; NoSic *Fr.* The Two Noble Kinsmen.

Roses used to bloom in spring. Crinagoras, *Greek.* GrAn, *tr. by* Alistair Elliot

Roses with the scent bred out. In Lieu. Louis MacNeice. CMoP

Roses, you are not so fair after all! (LL) The Flower's Name. Robert Browning. CTC; GaP; OBGa

Rosie-fingerd morne, no sooner shone, The. The Sacrifice. Homer. *Fr.* Odyssey. NAWM-1, *tr. by* Robert Fitzgerald

Rosie Nell. *Unknown.* AS

Rosina Alcona to Julius Brenzaida. Judith Wright. NALW

Roslyn Malamud the Coup. Anna Deavere Smith. OxWW *Fr.* Fires in the Mirror.

Ross's Poems. Geoffrey Lehmann. CBAP

"What's that bird, Mr Long?" BMAP

Rostov. George Sutherland Fraser. PoWW

Rosy Apple, Lemon or Pear. *Unknown.* CH

Rosy Bosom'd Hours, The. Coventry Patmore. EnLoPo; NOBVV

Rosy Days Are Numbered, The. Moses ibn Ezra. *Fr.* Wine-Songs. TrJP, *tr. by* Solomon Solis-Cohen

Rosy Ear. Zbigniew Herbert, *Polish.* EP, *tr. by* Czeslaw Milosz

Rosy shield upon its back, A. The Dead Crab. Andrew Young. FaBoTw; RB

Rot on the vine: in that land were we born. (LL) The Mediterranean. Allen Tate. FaBoMo; FuPo; HAP; ImPo; LiTM; MoAmPo; VGW

Rotation. Julian Bond. PFE

Rotation (1). Un-gyo Kang, *Korean.* CKP, *tr. by* Jaihiun Kim

Rothko's Yellow. Dean Young. WeT

Rotogravure. Errol Francis. NBiP

Rotten wood is unfit for carving, so I slept at noon. For Guests after Their Visit. Liu Ya-tzu, *Chinese.* SuSp, *tr. by* Wu-chi Liu

Rottnest Island. Nicholas Hasluck.

"All day the bicycles come and go." NOBAu

"Christmas Day. 1696." NOBAu

Rotund, stubby fingered. Tale. Jennifer Rankin. BMAP

Rou-cou spoke the dove. Song of Fixed Accord. Wallace Stevens. InPS-3; SAmP

Rouen. May Wedderburn Cannan. NAEL-2; OBWP; OxBTC

Rouen, Place de la Pucelle. Maria White Lowell. APN-2

("Here blooms the legend fed with time and chance.") APAD

(Rouen.) APAD

Rough. Stephen Spender. PBMP

Rough fir, hauled from the hills. The Making of the Cross. William Everson. VGW

Rough Music. Deborah Digges. PUP-18

Rough Ridge. Yüan Mei, *Chinese.* CoBLCP, *tr. by* Jonathan Chaves

Rough Sunday. Wooded plains underwater, seaweed, urchin, sea-horse. Olga Broumas, Jane Miller. WeT *Fr.* Black Holes, Black Stockings.

Rough wind, that moanest loud. A Dirge. Shelley. NAEL-2; NOBE; PFE; PoRA; SAGP; SCGP

Roughly estimated ones, who do not sort well, The. The Monuments of Hiroshima. D. J. Enright. OxBSP

Roughly figured, this man of moderate habits. Life Cycle of Common Man. Howard Nemerov. NBLV

Roughly-silvered leaves that are the snow. A Song from Armenia. Geoffrey Hill. FaBoMo

Roun a rocky corner. Dreamer. Jean Binta Breeze. HCP

Round, The. Stanley Kunitz. PiM

Round: " 'Wondrous life!' cried Marvell at Appleton House." Weldon Kees. CoAP

Round a cleft in the cliffs to come upon. Venus of the Salty Shell. Denis Devlin. BIrV; NOIV

Round about in a fair ring-a. *Unknown.* BoTP

Round about Me. Sappho, *Greek.* AWP, *tr. by* William Ellery Leonard

Round about, round about, / Catch a wee mouse. *Unknown.* OxNR

Round about, round about, here sits the hare. *Unknown.* OxNR

Round about, round about/ In a fair ring-a. The Elves' Dance. John Lyly *and* Thomas Ravenscroft. CH *Fr.* The Mayde's Metamorphosis.

Round about, round about, / maggotty pie. *Unknown.* OxNR

Round about the cauldron go! Edward Abbott Parry. BXAP

Round about the rosebush. *Unknown.* OxNR

Round about there / Sat a little hare. *Unknown.* OxNR

Round and round. Private Transport. Adrian Mitchell. FaBoEE

Round and round our lavatory. The Thinker. Anthony Delius. PeSA

Round and round the cornfield. *Unknown.* LB

Round and round the garden. *Unknown.* OxNR

Round and round the rugged rock. *Unknown.* OxNR

Round blazing sun, The. What She Said, Thinking of Him Crossing the Wilderness Alone. Auvaiyar, *Tamil.* PLW, *tr. by* A. K. Ramanujan

Round-bottomed babe from Mobile, A. Limerick. *Unknown.* PeLi

Round– / cheeked girlchild comes awake, A. Galway Kinnell. MoLi *Fr.* Under the Maud Moon. NNaP

Round dance of day has gone. Sitting Alone in Tulsa Three A.M. Lance Henson. VoR

Round her red garland and her golden hair. Of His Last Sight of Fiammetta. Giovanni Boccaccio. AWP *Fr.* Sonnets.

Round Midnight. Clarence Major. NAAL

Round mounds of the dead in the graveyard, The. Hymn to the Graveyard. Tujin Park, *Korean.* CKP, *tr. by* Jaihiun Kim

Round my neck a rosary of fine beads. "Anna Akhmatova," *Russian.* TCRP, *tr. by* Daniel Weissbort

Round Nights black Axle-tree, bright Stars, farewel. (LL) The Enchantment. Theocritus. HePo, *tr. by* Barbara Hughes Fowler; CTC; OBVE, *tr. by* Thomas Creech

Round—oblong—like jam. Contours. Noël Coward. UV

Round shape water takes inside the gourd, A. Nguyễn Trãi, *Vietnamese.* AVP, *tr. by* Huỳnh Sanh Thông

Round Song, A. Rhyll McMaster. CBAP

'Round that little old sod shanty on the claim. (LL) Little Old Sod Shanty. *Unknown.* AS; AmFP

Round the cape of a sudden came the sea. Parting at Morning. Robert Browning. AWP; CABP; EBEvV; EnVR; FHYEP; HeIP-4; ImPo; InPS-3; NAEL-2; NOBE; OBEV; OBNC; OxBSP; PFE; SAGP; SCGP; SoSe-8; TFi; UnPo

Round the house and round the house / and there lies a black glove in the window. Riddle. *Unknown.* FaBoVe

Round the house and round the house / and there lies a white glove in the window. Riddle. *Unknown.* FaBoVe

Round the island of Zipangu. The Mimshi Maiden. Hugh Raymond McCrae. NOBAu

Round the lone spar where mid-sea surges pour. (LL) A Requiem[:] for Soldiers Lost in Ocean Transports. Herman Melville. APN-2; PoEL-5

Round the streets of this city I rode you. Farewell to My Scooter. Mbuyiseni Oswald Mtshali. PeSAV

Round the world and back again. (LL) Dr. Foster. *Unknown.* ACTP

Round the Year. Coventry Patmore. BoTP

(Year, The.) EBVV

Round this particular date I have drawn a circle. Sulpicia. Michael Longley. RACG

Rounded Catalogue Divine Complete, The. Walt Whitman. NAAL-1; NAAL-3

Rounded world is fair to see, The. Nature [1844]. Ralph Waldo Emerson. APN-1

Roundel: "Now welcom[e], Somer [*or* Summer] with thy sunne soft." Chaucer. CTC; OAEL-1; OPOU; OxBSP *Fr.* The Parlement of Foules. (Qui Bien Aime a Tard Oublie.) EnLoPo

Roundelay: "*Motto* Tell me, thou skilful shepherd's swain." Michael Drayton. *Fr.* The Shepherd's Garland.

Roundelay Between Two Shepherds, A. Michael Drayton. NoP-4

Roundhouse in Cheyenne is filled every night, The. The Dreary Black Hills. *Unknown.* AS

Roundhouse Voices, The. Dave Jeddie Smith. MT; NoAM; VCAP ("In full glare of sunlight I came here, man-tall but thin.") ColAP; GM

Rounding a slip of the marsh, the boat skids. Looking for the Melungeon. Dave Jeddie Smith. HCAP

Rounding steeps and jostles were one thing, The. The Ferris Wheel. Wyatt Prunty. RA

Rounding the Cape. Roy Campbell. PeSA

Rounding the Horn. John Masefield. MoBrPo *Fr.* Dauber.

Rounding the sand spits, circling rocks, a rippling, murmuring green. Po Chü-i. *See* The Spring River.

Rouse for Stevens, A. Theodore Roethke. OBAL

Rousecastle. David Wright. MoBS

Roused by November seas, wrecked on Italian rocks. Theodoridas, *Greek.* GrAn, *tr. by* W. G. Shepherd

Rousseau in His Day. Donald Davie. DiPo

Rousseau, Voltaire, our Gibbon, and De Staël. Sonnet to Lake Leman. Byron. Son

Route. George Oppen.

("Tell the beads of the chromosomes like a rosary.") AF

"And if at 80." APSN

"Cars on the highway filled with speech." APSN

"Cars run in a void of utensils, The." APSN

"Department of Plants and Structures— obsolete, the old name." APSN

"In Alsace, during the war." APSN

"Not the symbol but the scene this pavement leads." APSN

"Not to reduce the thing to nothing." APSN

"Tell the beads of the chromosomes like a rosary." APSN

"Tell the life of the mind, the mind creates the finite." APSN

"To insist that what is true is good, no matter, no matter." APSN

"Troubled that you are not, as they say." APSN

"Wars that are just? A simpler question: In the event." APSN

"Words cannot be wholly transparent. And that is the." APSN

Route. Philippe Soupault. PFTM

Route of Evanescence, A. A Hummingbird. Emily Dickinson. APN-2; HeIP-4; NAAL-1; NAAL-3; NoP-4; PoEL-5; SoSe-8

Route of the Táin, The. Thomas Kinsella. PBCIP

Routes. Peter Everwine. NNaP

Routine Things Around the House, The. Stephen Dunn. CMAP; NAmP90 ("Doing the routine things / around the house.") (LL) FiLi

Rover killed the goat. Brave Rover. Max Beerbohm. NBLV

Rover or The Banished Cavaliers, The. Aphra Behn. BWW

Rover, with the good brown head. Matthias. Matthew Arnold. PC *Fr.* Poor Matthias. PoEL-5

Rovers, The. George Canning, George Ellis, *and* John Hookham Frere. Rogero's Song. NOEC; OBCoV

(Song of One Eleven Years in Prison.) PeLV

Rover's Adieu [*or* Farewell], The. Sir Walter Scott. NOBE; OBEV *Fr.* Rokeby.

(Song.) EnLoPo; OBNC

Roving breezes come and go, the reed-beds sweep and sway, The. The Travelling Post Office. Andrew Barton Paterson. CBAP; NOBAu

Roving Gambler, The. *Unknown.* AS

Roving Shanty Boy, The. *Unknown.* AmFP

Row after row. The Mule. Boynton Merrill Jr. CRP

Row after row with strict impunity. Ode to the Confederate Dead. Allen Tate. AiP; CBCWP; ColAP; FaBoMo; FuPo; HeIP-4; LiTM; MoAmPo; MoP; NAAL-2; NOBA; NoAM; NoP-4; OBWP; OxBA; TAP; TFi; UnPo

Row gently here, my gondolier; so softly wake the tide. Venetian Air. Thomas Moore. OxBSP

Row of Stalls, A. Raymond Knister.

"Nellie Rakerfield." NOBC

Row of willow trees, almost green for the spring, A. Two Fish by a Willow Embankment. Hsü Wei, *Chinese.* CoBLCP, *tr. by* Jonathan Chaves

Row us out from Desenzano, to your Sirmione row! Frater Ave Atque Vale. Tennyson. EBVV; GTBS-P; HAP; InPS-3; NAEL-2; NoP-4; OxBSP

Rowan County Crew, The. James William Day. AmFP

Rowan like a lip-sticked girl, A. Song. Seamus Heaney. TRP

Rowan Tree Fire, The. Sergey Yesenin, *Russian*. TCRP, tr. by Geoffrey Thurley

Rowed us out to the anchored boat. (LL) Letter to Derek Mahon. Michael Longley. CABP

Rowing. Larry Gates. HA

Rowing. Anne Sexton. BoWoP; LCAP-2

Rowing between Pond and Western Islands. A Loon Call. Richard Eberhart. ColAP

Rowing downstream. Michael McClintock. HA

Rowing in Familiar January. Milo De Angelis, *Italian*. NeIt, tr. by Lawrence Venuti

Rows of babies in plastic boxes. The Nursery. Laurel Trivelpiece. BAP-95

Rows of carriages, grooms at rest. Occasional Verse. Wang Ts'an, *Chinese*. SuSp, tr. by Ronald C. Miao

Rows of cells are unroofed, The. The Old Prison. Judith Wright. BMAP

Rows of Cold Trees, The. Yvor Winters. NOBA

Rowzing him up; and nought shall me dismay. Bible, *O.T. See* Psalm 55.

Roy Bean. *Unknown*. OBAL

Roy Kloof. Sydney Clouts. PeSAV

Royal and saintly Cashel! I would gaze. The Rock of Cashel. Sir Aubrey De Vere. IIP

Royal Angler, The. *Unknown*.
  "Me thinks I see our mighty monarch stand." OBSV

Royal Banquet, The. William Edmonstoune Aytoun *and* Sir Theodore Martin (1816–1909). OBCoV

Royal blue azure blue. Of Colours and Shadows. Ahmed Tidjani-Cissé. PBMAP

Royal Charlie's now awa. Will He No Come Back Again? *Unknown*. OBEV

Royal Crown, The. Solomon ibn Gabirol, *Hebrew*. AWP, tr. by Israel Zangwill
  "My God, I know that those who plead." TrJP, tr. by Alice Lucas

Royal Education. Winthrop Mackworth Praed. OBSV

Royal feast was done; the King, The. The Fool's Prayer. Edward Rowland Sill. APN-2; FaBoBe; PoLF

Royal Mischeif, The. Mary de la Rivière Manley.
  Epilogue: "Our Poet tells me I am very pretty." KTR
  Prologue: "Criticks, ye are grown so much unkind of late." KTR
  "What to conceal desire, when every." KTR

Royal Palm. Hart Crane. CMoP; MoAmPo; MoP; NoAM

Royal Portraits, The. William Dean Howells. APN-2

Royal Princess, A. Christina Rossetti. BrRo

Royal Progress. Antonin Bartusek, *German*. CEEP, tr. by Ewald Osers

Royal Stag, The. "Hugh MacDiarmid." FaBoMo

Royal Tour, The. "Peter Pindar." OxBoLi; PeLV

Royal Tour, and Weymouth Amusements, The, *abr*. "Peter Pindar." OxBoLi
  George III and the Sailor. NOEC

Royals. James Schuyler. FTOS

Royalties. D. J. Enright. NOBL; PeLV

Roye Robert the Bruss the rayke he avowit, The. Douglas and the Bruce's Heart. Sir Richard Holland. OxBS *Fr.* The Buke of the Howlat.

Roys, The. Arvind Krishna Mehrotra. OMIP

Rrrrrrrraaarghr / We have paid you back. Fury against the Moslems at Uhud. Hind bint Utba, *Arabic*. WPOW, tr. by Bridget Connelly *and* Deirdre Lashgari

Rt. Rev. Richard Allen. Josephine D. Henderson Heard. CBWP-4

Rub, A. John Banister Tabb. OBAL

Rub a dub dub. Mother Goose. NOBL; OxNR
  ("Turn 'em out, knaves all three!") (LL) LB

Rub-a-dub-dub. *Unknown*. ACTP

Rubáiyát, The. Anna Bunston DeBary, *Persian*.
  "Tomorrow I will haul down the flag of hypocrisy." LiLi, tr. by Peter Avery *and* John Heath-Stubbs

Rubáiyát of Omar Khayyám [of Naishápúr], The. Omar Khayyám, *Persian*. ad. by Edward Fitzgerald AWP; EBVV; FaBoBe; FaPoR; HAP; NAEL-2; NoP-4; PoEL-5
  "Ah, with the grape my fading life provide." EBVV; GTBS-P
  "And when like her, oh Sákí, you shall pass." TRP
  "Awake! for morning in the bowl of night." PeVV, *sect*. I–XII; EBEvV; NOBVV; OxAEP-2; TAL; UV
  "Come, fill the cup, and in the fire of spring." TRP; UV
  "For some we loved, the loveliest and the best." TRP

  "Here with a Loaf of Bread beneath the Bough." UV
  "'How sweet is mortal Sovranty!' — think some." UV
  "I sent my Soul through the Invisible." APAD
  "I sometimes think that never blows so red." TRP
  "Iram indeed is gone with all his rose." OBVE
  "Moving Finger writes; and, having writ, The." TRP
  "Myself when young did eagerly frequent." TRP
  "Oh, come with old Khayyam and leave the Wise." UV
  "Some for the Glories of This World; and some." TRP
  "They say the lion and the lizard keep." EBEV
  "Wake! for the sun, who scattered [*or* scatter'd] into flight." EnVR; ImPo; OBNC; TRP
  "Yon rising Moon that looks for us again." TRP

Rubber. Rolf Jacobsen, *Norwegian*. BLT, tr. by Roger Greenwald

Rubber penis, the wig, false breasts, The. Poggio. Lawrence Durrell. OxBTC

Rubens. Washington Allston. APN-1

Rubens, de Vos, Memling—room after room. Antwerp: Musée Des Beaux-Arts. Alan Ross. NYBP

Rubin. Charles Cooper. PoBA

Rublyov XVth Century. Ksenya Nekrasova, *Russian*. TCRP, tr. by Vera Rich

Rubric, The, *see also* "Now manhood and garbroyls I chaunt, and martial horror" tr. by Richard Stanyhurst, "Arms, and the Man I sing, who, forc'd by Fate" tr. by John Dryden, "I sing of warfare and a man at war" tr. by Robert Fitgerald, *and* "Arms, and the Man I sing, the first who bore." Virgil. OBVE, tr. by Gawin Douglas *Fr.* The Aeneid [*or* Eneados, *Aeneis*].

Ruby and amethyst eyes of anemones, The. Winter Anemones. Charles Brasch. PeNZ *Fr.* Night Cries, Wakari Hospital.

Ruby and me, stalking savannah. Catching Crabs. David Dabydeen. HCP

Ruby Tells All. Miller Williams. MT

Ruckled lips gaped slightly, but when, The. Six Belons. Chase Twichell. NAmP90

Ruddigore. Sir William Schwenck Gilbert.
  Darned Mounseer, The. NOBL
  Thought from Ruddigore, A. OBCoV

Ruddy fire-glow, like her sister's eyes, The. Lot and His Daughters I. Alec Derwent Hope. ChIV-1

Rude mass of earth, from which moilèd hands. On a Piece of Unwrought Pipeclay. John Frederick Bryant. NOEC

Rude unwelcome guest. Blackbird: Elegy for William Gordon Calvert. Barry MacSweeney. NBrP

Rudely thou wrongst my dear heart's desire. Sonnet 5. Edmund Spenser. *Fr.* Amoretti. AAS

Rudolph Reed was oaken. The Ballad of Rudolph Reed. Gwendolyn Brooks. PFE; RB

Rueful Lamentation on the Death of Queen Elizabeth, A. Sir Thomas More. AAS
  (Lamentation of Queen Elizabeth, A.) NoSic

Ruffed blue-green garden, red blossoms. Tune: "Butterflies Lingering over Flowers." Ou-yang Hsiu, *Chinese*. SuSp, tr. by Jerome P. Seaton

"Rufinianus" was once just Rufus. *Unknown, Greek*. GrAn, tr. by Peter Jay

Rufty and Tufty. Isabell Hempseed. BoTP

Rufus Mitchell's Confession. *Unknown*. AmFP

Rufus Prays. Leonard Alfred George Strong. MoBrPo

Rug, The. Michael McClure. NeAP

Rug of dead butterflies at my feet, A. Ghost. Nina Cassian, *Romanian*. PoSu, tr. by Christopher Hewitt

Rugby Chapel. Matthew Arnold. EBVVPR; EnVR; PeECV; PoEL-5

Rugged forhead that with grave foresight, The. Love. Edmund Spenser. OAEL-1 *Fr.* Wood Of Error. AEP

Rugged Pyrrhus, he whose sable arm, The. Shakespeare. *Fr.* Hamlet. NAWM-1

Rugged Pyrrhus, like th' Hyrcanian beast, The. Shakespeare. *Fr.* Hamlet. NAWM-1

Ruin, The. Dafydd ap Gwilym, *Welsh*. OBWVE, tr. by Rolfe Humphries

Ruin, The. Richard Hughes. OBMV

Ruin, The. *Unknown, Anglo-Saxon*. AnOE, tr. by Charles W. Kennedy

Ruin, The. *Unknown, Anglo-Saxon*. EBEV, tr. by Gavin Bone

Ruin, at least, was something; the yard, The. Late Return. E. A. Markham. PBCV

Ruin, now so intolerably sad, The. (LL) November. William Dean Howells. APN-2; GaP

Ruin seize thee, ruthless King! Thomas Gray. *Fr.* Bard, The [A Pindaric Ode]. GTBS-P; NOBE; NOEC; OAEL-1; OxAEP-1

Ruined and ill—a man of two score. Remembering Golden Bells. Po Chü-i, *Chinese*. AWP; ChiP, tr. by Arthur Waley

Ruined Chapel. George Mackay Brown. FaBoTC *Fr.* Runes from a Holy Island.

Ruined Cottage, The. Wordsworth. NoP-4 *See see also* The Wanderer, *Book 1 of* The Excursion. OAEL-2

Ruined Maid, The. Thomas Hardy. BoLoP; CMoP; FaBoSe; FaBoVe; HeIP-4; NAEL-2; NBLV; NOBL; OxBTC; PeLV; PeVV; SCV; TFi; TRP

("O'Melia, my dear, this does everything crown!") NoP-4; PoPoPo

Ruined, time ruined, all these once good things. Rimrock, Where It Is. Hayden Carruth. NNaP

Ruines of Rome: by Bellay. Edmund Spenser.

"Who lists to see, what ever nature, arte." PBRV

Ruines of Time, The. Edmund Spenser. OxAEP-1

Ruinous Rains. Fu Hsien, *Chinese.* CoBCP, *tr. by* Burton Watson

Ruins, The. Marcia Southwick. CMAP

Ruins of a Great House. Derek Walcott. TwCP

("Stones only, the disjecta membra of this.") PoPoPo

Ruins of Corinth, The. Antipater of Sidon, *Greek.* GrAn, *tr. by* Peter Jay

Ruins of Lo-yang, The. Ts'ao Chih, *Chinese.* ChiP, *tr. by* Arthur Waley

Ruins of Rome. Joachim Du Bellay, *French.*

Antiquitez de Rome. NNPT, *tr. by* Edmund Spenser

"Hope ye, my verses, that posterity." PoE

"Who list the Romane greatnes forth to figure." OBVE

Ruins of the City of Hay. Randolph Stow. CBAP

Ruins of Walsingham, The. *Unknown. See* A Lament for Our Lady's Shrine at Walsingham.

Ruins under the Stars. Galway Kinnell. LCAP-2

Rule, Britannia! James Thomson *and* David Mallet. EBEvV; FaPoR; GTBS-P; NOEC; OBWP *Fr.* Alfred: A Masque.

(Ode: Rule, Brittania!) NAEL-1

Rule well v, and come to hevyn. (LL) Ten Commandments, Seven Deadly Sins, and Five Wits. *Unknown.* FaBoEE; MiEL

Rule which by obeying grows. Intellect. Emerson. APN-1; NoP-4

Ruler, The. Robin Blaser. FTOS

Rules and Lessons. Henry Vaughan. ESCV

Rules and Regulations. "Lewis Carroll." NOBVV; PeVV

Rules break like a thermometer, The. Adrienne Rich. *Fr.* Twenty-one Love Poems. GLP

Rules of Sleep. Howard Moss. VCAP

Rules to Live By. Paula Del Giudice. CTV

Rum Mort's Praise of Her Faithless Maunder, The. *Unknown.* CBNP

Rum Tum Tugger is a Curious Cat. T. S. Eliot. NTP; PeP

Rumanian of Maria Banus, The. George MacBeth.

Poem of Death, A. HP

Rumba. José Zacarías Tallet, *Spanish.* TTY, *tr. by* Sangodare Akanji

Rumble, A. Virginia Schonborg. SSCS

Rumble of thunder brings evening rain, The. Chu Yün-ming. *Fr.* Miscellaneous Poems Written in My Studio on an Autumn Day. CoBLCP, *tr. by* Jonathan Chaves

Rumble on, machines of the gold mines. In the Gold Mines. B. W. Vilakazi. PeSA; TTY

Rumble, rumble in the pot. *Unknown.* CBNP

Rumbling in the chimneys. Windy Nights. Rodney Bennett. KaS

Rumbling sound of man. Buzz. Jim Tollerud. VoR

Rumbling under blackened girders, Midland, bound for Cricklewood. Parliament Hill Fields. John Betjeman. FaBoTw; NOBE

Ruminant pillows! Gregarious soft boulders! Donald Hall. LCAP-2

Rumination. Richard Eberhart. LiTM

Rummle an' dunt o' watter. Sumburgh Heid. George Bruce. OxBS

Rumor, stir of ripeness. Song IV: The Calling-Up. Muriel Rukeyser. NMM-2

Rumored Conversation with Oneself Continues in Pittsburgh, The. Diane Ackerman. WWSi

Rumors from an Aeolian Harp. Henry David Thoreau. APN-1; PAR

Rumors of liberation. We could not believe it. Richard Eberhart. *Fr.* Brotherhood of Men. PoWW

Rumors open up. The Morning Star. Primus St. John. PoBA

Rumor's rooster / halloos the distorted. Ray DiPalma. PmAP

Rumour. Owen Rutter. NSI *Fr.* The Song of Tiadatha.

Rumours that you lodge in a mountain temple. Tu Fu. PLT, *tr. by* A. C. Graham *Fr.* To My Younger Brother.

Rumpled river, The. River Rhyme. William Carlos Williams. PoA

Rumplestiltskin. Glyn Maxwell. OBCoV

Rumpty-iddity, row, row, row. *Unknown.* OxNR

Run down by fate's spite. Lament for Five Sons Lost in a Plague. Abu Dhu'ayb al-Hudhali, *Arabic.* ArPe, *tr. by* Omar S. Pound

Run, Great Excursioner. Run if you can. (LL) To William Wordsworth from Virginia. Julia Randall. NMM-2

Run like rats from the plague in you. Saint Coleman's Song for Flight/ An Ite Missa Est. Padraic Fiacc. PNI

Run My Hand Under. Andrew Schelling. PT

Run, my verse, my hound—fetch it!—. Prelude, Spoken to My Work Tools. Aleksey Parshchikov, *Russian.* TCRP, *tr. by* John High

Run, Nigger, Run! *Unknown.* BPo

("Run, nigger, run; de patter-roller catch you.") NAAAL

Run on a Warehouse. Susan Wheeler. BAP-96

Run out the boat, my broken comrades. Thalassa. Louis MacNeice. BIrV; FaBoMo; NOBE

Run! Run! Lu'u Văn Vong, *Vietnamese.* AVP, *tr. by* Huỳnh Sanh Thông

Run, tailors, run / or she'll kill you all e'en now. (LL) The Snail. Mother Goose. LB; OxNR; ReMoGo

Run to Mourne End Wood, The. John Masefield. EBNV *Fr.* Reynard the Fox.

Run toward the Nightland. *Unknown, Cherokee Indian.*

"Now! The Red Tobacco has come to strike your soul." STP

Runagate Runagate. Robert Earl Hayden. BPo; GM; InPS-3; LCAP-2; NAAAL; PoBA; SSLK

("I runs falls rises stumbles on from darkness into darkness.") ISC

Runaway, The. Robert Frost. AWP; CH; FaBoCh; MoAmPo; SAmP; TwCP; VGW

Runaway, The. Albery Allson Whitman. AAP

Runaway Slave, The. Walt Whitman. *Fr.* Song of Myself. AmPP; MoAmPo; NAAL-3; NOBA; OxBA

Runaway Slave at Pilgrim's Point, The. Elizabeth Barrett Browning. BrRo; NALW; VWP

Runaway Teen. William Stafford. LiLi

Runaways, The. Mark Van Doren. PoRA

Runaways Café I. Marilyn Hacker. CPO

Runaways Café II. Marilyn Hacker. NoAM

Rundown Church (Ballad of the First World War). Federico García Lorca, *Spanish.* RaBo

(Rundown Church.) AF, *tr. by* Robert Bly

Rune, A. Caroline Knox. BAP-94

Rune. Michael Longley. IIP

Rune for C, A. Barbara Howes. NYBP

Rune-Maker, The. Frederick Feirstein. RA

Rune of Riches, A. Florence Converse. BoTP

Rune of the Finland Woman. Marilyn Hacker. RA

Runes, The. Denise Levertov. SAGP

Runes for an Old Believer. Rolfe Humphries. NYBP

Runes from a Holy Island. George Mackay Brown.

Books. FaBoTC

Fish and Corn. FaBoTC

Harpoonist. FaBoTC

Hierarchy. FaBoTC

Press-Gang. FaBoTC

Ruined Chapel. FaBoTC

Saint. FaBoTC

Runes on Weland's Sword, The. Rudyard Kipling. NoAM; PoEL-5 *Fr.* Old Men at Pevensey. NoAM; PoEL-5, *tr. by* Smith makes me, A, *ad. by* Runes on Weland's Sword, The *Fr.* Puck of Pook's Hill.

Rung from their marble [*or* flinty] caves "Repent! Repent!" (LL) Saint John Baptist. William Drummond, of Hawthornden. ChIV-2; GTBS-P; NOBE; OBEV; OxAEP-1; SCGP; TrCP

Runnable Stag, A. John Davidson. EBEvV; EBNV; FaPoR; HAP; OBEV; OxBTC

Runner, The. Gary Gildner. TAP

Runner, The. Louis Simpson. AF

Runner, The. Walt Whitman. BLT; InPK-6; InPS-3; SAmP

("On a flat road runs the well-trained runner.") KaS

("With lightly closed fists and arms partially raised.") (LL) KaS

Runner in the Skies, The. James Oppenheim. TrJP

"*Runnin' space. . .*". (LL) After Winter. Sterling Brown. GT

Running. Leslie Ullman. PBCAP

Running. Richard Wilbur. CoAP

Running Away from Home. Carolyn Kizer.

"Most people from Idaho are crazed rednecks." PaTW

Running Battle, A. Brendan Kennelly. BiHa

Running downhill, spilling over, searching and spilling. Flood Water. *Unknown, Aborigine.* NOBAu, *tr. by* Mungayana Nundhirribala

Running from death. Death and the Dancer. Muriel Rukeyser. AF

Running Lightly over Spongy Ground. Theodore Roethke. RB

Running on Empty. Robert Phillips. InPK-6

Running over the fields. (LL) Days. Philip Larkin. EBEV; FaBoMo; NTP; OxAEP-2; OxBC; OxBSP; PeECV; PiM; RB; TOF

Running through the thick wiry grasses to the pond. Shore. Jean Garrigue. TAP

Running to Paradise. W. B. Yeats. NTP; OxBoLi

Runoff. William Everson. NoAM

Runs backwards toward chaos. (LL) Thief. Novica Tadic, *Serbo-Croatian.* CEEP; HSix, *tr. by* Charles Simic

Runs falls rises stumbles on from darkness into darkness. Runagate Runagate. Robert Earl Hayden. BPo; GM; InPS-3; LCAP-2; NAAAL; PoBA; SSLK

Runs on the standing windows and away. (LL) Storm Windows. Howard Nemerov. CoAmPo; InPK-6; VCAP

Rupert Murdoch, with glee, shouted: "What." Limerick. Frank Richards. PeLi

Ruptured underbelly of a black horse flew overhead. The Apocrypha of Jacques Derrida. Norman Dubie. NAmP90

Rural Carrier Stops to Kill a Nine-Foot Cottonmouth, The. T. R. Hummer. Poetr

Rural Colloquy with a Painter. Timothy Steele. CRP

Rural Dance about the Maypole, The. *Unknown.* OxBoLi

Rural Journey, The. Theocritus, *Greek.*
"We had not got half way, nor yet discerned." OBCVT, *tr. by* Leigh Hunt

Rural Lass, The. Catherine Jemmat. ECWP; NOEC

Rural letter box said Toffile Lajway, The. (LL) The Witch of Coös. Robert Frost. InPS-3; LiTM; MeMAP; MoP; NOBA; NoAM; PoE

Rural Life. George Crabbe. NOBE *Fr.* The Village. *See* Truth in Poetry.

Rural Mail, The. John Glassco. MoCV

Rural Recreation. Lillian Morrison. KaS

Rural Route. Charles Wright. WeT

Rural Sights and Sounds. William Cowper. NOEC, *book* 1, *ll.* 109–210 *Fr.* The Sofa. *Fr.* The Task.

Rural Simplicity. Henry James Byron. NOBL

Rush fields can be made good by draining: dry hill pastures. The Unfertile Heart. Naomi Mitchison. WPN

Rush Hour. Laurie Sheck. PuP-15

Rushed out when the bullock carts. Gasparillo Remembered. Anson Gonzalez. HCP

Rushes daily grow taller, The. Farm Routine. Ch'u Kuang-hsi, *Chinese.* SuSp, *tr. by* Joseph J. Lee

Rushes in a watery place. Summer. Christina Rossetti. AYFP

Rushing. Ray A. Young Bear. CDW

Rushing at times. Rushing at Times Like Flames. Nelly Sachs, *German.* WPoS, *tr. by* Ruth and Matthew Mead

Russia. Aleksandr Blok, *Russian.* AWP, *tr. by* Babette Deutsch and Avrahm Yarmolinsky

Russia. Maksimilian Aleksandrovich Voloshin, *Russian.*
"Peter the Great, first Bolshevik." TCRP, *tr. by* Bernard Meares

Russia. William Carlos Williams. VGW

Russia can't be grasped by the mind. Mariya Avakkumova, *Russian.* TCRP, *tr. by* Albert C. Todd

Russia 1812. Victor Hugo, *French.* OBWP, *tr. by* Robert Lowell

Russia has lost Russia in Russia. Loss. Yevgeny Yevtushenko, *Russian.* TCRP, *tr. by* James Reagan and Yevgeny Yevtushenko

Russia 1914/Bolinas 1988. Gail Shafarman. LoHo

Russia, 1927. Ai. NoAM

Russian Asylum. Marilyn Bowering. NOBC

Russian Cradle Song, A. David Nomberg, *Yiddish.* TrJP, *tr. by* Alter Brody

Russian Gods, The. Daniil Leonidovich Andreyev, *Russian.*
"Night winds! Dark mountainous skies." TCRP, *tr. by* Rose Styron and Olga Carlisle

Russian Mind, The. Vyacheslav Ivanov, *Russian.* TCRP, *tr. by* Albert C. Todd

Russian New Year. Bill Berkson. PmAP

Russian sailed over the blue Black Sea, A. "Soldier, Rest!" Robert Jones Burdette. OBAL

Russian Soul II, The. John Hollander. NBLV

Russian Student's Tale, The. Mathilde Blind. VWP

Russian Woman. "Igor Severyanin," *Russian.* TCRP, *tr. by* Bernard Meares

Russians. Keith Douglas. OxBTC

Russians Breathing. Philip Hammial. NOBAu

Russia's Resentment. Lizelia Augusta Jenkins Moorer. CBWP-3

Rust and silence fill the thatch. Wole Soyinka. HBAPE

Rust is ripeness, rust. Season. Wole Soyinka. PBMAP *Fr.* Idanre and Other Poems (1967).

Rust moth fungus mildew. Worm. Bob Cobbing. NBrP

Rustic Childhood. William Barnes. OBNC

Rustic Courtship. Robert Dodsley. ECEV *Fr.* Agriculture.

Rustic inn, our evening resting place, A. (LL) *see also* The Wanderer, *Book 1 of* The Excursion. Wordsworth. NoP-4; OAEL-2

Rustic mango-stone, The. Family Pride. T. S. Venugopalan, *Tamil.* OMIP, *tr. by* Rajagopal Parthasarathy

Rustic person like me seldom spends a night in a mountain home, A. Viewing Mr. Yü's Landscape Painting on the Wall. Wang Chi, *Chinese.* SuSp, *tr. by* Joseph J. Lee

Rustic temple is hidden, The. Chu Chen Po, *Chinese.* OHMPC, *tr. by* Kenneth Rexroth

Rustily creak the crickets: Jack Frost came down last night. Jack Frost. Celia Laighton Thaxter. OBCA

Rustin Steel is driving the crew to the river. A long. James Tate. CMAP

Rustle of each falling leaf, The. Love. Samuele Romanelli, *Hebrew.* TrJP, *tr. by* A. B. Rhine

Rustle of whispering wind over leaves, A. Kingfisher Flat. William Everson. PoM

Rustler. William Stroud. Spl

Rustling of leaves under the feet in woods and under hedges, The. Pleasant Sounds. John Clare. NTP

Rustling of the silk is discontinued, The. Liu Ch'e. Ezra Pound. OBVE; VGW

Rustling voices, / leaves, birds, I came, The. Shadowland. Johannes Bobrowski, *German.* CEEP, *tr. by* Ruth Mead and Matthew Mead

Rusty Man, The. Herman Melville. NCAP

Ruth. Bible, *O.T.*
Naomi and Ruth. TrJP

Ruth. Jacob Glatstein, *Yiddish.* CEEP, *tr. by* Ruth Whitman

Ruth. Thomas Hood. BoLoP; ChIV-1; EnLoPo; GLoP; NOBE; OBEV; OBNC

Ruth. Diane Q. Lewis. CrSp

Ruth. Colleen J. McElroy. BlSi

Ruth [or, The Influences of Nature]. Wordsworth. GTBS-P; PoEL-4

Rutherford McDowell. Edgar Lee Masters. OxBA *Fr.* Spoon River Anthology.

Ruthie, I'd like. Eve's Commentary. Michelene Wandor. NBrP

Ruth's Story, As Told to Lilith. Michelene Wandor. NBrP

Rwose in the Dark, The. William Barnes. NOBVV

Rye Bread. W. S. Braithwaite. GT

Rye, flax, horses, platinum, timber, and fur. (LL) The Monkeys. Marianne Moore. CMoP; MeMAP; NOBA; OxBA

Rye-sheaves are stacked, The. Alone with the Sea. Marie Under, *Estonian.* CEEP, *tr. by* Ivar Ivask

Rye Whisky. *Unknown.* AS; OxBoLi
("'Twill be all forgotten a hundred years hence.") (LL) APN-2

Ryght as the stern of day begouth to schyne. William Dunbar. *See* The Poet's Dream.

S

s. Richard Crashaw. *See* The Flaming Heart.

S.F. Southward. Allen Ginsberg. NAAL-2 *Fr.* Continuation of a Long Poem of These States.

S M. Alice Walker. CrSp

S.O.S. Léon Damas, *French.* PFTM, *tr. by* Norman R. Shapiro

S sz sz SZ sz SZ sz ZS zs Zs zs zs z. Siesta of a Hungarian Snake. Edwin Morgan. InPK-6

S—uche Is the Love I beare thy Honest Hart. Elizabeth Middleton. KTR

'S Wonderful. Ira Gershwin. CBLP

Saadi. Ralph Waldo Emerson. APN-1; MeMAP; OxBA

Sabbath. John Berryman. LCAP-2 *Fr.* Dream Songs.

Sabbath and sweet spices. Susan Howe. PmAP *Fr.* Speeches at the Barriers.

Sabbath Bells. John Clare. FHYEP

Sabbath Bells. Josephine D. Henderson Heard. CBWP-4

Sabbath Day Was By, The. Howard Chandler Robbins. AH

Sabbath day was ending in a village by the sea, The. The Last Hymn. "Marianne Farningham." BLPA

Sabbath, My Love. Judah Halevi, *Hebrew.* TrJP, *tr. by* Solomon Solis-Cohen

Sabbath of Mutual Respect, The. Marge Piercy. CrSp

Sabbath of Rest, A. Isaac Luria, *Hebrew.* TrJP, *tr. by* Nina Davis Salaman

Sabbath Sonnet. Felicia Dorothea Hemans. Son

Sabbath, the pious carry no money. A Voice out of the Sabbaths. Derek Walcott. WeW-3

Sable arrested a fine comb. 6. Jack Spicer. FTOS *Fr.* Love Poems.

Saboteur autumn has riddled the pampered folds. Wild Honey. Francis Webb. NOBAu

Sabrina. Milton. CH; NOBE; OBEV *Fr.* Comus; a Masque Presented at Ludlow Castle. FHYEP; OAEL-1

(Song.) OxAEP-1

Sabrina. Milton. *Fr.* Comus; a Masque Presented at Ludlow Castle. FHYEP; OAEL-1

Sabrina fair. Sabrina. Milton. CH; EBEV; FaBoCh; NOBE; OBEV; OxAEP-1; PoEL-3 *Fr.* Comus; a Masque Presented at Ludlow Castle. FHYEP; OAEL-1

Sabrina's Song. Milton. NOSC *Fr.* Comus; a Masque Presented at Ludlow Castle. FHYEP; OAEL-1

Sack of kittens, The. Nicholas Virgilio. HA

Sacrament of Poverty, The. Marilyn Nelson Waniek. GT

Sacrament of Sleep, The. John Oxenham. PoLF

Sacrament of the Altar, The. *Unknown.* NoP-4

Sacramento. Luke Breit. EC2

Sacramento. The Californian. *Unknown.* AmFP

Sacred. Gertrude Stein. OBAL

Sacred and Profane Love, or, There's Nothing New under the Moon Either. Peter De Vries. NBLV; OBCoV

Sacred Book, The. Zoroaster, *Persian.* AWP, *tr. by* A. V. Williams Jackson

Sacred Chant for the Return of Black Spirit and Power. Imamu Amiri Baraka. NBV

Sacred Children, The. Hoffman Reynolds Hays. SPE

Sacred Grove, A. Edward Cracroft Lefroy. AWP *Fr.* Echoes from Theocritus.

Sacred Grove, A. Fran Winant. BrRo

Sacred Hearth, The. David Gascoyne. FaBoTw

Sacred Heliconian spring, The. Clara Reeve. ECWP *Fr.* To My Friend Mrs.—, on Her Holding an Argument in Favour of the Natural Equality of Both the Sexes.

Sacred marble, clothed in spirit and strength. Venus de Milo. Charles Marie René Leconte de Lisle, *French.* GS, *tr. by Unknown*

Sacred Marriage of Shiva and Parvati, The. Parancoti Munivar, *Tamil.* "On the marriage platform made of gold." ITG, *tr. by* William P. Harman

Sacred mouthpiece of the Muses Pindar. The Nine Lyric Poets. *Unknown, Greek.* GrAn, *tr. by* Peter Jay

Sacred Mt. Hua, terrace of clouds. Seeing Off Han Ju-ch'ing as He Returns to the Land Within the Passes. Ho Ching-ming, *Chinese.* CoBLCP, *tr. by* Jonathan Chaves

Sacred muse that first[e] made love divine [*or* devine]. Sir John Davies. NoSic; PBRV *Fr.* The Gulling[e] Sonnets. Son

Sacred Nine delight in cruel *Love,* The. The Power of Love. Bion, *Greek.* OBCVT, *tr. by* Francis Fawkes

Sacred Religion, mother of form and fear. Samuel Daniel. NoSic *Fr.* Musophilus; or, Defence of All Learning.

Sacred Songs of the Konkau. *Unknown, Konkau.*

    Acorn Song, The. APN-2, *tr. by* Stephen Powers

    Ki-u-nad'-dis-si's Song. APN-2, *tr. by* Stephen Powers

    Red Cloud's Song. APN-2, *tr. by* Stephen Powers

Sacred thro' time, from age to age it stood. A Forest felled. Publius Papinius Statius, *Latin.* OBCVT, *tr. by* Walter Harte

Sacred tree midst the fair orchard grew, The. The Tree of Knowledge. Abraham Cowley. ChIV-1

Sacred wood, The. Lucan, *Latin.* OBCVT, *tr. by* Thomas May

Sacred words?, The. (LL) Ka 'Ba. Imamu Amiri Baraka. BPo; CAPP-1; CrDW; ISC; NBV; PmAP; TAP

Sacred Wrath. Vahan Tekeyan, *Armenian.* GI, *tr. by* Diana Der Hovanessian *and* Marsbed Margossian

Sacrifice, The. Frank Bidart. GLP; VCAP

Sacrifice, The. Chana Bloch.

    "In wings and starched." CrSp

    "Patriarch in black takes, The." CrSp

Sacrifice, A. Robert Davenport. NOSC

Sacrifice, The. George Herbert. GeHe; PoEL-2

Sacrifice, The. Homer. *Fr.* Odyssey. NAWM-1, *tr. by* Robert Fitzgerald

Sacrifice. Nana Issaia, *Modern Greek.* BoWoP, *tr. by* Helle Barnstone

Sacrifice, The. Gertrud Kolmar, *German.* AF, *tr. by* David Kipp

Sacrifice. Léon Laleau. NegPo, *tr. by* Ellen Conroy Kennedy *Fr.* Black Music.

Sacrifice. Christopher Okigbo. PBMAP

Sacrifice: An Epistle to Celia, The. Mary Leapor. PEW

Sacrifice of a Red Squirrel. Joseph Langland. NYBP

Sacrifice of Er-Heb, The. Rudyard Kipling. PeVV

Sacrifice to Apollo, The. Michael Drayton. NOSC

Sacrifice to Apollo, The. Homer. OBVE, *tr. by* Dryden *Fr.* The Iliad.

Sacrificed Author, A. Howard Nemerov. GI *Fr.* Gnomes.

Sacrificial Victim. Rie Yoshiyuki, *Japanese.* WPJ, *tr. by* Kenneth Rexroth *and* Ikuko Atsumi

Sacristans. Elizabeth Cook-Lynn. *Fr.* Journey. HATNAP

Sad, All Alone, Not Long I Musing Sat. Giles, the Elder Fletcher. Son *Fr.* Licia.

Sad and great evil is the expectation of death, A. Palladas, *Greek.* GrAn, *tr. by* Ezra Pound

Sad and mournful history, A. The Cabin Creek Flood. *Unknown.* AmFP

Sad and solemn night, The. Hymn to the North Star. William Cullen Bryant. NCAP

Sad and solemn verse doth please the mind, A. A Discourse of Melancholy. Margaret Cavendish, Duchess of Newcastle. GEA; NOSC

Sad Birds, The. Harry Mathews. PmAP

Sad Boy, The. Laura Riding Jackson. CBNP; RB

Sad Children's Song, The. Grace Paley. NMM-2; SoSe-8

Sad Day, The. Thomas Flatman. OBEV

Sad Day in Berlin. Sarah Kirsch, *German.* PBWP, *tr. by* Gerda Mayer

Sad for those without sweet Anglo-Saxon. The Change. David O'Bruadair, *Irish.* BIrV, *tr. by* Austin Clarke

Sad Green. Sylvia Townsend Warner. MoBrPo

Sad heart, the gymnast of inertia, does not count. The Sad Indian. Hart Crane. PoA

Sad Hesper o'er the buried sun. Tennyson. EBVV; EnVR *Fr.* In Memoriam A. H. H.

Sad Indian, The. Hart Crane. PoA

Sad is the man who is asked for a story. A Story. Li-Young Lee. IFJA; LoL; RaBo

Sad Is the Seagull. Larin Paraske, *Finnish.* PBWP, *tr. by* Jaakko A. Ahokas

Sad Joke on a Marae. Apirana Taylor. PeNZ

Sad lagoons. Film Vermouth: Six o'Clock Show. Magda Portal, *Spanish.* PBWP, *tr. by* Allan Francovich *and* Kathleen Weaver

Sad, lost in thought, and mute I go. *Unknown, French.* AWP, *tr. by* John Addington Symonds

Sad Love. Vidyapati, *Sanskrit.* EP, *tr. by* Deben Bhattacharya

Sad Lover, The. George Crabbe. OBNC *Fr.* Tales of the Hall.

Sad memento of the past, A. Philip Freneau. *See* On Observing a Large Red-Streak Apple.

Sad memories held in my heart, truly from another incarnation. (LL) I Had Occasion to Tell a Visitor about an Old Trip I Took. Lu Yu, *Chinese.* CoBCP, *tr. by* Burton Watson

Sad music from vermilion strings. Telling My Feelings. Yü Hsüan-chi. BoWoP, *tr. by* Geoffrey Waters

Sad / Nation, ah, A. Freedom is Walking toward Us. Tien Ch'ien, *Chinese.* ChiPo, *tr. by* Kai-yu Hsu

Sad old / umbrella, A. Old Age. Jerzy Harasymowicz, *Polish.* CEEP, *tr. by* Victor Contoski

Sad, purple well! whose bubbling eye. Abel's Blood. Henry Vaughan. KSG; OBWVE

Sad refrain I heard, from poet sad, A. Forevermore. Jones Very. NCAP

Sad Remembrance. Harry Mathews, *Chinese.* CoBCP, *tr. by* Burton Watson

Sad Remembrance. Mei Yao Ch'en, *Chinese.* CoBCP, *tr. by* Burton Watson

Sad, sad—lean with long illness. Illness. Po Chü-i, *Chinese.* ChiP, *tr. by* Arthur Waley

Sad, sad they leave their old village. Tu Fu, *Chinese.* SuSp, *tr. by* Ronald C. Miao *Fr.* Frontier Songs, First Series.

Sad seamstress, The. House Guest. Elizabeth Bishop. NYBP; TAP

Sad Shepherd, The. Ben Jonson.

    Death and Love. NOBE

    Here She Was Wont to Go. BeJo; OxBSP

    (Aeglamour's Lament.) CH

Sad Song, The. Francis Beaumont *and* John Fletcher. *See* Away, Delights.

Sad Song, A. Stephen Vincent Benét. *See* A Nonsense Song.

Sad Song. *Unknown, Chinese.* CoBCP, *tr. by* Burton Watson

Sad songs of Autumn mirth. (LL) Digging. Edward Thomas. GaP; MoBrPo; OxBTC

Sad Spring-Song. Sarah Morgan Bryan Piatt. NCAP

Sad State of Freedom, A. Nazim Hikmet, *Turkish.* NNPT, *tr. by* Taner Baybars

Sad Steps. Philip Larkin. NoAM; NoP-4

Sad Story of a Little boy That Cried, The. *Unknown.* OBSP

Sad Strains of a Gay Waltz. Wallace Stevens. OxBA

Sad Thyrsis weeps till his blue eyes are dim. Thyrsis. Edward Cracroft Lefroy. AWP *Fr.* Echoes from Theocritus.

Sad was his countenance, if we can call. Philip Freneau. NAAL-1; NAAL-3 *Fr.* The House of Night.

Sad Words. René Vivien. CPO

Sadde all alone, not long I musing satte. Giles, the Elder Fletcher. *See* Sad, All Alone, Not Long I Musing Sat.

Saddest day will have an eve, The. Hope. Clara Ann Thompson. CBWP-2

Saddest noise, the sweetest noise, The. Emily Dickinson. MeMAP

Saddest Words, The. John Greenleaf Whittier. ImPo *Fr.* Maud Muller on a summer's day. APN-1; FaBoBe; PoLF; TAP

Saddle and Cell. The Three Marias, *Portuguese.* BoWoP, *tr. by* Helen R. Lane

Saddled and briddled. Bonnie James Campbell. *Unknown.* ESPB

Saddled Ass, The. Jean de La Fontaine, *French.* NBLV, *tr. by* Deems Taylor

Saddlesore I came. Jerome Rothenberg. *Fr.* Cokboy. PmAP

Sadie. Philip Hammial. BMAP

Sadie and Maud. Gwendolyn Brooks. InPK-6; MoP; NAAAL; NOBA; NoAM; TAP *Fr.* A Street in Bronzeville. BPo; BlSi; FaBoWP

Sadie went into the bar-room, and she ordered up a big glass of beer. *Unknown.* AS

Sadie's Playhouse. Margaret Danner. PoBA

Sadly. Tanka. Ishikawa Takuboku, *Japanese.* MJT, *tr. by* Makoto Ueda

Sadly, sadly the season draws to an end. Hsü Kan. SuSp, *tr. by* Ronald C. Miao *Fr.* Boudoir Thoughts.

Sadly the dead leaves rustle in the whistling wind. The Church of a Dream. Lionel Pigot Johnson. ADE; CABP; OAEL-2; OBMV

Sadly unroll sleepingbag. 25:I:68. Philip Whalen. PoM

Sadness. Tanikawa Shuntaro, *Japanese.* VCWP, *tr. by* Harold Wright

Sadness. Tennyson. FaBoEE

Sadness, An Improvisation. Donald Justice. PUP-20

Sadness at the hairs in the miror is new no longer. On the Road. Tu Mu, *Chinese.* PLT, *tr. by* A. C. Graham

Sadness in Spring. *Unknown, Welsh.* OBWVE, *tr. by* Gwyn Jones

Sadness in the Autumn Chambers. Yün Shou-p'ing, *Chinese.* CoBLCP, *tr. by* Jonathan Chaves

Sadness in the human visage stares, The. At an Exhibition of Historical Paintings, Hobart. Vivian Smith. CBAP; NOBAu

Sadness of afternoons was unmistakable, The. After the War; When Coltrane Only Wanted to Play Dance Tunes. Matthew Graham. SeSe

Sadness of Leaving, The. Eileen Myles. PmAP

Sadness of our lives, The. Brooding. David Ignatow. PBMP

Sadness of the Gorges. Meng Chiao, *Chinese.*

"Above the gorges, one thread of sky." PLT, *tr. by* A. C. Graham

Sadness of the Sea, The. William Carlos Williams. ColAP

Sae let the Lord be thankit. (LL) Grace at Kirkudbright. Robert Burns. NTP; OxBSP

Safari to Bwagamoyo. Bwagamoyo. Lebert Bethune. PoBA

Safe. James Walker. AYFP; OBCP

Safe-Conduct. Ingeborg Bachmann, *German.* PoSu, *tr. by* Daniel Huws

Safe from the wolf's [*or* wolves] black jaw, and the dull ass's [*or* Asses] hoof[e]. (LL) An Ode To Himself. Ben Jonson. BeJo; CABP; HAP; NOBE; NOSC; OxAEP-1; PoEL-2; SCGP; SeCP

Safe in firelight sit. (LL) Safe. James Walker. AYFP

Safe in their Alabaster Chambers. Emily Dickinson. APN-2; AmPP; NAAL-1; NAWM-2; NOBA; OxBA; PAR; RaBo; WPE

("Ah, what sagacity perished here!") (LL) NAAL-3; NoP-4; PoPoPo

Safe upon the solid rock the ugly houses stand. Second Fig. Edna St. Vincent Millay. NALW; NoP-4; PoA

Safety. Rupert Brooke. EnLoPo *Fr.* 1914.

Safety-Clutch. Ambrose Bierce. APN-2; OBAL *Fr.* The Devil's Dictionary.

Safety deposit box, The. Dead Letters. Frank Manley. Poetr

Safety light seeps, The. The Summer My Mother Fell in Love and Wanted to Leave My Father. Adora Phillips. CMAP

Sag', wo ist dein schönes Liebchen. Heinrich Heine, *German.* AWP, *tr. by* James Thomson

Saga. Maxine W. Kumin. AFr

Saga. Andrey Andreievich Voznesensky, *Russian.* TCRP, *tr. by* William Jay Smith *and* Vera Dunham

Saga of Gisli, The. *Unknown, Icelandic.* OBVE, *tr. by* George Johnston

Sagacity. William Rose Benét. MoAmPo

Sage and the ordinary man both have bodies, The. A Poem on Buddha's Begging Bowl—For Hui-ku, His Holiness Ming. Hsü Pen, *Chinese.* CoBLCP, *tr. by* Jonathan Chaves

Sage Counsel. Sir Arthur Thomas Quiller-Couch. NBLV

Sage has the Six Classics, The. Hsieh Chin. *Fr.* What Does the Little Boy Love? CoBLCP, *tr. by* Jonathan Chaves

Sage high, Four then. Chinese Temple. Sándor Weöres, *Hungarian.* CEEP, *tr. by* Emery E. George

Sage in Unison, The. Harold Stewart. NOBAu

Sage lectured brilliantly, The. Stephen Crane. MeMAP

Sage nor saint nor soldier—these were not. At the Monument to Pierre Louÿs. Richard Howard. EOEF; VCAP

Sage Philosophy. Richard Jago. ECEV *Fr.* Edge-Hill; or, The Rural Prospect Delineated and Moralised.

Sagebrush (*Artemisia*) is of the sunflower family, or Compositae. It is. Earrings Dangling and Miles of Desert. Gary Snyder. APSN *Fr.* Mountains and Rivers without End: The Market.

Sagesse. Hilda Doolittle.

"Or is it a great tide that covers the rock-pool." WPoS

"You look at me, a hut or cage contains." NOCV

Sagesse. Paul Verlaine, *French.*

"Sky is up above the roof, The." AWP, *tr. by* Ernest Dowson

"Slumber dark and deep." AWP, *tr. by* Arthur Symons

Sagest of women, even of widows, she. Byron. NOBL; PeLV *Fr.* Canto the First. NAEL-2; OAEL-2; PoE *Fr.* Don Juan.

Sagging Bough, The. Louis Untermeyer. BXAP

Sagimusume: The White Heron Maiden. Jonny Kyoko Sullivan. WPOW

Saginaw Song, The. Theodore Roethke. NBLV; RB

Sah gimme ah wuk nah. Wukhand. Paul Keens-Douglas. HCP; PBCV

Sahara. Coventry Patmore. EBVV *Fr.* The Angel in the House.

Sahara to America, The. Aleksei Eliseievich Kruchyonykh. PFTM, *tr. by* Bruce McClelland

Said. George Starbuck. OBAL

Said a boastful young student from Hayes. Limerick. Frank Richards. PeLi

Said a diffident lady named Drood. Limerick. *Unknown.* PeLi

Said a dreadfully literate cat. Limerick. Conrad Potter Aiken. PeLi

Said a fair-headed maiden of Klondike. Limerick. Langford Reed. PeLi

Said a famous old writer called Fender. Limerick. Victor Gray. PeLi

Said a fervent young lady of Hammels. Limerick. Morris Gilbert Bishop. PeLi

Said a foolish young lady of Wales. Limerick. Langford Reed. PeLi

Said a frog on a log. *Unknown.* BoTP

Said a girl in green Mansfield Park. Limerick. E. O. Parrott. PeLi

Said a gloomy young fellow called Fart. Limerick. Victor Gray. PeLi

Said a God-fearing lady called Whitehouse. Limerick. Roger Woddis. PeLi

Said a herring one day to a sole. Limerick. Stanley J. Sharpless. PeLi

Said a luscious young lady called Wade. Limerick. *Unknown.* PeLi

Said a maid: "I will marry for lucre." Limerick. *Unknown.* PeLi

Said a Marxist who stood on the pier. Limerick. W. H. G. Price. PeLi

Said a medical student, unmanned. Limerick. Allan M. Laing. PeLi

Said a parson, addressing his flock. Limerick. W. J. Strachan. PeLi

Said a practical thinker: "One should." Limerick. Frank Watson. PeLi

Said a pupil of Einstein: "It's rotten." Limerick. C. F. Best. PeLi

Said a Tripper: "O joy, to have found." Limerick. Thomas Thorneley. PeLi

Said a wife to her husband near Scole. Limerick. Ida Thurtle. PeLi

Said Abner, "At last thou art come! Ere I tell, ere thou speak." Saul. Robert Browning.

Said active priest, "My work has increased." There Is None to Help. Chad Walsh. *Fr.* The Psalm of Christ. TrCP

Said / Agatha Christie to. George Starbuck. OBCoV

Said an ape as he swung by his tail. Limerick. *Unknown.* PeLi

Said an elderly Bishop called Greville. Limerick. "Little Billee." PeLi

Said an eminent, erudite ermine. Limerick. *Unknown.* PeLi

Said an erudite sinologue: "How." Limerick. R. J. P. Hewison. OBCoV; PeLi

Said Arnold to Arthur Hugh Clough. Limerick. Victor Gray. PeLi

Said Dorothy Hughes to Helen Hocking. William Jay Smith. KaS

Said Fading-leaf to Fallen-leaf. Fading-Leaf and Fallen-Leaf. Richard Garnett. EBVV

Said Freud: "I've discovered the Id." Limerick. Frank Richards. PeLi

Said God, "You sisters, ere ye go." Hope and Despair. Lascelles Abercrombie. OBMV

Said Harry Fat to Holyoake. The Private Conference of Harry Fat. James Keir Baxter. PeLV

Said, I, Oh, give me simplicity. Rural Simplicity. Henry James Byron. NOBL

Said Isolde to Tristan: "How curious!" Limerick. Conrad Potter Aiken. PeLi

Said Jerome K. Jerome to Ford Madox Ford. Mutual Problem. William Cole. OBAL; OBCoV

Said King Pompey, the emperor's ape. Dame Edith Sitwell. BWW; UV

Said lady once to lover. The Three Bushes. W. B. Yeats. EBNV

Said Little Boy Blue. W. S. Brownlee. PeLi

Said Mario Praz to Mario Pei. Miniature Dialogue. Edmund Wilson. OBCoV

Said Marlowe: "Bay City's a drag." Limerick. Peter Alexander. PeLi

Said Mars when entangled with Venus. Limerick. Mary Holtby. PeLi

Said Miss Farrow, on one of her larks. Limerick. *Unknown.* PeLi

Said Nelson at his most la-di-da-di. Limerick. A. Cinna. PeLi

Said Old Father William: "I'm humble." Limerick. Conrad Potter Aiken. PeLi

Said Old Gentleman Gay, "On a Thanksgiving Day." A Good Thanksgiving. "Marian Douglas." PoLF

Said Old Nick: "Mister Lewis and me." Limerick. M. Cassell. PeLi

Said Orville to Wilbur "Hold tight!" Limerick. Stanley J. Sharpless. PeLi

Said Paisley: "I've given up hope." Limerick. Frank Richards. PeLi

Said Philip Sidney, buttoning his jerkin. Scène de Boudoir. Edmund Wilson. OBCoV *Fr.* Easy Exercises in the Use of Difficult Words.

Said philosopher-physicist Jeans. Limerick. R. C. Owen. PeLi

Said Plato: "The things that we feel." Limerick. Basil Ransome-Davies. PeLi

Said Powell: "Don't call me insane." Limerick. Roger Woddis. PeLi

Said, Pull her up a bit will you, Mac, I want to unload there. Reason. Josephine Miles. InPK-6; NALW; NoAM; PFE; Poetr; TAP

Said Queen Isabella of Spain. Limerick. *Unknown.* PeLi

Said Tebbitt: "I don't understand 'em." Limerick. Gerry Hamill. PeLi

Said Tennyson: "Yes, *Locksley Hall's*." Limerick. Victor Gray. PeLi

Said the boy driving home towards Clere. Limerick. Ida Thurtle. PeLi

Said the Canoe. Isabella Valancy Crawford. NOBC

Said the chief of the marriage feast to the groom. The Wedding Feast. Edgar Lee Masters. ChIV-2

Said the Chinese philosopher, Lin. Limerick. Len. PeLi

Said the Duchess of Alba to Goya. Limerick. *Unknown.* PeLi

Said the Duck to the Kangaroo. The Duck and the Kangaroo. Edward Lear. OxBChV

Said the Englishman: "W'at's all this bloomin' wow?" Foreigners at the Fair. Fred Emerson Brooks. OBAL

Said the famous philosopher, Russell. Limerick. Victor Gray. PeLi

Said the first little chicken. Five Little Chickens. *Unknown.* BoTP; CTAV; TLR

Said the lady, Can you do. Question. Langston Hughes. APSN

Said the Lion: "On music I dote." The Musical Lion. Oliver Herford. OBCA

Said the Lion to the Lioness—'When you are amber dust'. Heart and Mind. Dame Edith Sitwell. LW; OxBTC; TwCP

Said the mythical King of Algiers. Limerick. *Unknown.* PeLi

Said the newly-weds staying near Kitely. Limerick. *Unknown.* PeLi

Said the Queen to her favourite ghillie. Limerick. A. Cinna. PeLi

Said the Robin to the Sparrow. Overheard in an Orchard. Elizabeth Cheney. CTV

Said the Rose. George Henry Miles. BLPA

Said the Stoic, tormented by gout. Limerick. Thomas Thorneley. PeLi

Said the Undertaker to the Overtaker. Tweedledee and Tweedledoom. Ogden Nash. OBCoV

Said the vet as he looked at my pet. Limerick. Frank Richards. PeLi

Said the Wind to the Moon, "I will blow you out." The Wind and the Moon. George Macdonald. NOxBChV

Said Uncle Sam to Harry Fat. Harry Fat and Uncle Sam. James Keir Baxter. PeLV

Said Wellington: "What's the location." Limerick. Frank Richards. PeLi

Said Wilbur Wright, "Oh, this is grand." Limerick. Frank Richards. PeLi

Said Wittgenstein: "Don't be misled!" Limerick. Peter Alexander. PeLi

Said Zwingli to Muntzer. How to Start a War. Phyllis McGinley. OBSV

Saies, "Come here, cuzen Gawaine so gay." King Arthur and King Cornwall. *Unknown.* ESPB

Saigon Bar Girls, 1975. Yusef Komunyakaa. MT

Sail, A. Mikhail Yuryevich Lermontov, *Russian.* AWP, *tr. by* Max Eastman

"Sail, A! a sail! Oh, whence away." Heart's Content. *Unknown.* PoLF

Sail Away. Robert Adamson. CBAP

Sail before the morning breeze. The Archipelago. Melville. APN-2

Sail is up, Fortune ruleth our helm, The. John Skelton. NoSic *Fr.* The Bouge of Court.

Sail, Monarchs, rising and falling. Roots and Branches. Robert Duncan. FTOS; VGW

Sail of Claustra, Aelis, Azalais. The Alchemist. Ezra Pound. CMoP

Sail On, O Ship of State. Henry Wadsworth Longfellow. *See* The Ship of State.

Sail Peacefully Home. Simeon Grigoryevich Frug, *Yiddish.* TrJP

Sailed. Aaron Shurin. FTOS

Sailing. Henrik Nordbrandt, *Danish.* VCWP, *tr. by* Henrik Nordbrandt and Alexander Taylor

Sailing along the Tai Stream from Stone Bridge to the Foot of Mo-ho Peak. Wang Shih-chieng, *Chinese.* SuSp, *tr. by* Chang Yin-nan *and* Lewis C. Walmsley

Sailing at Dusk from T'u-sung. Wu Wei-yeh, *Chinese.* SuSp, *tr. by* Chang Yin-nan *and* Lewis C. Walmsley

Sailing at Night on Flowing-sand River. Lin Hung, *Chinese.* SuSp, *tr. by* Irving Y. Lo

Sailing from the United States. Stanley Moss. VGW

Sailing Home from Rapallo. Robert Lowell. HCAP; PoPoPo; TAP ("Corpse / was wrapped like *panettone* in Italian tinfoil, The.") (LL) FiLi

Sailing Homeward. Chan Fang-sheng, *Chinese.* AWP; ChiP; FaBoCh, *tr. by* Arthur Waley

Sailing in the boat when the tide runs high. Rose in the Garden. *Unknown.* AmFP

Sailing of the Fleet, The. Noel Marcus Francis Corbett. NSI

Sailing on the Lake to the Ching River. Lu Yu, *Chinese.* OHPC, *tr. by* Kenneth Rexroth

Sailing Pine, The; the Cedar, proud and tall. Kinds of Trees to Plant. Edmund Spenser. *Fr.* Wood Of Error. AEP

Sailing, Sailing. Gray Burr. NYBP

Sailing the Back River. Dave Jeddie Smith. MT

Sailing to an Island. Richard Murphy. PBCIP

Sailing To Bien Hoa. Bruce Weigl. CDa

Sailing To Byzantium. W. B. Yeats. APAD; CABP; CMoP; ClHu; GTBS-P; GrIP; HAP; HeIP-4; HoPM; IIP; ImPo; InPK-6; InPS-3; LiTM; MoBrPo; MoP; NAEL-2; NAWM-2; NIP-4; NOBE; NoAM; NoP-4; OAEL-2; OBMV; OxBTC; PoE; PoPoPo; PoRA; RaBo; SAGP; SCGP; SoSe-8; TFi; TIRV; TOF; UnPo; WeW-3

Sailing to Italy—fitting out / commissioning—to see the friends. Crinagoras, *Greek.* GrAn, *tr. by* Alistair Elliot

Sailing upon the River. George Crabbe. OBNC *Fr.* The Borough.

Sailor. Langston Hughes. PoA

Sailor, The. Raymond Roseliep. HA

Sailor, The. Sylvia Townsend Warner. OBMV

Sailor and His Bride, The. *Unknown.* AmFP

Sailor and the Shark, The. Paul Fort, *French.* OBMV, *tr. by* Frederick York Powell

Sailor, ask not whose this tomb. *Unknown, Greek.* GrAn, *tr. by* Peter Jay

Sailor Boy, The. Tennyson. OxBoS; SCGP

Sailor Boy's Song. *Unknown.* CA

Sailor leaning on the rail thinks of home, The. One Day. Ray Mathew. NOBAu

Sailor pops upon the Royal Pair, A. George III and the Sailor. "Peter Pindar." NOEC *Fr.* The Royal Tour, and Weymouth Amusements. OxBoLi

Sailor rescued from his buffeting, The. Alcuin, *Latin.* MLL, *tr. by* Helen Waddell

Sailor, we all stare at you. Wynyard Sailor. Ray Mathew. CBAP

Sailor who had Served in the Slave-Trade, The. Robert Southey. Ro *Fr.* Poems.

"Sailorman, I'll give to you." The Silver Penny. Walter De la Mare. CMoP; NOxBChV; NTP; OBMV

Sailors. Louis Simpson. NYBP

Sailors' Alphabet, The. *Unknown.* AmFP

Sailor's Carol. Charles Causley. OBCP; PeECV

Sailors come / To the drum. Hornpipe. Dame Edith Sitwell. FaBoMo; GTBS-P; OAEL-2 *Fr.* Façade.

Sailor's Grave, The. Eliza Cook. BLPA

Sailor's Harbor. Henry Reed. MoBrPo

Sailors, I wish you safety on sea and land. *Unknown, Greek.* GrAn, *tr. by* Peter Jay

Sailor's Return, The. *Unknown.* OxBoLi

Sailors' Song. Thomas Lovell Beddoes. OxAEP-2 *Fr.* Death's Jest Book. (Sea Song.)

Sailors there are of gentlest breed. Commemorative of a Naval Victory. Herman Melville. HAP; UnPo

Sailor's trade is a weary life, A. The Rocky Island. *Unknown.* AmFP

Sailor's Wife, The. William Julius Mickle. *See* There's Nae Luck about the House.

Sails falshing to the wind like weapons. Robert Earl Hayden. *See* Middle Passage.

Sails flashing to the wind like weapons. Middle Passage. Frederick Douglass. CrDW

Sainless. Douglas Young. FaBoTC

Saint. George Mackay Brown. FaBoTC *Fr.* Runes from a Holy Island.

Saint. Robert Graves. CMoP

St Agnes' Eve—Ah, bitter chill it was! The Eve of St Agnes. Keats. CABP; EBNV; EP; FHYEP; HAP; HoPM; ImPo; NAEL-2; NOBRP; NoP-4; OAEL-2; OBNC; OBNV; OxAEP-2; PoE; PoEL-4; PoLF; Poetr; Ro; TFi; TRP

St Andrew's Day, blind November fumbling. Robert Greacen. PNI

St. Andrew's Voyage to Mermedonia. *Unknown.* AnOE, *tr. by* Charles W. Kennedy *Fr.* Andreas.

Saint Anfaidh walked alone. Saint, Bird, Angel. *Unknown, Irish*. TIRV, *tr. by* Brendan Kennelly

St. Anthony and His Pig; a Cantata. Frederick Forrest. NOEC

St. Anthony's Township. Gilbert Sheldon. CH

St. Anzas IX. B. P. Nichol. FTOS

St. Anzas VI. B. P. Nichol. FTOS

St. Aubin d'Aubigne. Paul Dehn. OBWP

Saint Augustine. Joseph Mary Plunkett. TIRV

Saint Augustine, thy praise was sung by one. Richard Henry Wilde. APN-1 *Fr.* Hesperia.

St. Bartholomew's Night. Bella Akhatovna Akhmadulina, *Russian*. TCRP, *tr. by* Albert C. Todd

Saint, Bird, Angel. *Unknown, Irish*. TIRV, *tr. by* Brendan Kennelly

Saint Bridget? Or her near and dear? (LL) The Giveaway. Phyllis McGinley. PBMP; PoRA

Saint Bridget was / A problem child. The Giveaway. Phyllis McGinley. PBMP; PoRA

St. Bridget's Cross. Anne Hartigan. CIP-2

Saint Called "Truth," A, *mod. by* Donald Attwater. William Langland. NOCV *Fr.* The Vision of Piers Plowman.

St Cecilia's Day Epigram. Peter Porter. PeLV

Saint Coleman's Song for Flight/ An Ite Missa Est. Padraic Fiacc. PNI

Saint Colm-Cille and the Cairn of Farewell. John Irvine. TIRV

Saint Columba. Lionel Pigot Johnson. TIRV

St. Crispin's Day. Shakespeare. *See* Henry V before Agincourt.

St. Dunstan, as the story goes. *Unknown*. OxNR

St. Eustace. Derek Mahon. BiHa

Saint Fiacre. John Irvine. TIRV

St Francias came to me alive last night and tole me. I Dream of St. Francis. Peter Orlovsky. BB

Saint Francis and the Birds. Seamus Heaney. NTP; TIRV

Saint Francis and the Sow. Galway Kinnell. AFr; ChAP; FYAP; InPK-6; RB

St. George. Charlie Walker. AmFP

Saint George's Fields are fields no more. New Buildings. Horace, *Latin*. OBCVT, *tr. by* James Smith

Saint Govan. A. G. Prys-Jones. OBWVE

Saint Harmony, many / years I have stript. Freedom and Discipline. Hayden Carruth. MoNo

Saint Harmony my patroness. Paul Goodman. VGW

St. Helena Lullaby, A. Rudyard Kipling. EBEV; FaBoCh; OBMV; PoEL-5

St. Isaac's Church, Petrograd. Claude McKay. NAAAL; PoBA

St. James Infirmary. *Unknown*. AmFP

Saint Jerome and his lion. Leonardo Da Vinci's. Marianne Moore. NYBP

Saint Jerome and his Lion. *Unknown*. PeP

St Jerome in his study kept a great big cat. Saint Jerome and his Lion. *Unknown*. PeP

Saint Jerome lived with a community. Elegy for Wright & Hugo. Norman Dubie. NoAM

St. John. Bible, *N.T. See also* John *and* Bible, John.

"I am the true vine, and my Father is the husbandman." OBVE

"In the beginnin o aa things the Wurd wis there ense." FaBoVe

John 3; But Men Loved Darknesse Rather than Light. ChIV-2, *tr. by* Richard Crashaw

St. John. Jorge Luis Borges.

John 1:14; And the Word became flesh and dwelt among us. GI

St. John. Mary Elizabeth Fullerton.

John 14:1–2. GI

St. John. Gail Holst-Warhaft.

John 1:1 and 14. GI

St. John. Nina Kossman.

John 13:21–30; When Jesus had thus said, he was troubled. GI

St. John. Howard Nemerov.

John 3:1–15; Now there was a man. GI

St. John. Pier Paolo Pasolini.

John 12:24–25; Truly, truly, I say to you. GI

St. John. Rilke.

John 11:30–44; Now Jesus had not yet come to the village. GI

John 20:11–18; But Mary stood weeping outside the tomb. GI

John 2:1–12; On the third day there was a marriage. GI

Saint John Baptist. William Drummond, of Hawthornden. GTBS-P; NOBE; OBEV; OxAEP-1; TrCP

(For the Baptist.) ChIV-2; SCGP

Saint John did lean on Jesus's breast. For Saint John's Day. Luke Wadding. TIRV

Saint John divinely counsels us. The Praise of Godly Love Out of 1 John. John Hall. ChIV-2

St John of the Cross: Song of the Soul That Is Glad to Know God by Faith. Roy Campbell. PeECV

St John of the Cross: Songs of the Soul in Rapture. Roy Campbell. PeECV

St. John tells how, at Cana's wedding-feast. A Wedding Toast. Richard Wilbur. ITG

St. John, whose love indulg'd my labours past. The First Epistle of the First Book of Horace Imitated. Alexander Pope.

Saint Judas. James Wright. CoAmPo; GI; LCAP-2; NOBA; WeT

Saint-Just: his name seems stolen from the Missal. Saint-Just 1767-93. Robert Lowell. FaBoMo

St. Kilda-Wren, 1957. Colin Simms. NBrp

St. Lawrence and the Saguenay. Charles Sangster. Thousand Islands, The. NOBC

Saint-Lô. Samuel Beckett. NOIV

St. Louis Blues. William Christopher Handy. CrDW; NAAAL

("But a red headed woman make a boy slap his papa down.") (LL) NAAAL

("I hate to see de evenin' sun go down.") NAAAL

St. Louis Blues. *Unknown*. BkSV

St. Louis / such a colored town / a whiskey. Nappy Edges (A Cross Country Sojourn). Ntozake Shange. BlSi

St. Luke. Bible, *N.T. See also* Luke *and* Bible, Luke.

"And it came to pass in those days, that there went out a decree from Caesar Augustus." NAWM-1

"And there were in the same country shepherds abiding in the field." PChr

Blessed be the Paps which Thou hast Sucked. BXAP; ChIV-2; NOSC, *tr. by* Richard Crashaw

"Feare not, litle flocke, for it is your fathers good pleasure to give you the kingdome." OBVE

Luke 7; She Began To Wash His Feet with Teares and Wipe Them with the Haires of Her Head. NOSC, *tr. by* Richard Crashaw

Magnificat, The. BoWoP; OBVE

("And Marie said, My soule doth magnifie the Lord.") OBVE

"Then drew near unto him all the publicans and sinners." NAWM-1

St. Luke. W. H. Auden.

Luke 23:26–38; And as they led him away. GI

St. Luke. Jorge Luis Borges.

Luke 23:39–43; One of the criminals. GI

St. Luke. Bertolt Brecht.

Luke 2:8–20; And in that region there were shepherds. GI

St. Luke. Ernesto Cardenal.

Luke 16:1–9; He also said to the disciples. GI

St. Luke. T. S. Eliot.

Luke 2:21–40; And at the end of eight days, when he was circumcised. GI

St. Luke. Robert Frost.

Luke 16:19–26; "There was a rich man." GI

St. Luke. Louise Glück.

Luke 2:1–7; In those days a decree went out from Caesar Augustus. GI

St. Luke. Alec Derwent Hope.

Luke 24:36–49; As they were saying this, Jesus. GI

St. Luke. Anna Kamienska.

Luke 10:38–42; Now as they went on their way. GI

Luke 1:26–38; In the sixth month the angel Gabriel. GI

St. Luke. Czeslaw Milosz.

Luke 5:1–11; While the people pressed upon him. GI

St. Luke. Stephen Mitchell.

Luke 10:25–37; And behold, a lawyer. GI

St. Luke. Eric Pankey.

Luke: 24:13–32; That very day two of them. GI

St. Luke. Rilke.

Luke 1:39–56; In those days Mary arose. GI

Luke 15:11–19; And he said, "There was a man." GI

St. Luke. Edwin Arlington Robinson.

Luke 15:20–32; And he arose and came. GI

St. Malachy. Thomas Merton. VGW

Saint Malcolm. Jewel C. Latimore. BPo

St. Mark. Bible, *N.T. See also* Mark.

"Aa this while, Peter wis doun ablò i the yaird." FaBoVe

"And he said, So is the kingdome of God." OBVE

And he said, So soule doth magnifie the Lord. OBVE

St. Mark. Czeslaw Milosz.

Mark 5:21–43; And when Jesus had crossed. GI

St. Mark. Boris Pasternak.

Mark 14:26–42; And when they had sung. GI

Saint Martha. Anna Kamienska, *Polish*. GI, *tr. by* David Curzon and Grazyna Drabik

St. Martin and the Beggar. Thom Gunn. MoBS

Saint Mary Magdalene. Richard Crashaw. GeHe; MeLP; OBEV; SeCP

(The Weeper.) ESCV; OAEL-1; OBEV; SeCP

Saint Mary Magdalene or the Weeper. ChIV-2

St. Matthew. Bible, *N.T. See also* Matthew *and* Bible, Matthew.
"And seeing the multitudes, he went up." NAWM-1
"In the end of the sabbath, as it began to dawn toward the first day of the week." NAWM-1
"No man can serve two masters." OBVE
Parable of the Good Seed, The. InPK-6
Prayer of-Lord. PeSAV, *tr. by* Sol T. Plaatje
("Father our, he-who is at-the-height, name Thy let-it-be.") PeSAV
"Then one of the twelve, called Judas Iscariot." NAWM-1
"When morning has come, all the chief priests and elders of the people." NAWM-1
St. Matthew. Philip Appleman.
Matthew 1:18–25: Now the birth of Jesus Christ took place. GI
St. Matthew. Jorge Luis Borges.
Matthew 25:14–30; "For it will be as when a man." GI
Matthew 5:1–12; Seeing the crowds, he went up on the mountain. GI
St. Matthew. René Daumal.
Matthew 27:11–24; Now Jesus stood before. GI
St. Matthew. T. S. Eliot.
Matthew 2:1–12; Now when Jesus was born. GI
St. Matthew. Jacob Glatstein.
Matthew 5:38–48; "You have heard that it was said, 'An eye'." GI
St. Matthew. Donald Hall.
Matthew 21:18–22; In the morning. GI
St. Matthew. Julia Hartwig.
Matthew 2:16–18; Then Herod, when he saw. GI
St. Matthew. Zbigniew Herbert.
Matthew 27:3–10; When Judas, his betrayer, saw. GI
St. Matthew. Gail Holst-Warhaft.
Matthew 5:13; You are the salt of the earth. GI
Matthew 5:27–30; You have heard that it was said. GI
St. Matthew. Ted Hughes.
Matthew 27:45–56; Now from the sixth hour there was darkness. GI
St. Matthew. Anna Kamienska.
Matthew 19:16–24; And behold, one came up to him. GI
St. Matthew. Karl Kirchwey.
Matthew 8:20; And Jesus said to him. GI
St. Matthew. Philip Larkin.
Matthew 10:1. GI
St. Matthew. D. H. Lawrence.
Matthew 6:7–15; "And in praying do not heap up empty." GI
St. Matthew. Desanka Maksimovic.
Matthew 22:15–22; Then the Pharisees went and. GI
St. Matthew. Czeslaw Milosz.
Matthew 28:1–6; Now after the sabbath. GI
Matthew 4:1–11; Then Jesus was led up by the spirit. GI
St. Matthew. Stephen Mitchell.
Matthew 13:1–9; That same day Jesus. GI
St. Matthew. Boris Pasternak.
Matthew 21:1–11. GI
Matthew 26:47–56; While he was still speaking, Judas came. GI
St. Matthew. Rilke.
Matthew 26:17–29. GI
Matthew 27:57–61; When it was evening, there came a rich man. GI
St. Matthew. Edwin Arlington Robinson.
Matthew 22:1–14; And again Jesus spoke to them. GI
St. Matthew. Theodore Roethke.
Matthew 7:1–2; "Judge not, that you be not." GI
St. Matthew. Richard Wilbur.
Matthew 8:28–34; And when he came to the other side. GI
St. Matthew. W. B. Yeats.
Matthew 24:15–31. GI
Matthew 28:16–20; Now the eleven disciples went to Galilee. GI
St. Matthew; He also told them a parable. William Carlos Williams. Luke 6:39. GI
St Merri district, The. Robert Desnos, *French.* MFP, *tr. by* Martin Sorrell
Saint Nicholas. Marianne Moore. NYBP; WPE
Saint Patrick. Sir Shane Leslie. TIRV
St Patrick's Breastplate. Saint Patrick, *Irish.* FaBoCh, *tr. by* Frances Alexander
Saint Patrick's Breastplate. *Unknown.* NOIV
Saint Patrick's Breastplate; or, The Deer's Cry. Saint Patrick, *Irish.* TIRV, *tr. by* Kuno Meyer
Saint Patrick's Day, 1973. Wendy Rose. CDW
St. Patrick's Dean, your country's pride. To Dr. Swift on His Birthday, 30th November 1721. Esther Johnson. EnLoPo
St. Paul. Thomas Merton. ChIV-2

St. Paul's Steeple. *Unknown.* ACTP
St. Paulinus to his Wife Therasia. Paulinus of Nola, *Latin.*
"Come my true Consort in my Joyes and Care!" OBCVT, *tr. by* Henry Vaughan
St. Peregrinus' Cancer. Judith Hall. BAP-95
St. Peter at the Gate. Joseph Bert Smiley. BLPA
St. Peter Claver. Toi Derricotte. LTA; PBCAP
St. Peter once: "Lord, dost Thou wash my feet?" Christina Rossetti. ChIV-2; NOCV
Saint Peter sat by the celestial gate. The Vision of Judgment. Byron. FHYEP; OAEL-2; OBSV; OxAEP-2; OxBSn; OxBoLi
St. Peter stood guard at the golden gate. St. Peter at the Gate. Joseph Bert Smiley. BLPA
St. Peter's Day was celebrated by St. Brendan at sea. The Fish at Mass. *Unknown, Latin.* BIrV, *tr. by* J. F. Webb
St. Philip and St. James. Christopher Smart. NOCV; NOEC
Saint Pumpkin. Nancy Willard. LCAP-2
Saint Ras. Anthony McNeill. PBCV
St. Roach. Muriel Rukeyser. GLP
St Sava's Spring. Vasco [*or* Vasko] Popa, *Serbo-Croatian.*
Life of St Sava, The. PoSu, *tr. by* Anne Pennington
St Sava's Forge. PoSu, *tr. by* Anne Pennington
St Sava's Journey. PoSu, *tr. by* Anne Pennington
St. Simeon Stylites. Tennyson. NOBVV; OAEL-2
St. Sophia. John Fuller. DiPo
St. Stephen and King Herod. *Unknown. See* Seynt Stevyn and Herowdes.
Saint Stephen had an angel's face. For Saint Stephen's Day. Luke Wadding. TIRV
St. Stephen's Day. Patric Dickinson. OBCP
Saint Stephen's Day. John Hewitt. CIP-2
St. Stephen's is a stage. The Patriot's Progress. Horace Twiss. UV
Saint Steven Was a Clerk. *Unknown. See* Seynt Stevyn and Herowdes.
St. Swithin's Day, if thou dost rain. *Unknown.* LB
St. Thomas. Christopher Smart. ChIV-2
St. Thomas Aquinas thought. Vulture. Kenneth Rexroth. NNaP *Fr.* A Bestiary. OBAL
St. Thomas's Day is past and gone. *Unknown.* OxNR
St. Ursanne. Michael Roberts. LiTM
St. Valentine. Marianne Moore. NYBP
St. Valentine's Day. Wilfrid Scawen Blunt. EnLoPo; GLoP *Fr.* The Love Sonnets of Proteus.
("Today, all day, I rode upon the Down.") GLoP
Saint Valentine's Day. Coventry Patmore. OBNC
St. Vincent's. W. S. Merwin. VCAP
Saint Wears a Halo, The. "Peter." BoTP
Saint, who overlaps. John Logan. CRP *Fr.* A Cycle for Mother Cabrini.
Sainte-Chapelle. John Taggart. FTOS
Sainte Lucie. Derek Walcott.
"Pomme arac." FaBoVe
Sainthood. Cristoir O'Flynn. TIRV
Saints and Strangers. Andrew Hudgins. RA
Saints are gathering at the real, The. The Confirmers. A. R. Ammons. TAP
Saints are in such wise from God's own godhead drunk, The. The More Abandoned, The More Divine. "Angelus Silesius." GePo, *tr. by* George C. Schoolfield *Fr.* The Cherubical Wanderer.
Saint's Bridge. Lola Ridge. WPE
Saints have adored the lofty soul of you. Charles Hamilton Sorley. NSI; PeFWW *Fr.* Two Sonnets. MoBrPo
Saints, I give myself up on. Two Hundred and Nineteenth Chorus. Jack Kerouac. NeAP *Fr.* Mexico City Blues.
Saints in Glory, We Together. Nehemiah Adams. AH
Saints of Jazz are playing, The. Yevgeny Yevtushenko. SeSe
Sakhara. Robert Arthur Douglas Ford. NOBC
Saki, for God's love, come and fill my glass. Hafiz. AWP, *tr. by* Richard Le Gallienne *Fr.* Odes.
Salaam Alaikum. *Unknown.* PoLF
Salaam, / to everyone, salaam. Mangesh Padgaonkar, *Marathi.* OMIP, *tr. by* Vinay Dharwadker
Salad, A. Sydney Goodsir Smith. NBLV
(Recipe for a Salad.) OBCoV
Salad Days. Susan Musgrave. NoAM
Salad La Raza. Janet Campbell Hale. VoR
Salad of greens! Salad of greens! The Universal Favorite. Carolyn Wells. NBLV
Salami. Philip Levine. NNaP; NOBA; TAP; TRP
Salamis. Lawrence Durrell. NYBP

Salaziennes, Les. Auguste Lacaussade, *French.*
  "My lips from this day forgot how to smile." TTY
Sale. Josephine Miles. WPE
Sale began—young girls were there, The. The Slave Auction. Frances Ellen Watkins Harper. APN-2; BPo; ColAP; ISC; TTY
Sale of Saint Thomas, The. Lascelles Abercrombie.
  "They say the land is full of apes, which have." NSI
Sale of Smoke, A. Roberta Spear. AmPA
Sale of Souls. Adah Isaacs Menken. CBWP-1
Sale of the Pet Lamb, The. Mary Howitt. CH
Salem. Robert Lowell. AiP; Son
Sales Talk for Annie. Morris Gilbert Bishop. NBLV
Salesgirl. Henrikas Radauskas, *Lithuanian.* CEEP, *tr. by* Jonas Zdanys
Salesman is an it that stinks excuse, A. E. E. Cummings. NoAM; OxBA; Poetr
Salina sauntering in a shade. The Slattern. Sarah Dixon. ECWP
Salisbury; the Cathedral Close. Coventry Patmore. *See* The Cathedral Close.
Sallad, The. Virgil, *Latin.* OBCVT, *tr. by* William Cowper
Sally Brown. *Unknown.* AmFP
Sally go round the sun. *Unknown.* OxNR
Sally Goodin. *Unknown.* AmFP
Sally, having swallowed cheese. Cruel, Clever Cat. Geoffrey Taylor. FaBoEE
Sally in Our Alley. Henry Carey. AWP; BoLoP; FaBoBe; GLoP; GTBS-P; NOBE; OBEV; OxAEP-1
  (Ballad of Sally in Our Alley, The.) NOEC
Sally is gone that was so kindly. Ha'nacker Mill. Hilaire Belloc. FaPoR; MoBrPo; OxBTC; RB
Sally is the laundress, and every Saturday. The Dolls' Wash. Juliana Horatia Ewing. OxBChV
Sally, Sally Waters. *Unknown.* OxNR
Sally, Sally Waters, sprinkle in the pan. *Unknown.* LiLi
Sally Simpkin's Lament, [*or* John Jones's Kit-Cat-astrophe]. Thomas Hood. CABP; CBNP
Sally: Twelfth Street. Naomi Long Madgett. NBV
Sally's Garden. *Unknown.* AmFP
Salmo: Para El. Ramon Garcia. BAP-96
Salmon. Jorie Graham. NAmP90
Salmon came to search for a dancer, The. Song of a Salmon Dancer. *Unknown. Fr.* Dances and Songs of the Winter Ceremonial. APN-2, *tr. by* Franz Boas
Salmon Courage. Marlene Philip. PBCV
Salmon Drowns Eagle. Malcolm Lowry. MoCV
Salmon lying in the depths of Llyn Llifon, The. The Ancients of the World. Ronald Stuart Thomas. OPOU; RB
Salome. Ai. NoAM
Salome. Charles Lamb. ChIV-2
Salon d'Automne. Stevie Smith. WPN
Salonika Campaign. Owen Rutter. NSI *Fr.* The Song of Tiadatha.
Salonikan Grave. Rudyard Kipling. *Fr.* Epitaphs of the War [1914–1918]. OBWP
Saloon is gone up the creek, The. Hemmed-in Males. William Carlos Williams. PoRA *Fr.* A Folded Skyscraper.
Saloon is sometimes called a Bar, The. The Bar. *Unknown.* PoToHe
Salopian student of Greek, A. Limerick. Martin Fagg. PeLi
Salsabîl. Jamîl, *Arabic.* ArPe, *tr. by* Omar S. Pound
Salt. George Barlow. GT
Salt. Viktor Fiodorovich Bokov, *Russian.* TCRP, *tr. by* Bernard Meares
Salt. Linda Gregerson. PUP-19
Salt. Anne Hartigan. CIP-2
Salt. Yusef Komunyakaa. UnSA
Salt, The. May Swenson. DeD *Fr.* Poet to Tiger. GLP
Salt creek mouths unflushed by the sea. The South Coast. William Everson. NeAP
Salt Garden, The. Howard Nemerov. OBGa
Salt grass silent of hooves, the lake stinks. Vestiges. Basil Bunting. PFTM *Fr.* Vestiges.
Salt over the shoulder. Airy Hall's Exits. Frederick D'Aguiar. IICP
Salt Pork, The. Robert Clayton Casto. HeIP-4
Salt Riot, The. Pavel Nikolaevich Vasilyev, *Russian.*
  Wedding, The. TCRP, *tr. by* David Macduff
Salt Sea, The. Chongsam Kim, *Korean.* CKP, *tr. by* Jaihiun Kim
Salt Water Story. Richard Hugo. NAAL-2; NoAM
Salt wave sings, The. Fingernail Sunrise. Vernon Watkins. NYBP
Saltmarsh on the horizon, The. The Estuarial Republic. Douglas Dunn. FaBoMo

Salt'peanuts! / De-dop! (LL) Children's Rhymes. Langston Hughes. BPo; InPS-3
Saltpetre sucked up the cigarette with. Paul Brown. NBrP *Fr.* De Rebus.
Salty spray glistens on the fence, The. Sleep, My Beloved. Yevtushenko, *Russian.* TCRP, *tr. by* Geoffrey Dutton *with* Tina Tupkina-Glaessner
Saluste du Bartas' Devine Weekes. Joshua Sylvester.
  "Cunning Painter, that with curious care, The." PBRV
Salutation, A. Louise Imogen Guiney. APN-2
Salutation. Robert Herrick. CavPo; ChIV-2
Salutation. Ezra Pound. HeIP-4; MeMAP; MoAmPo; NOBA; OxBA; TAP; VGW
Salutation [*or* Salutations], The. Thomas Traherne. ESCV; EnlH; GeHe; NOCV; SeCP
  ("These little limbs.") NoP-4
Salutation of the Dawn, The. *Unknown.* PoLF
Salutation the Second. Ezra Pound. NOBA; OxBA
Salutation to the Dawn. Kalidasa, *Sanskrit.* PoToHe
Salutations. Shanmuga Subbiah, *Tamil.* OMIP, *tr. by* T. K. Doraiswamy
Salutations to Fernando Pessoa. Allen Ginsberg. BAP-95
Salute. Oliver Pitcher. PoBA
Salute. James Schuyler. FYAP; NeAP
Salute, Friends! Vladimir Salimon, *Russian.* TCRP, *tr. by* Albert C. Todd
Salute from the Fleet, A. Alfred Noyes.
  Search-Lights, The. NSI
Salute the last and everlasting day. Ascension [*or* Ascension]. Donne. *Fr.* La Corona. ChIV-2; ESCV; Son *Fr.* Holy Sonnets.
Salute to Icheke. Okogbule Wonodi. PBMAP
Salute we must, nor strangers, kin, or friends. (LL) Salutation. Robert Herrick. CavPo; ChIV-2
Salute Your Partner. *Unknown.* AmFP
Saluting strange new women and grandfather clocks. (LL) Peekaboo, I Almost See You. Ogden Nash. EBEvV; PeLV; PoLF
Salvador Dali. David Gascoyne. OxBTC; SPE
  (In Defence of Humanism.) FaBoMo
Salvation. George Ella Lyon. CrSp
Salvation Army lass, The. Lola Ridge. WPE *Fr.* Ward X.
Salvation belongeth unto the Lord: thy blessing is upon thy people. Selah. (LL) Psalm 3. Bible, *O.T.* OBVE
Salvation comes by Christ alone. Evening Thought, An [: Salvation by Christ with Penetential Cries]. Jupiter Hammon. CrDW
Salvation lassie named Claire, A. Limerick. *Unknown.* PeLi
Salvation to all that will is nigh. Annunciation. Donne. TrCP *Fr.* La Corona. ChIV-2; ESCV; Son *Fr.* Holy Sonnets.
Salve! Thomas Edward Brown. OBEV
Salve Deus Rex Judaeorum. Emilia Lanier.
  Eves Apologie. BoWoP
  From Salve Deus Rex Judaeorum. NoP-4
  "Now Pontius Pilate is to judge the cause." NALW; NOSC
  "Our Mother *Eve,* who tasted of the Tree." PBRV
Salve Regina. *Unknown.* MiEL
Sam. Lucille Clifton. MoLi; UnSA
Sam. Walter De la Mare. MoBrPo
Sam and Bob. William Barnes. PeVV, *tr. by* Hualing Nieh, (*Eclogue*) *Fr.* The Best Man in the Vield.
Sam Bass. *Unknown.* AS; AmFP
Sam Hall. *Unknown.* AmFP
Sam, Sam, the butcher man. *Unknown.* ACTP; TLR
Sam Smiley. Sterling Brown. NAAAL
Sam, The Sportsman. Mother Goose. OxNR
  ("And knocked it off his head, head, head.") (LL) LB
  ("And the drake flew away with a quack, quack, quack.") (LL) ReMoGo
Samantha is my. Samantha Is My Negro Cat. William J. Harris. GT
Same as ever to the sight, The. (LL) The Miller's wife had waited long. Edwin Arlington Robinson. CMoP; HAP; MeMAP; NAAI -2; NoAM; NoP-4; Poetr; TAP; WeW-3
Same as from the start?, The. (LL) Common Dust. Georgia Douglas Johnson. PoBA; TTY
Same Corpse, The. Kojo Laing. HBAPE
Same Cottage—But Another Song, of Another Season. Max Beerbohm. UV
Same Gesture, The. John Montague. BIrV; PNI
Same in Blues. Langston Hughes. APSN; InPS-3; SAGP; SSLK *Fr.* Lenox Avenue Mural. HoPM
Same Inside, The. Anna Swirszczynska, *Polish.* BLT, *tr. by* Czeslaw Milosz *and* Leonard Nathan
Same leaves over and over again, The! In Hardwood Groves. Robert Frost. HAP

Same look which she turned when he rose!, The. (LL) Believe me, if all those endearing young charms. Thomas Moore. Ro

Same Month They Bombed Cambodia, The. Amy Uyematsu. OpBo

Same old crossing, same old boat. Gold Braid. A. A. Milne. NSI

Same Old Jazz, The. Philip Whalen. NeAP

Same Old Way, The. "Igor Severyanin," *Russian*. TCRP, *tr. by* Bernard Meares

Same place; never / stop!, The. (LL) Ho Ho Ho Caribou. Joseph Ceravolo. PmAP

Same Side of the Canoe, The. Alda do Espírito Santo, *Portuguese*. PBWP, *tr. by* Allan Francovich *and* Kathleen Weaver

Same Trouble with Beauty You've Always Had, The. Michael Atkinson. BAP-93

Sam'el Down vrom Lon'on. William Barnes. PeVV

Samela. Robert Greene. GBL; NOBE; OBEV *Fr.* Menaphon.

  (Doron's Description of Samela.) PoEL-2

  ("For beautie, wit, and matchlesse dignitie / yeeld to *Samela*.") (LL) PBRV

  ("Like to *Diana* in her Summer weede.") PBRV

Sammy Lou of Rue. Revolutionary Petunias. Alice Walker. BlSi

Samos. James Merrill. HCAP *Fr.* Scripts for the Pageant.

Sampler from Haworth. Frances Minturn Howard. WPE

Sampson Imitated. Benjamin Franklin. *See* Jack and Roger.

Sam's World . Sam Cornish. MBE

Samson Agonistes. Milton. FHYEP; OAEL-1; PoEL-3

  All Is Best. NOBE; NOSC; OBEV

  "Blind among enemies, O worse than chains." KSG

  Blindness of Samson, The. ImPo

  "But see here comes thy reverend Sire." EBEV

  "But what is strength without a double share." ChIV-1

  Consolation. LBC

  "Feast and noon grew high, and Sacrifice, The." EBEV

  "Let me obtain forgiveness of thee, Samson." EBEV

  Samson before the Prison in Gaza. FaBoPV

  Samson's Complaint. NOSC

  "Wilt thou then serve the Philistines with that gift." EBEV

Samson Agonistes. Ogden Nash. OBCoV

Samson, Our Hero. David Avidan, *Hebrew*. IP, *tr. by* Warren Bargad *and* Stanley F. Chyet

  General Truths. IP, *tr. by* Bargad, Warren and Stanley Chyet

Samson to His De [*or a*] lilah. Richard Crashaw. ChIV-1

Samson wasn't the brightest. The Moral. David Avidan. *Fr.* Samson, Our Hero. IP, *tr. by* Warren Bargad *and* Stanley F. Chyet

Samson's Hair. Natan Zach, *Hebrew*. IP, *tr. by* Warren Bargad *and* Stanley F. Chyet

Samuel Allen. *Unknown*. AmFP

Samuel Brown. Phoebe Cary. APN-2; OBAL

Samuel Hearne in Wintertime. John Newlove. NOBC

Samuel Sewall. Anthony Hecht. LiTM; NBLV; PeLV; PoRA; TwCP

  ("Samuel Sewall, in a world of wigs.") CoAmPo

Samuel's Prayer. John Keble. ChIV-1

San Antonio de Padua. W. S. Di Piero. PaTW

San Diego Poem, A. Simon J. Ortiz. CDW

San Francisco Company, The. *Unknown*. AmFP

San Francisco County Jail Cell B-6. Conyus. PoBA

San Francisco/New York. August Kleinzahler. WWSi

San Francisco Poem. John Logan. NNaP

San Fransisco. Miguel Algarin. PmAP

San Fransisco Ward. Charles Plymell. EC3

San Gloria. Thomas MacDermot.

  "Dark foreboding haunts me lest I die, A." PBCV

San Joaquin Valley Poems: 1969. Ed Webster. BAP-95

San Juan: 1979. Cheryl Clarke. CPO

San Martino del Carso. Giuseppe Ungaretti, *Italian*. PeFWW, *tr. by* David McDuff *and* Jon Silkin

San Miniato. Oscar Wilde. TIRV

San Sepolcro. Jorie Graham. HCAP; PoPoPo; VCAP

  ("Nimble-fingered / finding all of the stops.") (LL) PoPoPo

Sanct Christopher II ("Sanct Christopher's a muckle sanct and strang"). Robert Garioch, *after the Italian of* Giuseppe Belli. OBVE

Sanctification. Joseph Ibn Abithur, *Hebrew*. TOF, *tr. by* David Goldstein

Sanctity. Patrick Kavanagh. BIrV; NOIV; NoP-4

Sanctuary. Johannes Bobrowski, *German*. CEEP, *tr. by* Ruth Mead *and* Matthew Mead

Sanctuary. Bruce Boyd. NeAP

Sanctuary. Donald Davidson. FuPo

Sanctuary. Clifford Dyment. PoA

Sanctuary, The. Ford Madox Ford. PoA

Sanctuary. Dorothy Hewett. CBAP

Sanctuary. Dorothy Parker. NBLV

Sanctuary. Judith Wright. WPE

Sanctuary. Elinor Wylie. BoWoP; MoAmPo

Sanctuary of Spirits. Alistair Campbell.

  Against Te Rauparaha. PeNZ

Sanctuary should exist on earth. To Any M.F.H F. H. Vita Sackville-West. WPN

Sand. Nina Cassian, *Romanian*. PoSu, *tr. by* Nina Cassian *and* Naomi Lazard

Sand, The. May Swenson. DeD *Fr.* Poet to Tiger. GLP

Sand birds fly east, they flee the spread net. Following the Rhymes of Bamboo Branch Songs in Response to Yüan Po-chang. Yü Chi, *Chinese*. CoBLCP, *tr. by* Jonathan Chaves

Sand Creek. Charles G. Ballard. UnPo; VoR

Sand dollars in shallow waves. Naming the Shells. Judith C. Root. CMAP

Sand Dunes. Robert Frost. MoAmPo

Sand is a fine grit, The. Dry Root in a Wash. Simon J. Ortiz. HATNAP

Sand joins them together, / Enlisted on the other front, The. Kenneth Slessor. *See* Beach Burial.

Sand modeller always began by heaping the sand, The. The Entertainer. Bruce Beaver. NOBAu

Sand Nigger. Lawrence Joseph. LTA; WWSi

  ("Against the stranger.") (LL) LTA

Sand of Palestine, The. T. Hodgkinson. NSI

Sand of the Desert in an Hour-Glass. Henry Wadsworth Longfellow. NCAP

Sand one meets in Palestine's an all-pervading sediment, The. The Sand of Palestine. T. Hodgkinson. NSI

Sand pyramid, size of a child, each September. The Ant Hill. Cynthia Zarin. NoP-4

Sand-Quarry with Moving Figures. Muriel Rukeyser. MoLi; NoP-4

Sand Roads. Marge Piercy.

  Development, The. NBLV

Sand Seer, The. Niyi Osundare. PBMAP

Sand wet and cool, The. Dennis Brutus. GT

Sandal and garment of yellow and lotus garlands upon his body of blue. Jayadeva, *Sanskrit*. TAL, *tr. by* George Keyt *Fr.* The Gita Govinda.

Sandal Mountain. Hsieh Chin, *Chinese*. CoBLCP, *tr. by* Jonathan Chaves

Sandalwood comes to my mind. Carl Rakosi. *See* Sandlewood comes to my mind.

Sandalwood the hawser-ties, silk the puller ropes. Song to the Tune "Perching Crows." Wu Wei-yeh, *Chinese*. CoBLCP, *tr. by* Jonathan Chaves

Sandbags of sugar cannot conceal the gloomy fact. And the World was Calm. Chris Wallace-Crabbe. BMAP

Sandhill People. Carl Sandburg. CMoP

Sandinista Avioncitos. Lawrence Ferlinghetti. PiM

Sandlewood comes to my mind. Carl Rakosi. ChIV-1; KSG *Fr.* Exercises in Scriptural Writing.

Sandlot Days. M. P. Flynn. CTV

Sandpile Town. Aileen Fisher. CTV

Sandpiper. Elizabeth Bishop. AFr; AiP; HeIP-4; NYBP; RB; TOF

Sandpiper, The. Celia Laighton Thaxter. ImGa

  ("Thou, little sandpiper, and I?") (LL) CTAV

Sandpiper, The. Celia Laighton Thaxter. CTV; FaBoBe; OBCA; OxBChV; PWR

Sandra: At the Beaver Trap. Michael S. Harper. NoAM

Sands at my feet, The. (LL) Venus Transiens. Amy Lowell. CPO

Sands of Dee, The. Charles Kingsley. CH; EBEvV; EBVV; FaPoR; OxAEP-2 *Fr.* Alton Locke.

Sandwich Man, The. Ron Padgett. CoAmPo

Sandwiches. David Donnell. NoAM

Sandy cat by the Farmer's chair, The. Summer Evening. Walter De la Mare. MoBrPo

Sandy he belongs to the mill. *Unknown*. OxNR

Sandy Kildandy. *Unknown*. OxNR

Sanford Barney. *Unknown*. AmFP

Sang. John Hollander. *See* Swan and Shadow.

Sang. Robert MacLellan. OxBS

Sang a maiden in a meadow. Reunited. Henrietta Cordelia Ray. CBWP-3

Sang of the Outlaw Murray, The. *Unknown*. IBB

Sang Solomon to Sheba. Solomon to Sheba. W. B. Yeats. CMoP; KSG

Sang unmeanig down the stream. (LL) Orpheus. Yvor Winters. NOBA; VGW

Sangaree Kill de Captain. *Unknown*. PBCV

Sango. Gabriel Gbadamosi.

"Sango's son came down to the river." HBAPE

Sanitized Sonnets, The. Peter Porter.

"Now it's in all the novels, what's pornography to do?" OBCoV

Sank through easeful. The Diver. Robert Earl Hayden. AmPP; BPo; NAAAL

Sanquhar, whom this earth could scarce contain. William Drummond of Hawthornden. FaBoEE

Sans Culotte. Pavel Antokolsky, *Russian.* TCRP, *tr. by* Bernard Meares

Sans Equity and sans Poise. Confucius. *Fr.* Yung Wind. CTC, *tr. by* Ezra Pound

Sans teeth, sans eyes, sans taste, sans everything. (LL) The Seven Ages of Man. Shakespeare. APAD; EBEvV; FaPoR; ImPo; PoLF; RB; SAGP; UV

Sanskrit. Jayanta Mahapatra. VCWP

Santa. Anne Sexton. AFr *Fr.* The Death of the Fathers.

Santa Anna *or* Ana came storming, as a storm might come. The Defense of the Alamo. Joaquin Miller. FaBoBe

Santa Barbara Earthquake, The. *Unknown.* AmFP

Santa Claus. Walter De la Mare. PChr

Santa Claus. Christopher Vernon Hassall. OxBTC

Santa Claus. Dom Moraes. NoAM

Santa Claus. Howard Nemerov. HAP

Santa Claus. *Unknown.* BoTP

Santa Fe. Joy Harjo. NAmP90; PoPoPo

("And space is as solid as the bronze statue of St. Francis, the fox breaking through the lilacs, my invention of this story, the wind blowing.") (LL) PoPoPo

Santa Fe, still the one, The. American Trains. Reginald Gibbons. GM

Santa Fe Trail. Barbara Guest. FTOS; NeAP; PoM

Santhal Poems, 1. Bishnu De, *Bengali.* OMIP, *tr. by* Samir Dasgupta *and* Stephen N. Hay

Santo Domingo, DemRep, March 1965. War Poem. Simon J. Ortiz. CDa

Santorin. James Elroy Flecker. FaBoTw; OBMV

Santos and Stones. J. Delayne Barber. LoHo

Saon of Acanthus. Callimachus, *Greek.* AWP, *tr. by* John Addington Symonds

Sap, The. Henry Vaughan. ESCV

Sap is going out of my fingers, The. In Autumn. Charles Hubert Sisson. PeECV

Sap rises from the sodden ditch. For Jane Myers. Louise Glück. FaBoWP

Sap weeps, The. The Why the Wind Comes. Hirini Melbourne. PeNZ

Saphire (Metamorpho's Chick). Joe Rosenblatt. MoCV

Sapho and Phao. John Lyly.

Vulcan's Song. EBEV

(Song in Making of the Arrows, The.) NoSic

Sapho To Philaenis. Donne. RACG *Fr.* Elegies.

Sapho's Ode out of Longinus. Sappho, *Greek.* OBCVT, *tr. by* William Lisle Bowles

Saplings of the green-tipped birch, The. Never Tell. *Unknown, Welsh.* OBWVE, *tr. by* Anthony Conran

Sapphic Fragment, *fr. the Greek of* Sappho. Thomas Hardy. OBCVT; OBVE

(Achtung.) CTC

Sapphics. George Canning *and* John Hookham Frere. *See* The Friend of Humanity and the Knife Grinder.

Sapphics. Wyndham Lewis. NOBL; PeLV

Sapphics. Sappho, *Greek.* OBCVT; PoEL-5, *tr. by* Algernon Charles Swinburne

Sapphics. Sir Philip Sidney. SiPS *Fr.* Arcadia.

Sapphics: At the Mohawk-Castle, Canada. Thomas Morris. NOEC

Sapphics for Patience. Annie Finch. FFC

Sapphire, The. W. S. Merwin. PoA

Sapphire's lyre styles. Muse & Drudge. Harryette Mullen. BAP-94

Sappho. Catullus, *Latin.* AWP, *tr. by* William Ellery Leonard *Fr.* Carmina.

("And feels a temporary death.") (LL) OBCVT, *tr. by* Byron

("Equal to Jove that youth must be.") OBCVT, *tr. by* Byron

(Translation from Catullus: Ad Lesbiam.) OBCVT, *tr. by* Byron

Sappho. Jack Cope. PeSA

Sappho. Marie-Madeleine, *German.* CPO, *tr. by* Lillian Faderman, Brigitte Eriksson *and* Frankie Hucklenbroich

Sappho. Plato, *Greek.* GrAn, *tr. by* Peter Jay

Sappho. Christina Rossetti. VWP

Sappho. James Wright. NoAM

Sappho Burns Her Books and Cultivates the Culinary Arts. Elizabeth Moody. ECWP

"Sappho, if you do not come out." Sappho, *Greek.* BoWoP, *tr. by* Willis Barnstone

Sappho kisses softly. Paulus Silentiarius, *Greek.* InMo, *tr. by* Sam Hamill

Sappho; or, The Resolve. Charlotte Dacre. NOBRP

Sappho to Philaenis. Donne. *See* Sapho To Philaenis.

Sappho's Reply. Rita Mae Brown. OxWW

Sappho's Song. Letitia Elizabeth Landon. VWP *Fr.* The Improvisatrice and Other Poems.

Sara in Her Father's Arms. George Oppen. NNaP

Sarah. Delmore Schwartz. ChIV-1; KSG

Sarah Byng Who Could Not Read and Was Tossed into a Thorny Hedge by a Bull. A Cautionary Tale. Hilaire Belloc. CBNP

("Of Sarah Byng the tale is told.") CBNP

(Sarah Byng.) NoAM

Sarah Cynthia Sylvia Stout Would Not Take the Garbage Out. Shel Silverstein. OBCA

Sarah Hazard's Love Letter. John Ellis. NOEC

Sarah's Choice. Eleanor Wilner. NMM-2

Sarajevo. Lawrence Durrell. GTBS-P

Sardanapalus. Henry Howard, Earl of Surrey. SiPS

("Thassyrrans king, in peas with fowle desyre.") AAS

Sardines seem to get out of hand. Limerick. Leslie Johnson. PeLi

Sardis. William Cowper. ChIV-2 *Fr.* Olney Hymns.

Sardis, the old city of Gyges and Alyattes. Bianor, *Greek.* GrAn, *tr. by* Richard Evans

Saris go by me from the embassies, The. The Woman at the Washington Zoo. Randall Jarrell. CoAP; HAP; HCAP; LiTM; OxBC; TAP; TwCP; UnPo; VCAP

Sarmèd, whom they intoxicated from the cup of love. Quatrain. Sarmèd the Yahud, *Persian.* TrJP, *tr. by* David Shea

Sarolla's women in their picture hats. Lawrence Ferlinghetti. NeAP; PoM *Fr.* Pictures of a Gone World.

Sarpedon of the mighty war. (LL) A Dirge for McPherson. Herman Melville. CBCWP; PoEL-5

Sarpedon's Speech. Homer, *Greek.* NOSC, *tr. by* George Chapman *Fr.* The Iliad.

(". . . as ye see a mountaine Lion fare.") OBCVT, *tr. by* George Chapman

(Sarpedon to Glaucus.) OBCVT, *tr. by* George Chapman

Sarpedon's Speech to Glaucus. OBVE, *tr. by* Sir John Denham

(Sarpedon's Speech to Glaucus in the 12th of Homer.) OBCVT, *tr. by* Sir John Denham

("Thus to *Glaucus* spake.") OBCVT, *tr. by* Sir John Denham

Sasha and the Poet ("Sasha: I dreamed you and he"). Jean Valentine. VGW

Sassafras. Barbara Guest. FTOS

Sat a damsel on the hillside. The Messengers. Henrietta Cordelia Ray. CBWP-3

Sat down. Michael McClintock. HA

Sat for three days in a white room. Heroin. Jim Carroll. OBCoV

Sat in the pub. The Diet. Maureen Burge. BrRo

Sat in the sun. Virginia. Elouise Loftin. PoBA

Sat singing spirituals to sons. (LL) Ghetto Lovesong—Migration. Carole C. Gregory Clemmons. PoBA

Sat up all night and lugged at the moon. Critter. W. M. Ransom. CDW

Sat Will & Kate. Those Troublesome Disguises. Jonathan Williams. NeAP

Satan ("He ceased; and Satan stayed not to reply"). Milton. *Fr.* Book II. FHYEP; NAEL-1; OxAEP-1 *Fr.* Paradise Lost.

Satan ("His pride / Had cast him out from Heaven, with all his host"). Milton. *Fr.* Book I. FHYEP; NAEL-1; OAEL-1; OxAEP-1 *Fr.* Paradise Lost.

Satan and His Host. Milton. *Fr.* Book I. FHYEP; NAEL-1; OAEL-1; OxAEP-1 *Fr.* Paradise Lost.

Satan and the Fallen Angels. Milton. *See* Satan's Summons.

Satan as Rebel-Liberator. Milton. *Fr.* Book I. FHYEP; NAEL-1; OAEL-1; OxAEP-1 *Fr.* Paradise Lost.

Satan Beholds Adam and Eve in Eden. Milton. *Fr.* Book IV. OAEL-1 *Fr.* Paradise Lost.

Satan Defiant. Milton. *Fr.* Book I. FHYEP; NAEL-1; OAEL-1; OxAEP-1 *Fr.* Paradise Lost.

Satan has enough in hell. (LL) For a Mouthy Woman. Countee Cullen. ChIV-1; OBAL; PoBA

Satan Is on Your Tongue. George Barker. MoBrPo *Fr.* Secular Elegies.

Satan Journeys to the Garden of Eden. Milton. *Fr.* Book IV. OAEL-1 *Fr.* Paradise Lost.

Satan Says. Sharon Olds. PBCAP

Satan tempts Eve. Milton. FaBoSE *Fr.* Paradise Lost.

Satan Views the World. Milton. *See* Satan ("He ceased; and Satan stayed not to reply").

Satan's a Liah. *Unknown.* AS

Satan's Adjuration. Milton. *Fr.* Book I. FHYEP; NAEL-1; OAEL-1; OxAEP-1 *Fr.* Paradise Lost.

Satan's Journey. Milton. NOSC *Fr.* Book II. FHYEP; NAEL-1; OxAEP-1 *Fr.* Paradise Lost.

Satan's Legions and the Beech Leaves of the Casentino. Milton. *Fr.* Book I. FHYEP; NAEL-1; OAEL-1; OxAEP-1 *Fr.* Paradise Lost.

Satan's Soliloquy. Milton. *Fr.* Book IV. OAEL-1 *Fr.* Paradise Lost.

Satan's Summons. Milton. NOSC *Fr.* Book I. FHYEP; NAEL-1; OAEL-1; OxAEP-1 *Fr.* Paradise Lost.

Satchmo. Melvin Beaunearus Tolson. BPo; NAAAL

Sated with home, of wife, of children tired. Cui Bono? Horace Smith *and* James Smith.

Sather Gate Illumination. Allen Ginsberg. NeAP

Satia Te Sanguine. Swinburne. PeVV

Satie, at the End of Term. Simon Curtis. NOBL; PeLV

Satiety. Theodore Wratislaw. ADE

Satin-clad, with many a pearl. Stevie Smith. OxBC

Satin Doll. David Wojahn. PBCAP

Satire, A. John Oldham.
"On Butler who can think without rage." OBSV

Satire 1. Donne. *See* A London Street.

Satire 2. Donne. *See* The Poet Turned Lawyer.

Satire 3. Donne. EBEV; ESCV; FHYEP; MeLP; NAEL-1; OAEL-1; PoE; PoEL-2 *Fr.* Satires.
("Kind pity chokes my spleen brave scorn forbids.") FMP; FSCP; NoP-4
("Power from God claym'd, then God himselfe to trust.") (LL) PBRV
(Religion.)
(Satyre 3.) PBRV
(Satyre [*or* Satire] III.) MeLP; OxAEP-1
(Search for True Religion, The.) NoSic
("Though Truth and Falsehood be.") NOBE

Satire 4. Donne. OBSV *Fr.* Satires.
". . . Then, as if he would have sold." PBRV

Satire 5. Donne. OBSV *Fr.* Satires.

Satire [*or* Satyre] against [Reason and] Mankind, A. John Wilmot, 2d Earl of Rochester. CABP; NOSC; OAEL-1; OBSV; PoEL-3; SCV
(Homo Sapiens.) NOBE

Satire against Reason and Mankind, A. Grace Buchanan Sherwood. NoP-4

Satire on an Inconstant Lover, A. Jonathan Swift. CBLP

Satire on Charles II, A. John Wilmot, 2d Earl of Rochester. NOSC; PeLV
"Restless he rolls about from whore to whore." OBSV

Satire on London, A. Henry Howard, Earl of Surrey. AAS; SiPS

Satire on Paying Calls in August. Ch'ëng Hsiao, *Chinese.* ChiP, *tr. by* Arthur Waley

Satire on the O'Haras, A. Tadhg Dall O'Huiginn. NOIV

Satire upon the Licentious Age of Charles II. Samuel Butler.
"How silly were those sages heretofore." NOBL

Satire VIII. Joseph Hall. ChIV-2

Satires. Donne.
London Street, A. NoSic
Poet Turned Lawyer, The. OBSV
Satire 3. EBEV; ESCV; FHYEP; FSCP; MeLP; NAEL-1; OAEL-1; PoE; PoEL-2
("Kind pity chokes my spleen brave scorn forbids.") FMP; FSCP; NoP-4
("Power from God claym'd, then God himselfe to trust.") (LL) PBRV
(Religion.)
(Satyre 3.) PBRV
(Satyre [*or* Satire] III.) MeLP; OxAEP-1
(Search for True Religion, The.) NoSic
("Though Truth and Falsehood be.") NOBE
Satire 4. OBSV
Satire 5. OBSV

Satires, The. Horace, *Latin.*
Horatian Canons of Friendship, The. OBCVT, *tr. by* Christopher Smart

Satires. Juvenal, *Latin.*
"But of all the plagues, the greatest is untold." OBSV, *tr. by* Dryden
Celestial Wisdom. AWP, *tr. by* Samuel Johnson
"Give store of days, good Jove, give length of years." OBSV, *tr. by* Henry Vaughan
Hannibal ("Produce the urn that Hannibal contains"). OBVE, *tr. by* William Gifford
Hannibal ("Put Hannibal i' th' scale"). OBVE, *tr. by* Henry Vaughan
Hannibal ("Throw Hannibal on the scales, how many pounds"). OBVE, *tr. by* Robert Lowell
"In Saturn's reign, at Nature's early birth." OAEL-1; OBSV; OBVE, *tr. by* Dryden

"'Life! length of life!' for this, with earnest cries." OBVE, *tr. by* William Gifford
"Return we to the dangers of the night." OAEL-1, *tr. by* Dryden
Sejanus ("How many men are killed by power, by power"). OBVE, *tr. by* Robert Lowell
Sejanus ("Some ask for envy'd pow'r; which publick hate"). OBVE, *tr. by* Dryden
Sejanus ("What crowds by envied power, the wish of all"). OBVE, *tr. by* William Gifford
"When the last Flavius, drunk with fury, tore." OBVE, *tr. by* William Gifford

Satires. John Marston.
Cynic Satire, A. NoSic
Humours. NoSic

Satires. John Oldham, *after the French of* Boileau.
"Of all the creatures, in the world, that be." OBVE

Satires. Persius, *Latin.*
Prologue to the First Satire. AWP, *tr. by* Dryden

Satires. Sir Thomas Wyatt.
"My mother's maids [*or* maydes] when they did sew [*or* sowe] and spin [*or* spynne]." AAS; NoSic; SiPS
Myn owne John poyntz sins ye delight to know. PBRV
("Mine own John Poins, since ye delight to know.") NoP-4
("Thou shalt be judge how I do spend my time.") (LL) NoP-4
("Thou shalt be Judge how I do spend my tyme.") (LL) PBRV
To Sir Francis Brian. SiPS

Satires. Edward Young. ECEV
On Women ("Britannia's daughters"). ECEV
On Women ("Lavinia is polite"). ECEV

Satires of Circumstance in Fifteen Glimpses. Thomas Hardy.
At a Watering-Place. CMoP
At the Altar-Rail. MoBrPo
At the Draper's. MoBrPo; OxBM
By Her Aunt's Grave. MoBrPo; PFE
In Church. InPK-6; MoBrPo; SCV
In the Cemetery. InPK-6; Son
In the Moonlight. NoAM
In the Nuptial Chamber. InPK-6
In the Restaurant. MoBrPo
In the Room of the Bride-Elect. InPK-6

Satirical Elegy on the Death of a Late Famous General, A. Jonathan Swift. HoPM; NBLV; NoP-4; OBSV; PBMP; PoE; PoEL-3; Poetr
(On the Death of a Late Famous General.) PFE
("Turned to that dirt from whence he sprung.") (LL) NoP-4
("Turned to that dust from whence he sprung.") (LL) PBMP

Satirical Romance, A. Sister Juana Inés de la Cruz, *Spanish.* PBWP, *tr. by* Judith Thurman

Satisfaction Coal Company, The. Rita Dove. LCAP-2; WWSi

Satisfaction—is the Agent. Emily Dickinson. NOBA

Satori. Gayl Jones. BlSi

Saturated. Aaron Shurin. FTOS

Saturday Afternoon at the Movies. John Logan. NNaP

Saturday afternoon. The barracks is almost empty. The Soldier. David Ferry. WeT

Saturday Afternoon, When Chores Are Done. Harryette Mullen. ISC

Saturday, April 26, 1973. A Poem to Galway Kinnell. Etheridge Knight. NNaP

Saturday Market. Charlotte Mew. WPE

Saturday Morning. Marilyn Hacker. CPO

Saturday mornings, before. The Bait. Eric Chock. OpBo

Saturday Night. Clark Coolidge. FTOS

Saturday Night. Toi Derricotte. DeD

Saturday Night. Sir Alan Patrick Herbert. NBLV

Saturday Night. Langston Hughes. MoAmPo

Saturday Night. Anne Hussey. WeT

Saturday Night. I Can't Get Started. Ai. GT

Saturday Night. Antigone Kefala. CBAP

Saturday Night. Victoria Wood. OBCoV

Saturday night in August when, A. Last Meeting. Robert Penn Warren. DiPo

Saturday Night in the Parthenon. Kenneth Patchen. SPE

Saturday Night in the Village. Giacomo Leopardi, *Italian.* OBVE, *tr. by* Robert Lowell

Saturday night she comes in her little boat. Music on the Water. George Johnston. MoCV

Saturday Night Worship. Ann Carhart. CrSp

Saturday on Seventh Street. The Fields. W. S. Merwin. HCAP

Saturday Review, The. Dora Greenwell. EBVV

Saturday, Sunday. Mother Goose. ReMoGo

Saturday: The Small-Pox. Lady Mary Wortley Montagu. BWW; ECWP; NOEC; PEW; WPE *Fr.* Six Town Eclogues.

("Ye operas, circles, I no more must view!") PEW

Saturday, the sorrow's killing me. To My Dead Sister. Momcilo Nastasijevic, *Serbo-Croatian.* HSix, *tr.* by Charles Simic

Saturday Tub, The. Mary Gilmore. NOBAu

Saturday's Child. Countee Cullen. LiTM; NAAAL; PoBA

Saturn. Norma Cole. PT

Saturn. Günter Grass, *German.* AF, *tr.* by Michael Hamburger *and* Christopher Middleton

Saturn. Keats. OBNC *Fr.* Hyperion. OAEL-2; Ro

Saturn. Sharon Olds. RaBo

Saturn Sinking. Sándor Weöres, *Hungarian.* CEEP, *tr.* by Emery E. George

Saturnian Age, the Golden! Herman Melville. *See* Afterward.

Saturn's Three Sons. Robert Hayman. NOSC *Fr.* Owen's Epigrams.

Satyr. Charles Gullans. PoA

Satyr, A. John Oldham.

London. NOSC

"One night, as I was pondering of late." NOSC

Satyr, A. Elizabeth Tipper. KTR *Fr.* Pilgrim's Viaticum; or, The Destitute, But Not Forlorn.

Satyr by Diodorus, A. Plato the Younger, *Greek.* GrAn, *tr.* by G. R. H. Wright

Satyr, Cunnilinguet: To Herman Melville. Charles Martin. RA

Satyr O never ask how I came to this place. Michael Drayton. AEP *Fr.* The Muses' Elysium X.

Satyre 3. Donne. *See* Satire 3.

Satyre [*or* Satire] III. Donne. *See* Satire 3.

Satyretericall Character of a Proud Upstart, A. John Saffin. SCAP

Satyricon. Petronius Arbiter, *Latin.*

"Fate brought three men to birth." MLL, *tr.* by Helen Waddell

"From the high Alpine pass." MLL, *tr.* by Helen Waddell

"Roman was the victor of the world., The." MLL, *tr.* by Helen Waddell

"Such flowers as Earth our Mother." MLL, *tr.* by Helen Waddell

Satyr's Song. John Fletcher. *Fr.* The Faithful Shepherdess.

Satyr's Song, The ("Softly Gliding as I Go"). John Fletcher. NOSC *Fr.* The Faithful Shepherdess.

Satyrs used to fall for nymphs. Love-Songs, at Once Tender and Informative. Samuel Hoffenstein. OBAL

Satyrus Peregrinans. William Rankins.

"By this time long-gowned Lumen walked abroad." OBSV

Sauchs in the Reuch Heuch Hauch, The. "Hugh MacDiarmid." NoAM

Saul. Nathan Alterman, *Hebrew.* TrJP, *tr.* by Dov Vardi

Saul. Robert Browning.

Youth. BoTP

Saul. Byron. KSG

Saul did much care and diligence express. Rowland Watkyns. FaBoEE

Saul Re-enthroned. Meir Wieseltier, *Hebrew.* IP, *tr.* by Warren Bargad *and* Stanley F. Chyet

Sauna. Luchezar Elenkov, *Bulgarian.* CEEP, *tr.* by Jascha Kessler *and* Aleksandar Shurbanov

Sauntering home from church we lingered. Mary Ursula Bethell. PeNZ *Fr.* By the River Ashley.

Sauntering the pavement or riding the country by-road, lo, such faces! Faces. Walt Whitman. PoEL-5

Sausage. E. A. Guest. OBAL

Sausalito, / Little Willow. Sausalito Trash Prayer. Lew Welch. BB

Savage servility / slides by on grease, A. Robert Lowell. *See* For the Union Dead.

Savages, The. Josephine Miles. LiTM

Savage's romance, The. New York. Marianne Moore. FaBoA; NAAL-2

Save breed to brave him when he takes thee hence. (LL) Sonnet 12. Shakespeare. AWP; GSo; HeIP-4; InPS-3; NAEL-1; NoSic; OAEL-1; SCGP; Son

Save by the Old Road none attain the new. Coventry Patmore. FaBoEE

Save desiring and a yearning heart. (LL) The Lark. Bernard de Ventadour, *Provençal.* CTC; NNPT, *tr.* by Ezra Pound

Save it all; you do not know. 1915: A Pre-Raphaelite Ending, London. Richard Howard. RACG

Save me from such as me assail, *par.* by Countess of Pembroke, Mary Sidney Herbert. Psalm 59. Bible, *O.T.* NoSic *Fr.* Psalms.

Save of peace alone. (LL) To My Brother: Killed: Hammont Wood: October, 1918. Louise Bogan. AiP; NYBP

Save only that of death. (LL) Prospect. Ambrose Bierce. APN-2; OBAL

Save that to die . . . to die[dye], I leave my love alone. (LL) Sonnet 66. Shakespeare. AWP; CABP; CTC; EBEV; FaBoPV; GTBS-P; HAP;

ImPo; InPS-3; NOBE; NoSic; OAEL-1; OxAEP-1; PFE; PoEL-2; TFi; WeW-3

Save the Boys. Frances Ellen Watkins Harper. AAP; PWR

Save thou, my rose; it is thou art my all. (LL) Sonnet 109. Shakespeare. GTBS-P; NOBE; OBEV; OxAEP-1

Save your douth and your story. (LL) Troy. Agathias, *Greek.* GrAn; OBCVT, *tr.* by Ezra Pound

Save yourself. Run and leave me. I must go back. C. S. Lewis. EBEV *Fr.* Epigrams and Epitaphs.

Saved. Maria Teresa Horta, *Portuguese.* PBWP, *tr.* by Suzette Macedo

Saved. Adah Isaacs Menken. CBWP-1

Saville in Trouble. Albery Allson Whitman. AAP *Fr.* Not a Man and Yet a Man.

Saving the Harvest. Geoffrey Lehmann. CBAP

Savior Is Abducted in Puerto Rico, The. Martín Espada. TRP

Savior! I've no one else to tell. Emily Dickinson. TrCP

Savior looked on Peter. Ay, no word, The. The Look. Elizabeth Barrett Browning. TrCP

Saviour, Sprinkle Many Nations. Arthur Cleveland Coxe. AH

Saviour, Thy Dying Love. Sylvanus D. Phelps. AH

Saviour, Who Thy Flock Art Feeding. William Augustus Mühlenberg. AH

Sâvitrî; or, Love and Death. *Unknown.* TAL, *tr.* by Sir Edwin Arnold *Fr.* The Mahabharata.

Savoir Faire. Claribel Alegría, *Spanish.* VCWP, *tr.* by D. J. Flakoll

Savonarola. Clerihew. Edmund Clerihew Bentley. CBNP *Fr.* Clerihews.

Savonarola ("Savonarola / Declined to wear a bowler"). Edmund Clerihew Bentley. OxBoLi

Savonarola ("Savonarola looks more grim today"). Max Beerbohm. BXAP

Savouring the shade of our teacher's willow. Dog Day Lesson. John Hughes. PNI

Saw a lamb being born. Lamb. Michael Dennis Browne. RaBo

Saw my shadow on the wall. The Shadow Returns. Phillis Levin. RA

Saw the Cloud Lynx. Samuel Makidemewabe, *Cree Indian.* STP, *tr.* by Howard Norman

Saw the glass towers / slip. Violet City: Aspects of the Transitive. Gustaf Sobin. PT

Saw whites clap during a sacred dance. Today Was a Bad Day Like TB. "Chrystos." UnSA

Saw ye aught of my love a-coming from the market? My Love. *Unknown.* ReMoGo

Saw Ye Bonny Lesley. Robert Burns. *See* Bonnie Lesley.

Sawmill. Richard Kenney. NoP-4

Saxifrage is my flower that splits / the rocks. (LL) A Sort of a Song. William Carlos Williams. HoPM; NAAL-2; OxBSP; TAP

Saxon Legend of Language, The. Mary Weston Fordham. AAP; CBWP-2

Saxons of Flint, The. *Unknown, Welsh.* OBWVE, *tr.* by Mary C. Llewelyn

Saxophone turned into a dolphin, The. Albert Ayler: Eulogy for a Decomposed Saxophone Player. Stanley Crouch. PoBA

Say About Seven or Seven-Fifteen. Ogden Nash. FP

Say, "All flesh is grass." *Unknown.* *See* On a Clergyman's Horse Biting Him.

Say, crimson rose and dainty daffodil. A Nosegay. John Reynolds. OBEV

Say, darkeys hab you seen de massa. Kingdom Coming. Henry Clay Work. APN-2

Say, dear Maria! is the modish life. A Familiar Epistle. Ann Murry. WPE

Say, dwarf, for it seems to me. *Unknown.* OBVE, *tr.* by W. H. Auden *and* Paul B. Taylor *Fr.* The Words of the All-Wise.

Say, friend, if all is well still with the bowers. Vidya. PBWP, *tr.* by Daniel H. H. Ingalls *Fr.* The Wanton.

Say Girls in Shoe Ads: "I Go for a Man Who's Tall!" Robley Wilson Jr. PBCAP

Say good-by er howdy-do. Good-by er Howdy-do. James Whitcomb Riley. CTC

Say happiness is possible, or more than possible. On Track. Kathleene West. FFC

Say Hello to John. Sherley Anne Williams. BISi

Say, how shall thoughtless, easy-natured youth. Stanzas Imitated From Psalm CXIX. Thomas, the Elder Warton. ChIV-1

Say, I come tomorrow [*or* to-morrow]. (LL) Westphalian Song. *Unknown, German.* AWP; OBVE, *tr.* by Samuel Taylor Coleridge

Say it and cry aloud. I Am a Negro. Muhammad Al-Faituri, *Arabic.* TTY, *tr.* by Halim El-Dabh

Say it loud, I'm black and I'm proud. James Brown *and* Alfred Ellis. ISC

Say It Now. *Unknown.* *See* Seeds of Kindness.

Say it's an important event like this. Off to Patagonia. Theodore Weiss. TAP

Say itself inside our heads. (LL) Newark. Robert Kelly. MoNo

Say Ja. Tom Mandel. PmAP

Say life is the one-way trip, the one-way flight. Watchmaker God. Robert Lowell. HCAP; SoSe-8

Say, light proceeding edgewise, like a sword. (LL) Gardens No Emblems. Donald Davie. GaP; LiTM; OAEL-2; OBGa

Say, lovely Tory, why the jest. To Miss Eleanor Ambrose on the Occasion of Her Wearing an Orange Lily at a Ball in Dublin Castle on July the 12th. Philip Dormer Stanhope, 4th Earl of Chesterfield. EnLoPo

"Say me, wight in the brom [or broom]." Tell Me, Wight in the Broom. Unknown. MiEL; NAEL-1

Say, mighty Love, and teach my song. Few Happy Matches. Isaac Watts. NOEC

Say Muses, say; who now in those rich fields. Phineas Fletcher. ChIV-1 Fr. The Locusts, or Appolyonists.

Say nay. (LL) The Lover's Appeal. Sir Thomas Wyatt. AAS; EBEvV; EnLoPo; GLoP; GTBS-P; NAEL-1; NoSic; SCGP; SiPS

Say not, because no more you see. On the Death of Mr. Persall's Little Daughter, in the Beginning of the Spring, at Amsterdam. Unknown. NOSC

Say not of beauty she is good. Beauty. Elinor Wylie. NAAL-2; OxBA

Say not of me that weakly I declined. Robert Louis Stevenson. OBNC; PeVV

Say not the age is hard and cold. The Present Age. Frances Ellen Watkins Harper. AAP; PWR

Say not the mermaid is a myth. The Mermaid. Ogden Nash. Spl

Say not the struggle nought [or naught] availeth. Arthur Hugh Clough. APAD; AWP; EBEvV; EBVV; EnVR; FaPoR; GTBS-P; ImPo; NAEL-2; NOBE; NOBVV; NoP-4; NTP; OAEL-2; OBEV; OBNC; PFE; SCGP; TFi

Say of them / They knew no Spanish. To the Veterans of the Abraham Lincoln Brigade. Genevieve Taggard. NMM-2

Say over again, and yet once over again. Sonnet. Elizabeth Barrett Browning. NAEL-2 Fr. Sonnets from the Portuguese.

Say, reverend man, why midst this stormy night. The Blind Man. Anne Batten Cristall. ECWP

Say, stranger, that this is the tomb of the mare Aethyia. Mnasalcas. HePo, tr. by Barbara Hughes Fowler Fr. Epigrams.

Say, sweet, my grief and I, we may not brook. Je ne veux de personne aupres de ma tristesse. Henri De Regnier, French. AWP, tr. by "Seumas O'Sullivan"

Say (sweetest) whether thou didst use me well. To Cynthia on Her Being an Incendiary. Sir Francis Kynaston. HAP

Say that a ballad. Susan Howe. PmAP Fr. Speeches at the Barriers.

Say that I should say I love ye. An Assurance. Nicholas Breton. CBLP; SCGP

Say that the men of the old black tower. The Black Tower. W. B. Yeats. CMoP

Say that thou didst forsake me for some fault. Sonnet 89. Shakespeare. OxAEP-1 Fr. Sonnets.

Say that you're lying comfortably under. Journey Out. Rachel Hadas. RA

Say the bells at St. Paul's. Unknown. See The Bells of London.

Say the need's born within the tree. Gum-trees Stripping. Judith Wright. BMAP

Say, there's a lamb in the daisies. (LL) For a Lamb. Richard Eberhart. CMoP; ColAP; LiTM; OxBSP; RB; SoSe-8

Say this city has ten million souls. Refugee Blues. W. H. Auden. LiTM Fr. Ten Songs.

Say This of Horses. Minnie Hite Moody. PoLF

Say to them. Speech to the Young Speech to the Progress-Toward (Among Them Nora and Henry III). Gwendolyn Brooks. PiM

Say tyrant Custom, why must we obey. The Emulation. Sarah Fyge Egerton. CABP; ECWP; NOEC; PEW

Say well and do well. Unknown. OxNR

Say! what is life? 'Tis to be born. The Story of Life. John Godfrey Saxe. PoToHe

Say what remains when Hope is fled? The Boy of Egremond. Samuel Rogers. NOBRP

Say what we will, at times it seems the rarest. Inspiration. Sherod Santos. NAmP90

"Say what you did for me, too, only last Christmas Day." (LL) Christmas Day in the Workhouse. George R. Sims. BLPA; EBNV; OBCP

Say what you please. Rondelet. May Probyn. VWP

Say what you want about doctors or priests. The Lightning Rod Salesman. M. L. Hester. CRP

Say what you will in two. Air: Sentir avec Ardeur. Marie-Françoise-Catherine de, Marquise de Boufflers Beauveau, French. CTC; WPOW, tr. by Ezra Pound

"Say, where is the maiden sweet." Sag', wo ist dein schönes Liebchen. Heinrich Heine, German. AWP, tr. by James Thomson

Say who you are and where you're going. (LL) Advice to Travelers. Walker Gibson. KaS

"Say why are beauties praised and honoured most." Alexander Pope. ECEV Fr. The Rape of the Lock[, an Heroi-Comical Poem]. FHYEP; HAP; ImPo; OAEL-1; OBNV; PeLV; PoEL-3

Say, why is this? wherefore? what should we do? Shakespeare. See Angels and ministers of grace defend us!

Say, wilt thou go with me, sweet maid. Invite to Eternity. John Clare. NAEL-1; NOBVV; OAEL-2; OBNC; PoEL-4

Say, wilt thou more of scenes so sordid know? A Slum Dwelling. George Crabbe. OBNC Fr. The Borough.

Say witty fair one, from what sphere. To the Most Excellently Accomplished Mrs. Katherine Philips. Henry Vaughan. CABP

Say, wouldst thou guard thy son. Of Caution. Francesco da Barberini, Italian. AWP, tr. by D. G. Rossetti

Say Yes Quickly. Jelaluddin Rumi, Persian. EnlH, tr. by Coleman Barks and A. J. Arberry; RaBo, tr. by Coleman Barks and John Moyne

Say You Love Me. Molly Peacock. NAmP90

Say you were the kid who could not sleep. The Actor. Thomas Snapp. NYBP

Sayes "Christ thee saue, good Child of Ell!" Earl Brand. Unknown. ESPB

Saying blackberry, blackberry, blackberry. (LL) Meditation at Lagunitas. Robert Hass. ColAP; NoP-4; VCAP

Saying Dante Aloud. James Wright. InPK-6

Saying Dear child, and all time has disproved. (LL) Faith Healing. Philip Larkin. ChIV-2; GI; NoAM

Saying Farewell to a Friend. Li Po, Chinese. TAL, tr. by Robert Payne

Saying Farewell to Magistrate Ch'en Ta-yu. Lin Hung, Chinese. SuSp, tr. by Irving Y. Lo

Saying Good-bye to a Singing Girl Who Has Decided to Become a Nun. Mo Shih-lung, Chinese. CoBLCP, tr. by Jonathan Chaves

Saying Good-Bye to Feng the Hermit. Mo Shih-lung, Chinese. CoBLCP, tr. by Jonathan Chaves

Saying Goodby to the Monk Ling-ch'e. Liu Ch'ang-ch'ing, Chinese. SuSp, tr. by Dell R. Hales

Saying Goodbye to a Monk from Japan. Hsü Pen, Chinese. CoBLCP, tr. by Jonathan Chaves

Saying It to Keep It from Happening. John Ashbery. FTOS

Saying One Thing. Robert Long. NAmP90

Saying to himself. What her Girl Friend Said. Peyanar. PLW Fr. Nine on Happy Reunion. PLW, tr. by A. K. Ramanujan

Says a Reverend Priest to a less Rev'rend friend. Epigram. Unknown. NOBRP

Says Body to Mind, "'Tis amazing to see." A Dialogue. Elizabeth Carter. CABP; ECWP

Says it. His is. Zeimbekiko. Robin Magowan. SPE

Says Jone to his woife on a whot summer's day. Jone o' Grinfilt. Joseph Lees. NOBRP

Says my Uncle, I pray you discover. Molly Mog [or The Fair Maid of the Inn]. John Gay. OBCoV

Says the great bell of Bow. (LL) The Bells of London. Unknown. BoTP; CBNP; LB; OxBoLi; PeLV

Says the Miner to the Mucker. Unknown. AmFP

Says the Shan Van Vocht. (LL) The Shan Van Vocht. Unknown. FaBoPV; OxBoLi

Says the window. Indoors. George Johnston. PoA

Says Tom to Jack, ''Tis very odd,'. The Methodist. Thomas Chatterton. ECEV

Says Tweed to [tae] Till. Tweed and Till. Unknown. FaBoCh; FaBoVe; OBEV; OxBSP

Says William to Henry, "I cannot conceive." Henry's Secret. Dorothy Kilner. OxBChV

Scaffold in Winter. János Pilinszky, Hungarian. PoSu, tr. by Peter Jay

Scaffolding. Seamus Heaney. ChAP

Scala Coeli. Kathleen Jessie Raine. NYBP

Scald it and scour it like a doorstep. (LL) View of a Pig. Ted Hughes. LiTM; OxAEP-2; OxBTC; TwCP

Scale of dragon, tooth of wolf. Shakespeare. UV Fr. Macbeth.

Scales, The. William Empson. CBLP; CMoP; FaBoMo; LiTM

Scales. Libby Houston. NBrP

Scales of pearly cloud inlay. Holiday at Hampton Court. John Davidson. EBVV

Scales of the Eyes, The. Howard Nemerov. CMoP

Scaling small rocks, exhaling smog. Central Park. Robert Lowell. LiTM

Scallion stands, gruel shops—half are run by ex-scholars! Inscribed on the Wall of a Rice Cake Shop. Chin Nung, Chinese. CoBLCP, tr. by Jonathan Chaves

Scalpel in Hand. Marjorie Welish. FTOS

Scalpel on the napkin, The. (LL) Entry in an Unknown Hand. Franz Wright. CMAP; NAmP90

Scampering over saucers—. The Sound of a Rat. Buson, *Japanese.* APo, *tr. by* Geoffrey Bownas *and* Anthony Thwaite

Scandal among the Flowers, A. Charles S. Taylor. BLPA

Scandal or two, A. Tattle. Godfrey Turner. NOBL

Scandalous man, A. Mr. Tom Narrow. James Reeves. OBSP

Scant and straggling her yellow hair, from her lip. An Old Woman. David Gwenallt Jones, *Welsh.* OBWVE, *tr. by* H. Idris Bell

Scantext stutters, The. Message Understood. Gareth Owen. SpW

Scape-Goat, The. Agnes Mary Frances Robinson. VWP

Scaped. Stephen Crane. *Fr.* The Black Riders [and Other Lines].

Scapegoat. William Robert Rodgers. CIP-2

Scapular of birds hung fast, A. Eclipses. Nancy Sullivan. TAP

Scar, The. John Hewitt. CIP-2; PNI

Scar[e]-Fire, The. Robert Herrick. HAP

Scaramouche waves a threatening hand. Fantoches. Paul Verlaine. AWP; OBMV, *tr. by* Arthur Symons

Scarborough Fair. *Unknown.* OxBoLi; PeLV

Scarce a breeze on the lake, with four oars to our boat. On Loch Leven. Christian Carstairs. ECWP

Scarce do I pass a day, but that I hear. Meditation 8. Philip Pain. NOBA; NOSC; OxBSP

Scarce had I slept my wonted round. A Dream. John Suckling. ChIV-2

SCARCE had the morning star hid from the light. The Affectionate Shepherd. Richard Barnfield. CABP; NoSic

Scarce images of life, one here, one there. A Recollection of the Stone Circle near Keswick. Keats. *Fr.* Hyperion. OAEL-2; Ro

Scarcely Spring. Louis Untermeyer. AYFP

Scarecrow, The. Walter De la Mare. MoBrPo; OxBTC

Scarecrow. Alan Pizzarelli. HA

Scarecrow, The. Andrew Young. FaBoTw

Scarecrow stood in a field one day, A. Michael Franklin. BoTP

Scarecrows. James Kirkup. NOxBChV

Scared? / are responsible negros running. Concerning One Responsible Negro with Too Much Power. Nikki Giovanni. BPo

Scared Cows. Douglas Messerli. FTOS

Scarf, The. Ivy O. Eastwick. BoTP

Scaring Crows. *Unknown.* BoTP; OxNR

Scarlet, warm and heavy in black velvet leaves. Leah Goldberg. MHP, *tr. by* Ruth Finer Mintz *Fr.* On Blossoming.

Scarlet Woman, The. Fenton Johnson. NAAAL; RACG

("Gin is better than the water in Lethe.") (LL) PoBA

Scarred by flame, hollowed out by waves. To the Wooden Hermit. Han Yü, *Chinese.* SuSp, *tr. by* Kenneth O. Hanson

Scarronides; or, Virgile Travestie. Virgil, *Latin.*

"I Sing the man, (read it who list)." OBCVT, *tr. by* Charles Cotton

Scars Remaining, The. Coleridge. OBNC *Fr.* Christabel. FHYEP; NAEL-2; NOBRP; OAEL-2; Ro

Scat cat! That Cat! Robert Fisher. PeP

Scatter. Paul Violi. BAP-95

Scattered, aslant. Fathers. Robert Creeley. FTOS

Scattered clouds. Tanka. Miyazawa Kenji, *Japanese.* MJT, *tr. by* Makoto Ueda

Scattered Congregation, The. Tomas Tranströmer, *Swedish.* RaBo; VCWP, *tr. by* Robert Bly

("Don't know. But that's where we're going.") (LL) VCWP, *tr. by* Robert Bly

Scattered Leaves. Lance Henson. VoR

Scattered Light. Fanny Howe. FTOS

Scattered Moluccas. Ezra Pound. *Fr.* Mauberly. *Fr.* Hugh Selwyn Mauberley. (Life and Contacts). AmPP; CMoP; InPS-3; LiTM; NOBA; NoAM; TAP

Scattered petals gather on the road. Hatsui Shizue, *Japanese.* WPJ, *tr. by* Kenneth Rexroth *and* Ikuko Atsumi

Scattered pomp has fallen to the scented dust. Shih Ch'ung's 'Golden Valley' Garden. Tu Mu, *Chinese.* PLT, *tr. by* A. C. Graham

Scatterghost, / it can't float away. The Rabbit. Mary Oliver. CMAP

Scattering bloom, The. Buson, *Japanese.* TAL, *tr. by* Harold G. Henderson

Scattering Flowers. George Hitchcock. CDa

Scazons. C. S. Lewis. EBEV

Scel Lem Duib. *Unknown. See* Season Song.

Scene, The. Agnes Nemes Nagy, *Hungarian.* PoSu, *tr. by* Bruce Berlind

Scene after Hunting at Swallowfield in Berkshire, A. Sneyd Davies. NOEC

Scene at Heaven Gate, The. T'ang Yin, *Chinese.* CoBLCP, *tr. by* Jonathan Chaves

Scène de Boudoir. Edmund Wilson. OBCoV *Fr.* Easy Exercises in the Use of Difficult Words.

Scene from a Play, Acted at Oxford, Called "Matriculation." Thomas Moore. OBSV

Scene is different, and the place, The. Arthur Hugh Clough. PeVV, *scene* I *Fr.* Dipsychus [and the Spirit].

Scene is set now: in a silent room, The. Transfusion. Merrill Moore. PoA

Scene of a Summer Morning. Irving Feldman. NYBP

Scene of superfluous grace, and wasted bloom. Anna Seward. PEW *Fr.* Colebrook Dale.

Scene 6 The Boat Passage. Gabriel Gbadamosi. NBrP *Fr.* No Blacks, No Irish.

Scene with Figure. Babette Deutsch. TrJP

Scene within the paperweight is calm, The. The Paperweight. Gjertrud Schnackenberg. VCAP

Scenery. Ted Joans. PoBA

Scenes. Yang Chi, *Chinese.*

"Eastern neighbor, western neighbor." CoBLCP, *tr. by* Jonathan Chaves

Scènes de la Vie de Bohème. Arthur Symons.

Episode of a Night of May. PeVV

Scenes from the Door. Gertrude Stein. AF

Scenes from the Life of the Peppertrees. Denise Levertov. LiTM; NeAP; NoP-4; PoM

("Peppertrees, the peppertrees!, The.") NoP-4

Scenes from the Mesozoic. Clarence Day.

"Yesterday explorers found." OBCoV

Scenes of Childhood. James Merrill. CoAP

Scenes of Childhood. Carl Morse. GLP

Scenes of magnificence! your powerful charms. Cumberland Rocks. Barbara Hoole. Ro *Fr.* Poems.

Scenes of my childhood, how oft I recall, The My Infundibuliform Hat. Charles Follen Adams. OBAL

Scent of ripeness from over a wall, A. Unharvested. Robert Frost. SAmP

Scent of unseen jasmine on the warm night beach, The. Malaga. Pearse Hutchinson. DIrV; PDCIP

Scented, cool, and marble dark. Lemons. Ted Walker. NYBP

Scented herbage of my breast. Walt Whitman. APN-1; NAAL-1; NAAL-3

Scentless laurel a broad leaf displays, The. Walter Savage Landor. FaBoEE

Schadenfreude. Stephanie Brown. BAP-95

Sche broghte him to his chambre tho. The Rape of Lucrece. Ovid, *Latin.* OBCVT, *tr. by* John Gower

Schemmelfennig. Bret Harte. OBAL

Scherzo, A. Dora Greenwell. NOBVV; SDW

(Scherzo A Shy Person's Wishes, A.) PEW

Schir William Wallace. Henry the Minstrel. OxBS *Fr.* The Wallace.

Schir, ye have mony servitouris. Remonstrance to the King. William Dunbar. OxBS

Schism, A/ Nurtured by foppery and barbarism. Keats. EPCY *Fr.* Sleep and Poetry.

Schizophrenic. Patricia K. Page. HeIP-4

Schizophrenic, wrenched by two styles. Codicil. Derek Walcott. MoP; NoAM

Schluf mine faygele. Lullaby. Breyten Breytenbach, *Afrikaans.* VCWP, *tr. by* Breyten Breytenbach

Schoenberg Op. 11. Thomas William Shapcott. *Fr.* Piano Pieces. CBAP

Scholar, The. Austin Clarke. RB

Scholar, The. Frances Darwin Cornford. BrRo

Scholar, The. Robert Southey. GTBS-P

(Among His Books.) OxAEP-2

Scholar and the Cat, The. *Unknown, Irish.* PC, *tr. by* Frank O'Connor

Scholar Chang Tuan was fond of cats. Chang Tuan's Cats. Felicity Bast. PC

Scholar first my Love implor'd, A. Song. Dorothea Du Bois. ECWP; LW

Scholar-Gipsy, The. Matthew Arnold. EBEV; EBVV; EBVVPR; EnVR; FHYEP; HAP; ImPo; NAEL-2; NOBE; NOBVV; OAEL-2; OBEV; OBNC; OxAEP-1; PoE; PoEL-5; SCGP; TFi

(Scholar-Gypsy, The.) NoP-4

Scholar I. Seamus Deane. NOIV

Scholar II. Seamus Deane. CIP-2; NOIV

Scholar in the Narrow Street, The. Tso Ssu, *Chinese.* AWP; ChiP, *tr. by* Arthur Waley

Scholar-Laureate in Retirement, A. Nguyễn Khuyến, *Vietnamese.* AVP, *tr. by* Huỳnh Sanh Thông

Scholar of Oxford, while tipsy, A. A Tribute to Matthew Arnold in a Moment of Self-Abuse. Richard Shepherd. PeLi

Scholars. Walter De la Mare. NoAM; Poetr

Scholars, The. W. B. Yeats. APAD; CMoP; NoP-4; OAEL-2; PoA

Scholars and soldiers marshaled in two files! Nguyễn Công Trú', *Vietnamese.* AVP, *tr. by* Huỳnh Sanh Thông

Scholars at the Orchid Pavilion. John Berryman. PoE

Scholar's Life, The. Samuel Johnson. NOBE *Fr.* The Vanity of Human Wishes [The Tenth Satire of Juvenal Imitated]. EBEV; ECEV; NOEC; OAEL-1; OxAEP-1; PoEL-3; TFi

Scholar's Life, The. *Unknown, Irish.* NOIV, *tr.* by Thomas Kinsella

School and Nature. Jean Follain, *French.* BLT, *tr.* by W. S. Merwin

School and Schoolfellows. Winthrop Mackworth Praed. FP; OxAEP-2 (Schools and Schoolfellows.)

School-bell rings, The. Nine o'Clock. Katharine Pyle. *Fr.* The Wonder Clock. OBCA

School-Boy, The. William Blake. CH; FHYEP; FaBoCh; OxAEP-2 *Fr.* Songs of Experience. ("When the blasts of winter appear?") (LL) AYFP

School Cadets. Anne Elder. CBAP

School Children, The. Louise Glück. AmPA; ColAP; HCAP; PoPoPo; Poetr; WeW-3

School Creed. *Unknown.* BoTP

School Days. Maltbie Davenport Babcock. PWR

School Days. William Stafford. LCAP-2

School for calves. Virgil, *Latin.* OBCVT, *tr.* by John Dryden

School for Satire, The. Lady Sophia Burrell. ECWP

School for Scandal, The. Richard Brinsley Sheridan.
Song: "Here's to the maiden [*or* maid] of bashful fifteen." EBEvV; NOEC; OxAEP-1; OxBoLi; PeLV; PoRA (Drinking Song.) NOIV

School Globe, The. James Reaney. NOBC

School is over. Kate Greenaway. CTV

School is over. It is too hot. The Lonely Street. William Carlos Williams. PoA; TwCP

School Lesson Based on Word of Tragic Death of Entire Gillum Family. Robert Penn Warren. FuPo

School-Master and the Truants, The. "John Brownjohn." OBCA

School-Mistress, The. William Shenstone. NOEC

School of Beauty's a tavern now, The. Southeast Corner. Gwendolyn Brooks. VGW *Fr.* A Street in Bronzeville. BPo; BlSi; FaBoWP

School of Eloquence, The. Tony Harrison. NoAM
Book Ends. DiPo; NAEL-2
Classics Society. NoP-4
Marked with D. NAEL-2
National Trust. NAEL-2
On Not Being Milton. CABP; FaBoPV; NoP-4

School Of Night, The. Alec Derwent Hope. PoA

School of Pain, The. Donna Brook. EC2

School Parted Us. "George Eliot." Son *Fr.* Brother and Sister. NALW

School-Time. Wordsworth. FHYEP *Fr.* The Prelude; Growth of a Poet's Mind
"Blest the infant Babe." TOF
"But who shall parcel out." TOF
"Those incidental charms which first attached." OAEL-2

Schoolbag, The. Seamus Heaney. BiHa

Schoolbags in Winter. John Clare. PoEL-4

Schoolboys still their morning rambles take, The. Schoolboys in Winter. John Clare. PoEL-4

Schoolcraft's Diary Written on the Missouri: 1830. Robert Bly. ImGa

Schoolgirls dance on the cold grass, The. The Ballet of the Twelve Dancing Princesses. Stevie Smith. WPN

Schoolgirls Hastening. John Shaw Neilson. NOBAu

Schooling, A. Seamus Deane. CIP-2; PNI

Schoolmaster. George Rostrevor Hamilton. FaBoEE

Schoolmaster, The. Herodas, *Greek.* HePo, *tr.* by Barbara Hughes Fowler

Schoolmaster Abroad with His Son, The. Charles Stuart Calverley. NOBL; PeLV

Schoolmaster's Admonition, A. *Unknown.* OxBChV

Schoolmaster's Precepts, A. John Penkethman. OxBChV

Schools. George Crabbe. CTC *Fr.* The Borough.

Schools and Schoolfellows. Winthrop Mackworth Praed. *See* School and Schoolfellows.

Schools break up tonight, The. Lament for Fearghal Ruadh. Tadhg Og O'Huiginn. NOIV

School's Out. W. H. Davies. OBMV

Schoolyard in April. Kenneth Koch. PoA

Schooner. Edward Kamau Brathwaite. PBCV

Schooner *Fred Dunbar*, The. Amos Hanson. AmFP

Schooner *The Mother of Parliaments* has anchored in the bay, The. Tom Leonard. NBrP *Fr.* Situations Theoretical and Contemporary.

Schooners with their pale green lights, The. A Dream within a Song. Henrietta Cordelia Ray. CBWP-3

Schreckhorn, The. Thomas Hardy. OAEL-2

Schule Laddie's Lament on the Lateness o' the Season, A. James Logie Robertson. NOBVV

Schumann's Sonata in A Minor. Celia Laighton Thaxter. AiP

Schute, Bell, Badgery, Lumby. A Country Song. Douglas Stewart. NOBAu

Schwerner, Chaney, Goodman. Raymond R. Patterson. NBV

Sci-fi Horrorscopes. Geoffrey Summerfield. SpW

Science. Robinson Jeffers. OxBA

Science and Poetry. James Russell Lowell. NCAP

Science as Art. Hugh Seidman. AmPA

Science Fiction. Kingsley Amis. NoAM

Science Fiction. Reed Whittemore. KaS

Science finds out ingenious ways to kill. The Modern World. Colin Ellis. FaBoEE

Science! meet daughter of old time thou art. Sonnet—To Science. Edgar Allan Poe. NAAL-1; NAAL-3

Science of the Night, The. Stanley Kunitz. ColAP; MoAmPo; TwCP

Science, the agile ape, may well. Coventry Patmore. FaBoEE

Science! thou fair effusive ray. Hymn to Science. Mark Akenside. ECEV; PoEL-3

Science! true daughter of Old Time thou art! Sonnet—To Science. Edgar Allan Poe. APN-1; AmPP; GSo; MeMAP; NCAP; NoP-4; OxBA; PAR; PBMP; Son; TAP

Scientific inquiry, seen in a very broad perspective may. Not a Cage. Joan Retallack. FTOS

Scientific Wooing. Constance Naden. VWP

Scientist has a test tube full of sheep, A. Counting Sheep. Russell Edson. LCAP-2

Scientist living at Staines, A. Genius. R. J. P. Hewison. PeLi

Scientists are in terror, The. From 115. Ezra Pound. APSN; FaBoMo *Fr.* Cantos.

Scientists Are Mistaken, The. Abba Kovner, *Hebrew.* IP, *tr.* by Warren Bargad *and* Stanley F. Chyet

"Scientists find universe awash in tiny diamonds." Pat Mayne Ellis. CrSp

Scientists plunge into matter looking for the. A. R. Ammons. BAP-93 *Fr.* Garbage. BAP-93

Scilian Muse, begin a loftier strain. The Messiah. Virgil. AWP, *tr.* by Dryden *Fr.* Eclogues.

Scillaes Metamorphosis. Thomas Lodge.
"Minde through thee divines on endlesse things, The." PBRV

Scion of Boston society, A. Limerick. Conrad Potter Aiken. PeLi

'Sciplinin' Sister Brown. James Edwin Campbell. AAP

Scissor-Man. George MacBeth. FaBoMo

Scissor-Man, The. Madeleine Nightingale. BoTP

Scissors. Tanka. Kondō Yoshimi, *Japanese.* MJT, *tr.* by Makoto Ueda

Scissors and string, scissors and string. *Unknown.* OxNR

Scissors cut the long-grown hair, The. Upon Shaving Off One's Beard. John Updike. OxBSP

Scissors cut you? What tender ears! On Words and Concepts and Things. Paul Ramsey. CRP

Scobble for whoredom[e] whips his wife, and cries [*or* cryes]. Upon Scobble [Epigram]. Robert Herrick. BeJo; CaPo; FaBoEE

Scolded like an impolite child. Saint Martha. Anna Kamienska, *Polish.* GI, *tr.* by Curzon, David and Grazyna Drabik

Scolding Some Dunces. Ho Xuan Huong, *Vietnamese.* AVP, *tr.* by Huỳnh Sanh Thông

Scones. *Unknown.* OBCoV

Scoops in the sea rock full of natural water. Bathtubs. Richmond Lattimore. NYBP

Scorched with love, the cicada. Kenneth Rexroth. APSN *Fr.* The Love Poems of Marichiko.

Scorching sun, enough to parch the Yangtze!, A. Tsung Ch'en. *Fr.* Miscellaneous Words on the Lake. CoBLCP, *tr.* by Jonathan Chaves

Scorn not the Sonnet; Critic, you have frowned. Sonnet Wordsworth. EBEV; EPCY; GSo; HeIP-4; NoP-4; OBEV; Son

"Scorn not the sonnet," though its strength be sapped. On a Magazine Sonnet. Russell Hillard Loines. OBAL

Scorned, to be scorned by one that I scorn. Tennyson. *Fr.* Maud [A Monodrama]. EnVR

Scorner, The. U Tam'si Tchicaya. PBMAP *Fr.* Epitomé (1962).

Scorner, The. Felix Tchicaya U'Tamsi, *French.* TTY, *tr.* by Gerald Moore *and* Ulli Beier
("I drink to your glory, God.") NegPo, *tr.* by Ellen Conroy Kennedy

Scorning religion all thy lifetime past. On Mr. Dryden, Renegade. Aphra Behn. FaBoVe

Scorpion, The. William Plomer. OBMV; PeSAV

Scorpion. Stevie Smith. EBEV; FaBoWP; OxAEP-2; PeECV; PoE

Scorpion so wishes to be gone. (LL) Scorpion. Stevie Smith. EBEV; FaBoWP; OxAEP-2; PeECV; PoE

Scorpion's tails, silver hooks. Yün Shou-p'ing. CoBLCP, *tr. by* Jonathan Chaves *Fr.* In the Tenth Month of the Year Jen-tzu (1672) the Imperial Censor Tan Chiang-shang, Mountain Man Wang Shih-ku and I Traveled by Boat to Pi-ling and Moored There. We Lingered Among the Frosty Trees and Red Leaves. Wang Was Entrusted with the Task of Painting a Picture, and We Each Wrote Twelve Poems to Record Our Delightful Experience.

Scotch Drink. Robert Burns. ChIV-1

Scotch God / Kent His / Faither. Alexander Scott. OBCoV *Fr.* Scotched.

Scotch Rhapsody. Dame Edith Sitwell. TwCP

Scotch Te Deum. Bible, *O.T. See* Psalm 100.

Scotched. Alexander Scott.

"Scotch God / Kent His / Faither." OBCoV

Scot[t]ish Field[e]. *Unknown.*

Battle of Flodden, The. NoSic

Scotland. Sir Alexander Gray. FaBoTC; OxBS

Scotland. Alastair Reid. FaBoTC

Scotland. William Soutar. OxBS

Scotland in the 1890s. Robert Crawford. FaBoTC

Scotland 1941. Edwin Muir. CABP; FaBoTC; OxBS

Scotland small? Out multiform, our infinite Scotland *small*? "Hugh MacDiarmid." RB

Scotland, when it is given to me. With a Lifting of the Head. "Hugh MacDiarmid." MoBrPo

Scotland's Winter. Edwin Muir. OxBS; OxBTC

Scots steel tempered wi' Irish fire. The Weapon. "Hugh MacDiarmid." RB

Scots, wha hae wi' Wallace bled. Robert Burns. EBEvV; FaBoCh; FaPoR; NAEL-2; OAEL-1; OxBS

Scott, your last fragments I arrange tonight. On Editing Scott Fitzgerald's Papers. Edmund Wilson. NYBP

Scotts, Kerrs, and Murrays, and Deloraines all, The. A Border Ballad. Thomas Love Peacock. BXAP

Scottsboro. *Unknown.* APAD; InPK-6

Scottsboro, Too, Is Worth Its Song. Countee Cullen. PoBA

Scoundrel carries his baseness around like an ID card, The. Answer. Zhao Zhenkai, *Chinese.* VCWP, *tr. by* Donald Finkel

Scourge deep, and quick be done. Martyr. Mary Elizabeth Fullerton. CBAP

Scourge of Folly, The. John, of Hereford Davies.

Author Loving These Homely Meats, The. CBLP; CBNP; OBCoV; Son (Homely Meats.) FaBoCh

Scourge of Villainy [*or* Villanie], The. John Marston.

"Fy Satyre fie, shall each mechanick slave." PBRV

To Detraction I Present My Poesie. NoSic

To Everlasting Oblivion. NoSic; SCGP

Scouring pans. Larry Wiggin. HA

Scrap. Tomasz Jastrun, *Polish.* AF, *tr. by* Daniel Bourne

Scrap of iron jerks its arms upright, A. A Shoe. Tongjip Shin, *Korean.* CKP, *tr. by* Jaihiun Kim

Scrape the bottom of the hole: gather up the stuff! The Digger's Song. Barcroft Henry Boake. NOBAu

Scraps of Time. Mrs. Henry Linden. CBWP-4

Scraptures: 7th Sequence. B. P. Nichol. FTOS

Scratch a Jew and you'll find a Wailing Wall. The Wall. Eve Merriam. TrJP

Scratch Music. C. D. Wright. CMAP; NAmP90

Scrawled in a rage by Dublin's poor. (LL) Inscription for a Headstone. Austin Clarke. BIrV; CIP-2; IIP

Scrawled in Pencil in a Sealed Car. Dan Pagis, *Hebrew.* PoSu, *tr. by* Robert Friend

Scream, The. Donald Hall. GS

Scream, A. Tom Leonard. FaBoTC

Scream, The. May Miller. Poetr

Scream that climbs a candle, A. Screams in the Dark. Slavko Mihalic. PoSu, *tr. by* Charles Simic

Screamer Discusses Methods of Screaming, A. James Schevill. TAP

Screaming My Head Off. Vladimir Mayakovsky. PFTM

Screams in the Dark. Slavko Mihalic. PoSu, *tr. by* Charles Simic

Screams round the Arch-druid's brow the sea-mew—white. Trepidation of the Druids. Wordsworth. Son *Fr.* Ecclesiastical Sonnets.

Screech owls moan in the yellowing. Travelling Northward. Tu Fu, *Chinese.* BLT; OHPC, *tr. by* Kenneth Rexroth

Screen of the world for another audience, The. (LL) Evening Ebb. Robinson Jeffers. BLT; NoAM

Screened Porch in the Country, A. James Dickey. WeT

Screens will be set there. Czeslaw Milosz, *Polish.* CEEP, *tr. by* John Carpenter *and* Bogdana Carpenter

Screw you. I don't give a rat's ass. The Zouave. Peter Cooley. NAmP90

Scribbled at a Cabinet Meeting. Sir Edward Carlson. FaBoVe

Scribblers, The. Walter Savage Landor. OBSV

("Why should scribblers discompose.") FaBoEE

Scribe, The. Walter De la Mare. CMoP; EBEvV; FaBoCh; OBMV; TrCP

Scribe, The. *Unknown, Irish.* TIRV, *tr. by* Robin Flower

Scribe, to the vulgar inclined, A. Limerick. Douglas Catley. PeLi

Scribes, The. Suzanne Noguere. FFC

Scrimmage of appetite everywhere, The. (LL) The Heavy Bear. Delmore Schwartz. ColAP; ImPo; LiTM; NOBA; NoAM; PFE; Poetr; TAP; TrJP; TwCP; UnPo

Scripts for the Pageant. James Merrill.

Samos. HCAP

Scripts I used to write for the young actor, The. Written, Directed by and Starring. James Simmons. PBCIP

Scripture of the Golden Eternity, The. Jack Kerouac.

"Did I create that sky? Yes, for, if it was." CLPP

Scroll. Geoffrey O'Brien. PT

Scroll of blue, an exquisite thought, A. Ball. Birago Diop. PBMAP

Scroobious Pip went out one day, The. Edward Lear. CBNP

Scrub woman for the old bank and jailhouse, The. Lamentations. Norman Dubie. NoAM

Scruffy one, The. Hyena. *Unknown, Yoruba. Fr.* Hunter Poems of the Yoruba. RB, *tr. by* Ulli Beier

Scrutiny [*or* Scrutinie], The. Richard Lovelace. BeJo; BoLoP; CaPo; EnLoPo; GBL; MeLP; SeCP

("Ev'n sated with variety.") (LL) CavPo; FMP; GLoP

(Song.) CavPo

("Why should you swear I am forsworn.") CavPo; FMP; GLoP

Scuba Diver Recovers the Body of a Drowned Child, The. Gerald William Barrax. GT; NBV

Scudamor in the Temple of Venus. Edmund Spenser. PoE *Fr.* Wood Of Error. AEP

Sculler, The. John Taylor.

"As Gold is better that's in fire tride." PBRV

Sculptor, The. Cornelius Mathews. APN-1 *Fr.* Poems on Man in His Various Aspects under the American Republic.

Sculptor, The. *Unknown. See* Sculpture.

Sculptor musing sat one eve, A. The Sculptor's Vision. Henrietta Cordelia Ray. CBWP-3

Sculptor remarked: "I'm afraid," A. Limerick. *Unknown.* PeLi

Sculptor's Vision, The. Henrietta Cordelia Ray. CBWP-3

Sculpture. *Unknown.* PoLF

(Sculptor, The.) PoToHe

Sculpture in a bare white gallery, A. The Field. Jean Valentine. LCAP-2

Scum & Slime. John Giorno. PmAP

Scunner. "Hugh MacDiarmid." FaBoTC; FaBoTw

Scyld was still a strong man when his time came. A Ship of Death. Seamus Heaney. NoP-4

Scylla and Charybdis. Homer. *Fr.* Odyssey. NAWM-1, *tr. by* Robert Fitzgerald

Scylla and Charybdis. Thomas Kinsella. OxBTC

Scyros. Karl Shapiro. HoPM; ImPo; LiTM

Scythian winters. Virgil, *Latin.* OBCVT, *tr. by* Joseph Trapp

Scythians, The. Aleksandr Blok, *Russian.* AWP, *tr. by* Babette Deutsch *and* Avrahm Yarmolinsky; TCRP, *tr. by* Babette Deutsch

Se Aprovechan. Irving Feldman. GS

Sè Stesso, A. Giacomo Leopardi, *Italian.* AWP, *tr. by* Lorna De' Lucchi

Sea, The. E. M. Adams. BoTP

Sea. Marie-Claire Bancquart, *French.* MFP, *tr. by* Martin Sorrell

Sea, The. Byron. FaBoBe; ImPo *Fr.* The Ocean. PoEL-4 *Fr.* Childe Harold's Pilgrimage.

(Ocean, The.) TFi

Sea, The. W. H. Davies. FaBoTw

Sea, The. Keats. *See* On the Sea.

Sea, The. Kalju Lepik, *Estonian.* CEEP, *tr. by* Ivar Ivask

Sea, The. Phạm Hổ, *Vietnamese.* AVP, *tr. by* Huỳnh Sanh Thông

Sea, The. Swinburne. *See* I Will Go Back to the Great Sweet Mother.

Sea, The. *Unknown.* PFE

Sea, The. Francis Webb. CBAP

Sea and a crescent strip of beach, The. And Their Winter and Night in Disguise. George Oppen. APSN; NNaP *Fr.* Some San Francisco Poems.

Sea and Other Stories, The. Jennifer Rankin. NOBAu

Sea and Ourselves at Cape Ann, The. Lawrence Ferlinghetti. PoM

Sea and the Butterfly, The. Kirim Kim, *Korean.* CKP, *tr. by* Jaihiun Kim

Sea and the Eagle, The. Sydney Clouts. PeSA

Sea and the Hills, The. Rudyard Kipling. OxBoS; SCGP

Sea and the Man, The. Anna Swirszczynska, *Polish*. BLT, *tr. by* Czeslaw Milosz *and* Leonard Nathan

Sea and the Sands, The. H. H. T., *Vietnamese*. AVP, *tr. by* Huỳnh Thông

Sea and the Skylark, The. Gerard Manley Hopkins. OBMV

Sea Anemones, The. Gwen Harwood. BMAP

Sea at Evening, The. Christopher Laird. PBCV

Sea at evening moves across the sand, The. Soldiers Bathing. Frank Templeton Prince. GTBS-P; ImPo; LiTM; MoBrPo; NOCV; OBWP; OxBTC; PeSA

Sea at night is endlessly dark, The. Pathos. Kwangsop Kim, *Korean*. CKP, *tr. by* Jaihiun Kim

Sea at this town's neat threshold spills its gloss. At the Sea's Edge. Gwen Harwood. CBAP

Sea awoke at midnight from its sleep, The. The Sound of the Sea. Henry Wadsworth Longfellow. APAD

Sea Before I Start Dreaming, The. Branko Miljkovic, *Serbo-Croatian*. HSix, *tr. by* Charles Simic

Sea bird knows the coming of storm, A. To Secretary Lu Ch'ien of Jen City. Li Po, *Chinese*. SuSp, *tr. by* Joseph J. Lee

Sea-Birds. Elizabeth Akers Allen. FaBoBe

Sea Birds, The. Van K. Brock. NYBP

Sea-Breeze at Matanzas, The. Epes Sargent. APN-1

Sea Breeze, Bombay. Adil Jussawalla. OMIP

Sea-bundle. Jennifer Rankin. BMAP

Sea Burial from the Cruiser *Reve*. Richard Eberhart. NYBP

Sea Cadences. Henrietta Cordelia Ray. AAP; CBWP-3

Sea Calm. Langston Hughes. OxBoS

Sea Canes. Derek Walcott. FP; HeIP-4

Sea Change. John Masefield. FaBoTw; OBMV; RB

Sea-Change: For Harold, A. Joseph Langland. LiTM

Sea-Chantey, A. Derek Walcott. RB

"In the middle of the harbour." TTY

Sea Chanty. Gregory Corso. BB

Sea-Chaplain's Petition to the Lieutenants in the Ward-Room, for the Use of the Quarter-Gallery, A. "J. T." NOEC

Sea-Chill. Arthur Guiterman. BXAP; UV

Sea contains a destiny, The. The Sea and the Eagle. Sydney Clouts. PeSA

Sea creeps to pillage, The. Sea Lullaby. Elinor Wylie. OxBoS

Sea cries with its meaningless voice, The. Pibroch. Ted Hughes. FaBoMo; OAEL-2

Sea-Cucumber, The. Martin Johnston. BMAP

Sea dark, The. The Call of Two Birds. Basho *and* Shita Yaba, *Japanese*. APo, *tr. by* Geoffrey Bownas *and* Anthony Thwaite

Sea Dialogue, A. Oliver Wendell Holmes. OBAL

Sea Dirge. Archias of Byzantium, *Greek*. AWP, *tr. by* Andrew Lang

Sea Dirge, A. Shakespeare. *See* Ariel's Song ("Full fathom [*or* fadom] five thy father lies").

Sea does not, The. Those Others. Ian Wedde. PeNZ

Sea Dreams. Tennyson.

Cradle Song: "What does little birdie say?" BoTP; OxBChV

Sea drew back uninjured with the blood of giant squids, The. Beat It Night Dog. Aimé Césaire, *French*. NegPo, *tr. by* Clayton Eshleman *and* Denis Kelly

Sea Eats the Land at Home, The. Kofi Awoonor. PBMAP

Sea-Elephant, The. William Carlos Williams. MeMAP; SAmP

Sea-Fever. John Masefield. CABP; CTV; ChAP; EBEvV; FaBoBe; FaPoR; MoBrPo; NTP; OxAEP-2; OxBTC; OxBoS; PoLF; UV

("I must down to the seas again, to the lonely sea and the sky.") SAGP

Sea flat out / the light far out, The. Mazatlan: Sea. Robert Creeley. APSN

Sea Flower. Mary Dorcey. BrRo

Sea Fog, The. Josephine Jacobsen. NYBP

Sea gleamed deep blue in the sunlight, The. Homage to Marcel Proust. Thomas MacGreevy. CIP-2

Sea go dark, dark with wind. Wild Iron. Allen Curnow. NTP; RB

Sea-Goddess, The. Margaret Lucas Cavendish, Duchess of Newcastle. *See* Song: "My cabinets are oyster-shells."

Sea goes flick-flack or the light does, The. Sheep Dipping. Norman MacCaig. OxBC

Sea Grapes. Derek Walcott. TRP

Sea guards warily its treasures, The. The Heart. Jakov Steinberg, *Hebrew*. TrJP, *tr. by* Harry H. Fein

Sea-Gull, The. Mary Howitt. BoTP; OxBChV

("Waves leap up, the wild wind blows, The.") CTAV

Sea-Gull, The. Ogden Nash. ImPo

Sea-gull *is* so sorry!, The. The Sorrowful Sea-Gull. Menella Bute Smedley. VWP

Sea gull / who flaps his wings. Magic Words to Feel Better. Nakasuk, *Eskimo*. STP, *tr. by* Jerome Rothenberg

Sea gulls whiten and dip, The. In the Bay. Arthur Symons. OBNC *Fr.* Amorix Exsul.

Sea Gypsy, The. Richard Hovey. ChAP

Sea has invaded the kitchen, The. Fish Cooking. Huran Kim, *Korean*. CKP, *tr. by* Jaihiun Kim

Sea has it this way: if you see, The. Cormorants. John Blight. CBAP

Sea has made a wall for its defence, The. Shoreline. Mary Barnard. PoA

Sea Hath Its Pearls, The. Heinrich Heine, *German*. AWP, *tr. by* Longfellow

Sea hath tempered it, the mighty sunm The. The Fountain. Don Allen Johnson, *Arabic*. AWP, *tr. by* Dulcie L. Smith

Sea-Hawk. Richard Eberhart. RB

Sea Holly. Conrad Potter Aiken. LiTM

Sea Horse, The. Robert Graves. FaBoMo

Sea Horse, The. Ruthven Todd. APo

Sea howling and moaning by itself, The. Listen to the sea. Guillaume Apollinaire. PFTM, *tr. by* David Antin *Fr.* Victoire.

Sea inside my heart, The. Tanka. Akiko Yosano, *Japanese*. MJT, *tr. by* Makoto Ueda

Sea is a circuit of holes, The. The Coral Reef. Laurence Lieberman. CoAP

Sea is a hungry dog, The. James Reeves. NOxBChV; NTP

Sea is an acre of dull glass, the land is a table, The. Lusty Juventus. Charles Madge. FaBoMo

Sea is awash with roses O they blow, The. 'Sea is Awash with Roses, The'. Kenneth Patchen. CLPP

Sea is calm tonight, The. Dover Beach. Matthew Arnold. APAD; AWP; BLPA; CABP; ClHu; EBVV; EBVVPR; FaBoBe; GTBS-P; HAP; HeIP-4; HoPM; ImPo; InPK-6; InPS-3; NAEL-2; NIP-4; NOBE; NOBVV; NoP-4; OAEL-2; OBNC; OxBoS; PBMP; PFE; PeVV; PoE; PoEL-5; PoPoPo; PoRA; SAGP; SCGP; SCV; TFi; TOF

Sea is covered with adolescents, The. Adolescents on the Sea. Nichita Stanescu, *Romanian*. CEEP, *tr. by* Mariana Carpinisan *and* Mark Irwin

Sea is flecked with bars of grey, The. Les Silhouettes. Oscar Wilde. EBVV *Fr.* Impressions.

Sea is History, The. Derek Walcott. OxBoS

Sea / isn't a place, The. The Waves. Mary Oliver. OxBoS

Sea Knell. John Updike. OxBoS

Sea-lashed coast outside the gate reaches to the hedge. Bamboo Branch Song of the Seacoast. Yang Wei-chen, *Chinese*. CoBLCP, *tr. by* Jonathan Chaves

Sea Legs. Susan Feldman. AmPA

Sea-Limits, The. D. G. Rossetti. EnVR; NAEL-2; OAEL-2 *Fr.* The House of Life.

Sea limps up here twice a day, The. Paphos. Lawrence Durrell. NYBP

Sea Love. Charlotte Mew. LW; MoBrPo; OxAEP-2; OxBTC

Sea Lullaby. Elinor Wylie. OxBoS; PBMP

Sea-Marge. Ivor Gurney. NTP

Sea Marke. John Smith. SCAP

Sea Monsters. Edmund Spenser. *Fr.* Wood Of Error. AEP

Sea-mutterings and me. (LL) The Souls of the Slain. Thomas Hardy. CMoP; PoEL-5

Sea Nocturne. U Tam'si Tchicaya, *French*. NegPo, *tr. by* Ellen Conroy Kennedy

Sea Nymphs, The. Edmund Spenser. *Fr.* Wood Of Error. AEP

Sea of Death, The. Thomas Hood. OBNC; PoEL-4

Sea of Death, The. *Unknown*. CH

Sea of Lemon, The. Yojong Kim, *Korean*. CKP, *tr. by* Jaihiun Kim

Sea or Sky? Medbh McGuckian. PBCIP

Sea Owl. Dave Jeddie Smith. HCAP

Sea pearl, western star. On Leaving. Gertrudis Gomez de Avellaneda, *Spanish*. PBWP, *tr. by* Frederick Sweet

Sea-perch over paddocks. Dunes. Salt light everywhere low down. The Greenhouse Vanity. Les A. Murray. FaBoVe

Sea Poppies. Hilda Doolittle. NALW

Sea-preserved, heaped with sea-spoils. Picture of a Nativity. Geoffrey Hill. NoAM; OxBC

Sea pursued, The. The Shore Road. Norman MacCaig. FaBoTC

Sea Replies to Byron, The. G. K. Chesterton. UV

Sea retreats as I advance, The. Sea Nocturne. U Tam'si Tchicaya, *French*. NegPo, *tr. by* Ellen Conroy Kennedy

Sea-Ritual, The. George Darley. BIrV; OBNC *Fr.* Syren Songs. (Deadman's Dirge.) CH

Sea Rose. Hilda Doolittle. FaBoMo; HeIP-4; NoAM; NoP-4; OxWW; TRP

Sea School. Barbara Howes. NYBP

Sea Shell. Amy Lowell. BoTP

Sea-Shore. Ralph Waldo Emerson. APN-1; ColAP; OxBA

Sea Shroud, The. Jack Kerouac. PoM

Sea-Side Cave, The. Alice Cary. APN-2; ColAP

Sea Similized to Meadows and Pastures: the Mariners, to Shepherds: the Mast, to a May-Pole: the Fish, to Beasts, The. Margaret Lucas Cavendish, Duchess of Newcastle. NoP-4

Sea slaps the sleeping beach's ear, The. Beyond the breakers. Joyce Mansour, *French, tr. by* Martin Sorrell

Sea-Song, A. Allan Cunningham. BoTP; FaBoBe; FaPoR

Sea Song, A. Digby Mackworth Dolben. EBVV

Sea Song, A: "Master, the swabber, the boatswain and I, The." Shakespeare. NBLV; OBCoV; PeLV *Fr.* The Tempest. OAEL-1 (Song.) NOBL; OxBSP

Sea-Song from the Shore, A. James Whitcomb Riley. BoTP; FPC

Sea still plunges where as naked boys, The. The Grotto. Francis Scarfe. PoA

Sea sucks at its own, The. Landcrab II. Margaret Atwood. NIP-4

Sea Surface Full of Clouds. Wallace Stevens. AmPP; CMoP; MoAmPo; VGW

Sea, The—quick pugilist. Training. Herrera S. Demetrio, *Spanish.* TTY, *tr. by* Dudley Fitts

Sea, the World, and the Boat People, The. Hà Huyền Chi, *Vietnamese.* AVP, *tr. by* Huỳnh Sanh Thông

Sea Things. Gwendolyn MacEwen. FaBoWP

Sea took a sailor to its deep.—, The. Supplication. Constantine P. Cavafy, *Greek.* BLT, *tr. by* Rae Dalven

Sea-Turtle and the Shark, The. Melvin Beaunearus Tolson. PoBA *Fr.* Harlem Gallery.

Sea Unicorns and Land Unicorns. Marianne Moore. NALW; PFTM

Sea View, The. Charlotte Smith. ECWP

Sea Violet. Hilda Doolittle. NoP-4

Sea Voyage. William Empson. CMoP

Sea-Voyage from Tenby to Bristol, A. Katherine Philips. WPE

Sea voyagers talk about fairy islands. T'ien-mu Mountain Ascended in a Dream: A Farewell Song. Li Po, *Chinese.* SuSp, *tr. by* Wu-Chi Liu

Sea Wall. Velma Pollard. HCP *Fr.* Belize Suite.

Sea was as blue as the sky, The. The Real Thing. Ronald Wallace. IFJA

Sea was sapphire coloured, and the sky, The. Impression du Voyage. Oscar Wilde. GrIP

Sea-wash never ends, The. Carl Sandburg. OBCA

Sea waves are green and wet. Sand Dunes. Robert Frost. MoAmPo

Sea-weed sways and sways and swirls. D. H. Lawrence. RB

Sea whisper'd me, The. (LL) Out of the cradle endlessly rocking. Walt Whitman. ColAP; NCAP; NoP-4; PAR

Sea-Wind. Stéphane Mallarmé, *French.* AWP, *tr. by* Arthur Symons

Sea-wind salts your head white. (LL) Watch the Lights Fade. Robinson Jeffers. CMoP; NOBA

Sea Without Poets. Branko Miljkovic, *Serbo-Croatian.* HSix, *tr. by* Charles Simic

Sea would flow no longer, The. The Frozen Ocean. Viola Meynell. CH

Seacoast at Mera, The. Takada Toshiko, *Japanese.* WPJ, *tr. by* Kenneth Rexroth *and* Ikuko Atsumi

Seacoast wears you out with damp and heat. White Crane Hill. Su Tung-p'o, *Chinese.* CoBCP, *tr. by* Burton Watson

Seaconk or Rehoboths Fate. Benjamin Tompson. SCAP

Seaconk Plain Engagement. Benjamin Thompson. SCAP

Seafarer. Archibald MacLeish. Poetr

Seafarer, The. Henry Howard, Earl of Surrey. *See* Complaint of the Absence of Her Lover Being upon the Sea.

Seafarer, The. *Unknown, Anglo-Saxon. See also* "May I, for my own self, song's truth reckon," CTC; FaBoTw; HeIP-4; NoP-4; OXBA, *tr. by* Ezra Pound; PoE, *tr. by* Kemp Malone; OBVE

("I can sing a true song about myself.") ASW; OxBoS, *tr. by* Kevin Crossley-Holland

"I can sing of myself a true song." PoRA, *tr. by* L. Iddings

"Mæg ic be me sylfum sothgied wrecan." CABP

"My purpose is to tell my own true tale." EBEV, *tr. by* John Wain

"Song I sing of my sea adventure, A." AnOE, *tr. by* Charles W. Kennedy

"Tale I frame shall be found to tally." OBVE, *tr. by* Michael Alexander

("Song I sing of my sea-adventure, A.") AnOE, *tr. by* Charles W. Kennedy

("That He has raised us up forever. Amen.") (LL) EEP, *tr. by* Michael Alexander

Seafarers tell of the Isles of Ying. Song of a Dream Visit to T'ien-mu. Li Po, *Chinese.* CoBCP, *tr. by* Burton Watson

Seagull, The. Dafydd ap Gwilym, *Welsh.* OBWVE, *tr. by* Glyn Jones

Seagull, The. Siôn Phylip, *Welsh.* OBWVE, *tr. by* Joseph P. Clancy; PBRV

("Fair seagull on the water's edge, bright-feathered breast, rich your state.") PBRV

Seagull flying from the sea. A Feather for My Cap. Ivy O. Eastwick. BoTP

Seagull, spreadeagled, splayed on the wind, The. Memorial for Two Young Seamen. George Barker. ImPo; LiTM *Fr.* Pacific Sonnets.

Seagulls. John Updike. Poetsp

Seal, The. Guillaume Apollinaire, *French.* CBNP

Seal at Stinson Beach. Roberta Hill Whiteman. VoR

Seal up the book, all vision's at an end. On the Death of Mr. Pope. *Unknown.* NOEC

Sealed epistle submitted / at dawn to Nine-fold Heaven, A. Demoted I Arrive at Lan-t'ien Pass and Show This Poem to My Brother's Grandson Han Hsiang. Han Yü, *Chinese.* SuSp, *tr. by* Charles Hartman

Sealed in rainlight one. The Magic Apple Tree. Elaine Feinstein. BrRo

Seals all flap, The. Dorothy Aldis. CTV

Seals at High Island. Richard Murphy. BiHa; CIP-2; PBCIP

Seals at play off Western Isle, The. Seals, Terns, Time. Richard Eberhart. LiTM; MoAmPo

Seals in Penobscot Bay, The. Daniel Gerard Hoffman. TwCP

Seals in the Inner Harbor. Brendan Galvin. CMAP

Seals of love, but seal'd in vain, seal'd in vain! (LL) At the Moated Grange. Shakespeare. AWP; EBEV; EnLoPo; GBL; GTBS-P; ImPo; InPS-3; NOBE; NoSic; OAEL-1; OBEV; PoEL-2; SCGP; TFi

Seals, Terns, Time. Richard Eberhart. LiTM; MoAmPo

Seal's wide spindrift gaze toward paradise, The. (LL) —And yet this great wink of eternity. Hart Crane. AmPP; HAP; ImPo; LiTM; MoAmPo; OxBA; PoE; RaBo; TRP; UnPo; VGW

Seaman, 1941. Molly Holden. FaBoWP

Seamen Three. Thomas Love Peacock. *See* Three Men of Gotham.

Seamen's Mission. Gerald Dawe. PNI

Seamstress, The. Harry Clifton. BiHa

Seamus, Light hearted and Loving Friend of My Brea . Owen Roe O'Sullivan, *Irish.*

"Seamus, light-hearted and loving friend of my breast." NOIV, *tr. by* Thomas Kinsella

Séance. William Abrahams. NYBP

Séance. Francis King. PoA

Seance. Edouard Roditi. SPE

Seance. Raymond Roseliep. HA

Search. Claribel Alegría, *Spanish.* BoWoP, *tr. by* Aliki *and* Willis Barnstone

Search, The. Kwesi Brew. PBA

("The Past.") PBMAP

Search. Jane Draycott. LBC

Search, The. George Herbert. ESCV

Search, The. John Hewitt. PNI

Search, The. Nancy Peterson. LoHo

Search. Yannis Ritsos, *Greek.* NNPT, *tr. by* Nikos Stangos

Search, The. Charles Shaw. NOBAu

Search, The. Henry Vaughan. ChIV-2; ESCV; GeHe; SeCP

Search after Happiness, The. Hannah More.

Epilogue: "Child! we must quit these visionary scenes." ECWP

Search all the Christian climes from pole to pole. Daniel Defoe. OBSV *Fr.* Reformation of Manners.

Search and Destroy. Dale Ritterbusch. CDa

Search for Apollo, A. Agnes Mary Frances Robinson. VWP

Search for Love. D. H. Lawrence. CBLP

Search for True Religion, The. Donne. *See* Satire 3.

Search-Lights, The. Alfred Noyes. NSI *Fr.* A Salute from the Fleet.

Search. Search. Seek. Seek. A Weary Song to a Slow Sad Tune. Li Ch'ing-chao, *Chinese.* BoWoP; OIIMPC, *tr. by* Kenneth Rexroth

Searcher of souls, you who in heaven abide. A Prayer. Samuel Butler. FaBoEE

Searching, The. Alice S. Cobb. BlSi

Searching for Grandfather. Olive Senior. HCP

Searching for Herb Brazier and Cinnabar Well, I Also Saw the Waterfall of Singing Strings. Alongside Was the Cliff of the Lord of the Mountain. Tao-chi, *Chinese.* CoBLCP, *tr. by* Jonathan Chaves

Searching for Schüpfen. Dona Luongo Stein. LoHo

Searching for souvenirs among some rubble. A Post-Mortem. Siegfried Sassoon. PBMP

Searching for the Ruins of the Pavilion of the Drunken Old Man. Yang Shih-ch'i, *Chinese.* CoBLCP, *tr. by* Jonathan Chaves

Searching my heart for its true sorrow. Exiled. Edna St. Vincent Millay. PoRA

Searching on the wind. J. W. Hackett. HA

Searchlights. Kenneth Mackenzie. BMAP

Sea's Abundant Progeny, The. William Wood. NOSC

Seas are quiet when the winds give o'er, The. Old Age. Edmund Waller. NOBE; NOCV; OBEV *Fr.* Of The Last Verses in the Book. BeJo; EBEV; HAP; NOSC; NoP-4; PeECV; PoPoPo; SCGP; SeCP

Sea's Wash in the Hollow of the Heart, The. Denise Levertov. LW

Seascape. Elizabeth Bishop. ColAP; FaBoWP; OxBC; OxBoS

Seascape. Langston Hughes. GT

Seascape. Stephen Spender. NoP-4

Seascape. Francis Brett Young. OxBTC

Seascape shifts, The. Distinctions. Charles Tomlinson. CMoP

Seashore, The. Leonid Martynov, *Russian.* TCRP, *tr. by* J. R. Rowland

Seaside: In and Out of the Season, The. Charles Tennyson Turner. Son

Season. Wole Soyinka. PBMAP *Fr.* Idanre and Other Poems.

Season, ending, makes no sign, but the wind. Conserves. David Mus. PoA *Fr.* The Joy of Cooking.

Season is fall and the moon's full too, The. An Accidental Meeting with an Old Friend While Traveling at Night. Tai Shu-lun, *Chinese.* SuSp, *tr. by* William H. Nienhauser

Season late, day late, sun just down, and the sky. Birth of Love. Robert Penn Warren. GEA; UnPo; VCAP

Season of changing clothes, The. Teijo Nakamura, *Japanese.* WPJ, *tr. by* Kenneth Rexroth *and* Ikuko Atsumi

Season of Loss, A. Jim Barnes. HATNAP

Season of mists and mellow fruitfulness[!]. To Autumn. Keats. AWP; BoTP; CH; ClHu; EBEV; EBEvV; FHYEP; GTBS-P; HAP; HeIP-4; ImPo; InPK-6; InPS-3; NAEL-2; NAWM-2; NIP-4; NOBE; NOBRP; NTP; OAEL-2; OBEV; OBNC; OxAEP-2; PBMP; PoE; PoEL-4; PoLF; Poetr; RB; RaBo; SCGP; SCV; SoSe-8; TFi; TRP; UnPo; WeW-3

Season of Omens. J. P. Clark Bekedermo. PBMAP *Fr.* Casualties (1970).

Season of Phantasmal Peace, The. Derek Walcott. AFr; HCP; PoPoPo; VCWP

Season of rains: the horizon like an illness. Autumn 1942. Roy Fuller. PoWW

Season of ships is here, The. Spring on the Coast. Leonidas of Tarentum, *Greek.* GrAn, *tr. by* Clive Sansom

Season of the rains, The. Simon Mpondo. PBMAP

Season Song. Judith Nicholls. Spl

Season Song. Unknown, *Irish.* RB, *tr. by* Flann O'Brien (Scel Lem Duib.) BIrV

Season 'tis, my lovely lambs, The. E. E. Cummings. UnPo

Season when Nothing's in Place, A. Ory Bernstein, *Hebrew.* IP, *tr. by* Warren Bargad *and* Stanley F. Chyet

Seasonal Poems on Fields and Gardens. Fan Ch'eng-ta, *Chinese.*

Autumn. SuSp, *tr. by* Irving Y. Lo

Late Spring. SuSp, *tr. by* Irving Y. Lo

Summer. SuSp, *tr. by* Irving Y. Lo

Winter. SuSp, *tr. by* Irving Y. Lo

Seasoned with sage and onions, and port wine. (LL) To a Goose [*or* Gosse]. Robert Southey. BXAP; NOBL; PeLV; Son

Seasons, The. Thomas Holcroft. NOEC

Seasons, The. Rolfe Humphries. NYBP

Seasons, The. Kalidasa, *Sanskrit.* AWP, *tr. by* Arthur W. Ryder

Seasons, The. James Thomson.

Hymn on the Seasons, A. CABP

Seasons and Times. William Barnes. NOBVV

Season's anguish, crashing whirlwind, ice, The. Winter Garden. David Gascoyne. GTBS-P

Seasons burn, The. The wind is dry. Earthquake. Robert Arthur Douglas Ford. NOBC

Seasons Come and Go, The. T'ao Ch'ien, *Chinese.*

"Bank to bank, the stream is wide." SuSp, *tr. by* Eugene Eoyang

"By and by, the seasons come and go." SuSp, *tr. by* Eugene Eoyang

"In the morning and at night." SuSp, *tr. by* Eugene Eoyang

"Peering into the depths of the stream." SuSp, *tr. by* Eugene Eoyang

Seasons four, The. Keats. LaPo *Fr.* Endymion.

Seasons Greetings, Love and Revolution. Judy Miles. PBCV

Seasons in Santa Fe. Gerald Vizenor. HATNAP

Season's Lovers, The. Miriam Waddington. MoCV

Seasons of Fire. Billy Marshall-Stoneking. NOBAu

Seasons of the Soul. Allen Tate. FuPo; OxBA

Seasons: Winter, The. Virgil, *Latin.*

"When from the palid Sky the Sun descends." OBCVT, *tr. by* James Thomson

Seated on her bed legs spread open. Joyce Mansour, *French.* BoWoP, *tr. by* Willis Barnstone

Seated once by a brook, watching a child. The Brook. Edward Thomas. OAEL-2

Seated one day at the organ. The Lost Chord. Wyndham Lewis. UV

Seated one day at the Organ, / I was weary and ill at ease. A Lost Chord. Adelaide Anne Procter. EBEvV; SDW; UV

Seated their fellow-traveller on a cloud. (LL) The Vision of Judgment. Byron. FHYEP; OBSV; OxAEP-2; OxBoLi

Seattle, Autumn, 1933. Alfred Encarnacion. OpBo

Seaweed. Henry Wadsworth Longfellow. APN-1; ColAP; OxBA; TAP

Seaweeds. Sandra McPherson. AmPA; PoA

Sebastian. Yona Wallach, *Hebrew.* IP, *tr. by* Warren Bargad *and* Stanley F. Chyet

Sebastian. Yona Wollach, *Hebrew.* IP, *tr. by* Warren Bargad *and* Stanley F. Chyet

Sebastian's Lament, 1943. Sigitas Geda, *Lithuanian.* CEEP, *tr. by* Jonas Zdanys

Sebastopol. Ilya L'vovich Selvinsky, *Russian.* TCRP, *tr. by* Daniel Weissbort

Seboulisa, mother of power. Audre Lorde. CrSp *Fr.* October.

Secluded from domestic strife. The Double Transformation. Oliver Goldsmith. OBCoV; OBNV

Secluded within the women's quarters—that was sad enough. The Tomb of the Singing Girl Ch'iung-i. Hsü Pen, *Chinese.* CoBLCP, *tr. by* Jonathan Chaves

Second after, / the first boat touched the shore, A. The Settlers. Margaret Atwood. MoCV

2nd afternoon I come, The. A Poem for the Insane. John Weiners. BB; NeAP; PmAP; PoM

Second Air Force. Randall Jarrell. CMoP; LiTM; NAAL-2

Second and third month of sunny spring, The. Song of the Thoroughfare. Hsieh Shang, *Chinese.* CoBCP, *tr. by* Burton Watson

Second Anniversary [*or* Anniversarie], The. Donne. ESCV; SeCP *Fr.* Of the Progres[se] of the Soule; the Second Anniversarie.

("We see in authors, too stiff to recant.") NOSC, *ll.* 281–300

"We now lament not, but congratulate." NOSC

Second Ascension of Christ, The. John Wheelwright. NOCV *Fr.* Forty Days.

Second Attempt, A. Thomas Hardy. CBLP

Second batch of verses by that naughty provincial, A. Elegies 2.i. Ovid, *Latin.* EP, *tr. by* Peter Green

Second Best. Rupert Brooke. MoBrPo

Second Book of Virgil's Aeneid, The. Virgil. SiPS, *tr. by* Henry Howard, Earl of Surrey *Fr.* The Aeneid [*or* Eneados, Aeneis].

"It was the time when, granted from the gods." NAEL-1, *tr. by* Henry Howard, Earl of Surrey

Laocoön. OBVE, *tr. by* Henry Howard, Earl of Surrey

Trojan Horse, The. OAEL-1, *tr. by* Henry Howard, Earl of Surrey

"Whom when I saw assembled in such wise." PoE, *tr. by* Henry Howard, Earl of Surrey

Second bounding snow, The. (LL) A Mill. William Allingham. FaBoEE; OxBSP

Second Brother, The. Thomas Lovell Beddoes.

Song: "Strew not earth with empty stars." OxBSP

Second Carolina Said-Song. A. R. Ammons. OBAL

Second Childhood. Robin Boody Galguera. IFJA

Second Class Citizen. Jennifer Lagier. UnSA

Second-Class Citizen. Slavko Mihalic. PoSu, *tr. by* Charles Simic

Second class is the second grade, The. Primary Lesson: The Second Class Citizens. Sun-Ra. PoBA

Second Coming, The. John William Corrington. HoPM

Second Coming. Adam Small, *Afrikaans.* PeSAV, *tr. by* Carrol Lasker

Second Coming, The. W. B. Yeats. APAD; BIrV; CABP; CMoP; ChIV-2; ClHu; EBEvV; FaBoMo; FaBoPV; GI; GTBS-P; HAP; HeIP-4; HoPM; ImPo; InPK-6; InPS-3; LiTM; MoBrPo; NoP; NAEL-2; NAWM-2; NIP-4; NOBE; NoAM; NoP-4; OAEL-2; OxAEP-2; OxBTC; PBMP; PoE; PoPoPo; Poetr; RaBo; SCV; SoSe-8; TFi; TRP; UnPo

("Slouches toward Bethlehem to be born?") (LL) SAGP

Second Cycle of Love Poems. George Barker.

O Tender under Her Right Breast. MoBrPo

Second Dream, The. Jean Valentine. LCAP-2

Second Duino Elegy, The. Rilke, *German.*

"Lovers, gratified in each other, I am asking *you.*" ITG, *tr. by* Stephen Mitchell

Second Eclogue, The. Virgil, *Latin.*

"Young *Corydon* (hard Fate) an humble Swain." OBCVT, *tr. by* Thomas Creech

Second Elegy, Getic. Nichita Stanescu, *Romanian.* CEEP, *tr. by* Petru Popescu *and* Peter Jay

Second Epistle of the Second Book of Horace Imitated, The. Alexander Pope. TOF

Second Fig. Edna St. Vincent Millay. NALW; NoP-4; PoA

Second Glance at a Jaguar. Ted Hughes. NYBP; NoAM

Second-Hand Elegy, A. Michael Anania. CDa
Second-hand platitudes like antique watches. Catching One Clear Thought Alive. Paula Gunn Allen. WPOW
Second-hand sights, like crumpled. Newark, for Now (68). Carolyn M. Rodgers. PoBA
Second Honeymoon. *Unknown, Irish.* BIrV, *tr. by* Augustus Young
Second Hymn to Lenin. "Hugh MacDiarmid."
 "Ah, Lenin, you were richt. But I'm a poet." OAEL-2
 "Freend, foe; past, present, future." OAEL-2
Second Image Sequence. Umberto Piersanti, *Italian.* NeIt, *tr. by* Stephen Sartarelli
Second Inaugural Address. Abraham Lincoln. CTV
Second Language. Christine Dumaine. LoHo
Second Life, The. Edwin Morgan. FaBoTC; OxBS
Second Life of Lazarus, The. Gwen Harwood. CBAP
2nd Light Poem: For Diane Wakoski. Jackson MacLow. PoM
Second Madrigal, The. Anna Swirszczynska, *Polish.* BLT, *tr. by* Czeslaw Milosz *and* Leonard Nathan
Second man I love, The. Spring. Carole C. Gregory Clemmons. PoBA
Second Marriage. Mei Yao Ch'en, *Chinese.* SuSp, *tr. by* Jonathan Chaves
Second Merseburg Spell. *Unknown, German.* GePo, *tr. by* Carroll Hightower
Second Ode to Persephone. Robert Kelly. *Fr.* The Book of Persephone. PoM
Second Olympique Ode of Pindar, The. Pindar, *Greek.*
 "Greatness of *Mind* and *Fortune* too." OBCVT, *tr. by* Abraham Cowley
Second passerby (he reads): "The Tables of Destiny! I carve you in letters." Plane Four. Velemir Khlebnikov. PFTM *Fr.* Zangezi.
Second Pastoral. Or, Alexis, The. Virgil, *Latin.*
 "Come to my longing Arms, my lovely care." OBCVT, *tr. by* John Dryden
Second Philosopher's Song. Aldous Leonard Huxley. OBCoV
Second Poem. Peter Orlovsky. NeAP
Second Poem from Nicaragua Libre: War Zone. June Jordan. NoAM
Second Poem the Night-Walker Wrote, The. Goethe. *Fr.* Wanderer's Night-Songs.
Second Rapture, The. Thomas Carew. CaPo
Second Review of the Grand Army, A. Bret Harte. CBCWP
Second Rondeau. Johann Nikolaus Götz, *German.* GePo, *tr. by* George C. Schoolfield
Second Samuel. Bible, *O.T.*
 David's Lament. TrJP
 (David's Lament for Saul and Jonathan.) AWP
Second Satire of the Second Book of Horace Imitated, The. Alexander Pope.
 "With all a woman's virtues but the pox." OBSV
Second Sermon on the Warpland, The. Gwendolyn Brooks. BPo; NOBA; PoBA
Second Shadow. Theodore Roethke. PoA
Second Shaman Song. Gary Snyder. NOBA; NeAP; PoM *Fr.* Burning. NeAP; PoM *Fr.* Myths and Texts.
Second Shepherd's Play, The. *Unknown.* NAEL-1; PoEL-1
 (Wakefield Second Shepherd's Play.) OAEL-1
 Haylle, Comly and Clene. OBEV; OxBoLi
Second Sight. Felicia Dorothea Hemans. Ro
Second Skins—a Peyote Song. Joseph Bruchac. CDW
Second Song. T. Carmi. MHP, *tr. by* Ruth Finer Mintz *Fr.* René's Songs.
Second Song. Sir Philip Sidney. NoSic *Fr.* Astrophil and Stella. AAS; SiPS
Second Stanza for Dr. Johnson, A. Donald Hall. KaS
Second Test and West Indies won! (LL) Victory Calypso, Lord's 1950. Egbert Moore, ("Lord Beginner"). OBCoV; PeLV
Second Thoughts. "Michael Field." LW
Second Voice, The. "Lewis Carroll." *Fr.* The Three Voices. BXAP
Second Wind. Fred Chappell. MT
2nd Wind. Barbara Howes. FiLi
Second year of the emperor's reign, in autumn, The. Journey North. Tu Fu, *Chinese.* SuSp, *tr. by* Hugh M. Stimson
(Secondary experience, nouns). Zen Buddhism and Psychoanalysis / Psychoanalysis and Zen Buddhism. Jackson MacLow. PoM
Secondhand Coat. Ruth Stone. NALW; NIP-4
Secrecy [or Secresie] Protested. Thomas Carew. CaPo; PFE; SeCP
Secret, The. "Æ." MoBrPo
Secret. Gwendolyn B. Bennett. BlSi; FiLi
Secret, The. Charles Bukowski. RaBo
Secret, The. John Clare. GBL; GLoP
Secret, The. Elizabeth Fleming. BoTP
Secret, The. Denise Levertov. CrSp; PBMP; Poetr

Secret, The. Suzanne Noguere. FFC
Secret. Pierre Reverdy, *French.* PFTM, *tr. by* Kenneth Rexroth
Secret, The. *Unknown.* CTV
Secret, The. Mary Morison Webster. PeSA
Secret behind locks and double bars, covered with green moss. First Month: at Ch'ung-jang House. Li Shang-yin, *Chinese.* PLT, *tr. by* A. C. Graham
Secret Flowers. Katherine Mansfield. LW
Secret Garden, The. Rita Dove. NoAM
Secret Garden, The. Thomas Kinsella. TwCP
Secret Gratitude, A. James Wright. NoAM
Secret History of the Dividing Line. Susan Howe.
 "In its first dumb form." FTOS
Secret Joy, The. Mary Webb. BoTP
Secret Kept, A. Judah Al-Harizi, *Hebrew.* NNPT, *tr. by* David Goldstein
Secret kept from all the rest, / Between yourself and me, A. (LL) Evidence Read at the Trial of the Knave of Hearts. "Lewis Carroll." CBNP; GTBS-P; NOBVV; OxBoLi; PBMP; PeLV
Secret Life of Gilbert Bond, The. Joan Retallack. FTOS
Secret Love. John Clare. FHYEP; OBNC; PoE; PoEL-4; SCGP
 (Song.) NOBVV; NTP; OAEL-2; RB
Secret Love. Milton Kessler. UnSA
Secret Love. Lyubomir Levchev, *Bulgarian.* CEEP, *tr. by* Jascha Kessler *and* Aleksandar Shurbanov
Secret Love; or, The Maiden Queen. Dryden.
 Prologue: "He who writ [or wrote] this, not without pains and thought." PeLV
 Song: "I feed a flame within, which so torments me." AWP
 (Hidden Flame.) OBEV
Secret love or two, I must confess[e], A. Thomas Campion. AAS
Secret many years unseen, A. The Chess Play. Nicholas Breton. NoSic
SECRET murder hath been done of late. *Unknown.* NoSic
Secret Muse, The. Roy Campbell. PeSA
Secret of movement, The. The Time before You. Medbh McGuckian. CBLP
Secret of the Legal Secretary's Cigarette Smoke, The. Martín Espada. FiLi
Secret of the Quartz Pebble, The. Vasco [or Vasko] Popa. PoSu, *tr. by* Anne Pennington *Fr.* The Quartz Pebble.
Secret of these hills was stone, and cottages, The. The Pylons. Stephen Spender. AWP; NoAM
Secret People, The. G. K. Chesterton. FaPoR; OxBTC
Secret Places. Irene Thompson. BoTP
Secret Rose, The. W. B. Yeats. ADE; NAEL-2
Secret Sits, The. Robert Frost. InPK-6
Secret Song, The. Margaret Wise Brown. OBCA
Secret strangers, The. At Home. Linda Pastan. CMAP
Secret they are, sealed, annealed, and brainless. Oystering. Richard Howard. NoAM
Secret Thoughts. Ella Wheeler Wilcox. PWR
Secret Town, The. Abraham Sutskever, *Yiddish.* TrJP, *tr. by* Jacob Sonntag
Secret Virginity, The. "Angelus Silesius." GePo, *tr. by* George C. Schoolfield *Fr.* The Cherubical Wanderer.
Secret was the garden. The Mistress of Vision. Francis Thompson. CH
Secretary, The. Peter Redgrove. OxBTC
Secretary Chant, The. Marge Piercy. IFJA
Secrets, sels. Jessie Orton Jones. CTV
Secrets. Letitia Elizabeth Landon. VWP *Fr.* Fragments.
Secrets of the Earth, The. William Blake. NOBE *Fr.* The Book of Thel. NAEL-2; OAEL-2; OBNC; PoE; PoEL-4
Section: America (2). Seen as a Bird. Nathaniel Tarn. APSN *Fr.* Lyrics for the Bride of God.
Section VI. George Barker. SPE *Fr.* Calamiterror.
Secular, The. Chris Wallace-Crabbe. NOBAu
Secular Elegies. George Barker.
 O Golden Fleece ("O Golden Fleece she is where she lies tonight"). LiTM; MoBrPo
 (Secular Elegy V.) EP *See* O Golden Fleece.
 Satan Is on Your Tongue. MoBrPo
Secular Games. Richard Howard. PoA
Secular Masque, The. Dryden. NAEL-1; PoE; PoEL-3; SCGP
 ("Chronos, Chronos, mend thy pace.") OxAEP-1
 Chorus to the Gods. OxBSP
 Diana's Hunting-Song. NOBE
 Momus' Song to Mars. OxBSP
 Song: "All, all of a piece throughout." WeW-3
Secure in death he keeps the hearts he had. Death's Guerdon. Lizette Woodworth Reese. APN-2

Seder, The. Enid Dame. UnSA

Seder-Night. Israel Zangwill. TrJP

Sediment. David Ignatow. NYBP

Sedley has that prevailing, gentle art. John Wilmot, 2d Earl of Rochester. EPCY *Fr.* An Allusion to Horace.

Seduced by Analogy. Bob Perelman. FTOS

Seduced Girl. Hedylos, *Greek.* BoLoP, *tr. by* Louis Untermeyer

Seduction. Nikki Giovanni. NMM-2

Seduction. Jo Ann Hall-Evans. BlSi

See a man who so loves you as your lord S. T. COLERIDGE. (LL) Metrical Feet. Coleridge. FHYEP; NIP-4; OxBChV; Poetr

See a man with sound eyes. Ingrown. James Berry. PBCV

See a pin and pick it up. Pins. *Unknown.* FaBoBe; LB; ReMoGo

See a traveler in isorrow: deeper is his grief. Random Pleasures. Tu Fu, *Chinese.* SuSp, *tr. by* Irving Y. Lo

See an old unhappy bull. The Bull. Ralph Hodgson. LiTM; MoBrPo; NSI; OBMV; OxBTC

See, and not see; and if thou chance t' espy [*or* espie]. To the Generous Reader. Robert Herrick. CaPo

See, Ben, the water. To Ben, at the Lake. Cilla McQueen. PeNZ

See, Chloris, how the clouds. To Chloris. William Drummond, of Hawthornden. OxBSP

See columns rang'd in proud Palladian style! *Unknown.* FaBoEE

See commons, peers, and ministers of state. Edward Young. *Fr.* Love of Fame, the Universal Passion. OBSV

See dear Pater with the bills. Christmas Bills. Joseph Hatton. OBCP

See Florio in his *vis-à-vis.* The Picture of a Fine Gentleman. Lady Sophia Burrell. ECWP

'See for yourself?'. (LL) Telephone Conversation. Wole Soyinka. NoP-4; PBMAP

See! from the brake the whirring Pheasant springs. Hunting and Fishing. Alexander Pope. ECEV; FHYEP; PoEL-3 *Fr.* Windsor-Forest [*or* Windsor Forest].

See her caught in the throb of a drum. Agbor Dancer. J. P. Clark Bekederemo. PBA

See her come bearing down, a tidy craft! A Note on Wyatt. Kingsley Amis. WeW-3

See her there, Francie-the-Mad. Francie-the-Possessed. Oswald Durand, *French.* NegPo, *tr. by* Ellen Conroy Kennedy

See here an easy [*or* easie] Feast that know[e]s no wound. On the Miracle of Multiplied [*or* Multiplyed] Loaves. Richard Crashaw. OxBSP

See! Here, My Heart. *Unknown.* NoP-4

See here, nice Death, to please his palate. Epitaph. Alexander Pope. FaBoEE

See: here, the bougainvillea. Floating Petals. Jan Barry. CDa

See, here's the grand approach. Verses on Blenheim. Martial, *Latin.* AWP, *tr. by* Swift

See, here's the workbox, little wife. The Workbox. Thomas Hardy. InPK-6; NAEL-2; UnPo

See him go / little scrabble rat. Verbal Gerbil. Philip Gross. PeP

See His face, and sing His praise! (LL) A Cradle Hymn. Isaac Watts. OBEV; OxBChV; PoEL-3; SCGP

See how Flora smiles to see. On Clarastella walking in Her Garden. Robert Heath. NOSC

See how far upon the eastern road. The Magi. Milton. *Fr.* On the Morning of Christ's Nativity. MeLP; NOCV; NoP-4; PBRV; PoEL-3; SCGP

See how He watches? He snatches the bad ones. (LL) Fräulein Reads Instructive Rhymes. Maxine W. Kumin. NYBP; Poetsp

See how it circles. *Ambo Oral Tradition. Fr.* Five Ghost Songs. TTTS

See how she strips her lily for the sun. The Double Looking Glass. Alec Derwent Hope. CBAP

See how that pair of billing doves. Verses Written in a Garden. Lady Mary Wortley Montagu. ECWP

See how the brown kelp withers in air. Landed: A Valentine. Richard Howard. PoA

See how the flowers, as at parade. A Garden. Andrew Marvell. OBEV *Fr.* Upon Appleton House [To My Lord Fairfax]. FaBoPV; GeHe; SeCP

See, how the human animal is fed. The Digestive System. Sir Richard Blackmore. ECEV *Fr.* Creation.

See how the Orient Dew. *see also* Ros. Andrew Marvell. ESCV; FMP; FSCP; GeHe; HAP; MeLP; NOSC; SCGP; SeCP

See how the rainbow in the sky. Justification. William Strode. NOSC

See How the Rising Sun. Elizabeth Scott. AH

See,—how the shining share. God Save the Plough. Lydia Huntley Sigourney. OBAL

See how the sun has somewhat not of light. El Greco. Edward Leslie Mayo. HoPM

See how the willing earth gave way. The Fall. Edmund Waller. NOSC

See how they hurry. At Luca Signorelli's Resurrection of the Body. Jorie Graham. HCAP

See, / how they trace. Birds in Snow. Hilda Doolittle. PoA

See how this ivy strives to twine. Love's Innocence. Thomas Stanley. BeJo

See how this violet which before. On a Violet in Her Breast. Thomas Stanley. NOSC

See! Hymen comes; how his torch blazes! Sir Charles Sedley. NOSC

See, I have climbed the mountain side. San Miniato. Oscar Wilde. TIRV

See, I was raised on the wild side, border country. How the Wild South East Was Lost. Kit Wright. OBCoV

See lightning is flashing. The Storm. Sara Coleridge. NOxBChV

See Lucifer like lightning fall. John Keble. ChIV-2

See me, the lord of deep-bosomed earth, who turned Acmonides upside down. Wings. *Unknown, Greek.* HePo, *tr. by* Barbara Hughes Fowler

See me with all the terrors on my roads. The Face. Edwin Muir. GTBS-P

See, Mignonne, hath not the Rose. The Rose. Pierre de Ronsard, *French.* AWP, *tr. by* Andrew Lang

"See, nothing has happened to her," said my guide. Seeing Oloalok. Marilyn Bowering. NOBC

See now the Trumpets and the Torches!—see. A Bitter end. Persius, *Latin.* OBCVT, *tr. by* Thomas Brewster

See on one hand. The Rainbow. Gerard Manley Hopkins. OxBSP

See on yon verdant lawn, the gathering crowd. On the Village Green. William Somervile. ECEV *Fr.* Hobbinol.

See, one physician, like a sculler, plies. Joseph Jekyll. FaBoEE

See-saw, down in my lap. *Unknown.* OxNR

See-saw, Margery Daw. *Unknown.* ACTP; LB

See-saw, Margery Daw, / Jack[y] shall have a new master. Mother Goose. OxNR; ReMoGo

See-saw, Margery Daw, / Sold her bed and lay upon straw. *Unknown.* OxNR

See-saw, Margery Daw, / The old hen flew over the malt house. Mother Goose. OxNR

See-saw, sacradown [*or* Sacaradown]. Mother Goose. CBNP; OxNR

See See Rider, see what you done done! Gertrude "Ma" Rainey. NAAAL

See, see, she wakes, Sabina wakes! William Congreve. NOEC; OxBSP

See, see, what shall I see? Mother Goose. OxNR; ReMoGo

See sin, but through my tears. (LL) Hymn: "Drop, drop, slow tears." Phineas Fletcher. OxBSP; PeECV

See that brave and trembling motorman. The Dying Mine Brakeman. Orville Jenks. AmFP

See that [*or* the] building which, when my mistress living. A Well-wishing to a Place of Pleasure. *Unknown.* GBL

See the bunnies sitting there. Timid Bunnies. Jeannie Kirby. BoTP

See the chariot at hand here of Love. Her Triumph. Ben Jonson. CBLP; CTC; EBEV; NOBE; NOSC; NoP-4; OBEV; PoEL-2; TFi *Fr.* A Celebration of Charis in Ten Lyric[k] Pieces [*or* Peeces]. BeJo; OxAEP-1; SeCP

See the day begins to break. Satyr's Song. John Fletcher. SCGP *Fr.* The Faithful Shepherdess.

See the dazzled stripling stand. Goliath and David. Louis Untermeyer. TrJP

See the fountain opened wide. Zion's Sons and Daughters. *Unknown.* AmFP

See! The gleam. Chiyojo, *Japanese.* WPJ, *tr. by* Kenneth Rexroth *and* Ikuko Atsumi

See the handsome hippopotamus. Hippopotamus. Joanna Cole. NTCP

See the house took flight. Daniil Kharms, *Russian.* CBNP, *tr. by* Alice Stone Nakhamovsky

See the kitten on the wall. The Kitten at Play. Wordsworth. ChAP *Fr.* The Kitten and [the] Falling Leaves.

See! the moon is smiling. Eliza in Uncle Tom's Cabin. Eloise Bibb. CBWP-4

See the pretty snowflakes. Falling Snow. *Unknown.* CTV

See the Rat—at Least It's Got a Hide. *Unknown, Chinese.* CoBCP, *tr. by* Burton Watson

See the shark with teeth like razors. Bertolt Brecht. OxBoV, *tr. by* Ralph Manheim *and* John Willett *Fr.* The Threepenny Opera.

See, the smelle of my sone is as the smell of a feld. Bible, *O.T.* OBVE, *tr. by* William Tyndale *Fr.* Genesis.

See the smoking bowl before us. Drinking Song. Robert Burns. NBLV; PoE *Fr.* Love and Libery—A Cantata. NOBRP; NOEC

See the Spring herself discloses. Spring. Anacreon, *Greek.* AWP, *tr. by* Thomas Stanley

See the whole panoply of love. (LL) Past fifty and cloyed at last. Philetas, *Greek.* GrAn; PGA, *tr. by* Kenneth Rexroth

See the world! the tussles. The Annunciation. Douglas Messerli. FTOS

See the yellow catkins cover. A Spring Song. Mary Howitt. BoTP

See the young man I've laid out. Funeral Lament (Kommos) from Epiros. *Unknown, Modern Greek.* BoWoP, *tr. by* Elene Margot Kolb

See—the young, the rosy Spring. Ode 46. Anacreon, *Greek.* OBCVT, *tr. by* Thomas Moore

See them joined by strings to history. Puppets. Patricia K. Page. MoCV

See them sprawl with earth for bed. Angry Dusk. Jack Lindsay. NOBAu

See! There he stands; not brave, but with an air. Brothers. James Weldon Johnson. NAAAL

See! there she goes. William Somervile. ECEV *Fr.* The Chase.

See these happy youths, now made. Sung at Table by the Same Choir. Anne Penny. ECWP *Fr.* Odes Sung in Commemoration of the Marine Society.

See, they are clearing the sawdust course. Equestrienne. Rachel Lyman Field. OBCA *Fr.* A Circus Garland.

See, they return; ah, see the tentative. The Return. Ezra Pound. AmPP; CMoP; ColAP; HAP; MoAmPo; MoP; NOBA; NoAM; OxBA; PFTM; PoE; Poetr; RB; TRP; VGW; WeW-3

See this air, how empty it is of angels. Five for the Grace of Man. Winfield Townley Scott. VGW

See those cherries, how they cover. The Cherries; a Parable. Thomas Moore. OBSV

See those resplendent creatures, as they glide. Fashion. Ada Cambridge. NOBAu

See what a clouded Majesty. To My Worthy Friend Mr. Peter Lely [*or* Lilly]. Richard Lovelace. CaPo; GS; NOSC

See what a lovely shell. The Shell. Tennyson. PoEL-5 *Fr.* Maud [A Monodrama]. EnVR

See what a mass of gems the city wears. Impression de Nuit; London. Lord Alfred Bruce Douglas. ADE; OBEV

See when my English cousin comes. English Cousin Comes to Scotland. Jackie Kay. NOxBChV

See where Capella with her golden kids. Edna St. Vincent Millay. CMoP; MoAmPo *Fr.* Epitaph for the Race of Man.

See where she sits upon the grassie [*or* grassy] green[e]. Ditty, A: In Praise of Eliza, Queen of the Shepherds. Edmund Spenser. FaBoCh; OBEV *Fr.* Aprill. NAEL-1; OBEV; PoEL-1 *Fr.* The Shepheardes [*or* Shepeards *or* Shepherd's] Calender.

See where the falling day. Tomorrow. Anna Laetitia Barbauld. ECWP; PEW

See where the silver walls enclose. My Lady's Bath. John Barlas. ADE

See where the windows are boarded up. Where Are the Waters of Childhood? Mark Strand. HCAP; LCAP-2; VCAP; WeW-3

See where they blur, and die, and are outsoared. (LL) Camping Out. William Empson. CMoP; FaBoMo; OxBTC

See with what constant Motion. Gratiana Dancing [*or* Dauncing] and [*or* &] Singing. Richard Lovelace. BeJo; CaPo; CavPo; MeLP; PBRV

See with what simplicity. The Picture of Little T. C. in a Prospect of Flowers. Andrew Marvell. ESCV; FMP; FSCP; GeHe; MeLP; NAEL-1; NOBE; NoP-4; OAEL-1; OBEV; OxAEP-1; PoE; SCGP; SeCP; TFi

See yonder hallow'd fane, the pious work. The Grave-yard on a Stormy Night. Robert Blair. OxAEP-1 *Fr.* The Grave.

See yonder, where a gem of night. Es fällt ein Stern herunter. Heinrich Heine, *German.* AWP, *tr. by* Richard Garnett

See you not Heng Mountain towering over Hunan hills. Song of the Vermeil Phoenix. Tu Fu, *Chinese.* TAL, *tr. by* Robert Payne

See you the ferny ride that steals. Puck's Song. Rudyard Kipling. FaBoCh; OxBChV *Fr.* Puck of Pook's Hill.

See young John Sutton with his Kathaleen. Speaks the Whispering Grass. Jesse Stuart. FYAP

Seed. Herman Charles Bosman. PeSA

Seed. Charles Buckmaster. BMAP

Seed, The. Tomasz Jastrun, *Polish.* AF, *tr. by* Michael March *and* Jaroslaw Anders

Seed, The. Vasco [*or* Vasko] Popa. PoSu *Fr.* Games. RB, *tr. by* Anne Pennington

Seed catalog in the mailbox cold drizzle. Marlene Mountain. HA

Seed Cutters, The. Seamus Heaney. PNI *Fr.* Mossbawn. CIP-2; PNI

Seed dazzled over the footbattered blaze of the earth. (LL) Vapor Trail Reflected in the Frog Pond. Galway Kinnell. AF; OBWP; VCAP; VGW

Seed Growing Secretly, The. Henry Vaughan. ChIV-2; ESCV; GeHe

Seed is dug under, A. Shekhinah. Karl Wolfskehl, *German.* TrJP, *tr. by* Carol North Valhope *and* Ernst Morwitz

Seed is in Me, The. José Craveirinha. PBMAP

Seed Is the Light of the Earth, The. Christina Pacosz. LoHo

Seed Journey. Gregory Corso. VGW

Seed, leaf, flower, fruit, herb, bee, and tree, and more than I may sing. Nicholas Grimald. *See* The Garden.

Seed Leaves. Richard Wilbur. NoP-4

Seed of Nimrod, The. De Leon Harrison. PoBA

Seed-Picture, The. Medbh McGuckian. PNI

Seed pods of frost falling in autumn. A Trail among the Pines. Lin Pu, *Chinese.* SuSp, *tr. by* Irving Y. Lo

Seeded in the mud on turtle's back. Sweetgrass. Maurice Kenny. HATNAP

Seeds clutched in my hand. Hunting. "Yehoash," *Yiddish.* TrJP, *tr. by* Isidore Goldstick

Seeds in a dry pod, tick, tick, tick. Petit, the Poet. Edgar Lee Masters. CMoP; ColAP; MoAmPo; NOBA; NoAM; OxBA; TAP *Fr.* Spoon River Anthology.

Seeds of certain grasses that once grew, The. Metaphor of Grass in California. Charles Martin. RA

Seeds of Flight. Anghel Dumbrveanu, *Romanian.* CEEP, *tr. by* Adam J. Sorkin *and* Irina Grigorescu Pan

Seeds of Kindness. *Unknown.* PoToHe
(Say It Now.) BLPA

Seeds of Love, The. Mrs. Fleetwood Habergham. FaBoCh; OxBoLi
("I loved one flower too much.") (LL) LW
(Unfortunate Damsel, The.) LW

Seeds of Love, The. *Unknown.* GaP

Seeds of the grass. Tanka. Fumi Saito, *Japanese.* MJT, *tr. by* Makoto Ueda

Seedsman of old Saturn's land. Afterward. Herman Melville. APN-2 *Fr.* Clarel: A Poem and Pilgrimage in the Holy Land.

Seedy Henry rose up shy in de world. John Berryman. HCAP; VCAP *Fr.* Dream Songs.

Seeing. At the Castle. Jerome Rothenberg. FTOS

Seeing a Friend Off. Li Po, *Chinese.* CoBCP, *tr. by* Burton Watson

Seeing as the father saw the rosy morn. Ovid. OBVE, *tr. by* Joseph Addison *Fr.* Metamorphoses.

Seeing Auden Off. Philip Booth. PoA

Seeing Cousin Phyllis Off. Richard Howard. WeT

Seeing Flowers I Remember My Late Daughter, Shu. Kao Ch'i, *Chinese.* CoBLCP, *tr. by* Jonathan Chaves

Seeing for a Moment. Denise Levertov. VCAP

Seeing good places / in my hands. The Time We Climbed Snake Mountain. Leslie Marmon Silko. VoR

Seeing Her Dancing. Robert Heath. NOSC; OxBSP

Seeing Hsia Chan off by River. Po Chü-i, *Chinese.* TAL, *tr. by* Robert Payne

Seeing in all things around, types of the Infinite Mind. (LL) Correspondences. Christopher Pearse Cranch. APN-1; PAR

Seeing in flight along the lifting wind. Message. Dorothy M. Richardson. PoA

Seeing is believing. On Sir Henry Ferrett, M.P. John Bingham Morton. OBCoV

Seeing means going far off, going off down the road. Recurring Opportunity. David Avidan, *Hebrew.* IP, *tr. by* Warren Bargad *and* Stanley F. Chyet

Seeing Meng Hao-jan Off to Kuang-ling. Li Po, *Chinese.* SuSp, *tr. by* Paul W. Kroll

Seeing / movies you wouldn't let them see when they were young. Frank O'Hara. *See* Ave Maria.

Seeing Off Commander In Chief Li to Yün-chung. Li Meng-yang, *Chinese.* CoBLCP, *tr. by* Jonathan Chaves

Seeing Off Editor Wang Chou-tz'u and Secretary Lin Shih-lai on Their Mission as Envoys to the Ryūkyū Islands. Wang Shih-chieng, *Chinese.* CoBLCP, *tr. by* Jonathan Chaves

Seeing Off Han Ju-ch'ing as He Returns to the Land Within the Passes. Ho Ching-ming, *Chinese.* CoBLCP, *tr. by* Jonathan Chaves

Seeing Off Master Tan. Meng Chiao, *Chinese.* SuSp, *tr. by* Stephen Owen

Seeing Off Mr. Yang on His Journey to Wu-wei Prefecture. Yün Shou-p'ing, *Chinese.*
War ships, cold tides. CoBLCP, *tr. by* Jonathan Chaves

Seeing Off Sun Ling-hsiu on His Journey to Chen-ting. Wu Wei-yeh, *Chinese.* CoBLCP, *tr. by* Jonathan Chaves

Seeing Off Wang Yüan-chao—Reprise. Wu Wei-yeh, *Chinese.* CoBLCP, *tr. by* Jonathan Chaves

Seeing Oloalok. Marilyn Bowering. NOBC

Seeing Someone Off. Wang Wei, *Chinese.* CoBCP, *tr. by* Burton Watson; SuSp, *tr. by* Irving Y. Lo

Seeing St. James's. Ray Mathew. NOBAu

Seeing the Bones. Maxine W. Kumin. NoAM

Seeing the crowds, he went up on the mountain. Matthew 5:1–12; Seeing the crowds, he went up on the mountain. Bible, N.T., GI *tr. by* Jorge Luis Borges. *Fr.* St. Matthew.

Seeing the frog. May Swenson. APo

Seeing the infinite world. Life. Ch'ihwan Yu, *Korean.* CKP, *tr. by* Jaihiun Kim

Seeing the Plum Blossoms by the River. Lady Ise, *Japanese.* BoWoP, *tr. by* Etsuko Terasaki *and* Irma Brandeis

'SEEING the plum-tree I thought of the Western Island'. Ballad of the Western Island in the North Country. *Unknown, Chinese.* ChiP, *tr. by* Arthur Waley

Seeing the Returning Geese. Lady Ise. BoWoP, *tr. by* Etsuko Terasaki *and* Irma Brandeis

Seeing the snowman standing all alone. Boy at the Window. Richard Wilbur. RaBo

Seeing them like this. Toys. Carl Phillips. BAP-95

Seeing thou art fair, I bar not thy false playing. Ode 3.13. Ovid. OBVE, *tr. by* Marlowe *Fr.* Elegies.

Seeing through the Sun. Linda Hogan. HATNAP

Seeing You. Jean Valentine. PuP-16

Seeing you stand once more before my eyes. Amy Lowell. SAGP *Fr.* Eleanora Duse.

Seek[e] Flowers of Heaven. Robert Southwell. TrCP

Seek lovers only among them that sleep?' (LL) Moonrise Over Battlefield. Edgell Rickword. NSI; PoWW

Seek not, Leuconöe, to know how long you're going to live yet. Ode 1.11. Horace. AWP, *tr. by* F. P. Adams *Fr.* Odes.

Seek not man to please, for that. Isabella Whitney. *Fr.* Sweet Nosegay, A, or Pleasant Posy. WPE

Seek not the spirit, if it hide. Sursum Corda. Ralph Waldo Emerson. APN-1

Seek[e] not to know my love, for she. To One That Desired to Know My Mistress [*or* Mistris]. Thomas Carew. SeCP

Seek on his cross: there, then, thus Love stands nail'd with love. (LL) Ocean of Light. Phineas Fletcher. PBRV

Seek, roseate net, inchanting Zara's hand. To Miss Ponsonby. Anna Seward. CPO

Seek the Lord, and in His ways persever. Thomas Campion. TrCP

Seeker, The. Matthew Green. ECEV

Seeking a bearing point on hurt I find. Ospita. Peter Riley. NBrP

Seeking a Mooring. Wang Wei, *Chinese.* BoWoP; ChiPo; WPOW, *tr. by* Kenneth Rexroth *and* Ling Chung

Seeking an Explanation. Richard Emil Braun. NoAM

Seeking heat men become cold, and look for meaning. David Foster. NOBAu *Fr.* The Fleeing Atalanta.

Seeking Hsin E in the Western Hills. Meng Hao Jan, *Chinese.* SuSp, *tr. by* Daniel Bryant

Seeking in squalor lean, elusive youth. Nightwood. William Jay Smith. PoA

Seeking out Hermit Hu. Kao Ch'i, *Chinese.* CoBLCP, *tr. by* Jonathan Chaves

Seeking Out His face in a Cup. Fanny Howe. FTOS

Seeking Spring Beyond the city. Su Tung-p'o, *Chinese.* TAL, *tr. by* Robert Payne

Seeking Te Iwi-ika's death. Lament for Te Iwi—ika. *Unknown, Maori.* PeNZ, *tr. by* Margaret Orbell

Seeking the words. Poem for Jan. Joseph Bruchac. CDW

Seekonk Woods, The. Galway Kinnell. NoAM

Seele im Raum. Randall Jarrell. LCAP-2

Seem with their quiet to have stilled in life's dream / All sorrowing now. (LL) The Ghost. Walter De la Mare. CMoP; EnLoPo; LiTM; MoBrPo; NOBE; OAEL-2; OxBTC

Seems lak to me de stars don't shine so bright. Sence You Went Away. James Weldon Johnson. ISC; NAAAL

Seems like I heard. Sunnyland. Elmore James. NAAAL

Seems, madam? Nay, it is. I know not "seems." Shakespeare. *Fr.* Hamlet. NAWM-1

Seen from Above. Wislawa Szymborska, *Polish.* BLT, *tr. by* Magnus J. Krynski *and* Robert A. Maguire

Seen From Above. Wislawa Szymborska, *Polish.* PoSu, *tr. by* Grazyna Drabik *and* Sharon Olds

Seen from the air. (LL) Lamentations. Louise Glück. BoWoP; HCAP; VCAP

Seen my lady home las' night. A Negro Love Song. Paul Laurence Dunbar. AAP; APAD; APN-2; ColAP; CrDW; NAAAL; SSLK

Seen on the sea, no sign; no sign, no sign. The Dead Wingman. Randall Jarrell. PoWW

Seen Words. Hannah Weiner. FTOS *Fr.* Spoke Aug 19.

Seepage of time rots judgment, makes it slip. Darkened Windows. Ronald Bottrall. PoA

Seer foretold that I would love one day, A. Sonnet. Louise Labé, *French.* PBWP, *tr. by* Judith Thurman

Sees not my love how time resumes. To a Lady in a Garden. Edmund Waller. BeJo

See'st thou o'er my shoulders falling. Love Song. Judah Halevi, *Hebrew.* TrJP, *tr. by* Emma Lazarus

See'st thou that Cloud as silver cleare. Her Bed. Robert Herrick. PBRV

Seest thou those diamonds which she wears. Robert Herrick. NOSC

See'st thou yon mountains laden with deep snow. Horace. *See* Odes 1.9.

Seferis. Lawrence Durrell. EBEV

Segment, A. Martin Sorescu, *Romanian.* CEEP, *tr. by* Dan Duescu

Segregated Railway Diner—1946. Robert Winner. LTA

Sehnsucht. Anna Wickham. MoBrPo

Seil o'yer face! the send has come. The Fleggit Bride. "Hugh MacDiarmid." OxBS

Seine / transcend, be real, The. Grand Duo. James Schuyler. FTOS

16 heures / l'Etoile. Two X. E. E. Cummings. FaBoMo

Seized with a fancy for fresh meat. Hymn to Mercury. *Unknown.* OBVE *Fr.* Homeric Hymns.

Seizure. Linda Bierds. PUP-20

Sejanus his Fall. Claudian, *Latin.*

"Old Men not staid with Age, Virgins with shame." OBCVT, *tr. by* Ben Jonson

Sejanus ("How many men are killed by power, by power"). Juvenal. OBVE, *tr. by* Robert Lowell *Fr.* Satires.

Sejanus ("Some ask for envy'd pow'r; which publick hate"). Juvenal. OBVE, *tr. by* Dryden *Fr.* Satires.

Sejanus ("What crowds by envied power, the wish of all"). Juvenal. OBVE, *tr. by* William Gifford *Fr.* Satires.

Selah. Ronald Stuart Thomas. FaBoMo

Seldom "can't." Christina Rossetti. CTV

"Seldom we find," says Solomon Don Dunce. An Enigma. Edgar Allan Poe. Son

Select fine arrows and call for falcons. Lu Lun. SuSp, *tr. by* Ronald C. Miao *Fr.* Frontier Songs.

Selected Epigrams. Kassia, *Byzantine Greek.* PBWP, *tr. by* Patrick Diehl

Selecting a loose vibration from the taut air. Soundwaves. Andrew Sant. NOBAu

Selecting a Reader. Ted Kooser. PBCAP

Selection of Heaven, The. Paul Blackburn.

"Mind returns to it always, The." APSN

Selective Service. Carolyn Forché. Poetr

Selenologist, The. Bill Manhire. PeNZ

Self. Sharon Doubiago. NMM-2

Self. Norman Henry, II Pritchard. PoBA

Self-abandonment. Li Po, *Chinese.* ChiP, *tr. by* Arthur Waley

Self[e] Accuser, A. Donne. FaBoEE; PeLV

Self-Acquaintance. William Cowper. NOCV *Fr.* Olney Hymns.

Self-analysis. Michael Dransfield. BMAP

Self-Analysis. Anna Wickham. MoBrPo

Self-brewing of the amaryllis rising before me, The. Opulence. Jorie Graham. NoP-4

Self-Consciousness Makes All Changes Happy; Ode. Jonathan Richardson. NOEC

Self-Criticism in February. Robinson Jeffers. AmPP

Self crowned the day displays its plumage. Hymn Among the Ruins. Octavio Paz, *Spanish.* PFTM, *tr. by* William Carlos Williams

Self-Deceaver, The. Thomas Stanley. OBVE

Self-Defense. Santob De Carrion, *Spanish.* TrJP, *tr. by* George Ticknor

Self-Dependence. Matthew Arnold. PBMP

Self Dirge. Wendy Rose. CDW

Self-Discipline. "Æ." MoBrPo

Self-educated WILLIAM BLAKE. W. H. Auden. EPCY *Fr.* New Year Letter.

Self-employed. David Ignatow. NNaP

Self-Evident. James Robinson Planché. OBCoV

Self-Examination, The. *Unknown.* ECWP

Self-Hatred of Don L. Lee, The. Haki Madhbouti. BPo

Self, I want you now to be. The Thing is Violent. Gwendolyn MacEwen. MoCV; NOBC

Self in 1958. Anne Sexton. HCAP

Self-Interrogation. Emily Jane Brontë. BWW

Self Justification. Tony Harrison. *Fr.* The School of Eloquence. NAEL-2; NoAM

Self-Mastery. Henrietta Cordelia Ray. CBWP-3

Self-mockery. "Lu Hsün," *Chinese.* SuSp, *tr. by* William R. Schultz

Self-Pity. Philip Hodgins. NOBAu

Self-Pity. D. H. Lawrence. OxBTC; RB

Self-Pity Is a Kind of Lying, Too. James Schuyler. PoM

Self-Portrait. Frank Bidart. HCAP

Self-Portrait. Cecil Bødker, *Danish.* BoWoP, *tr. by* Nadia Christensen

Self-Portrait. Robert Creeley. NoAM; PmAP

Self-Portrait. Moses Mendelsohn, *German.* TrJP

Self-Portrait. A. K. Ramanujan. NoP-4

Self-Portrait. Lloyd Schwartz. WeT

Self-Portrait ("Someday they'll find me out, and my lavish hands"). Charles Wright. PoPoPo

Self-portrait, A. Tanka. Saitō Mokichi, *Japanese.* MJT, *tr. by* Makoto Ueda

Self-Portrait. William Carlos Williams. LCAP-2 *Fr.* Pictures from Brueghel.

Self-Portrait Approaching Promontory, Utah. Michael Pettit. GM

Self-Portrait as Van Gogh. Peter Cooley. NAmP90

Self-Portrait at Eighteen. Lynn Emanuel. CMAP

Self-Portrait at Thirty-Nine. Ted Kooser. PBCAP

Self Portrait 4. Tove Ditlevsen, *Danish.* WPOW, *tr. by* Ann Freeman

Self Portrait II. Tove Ditlevsen, *Danish.* IMW, *tr. by* Ann Freeman

Self-Portrait in a Convex Mirror. John Ashbery. HCAP; NAAL-2

Self-Portrait of the Laureate of Nonsense. Edward Lear. FaBoCh

Self-Portrait of the Other. Herberto Padilla, *Spanish.* VCWP, *tr. by* Alastair Reid *and* Andrew Hurley

Self-Portrayal. Nguyễn Khuyến, *Vietnamese.* AVP, *tr. by* Huỳnh Sanh Thông

Self-praise is a wonderful thing! The Unawkward Singer. David Ferry. PFE

Self-Protection. D. H. Lawrence. NoP-4

Self-Reflection. Nguyễn Bỉnh Khiêm, *Chinese.* AVP, *tr. by* Huỳnh Sanh Thông

Self-Reliance. Ralph Waldo Emerson. APN-1 *Fr.* Quatrains.

Self-Reliance. James M. Whitfield. NAAAL

Self-same Power that brought me there brought you, The. (LL) Rhodora, The [On Being Asked Whence Is the Flower]. Ralph Waldo Emerson. APN-1; AWP; AmPP; GEA; MeMAP; NAAL-1; NAAL-3; NOBA; NoP-4; OxBA; PAR; PFE; PWR; PoE; TAP; TFi

Self-slaved, The. Patrick Kavanagh. MoBrPo

Self-Storage. Alice Fulton. NAmP90

Self Unsatisfied Runs Everywhere, The. Delmore Schwartz. PoA

Self-Unseeing, The. Thomas Hardy. EBEV; HAP; MoBrPo; NOBE; NOBVV; OBNC; OxAEP-2; RB; WeW-3

Self World. Clarence Major. NBV

Selfish woman. Tanka. Kanoko Okamoto, *Japanese.* MJT, *tr. by* Makoto Ueda

Selfishness. Margaret E. Bruner. PoToHe

Self's the Man. Philip Larkin. NOBL; PeLV

Selfsame Song, The. Thomas Hardy. CMoP

Selfsame surface that billowed once with, The. Skin Flick. Fred Chappell. InPK-6

Selfsame toothless voice for death or bridal, The. Bell Speech. Richard Wilbur. MoAmPo

Sell it, though it sleeps still at its mother's breast! Meleager. HePo, *tr. by* Barbara Hughes Fowler *Fr.* I'll Twine White Violets. NIP-4, *tr. by* Goldwin Smith

Sell Out. Léon Damas, *French.* NegPo, *tr. by* Ellen Conroy Kennedy

Sellin biscuit an salfish in de plantation shop at pie. Horse Weebles. Edward Kamau Brathwaite. PBCV

Selling calico cloth on the mercantile shame-rock. Miss Own. Edward Kamau Brathwaite. HCP

Selling My Official Robe. Yang Chi, *Chinese.* CoBLCP, *tr. by* Jonathan Chaves

Selling My Soul. Minh Đức Hoài Trinh, *Vietnamese.* AVP, *tr. by* Huỳnh Sanh Thông

Selling Ruined Peonies. Yü Hsüan-chi, *Chinese.* BoWoP, *tr. by* Geoffrey Waters

Selves eternal. Thomas Campion. *See* Laura.

Semantic Limerick According to Dr. Johnson's Dictionary (Edition of 1765), The. Gavin Ewart. OBCoV

Semantic Limerick According to the Shorter Oxford English Dictionary (1933), The. Gavin Ewart. OBCoV

Semblables, The. William Carlos Williams. FaBoMo; NOBA

Semele Recycled. Carolyn Kizer. InPS-3; NALW; Poetr

Semele to Jupiter. William Congreve. OBCoV

Semen. Martha Paley Francescato, *Spanish.* BoWoP, *tr. by* Willis Barnstone

Semi-private inducement. Ezra Pound. OxBoV *Fr.* Cantos.

Semi-Revolution, A. Robert Frost. LiTM

Semi-Skilled Lover. Maureen Duffy. LW

Seminar for Backward Pupils. Günter Eich, *German.* AF, *tr. by* David Young

Semiramis. Anne Bradstreet. KTR *Fr.* The Four[e] Monarchies.

Semmes in the Garden. George Marion O'Donnell. NYBP

Semphill, his hat stuck full of hooks. Trout Fisher. George Mackay Brown. FaBoTC; OxBC

Sempronius,/ Sends greeting, warden of this Roman shore. A Roman Officer Writes. Charles Montague Doughty. FaBoTw *Fr.* The Dawn in Britain.

Senate Hearings. Michael McClure. BB

Senator Smoot (Republican, Ut.) Invocation. Ogden Nash. OBAL

Sence You Went Away. James Weldon Johnson. ISC; NAAAL

Sence you went away. (LL) Sence You Went Away. James Weldon Johnson. ISC; NAAAL

Send for Lord Timothy. John Heath-Stubbs. OxBC

Send Forth, O God, Thy Light and Truth. John Quincy Adams. AH

Send forth your songs like the doe and the fawn. Memento of Roads. Nathan Alterman, *Hebrew.* MHP, *tr. by* Ruth Finer Mintz

Send mine my long strayed [or long-strayed or long-strayd] eyes to me[e]. The Message. Donne. MeLP

Send me jewels from starboard. What It Takes. John Godfrey. FTOS

Send me no flowers, for they will die before they leave America. Junglegrave. S. E. Anderson. PoBA

Send me your pity bounteous Shepherdess. To Mrs. B. from a Lady Who Had a Desire to See Her. *Unknown.* KTR

Send my spinach. Douglas Florian. NOxBChV

Send-Off, The. Wilfred Owen. MoBrPo; NSI; OBWP; OBWVE; OxBTC; PeFWW; PoWW; RB; SAGP

Send Pictures, You Said. . . . Laurie Duesing. DeD

Send us new Nymphs with each new Moon. (LL) The Progress of Beauty. Jonathan Swift. GEA; PFE

Sending Off O.E. Who Brought an Orchid Home to Japan. "Lu Hsün," *Chinese.* SuSp, *tr. by* William R. Schultz

Sending Off Spring. Kuan Yun She, *Chinese.* ChiPo, *tr. by* Lynn, Richard John

Sending Tzu-lung Off to a Post in Chi-chou. Lu Yu, *Chinese.* CoBCP, *tr. by* Burton Watson

Senec. Traged. ex Thyeste Chor. 2. Seneca, *Latin.* OBCVT, *tr. by* Andrew Marvell *Fr.* Thyestes.

("Climb at *Court* for me that will.") OBCVT; OBVE, *tr. by* Andrew Marvell

("Death to him 's a Strange surprise.") (LL) OBCVT, *tr. by* Andrew Marvell

("Let who so lyst with might mace to raygne.") OBVE, *tr. by* Jasper Heywood

(Of the meane and sure estate.) OBCVT, *tr. by* Sir Thomas Wyatt

("Stond who so list upon the Slipper toppe.") OBCVT, *tr. by* Sir Thomas Wyatt

Seneca Journal 1: "A Poem of Beavers." Jerome Rothenberg. APSN

Seneca's Troas, Act 2. Chorus. Seneca, *Latin.* OBCVT, *tr. by* John Wilmot, 2d Earl of Rochester *Fr.* Troades.

("*Dreams, Whimsies,* and no more.") (LL) OBCVT, *tr. by* John Wilmot, 2d Earl of Rochester

Senex. John Betjeman. RB

Senful man, bethink and see. *Unknown.* MiEL

Senile bat with nicotine-streaked hair, The. Visitors. Katha Pollitt. PuP-16

Senilio Passes, Singing. Martin Bell. OBCoV

Senilio's Weather Saw. Martin Bell. PeLV

Senior Lady Sells Garden Eggs. Kojo Laing. HBAPE

Senior Members. Sean Lucy. CIP-2

Senlin; a Biography. Conrad Potter Aiken.

   Morning Song of Senlin. ImPo; MoAmPo; OxBA

   (Morning Song.) CMoP

Señora, it is true the Greeks are dead. Invocation to the Social Muse. Archibald MacLeish. LiTM

Señora X No More. Pat Mora. UnSA

Señorita who strolled on the Corso, A. Limerick. *Unknown.* PeLi

Sensation. Rimbaud, *French.* AWP, *tr. by* Jethro Bithell; TTTS, *tr. by* Kenneth Koch

Sensation Type and His Friends, The. Michael Davidson. FTOS

Sense. Rae Armantrout. FTOS

Sense of Coolness, A. Quincy Troupe. GT; PoBA

Sense of danger must not disappear, The. Leap Before You Look. W. H. Auden. NoAM

Sense of History, A. Nhu'ọ'ng Tống, *Vietnamese.* AVP, *tr. by* Huỳnh Sanh Thông

Sense of Identity. Zbigniew Herbert, *Polish.* CEEP, *tr. by* John Carpenter *and* Bogdana Carpenter

Sense of Smell, The. Louis MacNeice. NYBP

Sense of the Sleight-of-Hand Man, The. Wallace Stevens. HAP; ImPo; LiTM; MoAmPo; NOBA; NoAM; PoA; TwCP; WeW-3

Sense of the world is short, The. Eros. Ralph Waldo Emerson. APN-1; FaBoBe

Sense with keenest edge unused. Pater Filio. Robert Bridges. CMoP; OBEV

Senseless prof, A. *Unknown, French.* CBNP

Senseless school, where we must give, A. A Young Man's Epigram on Existence. Thomas Hardy. MoP

Sensemayá. Nicolás Guillén, *Spanish.* PFTM, *tr. by* Langston Hughes

Sensibility: A Poetical Epistle to the Hon. Mrs Boscawen. Hannah More. ("Sweet Sensibility, thou soothing pow'r.") Ro

Sensible Girl's Reply to Moore's, A. Walter Savage Landor. FaBoEE

Sensible Is the Label. Eldon Grier. MoCV

Sensible Qualities. Fred Muratori. BAP-94

Sensing the next. Re-Verse. Diane Ward. FTOS

Sensitive girl called O'Neill, A. Limerick. *Unknown.* PeLi

Sensitive Plant in a garden grew, A. Shelley. FHYEP
   "Whether the sensitive plant, or that." OAEL-2

Sensitive, Seldom and Sad. Mervyn Laurence Peake. OTCP

Sensitiveness. John Henry, Cardinal Newman. TrCP

Sensualists, The. Theodore Roethke. EP

Sensuous / sloe eyed. Seduction. Jo Ann Hall-Evans. BlSi

Sent as a present from Annam—. The Red Cockatoo. Po Chü-i, *Chinese.* ChiP, *tr. by* Arthur Waley

Sent for You Yesterday. Jimmy Rushing. NAAAL

Sent forth the beams which made so fair my race. (LL) Sonnet 41: "Having this day my horse, my hand, my lance." Sir Philip Sidney. AEP; HAP; NAEL-1; PoE; Son

Sent from Egypt with a Fair Robe of Tissue to a Sicilian Vinedresser. Thomas Sturge Moore. OBEV

Sent from the Capital to Her Elder Daughter. Lady Otomo no Sakanoé, *Japanese.* BoWoP; MDDM; WPOW, *tr. by* Geoffrey Bownas *and* Anthony Thwaite

Sent from the Power. *Unknown.* WPoS *Fr.* The Thunder: Perfect Mind.

Sent in Lieu of a Letter to Shih-wu, Lan-ku, and Other Friends. Huang Tsun-hsien, *Chinese.* SuSp, *tr. by* An-yan Tang

Sent in Parting. Tu Mu, *Chinese.* CoBCP, *tr. by* Burton Watson

Sent in Parting to Yen Kung-su. Shen Chou, *Chinese.* CoBLCP, *tr. by* Jonathan Chaves

Sent myself the length. Eleven Rock Poems. Gustaf Sobin. PmAP

Sent out of sight, somewhere becoming rain. (LL) The Whitsun Weddings. Philip Larkin. FaBoMo; HeIP-4; MoP; NoAM; NoP-4; OxAEP-2; OxBM; OxBTC

Sent to a Ch'an Master. Han Wo, *Chinese.* SuSp, *tr. by* Irving Y. Lo

Sent to All My Nephews and Nieces at Tung-ch'eng. Yang Shih-ch'i, *Chinese.*
   "I've drawn a salary in the capital for forty years now." CoBLCP, *tr. by* Jonathan Chaves

Sent To Be Inscribed on the Temple of P'u-jun (Universal Fructification) at Lou-fu Mountain. Yü Chi, *Chinese.* CoBLCP, *tr. by* Jonathan Chaves

Sent to Chief Abbot of Tung-lin Monastery. Su Shih, *Chinese.* SuSp, *tr. by* Chiang Yee

Sent to Lo-t'ien for Thinking of Me after the Rainfall. Yüan Chen, *Chinese.* SuSp, *tr. by* Angela Jung Palandri

Sent to My Two Little Children in the East of Lu. Li Po, *Chinese.* CoBCP, *tr. by* Burton Watson

Sent to Recluse Ch'eng. Wang Chi, *Chinese.* SuSp, *tr. by* Hellmut Wilhelm

Sent to the Ch'an Master Wu-hsiang. Lo Yin, *Chinese.* SuSp, *tr. by* Geoffrey R. Waters

Sent to the Hsiu-ts'ai on His Entry into the Army. Hsi K'ang, *Chinese.* CoBCP, *tr. by* Burton Watson

Sent to the Master Physician, "Almond Orchard" Shih. Li K'ai-hsien, *Chinese.* CoBLCP

Sent to the Painter, Lu Hsiao-feng. Li K'ai-hsien, *Chinese.* CoBLCP, *tr. by* Jonathan Chaves

Sent to the Taoist Holy Man of Ch'üan-chiao. Wei Ying-wu, *Chinese.* CoBCP, *tr. by* Burton Watson

Sent to the Taoist of Dragon Mountain, Hsü Fa-leng. Liu Ch'ang-ch'ing, *Chinese.* SuSp, *tr. by* William H. Nienhauser

Sent to Wen T'ing-yün on a Winter Night. Yü Hsüan-chi, *Chinese.* BoWoP, *tr. by* Geoffrey Waters

Sent to Yü Te-fu upon His Receipt of an Official Commission to the Two Che's. Tsung Ch'en, *Chinese.*
   "When you enter Chin-hua Mountain." CoBLCP, *tr. by* Jonathan Chaves

Sentence. Antonin Bartusek, *German.* CEEP, *tr. by* Ewald Osers

Sentence, The. Yuly Markovich Daniel, *Russian.* TCRP, *tr. by* David Burg *and* Arthur Boyars

Sentence in the evening. Today the boxscores are green. Tonight, A. Ron Silliman. PmAP *Fr.* Paradise.

Sentence—Life without a prison—struck, The. Divorcee. C. Webster Wheelock. SoSe-8

Sentence, unapproved, and overruled by Heaven, A. (LL) The Prisoner. Emily Jane Brontë. NALW; NOBVV

Sentence undulates, The. The End of the Parade. William Carlos Williams. NYBP

Sentences. Nicanor Parra, *Spanish.* AF, *tr. by* Miller Williams

Sentences. David Shapiro. PT

Sentences While Remembering Hiraethog. T. Glynne Davies, *Welsh.* OBWVE, *tr. by* R. Gerallt Jones

Sententiae: Maxims. Publilius Syrus, *Latin.* OBCVT, *tr. by* Gilbert Highet

Sentience. Sandra McPherson. PoA

Sentiment. Thomas Chatterton. NOEC

Sentimental Education. Rachel Hadas. RA

Sentimental Poem. Po Chü-i, *Chinese.* CoBCP, *tr. by* Burton Watson

Sentimental Voyage Around My Room, A. Jovan Hristic, *Serbo-Croatian.* HSix, *tr. by* Charles Simic

Sentiments at Autumn. Han Yü, *Chinese.* SuSp, *tr. by* Charles Hartman

Sentiments on New Year's Eve in the Year Kuei-ssu. Huang Ching-jen, *Chinese.* SuSp, *tr. by* Chang Yin-nan *and* Lewis C. Walmsley

Sentimientos pour into your teeth. Tato—Reading at the Nuyorican Poets' Cafe. Miguel Algarin. PmAP

Sentinel of the grave who counts us all! (LL) Ode to the Confederate Dead. Allen Tate. AiP; CBCWP; ColAP; FaBoMo; FuPo; HeIP-4; LiTM; MoAmPo; MoP; NAAL-2; NOBA; NoAM; NoP-4; OBWP; OxBA; TAP; TFi; UnPo

Sentry, The. Alun Lewis. PoWW

Sentry, The. Wilfred Owen. EBNV; PeFWW; PoWW

Sentry! What of the night? *Unknown.* NSI

Separate Parties. Dabney Stuart. NYBP

Separated East, The. Ernest Francisco Fenollosa. APN-2 *Fr.* East and West.

Separated Lovers. *Unknown.* OAEL-1

Separately I still recall. Portrait. Adèle Naudé. PeSA

Separating one by one. Island Waters. Tony Beyer. PeNZ

Separation, A. William Johnson Cory. OBNC

Separation. W. S. Merwin. HAP; NoP-4; SAGP

Separation. Po Chü-i, *Chinese.* ChiP, *tr. by* Arthur Waley

Separation by Death. Ibn Hazm al-Andalusi, *Arabic.* RaBo, *tr. by* A. R. Nykl, *ad. by* Robert Bly

Separation from the Torah. Solomon ibn Gabirol, *Hebrew.* TOF, *tr. by* David Goldstein

Separation in Succasunna. Sander Zulauf. EC3

Separation on the River Kiang. Li Po, *Chinese.* InPS-3; UnPo, *tr. by* Ezra Pound

Separations begin with placement. River Road Studio. Barbara Guest. PmAP; PoM

Sephestia's Song to Her Child[e]. Robert Greene. NoSic; OxAEP-1; PoEL-2 *Fr.* Menaphon.
   (Sephestia's Lullaby.) NOBE; OBEV

Sepia Fashion Show. Maya Angelou. BlSi

September. Mary Howitt. BoTP

September. Ted Hughes. BoLoP

September. Aldous Leonard Huxley. EBEV

September [Days Are Here]. Helen Hunt Jackson. APN-2; AYFP; OBCA; PoLF

September. Linda Pastan. Poetsp

September. Henrietta Cordelia Ray. CBWP-3

September. Folgore da San Geminiano. *Fr.* Sonnets of the Months. AWP, *tr. by* D. G. Rossetti

September. John Updike. KaS

September 1, 1923. Toki Zenmaro, *Japanese.* MJT, *tr. by* Makoto Ueda

September 1939. Vita Sackville-West. WPN

September Afternoon at Four O'Clock. Marge Piercy. NIP-4

September has come and I wake. Louis MacNeice. NoP-4 *Fr.* Autumn Journal.

September in Kittery. Gilbert Sorrentino. FTOS

September Midnight. Sara Teasdale. PoA

September Night, A. George Marion McClellan. AAP

September 1913. W. B. Yeats. CMoP; FaBoPV; GTBS-P; HAP; MoP; NAEL-2; NoAM; OBWP

September 1, 1939. W. H. Auden. AF; CMoP; ImPo; MoBrPo; OxAEP-2; OxBA; PoE

September rain falls on the house. Sestina. Elizabeth Bishop. ChAP; InPK-6; LCAP-2; NoP-4; PoE; PoPoPo; Poetr

September Song. Geoffrey Hill. HP; NAEL-2; NoAM; NoP-4; OBWP

September, the First Day of School. Howard Nemerov. OxBC

September. The gypsy and the nightingale. Autumn. Itsik Manger, *Yiddish.* CEEP; TrJP, *tr.* by Ruth Whitman

SEPTEMBER *twenty-second,* Sir: today. After the Surprising Conversions. Robert Lowell. AmPP; CoAmPo; HAP; NAAL-2; NoAM; TRP

September 2. Wendell Berry. PoA

September was when it began. The Coming of the Plague. Weldon Kees. ChIV-1; VGW

Septimius and Acme. Catullus. *See* Carmen 45 ("Phyllis Corydon clutched to him").

Sepulchre. George Herbert. ESCV; MiEL

Sepulchres, how thick they stand, The. Meditations on the Sepulchre in the Garden. Philip Doddridge. NOCV; NOEC; OBGa

Sepulchrum Domus Mea Est. William Austin. NOSC

Sequaire. Godeschalk, *Latin.* CTC, *tr.* by Ezra Pound

Sequel, The. Theodore Roethke. NYBP

Sequel, The. Delmore Schwartz. LiTM

Sequel of Appomattox. Donald Davidson. CBCWP; FuPo

Sequel to 'A Reminiscence," The. Amy Levy. VWP

Sequence. George Barker. PoA

Sequence. Ken Irby. FTOS

Sequence, The. C. S. Lewis. LBC

Sequence. Marilyn Nelson Waniek. PuP-14

Sequence for Saint Michael, A. Alcuin, *Irish.* TIRV, *tr.* by Helen Waddell

Sequence of Sonnets, A. Dylan Thomas.
  "Altarwise by owl-light in the half-way house." CMoP; FaBoMo; Son
  "And from the windy West came two-gunned Gabriel."
  "Cartoon of slashes on the tide-traced crater."
  "Death is all metaphors, shape in one history." CMoP; Son
  "First there was the lamb on knocking knees." CMoP
  "From the oracular archives and the parchment." CMoP
  "Let the tale's sailor from a Christian voyage." CMoP; FaBoMo; OAEL-2
  "Now stamp the Lord's Prayer on a grain of rice." FaBoMo
  "This was the crucifixion on the mountain." CMoP
  "What is the metre of the dictionary?" CMoP; FaBoMo

Sequins. Cornelius Eady. *See* The Supremes.

Seravezza. Hoyt W. Fuller. PoBA

Sere of the sun exploded in the sea. (LL) O Carib Isle! Hart Crane. NoAM; PFTM; PoA; VGW

Serenade, A: "Ah! County Guy, the hour is nigh." Sir Walter Scott. GTBS-P *Fr.* Quentin Durward.
  (Song.) CH

Serenade: "Come now, and let us wake them: time." *Unknown, German.* AWP, *tr.* by Jethro Bithell

Serenade: "Look out upon the stars, my love." Edward Coote Pinkney. APN-1

Serenade: "Sleep, love sleep." Mary Weston Fordham. CBWP-2

Serenade: "Softly, O midnight Hours!" Aubrey Thomas De Vere. OBEV

Serenade: "Stars of the summer night!" Henry Wadsworth Longfellow. FaBoBe *Fr.* The Spanish Student.

Serenade, A. Thomas Hood. NBLV *Fr.* Domestic Poems.

Serenade: Any Man to Any Woman. Dame Edith Sitwell. NALW

Serenade for Winds. T. Alan Broughton. CMAP

Serenade of a Loyal Martyr. George Darley. NOBE; OBNC
  ("Bleeds with its death-wound, but deeper yet for thee.") (LL) Ro
  (Song.) OBEV
  ("Sweet in her green cell the flower of beauty slumbers.") Ro

Serenader, The. *Unknown, Greek.* GrAn, *tr.* by Dudley Fitts

Serenades in Virginia. Andrew Hudgins. CBCWP

Serenata. Federico Garcia Lorca, *Spanish.* EP, *tr.* by Derek Parker

Serene and outraged in a trenchcoat. Severances. Aidan Carl Mathews. CIP-2

Serene descent, as a red leaf's descending. Epitaph. Sara Teasdale. PoA

Serene, I fold my hands [*or* arms] and wait. Waiting. John Burroughs. BLPA; FaBoBe

Serenely in the crystal jet, *subsel.* Canto 74. Ezra Pound. PoE *Fr.* Cantos.

Serenity. Philippe Jaccottet, *French.* MFP, *tr.* by Martin Sorrell

Serenity in Stones, The. Simon J. Ortiz. CDW; ColAP

Serenity so arduously maintained, and at such, A. Ann Lee. Lynne McMahon. NAmP90

Serf, The. Roy Campbell. GTBS-P; MoBrPo; OBMV

Sergeant Brandon Just, U. S. M. C. Bryan Alec Floyd. CDa

Sergeant Brown's Parrot. Kit Wright. OPOU

Sergeant, He Is the Worst of All, The. *Unknown.* AS

Sergeant laughs with strong teeth, The. At Rest from the Grim Place. Arthur Nortje. PBMAP

Sergeant-Major Money. Robert Graves. OBWP

Sergeant of the Lawe, war and wys, A. Chaucer. CTC *Fr.* The General Prologue. FHYEP; NAEL-1; NAWM-1; OAEL-1; PoE *Fr.* The Canterbury Tales.

Sergeant to Enyalios. Archilochus, *Greek.* GrAn, *tr.* by Guy Davenport

Sergeant's Weddin', The. Rudyard Kipling. OBCoV; OxBTC

Series—3, The. Leslie Scalapino. PmAP *Fr.* Crowd and Not Evening Or Light.

Serious and a Curious Night-Meditation, A. Thomas Traherne. SeCP

Serious Concerns. Wendy Cope. NoP-4; OBCoV
  ("Indigestion.") (LL) NoP-4

Serious Merriment of Women, The. Patricia Goedicke. TAP

Serious over my cereals I broke one breakfast my fast. Breakfast with Gerard Manley Hopkins. Anthony Brode. BXAP; NOBL

Serious Readers. Peter Redgrove. OxBC

Serious young lady from Welwyn, A. Limerick. C. Armstrong Gibbs. PeLi

Seriously, these sorts. Gradation. Charles Bernstein. FTOS

Sermon, The. Richard Hughes. OBMV

Sermon at Clevedon, A. Thomas Edward Brown. NOBVV

Sermon in a Stocking. Ellen A. Jewett. BLPA

Sermon on Swift, A. Austin Clarke. BIrV

Sermon on the Warpland, The. Gwendolyn Brooks. BPo; LiTM; NOBA; PoBA

Sermon our Pastor, Rt. Rev., The. Limerick. *Unknown.* PeLi

Sermonette. Ishmael Reed. PoBA

Serpent, The. Theodore Roethke. NOxBChV

Serpent, The. Jones Very. NCAP

Serpent Country. A. R. Ammons. EOEF

Serpent is shut out from Paradise, The. Stanzas to Edward Williams. Shelley. OBNC

Serpent Knowledge. Robert Pinsky. ColAP; NAAL-2 *Fr.* An Explanation of America.

Serpent with a voyce, so slie and fine, The. Samuel Gorton. SCAP

Serpent with the eagle in the boughs, The. (LL) The Dance. Hart Crane. LiTM; MoAmPo; OxBA

Serried hosts stood man to man, The. The Oranges. Abu Dharr, *Arabic.* TTY, *tr.* by A. J. Arberry

"Serva tibi minas!" The Judge with the Sore Rump. St. George Tucker. OBAL

Servant, A. Rudyard Kipling. PeFWW *Fr.* Epitaphs of the War [1914–1918]. OBWP

Servant Man, The. *Unknown.* AmFP

Servant of the House. "Sagittarius." UV

Servant to Servants, A. Robert Frost. CMoP; NAAL-2

Servant When He Reigneth, A. Rudyard Kipling. ChIV-1
  ('Servant When He Reigneth, A.") KSG

Servants then (commanded) soone obaid, The. Nausicaa. Homer. *Fr.* Odyssey. NAWM-1, *tr.* by Robert Fitzgerald

Served human liberty. (LL) Swift's Epitaph. W. B. Yeats. CMoP; OBVE

Service is joy, to see or swing. Allow. Tennis. Margaret Avison. MoP

Service Is No Heritage. Nicholas Breton. NoSic

Service of All the Dead. D. H. Lawrence. NSI

Service, or Latin *sorbus,* European. The Life of Service. Donald Davie. NYBP

Services. Carl Rakosi. ChIV-1

Servile Blood. Vasily Fyodorov, *Russian.* TCRP, *tr.* by Lubov Yakovleva

Servile Herd, The. Alexander Pope. OBSV *Fr.* An Essay on Criticism. NAEL-1; PoEL-3; TFi

Serving in endless bounty. What He Said after a Quarrel, Remembering His Wedding Night. Viṟṟuṟṟu Mūteyiṉaṉār, *Tamil.* PLW, *tr.* by A. K. Ramanujan

Serving Maid, The. Arthur Joseph Munby. NOBVV

Serving-man to be a queen, A. (LL) The Famous Flower of Serving-Men; or, The Lady Turn'd Serving-Man. *Unknown.* ESPB; OxBB

Serving Men's Song, A. John Lyly. NOBE *Fr.* Alexander and Campaspe.
  ("Oh, for a bowl of fat Canary.") NoP-4

Serving with Gideon. William Stafford. LCAP-2

Sesame. Jack Marshall. PuP-16

Session[s] of the Poets, A. Sir John Suckling. BeJo
  ("Sessions was held the other day, A.") CABP
  ("When he lends any poet about the town.") (LL) CABP
  (Wits, The.) CaPo
  "First that broke silence was good old Ben, The." EPCY

Session was held the other day, A. A Session[s] of the Poets. Sir John Suckling. BeJo; CaPo

Sestina: "Body of my love is a familiar country, The." Mary Stanley. PeNZ

Sestina: "Is this the object." Judith Kroll. AmPA

Sestina: "September rain falls on the house." Elizabeth Bishop. InPK-6; LCAP-2; NoP-4; PoE; PoPoPo; Poetr
("Child draws another inscrutable house, The.") (LL) ChAP

Sestina. James Cummins. BAP-94

Sestina: Altaforte. Ezra Pound. CMoP; ColAP; FaBoTw; ImPo; MoAmPo; NOBA

Sestina d'Inverno. Anthony Hecht. NoAM

Sestina for Jaime. Katherine Alice Power. BAP-96

Sestina for the House. Ronald Wallace. PBCAP

Sestina for the Ladies of Tehuántepec. Earle Birney. PeLV

Sestina from the Home Gardener. Diane Wakoski. MoP

Sestina in a Cantina. Malcolm Lowry. MoCV

Sestina in Time of Winter. Patrick Anderson. PoA

Sestina of the Tramp-Royal. Rudyard Kipling. ImPo; MoBrPo

Sestina with Refrain. Thomas William Shapcott. CBAP

Set down, set down your honourable load. Shakespeare. FaBoSe *Fr.* Richard III.

Set foot once beyond Nilotic Meroë. Paulus Silentiarius, *Greek.* GrAn, *tr.* by Andrew Miller

Set golden butter out in a dish. Fanny Howe. FTOS *Fr.* "O'clock."

Set in the tryst-ring but worn more bright. (LL) Carrier Letter. Hart Crane. BoLoP

Set in this stormy northern sea. Ave Imperatrix! Oscar Wilde. PeVV

Set Love in order, thou that lovest Me. Cantica: Our Lord Christ: Of Order. Saint Francis of Assisi, *also at.* to Jacopone da Todi, *Italian,* . AWP; OBVE, *tr.* by D. G. Rossetti

Set me as a seal on your heart. As a Seal upon Thy Heart. Bible, *O.T.* BoWoP, *tr.* by Willis Barnstone *Fr.* The Song of Songs. AWP

Set me to sound for you. Ark Anatomical. Jay Macpherson. NOBC *Fr.* The Ark.

Set me whereas the sun[ne] doth[e] parch [*or* perche] the green [*or* grene], *see also* trans. by Charlotte Smith, "Oh! place me where the burning noon." Love's Fidelity. Petrarch. AAS; HAP; NoSic; SiPS, *tr.* by Henry Howard, Earl of Surrey *Fr.* Sonnets to Laura.

Set on this bubble of dead stone and sand. On an Engraving by Casserius. Alec Derwent Hope. CBAP

Set silver cone to tulip flame! Inscription for a Mirror in a Deserted Dwelling. William Rose Benét. MoAmPo

Set up the drum. December. Maurice Kenny. HATNAP

Set where the upper streams of Simois flow. Palladium. Matthew Arnold. GTBS-P; OAEL-2; OBNC

Set your fir-tree / In a pot. Advice to a Child. Eleanor Farjeon. OTCP

Setting a trotline after sundown. In the Deep Channel. William Stafford. RB

Setting in the house with everything on my mind. In the House Blues. Bessie Smith. NAAAL

Setting out at dawn from T'ung-lu county. Wu Wei-yeh, *Chinese.* CoBLCP, *tr.* by Jonathan Chaves

Setting sun about to vanish west of the Hsien Hill, The. Song of Hsiang-yang. Li Po, *Chinese.* SuSp, *tr.* by Joseph J. Lee

Setting sun illuminates half the river, The. A Walk to the Eastern River Bank. Kao Ch'i, *Chinese.* CoBLCP, *tr.* by Jonathan Chaves

Setting sun is two rods high on the bridge over the brook, The. Tu Mu. PLT, *tr.* by A. C. Graham *Fr.* In Ch'i-an, on a Chance Theme.

Setting their country free. Mnasalcas, *Greek.* GrAn, *tr.* by Edward Lucie-Smith

Settlement. Ingeborg Bachmann, *German.* PoSu, *tr.* by Daniel Huws

Settler. Stewart Lindh. PoA

Settler, The. Alfred Billings Street. FaBoBe

Settlers, The. Margaret Atwood. MoCV

Settlers. Tom Paulin. IIP; PNI

Settlers abandoned our country long ago. Pauper Woodland. Ronald G. Everson. NOBC

Settling. Denise Levertov. PaTW

Seumas Beg. James Stephens. FuFo; OxBTC

Seven, The. *Unknown, Sumerian.* RB, *tr.* by Jerome K. Rothenberg

Seven Activities for a Young Child. Alan Brownjohn. OTCP

Seven against Thebes, The. Aeschylus, *Greek.*
Lament for the Two Brothers Slain by Each Other's Hand. AWP

Seven ageing pine tree hide. Allen Curnow. *Fr.* A Small Room with Large Windows. PeNZ

Seven ages, first puking and mewling. "All the World's a Stage." Victor Gray. NBLV; PeLi

Seven Ages of Man, The. Shakespeare. ImPo *Fr.* As You Like It.

Seven Beginnings. Olesya Nikolayeva, *Russian.* TCRP, *tr.* by Vera Dunham

Seven Black Friars sitting back to back. Blackfriars. Eleanor Farjeon. OxBChV

Seven candles in silver sticks. Planter. Richard Murphy. BIrV *Fr.* The Battle of Aughrim.

Seven Days of Creation, The. James McAuley.
Seventh Day, The. BMAP

Seven Days of the Sun, The. Walter James Turner. OBMV

Seven dead men, Brigit. The Celtic Lyric. Sir John Collings Squire. BXAP

Seven Deadly Sins, The. Stephen Hawes. PoEL-1 *Fr.* The Pastime of Pleasure. OBGa

Seven dog-days we let pass. Queens. John Millington Synge. GBL; MoBrPo; OBMV; PeVV

Seven Doors Away. Virginia Hooper. PT

Seven Dreams. John Clifford Bayliss. SPE

Seven Epigrams. Gerard Manley Hopkins.
"Of virtues I most warmly bless." FaBoEE

Seven Fiddlers, The. Sebastian Evans. EBVV

Seven fish dream of a lost king's daughter. (LL) A Spell for Sleeping. Alastair Reid. NOxBChV; NTP

7:v:60 (an interesting *lapsus calami*). For Kai Snyder. Philip Whalen. PoM

747 (London–Chicago). Robert Conquest. OxBC

Seven Good Germans. Hamish Henderson. FaBoTC

Seven Hells of Jigoku Zoshi, The. Jerome Rothenberg. NNaP

700 years ago. Slim Man Canyon. Leslie Marmon Silko. VoR

Seven ladies / and seventeen gentlemen. Parade. Langston Hughes. PFTM

Seven lang years I hae served the King. The Whummil Bore. *Unknown.* CH; ESPB

Seven lean cows, The. Glimpse of an Open Dream. David Avidan, *Hebrew.* IP, *tr.* by Warren Bargad *and* Stanley F. Chyet

Seven Little Pigs. *Unknown.* BoTP

Seven Long Years in State Prison. *Unknown.* AS

Seven lovely poplars. Poplars. Helen Leuty. BoTP

Seven Metal Mountains. Bible, Pseudepigrapha. TrJP *Fr.* Enoch. TrJP

Seven Months. Cleopatra Mathis. FiLi

Seven nuns went wading in the sea. Beach Party Given by T. Shaughnessy for the Sisters. Josephine Miles. LiLi

Seven of Pentacles, The. Marge Piercy. CrSp *Fr.* Laying Down the Tower.

Seven of the Clock. Roy Macnab. PeSA

Seven Old Men, The. Charles Baudelaire, *French.* OBVE, *tr.* by Roy Campbell

Seven pairs of leopard-skin underpants. Leopard Skin. Douglas Stewart. NOBA

Seven Pilgrims: A Clerk. Chaucer. *See* The Canterbury Tales.

Seven Pilgrims: A Knight. Chaucer. *See* The Knighthood.

Seven Pilgrims: A Miller. Chaucer. *Fr.* The General Prologue. FHYEP; NAEL-1; NAWM-1; OAEL-1; PoE *Fr.* The Canterbury Tales.

Seven Pilgrims: A Monk. Chaucer. *Fr.* The General Prologue. FHYEP; NAEL-1; NAWM-1; OAEL-1; PoE *Fr.* The Canterbury Tales.

Seven Pilgrims: A Prioress[e]. Chaucer. *See* Madame Eglantine.

Seven Pilgrims: A Squire [*or* Squyer]. Chaucer. *Fr.* The General Prologue. FHYEP; NAEL-1; NAWM-1; OAEL-1; PoE *Fr.* The Canterbury Tales.

Seven Pilgrims: A Wyf of Bathe. Chaucer. *Fr.* The General Prologue. FHYEP; NAEL-1; NAWM-1; OAEL-1; PoE *Fr.* The Canterbury Tales.

Seven plus thirty years are gone. Philodemus, *Greek.* GrAn, *tr.* by William Moebius

Seven Poems of Lament. Ts'ao Chih, *Chinese.* SuSp, *tr.* by Ronald C. Miao

Seven Poems of Lament. Wang Ts'an, *Chinese.*
"Land of the Ching tribes is not my home, The." SuSp, *tr.* by Ronald C. Miao
"This frontier post brings me sorrow." SuSp, *tr.* by Ronald C. Miao
"Western Capital is in turmoil, The." SuSp, *tr.* by Ronald C. Miao

Seven Poems on Living in the Mountains: Seeing Off. Chang Yü, *Chinese.* CoBLCP, *tr.* by Jonathan Chaves

Seven Rainy Months. William Plomer. OxBTC

Seven Sages, The. W. B. Yeats. NOIV

Seven Said by the Foster-Mother. Peyanar, *Tamil.*
"Embracing this woman." PLW, *tr.* by A. K. Ramanujan
"Evening in the yard." PLW, *tr.* by A. K. Ramanujan
"His heart swells." PLW, *tr.* by A. K. Ramanujan
"Like the red flame." PLW, *tr.* by A. K. Ramanujan
"Minstrels sing the jasmine songs." PLW, *tr.* by A. K. Ramanujan

Seven scythes leaned at the wall. Taxman. George Mackay Brown. FaBoTC

Seven Seages, The. John Rolland.
"In haist ga hy thee to sum hoill." OxBS

Seven-Sided Poem. Carlos Drummond de Andrade, *Portuguese.* VCWP, *tr.* by Elizabeth Bishop

Seven Sides and Seven Syllables. Edouard J. Maunick, *French.* NegPo; VCWP, *tr. by* Carolyn Kizer

Seven Skins. Sarah Kirsch, *German.* CEEP, *tr. by* Tanaquil Taubes

Seven Sleepers, The. Mark Van Doren. FYAP

Seven Songs. Cheng Hsieh, *Chinese.* CoBLCP, *tr. by* Jonathan Chaves

Seven Songs and Song Pictures. *Unknown.* PFTM

Seven Songs Written During the Ch'ien-yüan Era. Tu Fu, *Chinese.*
   "I have a sister, little sister, living in Chung-li." CoBCP, *tr. by* Burton Watson
   "I have brothers, younger brothers in a place far away." CoBCP, *tr. by* Burton Watson
   "Long hoe, long hoe, handle of white wood." CoBCP, *tr. by* Burton Watson
   "To the south there is a dragon living in a mountain pool." CoBCP, *tr. by* Burton Watson
   "Traveler, a traveler, Tzu-mei his name, A." CoBCP, *tr. by* Burton Watson

Seven Songs Written while Living at T'ung-ku in 759. Tu Fu, *Chinese.* SuSp, *tr. by* Goeffrey Waters

Seven Sorrows, The. Ted Hughes. NAEL-2

Seven Sorrows. Wang Ts'an, *Chinese.* CoBCP, *tr. by* Burton Watson
   "Tribes of Ching—that's not my home." CoBCP, *tr. by* Burton Watson

Seven South African Poems. David Wright. PeSA

Seven Spiritual Ages of Mrs. Marmaduke Moore, The. Ogden Nash. MoAmPo

Seven Stanzas at Easter. John Updike. TrCP

Seven stars in the still water. The Dole of the King's Daughter. *Unknown, French.* AWP, *tr. by* Oscar Wilde

Seven Strophes. Joseph Brodsky, *Russian.* EP, *tr. by* Paul Graves

Seven sweet singing birds up in a tree. The Dream of a Girl Who Lived at Sevenoaks. William Brighty Rands. OxBChV

Seven threads make the shroud. Shroud. George Mackay Brown. NoP-4; RB

7 : 3. "Alta."
   "Love is believable." CrSp

Seven Times One--Exultation. Jean Ingelow. BLPA; OBNC *Fr.* Songs of Seven.

Seven Times Three—Love. Jean Ingelow. PoLF *Fr.* Songs of Seven.

Seven Virgins, The. *Unknown.* CH; OBEV

Seven wealthy towns contend for Homer dead. A Cure for Poetry. *Unknown, after the Latin of* George Buchanan. FaBoEE

Seven weeks of sea, and twice seven days of storm. Gibraltar. Wilfrid Scawen Blunt. OBEV

Seven white peacocks against the castle wall, The. What the Orderly Dog Saw. Ford Madox Ford. CTC

Seven Wonders of North Wales, The. *Unknown, Welsh.* OBWVE

Seven Wonders of the World. Christopher Pearse Cranch.
   Locomotive, The. APN-1; GM
   Photograph, The. APN-1
   Printing-Press, The. APN-1

Seven Woodland Crows. Gerald Vizenor. VoR

Seven Words, The. Jerzy Ficowski, *Polish.* PoSu, *tr. by* Keith Bosley *and* Krystyna Wandycz

Seven years ago / at forty five. Now or Never. "Astra." BrRo

Seven years I have kept him, dead. The Corpse-Keeper. *Unknown, Catalan.* BoWoP, *tr. by* W. S. Merwin

Seven years lived in Italy leave me convinced. The Oak and the Olive. George Barker. FaBoMo

Seven years the boar's ham has been drying. Dedication. Māris aklais, *Latvian.* CEEP, *tr. by* Inara Cedrins

Seven years without milk. Ethiopia for Tita. Audre Lorde. LiLi

"Seven years ye shall be a stone." The Maid and the Palmer. *Unknown.* ESPB

Seventeen. Jonathan Holden. Poetsp

Seventeen. Andrew Hudgins. BAP-95

1780 a.d. in the street they flung foam about and a young. Poems. Philip O'Connor. SPE

1789. Jackson MacLow. APSN *Fr.* The Presidents of the United States of America

17. IV. 71. Paul Blackburn. PoM

Seventeen hundred and sixty yards. Enigma No. 6. Augusta Davies Webster. VWP

Seventeen hundred and thirty-nine. Ballad of 'Beau Brocade,' The. Austin Dobson. OxAEP-2

1797. Jackson MacLow. APSN *Fr.* The Presidents of the United States of America.

Seventeen Old Poems. *Unknown, Chinese.*
   "Bright moon, oh how white it shines, The." ChiP, *tr. by* Arthur Waley

"Crossing the river I pluck the lotus flowers;." ChiP, *tr. by* Arthur Waley

"Dead are gone and with them we cannot converse;, The." ChiP, *tr. by* Arthur Waley

"Eastern Wall stands high and long;, The." ChiP, *tr. by* Arthur Waley

"Green, green." ChiP, *tr. by* Arthur Waley

"In the north-west there is a high house." ChiP, *tr. by* Arthur Waley

"Of this day's glorious feast and revel." ChiP, *tr. by* Arthur Waley

"On and on, always on and on." ChiP, *tr. by* Arthur Waley

"Turning my chariot I yoke my horses and go." ChiP, *tr. by* Arthur Waley

"years of a lifetime do not reach a hundred, the." ChiP, *tr. by* Arthur Waley

17:II:82. David Meltzer. MoNo; SeSe

Seventeen Warnings in Search of a Feminist Poem. Erica Jong. AmPA

Seventeen years ago come March. (LL) Crusoe in England. Elizabeth Bishop. FaBoVe; HCAP; PoPoPo; RACG

Seventeen years ago you said. À Quoi Bon Dire. Charlotte Mew. LBC; OxBTC; VWP

Seventeenth stanza, The. My heart aches, my tears fall. Ts'ai Yen. WPOW *Fr.* Eighteen Verses Sung to a Tatar Reed Whistle.

Seventh, The. Attila József, *Hungarian.* AF; NNPT; RB, *tr. by* John Batki

Seventh Avenue. Mark Halliday. NAmP90

Seventh Birthday of the First Child. Sharon Olds. PBCAP

Seventh Day, The. James McAuley. BMAP *Fr.* The Seven Days of Creation.

Seventh Day Seventh Month. Kuan Yun She, *Chinese.* OHMPC, *tr. by* Kenneth Rexroth

Seventh Duino Elegy, The. Rilke, *German.*
   "Isn't the secret intent." ITG, *tr. by* Stephen Mitchell

Seventh Eclogue. Miklós Radnóti, *Hungarian.* AF, *tr. by* Emery E. George; PFTM, *tr. by* Clayton Eshleman *and* Gyula Kodolanyi

7th Light Poem: For John Cage—17 June 1962. Jackson Mac Low. FTOS

Seventh of July, the suith to say, The. The Raid of the Reidswire. *Unknown.* IBB

Seventh Son. Ed Roberson. PoBA

Seventh Song. Sir Philip Sidney. NoP-4 *Fr.* Astrophil and Stella. AAS; SiPS

Seventh Street. Jean Toomer. NAAL-2

Seventh Vertical Poetry. Roberto Juarroz, *Spanish.*
   "Prompting of my shadow, The." VCWP, *tr. by* W. S. Merwin

Seventies, The. Louis Johnson. PeNZ

70. Edward Fitzgerald. CABP

78's. Lloyd Schwartz. WeT

Seventy Feet Down. Philip Larkin. RB *Fr.* Livings.

Seventy-five are my abyssed forests. Shimon Halkin, *Hebrew.* MHP, *tr. by* Ruth Finer Mintz

75 lbs.—Get serious. José Cruz. Mel Glenn. LiLi

74. Edward Fitzgerald. CABP

74th Street. Myra Cohn Livingston. SSCS

71. Edward Fitzgerald. CABP

Seventy-six Hokku. Basho, *Japanese.*
   "Old pond, / frog jumps in." EnlH, *tr. by* Michael Katz

73. Edward Fitzgerald. CABP

72. Edward Fitzgerald. CABP

Several months after we lost our way. The Natives. David Mura. CDa; WeW-3

Several Questions Answered. William Blake.
   Eternity ("He who binds to himself a joy"). APAD; AWP; EBEV; EnlH; FaBoEE; ImPo; NOBE; NTP; NoP-4; OBNC; OxBSP; Poetr; RB; SCGP; SoSe-8; Spl
   Question Answered, The [*or* A]. FaBoEE; GBL; OxBM
   (*From* Several Questions Answered.) ITG

Several Voices Out of a Cloud. Louise Bogan. NALW

Severance. Kit Robinson. FTOS

Severance of Connections, 1946. Louis Edward Sissman *See* In and Out.

Severances. Aidan Carl Mathews. CIP-2

Sever'd from sweete Content, my live's sole light. Diana. Henry Constable.

Severed Selves. D. G. Rossetti. BoLoP; GLoP *Fr.* The House of Life.

Severer Service of myself. Emily Dickinson. TRP

Sew a Pocket. Jessie Welborn Smith. PWR

Sewing-Box, The. Gabriel Gbadamosi. NBrP

Sewing Lesson, The. Kate Lilley. BMAP

Sewing the long white seam. (LL) The Long White Seam. Jean Ingelow. NOBVV; SDW

Sex. Stefan Brecht.
   "Here then is the life-giving activity given to every man: the sexual / act, vivificator." CLPP

Sex. Jean Valentine. FaBoWP

Sex and the Over Forties. Peter Porter. BMAP; CBLP

Sex, as they harshly call it. Two Songs. Adrienne Rich. NIP-4; NOBA; PFE; TAP *Fr.* Two Songs.

Sex, consolation for misery! Pier Paolo Pasolini, *Italian.* CLPP, *tr. by* Lawrence Ferlinghetti *and* Francesca Valente

Sex fingers toes. Dear John, Dear Coltrane. Michael S. Harper. AmPA; ISC; LoL; NAAAL; NIP-4; VCAP

Sex floated like a moon. A Circle, a Square, a Triangle and a Ripple of Water. Jane Cooper. TAP

Sex-life of Fish, The. William Diaper. ECEV *Fr.* Halieutica. (Eels and Tortoises.) NOEC

Sex without Love. Sharon Olds. DeD; HeIP-4; NIP-4; Poetr; TRP

Sexes waking, now separate and sore, The. The Martyrs. Jay Macpherson. MoCV

Sext. Donald Davie. *Fr.* Horae Canonicae. CRP

Sextain: "Sith gone is my delight and only pleasure." William Drummond, of Hawthornden. NOSC

Sextain: "With elegies, sad songs, and mourning lays." William Drummond, of Hawthornden. NOSC

Sextet. Joseph Brodsky, *Russian.* TCRP, *tr. by* Joseph Brodsky

Sexton is opening up the grave, The. The Third Light. Michael Longley. PNI

Sexton tolled the bell, The. (LL) Faithless Sally Brown. Thomas Hood. NOBL; OBNV

Sextus the Usurer. Martial, *Latin.* AWP, *tr. by* Kirby Flower Smith

Sexual Couplets. Craig Raine. EP

Sexual intercourse began. Annus Mirabilis. Philip Larkin. NBLV; NIP-4; NOBL; OBAL

Sexual Privacy of Women on Welfare. Pinkie Gordon Lane. BlSi

Sexual Water. Pablo Neruda, *Spanish.* PFTM, *tr. by* Clayton Eshleman

Sexy young student once toyed, A. Limerick. Richard Taylor. PeLi

Seynt Stevyn and Herowdes. *Unknown.* CH; OxBB
(St. Stephen and King Herod.) ESPB; OxBoLi
(Saint Steven Was a Clerk.) EnVB

Seyton!—I am sick at heart. Shakespeare. OxAEP-1 *Fr.* Macbeth.

Sez I: My Country Calls? Well, let it call. The Volunteer. Robert W. Service. NSI

Sgt. Christopher and I are. OK Corral East Brothers in the Nam. Horace Coleman. CDa

Sgt. stands so fluently in leather, The. On a Photo of Sgt. Ciardi a Year Later. John Ciardi. AiP

Sh-Ta-Ra-Dah-Dey. *Unknown.* AS

Sha-ch'eng, "Sand City" ("In former years I passed this city"). Yang Shih-ch'i, *Chinese.* CoBLCP, *tr. by* Jonathan Chaves

Sha-ch'eng, "Sand City" ("Overlooking the water, a desolate city"). Yang Shih-ch'i, *Chinese.* CoBLCP, *tr. by* Jonathan Chaves

Shabby Old Dad. Anne Campbell. PoToHe

Shack and a few trees, The. After Work. Gary Snyder. HoPM; NNaP; PFE

Shack Outside Boise, The. Vern Rutsala. CMAP

Shade, The. Tom Mandel. PT

Shade-Catchers, The. Charlotte Mew. NTP

Shade of a Grammarian. Andrew Joron. PT

Shade of Columbus, here thy relics rest. Maria Gowen Brooks. PAR *Fr.* Zóphiël, or the Bride of Seven.

Shade of His hand shall cover us, The. His Hand Shall Cover Us. Isaac ben Samuel of Dampière, *Hebrew.* TrJP, *tr. by* Nina Davis Salaman

Shade-Seller, The. Josephine Jacobsen. TAP

Shade springs open, The. Alan Pizzarelli. HA

Shade upon the mind there passes, A. Emily Dickinson. APN-2

Shaded lamp and a waving blind, A. An August Midnight. Thomas Hardy. NOBVV

Shades of Callimachus, Coan ghosts of Philetas. Homage to Sextus Propertius. Ezra Pound. CMoP; HAP; NOBA; OBVE; OxBA *Fr.* Homage to Sextus Propertius.

Shades of eve are quickly closing in, The. Night. Josephine D. Henderson Heard. CBWP-4

Shades of Grand Central, The. Chase Twichell. NAmP90

Shades of night were falling fast, The. Excelsior. Henry Wadsworth Longfellow. EBEvV; FaPoR; NAAL-1; NAAL-3; OBCA; OBSP; PFE; UV

Shades of night were falling fast, The. A. E. Housman. BXAP; NBLV; OBCoV; UV

Shades of Pharoah Sanders Blues for My Baby. John O'Neal. NBV

Shading his eyes. Cor Van den Heuvel. HA

Shadow. Guillaume Apollinaire, *French.* AF, *tr. by* Anne Greet

Shadow. Guillaume Apollinaire, *French.* PeFWW, *tr. by* Christopher Middleton

Shadow. Mary Elizabeth Coleridge. VWP

Shadow, The. Ben Jonson. *See* Song. That Women Are But Men's Shadows.

Shadow, The. John Banister Tabb. APN-2

Shadow and caress- / ing a disguise!, A. (LL) An Image of Leda. Frank O'Hara. HCAP; LCAP-2

Shadow and Shade. Allen Tate. VGW

Shadow and Sunrise. Henrietta Cordelia Ray. CBWP-3

Shadow boxer, fighting. Father of Famine. Richard Ryan. PBCIP

Shadow does not leave my feet, The. David. Charles Reznikoff. ChIV-1

Shadow faces / In the shadow night. Chord. Langston Hughes. APSN

Shadow for shadow, stripped for fight. The Search-Lights. Alfred Noyes. NSI *Fr.* A Salute from the Fleet.

Shadow fruit is falling from the walls. Songs from an Island. Ingeborg Bachmann, *German.* VCWP, *tr. by* Mark Anderson

Shadow his father makes with joined hands, A. Alphabets. Seamus Heaney. NoAM

Shadow in Stone. Janice Mirikitani. OpBo

Shadow in the folded napkin, The. Cor Van den Heuvel. HA

Shadow is floating through the moonlight, A. The Bird of Night. Randall Jarrell. KaS

Shadow, killer of doves. Anthony Delius. PeSA

Shadow-Love. Heinrich Heine. *Fr.* Songs to Seraphine. TrJP, *tr. by* Emma Lazarus

Shadow of a Branch, The. Edith Marcombe Shiffert. WPE

Shadow of a fat man in the moonlight, The. Things to Come. James Reeves. OxBSP

Shadow of Cain, The. Dame Edith Sitwell. OxBTC

Shadow of Darkness. Gladys May Casely Hayford. PBA

Shadow of Flowers, The. Su Tung-p'o, *Chinese.* OHPC, *tr. by* Kenneth Rexroth

Shadow of her profile lay stringent, The. Woman, Gallup, N. M. Karen Swenson. NYBP

Shadow of Himself, The. William Renton. NOBVV

Shadow of Night, The. George Chapman. PoEL-2
Hymnus in Noctem. PoEL-2

Shadow of Night, The. Coventry Patmore. *See* Night and Sleep.

Shadow of the little fishing launch, The. The Parrot Fish. James Merrill. NOBA

Shadow of the night comes on. . . , The. (LL) You, Andrew Marvell. Archibald MacLeish. AWP; CMoP; ColAP; FYAP; GEA; HAP; HeIP-4; HoPM; LiTM; MeMAP; MoAmPo; MoP; NAAL-2; NOBA; NoAM; NoP-4; OxBA; PoRA; Poetr; SAGP; SoSe-8; TFi; TRP; TwCP

Shadow of the trees, The. Kenneth Yasuda. HA

Shadow of the Venetian blind on the painted wall, The. Forties Flick. John Ashbery. FTOS; NoAM

Shadow of War, 1941. Thomas William Shapcott. BMAP

Shadow of wings grew, The. Fight With An Angel. Tadeusz Rózewicz, *Polish.* PoSu, *tr. by* Victor Contoski

Shadow on shadow his mind. Remembering Yeats. Francis Stuart. BiHa

Shadow Play. Ralph Angel. NAmP90

Shadow Replies to Substance. T'ao Ch'ien. *Fr.* Substance, Shadow, and Spirit. CoBCP, *tr. by* Burton Watson

Shadow Returns, The. Phillis Levin. RA

Shadow sits and waits for me, The. (LL) Path by which we twain did go, The. Tennyson. EBVV; PeECV; SCV

Shadow streamed into the wall, The. Shadow and Shade. Allen Tate. VGW

Shadow Train. John Ashbery. LCAP-2

Shadow within the light, The. Serenity. Philippe Jaccottet, *French.* MFP, *tr. by* Martin Sorrell

Shadowed by your dear hair, your dear kind eyes. The Sanctuary. Ford Madox Ford. PoA

Shadowgraphs, The. Richmond Lattimore. NYBP

Shadowing the snow-limbed Eve from whom she came. Tennyson. *See* I have led her home, my love, my only friend.

Shadowland. Johannes Bobrowski, *German.* CEEP, *tr. by* Ruth Mead *and* Matthew Mead

Shadows. Samuel Daniel. NOBE *Fr.* Tethy's Festival.
(Song: "Are they shadowes that we see?") PoEL-2
("Thought must length it in the heart.") (LL) NoP-4

Shadows. Patricia Hubbell. Spl

Shadows. Richard Jackson. SeSe

Shadows. D. H. Lawrence. LBC; OxBTC

Shadows. Victor Gustave Plarr. NOBVV

Shadows. "Yehoash," *Yiddish.* TrJP, *tr. by* Elias Lieberman

Shadows are bodiless shapes, yet they have a song. (LL) Transaction. A. R. Ammons. HCAP; PoA

Shadows are descending, The. Outgoing Sabbath. *Unknown, Yiddish.* TrJP, *tr.* by Joseph Leftwich

Shadows become familiar. My Neighborhood. Stuart Dybek. PBCAP

Shadows blown from trees, The. Vain Advice at the Year's End. James Wright. NYBP

Shadows in his eye sockets like shades, The. Richmond. John Updike. CBCWP

Shadows in the grass. Rod Willmot. HA

Shadows in the Water. Thomas Traherne. CABP; GeHe; HAP; NoP-4; OAEL-1; PoEL-2; SCGP; SeCP

Shadows lay along Broadway, The. Unseen Spirits. Nathaniel Parker Willis. APN-1

Shadows, like Navahoes, wear velvet. Tourist Country. William Stafford. NoAM

Shadows of His Lady. Jacques Tahureau, *French.* AWP, *tr.* by Andrew Lang

Shadows of ringdoves chanting, but easing nothing, The. (LL) Winter Trees. Sylvia Plath. HCAP; LCAP-2

Shadows of Taste. John Clare.
 "In poesy's spells some all their raptures find." EPCY

Shadows of the cypresses, The. Wind Tossed Dragons. Hsieh Ngao, *Chinese.* OHMPC, *tr.* by Kenneth Rexroth

Shadows of the sails pass across his windows. Visiting the Garden at Monk Wen Ko's Home. Wu Wei-yeh, *Chinese.* SuSp, *tr.* by Chang Yin-nan and Lewis C. Walmsley

Shadows of the t'ung tree, glistening and clear. In a Dream. Lu Yu, *Chinese.* SuSp, *tr.* by Irving Y. Lo

Shadows on the wall. Life Doesn't Frighten Me. Maya Angelou. ChAP

Shadows, shadows, / Hug me round. Escape. Georgia Douglas Johnson. PoBA

Shadowy daughter of Urthona stood before red Orc, The. America; a Prophecy. William Blake. OAEL-2

Shadwell Stair. Wilfred Owen. FaBoTw

Shady grove, my true love. *Unknown.* APN-2

Shady, Shady. T'ao Ch'ien, *Chinese.* AWP, *tr.* by Arthur Waley

Shady, shady the wood in front of the Hall;. Ch'ien T'ao, *Chinese.* ChiP, *tr.* by Arthur Waley

Shady Woods. E. M. Adams. BoTP

Shaemus. Conrad Potter Aiken. OxBA

Shaft seemed like a place of sacrifice, The. Charles Tomlinson. DiPo

Shaft we raise to them and thee, The. (LL) Concord Hymn. Ralph Waldo Emerson. APN-1; AWP; AiP; AmPP; BLPA; CTV; ClHu; EBEvV; FaBoA; FaBoBe; FaPoR; HAP; HeIP-4; MeMAP; NAAL-1; NAAL-3; NOBA; NoP-4; OBWP; OxBA; PAR; PeECV; PoPoPo; TAP; TFi

Shag, The. Eileen Duggan. PeNZ

Shag Rock. "Paul Henderson." PeNZ

Shahnamah, The. Firdausi, *Persian.*
 Birth of Sohráb, The. TAL, *tr.* by James Atkinson
 Death of Sohráb, The. TAL, *tr.* by James Atkinson

Shaka, King of the Zulus. *Unknown, Zulu.* PBA; TTY, *tr.* by A. C. Jordan

Shake hands, we shall never be friends, all's over. A. E. Housman. CBLP

Shake off this sadness, and recover your spirit. Throw Yourself Like Seed. Miguel de Unamuno, *Spanish.* RaBo, *tr.* by Robert Bly

Shake off your heavy trance! Song for a Dance. Francis Beaumont. FaBoCh; NTP *Fr.* The Masque of the Inner Temple and Gray's Inne.

Shaken already, I know. Goodbye, Sally. James Simmons. BIrV

Shake'nbake Ballad. Peter Van Toorn. NOBC

Shakeout. Diane Ward. FTOS

Shakespeare. Matthew Arnold. EBVVPR; EPCY; FHYEP; HeIP-4; OBEV; OxAEP-2; SCGP; Son
 ("Find their sole speech in that victorious brow.") (LL) NoP-4; PoPoPo
 ("Find their sole voice in that victorious brow.") (LL) GSo

Shakespeare. Walter Savage Landor.
 "He lighted with his golden lamp on high." EPCY

Shakespeare. Henry Wadsworth Longfellow. AWP

Shakespeare. Henrietta Cordelia Ray. CBWP-3

Shakespeare. Swinburne. EPCY

Shakespeare; an Epistle to David Garrick, Esq. Robert Lloyd.
 True Genius. NOEC

Shakespeare created the world in seven days. Martin Sorescu, *Romanian.* CEEP, *tr.* by Donald Eulert and Stefan Avadanei

Shakespeare stand-ins, same string hair, gay, dirty. Ulysses. Robert Lowell. NAAL-2

Shakespeare: The Fairies' Advocate. Thomas Hood. *Fr.* The Plea of the Midsummer Fairies. OBNC

Shakespeare (whom you and every playhouse bill). Alexander Pope. EPCY *Fr.* The First Epistle of the Second Book of Horace Imitated.

Shakespeare, whose heartfelt scenes shall ever give. To Shakespeare. Thomas Edwards. Son

Shakespearean fish swam the sea, far away from land. Three Movements. W. B. Yeats. CMoP; FaBoEE

Shaking Hands with Mongo. Martín Espada. SeSe

Shaking my head, I let the world of red dust. Tune: "Happy Events Approaching." Chu Tun-ju, *Chinese.* SuSp, *tr.* by James J. Y. Liu

Shaking the snow from your hair, bowl cut. Huy Nguyen: Brothers, Drowning Cries. David Mura. CDa

Shako, The. Robert Lowell. Son

Shakti. Rae Desmond Jones. BMAP

Shall ancient worth, or ancient fame. True Genius. Robert Lloyd. NOEC *Fr.* Shakespeare; an Epistle to David Garrick, Esq.

Shall answer for yours in hell. (LL) Emmy ("Emmy's exquisite youth and her virginal air"). Arthur Symons. ADE

Shall be a soldier's sepulchre. (LL) Hohenlinden. Thomas Campbell. CABP; CH; FaBoCh; FaPoR; GTBS-P; NOBE; NOBRP; OBNC; OBWP; TFi

Shall be lifted—nevermore! (LL) The Raven. Edgar Allan Poe. APN-1; AmPP; BLPA; ChAP; ColAP; EBEvV; EBNV; FaBoBe; FaBoCh; HeIP-4; ImGa; NAAL-1; NAAL-3; NCAP; NIP-4; NOBA; NoP-4; OBCA; OBNV; OxBA; PWR; PoRA; TAP; TFi; UV

Shall be the Psalms sung forth in gracious layes. (LL) Like to the marigold, I blushing close. Edward Taylor. ChIV-2; SCAP

Shall both rise with me. (LL) The Cherry-Tree Carol. *Unknown.* AmFP; EBEV; ESPB; EnSB; HeIP-4; OAEL-1; OBCP; OxBB; OxBSn; OxBoLi; PeECV; SCGP; TFi

Shall bring my boats ashore. (LL) Where Go the Boats? Robert Louis Stevenson. CTV; FaBoBe; FaBoCh; NOxBChV; NTCP; NTP; OxBChV; TLR; WHSW

Shall brothers [or brithers] be for a' that. (LL) For A' That and A' That ["Is there, for honest poverty"]. Robert Burns. FaBoBe; FaBoPV; FaPoR; ImPo; NAEL-2; NOEC; OAEL-1; OxAEP-2; OxBS; TFi; UV

Shall buffet the vexed forests in his rage. (LL) A Winter Piece. William Cullen Bryant. APN-1; AmPP; ColAP; OxBA

Shall do it reverence. (LL) The City in the Sea. Edgar Allan Poe. APN-1; AmPP; KSG; MeMAP; NAAL-1; NAAL-3; NCAP; NOBA; NoP-4; OxBA; PAR; PoE; PoEL-4; SCV; TAP; TFi; TRP

Shall draw me safe to the land. (LL) The Widower. Rudyard Kipling. CBLP; LBC; OxBM

Shall draw the Thing as he sees It for the God of Things / as They are! (LL) When Earth's last picture is painted and the tubes are twisted / and dried. Rudyard Kipling. PWR; SAGP; UV

Shall Dumpish Melancholy spoil my Joys. On Christmas-Day. Thomas Traherne. PoEL-2

Shall Earth no more inspire thee. Emily Jane Brontë. BWW; VWP

Shall fear to seem untrue. The Rejection. Sir Robert Ayton. NOSC

Shall fill his mouth with mould. (LL) Ho, everyone that thirsteth. A. E. Housman. ChIV-1; OAEL-2

Shall find wings waiting there. (LL) Going Down Hill on a Bicycle. Henry Charles Beeching. NOxBChV; OBEV

Shall fly, the feathered arrow of the foam. (LL) Choosing a Mast. Roy Campbell. NoP-4

Shall Gaelic Die? Iain Crichton Smith. FaBoTC

Shall gentle Coleridge pass unnoticed here. Byron. EPCY *Fr.* English Bards and Scotch Reviewers.

Shall have a [or the] gold fiddle. (LL) Rock, Ball, Fiddle. *Unknown.* CBNP; CH; OxBoLi; OxNR

Shall hearts that beat no base retreat. The Enthusiast. Herman Melville. ChIV-1; NAAL-1; NAAL-3

Shall henceforth wash the river Rhine? (LL) Cologne. Coleridge. FaBoEE; NBLV; PBMP

Shall hog with holy child converse? Hog at the Manger. Norma Farber. PChr

Shall I abide this jesting? *Unknown.* GBL

Shall I ask the willow trees on the dike. Longing in My Heart. Wei Ying-wu, *Chinese.* SuSp, *tr.* by Irving Y. Lo

Shall I be one of those obsequious Fools. The Liberty. Sarah Fyge Egerton. KTR; PEW

Shall I charge like a bull. Auvaiyar, *Tamil.* WPOW, *tr.* by A. K. Ramanujan

Shall I come, if I swim? wide are the waves, you see. Thomas Campion. EnLoPo

Shall I come, sweet love, to thee. Thomas Campion. AAS; CBLP; EBEV; GBL; HAP; NOBE; OxAEP-1; OxBoLi; PoEL-2

Shall I come there, or you here? Hafsa bint al-Hajj, *Arabic.* WPOW, *tr.* by Michael Scott

Shall I come to see. Lady Ise, *Japanese.* WPJ, *tr.* by Kenneth Rexroth *and* Ikuko Atsumi

Shall I compare her to a summer play? Sonnet on Famous and Familiar Sonnets and Experiences. Delmore Schwartz. Son; TRP

Shall I Compare Thee to a Summer's Day? Howard Moss. InPK-6

Shall I compare thee to a summer's day? Sonnet 18. Shakespeare. AEP; APAD; BoLoP; CABP; CTC; ClHu; EnLoPo; FaBoBe; GBL; GLoP; GTBS-P; HAP; HeIP-4; ImPo; InPK-6; InPS-3; NOBE; NoSic; OAEL-1; OBEV; PBMP; PoE; PoEL-2; PoLF; PoPoPo; PoRA; SCGP; SCV; Son; TFi; WeW-3 *Fr.* Sonnets.

Shall I complain because the feast is o'er. Louise Chandler Moulton. PoToHe

Shall I complain or not? Or shall I mask. Ovid. *Fr.* De Ponto. OBVE, *tr.* by Henry Vaughan

Shall I connect for this world's eyes. The Dumb World. W. H. Davies. OxBTC

Shall I Do This. Swami Purohit. OBMV

Shall I embrace my disease. Monologue of a Dying Beast. Mark Ameen. GLP

Shall I ever see it, the Queen's River. Flyfisherman in Wartime. Leonard Bacon. FYAP

Shall I get drunk or cut myself a piece of cake. Cairo Jag. Keith Douglas. PoWW

"Shall I go with you [*or* thee]?" "Ay, by-and-by." (LL) Old Woman, Old Woman. Mother Goose. LB; OxNR

Shall I have jealous thoughts to nurse. No Man's Wood. W. H. Davies. OBGa

Shall I, I wonder, ever find. Peace. Irwin Edman. TrJP

Shall I love God for causing me to be? The Proof. Richard Wilbur. CRP; OxBSP

Shall I place a tin wreath upon! (LL) Tea-rose tea-gown, etc. Ezra Pound. ColAP; MoAmPo; NOBE

Shall I Repine. Jonathan Swift. *See* The Power of Time.

Shall I rise and go to the Isle of Ulung that lies. The Isle of Ulung. Ch'ihwan Yu, *Korean.* CKP, *tr.* by Jaihiun Kim

Shall I say how it is in your clothes? How It Is. Maxine W. Kumin. IMW; NALW; NoAM; Poetr

Shall I sit face to face with thee, Rabboni. Before Thy Love. Tujin Park, *Korean.* CKP, *tr.* by Jaihiun Kim

Shall I sonnet-sing you about myself? House. Robert Browning. NAEL-2

Shall I strew on thee rose or rue or laurel. Ave atque Vale. Swinburne. NAEL-2; NOBE; OAEL-2; OBEV; OBNC

Shall I tell you the signs of a New Age coming? The New Age. Stevie Smith. NAEL-2

Shall I tell you who [*or* what] will come. Words from an Old Spanish Carol. *Unknown, Spanish.* PChr, *tr.* by Ruth Sawyer

Shall I tell you whom I love? William Browne. NOSC *Fr.* Britannia's Pastorals.

Shall I then hope when faith is fled? Thomas Campion. AAS

Shall I then praise the heavens, the trees, the earth. Anne Bradstreet. NOSC; PBWP *Fr.* Contemplations. AmPP; NAAL-3; PoEL-3; SCAP; WPE

Shall I thus ever long, and be no whit the near? The Lady Prayeth the Return of Her Lover Abiding on the Seas. *Unknown.* GBL; OBEV

Shall I, wasting in despair. The Author's Resolution. George Wither. AWP; BoLoP; GTBS-P; NOBE; OBEV; OxAEP-1; SCGP *Fr.* Fair Virtue, the Mistress of Philarete.

Shall join my soul to thee. (LL) Ode: "How are thy servants blest, O Lord!" Joseph Addison. OxAEP-1; OxBoS

Shall last and shine when all of these are gone. (LL) Contemplations. Anne Bradstreet. ColAP; PBWP; WPOW

Shall lead the world the way to rest. (LL) Evening Quatrains. Charles Cotton. NOSC; PoEL-3; SCGP

Shall, like a hallowed [*or* hallow'd] Lamp, for ever burn. (LL) Eternity of Love Protested. Thomas Carew. BeJo; MeLP; NOSC

Shall live my Highland Mary. (LL) Highland Mary. Robert Burns. AWP; GTBS-P; OBEV; SAGP

Shall Man, O God of Light. Timothy Dwight. AH

Shall mine eyes behold the glory, O my country? After Death. Fanny Parnell. IIP

Shall never be by woman loved, *Lines* 1–32. William Blake. *See* To see a World in a Grain of Sand.

Shall no more blackened and obscured be. (LL) October. Edward Thomas. CABP

Shall not be seen upon thy hand again. (LL) Thy Brother's Blood. Jones Very. APN-1; NOBA; PAR; PoEL-4; TAP

Shall one be sorrowful because of love. De Amore. Ernest Christopher Dowson. OBNC

Shall one day mark the Port which ruled the Western seas. (LL) The Cotton Boll. Henry Timrod. APN-2; AmPP

Shall plough the wave no more. William Cowper. *See* On the Loss of the *Royal George.*

Shall pour such splendour as your heart to me. (LL) Most Lovely Shade. Dame Edith Sitwell. FaBoTw; GTBS-P

Shall pride a heap of sculptur'd marble raise. Epitaph on Laurence Sterne. David Garrick. FaBoEE

Shall *Reason* rule where *Reason* hath no right? To his Love that sent him a Ring wherein was gravde, / Let Reason rule. George Turberville. PBRV

Shall royal praise be rhym'd by such a ribald. On the Candidates for the Laurel. Alexander Pope. FaBoEE

Shall silence shroud such sin. A Declaration of the Death of John Lewes. Thomas Gilbart. NoSic

Shall spring to seize thee like an ambush'd foe. (LL) *ad. fr.* the Bible, Proverbs, 6, 6. Samuel Johnson. ChIV-1

Shall the Dead Praise Thee? George Macdonald. TrCP

Shall the embraces of our bodyes taste. Thomas Carew. *See* A Rapture.

Shall the voice of peace bring sweet release to the men behind the guns! . (LL) The Men behind the Guns. John Jerome Rooney. BLPA; FaBoBe

Shall the water not remember Ember. Narcissus and Echo. Fred Chappell. MT

Shall then another do what I have done. Kenneth Mackenzie. NOBAu

Shall turn and welcome me at the door. (LL) The Wizard's Funeral. Richard Watson Dixon. NOBVV; PeVV

Shall we come out of it all, some day, as one does from a tunnel? Claude to Eustace. Arthur Hugh Clough. EBVVPR *Fr.* Amours de Voyage. NOBVV

Shall we forget the shiver. Yury Ivask, *Russian.* TCRP, *tr.* by John Glad

Shall we gather at the river. Beautiful River. Robert Lowry. APN-2

Shall We Go A-Shearing? Mother Goose. ReMoGo

Shall we go dance the hay? The hay? A Report Song [in a Dream]. Nicholas Breton. GBL; NOBE; NoSic

Shall we go to the sea. Going by far. Hyon-jong Chong, *Korean.* CKP, *tr.* by Jaihiun Kim

Shall we have a family born. For Walter Lowenfels. Wendy Rose. CDW

Shall we make love. *Unknown.* AWP, *tr.* by Arthur Waley *Fr.* Manyo Shu, Part 3 of 4.

Shall we play barley-break? (LL) Now is the month of maying. *Unknown.* LiLi

Shall we play barley-break? *Unknown.* *See* Now is the month of maying.

Shall we sit here some more. August at the Lake. David Young. AmPA

Shall we stay in the. *Unknown, Japanese.* OHMPJ, *tr.* by Kenneth Rexroth

Shall we win at love or shall we lose. Hôtel Transylvanie. Frank O'Hara. NeAP; PoM

Shall well appear and by my death be seen. (LL) The Restless State of a Lover. Henry Howard, Earl of Surrey. AAS; SiPS

Shall whet their knives, and think of you. (LL) What, still alive at twenty–two. Hugh Kingsmill. BXAP; InPK-6; NBLV; NOBL; UV

Shall you complain who feed the world? To Labor. Charlotte Perkins Stetson Gilman. PoLF

Shallows, brighter, The. The Pier: Under Pisces. James Merrill. LCAP-2; NoAM

Shalom Aleichem. *Unknown, Hebrew.* TrJP

Shaman. María Sabina, *Spanish.* WPOW, *tr.* by Henry Munn

Shaman Breaks. Gerald Vizenor. HATNAP

Shaman Song. Luswat, *Tlingit Indian.* STP, *tr.* by James Koller

Shamash of the glade, The. The Venerable Bee. Abraham Moses Klein. TrJP

Shame. Sang Ku, *Korean.* CKP, *tr.* by Jaihiun Kim

Shame. Richard Wilbur. CoAmPo; FaBoMo; OBCoV; OxBC

Shame is a bad attendant to a State. Shame, no Statist. Lucan, *Latin.* OBCVT, *tr.* by Robert Herrick

Shame kept my tears away. Mutanabbi, *Arabic.* ArPe, *tr.* by Omar S. Pound

Shame, no Statist. Lucan, *Latin.* OBCVT, *tr.* by Robert Herrick

Shame to all my thoughts now. On the Flightiness of Thought. *Unknown, Irish.* TIRV, *tr.* by Brendan Kennelly

Shamed by the Creature. Mildmay Fane, 2d Earl of Westmorland. NOSC

Shameful Death. William Morris. GTBS-P; PeVV

Shameful mask hid his teeth, The. Squares. Pierre Reverdy, *French.* PFTM, *tr.* by Mary Ann Caws

Shampoo, The. Elizabeth Bishop. FaBoWP; OxBC; VCAP

Shan Van Vocht, The. *Unknown.* FaBoPV; OxBoLi

Shancoduff. Patrick Kavanagh. BIrV; CIP-2; FaBoTw; IIP

Shandon Bells, The. Francis Sylvester Mahony. *See* The Bells of Shandon.

Shane O'Neill's Cairn. Robinson Jeffers. NOBA; NoAM

Shaneen and Maurya Prendergast. Patch-Shaneen. John Millington Synge. FaBoVe

Shang ya! Oath of Friendship. *Unknown, Chinese.* TTTS, *tr. by* Arthur Waley

Shango ("Shango is an animal like the gorilla"). *Unknown, Yoruba.* PBA; TTY, *tr. by* Gbadamosi *and* Ulli Beier, *(st. 1)*

Shango ("Shango is the death who kills money with a big stick"). *Unknown, Yoruba.* TTY, *tr. by* Gbadamosi *and* Ulli Beier

Shannon Estuary Welcoming the Fish, The. Nuala Ni Dhomhnaill, *Irish.* CIP-2, *tr. by the author*

Shantih shantih shantih. "Edward Pygge." BXAP

Shantih shantih shantih. (LL) The Waste Land. T. S. Eliot. AmPP; CMoP; FaBoMo; HAP; LiTM; MoAmPo; MoP; NAAL-2; NAEL-2; NAWM-2; NOBA; NOBE; NoAM; NoP-4; OAEL-2; OxAEP-2; OxBA; OxBTC; PoE; TAP; TFi; UnPo

Shanty Boys and the Pine, The. *Unknown.* AmFP

Shantyman's Life, A. *Unknown.* AS; AmFP

Shao and the South. Confucius, *Chinese.* CTC, *tr. by* Ezra Pound

Shapcot, to thee the Fairy [or faery] State. Oberon's Feast. Robert Herrick. BeJo; CaPo; NOSC

Shape-Changer, The. Chris Wallace-Crabbe. NOBAu

Shape, like folded light, embodied air, A. Aishah Schechinah. Robert Stephen Hawker. OBNC

Shape of a Roethke, The? Theodore Roethke Foots It. David Chapman Berry. BXAP

Shape of Death, The. May Swenson. TAP

Shape of History, The. Charles Henry Webb. BAP-95

Shape of the Fire, The. Theodore Roethke. CMoP; LCAP-2; VCAP

Shape ships to seek some shining shore. Vladislav Felitsianovich Khodasevich, *Russian.* TCRP, *tr. by* Michael Frayn

Shape the lips to an *o*, say *a*. Ö. Rita Dove. HCAP; WeW-3

Shaped and vacated. The Event. Thomas Sturge Moore. OBMV

Shaped new to your measure. Ark Articulate. Jay Macpherson. NOBC *Fr.* The Ark.

Shapeless mass of wreck and rubbish lies, A. (LL) The Warning. Henry Wadsworth Longfellow. APN-1; ChIV-1; NCAP; PAR

Shapes of Death, The. Stephen Spender. OBMV

Shapes of Leaves, The. Arthur Sze. IFJA

Shapeshifter Poems. Lucille Clifton. LoL

Shards, The. Michael O'Loughlin.
    Bunkers, The. PBCIP

Shards of sunlight touch me here. Massacre, October '66. Wole Soyinka. AF; PBMAP

Share-Croppers. Langston Hughes. SAmP

Share in perdition. (LL) A Lost Soul. Jay Macpherson. NoP-4

Share my harvest and my home. (LL) Ruth. Thomas Hood. BoLoP; ChIV-1; EnLoPo; GLoP; NOBE; OBEV; OBNC

Sharing, The. Bruce Weigl. CDa

Sharing Eve's Apple. Keats. ChIV-1; NBLV; PeLV

Sharing Lodging with Hsieh Shih-hou. Harry Mathews, *Chinese.* CoBCP, *tr. by* Burton Watson

Sharing Lodging with Hsieh Shih-hou. Mei Yao Ch'en, *Chinese.* CoBCP, *tr. by* Burton Watson

Sharing the gentleness. Tanka. Nakajō Fumiko, *Japanese.* MJT, *tr. by* Makoto Ueda

Shark, The. Edwin John Pratt. NOBC

Shark, with your mouth tucked under. Cannibal. Thom Gunn. NOxBChV *Fr.* Three for Children.

Sharks, The. Denise Levertov. NeAP

Sharks at the New York Aquarium. Charles Martin. RA

Sharks in Shallow Water. Fred Levinson. AmPA

Shark's Parlor, The. James Dickey. MT; NYBP

Sharks tooth is perfect for biting, The. Canticle. Michael McClure. NeAP; PoM

Sharp. To a Set of Drawing Pencils. Fay Lipshitz. IFJA

Sharp as an arrow Orpheus. Orfeo. Jack Spicer. APSN

Sharp Ridge, The. Robert Graves. FaBoEE

Sharp winter melts and changes into spring. Spring. Horace. OBCVT, *tr. by* Robert Lowell *Fr.* The Odes.

Sharpen the sword in the Sobbing Waters. Tu Fu. SuSp, *tr. by* Irving Y. Lo *Fr.* Frontier Songs, First Series.

Sharpeville Inquiry. Anne Welsh. PeSA

Shatterday nite aucung lau town. My Deery Honey. *Unknown.* PBCV

Shattered Lute, A. Alice Thompson Meynell. SDW

Shattered membranes of the fly, The. (LL) The Range in the Desert. Randall Jarrell. PoWW

Shattered tree tops crackle beneath our feet, The. Over the Pass. Julie Convisser. IFJA

Shattered water made a misty din, The. Once by the Pacific. Robert Frost. CMoP; GSo; HAP; HeIP-4; LiTM; MeMAP; MoAmPo; NAAL-2; NOBA; PFE; Son; TRP; VGW; WeW-3

Shaving. Stephen Dobyns. NAmP90

Shavings, fall from the carved stick. Working Song. Buluguru, *Yaoro.* CBAP, *tr. by* E. A. Worms

She. Jean-Joseph Rabéarivelo. *See* Here is.

She. Theodore Roethke. BoLoP

She. Richard Wilbur. AmPP; CoAmPo

She, alone in her tower. (LL) The Return of the Greeks. Edwin Muir. NoP-4

She always had to burn a light. Five Nocturnes. Robert Frost.

She always said "*tu*" in such a way. A Dark Portrait. Lawrence Ferlinghetti. PmAP

"She always seems so tied" is what friends say. Just to Be Needed. Mary Eversley. PoToHe

She and I. Norman Cameron. OxBSP; RB

("She and I, we thought and fought.") FaBoTC

She and the Muse. Denise Levertov. CrSp

She answers the bothersome telephone, takes the message, forgets the message, forgets who called. Alzheimer's: The Wife. Charles Kenneth Williams. VCAP

She appears, present there. (LL) Autumn Garden. Dino Campana, *Italian.* GaP; STV, *tr. by* John Frederick Nims

She as a veil down to the slender waist. Before the Fall. Milton. *Fr.* Book IV. OAEL-1 *Fr.* Paradise Lost.

She asked brown eyes, "Burn me loose." Seal at Stinson Beach. Roberta Hill Whiteman. VoR

She asked me to luncheon in fur. Far from. Oppenheim's Cup and Saucer. Carol Ann Duffy. LW

She asked me twice. Pity. William Mills. MT

She asks his sister to taste. (LL) Words of the Newly Wed Wife. Wang Chien, *Chinese.* BLT, *tr. by* J. P. Seaton

She Attempts to Refute the Praises That Truth, Which She Calls Passion, Inscribed on a Portrait of the Poet. Sister Juana Inés de la Cruz, *Spanish.* BoWoP

She Begining to Study Phisick, Takes Her Leave of Poetry. Jane Barker. KTR

She begins, and my grandmother joins her. I Ask My Mother to Sing. Li-Young Lee. LoL; OpBo; UnSA

She being Brand. E. E. Cummings. MoP; NOBA; OxBA; PeLV

She Bewitched Me. Mary Burbidge. EnLoPo

She bites into the red skin. My Love Eats an Apple. Ralph Gustafson. MoCV

She Boasts of Her Constancy. Johann Rist, *German.* GePo, *tr. by* George C. Schoolfield

She bounded o'er the graves. Anna Playing in a Graveyard. Caroline Gilman. OBCA

She bows her head. The Annunciation. Samuel Menashe. GI

She brings that breath, and music too. The Visitor. W. H. Davies. GBL; OBWVE

She brings the surprise of being. Fernando Pessoa, *Portuguese.* EP, *tr. by* Jonathan Griffin

She brought a drinking-cup to him. Two. Hugo von Hofmannsthal, *German.* TrJP, *tr. by* Jethro Bithell

She brought her to her ioyous Paradize. Edmund Spenser. *See* The Garden of Adonis.

She brought us a month noisy with rain. Full Moon in Malta. "Asphodel." BrRo

She burnt like ho[ll]y gren. (LL) Young Hunting. *Unknown.* ESPB; OxBB

She by the river sat, and sitting there. Upon Julia Weeping. Robert Herrick. PFE

She calved in the ravine, beside. November Calf. Jane Kenyon. InPS-3

She came among us from the South. Enrica, 1865. Christina Rossetti. NALW

She came and spoke low. Velemir Khlebnikov. TCRP, *tr. by* Gary Kern *Fr.* The Night Before the Soviets.

She came as a falling star to the lakes. She the lithesome virgin not to be turned into. My Mother, Life. John Godfrey. ITOS

She came every morning to draw water. A Drink of Water. Seamus Heaney. OxBC; TRP

She came home, my Lord, and smashed-in the television. Wife Who Smashed Television Gets Jail. Paul Durcan. CABP; CIP-2

She came in from the snowing air. Ice. Stephen Spender. FaBoMo; GTBS-P

She came on Earth soon after the creation. The Fairy Maimounè. John Moultrie. NOBRP

She came through the room like an answer in long division. A Victorian Idyll. David Wagoner. NoAM

She came to America with him. The Passion and Woe in Marriage: A Ukrainian Love Story. Peter Oresick. IFJA

She came to him in dreams—her ears. Cowper's Tame Hare. Norman Nicholson. RB

She came to show her beauties dear. The Sister. Rose Cecil O'Neill. CPO

She came to the village church. Tennyson. EBVV; NAEL-2 *Fr.* Maud [A Monodrama]. EnVR

She came to us walking, at night. The Shoemaker's Wife. Lotte Kramer. HP

She came up the hill carrying water. The Achill Woman. Eavan Boland. BiHa

She came walking. Parable. Bob Orr. PeNZ

She cannot leave it alone. The New Toy. Thomas Hardy. ChAP

She carried a book, either to imply. Hilda Doolittle. NALW *Fr.* Tribute to the Angels.

She carried books. Margaret Fuller. Lorine Niedecker. NMM-2

She carries it unsteadily, warily. A Young Girl with a Pitcher Full of Water. David Wagoner. NoAM

She chooses her clothes in subdued colours. The Other Woman. Marion Lomax. LW

She clasps the cup with both her hands. In a Café. Rosemary Dobson. CBAP

She cleaned house, and then lay down long. A Secret Gratitude. James Wright. NoAM

She climbs the stairs to the fifth floor. Portrait of My Mother. Ilya L'vovich Selvinsky, *Russian.* TCRP, *tr. by* Daniel Weissbort

She coaxes her fat in front of her. New Day. Naomi Long Madgett. BlSi

She combs his head, and finds him horn. (LL) Three Epigrams. Jonathan Swift. FaBoEE; NBLV

She comes, and straight therewith her shining twins do move. Sonnet 76. Sir Philip Sidney. *Fr.* Astrophil and Stella. AAS; SiPS

She comes in late, then settles like a sigh. Introduction to Poetry. Paul Lake. RA

She comes level with him at. Donahue's Sister. Thom Gunn. NoAM

She Comes Not When Noon Is on the Roses. Herbert Trench. LBC; OBEV

She comes on drenched in a perfume called Self Satisfaction. Mae West. Edward Field. FYAP

She comes! she comes! the sable throne behold. Alexander Pope. ECEV *Fr.* Yet, yet a moment, one dim ray of light. NAEL-1; OAEL-1; PoEL-3 *Fr.* The Dunciad.

She comes to me. (LL) She Comes Not When Noon Is on the Roses. Herbert Trench. LBC

She could bind the world's winds in a single strand. Rune of the Finland Woman. Marilyn Hacker. RA

She could die laughing. Minnie and Mrs. Hoyne. Kenneth Fearing. PoRA

She could not remember anything about the voyage. The Migrant. A. L. Hendriks. PBCV

She cried out for Mama, who did not. Persephone Abducted. Rita Dove. NAAAL *Fr.* Mother Love.

She Cries. John Montague. BiHa

She cursed the circumstance. (LL) The Ballad of Sue Ellen Westerfield. Robert Earl Hayden. AmPP; NoAM

She danced, near nude, to tom-tom beat. Zalka Peetruza. Ray Garfield Dandridge. PoBA

She danced topless, the light-eyed drunken girl. To the Muse. Carol Muske. PuP-17

She dealt her pretty words like Blades. Emily Dickinson. HAP

She dens in a garret. Fruit and Flower Painter. Herman Melville. NCAP

She deserted you. Horse on the Wall. Marcia Southwick. CMAP; NAmP90

She did not climb the April hill. The April Hill. Janet Lewis. CRP

She did not love to love, but hated him. The End of It. Francis Thompson. NOBVV; OxBSP

She did till she died. (LL) A Nonsense Song. Stephen Vincent Benét. NOxBChV

She Didn't Even Wave. Ai. NMM-2

She didn't know she was beautiful. On Getting a Natural. Dudley Randall. PoBA

She didn't wear a crown. (LL) The Queen Bee. Mary K. Robinson. CTAV

She died after the beautiful snow had melted. In Memorial. J. Gordon Coogler. OBAL

"She died as she lived, sniffing cocaine." (LL) Cocaine Lil [and Morphine Sue]. *Unknown.* AS; CBNP; OxBoLi; RB

She died full long agone! (LL) Meg Merrilies [*or* Merrilees]. Keats. BoTP; FHYEP; FaBoCh; NOxBChV; OxBChV

She died in the upstairs bedroom. Death in Leamington. John Betjeman. NoP-4; OxAEP-2; RB

She died, she died; yet still to me. Stanzas. Caroline Anne Bowles. Ro *Fr.* Ellen Fitzarthur: A Metrical Tale.

She does not know. No Images. Waring Cuney. ISC; NIP-4; PFE; SAGP; SSLK; TTY

She does not move. Takes the man's. Jean Daive, *French.* MFP, *tr. by* Martin Sorrell

She Does Not Remember. Anna Swirszczynska, *Polish.* BLT, *tr. by* Czeslaw Milosz *and* Leonard Nathan

She doesn't say a word, concentrating on one thing only. Balgu Song. *Unknown, Balgu.* CBAP, *tr. by* Clancy McKenna

She done put huh little hands. Conjured. Sterling Brown. NoP-4

She don't have no sense. (LL) Admonitions. Lucille Clifton. BPo; NALW; NMM-2

She drank good ale, strong punch and wine. *Unknown.* LiLi *Fr.* Epitaph to Mrs Freland, in Edwelton churchyard, Nottinghamshire, 1741.

She drawled, When Ah itchez, Ah scratchez! (LL) Requiem: "There was a young belle of old Natchez." Ogden Nash. KaS; NoP-4

She dreamed along the beaches of this coast. Palo Alto. Robert Hass. PaTW

She dreams the baby's so small she keeps. Motherhood. Rita Dove. NAAAL

She drew an angel down[!]. (LL) Alexander's Feast; or, The Power of Music [*or* Musique]. Dryden. FaPoR; GTBS-P; NAEL-1; NOBE; OAEL-1; PeECV; TFi

She drew back; he was calm. The Subverted Flower. Robert Frost. CMoP; ColAP; HAP; MeMAP; MoP; NOBA; NoAM; OxBA; PoE; Poetr

She dried her tears, and they did smile. Emily Jane Brontë. NOBVV

She Drives. Sophie Cabot Black. LoHo

She dwelt among the untrodden ways. Song. Wordsworth. AWP; BLPA; BoLoP; EBEvV; EnLoPo; GTBS-P; HAP; HeiP-4; IMW; ImPo; NIP-4; NOBRP; OxAEP-2; OxBSP; PBMP; PWR; Poetr; UV; UnPo; WeW-3 *Fr.* Lucy. FHYEP; NOBE; OAEL-2; OBEV; OBNC; SCGP; TFi

She Dwelt among the Untrodden Ways. Sir John Collings Squire. BXAP

She even thinks that up in heaven. For a Lady I Know. Countee Cullen. HeiP-4; InPK-6; MoAmPo; NIP-4; OBAL; SSLK; TAP; TRP *Fr.* Four Epitaphs. PoBA

She fears him, and will always ask. Eros Turannos. Edwin Arlington Robinson. CMoP; GBL; GLoP; HAP; HeiP-4; LiTM; MeMAP; MoAmPo; MoP; NAAL-2; NOBA; NoAM; NoP-4; OxBA; PoA; PoE; PoPoPo; Poetr; TAP; TFi; TRP

She feels her hands, scabrous as fish. The Washerwoman. Veronica Volkow, *Spanish.* VCWP, *tr. by* Forrest Gander

She fell asleep on Christmas Eve. My Sister's Sleep. D. G. Rossetti. EnVR; NAEL-2

She fell away in her first ages spring. An Elegy. Edmund Spenser. OBEV *Fr.* Daphnaïda.

She filled her arms with wood, and set her chin. Edna St. Vincent Millay. *Fr.* Sonnets from an Ungrafted Tree. NALW

She finds grief, her meat. Hyena. Carol Muske. AmPA

She Finds Herself in a Garden. Angelo Poliziano, *Italian.* GaP, *tr. by* John Hollander

She flees, she flees through flat white lands, as patiently I take my aim. Song of the Initiate. Léopold Sédar Senghor, *French.* NegPo, *tr. by* Ellen Conroy Kennedy

She flourished in the 'Twenties, "hectic" days of peace. Mews Flat Mona. William Plomer. FaBoTw

She folds her wings about her sleeping child. (LL) Bats. Randall Jarrell. ChAP; NTCP; OBCA

She followed him all afternoon. Looking for Camels. Selima Hill. NBrP

She found him drownd in Yarrow. (LL) Rare Willie Drowned in Yarrow; or, The Water o Gamrie. *Unknown.* ESPB; OxBB

She Found Me Roots. R. W. Ransford. BXAP

She gave it out as if it were. The Aphrodisiac. Medbh McGuckian. PBCIP

She gave me childhood's flowers. Heirloom. Kathleen Jessie Raine. NALW

"She gives herself;" there's a poetic thought. Portrait in Black Paint, with a Very Sparing Use of Whitewash. Elinor Wylie. NALW

She goes but softly, but she goeth sure. Upon the [*or* a] Snail. John Bunyan. CTAV; OxBSP

She goes on with her story. Mother and Son. Alden Nowlan. RaBo

She goes out in the night again. The Wastrel-Woman Poem. Brenda Marie Osbey. MT

She goes to different bars. There Is a Woman in This Town. Patricia Parker. BlSi

She goes upstairs early. Double Bed. Carol Rumens. LW

She grew ninety years through sombre winter. Epitaph on a Fir-Tree. Richard Murphy. FaBoTw

She grew up in bedeviled southern wilderness. The Ballad of Sue Ellen Westerfield. Robert Earl Hayden. AmPP; NoAM

She grew within his heart as the flushed rose. Extract from Romance. Dame Edith Sitwell. WPN *Fr.* Extract from Romance.

She had a horror he would die at night. Edna St. Vincent Millay. *Fr.* Sonnets from an Ungrafted Tree. NALW

She had a little time to think. Leda Reconsidered. Mona Van Duyn. NMM-2

She had a name among the children. A Cat. Edward Thomas. OxBSP; PC

She had corn flowers in her ear. Gipsy Jane. William Brighty Rands. BoTP

She had forgotten how the August night. Edna St. Vincent Millay. *Fr.* Sonnets from an Ungrafted Tree. NALW

She Had Known Brothers. Sherley Anne Williams. GT

She had no saying dark enough. The Oft-Repeated Dream. Robert Frost. Poetr *Fr.* The Hill Wife. CMoP; HAP; InPS-3; LiTM; NoP-4; RACG

She had no shoes on, she had freed her hair. Victor Hugo, *French.* FLP, *tr. by* Alistair Elliot

She had not held her secret long enough. The Visitation. Elizabeth Jennings. MoBS

She had nothing. A Girl of Six from the Ghetto Begging in Smolna Street in 1942. Jerzy Ficowski, *Polish.* HP, *tr. by* Keith Bosley

She had raised the window. Destination: Tule Lake Relocation Center, May 20, 1942. Jim Mitsui. OpBo

She Had Some Horses. Joy Harjo. HATNAP; LoL

She had the fewer for what she did. (LL) Riddle: Cuckoo. Cynewulf. AnOE, *tr. by* Charles W. Kennedy; ASW, *tr. by* Kevin Crossley-Holland

She had thought the studio would keep itself. Living in Sin. Adrienne Rich. NIP-4; NYBP; NoP-4; Poetr; SoSe-8; TAP; UnPo

She had to be Milked by a Man and his Wife. (LL) The Cow. Theodore Roethke. OBAL; OBCA

She had travelled through nights and days. The End of the Journey. May Probyn. VWP

She hadn't found a speck of death. (LL) How I Learned to Sweep. Julia Alvarez. FFC; RA

She has been burning palaces. "To ———." The Palace-Burner. Sarah Morgan Bryan Piatt. NCAP

She has been condemned to death by hanging. Marrying the Hangman. Margaret Atwood. NOBC

She has begun to see men invite themselves. The Professional. David Ignatow. NNaP

She has but one eye. Mother Goose. *See* I have a little sister, they call her Peep-Peep.

She has calld to her her bower-maidens. Young Hunting. *Unknown.* ESPB

She has come next door to practice our piano. The "Wife Takes a Child." Ellen Bryant Voigt. CrSp

She has decided that she no longer loves me. The Wind in the Tree. Frank Templeton Prince. OxBSP

She has gone. Richard Crist. HA

She has gone to the valley. Lament for an Old Woman. Albert Huffstickler. IFJA

She has had to bear. (LL) The Whipping. Robert Earl Hayden. FiLi; PoBA; PoE; SSLK; SoSe-8

She has left me, my pretty. Song. Sylvia Townsend Warner. MoBrPo

"She has no heart," they said, and turned away. In Time of Famine. Helen Hunt Jackson. PAR

She has not come. Paulus Silentiarius, *Greek.* GrAn, *tr. by* Andrew Miller

She has not imbibed LSD in many years until today. Evangele. Anne Waldman. PT

She has taken a woman lover. Carol, in the Park, Chewing on Straws. Judy Grahn. WPOW *Fr.* The Common Woman.

She has withdrawn from us. Maude Meehan. MDDM *Fr.* Small Wings.

She hath an art[e] to break[e] them with her eyes. (LL) Thrice toss[e] these oaken ashes in the air [*or* ayre]. Thomas Campion. CBLP; EBEV; EnLoPo; FaBoCh; HAP; NOBE; OAEL-1; OxBSP; PoEL-2; PoRA; SCGP; TFi; WeW-3

She hath her reward. (LL) The Man Who Married Magdalene. Anthony Hecht. ChIV-2; PeLV

She having gainèd both the Wind and Sun. (LL) The Fair Singer. Andrew Marvell. EnLoPo; FSCP; MeLP; NOBE; NoP-4; PoEL-2; SCGP

She heard with patience all unto the end. Prince Arthur. Edmund Spenser. *Fr.* Wood Of Error. AEP

She hears me strike the board and say Father and Child. W. B. Yeats. PFE

She hears the infantry of eyes advance. (LL) The Retreat of Ita Cagney. Michael Hartnett. CIP-2; PBCIP

She Hears The Storm. Thomas Hardy. LoP; NAEL-2

She held me for a night against her bosom. Macon Prairie. Willa Silbert Cather. PaTW

She hers, he his, pursuing. (LL) The Dalliance of the Eagles. Walt Whitman. APo; AmPP; HAP; HeIP-4; NAAL-1; NAAL-3; NoP-4; SAGP; SAmP; TAP; TRP

She / holds th mirror to her eye. My Lai / Remuera / Ponsonby. David Mitchell. PeNZ

She holds things together, collects bail. Judy Grahn. NALW *Fr.* The Common Woman.

She holds to the idea. Visit. Gerald William Barrax. GT

She holds you by the hair. How She Operates. Grace Caroline Bridges. LoHo

She hopes to hear a word from her. Adoration of the Anchor. Laura Jensen. LCAP-2

She hovered hooded, blue-eyed. Catechism, 1958. W. M. Ransom. CDW

She Hugged Me and Kissed Me. *Unknown.* BPo

She hung away her years, her eyes grew young. Waiting for the Bus. D. J. Enright. OxBTC

She, in dowdy dress and dumpy. Still Life: Lady with Birds. Quandra Prettyman. PoBA

She in whose lipservice. The Goddess. Denise Levertov. LiTM; NALW; NOBA; NeAP; PoM

She is a black crow being driven out of sight. Drinking the Wind. "Tan Ying," *Chinese.* WPOW, *tr. by* Kenneth Rexroth *and* Ling Chung

She is a mother, and her heart / Is breaking to despair. Frances Ellen Watkins Harper. *See* The Slave Mother.

She is a reed swaying in blue. Love Song. Earle Thompson. HATNAP

She is a rich and rare land. This Native Land. Thomas Osborne Davis. BoTP

She is all so slight. After Two Years. Richard Aldington. MoBrPo

She is all there. For My Lover, Returning to His Wife. Anne Sexton. CBLP; HCAP; NMM-2; Poetr; SAGP; UnPo; WPE

She is as in a field a silken tent. The Silken Tent. Robert Frost. AmPP; ColAP; ImPo; InPK-6; NOBA; NoP-4; Son; TAP; TRP; TwCP; WeW-3

She is building a model of a concentration camp complex. She has. Harriet Feigenbaum is a Sculptor. Phyllis Koestenbaum. BAP-93

She is carried in with half her buttocks gone. Kim-San. Steve Denning. CDa

She is committed to the earth and the earth. Canaan. Muriel Spark. NYBP

She is dead. Birthdays. Hilde Domin, *German.* BoWoP, *tr. by* Tudor Morris

"She is dead!" they said to him. "Come away." He and She. Sir Edwin Arnold. BLPA

She is facetious, of a gentle nature. Epigram VII: Winifred. Hugh Crompton. NOSC

She Is Far from the Land. Thomas Moore. NOIV; OBNC; OxAEP-2

She is flat on her back. E. Ethelbert Miller. GT

She is gathering lotos-seed in the river of Yueh. The Girl of Yueh. Li Po, *Chinese.* TAL, *tr. by* Robert Payne

She is gone! The occasion for ever is past! Lines Written Immediately after Parting from a Lady. Sir Samuel Egerton Brydges. NOEC

She is in your painting the one you bought when the taxi. Framed. Claire Harris. PBCV

She is large and matronly. Lui et Elle. D. H. Lawrence. NoAM

She is liquid darkness occult with desire. Christopher Dewdney. FTOS *Fr.* Concordat Proviso Ascendant.

She Is More to Be Pitied than Censured. William B. Gray. BLPA

She is most fair. The Unknown. Edward Thomas. GBL

She is no liar, yet she will wash away. Robert Graves. OxBSP

She is no woman, but a sencelesse stone. (LL) Sonnet 54: "Of this world's Theatre in which we stay." Edmund Spenser. NAEL-1; NoP-4; OAEL-1

She is not dead, but sleepeth. Mrs. Rebecca Weston. Mary Weston Fordham. CBWP-2

She is not fair to outward view. Hartley Coleridge. GTBS-P; OBEV; OxAEP-2

She is not happy as the Poets say. On Sandro's Flora. Trumbull Stickney. APN-2

She Is Not Satisfied. Charles Baudelaire, *French.* EP; FLP, *tr. by* Alistair Elliot

She is not sure. An Old Thought for a New Couple. E. A. Markham. PBCV

She is now water and air. Sea Burial from the Cruiser *Reve.* Richard Eberhart. NYBP

She is old, and bent, and wrinkled. Marching Still. Minna Irving. CBCWP

She is older than the rocks among which she sits. Mona Lisa. Walter Pater. OBMV

She is purposeless as a cyclone; she must move. Cubist Portrait. Marjorie Allen Seiffert. PoA

She is shameless, despicable, vile. Zinaida Nikolayevna Gippius, *Russian.* WPOW, *tr. by* Dianne Levitin

She is singing to Thee, *Domine!* "Michael Field." CPO; VWP

She is sixty. She lives. The Greatest Love. Anna Swirszczynska, *Polish.* BLT; PoSu, *tr. by* Czeslaw Milosz *and* Leonard Nathan

She is slim again. A Baby in the House. Patrick Williams. PNI

She is so proper and so pure. My Sweet Sweeting. *Unknown.* CH

She is standing on my lids. Lady Love. Paul Éluard, *French.* OBVE, *tr. by* Samuel Beckett

She is still unborn. Silentium. Osip Emilevich Mandelstam, *Russian.* TCRP, *tr. by* Albert C. Todd

She Is the Greatest Wealth. Georg Rudolph Weckherlin, *German.* GePo, *tr. by* George C. Schoolfield

She is the one you call sister. The Mirror in Which Two Are Seen as One. Adrienne Rich. NAAL-2; NNaP

She is the thing that she despises. (LL) A Hue and Cry after Fair Amoret. William Congreve. NOEC; OBEV

She is the woman hanging from the 13th floor. The Woman Hanging from the Thirteenth Floor Window. Joy Harjo. GLP; HATNAP; UnSA

She is thinking of the delta. After Dark. Allison Funk. BAP-94

She is tougher than me, harder. For My Mother. Iain Crichton Smith. OxBS

She is washed by white-water, white if she looked up. Fish. Daniel Halpern. AmPA

She is weeping for her lost right arm. Weeping Woman. Denise Levertov. AF

She is without longinge. *Unknown. See* I Have a Young Sister.

She isn't straight. Photograph & Story in *The Press*: The Mother Whose Children Burned to Death. Adora Phillips. FTOS

She issues radiant from her dressing-room. George Meredith. EnVR; NOBVV *Fr.* Modern Love.

She jes' gits hold of us dataway. (LL) Ma Rainey. Sterling Brown. ISC; NAAAL

She juliets him from a window in Soho. Short Time. Gavin Ewart. NoAM

She just hauls out and smacks him. Homeric. Richard Jackson. NAmP90

She keeps the memory-game. The Net. Fleur Adcock. PeNZ

She kept an antique shop—or it kept her. My Grandmother. Elizabeth Jennings. NoP-4

She kept her secret well, oh, yes. My Angeline. Harry Bache Smith. NBLV

She-kin, show our force. Join hands! Aeschylus. OBCVT, *tr. by* Tony Harrison *Fr.* The Eumenides.

She kneads / deep into the night. Don't Talk to Me about Bread. E. A. Markham. HCP; PBCV

She kneels behind her best friend. The Backup. Wing Tek Lum. IFJA

She knew more about me *than* let us say. Isolate. Clarence Major. PmAP

She knows nothing about babies. (LL) The Cherry Tree. Thom Gunn. GLP; Poetsp

She knows them all. Urchins. Beggars. The Left Eye of Odin. Regina DeCormier-Shekejian. LoHo

She knows where to get cracked eggs, does Nelly. Old Nelly's Birthday. Ruth Pitter. NALW

She languorously swings her tongue. The Domesticity of Giraffes. Judith Beveridge. BMAP

She Lay All Naked in Her Bed. *Unknown.* BoLoP; EP

She lay all night beside me. Paulus Silentiarius, *Greek.* GrAn, *tr. by* Andrew Miller

She lay, and serving-men her lithe arms took. Abishag. Rilke, *German.* AWP, *tr. by* Jethro Bithell

She lay beside me in the dawn. (LL) Alba ("As cool as the pale wet leaves"). Ezra Pound. GBL; HAP; WeW-3

She lay beside the bridge. The German troops had reckoned. Retribution. Ilya Grigoryevich Ehrenburg, *Russian.* TCRP, *tr. by* Gordon McVay

She lay in her girlish sleep at ninety-six. Castoff Skin. Ruth Whitman. InPK-6

She Lay Wrapped. Gail Fox. NOBC

She Lays ("She lays each beautifully mooned finger"). Molly Peacock. EOEF

She lays each beautifully mooned finger. She Lays. Molly Peacock. EOEF

She leaned her back unto a thorn. The Cruel Mother. *Unknown.* ESPB

She leaned her head upon her hand. Vashti. Frances Ellen Watkins Harper. AAP; BlSi; NAAAL; NALW

She leaned in a small fist on the cushions, buds in her pajamas. "Make me a story." Blue Shade. Aaron Shurin. FTOS

She leans across a golden table. For Amy Lowell. Countee Cullen. PoA

She leaves. Michael McClintock.

She leaves the motor running. Shadow Play. Ralph Angel. NAmP90

She left a bit of her tail in a trap. Mother Goose. *See* Old Mother Twitchett had [*or* has] but one eye.

She left me at the silent time. Lines Written in the Bay of Lerici. Shelley. OAEL-2

She let them leave their jellies at the door. Edna St. Vincent Millay. *Fr.* Sonnets from an Ungrafted Tree. NALW

She licked my salty nose. Old People. Michael Davitt, *Irish.* PBCIP, *tr. by* Michael Hartnett

She lies far inland, and no stick nor stone of her. Inland City. John Crowe Ransom. CMoP

She liked mornings the best—Thomas gone. Weathering Out. Rita Dove. CMAP; LCAP-2; NoAM

She Lived. Lucille Clifton. LoL

She lived in storm and strife. That the Night Come. W. B. Yeats. PoEL-5

She lived in the hovel alone, the beautiful child. The Scape-Goat. Agnes Mary Frances Robinson. VWP

She lived too much alone to be aware of it. Death of an Old Woman. Alasdair Maclean. FaBoTC

She lives a prisoner within. The Shut-In. Nellie De Hearn. PoToHe

She lives alone now. The Poet Reflects On Her Solitary Fate. Sandra Cisneros. FFC

She lives in the porter's room; the plush is nicotined. Bitter Sanctuary. Harold Monro. FaBoMo; OBMV

She Looked At the Sun. Tadeusz Różewicz, *Polish.* PoSu, *tr. by* Magnus F. Krynski

She looked over his shoulder. The Shield of Achilles. W. H. Auden. EBEV; FaBoMo; FaBoPV; GTBS-P; HAP; NAEL-2; NOBE; NOCV; NoAM; NoP-4; OxAEP-2; PeECV; PoA; PoE; WeW-3

She looked to east, she looked to west. Mater Dei. Katharine Tynan. TIRV

She looks out in the blue morning. The Window. Conrad Potter Aiken. CMoP

She love me, loves me not. Vladimir Mayakovsky. *See* Mayakovsky's Suicide Note.

She Loves. Olga Broumas. GLP

She loves, and she confesses too. Honour. Abraham Cowley. BoLoP

She loves him. . . and what small child could deny. Americanized. Bruce Dawe. CBAP

She loves me? She loves me not? Mayakovsky's Suicide Note. Vladimir Mayakovsky, *Russian.* TCRP, *tr. by* Bernard Meares

She Loves Me, She Loves Me Not. Dmitry Sergeievich Merezhkovsky, *Russian.* TCRP, *tr. by* Albert C. Todd

She makes her way through the dark trees. The Country Wife. Dana Gioia. RA

She may count three little daisies very well. From Stanzas in Meditation. Gertrude Stein. NoP-4 *Fr.* Stanzas in Meditation.

She may not accuse me. Friedrich von Hausen, *German.* GePo, *tr. by* Sylvia Stevens

She Mends an Ancient Wireless. Paul Durcan. PBCIP

She met me, Stranger, upon life's rough way. Shelley. EP *Fr.* Epipsychidion.

She might, so noble from head. A Thought from Propertius. W. B. Yeats. OAEL-2; OxBSP

She mixes blue and mauve and green. The Patchwork Quilt. Elizabeth Fleming. BoTP

She Moved through the Fair. Padraic Colum. BIrV; NOIV

She must have been kicked unseen or brushed by a car. Dog's Death. John Updike. Poetr; Poetsp

She never brought flowers. My Mother's Blue Vase. Jeannette Doob. IFJA

She never puts her toys away. Patty-Poem. Nick Kenny. PoToHe

She never saw. Orpheus and Eurydice. Virgil. OBCVT, *tr. by* Lewis, C. Day

She never was quite one of us. Sleep-Walking Child. Elisabeth Eybers, *Afrikaans.* PeSA, *tr. by* Jack Cope, Uys Krige, *and* Adèle Naudé

She / not to be confused with she, a dog. Lady Tactics. Anne Waldman. PoM

She of the Impudent Face. Bible, *O.T.* TrJP *Fr.* Proverbs.

She only knew the birth and death. At Dawn. Arthur Symons. OBNC

She, only she, can please the taste! (LL) To an Author. Philip Freneau. AmPP; ColAP; NOBA; OxBA

She packs her suitcase. Snow. Donna Trussell. IFJA

She passed away like morning dew. Early Death. Hartley Coleridge. OBEV

She passively nods. And they go that way. (LL) By Her Aunt's Grave. Thomas Hardy. MoBrPo; PFE

She peeked out from under. The Missing Patriarch. Michael S. Weaver. PBCAP

She played her game of chess, alone, when day was done. Spinster. Vita Sackville-West. WPN

She played me false, but that's not why. Our Photograph[s]. Frederick Locker-Lampson. NBLV; NOBL; PeLV

She plucked one thread. Paulus Silentiarius, *Greek.* GrAn, *tr. by* Andrew Miller

She plucks a harp, ascends a stair. Memory. Eve Shelnutt. CMAP

She practices a fugue, though it can matter. Suburban Sonnet. Gwen Harwood. CBAP

She pricked hard [*or* herd] and made her self to ble[e]d[e]. (LL) Who hath he[a]rd of such[e] cruelty before. Sir Thomas Wyatt. AAS; SiPS

She Promised She'd Meet Me. *Unknown.* AS

She Proves the Inconsistency of the Desires and Criticism of Men Who Accuse Women of What They Themselves Cause. Sister Juana Inés de la Cruz, *Spanish.* BoWoP, *tr. by* Aliki *and* Willis Barnstone

She put her arms around me and we cried. (LL) The Truth. Randall Jarrell. FiLi; OxBC

She puts her face against the wall. She Cries. John Montague. BiHa

She puts on a silken blouse and comes down from the western chamber. Su Man-shu. SuSp, *tr. by* Wu-chi Liu *Fr.* Poems Written during My Sojourn in Japan.

She re-enters her life. Returning. Linda Pastan. WeW-3

"She reaped as she sowed, Lo! this is her son." (LL) To My Son. Margaret Johnston Grafflin. BLPA; PoToHe

She recognizes miner's lettuce. Ellen Bass. MDDM

She remarks how the style of a whole age. The Moment of Waking. John Tranter. BMAP

She returned from the clinic. Unhappy Diary Days. Gerald Vizenor. VoR

She roamed the meadows long in hope. Recompensed? Henrietta Cordelia Ray. CBWP-3

She rose to His Requirement—dropt. Emily Dickinson. APAD; NALW

She rose upon her toes. A Minor Elegy. "Igor Severyanin," *Russian.* TCRP, *tr. by* Bernard Meares

She said, "I was not born to mope at home in loneliness." The Ride round the Parapet. Friedrich Rückert, *German.* AWP, *tr. by* James Clarence Mangan

She said, If tomorrow my world were torn in two. The 5:32. Phyllis McGinley. NMM-2; OxBM; WPE *Fr.* I Know a Village.

She said. "I'm god and all." Against a Sickness. To the Female Double Principle God. Alan Dugan. NoAM

She said, it's not as though. Ask This of a Mother Whose Daughter Has Been Tortured. Barbara Jamison. EC3

She said she don't love me anymore because I drink whiskey. *Unknown.* STP *Fr.* Kiowa "49" Songs.

She said she forgave me. Parted. Clara Ann Thompson. CBWP-2

She said she / woke up with him in. Dreaming Frankenstein. Liz Lochhead. FaBoTC

She said she would come. Sosei, *Japanese.* OHPJ, *tr. by* Kenneth Rexroth

She said she would marry him. Listen. Marylin Butler. CDa

She said, "That's what / You think." (LL) Myth. Muriel Rukeyser. CrSp; FaBoWP; NALW; NNaP

She said the Jehovah Witness man. Ode 3-31-70. Gayl Jones. BlSi *Fr.* Journal.

She said: the pitying audience melt in tears. Alexander Pope. EBNV, *canto* V, *abr. Fr.* The Rape of the Lock[, an Heroi-Comical Poem]. FHYEP; HAP; ImPo; OAEL-1; OBNV; PeLV; PoEL-3

She Said the Same to Me. *Unknown.* AS

She said, "They gave me of their best." After Aughrim. Emily Lawless. OBEV

She said to one: "How glows." Subalterns. Elizabeth Daryush. OBWP

She said, Wear my leather jacket, a looser. How to Dress like a Scary Dyke. Jane Barnes. GLP

She said: "When I was with him." Alice Walker. DeD

She sang beyond the genius of the sea. The Idea of Order at Key West. Wallace Stevens. CMoP; ColAP; HAP; HCAP; HeIP-4; MeMAP; MoAmPo; MoP; NAAL-2; NAWM-2; NIP-4; NOBA; NoAM; NoP-4; OxBA; PoE; PoPoPo; Poetr; SAmP; TAP; TFi

She sang this "Song of the Shirt!" (LL) The Song of the Shirt. Thomas Hood. EBEvV; EBVV; FaPoR

She sat and looked at a picture. Her Son. Ebba M. Leaf. PWR

She sat and sang alway. Song. Christina Rossetti. GBL; NAEL-2

She sat at tea just like the others. First. Going Blind. Rilke, *German.* BLT, *tr. by* Walter Arndt

She sat by me and eyed me craftily. Dinner at the Mongoloid's. Larry Rubin. MT

She sat by the fire and told many a fine tale. (LL) The Clever Hen. *Unknown.* BoTP; LB; ReMoGo

She sat down below a thorn. The Cruel Mother. *Unknown.* AmFP; ESPB; InPK-6; OxBB

She sat on a shelf. Motherhood. May Swenson. CoAP; NoP-4

She sat on a willow-trunk. The Fly. Miroslav Holub, *Czech.* PoSu; RB, *tr. by* Milner *and* George Theiner

She sat on the willow bark. Miroslav Holub. *See* The Fly.

She sat up on her pillows, receiving guests. Douglas Dunn. NoP-4 *Fr.* Elegies.

She saw Africa as a continent. White Poetess. Musaemura Bonus Zimunya. PeSAV

She Saw Me in Church. *Unknown.* MiEL

She Says, Cocks Are Crowing! *Unknown, Chinese.* CoBCP, *tr. by* Burton Watson

She says "How was you?" Kissing. "Come on in." Unrecorded Speech. Anna Adams. BrRo

She says hows bachelor life. Brandon Kershner. *Fr.* 3 Dialogues. EC2

She says the book she is reading is gross. Condoms. Ronald Wallace. MoLi

She says the coffin to be opened. Lady Alice. *Unknown.* AmFP

She schools the flighty pupils of her eyes. Gerard Manley Hopkins. OxBSP

She seemed to be a witch. (LL) Then Margery [*or* Marjorie] Milkduck. John Skelton. EBEV; OAEL-1; PoE

She sees him on her way home from work. Steps. Michael Cuddihy. CMAP

She sells sea-shells on the sea shore. *Unknown.* OTCP

She Sent Him Away. Clara Ann Thompson. CBWP-2

She serves me a piece of it a few minutes. My Daughter and Apple Pie. Raymond Carver. MoLi

She shakes feathers toward him. Pay Cash Only. James Sherry. FTOS

She shakes in the take-off lounge. The Frightened Flier Goes North. Judith Kazantzis. BrRo

She shall have music wherever she goes. Mother Goose. *See* Ride a cock-horse [*or* a-cock horse] to Banbury Cross, / To see a fine lady upon a white horse.

She shall live in the proud memorial of your arms! (LL) Appeal. Noémia da Sousa, *Portuguese.* PBMAP

She shall sing me a song. A Song Composed for Fanny Burney. Samuel Johnson. CBNP

She sharpened her knife both sharp and keen. Young Hunting. *Unknown.* OxBoLi

She, she is dead; she's dead; when thou knowest [*or* know'st] this. Donne. *Fr.* The First Anniversary [*or* Anniversarie]. NAEL-1 *Fr.* Anatomy [*or* Anatomie] of the World, An[: The First Anniversary].

She should have died hereafter. Tomorrow, and Tomorrow, and Tomorrow. Shakespeare. SoSe-8 *Fr.* Macbeth.

She sights a Bird—she chuckles—. Cat. Emily Dickinson. APo; SAmP

She sits beside: through four low panes of glass. Nightfall. "Michael Field." VWP

She sits by the lodge fire. Making the Snowshoes. R. T. Smith. EC2

She sits down to eat, breaks off a piece. Yevgeny Mikhailovich Vinokurov, *Russian.* TCRP, *tr. by* Daniel Weissbort

She sits home [*or* in the house] for days on end. Portrait. Dahlia Ravikovitch, *Hebrew.* IP, *tr. by* Warren Bargad *and* Stanley F. Chyet

She sits home for days on end. Dahlia Ravikovitch. *See* Portrait.

She sits in her glass garden. The One Whose Reproach I Cannot Evade. George Hitchcock. SPE

She sits in the marketplace. Pearle's Poem. Primus St. John. GT

She sits in the park. Her clothes are out of date. In The Park. Gwen Harwood. BMAP; CBAP; GEA

She sits in the tawny vapour. A Wife in London. Thomas Hardy. NOBVV; OBWP

She sits naked on a rock. Last Gods. Galway Kinnell. RaBo

She sits on a smoldering couch. The Woman on the Dump. Elizabeth Spires. WWSi

She sits on the mountain that is her home. Night Music. Linda Gregg. BLT

She sits on tumulus Savoor, and stares. Flax. Ivan Alekseievich Bunin, *Russian.* AWP, *tr. by* Babette Deutsch *and* Avrahm Yarmolinsky

She sits there. Girl at the Window. Pinkie Gordon Lane. GT

She sits with one hand poised against her head, the. Dialogue. Adrienne Rich. TAP

She skimmed the yellow water like a moth. My Grandmother's Ghost. James Wright. Son

She skips on to the day's next blue radius. Maggie. Duane Niatum. HATNAP

She sleeps and rests on the candor of the sand. Negro Mask. Léopold Sédar Senghor, *French.* NegPo, *tr. by* Ellen Conroy Kennedy

She sleeps on a cot in the living room. Silence. She Is Six Years Old. Lynn Emanuel. CrSp

She sleeps: yet is her hand awake. T. Carmi, *Hebrew.* MHP, *tr. by* Ruth Finer Mintz

She slid down through the straw and fell in. *Unknown. See* There was a young lady from Lynn.

She slipped. Heels over head she landed. Portrait. Gail Fox. NOBC

She slipped through the straw and / fell in. (LL) There was a young lady from Lynn. *Unknown.* CTV

She slowly came, I knew her by the sign. A Dream of Sappho. Rose Cecil O'Neill. CPO

She smiled behind a lawny cloud. Fancy Dress. Dorothea MacKellar. NOBAu

She Smiled like a Holiday. *Unknown.* OxBoLi

She / somersaulted. Joyce Carol Thomas. MDDM *Fr.* Bittersweet.

She sought him east, she sought him west. Rare Willie Drowned in Yarrow; or, The Water o Gamrie. *Unknown.* ESPB

She speaks always in her own voice. The Portrait. Robert Graves. CMoP; LoP; PBMP

She Speaks the Morning's Filigree. Philip Lamantia. VGW

She spends the afternoon in a deckchair. Summer Afternoon. Stewart Conn. FaBoTC

She spent her money with such perfect style. The Rapist's Villanelle. Thomas M. Disch. RA

She spent three hundred and sixty four days a year. Grandmother Jackson. David Jackson. OBCP

She spreads her pale legs. In the Purple Bar. Gig Ryan. BMAP

She springs from the ground-clinging thicket, her face. Veneris Venefica Agrestis. Lucio Piccolo, *Italian.* OBVE, *tr. by* Charles Tomlinson

She stands as pale as Parian statues stand. A Soul. Christina Rossetti. NALW; WPOW

She stands as pale as Parian statues stand. A Study (A Soul). Christina Rossetti. VWP

She stands at the intersection, waiting. The Pedestrian Woman. Robin Morgan. CrSp

She stands beside me, stands away. Like Rousseau. Imamu Amiri Baraka. PoA

She stands by the table, poised. Vermeer. Stephen Mitchell. GI

She started up from where the lizard lies. On Rodin's "L'Illusion, Sœur d'Icare." Trumbull Stickney. APN-2

She stepped out of the framing circle of the dark. Coda, Overture. Eleanor Wilner. NMM-2

She stitched her story on black. The Constellation Quilt. Mei-Mei Berssenbrugge. OpBo

She stole my pencil-case, red leather. The Thief. Josephine Jacobsen. WPE

She stood at the bar of justice. "Guilty or Not Guilty?" *Unknown.* BLPA

She stood breast-high amid the corn. Ruth. Thomas Hood. BoLoP; ChIV-1; EnLoPo; GLoP; NOBE; OBEV; OBNC

She stood close to a tree and wrinkled. Tree Old Woman. Samuel Makidemewabe, *Cree Indian.* STP, *tr. by* Howard Norman

She stood hanging wash before sun. Ghetto Lovesong—Migration. Carole C. Gregory Clemmons. PoBA

She stood in her scarlet gown. *Unknown, Latin.* MLL, *tr. by* Helen Waddell *Fr.* Carmina Burana.

She stood nakedly. After Her Man Had Left Her for the Sixth Time That Year / (An Uncommon Occurrence). Haki R. Madhubuti. GT

She Stoops to Conquer. Oliver Goldsmith.

   Song: "Let school-masters puzzle their brain." BIrV; NOIV

   (Three Jolly Pigeons, The.) PoRA

She stops combing her hair, Tune: "Dreaming of the South." Tune: Dreaming of the South. Wen T'ing-yün, *Chinese.* CoBCP, *tr. by* Burton Watson

She strolls in the valley, alone. Madwoman at Rodmell. Michele Roberts. BrRo

She suffers like a red stone, small as a carat. Sisters. Sandra McPherson. AmPA

She swam smiling in the river. Waiting to Be Fed. Ray A. Young Bear. CDW

She sweeps with many-colored Brooms. Evening. Emily Dickinson. BoTP

She talks not, plays not, visits not, in bed. *Unknown.* FaBoEE

She tells her love while half asleep. Robert Graves. BoLoP; EBEV; FaBoTw; GBL; LoP; NOBE; OxBTC

She tells me with claret she cannot agree. Drinking Song. *Unknown.* NOBL

She tells us an interminable story, from television. The Somerset Dam for Supper. John Holmes. NYBP

She tests the curb with a chubby boot. For Heather, Entering Kindergarten. Roberta Hill Whiteman. HATNAP; NoAM

She that but little patience knew. On a Political Prisoner. W. B. Yeats. FaBoPV; IIP; OAEL-2; OBMV

She that holds me under the laws of love. Sir Arthur Gorges. GBL

She That Is Memory's Daughter. Vernon Watkins. NYBP

She that, oh, broke her faith, would soon break thee. (LL) A Jet Ring Sent. Donne. CBLP; OxBSP; PoEL-2

She, the mirror. Old Magic. Grace Nichols. PBCV

She, the river. Woman. Hira Bansode, *Marathi.* OMIP, *tr. by* Vinay Dharwadker

She, the sensual creature, the green singer. Slow Dancer That No One Hears but You. Duane Niatum. CDW

She Thinks of Her Beloved. Lu Chi, *Chinese.* OHMPC, *tr. by* Kenneth Rexroth

She thus; when I had great desire to prove. Homer. OBVE, *tr. by* George Chapman *Fr.* Odyssey. NAWM-1, *tr. by* Robert Fitzgerald

She Tied Up Her Few Things. John Clare. HAP

She, to Him. Thomas Hardy. EnVR

   "This love puts all humanity from me." TOF

   "When you shall see me in the toils of Time." OxBTC

She told how they used to form for the country dances. One We Knew. Thomas Hardy. NAEL-2

She told me she opened up. Blossoming. Laurie Duesing. DeD

She told the story, and the whole world wept. Harriet Beecher Stowe. Paul Laurence Dunbar. AAP; BPo; PoPoPo

She, too, the voyaging in doors and Keys. This Alice. Herbert Morris. PoRA

She too went dark as dusk began, though rising. On the Death of Cleopatra-Selene. Crinagoras, *Greek.* GrAn, *tr. by* Alistair Elliot

She took. Medusa Cement. Alise Alousi. IFJA

She took a last and simple meal when there were none to see. The Lost Cat. Emile Victor Rieu. PC

She took from her basket four fishes. The Fisherwoman. David Ignatow. LiLi

She took her name beneath according skies. The Ritual. Edwin John Pratt. MoP

She took the dappled partridge flecked [*or* fleckt] with blood. Sonnet. Tennyson. NAEL-2

She took the Hint; (what Lovers now can find). Courtship. Musaeus, *Greek.* OBCVT, *tr. by* Unknown

She tosses and rumples alone on the double bed. Flying Fox. Thomas William Shapcott. CBAP

She Touched Me. Erin Mouré. DeD

She touches me. Her fingers nibble gently. In Love. David Wevill. MoCV

She transplanted each spruce, blue as the. Spruce. Phillip William George. VoR

She trips across the meadows. April. Henrietta Cordelia Ray. CBWP-3

She turned in the high pew, until her sight. A Church Romance. Thomas Hardy. FaBoTw; NOBE; OxAEP-2; OxBTC; PeECV

She turned her to descend the stair, her heart. Penelope hesitates. Homer. OBCVT, *tr. by* Robert Fitzgerald *Fr.* The Odyssey.

She turns and calls him by name. His Wife. "Rachel," *Hebrew.* WPOW, *tr. by* Sholom J. Kahn

She turns the child. Anita Virgil. HA

She turns them over in her slow hands. A Mongoloid Child Handling Shells on the Beach. Richard Snyder. InPK-6

She used to let her golden hair fly free. Petrarch. NAWM-1, *tr. by* Morris Bishop *Fr.* Sonnets to Laura.

She wadna bake, she wadna brew. The Wife Wrapt in Wether's Skin. *Unknown.* ESPB

She Waited. Tania Van Zyl. PeSA

She waited on the 7th floor. Frank Albert and Viola Benzena Owens. Ntozake Shange. BISi

She walked nude beside them. Springtime. Norman Henry, II Pritchard. GT

She Walked Unaware. Patrick MacDonogh. BoLoP; FaBoTw

She walks down the road. Girl with the Green Skirt. Dana Naone. CDW

She walks in Beauty like the night. Byron. APAD; AWP; BLPA; BoLoP; CABP; CBLP; EBEvV; FHYEP; FaBoBe; GLoP; GTBS-P; HeIP-4; ImPo; InPS-3; LoP; NAEL-2; NOBE; NOBRP; NoP-4; OBEV; OBNC; OxAEP-2; PBMP; PFE; PoE; PoEL-4; PoPo; Ro; SCGP; TFi

She walks, slow and solemn. A Woman Pregnant. Blaga Dimitrova, *Bulgarian.* CEEP, *tr. by* Jascha Kessler *and* Aleksandar Shurbanov

She walks—the lady of my delight. The Shepherdess. Alice Thompson Meynell. AWP; CABP; MoBrPo; NOBVV; OBEV; RACG

She wanted a little room for thinking. Daystar. Rita Dove. LCAP-2; NAAAL; NIP-4; OxWW

She wanted pretty fine. Aunt Jessie. Wanda Coleman. GT

She wanted rain. Dust. Kathleen Spivack. BoWoP

She wants a man she can just. Roadmap. Harryette Mullen. ISC

She wants to hear. Sunday Greens. Rita Dove. GT; LCAP-2

She Warns Him. Frances Darwin Cornford. EnLoPo

She was a child's purse, full of useless things. (LL) Death of an Irishwoman. Michael Hartnett. CIP-2; IIP; PBCIP

She was a dear little dicky bird. She Was One of the Early Birds. T. W. Connor. OBCoV

She was a maid of high degree. He Took Her. Tom Masson. OBAL

She was a Phantom of delight. Wordsworth. APAD; CTV; FaBoBe; GTBS-P; HeIP-4; ImPo; NoP-4; OAEL-2; OBEV; PBMP; PWR; PoEL-4; SCGP; TFi

   ("With something of an angel-light.") (LL) APAD

She was a queen of noble Nature's crowning. Hartley Coleridge. OxAEP-2

She was a small dog, neat and fluid. Praise of a Collie. Norman MacCaig. RB

She was a woman obsessed by an old book;. Beyond Phigalia. Alec Derwent Hope. BMAP

She was a year younger. Picture Bride. Cathy Song. AiP

She was able to kill herself. The Way Down. Ernest Sandeen. CRP

She was all around me. The Blue Wing. Donald Hall. CoAmPo

She was alone that evening—and alone. The Lonely Lady. Charlotte Brontë. VWP

She was already lean when. Parting. A. R. Ammons. NoAM

She was an evil stepmother. She Does Not Remember. Anna Swirszczynska, Polish. BLT, tr. by Czeslaw Milosz and Leonard Nathan

She was at work on a poem about breath. Poem about Breath. David Wagoner. NoAM

She was blushing in the misty green of August. Good Night! Gilbert Sorrentino. FTOS

She was buying an elixir. Buying. Jean Follain, Spanish. BLT, tr. by Heather McHugh

She was caught, a young girl of Uttoxeter. Limerick. Tim Hopkins. PeLi

She was cleaning—there is always. Black Silk. Tess Gallagher. FaBoWP

She was going on the bus he could see. Woman Looking Through a Viewmaster. C. D. Wright. LCAP-2

She was in terrible pain the whole day. A Wedding. James Tate. NoAM

She was just a parson's daughter. It's the Syme the Whole World Over. Unknown. AS

She was just risen from her bended knee. A Girl at Her Devotions. Letitia Elizabeth Landon. VWP

She was left with two sons. Ruth's Story, As Told to Lilith. Michelene Wandor. NBrP

She Was Mine. Coventry Patmore. LBC

She was my staff and I am blind. Jana Bai, Marathi. BoWoP, tr. by Willis Barnstone

She Was One of the Early Birds. T. W. Connor. OBCoV

She Was Poor but She Was Honest. Poor But Honest. Unknown. NBLV; NOBL; OxBoV; RB

She was pure and white, resembling the sun as it rises. Separation by Death. Ibn Hazm al-Andalusi, Arabic. RaBo, tr. by A. R. Nykl, ad. by Robert Bly

She was skilled in music and the dance. Alas! Poor Queen. Marion Angus. FaBoTC

She was sleeping in the woodpile. The Lizard's Tango. Lucia Casalinuovo. IFJA

She was so aesthetic and culchud. The Cultured Girl Again. Ben King. OBAL

She was the daughter of a fishmonger, she stood. Theatrical Venus. George Buchanan. PNI

She was the one who lived up country. After Reading "The Country of the Pointed Firs." Jean Garrigue. VCAP

She was thinner, with a mannered gauntness. The Bistro Styx. Rita Dove. NoP-4

She was untouched by lust, which they might. Passion at the Chat 'n Chew Diner. Karen Zealand. CMAP

She was urgent to speak of the moon: she offered delight. An Old Woman Speaks of the Moon. Ruth Pitter. WPE

She was wearing the coral taffeta trousers. Full Moon. Vita Sackville-West. NTP

She was young! She was pure! She was new! She was nice! Have Some Madeira, M'dear? Michael Flanders. OBCoV

She washed and washed the pity from her hands. (LL) The Intruder. Carolyn Kizer. BoWoP; InPK-6

She watched all day that she might see him pass. How Lisa Loved the King. "George Eliot." LW Fr. How Lisa Loved the King.

She wears her middle age like a cowled. From a Correct Address in a Suburb of a Major City. Helen Sorrells. WPE

She wears the sailor suit—a blouse with anchors. Shore Leave. Lynda Hull. NAmP90

She went along the road. Hagar. Francis Lauderdale Adams. OxBS

She Went to Stay. Robert Creeley. OBAL

She went up the hill to pick angelica. Old Poem. Unknown, Chinese. AWP, tr. by Arthur Waley; CoBCP, tr. by Burton Watson

She went up the mountain to pluck wild herbs;. Old and New. Unknown, Chinese. AWP; ChiP, tr. by Arthur Waley

She wept, she railed, she spurned the meat. Stanley Kunitz. VGW

She who carries / in her heart a love. Akiko Yosano, Japanese. WPJ, tr. by Kenneth Rexroth and Ikuko Atsumi

She, who could neither rest nor sleep. Alas! Sadi. AWP, tr. by L. Cranmer-Byng Fr. The Gulistan.

She Who First Bore Our People. Unknown, Chinese. CoBCP, tr. by Burton Watson

She who had eyes but had not wherewithal. "If the Lord Would Make windows in Heaven." Edwin Arlington Robinson. MeMAP

She who has no love for women. Calliope in the Labour Ward. Elaine Feinstein. BrRo

She who hath felt a real pain. John Gay. EnLoPo

She who in the beginning gave birth to the people. Origin-Legend of the Chou Tribe. Unknown, Chinese. ChiP, tr. by Arthur Waley

She who is always in my thoughts prefers. Bhartrihari, Sanskrit. BoLoP; LoP, tr. by John Brough

She who shook and swayed among the chorus. Macedonius, Greek. GrAn, tr. by Adrian Wright

She who to Heaven more Heaven doth annex. On a Virtuous Young Gentlewoman That Died Suddenly. William Cartwright. HAP; OBEV

She who usually feeds us. Teeth. Susan Griffin. CrSp

She who was burned more than half her body skipped out of death. The Praises. Charles Olson. VGW

She will be bound with garlands of her own. (LL) On the Sonnet. Keats. NIP-4; NoP-4; OAEL-2

She will know. (LL) The Scuba Diver Recovers the Body of a Drowned Child. Gerald William Barrax. GT; NBV

She will lie naked. Rachel Blau DuPlessis. DeD Fr. Eurydice.

She will run to you for love whoever. Children. Sandra McPherson. FaBoWP

She will sell you six for three. (LL) Lydia Pinkham. Unknown. AS; OBCoV

She with her friends, the full-breasted daughters of the ocean. To Demeter. Unknown, Greek. GrIP, tr. by Thelma Sargent Fr. Homeric Hymns.

She Wolf, The. Muriel Spark. NYBP

She wonders how people get babies. The Facts of Life. Ronald Wallace. PBCAP

She wonders / why I'm still here. A Man in the House. Mark McWatt. HCP

She wore a new 'terra-cotta' dress. A Thunderstorm in Town. Thomas Hardy. APAD; BoLoP; CBLP; EnLoPo; GBL; GLoP; OxBSP

She worked in the newsagent, redhaired. Graffiti. Julian Croft. NOBAu

She works and works against sadness. The Gardener. Robin Becker. CrSp

She works with the Moors. Showing some skin she lures a. Sadie. Philip Hammial. BMAP

She Would Have Roses. Nicholas Lloyd Ingraham. PWR

She would not see. (LL) A Leave-taking. Swinburne. CBLP; CH; NOBE; NOBVV; OBNC; PoEL-5; PoLF

She wreaks such havoc in my library. Minding Ruth. Aidan Carl Mathews. BiHa; CIP-2; PBCIP

Sheaf Mark. Ray DiPalma. FTOS

Sheafe of snakes used heretofore to be, A. To Mr. George Herbert. Donne. OBVE

Shealtiel, governor of Judah. Haggai. John Chagy. ChIV-1

Sheapherd who noe care did take, A. Mary Sidney, Countess of Montgomery Wroth. Fr. Urania.

Shearer man like toast and butter. Indian Bagman's Toast. Unknown. FaBoVe

Shearer's Wife, The. Louis Esson. NOBAu

Shearing, The. Unknown, Welsh. OBWVE, tr. by Glyn Jones

Shearing, as the gardener. That's All? Anna Hajnal, Hungarian. CEEP; PBWP, tr. by Jascha Kessler

Sheath and Knife. Unknown. CH; ESPB

Sheaves, The. Edwin Arlington Robinson. AWP; CMoP; HAP; ImGa; MoAmPo; MoP; NOBA; NoAM; OxBA; Poetr; SoSe-8; TAP

Sheaves of drooping dandelions to the courts of Kentish town. (LL) Parliament Hill Fields. John Betjeman. FaBoTw; NOBE

Shed, The. Frank Flynn. OTCP

Shed a tear for the WREN named McGinnis. Limerick. Unknown. PeLi

Shed all the blood, felt all the smart. (LL) Celia Bleeding, to the Surgeon. Thomas Carew. CavPo; SeCP

She'd always been there. Interface. Gloria Anzaldúa. GLP

Shed in Space. Gareth Owen. SpW

Shed no tear! O, shed no tear! Faery Song. Keats. CH

She'd Say. Frank Davey. NOBC

She'd start the fires under the bed. The Split. Marie Howe. NAmP90

Shed the Fear. Anselm Hollo. PmAP

Shed, the wall, and the anonymous cross. (LL) Here is another poem in a picture. Daryl Hine. GS

She'd want, if we were given what we want. (LL) What Do Women Want? Mary Jo Salter. FFC; RA

Sheding the saut, saut tear. (LL) Proud Margret. Unknown. ESPB; OxBB

Sheds doubled darkness up the labouring hill. (LL) Without Her. D. G. Rossetti. GBL; GLoP; OBNC; PoEL-5; Son

Shee brought her to her joyous paradize. The Garden of Adonis. Edmund Spenser. NOBE; PoEL-1 *Fr.* Wood Of Error. AEP

Sheen of the willows spreads ten thousand feet, The. "Song of Farewell" in the Tartar Mode. Chang Yü, *Chinese.* SuSp, *tr. by* Irving Y. Lo

Sheep. W. H. Davies. LiTM; MoBrPo; NTP; RB

Sheep. Robert Francis. LCAP-2

Sheep. Samuel Hoffenstein. TrJP

Sheep, The. Ann Taylor. BoTP; CTAV; OxBChV

Sheep and Lambs. Katharine Tynan. BoTP; OBEV; TIRV

Sheep and the Goat, The. George Macdonald. EBVV

Sheep-bell tolleth curfew time, The. An Evening Scene. Coventry Patmore. ACTP

Sheep Child, The. James Dickey. HCAP; MT; MoP; NOBA; NoAM; TAP; VCAP

Sheep Dipping. Norman MacCaig. OxBC

Sheep-folds, holy spring of the Nymphs. Leonidas of Tarentum, *Greek.* GrAn, *tr. by* Peter Levi

Sheep in Fog. Sylvia Plath. FaBoWP; HCAP; LCAP-2

Sheep is blind; a passing Owl, The. The Blind Sheep. Randall Jarrell. NYBP; OBAL

Sheep was. And a purse dangled from his arm. A sporran jogged between his lies, A. Tune. Robert Kelly. FTOS

Sheepdog Trials in Hyde Park. C. Day Lewis. MoP; NoAM; OxBTC

Sheer cliff, far mountains. Inscribed on My Large Landscape Hanging Scroll "Listening to a Waterfall." Tao-chi, *Chinese.* CoBLCP, *tr. by* Jonathan Chaves

Sheer rock, four walls stand. Dragon Mouth Cliff. Chao Meng-fu. *Fr.* Twenty-Eight Poems Inscribed on T'ien-kuan Mountain. CoBLCP, *tr. by* Jonathan Chaves

Sheet lightning. Chuck Brickley. HA

Sheet of paper, placed, A. Lakshmi. Padraic Fallon. NOIV

Sheet of writing paper, The. The Alchemist. Richard Church. OxBTC

Sheeted in steel, embedded face to face. At a Low Mass for Two Hot-Rodders. X. J. Kennedy. Poetsp

Sheets, The. Timothy Steele. DiPo

Sheets of night mist travel a long valley, The. Mist Forms. Carl Sandburg. CMoP

Sheets were frozen hard, and they cut the naked hand, The. Christmas at Sea. Robert Louis Stevenson. CH; EBVV; FaBoBe; PeVV

Sheffield 'Prentice, The, *diff. version. Unknown.* AmFP

Sheffield 'Prentice, The. *Unknown.* AmFP

Shekhinah. Karl Wolfskehl, *German.* TrJP, *tr. by* Carol North Valhope *and* Ernst Morwitz

Shell. Federico García Lorca, *Spanish.* CBNP

Shell, The. H. M. Sarson. NSI; PoWW

Shell, The. James Stephens. BoTP; CH; CMoP; MoBrPo

She'll Be Comin' Round the Mountain. *Unknown.* AS

She'll be comin' 'round the mountain when the shell sometimes is empty. James Sherry. FTOS

Shell-less, on your slimey trail. After Tempest. Percy MacKaye. FYAP

Shell of objects inwardly consumed, The. My Last Dance. Julia Ward Howe. APN-1

Shell Secrets. *Unknown.* BoTP

Shellbrook. William Barnes. OBNC

Shelley. Charles Simic. TRP

Shelley. James Thomson.
    "Voice of right amidst a world gone wrong, A." EPCY

Shelley. Thomas Wade. EPCY

Shelley and jazz and lieder and love and hymn-tunes. Louis MacNeice. NOBL *Fr.* Autumn Journal.

Shelley's "Arethusa" Set to New Measures. Robert Duncan. CMoP

Shelley's death—was it really his wish. Limerick. Bill Greenwell. PeLi

Shelley's Skylark. Thomas Hardy. CABP

Shelley's Vision. Herman Melville. APN-2

Shellfish. Rin Ishigaki, *Japanese.* WPJ, *tr. by* Kenneth Rexroth *and* Ikuko Atsumi

Shelly Beach. Christopher Koch. NOBAu

Shelter. Louise Erdrich. FiLi

Shelter. Bruce Weigl. PUP-18

Sheltered from the spring wind by. The Old Anguish. Chu Shu-chen, *Chinese.* BoWoP; OHPC, *tr. by* Kenneth Rexroth

Sheltered Garden. Hilda Doolittle. NMM-2

Sheltered garden sleeps among the tall, The. Battledore. John Gray. NOBVV

Sheltering Ground, The. Sherod Santos. Son

Sheltering Places. Gerald Dawe. PNI

Shemà. Primo Levi, *Italian.* AF; HP; NNPT, *tr. by* Ruth Feldman *and* Brian Swann

Shema Yisrael. *Unknown.* TrJP

Shen is very sick these days, he's fading away. On the Road Through the Wu-i Mountains—Making Fun of Chia-tse for Falling Off His Horse. Hsü Wei, *Chinese.* CoBLCP, *tr. by* Jonathan Chaves

Shenandoah. Delmore Schwartz.
    Let Us Consider Where the Great Men Are. MoAmPo

Shenandoah. *Unknown.* APN-2
    ("Ah-ha, I'm bound away 'cross the wide Missouri.") (LL) FaBoA
    ("Oh, Missouri, she's a mighty river.") FaBoA

Shep lies long-bodied upon the auburn grass. February's Forgotten Mitts. Raymond Knister. NOBC

Shep'erd Bwoy, The. William Barnes. EBVV

Shephard loveth thow me vell? Song. Jean Passerat, *French.* OBVE, *tr. by* William Drummond of Hawthornden

Shepheard *Paris* bore the *Spartan* Bride, The. Theocritus. *See* Idyll.

Shepheardes [*or* Shepeards *or* Shepherd's] Calender, The. Edmund Spenser.

Shepheardes Calender, The. Edmund Spenser.
    April. NAEL-1; PoEL-1
    ("Tell me, good Hobbinoll, what garres thee greete?") OBEV; PoEL-1
    Ditty, A: In Praise of Eliza, Queen of the Shepherds. OBEV
    (Ditty, A: "See where she sits upon the grassy green.") FaBoCh
    Lay to Eliza, The. NOBE
    "Is not thilke the mery moneth of May." PBRV
    November. PoEL-1
    October. NAEL-1; OAEL-1

Shepheard's Daffodil, The. Michael Drayton. *See* The Daffodil Song.

Shepherd, The. William Blake. BoTP; ChAP; FHYEP; Ro *Fr.* Songs of Innocence.

Shepherd. Avraham Shlonsky, *Hebrew.* MHP, *tr. by* Ruth Finer Mintz

Shepherd. William Stafford. PoA

Shepherd and Shepherdess. Nicholas Breton. *See* The Merry Country Lad.

Shepherd and Shepherdess. Thomas Hennell. FaBoTw

Shepherd and the Nymph, The. Walter Savage Landor. OBNC *Fr.* Gebir.

Shepherd Boy, The. John Clare. CABP; NOBVV

Shepherd Boy, The. Heinrich Heine, *German.* BoTP

Shepherd-Boy and the Wolf, The. Aesop, *Greek.* AWP, *tr. by* William Ellery Leonard

Shepherd Boy Sings [in the Valley of Humiliation], The. John Bunyan. NOBE; OBEV *Fr.* The Pilgrim's Progress.
    (Shepherd Boy's Song, The.) BoTP; NTP

Shepherd cheerfully, The. Hildebert, *Latin.* MLL, *tr. by* Helen Waddell

Shepherd Left Behind, The. Mildred Plew Meigs. TrCP

Shepherd, Ned Vaughan, A. Ned Vaughan. Walter De la Mare. FaBoEE

Shepherd Paris bore the Spartan bride, The. Idyll. Theocritus, *Greek.* OBVE, *tr. by* Dryden *Fr.* Idylls.

Shepherd plays his flute, The. Hollow Echo. Fazil Hüsnü Daglarca. CRP

Shepherd, Shepherd, Hark. Saint, of Avila Theresa, *Spanish.* AWP, *tr. by* Arthur Symons

Shepherd, Show Me How to Go. Mary Baker Eddy. AH

Shepherd-Song ("All men may hasty-gone happiness find"). Sigmund von Birken, *German.* GePo, *tr. by* George C. Schoolfield

Shepherd-Song ("I sit here at your edge, in your embankment's screen"). Sigmund von Birken, *German.* GePo, *tr. by* George C. Schoolfield

Shepherd Song. Sir Philip Sidney. SiPS *Fr.* Arcadia.

Shepherd Speaks, The. John Erskine. TrCP

Shepherd stands at one end of the arena, A. Sheepdog Trials in Hyde Park. C. Day Lewis. MoP; NoAM; OxBTC

Shepherd who lived up in Gwent, A. Limerick. E. O. Parrott. PeLi

Shepherd Who Stayed, The. Theodosia Pickering Garrison. PChr

Shepherd, why creep we in this lowly vein. Michael Drayton. NoSic *Fr.* The Shepherd's Garland.

Shepherdess. Norman Cameron. GBL; OxBS *Fr.* Three Love Poems. FaBoTw; GTBS-P

Shepherdess, The. Alice Thompson Meynell. *See* The Shepherdress.

Shepherdess--/ A fair one are you. Shakespeare. PoE *Fr.* The Winter's Tale.

Shepherdess of sheep, A. (LL) The Shepherdress. Alice Thompson Meynell. AWP; CABP; MoBrPo; NOBVV; OBEV; RACG

Shepherdess, show me now where I may sleep. (LL) Shepherdess. Norman Cameron. GBL; OxBS

Shepherdress, The. Alice Thompson Meynell. AWP; MoBrPo; NOBVV; OBEV
    (Shepherdess, The.) CABP; RACG

Shepherds [*or* Shepheards], The. Henry Vaughan. ChIV-2; ESCV

Shepherds all, and maidens fair. Folding the Flocks. John Fletcher. CH *Fr.* The Faithful Shepherdess.

Shepherds almost wonder where they dwell, The. November. John Clare. AYFP

Shepherds and angels sing in unison. Harmony. *Unknown, Greek.* GrAn, *tr. by* William J. Philbin

Shepherds armed with staff and sling. Carol of Patience. Robert Graves. OBCP

Shepherd's brow, fronting forked lightning, owns, The. Sonnet. Gerard Manley Hopkins. KSG

Shepherd's [*or* Shepheards] Calendar, The. John Clare.

February. NOBE; OBNC

January. Ro

Shepherd's Calendar, 'June,' The. Edmund Spenser. AEP

Shepherds' Carol. Norman Nicholson. OBCP

Shepherd's daughter watching sheep, A. The Knight and the Shepherd's Daughter. *Unknown.* AmFP

Shepherd's Dochter, The. Douglas Young. FaBoTC

Shepherd's Dog, The. Leslie Norris. OBCP

Shepherd's Flute. Branko Miljkovic, *Serbo-Croatian.* HSix, *tr. by* Charles Simic

Shepherd's Garland, The. Michael Drayton.

Daffodil Song, The. AEP

Roundelay: "*Motto* Tell me, thou skilful shepherd's swain." "Shepherd, why creep we in this lowly vein." NoSic

Shepherd's Gift, A. Anyte, *Greek.* AWP, *tr. by* John William Burgon

Shepherd's Gratitude, The. Virgil. AWP, *tr. by* Charles Stuart Calverley *Fr.* Eclogues.

Shephe[a]rd's Hunting, The. George Wither.

Sonnet: "I that erstwhile the world's sweet air did draw." NOSC

Shepherd's Hut, The. Andrew Young. FaBoTC; OxBTC

Shepherds' Hymn, The. Richard Crashaw. NOBE *Fr.* In the Holy Nativity of Our Lord God. GeHe; PoEL-2

Shepherd's Lament, The. Goethe, *German.* AWP, *tr. by* Bayard Taylor

Shepherd's Night Count. Jane Yolen. TLR

Shepherds on old hills, with robber. Gallery Shepherds. Patricia Beer. OxBC

Shepherd's Pipe: The thing is magic, unimaginable. *Unknown.* EEP, *tr. by* Michael Alexander *Fr.* Riddles (Exeter Book).

Shepherd's Praise of Diana, The. Sir Walter Ralegh. SiPS

("Praisd be Dianas faire and harmles light.") PBRV

("With Circes let them dwell that thinke not so.") (LL) PBRV

Shepherd's Sirena, The. Michael Drayton.

Trent, The. OBEV

(Jovial Shepheard's Song, The.) PoEL-2

Shepherd's Song at Christmas. Langston Hughes. PChr

Shepherd's Sorrow, Being Disdained in Love, The. Thomas Lodge. NoSic

Shepherd's star with trembling glint, The. En Bateau. Paul Verlaine, *French.* AWP, *tr. by* Arthur Symons

Shepherd's Tale, The. James Kirkup, *after the French of* Raoul Ponchon. OBCP

Shepherd's Tale, A. Sir Philip Sidney. SiPS *Fr.* Arcadia.

Shepherds that on this mountain ridge abide. Cleitagoras. Leonidas of Tarentum, *Greek.* AWP, *tr. by* William M. Hardinge

Shepherd's warning. (LL) Red sky at night. *Unknown.* ACTP; OxNR

Shepherd's Week, The. John Gay.

Thursday; or, The Spell. PoEL-3

Tuesday; or, the Ditty. NOEC

Wednesday; or, The Dumps. OAEL-1

Shepherd's Wife's Song, The. Robert Greene. HAP; NoSic; RACG *Fr.* Greene's Mourning Garment.

Sherbet. Cornelius Eady. CMAP; GT; LTA

Sheridan at Cedar Creek. Herman Melville. CBCWP

Sheridan's Ride. Thomas Buchanan Read. APN-2; CBCWP; FaBoBe

Sherman Cyclone, The. *Unknown.* AmFP

Sherwood in the twilight, is Robin Hood awake? Alfred Noyes. MoBrPo

She's a big teaser. She took him half the way there. Big Tease. Ania Walwicz. BMAP

She's a copperheaded waitress. Ella, in a Square Apron, Along Highway 80. Judy Grahn. NALW; NMM-2 *Fr.* The Common Woman.

She's a young thing, and cannot leave her mother . (LL) Billy Boy. *Unknown.* AmFP; BLPA; HoPM; OxNR

She's black: what then? so are dead coales, but cherish. Asclepiades, *Greek.* OBCVT, *tr. by* Phineas Fletcher

She's combed his neckties out of her hair. A Widow. Ted Kooser. PBCAP

She's dreaming. Nightmare. Rita Dove. GT

She's empty: hark, she sounds: there's nothing there. Nahum 2.10. Francis Quarles. ChIV-1

She's Free! Frances Ellen Watkins Harper. BlSi; Son

She's gone! Call Rape! Call Robbers! Violence!. Meleager, *Greek.* GrAn, *tr. by* Peter Whigham

She's gone. She was my love, my moon or more. Complaint. James Wright. NOBA; SAGP; TAP; VGW

She's looking out of the picture. The bars across her face hold her in the picture and . A Motive for Mayhem. Abigail Child. FTOS

She's loveliest of the festal throng. The Rose and the Thorn. Paul Hamilton Hayne. FaBoBe

She's my lover. One or More Together. John Godfrey. FTOS

She's not a faultless woman; no! James Kenneth Stephen. EBVV; NOBVV; OxBM *Fr.* After the Golden Wedding.

She's not and never can be mine. (LL) The Married Lover. Coventry Patmore. OBEV; OxAEP-2

She's now yo' own. Salute yo' bride! (LL) Slave Marriage Ceremony Supplement. *Unknown.* BPo; CrDW; TAP

She's resting in the bosom of Jesus. (LL) Go Down Death. James Weldon Johnson. BkSV; ISC

She's somewhere in the sunlight strong. Song. Richard Le Gallienne. OBEV

She's the camera. Judy-One. Don L. Lee. TAP

She's the plaything of the Navy, she's the nightmare of the Hun. The Q-Boat. H. E. Wilkes. NSI

She's to me a Paragon. (LL) No Loathsomnesse in Love. Robert Herrick. BeJo; GBL

Shet up dat noise, you chillen! Dar's some one at de do'. 'Sciplinin' Sister Brown. James Edwin Campbell. AAP

Shew, weakenes speaks in prose, but powre in verse. (LL) Poet and Critic. Samuel Daniel. PBRV

Shi King. *Unknown, Chinese.*

Chou and the South. CTC, *tr. by* Ezra Pound

How Goes the Night? AWP, *tr. by* Helen Waddell

I Wait My Lord. AWP, *tr. by* Helen Waddell

Maytime. AWP, *tr. by* L. Cranmer-Byng

Morning Glory, The. AWP, *tr. by* Helen Waddell

Pear-Tree, The. AWP, *tr. by* Allen Upward

Under the Pondweed. AWP, *tr. by* Helen Waddell

Woman. AWP, *tr. by* H. A. Giles

You Will Die. AWP, *tr. by* H. A. Giles

Shickered As He Could Be. *Unknown.* NOBAu

Shield, The. Archilochus, *Greek.* GrIP, *tr. by* H.D.E. Kitto

Shield: I'm by nature solitary, scarred by spear. Cynewulf. ASW, *tr. by* Kevin Crossley-Holland *Fr.* Riddles (Exeter Book).

Shield: "Lonely wanderer, wounded with iron, A." Cynewulf. AnOE, *tr. by* Charles W. Kennedy *Fr.* Riddles (Exeter Book).

Shield of Achilles, The. W. H. Auden. EBEV; FaBoMo; FaBoPV; GTBS-P; HAP; NAEL-2; NOBE; NOCV; NoAM; NoP-4; OxAEP-2; PeECV; PoA; PoE; WeW-3

Shield of Achilles, The. Homer. NOSC, *tr. by* George Chapman *Fr.* The Iliad.

Shield of Achilles, The. Tomas Venclova, *Lithuanian.* CEEP, *tr. by* David McDuff

Shield of War, The. Thomas, 1st Earl of Dorset Sackville. *Fr.* Induction to "A Mirror for Magistrates." AAS

Shift[,] here, in town, not meanest among squires. On Lieutenant Shift. Ben Jonson. OBSV

Shifting Colors. Robert Lowell. HCAP

Shifting riddle glitters, The. The Highest Sickness. Boris Pasternak, *Russian.* TCRP, *tr. by* Mark Rudman *and* Bohdan Boychuk

Shiftless young fellow of Kent, A. Limerick. *Unknown.* PeLi

Shih Ching. *Unknown, Chinese.*

"Very handsome gentleman, A." BoWoP

Widow's Lament. BoWoP

("Cloth-plant grew till it covered the thorn bush, The.") ChiP, *tr. by* Arthur Waley

Shih Ch'ung's 'Golden Valley' Garden. Tu Mu, *Chinese.* PLT, *tr. by* A. C. Graham

Shih-hou Pointed Out to Me That from Ancient Times There Had Never Been a Poem on the Subject of Lice. Mei Yao Ch'en, *Chinese.* CoBCP, *tr. by* Burton Watson

Shih-hou Pointed Out to Me that from Ancient Times There Had Never Been a Poem on the Subject of Lice. Harry Mathews, *Chinese.* CoBCP, *tr. by* Burton Watson

Shillin' a Day. Rudyard Kipling. NoAM

Shilling life will give you all the facts, A. Who's Who. W. H. Auden. MeMAP; MoBrPo; MoP; NoAM; Son

Shillong. Bernard Gutteridge. PoWW

Shilly-Shally. Hồ Dzếnh, *Vietnamese.* AVP, *tr. by* Huỳnh Sanh Thông

Shiloh [A Requiem]. Herman Melville. APN-2; CBCWP; NOBA; OBWP; OxBA; SCV

(Shiloh.) APAD; ColAP; NoP-4

Shimmer. James Schuyler. VCAP

Shimmering beneath the glaze. Elizabeth Searle Lamb. HA

Shimmering water at its full—sunny day is best. Drinking at the Lake, First It's Sunny, Then It Rains. Su Shih, *Chinese.* SuSp, *tr.* by Irving Y. Lo

Shine. Léon Damas, *French.* NegPo, *tr.* by Ellen Conroy Kennedy

Shine alone, shine nakedly, shine like bronze. Nuances of a Theme by Williams. Wallace Stevens. CMoP

Shine and the Titanic. *Unknown.* CrDW

  (Sinking of the *Titanic.*) NAAAL

Shine, "O world!" don't weary the gulping Pole. Frank O'Hara. UnPo *Fr.* Life on Earth.

Shine out, resplendent God of day. A Laplander's Song to His Mistress. Elizabeth Singer Rowe. ECWP

Shine, Perishing Republic. Robinson Jeffers. CMoP; ColAP; LiTM; MoP; NAAL-2; NOBA; NoAM; NoP-4; OxBA; PoPoPo; TAP; TFi; UnPo; VGW

  ("God, when he walked on earth.") (LL) NoP-4

  ("Mortal splendor: meteors are not needed less than mountains: shine, / perishing republic, A.") (LL) ColAP

Shine, Republic. Robinson Jeffers. FaBoPV

Shine was in Sugar Ray's Bar drinking Seagrams Seven. (LL) Shine and the Titanic. *Unknown.* CrDW; NAAAL

Shine was up in Harlem damn near drunk. (LL) Dark Prophecy: I Sing of Shine. Etheridge Knight. BPo; LTA; PBCAP

Shines / in the mind of heaven God. Canto 51. Ezra Pound. PFTM

Shining, A. Theodore Roethke. *See* Meditation at Oyster River.

Shining and whole. (LL) Gold. Donald Hall. CoAmPo; SAGP

Shining Eye of Horus cometh, The. He Kindleth a Fire. *Unknown.* AWP *Fr.* Book of the Dead.

Shining fauna of that fire, The. (LL) Burning the Christmas Greens. William Carlos Williams. LiTM; MeMAP; MoP; NAAL-2; NOBA; NoAM

Shining in his stickiness and glistening with honey. The Friendly Cinnamon Bun. Russell Hoban. OTCP

Shining like a star. Hunting Song. *Unknown, Chippewa Indian.* STP, *tr.* by Jerome Rothenberg

Shining neutral summer has no voice, The. In Memoriam: Ernst Toller. W. H. Auden. NYBP

Shining Things. Elizabeth Gould. BoTP

Shiny Little House, The. Nancy M. Hayes. BoTP

Shiny record albums scattered over. As You Leave Me. Etheridge Knight. CoAmPo; ISC; MT; NNaP

Ship, The. Charles MacKay. BLPA

Ship, The. Sir John Collings Squire. CH

Ship, A. Gregor Strnisa, *Slovenian.* CEEP, *tr.* by Vasa D. Mihailovich

Ship, The. *Unknown.* PoLF

Ship, A chain. I Sing This Song for Our Mothers: Ruise. Sherley Anne Williams. MDDM

Ship An-Nam, The. Tản Đà, *Vietnamese.* AVP, *tr.* by Huỳnh Sanh Thông

Ship at rock, wakes, terns, A. Going to Sea. Douglas Messerli. FTOS

Ship Burning and a Comet All in One Day, A. Richard Eberhart. NYBP

Ship I have got in the North Country, A. The *Golden Vanity.* *Unknown.* FaBoCh; OxBoV

Ship Is Lost, The. William Falconer. OxAEP-1 *Fr.* The Shipwreck.

Ship, leaving or arriving, of my lover. After a Passage in Baudelaire. Robert Duncan. CMoP; PoA; PoE

Ship moves, The. 4th of July. William Carlos Williams. PoA

Ship of Death, A. Seamus Heaney. NoP-4

Ship of Death, The. D. H. Lawrence. CMoP; FaBoTw; GTBS-P; MoBrPo; MoP; NAEL-2; NoAM; NoP-4; OAEL-2; OxAEP-2

  "Build then the ship of death, for you must take." APAD

Ship of State, The. Henry Wadsworth Longfellow. FaBoBe *Fr.* The Building of the Ship.

Ship Sails Up to Bideford, A. Herbert Asquith. BoTP

Ship Sets out, the. William Falconer. OxAEP-1 *Fr.* The Shipwreck.

Ship sets sail, the ship is journeying, The. The Stoker. Shin Shalom, *Hebrew.* MHP, *tr.* by Ruth Finer Mintz

Ship That Never Returned, The. Henry Clay Work. BLPA

  ("On a summer's day while the waves were rippling, with a quiet and gentle breeze.") AS

Ship That Sails, The. *Unknown.* PoToHe

Ship That Went Down, The. Adah Isaacs Menken. CBWP-1

Ship was large, The. Ode to a Lost Cargo in a Ship Called *Save.* José Craveirinha, *Portuguese.* PeSAV, *tr.* by Chris Searle

Ship weighed twenty thousand ton, The. Passenger Shanty. W. H. Auden. OBCoV

Ship with shields before the sun, A. Near Avalon. William Morris. OAEL-2

Ship you've boarded, The. Ark. Gu Cheng, *Chinese.* VCWP, *tr.* by Donald Finkel

Shiperd-boy, what is yer trade? The Beggar-Laddie. *Unknown.* ESPB

Shipman, The ("Shipman was ther, woning fer by weste, A"). Chaucer. *Fr.* The General Prologue. FHYEP; NAEL-1; NAWM-1; OAEL-1; PoE *Fr.* The Canterbury Tales.

Shipment to Maidanek. Ephraim Fogel. HP; OBWP; TrJP

Ships, The. J. J. Bell. BoTP

Ship's Cook, a Captive Sings, The. Hugo von Hofmannsthal, *German.* TrJP, *tr.* by Charles Wharton Stork

Ship's master:/ before him, in the waist and before it. David Jones. FaBoTw *Fr.* The Anathemata.

Ship's Nail, A. *Unknown.* ReMoGo

Ships of state, The. Australorp. Edith Speers. NOBAu

Ships That Pass in the Night. Paul Laurence Dunbar. ColAP

Ships that sail forth. Yury Konstantinovich Terapiano, *Russian.* TCRP, *tr.* by Bradley Jordan

Shipwreck, The. William Falconer.

  "'All hands unmoor!' proclaims a boisterous cry." OxBoS

  "Amid this fearful trance, a thundering sound." ECEV

  Ship Is Lost, The. OxAEP-1

  Ship Sets out, the. OxAEP-1

Shipwreck. Mary Weston Fordham. CBWP-2, *tr.* by Mary Ann Caws

Shipwreck in Haven, A. Keith Waldrop.

  "Balancing. Austere. Life." PmAP

Shirt. Robert Pinsky. ColAP; NAmP90

Shirt. Carl Sandburg. CA

Shirt. Charles Simic. AFr; HCAP

Shirt of a Lad, The. *Unknown, Welsh.* OBWVE, *tr.* by Anthony Conran

Shirt races in the meadow, A. Storm. Agnes Nemes Nagy, *Hungarian.* CEEP; PBWP, *tr.* by Laura Schiff

Shitting in the winter turnip field. Masaoka Shiki, *Japanese.* OHMPJ, *tr.* by Kenneth Rexroth

Shitty. Kingsley Amis. OxBC

Shiva. Robinson Jeffers. NOBA; NoAM; Son

Shivering and hoping no one. Grandma's Bureau. Robert Morgan. EOEF; WeW-3

Shlup, shlup, the dog. Denise Levertov. HeIP-4; InPK-6; Poetr *Fr.* Six Variations. AmPP; CoAmPo; LCAP-2

Shock. Rudyard Kipling. *Fr.* Epitaphs of the War [1914–1918]. OBWP

Shocked that she missed the footbridge! The Suicide. V. R. Lang. PoA

Shocks Reason, and the rules of common Sence. (LL) Should some ill Painter in a wild design. Horace, *Latin.* OBCVT, *tr.* by John Oldham

Shoe. John Perreault. SPE

Shoe, A. Tongjip Shin, *Korean.* CKP, *tr.* by Jaihiun Kim

Shoe a little horse. *Unknown.* OxNR

Shoe Shop. Barton Sutter. EC3; SoSe-8

Shoe the colt, shoe the colt. Shoeing. Mother Goose. OxNR; ReMoGo

Shoe the little horse. *Unknown.* LB

Shoe the steed with silver. Sheridan at Cedar Creek. Herman Melville. CBCWP

Sho[o]e Tying, The. Robert Herrick. CaPo

Shoe with legs, A. Lobster. Anne Sexton. ChAP

Shoeing. Mother Goose. ReMoGo

Shoelace. Roger Fanning. BAP-93

Shoemaker makes shoes without leather, A. Riddle. *Unknown.* OxNR

Shoemaker's Holiday, The. Thomas Dekker *and others.*

Shoemaker's Wife, The. Lotte Kramer. HP

Shoemakker, The. *Unknown.* FaBoVe

Shoes and he wonder'd. Keats. *See* The Naughty Boy.

Shoes, secret face of my inner life. My Shoes. Charles Simic. CoAP; HCAP; VCAP

Sholom Aleichem. Elias Lieberman. TrJP

Sholto Peach Harrison you are no son of mine. Correspondence between Mr. Harrison in Newcastle and Mr. Sholto Peach Harrison in Hull. Stevie Smith. NBLV; OxBC

Shon a Morgan. *Unknown.* OxNR

Shona married a Ndebele, A. A Maze of Blood. N. C. G. Mathema. PeSAV

Shone through her body visibly. (LL) Phantom. Samuel Taylor Coleridge, *Unknown, sometimes at. to.* NAEL-2; OAEL-2; OxBSP; PoEL-1

Shoo the orioles, drive them away. Spring Grievance. Chin Ch'ang-hsü, *Chinese.* CoBCP, *tr.* by Burton Watson

Shoofly, The. Felix O'Hare. AmFP

Shoot from above. The Dart. "Eliza." KTR

Shooter's Hill. Robert Bloomfield.

  "Health! I seek thee; dost thou love." OBNC

Shooting a Farmhouse. Ted Kooser. PBCAP

Shooting Back. Thomas Sayers Ellis. GT

Shooting for Line, for Bob Hershon. Charles North. BAP-95

Shooting of Dan McGrew, The. Robert W. Service. EBEvV; EBNV; FaBoBe; PoLF; PoRA; RB; UV

("Was the lady that's known as Lou.") (LL) SAGP

Shooting of His Dear. *Unknown*. OxBoLi

Shooting of John Dillinger outside the Biograph Theater July 22, 1934, The. David Wagoner. CoAP; FYAP; RB

Shooting Script. Adrienne Rich.

"Mare's skeleton in the clearing: another sign of life, The." FaBoWP

Newsreel. FaBoWP; HCAP

"Of simple choice they are the villagers; their clothes come." HCAP

"Old blanket. The crumbs of rubbed wool turning up, The." HCAP

"They come to you with their descriptions of your soul." HCAP

"We are driven to odd attempts; once it would not have occurred to." HCAP

"Whatever it was: the grains of the glacier caked in the boot-cleats." FaBoWP; HCAP

Shooting Song, A. William Brighty Rands. OxBChV

Shooting Star, A. Edith Matilda Thomas. ChAP

Shooting the Dogs. Philip Hodgins. BMAP

Shooting the Horses. Pamela Mordecai. PBCV

Shooting the rapids! Robert Spiess. HA

Shooting Whales. Mark Strand. ColAP

Shop o' Meat-Weare. William Barnes. NOBVV

Shop Talk. Roy Fuller. OxBC

Shopkeepers at the Party Meeting. Thomas McCarthy. BiHa

Shoplifters. Maura Stanton. CMAP

Shopping-Bag Lady, The. Linda Gregg. WWSi

("Fading in the most important place we have yet devised.") (LL) AFr

Shopping for Meat in Winter. Oscar Williams. LiTM

Shops, the streets are full of old men, The. Talk. Roo Borson. NIP-4; NOBC

Shore. Jean Garrigue. TAP

Shore Leave. Lynda Hull. NAmP90

Shore of Life, The. Robert Fitzgerald. VGW

Shore repels it; it returns again, The. (LL) My hopes retire; my wishes as before. Walter Savage Landor. GBL; OBNC

Shore Road, The. Norman MacCaig. FaBoTC

Shore seemed suddenly more distant. Or had the other slid close?, The. A Summer on the Lake. Otto Orban, *Hungarian*. CEEP, *tr. by* Jascha Kessler

Shore Tullye. Robert Rendall. OxBS

Shore wind is cold on my travel clothes, The. Abutsu the Nun [*or* Abutsu-Ni]. PBWP, *tr. by* Edwin O. Reischauer *Fr.* The Diary of the Waning Moon.

Shoreham: Twilight Time. Samuel Palmer. OAEL-2

(Twilight Time.) NTP

Shoreless breeze from heaven over an endless road. In a Dream I Traveled among Ten Thousand Acres of Lotuses. Lu Yu, *Chinese*. SuSp, *tr. by* Irving Y. Lo

Shoreline. Mary Barnard. PoA

Shores are crown'd with people, The. Luis de Camões. *Fr.* The Lusiads. OBVE, *tr. by* Sir Richard Fanshawe

Shores of anguish. Magda Portal, *Spanish*. PBWP, *tr. by* Allan Francovich *and* Kathleen Weaver

Shores of my native land. Farewell. Isaac Toussaint L'Ouverture, *French*. TTY, *tr. by* Edna Worthley Underwood

Shores of Styx are lone for evermore, The. Idle Charon. Eugene Lee-Hamilton. NOBVV

Shoriken. Charles Brasch. PeNZ

Shoring up the ocean. A railroad track. Blood-Sister. Adrienne Rich. NAAL-2

Shorn of landmarks, glued to a sere promontory. "No!" He Said. Wole Soyinka. HBAPE

Short and dirty, is all the fun of it. Petronius Arbiter, *Latin*. OBCVT, *tr. by* Judy Spink

Short, big-nosed men with nasty conical caps. The Hittites. Roy Fuller. OxBSP

Short cut home lay through the cemetery, The. The Mistress. Joan Barton. OxBTC

Short day has grown, A. The Place of V. Ray A. Young Bear. VoR

Short direction / To avoid dejection, A. Rules and Regulations. "Lewis Carroll." NOBVV; PeVV

Short History of British India, A. Geoffrey Hill. OxBC

Short History of the Bourgeoisie. Hans Magnus Enzensberger, *German*. VCWP, *tr. by* Enzensberger, Hans Magnus *and* Michael Hamburger

Short History of the Vietnam War Years, A. Dick Allen. BAP-94

Short in measure, narrow in theme. Erinna's *Distaff*. Antipater of Sidon, *Greek*. GrAn, *tr. by* Peter Jay

Short is my say, O stranger. Stay and read. Inscription. Terence, *Latin*. OBCVT, *tr. by* Frank Lawrence Lucas

Short is perhaps our date of life. Stanzas on Hearing for Certainty that we were to be Tried for High Treason. John Thelwall. Ro *Fr.* Poems Written in Close Confinement in the Tower and Newgate upon a Charge of Treason.

Short Lexicon of Torture in the Eighties, A. Edward Hirsch. VCAP

Short Life of the Hermit, A. John Logan.

"He told the crowd 'The devils'." CRP

Short Note on the Sparseness of the Language. Diane Di Prima. BB

Short on brains, long on stupidity, the mantis seizes the cicada. Huang T'ing-chien. SuSp, *tr. by* Michael E. Workman *Fr.* In My Study in Monastery, Rising after a Nap.

Short Order. Charles Bukowski. HoPM

Short Poem. William Carlos Williams. SAmP

Short Poem for Armistice Day, A. Sir Herbert Read. PeFWW

Short Revelation Concerning Death and Chaos. René Daumal, *French*. PFTM, *tr. by* Pierre Joris

Short Sermon. *Unknown, German*. CTV, *tr. by* Louis Untermeyer

Short service, to be sure, A. Lament for a Leg. John Ormond. NoP-4; OBWVE

Short Song of Congratulation [*or* To a Young Heir], A. Samuel Johnson. EBEV; HAP; InPK-6; InPS-3; NOBE; NOEC; OBCoV; OBSV; OxAEP-1; PeLV; PoE; PoEL-3; TFi; UnPo

("Show the spirit of an heir.") (LL) LiLi

(To a Young Heir.) SCGP

Short space my feet had traversed ere. Guillaume de Lorris *and* Jean de Meun. OAEL-1, *tr. by* F. S. Ellis *Fr.* The Romance [*or* Romaunt] of the Rose.

Short Story, A. David Escobar Galindo, *Spanish*. ChAP, *tr. by* Jorge Piche.

Short the way, but pitiless. Alcman, *Greek*. OBCVT, *tr. by* Guy Davenport

Short Time. Gavin Ewart. NoAM

Short-Wave. Christopher Cokinos. IFJA

Short Wave In Shanghai. Sibyl James. LoHo

Short Year, The. Paavo Haavikko, *Finnish*.

"One who writes us is now doing four plays a year, The." VCWP, *tr. by* Herbert Lomas

Shortening the Road. Michael Davitt, *Irish*. PBCIP, *tr. by* Philip Casey

Shorter American Memory of the American Character According to Santayana. Rosemarie Waldrop. EOEF

Shorter and shorter now the twilight clips. Autumn. Alice Cary. APN-2

Shorter she grows, The. (LL) A Candle. Mother Goose. LB; OxNR; ReMoGo

Shortest and Sweetest of Songs, The. George Macdonald. NOBVV

Shortest Day, The. William Dickey. IMW

Shortness and Misery of Life, The. Isaac Watts. NOCV

Shortness of Life. Thomas Fairfax. NOSC

Shorts [1948–1957]. W. H. Auden.

Aesthetic Point of View, The. NBLV; OBAL; OBCoV

(Limerick.) PeLi

"Behold the manly mesomorph." OxBSP

Dedication: "Let us honour if we can." PeLV

Dedication: "Private faces in public places." PeLV

"Give me a doctor, partridge-plump." OBCoV

Statesmen. OBCoV

Words. PeLV

Shorts / Excerpts ("I keep a TV monitor on my chest"). Bill Knott. PBCAP

Shorts I. W. H. Auden.

"Lost on a fog-bound spit of sand." FaBoEE

Shoshone Wedding Song. Mary Austin, *Shoshone*. ITG, *tr. by* Robert Hass

Shot at Random, A. Wyndham Lewis. UV

Shot down from its enskied formation. An Angel in Blythburgh Church. Peter Porter. NoP-4

Shot of War, A. J. S. Harry. BMAP

Shot Who? Jim Lane! Merrill Moore. MoAmPo

Shotgun / blossoming / outward. Amble. Maxine Chernoff. PmAP *Fr.* Japan. PmAP

Should all my life employ, and busy [*or* busie] me. (LL) The Odour. 2. Cor. 2. George Herbert. ChIV-2; ESCV

Should all our churchmen foam in spite. At Farringford. Tennyson. *Fr.* To the Rev. F. D. Maurice. GTBS-P; NOBVV; PeECV

Should any ask me on His form to dwell. He Hath No Parallel. Sadi. AWP, *tr. by* L. Cranmer-Byng *Fr.* The Gulistan.

Should auld acquaintance be forgot. Auld Lang Syne. Robert Burns. APAD; AWP; EBEvV; ImPo; NAEL-2; NOBE; OBEV; OxAEP-2; OxBS; PoLF; SCGP

Should be her proper text. G. K. Chesterton. *See* The Song against Grocers.

Should be very quiet this morning. Sunday Morning. Robert Grenier. PmAP

Should be written out on air & running water. (LL) Carmen 70 ("Lesbia says she'ld rather marry me"). Catullus, *Latin.* OBVE, *tr. by* Richard Lovelace

Should blaze the path of thunder. (LL) Tableau. Countee Cullen. NAAAL; PoBA

Should Dennis print how once you robb'd your brother. On Dennis. Alexander Pope. FaBoEE

Should ever be forgot. (LL) Gunpowder Plot Day. *Unknown.* FaBoPV; LB; OxNR

Should find brief solace there, as I have found. (LL) Nuns fret not at their convent's narrow room. Wordsworth. EBEV; GSo; NIP-4; NoP-4; OBEV; Poetr; Son

Should fright us from the shore. (LL) A Prospect of Heaven Makes Death Easy. Isaac Watts. NOCV; NoP-4; PeECV; TOF

Should Heaven send me any son. Alfred, Lord Tennyson. Dorothy Parker. NALW *Fr.* A Pig's-Eye View of Literature.

Should I Be a Rabbi? Hayyim Nahman Bialik, *Hebrew.* TrJP, *tr. by* Grace Goldin

Should I be troubled when the purblind knight. John Wilmot. EPCY *Fr.* An Allusion to Horace.

Should I believe you, e'en my oaths are witty. *Unknown.* FaBoEE

Should I ever fall ill. Yaroslav Vasilevich Smelyakov, *Russian.* TCRP, *tr. by* Albert C. Todd

Should I forget your scales. Walking Buddha. Barbara Guest. FTOS

Should I get married? Should I be good? Marriage. Gregory Corso. CBLP; CoAP; LiTM; MoP; NeAP; NoP-4; OBAL; PeLV; PmAP; TAP; TRP

Should I give in to sleep? This fire's warm. Reading *Paradise Lost* in Protestant Ulster 1984. Seamus Deane. BiHa; PBCIP

Should I greet you. The Kama Sutra of Kindness: Position No. 2. Mary Mackey. DeD

Should I know this room. Locale. Penelope Shuttle. BrRo

Should I not be ashamed. The Ending. Paul Engle. NYBP

Should I see a cloud high up in the sky. Yury Kuznetsov, *Russian.* TCRP, *tr. by* Lubov Yakovleva

Should I stroke it. Tanka. Mori Ōgai, *Japanese.* MJT, *tr. by* Makoto Ueda

Should I tell what a miracle she was. (LL) The Relic. Donne. ESCV; FHYEP; FMP; FSCP; GBL; GEA; HAP; HeIP-4; ImPo; MeLP; NOBE; NOSC; NoP-4; OAEL-1; PoEL-2; SCGP; SeCP; TFi

Should I thee ranke with Radamanthus fell. A Satyrete ricall Charracter of a Proud Upstart. John Saffin. SCAP

Should I wear a shadowed eye. Acceptance. John Wieners. FTOS

Should I with silver tooles delve through the hill. Edward Taylor. ChIV-2, *sect.* II, lvi; OxBA; SCAP, *sect.* LVI; MeMAP *Fr.* Preparatory Meditations Before My Approach to the Lord's Supper.

Should Latin, Greek, and Hebrew fail. *Unknown.* OxBSn

Should make men atheists and not women whores[?]. (LL) A Rapture. Thomas Carew. BeJo; CaPo; NAEL-1; OAEL-1; OxAEP-1; SeCP

Should old acquaintance be forgot. Auld Lang Syne. *Unknown.* NOSC

Should rejoice. Robert Penn Warren. *See* Colder Fire.

Should smile like you, and perish as they smile! (LL) Sonnet 5: "Evening, as slow thy placid shades descend." William Lisle Bowles. NOBRP; NOEC

Should some ill Painter in a wild design. Horace, *Latin.* OBCVT; OBVE, *tr. by* John Oldham *Fr.* The Art of Poetry.

Should steal her quite from *Me.* (LL) Platonic[k] Love. Abraham Cowley. BeJo; NoP-4

Should the building totter, run for an archway! The Fallen Tower of Siloam. Robert Graves. ChIV-2

Should the cold Muscovit, whose furre and stove. To the Right Honourable the Countess of C. William Habington. SeCP

Should the pillar sing, should salt. Lot. David Helwig. NIP-4

Should the shade of Plato. On Installing an American Kitchen in Lower Austria. W. H. Auden. NYBP *Fr.* Thanksgiving for a Habitat.

Should the wide world roll away. Stephen Crane. APN-2; AmPP *Fr.* The Black Riders [and Other Lines].

Should toss with tangle and with shells. (LL) I hear the noise about thy keel. Tennyson. EBVV; EnVR

Should wear all Time's destructions for a dress. (LL) The Poet Laments the Coming of Old Age. Dame Edith Sitwell. NAEL-2; NoAM

Should you ask me, whence these stories? Introduction. Henry Wadsworth Longfellow. ColAP; MeMAP; NOBA; PoE; Poetr *Fr.* The Song of Hiawatha.

Should You Go First. Albert K. Rowswell. PoLF; PoToHe

Should you, my lord, while you pursue my song. Phillis Wheatley. BPo; ImGa; TTY *Fr.* To the Right Honourable William, Earl of Dartmouth. AmPP

Should you revisit us. New Approach Needed. Kingsley Amis. NoAM; OxBTC

Shoulder-bag, cloak, unleavened barley-cake, stick. On Diogenes the Cynic. Antiphilus, *Greek.* GrAn, *tr. by* W. S. Merwin

Shoulder of rock, A. High Island. Richard Murphy. CIP-2; NOIV

Shouldered box has nested deep, The. Farewell to a Jovial Friend. Gloria Escoffery. PBCV

Shouldering its way and shedding the earth crumbs. (LL) Putting in the Seed. Robert Frost. NoAM; OxBA

Shouldering shapes of the skies of Broceliande. Taliessin's Song of the Unicorn. Charles Williams. FaBoTw

Shouldn't I pilfer wantonly this famed fragrance of a foreign land? Su Man-shu. SuSp, *tr. by* Wu-chi Liu *Fr.* Poems Written during My Sojourn in Japan.

Shouldn't we finally get started? California. Leon Stokesbury. PFE

Shout came from the loquacious ones, A. A Welsh Ballad. Edmwnd Prys, *Welsh.* OBWVE, *tr. by* Gwyn Williams

Shout for Joy. *Unknown.* AmFP

Shout, Little Lulu. *Unknown.* AmFP

Shout, shout, up with your song! The March of the Women. Cicely Hamilton. BrRo

Shout the Redeemer. Isaac Watts. *See* The Day of Judgement [*or* Judgment]; an Ode.

Shouting Song. *Unknown.* AmFP

Shouting the battle cry of Freedom. (LL) The Battle-Cry of Freedom. George Frederick Root. CBCWP; FaBoBe

Shouting through the town? (LL) Mirror mirror tell me. Robert Graves. NOxBChV

Shovel Man, The. Carl Sandburg. HAP

Shovelling Iron Ore. *Unknown.* AS

Show, The. Wilfred Owen. ImPo; LiTM; MoBrPo; NSI; OBWVE; OxBTC; PeFWW

Show an affirming flame. (LL) September 1, 1939. W. H. Auden. AF; CMoP; ImPo; MoBrPo; OxAEP-2; OxBA; PoE

Show is not the Show, The. Emily Dickinson. AmPP

Show Me a Rose. John Godfrey. FTOS

Show me again the time. Lines to a Movement in Mozart's E-Flat Symphony. Thomas Hardy. NoAM

Show me dear[e] Christ, thy spouse, so bright and clear. Show me dear Christ. Donne. MeLP; NAEL-1; NOSC; PoE; Son *Fr.* Holy Sonnets. ESCV

("Show me dear Christ, Thy Spouse so bright and clear.") FSCP; NoP-4; PeECV

("When she is embrac'd and open to most men.") (LL) PBRV

("When she's embraced and open to most men.") (LL) NoP-4

Show me himself, himself (bright Sir) O show. Come See the Place Where the Lord Lay. Richard Crashaw. ChIV-2

Show me the flames you brag of, you that be. On the Great Frost (1634). William Cartwright. NOSC

Show Me The Way. *Unknown, Burmese.* LiLi; PBWP, *tr. by* U Win Pe

Show [*or* Shew] me thy feet; show [*or* shew] me thy legs, thy thighs. To Dianeme. Robert Herrick. CaPo; NOSC

"Show me your God!" the doubter cries. Blind. John Kendrick Bangs. PoToHe

Show of arrogant spirit fills the road, A. Light Furs, Fat Horses. Po Chü-i, *Chinese.* CoBCP, *tr. by* Burton Watson

Show the runner coming through the shadows. The Runner. Gary Gildner. TAP

Show the spirit of an heir. Samuel Johnson. *See* A Short Song of Congratulation [*or* To a Young Heir].

Show us there's chance at least of winning through. (LL) To Whistler, American. Ezra Pound. FaBoA

Show weakness speaks in prose, but power in verse. (LL) Poetry in England. Samuel Daniel. EPCY; NOBE; NoSic

Shower, A. Amy Lowell. CPO

Shower, The. Linda Smukler. GLP

Shower [*or* Showre], The. Henry Vaughan. ESCV; GeHe; SeCP

Shower and Sunshine. Maud Morin. BoTP

Shower of Secret Things, The. Nathaniel Mackey. PmAP

Showered on the shining pavement where he lay. (LL) Again I find myself alone, and ever. Charlotte Brontë. PEW; VWP

Showing. Liam Rector. TRP

Showing no visible sign, for such things are untold. (LL) The Eve of Waterloo. Byron. EBEV; EBEvV; FaBoBe; FaBoCh; NOBE; OBNC; OBWP; OxAEP-2; TFi

Shown to My Son Yü. Lu Yu, *Chinese.* SuSp, *tr. by* Irving Y. Lo

Showre, The. Henry Vaughan. SeCP

Shows. Yevgeny Mikhailovich Vinokurov, *Russian.* TCRP, *tr. by* Daniel Weissbort

Shows most true mettle when you check his course. (LL) First follow Nature, and your judgment frame. Alexander Pope. EPCY; FHYEP

Shrapnel lives in Morton's neck, so his head stays. Refuge at the One Step Down. Belle Waring. PBCAP; SeSe

Shred in his little fist. (LL) Balloons. Sylvia Plath. FaBoWP; PoE

Shrewish, barren, bony, nosy servant, A. David O'Bruadair, Irish. NOIV, tr. by Thomas Kinsella

Shriek said the saw smile said the mice. To the Age's Insanities. Marie Ponsot. VGW

Shrieking its message the flying death. The Shell. H. M. Sarson. NSI; PoWW

Shrieking, sobbing, shaking. Separation in Succasunna. Sander Zulauf. EC3

Shrieks in dark leaves. The rumpled owl. Hunger and Thirst. John Peale Bishop. PoA

Shrill sentence: God is love, The. (LL) On the Farm. Ronald Stuart Thomas. NoP-4

Shrill the fife, kettle the drum. Baldy Bane. W. S. Graham. FaBoTC

Shrilling cicada, drunk on drops of dew, you sing. Meleager. HePo, tr. by Barbara Hughes Fowler Fr. I'll Twine White Violets. NIP-4, tr. by Goldwin Smith

Shrimp, The. Moses Browne.
   "Shrimp, A! Black thing as widow's crape." NOEC

Shrimp. Nguyễn Văn Lạc, Vietnamese. AVP, tr. by Huỳnh Sanh Thông

Shrimp, A! Black thing as widow's crape. Moses Browne. NOEC Fr. The Shrimp.

Shrimp plant on my desk had one long low branch, The. Plant Poem. Edward Field. IFJA

Shrimp who sought his lady shrimp, A. Ogden Nash. CBNP

Shrine, The. Hilda Doolittle. ColAP

Shrine and the Burning Wheel, The. Mark Jarman. NAmP90

Shrine Festival. Wang Chia, Chinese. CoBCP, tr. by Burton Watson

Shrine is vowed to freedom, but, my friend, The. Freedom and Truth. Margaret Fuller. PAR

Shrine of General Pien, The. Chu Yün-ming, Chinese. CoBLCP, tr. by Jonathan Chaves

Shrine of Ts'en Yi-tung, The. Ho Xuan Huong, Vietnamese. AVP, tr. by Huỳnh Sanh Thông

"Shrink" is a misnomer. The religious. Some Terms. Robert Pinsky. HCAP Fr. Essay on Psychiatrists.

Shrinking brain, sick of an inner war, The. (LL) Moon is a poor woman, The. Sidney Keyes. NoP-4

Shropshire Lad, A. John Betjeman. MoBS

Shropshire Lad's Cousin, The. Samuel Hoffenstein. BXAP

Shroud. George Mackay Brown. NoP-4; RB

Shroud, The. Galway Kinnell. LCAP-2

Shroud of Color, The. Countee Cullen. NAAAL

Shrouded Stranger, The. Allen Ginsberg. NeAP

Shrouding of the Duchess of Malfi, The. John Webster. NOBE; OBEV Fr. The Duchess of Malfi. NAEL-1
   (Hearke, Now Every Thing Is Still.)

Shrubbery, The. William Cowper. NOBE; OBGa

Shu Has Gone Hunting. Unknown, Chinese. CoBCP

Shu' Shu' of Delgo. Albert Brodrick. PeSAV

Shua-O! Shua-O! (LL) Scaring Crows. Unknown. BoTP; OxNR

Shubble, The. Walter De la Mare. OBCoV

Shudder [, The]. Donald Hall. NYBP

Shuddering the Spectre howls, his howlings terrify the night. William Blake. OAEL-2 Fr. Jerusalem; The Emanation of the Giant Albion.

Shuffle and shudder of Autumn, The. Autumn Imagined. Donald Davie. PoA

Shuffling papers. Certificate of Live Birth. Kimberly M. Blaeser. UnSA

Shui Shu. Various authors, Japanese.
   River-Fog. AWP, tr. by Arthur Waley

Shun[ne] delay[e]s, they breed[e] remorse. Loss[e] in Delay[e]. Robert Southwell. NoSic

Shut-In, The. Nellie De Hearn. PoToHe

Shut In. Robert B. Shaw. SoSe-8

Shut in behind the window, a glittering candle. Yang Chi. Fr. Living in the Country at Kou-ch'ü in Autumn—mdash;Miscellaneous Impressions. CoBLCP, tr. by Jonathan Chaves

Shut in from all the world without. Firelight. John Greenleaf Whittier. OBCP, ll. 155–163 Fr. Snow-Bound [or Snow-Bound; a Winter Idyl]. APN-1; AiP; AmPP; NAAL-3; NOBA; OxBA; TAP; TFi

Shut not me alive away. The Commuted Sentence. Stevie Smith. OxAEP-2

Shut not so soon; the dull-eyed night. To Daisies, Not to Shut So Soon[e]. Robert Herrick. BeJo; CH; CaPo; GBL; OBEV; OxBSP

Shut not your doors to me proud libraries. Walt Whitman. NOBA; OxBA

Shut Out. Christina Rossetti. NALW

Shut Out That Moon. Thomas Hardy. CMoP; NOBE; NoAM

Shut, shut the door, good John! fatigu'd I said. Epistle to Dr. Arbuthnot. Alexander Pope. FHYEP; InPS-3; NOEC; OAEL-1; OBCoV; OxAEP-1; OxBoLi; PoE; PoEL-3; TFi

Shut the gallery lock the door. Mouth. Dennis Scott. PBCV

Shut the Seven Seas against Us. George Barker. MoBrPo Fr. Third Cycle of Love Poems.

Shut up. Shut up. There's nobody here. The Beast in the Space. W. S. Graham. FaBoTw; OxAEP-2; PoA

Shut your eyes then. Nursery Rhyme. May Sarton. NOxBChV

"Shut your trap, you. The question is, what about Karl Marx?" (LL) Cultural Notes. Kenneth Fearing. CMoP; PoE

Shutter of time darkening ceaselessly, The. August. Louis MacNeice. LiTM

Shuttle in the Crypt, The. Wole Soyinka.
   Bearings III: Amber Wall. PBMAP
   Ujamaa. PBMAP

Shuttles of trains going north, going south, drawing threads of blue. Morning Sun. Louis MacNeice. MoBrPo; TwCP

Shy and timid, Gloom to me. The Outcast. James Stephens. MoBrPo

Shy Geordie. Helen B. Cruickshank. OxBS

Shy in their herding dwell the fallow deer. Deer. John Drinkwater. CH

Shy one, shy one. To an Isle in the Water. W. B. Yeats. AWP; TTTS

Shy speechless sound, The. Osip Emilevich Mandelstam, Russian. Spl, tr. by Clarence Brown and W. S. Merwin

Shyly the silver-hatted mushrooms make. May. John Shaw Neilson. NOBAu

Shyness and modesty, they said. Disillusionment. Virginia Graham. NBLV

Si Hubbard. Unknown. AS

Si Monumentum Requiris. Daryl Hine. EOEF

Si, señor, is halligators here, your guidebook say it. Sinalóa. Earle Birney. MoCV; OxBC; PeLV

Siamese twins: one, maddened by. Twins. Robert Graves. FaBoEE; OBCoV

Siberia. James Clarence Mangan. BIrV; NOBVV; NOIV

Siberian Wooing. Yevtushenko, Russian. VCWP, tr. by Albert C. Todd and James Ragan

Sibilla's Dirge. Thomas Lovell Beddoes. See Dirge: "We do lie beneath the grass."

Siblings, The. Odysseus Elytis, Greek.
   Psalm and Mosaic for a Springtime in Athens. GrIP, tr. by Nanos Valaortis

Sibrandus Schafnaburgensis. Robert Browning. CTC; EBVV Fr. Garden Fancies.
   ("Plague take all your pendants, say I!") OBGa

Sibyl. Robert Adamson. BMAP

Sibyl, The. Agnes Mary Frances Robinson. VWP

Sibylla Palmifera. D. G. Rossetti. See Soul's Beauty.

Sibylline, yet benign. (LL) Formerly a Slave. Herman Melville. APN-2; TAP

Sibyl's Song, The. Michele Roberts. BrRo

Sic counsels ye gave to me, O. Unknown. See Edward [or Edward, Edward].

Sic et Non. Sir Herbert Read. FaBoTw

Sic Itur. Arthur Hugh Clough. EBVV

Sic Transit Gloria Scotia. "Hugh MacDiarmid." CMoP

Sic Vita. W. S. Braithwaite. NAAAL

Sic Vita. Henry, Bishop of Chichester King. NOBE; NOSC; OxBSP; SCGP; SeCP

Sich a Nice Man Too! Albert Chevalier.
   "There's parties ad yer meets about." UV

Sicilian Cyclamens. D. H. Lawrence. NoAM

Sicilian Muse, I Would Try Now a Somewhat Grander Theme. Virgil. See The Messiah.

Sicilian Muses, sing we greater things. Virgil. See The Messiah.

Sick. Shel Silverstein. ChAP

Sick, am I sick of a jealous dread? Tennyson. Fr. Maud [A Monodrama]. EnVR

Sick Assailant, The. Anna Wickham. WPN

Sick Child, A. Randall Jarrell. InPK-6; NoP-4; OxBC; VGW

Sick Child, The. Robert Louis Stevenson. CH

Sick cicada, unable now to fly, A. Chia Tao, Chinese. SuSp, tr. by Stephen Owen

Sick image of my father fades, The. John Horder. RaBo

Sick Leave. Po Chü-i, Chinese. ChiP, tr. by Arthur Waley

Sick Love. Robert Graves. BoLoP; CMoP; EBEV; GTBS-P; HAP; NOBE; OAEL-2; OxAEP-2

(O Love in Me.) FaBoMo

Sick Men Sleeping. Kenneth Mackenzie. BMAP

Sick Nought, The. Randall Jarrell. OxBA

Sick of the piercing company of women. A Country Walk. Thomas Kinsella. CIP-2; CMoP

Sick of thy northern glooms, come, shepherd, seek. Philip Freneau. AmPP *Fr.* The Beauties of Santa Cruz.

Sick Rose, The. William Blake. AWP; BoLoP; ClHu; EBEvV; EnLoPo; FHYEP; HAP; HeIP-4; InPK-6; InPS-3; NAEL-2; NAWM-2; NIP-4; NOBE; NOBRP; NOEC; OAEL-2; OBNC; OPOU; OxAEP-2; OxBSP; PoE; PoEL-4; Poetr; RB; Ro; SCGP; SoSe-8; TFi; TRP; WeW-3 *Fr.* Songs of Experience.

("O Rose thou art sick!") APAD; CABP; EP; FaBoSe; GEA; NoP-4; PFE; PoPoPo

Sick. . . Sick. . . I will lie down and die. How. Isaac Rosenberg. PeFWW *Fr.* The Unicorn.

Sick Stockrider, The. Adam Lindsay Gordon. CBAP

Sick to our souls we dumbly wait. September 1939. Vita Sackville-West. WPN

Sick Woman. John Kinsella. BMAP

Sick, you said goodbye to me. Lamenting for My Wife. Wang Shih-chieng, *Chinese.* CoBLCP, tr. by Jonathan Chaves

Sickens my gut, Yellow Bittern. The Yellow Bittern. *Unknown, Irish.* CIP-2; PBCIP, tr. by Tom MacIntyre

Sickles mount. Harvest Song. Ludwig Heinrich Christoph Hölty, *German.* AWP, tr. by Charles T. Brooks

Sickly taper / By glimmering through thy low-browed misty vaults, The. Robert Blair. ECEV *Fr.* The Grave.

Sickness. William Thompson.
"Next, in a low-browed cave, a little hell." ECEV

Sickness, intending my love to betray. Sir John Davies. *Fr.* Sonnets to Philomel. SiPS

Sickness of Adam, The. Karl Shapiro. CRP *Fr.* Adam and Eve.

Sickness of desire, that in dark days, The. Melancholia. Robert Bridges. CMoP

Sickness of Friends, The. Henri Coulette. NYBP

Side by side after the meal. Valerio Magrelli, *Italian.* NeIt, tr. by Dana Gioia

Side by side on the narrow bed. That Room. John Montague. CIP-2

Side by side, their faces blurred. An Arundel Tomb. Philip Larkin. NoP-4; OxAEP-2; OxBM

Side by side, we ride out of the city. Tsung Ch'en. CoBLCP, tr. by Jonathan Chaves *Fr.* An Excursion to the Suburbs.

Side-canyon, A. Michael McClintock. HA

Side-room has sweated years and patience, rolls its one eye, The. Hospital Night. Francis Webb. BMAP

Side street in the French Quarter through. Urban Cowboy Hat. Maureen Owen. DeD

Side Window. John James. ImPo

Sidera Cadentia. Ford Madox Ford. OxBSP

Sidewalk joins the concrete wall around the vacant lot, The. Where or When. Philip Whalen. PoM

Sidewalk Racer Or, On the Skateboard, The. Lillian Morrison. NTCP
("Skimming.") KaS

Sidewalks of New York, The. James W. Blake. BLPA; FaBoBe

Sidney, Looking for her Mother. Dolores Kendrick. ISC

Sidrophel, the Rosicrucian Conjurer. Samuel Butler. OxBoLi *Fr.* Hudibras.

Siege. Dan Pagis, *Hebrew.* IP, tr. by Warren Bargad *and* Stanley F. Chyet

Siege and the assault being ceased at Troy, The. Sir Gawain and the Green Knight. *Unknown, Middle English.* OAEL-1, tr. by Brian Stone

Siege of Thebes, The. John Lydgate.
"When brighte Phoebus passed was the Ram." EPCY

Siege of Valencia, The. Felicia Dorothea Hemans.
Dirge: "Calm on the bosom of thy God." OBEV; WoRP

Siena. Lily Thicknesse. LW

Siena Mi Fe'; Disfecemi Maremma. Ezra Pound. MoAmPo *Fr.* Hugh Selwyn Mauberley. (Life and Contacts). AmPP; CMoP; InPS-3; LiTM; NOBA; NoAM; TAP

Sierra. Alfonsina Storni, *Spanish.* PBWP, tr. by Rachel Benson

Sierra Kid. Philip Levine.
He Faces the Second Winter. PoA

Sierras. Joaquin Miller. APN-2

Siesta, The. *Unknown, Spanish.* AWP, tr. by Bryant

Siesta in Xbalba. Allen Ginsberg.
"So I dream nightly of an embarkation." CLPP

Siesta of a Hungarian Snake. Edwin Morgan. InPK-6

Sieve, A. Mother Goose. ReMoGo

Sigh. Stéphane Mallarmé, *French.* AWP, tr. by Arthur Symons

Sigh, A. Anne Finch, Countess of Winchilsea. ECWP

Sigh, heart, and break not; rest, lark, and wake not! Nuptial Song. John Byrne Leicester Warren. GTBS-P; PeVV; RACG

Sigh, in the wind fall flowers, their petals dance. Selling Ruined Peonies. Yü Hsüan-chi, *Chinese.* SuSp, tr. by William H. Nienhauser

Sigh no more, ladies [sigh no more]. Song: "Sigh no more, ladies, sigh no more." Shakespeare. AWP; CTC; NoSic; PoEL-2; UV *Fr.* Much Ado about Nothing.

Sigh no more ladies nor gentlemen at all. Stevie Smith. WPN

Sigh sounds and a sough replies, A. The Ballad of Mulan. *Unknown, Chinese.* SuSp, tr. by William H. Nienhauser

Sigh that heaves the grasses, The. A. E. Housman. NOBVV

Sigh then beyond my song: whirl & rejoice! (LL) Canto Amor. John Berryman. CoAP; MoAmPo; VGW

Sigh, wind in the pine. Douglas Stewart. CBAP *Fr.* Glencoe.

Sighed a dear little shipboard divinity. Limerick. Conrad Potter Aiken. OBAL; PeLi

Sighing, and Sadly Sitting by My Love. Richard Barnfield. PBRV; Son *Fr.* Cynthia.

Sighing high and / again a sigh! Weaving at the Window. Wang Chien, *Chinese.* SuSp, tr. by William H. Nienhauser

Sighing I murmur, 'O mihi pratteritos!' (LL) Eheu Fugaces. "Thomas Ingoldsby." FaBoEE; OxBoLi

Sighing over Flowers. Tu Mu, *Chinese.* SuSp, tr. by Eddie Tsang

Sighing, sleeping alone all night. The Mother of Michitsuna, *Japanese.* WPJ, tr. by Kenneth Rexroth *and* Ikuko Atsumi

Sighioara 1982. Grete Tartler, *Romanian.* CEEP, tr. by Fleur Adcock

Sighs and Groans [or Grones]. George Herbert. PoEL-2

Sighs are my food, drink are my tears. Sir Thomas Wyatt. NoSic; OxBSP; SiPS

Sighs of the Gunner from Dakar, The. Guillaume Apollinaire, *French.* PeFWW, tr. by Anne Hyde Greet

Sight. Wilfred Wilson Gibson. MoBrPo

Sight and hearing finely tuned. When I Was Young, I Stopped by a Wine Shop in Chi-men and Wrote This Poem, Inscribed It and Signed It, "Written by Lien the Eighteenth." The People of That District Have Since Taken It To Be a Poem of [the God] Lü Tung-pin! I Have Recorded It Here as an Amusement. Yü Chi, *Chinese.* CoBLCP, tr. by Jonathan Chaves

Sight grows dim—my power. Arseny Aleksandrovich Tarkovsky, *Russian.* TCRP, tr. by Albert C. Todd

Sight in camp in the daybreak gray and dim, A. Walt Whitman. AmPP; BLT; CBCWP; MoP; NAAL-1; NAAL-3; NoAM; OxBA; PoE; PoEL-5; SAmP; TAP

Sight of a lark's, The. Virginia Brady Young. HA

Sight of the coffee was good for sore eyes, The. Upon Receipt of a Pound of Coffee in 1863. Mary E. Tucker. CBWP-1

Sight of the English is getting me down, The. Hiraeth in N.W.3. Wynford Vaughan-Thomas. NOBL

Sight Unseen. Kingsley Amis. NoAM

Sighting, The. Jonathan Aaron. WeT

Sighting down the long black barrel. Hunting. William Daniel Ehrhart. CDa

Sightseeing. Rita Dove. GT

Sightseers, The. Paul Muldoon. BiHa; CIP-2

Sightseers in a Courtyard. Nicolás Guillén, *Spanish.* TTY, tr. by Langston Hughes

Sigil. Hilda Doolittle.
Moon in Your Hands, The. BoWoP; NYBP
"Now let the cycle sweep us here and there." VGW

Sigismundo. Linda Gregg. AmPA

Sigmund Freud. Howard Nemerov. PoA

Sigmund Freud says that one who reflects. Limerick. Peter Alexander. PeLi

Sign for father, The. (LL) Quinnapoxet. Stanley Kunitz. AFr; LoL

Sign for My Father, Who Stressed the Bunt. David Bottoms. MT

Sign for our town, The. Proposal. Kim R. Stafford. IFJA

Sign of brotherhood which comes to nourish the dreams of men, The. (LL) Listen, comrades of the flaming centuries. David Diop, *French.* PBMAP

Sign of Saturn, The. Sharon Olds. InPS-3

Sign your name in the book. It's just ink. Limerick. Sydney Bernard Smith. PeLi

Signal, The. David Ignatow. NNaP

Signal Fire, The. Aeschylus. CTC, tr. by Dallam Simpson *Fr.* Agamemnon. NAWM-1, tr. by Robert Fagles

Signal flutters at the Flagship's fore, A. The Sailing of the Fleet. Noel Marcus Francis Corbett. NSI

Signal Gun, The. Mary E. Tucker. CBWP-1

Signal Hill. Sharon Doubiago. MoLi

Signal; or, A Satire against Modesty, The. Francis Hawling.
  Author Consults a Critic and Sells His Manuscript, The. NOEC

Signals. Jewel C. Latimore. PoBA

Signature for Tempo. Archibald MacLeish. CRP; VGW

Signature of All Things, The. Kenneth Rexroth. APSN; TRP
  ("Eternally in summer air.") (LL) BLT
  "When I dragged the rotten log." NNaP

Signatures. Daniel Gerard Hoffman. VGW

Signboard, The. Robert Creeley. CoAmPo

Significance of a Water Animal, The. Ray A. Young Bear. HATNAP

Significant Fevers. Alison Fell. BrRo

Signify the strength of the waves' lash. (LL) Lear. William Carlos
  Williams. MeMAP; NAAL-2; NOBA; PoA

Signifying Monkey, The. *Unknown.* CrDW; NAAAL

Signifying nothing. (LL) To-morrow, and to-morrow, and to-morrow.
  Shakespeare. EBEV; EBEvV; ImPo; OxAEP-1

Signpost. Toksu Moon, *Korean.* CKP, *tr. by* Jaihiun Kim

Signs, The. Norman Henry. NBV

Signs. Gjertrud Schnackenberg. InPK-6; PoA; VCAP

Signs of Love. Petrarch. AWP *Fr.* Sonnets to Laura.

Signs of Rain. Edward Jenner. BLPA

Signs of Rain. Virgil. APo, *tr. by* John Dryden *Fr.* The Georgics.

Signs of Spring. Sir Thomas Browne. NOSC

Signs of Storm. James Thomson. APo

Signs of the Times. Paul Laurence Dunbar. APN-2

Signs of the Zodiac are fading, The. Nikolai Alekseievich Zabolotsky,
  Russian. TCRP, *tr. by* Daniel Weissbort

Signs of wear. Monogram 29. Martina Werner, *German.* BoWoP, *tr. by*
  Rosemarie Waldrop

Signs of Winter. John Clare.
  "Cat runs races with her tail, The." OAEL-2

Signs on 42nd Street. Flash. Lee Bennett Hopkins. SSCS

Sigurd of yore. The Lay [*or* Short Lay] of Sigurd. *Unknown.* AWP, *tr. by*
  William Morris *and* Eirikr Magnusson *Fr.* The Elder Edda.

Sigurd Rideth to the Glittering Heath. William Morris. PoEL-5 *Fr.* The
  Story of Sigurd the Volsung.

Sila. Robert Penn Warren. NoP-4

Silence. Bella Akhatovna Akhmadulina, *Russian.* BoWoP, *tr. by* Daniel
  Halpern

Silence. Eugenio de Andrade, *Portuguese.* VCWP, *tr. by* Alexis Levitin

Silence. Alvin Aubert. MT

Silence. Stefan Brecht. CLPP

Silence. Miroslav Holub, *Czech.* PoSu, *tr. by* Ian *and* Jarmila Milner

Silence. Thomas Hood. CH; EBEV; GSo; NOBE; OBEV; PoEL-4; Son
  (Sonnet: Silence.) OBNC

Silence, The. Tomas Mac Siomoin, *Irish.* TIRV, *tr. by the author*

Silence. René Maran, *French.* NegPo, *tr. by* Ellen Conroy Kennedy

Silence. Edgar Lee Masters. MoAmPo; PoToHe

Silence. Marianne Moore. CMoP; FaBoMo; FaBoWP; InPS-3; NALW;
  NOBA; TRP

Silence. Violeta Palinskaite, *Lithuanian.* CEEP, *tr. by* Irene Pogoželskyte
  Suboczewski

Silence. Edgar Allan Poe. APN-1; NCAP; PAR
  ("No foot of man,) commend thyself to God!") (LL) GSo
  (Sonnet—Silence.) ColAP; MeMAP; NOBA

Silence. James Whitcomb Riley. GSo

Silence, The. Vern Rutsala. CDa

Silence, The. Myra Scovel. HA

Silence. Walter James Turner. MoBrPo

Silence. John Hall Wheelock. LiTM

Silence. William Carlos Williams. SAmP

Silence, The. Virginia Brady Young. HA

Silence, 2. Stefan Brecht. CLPP

Silence: 2. Sipho Sepamla. AF

Silence a droplet of water trickles down a stone, The. Matsuo Allard. HA

Silence: A Sonnet. Henry, Bishop of Chichester King. NOSC

Silence all flesh, your selves prepare. A Judicious Observation of That
  Dreadful Comet. Ichabod Wiswall. SCAP

Silence, an Eloquent Applause. Leona Gregory. TrCP

Silence and aura. An ancient Yemenite woman gathers dry. Gleaning.
  David Shimoni, *Hebrew.* MHP, *tr. by* Ruth Finer Mintz

Silence and sleep like fields / Of amaranth lie. (LL) All That's Past. Walter
  De la Mare. NOBE; OAEL-2; OBMV; OxBTC

Silence and Solitude may hint. An Uninscribed Monument on One of the
  Battlefields of the Wilderness. Herman Melville. CBCWP

Silence and solitude were vacancy? (LL) Mont Blanc. Shelley. InPS-3;
  NAEL-2; NIP-4; NOBRP; NoP-4; OAEL-2; Ro

Silence, and stealth of day[e]s! 'tis now. Henry Vaughan. ESCV; NAEL-1

Silence augmenteth grief, writing increaseth rage. Epitaph on Sir Philip
  Sidney. Greville Fulke. SCGP

Silence brought by the dark night: Eryri's. Nightfall. Walter Davies,
  Welsh. OBWVE, *tr. by* Anthony Conran

Silence. Coffee. The dusky ceiling. Cigars. Olafs Stumbrs. CEEP

Silence Concerning an Ancient Stone. Rosario Castellanos, *Spanish.* PBWP,
  tr. by George D. Schade

Silence, cooked like gold, in. Alchemical. Paul Celan, *German.* VCWP, *tr.
  by* Michael Hamburger

Silence I speak of, The. Silence: 2. Sipho Sepamla. AF

Silence, in truth, would speak my sorrow best. Tears at the Grave of Sir
  Albertus Morton. Sir Henry Wotton. SeCP

Silence / is / a / looking. E. E. Cummings. CMoP; PoE

Silence is harder, Una said. The Cup. Judith Wright. FaBoWP

Silence is sucking the earth dry. Tymoteusz Karpowicz, *Polish.* PoSu, *tr.
  by* Jan Darowski

Silence of Love, The. Yong-un Han, *Korean.* CKP, *tr. by* Jaihiun Kim

Silence of our watching, waiting springs, A. A View. Beverly Quint.
  NYBP

Silence on silence treads at each low morn. Philoctetes. John Byrne
  Leicester Warren. NOBVV

Silence. She Is Six Years Old. Lynn Emanuel. CrSp

Silence slipping around like death, A. A Winter Twilight. Angelina Weld
  Grimké. NAAAL; PoBA

Silence! "The best" (he said) "are silent now." On the Death of Lord
  Tennyson. Andrew Lang. EPCY

Silence Wager Stories. Susan Howe. FTOS

Silences, Agnes Gergely, *Hungarian.* CEEP, *tr. by* Timea K. Szell

Silences. David Mitchell. PeNZ

Silences. Arthur William Edgar O'Shaughnessy. OBNC

Silences. Edwin John Pratt. NOBC

Silences; a Dream of Governments. Jean Valentine. LCAP-2

Silent, The. Jones Very. NCAP; PAR

Silent, about-to-be-parted-from house. Invocation. Denise Levertov. PoA

Silent alone, where none or saw, or heard. Anne Bradstreet. PBWP *Fr.*
  Contemplations. AmPP; NAAL-3; PoEL-3; SCAP; WPE

Silent and small in your wet sleep. A Winter's Tale. Wyatt Prunty. RA

Silent are the woods, and the dim green boughs are. On Eastnor Knoll.
  John Masefield. CH

Silent at last, beneath the silent ground. On the Death of Echo, A Favourite
  Beagle. Hartley Coleridge. APo

Silent Buddha, The. Larry Gates. HA

Silent conquering army, A. Kirkyard. George Mackay Brown. FaBoTC

Silent cortège, The. (LL) Coming of War, The; Actaeon. Ezra Pound.
  CMoP; PoA; PoE

Silent crowd, The. L. A. Davidson. HA

Silent deer the sound of a waterfall. Lenard D. Moore. HA

Silent friend of many distances, feel. Rilke. EnlH, *tr. by* Stephen Mitchell
  Fr. Sonnets to Orpheus.

Silent girl, The. In the Library. Ed Ochester. Poetsp

Silent Grief. Elizabeth Barrett Browning. *See* Grief.

Silent hammers of decay. (LL) The Hammers. Ralph Hodgson. MoBrPo;
  NOBE; OxBTC

Silent Hour. Rilke, *German.* AWP, *tr. by* Jessie Lemont

Silent hush, the stated hinges, The. Who Will Live in Our Houses When
  We Die? Michael C. Blumenthal. NoAM

Silent I gaze at the cataract. By the Waterfall. Friedrich Adler, *German.*
  TrJP, *tr. by* Jethro Bithell

Silent, I go up alone to the Western Pavilion. Tune: "Joy at Meeting." Li
  Yü, *Chinese.* SuSp, *tr. by* Eugene Eoyang

Silent Icicles, The. Coleridge. *Fr.* Frost at Midnight. CABP; EBEV;
  FHYEP; HAP; NAEL-2; NOBE; NOBRP; NoP-4; OAEL-2; OBNC; PoE;
  PoEL-4; Poetr; Ro; TFi; TOF
  ("All seasons shall be sweet to thee.")

Silent is the house: all are laid asleep. The Visionary. Emily Jane Brontë.
  BiRo; CH; NOBE; NOBVV; OBNC; PBWP; SCGP; SCV

Silent Love. John Clare. Ro

Silent Lover, The. Sir Walter Ralegh. OBEV

Silent Night, The. Mrs. Henry Linden. CBWP-4

Silent Noon. D. G. Rossetti. EnVR; GLoP; GSo; GaP; HAP; NAEL-2;
  OBNC; PoEL-5 *Fr.* The House of Life.
  (19. Silent Noon.) NoP-4

Silent Nymph, with curious eye! Grongar Hill. John Dyer. CABP; NOEC;
  NoP-4; OxAEP-1; PoEL-3

Silent, O Moyle, be the roar of thy water. The Song of Fionnuala. Thomas Moore. BIrV

Silent on the subject of vengeance. Sappho, *Greek.* InMo, *tr. by* Sam Hamill

Silent One, The. Ivor Gurney. NoP-4

Silent Poem. Robert Francis. CRP; LCAP-2

Silent Prophet, The. Norman Jordan. NBV

Silent Room, The. Kingsley Amis. OxBC

Silent room—gray with a dusty blight, A. Among His Books. Edith Nesbit. NOBVV

Silent Singer, The. Anna Wickham. WPN

Silent slain, The. (LL) The Too-Late Born. Archibald MacLeish. CMoP; LiTM; MeMAP; MoAmPo; OxBA; PeFWW

Silent Snake, The. *Unknown.* BoTP
　("Silent snake goes creepy-creep!, The.") CTAV

Silent, thatched hut deep among the trees, A. A Little Landscape. Chu Yün-ming, *Chinese.* CoBLCP, *tr. by* Jonathan Chaves

Silent, the autumn river, fishermen's fires sparse. Spending the Night on the River. T'ang Hsien-tsu, *Chinese.* CoBLCP, *tr. by* Jonathan Chaves

Silent the maid with the spindle spun. The Maid. Nathan Alterman, *Hebrew.* MHP, *tr. by* Ruth Finer Mintz

Silent, the Savoy. Harlem Suite. Raymond R. Patterson. BAP-96

Silent Town, The. Richard Dehmel, *German.* AWP, *tr. by* Jethro Bithell

Silent, upon a peak in Darien. (LL) On First Looking into Chapman's Homer. Keats. APAD; BLPA; CABP; CH; ClHu; EBEvV; EPCY; FHYEP; FaBoBe; FaBoCh; GSo; GTBS-P; HAP; HeIP-4; HoPM; ImPo; InPK-6; NAEL-2; NAWM-2; NIP-4; NOBE; NOBRP; NoP-4; OAEL-2; OBAL; OBEV; OBNC; OPOU; OxAEP-2; PFE; PoE; PoEL-4; PoPoPo; Poetr; Ro; SCGP; SoSe-8; Son; TFi; TRP; UV

Silent wind / settles in / behind the motion of naming, A. Inside Language. Charles Borkhuis. PT

Silent Woman to the University of Oxford, The. Dryden.
　"What Greece, when learning flourished, only knew." NOSC

Silent Wood, A. Elizabeth Siddal. NOBVV

Silent Words, The. Haim Guri, *Hebrew.* MHP, *tr. by* Ruth Finer Mintz

Silent World Is Our Only Homeland, The. Francis Ponge, *French.* AF, *tr. by* Beth Archer

Silent, you say, I'm grown of late. Walter Savage Landor. GBL

Silentium. Osip Emilevich Mandelstam, *Russian.* TCRP, *tr. by* Albert C. Todd

Silently and very fast. (LL) The Fall of Rome. W. H. Auden. InPS-3; OAEL-2; OxBTC; PFE; UnPo

Silently my wife walks on the still wet furze. Berry Picking. Irving Layton. HeIP-4; MoCV; NIP-4; NoP-4

Silently / or LOUD. (LL) Black Art. Imamu Amiri Baraka. NAAAL

Silently / she was quieter than breathing now. Juliet's Garden. Charles Tomlinson. OBGa

Silently, slowly falls the snow from an ashen sky. Snowfall. Giosuè Carducci, *Italian.* AWP, *tr. by* Romilda Rendel

Silently the sleepy dray cart crawls. In the Moldavian Steppe. Aleksandr Vertinsky, *Russian.* TCRP, *tr. by* Daniel Weissbort

Silently / time passes. Hatsui Shizue, *Japanese.* WPJ, *tr. by* Kenneth Rexroth *and* Ikuko Atsumi

Silenus sings. Virgil, *Latin.* OBCVT, *tr. by* Wentworth Dillon.

Silet. Ezra Pound. MoAmPo; Son

Silhouette. Marc Cohen. EOEF

Silhouette. Annette M'Baye, *French.* PBWP, *tr. by* Kathleen Weaver

Silhouettes, they lean against a ringed moon. Paiute Ponies. Jim Barnes. CDW

Silk and Silence. Haim Guri, *Hebrew.* IP, *tr. by* Warren Bargad *and* Stanley F. Chyet

Silk Robe. Jeffrey Skinner. PBCAP

Silk, / Satin. *Unknown.* OxNR

Silk tatters, "Nec Spe Nec Metu." (LL) Canto 3. Ezra Pound. MeMAP; TAP

Silk Threads of Memory. Chế Lan Viên, *Vietnamese.* AVP, *tr. by* Huỳnh Sanh Thông

Silk Weaver's Daughter, The. *Unknown.* AmFP

Silken Snake, The. Robert Herrick. OxBSP; PBRV

Silken Tent, The. Robert Frost. AmPP; ColAP; ImPo; InPK-6; NOBA; NoP-4; Son; TAP; TRP; TwCP; WeW-3

Silken threads by viewless spinners spun, The. Crossed Threads. Helen Hunt Jackson. PAR; SDW

Silkworm, The. Vincent Bourne, *Latin.* APo, *tr. by* William Cowper

Silkworm Song of Torchlit Fields. Kao Ch'i, *Chinese.* CoBLCP, *tr. by* Jonathan Chaves

Silkworms, The. Douglas Stewart. CBAP

Siller Croun, The. Susanna Blamire. ECWP; LW

Silly boy, 'tis ful[l] moon[e] yet, thy night as day shines clearly [*or* clearely]. First Love. Thomas Campion. GBL; OxBoLi

Silly boy, wert you but wise. *Unknown.* NOSC

Silly country maiden went, A. Leda in Stratford, Ont. Anne Wilkinson. MoCV

Silly fool, the silly fool, The. W. H. Auden. OBMV

Silly girl! Yet morning lies. To a Pretty Girl. Israel Zangwill. TrJP

Silly Song. Federico García Lorca, *Spanish.* TTTS, *tr. by* M. D. Herter Norton

Silly Sweetheart. *Unknown.* CH

Silo Treading. Bruce Beaver. BMAP

Silos, The. Nancy Paddock. LoHo

Silos. Paul Zarzyski. PaTW

Silvae. Publius Papinius Statius, *Latin.*
　"And so Death took him. Yet be comforted." OBCVT, *tr. by* Heathcote William Garrod

Silver. A. R. Ammons. NoP-4

Silver. Walter De la Mare. BoTP; CTV; MoBrPo; PoRA; SAGP; TTTS

Silver against blue sky. Thistledown. Andrew Young. AYFP

Silver answer rang,—"Not Death, but Love," The. (LL) Sonnet: "I thought once how Theocritus had sung." Elizabeth Barrett Browning. BWW; EBVV; EnVR; GBL; NOBE; OBEV; OBNC; OxAEP-2; PoPoPo; WPE

Silver as / The needle's eye. George Oppen. NNaP　*Fr.* Some San Francisco Poems.

Silver bark of beech, and sallow. Counting-out Rhyme. Edna St. Vincent Millay. InPK-6; NOxBChV; Poetr; SoSe-8; TTTS

Silver Bells. Hamish Hendry. BoTP

Silver birch is a dainty lady, The. Child's Song in Spring. Edith Nesbit. BoTP; NOxBChV; OxBC

Silver Bowl, The. Joseph Ezobi, *Spanish.*
　Barren Soul, A. TrJP, *tr. by* D. I. Friedmann

Silver Dagger, The. *Unknown.* AmFP

Silver dust, / lifted from the earth. Pear Tree. Hilda Doolittle. BoWoP; CMoP; MoAmPo; NOBA; PoE; UnPo

Silver Eros the ankle bracelet, The. Leonidas of Tarentum, *Greek.* GrAn, *tr. by* Peter Levi

Silver fish swarms into the rapids. Gang-gang-suwole. Tongju Yi, *Korean.* CKP, *tr. by* Jaihiun Kim

Silver Flask, The. John Montague. CIP-2; PNI

Silver-footed girl was bathing, letting the water, The. Rufinus Domesticus. HePo, *tr. by* Barbara Hughes Fowler　*Fr.* Epigrams.

Silver greeting. Tanka. Miyazawa Kenji, *Japanese.* MJT, *tr. by* Makoto Ueda

Silver herring throbbed thick in my seine, The. Sonnet: "Silver herring throbbed thick in my seine, The." Kenneth Leslie. NOBC　*Fr.* By Stubborn Stars.

Silver House, The. John Lea. BoTP

Silver Jubilee. Llewelyn Wyn Griffith. OBWVE

Silver Lake. Brigit Pegeen Kelly. NAmP90

Silver Love, an anklet, A. Leonidas of Tarentum, *Greek.* PGA, *tr. by* Kenneth Rexroth

Silver Lucifer, A. Lunar Baedeker. Mina Loy. VGW

Silver mist more lowly swims, The. John Clare. FHYEP

Silver Penny, The. Walter De la Mare. CMoP; NOxBChV; NTP; OBMV

Silver rain, the shining sun, The. The Harvest. Alice Corbin. BoTP

Silver Road, The. Hamish Hendry. BoTP

Silver-scaled Dragon with jaws flaming red, A. The Toaster. William Jay Smith. NOxBChV; OTCP

Silver Spoon, The. Po Chü-i, *Chinese.* ChiP, *tr. by* Arthur Waley

Silver swan, who living had no note, The. Orlando Gibbons. FaBoCh; HAP; HeIP-4; IMW; InPK-6; NAEL-1; NoP-4; OPOU; OxBSP; PoEL-2; PFE; RB

Silver Tassie, The. Robert Burns. NOBE; OBEV

Silver trumpets rang across the Dome, The. Easter Day. Oscar Wilde. OxAEP-2

Silver-vested monkey trips, A. Cortège. Paul Verlaine, *French.* AWP; OBVE, *tr. by* Arthur Symons

Silver wasp-nest hang like fruit., The. (LL) Escape. Elinor Wylie. MoAmPo

Silver watch you've worn for years, A. Some Slippery Afternoon. Daniela Gioseffi. CrSp

Silver Wedding. Ralph Hodgson. CBLP; OxBTC

Silverthorn Bush. Robert Finch. NOBC

Silvertoed virgin, A. Rufinus, *Greek.* GrAn, *tr. by* Alan Marshfield

Silvery autumn candlelight chills the painted screen. Autumn Evening. Tu Mu, *Chinese.* PLT, *tr. by* A. C. Graham

Silvery Fountain. Mary E. Tucker. CBWP-1

Silvery Tide, The. *Unknown.* AmFP

Silvia. Shakespeare. OBEV *Fr.* The Two Gentlemen of Verona. (Song.) EBEvV

Silvia pretty nymph! within this shade. A Pastoral Dialogue between Two Shepherdesses. Anne Finch, Countess of Winchilsea. ECWP

Silvio's Complaint: A Song, To a Fine Scotch Tune. Aphra Behn. KTR ("In the Blooming Time o'th'year.") RACG

Simchas Torah. Morris Jacob Rosenfeld, *Yiddish.* TrJP

Simcox was one of several rather uninteresting. John Heath-Stubbs. OBCoV

Simhat Torah. Judah Leib Gordon, *Hebrew.* TrJP, *tr. by* Alice Lucas *and* Helena Frank

Similar Cases. Charlotte Perkins Stetson Gilman. PoLF

Simile. N. Scott Momaday. CDW

Simile. Agnes Nemes Nagy, *Hungarian.* PoSu, *tr. by* Frederic Will

Simile, A. Matthew Prior. NOEC

Simile for Her Smile, A. Richard Wilbur. HoPM; InPK-6; SAGP

Similes for Two Political Characters of 1819. Shelley. FaBoPV; RB (To Sidmouth and Castlereagh.) NAEL-2

Similie. Charlotte Dacre. NOBRP

Simmer's a pleasant time. Robert Burns. NOEC; PoEL-4

Simon and Susan. *Unknown.* OxBoLi

Simon and the Tarantula. James Wright. NNaP

Simon Gerty. Elinor Wylie. OBAL

Simon Lee [the Old Huntsman]. Wordsworth. GTBS-P; NAEL-2 ("Has oft'ner left me mourning.") (LL) Ro (Simon Lee, the Old Huntsman, with an Incident in which he was Concerned.) Ro

Simon Legree—A Negro Sermon. Vachel Lindsay. MeMAP; TAP *Fr.* The Booker Washington Trilogy. (Negro Sermon—Simon Legree, A.) MoAmPo

Simon my son, son of my Nuptiall knot. A Lamentation on My Dear Son Simon. John Saffin. SCAP

Simon the Cyrenian Speaks. Countee Cullen. BPo; ChIV-2; HAP; MoAmPo; TTY; TrCP

Simple. Naomi Long Madgett. GT; PoBA

Simple and extraordinary wall. Wall. Gabriela Mistral, *Spanish.* PiM, *tr. by* Maria Giachetti

Simple Autumnal. Louise Bogan. MoAmPo; Son

Simple child, dear brother Jim, A. We Are Seven. Wordsworth. BLPA; NAEL-2; NOBRP; OxBChV; Ro

Simple contact with a wooden spoon and the word, The. Words. Barbara Guest. FTOS

Simple Faith. William Cowper. FHYEP

Simple food, coarse clothing are all you need. The Bamboo Villa. Shen Chou, *Chinese.* CoBLCP, *tr. by* Jonathan Chaves

Simple Gifts. *Unknown.* APAD; APN-2

Simple living was clearly the nub. Limerick. Joyce Johnson. PeLi

Simple lust is all my woe, A. Dennis Brutus. HBAPE

Simple Man, A. Nikolai Ivanovich Glazkov, *Russian.* TCRP, *tr. by* Daniel Weissbort

Simple Matter, A. Gloria Rawlinson. PeNZ

Simple Nature. George John Romanes. PFE

Simple nosegay! was that much to ask?, A. The Troll's Nosegay. Robert Graves. Son

Simple outlines, human shapes, daily acts, plain poses. Irving Feldman. VCAP *Fr.* All of Us Here.

Simple Pastoral, A. George Alexander Stevens. NOEC

Simple Ploughboy, The. *Unknown.* FaBoCh

Simple Poem. Anthony Thwaite. DiPo

Simple Prayer, A. Saint Francis of Assisi. *See* Prayer of St. Francis of Assisi for Peace.

Simple Purification, The. Kabir, *Hindi.* EnIH, *tr. by* Robert Bly

Simple rustic you seemed, A. *Unknown, Chinese.* SuSp, *tr. by* Wu-Chi Liu

Simple Simon. Tom Leonard. FaBoTC

Simple Simon met a pieman. Mother Goose. BoTP; FaBoBe; LB; OTCP; OxNR; ReMoGo

Simple Story, A. Gwen Harwood. FaBoWP; NOBAu

Simple Truth, The. Philip Levine. NoP-4

Simple Verses. José Martí, *Spanish.* TTY, *tr. by* Seymour Resnick

Simplex Munditiis. Ben Jonson. AWP; HoPM; NOBE; OBEV; PBMP *Fr.* Epicoene; or, The Silent Woman. (Clerimont's Song.) NOSC; OAEL-1; PoE; SeCP (Simplicity and Sweet Neglect.) OxAEP-1 ("Still to be neat, still to be dressed.") NoP-4; PoPoPo

Simplicity. Horace, *Latin.* OBVE, *tr. by* Gerard Manley Hopkins; InPK-6; NBLV, *tr. by* William Cowper ("Boy, I detest the Persian pomp.") InPK-6; NBLV, *tr. by* Eugene Field (Fie on Eastern Luxury.) InPK-6, *tr. by* Hartley Coleridge

(Myrtle for Two.) NBLV, *tr. by* George F. Whicher ("Nay, nay, my boy—'tis not for me.") InPK-6, *tr. by* Hartley Coleridge ("Persian flummery.") NBLV, *tr. by* George F. Whicher ("Persian pomps, boy, ever I renounce them.") OBVE, *tr. by* Christopher Smart (Persicos Odi: Pocket Version.) NBLV, *tr. by* Austin Dobson (Preference Declared, The.) InPK-6; NBLV, *tr. by* Eugene Field

Simplicity. Henri Michaux, *Belgian.* NNPT, *tr. by* Richard Ellmann

Simplicity. Valentine. Tom Pickard. NBrP

Simplicity Aims Circularly. Anna Wickham. VoR

Simplicity and Sweet Neglect. Ben Jonson. *See* Simplex Munditiis.

Simplicity sings it and 'sperience doth prove. Simplicity's Song. Robert Wilson. CTC *Fr.* The Three Ladies of London.

Simplicity so graven hurts the sense. So Graven. Josephine Miles. NoAM

Simplicity's Song. Robert Wilson. CTC *Fr.* The Three Ladies of London.

Simplification, A. Richard Wilbur. CMoP

Simplify Me When I'm Dead. Keith Douglas. NoAM; OxBTC

Simply by sailing in a new direction. Landfall in Unknown Seas. Allen Curnow. NoP-4

Simply to breathe. An Emblem of Two Foxes. Barry Spacks. HoPM

Simply to leave him out of the scene forever. (LL) Anonymous Drawing. Donald Justice. CoAP; HeIP-4

Simulated Eden. Tropical Greenhouse. Dan Pagis, *Hebrew.* IP, *tr. by* Warren Bargad *and* Stanley F. Chyet

Simultaneously, as soundlessly. Prime. W. H. Auden. CMoP; PoE *Fr.* Horae Canonicae.

Simultaneously, five thousand miles apart. David Ignatow. TwCP ("Standing straight / sprouting leaves.") (LL) PFE

Sin. "Angelus Silesius." GePo, *tr. by* George C. Schoolfield *Fr.* The Cherubical Wanderer.

Sin: "O that I could a sin once see!" George Herbert. OxBSP

Sin!/ O only fatal Woe. Thomas Traherne. ESCV *Fr.* The Third Century.

Sin Adam's days begun. (LL) Sir Hugh; or, The Jew's Daughter. *Unknown.* CH; ESPB; EnSB; OxBB

Sin and Death. Milton. OBNV, *ll.* 629–889 *Fr.* Book II. FHYEP; NAEL-1; OxAEP-1 *Fr.* Paradise Lost.

Sin and despair have so possess'd my heart. Anne Vaughan Locke. CABP

Sin' auld lang syne. (LL) Auld Lang Syne. Robert Burns. AWP; EBEvV; ImPo; NAEL-2; NOBE; OBEV; OxAEP-2; OxBS; PoLF; SCGP

Sin, Despair, and Lucifer. Phineas Fletcher. *Fr.* The Locusts, or Appolyonists.

Sin (I). George Herbert. *See* Sin (1).

Sin I am free, I counte him not a bene. (LL) Merciless Beauty. Chaucer. BoLoP; EnVB; NAEL-1; SCGP

Sin of Omission, The. Margaret Elizabeth Munson Sangster. BLPA; PoToHe (At Sunset.) PWR

Sin[ne] of self[e]-love possesseth all mine eye [*or* eie]. Sonnet 62. Shakespeare. EBEV; OxAEP-1; PoEL-2 *Fr.* Sonnets.

Sin (1). George Herbert. GeHe; OxAEP-1 (Sin (I).) NoP-4

Sin' they nailed him to the tree. (LL) Ballad of the Goodly Fere. Ezra Pound. CMoP; ChIV-2; ImPo; LiTM; MeMAP; MoAmPo; MoBS; PoRA; TrCP

Sin! wilt thou vanquish me! The Recovery. Thomas Traherne. ESCV *Fr.* The Third Century.

Sinalóa. Earle Birney. MoCV; OxBC; PeLV

Since. W. H. Auden. CBLP; InPS-3

Since 1619. Margaret Abigail Walker. NoP-4

Since 1915/ the walled monastery. Radio Yerevan. Diana Der Hovanessian. LoHo

Since Adam's days begun. (LL) Hugh of Lincoln. *Unknown.* ESPB; EnSB; OxBB

Since all our keys are lost or broken. An Art of Poetry. James Philip McAuley. NOCV

Since all shall be nothing a hundred years hence. (LL) The Careless Gallant. Thomas Jordan. HAP; NOBE; OBEV; OxBoLi; PeLV

Since all that beat about in Nature's range. Constancy to an Ideal Object. Coleridge. NAEL-2; NOBRP

Since all that I can ever do for thee. The Last Wish. "Owen Meredith." OxBSP

Since all the Riches of this World. William Blake. OAEL-2

Since apes are still able to learn. Shih Te, *Chinese.* SuSp, *tr. by* James M. Hargett

Since as in night's deck-watch ye show. Herman Melville. APN-2 *Fr.* John Marr.

Since Bonny-Boots Was Dead. *Unknown.* OxBoLi; PoEL-2

Since brass, nor stone, nor earth, nor boundless sea. Sonnet 65. Shakespeare. AEP; AWP; GTBS-P; HAP; ImPo; InPS-3; NAEL-1; NOBE; NoSic; OxAEP-1; PoRA; RaBo; SCGP; Son; TFi; UnPo *Fr.* Sonnets.

Since Cassius first did whet me against Cæsar. Shakespeare. OxAEP-1 *Fr.* Julius Caesar.

Since Christmas they have lived with us. Balloons. Sylvia Plath. FaBoWP; PoE

Since clarity suggests simplicity. The Counterpart. Elizabeth Jennings. LiTM; TOF

Since coming to Huang-chou. Su Shih. SuSp, *tr. by* Irving Y. Lo *Fr.* Rain at Cold-Food Festival.

Since cruel seas and angry winds parted my love and me. (LL) The Lowlands o' [*or of*] Holland. *Unknown.* AmFP; CH; OxBB

Since death in misery is a release. (LL) A Discourse of Melancholy. Margaret Lucas Cavendish, Duchess of Newcastle. GEA; NOSC

Since earnestly studying the Buddhist doctrine of emptiness. Idle Droning. Po Chü-i, *Chinese.* CoBCP, *tr. by* Burton Watson

Since earth has put you away, O sons of Barmak. Abu Nowas for the Barmacides. *Unknown.* AWP *Fr.* The Thousand and One Nights.

Since every quill is silent to relate. A Monumental Memorial of Marine Mercy. Richard Steere. SCAP

Since feeling is first. E. E. Cummings. MoAmPo; NoP-4

Since first break of dawn the fiend. The Tempter Disarmed. Milton. NOSC *Fr.* Book IX. FHYEP; NAEL-1; NAWM-1; OAEL-1 *Fr.* Paradise Lost.

Since first I saw your face I resolved to honor and reknown. *Unknown.* OBEV; OxBSP

Since first my little one lay on my breast. Augusta Davies Webster. VWP

Since first to exhibit his Plays he began. Aristophanes. OBCVT, *tr. by* Rogers, Benjamin Bickley *Fr.* The Acharnians.

Since first you knew my am'rous smart. Epigram. Robert, Earl Nugent Nugent. NOEC

Since fortune's wrath envieth the wealth. Henry Howard, Earl of Surrey. SiPS

Since foul I fare and painting is my shame. (LL) To Giovanni da Pistoia When the Author Was Painting the Vault of the Sistine Chapel, 1509. Michelangelo Buonarroti, *Italian.* NNPT, *tr. by* John Addington Symonds

Since gracious Heven, you have bestow'd on me. A Virgin Life. Jane Barker. KTR

Since he came back. Private Jack Smith, U. S. M. C. Bryan Alec Floyd. CDa

Since he kissed them and put them /there. there. (LL) Little Boy Blue. Eugene Field. CTV; ChAP; FPC; OBAL; OBCA; PoLF; SoSe-8

Since heaven helpes not, deepest hell weele try. Lucan. OBCVT, *tr. by* John Marston *Fr.* The Wonder of Women, or The Tragedie of Sophonisba.

Since I am coming [*or* comming] to that holy room[e]. Hymn[e] to God My God, In My Sickness[e]. Donne. EBEV; ESCV; HeIP-4; ImPo; InPS-3; MeLP; NAEL-1; NOSC; OAEL-1; OxAEP-1; PoE; PoEL-2; SeCP; SoSe-8; TFi; TOF

Since I am convinced. Saigyo, *Japanese.* AWP, *tr. by* Arthur Waley

Since I believe in God the Father Almighty. Johannes Milton, Senex. Robert Bridges. CMoP; PeECV; PoEL-5

Since I do trust Jehova still, *par. by* Sir Philip Sidney. Psalm 11. Bible, *O.T.* OBVE *Fr.* Psalms.

Since I don't know my mother. Akiko Baba, *Japanese.* WPJ, *tr. by* Kenneth Rexroth *and* Ikuko Atsumi

Since I don't wake with her. A Thin, Black Band. Sandor Csoori, *Hungarian.* VCWP, *tr. by* Len Roberts *and* Tibor Tengerdi

Since I emerged that day from the labyrinth. The Labyrinth. Edwin Muir. CMoP; FaBoTC; MoBrPo

Since I entered the inner rooms. Written on a Leaf. *Unknown, Chinese.* BoWoP, *tr. by* Geoffrey Waters

Since I got my cat Five White. An Offering for the Cat. Mei Yao Ch'en, *Chinese.* CoBCP; PC, *tr. by* Burton Watson

Since I have lacked the comfort of that light. Sonnet 87. Edmund Spenser. *Fr.* Amoretti. AAS

Since I have seen a bird one day. The Truth. W. H. Davies. FaBoTw

Since I have set my lips to your full cup, my sweet. More Strong Than Time. Victor Hugo, *French.* AWP, *tr. by* Andrew Lang

Since I heard. Mitsune. AWP, *tr. by* Arthur Waley *Fr.* Kokin Shu.

Since I in storms used most to be. The Wreath. Henry Vaughan. FMP

Since I lately came to live. Forest. Angus Martin. FaBoTC

Since I lay ill, how long has passed? Po Chü-i, *Chinese.* ChiP, *tr. by* Arthur Waley

Since I left her. Mibu no Tadami, *Japanese.* OHPJ, *tr. by* Kenneth Rexroth

Since I left you, mine eye is in my mind. Sonnet 113. Shakespeare. SCGP *Fr.* Sonnets.

Since I lived a stranger in the City of Hsün-yang. Rain. Po Chü-i, *Chinese.* BLT; ChiP, *tr. by* Arthur Waley

Since I must love your north. To My Mountain. Kathleen Jessie Raine. OxBS

Since I must needs into thy school[e] return[e]. A Lady's Prayer to Cupid. Thomas Carew, *after* Giovanni Battista Guarini. CaPo; OBVE

Since I noo mwore do zee your feäce. The Wife A-Lost. William Barnes. BoLoP; EBVV; EnLoPo; EnVR; GLoP; HAP; OBEV; OxBM; SCGP

Since I parted from you, immortal bird. For Several Days I Have Not Visited the Garden Pavilion—A Poem Sent to My Pet Crane. Wang Chiu-ssu, *Chinese.* CoBLCP, *tr. by* Jonathan Chaves

Since I was in Syracuse is a month ago. Quarries in Syracuse. Louis Golding. TrJP

Since I was thrown inside. Nazim Hikmet, *Turkish.* AF, *tr. by* Randy Blasing *and* Mutlu Konuk

Since I work with those. Tanka. Kondō Yoshimi, *Japanese.* MJT, *tr. by* Makoto Ueda

Since I'm a girl. *Unknown, Spanish.* BoWoP, *tr. by* Willis Barnstone

Since in a land not barren still. Love and Discipline. Henry Vaughan. GeHe

Since in religion all men disagree. To Caelia. *Unknown.* FaBoEE

Since ista possum is a goner! (LL) Carmen Possum. *Unknown.* BLPA; NBLV

Since I've been in this colony I've written many a song. The Flash Colonial Barman. William W. Coxon. NOBAu

Since I've felt this pain. Ono no Komachi, *Japanese.* WPOW, *tr. by* Rob Swigart

Since I've lost you. (LL) I've lost my rifle and bayonet. *Unknown.* NSI; PoWW

Since last September I've been trying to describe. Edward Lear in February. Christopher Middleton. TwCP

Since last the tutelary hearth. Christmas Family Reunion. Peter De Vries. NBLV; NOBL

Since laws were made for ev'ry degree. Air. John Gay. NOEC *Fr.* The Beggar's Opera. OAEL-1

Since life is nothing in your philosophy. Nothing. Julia De Burgos. BoWoP, *tr. by* Aliki *and* Willis Barnstone

Since, Lord, to thee / A narrow way and little gate. Holy Baptism (2). George Herbert. ChIV-2; PoEL-2

Since Love is shivering. Sister Juana Inés de la Cruz. WPoS, *tr. by* Alan S. Trueblood *Fr.* The First Villancico, Written for the Nativity of Our Lord, Puebla, 1689.

Since love is such that, as ye wot. Sir Thomas Wyatt. SiPS

Since Love will needs that I shall love. Sir Thomas Wyatt. SiPS

Since / Malcolm died / That old aardvark. Aardvark. Julia Fields. MBE

Since man has been articulate. Every Thing. Harold Monro. MoBrPo

Since man went out from the fields of paradise. On the Killing at Lindisfarne. Alcuin, *Latin.* MLL, *tr. by* Helen Waddell

Since man with that inconstancy was born. To Alexis in Answer to His Poem Against Fruition. Aphra Behn. LW

Since Man's a little world, to make it great. An Epigram on Woman. Philip Ayres. FaBoEE

Since Mars and she played even and odd. (LL) Love. George Peele. CBLP; NOBE

Since men grow diffident at last. Youth Sings a Song of Rosebuds. Countee Cullen. PoLF

"Since mountains sink to vales, and valleys die." The Bathos. Richard Porson. FaBoEE

Since my first infant term I remember. Tadpoles. Barrie Wade. AYFP

Since my hair was plaited and we became man and wife. To His Wife. Su Wu, *Chinese.* ChiP, *tr. by* Arthur Waley

Since my life's been spent. Côte d'Azur. Katherine Hoskins. NYBP

Since my Love died for me. *Unknown. See* Helen of Kirconnell.

Since my overdraft threatens to be. Limerick. S. Tonkin. PeLi

Since my smeared blood has registered *beep beep beep.* Spike Logic. James McManus. BAP-94

Since my Vivian left me. The Barrel Organ. Daniel Mark Epstein. DiPo *Fr.* Homage to Mallarmé.

Since my wife was born. Notes for the Legend of Salad Woman. Michael Ondaatje. NoAM

Since Naturally Black is Naturally Beautiful. Naturally. Audre Lorde. BlSi; ISC

Since Nature's works be good, and death doth serve, *speech of Musidorus.* Why Fear to Die? Sir Philip Sidney. SiPS *Fr.* Arcadia.

Since no one has ever told her. The Sea and the Butterfly. Kirim Kim, *Korean.* CKP, *tr. by* Jaihiun Kim

Since nought avails, let me arise and leave. Love's Last Resource. Sadi. AWP, *tr. by* L. Cranmer-Byng *Fr.* The Gulistan.

Since now I dare not ask. The Sharp Ridge. Robert Graves. FaBoEE

Since now I have a mind to sing. William of Aquitaine, *Provençal*. MLL, *tr. by* Helen Waddell

Since now in every public place. The Sea Horse. Robert Graves. FaBoMo

Since now, once more beside this mound. Sing Again Together. William Barnes. SCGP

Since, O good Heavens! you have bestow'd on me. Jane Barker. *See* A Virgin Life.

Since observed by Yours faithfully, God. (LL) A Reply. *Unknown*. NBLV; NOBL; PeLi

Since of no creature living the last breath. Edna St. Vincent Millay. HeIP-4; VGW

Since one anthologist put in his book. Anthologistics. Arthur Guiterman. NBLV

Since our Country, our God—Oh, my Sire! Jephtha's Daughter. Byron. ChIV-1

Since our relations / are like the crumbling. Sei Shonagon, *Japanese*. WPJ, *tr. by* Kenneth Rexroth *and* Ikuko Atsumi

Since Potiphar made you his overseer. Israel II. Charles Reznikoff. ChIV-1

Since puberty. Tanka. Sasaki Yukitsuna, *Japanese*. MJT, *tr. by* Makoto Ueda

Since Reverend Doctors now declare. The Respectable Burgher. Thomas Hardy. CMoP; ChIV-2; NoAM

Since she gives so little pay. Steinmar, *German*. GePo, *tr. by* J. W. Thomas

Since she must go, and I must mourn, come night. His Parting from Her. Donne. EBEV *Fr.* Elegies.

Since she was lovelier than any of you. (LL) Blue Girls. John Crowe Ransom. CMoP; ColAP; FuPo; GBL; MeMAP; MoAmPo; NoAM; NoP-4; RB; TAP; VGW; WeW-3

Since she whom I loved [*or* lov'd] hath paid [*or* payd] her last debt. Since she whome I lovd, hath payd her last debt. Donne. FMP; FSCP; NAEL-1; NOSC; Son *Fr.* Holy Sonnets. ESCV

("Least the World, fleshe, yea Devill putt thee out.") (LL) PBRV

Since she's all winter, with a heart of snow. Sonnet For Helen. Pierre de Ronsard, *French*. LoP, *tr. by* Alistair Elliot

Since Shylock's book has walk'd the circles here. To a Noisy Politician. Philip Freneau. TAP

Since so mine eyes are subject to your sight. Sir Philip Sidney. *Fr.* Arcadia.

Since so ye please to hear me plain. Sir Thomas Wyatt. SiPS

Since Sturdee cleared the Southern Seas. Off Coronel. Austin Threlfall Nankivell. NSI

Since that evening. Tanka. Nakajō Fumiko, *Japanese*. MJT, *tr. by* Makoto Ueda

Since that night / I cannot know myself. Lady Izumi, *Japanese*. BoWoP, *tr. by* Willis Barnstone

Since that our Deares wee cannot have. The 3 Sad Sheppards Sings This in Parts. Lady Jane Cavendish. KTR *Fr.* A Pastorall.

Since that this thing we call the world. An Epicurean Ode. John Hall. CBLP; MeLP; NOSC

Since the Conquest none of us. The Conquest. Oliver St. John Gogarty. OBMV

Since the good Bishop left his name. To Mr. Wren, My Valentine Six Year Old. Jane Holt. ECWP

Since the images you demand. Revolution. Junko Nishi, *Japanese*. WPJ, *tr. by* Kenneth Rexroth *and* Ikuko Atsumi

Since the narcissus bud. Rachel Blau DuPlessis. DeD *Fr.* Eurydice.

Since the narcissus bud. *Unknown*. DeD *Fr.* Kiowa "49" Songs.

Since the night is dark. *Unknown, Spanish*. BoWoP, *tr. by* Willis Barnstone

Since "the pillow knows all." Lady Ise, *Japanese*. WPJ, *tr. by* Kenneth Rexroth *and* Ikuko Atsumi

Since the / Spirit's omnipresent, there's a difference. John Cage. APSN *Fr.* Diary: How to Improve the World (You Will Only Make Matters Worse).

Since the storm two nights ago. The Recognition. Denise Levertov. VGW

Since the wise men have not spoken, I speak that am only a fool. The Fool. Padraic Pearse. TIRV

Since the world, the base world has no pleasure for me. (LL) Stanzas: "In this vain, busy world, where the good and the gay." Mary Robinson. ECWP; WoRP

Since their dream has / come true. (LL) Passing. Langston Hughes. APSN; SAmP

Since Then. D. J. Enright. OBSV

Since then I was. The Significance of a Water Animal. Ray A. Young Bear. HATNAP

Since then, inside me, summer has blazed up. Tố Hū'u, *Vietnamese*. AVP, *tr. by* Huỳnh Sanh Thông

Since ther's no helpe, Come let us kisse and part. The Parting. Michael Drayton. AAS; AEP; AWP; BoLoP; CABP; ClHu; EnLoPo; GBL;

GLoP; GSo; GTBS-P; HAP; HeIP-4; ImPo; InPS-3; LoP; NAEL-1; NOBE; NOSC; OAEL-1; OBEV; OPOU; PBMP; PFE; PoEL-2; PoPoPo; SAGP; SCGP; SCV; SoSe-8; Son; TFi *Fr.* Idea.

(Love's Farewell.) GTBS-P

(Parting, The.) GLoP; OBEV; SCV

("Since ther's no helpe, Come let us kisse and part.") GEA

Since those bards. Aỹ: A Gift of Elephants. Mutamociyar, *Tamil*. PLW, *tr. by* A. K. Ramanujan

Since Those We Love and Those We Hate. William Ernest Henley. OBMV

Since thou art gone, my friend, I seek in vain for peace. On Parting with Moses ibn Ezra. Judah Halevi, *Hebrew*. TrJP, *tr. by* Solomon Solis-Cohen

Since thou hast viewed [*or* view'd] some Gorgon, and art grown. The Double Rock. Henry, Bishop of Chichester King. CBLP; NOSC; SeCP

Since thou wou'dst [*or* wouldst] needs, bewicht [*or* bewitched] with some ill charms. To One Married to an Old Man. Edmund Waller. FaBoEE; OxBSP; SeCP

Since Thursday last the bare living-room. Bicycle. David Malouf. BMAP

Since thy third curing of the French infection. Against an Old Lecher. Sir John Harington. FaBoEE

Since time began, when people leave. The Dawn of a New Humankind. Du Tử' Lê, *Vietnamese*. AVP, *tr. by* Huỳnh Sanh Thông

Since 'tis my doom, Love's undershrieve. To Julia to Expedite Her Promise. John Cleveland. CBLP

Since to obtaine thee, nothing me will sted. His Remedie for Love. Michael Drayton. AAS *Fr.* Idea.

Since tonight the wind is high. The Viking Terror. *Unknown, Old Irish*. IIP, *tr. by* Frank O'Connor

Since we approached the road between us. No Road. Philip Larkin. CBLP; EBEV; MoBrPo; OxAEP-2

Since we can die but once, what matters it. Sentiment. Thomas Chatterton. NOEC

Since we had changed. Message. Allen Ginsberg. CoAmPo; NeAP; VGW

Since we halved the hairpin. Tune: "Slow Song of Chu Ying-t'ai" Late Spring. Hsin Ch'i-chi, *Chinese*. SuSp, *tr. by* Irving Y. Lo

Since we parted, spring half over, Tune: "Pure Serene Music." Li Yü, *Chinese*. CoBCP, *tr. by* Burton Watson

Since we through war awhile must part. At Parting. Anne Ridler. APAD; LW

Since we were first married. On the Death of His Wife. Mei Yao Ch'en, *Chinese*. OHPC, *tr. by* Kenneth Rexroth; OxBM

Since we'd always sky about. Can. Lit. Earle Birney. NOBC

Since we're not young, weeks have to do time. Adrienne Rich. CPO *Fr.* Twenty-one Love Poems.

Since when have you existed, green bamboos. Bamboos of Vietnam. Nguyễn Duy Nhuệ, *Vietnamese*. AVP, *tr. by* Huỳnh Sanh Thông

Since worms and dust must be your fate. Ausonius, *Latin*. MLL, *tr. by* Helen Waddell

Since ye delight to know. Sir Thomas Wyatt. SiPS

Since you are dead, and I am gone. White Valentine. Winifred Welles. WPN

Since you are dead, Timon, tell me which. Callimachus, *Greek*. GrAn, *tr. by* Peter Jay

Since you ask, most days I cannot remember. Wanting to Die. Anne Sexton. CoAmPo; ColAP; MoP; NoAM; TAP; TRP; VCAP

Since you dare Brave me, with a Rivals Name. To My Rival. "Ephelia." LW

Since you have been. (LL) Birthday Poem for Thomas Hardy. C. Day Lewis. EBEvV; EPCY

Since you have turned unkind. To a Lady Friend. W. H. Davies. MoBrPo

Since you left, my lover. Chang Chiu-ling, *Chinese*. OHMPC, *tr. by* Kenneth Rexroth

Since you lie buried in the hill. To Senna Hoy. Else Lasker-Schüler, *German*. IMW, *tr. by* Glauco Cambon

Since you walked out on me. Lady of Miracles. Nina Cassian, *Romanian*. WPOW, *tr. by* Laura Schiff

Since you went away. In Imitation of Hsü Kan. Liu Chün, *Chinese*. SuSp, *tr. by* Jan W. Walls

Since you weds mean that I shall sing. Sir Thomas Wyatt. SiPS

Since you wrote a poem. What Color Is Lonely. Carolyn M. Rodgers. BPo

Since your marriage you have lost the look. Martial, *Greek*. PGA, *tr. by* Kenneth Rexroth

Since you're asking so many questions I'll be off to Tuia and seek ship. Song by a Woman Accused of Adultery. Kie Tapu, *Maori*. PeNZ, *tr. by* Margaret Orbell

Sincere and most Peruvian mechanics. Telluric and Magnetic. César Vallejo, *Spanish*. PFTM, *tr. by* Clayton Eshleman

Sincere Flattery of R. B. James Kenneth Stephen. NOBL

Sincere Flattery of W. W. (Americanus.) James Kenneth Stephen. NOBL

Sincere Man, The. Alfred Grant Walton. PoToHe

Sincerity. Agnes Nemes Nagy, *Hungarian.* VCWP, *tr. by* Hugh Maxton

Sindhi Woman. Jon Stallworthy. OxBC

Sine qua non of bed wetting. Air and Angels. Charles North. FTOS

Sinfonia Domestica. Jean Starr Untermeyer. MoAmPo

Sinful to Flirt. *Unknown.* AmFP

Sing!/ Great dark oak. Lines to the Black Oak. Oliver La Grone. NBV

Sing a last song. The Locket. John Montague. BiHa; PBCIP

Sing a song of cobbler! Jeremy Hobbler. *Unknown.* BoTP

Sing a song of critics. Valentine. Ernest Hemingway. OBAL

Sing a song of hollow logs. Song of Summer Days. James William Foley. BoTP

Sing a song of mincemeat. Mincemeat. Elizabeth Gould. BoTP

Sing a Song of People. Lois Lenski. NOxBChV; OTCP

Sing a song of Scissor-men. The Scissor-Man. Madeleine Nightingale. BoTP

Sing a song of sixpence. Mother Goose. FaBoBe; OxNR

("And popped it on again.") (LL) LB

Sing a Song of Sixpence. *Unknown.* CBNP; ReMoGo

(Song of Sixpence.) OxBoLi

Sing a Song of Subways. Eve Merriam. KaS

Sing a song of washing-up. The Washing-Up Song. Elizabeth Gould. BoTP

Sing Again Together. William Barnes. SCGP

Sing agreeably, agreeably, agreeably of love. (LL) Carry her over the water. W. H. Auden. FaBoTw; RB

Sing, birds, in every furrow! (LL) Matin Song. Thomas Heywood. BoTP; CH; GBL; GLoP; GTBS-P; ITG; OBEV

Sing, Brothers, Sing! William Robert Rodgers. MoBrPo

Sing cuccu [*or* cuckoo]! Sing cuccu [*or* cuckoo] nu [*or* now]! (LL) Sumer is icumen in. *Unknown.* AWP; EBEV; EBEvV; HAP; HeIP-4; ImPo; InPK-6; InPS-3; MiEL; NBLV; NOBE; OAEL-1; OBEV; OPOU; PBMP; PeLV; TFi; UV

Sing dum de whickerty, dum de way. (LL) The Factory Girl's Come-All-Ye. *Unknown.* AmFP; OBAL

Sing first the heroe in his goodly ship. *Unknown.* PBCV *Fr.* A Pindarique Ode on the Arrival of His Excellency.

Sing goddamm, sing goddamm, DAMM. (LL) Ancient Music. Ezra Pound. BXAP; HeIP-4; LiTM; NBLV; OBAL; OBCoV; OxBA; PBMP; PeLV; UV

Sing, hey! Sing, hey! / For Christmas Day. *Unknown.* PChr

Sing his praises that doth keep. Hymn to Pan. John Fletcher. NOBE; OBEV *Fr.* The Faithful Shepherdess.

Sing ho! for a brave and a gallant ship. Ten Thousand Miles Away. *Unknown.* AS

Sing holly, go whistle and ivy! (LL) Sing Ivy. *Unknown.* BoTP; OxNR

Sing I for a brave and gallant barque, and a stiff and a rattling breeze. Ten Thousand Miles Away. *Unknown.* AS

Sing in me, Muse, and through me tell the story. Odyssey. Homer, *Greek.* NAWM-1, *tr. by* Robert Fitzgerald

Sing Ivy. *Unknown.* BoTP; OxNR

Sing jigmijole, the pudding bowl. Kissing of My Dame. *Unknown.* OxNR

Sing little box. The Admirers of the Little Box. Vasco [*or* Vasko] Popa, *Serbo-Croatian.* HSix, *tr. by* Charles Simic

Sing Loud. Li Ho, *Chinese.* PLT, *tr. by* A. C. Graham

Sing loudly this my Lady-day. (LL) On a Birthday. John Millington Synge. GBL; OBMV

Sing lullaby [*or* lullabie] as women do[e]. The Lullaby [*or* Lullabie] of a Lover. George Gascoigne. AAS; EBEV; HAP; NAEL-1; NoSic; OBEV; PoEL-1; SCGP

Sing lullaby, mine only joy! (LL) Lullaby: "Upon my lap my sovereign sits." Richard Verstegan. CH; OBEV; SCGP

Sing, magnarello, merrily. The Leaf-picking. Frédéric Mistral, *French.* AWP, *tr. by* Harriet Waters Preston

Sing Me a New Song. John Henrik Clarke. PoBA

Sing me a song of a lad that is gone. Robert Louis Stevenson. CABP; NOBE; NTP

Sing me a sweet, low song of night. A Song. Hildegarde Hawthorne. FaBoBe

"Sing me something" is what the other keeps saying. Rapture. Susan Mitchell. BAP-93

Sing me the men ere this. He Would Have His Lady Sing. Digby Mackworth Dolben. EBEV

Sing me "Woe," you glades and Dorian water. Moschus. *See* Lament for Bion.

Sing, Muse, the Force, and all-informing Fire. *Unknown.* OBCVT, *tr. by* William Congreve *Fr.* Hymn to Aphrodite: Invocation.

Sing, Muse, the son of Maia and of Jove. *Unknown.* *See* Hymn to Mercury.

"Sing, my golden cock, I'll give thee grain!" Neidhart von Reuental, *German.* GePo, *tr. by* J. W. Thomas

Sing, my soul, his wondrous love. *Unknown.* AH

Sing on in the soul alway. (LL) The Human Touch. Spencer Michael Free. BLPA; FaBoBe; PoToHe

Sing on: somewhere, at some new moon. I Sing of Change. Niyi Osundare. PBMAP

Sing out, my soul, thy songs of joy. Songs of Joy. W. H. Davies. MoBrPo

Sing out pent soul[e]s, sing cheerfully! The Vintage to the Dungeon. Richard Lovelace. BeJo; CaPo

Sing, sing, / What shall I sing? Mother Goose. LB; ReMoGo

("Cat's run away / With the pudding too!, The.") (LL) OxNR

Sing-Song. Christina Rossetti.

Caterpillar, The. AYFP; CTAV; CTV; ChAP

("To live again as butterfly.") (LL) BoTP; FaBoVe; OxBChV

City Mouse and the Garden Mouse, The. BoTP; FaBoBe; NTCP

Ferry Me across the Water. NTP; OxBChV; TLR

(Ferryman, The.) BoTP

Flint. OxBChV

(Precious Stones.) ChAP

"Horses of the sea, The." NTCP

Hurt No Living Thing. OTCP

Let's Be Merry. TLR

Mix a Pancake. NTCP

(Pancake, The.) BoTP

"O sailor, come ashore." BoTP

Sing the names of the women sing. Crazy Horse Names His Daughter. Lucille Clifton. PaTW

Sing to Apollo, God of Day. Song of Apollo. John Lyly. NoSic *Fr.* Midas.

Sing to Ashtaroth and Bel. To Ashtaroth and Bel. Saul Tchernichowsky, *Hebrew.* TrJP, *tr. by* L. V. Snowman

Sing to the Lord, all creatures! Bible, *O.T. See* Psalm 100.

Sing to the Lord, for what can better be, *par. by* Mary Herbert. Psalm 147. Bible, *O.T.* NOCV *Fr.* Psalms.

Sing to the Lord Most High. Timothy Dwight. AH

Sing unto the Lord with Thanksgiving, *sel., vv. 7–9, 12, of sl. diff. vers.* Bible, *O.T. See* Psalm 147.

Sing unto the Lord with thanksgiving! / Praise ye the Lord. Bible, *O.T. See* Psalm 147.

Sing we and chant it. Thomas Morley. EBEV; NoSic

Sing we for love and idleness. An Immorality. Ezra Pound. CMoP; ImPo; LiTM; MoAmPo; NOBA; OBAL

Sing we now merily. Thomas Ravenscroft. PBRV

Sing what God doth, and do what men may sing. (LL) To the Thrice-Sacred Queen Elizabeth. Mary Herbert. NALW; NoP-4

Sing while you may, O bird upon the tree! Dark Wings. James Stephens. PoA

Sing with Your Body. Janice Mirikitani. MDDM; WPOW

Singe we alle and say we thus. My Purse. *Unknown.* EBEV

Singee a songee sick a pence. Song. *Unknown.* BXAP

Singer, The. Lizette Woodworth Reese. SDW

Singer, The. Diane Wakoski. HeIP-4

Singer, The. Anna Wickham. MoBrPo

Singer Asleep, A (Algernon Charles Swinburne). Thomas Hardy.
"Passionate pages of his earlier years, The." EPCY

Singer of sweet Colonus, and its child. (LL) To a Friend. Matthew Arnold. NAEL-2; Son

Singers, The. George Bruce. OxBS

Singers are gone from the Cornmarket-place, The. After the Fair. Thomas Hardy. CMoP; HAP *Fr.* At Casterbridge Fair.

Singers have hushed their notes of shrill song, The. The Five-string. Po Chü-i, *Chinese.* ChiP, *tr. by* Arthur Waley

Singer's House, The. Seamus Heaney. EBEV; IIP

Singers of serenades, The. Mandoline. Paul Verlaine, *French.* AWP; OBMV, *tr. by* Arthur Symons

Singers to Come. Alice Thompson Meynell. WPE

Singin': "Come, shove in your heids and growl!" (LL) With the Herring Fishers. "Hugh MacDiarmid." CABP; LiTM

Singing & Doubling Together. A. R. Ammons. NAAL-2; NoAM

Singing Bones, The. Randolph Stow. BMAP; CBAP

Singing Cat, The. Stevie Smith. OxBTC; PC

Singing, dancing—handsome actors entertain. On the Cold Food Festival, Entertaining at the Southern Estate—the Guests Were Li Chiu-ho, Ma Nan-yeh, Wei Tung-kao, Li Hu-ch'uan, Huang K'ung-ts'un, Li Lung-t'ang, and Hu Hu-shan. Li K'ai-hsien, *Chinese.* CoBLCP, *tr. by* Jonathan Chaves

Singing Death. Stan Rice. FYAP; IMW

Singing down the Breadfruit. Pauline Stewart. NOxBChV

Singing Flower, The. "Shu Ting," *Chinese.* VCWP, *tr. by* Carolyn Kizer

Singing Glory to God. (LL) Ballad of an Old Woman. Frank A. Collymore. NOxBChV

Singing Hallelujia. Fenton Johnson. NAAAL

Singing Image of Fire. Kukai, *Japanese.* EnlH, *tr. by* Stephen Mitchell

Singing in the Streets. Leonard Clark. NOxBChV

Singing is sweet; but be sure of this. James Thomson. NOBVV *Fr.* Art.

Singing Lesson, The. David Wagoner. NoAM

Singing my days. Passage to India. Walt Whitman. APN-1; AmPP; NAAL-1; NCAP; PoEL-5

Singing nature when I need sing my nature nevermore. (LL) Singing & Doubling Together. A. R. Ammons. NAAL-2; NoAM

Singing of Niagara, and the Huron squaws. The Possibility of New Poetry. Robert Bly. CoAmPo

Singing of Thoughts. Juan Chi, *Chinese.* CoBCP, *tr. by* Burton Watson

"In North Ward they do many strange dances." CoBCP, *tr. by* Burton Watson

"Long ago, at fourteen or fifteen." CoBCP, *tr. by* Burton Watson

"This summer's burning heat." CoBCP, *tr. by* Burton Watson

"Tung-ling melons—men say that long ago." CoBCP, *tr. by* Burton Watson

"Years ago, when I was young." CoBCP, *tr. by* Burton Watson

Singing School. Seamus Heaney. InPS-3

Constable Calls, A. FaBoPV; NOIV

Singing through the forests. Rhyme of the Rail[s]. John Godfrey Saxe. PoLF

Singing, today I married my white girl. Epithalamion. Dannie Abse. OBWVE

Singing under ice. (LL) The Uninvited. Dorothy Livesay. NoP-4

Singing we ride over the field. The Battle on the Blackbird's Field. Vasco [or Vasko] Popa. PoSu, *tr. by* Anne Pennington *Fr.* The Blackbird's Field.

Single clenched fist lifted and ready, The. Choose. Carl Sandburg. SpI

Single creature leads a partial life, The. Cats and Dog. W. H. Auden. APo *Fr.* Ten Songs.

Single Dram of Heaven!, A. (LL) I took one Draught of Life. Emily Dickinson. APN-2; NTP

Single Eye All Light, no Darkness, A. Laurence Clarkson.

"Behold, the King of glory now is come." PBRV

Single-eyed to child and sunbeam. Blue-eyed Mary. Mary Eleanor Wilkins Freeman. OBCA

Single fact is matter, The. Chronic Meanings. Bob Perelman. PmAP

Single flow'r he sent me, since we met, A. One Perfect Rose. Dorothy Parker. APAD; LoP; NALW; NBLV; NIP-4; NoP-4; OBAL; OBCoV; Poetr

Single Girl, The. *Unknown. See* I Wish I Were [or Was] Single Again.

Single illness has lasted three months, A. Written While Sick. Wen Cheng-ming, *Chinese.* CoBLCP, *tr. by* Jonathan Chaves

Single Life Most Secure. Robert Herrick. PFE

Single man stands like a bird-watcher, A. The Mouth of the Hudson. Robert Lowell. AiP; VCAP

Single pavilion looms dark against clouds and forest, A. Deepening-Green Pavilion. Chu Yi-tsun, *Chinese.* SuSp, *tr. by* Chang Yin-nan *and* Lewis C. Walmsley

Single pearl of dew suspended clear and chill, A. Tune: "Lotus-leaf Cup." Wen T'ing-yün, *Chinese.* SuSp, *tr. by* William R. Schultz

Single petal swirling diminishes the spring, A. Tu Fu. SuSp, *tr. by* Irving Y. Lo *Fr.* Meandering River.

Single post, a point of rusting, A. Marina Ivanovna Tsvetayeva. BrRo *Fr.* Poem of the End.

Single rock from Cinnabar Hill, A. On a Painting of Mushrooms. Yün Shou-p'ing, *Chinese.* CoBLCP, *tr. by* Jonathan Chaves

Single rock, vast, A. Rock among Bamboo. Hsü Wei. *Fr.* A Kite. CoBLCP, *tr. by* Jonathan Chaves

Single Screw of Flesh, A. Emily Dickinson. APN-2; PAR

Single sleeper lying here, The. Epitaph for the Poet. George Barker. OxBSP

Single slender crescent brow before her dressing mirror, A. Tune: "Echoing Heaven's Everlastingness." Li Ching, *Chinese.* SuSp, *tr. by* Daniel Bryant

Single Sonnet. Louise Bogan. Son

Single soul that lacks a sweet crystalline cry, A. (LL) Paudeen. W. B. Yeats. HAP; OxBSP; PoEL-5

Single spot slides the trumpet's flare then stops, A. Lost Fugue for Chet. Lynda Hull. PuP-17; SeSe

Single stench two winds have parted, A. Nicarchus of Alexandria, *Greek.* InMo, *tr. by* Sam Hamill

Single tulip!, A. Michael McClintock. HA

Single wild goose climbs into the void, A. (LL) Clear After Rain. Tu Fu, *Chinese.* BLT; OHPC, *tr. by* Kenneth Rexroth

Single Woman, The. Frances Darwin Cornford. WPN

Sings for us two / Especially. (LL) The Blackbird. Humbert Wolfe. BoTP; NOxBChV

Sings Harry. Denis Glover.

Once the Days. PeNZ

Song: "If everywhere in the street." PeNZ

Song: "These songs will not stand." PeNZ

Song: "When I am old." PeNZ

Thistledown. PeNZ

Singular Indeed. David McCord. OBCA

Singular Metamorphosis, A. Howard Nemerov. CoAmPo

Singularly and in pairs the decade has been ripped by bullets. Lines. Herbert Martin. PoBA

Sinister spacecraft came down on the field, A. Supposing. Eric Finney. SpW

Sinking into sound grief. Rebus Tact. Ray DiPalma. PmAP

Sinking of the Mendi, The. S. E. K. Mqhayi, *Xhosa.* PeSA, *tr. by* C. M. Mcanyangwa *and* Jack Cope

Sinking of the Titanic, The. Hans Magnus Enzensberger.

Reprieve, The. PoSu

Sixteenth Canto. PoSu

Thirty-third Canto. PoSu

Twenty-ninth Canto. PoSu

Sinking of the *Titanic.* *Unknown. See* Shine and the Titanic.

Sinking Rising. Dahlia Ravikovitch, *Hebrew.* IP, *tr. by* Warren Bargad *and* Stanley F. Chyet

Sinks the sun below the desert. Cleopatra Dying. Thomas Stephens Collier. BLPA; FaBoBe

Sinn Fein· Ourselves Alone. Isobel Marchbank. NSI

Sinner, The. Margaret E. Bruner. PoToHe

Sinner, Is Thy Heart at Rest? Jared Bell Waterbury. AH

Sinners, abhor the Fiend. Charles Wesley. NOCV *Fr.* The Horrible Decree.

Sinner's Lament, A. Edward Herbert. SeCP

Sinner's Rue. A. E. Housman. PeVV

Sinners, Will You Scorn the Message? Jonathan Allen. AH

Sinnes Heavie Loade. Robert Southwell. ESCV

Sins of Kalamazoo are neither scarlet nor crimson, The. Carl Sandburg. VGW

Sins of the Fathers. Mark Vinz. IFJA

Sin's Round. George Herbert. NOSC

Sion. George Herbert. ChIV-1; ESCV

Sion lies [or Syon lyes] waste, and thy Jerusalem. Greville Fulke. PeECV, *sect.* CX; ChIV-1; NoSic; PoEL-1 *Fr.* Caelica.

Sioux, The. Eugene Field. GoJo-1

Sioux Indians. *Unknown.* AmFP

Sioux Metamorphoses. *Unknown, Sioux Indian.* STP, *tr. by* James Koller

Sip a little. Baby's Drinking Song. James Kirkup. NTCP; OTCP

Sipping a Schlitz. Bullfrogs. David Allan Evans. Poetsp

Sipping whiskey and gin. Analysands. Dudley Randall. BPo

Sir, after you have wip'd the eyes. A Consolatory Poem Dedicated unto Mr. Cotton Mather. Nicholas Noyes. SCAP

Sir Aldingar. *Unknown.* ESPB; OxBB

Sir Andrew Bart[t]on. *Unknown.* AmFP; ESPB; EnSB; OxBB

Sir Anthony Habberton, Justice and Knight. Obiter Dicta. Hilaire Belloc. OBCoV

Sir—awaiting you. Waiting for the Emperor Tenji. Princess Nukada, *Japanese.* PBWP, *tr. by* Cid Corman *and* Susumu Kamaike

Sir Beelzebub. Dame Edith Sitwell. BoWP; FaBoMo; FaBoWP; HoPM; MoBrPo; NALW; OBCoV; OxBTC *Fr.* Façade.

Sir Brian had a battleaxe with great big knobs on. Bad Sir Brian Botany. A. A. Milne. NOxBChV

Sir Bumper was a baron bold. The Lover's Leap; a Tale. Andrew Macdonald. NOEC

Sir Cawline. *Unknown.* ESPB

Sir Charles into my chamber coming in. Courting the Faerie Queen. Margaret Lucas Cavendish, Duchess of Newcastle. NOSC

Sir Chaucer. Robert Greene. *See* The Description of Sir Chaucer.

Sir Christopher Wren. Edmund Clerihew Bentley. NBLV; PeLV *Fr.* Clerihews.

Sir Colin. *Unknown.* OxBB

Sir Dilberry Diddle, Captain of Militia. *Unknown.* NOEC

Sir *Drake* whom well the world's end knew. On Francis Drake. *Unknown.* NOSC; PBRV

Sir Eggnogg. Bayard Taylor. BXAP

Sir Eglamour. Samuel Rowlands. FaBoCh *Fr.* Melancholy Conceit. OxBSP

Sir Egrabell had sonnes three. Sir Lionel. *Unknown.* AmFP; ESPB

Sir, / Ere you pass this threshold, stay. To the King, at His Entrance into Saxham: By Master John Crofts. Thomas Carew. CaPo

Sir Eustace Grey. George Crabbe.
Frenzy. NOBE
"Peace, peace, my friend; these subjects fly." PoEL-4

Sir Francis Drake; or, Eighty-eight. *Unknown.* FaBoCh

Sir Francis, Sir Francis, Sir Francis is come. Upon Sir Francis Drake's Return from His Voyage about the World, and the Queen's Meeting Him. *Unknown.* FaBoCh

Sir *Frauncis* and *Sir Phillip* have noe Tombe. Of Sir Frauncis Walsingham Sir Phillipp Sydney, and Sir Christopher Hatton, Lord Chancelor. *Unknown.* PBRV

Sir Gawain and the Green Knight. *Unknown, Middle English.* OAEL-1, *tr.* by Brian Stone
Gawain and the Lady of the Castle. EBEV
"Mony klyf he overclambe in contrayes straunge." FaBoVe
"Now neghes the New Yere and the night passes." EnVB
Passage of a Year, The. PoEL-1

Sir Gawayn Goes to Receive His Return Blow from the Green Knight. OAEL-1, *tr.* by Brian Stone
"Sun rises red amid radiant clouds, The." FaBoSe
"This kyng lay at Camylot upon Krystmasse." PoE

Sir Gawain Encounters Sir Priamus. *Unknown.* PoEL-1 *Fr.* Morte Arthur.

Sir Gawaine and the Green Knight. Yvor Winters. MoP; NoAM; PoRA; VGW

Sir Gregory Nonsense's News from No Place. John Taylor.
"It was in June the eight and thirtieth day." CBNP; NOSC

Sir Halewyn. Sir Alexander Gray. OxBB

Sir Hudibras, his passing worth. The Argument. Samuel Butler. EBEV; NAEL-1; OAEL-1 *Fr.* Hudibras.

Sir Hudson Lowe, Sir Hudson *Low.* To Sir Hudson Lowe. Thomas Moore. OBSV

Sir Hugh; or, The Jew's Daughter. *Unknown.* AmFP; CH; ESPB
(Hugh of Lincoln.) EnSB; OxBB

Sir, I admit your general [*or* gen'ral] Rule. Epigram from the French. Alexander Pope, *also at. to* Matthew Prior *and to* Coleridge. FaBoEE; NBLV

Sir, I am not a bird of prey. A Reply From His Coy Mistress. Annie Finch. FFC

Sir, *I Ham a very Bad Hand at Righting.* (LL) On Not Being Milton. Tony Harrison. CABP; NoP-4

Sir Inigo doth feare it as I heare. To a Friend an Epigram: Of him. Martial, *Latin.* OBCVT, *tr.* by Ben Johnson

Sir Isaac Newton. *Unknown.* WeW-3

Sir James the Rose. *Unknown.* ESPB

Sir John addressed the Snake-god in his temple. Robert Graves. PeLV *Fr.* Grotesques. CMoP

Sir John Butler. *Unknown.* ESPB

Sir John Raynsford's Confession. John Harington. NoSic

Sir John Shagbag (Conservative, Nore). Limerick. Victor Gray. PeLi

Sir Joseph's Song. Sir William Schwenck Gilbert. *See* The First Lord's Song.

Sir Joshua Reynolds. William Blake. FaBoEE; OxBoLi; PeLV

Sir Joshua Reynolds. Oliver Goldsmith. FaBoEE; NOEC; OBCoV *Fr.* Retaliation. OxBoLi

Sir knights, take heed hither in hie. The York Play of the Crucifixion. *Unknown.* NAEL-1

Sir, laugh no more at Pliny and the rest. Animal Weather-Forecasting. Thomas Lodge. NoSic

Sir Lionel, vers. A. *Unknown.* AmFP; ESPB

Sir Mordred, traitor false and vile. *Unknown, Middle English.* OxBoV, *tr.* by Brian Stone

Sir, more than kisses, letters mingle souls. To Sir Henry Wotton. Donne. NoSic

Sir Nicketty Nox. Hugh Chesterman. BoTP
("Sir Nicketty Nox was an ancient knight.") FuFo

Sir, no man's enemy, forgiving all. Petition. W. H. Auden. CMoP; MeMAP; NAEL-2; Son

Sir, / not that we did not hear the noise. What Her Girl Friend Said to Him. Kannan, *Tamil.* PLW, *tr.* by A. K. Ramanujan

Sir, now unravelled [*or* unravell'd] is the Golden Fleece. To Dr. F. B. on His Book of Chess[e]. Richard Lovelace. CaPo

Sir Olaf. Johann Gottfried von Herder, *German.* AWP, *tr.* by Elizabeth Craigmyle

Sir Oluf he rideth over the plain. The Elected Knight. *Unknown, Danish.* AWP, *tr.* by Longfellow

Sir Orfeo. *Unknown.* EnVB

Sir, / Our times are much degenerate from those. To His Noble Friend, Mr Richard Lovelace, upon His Poems. Andrew Marvell. EPCY

Sir Patient Fancy. Aphra Behn.
"What has poor Woman done, that she must be." WPOW

Sir Patrick Spens [*or* Spence]. *Unknown.* AWP; AmFP; BXAP; CH; ClHu; EBEV; ESPB; EnSB; FaBoCh; FaPoR; GEA; HAP; HoPM; InPK-6; InPS-3; NAEL-1; NIP-4; NOBE; OAEL-1; OBEV; OBSP; OxBB; OxBS; PBMP; PoE; PoEL-1; RB; SCGP; TFi; UnPo; WeW-3

Sir, / Pray discruciate what follows: / A long-eared beast, and a field-house for cattle. A Riddling Letter. Jonathan Swift. CBNP

Sir Proteus, a Satirical Ballad. Thomas Love Peacock.
"Even while he sung Sir Proteus rose." CBNP
"Poor Johnny looked exceeding blue." CBNP
"Ten thousand thousand fathoms down." CBNP

Sir Revel. Samuel Rowlands. NoSic; OBCoV

Sir Robert Bolton had three sons. Sir Lionel. *Unknown.* ESPB

Sir Roland; a Fragment. Robert Merry. NOEC

Sir S.J. Sir John Suckling. *See* Constant Lover, A [*or* The].

Sir, say no more. Trumbull Stickney. APN-2; InPK-6; OxBA; OxBSP *Fr.* Dramatic Fragments.

Sir, so suspicious. *Unknown, Irish.* NOIV, *tr.* by Thomas Kinsella

Sir Thopas. Chaucer. *See* The Tale of Sir Thopas.

Sir: though (I thank God for it) I do hate. The Poet Turned Lawyer. Donne. OBSV *Fr.* Satires.

Sir, to be short, in this expensive town. London. John Oldham. NOSC *Fr.* A Satyr.

Sir Tristrem. Thomas of Erceldoune.
Tristrem and the Hunters. OxBS

Sir Walter, oh, oh, my own Sir Walter. Lady Ralegh's Lament. Robert Lowell. OxBSP

Sir Walter Ra[u]le[i]gh to His Son[ne]. Sir Walter Ralegh. NAEL-1; NoSic; RB; Son
("Three things there be that prosper up apace.") GSo; NoP-4
(To His Son.) InPS-3; OxBSP; SCGP
("We part not with thee at this meeting day.") (LL) GSo; NoP-4

Sir Walter Ralegh to the Queen. Sir Walter Ralegh. NoSic
(To His Mistress.) SiPS

Sir Walter Raleigh has built a ship. Sir Walter Raleigh Sailing in the Lowlands. *Unknown.* OxBoLi

Sir Walter Scott at the Tomb of the Stuarts in St. Peter's. Richard Monckton, 1st Baron Houghton Milnes. EBVV

Sir Walter Scott's Tribute. Sir Walter Scott. *See* The Book of Books.

Sir, We Would See Jesus. Frances Ellen Watkins Harper. AAP

Sir, whatsoever you are pleas'd to do. Dedications, II: To the Prince. Sir John Davies. SiPS *Fr.* Orchestra; or, A Poem[e] of Da[u]ncing. NoSic; SiPS

Sir! when I flew to seize the bird. Beau's Reply. William Cowper. FaBoCh

Sir, when you say. 15th Raga: For Bela Lugosi. David Meltzer. *Fr.* Ragas. NeAP

Sir, / Whether these lines do find you out. A Summons to Town. Sir John Suckling. NOSC

Sir William Dyer, Knight. Lady Catherine Dyer.
Epitaph on the Monument of Sir William Dyer at Colmworth, 1641. BoLoP; EnLoPo; OxBM

Sir William of Deloraine at the Wizard's Tomb. Sir Walter Scott. *See* Melrose Abbey.

Sir Winston Churchill advised against suicide. Enigma Variations. David Lehman. NAmP90

Sir, you are tough, and I am tough. Joseph Brodsky. PiM

Sir, / You need no Parian or Egyptian stone. To Sir Henry Newton, upon His Re-edifying the Church of Charleton in Kent. Thomas Philipott. NOSC

Sir, you should notice me: I am the Man. Epitaph. Lascelles Abercrombie. MoBrPo

Sir, you were a credit to whatever. To a Teacher of French. Donald Davie. OxBC

Sire. W. S. Merwin. CoAP; VGW

Siren, The. "Violet Fane." VWP

Siren. Anna Semionovna Prismanova, *Russian.* TCRP, *tr.* by Bradley Jordan

Siren Bird, The. Henrietta Cordelia Ray. CBWP-3

Siren Chorus. George Darley. *See* The Mermaidens' Vesper-Hymn.

Siren: I was in one hour an ashen crone. *Unknown.* EEP, *tr.* by Michael Alexander *Fr.* Riddles (Exeter Book).

Siren sang, and Europe turned away, A. To the Western World. Louis Simpson. CoAP; CoAmPo; LiTM; NOBA; PFE; TAP; TRP

Siren Song. Margaret Atwood. HAP; NIP-4; PoA; WeW-3 *Fr.* Songs of the Transformed.

Siren waits thee, singing song for song, The. (LL) To Robert Browning. Walter Savage Landor. EPCY; NoP-4

Sirens, The. Gordon Challis. PeNZ

Sirens, The. John Streeter Manifold. LiTM; MoBrPo; Son

Sirens' Song, The. William Browne. NOBE; OBEV *Fr.* The Inner Temple Masque.

(Syrens' Song, The.) GBL

Sirhan Drinks His Coffee in the Cafeteria. Mahmoud Darwish, *Arabic*. VCWP, *tr. by* Rana Kabbani

Sirius. Donald Revell. PT

Sirius: / what mystery is this? Hilda Doolittle. PBWP *Fr.* The Walls Do Not Fall. NAAL-2

Sirmio, thou dearest dear of strands. Catullus. *See* Carmen 31 ("Apple of islands, Sirmio, & bright peninsulas, set").

Sirocco. Robert Penn Warren. FuPo *Fr.* To a Little Girl, One Year Old, in a Ruined Fortress.

Sirs—though we fail you—let us live. To Men. Anna Wickham. MoBrPo

Sirventes. Paul Blackburn. NeAP; PoM

Sis Boom Ba. Tina Darragh. FTOS

Sis co wet. Sis Boom Ba. Tina Darragh. FTOS

Sisley / Walked so nicely. Bag-Snatching in Dublin. Stevie Smith. OxBoV

Sissinghurst. Vita Sackville-West. WPN

Sister. Langston Hughes. APSN

Sister. Gabriela Mistral, *Spanish*. BoWoP, *tr. by* Langston Hughes

Sister, The. Rose Cecil O'Neill. CPO

Sister. John Greenleaf Whittier. *Fr.* Snow-Bound [*or* Snow-Bound; a Winter Idyl]. APN-1; AiP; AmPP; NAAL-3; NOBA; OxBA; TAP; TFi

Sister, a sister calling. Gerard Manley Hopkins. FaBoVe *Fr.* The Wreck of the Deutschland. CMoP; EnVR; FaBoMo; ImPo; LiTM; NOBE; NoAM; OBNC; OxAEP-2; PeECV; PoEL-5

Sister Agnes Writes to Her Beloved Mother. Paul Durcan. OBCoV

Sister and mother and diviner love. To the One of Fictive Music. Wallace Stevens. MeMAP; MoAmPo; NoP-4

Sister, Awake! *Unknown*. BoTP; CH; NOBE; OBEV

Sister, come to the chestnut toll. The Last Night. Alfred Austin. PeVV

Sister darling, ope the window, let the balmy air once more. The Dying Girl. Mary Weston Fordham. CBWP-2

Sister Emma, O you must come down to the mire. Down to the Mire. *Unknown*. WPoS

Sister Johnson's Speech. Maggie Pogue Johnson. CBWP-4

Sister Lou. Sterling Brown. BkSV; GM; ISC; PoBA

Sister Midnight. John James. NBrP

Sister of Mercy, The. Constance Naden. VWP

Sister on the Tracks, A. Donald Hall. GM

Sister saying—"Soon you'll be back in the ward—." In the Theatre. Dannie Abse. NoAM

Sister, sister go to bed! Brother and Sister. "Lewis Carroll." NOxBChV

Sister Songs. Francis Thompson.

"But lo! at length the day is lingered out." OBMV

Sister Swallow to Swinburne. Mary Holtby. UV

Sister! the sundering sea. Cuba. Thomas MacDermot. PBCV

Sister was wedged beside the wicker basket. The Burned Bridge. Ruth Stone. WPE

Sister Water. Robert Penn Warren. MT

Sisters, The. Roy Campbell. BoLoP; EP; FaBoTw; NoP-4; OBMV

Sisters, The. Melissa Cannon. FFC

Sisters, The. Alexis De Veaux. GLP

Sisters. (LL) For the Record. Audre Lorde. LoHo

Sisters, The. Nicki Jackowska. BrRo

Sisters, The. Josephine Jacobsen. NMM-2

Sisters, The. Amy Lowell. NALW; NMM-2

Sisters. Sandra McPherson. AmPA

Sisters? Lotte Moos. NBrP

Sisters. Saleem Peeradina. OMIP

Sisters, The. John Banister Tabb. APN-2

Sisters, The. John Greenleaf Whittier. AWP

Sisters, The. Judith Wright. NALW

Sisters are always drying their hair. Triolet Against Sisters. Phyllis McGinley. KaS; OBCA

Sisters! / I love you. / Because you love you. To Those of My Sisters Who Kept Their Naturals. Gwendolyn Brooks. NMM-2

Sisters in Arms. Audre Lorde. NMM-2

Sisters of Sexual Treasure, The. Sharon Olds. PBCAP

Sistine Chapel. Raymond Roseliep. HA

Sistrum. Margaret Fuller. APAD; APN-1; PAR

Sisyphus. Josephine Miles. NYBP

Sit as close to the stage as possible. How to Find Love in an Instant. Michael Lassell. GLP *Fr.* Times Square Poems.

Sit by the fire, and spare shoe leather. (LL) Winter Wise. *Unknown*. AYFP; Spl

Sit down by the side of your mother, my boy. Mother's Advice. *Unknown*. AmFP

Sit down in the shade of this fine spreading laurel. Anyte, *Greek*. GrAn, *tr. by* Sally Purcell

Sit down under the high crown. Plato, *Greek*. PGA, *tr. by* Kenneth Rexroth

Sit down with me awhile beside the heath-corner. Erica. Mary Ursula Bethell. PeNZ

Sit on the bed. I'm blind, and three parts shell. A Terre. Wilfred Owen. LiTM; NSI; OxBTC; PeFWW; PoWW

Sit: sit all. Lucan. OBCVT, *tr. by* John Fletcher *Fr.* The False One.

Sit too close. My Mother Spinning. Peter Olds. PeNZ

Site. Meir Wieseltier, *Hebrew*. IP, *tr. by* Warren Bargad *and* Stanley F. Chyet

Site of Ambush. Eiléan Ní Chuilleanáin.
"At alarming bell daybreak, before." CIP-2

Sith Cynthia is ascended to that rest. From Salve Deus Rex Judaeorum. Aemilia Bassano Lanyer. NoP-4

Sith eyes from love, and hope from heart, is wrought. (LL) When we in kind embracements had agre'd [agreed]. *Unknown*. AAS; Son

Sith gone is my delight and only pleasure. Sextain. William Drummond, of Hawthornden. NOSC

Sith, in dark speech, Carvilios hymn unfolds. Hymn to the Sun. Charles Montague Doughty. FaBoTw *Fr.* The Dawn in Britain.

Sith my life from life is parted. Marie [*or* Mary] Magdalens Complaint at Christs Death. Robert Southwell. ChIV-2; ESCV

Sith passèd pleasures double but new woe? (LL) Sonnet: "Alexis, here she stayed; among these pines." William Drummond, of Hawthornden. NOSC; OBEV

Sith sickles and the shearing scythe. Hawking for the Partridge. Thomas Ravenscroft. OxBoLi

Sith Venus had her mole, Helen her stain. Against Proud Poor Phryna. John, of Hereford Davies. FaBoEE

Sits till evening and will not move from the place! (LL) Planting Flowers on the Eastern Embankment. Po Chü-i, *Chinese*. ChiP; OBGa, *tr. by* Arthur Waley

Sitter Bitter. Miss Bitter. N. M. Bodecker. NTCP

Sitters on the mead-bench, quaffing among questions. An Exeter Riddle. Gavin Ewart. OxBC

Sitteth alle stille and herkneth to me. The Song of Lewes. *Unknown*. OxBoLi

Sitting. Bob Boldman. HA

Sitting, The. Medbh McGuckian. CABP; PNI

Sitting alone (as one forsook). The Vision. Robert Herrick. CaPo; CavPo; PBRV; SCGP; SeCP

Sitting Alone in Ching-t'ing Mountain. Li Po, *Chinese*. SuSp, *tr. by* Irving Y. Lo

Sitting Alone in the Courtyard. Yü Chi, *Chinese*. CoBLCP, *tr. by* Jonathan Chaves

Sitting Alone in Tulsa Three A.M. Lance Henson. VoR

Sitting alone upon my thought, in melancholy mood. Edward De Vere, 17th Earl of Oxford. NoSic

Sitting, and ready to be drawn. The Picture of the Body. Ben Jonson. NOSC *Fr.* Eupheme.

Sitting at crossings and waiting for freights to pass, we have all noticed. A Project for Freight Trains. David Young. GM

Sitting at her table, she serves. Nani. Alberto A. Ríos. SoSe-8; UnSA

Sitting at her / or] window / in her cloak and hat. Mother Tabbyskins. Elizabeth Anna Hart. OxBChV

Sitting at Night. Om Ui-Gil, *Chinese*. FP, *tr. by* Jong-Gil, Kim

Sitting at Night. Po Chü-i, *Chinese*. TAL, *tr. by* Robert Payne

Sitting at Night on the Front Porch. Charles Wright. ColAP; LCAP-2

Sitting at Night on the Moon-viewing Terrace. Yang Wan-li, *Chinese*. SuSp, *tr. by* Jonathan Chaves

Sitting at Night on the Moonlit Terrace. Yang Wan-li, *Chinese*. CoBCP, *tr. by* Burton Watson

Sitting at Night with My Nephew Who Has Just Come from Afar. Su Tung-p'o, *Chinese*. TAL, *tr. by* Robert Payne

Sitting Bard, The. Sir Owen Seaman. NOBL

Sitting between the sea and the buildings. The Painter. John Ashbery. HCAP; NOBA; NoP-4; PoE; PoPoPo

Sitting Bull's Will versus the Sioux Treaty of 1868 and Monty Hall. A. K. Redwing. VoR

Sitting by a Bush in Broad Daylight. Robert Frost. ChIV-1

Sitting by Myself. K'ang Hai, *Chinese*. CoBLCP, *tr. by* Jonathan Chaves

Sitting by the riverside with a torn net. Li K'ai-hsien. *Fr.* Impromptu Poems. CoBLCP, *tr. by* Jonathan Chaves

Sitting by the streams that glide, *par. by* Thomas Carew. Bible, *O.T. See* Psalm 137.

Sitting dead in 'Death Valley'. Death Valley. Sorley MacLean. FaBoTC

Sitting Here. Robert Creeley. MoLi

Sitting here alone, in peace. Private Sadness. Bob Kaufman. ISC

Sitting here by the foreshore day after day. Iain Crichton Smith. FaBoTC *Fr.* By the Sea.

Sitting in an alcove. Gypsy Music in Krakow. Tom Pickard. NBrP

Sitting in cold fear, boys, waiting for the end? (LL)　Just a Smack at Auden. William Empson. LiTM; MoBrPo; PeLV; UV; UnPo

Sitting in sunlight, the child. Eleven A.M. on My Day Off, My Sister Phones Desperate for a Babysitter. Sharon Hashimoto. OpBo

Sitting in the dusk, weeping. Circles. Celia Gilbert. MDDM

Sitting, legs crossed, copper-toned old man. My Song. King D. Kuka. VoR

Sitting on a Rock by Mountain Stream. Ch'en Yü-yi, *Chinese.* SuSp, *tr. by* Irving Y. Lo

Sitting on the grass. In the Park. Judith Beveridge. BMAP

Sitting Out New Year With My Wife. Hsü Chün-ch'ien, *Chinese.* EP, *tr. by* Anne Birrell

Sitting Outdoors. Lu Yu, *Chinese.* CoBCP, *tr. by* Burton Watson

Sitting over words. Utterance. W. S. Merwin. BLT

Sitting Pretty. Margaret Fishback. PoLF

Sitting straightbacked, a modest Irish miss. A Lesson in Love. Philip Hobsbaum. OxBTC

Sitting Up at Night. Lu Yu, *Chinese.* CoBCP, *tr. by* Burton Watson

Sitting Up with My Wife on New Year's Eve. Hsü Chün-ch'ien, *Chinese.* CoBCP, *tr. by* Burton Watson

Sitting with Lester Young. Paul Zimmer. SeSe

Situation. Langston Hughes. APSN; OBAL

Situation. Kaa Naa Subramanyam, *Tamil.* OMIP, *tr. by* Kaa Naa Subramanyam

Situation is not going to change, The. For Example (5): Song of the Already Sung. Anne Lauterbach. PT

Situations Theoretical and Contemporary. Tom Leonard.
"And their judges spoke with one dialect." NBrP
"Schooner *The Mother of Parliaments* has anchored in the bay, The." NBrP
"We have decided to make Scotland secure." NBrP

Siwashing it out once in Siuslaw Forest. Miyazawa Kenji, *Japanese.* SAGP, *tr. by* Gary Snyder

6:00 A.M. Invasions. Jimmy Santiago Baca. PaTW

6 A.M. Thoughts. Dick Davis. APAD

Six beds in a square room: you give your name. Wait. Timothy Steele. PoA

Six Belons. Chase Twichell. NAmP90

Six Commissioned Texts. W. H. Auden.
Ballad of Barnaby, The. OBNV

Six-cylinder car and two Fords in the middle of / the fields, A. Harvest. Blaise Cendrars, *French.* BLT, *tr. by* Monique Chefdor

Six days ago the water fell. A Peacock's Feather. Seamus Heaney. DiPo

Six discs / with Decca. (LL)　Be-Bop Boys. Langston Hughes. APSN; MoNo; OBAL

Six Eagles. Thomas Love Peacock. VoR

Six Feet of Earth. *Unknown.* BLPA

Six Feet Under. Janet Campbell Hale. VoR

Six-foot nest of the sea-hawk, The. Sea-Hawk. Richard Eberhart. RB

Six girls in red skirts and red sweaters. The Cheerleaders. Jack Matthews. CMAP

Six Glasgow Poems. Tom Leonard. FaBoTC

Six green plums bottoms. Wickson Plums. William Corbett. PmAP

Six hundred dark feet from the cliffs. "But Still in Israel's Paths They Shine." Carter Revard. VoR

Six Lectures in Verse. Czeslaw Milosz, *Polish.*
"'Christ has risen.' Whoever believes that / Should not behave as we do." GI, *tr. by* Czeslaw Milosz *and* Leonard Nathan

Six little mice sat down to spin;. Mother Goose. BoTP; CTAV; OxNR; PC
("And Pussy soon had them all dead on the floor.") (LL)　PC
("'Oh, no, Mistress Pussy, you'd bite off our heads!'.") (LL)　CTAV

Six long-headed jazzers play. (LL)　Jazzonia. Langston Hughes. ColAP; NAAAL

Six men turned to smoke in the next square. The Parachutist's Wife. Sandra M. Gilbert. LoHo

6 months I was in. My Seasonal Body, My Ears. Clarence Major. WeT

Six Movements on a Theme. David Ignatow. NNaP

Six Nations Museum Onchiota, New York—January. Wendy Rose. HATNAP

Six o'Clock. Trumbull Stickney. APN-2; OxBA

6:00 a.m. / awake and leave to fish. 43. Jimmy Santiago Baca. PuP-14

6: o' clock our passageway. Travois of the Nameless. Sotère Torregian. NBV

Six o'clock: the kitchen bulbs which blister. Ode to Suburbia. Eavan Boland. PBCIP

Six of them, The. These Six. Sean Lucy. CIP-2

Six on the Desert Ways. Otalantaiyar, *Tamil.* PLW, *tr. by* A. K. Ramanujan

Six or seven rows of waves struggle landward. On the Oregon Coast. Galway Kinnell. NoAM

Six Poems of Loneliness. Enrique Lihn, *Spanish.* VCWP, *tr. by* David Unger

Six Poems on Remembering. Shen Yüeh, *Chinese.* CoBCP, *tr. by* Burton Watson

Six Poets in Search of a Lawyer. Donald Hall. NYBP

Six-Quart Basket, The. Raymond Souster. MoCV

Six Reasons for Drinking. Vernon Scannell. OxBC

Six Religious Lyrics. Karl Shapiro.
"I sing the simplest flower." CMoP

Six Said by the Concubines to Him. Ammuvanar, *Tamil.* PLW, *tr. by* A. K. Ramanujan

Six street ends come together here. Blue Island Intersection. Carl Sandburg. MoAmPo

Six Strings, The. Federico García Lorca, *Spanish.* RB, *tr. by* Donald Hall

Six Ten Sixty-Nine. Conyus. GT; PoBA

Six times faster than the fool can weep. The Peasant. Leonard Wolf. NYBP

Six to Six. *Unknown, Xhosa.* PBA, *tr. by* A. C. Jordan

Six Town Eclogues. Lady Mary Wortley Montagu.
Saturday: The Small-Pox. BWW; ECWP; NOEC; PEW; WPE
("Ye operas, circles, I no more must view! / My toilette, patches, all the world, adieu!") (LL)　PEW

Six Underrated Pleasures. Marge Piercy. EC2

Six Variations. Denise Levertov. AmPP; CoAmPo; LCAP-2
"Shlup, shlup, the dog." HeIP-4; InPK-6; Poetr

Six Winter Privacy Poems. Robert Bly. LCAP-2
"About four, a few flakes."
Listening to Bach.
"More of the fathers are dying each day."
"My shack has two rooms; I use one."
On Meditation.
"When I woke, a new snow had fallen."

Six Years. Gary Snyder.
December. InPS-3

Six Years Later. Joseph Brodsky, *Russian.* TCRP; VCWP, *tr. by* Richard Wilbur
("Through them into the future, into night.") (LL)　SAGP, *tr. by* Richard Wilbur

Six years the moon shone at mid-autumn. Mid-Autumn Moon. Su Tung-p'o, *Chinese.* CoBCP, *tr. by* Burton Watson

Six Young Men. Ted Hughes. NSI; OBWP; PoWW

"Sixpence a week," says the girl to her lover. By Her Aunt's Grave. Thomas Hardy. MoBrPo; PFE *Fr.* Satires of Circumstance in Fifteen Glimpses.

Sixt Nimphall, The. Michael Drayton. *Fr.* Muses' Elysium [*or* Elizium].

Sixteen Dead Men. W. B. Yeats. FaBoPV; OBWP

Sixteen Poems in Eight Pairings. John Crowe Ransom.
Agitato Ma Non Troppo ("I have a grief"). OxBA
Conrad in Twilight. FuPo; MeMAP; OxBA
("By the summer's flare and winter's flaw.") (LL)　FuPo
"Here lies a lady of beauty and high degree." AWP; CMoP; HAP; LiTM; MeMAP; MoAmPo; MoP; NAAL-2; NoAM; PoRA; RB; TAP; VGW
Prelude to an Evening. MoAmPo; OxBA; SPE
Vanity of the Bright Young Men, The. FuPo
("Grim in my little black coat as the sleazy beetle.")
(Tom, Tom, the Piper's Son.)

Sixteen Sonnets. Thomas A. Clark.
"As I walked out early." NBrP
"Each colour sits beside." NBrP
"Our boat touches the bank." NBrP
"Stag comes home at last, The." NBrP
"What the day weaves." NBrP

16 years old. My Old Man. Charles Bukowski. PmAP

Sixteen years old and crooked. Meeting Mescalito at Oak Hill Cemetery. Lorna Dee Cervantes. PBCAP

Sixteenth Canto. Hans Magnus Enzensberger. PoSu *Fr.* The Sinking of the Titanic.

6th Dance—Doing Things With Pencils—17-18 February 1964. Jackson MacLow. PmAP

6th grade—our lady of pompeii. Vittoria Repetto. UnSA

Sixth-Month Song in the Foothills. Gary Snyder. HCAP

Sixth Pearle, The: Justice. Lady Diana Primrose. KTR *Fr.* A Chain of Pearl.

Sixth Psalm. Anne Sexton. LCAP-2

Sixth Sense, The. Nikolai Stepanovich Gumilyov, *Russian.* TCRP, *tr. by* Yakov Hornstein

Sixth Song of the Holy Young Men. *Unknown.* APN-2, *tr. by* Washington Matthews *Fr.* The Mountain Chant.

Sixth Vertical Poetry. Roberto Juarroz, *Spanish.*
   "Bell is full of wind, The." VCWP, *tr. by* W. S. Merwin

Sixties brought a clash of arms, The. Emancipation Day. Lizelia Augusta Jenkins Moorer. CBWP-3

Sixties, I think, were not a total loss, The. January 15 as a National Holiday. Carter Revard. VoR

Sixties, / I told Black people, it would be all right, The. Clinton. Sterling Plumpp. BkSV

68. Edward Fitzgerald. CABP

Sixty-Eighth Birthday. James Russell Lowell. OxBSP; PFE; PoEL-5

64 Panoramic Way. Carol Moldaw. WWSi

Sixty-four Tanka. Saigyo, *Japanese.*
   In Winter. GaP, *tr. by* Burton Watson

69. Edward Fitzgerald. CABP

Sixty second / August. Black. Maxine Chernoff. PmAP *Fr.* Japan. PmAP

Sixty-Six Poems for a Blackfoot Bundle. *Unknown, Blackfoot Indian.* STP, *tr. by* Jerome Rothenberg

Sixty sun-decked years Charito has gotten to. Philodemus, *Greek.* OiAii, *tr. by* William Moebius

62. You would have been 62. Sweet Daddy. Patricia Smith. MoLi

Sixty was hardly the age for such youthful excesses! Ulysses. John Holloway. PFE

Sixty years after the fall of Troy. Proem. Richard Aldington. PoFWW

Size, The. George Herbert. GeHe

Size and Sheer Will. Sharon Olds. Poetr

Size Is Relative. Chuck Martin. IFJA

Size of a cavern for men to crouch in, The. Dawn Hippo. Sydney Clouts. PeSA

Sizeline. Felix Mnthali. PeSAV

Skaian Gate, The. Geoffrey Scott.
   "Hector, the captain bronzed, from simple fight." OBMV

Skara Brae. Michael Longley. PBCIP

Skater, The. Sir Charles G. D. Roberts. NOBC

Skaters, The. John Ashbery.
   "These decibels / Are a kind of flagellation, an entity of sound." PmAP
   "Wind thrashes the maple seed-pods, The." APSN

Skaters, The. John Gould Fletcher. KaS; MoAmPo

Skaters. Vern Rutsala. CMAP

Skating. Wordsworth. CH *Fr.* Introduction—Childhood and School-Time. FHYEP *Fr.* The Prelude; Growth of a Poet's Mind [1850 vers.]

Skein, The. Carolyn Kizer. VGW

Skeleton, The. G. K. Chesterton. FaBoTw

Skeleton House. Laurence Smith. OTCP

Skeleton in Armor [or Armour], The. Henry Wadsworth Longfellow. APN-1; AWP; AmPP; CTV; FaBoBe

Skeleton in the Cupboard, The. Dora Sigerson Shorter. VWP

Skeleton is hiding in the closet as it should, The. Everything in Its Place. Arthur Guiterman. NBLV; OBAL; OBCoV

Skeleton of the Future, The. "Hugh MacDiarmid." MoBrPo; OBMV

Skeleton of the Great Moa in the Canterbury Museum, Christchurch, The. Allen Curnow. PeNZ

Skeleton of Winter. Joy Harjo. LoL

Skeleton Parade. Jack Prelutsky. NTCP

Skeltoniad, A. Michael Drayton. PoEL-2

Skeptic, The. Clara Ann Thompson. CBWP-2

Sketch, A. Christina Rossetti. GTBS-P; VWP

Sketch, A. Dorothy Wordsworth. Ro

Sketch for a Job Application Blank. James Harrison. AmPA; MoP

Sketch for a Modern Love Poem, A. Tadeusz Różewicz. *See* Draft of a Modern Love Poem.

Sketch for an Aesthetic Project. Jay Wright. GT

Sketch from Private Life, A. Byron. OBNC

Sketch in October. Tomas Tranströmer, *Swedish.* VCWP, *tr. by* Robin Fulton

Sketch of Lord Byron's Life. Julia A. Moore. OBAL

Sketch of Mount Chung, A. Wang An-shih, *Chinese.* SuSp, *tr. by* Jan W. Walls

Sketches. Federico García Lorca. PFTM

Sketches from History. Sergey Drofenko, *Russian.* TCRP, *tr. by* Lubov Yakovleva

Skialetheia Satire 5. Everard Guilpin.
   "What more variety of pleasures can." PBRV

Skies and god's mystery look on, The. Another Alexandra. Mongane Wally Serote. PeSAV

Skies are cold and hard; the dead lights trail, The. The Departure. Trumbull Stickney. ColAP

Skies contain still groves of silver clouds, The. Spring 1943. Roy Fuller. LiTM

Skies gan scowl, o'ercast with misty clouds, The. George Gascoigne. ChIV-1 *Fr.* De Profundis.

Skies have sunk and hid the upper snow, The. Les Vaches. Arthur Hugh Clough. CBLP

Skies o'ercast and fierce winds blow, The. December. Josephine D. Henderson Heard. CBWP-4

Skies remind one of one of those mounds of custard, The. Lollipops of the Pomeranian Baroque. James Fenton. PeLV

Skies they were ashen and sober, The. Ulalume [*or* Ulalume—a Ballad]. Edgar Allan Poe. APN-1; AWP; AmPP; ImPo; MeMAP; NAAL-1; NAAL-3; NCAP; NOBA; OxBA; PAR; TAP

Skies they were ashen and sober, The. The Willows. Bret Harte. BXAP

Skiing on Russian Christmas. Nora Dauenhauer. HATNAP

(skilfully curled) / all worlds. E. E. Cummings. *See* Love is a place.

Skill'd to deceive our ears and eyes. The County Member. Winthrop Mackworth Praed. OBNC *Fr.* The County Ball.

Skilled to pull wires, he baffles Nature's hope. The Boss. James Russell Lowell. NCAP; OBAL

Skillful mistress of guilty glances. Osip Emilevich Mandelstam, *Russian.* TCRP, *tr. by* Bernard Meares

(Skillfully curled) / all worlds. (LL) Love is a place. E. E. Cummings. FaBoEE

Skim from curb to curb like regatta. The Island Women of Paris. Rita Dove. LoL

Skimbleshanks: The Railway Cat. T. S. Eliot. NOBL

Skimmers. Ted Walker. NYBP

Skimming / an asphalt sea. The Sidewalk Racer Or, On the Skateboard. Lillian Morrison. NTCP

Skimming lightly, wheeling still. Shiloh [A Requiem]. Herman Melville. APAD; APN-2; CBCWP; ColAP; NOBA; NoP-4; OBWP; OxBA; SCV

Skimming the waves, deep in the night. Sandal Mountain. Hsieh Chin, *Chinese.* CoBLCP, *tr. by* Jonathan Chaves

Skin. Lucia Maria Perillo. BAP-93

Skin. Marjorie Welish. PmAP

Skin-and-Bone Lady, The. *Unknown.* AmFP

Skin Color from the Sun. Daryl Ngee Chinn. LTA

Skin deep, you son of a bitch, I thought, *no more*—but the impure. Worldly Beauty. T. R. Hummer. PuP-17

Skin Divers, The. George Starbuck. NYBP

Skin Diving in the Virgins. John Malcolm Brinnin. NYBP; TAP

Skin Flick. Fred Chappell. InPK-6

Skin is broken. The hotel breakfast china, The. Houseboat Days. John Ashbery. FTOS

Skin / Meat / BONES. Anne Waldman. PmAP

Skin meeting skin, we want to think. Touching Each Other's Surfaces. Carol Jane Bangs. NIP-4

Skin quickens to noises, The. One Eyed Black Man in Nebraska. Sam Cornish. PoBA

Skin ripples over my body like moon-wooed water, The. Prison Song. Alan Dugan. PoA

"Skin Skin, Yuh Na Know Meh." John C. M. Lyons. NBrP

Skin that is a closed curtain. Poll. Ed Roberson. PoBA

Skin the Goat's Curse on Carey. *Unknown.* BIrV

Skin Trade. Reginald Shepherd. BAP-96

Skinful of bowls, he bowls them. Second Glance at a Jaguar. Ted Hughes. NYBP; NoAM

Skinny Girl, The. Anne Hébert, *French.* BoWoP, *tr. by* Willis Barnstone

Skinny Mrs. Snipkin. Mrs. Snipkin and Mrs. Wobblechin. Laura Elizabeth Richards. OxBChV

Skinny / poem, / all your / ribs. Lou Lipsitz. PFE

Skinny rocks—verdigris green. Crossing Ts'en River. Yang Wan-li, *Chinese.* SuSp, *tr. by* Jonathan Chaves

Skinny waterfalls, footpaths, The. Lastness. Galway Kinnell. NNaP

Skins. Charles Wright. HCAP

Skins. Judith Wright. BMAP

Skip to My Lou. *Unknown.* AmFP

Skipper Ireson's Ride. John Greenleaf Whittier. APN-1; NCAP; NOBA; OBAL; OBCA; OxBA; PoLF

Skippets, the Bad One. Christine E. Bradley. BoTP

Skipping along the footpath. The Wind Debates Asian Immigration. Peter Rose. BMAP

Skirting the river road, (my forenoon walk, my rest,). The Dalliance of the Eagles. Walt Whitman. APo; AmPP; HAP; HeIP-4; NAAL-1; NAAL-3; NoP-4; SAGP; SAmP; TAP; TRP

Skokie Theatre, The. Edward Hirsch. IFJA

Skunk, The. Philip Dow. BXAP

Skunk, The. Seamus Heaney. NAEL-2; NoP-4; OxBC; PoE

Skunk cabbage with its smug and opulent smell, The. Eric Ormsby. NoP-4

Skunk Hour. Robert Lowell. AmPP; CMoP; CoAP; CoAmPo; ColAP; FaBoMo; HAP; HCAP; HeIP-4; InPK-6; InPS-3; LCAP-2; MoAmPo; MoP; NAAL-2; NIP-4; NOBA; NoAM; NoP-4; OxBC; PoE; PoPoPo; Poetr; SAGP; SCV; TAP; TFi; TRP; VCAP

Skunks fight under the house and keep us. Bureau 2. Josephine Miles. NALW

Sky. Richard Katrovas. LTA

Sky, The. Un Ko, *Korean.* CKP, *tr. by* Jaihiun Kim

Sky, The. Vladimir Nikolaevich Kornilov, *Russian.* TCRP, *tr. by* Daniel Weissbort

Sky. Grace Nichols. AYFP

Sky, The. Elizabeth Madox Roberts. MoAmPo

Sky. Raymond Roseliep. KaS

Sky. Robert Penn Warren. AFr

Sky a black sphere, The. Lighthouse in the Night. Alfonsina Storni, *Spanish.* BoWoP, *tr. by* Aliki *and* Willis Barnstone

Sky, a deep blue sea, The. A Falling Leaf. Trần Gia Thoại, *Vietnamese.* AVP, *tr. by* Huỳnh Sanh Thông

Sky and earth and one sandy gull. (LL) A Traveler at Night Writes His Thoughts. Tu Fu, *Chinese.* ChiPo; CoBCP, *tr. by* Burton Watson

Sky at night is like a big city, The. *Unknown, Ewe.* TTY, *tr. by* Ulli Beier

Sky became a still and woven blue, The. (LL) Merlin Enthralled. Richard Wilbur. CMoP; NYBP

Sky becomes one with its clouds, The. "Fisherman's Honor," The. Li Ch'ing-chao, *Chinese.* WPoS, *tr. by* Jane Hirshfield

Sky bends over the earth, The. Paul-Eerik Rummo, *Estonian.* CEEP, *tr. by* Ivar Ivask

Sky-black gull. Interstices. William J. Higginson. HA

Sky, blue and ever / imitates her. Bent. (LL) Bent. Martin Carter. HCP; PBCV

Sky ceases. There is only. Michael Dransfield. CBAP *Fr.* Geography.

Sky Clears, The. *Unknown.* OBVE, *tr. by* Frances Densmore

Sky extends upwards for ninety thousand miles, The. A Buddhist Monk Cut and Burned with His Own Flesh to Make The Rains Stop—A Man From His Native Place Asked Me to Write a Poem to Send to Him. Hsü Wei, *Chinese.* CoBLCP, *tr. by* Jonathan Chaves

Sky full of cymbals, of fiddles and lutes. Spring Joy Praising God. Catharina Regina von Greiffenberg, *German.* GePo, *tr. by* George C. Schoolfield

Sky Full of Swallows. Hanns Cibulka, *German.* CEEP, *tr. by* Ewald Osers

Sky glows one side black, three sides purple, The. The Northern Cold. Li Ho, *Chinese.* PLT, *tr. by* A. C. Graham

Sky grew darker with each minute, The. Before the Storm. Richard Dehmel, *German.* AWP, *tr. by* Ludwig Lewisohn

Sky hangs heavy tonight, The. Lighthouse in the Night. Lewis Alexander. PoBA

Sky has been dark, The. The Youngest Daughter. Cathy Song. NoAM

Sky has recovered its haze-blue tints, The. Louise Herlin, *French.* MFP, *tr. by* Martin Sorrell

Sky Is Blue, The. David Ignatow. IFJA; NNaP

Sky is changed!—and such a change! Oh night, The. Byron. NOBRP *Fr.* Childe Harold's Pilgrimage Canto III. Ro *Fr.* Childe Harold's Pilgrimage.

Sky is dark, and the hills are white, The. Norse Lullaby. Eugene Field. BoTP

Sky is dotted like th' unleavened bread, The. Haggadah. Abraham Moses Klein. TrJP

Sky Is Full of Blue and Full of the Mind of God, The. Kathleen Norris. CrSp

Sky is gray with rain that will not fall, The. At the Zoo. Israel Zangwill. TrJP

Sky is green, and there is no book to tell us what it means. It has. Engines of Gloom and Affection. John Yau. PmAP

Sky is heavy, it is raining stars, The. The Cannibal Hymn. *Unknown, Egyptian.* TTY, *tr. by* Samuel A. B. Mercer

Sky is hot and yellow, filled, The. The Brides Come to Yuba City. Chitra Divakaruni. OpBo; UnSA

Sky is low—the Clouds are mean, The. Emily Dickinson. MeMAP; MoAmPo; OxBA; PBMP; PoEL-5

Sky is overcast and behind it an infinite regress, The. Within This Book, Called Marguerite. Marjorie Welish. FTOS; PmAP

Sky is strewn with stars, The. *Unknown, Serbo-Croatian.* HSix, *tr. by* Charles Simic

Sky is such a softness, is such dark. No Moon, No Star. Babette Deutsch. NYBP

Sky is up above the roof, The. Paul Verlaine. AWP, *tr. by* Ernest Dowson *Fr.* Sagesse.

Sky, lazily disdaining to pursue, The. Georgia Dusk. Jean Toomer. BPo; NAAL-2; NoAM; NoP-4; PoBA; Poetr

Sky like pigeon's little belly. Village for a Wedding. Jan Bolesw Ozog, *Polish.* CEEP, *tr. by* Leonard Kress

Sky links cloud waves, links dawn fog. Li Ch'ing-chao, *Chinese.* BoWoP, *tr. by* Willis Barnstone *and* Sun Chu-chin

Sky looks down on me in aimless blues, The. Uncertain Admission. Frances Bazil. LiLi

Sky low down in distant West, The. To Mary. Mary E. Tucker. CBWP-1

Sky lowers itself to my book, The. Blue Crêpe. Asa Benveniste. NBrP

Sky of churning cogs and work without weekends, A. The First Circle. S. K. Kelen. BMAP

Sky or an edge or a beach or a wall or a room or a, A. Nursery Rhyme. Kit Robinson. FTOS

Sky Picture. Henrietta Cordelia Ray. CBWP-3

Sky scrape, / City scape. Jane Yolen. SSCS

Sky Seasons. John Rice. SpW

Sky so pale, and the trees, such frail things, The. A la Promenade. Paul Verlaine. AWP; OBVE, *tr. by* Arthur Symons

Sky the color of a wren's [*or* wrens] breath, A. At Chadwicks Bar and Grill. Lance Henson. HATNAP

Sky unshaken, smokeless ashless, A. Of All My Loves. Abba Kovner, *Hebrew.* IP, *tr. by* Warren Bargad *and* Stanley F. Chyet

Sky was a street map with stars for, The. Ode. Elizabeth Alexander. GT; PoPoPo

Sky was battered down, The. On Galveston Beach. Barbara Howes. MoAmPo

Sky was blue, so blue, that day, The. For the Candle Light. Angelina Weld Grimké. BlSi; NAAAL

Sky was carpeted with Italian flak. Crump!, The. Malta. John Forbes. NOBAu

Sky was gold in those days, The. In the Beginning. Valerie Sinason. BrRo

Sky was low, the sounding rain was falling dense and dark, The. The Late Passenger. C. S. Lewis. TrCP

Sky widens to Cornwall. A sense of sea, The. Old Friends. John Betjeman. FP

Sky widens to Cornwall, The. A sense of sea. In Memoriam: A. C., R. J. O., K. S. John Betjeman. *Fr.* Old Friends. FP

Sky will extinguish its stars, and the sun, The. Philip of Thessalonica, *Greek.* GrAn; OBCVT, *tr. by* Edwin Morgan

Sky, with all those eyes to stare at you!, The. (LL) Aster. Plato, *Greek.* GrAn; OBCVT, *tr. by* Peter Jay

Skykomish River Running. Richard Hugo. PoA

Skylark, The. Christina Rossetti. *See* A Green Cornfield.

Skylark, what prompts your silver song. Nature Poem. Adrian Mitchell. Spl

Skylarks. Ted Hughes.
"All the dreary Sunday morning." HAP, *sect.* 6
"Crueller than owl or eagle." HAP
"I suppose you just gape and let your gaspings." HAP
"Lark begins to go up, The." HAP
"Like those flailing flames." HAP, *sect.* 7
"My idleness curdles." HAP, *sect.* 5

Skylarks and Fuji. Kusano Shimpei, *Japanese.* PFTM, *tr. by* Cid Corman

Skylarks are far behind that sang over the down. Good-Night. Edward Thomas. FP

Skylark's nest among the grass, The. Birds' Nests. *Unknown.* BoTP

Skylike limpid eyes, The. Brennbaum. Ezra Pound. MoAmPo *Fr.* Hugh Selwyn Mauberley. (Life and Contacts). AmPP; CMoP; InPS-3; LiTM; NOBA; NoAM; TAP

Skyline of New York does not excite me, The. Review from Staten Island. Gloria C. Oden. GT; PoBA

Skymen coming down out the clouds land. A Poem for Deep Thinkers. Imamu Amiri Baraka. APSN

Sky's are a pitiful lot, The. Limerick. Bob Scott. PeLi

Sky's as blue and black as ink, The. Calligram, 15 May 1915. Guillaume Apollinaire, *French.* OBWP, *tr. by* O. Bernard

Sky's blue lapels flap open, The. Flying Home. Gabriel Gbadamosi. NBrP

Sky's lip and the sea's lip shut in peace, The. Lines on the Sea. Dilys Bennett Laing. NYBP

Sky's unresting cloudland, that with varying play, The. Robert Bridges. EBEV *Fr.* The Testament of Beauty.

Skyscraper. Carl Sandburg. ImGa

Skyscraper, skyscraper. Dennis Lee. SSCS

Skyscrapers. Rachel Lyman Field. ChAP; NOxBChV; SSCS

Slack your rope, hangs—a—man. The Maid Freed from the Gallows. *Unknown.* AS

Slag. Charles David Wright. MT

Slain. T. W. H. Crosland. OBWP

Slain Lamb of God. Nikolaus Ludwig, Graf von Zinzendorf, *German.* AH, *tr. by* Sheema Z. Buehne.

Slam, Dunk, and Hook. Yusef Komunyakaa. ISC

Slander. "Anna Akhmatova," *Russian.* TCRP, *tr. by* Daniel Weissbort

Slant of sun on dull brown walls, A. Stephen Crane. LiTM; MeMAP; NAAL-2 *Fr.* War Is Kind.

Slant rays of the setting sun feel sorry, The. It is Not Time Yet to Light the Candle. Sokchong Shin, *Korean.* CKP, *tr. by* Jaihiun Kim

Slanted. Tanka. Miya Shūji, *Japanese.* MJT, *tr. by* Makoto Ueda

Slanting ray of evening light, A. The Squire's Pew. Jane Taylor. PEW

Slanting rays shine on the hamlet. The Farms at Wei River. Wang Wei, *Chinese.* SuSP, *tr. by* Paul W. Kroll

Slap in the Face of Public Taste, A. D. Burliuk, Aleksandr Kruchenykh, V. Mayakovsky, *and* Viktor Khlebnikov. PFTM, *tr. by* Anna Lawton *and* Herbert Eagle

Slate I picked from a nettlebed. Richard Murphy. PBCIP *Fr.* The Battle of Aughrim.

Slate Street School. Ciaran Carson. CABP

Slated for demolition. The Cathedral Is. John Ashbery. InPK-6

Slattern, The. Sarah Dixon. ECWP

Slaughter-House, The. Alfred Hayes. ImPo; PTE

Slaughter of the Laird of Mellerstain, The. *Unknown.* ESPB

Slaughterhouse. Masako Takiguchi, *Japanese.* WPJ, *tr. by* Kenneth Rexroth *and* Ikuko Atsumi

Slave. Langston Hughes. LiTM

Slave, The. James Oppenheim. TrJP

Slave, The. Jones Very. TAP

Slave and the Iron Lace, The. Margaret Danner. BPo

Slave Auction, The. Frances Ellen Watkins Harper. APN-2; BPo; ColAP; ISC; TTY

Slave Cabin, Sotterly Plantation, Maryland, 1989. Lucille Clifton. LoL

Slave Girl, The. Rufinus, *Greek.* GrAn, *tr. by* Alan Marshfield

Slave Girl's Song. *Unknown, Maori.* PeNZ, *tr. by* Margaret Orbell

Slave Marriage Ceremony Supplement. *Unknown.* BPo; CrDW; TAP

Slave Mother, The. Frances Ellen Watkins Harper. APN-2; ColAP; CrDW; NAAAL; PAR

("Heard you that shriek? It rose.") PAR

("Oh, Father! must they part?") (LL) APN-2

("She is a mother, and her heart / Is breaking to despair.") (LL) CrDW

Slave Quarters. James Dickey. CAPP-1; NYBP

Slave Ritual. Carolyn M. Rodgers. ISC

Slave Song. David Dabydeen. PBCV

Slave Song. *Unknown. See* Song: "We raise de wheat."

Slave systems of Rome and Greece, and no one agreed, The. (LL) Sleet Storm on the Merritt Parkway. Robert Bly. CoAmPo

Slave Trade, The. Hannah More. NoP-4

From The Slave Trade. NoP-4

Slavery. Hannah More. WoRP

Slavery. Jones Very. NCAP

Slavery, a Poem. Hannah More.

"Perish th' illiberal thought which would debase." ECWP

Slavery chain done broke at last, broke at last, broke at last. *Unknown.* BkSV

Slaves. James Grainger. NOEC *Fr.* The Sugar Cane.

Slaves, *last st.* James Russell Lowell. *See* On Freedom.

Slave's Complaint, The. George Moses Horton. AAP; CrDW

Slave's Dream, The. Henry Wadsworth Longfellow. FaPoR; NAAL-1; NAAL-3

Slaves / Humming in the twilight by the shanty door. A. J. Seymour. PBCV

Slave's Lament, The. Massillon Coicou, *French.* NegPo, *tr. by* Ellen Conroy Kennedy

Slaves of fools, The. (LL) The Search. Kwesi Brew. PBMAP

Slaves to London, I'll deceive you. A Song. Peter Anthony Motteux. NOSC

Sled Burial, Dream Ceremony. James Dickey. NoP-4

Sledburn Fair. *Unknown.* CH

Sleek, dark-suited. The Elegist. Geoff Page. BMAP

Sleep, The. Elizabeth Barrett Browning. ChIV-1; OxAEP-2

Sleep. Theophile De Viau, *French.* AWP, *tr. by* Sir Edmund Gosse

Sleep. Robert Farren.

"While now I lay me down to sleep." TIRV

Sleep. Bartholomew Griffin. *Fr.* Fidessa, More Chaste than Kind[e].

Sleep. John Haines. WeT

Sleep. Bravig Imbs. SPE

Sleep. Bill Knott. SPE

Sleep. Dana Naone. CDW

Sleep. Publius Papinius Statius, *Latin.* AWP, *tr. by* W. H. Fyfe

Sleep. James Schuyler. GLP

Sleep. Sir Philip Sidney. SiPS *Fr.* Arcadia.
(Sonnet.)

Sleep. Sir Philip Sidney. *See* Sonnet 39: "Come Sleep, O Sleep."

Sleep. Charles Simic. CoAP

Sleep. Kenneth Slessor. BMAP

Sleep after Toil. Edmund Spenser. *Fr.* Wood Of Error. AEP

Sleep, America. Bedtime Story. Gustav Hasford. CDa

Sleep and death, the dusky eagles. Lament. Georg Trakl, *German.* PeFWW, *tr. by* Michael Hamburger

Sleep and oblivion / Reign over all. (LL) Curfew. Henry Wadsworth Longfellow. APN-1; MeMAP; OxBA

Sleep and Poetry. Keats.

"And can I ever bid these joys farewell?" TOF

"O for ten years, that I may overwhelm." NAEL-2; OAEL-2

"O Poesy! for thee I hold my pen." FHYEP

"Schism, A/ Nurtured by foppery and barbarism." EPCY

Sleep, angry beauty, sleep, and fear[e] not me. Thomas Campion. OxBSP

Sleep Apnea. Mark Cox. PUP-18

Sleep, baby mine, Desire; nurse Beauty singeth. Sir Philip Sidney. OxBSP

Sleep, baby, sleep. Lullaby. *Unknown, Japanese.* NOBE, *tr. by* Geoffrey Bownas *and* Anthony Thwaite

Sleep, baby, sleep. *Unknown.* LB

Sleep, baby, sleep, / Our cottage vale is deep. *Unknown.* ReMoGo

Sleep baby sleep! / Thy father watches the sheep. A Cradle Song. *Unknown.* BoTP

Sleep, Big Baby, sleep your fill. (LL) Lullaby: "The Din of work is subdued." W. H. Auden. FaBoMo; GLP; NoAM

Sleep Brought Me Vision. John Peale Bishop. Son

Sleep, calm winter sleep, the rides are woollen. Calm Winter Sleep. Hilary Corke. NYBP

Sleep, Christian warrior, sleep. To Rev. Thaddeus Saltus. Mary Weston Fordham. CBWP-2

Sleep Close to Me. Gabriela Mistral, *Spanish.* PBWP, *tr. by* D. M. Pettinella

Sleep cold at someone's. Callimachus, *Greek.* GrAn, *tr. by* Edward Lucie-Smith

Sleep, Ellen Aubrey, sleep, and dream of me. Tennyson. CBLP *Fr.* Audley Court. NOBVV; PeVV

Sleep, grandmother, sleep. Mark Van Doren. ImGa

Sleep, grim Reproof; my jocund muse doth sing. Humours. John Marston. NoSic *Fr.* Satires.

Sleep in the Heat. Laura Jensen. AmPA

Sleep in the Mojave Desert. Sylvia Plath. AiP

Sleep is a country of water. Country of Water. Bernice Ames. WPE

Sleep is a Deep and Many Voiced Dream. Robert Duncan. CLPP

Sleep is 20. 20. Barbara Guest. PoM

Sleep, King Jesus. Mary's Song. Charles Causley. OBCP

Sleep late with your dream. Owen Dodson. PoBA *Fr.* Poems for My Brother Kenneth.

Sleep, little Baby, kip in peace through the night. Radio Cradle-song. Eugène Marais, *Afrikaans.* PeSAV, *tr. by* Stephen Gray

Sleep, love sleep. Serenade. Mary Weston Fordham. CBWP-2

Sleep, McKade. Evening Song. Kenneth Fearing. SPE

Sleep, Mr. Speaker! it's surely fair. Stanzas to the Speaker Asleep. Winthrop Mackworth Praed. OBSV

Sleep, my babe, lie still and slumber. All Through the Night. *Unknown.* ACTP

Sleep, My Beloved. Yevtushenko, *Russian.* TCRP, *tr. by* Geoffrey Dutton *with* Tina Tupkina-Glaessner

Sleep, My Child. "Sholom Aleichem," *Yiddish.* TrJP, *tr. by* Alter Brody

Sleep, my child, my little daughter. Cradle Song. *Unknown, Yiddish.* TrJP, *tr. by* Joseph Leftwich

Sleep, my child, sleep. Lullaby. Elolongue Epanya Yondo, *French.* NegPo, *tr. by* Ellen Conroy Kennedy

Sleep, my little baby, sleep. Lullaby. Samuel Hoffenstein. TrJP

Sleep my little love. Breyten Breytenbach, *Afrikaans.* PeSAV, *tr. by* Stephen Gray *and* A. J. Coetzee

Sleep, my sweet girl! and all the sleep. La Promessa Sposa. Walter Savage Landor. NOBVV

Sleep now, O sleep now. James Joyce. GBL

Sleep of Adam, The. John Hejduk. ChIV-1

Sleep of My Lions, The. Douglas Livingstone. PeSAV

Sleep of the Brave, The. Odysseas Elytis, *Greek.* AF, *tr. by* Edmund Keeley *and* Philip Sherrard

Sleep of the Painted Ladies, The. Nancy Willard. LCAP-2

Sleep of this night deepens, The. Under Stars. Tess Gallagher. InPK-6

Sleep on, and dream of Heaven awhile. The Sleeping Beauty. Samuel Rogers. GTBS-P; OxAEP-2

Sleep on, beloved, sleep and take thy rest. The Christian's "Good-Night." Sarah Doudney. BLPA

Sleep on, I lie at heaven's high oriels. Nirvana. John Hall Wheelock. MoAmPo

Sleep on my Love in thy cold bed. Stay For Me There. Henry King, Bishop of Chichester. CH; LBC *Fr.* The Exequy. GBL; GLoP; HAP; LoP; MeLP; OxBM; PoEL-2; SCGP; SeCP

Sleep, our lord, and for thy peace. Night Song for a Child. Charles Williams. OBEV

Sleep, Silence' Child. Sonet to Sleepe. William Drummond, of Hawthornden. NOSC; OxBS; Son

Sleep, sleep again, my Lyre, and let thy master die. (LL) A Supplication. Abraham Cowley. GTBS-P; OxAEP-1

Sleep, sleep, beauty bright. A Cradle Song. William Blake. OBEV; PoLF

Sleep sleep old sun, thou canst not have repast [*or* repassed]. Resurrection, Imperfect. Donne. ChIV-2

Sleep softly. . . eagle forgotten. . . under the stone. The Eagle That Is Forgotten. Vachel Lindsay. AWP; CMoP; MeMAP; MoAmPo; NOBA; OxBA

Sleep Song. John Fletcher. NOSC *Fr.* The Tragedy of Valentinian.
  (Song to Sleep.) OxBoLi
  (To Sleep.) PoRA

Sleep Sweet. Ellen M. Huntington Gates. BLPA; FaBoBe

Sleep sweetly in your humble graves. Ode. Henry Timrod. AH; APN-2; CBCWP; ColAP; NOBA; OxBA; PAR; TAP

Sleep tried to split us apart. A Meeting with Vilakazi, the Great Zulu Poet. Raymond Mazisi Kunene, *Zulu.* PeSAV, *tr. by the author*

Sleep-Walking Child. Elisabeth Eybers, *Afrikaans.* PeSA, *tr. by* Jack Cope, Uys Krige, *and* Adèle Naudé

Sleep-walking vapor, like a visitant ghost. Still Life. Anthony Hecht. NoP-4

Sleep was only a dream. Chicago: Near West-Side Renewal. Dennis Schmitz. AmPA

Sleep Watch. Lance Henson. VoR

Sleep well, my child—a shadow, not mama. The New Lullaby. Trần Dạ Tửu', *Vietnamese.* AVP, *tr. by* Huỳnh Sanh Thông

Sleep well, my love, sleep well. Nightsong: City. Dennis Brutus. HBAPE; PBMAP

Sleep will He give His beloved? Nirvana. Rosamund Marriott Watson. VWP

Sleepe after our short light / One everlasting night. (LL) Lines from Catullus. Catullus, *Latin.* FaBoEE; NoSic; OBVE; SiPS, *tr. by* Sir Walter Raleigh

Sleeper, The. Sydney Clouts. PeSA

Sleeper, The. Walter De la Mare. MoBrPo

Sleeper, The. Edgar Allan Poe. AmPP; MeMAP; NAAL-1; NAAL-3; NCAP; NOBA; OxBA; PAR; PoEL-4; TAP

Sleeper in the Valley, The. Rimbaud. OBWP, *tr. by* Robert Lowell *Fr.* Eighteen-Seventy.
  ("There's a green hollow where a river sings.") AWP, *tr. by* Ludwig Lewisohn

Sleeper, the palm-trees drink the breathless noon. *Unknown.* AWP *Fr.* The Thousand and One Nights.

Sleepers, The. Peter Kocan. CBAP

Sleepers. Branko Miljkovic, *Serbo-Croatian.* HSix, *tr. by* Charles Simic

Sleepers, The. Randolph Stow. *Fr.* Thailand Railway. CBAP

Sleepers, The. Walt Whitman. AmPP; NAAL-1; NAAL-3
  (Leaves of Grass (1855).) APN-1
  ("Not the womb yields the babe in its time more surely than I shall be / yielded from you in my time.") (LL) APN-1; PAR

SLEEPERS AWAKE. Text for a Poster (2). Lee Harwood. NBrP

Sleepers humped down on the benches, The. Night Raid. Desmond Hawkins. PoWW

"Sleepers," The. Walt Whitman.
  "Now what my mother told me one day as we sat at dinner / together." BLT

Sleepin' at the Foot o' the Bed. Luther Patrick. BLPA

Sleeping, The. Lynn Emanuel. AiP; WWSi

Sleeping. (LL) Weep you no more, sad fountains. *Unknown.* CH; EBEV; EnLoPo; GBL; HAP; NOSC; NTP; NoSic; PoE; PoEL-2; TFi

Sleeping armies of the living God, The. The Death of Saul. Philip Levine. ChIV-1

Sleeping at last, the trouble and tumult over. Christina Rossetti. NAEL-2

Sleeping Beauty. Olga Broumas. CPO

Sleeping Beauty, The. Samuel Rogers. GTBS-P; OxAEP-2

Sleeping Beauty, The. Dame Edith Sitwell.
  Governante, The. BWW
  Innocent Spring, The. NOBE
  "Mauve summer rain, The." BWW
  Princess, The. BWW
  "When we come to that dark house." OBMV

Sleeping Beauty: Variation of the Prince, The. Randall Jarrell. PoA

Sleeping Fury, The. Louise Bogan. LiTM; NALW

Sleeping Giant, The. Donald Hall. NYBP; Poetsp; TwCP

Sleeping Heroes. Edward Richard Burton Shanks. OBMV

Sleeping House, The. Tennyson. OBNC *Fr.* Maud has a garden of roses. FHYEP *Fr.* Maud [A Monodrama]. EnVR

Sleeping in fever, I am unfit. For God While Sleeping. Anne Sexton. CAPP-1

Sleeping in the Forest. Mary Oliver. InPS-3

Sleeping in their sheen'. (LL) Willie Macintosh. *Unknown.* ESPB; OxBB; OxBoLi

Sleeping Lord, The. David Jones.
  "Tawny-black sky-scurries." OBWVE

Sleeping on Horseback. Po Chü-i, *Chinese.* BLT; ChiP, *tr. by* Arthur Waley

Sleeping on the Bus. Martín Espada. BAP-96

Sleeping on the Ceiling. Elizabeth Bishop. OBGa; TTTS

Sleeping on the Wing. Frank O'Hara. InPS-3; NAAL-2

Sleeping or waking, thou sweet face. *Unknown. Fr.* Popular Songs of Tuscany. AWP, *tr. by* John Addington Symonds

Sleeping Out with My Father. Gibbons Ruark. MT

Sleeping They Bear Me. Alfred Mombert, *German.* AWP, *tr. by* Jethro Bithell

Sleeping, turning in turn like planets. Adrienne Rich. TRP *Fr.* Twenty-one Love Poems. GLP

Sleeping with Boa. May Swenson. BAP-94

Sleeping with Cats. Marge Piercy. *Fr.* Six Underrated Pleasures. EC2

Sleeping with Foxes. Roberta Hill Whiteman. CDW

Sleeping with One Eye Open. Mark Strand. NYBP

Sleeping with Women. Kenneth Koch. PoM

Sleeping woman dreams she wakes, A. Nightmare. Isabella Gardner. CoAP

Sleeping Youth. Vesna Parun, *Croatian.* CEEP, *tr. by* Peter Kastmiler

Sleepless. Al-Khansa, *Arabic.* BoWoP, *tr. by* Willis Barnstone

Sleepless. Sara Teasdale. SAGP

Sleepless as Prospero back in his bedroom. Darwin in 1881. Gjertrud Schnackenberg. NoAM; NoP-4

Sleepless at Crown Point. Richard Wilbur. InPK-6; WeW-3

Sleepless ghost perpetually striving, The. Eros Out of the Sea. Dilys Bennett Laing. PoA

Sleepless Hours who watch me as I lie, The. Hymn of Apollo. Shelley. NAEL-2; OAEL-2

Sleepless, I stare. The Broken Dark. Robert Earl Hayden. GT

Sleepless Night. Léon Damas, *French.* NegPo, *tr. by* Ellen Conroy Kennedy

Sleepless Night, A. Philip Levine. BLT

Sleepless nights, The. I Wish I Were in Love Again. Lorenz Hart. OBCoV

Sleepless Nights. Marilyn Nelson Waniek. ISC

Sleepless with cold commemorative eyes. (LL) A Superscription. D. G. Rossetti. EBVV; GSo; GTBS-P; NAEL-2; NoP-4; OAEL-2; OBNC; PoEL-5

Sleepless, with pleasure and expiring fears. Walter Savage Landor. NOBRP *Fr.* Gebir.

Sleepless, you hear the neighboring temple bell. A Poem Making Fun of Chi-ti for His Eye Illness. Yang Chi, *Chinese.* CoBLCP, *tr. by* Jonathan Chaves

Sleeplessness. Luigi Fontanella, *Italian.* NeIt, *tr. by* W. S. Di Piero

Sleep'ry Sim of the Lamb-kill. The Fray of Suport. *Unknown.* IBB

Sleeps as thy lover for a little while. (LL) Hymn to Earth. Elinor Wylie. LiTM; MoAmPo

Sleep's dream / the nerve-flash in the blood. Subliminal. Lorine Niedecker. PFTM

Sleepwalkers. Bella Akhatovna Akhmadulina, *Russian*. BoWoP, *tr. by* Barbara Einzig

Sleepwalkers' Ballad. Federico García Lorca, *Spanish*. STV; WeW-3, *tr. by* John Frederick Nims

Sleepy Giant, The. Charles Edward Carryl. NOxBChV; OTCP

Sleepy world of streams, A. (LL) The Garden of Proserpine. Swinburne. AWP; BLPA; FaPoR; HAP; NAEL-2; NOBE; NOBVV; OBNC; PoE; PoEL-5; PoRA; SCV

Sleet. Norman MacCaig. AYFP; OBCP

Sleet Storm on the Merritt Parkway. Robert Bly. CoAmPo; NOBA

Slender as a needle. If a Suite in Praise of the Yoruba Oracle. Awotunde Aworinde. PFTM, *tr. by* Judith Gleason *and* John Olaniyi Ogundipe

Slender bamboo is like a hermit, The. On a Painting by Wang the Clerk of Yen Ling. Su Tung-p'o, *Chinese*. BLT, *tr. by* Kenneth Rexroth

Slender breath of the piper, The. (LL) Elevator Man, 1949. Rita Dove. NAmP90

Slender, delicate, soft jade. Slender Fingers. Chao Luan-luan, *Chinese*. BoWoP, *tr. by* Kenneth Rexroth *and* Ling Chung

Slender glow of minaret and silent muezzins. Landscapes. Husein Tahmisic, *Serbian*. CEEP, *tr. by* Ewald Osers

Slender Lad, The. *Unknown, Welsh*. OBWVE, *tr. by* Kenneth Hurlstone Jackson

Slender plank above a waterhole, A. The Founding of New Hampshire. Carl Rakosi. FTOS

Slender, shy, and sensitive young girl, The. For Gwen, 1969. Margaret Abigail Walker. NMM-2

Slender young blackbird built in a thorn-tree, A. The Blackbird. Dinah Maria Mulock Craik. BoTP

Slept, and there was no pursuit. (LL) Hell Gate. A. E. Housman. NoAM; SCGP; UnPo

Sliab Cua, dark and broken, is full of wolf packs. *Unknown*. *Fr.* Toward Winter. NOIV

Slice of Wedding Cake, A. Robert Graves. BoLoP; NAEL-2; NOBE; OxBTC

Slices of Knowledge. Henri Michaux, *French*.

"He who knows how to shave the razor, will know how to erase the." PFTM, *tr. by* Pierre Joris

Slicing my head off shaving I think of Charles I. Notes for a Revised Sonnet. "Edward Pygge." BXAP *Fr. Robert Lowell's Notebook*. OBCoV

—slide and— / pass on. Vagabond's Arising. Aina Kraujiete, *Latvian*. CEEP, *tr. by* Inara Cedrins

Slide soft, fair forth, and make a crystal plain. Sonnet. William Drummond, of Hawthornden. NOSC

Slides. Jennifer Maiden. CBAP

Slides by on grease. (LL) For the Union Dead. Robert Lowell. AmPP; CBCWP; CoAP; ColAP; FYAP; FaBoPV; HAP; HCAP; HeIP-4; InPS-3; LCAP-2; LiTM; MoP; NAAL-2; NOBA; NoAM; NoP-4; OBWP; PoE; Poetr; SCV; TFi; TRP; TwCP; UnPo; VCAP; WeW-3

Sliding down the banisters. On the Banisters. Margaret E. Gibbs. BoTP

Sliding Trombone. Georges Ribemont-Dessaignes, *French*. SPE, *tr. by* David Gascoyne

Slight accent, A. Emigrant/Immigrant. Rina Ferrarelli. LoHo

Slight as thou art, thou art enough to hide. To a Daisy. Alice Thompson Meynell. MoBrPo; Son; VWP

Slight Confusion, A. James Reiss. AmPA

Slight infection of the ear, A. Seven Months. Cleopatra Mathis. FiLi

Slight neglects of conversation, the. (LL) Carmen 10 ("Varus, whom I chanced to meet"). Catullus. AWP; OBVE, *tr. by* John Hookham Frere

Slight unpremeditated Words are borne. Love's Witness. Aphra Behn. BoWoP; LW

Slighted Lady, The. Anna Wickham. LW

Slighted Wife, The. Aaron Hodza, *Shona*. PeSAV, *tr. by* George Fortune

Slightly before the middle of Congressman Pudd. E. E. Cummings. FaBoEE; OBAL

Slightly simpering sparkle of the eye, The. (LL) L'Allée. Paul Verlaine, *French*. GaP; OBGa, *tr. by* Arthur Symons

Slim and singing copper girl, A. Early Copper. Carl Sandburg. HeIP-4

Slim cunning hands at rest, and cozening eyes. Walter De la Mare. FaBoEE; NIP-4; WeW-3

Slim Greer. Sterling Brown. NAAAL

Slim Greer went to heaven. Slim in Hell. Sterling Brown. BPo

Slim in Atlanta. Sterling Brown. NoP-4

Slim Man Canyon. Leslie Marmon Silko. VoR

Slim sentinels. Trees at Night. Helene Johnson. BlSi

Slim / young fascist, A. On the Yard. Etheridge Knight. RaBo

Slime clung, The. Isaac Rosenberg. PeFWW *Fr.* The Amulet.

Slimy obscene creatures, insane. The Nigga Section. Welton Smith. BPo

Slip, The. Wendell Berry. NOCV

Slip / from my arm. (LL) Balboa, the Entertainer. Imamu Amiri Baraka. AF

Slip of loveliness, slim, seemly. In Praise of a Girl. Huw Morus, *Welsh*. OBWVE, *tr. by* Gwyn Williams

Slip of the tong. (LL) Lapsus Linguae. Keith Preston. NBLV; OBAL; OBCoV

Slip off that gown. Paulus Silentiarius, *Greek*. GrAn, *tr. by* Andrew Miller

Slip out of darkness, it is time. (LL) The Second Life. Edwin Morgan. FaBoTC

Slipped Quadrant. Nathaniel Mackey. FTOS; PT

("As if by late light shaped of its / arrival.") PT

Slipping in blood, by his own hand, through pride. To an Artist, to Take Heart. Louise Bogan. NYBP; TRP

Slipping in the snow. Chuck Brickley. HA

Slipping into my black patent leather shoes. Black Patent Leather Shoes. Karen L. Mitchell. IFJA

Slipping—is Crash's law. (LL) Crumbling is not an instant's Act. Emily Dickinson. AmPP; NOBA

Slithergadee has crawled out of the sea, The. Shel Silverstein. KaS; NBLV; NTCP; OBCoV

Sloe Gin. Seamus Heaney. PNI

Sloe was lost in flower, The. A. E. Housman. CBLP

Slog brute streets with rebel tramping! Our March. Vladimir Mayakovsky, *Russian*. AWP, *tr. by* Babette Deutsch *and* Avrahm Yarmolinsky

Slogan, The. Paul Blackburn. PoM

Slogan Will Not Suffice, A. Kelvin Corcoran. NBrP

Slop Barrel, The. Philip Whalen. PmAP

Slope like a path for, A. Marina Tsvetayeva, *Russian*. PFTM, *tr. by* Elaine Feinstein *Fr.* Poem of the End.

Slope of it. Body. Robert Creeley. FTOS

Slope woods' snows melt. Easter Sunday. Allen Ginsberg. FTOS

Slopes of the sun and vine, and thou dark stream. Pastoral. George Cabot Lodge. APN-2

Sloth, The. Theodore Roethke. ChAP; OBAL; OBCA; PiM; TRP

Slouches towards Bethlehem to be born? (LL) The Second Coming. W. B. Yeats. APAD; BIrV; CABP; CMoP; ChIV-2; ClHu; EBEvV; FaBoMo; FaBoPV; GI; GTBS-P; HAP; HeIP-4; HoPM; ImPo; InPK-6; InPS-3; LiTM; MoBrPo; MoP; NAEL-2; NAWM-2; NIP-4; NOBE; NoAM; NoP-4; OAEL-2; OxAEP-2; OxBTC; PBMP; PoE; PoPoPo; Poetr; RaBo; SCV; SoSe-8; TFi; TRP; UnPo

Slough. John Betjeman. APAD; MoBrPo; NoAM; OxAEP-2

Slow bleak awakening from the morning dream. Living. Harold Monro. ImPo

Slow burn, A. Pit Viper. George Starbuck. NYBP

Slow, cold breathing, The. The Marsh, New Year's Day. Peter Everwine. NNaP

Slow Dance. David St. John. AmPA; LCAP-2

Slow Dancer That No One Hears but You. Duane Niatum. CDW

Slow dirty tears. Pablo Neruda. *See* Walking [*or* Walkin'] Around.

Slow-footed stockman called Beales, A. Limerick. Cyril Mountjoy. PeLi

Slow for the sake of flowers as they turn. Release. R. S. Gwynn. RA

Slow Giving. Ibn al-Rumi, *Arabic*. ArPe, *tr. by* Omar S. Pound

Slow, horses, slow. Night of Spring. Thomas Westwood. BoTP

Slow Men Working in Trees. Anne C. Bromley. CMAP

Slow Movement. Louis MacNeice. CBLP

Slow Movement. William Carlos Williams. PoA

Slow moves the acid breath of noon. Field of Autumn. Laurie Lee. LiTM

Slow moves the pageant of a climbing race. Slow Through the Dark. Paul Laurence Dunbar. GSo

Slow on tle leash / Pallid the leash-men! (LL) The Return. Ezra Pound. AmPP; CMoP; HAP; MoAmPo; MoP; NOBA; NoAM; OxBA; PoE; Poetr; RB; TRP; VGW; WeW-3

Slow overture of rain, The. Mind. Jorie Graham. HCAP; Poetr

Slow Pacific Swell, The. Yvor Winters. ColAP; NOBA

Slow pass the hours—ah, passing slow! Ballade Tragique à Double Refrain. Max Beerbohm. OBSV

Slow Rain. Gabriela Mistral. PBWP, *tr. by* Gunda Kaiser *and* James Tipton

Slow, rigid, is this masquerade. Spring 1916. Isaac Rosenberg. NSI

Slow sinks, more lovely ere his race be run. Sunset over the Aegean. Byron. OBNC *Fr.* The Corsair.

Slow, slow, fresh fount, keep time with my salt tears. Song: "Slow, slow fresh fount, keep time with my salt tears." Ben Jonson. BeJo; CH; InPS-3; NAEL-1; NIP-4; NOSC; NoP-4; OAEL-1; OxAEP-1; OxBSP; PoEL-2; RB; SCGP; SeCP; TFi *Fr.* Cynthia's Revels.

Slow—slow—slow—slow. (LL) A Swing Song. William Allingham. CTV; OTCP; TLR

Slow Spring. Katharine Tynan. BoTP

Slow Summer Twilight. John Hall Wheelock. LiTM

Slow the Kansas sun was setting o'er the wheat fields far away. Towser Shall Be Tied Tonight. *Unknown.* BLPA

Slow the limpid currents twining. Canzonet. Mary Robinson. NOBRP

Slow Through the Dark. Paul Laurence Dunbar. GSo

Slow to Come, Quick a-Gone. William Barnes. NOBVV

Slow toiling upward from the misty vale. Nearing the Snow-Line. Oliver Wendell Holmes. APN-1

Slow wand'ring came the sightless sire and she. Antigone and Oedipus. Henrietta Cordelia Ray. AAP; BlSi; CBWP-3

Slowest animals [or beasts] are, The. Armchairs. Dan Pagis, *Hebrew.* IP, *tr. by* Warren Bargad *and* Stanley F. Chyet

Slowly a hundred miles through the powerful rain. You Drive in a Circle. Ted Hughes. NYBP

Slowly, and flake by flake. . . At the drifted fond. Winter Night: Mount Royal. Abraham Moses Klein. NoAM

Slowly beginning to wake. (LL) The Kite. Mark Strand. ColAP

Slowly, by God's hand unfurled. Evening Hymn. William Henry Furness. AH; FaBoBe

Slowly England's sun was setting o'er the hilltops far away. Curfew Must Not Ring Tonight. Rose Hartwick Thorpe. BLPA; FaBoBe

Slowly flutters the snow from ash-coloured heavens in silence. Snowfall. Giosuè Carducci, *Italian.* AWP, *tr. by* Romilda Rendel

Slowly he sways that head that cannot hear. Rattler, Alert. Brewster Ghiselin. HAP; WeW-3

Slowly he turns himself round and round. The Dancing Bear. Rachel Lyman Field. KaS; NTCP

Slowly I walk the gully path, alone. Painting. Chang Yü. *Fr.* Twelve Miscellaneous Poems on the Fang Garden. CoBLCP, *tr. by* Jonathan Chaves

Slowly in three to four weeks. My Girlfriends. Erich Fried, *German.* AF, *tr. by* Georg Rapp

Slowly inside me. Tanka. Miya Shūji, *Japanese.* MJT, *tr. by* Makoto Ueda

Slowly / like a crippled cow. Jean-Joseph Rabéarivelo, *French.* NegPo, *tr. by* Ellen Conroy Kennedy

Slowly now, and softly now, and sweetly. Dark and Dark. William Robert Moses. WeT

Slowly out of the sun-blackened landscape. (LL) Rivers and Mountains. John Ashbery. CoAP; NOBA; NoAM; TRP

Slowly, silently, now the moon. Silver. Walter De la Mare. BoTP; CTV; MoBrPo; PoRA; SAGP; TTTS

Slowly, slowly. Donne. ITG

"Slowly, Slowly" Poem, The. Yüan Hung-tao, *Chinese.* CoBLCP, *tr. by* Jonathan Chaves

Slowly, slowly, swinging low. Swinging. Irene Thompson. BoTP

Slowly, Slowly Wisdom Gathers. Mark Van Doren. PoA

Slowly the Moon her banderoles of light. A Battle. Isabella Valancy Crawford. NOBC

Slowly the moon is rising out of the ruddy haze. Aware. D. H. Lawrence. MoBrPo; NoAM

Slowly the night blooms, unfurling. Flowers of Darkness. Frank Marshall Davis. PoBA

Slowly the poison the whole blood stream fills. Missing Dates. William Empson. CMoP; HAP; LiTM; MoBrPo; MoP; NOBE; NoAM; OAEL-2; PoE; UnPo

Slowly the ponderous doors of lead imponderous. Sleep. Bravig Imbs. SPE

Slowly the sugar dissolves in the tall glass of tea. Comfortable Words. Gillian Allnutt. NBrP

Slowly, the summer was ending with a shower. We were. A Sentimental Voyage Around My Room. Jovan Hristic, *Serbo-Croatian.* HSix, *tr. by* Charles Simic

Slowly the tide creeps up the sand. James Reeves. NOxBChV; NTP

Slowly the vision grows. Lakeside Incident. Robin Skelton. NOBC

Slowly the women file to where he stands. Faith Healing. Philip Larkin. ChIV-2; GI; NoAM

Slowly the world contracts about my ears. The Flagpole Sitter. Donald Finkel. CoAP

Slowly thy flowing tide. The Ebb Tide. Robert Southey. OBNC

Slowly we learn; the oft repeated line. On National Vanity. J. E. Clare McFarlane. PBCV

Slowness of Belief in a Spiritual World, The. Jones Very. NCAP

Slug. Theodore Roethke. APo

Slug in Woods. Earle Birney. NOBC; NoP-4

Slugabed. Sydney Goodsir Smith. FaBoTC *Fr.* Under the Eildon Tree.

Sluggard, The. W. H. Davies. OBMV

Sluggard, The. Isaac Watts. CH; EBEvV; ECEV; HAP; NOEC; OxBChV; OxBoLi; PoEL-3; UV

Sluggish morne as yet undrest, The. Upon Phillis Walking in a Morning before Sun-Rising. John Cleveland. MeLP

Sluggy and slowe, in spetinge muiche. *Unknown.* MiEL

Slum Dwelling, A. George Crabbe. OBNC *Fr.* The Borough.

Slum man they killed, the mountain man lives on, The. (LL) Early Lynching. Carl Sandburg. ChIV-2; MoAmPo

Slumber dark and deep. Paul Verlaine. AWP, *tr. by* Arthur Symons *Fr.* Sagesse.

Slumber *did* my spirit *seal*, A. Wordsworth. AWP; EBEvV; EnLoPo; FaBoCh; GTBS-P; HAP; HeIP-4; ImPo; InPK-6; InPS-3; NOBRP; NoP-4; PBMP; PoEL-4; PoRA; SCV; UnPo; WeW-3 *Fr.* Lucy. FHYEP; NOBE; OAEL-2; OBEV; OBNC; SCGP; TFi

("With rocks and stones and trees!") (LL) LaPo; NoP-4; PFE; PoPoPo; Ro

Slumber in Spring. Elizabeth Gould. BoTP

Slumber Party. Carson McCullers. CTV

Slumber Song of the Gardens, A. John Runcie. PeSAV

Slumbering Passion. Josephine D. Henderson Heard. CBWP-4

Slumnight. Colette Inez. CMAP

Slump. Vassar Miller. BoWoP

Slumped on a chair, his body is an S. The Lavatory Attendant. Wendy Cope. UV

Slumped on a pallet of winter-withered grass. Cross Cut. Peter Davison. ColAP

Slumped under the impressive genitals. Boston Common. John Berryman. CBCWP

Sly Mongoose. *Unknown add. verses by* Knolly La Fortune. PBCV

Sma' was I, amang brother o' mine. David and Goliath. P. Hately Waddell. ChIV-1

Small Aircraft. Bella Akhatovna Akhmadulina, *Russian.* BoWoP, *tr. by* Daniel Halpern

Small and emptied woman you lie here a thousand years dead. In the Museum. Isabella Gardner. NYBP; SoSe-8

Small / & with intensely. Parents. Hilda Morley. PmAP

Small bird, forgive me. *Unknown, Japanese.* KaS, *tr. by* Harry Behn

Small bird / tracks. Rain. Lance Henson. VoR

Small Birds. Leonard Clark. AYFP

Small Bird's Nest Made of White Reed Fiber, A. Robert Bly. NNaP

Small Boy, Dreaming, A. Albert Herzing. NYBP

Small boy drove the shaggy ass, The. Turf-Carrier [or Turf Carrier] on Aranmore. John Hewitt. PoRA

Small, busy flames play through the fresh-laid coals. To My Brothers. Keats. Son

Small car distant, no life in it. Cross Divide. Tom Raworth. NBrP

Small change, when we are [or we are or we're] to bodies gone. (LL) The Ecstasy. Donne. BoLoP; CBLP; ESCV; EnLoPo; FHYEP; HAP; ImPo; InPS-3; MeLP; NAEL-1; NOBE; OAEL-1; OBEV; PoE; PoEL-2; SeCP; TFi; TOF

Small child of a wind, A. Requiem for Sonora. Richard Shelton. Poetsp

Small Comfort. Katha Pollitt. CrSp

Small Country. Claribel Alegría, *Spanish.* BoWoP, *tr. by* Aliki *and* Willis Barnstone

Small Dark Song. Philip Dacey. CMAP

Small Differences. Judith C. Root. CMAP

Small doses, effleurage will do. Sea or Sky? Medbh McGuckian. PBCIP

Small eyes water on the branch. Another Face. Ray A. Young Bear. CDW

Small fact and fingers and farthest one from me. A Poem for Emily. Miller Williams. MT; MoLi; WeW-3

Small Faculty Stag for the Visiting Poet, A. Earle Birney. OxBC; PeLV

Small Farm, A. Michael Hartnett. CIP-2; PBCIP

Small Fat Boy Walking Backwards, A. Gerry Murphy. BiHa

Small Fig Tree, A. Donald Hall. ChIV-2; GI

Small fists waving. The Baby Hilary, Sir Edmund. Kathleen Leland Baker. NBLV

Small Fountains. Lascelles Abercrombie. CH *Fr.* Epilogue: "What shall we do for Love these days?" CH; MoBrPo *Fr.* Emblems of Love.

Small Frogs Killed on the Highway. James Wright. HCAP; NNaP; NoAM; PoPoPo

Small gal, Jamaican, she came to me. Jamaican Small Gal. A. L. Hendriks. HCP

Small Garden, The. Cheng Hsieh, *Chinese.* SuSp, *tr. by* Wu-chi Liu

Small girl, A. Michael McClintock. HA

Small girls hurried to the hilltop church, The. Whit Monday. John Hewitt. TIRV

Small girls on trikes. Christmas Day. Roy Fuller. OBCP

Small gleams on the bank. (LL) Bog Queen. Seamus Heaney. NoAM; RACG

Small gnats that fly. One Hard Look. Robert Graves. MoBrPo

Small grey bird that fit inside the hand, The. Peddler's Village. Gerald Stern. CMAP

Small grey cloudy louse that nests in my beard, The. James Keir Baxter. NoP-4; PeNZ *Fr.* Jerusalem Sonnets.

Small householder now comes out warily, The. Spring Voices. Louis MacNeice. Son

Small Joys. May Sarton. FFC

Small justice shown, and still less pity. (LL) Hell is a city much like London. Shelley. OBSV; OxBSn

Small Kulak Landowner. Innokenty Fiodorovich Annensky, *Russian.* TCRP, *tr. by* Lubov Yakovleva *with* Daniel Weissbort

Small Light, A. Cathy Song. TRP

Small lights pirouette. Peterhead in May. Burns Singer. FaBoTC; OxBS

Small Love Song, A. Tong-gyu Hwang, *Korean.* CKP, *tr. by* Jaihiun Kim

Small man suffers the indignities of childhood, The. Paul Klee. Ruthven Todd. SPE

Small men make love on stilts, and hold their poise. A Forked Radish. Jonathan Price. CBLP

Small. Miniaturized, yet you insist. The Country of Dust. Vahan Tekeyan, *Armenian.* AF, *tr. by* Diana Der Hovanessian and Marzbed Margossian

Small Miseries. Letitia Elizabeth Landon. VWP

Small moon. Prayer to the Young Moon. *Unknown, Bushman.* PeSA, *tr. by* W. H. I. Bleek *and* Jack Cope

Small-mouth bass breaks water, gorged with spawn, The. (LL) After the Surprising Conversions. Robert Lowell. AmPP; CoAmPo; HAP; NAAL-2; NoAM; TRP

Small noise, A. Rod Willmot. HA

Small of the back has its answers. Cuba Night. Dave Jeddie Smith. NAmP90

Small part of it will die if I'm not around / feeding it anymore, A. (LL) Chicago Poem. Lew Welch. BB

Small Patch of Ice, A. Betsy Sholl. PBCAP

Small Paths. Henriëtte Roland-Holst, *Dutch.* WPOW, *tr. by* Jonathan Crewe

Small poems, The. Robert Burlingame. IFJA

Small Prayer. Weldon Kees. IMW; PoA; VGW

Small Rains. N. M. Bodecker. Spl

Small Room with Large Windows, A. Allen Curnow. PeNZ

"In the interim, how the children should be educated."

"Kingfisher's naked arc alight, A."

"Seven ageing pine tree hide."

"What it would look like if really there were only."

Small room with one table and one chair, A. Poet in Winter. Edward Lucie-Smith. TwCP

Small sad man with a hat, A. At Last. John Montague. PBCIP

Small Sad Song. Alastair Reid. NYBP

Small-scale Reflections on a Great House. A. K. Ramanujan. OxBC

Small Score, A. Delmore Schwartz. PBMP

Small script take thy swift way across the sea. For His Friends. Alcuin, *Latin.* MLL, *tr. by* Helen Waddell

Small service is true service while it lasts. To a Child [Written in Her Album]. Wordsworth. OxBChV; OxBSP; Spl

Small, Smaller. Russell Hoban. NOxBChV

Small Song. A. R. Ammons. NoAM

Small space. Two Tile Beaks. Maria Amalia Fonte Boa. BoWoP, *tr. by* Willis Barnstone *and* Nelson Cerqueira

Small Square, The. Sophia de Mello Breyner Andresen, *Portuguese.* WPOW, *tr. by* Alexis Levitin

Small Square, The. Sophia De Mello Breyner, *Portuguese.* VCWP, *tr. by* Ruth Fainlight

Small Talk in a Garden. O. B. Hardison Jr. CRP

Small thing and moreover black is she, A. Philodemus, *Greek.* GrAn, *tr. by* William Moebius

Small things, like the turning of a key. Chimes. Michael Smith. PBCIP

Small thunder cuts my autumn doze on the porch. Museum. Sydney Lea. NAmP90

Small Town. Rita Dove. GT

Small town Gladys. David Campbell. BMAP

Small Town with One Road. Gary Soto. SoSe-8

Small traveller from an unseen shore. To a New-Born Child. Cosmo Monkhouse. LiLi

Small type of great ones, that do him, A Fly Caught in a Cobweb. Richard Lovelace. BeJo; CaPo; SeCP

Small vampire, gorger at your mother's teat. Last Child. X. J. Kennedy. OxBSP

Small Variation. Octavio Paz, *Spanish.* VCWP, *tr. by* Mark Strand

Small Vases from Hebron, The. Naomi Shihab Nye. BAP-96

Small wax candles melt to light, The. Poor Women in a City Church. Seamus Heaney. TIRV

Small wheel, A. Watch Repair. Charles Simic. NoP-4

Small wind lightly, A. Count Carrots. Gerda Mayer. OBSP

Small Wings. Maude Meehan.

"She has withdrawn from us." MDDM

Small Woman on Swallow Street. W. S. Merwin. CoAmPo; CoAP

Small Wonder. Brock. Paul Muldoon. NoAM; NoP-4

Smaller and clearer as the years go by. (LL) Lines on a Young Lady's Photograph Album. Philip Larkin. EnLoPo; HAP; OAEL-2

Smaller Love Song, A. Tong-gyu Hwang, *Korean.* CKP, *tr. by* Jaihiun Kim

Smaller—that Covered Vision—Here. (LL) Renunciation—is a piercing Virtue. Emily Dickinson. APN-2; NoP-4

Smallest bark on life's tumultuous ocean, The. Influence. Sarah Knowles Bolton. PWR

Smallest basil leaf was heard to whimper, The. *Unknown, Serbo-Croatian.* HSix, *tr. by* Charles Simic

Smalltown Memorials. Geoff Page. BMAP

Smart and cannot fish there. (LL) Limbo. Seamus Heaney. CIP-2; NoAM; OxBC

Smart man was Bishop Colenso, A. Colenso Rhymes for Orthodox Children. Bret Harte. OBAL

Smash me looking-glass glass. Mirror's Song. Liz Lochhead. FaBoTC; NBrP

Smear of blue peat smoke, The. The Shepherd's Hut. Andrew Young. FaBoTC; OxBTC

Smeared with the gold of the opulent sun. (LL) A Postcard from the Volcano. Wallace Stevens. GEA; HAP; HCAP; MeMAP; NoAM; SAmP; WeW-3

Smears re-bop / sound. (LL) Neon Signs. Langston Hughes. APSN

Smell. Molly Peacock. NMM-2

Smell. William Carlos Williams. MoAmPo; RaBo; TAP

(Smell!) SAmP

Smell of canyon rain storm. Eric Mottram. NBrP

Smell of cigar smoke, Sunday, after dinner. Cigar Smoke, Sunday, after Dinner. Louise Townsend Nicholl. FYAP

Smell of Coal Smoke, The. Les A. Murray. NOBAu

Smell of death is so powerful, The. Marguerite de Navarre, *French.* PBWP, *tr. by* Aline Allard

Smell of death was in the air, The. Farewell. John Press. PoRA

Smell of gasoline. (LL) The Moose. Elizabeth Bishop. DiPo; FaBoWP; NAAL-2; NALW

Smell of Old Newspapers Is Always Stronger after Sleeping in the Sun, The. Mike Lowery. Poetsp

Smell of piss guides us down the halls. The Hospital State. Betsy Sholl. PBCAP

Smell of potatoes just taken out of the earth, The. Chilean Elegies: 5, The. The Interior. Tom Wayman. NOBC

Smell of snow, stinging in nostrils as the wind lifts it from a beach, The. The Crystal Lithium. James Schuyler. PmAP; PoM; VCAP

Smells. Yelena Sergeievna, Countess de Carli Shchapova, *Russian.* TCRP, *tr. by* Bradley Jordan

Smells. Kathryn Worth. AYFP

Smells—how many. The Sense of Smell. Louis MacNeice. NYBP

Smelt! (LL) At the Zoo. William Makepeace Thackeray. NTCP; OxBChV

Smilax in our homes entwine, The. Christmas Eve. Lizelia Augusta Jenkins Moorer. CBWP-3

Smile, The. William Blake. RB

Smile, The. Robert Frost. *Fr.* The Hill Wife. CMoP; HAP; InPS-3; LiTM; NoP-4; RACG

Smile, A. *Unknown.* BLPA

Smile. *Unknown.* BLPA

Smile at us, pay us, pass us; but do not quite forget. The Secret People. G. K. Chesterton. FaPoR; OxBTC

Smile costs nothing but gives much—, A. *Unknown.* PoToHe

Smile, Death. Charlotte Mew. WPE; WPOW

Smile fell in the grass, A. The Night Dances. Sylvia Plath. LCAP-2

Smile is quite a funny thing, A. Growing Smiles. *Unknown.* PoLF

Smile of iceboxes annihilates me, The. An Appearance. Sylvia Plath. CAPP-1

Smile of the Goat has a meaning that few, The. Oliver Herford. OBCoV; PeLV

Smile of the Walrus is wild and distraught, The. Oliver Herford. OBCoV

Smile on the famed Mona Lisa, The. The Limerick. Stanley J. Sharpless. PeLi

Smile, smile / Blest isle! A Lilliputian Ode on Their Majesties' Accession. Henry Carey. FaBoVe; NOEC; OBCoV

Smile, Smile, Smile. Wilfred Owen. PeFWW

Smile / to see the lake. Lorine Niedecker. VGW

Smiling and haunted, to a dark morning. (LL) To the Snake. Denise Levertov. AmPP; LiTM; NMM-2; PoA

Smiling Dawn, with diadem of dew, The. The Poet's Ministrants. Henrietta Cordelia Ray. CBWP-3

Smiling girls, rosy boys. The Gingerbread Man. *Unknown.* ACTP

Smiling girls, rosy boys. Mother Goose. OxNR

Smiling Mouth and Laughing Eyen Grey, The. Charles, Duc d' Orléans. HAP; MiEL; NoP-4

Smiling, sweet girl, this proffered toy approve. To a Lady, with a Present of a Fan. Charles Brandling. NOEC

Smiling the boy fell dead. (LL) Incident of the French Camp. Robert Browning. FaPoR; OBWP

Smiling through my own memories of painful excitement your wide eyes. Ode to Tanaquil Leclercq. Frank O'Hara. FTOS

Smiling, we set the testing tray before the hall. Wen Cheng-ming. CoBLCP, *tr. by* Jonathan Chaves *Fr.* My Son's One-Year Test: Improvised.

Smith at the organ is like an anvil being. The Sound of Afroamerican History Chapt II. S. E. Anderson. PoBA

Smith makes me, A. The Runes on Weland's Sword. Rudyard Kipling. NoAM; PoEL-5 *Fr.* Old Men at Pevensey.

Smith of Maudlin. George Walter Thornbury. PeVV

Smithereens. D. G. Rossetti. NOBVV

Smithfield Ham. Dave Jeddie Smith. HCAP

Smiths, The. E. G. Murphy. NOBAu

Smoke. Rubén Bonitaz Nuño, *Spanish.* STV, *tr. by* John Frederick Nims

Smoke. Smoke Rose. Itamar Ya'oz-kest, *Hebrew.* HP, *tr. by* Abramson, Glenda

Smoke. Henry David Thoreau. AWP; NoP-4; OxBA *Fr.* Walden.

Smoke. Charles Wright. NYBP

Smoke and Steel. Carl Sandburg.
  "Bar of steel--it is only, A." AiP
  "Smoke of the fields in spring is one." MoAmPo

Smoke Animals. Rowena Bastin Bennett. CA

Smoke-Blackened Smiths. *Unknown.* OBCoV
  (Blacksmiths, The.) CABP
  ("May no man for brenwaters on night han his rest.") (LL) CABP

Smoke contending with smoke which will be maddest. Portrait of an Engine Driver. Bobi Jones, *Welsh.* OBWVE, *tr. by* Joseph P. Clancy

Smoke from a neighbor's chimney loneliness. Marlene Mountain. HA

Smoke from the train-gulf hid by hoardings blunders upward. Birmingham. Louis MacNeice. CMoP; MoBrPo; OxAEP-2

Smoke of the fields in spring is one. Carl Sandburg. MoAmPo *Fr.* Smoke and Steel.

Smoke rises from the stones: no, it is mist. (LL) An Airstrip in Essex, 1960. Donald Hall. LCAP-2; LiTM

Smoke rises. Never before, The. The Achaian Invasion of Sparta. *Unknown, Greek.* GrAn, *tr. by* Peter Jay

Smoke Rose. Itamar Ya'oz-kest, *Hebrew.* HP, *tr. by* Abramson, Glenda

Smoke should dry me well before I slept, The. (LL) The Author Loving These Homely Meats. John, of Hereford Davies. CBLP; CBNP; FaBoCh; OBCoV; Son

Smoke when the sun fell and when it rose. Peter Levi. FaBoTw *Fr.* Life Is a Platform.

Smokehouse, The. Yusef Komunyakaa. NoP-4

Smokey's Getting Old. Jessica Hagedorn. OpBo

Smoking in an Open Grave. David Bottoms. InPK-6

Smoking swamp before a cottage door, A. An Irish Picture. J. Stanyan Bigg. NOBVV

Smoky as peat your lank hair on my pillow. A Nest in a Wall. Richard Murphy. BiHa; CIP-2

Smoky rain riddles the ocean plains, A. My Father Paints the Summer. Richard Wilbur. NOBA

Smoky smell of menses—Ma always, The. Smell. Molly Peacock. NMM-2

Smoky summer evening, The. The Window. Dino Campana, *Italian.* STV, *tr. by* John Frederick Nims

Smoky sunset. I dab my eyes, A. Required of You This Night. Peter Redgrove. PoE

Smoldering dry fern. And What of Me? Liz Sohappy Bahe. CDW

Smooth Divine, The. Timothy Dwight. *Fr.* Here stood Hypocrisy, in sober brown. NOCV *Fr.* The Triumph of Infidelity.

Smooth simple path! whose undulating line. To a Gravel Walk. William Mason. OBGa

Smooth smell of Manhattan taxis, The. Dance of the Infidels. Al Young. MoNo; NBV; PoBA; SeSe

Smoothing the heads of the hungry children. (LL) Prelude to an Evening. John Crowe Ransom. MoAmPo; OxBA

Smoothness of onions infuriates him, The. The Onion. Katha Pollitt. RaBo

Smothered Fires. Georgia Douglas Johnson. BlSi

Smothering dark engulfs relentlessly, The. A Child's Winter Evening. Gwen John. CH

Smudging. Diane Wakoski. AmPA

Smuggled human hair from Mexico. The Assassination of John Lennon as Depicted by the Madame Tussaud Wax Museum, Niagara Falls, Ontario, 1987. David Wojahn. NAmP90; PBCAP *Fr.* Mystery Train: A Sequence.

Smugglers. "Eduard Georgievich Bagritzky," *Russian.* TCRP, *tr. by* Vera Dunham

Sn wfl k s. Marlene Mountain. HA

Snack, The. L. L. Zeigler. BXAP

Snail, The. Vincent Bourne, *Latin.* BoTP; CTAV; OBVE, *tr. by* William Cowper

Snail. Elisabeth Eybers, *Afrikaans.* PeSA; PeSAV, *tr. by* Elisabeth Eybers

Snail. Ho Xuan Huong, *Vietnamese.* AVP, *tr. by* Huỳnh Sanh Thông

Snail [*or* Snayl], The. Richard Lovelace. BeJo; CaPo; OAEL-1; PoEL-3
  ("Upward, and rarefy the air.") (LL) APo
  ("Upward, and Rarifie the Air.") (LL) PBRV
  ("Wise emblem of our politic world.") APo

Snail, The. Mother Goose. ReMoGo

Snail Garden. Janet Lewis. PaTW

Snail moves like a, The. Hedgehog. Paul Muldoon. BIrV; NoAM; PBCIP

Snail Poem. Peter Orlovsky. BB

Snail pushes through a green, The. Considering the Snail. Thom Gunn. LiTM; NAEL-2; TwCP

Snail says, "Alas!," The. The Poor Snail. J. M. Westrup. BoTP

Snail, snail, put out your horns. *Unknown.* OxNR

Snail who had a way, it seems, A. The Snail's Dream. Oliver Herford. CTV

Snail Winter. Judith C. Root. CMAP

Snails. E. D. Blodgett. NoAM

Snails. Philip Levine. PaTW

Snails. Liagarang, *Dharlwangu dialect.* CBAP, *tr. by* Ronald M. Berndt

Snail's Dream, The. Oliver Herford. CTV

Snails have made a garden of green lace, The. After Rain. Patricia K. Page. NOBC; PoE

Snails lead slow idyllic lives. The Widow's Yard. Isabella Gardner. Poetr

Snail's Lesson, The. Priscilla Jane Thompson. CBWP-2

Snaith Marsh; a Yorkshire Pastoral. "Ophelia." ECWP

Snake. Dannie Abse. NoAM

Snake. Desanka Maksimovic, *Serbo-Croatian.* HSix, *tr. by* Charles Simic

Snake. J. D. McClatchy. APo

Snake, The. Vance Palmer. NOBAu

Snake. Paresh Chandra Raut, *Oriya.* OMIP, *tr. by* Jayanta Mahapatra

Snake. Theodore Roethke. NOBA; NYBP

Snake, The. Andrew Suknaski. NOBC

Snake. Tanka. Yosano Tekkan, *Japanese.* MJT, *tr. by* Makoto Ueda

Snake-Back Solo. Quincy Troupe. MoNo

Snake came to my water-trough, A. D. H. Lawrence. CABP; CMoP; ChAP; EBEvV; EBNV; FaBoMo; HeIP-4; HoPM; LiTM; NOBE; NTP; NoAM; NoP-4; OAEL-2; PoRA; Poetr; TFi; UV

Snake-Charmer, The. Sarojini Naidu [*or* Nayadu]. PBWP

Snake Dance, (Hotevilla). Witter Bynner. PaTW

Snake emptied itself into the grass, A. Monsoon. David Wevill. NYBP

Snake Eyes. Imamu Amiri Baraka. VGW

Snake in the Garden Considers Daphne, The. William Wadsworth. BAP-94

Snake on D. H. Lawrence, The. N. J. Warburton. UV

Snake snatched, The. The Horned Snake. Louis Oliver. HATNAP

Snake tooth pinches his own mail, The. Remorse. Richmond Lattimore. PoA

Snake Trying, The. W. W. Eustace Ross. MoCV; NOBC

Snakecharmer. Sylvia Plath. PFE

Snakes. A. K. Ramanujan. NoP-4

Snakes. Virgil, *Latin.* OBCVT, *tr. by* David R. Slavitt

Snakes. Peter Wild. AmPA

Snake's Destiny, The. Hy Sobiloff. PFE

Snakes, Mongooses, Snake-Charmers and the Like. Marianne Moore. CMoP

Snakes of September, The. Stanley Kunitz. AFr; ColAP
  ("Braid of creation / Trembles.") (LL) ColAP

Snap tempered tooth chips. Sawmill. Richard Kenney. NoP-4

Snapper, The. William Heyen. AmPA

Snapping of the Bow, The. James David Corrothers. NAAAL

Snaps for Dinner, Snaps for Breakfast, and Snaps for Supper. George Moses Horton. OBAL

Snaps its twig-tethermounts. A Dove. Ted Hughes. OxBC

Snapshot. Charles Wright. WeT

Snapshot of a Crab-Picker among Barrels Spilling Over, Apparently at the End of Her Shift. Dave Jeddie Smith. NoAM

Snapshot of Adam. James Merrill. EOEF

Snapshots. John Updike. NoP-4

Snapshots of a Daughter-in-Law. Adrienne Rich. FaBoWP; HCAP; NAAL-2; NALW; NIP-4; NoAM; NoP-4; Poetr; VCAP

("No promise then: / delivered / palpable / ours.") (LL) NMM-2

("Ours.") (LL) PoPoPo

Snapshots of the Cotton South. Frank Marshall Davis. PoBA

Snare, The. James Stephens. BoTP; CH; CMoP; SCGP

Snatch out of time the passionate transitory. (LL) The Hospital. Patrick Kavanagh. CABP

Sneaked about here. By the Road. Geoffrey Grigson. OxBTC

Sneeze, A. So Chong-Ju, *Korean*. VCWP, *tr. by* David R. McCann

Sneeze on [a] Monday, [You] sneeze for danger. Sneezing. *Unknown*. LB; NBLV; OTCP

Sneeze on [a] Saturday, see your true love tomorrow. (LL) Sneezing. *Unknown*. LB; NBLV; OTCP

Sneezing. *Unknown*. ReMoGo

Sniff of the real, that's, The. Autobiography. Thom Gunn. NoAM

Sniffed, dilating my nostrils. Elvin's Blues. Michael S. Harper. BPo; LoL

Snobby Roberts' Message. Ken Smith. NBrP

Snore in the foam: the night is vast and blind. Tristan da Cunha. Roy Campbell. MoBrPo; PeSA

Snoring Bedmate, The. *Unknown, Irish*. BIrV, *tr. by* John V. Kelleher

Snot goes down. Pieces of Snot. *Unknown, Bella Bella Indian*. STP, *tr. by* Franz Boas

Snow. Innokenty Fiodorovich Annensky, *Russian*. TCRP, *tr. by* Lubov Yakovleva *with* Daniel Weissbort

Snow. Margaret Avison. NOBC

Snow. John Davidson. FaBoTC

Snow. Walter De la Mare. OxAEP-2

Snow, The. Emily Dickinson. ACTP

Snow, The. F. Ann Elliott. BoTP

Snow, The. June Jordan. GLP

Snow. Vladimir Nikolaevich Kornilov, *Russian*. TCRP, *tr. by* Daniel Weissbort

Snow. Philip Levine. ColAP

Snow. Henry Wadsworth Longfellow. *See* Snow-Flakes.

Snow. Louis MacNeice. CIP-2; CMoP; FaBoMo; LiTM; MoP; NOBE; NoAM; OPOU; OxAEP-2; OxBSP; PNI

Snow. David Malouf. CBAP

Snow. Ralph Pomeroy. Poetsp

Snow. William Robert Rodgers. LiTM

Snow. Ruth Stone. NYBP

Snow. Edward Thomas. FaBoTw; NTP; OPOU; PFE

Snow. Donna Trussell. IFJA

Snow. David Wevill. MoCV

Snow. Charles Wright. ColAP; LCAP-2

Snow? Absolutely not. A Peculiar Christmas. Roy Fuller. AYFP

Snow and then rain. The roads are wet. A car. Edgar Bowers. VCAP *Fr.* Autumn Shade.

Snow at dusk. Betty Drevniok. HA

Snow-Ball, The. Soame Jenyns. OBVE

Snow-Ball, The. Thomas Stanley. CBLP

Snow-Bound [*or* Snow-Bound; a Winter Idyl]. John Greenleaf Whittier. APN-1; AmPP; NAAL-3; NOBA; OxBA; PAR; TAP; TFi

("Looked in like tall and sheeted ghosts.") (LL) AiP

Snow-bound in woodland, a mournful word. Postponement. Thomas Hardy. EnVR

Snow by Morning. May Swenson. NYBP

Snow by the window paper flowers gathering dust. Matsuo Allard. HA

Snow came down last night like moths, The. First Snow in Alsace. Richard Wilbur. NoP-4; OBWP

Snow came early here, and hard. The Blizzard of Sixty-Six. William Daniel Ehrhart. CDa

Snow, clothing sky & mountain. Apollonides, *Greek*. GrAn, *tr. by* Peter Whigham

Snow Country Weavers. James Welch. CDW; HATNAP

Snow-covered and bleeding, he came home. Feeding Ground. Thomas McCarthy. CIP-2

Snow crept up overnight as we slept. The Vanishing Point. Peter Davison. DiPo

Snow Curlew, The. Vernon Watkins. NYBP

Snow dances and the frost flies, The. Plum Blossoms. Chu Shu-chen. PBWP, *tr. by* Kenneth Rexroth *and* Ling Chung

Snow dissolv'd no more is seen, The. Ode: 4.7. Horace, *Latin*. NAEL-1; OBVE, *tr. by* Samuel Johnson *Fr.* Odes.

Snow down, snow down, you little white flakes. Tennessee Snow. Naomi Mitchison. WPN

Snow drifts noiselessly in the middle of the night. Snowy Night. Kwanggun Kim, *Korean*. CKP, *tr. by* Jaihiun Kim

Snow falling. Eric Amann. HA

Snow Falling. Gillian Hughes. NTP

Snow falling. Snowfall. Artis Bernard. NTCP

Snow falling and night falling fast oh fast. Desert Places. Robert Frost. AFr; AmPP; CMoP; InPK-6; MoAmPo; MoP; NAAL-2; NOBA; NoAM; OxBA; PFE; PoE; RB; SoSe-8; TAP; TRP; UnPo

Snow falls and falls, The. Ōkura Ichijitsu, *Japanese*. OHMPJ, *tr. by* Kenneth Rexroth

Snow falls deep; the forest lies alone, The. Gipsies. John Clare. CH; NoP-4; PoEL-4

Snow falls from trees. Alan Pizzarelli. HA

Snow falls on the cars in Doctors' Row and hoods the headlights. Doctors' Row. Conrad Potter Aiken. HAP

Snow fell, and its power was multiplied, The. Russia 1812. Victor Hugo, *French*. OBWP, *tr. by* Robert Lowell

Snow Figure. David Baker. PuP-17

Snow-filled Nest, The. Rose Terry Cooke. OBCA

Snow fills heaven and earth. On a Painting of a Knight-Errant. Cheng Hsieh, *Chinese*. CoBLCP, *tr. by* Jonathan Chaves

Snow-Flakes. Henry Wadsworth Longfellow. APN-1; GEA; NCAP; NOBA; NoP-4; PoEL-5; TAP; UnPo

("Descends the snow.") (LL) CA

(Snow.) BoTP

Snow-Flakes, The. Priscilla Jane Thompson. CBWP-2

Snow had begun in the gloaming, The. The First Snowfall [*or* Snow-Fall]. James Russell Lowell. BLPA; FaBoBe; TAP

Snow had fallen many nights and days, The. The End of the World. Gordon Bottomley. CH; MoBrPo

Snow, hail and smut the sky. Asclepiades, *Greek*. GrAn, *tr. by* Alan Marshfield

Snow! Hail! Lower! Lightning! Thunder! Asclepiades, *Greek*. PGA, *tr. by* Kenneth Rexroth

Snow has covered the next line of tracks. Looking at New Fallen Snow from a Train. Robert Bly. GM

Snow has drifted. Quietness descends, The. Twilight. Vladislav Felitsianovich Khodasevich, *Russian*. TCRP, *tr. by* Michael Frayn

Snow has fallen. Tanka. Miyazawa Kenji, *Japanese*. MJT, *tr. by* Makoto Ueda

Snow has fallen all night. The Snow Curlew. Vernon Watkins. NYBP

Snow has gone from Chung-nan; spring is almost come, The. Passing T'ien-mên Street in Ch'ang-an and Seeing a Distant View of Chung-nan Mountains. Po Chü-i, *Chinese*. ChiP, *tr. by* Arthur Waley

Snow has left the cottage top, The. February. John Clare. NOBE; OBNC *Fr.* The Shepherd's [*or* Shepheards] Calendar.

Snow has melted now, The. January. Douglas Gibson. OBCP

Snow: II. Charles Kenneth Williams. NoP-4

Snow immaculate upon that mountain's brow!, The. (LL) Mount Shasta. John Rollin Ridge. APN-2; PAR

Snow in October. Alice Moore Dunbar-Nelson. BlSi

Snow in the Suburbs. Thomas Hardy. CMoP; EBEvV; MoBrPo; OAEL-2; OBMV; OxBTC

Snow in Town. Rickman Mark. BoTP

Snow is a mind. Revival. Steve Crow. HATNAP; PiM

Snow is a strange white word. On Receiving News of the War. Isaac Rosenberg. MoBrPo; NSI; OBWP; OxAEP-2; PeFWW; PeSAV; PoWW

Snow is falling, snow is falling. Boris Pasternak, *Russian*. ChAP, *tr. by* Jon Stallworthy *and* Peter France

Snow is gone from cottage tops, The. John Clare. *See* February.

Snow is knee-deep in the courtyard, The. The Cucumber. Nazim Hikmet, *Turkish*. VCWP, *tr. by* Randy Blasing *and* Mutlu Konuk

Snow is sick, The. The pure. March Snow. Don McKay. NOBC

Snow is weaving a soft, white, shroud, The. The Dying Year. Clara Ann Thompson. CBWP-2

Snow is white on wood and wold, The. The Kiss. Edith Nesbit. LW

Snow is witherin' off'n the' gress, T'. The Drained Cup. D. H. Lawrence. FaBoVe

Snow-laden bushes. O. Mabson Southard. HA

Snow Landscape, in a Glass Globe. Jean Valentine. NMM-2

Snow-Leopard, The. Randall Jarrell. APo; LiTM; TwCP

Snow lies deep, The. nor melting shower. Winter at Tomi. Ovid, *Latin*. AWP, *tr. by* F. A. Wright

Snow lies in long bright fingers, frigid melt–water in pools. April Fool's Day, Mount Pleasant Cemetary. A. F. Moritz. BAP-93

Snow Lies Sprinkled on the Beach, The. Robert Bridges. NoAM

Snow lies there—ro' rãni'!, The. Songs of the Paiute. *Unknown, Paiute*. APN-2 *Fr.* Ghost-Dance Songs.

Snow Light, The. May Sarton. NBLV

Snow-Man, The. "Marian Douglas." OBCA

Snow Man, The. Wallace Stevens. AFr; CMoP; ColAP; EnlH; HAP; HCAP; HeIP-4; NAAL-2; NoAM; NoP-4; PoE; PoPoPo; Poetr; SoSe-8; TRP; WeW-3

Snow melting and the dog. Tremayne. Donald Justice. MT

Snow on a Mountain. Dom Moraes. NoP-4

Snow on Lotus Mountain. Liu Ch'ang-ch'ing, *Chinese.* OHMPC, *tr. by* Kenneth Rexroth

Snow on Saddle Mountain, The. Miyazawa Kenji, *Japanese.* ColAP; NOBA; NoAM, *tr. by* Gary Snyder

Snow on Stone Gate. Crossing the Lang-yeh Mountain with a Friend. Wei Ying-wu, *Chinese.* SuSp, *tr. by* Wu-Chi Liu

Snow panels, ice pipes, house the afternoon. The January of a Gnat. Carl Rakosi. FTOS

Snow Party, The. Derek Mahon. CIP-2; FaBoPV; OxBC; PBCIP; PNI

Snow Poem. Rodolfo Di Biasio, *Italian.* NeIt, *tr. by* Stephen Sartarelli

Snow Poem. Roger McGough. Spl

Snow powder, flowery. Kuan Han-ch'ing. SuSp, *tr. by* Jerome P. Seaton *Fr.* Tune: "Song of Great Virtue"—Winter.

Snow Queen comes on dazzling feet, The. The North Wind. Dorothy Graddon. BoTP

Snow relents, the. Diffugere nives, redeunt iam gramina campis. Horace, *Latin.* OBCVT, *tr. by* Jim McCulloch

Snow seeping. Tanka. Fumi Saito, *Japanese.* MJT, *tr. by* Makoto Ueda

Snow Signs. Charles Tomlinson. NoAM

Snow, snow faster. *Unknown.* OxNR

Snow, snow, more snow! (LL) Winter. Walter De la Mare. OAEL-2; OBMV

Snow Song. Henrietta Cordelia Ray. CBWP-3

Snow Songs. W. D. Snodgrass. BAP-94

Snow-Stars. Frances Mary Frost. CTV

Snow-Storm, The. Ralph Waldo Emerson. APN-1; AmPP; FaBoBe; MeMAP; NAAL-1; NAAL-3; NCAP; NOBA; NoP-4; OxBA; PAR; PoE; PoEL-4; PoLF; PoPoPo; TAP; TFi; UnPo

Snow Storm, The. Mary Weston Fordham. CBWP-2

Snow Storm, The. Edna St. Vincent Millay. NAAL-2; PoA

Snow Storm. Tu Fu, *Chinese.* BLT; OHPC, *tr. by* Kenneth Rexroth

Snow thick and wet, porous. Spring. James Schuyler. FTOS

Snow visits us, The. Storm. James Tate. WeT

Snow whispers about me, The. Falling Snow. Amy Lowell. ColAP

Snow White. Olga Broumas. CPO

Snow White and the Seven Deadly Sins. R. S. Gwynn. SoSe-8

Snow White and the Seven Dwarfs. Anne Sexton. HCAP; PoPoPo

Snow-white terrier brushes the ground as it walks. Palace Poem. Wang Ya, *Chinese.* SuSp, *tr. by* Irving Y. Lo

Snow White was nude at her wedding, she's so white. Lessons from a Mirror. Thylias Moss. LTA

Snow wind-whipt to ice. Winter. Richard Hughes. OBMV; OBWVE

Snowbanks North of the House. Robert Bly. AiP; LCAP-2; RaBo

Snowbound City, The. John Haines. SPE

Snowdonia at a Distance. Douglas Oliver. NBrP

Snowdonia water falls in a memory. Snowdonia at a Distance. Douglas Oliver. NBrP

Snowdrop, The. Anna Bunston DeBary. BoTP

Snowdrop, The. Mary Weston Fordham. CBWP-2

Snowdrop. Ted Hughes. FaBoMo

Snowdrop of dogs, with ear of brownest dye. Sonnet: To Tartar, a Terrier Beauty. Thomas Lovell Beddoes. NOBVV; OBNC

Snowdrop, who, in habit white and plain, The. The Poet as King of Gotham. Charles Churchill. *Fr.* Gotham. NOEC

Snowdrops. Laurence Alma-Tadema. BoTP

Snowdrops. Margiad Evans. OBWVE

Snowdrops. George MacBeth. OBCP

Snowdrops. Mary Vivian. BoTP

Snowfall. Artis Bernard. NTCP

Snowfall. Giosuè Carducci, *Italian.* AWP, *tr. by* Romilda Rendel

Snowfall, The. Gwerfyl Mechain, *Welsh.* OBWVE, *tr. by* Kenneth Hurlstone Jackson

Snowfall, The. Donald Justice. CRP; Poetr; VGW

Snowfall. W. S. Merwin. NNaP

Snowfall; a Poem about Spring. James Wright. NoAM

Snowfall began its thing, The. Bella Akhatovna Akhmadulina, *Russian.* TCRP, *tr. by* Albert C. Todd

Snowfall: Four Variations. George Amabile. NYBP

Snowfall in Boston. Otto Orban, *Hungarian.* CEEP, *tr. by* Timea K. Szell

Snowfall in the Afternoon. Robert Bly. NOBA; SPE

Snowfall on a College Garden. C. Day Lewis. OBGa

Snowfall on the Seas. Hyongman Ho, *Korean.* CKP, *tr. by* Jaihiun Kim

Snowflake. First Snowflake. N. M. Bodecker. TLR

Snowflake on asphodel, clear ice on rose. Conrad Potter Aiken. CMoP

Snowflake Which Is Now and Hence Forever, The. Archibald MacLeish. NoP-4

Snowflakes. Ruth M. Arthur. BoTP

Snowflakes. Penny Harter. HA

Snowflakes. Howard Nemerov. HCAP

Snowflakes. Clive Sansom. OBCP

Snowflakes. Tanka. Saitō Mokichi, *Japanese.* MJT, *tr. by* Makoto Ueda

Snowflakes Sail Gently Down, The. Gabriel Okara. PBMAP

Snowflakes were teeming down. The Assumption of Miriam from the Street in the Winter of 1942. Jerzy Ficowski. HP, *tr. by* Keith Bosley

Snowing. Snowing. Snowing. Olive Dove. AYFP

Snowman, The. E. M. Adams. BoTP

Snowman, The. Roger McGough. OTCP

Snowman, The. Patricia K. Page. NOBC

Snowman, The. *Unknown.* OTCP

Snowman in a field. Roger McGough. Spl

Snowman Sniffles. N. M. Bodecker. TLR

Snowmelt pond warm granite. Bedrock. Gary Snyder. PoE

Snowmen. Agha Shahid Ali. IFJA

Snow's on the fellside, look! How deep. Horace, *Latin.* OBCVT, *tr. by* Basil Bunting

Snows that glittered on the disk of Mars, The. Sympathies. Oliver Wendell Holmes. APN-1 *Fr.* Wind-Clouds and Star-Drifts.

Snow's white pencil outlining the buildings. . . . Vladimir Nikolaevich Sokolov, *Russian.* TCRP, *tr. by* Simon Franklin

Snowstorm: At a Gathering at Chang Chu-fu's House, with Tzu-yeh Attending, We All Wrote Poems on This Subject—I Got the Ryhme-Word, "Hu." Tsung Ch'en, *Chinese.* CoBLCP, *tr. by* Jonathan Chaves

Snowstorm shook its cloak––, The. Ballad about the Circus. Aleksandr Petrovich Mezhirov, *Russian.* TCRP, *tr. by* Deming Brown

Snowy Benches. Aileen Fisher. KaS

Snowy coats and snowy crests and beaks of blue jade. Egrets. Tu Mu, *Chinese.* PLT, *tr. by* A. C. Graham

Snowy Day, A. *Unknown, Welsh.* OBWVE, *tr. by* H. Idris Bell

Snowy, Flowy, Blowy. The Twelve Months. *Unknown. at. to* "Sir Gregory Gander." AYFP; CTV

Snowy morning, A. Den Sute-Jo, *Japanese.* WPJ, *tr. by* Kenneth Rexroth *and* Ikuko Atsumi

Snowy Mountains. Tsung Ch'en, *Chinese.* CoBLCP, *tr. by* Jonathan Chaves

Snowy Night. Kwanggun Kim, *Korean.* CKP, *tr. by* Jaihiun Kim

Snowy owl, storm cast from the arctic tundra. Snowy Owl near Ocean Shores. Duane Niatum. HATNAP

Snub-nosed, bone-fingered, deft with engraving tools. Death the Painter. Anthony Hecht. NoP-4

Snug at hearthside, while heart of the backlog. Heart of the Backlog. Robert Penn Warren. MT

Snug at the club two fathers sat. The Fathers. Siegfried Sassoon. MoP

So. Citadel. Edward Kamau Brathwaite. VCWP

So Abram rose, and clave the wood, and went. The Parable of the Old Man and the Young. Wilfred Owen. ChIV-1; PoFWW

So all day long the noise of battle rolled. Morte d'Arthur. Tennyson. EBNV; EBVVPR; EnVR; FaBoBe; NIP-4; NOBVV; OAEL-2; OBNV; OxAEP-2; PoEL-5

So all day long the noise of battle rolled. The Passing of Arthur. Sir John Collings Squire. BXAP

So all day long the noise of battle rolled. Tennyson. *Fr.* The Passing of Arthur. FHYEP; NAEL-2; OBNC *Fr.* Idylls of the King.

So all waited for manna. Manna. Jared Angira. PBMAP

So all within be livelier than before. (LL) The Forerunners. George Herbert. ESCV; GeHe; NAEL-1; NoP-4; TOF

So am I as the rich, whose blessed key. Sonnet 52. Shakespeare. OxAEP-1 *Fr.* Sonnets.

So an age ended, and its last deliverer died. W. H. Auden. CMoP; PoE *Fr.* Sonnets from China.

("And the age ended, and the last deliverer died.") Son

So and no otherwise—so and no otherwise—hillmen desire their Hills. (LL) The Sea and the Hills. Rudyard Kipling. OxBoS; SCGP

So-and-So Reclining on Her Couch. Wallace Stevens. AmPP; LiTM; NOBA

So are you to my thoughts as food to life. Sonnet 75. Shakespeare. PoEL-2 *Fr.* Sonnets.

So as they travelled, the drouping night. Edmund Spenser. OAEL-1 *Fr.* Wood Of Error. AEP

So, back again? To a Dog. Josephine Preston Peabody. BLPA

So bandit-eyed, so undovelike a bird. Blue Jay [*or* Bluejay]. Robert Francis. LCAP-2; WeT

So be it. I am. Hayden Carruth. VGW

So beautiful—God himself quailed. The Woman. Ronald Stuart Thomas. OxBC

So Beautiful Is the Tree of Night. Pauline Hanson. TAP

So beautiful that couple. Indran Amirthanayagam. OpBo

So beautiful the lungs. From "Songs of a Wanderer." Aleksander Wat, Polish. BLT, tr. by Czeslaw Milosz and Leonard Nathan (b. 1924)

So, because you chose to follow me into the subtle sadness of night. Giving Back the Flower. Sarah Morgan Bryan Piatt. APN-2

So, behind the heavy backyard orchard. We Wondered about the Mellow Peaches. Jack A. Mapanje. HBAPE

So blest are they who round a family board. The Family. Donna R. Lydston. PoToHe

So bondage is a big part of it, after all—. Sestina. James Cummins. BAP-94

So, bored with dragons, he lay down to sleep. Beowulf. Kingsley Amis. OxBC

So Bring the Order for My Execution. Faiz Ahmad Faiz, Urdu. VCWP, tr. by Agha Shahid Ali

"So careful of the type?" but no. Tennyson. EBVV; EBVVPR; EnVR; FHYEP; HAP; OAEL-2; OBNC; TOF   Fr. In Memoriam A. H. H.

So, circling about my head, a fly. For Mao Tse-tung; a Meditation on Flies and Kings. Irving Layton. NOBC

So cold? (LL) The Warning. Adelaide Crapsey. Spl; WPE; WeW-3

So cold and lost for ever evermore. (LL) Dead before Death. Christina Rossetti. NAEL-2; NALW

So confortand his levis unto me bene. (LL) To a Lady[e]. William Dunbar. EBEV; GBL; OBEV; OxBS; PeLV

So covetous Ballaam with fond intent. Abraham Cowley. ChIV-1   Fr. Davideis.

So cruel [or cruell or crewell] prison how could betide [or howe coulde betyde], alas. In Windsor Castle. Henry Howard, Earl of Surrey. AAS; HAP; NOBE; NoSic; SCGP; SiPS

So cruel prison how could betide, alas. Prisoned in Windsor, He Recounteth His Pleasure There Passed. Henry Howard, Earl of Surrey. NAEL-1   Fr. Windsor Castle.

So dark a mind within me dwells, sels. Tennyson. Fr. Maud [A Monodrama]. EnVR

So Davies wrote: "This leaves me in the pink." "In the Pink." Siegfried Sassoon. CMoP

So dawn. A morcellation of the dark. A.M.: The Hopeful Monster. Alice Fulton. PUP-18

So dear, so dainty, so demure. To a Persian Cat. F. C. W. Hiley. PC

So delicate, so airy. Pink Almond. Katharine Tynan. BoTP

So died John So. On John So. Unknown. FaBoEE

So different, this man. Marriage. William Carlos Williams. ITG; PoA

So does the sun withdraw his beam[e]s. On His Mistress Going from Home [Song]. Unknown. NOSC

So dream thy sails, O phantom bark. The Phantom Bark. Hart Crane. CMoP

So earth's inclined toward the one invisible. Winter Scene. Marguerite Young. WPE

So easie to part, or so equally join'd. (LL) Mercury's Song [to Phaedra]. Dryden. AWP; NOSC; OxBSP; PBMP; PoEL-3

So easy to repair. (LL) Softened by Time's consummate plush. Emily Dickinson. CrDW; NOBA

So ended Saturn; and the God of the Sea. Keats. FHYEP   Fr. Hyperion. OAEL-2; Ro

So even he was not so lazy as I. (LL) Lazy Man's Song. Po Chü-i, Chinese. ChiP, tr. by Arthur Waley

So fair thy vision that the night. Milton. John Banister Tabb. APN-2

So fallen! so lost! the light withdrawn. Ichabod[!]. John Greenleaf Whittier. APN-1; NAAL-1; NAAL-3; NOBA; OxBA; PAR; PBMP; PoEL-4; TAP

So far as our story approaches the end. A Light Woman. Robert Browning. FP

So. Farewell Krishna. In Memoriam Krishna Menon. E. J. Thribb. OBCoV

So. Farewell / Then / Larry Parnes. In Memoriam Larry Parnes ("Mr Parnes Shillings and Pence"). E. J. Thribb. OBCoV

So few, really. What Her Friend Said to Her, within the Lover's Hearing. Paranar, Tamil. PLW, tr. by A. K. Ramanujan

So finally I came to it the spring. Revelations, First Time. Roger Jones. IFJA

So fine, the boards of magnolia. Wrecked Boat on the River Shore. Chiang Lu, Chinese. CoBCP, tr. by Burton Watson

So flies love's meteor to her shroud of winds. The Dead Words. Vernon Watkins. LiTM

So for your arrogance. Hilda Doolittle. NMM-2   Fr. Eurydice.

So, forth issued [or issew'd] the Seasons of the year(e). The Pageant of the Seasons and the Months. Edmund Spenser. OxAEP-1   Fr. Wood Of Error. AEP

So forth she comes, and to her coche does clyme. Edmund Spenser. NAEL-1; OAEL-1   Fr. Wood Of Error. AEP

So foul is sin and loathsome in thy sight. Anne Vaughan Locke. CABP

So friendly, and so rich. (LL) On the Circuit. W. H. Auden. FaBoA; NOBL; OxBTC

So frisky and fit. Simchas Torah. Morris Jacob Rosenfeld, Yiddish. TrJP

So from the ground we felt that virtue branch. The Transfiguration. Edwin Muir. ChIV-2; OxBS

So from the years their gifts were showered: each. W. H. Auden. CMoP   Fr. Sonnets from China.

So from this life, male in its first motion. Vittoria Colonna. Roy Marz. PoA

So full my thoughts are of thee, that I swear. Il Trionfo del Amor. Charlotte Dacre. Ro   Fr. Hours of Solitude.

So full of courtly reverence. Air. Dudley North. OxBSP

So full of sleep are those who lose the way. William Dickey. WeT

So gentle and so beautiful, should perish with the flowers. (LL) The Death of the Flowers. William Cullen Bryant. OBCA; PoLF

So gentle and so virtuous she appears. Dante. ItIP

So God send to my foes all they have thought. (LL) Written on a Wall at Woodstock. Elizabeth I, Queen of England. CABP; PBWP; PEW; WPE

So God spoke to her. Ann Griffith. Ronald Stuart Thomas. PeECV

So good luck came, and on my roof[e] did light. The Coming of Good Luck. Robert Herrick. FaBoEE; OxBSP; Spl

So, good night, with lullaby. (LL) Fairy Land, 2. Shakespeare. BoTP; NOBE; NoSic; OBEV; PoRA; SCGP

So goodbye, Mrs. Brown. To-Day I Leave Mrs. Brown's Lodgings. Sir Walter Scott. FaBoEE

So goodly wonne with her owne will beguyld. (LL) Sonnet 67: "Like a huntsman after weary chase." Edmund Spenser. GBL; HeIP-4; NAEL-1; NoP-4; PBRV; PoE; PoEL-1; Son

So Graven. Josephine Miles. NoAM

So hallow'd and so gracious is the time. Shakespeare.   See Hamlet.

So Han-shan writes you these words. Unknown, Chinese. CoBCP, tr. by Burton Watson

So hard for women to believe each other. Apron Strings. Marge Piercy. TAP

So hard to say I love you madly. Love Song for Difficult Times. Maria Elena Cruz Varela, Spanish. VCWP, tr. by Mairym Cruz-Bernal and Deborah Digges

So hath been dawning another blue day. Today. Thomas Carlyle. PWR

So have I heard and do in part believe it. (LL) Hamlet. Shakespeare. PeECV, sect. I, i; TOF

So have I seen a little silly fly. A Quarrel with Fortune. Benjamin Colman. SCAP

So having ended, silence long ensewed. Nature's Reply to Mutability. Edmund Spenser. NOBE   Fr. Wood Of Error. AEP

So he came to write again. Burning Hills. Michael Ondaatje. NOBC; NoAM

So he said / on radio. Lorine Niedecker. NMM-2

So he that saileth in this world of pleasure. Anne Bradstreet. WPOW   Fr. Contemplations. AmPP; NAAL-3; PoEL-3; SCAP; WPE

So he threw down his pitchfork and went to his work. (LL) The Riot; or, Half a Loaf Is Better than No Bread. Hannah More. PEW

So he was exiled from rome. Ovid Twice Exiled. Jerzy Ficowski, Polish. PoSu, tr. by Frank J. Corliss, Jr., and Grazyna Sandel

So he were like him, and by Venus side. Shakespeare.   See Even as the sun with purple-colour'd face.

So Hector Protector was sent back again. (LL) Hector Protector was dressed all in green. Mother Goose. OxNR; ReMoGo

So Hector spake; the Trojans roar'd applause. Specimen of a Translation of the Iliad in Blank Verse. Homer, Greek. OBCVT, tr. by Alfred Tennyson, 1st Baron Tennyson   Fr. The Iliad.

So. / Hello then / Dali. In Memoriam Salvador Dali. E. J. Thribb. OBCoV

So here goes an I shell try. The Testimony. Kay Boyle. NMM-2

So here hath been dawning. Today. Thomas Carlyle. PFE

So here we are. Song of Calling Souls. Wang Ping. BAP-96

So him at first De Nance commanded was to kill;. Anne Dowriche. PBRV   Fr. The French Historie.

So how is life with your new bloke? An Attempt at Jealousy. Craig Raine. NoAM

So, how was I to know, when he invited. Helen. James Harrison. NBLV

So Hrothgar's men lived happy in his hall. Unknown. PoE, tr. by Burton Raffel   Fr. Beowulf. OAEL-1, tr. by Charles W. Kennedy; ASW, tr. by Kevin Crossley-Holland

So huge is God's despair. Death of a Oaxaquenian. Malcolm Lowry. CLPP

So humble things thou hast borne for us, O God. Veni Creator. Alice Thompson Meynell. WPE

So I came down the steps to Lenin. Dorothy Wellesley. OBMV *Fr.* Lenin

"So I don't have to think / any / more." (LL) How to Meditate. Jack Kerouac. BB; CLPP

So I dream nightly of an embarkation. Allen Ginsberg. CLPP *Fr.* Siesta in Xbalba.

So I experienced. Easter Roses. Robert Grenier. FTOS *Fr.* Phantom Anthems.

So, I have seen a man killed! Arthur Hugh Clough. EBVV; PeVV *Fr.* Amours de Voyage. NOBVV

So I Let Her Go. *Unknown.* AmFP

So I Lost My Temper. Rose Romano. UnSA

So I Said I Am Ezra. A. R. Ammons. ColAP; NAAL-2; NOBA; NoAM

So I say what the hell could it matter. Brandon Kershner. *Fr.* 3 Dialogues. EC2

So I See You Still. Aleksis Rannit, *Estonian.* CEEP, *tr. by* Henry Lymann

So, I shall see her in three days. In Three Days. Robert Browning. CBLP

So I took her to the riverside. The Unfaithful Wife. Federico García Lorca. OxBM

So I wait—bereft of 2,000 years and the bath of life. (LL) Marriage. Gregory Corso. CBLP; CoAP; LiTM; MoP; NeAP; NoP-4; OBAL; PeLV; PmAP; TAP; TRP

So I walked her down to the river. The Unfaithful Wife. Federico García Lorca, *Spanish.* STV, *tr. by* John Frederick Nims

So I would hear out those lungs. Buckdancer's Choice. James Dickey. HeIP-4; NOBA; NYBP; NoAM; NoP-4; WeT

So if all do their duty, they need not fear harm. (LL) The Chimney Sweeper ("When my mother died I was very young"). William Blake. CH; FHYEP; FaBoPV; HeIP-4; InPK-6; NAEL-2; NAWM-2; NOEC; OAEL-2; OxAEP-2; OxBChV; PoE; Poetr; Ro; SCGP; SoSe-8; TFi

So I'le not feare the Judge, or thee. (LL) To His Conscience. Robert Herrick. BeJo; ChIV-1; NAEL-1; PoEL-3

So I'm an alcoholic Catholic mother-lover. Jack Would Speak Through the Imperfect Medium of Alice. Alice Notley. PT; PmAP

So in Pieria, from the wedded bliss. In Memory of Bryan Lathrop. Edgar Lee Masters. PoA

So, in the evening, to the simple cloister. Cloister. Conrad Potter Aiken. MoAmPo *Fr.* Preludes for Memnon; or, Preludes to Attitude.

So, in the nocturnal stream. Daedalus. Leonid Nikolaevich Martynov, *Russian.* TCRP, *tr. by* J. R. Rowland

So insular, so quiet, it enters the earth. (LL) The Black Riviera. Mark Jarman. NAmP90; WeT

So is coal, but alight it shines like roses. (LL) Didyme waved her wand at me. Asclepiades, *Greek.* GrAn; PGA, *tr. by* Kenneth Rexroth

So is it not with me as with that Muse. Sonnet 21. Shakespeare. HeIP-4 *Fr.* Sonnets.

So it always was, so shall ever be! (LL) De Gustibus. Robert Browning. FHYEP; InPS-3; SCGP

So it begins. Adam is in his earth. James Agee. *Fr.* Sonnets. MoAmPo

So it is. Coleman Barks. CRP *Fr.* New Words.

So it is given: we follow as through a tunnel down through. The Tearing and Merging of Clouds. Russell Edson. WeT

So it is, my dear. Even So. D. G. Rossetti. NOBE; NOBVV; OBNC

So it is whispered here and there. A Lesson in a Picture. Sarah Morgan Bryan Piatt. NCAP

So it's hullo now. Rufinus, *Greek.* GrAn, *tr. by* Alan Marshfield

So it's today, and in the chokecherry this year. Fall. Laure-Anne Bosselaar. APAD

So I've thought the matter over and think I'll marry Bill. (LL) Common Bill. *Unknown.* AS; AmFP

So jealous of your beauty. "Michael Field." VWP

So joyful he to Alma Mater went. The Student. James Hurdis. *Fr.* Adriano; or, The First of June. ECEV

So late, so late, so haunting. On the Threshold. Karl Kraus, *German.* TrJP, *tr. by* Albert Bloch

So lay the youth with Mary in his arms. Sir John Collings Squire. BXAP *Fr.* Country Wooing.

So learned men in controversies spend. Learning. So Learned Men in Controversies Spend. George Chapman. NOSC *Fr.* Euthymiae Raptus; or, The Teares of Peace.

So leave her, and cast care from thy heart. His Camel. Alqamah. *Fr.* The Mufaddaliyat. AWP, *tr. by* Sir Charles Lyall

So let all thine enemies perish, O Lord: but let them that love him be as the sun when he goeth forth in his might. And the land had rest forty years. (LL) The Song of Deborah. Bible, *O.T.* AWP; BoWoP; PBWP; TrJP

So let's live—really live!—for love and loving. Catullus. *See* Carmen 5 ("My sweetest Lesbia, let us live and love").

So Let's Look at It Another Way. John Godfrey. PmAP

So light no one noticed. The Song. Edward Dorn. VGW

So like a harrow pin. Iron Spike. Seamus Heaney. TRP

So Live. William Cullen Bryant. *See* Thanatopsis.

So live, so love, so use that fragile hour. Robert Louis Stevenson. NOBVV

So lonely am I. Ono no Komachi, *Japanese.* BoWoP; PBWP, *tr. by* David Keene

So Long. Jayne Cortez. BoWoP; LW

So long. James Dickey. AiP *Fr.* For the First Manned Moon Orbit.

So Long! Walt Whitman. PAR

So Long Ago. Morris Jacob Rosenfeld, *Yiddish.* TrJP, *tr. by* Elbert Aidline

So long ago my father led me to. Time of Mountains. Thomas Hornsby Ferril. PaTW

So long as I loved shadows, the shadows of vain gods. Christian Rome. Hildebert, *Latin.* MLL, *tr. by* Helen Waddell

So long as this breath fills your nostrils. Mahadevi, *Kannada.* WPoS, *tr. by* Jane Hirshfield

So long as we speak the same language and never understand each other. Useless Words. Carl Sandburg. PBMP

So long as you live and move. Teach Us to Mark This, God. Franz Werfel, *German.* TrJP, *tr. by* Jacob Sloan

So long gone from life itself, so many things have changed. (LL) Immigrants in Our Own Land. Jimmy Santiago Baca. AF; UnSA

So long had life together been that now. Six Years Later. Joseph Brodsky, *Russian.* SAGP; TCRP; VCWP, *tr. by* Richard Wilbur

So *long* / is in the song. Langston Hughes. APSN

So long lives this, and this gives life to thee. (LL) Sonnet 18. Shakespeare. AEP; APAD; BoLoP; CABP; CTC; ClHu; EnLoPo; FaBoBe; GBL; GLoP; GTBS-P; HAP; HeIP-4; ImPo; InPK-6; InPS-3; NOBE; NoSic; OAEL-1; OBEV; PBMP; PoE; PoEL-2; PoLF; PoPoPo; PoRA; SCGP; SCV; Son; TFi; WeW-3

So long since I've enjoyed the hills and ponds. Returning to My Home in the Country. T'ao Ch'ien, *Chinese.* CoBCP, *tr. by* Burton Watson

So long, / So far away. Afro-American Fragment. Langston Hughes. PBMP

So Long Solon. Jack Myers. AmPA

So Long? Stevens. John Berryman. HAP; HCAP; NOBA *Fr.* Dream Songs.

So long to love / so long. (LL) So Long. Jayne Cortez. LW

So long you stay on shore. (LL) The Wreck of the *Julie Plante* [*or* The *Julie Plante*]. William Henry Drummond. BLPA; FaBoBe

So long you wandered on the dusky plain. To His Friend in Elysium. Joachim Du Bellay, *French.* AWP, *tr. by* Andrew Lang

So looks Anthea, when in bed she lyes. To Anthea Lying in Bed. Robert Herrick. BeJo; SeCP

So lost a thing as thou hadst been. (LL) Upon My Lady Carlisle's [*or* Carlile's] Walking in Hampton Court Garden. Sir John Suckling. BeJo; CaPo; CavPo; NoP-4

So Love and Folly were in hell. (LL) A Barley-Break . Sir John Suckling. CaPo; CavPo

So lovely. . . / so tender. Alcaeus, *Greek.* InMo, *tr. by* Sam Hamill

So luminous around them lay the air. Oystercatchers. Christopher Middleton. FaBoTW

So. Magnus / Magnusson. Lines on the Award "Pipe Man of the Year" to Magnus Magnusson. E. J. Thribb. OBCoV

So manifold, all pleasing in their kind. The Work of Gardening. William Cowper. GaP

So many cloisters closed. John Skelton. PeECV *Fr.* The Manner of the World Nowadays.

So many convolutions and not enough simplicity! To Marina. Kenneth Koch. NoAM

So many delights the excitement has no end. Sitting Up with My Wife on New Year's Eve. Hsü Chün-ch'ien, *Chinese.* CoBCP, *tr. by* Burton Watson

So Many Feathers. Jayne Cortez. BlSi; ISC

So many new crimes since then! Since Then. D. J. Enright. OBSV

So many nights the solitary lamp had burned. Rousseau in His Day. Donald Davie. DiPo

So many pangs of the tender heart for those. Pity Wasted. Freda C. Bond. WPN

So many people lie in this alley. The Neighborhood House. Jay Wright. NBV

So many people, not to speak of the dog. (LL) The Taxis. Louis MacNeice. OxBTC; PNI

So many pigeons at Columbus. Poem. Arthur Gregor. VGW

So many poems with kimonos. Another Kimono. Nancy Eimers. WeT

So many theories of east and west abound. Africa, Music and Show Business. Abdullah Ibrahim. MoNo

So many things happen. The War of the Worlds. Vern Rutsala. Poetsp

So many thousands for a house! On a Certain Lord Giving Some Thousand Pounds for a House. David Garrick. FaBoEE

So many times I've seen hand-to-hand combat. Yuliya Vladimirovna Drunina, *Russian.* TCRP, *tr. by* Albert C. Todd

So many traces, fragile monuments. Louise Herlin, *French.* MFP, *tr. by* Martin Sorrell

So many want to be lifted by song and dancing. A Dark Thing Inside the Day. Linda Gregg. BLT

So many women are murdered because some man. Body Count. Leonard Nathan. PBCAP

So many years I've seen the sun. The Mystery of Life. John Gambold. NOEC

So Mary died last night! To-day. Twilight. Amy Levy. VWP

So may the auspicious Queen of Love. Ode: 1.3: To the Ship on Which Virgil Sailed to Athens ("Sic te diva potens Cyri"). Horace. AWP, *tr. by* John Dryden *Fr.* Odes.

So me saary. Men and Women. David Dabydeen. PBCV

So mean I. (LL) Waiting Both. Thomas Hardy. MoBrPo; OxBoLi; TTTS

So merrily march the merchant men. (LL) The Merchants of London. Mother Goose. OxNR; ReMoGo

So merrily we'll run around. (LL) Fool's Song. Thomas Holcroft. CBNP; NOEC

So Mexicans Are Taking Jobs from Americans. Jimmy Santiago Baca. LTA; UnSA

So, midst the wither'd waste of life, those tears would flow to me. (LL) Stanzas for Music ("There's not a joy the world can give like that it takes away"). Byron. GTBS-P; HAP; NOBRP

So Might is Right, you say; I fight in vain. "Might Is Right." Israel Zangwill. TrJP

So Might It Be. John Galsworthy. PoLF

So mine be your eyes!. (LL) To Morfydd. Lionel Pigot Johnson. MoBrPo; OAEL-2; OBMV

So Miss Myrtle is going to marry? The Charming Woman. Helen Selina Blackwood, Countess of Dufferin. VWP

So Miss Myrtle is going to marry? The Charming Woman. Helen Selina Sheridan. WPE

So, Mister Moneybags, you're loaded? So'? Palladas, *Greek.* GrΛn, *tr. by* Tony Harrison

So moping flat and low our valleys lie. Winter in the Fens. John Clare. EnVR

So Motown taught me all about men. Men worshipped. Patricia Smith. UnSA *Fr.* Sweet Daddy.

So much could stay a moment in so little. (LL) On a Child Who Lived One Minute. X. J. Kennedy. HoPM; NYBP; Poetr

So much depends. The Red Wheelbarrow. William Carlos Williams. BLT; CMoP; ChAP; HeIP-4; HoPM; InPK-6; LiTM; MoAmPo; MoP; NAAL-2; NIP-4; NOBA; NoAM; NoP-4; PoE; Poetr; SAmP; SoSe-8; TAP; TFi; TRP; TTTS; UnPo; WeW-3

So much for the elves' wergild, the true governance. Geoffrey Hill. NoAM *Fr.* Mercian Hymns.

So much I have forgotten in ten years. Flame-Heart. Claude McKay. GT

So much is parchment where I gloom. The Black Mesa. James Merrill. PoA

So much sweeter here than in other lands? (LL) Columbus Day. Jimmie Durham. LTA

So much to tell you. 2 Variations: All About Love. Philip Whalen. NeAP

So—Murray to Byron in Italy. Kaleidoscope. G. K. Page. NoAM

So my mother begins. The Nice Thing About Counting Stars. Dwight Okita. UnSA

So my soul can sing. (LL) Feeling Fucked/Up Up. Etheridge Knight. GT; NNaP; PBCAP; RaBo

So my wild words are addressed to my nephews and nieces. (LL) A Mad Poem Addressed to My Nephews and Nieces. Po Chü-i, *Chinese.* ChiP; NNPT, *tr. by* Arthur Waley

So Near and Yet So Near. Lemn Sissay. NBrP

So near / no room for fear. (LL) Subway Rush Hour. Langston Hughes. InPK-6

So nigh is grandeur to our dust. I Can. Ralph Waldo Emerson. CTV *Fr.* In an age of fops and toys. PoLF *Fr.* Voluntaries. APN-1; CBCWP

So night sits me down be- / fore braided Isis. Memphite Recension. Nathaniel Mackey. PT

So not doing anything, how much. Mountain Forest. " Aleksandr Borisovich Kusikov," *Russian.* TCRP, *tr. by* Albert C. Todd

So, now I have confess'd that he is thine. Sonnet 134. Shakespeare. HeIP-4; OxAEP-1 *Fr.* Sonnets.

So now i have to pack my forests. Leaving. Pamela Brown. BMAP

So now I'm brooding moodily upon. A Simple Matter. Gloria Rawlinson. PeNZ

So now it's your turn. Instructions to the Double. Tess Gallagher. FaBoWP; NMM-2

So now just suppose that someone wanted to know. Surgery. Kenneth Pitchford. GLP

So now the sun moves to die at mid-morning. Harvest of Hate. Wole Soyinka. AF

So now the very bones of you are gone. Doricha. Poseidippus, *Greek.* AWP; FaBoEE; OBCVT; OBVE, *tr. by* E. A. Robinson

So now, this poet, who forsakes the stage. Prologue to "Love Triumphant." Dryden. OxBoLi *Fr.* Love Triumphant.

So obese is my cousin from Hendon. Limerick. A. H. Baynes. PeLi

So oft as I her beauty do behold. Sonnet 55. Edmund Spenser. Son *Fr.* Amoretti. AAS

So oft as I with state of present time. Edmund Spenser. OAEL-1 *Fr.* Wood Of Error. AEP

So oft have I invok'd thee for my muse. Sonnet 78. Shakespeare. AEP *Fr.* Sonnets.

So often and with such cruel fascination I have dreamed the implacable void that contains dream. A Dream of Mind: The Gap. Charles Kenneth Williams. BAP-93

So often it appears like an escape. Works of Art. Elizabeth Jennings. PeECV

So often my feeling of race. Léon Damas, *French.* NegPo, *tr. by* Ellen Conroy Kennedy

So often, so long I have thought of death. Song: So Often, So Long I Have Thought. Hayden Carruth. AFr

So often we hear of the vacant chair. The Chair That Is Filled. Carrie Biggs. PWR

So on he pricked, and loe, he gan espy. Ride a Cock Horse. Barry Pain. BXAP

So on she goes, and in her idle flight. Marlowe. PoE *Fr.* Hero and Leander. AAS

So, on the bloody sand, Sohrab lay dead. Sohrab Dead. Matthew Arnold. EBEvV; GTBS-P; NOBE; PeVV *Fr.* Sohrab and Rustum. EBNV; OBNV

So once again, hearing the tired aunts. In the House of the Dying. Jane Cooper. CrSp

So open was his mind, so wide. The Independent. Phyllis McGinley. FaBoEE

So Paradise was brightened, so 'twas blest. To Philomela. Benjamin Colman. SCAP

So passed they naked on, nor shunned the sight. Adam and Eve. Milton. PeECV, *ll.* 319–334 *Fr.* Book IV. OAEL-1 *Fr.* Paradise Lost.

So Pleasant It Is To Have Money. Arthur Hugh Clough. *See* So Pleasant It Is to Have Money.

So pleasing a light. The Moon. Robert Duncan. APSN, *sect.* 5 *Fr.* Passages.

'So pray, Sir—step outside!'. (LL) Outside. Hugh Chesterman. AYFP

So prayis me as ye think caus quhy. Remeidis of Luve. *Unknown.* OxBS

So proud in his furry robe. Baboon. *Unknown. Fr.* Hunter Poems of the Yoruba. RB, *tr. by* Ulli Beier

So proud she was to die. Emily Dickinson. NOBA

So prudent and so young a wife! To Geron. Hildebrand Jacob. NOEC

So quicke, so hot, so mad is thy fond sute. Thomas Campion. PoEL-2

So quiet it was in that high, sun-steeped room. Nuremberg. Kenneth Slessor. BMAP

So Quietly. Leslie Pinckney Hill. PoBA

So sang he: and as meeting rose and rose. Willowwood. D. G. Rossetti. NAEL-2; OAEL-2 *Fr.* The House of Life.

So sang the gallant glorious chronicle. The Princess. Tennyson. OBGa

So Sat the Muses. William Browne. *Fr.* Caelia. Son

So Satan spake, and him Bëëlzebub. The Council of Satan. Milton. PoEL-3 *Fr.* Book I. FHYEP; NAEL-1; OAEL-1; OxAEP-1 *Fr.* Paradise Lost.

So saying, light-foot Iris pass'd away. Achilles Over the Trench. Homer, *Greek.* OBVE, *tr. by* Tennyson *Fr.* The Iliad.

"So serious. Why don't you smile?" Handful of Pebbles, Mouthful of Stones. Pegatha Hughes. LoHo

So several factions from this first ferment. Achitophel: The Earl of Shaftsbury. Dryden. NOBE *Fr.* Absalom and Achitophel, Pt. I. EBEvV; FHYEP; FaBoPV; HAP; NOSC; OAEL-1; PoE

So shaken as we are, so wan with care. Shakespeare. OxAEP-1 *Fr.* King Henry IV, Pt. I. NAEL-1

So shall ye waste to dust. (LL) The Aged Lover Renounceth Love. Thomas Vaux. NoSic, OAEL-1; PoEL-1; SCGP

So she became a bird and bird-like danced. Procne. Peter Quennell. LiTM; MoBrPo

So she came back into his house again. Edna St. Vincent Millay. ColAP *Fr.* Sonnets from an Ungrafted Tree. NALW

So she must have been pleased with us. Hilda Doolittle. NALW *Fr.* Tribute to the Angels.

So she sat down. For P—Celtic: found text from Machen. Bill Griffiths. NBrP

So she sd, if u lose me, u lose a good thing. Next Door. Laini Mataka. ISC

So, she thought, where did he go? Reach. Phyllis Janowitz. IFJA

So she went into the garden. The Great Panjandrum [Himself]. Samuel Foote. CBNP; FaBoCh; PoLF

So shoots a star as doth my mistress glide. Sonnet. John, of Hereford Davies. CBLP

So-shu dreamed. Ancient Wisdom, Rather Cosmic. Ezra Pound. NOBA

So shuts the marigold her leaves. Memory. William Browne. OBEV *Fr.* Britannia's Pastorals.

So shy shy shy(and with a). E. E. Cummings. MeMAP

So, since your heart is set on those sweet fields. To Colman Returning. *Unknown.* BIrV, *tr. by* Helen Waddell

So sits enthroned in vegetable pride. Kew. Erasmus Darwin. OBGa *Fr.* The Botanic Garden.

"So small and young" the silver moon with its spoons hung. Donagh MacDonagh. James Liddy. BiHa

So small are the flowers of Seamu. *Unknown, Egyptian hieroglyphics into Italian.* BoWoP; PBWP, *tr. by* Boris de Rachewiltz; *English vers. by* Ezra Pound *and* Noel Stock

So smell those odours that do rise. To the Most Fair and Lovely Mistress Anne Soame, Now Lady Abdie. Robert Herrick. CaPo; NOBE; NOSC

So smooth, so sweet, so silv'ry is thy voice. Upon Julia's Voice. Robert Herrick. InPK-6; NOBE; SeCP; SoSe-8

So, so, break[e] off this last lamenting kiss[e]. The Expiration. Donne. CBLP; MeLP; OxBSP

So soft in the hemlock wood. Pastoral. Robert Silliman Hillyer. MoAmPo

So soft streams meet, so springs with gladder smiles. The Welcome to Sack. Robert Herrick. BeJo; CaPo; CavPo; SeCP

So soon as day, forth dawning from the East. Artegall and Radigund. Edmund Spenser. *Fr.* Wood Of Error. AEP

So Sound You Sleep. A. E. Housman. LBC

So spake the enemy of mankind, enclosed. Milton. *Fr.* Book IX. FHYEP; NAEL-1; NAWM-1; OAEL-1 *Fr.* Paradise Lost.

So spends a summer's jasper century. (LL) Slug in Woods. Earle Birney. NOBC; NoP-4

So stretched out huge in length the Arch-Fiend lay. Milton. *Fr.* Book I. FHYEP; NAEL-1; OAEL-1; OxAEP-1 *Fr.* Paradise Lost.

So strong you thump O terrible drums—so loud you bugles blow. (LL) Beat! beat! drums!—blow! bugles! blow! Walt Whitman. NoP-4

So summer comes in the end to these few stains. The Beginning. Wallace Stevens. VGW

So sung the BARD—and Nansie's waws. Robert Burns. PoE *Fr.* Love and Libery—A Cantata. NOBRP; NOEC

So sweet, all sweet—the body as the shyer. Sweet-Briar in Rose. "Michael Field." VWP

So Sweet Is She. Ben Jonson. *See* So White, So Soft, So Sweet.

So sweet, so golden. Christian Hofmann von Hofmannswaldau, *German.* GePo, *tr. by* Alexander Gode

So swete a kis yistrene fra thee I reft. To His Maistres [*or* Mistress]. Alexander Montgomerie. GBL; OxBS

So take a happy view. A Happy View. C. Day Lewis. CMoP

So talks as it's most used to do. (LL) Christabel. Coleridge. FHYEP; NAEL-2; NOBRP; OAEL-2; Ro

So tell me what you have. Tell Me. Pamela Mordecai. PBCV

So Terrifyingly Melancholy. Hagiwara Sakutaro, *Japanese.* PFTM, *tr. by* Hiroaki Sato

So thank Mum for the book of poetry. 1916. R. S. Gwynn. MT

So that each person may quickly find that. Johann Joachim Quantz's Five Lessons. W. S. Graham. FaBoMo; FaBoTC

So, that girl with the gazelle eyes. Tanka. Nikolai Stepanovich Gumilyov, *Russian.* TCRP, *tr. by* Simon Franklin

So that good and evil may die in equal hope. (LL) May, 1945. Peter Porter. HP

So that I can't refuse. (LL) My Garden, My Daylight. Jorie Graham. HCAP; Poetr

So that I understand it, ladies mine. (LL) Beyond the sphere which spreads to widest space. Dante. AWP; CTC

So that is his mother. Born of Woman. Wislawa Szymborska, *Polish.* GI, *tr. by* Magnus J. Krynski *and* Robert A. Maguire

So that now when I think of love / I think of this. (LL) China. Dorianne Laux. DeD; LW

So that suddenly I might find you standing at my side! (LL) Hearing That His Friend Was Coming Back from the War. Wang Chien, *Chinese.* ChiP, *tr. by* Arthur Waley; FP

So that the cheek blanches and then blushes. (LL) At First Sight. Robert Graves. FaBoEE; OxBSP

So that the vines burst from my fingers. Canto 17. Ezra Pound. InPS-3; MeMAP; NAAL-2; OBMV *Fr.* Cantos.

So that's what you've got in your back pocket. Journal of the Thousand Choices. Susan Wheeler. PUP-19

So That's Who I Remind Me Of. Ogden Nash. PoLF

So the committee met again, and again. The Committee. C. Day Lewis. CMoP

So. The curtain has come. In Memoriam the Master—Noel Coward (1900-1973). E. J. Thribb. PeLV

So the cyclo driver. Dead for Two Years, Erhart Arranges to Meet Me in a Dream. John Balaban. CDa

So the distances are Galatea. The Distances. Charles Olson. NAAL-2; NeAP

So. The game was worth the candle. Clichés for an Unfaithful Husband. Jane King. HCP

So the last day's come at last, the close of my fifteen year. The Old Place. Blanche Edith Baughan. PeNZ

So the little children sing. (LL) Christmas Song: "Why do the bells for Christmas ring?" Eugene Field. BoTP

So the man spread his blanket on the field. A Tall Man Executes a Jig. Irving Layton. MoCV; NOBC; NoAM

So, the next parson stubbed and burnt it. (LL) Baucis and Philemon. Jonathan Swift. NOEC; OAEL-1

So the plastic conduits for the new. Cracking a Few Hundred Million Years. A. R. Ammons. EC3

So the rain falls. Cornkind. Frank O'Hara. CLPP

So the river—yes, the river; I have come to that at last. Emily Jane Pfeiffer. VWP *Fr.* Out of the Night.

So the sky wounded you, jagged at the heart. Daylights. Rosanna Warren. NoAM

So the storms bore the daughters of Pandarus out into thrall, *diff. vers.* Homer. *See* The Daughters of Pandarus.

So the World Changes. Kofi Awoonor. VCWP

So the world woos its children back for an evening kiss. (LL) Letters from a Father. Mona Van Duyn. FYAP; NoP-4

So, the year's done with! Love. Robert Browning. EnLoPo; GLoP *Fr.* Earth's Immortalities.

So then came his word here. Beginnings. *Unknown. Fr.* The Popol Vuh. STP, *tr. by* Munro Edmonson

So then naturally / This Count Rainuv I speak of. Rainuv; a Romantic Ballad from the Early Basque. Margaret Widdemer. BXAP

So then the Lord Jesus. Mark 16:19–20; So then the Lord Jesus, after. A. E. Housman. GI

So, then, the soul craves an earthly body. Flora Imre, *Hungarian.* CEEP, *tr. by* Emery E. George

So then you won't fight? Dooley Is a Traitor. James Michie. OxBTC

So there stood Matthew Arnold and this girl. The Dover Bitch. Anthony Hecht. BXAP; NBLV; NIP-4; NOBA; NOBL; OBAL; PFE; PeLV; Poetr; TRP; UnPo; VGW

So there was no one left but me. (LL) A Good Play. Robert Louis Stevenson. ACTP; OTCP; PWR

So there we were stuck. The Life of. . . . Theodore Weiss. NYBP

So there you are, in wispy veil and hat. Tea Party. Nancy Vieira Couto. PBCAP

So these then are the deeds of Alligator in turn. Alligator's Struggles with the 400 sons. *Unknown. Fr.* The Popol Vuh. STP, *tr. by* Munro Edmonson

So these two faced each other there. A Portrait in the Guards. Laurence Whistler. GTBS-P

So. They and I are back from the outside. Requiem. Carl Bode. IMW

So they appeared before their lord the king. Dynastic Hymn. *Unknown, Chinese.* ChiP, *tr. by* Arthur Waley

So they are satisfied with our Brigade. After the Battle. Audrey Herbert. PoFWW

So they are satisfied with our Brigade. After the Battle. Sir Alan Patrick Herbert. NSI

So they begin. With two years gone. Poem. Boris Pasternak, *Russian.* TrJP, *tr. by* C. M. Bowra

So they came. The Animals' Arrival. Elizabeth Jennings. PBWP

So they canonized him by the name of Jem Crow! (LL) The Jackdaw of Rheims. *Unknown.* EBNV; OBCoV; OBNV; OBSP

So they get this and we're coming off some it's like and. Et in Leucadia Ego. Michael Davidson. PmAP

So they have got you down at last, omera. Omera. Marjorie Oludhe Macgoye. HBAPE

So they passed. Group Shot. Basil T. Paquet. CDa

So they smashed that old man of Whitehaven. (LL) Limerick: "There was an old man of Whitehaven." Edward Lear. CBNP; EBEV; OxAEP-2

So they went, leaving a picnic-litter of talk. The Party. William Robert Rodgers. BIrV; PNI

So this is, Jimmy, where we live. An Urgent Letter. Hugh Maxton. PBCIP

So this is love, a kind of sad dance. Lorna Crozier. LW

So this is the dust that passes through porcelain. The Iron Lung. Stanley Plumly. AmPA; LCAP-2

So this is utopia, is it? Well. In a Copy of More's (or Shaw's or Wells's or Plato's or Anybody's) Utopia. Max Beerbohm. OBCoV

So thou art come again, old black-winged night. To Night. Thomas Lovell Beddoes. Son

So through that unripe day you bore your head. Philip Larkin. NoAM

So through the darkness and the cold we flew. Skating. Wordsworth. CH *Fr.* Introduction—Childhood and School-Time. FHYEP *Fr.* The Prelude; Growth of a Poet's Mind [1850 vers.]

So through the night rode Paul Revere. Henry Wadsworth Longfellow. *See* Paul Revere's Ride (The Landlord's Tale).

So thus he sorrowed till it was day. David Jones. NoAM *Fr.* King Pellam's Launde. OAEL-2 *Fr.* In Parenthesis.

So tired! so weary. Catharine of Arragon. Eloise Bibb. CBWP-4

So, 'tis enough. (LL) Kissing. Edward Herbert. EnLoPo; NOSC

So, to begin with, ghosts of rain arise. The Dance of Dust. Louis Untermeyer. BXAP

So to Tell the Truth. Janet Dubé. BrRo

So Touch Our Hearts with Loveliness. Gail Brook Burket. AH

So turne they still about, and change in restlesse wise. (LL) Dame Nature. Edmund Spenser. PoEL-1

So unwarely was never no man caught. Sir Thomas Wyatt. SiPS

So, up the steep side of the rugged hill. Jack and Jill. A. E. Housman. UV

So very sad. (LL) The First Circle. Kofi Awoonor. HBAPE; PBMAP; VCWP

So vile was poor Wat, such a miscreant slave. Robert Burns. FaBoEE

So warm I may melt. Sunday Morning. Christina Jenkins. BrRo

So was it even then. So soundlessly. A Trysting. Richard Dehmel, *German.* AWP, *tr. by* Jethro Bithell

So we are taking off our masks, are we, and keeping. Homosexuality. Frank O'Hara. LCAP-2; PoA; TAP

So we came at last to meet, after the lights were out. John Hollander. VCAP *Fr.* Powers of Thirteen.

So, we got you in the heel. Goodnight, Achilles. Enrique Lihn, *Spanish.* VCWP, *tr. by* Alastair Reid

So we move now. Sam Hamod. UnSA *Fr.* Moving.

So we must part, my body, you and I. Any Soul to Any Body. Cosmo Monkhouse. NOBVV

So we must say Goodbye, my darling. Goodbye. Alun Lewis. BoLoP; NAEL-2; NoP-4; OBWP; OxBM; OxBTC; PoWW

So we pass our time together, calm and delighted. (LL) For My Son Noah, Ten Years Old. Robert Bly. InPS-3; LoL; RaBo

So we ride, and ride through milked heaven. Rides. Gene Derwood. LiTM

So we tumble to bed. (LL) Tumbling. *Unknown.* ACTP

So we wait on the verge of. Sequence. Ken Irby. FTOS

So we were together. Hilda Doolittle. FaBoWP *Fr.* Winter Love.

So we'll go no more a-roving. Byron. APAD; AWP; BoLoP; CABP; CBLP; CH; ChAP; ClHu; EBEvV; FHYEP; FaPoR; GLoP; HAP; HeIP-4; ImPo; NAEL-2; NOBE; NoP-4; OAEL-2; OBEV; OPOU; OxBS; OxBSP; PoE; PoEL-4; PoLF; PoRA; Poetr; Ro; SAGP; SCGP; TFi; TTTS

So well I love thee[, as without thee I]. These verses weare made By Michaell Drayton Esquier Poett Lawreatt the night before hee dyed. Michael Drayton. GBL; NOBE

So well is me begone. *Unknown.* MiEL

So/ Went this little pig from the mainland to the market. Archibald MacLeish Suspends the Five Little Pigs. Louis Untermeyer. MoAmPo *Fr.* Mother Goose Up-to-Date.

So, we're estranged again—how it goes on! Drought. David Holbrook. OxBTC

So What. Philip Appleman. BXAP

So what if clowns and gnomes. The Golden Age. Artur Miedzyrzecki, *Polish.* PoSu, *tr. by* Stanislaw Baranczak *and* Clare Cavanagh

So what if Lowry got spooked by sea-birds and volcanoes crossing. Imperfect Sestina. Phyllis Webb. NOBC

So what if the underside of it's / not silver. Coin of the Realm. Patricia Goedicke. CMAP

So what said the others and the sun went down. Mrs. Alfred Uruguay. Wallace Stevens. TwCP

So what would you do? (LL) What? Langston Hughes. NBLV; OBAL

So when from hence we shall be gone. One Another's Mystery. Edward Herbert, 1st Baron Herbert of Cherbury. LBC

So, when *he* lost his temper, the Owl lost its life. "Lewis Carroll." *See* The Lobster.

So, When I Swim to the Shore. Molly Peacock. NMM-2

So when you see the desolating sacrilege spoken of by the prophet Daniel. Matthew 24:15–31. W. B. Yeats. GI *Fr.* St. Matthew.

So White, So Soft, So Sweet. Ben Jonson. *Fr.* The Devil Is an Ass. OxBSn

So wild it was when first we settled here. (LL) Domicilium. Thomas Hardy. GaP; OBGa

So wild yet candle-calm. The Grave's Cherub. Sydney Clouts. PeSA

So winter closed its fist. Rite of Spring. Seamus Heaney. OxBC

So would I to the hills again. Lustra. Christopher Okigbo. PBMAP *Fr.* Heavensgate (1961).

So write, before I end, " 'E liked it all!" (LL) Sestina of the Tramp-Royal. Rudyard Kipling. ImPo; MoBrPo

So ye're runnin' fer Congress, mister? Le' me tell ye 'bout my son. Whisperin' Bill. Irving Bacheller. PoLF

So, you and I are dethroned, divorced. The Garland. Vladimir Nikolaevich Sokolov, *Russian.* TCRP, *tr. by* Albert C. Todd

So you are married, girl. It makes me sad. Epithalamium. Roy McFadden. PNI

So you aren't Tolstoy or Saint Francis. Leonard Nathan. PBCAP

So you beg for a story, my darling, my brown-eyed Leopold. How He Saved St. Michael's. Mary Anna Phinney Stansbury. BLPA

So, you to ole Kentucky. Answer to Dunbar's "After a Visit." Joseph Cotter, Sr.. AAP

So you come with these maps in your head. The Man Who Makes Brooms. Naomi Shihab Nye. LoL

So you have swept me back. Hilda Doolittle. NALW; NMM-2; VGW *Fr.* Eurydice.

("I had forgot you / and the past.") (LL) NMM-2

So you haven't had a very. Easy Life. Pamela Mordecai. HCP

So you said you'd go home to work on your father's farm. To a Young Poet Who Died. John Logan. CAPP-1

So. You were. Lines on the Hundredth Anniversary of the Birth of W. Somerset Maugham. E. J. Thribb. PeLV

So you were David's father. In Memoriam[, Private D. Sutherland]. Ewart Alan Mackintosh. PoWW

So you will presently my loving hands abjure. To This Book. Martin Opitz, *German.* GePo, *tr. by* George C. Schoolfield

So, you've come to the tropics, heard all you had to do. Down and Out. Clarence Leonard Hay. BLPA

So you've reached your thirty-eighth birthday. My Husband's Birthday. Josephine D. Henderson Heard. CBWP-4

So zestfully canst thou sing? The Blinded Bird. Thomas Hardy. CMoP; LiTM

Soaked to the skin I peer through the drizzle, and I perceice. Thirty-third Canto. Hans Magnus Enzensberger. PoSu *Fr.* The Sinking of the Titanic.

Soap Box Derby, The. Michael L. Kane. CTV

Soap Bubbles. Bùi Khải Nguyễn, *Vietnamese.* AVP, *tr. by* Huỳnh Sanh Thông

Soap (II). Jerome Rothenberg. NNaP

Soap-Pig, The. Paul Muldoon. PBCIP

Soap Suds. Louis MacNeice. FaBoMo; NAEL-2; NOIV; NTP; SCV

Soap, the Oppressor. Burges Johnson. PoLF

Soar[e] up[p], my soul[e], unto thy rest[e]. Seek[e] Flowers of Heaven. Robert Southwell. TrCP

Soaring hawk from fist that flies, The. The Lover Compareth Himself to the Painful Falconer. *Unknown.* NoSic

Soaring into the distant sky, a lone bird disappears. Climbing Up to the Lo-yu Plain. Tu Mu, *Chinese.* SuSp, *tr. by* Irving Y. Lo

Sober, he thinks of her; so he gets drunk. Man and Woman. Robert Conquest. OxBTC

Sober man, I'll take the wine, A. Paulus Silentiarius, *Greek.* InMo, *tr. by* Sam Hamill

Sobering Up. Yüan Chen, *Chinese.* SuSp, *tr. by* Dell R. Hales

Soccer. Nikolai Alekseievich Zabolotsky, *Russian.* TCRP, *tr. by* Daniel Weissbort

Social Glass, The. Lizelia Augusta Jenkins Moorer. CBWP-3

Social Life, The. Lizelia Augusta Jenkins Moorer. CBWP-3

Social Note. Dorothy Parker. LW *Fr.* Some Beautiful Letters.

Social Virtue's liberal plan. Sung by a Choir of Boys Marching Round the Room. Anne Penny. ECWP *Fr.* Odes Sung in Commemoration of the Marine Society.

Society. Tom Clark. PmAP

Society, gregarious dame! An Ode to Society. Hester Lynch Salusbury Thrale [*later* Mrs. Piozzi]. ECWP

Society has quite forsaken all her wicked courses. Utopia Anglicized. Sir William Schwenck Gilbert. OBSV *Fr.* Utopia Limited.

Society Upon the Stanislaus, The. Bret Harte. OBAL; PaTW

Socrates' Death. Michael Jackson. PeNZ

Socrates' Ghost Must Haunt Me Now. Delmore Schwartz. LiTM

Socrates Snooks. Fitz Hugh Ludlow. BLPA

Socratic. Hilda Doolittle. HoPM *Fr.* Child Poems.

Sodden on her bed. 1975. Wayne Koestenbaum. BAP-95

Sodger laddie's socht a hoose, A. Under the Greenwood Tree. "Hugh MacDiarmid," *after the Cretan.* OBVE

Sodom. Chaim Grade, *Yiddish.* TrJP, *tr. by* Joseph Leftwich

Sodom. Herman Melville. AmPP *Fr.* Clarel: A Poem and Pilgrimage in the Holy Land.

Sodom. John Wilmot, 2d Earl of Rochester.
"Twelve months must pass ere you can yet arrive." FaBoSe

Soe well I love thee, as without thee I. Michael Drayton. *See* These verses weare made By Michaell Drayton Esquier Poett Lawreatt the night before hee dyed.

Soeur Louise de la Miséricorde (1674). Christina Rossetti. VWP

Sofa, The. William Cowper. *Fr.* The Task.
Ease.
Rural Sights and Sounds. NOEC, book 1, *ll.* 109–210
"Thou knowest my praise of nature most sincere." NAEL-1

Sofa, The. Medbh McGuckian. PBCIP; PNI

Sofa Book, The. Paul Evans.
"Blair Peach died with a broken head." NBrP
"City is a crowded lift, The." NBrP
"Hail, Garcia, hammer of pigeons." NBrP
"Man points with his umbrella, A." NBrP
"Poets detained by Thought Police." NBrP

Soft answer turneth away wrath, A. The Bible, Proverbs 15:1. Bible, *O.T.* CTV *Fr.* Proverbs.

Soft are Sappho's kisses. Paulus Silentiarius, *Greek.* GrAn, *tr. by* Andrew Miller

Soft as old silk. Loving You. Frances Horovitz. LW

Soft as yon silver ray that sleeps. Rondeau. Ann Radcliffe. Ro *Fr.* The Mysteries of Udolpho.

Soft Black Eyes. Priscilla Jane Thompson. CBWP-2

Soft cat and the scratchy cat, The. Concord Cats. Richard Eberhart. PC

Soft colored clouds obscured by the sun. Tune: "Song of the Southern Country"—Spring Thoughts at Pearl River. Chu Yi-tsun, *Chinese.* SuSp, *tr. by* Irving Y. Lo

Soft falls the night. Evening Song. Edith King. BoTP

Soft falls the sweet evening. Song. John Clare. NOBVV

Soft grasses, a plain of sedge fresh with passing rain. Tune: Sand of Silk-washing Stream. Su Tung-p'o, *Chinese.* CoBCP, *tr. by* Burton Watson *Fr.* Along the Road to Stone Lake.

Soft greens, deep reds, really fresh colors. On the Butterflies. T'ang Yin, *Chinese.* CoBLCP, *tr. by* Jonathan Chaves

Soft hangs the opiate in the brain. An Opium Fantasy. Maria White Lowell. APN-2; InPK-6

Soft haze upon the mountain and a haze upon the sea. A Slumber Song of the Gardens. John Runcie. PeSAV

Soft kisses may be innocent. The Caution. Catherine Cockburn. LW

Soft, lovely, rose-like lips, conjoined with mine. Barnabe Barnes. EnLoPo *Fr.* Parthenophil and Parthenophe.

Soft misty rain and a drop of thirty degrees. Bruce Beaver. *Fr.* Letters to Live Poets. CBAP

Soft new grass is creeping o'er the graves, The. By the Potomac. Thomas Bailey Aldrich. Son

Soft on the wave the oars at distance sound. Netley Abbey; Midnight. William Sotheby. NOEC

Soft *quem quam* will be Scops the Owl, The. Acropolis. Lawrence Durrell. OxAEP-2

Soft Sea washed around the House, A. Emily Dickinson. SAmP

Soft Snow. William Blake. SoSe-8

Soft sound of his steps on the pier, The. Photograph of a Child, Japanese-American Evacuation, Bainbridge Island, Washington, March 30, 1942. Jim Mitsui. OpBo

Soft sounds and odours brim up through the night. Guided Missiles Experimental Range. Robert Conquest. OxBC

Soft Targets. Essex Hemphill. GT

Soft: the way her eyes view her children. Don L. Lee. MBE *Fr.* Blackwoman Poems.

Soft through the silent air descend the feathery snow-flakes. Fragment: December 18, 1847. Henry Wadsworth Longfellow. APN-1

Soft toys that make to seem girls. Strip-tease. Lawrence Durrell. OxAEP-2

Soft Warm Breeze, A. Natan Zach, *Hebrew.*
("Soft warm breeze and the summer land awakes, A.") IP, *tr. by* Warren Bargad *and* Stanley F. Chyet

Soft White. Lee Harwood. SPE

Soft Wood. Robert Lowell. LiTM

Soft you; a word or two before you go. Death of Othello. Shakespeare. OxAEP-1 *Fr.* Othello.

Softened by Time's consummate plush. Emily Dickinson. CrDW; NOBA

Softly along the road of evening. Nod. Walter De la Mare. BoTP; MoBrPo; OxBTC

Softly and humbly to the Gulf of Arabs. Beach Burial. Kenneth Slessor. BMAP; CBAP

Softly croons the radiogram, loudly hoot the owls. Invasion Exercise on the Poultry Farm. John Betjeman. NOBL

Softly Fades the Twilight Ray. Samuel Francis Smith. AH

Softly gliding I go. Satyr's Song, The ("Softly Gliding as I Go"). John Fletcher. NOSC *Fr.* The Faithful Shepherdess.

Softly, in the dusk, a woman is singing to me;. Piano. D. H. Lawrence. APAD; CABP; CMoP; GEA; GTBS-P; HAP; HeIP-4; InPK-6; MoBrPo; MoP; NAEL-2; NOBE; NoAM; NoP-4; OAEL-2; OPOU; OxBSP; PoE; Poetr; RB; SAGP; SCGP; TFi; TRP; UnPo; WeW-3

Softly, now softly lies / Sleeping. *Unknown. See* Weep you no more, sad fountains.

Softly now the day is dawning. The Signal Gun. Mary E. Tucker. CBWP-1

Softly now the light of day. Evening Contemplation. George Washington Doane. AH; BLPA; FaBoBe

Softly, O midnight Hours! Serenade. Aubrey Thomas De Vere. OBEV

Softly rustled the oaks, whispered low in my ear. The Graveyard. Hayyim Nahman Bialik, *Hebrew.* TrJP, *tr. by* Bertha Beinkinstadt

Softly sighs the April air. Bel m'es quan lo vens m'alena. Arnaut Daniel, *French.* AWP, *tr. by* Harriet Waters Preston

Softly, softly, through the darkness. Christmas Night. B. E. Milner. BoTP

Softly the Evening. William Hurrell Mallock. BXAP

Softly the linden grows green in the opening summer. Early Noon. Ingeborg Bachmann, *German.* AF, *tr. by* Mark Anderson

Softly the waters ripple. Ares. Albert Ehrenstein, *German.* TrJP, *tr. by* Babette Deutsch *and* Avrahm Yarmolinsky

Soggarth Aroon. John Banim. TIRV

Soho Hospital for Women, The. Fleur Adcock. NoP-4

Sohrab and Rustum. Matthew Arnold. EBNV; OBNV
Sohrab Dead. NOBE
"Then Sohrab with his sword smote Rustum's helm." OBWP

Soil between balls of thumb and forefinger crumbled / falls. Skylarks and Fuji. Kusano Shimpei, *Japanese.* PFTM, *tr. by* Cid Corman

Soil is freshly dug, the half-faded wreaths of leaves, The. Heraclitus of Halicarnassus, *Greek.* GrAn, *tr. by* Edwin Morgan

Soil now gets a rumpling soft and damp, The. The Strong Are Saying Nothing. Robert Frost. CMoP

Soil was deep and the field well-sited, The. A Failure. C. Day Lewis. NOBE

Soiled Dove. Carl Sandburg. SAGP

Soil's fertility from wholesome flowers, The. Shakespeare. *See* Richard II.

Soirée. Ezra Pound. OBCoV

Sois sage, ô ma doleur. . . I don't. Michael Foley. PNI *Fr.* True Life Love Stories.

Soissons. Keith Douglas. NoAM

Sojourn in the Whale. Marianne Moore. NALW

Sojourner Truth. Robert Earl Hayden. *Fr.* Stars. LCAP-2

Sokoya, I said, looking through. There Is No Word for Goodbye. Mary TallMountain. HATNAP; LoL

Sokrates to Agathon. Plato, *Greek.* GrAn, *tr. by* Peter Jay

Sokrates to his Lover. Plato, *Greek.* OBCVT, *tr. by* Willis Barnstone

Sokrates to Xanthippé. Plato, *Greek.* GrAn, *tr. by* Peter Jay

Sol through white curtains shot a tim'rous ray. Alexander Pope. ECEV *Fr.* The Rape of the Lock[, an Heroi-Comical Poem]. FHYEP; HAP; ImPo; OAEL-1; OBNV; PeLV; PoEL-3
("And Betty's praised for labours not her own.") (LL) EP

Sol took his nightcap off and gazed. After the Storm. Henrietta Cordelia Ray. CBWP-3

Solace. Clarissa Scott Delany. PoBA

Solace. Josephine D. Henderson Heard. CBWP-4

Solace hast thou for pain! (LL) The Dying Words of Stonewall Jackson. Sidney Lanier. APN-2; CBCWP

Solace in Age. Sir Richard Maitland. OxBS

Solar Creation. Charles Madge. APAD; FaBoMo; OBMV; OxBTC

Solar Loneliness. "Strannik," *Russian.* TCRP, *tr. by* April FitzLyon

Solar Myth. Genevieve Taggard. MoAmPo

Solar Years. David Rokeah, *Hebrew.* MHP, *tr. by* Ruth Finer Mintz

Soldier, The. Rupert Brooke. APAD; CABP; EBEvV; FaPoR; GSo; HeIP-4; LiTM; MoBrPo; NAEL-2; NOBE; NSI; NoP-4; OBEV; OBWP; OxBTC; PeFWW; PoA; PoFWW; PoLF; PoRA; PoWW; Son *Fr.* 1914.

Soldier, The. David Ferry. WeT

Soldier, The. Uys Krige, *Afrikaans.* PeSA, *tr. by the author*

Soldier, A. Sir John Suckling. CavPo; PoE
("You would be hurt so night and day, / Yet love me.") (LL) CavPo

Soldier, The. J. Y. Watson. BXAP

Soldier Addresses his Body, The. Edgell Rickword. PeFWW; PoWW

Soldier and a Sailor, A. John Gay. *See* Air: "A Fox may steal your hens, sir."

Soldier Bathing. Frank Ormsby. PNI *Fr.* A Northern Spring.

Soldier,beware of mrs smith. (LL) In heavenly realms of hellas dwelt. E. E. Cummings. NOBA; OBSV

Soldier Boy for Me. *Unknown.* AmFP

Soldier Boy's Dream, The. Mary E. Tucker. CBWP-1

Soldier brave, sailor true. *Unknown.* OxNR

Soldier came back home one day, A. Ground Glass. Irina Odoyevtseva, *Russian.* TCRP, *tr.* by Bradley Jordan

Soldier from the Wars Returning. A. E. Housman. OBMV

Soldier Going to the Field, The. Sir William Davenant. NOBE; OBWP

Soldier in the Park, The. Elizabeth Riddell. CBAP

Soldier Is Home, The. John Shaw Neilson. CBAP

Soldier maimed and in the beggars' list, A. The Pluralist and Old Soldier. John Collier. NOEC

Soldier of the Legion lay dying in Algiers, A. Bingen on the Rhine. Caroline Elizabeth Norton. BLPA

Soldier on the Marsh, A. Andrew Hudgins. CBCWP

Soldier passed me in the freshly fallen snow, A. To a Conscript of 1940. Sir Herbert Read. LiTM; NSI; OBWP; PoWW

Soldier, past full retreat, is marching out of the grave, The. Go Ask the Dead. Thomas McGrath. AF; CDa

"Soldier, Rest!" Robert Jones Burdette. OBAL

Soldier Rest! [Thy Warfare O'er]. Sir Walter Scott. AWP; NOBE; PoRA *Fr.* The Lady of the Lake.

(Song: "Soldier rest! thy warfare o'er.") OBNC

Soldier stalks before my door, A. (LL) Contrary Theses (I). Wallace Stevens. OxBA; SAmP

Soldier That Has Seen Service, The. *Unknown.* NOEC

Soldier, the only one in sight, The. San Antonio de Padua. W. S. Di Piero. PaTW

Soldier, there is a war between the mind. Epilogue. Wallace Stevens. ColAP; NoAM *Fr.* Notes toward a Supreme Fiction.

Soldier, think before you marry. John Gay. PeLV *Fr.* Achilles.

Soldier: Twentieth Century. Isaac Rosenberg. PoWW

Soldier waits until he's called—then, A. Alfonzo Prepares to Go Over the Top. Rita Dove. LoL

Soldier Walks under the Trees of the University, The. Randall Jarrell. OxBA

Soldier, Won't You Marry Me? *Unknown.* AmFP; OxBoLi; PeLV

Soldiers. Padraic Fiacc. PNI

Soldiers. Giuseppe Ungaretti. PFTM

Soldiers and poor, unable to rejoice. (LL) The Owl. Edward Thomas. AF; APo; ChAP; EBEV; FaBoTw; GTBS-P; MoP; NAEL-2; NIP-4; NOBE; NoAM; NoP-4; OAEL-2; OBWVE; OxAEP-2; PeFWW; PoE; Poetr; RB; SCGP; TFi; TRP; UnPo

Soldiers are citizens of death's grey land. Dreamers. Siegfried Sassoon. MoBrPo; NoAM; Son

Soldiers Bathing. Frank Templeton Prince. GTBS-P; ImPo; LiTM; MoBrPo; NOCV; OBWP; OxBTC; PeSA

Soldiers came, brewed tea in Snoddy's field, The. After the War. Douglas Dunn. OxBC

Soldiers' Chorus from Faust. *Unknown.* NOBAu

Soldier's Cigarette, The. Harold Beckh. NSI

Soldier's Ditty, A. Bulat Shalvovich Okudzhava, *Russian.* TCRP, *tr.* by Deming Brown

Soldier's Dream, The. Thomas Campbell. FaPoR; GTBS-P; OxAEP-2

Soldiers have to fight and swear. Unequal Distribution. Samuel Hoffenstein. TrJP

Soldiers in a Small Camp. Walter James Turner. NSI

Soldiers in the air. (LL) Song My. Susan Griffin. NMM-2

Soldiers never do die well. Champs d'Honneur. Ernest Hemingway. AiP; PoA

Soldiers of Christ, arise. The Whole Armour of God. Charles Wesley. NOCV

Soldiers on the ground. Tanka. Kondō Yoshimi, *Japanese.* MJT, *tr.* by Makoto Ueda

Soldier's Song. Goethe. AWP, *tr.* by Bayard Taylor *Fr.* Faust.

Soldier's Song. *Unknown, Sioux Native American.* APN-2, *tr.* by Stephen Return Riggs

Soldiers' Songs of the First World War. *Unknown.*

"Bells of hell go ting-a-ling-a-ling, The." OBCoV

"I don't want to be a soldier." NSI; OBCoV; PoWW

("And———my bloody life away.") (LL) OBCoV

"I have no pain, dear mother, now." OBCoV

"Sure, a little bit of shrapnel fell from out the sky one day." OBCoV

"Wash me in the water." OBCoV

"We are Fred Karno's army." OBCoV

Soldier's Tale, The. *Unknown.* PeLV

Soldiers who wish to be a hero. *Unknown.* FaBoEE

Soldier's Wife, The. Robert Southey. OxBSP

Soldier's Wooing, The. *Unknown.* AmFP

Soldier's Wound, The. Wallace Stevens. *Fr.* Esthétique du Mal. LiTM

Sole heir of virtue, and of beauty both. Sir John Davies. NAEL-1 *Fr.* Orchestra; or, A Poem[e] of Da[u]ncing. NoSic; SiPS

Sole necessity of Earth and Heaven!, The. (LL) Prelude: "Along the roadside, like the flowers of gold." John Greenleaf Whittier. APN-1; NAAL-1; NAAL-3; OxBA; PoEL-4

Sole Positive of Night! Ne Plus Ultra. Coleridge. OAEL-2

Sole true something—This! In Limbo's den, The. Limbo. Coleridge. OAEL-2

Sole watchman of the flying stars, guard me. John Berryman. UnPo *Fr.* Eleven Addresses to the Lord. OxBC

Solea. Jessica Hagedorn. MoNo; WWSi

("There are rapists.") MoNo

Soledad. Robert Earl Hayden. MoNo; NAAAL

Solemn Douglas firs stride slowly. A Confirmation. William Daniel Ehrhart. CDa

Solemn Hour. Rilke, *German.* TrJP, *tr.* by C. F. MacIntyre

Solemn Meditation, A. William Shenstone. NOEC

Solemn plain-faced child stands gazing there, A. A Portrait. Walter De la Mare. NoAM

Solemn, solemn the coachman gets ready to go;. To His Wife. Ch'in Chia, *Chinese.* ChiP, *tr.* by Arthur Waley

Solemn thing—it was—I said, A. Emily Dickinson. NALW

Solemn whip-poor-will, The. The Queens. Robert Fitzgerald. NYBP

Solemnly, mournfully, / Dealing its dole. Curfew. Henry Wadsworth Longfellow. APN-1; MeMAP; OxBA

Solicitudes canine, four-footed amities. (LL) Sonnet: To Tartar, a Terrier Beauty. Thomas Lovell Beddoes. NOBVV; ODNC

Solid citizens, The. Undertow. Langston Hughes. LiTM

Solid houses in the mist, The. New Year's. Charles Reznikoff. VGW

Solid man and the coxcomb, The. (LL) Crazy Jane and the Bishop. W. B. Yeats. CMoP; LiTM

Soliloquies on Temporal Indigence. Mary Latter.

"Now calumnies arise, and black reproach." ECWP

"Strangers to meek compassion's tender touch." ECWP

"With tearful eye, how frequent have I seen." ECWP

Soliloquy. Francis Ledwidge. HoPM

Soliloquy. George Sewell. *See* The Dying Man in His Garden.

Soliloquy: "What folly to complain." Ann Yearsley. NOBRP

Soliloquy 2. Richard Aldington. PoFWW

Soliloquy at Potsdam. Peter Porter. NOBAu

Soliloquy from "Hamlet." Shakespeare. *See* Hamlet's Soliloquy.

Soliloquy in an Air-Raid. Roy Fuller. PoA

Soliloquy in the Suburbs, A. Charles Jenner. NOEC *Fr.* Eclogue IV: The Poet. AWP

Soliloquy of a Beauty in the Country. George Lyttelton. ECEV

Soliloquy of a Maiden Aunt. Dollie Radford. NOBVV

Soliloquy of a Turkey. Paul Laurence Dunbar. BPo

Soliloquy of One of the Spies Left in the Wilderness, A. Gerard Manley Hopkins. TrCP

Soliloquy of the Spanish Cloister. Robert Browning. FHYEP; FaBoVe; ImPo; InPK-6; NAEL-2; NIP-4; NOBL; NOBVV; NoP-4; OAEL-2; OxBoV; PeVV; TOF; UV

Soliloquy on an Empty Purse. Mary Jones. ECWP

("Alas! my Purse! how lean and low!") PEW

Soliloquy on Death. F. K. Fiawoo. PBA

Soliloquy to Absent Friends. Douglas G. Jones. MoCV

Solipsist with triplets said: "Though," A. Limerick. Lupellus. PeLi

Solitaire. Conrad Potter Aiken. ColAP

Solitaire. Amy Lowell. MoAmPo

Solitariness. Sir Philip Sidney. SCGP; SiPS *Fr.* Arcadia.

(Delight of Solitariness, The.)

Sweetly Empty Woods.

Solitary. Lance Henson. HATNAP

Solitary, The. Sylvia Lynd. WPN

Solitary, The. Friedrich Wilhelm Nietzsche, *German.* AWP, *tr.* by Ludwig Lewisohn

Solitary. Sharon Olds. NMM-2

Solitary, The. Rilke, *German.* TrJP, *tr.* by C. F. MacIntyre

Solitary, The. Sara Teasdale. MoAmPo

Solitary bird of night, The. Ode to Wisdom. Elizabeth Carter. CABP; ECWP

Solitary Canto to Chloris the Disdainful, A. John Smith. NOEC

Solitary Confinement. Robert Walker. NOBAu

Solitary crow. Norman MacCaig. NoP-4

Solitary Falcon above the Buddha Hall of the Monastery of Universal Purity, A. Mei Yao Ch'en, *Chinese*. SuSp, *tr. by* Jonathan Chaves

Solitary invalid in a fuchsia garden, A. The Philosopher and the Birds. Richard Murphy. CIP-2

Solitary molar of a whore, The. Cycle. Gottfried Benn, *German*. PFTM, *tr. by* Francis C. Golffing

Solitary peak, A. April. Mogwol Park, *Korean*. CKP, *tr. by* Jaihiun Kim

Solitary prospector, A. Sunstrike. Douglas Livingstone. PeSA

Solitary Reaper, The. Wordsworth. APAD; AWP; CABP; CH; ClHu; EBEvV; FHYEP; FaBoCh; FaPoR; HAP; HeIP-4; ImPo; InPS-3; NAEL-2; NOBE; NOBRP; NoP-4; OAEL-2; OBEV; OBNC; OxAEP-2; PoEL-4; PoPoPo; PoRA; Poetr; Ro; SCGP; SCV; SoSe-8; TFi; UnPo; WeW-3 (Reaper, The.) GTBS-P

Solitary wayfarer! Hoopoe. George Darley. OBNC   *Fr. Nepenthe.*

Solitude. John Clare. OxBSP

Solitude. Abraham Cowley. *See* On Solitude.

Solitude. Walter De la Mare. CMoP

Solitude. Babette Deutsch. LW

Solitude. Andreas Gryphius, *German*. GePo, *tr. by* George C. Schoolfield

Solitude. Mary Mollineux. NOSC

Solitude. Harold Monro. LBC; MoBrPo

Solitude. Tomas Tranströmer, *Swedish*. RB, *tr. by* Robert Bly

Solitude. Ella Wheeler Wilcox. EBEvV; PWR; PoLF; SDW

Solitude: An Ode. James Grainger. ECEV

Solitude flared out, The. Lyn Hejinian. FTOS   *Fr.* The Person.

Solitude is like rain. Rilke, *German*. TrJP, *tr. by* C. F. MacIntyre

Solitude Late at Night in the Woods. Robert Bly. VGW

Solitude of Alexander Selkirk, The. William Cowper. *See* Verses Supposed to Be Written by Alexander Selkirk during His Solitary Abode on the Island of Juan Fernandez.

Solitude supporting solitude on two pergolas. Poem for a Guerrilla Leader. Syl Cheney-Coker. PBMAP

Solitude that unmakes one of men. Compensation. Robinson Jeffers. MoAmPo

Solitude walks one heavy step more near. (LL) Solitude. Harold Monro. LBC

Solitude: you must be very strong. Lines from the Testament. Pier Paolo Pasolini, *Italian*. VCWP, *tr. by* Norman MacAfee *and* Luciano Martinengo

Solo. Mary Elizabeth Coleridge. VWP

Solo by Moonlight. Jules Laforgue, *French*. FLP, *tr. by* Alistair Elliot

Solo Finger Solo. Jayne Cortez. MoNo

Solo for Ear-Trumpet. Dame Edith Sitwell. MoBrPo

Solo for Two Voices. Octavio Paz, *Spanish*. STV, *tr. by* John Frederick Nims

Solo Native. Thomas Lux. CMAP; LCAP-2

Solo, New Orleans. Diann Blakely Shoaf. PUP-20

Solo or in the ride out gliding and. Barney Bigard. Suzanne Noguere. FFC

Solo: The Good Blues. Dolores Kendrick. FFC

Solo with Chorus. Rose Fyleman. NOxBChV

Soloing. Philip Levine. FiLi

Soloists, The. Mingus Speaks: Found Poems. George Barlow. ISC

Solomon. Heinrich Heine, *German*. TrJP, *tr. by* Emma Lazarus

Solomon and Balkis. Robert Browning. ChIV-1; NoAM

Solomon and the Witch. W. B. Yeats. ChIV-1; NoAM

Solomon Grundy. Mother Goose. CBNP; LB; NBLV; OTCP; OxBoLi; OxNR; PeLV; ReMoGo

Solomon Grundy / Bored on Tuesday. Senilio Passes, Singing. Martin Bell. OBCoV

Solomon King of the Jews and the Queen of Sheba, Balkis. Solomon and Balkis. Robert Browning. ChIV-1

Solomon on the Vanity of the World. Matthew Prior.
"Pass we the ills, which each man feels or dreads." NOEC; PoEL-3

Solomon Redivivus, 1886. Constance Naden. VWP

Solomon to Sheba. W. B. Yeats. CMoP; KSG
("'World a narrow pound,' The.") (LL) KSG

Solomon! where is thy throne? It is gone in the wind. Gone in the Wind. James Clarence Mangan, *after the German of* Friedrich Rückert. TIRV

Solomon's Seal, False and True. Graveyard at Bald Eagle Ridge. John Balaban. CDa

Solsequium, The. Alexander Montgomerie. OxBS

Solstice. Gerald Dawe. PNI

Solstice Poem. Margaret Atwood.
"In this house (in a dying orchard)." CrSp

Soluble Noughts and Crosses; or, California, Here I Come. Roger Roughton. SPE

Solum Mihi Superest Sepulchrum. William Habington. ChIV-1; NOSC

Solution, The. Bertolt Brecht, *German*. PoSu, *tr. by* Dereck Bowman

Solution. Ralph Waldo Emerson. OBAL

Solution, The. Brian Merriman. BIrV, *tr. by* Arland Ussher   *Fr.* The Midnight Court. NOIV, *tr. by* Thomas Kinsella

"Solution," they said to my friend, The. The Long Way Round. Denise Levertov. NMM-2

Soma. Suzanne Noguere. FFC

"Sombra?" The Shade-Seller. Josephine Jacobsen. TAP

Sombre [or Somber] and rich, the skies. By the Statue of King Charles [or I] at Charing Cross. Lionel Pigot Johnson. MoBrPo; NOBE; OBEV; OBMV; OBNC; PeVV; PoEL-5

Sombre as the heavens when morning clouds arise. The Lychee-tree. Wang I, *Chinese*. ChiP, *tr. by* Arthur Waley

Sombre the night is. Returning, We Hear the Larks. Isaac Rosenberg. FaBoMo; NAEL-2; NSI; NoAM; OAEL-2; OBWP; PeFWW; PoWW

Some act of Love's bound to rehearse. Why I Write Not of Love. Ben Jonson. BeJo; OxBSP

Some affairs are hard to relate and painful to hear. On the Second Day of the Fifth Month—Written after Drink. Liu Ya-tzu, *Chinese*. SuSp, *tr. by* Wu-chi Liu

Some ages hence, for it must not decay. Under a Lady's Picture. Edmund Waller. EnLoPo

Some are & are going to my howinouse. The 12th Horse Song of Frank Mitchell (Blue). Frank Mitchell, *Navajo Indian*. APSN; FTOS; STP, *tr. by* Jerome Rothenberg

Some are bewildered in the maze of Schools. Plain Fools. Alexander Pope. OBSV   *Fr.* An Essay on Criticism. NAEL-1; PoEL-3; TFi

Some are coming on the passenger. They're Leaving Memphis in Droves. *Unknown*. CrDW

Some are dogs, you see! (LL) Mother Tabbyskins. Elizabeth Anna Hart. NOxBChV

Some are drunk. Some are mumbling. Thirty-Six Poets. Judith Baumel. WeT

Some are in prison; some are dead. The Chums. Theodore Roethke. FP

Some are nights others stars. Ashes. Vasco [or Vasko] Popa. HSix, *tr. by* Charles Simic   *Fr.* Games. RB, *tr. by* Anne Pennington

Some are plain lucky—we ourselves among them. A Lost Soul. Jay Macpherson. NOBC; NoP-4

Some are teethed on a silver spoon. Saturday's Child. Countee Cullen. LiTM; NAAAL; PoBA

Some ask for envy'd pow'r; which publick hate. Sejanus. Some ask for envy'd pow'r; which publick hate. Juvenal. OBVE, *tr. by* Dryden   *Fr.* Satires.

Some autumn leaves a painter took. The Sumach Leaves. Jones Very. ColAP; NOBA

Some banks cropped close, and lawns smooth mown and green. The Hill-Side Park. W. H. Davies. OBGa

Some beating in there. Night Bird. James Dickey. WeT

Some beauties yet no precepts can declare. Alexander Pope. HAP   *Fr.* An Essay on Criticism. NAEL-1; PoEL-3; TFi

Some Beautiful Letters. Dorothy Parker.
Comment. LW; NBLV; NIP-4; OBAL; OBCoV
("And I am Marie of Rumania.") (LL) LW
News Item. NALW; OBAL
Résumé. HeIP-4; InPK-6; NAAL-2; NALW; NBLV; NoP-4; OBAL; PFE; Poetr; TrJP; UV
Social Note. LW

Some bite off the others. He. Vasco [or Vasko] Popa, *Serbian*. CBNP; PoSu   *Fr.* Games. RB, *tr. by* Anne Pennington

Some Blaze the Precious Beauties of Their Loves. John, of Hereford Davies. Son   *Fr.* Wit's Pilgrimage.

Some bloodied sea-bird's hovering decay. The Lie. Howard Moss. LiTM

Some books are lies frae end to end. Death and Doctor Hornbook [A True Story]. Robert Burns. OxBS

Some Boys. Chuck Ortleb. GLP

Some Boys. John Penkethman. OxBChV

Some broken. A State of Nature. John Hollander. AiP

Some by their friends, more by themselves thought wise. Dryden. ChIV-1; OBSV   *Fr.* Absalom and Achitophel, Pt. I. EBEvV; FHYEP; FaBoPV; HAP; NOSC; OAEL-1; PoEL

Some call Experience. (LL) I stepped from Plank to Plank. Emily Dickinson. CMoP; NOBA; NOCV; OxBSP; SAmP; SDW

Some call that deep-deep bell. Hilda Doolittle. NALW   *Fr.* Tribute to the Angels.

Some can gaze and not be sick. A. E. Housman. FaBoEE; NOBVV; OBSV

Some can leave the truth unspoken. Truth. Eileen Duggan. PeNZ

Some candle clear burns somewhere I come by. The Candle Indoors. Gerard Manley Hopkins. ChIV-2; ImPo; LiTM; OxAEP-2; PoEL-5

Some celebration. / One by one they all left me. On the Carpet, Staring at Myself. Slavko Mihalic. PoSu, tr. by Peter Kastmiler

Some Contemplations of the Poor, and Desolate State of the Church at Deerfield. John Williams. SCAP

Some creep came to my water trough. The Snake on D. H. Lawrence. N. J. Warburton. UV

Some cry up Haydn, some Mozart. Free Thoughts on Several Eminent Composers. Charles Lamb. OxBoLi; PeLV

Some curse that traitor Judas life and limb. On Judas Iscariot. Francis Quarles. FaBoEE

Some day.—Alas, alas! (LL) Near Lanivet, 1872. Thomas Hardy. AWP; CMoP; NoAM

Some day, all unawares, alone in the deep forest. My Death. Carl Zuckmayer, German. TrJP, tr. by E. B. Ashton

Some day I will go to Aarhus. The Tollund Man. Seamus Heaney. BIrV; CABP; CIP-2; EBEV; FaBoMo; PBCIP; PNI

Some day I'm going to have a store. General Store. Rachel Lyman Field. ChAP

Some day in six inches of. Kenneth Rexroth. APSN   Fr. The Love Poems of Marichiko.

Some day shall I be the one who let. Jules Supervielle, French. MFP, tr. by Martin Sorrell

Some Day, Some Day. Cristóbal de Castillejo, Spanish. AWP, tr. by Longfellow

Some day when I leave. Lilies. Bozhidar Bozhilov, Bulgarian. CEEP, tr. by Jascha Kessler and Aleksandar Shurbanov

Some day, when trees have shed their leaves. After the Winter. Claude McKay. PoBA

Some days ago I remarried. Marrying Again. Mei Yao Ch'en, Chinese. CoBCP, tr. by Burton Watson

Some days, although we cannot pray, a prayer. Prayer. Carol Ann Duffy. NoP-4

Some days he would wander around his attic-room. The Wisdom of AE. Thomas McCarthy. PBCIP

Some days, I'm sorely tempted to throw out the baby. Lamentations of an Au Pair Girl. Susan Feldman. AmPA

Some days in May, little stars. A Long Branch Song. Robert Pinsky. NoP-4

Some days it is my one inescapable wish to live / alone. Change My Evil Ways. David Rivard. PUP-18

Some days must be dark and dreary. (LL) The Rainy Day. Henry Wadsworth Longfellow. AWP; PoLF

Some Days / Out Walking Above. De Leon Harrison. PoBA

Some define the happening. (LL) Native's Letter. Arthur Nortje. HBAPE; PeSAV

Some depature from the norm. Saying It to Keep It from Happening. John Ashbery. FTOS

Some die too late and some too soon. The Lost Occasion. John Greenleaf Whittier. NOBA

Some distance away. Letter from An Hoc (4), by a Seedbed. R. L. Barth. CDa

Some Dreams They Forgot. Elizabeth Bishop. NoAM

Some dreams we have are nothing else but dreams. The Haunted House. Thomas Hood. EBEV

Some Early gardenists. William Mason. OBGa   Fr. The English Garden.

Some Eyes Condemn. Edward Thomas. NoAM

Some Feelings. Michael Benedikt. CoAmPo

Some Fishy Nonsense. Laura Elizabeth Richards. CTV

Some flecks of sun, some drops of chilly dew. Spring Out of Season. Xuân Diệu, Vietnamese. AVP, tr. by Huỳnh Sanh Thông

Some folk like the chaffinch. The Robin. O. M. Bent. BoTP

Some folks are drunk, yet do not know it. An English Ballad, on the Taking of Namur by the King of Great Britain, 1695. Matthew Prior. PoEL-3

Some folks as can afford. Under a Wiltshire Apple Tree. Anna Bunston DeBary. CH

Some folks in looks take so much pride. Unknown. PoToHe

Some for everyone. Snow by Morning. May Swenson. NYBP

Some for the Glories of This World; and some. Omar Khayyám, Persian; Ad. by Edward Fitzgerald. TRP   Fr. The Rubáiyát of Omar Khayyám [of Naishápúr]. AWP; CABP; EBVV; FaBoBe; FaPoR; HAP; NAEL-2; PoEL-5

Some Foreign Letters. Anne Sexton. MoAmPo

Some fowls there be that have so perfect sight. How the Lover Perisheth in His Delight, As the Fly in the Fire. Petrarch. SCGP, tr. by Sir Thomas Wyatt   Fr. Sonnets to Laura.

Some Frenchmen. John Updike. NBLV

Some Futureplans. David Avidan, Hebrew. IP, tr. by Warren Bargad and Stanley F. Chyet

Some Gangster Pain. Gillian Conoley. CMAP

Some generous painter now assist my pen. The True Effigies of a Certain Squire: Inscribed to Clemena. Elizabeth Thomas. ECWP

Some Girls. Susanne Doyle. FFC

Some Glow on the Sill. Clark Coolidge. FTOS

Some glowing in the common blood. / Some specialness within. (LL) Of Robert Frost. Gwendolyn Brooks. MoP; NOBA; NoAM

Some go local. Yes. Muriel Rukeyser. PiM   Fr. Yes.

Some gold lies veiled behind each evening cloud. Hidden Essence. Henrietta Cordelia Ray. CBWP-3

Some good account at last. Isaac Watts. See How doth the little busy bee.

Some good people, daring and subtle voices. John Berryman. HCAP   Fr. Dream Songs.

Some Good Things to Be Said for the Iron Age. Gary Snyder. HoPM; TTTS

Some Grand River Blues. Daniel David Moses. HATNAP

Some guy in the miserable convoy. The Last Lie. Bruce Weigl. AF

Some guys show up. Lawrence Ferlinghetti. See Sometime during eternity / some guys show up.

Some hae meat that canna eat. A Child's Grace. Unknown. FaBoCh   Fr. Two Graces.

Some Harvard men, stalwart and hairy. Limerick. Edward Gorey. OBAL; OBCoV

Some have [or hae] meat and cannot [or canna] eat. Grace at Kirkudbright. Robert Burns. NTP; OxBSP

Some heaps of trash upon a vacant lot. Hypochondriasis. Ambrose Bierce. APN-2   Fr. The Devil's Dictionary.

Some hearts go hungering thro' the world. Hungering Hearts. Unknown. PoToHe

Some in the Godspeed, the Susan C. Enough. Marianne Moore. NOBA

Some in their harts their mistris colours bears. William Smith. AAS   Fr. Chloris [or the Complaint of the Passionate Despised Shepheard].

Some Indian Uses of History on a Rainy Day. A. K. Ramanujan. OxBC

Some intense event dictated a poem. Events by Moonlight. Michael Benedikt. WeT

Some keep the Sabbath going to Church. Emily Dickinson. HeIP-4; MoAmPo; PBMP

Some kinds of trees seem ever eager. The Mast Year. Medbh McGuckian. CIP-2

Some Kisses from The Kama Sutra. Hugo Williams. BoLoP

Some ladies smoke too much and some ladies drink too much and some ladies pray too much. Curl Up and Diet. Ogden Nash. OBCoV

Some Last Questions. W. S. Merwin. HCAP; VCAP

Some leading thoroughfares of man. Via Crucis. Herman Melville. APN-2; NCAP   Fr. Clarel: A Poem and Pilgrimage in the Holy Land.

Some like cats, and some like dogs. Cats and Dogs. N. M. Bodecker. TLR

Some like drink. Not I. Robert Louis Stevenson. NOBL

Some like them gentle and sweet. I Like Them Fluffy. Sir Alan Patrick Herbert. NBLV

Some Lines on My Mother's Illness. Yunna Petrovna Moritz, Russian. TCRP, tr. by Bernard Meares

Some Litanies. Michael Benedikt. CoAP; TwCP

Some Little Bug. Roy Atwell. PoLF

Some lives are so odd—you agree? Limerick. Unknown. PeLi

Some love a laundress and others love a duchess. My Love. "Sasha Chorny," Russian. TCRP, tr. by Bernard Meares

Some lovers speak, when they their Muses entertain. Sonnet 6. Sir Philip Sidney. AEP; NAEL-1; NoSic; Son   Fr. Astrophil and Stella. AAS; SiPS

Some lucky day each November great waves awake and are drawn. November Surf. Robinson Jeffers. NAAL-2; OxBA

Some lucky Thracian has my noble shield. The Shield. Archilochus, Greek. GrIP, tr. by H.D.E. Kitto

Some Magic. James Koller. PoM

Some Magnetism in the Sea. Rodney Hall. Fr. The Owner of My Face. CBAP

Some Make This Answer. Sylvia Townsend Warner. WPN

Some may occasion snatch to carp. The Harp. Ralph Knevet. ChIV-2

Some may wish for city streets, jewels or silken gown. Wishes. A. C. Child   PoToHe

Some Me of Beauty. Carolyn M. Rodgers. NMM-2

Some medals. Tanka. Mori Ōgai, Japanese. MJT, tr. by Makoto Ueda

Some men break your heart in two. Experience. Dorothy Parker. NAAL-2

Some men deem. Ideals. Robert Greene. PoToHe

Some men marriage do commend. De Se. John Weever. FaBoEE

Some men never think of it. Flowers. Wendy Cope. NoP-4

Some men say there is a God. God? Cristoir O'Flynn. TIRV

Some men, 'tis said, prefer a woman fat. Nathaniel Parker Willis. *Fr.* Lady Jane, The; a Humorous Novel in Rhyme. OBAL

Some Metaphysics of Junior Wells. Sandra McPherson. SeSe

Some, Milton-mad (an affectation). Robert Lloyd. EPCY *Fr.* On Rhyme.

Some, misbelieving and profane in love. Sonnet 35: 'Some, misbelieving and profane'. Michael Drayton. AEP *Fr.* Idea.

Some moments stolen by a slave. The Frozen Witness. Nick Piombino. FTOS

Some moralist or mythological poet. W. B. Yeats. PoE *Fr.* Nineteen Hundred and Nineteen.

Some morning, while you and I are dozing. Intruder. Susan Feldman. AmPA

Some motes of sunlight cathedralled beaming. (LL) Buffalo. Molly Peacock. MoLi; WWSi

Some musical intervals survive. Geoffrey Lehmann. *Fr.* Ross's Poems. CBAP

Some must employ the scythe. The Dedicated. Philip Larkin. OxBC

Some names are ominous, wherein wise fate. Of St Stephen. Francis Quarles. NOSC

Some names there are that win the best applause. William Lloyd Garrison. Henrietta Cordelia Ray. CBWP-3

Some ne'er advance a judgment of their own. The Servile Herd. Alexander Pope. OBSV *Fr.* An Essay on Criticism. NAEL-1; PoEL-3; TFi

Some Nets. B. P. Nichol. FTOS

Some newness of the heart I would discern. Mid Winter. Hubert Witheford, *Maori*. PeNZ, *tr. by* Sam Karetu.

Some nieces won't, some nieces can't. Aunts and Nieces or Time and Space. A. E. Housman. CBNP

Some nights it's bound to be your best way out. Insomnia I. Howard Nemerov. DiPo

Some nights / the rat with pointed teeth. Hello. Naomi Shihab Nye. MT; NAmP90

Some nights when you're off. The Avenues. David St. John. WWSi

Some nights you need to get into the car and drive. We Never Close. David Clewell. NAmP90

Some nineteen German planes, they say. Reprisals. W. B. Yeats. OBWP; PoWW

Some Notes on Courage. Susan Bartels Ludvigson. MT

Some Odes of the Excellent and Knowing Severinus, Englished: Metrum 12. Lib. 3. Boethius, *Latin*.
  "Happy is he, that with fix'd Eyes." OBCVT, *tr. by* Henry Vaughan

Some of my best friends are white boys. Friends. Ray Durem. PoBA

Some of Our Koorawatha Saints. Geoffrey Lehmann. *Fr.* Ross's Poems. CBAP

Some of the ears on the floor were / pressed to the ground. Carolyn Forché. *See* The Colonel.

Some of the girls are playing jacks. Narcissa. Gwendolyn Brooks. CA; NTCP

Some of the time. Working with Mother. Myra Cohn Livingston. TLR

Some of their chiefs were princes of the land. Zimri. Dryden. AWP; EBEV; SCV *Fr.* Absalom and Achitophel, Pt. I. EBEvV; FHYEP; FaBoPV; HAP; NOSC; OAEL-1; PoE

Some of them with staves. Basho, *Japanese*. TAL, *tr. by* Harold G. Henderson

Some of us barefoot. (LL) Group Photo from Pretoria Local on the Occasion of a Fourth Anniversary (Never Taken). Jeremy Cronin. AF; PeSAV

Some of us stayed forever, under the lough. Frank Ormsby. CIP-2 *Fr.* A Northern Spring.

Some of us / these days. Resurrection. Frank Horne. PoBA

Some "old Robin Down" they call me. Ibby Damsel. *Unknown.* AmFP

Some One. Walter De la Mare. TLR

Some one calls out, and some one else. Sick Men Sleeping. Kenneth Mackenzie. BMAP

Some One Liked Me when I Was Twelve. Peter Orlovsky. GLP

Some one prepared this mighty show. Emily Dickinson. SAmP

Some Opposites. Richard Wilbur. OBCA

Some other day, my love. (LL) France. Douglas Dunn. LBC; OxBM

Some owls have big eyes. Owls. Bob Merkel. CTV

Some patios won't allow the shadow of a maid. Scattered Light. Fanny Howe. FTOS

Some People. Rachel Lyman Field. ChAP; NTCP

Some People. A. K. Ramanujan. VCWP

Some people admire the work of a Fool. William Blake. OAEL-2

Some people are incurably gentle. Portrait of a Lady. Elizabeth Nannestad. PeNZ

Some people as they die grow fierce, afraid. The Hereafter. Andrew Hudgins. RA

Some people cannot endure. Going the Rounds; a Sort of Love Poem. Anthony Hecht. BoLoP

Some people despise me be- / cause I have a Venus mound. June Jordan. NMM-2

Some people hang portraits up. A Likeness. Robert Browning. CTC

Some people in the sky. Song for a Scalp Dance. *Unknown, Chippewa Indian*. STP, *tr. by* Jerome Rothenberg

Some people know how to love. Poem of Explanations. Dahlia Ravikovitch, *Hebrew*. BoWoP, *tr. by* Chana Bloch

Some People Laugh, Some People Cry. Sri Sri, *Telugu*.
  "Man walks on the bridge and gives away the change in his, A." OMIP, *tr. by* V. Narayana Rao *and* A. K. Ramanujan (1929–93)

Some people may think I'm a bit la-di. Limerick. C. Vita-Finzi. PeLi

Some people, / no matter what you give them. Adam's Complaint. Denise Levertov. BoWoP; NNaP

Some people on the moon are so idle. Moon-transport. Ted Hughes. SpW

Some people say the world's all a stage. The Gate at the End of Things. *Unknown*. BLPA

Some people see only you. The Couple. Ana Blandiana, *Rumanian*. WPOW, *tr. by the author and* William M. Murray

Some people understand all about machinery. Up from the Wheelbarrow. Ogden Nash. FaBoBe

Some pimps wear summer hats. What? Langston Hughes. NBLV; OBAL

Some pleasant tales of thee. (LL) To Mary: 'I Sleep with Thee, and Wake with Thee.' John Clare. EnLoPo; GBL; GLoP

Some pleasure for our punishment! (LL) An Argument. Thomas Moore. BoLoP; EnLoPo; GLoP; OxBSP

Some prefer a glory of horsemen; warships. Sappho, *Greek*. STV, *tr. by* John Frederick Nims

Some primal termite knocked on wood. The Termite. Ogden Nash. KaS; OBCA

Some questions have no answers. The Question. Tony Hoagland. EC2

Some Questions You Might Ask. Mary Oliver. ColAP

Some 're lovely N nawu nnnn but some 're & are at my hawuz nawu wnn. The 13th Horse Song of Frank Mitchell (White). Frank Mitchell, *Navajo Indian*. STP, *tr. by* Jerome Rothenberg *and* David P. McAllester

Some Reflections. Anne Finch, Countess of Winchilsea. ChIV-1

Some rose from the underground. Civil War. Maksimilian Aleksandrovich Voloshin, *Russian*. TCRP, *tr. by* Albert C. Todd

Some rows of cages under those green trees. Zoo Cages. Hải Âu Tử', *Vietnamese*. AVP, *tr. by* Huỳnh Sanh Thông

Some rub their shingles, others scratch their mange. Opera Actors. Phan Văn Trị, *Vietnamese*. AVP, *tr. by* Huỳnh Sanh Thông

Some Ruthless Rhymes. Harry Graham.
  Calculating Clara. PeLV
  Compensation. CBNP; PeLV
  Englishman's Home, The. CBNP; PeLV
  Mr Jones. PeLV
  Necessity. PeLV
  Stern parent, The. CBNP; PeLV
  Tender-Heartedness. CBNP; FPC; NBLV; NOxBChV; PeLV
    ("But no one liked to poke up Willie.") (LL) FPC
    ("Little Willie, in the best of sashes.") FPC

Some San Francisco Poems. George Oppen.
  And Their Winter and Night in Disguise. APSN; NNaP
  Anniversary Poem. APSN; NNaP
  But So As by Fire. NNaP
  Impossible Poem, The. NNaP
  Morality Play: Preface, A. APSN; NNaP
  "Moving over the hills, crossing the irrigation." APSN; NNaP
  "O withering seas." NNaP
  "Silver as / The needle's eye." FTOS; NNaP
  Taste, The. NNaP
  Translucent Mechanics, The. NNaP

Some say because the tallest pine. The Doomsayers. Pattiann Rogers. LoHo

Some say cavalry and others claim. Sappho, *Greek*. BoWoP, *tr. by* Willis Barnstone

Some say, compar'd to Bononcini. Epigram on the Feuds between Handel and Bononcini. John Byrom. FaBoEE; NOBL; NOEC

Some say he's from Georgia. John Henry. *Unknown*. CrDW

Some say my love has proved unfaithful. The Weeping Willow. *Unknown*. AmFP

Some say nothing on earth excels in beauty. Sappho, *Greek*. OBCVT, *tr. by* David Constantine

Some say that Chattanooga is the. Chattanooga. Ishmael Reed. NAAAL

Some say that ever 'gainst that season comes. The Bird of Dawning. Shakespeare. PChr *Fr.* Hamlet. NAWM-1

Some say that my teaching is nonsense. Lao Tzu. EnlH *Fr.* Tao Te Ching.

Some say the deil's deid. *Unknown.* FaBoCh

Some say the radiance around the body. 11/10 Again. Lucille Clifton. GT

Some say the world will end in fire. Fire and Ice. Robert Frost. AmPP; CMoP; ColAP; EBEvV; FaBoEE; HeIP-4; HoPM; InPK-6; LiTM; MoAmPo; MoP; NAAL-2; NOBA; NoAM; OxBA; PFE; Poetr; RaBo; SoSe-8; TAP; TFi

Some say the world's / A hopeless case. How I See It. Kit Wright. OTCP

Some say there are nine Muses: but they're wrong. Sappho. Plato, *Greek.* GrAn, *tr. by* Peter Jay

Some say thy fault is youth, some wantonness. Shakespeare. *See* Sonnet: "Let me confesse that we two must be twaine."

Some say you dye your hair, Nikylla. Lucilius, *Greek.* GrAn, *tr. by* Peter Jay

Some seven score Bishops late at Lambeth sat. Lambeth Lyric. Lionel Pigot Johnson. NOBVV

Some shapes cannot be seen in a glass. Holding the Mirror Up to Nature. Howard Nemerov. PoA

Some Sights Sometimes Seen and Seldom Seen. William Cole. TLR

Some silent movie star. The Flicker. Lew Blockcolski. VoR

Some sit and stare. The Common Grave. James Dickey. CoAP

Some Slippery Afternoon. Daniela Gioseffi. CrSp

Some slumbering thoughts possess'd my brain. The Golden Island; or, the Darian Song. *Unknown.* KTR

Some small grey fur is pulsing in its grip. (LL) The End of the Weekend. Anthony Hecht. CoAmPo; FaBoMo; HAP; LiTM; WeW-3

Some Small Shells from the Windward Islands. May Swenson. FYAP

Some songs by women. Some Songs Women Sing. Peter Harris. ISC

Some specialness within. Gwendolyn Brooks. *See* Of Robert Frost.

Some springs song was sweeter even so. (LL) C.T.'s variation. Thulani Davis. MoNo; SeSe; WeT

Some springs the mississippi rose up so high. C.T.'s variation. Thulani Davis. MoNo; SeSe

Some starry head. . . not. Condition of Desire. Harry Mathews. EOEF

Some Stories of the Beauty Wapiti. Ebbe Borregaard. NeAP

Some stormy council hold in the high trees. (LL) The Garden in September. Robert Bridges. GaP; OBGa

Some, striving knowledge to refine. A Thought on Human Life. *Unknown.* OxBSP

Some Syrian rainmaker. Assumption. Padraic Fallon. BIrV; NOIV

Some talk of Alexander, and some of Hercules. The British Grenadiers. *Unknown.* OxBoLi

Some talk of trade as low and mean. Trade. Egbert Martin. PBCV

Some Terms. Robert Pinsky. HCAP *Fr.* Essay on Psychiatrists.

Some that have deeper digged love's mine than [*or* myne then] I. Love's Alchemy [*or* Alchemie]. Donne. ESCV; NAEL-1; OAEL-1; PoE; SeCP

Some that reporte great Alexanders life. Thomas Watson. AAS *Fr.* Hecatompathia; or, Passionate Century of Love.

Some—the ones with fish names—grow so north. Wildflower. Stanley Plumly. LCAP-2

Some there are who are present at such occasions. On the Suicide of a Friend. Reed Whittemore. CoAmPo

Some there are who say that the fairest thing seen. Sappho, *Greek.* WPOW, *tr. by* Richmond Lattimore

Some they will talk of bold Robin Hood. Robin Hood and the Bishop of Hereford. *Unknown.* ESPB

Some thing is lost in me. Man Thinking about Woman. Don L. Lee. MoP

Some things a man must surely know. Recipe for Living. Alfred Grant Walton. PoToHe

Some things are truly lost. Think of a sun-hat. The Mind-Reader. Richard Wilbur. LCAP-2; NAAL-2; NoAM

Some things are very dear to me—. Sonnet—2. Gwendolyn B. Bennett. NAAAL

Some things go to sleep in such a. How They Sleep. *Unknown.* CTV

Some things I do not profess. The Abduction. Stanley Kunitz. WeW-3

Some things I have to say aren't getting said. Bilingual Sestina. Julia Alvarez. FFC

Some things persist by suffering change, others. Homage to the Philosopher. Babette Deutsch. TrJP

Some things that by there be. Emily Dickinson. NCAP; OxBA

Some things we cannot translate. Yahrzeit. Larry Moffi. EC3

Some things you should forget. But Bird. Paul Zimmer. PuP-17; SeSe

Some think that in the Christian scheme. Mutual Subjection. Christopher Smart. NOCV; OxBChV *Fr.* Hymns for the Amusement of Children.

Some three or four mile out of town. Robert Lloyd. *See* The Cit's Country Box.

Some time after / and in shallower water. (LL) One Time. Douglas Livingstone. NoP-4

Some Time at Eve. Elizabeth Clark Hardy. PoLF

Some time in the dark hours. Snowfall. W. S. Merwin. NNaP

Some time later, in Provence. John Ashbery. BAP-93 *Fr.* Baked Alaska. BAP-93

Some time now past in the autumnal tide. Anne Bradstreet. *See* Contemplations.

Some time when the river is ice ask me. Ask Me. William Stafford. LoL

Some Tips on Watching Birds. Deatt Hudson. NYBP

Some to Conceit alone their taste confine. Alexander Pope. OxAEP-1, *ll.* 289–393; EPCY *Fr.* An Essay on Criticism. NAEL-1; PoEL-3; TFi ("As bodies perish through excess of blood.") (LL) EPCY

Some Trees. John Ashbery. CAPP-1; CoAmPo; HCAP; NAAL-2 ("These accents seem their own defense.") (LL) ColAP

Some trees loft their heads. Pitch Pines. Brendan Galvin. AFr

Some truck was gunning the night before up Pippin Hill's steep grade. All Wild Animals Were Once Called Deer. Brigit Pegeen Kelly. BAP-95

Some truths may pierce the spirit's deeper gloom. Frederick Goddard Tuckerman. APN-2 *Fr.* Sonnets.

Some tyme I fled the fyre that me brent. Sir Thomas Wyatt. AAS

Some unknown sound. Foster Jewell. HA

Some vex their souls with jealous pain. On One Who Died Discovering Her Kindness. John Sheffield, Duke of Buckingham and Normandy. OBEV

Some Walks with You. John Hollander. NoAM

Some We Loved. Edward Fitzgerald. LBC

Some were for setting up a king. Samuel Butler. EBEV *Fr.* Hudibras.

Some with sharp swords, to tell O most accursed! Margaret Lucas Cavendish. PEW *Fr.* The Fort or Castle of Hope.

Some without remote interview. Shakeout. Diane Ward. FTOS

Some women marry houses. Housewife. Anne Sexton. NALW; NMM-2

Some women save their sanity with needles. Mr. McGregor's Garden. Medbh McGuckian. CIP-2; PNI

Some write of angels, some of goddess. The Gentleman's Study, in Answer to The Lady's Dressing-Room. "Miss W——." ECWP

Some years ago, ere time and taste. The Vicar. Winthrop Mackworth Praed. OBEV; OBNC; OxAEP-2; PoEL-4 *Fr.* Every-Day Characters.

Some years ago you heard me sing. Sarah Byng Who Could Not Read and Was Tossed into a Thorny Hedge by a Bull. A Cautionary Tale. Hilaire Belloc. NoAM

Some years of late, in eighty-eight. Sir Francis Drake; or, Eighty-eight. *Unknown.* FaBoCh

Some young and saucy dandelions. The Dandelions. *Unknown.* BoTP

Somebodies walked the woods. The North. Barry McKinnon. NOBC

Somebody ("Somebody's tall and handsome"). *Unknown.* AS

Somebody. *Unknown.* OxBS

Somebody almost walked off wid alla my stuff. Ntozake Shange. NAAAL; WPOW

Somebody being a nobody. Tennyson. FaBoEE; NOBL; OxBSP

Somebody, / Cut his hair. Young Poet. Myron O'Higgins. PoBA

Somebody Died. Robert Creeley. LCAP-2

Somebody has given my. Proust's Madeleine. Kenneth Rexroth. NoAM; TRP

Somebody is hanging. A Wreath for the Suicide Heart. Anthony McNeill. PBCV

Somebody is shooting at something in our town. The Swarm. Sylvia Plath. NALW

Somebody loses whenever somebody wins. Crapshooters. Carl Sandburg. VGW

Somebody loves us all. (LL) Filling Station. Elizabeth Bishop. FaBoMo; HAP; HCAP; InPK-6; NYBP; NoP-4; VCAP; WeW-3

Somebody muffed it? Somebody wanted to joke. (LL) A Sunset of the City. Gwendolyn Brooks. FaBoWP; GT; LCAP-2; PBWP

Somebody said that it couldn't be done. It Couldn't Be Done. E. A. Guest. BLPA; FaBoBe

Somebody Said That It Couldn't Be Done. Optimist / "Somebody Said That It Couldn't Be Done." *Unknown.* FuFo

Somebody said wrecks. The Drowned. Norman MacCaig. OxBC

Somebody threw away a piano. Street Music. Barbara Angell. AiP

Somebody told me you were dead. Callimachus, *Greek.* PGA, *tr. by* Kenneth Rexroth

Somebody treat her real bad. Lady on a Bus. Jeanne Lohmann. CrSp

Somebody, when I was young, stole my toy horse. The Toy Horse. Valentin Iremonger. NOIV

Somebody who should have been born. The Abortion. Anne Sexton. LCAP-2; Poetr; VGW

Somebody's Darling. Marie La Coste. BLPA; UnPo

Somebody's done for. (LL) Death and Co. Sylvia Plath. CMoP; CoAmPo; LCAP-2

Somebody's Gone. Charles Henri Ford. SPE

Somebody's in there. Saint Pumpkin. Nancy Willard. LCAP-2

Somebody's knockin' at th' door. The Collier's Wife. D. H. Lawrence. FaBoVe; OxBTC

Somebody's Mother. Mary Dow Brine. BLPA

Somebody's Mother. *Unknown*. ChAP

Somebody's tall and handsome. Somebody. *Unknown*. AS

Someday, if you are lucky. Man. Kenneth Rexroth. *Fr.* A Bestiary. OBAL

Someday there will be girls and women whose name will no longer mean. Rilke. ITG, *tr. by* Stephen Mitchell *Fr.* Letters to a Young Poet.

Someday they'll find me out, and my lavish hands. Self-Portrait. Charles Wright. PoPoPo

Someday you will be dead. Sappho, *Greek*. InMo, *tr. by* Sam Hamill

Somehow. Tanka. Ishikawa Takuboku, *Japanese*. MJT, *tr. by* Makoto Ueda

Somehow began the / measured rise. (LL) The Diver. Robert Earl Hayden. AmPP; BPo

Somehow myself survived the Night. Emily Dickinson. APN-2

Somehow the tutorial takes an unplanned direction. How Come the Truck-Loads? Judith Rodriguez. FaBoWP

Somehow this impulse. Tanka. Tawara Machi, *Japanese*. MJT, *tr. by* Makoto Ueda

Someone. Man Cursing the Sea. Miroslav Holub, *Czech*. VCWP, *tr. by* Stuart Friebert *and* Dana Hábová

Someone. Nelly Sachs, *German*. WPoS, *tr. by* Ruth and Matthew Mead

Someone approaches to say his life is ruined. The Dream. David Ignatow. CoAP; NNaP

Someone asked me in passing. Spring Comes to the Hills and Fields. Namju Kim, *Korean*. CKP, *tr. by* Jaihiun Kim

Someone asked the publisher. John Bingham Morton. UV *Fr.* When We Were Very Silly.

Someone be a rose tree. Vasco [*or* Vasko] Popa. *See* The Rose Thieves.

Someone came knocking. Walter De la Mare. MoBrPo

Someone comes knocking, he wants lodging. A Stranger. Sandor Csoori, *Hungarian*. CEEP, *tr. by* Jascha Kessler

Someone dancing inside us. Advice. Bill Holm. RaBo

Someone Digging in the Ground. Jelaluddin Rumi, *Persian*. RaBo, *tr. by* Coleman Barks

Someone drove a two-by-four. Child's Grave, Hale County, Alabama. Jim Simmerman. WeW-3

Someone Else. Sophie Behrens. NBrP

Someone else cut off my head. Bread. Brendan Kennelly. PBCIP

Someone else / looked at the sky. Lady Izumi, *Japanese*. BoWoP, *tr. by* Willis Barnstone

Someone else was afraid and spoke to me. Apple Rind. Carol Frost. PuP-17

Someone enters without knocking. Hunter. Vasco [*or* Vasko] Popa. HSix, *tr. by* Charles Simic *Fr.* Games. RB, *tr. by* Anne Pennington

Someone fits a flute to his lips, and. Deception. Alfred Corn. PoA

Someone had been walking in and out. The Origin of Baseball. Kenneth Patchen. CLPP

Someone has remembered to dry the dishes. Red Lilies. Barbara Guest. FTOS; PmAP; PoM

Someone has shut the shining eyes, straightened and folded. Beside the Bed. Charlotte Mew. BWW; MoBrPo; OxBSP; WPE

Someone hides from someone. Hide-and-Seek. Vasco [*or* Vasko] Popa. HSix, *tr. by* Charles Simic *Fr.* Games. RB, *tr. by* Anne Pennington

Someone, I tell you, / will remember us. Sappho, *Greek*. BoWoP, *tr. by* Willis Barnstone

Someone in Quaker meeting talks about greed and aggression. Greed and Aggression. Sharon Olds. DeD; RaBo

Someone in the next apartment. Room. Ruth Stone. BoWoP

Someone is a rose bush. The Rose Thieves. Vasco [*or* Vasko] Popa. HSix *Fr.* Games. RB, *tr. by* Anne Pennington

Someone is beating a woman. Andrey Andreievich Voznesensky, *Russian*. VCWP, *tr. by* Jean Garrigue

Someone is breathing in the room. Waking. Hugh Maxton. BIrV; CIP-2

Someone is dead. Lament. Anne Sexton. CoAmPo; WPE

Someone is locking out the stars and the yellow flowers. Old Man in a Moon Loft. T. Glynne Davies, *Welsh*. OBWVE, *tr. by the author*

Someone is sitting in the red house. Small Town. Rita Dove. GT

Someone is walking through the snow. Hearing Steps. Charles Simic. HCAP

Someone Knocks. Peter Everwine. NNaP

Someone later may hear these playthings, thinking. Strato, *Greek*. GrAn, *tr. by* Teddy Hogge

Someone lightly brushed the penis. Nude Study. Yusef Komunyakaa. BAP-96

Someone like No One Else. Forugh Farrokhzad, *Farsi*. WPOW, *tr. by* Deirdre Lashgari

Someone on Walnut Hill has taken a picture. The Prospect Before Us. Constance Carrier. AFr

Someone passes. Murasaki Shikibu, *Japanese*. OHPJ, *tr. by* Kenneth Rexroth; BoWoP, *tr. by* Kenneth Rexroth and Ikuko Atsomi

Someone runs about. Bullfight. Miroslav Holub, *Czech*. RB, *tr. by* Ian *and* Jarmila Milner

Someone said dead men make islands in the sea. Fishermen, Drowned beyond the West Coast. Vivian Smith. CBAP

Someone said, I remember the first hard crack. After the Last Practice. Edward Hirsch. NAmP90

Someone said, "Our right hand is in the book. But the left has the / privilege of opening and closing." The Book. Edmond Jabès, *French*. AF, *tr. by* Rosemarie Waldrop

Someone sows someone. The Seed. Vasco [*or* Vasko] Popa. PoSu *Fr.* Games. RB, *tr. by* Anne Pennington

Someone spoke of your death, Herakleitos. It brought me. Callimachus, *Greek*. GrAn, *tr. by* Peter Jay

Someone told me. Patrizia Cavalli, *Italian*. NeIt, *tr. by* Judith Baumel

Someone told me, Heracleitus. Callimachus, *Greek*. HePo *Fr.* Epigrams.

("For Death, he taketh all away, but them he cannot take.") (LL) OBCVT, *tr. by* William Johnson Cory

("They told me, Heraclitus, they told me you were dead.") OBCVT, *tr. by* William Johnson Cory

Someone who well knew how she'd toss her chin. Loose Woman. X. J. Kennedy. WeW-3

Someone, whose morals need mending. Time's Betrayal. Herman Melville. NCAP

Someone would like to have you for her child. Lullaby. *Unknown*. TTTS

Someone writes kike on. Being Jewish in a Small Town. Lyn Lifshin. UnSA

Someone's hiding in the graveyard. Anyone, Lifting. Alberta Turner. CMAP

Someone's licked a finger, touched it to the mirror. Ghazal on signs of Love and Occupation. Philip Salom. BMAP

Someone's lifeless body lies in the street. The Corpse. Jagannath Prasad Das, *Oriya*. OMIP, *tr. by* Jayanta Mahapatra

Someone's newspaper. Jack Cain. HA

Somer is comen and winter gon. *Unknown*. MiEL

Somer is comen with love to toune. *Unknown*. MiEL

Somersby, Lincolnshire; after Leaving the Refectory. Tennyson. *Fr.* In Memoriam A. H. H.

("Unwatched, the garden bough shall sway.") GaP

Somerset Dam for Supper, The. John Holmes. NYBP

Something. Witchgrass. Louise Glück. AFr

Something About Being an Indian. Adrian C. Louis. UnSA

Something about pumpkins caused. What Brings Us Out. Naomi Shihab Nye. NAmP90

Something about the idea. Abandonment of Autos. Bruce Dawe. CBAP

Something about You. Jessica Hagedorn. PmAP

Something cracks every moment because. Brief Thoughts on Cracks. Miroslav Holub, *Czech*. PoSu, *tr. by* Ian *and* Jarmila Milner

Something drained our blood and it wasn't the leeches. Anorexia. Peter Hollenbeck. CDa

Something for her lips. oh dare, oh share. something. Bernice Got Next to Isis. Leslie Simon. FFC

Something for My Russian Friends. Edmund Wilson. OBAL

Something for Supper. Carroll Arnett. VoR

Something forgotten for twenty years: though my fathers. A Map of the Western Part of the County of Essex in England. Denise Levertov. CoAP; NAAL-2

Something hangs in back of me. The Wings. Denise Levertov. APSN; NALW

Something happened the other day that never happened before. Shovelling Iron Ore. *Unknown*. AS

Something has ceased to come along with me. Death of a Son. Jon Silkin. GTBS-P; MoP; OxBTC

Something has happened to me. Kofi Awoonor. HBAPE

Something has reached out and taken in the beams of my eyes. All I Was Doing Was Breathing. Mirabai, *Rajasthani*. WPoS, *tr. by* Robert Bly

Something / holds up two or three leaves. In One Place. Robert Wallace. Poetsp

Something I saw or thought I saw. On the Heart's Beginning to Cloud the Mind. Robert Frost. CMoP; GM

Something immense and lonely. Foreboding. John Haines. CoAmPo

Something in my soul. Meleager, *Greek*. InMo, *tr. by* Sam Hamill

Something / in the way these alleys twist and. Reggae Cat (for Boston Jack). Kendel Hippolyte. HCP

Something inspires the only cow of late. The Cow in Apple Time. Robert Frost. APo; MoAmPo; OxBSP; PoLF

Something is going to go, baby. Cyril Connolly. OBCoV *Fr.* Where Engels Fears to Tread.

Something is pushing against my blood. Posthumous. Michael O'Loughlin. PBCIP

Something is shattering high in the frozen. A Heart Attack in the Country. Terry Hummer. NAmP90

Something is very gently. The Thread. Denise Levertov. CrSp

Something Like Happiness. Stephen Dunn. PUP-20

Something like radiance is crossing my wife's face. Macular Degeneration. Peter Cooley. BAP-93

Something muffled / barely audible. The String. Momcilo Nastasijevic, *Serbo-Croatian.* HSix, tr. by Charles Simic

Something must be done right away. Song for Those Who Know. Hans Magnus Enzensberger, *German.* VCWP, tr. by Hans Magnus Enzensberger and Michael Hamburger; PoSu

Something occurred after the operation. Surgical Ward: Men. Robert Graves. FaBoMo

Something of a Departure. Paul Muldoon. PBCIP

Something of desk work and pornography. Sonogram. Karl Kirchwey. BAP-95

Something of glass about her, of dead water. Circe. Louis MacNeice. OBMV

Something old and tyrannical burning there. A Coal Fire in Winter. Thomas McGrath. RaBo

Something Old, Something New. Carl H. Greene. NBV

Something or Other. Ron Padgett. FTOS

—Something out of it, I think. (LL) The Best Thing in the World. Elizabeth Barrett Browning. EBVV; NOBVV; OxBSP; SDW; VWP

Something startles me where I thought I was safest. This Compost. Walt Whitman. AWP; MoAmPo; NAAL-1; NAAL-3; OBGa; PFTM

Something strange I do not comprehend. Literature: The God, Its Ritual. Merrill Moore. FuPo

Something there is that doesn't love a wall. Mending Wall. Robert Frost. AFr; AmPP; CMoP; ChAP; ClHu; EBEvV; FP; FaBoPV; HAP; HeIP-4; HoPM; ImGa; InPS-3; LiTM; MeMAP; MoAmPo; MoP; NAAL-2; NOBA; NoAM; NoP-4; OxBA; PoE; PoPoPo; Poetr; SAmP; SCV; SoSe-8; TAP; TFi; VGW; WeW-3

Something this foggy day, a something which. Christina Rossetti. NAEL-2 *Fr.* Later Life: A Double Sonnet of Sonnets.

Something to be tinkered with at their leisure. (LL) Talk. Roo Borson. NIP-4; NOBC

Something to Look Forward To. Marge Piercy. NMM-2

Something told the wild geese. Rachel Lyman Field. CTV; ChAP; NTCP; OBCA

Something uncertain moves. Again. Lenard D. Moore. GT

Something went crabwise. The Presence. Maxine W. Kumin. WPE

Something Whispered in the *Shakuhachi.* Garrett Kaoru Hongo. InPS-3

Something you said—I found it written down. A Postcard to Send to Sumer. William Bronk. VGW

Something's dead in that stand of fir. Ravens at Deer Creek. Robert Wrigley. PuP-16

Something's nested / In his tomb. Hat-Tomb. Guillaume Apollinaire, *French.* CBNP

Something's there, by Pan there's something hidden—. Callimachus, *Greek.* GrAn, tr. by Peter Jay

Something during eternity / some guys show up. Lawrence Ferlinghetti. NoAM; Poetr

  ("Real dead.") (LL) NoP-4

  ("Some guys show up.") NoP-4

Sometime during the night there are three mushrooms which are the. Moon Poem. Max Jacob, *French.* AF, tr. by Michael Brownstein

Sometime I fled the fire that me brent. Sir Thomas Wyatt. NoSic

Sometime I sigh, sometime I sing. Sir Thomas Wyatt. SiPS

Sometime I sit and wonder long. Dis Time No Stan' Like befo' Time. James Martinez. PBCV

Sometime in the night I stir, rain. Loft. Michael Dransfield. CBAP

Sometime let gorgeous Tragedy. Poetry and the Melancholy Man. Milton. EPCY *Fr.* Il Penseroso. AWP; FHYEP; GTBS-P; HAP; HoPM; ImPo; NOSC; NoP-4; OAEL-1; OBEV; TFi

Sometime the world seems sad and lonely. Lonely World. Mrs. Henry Linden. CBWP-4

Sometime this world was so steadfast and stable. Lack of Steadfastness. Chaucer. PBMP

Sometime, when all life's lessons have been learned. May Riley Smith. BLPA

Sometimes. Maggie Pogue Johnson. CBWP-4

Sometimes. P. J. Kavanagh. OxBSn

Sometimes. Greg Kuzma. Poetsp

Sometimes Fat. Moon. Jean Kenward. SpW

Sometimes. Lilian Moore. TLR

Sometimes. Woman, 2. Jyotsna Milan, *Hindi.* OMIP, tr. by Mrinal Pande and Arlene Zide

Sometimes (/ when the night air feels *chevere*). Oye Mundo/Sometimes. Jesús Papoleto Meléndez. UnSA

Sometimes a crumb falls. Luck. Langston Hughes. PiM; SAmP

Sometimes a lantern moves along the night. The Lantern Out of Doors. Gerard Manley Hopkins. CMoP; TrCP

Sometimes a light surprizes. Joy and Peace in Believing. William Cowper. NOCV *Fr.* Olney Hymns.

Sometimes a man stands up during supper. Rilke, *German.* RaBo, tr. by Robert Bly

Sometimes a mesh of ideas. Dennis Brutus. HBAPE

Sometimes / A night funeral. Dead in There. Langston Hughes. APSN

Sometimes a rain comes. A Rain of Rites. Jayanta Mahapatra. PoA

Sometimes alone at night. Vanderdecken. Douglas Livingstone. PeSAV

Sometimes and always, with mixed feelings? (LL) At North Farm. John Ashbery. ColAP; HCAP; PoE; Poetr

Sometimes, apart in sleep, by chance. The Trance. Stephen Spender. OxBM

Sometimes at night when the heart stumbles and stops. Caesura. Kenneth Mackenzie. CBAP; NOBAu

Sometimes, avoiding trouble, we accept defeat. Joseph of Arimathaea. Mervyn Morris. HCP

Sometimes before great events a person will try. Things That Happen. William Stafford. NNaP

Sometimes, childishly watching a beetle, thrush or trout. Clarence Mangan. Thomas Kinsella. CIP-2

Sometimes colored tears play. George Grosz. Else Lasker-Schüler, *German.* PFTM, tr. by Audri Durchslag and Jeanette Litman-Demeestère

Sometimes Even Parents Win. John Ciardi. NOxBChV

Sometimes he walked to occupy / his feet. Generations 2. Sam Cornish. GT

Sometimes I catch a glimpse of it. The Presence. Dana Naone. CDW

Sometimes I do despatch my heart. "Michael Field." VWP

Sometimes I dont understand you, sometimes i sit helpless in. Lorelei. "Alta." CrSp

Sometimes I dress, with women sit. Matthew Green. ECEV; OBCoV *Fr.* The Spleen.

Sometimes I feel like a motherless child. *Unknown.* APN-2

  ("Long ways from home, A.") (LL) BkSV

Sometimes I feel [like] I will never stop. To Satch. Samuel Allen. PoBA; TTY

Sometimes I fly at dawn above the sea. The Dawn Patrol. Paul Bewsher. NSI

Sometimes I Get Distracted, *for Philip Whalen.* Elaine Equi. BAP-95

Sometimes I get the feeling that I have been here before. Reincarnation. Mae Jackson. PoBA

Sometimes / I go about pitying myself. Song of the Thunders. *Unknown, Chippewa.* OBVE; RaBo, tr. by Frances Densmore

Sometimes I Go to Camarillo and Sit in the Lounge. K. Curtis Lyle. NBV; PoBA

Sometimes I go to the pornos. No God. Dennis Cooper. PmAP

Sometimes I have supposed seals. Soft Wood. Robert Lowell. LiTM

Sometimes I have wanted. Coat. Vicki Feaver. LW

Sometimes I hear God's whisper in. Jessie Orton Jones. CTV *Fr.* (V from Secrets).

Sometimes I know the way. Absence. Charlotte Mew. CPO; MoBrPo

Sometimes I pause and sadly think. It Might Have Been Worse. G. J. Russell. PoToHe

Sometimes I plunge into the ocean, for a long time. Herberto Padilla, *Spanish.* AF, tr. by Alastair Reid

Sometimes I recall how, in the early eighteen-eighties. Stars in Sand. Francis Carey Slater. PeSAV

Sometimes I remember you, little Ruth. Little Ruth. Yehuda Amichai, *Hebrew.* VCWP, tr. by Benjamin Harshav and Barbara Harshav

Sometimes I see a light in her kitchen. Friday Night. Linda Hogan. NMM-2

Sometimes I see churches. Winter Walking. Alfred Wellington Purdy. NoAM

Sometimes I see them. Galway Kinnell. *Fr.* Ruins under the Stars. LCAP-2

Sometimes I stare into an awning of spirit. Sometimes I Go to Camarillo and Sit in the Lounge. K. Curtis Lyle. NBV; PoBA

Sometimes I think that nothing. Small-scale Reflections on a Great House. A. K. Ramanujan. OxBC

Sometimes I walk where the deep water dips. Frederick Goddard Tuckerman. APN-2; NOBA; PAR *Fr.* Sonnets.

Sometimes I watch the moon at night. The Moon and a Cloud. W. H. Davies. RB

Sometimes I wish that I his pillow were. Richard Barnfield. PBRV *Fr.* Sonnets.

Sometimes I wish that I were Helen-fair. Poem. Lesbia Harford. NOBAu

Sometimes, in morning sunlights by the river. Resurrection. Sidney Lanier. PoEL-5

Sometimes in summer months, the gestate earth. Summer Idyll. George Barker. FaBoMo

Sometimes in the dark I fear trampling. Fear of Subways. Maureen Seaton. FFC

Sometimes in the evening. Marriage. Joan Logghe. IFJA

Sometimes in the over-heated house, but not for long. Fame. Charlotte Mew. BrRo; InPK-6; PBWP; VWP

Sometimes, in very joy of shame. A Decadent's Lyric. Lionel Pigot Johnson. ADE

Sometimes in weariness I stop. Years. Jon Anderson. AmPA

Sometimes in Winter. Marc Cohen. BAP-93

Sometimes it seems almost beyond belief. Whirling Round the Sun. Suzanne Noguere. FFC

Sometimes I've seen. A Little Bird's Song. Margaret Rose. BoTP

Sometimes memory fails: meanings get forgotten. Earlobe. Leonid Andreievich Zavalnyuk, *Russian.* TCRP, *tr. by* Albert C. Todd

Sometimes my daughter looks at me with an. The Sign of Saturn. Sharon Olds. InPS-3

Sometimes, my little son, I have become. To David—At Six Months. Eleanor Cameron. LiLi

Sometimes, old pal, in the morning. Is It Really Worth the While? *Unknown.* BLPA

Sometimes / on windless nights. After the Vietnam War. Steven Ford Brown. CDa

Sometimes one of Erickson's patients phoned him in the middle of. The Urinating Man. Lisa Lewis. BAP-93

Sometimes pus / Sometimes a poem. Ibn Gabirol. Yehuda Amichai, *Hebrew.* AF, *tr. by* Assia Gutmann

Sometimes, riding in a car, in Wisconsin. Three Kinds of Pleasures. Robert Bly. AiP

Sometimes she is a child within mine arms. Heart's Haven. D. G. Rossetti. Son *Fr.* The House of Life.

Sometimes she is like sherry, like the sun through a vessel of glass. Polarities. Kenneth Slessor. CBAP

Sometimes, she remembers, a chipped flint. Imago. Amy Clampitt. VCAP

Sometimes she wished they were travelling again. Wedding in the Port. Sophie Behrens. NBrP

Sometimes still in my deepest sleep. Vietnam Dream. Ron Carter. CDa

Sometimes the lake water writes and writes and gets. To a Girl Writing Her Father's Death. Beckian Fritz Goldberg. NAmP90

Sometimes the light falls here too as at Florence. The Old Age of Michelangelo. Frank Templeton Prince. PeSA

Sometimes the mountain. Witness. Denise Levertov. BLT

Sometimes the night echoes to prideless wailing. John Berryman. NoAM *Fr.* Sonnets to Chris.

Sometimes the night is not enough. I rise remembering. The Biplane. Steve Orlen. WeT

Sometimes the pencil, in cool airy halls. James Thomson. PoEL-3 *Fr.* The Castle of Indolence.

Sometimes the sea lays. Dragging in Winter. David McElroy. AmPA

Sometimes the weather goes on for days. The Mystery of Emily Dickinson. Marvin Bell. CMAP

Sometimes the words are so close I am. Sonnet 42. Julia Alvarez. FFC *Fr.* ("33").

Sometimes there are airs grave and gentle. Limerick. *Unknown.* PeLi

Sometimes they cross an avenue at dusk. Survivors. Frank Ormsby. CIP-2

Sometimes they smear the evening on the air. Bat Angels. Larry Levis. AmPA

Sometimes things don't go, after all. Sheenagh Pugh. OPOU

Sometimes, tired, I imagine your death. To L. B. S. Winfield Townley Scott. SAGP

Sometimes to think about age. Age. Rae Desmond Jones. CBAP

Sometimes too personal, sun, you. Sun. John Blight. BMAP

Sometimes up out of this land. Bi-Focal. William Stafford. RB

Sometimes waking, sometimes sleeping. Nestus Gurley. Randall Jarrell. HeIP-4; TwCP

Sometimes walking late at night. Butcher Shop. Charles Simic. AF; AmPA; InPK-6; LCAP; NNaP

Sometimes we get up. Resurrection. Marie Luise Kaschnitz, *German.* WPOW, *tr. by* Michael Hamburger

Sometimes we go our way carefree. Rebirth. Margaret E. Bruner. PoToHe

Sometimes we sit in Phil's. My Care. Peter Fallon. CIP-2

Sometimes when alone. Outcast[, The]. "Æ." OxBSP

Sometimes when clouds float. At the Edge of Town. William Stafford. NNaP

Sometimes when I feel hurried or dismayed. For One Who Is Serene. Margaret E. Bruner. PoToHe

Sometimes when I have dropped to sleep. The Room beneath the Rafters. Ella Wheeler Wilcox. PWR

Sometimes when I hold. The School Globe. James Reaney. NOBC

Sometimes when I see the bare arms of trees in the evening. The Bare Arms of Trees. John Tagliabue. Poetsp

Sometimes when I'm lonely. Hope. Langston Hughes. OBAL; OBCA; TRP

Sometimes when my eyes are red. My Sad Self. Allen Ginsberg. Poetr; UnPo; VCAP

Sometimes When Night. Vita Sackville-West. WPE

Sometimes, when winding slow by brook and bower. Sonnets: First Series. Frederick Goddard Tuckerman. NCAP

Sometimes, when you're asleep, I want to do. Marilyn Hacker. *See* Another Sunday.

Sometimes, when you're away from home. Away from Home. *Unknown.* PWR

Sometimes, when you're called a bastard. When Something Happens. James A. Randall Jr. BPo; SSLK

Sometimes, when you're sleep, I want to do. Another Sunday. Marilyn Hacker. DeD *Fr.* Love, Death and the Changing of the Seasons.

Sometimes while I sleep. 1925. Edwin Honig. NoAM *Fr.* To Restore a Dead Child.

Sometimes with one I love I fill myself with rage for fear I effuse unreturn'd love. Walt Whitman. APN-1; GBL; OxBSP; SAmP

Sometimes / you feel / like / a / bottle. No Deposit. Earle Thompson. HATNAP

Sometimes, you give way to sickness. Igor Vladimirovich Chinnov, *Russian.* TCRP, *tr. by* Thomas E. Bird

Sometimes you hear, fifth-hand. Poetry of Departures. Philip Larkin. CMoP; HeIP-4; OxBC; PoE; TwCP

Somewhat back from the village street. The Old Clock on the Stairs. Henry Wadsworth Longfellow. PWR

Somewhat more splendid in dress, in a waistcoat work of a lady. Arthur Hugh Clough. FaBoVe *Fr.* Bothie of Tober-na-Vuolich, The [A Long-Vacation Pastoral].

Somewhere. Robert Creeley. NoAM

Somewhere. A Sneeze. So Chong-Ju, *Korean.* VCWP, *tr. by* David R. McCann

Somewhere a forest, every. These Leaves. William Stafford. NNaP

Somewhere a man puts on his shorts. Andrey Andreievich Voznesensky, *Russian.* CBNP, *tr. by* William Jay Smith *and* Vera Dunham

Somewhere / a niche. Wish. Lance Henson. CDW

Somewhere a poem. Elegy. Linda Pastan. IFJA

Somewhere a white horse gallops with its mane. Elsewhere. Derek Walcott. HCP

Somewhere afield here something lies. Shelley's Skylark. Thomas Hardy. CABP

Somewhere Along the Line. "Antler." PUP-18

Somewhere along the Way. Henry Taylor. Poetr

Somewhere around. Tanka. Shaku Chōkū, *Japanese.* MJT, *tr. by* Makoto Ueda

Somewhere behind me. Foster Jewell. HA

Somewhere bells are ringing. Somewhere far away bells / are ringing. Bells. Mateja Matevski, *Macedonian.* CEEP, *tr. by* Dragan Milivojevic

Somewhere beneath that piano's superb sleek black. The Piano. D. H. Lawrence. WeW-3

Somewhere between *Amazing Grace*. The Death of Chet Baker. Miller Williams. SeSe

Somewhere does the sky bend into itself. Show Me a Rose. John Godfrey. FTOS

Somewhere East of Suez. H. W. Berry. NSI

Somewhere his number must have been betrayed. The Common Man. Arthur James Marshall Smith. NOBC

Somewhere i have never travelled, gladly beyond. E. E. Cummings. BoLoP; InPS-3; LiTM; MoAmPo; NAAL-2; NoP-4; Poetr; TwCP; VGW

Somewhere I read that high and loe notes. Comfort. Maura Stanton. SoSe-8

Somewhere, I think in Dakota. A Sound from the Earth. William Stafford. NNaP

Somewhere in a field near Magadan. Nikolai Alekseievich Zabolotsky, *Russian.* TCRP, *tr. by* Daniel Weissbort

Somewhere in Africa. Anne Sexton. NALW

Somewhere in his body a blood-clot is moving. Little Death. Gwyn Thomas, *Welsh.* OBWVE, *tr. by* Joseph P. Clancy

Somewhere in India, upon a time. An Oriental Apologue. James Russell Lowell. PoEL-5

Somewhere in Mauriac a girl. Frank Templeton Prince. PeSAV *Fr.* Memoirs in Oxford.

Somewhere in the next block. Early Sunday Morning. John A. Stone. MT

Somewhere in the world my tree stands, for I know that every person. Mail. Sarah Kirsch, *German.* AF, *tr. by* Wayne Kvam

Somewhere inside me. Coming Back Home. Ray A. Young Bear. CDW

Somewhere Is Such a Kingdom. John Crowe Ransom. CMoP

Somewhere it being yesterday. A Song of Mary. Lucille Clifton. NALW

Somewhere Near Phu Bai. Yusef Komunyakaa. CDa

Somewhere near the end of a snowshoe trail. A Baby Ten Months Old Looks at the Public Domain. William Stafford. NYBP

Somewhere now she takes off the dress I am putting. Palindrome. Lisel Mueller. WeW-3

Somewhere nowhere in Utah, a boy by the roadside. Utah. Anne Stevenson. FaBoVe

Somewhere on his travels the strange Child. Santa Claus. Howard Nemerov. HAP

Somewhere or other there must surely be. Christina Rossetti. FaBoVe; LoP; NOBE; NOBVV

Somewhere outside your window. A Sense of Coolness. Quincy Troupe. GT; PoBA

Somewhere she waits to make you win, your soul in her firm, white hands. The Woman Who Understands. Everard Jack Appleton. PoLF

Somewhere someone is traveling furiously toward you. At North Farm. John Ashbery. ColAP; HCAP; PoE; Poetr

Somewhere, sometime, in an April twilight. Willa Cather. WPE

Somewhere, somewhen I've seen. The Parrots. Wilfrid Wilson Gibson. CH

Somewhere the deer lies on the ground, I think; I walk about. Hunter's Song. *Unknown, Hitchiti (Creek).* APN-2, *tr. by* Albert S. Gatschet

Somewhere the Equation Breaks Down. Daniel Berrigan. NYBP

Somewhere there figures a man. In uniform. Kings' Daughters, Home for Unwed Mothers, 1948. C. D. Wright. NAmP90

Somewhere there is Grace, Lord. Latter Day Psalms. Cliff Ashby. NOCV

Somewhere there waiteth in this world of ours. Destiny. Sir Edwin Arnold. PoLF; PoToHe

Somewhere under sand. Primitive Place. Mildred Weston. FFC

Somewhere / without me / my life begins. In the Mountains. Agha Shahid Ali. WeT

Somewhere you are always going home. The Sums. Lauris Edmond. FaBoWP

Somnolence of star-stones, ice-tears, The. Laurentia. Medbh McGuckian. BiHa

Somnolent through landscapes and by trees. The Permanent Tourists. Patricia K. Page. LiTM; NOBC

Somnus, the humble god, that dwells. A Song. Sir John Denham. BeJo

Somonour was ther with us in that place, A. Chaucer. OBCoV *Fr.* The General Prologue. FHYEP; NAEL-1; NAWM-1; OAEL-1; PoE *Fr.* The Canterbury Tales.

Somtyme this world was so stedfast and stable. Lak of Stedfastnesse. Chaucer. AWP; MiEL

Son, The. Donne. NOCV *Fr.* The Litanie. PoEL-2

Son[ne], The. George Herbert. GeHe; PeECV; SeCP

Son, A. Rudyard Kipling. FaBoEE; PeFWW *Fr.* Epitaphs of the War [1914–1918]. OBWP

Son, The. Denise Levertov. FiLi; NALW

Son. Father and I in the Woods. David McCord. NOxBChV

Son, The. Jones Very. NCAP

Son and Heir. Philip Gross. APAD

Son, come tell me 'bout the meetin. The Old and the New. Clara Ann Thompson. CBWP-2

Son Cotton! these light idle brooks. Izaac Walton, Cotton, and William Oldways. Walter Savage Landor. PoEL-4

Son David. *Unknown.* OxBB; OxBS

Son-Days [dayes]. Henry Vaughan. GeHe; NOSC; ScCP

Son learns how to beat his father, The. Aristophanes, *Greek.* OBCVT, *tr. by* Thomas Stanley

Son, my son! Lament of a Man for His Son. *Unknown, Paiute.* AWP; IMW, *tr. by* Mary Austin

Son of a Gambolier, The. *Unknown.* AS

Son of a mystic race, he came. Heinrich Heine. Ludwig Lewisohn. TrJP

Son of a whore, God dam you: Can you tell. Rochester to the Post Boy. John Wilmot. OxBoV

Son of Enops, Thestor next he smote, The. Patroclus Spears Thestor. Homer. OBVE, *tr. by* William Cowper *Fr.* The Iliad.

Son[ne] of God hear[e] us, and since thou. Donne. *Fr.* The Litanie. PoEL-2

Son, of great fortune have I none. Christine to Her Son. Christine de Pisan, *French.* BoWoP, *tr. by* Barbara Howes

Son of the Bone Speaks, The. Roger Gilbert-Lecomte, *French.* PFTM, *tr. by* Pierre Joris

Son of the ocean isle! England's Dead. Felicia Dorothea Hemans. NoP-4

Son of the righteous one, he who thunders on the ground. Praises of the King Tshaka. *Unknown, Zulu.* PeSA

Son of the Romanovs, A. Louis Simpson. OxBC

Son of the Thundercloud. Song of the Thunder. *Unknown, Hottentot.* PeSA

Son replied, "For all your good advice," The. To His Father on Praising the Honest Life of the Peasant. Parvin E'tesami, *Persian.* WPOW, *tr. by* Deirdre Lashgari

"Son," said my mother. The Ballad of the Harp-Weaver. Edna St. Vincent Millay. PBMP

Son singin. Wise 3. Imamu Amiri Baraka. FTOS *Fr.* Why's/Wise.

Son who came forth on a winter's morning. Song for Te Hauapu. Noho-mai-te-Rangi, *Maori.* PeNZ, *tr. by* Margaret Orbell

Son'ahchi. The Boy and the Deer. Andrew Peynetsa. STP, *tr. by* Dennis Tedlock

Sonata. John Fuller. DiPo

Sonata for the Invisible. Joy Harjo. PaTW

Sonatina in Yellow. Donald Justice. ColAP; LCAP-2

Sonet: "Fra bank [*or* banc] to bank [*or* banc], fra wood [*or* wod] to wood [*or* wod] I rin." Mark Alexander Boyd. EBEV; OBEV

(Fra Bank to Bank, Fra Wood to Wood I Rin.) Son

("Let be a blind and teichit be a bairn.") (LL) PBRV

(Venus and Cupid.) HAP

Sonet to Sleepe. William Drummond, of Hawthornden. OxBS

Sonet Written in Prayse of the Browne Beautie, A. George Gascoigne. AAS; PBRV

Sonetto XXXV; To Guido Orlando. Guido Cavalcanti, *Italian.* CTC, *tr. by* Ezra Pound

Song 385. John Berryman. MoLi *Fr.* Dream Songs.

Song. Anne Brontë. PEW

Song. Thomas Dekker *and others.* NOSC *Fr.* The Sun's Darling.

Song, A. Edward Dorn. CoAmPo

Song, A. Richard Duke. BoLoP; ECEV

Song. Cornelius Eady. GT

Song, A. George Farquhar. NOSC

Song. John Fletcher *and others.* PoEL-2 *Fr.* The Bloody Brother.

Song. Thomas Hood. CBNP

Song. Letitia Elizabeth Landon. VWP

Song. Philip Massinger. OxAEP-1 *Fr.* The Emperor of the East.

Song. John McGrath. APAD

Song. Gabriela Mistral, *Spanish.* WPoS, *tr. by* Langston Hughes

Song, A. Laetitia Pilkington. PEW

Song. Primus St. John. GT

Song. Gunars Salis, *Latvian.* CEEP, *tr. by* Laris Salinš

Song. Sir Walter Scott. *See* A Serenade: "Ah! County Guy, the hour is nigh."

Song. Sir Walter Scott. *See* Fitz-Eustace's Song.

Song. Sir Walter Scott. *See* The Rover's Adieu [*or* Farewell].

Song. Shakespeare. *See* A Sea Song: "The Master, the swabber, the boatswain and I."

Song. Shakespeare. *See* At the Moated Grange.

Song. Shakespeare. *See* Silvia.

Song. Nichita Stanescu, *Romanian.* CEEP, *tr. by* Irina Livezeanu

Song. *Unknown.* BXAP

Song. Cynthia Zarin. NoP-4

Song: "Absent from thee, I languish still." John Wilmot. BoLoP; EnLoPo; GBL

(Return.) GLoP; NOBE; OBEV

Song: "Ae fond kiss, and then we sever." Robert Burns. BoLoP; NOBRP; NOEC

Song: "Afternoon cooking in the fall sun." Robert Hass. AmPA; LoL

Song: "Age is when to a man." Samuel Beckett. BIrV *Fr.* Words and Music.

Song: "Ah, Dangerous Swain, tell me no more." Delariviere Manley. KTR; LW *Fr.* The Lost Lover.

Song: "Ah false Amyntas, can that hour." Aphra Behn. WPE *Fr.* The Dutch Lover.

Song: "Ah, vale of woe, of gloom and darkness moulded." Rachel Morpurgo, *Hebrew.* TrJP, *tr. by* Nina Davis Salaman

Song: "All, all of a piece throughout." Dryden. WeW-3 *Fr.* The Secular Masque. NAEL-1; OxAEP-1; PoE; PoEL-3; SCGP

(Chorus to the Gods.) OxBSP

Song: "All joy to mortals, joy and mirth." Aphra Behn. WPE *Fr.* Emperor of the Moon.

Song: "April, April, / Laugh thy girlish laughter." Sir William Watson. OBEV

Song, [A]: "Ask me no more where Jove bestows." Thomas Carew. BeJo; CH; CaPo; EnLoPo; GBL; HoPM; ImPo; InPS-3; MeLP; NOBE; NOSC; OBEV; PoEL-3; SCGP; SeCP; TFi

("And in your fragrant bosom dies.") (LL) CavPo; GEA; GLoP; LoP; NoP-4

Song: "At night on my bed I longed for." Bible, *O.T.* WPoS, *tr. by* Chana Bloch *and* Ariel Bloch *Fr.* The Song of Solomon.

Song: "At the center of the earth." *Unknown, Chippewa.* STP, *tr. by* Jerome Rothenberg

Song. W. H. Auden. *See* Refugee Blues.

Song: "Balkis was in her marble town." Lascelles Abercrombie. MoBrPo *Fr.* Judith.

Song, The: "Beauty no more the subject be." Thomas Nabbes. NOSC

Song: "Because I know deep in my own heart." Pauli Murray. BlSi

Song: "Before the barn-door crowing." John Gay. OxBSP; PoEL-3 *Fr.* The Beggar's Opera. OAEL-1

Song, A. Aphra Behn. CPO

Song. Ana Blandiana, *Romanian.* CEEP, *tr. by* Irina Livezeanu

Song: "Blow, blow, thou winter wind." Shakespeare. CTC; EBEvV; OxAEP-1; PoEL-2 *Fr.* As You Like It.

Song: "Boat is chafing at our long delay, The." John Davidson. OBEV

Song: "But I'm the one from whom they stole a button from his trouser leg." Milorad Pavic. HSix *Fr.* Holy Mass For Relja Krilatica.

Song: "But I'm the one to whom others spit in the hand when he works." Milorad Pavic. HSix *Fr.* Holy Mass For Relja Krilatica.

Song: "But I'm the one who carries a garlic clove in the ear." Milorad Pavic. HSix *Fr.* Holy Mass For Relja Krilatica.

Song: "Can love be controlled by advice?" John Gay. OxBSP *Fr.* The Beggar's Opera. OAEL-1

Song: "Chloris, forbear a while." Henry Bold. GBL; NOSC

Song: "Chloris, it is not thy disdaine." Sidney Godolphin. MeLP

Song: "Christ keep the Hollow Land." William Morris. PoEL-5 *Fr.* The Hollow Land.

Song: "Choose now among this fairest number." William Browne. GBL

Song: "Clawed green-eyed." Lenrie Peters. PBMAP

Song: "Cloris misfortunes that can be exprest." Elizabeth Wilmot, Countess of Rochester. KTR

Song. Anne Collins. PEW

Song: "Come into the garden, Maud." Tennyson. AWP *Fr.* Maud [A Monodrama]. EnVR

("And the lily whispers, 'I wait'.") (LL) GaP

(Maud.) OBGa

Song: "Come, live with me and be my love." C. Day Lewis. NIP-4; Poetr *Fr.* Two Songs. HAP; NoAM

Song: "Come, my beloved." Bible, *O.T.* WPoS, *tr. by* Chana Bloch *and* Ariel Bloch *Fr.* The Song of Solomon.

Song: "Come unto these yellow sands." Shakespeare. *See* Ariel's Song: "Come unto these yellow sands."

Song: "Curse upon that faithless maid, A." Aphra Behn. WPE *Fr.* Emperor of the Moon.

Song: "Day will rise and the sun from eastward." George Campbell Hay. OxBS

Song: "Deftly, admiral, cast your fly." W. H. Auden. GTBS-P *Fr.* Five Songs.

Song: "Did you see me walking by the Buick Repairs?" Frank O'Hara. TTTS

Song: "Distil not poison in mine ears." John Hall. OxBSP

Song: "Do not fear to put thy feet." John Fletcher. *See* The River[-]God's Song.

Song: "Do your balls hang low?" *Unknown.* NSI

Song: "Does the policeman sleep with his boots on." Gerda Mayer. PeLV

Song: "Donought would have everything." Ebenezer Elliot. NOBVV

Song, The: "Drink and be merry, merry, merry boys." Thomas Morton. NAAL-3; SCAP

Song. Dryden. *See* Love's Despair.

Song. Dryden. *See* One Happy Moment.

Song. Dryden. *See* Song from The Indian Emperor.

Song. Dryden. *See* Song from Troilus and Cressida.

Song. Dryden. *See* Song: "SYLVIA the fair, in the bloom of fifteen."

Song: "Fair Chloris in a pigsty lay." John Wilmot. NOSC

("Fair Chloris in a pigsty lay.") FaBoSe

Song, A: "Fairest Nymph that ever bless'd our Shore." Mary Pix. KTR *Fr.* The Spanish Wives.

Song: "Fairest things are those which live, The." Mary Russell Mitford. NOBRP

Song, A: "Fame let thy trumpet sound." Joel Barlow. AmPP

Song, A: "Farewell, adieu, that court-like life!" John Pickering. *See* Haltersick's Song.

Song, A: "Farewell my Betty, and farewell my Annie." Christian Carstairs. ECWP

Song: "Fear no more the heat o' the Sun." Shakespeare. CTC; EBEvV; NOSC; PoE; PoEL-2 *Fr.* Cymbeline.

("Consign to thee and come to dust.") (LL) GTBS-P; PFE

(Dirge.) OAEL-1

(Fidele.) GTBS-P; OBEV

Song: "Feathers of the willow, The." Richard Watson Dixon. CH; FaBoCh; GTBS-P; NOBE; OBNC; PFE

(Willow.) OBEV

Song: "Fire, fire." Henry Bold. GBL

Song: "Flowers that in thy garden rise, The." Sir Henry John Newbolt. FaBoTw

Song: "Fool, take up thy shaft again." Thomas Stanley. EnLoPo

Song: "Foolish eyes, thy streams give over." Martha Sansom. ECWP

Song: "For her gait, if she be walking." William Browne. OBEV

(Sonnet.) NOSC

Song, A: "For mercy, courage, kindness, mirth." Laurence Binyon. BoTP; MoBrPo

Song: "Four arms, two necks, one wreathing." *Unknown.* CBLP

Song: "Fresh from the dewy hill, the merry year." William Blake. PeECV

Song: "Give Isaac the nymph who no beauty can boast." Richard Brinsley Sheridan. NOIV *Fr.* The Duenna.

Song: "Give me leave to rail at you." John Wilmot, 2d Earl of Rochester. NOSC

Song: "Go and catch a falling star." Donne. AWP; ClHu; EBEV; EBEvV; FHYEP; FSCP; HAP; HeIP-4; ImPo; InPK-6; InPS-3; NAEL-1; NAWM-1; NIP-4; NOBE; NOSC; NoP-4; NoSic; OBEV; OxAEP-1; PBMP; PFE; PoE; SoSe-8; TFi

("Goe and catche a falling starre.") CBNP; ESCV; HoPM; MeLP; NBLV; PoEL-2; SeCP

Song: "Go[e], lovely rose[—ous sweet and fair]." Edmund Waller. GBL; GLoP; NOSC; NoP-4; OAEL-1; OxAEP-1; PBRV; PFE; PoEL-3; PoPoPo; Poetr; SeCP; SoSe-8

Song: "Great friend and servant of the good." Ben Jonson. *Fr.* Pleasure Reconciled to Virtue. NAEL-1; OAEL-1

Song: "Hang sorrow, cast away care." *Unknown.* NOSC

Song: "Hark, hark!/ Bow-wow./ The watch-dogs bark." Shakespeare. *Fr.* The Tempest. OAEL-1

Song: "Hark! hark! the lark at heaven's gate sings." Shakespeare. EBEvV; NOSC *Fr.* Cymbeline.

(Aubade: "Hark! hark! the lark at heaven's gate sings.") OBEV

Song: "Heap cassia, sandal-buds and stripes." Robert Browning. OBEV *Fr.* Paracelsus.

Song: "Hear me, ye smokeless skies and grass-green earth." Charles Mair. NOBC *Fr.* The Last Bison.

Song: "Heare ye Ladies that despise." John Fletcher. PoEL-2 *Fr.* The Tragedy of Valentinian.

Song: "Hears not my Phillis how the birds." Sir Charles Sedley. EnLoPo

Song: "Here's to the maiden [*or* maid] of bashful fifteen." Richard Brinsley Sheridan. EBEvV; NOEC; OxAEP-1; OxBoLi; PeLV; PoRA *Fr.* The School for Scandal.

(Drinking Song.) NOIV

Song: "Hold back thy hours, dark night, till we have done." Francis Beaumont *and* John Fletcher. OxBSP *Fr.* The Maid's Tragedy.

(Bridal Song.)

Song: "How hardly I concealed my tears." Anne Wharton. LW

Song: "How many times do I love thee, dear?" Thomas Lovell Beddoes. ImPo *Fr.* Torrismond.

Song: "How pleasant it is that always." Florence Smith. BLPA

Song: "How strongly does my passion flow." Aphra Behn. OxAEP-1

Song: "I am dark, daughters of Jerusalem." Bible, *O.T.* WPoS, *tr. by* Chana Bloch *and* Ariel Bloch *Fr.* The Song of Solomon.

Song: "I am weaving a song of waters." Gwendolyn B. Bennett. BlSi

Song: "I can't be talkin' of love, dear." Esther Mathews. ImPo

Song: "I feed a flame within, which so torments me." Dryden. AWP *Fr.* Secret Love; or, The Maiden Queen.

(Hidden Flame.) OBEV

Song: "I had a dove, and the sweet dove died." Keats. *Fr.* I Had a Dove [and the Sweet Dove Died]. CH; PeP

Song: "I have so little sorrow." Patricia Jones. ISC

Song: "I keep running around." *Unknown, Chippewa.* STP, *tr. by* Jerome Rothenberg

Song: "I know that any weed can tell." Louis Ginsberg. TrJP

Song: "I love you, Mrs. Acorn. Would your husband mind." Kath Fraser. LW

Song: "I made another garden, yea." Arthur William Edgar O'Shaughnessy. OBEV

Song: "I peeled bits of straw and I got switches too." John Clare. NAEL-2

Song: "I placed my dream in a boat." Cecília Meireles, *Portuguese.* WPOW, *tr. by* Eloah F. Giacomelli

Song: "I prithee let my heart alone." Thomas Stanley. BeJo

Song: "I prithee spare me, gentle boy." Sir John Suckling. BeJo; CavPo

Song: "I, that ame of all most crost." Mary Sidney Wroth. KTR *Fr.* Pamphilia to Amphilanthus.

Song, A: "I thought no more was needed." W. B. Yeats. CBLP

Song: "I was asleep but my heart stayed awake." Bible, *O.T.* WPoS

Song: "I was so chill, and overworn, and sad." Anna Wickham. MoBrPo

Song: "I watered my horse at the Long Wall caves." Susan Ch'en Lin, *Chinese.* CoBCP, *tr. by* Burton Watson

Song: "I went my Sunday mornings round." John Clare. NOBVV

Song: "I went to her who loveth me no more." Arthur William Edgar O'Shaughnessy. OBNC

Song: "I would not feign a single sigh." John Clare. GBL

Song: "If any wench Venus's girdle wear." John Gay. PeLV; PoEL-3 *Fr.* The Beggar's Opera. OAEL-1

Song: "If everywhere in the street." Denis Glover. PeNZ *Fr.* Sings Harry.

Song: "If I freely may discover." Ben Jonson. *Fr.* The Poetaster.

Song: "If she be not as kind as fair." William Walsh *and* Sir George Etherege (1653–91). NOSC

Song: "If the scorn of your bright eyne." Shakespeare. CTC *Fr.* As You Like It.

Song: "If thou art sleeping, maiden." Gil Vicente, *Spanish.* AWP; CTC, *tr. by* Longfellow

Song: "If to be absent were to be." Richard Lovelace. CavPo

("To *Lucasta, Going Beyond the Seas*.") CavPo

Song: "I'm about to go shopping." James Schuyler. TTTS

Song: "I'm living in a cave." *Unknown, Chippewa.* STP, *tr. by* Jerome Rothenberg

Song: "In a maiden-time professed." Thomas Middleton. OxBSP *Fr.* The Witch.

Song: "In mine one [*or* own] monument I lie [*or* lye]." Richard Lovelace. CBLP; OxBSP

Song: "In the middle of the sea." *Unknown, Chippewa.* STP, *tr. by* Jerome Rothenberg

Song: "Isle!/ Island of the syllables of flame!" Jacques Rabémanganjara, *French.* NegPo, *tr. by* Ellen Conroy Kennedy

Song, A: "It is not Beauty [*or* beautie] I demand[e]." George Darley. NOBRP; OBNC

("Hers could not staye for sympathie.") (LL) Ro

(Loveliness of Love, The.) GTBS-P; OxAEP-2

Song: "It was a lover and his lass." Shakespeare. APAD; CTC; EBEvV; OxAEP-1 *Fr.* As You Like It.

Song: "It was upon a Lammas night." Robert Burns. BoLoP; NOBRP; PeLV

(Corn Rigs Are Bonnie.) OxBS

Song: "Jog on, jog on, the footpath way." Shakespeare. OxBSP *Fr.* The Winter's Tale.

(Merry Heart, The.) BoTP

Song: "Keep the dream alive and growing always." Edwin Rolfe. TrJP

Song: "Kind lovers, love on." John Crowne. OxBSP *Fr.* Calisto.

Song: "Know what I'll promise you?" *Unknown, Chippewa.* STP, *tr. by* Jerome Rothenberg

Song: "Ladies, though to your conquering eyes." Sir George Etherege. OxBSP *Fr.* The Comical Revenge.

Song: "Leave this gaudy gilded stage." John Wilmot, 2d Earl of Rochester. OxBSP

Song: "Let it be forgotten, as a flower is forgotten." Sara Teasdale. MoAmPo; PoA

Song: "Let not the sluggish sleep." *Unknown.* OxBSP

Song: "Let school-masters puzzle their brain." Oliver Goldsmith. BIrV; NOIV *Fr.* She Stoops to Conquer.

(Three Jolly Pigeons, The.) PoRA

Song: "Life is ours in vain." Oodgeroo of the tribe Noonuccal. APAD

Song: "Linnet in the rocky dells, The." Emily Jane Brontë. HAP; OBNC; RACG

(My Lady's Grave.) OxAEP-2

Song: "Listen: there was a goat's head hanging by ropes in a tree." Brigit Pegeen Kelly. PUP-19 *Fr.* The Southern Review.

Song: "Little onion lay by the fireplace, A." Nicholas Moore. SPE

Song: "Love a child is ever criing [*or* crying]." Mary Sidney Wroth. KTR; LW; NOSC; NoP-4 *Fr.* Pamphilia to Amphilanthus.

Song: "Love a woman? You're [*or* Y'are] an ass." John Wilmot, 2d Earl of Rochester. GBL; NBLV; NOBL; NOSC; PeLV

Song: "Love is a green girl." Michael Stillman. TLR

Song: "Love, love today, my dear." Charlotte Mew. MoBrPo

Song: "Love that is hoarded, moulds at last." Harold C. Sandall. PoToHe

Song: "Lovely hill-torrents are." Walter James Turner. MoBrPo

Song: "Lovers in ladies' magazines." Thomas McGrath. VGW

Song, A: "Lying is an occupation." Laetitia Pilkington. PEW; WPE

Song: "Man's a poor deluded bubble." Robert Dodsley. OxBSP

Song: "Memory, hither come." William Blake. NAEL-2; PoEL-4

Song, A: "Men of England." Shelley. *See* Song to the Men of England.

Song: "Might have known it." *Unknown, Chippewa.* STP, *tr. by* Jerome Rothenberg

Song. Milton. *See* Sabrina.

Song. Milton. *See* Song: on [*or* of] May Morning.

Song: "Mist rauk is hanging, The." John Clare. NOBVV

Song, A: "Morpheus, the humble god, that dwells." Sir John Denham. NOSC

Song: "Mother Mother shave me." *Unknown, Nyasa.* BoWoP, *tr. by* Ulli Beier

Song: "Moth's kiss, first, The!" Robert Browning. *See* In a Gondola.

Song, A: "Music, thou queen of souls, get up and string." Thomas Randolph. OxBSP

Song: "My cabinets are oyster-shells." Margaret Lucas Cavendish, Duchess of Newcastle. WPE *Fr.* The Convent of Pleasure.

(Sea-Goddess, The.) OxBoS

Song, A: "My head on moss reclining." *Unknown.* NOEC

Song: "My heart is like the failing hearth." Letitia Elizabeth Landon. NOBRP *Fr.* The Golden Violet.

Song: "My silks and fine array." William Blake. OBNC; RACG; SCGP

Song: "My straying thoughts, reduced stay." Anne Collins. WPE

Song: "Neath blue-bell or streamer." Edgar Allan Poe. AmPP; NOBA; OxBA *Fr.* Al Aaraaf. APN-1

Song: "No, no, fair heretic[k], it needs must be." Sir John Suckling. BeJo; CaPo; CavPo *Fr.* Aglaura.

("No, no, fair heretic, it needs must be.") CavPo

Song: "No, no, no, no, I cannot hate my foe." Sir Philip Sidney. SiPS

Song, A: "No riches from his scanty store." Helen Maria Williams. WoRP

Song: "Noe more unto my thoughts appeare." Sidney Godolphin. MeLP

Song: "Nothing ades to Loves fond fire." Elizabeth Wilmot. KTR; LW

Song: "Now and then there will arise." *Unknown, Chippewa.* OBVE, *tr. by* Frances Densmore

Song: "Now that Fate is dead and gone." Dame Edith Sitwell. MoBrPo

Song: "Now this bloody war is over." George Barker. PeLV

Song, A: "Nymph in vain bestows her pains, The." Anne Finch. OxBSP

Song: "O fair! O sweet! when I do look on thee." Sir Philip Sidney. SiPS

Song: "O lovely April, rich and bright." Gustave Kahn, *French.* TrJP, *tr. by* Ludwig Lewisohn

Song: "O Mary sing thy songs to me." John Clare. CBLP

Song: "O[h] me[e], the time is [*or* has] come to part." Mary Sidney, Countess of Montgomery Wroth. NOSC *Fr.* Pamphilia to Amphilanthus.

Song: "O more, and more! this was so well." Ben Jonson. *Fr.* Pleasure Reconciled to Virtue. NAEL-1; OAEL-1

Song: "O sweet delight, O more than human[e] bliss[e]." Thomas Campion. CBLP

Song: "O sweet, sad, singing river." Henrietta Cordelia Ray. CBWP-3

Song: "Oh, blush not so, oh, blush not so." Keats. APAD; CBLP

Song: "Oh, baby, baby, baby dear." Edith Nesbit. NOBVV; PEW

("My baby dear.") (LL) VWP

Song: "Oh, dear! Oh, me! Oh, my!" Gregory Corso. BB

Song, A: "Oh do[e] not wanton with those eyes." Ben Jonson. CBLP; SeCP

Song: "Oh [*or* O] fair[e] sweet face, oh [*or* O] eyes celestial[l] bright." John Fletcher. PoEL-2 *Fr.* Women Pleased.

(To His Sleeping Mistress.) NOSC

Song: "Oh for the wings of a dove." Agnes Mary Frances Robinson. VWP

Song, The: "Oh, foully slighted Ethiope maid!" Priscilla Jane Thompson. CBWP-2

Song of the Reverend Gatemouth Moore. Etheridge Knight. BkSV *Fr.* Three Songs.

Song: "Oh! Love, that stronger art than wine." Aphra Behn. LW; WPE; WPOW *Fr.* The Lucky Chance.

Song: "Oh no more, no more, too late." John Ford. *See* Love's Martyrs.

Song: "Oh roses for the flush of youth." Christina Rossetti. GTBS-P; NOBVV

Song: "Oh say not that my heart is cold." Charles Wolfe. OxAEP-2

Song: "Oh the charming month of May!" Joseph Addison. NOEC

Song: "Oh, you powerful Gods, if I must be." Frances Boothby. KTR *Fr.* The Marcelia; or, Treacherous Friend.

Song: "Old England is eaten by Knaves." Alexander McLachlan. NOBC *Fr.* The Emigrant.

Song: "Old Farmer Oats and his son Ned." John Jay Chapman. PoEL-5

Song, A: On His Mistress. Sir Robert Ayton. NOSC

Song: "Ope, aged Atlas, open then thy lap." Ben Jonson. *Fr.* Pleasure Reconciled to Virtue. NAEL-1; OAEL-1

Song: "Or love me less, or love me more." Sidney Godolphin. NOSC

Song: "O're [*or* O'er] the smooth enamel'd [*or* enameled *or* enamelled] green." Milton. OxBSP *Fr.* Arcades.

Song: "Orpheus with his Lute made Trees." John Fletcher *and* Shakespeare. *See* Music.

Song: "Pardon, goddess of the night." Shakespeare. CTC *Fr.* Much Ado about Nothing.

Song: "Phillis is my only joy." Sir Charles Sedley. EnLoPo

Song: "Pious Selinda goes to prayers." William Congreve. BoLoP; ECEV; NBLV; NOEC; OxBSP

Song: "Place in thy memory, dearest, A." Gerald Griffin. BLPA

Song: "Platinum fur and brass revolver shine." Michael McClure. BB

Song: "Pursuing beauty, men descry." Thomas Southerne. NOSC

Song: "Rarely, rarely, comest thou." Shelley. FHYEP; LaPo; OBNC

("Barely, rarely, comest thou.") CH

(Invocation.) GTBS-P

Song: "Red young men under the ground, The." *Unknown.* STP, *tr. by* Jerome Rothenberg *Fr.* Red Ant Way.

Song: "Rejoice bather between two waters." Milorad Pavic, *Serbo-Croatian.* HSix, *tr. by* Charles Simic *Fr.* Holy Mass For Relja Krilatica.

Song: "Rejoice eleventh finger reckoner of stars." Milorad Pavic, *Serbo-Croatian.* HSix, *tr. by* Charles Simic *Fr.* Holy Mass For Relja Krilatica.

Song: "Rejoice mason of years." Milorad Pavic, *Serbo Croatian.* HSix *tr. by* Charles Simic. *Fr.* Holy Mass For Relja Krilatica.

Song: "Rejoice singer of songs for the deaf." Milorad Pavic, *Serbo Croatian.* HSix *tr. by* Charles Simic. *Fr.* Holy Mass For Relja Krilatica.

Song: "Rejoice you who sleep with a finger in your ear." Milorad Pavic, *Serbo Croatian.* HSix *tr. by* Charles Simic. *Fr.* Holy Mass For Relja Krilatica.

Song: "Rowan like a lip-sticked girl, A." Seamus Heaney. TRP

Song: "Scholar first my Love implor'd [*or* implored], A." Dorothea Du Bois. ECWP; LW

Song: "She dwelt among the untrodden ways." Wordsworth. NOBRP *Fr.* Lucy. FHYEP; NOBE; OAEL-2; OBEV; OBNC; SCGP; TFi

(Lost Love, The.) GTBS-P

("She dwelt among th' untrodden ways.") Ro

Song: "She has left me, my pretty." Sylvia Townsend Warner. MoBrPo

Song: "She sat and sang alway." Christina Rossetti. GBL; NAEL-2

Song: "Shephard loveth thow me vell?" Jean Passerat, *French.* OBVE, *tr. by* William Drummond of Hawthornden

Song: "She's somewhere in the sunlight strong." Richard Le Gallienne. OBEV

Song: "Sigh no more, ladies, sigh no more." Shakespeare. PoEL-2 *Fr.* Much Ado about Nothing.

("Into Hey nonny, nonny.") (LL) APAD

("Sigh no more, ladies, sigh no more.") APAD

Song, A: "Sing me a sweet, low song of night." Hildegarde Hawthorne. FaBoBe

Song, A: "Slaves to London, I'll deceive you." Peter Anthony Motteux. NOSC

Song: "Slow, slow fresh fount, keep time with my salt tears." Ben Jonson. OxBSP; PoEL-2; SeCP *Fr.* Cynthia's Revels.

(Echo's Lament for Narcissus.) CH; OxAEP-1

Song, The: "So light no one noticed." Edward Dorn. VGW

Song: "Soft falls the sweet evening." John Clare. NOBVV

Song, A: "Somnus, the humble god, that dwells." Sir John Denham. BeJo

Song: "Soules joy, now I am gone." William Herbert, Earl of Pembroke. ESCV

Song: "Sound is fading out." *Unknown, Chippewa.* STP, *tr. by* Jerome Rothenberg

Song: "Spirit haunts the year's last hours, A." Tennyson. GTBS-P; GaP; HeIP-4; LaPo; OBGa; OBNC

Song: "Stay Phoebus, stay." Edmund Waller. BeJo; SeCP

Song: "Stop all the clocks, cut off the telephone." W. H. Auden. MoBrPo; OPOU *Fr.* Twelve Songs.

Song: "Stranger, you who hide my love." Stephen Spender. FaBoTw

Song: "Strephon has fashion, wit and youth." Elizabeth Taylor. KTR

("Strephon hath Fashion, Wit and Youth.") LW

Song, A: "Strephon, your breach of faith and trust." Laetitia Pilkington. LW

Song: "Strew not earth with empty stars." Thomas Lovell Beddoes. OxBSP *Fr.* The Second Brother.

Song: "Strive not, vain Lover, to be fine." Richard Lovelace. CavPo

Song: "Sun sets in night, and the stars shun the day, The." Royall Tyler. NAAL-3 *Fr.* The Contrast.

Song: "Sure thing / I'm a spirit!" *Unknown, Chippewa.* STP, *tr. by* Jerome Rothenberg

Song: "Sweet are the thoughts that savour of content." Robert Greene. PoEL-2; PoToHe *Fr.* Greene's Farewell to Folly.

Song: "Sweet beast, I have gone prowling." W. D. Snodgrass. MoAmPo; NYBP

Song: "Sweetest love, I do not go[e]." Donne. AWP; BoLoP; ESCV; FHYEP; FSCP; HeIP-4; InPS-3; MeLP; NOBE; NoSic; OAEL-1; PoEL-2; SeCP; TFi

("Sweetest love, I do not go.") FMP; GLoP; LoP; NoP-4

Song: "SYLVIA the fair, in the bloom of fifteen." Dryden. EBEV; OxAEP-1

Song: "Tell me where is fancy [*or* Fancie] bred." Shakespeare. CTC; EBEvV; PoEL-2 *Fr.* The Merchant of Venice.

(Love.) OBEV

Song, The: "That day, in the slipping of torsos and straining flanks." Lola Ridge. WPE

Song: "There is no joy in water apart from the sun." Ralph Nixon Currey. PeSA

Song: "There stands a lonely pine-tree." Heinrich Heine, *German.* TrJP, *tr. by* Emma Lazarus

Song: "There was a Knight of Bethlehem." Henry Neville Maughan. BoTP *Fr.* The Husband of Poverty.

Song: "There's a barrel of porter at Tammany Hall." Fitz-Greene Halleck. OBAL

Song: "These songs will not stand." Denis Glover. PeNZ *Fr.* Sings Harry.

Song: "Think of dress in every light." John Gay. OxBSP *Fr.* Achilles.

Song: "This is the song of those who live alone." William Justema. NYBP

Song: "Those rivers run from that land." Robert Creeley. VGW

Song: "Three little maidens whom have slain." Maurice Maeterlinck, *French.* AWP, *tr. by* Jethro Bithell

Song: "Through springtime walks, with flowers perfumed." Anne Batten Cristall. ECWP

Song: "Thus when the swallow, seeking prey." John Gay. PoEL-3 *Fr.* The Beggar's Opera. OAEL-1

Song: "'Tis affection but dissembled." Sidney Godolphin. BeJo

Song: "'Tis light to love thee living, girl, when hope is full and fair." Thomas Tod Stoddart. NOBRP *Fr.* Death-Wake, The; or, Lunacy.

Song: "'Tis true our life is but a long dis-ease." Katherine Philips. OxBSP

Song: "To the old, long life and treasure." Ben Jonson. OxBSP *Fr.* The Gypsies Metamorphosed.

Song: "Tomorrow is Saint Valentine's Day." Shakespeare. EnLoPo; NoSic *Fr.* Hamlet. EBEvV; NAWM-1; NTCP

Song: "Turn, turn thy beauteous face away." Francis Beaumont *and* John Fletcher. NOSC; PoEL-2 *Fr.* Love's Cure.

Song: "Two doves upon the selfsame branch." Christina Rossetti. CBLP

Song: "Under the greenwood tree." Shakespeare. EBEvV *Fr.* As You Like It.

(Amiens's Song.)

("But winter and rough weather.") (LL) APAD; CTV; NoP-4

Song: "Victorious men of earth, no more." James Shirley. BeJo *Fr.* Cupid and Death.

(Last Conqueror, The.) GTBS-P

Song: "Wake, Hercules, awake: but heave up thy black eye." Ben Jonson. *Fr.* Pleasure Reconciled to Virtue. NAEL-1; OAEL-1

Song: "Water's flowing." *Unknown, Chippewa.* STP, *tr. by* Jerome Rothenberg

Song: "We are the darkness in the heat of the day." Dame Edith Sitwell. BWW

Song: "We raise de wheat." *Unknown.* BPo; TAP

("Poor nigger you can't get over dat; / Walk over!") (LL) APN-2

(Slave Song.) CrDW

Song: "We'll, placed in Love's triumphant chariot high." William Cavendish, Duke of Newcastle. OxBSP *Fr.* The Humorous Lovers.

Song: "Were I laid on Greenland's coast." John Gay. EBEvV, *sect.* I, *pt.* i; CBLP; EnLoPo; NAEL-1; OxBoLi; PeLV; PoEL-3 *Fr.* The Beggar's Opera. OAEL-1

(Macheath and Polly.) NOEC

Song: "What a dainty life the milkmaid leads!" Thomas Nabbes. NOSC

Song: "What I took in my hand." Robert Creeley. FTOS; PoA

Song: "What is there hid in the heart of a rose." Alfred Noyes. CH

Song: "What means this strangeness now of late." Sir Robert Ayton. NOSC

Song: "What shall he have that kill'd the deer?" Shakespeare. CTC *Fr.* As You Like It.

Song, A: "What torments must the virgin prove." Charlotte Lennox. ECWP

Song: "What voice is this, thou evening gale!" Joanna Baillie. WoRP

Song: "What's in the body you've forgotten." Robert Creeley. PuP-14

Song: "Whaur yon broken brig hings owre;.." William Soutar. FaBoTC; OxBS

Song: "When as [or whenas] the rye [or rie] reach to the chin." George Peele. CBNP; FaBoVe; NoP-4; OxBoLi; PoEL-2 *Fr.* The Old Wives' [or Wife's] Tale.

(Summer Song, A.) GLoP; NOBE; OBEV

Song: "When daffodils begin to peer." Shakespeare. *See* The Pedlar's Song.

Song: "When, dearest, I but think on [or of] thee." Sir John Suckling *and* Owen Felltham (c.1602–1668). OBEV

(Ensuing Copy the Late Printer Hath Been Pleased to Honour, by Mistaking It Among Those of the Most Ingenious and Too Early Lost Sir John Suckling, The.) NOSC

Song: "When I am dead, my dearest." Christina Rossetti. APAD; AWP; BoLoP; CABP; CH; EBEV; EBEvV; GBL; InPS-3; NAEL-2; NOBE; NOBVV; NoP-4; OAEL-2; OBEV; OxAEP-2; PoLF; PoRA; Poetr; SCV; SDW; TFi; VWP; WPE

Song: "When I am old." Denis Glover. PeNZ *Fr.* Sings Harry.

Song: "When I show up." *Unknown, Chippewa.* STP, *tr. by* Jerome Rothenberg

Song: "When I was a greenhorn and young." Charles Kingsley. NOBVV

Song, The: "When I would sing of crooked streams and fields." Jones Very. APN-1

Song: "When lovely woman stoops to folly." Oliver Goldsmith. AWP; BoLoP; EBEvV; FHYEP; FaBoSe; NOBE; NOEC; OxAEP-1 *Fr.* The Vicar of Wakefield.

(Woman.) ImPo; OBEV

Song: "When o'er the wold the heedless lamb." Thomas Holcroft. NOEC

Song: "When that I was and a little tiny boy." Shakespeare. CH; EBEV; FaBoCh; ImPo; NOBE; NoSic; OAEL-1; PoRA, SCGP; TFi *Fr* Twelfth Night.

(Feste's Song.) PFE

(Feste's Song ("When that I was and a little tiny boy").) CBNP; NBLV; OxBoLi

(Wind and the Rain, The.)

Song: "When the echo of the last footstep dies." Eli W. Mandel. MoCV

Song: "When the heart's feeling." Thomas Moore. OxBSP

Song: "When the Sex War ended with the slaughter of the Grandmothers." W. H Auden. PeLV

Song: "When the water's calm." *Unknown, Chippewa.* STP, *tr. by* Jerome Rothenberg

Song: "When thy beauty appears." Thomas Parnell. OBEV; OxAEP-1

Song: "When working blackguards come to blows." Ebenezer Elliot. EBEV; OxAEP-2

Song: "Whenever, Chloe, I begin." Philip Dormer Stanhope. NOEC

Song: "Where did you borrow that last sigh." Sir William Berkeley. OxBSP *Fr.* The Lost Lady.

Song: "Where in blind files." Eavan Boland. CIP-2; IIP

Song: "Where is all the bright company gone." Dame Edith Sitwell. NALW

Song: "Where is the nymph, whose azure eye." Thomas Moore. EnLoPo

Song: "Where, O! where's the chain to fling." Letitia Elizabeth Landon. NOBRP *Fr.* The Golden Violet.

Song: "Where shall Celia fly for shelter." Christopher Smart. EnLoPo

Song, A: "While a thousand fine projects are planned ev'ry day." *Unknown.* NOEC

Song: "While Morpheus thus doth gently lay." Henry Killigrew. CH

Song: "Who can say." Tennyson. FaBoCh

Song: "Who hath his fancy [or fancie] pleasèd." Sir Philip Sidney. PoEL-1

Song: "Why Damon, why, why, why so pressing?" Mary Lee, Lady Chudleigh. LW

Song: "Why should your face so please me." Edwin Muir. OxBM

Song: "Why so pale and wan, fond lover?" Sir John Suckling. BeJo; BoLoP; CaPo; CavPo; ClHu; EBEvV; EnLoPo; HeIP-4; InPS-3; NAEL-1; NBLV; NIP-2; NoP-4; OxAEP-1; PoEL-3; SeCP; TFi *Fr.* Aglaura.

(Encouragements to a Lover.) GTBS-P; PBMP

Song, A: "Widow bird sate mourning for her love, A." Shelley. NOBE; OBNC; OxBSP; PoEL-4 *Fr.* Charles the First.

Song: "Woman sits on her porch." Earle Thompson. HATNAP

Song: "World is full of loss; bring, wind, my love, The." Muriel Rukeyser. PFE

Song, A: "World is young today, The." Digby Mackworth Dolben. NOBVV; OBNC

Song: "Ye Virgin Pow'rs defend my heart." Elizabeth Taylor. KTR

Song: "You are as gold." Hilda Doolittle. LiTM; MoAmPo

Song: "You wear the morning like your dress." Hilaire Belloc. OBEV

Song: "Young flowers were whispering in melody." Edgar Allan Poe. NOBA *Fr.* Al Aaraaf. APN-1

Song: "'Neath blue-bell or streamer." AmPP; OxBA

Song: "You're wondering if I'm lonely." Adrienne Rich. InPK-6; PBWP

Song 2: "All night I weep[e], all day I cry, Ay me[e]." Mary Sidney Wroth. NOSC *Fr.* Pamphilia to Amphilanthus.

Song, a poem of itself—the word itself a dirge, A. Yonnondio. Walt Whitman. NAAL-1; NAAL-3

Song about a Dead Person—or Was It a Mole?, A. *Unknown, Seneca.* STP, *tr. by* Jerome Rothenberg *and* Richard Johnny John

Song about Major Eatherly, A. John Wain. OxBTC

Song about Myself, A. Keats. *See* The Naughty Boy.

Naughty Boy, The. CTV

("And he wondered.") (LL) CTV

Song against Grocers, The. G. K. Chesterton. OBCoV

("Should be her proper text.") (LL) UV

Song and Poetry. *Unknown, Welsh.* OBWVE, *tr. by* Gwyn Jones

Song and Story. Ellen Bryant Voigt. BAP-93

Song as Yet Unsung, A. "Yehoash," *Yiddish.* TrJP, *tr. by* Isidore Goldstick

Song at Graveside. Ewald von Kleist, *German.* GePo, *tr. by* George C. Schoolfield

Song at Midnight. Lucille Clifton. UnSA

Song at Morning, A. Dame Edith Sitwell. CMoP

Song at Night. Norman Nicholson. FaBoTw

Song at the African Middle Class, (*for Augustinho Neto).* Molara Ogundipe-Leslie. HBAPE; PBMAP

Song at the Beginning of Autumn. Elizabeth Jennings. OxBTC

Song at the Ruin'd Inn. Tennyson. PoEL-5 *Fr.* The Vision of Sin. EBVVPR; OAEL-2

Song Ballet (I Was Sixteen Years of Age). *Unknown.* AmFP

Song Bewailing the Time of Christmas, So Much Decayed in England, A. *Unknown.* NoP-4

Song by a Woman Accused of Adultery. Kie Tapu, *Maori.* PeNZ, *tr. by* Margaret Orbell

Song By an Old Shepherd. William Blake. NTP

Song by Isbrand. Thomas Lovell Beddoes. NOBVV; OBNC *Fr.* Death's Jest Book.

Song by Klipstein and Krumpacker. T. S. Eliot. *Fr.* Two Songs from *Sweeny Agonistes.* UnPo *Fr.* Sweeney Agonistes.

Song by Mr. Cypress. Thomas Love Peacock. OAEL-2; OBNC *Fr.* Nightmare Abbey.

Song by Mrs. P—, A. Mary Pix. KTR *Fr.* The Innocent Mistress.

Song by the Brook. Sowol Kim, *Korean.* CKP, *tr. by* Jaihiun Kim

Song by the Shore, A. Richard Hovey. APN-2

Song by Wauchope and Horsfall. T. S. Eliot. *Fr.* Two Songs from *Sweeny Agonistes.* UnPo *Fr.* Sweeney Agonistes.

Song Composed for Fanny Burney, A. Samuel Johnson. CBNP

Song Cycle of Jacky, The. Mudrooroo.

Song Thirty-Four. BMAP

Song Cycle of the Moon-Bone. *Unknown, Aborigine.* NOBAu, *tr. by* Ronald M. Berndt

Song XI: "Lay your sleeping head, my love." W. H. Auden. *See* Lullaby: "Lay your sleeping head, my love."

Song for a Ball-Game. Wilfrid Thorley. BoTP

Song for a Birth or a Death. Elizabeth Jennings. EBEV

Song for a Dance. Francis Beaumont. FaBoCh *Fr.* The Masque of the Inner Temple and Gray's Inne.

Song for a Dance. Abraham Sutskever, *Yiddish.* CEEP, *tr. by* Ruth Whitman

Song for a Dancer. Kenneth Rexroth. TAP

Song for a Dark Girl. Langston Hughes. AmPP; NAAAL; NAAL-2; NoP-4; PoBA; SAmP

Song for a Fallen Warrior. *Unknown, Blackfeet.* APN-2, *tr. by* John Mason Browne

Song for a Girl on Her First Menstruation. *Unknown, Boikin.* BoWoP, *tr. by* Joe Prentuo

Song for a Jewess. Iwan Goll, *French.* TrJP, *tr. by* Joseph T. Shipley

Song for a Little House. Christopher Darlington Morley. BoTP; CTV

Song for a Scalp Dance. *Unknown, Chippewa.* STP, *tr. by* Jerome Rothenberg

Song for a Street-Song. Sylvia Townsend Warner. WPN

Song for a Thin Sister. Audre Lorde. OxWW

Song For a Tourist. Wayne Brown. HCP

Song for a Young Girl's Puberty Ceremony. *Unknown, Papago.* ChAP, *tr. by* Frances Densmore

Song for All Seas, All Ships. Walt Whitman. APN-1; CH; FaBoBe

Song for Apollo. Matthew Arnold. *See* The Song of Callicles ("Through the black, rushing smoke-bursts").

Song for Autumn. Andrew Young. GBL

Song For Baby-O, Unborn. Diane Di Prima. BB

Song for Billie Holiday. Langston Hughes. MoNo

Song for Bird and Myself. Jack Spicer. MoNo

Song for "Buvez les Vins du Postillion"—Advt. Jean Garrigue. TAP

Song for Empty Cup. Hijin Park, *Korean*. CKP, *tr. by* Jaihiun Kim

Song for England, A. Andrew Salkey. HCP; PBCV

Song for February, A. Thomas Given. FaBoVe

Song for Fine Weather. *Unknown, Haida.* AWP, tr. by Constance Lindsay Skinner. *Fr.* Three Songs from the Haida.

Song for Girls' Puberty Rites. *Chiricahua Apache Oral Tradition, Chiricahua Apache.* PaTW, *tr. by* Morris Edward Opler

Song for Grass Leaf. Toksu Moon, *Korean*. CKP, *tr. by* Jaihiun Kim

Song for Healing. Roberta Hill Whiteman. CDW

Song for Ilva Mackay and Mongane. Keorapetse Kgositsile. PBMAP

Song for Ishtar. Denise Levertov. MoP; NALW; NoAM; PoM

Song for Joseph. *Unknown, Maori.* PeNZ, tr. by Margaret Orbell

Song for Medicine Hunting—Rarely for the Metai. *Unknown. Fr.* Music and Poetry of the Indians. APN-2, *tr. by* John Tanner

Song for My Father. Jessica Hagedorn. MoLi

Song for My Lady. A. Godwin. OxBoLi

Song for occupations!, A. Walt Whitman. *See* Leaves of Grass (1855).

Song for Pacifying the Excited Nū′ LmaL. *Unknown. Fr.* Dances and Songs of the Winter Ceremonial. APN-2, *tr. by* Franz Boas

Song for Past Midnight. Geoffrey Lehmann. CBAP

Song for Ranelagh. William Whitehead. ECEV

Song for St. Cecilia's Day. W. H. Auden. FaBoTw; TwCP

Song for St Cecilia's Day [1687], A. Dryden. AWP; CABP; FHYEP; FaBoTw; GTBS-P; HAP; ImPo; InPS-3; NoP-4; NOSC; OAEL-1; OBEV; OxAEP-1; PoEL-3; SCGP; TFi

Song for September. Robert Fitzgerald. VGW

Song for Simeon, A. T. S. Eliot. ChIV-2; GI; NOCV

Song for Smooth Waters. Haida. CA

Song for Straphangers. George Buchanan. PNI

Song for Te Hauapu. Noho-mai-te-Rangi, *Maori.* PeNZ, tr. by Margaret Orbell

Song for the Cattle. David Campbell. NOBAu

Song for the Clatter-Bones. Frederick Robert Higgins. ChIV-1; ImPo; OBMV

Song for the Dead, III. *Unknown.* TTY, *tr. by* Frances S. Herskovits

Song for the Deer and Myself to Return On. Joy Harjo. WeT

Song for the Festival of Tlaloc, the Rain God. *Nahuatl Oral Tradition.* PaTW

Song for the Goddess of Love. Sappho, *Greek.* ITG, *tr. by* Jane Hirshfield

Song for the Head. George Peele. *See* The Voice from the Well [of Life Speaks to the Maiden].

Song for the Heroes. Alex Comfort. MoBrPo

Song for the In-Itself and For-Itself. Henry Weinfield. BAP-94

Song for "The Jacquerie." Sidney Lanier. NCAP

Song for the Last Act. Louise Bogan. NYBP; NoP-4; UnPo; WPE

Song for the Lost Private. Bruce Weigl. CDa

Song for the Metai Only. *Unknown. Fr.* Music and Poetry of the Indians. APN-2, *tr. by* John Tanner

Song for the Metai, or for Medicine Hunting. *Unknown. Fr.* Music and Poetry of the Indians. APN-2, *tr. by* John Tanner

Song for the Middle of the Night, A. James Wright. WeW-3

Song for the Newborn. *Unknown, Grande Pueblo.* WPE

Song for the Richest Woman in Wrangell. Guxnawu, *Tlingit.* STP, tr. by James Koller

Song for the Single Table on New Year's Day, A. Elizabeth Frances Amherst. ECWP

Song for the Squeeze-Box. Theodore Roethke. NBLV

Song for the Sun That Disappeared behind the Rainclouds. *Hottentot Oral Tradition.* ChAP; TTTS; TTY, *tr. by* Ulli Beier

Song for the unsung heroes who rose in the country's need, A. The Unsung Heroes. Paul Laurence Dunbar. BPo; CBCWP

Song for the Workers, A. Eliza Cook. VWP

Song for Those Who Know. Hans Magnus Enzensberger, *German.* VCWP, *tr. by* Hans Magnus Enzensberger and Michael Hamburger; PoSu

Song for Unbound Hair. Genevieve Taggard. PoRA

Song for Wei City, A. Wang Wei, *Chinese.* TAL, tr. by Robert Payne

Song Form. Imamu Amiri Baraka. ChAP; TTTS

Song IV: The Calling-Up. Muriel Rukeyser. NMM-2

Song from a Two-Desk Office. Byron Buck. NYBP

Song from Armenia, A. Geoffrey Hill. FaBoMo

Song from "Chartivel." Marie de France. AWP *Fr.* Chartivel.

Song from *Mardi*. Herman Melville. APN-2

Song from Poetaster, or The Arraignment. Martial, *Latin.* OBCVT, *tr. by* Ben Jonson

Song from Shakespeare's Cymbeline, A. William Collins. *See* Dirge in "Cymbeline."

Song from Sylvan, A. Elizabeth Barrett Browning. BLPA

Song from the Bride of Smithfield. Sylvia Townsend Warner. MoBrPo

Song from the Coptic, A. James Clarence Mangan. NOIV

Song from The Indian Emperor. Dryden. NoP-4 *Fr.* The Indian Emperor. (Song.)

Song from the Occupation Time. Ion Caraion, *Romanian.* AF, *tr. by* Marguerite Dorian *and* Elliott B. Urdang

Song from the Waters. Thomas Lovell Beddoes. *See* Dirge: "Swallow leaves her nest, The."

Song from Troilus and Cressida. Dryden. NoP-4 *Fr.* Troilus and Cressida. (Song.)

Song gives birth to. . . The woman with white hair. The Song of Ancient Ways. William Oandasan. HATNAP

Song: Good Counsel to a Young Maid. Thomas Carew. CaPo

("Gaze not on thy beauty's pride.") CavPo

(Good Counsel to a Young Maid.) CavPo

Song, *Hamlet.* John F. Poole. BXAP

Song: How Can I Care? Robert Graves. GBL

Song I sing of my sea-adventure, A. The Seafarer. *Unknown, Anglo-Saxon.* AnOE, *tr. by* Charles W. Kennedy

Song I sing of my sea adventure, A. *Unknown.* AnOE, tr. by Charles W. Kennedy *Fr.* The Seafarer.

Song I sing of sorrow unceasing, A. The Wife's Lament. *Unknown.* AnOE, *tr. by* Charles W. Kennedy; BoLoP, *tr. by* Michael Alexander

Song: I Want a Witness. Michael S. Harper. LTA; UnSA

("As they wave their tongues.") (LL) UnSA

Song: I Watered My Horse at the Long Wall Caves. Susan Ch'en Lin. *See* Song: "I watered my horse at the Long Wall caves."

Song in a windless night. . . , A. The Toad. Tristan Corbière, *French.* APo, *tr. by* Vernon Watkins

Song in Making of the Arrows, The. John Lyly. *See* Vulcan's Song.

Song in Passing, A. Yvor Winters. CRP; VGW

Song in Praise of a Favourite Humming-Top, A. Hone Tuwhare. PeNZ

Song In Space. Adrian Mitchell. SpW

Song in Spite of Myself. Countee Cullen. ISC

Song in the Blood. Jacques Prévert, *French.* AF, *tr. by* Lawrence Ferlinghetti

Song in the Cold Season. Samuel French Morse. PoA

Song in the Front Yard, A. Gwendolyn Brooks. NAAAL; NAAL-2; NOBA; NOxBChV; NoAM; PoBA *Fr.* A Street in Bronzeville. BPo; BlSi; FaBoWP

Song in the valley of Nemea, A. Nemea. Lawrence Durrell. FaBoTw; GTBS-P

Song in the Wood. John Fletcher. NOSC *Fr.* The Little French Lawyer.

Song in Time of Plague. Thomas Nashe. *See* A Litany in Time of Plague.

Song is gone; the dance, The. Bora Ring. Judith Wright. NoAM

Song—Last Day. John Clare. EnVR

Song: Lift-Boy. Robert Graves. NTP; OxAEP-2

Song: Little Black Rose, The. Aubrey Thomas De Vere. BIrV

Song: Love Armed. Aphra Behn. NOSC; Poetr; WeW-3 *Fr.* Abdelazer. (Love Armed.) NALW

("Love in fantastic triumph sat.") NoP-4; PEW

(Song: "Love in fantastic triumph sate.") OBEV; OxAEP-1

("While thine the victor is and free.") (LL) LW

Song: Love Lives Beyond the Tomb. John Clare. *See* Loves Lives Beyond the Tomb.

Song: Love Still Has Something of the Sea. Sir Charles Sedley. GBL; NOBE; OxAEP-1

Song-Maker. Anita Endrezze-Danielson. HATNAP

Song-Maker, The. Anna Wickham. MoBrPo

Song Making. Sara Teasdale. SAGP

Song: Mary Morison. Robert Burns. *See* Mary Morison.

Song—Molly Magee. John Clare. EnVR

Song: Montrose. Charles Cotton. NOSC

Song: Murdring Beautie. Thomas Carew. SeCP

Song My. Susan Griffin. NMM-2; WPOW

Song No. 2: "I say. all you young girls waiting to live." Sonia Sanchez. FFC

Song No. 3: "Cain't nobody tell me any different." Sonia Sanchez. FFC; NOxBChV

Song of a Bear Dancer Named Walas Nā′ nē (Great Bear). *Unknown. Fr.* Dances and Songs of the Winter Ceremonial. APN-2, *tr. by* Franz Boas

Song of a Common Lover. Flavien Ranaivo, *French.* TTY, *tr. by* Alan Ryder; PBMAP

Song of a Cotton Yarn, The. Ho Chi Minh, *Vietnamese.* AVP, *tr. by* Huỳnh Sanh Thông

Song of a Dream Journey over the Vast Sea. Yang Wei-chen, *Chinese.* CoBLCP, *tr. by* Jonathan Chaves

Song of a Dream Visit to T'ien-mu. Li Po, *Chinese.* CoBCP, *tr. by* Burton Watson

Song of a Farmer. P'i Jih-hsiu, *Chinese.* SuSp, *tr. by* William H. Nienhauser

Song of a Jewish Boy. "M. J.," *Polish.* TrJP, *tr. by* A. Glanz-Leyeles

Song of a Man About to Die in a Strange Land. Mary Austin. PaTW

Song of a Man in the Dark. "Adunis," *Arabic.* VCWP, *tr. by* Samuel Hazo

Song of a Man Who Has Come Through. D. H. Lawrence. APAD; CMoP; FaBoMo; GTBS-P; InPS-3; LiTM; OxBTC; PeFWW; PoE; RaBo; TRP

Song of a Man Who Is Loved. D. H. Lawrence. OxBM

Song of a Prisoner. Jack Spicer. APSN

Song of a Rat. Ted Hughes. CMoP

Song of a Salmon Dancer. *Unknown. Fr.* Dances and Songs of the Winter Ceremonial. APN-2, *tr. by* Franz Boas

Song of a Second April. Edna St. Vincent Millay. CMoP; OxBA

Song of a Soldier's Wife, The. Đng Trần Côn *and* Phan Huy Ích, *Chinese.* AVP, *tr. by* Huỳnh Sanh Thông

Song of a Spirit. Ann Radcliffe. ECWP

Song of a Traveller, The. Robert Louis Stevenson. BoTP

Song of a Woman Abandoned by the Tribe. *Unknown, Shoshone.* WPE, *tr. by* Mary Austin

Song of a Young Girl. Flavien Ranaivo. PBMAP

Song of a Young Lady to Her Ancient Lover, A. John Wilmot. APAD; BoLoP; EBEV; GBL; GLoP; NOSC; OxAEP-1

Song of a Young Lady to Her Ancient Lover, A. Grace Buchanan Sherwood. NoP-4

Song of Absinthe Granny, The. Ruth Stone. NAIW

Song of Ale, A. William Stevenson *and* John Still. *See* Back and Side Go Bare, Go Bare.

Song of an Autumn Night. Chao Meng-fu, *Chinese.* CoBLCP, *tr. by* Jonathan Chaves

Song of an Old Gray Wolf. *Unknown, Cheyenne.* APN-2, *tr. by* Alfred Kroeber

Song of Ancient Ways, The. William Oandasan. HATNAP

Song of Apelles. John Lyly. *See* Cards and Kisses.

Song of Apollo. John Lyly. *Fr.* Midas.

Song of Apollo. Shelley. *See* Hymn of Apollo.

Song of Autumn Night. Wang Ya, *Chinese.* SuSp, *tr. by* Irving Y. Lo

Song of Battle. Bertrans de Born. AWP
(War Song, A.) CTC

Song of Becoming. Fadwa Tuqan, *Arabic.* AF, *tr. by* Naomi Shihab Nye

Song of Bekotsidi, The. *Unknown, Navajo.* OBVE, *tr. by* Washington Matthews

Song of Bliss. Edmund Spenser. *Fr.* Wood Of Error. AEP

Song of Blodeuwedd, The. Robert Graves. NoP-4

Song of Blood, A. Sidney Walter Powell. NSI *Fr.* Gallipoli.

Song of Blue and Red, A. Amir Gilbo'a, *Hebrew.* MHP, *tr. by* Ruth Finer Mintz

Song of Breath. Peire Vidal, *French.* AWP, *tr. by* Ezra Pound

Song of Callicles, The ("Far far from here"). Matthew Arnold. *Fr.* Empedocles on Etna.

Song of Callicles, The ("Through the black, rushing smoke-bursts"). Matthew Arnold. NOBE; OAEL-2; OBEV *Fr.* Empedocles on Etna.

Song of Calling Souls. Wang Ping. BAP-96

Song of canaries, The. The Canary. Ogden Nash. PeLV

Song of Catching Tigers. Hsü Chung-hsing, *Chinese.*
"How brave the peasant who lives beside the lake." CoBLCP, *tr. by* Jonathan Chaves

Song of Cayetano's Circus, The, *tr. of Creole slave song.* George Washington Cable. APN-2

Song Of Chang Ching-Yüan Picking Lotus Flowers, A. Wen T'ing-yün, *Chinese.* LoP; SuSp, *tr. by* William R. Schultz

Song of Chess, The. Abraham ibn Ezra, *Hebrew.* TrJP, *tr. by* Nina Davis Salaman

Song of Chiang-nan. Tsung Ch'en, *Chinese.*
"On the spring river, you depart." CoBLCP, *tr. by* Jonathan Chaves

Song of Childbirth, The. *Unknown, Irish.* TIRV, *tr. by* Eleanor Hull

Song of Cove Creek Dam, The. *Unknown.* AmFP

Song of Creation. *Hopi Oral Tradition.* PaTW, *tr. by* Frank Waters

Song of Crede, The. *Unknown, Middle Irish.* BIrV, *tr. by* Alfred Perceval Graves

Song of Cricket. Hyonggi Yi, *Korean.* CKP, *tr. by* Jaihiun Kim

Song of Cursive Calligraphy. Hsieh Chin, *Chinese.* CoBLCP, *tr. by* Jonathan Chaves

Song of Dalliance, A. William Cartwright. NOSC

Song of Daphne to the Lute, A. John Lyly. *See* Daphne.

Song of Deborah, The. Bible, *O.T.* AWP; BoWoP; PBWP *Fr.* Judges.
(Then Sang Deborah and Barak.) TrJP
"Blessed above women/ shall Jael the wife of Heber the Kenite be." WPOW

Song of Delight. Shao Yung, *Chinese.* CoBCP, *tr. by* Burton Watson

Song of Derivations, A. Alice Thompson Meynell. CABP

Song of Devotion to the Forest, *after the pygmies of the Ituri Forest.* David Henderson. GT

Song of Distant Waters, A. Wen T'ing-yün, *Chinese.* SuSp, *tr. by* William R. Schultz

Song of Dust, A. John Byrne Leicester Warren. EnLoPo

Song of Emigration. Felicia Dorothea Hemans. VWP

Song of Emptiness to Fill up the Empty Pages Following, A. Michael Wigglesworth. SCAP

Song of Enitharmon. William Blake. OAEL-2 *Fr.* Vala; or The Four Zoas.

Song of Esechia, The. John Hall. ChIV-1

Song of Exile, A. Bible, *O.T. See* Psalm 137.

Song of Exile. Antônio Gonçalves Dias, *Portuguese.*
"There are palm trees in my homeland." TTY, *tr. by* Frances Ellen Buckland

Song of Expectancy. George Hitchcock. SPE

Song of Faith Forsworn, A. John Byrne Leicester Warren, 3d Baron De Tabley. PeVV

"Song of Farewell" in the Tartar Mode. Chang Yü, *Chinese.* SuSp, *tr. by* Irving Y. Lo

Song of Finis, The. Walter De la Mare. MoBrPo

Song of Fionnuala, The. Thomas Moore. BIrV

Song of Fixed Accord. Wallace Stevens. InPS-3; SAmP

Song of grass, A, / A song of earth. "Yehoash," *Yiddish.* TrJP, *tr. by* Isidore Goldstick

Song of Greatness, A. *Unknown, Chippewa.* ImGa, *tr. by* Mary Austin

Song of "Hand-in-Hand," A. Ou-yang Hsiu, *Chinese.* SuSp, *tr. by* Irving Y. Lo

Song of Hannah, The. Bible, *O.T. See* Hannah's Song of Thanksgiving.

Song of Hate. Jacob ben David Frances, *Hebrew.* TrJP, *tr. by* A. B. Rhine

Song of Hate for Eels. Arthur Guiterman. OBAL

Song of Heavenly Ascent. Ts'ao Chih, *Chinese.* SuSp, *tr. by* Ronald C. Miao

Song of Hiawatha, The. Henry Wadsworth Longfellow.
Hiawatha's Wooing. EBNV
Introduction: "Should you ask me, whence these stories?" ColAP; MeMAP; NOBA; PoE; Poetr
Picture-Writing. APN-1

Song of Honor [*or* Honour], The. Ralph Hodgson. MoBrPo

Song of Hope. Mary Artemisia Lathbury. BLPA

Song of Hsiang-yang. Li Po, *Chinese.* SuSp, *tr. by* Joseph J. Lee

Song of Hungarrda, The. Ngunaitponi. NOBAu

Song of Hybrias the Cretan. Hybrias The Cretan, *Greek.* OBCVT, *tr. by* Thomas Campbell

Song of Instruction, A. Te Kooti Rikirangi, *Maori.* PeNZ, *tr. by* Margaret Orbell

Song of Jed Smith, The. John Gneisenau Neihardt.
"One more rendezvous." FYAP

Song of Jehane du Castel Beau, The. William Morris. *Fr.* Golden Wings. OBNC

Song of Jonah in the Whale's Belly, The. Michael Drayton. ChIV-1

Song of Kai-hsia. Hsiang Chi, *Chinese.* SuSp, *tr. by* Ronald C. Miao

Song of Kuk-ook, the Bad Boy, The. *Eskimo Oral Tradition.* TTTS

Song of Lament, A. Ts'ao Chih, *Chinese.* SuSp, *tr. by* Hans H. Frankel

Song of Lazarus, The. Alex Comfort.
Notes for My Son. LiTM; MoBrPo

Song of Lewes, The. *Unknown.* OxBoLi

Song of Liang Chou. Ou-yang Hsiu, *Chinese.* OHPC, *tr. by* Kenneth Rexroth

Song of Liberty, A. William Blake. *Fr.* The Marriage of Heaven and Hell. NAEL-2; NOBRP; OAEL-2

Song of Lies, The. *Unknown, Irish.* CBNP, *tr. by* Donal O'Sullivan

Song of Lies on Sabbath Eve, A. Yehuda Amichai, *Hebrew.* PoSu, *tr. by* Chana Bloch

Song of Life, A. Franz Werfel, *German.* TrJP, *tr. by* Edith Abercrombie Snow

Song of Lin Liang's Painting "Two Horned Falcons." Li Meng-yang, *Chinese.* CoBLCP, *tr. by* Jonathan Chaves

Song of Lo-fu, The. *Unknown, Chinese.* AWP; ChiP, *tr. by* Arthur Waley

Song of Loneliness. Judah Halevi, *Hebrew.* TrJP, *tr. by* Nina Davis Salaman

Song of Love, The. Rilke, *German.* AWP, *tr. by* Ludwig Lewisohn

Song of Lung-hsi. Ch'en Tao, *Chinese.* CoBCP, *tr. by* Burton Watson

Song of Man Chipping an Arrowhead. W. S. Merwin. InPK-6

Song of Mary, A. Lucille Clifton. NALW

Song of Meeting. Tsung Ch'en, *Chinese.* CoBLCP, *tr. by* Jonathan Chaves

Song of Mehitabel, The. Don Marquis. OBCoV *Fr.* Archy and Mehitabel.

Song of Milkanwatha, The, *parody.* George A. Strong.
  Modern Hiawatha, The. EBEvV; OBCoV; PeLV; UV
  (Hiawatha Revisited.) BXAP

Song of Mr Toad, The. Kenneth Grahame. NOBL; NOxBChV *Fr.* The Wind in the Willows.

Song of My Song, in Three Parts, A. *Unknown, Seneca Indian.* STP, *tr. by* Jerome Rothenberg *and* Richard Johnny John

Song of Myself. Walt Whitman. AmPP; MoAmPo; NAAL-3; NCAP; NOBA; OxBA; PoPoPo; SAGP
  ("I celebrate myself, / And what I assume you shall assume.") HeIP-4
  (Myself.) FaBoBe
  ("Nature without check with original enery.") (LL) ColAP
  "All goes onward and outward, nothing collapses." IMW
  "All truths wait in all things." ColAP
  "Alone far in the wilds and mountains I hunt." SAmP
  "And as to you Death, and you bitter hug of mortality, it is idle to try to alarm." ColAP
  Animals. ImPo
    ("I think I could turn and live with animals, they're so placid and self- / contain'd.") PFE
  Battle of the *Bonhomme Richard* and the *Serapis.* RB; UnPo, *sect.* XXXV-XXXVI
    (Old-Time Sea-Fight, An.)
    ("Stretch'd and still lies the midnight.") ColAP
  "Big doors of the country barn stand open and ready, The." ColAP
  "Dazzling and tremendous how quick the sun-rise would kill me." ColAP
  "Did you read in the seabooks of the oldfashioned frigate-fight?" PAR
  "Gigantic beauty of a stallion, fresh and responsive to my caresses, A." ImGa
  Grass. ImPo
    ("Child said *What is the grass?*, A.") ImPo; SAmP
  Has Any One Supposed It Lucky to Be Born?
  "Houses and rooms are full of perfumes." EBEvV; UnPo
    ("Houses and rooms are full of perfumes, the shelves are crowded with perfumes.") ColAP
  Hub of the Universe, The. ImPo
  "I am of old and young, of the foolish as much as the wise." ImGa
  "I am the poet of the Body and I am the poet of the Soul." ColAP; WeW-3
  "I am the teacher of athletes." ColAP
  "I believe a leaf of grass is no less than the journey-work of the stars." ColAP; SAmP
    ("Boiling her iron tea-kettle and baking shortcake.") (LL) PAR
    ("I believe a leaf of grass is no less than the journeywork of the stars.") PAR
    ("I follow quickly, I ascend to the nest in the fissure of the cliff.") (LL) ColAP
  "I believe in you my soul, the other I am must not abase itself to you." APAD; ColAP; PAR
    ("And elder and mullen and pokeweed.") (LL) PAR
  Swiftly Arose. TrCP
    ("I celebrate myself.") APN-1
  "I have heard what the talkers were talking, the talk of the beginning and the end." ColAP
    ("Exactly the contents of one, and exactly the contents of two, and which is / ahead?") (LL) PAR
    ("I have heard what the talkers were talking.. . . the talk of the beginning.") PAR
  "I have said that the soul is not more than the body." ColAP
    (Leaves of Grass (1855).) APN-1
  "Little one sleeps in its cradle, The." SAmP
    ("Has any one supposed it lucky to be born?") ColAP
    ("I mind them or the show or resonance of them—I come and I depart.") (LL) PAR
  "Now I will do nothing but listen." HoPM; SAmP
  "Past and present wilt—I have fill'd them, emptied them, The." ColAP
    ("Past and present wilt.. . . I have filled them and emptied them, The.") PAR
  Song of Myself. NCAP; PoPoPo; SAGP
    ("I celebrate myself, / And what I assume you shall assume.") HeIP-4
    (Myself.) FaBoBe

("Nature without check with original enery.") (LL) ColAP

Song of Myself [15]. FaBoA

"Spotted hawk swoops by and accuses me, The." SAmP
  ("Spotten hawk swoops by and accuses me, he complains of my gab and my, The.") ColAP

"Swift wind! Space! My Soul! Now I know it is true what I guessed at." PAR

"There is that in me.. . . I do not know what it is.. . . but I know it is in me." ColAP; PAR
  ("It is eternal life.. . . it is happiness.") (LL) PAR

"Trippers and askers surround me." ColAP; EnlH; PAR; UnPo

"Twenty-eight young men bathe by the shore." ColAP; HAP; NoP-4; PAR; SAmP

Walt Whitman. NoAM
  ("I know I have the best of time and space, and was never measured and never.") ColAP
  ("Laughingly dash with your hair.") (LL) ColAP

"Walt Whitman, a kosmos, of Manhattan the son." ColAP; NoP-4; SAmP; SCV

"Walt Whitman, an American, one of the roughs, a kosmos." PAR

"Who goes there! hankering, gross, mystical, nude?" ColAP; PAR
  ("I laugh at what you call dissolution, / And I know the amplitude of time.") (LL) PAR

"Wild gander leads his flock through the cool night, The." ColAP

"You sea! I resign myself to you also—I guess what you mean." OxBoS

Song of Napalm. Bruce Weigl. CDa

Song of Nature. Ralph Waldo Emerson. APN-1

Song of "Night After Night," A. Ou-yang Hsiu, *Chinese.* SuSp, *tr. by* Irving Y. Lo

Song of Nü' LmaL, La' Lasiqoala. *Unknown. Fr.* Dances and Songs of the Winter Ceremonial. APN-2, *tr. by* Franz Boas

Song of Nu-Numma-Kwiten, The. *Unknown, Bushman.* PeSA

Song of Obstacles. Louise Glück. LW *Fr.* Marathon.

Song of One Eleven Years in Prison. George Canning, George Ellis, *and* John Hookham Frere. *See* Rogero's Song.

Song of One of the Girls. Dorothy Parker. NALW

Song of Ophelia the Survivor. Anna Wickham. WPN

Song of Pajaro. Jeff Tagami. OpBo

Song of Parable, A. *Unknown, Chinese.* SuSp, *tr. by* Jan W. Walls

Song of Parents Who Want to Wake Up Their Son. *Unknown, Kwakiutl.* TTTS

Song of Peach Blossom Retreat. T'ang Yin, *Chinese.* CoBLCP, *tr. by* Jonathan Chaves

Song of P'eng-ya. Tu Fu, *Chinese.* CoBCP, *tr. by* Burton Watson

Song of Picking Mulberry ("Ten years ago I was a visitor at the wine jar"). Ou-yang Hsiu, *Chinese.* CoBCP, *tr. by* Burton Watson

Song of Quavering, A. Jerome Rothenberg. FTOS

Song of Reasons. Robert Pinsky. HCAP

Song of Regret. Pan Chieh-yû, *Chinese.* CoBCP, *tr. by* Burton Watson

Song of Resignation. Yehuda Amichai, *Hebrew.* NYBP, *tr. by* Assia Gutmann

Song of Roland, The. *Unknown, Old French.* NAWM-1, *tr. by* Frederick Goldin, *abr.*
  "In wrath and grief away the Paynims fly." OBWP, *tr. by* Dorothy L. Sayers

Song of Samuel Sweet, The. Charles Causley. OBNV

Song of Saul before His Last Battle. Byron. ChIV-1

Song of Selling Flowers. Tsung Ch'en, *Chinese.* CoBLCP, *tr. by* Jonathan Chaves

Song of Seyd [*or* Seid] Nimetollah of Kuhistan. Seid Nimatullah, *Persian.* NOBA

Song of shadows: never glory was, A. Shadows. Victor Gustave Plarr. NOBVV

Song of Shem. James Philip McAuley. ChIV-1 *Fr.* The Family of Love.

Song of Sixpence. *Unknown. See* Sing a Song of Sixpence.

Song of Slaves in the Desert. John Greenleaf Whittier. APN-1; OxBA

Song of Snow-white Heads. Chuo Wen-chün. BoWoP, *tr. by* Arthur Waley

Song of Solomon, The. Bible, *O.T. See also* The Song of Songs.
  Song: "At night on my bed I longed for." WPoS, *tr. by* Chana Bloch *and* Ariel Bloch
  Song: "Come, my beloved." WPoS, *tr. by* Chana Bloch *and* Ariel Bloch
  Song: "I am dark, daughters of Jerusalem." WPoS, *tr. by* Chana Bloch *and* Ariel Bloch

Song of Solomon, The. OBGa
  "Voice of my beloved! behold, he cometh leaping, The." PiM

Song of Songs, The. Bible, *O.T.* AWP

Song of Songs. Bible, *O.T.* AWP
  As a Seal upon Thy Heart. BoWoP, *tr. by* Willis Barnstone; TrJP

"Awake! Oh, north wind."

"Behold, thou art fair." OxBM; TrJP

"Hark! My beloved!" TrJP

("Voice of my beloved, The.") PBMP

"I am come into my garden, my sister, my spouse." OBVE; TOF

I Am My Beloved's. BoWoP, tr. by Willis Barnstone; TrJP

"I am the rose of Sharon, and the lily of the valleys." BoLoP; GBL; OBVE

I Sleep, but My Heart Waketh. BoWoP, tr. by Willis Barnstone; TrJP

"My beloved spake, and said unto me, Rise up, my love." OPOU

"My love has gone down to his garden." BoWoP, tr. by Willis Barnstone

"My love is white and ruddy." BoWoP, tr. by Willis Barnstone

("I am come into my garden, my sister, my spouse: I have gathered my.") APAD

("Is my friend, O daughters of Jerusalem.") (LL) APAD

On My Bed I Sought Him. TrJP

("In my bed at night.") BoWoP, tr. by Willis Barnstone

Return, Return, O Shulammite. TrJP

Song of Songs. OPOU

"Song of songs, which is Solomon's, The." OBVE

"Turning to him, who meets me with desire." PBWP, tr. by Marcia Falk

"Under the quince tree." PBWP, tr. by Marcia Falk

"Yes, I am black! and radiant." PBWP, tr. by Marcia Falk

Song of Songs. Yelena Kryukova, Russian. TCRP, tr. by Albert C. Todd

Song of Songs, 7. Unknown. NNPT, tr. by Unknown

Song of Sorrow. Unknown, Chinese. CoBCP, tr. by Burton Watson

Song of Sorrow Inside the Royal Harem, A. Nguyễn Gia Thiều, Vietnamese. AVP, tr. by Huỳnh Sanh Thông

Song of Spring. Keats. BoTP

Song of Spring. Wu Chün, Chinese. CoBCP, tr. by Burton Watson

Song of Spring at West Lake, A, Sent to Circuit Officer Hsieh. Ou-yang Hsiu, Chinese. SuSp, tr. by Irving Y. Lo

Song of Spring Journeying. Wang Ya, Chinese. SuSp, tr. by Irving Y. Lo

Song of Spring Replying to a Poem by Po Chü-yi, A. Liu Yü Hsi, Chinese. SuSp, tr. by Daniel Bryant and Ronald C. Miao

Song of Starvation. Unknown, Chippewa. STP, tr. by Jerome Rothenberg

Song of Summer. Paul Laurence Dunbar. APN-2

Song of Summer Days. James William Foley. BoTP

Song of Supplication, A. Bible, O.T. See Psalm 130.

Song of Surfing on the Bore. Cheng Hsieh, Chinese. CoBLCP, tr. by Jonathan Chaves

Song of the Aged Mother which shook the heavens with wrath, The. Vala; or The Four Zoas. William Blake.

Song of the Air, A. Gordon Alchin. NSI

Song of the Andoumboulou. Nathaniel Mackey. NAAAL

Song of the Andoumboulou: 12. Nathaniel Mackey. FTOS

Song of the Andoumboulou: 6. Nathaniel Mackey. FTOS

Song of the Andoumboulou: 7. Nathaniel Mackey. FTOS

Song of the Angels. Lizelia Augusta Jenkins Moorer. CBWP-3

Song of the Autumn Wind. Emperor Wu of Han, Chinese. CoBCP, tr. by Burton Watson

Song of the Bald Eagle. Unknown. APN-2; STP Fr. Minnetare Songs.

Song of the Banana Man, The. Evan Jones. PBCV

Song of the Banjo, The. Rudyard Kipling. FaBoCh

Song of the Bath, The. Margaret E. Gibbs. BoTP

Song of the Bay Steed of Governor Wei, A. Ts'en Shen, Chinese. SuSp, tr. by Daniel Bryant

Song of the Bear. Unknown. APN-2 Fr. Minnetare Songs.

Song of the Beasts (Sung, on one night, in the cities, in the darkness), The. Rupert Brooke. APo

Song of the Beautiful Ladies. Tu Fu, Chinese. CoBCP, tr. by Burton Watson

Song of the Beggars. W. H. Auden. PeLV Fr. Twelve Songs.

Song of the Bird, The. Henry Wadsworth Longfellow. BoTP

Song of the Black Bear, The. Unknown, Navajo. RaBo

Song of the Boat-Pullers. Pien Kung, Chinese. CoBLCP, tr. by Jonathan Chaves

Song of the Boatswain of Yüeh. Unknown, Chinese. SuSp, tr. by Irving Y. Lo

Song of the Borderguard, The. Robert Duncan. NeAP; PoM

Song of the Bounder, The. Edgar Wallace. PeSAV

Song of the Bowmen of Shu. Ezra Pound, after the Chinese. OBVE

Song of the boy who was brave and fair, The. The Song of the Happy Warrior. Donald S. Cox. NSI

Song of the Breaking of the Willow. Unknown, Chinese. CoBCP, tr. by Burton Watson

Song of the Breed. Carroll Arnett. LTA

Song of the Brightness of Water. Karol Wojtyla. CRP

Song of the Broad-Axe. Walt Whitman. CA

(Song of the Broad-Axe [or Broad-Ax].)

("Weapon shapely, naked, wan.")

Song of the Broad-Axe [or Broad-Ax]. Walt Whitman. See Song of the Broad-Axe.

Broad-Ax, The. MoAmPo

"Place where a great city stands is not the place of stretch'd wharves, docks, The." ImGa

Song of the Bush-Shrike. Unknown, Zulu. PeSA

Song of the Camel, The. Charles Edward Carryl. See The Camel's Complaint.

Song of the Cannibals, A. Anne Finch, Countess of Winchilsea. PoE

Song of the Cat, The. Tristan Klingsor, French. PC, tr. by Felicity Bast

Song of the Chattahoochee. Sidney Lanier. APN-2; ColAP; FaBoBe

Song of the Ch'in-Dynasty Mirror—Written for Yüan Sung-li. Wang Shih-chieng, Chinese. CoBLCP, tr. by Jonathan Chaves

Song of the Clear River. Huang T'ing-chien, Chinese. CoBCP, tr. by Burton Watson

Song of the Clouds. Aristophanes. AWP, tr. by Oscar Wilde Fr. The Clouds.

("Cloud-maidens that float on for ever.") OBCVT, tr. by Oscar Wilde

Song of the Corn. James Edwin Campbell. AAP

Song of the Crab Medicine-Bag. Unknown, Chippewa. STP, tr. by Jerome Rothenberg

Song of the Cricket. Lo Fu, Chinese. ChiPo, tr. by Dominic Cheng

Song of the Crow Pecking at My Scarred Donkey. Wang Yü-ch'eng, Chinese. SuSp, tr. by Jonathan Chaves

Song of the Cuban Blacks. Federico García Lorca, Spanish. RaBo, tr. by Robert Bly

Song of the Decanter. Alfred Gibbs Campbell. AAP

Song of the Desert. Eliza R. Snow. PaTW

Song of the Dew. Unknown, Hebrew. TrJP, tr. by Solomon Solis-Cohen

Song of the Duck Hunters. Kao Ch'i, Chinese. CoBLCP, tr. by Jonathan Chaves

Song of the Dying Gunner A.A.1. Charles Causley. PoWW

Song of the Elk. Unknown. APN-2 Fr. Minnetare Songs.

Song of the Emigrants in Bermuda. Andrew Marvell. See Bermudas.

Song of the Engine, The. H. Worsley-Benison. BoTP

Song of the Eternal Sailor, The. Slavko Janevski, Macedonian. CEEP, tr. by Vasa D. Mihailovich

Song of the Exposition. Walt Whitman.

Muse in the New World, The. MoAmPo

Song of the Faithful. Michael Drayton. ChIV-1

Song of the Fallen Deer. Unknown, Pima. NNPT; OBVE, tr. by Frank Russell

Song of the Field. Jan Bolesw Ozog, Polish. CEEP, tr. by Leonard Kress

Song of the Fire-Charm. Unknown, Chippewa. STP, tr. by Frances Densmore; English vers. by Jerome Rothenberg

Song of the Flea. Judah Al-Harizi, Hebrew. TrJP

Song of the Flood. Unknown, Navajo. TTTS

Song of the flute, O sister, is madness, The. Mirabai, Indian. WPoS, tr. by Jane Hirshfield

Song of the Freedman. Unknown. PBMP

Song of the Fucked Duck. Marge Piercy. BoWoP; LW

("With a pocketful of words and plastic tokens.") (LL) LW

Song of the Galley, The. Unknown, Spanish. AWP, tr. by John Gibson Lockhart

Song of the Galley-Slaves. Rudyard Kipling. GTBS-P; HAP; NTP; PoEL-5; SCGP

Song of the Ghost Dancer of the La' Lasiqoala, A. Unknown. Fr. Dances and Songs of the Winter Ceremonial. APN-2, tr. by Franz Boas

Song of the Good Samaritan, The. Vernon Watkins. LiTM

Song of the GPO, A. Gerry Hamill. NOBL

Song of the Grass, The. Leigh Hunt. BoTP

Song of the Graves, The. Unknown. OBMV, tr. by Ernest Rhys Fr. The Black Book of Carmarthen.

Song of the Great Wind. Liu Pang, Chinese. SuSp, tr. by Ronald C. Miao

Song of the Gun. Unknown. APN-2 Fr. Minnetare Songs.

Song of the Hanged. Eléni Vakaló, Modern Greek. PBWP, tr. by James Damaskos

Song of the Happy Shepherd, The. W. B. Yeats. NoAM

Song of the Happy Warrior, The. Donald S. Cox. NSI

Song of the Harlot. Bible, O.T. TrJP Fr. Isaiah.

Song of the Hat-Raising Doll. John Mole. OBCoV Fr. Penny Toys.

Song of the Highest Tower. Rimbaud, French. AWP, tr. by Edgell Rickword

Song of the Horse. Unknown, Navajo. AWP, tr. by Natalie Curtis Burlin

Song of the Ia′ kĭm. *Unknown. Fr.* Dances and Songs of the Winter Ceremonial. APN-2, *tr. by* Franz Boas

Song of the Ill-Married. *Unknown, French.* BoWoP, *tr. by* Patricia Terry

Song of the Imprisoned Bird. Eliza Cook. VWP

Song of the Indian Maid, The ("Beneath my palm-trees, by the riverside"). Keats. NOBE; OBEV *Fr.* Endymion: Poetic Romance.

Song of the Indian Wars, The. John Gneisenau Neihardt.

"III. THE COUNCIL ON THE POWDER." PaTW

"Summer turned." GM

Song of the Initiate. Patrice Kayo. PBMAP

Song of the Initiate. Léopold Sédar Senghor, *French.* NegPo, *tr. by* Ellen Conroy Kennedy VCWP, *tr. by* Melvin Dixon

Song of the Jellicles, The. T. S. Eliot. EBEvV; FaBoCh; ImGa; OxBChV

Song of the Juggler. Herberto Padilla, *Spanish.* AF, *tr. by* Alastair Reid

Song of the King of the Eboes. *Unknown.* PBCV

Song of the last soldier, A. Meir Wieseltier, *Hebrew.* IP, *tr. by* Bargad, Warren *and* Stanley Chyet

Song of the Lenape Warriors Going against the Enemy, The. *Unknown, Delaware.* APN-2, *tr. by* John Heckwelder

Song of the Lioness for Her Cub. *Unknown, Hottentot.* BoWoP, *tr. by* Thomas Hahn

Song of the Lonely Shepherd. Anna Wickham. WPN

Song of the Lotus-Eaters. Tennyson. NOBE; OBEV *Fr.* The Lotus-Eaters. EnVR; NAEL-2; OAEL-2; PoEL-5; SCGP

(Choric Song.) HeIP-4; OBNC

(Choric Song of the Lotus-Eaters.)

Song of the Love of Jesus, A. Richard Rolle of Hampole.

Love is Life. PoEL-1

Song of the Low, The. Ernest Charles Jones. NOBVV

Song of the Lute. Po Chü-i, *Chinese.* CoBCP, *tr. by* Burton Watson

Song of the Mad Prince, The. Walter De la Mare. EBEV; FaBoCh; MoP; NOBE; NTP; NoAM; OxAEP-2; OxBChV

Song of the Maidens. Yüan Hao-wen, *Chinese.* SuSp, *tr. by* Stephen West

Song of the Man of Green Hill, The. Kao Ch'i, *Chinese.* CoBLCP, *tr. by* Jonathan Chaves

Song of the Man Who Succeeded. *Unknown, Chippewa.* STP, *tr. by* Jerome Rothenberg *from* Frances Densmore

Song of the Maverick. Mary Austin. PaTW

Song of the Mayers [*or* The Mayers' Song]. *Unknown.* CH

Song of the Men of Chin-ling. Hsieh T'iao, *Chinese.* ChiP, *tr. by* Arthur Waley

Song of the Merchant's Wife. Yang Shih-ch'i, *Chinese.* CoBLCP, *tr. by* Jonathan Chaves

Song of the Militant Romance, The. Percy Wyndham Lewis. FaBoTw; OxBTC

Song of the Mischievous Dog, The. Dylan Thomas. OBCoV

Song of the Mock Turtle, The. "Lewis Carroll." UV *Fr.* Alice's Adventures in Wonderland.

Song of the Modern Time. Eliza Cook. VWP

Song of the Moderns. John Gould Fletcher. AWP

Song of the Moon. Priscilla Jane Thompson. CBWP-2

Song of the Narcissus, The. *Unknown.* AWP *Fr.* The Thousand and One Nights.

Song of the Night at Daybreak. Alice Thompson Meynell. CH

Song of the Oktahutchee. Alexander L. Posey. APN-2

Song of the Old Man of the Hills. Meng Chiao, *Chinese.* PLT, *tr. by* A. C. Graham

Song of the Old Mother, The. W. B. Yeats. MoBrPo

Song of the Old Oak. Chang Yü, *Chinese.* CoBLCP, *tr. by* Jonathan Chaves

Song of the Old Woman. *Unknown, Eskimo in French.* BoWoP, *tr. by* Paul-Emile Victor; *English vers. by* Armand Schwerner

Song of the Open Road. Ogden Nash. EBEvV; OBAL

Song of the Open Road, A. *Unknown, Latin.* AWP, *tr. by* John Addington Symonds

Song of the Open Road. Walt Whitman. NOBA

Song of the Owl, The. Richard Kendall Munkittrick. OBCA

Song of the Owl. *Unknown, Ojibwa.* APN-2, *tr. by* Henry Wadsworth Longfellow

Song of the Painting "Catching Fish." Li Tung-yang, *Chinese.* CoBLCP, *tr. by* Jonathan Chaves

Song of the Painting of the Long-Life Star. Wang Chiu-ssu, *Chinese.* CoBLCP, *tr. by* Jonathan Chaves

Song of the Painting "River and Mountains," by Wu Wei. Ho Ching-ming, *Chinese.* CoBLCP, *tr. by* Jonathan Chaves

Song of the Pen, The. Judah Al-Harizi, *Hebrew.* TrJP, *tr. by* J. Chotzner

Song of the Pheasant. *Unknown.* APN-2 *Fr.* Minnetare Songs.

Song of the pines. Po Chü-i, *Chinese.* TAL, *tr. by* Robert Payne

Song of the Poor Man. *Unknown.* TTY, *tr. by* Anselm Hollo

Song of the Pop-Bottlers. Morris Gilbert Bishop. KaS

Song of the Promise of the Buffalo. *Unknown.* APN-2, *tr. by* Alice C. Fletcher *Fr.* The Hako.

Song of the Prophet. *Unknown.* APN-2, *tr. by* Washington Matthews *Fr.* The Mountain Chant.

Song of the Queen Bee. Elwyn Brooks White. NYBP

Song of the Rabbits outside the Tavern, The. Elizabeth Jane Coatsworth. OBCA; SoSe-8

Song of the Radiant Lady. Wang An-shih, *Chinese.* SuSp, *tr. by* Jan W. Walls

Song of the Radiant Lady, Replying to a Poem by Wang Chieh-fu. Ou-yang Hsiu, *Chinese.* SuSp, *tr. by* Irving Y. Lo

Song of the Rain. Hugh Raymond McCrae. CBAP

Song of the Rain Chant. *Unknown, Navajo.* AWP, *tr. by* Natalie Curtis Burlin

Song of the Rear Palace. Po Chü-i, *Chinese.* SuSp, *tr. by* Ronald C. Miao

Song of the Red & Green Buffalo, A. *Unknown, Oto.* STP, *tr. by* William Whitman

Song of the Redwood-Tree. Walt Whitman. AmPP

Song of the Reed Sparrow, The. *Unknown.* OxBChV

Song of the Reim-Kennar, The. Sir Walter Scott. OAEL-2; OBNC *Fr.* The Pirate.

Song of the Rejected Woman. Kibkarjuk, *Eskimo into Danish.* WPOW, *tr. by* Knud Rasmussen; *English vers. by* Tom Lowenstein

Song of the Riders. Stephen Vincent Benét. MoAmPo *Fr.* John Brown's Body.

Song of the Rising Sun Dance. *Unknown.* APN-2, *tr. by* Washington Matthews *Fr.* The Mountain Chant.

Song of the Running Horse River, A: Presented on Seeing General Feng Off on a Campaign to the West. Ts'en Shen, *Chinese.* SuSp, *tr. by* Daniel Bryant

Song of the Rushlight. Eliza Cook. VWP

Song of the Sabbath. Kadya Molodovsky, *Yiddish.* PBWP; WPOW, *tr. by* Jean Valentine

Song of the Sacred Strings. Li Ho, *Chinese.* CoBCP, *tr. by* Burton Watson

Song of the Sad Guitar. Marilyn Chin. WWSi

Song of the Seeress. *Unknown, Norse.* NAWM-1, *tr. by* Paul B. Taylor *and* W. H. Auden

Song of the Self-Made Orphans. David Avidan, *Hebrew.* IP, *tr. by* Warren Bargad *and* Stanley F. Chyet

Song of the Shadows, The. Walter De la Mare. CMoP; MoBrPo

Song of the Sheet. *Unknown.* BXAP

Song of the Shirt, The. Thomas Hood. EBEvV; EBVV; FaPoR

Song of the Silent Land. Johann Gaudenz von Salis-Seewis, *German.* AWP, *tr. by* Longfellow

Song of the Sky Loom. *Tewa Oral Tradition.* PaTW, *tr. by* Herbert J. Spinden

Song of the Smoke, The. W. E. B. DuBois. ISC; NAAAL; PoBA; SSLK; UnPo

("I am black.") (LL) NAAAL

Song of the snails on their way to a funeral. Jacques Prévert, *French.* MFP, *tr. by* Martin Sorrell

Song of the Snow. Zalman Schneour, *Hebrew.* MHP, *tr. by* Ruth Finer Mintz

Song of the Snow-white Heads. *Unknown, Chinese.* ChiP, *tr. by* Arthur Waley

Song of the Son. Jean Toomer. CrDW; ISC; NIP-4; PoBA

Song of the Soul That Knows [*or* Rejoices in Knowing] God by Faith. Saint John of the Cross, *Spanish.* TIRV, *tr. by* Seamus Heaney; TOF, *tr. by* K. Kavanaugh *and* O. Rodrigues

Song of the spheres in their revolutions, The. Jelaluddin Rumi, *Persian.* TOF, *tr. by* E. H. Whinfield

Song of the Springbok Does. *Unknown, Hottentot.* PeSA, *tr. by* W. H. I. Bleek

Song of the Stars, The. *Unknown, Passamaquoddy.* APN-2, *tr. by* Charles Godfrey Leland

Song of the Stormy Petrel. "Maksim Gorky," *Russian.* TCRP, *tr. by* Albert C. Todd

Song of the Stricken Twins. *Unknown. Fr.* The Night Chant. APN-2, *tr. by* Washington Matthews

Song of the Stygian Naiades. Thomas Lovell Beddoes. OAEL-2

Song of The Suffering Servant, The. Bible, *O.T.* NAWM-1 *Fr.* Isaiah.

Song of the Syrens. William Browne. See The Sirens' Song.

Song of the Taste. Gary Snyder. LCAP-2

Song of the Third Generation. Julia Lisella. UnSA

Song of the Thoroughfare. Hsieh Shang, *Chinese.* CoBCP, *tr. by* Burton Watson

Song of the Thunder. *Unknown, Hottentot.* PeSA

Song of the Thunders. *Unknown, Chippewa.* OBVE, *tr. by* Frances Densmore

Song of the Tortured Girl, The. John Berryman. CoAP

Song of the Train. David McCord. NTCP

Song of the Transport Workers—Seeing Off Fang Wen-yü on His Way to His Post as Inspector of Transportation. Pien Kung, *Chinese.* CoBLCP, *tr. by* Jonathan Chaves

Song of the Transportationist, The. *Unknown.* NOBAu

Song of the Traveler at Evening. Goethe, *German.* STV, *tr. by* John Frederick Nims

Song of the Trees. *Unknown, Chippewa.* OBVE, *tr. by* Frances Densmore

Song of the Ts'ē'k'ois, A. *Unknown. Fr.* Dances and Songs of the Winter Ceremonial. APN-2, *tr. by* Franz Boas

Song of the Turkey Buzzard. Lew Welch. BB; PoM

("Praises, Tamalpais, / Perfect in Wisdom and Beauty.") BB

Song of the Ugly Maiden. Eliza Cook. VWP

Song of the Ungirt Runners, The. Charles Hamilton Sorley. MoBrPo; OBEV

Song of the Unloved. *Unknown, Sotho.* PeSA, *tr. by* Jack Cope *and* Dan Kunene

Song of the Vermeil Phoenix. Tu Fu, *Chinese.* TAL, *tr. by* Robert Payne

Song of the Virgin Mary, The. Miles Coverdale. ChIV-2

Song of the Virgin Mother, A. Félix Lope de Vega Carpio, *Spanish.* AWP, *tr. by* Ezra Pound

Song of the Wagon-whip, A. Samuel Cron Cronwright. PeSAV

Song of the Wanderer. Wang T'ing-hsiang, *Chinese.* CoBLCP, *tr. by* Jonathan Chaves

Song of the Wandering Ængus, The. W. B. Yeats. *See* The Song Of Wandering Aengus.

Song of the Waterfall at Mount Lu. Yang Wei-chen, *Chinese.* CoBLCP, *tr. by* Jonathan Chaves

Song of the Weasel. *Unknown.* APN-2 *Fr.* Minnetare Songs.

Song of the Weaving Woman. Yüan Chen, *Chinese.* SuSp, *tr. by* Wu-chi Liu

Song of the Well. Bible, *O.T.* TrJP *Fr.* Numbers.

Song of the Western Men, The. Robert Stephen Hawker. EBEvV; FaPoR; OBNC

(And Shall Trelawny Die?) OxAEP-2

Song of the Whirlwind. Fenton Johnson. NAAAL

Song of the White Man. *Unknown.* APN-2 *Fr.* Minnetare Songs.

Song of the White Snow: Saying Farewell to Supervisor Wu Returning to the Capital. Ts'en Shen, *Chinese.* SuSp, *tr. by* C. H. Wang

Song of the Wind and the Rain. Solomon ibn Gabirol, *Hebrew.* TrJP, *tr. by* Solomon Solis-Cohen

Song of the Witches. Shakespeare. *Fr.* Thrice the Brinded Cat Hath Mewed. RB *Fr.* Macbeth.

Song of the Woman, The. *Unknown.* TIRV *Fr.* The Voyage of Bran.

Song of the Woman with Her Parts Coming Out, The. Susan Griffin. GLP

Song of the Woodcutter of the Sea. Pien Kung, *Chinese.* CoBLCP, *tr. by* Jonathan Chaves

Song of the Yellow Cedar Face, A. George Clutesi. HATNAP

Song of the Zambra Dance. Dryden. PoEL-3 *Fr.* The Conquest of Granada.

Song of Those Who Died, A. Donald McDonald. PBCV

Song of Three Smiles. W. S. Merwin. CoAP; NOBA; VGW

Song of Tiadatha, The. Owen Rutter.

"In this war the Hun has brought us." NSI

Rumour. NSI

Salonika Campaign. NSI

Trenches. NSI

Song of Troylus, The. Chaucer. AWP *Fr.* Troilus and Criseyde [*or* Criseide]. EnVB

("For hoot of cold, for cold of hoot I die.") (LL) NoP-4

("If no love is, O God, what feele I so?") NoP-4

Song of Tzu-yeh. *Unknown, Chinese.* SuSp, *tr. by* Ronald C. Miao

Song of Ullikummi, The. Charles Olson. PFTM

Song of Venus. Dryden. OxBoLi; PoEL-3 *Fr.* King Arthur.

Song Of Wandering Aengus, The. W. B. Yeats. ADE; APAD; CH; CMoP; ChAP; FaBoCh; MoBrPo; NTP; OTCP; PBMP; PoEL-5; PoRA; RaBo; TFi; TTTS

(Song of the Wandering Ængus, The.) SAGP

Song of War. Kofi Awoonor. *See* Songs of Sorrow.

Song of War, A. Li Po, *Chinese.* TAL, *tr. by* Robert Payne

Song of Wildfire, A. Wen T'ing-yün, *Chinese.* SuSp, *tr. by* William R. Schultz

Song of Winter, A. Emily Jane Pfeiffer. OBWVE

Song of Winter, A. *Unknown, Middle Irish.* CH, *tr. by* Kuno Meyer

Song of Woe. Shen Yüeh, *Chinese.* SuSp, *tr. by* Richard B. Mather

Song of Words. Konstantin Konstantinovich Vaginov, *Russian.* TCRP, *tr. by* Nina Kossman

Song of Wu-ch'eng. Wang T'ing-hsiang, *Chinese.*

"Don't ask about the Six Dynasties of the Sui Palace." CoBLCP, *tr. by* Jonathan Chaves

Song of Yearning, A. Kohine Whakarua Ponika, *Maori.* PeNZ, *tr. by the author*

Song of Yen. Kao Shih, *Chinese.* SuSp, *tr. by* Joseph J. Lee

Song of Yen. Ts'ao P'i, *Chinese.* SuSp, *tr. by* Ronald C. Miao

Song on Being Too Lazy to Get Up. Shao Yung, *Chinese.* CoBCP, *tr. by* Burton Watson

Song on Climbing the Gate Tower at Yu-chou, A. Ch'en Tzu-ang, *Chinese.* SuSp, *tr. by* Wu-Chi Liu

(Song on Climbing Yu-chou Gate Tower.) CoBCP, *tr. by* Burton Watson

Song on Enduring the Cold. Ts'ao Ts'ao, *Chinese.* CoBCP, *tr. by* Burton Watson

Song: on [*or* of] May Morning. Milton. CH; PBRV

Song (On Seeing Dead Bodies Floating Off the Cape). Alun Lewis. LiTM; NAEL-2; NoP-4; OBWP

Song on the River of Perfumes, The. Tô Hū'u, *Vietnamese.* AVP, *tr. by* Huỳnh Sanh Thông

Song on the South Sea, A. Anne Finch. ECWP; NOEC

Song on the Water. Thomas Lovell Beddoes. FaBoCh *Fr.* Death's Jest Book.

Song on the Way to Jail. Kakayek, *Tlingit.* STP, *tr. by* James Koller

Song Out of Season, A. May Probyn. VWP

Song: Persuasions to Enjoy. Thomas Carew. *See* Persuasions to Enjoy.

Song Set by John Farmer. *Unknown.* CTC; NoSic

Song: So Often, So Long I Have Thought. Hayden Carruth. AFr

Song Sung by Egistus and Clytemnestra. John Pickering. NoSic *Fr.* Horestes.

Song Taught to Joseph, The. Ray A. Young Bear. AF

Song that I'm going to sing, The. The Crafty Farmer. *Unknown.* ESPR

Song that she sang was all written, The. The Moon of Mobile. Thomas Holley Chivers. OBAL

Song. That Women Are But Men's Shadows. Ben Jonson. BeJo; OxBSP; SeCP

(Shadow, The.) NOBE; OBEV

Song the First. *Unknown. Fr.* Two Cherokee Songs of Friendship. APN-2, *tr. by* Samuel L. Mitchill

Song: The Railway Train. *Unknown.* NOBAu, *tr. by* George Taplin

Song the Second. *Unknown. Fr.* Two Cherokee Songs of Friendship. APN-2, *tr. by* Samuel L. Mitchill

Song: The Willing Prisoner to His Mistress. Thomas Carew. CaPo

Song Thirty-Four. Mudrooroo. BMAP *Fr.* The Song Cycle of Jacky.

Song, 'tis my will that thou do seek out Love. Dante. AWP *Fr.* La Vita Nuova.

Song to a Fair Young Lady, Going Out of the Town in the Spring. Dryden. OBEV

Song to a Lover. *Unknown, Amharic.* BoWoP, *tr. by* Willis Barnstone

Song to a Lover. *Unknown, Amharic.* BoWoP, *tr. by* Willis Barnstone

Song to a Lute, A. Sir John Suckling. BeJo; CaPo

(Song: "Hast thou seen the down i' th' air.") EnLoPo

Song: To Amarantha, That She Would Dishevel Her Hair. Richard Lovelace. *See* To Amarantha, That She Would Dishevel[l] Her Hair[e].

Song to be Shouted Out. Nissim Ezekiel. OBCoV *Fr.* Songs for Nandu Bhende.

Song to Be Sung by the Father of Infant Female Children. Ogden Nash. MoAmPo

Song to Be Written on a Wave. José Emilio Pacheco, *Spanish.* STV, *tr. by* John Frederick Nims

Song to Celia. Catullus. *See* Carmen 5 ("My sweetest Lesbia, let us live and love").

Song. To Celia ("Come my Celia, let us prove"). Ben Jonson. BeJo; OAEL-1 *Fr.* Volpone. NAEL-1 *See also* To the Same [Celia].

(Carmina V [To Celia].) OBVE

(Song.) PFE

("These have crimes accounted been.") (LL) AEP; FMP; NoP-4; PFE; PoPoPo

(To Celia.) FMP; OxAEP-1

Song to David, A. Christopher Smart. ImPo; NAEL-1; NOBE; OAEL-1; OBWVE; PoE; PoEL-3

David's Song to Saul. KSG

"Glorious the sun in mid career." FaBoCh

"O David, highest in the list." NOEC

"O thou, that sit'st upon a throne." EBEV; OxAEP-1

("Frantic throes of Saul, The.") (LL) EBEV

"Strong is the lion — like a coal." HAP

"Sublime – invention ever young." OBEV

Song to Erin. Mary Weston Fordham. CBWP-2

Song: To Her Again[e], She Burning in a Fe[a]ver. Thomas Carew. SeCP

Song to Hymen: 1942. Anthony Richardson. PoWW

Song to Imogen [in Basic English]. Richard Leighton Greene. BXAP

Song to Imogen. Shakespeare. *See* Song: "Hark! hark! the lark at heaven's gate sings."

Song: To Lucasta, Going to the War[re]s. Richard Lovelace. CABP; CavPo; GLoP; NoP-4; NOSC; PBRV; PFE; PoE; PoPoPo

Song: To Mary. Charles Wolfe. *See* To Mary.

Song to Promote Growth. *Unknown, Navajo.* OBVE, *tr. by* Washington Matthews

Song to Sleep. John Fletcher. OxBoLi *Fr.* The Tragedy of Valentinian. (To Sleep.) PoRA

Song to the Creator. Hildegard von Bingen, *German.* WPoS, *tr. by* Barbara Newman

Song to the Lamb. Novica Tadic, *Serbo-Croatian.* HSix, *tr. by* Charles Simic

Song to the Masquers. James Shirley. OxBSP *Fr.* The Triumph of Peace.

Song to the Men of England. Shelley. CABP; InPS-3; PBMP (Song, A: "Men of England.") NAEL-2

Song to the Mountains. *Unknown, Pawnee.* AWP, *tr. by* Alice C. Fletcher

Song to the oak, the brave old oak, A. The Brave Old Oak. Henry Fothergill Chorley. FaBoBe

Song to the Runaway Slave. *Unknown.* BPo

Song to the Trees and Streams. *Unknown.* APN-2, *tr. by* Alice C. Fletcher *Fr.* The Hako.

Song to the Tune "Perching Crows." Wu Wei-yeh, *Chinese.* CoBLCP, *tr. by* Jonathan Chaves

Song to the Wife of His Youth, The. Nathan Alterman. MHP, *tr. by* Ruth Finer Mintz *Fr.* The Joy of the Poor.

Song to the Wind, A. Taliesin, *Welsh.* FaBoCh, *tr. by* A. P. Graves

Song Tournament: New Style. Louis Untermeyer. OBAL

Song upon Miss Harriet Hanbury, Addressed to the Revd Mr Birt. Sir Charles Hanbury Williams. OBCoV

Song went to the garden, The. Where the Song Went Where She Went & What Happened When They Met. *Unknown, Seneca Indian.* STP, *tr. by* Jerome Rothenberg *and* Richard Johnny John

Song will deceive you, the scent will incite you to sing, The. You Cannot Go Down to the Spring. John Shaw Neilson. CBAP

Song with Words. James Agee. ChIV-1; MoAmPo

Song: Woo'd and married and a'. Joanna Baillie. NoP-4

Song Written at Sea in the First Dutch War (1665), the Night before an Engagement. Charles, 6th Earl of Dorset Sackville. EnLoPo; NOBE; OBEV; OBWP; OxAEP-1 (Written at Sea, in the First Dutch War.) NOSC

Song—Written at the North. Samuel Henry Dickson. APN-1

Song Yet Song. Amir Gilbo'a, *Hebrew.* MHP, *tr. by* Ruth Finer Mintz

Songe 17: "Sun is set, and masked night, The." Robert Sidney. PBRV

Songe bewailinge the tyme of Christmas, So much decayed in Englande, A. *Unknown.* PBRV

Songless Land, The. Francis Carey Slater. PeSAV

Songs. Steve Crow.
  "They say a man dies." HATNAP

Songs. *Unknown.* PBCV
  "New-come buckra/ He get sick."
  "One, two, tree/ All de same."

Songs about Life and Brighter Things Yet. Samuel Hoffenstein. NBLV

Songs and Chants. *Unknown, Southern Paiute Native American.* APN-2, *tr. by* John Wesley Powell

Songs Anthome. Lady Jane Cavendish. KTR *Fr.* A Pastorall.

Songs are thoughts, sung out with the breath when people are moved by great forces and ordinary speech no longer suffices. Orpingalik. PFTM

Song's Eternity. John Clare. FaBoCh

Songs for a Colored Singer. Elizabeth Bishop. RB
  "Washing hangs upon the line, A." FaBoVe; FaBoWP

Songs for a Three-String Guitar. Léopold Sédar Senghor, *French.* PBA, *tr. by* Miriam Koshland

Songs for Eve. Archibald MacLeish.
  What the Serpent Said to Adam. ChIV-1; MeMAP

Songs for Nandu Bhende. Nissim Ezekiel.
  Family. OBCoV
  Song to be Shouted Out. OBCoV

Songs for Signare. Léopold Sédar Senghor, *French.*
  "I walked into the village where the granaries are at the threshold of Night." NegPo, *tr. by* Ellen Conroy Kennedy
  "Long, long between your hands you held the warrior's black face." NegPo, *tr. by* Ellen Conroy Kennedy

"We shall bathe, my love, in an African presence." NegPo, *tr. by* Ellen Conroy Kennedy

"Your face, the beauty of a time long past evokes the perfumed robes in faded hues." NegPo, *tr. by* Ellen Conroy Kennedy

Songs for the Cisco Kid; or, Singing for the Face. K. Curtis Lyle. PoBA

Songs for the Cisco Kid; or, Singing: Song #2. K. Curtis Lyle. PoBA

Songs for the Four Parts of the Night. Owl Woman, *Papago Indian.* PBWP, *tr. by* Frances Densmore

Songs for the People. Frances Ellen Watkins Harper. AAP; NAAAL; PWR

Songs from an Island. Ingeborg Bachmann, *German.* VCWP, *tr. by* Mark Anderson

Songs from Cyprus. Hilda Doolittle.
  "Gather for festival." MoAmPo
  "Where is the nightingale." MoAmPo, *sect.* 2

Songs from the Great Feast to the Dead. *Unknown, Eskimo.* APN-2, *tr. by* Edward William Nelson

Songs from The Princess. Tennyson. *See* Blow, Bugle, Blow.

Songs from the Society of the Mystic Animals. Richard Johnny John, Jerome Rothenberg, *and* Ian Tyson.
  Two Songs About a Dead Person or a Mole—Whichever It Was. PFTM

Songs I had are withered, The. Ivor Gurney. NTP

Songs I wrote when I was young and ardent, The. Boethius, *Latin.* MLL, *tr. by* Helen Waddell *Fr.* Consolation of Philosophy, The ("De Consolacione Philosophie").

Songs in Absence. Arthur Hugh Clough.
  Mari Magno II.

Songs in Flight. Ingeborg Bachmann, *German.*
  "Instructed in love." WPOW, *tr. by* Daniel Huws

Songs of a Stranger (1825). Louisa Costello.
  Lines: "If we should ever meet again." Ro

Songs of an Other. Robert Duncan. PmAP

Songs of Ch'ang-kan. Ts'ui Hao, *Chinese.* CoBCP, *tr. by* Burton Watson

Songs of Ch'en. Confucius, *Chinese.* CTC, *tr. by* Ezra Pound

Songs of Cheng. Confucius, *Chinese.* CTC, *tr. by* Ezra Pound

Songs of Chiang-nan. Wang T'ing-hsiang, *Chinese.* CoBLCP, *tr. by* Jonathan Chaves

Songs of Ch'iu-p'u. Li Po, *Chinese.*
  "Ch'iu-p-u teems with white gibbons." SuSp, *tr. by* Irving Lo
  "Furnace fire lights up earth and sky, The." SuSp, *tr. by* Irving Lo
  "How like a bolt of white silk is this water." SuSp, *tr. by* Irving Lo
  "My white hair of thirty thousand feet." SuSp, *tr. by* Irving Lo

Songs of Conn the Fool, The. Fannie Stearns Gifford.
  Moon Folly. RACG

Songs of Courtship. *Unknown, Chinese.* ChiP, *tr. by* Arthur Waley

Songs of Degrees. Louis Zukofsky.
  "William / Carlos / Williams / alive!" PFTM

Songs of Depression. Yang Wan-li, *Chinese.*
  "I don't feel like reading another book." SuSp, *tr. by* Jonathan Chaves
  "I finish chanting my new poems." SuSp, *tr. by* Jonathan Chaves

Songs of Divers Airs and Natures. Thomas Vautor.
  "Mother, I will have a husband." CBLP

Songs of Divorce. Jane Green, *Ojibwa Indian.* WPOW, *tr. by* Frances Densmore

Songs of Education. G. K. Chesterton.
  Geography. OBSV
  History. OBSV

Songs of Experience. William Blake.
  Ah Sun-flower. NoP-4; PoPoPo
    ("Ah, sunflower! weary of time.") Ro
    (Sunflower, The.)
    ("Where my sunflower wishes to go.") (LL) Ro
  Angel, The. CH; FHYEP; RACG; Ro
  Chimney Sweeper, The ("Little black thing among the snow, A"). EBEvV; FHYEP; NAEL-2; NAWM-2; NOEC; OAEL-2; RB; Ro
  Clod and [*or* &] the Pebble, The. EnLoPo; FHYEP; InPS-3; NAEL-2; NOBE; OBNC; OxAEP-2; OxBSP; PoE; RB; SCGP; SCV; TFi
    (Clod and the Pebble, The.) APAD; GLoP; NoP-4; Ro
  Divine Image, A ("Cruelty has a Human heart"). ChIV-1; NAEL-2; NoP-4; OBNC; RB; Ro
  Earth's Answer. ChIV-1; FHYEP; InPS-3; NAEL-2; NAWM-2; NOBRP; NOEC; OAEL-2; PoE; Ro
    ("Earth raised up her head.") Ro
  Fly, The. CTAV; FHYEP; NOBRP; NOxBChV; OxAEP-2; PBMP; Ro
    ("If I live / Or if I die.") (LL) CTAV
    ("Little fly.") Ro

Garden of Love, The. APAD; AWP; EnLoPo; FHYEP; GBL; GLoP; GaP; HAP; NAEL-2; NoP-4; OBGa; OxAEP-2; PoE; PoPoPo; RB; Ro; SCGP; TFi; TOF; TRP

Holy Thursday [II.] ("Is this a holy thing to see"). FHYEP; InPS-3; NAEL-2; NOBRP; NOEC; NoP-4; OAEL-2; Ro

(Holy Thursday (Experience).) NOxBChV

("Nor poverty the mind appal.") (LL) Ro

Human Abstract, The. FHYEP; NAEL-2; NOBRP; NOEC; OAEL-2; OxAEP-2; PoE; PoEL-4; Ro

Infant Sorrow. APAD; EBEvV; FHYEP; InPS-3; NAEL-2; OBNC; OxAEP-2; OxBM; OxBSP; PFE; PoEL-4; PoPoPo; RB; Ro

("And grey hairs are on my head.") (LL) PFE

("My mother groaned, my father wept!") PoPoPo; Ro

Introduction: "Hear the voice of the Bard!" APAD; ChIV-1; EBEV; FHYEP; HAP; InPS-3; NAEL-2; NAWM-2; NOBE; NOBRP; NOEC; NoP-4; OAEL-2; PoE; PoEL-4; RB; Ro; TFi

(Bard, The.)

Lily, The. FHYEP; NOBRP; Ro

Little Boy Lost, A ("Nought loves another as itself"). FHYEP; PeECV; Ro

Little Girl Found, The. FHYEP; NOBRP

Little Girl Lost, A. FHYEP; Ro

Little Girl Lost, The. FHYEP; NOBRP

Little Vagabond, The. FHYEP; NBLV; OBSV; Ro

London ("I wander through [or thro'] each chartered [or charter'd] street"). APAD; AWP; CABP; ClHu; FHYEP; FaBoPV; HAP; HeIP-4; InPK-6; InPS-3; NAEL-2; NAWM-2; NIP-4; NOBE; NOBRP; NOEC; NoP-4; OAEL-2; OBNC; OxAEP-2; PBMP; PFE; PoE; PoEL-4; PoPoPo; Poetr; RB; Ro; SAGP; SCGP; SCV; TFi; TRP; UnPo; WeW-3

("I wander thro' each charter'd street.") CABP; NoP-4; PFE; PoPoPo

My Pretty Rose-Tree. BoLoP; FHYEP; NAEL-2; NOBRP; Ro

("Flower was offered to me, A.") Ro

Nurse's Song ("When the voices of children are heard on the green / And whisperings [or whisprings] are in the dale") FHYEP

Poison Tree, A. APAD; AWP; FHYEP; HAP; HoPM; ImPo; NAEL-2; NTP; NoP-4; OxAEP-2; PFE; PoEL-4; RB; Ro; SCV; SoSe-8; TFi; WeW-3

("My foe outstretch'd beneath the tree.") (LL) APAD; NoP-4; PFE

("My foe outstretched beneath the tree.") (LL) Ro

School-Boy, The. AYFP; CH; FHYEP; FaBoCh; OxAEP-2

("When the blasts of winter appear?") (LL) AYFP

Sick Rose, The. APAD; AWP; BoLoP; CABP; ClHu; EBEvV; EP; EnLoPo; FHYEP; FaBoSe; GEA; HAP; HeIP-4; InPK-6; InPS-3; NAEL-2; NAWM-2; NIP-4; NOBE; NOBRP; NOEC; NoP-4; OAEL-2; OBNC; OPOU; OxAEP-2; OxBSP; PFE; PoE; PoEL-4; PoPoPo; Poetr; RB; Ro; SCGP; SoSe-8; TFi; TRP; WeW-3

("O Rose thou art sick!") APAD; CABP; EP; FaBoSe; GEA; NoP-4; PFE; PoPoPo

To Tirzah. FHYEP; NAEL-2; NOBE; OAEL-2; Ro

Tyger, The. APAD; CTAV; ChAP; FPC; NOxBChV; NoP-4; PFE; PoPoPo

("Tyger! Tyger! burning bright.") NoP-4

Voice of the Ancient Bard, The. FHYEP; Ro

Songs of Fairly Utter Despair. Samuel Hoffenstein.

"Now, alas, it is too late." OBCoV

Songs of Innocence. William Blake.

Blossom, The. CTAV; FHYEP; Ro

Chimney Sweeper, The ("When my mother died I was very young"). CH; FHYEP; FaBoPV; HeIP-4; InPK-6; NAEL-2; NAWM-2; NOEC; OAEL-2; OxAEP-2; OxBChV; PoE; Poetr; Ro; SCGP; SoSe-8; TFi

Cradle Song, A: "Sweet dreams form a shade." FHYEP; OBCP; Ro

("Heaven and earth to peace beguiles.") (LL) Ro

Divine Image, The ("To Mercy, Pity, Peace and Love"). APAD; BoTP; ChAP; FHYEP; NAEL-2; NOBE; NOBRP; NOEC; NoP-4; OAEL-2; OBNC; PeECV; PoE; PoEL-4; Ro

Dream, A. CH; FHYEP; NOBRP; Ro

Echoing [or Ecchoing] Green, The. BoTP; CH; FHYEP; NAEL-2; NTP; OxAEP-2; PoE; Ro; UnPo

("Sun does arise, The.") Ro

Holy Thursday [I.] ("'Twas on a Holy Thursday, their innocent faces clean"). FHYEP; InPS-3; NAEL-2; NAWM-2; NOBE; NOBRP; NOEC; NoP-4; OAEL-2; PeECV; PoE; Ro; SCV; TFi; TrCP

(Holy Thursday (Innocence).) NOxBChV

Infant Joy. APAD; FHYEP; LiLi; NAEL-2; NTP; OxAEP-2; OxBSP; PoLF; PoPoPo; Ro

("I have no name, / I am but two days old.") PoPoPo

Introduction: "Piping down the valleys wild." NOBRP; Ro

(From Songs of Innocence.) NoP-4

(Reeds of Innocence.) ImPo; OBEV

Lamb, The. BoTP; CH; CTAV; ChIV-2; EBEvV; FHYEP; FaBoBe; FaBoCh; HeIP-4; ImPo; InPS-3; NAEL-2; NAWM-2; NIP-4; NOBRP; NOEC; NoP-4; OAEL-2; OxAEP-2; OxBChV; PoE; PoPoPo; Poetr; Ro; SAGP; SoSe-8; TFi; TRP; TrCP; UnPo

("Little Lamb, who made thee?") CTAV; NoP-4; PoPoPo; Ro; SAGP

Laughing Song. BoTP; FHYEP; FPC; NAEL-2; Ro

("When the green woods laugh with the voice of.") FPC

Little Black Boy, The. AWP; CABP; CH; ChAP; FHYEP; HeIP-4; NAEL-2; NAWM-2; NOBRP; NOEC; NoP-4; OAEL-2; OBEV; OBNC; OxBChV; PeECV; PoE; PoEL-4; PoPoPo; Ro; SCGP; TFi

Little Boy Found, The. FHYEP; NoP-4; Ro

Little Boy Lost, The ("Father, father, where are you going?"). FHYEP; NoP-4; Ro

("And away the vapor flew.") (LL) NoP-4

Little Girl Found, The. FHYEP; NOBRP; Ro

Little Girl Lost, The. FHYEP; NOBRP

Night. BoTP; CH; FHYEP; FaBoBe; OBEV; OxBChV; PoLF; Ro

Nurse's Song ("When the voices of children are heard on the green / And laughing is heard on the hill"). AWP; CH; FHYEP; FaBoBe; NAEL-2; OxBChV; PeLV; RACG; SCGP

("And all the hills echoed.") (LL) RACG

("When the voices of children are heard on the green.") RACG

On Another's Sorrow. AWP; FHYEP; OxAEP-2; PoEL-4; Ro

Shepherd, The. BoTP; ChAP; FHYEP; Ro

Spring. BoTP; FHYEP; FaBoCh; NOxBChV; NTP; Ro; TTTS

Songs of Joy. W. H. Davies. MoBrPo

Songs of Lake Tung-t'ing. Yang Wei-chen, *Chinese*. CoBLCP, *tr. by* Jonathan Chaves

Songs of Maximus. Charles Olson. NeAP *Fr.* The Maximus Poems.

All/ wrong. NoAM

"Colored pictures/ of all things to eat: dirty." NeAP; NoAM

Songs of Rescue. Jacques Dupin, *French*.

"From a thread in space, endless and unbroken. Without unravelling." VCWP, *tr. by* Paul Auster

Songs of Seven. Jean Ingelow.

Seven Times One--Exultation. BLPA; OBNC

Seven Times Three--Love. PoLF

Songs of shepherds and rustical roundelays. The Hunting of the Gods. *Unknown*. OxBoLi

Songs of Sorrow. Kofi Awoonor. HBAPE; PBMAP

("And strangers walk over our portion.") (LL) PBMAP

("I shall sleep in white calico.") PBMAP

(Song of War.) PBMAP

("We shall die on the battlefield.") (LL) PBMAP

Songs of Spirits. *Unknown, Wintu*. APN-2, *tr. by* Jeremiah Curtin

Songs of T'ang. Confucius, *Chinese*.

Alba. CTC, *tr. by* Ezra Pound

Songs of the Affections, with Other Poems. Felicia Dorothea Hemans.

Land of Dreams, The. Ro

Songs of the Arapaho. *Unknown, Arapaho*. APN-2, *tr. by* James Mooney *Fr.* Ghost-Dance Songs.

"My children, when at first I liked the whites." STP

Songs of the Common Day. Sir Charles G. D. Roberts.

Herring Weir, The. NOBC

Pea-Fields, The. NOBC

Songs of the Frontier. Li K'ai-hsien, *Chinese*. CoBLCP, *tr. by* Jonathan Chaves

Songs of the Fruits and Sweets of Childhood. Lorna Goodison. VCWP

Songs of the Ghost Dance. *Unknown, Paiute*. *Fr.* Songs of the Paiute. APN-2 *Fr.* Ghost-Dance Songs.

Songs of the Kiowa. *Unknown, Kiowa*. APN-2, *tr. by* James Mooney *Fr.* Ghost-Dance Songs.

Songs of the Kwakiutl Indians. *Unknown, Kwakiutl*.

Girl's Song, A. APN-2, *tr. by* Franz Boas

Love Song: "Like pain of fire runs down my body my love to you, my dear!" APN-2, *tr. by* Franz Boas

Warsong of the Kwakiutl. APN-2, *tr. by* Franz Boas

Songs of the Land of Zion Jerusalem. Yehuda Amichai, *Hebrew*. IP, *tr. by* Warren Bargod *and* Stanley F. Chyet

Songs of the Paiute. *Unknown, Paiute*. APN-2 *Fr.* Ghost-Dance Songs.

Songs of the Ghost Dance.

Songs of the People. Hayyim Nahman Bialik, *Hebrew*. AWP, *tr. by* Maurice Samuel

Songs of the Psyche. Thomas Kinsella.

"Character, indistinct, entered, A." NoAM

Songs of the Sacred Mysteries. *Unknown, Sioux Native American*. APN-2, *tr. by* Alfred Longley Riggs

Songs of the shepherds. The Wild Swan. Johannes Bobrowski, *German.* CEEP, *tr. by* Juliette Victor-Rood

Songs of the Sioux. *Unknown, Sioux.* APN-2 *Fr.* Ghost-Dance Songs.

Songs of the Squatters. Robert, Viscount Sherbrooke Lowe. NOBAu

"Commissioner bet me a pony, The—I won, The." NOBAu

"Gum has no shade, The." NOBAu

Songs of the Stream. Leah Goldberg, *Hebrew.*

Blade of Grass Sings to the River, The. TrJP, *tr. by* Robert Friend

Blade of Grass Sings to the Stream, The. MHP, *tr. by* Ruth Finer Mintz

Girl Sings to the Stream, The. MHP, *tr. by* Ruth Finer Mintz

Moon Sings to the Stream, The. MHP, *tr. by* Ruth Finer Mintz

Stream Sings to the Stone, The. MHP, *tr. by* Ruth Finer Mintz

Tree Sings to the Stream, The. MHP, *tr. by* Ruth Finer Mintz

Songs of the Transformed. Margaret Atwood.

Rat Song. NIP-4

Siren Song. HAP; NIP-4; PoA; WeW-3

Songs of Yen-ching. Hsü Wei, *Chinese.* CoBLCP, *tr. by* Jonathan Chaves

Songs, so old and bitter, The. The Coffin. Heinrich Heine, *German.* AWP, *tr. by* Louis Untermeyer

Songs to Seraphine. Heinrich Heine, *German.* TrJP, *tr. by* Emma Lazarus

Songs to Survive the Summer. Robert Hass. AmPA

Songs to Welcome the Society of the Mystic Animals. *Unknown, Seneca Indian.* STP, *tr. by* Jerome Rothenberg *and* Richard Johnny John

Songs without Words. John Ashbery. NAAL-4

Songs you sent me I have read, The. Hildebert, *Latin.* MLL, *tr. by* Helen Waddell

Sonja Henie, the young girl. Preface. Theodore Weiss. VGW

Sonnet, The. Richard Watson Gilder. APN-2

Sonnet. James Russell Lowell. NCAP

Sonnet. Ed Roberson. GT

Sonnet. Sir Philip Sidney. *See* Sleep.

Sonnet, The. Ella Wheeler Wilcox. APN-2

Sonnet: "After dark vapours have oppress'd our plains." Keats. OBNC

Sonnet: "Ah, sweet Content! where is thy mild abode." Barnabe Barnes. *See* Content.

Sonnet: "Alexis, here she stayed; among these pines." William Drummond, of Hawthornden. NOSC

(Spring Bereaved.) OBEV

Sonnet ("All my senses, like beacon's flame"). Fulke Greville. NOSC *Fr.* Caelica.

Sonnet: "All my thoughts always speak to me of love." Dante. AWP *Fr.* La Vita Nuova.

Sonnet: "And so, as this great sphere (now turning slow)." Frederick Goddard Tuckerman. ColAP

Sonnet: "And then I sat me down, and gave the rein." Gustav Rosenhane, *Swedish.* AWP, *tr. by* Sir Edmund Gosse

Sonnet: "And wilt thou have me fashion into speech." Elizabeth Barrett Browning. BWW; BrRo; EnVR; VWP *Fr.* Sonnets from the Portuguese.

(Sonnet 13.) CABP

Sonnet: "As in a duskie [or dusky] and tempestuous night." William Drummond, of Hawthornden. NOSC; OxAEP-1

Sonnet: "As long as I continue weeping." Louise Labé, *French.* PBWP, *tr. by* Joan Keefe *and* Richard Terdiman

Sonnet: "As when, to one who long hath watched, the morn." John Codrington Bampfylde. NOEC

Sonnet: "Beauty of songs your absence I should not show." Bernadette Mayer. PmAP

Sonnet: "Beauty, sweet love, is like the morning dew." Samuel Daniel. *Fr.* To Delia.

Sonnet: "Because my grief seems quiet and apart." Robert Nathan. TrJP

Sonnet: "Beckie, my luve!—What is't, ye twa-faced tod?" George Campbell Hay. OxBS

Sonnet: "Belovéd, my Belovéd, when I think." Elizabeth Barrett Browning. Son; WPE *Fr.* Sonnets from the Portuguese.

Sonnet: "Belovèd, thou hast brought me many flowers." Elizabeth Barrett Browning. EBVV; EnVR; LW; OBNC; WPE *Fr.* Sonnets from the Portuguese.

Sonnet: "Bible says Sennacherib's campaign was spoiled, The." C. S. Lewis. TrCP

Sonnet: "Caelica, I overnight was finely used." Fulke Greville. *Fr.* Caelica.

Sonnet: "Can it be right to give what I can give?" Elizabeth Barrett Browning. CTC *Fr.* Sonnets from the Portuguese.

Sonnet: "Care-charmer Sleep[e], son[ne] of the sable night." Samuel Daniel. CABP; GSo; NoP-4; PoEL-2 *Fr.* To Delia.

Sonnet: "Cleare moving cristall, pure as the Sunne beames." Sir William Alexander, Earl of Stirling. OxBS *Fr.* Aurora.

Sonnet: "Crumbled rock of London is dripping under, The." Roy Fuller. PoA

Sonnet: "Cry, crow." Hayden Carruth. NNaP; Son

Sonnet: "Dear [or Deere], why should you command me to my rest." Michael Drayton. *See* Night and Day.

Sonnet: "Deep in a vale where rocks on every side." Gustav Rosenhane, *Swedish.* AWP, *tr. by* Sir Edmund Gosse

Sonnet: "Depose your finger of that Ring." Richard Lovelace. CavPo

Sonnet: "Dost see how unregarded now." Sir John Suckling. BeJo; CaPo; CavPo; NOSC

Sonnet: "Down[e] in the depth of mine iniquity." Fulke Greville. NOSC *Fr.* Caelica.

("Thus hath his death rais'd up this soule of mine.") (LL) PBRV

Sonnet: "Each man me telleth." Sir Thomas Wyatt. AEP

Sonnet: "Earth with thunder torn, with fire blasted, The." Fulke Greville. *Fr.* Caelica.

Sonnet: "England! the time is come when thou shouldst wean." Wordsworth. Son

Sonnet: "Ere I had known the world and understood." John Clare. Ro

Sonnet: "Eternall Truth, almighty, infinite." Fulke Greville. *Fr.* Caelica.

Sonnet: "Face of all the world is changed, I think, The." Elizabeth Barrett Browning. CTC *Fr.* Sonnets from the Portuguese.

Sonnet: "Fair is my love, and cruel as she's fair." Samuel Daniel. *See* Beauty, Time and Love.

Sonnet: "Farewell, Love." Sir Thomas Wyatt. *See* A Renouncing of Love.

Sonnet: "First time he kissed me, he but only kissed." Elizabeth Barrett Browning. BLPA; CTC; FaBoBe; LW *Fr.* Sonnets from the Portuguese.

Sonnet: "First time that the sun rose on thine oath, The." Elizabeth Barrett Browning. EnVR; NAEL-2; WPE *Fr.* Sonnets from the Portuguese.

Sonnet: "From a rived tree, that stands beside the grave." Anna Seward. ECWP

Sonnet: "Go from me. Yet I feel that I shall stand." Elizabeth Barrett Browning. BWW; CBLP; LW; OBEV; OxAEP-2 *Fr.* Sonnets from the Portuguese.

Sonnet: "Go, thou that vainly dost mine eyes invite." Henry, Bishop of Chichester King. OxBSP

Sonnet: "Guido, I wish that you and Lapo and I." Dante, *Italian.* RB; TTTS, *tr. by* Kenneth Koch

Sonnet: "He came in silvern armor, trimmed with black." Gwendolyn B. Bennett. PoBA

Sonnet: "Here in the self is all that men can know." John Masefield. AWP *Fr.* Lollingdon Downs.

Sonnet: "Here lies the noble flesh of Spartacus the knave." Daniel Casper von Lohenstein. GePo *Fr.* Arminius.

Sonnet, A: "His golden locks time hath to silver turned." George Peele. *See* A Farewell to Arms.

Sonnet: "How do I hate you? Let me count the ways." Stanley J. Sharpless. UV

Sonnet: "How do I love thee? Let me count the ways." Elizabeth Barrett Browning. BWW; BoLoP; CTC; EBEvV; EBVV; EnVR; FaBoBe; HeIP-4; HoPM; InPK-6; NAEL-2; NALW; NIP-4; OPOU; OxAEP-2; OxBM; PoE; PoLF; PoRA; Poetr; Son; TFi; UV; UnPo; VWP; WPE *Fr.* Sonnets from the Portuguese.

("How Do I Love Thee? Let Me Count The Ways.") APAD; GSo

(Sonnet: "How Do I Love Thee? Let Me Count the Ways.") GLoP

Sonnet: "How many faults you might accuse me of." Elinor Wylie. NAAL-2

Sonnet: "How soon hath Time the suttle [or subtle] theef [or thief] of youth." Milton. NOSC

(On His Being Arrived to the Age of Twenty-Three.) GSo

(Sonnet.) NOSC

Sonnet: "I dreamed the nymph that o'er my fancy reigns." Sir William Alexander, Earl of Stirling. NOSC *Fr.* Aurora.

Sonnet: "I had no thought of violets of late." Alice Moore Dunbar-Nelson. BlSi; PoBA; Son

Sonnet: "I hate the Spring in parti-coloured vest." Mary Locke. ECWP

Sonnet: "I have not spent the April of my time." Bartholomew Griffin. *Fr.* Fidessa, More Chaste than Kind[e].

Sonnet: "I hereby swear that to uphold your house." Elinor Wylie. NAAL-2; OxBA; Son *Fr.* One Person.

(Sonnet from "One Person.") MoAmPo

Sonnet: "I lift my heavy heart up solemnly." Elizabeth Barrett Browning. NALW *Fr.* Sonnets from the Portuguese.

("Hair beneath. Stand further off then! Go, The.") (LL) LW

(Sonnet 5.) VWP

Sonnet: "I lived with visions for my company." Elizabeth Barrett Browning. BWW *Fr.* Sonnets from the Portuguese.

Sonnet: "I never gave a lock of hair away." Elizabeth Barrett Browning. EBVV; HAP *Fr.* Sonnets from the Portuguese.

Sonnet: "I saw magic on a green country road." Michael Hartnett. BIrV *Fr.* Thirteen Sonnets.

Sonnet: "I still shall smile and go my careless way." Mamie A. Richardson. LW

Sonnet: "I that erstwhile the world's sweet air did draw." George Wither. NOSC *Fr.* The Shephe[a]rd's Hunting.

Sonnet: "I thought once how Theocritus had sung." Elizabeth Barrett Browning. BWW; EBVV; EnVR; GBL; NOBE; OBEV; OBNC; OxAEP-2; WPE *Fr.* Sonnets from the Portuguese.

("Silver answer rang,—'Not Death, but Love,' The.") (LL) GLoP; LBC; NoP-4

(Sonnet: "I Thought Once How Theocritus Had Sung.") GLoP

(Sonnets from the Portuguese.) NoP-4; PoPoPo

Sonnet: "I wandered out a while agone." George Wither. NOSC *Fr.* Fair Virtue, the Mistress of Philarete.

Sonnet: "If I leave all for thee, wilt thou exchange." Elizabeth Barrett Browning. Son *Fr.* Sonnets from the Portuguese.

Sonnet: "If it be night. . . ." Alec Brock Stevenson. FuPo

Sonnet: "If love is chaste, what bears adultery?" Sibylla Schwarz, *German.* GePo, tr. by George C. Schoolfield

Sonnet: "If there were any power in human love." Frances Anne Kemble. VWP

Sonnet: "If thou must love me, let it be for nought." Elizabeth Barrett Browning. BWW; CTC; HeIP-4; InPS-3; LW; OBEV; OBNC; OxAEP-2; SoSe-8 *Fr.* Sonnets from the Portuguese.

(For Love's Sake Only.) PoToHe

("If thou must love me, let it be for naught.") SAGP

Sonnet: "Ile give thee leave my love, in beauties field." Sir William Alexander, Earl of Stirling. OxBS *Fr.* Aurora.

Sonnet: "In every dream thy lovely features rise." William Barnes. BoLoP

Sonnet: "Innumerable Beauties, thou white haire." Edward Herbert, 1st Baron Herbert of Cherbury. PoEL-2

Sonnet: "It is not death, that sometime in a sigh." Thomas Hood. OBNC (Death.) GSo

Sonnet: "Leave me, all sweet refrains my lip hath made." Luis de Camões, *Spanish.* AWP, tr. by Richard Garnett

Sonnet: "Let me confesse that we two must be twaine." Shakespeare. PBRV *Fr.* Sonnets.

Sonnet: "Let others sing of knights and paladin[e]s." Samuel Daniel. *See* To Delia.

Sonnet: "Let the world's sharpness, like a clasping knife." Elizabeth Barrett Browning. NOBVV *Fr.* Sonnets from the Portuguese.

Sonnet: "Let us leave talking of angelic hosts." Elinor Wylie. OxBA *Fr.* One Person.

Sonnet: "Lift not the painted veil which those who live." Shelley. NOBRP; OBNC; Son

("Lift not the veil which those who live.") FHYEP

Sonnet: "Light-spring, oh sun, in light our wedding joys immure." Daniel Casper von Lohenstein. GePo *Fr.* Arminius.

Sonnet: "Like Memnon's rock, touched with the rising sun." Giles Fletcher, the Elder. *Fr.* Licia.

Sonnet: "Long love, The." Sir Thomas Wyatt. AEP

("Long love that in my thought doth harbor, The.") GSo

Sonnet: "Look, Delia, how we esteem the half-blown rose." Samuel Daniel. *See* The Half-blown Rose.

Sonnet: "Love and the gentle heart are one same thing." Dante. AWP *Fr.* La Vita Nuova.

Sonnet: "Love is the peace, whereto all thoughts do strive." Fulke Greville. *Fr.* Caelica.

Sonnet: "Man, dream[e] no more of curious mysteries." Fulke Greville. NOSC *Fr.* Caelica.

Sonnet: "Master and the slave go hand in hand, The." Edwin Arlington Robinson. APN-2

Sonnet: "My dream a drink with Lonnie Johnson we discuss the code." Ted Berrigan. NoAM *Fr.* The Sonnets.

Sonnet: "My future will not copy fair my past." Elizabeth Barrett Browning. EnVR *Fr.* Sonnets from the Portuguese.

Sonnet: "My galley charged." Sir Thomas Wyatt. AEP

Sonnet: "My God, where is that ancient heat towards Thee." George Herbert. ESCV; GeHe; NOSC; OAEL-1

(Sonnet 1.) FSCP

Sonnet: "My letters! all dead paper, mute and white." Elizabeth Barrett Browning. HAP; OxAEP-2 *Fr.* Sonnets from the Portuguese.

Sonnet: "My poet, thou canst touch on all the notes." Elizabeth Barrett Browning. BrRo *Fr.* Sonnets from the Portuguese.

Sonnet: "My soul surcharged with grief now loud complains." Rachel Morpurgo, *Hebrew.* TrJP, tr. by Nina Davis Salaman

Sonnet: "No worst, there is none. Pitched past pitch of grief." Gerard Manley Hopkins. OBNC

Sonnet: "Not wrongly moved by this dismaying scene." William Empson. LiTM

Sonnet: "Now the bat circles on the breeze of eve." Ann Radcliffe. WPE

Sonnet: "Nurse-life wheat within his green husk growing, The." Fulke Greville. NoP-4 *Fr.* Caelica.

("Turnes all the spirits of Man into desire.") (LL) PBRV

Sonnet: "O false and treacherous Probability." Fulke Greville. *Fr.* Caelica.

Sonnet: "O[h]! for some honest lover's ghost." Sir John Suckling. BXAP; BeJo; CavPo; MeLP; PoEL-3; SeCP

(Doubt of Martyrdom, A.) BoLoP; CaPo; NOBE; OBEV

("Give me the woman here.") (LL) CavPo

Sonnet, A: "O lovely O most charming pug." Marjory Fleming. NBLV

Sonnet: "O thou who never harbored fear." Eloise Bibb. CBWP-4

Sonnet: "October's gold is dim—the forests rot." David Gray. OxAEP-2

Sonnet: "Of thee, kind boy, I ask no red and white." Sir John Suckling. BeJo; CaPo; CavPo; MeLP; NOSC; OxBoLi; SeCP

(Sonnet II.) NoP-4

Sonnet: "Oh! Death will find me, long before I tire." Rupert Brooke. NoP-4; PoRA

(Sonnet: Death Will Find Me.) MoBrPo; Son

Sonnet: "Oh for a poet—for a beacon bright." Edwin Arlington Robinson. APN-2; NCAP; OxBA

Sonnet: "Oh, my belovèd, have you thought of this." Edna St. Vincent Millay. LW

Sonnet: "Orgasm completely, The." Tom Clark. CoAP

Sonnet: "Patience, hard thing! the hard thing but to pray." Gerard Manley Hopkins. NOBVV; OBNC

Sonnet: "Record is nothing, and the hero great." John Byrne Leicester Warren, 3d Baron De Tabley. EBVV

Sonnet: "Say over again, and yet once over again." Elizabeth Barrett Browning. NAEL-2 *Fr.* Sonnets from the Portuguese.

Sonnet: "Scorn not the sonnet, critic, you have frowned." Wordsworth. OBEV

Sonnet: "Seer foretold that I would love one day, A." Louise Labé. *See* Sonnet XX.

Sonnet: "She took the dappled partridge flecked [*or* fleckt] with blood." Tennyson. NAEL-2

Sonnet: "Shepherd's brow, fronting forked lightning, owns, The." Gerard Manley Hopkins. KSG

Sonnet: "Silver herring throbbed thick in my seine, The." Kenneth Leslie. NOBC *Fr.* By Stubborn Stars.

Sonnet: "Slide soft, fair forth, and make a crystal plain." William Drummond, of Hawthornden. NOSC

Sonnet, A [*or* The: "Sonnet is a moment's monument"]. D. G. Rossetti. EnVR; NAEL-2; Son *Fr.* The House of Life.

Sonnet: "So shoots a star as doth my mistress glide." John, of Hereford Davies. CBLP

Sonnet: "Stranger, when o'er yon slant, warm field no cloud." Anna Seward. NOBRP

Sonnet: "Sure Lord, there is enough in thee to dry." George Herbert. GeHe; NOSC

(Sonnet 2.) FSCP

Sonnet: "Tell me[e] no more how fair[e] she[e] is." Henry, Bishop of Chichester King. EnLoPo; GLoP; MeLP; SeCP

Sonnet: "There, on the darkened deathbed, dies the brain." John Masefield. EBEV

Sonnet: "There was an Indian, who had known no change." Sir John Collings Squire. CH

Sonnet: "Thou comest! all is said without a word." Elizabeth Barrett Browning. BWW *Fr.* Sonnets from the Portuguese.

Sonnet: "Thou hast thy calling to some palace-floor." Elizabeth Barrett Browning. OxAEP-2; Son *Fr.* Sonnets from the Portuguese.

(Sonnet 4.) VWP

("That weeps. . . as thou must sing. . . alone, aloof.") (LL) VWP

Sonnet: "Thousand apples you might put in your theories." Bernadette Mayer. PmAP

Sonnet: "Three silences made him a single word." Richard Palmer Blackmur. PoA

Sonnet: "Three things there be in mans opinion dear[e]." Fulke Greville. NOSC *Fr.* Caelica.

Sonnet: "Time and the mortal will stand never fast." Luis de Camões, *Spanish.* AWP, tr. by Richard Garnett

Sonnet: "Tis dead of night; storms rend the troubled air." Mary Locke. ECWP

Sonnet: "To work away in art's traditional measure." Goethe, *German.* STV, tr. by John Frederick Nims

Sonnet: "Triumphing chariots, statues, crowns of bay." William Drummond, of Hawthornden. NOSC *Fr.* Urania, or Spiritual Poems.

Sonnet, A: "Two voices are there: one is of the deep." James Kenneth Stephen. BXAP; CABP; EPCY; NOBL; UV

(Sonnet, A.) PeLV

Sonnet: "Unlike are we, unlike, O princely Heart!" Elizabeth Barrett Browning. BWW; EnVR; OBEV; OxAEP-2 *Fr.* Sonnets from the Portuguese.

(Sonnet 3.) CABP

Sonnet: "Way the world is not, The." Bill Knott. PBCAP

Sonnet: "We will not whisper, we have found the place." Hilaire Belloc. MoBrPo

Sonnet, A: "Weeping, murmuring, complaining." Oliver Goldsmith. NOIV

Sonnet: "What can I give thee back, O liberal." Elizabeth Barrett Browning. BWW; OxAEP-2 *Fr.* Sonnets from the Portuguese.

Sonnet: "What's in the braine that Inck my character." Shakespeare. PBRV *Fr.* Sonnets.

Sonnet: "When I catch sight of your fair head." Louise Labé. PBWP, *tr. by Joan Keefe and Richard Terdiman.*

Sonnet: "When I was marked for suffering, Love forsworse." Miguel de Cervantes Saavedra, *Spanish.* AWP, *tr. by Sir Edmund Gosse.*

Sonnet: "When our two souls stand up erect and strong." Elizabeth Barrett Browning. BWW; BoWoP; EnVR; LW; NAEL-2; NALW; NOBE; OBEV; WPE *Fr.* Sonnets from the Portuguese.

Sonnet: "When Phoebe formed a wanton smile." William Collins. EnLoPo; OxBSP

Sonnet: "When you see millions of the mouthless dead." Charles Hamilton Sorley. OBWP; PeFWW; PoWW

(Sonnet.) NSI

Sonnet: "Where are we to go when this is done?" Alfred A. Duckett. PoBA

Sonnet: "Wisest of all men lies buried on this spot, The." Daniel Casper von Lohenstein. GePo *Fr.* Arminius.

Sonnet: "World is too much with us; late and soon, The." Wordsworth. PWR

Sonnet: "World's bright comforter, whose beamsome light, The." Barnabe Barnes. *See* God's Virtue.

Sonnet: "Yet, love, mere love, is beautiful indeed." Elizabeth Barrett Browning. BWW; CTC; OxAEP-2 *Fr.* Sonnets from the Portuguese.

Sonnet: "You were born; must die; were loved; must love." Stephen Spender. MoBrPo

Sonnet 1: "Everything that happens to me these days." Julia Alvarez. FFC *Fr.* ("33").

Sonnet 1: "Happy ye leaves! whenas those lily hands." Edmund Spenser. EBEV; NAEL-1; OAEL-1; PoE; Son *Fr.* Amoretti. AAS

("Happy ye leaves when as those lilly hands.") NoP-4

Sonnet I: "His piercing pince-nez. Some dim frieze." Ted Berrigan. FTOS *Fr.* The Sonnets.

Sonnet I: "If it must be; if it must be, O God!" David Gray. OxBS *Fr.* In the Shadows.

Sonnet 1: "Loving in truth, and fain[e] in verse my love to show." Sir Philip Sidney. AWP; EBEV; EPCY; GBL; GSo; HAP; ImPo; InPS-3; LoP; NAEL-1; NoP-4; NoSic; OAEL-1; OxAEP-1; PoE; Poetr; SCGP; Son; TFi *Fr.* Astrophil and Stella. AAS; SiPS

(Astrophil and Stella.) GLoP

("'Fool,' said my Muse to me, "look in thy heart and write.""") (LL) CABP; NoP-4; PBRV

Sonnet 1: "Not Ulysses, no, nor any other man." Louise Labé, *French.* BoWoP, *tr. by Willis Barnstone*

Sonnet 1: "When night's [or nights] black mantle could most darknes prove." Mary Sidney, Countess of Montgomery Wroth. Son *Fr.* Pamphilia to Amphilanthus.

("Yet since, (O me!), a lover have I been.") (LL) CABP

Sonnet 2: "Deep in her seventh month, my sister dozes." Debra Bruce. FFC *Fr.* ("Light They Make, The").

Sonnet 2: "Late in the Forest I did Cupid See." Mary Sidney, Countess of Montgomery Wroth. KTR *Fr.* Pamphilia to Amphilanthus.

("Burning my heart who had him kindly warmed.") (LL) LW

(Cupid Lost.) LW

Sonnet 2: "My own heart let me have. More pity on." Nell Altizer. FFC *Fr.* ("Love Letters to Her Who Lives [Alas!] Away").

Sonnet 2: "Not at [the] first sight, nor a dribbed shot." Sir Philip Sidney. NAEL-1; OAEL-1; PBRV *Fr.* Astrophil and Stella. AAS; SiPS

Sonnet 2: "O handsome chestnut eyes, evasive gaze." Louise Labé, *French.* BoWoP, *tr. by Willis Barnstone*

Sonnet—2: "Some things are very dear to me—." Gwendolyn B. Bennett. NAAAL

Sonnet 3: "Let dainty wits cry on the sisters nine." Sir Philip Sidney. NoSic; OAEL-1; Son *Fr.* Astrophil and Stella. AAS; SiPS

Sonnet 3: "O interminable desires, O futile hope." Louise Labé, *French.* BoWoP, *tr. by Willis Barnstone*

Sonnet III: "O world, thou choosest not the better part!" George Santayana. APN-2 *Fr.* Sonnets.

Sonnet III: "Stronger than alcohol, more great than song." Ted Berrigan. FTOS *Fr.* The Sonnets.

Sonnet (III), The. John Addington Symonds. GSo

Sonnet III. Written at Midnight, on Helm Crag. John Wilson. Ro *Fr.* The Isle of Palms and Other Poems.

Sonnet IV. E. E. Cummings. ChIV-1

(Sonnet IV: This Is The Garden.) KSG

("This is the garden: colors come and go.") KSG

Sonnet IV. Chris Wallace-Crabbe. BMAP *Fr.* Sonnets to the Left.

Sonnet 4: "From that first flash when awful Love took flame." Louise Labé, *French.* BoWoP, *tr. by Willis Barnstone*

Sonnet 4: "New year, forth looking out of Janus' gate." Edmund Spenser. NoSic *Fr.* Amoretti. AAS

Sonnet 4: "Virtue, alas, now let me take some rest." Sir Philip Sidney. *Fr.* Astrophil and Stella. AAS; SiPS

Sonnet 4: "Wet streets, black trees, a gold leaf smacked." Debra Bruce. FFC *Fr.* ("Light They Make, The").

Sonnet V: "Dreamt I today [or to-day] the dream of yesternight." George Santayana. APN-2 *Fr.* Sonnets.

Sonnet 5: "Evening, as slow thy placid shades descend." William Lisle Bowles. NOBRP; NOEC

Sonnet 5: "It is most true that eyes are formed to serve." Sir Philip Sidney. NAEL-1; NoSic; OAEL-1; Son *Fr.* Astrophil and Stella. AAS; SiPS

Sonnet 5: "No, I'll not, carrion, comfort you. Comfort." Nell Altizer. FFC

Sonnet 5: "Rudely thou wrongst my dear heart's desire." Edmund Spenser. *Fr.* Amoretti. AAS

Sonnet V. To the South Downs: "Ah, hills beloved!—where once, an happy child." Charlotte Smith. Ro

Sonnet 5: 'Whilst Youth and Error'. Samuel Daniel. AEP *Fr.* Delia.

Sonnet 5: "White Venus limpid wandering in the sky." Louise Labé, *French.* BoWoP, *tr. by Aliki and Willis Barnstone*

Sonnet 6: "Coming of that limpid star is twice, The." Louise Labé, *French.* BoWoP, *tr. by Willis Barnstone*

Sonnet 6: 'How many paltry, foolish, painted things'. Michael Drayton. AEP *Fr.* Idea.

(Sonnet: "How many paltry. . . .")

Sonnet 6: "My pain[e], still smothered [or smother'd] in my grievèd bre[a]st." Mary Sidney, Countess of Montgomery Wroth. NOSC; PEW *Fr.* Pamphilia to Amphilanthus.

(Sonnet 68.) PEW

("Yet faith still cries, Love will not falsify.") (LL) PEW

Sonnet 6: "Ô[h] strive not[t] still to heape[e] disdain[e] on me[e]." Mary Sidney, Countess of Montgomery Wroth. NOSC *Fr.* Pamphilia to Amphilanthus.

Sonnet 6: "Some lovers speak, when they their Muses entertain." Sir Philip Sidney. NAEL-1; NoSic; Son *Fr.* Astrophil and Stella. AAS; SiPS

(Sonnet 6: 'some lovers speak'.) AEP

Sonnet VI. To the Torrid Zone. Helen Maria Williams. NOBRP

(To the Torrid Zone.) NoP-4

Sonnet VII: "By Derwent's rapid stream as oft I strayed." Anna Seward. Ro *Fr.* Sonnets.

Sonnet 7: "Like an enfranchised bird, who wildly springs." Caroline Elizabeth Norton. VWP

Sonnet 7: "Love leave to urge, thou know'st thou hast the hand." Mary Sidney, Countess of Montgomery Wroth. Son *Fr.* Pamphilia to Amphilanthus.

Sonnet 7: "We see each living thing finally die." Louise Labé, *French.* BoWoP, *tr. by Willis Barnstone*

Sonnet 7: "When Nature made her chief work, Stella's eyes." Sir Philip Sidney. NAEL-1; NIP-4; Son *Fr.* Astrophil and Stella. AAS; SiPS

Sonnet [or Sonetto] 7: "Who is she that comes, makyng turn every man's eye." Guido Cavalcanti. CTC; OBVE, *tr. by Ezra Pound*

Sonnet VII. Written on Skiddaw, during a Tempest. John Wilson. Ro

Sonnet 8: "I live, I die, I burn myself and drown." Louise Labé, *French.* BoWoP, *tr. by Willis Barnstone*

Sonnet 8: "Love, born in Greece, of late fled from his native place." Sir Philip Sidney. *Fr.* Astrophil and Stella. AAS; SiPS

Sonnet 8: "More than most fair [or fayre], full of the living fire [or fyre]." Edmund Spenser. PoE; Son *Fr.* Amoretti. AAS

("Well is he borne, that may behold you ever.") (LL) NoP-4

Sonnet 9: "As soon as I lie down in my soft bed." Louise Labé, *French.* BoWoP, *tr. by Willis Barnstone*

Sonnet 9: "Be[e] you all pleased [or pleas'd]? your pleasures grieve not[t] me[e]." Mary Sidney Wroth. BWW; NOSC *Fr.* Pamphilia to Amphilanthus.

Sonnet 9: "Queen Virtue's court, which some call Stella's face." Sir Philip Sidney. NAEL-1 *Fr.* Astrophil and Stella. AAS; SiPS

("Of touch they are, and poore I am their straw.") (LL) PBRV

("Queene *Vertues* court, which some call *Stellas* face.") PBRV

Sonnet 10: 'Unrighteous Lord of Love'. Edmund Spenser. AEP *Fr.* Amoretti. AAS

("As she doth laugh at me and makes my pain her sport.") (LL) NoP-4

Sonnet 10: "Reason, in faith thou art well served, that still." Sir Philip Sidney. NAEL-1 *Fr.* Astrophil and Stella. AAS; SiPS

Sonnet 10: "When I perceive your blond and graceful head." Louise Labé, *French.* PBWP, tr. by Joan Keefe and Richard Terdiman; BoWoP, tr. by Willis Barnstone

Sonnet 11: "In truth, O love, with what a boyish kind." Sir Philip Sidney. CBLP; PoE *Fr.* Astrophil and Stella. AAS; SiPS

Sonnet 11: "O eyes clear with beauty, O tender gaze." Louise Labé, *French.* BoWoP, tr. by Willis Barnstone.

Sonnet 12: "Cupid, because thou shin'st in Stella's eyes." Sir Philip Sidney. *Fr.* Astrophil and Stella. AAS; SiPs

Sonnet 12: "I saw an ugly beast come from the sea." Edmund Spenser. ChIV-2

Sonnet 12: "Lute, companion of my calamity." Louise Labé, *French.* BoWoP, tr. by Aliki and Willis Barnstone.

Sonnet XII. Pablo Neruda, *Spanish.*

"Loving is a journey with water and with stars." ITG, tr. by Stephen Mitchell

Sonnet 12. Anna Seward. CPO

Sonnet 13: "I saw a woman sitting on a beast." Edmund Spenser. ChIV-2

Sonnet 13: "If I could linger on his lovely chest." Louise Labé, *French.* BoWoP, tr. by Aliki and Willis Barnstone

Sonnet 13: "In That proud port, which her so goodly graceth." Edmund Spenser. Son *Fr.* Amoretti. AAS

Sonnet 13: "Phoebus was judge between Jove, Mars, and Love." Sir Philip Sidney. *Fr.* Astrophil and Stella. AAS; SiPS

Sonnet 13. Anna Seward. CPO

Sonnet 14: "Alas, have I not pain enough, my friend." Sir Philip Sidney. NoSic; OAEL-1 *Fr.* Astrophil and Stella. AAS; SiPS

Sonnet XIV. Louise Labé, *French.* BoWoP, tr. by Willis Barnstone

Sonnet 14: "Not Wordsworth's genius, Pestalozzi's love." Amos Bronson Alcott. APN-1

Sonnet 14: "Then might I see upon a white horse set." Edmund Spenser. ChIV-2

Sonnet 15: "I saw new Earth, new Heaven, said Saint John." Edmund Spenser. ChIV-2

Sonnet 15. "To honor the return of sparkling sun." Louise Labé, *French.* BoWoP, tr. by Willis Barnstone

Sonnet 15: "Ye tradeful merchants that, with weary toil." Edmund Spenser. HeIP-4; NIP-4; OAEL-1; Son *Fr.* Amoretti. AAS

("Her mind adornd with vertues manifold.") (LL) NoP-4

("Ye tradefull Merchants that with weary toyle.") NoP-4

Sonnet 15: "You that do search for every purling spring." Sir Philip Sidney. NAEL-1; NoSic; OAEL-1; OxAEP-1; Son *Fr.* Astrophil and Stella. AAS; SiPS

("Stella behold, and then begin to endite.") (LL) CABP

Sonnet XVI: "After an age when thunderbolts and hail." Louise Labé, *French.* BoWoP, tr. by Willis Barnstone

Sonnet 16: "In nature apt to like when I did see." Sir Philip Sidney. NAEL-1 *Fr.* Astrophil and Stella. AAS; SiPS

Sonnet 16: "One day as I unwarily did gaze." Edmund Spenser. OAEL-1 *Fr.* Amoretti. AAS

Sonnet 17: "His mother dear Cupid offended late." Sir Philip Sidney. *Fr.* Astrophil and Stella. AAS; SiPS

Sonnet 17: "I flee the city, temples, and each place." Louise Labé, *French.* BoWoP, tr. by Willis Barnstone

Sonnet XVII. Pablo Neruda, *Spanish.* ITG, tr. by Stephen Mitchell

Sonnet 18: "Adventurous mariner! in whose gray skiff." Amos Bronson Alcott. APN-1

Sonnet 18: "Kiss me again, re-kiss and kiss me whole." Louise Labé, *French.* WPOW, tr. by Raymond Oliver

(Sonnet XVIII: "Kiss me again, rekiss, kiss me more.") BoWoP, tr. by Willis Barnstone

Sonnet 18: "With what sharp checks I in myself am shent." Sir Philip Sidney. NAEL-1; NoSic *Fr.* Astrophil and Stella. AAS; SiPS

Sonnet XIX: "After having slain very many beasts." Louise Labé, *French.* BoWoP, tr. by Willis Barnstone

Sonnet 19: "Come darkest night, be[e]coming sorrow best." Mary Sidney Wroth. NOSC *Fr.* Pamphilia to Amphilanthus.

Sonnet 19: "Merry cuckoo, messenger of spring, The." Edmund Spenser. *Fr.* Amoretti. AAS

Sonnet 19: "On Cupid's bow how are my heart-strings bent." Sir Philip Sidney. NoSic *Fr.* Astrophil and Stella. AAS; SiPS

Sonnet 19: "Romancer, far more coy than that coy sex!" Amos Bronson Alcott. APN-1

Sonnet 19. Anna Seward. CPO

Sonnet 20: "Fly, fly, my friends." Sir Philip Sidney. NoSic; OAEL-1 *Fr.* Astrophil and Stella. AAS; SiPS

("But ere I could fly thence, it pierc'd my heart.") (LL) AEP

Sonnet 21. Mark Ameen. GLP

Sonnet XX. Louise Labé, *French.* BoWoP, tr. by Willis Barnstone

(Sonnet: "Seer foretold that I would love one day, A.") PBWP, tr. by Joan Keefe and Richard Terdiman

Sonnet 21: "What grandeur makes a man seem venerable?" Louise Labé, *French.* BoWoP, tr. by Willis Barnstone

Sonnet 21: "Your words my friend (right healthful caustics) blame." Sir Philip Sidney. NAEL-1; NoSic; PoE *Fr.* Astrophil and Stella. AAS; SiPS

("Hath this world ought so fair as Stella is?") (LL) NoP-4

Sonnet 22: "In highest way of heav'n the sun did ride." Sir Philip Sidney. Son *Fr.* Astrophil and Stella. AAS; SiPS

Sonnet 22: "O blazing Sun, how happy you are there." Louise Labé, *French.* BoWoP, tr. by Willis Barnstone

Sonnet 22: "This holy season, fit to fast and pray." Edmund Spenser. PoE *Fr.* Amoretti. AAS

Sonnet 23: "Curious wits, seeing dull pensiveness, The." Sir Philip Sidney. *Fr.* Astrophil and Stella. AAS; SiPS

Sonnet 23: "What good is it to me if long ago." Louise Labé, *French.* BoWoP, tr. by Willis Barnstone

Sonnet 23: "When every one to pleasing pastime hies." Mary Sidney, Countess of Montgomery Wroth. WPE *Fr.* Pamphilia to Amphilanthus.

("Or musique bee butt in deere thoughts of love?") (LL) PBRV

Sonnet 24: "Don't blame me, ladies, if I've loved. No sneers." Louise Labé, *French.* BoWoP, tr. by Willis Barnstone

("Don't scold me, ladies, if I have loved'.") PBWP, tr. by Carol Cosman

Sonnet 24: "Rich fools there be, whose base and filthy heart." Sir Philip Sidney. *Fr.* Astrophil and Stella. AAS; SiPS

Sonnet 24: "When last I saw thee, I did not[t] thee see." Mary Sidney Wroth. PEW *Fr.* Pamphilia to Amphilanthus.

Sonnet XXV: "As in the midst of battle there is room." George Santayana. APN-2 *Fr.* Sonnets.

Sonnet 25: "How long shall this like dying life endure." Edmund Spenser. AAS *Fr.* Amoretti. AAS

Sonnet 25: "Wisest scholar of the wight most wise, The." Sir Philip Sidney. OAEL-1 *Fr.* Astrophil and Stella. AAS; SiPS

Sonnet 25: "Yow that take pleasure in yowr cruelty." Robert Sidney. PBRV

Sonnet 26: "Deare cherish this, and with it[t] my soules will." Mary Sidney Wroth. BWW *Fr.* Pamphilia to Amphilanthus.

Sonnet 26: "Sweet is the rose, but grows upon a brere." Edmund Spenser. *Fr.* Amoretti. AAS

Sonnet 26: "This Life is full of numbness and of balk." Christina Rossetti. VWP *Fr.* Later Life: A Double Sonnet of Sonnets.

Sonnet 26: "Though dusty wits dare scorn astrology." Sir Philip Sidney. OAEL-1; Son *Fr.* Astrophil and Stella. AAS; SiPS

Sonnet 27: "Because I oft, in dark abstracted guise." Sir Philip Sidney. NoSic *Fr.* Astrophil and Stella. AAS; CABP; SiPS

Sonnet 27: "Fair proud, now tell me, why should fair be proud." Edmund Spenser. Son *Fr.* Amoretti. AAS

Sonnet 27: "Fie [or Fy] tedious Hope, why do[e] you still rebel[l]?" Mary Sidney Wroth. NOSC *Fr.* Pamphilia to Amphilanthus.

Sonnet 28: "Griefe, killing griefe: have nott my torments binn." Mary Sidney, Countess of Montgomery Wroth. KTR *Fr.* Pamphilia to Amphilanthus.

Sonnet 28: "You that with allegory's curious frame." Sir Philip Sidney. NoSic; OAEL-1 *Fr.* Astrophil and Stella. AAS; SiPS

Sonnet 29: "Am I failing? For no longer can I cast." George Meredith. PFE *Fr.* Modern Love.

Sonnet XXIX. Elizabeth Barrett Browning. PEW *Fr.* Sonnets from the Portuguese.

Sonnet 29: "Fly hence O! joy noe longer heere abide." Mary Sidney, Countess of Montgomery Wroth. KTR *Fr.* Pamphilia to Amphilanthus.

Sonnet 29: "Like some weak lords, neighboured by mighty kings." Sir Philip Sidney. *Fr.* Astrophil and Stella. AAS; SiPS

Sonnet 30: "My love is like to ice, and I to fire." Edmund Spenser. ImPo *Fr.* Amoretti. AAS

Sonnet 30: "Whether the Turkish new moon minded be." Sir Philip Sidney. NoSic; PoE *Fr.* Astrophil and Stella. AAS; SiPS

Sonnet 30: "You blessed shades, which give mee silent rest." Mary Sidney Wroth. KTR *Fr.* Pamphilia to Amphilanthus.

Sonnet 31: "After long trouble in a taedious way." Mary Sidney, Countess of Montgomery Wroth. KTR *Fr.* Pamphilia to Amphilanthus.

Sonnet 31: "With how sad steps, O Moon, thou climb'st the skies!" Sir Philip Sidney. AEP; AWP; BoLoP; CABP; CH; EnLoPo; GBL; HAP; HeIP-4; InPS-3; NAEL-1; NoSic; OxAEP-1; PBMP; PoE; PoEL-1; PoRA; SCGP; Son; TFi; TRP *Fr.* Astrophil and Stella. AAS; SiPS

("Do they call virtue there ungratefullness?") (LL) NoP-4

(His Lady's Cruelty.) OBEV

("With how sad steps, Oh Moon, thou climb'st the skies.") NoP-4

Sonnet 32: "How fast thou fliest, O Time, on loves swift wings." Mary Sidney, Countess of Montgomery Wroth. NOSC *Fr.* Pamphilia to Amphilanthus.

Sonnet 32: "Morpheus, the lively son of deadly sleep." Sir Philip Sidney. *Fr.* Astrophil and Stella. AAS; SiPS

Sonnet 32. Anna Seward. CPO

Sonnet XXXII. (To Melancholy. Written on the Banks of the Arun, October 1785). Charlotte Smith. Ro

Sonnet 33: "I might, unhappy word, O me, I might." Sir Philip Sidney. OAEL-1 *Fr.* Astrophil and Stella. AAS; SiPS

Sonnet 33: 'When men shall find thy flower'. Samuel Daniel. AEP *Fr.* To Delia.

("When men shall find thy flower, thy glory pass.") AEP; NoP-4

("When Winter snows upon thy golden hairs.") (LL) NoP-4

Sonnet 34: "Come, let me write. 'And to what end?' To ease." Sir Philip Sidney. *Fr.* Astrophil and Stella. AAS; SiPS

Sonnet 34: "Like as a ship, that through the ocean wide." Edmund Spenser. NAEL-1; PoE *Fr.* Amoretti. AAS

Sonnet XXXIV: "Time flies by like a great whale." Ted Berrigan. FTOS *Fr.* The Sonnets.

Sonnet 35: "False [*or* Faulce] hope which feeds but[t] to destroy, and spill." Mary Sidney Wroth. KTR; NAEL-1; PEW *Fr.* Pamphilia to Amphilanthus.

("Of our desires, the farther down to slide.") (LL) PEW

(Sonnet 40.) PEW

Sonnet 35: "Some, misbelieving and profane." Michael Drayton. AEP *Fr.* Idea.

Sonnet 35: "What may words say, or what may words not say." Sir Philip Sidney. *Fr.* Astrophil and Stella. AAS; SiPS

Sonnet XXXV: "You can make this swooped transition on your lips." Ted Berrigan. FTOS *Fr.* The Sonnets.

Sonnet 36: "Stella, whence doth this new assault arise." Sir Philip Sidney. *Fr.* Astrophil and Stella. AAS; SiPS

Sonnet 37: "I'd decided I initiate most." Phyllis Koestenbaum. FFC

Sonnet 37: "My mouth doth water, and my breast doth swell." Sir Philip Sidney. NAEL-1; Son *Fr.* Astrophil and Stella. AAS; SiPS

Sonnet 37: "What guile [*or* guyle] is this, that those her golden tresses." Edmund Spenser. NAEL-1; NoP-4; Son *Fr.* Amoretti. AAS

Sonnet 38: "This night, while sleep begins with heavy wings." Sir Philip Sidney. *Fr.* Astrophil and Stella. AAS; SiPS

Sonnet 39: "Come Sleep, O Sleep." Sir Philip Sidney. NAEL-1; NoSic; OxAEP-1; PoE; PoRA; SCGP; SCV; Son; TFi *Fr.* Astrophil and Stella. AAS; SiPS

("Come sleep, Oh sleep, the certain knot of peace.") NoP-4

(Sleep.) OBEV; SAGP

Sonnet 40: "As good to write as for to lie and groan." Sir Philip Sidney. NoSic *Fr.* Astrophil and Stella. AAS; SiPS

Sonnet 40: "Mark when she smiles with amiable cheer." Edmund Spenser. *Fr.* Amoretti. AAS

Sonnet 41: "Having this day my horse, my hand, my lance." Sir Philip Sidney. AEP; HAP; NAEL-1; PoE; Son *Fr.* Astrophil and Stella. AAS; SiPS

Sonnet 42: "If ever love had force in huma[i]ne brest?" Mary Sidney Wroth. BWW *Fr.* Pamphilia to Amphilanthus.

Sonnet 42: "O eyes, which do the spheres of beauty move." Sir Philip Sidney. *Fr.* Astrophil and Stella. AAS; SiPS

Sonnet 42: "Sometimes the words are so close I am." Julia Alvarez. FFC *Fr.* ("33").

Sonnet XLIII: "Candour of the gods is in thy gaze, The." George Santayana. APN-2 *Fr.* Sonnets.

Sonnet 43: "Fair eyes, sweet lips, dear heart, that foolish I." Sir Philip Sidney. *Fr.* Astrophil and Stella. AAS; SiPS

Sonnet 44: "My words I know do well set forth my mind." Sir Philip Sidney. *Fr.* Astrophil and Stella. AAS; SiPS

Sonnet 44: "When those renowned noble peers of Greece." Edmund Spenser. PoE *Fr.* Amoretti. AAS

Sonnet 45: "Stella oft sees the very face of woe." Sir Philip Sidney. InPS-3; NAEL-1; NoSic; PoE *Fr.* Astrophil and Stella. AAS; SiPS

Sonnet 46: "I cursed thee oft, I pity now thy case." Sir Philip Sidney. *Fr.* Astrophil and Stella. AAS; SiPS

Sonnet 47: "Trust not the treason of those smiling looks." Edmund Spenser. *Fr.* Amoretti. AAS

Sonnet 47: "What, have I thus betrayed my liberty?" Sir Philip Sidney. GBL; NAEL-1; PoEL-1 *Fr.* Astrophil and Stella. AAS; SiPS

Sonnet 48: "How like a fire doth love increase in me[e]." Mary Sidney Wroth. NOSC *Fr.* Pamphilia to Amphilanthus.

Sonnet XLVIII. Pablo Neruda, *Spanish.*

"Two happy lovers make one single bread." ITG, *tr. by* Stephen Mitchell

Sonnet XLVIII: "Of Helen's brothers, one was born to die." George Santayana. APN-2 *Fr.* Sonnets.

Sonnet 48: "Soul's joy, bend not those morning stars from me." Sir Philip Sidney. *Fr.* Astrophil and Stella. AAS; SiPS

Sonnet 49: "I on my horse, and Love on me doth try." Sir Philip Sidney. NAEL-1; OAEL-1; PoE *Fr.* Astrophil and Stella. AAS; SiPS

Sonnet 50: "Stella, the fullness of my thoughts of thee." Sir Philip Sidney. *Fr.* Astrophil and Stella. AAS; SiPS

Sonnet 51: "Pardon mine ears; both I and they do pray." Sir Philip Sidney. *Fr.* Astrophil and Stella. AAS; SiPS

Sonnet 52: "Strife is grown between Virtue and Love, A." Sir Philip Sidney. NAEL-1 *Fr.* Astrophil and Stella. AAS; SiPS

Sonnet 53: "In martial sports I had my cunning tried." Sir Philip Sidney. NAEL-1; NoSic *Fr.* Astrophil and Stella. AAS; SiPS

Sonnet 53: "Panther, knowing that his spotted hide, The." Edmund Spenser. *Fr.* Amoretti. AAS

Sonnet 54: "Because I breathe not love to every one." Sir Philip Sidney. ImGa; InPS-3; NoSic *Fr.* Astrophil and Stella. AAS; SiPS

("Because I breathe not love to ev'ry one.") CABP

Sonnet 54: "Of this world's Theatre in which we stay." Edmund Spenser. NAEL-1; OAEL-1 *Fr.* Amoretti. AAS

("She is no woman, but a senseless stone.") (LL) CABP

Sonnet LV: "Grace to be born and live as variously as possible." Ted Berrigan. FTOS *Fr.* The Sonnets.

Sonnet 55: "Muses, I oft invoked your holy aid." Sir Philip Sidney. *Fr.* Astrophil and Stella. AAS; SiPS

Sonnet 55: "So oft as I her beauty do behold." Edmund Spenser. Son *Fr.* Amoretti. AAS

Sonnet 56: "Fair ye be sure, but cruel and unkind." Edmund Spenser. Son *Fr.* Amoretti. AAS

Sonnet 56: "Fie, school of Patience, fie; your lesson is." Sir Philip Sidney. NAEL-1 *Fr.* Astrophil and Stella. AAS; SiPS

Sonnet 57: "Woe, having made with many fights his own." Sir Philip Sidney. *Fr.* Astrophil and Stella. AAS; SiPS

Sonnet 58: "Doubt there hath been, when with his golden chain." Sir Philip Sidney. *Fr.* Astrophil and Stella. AAS; SiPS

Sonnet 58: "Weak is the assurance that weak flesh reposeth." Edmund Spenser. *Fr.* Amoretti. AAS

Sonnet 59: "Dear, why make you more of a dog than me?" Sir Philip Sidney. GBL *Fr.* Astrophil and Stella. AAS; SiPS

Sonnet 60: "When my good angel guides me to the place." Sir Philip Sidney. *Fr.* Astrophil and Stella. AAS; SiPS

Sonnet 61: "Glorious image of the Maker's beauty, The." Edmund Spenser. Son *Fr.* Amoretti. AAS

Sonnet 61: "Oft with true sighs, oft with uncalled tears." Sir Philip Sidney. NAEL-1 *Fr.* Astrophil and Stella. AAS; SiPS

Sonnet 62: "Late tired with woe, e'en ready for to pine." Sir Philip Sidney. *Fr.* Astrophil and Stella. AAS; SiPS

Sonnet 62: "Weary year his race now having run, The." Edmund Spenser. *Fr.* Amoretti. AAS

Sonnet 63: "After long storms and tempests sad assay." Edmund Spenser. OAEL-1 *Fr.* Amoretti. AAS

Sonnet 63: "O Grammer rules, ô now your virtues show." Sir Philip Sidney. *Fr.* Astrophil and Stella. AAS; SiPS

Sonnet 64: "Coming [*or* Comming] to kiss[e] her lips [*or* lyps], (such grace I found)." Edmund Spenser. EBEV; NAEL-1; OAEL-1; Son *Fr.* Amoretti. AAS

("But her sweet odour did them all excell.") (LL) PBRV

Sonnet 64: "No more, my dear, no more these counsels try." Sir Philip Sidney. SCGP *Fr.* Astrophil and Stella. AAS; SiPS

Sonnet 65.: "Doubt which ye misdeeme, fayre love, is vaine, The." Edmund Spenser. AEP; NAEL-1 *Fr.* Amoretti. AAS

Sonnet 65: "Love, by sure proof I may call thee unkind." Sir Philip Sidney. Son *Fr.* Astrophil and Stella. AAS; SiPS

Sonnet 66: "And do I see some cause a hope to feed." Sir Philip Sidney. *Fr.* Astrophil and Stella. AAS; SiPS

Sonnet 67: "Hope, art thou true, or dost thou flatter me?" Sir Philip Sidney. *Fr.* Astrophil and Stella. AAS; SiPS

Sonnet 67: "Like a huntsman after weary chase." Edmund Spenser. GBL; HeIP-4; NAEL-1; PoE; PoEL-1; Son *Fr.* Amoretti. AAS

("Lyke as a huntsman after weary chace.") NoP-4; PBRV

("So goodly won, with her own will beguil'd.") (LL) CABP

Sonnet 68: "Most glorious Lord of Life that on this day." Edmund Spenser. ChIV-2; HAP; InPS-3; NAEL-1; NOBE; NOCV; NoSic; OBEV; PoE; Son *Fr.* Amoretti. AAS

(Easter.) NOBE; OBEV; PeECV

("Most Glorious Lord of lyfe that on this day.") NoP-4; PeECV

Sonnet 68: "Stella, the only planet of my light." Sir Philip Sidney. *Fr.* Astrophil and Stella. AAS; SiPS

Sonnet 69: "O joy, too high for my low style to show." *Sir Philip Sidney.* NAEL-1; OxAEP-1 *Fr.* Astrophil and Stella. AAS; SiPS

Sonnet 70: "Fresh Spring the herald of love's mighty king." *Edmund Spenser.* AWP; HAP; InPS-3; OBEV; PoE; Son *Fr.* Amoretti. AAS

("For none can call againe the passèd time.") (LL) NoP-4; PBRV

Sonnet 70: "My Muse may well grudge at my heav'nly joy." *Sir Philip Sidney. Fr.* Astrophil and Stella. AAS; SiPS

Sonnet LXX: "Sweeter than sour apples flesh to boys." *Ted Berrigan.* FTOS *Fr.* The Sonnets.

Sonnet 71: "I joy to see how in your drawen work." *Edmund Spenser.* PoE *Fr.* Amoretti. AAS

Sonnet 71: "Soverayne beauty which I doo admire, The." *Edmund Spenser.* PoEL-1 *Fr.* Amoretti. AAS

("Sovereign beauty which I do admire, The.") AEP

Sonnet 71: "Who will in fairest book of Nature know." *Sir Philip Sidney.* InPS-3; NAEL-1; NoSic; OAEL-1; PoE; Poetr *Fr.* Astrophil and Stella. AAS; SiPS

Sonnet 72: "Desire, though thou my old companion art." *Sir Philip Sidney.* NAEL-1 *Fr.* Astrophil and Stella. AAS; SiPS

("Now banish'd art—but yet, alas, how shall?") (LL) AEP

("Now banisht art, but yet alas how shall?") (LL) PBRV

Sonnet 73: 'Being my self captived here'. *Edmund Spenser.* AEP

Sonnet 72: "Oft when my spirit doth spread her bolder wings." *Edmund Spenser.* Son *Fr.* Amoretti. AAS

Sonnet 74: "I never drank of Aganippe well." *Sir Philip Sidney.* NAEL-1; NoSic; Son *Fr.* Astrophil and Stella. AAS; SiPS

Sonnet 74: "Love still a boy, and oft a wanton is." *Sir Philip Sidney.* Son *Fr.* Astrophil and Stella. AAS; SiPS

Sonnet 74: "Most happy letters framed by skilfull trade." *Edmund Spenser.* NAEL-1 *Fr.* Amoretti. AAS

Sonnet 75: "Of all the kings that ever here did reign." *Sir Philip Sidney.* NoSic *Fr.* Astrophil and Stella. AAS; SiPS

Sonnet 75: "One day I wrote her name upon the strand." *Edmund Spenser.* AWP; BoLoP; CABP; CBLP; EBEV; EPCY; GBL; HAP; HeIP-4; ImPo; InPS-3; NAEL-1; NoSic; OAEL-1; PBMP; PoE; PoPoPo; Son; TFi; WeW-3 *Fr.* Amoretti. AAS

Sonnet 75: "Was it a dream, or did I see it plain?" *Edmund Spenser.* CBLP; NIP-4 *Fr.* Amoretti. AAS

Sonnet 76: "Fair bosom! fraught with virtue's richest treasure." *Edmund Spenser.* NIP-4 *Fr.* Amoretti. AAS

Sonnet 76: "She comes, and straight therewith her shining twins do move." *Sir Philip Sidney. Fr.* Astrophil and Stella. AAS; SiPS

Sonnet LXXVII: "It is 3:17 a.m. in New York city, yes, it is." *Ted Berrigan.* FTOS *Fr.* The Sonnets.

Sonnet 77: "Those looks, whose beams be joy, whose motion is delight." *Sir Philip Sidney. Fr.* Astrophil and Stella. AAS; SiPS

Sonnet 78: "Lacking my love, I go from place to place." *Edmund Spenser.* NoSic *Fr.* Amoretti. AAS

Sonnet 78: "Little Hearts, where light-wing'd Passion raignes, The." *Greville Fulke.* PBRV *Fr.* Cælica.

Sonnet 78: "O how the pleasant airs of true love be." *Sir Philip Sidney. Fr.* Astrophil and Stella. AAS; SiPS

Sonnet 79: "Men call you fair [or fayre], and you do[e] credit it." *Edmund Spenser.* AWP; FaBoBe; NAEL-1; Son *Fr.* Amoretti. AAS

("All other fayre lyke flowres untymely fade.") (LL) NoP-4

Sonnet 79. *Sir Philip Sidney. See* Stella's Kiss.

Sonnet 80: "Sweet swelling lip, well mayst thou swell in pride." *Sir Philip Sidney. Fr.* Astrophil and Stella. AAS; SiPS

Sonnet 81: "Fair [or Fayre] is my love, when her fair [or fayre] golden heares." *Edmund Spenser.* Son *Fr.* Amoretti. AAS

("But this the worke of harts astonishment.") (LL) NoP-4

("Fair is my love, when her fair golden hairs.") GSo

Sonnet 81: "O kiss, which doest those ruddy gems impart." *Sir Philip Sidney.* NAEL-1; Son *Fr.* Astrophil and Stella. AAS; SiPS

("O kisse, which doest those ruddie gemmes impart.") PBRV

Sonnet 82: "Joy of my life, full oft for loving you." *Edmund Spenser.* HeIP-4 *Fr.* Amoretti. AAS

Sonnet 82: "Nymph of the garden where all beauties be." *Sir Philip Sidney.* PoE *Fr.* Astrophil and Stella. AAS; SiPS

Sonnet 83: "Good brother *Philip,* I have borne you long." *Sir Philip Sidney. Fr.* Astrophil and Stella. AAS; SiPS

Sonnet 83: "Let not one sparke of filthy lustfull fyre." *Edmund Spenser. Fr.* Amoretti. AAS

Sonnet 84: "Highway, since you my chief Parnassus be." *Sir Philip Sidney.* SCGP *Fr.* Astrophil and Stella. AAS; SiPS

Sonnet 85: "I see the house; my heart thyself contain." *Sir Philip Sidney. Fr.* Astrophil and Stella. AAS; SiPS

Sonnet 86: "Alas, whence came this change of looks? If I." *Sir Philip Sidney. Fr.* Astrophil and Stella. AAS; SiPS

Sonnet 87: "Since I have lacked the comfort of that light." *Edmund Spenser. Fr.* Amoretti. AAS

Sonnet 87: "When I was forced from Stella ever dear." *Sir Philip Sidney.* NAEL-1 *Fr.* Astrophil and Stella. AAS; SiPS

Sonnet 88: "Out, traitor absence: dar'st thou counsel me." *Sir Philip Sidney. Fr.* Astrophil and Stella. AAS; SiPS

Sonnet 89: "Like as the culver on the bared bough." *Edmund Spenser.* GBL; PoE *Fr.* Amoretti. AAS

("And dead my life that wants such lively blis.") (LL) NoP-4

("Lyke as the Culver on the barèd bough.") NoP-4

Sonnet 89: "Now that of absence the most irksome night." *Sir Philip Sidney.* NAEL-1 *Fr.* Astrophil and Stella. AAS; SiPS

Sonnet 90: "Stella, think not that I by verse seek fame." *Sir Philip Sidney.* NoSic *Fr.* Astrophil and Stella. AAS; SiPS

Sonnet 91: "Stella, while now by honour's cruel might." *Sir Philip Sidney.* NAEL-1; PoE *Fr.* Astrophil and Stella. AAS; SiPS

Sonnet 92: "Be your words made (good sir) of Indian ware." *Sir Philip Sidney.* NoSic *Fr.* Astrophil and Stella. AAS; SiPS

Sonnet 93: "O fate, O fault, O curse, child of my bliss." *Sir Philip Sidney. Fr.* Astrophil and Stella. AAS; SiPS

Sonnet 94: "Grief, find the words, for thou hast made my brain." *Sir Philip Sidney. Fr.* Astrophil and Stella. AAS; SiPS

Sonnet 95: "Yet sighs, dear sighs, indeed true friends you are." *Sir Philip Sidney. Fr.* Astrophil and Stella. AAS; SiPS

Sonnet 96: "Thought, with good cause thou lik'st so well the night." *Sir Philip Sidney. Fr.* Astrophil and Stella. AAS; SiPS

Sonnet 97: "Dian, that fain would cheer her friend the Night." *Sir Philip Sidney. Fr.* Astrophil and Stella. AAS; SiPS Sonnet 97: 'How like a winter'. *Shakespeare. See* Sonnet 97.

Sonnet 98: "Ah bed, the field where joy's peace some do see." *Sir Philip Sidney.* EnLoPo *Fr.* Astrophil and Stella. AAS; SiPS

Sonnet 99: "When far-spent night persuades each mortal eye." *Sir Philip Sidney;* PoE; Son *Fr.* Astrophil and Stella. AAS; SiPS

Sonnet 100: "O tears, no tears, but rain from beauty's skies." *Sir Philip Sidney.* Son *Fr.* Astrophil and Stella. AAS; SiPS

Sonnet 101: "Stella is sick, and in that sick-bed lies." *Sir Philip Sidney. Fr.* Astrophil and Stella. AAS; SiPS

Sonnet 101. *Mary Sidney, Countess of Montgomery Wroth.* PEW *Fr.* Pamphilia to Amphilanthus.

Sonnet 102: "Where be those roses gone, which sweetened so our eyes?" *Sir Philip Sidney. Fr.* Astrophil and Stella. AAS; SiPS

Sonnet 103: "O happy Thames, that didst my Stella bear." *Sir Philip Sidney.* OxAEP-1 *Fr.* Astrophil and Stella. AAS; SiPS

Sonnet 104: "Envious wits, what hath been mine offence." *Sir Philip Sidney.* PoE; Son *Fr.* Astrophil and Stella. AAS; SiPS

Sonnet 105: "Unhappy sight, and hath she vanished by." *Sir Philip Sidney. Fr.* Astrophil and Stella. AAS; SiPS

Sonnet 106: "O absent presence, Stella is not here." *Sir Philip Sidney. Fr.* Astrophil and Stella. AAS; SiPS

Sonnet 107: "Stella, since thou so right a Princess art." *Sir Philip Sidney.* OxAEP-1 *Fr.* Astrophil and Stella. AAS; SiPS

Sonnet 108: "When sorrow (using mine own fire's might)." *Sir Philip Sidney. Fr.* Astrophil and Stella. AAS; SiPS

Sonnet: A Rapture Concerning His Lady. *Guido Cavalcanti, Italian.* AWP, *tr. by* D. G. Rossetti

Sonnet; A Still Place. "Barry Cornwall." NOBRP

Sonnet: A Trance of Love. *Cino da Pistoia.* AWP, *tr. by* D. G. Rossetti

Sonnet Addressed to My Mother. *Mary Tighe.* NoP-4

Sonnet: At Ostend. *William Lisle Bowles.* NOEC

Sonnet: Death Is Not without but within Him. *Cino da Pistoia, Italian.* AWP, *tr. by* D. G. Rossetti

Sonnet: Death Warnings. *Francisco de Quevedo y Villegas, Spanish.* AWP, *tr. by* John Masefield

Sonnet: Death Will Find Me. *Rupert Brooke. See* Sonnet: "Oh! Death will find me, long before I tire."

Sonnet: Equality of the Sexes. *Gavin Ewart.* Son

Sonnet for a Picture. *Swinburne.* BXAP; OAEL-2; UV *Fr.* The Heptalogia.

Sonnet for Christmas. *Judith Wright.* LW

Sonnet For Helen. *Pierre de Ronsard, French.* LoP, *tr. by* Alistair Elliot (Sonnets for Helen.) FLP

Sonnet for Iva. *Marilyn Hacker.* NMM-2

Sonnet for Minimalists. *Mona Van Duyn.* FFC; WeW-3

Sonnet for the Season. *Art Lange.* PmAP

Sonnet from Below the Age Gap. *Keith Sinclair.* PeNZ

Sonnet from "One Person." *Elinor Wylie. See* Sonnet: "I hereby swear that to uphold your house."

Sonnet: He Argues His Case with Death. *Cecco Angiolieri, da Siena, Italian.* AWP, *tr. by* D. G. Rossetti

Sonnet: He Compares All Things with His Lady, and Finds Them Wanting. Guido Cavalcanti, *Italian.* AWP, *tr. by* D. G. Rossetti

Sonnet: He Craves Interpreting of a Dream of His. Dante da Maiano, *Italian.* AWP, *tr. by* D. G. Rossetti

Sonnet: He Is Past All Help. Cecco Angiolieri, da Siena, *Italian.* AWP, *tr. by* D. G. Rossetti

Sonnet: He Jests Concerning His Poverty. Bartolomeo di Sant' Angelo, *Italian.* AWP, *tr. by* D. G. Rossetti

Sonnet: He Rails against Dante, Who Had Censured His Homage to Becchina. Cecco Angiolieri, da Siena, *Italian.* AWP, *tr. by* D. G. Rossetti

Sonnet: He Speaks of a Third Love of His. Guido Cavalcanti, *Italian.* AWP, *tr. by* D. G. Rossetti

Sonnet: He Will Not Be Too Deeply in Love. Cecco Angiolieri, da Siena, *Italian.* AWP, *tr. by* D. G. Rossetti

Sonnet: He Will Praise His Lady. Guido Guinicelli, *Italian.* AWP, *tr. by* D. G. Rossetti

Sonnet: In Absence from Becchina. Cecco Angiolieri, da Siena, *Italian.* AWP, *tr. by* D. G. Rossetti

Sonnet in Praise of Mr. Thomas the Deceased. John Taylor. CBNP *Fr.* Odcomb's Complaint.

Sonnet in Primary Colors. Rita Dove. NAmP90

Sonnet: In Time of Revolt. Rupert Brooke. OBCoV

Sonnet: Ingratitude. Anna Seward. ECWP; NOEC

Sonnet is a moment's monument,—A A. Sonnet, A [*or* The: "Sonnet is a moment's monument"]. D. G. Rossetti. EnVR; GSo; NAEL-2; Son *Fr.* The House of Life.

Sonnet is a world, where feelings caught, The. The Sonnet (III). John Addington Symonds. GSo

Sonnet: Kamikaze: "Dawn and night of fighting, lovers like actual wars." Bernadette Mayer. FTOS

Sonnet: Lady, That in the Prime. Milton. *See* Lady That in the Prime.

Sonnet: Leaves. William Barnes. OBNC

Sonnet Macabre. Theodore Wratislaw. ADE

Sonnet Made upon the Groves near Merlou [*or* Merlow] Castle. Edward Herbert, 1st Baron Herbert of Cherbury. NOSC

Sonnet: Of All He Would Do. Cecco Angiolieri, da Siena, *Italian.* AWP, *tr. by* D. G. Rossetti

("And leave the old and ugly for others.") (LL) ItIP

("If I were fire, I would set the world aflame.") ItIP

Sonnet: Of an Ill-Favored Lady. Guido Cavalcanti, *Italian.* AWP, *tr. by* D. G. Rossetti

Sonnet: Of Beatrice de' Portinari, on All Saints' Day. Dante, *Italian.* AWP, *tr. by* D. G. Rossetti

Sonnet: Of Beauty and Duty. Dante, *Italian.* AWP, *tr. by* D. G. Rossetti

Sonnet: Of Becchina in a Rage. Cecco Angiolieri, da Siena, *Italian.* AWP, *tr. by* D. G. Rossetti

Sonnet: Of Becchina, the Shoemaker's Daughter. Cecco Angiolieri, da Siena, *Italian.* AWP, *tr. by* D. G. Rossetti

Sonnet of Black Beauty. Edward Herbert. NOSC

Sonnet of Brotherhood. Ronald Allison Kells Mason. PeNZ

Sonnet of Fishes. George Barker. FaBoMo; Son

Sonnet: Of His Lady's Face. Jacopo da Lentino, *Italian.* AWP

Sonnet: Of His Pain from a New Love. Guido Cavalcanti, *Italian.* AWP, *tr. by* D. G. Rossetti

Sonnet: Of Love, in Honor of His Mistress Becchina. Cecco Angiolieri, da Siena, *Italian.* AWP, *tr. by* D. G. Rossetti

Sonnet: Of Love in Men and Devils. Cecco Angiolieri, da Siena, *Italian.* AWP, *tr. by* D. G. Rossetti

Sonnet: Of Moderation and Tolerance. Guido Guinicelli, *Italian.* AWP, *tr. by* D. G. Rossetti

Sonnet: Of the Eyes of a Certain Mandetta. Guido Cavalcanti, *Italian.* AWP, *tr. by* D. G. Rossetti

Sonnet: Of the Grave of Selvaggia, on the Monte della Sambuca. Cino da Pistoia, *Italian.* AWP, *tr. by* D. G. Rossetti

Sonnet: Of the Making of Master Messerin. Rustico Di Filippo, *Italian.* AWP, *tr. by* D. G. Rossetti

Sonnets of the Months: Conclusion. Folgore da San Geminiano. AWP, *tr. by* D. G. Rossetti

Sonnets of the Months: September. Folgore da San Geminiano, *Italian.* AWP, *tr. by* D. G. Rossetti

Sonnet of the Moon, A. Charles Best. CH

Sonnet of the Mountain, The. Mellin de Saint-Gelais, *French.* AWP, *tr. by* Austin Dobson

Sonnet: Of the 20th of June 1291. Cecco Angiolieri, da Siena, *Italian.* AWP, *tr. by* D. G. Rossetti

Sonnet: Of Virtue. Folgore da San Geminiano, *Italian.* AWP, *tr. by* D. G. Rossetti

Sonnet: Of Why He Is Unchanged. Cecco Angiolieri, da Siena, *Italian.* AWP

Sonnet: Of Why He Would Be a Scullion. Cecco Angiolieri, da Siena, *Italian.* AWP, *tr. by* D. G. Rossetti

Sonnet on a Family Picture. Thomas Edwards. NOEC

Sonnet on a Still Night. James Vincent Cunningham. PoA

Sonnet on Chillon. Byron. GSo; PBMP *Fr.* The Prisoner of Chillon. PoLF

(On the Castle of Chillon.) GTBS-P

Sonnet on Famous and Familiar Sonnets and Experiences. Delmore Schwartz. Son; TRP

Sonnet: on Loss. Sir Robert Ayton. NOSC

Sonnet on Mr Haydon's Portrait of Mr Wordsworth. Elizabeth Barrett Browning. *See* On a Portrait of Wordsworth by B. R. Haydon.

Sonnet on Reading the Poem upon the Mountain Daisy, by Mr. Burns. Helen Maria Williams. ECWP

Sonnet on Sir William Alexander's Harsh Verses after the English Fashion, A. James I, King of England. Son

Sonnet: On the 9th of June 1290. Dante, *Italian.* AWP, *tr. by* D. G. Rossetti

Sonnet on the Crimean War. William Forster. CBAP

Sonnet: On the Late Massacre in Piedmont. Milton. *See* On the Late Massacre [*or* Massacher] in Piedmont [*or* Piemont].

Sonnet [on the Death of Mr. Richard West]. Thomas Gray. NOEC; PoE; PoEL-3

(On the Death of Mr. Richard West.) GSo; NOBE; Son

Sonnet on the Death of the Man Who Invented Plastic Roses. Peter Meinke. PBCAP

Sonnet on the Death of the Poet J. Keats. John Taylor. Ro *Fr.* London Magazine, 3 526.

Sonnet: On the Detection of a False Friend. Guido Cavalcanti, *Italian.* AWP, *tr. by* D. G. Rossetti

Sonnet: On the Religious Memorie of Mrs. Catherine Thomason My Christian Freind Deceas'd Decem. 1646. Milton. ChIV-2

(Sonnet.) OxAEP-1

Sonnet: On the River Tweed. Sir Robert Ayton. NOSC

Sonnet Reversed. Rupert Brooke. NOBL; PeLV

Sonnet Right off the Bat. Félix Lope de Vega Carpio, *Spanish.* STV, *tr. by* John Frederick Nims

Sonnet sent to Blackness to Mr. John Welsch, by the Lady Culross, A. Elizabeth, Lady Culross Melvill. KTR

Sonnet: Silence. Thomas Hood. *See* Silence.

Sonnet—Silence. Edgar Allan Poe. *See* Silence.

Sonnet: Supernatural Beings. Gavin Ewart. Son

Sonnet: Suppos'd to Be Written at Lemnos. Thomas Russell. NOBRP; NOEC

Sonnet, to a Child. Wilfred Owen. NOxBChV

Sonnet: To a Friend. Hartley Coleridge. *See* To a Friend.

Sonnet: To a Friend Who Does Not Pity His Love. Guido Cavalcanti, *Italian.* AWP, *tr. by* D. G. Rossetti

Sonnet to a Negro in Harlem. Helene Johnson. NAAAL; NIP-4; SSLK

Sonnet: To a Portrait of Hart Crane. Allen Tate. GS

Sonnet—To an American Painter Departing for Europe. William Cullen Bryant. *See* To Cole, the Painter, Departing for Europe.

Sonnet to Be Written from Prison. Robert Adamson. CBAP

Sonnet: To Brunetto Latini. Dante, *Italian.* AWP, *tr. by* D. G. Rossetti

Sonnet to Byron. Shelley. EPCY

(Lines to Lord Byron.) Ro

("May lift itself in worship to the god.") (LL) Ro

Sonnet: To Certain Ladies; When Beatrice Was Lamenting Her Father's Death. Dante, *Italian.* AWP, *tr. by* D. G. Rossetti

Sonnet: To Dante (He Writes to Dante, Then in Exile at Verona, Defying Him as No Better Than Himself). Cecco Angiolieri, da Siena, *Italian.* AWP, *tr. by* D. G. Rossetti

Sonnet: To Dante on the Last Sonnet of the Vita Nuova. Cecco Angiolieri, da Siena, *Italian.* AWP, *tr. by* D. G. Rossetti

Sonnet to Gath. Edna St. Vincent Millay. BoWoP; CMoP; MoAmPo

Sonnet: To Guido Cavalcanti. Dante, *Italian.* AWP, *tr. by* Shelley

(Sonnet: [From the Italian of Dante.] Dante to Guido Cavalcanti.) OBVE

Sonnet to Heavenly Beauty, A. Joachim Du Bellay, *French.* AWP; CTC, *tr. by* Andrew Lang

Sonnet: To His Lady Joan, of Florence. Guido Cavalcanti, *Italian.* AWP, *tr. by* D. G. Rossetti

Sonnet to Hope. Helen Maria Williams. ECWP

Sonnet to Lake Leman. Byron. Son

Sonnet: To Love, In Great Bitterness. Cino da Pistoia, *Italian.* AWP, *tr. by* D. G. Rossetti

Sonnet: To Mr. H. Lawes, on His Air[e]s. Milton. *See* To Mr. H. Lawes On His Airs.

Sonnet to My First Born. Mary Weston Fordham. CBWP-2
Sonnet to My Mother. George Barker. *See* To My Mother.
Sonnet to My Mother, A. Heinrich Heine. TrJP, *tr. by* Emma Lazarus
Sonnet to My Mother, A. Heinrich Heine. *See* To My Mother.
Sonnet to Negro Soldiers. Joseph Cotter, Sr.. PoBA
Sonnet to Nothing. Thomas Beck. NOBRP
Sonnet to Opium; Celebrating Its Virtues, A. "Orestes." NOEC
Sonnet—To Science. Edgar Allan Poe. AmPP; MeMAP; NAAL-1; NAAL-3; OxBA; PBMP; Son; TAP
  ("Summer dream beneath the tamarind tree?, The.") (LL) GSo; NCAP; NoP-4; PAR
  (To Science.) APN-1; GSo; PAR
Sonnet to Sleep. Keats. *See* To Sleep.
Sonnet: To Tartar, a Terrier Beauty. Thomas Lovell Beddoes. NOBVV; OBNC
Sonnet to the Lady Pietra degli Scrovigni. Dante, *Italian.* AWP, *tr. by* D. G. Rossetti
Sonnet to the "Most Distinguished Chancellor" that Oxford Has Had. Max Beerbohm *and* William Rothenstein. UV
Sonnet to the Noble Lady, the Lady Mary Wroth, A. Ben Jonson. BeJo; NoP-4
Sonnet: To the River Lodon. Thomas, the Younger Warton. NOEC
  (Sonnet IX. To the River Lodon.) Ro
Sonnet to the River Otter. Coleridge. OAEL-2
  ("Ah, that once more I were a careless child!") (LL) Ro
  (To the River Otter.) Son
Sonnet: To the Same Ladies; With Their Answer. Dante, *Italian.* AWP, *tr. by* D. G. Rossetti
Sonnet to Twilight. Helen Maria Williams. Ro *Fr.* Poems.
Sonnet to Valclusa. Thomas Russell. NOBRP
Sonnet to Vauxhall. Thomas Hood. OBCoV; PoEL-4
Sonnet upon Sonnets, A. Robert Burns. GSo; Son
Sonnet Variations. Peyton Houston. Son
Sonnet: When I Consider. Milton. *See* On His Blindness.
Sonnet: "Whenas [*or* When as] man's life, the light of human lust." Greville Fulke. NOSC *Fr.* Caelica.
Sonnet with a Different Letter at the End of Every Line. George Starbuck. OBAL
Sonnet Written at the Close of Spring [*or* Elegiac Sonnet]. Charlotte Smith. ECWP
Sonnet Written in Keats's *Endymion.* Thomas Hood. EPCY; Ro
Sonnet Written in the Church-Yard at Middleton in Sussex. Charlotte Smith. ECWP; NOEC; WPE; WoRP
  ("Press'd by the Moon, mute arbitress of tides.") CABP
  (Written in the churchyard at Middleton in Sussex.) PEW
Sonnet Written in Tintern Abbey, Monmouthshire. Edmund Gardner. NOEC
Sonnet Written upon My Lord Admiral Seymour, A. John Harington. NoSic
Sonneteering Made Easy. S. B. Botsford. NYBP
Sonnets. James Agee. MoAmPo
Sonnets. Richard Barnfield.
  "Sighing, and sadly sitting by my Love." PBRV
  "Sometimes I wish that I his pillow were." PBRV
Sonnets, The. Ted Berrigan.
  "Dear Margie, hello. It is 5:15 a.m." PmAP
  Final Sonnet, A. FTOS; PmAP
  Real Live. FTOS
  Sonnet: "My dream a drink with Lonnie Johnson we discuss the code." NoAM
  Sonnet I: "His piercing pince-nez. Some dim frieze." FTOS
  Sonnet III: "Stronger than alcohol, more great than song." FTOS
  Sonnet LV: "Grace to be born and live as variously as possible." FTOS
  Sonnet LXX: "Sweeter than sour apples flesh to boys." FTOS
  Sonnet LXXVII: "It is 3:17 a.m. in New York city, yes, it is." FTOS
    ("DEAR CHRIS / It is 3:17 a.m. in New York city, yes, it is.")
  Sonnet XXXIV: "Time flies by like a great whale." FTOS
  Sonnet XXXV: "You can make this swooped transition on your lips." FTOS
Sonnets. John Berryman. Son
Sonnets. Giovanni Boccaccio, *Italian.*
  Inscription for a Portrait of Dante. AWP
  Of Fiammetta Singing. AWP
  Of His Last Sight of Fiammetta. AWP
  Of Three Girls and of Their Talk. AWP
  To Dante in Paradise, after Fiammetta's Death. AWP
  To One Who Had Censured His Public Exposition of Dante. AWP
Sonnets. John Masefield.

Flesh, I Have Knocked at Many a Dusty Door. LiTM
"Is there a great green commonwealth of Thought." LiTM; MoBrPo
"There is no God, as I was taught in youth." CMoP
Sonnets. George Santayana.
  Sonnet III: "O world, thou choosest not the better part!" APN-2
  Sonnet V: "Dreamt I today [*or* to-day] the dream of yesternight." APN-2
  Sonnet XLIII: "Candour of the gods is in thy gaze, The." APN-2
  Sonnet XLVIII: "Of Helen's brothers, one was born to die." APN-2
  Sonnet XXV: "As in the midst of battle there is room." APN-2
Sonnets. Anna Seward.
  "Behold that tree, in Autumn's dim decay." WoRP
  "On the fleet streams, the Sun, that late arose." WoRP
  Sonnet VII: "By Derwent's rapid stream as oft I strayed." Ro
  "While one sere leaf, that parting autumn yields." WoRP
Sonnets. Shakespeare.
  Blind Love. GTBS-P
  Post Mortem. GTBS-P
  Sonnet: "Let me confesse that we two must be twaine." PBRV
  Sonnet: "What's in the braine that Inck may character." PBRV
  Sonnet 1. CTC; HeIP-4; ImPo
    (From Sonnets.) NoP-4
  Sonnet 2. HeIP-4; ImPo; NoSic; SCGP; Son
  Sonnet 3. ImPo; NAEL-1; SCGP
  Sonnet 5: "Those hours that with gentle work." AEP
  Sonnet 8. PoEL-2
  Sonnet 12. AWP; HeIP-4; InPS-3; NAEL-1; NoSic; OAEL-1; SCGP; Son
    (When I Do Count the Clock.)
  Sonnet 14. Son
  Sonnet 15. AWP; NAEL-1; NoSic; SCGP; Son
  Sonnet 18. APAD; BoLoP; CABP; CTC; ClHu; EnLoPo; FaBoBe; GBL; HAP; HeIP-4, ImPo, InPK 6; InPS-3; NOBE; NoSic; OAEL-1; OBEV; PBMP; PoE; PoEL-2; PoLF; PoPoPo; PoRA; SCGP; SCV; Son; TFi; WeW-3
    (Sonnet 18: 'Shall I compare thee'.) AEP
    (To His Love.) Son
  Sonnet 19. AWP; EBEV; HeIP-4; ImPo; NAEL-1; NoSic; OAEL-1; OxAEP-1; PoE; PoEL-2; SCGP
    ("Devouring time blunt thou the Lyons pawes.") PBRV
    (Sonnet.) PBRV
  Sonnet 20. HeIP-4; NAEL-1; NoSic; OAEL-1; OxAEP-1
    (Sonnet.) PBRV
    ("Womans face with natures owne hand painted, A.") PBRV
  Sonnet 21. HeIP-4
  Sonnet 22. Son
  Sonnet 23. CABP; NoSic; Son
    ("To hear with eyes belongs to love's fine wit.") (LL) CABP
  Sonnet 25. OxAEP-1; SCGP
  Sonnet 26. HeIP-4
  Sonnet 27. HeIP-4; NoSic; SCGP
  Sonnet 29. APAD; AWP; CTC; EBEV; GBL; HAP; HeIP-4; ImPo; InPK-6; InPS-3; NAEL-1; NOBE; NoSic; OAEL-1; OBEV; OPOU; OxAEP-1; PoEL-2; PoPoPo; Poetr; SCGP; Son; TFi; WeW-3
    ("That then I skorne to change my state with Kings.") (LL) PBRV
    (When In Disgrace.) LoP
  Sonnet 30. AWP; CTC; ClHu; EBEV; EBEvV; GBL; HAP; HeIP-4; ImPo; InPS-3; NAEL-1; NOBE; NoSic; OAEL-1; OBEV; OxAEP-1; PoE; PoEL-2; PoLF; PoRA; SCGP; TFi
    ("All losses are restor'd and sorrows end.") (LL) APAD; GSo
    ("All losses are restored and sorrows end.") (LL) CABP; NoP-4; PFE; PoPoPo
    (Remembrance.) GTBS-P
  Sonnet 31. NOBE; OBEV; PoEL-2
  Sonnet 33. AWP; EBEV; EBEvV; HAP; ImPo; NIP-4; NoSic; OAEL-1; OxAEP-1; PoRA; SCGP; Son; TFi; WeW-3
    ("Full many a glorious morning have I seen.") NoP-4
  Sonnet 34. HeIP-4; OxAEP-1
  Sonnet 35. AWP; ImPo; NAEL-1; NoSic; OxAEP-1; PoE; SCGP; UnPo
    ("No more bee greev'd at that which thou hast done.") PBRV
    ("To that sweet theefe which sourely robs from me.") (LL) PBRV
  Sonnet 36. HeIP-4
  Sonnet 40. HeIP-4; OxAEP-1; SCGP
  Sonnet 41. OxAEP-1
  Sonnet 42. CBLP; HeIP-4; OxAEP-1
  Sonnet 44. Son
  Sonnet 46. HeIP-4
  Sonnet 49. OxAEP-1

Sonnet 50. OxAEP-1

Sonnet 52. OxAEP-1

Sonnet 53. CTC; EBEV; ImPo; NoSic; OAEL-1; OBEV; OxAEP-1; SCGP

Sonnet 54. AWP; OBEV; PoE; SCGP

("O how much more cloth beauty beauteous seem.") AEP

(Sonnet 54: 'O how much more doth beauty'.) AEP

("When that shall vade, by verse distils your truth.") (LL) AEP

Sonnet 55. AWP; CABP; CTC; EPCY; HeIP-4; ImPo; NAEL-1; NIP-4; NOBE; NoSic; OAEL-1; OxAEP-1; PoE; PoEL-2; PoRA; Poetr; SCGP; Son

("Not marble, nor the guilded monuments.") PBRV

(Sonnet.) PBRV

("You live in this, and dwell in lovers eies.") (LL) PBRV

Sonnet 56. PoLF; SCGP

("Makes Sommers welcome, thrice more wish'd, more rare.") (LL) PBRV

Sonnet 57. HAP; NoSic; OBEV; PoEL-2

(Absence.) GTBS-P

Sonnet 60. CABP; EBEV; NIP-4; NOBE; NoSic; OxAEP-1; PoRA; SCGP; Son; TFi; UnPo

("'Like as the waves make toward the pebbled shore'.") PoPoPo

(Revolutions.) GTBS-P

Sonnet 61. PoEL-2

Sonnet 62. EBEV; OxAEP-1; PoEL-2

Sonnet 64. AWP; EnLoPo; HAP; HeIP-4; ImPo; NOBE; NoSic; OAEL-1; OxAEP-1; PoE; PoRA; SCGP; Son

(Time and Love, I.) GTBS-P

("When I have seen by Time's fell hand defac'd.") AEP

Sonnet 65. AWP; HAP; InPS-3; NAEL-1; NOBE; NoSic; OxAEP-1; PoRA; RaBo; SCGP; Son; TFi; UnPo

("That in blank ink my love may still shine bright.") (LL) AEP

(Time and Love, II.) GTBS-P

Sonnet 66. AWP; CTC; EBEV; FaBoPV; HAP; InPS-3; NOBE; NoSic; OAEL-1; OxAEP-1; PoEL-2; TFi; WeW-3

("And right perfection wrongfully disgraced.") (LL) PoPoPo

("Save that to dye, I leave my love alone.") (LL) PBRV

("Tired with all these, for restful death I cry.") CABP; PFE; PoPoPo

(World's Way, The.) GTBS-P

Sonnet 67. SCGP

Sonnet 68. SCGP

Sonnet 70. OxAEP-1; SCGP

Sonnet 71. AWP; EBEV; GBL; HAP; HeIP-4; IMW; ImPo; LBC; NAEL-1; NoSic; OxAEP-1; PoRA; SCGP; Son; TFi

(Triumph of Death, The.) GTBS-P

Sonnet 72. OxAEP-1

Sonnet 73. APAD; AWP; BoLoP; CABP; CTC; ClHu; EBEV; GTBS-P; HAP; HeIP-4; HoPM; ImPo; InPK-6; InPS-3; LiLi; NAEL-1; NIP-4; NOBE; NoSic; OAEL-1; OBEV; PFE; PoE; PoEL-2; PoRA; SCGP; SoSe-8; Son; TFi; UnPo; WeW-3

(Sonnet 73: "That Time of Year Thou Mayst in Me Behold.") GLoP

("That time of year thou mayst in me behold.") AEP; APAD; CABP; GLoP; LiLi; NoP-4; SAGP

Sonnet 74. NAEL-1; OxAEP-1; Son

("And that is this, and this with thee remaines.") (LL) PBRV

("But be contended when that fell arest.") PBRV

Sonnet 75. PoEL-2

Sonnet 76. EBEV; NoSic; OxAEP-1

Sonnet 77. HeIP-4

Sonnet 78. "So oft have I invok'd thee." AEP

Sonnet 80. OxAEP-1

Sonnet 81. OxAEP-1

Sonnet 85. Son

Sonnet 86. CABP; NoSic; OAEL-1; OxAEP-1; SCGP; Son

Sonnet 87. CBLP; EBEV; EBEvV; GTBS-P; ImPo; InPS-3; NAEL-1; NOBE; NoSic; OAEL-1; OBEV; OxAEP-1; PoEL-2; Son; TFi

("Farewell! thou art too dear for my possessing.") LoP

Sonnet 88. OxAEP-1

Sonnet 89. OxAEP-1

Sonnet 90. AWP; EBEV; NOBE; NoSic; OBEV; OxAEP-1; PoEL-2

Sonnet 92. HeIP-4

Sonnet 94. CABP; CBLP; ImPo; InPS-3; NAEL-1; NOBE; NoSic; OAEL-1; OBEV; OxAEP-1; PoE; PoEL-2; SCGP; SCV; Son; TRP

(Life without Passion, The.) FP

("Lilies that fester, smell far worse then weeds.") (LL) LoP

("Lillies that fester, smell far worse then weeds.") (LL) PBRV

("They that have power to hurt and will do none.") LoP; NoP-4; OxBoV

("They that have powre to hurt, and will doe none.") PBRV

Sonnet 95. HeIP-4; SCGP

Sonnet 97. AEP; AWP; EnLoPo; GTBS-P; HeIP-4; NAEL-1; NOBE; NoSic; OAEL-1; OxAEP-1; PoRA; SCGP; Son; TFi

("How like a winter hath my absence been.") GEA

(Sonnet 97: 'How like a winter'.) AEP

("That leaves look pale, dreading the winter's near.") (LL) AEP; GEA

Sonnet 98. AWP; EBEV; ImPo; NAEL-1; NOBE; NoSic; OBEV; OxAEP-1

(Sonnet 98: "From You Have I Been Absent in the Spring.") GLoP

Sonnet 99. OxAEP-1

Sonnet 102. AWP; OBEV

Sonnet 104. GBL; GTBS-P; HeIP-4; NoSic; OBEV; OxAEP-1; SCGP

("To me, fair friend, you never can be old.") FP

Sonnet 106. AWP; CTC; EBEvV; EnLoPo; FaBoCh; ImPo; NAEL-1; NOBE; NoSic; OBEV; OxAEP-1; PoRA; SCGP; Son

(To His Love.) GTBS-P

Sonnet 107. AWP; CTC; EBEV; HAP; ImPo; NAEL-1; NoSic; OAEL-1; OxAEP-1; SCGP

Sonnet 109. NOBE; OBEV; OxAEP-1

(Unchangeable, The.) GTBS-P

Sonnet 110. EBEV; NoSic; OxAEP-1

(Sonnet 110: 'Alas, 'tis true'.) AEP

Sonnet 111. OxAEP-1

Sonnet 113. SCGP

Sonnet 114. SCGP

Sonnet 116. APAD; AWP; CABP; ClHu; EBEvV; EnLoPo; GBL; HAP; HeIP-4; ITG; InPS-3; NAEL-1; NIP-4; NOBE; NoSic; OAEL-1; OBEV; OxAEP-1; OxBM; PBMP; PFE; PoE; PoEL-2; PoPoPo; PoRA; Poetr; SCGP; SCV; SoSe-8; Son; TFi; TRP; UnPo; WeW-3

("I never writ, nor no man ever lov'd.") (LL) AEP; GLoP; GSo

(Marriage of True Minds, The.) ImPo

(Sonnet 116: "Let Me Not to the Marriage of True Minds.") GLoP

Sonnet 118. SCGP

Sonnet 119. OxAEP-1

Sonnet 120. OxAEP-1

Sonnet 121. NoSic; OAEL-1; OxAEP-1; PoEL-2; SCGP

("All men are bad and in their badnesse raigne.") (LL) PBRV

("'Tis better to be vile then vile esteemed.") PBRV

Sonnet 123. OxAEP-1; Son

Sonnet 124. NoSic

("Which die for goodnes, who have liv'd for crime.") (LL) PBRV

("Yf my deare love were but the childe of state.") PBRV

Sonnet 125. NoSic

(Sonnet 125: 'Were't aught to me'.) AEP

Sonnet 126. HeIP-4; NAEL-1

Sonnet 127. OxAEP-1

Sonnet 128. NAEL-1; OxAEP-1; PoE

Sonnet 129. AWP; EBEV; GBL; HAP; HeIP-4; ImPo; InPS-3; NAEL-1; NIP-4; NOBE; NoSic; OAEL-1; OBEV; OxAEP-1; PoE; PoEL-2; PoPoPo; Poetr; SCGP; SCV; Son; TFi; UnPo

("Expense of spirit in a waste of shame, The.") APAD; PFE

(Sonnet.) PBRV

("Th'expense of spirit in a waste of shame.") CABP

("To shun the heav'n that leads men to this hell.") (LL) CABP

Sonnet 130. AWP; BoLoP; CABP; EBEV; HAP; HeIP-4; HoPM; ImPo; InPK-6; InPS-3; NAEL-1; NIP-4; NoSic; OAEL-1; OxAEP-1; PBMP; PFE; PoE; PoPoPo; Poetr; SoSe-8; Son; TFi; WeW-3

(Sonnet 130: "My Mistress' Eyes Are Nothing Like the Sun.") GLoP

Sonnet 132. OxAEP-1

Sonnet 133. OxAEP-1

Sonnet 134. HeIP-4; OxAEP-1

Sonnet 135. NAEL-1; OAEL-1

("Thinke all but one, and me in that one *Will*.") (LL) PBRV

("Who ever hath her wish, thou hast thy *Will*,.") PBRV

Sonnet 138. AWP; CABP; EBEV; HeIP-4; NAEL-1; NoSic; OAEL-1; OxAEP-1; PoEL-2; Poetr; SoSe-8

("And in our faults by lies we flattered be.") (LL) CABP; NoP-4

("And in our faults by lyes we flattered be.") (LL) PBRV

("When my love swears that she is made of truth.") CABP; NoP-4

Sonnet 140. NoSic

Sonnet 144. EBEV; HeIP-4; NAEL-1; NIP-4; OAEL-1; PoEL-2; Son

(Sonnet.) PBRV

("Two loves I have of comfort and dispaire.") PBRV

Sonnet 145. Son

Sonnet 146. AWP; HAP; HeIP-4; ImPo; InPS-3; NAEL-1; NOBE; NOCV; OAEL-1; OBEV; OxAEP-1; PoE; PoEL-2; SCGP; Son; TFi

("Poor soul, the center of my sinful earth.") NoP-4

(Soul and Body.) GTBS-P

Sonnet 147. EBEV; HoPM; NAEL-1; OxAEP-1; PoEL-2

("My love is as a fever, longing still.") AEP

(Sonnet 147: 'My love is as a fever'.) AEP

Sonnet 148. SCGP

Sonnet 150. OxAEP-1; SCGP

Sonnet 151. EBEV; HeIP-4; NoSic; OxAEP-1; PoE; PoEL-2

Sonnet 151. HeIP-4; OxAEP-1; PoEL-2

Sonnets: "Starry flower, the flower-like stars that fade, The." Frederick Goddard Tuckerman. APN-2

(Sonnet.) ColAP

("Stippled Orion on the midnight blue.") (LL) ColAP

Sonnets. Frederick Goddard Tuckerman.

"And change[,] with hurried hand, has swept these scenes." APN-2; HAP; NOBA; TAP

"And two I knew, an old man and a boy." APN-2

"As when, down some broad River dropping,we." APN-2

"But war his overturning trumpet blew." APN-2

"But we are set to strive to make our mark." TrCP

"Dark fens of cedar; hemlock-branches gray." APN-2

("Dank fens of cedar; hemlock-branches gray.") PAR

"Gertrude and Gulielma, sister-twins." HAP

"Hast thou seen reversed the prophet's miracle." NOBA

"Here, where the red man swept the leaves away." NOBA; TAP

"His heart was in his garden; but his brain." APN-2; NoP-4

"How oft in schoolboy-days, from the school's sway." APN-2; NoP-4; Son

"How well do I recall that walk in state." APN-2

"Let me give something!—as the years unfold." APN-2

"Let me give something!—though my spring be done." APN-2

"Morning comes; not slow, with reddening gold, The." APN-2

"Nor strange it is, to us who walk in bonds." APN-2

"Roll on, sad world! Not Mercury or Mars." APN-2

"Some truths may pierce the spirit's deeper gloom." APN-2

"Sometimes I walk where the deep water dips." APN-2; NOBA; PAR

"Still pressing through these weeping solitudes." NOBA

"Thin little leaves of wood fern, ribbed and toothed." APN-2; TAP

"Under the mountain, as when first I knew." APN-2; HAP; TAP

"Upper chamber in a darkened house, An." GSo

("Tiny petals of the mountain-ash, The.") (LL) GSo; NoP-4; PAR

"Yes: though the brine may from the desert deep." HAP

"Yet, even 'mid merry boyhood's tricks and scapes." APN-2

Sonnets: A Sequence on Profane Love. George Henry Boker.

"Ah, lute, how well I know each tone of thee." APN-2

"As stands a statue on its pedestal." APN-2

"Farewell once more,—and yet again farewell!" APN-2

"If she should give me all I ask of her." APN-2

"Leaden eyelids of wan twilight close, The." APN-2

"My darling's features, painted by the light." APN-2

Sonnets at Christmas. Allen Tate. HAP; LiTM; NOBA; OxBA; VGW

"Ah, Christ, I love you rings to the wild sky." Son

"This is the day His hour of life draws near." NAAL-2; Son

Sonnets Attempted in the Manner of Contemporary Writers. Coleridge. Son

House That Jack Built, The. CBNP

Sonnets: First Series. Frederick Goddard Tuckerman. NCAP

Sonnets for Roberta (1954). John Hewitt.

"How have I served you? I have let you waste." PNI

"If I had given you that love and care." PNI

Sonnets for Stan Gage (1945–1992). Sascha Feinstein. SeSe

Sonnets for the Novachord. "Ern Malley." BMAP

Sonnets from a Lock Box. Anna Hempstead Branch.

"I say that words are men and when we spell." NALW

"Into the void behold my shuddering flight." NALW

"What witchlike spell weaves here its deep design." NALW

Sonnets from an Ungrafted Tree. Edna St. Vincent Millay. NALW

"So she came back into his house again." ColAP

Sonnet 17. NMM-2

Sonnets from China. W. H. Auden.

Embassy. LiLi

"Far from a cultural centre he was used." CMoP; NoAM

"He stayed, and was imprisoned in possession." CMoP

"He turned his field into a meeting-place." SCV

"He was their servant (some say he was blind)." CMoP

"He watched the stars and noted birds in flight." CMoP

"Here war is harmless like a monument." OBWP

"His care-free swagger was a fine invention." CMoP

"So an age ended, and its last deliverer died." CMoP; PoE

("And the age ended, and the last deliverer died.") Son

"So from the years their gifts were showered: each." CMoP

"They wondered why the fruit had been forbidden." CMoP; ChIV-1; Son

Sonnets from Greece. Trumbull Stickney. APN-1

Mount Lykaion. OxBA; Son

Sonnets from Mother and Daughter. Augusta Davies Webster.

"Little child she, half defiant came, A." VWP

Sonnets from Scotland. Edwin Morgan.

After a Death. FaBoTC

Coin, The. FaBoTC

De Quincey in Glasgow. FaBoTC

Pilate at Fortingall. FaBoTC

Post-Referendum. FaBoTC

Sonnets from the Portuguese. Elizabeth Barrett Browning.

Sonnet: "And wilt thou have me fashion into speech." BWW; BrRo; EnVR; VWP

(Sonnet 13.) CABP

Sonnet: "Belovéd, my Belovéd, when I think." Son; WPE

Sonnet: "Belovèd, thou hast brought me many flowers." EBVV; EnVR; LW; OBNC; WPE

Sonnet: "Can it be right to give what I can give?" CTC; Son

Sonnet: "Face of all the world is changed, I think, The." CTC

Sonnet: "First time he kissed me, he but only kissed." BLPA; CTC; FaBoBe; LW

Sonnet: "First time that the sun rose on thine oath, The." EnVR; NAEL-2; WPE

Sonnet: "Go from me. Yet I feel that I shall stand." BWW; CBLP; LW; OBEV; OxAEP-2

Sonnet: "How do I love thee? Let me count the ways." BWW; BoLoP; CTC; EBEVV; EBVV; EnVR; FaBoBe; HeIP-4; HoPM; InPK-6; NAEL-2; NALW; NIP-4; OxAEP-2; OxBM; PoE; PoLF; PoRA; Poetr; Son; TFi; UV; UnPo; VWP; WPE

("How Do I Love Thee? Let Me Count The Ways.") APAD; GSo

(Sonnet: "How Do I Love Thee? Let Me Count the Ways.") GLoP

Sonnet: "I lift my heavy heart up solemnly." LW; NALW

("Hair beneath. Stand further off then! Go, The.") (LL) LW

(Sonnet 5.) VWP

Sonnet: "I lived with visions for my company." BWW

Sonnet: "I never gave a lock of hair away." EBVV; HAP

Sonnet: "I thought once how Theocritus had sung." BWW; EBVV; EnVR; GBL; NOBE; OBEV; OBNC; OxAEP-2; WPE

("Silver answer rang,—'Not Death, but Love,' The.") (LL) GLoP; LBC; NoP-4

(Sonnet: "I Thought Once How Theocritus Had Sung.") GLoP

(Sonnets from the Portuguese.) NoP-4; PoPoPo

Sonnet: "If I leave all for thee, wilt thou exchange." Son

Sonnet: "If thou must love me, let it be for nought." BWW; CTC; HeIP-4; InPS-3; LW; OBEV; OBNC; OxAEP-2; SoSe-8

(For Love's Sake Only.) PoToHe

("If thou must love me, let it be for naught.") SAGP

Sonnet: "Let the world's sharpness, like a clasping knife." NOBVV

Sonnet: "My future will not copy fair my past." EnVR

Sonnet: "My letters! all dead paper, mute and white." HAP; OxAEP-2

Sonnet: "My poet, thou canst touch on all the notes." BrRo

Sonnet: "Say over again, and yet once over again." NAEL-2

Sonnet: "Thou comest! all is said without a word." BWW

Sonnet: "Thou hast thy calling to some palace-floor." OxAEP-2; Son

(Sonnet 4.) VWP

("That weeps. . . as thou must sing. . . alone, aloof.") (LL) VWP

Sonnet: "Unlike are we, unlike, O princely Heart!" BWW; EnVR; OBEV; OxAEP-2

(Sonnet 3.) CABP

Sonnet: "What can I give thee back, O liberal." BWW; OxAEP-2

Sonnet: "When our two souls stand up erect and strong." BWW; BoWoP; EnVR; LW; NAEL-2; NALW; NOBE; OBEV; WPE

Sonnet: "Yet, love, mere love, is beautiful indeed." BWW; CTC; OxAEP-2

Sonnet XXIX. PEW

Sonnets in Quaker Language. Hildegarde Flanner. WPE

Sonnets of English Dramatic Poets. Swinburne. Son

Ben Jonson. EPCY

Marlowe. EPCY

Sonnets of Michelangelo, The. Elizabeth Jennings.

"I wish, God, for some end I do not will." PeECV; TOF

Sonnets of the Blood. Allen Tate.

"Fire I praise was once perduring flame, The." PoA

"Near to me as my flesh, my flesh and blood." PoA

"Not power nor the casual [*or* storied] hand of God." PoA

"Times have changed, there is not left to us, The." PoA

"What is this flesh and blood compounded of." PoA

Sonnets of the Months. Folgore da San Geminiano, *Italian*. AWP, *tr. by* D. G. Rossetti

    August. CTC

Sonnets of the Triple-headed Manichee. George Barker.

    "Keelhauled across the star-wrecked death of God." PoA

Sonnets to Aurelia. Robert Malise Bowyer Nichols. OBMV

Sonnets to be Written from Prison. Robert Adamson.

    "O to be in the news again—now as fashion runs." BMAP

Sonnets to Chris. John Berryman.

    "Ah when you drift hover before you kiss." EP

    "I wished, all the mild days of middle March." LoP

    "I've found out why, that day, that suicide." PoE

    "Nothing there? nothing up the sky alive." BoLoP

    "Sometimes the night echoes to prideless wailing." NoAM

    Sonnet 115: "All we were going strong last night this time." APAD

    Sonnet 115: "As usual I'm up before the sun." SAGP

    "Your shining—where?—rays my wide room with gold." EP

Sonnets to Laura. Petrarch, *Italian*.

    Alas, So All Things Now.

    ("Alas, so all things now do hold their peace.") NoSic, *sect.* CIX, *tr. by* the Earl of Surrey

    "Blest be the day, and blest the month and year." NAWM-1, *tr. by* Joseph Auslander

    ("Father in heaven, after each lost day.") NAWM-1, *tr. by* Bernard Bergonzi

    Complaint of a Lover Rebuked. AWP; Son

    ("Love that liveth and reigneth in my thought.") AWP; SiPS; Son

    Description of the Contrarious Passions in a Lover. Son

    "Eyes that drew from me such fervent praise, The." NAWM-1, *tr. by* Edwin Morgan

    "First day she passed up and down through the Heavens, The." OBMV

    Galley, The. GBL; PoEL-1

    (Lover Compareth His State to a Ship in Perilous Storm Tossed on the Sea, The.) GBL; PoEL-1

    "Go, grieving rimes of mine, to that hard stone." NAWM-1

    "Great is my envy of you, earth, in your greed." NAWM-1, *tr. by* Edwin Morgan

    He Understands the Great Cruelty of Death. BIrV

    Heart on the Hill, The. AWP

    How the Lover Perisheth in His Delight, As the Fly in the Fire. Son

    I saw a Phoenix in the Wood Alone. AWP, *tr. by* Spenser

    If It Be Destined. AWP; SiPS, *tr. by* Edward Fitzgerald

    "In the years of her age the most beautiful." OBMV, *tr. by* J. M. Synge

    "It was the morning of that blessed day." NAWM-1

    Lover for Shamefastness[e] Hideth His Desire Within His Faithful[l] Heart [*or* Hart], The. AAS; Son

    Love's Fidelity. AWP

    "She used to let her golden hair fly free." NAWM-1, *tr. by* Morris Bishop

    Signs of Love. AWP

    Translation from Petrarch, A. MoBrPo, *tr. by* J. M. Synge

    Visions, The. AWP

Sonnets to Miranda. Sir William Watson.

    "If I had never known your face at all." FaBoBe

Sonnets to Orpheus. Rilke, *German*.

    "As once the winged energy of delight." EnlH, *tr. by* Stephen Mitchell

    "Be ahead of all parting, as though it already were." EnlH

    "Call me to the one among your moments." EnlH, *tr. by* Stephen Mitchell

    "Silent friend of many distances, feel." EnlH, *tr. by* Stephen Mitchell

    Sonnets to Orpheus, The. ITG, *tr. by* Stephen Mitchell; APAD

    ("But the winds. . . But the spaces. . . .") (LL) ITG, *tr. by* Stephen Mitchell

    ("O you tender ones, walk now and then.") ITG, *tr. by* Stephen Mitchell

    "This is the creature there has never been." OBVE, *tr. by* James Blair Leishman

    "Tree ascending there. O pure transcension, A." TOF, *tr. by* James Blair Leishman

    "We are the driving ones." EnlH, *tr. by* Stephen Mitchell

    "Where in what ever-blissfully watered gardens, upon what trees." OBVE, *tr. by* James Blair Leishman

"Where praise already is is the only place Grief." RaBo, *tr. by* Robert Bly

Sonnets to Philomel. Sir John Davies. SiPS

Sonnets to the Left. Chris Wallace-Crabbe.

    Sonnet IV. BMAP

Sonnets to the Seasons. Hartley Coleridge.

    November. LaPo; OBNC

Sonnet's Voice, The, (A Metrical Lesson by the Seashore). Theodore Watts-Dunton. GSo

Sonnets Written in the Orillia Woods. Charles Sangster.

    "Our life is like a forest, where the sun." NOBC

Sonny grows up in Fukien. Ku K'uang, *Chinese*. SuSp, *tr. by* Irving Y. Lo

Sonny rollins seeking. David Henderson. MoNo

Sonogram. Karl Kirchwey. BAP-95

Sonora for Sale. Richard Shelton. PaTW

Sonrisas. Pat Mora. NIP-4

Sons. Jack Cope. PeSA

Sons, my sons. Black Star Line. Henry Dumas. PoBA

Sons of freedom, listen to me, and ye daughters, too, give ear. James Bird. *Unknown*. AmFP

Sons of Martha, The. Rudyard Kipling. ChIV-2; GI

    ("Lord He lays / it on Martha's Sons!, The.") (LL) GI

    ("Sons of Mary seldom bother, The.") GI

Sons of mine, I hear you thrilling. England to Her Sons. William Noel Hodgson. PoFWW

Sons of Our Sons, The. Ilya Ehrenburg, *Russian*. TrJP, *tr. by* Babette Deutsch

Sons of Promise. Thomas Curtis Clark. PoToHe

Sons of Saint Crispin, 'tis in vain! "Peter Pindar." NOEC *Fr.* Resignation; an Ode to the Journeyman Shoemakers.

Sons of the King. Joan Agnew. BoTP

Sons of the prophet are hardy and bold, The. Abdul, the Bulbul Ameer. *Unknown*. AS

Sons of War sometimes are known, The. Evan Lloyd. OBSV *Fr.* The Methodist.

Soon after, he a crystal stream espying. Ludovico Ariosto, *Italian*. NoSic, *tr. by* Sir John Harington *Fr.* Orlando Furioso.

Soon as the Azure-colored Gates. Richard Lynche. Son *Fr.* Diella.

Soon as the harvest hath laid bare the plains. Stephen Duck. NOEC *Fr.* The Thresher's Labour.

Soon as the sound had ceased whose thunder filled. Shelley. *Fr.* Prometheus Unbound. NOBRP; OAEL-2

Soon as the sun forsook the eastern main. An Hymn to the Evening. Phillis Wheatley. WPE

Soon as / you stop. Cleavage. A. R. Ammons. OBAL

Soon at Last My Sighs and Moans. Louis Ginsberg. TrJP

Soon I foresee few acres for harrowing. Conservation. Horace, *Latin*. GaP, *tr. by* James Michie

Soon I will be done with the troubles of the world. *Unknown*. NAAAL

Soon I will climb the hill to the sunlight. From the Rain Forest. Desiré Flynn. BrRo

Soon it will be thirteen years since the nightingale. Letters from the Ming Dynasty. Joseph Brodsky, *Russian*. TCRP, *tr. by* Derek Walcott

Soon kindled and soon spent, we that were the pick of many. (LL) An Old Woman's Lamentations. François Villon, *French*. MoBrPo; OBMV, *tr. by* J. M. Synge

Soon now that day is coming. Two Worlds. Matija Beckovic, *Serbo-Croatian*. HSix, *tr. by* Charles Simic

Soon, summer's drum will shake the earth no longer. Fall of Leaves. Derek S. Savage. PoA

Soon the last trains will be backed. The Last Trains. C. G. Hanzlicek. GM

Soon the night in mantle dark. The Ploughboy. John Clare. PoEL-4

Soon to bloom / in splendour. Little Rosebud Girl. Anson Gonzalez. HCP

Soon we entered in the woods. The Arrival. Alexander McLachlan. NOBC *Fr.* The Emigrant.

Sooner I may some fixed statue be. On the Duke of Buckingham, Slain by Felton, the 23rd August, 1628. Owen Felltham [*or* Feltham]. NOSC

Sooner or later. The Rewaking. William Carlos Williams. ITG

Sooner or later the sun cracks rebecca. Fragment. Ray DiPalma. FTOS

Sooner tears than sleep this midnight. The Wind's Lament. John Morris-Jones, *Welsh*. OBWVE, *tr. by* Anthony Conran

Soote season, that bud and bloom forth brings, The. Description of Spring, Wherein Each Thing Renews Save Only the Lover. Henry Howard, Earl of Surrey, *after* Petrarch. AAS; InPS-3; NAEL-1; NoP-4; NoSic; OBEV; SCGP; Son

Sooth-Sayer, The. Sadi. AWP, *tr. by* Sir Edwin Arnold *Fr.* The Gulistan.

Soothed by the murmurs on the sea-boat shore. To the Curlew. Helen Maria Williams. WoRP

Sooty, swart smiths, smattered with smoke. Swarte-smeked Smithes. *Unknown.* HAP

Sopha'd on silk, amid her charm-built towers. The Poppy. Erasmus Darwin. GaP

Sophia! Antiphon for Divine Wisdom. Hildegard von Bingen, *German.* WPoS, *tr. by* Barbara Newman

Sophocles. *Unknown, Greek.* GrAn, *tr. by* Lee T. Pearcy

Sopolis. Callimachus, *Greek.* AWP, *tr. by* William M. Hardinge

Soracte. Horace, *Latin.* OBCVT, *tr. by* Charles Stuart Calverley

Soraidh Slan Don Oidhche Areir. Niall Mor MacMuireadach, *Irish.* BIrV, *tr. by* Maire Cruise O'Brien

Sorcerer sang the spring to sleep, The. Aleksandr Blok, *Russian.* TCRP, *tr. by* Yakov Hornstein

Sorceress, The. Eugène Marais, *Afrikaans.* PeSA, *tr. by* Jack Cope *and* Uys Krige

Sorceress, The. Theocritus. *See* The Enchantment.

Sordello. Robert Browning. OBGa *Fr.* Sordello.

"In Mantua-territory half is slough." EBVVPR

Sordid, unfeeling, reprobate, degraded / Spiritless outcast! (LL) The Friend of Humanity and the Knife Grinder. George Canning *and* John Hookham Frere. BXAP; NOBRP; NOEC; OBCoV; UV

Sorrow. Chu Shu-chen, *Chinese.* BoWoP; OHMPC, *tr. by* Kenneth Rexroth

Sorrow. Aubrey Thomas De Vere. BLPA

Sorrow. T. R. Hummer. MT

Sorrow. D. H. Lawrence. CMoP; GTBS-P; OBMV

Sorrow. Mei Yao Ch'en, *Chinese.* OHPC, *tr. by* Kenneth Rexroth

Sorrow. Josephine Miles. IMW

Sorrow. Laetitia Pilkington. FCWP

Sorrow. Tanka. Ishikawa Takuboku, *Japanese.* MJT, *tr. by* Ueda, Makoto

Sorrow. *Unknown, Russian.* AWP, *tr. by* W. R. S. Ralston

Sorrow and mourn and fast. (LL) Mirie it is, while sumer ilast. *Unknown.* HAP; MiEL

Sorrow Garden, The. Thomas McCarthy. BiHa

Sorrow heaped on sorrow, ruin on disaster. On My Sorrowful Life. Moses ibn Ezra, *Hebrew.* TrJP, *tr. by* Solomon Solis-Cohen

Sorrow I'll [*or* I'le] wed: Despair [*or* Dispaire] thus governs me[e]. (LL) Sonnet 9: "Be[e] you all pleased [*or* pleas'd]? your pleasures grieve not[t] me[e]." Mary Sidney, Countess of Montgomery Wroth. BWW; NOSC

Sorrow in the Harem, A. Wang Ch'ang-ling, *Chinese.* OHMPC, *tr. by* Kenneth Rexroth

Sorrow is eternally / silent as stone. Late Autumn. Hanmo Chong, *Korean.* CKP, *tr. by* Jaihiun Kim

Sorrow is my own yard. The Widow's Lament in Springtime. William Carlos Williams. CMoP; GaP; HAP; IMW; LiTM; MoP; NAAL-2; NOBA; NoAM; PoE; SAGP; SAmP; SoSe-8; TAP

Sorrow lay upon my breast more heavily than winter clay. "Desolation Is a Delicate Thing." Elinor Wylie. MoAmPo

Sorrow of Kodio, The. *Unknown, Baule.* PBA, *tr. by* Miriam Koshland

Sorrow of Love, The ("Quarrel of the sparrows in the eaves, The"), *see also* The Sorrow of Love ("The brawling of a sparrow in the eaves"). W. B. Yeats. MoBrPo; NOBVV; NoAM; OAEL-2; PoEL-5

Sorrow of Mydath. John Masefield. MoBrPo

Sorrow of Troilus, The. Chaucer. PoEL-1 *Fr.* Troilus and Criseyde [*or* Criseide]. EnVB

Sorrowful Sea-Gull, The. Menella Bute Smedley. VWP

Sorrowing for the Past at Western Pass Mountain. Liu Yu Hsi, *Chinese.* SuSp, *tr by* Daniel Bryant

Sorrowing mother was, The. The Stabat Mater. Jacopone da Todi, *Italian.* NNPT, *tr. by* George Barker

Sorrows of my heart enlarged are, The. Some Contemplations of the Poor, and Desolate State of the Church at Deerfield. John Williams. SCAP

Sorrows of Sunday; an Elegy, The. "Peter Pindar."

"Susan, the constant slave to mop and broom." NOEC

Sorrows of thy line!, The. (LL) The Ballad of Keith of Ravelston. Sydney Thompson Dobell. CH; OBEV

Sorrows of Werther, The. William Makepeace Thackeray. BLPA; NBLV; NOBL; NOBVV; OBCoV; PFE; PeLV

Sorrows of Yamba, or the Negro Woman's Lamentation, The. Hannah More. Ro

Sorrows play at the edge of these willow leaf curves. Willow Eyebrows. Chao Luan-luan, *Chinese.* ChiPo, *tr. by* Kenneth Rexroth *and* Ling Chung

Sorry, Hank. / Found out / The Hard / Way. Hank Mobley's. Cornelius Eady. SeSe

Sorry I am, my God, sorry I am. Sin's Round. George Herbert. NOSC

Sort of a Song, A. William Carlos Williams. HoPM; NAAL-2; OxBSP; TAP

("Rocks, The.") (LL) NoP-4

Sort of extra hunger, A. Poet Wondering What He Is Up To. D. J. Enright. OxBC

Sort of Language, A. Burns Singer. FaBoTC

Sort of meaning that comes back, A. (LL) Sonatina in Yellow. Donald Justice. ColAP

Sorting Laundry. Elisavietta Ritchie. SoSe-8

Sorting out letters and piles of my old. Mementos, 1. W. D. Snodgrass. MoAmPo; NoP-4; SAGP; UnPo; VCAP

Sory beverech [*or* beverech] it is, and sore it is abought [*or* abouth], A. *Unknown.* MiEL

So's Liberty. (LL) No Rack can torture me. Emily Dickinson. MeMAP; NALW

SOS Lifescene. Burns Singer. FaBoTC

Sosicles the farmer dedicated these sheaves. Philip of Thessalonica, *Greek.* GrAn, *tr. by* Edwin Morgan

Sōsos the cattleman slew the lion. Leonidas of Tarentum, *Greek.* GrAn, *tr. by* W. G. Shepherd

Soto, a Character. Mary Leapor. ECWP

Soucouyant. LeRoy Clarke. HCP

Soucouyant, Soucouyant. "Skin Skin, Yuh Na Know Meh." John C. M. Lyons. NBrP

Soufrière. Ellsworth McGranahan Keane. HCP; PBCV *Fr.* Volcanoe Suite.

Sought by the world, and hath the world disdained. *Unknown.* NoSic

Soul, The. Peter Cooley. NAmP90

Soul, A. Randall Jarrell. CMoP

Soul, A. Christina Rossetti. NALW; WPOW

Soul. Walt Whitman. *See* A Noiseless patient spider.

Soul a crystal is, the Godhead is its shine, The. Body, Soul, And Godhead. "Angelus Silesius." GePo, *tr. by* George C. Schoolfield *Fr.* The Cherubical Wanderer.

Soul and Body, *epigram.* Friedrich von Logau, *German.* GePo, *tr. by* George C. Schoolfield

Soul and Body. Shakespeare. *See* Sonnet 146.

Soul and Body: I've heard tell of a noble guest. Cynewulf. ASW, *tr. by* Kevin Crossley-Holland *Fr.* Riddles (Exeter Book).

Soul and Body of John Brown, The. Muriel Rukeyser. CBCWP; MoAmPo

Soul and race. Here Where Coltrane Is. Michael S. Harper. NAAAL; PoBA

Soul and the Body, The. Sir John Davies. CTC; NOBE *Fr.* Nosce Teipsum. NoSic; SiPS

(In What Manner the Soule Is United to the Body.) PoEL-2

Soul-animating strains—alas, too few! (LL) Sonnet: "Scorn not the sonnet; critic, you have frowned." Wordsworth. EBEV; EPCY; GSo; HeIP-4; NoP-4; OBEV; Son

Soul counsels flight. Meleager, *Greek.* GrAn, *tr. by* Peter Whigham

Soul Food. Janice Mirikitani. NMM-2; OpBo

Soul has Bandaged moments, The. Emily Dickinson. NALW; TRP

Soul-Hunter, The. Julia Ward Howe. PAR

Soul is a prisoner, and body is its jail. Soul and Body. Friedrich von Logau, *German.* GePo, *tr. by* George C. Schoolfield

Soul is a region without definite boundaries, The. Terrain. A. R. Ammons. CoAmPo; VCAP

Soul is its own monument, The. (LL) Song by Mr. Cypress. Thomas Love Peacock. OAEL-2; OBNC

Soul is kissed by God, The. Hildegard von Bingen, *Latin.* CrSp

Soul is lonely, The. La Selva. Cid Corman. VGW

Soul lies buried in the ink that writes, The. (LL) Fragment: "Language has not the power to speak what love indites." John Clare. FaBoEE; OAEL-2; OBNC; OxBSP; PoEL-4

Soul, like the moon, The. Lal Ded, *Kashmiri.* WPoS, *tr. by* Coleman Barks

Soul lonely comes and goes; for each our theme. Lachesis. Kathleen Jessie Raine. NYBP

Soul Longs to Return Whence It Came, The. Richard Eberhart. CMoP

Soul Make A Path Through Shouting, *for Elizabeth Eckford / Little Rock, Arkansas, 1957.* Cyrus Cassells. GT; UnSA

Soul Music. Baron Wormser. LTA

Soul Music: The Derry Air. Eamon Grennan. BiHa; PBCIP

Soul of Jesus Is Restless, The. Cyprus R. Mitchell. TrCP

Soul of man is cast, The. (LL) A Creed. Edwin Markham. BLPA; FaBoBe

Soul of Man is larger than the sky, The. To Shakespeare. Hartley Coleridge. EPCY

Soul[e] of my soul[e]! my Joy, my crown, my friend! L'Amitie: To Mrs. M. Awbrey. Katherine Philips. KTR; NOSC

Soul of the Black Land, The. Guy Tirolien, *French*. NegPo, *tr. by* Ellen Conroy Kennedy

Soul of the nineteenth century, The. (LL) The Spirit of the Age. Christopher Pearse Cranch. APN-1; PAR

Soul of the Village, The. Lucian Blaga, *Romanian*. CEEP, *tr. by* Don Eulert, Stefan Avădanei, *and* Mihail Bogdan

Soul Says. Jorie Graham. PoPoPo

Soul selects her own Society, The. Emily Dickinson. APN-2; AWP; AmPP; BoWoP; CMoP; HeIP-4; ImPo; InPK-6; InPS-3; MeMAP; MoAmPo; NAAL-1; NAAL-3; NALW; NAWM-2; NOBA; NoAM; OxBA; OxWW; PAR; PoE; PoEL-5; Poetr; SAGP; SAmP; TAP; TFi; UnPo; WPE

("Like Stone—.") (LL) NoP-4; OxWW; PoPoPo; SAGP

Soul-soothing drug! your virtues let me laud. A Sonnet to Opium; Celebrating Its Virtues. "Orestes." NOEC

Soul Speaks, The. *Unknown, French*.

"Beguines who hear these words." WPoS, *tr. by* Jane Hirshfield *and* Mariko Aratani

Soul that hath a Guest, The. Emily Dickinson. APN-2

Soul that's fed on Nature is content, The. Nature's Uplifting. Henrietta Cordelia Ray. CBWP-3

Soul, thou must seek thyself in Me. Saint, of Avila Theresa, *Spanish*. TOF, *tr. by* E. Allison Peers

Soul to be strong?, The. Marianne Moore. *See* What Are Years?

Soul which doth with God unite, The. Cupio Dissolvi. William Habington. ChIV-2

Soules joy, now I am gone. Song. William Herbert, Earl of Pembroke. ESCV

Soulfolk, think a minute. To Soulfolk. Margaret Goss Burroughs. BlSi

Souls. Paul Wertheimer, *German*. TrJP, *tr. by* Jethro Bithell

Soul's Beauty. D. G. Rossetti. OBEV *Fr.* The House of Life.

(Sibylla Palmifera). OxAEP-2

Soul's Courts, The. Henrietta Cordelia Ray. CBWP-3

Soul's Dark Cottage, The. Edmund Waller. *Fr.* Of The Last Verses in the Book. BeJo; EBEV; HAP; NOSC; NoP-4; PeECV; PoPoPo; SCGP; SeCP

Soul's Desire, The. *Unknown, Irish*. TIRV, *tr. by* Eleanor Hull

Soul's distinct connection, The. Emily Dickinson. SAmP

Soul's Groan to Christ for Succo[u]r, The. Edward Taylor. NAAL-1; NAAL-3; PoEL-3 *Fr.* God's Determinations [touching his Elect].

Soul's joy, bend not those morning stars from me. Sonnet 48. Sir Philip Sidney. NoP-4 *Fr.* Astrophil and Stella. AAS; SiPS

Soul's joy, when thou art gone. A Parody [or Parodie]. George Herbert. ESCV

Souls of Poets dead and gone. Lines on the Mermaid Tavern. Keats. FHYEP; FaBoBe; GTBS-P; PoRA; SCGP

Souls of the Slain, The. Thomas Hardy. CMoP; PoEL-5

Souls of Women at Night, The. Wallace Stevens. CMoP

Soul's Soliloquy, A. Wenonah Stevens Abbott. BLPA

Soul's Superior instants, The. Emily Dickinson. APN-2; EnlH

Sound, A. Gertrude Stein. TTTS *Fr.* Tender Buttons.

Sound Advice. *Unknown*. NBLV

Sound, and the imagination of the sound—a place, The. (LL) Triphammer Bridge. A. R. Ammons. ColAP

Sound from the Earth, A. William Stafford. NNaP

Sound grates on the river tower, one blast of the horn, The. The Gate Tower of Ch'i-an City. Tu Mu, *Chinese*. PLT, *tr. by* A. C. Graham

Sound I Listened For, The. Robert Francis. AFr

Sound is fading out. Song. *Unknown, Chippewa Indian*. STP, *tr. by* Jerome Rothenberg

Sound is forced [or forc'd], the notes are few!, The. (LL) To the Muses. William Blake. EPCY; HAP; HeIP-4; ImPo; NAEL-2; NOBE; NOEC; OAEL-2; OBEV; SCGP

Sound is sea: pattern lapping pattern. If we erase the air and slow the. Beam 7. Ronald Johnson. APSN *Fr.* Ark.

Sound like a great big crowd. (LL) Morning After. Langston Hughes. MoP; NAAL-2; NBLV; NoAM; OBCoV

Sound like a rusty pump beneath our window, A. Blue Jay. Paul Lake. RA

Sound like hundreds of barbers, A. Night Dust-off. Basil T. Paquet. CDa

Sound of a Rat, The. Buson, *Japanese*. APo, *tr. by* Geoffrey Bownas *and* Anthony Thwaite

Sound of Afroamerican History Chapt I, The. S. E. Anderson. PoBA

Sound of Afroamerican History Chapt II, The. S. E. Anderson. PoBA

Soundlessly, a tide at the ear. Awakening. John Haines. SPE

Soundly they slept in midst of all their rest. (LL) Midnight ("Midnight was come, when every vital thing"). Thomas Sackville. CH

Sounds. Wassily Kandinsky, *Russian*. PFTM, *tr. by* Elizabeth R. Napier

Sound of autumn from a stretch of reed flowers, The. Tune: "Song of Plucking Cassia." Ch'iao Chi, *Chinese*. SuSp, *tr. by* Sherwin S. S. Fu

Sound of Birds at Noon, The. Dahlia Ravikovitch, *Hebrew*. VCWP, *tr. by* Chana Bloch *and* Ariel Bloch

Sound of Breaking. Conrad Potter Aiken. AWP

Sound of gunfire—dilutes the bloody terror of revolution, The. When the People Stand Up out of the Hard Cheese. Duoduo. AF, *tr. by* Gregory Lee *and* John Cayley *Fr.* Thoughts and Recollections.

Sound of Guns, The. Gerald McCarthy. CDa

Sound of guns from beleaguered Donelson, The. Lines Written for Allen Tate on His Sixtieth Anniversary. Donald Davidson. FuPo

Sound of happy laughter leap with shadows on the walls. Taos Winter. Patty L. Harjo. VoR

Sound of her silk skirt has stopped, The. Li Fu-Jên. Emperor Wu of Han, *Chinese*. ChiP, *tr. by* Arthur Waley

Sound of its thump at dawn hurries the circling sun, The. The Watchman's Drum in the Streets of Officials. Li Ho, *Chinese*. PLT, *tr. by* A. C. Graham

Sound of My Sneezing Nose, The. Te Whetu, *Maori*. PeNZ, *tr. by* Margaret Orbell

Sound of Rain, The. Bella Akhatovna Akhmadulina, *Russian*. BoWoP, *tr. by* Daniel Halpern *and* Albert Todd

Sound of Rain, The. Yohan Chu, *Korean*. CKP, *tr. by* Jaihiun Kim

Sound of Silence, The. Paul Simon. PBMP

Sound of snails—crying. Snails. Liagarang, *Dharlwangu dialect*. CBAP, *tr. by* Ronald M. Berndt

Sound of tears the moment after, A. (LL) Dream, A [or The]. William Allingham. BIrV; NOBVV

Sound of the Horn, The. Alfred de Vigny, *French*. AWP, *tr. by* Wilfred Thorley

Sound of the Sea, The. Henry Wadsworth Longfellow. APAD

Sound of the Trees, The. Robert Frost. *See* The Sound of Trees.

Sound of the Wind That Is Blowing, The. J. Kitchener Davies, *Welsh*.

"Today,/ there came a breeze thin as the needle of a syringe." OBWVE, *tr. by* Joseph P. Clancy

Sound of Trees, The. Robert Frost. NoAM

(Sound of the Trees, The.) OxBA

Sound of Water. Mary O'Neill. NTCP

Sound of words as they fall away from our mouths, The. Duet for a Chair and a Table. Jack Spicer. APSN

Sound on, thou dark unslumbering sea! The Last Song of Sappho. Felicia Dorothea Hemans. VWP

Sound out, sound over Hirta sound rare. St Kilda-Wren, 1957. Colin Simms. NBrP

Sound secreted the form, / blew. Notes on Sound, Speech, Speech-Crystals and the Celestial Echo. Gustaf Sobin. PT

Sound, Sound the Clarion. T. O. Mordaunt, *formerly at. to* Scott. EBEV; FaBoEE; FaPoR; NOBE; OxAEP-2 *Fr.* Verses Written during the War, 1756–1763.

(Call, The.) OBEV

Sound the Flute! Spring. William Blake. BoTP; FHYEP; FaBoCh; NOxBChV; NTP; Ro; TTTS *Fr.* Songs of Innocence.

Sound the Loud timbrel o'er Egypt's dark sea! Thomas Moore. ChIV-1

Sound the trumpet, beat the drum. Dryden. *Fr.* The Secular Masque. NAEL-1; OxAEP-1; PoE; PoEL-3; SCGP

Sound trumpets, ho!—weigh anchor—loosen sail. The Voyager's Song. Edward Coote Pinkney. APN-1

Sound variegated through beneath lit. Gyre's Galax. Norman Henry, II Pritchard. PoBA

Sound Waves. Mary Kinzie. FFC

Sounding brass of my heart says / "Love," The. (LL) Thing Language. Jack Spicer. APSN

Sounding cataract, The/ Haunted me like a passion. Wordsworth. *Fr.* Lines Composed a Few Miles above Tintern Abbey on Revisiting the Banks of the Wye During a Tour. EBEvV; FHYEP; HeIP-4; InPS-3; NoP-4; OAEL-2; OBNC; OxAEP-2; PoEL-4; Poetr; SCGP; TFi

Sounding down this world. (LL) We Dance Like Ella Riffs. Carolyn M. Rodgers. PoBA

Soundings. Paula Gunn Allen. HATNAP

Soundless / light drifts over, The. The Light of the World. B. Alquit, *Yiddish*. CEEP, *tr. by* Howard Schwartz

Soundlessly, a tide at the ear. Awakening. John Haines. SPE

Soundly they slept in midst of all their rest. (LL) Midnight ("Midnight was come, when every vital thing"). Thomas Sackville. CH

Sounds. Wassily Kandinsky, *Russian*. PFTM, tr. by Elizabeth R. Napier

Sounds are heard too high for ears. Watching Television. Robert Bly. CoAP

Sounds Begin Again, The. Dennis Brutus. HBAPE

Sounds in the dim washed room. Learning to Count. Sara Berkeley. BiHa

Sounds like big. Waking from a Nap on the Beach. May Swenson. NTCP

Sounds of Autumn. Lu Yu, *Chinese*. SuSp, tr. by Irving Y. Lo

Sounds of Ireland, The. Windharp. John Montague. CIP-2; IIP; PNI

Sounds of love are needles in my ears, The. Meleager, *Greek*. InMo, tr. by Sam Hamill

Sounds of the Day, *sonnet*. Norman MacCaig. RB

Sounds of the winter dance are heard wherever you are, great one, The. Kí′ nqalaLala Song. *Unknown*. Fr. Dances and Songs of the Winter Ceremonial. APN-2, tr. by Franz Boas

Sounds our parents heard echoing over, The. Strangers Like Us: Pittsburgh, Raleigh, 1945–1985. Gerald William Barrax. ISC

Sounds That Arrived, The. Milo De Angelis, *Italian*. Nelt, tr. by Lawrence Venuti

Soundwaves. Andrew Sant. NOBAu

Soup. Carl Sandburg. NOBA; NOBE; OBCA

Soup, The. Gary Soto. NoP-4

Soup Jar, The. Dabney Stuart. MT

Soup Kitchen. Betsy Sholl. PBCAB

Soup Kitchen Song. *Unknown*. NOBAu

Soup of Venus, The. James Tate. AmPA

Sour-Cherry Trees. Gyula Illyés, *Hungarian*. CEEP, tr. by Emery E. George

Sour daylight cracks through my sleep-caked lids, The. The Distant Winter. Philip Levine. VGW

Sour fiend, go home and tell the Pit. Ghoul Care. Ralph Hodgson. MoBrPo

Sour smell, The. Getting in the Wood. Gary Snyder. NoAM

Source, The. Jon Stallworthy. CBLP

Source, The. David Wagoner. VCAP

Source immaterial of material naught. "Orpheus C. Kerr." Fr. The Rejected "National Hymns." OBAL

Source unfolding bodily rhythm, impulse, local current, The. Ars Poetica. James ("Jim") Grabill. EC2

Sources. Marilyn Hacker. DeD Fr. Love, Death and the Changing of the Seasons.

Sources of My Being, The. Moses ibn Ezra, *Hebrew*. TOF, tr. by David Goldstein

Sourdough mountain called a fire in. The Text. Gary Snyder. NAAL-2 Fr. Burning. NeAP; PoM Fr. Myths and Texts.

Sourdough Mountain Lookout. Philip Whalen. BB; NeAP; PoM

Sourwood Mountain. *Unknown*. AmFP

South. Blaise Cendrars, *French*. BLT, tr. by Monique Chefdor

South, The. Emma Lazarus. APN-2; ColAP

South, The. Wang Chien, *Chinese*. AWP; BLT; ChiP; PNI, tr. by Arthur Waley

South African Broadsheets. David Wright.

"Under the African lintel, Table Mountain." PeSA

South African Exhibition, 1907. Kingsley Fairbridge. PeSAV

South America. Tom Raworth.

South America Mi Hija. Sharon Doubiago.

"Out the window, Colombia, out the window." PBCAP

South Bronx Testimonial. Sandra Maria Esteves. UnSA

South China Sea drives in, The. A Break from the Bush. Yusef Komunyakaa. CDa

South Coast, The. William Everson. NeAP

South Coast Haiku. Laurie Duggan. BMAP Fr. Dogs.

South Country, The. Hilaire Belloc. MoBrPo; OxAEP-2

South Mount soaring high. *Unknown, Chinese*. SuSp, tr. by C. H. Wang

South Mountain! So full of sorrows! In Protest. Li Ho, *Chinese*. SuSp, tr. by Maureen Robertson

South Mountain stuffs all heaven and earth. Wandering on Mount Chung-nan. Meng Chiao, *Chinese*. PLT, tr. by A. C. Graham

South Mountains, The. Han Yü, *Chinese*.

"Fine weather since yesterday." PLT, tr. by A. C. Graham

"Gazing as I climbed a high peak." PLT, tr. by A. C. Graham

"North of the great lake of K'un-ming." PLT, tr. by A. C. Graham

South, North, East, West, inland and seaboard, we will surely awake. (LL) To the States, To Identify the 16th, 17th, or 18th Presidentiad. Walt Whitman. CTC; NAAL-1; NAAL-3; RaBo

South of Boston, south of Washington. Robert Lowell. HCAP Fr. Mexico.

South of My Days. Judith Wright. FaBoWP; WPE

South of success and east of gloss and glass are. The Wall. Gwendolyn Brooks. Fr. The Wall. PoBA Fr. Two Dedications.

South of the Bridge. Shen Chou. CoBLCP, tr. by Jonathan Chaves Fr. The Stone Bridge.

South of the fabled pillars of Hercules. Volubilis, North Africa. Ralph Nixon Currey. PeSA

South of the Great Sea. *Unknown, Chinese*. ChiP, tr. by Arthur Waley

South of the house, north of the house. Tai Piao-yüan. CoBLCP, tr. by Jonathan Chaves Fr. Following His Rhymes and Answering the Poems of My Friend Next Door on Recent Events.

South of the Line, inland from far Durban. A Christmas Ghost-Story. Thomas Hardy. OBWP

South Parks Road. James Fenton. PeLV Fr. Exempla.

South Sea Ballad, A. Edward Ward. OBCoV

South-west wind is blowing, The. Autumn Morning. Adeline White. BoTP

South Wind. Siegfried Sassoon. BoTP

South Wind. Tu Fu, *Chinese*. BLT; OHPC, tr. by Kenneth Rexroth

South-wind brings, The. Threnody. Ralph Waldo Emerson. APN-1

South wind does not shed so great a cast, The. Callimachus. HePo, tr. by Barbara Hughes Fowler Fr. Hecale.

South-wind strengthens to a gale, The. Low Barometer. Robert Bridges. CABP; CMoP; MoP; NOCV; NoAM; OBNC; Poetr; SCGP

South wind's gust against the hill will make it flat land, The. Sing Loud. Li Ho, *Chinese*. PLT, tr. by A. C. Graham

South wind's molded by a spine of hill, The. Another Kind of Burning. Ruth Fox. NYBP

Southbound. Betty Adcock. MT

Southbound on the Freeway. May Swenson. ImGa; NTCP; NYBP

Southeast, and storm, and every weathervane. Hatteras Calling. Conrad Potter Aiken. ColAP; NOBA; TAP

Southeast at low tide. Skiing on Russian Christmas. Nora Dauenhauer. HATNAP

Southeast Corner. Gwendolyn Brooks. VGW Fr. A Street in Bronzeville. BPo; BlSi; FaBoWP

Southeast the Peacock Flies. *Unknown, Chinese*. CoBCP, tr. by Burton Watson

Southern Africa. Nguno Wakolele. PeSAV

Southern Blues, The. Big Bill Broonzy. GM

Southern Blues, The. *Unknown*. BkSV

Southern Cop. Sterling Brown. SoSe-8

Southern Crescent Was on time, The. Andrew Hudgins. GM

Southern Cross. Hart Crane. Fr. Three Songs. NAAL-2 Fr. The Bridge. NAAL-2

Southern Dawn. Pier Paolo Pasolini, *Italian*. VCWP, tr. by Norman MacAfee and Luciano Martinengo

Southern emperor rules the Southern land, The. Lý Thu'ò'ng Kiệt, *Chinese*. AVP, tr. by Huỳnh Sanh Thông

Southern hill-billy named Hollis, A. Limerick. *Unknown*. PeLi

Southern hills, how mournful!, The. Li Ho. PLT, tr. by A. C. Graham Fr. Criticisms.

Southern Mansion. Arna Bontemps. AiP; GT; LiTM; NAAAL; PoBA; TTY

Southern Mountains. Han Yü, *Chinese*. SuSp, tr. by Charles Hartman

Southern Pacific. Carl Sandburg. GM

Southern Paiute Poetry. *Unknown, Southern Paiute Native American*. APN-2, tr. by John Wesley Powell

Southern Press, The. Lizelia Augusta Jenkins Moorer. CBWP-3

Southern Pulpit, The. Lizelia Augusta Jenkins Moorer. CBWP-3

Southern Review, The. Brigit Pegeen Kelly.

Song: "Listen: there was a goat's head hanging by ropes in a tree." PUP-19

Southern Road. Sterling Brown. BPo; PoBA

("Evahmo'. . . .") (LL) GM; NAAAL

Southern Road. Mwatabu Okantah. SeSe

Southern Road, The. Dudley Randall. GM; PoBA

Southern Room Over the River, The. Su Tung-p'o, *Chinese*. OHPC, tr. by Kenneth Rexroth

Southern Work of Dr. and Mrs. L. M. Dunton. Lizelia Augusta Jenkins Moorer. CBWP-3

Southey and Wordsworth. Byron. See Don Juan.

Southward bound over sixty days. The Officer at the Rapids. Han Yü, *Chinese.* SuSp, *tr. by* Charles Hartman

Southward from hence ten miles, where Derwent laves. Chatsworth. Charles Cotton. OBGa *Fr.* The Wonders of the Peak.

Southward I once traveled, crossing mountain passes. Plum Blossoms. Su Shih. SuSp, *tr. by* Irving Y. Lo *Fr.* On Chao Ch'ang's Flower Paintings in Wang Po-yang's Collection.

Southward through Eden went a river large. Milton. *See* Eden.

Southwest Passage. Dudley Fitts. PoA

Souvenir. Naomi Long Madgett. NBV

Souvenir. Alfred de Musset, *French.* AWP, *tr. by* George Santayana

Souvenir. Edwin Arlington Robinson. NoAM

Souvenir de Monsieur Poop. Stevie Smith. NALW

Souvenir of the Ancient World. Carlos Drummond de Andrade, *Portuguese.* ChAP; VCWP, *tr. by* Mark Strand

Souvenirs. Jane Cooper. *Fr.* Dispossessions. FaBoWP

Souvenirs. Dudley Randall. BPo

Sou'wester whips the day awake, The. Bruce Beaver. *Fr.* Letters to Live Poets. CBAP

Sovereign and Transforming Grace. Frederic Henry Hedge. AH

Sovereign beauty which I do admire, The. Sonnet 71. Edmund Spenser. PoEL-1 *Fr.* Amoretti. AAS

Sovereign Queen. Padeshah Khatun, *Farsi.* WPOW, *tr. by* Deirdre Lashgari

Sovereign soul, The/ Of him who lives self-governed and at peace. *Unknown.* TOF, *tr. by* Sir Edwin Arnold *Fr.* The Bhagavad-Gita.

Sovereignty, His. Kalonymos ben Moses of Lucca, *Hebrew.* TrJP, *tr. by* Nina Davis Salaman

Soviet Union, The. John Berryman. FaBoPV

Sow came in with the saddle, The. Mother Goose. OxNR

Sow charlock around the ears. From Bosch's Hill. Tymoteusz Karpowicz, *Polish.* CEEP, *tr. by* Ewa Zak

Sow of Feeling, The. Robert Fergusson. NOEC

Sower, The. Mathilde Blind. WPE

Sower, The. William Cowper. ChIV-2 *Fr.* Olney Hymns.

Sower went forth to sow, A. The Parable of the Sower. Stephen Mitchell. GI

Sower's Song, The. Thomas Carlyle. SCGP

Sowing Seeds. Ursula Cornwall. BoTP

Sown in dishonor! Emily Dickinson. ChIV-2

Soyer is gone! Then be it said. On the Death of the Great Chef Alexis Soyer. *Unknown.* FaBoEE

Soyŏng Problems. Sang Yi, *Korean.* PFTM, *tr. by* Walter Lew

Sozzled, Mo-tsu, after a silence, vouchsafed. Scholars at the Orchid Pavilion. John Berryman. PoE

Space. Shindo Chie, *Japanese.* WPJ, *tr. by* Kenneth Rexroth *and* Ikuko Atsumi

Space. Jenny Thomas. SpW

Space. Urdeath. August Stramm, *German.* PFTM, *tr. by* Rothenberg, Jerome *and* Pierre Joris

Space and stars. Below. Federico García Lorca. PFTM

Space beats the ruddy freedom of their limbs. Daughters of War. Isaac Rosenberg. PeFWW

Space being(don't forget to remember)Curved. E. E. Cummings. NoAM

Space Between, The. Ana Luisa Ortiz de Montellano. LoHo

Space Captain. John Kitching. SpW

Space Explorer's Story, The. David Harmer. SpW

Space in the light said to be where one / comes from. Stephen Ratcliffe. PT

Space in the lives of their friends, A. Ishmael Reed. *See* Beware: Do Not Read This Poem.

Space instead of furniture. Jean Daive, *French.* MFP, *tr. by* Martin Sorrell

Space Invaders Machine, The. Pita Sharples, *Maori.* PeNZ, *tr. by the author*

Space is too full. Did nothing happen here? American Farm, 1934. Genevieve Taggard. VGW

Space Men. Charles Connell. SpW

Space News Agency Atmos report, The. Here is the News from space. Michael Rosen. SpW

Space Settlement. Albert Rowe. SpW

Space Shot. Gareth Owen. SpW

Space-Shuttle. Judith Nicholls. SpW

Space Spot. Max Fatchen. SpW

Space Trip. James Kirkup. SpW

Space Walk. Raymond Wilson. SpW

Space was, The / magnificent & dry, The. On a Line by John Ashbery. James Bertolino. CMAP

Spaces. Judy Page Heitzman. CMAP

Spaceship drifting up, The. Christmas. Peter McDonald. PNI

Spacious Encounter. Tess Gallagher. NMM-2

Spacious firmament on high, The. Ode. Joseph Addison. BLPA; ChIV-1; ECEV; FaBoBe; FaPoR; NOCV; NOEC; PoEL-3; TOF

Spade and the Wreath, The. George Wither. NOSC *Fr.* A Collection of Emblems, Ancient and Moderne.

Spade-bearded grandfather, squat Lenin. Summer Pogrom. Fay Zwicky. CBAP

Spade, for labour stands. The ball with wings, The. George Wither. NOSC *Fr.* A Collection of Emblems, Ancient and Moderne.

Spade Scharnweber was a white Watusi. His mother. Don Welch. Poetsp

Spades take up leaves. Gathering Leaves. Robert Frost. RB; VGW

Spading earth. Animal Kingdom. Sydney Clouts. PeSA

Spaewife, The. Robert Louis Stevenson. OxBS

Spaghetti Nut, The. Jack Prelutsky. ChAP

Spain. Dorothy Livesay. NOBC

Spain, 1809. Frank Lawrence Lucas. EBNV

Spain! much more beautiful than Egypt! Madrid. Frank O'Hara. FTOS

Spain 1937. W. H. Auden. AF; FaBoPV; NAEL-2; NoP-4; OBWP

Spain. The wild dust, the whipped corn, earth easy for. Teresa of Avila. Elizabeth Jennings. PeECV; TOF

Span of Life, The. Robert Frost. HoPM; LiTM; SoSe-8 *Fr.* Ten Mills.

Spaniard That Blighted My Life, The. Billy Merson. OBCoV

Spaniards' dispatch, Danes' wit, are mainly seen in thee. John Wilmot, 2d Earl of Rochester. *See* Upon Nothing.

Spaniel, Beau, that fares like you, A. On a Spaniel Called Beau Killing a Young Bird. William Cowper. FaBoCh

Spanish Blue. Herbert Morris. NYBP

Spanish Curate, The. John Fletcher.

  "Let the bells ring, and let the boys sing." SCGP

Spanish Descent, The. Daniel Defoe.

  "Word's gone out, and now they spread the main, The." OBWP

Spanish expression, The, *Cuando yo era muchacho.* Habla Usted Español? James Reiss. AmPA

Spanish Folk Songs. Antonio Machado Ruiz, *Spanish.* AWP, *tr. by* Havelock Ellis

Spanish Friar [*or* Fryar], The. Dryden.

  Love's Despair.

    ("Farewell, ungrateful traitor!") GLoP; RACG

    ("When loving is a pain.") (LL) RACG

  "'Twere well your judgments but in plays did range." OBSV

Spanish Jew's Tale: Azrael, The. Henry Wadsworth Longfellow. APN-1 *Fr.* Tales of a Wayside Inn.

Spanish Johnny. Willa Cather. AiP; PaTW

Spanish noon is a blaze of azure fire, and the dusty pilgrims, The. The Exodus (August 3, 1492). Emma Lazarus. *Fr.* By the Waters of Babylon. WPE

Spanish of Our Out–Loud Dreams, The. Martín Espada. MoLi

Spanish record turns, The. By the Campfire. Konstantin Mikhailovich Simonov, *Russian.* TCRP, *tr. by* Lubov Yakovleva

Spanish Student, The. Henry Wadsworth Longfellow.

  Serenade: "Stars of the summer night!" FaBoBe

Spanish Wives, The. Mary Pix.

  Song, A: "Fairest Nymph that ever bless'd our Shore." KTR

Sparafucile fought his peasant war. Dead Fly. Eiléan Ní Chuilleanáin. CIP-2

Spare, gen'rous victor, spare the slave. To a Lady: She Refusing to Continue a Dispute with Me, and Leaving Me in the Argument. Matthew Prior. NoP-4

Spare me the man. Anacreon, *Greek.* InMo, *tr. by* Sam Hamill

Spare not but play thee! Thomas Lodge. *See* Rosalind's [*or* Rosalynd's] Madrigal[l].

Spare Professor, grave and bald, The. At a Reading. Thomas Bailey Aldrich. OBAL

Spare the mother of acorns, man. Cut down some paliurus. Diodorus Zonas, *Greek.* GrAn, *tr. by* Alistair Elliot

Spare then the person, and expose the vice. Alexander Pope. OBSV *Fr.* Epilogue to the Satires, in Two Dialogues. OAEL-1

Spare Us, O Lord, Aloud We Pray. Isaac Watts. AH

"Spare us of dying beauty," cries out Youth. Of Dying Beauty. Louis Zukofsky. PoA

Spared by a car- or airplane-crash or. Accidents of Birth. William Meredith. APAD

Sparhawk [*or* Sparrow-hawk] proud did hold in wicked jail, A. A Sparrow-Hawk. *Unknown.* CH; EBEV

Spark, A. Alan Pizzarelli. HA

Spark, A. Springburst. John Travers Moore. AYFP

Spark in Your seeing, A. (LL) Day of Atonement. Charles Reznikoff. ChIV-1; KSG

Sparkle and fall to the power of a thousand from her body. (LL) The One Girl at the Boys Party. Sharon Olds. SAGP

Sparkler goes out, The. Lorraine Ellis Harr. HA

Sparkles from the wheel. (LL) Sparkles from the Wheel. Walt Whitman. InPS-3; NAAL-1; NAAL-3; SAmP

Sparkles from the Wheel. Walt Whitman. InPS-3; NAAL-1; NAAL-3; SAmP

Sparkling light of heaven fills the well, The. The Well. Nguyễn Thiên Túng, Chinese. AVP, tr. by Huỳnh Sanh Thông

Spark's Farewell to Its Clay, The. Ronald Allison Kells Mason. PeNZ

Sparrow, The. William Carlos Williams. InPS-3; LCAP-2; Poetr; VGW

Sparrow dips in his wheel-rut bath, The. The Five Students. Thomas Hardy. CMoP; GTBS-P; PoEL-5

Sparrow-Hawk, A. Unknown. CH; EBEV

Sparrow hawk drops to the cornfield, The. The Sound of Guns. Gerald McCarthy. CDa

Sparrow Hills. Robley Wilson Jr. PBCAP

Sparrow in the Zoo, The. Howard Nemerov. MoP Fr. Epigrams. OBAL (Epigram: Political Reflexion.) NIP-4

Sparrow of Espanola. Michael Pettit. NAmP90

Sparrows among Dry Leaves. William Carlos Williams. NYBP

Sparrows by the iron fence post, The. Sparrows among Dry Leaves. William Carlos Williams. NYBP

Sparrow's Dirge, The. John Skelton. FaBoCh Fr. Phyllyp Sparowe [or Philip Sparrow]. AAS; PoEL-1

Sparrow's Fall, The. Frances Ellen Watkins Harper. PWR

Sparrow's Feather, A. George Barker. NYBP

Sparrow's Flight, A. The Venerable Bede. LBC

Sparrows in a Hillside Drift. James Wright. ColAP

Sparrows pitch at the wooden walls. Birds. Ralph Hawkins. NBrP

Sparrow's Skull, The. Ruth Pitter. FaBoWP

Sparrows sunning. Martin Shea. HA

Sparrows were feeding in a freezing drizzle. Because You Asked about the Line between Prose and Poetry. Howard Nemerov. VCAP; WeW-3

Sparse fence, winding path, a small farmhouse. Chou Pang-yen. SuSp, tr. by Irving Y. Lo Fr. Tunc: "Beautiful Lady Yü, The."

Spasibo. Thanks. O.K. Adrienne Rich. See Two Songs.

Spate in Winter Midnight. Norman MacCaig. GTBS-P

Spatial depths of being survive. The Lost Dancer. Jean Toomer. PoBA

Spattering of the rain upon pale terraces, The. John Gould Fletcher. Fr. Irradiations. MoAmPo

Spawn of fantasies. Love Songs. Mina Loy. VGW; WPE

Spawn of Slums, The. James W. Thompson. BPo

Spawning in Northern Minnesota. David McElroy. AmPA

Speak! Wordsworth. See To a Distant Friend.

Speak. James Wright. HAP; NoP-4; TAP

Speak, daughter, speak; art speaking now? Demeter and Cora. Dora Greenwell. VWP

Speak earth and bless me with what is richest. Love Poem. Audre Lorde. GLP; NoAM

Speak! fairy Moon, interpret this! (LL) The Dawn of Love. Henrietta Cordelia Ray. BlSi; CBWP-3

"SPEAK, gentlemen, what shall we do today?" Sir Revel. Samuel Rowlands. NoSic; OBCoV

Speak Gently. David Bates. PWR

Speak gently; it is better far. G. W. Langford. PoToHe; UV

Speak not ill of womankind. Against Blame of Woman. Gerald Fitzgerald. BIrV, tr. by the Earl of Longford

Speak not of niceness, when there's chance of wreck. Sir Walter Scott. FaBoEE Fr. Peveril of the Peak.

Speak not of passion, for my heart is tired. The Sister of Mercy. Constance Naden. VWP

Speak out your secret, bellowing waves. Lines: Composed at the Old Temples of Maralipoor. Charles Timothy Brooks APN-1

Speak [or Speke], Parrot, sels. John Skelton.
　"Now, Parrot, my sweet bird, speak out yet once again." NoSic
　　Parrot's Soliloquy. PoEL-1
　"My name is Parrot, a bird of Paradise." OBCoV; NOSIC

Speak roughly to your little boy. The Duchess's Lullaby. "Lewis Carroll." CBNP; FaBoCh; NBLV; NOxBChV; UV Fr. Alice's Adventures in Wonderland.

Speak, Satire, for there's none can tell like thee. The True-born Englishman. Daniel Defoe.

Speak! speak! thou fearful guest! The Skeleton in Armor [or Armour]. Henry Wadsworth Longfellow. APN-1; AWP; AmPP; CTV; FaBoBe

Speak, that my torturing doubts their end may know! (LL) To a Distant Friend. Wordsworth. GTBS-P; OBEV

Speak[e] to dead walls: but[t] thos[e] hear not my moan [or mone]. (LL) My Body in the Walls Captived. Sir Walter Ralegh. CABP; SiPS

Speak to Her Tenderly. Mary E. Tucker. CBWP-1

Speak to me. Take my hand. What are you now? Effort at Speech between Two People. Muriel Rukeyser. FYAP; MoAmPo; Poetr; TrJP; TwCP

Speak when you're spoken to, / Come for one call. Mother Goose. OxNR

Speake gentle heart, where is thy dwelling place? Thomas Watson. AAS Fr. Hecatompathia; or, Passionate Century of Love.

Speaker, The. Charles G. Ballard. VoR

Speaker in the Square, A. George Buchanan. PNI

Speakin' in general, I 'ave tried 'em all. Sestina of the Tramp-Royal. Rudyard Kipling. ImPo; MoBrPo

Speaking. Michael Ryan. AmPA; SoSe-8

Speaking and Kissing. Thomas Stanley. BeJo

Speaking in a state of fidelity to the subject, living flesh though it may. My Story. Carla Harryman. PmAP

Speaking like wind. Swimmer. Gladys Cardiff. CDW

Speaking of Gethsemane in Yoruba Land. Edouard J. Maunick. NegPo, tr. by Ellen Conroy Kennedy Fr. As Far as Yoruba Land.

Speaking of peaceful trees / another village explodes. (LL) It Is Dangerous to Read Newspapers. Margaret Atwood. CrSp; HeIP-4; OBWP

Speaking of Places. Rajagopal Parthasarathy. OMIP

Speaking of Television. Phyllis McGinley.
　Robin Hood. OBSV

Speaking Through White: For My Mother. Kyoko Mori. UnSA

Speaking to My Photo. Tản Đà, Vietnamese. AVP, tr. by Huỳnh Sanh Thông

Speaking with Hands. Luis J. Rodriguez. UnSA

Speaks Bito's tomb to whomsoever reads. Nicaenetus, Greek. GrAn, tr. by Peter Whigham

Speaks the Whispering Grass. Jesse Stuart. FYAP

Speargrass crackles under the billy and overhead is the winter sun, The. While the Billy Boils. David McKee Wright, Maori. PeNZ, tr. by Margaret Orbell

Spearmen and the bowmen, The. (LL) The War Song of Dinas Vawr. Thomas Love Peacock. AWP; EBEvV; FaBoCh; FaPoR; HAP; NAEL-2; NOBE; NTP; OAEL-2; OxAEP-2

Spearmen heard the bugle sound, The. Beth Gêlert; or, The Grave of the Greyhound. William Robert Spencer. BLPA; EBNV; OBNV

Spearo's Blues (or: Ode to a Grecian Yearn). Eugene B. Redmond. NBV

Special Bulletin. Langston Hughes. PoBA

Special Jurymen of England! who admire your country's laws. Damages, Two Hundred Pounds. William Makepeace Thackeray. OBSV

Special Rider Blues. Unknown. AmFP

Special Theory of Relativity, A. Alan Bold. FaBoTC

Special Train, A. Daniel Gerard Hoffman. CDa

Specially for me, she had some breaded. Breaded Fish. A. K. Ramanujan. NoP-4

Species. Philip Booth. AFr

Species means guilt. Slave ship somatism grease their wings wrencher. Bruce Andrews. PmAP

Specifically the rose window specifically the center. Sainte-Chapelle. John Taggart. FTOS

Specifications for a Perfect Lover. Richard Crashaw. Fr. Wishes. To His (Supposed) Mistresse. BoLoP; EBEV; ImPo; MeLP; NOSC; OBEV; OxAEP-1; PoEL-2; SeCP

Specimen of a Translation of the Iliad in Blank Verse. Homer, Greek. OBCVT, tr. by Alfred Tennyson, 1st Baron Tennyson Fr. The Iliad.

Specimens of Indian Songs. Unknown, Miami. APN-2; tr. by Lewis Cass

Speck of protoplasm in a finch's egg, The. Birdsong. Burns Singer. FaBoTw

Speck Speaks, A. Adrian Mitchell. OBSP

Speck that would have been beneath my sight, A. A Considerable Speck. Robert Frost. MoAmPo; OBAL; PBMP; SAmP

Speckled bird sings in the tree, The. The Nightingale. Katharine Tynan. BoTP

Speckled cat and a tame hare, A. Two Songs of a Fool. W. B. Yeats. CMoP; RB

Speckled Hen's Morning Song to Biddy Early, The. Nancy Willard. FFC

Spectacular. Lilian Moore. KaS

Spectacular Blossom. Allen Curnow. PeNZ

Spectator ab Extra. Arthur Hugh Clough. OxBoLi; PeLV; PeVV

How Pleasant It Is to Have Money. NOBE; OAEL-2

Le Diner. OBCoV

Parvenant. OBCoV

Spectator's Guide to Contemporary Art. Phyllis McGinley.

On the Farther Wall, Marc Chagall. OBSV

Squeeze Play. FaBoEE; OBCoV; OBSV

Spectators only on this bustling stage. Charles Churchill. OBSV *Fr.* Night; an Epistle to Robert Lloyd.

Specter, The. "Anna Akhmatova," *Russian.* TCRP, *tr.* by Daniel Weissbort

Spectral Attitudes, The. André Breton, *French.* SPE, *tr.* by David Gascoyne

Spectre, fiercely staring, thus reply'd, The. Dryden. OxBSn *Fr.* Theodore and Honoria.

Spectre is haunting America—the spectre of hoodooism, A. Black Power Poem. Ishmael Reed. BPo

Spectrum. Mari E. Evans. BPo

Spectrum. Aidan Carl Mathews. PBCIP

Spectrum Trench. Autumn. Nineteen-Sixteen. The Dead Soldiers. Max Plowman. PoWW

Speculation. Howard Nemerov. TAP

Speculations. Marcel Duchamp. PFTM

Speculations on the Present through the Prism of the Past, *for Haruko.* June Jordan. GT

Speculations on the Subject of Barabbas. Zbigniew Herbert, *Polish.* GI, *tr.* by John Carpenter *and* Bogdana Carpenter

Speculators, The. William Makepeace Thackeray. OBCoV; OBSV

Speech. Chief Mothibi. PeSAV

Speech. Leopold Staff, *Polish.* PoSu, *tr.* by Adam Czerniawski

Speech. Henry Taylor. NBLV

Speech after long silence; it is right. After Long Silence. W. B. Yeats. BoLoP; CMoP; EnLoPo; HeIP-4; HoPM; LiTM; NAEL-2; OAEL-2; OBMV; UnPo

Speech Against Stone. Charles Martin. RA

Speech and Image: An African Tradition of the Surreal. Léopold Sédar Senghor, *French.* PFTM, *tr.* by John Reed *and* Clive Wake

Speech of Ajax. Sophocles, *Greek.* OBCVT, *tr.* by Charles Stuart Calverley

speech of Charita. The Bargain. Sir Philip Sidney. AWP; BoLoP; CH; EBEvV; FaBoBe; GBL; GTBS-P; NOBE; NoSic; OBEV; OxAEP-1; PoE; PoEL-1; SCGP; SiPS; TFi; UV *Fr.* Arcadia.

Speech of Sarpedon (an Ally of the Trojans) to Glaucus, The. Homer. OBVE, *tr.* by Alexander Pope *Fr.* The Iliad.

Speech of the Nymph. Anna Seward. NOBRP

Speech seems to us the main instrument of thought, emotion and action. Speech and Image: An African Tradition of the Surreal. Léopold Sédar Senghor, *French.* PFTM, *tr.* by John Reed *and* Clive Wake

Speech to a Crowd. Archibald MacLeish. MoAmPo

Speech to the Young Speech to the Progress-Toward (Among Them Nora and Henry III). Gwendolyn Brooks. PiM

Speeches at the Barriers. Susan Howe.

"Right or ruth." PmAP

"Sabbath and sweet spices." PmAP

"Say that a ballad." PmAP

"Twenty lines of." PmAP

Speeches in the Interior. Juhan Viiding, *Estonian.* CEEP, *tr.* by Ivar Ivask

Speechless [upon the Marriage of Two Deaf and Dumb Persons]. Philip Bourke Marston. EBVV

Speechless, speechless, you testify against us. (LL) On the Wall of a KZ-Lager. János Pilinszky, *Hungarian.* PoSu, *tr.* by Janos Csokits *and* Ted Hughes; HP, *tr.* by Ted Hughes; AF, *tr.* by Ted Hughes *and* Janos Csokits

Speechlesse still, and never crie. John Cleveland. See Epitaph on the Earl of Strafford.

Speechlesse still, and never crie[y]. (LL) Epitaph on the Earl of Strafford. John Cleveland. FaBoEE; FaBoPV; NOBE; NOSC; PeECV

Speed, a Pastoral. John Forbes. BMAP

Speed Ball. Yusef Komunyakaa. SeSe

Speed it, o[h] Father! Let thy Kingdom come! (LL) Reflections on Having Left a Place of Retirement. Coleridge. LaPo; Ro

Speed of Darkness, The. Muriel Rukeyser. APSN; GLP; LCAP-2

Speed Track, The. "Peter." BoTP

Speeding carriage climbs through eastern gate, A. Unknown, *Chinese.* SuSp, *tr.* by Charles Hartman

Speeding flowers along the shores mirror my boat red. Journeying to Hsiang-yi. Ch'en Yü-yi, *Chinese.* SuSp, *tr.* by Irving Y. Lo

Spell. Robert Herrick. CaPo; OxBSn

Spell. Anuradha Mahapatra, *Bengali.* OMIP, *tr.* by Jyotirmoy Dutta *and* Carolyne Wright

Spell, The. Molly Peacock. FFC

Spell Against Sorrow. Kathleen Jessie Raine. PBWP

Spell against Spelling, The. George Starbuck. FYAP

Spell for Making the First Man. Unknown, *Maori.* PeNZ, *tr.* by Margaret Orbell

Spell for Sleeping, A. Alastair Reid. NOxBChV; NTP

Spell me that in four letters. Mother Goose. See Pease porridge [or pudding] hot.

Spell of Creation. Kathleen Jessie Raine. FaBoCh; OxBS

Spell of the Yukon, The. Robert W. Service. BLPA; FaBoBe

Spell of Weather, A. Eve Merriam. CA

Spell, treasure-bearing spell, prop up the sky standing above. Lament. Unknown, *Maori.* PeNZ, *tr.* by Margaret Orbell

Spellbound. Emily Jane Brontë. NOBE

Spellbound. Homer. Fr. Odyssey. NAWM-1, *tr.* by Robert Fitzgerald

Spelling. Margaret Atwood. NALW; NoAM

Spelling reformer indicted, A. Orthography. Ambrose Bierce. APN-2; OBAL; PeLi Fr. The Devil's Dictionary.

Spells. James Reeves. NTP

Spend the years of learning squandering. Gnome. Samuel Beckett. BIrV; OxBSP

Spende and god schall sende. Penny. Unknown. EnVB; FaBoVe; MiEL

Spending beyond their income on gifts for Christmas. Christmas Shopping. Louis MacNeice. OBCP

Spending hand that alway poureth [or powreth] out [or owte], A. To Sir Francis Brian. Sir Thomas Wyatt. AAS; NoSic; SiPS Fr. Satires.

Spending the Night at a Mountain Temple. Chia Tao, *Chinese.* SuSp, *tr.* by Stephen Owen

Spending the Night at the Hillside Lodge of Master Yeh and Waiting for My Friend Ting. Meng Hao Jan, *Chinese.* SuSp, *tr.* by Daniel Bryant

Spending the Night in an Inn at Swatow and Writing about My Feelings, Sent to Liang Shih-wu. Huang Tsun-hsien, *Chinese.* SuSp, *tr.* by An-yan Tang

Spending the Night in the Eastern Park. Shen Yüeh, *Chinese.* SuSp, *tr.* by Richard B. Mather

Spending the Night on Stone Gate Mountain. Hsieh Ling-yün, *Chinese.* SuSp, *tr.* by Francis Westbrook

Spending the Night on the River. T'ang Hsien-tsu, *Chinese.* CoBLCP, *tr.* by Jonathan Chaves

Spendthrift, disinherited and graceless, The. Remittance Man. Judith Wright. NoAM

Spendthrifts. Lotte Moos. NBrP

Spenser! a jealous honourer of thine. Keats. EPCY

Spent purpose of a perfectly marvellous, The. In Favor of One's Time. Frank O'Hara. NeAP; PoA

Spermal Chimney. Francis Picabia, *French.* PFTM, *tr.* by Jerome Rothenberg

Sperrins surround it, the Faughan flows by, The. Claudy. James Simmons. BiHa; CIP-2; PBCIP

Sphere. A. R. Ammons.

"I don't know about you,/ but I'm sick of good poems." HCAP

"I was pulling veronica out of the lawn when this hornet came." NoAM

"There is a faculty or knack, smallish, in the mind that can turn." NoAM

Sphere. Jules Supervielle, *French.* MFP, *tr.* by Martin Sorrell

Sphere, which is as many thousand spheres, A. Shelley. Fr. Prometheus Unbound. NOBRP; OAEL-2

Spheres, The. Jones Very. PAR

Sphinx. Robert Earl Hayden. GT; HCAP

Sphinx, The. Oscar Wilde.

"How subtle-secret is your smile! Did you love none then? Nay, I know." MoBrPo

Sphinx is drowsy, The. Ralph Waldo Emerson. APN-1; AmPP; NOBA; OxBA

Sphinxes Inclined to Be. Olga Orozco, *Spanish.* WPOW, *tr.* by Leslie Keffer

Spice and pungent air of the earth, The. The Confession of Cleopas. Eric Pankey. GI

Spicewood. Lizette Woodworth Reese. MoAmPo

Spicy grove, cinamon tree, / What is Africa to me? Countee Cullen. See Heritage.

Spider. Basho, *Japanese.* TTTS

Spider. Thomas Cole. PoA

Spider. Norma Farber. PChr

Spider, The. Hannah Flagg Gould. OBCA

Spider, The. César Vallejo, *Spanish.* RaBo, *tr.* by Robert Bly

Spider and the Fly, The. Mary Howitt. OTCP; OxBChV; PWR; UV

("'Will you walk into my parlour?' said the Spider to the Fly.") ACTP

("Within his little parlour—but she ne'er came out again!") (LL) ACTP

Spider and the Ghost of the Fly, The. Vachel Lindsay. VGW

Spider bite the size of a dinner plate, A. Into the Dark. Paul Monette. AmPA

Spider crouching on the ledge above the sink, The. James Keir Baxter. PeNZ *Fr.* Autumn Testament.

Spider Crystal Ascension. Charles Wright. HCAP; LCAP-2; VCAP

Spider expects the cold of winter, The. Richard Eberhart. NoAM; PoA

Spider has more eyes than I have money, The. Robert Penn Warren. MT

Spider holds a Silver Ball, The. Emily Dickinson. WPOW

Spider in the bath, A. The image noted. The Image. Roy Fuller. GTBS-P; OxBTC

Spider, juiced crystal and Milky Way, drifts on his web through the night sky, The. Spider Crystal Ascension. Charles Wright. HCAP; LCAP-2; VCAP

Spider sewed at Night, A. Emily Dickinson. NAAL-1; NAAL-3; NALW

Spider spreads her webs, whether she be, The. Letter to Maria Gisborne. Shelley.

Spider Webster's Declaration: He Is Singing the End of the World Again. Judy Grahn. EC2

Spiders. David Wevill. MoCV

Spiders started out to go with the wind on its pilgrimage, The. The Broken. W. S. Merwin. LCAP-2

Spiderwebs on the casement. Old Times. Daniel Mark Epstein. DiPo

Spiel of [the] Three Mountebanks. John Crowe Ransom. MoAmPo

Spies whisper through my air condition units. Light Reading. Vassar Miller. FFC

Spies, you are lights in state, but of base stuff. On Spies. Ben Jonson. BeJo; FaBoVe; NoP-4; OxBSP

Spike Logic. James McManus. BAP-94

Spiked thorns all over, and a thirty-foot wall. Ballad of the Government Granary Clerk. Ho Ching-ming, *Chinese.* CoBLCP, *tr. by* Jonathan Chaves

Spikes of new smell driven up nostrils. Gary Snyder. *Fr.* Burning. NeAP; PoM *Fr.* Myths and Texts.

Spilled. Heather McHugh. WeT

Spilled into the cup. Bubbling Wine. Abu Zakariya, *Arabic.* TTY, *tr. by* A. J. Arberry

Spilling out / into the world. (LL) Where Mountain Lion Lay [*or* Laid] Down with Deer. Leslie Marmon Silko. ImGa; Poetr; TRP; VoR; WPOW

Spilt Milk. Sarah Maguire. LW

Spilt Milk. W. B. Yeats. OxBSP

Spin a coin, spin a coin. Queen Nefertiti. *Unknown.* OTCP; TLR

Spin, a hardy spin, and here's the globe, A. A Small Boy, Dreaming. Albert Herzing. NYBP

Spin, Dame, spin. *Unknown.* OxNR

Spin him like a top! (LL) Homage to My Hips. Lucille Clifton. NAAAL

Spin the ball! I reel, I burn. Song of Seyd [*or* Seid] Nimetollah of Kuhistan. Seid Nimatullah, *Persian.* NOBA

Spindle, The. Peter Huchel, *German.* CEEP, *tr. by* Rich Ives

Spindrift. Galway Kinnell. NYBP

Spine doesn't give or arch to it, The. Not-loving. Sylvia Kantaris. LW

Spine has been tingled; the horn has been swoggled, The. Woolly Words. Robert N. Feinstein. NBLV

Spinner'' lights from house to house brighten the deep night. Sitting Up at Night. Lu Yu, *Chinese.* CoBCP, *tr. by* Burton Watson

Spinning Song. Dame Edith Sitwell. MoBrPo

Spinning top. (LL) Philokles offers his bouncing. Leonidas, *Greek.* GrAn; PGA, *tr. by* Kenneth Rexroth

Spinning Woman, The. Leonidas of Tarentum. AWP, *tr. by* Andrew Lang *Fr.* Epigrams.

Spinoza / Collected curiosa. Clerihew. *Unknown.* NOBL

Spinoza Was a Bee. Jaroslaw Marek Rymkiewicz, *Polish.* CBNP, *tr. by* Czeslaw Milosz

Spinster. Sylvia Plath. FaBoWP; LW; SoSe-8

Spinster. Vita Sackville-West. WPN

Spinster with a mouth like a dam and a heart, A. Lizzie. Nancy Vieira Couto. PBCAP

Spinster's Sweet-Arts, The. Tennyson.

"Robby, git down wi'tha, wilt tha?" FaBoVe

Spiral Shell, A. Howard Nemerov. *Fr.* Epigrams. OBAL

Spiralwise it spins. Time. Ralph Hodgson. GTBS-P

Spire, The. Ellen Bryant Voigt. NoAM

Spire cranes, The. Its statue is an aviary. Dylan Thomas. PoA

Spires, firm on their monster feet rose light and thin, The. Denis Devlin. CIP-2 *Fr.* The Heavenly Foreigner.

Spires of Oxford, The. Winifred M. Letts. PoLF; PoRA

Spirit, The. Jones Very. NCAP

Spirit appeared to me, and said, A. Herman Melville. ChIV-1

Spirit Craft, The. Charles G. Ballard. VoR

Spirit cries *Be strong!* and cries *Be still!*, A. (LL) Dead. Lionel Pigot Johnson. OBNC; PoEL-5

Spirit Epiloguizes, The. Milton. *See* The Spirit's Epilogue.

Spirit Expounds. T'ao Ch'ien. *Fr.* Substance, Shadow, and Spirit. CoBCP, *tr. by* Burton Watson

Spirit Flowers. Della Burt. BlSi

Spirit from Perfecter Ages. Arthur Hugh Clough. OBNC *Fr.* Amours de Voyage. NOBVV

Spirit haunts the year's last hours, A. Song. Tennyson. GTBS-P; GaP; HeIP-4; LaPo; OBGa; OBNC

Spirit in Our Hearts, The. Henry Ustic Onderdonk. AH

Spirit is too blunt an instrument, The. Anne Stevenson. ColAP

Spirit lasts, but in what mode, The. Emily Dickinson. APN-2

Spirit of dreams, that when the dark hours steep. Invocation, To the Genius of Slumber Written Oct. 1787. Anna Seward. PEW

Spirit of Evil, The. Arrigo Boito. OxBoV, *tr. by* Andrew Porter *Fr.* Otello.

Spirit of Evil, The. Goethe. OxBoV, *tr. by* Bayard Taylor *Fr.* Faust.

Spirit of Gama! round the stormy Cape. The Cape of Storms. John Wheatley. PeSAV

Spirit of God, The. Antiphon for the Holy Spirit. Hildegard von Bingen, *German.* WPoS, *tr. by* Barbara Newman

Spirit of Life, in This New Dawn. Earl Bowman Marlatt. AH

Spirit of Poetry, The. Henry Wadsworth Longfellow. APN-1

Spirit of spirits, who, through ev'ry part. A Hymn to Na'ra'yena. Sir William Jones. NOBRP

Spirit of the Age, The. Christopher Pearse Cranch. APN-1; PAR

Spirit of the Mountain, The. Ch'u Yüan, *Chinese.* ChiPo, *tr. by* Rewi Alley

Spirit of the Wind. Gabriel Okara. PBMAP

Spirit of Wrath, The. William Heyen. AmPA

Spirit pass'd before me: I beheld, A. Byron. ChIV-1

Spirit Pool is never polluted, The. Chao Meng-fu. *Fr.* Twenty-Eight Poems Inscribed on T'ien-kuan Mountain. CoBLCP, *tr. by* Jonathan Chaves

Spirit seems to pass, A. Lausanne: In Gibbon's Old Garden: 11–12 p.m. Thomas Hardy. FaBoTw

Spirit, Silken Thread. Margot Ruddock. OBMV

Spirit Voice, The; or Liberty Call to the Disfranchised (State of New York). Charles Lewis Reason. AAP

Spirit! What art thou erecting. The Poet's Ideal. Henrietta Cordelia Ray. CBWP-3

Spirit whose work is done—spirit of dreadful hours! Walt Whitman. CBCWP; NAAL-1; NAAL-3

Spirited light! on the edge. Antiphon for the Angels. Hildegard von Bingen, *German.* WPoS, *tr. by* Barbara Newman

Spirits. Birago Diop, *French.* NegPo, *tr. by* Ellen Conroy Kennedy

Spirits and illusions have died. Life from the Lifeless. Robinson Jeffers. CMoP

Spirit's Epilogue, The. Milton. NOSC *Fr.* Comus; a Masque Presented at Ludlow Castle. FHYEP; OAEL-1

(Spirit Epiloguizes, The.) NOBE

Spirit's Epochs, The. Coventry Patmore. EBEV; GBL; OxBSP *Fr.* The Angel in the House.

Spirits Everywhere. Ludwig Uhland, *German.* AWP, *tr. by* James Clarence Mangan

Spirit's Odyssey, The. M. Krishnamurti. InPK-6

Spirits of children are remote and wise, The. Ode on the Whole Duty Of Parents. Frances Darwin Cornford. WPN

Spirits of Movement. James Berry. NBrP

Spirits of old that bore me. The Knight Errant. Louise Imogen Guiney. RACG

Spirits of well-shot woodcock, partridge, snipe. "New King Arrives in His Capital by Air. . ."—Daily Newspaper. John Betjeman. NOBE; OxBoLi

Spirits perceive his presence. Coleridge. *See* This Lime-Tree Bower My Prison.

Spirit's Song. Louise Bogan. NYBP

Spirit's Song. Louisa Costello. Ro

Spirits Unchained. Keorapetse Kgositsile. PoBA

Spirits walking everywhere. Walter James Turner. *Fr.* The Seven Days of the Sun. OBMV

Spiritual Alchemy, The. "Angelus Silesius." GePo, *tr. by* George C. Schoolfield *Fr.* The Cherubical Wanderer.

Spiritual Ark And The Manna-Vessel, The. "Angelus Silesius." GePo, *tr. by* George C. Schoolfield *Fr.* The Cherubical Wanderer.

Spiritual athlete often changes the color of his clothes, The. The Hopeful Spiritual Athlete. Kabir, *Hindi*. RaBo, *tr. by* Robert Bly

Spiritual Canticle, The. Saint John of the Cross, *Spanish*. STV, *tr. by* John Frederick Nims

Spiritual for Nine Voices, The. Kay Boyle. NMM-2

Spiritual Impregnation, The. "Angelus Silesius." GePo, *tr. by* George C. Schoolfield *Fr.* The Cherubical Wanderer.

Spiritual Isolation. Isaac Rosenberg. TrJP

Spiritual Laws. Ralph Waldo Emerson. APN-1

Spiritual, the carnal, are one, The. Dorothy, Duchess of Wellington Wellesley. OBMV *Fr.* Matrix.

Spit in my face ye [*or* you] Jew[e]s, and pierce my side. Donne. Son; TOF *Fr.* Holy Sonnets. ESCV

Spite Fence. Richard Eberhart. AFr

Spite hath no power to make me sad. Sir Thomas Wyatt. SiPS

Spitfire! from *BlackFleshMotors*. Dance Bodies #1. Eugene B. Redmond. ISC

Spits of glitter in lowgrade ore. Conserving the Magnitude of Uselessness. A. R. Ammons. NoAM

Spitting—from lips once sanctified by Hers. (LL) To Edward FitzGerald. Robert Browning. NAEL-2; OxBSP

Spitting in the Leaves. Maggie Anderson. PBCAP

Spittle beads as ice along. The Wrong Way Will Haunt You. Sydney Lea. RA

Splashing paint from a glass. But Could You? Vladimir Mayakovsky, *Russian*. TCRP, *tr. by* Bernard Meares

Splat of bare feet on wet tile, The. Women's Locker Room. Marilyn Nelson Waniek. LTA; Poetr

Spleen. Ernest Christopher Dowson. ADE; APAD; MoBrPo; NOBVV

Spleen. John Gray. NOBVV

Spleen, The. Matthew Green.
  "But now more serious let me grow." PoEL-3
  "First know, my friend, I do not mean." ECEV; NOEC
  "Forced by soft violence of prayer." ECEV
  "Sometimes I dress, with women sit." ECEV; OBCoV
  "This motley piece to you I send." NoP-4
  "To cure the mind's wrong bias, Spleen." ECEV
  "When by its magic lantern Spleen." OxAEP-1

Spleen. August Kleinzahler. PmAP

Spleen, The. Anne Finch. NALW; NOSC
  ("And sunk beneath thy chain to a lamented grave.") (LL) NoP-4

Power of Spleen, The. ECWP

Splendid Bankrupt, The. Arthur A. Sykes. UV

Splendid fellow in the grass, A. Feathered Friends. Robert Peters. BXAP

Splendid Shilling, The. John Phillips. BXAP; OAEL-1
  "Happy the man, who, void of cares and strife." NOEC

Splendid sun hath set! When shall our eyes, A. Lord Byron. John Clare. EPCY

Splendid Village, The. Ebenezer Elliot.
  "Village! thy butcher's son, the steward now." OBSV

Splendidly-shining darkness. Geoffrey Hill. HAP *Fr.* The Pentecost Castle.

Splendor of the moon shines down on quiet night. A Response to Wang Ssu-yüan's Poem on the Moon. Shen Yüeh, *Chinese*. SuSp, *tr. by* Richard B. Mather

Splendour falls on castle walls, The. Blow, Bugle, Blow. Tennyson. AWP; CH; CTV; ClHu; EBEvV; EBVV; FHYEP; FaBoCh; GTBS-P; HeIP-4; ImPo; InPK-6; NAEL-2; NOBE; NoP-4; OAEL-2; OBEV; OBNC; PFE; PeVV; PoEL-5; TFi; UnPo *Fr.* The Princess.

Splendour of life so splendidly contained. The Masque of Blackness. Geoffrey Hill. NoAM *Fr.* Lachrimae; or Seven Tears Figured in Seven Passionate Pavans.

Splendour of my Spring I destroy here, The. Not knowing. Abishag. Jacob Fichman, *Hebrew*. TrJP, *tr. by* Sholom J. Kahn

Splendour recurrent. Fraternitas. Confucius. CTC; OBVE *Fr.* Deer Sing.

Splinter. Carl Sandburg. KaS; OBCA; SoSe-8; Spl

Splinters of information, stones of information. Minerals of Cornwall, Stones of Cornwall. Peter Redgrove. FaBoMo

Splish splosh, February-fill-the-dike. February. John Heath-Stubbs. AYFP; OBCP

Split, The. Marie Howe. NAmP90

Split open the massive chaos to obtain black gold. A Poem on Coal. Yü Ch'ien, *Chinese*. SuSp, *tr. by* Wu-chi Liu

Split the Lark—and you'll find the Music. Emily Dickinson. APN-2; ChIV-2; NoP-4

Splitting birches, spiky thicket, kinship. Black Bread. Tom Paulin. CIP-2

Splitting from Jack Delaney's, Sheridan Square. God Rest Ye Merry, Gentlemen. Derek Walcott. GT

Splitting the Infinite. Yona Wallach, *Hebrew*. IP, *tr. by* Warren Bargad *and* Stanley F. Chyet

Splitting the Infinite. Yona Wallach, *Hebrew*. IP, *tr. by* Warren Bargad *and* Stanley F. Chyet

Spluttering burnt-out lamp blazes in the dusk. Ch'ien Ch'ien-i. SuSp, *tr. by* Irving Y. Lo *Fr.* Poems Written in Prison.

Spoiler's Return, The. Derek Walcott. PBCV

Spoiling daylight inched along the bar-top, The. The Mill. Richard Wilbur. FP; Poetsp

Spoils. Robert Graves. HAP; Son; WeW-3

(Spoils of Love, The.) NYBP

Spoils of Youth, The. Robert Browning. *Fr.* A Likeness. CTC

Spokane Falls. Phillip William George. VoR

Spoke Aug 19. Hannah Weiner.
  Seen Words. FTOS

Spoken Extempore on the Death of Mr. Pope. *Unknown*. NOEC

Spoken in response. Tanka. Miya Shūji, *Japanese*. MJT, *tr. by* Makoto Ueda

Spoken to Pines and Bamboos. Wei Chuang, *Chinese*. SuSp, *tr. by* Robin D. S. Yates

Spontaneous Combustion. David Lehman. NAmP90

Spontaneous me, Nature. Walt Whitman. NAAL-1; NAAL-3; OxBA; PAR

Spontaneous momentum, A. Sheaf Mark. Ray DiPalma. FTOS

Spontaneous Requiem For the American Indian. Gregory Corso. BB; PoM

Spoon. Conrad Hilberry. IFJA

Spoon, The. Charles Simic. NNaP

Spoon, A. Tanka. Kondō Yoshimi, *Japanese*. MJT, *tr. by* Makoto Ueda

Spoon of your head, The. Rain. John Ashbery. FTOS

Spoon River Anthology. Edgar Lee Masters.
  Amanda Barker. NoAM
  Anne Rutledge. CBCWP; CMoP; HAP; ImPo; LiTM; MoAmPo; MoP; NOBA; NoAM; OxBA; TFi
  Arlo Will. PBMP
  Carl Hamblin. CMoP; LiTM; OBSV
  Cassius Hueffer. OxBA
  Circuit Judge, The. FaBoEE
  Daisy Fraser. CMoP; HAP; PoE
  Davis Matlock. LiTM
  Dora Williams. HAP
  "Earth keeps some vibration going, The." CMoP; NoAM; OxBA; TAP
  Editor Whedon. CMoP; FaBoEE; NOBA; OBSV; OxBA; PoE
  Elliott Hawkins. OxBA
  Elsa Wertman. MoP; NoAM; OxBA
  English Thornton. OxBA
  Father Malloy. OxBA
  Hamilton Greene. MoP; NoAM; OxBA
  Henry C. Calhoun. LiTM
  Herman Altman. OxBA
  Hill, The. CMoP; ColAP; FYAP; LiTM; NOBA; NoAM; OxBA; TAP
  Jonathan Houghton. OxBA
  Jonathan Swift Somers. OBAL
  Judge Somers. FaBoEE; OBSV
  Knowlt Hoheimer. OxBA
  Lucinda Matlock. CMoP; HAP; LiTM; MoAmPo; MoP; NOBA; NoAM; OxBA; PBMP
  Petit, the Poet. CMoP; ColAP; MoAmPo; NOBA; NoAM; OxBA; TAP
  Rutherford McDowell. OxBA
  Spooniad, The. OBAL

Spoons with Realistic Dead Flies on Them. Charles Simic. FiLi

Sport. (LL) Sonnet 10: 'Unrighteous Lord of Love'. Edmund Spenser. AEP

Sportif. David McCord. *See* Ascot Waistcoat.

Sporting Acquaintances. Siegfried Sassoon. OxBTC

Sporting and capering high in the breeze. The Man on the Flying Trapeze. Jack Prelutsky. FuFo

Sporting Beasley. Sterling Brown. NAAAL

Sporting the Plaid. Chris Wallace-Crabbe. NOBAu

Sports and gallantries, the stage, the arts, the antics of dancers. Boats in a Fog. Robinson Jeffers. BLT; NAAL-2; NoP-4; OxBA

Sportsman, The. Anna Wickham. WPN

Sportsmen in Paradise. T. P. Cameron Wilson. PoFWW

Sportsmen keep hawks, and their quarry they gain, The. Air. John Gay. NOEC *Fr.* Polly; an Opera.

Sporus. Alexander Pope. AWP; NOBE; OBSV *Fr.* Epistle to Dr. Arbuthnot. FHYEP; InPS-3; NoP-4; OAEL-1; OxAEP-1; PoE; PoEL-3; TFi

("Let Sporus tremble—A. What? that thing of silk.") OxBoV

Spot the Ball. Frank Ormsby. CIP-2; PBCIP; PNI

Spotlights had you covered, The. A Poem about Poems about Vietnam. Jon Stallworthy. NoAM

Spots in the Sun. Coleridge. Ro *Fr.* Morning Post, no.

Spots of Blood. Phyllis Webb. NOBC

Spots on black skin. Blind Old Woman. Clarence Major. PoBA

Spot's unconsciousness of you! The. (LL) In a Cathedral City. Thomas Hardy. EnLoPo

Spotted hawk swoops by and accuses me, The. Walt Whitman. SAmP *Fr.* Song of Myself. AmPP; MoAmPo; NAAL-3; NOBA; OxBA

("Spotten hawk swoops by and accuses me, he complains of my gab and my, The.") ColAP

Spouse of Jesus Laments Her Heart's Flame, The. Friedrich Spee, *German.* GePo, *tr. by* George C. Schoolfield

Spouse! Sister! Angel! Pilot of the Fate. Shelley. CBLP *Fr.* Epipsychidion.

Spraeta tamen vivunt. (LL) Gascoigne's Woodmanship. George Gascoigne. AAS; NoSic; PoEL-1

Spraggy cod'll grow ni fatter, A. Fisherman's Rhyme. *Unknown.* FaBoVe

Sprawl is the quality. The Quality of Sprawl. Les A. Murray. NoP-4

Sprawled in the pigsty. For a Young Artist. Robert Earl Hayden. NoAM

Sprawled, like park derelicts, about. The Sleepers. Peter Kocan. CBAP

Sprawled / on our faces in the spring. The Hen Flower. Galway Kinnell. NNaP

Sprawled on the crates [*or* bags] and sacks [*or* crates] in the rear of the truck. Green, Green Is El Aghir. Norman Cameron. FaBoTW; MoB3, OBWP; OxBTC

Spray. D. H. Lawrence. AYFP

Spray made as it hit the front of the boat, The. (LL) Two Sonnets. John Ashbery. VGW; WeT

Spray sprang up across the cusps of the moon, The. Once at Swanage. Thomas Hardy. CBLP

Sprayed with strong poison. Paul Goodman. InPK-6

Spread, The. Spencer Selby. PT

Spread eagle sheep legs wide. Mantanza to Welcome Spring. Jimmy Santiago Baca. PmAP

Spread like a field of death, gold on the sea. (LL) Annual Legend. Winfield Townley Scott. CoAP; LiTM

Spread on the roadway. The Cyclists. Amy Lowell. WPE

Spread out, unbuttoned, grateful, under the trees. (LL) The Wife's Tale. Seamus Heaney. CIP-2; SAGP

Spread Rhythm. C. D. Wright. LCAP-2

Spread, table, spread. George Peele. NoSic *Fr.* The Old Wives' [*or* Wife's] Tale.

Spread the board with linen snow. Invitation to the Dance. Apollinaris Sidonius, *Latin.* AWP, *tr. by* Howard Mumford Jones

Spread their gay wings before the Throne, and smile. (LL) Epitaph on the Tombstone of a Child, the Last of Seven That Died Before. Aphra Behn. CABP; KTR; NOSC

Spreading fragrant grass, random spring clouds. Tune: "Full Moon in the Human World"—Spring Evening: Replying to a Song. *Unknown, Chinese.* SuSp, *tr. by* Sherwin S. S. Fu

Spreading here, spreading there, the grasses on the plain. Grass on Ancient Plain, a Song of Farewell. Po Chü-i, *Chinese.* SuSp, *tr. by* Irving Y. Lo

Spreading Wings on Wind. Simon J. Ortiz. HATNAP

Spree. Maxine W. Kumin. NoAM

Sprig of Karo, A. Murray Edmond. PeNZ

Sprig of Rosemary, A. Amy Lowell. CPO

Spring. Anacreon, *Greek.* AWP, *tr. by* Thomas Stanley

Spring. William Blake. BoTP; FHYEP; FaBoCh; NOxBChV; Ro; TTTS *Fr.* Songs of Innocence.

Spring. Robert Bloomfield. Ro *Fr.* The Farmer's Boy.

Spring. Pat Brennen. CTV

Spring, The. Thomas Carew. BeJo; CaPo; CavPo; NoP-4; PBRV; PoE; PoEL-3

Spring. Chang Yü. *Fr.* The Four Seasons in the Mountains. CoBLCP, *tr. by* Jonathan Chaves

Spring. Carole C. Gregory Clemmons. PoBA

Spring, The. Abraham Cowley. BeJo; HAP; MeLP; OxAEP-1 *Fr.* The Mistress.

Spring. Patricia Cumming. MDDM

Spring. Aubrey Thomas De Vere. OBNC *Fr.* A Year of Sorrow.

Spring. Ebenezer Elliot. OxAEP-2

Spring. Marjorie Frost Fraser. ImGa

Spring. Giovanni Battista Guarini, *Italian.* AWP, *tr. by* Leigh Hunt

Spring. Michael Hogan. InPK-6

Spring. Gerard Manley Hopkins. APAD; EBVV; GSo; HAP; LiTM; MoBrPo; NAEL-2; NOBE; NOBVV; NoAM; OAEL-2; OBMV; OBNC; RB; TFi; TrCP

Spring. Horace. OBCVT, *tr. by* Robert Lowell *Fr.* The Odes.

Spring. Kirim Kim, *Korean.* CKP, *tr. by* Jaihiun Kim

Spring. Pinkie Gordon Lane. GT

Spring. Meleager, *Greek.* AWP, *tr. by* William M. Hardinge

Spring. Edna St. Vincent Millay. BoWoP; MeMAP; MoAmPo; NoP-4; SAGP

Spring. Thomas Nashe. GTBS-P; NOBE; OBEV; SCGP *Fr.* Summer's Last Will and Testament.

Spring. Charles, Duc d' Orléans, *French.* AWP; CTC, *tr. by* Andrew Lang

Spring. Papyrus. Ezra Pound. PFTM

Spring. Helen G. Quigless. BkSV *Fr.* Childhood Scenes in Four Seasons.

Spring. Isaac Rosenberg. TrJP

Spring. James Schuyler. FTOS

Spring. Shakespeare. HAP; ImPo; InPK-6; NAEL-1; NBLV; NIP-4; NOBE; NoSic; OAEL-1; OBEV; PoEL-2; PoRA; TFi; UnPo *Fr.* Love's Labour's Lost.

("Now daisies pied, and violets blue.") BoTP

(Ver.)

Spring. Charles Simic. AFr

Spring. André Spire, *French.* AWP, *tr. by* Jethro Bithell

Spring. James Still. MT

Spring. Su Tung-p'o, *Chinese.* OHPC, *tr. by* Kenneth Rexroth

Spring. Tu Fu, *Chinese.* TAI, *tr. by* Robert Payne

Spring. Mary E. Tucker. CBWP-1

Spring. *Unknown.* SuSp *Fr.* Tzu-yeh Songs of the Four Seasons.

"Before jade pavilions the new moon dims." SuSp, *tr. by* Michael E. Workman

"Bewwitching the blossoms of the spring grove." SuSp, *tr. by* Ronald C. Miao

"Luminous winds flicker in the moonrise." SuSp, *tr. by* Michael E. Workman

"Plum flowers all fallen and gone." SuSp, *tr. by* Michael E. Workman

"Spring breeze stirs a springtime heart." SuSp, *tr. by* Ronald C. Miao

"Young swallows trill their new tune." SuSp, *tr. by* Michael E. Workman

Spring. Walt Whitman. LBC *Fr.* Memories of President Lincoln.

("And thought of him I love.") (LL) LBC

("I give you my sprig of lilac.") (LL)

Carol of Death, The.

"In the swamp in secluded recesses."

Spring 1916. Isaac Rosenberg. NSI

Spring 61. Lenore Kandel. BB

Spring And. Elizabeth Libbey. CMAP

Spring, and a new pair of moccasins! Sunflower Moccasins. Phillip William George. VoR

Spring and Autumn. William James Linton. EBVV

Spring and Fall. Gerard Manley Hopkins. CABP; CMoP; EBEV; GTBS-P; HAP; HeIP-4; InPK-6; InPS-3; LiTM; NAEL-2; NIP-4; NOBE; NoAM; NoP-4; OPOU; PeVV; PoE; PoEL-5; PoPoPo; Poetr; RB; SAGP; SCGP; SCV; TFi; TOF; TRP

(Spring and Fall: To a Young Child.) ClHu; IMW; ImPo; LiLi; OxAEP-2; PFE

Spring and the Ashura. Miyazawa Kenji, *Japanese.* PFTM, *tr. by* Gary Snyder

Spring, and the Blind Children. Alfred Noyes. OxBTC

Spring and the girls are twirling batons. Twirling. Jane Flanders. PBCAP

Spring appears, in which the earth, The. The Vigil of Venus. *Unknown, Latin.* GBL, *tr. by* Allen Tate; AWP, *tr. by* Thomas Stanley

Spring at Fort Okanogan. Ramona Wilson. VoR

Spring at Nant Dywelan. Bobi Jones, *Welsh.* OBWVE, *tr. by* Joseph P. Clancy

Spring at Yesan Station. Sub-ok, *Korean.* WPoS, *tr. by* Julie Pickering

Spring Bank. Geraldine Monk. NBrP

Spring Bereaved. William Drummond, of Hawthornden. OBEV *See* Sonnet: "Alexis, here she stayed, among these pines."

Spring Bereaved 2. William Drummond, of Hawthornden. OBEV

Spring bird. Tanka. Kitahara Hakushū, *Japanese.* MJT, *tr. by* Makoto Ueda

Spring blooms, autumn moon, when will they end? Tune: "Beautiful Lady Yü, The." Li Yü, *Chinese.* SuSp, *tr. by* Eugene Eoyang

Spring blossoms, honey-bee, in the colours you parade. Nicias, *Greek.* GrAn, *tr. by* Anthony Holden

Spring Breeze. Ho Hsun, *Chinese.* OHMPC, *tr. by* Kenneth Rexroth

Spring breeze. Anita Virgil. HA

Spring breeze blows the rain, A. Wang Chien. SuSp, *tr. by* William H. Nienhauser *Fr.* Palace Poems.

Spring breeze stirs a springtime heart. *Unknown.* SuSp, *tr. by* Ronald C. Miao *Fr.* Spring. SuSp *Fr.* Tzu-yeh Songs of the Four Seasons.

Spring breezes early along the avenue. The Horseman at the Roadside. Yang Wei-chen, *Chinese.* CoBLCP, *tr. by* Jonathan Chaves

Spring Burning. Patrick Roland. PeSA

Spring came, with orioles singing. A Farmer's Thoughts. Ch'u Kuang-hsi, *Chinese.* CoBCP, *tr. by* Burton Watson

Spring Cleaning. Phillip William George. VoR

Spring clouds look like beasts. Random Thoughts Written in Spring. Wang Yü-ch'eng, *Chinese.* SuSp, *tr. by* Irving Y. Lo

Spring comes early to the gardens. Green Jade Plum Trees in Spring. Ou-yang Hsiu, *Chinese.* OHPC, *tr. by* Kenneth Rexroth

Spring comes in with all her hues and smells, The. A Spring Morning. John Clare. GBL

Spring comes: the flowers learn their coloured shapes. A Vision. Maria Konopnicka, *Polish.* WPOW, *tr. by* Jerzy Peterkiewicz *and* Burns Singer

Spring Comes to Mid-Ohio in a Holy Shower of Stars. Terry Hummer. NAmP90

Spring Comes to the Hills and Fields. Namju Kim, *Korean.* CKP, *tr. by* Jaihiun Kim

Spring Day. John Ashbery. ColAP; NOBA

Spring Day. "Igor Severyanin," *Russian.* TCRP, *tr. by* Bernard Meares

Spring Day. Su Shih, *Chinese.* SuSp, *tr. by* Irving Y. Lo

Spring day at the edge of the world, A. Exile. Li Shang-yin, *Chinese.* PLT, *tr. by* A. C. Graham

Spring Day in the Countryside, A. Wen T'ing-yün, *Chinese.* SuSp, *tr. by* William R. Schultz

Spring Day on West Lake. Ou-yang Hsiu, *Chinese.* OHPC, *tr. by* Kenneth Rexroth

Spring Day—Remembering Living on the River, A. Kao Ch'i, *Chinese.* CoBLCP, *tr. by* Jonathan Chaves

Spring Days in My Home Town. Yang Chi, *Chinese.*
"Thousands of flowers, thousands of petals." CoBLCP, *tr. by* Jonathan Chaves

Spring dreams, more spring dreams. Yang Chi, *Chinese.* CoBLCP, *tr. by* Jonathan Chaves

Spring Ecstasy. Lizette Woodworth Reese. MoAmPo

Spring Equinox. Peter Blue Cloud. ChAP *Fr.* Within the Seasons. HATNAP

Spring evening. Chuck Brickley. HA

Spring Evening. Frederick Turner. RA

Spring Fancies. Christina Rossetti.
Spring Quiet. BoTP; CH; GTBS-P; InPS-3; PoE; PoEL-5; WPE

Spring Fever. Yunsuk Hong, *Korean.* CKP, *tr. by* Jaihiun Kim

Spring Fiord. *Unknown, Eskimo.* STP, *tr. by* Armand Schwerner

Spring flood is coming up to my door. Su Shih. SuSp, *tr. by* Irving Y. Lo *Fr.* Rain at Cold-Food Festival.

Spring Flower, The. Stanley Cook. AYFP

Spring flowers and autumn moon enter poems. For Hidden Mist Pavilion. Yü Hsüan-chi. BoWoP, *tr. by* Geoffrey Waters

Spring flowers, Autumn moons. Plaint. Chu Shu-chen, *Chinese.* OHPC, *tr. by* Kenneth Rexroth

Spring Fragments. Betsy Sholl.
"Dogwood blossoms, lovely and full—." CrSp

Spring garden is *Irish* green, The. A British Garden. Wes Magee. OBGa

Spring garlands the earth with leaves. *Unknown, Greek.* GrAn, *tr. by* Peter Jay

Spring goes, spring comes, spring again will be spring. Tune: "Willow Branches." *Unknown, Chinese.* SuSp, *tr. by* Hellmut Wilhelm

Spring Goeth All in White. Robert Bridges. BoTP

Spring Grievance. Chin Ch'ang-hsü, *Chinese.* CoBCP, *tr. by* Burton Watson

Spring hailstones would drive us. Because of My Father's Job. Jim Mitsui. OpBo; UnSA

Spring has come and the snow has gone. Captive. Peretz Hirshbein, *Yiddish.* TrJP, *tr. by* Joseph Leftwich

Spring has come. I try to forget. Chu Shu-chen, *Chinese.* OHPC, *tr. by* Kenneth Rexroth

Spring has come to the gate—spring's grasses green. Tune: "Manifold Little Hills." Li Ch'ing-chao, *Chinese.* SuSp, *tr. by* Eugene Eoyang

Spring has come to the Pass. Two Springs. Li Ch'ing-chao, *Chinese.* BoWoP; OHPC, *tr. by* Kenneth Rexroth

Spring has come to the women's quarters. To the Tune "A Hilly Garden." Li Ch'ing-chao, *Chinese.* ChiPo, *tr. by* Kenneth Rexroth *and* Ling Chung

Spring has darkened with activity, The. Time and the Garden. Yvor Winters. GaP; MoAmPo; NoAM; VGW

Spring has passed. The Sudden Appearance of Cherry Blossoms. Empress Jito, *Japanese.* WPJ, *tr. by* Kenneth Rexroth *and* Ikuko Atsumi *Fr.* Manyo Shu, Part 3 of 4.

Spring has swept the ice from all my frozen rivers, The. Blues. Léopold Sédar Senghor, *French.* PBMAP

Spring-heeled Jack. James Keir Baxter. FuFo

Spring here in Tien-nan, The. To the Tune "Chiang ch'eng tzu." Yang Shen, *Chinese.* CoBLCP, *tr. by* Jonathan Chaves

Spring I was failing the blackboard test, The. The Era of the Vari-Vue. Gary Fincke. PUP-20

Spring in Chiang-nan. Tu Mu, *Chinese.* PLT, *tr. by* A. C. Graham

"Spring in Ch'in's Garden" ("Alone I stand in autumn cold"). Mao Tse-tung, *Chinese.* SuSp, *tr. by* Eugene Eoyang

Spring in London. John Bingham Morton. OBCoV

Spring in New Hampshire. Claude McKay. BPo; ChAP; CrDW

Spring in the Bronx. *Unknown.* OBCoV

Spring in the City. Ruth Fainlight. CMAP

Spring in the Garden. Edna St. Vincent Millay. GaP

Spring in the Students' Quarter. Henry Murger, *French.* AWP, *tr. by* Andrew Lang

Spring in This World of Poor Mutts. Joseph Ceravolo. FTOS

Spring in Tien is fine! To the Tune "Spring in Tien Is Fine." Yang Shen, *Chinese.* CoBLCP, *tr. by* Jonathan Chaves

Spring is a Cat, The. Jang-hi Lee, *Korean.* PC, *tr. by* Koh Chang-soo

Spring is come at last, my freens, cheer up, you sons of toil, The. The Working Man. Ellen Johnston. VWP

Spring is coming, spring is coming. May Day. *Unknown.* BoTP; CTV

Spring is early this year. Kenneth Rexroth. APSN *Fr.* The Love Poems of Marichiko.

Spring is here, and everywhere they pursue the sweet fragrance. Butterflies. Chang Yü. *Fr.* Twelve Miscellaneous Poems on the Fang Garden. CoBLCP, *tr. by* Jonathan Chaves

Spring is icummen in—. (LL) The Sea-Elephant. William Carlos Williams. MeMAP; SAmP

Spring is like a perhaps hand. E. E. Cummings. AmPP; MeMAP; NoP-4; TAP; VGW

Spring is not so beautiful there, The. Water-Front Streets. Langston Hughes. SAmP

Spring is passing and. Empress Jito, *Japanese.* PBWP, *tr. by* Cid Corman *and* Susumu Kamaike

Spring is past and over these many days. September. Aldous Leonard Huxley. EBEV

Spring is short. Akiko Yosano, *Japanese.* BoWoP; PBWP, *tr. by* Geoffrey Bownas *and* Anthony Thwaite

Spring is showery, flowery, bowery;. Mother Goose. CTV

Spring is sprung. Spring in the Bronx. *Unknown.* OBCoV

Spring is the Period. Emily Dickinson. TAP

Spring is when. Bobbi Katz. AYFP

Spring is when the grass turns green and glad. Lines Written for Gene Kelly to Dance To. Carl Sandburg. AiP

Spring Joy. Chu Shu-chen, *Chinese.* ChiPo, *tr. by* Kenneth Rexroth *and* Ling Chung

Spring Joy Praising God. Catharina Regina von Greiffenberg, *German.* GePo, *tr. by* George C. Schoolfield
Spring-Joy Praising God; Praise of the Sun. WPOW, *tr. by* George C. Schoolfield

Spring Liturgy for Branko Miljkovic. Ivan V. Lalic, *Serbo-Croatian.*
"Tree in the wind remembered like a letter." HSix, *tr. by* Charles Simic

Spring Memorandum, A. Robert Duncan. PoA

Spring moon—. Basho, *Japanese.* Spl, *tr. by* Lucien Stryk

Spring moon, The. (LL) The Springtime. Denise Levertov. CoAmPo

Spring Morning. Ch'en Yü-yi, *Chinese.* OHMPC, *tr. by* Kenneth Rexroth

Spring Morning, A. John Clare. GBL

Spring Morning. Frances Darwin Cornford. BoTP

Spring, my dear, The. Out of Tune. William Ernest Henley. MoBrPo

Spring Night. Chang Yü. *Fr.* Twelve Miscellaneous Poems on the Fang Garden. CoBLCP, *tr. by* Jonathan Chaves

Spring Night. Hagiwara Sakutaro, *Japanese.* PFTM, *tr. by* Hiroaki Sato

Spring night. Masaoka Shiki, *Japanese.* OHMPJ, *tr. by* Kenneth Rexroth

Spring Night. Sara Teasdale. FaBoBe; MoAmPo

Spring Night, A—Rejoicing in Rain. Tu Fu, *Chinese.* SuSp, *tr. by* William H. Nienhauser

Spring Night in Lo-Yang—Hearing a Flute. Li Po, *Chinese.* CoBCP; TTTS, *tr. by* Burton Watson

Spring Night in Shokoku-ji, A. Gary Snyder. VGW *Fr.* Four Poems for Robin. MoP; NNaP; NOBA; NoAM

Spring night—one hour worth a thousand gold coins. Su Tung-p'o, *Chinese.* CoBCP, *tr. by* Burton Watson

Spring night's, The. Teika, *Japanese.* OHMPJ, *tr. by* Kenneth Rexroth

Spring 1943. Roy Fuller. LiTM

Spring 1942. Roy Fuller. LiTM; OxBTC

Spring Nocturne. Abraham Liessin, *Yiddish.* TrJP

Spring of Work Storm. Joseph Ceravolo. FTOS

Spring Offensive of the Snail, The. Marge Piercy. TAP

Spring omnipotent goddess thou dost. E. E. Cummings. NBLV; OxBA

Spring on the Coast. Leonidas of Tarentum, *Greek.* GrAn, *tr. by* Clive Sansom

Spring once said to the nightingale. The Birds' Ball. Charles William Bardeen. BLPA

Spring Out of Season. Xuân Diệu, *Vietnamese.* AVP, *tr. by* Huỳnh Sanh Thông

Spring pigeons bill and coo under the rocks. Composed on a Spring Day on the Farm. Wang Wei, *Chinese.* ChiPo, *tr. by* Chang Yin-nan and Lewis C. Walmsley

Spring Planting. Gail Mazur. NAmP90

Spring Poem, The. Dave Jeddie Smith. PoPoPo

Spring Pools. Robert Frost. AmPP; ColAP; NAAL-2; NOBA; NoAM; OxBA

Spring Prospect. Tu Fu, *Chinese.* CoBCP, *tr. by* Burton Watson

Spring Quiet. Christina Rossetti. BoTP; CH; GTBS-P; InPS-3; PoE; PoEL-5; WPE *Fr.* Spring Fancies.

Spring Rain. Ch'in Kuan, *Chinese.* SuSp, *tr. by* Stephen West

Spring rain. Haiku. Chiyojo, *Japanese.* PBWP, *tr. by* R. H. Blyth

Spring Rain. Robert Hass. PaTW

Spring Rain. William Hawkins. MoCV

Spring Rain. Li Shang-yin, *Chinese.* CoBCP, *tr. by* Burton Watson

Spring Rain. Yongno Pyon, *Korean.* CKP, *tr. by* Jaihiun Kim

Spring Rain. Tu Fu, *Chinese.* OHMPC, *tr. by* Kenneth Rexroth

Spring rain! And as yet. Buson, *Japanese,* TAL, *tr. by* Harold G. Henderson

Spring—River—Flower—Moon—Night. T'ang Yin, *Chinese.*

"Fog of night envelops the flowering trees, The." CoBLCP, *tr. by* Jonathan Chaves

Spring River Flowers Moon Night. Emperor Yang of Sui, *Chinese.* OHMPC, *tr. by* Kenneth Rexroth

Spring said nothing to me—it couldn't. Georgy Vladimirovich Ivanov, *Russian.* TCRP, *tr. by* Daniel Weissbort

Spring scarlet of the forest blossoms fades and falls, The. Tune: "Crows Crying at Night." Li Yü, *Chinese.* SuSp, *tr. by* Daniel Bryant

Spring Scene. Buson, *Japanese.* TTTS, *tr. by* Kenneth Koch and Harold Henderson

Spring Scene. Su Tung-p'o, *Chinese.* TAL, *tr. by* Robert Payne

Spring Sentiments. Chao Yi, *Chinese.* SuSp, *tr. by* Chang Yin-nan and Lewis C. Walmsley

Spring shakes the windows; doors whang to. A Spring Wind. Bernard Spencer. GTBS-P

Spring / slips / silent / snowdrops. Hugo Majer. Spl

("Spring slips silent.") AYFP

Spring Snow and Tui. Mary Ursula Bethell. PeNZ

Spring Song. Lucille Clifton. CrSp

Spring Song. Peter Fallon. CIP-2; PBCIP

Spring Song. Hermann Hesse, *German.* AWP, *tr. by* Ludwig Lewisohn

Spring Song, A. Mary Howitt. BoTP

Spring Song. John Milton, *Latin.* MLL, *tr. by* Helen Waddell

Spring Song. Nahum, *Hebrew.* TrJP, *tr. by* Emma Lazarus

Spring Song, A. *Unknown.* PoLF

Spring Song of A Civil Servant. James Keir Baxter. PeLV

Spring Song of the Birds. James I, King of Scotland. OBEV

Spring Song of Tzu-yeh, A. Hsiao Yen, *Chinese.* SuSp, *tr. by* Jan W. Walls

Spring Sorrow. Chin Ch'ang-hsü, *Chinese.* OHMPC, *tr. by* Kenneth Rexroth

Spring stirs slowly, shuffles, hops;. Season Song. Judith Nicholls. Spl

Spring Sun. Chu Hsi, *Chinese.* OHPC, *tr. by* Kenneth Rexroth

Spring that I was six I found in the woods, The. Paul Smyth. CRP *Fr.* A Frame for the Angels.

Spring: The Lover and the Birds. William Allingham. OBNC

Spring, the new, the warb'ling Spring appears, The. Pervigilium Veneris. OBCVT, *tr. by* Thomas Parnell *Fr.* The Vigil of Venus.

Spring the purple Violet. (LL) Upon Prue [or Prew], His Maid. Robert Herrick. BeJo; CaPo; NAEL-1; NoP-4

Spring, the sweet spring! (LL) Spring. Thomas Nashe. CH; GTBS-P; ImPo; NAEL-1; NOBE; NoP-4; NoSic; OBEV; SCGP; TFi

Spring, the sweet spring, is the year's pleasant king. Spring. Thomas Nashe. CH; GTBS-P; ImPo; NAEL-1; NOBE; NoP-4; NoSic; OBEV; SCGP; TFi *Fr.* Summer's Last Will and Testament.

Spring, the Travelling Man. Winifred M. Letts. BoTP

Spring Thoughts Sent to Tzu-an. Yü Hsüan-chi. BoWoP, *tr. by* Geoffrey Waters

Spring Time. John Milton, *Latin.* MLL, *tr. by* Helen Waddell

Spring Trances in the Control Emerald Night. Christopher Dewdney.

"August a haze amniotic our dream aether and lens of distance. Tree sentinels in." FTOS

Spring twilight. Noin, *Japanese.* OHMPJ, *tr. by* Kenneth Rexroth

Spring up, O well—sing ye unto it. Song of the Well. Bible, *O.T.* TrJP *Fr.* Numbers.

Spring Vacation, The. Derek Mahon. PNI

Spring violet fragment. Psalm and Mosaic for a Springtime in Athens. Odysseus Elytis. GrIP, *tr. by* Nanos Valaortis *Fr.* The Siblings.

Spring Vista from the Tower of Illuminated Distance. Li Meng-yang, *Chinese.* CoBLCP, *tr. by* Jonathan Chaves

Spring Voices. Louis MacNeice. Son

Spring Walk to the Pavilion of Good Crops and Peace. Ou-yang Hsiu, *Chinese.* OHPC, *tr. by* Kenneth Rexroth

Spring Waters. "Ping Hsin," *Chinese.*

"Falling Star, The." PBWP

"In shaping the snow into blossoms." BoWoP; WPOW

"O, Lord/ If in life eternal." WPOW

Spring we went into the heat of lilacs. For My Father. Philip Schultz. IFJA

Spring when the world is mud. E. E. Cummings. *See* In Just- / spring when the world is mud-.

Spring—where has it come from. Song of Spring. Wu Chün, *Chinese.* CoBCP, *tr. by* Burton Watson

Spring will be reborn under our bright steps. (LL) The Vultures. David Diop, *French.* NegPo, *tr. by* Ellen Conroy Kennedy; PBA; TTY, *tr. by* Ulli Beier; PBMAP

Spring Wind, A. Bernard Spencer. GTBS-P

Spring wind on the Bowery, A. Lola Ridge. WPE

Spring wind, proud rider! To the Tune "Shui hsien-tzu." Ma Chih-yüan, *Chinese.* CoBLCP

Spring wind will never reach, The. An Answer to Ting Yuan Ch'en. Ou-yang Hsiu, *Chinese.* OHPC, *tr. by* Kenneth Rexroth

Spring Work at the Farm. Thirza Wakley. BoTP

Springbok doe mothers sang, The. Song of the Springbok Does. *Unknown, Hottentot.* PeSA, *tr. by* W. H. I. Bleek

Springburst, (to be read from the bottom). John Travers Moore. AYFP

Springfield Mountain. *Unknown.* AmFP

Springing, full-grown, from your own head, Athena? Carolyn Kizer. *See* Two.

Spring's second month. Things Seen on Spring Days. Yüan Mei, *Chinese.* CoBLCP, *tr. by* Jonathan Chaves

Spring's Welcome. John Lyly. *See* Trico's Song.

Springtime. Nikki Giovanni. TLR

Springtime, The. Denise Levertov. CoAP; CoAmPo

Springtime. Norman Henry, II Pritchard. GT

Springtime—and the green willow catkins. To the Tune "Bamboo at West Lake." Shen Chou, *Chinese.* CoBLCP, *tr. by* Jonathan Chaves

Springtime Embroidery. Yang Chi. CoBLCP, *tr. by* Jonathan Chaves *Fr.* Paintings of Ladies Engaged in Four Springtime Occupations.

Springtime it brings on the shearing, The. E. J. Overbury. NOBAu

Springtime of low walls and flowery darkness. In Harmony with Kao "The Second" Ch'i's Poem "On Hearing a P'i-p'a Played Next Door." Hsü Pen, *Chinese.* CoBLCP, *tr. by* Jonathan Chaves

Sprinkler twirls, The. August. John Updike. AYFP; OBCA *Fr.* A Child's Calendar.

Spritely Dead, The. Oscar Williams. Son *Fr.* Variations on a Theme.

Sprouting grass waiting for spring, The. The Lady Gio, *Japanese.* WPJ, *tr. by* Kenneth Rexroth and Ikuko Atsumi

Sprouting two small wings. (LL) Wingfoot Lake. Rita Dove. PoPoPo; UnSA

Spruce. Phillip William George. VoR

Sprung from a race that had long till'd the soil. The Adventures of Simon Swaugum, a Village Merchant. Philip Freneau. PoEL-4

Spry, wry, and gray as these March sticks. Among the Narcissi. Sylvia Plath. FaBoMo; RB; SCV

Spur, The. W. B. Yeats. OxAEP-2; WeW-3

Spur the others to fey elation; no mad dogs in the house for me. Catullus. See Attis.

Spurt of Blood, The. Antonin Artaud, *French*. PFTM, tr. by Helen Weaver

Spy bears his bald intent like a maniac, The. John Tranter. CBAP *Fr.* Crying in Early Infancy.

Spyglass Conversations. *Unknown, Tule Indian*. STP, tr. by Frances Densmore

Squalid, empty-headed hen, A. Hen under Bay-Tree. Ruth Pitter. OxBTC

Squalid street after squalid street. A Great Industrial Centre. Edith Nesbit. VWP

Squalid village set in wintry mud, A. Born without a Chance. Edmund Vance Cooke. BLPA

Squall. Stanley Moss. CoAP

Squander for me no scent of myrrh. Epitaph on a Tomb near Rome. *Unknown, Greek*. GrAn, tr. by Frank Kuenstler

Square along the couch, and stark. George Meredith. PeVV *Fr.* The Nuptials of Attila.

Square as a seed-box, in their attic stands. The Handloom. Judith Rodriguez. FaBoWP

Square Dance, A. Roger McGough. NSI

Square, squat room (a cellar on promotion), A. Waiting. William Ernest Henley. NAEL-2; NOBVV *Fr.* In Hospital.

Squares. Pierre Reverdy, *French*. PFTM, tr. by Mary Ann Caws

Squares of tended grass, roses. Moment. John Daniel. PaTW

Squash in Blossom. Robert Francis. FYAP

Squat Down, Josey. *Unknown*. AmFP

Squat in swamp shadows. Second Shaman Song. Gary Snyder. NOBA; NeAP; PoM *Fr.* Burning. NeAP; PoM *Fr.* Myths and Texts.

Squats on a toad-stool under a tree. Song by Isbrand. Thomas Lovell Beddoes. NOBVV; OBNC *Fr.* Death's Jest Book.

Squats on a toadstool under a tree. Thomas Lovell Beddoes. *See* Song by Isbrand.

Squatter in the Foreground. Kenward Elmslie. FTOS

Squatting a day in the sun. Fire in the Hole. Gary Snyder. NAAL-2

Squeal. Louis Simpson. BXAP; UnPo

Squealing under city stone. Rapid Transit. James Agee. MoAmPo

Squeeze. Abigail Child. FTOS

Squeeze Play. Phyllis McGinley. FaBoEE; OBCoV; OBSV *Fr.* Spectator's Guide to Contemporary Art.

Squeezes. Brian Patten. OTCP; Spl

Squinting against neon signs. Eclipse. Anita Endrezze-Danielson. CDW

Squire and Milkmaid; or, Blackberry Fold. *Unknown*. OxBB

Squire he had whose name was Ralph, A. Independent Squire. Samuel Butler. NOBE *Fr.* Hudibras.

Squire is in his library, The. He is rather worried. Send for Lord Timothy. John Heath-Stubbs. OxBC

Squire Meldrum at Carrickfergus. Sir David Lindsay. OxBS *Fr.* The Historie of Squyer William Meldrum.

Squire nagged and bullied till I went to fight. Memorial Tablet. Siegfried Sassoon. PoWW

Squire sat alone beside the board, The. Little Fay's Thanksgiving. Henrietta Cordelia Ray. CBWP-3

Squire Squint, shooting at a pheasant. G. J. Blundell. UV

Squire's Pew, The. Jane Taylor. PEW

Squirrel, The. Mary Howitt. BoTP

Squirrel, The. *Unknown*. BoTP; OxNR
("To rest my tiny back.") (LL) CTAV

Squirrel crosses / my way while on a trip, A. If. Jared Angira. PBMAP

Squirrel, flippant, pert and full of play, The. William Cowper. CTAV

Squirrel in his shirt, The. Ground-Squirrel Song. *Navajo Oral Tradition*. TTTS

Squirrel is digging up the bulbs, A. Better Be Kind to Them Now. D. J. Enright. PeP

Squirrel is the curliest thing, The. The Curliest Thing. *Unknown*. BoTP

Squirrel Stand. Jim Wayne Miller. MT

Sssnnnwhufffffl? The Loch Ness Monster's Song. Edwin Morgan. OPOU

Ssǔ-ma Hsiang-ju pondered Leafy Mound. Li Ho. PLT, tr. by A. C. Graham *Fr.* Musing.

Stab me with sword, or poison strong. Propertius, *Latin*. *Fr.* Elegies. AWP

Stabat Mater, The. Jacopone da Todi, *Italian*. NNPT, tr. by George Barker

Stable Cat, The. Leslie Norris. PChr

Stable-lamp is lighted, A. A Christmas Hymn. Richard Wilbur. ChIV-2; OBCP; PChr; TrCP

Stable Straw. Robert Farren. TIRV

Stackalee. *Unknown, comp.* by Onah L. Spencer. APN-2; CrDW

Stacking the Straw. Amy Clampitt. VCAP

Stackolee. *Unknown*. NAAAL

Staff. John Engman. NAmP90

Staff and slippers hang here, Kypris, A. Leonidas, *Greek*. PGA, tr. by Kenneth Rexroth

Staff[e] is now greased [or greas'd], The. The Hag. Robert Herrick. CaPo

Staff slips from the hand, The. Outward. Louis Simpson. NYBP

Staffs and Hats. *Unknown, Vietnamese*. AVP, tr. by Huỳnh Sanh Thông

Stag comes home at last, The. Thomas A. Clark. NBrP *Fr.* Sixteen Sonnets.

Stag, the runnable stag, The. (LL) A Runnable Stag. John Davidson. EBEvV; EBNV; FaPoR; HAP; OBEV; OxBTC

Stage-Driver's Story, The. Bret Harte. EBNV

Stage Duo. Kenward Elmslie. FTOS

Stage is about to be swept of corpses, The. Horatian Epode to the Duchess of Malfi. Allen Tate. FaBoMo

Stage-lit streets. S.F. Southward. Allen Ginsberg. NAAL-2 *Fr.* Continuation of a Long Poem of These States.

Stage Love. Swinburne. PoEL-5

Stage was set, the house was packed, The. Concert Party: Busseboom. Edmund Blunden. NSI; PoFWW

Stages on a Journey Westward. James Wright. LCAP-2

Staggering down the road at midnite. The Encounter. Paul Blackburn. NeAP

Stagnant pond, A. John Wills. HA

Stagolee. *Unknown*. OxBoLi; TTY

Staid schizophrenic named Struther, A. Limerick. *Unknown*. NIP-4

Staircase, The. Samuel Allen. PoBA

Stairs are dark, the steps are high, The. Up in Mabel's Room. Kenneth Slessor. BMAP

Stairs mount to his eternity, The. The Staircase. Samuel Allen. PoBA

Stairs of sleeping climbed against the first night with real gods, The. Temptation. Aaron Shurin. PT

Stairway is not, The. The Jacob's Ladder. Denise Levertov. APSN; AmPP; ChIV-1; KSG; PoM

Stairway to Heaven. Robert Creeley. FTOS

Stalagmites in spring caves rise to more stalactites. Red Embankment. Tu Mu, *Chinese*. SuSp, tr. by John M. Ortinau

Stalin. Robert Lowell. HCAP

Stalin Epigram, The. Osip Emilevich Mandelstam, *Russian*. AF; FaBoPV; NNPT, tr. by W. S. Merwin *and* Clarence Brown

Stalin Moy Golubchik. "Sagittarius." OBCoV

Stalin stood committed to peasant hunger. Reply to the Committed Intellectual. Francis Sparshott. NOBC

Stalingrad Theater. Mikhail Kuz'mich Lukonin, *Russian*. TCRP, tr. by Albert C. Todd

Stalin's falcons proudly soar. The Year 1937. Timur Kibirov, *Russian*. TCRP, tr. by Vera Dunham

Stalin's genius consisted of not french-kissing. Bruce Andrews. PmAP

Stalking. Where Seed Falls. Essex Hemphill. GT

Stalking before the lords of life, one came. Circumstance. John Townsend Trowbridge. APN-2

Stalks growing. Tanka. Miya Shūji, *Japanese*. MJT, tr. by Makoto Ueda

Stalks of Wild Hay. Harold Lenoir Davis. PoA

Stalky Jack. William Brighty Rands. BoTP

Stalled before my metal shaving mirror. Notes for a Sonnet. "Edward Pygge." BXAP; OBCoV

Stalled car. Gary Hotham. HA

Stallion, The. "Mikhail Semionovich Golodny," *Russian*. TCRP, tr. by Simon Franklin

Stallion, The. Tudur Aled, *Welsh*. OBWVE, tr. by Joseph P. Clancy

Stalls? I'd have wondered, Has he died at last? Over All. Thomas Rabbitt. PUP-19

Stalwartly. Tanka. Tsukamoto Kunio, *Japanese*. MJT, tr. by Makoto Ueda

Stamp, roar like our Russian poets, like Derzhavin. Ode for the Dancing Khlysty. Yury Ivask, *Russian*. TCRP, tr. by Burton Raffel *and* Alla Burago

Stamped out the fires. (LL) Place of Fire. Johannes Bobrowski, *German*. CEEP; PoSu, tr. by Ruth Mead *and* Matthew Mead

'Stand back, Tom Devil, I'm gonna rule Hell by myself'. (LL)   Stagolee. *Unknown.*   OxBoLi; TTY

Stand back, ye sleeping jacks at home.   The Vice's Song.   John Pickering. NoSic   *Fr.* Horestes.

Stand by Me.   *Unknown.*   NAAAL

Stand by me, Death, lest these dark days.   Three Pleas.   Henry Treece. PoWW

Stand close around, ye Stygian set.   Dirce.   Walter Savage Landor.   AWP; CTC; EBEV; FaBoEE; GBL; HAP; NOBE; NoP-4; OAEL-2; OBEV; OBNC; OxAEP-2; OxBSP; PoEL-4; PoRA; SCGP; TFi; WeW-3   *Fr.* Pericles and Aspasia.

Stand fast, my child, and after all.   Fortitude.   Christopher Smart.   ChIV-2 *Fr.* Hymns for the Amusement of Children.

Stand here, says the professional TV person.   Telyric.   Andrei Codrescu. PmAP

Stand here, you can see the hill;.   A Memory of the Hill.   Kapilar, *Tamil.* PLW, *tr. by* A. K. Ramanujan

Stand not uttering sedately.   Epitaphium Citharistriae.   Victor Gustave Plarr. EnLoPo; NBLV; PoRA

Stand of Queen Anne's Lace, A.   Mirage.   Richard Harteis.   CMAP

Stand off, daughter of the dusk.   Gwendolyn Brooks.   NALW   *Fr.* The Womanhood.

Stand off, physician! Let me frolic.   On Melancholy.   *Unknown.*   NOSC

Stand on the highest pavement of the stair.   La Figlia Che Piange.   T. S. Eliot.   CBLP; FaBoTw; GBL; HeIP-4; LoP; OxBTC; PoA; UnPo; VGW

Stand out, maids, and look on the land of Cynddylan.   *Unknown.*   OBWVE, *tr. by* Kenneth Hurlstone Jackson   *Fr.* The Elegy on Cynddylan.

Stand out the bright steamers / to kingdom come. (LL)   Away above a harborful.   Lawrence Ferlinghetti.   BoLoP; PoM

Stand still.   In the Fog.   Lilian Moore.   TLR

Stand still, and I will read to thee.   A Lecture upon the Shadow.   Donne. AWP; ESCV; ImPo; NAEL-1; NoSic; SCGP; SoCP; UnPo

Stand still. The trees ahead and bushes beside you.   Lost.   David Wagoner. PaTW; PoA

Stand still, true poet that you are!   Popularity.   Robert Browning.   OAEL-2

Stand still, you floods! do[e] not deface.   On Sight of a Gentlewoman's Face in the Water.   Thomas Carew.   CaPo

Stand! the ground's your own, my braves!   Warren's Address at Bunker Hill [*or to the American Soldiers*].   John Pierpont.   FaBoBe

Stand there and have a look at that poor map.   The Tattered Map.   Tản Đà, *Vietnamese.*   AVP, *tr. by* Huỳnh Sanh Thông

Stand-to: Good Friday Morning.   Siegfried Sassoon.   FaBoTw

Stand to one side. No, over here with me.   Venetian Interior, 1889.   Richard Howard.   VCAP

Stand up, but not for Jesus!   D. H. Lawrence.   OxBTC

Stand Up! Stand Up for Jesus.   George Duffield Jr.   AH

Stand! Who goes there?   John Lyly.   NoSic; OBCoV   *Fr.* Endimion.

Stand [*or* Stond] who so list upon the slipper top[pe].   Senec. Traged. ex Thyeste Chor. 2.   Seneca, *Latin.*   AAS; NoSic; OBVE; PoEL-1; SiPS, *tr. by* Sir Thomas Wyatt   *Fr.* Thyestes.

Stand whoso list upon the slipper top.   Sir Thomas Wyatt.   NoP-4

Stand with thy nose against.   Of One That Had a Great Nose.   George Turberville, *after the Greek of* Trajan.   FaBoEE

Stand with your lover on the ending earth.   E. E. Cummings.   MeMAP

Stand you here, murdering shaft, no longer.   Dedication: A Spear.   Anyte, *Greek.*   GrAn, *tr. by* John Heath-Stubbs *and* Carol A. Whiteside

Standards of the King go forth, The.   Saint Venantius Fortunatus, *Latin.* MLL, *tr. by* Helen Waddell

Standin' on the Walls of Zion.   *Unknown.*   AS

Standing all day on Lake View Tower.   Written on Lake View Tower.   P'an Lang, *Chinese.*   SuSp, *tr. by* Jonathan Chaves

Standing aloft on lotus blossoms.   Ode to Merciful Bodhisattva.   Hijin Park, *Korean.*   CKP, *tr. by* Jaihiun Kim

Standing aloof in giant ignorance.   To Homer.   Keats.   EBEV; NAEL-2; NoP-4; Son

Standing beside you, fiddler.   *Unknown, Greek.*   GrAn, *tr. by* Peter Jay

Standing Coffin.   Tamura Ryuichi, *Japanese.*   AF, *tr. by* Christopher Drake

Standing corn is green, the wild in flower, The.   Nunc Viridant Segetes. Sedulius Scottus, *Medieval Latin.*   BIrV; NAWM-1, *tr. by* Helen Waddell

Standing guests, a grotesque glade, The.   The Party.   Margaret Avison.   PoA

Standing high on the shoulders of all things, all things.   The Place at Albert Bay.   Muriel Rukeyser.   PoA

Standing in ribbons, over our heads, for an hour. (LL)   End of the Picnic. Francis Webb.   BMAP; NOBAu

Standing in the Doorway, I Watch the Young Child Sleep.   Sharon Hashimoto.   OpBo

Standing in the doorway of Cuba's Spanish.   The Flesh of the Young Men Is Burning.   Lance Jeffers.   BkSV

Standing in the garden.   Listen.   Linda Lancione Moyer.   CrSp

Standing in the hall against the / wall.   Listening to Grownups Quarreling. Ruth Whitman.   NTCP

Standing on the Corner.   Philip Levine.   NNaP

Standing on the mountaintop.   Lost Silvertip.   J. D. Reed.   NYBP

Standing on top of the hay.   The Farm.   Donald Hall.   LiTM

Standing still.   Tanka.   Tsukamoto Kunio, *Japanese.*   MJT, *tr. by* Makoto Ueda

Standing straight / sprouting leaves. (LL)   Simultaneously, five thousand miles apart.   David Ignatow.   PFE

Standing there they began to grow skins.   Pilgrims.   Jean Valentine.   LCAP-2; TAP

Standing Up.   Tomas Tranströmer, *Swedish.*
  "It's been a hard winter, but summer is here and the fields."   RaBo, *tr. by* Robert Bly

Standing up on lifted, folded rock.   By Frazier Creek Falls.   Gary Snyder. InPS-3

Standing upon a hill of fancies high.   A Landscape.   Margaret Lucas Cavendish, Duchess of Newcastle.   NOSC

Standing upon the margent of the Main.   The Tempest.   Charles Cotton. OxBoS

Stands be within me, let me be where it is. (LL)   Psalm Concerning the Castle.   Denise Levertov.   TwCP; WPE

Stands for hope.   Marianne Moore.   *See* The Steeple-Jack.

Stands / outside my door this morning.   A New Refugee.   Marisella Veiga. LoHo

Stanley Matthews.   Alan Ross.   OxBTC

Stanley Meets Mutesa.   James David Rubadiri.   PBA

Stanza Written in Jest.   Yang Wan-li, *Chinese.*   SuSp, *tr. by* Sherwin S. S. Fu

Stanzas: "Ah! think'st thou, Laura, then, that wealth."   Charlotte Smith. NoP-4

Stanzas.   Caroline Anne Bowles.   Ro   *Fr.* Ellen Fitzarthur: A Metrical Tale.

Stanzas: "How often we forget all time, when lone."   Edgar Allan Poe. APN-1

Stanzas: "How smooth that lake expands its ample breast!"   Ann Radcliffe. WPE

Stanzas: "I heard thy fate without a tear."   Byron.   PBMP

Stanzas: "I thought I woke: the midnight sun."   Paul Goodman.   PoA

Stanzas: "I'll not weep that thou art going to leave me."   Emily Jane Brontë.   WPE

Stanzas: "In this vain, busy world, where the good and the gay."   Mary Robinson.   ECWP; WoRP

Stanzas.   Osip Emilevich Mandelstam, *Russian.*
  "And then my country spoke to me."   TCRP, *tr. by* Bernard Meares
  "And you, my sister Moscow, are at ease."   TCRP, *tr. by* Bernard Meares

Stanzas.   Charles Newton.
  Wild Nature.   NOEC

Stanzas: "Often rebuked, yet always back returning."   Emily Jane Brontë. GEA; NALW; NOBVV; OAEL-2; OBEV; OBNC; PBWP; SCGP; VWP

Stanzas: "Oh, come to me in dreams, my love!"   Mary Wollstonecraft Shelley.   LW

Stanzas: "Passing of a dream, The."   John Clare.   NOBVV

Stanzas.   Edgar Allan Poe.   NCAP

Stanzas: "When a man hath no freedom to fight for at home."   Byron. FaBoEE; NAEL-2; NBLV; OxAEP-2; PoLF; Poetr; TRP
  ("And, if not shot or hanged, you'll get knighted.") (LL)   NoP-4

Stanzas: "With tears thy grief thou dost bemoan."   Solomon ibn Gabirol, *Hebrew.*   TrJP, *tr. by* Emma Lazarus

Stanzas: "With youthful toil and memory, in my voiceless land."   Viktor Korkiya, *Russian.*   TCRP, *tr. by* Vera Dunham

Stanzas: "You say you love; but with a voice."   Keats.   CBLP

Stanzas Addressed to Miss Landon, and suggested by her 'Stanzas on the Death of Mrs Hemans'.   Elizabeth Barrett Browning.   *See* Felicia Hemans.

Stanzas Against Forgetting.   Guillaume Apollinaire, *French.*   AF, *tr. by* Carolyn Forché

Stanzas Concerning an Ecstasy Experienced in High Contemplation.   Saint John of the Cross, *Spanish.*   TOF, *tr. by* K. Kavanaugh *and* O. Rodrigues

Stanzas Concerning Love.   Stefan George, *German.*   AWP, *tr. by* Ludwig Lewisohn

Stanzas for an Imaginary Garden.   Octavio Paz.   OBGa

Stanzas for Music.   Byron.   NAEL-2; OxBSP

Stanzas for Music ("There be none of Beauty's daughters").   Byron.   AWP; CBLP; GTBS-P; HAP; LaPo; NAEL-2; OAEL-2; PoRA

Stanzas for Music ("There's not a joy the world can give like that it takes away").   Byron.   HAP; NOBRP
  (Youth and Age.)   GTBS-P

Stanzas from "Child Harold." John Clare. OBNC *Fr.* Child Harold.

Stanzas from the Grande Chartreuse. Matthew Arnold. EBVV; EnVR; NAEL-2; OAEL-2; PoE; PoEL-5

"For rigorous teachers seized my youth." FHYEP

Stanzas Imitated From Psalm CXIX. Thomas, the Elder Warton. ChIV-1

Stanzas in Meditation. Gertrude Stein.

Stanzas in Meditation. Gertrude Stein.

From Stanzas in Meditation. NoP-4

"Full well I know that she is there." PoA

"How I wish I were able to say what I think." PBWP

Stanzas Occasioned by the Ruins of a Country Inn *or* On the Ruins of a Country Inn. Philip Freneau. OxBA

Stanzas of the Graves, The. *Unknown, Welsh.*

"Graves the rain makes wet and sleek, The." OBWVE, *tr. by* Gwyn Jones

Stanzas of the Soul that Suffers with Longing to See God. Saint John of the Cross, *Spanish.* TOF, *tr. by* K. Kavanaugh *and* O. Rodrigues

Stanzas on Freedom. James Russell Lowell.

On Freedom. ImGa

Stanzas on Hearing for Certainty that we were to be Tried for High Treason. John Thelwall. Ro *Fr.* Poems Written in Close Confinement in the Tower and Newgate upon a Charge of Treason.

Stanzas on Mutability. Hugo von Hofmannsthal, *German.* AWP; TrJP, *tr. by* Jethro Bithell

Stanzas on the Death of Lord Byron. Elizabeth Barrett Browning. Ro *Fr.* Globe and Traveller, no. 6733.

Stanzas on the Death of Lord Byron. Elizabeth Barrett Browning. Ro *Fr.* Globe and Traveller, no. 6733.

Stanzas on the Death of Mrs Hemans. Letitia Elizabeth Landon. Ro; VWP *Fr.* New Monthly Magazine, 44 286–8.

Stanzas on the Psalms. Thomas, the Elder Warton. ChIV-1

Stanzas Subjoined to the Yearly Bill of Mortality of the Parish of All Saints, Northampton; for the Year 1787. William Cowper. NOCV

Stanzas to———. Emily Jane Brontë. WPE

Stanzas to Edward Williams. Shelley. OBNC

Stanzas to the Po. Byron. OAEL-2

("To tear a heart which pants to be unmoved?") (LL) Ro

(To the Po. 2 June 1819.) Ro

Stanzas to the Speaker Asleep. Winthrop Mackworth Praed. OBSV

Stanzas Written between Dover and Calais, in July, 1792. Martha Robinson. ECWP

Stanzas Written in Dejection, near Naples [*or* —December 1818, near Naples]. Shelley. GTBS-P; NAEL-2; NAWM-2; PBMP; PoRA

(Stanzas Written in Dejection, Near Naples.) NoP-4

Stanzas Written in Dejection, Near Naples. Shelley. *See* Stanzas Written in Dejection, near Naples [*or* —December 1818, near Naples].

Stanzas Written on the Road between Florence and Pisa. Byron. NAEL-2

(All for Love.) GTBS-P

Stanzas Written under Aeolus' Harp. Amelia Alderson Opie. Ro *Fr.* Poems.

Star, A. Federico García Lorca. PFTM

Star, A. (LL) I have a little sister, they call her Peep-Peep. Mother Goose. BoTP; OxNR

Star. Pavel Davydovich Kogan, *Russian.* TCRP, *tr. by* Albert C. Todd

Star, The. Jane Taylor. ACTP; BoTP; CABP; CTV; FPC; FaBoBe; ImGa; NOBRP; NOxBChV; NTCP; OTCP; OxBChV; OxNR; UV

("Twinkle, twinkle, all the night.") (LL) CABP

Star. Derek Walcott. PFE; PiM

Star & Garter Theater. Dennis Schmitz. LCAP-2

Star and Sea. William Peskett. PNI

Star-breath descends. line. Iain Sinclair. NBrP

Star crashes in a small plaza and a bird loses its eyes, A. The Things I Say Are True. Blanca Varela, *Spanish.* BoWoP, *tr. by* Donald Yates

Star-crowned solitude of thine oblivious hours!, The. (LL) To One in Bedlam. Ernest Christopher Dowson. GSo; MoBrPo; OBMV; Son

Star-filled seas are smooth to-night, The. The Isle of Portland. A. E. Housman. MoBrPo

Star-Fix. Marilyn Nelson Waniek. LTA; NAmP90

Star frightens the steeple cross, A. Guard-Duty. August Stramm, *German.* PeFWW, *tr. by* Patrick Bridgwater

Star-Gazers. Wordsworth. Poetr

"What crowd is this? what have we here! we must not pass it by." Poetr

Star-Gazing. Ptolemy, *Greek.* GrAn, *tr. by* Dudley Fitts

Star, / If you are. A Christmas Tree. William Burford. SoSe-8

Star is gone, A! a star is gone! The Fallen Star. George Darley. OBEV

Star light, star bright. Wishing Poem. *Unknown.* ACTP; NTCP; OTCP; OxNR

Star looks down at me, A. Waiting Both. Thomas Hardy. MoBrPo; OxBoLi; TTTS

Star Morals. Friedrich Wilhelm Nietzsche, *German.* AWP, *tr. by* Ludwig Lewisohn

Star of Free Will, The. Maria Luisa Spaziani, *Italian.*

"I shall find in paradise that emaciated rose shoot." NeIt, *tr. by* Beverly Allen

"Sunday in the provinces, a plaintive Norman bell-peal." NeIt, *tr. by* Beverly Allen

"Traveling with too much baggage is not a good idea." NeIt, *tr. by* Beverly Allen

Star of peace the standard of the world, The. (LL) General Grant—the Hero of the War. George Moses Horton. AAP; CBCWP

Star of the North! though night winds drift. The Fugitive Slave's Apostrophe to the North Star. John Pierpont. APN-1

Star of the sea, surest point of brightness. Stella Maris. O. B. Hardison, Jr. CRP

Star over all. Christmas Tree. Laurence Smith. OBCP

Star Quilt. Roberta Hill Whiteman. CDW; NoAM

Star-sailor, with your eyes on space. The Astronaut. James Kirkup. SpW

Star-shell holds the sky beyond, A. Patrick MacGill. NSI

Star Song. Henrietta Cordelia Ray. CBWP-3

Star-Spangled Banner, The. Francis Scott Key. AiP; BLPA; CTV; EBEvV; FaBoBe; TAP; UV

(Defense of Fort McHenry.) APN-1

Star, Sun, Moon. Henrikas Radauskas, *Lithuanian.* CEEP, *tr. by* Jonas Zdanys

Star System, The. Richard Wilbur. NBLV *Fr.* Flippancies.

Star that bids the shepherd fold, The. Comus' Summons. Milton. FaBoCh; NOBE; NOSC; OBEV *Fr.* Comus; a Masque Presented at Ludlow Castle. FHYEP; OAEL-1

Star that bringest home the bee. To the Evening Star. Thomas Campbell. GTBS-P

Star-Tribes, The. *Aborigine Oral Tradition.* NOBAu, *tr. by* Fred Biggs

Star Watcher, The. Peter Davison. TwCP

Star Wish. *Unknown. See* Wishing Poem.

Starapple Tree. Pamela Mordecai. HCP

Stardust Sequence, The. Dermot Bolger.

"Last night in swirling colour we daced again." BiHa

Stare at the monster: remark. Famous Poet. Ted Hughes. LiTM

Stare at the stars, the stars say. Look at me. Ego. Norman MacCaig. GTBS-P

Stare from your pillow into the sun. People of Unrest. Margaret Walker Alexander. GT

Stared, astonied all. È, the Feasting Florentines. Daniel Gerard Hoffman. VGW

Stared Story, A. William Stafford. Son

Stare's Nest by My Window, The. W. B. Yeats. BIrV; FaBoPV; GTBS-P; InPS-3; NOBE *Fr.* Meditations in Time of Civil War.

("Bees in the crevices, The.") FaBoPV

Starfish. Eric Ormsby. NoP-4

Stargazer, The. *Unknown.* OxBChV

Staring at the almost. Mother's Day. Steve Hassett. CDa

Staring at the mud turtle's eye. Concepts and Their Bodies (The Boy in the Field Alone). Pattiann Rogers. MT

Staring back at him like a stranger's. (LL) Horse on the Wall. Marcia Southwick. CMAP; NAmP90

Stark Major. Hart Crane. FuPo; MeMAP

Stark naked. Tanka. Kanoko Okamoto, *Japanese.* MJT, *tr. by* Makoto Ueda

Starless and chill is the night. A Night by the Sea. Heinrich Heine. AWP, *tr. by* Howard Mumford Jones *Fr.* The North Sea.

Starless and fatherless, a dark water. (LL) Sheep in Fog. Sylvia Plath. FaBoWP; HCAP; LCAP-2

Starlight. Freda Downie. FaBoWP

Starlight Haven. Shirley Lim. UnSA

Starlight like Intuition Pierced the Twelve. Delmore Schwartz. ChIV-2

Starlight Night, The. Gerard Manley Hopkins. APAD; EnVR; GTBS-P; InPS-3; LiTM; MoBrPo; NAEL-2; PoE

Starlight Thought. Henrietta Cordelia Ray. *Fr.* A Group of Musings. CBWP-3

Starlight's intuitions pierced the twelve, The. Starlight like Intuition Pierced the Twelve. Delmore Schwartz. ChIV-2

Starling and a willow-wren, A. W. H. Auden. FaBoMo *Fr.* Five Songs.

Starling Lake, The. "Seumas O'Sullivan." AWP

Starling Migration, The. Jeffrey Skinner. PBCAP

Starlings in George Square, The. Edwin Morgan. FaBoTC

Starre, The. Henry Vaughan. ESCV

Starry flower, the flower-like stars that fade, The. Sonnets. Frederick Goddard Tuckerman. APN-2; ColAP

Starry frost descends, The. Suibne Geilt. NOIV

Starry hosts whose far-flung cohorts gleam, The. Human Greatness. Edwin Barclay. PBA

Starry Night, The. Anne Sexton. ColAP; NoAM; PoE; VCAP

Starrynightlenteryourmirror. Alexis Rotella. HA

Stars. Alan Bold. SpW

Stars. George Mackay Brown. OxBS

Stars, The. Madison Cawein. APN-2

Stars. Nikki Giovanni. KaS

Stars. Robert Earl Hayden. LCAP-2

Stars. Langston Hughes. GLP

Stars. Lenard D. Moore. HA

Stars, The. "Ping Hsin," Chinese. WPOW, tr. by Kai-yu Hsu

    Builder of Continents, The.

Stars. Oktay Rifat, Turkish. PC, tr. by Taner Baybars

Stars, The. Lydia Huntley Sigourney. ColAP

Stars, about to fade, are straggling east, The. The Morning Bell at Tiêu Monastery. Mạc Thiên Tích, Chinese. AVP, tr. by Huỳnh Sanh Thông

Stars all fell out of the sky, The. Guy Fawkes '58. Fiona Kidman. PeNZ

Stars and Moon on the River. Tu Fu. See Stars and Moon on the Yangtse.

Stars and Moon on the Yangtse. Tu Fu, Chinese. PLT, tr. by A. C. Graham

    ("Autumn night is clear, The.") OHPC, tr. by Kenneth Rexroth

    ("Frost glitters on the chrysanthemums.") (LL) OHPC, tr. by Kenneth Rexroth

    (Stars and Moon on the River.) OHPC, tr. by Kenneth Rexroth

Stars and Planets. Norman MacCaig. OPOU; OxBSP

Stars and trouble, stars and trouble. Walk out. One Reason for Stars. Jack Butler. MT

Stars are a memory system, The. Notes on the Art of Memory, Diane Di Prima. SeSe

Stars are circles of children. Everything Is Round. Gabriela Mistral, Spanish. PBWP, tr. by D. M. Pettinella

Stars are dropping thick as stones into the twiggy. Stars over the Dordogne. Sylvia Plath. PoA

Stars are forth, the moon above the tops, The. Byron. OAEL-2 Fr. The Lamp must be replenish'd, but even then. NAEL-2; NOBRP

Stars Are Glittering in the Frosty Sky, The. Winter Galaxy. Charles Heavysege. NOBC

Stars are Lit, The. Hayyim Nahman Bialik, Hebrew. TrJP, tr. by Florence L. Friedman

Stars are only a backdrop for, The. Notes on a Life to Be Lived. Robert Penn Warren. NYBP

Stars are pinned against the sky, The. It Is the Stars That Govern Us. Michael Magee. PoA

Stars are shining / the eyes of men are closed. Rabi'a al-Adawiyya, Arabic. WPOW, tr. by Margaret Smith, ad. by Deirdre Lashgari

Stars are too many to count. Carl Sandburg. NOxBChV

Stars around the luminous moon—how soon they. Sappho, Greek. OBCVT; STV, tr. by John Frederick Nims

Stars come out to graze, wild-eyed in the new dark, The. Rural Route. Charles Wright. WeT

Stars crickets. George Swede. HA

Stars dead heroes in the sky, The. The Offensive. Keith Douglas. PoWW

Stars / Expanding with the starr'd nocturnal flowers. (LL) From My Diary, July 1914. Wilfred Owen. FaBoMo; LiTM; MoBrPo

Stars Fade. Peretz Hirshbein, Yiddish. TrJP, tr. by Joseph Leftwich

Stars Go Over the Lonely Ocean, The. Robinson Jeffers. LiTM

Stars had the look of dogs to him sometimes. The Star Watcher. Peter Davison. TwCP

Stars hang thick in the apple tree, The. Hora Stellatrix. Amy Lowell. SDW

Stars have given me a hard fate, The. Gaspara Stampa, Italian. PBWP, tr. by Lynne Lawner

Stars have not dealt me the worst they could do, The. A. E. Housman. EBEV; GTBS-P; OxBoLi

Stars have not yet retired, and the sky is still dark, The. Women Transport Corps. Unknown, Chinese. WPOW, tr. by Kai-yu Hsu

Stars Heng and Chi never halt their courses, The. Fulling Cloth for Clothes. Hsieh Hui-lien, Chinese. CoBCP, tr. by Burton Watson

Stars hidden by dark clouds. Boethius, Latin. MLL, tr. by Helen Waddell Fr. Consolation of Philosophy, The ("De Consolacione Philosophie").

Stars, I Have Seen Them Fall. A. E. Housman. OxBSP

Stars in Apple Cores. Luci Shaw. TrCP

Stars in profusion. A World to Come. Bernard Dadié, French. NegPo, tr. by Ellen Conroy Kennedy

Stars in Sand. Francis Carey Slater. PeSAV

Stars in the sky are as big as coins. Turkish Love Songs. Unknown. BoWoP, tr. by Reza Baraheni and Zahra-Soltan Shokoohtaezeh

Stars in their calm, The. (LL) The Song of Callicles ("Through the black, rushing smoke-bursts"). Matthew Arnold. NOBE; OAEL-2; OBEV

Stars in your face, The. In Missing. Ray A. Young Bear. CDW

Stars must make an awful noise, The. One Blackbird. Harold Monro. BoTP

Stars of Night contain the glittering Day, The. The Dying Words of Stonewall Jackson. Sidney Lanier. APN-2; CBCWP

Stars of the summer night! Serenade. Henry Wadsworth Longfellow. FaBoBe Fr. The Spanish Student.

Stars over snow. Night. Sara Teasdale. NOxBChV

Stars over the Dordogne. Sylvia Plath. PoA

Stars pass, The. Empress Jito, Japanese. WPJ, tr. by Kenneth Rexroth and Ikuko Atsumi

Stars rest cold by shoals of cloud. For the Examination at Ho-nan-fu: Songs of the Twelve Months. Li Ho, Chinese. CoBCP, tr. by Burton Watson Fr. For the Examination at Ho-nan-fu: Songs of the Twelve Months.

Stars Sang in God's Garden, The. Joseph Mary Plunkett. TIRV

Stars stand up in the air, The. Unknown, Irish. BIrV, tr. by Thomas Macdonagh

Stars, the implacable stars, The. The Blueness of Stars. Elizabeth Kirschner. CMAP

Stars walk downhill. Concert. Robert Sward. VGW

Stars wheel in purple, yours is not so rare. Hilda Doolittle. MoAmPo; NOBA; TAP Fr. Let Zeus Record.

Stars Which See, Stars Which Do Not See. Marvin Bell. CMAP

Start. Martin Sorescu, Romanian. VCWP, tr. by Michael Hamburger

Start from death's slumbers to eternity. (LL) The New Birth. Jones Very. APN-1; NCAP; NOBA; PAR

Start it well and carry it through. (LL) One, two, whatever you do. Unknown. CTV

Start like pieces of string. Advice to the Orchestra. David Wagoner. NoAM

Start of summer, grass and trees grown tall. Reading The Classic of Hills and Seas. T'ao Ch'ien, Chinese. CoBCP, tr. by Burton Watson

Start where you stand and never mind the past. Berton Braley. PoToHe

Start with a simple room. Plucking Out a Rhythm. Lawson Fusao Inada. AmPA

Started as arr. Crow. Robert Grenier. PmAP

Starting 1973: What to Do Now that Peace Has Been Announced. Joseph Cady. CDa

Starting a Pasture. Walter McDonald. MT

Starting again. A Dark Country. Derek Mahon. BIrV

Starting at Dawn. Sun Yün-feng, Chinese. PBWP, tr. by Kenneth Rexroth and Ling Chung

Starting at the center. Tables in Pictures. Diane Ward. FTOS

Starting Early. Po Chü-i. See Starting Early from the Ch'u-ch'êng Inn.

Starting Early from the Ch'u-ch'êng Inn. Po Chü-i, Chinese. ChiP; OBVE, tr. by Arthur Waley

    (Starting Early.) BLT, tr. by Arthur Waley

Starting Early from Yü-p'u Deep. Meng Hao Jan, Chinese. SuSp, tr. by Daniel Bryant

Starting from Central Station. David Campbell.

    I Starting from Central Station. BMAP

Starting to rise. Cor Van den Heuvel. HA

Starting. Words which begin, A. Zoetropes. Bill Manhire. PeNZ

Startled awake, back from a dream. Ni Tsan. Fr. Two Poems to the Tune "Jen-yüeh yüan." CoBLCP, tr. by Jonathan Chaves

Startled / By a single scream. Saigyo, Japanese. AWP, tr. by Arthur Waley

Startled by his own thoughts, he looked around. Shelley. OxBoS Fr. Alastor; or, The Spirit of Solitude. OAEL-2; Ro

Startled into Life Like Fire. Charles Bukowski. PmAP

Startled stag, the blue-grey night, A. The Dark Stag. Isabella Valancy Crawford. NOBC

Startling reality of things / Is my discovery every single day, The. "Startling Reality of Things," The. Fernando Pessoa, Portuguese. PFTM, tr. by Edwin Honig and Susan M. Brown

"Startling Reality of Things," The. Fernando Pessoa, Portuguese. PFTM, tr. by Edwin Honig and Susan M. Brown

Starvation and Blues. Edward Kamau Brathwaite. PBCV

Starvation Camp near Jaslo. Wislawa Szymborska, Polish. WPOW, tr. by Jan Darowski

    (Hunger Camp at Jaso.) AF, tr. by Grazyna Drabik and Austin Flint

    ("Write it. Write. In ordinary ink.") AF, tr. by Grazyna Drabik and Austin Flint

Starved. Laura Riding Jackson. FuPo

Starved island, Cormack, A. Saint. George Mackay Brown. FaBoTC Fr. Runes from a Holy Island.

Starved Lovers. Archibald MacLeish. MeMAP

Starved old gelding, blind and lamed, A. An Irish Marriage Night. Brian Merriman. BIrV, *tr. by* Frank O'Connor *Fr.* The Midnight Court. NOIV, *tr. by* Thomas Kinsella

"Starved to death." In Memoriam. Bernard Dadié, *French.* NegPo, *tr. by* Ellen Conroy Kennedy

Starving to Death on a Government Claim. *Unknown.* APN-2; AmFP; OBAL

(Lane County Bachelor, The.) AS

Stasis in darkness. Ariel. Sylvia Plath. CMoP; ColAP; HCAP; HeIP-4; LCAP-2; MoP; NAAL-2; NALW; NOBA; NoAM; NoP-4; PBWP; PoE; Poetr; VCAP

State, The. Randall Jarrell. LiTM

State, a state, oh! dungeon state indeed, A. Edward Taylor. ChIV-1, *sect.* LXXVII, Division II *Fr.* Preparatory Meditations Before My Approach to the Lord's Supper.

State Funeral. Thomas McCarthy, *Irish.* CIP-2

State of Arkansas, The, *see also* The Arkansaw Traveler. *Unknown.* APN-2

State of Innocence, The. Dryden. NOCV

Death the Consequence of the Fall.

Predestination and Free Will.

State of Nature, A. John Hollander. AiP

State of Preservation. Celeste Turner Wright. FFC

State of the Nation, The. Kenneth Patchen. CLPP

State of the Union. Aimé Césaire, *French.* NegPo, *tr. by* Denis Kelly

State of the World, The. T(stilde;a)n Đà, *Vietnamese.* AVP, *tr. by* Huỳnh Sanh Thông

State Poetry Day. Ronald Wallace. PBCAP

State Quiz. *Unknown.* CTV

State Street is lonely today. Aunt Jane Allen. Fenton Johnson. PoBA

State with the prettiest name, The. Florida. Elizabeth Bishop. FaBoA; TwCP

State you must dare not enter, A. Happiness. Stephen Dunn. PiM

State/meant. Imamu Amiri Baraka. BB

Stately as a Galleon. Joyce Grenfell. OBCoV

Stately home where doves, in dovecotes, coo—, A. The Owl Writes a Detective Story. Gavin Ewart. OBCoV

Stately Homes of England, The. Noël Coward. UV *Fr.* The Stately Homes of England. OBCoV

Stately Homes of England, The. Noël Coward. UV

("Lord Elderley, Lord Borrowmere, Lord Sickert and Lord Camp.") OBCoV

Stately homes of England, The. The Homes of England. Felicia Dorothea Hemans. FaPoR; NOBRP; PEW; UV; WPE

Stately, kindly, lordly friend. To a Cat. Swinburne. PC

Stately Lady, The. Flora Sandstrom. BoTP

Stately palace in which the queen dwells, The. Her Descending Down. Margaret Lucas Cavendish, Duchess of Newcastle. NOSC

Stately rainbow came and stood, A. The Rainbow. Coventry Patmore. GTBS-P *Fr.* The Angel in the House.

Stately Southerner, The. *Unknown.* AmFP *See also* The Yankee Man-of-War.

Stately stand the sunflowers, glowing down the. The Mill Garden. Swinburne. GaP

Stately Structure of This Earth, The. Martha Brewster. AH

Stately you came to town in my opening dream. Midwinter Day. Bernadette Mayer. PT *Fr.* Midwinter Day.

Statement on Our Higher Education. W. M. Ransom. CDW

States when they black out and lie there rolling when they turn, The. Falling. James Dickey. LCAP-2; MT; NYBP; NoAM

Statesman, The. Hilaire Belloc. NOBE

Statesman is an easy man, A. The Old Stone Cross. W. B. Yeats. PBMP

Statesman's Holiday, The. W. B. Yeats. CMoP; OxBTC

Statesmen. W. H. Auden. OBCoV *Fr.* Shorts [1939–1947].

Statesmen, The. Ambrose Bierce. APN-2

Static, The. Lewis Warsh. FTOS

Static Autumn. Yvor Winters. PoA

Static from the radio stippled grey as anesthesia dream. Fiat Lux. Lynda Hull. WWSi

Station. Sharon Olds. PBCAP

Station Island. Seamus Heaney.

"Black water. White waves. Furrows snowcapped." NoAM

"I had come to the edge of the water." PBCIP

"Like a convalescent, I took the hand." FaBoPV; NAEL-2; NoAM; TOF

"My brain dried like spread turf, my stomach." CIP-2

Stationmaster is garrulous in, The. Daphne Stillorgan. Denis Devlin. CIP-2

Stations. Philip Booth. GM

Stations. Ted Hughes.

"I can understand the haggard eyes." NoAM

"Suddenly his poor body." NoAM

"Whether you say it, think it, know it." NoAM

"You are a wild look—out of an egg." NoAM

Statistic. Michelle Parkerson. ISC

Statistic: The Witness. Rita Dove. NAAAL *Fr.* Mother Love.

Statistics. Stephen Spender. MoBrPo

Statistics. Barrett Watten. PmAP

Statuary. John Ashbery. NoAM

Statue, The. Kenneth Allott. SPE

Statue, The. Hilaire Belloc. OxAEP-2

Statue. Tom Clark. BAP-93

Statue, The. Robert Creeley. LCAP-2

Statue, The. John Fuller. NOBE

Statue of Bereniké, A. Callimachus, *Greek.* GrAn, *tr. by* Peter Jay

Statue Of Eros, A. Zenodotus, *Greek.* GrAn, *tr. by* Peter Jay

("Who carved Love.") LoP, *tr. by* Peter Jay

Statue of Medusa, The. William Drummond of Hawthornden. GS

Statue of Nemesis at Rhamnus, The. Parmenion of Macedon, *Greek.* GrAn, *tr. by* Alistair Elliot

Statue of Old Andrew Jackson, The. Vachel Lindsay. CA

Statue painted gold, tea on the white table. (LL) After Yeats. Allen Ginsberg. FTOS; PFE

Statues, The. Laurence Binyon. OBEV

Statues. Olive Custance. ADE

Statues. Kathleen Jessie Raine. NYBP

Statues, The. W. B. Yeats. NoAM; OAEL-2; WeW-3

Statues left first. A little later, The. Return. Yannis Ritsos, *Greek.* GrIP, *tr. by* Edmund Keeley

Statues with exposed hearts and barbed-wire crowns. The Mud Vision. Seamus Heaney. PBCIP

Status Symbol. Mari E. Evans. NAAAL

Stavrogin's Farewell. János Pilinszky. CEEP, *tr. by* Jascha Kessler *Fr.* Three Poems.

Stavrogin's Return. János Pilinszky. CEEP, *tr. by* Jascha Kessler *Fr.* Three Poems.

Stay All Night, Stay a Little Longer. *Unknown.* AmFP

Stay beautiful / but dont stay down underground too long. For Poets. Al Young. PoBA

Stay Behind, The. Andrew Elliott. PNI

Stay! Beneath your feet is a wonder of women. On a Woman. Robert Williams, *Welsh.* OBWVE, *tr. by* H. Idris Bell

Stay, Death. Not mine the Christus-wand. Dirge. Herman Melville. APN-1; NCAP *Fr.* Clarel: A Poem and Pilgrimage in the Holy Land.

Stay, fairest Chari[e]ssa, stay and mark. The Glowworm. Thomas Stanley. BeJo; NOSC

Stay For Me There. Henry King. LBC *Fr.* The Exequy. GBL; GLoP; HAP; LoP; MeLP; OxBM; PoEL-2; SCGP; SeCP

Stay, gentle Child of Taste! who'er thou art. A Prefatory Epistle. Maria Falconar. ECWP

Stay here, fond youth, and ask no more. Against Fruition. Sir John Suckling. BeJo; CaPo; CavPo; NOSC

Stay My Steps in Thy Paths, That My Feet Do Not Slide. Francis Quarles. NOSC *Fr.* Emblems.

Stay, my tendrils, where hung. Asclepiades, *Greek.* GrAn, *tr. by* Alan Marshfield

Stay near me—do not take thy flight! To a Butterfly. Wordsworth.

Stay near me. Speak my name. Oh, do not wander. Midcentury Love Letter. Phyllis McGinley. LW; OxBM

Stay now with me, and listen to my sighs. Dante. AWP *Fr.* La Vita Nuova.

Stay, O sweet, and do not rise! Aubade. *Unknown, at. to* John Donne. BoLoP; NOBE; OBEV

Stay off from me, wild sea. A Tomb on the Shore. Asclepiades, *Greek.* GrAn, *tr. by* Alan Marshfield

Stay, passenger, and lend a tear. On a Hopeful Youth. Owen Feltham [*or* Feltham]. NOSC

Stay Phoebus, stay. Song. Edmund Waller. BeJo; SeCP

"Stay!" said the child. The bird said, "No." A Footprint on the Air. Naomi Lewis. NOxBChV

Stay, shade of my shy treasure! Oh, remain. Sister Juana Inés de la Cruz, *Spanish.* WPOW, *tr. by* Alice Stone Blackwell

Stay, should I answer, Lady, then. To Mrs K. T. (Who Asked Him Why He Was Dumb). John Cleveland. CBLP

Stay, Spring. Andrew Young. FaBoTw

Stay, Thames, to heare my Song, thou great and famous Flood. Michael Drayton. PoEL-2 *Fr.* The Third Eclogue.

Stay weary traveler, stay! The Fountain at the Tomb. Nicias, *Greek.* AWP, *tr. by* Charles Merivale

Stay with Me. Garrett Kaoru Hongo. WeT

Stay with me, Marguerite, still! (LL) Absence. Matthew Arnold. EnVR; GLoP

Stay yet, pale flower, though coming storms will tear thee. On a Rose in December. Ebenezer Elliot. FaBoEE

Stay, you that bear the corse, and set it down. Shakespeare. OxBoV *Fr.* Richard III.

Stayed late in town, sped home in my boat. On the Fifteenth Day of the Seventh Month I Came Home Late from the City. Shen Chou, *Chinese.* CoBLCP, *tr. by* Jonathan Chaves

Staying Alive. Denise Levertov.

"Went with some of my students to work in the People's." CDa

Staying Alive. David Wagoner. CoAP; InPK-6; NYBP

Staying at Ed's Place. May Swenson. SAGP; VCAP

Staying in a Mountain Pavilion on a Summer Night. Ma Chih-yüan. *Fr.* Two Poems to the Tune "Po pu tuan." CoBLCP, *tr. by* Jonathan Chaves

Staying in the Mountains in Summer. Yü Hsüan-chi, *Chinese.* BoWoP, *tr. by* Geoffrey Waters

Staying Overnight at Blue Cloud Temple. Mo Shih-lung, *Chinese.* CoBLCP, *tr. by* Jonathan Chaves

Staying Overnight at the Temple of the Holy Vulture. Yang Wan-li, *Chinese.* SuSp, *tr. by* Sherwin S. S. Fu

Staying Overnight at T'ien-ning Ch'an Temple. Chang Yü, *Chinese.* CoBLCP, *tr. by* Jonathan Chaves

Steadfast a lamp burns sheltered from the wind. *Unknown.* TOF, *tr. by* Sir Edwin Arnold *Fr.* The Bhagavad-Gita.

Steadily it snows. O. Mabson Southard. HA

Steady. Blaga Dimitrova, *Bulgarian.* CEEP, *tr. by* Jascha Kessler *and* Aleksandar Shurbanov

Steady advance of the darkness. Night. Boris Pasternak, *Russian.* TCRP, *tr. by* Edwin Morgan

Steady in the darkness. Put a Woman into the Memory Box. Brigitte Frase. LoHo

Steadying, The. William Heyen. BAP-96

Steal away, steal away, steal away to Jesus! Steal Away to Jesus. *Unknown.* APN-2; BPo; BkSV; CrDW; ISC; NAAAL; NoP-4

Stealing the Golden Fleece. Apollonius Rhodius, *Greek.* OBCVT, *tr. by* William Preston

Stealing Trout. Ted Hughes. NYBP

Steam / breathing from burnt saucepans. Home. Antonin Bartusek, *German.* CEEP, *tr. by* Ewald Osers

Steam Engine; or, The Power of the Flame, The. Thomas Baker.

"I dream'd I walk'd in raptures high." BXAP

Steam in Sacrifice. Robert Herrick. CaPo

Steam rises over my nose. Coffee. Wanda Coleman. ISC

Steam whistle cleaves to the wind, The. Spring at Yesan Station. Sub-ok, *Korean.* WPoS, *tr. by* Julie Pickering

Steamboat Whistle, The. Archibald MacLeish. MeMAP

Steamboats, Viaducts and Railways. Wordsworth. NAEL-2 *Fr.* Poems Composed or Suggested During a Tour, in the Summer of 1833.

Steamboats, Viaducts, and Railways. Wordsworth. NAEL-2

Steamer left he black and oozy wharves, The. Alexander Smith. PeVV *Fr.* A Boy's Poem.

Steaming hunk of meat, A. Hero's Portion. John Montague. NOIV

Stedefast [*or* Steddefast *or* Steadfast] cross[e], inmong [*or* among] alle [*or* all] other. Venantius Fortunatus. MiEL

Stedfast and enduring bone, The. (LL) The Immortal Part. A. E. Housman. MoBrPo; SCGP; SoSe-8; UnPo

Steed bit his master, The. On a Clergyman's Horse Biting Him. *Unknown.* ChIV-1; FaBoEE; NBLV; OxBoLi; PFE

Steekit, consecrat, fou o fire but fuel. Douglas Young. OBVE *Fr.* The Kirkyaird by the Sea.

Steel blue clouds and the enormous brown Delaware river. The Franklin Bridge in Philadelphia. Miroslav Holub, *German.* CEEP, *tr. by* Stuko, Daniel

Steel fibrous slant & ribboned glint, The. The Turncoat. Imamu Amiri Baraka. NeAP; PoE

Steel pen. Tanka. Miyazawa Kenji, *Japanese.* MJT, *tr. by* Makoto Ueda

Steel-Rod Benders. Miroslav Valek, *German.* CEEP, *tr. by* Ewald Osers

Steel Usurps the Forests; Silence Dethrones Dialogue. Bible, Apocrypha. HBAPE

Steel voice of a steel god. Pans at Carnival. Henry Beissel. PBCV

Steele Glas, The. George Gascoigne. AAS

Steely train in the stupid green, The. Train: Abstraction. Genevieve Taggard. WPE

Steelyards, the long lines of workers, The. Meditation at Pearl Street. Bruce Weigl. NAmP90

Steep cliffs pierce the sky. Mount T'ai P'ing. Ch'ien Ch'i, *Chinese.* OHMPC, *tr. by* Kenneth Rexroth

Steep eyes of wooden gods. Sigitas Geda, *Lithuanian.* CEEP, *tr. by* Jonas Zdanys

Steep, steep the lofty mountain peak. Hsü Kan. SuSp, *tr. by* Ronald C. Miao *Fr.* Boudoir Thoughts.

Steep valley overhung by trees, A. Plea for Peace. Frank Prewett. HATNAP

Steeped in ecstasies of perfume. Spring Nocturne. Abraham Liessin, *Yiddish.* TrJP

Steepies for the bairnie. Supper. William Soutar. OxBS

Steeple-Jack, The. Marianne Moore. BoWoP; CMoP; FaBoMo; FaBoWP; HAP; InPS-3; NOBA; NoAM; OxBA; PBWP; Poetr; WPE *Fr.* Part of a Novel, Part of a Poem, Part of a Play.

("Stands for hope.") (LL) ColAP; PoPoPo

("Which on a steeple / stands for hope.") (LL) NoP-4

Steer hither, steer your wingéd pines. The Sirens' Song. William Browne. GBL; NOBE; OBEV *Fr.* The Inner Temple Masque.

Steered straight into this century I see narrowboats. Homage to the Canal People. Andrew Sant. NOBAu

Stefansson: a walrus of a man. Stefansson Island. Philip Booth. SoSe-8

Stefansson Island. Philip Booth. SoSe-8

(Steingeröll) new signs putting. The Dance of the Greased Women. Tristan Tzara. PFTM, *tr. by* Pierre Joris *Fr.* Poemes Negres.

Stele and my Sirens and mournful pitcher that hold. Erinna. HePo, *tr. by* Barbara Hughes Fowler *Fr.* Epigrams.

Stella and Flavia every hour. Mary Barber. ECWP

Stella at Wood-Park. Jonathan Swift. BIrV

Stella behold, and then begin t'indite. (LL) Sonnet 15: "You that do search for every purling spring." Sir Philip Sidney. NAEL-1; NoSic; OAEL-1; OxAEP-1; Son

Stella is sick, and in that sick-bed lies. Sonnet 101. Sir Philip Sidney. *Fr.* Astrophil and Stella. AAS; SiPS

Stella Maris. O. B. Hardison Jr. CRP

Stella oft sees the very face of woe. Sonnet 45. Sir Philip Sidney. InPS-3; NAEL-1; NoSic; PoE *Fr.* Astrophil and Stella. AAS; SiPS

Stella, since thou so right a Princess art. Sonnet 107. Sir Philip Sidney. NoP-4; OxAEP-1 *Fr.* Astrophil and Stella. AAS; SiPS

Stella, the fullness of my thoughts of thee. Sonnet 50. Sir Philip Sidney. *Fr.* Astrophil and Stella. AAS; SiPS

Stella, the only planet of my light. Sonnet 68. Sir Philip Sidney. *Fr.* Astrophil and Stella. AAS; SiPS

Stella, think not that I by verse seek fame. Sonnet 90. Sir Philip Sidney. NoP-4; NoSic *Fr.* Astrophil and Stella. AAS; SiPS

Stella this day is thirty-four. On Stella's Birthday, 1718/1719. Jonathan Swift. CBLP; EnLoPo; IIP; InPK-6; NIP-4; NOIV; OAEL-1

Stella, whence doth this new assault arise. Sonnet 36. Sir Philip Sidney. *Fr.* Astrophil and Stella. AAS; SiPS

Stella, while now by honour's cruel might. Sonnet 91. Sir Philip Sidney. NAEL-1; PoE *Fr.* Astrophil and Stella. AAS; SiPS

Stellar Hour. Betti Alver, *Estonian.* CEEP, *tr. by* Ivask, Astrid

Stellar sea crawler, maw, The. Starfish. Eric Ormsby. NoP-4

Stella's Birthday ([March 13,] 1727). Jonathan Swift. OAEL-1; PoE; PoEL-3; SCGP

(Stella's Birthday.) NoP-4

Stella's Birthday; Written in the Year 1718[/9]. Jonathan Swift. *See* On Stella's Birthday, 1718/1719.

Stella's Epitaph. Mary Jones. ECWP

Stella's Kiss. Sir Philip Sidney. NoSic *Fr.* Astrophil and Stella. AAS; SiPS

Stem heaped up, heaped, heaped up. Spell for Making the First Man. *Unknown, Maori.* PeNZ, *tr. by* Margaret Orbell

Stendhal. Sergey Nikolaevich Markov, *Russian.* TCRP, *tr. by* Lubov Yakovleva

Step aside, you ornery tenderfeet. I'm an Old Cowhand. Johnny Mercer. OBAL

Step Away from Them, A. Frank O'Hara. CoAmPo; HCAP; InPS-3; NAAL-2; VCAP; VGW

Step by step. Tanka. Mori Ōgai, *Japanese.* MJT, *tr. by* Makoto Ueda

Step carefully please. War Rug. Natasha Waxman. IFJA

Step on His Head. James Laughlin. IFJA; VGW

"Step on it," said Aunt Alice, "for God's sake." The Ascension: 1925. John Malcolm Brinnin. InPK-6

Step One. Albert Mobilio. PT

Step Seven. Albert Mobilio. PT

Stepfathers. David Donnell. NOBC

Stéphane Mallarmé. Arthur Symons.

I. Hérodiade. ADE

Stephano Remembers. James Simmons. PBCIP; PNI

Stephen Smith, University of Iowa sophomore, burned what he said was his draft card. Of Late. George Starbuck. VGW

Stephen to Lazarus. C. S. Lewis. ChIV-2

Stepping gingerly. Cat in the Snow. Aileen Fisher. NTCP

Stepping Out. Michael Brownstein. FTOS

Stepping Out of the World. *Unknown, Vietnamese.* AVP, *tr. by* Huỳnh Sanh Thông

Stepping out through the west-wall gate. Leaving West Archery Hall at Dusk. Hsieh Ling-yün, *Chinese.* SuSp, *tr. by* Francis Westbrook

Stepping Stones, The. W. S. Graham. FaBoTC

Stepping Westward. Denise Levertov. CrSp; NALW; Poetr; VGW ("Eat as I go.") (LL) NMM-2

Stepping Westward. Wordsworth. CH; PoEL-4; Ro; SCGP

Steps. Michael Cuddihy. CMAP

Steps. Frank O'Hara. CoAmPo; PmAP

Steps in the Night. Mahmoud Darwish, *Arabic.* VCWP, *tr. by* Denys Johnson-Davies

Steps out / from a lily. Woman. Carl Rakosi. TAP

Stereo Time with Booker Little. Rick Madigan. SeSe

Sterile line glows, The. Poem for Claude. Ray DiPalma. FTOS

Sterilization. Stevie Smith. WPN

Sterkfontein. Ruth Miller. PeSA; PeSAV

Sterling believes that chaos arises from deep intrinsic order. White Boot. Michael McClure. PuP-16

Stern Brow, The. Walter Savage Landor. CBLP

Stern Daughter of the Voice of God! Ode to Duty. Wordsworth. AWP; FHYEP; GTBS-P; ImPo; NAEL-2; NOBRP; OAEL-2; OBEV

Stern eagle of the far north-west. The Song of the Reim-Kennar. Sir Walter Scott. OAEL-2; OBNC *Fr.* The Pirate.

Stern Master Munchem, rod in hand, stole out of school one day. The School-Master and the Truants. "John Brownjohn." OBCA

Stern Miss Frugle always said. What Happened to Miss Frugle. Brian Patten. OBSP

Stern parent, The. Harry Graham. CBNP; PeLV *Fr.* Some Ruthless Rhymes.

Stern Truth. Letitia Elizabeth Landon. VWP

Stethoscope tells what everyone fears, The. Academic. Theodore Roethke. FaBoEE; OBAL

Steve Biko is Dead. Jack A. Mapanje. PeSAV

Steven Pudenz. Paul Bonin-Rodriguez. IFJA

Steveston. Daphne Marlatt.
Imagine: A Town. NOBC

Sthenelais. *Unknown, Greek.* GrAn, *tr. by* Guy Davenport

Sticheron for Matins, Wednesday of Holy Week. Kassia, *Greek.* WPOW, *tr. by* Patrick Diehl

Stick, The. Edvard Kocbek, *Slovenian.* CEEP, *tr. by* Veno Taufer *and* Michael Scammell

Stick goes over the falls at sunset, A. Cor Van den Heuvel. HA

Stick he used to tap out feet, The. Phanias, *Greek.* GrAn, *tr. by* Peter Porter

Stick-nest in Ygdrasil, A. "Hugh MacDiarmid." FaBoTC *Fr.* A Drunk Man Looks at the Thistle.

Stick of Incense, A. W. B. Yeats. ChIV-2

Stick one in the old man's crown. (LL) A Baby Verse. *Unknown.* BoTP; OxNR

Stick the finger inside. Black Mail. Alice Walker. AmPA

Stick your patent name on a signboard. The River. Hart Crane. AmPP; CMoP; GM; MoAmPo; NOBA; OxBA *Fr.* Powhatan's Daughter. *Fr.* The Bridge. NAAL-2

Sticking morphine in the arm and eating meat. (LL) Last Night in Calcutta. Allen Ginsberg. FTOS; NoAM

Sticks and stones are hard on bones. A Choice of Weapons. Phyllis McGinley. PFE

Sticks and stones may break my bones. Truth. Barrie Wade. OTCP

Sticks-in-a-drowse droop over sugary loam. Cuttings. Theodore Roethke. ColAP; HCAP; LCAP-2; MoP; NAAL-2; NOBA; NoAM; OBGa; TAP; UnPo

Sticky inside their winter suits. Thaw. Margaret Avison. FaBoWP; NOBC

Stiff in a white coat. A Child's Visit to the Biology Lab. Kathleen Spivack. AmPA

Stiff spokes of this wheel, The. July in Washington. Robert Lowell. LCAP-2; NAAL-2

Stiff standing on the bed. Riddle. *Unknown.* GBL

Stiff, still features, The. (LL) Canto 7. Ezra Pound. NOBA; NoAM

Stiff wind off the channel, A. Wet Thursday. Weldon Kees. NYBP

Stiff winds blow. *Unknown, Japanese.* OHMPJ, *tr. by* Kenneth Rexroth

Stigmata. Patrick Lane. NOBC

Stiles. John Pudney. NYBP

Still. Aila Meriluoto, *Finnish.* PBWP, *tr. by* Jaakko A. Ahokas

Still. Wislawa Szymborska, *Polish.* AF, *tr. by* Robert A. Maguire *and* Magnus Jan Krynski

Still. James Wright. *See* Small Frogs Killed on the Highway.

Still a virgin. Ashtray (two poems). Ōkuma Nobuyuki, *Japanese.* MJT, *tr. by* Makoto Ueda

Still and All. Burns Singer. OxBS

Still and was a flower. (LL) Winter Poem. Nikki Giovanni. MBE; PiM

Still are there wonders of the dark and day. To Keep the Memory of Charlotte Forten Grimké. Angelina Weld Grimké. BlSi

Still At Play. Tản Đà, *Vietnamese.* AVP, *tr. by* Huỳnh Sanh Thông

Still be renownëd. (LL) A Prayer to the Holy Trinity. Richard Stanyhurst. PoEL-2; TIRV

Still blooming on, when Summer-flowers all fade. Autumn Flowers. Jones Very. APN-1

Still-born silence, thou that art. Invocation of Silence. Richard Flecknoe. OxBSP

Still burning. Stanley Kunitz. *See* The Portrait.

Still, citizen sparrow, this vulture which you call. Richard Wilbur. AmPP; CMoP; ColAP; HoPM; LiTM; MoP; NoAM; PFE; TRP

Still clinging to your shirt. (LL) My Papa's Waltz. Theodore Roethke. CMoP; ChAP; ClHu; ColAP; HAP; HCAP; HeIP-4; HoPM; InPK-6; InPS-3; LCAP-2; LiTM; MoP; NAAL-2; NBLV; NIP-4; NOBA; NOxBChV; NTP; NoAM; NoP-4; PBMP; PoE; PoPoPo; Poetr; RaBo; SAGP; TAP; TFi; TRP; VGW

Still craving a robust / Tenderness and justice. Sung From A Hospice. Cyrus Cassells. PUP-20

Still do the stars impart their light. Falsehood. William Cartwright. OBEV

Still drifting together. The Unpossessed. Adèle Naudé. PeSA

Still explosions on the rocks, The. The Shampoo. Elizabeth Bishop. FaBoWP; OxBC; VCAP

Still fainter as the dewdrops settle on the flowers. (LL) Stars and Moon on the Yangtse. Tu Fu, *Chinese.* PLT, *tr. by* A. C. Graham

Still falls the Rain—. Dame Edith Sitwell. BoWoP; CABP; LiTM; MoBrPo; MoP; NAEL-2; NOBE; NoAM; OBWP; PFTM; PeECV; TFi; TwCP

Still far from patriarch or sage. Osip Emilevich Mandelstam, *Russian.* TCRP, *tr. by* Bernard Meares

Still fettered, still unconquered, still in pain. Prometheus Unbound. Alec Derwent Hope. OxBC

Still for the world he lives, and lives in bliss. Written on the Anniversary of Our Father's Death. Hartley Coleridge. Son

Still green on the limbs o' the woak wer the leaves. Which Road? William Barnes. NOBVV

Still green with bays each ancient altar stands. Alexander Pope. EPCY *Fr.* An Essay on Criticism. NAEL-1; PoEL-3; TFi

Still Here. Langston Hughes. BPo; SAmP
("I been scarred and battered.") BPo

Still holding and feeding the stem of the contained flower. (LL) The Shape of the Fire. Theodore Roethke. CMoP; LCAP-2; VCAP

Still I complain; I am complaining still. Was Ever Heart Like Mine? Edward Taylor. MeMAP; OxBA; PoEL-3 *Fr.* Preparatory Meditations Before My Approach to the Lord's Supper.

Still, I lay awake in the dark. The Call. Robert Harris. BMAP

Still I Rise. Maya Angelou. BlSi; NAAL
("I rise.") (LL) APAD; ISC

Still, I would leap too. Small Frogs Killed on the Highway. James Wright. HCAP; NNaP; NoAM

Still in an amorphous world she moves. The Idiot. Adèle Naudé. PeSA

Still in his mother's lap the baby Love played. Meleager. HePo, *tr. by* Barbara Hughes Fowler *Fr.* I'll Twine White Violets. NIP-4, *tr. by* Goldwin Smith

Still in October, the woodcock. On the Mountain. Ruth Stone. BoWoP

Still in sleeping bags, the promised delivery. Bats. Dave Jeddie Smith. NoAM

Still, in some hidden towns of our Dispersion. The Talmud Student. Hayyim Nahman Bialik, *Hebrew.* TrJP, *tr. by* Helena Frank

Still in the published city but not yet. John Ashbery. PmAP *Fr.* Flow Chart.

Still is my love telling what is told. (LL) Sonnet 76. Shakespeare. EBEV; NoSic; OxAEP-1

Still it is raining lightly. A Love Medicine. Louise Erdrich. HATNAP

Still / it was nice. Lucille Clifton. InPS-3

Still Later There Are War Stories. D. F. Brown. CDa

Still, leagues beyond those leagues, there is more sea. (LL) The Choice. D. G. Rossetti. GTBS-P; OBEV

Still let my tyrants know, I am not doomed to wear. The Prisoner. Emily Jane Brontë. NOBE; NoP-4; OBEV; OBNC *Fr.* The Prisoner. NALW; NOBVV

Still letters reach us. News from Behind the Seven Hills. Günter Kunert, *German.* CEEP, *tr. by* Michael Hamburger

Still-Life. Elizabeth Daryush. FaBoWP; WPE; WPN

Still-Life. Anthony Hecht. NoP-4

Still-Life. Ted Hughes. NYBP

Still Life. Veronica Morgan. CMAP

Still Life. "Shahryar," *Urdu.* OMIP, *tr. by* Gopi Chand Narang *and* David Paul Douglas

Still Life. Sharan Strange. GT

Still Life. Francis Sullivan. CRP

Still Life. Reed Whittemore. CoAP; CoAmPo

Still-Life in the Coat Factory Office. Vickie Karp. WWSi

Still Life: Lady with Birds. Quandra Prettyman. PoBA

Still Life, Symbolic of Lines, A. Albert Goldbarth. BAP-95

Still Life: The Table. Theo Van Doesburg, *Dutch.* PFTM, *tr. by* Jerome Rothenberg

Still Life, Untitled, A. Karen Zealand. CMAP

Still Life with Cleaning Lady. Kurt Bartsch, *German.* CEEP, *tr. by* Wayne Kvam

Still must I hear?—shall hoarse Fitzgerald bawl. English Bards and Scotch Reviewers. Byron.

Still night. The old clock Ticks. Last Night in Calcutta. Allen Ginsberg. FTOS; NoAM

Still Night Thoughts. Li Po, *Chinese.* CoBCP; TTTS, *tr. by* Burton Watson

Still on my cheeks I feel their fondling breath. Stanzas on Mutability. Hugo von Hofmannsthal, *German.* AWP; TrJP, *tr. by* Jethro Bithell

Still, passed through the spokes of an old wheel, on and around. Reincarnation (I) ['Still, passed through the spokes of an old wheel, on and around"]. James Dickey. HoPM

Still Poem 9. Philip Lamantia. NeAP

Still Pond, No More Moving. Howard Moss. NYBP

Still pressing through these weeping solitudes. Frederick Goddard Tuckerman. NOBA *Fr.* Sonnets.

Still round thy towers descend the fertile rain! Cordova. Ibn Zaydun, *Arabic.* AWP, *tr. by* H. A. R. Gibb

Still salt pool locked in with bars of sand, A. Lincolnshire Shores. Tennyson. *Fr.* The Palace of Art. EnVR; NOBRP

Still Shines When You Think of It. Vincent O'Sullivan. PeNZ

Still sits the school-house by the road. In School-Days. John Greenleaf Whittier. BLPA; FaBoBe; OBCA

Still small voice unto, The. A Successful Summer. David Schubert. ChIV-1

Still. . . some echo. Elizabeth Searle Lamb. HA

Still south I went and west and south again. Prelude. John Millington Synge. AWP; IIP; MoBrPo; OBMV

Still sparkles here the glory of the west. M. J. Chapman. *Fr.* Barbadoes. PBCV

Still, still my eye will gaze long-fixed on thee. The Columbine. Jones Very. ColAP; GSo; NOBA; PAR

Still, Still, with Thee. Harriet Beecher Stowe. AH

Still sunlit, one tree. O. Mabson Southard. HA

Still-surviving funerall, A. (LL) Hymn to Saint Teresa. Richard Crashaw. EBEV; ESCV; GeHe; HAP; MeLP; NOSC

Still the loud death drum, thundering from afar. Eighteen Hundred and Eleven. Anna Laetitia Barbauld. NOBRP

Still the mighty mountains stand. Epilogue to Alun Mabon. John Ceiriog Hughes, *Welsh.* OBWVE, *tr. by* H. Idris Bell

Still the mind smiles at its own rebellions. Robinson Jeffers. CMoP

Still the world is wondrous large,—seven seas from marge to marge. The Wide, Wide World. Rudyard Kipling. *Fr.* In the Neolithic Age savage warfare did I wage. NOBVV

Still therefore of Thy Graces shall be my / Song's Ditty, *par. by* Sir Philip Sidney. Bible, *O.T. See* Psalm 13.

Still There's No Trace. Zim Mnotoza. PeSAV

Still to be neat, still to be dressed [*or* Drest]. Simplex Munditiis. Ben Jonson. AWP; BeJo; EBEvV; GBL; HAP; HoPM; InPS-3; NAEL-1; NOBE; NOSC; OAEL-1; OBEV; OxAEP-1; OxBSP; PRMP; PoE; Poetr; SeCP; TFi; WeW-3 *Fr.* Epicoene; or, The Silent Woman.

Still to survive in my immortal song. (LL) Sonnet 6: 'How many paltry, foolish, painted things'. Michael Drayton. AAS; AEP; EnLoPo; GBL; HAP; HeIP-4; NAEL-1; NIP-4; NOSC; OAEL-1; SCGP

Still to the full-grown plant is added care. Weeds. Virgil, *Latin.* OBCVT, *tr. by* Hoblyn, Robert

Still Trees. Momcilo Nastasijevic, *Serbo-Croatian.* HSix, *tr. by* Charles Simic

Still unable to pronounce the months. Ice Cream. Peter Wild. Poetsp

Still visioning the stars! (LL) Oriflamme. Jessie Redmond Fauset. BlSi; PoBA

Still was the night, serene and bright. Michael Wigglesworth. NAAL-3 *Fr.* The Day of Doom. NAAL-1; SCAP

("This was their song, their cups among, / the evening before.") (LL) ColAP

Still waters of the air, The. Variations. Federico García Lorca, *Spanish.* PiM, *tr. by* Lysander Kemp

Still young and fine! but what is still in view. The Rainbow. Henry Vaughan. GeHe

Still your people and mine were tearing each other to pieces when we. Letter to the Actor Charles Laughton concerning the Work on the Play "The Life of Galileo." Bertolt Brecht, *German.* PoSu, *tr. by* Michael Hamburger

Stillborn [*or* Still-born] Silence! thou that art. Invocation of Silence. Richard Flecknoe. NOSC

Stilled room to which I am called, A. The Call. Dennis Haskell. NOBAu

Stillness. Exclamation. Octavio Paz, *Spanish.* ChAP, *tr. by* Eliot Weinberger

Stillness. James Elroy Flecker. CH; MoBrPo

Stillness is highest act. The Seventh Day. James McAuley. BMAP *Fr.* The Seven Days of Creation.

Stillness of dawn, The. J. W. Hackett. HA

Stillness of the jungle, The. The Stillness of the Poem. Ron Loewinsohn. NeAP; PoM

Stillness of the Poem, The. Ron Loewinsohn. NeAP; PoM

Stillness of the rose, The. The Rose. William Carlos Williams. NOBA

Stillness, / of the wood, The. The Figures. Robert Creeley. UnPo

Stillness, the Dancing, The. Linda Bierds. NAmP90

Stimulus beyond the Grave, The. Emily Dickinson. OxBSP

Stincher, The. Jackie Kay. NOxBChV

Stingier your suppers, The. Karl Marx. Alfred M. Lee. AmPA

Stinging / gold swarms. Sunset. E. E. Cummings. MoAmPo

Stingo! to thy bar-room skip. Anacreontic to Flip. Royall Tyler. OBAL

Stink and are thrown away. End fair enough. (LL) On Spies. Ben Jonson. BeJo; FaBoVe; NoP-4; OxBSP

Stippled Orion on the midnight blue. Frederick Goddard Tuckerman. *See* Sonnets: "The Starry flower, the flower-like stars that fade."

Stir not the sand too much, for there lies Stuyvesant. Epitaph for Peter Stuyvesant. Henricus Selyns. SCAP

Stir of the world, the music of the mountain, The. (LL) Fawn's Foster-Mother. Robinson Jeffers. MoP; NOBA; NoAM

Stir the holy grains, set. Denise Levertov. APAD *Fr.* Matins.

Stirling's Hotel. *Unknown.* AmFP

Stirring as among / cattle, A. Snow. David Malouf. CBAP

Stirring of a feathering cloud, The. Nature's Minor Chords. Henrietta Cordelia Ray. CBWP-3

Stirring the red: a single boat. Tune: "Charm of Nien-nu." Chiang K'uei, *Chinese.* SuSp, *tr. by* James J. Y. Liu

Stirs its ashes and embers, its burnt sticks. Old Age Gets Up. Ted Hughes. NoAM

Stirs the Culprit—Life! (LL) Surgeons must be very careful. Emily Dickinson. MeMAP; SAmP; TAP

Stitch in the side. Want of

&$ Want of —+. Anne Szumigalski. FaBoWP

Stock of man, the Root, the body, Boughs, The. Boetius. Libr. 3. Metr. 6. Boethius, *Latin.* OBCVT, *tr. by* Phineas Fletcher

Stockdoves, The. Andrew Young. FaBoTC

Stocking Up. Sylvia Kantaris. LW

Stockpiling of frozen trees, The. Jayne Cortez. NMM-2

Stocky woman at the door, The. The Last Day and the First. Theodore Weiss. TwCP; VGW

Stoic. Lawrence Durrell. NYBP

Stoker, The. Shin Shalom, *Hebrew.* MHP, *tr. by* Ruth Finer Mintz

Stoklewath; or, the Cumbrian Village. Susanna Blamire.

"From where dark clouds of curling smoke arise." ECWP; NOEC

Stolen Away. Joseph Ceravolo. FTOS

Stolen Child, The. W. B. Yeats. CMoP; NAEL-2; NoP-4

Stolen Heart, The. Rimbaud, *French.* NNPT, *tr. by* Wallace Fowlie

Stolen Kiss, The. Robert Dodsley. ECEV

Stolen Pleasure. William Drummond, of Hawthornden. EnLoPo

Stolen White Girl, The. John Rollin Ridge. PAR; PaTW

("Let Happiness smile, as she wings their sweet dreams.") (LL) APN-2

Stomach. Kathleen Norris. OBAL

Stomach of goat, crushed. Salami. Philip Levine. NNaP; NOBA; TAP; TRP

Stomp of feet, A bevy of swift hands, A. (LL) Woman Me. Maya Angelou. BlSi; OxWW

"Stond well, moder, under Rode." *Unknown.* MiEL

Stond who so list upon the Slipper toppe. Seneca. *See* Senec. Traged. ex Thyeste Chor. 2.

Stone, A. Yves Bonnefoy, *French.* VCWP, *tr. by* John Naughton

Stone, The. Walter De la Mare. WeW-3

Stone. Luchezar Elenkov, *Bulgarian.* CEEP, *tr. by* Jascha Kessler *and* Aleksandar Shurbanov

Stone. Donald Justice. CRP *Fr.* Things.

Stone. Mark McWatt. HCP

Stone, The. Henry Vaughan. ChIV-1

Stone, The. Thomas Vaughan. OBWVE

Stone and Ashes. Husein Tahmisic, *Serbian.* CEEP, *tr. by* Ewald Osers

Stone and Light. Tanikawa Shuntaro, *Japanese.* VCWP, *tr. by* Harold Wright

Stone at dawn, A. Easter Morning. Amy Clampitt. ChIV-2

Stone at the Bottom, The. Manuel Ulacia, *Spanish.* VCWP, *tr. by* Reginald Gibbons

Stone Bridge, The. Shen Chou, *Chinese.*
   "South of the Bridge." CoBLCP, *tr. by* Jonathan Chaves

Stone, bronze, stone, steel, stone, oakleaves, horses' heels. Triumphal March. T. S. Eliot. OBWP *Fr.* Coriolan.

Stone Buddha (two poems). Ōkuma Nobuyuki, *Japanese.* MJT, *tr. by* Makoto Ueda

Stone Castle Music. *Unknown, Chinese.* CoBCP, *tr. by* Burton Watson

Stone cliffs, no clouds. Early Summer in the Year Jen-tzu (1672)—Playfully Painted in the Manner of Ts'ao Yün-hsi. Yün Shou-p'ing, *Chinese.* CoBLCP, *tr. by* Jonathan Chaves

Stone / cold / daylight. Poem for Etheridge. Sonia Sanchez. BPo

Stone cries from the wall, The. Epitaph. *Unknown.* TrJP

Stone-cutters fighting time with marble, you foredefeated. To the Stone-Cutters. Robinson Jeffers. AmPP; ColAP; MoAmPo; NAAL-2; NOBA; NoP-4; OxBA; PoRA

Stone doesn't repel the light, The. Stone and Light. Tanikawa Shuntaro, *Japanese.* VCWP, *tr. by* Harold Wright

Stone Dolphin, The. Fay Zwicky. BMAP *Fr.* Three Songs of Love and Hate.

Stone Fish Lake. Yüan Chieh, *Chinese.* ChiP, *tr. by* Arthur Waley

Stone-flake and salmon. Gary Snyder. *Fr.* Burning. NeAP; PoM *Fr.* Myths and Texts.

Stone For A Statue. Sarah Morgan Bryan Piatt. NCAP

Stone found me in bright sunlight, The. Paul Blackburn. NYBP

Stone Gentleman, The. James Reeves. OxBSP

Stone Giant. Joseph Bruchac. CDW

Stone goes straight, The. Washington Monument by Night. Carl Sandburg. CMoP; ImGa

Stone gullets among. May Swenson. VCAP

Stone Hammer Poem. Robert Kroetsch. NOBC

Stone Horse Shoals. Malcolm Cowley. NYBP

Stone Idol, The. Ivan Alekseievich Bunin, *Russian.* TCRP, *tr. by* Simon Franklin

Stone Knife, A. James Schuyler. FTOS

Stone. Love this man. (LL) The Distances. Charles Olson. NAAL-2; NeAP

Stone Man Peak. Chao Meng-fu. *Fr.* Twenty-Eight Poems Inscribed on T'ien-kuan Mountain. CoBLCP, *tr. by* Jonathan Chaves

Stone-masons give stones dreams to dream. Stone-masons, My Father, and Me. Namdeo Dhasal, *Marathi.* OMIP, *tr. by* Vinay Dharwadker

Stone-masons, My Father, and Me. Namdeo Dhasal, *Marathi.* OMIP, *tr. by* Vinay Dharwadker

Stone of Megakles who's dead, The. Simonides, *Greek.* GrAn, *tr. by* Peter Jay

Stone says that it covers here the white dog, The. Tymnes. HePo *Fr.* Epigrams.

Stone strikes the body, because, The. A Parable. Gregory Orr. WeT

Stone turns over slowly, The. A Fit against the Country. James Wright. WeT

Stone Wall and Celebration. János Pilinszky, *Hungarian.* PoSu, *tr. by* Peter Jay

Stone, who was his father that lies beneath you? Hektor of Troy. Archias of Macedon, *Greek.* GrAn, *tr. by* Dudley Fitts

Stone within stone, and man, where was he? Pablo Neruda. VCWP, *tr. by* Nathaniel Tarn *Fr.* The Heights of Macchu Picchu.

Stonebridge Park Estate. Pauline Melville. HCP

Stoned & / singing Indian scat. A River Still To Be Found. Lawrence Ferlinghetti. BB

Stoned cheek turned again. March. Roy McFadden. TIRV

Stonemason, stonemason, in your white apron. Valery Yakovlevich Bryusov, *Russian.* TCRP, *tr. by* April FitzLyon

Stonemason wanted. . . he dared to want, A. Tomb of the Imagination. Miguel Hernández, *Spanish.* AF, *tr. by* Tom Jones

Stones, The. Sylvia Plath. CAPP-1

Stones. Charles Hamilton Sorley. NSI

Stones (a miracle to mortal view), The. Ovid. OBVE, *tr. by* Dryden *Fr.* Metamorphoses.

Stones and Snow. Homer. OBVE, *tr. by* Alexander Pope *Fr.* The Iliad.

Stones in Jordan's stream, The. William Jeffrey. OxBS

Stones must form a circle first not a wall. First Rule. Maurice Kenny. HATNAP

Stones of Rome to rise and mutiny, The. (LL) Mark Antony Addresses the Mob. Shakespeare. EBEvV; FaPoR

Stones of Time, The. Kenneth Koch. NoAM *Fr.* Days and Nights.

Stones only, the disjecta membra° of this. Derek Walcott. *See* Ruins of a Great House.

Stones only, the disjecta membra of this Great House. Ruins of a Great House. Derek Walcott. TwCP

Stones watch the sea like cats: the stone of sleep. The Desire to be in Two Places at Once. Charles Henri Ford. PC

Stones Where the Haft Rotted, The. Meng Chiao, *Chinese.* PLT, *tr. by* A. C. Graham

Stonewall Jackson. Herman Melville. NCAP

Stoney Ridge Dance Hall. Alden Nowlan. MoCV

Stony Grey Soil. Patrick Kavanagh. CIP-2

Stony Lonesome. Langston Hughes. NOBA; SAmP

Stony rock of death's insensibility, The. Tired Memory. Coventry Patmore. EnVR *Fr.* The Unknown Eros.

Stood, at the closed door. Prelude LII. Conrad Potter Aiken. LiTM *Fr.* Preludes for Memnon; or, Preludes to Attitude.

Stood off shrouded in his loneliness. (LL) Watchmaker God. Robert Lowell. HCAP; SoSe-8

Stood on the top of a spur once. Still Shines When You Think of It. Vincent O'Sullivan. PeNZ

Stood there then among. Stars. Robert Earl Hayden. LCAP-2

Stood watching the boat disappear on the black waters of Lethe? (LL) A Supermarket in California. Allen Ginsberg. AmPP; CoAP; FaBoA; HAP; HCAP; HeIP-4; InPK-6; InPS-3; LiTM; NAAL-2; NOBA; NeAP; NoAM; PBMP; PmAP; PoM; SAGP; TAP; TFi; TwCP; UnPo; WeW-3

Stool Ball. *Unknown.* CH

Stoop, and begin the ancient croaking. (LL) The Poets Agree to Be Quiet by the Swamp. David Wagoner. CoAP; VGW

Stoop on the log-house is brown with sweet rain-rot, The. Joan Finnigan. WPE *Fr.* May Day Rounds: Renfrew County.

Stop. Richard Wilbur. LCAP-2

Stop All the Clocks, Cut Off the Telephone. W. H. Auden. MoBrPo; RB

Stop all the clocks, cut off the telephone. Song. W. H. Auden. MoBrPo; OPOU; RB; SAGP *Fr.* Twelve Songs.

Stop. Along this path, in phrases of light. Plainsong. Carol Ann Duffy. FaBoTC

Stop bleeding said the knife. Bleeding. May Swenson. NALW

Stop, Christian passer-by!—Stop, child of God. Epitaph. Coleridge. CH; NAEL-2; NOCV; OAEL-2; PeECV

"Stop!" cried the Knight. "No more of this, good sir!" The Nun's Priest's Prologue. Chaucer. NAWM-1 *Fr.* The Canterbury Tales.

Stop! Don't touch me. *Unknown, Spanish.* BoWoP, *tr. by* Willis Barnstone

Stop Fooling. Velemir Khlebnikov, *Russian.* TCRP, *tr. by* Gary Kern

Stop for a moment, driver. Let's Get the Coachman Drunk. Vesna Parun, *Croatian.* CEEP, *tr. by* Peter Kastmiler

Stop! for thy tread is on an empire's dust! Byron. InPS-3 *Fr.* Childe Harold's Pilgrimage.

Stop!—Gaze thro' this hushed gallery! The air. Benjamin Paul Blood. APN-2 *Fr.* The Bride of the Iconoclasts.

Stop, let me have the truth of that! Dîs Aliter Visum; or, Le Byron de Nos Jours. Robert Browning. CBLP; NAEL-2

STOP LOOK LISTEN / as gate stripes swing down. Crossing. Philip Booth. GM

Stop, my Augustine, stop: ere you will God explain. To St. Augustine. "Angelus Silesius." GePo, *tr. by* George C. Schoolfield *Fr.* The Cherubical Wanderer.

Stop singing motley tales of broken love. Against Tunes in a Minor Key. Nam Trân, *Vietnamese.* AVP, *tr. by* Huỳnh Sanh Thông.

Stop, stop and listen for the bough top. The Blackbird of Derrycairn. *Unknown, Irish.* BIrV, *tr. by* Austin Clarke

Stop that Alabama bus I don't wanna ride. Alabama Bus. William Hairston. FaBoPV

Stop you my mouth with still still kissing me. (LL) Sonnet 81: "O kiss, which dost those ruddy gems impart." Sir Philip Sidney. NAEL-1; PBRV; Son

Stopless wind, here are the columbine seeds I have. Of Forced Sightes and Trusty Ferefulness. Jorie Graham. PoPoPo

Stoplights edged the licorice street with ribbon. Leap in the Dark. Roberta Hill Whiteman. WPOW

Stopover. Sarah Kirsch, *German.* CEEP, *tr. by* Wayne Kvam

Stopped feet. He reached, and wound the clock. (LL) Original Sequence. Philip Booth. ChIV-1; KSG

Stopping at a Friend's Farm. Meng Hao Jan, *Chinese.* SuSp, *tr. by* Daniel Bryant

("My old friend prepared a chicken with millet.") FP, *tr. by* Innes Herdan

("To enjoy your chrysanthemums.") (LL) FP, *tr. by* Innes Herdan

Stopping at an otel with an Ibernian. Dropping Your Aitches. Joseph Warren Beach. NYBP

Stopping by Shadows. Robin Fulton. FaBoTC

Stopping by Woods on a Snowy Evening. Robert Frost. AmPP; CMoP; ChAP; ClHu; ColAP; FaBoCh; HAP; HeIP-4; HoPM; ImGa; ImPo; InPK-6; InPS-3; LiTM; MeMAP; MoAmPo; MoP; NAAL-2; NIP-4; NOBA; NTCP; NTP; NoAM; NoP-4; OBCA; OxBA; PFE; PoE; PoPoPo; PoRA; Poetr; RB; SAGP; SAmP; SCV; SoSe-8; TAP; TFi; TOF; TRP; TTTS

Stopping on a Journey at the East Water Pavilion at Lo-ch'eng. Meng Chiao, *Chinese.* PLT, *tr. by* A. C. Graham

Stopping the diary. Forget What Did. Philip Larkin. NoAM

Stopping the Night at Jung-yang. Po Chü-i, *Chinese.* ChiP, *tr. by* Arthur Waley

Stopping to Take Notes. Michael Smith. PBCIP

Stopping Wine. T'ao Ch'ien, *Chinese.* CoBCP, *tr. by* Burton Watson

Stopwatch and an Ordnance Map, A. Stephen Spender. MoBS

Stores and filling stations prefer a roof. Christmas Tree. Stanley Cook. OBCP

Stores lit up with their goods, The. (LL) The Dream. David Ignatow. CoAP; NNaP

Stories. J. Patrick Lewis. NOxBChV

Stories and Poems. Susan Griffin. CrSp

Stories have it that when the rebels. Ganaderia. Ricardo Pau-Llosa. CMAP

Stories of Snow. Patricia K. Page. NOBC; NoP-4; PoA

Stories / would be braided in my hair, The. Story Keeper. Wendy Rose. UnSA

Stork questioned the swan whose moving song, The. Aria Senza da Capo. Robert Finch. MoCV

Storks are coming now—, The. Spirit of the Wind. Gabriel Okara. PBMAP

Storks like elbows had a fit of falling, The. There's No Place to Sleep in This Bed, Tanguy. Charles Henri Ford. SPE

Storm, The. Alcaeus, *Greek.* AWP, *tr. by* John Hermann Merivale

Storm, The. Elizabeth Jane Coatsworth. OBCA

Storm, The. Sara Coleridge. NOxBChV

Storm, The. Walter De la Mare. NOxBChV; NTP

Storm[e], The. Donne. NoSic

("That though thine absence sterve me, I wish not thee.") (LL) OxBoS

Storm at Sea, A. NOBE

Storm, The. Heinrich Heine, *German.* AWP, *tr. by* Louis Untermeyer

Storm. Helga Marie Heinze, *German.* CEEP, *tr. by* Katherine Bradley

Storm, The. George Herbert. ESCV

Storm. Roger McGough. OTCP

Storm. Agnes Nemes Nagy, *Hungarian.* CEEP; PBWP, *tr. by* Laura Schiff

Storm, The. Nguyễn Đình Chiểu, *Vietnamese.* AVP, *tr. by* Huỳnh Sanh Thông

Storm, The. Coventry Patmore. EnLoPo

Storm, The. Margaret Stanley-Wrench. LW

Storm. James Tate. WeT

Storm, The. Henry Vaughan. ESCV

Storm, The. Robert Wallace. NYBP

Storm, The. John Greenleaf Whittier. *See* Snow-Bound [*or* Snow-Bound; a Winter Idyl].

Storm. Judith Wright. WPE

Storm and Calm: Sent from Embden to M. Edw. Ma. and M. Tho. Ly, The. Nicholas Murford. NOSC

Storm at Sea, A. Donne. NOBE *Fr.* The Storm[e]. NoSic; OxBoS

Storm at Sea: Sometimes I plunge through the press of waves. Cynewulf. ASW, *tr. by* Kevin Crossley-Holland *Fr.* Riddles (Exeter Book).

Storm-Beaten. Clara Ann Thompson. CBWP-2

Storm-beaten old watch-tower, A. Symbols. W. B. Yeats. OBMV

Storm blew in last night and knocked out, A. The Window. Raymond Carver. BLT

Storm blew up so suddenly, The. In Rough Weather. Paul Lake. RA

Storm Chasers, The. William Olsen. PUP-20

Storm clouds a smudge of damson. Tony Baker. NBrP

Storm-Cock's Song, The. "Hugh MacDiarmid." OxBTC

Storm Cone, The. Rudyard Kipling. NoAM; OxBTC

Storm cries every night, The. Spring Song. Hermann Hesse, *German.* AWP, *tr. by* Ludwig Lewisohn

Storm-dances of gulls, the barking game of seals, The. Divinely Superfluous Beauty. Robinson Jeffers. HeIP-4; MoAmPo

Storm Fear. Robert Frost. CMoP; ColAP; OxBA; SAGP

Storm from the East, A. Reed Whittemore. NYBP

Storm has passed, The. The Calm after the Storm. Giacomo Leopardi. ItIP

Storm hath ceased: yet still I have, The. The Ghona Widow's Lullaby. Thomas Pringle. PeSAV

Storm high. Rosellen Brown. FFC

Storm House, The. Elizabeth Jennings. WPE

Storm in Summer, A. Wilfrid Scawen Blunt. FaBoTw

Storm in the Black Forest. D. H. Lawrence. FaBoVe

Storm is over, the land hushes to rest, The. Robert Bridges. GTBS-P; LiTM; OBMV

Storm is sweeping o'er the land, The. A Wild Night. Julia Ward Howe. ColAP

Storm not, brave Friend, that thou hast never yet. To Scilla. Sir Charles Sedley. FaBoEE

Storm of Love, A. Hilary Corke. NYBP

Storm Pattern. Greg Pape. PBCAP

Storm splattering the tough magnolia, The. Eugenio Montale, *Italian.* AF, *tr. by* William Arrowsmith

Storm was coming, that was why it was dark, A. Sudden Things. Donald Hall. SPE

Storm-Wind, The. William Barnes. NOBE

Storm Windows. Howard Nemerov. CoAmPo; InPK-6; VCAP

Storm winds carry snow. Deer Song. Leslie Marmon Silko. VoR

Stormalong! *Unknown.* FaBoVe

Stormed at with shot and shell. Tennyson. Poetr *Fr.* The Charge of the Light Brigade. APAD; BLPA; CABP; CTV; ChAP; EBEvV; EnVR; FHYEP; FaBoBe; FaPoR; HoPM; NAEL-2; NOBVV; NoP-4; OBWP; OxAEP-2; PBMP; PeVV; TFi; UV

Stormeys' dead that good old man—. Stormalong! *Unknown.* FaBoVe

Storms. Dean Young. NAmP90

Storms are past, the [*or* these] clouds are overblown, The. Bonum Est Mihi Quod Humiliasti Me. Henry Howard, Earl of Surrey. SiPS

Storms lend you wings, destroyer of the lands. Inanna and Enlil. Enheduanna, *Sumerian.* BoWoP, *ad. by* Aliki *and* Willis Barnstone

Stormy are the waters of Waiapu. The Waters of Waiapu. Paraire Henare Tomoana, *Maori.* PeNZ, *tr. by* Margaret Orbell

Stormy Hebrides, The. William Collins. NOBE *Fr.* An Ode on the Popular Superstitions of the Highlands of Scotland. NOEC; OAEL-1; OxAEP-1

Stormy Night. William Robert Rodgers. PNI

Stormy Night in Autumn. Chu Shu-chen, *Chinese.* BoWoP; OHPC, *tr. by* Kenneth Rexroth

Stormy Scenes of Winter, The. *Unknown.* AmFP

Stornelli and Strambotti. Agnes Mary Frances Robinson. VWP

Story, A. Margaret Avison. MoCV

Story. John Balaban. CDa

Story, The. Kevin Hart. BMAP

Story, A. Jane Hirshfield. BLT

Story, A. Jean Ingelow. VWP

Story, A. Li-Young Lee. IFJA; LoL; RaBo

Story. Larry Levis. CMAP

Story, A. Susan Mitchell. WWSi

Story, The. Dan Pagis, *Hebrew.* PoSu, *tr. by* Stephen Mitchell

Story, a story!, A. Rowing. Anne Sexton. BoWoP; LCAP-2

Story, a story, a story anon, A. The Bishop of Canterbury. *Unknown.* AmFP

Story About Chicken Soup, A. Louis Simpson. NNaP; PoE; PoWW; TAP; UnSA

Story about Indians, A. The Climate of Paradise. Louis Simpson. NOBA

Story about the Body, A. Robert Hass. NAmP90; RaBo

Story Books on a Kitchen Table. Audre Lorde.

("For the vanished mother / of a Black girl.") (LL) GT

Story I Like to Tell, The. Robin Becker. PBCAP

Story I shall tell today, The. The Nightingale. Marie de France, *French.* BoWoP, *tr. by* Patricia Terry

Story is true, The. (LL) Bresson's Movies. Robert Creeley. NoP-4; PmAP

Story Keeper. Wendy Rose. UnSA

Story of a Hotel Room. Rosemary Tonks. APAD; LW; OxBTC

Story of a Story, The. Vasco [*or* Vasko] Popa, *Serbo-Croatian.* CBNP, *tr. by* Anne Pennington

Story of a Well-made Shield, The. N. Scott Momaday. CDW; HATNAP

Story of Canobie Dick, The. Libby Houston. OBSP
Story of Cephisa, The. Ovid, *Latin.*
　"While thus to unknown pow'rs *Cephisa* pray'd." OBCVT, *tr.* by John Gay
Story of Fidgety Philip, The. Heinrich Hoffmann, *German.* ACTP; OxBChV
Story of Frankie. . . My Man, The. Archie Weller. BMAP
Story of How a Wall Stands, A. Simon J. Ortiz. HATNAP
Story of Inkle and Yarico, The. Frances Seymour, Countess of Hertford. ECWP
Story of Joshua. Alicia Ostriker. ChIV-1
Story of Life, The. John Godfrey Saxe. PoToHe
Story of Lovers Leap, The. Maggie Pogue Johnson. CBWP-4
Story of Lucretia out of Ovid de Fastis. / Book II, The. Ovid. OBCVT, *tr.* by Thomas Creech *Fr.* Fasti (Roman Feast-Days).
Story of My Life, The. Liz Rosenberg. PBCAP
Story of Our Lives, The. Mark Strand. VCAP
Story of Phoebus and Daphne Applied, [etc.], The. Edmund Waller. NAEL-1; NOSC
　("He catcht at love, and fill'd his arm with bayes.") (LL) PBRV
　(Story of Phœbus and Daphne appli'd, The.) PBRV
　(*Thirsis* a youth of the inspired train.) PBRV
Story of Prince Agib, The. Sir William Schwenck Gilbert. CBNP
Story of replacement, The. (LL) 35/10. Sharon Olds. CrSp; MDDM; SAGP
Story of Rimini, The. Leigh Hunt. OBGa
　"One day—'twas on a gentle, autumn noon." NOBRP
Story of Sigurd the Volsung, The. William Morris.
　Sigurd Rideth to the Glittering Heath. PoEL-5
Story of the Ashes and the Flame, The. E. A. Robinson. MeMAP
Story of the Gadsbys, The. Rudyard Kipling.
　Winners, The. BLPA; FaPoR
　(L'Envoi: "What is the moral? Who rides may read.") MoBrPo
Story of the Zeros, The. Victor Hernandez Cruz. PoBA
Story of Uriah, The. Rudyard Kipling. NOBVV; PeVV; SCV
Story So Far, The. John Clarke. UV
Story That Could Be True, A. William Stafford. KaS; NTCP; RaBo
Story We Know, The. Martha Collins. SoSe-8
Storys to rede ar delitabill. John Barbour. OxBS *Fr.* The Bruce.
Storytime. Judith Nicholls. OBSP
Stove. Philip Booth. FYAP
Stove was grey, the coal was gone, The. Into Laddery Street. Laura Riding Jackson. *Fr.* Forgotten Girlhood. RB
Stow, birde, stow, stow! John Skelton. NoSic *Fr.* Magnificence.
Stowaway in a fold. The Witnesses. X. J. Kennedy. PChr
Stowe, the Gardens of the Rt. Hon. Richard Lord Viscount Cobham. Gilbert West. OBGa
Stowed away in a Montreal lumber room. O God! O Montreal! Samuel Butler. OBSV; OxBoLi; PeLV
Stown Bairn, The. Lewis Spence. FaBoTC
Straggled soldier halted—stared at Him, The. Christ and the Soldier. Siegfried Sassoon. NoP-4
Strahan, Tonson, Lintot of the times. To Mr. Murray. Byron. UV
Straight as a nun I sit. Señora X No More. Pat Mora. UnSA
Straight from the east the wind blows sharp with rain. April in Town. Lizette Woodworth Reese. APN-2
Straight-jacketing sprang to every lock. Austin Clarke. CMoP *Fr.* Mnemosyne Lay in Dust.
Straight out of the blue. Pigeon of My Childhood. Sergey Aleksandrovich Vasilyev, *Russian.* TCRP, *tr.* by Lubov Yakovleva *and* Max Hayward
Straight rye whiskey, 100 proof. Brooklyn Narcissus. Paul Blackburn. PmAP
Straight Seeking. Anthony McNeill. HCP
Straight Talk from Plain Women. Sherley Anne Williams. GT
Straight, the swift, the debonair, The. Magnets. Countee Cullen. PBMP
Straight up away from this road. Achieving Perspective. Pattiann Rogers. MT
Straight up from the mountain. Because the Moon Comes. Richard Shelton. PaTW
Straining at the padlock. Jack Kerouac. HA
Strand, The. Michael Longley. IIP
Strand at Lough Beg, The. Seamus Heaney. CIP-2; NoAM; OBWP
Strand Hotel, Rosslare, The. James Liddy. CIP-2
Strand-Thistle. Gustav Falke, *German.* AWP, *tr.* by Jethro Bithell
Stranded ashore from the sea. Archilochus, *Greek.* OBCVT, *tr.* by Michael Ayrton
Stranded in My Ontario. Ronald G. Everson. NOBC

Stranded on the moon. Moon-Man. Dorothy Hewett. CBAP
Stranded Whales, The. Geoffrey Dutton. CBAP
Strange. Kirby Doyle. NeAP
Strange. To a Fair Lady Playing with a Snake. Edmund Waller. CABP; CBLP; EBEV; HoPM; NOSC; PoE; PoEL-3
Strange Adventure. Rossana Ombres, *Italian.* NeIt, *tr.* by Ruth Feldman
Strange and slow work: they dig in turn. The Well. Philip Salom. NOBAu
Strange and unnatural! lets stay and see. Destinie. Abraham Cowley. MeLP
Strange are the feelings arising within me. The Love of Hell. Abraham Burstein. TrJP
Strange are the paths of mankind in the night. Revelation and Decline. Georg Trakl, *German.* PFTM, *tr.* by Keith Waldrop
Strange arrangement to comfort the heart—, A. Fragrant Hands. Faiz Ahmad Faiz, *Urdu.* VCWP, *tr.* by Agha Shahid Ali
Strange—as I sat brooding here. Lucy. Walter De la Mare. CMoP
Strange, beautiful girl, A. By T'ing Yang Waterfall. Hsieh Ling-yün, *Chinese.* OHMPC, *tr.* by Kenneth Rexroth
Strange beautiful woman, A. Marilyn Nelson Waniek. NMM-2
Strange beauty, eight-limbed and eight-handed. Octopus. Arthur Clement Hilton. BXAP; UV
Strange bed, whose recurrent dream we are, The. Hotel de l'Univers et Portugal. James Merrill. PoA
Strange Bird, A. Michael Dransfield. BMAP
Strange, bright dancers, the. Poppies. P. A. Ropes. BoTP
Strange Business. Jelaluddin Rumi, *Persian.* LoL, *tr.* by Coleman Barks
Strange but true is the story. The Sea-Turtle and the Shark. Melvin Beaunearus Tolson. PoBA *Fr.* Harlem Gallery.
Strange Case of Mr. Ormantude's Bride, The. Ogden Nash. OxBM
Strange church smelled a bit 'high,' of censers, The. Geoffrey Hill. PoE *Fr.* Mercian Hymns.
Strange fits of passion have I known. Lucy. Wordsworth. EBEV; GBL; GLoP; NAEL-2; NOBE; NOBRP; OAEL-2; OBEV; OBNC; PFE; PoE *Fr.* Lucy. FHYEP; NOBE; OAEL-2; OBEV; OBNC; SCGP; TFi
Strange Fits of Passion Have I Known. Wordsworth. EBEV; GBL; NAEL-2; NOBE; OAEL-2; OBEV; OBNC; PoE
Strange Fruit. Joy Harjo. SeSe
Strange grows the river on the sunless evenings! Vesperal. Ernest Christopher Dowson. OBMV
Strange Hells. Ivor Gurney. OxBTC; PeFWW
Strange House, The. Thomas Hardy. OxBSn
Strange Hurt. Langston Hughes. GT
Strange Legacies. Sterling Brown. PoBA; TTY
Strange Love. Moses ibn Ezra, *Hebrew.* TrJP, *tr.* by Solomon Solis-Cohen
Strange Meeting. Wilfred Owen. CMoP; EBEvV; FP; FaBoMo; GTBS-P; HeIP-4; HoPM; ImPo; MoBrPo; MoP; NAEL-2; NOBE; NoAM; NoP-4; OAEL-2; OBWP; OxAEP-2; PeFWW; PoE; PoFWW; PoWW; RB; SCV; TFi
Strange Meetings. Harold Monro.
　Birth. PoA
　Flower Is Looking, A. MoBrPo
　If Suddenly a Clod of Earth. MoBrPo
Strange Monsters. Rowland Watkyns. FaBoEE
Strange New Cottage in Berkeley, A. Allen Ginsberg. BLT
Strange news! a city full? will none give way. Upon Christ His Birth. Sir John Suckling. ChIV-2
Strange now to think of you, gone without corsets & eyes. Kaddish. Allen Ginsberg. HCAP; NAAL-2; NOBA; NeAP; PmAP; PoM
Strange old man, A. Hitomaro, *Japanese.* OHPJ, *tr.* by Kenneth Rexroth
Strange Old Woman, A. Mother Goose. ReMoGo
Strange one, who are you. Strangers. Iain Crichton Smith. SpW
Strange people, we who trust—. To a Despondent Evening. Iftiqar Arif. NBrP
Strange pie that is almost a passion. A Melton Mowbray Pork Pie. Richard Le Gallienne. BXAP
Strange Power! I trust thy might; trust thou my constancy. (LL) The Visionary. Emily Jane Brontë. BrRo; CH; NOBE; NOBVV; OBNC; PBWP; SCGP; SCV
Strange power of song! the strain that warms the heart. From The Slave Trade. Hannah More. NoP-4 *Fr.* The Slave Trade.
Strange race of critics, A. Antiphanes, *Greek.* InMo, *tr.* by Sam Hamill
Strange room, from this angle. The Soho Hospital for Women. Fleur Adcock. NoP-4
Strange spirit with inky hair. The Lion. Walter James Turner. MoBrPo
Strange, / Strange, / Is the little old man. Alone in the Grange. Gregory Harrison. FuFo
Strange Talk. L. E. Yates. BoTP
Strange Tears. Liu Ya-tzu, *Chinese.* SuSp, *tr.* by Wu-chi Liu

Strange Thanksgiving. Tess Gallagher. NAmP90

Strange that I did not know him then. An Old Story. E. A. Robinson. MoAmPo; OxBSP

Strange, that I felt so gay. Tennyson. *Fr.* Maud [A Monodrama]. EnVR

Strange that I should have grown so suddenly blind. (LL) The Book of Wisdom. Stephen Crane. HoPM; MoAmPo

Strange that in "crimes of passion" what results. Love and Murder. Roy Fuller. CBLP

Strange / That in this nigger place. Esthete in Harlem. Langston Hughes. BPo; ColAP

Strange that your image should occur to me. The Grudge. Dimitris Tsaloumas. BMAP

Strange the Formation of the *Eely* Race. The Loves of the Eel. Oppian. APo, *tr. by* William Diaper *Fr.* Halieutica.

Strange the formation of the eely race. The Sex-life of Fish. William Diaper. ECEV; NOEC; OBVE *Fr.* Halieutica.

Strange things hangs by man's hip, A. Three Riddles from *The Exeter Book.* Cynewulf. PeLV, *tr. by* Kevin Crossley-Holland *Fr.* Riddles (Exeter Book).

Strange to be torn away from your embrace. Stanley Burnshaw. TrJP

Strange to behold, unmingled with surprize. On the Civilization of the Western Aboriginal Country. Philip Freneau. APN-1; PaTW

Strange to step straight into the beautiful dawn. Miraculous Dawn. R. Williams Parry, *Welsh.* OBWVE, *tr. by* Joseph P. Clancy

Strange Type. Malcolm Lowry. NoP-4

Strange Visitor, The. *Unknown.* FaBoCh

Strange Western town at the round edge of night. Western Town. Karl Shapiro. NYBP

Strangely assorted, the shape of song and the bloody man. The Military Harpist. Ruth Pitter. FaBoTw; NALW

Strangeness of Heart. Siegfried Sassoon. TrJP

Stranger, The. Aleksandr Blok, *Russian.* TCRP, *tr. by* Jon Stallworthy *and* Peter France

Stranger, A. Sandor Csoori, *Hungarian.* CEEP, *tr. by* Jascha Kessler

Stranger, The. Jean Garrigue. LiTM; NOBA; TwCP

Stranger, The. W. S. Merwin. BAP-93

Stranger, The. Aldo Palazzeschi, *Italian.* PFTM, *tr. by* Jerome Rothenberg

Stranger, The. Adrienne Rich. NNaP

Stranger, The. Rilke, *German.* FP, *tr. by* J. B. Leishman

Stranger. Elizabeth Madox Roberts. MoAmPo

Stranger, A. Edith Jay Scovell. WPN

Stranger! Approach this spot with gravity! A Dentist *Unknown.* FaBoEE; OxBoLi

Stranger arrives at her door, A. The Widow. Susan Bartels Ludvigson. MT

Stranger, beware! This terrible tomb. Philip of Thessalonica, *Greek.* GrAn, *tr. by* Edwin Morgan

Stranger by the roadside, do not smile. Epitaph of a Dog. *Unknown, Greek.* FP; GrAn, *tr. by* Dudley Fitts

Stranger came one night to Yussouf's tent, A. Yussouf. James Russell Lowell. BLPA; BoTP; FaBoBe

Stranger came to the door at eve, A. Love and a Question. Robert Frost. MoBS

Stranger could ever happen. Elizabeth Bishop. *See* In the Waiting Room.

Stranger here, as all my fathers were, A. Motet. John Amner. OxBSP

Stranger, if thou hast learned [*or* learnt] a truth which needs. Inscription for the Entrance to a Wood. William Cullen Bryant. APN-1; AmPP; OxBA; TAP

Stranger in his own element. Penguin on the Beach. Ruth Miller. PeSA

Stranger in the Pumpkin, The. John Ciardi. NTCP

Stranger in This Land, A. Cliff Ashby. NOCV

Stranger it was never meant for, A. Mine. Frank Polite. NYBP

Stranger Not Ourselves, The. William Stafford. NNaP

Stranger passing, A. Alan Pizzarelli. HA

Stranger! Tell the people of Spoon River two things. Unknown Soldiers. Edgar Lee Masters. NoAM; TAP *Fr.* The New Spoon River.

Stranger than the Worst. Babette Deutsch. WPE

Stranger, the bark you see before you says. The Yacht. Catullus. AWP; OBVE, *tr. by* John Hookham Frere *Fr.* Carmina.

Stranger to Europe, waiting release. Guy Butler. PeSAV

Stranger walks into the dark room, The. Seance. Edouard Roditi. SPE

Stranger walls, that shell no violent presence. Zimbabwe. F. D. Sinclair. PeSA

Stranger was short: let my verse be such, The. Callimachus, *Greek.* GrAn, *tr. by* Peter Jay

Stranger, when o'er yon slant, warm field no cloud. Sonnet. Anna Seward. NOBRP

Stranger, when you come to / Lakedaimon. Simonides, *Greek.* OBVE; PGA, *tr. by* Kenneth Rexroth

Stranger, whoe'er thou art, whose ling'ring feet. Sonnet Written in Tintern Abbey, Monmouthshire. Edmund Gardner. NOEC

Stranger, wond'ring, stalks, and stares upon, The. Rome, Conqueror, Conquered. Joshua Sylvester. FaBoEE

Stranger, you who hide my love. Song. Stephen Spender. FaBoTw

Strangers. Iain Crichton Smith. SpW

Strangers are people we haven't seen before. Conversations with Strangers. George Buchanan. PNI

Strangers Are We All upon the Earth. Franz Werfel, *German.* TrJP, *tr. by* Edith Abercrombie Snow

"Strangers are we and pilgrims here!" At a Friends' Meeting. Mary Elizabeth Coleridge. WPE

Stranger's heart! Oh! wound it not!, The. Felicia Dorothea Hemans. VWP

Strangers Like Us: Pittsburgh, Raleigh, 1945–1985. Gerald William Barrax. ISC

Strangers on a train. Travels with the Band-Aid Army. Lance Henson. VoR

Strangers to meek compassion's tender touch. Mary Latter. ECWP *Fr.* Soliloquies on Temporal Indigence.

Strangers! your eyes are on that valley fixed. The Field of the Grounded Arms. Fitz-Greene Halleck. PoEL-4

Strangled, The. Antonin Bartusek, *German.* CEEP, *tr. by* Ewald Osers

Stranglehold of English Lit, The. Felix Mnthali. PBMAP

Strangling women in the suburban bush. Das Kapital. Imamu Amiri Baraka. PoM

Strapped at the center of the blazing wheel. A Pilot from the Carrier. Randall Jarrell. PoWW

Strapped down, / victim in an old comic book. Notes from the Delivery Room. Linda Pastan. NMM-2

Strapped helpless, monarchs and prelates, round they swung. The Wheel of Fortune. Thom Gunn. OxBC

Strapped to my seat, I turn. Above It All. Philip Levine. NOBA

Stratton Water. D. G. Rossetti. OxBB

Straw, The. Robert Graves. OxBTC

Straw, and figures of moulded clay. Stable Straw. Robert Farren. TIRV

Straw in the street where I pass to-day. Amy Levy. VWP

Straw rustling everywhere. Clearing-Station. Wilhelm Klemm, *German.* PeFWW, *tr. by* Patrick Bridgwater

Strawberries. W. S. Merwin. NoP-4

Strawberries. Edwin Morgan. BoLoP; NoP-4

Strawberries lie in a dish of cream, The. Coloring Book. Robert Farnsworth. IFJA

Strawberries that in gardens grow. Wild Strawberries. Robert Graves. FaBoCh

Strawberry Moon. Mary Oliver. InPS-3

Strawberry Shrub, old-fashioned, quaint as quinces. Edna St. Vincent Millay. CMoP; FaBoWP

Strawberrying. Maurice Kenny. HATNAP

Strawberrying. May Swenson. VCAP

Straws like tame lightnings lie about the grass. Summer Farm. Norman MacCaig. FaBoTC; OxBTC

Stray Animals. James Tate. NoAM

Stray Dog. Charlotte Mish. PoLF

Strayed Reveller, The. Matthew Arnold. EBVVPR; OAEL-2

Strayed Reveller to Ulysses, The. OBEV

Straying Student, The. Austin Clarke. BIrV; CIP-2; NOIV

Streak of Sappho, it is said, A. Mould of Castile. Jack R. Clemo. NOCV

Streaked and fretted with effort, the thick. The Street. Robert Pinsky. NoP-4

Stream, The. Mona Van Duyn. NMM-2; VCAP

Stream and hill once swore their solemn troth, The. The Troth Between the Hill and the Stream. Tản Đà, *Vietnamese.* AVP, *tr. by* Huỳnh Sanh Thông

Stream Flowing, The. Robert Mezey. WeT

Stream flowing steadily over a stone does not wet its core, A. An Elder's Reproof to his Wife. 'Abdillaahi Muuse, *Somali.* TTY, *tr. by* B. W. Andrzejewski *and* I. M. Lewis

Stream / piles out of the pile, The. The Crossing. Paul Blackburn. NYBP

Stream ripples pure, The. By a Stream on Mount T'ien-t'ung. Wang An-shih, *Chinese.* SuSp, *tr. by* Jan W. Walls

Stream Sings to the Stone, The. Leah Goldberg. MHP, *tr. by* Ruth Finer Mintz *Fr.* Songs of the Stream.

Stream sorrow, eyes. Elegy for Her Brother Sakhr. Al-Khansa, *Arabic.* WPOW, *tr. by* Bridget Connelly; BoWoP, *tr. by* Willis Barnstone

Stream swirls. The wind moans in, The. Jade Flower Palace. Tu Fu, *Chinese.* ChiPo; OHPC, *tr. by* Kenneth Rexroth

Stream was swift, and so cold, The. Captivity. Louise Erdrich. HATNAP; NoAM

Streamed from my eyes and fell on the collar of my dress. (LL) The Pitcher. Yüan Chen, *Chinese*. ChiP, *tr*. by Arthur Waley

Streamers. Sandra McPherson. VCAP

Streamful of flowing water, A. A Spring Day—Remembering Living on the River. Kao Ch'i, *Chinese*. CoBLCP, *tr*. by Jonathan Chaves

Streams are fettered, and with us as rare, The. Thomas Shipman. NOSC *Fr*. Frost, 1654, The: To Mr. W.L.

Streams fall down and through the darkness bear, The. Spate in Winter Midnight. Norman MacCaig. GTBS-P

Streams of Bunclody, The. *Unknown*. BIrV

Streams of Lovely Nancy, The. *Unknown*. OxBoLi

Stream's Song, The. Lascelles Abercrombie. OBMV

Streekit ahint the winbreak I let. Alastair MacKie. FaBoTC *Fr*. Back-Green Odyssey.

Street. Geoffrey Fraser Dutton. FaBoTC

Street, The. James Russell Lowell. GSo; Son

Street, The. Robert Pinsky. NoP-4

Street, The. Tanka. Kondō Yoshimi, *Japanese*. MJT, *tr*. by Makoto Ueda

Street climbs upward steeply, The. Gene Baro. NYBP

Street Corner College. Kenneth Patchen. CLPP; MoAmPo

Street Cries. Sidney Lanier.
To Richard Wagner. APN-2; NCAP

Street Cries. Marjorie Welish. EOEF

Street Demonstration. Margaret Abigail Walker. BPo

Street fills slowly with the thin, The. Walkers at Dusk. Hazel Hall. NMM-2

Street Fire. Daniel Halpern. AmPA

Street in Bronzeville, A. Gwendolyn Brooks. BPo; BlSi; FaBoWP
Ballad of Chocolate Mabbie, The. CAPP-1
Hunchback Girl: She Thinks of Heaven. ChAP
Independent Man, The.
Kitchenette Building. BPo; FaBoWP; GT; NAAAL; NAAL-2; NoP-4; PoE; PoPoPo; Poetr; UnPo
("Grayed in, and gray. . . .") (LL) GT
Mother, The. CrDW; CrSp; ISC; MDDM; NAAAL; NALW; NMM-2; PoPoPo
("All.") (LL) ISC
Of De Witt Williams on His Way to Lincoln Cemetery. NOBA; NoAM
Preacher: Ruminates Behind the Sermon, The. NAAAL; PBMP
Sadie and Maud. InPK-6; MoP; NAAAL; NOBA; NoAM; TAP
Song in the Front Yard, A. NAAAL; NAAL-2; NOBA; NOxBChV; NoAM; PoBA
Southeast Corner. VGW
Vacant Lot, The. NAAAL; NAAL-2; NOBA; NoAM

Street in our town, A. The Watchmaker's Shop. *Unknown*. BoTP

Street is soon there, The. To Ride. Paul Éluard, *French*. TTTS, *tr*. by Kenneth Koch

Street lamps streaming on, and the grey. Apologues of Winter Light. Christopher Buckley. PuP-15

Street Music. Barbara Angell. AiP

Street Music. Greg Pape. PBCAP

Street Musicians. John Ashbery. HCAP; PoPoPo

Street of Named Houses, The. Robert David Cohen. NYBP

Street of Nectar, Street of Contingency. Address. Bruce Smith. Son *Fr*. In My Father's House.

Street Performers, 1851. Terence Tiller. GTBS-P

Street perturbs my mind somehow, The. Ksenya Nekrasova, *Russian*. TCRP, *tr*. by Vera Rich

Street Scene. William Ernest Henley. BoTP

Street Song. Thom Gunn. HeIP-4; OxBC

Street Song. Dame Edith Sitwell. CMoP

Street there is in Paris famous, A. The Ballad of Bouillabaisse. William Makepeace Thackeray. APAD; OBEV; OxAEP-2

Street threatened, The. The Aerial. Reiner Kunze, *German*. PoSu, *tr*. by Ewald Osers

Street was strange. Things made me wonder, The. The Tram That Lost Its Way. Nikolai Stepanovich Gumilyov, *Russian*. TCRP, *tr*. by Yakov Hornstein

Streetcar, A. Tanka. Kondō Yoshimi, *Japanese*. MJT, *tr*. by Makoto Ueda

Streetcleaner's Lament, The. Patricia Hubbell. SSCS

Streets. Henrik Nordbrandt, *Danish*. VCWP, *tr*. by Henrik Nordbrandt and Alexander Taylor

Streets. Naomi Shihab Nye. NAmP90

Streets I walk down are an incorporating of English into proscriptions, The. Monuments to the Not Yet Lived. Leonard Schwartz. PT

Streets, in a poor district. Power, The Enchanted World. George Oppen. FTOS *Fr*. Power, the Enchanted World.

Streets of Air, The. Malcolm Cowley. PoA *Fr*. Blue Juniata.

Streets of Baltimore. *Unknown*. BLPA

Streets of Laredo, The. Louis MacNeice. MoBS; OBWP

Streets of the roaring town. On a Soldier Fallen in the Philippines. William Vaughn Moody. NOBA

Streets of your glances, The. Vasco [*or* Vasko] Popa. PoSu, *tr*. by Anne Pennington *Fr*. Far Within Us.

Strength. Christopher Smart. *Fr*. A Song to David. ImPo; NAEL-1; NOBE; OAEL-1; OBWVE; PoE; PoEL-3

Strength for To-Day. *Unknown*. PWR

Strength I had to uproot hills. Song of Kai-hsia. Hsiang Chi, *Chinese*. SuSp, *tr*. by Ronald C. Miao

Strength of Fate, The. Euripides. AWP *Fr*. Alcestis.

Strength of Fields, The. James Dickey. VCAP

Strengthen, my Love, this castle of my heart. Rondel. Charles, Duc d' Orléans, *French*. AWP, *tr*. by Andrew Lang

Strengthened to live, strengthened to die for. In Distrust of Merits. Marianne Moore. ColAP; LiTM; MeMAP; MoAmPo; NAAL-2; OBWP; OxBA

Strenuous Life, The. Henry Sidgwick. OBCoV

Strephon has fashion, wit and youth. Song. Elizabeth Taylor. KTR

Strephon I saw, and started at the sight. Love's First Approach. "Ephelia." KTR

Strephon kissed me in the spring. The Look. Sara Teasdale. LW

Strephon to Celia. Mary Leapor. ECWP; RACG

Strephon. Ye Goat-herd gods, that love the grassy. Sir Philip Sidney. *See* Double Sestine [*or* Sestina].

Strephon, your breach of faith and trust. A Song. Laetitia Pilkington. LW; PEW

Stretch cast out night's long,'d, The. Lakefront, Cleveland. Russell Atkins. GT

Stretch of wall, The. The Volga Towns. Johannes Bobrowski, *German*. PoSu, *tr*. by Ruth *and* Matthew Mead

Stretch out your hands to me. Bei Dao, *Chinese*. AF, *tr*. by Bonnie S. McDougall

Stretch'd and still lies the midnight. Walt Whitman. *See* Battle of the *Bonhomme Richard* and the *Serapis*.

Stretched in the shadow of the broad beech. The Shepherd's Gratitude. Virgil. AWP, *tr*. by Charles Stuart Calverley *Fr*. Eclogues.

Stretched out on the grass. Engaged. Octavio Paz, *Spanish*. PBMP, *tr*. by Muriel Rukeyser

Stretcher Case. Siegfried Sassoon. NSI

Stretching. Robert Morgan. WeW-3

Stretching and reaching. (LL) Transplanting. Theodore Roethke. GaP

Stretching before and after. (LL) Burnt Norton. T. S. Eliot. CMoP; LiTM; MoAmPo; NAAL-2; PoE

Stretching out / from my feet. (LL) Maximus, to Himself. Charles Olson. CMoP; NOBA; NeAP; PmAP; PoE; PoM; VGW

Strew me with blossoms when I die. *Unknown*. *Fr*. Popular Songs of Tuscany. AWP, *tr*. by John Addington Symonds

Strew not earth with empty stars. Song. Thomas Lovell Beddoes. OxBSP *Fr*. The Second Brother.

Strew on her roses, roses. Requiescat. Matthew Arnold. AWP; EBEvV; FHYEP; NOBE; OBEV; PBMP; PoRA

Strict hairshirt of circumstance tears the flesh. The Veterans. Donagh MacDonagh. CIP-2

Strife is grown between Virtue and Love, A. Sonnet 52. Sir Philip Sidney. NAEL-1; NoP-4 *Fr*. Astrophil and Stella. AAS; SiPS

Strike. Veronica Forrest-Thomson. FaBoTC

Strike, churl; hurl, cheerless wind, then; heltering hail. Hailstorm in May. Gerard Manley Hopkins. Spl

Strike his wakening, slap his eyes ajar. Dub Eleven. Jeff Nuttall. NBrP

Strike the concertina's melancholy string! The Story of Prince Agib. Sir William Schwenck Gilbert. CBNP

Strike up, you lusty gallants, with music [*or* musick] and sound of drum. Captain Ward and the *Rainbow*. *Unknown*. ESPB

Strikers in Hyde Park. Louise Imogen Guiney. APN-2

Striking two towns, and fed its flocks. (LL) The Children of Greenock. W. S. Graham. FaBoTC

String. Gary Gildner. CMAP

String, The. Momcilo Nastasijevic, *Serbo-Croatian*. HSix, *tr*. by Charles Simic

String. Dennis Schmitz. LCAP-2

String Bean. Luis J. Rodriguez. EC3

String-chewing bass players. Mingus. Bob Kaufman. PoBA

String of Pearls. Ted Berrigan. MoNo

String of Pearls, The. Đồng Hồ, *Vietnamese*. AVP, *tr*. by Huỳnh Sanh Thông

Stringer's Field. Roy McFadden. PNI

Stringing red serrano peppers, crushing. Desert Landscape. Agha Shahid Ali. OMIP

Strings' Excitement, The. W. H. Auden. MoBrPo

Stringybark Cockatoo, The. *Unknown.* NOBAu

"Strip," Leofric said, "and you'll find." Limerick. Harry Thomas. PeLi

Strip Me Naked, or Royal Gin for Ever; a Picture. *Unknown.* NOEC

Strip off your clothes and give them to a man. The Visiting Hour. David Wagoner. HoPM

Strip-tease. Lawrence Durrell. OxAEP-2

Striped blouse in a clearing by Bazille, A. Ceremony. Richard Wilbur. CoAP; MoP; NAAL-2; NoAM

Striped suit. The New Suit. Nidia Sanabria de Romero, *Spanish.* ChAP, *tr.* by Arnaldo D. Larrosa Morán and Naomi Shihab Nye

Stripped almond of the plane is gone, The. Between Two Worlds. Rosemary Thomas. NYBP

Stripped of all his dreams. (LL) Autumn. Itsik Manger, *Yiddish.* CEEP, *tr.* by Ruth Whitman

Stripped of his crown. The Bombax Tree. Fily-Dabo Sissoko, *French.* NegPo, *tr.* by Ellen Conroy Kennedy

Stripped of its leaves. Trees on a Frosty Night. Mairtin O Direain, *Irish.* TIRV, *tr. by the author*

Stripper, The. Anita Endrezze-Danielson. CDW

Stripping and Putting on. May Swenson. WeW-3

"Strive and thrive!" cry "Speed,—fight on, fare ever / There as here!" (LL) Epilogue: "At the midnight in the silence of the sleep-time." Robert Browning. EnVR; NAEL-1; NOBE; OBNC

Strive in this, and love the strife. (LL) The Banquet. George Herbert. ESCV; GeHe

Strive not, vain Lover, to be fine. Song. Richard Lovelace. CavPo

Strive not with Love; for if ye do, it will ye thus befall. (LL) Love's Rebel. Henry Howard, Earl of Surrey. AAS; SiPS

Striving to save the whole, by parcells dye. (LL) Distraction. Henry Vaughan. GeHe; SeCP

Stroke. Vincent Buckley.

"In the faint blue light." BMAP

Strokes. William Stafford. CoAmPo

Strokes are pulses: from my shapely cloud, The. A Minor Van Gogh (He Speaks). Alicia Ostriker. RACG

Stroll-Joy. Johann Klaj, *German.* GePo, *tr.* by George C. Schoolfield

Stroll on, thou dark not deep "blue" dandy, stroll. The Sea Replies to Byron. G. K. Chesterton. UV

Strolling along the Riverbank, Looking for Flowers. Tu Fu, *Chinese.*

"Masses of flowers and plants envelop the riverbanks." SuSp, *tr.* by Irving Y. Lo

"'Tis not I pity the flowers are about to die." SuSp, *tr.* by Irving Y. Lo

Strolling in the Countryside. Chao Yi, *Chinese.* SuSp, *tr.* by Chang Yin-nan *and* Lewis C. Walmsley

Strolling Musicians. Nikolai Alekseievich Zabolotsky, *Russian.* TCRP, *tr.* by Daniel Weissbort

Strong am I among mortals, not without a name. Hippolytus. Euripides, *Classical Greek.*

Strong and slippery, / built for the midnight grass-party. Peter. Marianne Moore. CMoP; NAAL-2; OxBA

Strong ankled, sun burned, almost naked. Vitamins and Roughage. Kenneth Rexroth. NoAM

Strong Are Saying Nothing, The. Robert Frost. CMoP

Strong Bond, The. Juana de Ibarbourou, *Spanish.* PBWP, *tr.* by Linda Scheer

Strong drink, hundred-year-old, A. Soul Music: The Derry Air. Eamon Grennan. BiHa; PBCIP

Strong extreme speed, that the brain burries with. Boulogne to Amiens and Paris. D. G. Rossetti. PeVV *Fr.* A Trip to Paris and Belgium.

Strong is the horse upon his speed. Strength. Christopher Smart. UV *Fr.* A Song to David. ImPo; NAEL-1; NOBE; OAEL-1; OBWVE; PoE; PoEL-3

Strong is the lion – like a coal. Christopher Smart. HAP *Fr.* A Song to David. ImPo; NAEL-1; NOBE; OAEL-1; OBWVE; PoE; PoEL-3

Strong Men. Sterling Brown. BPo; BkSV; CrDW; PoBA; TTY

("Stronger. . . .") (LL) ISC; NAAAL

(*They dragged you from homeland.*") BkSV; NAAAL

Strong men keep coming on, The. Upstream. Carl Sandburg. MoAmPo

Strong Men, riding horses. In the West. Gwendolyn Brooks. GT; PoBA

("Pasted to stars already. . . .") (LL) GT

Strong men. . . / Stronger. . . . (LL) Strong Men. Sterling Brown. BPo; BkSV; CrDW; PoBA; TTY

Strong Pomegranate Flowers and Seeds of the Mind. Linda Gregg. PuP-16

Strong rods for scepters to bear sway. On the Decease of the Religious and Honourable Jno Haynes Esqr. John James. SCAP

Strong Room of the House, The. William Bronk. APSN

Strong saturation of sea! O widely flown. George Cabot Lodge. APN-2

Strong scent, The. Tanka. Kitahara Hakushū, *Japanese.* MJT, *tr.* by Makoto Ueda

Strong-shouldered mole. A Dead Mole. Andrew Young. GTBS-P; OxBSP

Strong sob of the chafing stream, The. Orara. Henry Clarence Kendall. CBAP

Strong Son of God, immortal Love. Tennyson. EBVV; EBVVPR; EnVR; HAP; NAWM-2; OAEL-2; TrCP *Fr.* In Memoriam A. H. H.

Strong song tows, A. Basil Bunting. OAEL-2 *Fr.* Briggflatts [An Autobiography].

Strong strong sun, in that look. Pods Pop and Grin. James Berry. AYFP

Strong without rage, without o'er-flowing full. (LL) The Thames from Cooper's Hill. Sir John Denham. NAEL-1; NOSC; OAEL-1; OxAEP-1

Strong women told the faggots that there are two important, The. Women Wisdom. Larry Mitchell. GLP

Stronger. . . . Sterling Brown. *See* Strong Men.

Stronger than alcohol, more great than song. Sonnet III. Ted Berrigan. FTOS *Fr.* The Sonnets.

Strongest, The. "Yehoash," *Yiddish.* TrJP, *tr.* by Marie Syrkin

Strongest and the noblest argument, The. Dedication II. Sir John Davies. SiPS *Fr.* Nosce Teipsum. NoSic; SiPS

Strongly it bears us along in swelling and limitless billows. The Homeric Hexameter. Coleridge. OxAEP-2

Strongly worded to say on the subject. (LL) Seascape. Elizabeth Bishop. ColAP; FaBoWP; OxBC; OxBoS

Strong's Winter. Sidney Burris. BAP-96

Strophes. O. V. de L. Milosz, *French.* NNPT, *tr.* by Ezra Pound

Struck out of dim fluctuant forces and shock of electrical vapour. Chaunts of Life. Mathilde Blind. VWP *Fr.* The Ascent of Man.

Struck through such a dome. A Baroque Sunburst. Amy Clampitt. ColAP

Struck, was I, not yet by Lightning. Emily Dickinson. NCAP

Struck with huge Love, of what to be possest. Prefatory Poem, on. . . *Magnalia Christi Americana.* Nicholas Noyes. SCAP

Structural Study of Myth, The. Jerome Rothenberg. FTOS; PoM

Structure of process, The. Process. John Montague. CIP-2

Structure of Rime XVIII. Robert Duncan. FTOS

Structure, yes. You'd hardly say a house, A. At the Flyfisher's Shack. Sydney Lea. RA

Struggle, The. Toi Derricotte. IFJA; LTA; PBCAP

Struggle. Sidney Lanier. OxBA

Struggle, The. René François Armand Sully-Prudhomme, *French.* AWP, *tr.* by Arthur O'Shaughnessy

Struggle for the Taal, The. Breyten Breytenbach, *Afrikaans.* AF, *tr.* by Denis Hirson

Struggle-Road Dance. Ahmos, II Zu-Bolton. ISC

Strugnell's Bargain. Wendy Cope. UV

Strugnell's Rubáiyát. Wendy Cope. UV

Strumming and patter / the meaningful glances, The. Philodemus, *Greek.* GrAn, *tr.* by William Moebius

Strut for Roethke, A. John Berryman. NOBA

Stubborn. Ruth Fainlight. CMAP

Stubbs butters Freeman, Freeman butters Stubbs. (LL) On the Historians Freeman and Stubbs. J. E. Thorold Rogers. FaBoEE; OBCoV

Stuck in a bottle on the window-sill. Geraniums. Wilfrid Wilson Gibson. NSI

Stuck on the fridge, our favorite pin-up girl. The Oven Loves the TV Set. Heather McHugh. CrSp

Stud. Michael Lassell. GLP *Fr.* Times Square Poems.

Student. Cheng Min. PBWP, *tr.* by Kenneth Rexroth *and* Ling Chung

Student, The. James Hurdis. *Fr.* Adriano; or, the First of June. ECEV

Student, The. Marianne Moore. NAAL-2; TwCP

Student, do the simple purification. The Simple Purification. Kabir, *Hindi.* EnIH, *tr.* by Robert Bly

Student from Pembroke once said, A. Limerick. Andrew Stoker. PeLi

Student of nuclear fission, A. Limerick. W. Bernard Wake. PeLi

Student's life is pleasant, The. *Unknown, Early Modern Irish.* OBMV, *tr.* by Frank O'Connor

Students, like students, form and fly. "When the Students Resisted, a Minor Clash Ensued." David Knight. MoCV

Student's Tale, The. Henry Wadsworth Longfellow. AmPP *Fr.* Tales of a Wayside Inn.

Studies at Delhi, 1876. Sir Alfred Comyn Lyall. Badminton. PeVV

Studio Poem. Cilla McQueen. PeNZ

Studio Up Over In Your Ear. Al Young. GT

Studley Park. John Langhorne. OBGa

Study. Tony Harrison. CABP

Study, A. Alice Thompson Meynell. VWP

Study AA Soul), A. Christina Rossetti. VWP

Study in Aesthetics, A. Robert Peters. BXAP

Study in Aesthetics, The. Ezra Pound. CMoP; NOBA

Study in Blue. Evan Jones. NOBAu

Study of Reading Habits, A. Philip Larkin. InPK-6; NOBL; OBCoV

Study of Two Pears. Wallace Stevens. BLT; InPS-3; NAAL-2; NoAM; OxBA

Study Peace. Imamu Amiri Baraka. APSN; PoBA

Studying Horses. Robert Kelly. APSN

Studying Physics with My Daughter. Jeanne Murray Walker. WeW-3

Studying the ancient manuscript crumbly with age. Following the Rhymes of Chang Hsün, in My Study in Late Spring. Huang T'ing-chien, *Chinese.* SuSp, *tr. by* Michael E. Workman

Studying the Signs. Allen Ginsberg. FTOS

Stuff of Dreams, The. Shakespeare. *See* Epilogue.

Stuff of the moon. Nocturne in a Deserted Brickyard. Carl Sandburg. MoAmPo

Stuffed owls drum in my heart. Fear. Thomas Love Peacock. VoR

Stuffed quail, A. October Tune. Joseph Brodsky, *Russian.* VCWP, *tr. by* Joseph Brodsky

Stuffy chill of clouded Summer, crowdsmell, booksmell. Supervising Examinations. Sean Lucy. CIP-2

Stuffy Turkey. Dave Etter. SeSe

Stumpfoot on 42nd Street. Louis Simpson. NNaP; UnPo; VGW

Stunted / Figtrees. Figtrees. Agnes Nemes Nagy, *Hungarian.* CEEP, *tr. by* Bruce Berlind

Stuntman. Lionel Kearns. MoCV

Stupendious love! all saints astonishment. Edward Taylor. MeMAP; OxBA *Fr.* Preparatory Meditations Before My Approach to the Lord's Supper.

Stupid Catullus! Stubborn soul, endure. Catullus. *See* Carmen 8 ("Break off / fallen Catullus").

Stupid of me to think you were salmon. American Tourist. B. C. Ramachandra Sharma, *Kannada.* OMIP, *tr. by* A. K. Ramanujan

Stupidity. Mary Elizabeth Fullerton. CBAP

Stupidity achieves the crime. Martyr. Mary Elizabeth Fullerton. CBAP

Stupidity Street. Ralph Hodgson. CH; LiTM; MoBrPo; OxBTC

Sturdiest of forest trees, The. The Holly. Walter De la Mare. CMoP

Sturdy ploughman doth the soldier see, The. Joseph Hall. OBSV *Fr.* Virgidemiarum.

Stuttering rain at the window. Sister Midnight. John James. NBrP

Stwonen Steps, The. William Barnes. NOBVV

Stygian council thus disolved; and forth, The. Milton. OAEL-1 *Fr.* Book II. FHYEP; NAEL-1; OxAEP-1 *Fr.* Paradise Lost.

Style is the answer to everything. Charles Bukowski. HoPM

Style is the water out of Homer. The Garden God. Richard Eberhart. OBGa

Style of Prayer, A. Lynda Hull. PUP-19

Style of the new moon, stirrings of new love. New Love. Vidyapati, *Sanskrit.* EP, *tr. by* Deben Bhattacharya

Stylized Donkey, A. "Sasha Chorny," *Russian.* TCRP, *tr. by* Bernard Meares

Styro. Clark Coolidge. PmAP

Styx. Robert Duncan. VCAP

Su-chuang, a horse, won fame throughout the world. The Loyal Horse. Nguyễn Đình Chiều, *Vietnamese.* AVP, *tr. by* Huỳnh Sanh Thông

Su Su. Velma Pollard. HCP

Suave and paltry man, my enemy, A. In the Tail of the Scorpion. Genevieve Taggard. VGW

Suave Mari Magno. Lucretius. AWP, *tr. by* W. H. Mallock *Fr.* De Rerum Natura (On the Nature of Things).

Sub Specie Aeternitatis. Robert Earl Hayden. AmPP *Fr.* An Inference of Mexico.

Subalterns. Elizabeth Daryush. OBWP

Subalterns, The. Thomas Hardy. CMoP; MoBrPo; MoP; NOBVV; NoAM; OAEL-2; Poetr

Subaltern's Love-Song, A. John Betjeman. APAD; BoLoP; EBEvV; HAP; NOBL; NoAM; OxAEP-2; OxBTC; TwCP

Subject. Marie Ponsot. VGW

Subject chosen for tonight's discussion, The. An Evening of Russian Poetry. Vladimir Nabokov. NYBP

Subject for a Story. Nikolai Ivanovich Glazkov, *Russian.* TCRP, *tr. by* Daniel Weissbort

Subject of Heroic Song, The. Milton. *See* Higher Argument.

Subject to Change. Anne Lauterbach. PT

Subject to ev'ry mounter's bended knee. (LL) The H. Scriptures ("Oh Book! infinite sweetnesse! let my heart"). George Herbert. ChIV-1; ESCV; MiEL

Subject was put to bed at midnight, The. Operative No. 174 Resigns. Kenneth Fearing. NYBP

Subjection of Women, The. Austin Clarke. CIP-2

Subjectivity at Sestos. P. M. Hubbard. NYBP

Sublime – invention ever young. Christopher Smart. OBEV *Fr.* A Song to David. ImPo; NAEL-1; NOBE; OAEL-1; OBWVE; PoE; PoEL-3

Sublime was he, stupendous in invention. The Wangsun. Wang Yen-Shou, *Chinese, tr. by* Arthur Waley

Subliminal. Lorine Niedecker. PFTM

Submarine Tombs. Jean-Baptiste Tati-Loutard. PBMAP

Submarines. "Klaxon." NSI

Submerged, silent, rooted in water. Foetus. Phyllis Haring. PeSA

Submission. Clara Ann Thompson. CBWP-2

Submission to Afflictive Providences. Isaac Watts. NOCV

Submitting a Memorial Requesting Permission to Return Home and Care for My Parents. Yang Chi, *Chinese.* CoBLCP, *tr. by* Jonathan Chaves

Submitting to a sentry's fate. Common Dawn. Guy Butler. PeSA

Subscribe myself your servant / Francis Ben. (LL) A Messe of Nonsense. *Unknown.* CBNP; NOSC

Substance and Shadow. John Hewitt. PNI

Substance, Shadow, and Spirit. T'ao Ch'ien. ChiP, *tr. by* Arthur Waley; CoBCP, *tr. by* Burton Watson

Substance that stirs in my palm, The. Ash. Jayanta Mahapatra. VCWP

Substantiations. Vidya, *Sanskrit.*

One born to hardship in his place and station. PBWP, *tr. by* Daniel H. H. Ingalls

Substitute, The. Leslie Adrienne Miller. CMAP

Substitute for Time, The. John Koethe. EOEF

Substitution. Anne Spencer. BlSi

Subterfuge. Vassar Miller. NMM-2

Subtle almost beyond thought are these dim colours. Dun-Colour [*or* Dun-Color]. Ruth Pitter. PoRA

Subtle capering on a simple thought. Fleadh Cheoil. Pearse Hutchinson. PBCIP

Subtle chain of countless rings, A. Nature [1836]. Ralph Waldo Emerson. APN-1; AWP; NCAP

Subtlest strain a great musician weaves, The. Limitations. Henrietta Cordelia Ray. CBWP-3

Suburb, The. Anne Stevenson. NMM-2; WeT

Suburb Hilltop. Richard Moore. NYBP

Suburban. John Ciardi. NBLV

Suburban. William Dickey. WeT

Suburban Childhood, A. Liz Rosenberg. IFJA; PBCAP

Suburban Dreams. Edwin Muir. OxBTC

Suburban Dusk. Bert Meyers. SPE

Suburban Garden. Tennyson. GaP

Suburban Lovers. Bruce Dawe. NOBAu

Suburban Song. Elizabeth Riddell. CBAP; NOBAu

Suburban Sonnet. Gwen Harwood. CBAP

Suburban Wife's Song. Robert Hutchinson. NYBP

Suburbs on a Hazy Day. D. H. Lawrence. OBMV

Subverted Flower, The. Robert Frost. CMoP; ColAP; HAP; MeMAP; MoP; NOBA; NoAM; OxBA; PoE; Poetr

Subway. Susan Fawcett. CrSp

Subway Rush Hour. Langston Hughes. InPK-6
("No room for fear.") (LL) KaS

Subway train, the / subway train, The. Leland B. Jacobs. SSCS

Subway Witnesses, The. Lorenzo Thomas. GT; PoBA

Success. Rupert Brooke. OxBTC

Success. C. C. Cameron.
Don't Give Up. PoToHe

Success. Cornelius Eady. ISC

Success. William Empson. OxBTC

Success (If you want a thing bad enough). Berton Braley. PoToHe

Success and failure are not our affairs. Seeing Off Sun Ling-hsiu on His Journey to Chen-ting. Wu Wei-yeh, *Chinese.* CoBLCP, *tr. by* Jonathan Chaves

Success is counted sweetest. Emily Dickinson. APN-2; AWP; CMoP; ColAP; EBEvV; HeIP-4; ImPo; InPS-3; LiTM; MeMAP; MoAmPo; NAAL-1; NAAL-3; NOBA; NoP-4; OxBA; PAR; PFE; PoPoPo; PoRA; SAmP; TAP; TFi; WPE
("Break, agonized and clear.") (LL) ColAP

Success is like some horrible disaster. After Publication of Under the Volcano. Malcolm Lowry. CLPP; FaBoTw

Success is speaking words of praise. *Unknown.* CTV; PoToHe

Successful Summer, A. David Schubert. ChIV-1

Succubus, The. Robert Graves. EP; OAEL-2

Succulence by implication pinks the eye with condensation, A. Cris Cheek. NBrP *Fr.* Drawing on the Traditions.

Succulent flower bleeds molasses, The. Sugar Cane. Faustin Charles. PBCV

Such a Blustery Day! Elizabeth Gould. BoTP

Such a Boat of Land. Lamont B. Steptoe. UnSA

Such a calmness. Rest. Jacob Isaac Segal, *Yiddish.* CEEP, *tr. by* Seymour Mayne

Such a flow of language! Rebecca Cutlet. Bill Berkson. PmAP

Such a fool as I am you had better ignore. The Usk. Charles Hubert Sisson. NOCV

'Such a little king's eye,' said my mother. Roy Kloof. Sydney Clouts. PeSAV

Such a peculiar lot. Fantasy of an African Boy. James Berry. HCP; NTP; PBCV

Such a prelate, I trow. John Skelton. OBSV *Fr.* Why Come Ye Not to Court.

Such a result so soon—and from such a beginning! (LL) A Hand-Mirror. Walt Whitman. NAAL-1; NAAL-3; OxBA; PoPoPo

Such a time of it they had. Stanley Meets Mutesa. James David Rubadiri. PBA

Such a wide, still landscape, all cold and white! A Greenland Winter. Lucy Diamond. BoTP

Such a wizened creature. Old Age. E. Keary. NOBVV

Such accidents do happen. Blues 2. Barry Wallenstein. SeSe

Such an itch and tickle of slow. Stretching. Robert Morgan. WeW-3

Such are our habits. To My Friends. Nikolai Ivanovich Glazkov, *Russian.* TCRP, *tr. by* Daniel Weissbort

Such are the little memories of you. To Theodore. George Marion McClellan. AAP

Such as in God the Lord Do Trust. William Kethe. AH

Such as mine has been! (LL) May the men who are born. Hitomaro, *Japanese.* AWP; TAL, *tr. by* Arthur Waley

Such as, retired from sight of men, like thee. To Saint Mary Magdalen. Henry Constable. Son

Such as she was, such as she would become. (LL) The Gift Outright. Robert Frost. AiP; AmPP; CMoP; ColAP; FaBoA; LiTM; MeMAP; MoAmPo; MoP; NAAL-2; NOBA; NoAM; NoP-4; OxBA; PoPoPo; Poetr; TFi; TRP

Such be the dog, I charge, thou mean'st to train. Thomas Tickell. ECEV *Fr.* A Fragment of a Poem on Hunting.

Such beautiful, beautiful hands! My Mother's Hands. *Unknown.* PFE

Such bliss he on you lays, *par. by* Countess of Pembroke, Mary Sidney Herbert. Bible, *O.T. See* Psalm 148.

Such brazen slatterns. Dandelions. Gerda Mayer. Spl

Such closets to search, such alcoves to /importune! importune! (LL) Love in a Life. Robert Browning. CBLP; EBVVPR; FHYEP; NOBE; NOBVV; OBNC

Such counsels ye gave to me, O! (LL) Edward [*or* Edward, Edward]. *Unknown.* AmFP; CH; ClHu; EBEV; EBEvV; ESPB; FaPoR; HAP; HoPM; InPK-6; InPS-3; NAEL-1; NOBE; OBEV; OxBB; OxBS; PoEL-1; PoRA; SCGP; SoSe-8; TFi; TRP

Such earnestness! such wear and tear. Herman Melville. *See* Ungar and Rolfe.

Such eyes, such hair, such wit, and such a hand? (LL) Conquest [*or* His Lady's Might]. Philippe Desportes. AWP; NoSic

Such fine Employments our whole days divide. The Client, the patron, the age. Juvenal, *Latin.* OBCVT, *tr. by* John Dryden

Such flowers as Earth our Mother. Petronius Arbiter. MLL, *tr. by* Helen Waddell *Fr.* Satyricon.

Such grace, so self-contained, was the best escape to know. (LL) The Ballet of the Fifth Year. Delmore Schwartz. OxBA; TwCP

Such hap as I am happed in. Sir Thomas Wyatt. SiPS

Such haukes, such hounds, and such a leman. (LL) The Three Ravens. *Unknown.* AmFP; ESPB; HeIP-4; InPK-6; NAEL-1; OAEL-1; OBEV; OxBB; PFE; PoE; PoEL-1; SCGP; TFi; UnPo

Such icy kisses, anchorites that live. The Cold Kiss. Thomas Stanley. CBLP

Such ills attend. Advice to Lovers. John Armstrong. NOEC *Fr.* The Oeconomy of Love; a Poetical Essay.

Such is the Mode of these censorious Days. On Mr. Hobbs, and His Writings. John, Duke of Buckingham and Normandy Sheffield. PoEL-3

Such is the secret union, when we feel. The Creative Process. Mark Akenside. NOEC *Fr.* The Pleasures of Imagination.

Such is the way of the world. Anabasis. "St.-John Perse," *French.* OBVE, *tr. by* T. S. Eliot *Fr.* Anabasis.

Such is the worlde, who beares the swey. Horace, *Latin.* OBCVT, *tr. by* Thomas Drant

Such light in sense, with such a darkened [*or* darken'd] mind. (LL) Sonnet 99: "When far-spent night persuades each mortal eye." Sir Philip Sidney. NoSic; PoE; Son

Such light is in sea-caves. Musica No. 3. Richard Duerden. NeAP

Such love I cannot analyse. Friendship. Elizabeth Jennings. FP

Such maner time there was (what time I n'ot). Sir Philip Sidney. PBRV *Fr.* The Countesse of Pembrokes Arcadia.

Such marvellous ways to kill a man! The Bofors A. A. Gun. Gavin Ewart. PoWW

Such men as sideling ride the ambling Muse. Homer and the Brazen Head of Rumour. George Chapman. NOSC

Such moving sounds from such a careless touch. Of My Lady Isabella Playing on the Lute. Edmund Waller. HAP; SeCP

Such poor folk as to law do go. Isabella Whitney. *Fr.* Sweet Nosegay, A, or Pleasant Posy. WPE

Such pretious perils for mankind! (LL) Lib. 2. Metrum 5. Boethius, *Latin.* NOSC; OBCVT; OBVE, *tr. by* Henry Vaughan

Such radiance of green. Red Peonies. Wang Wei, *Chinese.* SuSp, *tr. by* Irving Y. Lo

Such shameless bards we have; and yet 'tis true. The Bookful Blockhead. Alexander Pope. OBSV *Fr.* An Essay on Criticism. NAEL-1; PoEL-3; TFi

Such should this day be, so the sun should hide. On the Marriage of T. K. and C. C.: The Morning Stormy. Thomas Carew. BoLoP

Such skill, matcht with such courage as he had. Edmund Spenser. OBWP *Fr.* Astrophel.

Such splendid icecaps and hard rills, such weights. Piano Practice. Howard Moss. NYBP

Such subtile filigranity and nobless of construccion. "Wellcome, to the Caves of Artá!" Robert Graves. NBLV; NOBL; NYBP; PeLV

Such, such is Death: no triumph: no defeat. Charles Hamilton Sorley. NSI; PeFWW *Fr.* Two Sonnets. MoBrPo

Such the drear roar of battle when they mixt. (LL) Battle. Homer, *Greek.* OBCVT, *tr. by* Alfred Tennyson, 1st Baron Tennyson; OBVE, *tr. by* Tennyson

Such Tophet was; so looked the grinning fiend. Tophet. Thomas Gray. ChIV-1; FaBoEE; NOEC; OxBSP

Such understanding that it seems like love. (LL) Celtic Cross. Norman MacCaig. FaBoTC

Such was old Chaucer. Such the placid mien. For a Statue of Chaucer at Woodstock. Mark Akenside. EPCY

Such was the Boy—but for the growing Youth. The Excursion. Wordsworth. LaPo *Fr.* The Excursion.

Such was thir song. Milton. PeECV *Fr.* Book X. FHYEP *Fr.* Paradise Lost.

Such[e] wayward[e] ways [*or* wais] hath love, that most[e] part[e] in discord[e]. Henry Howard, Earl of Surrey. AAS; SiPS

Such wrong, as when a married man doth woo[e]. (LL) Break[e] of Day. Donne. NAEL-1; SoSe-8

Suck, The. John Wieners. FTOS

Sucking Cider through a Straw. *Unknown.* AS

Sudden Appearance of a Monster at a Window. Lawrence Raab. BLT

Sudden Appearance of Cherry Blossoms, The. Empress Jito, *Japanese.* WPJ, *tr. by* Kenneth Rexroth *and* Ikuko Atsumi *Fr.* Manyo Shu, Part 3 of 4.

Sudden blow: the great wings beating still, A. Leda and the Swan. W. B. Yeats. CABP; CMoP; ClHu; EBEV; FaBoSe; GSo; GTBS-P; HAP; HeIP-4; ImPo; InPK-6; LiTM; MoBrPo; MoP; NAEL-2; NAWM-2; NIP-4; NOBE; NoAM; NoP-4; OAEL-2; OxABoV; OxBoV; PFE; PoE; PoPoPo; Poetr; SAGP; SCV; SoSe-8; Son; TFi; TRP; WeW-3

Sudden Journey. Tess Gallagher. NIP-4

Sudden Light. D. G. Rossetti. BoLoP; CABP; CTC; EBEvV; GLoP; NOBE; NOBVV; NoP-4; OAEL 2; OBNC; PoLF

Sudden / Quick as light. Life/Death. Ian McDonald. HCP

Sudden roar, a mighty rushing sound, A. On the Wings of the Morning. Jeffery Day. NSI

Sudden Shower. John Clare. OxAEP-2

Sudden snowfall comes in darkness, A. Snowy Mountains. Tsung Ch'en, *Chinese.* CoBLCP, *tr. by* Jonathan Chaves

Sudden strong squalls from the sou'-west. Leonidas of Tarentum, *Greek.* GrAn, *tr. by* Clive Sansom

Sudden Thaw. Andrew Young. FaBoTC; NTP

Sudden the desert changes. Bridge-Guard in the Karroo. Rudyard Kipling. OBWP

Sudden Things. Donald Hall. SPE

Sudden, unexpected movement; his hand, A. Audible and Inaudible. Yannis Ritsos, *Greek.* AF, *tr. by* Minas Savas

Sudden upriseth from her stately palace. Edmund Spenser. *Fr.* Wood Of Error. AEP

Sudden wakin', a sudden weepin', A. Man's Days. Eden Phillpotts. OBEV; OxBTC

Suddenly. Robin Blaser. FTOS; PoM

Suddenly. The Curative Powers of Silence. Al Young. GT

Suddenly. Louis Simpson. BAP-93

Suddenly. Tanka. Miya Shūji, *Japanese.* MJT, *tr. by* Makoto Ueda

Suddenly after a few years of abject misery, depression and paralysis. The Obvious. Anna Couani. BMAP

Suddenly, after the quarrel, while we waited. The Quarrel. Conrad Potter Aiken. MoAmPo

Suddenly an old man on the threshold of the age. Joseph Miezan Bognini. PBMAP *Fr.* Herbe Féconde (1973).

Suddenly as the riot squad moved in. Belfast Confetti. Ciaran Carson. BiHa; CIP-2; PNI

Suddenly aware that the good year is almost over. Autumn Thoughts. Ts'en Shen, *Chinese.* SuSp, *tr. by* C. H. Wang

Suddenly becoming talkative. Christopher Okigbo. PBMAP *Fr.* Limits (1962).

Suddenly drawn in through the thick glass plate. Sharks at the New York Aquarium. Charles Martin. RA

Suddenly everything stops. Slump. Vassar Miller. BoWoP

Suddenly half in jest. Album Leaf. Stéphane Mallarmé, *French.* OBVE, *tr. by* Keith Bosley

Suddenly he sang across the trenches. A Thrush In the Trenches. Humbert Wolfe. NSI

Suddenly her breast has never been larger. Impotence. Marvin Bell. AmPA

Suddenly his mouth filled with sand. Death of a Poet. Charles Causley. OxBTC

Suddenly his poor body. Ted Hughes. NoAM *Fr.* Stations.

Suddenly I meet your face. (LL) A Deep-sworn Vow. W. B. Yeats. CMoP; OAEL-2; PoE; UnPo

Suddenly I remember the holes. The Holes. Stephen Berg. NYBP

Suddenly I remembered. Lord of Nature. Leonid Nikolaevich Martynov, *Russian.* TCRP, *tr. by* J. R. Rowland

Suddenly I saw the cold and rook-delighting heaven. The Cold Heaven. W. B. Yeats. AWP; CTC; GTBS-P; HAP; NoAM; OAEL-2; OxBSP; RB

Suddenly I would like prison. (LL) Now that the time seems all mine. Patrizia Cavalli, *Italian.* NeIt; VCWP, *tr. by* Judith Baumel

Suddenly / in middle age. Icons. Miriam Waddington. NOBC

Suddenly in the dark wood. Her Voice Could Not Be Softer. Austin Clarke. NOIV

Suddenly in the midnight on mortal men. The Last Judgment. *Unknown.* AnOE, *tr. by* Charles W. Kennedy *Fr.* Christ 3.

Suddenly in the midst of a game of lotto with his sisters. Louis Armstrong. Ernst Moerman. SeSe

Suddenly leaves struck the street. Allenby. Meir Wieseltier, *Hebrew.* IP, *tr. by* Warren Bargad *and* Stanley F. Chyet

Suddenly my father lifted up his nightie, I. In the Hospital Near the End. Sharon Olds. NIP-4

Suddenly night crushed out the day and hurled. The Unreturning. Wilfred Owen. MoBrPo

Suddenly out of its still and drowsy lair, the lair of slaves. Leaves of Grass (1855). Walt Whitman. APN-1

Suddenly she slapped me, hard across the face. Elizabeth in Italy. Richard Weber. BoLoP

Suddenly the swallow's shadow reaped the glances of its nostalgia: / Noon. The Origin of Landscape or the End of Mercy. Odysseus Elytis, *Greek.* VCWP, *tr. by* Edmund Keeley *and* Philip Sherrard

Suddenly the window will open. The Return. Tadeusz Różewicz, *Polish.* HP, *tr. by* Adam Czerniawski

Suddenly there stirs in you the image of parks in polaroid colors like. To the Things That Are Immortal. Abba Kovner, *Hebrew.* IP, *tr. by* Warren Bargad *and* Stanley F. Chyet

Suddenly there was a dress. White Notes. Donald Justice. LCAP-2

Suddenly there were forms there. Horses. Gwyn Thomas, *Welsh.* OBWVE, *tr. by* Joseph P. Clancy

Suddenly they came flying, like a long scarf of smoke. The Thing. Theodore Roethke. CMoP

Suddenly to become John Benbow, walking down William Street. Metempsychosis. Kenneth Slessor. NOBAu

Suddenly, warm weather, I change to lighter clothes. Yang Chi. *Fr.* Living in a Riverside Village—Miscellaneous Impressions. CoBLCP, *tr. by* Jonathan Chaves

Suddenly we will wake from sleep at night. Shin Shalom, *Hebrew.* MHP, *tr. by* Ruth Finer Mintz

Sue asked, why is there a line. Spring. Patricia Cumming. MDDM

Suelick is the greatest Indian power. The Origin of the Skagit Indians. Lucy Williams, *Skagit Indian.* STP, *tr. by* Carl Cary

Suffenus, whom so well you know. To Varus. Catullus. AWP, *tr. by* Walter Savage Landor *Fr.* Carmina.

Suffenus whom you know, the Witty. Catullus. *See* To Varus.

Suffer, Poor Negro! David Diop, *French.* PBA, *tr. by* Langston Hughes

Suffer the Children. Audre Lorde. PoBA

Sufferance of her race is shown, The. Formerly a Slave. Herman Melville. APN-2; TAP

Suffering. Albert Ehrenstein, *German.* TrJP, *tr. by* Babette Deutsch

Suffering. Miroslav Holub, *Czech.* PoSu, *tr. by* Ian Milner *and* George Theiner

Suffering. Patricia K. Page. NoAM

Suffering from Heat. Wang Wei, *Chinese.* SuSp, *tr. by* Hugh M. Stimson

Suffering has settled like a sly disguise. A Korean Woman Seated by a Wall. William Meredith. Poetr

Suffering of the gods, The. Aristophanes, *Greek.* OBCVT, *tr. by* Thomas Randolph

Suffering The Sea Change: All My Pretty Ones. Lucinda Roy. GT

Suffice they show I lived, and loved thee dear. (LL) 46. Samuel Daniel. AAS; GSo; NOBE; NoSic; OBEV; SCGP

Suffice, thou shalt be loved as well as she. (LL) Thou canst not die whilst any zeal abound. Samuel Daniel. NoSic; Son

Sufficed not, madame, that you did tear. Sir Thomas Wyatt. SiPS

Sufficeth it to you [or yow] my joy[e]s interred. The Ocean's Love to Cynthia. Sir Walter Ralegh. NoSic; SiPS

Suffisant this flour to preyse aryght! (LL) And as for me, though that I konne [or can] but [or my wit be] lyte. Chaucer. CH; HeIP-4

Suffolk Miracle, The. *Unknown.* AmFP; ESPB

Suffused in April twilight. Redemption. Pauli Murray. GT

Sufi Quatrain. Rabi'a bint Isma'il of Syria, *Arabic.* WPOW, *tr. by* Deirdre Lashgari

Sugar Cane. Faustin Charles. PBCV

Sugar Cane, The. James Grainger.

    Compost. NOEC

    "On festal days; or when their work is done." PBCV

    Slaves. NOEC

    "Then earthquakes, nature's agonizing pangs." PBCV

Sugar Cane. Grace Nichols. HCP

Sugar in the Cane. Tennessee Williams. OBAL

Sugarfields. Barbara Mahone. PoBA

Suggested by a Picture of Peele Castle, in a Storm, Painted by Sir George Beaumont. Wordsworth. *See* Elegiac Stanzas Suggested by a Picture of Peele Castle, in a Storm [Painted by Sir George Beaumont].

Suggestion from a Friend. Jane Kenyon. BAP-93 *Fr.* Having It Out With Melancholy. BAP-93

    (3. Suggestion from a Friend.) LoL

Suicide, The. Kathleen de Azevedo. WWSi

Suicide, The. V. R. Lang. PoA

Suicide. Robert Lowell. PoE

Suicide, The. Edith Jay Scovell. WPN

Suicide. Anne Stevenson. FaBoWP

Suicide applicant, A. Ant Dodger. Bill Knott. PBCAP

Suicide in the Trenches. Siegfried Sassoon. *See* Suicide in [the] Trenches.

Suicide in [the] Trenches. Siegfried Sassoon. PoWW

    (Suicide in the Trenches.) PoFWW

Suicide is such a bore. one wishes one's friends would stop it. 3 : 1. "Alta." CrSp

Suicide Note. Janice Mirikitani. OxWW

Suicide Pond. Kathy McLaughlin. PoA

Suicide Rates, The. Lewis Warsh. FTOS

Suicide with Squirtgun. Tom Clark. PmAP

Suicides, The. Donald Justice. Poetr

Suilven. Andrew Young. OxBS

Suilven and the Eagle. Gordon Bottomley.

    Eagle Song. MoBrPo

Suit of Nettles, A. James Reaney.

    Branwell's Sestina. MoCV

Suitable for a gentleman with medals. War Lord in the Early Evening. Patricia K. Page. NoAM

Suite for Augustus, A. Rita Dove.

    Planning the Perfect Evening. GT

Suite for Celery and Blind Date. Philip Dow. BXAP

Suite for Marriage, A. David Ignatow. NNaP

Suite to Fathers. James Harrison. AmPA

Suitor, The. Jane Kenyon. InPK-6

Suitors watch Ulysses string the bow, The. Homer, *Greek.* OBCVT, *tr. by* Alexander Pope *Fr.* Odyssey. NAWM-1, *tr. by* Robert Fitzgerald

("Pierc'd thro' and thro', the solid gate resounds.") (LL) OBCVT, *tr. by* Alexander Pope

Sukey [*or* Suky], you shall be my wife. *Unknown.* ACTP; ITG; OxBM; OxNR; TLR

Sukhanovo. Natalya Gorbanevskaya, *Russian.* AF, *tr. by* Daniel Weissbort

Sulkily the sticks burn, and though they crackle. Under the Pot. Robert Graves. FaBoEE

Sulking in the Seventies. Kris Hemensley. BMAP

Sulky old gray brute!, The. The Bristol Channel. Thomas Edward Brown. NOBVV

Sulky Sue. Mother Goose. ReMoGo

Sullen, sullen, my brows are ever knit. To his Brother Hsing-chien, Who was Serving in Tung-ch'uan. Po Chü-i, *Chinese.* ChiP, *tr. by* Arthur Waley

Sullenness. "Michael Field." VWP

Sullivan arrived at the very lowest Heaven. John L. Sullivan Enters Heaven. Robert Frost. BXAP

Sulphur-yellow chord of the eleventh, A. On Hearing Prokofieff's Grotesque for Two Bassoons, Concertina and Snare-Drums. Louis Untermeyer. BXAP

Sulpicia. Michael Longley. RACG

Sulpicia to Cerinthus. Sulpicia, *Latin.* OBCVT, *tr. by* Allen Tate

Sulpicia to Cerinthus. Sulpicia, *Latin.* OBCVT, *tr. by* George Lyttelton

Sultry air, the smoke of shavings. A Night in a Village. Ivan Savvich Nikitin, *Russian.* AWP, *tr. by* P. E. Matheson

Sultry heat; dry, dead grass; endless steppes. The Stone Idol. Ivan Alekseievich Bunin, *Russian.* TCRP, *tr. by* Simon Franklin

Sultry noon, not in the summer's prime, A. Carlos Wilcox. APN-1 *Fr.* The Age of Benevolence.

Sum, A. "Lewis Carroll." Spl

Sum of Life, The, *abr.* Ben King. CTC *See* The Pessimist.

Sum of two and one: a cardinal number, The. Argument for Resurrection. Virginia Hooper. PT

Sum speiks of lords, sum speiks of lairds. Johnie Armstrang. *Unknown.* ESPB; IBB; OxBB

Sumac showing faint traces of red. Autumn Thoughts. Lu Yu, *Chinese.* SuSp, *tr. by* Burton Watson

Sumach Leaves, The. Jones Very. ColAP; NOBA

Sumburgh Heid. George Bruce. OxBS

Sumer is comen and winter gon. An Easter Song. *Unknown.* MiEL

Sumer is icumen in. *Unknown.* AWP; HAP; HeIP-4; ImPo; InPS-3; MiEL; NBLV; NOBE; OBEV; OPOU; PBMP; TFi

("Ne swik thu naver nu [*or* thou never now]!") (LL) EBEV; EBEvV; NoP-4; OAEL-1; UV

(Sing cuccu nu.) EBEV; EBEvV; NoP-4; OAEL-1; UV

(Summer is acoming in.) InPK-6

Summa is i-cumen in. Baccalaureate. David McCord. BXAP; NBLV; OBAL

Summah night an' sighin' breeze. Lover's Lane. Paul Laurence Dunbar. ColAP

Summary. Sonia Sanchez. BPo

Summary for Alastor. Laura Riding Jackson. FuPo

Summe men sayen that I am blac. *Unknown.* MiEL

Summer. Frank Asch. AYFP; NTCP

Summer. John Ashbery. NAAL-2

Summer. John Betjeman. PeLi

Summer. Robert Bloomfield. Ro

Summer. Robert Bloomfield. Ro

Summer. Chang Yü. *Fr.* The Four Seasons in the Mountains. CoBLCP, *tr. by* Jonathan Chaves

Summer, The. Change. Charlotte Zolotow. AYFP

Summer. Douglas Dunn. *See* France.

Summer. Fan Ch'eng-ta. SuSp, *tr. by* Irving Y. Lo *Fr.* Seasonal Poems on Fields and Gardens.

Summer. Hesiod. GrIP, *tr. by* Richard Lattimore *Fr.* Works and Days.

Summer. Moishe Kulbak, *Yiddish.* CEEP, *tr. by* Ruth Whitman

Summer, The. Morgan Llwyd.

1. What? summer now? divisions ring. PBRV

Summer. Tom Marshall. NOBC

Summer. Josephine Miles. FaBoWP; WPE

Summer. Walter Dean Myers. PiM

Summer. Helen G. Quigless. BkSV *Fr.* Childhood Scenes in Four Seasons.

Summer. Christina Rossetti. AYFP; PBMP

(Summer Days.) CTV

Summer. Edmund Spenser. *Fr.* Wood Of Error. AEP

Summer. Georg Trakl, *German.* NNPT, *tr. by* Robert Genier

Summer. *Unknown.* SuSp, *tr. by* Michael E. Workman *Fr.* Tzu-yeh Songs of the Four Seasons.

"All winds died this hot day."

"At dawn I stand on cool roof garden."

"Green lotus leaves, a canopy on the pond."

"These scanty clothes too drab."

"Though humid summer's unfit for excursions."

"Toss and turn on bamboo mat."

Summer 1983. Mary Jo Salter. RA

Summer, adieu. Ode to the End of Summer. Phyllis McGinley. NBLV

Summer Adjustments. Anne S. Perlman. CMAP

Summer Afternoon. Stewart Conn. FaBoTC

Summer Again. Yves Bonnefoy, *French.* VCWP, *tr. by* Lisa Sapinkopf

Summer again; / in the mirrors of this room. Margaret Atwood. *Fr.* The Circle Game. MoCV

Summer air is thick, is wads, The. Looking Down on Glen Canisp. Norman MacCaig. FaBoTC

Summer and [the] autumn had been so wet, The. Bishop Hatto. Robert Southey. OBNV; OBSP; OxAEP-2

Summer and Winter. Shelley. OxAEP-2; SCGP

Summer, At Home. Mary Clark. IFJA

Summer Band Concert. Vivian Smith. CBAP

Summer, betray this tree again! Misericordia. Margaret Mead. PoA

Summer blew its little drifts of sound, The. Army of Occupation. Sarah Morgan Bryan Piatt. NCAP

Summer Breeze. *Unknown.* BoTP

Summer breeze. Cor Van den Heuvel. HA

Summer Breezes. Frank O'Hara. FTOS

Summer brought fireflies in swarms. Childhood. Sharan Strange. GT

Summer come soon and turn the sickness from my house. Entreaty. Robert Fitzgerald. OxBSP

Summer comes / The ziczac hovers. Magalu. Helene Johnson. BlSi; PoBA

Summer Commentary, A. Yvor Winters. LiTM

Summer Countries, The. Henry Rago. VGW

Summer Dawn. William Morris. GSo; NOBE; NOBVV; OAEL-2; OBEV; OBNC; OxAEP-2

Summer Day, A. Joanna Baillie.

Evening. ECWP

Summer Day, A. Robert Greacen. PNI

Summer Day, A. Florence Harrison. BoTP

Summer Day. Yüan Mei, *Chinese.* OHMPC, *tr. by* Kenneth Rexroth

Summer Day in the Mountains. Li Po, *Chinese.* CoBCP, *tr. by* Burton Watson

Summer day suffocates, smothers, pants, The. Poem on Azure. Anna de Noailles, *French.* WPOW, *tr. by* Betty L. Schwimmer

Summer Days. Wathen Mark Wilks Call. EBVV

Summer Days. Christina Rossetti. *See* Summer.

Summer days are noticeably shortening, The. Margarita Iosifovna Aliger, *Russian.* TCRP, *tr. by* Daniel Weissbort

Summer days were sandlot days. Sandlot Days. M. P. Flynn. CTV

Summer delights the scholar. The Scholar. Austin Clarke. RB

Summer dream beneath the shrubbery? The. (LL) Sonnet—To Science. Edgar Allan Poe. NAAL-1; NAAL-3

Summer dream beneath the tamarind tree? The. (LL) Sonnet—To Science. Edgar Allan Poe. APN-1; AmPP; MeMAP; OxBA; PBMP; Son; TAP

Summer drizzle. John Wills. HA

Summer Drought. Phạm Quý Thích, *Chinese.* AVP, *tr. by* Huỳnh Sanh Thông

Summer Ending, The. Glenway Wescott. PoA

Summer ends now; now, barbarous in beauty, the stooks [a]rise. Hurrahing in Harvest. Gerard Manley Hopkins. CMoP; MoBrPo; NAEL-2; PeECV; PoE; TOF

Summer evening. Chuck Brickley. HA

Summer Evening. Walter De la Mare. MoBrPo

Summer Evening's Meditation, A. Anna Laetitia Barbauld. Ro *Fr.* Poems (1773).

Summer Eve's Vision, A. Maria Jane Jewsbury. VWP

Summer—five o'clock. In the Courtyard. Miriam Ulinover, *Yiddish.* CEEP, *tr. by* Seth L. Wolitz

Summer Garden. "Anna Akhmatova," *Russian.* BoWoP, *tr. by* Stephen Stepanchev

Summer goes, summer goes. Russell Hoban. AYFP

Summer grasses. Basho, *Japanese.* Spl *tr. by* Geoffrey Bownas, Anthony Thwaite *and* Lucien Stryk

Summer grasses grow, The. Basho, *Japanese.* TAL, *tr. by* Harold G. Henderson

Summer grows old, cold-blooded mother. Frog Autumn. Sylvia Plath. OxBSP; PFE

Summer Harvest Spreads the Fields, The. Nathan Strong. AH

Summer has doft his latest green. Winter. W. D. Landor. BoTP

Summer holds, The: upon its glittering lake. Chorus. W. H. Auden. *Fr.* The Dog beneath the Skin. OxBTC

Summer Holiday. Robinson Jeffers. MoAmPo; OxBA

Summer Home. Seamus Heaney. PBCIP

Summer I taught English to the French, The. Abigail Mozley. PeLV

Summer Idyll. George Barker. FaBoMo

Summer Images. John Clare. OBNC

Summer in England, 1914. Alice Thompson Meynell. BrRo; SoSe-8; WPE

Summer in the Arges, with plum trees bent low on the hills. Seeds of Flight. Anghel Dumbrveanu, *Romanian.* CEEP, tr. by Adam J. Sorkin and Irina Grigorescu Pan

Summer in the South. Paul Laurence Dunbar. GT

Summer in the trees! "It is time to strangle several bad poets." Kenneth Koch. *Fr.* Fresh Air. CAPP-1; NNaP; NeAP

Summer Is a Poem by Ovid. Douglas G. Jones. NIP-4

Summer is acoming in. *Unknown. See* Sumer is icumen in.

Summer is by. William Soutar, *Irish.* FaBoVe

Summer is come, and evening spreads its gold. Return. Theodore Spencer. PoA

Summer is coming, summer is coming. The Throstle. Tennyson. ACTP

Summer Is Ended. Christina Rossetti. NOBVV

Summer Is Gone. *Unknown, Old Irish.* FaBoCh, tr. by Kuno Meyer

Summer is gone with all its roses. Bitter for Sweet. Christina Rossetti. GBL

Summer is late, my heart. Touch Me. Stanley Kunitz. BAP-96; NoP-4

Summer Is Nigh. *Unknown.* BoTP

Summer is over and. Bashō, A Departure. Robert Hass. LoL

Summer is over, the old cow said. Moo! Robert Silliman Hillyer. OBAL

Summer journeys. Manhattan. Lorenz Hart. OBAL

Summer Landscape; or, The Dragon's Teeth, The. Rolfe Humphries. NYBP

Summer Lost. Harriet Hamilton King. VWP

Summer Lullaby, A. Eudora S. Bumstead. BoTP

Summer Malison, The. Gerard Manley Hopkins. CMoP; PoEL-5

Summer meant peeling: peaches. The Preserving. Kevin Young. GT

Summer moon. William J. Higginson. HA

Summer Morning, A. Rachel Lyman Field. ChAP

Summer Morning. Charles Simic. IFJA

Summer My Mother Fell in Love and Wanted to Leave My Father, The. Adora Phillips. CMAP

Summer near the River. Carolyn Kizer. CoAP; VGW

Summer Night, The. Friedrich Gottlieb Klopstock, *German.* GePo, tr. by George C. Schoolfield

Summer night. Peggy Lyles. HA

Summer Night. Antonio Machado Ruiz, *Spanish.* BLT, tr. by Willis Barnstone

Summer night. George Swede. HA

Summer Night. Tu Fu, *Chinese.* TAL, tr. by Robert Payne

Summer Night at the Pond Pavillion. Chang Yü. *Fr.* Twelve Miscellaneous Poems on the Fang Garden. CoBLCP, tr. by Jonathan Chaves

Summer night clothes whirling in a dryer. Marlene Mountain. HA

Summer Night. *Unknown, Chinese.* SuSp, tr. by Edward H. Schafer

Summer, 1970. Daniel Halpern. AmPA

Summer nineteen seventy. Lindiwe Mabuza. WPOW

Summer nineteen sixty nine. Seamus Heaney. CIP-2

Summer noon. Lenard D. Moore. HA

Summer Noon: 1941. Yvor Winters. ColAP

Summer, now we must live without your sweet weather. Neidhart von Reuental, *German.* GePo, tr. by Frederick Goldin

Summer of nineteen eighteen, The. The Bad Old Days. Kenneth Rexroth. NNaP; NoAM

Summer of 'sixty-three, sir, and Conrad was gone away. Kentucky Belle. Constance Fenimore Woolson. BLPA; CBCWP; FaBoBe

Summer on the Lake, A. Otto Orban, *Hungarian.* CEEP, tr. by Jascha Kessler

Summer or Its Ending. Yehuda Amichai, *Hebrew.* PoSu, tr. by Dennis Silk

Summer Oracle. Audre Lorde. BlSi; PoBA

Summer Palace burnt, the Winter Palace, wherever it was, The. 10:X:57, 45 Years Since the Fall of the Ch'ing Dynasty. Philip Whalen. NeAP; PoM

Summer passed through the cool rooms, violent. A Stone. Yves Bonnefoy, *French.* VCWP, tr. by John Naughton

Summer Poem, A. Jayanta Mahapatra. VCWP

Summer Pogrom. Fay Zwicky. CBAP

Summer Rain. Amy Lowell. CPO

Summer rain, and the voices of children. Richard Tillinghast. MT

Summer rain isn't here yet, The. The Language of Weather. Ray A. Young Bear. HATNAP

Summer Sabbath. Jessie E. Sampter. TrJP

Summer School. Barrie Wade. AYFP

Summer set lip to earth's bosom bare. The Poppy. Francis Thompson. MoBrPo

Summer Shower. David McCord. TLR

Summer Shower, A. *Unknown.* BoTP

Summer Sketches. Bessie Rayner Parkes. Lilian's Second Letter. VWP

Summer slams the tropic sun, The. A Country Club Romance. Derek Walcott. OxBC

Summer Solstice. Peter Blue Cloud. *Fr.* Within the Seasons. HATNAP

Summer Solstice. George Bowering. "I am slowly dying, water evaporating." NOBC

Summer Solstice. Alan Garner. NOxBChV

Summer Solstice. Dorothy Hewett. Sunset flames over the city, The. BMAP

Summer Solstice, New York City. Sharon Olds. NAmP90

Summer Song, A. George Peele. *See* Song: "When as [*or* whenas] the rye [*or* rie] reach to the chin."

Summer Song. *Unknown, Eskimo.* APN-2, tr. by Franz Boas

Summer Song. Emperor Wu of Han, *Chinese.* ChiP, tr. by Arthur Waley

Summer, splendid summer, nourishing the poet on the milk of your light. Midnight Elegy. Léopold Sédar Senghor, *French.* NegPo, tr. by Ellen Conroy Kennedy

Summer still plays across the street. Dying: An Introduction. Louis Edward Sissman. NYBP

Summer stillness. Peggy Lyles. HA

Summer Storm. Dana Gioia. RA

Summer Storm. Louis Simpson. OxBC

Summer sun bakes. Summer School. Barrie Wade. AYFP

Summer sun is sinking low, The. Sunset. Henry Wadsworth Longfellow. BoTP

Summer sun ray, The. Noon Walk on the Asylum Lawn. Anne Sexton. OBGa

Summer that I was ten—The, The. The Centaur. May Swenson. FaBoWP; NMM-2; NTP; TwCP

Summer, this is our flesh. Seasons of the Soul. Allen Tate. FuPo; OxBA

Summer Time on Bredon. Hugh Kingsmill. UV

Summer. Time to leave. Time to Leave. Ory Bernstein, *Hebrew.* IP, tr. by Warren Bargad and Stanley F. Chyet

Summer turned. John Gneisenau Neihardt. GM *Fr.* The Song of the Indian Wars.

Summer was dry, dry the garden. On the Debt My Mother Owed to Sears Roebuck. Edward Dorn. CoAmPo; TRP

Summer wilderness, a blue light. The Loon on Forrester's Pond. Hayden Carruth. AFr

Summer Wind. William Cullen Bryant. APN-1; PoEL-4

Summer wind, The. What Her Girl Friend Said before the Elopement. Kutavayir Kirattanar, *Tamil.* PLW, tr. by A. K. Ramanujan

Summer Wish, A. Christina Rossetti. OBNC

Summer with Monika. Roger McGough. "Away from you." OBCoV

Summerfield. Jim Barnes. HATNAP, *sect.* i *Fr.* An Ex-Deputy Sheriff Remembers the Eastern Oklahoma Murderers.

Summers and summers have come, and gone with the flight of the swallow. The Tantramar Revisited. Sir Charles G. D. Roberts. NOBC

Summer's Day, A. Joanna Baillie. WoRP

Summer's Day, A. Tom Leonard. NBrP

Summer's Dream, A. Elizabeth Bishop. OxBC

Summer's Early End at Hudson's Bay. Hayden Carruth. NYBP

Summer's Farewell. Thomas Nashe. PoEL-2 *Fr.* Summer's Last Will and Testament.

Summer's gone brown, and, with it. Me to You. Alastair Reid. NYBP

Summer's Last Will and Testament. Thomas Nashe. Autumn Hath All the Summer's Fruitful Treasure. Baning Summer. OxBSP; SCGP Litany in Time of Plague, A. ClHu; GEA; NAEL-1; NIP-4; OAEL-1; PoPoPo; PoRA ("Adieu, farewell earth's bliss.") PeECV (In Plague Time.) FaBoCh; FaPoR (In Time of Pestilence.) PeECV (Song in Time of Plague.) SCV

Spring. GTBS-P; NOBE; OBEV; SCGP

Summer's Farewell. PoEL-2

Summer's loneliness. At a hospital in Tokyo during the summer of 1911. Kitahara Hakushū, *Japanese*. MJT, *tr. by* Makoto Ueda

Summer's Night, A. Paul Laurence Dunbar. APN-2

("Fire-flies come stagg'ring down the dark, The.") (LL) NoP-4

Summer's sun is warm and bright. Pleasant Changes. Jane Euphemia Browne. OxBChV

Summer's sun was beaming hot, The. Mother's Songs. Frank Barbour Coffin. AAP

Summertime. Su Shun-ch'in, *Chinese*. SuSp, *tr. by* Michael E. Workman

Summertime and the Living. Robert Earl Hayden. PoBA; TwCP

Summing Up. Claribel Alegría, *Spanish*. LoL, *tr. by* D. J. Flakoll

Summing-up, The. Stanley Kunitz. OBAL

Summit, The. Chiyong Chong, *Korean*. CKP, *tr. by* Jaihiun Kim

Summit, The. Kathleen Jessie Raine. OxBS *Fr.* Beinn Naomh.

Summit gain'd how glorious the reward, The. Robert Dunbar. PBCV *Fr.* The Cruise.

Summit Temple, The. Li Po, *Chinese*. TAL, *tr. by* Robert Payne

Summon now the kings of the forest. Mmenson. Edward Kamau Brathwaite. OPOU

Summon the Earth (the fair Astrea's gone,). An Elegy upon the Death of Mrs. A. Behn, the Incomparable Astrea. *Unknown*. KTR

Summoned by Bells. John Betjeman.

"My dear deaf father, how I loved him then." OxBTC

Summoned by conscious recollection, she. Misery and Splendor. Robert Hass. VCAP

Summonee's Tale, The. Stanley J. Sharpless. BXAP

Summons, The. Milton. *See* Satan's Legions and the Beech Leaves of the Casentino.

Summons. David Rivard. NAmP90

Summons to Love, *sl. diff. vers.* William Drummond, of Hawthornden. *See* Invocation: "Pheobus, arise! / And paint the sable skies."

Summons to Town, A. Sir John Suckling. NOSC

Sums, The. Lauris Edmond. FaBoWP

Sun, The. Judah Al-Harizi, *Hebrew*. BLT, *tr. by* T. Carmi

Sun, The. Hugo Ball, *German*. PFTM, *tr. by* Christopher Middleton

Sun. John Blight. BMAP

Sun. James Dickey. CAPP-1

Sun, The. John Drinkwater. NTCP

Sun. Omer Hillel, *Hebrew*. MHP, *tr. by* Ruth Finer Mintz

Sun. Jean Kenward. SpW

Sun. Branko Miljkovic, *Serbo-Croatian*. HSix, *tr. by* Charles Simic

Sun, The. Czeslaw Milosz. ChAP

Sun. Michael Palmer. APSN; FTOS

("These Letters—humid, sunless. The writing occurs on their walls.") (LL) FTOS

Sun, The. Tujin Park, *Korean*. CKP, *tr. by* Jaihiun Kim

Sun, The. Marge Piercy. WPOW *Fr.* Laying Down the Tower.

(Total Influence of Outcome of the Matter: The Sun, The.) WPOW

Sun, The. Anne Sexton. NYBP; PBWP

Sun. Gary Soto. TRP

Sun, The. Francis Thompson. MoBrPo *Fr.* Ode to the Setting Sun.

Sun, The. Vidya, *Sanskrit*.

I praise the disk of the rising sun. PBWP; WPOW

Sun, The. William Carlos Williams. MeMAP *Fr.* Paterson.

Sun, The. Valerie Worth. NOxBChV

Sun—a shadow of a magnitude, A. (LL) On Seeing the Elgin Marbles. Keats. GSo; ImPo; NAEL-2; NIP-4

Sun a-shine an' rain a-fall. Sun-a-shine, Rain-a-fall. Valerie Bloom. NOxBChV

Sun a shine but tings noh bright. Dutty Tough. Louise Bennett. PBCV

Sun above the hills raged in the height, The. Lot and His Daughters II. Alec Derwent Hope. ChIV-1

Sun and Fog contested, the. Emily Dickinson. AYFP; NTP; Spl

Sun and Moon. Charlotte Druitt Cole. BoTP

Sun and moon. Gary Hotham. HA

Sun and Moon. Mary Kinzie. HFC

Sun and Moon: I saw a strange creature. Cynewulf. ASW, *tr. by* Kevin Crossley-Holland *Fr.* Riddles (Exeter Book).

Sun and moon refuse to slow their pace. Poem without a Category. T'ao Ch'ien, *Chinese*. CoBCP, *tr. by* Burton Watson

Sun and Moon So High and Bright, The. *Unknown*. AH

Sun and moon, that ceaselessly obey, The. Immortal Israel. Judah Halevi, *Hebrew*. TrJP, *tr. by* Solomon Solis-Cohen

Sun and Rain and Dew from Heaven. Adam Lindsay Gordon. PoLF *Fr.* Ye Wearie Wayfarer.

Sun and rain at work together. The Red-Gold Rain. Sacheverell Sitwell. MoBrPo

Sun and softness. Sun Song. Langston Hughes. MBE

Sun appearing, The: a pendant. Plainview: 3. N. Scott Momaday. CDW

Sun as a Spinning Top (I), The. Francis Ponge, *French*. AF, *tr. by* Serge Gavronsky

Sun at noon to higher air, The. March. A. E. Housman. FaBoCh

Sun-beams [*or* Sun-beames] in the east are spred [*or* spred], The. Epithalamion Made at Lincoln's Inn [*or* Lincolnes Inne]. Donne. SeCP

Sun, beholding so as he does pass, The. On a Fair Lady, Looking in the Glass. Richard Leigh. NOSC

Sun blazed while the thunder yet, The. The Mill-Pond. Edward Thomas, *German*. RB

Sun blooms in our bodies. Summer. Tom Marshall. NOBC

Sun brightens. Alan Pizzarelli. HA

Sun brightly beam'd, the birds sweetly sang, The. (LL) Who Was It, Tell Me. Heinrich Heine, *German*. TrJP, *tr. by* Richard Garnett

Sun came, Miss Brooks—, The. Etheridge Knight. PoBA

Sun Came Out in April, The. C. Day Lewis. MoBS

Sun came up, The. Rain Rain on the Splintered Girl. Ishmael Reed. PoBA

Sun cheers us for a pin-point, flicks, then westers. Mating Answer. Ronald Bottrall. PoA

Sun Children. Leslie Marmon Silko. VoR

Sun comes up, wind starts to ripple, The. Going to the Ministry with Chao Tzu-ch'i. Yü Chi, *Chinese*. CoBLCP, *tr. by* Jonathan Chaves

Sun-Day Hymn. Oliver Wendell Holmes. *See* Lord of All Being, Throned Afar.

Sun dazzle and black shadow. Mending the Adobe. Hayden Carruth. Poetsp

Sun descending in the west, The. Night. William Blake. BoTP; CH; FHYEP; FaBoBe; OBEV; OxBChV; PoLF; Ro *Fr.* Songs of Innocence.

Sun descending, the *Phæacian* train, The. Homer. *Fr.* Odyssey. NAWM-1, *tr. by* Robert Fitzgerald

Sun-Dial, The. Thomas Love Peacock. OBNC *Fr.* Melincourt.

Sun does [*or* doth] arise, The. The Echoing [*or* Ecchoing] Green. William Blake. BoTP; CH; FHYEP; NAEL-2; NTP; OxAEP-2; PoE; UnPo *Fr.* Songs of Innocence.

Sun drew off at last his piercing fires, The. Witchcraft: New Style. Lascelles Abercrombie. MoBrPo

Sun dries me as I dance, The. (LL) Second Shaman Song. Gary Snyder. NOBA; NeAP; PoM

Sun drops below the elms. Routes. Peter Everwine. NNaP

Sun drops luridly into the west, The. Circe. Augusta Davies Webster. PeVV; VWP *Fr.* Circe.

Sun etches out the minutes of my days, The. Hill Country. Olive Senior. HCP

Sun-Flower, The. Dora Greenwell. VWP; WPE

(Sunflower, The.) PEW

Sun frets, a fat wafer falling like a trap of failed mesh, The. Hole, Where Once in Passion We Swam. Dave Jeddie Smith. NoAM

Sun from the east tips the mountains with gold, The. Hunting Song. Paul Whitehead. OxBoLi *Fr.* Apollo and Daphne.

Sun-god was reclining on a couch of rosy shells, The. Sunset Picture. Henrietta Cordelia Ray. CBWP-3

Sun goes. David Chapman Berry. CDa

Sun goes down, The. Midsummer Night. Elizabeth Gould. BoTP

Sun goes down, The. Cor Van den Heuvel. HA

Sun goes down, and over all, The. Low Tide on Grand Pré. Bliss Carman. NOBC

Sun goes down for hours, taking more of her along, The. The Lady in the Pink Mustang. Louise Erdrich. HATNAP

Sun going down. Sundown Blues. Raymond R. Patterson. SeSe

Sun had grown on lessening day, The. Ballad: The Sun Had Grown on Lessening Day. John Clare. EnVR

Sun had wheeled from Grey's to Dammer's Crest, The. The Burghers. Thomas Hardy. EBNV

Sun has come, I know, the. Walter James Turner. MoBrPo

Sun has gone from the shining skies, The. A Summer Lullaby. Eudora S. Bumstead. BoTP

Sun has left the middle of the sky, The. Family. Eve Shelnutt. CMAP

Sun has long been set, The. A Night in June. Wordsworth. BoTP

Sun has risen on the eastern brim of the world, The. The Song of Lo-fu. *Unknown, Chinese*. AWP; ChiP, *tr. by* Arthur Waley

Sun has set, and the long grass now, The. Emily Jane Brontë. UnPo

Sun has set, the moon is in darkness, The. Swarming Mosquitoes. Mei Yao Ch'en, *Chinese*. APo; SuSp, *tr. by* Jonathan Chaves

Sun has sunk 'neath yonder distant hill, The. Belshazzar's Feast. Eloise Bibb. CBWP-4

Sun hath run his course through all the Signes, The. George Wither. PBRV *Fr.* Vox Pacifica.

Sun hath twice brought forth[e] the tender green, The. The Restless State of a Lover. Henry Howard, Earl of Surrey. AAS; SiPS

Sun, hung by a string, The. Diptych. Birago Diop, *French.* NegPo, *tr. by* Ellen Conroy Kennedy

Sun hung by a thread, The. Birago Diop. *See* Diptych.

Sun-Hunters, The. Mark O'Connor. NOBAu

Sun in Capricorn, The. Joyce Mansour, *French.* PBWP, *tr. by* Carol Cosman

Sun, in clownish yellow, but not a clown, The. Wallace Stevens. NOBA *Fr.* Esthétique du Mal. LiTM

Sun, / in her memory, The. Lost in the Desert. Clarence Major. FTOS

Sun in the mouth of the day. Envoi. Robley Wilson Jr. PBCAP

Sun is about to set when I board the boat, The. Sailing at Night on Flowing-sand River. Lin Hung, *Chinese.* SuSp, *tr. by* Irving Y. Lo

Sun is a Negro, The. Bob Kaufman. ISC

Sun is an orange dinghy, The. What is the Sun? Wes Magee. AYFP

Sun is blazing and the sky is blue, The. Pink Dog. Elizabeth Bishop. NALW

Sun is blue and scarlet on my page, The. Falling Asleep over the Aeneid. Robert Lowell. MoAmPo; OxBA

Sun is bright,—the air is clear, The. It Is Not Always May. Henry Wadsworth Longfellow. PWR

Sun is down, The. What the Passersby Said to the Lover Eloping with the Girl. Uraiyur Mutukorran, *Tamil.* PLW, *tr. by* A. K. Ramanujan

Sun is folding, cars stall and rise, The. The New World. Imamu Amiri Baraka. NoAM; NoP-4; PmAP

Sun is going down. The. Aranda Song. *Unknown, Aranda.* CBAP, *tr. by* T. G. H. Strehlow

Sun is going down. A few miles, The. Making a Great Space Small. Greg Pape. PaTW

Sun is going down behind the hills, The. The Buffalo Boy On a Field of Corpses. Phổ Đú'c, *Vietnamese.* AVP, *tr. by* Huỳnh Sanh Thông

Sun is gone down, The. Things We Can Depend On. George Macdonald. CTV

Sun is in the west. Fishing boats, The. Drinking at Night with Yen Kung-mou. Shen Chou, *Chinese.* CoBLCP, *tr. by* Jonathan Chaves

Sun is lord and god, sublime, serene, The. The Lake of Gaube. Swinburne. CABP; NAEL-2; OAEL-2

Sun is nigh the verge, The. Soon we must part. A Walk. Hedwig Lachmann, *German.* TrJP, *tr. by* Jethro Bithell

Sun is not in love with us, The. The Isles of Greece. Demetrios Capetanakis. GTBS-P

Sun is rising, The. Healing Song. *Unknown.* OBVE, *tr. by* Frances Densmore

Sun is setting—clouds still glow with red, The. Harvesting at Sunset. Anh Tho', *Vietnamese.* AVP, *tr. by* Huỳnh Sanh Thông

Sun is setting in another part of the city, The. Animal Mimicry. Robert Polito. WWSi

Sun is shining in my backdoor, The. Myself When I Am Real. Al Young. PoBA

Sun is sinking. Here on the pine-haunted bank, the mosquitoes, The. Sunset at a Lake. Robert Bly. WeT

Sun is the blind eyes of statues gilded, The. Andrew Oerke. PoA

Sun is warm, the sky is clear, The. Stanzas Written in Dejection, near Naples [*or* —December 1818, near Naples]. Shelley. GTBS-P; NAEL-2; NAWM-2; NoP-4; PBMP; PoRA

Sun kept setting—setting—still, The. Emily Dickinson. APN-2

Sun lights up a distant ridge another, The. John Wills. HA

Sun like a sleepy giant, The. Narcolepsy. Maureen Owen. TTTS

Sun like an orange mousse through the trees. Dog Day Vespers. Charles Wright. LCAP-2

Sun May Set, The. Catullus. *See* Lines from Catullus.

Sun moves south like a transient lover, The. The Yield. Gloria Frym. DeD

Sun now darts his fervid rays, The. Lines Written in the Dog-Days. William Woty. NOEC

Sun Now Risen, The. Johann Conrad Beissel. AH

Sun of Auschwitz, The. Tadeusz Borowski, *Polish.* AF, *tr. by* Larry Rafferty, Meryl Natchez *and* Tadeusz Pioro; HP, *tr. by* Tadeuszt Pióro

Sun of Our Existence, The. Mrs. Henry Linden. CBWP-4

Sun, of whose terrain we creatures are, The. Solar Creation. Charles Madge. APAD; FaBoMo; OBMV; OxBTC

Sun on hillsides, wind on seas. Desolation. *Unknown, Welsh.* OBWVE, *tr. by* Aneirin Talfan Davies

Sun on the faces. On the knotted rocks. Campaign. Muriel Rukeyser. GM

Sun on the tree-tops no longer is seen, The. Queen Sabbath. Hayyim Nahman Bialik, *Hebrew.* TrJP, *tr. by* Jessie Sampter

Sun on water now in my mouth memory rich as real. Your Tongue Sparkles. "Chrystos." CPO

Sun only a small bird flitting, The. Of Royal Issue. Brigit Pegeen Kelly. PUP-20

Sun plants a foot in the pasture, The. Goree. Niyi Osundare. HBAPE

Sun rises, The. In Fields of Summer. Galway Kinnell. VGW

Sun rises at the southeastern corner, The. Mulberry by the Path. *Unknown, Chinese.* SuSp, *tr. by* Hans H. Frankel

Sun rises red amid radiant clouds, The. *Unknown.* FaBoSe *Fr.* Sir Gawain and the Green Knight.

Sun rushed up the sky, The; the taxi flew. Parting as Descent. John Berryman. MoAmPo

Sun sank in the thunderous sky of the town, The. Marriage. Walter James Turner. NOBAu

Sun sends me wires of blue rain, The. Faustin Charles. HCP *Fr.* Letters from Home. HCP

Sun set, but set not his hope, The. Character. Ralph Waldo Emerson. OxBSP

Sun sets in night, and the stars shun the day, The. North American Death Song. Anne Hunter. ECWP

Sun sets in night, and the stars shun the day, The. Song. Royall Tyler. NAAL-3 *Fr.* The Contrast.

Sun sets in the cold without friends, The. Dusk in Winter. W. S. Merwin. BLT

Sun sets on the dike where I walk. A Song of "Hand-in-Hand." Ou-yang Hsiu, *Chinese.* SuSp, *tr. by* Irving Y. Lo

Sun sets on Tung-t'ing's waves. Yang Wei-chen. *Fr.* Songs of Lake Tung-t'ing. CoBLCP, *tr. by* Jonathan Chaves

Sun sets, the pagoda is darkened, The. Evening Bell from a Misty Temple. Wen Cheng-ming, *Chinese.* CoBLCP, *tr. by* Jonathan Chaves

Sun sets, The. The wind moans. Ts'ai Yen. BoWoP; WPOW *Fr.* Eighteen Verses Sung to a Tatar Reed Whistle.

Sun sets unevenly and the people, The. Chasing the Bird. Robert Creeley. MoNo

Sun shines, The. Tommies in the Train. D. H. Lawrence. PoWW

Sun shines bright, but sadly, The. Autumn. Priscilla Jane Thompson. CBWP-2

Sun shines bright in the old Kentucky home, The. My Old Kentucky Home[, Good Night!]. Stephen Collins Foster. APN-2; FaBoA; FaBoBe; PoLF

Sun shines high on yonder hill, The. The False Lover Won Back. *Unknown.* ESPB; OxBB

Sun shines in disarray, The. Maybe There's a God Around. Aleksandr Ivanovich Vvedensky, *Russian.* TCRP, *tr. by* Bradley Jordan

Sun Shines over the Mountain, The. *Unknown.* AmFP

Sun shone in my hut, The. He Who Has Lost All. David Diop, *French.* TTY, *tr. by* Anne Atik

Sun sinks softly to his ev'ning post, The. "Orpheus C. Kerr." *Fr.* The Rejected "National Hymns." OBAL

Sun sinks towards the horizon, The. Clear Evening after Rain. Tu Fu, *Chinese.* OHPC, *tr. by* Kenneth Rexroth

Sun Song. Langston Hughes. MBE

Sun sought thy dim bed and brought forth light, The. Africa. Claude McKay. NAAAL; Son

Sun Speaks, The. Marcia Southwick. CMAP

Sun Spots. Christopher Buckley. PuP-16

Sun stood still, The. The Day They Came for Our House. Don Mattera. PeSAV

Sun struts over the asphalt world, The. Noon of the Sunbather. Marge Piercy. NMM-2

Sun stuff, star fluff. John Rice. SpW

Sun-tanned men and women, toiling there together. Reapers. Mathilde Blind. WPE

Sun, that brave man, The. The Brave Man. Wallace Stevens. PBMP; SAmP

Sun that brief December day, The. Snow-Bound [*or* Snow-Bound; a Winter Idyl]. John Greenleaf Whittier. APN-1; AiP; AmPP; ColAP; NAAL-3; NOBA; OxBA; PAR; TAP; TFi

Sun that shines all day so bright, The. Night. *Unknown.* BoTP

Sun, the moon, the stars, the seas, the hills and the plains, The. The Higher Pantheism. Tennyson. CABP; EnVR

Sun, the rose, the lily, the dove, The. Love's Résumé. Heinrich Heine. TrJP, *tr. by* J. F. C.

Sun through the window, The. The Mullins Farm. Richard H. W. Dillard. MT

Sun-treader, life and light be thine for ever! Robert Browning. EPCY *Fr.* Pauline, mine own, bend o'er me—thy soft breast.

Sun Underfoot Among the Sundews, The. Amy Clampitt. NoP-4

Sun upon the lake is low, The. Datur Hora Quieti. Sir Walter Scott. GTBS-P

Sun upon the Weirdlaw Hill, The. The Dreary Change. Sir Walter Scott. NAEL-2; OAEL-2; OBNC

Sun used to shine while we two walked, The. Edward Thomas. FP; FaBoTw

Sun was down, and twilight grey, The. In the Room. James Thomson. NOBVV; PeVV

Sun was now withdrawn, The. Damon and Cupid. John Gay. EnLoPo

Sun was shining on the sea, The. The Walrus and the Carpenter. "Lewis Carroll." BLPA; CABP; CBNP; ChAP; EBEvV; FPC; FaBoBe; NAEL-2; NOBL; NOBVV; NoAM; OBSP; OTCP; OxAEP-2; OxBChV; PeLV; PoRA; SAGP; TFi *Fr.* Through the Looking-Glass.

Sun went down in beauty, The. George Marion McClellan. AAP

Sun, when he enamels day, The. Praise of a Yellow Skin, The, or An Elizabeth in Gold. John Collop. NOSC

Sun which doth the greatest comfort bring[e], The. Francis Beaumont's Letter from the Country to Jonson. Francis Beaumont. BeJo; SeCP

Sun whirls an axle on fire, The. Leonidas of Tarentum, *Greek.* GrAn, *tr. by* Peter Levi

Sun will never see you, The. On a Pet Grasshopper. Aristodicus of Rhodes, *Greek.* PGA, *tr. by* Kenneth Rexroth

Sun will rise, The. (LL) Giraffe. Stanley Plumly. ChAP

Sun woke me this morning loud, The. A True Account of Talking to the Sun at Fire Island. Frank O'Hara. HCAP; NNaP; RB; TTTS

Sunbather in Late October, A. Arthur Gregor. PFE

Sunbathing. Nancy Travis. ISC

Sunbeams. Avner Trainin, *Hebrew.* MHP, *tr. by* Ruth Finer Mintz

Sunbeams streamed without, The. In the Morgue. Israel Zangwill. TrJP

Sunburned, with lustre of her own. (LL) To the State of Love or The Senses' Festival. John Cleveland. CBLP

Suncoming. Oliver La Grone. NBV

Sunday. George Herbert. GeHe; PeECV; TrCP

Sunday. Josephine Miles. PoA

Sunday. Carl Phillips. GT

Sunday. Primus St. John. ISC

Sunday. James Schuyler. TTTS

Sunday. Philippe Soupault, *French.* PFTM, *tr. by* Anselm Hollo

Sunday. Ojars Vacietis, *Latvian.* CEEP, *tr. by* Inara Cedrins

Sunday: A Fragment Transcribed from a Ms. in Chatterton's Handwriting. Thomas Chatterton. ECEV

Sunday afternoon and the water. Fording the River. Seamus Deane. PBCIP; PNI

Sunday Afternoon at Fulham Palace. Elizabeth Spires. NAmP90

Sunday Afternoon at the State Hospital. Marilyn J. Boe. LoHo

Sunday afternoon in late September, one of the last, A. Sunday Afternoon at Fulham Palace. Elizabeth Spires. NAmP90

Sunday Afternoons. Herbert Asquith. NAAAL

Sunday Afternoons. Yusef Komunyakaa. NAmP90

("They'd latch the screendoors.") NoP-4

Sunday Afternoons. Anthony Thwaite. OxBTC

Sunday and sunlight ashen on the Square. The Self Unsatisfied Runs Everywhere. Delmore Schwartz. PoA

Sunday at Hampstead. James Thomson.

"How your eyes dazzle down into my soul!" EnVR

In the Train. BoTP; OBEV

"This is the Heath of Hampstead." EnVR

"Was it hundreds of years ago, my love." EnVR

Sunday at the End of Summer. Howard Nemerov. ImGa

Sunday at the State Hospital. David Ignatow. RaBo

Sunday Brunch. Reuben Jackson. ISC

Sunday Chicken. Gwendolyn Brooks. ColAP *Fr.* Notes from the Childhood and the Girlhood. LCAP-2

Sunday Chimes in the City. Louise Imogen Guincy. APN-2

Sunday, Churchbells. You stood outside. Coming Home. Daniel S. Simko. CEEP

Sunday Dreamer's Guide to Yarrow, Missouri, A. Jim Barnes. HATNAP

Sunday Evening. Barbara Guest. NeAP

Sunday Evening. Sam Hunt. PeNZ

Sunday Evening in the Common. John Hall Wheelock. MoAmPo

Sunday Graveyard. Maura Stanton. CMAP

Sunday Greens. Rita Dove. GT; LCAP-2

Sunday heavy potlid on the boiling blood. [Part One]. Tristan Tzara. PFTM, *tr. by* Jerome Rothenberg *Fr.* The Approximate Man.

Sunday in Glastonbury. Robert Bly. CoAmPo

Sunday in Great Tew. Peter McDonald. PNI

Sunday in the Park. William Carlos Williams. NAAL-2 *Fr.* Paterson.

Sunday in the provinces, a plaintive Norman bell-peal. Maria Luisa Spaziani. NeIt, *tr. by* Beverly Allen *Fr.* The Star of Free Will.

Sunday is the dullest day, treating. Sweeney in Articulo. "Myra Buttle." BXAP *Fr.* The Sweeniad.

Sunday lamb cracks in its fat, The. Mary's Song. Sylvia Plath. ChIV-2; FaBoMo; FaBoWP

Sunday Matinee. Sybil Kollar. FFC

Sunday Morning. Robert Grenier. PmAP

Sunday Morning. Susan Griffin. NMM-2

Sunday morning. B. Vincent Hernandez. IFJA

Sunday Morning. Christina Jenkins. BrRo

Sunday Morning. Wayne Moreland. PoBA

Sunday morning and her mother's hands. Birmingham 1963. Raymond R. Patterson. PoBA

Sunday morning at the marina. Common Prayer. Lynn Ungar. CrSp

Sunday Morning, 1950. Irene McKinney. PBCAP

Sunday Morning Through Binoculars. Eamon Grennan. PBCIP

Sunday News, The. Dana Gioia. WeW-3

Sunday Schools. Anna Sawyer. ECWP

Sunday shuts down on this twentieth-century evening. Boy with His Hair Cut Short. Muriel Rukeyser. LiTM; NALW; NoAM; TwCP; VGW; WPE

Sunday strollers along a sewage-choked Schuylkill. To Some Millions Who Survive Joseph E. Mander, Sr. Sarah E. Wright. PoBA

Sunday, Tarzan in His Hammock. Lewis Buzbee. BAP-95

Sunday the only day we don't work. A Walk. Gary Snyder. NOBA

Sunday up the River. James Thomson.

Gifts. OBEV

"Wine of Love is music, The." OBEV

Sunday Visit. Antigone Kefala. BMAP

Sunday's bad. Why do you bother. Too Bad. Gig Ryan. NOBAu

Sundays of Satin-Legs Smith, The. Gwendolyn Brooks. NAAAL; Poetr; SeSe

Sundays too my father got up early. Those Winter Sundays. Robert Earl Hayden. APAD; ChAP; ColAP; GEA; HAP; HCAP; ISC; InPK-6; LCAP-2; MoP; NIP-4; NoAM; NoP-4; PiM; PoBA; PoPoPo; Poetr; RaBo; SAGP; SSLK; SoSe-8; TFi; UnPo; WeW-3

Sunder me from my bones, O sword of God. The Sword of Surprise. G. K. Chesterton. MoBrPo

Sundered. Israel Zangwill. TrJP

Sundering ultimate kingdom of genesis' thunder, The. (LL) Ceremony after a Fire Raid. Dylan Thomas. AF; CMoP

Sunderland Children, The. Alice Thompson Meynell. NALW

Sundew, The. Swinburne. OBNC; PeVV

Sundial, The. Austin Dobson. OBGa

Sundown. Léonie Adams. MoAmPo

Sundown Blues. Raymond R. Patterson. SeSe

Sundown on the high stonefields! The Starlings in George Square. Edwin Morgan. FaBoTC

Sundown splendid and serene / Death, The. (LL) Margaritæ Sorori [I. M.]. William Ernest Henley. CABP; MoBrPo; NOBE; OBEV; OBNC; PoRA

Sundowner, The. John Shaw Neilson. CBAP

Sundry Christian Passions Contained in Two Hundred. Henry Lok. Son

It Is Not, Lord, the Sound of Many Words.

Sundry Notes. Nguyễn Chí Thiện, *Vietnamese.*

"Party holds you down and you lie still, The." VCWP, *tr. by* Huynh Sanh Thông

Sunfish Races. James Preston. InPK-6

Sunflakes. Frank Asch. NTCP

Sunflower, The. William Blake. *See* Ah Sun-flower.

Sunflower, The. Dora Greenwell. *See* The Sun-Flower.

Sunflower. Rolf Jacobsen, *Norwegian.* RaBo, *tr. by* Robert Bly

Sunflower. Kao Ch'i, *Chinese.* SuSp, *tr. by* Irving Y. Lo

Sunflower. Leonid Nikolaevich Martynov, *Russian.* TCRP, *tr. by* J. R. Rowland

Sunflower. Tuvia Rivner, *Hebrew.* MHP, *tr. by* Ruth Finer Mintz

Sunflower. Su Shih. SuSp, *tr. by* Irving Y. Lo *Fr.* On Chao Ch'ang's Flower Paintings in Wang Po-yang's Collection.

Sunflower ain't a daisy, De. Doan't You Be What You Ain't. Edwin Milton Royle. BLPA

Sunflower Moccasins. Phillip William George. VoR

Sunflower Sonnet Number Two. June Jordan. Son

Sunflower Sutra. Allen Ginsberg. AmPP; CoAP; GM; HCAP; InPS-3; NAAL-2; NOBA; NeAP; PaTW; PoPoPo; VCAP

("Evening sitdown vision.") (LL) PoPoPo

("Of the mad locomotive riverbank sunset Frisco hilly tincan / evening sitdown vision.") (LL) GM

("Riverbank sunset Frisco hilly tincan evening sitdown vision.") (LL) PaTW

Sung at Table by the Same Choir. Anne Penny. ECWP *Fr.* Odes Sung in Commemoration of the Marine Society.

Sung by a Choir of Boys Marching Round the Room. Anne Penny. ECWP *Fr.* Odes Sung in Commemoration of the Marine Society.

Sung From A Hospice. Cyrus Cassells. PUP-20

Sung-ling road in setting sunlight. Feelings Come As I Pass through Wu-chiang. Wu Wei-yeh, *Chinese.* CoBLCP, *tr. by* Jonathan Chaves

Sunheat was equivalent, The. Still There's No Trace. Zim Mnotoza. PeSAV

Sunium. Trumbull Stickney. *Fr.* Sonnets from Greece. APN-1

Sunk Lyonesse. Walter De la Mare. FaBoCh; LiTM

Sunk was each heart, and pale was ev'ry face. (LL) The Suitors watch Ulysses string the bow. Homer, *Greek.* OBVE, *tr. by* Pope

Sunk were his eyes, his voice was harsh and loud. Dryden. *Fr.* Absalom and Achitophel, Pt. I. EBEvV; FHYEP; FaBoPV; HAP; NOSC; OAEL-1; PoE

Sunken Gold. Eugene Lee-Hamilton. GSo; NOBVV

Sunken murmurs rise from the sea bottom. Blue Horse. Masako Takiguchi, *Japanese.* WPJ, *tr. by* Kenneth Rexroth *and* Ikuko Atsumi

Sunken road, / the sycamore pinion rustling above. The Spindle. Peter Huchel, *German.* CEEP, *tr. by* Rich Ives

Sunlicht still on me, you row'd in clood, The. At My Father's Grave. "Hugh MacDiarmid." GTBS-P

Sunlight. Seamus Heaney. *See* Mossbawn Sunlight.

Sunlight climbs the snowpeak. Late October Camping in the Sawtooths. Gary Snyder. BLT

Sunlight drawing from shadow, up and down the street. Passages. Larry Eigner. NeAP

Sunlight dried the last small patches of moisture. In Ferrara. John Jenkins *and* Ken Bolton. BMAP

Sunlight in spring explodes in your eyes. Verses about a Nightingale and a Poet. "Eduard Georgievich Bagritzky," *Russian.* TCRP, *tr. by* Vera Dunham

Sunlight in the house. Maritimes. Penelope Shuttle. BrRo

Sunlight lies along my table. Jane Cooper. *Fr.* The Weather of Six Mornings. NYBP

Sunlight on the garden, The. Louis MacNeice. CMoP; EBEV; FP; GTBS-P; HAP; InPS-3; NAEL-2; NOBE; NOIV; NoP-4; OxAEP-2; OxBTC; PNI; TRP; TwCP

Sunlight streaming on Incense Stone kindles violet smoke. Viewing the Waterfall at Mount Lu. Li Po, *Chinese.* CoBCP; TTTS, *tr. by* Burton Watson

Sunlight that has been chasing me, The. The Cross. Tongju Yun, *Korean.* CKP, *tr. by* Jaihiun Kim

Sunlight that pulls itself over the rooftops looks vacant, The. Inertia. Kirti Chaudhari. WPOW, *tr. by* Leonard Nathan

Sunlight the tall women may never have seen. Children, the Sandbar, That Summer. Muriel Rukeyser. LCAP-2

Sunlight thins, the view empties, the. Evening: for Chang Chi and Chou K'uang. Han Yü, *Chinese.* PLT, *tr. by* A. C. Graham

Sunne begins uppon my heart to shine, The. William Alabaster. ESCV *Fr.* Divine Meditations. Son

Sunne may set and rise, The. Lines from Catullus. Catullus, *Latin.* FaBoEE; NoSic; OBVE; SiPS, *tr. by* Sir Walter Raleigh

Sunny Gale. "Hugh MacDiarmid." FaBoVe

Sunny shaft did I behold, A, *ad. fr.* Tieck's Herbstlied. Glycine's Song. Coleridge. CH; OBEV *Fr.* Zapolya.

Sunnyland. Elmore James. NAAAL

Sunrise. Sidney Lanier. PoEL-5 *Fr.* Hymns of the Marshes. APN-2

Sunrise. Mary Oliver. CrSp

Sunrise. Henrietta Cordelia Ray. BlSi *Fr.* Idyl. CBWP-3

Sunrise. Jim Tollerud. VoR

Sunrise and Moonfall, Rosarito Beach. Campbell McGrath. WeT

Sunrise Comes to Second Avenue. Thylias Moss. TRP

Sunrise path. Ruth Yarrow. HA

Sunrise Sequence. *Unknown, Aborigine.* NOBAu, *tr. by* Ronald M. Berndt *Fr.* The Dulngulg Song Cycle.

Sunrise Thought. Henrietta Cordelia Ray. *Fr.* A Group of Musings. CBWP-3

Sunrise. . . & toward the sunrise stands the village of the Bow People. Muu's Way; or Pictures from the Uterine World. *Unknown, Cuna Indian.* STP, *tr. by* Jerome Rothenberg

Sunrise with Sea Monster. Charles North. FTOS

Sun's bright orb, declining all serene, The. Ship Sets out, the. William Falconer. OxAEP-1 *Fr.* The Shipwreck.

Sun's Darling, The. Thomas Dekker *and others.* Song. NOSC

Suns have set and suns will rise. Keep Cool. Marcus Garvey. PBCV

Sun's high, I've slept enough, still too lazy to get up, The. Writing Again on the Same Theme. Po Chü-i, *Chinese.* CoBCP, *tr. by* Burton Watson

Suns in a skein, the uncut stones of night. Roy Fuller. GTBS-P *Fr.* Mythological Sonnets.

Sun's low light splinters in a plastic gleam, The. On a Scooter. Desmond A. Greig. PeSA

Sun's oot. I sit, my pipe alunt and puff, The. Alastair MacKie. FaBoTC *Fr.* Back-Green Odyssey.

Sun's Perpendicular Rays, The. William Lort Mansel. FaBoEE

Sun's rays that shoot up, stretched out, The. An Old Song of Rejoicing. *Unknown, Maori.* PeNZ, *tr. by* Margaret Orbell

Sun's return is magical, The. Carnival. Primus St. John. CMAP; GT

Sunset. Joseph Ceravolo. FTOS

Sunset, A. Coleridge. OxBSP

Sunset. E. E. Cummings. MoAmPo

Sunset. Jim Handlin. HA

Sunset, A. Victor Hugo. AWP, *tr. by* Francis Thompson *Fr.* Feuilles d'Automne.

Sunset. Henry Wadsworth Longfellow. BoTP

Sunset. Henrietta Cordelia Ray. BlSi *Fr.* Idyl. CBWP-3

Sunset, a huge flower, wilts on the horizon, The. Flowers. Roo Borson. NOBC

Sunset after Rain. W. S. Merwin. PoA

Sunset and silence! A man: around him earth savage, earth broken. The Plower. Padraic Colum. MoBrPo

Sunset at a Lake. Robert Bly. WeT

Sunset at Twin Lake. Anita Endrezze-Danielson. HATNAP

Sunset. Blue peaks vanish in dusk. Snow on Lotus Mountain. Liu Ch'ang-ch'ing, *Chinese.* OHMPC, *tr. by* Kenneth Rexroth

Sunset by the lake. Lake Murry. Pinkie Gordon Lane. GT

Sunset dying. Gary Hotham. HA

Sunset flames over the city, The. Dorothy Hewett. BMAP *Fr.* Summer Solstice.

Sunset Frisco hilly tincan evening sitdown vision. (LL) Sunflower Sutra. Allen Ginsberg. AmPP; CoAP; HCAP; InPS-3; NAAL-2; NOBA; NeAP; VCAP

Sunset from Omaha Hotel Window. Carl Sandburg. AiP

Sunset glitters on the beads. Tu Fu, *Chinese.* BLT; OHPC, *tr. by* Kenneth Rexroth

Sunset-glow so beautiful, The. Namelessness. Sangbyong Ch'on, *Korean.* CKP, *tr. by* Jaihiun Kim

Sunset—God's face from which grief radiates. Sodom. Chaim Grade, *Yiddish.* TrJP, *tr. by* Joseph Leftwich

Sunset grand couturier. (LL) Canto 80. Ezra Pound. PoA

Sunset in the City. Richard Le Gallienne. ADE

Sunset is always disturbing. Afterglow. Jorge Luis Borges, *Spanish.* NYBP, *tr. by* Norman Thomas Di Giovanni

Sunset like the grasshopper flying. (LL) Canto 17. Ezra Pound. InPS-3; MeMAP; NAAL-2; OBMV

Sunset / molten bronze. Tune: Endless Union. Li Ch'ing-chao, *Chinese.* PBWP, *tr. by* C. H. Kwock *and* Vincent McHugh

Sunset over the Aegean. Byron. OBNC *Fr.* The Corsair.

Sunset Picture. Henrietta Cordelia Ray. CBWP-3

Sunset: the blaze of evening burns. Hospital Evening. Gwen Harwood. FaBoWP

Sunset, the cheapest of all picture-shows. Frederiksted, Dusk. Derek Walcott. NoAM

Sunset Thought. Henrietta Cordelia Ray. *Fr.* A Group of Musings. CBWP-3

Sunsets. Carl Sandburg. MoAmPo

Sunset's mounded cloud, A. An Evening. William Allingham. EnLoPo; NOBVV

Sunshine. Mother Goose. ReMoGo

Sunshine and Music. *Unknown.* PoToHe

Sunshine and shadow play amid the trees. July. Henrietta Cordelia Ray. CBWP-3

Sunshine, it seems, The. Flute Holes. Chaesam Park, *Korean.* CKP, *tr. by* Jaihiun Kim

Sunshine not yet through. (LL) Poem for Ben Barney. Leslie Marmon Silko. CDW; VoR

Sunshiny shower, A. *Unknown.* FaBoBe; LB; OxNR; ReMoGo

Sunstrike. Douglas Livingstone. PeSA

Sunt Leones. Stevie Smith. NoAM

Super-Brave. Teresa Whitman. LoHo

Super-cool / ultrablack. But He Was Cool; or, He Even Stopped for Green Lights. Haki Madhbouti. BPo; MoP; PoBA

Super-suburbia of the Southern Seas. Farewell to New Zealand. Wynford Vaughan-Thomas. NOBL

Superb and sole, upon a plumed spray. The Mocking Bird. Sidney Lanier. APN-2

Superballs. Tom Clark. SPE

Supercilious nabob of the East, A. A Modest Wit. Selleck Osborn. BLPA

Supererogatory divinations one is. The Unknown. Denise Levertov. NAAL-2

Superheated steam. Sauna. Luchezar Elenkov, *Bulgarian*. CEEP, tr. by Jascha Kessler and Aleksandar Shurbanov

Superhighway elegy in a pink convertible / It was 1956. Western CIV, 4 and 5. Joan Retallack. FTOS

Superintindint wuz Flannigan. Finnigin to Flannigan. Strickland W. Gillilan. FaBoBe

Superliminare. George Herbert. ESCV; NOSC; SeCP

Supermarket. Felice Holman. OTCP

Supermarket. Peter Meinke. PBCAP

Supermarket in California, A. Allen Ginsberg. AmPP; CoAP; CoAmPo; FaBoA; HAP; HCAP; HeIP-4; InPK-6; InPS-3; LiTM; NAAL-2; NOBA; NeAP; NoAM; PBMP; PmAP; PoM; SAGP; TAP; TFi; TwCP; UnPo; WeW-3

("Boat disappear on the black waters of Lethe?[, The].") (LL) CoAmPo

Supernatural Love. Gjertrud Schnackenberg. DiPo; NoAM; NoP-4; VCAP

Superscription, A. D. G. Rossetti. EBVV; GSo; GTBS-P; NAEL-2; OAEL-2; OBNC; PoEL-5 *Fr. The House of Life.*

(97. A Superscription.) NoP-4

Superseded, The. Thomas Hardy. LiLi

Superstition. Minji Karibo. WPOW

Superstitions. Maggie Pogue Johnson. CBWP-4

Supervising Examinations. Sean Lucy. CIP-2

Supper. Walter De la Mare. NYBP

Supper. William Soutar. OxBS

Supper at Apelles'/ was a garden-butcher's work. Ammianus, *Greek*. GrAn, tr. by Peter Jay

Supper at Marlo's Cafe. On the Road. William Kloefkorn. EC2

Supper is over, the hearth is swept, The. Sermon in a Stooking. Ellen A. Jewett. BLPA

Supper party is something at which you arrive either, A. Say About Seven or Seven-Fifteen. Ogden Nash. FP

Supper with Lindsay. Theodore Roethke. FP

Supplement, A. Benjamin Tompson. SCAP

Supplement of an Imperfect Copy of Verses of Mr. Will. Shakespeare's, by the Author, A. Sir John Suckling. CavPo

Supplementary to the account. The Wrong Side of the Door. Ray DiPalma. FTOS

Suppliant, The. Georgia Douglas Johnson. PoBA

Suppliant Women, The. Euripides, *Greek*.

"Nothing / Is worse for a city than an absolute ruler." GrIP, tr. by Frank Jones

Supplication. Constantine P. Cavafy, *Greek*. BLT, tr. by Rae Dalven

Supplication, A. Abraham Cowley. GTBS-P *Fr. Davideis.*

(Music.) OxAEP-1

Supplication. Edgar Lee Masters. TrCP

Supplication of the Black Aberdeen. Rudyard Kipling. BLPA

Supplied [or Supply'd] the epithalamy [or Epithalamie]. (LL) Upon a Maid That Died [or Dyed] the Day She Was Married [or Marryed]. Meleager, *Greek*. AWP; OBVE, tr. by Robert Herrick

Support act, The. A Nigger and Some Poofters. Nigel Roberts. BMAP

Support Your Local Police Dog. Carter Revard. VoR

Suppose an Eyes. Gertrude Stein. PFTM

Suppose Gauguin had never seen Tahiti. Suppose the. Wheatfield Under Clouded Sky. Campbell McGrath. PuP-17

Suppose he had been Tabled at thy Teates. Blessed be the Paps which Thou hast Sucked. Bible, *N.T.* BXAP; ChIV-2; NOSC, tr. by Richard Crashaw *Fr. St. Luke.*

Suppose his body was the meticulous layering. Suppose Your Father Was a Redbird. Pattiann Rogers. MT

Suppose I can convince myself this world. Summons. David Rivard. NAmP90

Suppose I make a timepiece of humanity. Velemir Khlebnikov, *Russian*. AF, tr. by Paul Schmidt

Suppose is, for the last time, in that moment. The Coming of the White Man. Patrick Anderson. MoCV *Fr. Poem on Canada.*

Suppose it is nothing but the hive. Davis Matlock. Edgar Lee Masters. LiTM *Fr. Spoon River Anthology.*

Suppose it is within a gate which open is open at the hour of closing summer that is to say so. Suppose an Eyes. Gertrude Stein. PFTM

Suppose me dead; and then suppose. Jonathan Swift. NOBE; NOEC; OxBoLi; PeLV; PoEL-3 *Fr. Verses on the Death of Dr. Swift, D.S.P.D.*

Suppose, my little lady. Phoebe Cary. BLPA

Suppose one thing. For Those Who Always Fear the Worst. *Unknown*. NBLV

Suppose the Ceiling went Outside. The Ceiling. Theodore Roethke. KaS

Suppose the dead could crown their wit. A Responsory, 1948. Thomas Merton. VGW

Suppose the little Cowslip. Deeds of Kindess. *Unknown*. CTV

Suppose the / veil could be lifted. (LL) Wheatfield Under Clouded Sky. Campbell McGrath. PaTW; PuP-17

Suppose This Moment Some Stupendous Question. Alden Nowlan. NOBC

Suppose we are standing together a minute. April. Jean Valentine. TAP

Suppose we could telephone the dead. Hotel De Dream. Jane Cooper. NMM-2

Suppose you screeve? or go cheap-jack? Villon's Straight Tip to All Cross Coves. William Ernest Henley, *after* Villon. AWP; CBNP; OxAEP-2; OxBoV

Suppose you want to write. Adrienne Rich. LoL *Fr. North American Time.*

Suppose you were dreaming about your family. Benign Neglect / Mississippi, 1970. Primus St. John. PoBA

Suppose Your Father Was a Redbird. Pattiann Rogers. MT

Suppose you're a solo native here. Solo Native. Thomas Lux. CMAP; LCAP-2

Supposing. Eric Finney. SpW

Supposing all the things on the playground. On a Cold Autumn Day. Bonnie Nims. TLR

Supposing that one walks out into the air. Kenneth Koch. OBCoV *Fr. Fresh Air.* CAPP-1; NNaP; NeAP

Supposing we could just go on and on as two. Sunflower Sonnet Number Two. June Jordan. Son

Supposition with Qualification. Philip Booth. AFr

Suppression. Jayne Cortez. NBV

Supremacy. Edwin Arlington Robinson. APN-2; NoAM

Supreme Fortune Falls Soonest. Robert Herrick. CaPo

Supreme my holdings, greater yet my need. John Berryman. CRP *Fr. Dream Songs.*

Supremes, The. Cornelius Eady. CMAP; LTA

("Sequins.") (LL) LTA

Supremes, The. Mark Jarman. CMAP

Supremes done gone, The. Memorial. Sonia Sanchez. BISi

SURcenSURE. Marcel Duchamp, *French*. PFTM, tr. by Jerome Rothenberg and Peggy Guggenheim

Sure. Naomi Shihab Nye. MT

Sure. Hugo Williams. CBLP

Sure, a little bit of shrapnel fell from out the sky one day. *Unknown*. OBCoV *Fr. Soldiers' Songs of the First World War.*

Sure an' twas a / fine st. patrick's day. Saint Patrick's Day, 1973. Wendy Rose. CDW

Sure, if those Babel-builders had thought good. On the Babel-Builders. Francis Quarles. ChIV-1

Sure It was so. Man in those early days. Corruption. Henry Vaughan. ESCV; GEA; GeHe; NAEL-1; NOCV; NOSC; OAEL-1; SeCP

Sure John and I are more than quit. (LL) Epigram: "To John I ow'd great obligation." Matthew Prior. AWP; FaBoEE; OBVE

Sure Lord, there is enough in thee to dry. Sonnet. George Herbert. FSCP; GeHe; NOSC

Sure *quondam* was I. (LL) *Quondam* was I in my lady's grace. Sir Thomas Wyatt. GBL; NoSic

Sure, Saul as little looked to be a king. On Saul and David. Francis Quarles. ChIV-1

Sure some malignant star diffused its ray. The Power of Destiny. Mary Whateley. ECWP

Sure Test, A. *Unknown*. ReMoGo

Sure the last end. Peace the End of the Good Man. Robert Blair. OxAEP-1 *Fr. The Grave.*

Sure, the need was simple. Tatters. Ralph Angel. WeT

Sure there are Poets which did never dream. Cooper's Hill. Sir John Denham. BeJo; CABP; PBRV; SeCP

Sure, there are times when one cries with acidity. To An Undiscerning Critic. Sir Arthur Conan Doyle. OBCoV

Sure there's a lethargy in mighty woe. Dryden. IMW *Fr. Threnodia Augustalis.*

Sure, there's a tie of bodies! and as they. Henry Vaughan. GeHe

Sure thing / I'm a spirit! Song. *Unknown, Chippewa Indian*. STP, tr. by Jerome Rothenberg

Sure thing / I'm a spirit! / see me becoming visible? Seven Songs and Song Pictures. *Unknown*. PFTM

Sure, this world is full of trouble. Ain't It [or It's] Fine Today. Douglas Malloch. FMP

Sure thou didst flourish once! and many springs. The Timber. Henry Vaughan. GeHe; OBEV; SeCP

Sure will he saint her in his calendar. (LL) Great is the folly of a feeble brain. Joseph Hall. FMP

Surely among a rich man's flowering lawns. Ancestral Houses. W. B. Yeats. OAEL-2; OBGa *Fr.* Meditations in Time of Civil War.

Surely by now. Tanka. Maekawa Samio, *Japanese.* MJT, *tr. by* Makoto Ueda

Surely I heard a voice—surely my name. Dreams. Caroline Elizabeth Norton. Ro

Surely in my eyes that light is now lost. The Photograph of Myself. Jon Anderson. AmPA

Surely it is death to come here. Tlanusi' Yi, the Leech Place. Gladys Cardiff. CDW

Surely My Soul. . . . Jacob Cohen, *Hebrew.* TrJP, *tr. by* I. M. Lask

Surely nobody has ever decided. Taking a Hot Bath. Marge Piercy. *Fr.* Six Underrated Pleasures. EC2

Surely now I'm out of danger. To the Tune—"But I Fancy Lovely Nancy." Patrick Carey. CBLP

Surely one of my finest days, I'd just. Extract from Memoirs. Howard Nemerov. OxBC

Surely, so alike, airborne wind gave birth. Spirits of Movement. James Berry. NBrP

Surely the air must still have human warmth. Air. Jennifer Maiden. BMAP

Surely there is a mine for silver. Price of Wisdom. Bible, *O.T.* *Fr.* Job. NAWM-1

Surely they're just so large as their burdens allow. Irving Feldman. VCAP *Fr.* All of Us Here.

Surely you paused at this roadside oasis. A Garage in Co. Cork. Derek Mahon. DiPo; PBCIP

Surely you would not ask me to have known. Question to Life. Patrick Kavanagh. MoBrPo

Surf. Lillian Morrison. KaS; NTCP

Surf-casting. W. S. Merwin. NOBA

Surf is a partial deafness islanders. Polynesia. Allen Curnow. PeNZ

Surface of the pond was mostly green, The. The Lotus Flowers. Ellen Bryant Voigt. MT

Surge, The. Molly Peacock. NAmP90

Surge of spirit that goes with using an axe, The. Felling a Tree. Ivor Gurney. FaBoVe

Surgeon's Knife, The. Eliza Cook. VWP

Surgeons must be very careful. Emily Dickinson. MeMAP; SAmP; TAP

Surgery. Kenneth Pitchford. GLP

Surgical Ward: Men. Robert Graves. FaBoMo

Surging sea of human life forever onward rolls, The. A Hundred Years from Now. Mary A. Ford. BLPA

Surplus. Abigail Child. FTOS

Surplus Blues. Raymond R. Patterson. IFJA

Surprise. Richard Brautigan. KaS

Surprise me on some ordinary day. John Berryman. *Fr.* Eleven Addresses to the Lord. OxBC

Surprise, Surprise. *Unknown, Arabic.* EP, *tr. by* Derek Parker

Surprised by Evening. Robert Bly. VGW; WeT

Surprised by Joy—impatient as the Wind. Wordsworth. BoLoP; CABP; GLoP; GSo; GTBS-P; HAP; IMW; LBC; NAEL-2; NOBE; NoP-4; OAEL-2; OBEV; PoE; SCGP; Son; TFi

Surprised by Me. Walter Darring. NYBP

Surprising my dupe by his egg of Oedipus. Dirge for Three Trumpets. *Unknown.* SPE

Surprisingly easy to cook a meal now. Turning Fifty. Thomas William Shapcott. BMAP

Surrealism, *n.* Psychic automatism in its pure state. Three Excerpts. André Breton. PFTM, *tr. by* Richard M. Seaver *and* Helen R. Lane *Fr.* Manifesto of Surrealism (1924).

Surrender, The. Henry King, Bishop of Chichester. BoLoP; CBLP; EBEV; NOSC

Surrender of the Hun Fleet, The. *Unknown.* NSI

Surrendered Names. Gerald Vizenor. HATNAP

Surrendering the joys that they condemn. (LL) Lachrimae Verae. Geoffrey Hill. NAEL-2; NoAM

Surrendering to a rain-washed stone. Alexis Rotella. HA

Surrey's Poetic Art. George Turberville. EPCY *Fr.* Verse in Praise of Lord Henry Howard, Earl of Surrey.

Surrounded by broken. For Farmers. Harley Elliott. EC2

Surrounded by scientists in a faculty. Homage to the New World. Michael S. Harper. LCAP-2

Surrounded by tigers. The Life of the Wolf. Gary Gildner. AmPA

Surrounding Blues on the Way Down. Bruce Weigl. CDa

Surrounding me. Claribel Alegría. *See* From the Bridge.

Surroundings. Joseph A. Soldati. CDa

Sursum Corda. Ralph Waldo Emerson. APN-1

Surveillances. Tom Paulin. CIP-2; PNI

Survey. Donald Revell. WeT

Survey of Literature. John Crowe Ransom. FaBoCh; MeMAP; NBLV; OBAL; TAP; TwCP; VGW

Survey of the Amphitheatre, A. Moses Browne. NOEC

Surveying Britain's battled coast. Servant of the House. "Sagittarius." UV

Survival, The. Edmund Blunden. OBEV; OBMV

Survival. Anne S. Perlman. CMAP

Survival, I know how this way. Survival This Way. Simon J. Ortiz. CDW

Survival: Infantry. George Oppen. FTOS

Survival Motion: Notice. Melvin E. Brown. ISC

Survival of the Fittest, The (In Memoriam, L.C. and T.) Sir John Collings Squire. NSI

Survival This Way. Simon J. Ortiz. CDW

Survivor, The. Robert Graves. CMoP

Survivor, The, to B. V. Primo Levi, *Hebrew.* HP, *tr. by* Ruth Feldman *and* Brian Swann

Survivor, The. Philip Levine. UnSA

Survivor, The. Tadeusz Rózewicz, *Polish.* HP; PoSu, *tr. by* Adam Czerniawski

Survivor, The. Ronald Stuart Thomas. FaBoTw

Survivor sole, and hardly such, of all. Yardley Oak. William Cowper. NOEC

Survivor speaks, A. Treblinka. Michael Hamburger. HP

Survivors. Chana Bloch. CrSp

Survivors, The. Daryl Hine. TwCP

Survivors. Frank Ormsby. CIP-2

Survivors, The. Adrienne Rich. NYBP

Survivors will be human. (LL) Deathwatch. Michael S. Harper. NAAAL

"Susaddah!" exclaimed Ibsen. Edmund Clerihew Bentley. OBCoV *Fr.* Clerihews.

Susan and Charlotte and Letty and all. The Welford Wedding. Elizabeth Frances Amherst. ECWP

Susan, the constant slave to mop and broom. "Peter Pindar." NOEC *Fr.* The Sorrows of Sunday; an Elegy.

Susanna. Stephen Collins Foster. *See* Oh! Susanna.

Susanna and the Elders. Adelaide Crapsey. WPE

Susanna: girl and bride. The Man-Fate. William Everson. NoAM

Susannah, (*Time of the Gingham Rooster,* collage by Romare Bearden). Thulani Davis. GT

Susannah and the Elders. *Unknown.* PeLV

Susannah the fair. Susannah and the Elders. *Unknown.* PeLV

Susans. Susan Clements. UnSA

Sushi. Paul Muldoon. CABP; CIP-2

Susie Asado. Gertrude Stein. NoAM; TAP

Susie Wong was at the Starlight Haven. Starlight Haven. Shirley Lim. UnSA

Susie's galoshes. Galoshes. Rhoda Warner Bacmeister. NTCP

Suspended. Denise Levertov. PiM

Suspended between lives, suspended between destinations. (LL) Turning Thirty. Katha Pollitt. LiLi

Suspended from the eaves. Wintersong. Lawson Fusao Inada. MoNo

Suspense. D. H. Lawrence. MoBrPo

Suspension: Junior Wells on a Small Stage in a Converted Barn. Sandra McPherson. SeSe

Suspicion, Discontent, and Strife. Single Life Most Secure. Robert Herrick. PFE

Suspicion in the capital: the ecstacy. The Materialization of Soap 1947. Robert Sheppard. NBrP

Suspiria. *Unknown.* OBEV

Suspiria Noctis. Henry Howard Brownell. APN-2

Sussex Street sleeps in mists of nickel moonlight. Night Flower. Geoffrey Lehmann. NOBAu

Sustain tomorrow's road. (LL) The Survival. Edmund Blunden. OBEV; OBMV

Sustains it from beneath, and kindles it above. Shelley. *See* Made One With Nature.

Susu su su   Susu su su. Su Su. Velma Pollard. HCP

Suum Cuique ("Wilt thou seal up the avenues of ill?"). Ralph Waldo Emerson. APN-1 *Fr.* Quatrains.

Suzanne takes you down to her place near the river. Leonard Cohen. APAD

Suzie, you picked a hell of a time. ". . . Light that cannot fade. . . , The." William Daniel Ehrhart. CDa

Swain, give o'er your fond pretension. Hildebrand Jacob. FaBoEE

Swallow, The. Sir John Collings Squire. BXAP
    Birds, trees and flow'rs they bring to me. BXAP

Swallow Creek. Trish Rucker. CMAP

Swallow has set her six young on the rail, The. In the Doorway. Robert Browning. SCGP *Fr.* James Lee's Wife.

Swallow leaves her nest, The. Thomas Lovell Beddoes. *See* Dirge: "Swallow leaves her nest, The."

Swallow, my sister, O sister swallow. Itylus. Swinburne. EBVVPR; UV

Swallow sings "Dawn," The. *Unknown, Egyptian hieroglyphics.* BoWoP, *tr. by* Ezra Pound *and* Noel Stock

Swallow, that on rapid wing. Lucy Aikin. OxBChV

Swallowing raindrops / clear from China. (LL) Prayer to the Pacific. Leslie Marmon Silko. NoP-4; PoPoPo

Swallows, The. Elizabeth Jane Coatsworth. TLR

Swallows are passing, The. (LL) They've Come. Alfonsina Storni, *Spanish.* BoWoP, *tr. by* Aliki *and* Willis Barnstone; WPOW, *tr. by* Marti Moody

Swallow's Flight, The. Louis Levy, *Danish.* TrJP, *tr. by* Martin S. Alwood *and* Sanford Kaufman

Swallows of Capistrano, The. Trish Rucker. CMAP

Swallows over the Camp. Uys Krige, *Afrikaans.* PeSA, *tr. by the author and* Jack Cope

Swallows travel to and fro. Robert Louis Stevenson. EBVV

Swam too far out: the swell took him. Elegy for a School-Friend. Augustus Young. BIrV

Swamp, The. Derek Walcott. GT

Swamp. Roberta Hill Whiteman. VoR

Swamp Angel, The. Herman Melville. APN-2

Swamp Fox, The. William Gilmore Simms. FaBoBe

Swamp is silent, The. Frog Voices. James Bertolino. EC2

Swamp reeds murmur the song, The. Marsh Leaf. David Wagoner. PoA

Swampland Mulberries Are Lovely. *Unknown, Chinese.* CoBCP, *tr. by* Burton Watson

Swamps, marshes, borrow-pits and other. Culture as Exhibit. "Ern Malley." BMAP

Swampy State of Illinois, The. Excelsior. *Unknown.* BXAP

Swan, The. Mei-Mei Berssenbrugge. OpBo

Swan, The. Cynewulf. RB, *tr. by* Geoffrey Grigson *Fr.* Riddles (Exeter Book).

Swan, The. Jay Macpherson. NoP-4

Swan, The. Rilke, *German.* APo, *tr. by* Stephen Mitchell; PFE, *tr. by* M. D. Herter Norton

Swan, The. William Robert Rodgers. PNI

Swan, The. Theodore Roethke. VGW

Swan and the Goose, The. Aesop, *Greek.* AWP, *tr. by* William Ellery Leonard

Swan Bathing, The. Ruth Pitter. MoBrPo

Swan her sweetest Notes sings as she dies, The. Martial, *Latin.* OBCVT, *tr. by* John Ogilby

Swan: Silent is my dress when I step across the earth. Swan, The: "Silent is my dress when I step across the earth." Cynewulf. ASW, *tr. by* Kevin Crossley-Holland *Fr.* Riddles (Exeter Book).

Swan Song. Swinburne. *Fr.* The Garden of Proserpine. AWP; BLPA; FaPoR; HAP; NAEL-2; NOBE; NOBVV; OBNC; PoE; PoEL-5; PoRA; SCV

Swan swam [*or* swan] over the sea. *Unknown.* OxNR; ReMoGo

Swan, tell my your old story. Kabir, *Hindi.* EnlH, *tr. by* Czeslaw Milosz *and* Robert Hass

Swan: When it is earth I tread, make tracks upon water. *Unknown.* EEP, *tr. by* Michael Alexander *Fr.* Riddles (Exeter Book).

Swans, The. Dame Edith Sitwell. CMoP; WPE

Swans. Leonora Speyer. FYAP

Swan's Feet, The. Edith Jay Scovell. FaBoWP; OxBTC

Swan's head, The. Anita Virgil. HA

Swans in Flight. Miroslav Holub, *Czech.* FaBoPV, *tr. by* Ewald Osers

Swans stir of his breath against my hair. Alexis Rotella. HA

Swansong. Carol Muske. AmPA

Swarm, The. Sylvia Plath. NALW

Swarm is copulating in the blood, A. Babel. Giuseppe Ungaretti. PFTM

Swarm of bees in May, A. *Unknown.* ACTP; FaBoBe; LB; OxNR; ReMoGo

Swarming Bees, The. James Laughlin. VGW

Swarming Mosquitoes. Mei Yao Ch'en, *Chinese.* APo; SuSp, *tr. by* Jonathan Chaves

Swarming over the damp ground with pocket lenses. Sweet Everlasting. Ellen Bryant Voigt. MT

Swarms of flies crowd my sick horse. Ballad of Ching Mountain. Meng Chiao, *Chinese.* SuSp, *tr. by* Stephen Owen

Swarms of minnows show their little heads. Keats. CTAV

Swart Italian with his breast of fur, The. Public Beach (Long Island Sound). Christopher Darlington Morley. NBLV

Swart swarthy smiths besmattered with smoke. *Unknown. See* The Blacksmiths.

Swarte smeked smethes smatered with smoke. The Blacksmiths. *Unknown.* FaBoVe; MiEL

Swarte-smeked smethes, smatered with smoke. Smoke-Blackened Smiths. *Unknown.* CABP; OBCoV

Swarte-smeked Smithes. *Unknown.* HAP

Swarthy bee is a buccaneer, The. A More Ancient Mariner. Bliss Carman. OBAL

Swarthy little statue, The. Naked War. Michael Heffernan. BXAP

Swath. Federico García Lorca. PFTM

Sway song. Eye of God. Jim Tollerud. VoR

Swear. Virtual Reality. Charles Bernstein. FTOS

Swear by what the sages spoke. Under Ben Bulben. W. B. Yeats. CMoP; HAP; IIP; LiTM; MoP; NAEL-2; NoAM; NoP-4; OxBTC

Swearest thou, ungracious boy, henceforth ne'er look on me. Villanious and Abominable Falstaff. Shakespeare. *Fr.* King Henry IV, Pt. I. NAEL-1

Swearing an oath to Demeter. Asclepiades, *Greek.* InMo, *tr. by* Sam Hamill

Sweat begins to ooze from Compass's forehead. Get Angry, Compass. Michiko Inoue, *Japanese.* WPJ, *tr. by* Kenneth Rexroth *and* Ikuko Atsumi

Sweat is a style of the body. John Tranter. NoAM *Fr.* Crying in Early Infancy.

Sweat is leaven for the earth. Ujamaa. Wole Soyinka. PBMAP *Fr.* The Shuttle in the Crypt.

Sweat like drops of blood run down, The. Dark Was the Night. *Unknown.* AmFP

Sweater, The. Gregory Orr. TRP

Sweaters, The. Lucia Maria Perillo. UnSA

Sweating between his fingers, the agricultural man. The Hunger of the Suffering Man. Syl Cheney-Coker. PBMAP

Sweating It Out on Winding Stair Mountain. Jim Barnes. CDW

Swedenborg's Skull. Vernon Watkins. FaBoTw

Swedes. Edward Thomas. OAEL-2; RB

Swedish Angel. Winfield Townley Scott. LiTM

Sweeney Agonistes, sels. T. S. Eliot.
    Two Songs from *Sweeny Agonistes.* UnPo
    "Well here again that don't apply." FaBoVe

Sweeney Erect. T. S. Eliot. OxBTC; VGW

Sweeney, Old and Phthisic, among the Hippopotami. David Cummings. BXAP

Sweeney Redivivus. Seamus Heaney.
    "I stirred wet sand and gathered myself." NoAM
    On the Road. TOF

Sweeney to Mrs. Porter in the Spring. Louis Edward Sissman. NYBP

Sweeniad, The. "Myra Buttle."
    Sweeney in Articulo. BXAP

Sweep. Rodney Jones. MT

Sweep Me through Your Many-Chambered Heart. Diane Ackerman. NIP-4

Sweep the house. The Dead Baby. William Carlos Williams. NAAL-2

Sweep the house clean. Love Song. William Carlos Williams. LoP; MoAmPo; SAmP

Sweep thy faint strings, Musician. The Song of the Shadows. Walter De la Mare. CMoP; MoBrPo

Sweeper collects dry leaves with his broom, The. Time Swept Up. Vasco [*or* Vasko] Popa. PoSu, *tr. by* Anne Pennington *Fr.* Raw Flesh.

Sweepers, The. William Whitehead. ECEV; NOEC

Sweeping. Leslie Monsour. FFC

Sweeping past the florist's came the baby and the girl. Girl and Baby Florist Sidewalk Plum Nineteen Seventy Something. Kenneth Koch. NoP-4

Sweet, a delicate white mouse, A. The Waltzer in the House. Stanley Kunitz. NYBP

Sweet, acidulous, down-reaching thrill, A. Ode on [*or* to] a Jar of Pickles. Bayard Taylor. BXAP

Sweet after showers, ambrosial air. Tennyson. EBVV *Fr.* In Memoriam A. H. H.

Sweet age of blest illusion! blooming boys. Written on Seeing Her Two Sons at Play. Henrietta O'Neill. ECWP

Sweet Amarillis, by a spring's. Upon Mistress Elizabeth Wheeler under the Name of Amarillis. Robert Herrick. CaPo

Sweet and calm the breezes stealing. Sabbath Bells. Josephine D. Henderson Heard. CBWP-4

Sweet and lovely, dimly in my dreams. An Oriole at Dawn. Li Meng-yang, *Chinese.* CoBLCP, *tr. by* Jonathan Chaves

Sweet and low, sweet and low, *see also alt. vers.* "Bright is the moon on the deep." Lullaby. Tennyson. BoTP; CTV; ChAP; FHYEP; FaBoBe; NAEL-2; OxBChV; PoLF; SCGP *Fr.* The Princess.

Sweet and sad / like love overwhelmed. Akiko Yosano, *Japanese.* WPJ, *tr. by Kenneth Rexroth and Ikuko Atsumi.*

Sweet-and-Twenty. Shakespeare. OBEV; PoE *Fr.* Twelfth Night. (Carpe Diem.) GTBS-P

("O mistress mine, where are you roaming?") AEP; APAD

Sweet antidote to sorrow, toil and strife. To a Segar. Samuel Low. OBAL

Sweet are the thoughts that savo[u]r of content. Maesia's Song. Robert Greene. CTC; PoEL-2; UnPo *Fr.* Farewell to Folly.

Sweet are the thoughts that savour of content. Song. Robert Greene. PoEL-2; PoToHe *Fr.* Greene's Farewell to Folly.

Sweet are the ways of death to weary feet. Chorus. Euripides. OBEV, *tr. by John Byrne Leicester Warren Fr.* Medea.

Sweet are the whispers of yon pine that makes. The Death of Daphnis. Theocritus. AWP, *tr. by Charles Stuart Calverley Fr.* Idylls.

Sweet are thy strains, celestial bard. To Cowper. Anne Brontë. EPCY

Sweet Armida tooke this charge on hand, The. Torquato Tasso. OBVE *Fr.* Godfrey of Bulloigne; or, The Recoverie of Jerusalem.

Sweet Auburn! parent of the blissful hour. The Deserted Village. Oliver Goldsmith. CABP; EBEV; ECEV; FHYEP; ImPo; NOBE; NoP-4; OxAEP-1; TFi *Fr.* The Deserted Village. NOEC; OAEL-1; PoEL-3

Sweet babe, that on thy mother's guardian breast. To the Infant Hampden. Written during a Sleepless Night. John Thelwall. Ro

Sweet baby sleep: What ail[e]s my dear? A Rocking Hymn. George Wither. OxBChV *Fr.* Hallelujah; or, Britain's Second Remembrancer.

Sweet baked apple dappled cinnamon speckled sin of mine. Love Child—a Black Aesthetic. Everett Hoagland. BPo

Sweet, be not proud of those two eyes. To Dianeme. Robert Herrick. BeJo; CaPo; GTBS-P; NOBE; NOSC; OBEV

Sweet beast, I have gone prowling. Song. W. D. Snodgrass. MoAmPo; NYBP

Sweet beats of jazz impaled on slivers of wind. Walking Parker Home. Bob Kaufman. MoNo; NAAAL; PoBA

Sweet beguilings. The Cheat. Joseph Beaumont. NOSC

Sweet Be'mi'ster, that bist a-bound. Be'mi'ster. William Barnes. EBVV

Sweet Benedict, whilst thou art young. To His Little Son Benedict from the Tower of London. John Hoskyns. NOSC; OxBChV

Sweet Betsey from Pike. *Unknown, sometimes att. to John A. Stone* ("Old Put"). APN-2; AS; AmFP; OBAL; OxBoLi

("Good-by, you big lummux, I'm glad you backed out!") (LL) APN-2

(Oh, don't you remember Sweet Betsey from Pike.) APN-2

Sweet bird that shunn'st the noise of folly. Milton. CH *Fr.* Il Penseroso. AWP; FHYEP; GTBS-P; HAP; HoPM; ImPo; NOSC; NoP-4; OAEL-1; OBEV; TFi

Sweet blackbird is silenced with chaffinch and thrush. Winter. Christina Rossetti. BoTP

Sweet-Briar in Rose. "Michael Field." VWP

Sweet Catullus's all-but-island, olive-silvery Sirmio! (LL) Frater Ave Atque Vale. Tennyson. EBVV; GTBS-P; HAP; InPS-3; NAEL-2; NoP-4; OxBSP

Sweet Chance, that led my steps abroad. A Great Time. W. H. Davies. ImPo; MoBrPo

Sweet cheat gone, The. (LL) The Ghost. Walter De la Mare. CMoP; EnLoPo; LiTM; LoP; MoBrPo; NOBE; OAEL-2; OxBSn; OxBTC

Sweet children amid the apple boughs. On the Picture of a Child. Henrietta Cordelia Ray. CBWP-3

Sweet Content. Thomas Dekker *and others. See* The Happy Heart.

Sweet country life, to such unknown. The Country Life, to the Honored Mr. Endymion Porter[, Groome of the Bed-Chamber to His Maj.] Robert Herrick. BeJo

Sweet Cupid, ripen her desire. William Corkine. OxBSP

Sweet cyder is a great thing. Great Things. Thomas Hardy. GTBS-P; NOBE

Sweet Daddy. Patricia Smith. MoLi

So Motown taught me all about men. Men worshipped. UnSA

Sweet daughter of a rough and stormy sire. Ode to Spring. Anna Laetitia Barbauld. OxAEP-1

Sweet day, so cool, so calm, so bright! Virtue [*or* Vertue]. George Herbert. APAD; AWP; CH; ClHu; FMP; FSCP; GeHe; HAP; HeIP-4; InPS-3; MeLP; NAEL-1; NOBE; NOCV; NOSC; NoP-4; OAEL-1; OBEV; OPOU; PFE; PeECV; PoE; PoRA; SCGP; SeCP; SoSe-8; TFi

Sweet, deep sense of mystery filled the wood, A. In Cool, Green Haunts. Mahlon Leonard Fisher. WeW-3

Sweet disorder in the dress[e], A. Delight in Disorder. Robert Herrick. AWP; BeJo; CaPo; ClHu; EBEV; EBEvV; EnLoPo; GTBS-P; HAP; HeIP-4; ImPo; InPK-6; InPS-3; NAEL-1; NIP-4; NOBE; NOSC; OAEL-1; OBEV; OxAEP-1; PBMP; PeLV; PoE; PoRA; Poetr; SCGP; SeCP; TFi; TRP; WeW-3

Sweet Disorder in the Dress, A. Harry Hooton. NOBAu

Sweet Dreams. Ogden Nash. OTCP

Sweet dreams form a shade. A Cradle Song. William Blake. FHYEP; OBCP; Ro *Fr.* Songs of Innocence.

Sweet earth, he ran and changed his shoes to go. Arrangements with Earth for Three Dead Friends. James Wright. NIP-4

Sweet Echo, sweetest Nymph, that livest unseen. Echo. Milton. NOBE; OBEV *Fr.* Comus; a Masque Presented at Ludlow Castle. FHYEP; OAEL-1

Sweet elfin music comes to me. A Dream of Elfland. Henrietta Cordelia Ray. CBWP-3

Sweet empty sky of June without a stain. Youth. Emma Lazarus. SDW

Sweet enthusiast, on a rock reclin'd, The. The Power of Love. Charlotte Dacre. NOBRP

Sweet especial rural scene. (LL) Binsey Poplars (Felled 1879). Gerard Manley Hopkins. APAD; EBVV; EnVR; InPS-3; NAEL-2; NoAM; RB

Sweet Ethel. Linda Piper. BlSi

Sweet Everlasting. Ellen Bryant Voigt. MT

Sweet father I have shrunk a bit. Father Father Son and Son. Jon Swan. NYBP

Sweet fever of wind-troubled flowers. Shepherd's Flute. Branko Miljkovic, *Serbo-Croatian.* HSix, *tr. by Charles Simic*

Sweet flattery! then she loves but me alone. (LL) Sonnet 42. Shakespeare. CBLP; HeIP-4; OxAEP-1

Sweet flocks, whose soft enamel's wing. Flying Fowl, and Creeping Things, Praise Ye the Lord. Isaac Watts. ChIV-1

Sweet flower, that art so fair and gay. *Unknown. Fr.* Medieval Norman Song. AWP, *tr. by John Addington Symonds*

Sweet for a little even to fear, and sweet. Erotion. Swinburne. PoEL-5

Sweet fore-warning?, A. (LL) Hester. Charles Lamb. GTBS-P; OBEV

Sweet friend, when you and I are gone. Patience with the Living. Margaret Elizabeth Munson Sangster. PoToHe

Sweet gentle angel, not that I aspire. To Miss M————, Written by Moonlight, July 18, 1782. Sir Samuel Egerton Brydges. Son

Sweet girl graduate, lean as a fawn, A. Nancy Hanks, Mother of Abraham Lincoln. Vachel Lindsay. CMoP

Sweet, harmles[s] livers [*or* lives]! (on whose holy leisure). The Shepherds [*or* Shepheards]. Henry Vaughan. ChIV-2; ESCV

Sweet heart, / A morning, climbing in its brass. Letter from an Island. John Malcolm Brinnin. TAP

Sweet Highland Girl, a very shower. To the Highland Girl of Inversneyde. Wordsworth. GTBS-P

Sweet in goodly fellowship. There's No Lust like to Poetry. *Unknown.* AWP, *tr. by John Addington Symonds*

Sweet in her green dell the flower of beauty slumbers. Serenade of a Loyal Martyr. George Darley. NOBE; OBEV; OBNC; OxAEP-2

Sweet in your antique body, not yet young. To a Child. Wilfred Owen. Son

Sweet in your sight the fiery stride. *Unknown. Fr.* Exile of the Sons of Uisliu. NOIV, *tr. by Thomas Kinsella*

Sweet infancy! The Rapture. Thomas Traherne. GeHe; NOSC

Sweet Innisfallen. Thomas Moore. OBNC

"Sweet is the fruit," say. Cillactor, *Greek.* GrAn, *tr. by Edward Lucie-Smith*

"Sweet is the holiness of Youth"—so felt. Edward VI. Wordsworth. EPCY *Fr.* Ecclesiastical Sonnets.

Sweet is the lore which Nature brings;. Wordsworth. PFE *Fr.* The Tables Turned.

Sweet is the rose, but grows upon a brere. Sonnet 26. Edmund Spenser. *Fr.* Amoretti. AAS

Sweet is the scholar's life. The Scholar's Life. *Unknown, Irish.* NOIV, *tr. by Thomas Kinsella*

Sweet is the whispering of that pine tree, goatherd. Theocritus. *See* The Death of Daphnis.

Sweet is your antique body, not yet young. Sonnet, to a Child. Wilfred Owen. NOxBChV

Sweet it is to be a child. "Tabitha." FaBoVe

Sweet joy befall thee! (LL) Infant Joy. William Blake. APAD; FHYEP; LiLi; NAEL-2; NTP; OxAEP-2; OxBSP; PoLF; PoPoPo; Ro

Sweet kiss, thy sweets I fain would sweetly indite. Stella's Kiss. Sir Philip Sidney. NoSiC *Fr.* Astrophil and Stella. AAS; SiPS

Sweet, Let Me Go! *Unknown.* OxBSP

Sweet Levinsky in the night. Allen Ginsberg. NBLV

Sweet little bell. *Unknown, Old Irish.* NOIV

Sweet little bird in russet coat. The Autumn Robin. John Clare. BoTP

Sweet Love dead. (LL) An Evening. William Allingham. EnLoPo; NOBVV

Sweet Love, mine only treasure. Where His Lady Keeps His Heart. "A. W." CTC

Sweet love renew thy force. Sonnet 56. Shakespeare. PBRV; PoLF; SCGP *Fr.* Sonnets.

Sweet lovely infant, innocently gay. Oh My Own Little Daughter, Four Years Old. *Unknown.* ECWP

Sweet Lovers love the spring. (LL) Song: "It was a lover and his lass." Shakespeare. APAD; AWP; CBLP; CH; CTC; EBEvV; GBL; GTBS-P; ImPo; InPS-3; NAEL-1; NOBE; NoSic; OBEV; OxAEP-1; RB; SCGP; TFi; TTTS

Sweet Lydia, take this mask, and shroud. A Mask for Lydia. Thomas Randolph. BeJo

Sweet maid, if thou wouldst charm my sight. A Persian Song of Hafiz. Hafiz, *Persian.* AWP, *tr. by* Sir William Jones

Sweet marmalade of kisses new gathered. A Dissert. Margaret Lucas Cavendish, Duchess of Newcastle. PEW

Sweet Mary was a servant girl. Edwin in the Lowlands Low. *Unknown.* AmFP

Sweet Meat Has Sour Sauce. William Cowper. ECEV; NOEC; OBSV (Sweet Meat has Sour Sauce, or The Slave-Trader in the Dumps.) Ro

Sweet mermaid of the incomparable eyes. The Mermaid. Ben King. OBAL

Sweet monster you hold death in your beak. Meetings. Paul Éluard, *French.* AF, *tr. by* Lloyd Alexander

Sweet Mother! rare in gifts of tenderness! To My Mother. Henrietta Cordelia Ray. CBWP-3

Sweet Mountains—Ye tell Me no lie. Emily Dickinson. NALW

Sweet mouth, that send'st a musky-rosed breath;. Joshua Sylvester. EnLoPo

Sweet Muse, Descend. Isaac Watts. NOBE

Sweet my musings used to be. Mot eran dous miei cossir. Arnaut Daniel. AWP, *tr. by* Harriet Waters Preston

Sweet nature, give me holy dreams. At Nature's Shrine. Henrietta Cordelia Ray. CBWP-3

Sweet Nicarete, who served Athene's shuttle. Nicarchus of Alexandria, *Greek.* GrAn, *tr. by* Peter Porter

Sweet nightingale! Once more, my friends, farewell! Coleridge. *See* The Nightingale.

Sweet "No! no!" with a sweet smile beneath, A. A Love-Lesson. Clément Marot, *French.* AWP, *tr. by* Leigh Hunt

Sweet Nosegay, A, or Pleasant Posy. Isabella Whitney. WPE

Sweet nymph, come to thy lover. *Unknown.* NoSic

Sweet orange grove, the fairest of the isle. The Beauties of Santa Cruz. Philip Freneau.

Sweet Oranges. Mary Logue. EC3

Sweet peace, where dost thou dwell? I humbly crave. Peace. George Herbert. AWP; ESCV; GeHe; NOCV; NOSC

Sweet Peas. Keats. FHYEP *Fr.* I stood tip-toe upon a little hill.

Sweet Phosphor tricks to a smile the brow of heaven. All's Right with the World. Gerald Massey. EBVV

Sweet poet of the woods, a long adieu! On the Departure of the Nightingale. Charlotte Smith. WoRP

Sweet Rain. Tony Hoagland. NAmP90
(Sweet Ruin.) PuP-16

Sweet Rivers of Redeeming Love. John A. Granade. AH

Sweet rose [*or* Sweit rois] of virtue [*or* vertew] and of gentleness [*or* gentilnes]. To a Lady[e]. William Dunbar. EBEV; GBL; OBEV; OxBS; PeLV

Sweet Ruin. Tony Hoagland. *See* Sweet Rain.

Sweet, sacred hill! on whose fair brow. Mount of Olives. Henry Vaughan. GeHe

Sweet semi-circled Cynthia played at maw. Sonnet in Praise of Mr. Thomas the Deceased. John Taylor. CBNP *Fr.* Odcomb's Complaint.

Sweet Sensibility! thou soothing pow'r. Sensibility: A Poetical Epistle to the Hon. Mrs Boscawen. Hannah More. ECWP

Sweet serene sky[e]-like Flower. To Lucasta: The Rose. Richard Lovelace. BeJo

Sweet she was, as kind a love. She Smiled like a Holiday. *Unknown.* OxBoLi

Sweet silence after bells! Christopher John Brennan. NOBAu

Sweet silver trumpets / Jesus! (LL) When Sue Wears Red. Langston Hughes. NAAAL; TTY

Sweet smell of earth and easy rain on. Sleeping Out with My Father. Gibbons Ruark. MT

Sweet smiling, and sweet spoken. (LL) To Sally. John Quincy Adams. APN-1; AWP; OBAL

Sweet smiling village, loveliest of the lawn. Oliver Goldsmith. NOIV *Fr.* The Deserted Village. NOEC; OAEL-1; PoEL-3

Sweet soul, which now with heavenly songs dost tell. To the Marquess of Piscat's Soul. Henry Constable. NoSic

Sweet sounds, oh, beautiful music, do not cease! On Hearing a Symphony of Beethoven. Edna St. Vincent Millay. LiTM; MoAmPo

Sweet Spenser, sweetest bard; yet not more sweet. Robert Southey. EPCY

Sweet Spirit, comfort me! (LL) His Litany to the Holy Spirit. Robert Herrick. BeJo; NOSC; OBEV; PeECV; PoLF

Sweet spouse, you must presently troop and be gone. Imitation of Martial, Book II Ep, An 105. "Captain H——." NOEC

Sweet Spring, thou turn'st with all thy goodly train. Spring Bereaved 2. William Drummond, of Hawthornden. OBEV; Son

Sweet Stay-at-Home. W. H. Davies. CH

Sweet stream, that dost with equal pace. On His Mistress Drown'd. Thomas Spratt. EnLoPo

Sweet stream, that winds through [*or* thro'] yonder glade. To a Young Lady. William Cowper. GTBS-P

Sweet Suffolk owl, so trimly dight. Thomas Vautor. CH; EBEV

Sweet Swan of Avon! what a sight it were. Ben Jonson. *Fr.* To the Memory of My Beloved, the Author Mr [*or* Master] William Shakespeare[: And What He Hath Left Us]. BeJo; EPCY; HAP; HeIP-4; NOSC; OAEL-1; OxAEP-1; PoEL-2; SeCP

Sweet, sweet, sweet, let me go. *Unknown.* GBL

Sweet sweet sweet sweet sweet tea. Susie Asado. Gertrude Stein. NoAM; TAP

Sweet swelling lip, well mayst thou swell in pride. Sonnet 80. Sir Philip Sidney. *Fr.* Astrophil and Stella. AAS; SiPS

Sweet Teviot! on thy silver tide. A Father's Notes of Woe. Sir Walter Scott. OBNC *Fr.* The Lay of the Last Minstrel.

Sweet[e] Thames! [*or* Themmes,] run[ne] softly, till I end my song. (LL) Prothalamion. Edmund Spenser. AAS; AWP; EBEV; GTBS-P; HAP; NoSic; OBEV; TFi; EBEvV; ImPo; OxAEP-1; SCGP

Sweet then the ploughman's slumbers, hale and young. The Ploughman's Horse. Robert Bloomfield. ECEV *Fr.* Winter.

Sweet things. Victor Hernandez Cruz. *See* Problems With Hurricanes.

Sweet, thou art pale. The Three Enemies. Christina Rossetti. TrCP

Sweet, though short, our. The Silver Flask. John Montague. CIP-2; PNI

Sweet-tied-tight-in-the-middle. His Praises. Swidi-Nonkamfela Mhlongo, *Zulu.* PeSAV, *tr. by* Elizabeth Gunner

Sweet to myself that am so sweet to you! (LL) The Azalea. Coventry Patmore. GBL; GLoP

Sweet to the morning traveller. The Traveller's Return. *Unknown.* BoTP

Sweet trees who shade this mould. *Unknown, Spanish.* GBL, *tr. by* James Mabbe

Sweet Trinity, The. *Unknown.* AmFP

Sweet Trinity (The Golden Vanity), The. *Unknown. See* The Golden Vanity.

Sweet Unsure. Sir Walter Ralegh. SiPS

Sweet voice of the Garb. Sulbne Geilt. NOIV

Sweet waft their rounds those tuneful brothers five. Balsham Bells. Kenrick Prescot. NOEC

Sweet Was the Song. *Unknown.* NOCV

Sweet was the sound, when oft at evening's close. Village, The . Oliver Goldsmith. IIP *Fr.* The Deserted Village. NOEC; OAEL-1; PoEL-3

Sweet were the day[e]s, when thou didst lodge with Lot. Decay. George Herbert. ESCV; SCGP; SeCP

Sweet[e] were the joy[e]s that both might like and last. Sweet Unsure. Sir Walter Ralegh. SiPS

Sweet [*or* Swete] were the sauce would please e[a]ch kind of tast[e]. In Commendation of George Gascoigne's Steel Glass. Sir Walter Ralegh. AAS; SiPS

Sweet western wind, whose luck it is. To the Western Wind. Robert Herrick. CaPo; OBEV

Sweet Will. Philip Levine. LCAP-2; VCAP

Sweet William. "Ern Malley." BMAP

Sweet William and May Margaret. *Unknown. See* Sweet William's Ghost.

Sweet William he married [him] a wife. The Wife Wrapt in Wether's Skin. *Unknown.* AmFP; ESPB

Sweet William rode up to the old man's gate. Earl Brand. *Unknown.* AmFP

Sweet william, silverweed, sally-my-handsome. A Spell for Sleeping. Alastair Reid. NOxBChV; NTP

Sweet William would [*or* he would] a wooing ride. Fair Margaret and Sweet William. *Unknown.* ESPB

Sweet William's Ghost *or* Sweet William and May Margaret. *Unknown.* AWP; CH; ESPB

Sweet William's gone over seas. Lord William; or, Lord Lundy. *Unknown.* ESPB

Sweet Willie was a widow's son. Willie and Lady Margerie [*or* Maisry]. *Unknown.* ESPB; OxBB

Sweet Willie's ta'en him o'er the faem. *Unknown.* OxBB

Sweet, winsome May, coy, pensive fay. May. Henrietta Cordelia Ray. CBWP-3

Sweet words that take. Sweet Words on Race. Langston Hughes. LTA

Sweetchile / dem will say dat. Revo Lyric. Kendel Hippolyte. HCP

Sweete Saynt: Thow better canst declare to me. To St Mary Magdalen. Henry Constable. PBRV

Sweete Themmes runne softly, till I end my Song. Edmund Spenser. *See* Prothalamion.

Sweeter Far than the Harp, More Gold than Gold. "Michael Field." OBMV; PeVV

Sweeter Saint I Serve, A. Sir Philip Sidney. SiPS *Fr.* Arcadia.

Sweeter than a song. Tanka. Fumi Saito, *Japanese.* MJT, *tr. by* Makoto Ueda

Sweeter than sour apples flesh to boys. Sonnet LXX. Ted Berrigan. FTOS *Fr.* The Sonnets.

Sweetest Heresy received, The. Emily Dickinson. CBLP; ITG ("Though the Faith accommodate but Two—.") (LL) ITG

Sweetest lives are those to duty wed, The. Reward of Service. Elizabeth Barrett Browning. BLPA; FaBoBe

Sweetest love, I do not go[e]. Song. Donne. AWP; BoLoP; ESCV; FHYEP; HeIP-4; InPS-3; MeLP; NOBE; NoSic; OAEL-1; PoEL-2; SeCP; TFi

Sweetest notes among the human heart-strings, The. Love Unexpressed. Constance Fenimore Woolson. APN-2

Sweetest of sweets, I thank you: when displeasure. Church-Music[k]. George Herbert. ESCV; GeHe; OxBSP

Sweetest Saviour, if my soul. A Dialogue. George Herbert. FSCP; GeHe; NOSC; OBEV

Sweetest Thing, The. *Unknown, Susu.* TTY, *tr. by* Ulli Beier

Sweetgrass. Maurice Kenny. HATNAP

Sweetheart, I wish you could tour my native land. Travelogue. Amy Gerstler. WWSi

Sweetheart / when you break through. Song For Baby-O, Unborn. Diane Di Prima. BB

Sweethearts. J. A. Phillips. DeD

Sweethearts, we felt the same pleasure. Parody of a Lover. Li Ch'ung, *Chinese.* EP, *tr. by* Anne Birrell

Sweetly Empty Woods. Sir Philip Sidney. *Fr.* Solitariness. SCGP; SiPS *Fr.* Arcadia.

Sweetly-favored face, The. Canzonetta: Of His Lady in Absence. Giacomino Pugliesi, *Italian.* AWP, *tr. by* D. G. Rossetti

Sweetly hath Dorcas of Lycaenis learnt. Meleager, *Greek.* GrAn, *tr. by* Peter Whigham

Sweetly (my Dearest) I left thee asleep. John Saffin. SCAP

Sweetness and wit, they are but mummy, possessed. (LL) Love's Alchemy [or Alchemie]. Donne. ESCV; NAEL-1; OAEL-1; PoE; SeCP

Sweetness of England, The. Elizabeth Barrett Browning. OxAEP-2 *Fr.* Aurora Leigh. VWP

Sweetness of poverty like this, The. Aspiration. Mário de Andrade, *Portuguese.* TTY, *tr. by* John Nist

Sweetness of the fruit, his hand eats hers, The. (LL) Love for a Hand. Karl Shapiro. CoAP; NYBP

Swell foams where they float and crawl, The. Girls Bathing, Galway 1965. Seamus Heaney. InPS-3

Swell me a bowl with lusty wine. Ben Jonson. BeJo *Fr.* The Poetaster.

Swell the Anthem, Raise the Song. Nathan Strong. AH

Swell'd with our late successes on the foe. Dryden. EBEV *Fr.* Annus Mirabilis.

Swells then thy feeling heart, and streams thine eye. The Dead Beggar, an Elegy Addressed to a Lady. Charlotte Smith. BWW

Swept all my pride away, and trembling I forgave! (LL) Forgiveness. John Greenleaf Whittier. GSo; TrCP

Swept into limbo is the host. A Ballad of Religion and Marriage. Amy Levy. VWP

"Swerve to the left, son Roger," he said. The Judgement of God. William Morris. PeVV

Swerving east, from rich industrial shadows. Here. Philip Larkin. CMoP; PoE

Swet Jesus. Friar Michael of Kildare. NOIV

Swete Jesu, king of blisse. *Unknown.* MiEL

Swete sone, reu on me. *Unknown.* MiEL

Swich fyn hath, lo, this Troilus for love! Chaucer. NOCV *Fr.* Troilus and Criseyde [or Criseide]. EnVB

Swift. Thomas Caulfield Irwin. "It was a dim October day." BIrV

Swift. Delmore Schwartz. PoA

Swift as a spirit hastening to his task. The Triumph of Life. Shelley. NAEL-2; NOBRP; OAEL; PoEL-4

Swift cloud, swift light, now dark, now bright, across the landscape played. An Idyl of Harvest Time. John Townsend Trowbridge. APN-2

Swift cold and deep. (LL) Charon's Cosmology. Charles Simic. HCAP; PoPoPo

Swift fleet the billowy clouds along the sky. On Passing Over a Dreary Tract of Country, and Near the Ruins of a Deserted Chapel, During a Tempest. Charlotte Smith. BoWoP; WPE *Fr.* Montalbert.

Swift Floods. Kata Szidónia Petröczi, *Hungarian.* WPOW, *tr. by* Laura Schiff

Swift had pains in his head. January 1940. Roy Fuller. HoPM; LiTM

Swift has sailed into his rest. Swift's Epitaph. W. B. Yeats. CMoP; OBVE

Swift Is That Falcon. *Unknown, Chinese.* CoBCP, *tr. by* Burton Watson

Swift is't in pace, light poiz'd, to look in clear. Description of a New England Spring. John Josselyn. SCAP

Swift red flash, a winter king, The. The Dance. Hart Crane. LiTM; MoAmPo; OxBA *Fr.* Powhatan's Daughter. *Fr.* The Bridge. NAAL-2

Swift shot the curlew 'thwart the rising blast. Ode on Lord Macartney's Embassy to China. William Shepherd. NOEC

Swift stream in the high mountains, dropping dental, lateral, A. The River That FLows through Our Land. Jeremy Cronin. PeSAV

Swift things are beautiful. Elizabeth Jane Coatsworth. ChAP

Swift through the yielding air I glide. The Lark. *Unknown.* NOSC

Swift to the western bounds of this wide land. On the Completion of the Pacific Telegraph. Jones Very. TAP

Swift wind! Space! My Soul! Now I know it is true what I guessed at;. Walt Whitman. PAR *Fr.* Song of Myself.

Swifter than hail. Akiko Yosano, *Japanese.* OHMPJ, *tr. by* Kenneth Rexroth

Swiftly Arose. Walt Whitman. TrCP *Fr.* I believe in you my soul, the other I am must not abase itself to you. APAD; ColAP; PAR *Fr.* Song of Myself. AmPP; MoAmPo; NAAL-3; NOBA; OxBA

Swiftly re-light the flame. Hilda Doolittle. NALW *Fr.* Tribute to the Angels.

Swiftly the years, beyond recall. New Corn. Ch'ien T'ao, *Chinese.* ChiP, *tr. by* Arthur Waley

Swiftly walk o'er the western wave. To Night. Shelley. AWP; CH; FHYEP; GTBS-P; NAEL-2; OAEL-2; OBEV; OBNC; PoLF; PoRA; TFi

Swifts. Philippe Jaccottet, *French.* VCWP, *tr. by* Derek Mahon

Swift's Epitaph. W. B. Yeats. CMoP; OBVE

Swifts turn in the heights of the air. Distances. Philippe Jaccottet, *French.* VCWP, *tr. by* Derek Mahon

Swim in petals. (LL) Heliodora's Brows. Meleager, *Greek.* GrAn, *tr. by* Peter Whigham

Swimmer. Gladys Cardiff. CDW

Swimmer. Robert Francis. WeW-3

Swimmer, The. Brendan Kennelly. PBCIP

Swimmer. Mervyn Morris. HCP

Swimmers, The. Allen Tate. FuPo; InPS-3; MoAmPo; NOBA; NoAM

Swimming. Clinton Scollard. FPC

Swimming By Night. James Merrill. ColAP; NYBP; VGW

Swimming Chenango Lake. Charles Tomlinson. FaBoMo; MoP; NoAM

Swimming Pool. Maria Teresa Horta, *Portuguese.* PBWP, *tr. by* Suzette Macedo

Swimming Pool. Myra Cohn Livingston. NOxBChV

Swinburne, old Swinburn, silly old Swinburne. Sister Swallow to Swinburne. Mary Holtby. UV

Swine gobble dead men's flesh. Han-shan, *Chinese.* SuSp, *tr. by* Edward H. Schafer

Swineherd. Eiléan Ní Chuilleanáin. BIrV; CIP-2; FaBoWP; WPOW

Swing, The. Mary I. Osborn. BoTP

Swing, The. Robert Louis Stevenson. CTV; ChAP; FPC; FaBoBe; LiLi; NOxBChV; NTCP; TLR

Swing dat hammer—hunh—. Southern Road. Sterling Brown. BPo; GM; NAAAL; PoBA

Swing low, sweet chariot. *Unknown.* APN-2; CrDW; NAAAL ("I looked over Jordan and [or an'] what did I see.") UnPo

Swing over the Calm Source of Our Names, The. Milorad Pavic, *Serbo-Croatian.* HSix, *tr. by* Charles Simic

Swing, swing. A Swing Song. William Allingham. CTV; OTCP; TLR

Swing up into the apple-tree. (LL) New Hampshire. T. S. Eliot. FaBoCh; GTBS-P; NoAM; WeW-3

Swinging. Ho Xuan Huong, *Vietnamese.* AVP, *tr. by* Huỳnh Sanh Thông

Swinging. Irene Thompson. BoTP

Swinging. *Unknown.* OxNR

Swinging on the hanger. George Swede. HA

Swirl and smash of waves against the legs. Mutoscope. Elizabeth Spires. NAmP90

Swirl sleeping in the waterfall! Chomei at Toyama. Basil Bunting. OxBTC

Swirling spring. Young Girl. Ricarda Huch, *German.* WPOW, *tr. by* Janine Canan *and* Deirdre Lashgari

Swirling, swirling—aloeswood-scented smoke. Young Noble at Night's End; a Song. Li Ho, *Chinese.* SuSp, *tr. by* Maureen Robertson

Swirling world stands still, The. John Kitching. SpW

Switch Blade; or, John's Other Wife, The. Jonathan Williams. NeAP

Switch on the Night. Ray Bradbury. OBSP

Switchblade. Michael Ryan. NAmP90

Switzerland. Matthew Arnold.

  Absence. EnVR; GLoP

  Dream, A. EnVR; GBL; GTBS-P

  Farewell, A: My horse's feet beside the lake. EnVR

  Lake, The. EnVR

  Parting. EnVR

  Terrace at Berne, The. EnVR

  To Marguerite. CABP; NoP-4; PoPoPo

    (To Marguerite—Continued.) GTBS-P; SoSe-8

    ("Unplumb'd, salt, estranging sea, The.") (LL) CABP

    ("Unplumbed, salt, estranging sea, The.") (LL) NoP-4; PoPoPo

    ("Yes! in the sea of life enisled.") CABP; NoP-4; PoPoPo

  To Marguerite. EnVR

  To My Friends, Who Ridiculed a Tender Leave-Taking. EnVR

Swollen river sang through the green hole, The. The Sleeper in the Valley. Rimbaud. OBWP, tr. by Robert Lowell Fr. Eighteen-Seventy.

Swoon of noon, a trance of tide, A. In a Bye-Canal. Herman Melville. APN-2; NCAP

Sword, The. Abu Bakr, Arabic. TTY, tr. by A. J. Arberry

Sword, A. Karin Boye, Swedish. WPOW, tr. by Joanna Bankier

Sword and the Sickle, The. William Blake. Fr. Gnomic Verses.

Sword in a Cloud of Light, A. Kenneth Rexroth. MoLi Fr. The Lights in the Sky are Stars.

Sword in length a reaping-hook amain. King Harald's Trance. George Meredith. EBNV; PeVV

Sword is a cold bride. Yuk!, The. Michael Foley. PNI Fr. True Life Love Stories.

Sword of Robert Lee, The. Abram Joseph Ryan. CBCWP

Sword of Surprise, The. G. K. Chesterton. MoBrPo

Sword sang [or sung] on the barren heath, The. The Sword and the Sickle. William Blake. FaBoEE Fr. Gnomic Verses.

Swordscape, tombscape, flame ploughed. After the Fall. Gloria Escoffery. HCP; PBCV

Swung torch scatters seeds, The. Night Piece. "Ern Malley." BMAP

Sybil, The. Virgil. OBVE, tr. by Gawin Douglas Fr. The Aeneid [or Eneados, Aeneis].

Sybil Sibelius! Yes, Belinda Brahms! The Great Women Composers. Gavin Ewart. OBCoV

Sybilline. "Ern Malley." BMAP

Sycamore Tree, The. Unknown. AmFP

Sycamores and sidewalks of, The. Adam's Dream. David Ferry. PFE

Sycophantic Fox and the Gullible Raven, The. Guy Wetmore Carryl. BLPA; NBLV; OBCA; PBMP

Sydney. Robert Harris. NOBAu

Sydney and the Bush. Les A. Murray. DiPo

Sydney Highrise Variations, The. Les A. Murray.

  Flight from Manhattan, The. BMAP

Syllables disintegrate ingrate alphabets. Phyllis Webb. NOBC Fr. The Kropotkin Poems.

Syllables shaped around the darkening day's. Cancer Winter. Marilyn Hacker. RA

Sylphs of the Seasons, The. Washington Allston.

  "And now, in accents deep and low." APN-1

Sylva. Abraham Cowley.

  To His Mistress. NOSC; OxAEP-1

Sylvan Revel, A. Edward Cracroft Lefroy. AWP Fr. Echoes from Theocritus.

Sylvester's Dying Bed. Langston Hughes. NAAAL; NoM; Poetr; SAmP; UnPo

  ("I work up this mornin'.") NAAAL

Sylvia. Samuel Croxall. NOEC

Sylvia; or, The May Queen. George Darley.

  "View like one of Fairy-land, A." NOBRP

SYLVIA the fair, in the bloom of fifteen. Song. Dryden. EBEV; OxAEP-1; PoPoPo

Sylvia's Death. Anne Sexton. LCAP-2; NAAL-2; NALW

Sylvie and Bruno. "Lewis Carroll."

  Mad Gardener's Song, The. OxBChV; PBMP

  Three Badgers, The. CBNP

Sylvie and Bruno Concluded. "Lewis Carroll."

  King-Fisher [or King-Fisher's] Song, The. CBNP

    (King-Fisher Song, The.) CTAV

  Little Man That Had a Little Gun, The. CBNP

(Manlet, The.) BXAP

Sylvius, your hands near my mouth are heady flowers. Marguerite Burnat-Provins, French. BoWoP, tr. by Cassia Berman

Sym of Lyntoun, be the ramis horn. King Berdok. Unknown. OxBS

Symbols. Christina Rossetti. NALW

Symbols. W. B. Yeats. OBMV

Symbols of Gross Experience. C. Day Lewis. Son Fr. Oh Dreams, Oh Destinations.

Symbols of Transformation. Ron Padgett. FTOS

Symbolum. Goethe, German. FaBoPV, tr. by Tom Paulin

Sympathies. Oliver Wendell Holmes. APN-1 Fr. Wind-Clouds and Star-Drifts.

Sympathy, sl. diff. Emily Jane Brontë. BWW

Sympathy. Paul Laurence Dunbar. AAP; APAD; APN-2; CrDW; GEA; GT; NAAAL; NoP-4; PoBA; SSLK

Sympathy. Viola Meynell. LW

Symphonies. Herman Melville. APN-2 Fr. Clarel: A Poem and Pilgrimage in the Holy Land.

Symphony, The. Sidney Lanier. AmPP

Symphony in Yellow. Oscar Wilde. ADE; EBVV; MoBrPo; NOBVV; NoAM; OPOU; OxBSP; PFE

Symphony No. 2. Daniil Kharms, Russian. AF, tr. by George Gibian

Symphony No. 3, in D Minor. Jonathan Williams. VGW Fr. Mahler.

Symposium, The. Leah Goldberg, Hebrew.

  "Outside the cats are wailing." PBWP, tr. by Robert Alter

Symptom. Dorothy Parker. LW

Symptoms Of Love. Robert Graves. BoLoP; LoP

Symptoms of plague in Athens. Lucretius, Latin. OBCVT, tr. by Charles Hubert Sisson

Syn I fro Love escaped am so fat. Chaucer. EnVB

Synagogue, The. Christopher Harvey.

  "What Church is this? Christ's Church. Who builds it?" EPCY

Synagogue in Prague. Alan Sillitoe. BLPA

Synchoresis. Godfrey Turner. OBCoV

Syng a song of Saxons. Old-Saxon Fragment. Unknown. CBNP; OBCoV

Syntax of the mind grips, The. Quincy Troupe. NBV

Syren Songs. George Darley.

  Mermaidens' Vesper-Hymn, The. GBL; NAEL-2; OBNC; PoEL-4

    (Siren Chorus.) BIrV

  Sea-Ritual, The. BIrV; OBNC

    (Deadman's Dirge.) CH

Syrens' Song, The. William Browne. See The Sirens' Song.

Syrian Hostesse, with a Greek Wreath crown'd, The. The Hostesse. Virgil, Latin. OBCVT, tr. by Thomas Stanley

Syringa. John Ashbery. APSN; HCAP; NoAM; VCAP

Syringe cloud of aspiration, The. Arthur Hugh Clough. EnVR

Syrinx. Amy Clampitt. NoP-4

Syrinx. John Lyly. See Pan's Song.

Syros. Tomas Tranströmer, Swedish. BLT, tr. by Swenson, May and Leif Sjöberg

Sons and Fathers. Larry Mitchell. GLP

Sons of Levi, The. Unknown. AmFP

"Sooeep!" Walter De la Mare. BoTP

Soon one more goes thither! (LL) Exeunt Omnes. Thomas Hardy. FaBoVe; UV

Sooner or Later. John Digby. SPE

Soonest Mended. John Ashbery. HCAP; NAAL-2; VCAP

Sorrow. Aubrey Thomas De Vere. BLPA

Sorrow of Love, The ("Brawling of a sparrow in the eaves, The"), see also The Sorrow of Love ("The quarrel of the sparrows in the eaves"). W. B. Yeats. NAEL-2; OAEL-2, PeVV

SOS. Imamu Amiri Baraka. BPo; NAAAL; PoBA

  ("Come on in.") (LL) MBE

Soufrière. Andrew Salkey. PBCV

Soul. D. L. Graham. PoBA

Soul and Body. Margaret Lucas Cavendish, Duchess of Newcastle. OxBSP

  (Soule, and Body.) PEW

Soul Incense. Henrietta Cordelia Ray. CBWP-3

Soul that knew It well, A. (LL) Happiest day—the happiest hour, The. Edgar Allan Poe. AmPP; ImPo; MeMAP; OxBA

Soul that must endure it, The. (LL) 'All Is Vanity, Saith the Preacher'. Byron. ChIV-1; KSG; TrCP

Soule, and Body. Margaret Lucas Cavendish, Duchess of Newcastle. See Soul and Body.

Soul's Garment, The. Margaret Lucas Cavendish, Duchess of Newcastle. WPE

Souls Lake. Robert Fitzgerald. TwCP

Soul's Liberty. Anna Wickham. MoBrPo; OxBSP

Sound. James Harrison. VGW

Sound, The. Robert Kelly. PoM

Sound of Night, The. Maxine W. Kumin. SoSe-8; WPE

Sound of rain, The. (LL) On Gay Wallpaper. William Carlos Williams. MeMAP; MoAmPo; TAP

Sources of Good Counsel. Peter Idley. OxBChV

Sourwood Mountain. *Unknown.* AS

Sous-Entendu. Anne Stevenson. LW; OxBSP

South Country. Kenneth Slessor. BMAP; CBAP

South End. Conrad Potter Aiken. CMoP; HoPM; OxBA

South-Folk in Cold Country. Ezra Pound, *after the Chinese.* OBVE

South Texas Summer Rain. Rebecca Gonzales. AiP

Southern Scene, A. Priscilla Jane Thompson. CBWP-2

Southerner, The. Karl Shapiro. NYBP

Souvenir, The. Dan Pagis, *Hebrew.* IP, *tr. by* Warren Bargad *and* Stanley F. Chyet

Space in the Air, A. Jon Silkin. TrJP

Spacepoem 3: Off Course. Edwin Morgan. SpW

Spade Is Just a Spade, A. Walter Everette Hawkins. PoBA

Spanish Ladies. *Unknown.* FaBoCh

Spanish Lions, The. Phyllis McGinley. NYBP

Spanish War, The. "Hugh MacDiarmid." CMoP; NOBC

Spark, The. Joseph Mary Plunkett. AWP

Sparrow in the Dust, A. Ruth Domino, *Italian.* BoWoP, *tr. by* Daniel Hoffman *and* Jerre Mangione

Speaking little, perhaps not a word. (LL) Glimpse through an interstice caught, A. Walt Whitman. EP

Speaking little, perhaps not a word. Walt Whitman. *See* A Glimpse through an interstice caught.

Speaking My Mind. Chung-ch'ang T'ung, *Chinese.* CoBCP, *tr. by* Burton Watson

Speaking of Poetry. John Peale Bishop. OxBA

Speaking Tree, The. Muriel Rukeyser. VGW

Specter, The. Ernst Hardt, *German.* AWP, *tr. by* Jethro Bithell

Spectral Lovers. John Crowe Ransom. GBL; HeIP-4

Speech for the Repeal of the McCarran Act. Richard Wilbur. CMoP

Speech to Those Who Say Comrade. Archibald MacLeish. OxBA

Speech Warts. Myra Sklarew. CRP

Spell before Winter, A. Howard Nemerov. LiTM

Spelt from Sibyl's Leaves. Gerard Manley Hopkins. CMoP; EnVR; FaBoMo; LiTM; NOBVV; OAEL-2; TOF

Spenser's Ireland. Marianne Moore. FaBoWP; IIP; LiTM; MeMAP; NOBA; NoAM; OxBA; TAP

Spider, The. Edward Littleton. NOEC

Spider Reeves. Henry Carlile. Poetsp

Spinning. Alfred Wellington Purdy. NOBC; NoAM

Spinster's Lullaby. Vassar Miller. BoWoP; NMM-2

Spirit Land, The. Jones Very. HAP

Spirit of Plato. *Unknown, Greek.* OBCVT, *tr. by* Shelley; AWP; OBVE, *tr. by* Shelley

   (Plato's Tomb.) FaBoCh

Spirits. Victor Hernandez Cruz. PoBA

Spirits, Dancing. Arthur Gregor. NYBP; VGW

Spiritual, A. Paul Laurence Dunbar. BPo

Spleen. Paul Verlaine, *French.* AWP, *tr. by* Ernest Dowson

Splendidis longum valedico nugis. Sir Philip Sidney. GSo; NOBE; OxAEP-1

   ('Leave Me, O Love'.) AEP; GBL; HeIP-4; NIP-4; PFE; PoE; Son; TFi

Splendor of Thine Eyes, The. Moses ibn Ezra, *Hebrew.* TrJP, *tr. by* Solomon Solis-Cohen

Splitting Wood Near Morris, Oklahoma on Robbie and Lesa McMurtry's Farm. Lance Henson. HATNAP

Spoken by Venus on Seeing Her Statue Done by Praxiteles. *Unknown, Greek.* FaBoEE

Sporting Goods. Philippe Soupault, *French.* TTTS, *tr. by* Rosemarie Waldrop; PFTM

   ("And there are lots of other things, too.") (LL) PFTM

Spotted Flycatcher, The. Walter De la Mare. OxBSP

Spraying the Potatoes. Patrick Kavanagh. BIrV; CABP; IIP

Sprig of Lime, The. Robert Malise Bowyer Nichols. GTBS-P

Spring. Reed Bye. TTTS

Spring. Philip Larkin. MoBrPo

Spring. Christina Rossetti. OBNC

Spring. Princess Shikishi, *Japanese.* PBWP, *tr. by* Hiroaki Sato

Spring and All. William Carlos Williams. CMoP; ChAP; ColAP; HAP; InPK-6; InPS-3; LiTM; MeMAP; MoP; NAAL-2; NOBA; NoAM; OxBA; PoE; PoPoPo; TAP; TFi; TRP

   (Poem: "By the road to the contagious hospital.") MoAmPo; UnPo

Spring Bereaved. William Drummond, of Hawthornden. *See* Sonnet: "Alexis, here she stayed; among these pines."

Spring Coming. A. R. Ammons. HeIP-4; InPK-6

Spring Festival on the River, The. John Peck. AmPA

Spring-gazing Song. Hsüeh T'ao, *Chinese.* BoWoP, *tr. by* Carolyn Kizer

Spring Has Come. *Unknown.* BoTP

Spring in Virginia. Ramona Wilson. VoR

Spring Morning. D. H. Lawrence. CMoP; MoBrPo

Spring of the Thief. John Logan. NNaP

Spring Offensive. Wilfred Owen. GTBS-P; NSI; PeFWW

Spring over the City. Anne Hébert, *French.* PBWP, *tr. by* Kathleen Weaver

Spring Prayer. Ralph Waldo Emerson. BoTP

Spring River, The. Po Chü-i, *Chinese.* ChiP, *tr. by* Arthur Waley; CoBCP, *tr. by* Burton Watson

   ("Heat and cold, dusk and dawn have crowded one upon the other.") ChiP, *tr. by* Arthur Waley

   ("Rounding the sand spits, circling rocks, a rippling, murmuring green.") (LL) CoBCP, *tr. by* Burton Watson

Spring river as it trickles over the stones and babbles past the rocks, The. (LL) The Spring River. Po Chü-i, *Chinese.* ChiP, *tr. by* Arthur Waley

Spring Song. Donald Finkel. NYBP

Spring Song. *Unknown, Chippewa Indian.* OBVE, *tr. by* Frances Densmore

Spring Street Bar. Mei-Mei Berssenbrugge. WPOW

Spring Whistles. Lucy Larcom. OBCA

Spring wind raises fine dust from the road, The. Su Tung-p'o. *See* Rhyming with Tzu-yu's "Treading the Green."

Springboard, The. Louis MacNeice. PoA

Springer Mountain. James Dickey. CAPP-1

Squaring the Circle. Louis O. Coxe. NYBP

Squirrel near Library. Genevieve Taggard. WPE

St. Agnes' Eve. Tennyson. OBEV

St. Asaph's. Kingsley Amis. OxBTC

St. Enda. Laurence David Lerner. PeSA

St. Gervais. Michael Roberts. FaBoCh

Stafford in Kansas. James Baker Hall. BXAP

Staircase with a Hundred Steps, The. Benjamin Péret, *French.* SPE, *tr. by* David Gascoyne

Stand in a row and learn. (LL) The Drunk in the Furnace. W. S. Merwin. LiTM; MoP; NAAL-2; NoAM; NoP-4; PoE; Poetr; TwCP

Stand still, yet we will make him run. (LL) To His Coy Mistress. Andrew Marvell. APAD; AWP; BoLoP; CABP; CBLP; ClHu; EBEV; EBEvV; ESCV; EnLoPo; FHYEP; FMP; FSCP; FaBoSe; GBL; GEA; GLoP; GeHe; HAP; HeIP-4; HoPM; ImPo; InPK-6; InPS-3; LoP; MeLP; NAEL-1; NIP-4; NOBE; NOSC; NoP-4; OAEL-1; OBEV; OxAEP-1; PBMP; PBRV; PFE; PoEL-2; PoLF; PoPoPo; PoRA; Poetr; SAGP; SCGP; SCV; SeCP; TFi; TRP; UV

Stand-To, The. C. Day Lewis. NoP-4; OBWP

Standing in a stillness that now is yours. (LL) Water Island. Howard Moss. CoAP; NYBP; NoP-4

Standing sentry for the avalanche. (LL) Strength through Joy. Kenneth Rexroth. FYAP; VGW

Stanzas: "And thou art dead, as young and fair." Byron. Ro

   (Stanzas.) Ro

Stanzas: "Black absence hides upon the past." John Clare. EnLoPo; NOBVV

Stanzas—April, 1814. Shelley. OBNC; SCGP

   (Remorse.) OBEV

Stanzas on Charles Armitage Brown. Keats. *See* A Portrait.

Star[re], The. George Herbert. ESCV; PeECV

Star, A. George MacBeth. NYBP

Star Blanket. Ray A. Young Bear. CDW

Star-Gazer. Louis MacNeice. NAEL-2; NoP-4

Star Journey. Naomi Long Madgett. BPo

Star of the Evening. James M. Sayles. UV

Star Song of the Bushman Women. *Unknown, Bushman.* PeSA, *tr. by* W. H. I. Bleek

Star-Talk. Robert Graves. MoBrPo; OxBTC

Star Trek III. Richard Harteis. GLP

Starlight Scope Myopia. Yusef Komunyakaa. AF; CDa; WeT

   ("Loaded on an oxcart.") (LL) WeT

Starry Night, The. George Starbuck. NYBP

Stars. Emily Jane Brontë. NAEL-2

Stars and Stripes. Mary Weston Fordham. CBWP-2

Starting from San Francisco. Lawrence Ferlinghetti. CAPP-1; GM

Statue and Birds. Louise Bogan. MoAmPo

Statues in the Public Gardens, The. Howard Nemerov. CoAmPo

Staying Overnight at Spirit-Source Temple. Wen Cheng-ming, *Chinese.* CoBLCP, *tr. by* Jonathan Chaves

Staying Overnight on the Banks of Embroidered River. Li K'ai-hsien, *Chinese.* CoBLCP, *tr. by* Jonathan Chaves

Steal from the world, and not a stone / Tell where I lie. (LL) Ode on Solitude. Alexander Pope. AWP; EBEvV; FHYEP; GTBS-P; HeIP-4; ImPo; NAEL-1; NOSC; PBMP; PoRA; PoToHe; SCGP

Steam Shovel. Charles Malam. NTCP

Steam Threshing-Machine, The. Charles Tennyson Turner. OBNC

Stella's Birthday, 1720. Jonathan Swift. *See* Stella's Birthday, 1721.

Stella's Birthday, 1725. Jonathan Swift. CABP; NOEC

Stella's Birthday, 1721. Jonathan Swift. NAEL-1; PoEL-3

(Stella's Birthday, 1720.) OxAEP-1

Stenographers, The. Patricia K. Page. HeIP-4; LiTM; NALW; NoAM

Stepping Outside. Tess Gallagher. AmPA

Steps. Roberta Hill Whiteman. VoR

Stiff with weapons, fighting back over the same ground. (LL) Thistles. Ted Hughes. APAD; FaBoVe; NoAM; OxBSP; OxBTC; SoSe-8

Still, and so on. Augustus De Morgan. *See* Great Fleas [have little fleas upon their backs to / bite 'em].

Still, and so on. (LL) Great Fleas [have little fleas upon their backs to / bite 'em]. Augustus De Morgan. FPC

Still Century. Tom Paulin. BiHa

Still Do I Keep My Look, My Identity. . . . Gwendolyn Brooks. PoA

Still-Heart. Frank Pearce Sturm. OBMV

Still in the cool[e], and silent shades of sleep. (LL) To Perilla. Robert Herrick. BeJo; CaPo; NOSC; SCGP; SeCP

Still seems to need. (LL) Memories of a Lost War. Louis Simpson. OBWP; VGW

Still Voice of Harlem, The. Conrad Kent Rivers. PoBA

Stings. Sylvia Plath. NALW

Stirrup-Cup, The. Sidney Lanier. AmPP

Stockyard, The. Sir John Collings Squire. OxBTC

Stoic: for Laura von Courten, The. Edgar Bowers. CoAP; MT

Stone, The. Wilfrid Wilson Gibson. MoBrPo

Stone. Charles Simic. ChAP; InPS-3

Stone Canyon Nocturne. Charles Wright. ColAP; HCAP; LCAP-2; VCAP; WeT

Stone Diary, A. Pat Lowther. NOBC

Stone on the Hilltop, The. Lu Yu, *Chinese.* CoBCP, *tr. by* Burton Watson

Stones: Avesbury. Daisy Aldan. PoA

Stonewall Jackson's Way. John Williamson Palmer. CBCWP

Storm, The. Robert David Cohen. NYBP

Storm Warnings. Adrienne Rich. AiP; NAAL-2; NIP-4

Story, The. Charles Simic. NNaP

Story, A. William Stafford. NNaP

Story of Augustus Who Would Not Have Any Soup, The. Heinrich Hoffmann, *German.* NBLV; OxBChV

Story of Johnny Head-in-Air, The. Heinrich Hoffmann, *German.* OxBChV

Story of Lava, The. David Allan Evans. Poetsp

Story of My Life, The. Carroll Arnett. VoR

Story of the Corn. K. Fisher. BoTP

Story of the Eaters, A. Santiago Mendes Zapata, *Tzeltal Indian.* STP, *tr. by* W. S. Merwin

Strains of Sight. Robert Duncan. CMoP; PoE

Strange People, The. Louise Erdrich. PoPoPo

Strange tropic warmth and hints of summer seas. (LL) Ethnogenesis. Henry Timrod. APN-2; AmPP; NOBA; OxBA

Stranger, The. Walter De la Mare. OxBTC

Stranger, A. Lionel Pigot Johnson. NOBVV

Strangers. William Stafford. NNaP

Strangers, The. Jones Very. APN-1; OxBA

Strategies. Welton Smith. PoBA

Straunge [or Strange] Passion of a Lover, A. George Gascoigne. AAS

Strawberries in Mexico. Ron Padgett. SPE

Strawberry, The. Maggie Pogue Johnson. CBWP-4

Stray Dog, near Ecully. Margaret Avison. PoA

Street Fight. Harold Monro. FaBoTw

Street Lanterns. Mary Elizabeth Coleridge. BoTP; PoRA

Street Scene. Robert Mezey. LiTM

Street Scene, A. Lizette Woodworth Reese. OBCA

Streets of Ch'ang-an, The. Ch'u Kuang-hsi, *Chinese.* CoBCP, *tr. by* Burton Watson

Streets of Forbes, The. Jack McGuire. CBAP; NOBAu

Streets of Laredo, The. *Unknown. See* The Cowboy's Lament.

Strength through Joy. Kenneth Rexroth. FYAP; VGW

Strictly for Posterity. Charles Simic. NNaP

Strictly Germ-proof. Arthur Guiterman. BLPA; TrJP

Stroke. Mike Lowery. Poetsp

Strong enough to trust to. (LL) The Paper Nautilus. Marianne Moore. FaBoWP; NALW; VGW

Strong is your hold O Love. (LL) The Last Invocation. Walt Whitman. MoAmPo; OBEV; OxBA; PAR; PoEL-5; SAGP

Strong Wind, A. Austin Clarke. RB

Studio for Listening to the Snow, The. Yang Chi, *Chinese.* CoBLCP, *tr. by* Jonathan Chaves

Study of a Spider, The. John Byrne Leicester Warren. APo; NOBVV

Stupid and abiding jelly, The. (LL) Bacchanal. Peter De Vries. BXAP; NBLV; NOBL; OBAL

Stutterer. Alan Dugan. CAPP-1; NYBP

Style. Howard Nemerov. NoAM

Style thee a most great fool, but no great man. (LL) On Don Surly. Ben Jonson. FaBoEE; NAEL-1

Styled [or Stil'd] but the shadows [or shaddowes] of us men? (LL) Song. That Women Are But Men's Shadows. Ben Jonson. BeJo; NOBE; OBEV; OxBSP; SeCP

Subplot. Jack Butler. MT

Subtlety. Bruce St. John. PBCV

Subway, The. Allen Tate. NOBA

Subway Wind. Claude McKay. PBCV

Succubus, The. Harriet Rose. BrRo

Such a King Harry? (LL) Agincourt. Michael Drayton. EBEvV; EBNV; FaBoBe; FaBoCh; NTP; OBEV; OxAEP-1

Such a Parcel of Rogues in a Nation. Robert Burns. OxBS

Such Cloe is, and common as the air. (LL) Cloe ("Bright as the day, and like the morning fair"). George, Baron Lansdowne Granville. FaBoEE; NIP-4

Such nice machines. (LL) Spring Coming. A. R. Ammons. HeIP-4, InPK 6

Such violence. And such repose. (LL) Tywater. Richard Wilbur. CMoP; CoAmPo; LiTM; TRP

Suddenly into flowers more lovely than the white moon. (LL) Train Journey. Judith Wright. NoP-4

Suet Dumpling, The. *Unknown.* BXAP

Sugar and cream. (LL) Curly Locks [!] Curly Locks [!] wilt thou be mine? Mother Goose. LB; OxNR; ReMoGo

Sugar-Plum Tree, The. Eugene Field. CTV; NBLV; OTCP; OxBChV

Suggestion Made by the Posters of the *Globe*, A. J. E. Thorold Rogers. FaBoEE

Suicide, The. Joyce Carol Oates. Poetsp

Suicide. Alice Walker. GT

Suicide's Note. Langston Hughes. PoPoPo; SAmP

Summer. Conrad Potter Aiken. NoAM; Poetr

Summerer. Diane Wakoski. VGW

Summer. Ramona Wilson. VoR

Summer Beach. Frances Darwin Cornford. BrRo

Summer Christmas in Australia, A. Douglas Brook Wheelton Sladen. OBCP

Summer Cloud, A. Waldo Williams, *Welsh.* OBWVE, *tr. by* Joseph P. Clancy

Summer Evening. John Clare. BoTP

Summer Matures. Helene Johnson. BlSi

Summer Morning, A. Richard Wilbur. FaBoMo; NBLV

Summer Rain. Sir Herbert Read. LiTM

Summer Reflection. Cyril Cusack. TIRV

Summer Sun. Robert Louis Stevenson. MoBrPo; PWR

Summer when our life was fair, The. (LL) Musings. William Barnes. HAP; NOBE; OBNC

Summer Words of [or for] a Sistuh [or Sister] Addict. Sonia Sanchez. BPo; BlSi; UnPo

(Summer Words of a Sistuh Addict.) NAAAL

Summer Words of a Sistuh Addict. Sonia Sanchez. *See* Summer Words of [or for] a Sistuh [or Sister] Addict.

Summer's Day, A. Alexander Hume. CH

Sun. Henry Rowe. OBEV

Sun is set, and masked night, The. Songe 17. Robert Sidney. NoSlc; PBRV

Sun[ne] Rising, The. Donne. APAD; BoLoP; CABP; CBLP; ClHu; EBEvV; ESCV; FHYEP; FMP; FSCP; GBL; GLoP; HAP; HeIP-4; InPS-3; LoP; MeLP; NAEL-1; NIP-4; NOBE; NOSC; NoP-4; OAEL-1; PBRV; PoE; PoEL-2; PoPoPo; Poetr; SCV; SeCP; TFi; WeW-3

Sun still prov'd the shadow still disdained, The. Thomas Campion. *See* Follow thy fair sun unhappy shadow.

Sun still prov'd the shadow still disdained, The. (LL)   Follow thy fair sun unhappy shadow. Thomas Campion. PBRV

Sun was black with judgment, and the moon, The. Femina Contra Mundum. G. K. Chesterton. OxAEP-2

Sun-Watchers. Abba Kovner, *Hebrew.* IP, *tr. by* Warren Bargad *and* Stanley F. Chyet.

Sun-Witch to the Sun, The. George Howe. NYBP

Sunday Afternoon. Denise Levertov. CoAmPo

Sunday Afternoon Service in St. Enodoc Church, Cornwall. John Betjeman. NOCV

Sunday Evenings. John Hollander. NYBP

Sunday Morning. Louis MacNeice. FaBoMo; MoBrPo; NAEL-2; NIP-4; OxAEP-2; Son

Sunday Morning. Wallace Stevens. AmPP; CMoP; ColAP; HAP; HCAP; HeIP-4; ImPo; InPS-3; LiTM; MeMAP; MoAmPo; MoP; NAAL-2; NAWM-2; NIP-4; NOBA; NoAM; NoP-4; OxBA; PoA; PoE; PoPoPo; Poetr; SAmP; SoSe-8; TAP; TFi; TRP

Sunday Morning, King's Cambridge. John Betjeman. PeECV

Sunday Service. Michael Heffernan. BXAP

Sundown at Darlington 1878. Lance Henson. VoR

Sunflower Sonnet Number One. June Jordan. Son

Sunflowers and Saturdays. Melba Joyce Boyd. BlSi

Sunken Evening [in Trafalgar Square]. Laurie Lee. LiTM; NYBP

Sunny Prestatyn. Philip Larkin. NoAM; OBCoV

Sunrise on Rydal Water. John Drinkwater. LiTM

Sunrise Trumpets. Joseph Auslander. TrJP

Sun's accomplice, the tree. / Maurice. (LL)   Dusting. Rita Dove. HCAP; HeIP-4; LCAP-2; Poetr

Sunset. Hayyim Nahman Bialik, *Hebrew.* TrJP, *tr. by* Helena Frank

Sunset. Mary Weston Fordham. CBWP-2

Sunset and evening star. Crossing the Bar. Tennyson. APAD; ChIV-2; ClHu; EBVV; EBVVPR; FaPoR; HeIP-4; ImPo; NAEL-2; NOBE; NOBVV; NoP-4; OAEL-2; OBEV; OBNC; OxBoS; PBMP; PFE; PWR; PeECV; PoLF; PoRA; SAGP; SoSe-8; TFi; TrCP

Sunset of the City, A. Gwendolyn Brooks. FaBoWP; LCAP-2; PBWP

   (Sunset of the City / Kathleen Eileen, A.) GT

Sunset of the City / Kathleen Eileen, A. Gwendolyn Brooks. *See* A Sunset of the City.

Sunshade, The. Thomas Hardy. OxBTC

Sunshine after Cloud. Josephine D. Henderson Heard. CBWP-4

Super Flumina Babylonis. Swinburne. PoEL-5

Supervisor, Han Chün-mei, Has Shown Me Five Poems He Has Written Called, the Trees Flourish in Early Summer. I Have Therefore Written Down My Own Ignoble Feelings and Sent Them Via Inspector Juan. At This Time, Chün-mei Is Lecturing to the Various Scholars on the I-ching, The. Tai Piao-yüan, *Chinese.* CoBLCP, *tr. by* Jonathan Chaves

Supper after the Last, The. Galway Kinnell. NOBA

Supplication, A. Sir Thomas Wyatt.

   ("Forget not this.") (LL) NoP-4; PoPoPo

   (Supplication, A.) GTBS-P

Supplication of the Black Aberdeen. Rudyard Kipling. BLPA

Supreme Death. Douglas Dunn. FaBoMo

Supremer Sacrifice, The. Suzanne Gardinier. CBAP

Surely You Remember. Dahlia Ravikovitch, *Hebrew.* IP, *tr. by* Warren Bargad *and* Stanley F. Chyet; VCWP, *tr. by* Chana Bloch *and* Ariel Bloch

Surfer, The. Judith Wright. WPE

Surge and thunder of the Odyssey, The. (LL)   The Odyssey. Andrew Lang. OBEV; OBNC; PoLF; PoRA

Surprised and ungrateful eye, The. (LL)   Cutting Greens. Lucille Clifton. GT

Surrexit Dominus de sepulchro. (LL)   On the Resurrection of Christ. William Dunbar. ChIV-2; EnVB; NOCV; OxBS; PoEL-1

Survey, A. William Stafford. RB

Surveyor. Guy Butler. PeSA

Surviving. James Welch. CDW; HATNAP

Survivor. Roger McGough. OBCoV

Susan. Robin Magowan. SPE

Susannah Prout. Walter De la Mare. FaBoEE

Suspense. Emily Dickinson. AWP

Sussex Legend, A. Charles Dalmon. BoTP

Swallow, The. Abraham Cowley. EBEV; OBEV; OxAEP-1

Swallow, The. Thomas Stanley. AWP

Swallow the Lake. Clarence Major. FTOS; GT; NAAAL; PmAP; PoBA; WeT

Swan. D. H. Lawrence. CMoP; PoE

Swan. Edward Lowbury. GTBS-P

Swan and Shadow. John Hollander. InPK-6; NoP-4; PoA; VCAP

   ("Sang.") (LL) NoP-4

Swans. Lawrence Durrell. MoBrPo

Swans Mating. Michael Longley. IIP; PNI

Swans of Vadstena, The. Ralph Gustafson. MoCV

Sway. Louis Simpson. NoAM

Sweat Song. Peter Blue Cloud. VoR

Sweeney Among the Nightingales. T. S. Eliot. AmPP; CMoP; FaBoMo; HAP; HeIP-4; LiTM; MoP; NAAL-2; NAEL-2; NOBA; NOBE; NoAM; NoP-4; OBMV; OxBA; Poetr; Poetr; TFi; WeW-3

Sweeney Praises the Trees. Seamus Heaney. RB

Sweeper of Ways, The. Howard Nemerov. HCAP

Sweet Apple. James Stephens. CMoP

Sweet Jane. *Unknown.* AmFP

Sweet Killen Hill. Tom MacIntyre. *See* On Sweet Killen Hill.

Sweet Lullaby, A. Nicholas Breton. *See* Cradle Song: "Come, little babe."

Sweet / May / again. (LL)   The Locust Tree in Flower. William Carlos Williams. Spl; TTTS

Sweet Peril. George Macdonald. BLPA; FaBoBe

Sweet Saints grant I live not long, The. (LL)   Riding Together. William Morris. EnVR; NOBE; OAEL-2

Sweet Surprises. Sarah Doudney. BoTP

Sweet William's Farewell to Black-Eyed [*or* Black-Ey'd] Susan. John Gay. AmFP; BoLoP; CBLP; NOEC

   ("'Adieu,' she cries, and waved her lily hand.") (LL) GLoP

   (Black-Eyed Susan.) GTBS-P

Sweet William's Ghost. *Unknown.* ESPB

Sweetness. *Unknown, Irish.* BIrV, *tr. by* John Montague

Sweetness of Nature, The. *Unknown, Irish.* IIP; TIRV, *tr. by* Frank O'Connor

Swift Love, Sweet Motor. Hildegarde Flanner. WPE

Swift! to the head of the army!—swift! spring to your places, / Pioneers! O pioneers! (LL)   Pioneers! O Pioneers! Walt Whitman. FaBoBe

Swim like a fish toward Rome. (LL)   Cleopatra to the Asp. Ted Hughes. EBEV; RACG

Swimmer's Moment, The. Margaret Avison. NOBC

Switchback. Dame Edith Sitwell. PBWP

Sydney Cove, 1788. Peter Porter. NoAM

Symon's Lesson of Wisdom for All Manner of Children. *Unknown.* OxBChV

Sympathy. Lizelia Augusta Jenkins Moorer. CBWP-3

Sympathy, A Welcome, A. John Berryman. NYBP; NoP-4

Synthesizing Several Abstruse Concepts with an Experience. Carol Poster. BXAP

Syrinx. James Merrill. HCAP

System. Robert Louis Stevenson. PWR

T

T-Bar. Patricia K. Page. NOBC; NoAM

T. E. Lawrence Poems, The. Gwendolyn MacEwen. NOBC

   There Is No Place to Hide.

'T is not to honor thee by verse of mine. On Michael Angelo. Washington Allston. APN-1

'T is [*or* 'Tis] time this heart should be unmoved. On This Day I Complete My Thirty-sixth Year. Byron. FHYEP; NOBRP; OAEL-2; OBWP; PoE

T. R. Donald Hall. PoA

T. S. Eliot. W. H. Auden. OBAL

T. S. Eliot. Robert Lowell. NOBA; NoAM

T. S. Eliot is quite at a loss. Limerick. W. H. Auden. PeLi

T' snow is witherin' off'n th' gress—. The Drained Cup. D. H. Lawrence. CBLP

T.V. John Forbes. *See* TV.

T.V. gunning down. Slumnight. Colette Inez. CMAP

'T was earliest morning in the early spring. The Bird and the Bell. Christopher Pearse Cranch. APN-1

'T were folly still to hope for higher Heaven. (LL)   Oh! that my young life were a lasting dream! Edgar Allan Poe. AmPP; MeMAP; OxBA; Poetr; TAP, *ll.* 1–12

Taana boy, how you do? Coolie Son. David Dabydeen. HCP

Tab, The. Clark Coolidge. FTOS

Tabernacle. D. H. Lawrence. ChIV-1; KSG

Tabernacle Thought, A. Israel Zangwill. TrJP

Tabitha Longclaws Tiddley Wink. (LL)   Choosing Their Names. Thomas Hood. ACTP; NOxBChV; PeP

Table, The. Ray DiPalma. FTOS

Table, The. Michael Heffernan. PoA

Table-Birds. Kenneth Mackenzie. BMAP; NOBAu

Table is spread, the lamp glitters and sighs, The. The Expected Guest. Sidney Keyes. PoWW

Table Laid with Horrors, A. Forrest Gander. PT

Table Manners. Frank Gelett Burgess. OBCA

(Table Manners I.) CTV

Table Manners I. Frank Gelett Burgess. See Table Manners.

Table Manners II. Frank Gelett Burgess. CTV

Table of Contents. Henry Lawes, *Italian*. CBNP, *tr. by* Peggy Forsyth

Table Rules for Little Folk[s]. *Unknown*. OxBChV

Table Talk. William Cowper.

"Contemporaries all surpassed, see one." EPCY

"Then Pope, as harmony itself exact." EPCY

"When Cromwell fought for power, and while he reigned." EPCY

Table Talk. Derek Mahon. DiPo

Table Talk. Wallace Stevens. NoP-4

Table was filled with many objects, The. "Utopia" The. Lee Harwood. SPE

Tableau. Countee Cullen. NAAAL; PoBA

Tableau. Judith Wright. CBAP

Tables in Pictures. Diane Ward. FTOS

Tables Turned, The. Wordsworth.

Tables Turned[: An Evening Scene, on the Same Subject], The. Wordsworth. APAD; FHYEP; NAEL-2; NOBRP; OAEL-2; Ro; TOF

"Sweet is the lore which Nature brings;." PFE

Tablet V. Armand Schwerner. PFTM

Tablets, The. Nicanor Parra, *Spanish*. VCWP, *tr. by* W. S. Merwin

Taboo to Boot. Ogden Nash. RB

Taches Jaunes, Les. Théophile Gautier, *French*. Clarimonde. AWP

Taciturn, oblivious—until the end of Time, (LL) The Widening Spell of the Leaves. Larry Levis. NAmP90; PBCAP

Tacking Ship Off Shore. Walter Mitchell. FaBoBe

Tact. Paul Pascal. WeW-3

Tact. Edwin Arlington Robinson. NoAM

Tadhg sat up on his hills. Senior Members. Sean Lucy. CIP-2

Tadoussac. Charles Bancroft. BLPA

Tadpole, The. E. E. Gould. BoTP

Tadpoles, For J. W. Barrie Wade. AYFP

Tae be wan o them Kings. Stars. George Mackay Brown. OxBS

Tae titly. *Unknown*. FaBoVe, OxNR

Taffy, the topaz-coloured cat. In Honour of Taffy Topaz. Christopher Darlington Morley. WHSW

Taffy was a Welshman, Taffy was a thief. Mother Goose. OxNR; RB; ReMoGo

Taffy was born. *Unknown*. OxNR

Taga for Mbaye Dyôb. Léopold Sédar Senghor. PFTM, *tr. by* Melvin Dixon

Tagus fare well that westward with thy strems. Sir Thomas Wyatt. *See* In Spayn.

Tagus farewell, that westward with thy streams. In Spayn. Sir Thomas Wyatt. AAS; NoSic; OPOU; SCGP

Tahirassawichi, I suppose, has said nothing to the Department of / State. (LL) Tahirassawichi in Washington. Ernesto Cardenal, *Spanish*. EC2

Tahirassawichi in Washington. Ernesto Cardenal, *Spanish*. VCWP, *tr. by* Carlos Altschul *and* Monique Altschul; EC2

("To the State Department.") (LL) VCWP, *tr. by* Carlos Altschul *and* Monique Altschul

Tahiti. Louis Johnson. PeNZ

Tahoe in August. Robert Hass. NoP-4

Taiaha Haka Poem. Apirana Taylor. PeNZ

Taid's Grave. Gillian Clarke. OPOU

Tail behind, a trunk in front, A. The Elephant, or the Force of Habit. A. E. Housman. NOBL

Tail of the See, A. Elizabeth T. Corbett. OBCA

Taill of the Foxe, That Begylit the Wolf, in the Schadow of the Mone, The. Robert Henryson. OxBS

Tailor, The. "S. Ansky," *Yiddish*. TrJP, *tr. by* Joseph Leftwich

Tailor. Eleanor Farjeon. OTCP; OxBChV

Tailor, The. Joseph Leftwich. TrJP

Tailor Called Sorrow, A. Betti Alver, *Estonian*. BoWoP, *tr. by* Willis Barnstone *and* Felix Oinas

Tailor of Bicester. *Unknown*. OxNR

Tailor's Wedding, The. Louis Simpson. NNaP

Tailpiece. Max Fatchen. OTCP

Tails and Heads. Suzanne Knowles. RB

Táin, The. *Unknown, Irish*. NOIV, *tr. by* Thomas Kinsella

Armies Enter Cuailnge, The.

Before the Last Battle.

Taisigh Agat Fein Do Phog. *Unknown, Irish*. BIrV, *tr. by* Maire Cruise O'Brien

Tajo, tajo, tajo! tajo, my mackey massa! *Unknown*. *Fr*. Dancing Songs. PBCV

Tak for Sidst. Babette Deutsch. PoA

Tak tyme in tym, or tym will not be tane. A Description of Tyme. Alexander Montgomerie. OxBS

Tak' Your Auld Cloak about Ye. *Unknown*. OxBS

Take a father's admonition, from a heart disturbed. A Father's Testament. Judah ibn Tibbon, *Hebrew*. TrJP, *tr. by* Israel Abrahams

Take a harp. Song of the Harlot. Bible, *O.T.* TrJP *Fr*. Isaiah.

Take a large olive, stone it and then stuff it. A Dish for a Poet. *Unknown*. OBCP

Take a Look at My Rebels. Meir Wieseltier, *Hebrew*. IP, *tr. by* Warren Bargad *and* Stanley F. Chyet

Take a model of the world so big. The Rescued Year. William Stafford. ColAP; LCAP-2

Take a note and spin it around spin it around don't. The Genie in the Jar. Nikki Giovanni. SeSe

Take a sheet of paper. How to Reach the Sun. . . on a Piece of Paper. Wes Magee. NOxBChV

Take a statement: the same as yesterday's dictation. Vowel Movements. Daryl Hine. PoA

Take a Whiff on Me. *Unknown*. NOBA

Take all my loves, my Love, yea, take them all. Sonnet 40. Shakespeare. HeIP-4; OxAEP-1; SCGP *Fr*. Sonnets.

Take all the rest the sun goes round! (LL) On a Girdle. Edmund Waller. AWP; BeJo; GLoP; GTBS-P; ImPo; InPK-6; NAEL-1; NOSC; NoP-4; OBEV; PoE; PoRA; SCGP; TFi

Take as a sign of the rising wind the swelling sea. Weather Signs. Aratus. HePo, *tr by* Barbara Hughes Fowler *Fr*. Phaenomena.

Take Away. Margot Ruddock. OBMV

Take away the stuff! Dry. Samuel Hoffenstein. BXAP

Take back the heart you with such caution give. To Lysander. Aphra Behn. LW

Take Back the Virgin Page. Thomas Moore. OBNC

Take back your suit. A Song of Faith Forsworn. John Byrne Leicester Warren, 3d Baron De Tabley. PeVV

Take breath in irregular / measure. (LL) Shlup, shlup, the dog. Denise Levertov. HeIP-4; InPK-6; Poetr

Take Care. Heather McHugh. WeT

Take care of that face! That Face. Mairtin Ó Direain. BiHa

Take care of this. It's all there is. I. Kenneth Rexroth. *Fr*. A Bestiary. OBAL

Take care to live out my hundred years! (LL) Lotus Lake. Ts'ao P'i, *Chinese*. CoBCP; GaP, *tr. by* Burton Watson

Take charge of me, and of my END. (LL) Dies Irae. Thomas of Celano, *Latin*. AWP; TIRV, *tr. by* Richard Crashaw

Take control! Margaret Abigail Walker. *See* For my people [everywhere singing their slave songs repeatedly: their]

Take Down the Fiddle, Karl! John Shaw Neilson. CBAP

Take eat take glowing coal eat. Body and Soul: Poem for Two Readers. John Taggart. FTOS

Take fortune as it falls, as one adviseth. The Author, of His Own Fortune. Sir John Harington. FaBoEE

Take, friend, Orthon of Syracuse' advice. Theocritus, *Greek*. GrAn, *tr. by* Anthony Holden

Take fright in his bewildering bower, and die. (LL) Winter Will Follow. Richard Watson Dixon. CH; GTBS-P

Take, gentle marble, to thy trust. An Elegy upon His Tomb in Herndon-Hill Church, Erected by His Wife, Who Speaks. James Howell. OBWVE

Take half thy canvass in. (LL) Odes 2.10. Horace. AWP; OBVE, *tr. by* William Cowper

Take hands. / There is no love now. Laura Riding Jackson. PiM

Take heart, monsieur, four-fifths of this province. For Jean Vincent d'Abbadie, Baron St.-Castin. Alden Nowlan. NOBC

Take heart, Prytherch. Aside. Ronald Stuart Thomas. OxBC

Take heart, the journey's ended. In the Town. *Unknown, French*. OBCP; PChr, *tr. by* Eleanor Farjeon

Take heed betime, lest ye be spied. Sir Thomas Wyatt. SiPS

Take heed mine eyes, how you your lookes doe cast. Mary Sidney, Countess of Montgomery Wroth. *See* Sonnet 39.

Take heed mine eyes, how you your looks do cast. Sonnet 39. Mary Sidney Wroth. PEW *Fr*. Pamphilia to Amphilanthus.

Take heed of loving me[e]. The Prohibition. Donne. GBL; MeLP; NOSC

Take heed of this small child of earth. The Poor Children. Victor Hugo, *French*. AWP, *tr. by* Swinburne

Take hence this tuneful trifler's lays! Ode: Written After Reading Some Modern Love-Verses. John Scott of Amwell. ECEV

Take Him away, he's dead as they die. Obituary. Kenneth Fearing. VGW

"Take him to the Gulley! Take him to the Gulley!" A Popular Negro Song. *Unknown.* PBCV

Take home Thy prodigal child, O Lord of Hosts! Birthday Sonnet. Elinor Wylie. MoAmPo

Take in hand the cup of delusion. Drink On. Mary E. Tucker. CBWP-1

Take it as earnest of a faith renewed. Nathaniel Lee. EPCY *Fr.* To the Unkown Author of *Absalom and Achitophel.*

Take It from Me. Kenneth O. Hanson. CoAP

Take it from me kiddo. Poem, or Beauty Hurts Mr. Vinal. E. E. Cummings. FaBoA; InPS-3; MoAmPo; NAAL-2; OBAL; OxBA; PFTM; PeLV; TRP

Take it not back! the priceless gift. Invocation to the Muse. Henrietta Cordelia Ray. CBWP-3

Take it out in vile whisky, take it out. Impromptu: The Suckers. William Carlos Williams. FaBoA

Take it to the hoop, "magic" johnson. A Poem for "Magic." Quincy Troupe. ISC; LoL

Take it up like a kite on the wing! (LL) Limerick: "Well, it's partly the shape of the thing." *Unknown.* KaS

Take, Lord, this soul of furred unblemished worth. Epitaph for a Good Mouser. Anne Stevenson. Spl

Take me back before everything. (LL) Being Aware. Dennis Cooper. GLP; PmAP

Take me in your arms, Miss Moneypenny-Wilson. Patrick Barrington. OBCoV

Take Me Out to the Ball Game. Jack Norworth. OBAL

Take me to the distant northlands. Tirzah and the Wide World. Dahlia Ravikovitch, *Hebrew.* IP, *tr. by* Warren Bargad *and* Stanley F. Chyet

Take My Hand, Precious Lord. Thomas A. Dorsey. ISC

Take My Hand, Precious Lord. *Unknown.* NAAAL

Take my song of love to heart. *Unknown, Irish.* NOIV, *tr. by* Thomas Kinsella

Take my tunic, woman. Goll Mac Morna Parts from His Wife. *Unknown.* NOIV

Take my word for it, Hanzlicek. C.G. Hanzlicek. C. G. Hanzlicek. CMAP

Take my word for jewel in your open light. Audre Lorde. *See* Coal.

Take note, passers-by, of the sharp erosions. The Circuit Judge. Edgar Lee Masters. FaBoEE *Fr.* Spoon River Anthology.

Take note who stoop. Nicarchus of Alexandria, *Greek.* GrAn, *tr. by* Peter Porter

Take, O take the cream away. Breakfast Song in Time of Diet. Stoddard King. OBAL

Take, O take those lips away. At the Moated Grange. Shakespeare. AWP; EBEV; EnLoPo; GBL; GTBS-P; ImPo; InPS-3; NOBE; NoSic; OAEL-1; OBEV; PoEL-2; SCGP; TFi *Fr.* Measure for Measure.

Take of me what is not my own. Envoi. Kathleen Jessie Raine. NOBE

Take off his hide and feed him to the crows. (LL) On Buying a Horse. *Unknown.* NBLV; RB

Take off those flimsy nets, Lysidice. Argentarius, *Greek.* GrAn, *tr. by* Fleur Adcock

Take off your clothes, my love! Paulus Silentiarius, *Greek.* InMo, *tr. by* Sam Hamill

Take off your hat. Pass Office Song. *Unknown, Afrikaans.* PBA; TTY, *tr. by* Peggy Rutherford

Take, oh, take those lips away. John Fletcher. NoP-4

Take, Oh, Take Those Lips Away. John Fletcher *and others. See* Song.

Take I, 4:11:58. Philip Whalen. NeAP

Take 1 green pepper and 2 tomatoes. Pour Commencer. Jon Stallworthy. NoAM

Take One Home for the Kiddies. Philip Larkin. OxBTC; PeP

Take poems, but don't read them. Meir Wieseltier, *Hebrew.* IP, *tr. by* Warren Bargad *and* Stanley F. Chyet

Take sackcloth of the darkest dye. Bible Defence of Slavery. Frances Ellen Watkins Harper. APAD; APN-2; PAR

Take that, damn you; and that! Mezzo Forte. William Carlos Williams. SAmP

Take the cloak of all my love. Song for a Jewess. Iwan Goll, *French.* TrJP, *tr. by* Joseph T. Shipley

Take the Crust. Sadi. AWP, *tr. by* L. Cranmer-Byng *Fr.* The Gulistan.

Take the night Myron Stout shut his sure blind eyes. Baby Vallejo. David Rivard. SeSe

Take the thanks of a boy. (LL) Prayers. Henry Charles Beeching. BoTP; OBEV

Take the Toys from the Boys. Ulli Freer. NBrP

Take the World As It Is. Charles Swain.
  "Take the world as it is!—with its smiles and its sorrow." PoToHe

Take then these nail and boards. Charles Bernstein. FTOS

Take, then your paltry Christ. To the Christians. Francis Lauderdale Adams. ChIV-2; OxBS

Take Therefore That You May Have. "Angelus Silesius." GePo, *tr. by* George C. Schoolfield *Fr.* The Cherubical Wanderer.

Take these who will as may be: I. Permit Me Voyage. James Agee. MoAmPo

Take this hammer—huh! *Unknown.* ISC

Take this hammer, (huh!) carry it to the captain, (huh!). "Leadbelly." GM

Take this kiss upon the brow! A Dream within A Dream. Edgar Allan Poe. AmPP; GBL; MeMAP; NCAP; NOBA; OxBA; TAP

Take this man with an axe. The Private. Robert Adamson. BMAP

Take this news to the Lakedaimonians, friend. For the Spartan Dead at Thermopylai (480 B.C.). Simonides, *Greek.* OBCVT, *tr. by* Peter Jay; GrAn

Take Thou Our Minds, Dear Lord. William H. Foulkes. AH

Take thou the world and all that will. (LL) The Flesh and the Spirit. Anne Bradstreet. AmPP; ChIV-2; NAAL-1; NAAL-3; NOBA; OxBA; OxWW; SCAP; TAP

Take Thy Bliss, O Man. William Blake. *Fr.* Visions of the Daughters of Albion. CABP; OAEL-2; Ro

Take time, my dear, ere Time takes wing. Fading Beauty. *Unknown.* FaBoEE

Take time to live. Thomas Curtis Clark. PoToHe

Take time while time doth last. Song Set by John Farmer. *Unknown.* CTC; NoSic

Take two people. Any two people. Necessary Story. Dionisio D. Martinez. WWSi

Take up the pen: fall into the net of law. Call to Arms. "Lu Hsün," *Chinese.* SuSp, *tr. by* William R. Schultz

Take up the song; forget the epitaph. (LL) To Inez Milholland. Edna St. Vincent Millay. AiP; NALW; WPE

Take up the White Man's burden. The White Man's Burden. Rudyard Kipling. FaBoPV

Take Ye Heed, Watch and Pray. Jones Very. ChIV-2

Take yesterday's worries and sort them all out. Worries. *Unknown.* PoToHe

Take your bucket, and take your spade. The Sea. E. M. Adams. BoTP

Take your first steps in a Walker. Poem for the Children. Carolyn Beard Whitlow. FFC

Take your own kisses; give me mine again. (LL) Kisses. William Strode. FaBoEE; NOSC

Taken away from her language. Island. Meredith Stricker. LoHo

Taken by storm, she is the girl you will marry. (LL) Courtship. Mark Strand. PoPoPo

Taken by surprise. Meeting Bida. Fily-Dabo Sissoko, *French.* NegPo, *tr. by* Ellen Conroy Kennedy

Taken from the. The Primitive. Don L. Lee. BPo

Taken in by none but Thee. (LL) To Julia ("Julia, when thy Herrick dies"). Robert Herrick. CaPo; NOSC

Takes a taste of green. The Moon. Wendy Mulford. NBrP

Takes in / the world / from the heart out. The Morning-Glory. Raymond Roseliep. HA

Takes one long slow step nearer. (LL) Golden Calf. Norman MacCaig. ChIV-1; OxBS

Taking a Captive / 1984. Barney Bush. HATNAP

Taking a Hot Bath. Marge Piercy. *Fr.* Six Underrated Pleasures. EC2

Taking a Look. David Shapiro. PT

Taking a Walk with You. Kenneth Koch. CAPP-1

Taking Ford's dictation on Samuel Butler. Ford Madox Ford. Robert Lowell. OxBC

Taking, giving back their lives. The Field Hospital. Paul Muldoon. CIP-2; PNI

Taking in Wash. Rita Dove. MoLi

Taking It Back. Dixie Salazar. UnSA

Taking Leave of a Friend. Li Po, *Chinese.* RB, *tr. by* Ezra Pound
  ("Blue hills over the north wall;.") FP, *tr. by* Innes Herdan
  ("Our horses whinnied to each other at parting.") (LL) FP, *tr. by* Innes Herdan

Taking me into your body. The Source. Jon Stallworthy. CBLP

Taking Notice. Marilyn Hacker.
  "And I shout at Iva, whine at you. Easily." VCAP
  "If we talk, we're too tired to make love; if we." VCAP
  "In the Public Theater lobby, I wait for Marie." VCAP
  "We work, play, don't cross-reference calendars." VCAP

Taking of the Koppie, The. Uys Krige. PeSAV

Taking Off My Clothes. Carolyn Forché. AmPA; NoAM

Taking recreation, seeing pleasant things. Nebamun's Cat. Felicity Bast. PC

Taking the air rifle from my son's hand. Cain. Irving Layton. MoCV

Taking the Census. Charles Robert Thatcher. NOBAu

Taking the Ferry at Ta-kao at Dawn. Yang Wei-chen, *Chinese*. SuSp, *tr. by* Jonathan Chaves

Taking the hands of someone you love. Robert Bly. IFJA; TRP

Taking the Night-Train. John James Piatt. APN-2

Taking the Plunge. John Mole. NOxBChV

Taking to the Woods. Henry Taylor. MT

Taking Turns. Norma Farber. TLR

Taking us by and large, we're a queer lot. The Sisters. Amy Lowell. NALW; NMM-2

Taku Skanskan. Paula Gunn Allen. HATNAP

Tale. Jennifer Rankin. BMAP

Tale About a Tale, The. Vasco [*or* Vasko] Popa. HSix *Fr.* The Yawn of Yawns.

Tale for Husbands, A. Sir Philip Sidney. SiPS *Fr.* Arcadia.

Tale half told and hardly understood, A. Pilgrims of the Plains. Joaquin Miller. PaTW

Tale I frame shall be found to tally, The. The Seafarer. *Unknown, Anglo-Saxon.* EEP; OBVE, *tr. by* Michael Alexander

Tale I frame shall be found to tally, The. The Seafarer. *Unknown.* OBVE, *tr. by* Michael Alexander

Tale I frame shall be found to tally. *Unknown.* OBVE, *tr. by* Michael Alexander *Fr.* The Seafarer.

Tale is told of long ago, A. A Song of the Yellow Cedar Face. George Clutesi. HATNAP

Tale of a Dog and a Bee, The. *Unknown.* BoTP

Tale of a Friar and A Shoemaker's Wife, a. Thomas Churchyard. NoSic

Tale of a Pony, The. Bret Harte. OBNV

Tale of Acadie, A. Henry Wadsworth Longfellow. MeMAP *Fr.* Evangeline.

From Evangeline. NoP-4

Tale of Custard the Dragon, The. Ogden Nash. OBCA; OTCP; PoRA

Tale of Genji, The. Murasaki Shikibu, *Japanese.*

"Lady Murasaki says." BoWoP; WPJ

"Troubled waters, The/ are frozen fast." WPJ; WPOW

Tale of Genji. Hugh Seidman. AmPA

Tale of Italy, A. Eloise Bibb. CBWP-4

Tale of Jorkyns and Gertie; or, Vice Rewarded, The. Richard Percival Lister. NYBP

Tale of Lord Lovell, The. *Unknown.* NOBL; PeLV

Tale of Mushrooms. Lynda Hiott. CTV

Tale of Red-Haired Motl, Mister Inspector, Rabbi Isaiah, and Commissar Blokh, The. Iosif Pavlovich Utkin, *Russian.* TCRP, *tr. by* Lubov Yakovleva

Tale of Sigemund, The. *Unknown.* AnOE, *tr. by* Charles W. Kennedy *Fr.* Beowulf. OAEL-1, *tr. by* Charles W. Kennedy; ASW, *tr. by* Kevin Crossley-Holland

Tale of Sir Thopas, The. Chaucer. BXAP, *ll.* 1–248; NAEL-1, *ll.* 1–252 *Fr.* The Canterbury Tales.

Tale of Sunlight, The. Gary Soto. NoAM

Tale of the Beginning of Friars and Cloisterers, A. William Warner. NoSic *Fr.* Albion's England.

Tale of the Cyclopses, The. Nikolai Ivanovich Glazkov, *Russian.* TCRP, *tr. by* Daniel Weissbort

Tale of the Miser and the Poet, A. Anne Finch, Countess of Winchilsea. ECWP

Tale of the Upland Mouse and the Burgess Mouse, The. Robert Henryson. OBNV

("Isope [*or* Aesoe] myn auctor makis mencioun.") EnVB

(Tale of the Uplandis Mous and the Borowstown Mous, The.) EnVB

Tale of the Uplandis Mous and the Borowstown Mous, The. Robert Henryson. *See* The Tale of the Upland Mouse and the Burgess Mouse.

Tale of Time. Robert Penn Warren. LCAP-2

Tale Told by a Head, A. Lois Moyles. NYBP

Talebearer revealeth secrets, A. The Bible, Proverbs 11:13. Bible, *O.T.* CTV *Fr.* The Bible, Proverbs 11:13.

Talent. Tadeusz Rózewicz, *Polish.* CEEP, *tr. by* Victor Contoski

Talent is what they say. For the Young Who Want To. Marge Piercy. Poetsp

Talented Man, The. Winthrop Mackworth Praed. CABP; NOBL; PeLV

(Letter, From a Lady in London to a Lady at Lausanne, A.) OBCoV

Tales. George Crabbe.

Jonas Kindred's Household. OBNC

Tales from a Family Album. Donald Justice. Poetr

Tales of a Wayside Inn, *sels.* Henry Wadsworth Longfellow.

Birds of Killingworth, The (The Poet's Tale). MeMAP; OxBA

Monk of Casal-Maggiore, The (The Sicilian's Tale). AmPP; OxBA

Paul Revere's Ride (The Landlord's Tale). AiP; BLPA; EBEvV; EBNV; FaBoBe; FaBoTw; FaPoR; ImGa; OBAL; OBCA; OBNV; PWR; TFi

("And the midnight message of Paul Revere.") (LL) ChAP; ColAP; NOxBChV; SAGP

(Paul Revere's Ride.) CTV; ChAP; ColAP; NOxBChV; SAGP

("So through the night rode Paul Revere.") CA

Prelude: The Wayside Inn. APN-1

Spanish Jew's Tale: Azrael, The. APN-1

Student's Tale, The. AmPP

Tales of Shatz. Dannie Abse. OxBC

Tales of the Hall. George Crabbe.

Sad Lover, The. OBNC

Tales of the Islands. Derek Walcott. OxBTC

Taliessin's Song of the Unicorn. Charles Williams. FaBoTw

Talisman, A. Marianne Moore. MoAmPo

Talk. Roo Borson. NIP-4; NOBC

Talk about the shade of the sheltering palms. Under the Anheuser Bush. Andrew B. Sterling. OBAL

Talk about your harbor girls around the corner, Sally. Haul Away, My Rosy. *Unknown.* AmFP

Talk all day and then keep silent. Parrot. Po Chü-i, *Chinese.* SuSp, *tr. by* Irving Y. Lo

Talk between the people and the soil. Clinton. Sterling Plumpp. BkSV *Fr.* Clinton.

Talk happiness. The world is sad enough. Optimism. Ella Wheeler Wilcox. BLPA; FaBoBe; PoToHe

Talk no more of the lucky escape of the head. On a Stone Thrown at a Very Great Man, But Which Missed Him. "Peter Pindar." NBLV

Talk not of strength, till your heart has known. *Unknown.* PoToHe

Talk not of wasted affection. Henry Wadsworth Longfellow. CTV

Talk of energy. Mayan sub-flower. Dangers of the Journey to the Happy Land. Joseph Ceravolo. PT

Talk of passion is a winter thing. The Kiss. Ned O'Gorman. FYAP

Talk to Me, Baby. Michael Dennis Browne. CMAP

Talk to the Peach Tree. Sipho Sepamla. PBMAP

Talk War. Albie Ollivierre. NBrP

Talk with My Cousin Alone, A. Hone Tuwhare. PeNZ

Talked to my father again in a dream he seemed happy. Le Jazz Hot. Anselm Hollo. SeSe

Talker, The. Benjamin Appel. TrJP

Talker, The. Mona Van Duyn. PiM

Talkers in a Dream Doorway. Judy Grahn. GLP

Talking. Robert Creeley. FTOS

Talking along in this not quite prose way. Near. William Stafford. CoAmPo

Talking Designs. Liz Sohappy Bahe. CDW

Talking Drums, The. Kojo Gyinaye Kyei. PBA

Talking Fish, The. Ruth Stone. BoWoP

Talking for yonks about babies and / washing machines. Grown-ups. Geoffrey Holloway. OTCP

Talking his cock, talking. Mr. Muscle-On. Faye Kicknosway. DeD

Talking in bed ought to be easiest. Philip Larkin. BoLoP; CBLP; NAEL-2; OxBM

("Or not untrue and not unkind.") (LL) LoP; NoP-4; PoPoPo

Talking of Ezra Pound and long-dead pantos. Robert Malise Bowyer Nichols. OBSV *Fr.* Fisbo.

Talking of poetry, hauling the books. In a Classroom. Adrienne Rich. LoL

Talking of sects quite late one eve. No Sects in Heaven. Elizabeth Hannah Jocelyn Cleaveland. BLPA

Talking of Sharp Things. Frank Mkalawile Chipasula. HBAPE

Talking to God. Garry Cleveland Myers. CTV

Talking to her, he knew it was the end. Hector. Valentin Iremonger. CIP-2

Talking to Patrizia. Kenneth Koch. BAP-93

Talking to strange men on the subway. My Mother. John Weiners. BB; GLP; PmAP

Talking to the Mule. Laura Jensen. AmPA

Talking to You Afterwards. Peter Porter. BMAP

Talking together between the wire grates of a cage. (LL) My Mother. John Weiners. GLP; PmAP

Talking with Soldiers. Walter James Turner. MoBrPo

Talking With the Pyramid. Huy Cận, *Vietnamese.* AVP, *tr. by* Huỳnh Sanh Thông

Talks and talks. (LL) Age. Robert Creeley. FTOS; PmAP

Tall Ambrosia. Henry David Thoreau. PoEL-4

Tall and blue. Sky. Grace Nichols. AYFP

Tall and clothed in samite. A White Iris. Pauline B. Barrington. PoLF

Tall and great-bearded: black and white. Anachronism. Oliver St. John Gogarty. FYAP

Tall as a foxglove spire, on tiptoe. Fox Dancing. Suzanne Knowles. RB

Tall Buildings. Munib-ur-Rahman, *Urdu*. OMIP, *tr. by* Kathleen Grant Jaeger *and* Baidar Bakht

Tall camels of the spirit, The. 'World Without Objects Is a Sensible Emptiness," A." Richard Wilbur. CoAmPo; LiTM; MoAmPo; MoP; NAAL-2; NOBA; NoAM; PoA

Tall dames go walking in grass-green Avalon. (LL) The Statesman's Holiday. W. B. Yeats. CMoP; OxBTC

Tall dancer dances, The. The Dancer. Joseph Campbell. OBMV

Tall ears. What Is It? Marie Louise Allen. CTV

Tall Girl, The. John Crowe Ransom. Son

Tall grows that pear-tree. Return from Battle. *Unknown, Chinese*. ChiP, *tr. by* Arthur Waley

Tall Hat. Victor James Daley. CBAP

Tall man and myself tonight, The. Grand Army Plaza. June Jordan. ISC

Tall Man Executes a Jig, A. Irving Layton. MoCV; NOBC; NoAM

Tall Nettles. Edward Thomas. BoTP; FaBoTw; FaBoVe; MoBrPo; OxBSP

Tall palm tree sixty feet high, The. Prayer to the God Thot. *Unknown, Egyptian*. TTY, *tr. by* Ulli Beier

Tall stand the peaks. Staying in a Mountain Pavilion on a Summer Night. Ma Chih-yüan. *Fr.* Two Poems to the Tune "Po pu tuan." CoBLCP, *tr. by* Jonathan Chaves

Tall stature of, A. Sorrow. Josephine Miles. IMW

Tall Story for Fred Dibnah. Geoffrey Summerfield. OTCP

Tall tall, the hundred foot tower. Imitating the Old Poems. T'ao Ch'ien, *Chinese*. CoBCP, *tr. by* Burton Watson

Tall terrace crumbled long ago, The. Dragon-Tiger Terrace. Yang Shih-ch'i, *Chinese*. CoBLCP, *tr. by* Jonathan Chaves

Tall-topped acacia, you, full of branches. Elephant. *Unknown*. PeSA

Tall tree talking with the wind, A. The Wind. Sara Teasdale. NMM-2

Tall Trees. Eileen Mathias. BoTP

Tall Trees. Phạm H(cfstilde;o), *Vietnamese*. AVP, *tr. by* Huỳnh Sanh Thông

Tall trees are full of sad wind, The. Ballad of the Orioles in the Fields. Ts'ao Chih, *Chinese*. SuSp, *tr. by* Hans H. Frankel

Tall unpopular men. Dedication. Oliver St. John Gogarty. OBMV

Tall Wind, The. K. O. Arvidson. PeNZ

Talla ly li oh / Freedom a come oh! Freedom a Come Oh! *Unknown*. FaBoVe; PBCV

Taller to-day, we remember similar evenings. W. H. Auden. CMoP

Tallest poet for his height. Arroyo. Tom Weatherly. PoBA

Tallness. Paulette Jiles. IFJA

Tallulah. James Matthew Legaré. APN-2

Tally. Josephine Miles. NoAM

Tally Stick, The. Jarold Ramsey. NIP-4

Talmud, The. Simeon Grigoryevich Frug, *Yiddish*. TrJP, *tr. by* Alice Stone Blackwell

Talmud, The. *Unknown, Hebrew*. TrJP

Talmud Student, The. Hayyim Nahman Bialik, *Hebrew*. TrJP, *tr. by* Helena Frank

Talmudist. Stanley Burnshaw. DiPo

Talysarn. Brenda Chamberlain. OBWVE

Tam Cari Capitis. Louis MacNeice. FP

Tam Glen. Robert Burns. AWP; OxBS

Tam i' the Kirk. Violet Jacob. GBL

Tam Lin. *Unknown*. ESPB; NOBE; OBEV; OBNV; OxBB; OxBS

Tam o' Shanter. [A Tale]. Robert Burns. CABP; EBNV; ImPo; NAEL-2; NoP-4; OAEL-1; OBNV; PeLV; Ro

"And, wow! Tam saw an unco sight!" OxBSn

Tam o' the linn cam up the gait. *Unknown*. FaBoCh

Tam Samson's Elegy. Robert Burns. PoEL-4

Tamaki of a Hundred Lovers. Hirini Melbourne. PeNZ

Tamaki of a Hundred Lovers. Merimeri Penfold, *Maori*. PeNZ, *tr. by* Margaret Orbell

Tamaracks swing light away. Swamp. Roberta Hill Whiteman. VoR

Tamar's Wrestling. Walter Savage Landor. *See* The Shepherd and the Nymph.

Tambour. István Vas, *Hungarian*. CEEP, *tr. by* Jascha Kessler

Tambourine song for Soldiers Going into Battle. Hind bint Utba, *Arabic*. WPOW, *tr. by* Bridget Connelly *and* Deirdre Lashgari

Tambourines! Langston Hughes. *See* Tambourines! / Tambourines! / Tambourines.

Tambourines! / Tambourines! / Tambourines. Langston Hughes. SAmP ("Tambourines!") NOxBChV

Tamburlaine the Great. Marlowe.
     Nature That Framed Us of Four Elements. PoEL-2
     "What is beauty, saith my sufferings, then?" ImPo

Tame Cat. Ezra Pound. OBAL

Tamed by *Miltown* we lie on Mother's bed;. Man And Wife. Robert Lowell. AmPP; BoLoP; CoAmPo; ColAP; LoP; NAAL-2; SAGP; VCAP

Tamer and Hawk. Thom Gunn. APAD; APo; FaBoTw

Tamer as prey. (LL) Tamer and Hawk. Thom Gunn. APAD; APo; FaBoTw

Tamil, it's true, is the breath of my life. Gnanakoothan, *Tamil*. OMIP, *tr. by* A. K. Ramanujan

Taming of the Shrew, The. Shakespeare.
     "Thy gown? Why, ay. Come, tailor, let us see't." OBCoV

Tammy Messer. *Unknown*. FaBoEE

Tamp 'em up solid. Tamping Ties. *Unknown*. AmFP; GM

Tampa Red's Contemporary Blues. K. Curtis Lyle. MoNo

Tamping Ties ("Tamp 'em up solid"). *Unknown*. AmFP; GM

Tampons. Ellen Bass. NMM-2

Tan like young mango leaf. What Her Girl Friend Said, Seeing Her Friend Suffer in Silent Dignity over Her Husband's Infidelity. Kayamanar, *Tamil*. PLW, *tr. by* A. K. Ramanujan

Tan ta ra: cries Mars on bloody rampier. Thomas Weelkes. CBLP

Tan tandinanan tandinane. Bob Cobbing. NBrP

Tan Tien. Mei-Mei Berssenbrugge. OpBo

Tanagra! think not I forget. Corinna, from Athens, to Tanagra. Walter Savage Landor. NOBE; OBEV; OBNC *Fr.* Pericles and Aspasia.

Tang! tang! went the gong's wild roar. Night-Quarters. Henry Howard Brownell. PAR

Tangled fine and light as our indecision. Within the Greenhouse Effect. Veronica Morgan. CMAP

Tangled [*or* Tanglid] I was [*or* was I] in [*or* yn] Love's snare. Sir Thomas Wyatt. AAS; SiPS

Tangled web indeed we weave, A. Women's Degrees. Alfred Denis Godley. NOBL

Tango. Ntozake Shange. GT

Tank Town. John Atherton. NYBP

Tanka: "Accidentally." Ishikawa Takuboku, *Japanese*. MJT, *tr. by* Makoto Ueda

Tanka: "After death." Tsukamoto Kunio, *Japanese*. MJT, *tr. by* Makoto Ueda

Tanka: "After enduring." Shaku Chōkū, *Japanese*. MJT, *tr. by* Makoto Ueda

Tanka: "After letting my wife." Kitahara Hakushū, *Japanese*. MJT, *tr. by* Makoto Ueda

Tanka: "After lunch." Kitahara Hakushū, *Japanese*. MJT, *tr. by* Makoto Ueda

Tanka: "After rainfall." Miya Shūji, *Japanese*. MJT, *tr. by* Makoto Ueda

Tanka: "Agonizing beyond words." Akiko Yosano, *Japanese*. MJT, *tr. by* Makoto Ueda

Tanka: "Ailing child, An." Kitahara Hakushū, *Japanese*. MJT, *tr. by* Makoto Ueda

Tanka: "All that past life." Saitō Mokichi, *Japanese*. MJT, *tr. by* Makoto Ueda

Tanka: "All the more." Tawara Machi, *Japanese*. MJT, *tr. by* Makoto Ueda

Tanka: "All the way." Tsukamoto Kunio, *Japanese*. MJT, *tr. by* Makoto Ueda

Tanka: "All the young men I know." Toki Zenmaro, *Japanese*. MJT, *tr. by* Makoto Ueda

Tanka: "Almost invisible." Kitahara Hakushū, *Japanese*. MJT, *tr. by* Makoto Ueda

Tanka: "Almost invisible." Kitahara Hakushū, *Japanese*. MJT, *tr. by* Makoto Ueda

Tanka: "Along a street." Kondō Yoshimi, *Japanese*. MJT, *tr. by* Makoto Ueda

Tanka: "Although." Tawara Machi, *Japanese*. MJT, *tr. by* Makoto Ueda

Tanka: "Although blooming." Nakajō Fumiko, *Japanese*. MJT, *tr. by* Makoto Ueda

Tanka: "Always loving." Sasaki Yukitsuna, *Japanese*. MJT, *tr. by* Makoto Ueda

Tanka: "Amid the waves of time." Sasaki Yukitsuna, *Japanese*. MJT, *tr. by* Makoto Ueda

Tanka: "Among the hundreds." Shaku Chōkū, *Japanese*. MJT, *tr. by* Makoto Ueda

Tanka: "Arriving." Tawara Machi, *Japanese*. MJT, *tr. by* Makoto Ueda

Tanka: "Arrowroot flowers." Shaku Chōkū, *Japanese*. MJT, *tr. by* Makoto Ueda

Tanka: "As I gaze upon." Kanoko Okamoto, *Japanese*. MJT, *tr. by* Makoto Ueda

Tanka: "As if in water." Ishikawa Takuboku, *Japanese*. MJT, *tr. by* Makoto Ueda

Tanka: "As if it came." Miya Shūji, *Japanese*. MJT, *tr. by* Makoto Ueda

Tanka: "As night falls." Tsukamoto Kunio, *Japanese*. MJT, *tr.* by Makoto Ueda

Tanka: "As the surgical knife." Nakajō Fumiko, *Japanese*. MJT, *tr.* by Makoto Ueda

Tanka: "As though to let loose." Tawara Machi, *Japanese*. MJT, *tr.* by Makoto Ueda

Tanka: "Aspiration." Saitō Mokichi, *Japanese*. MJT, *tr.* by Makoto Ueda

Tanka: "Aster, The." Akiko Yosano, *Japanese*. MJT, *tr.* by Makoto Ueda

Tanka: "At a corner." Miya Shūji, *Japanese*. MJT, *tr.* by Makoto Ueda

Tanka: "At dawn." Miyazawa Kenji, *Japanese*. MJT, *tr.* by Makoto Ueda

Tanka: "At last." Miyazawa Kenji, *Japanese*. MJT, *tr.* by Makoto Ueda

Tanka: "Autumn bellflower." Kitahara Hakushū, *Japanese*. MJT, *tr.* by Makoto Ueda

Tanka: "Beastly face." Ishikawa Takuboku, *Japanese*. MJT, *tr.* by Makoto Ueda

Tanka: "Because." Kondō Yoshimi, *Japanese*. MJT, *tr.* by Makoto Ueda

Tanka: "Because my room." Maekawa Samio, *Japanese*. MJT, *tr.* by Makoto Ueda

Tanka: "Because the folks." Tsukamoto Kunio, *Japanese*. MJT, *tr.* by Makoto Ueda

Tanka: "Beyond doubt." Sasaki Yukitsuna, *Japanese*. MJT, *tr.* by Makoto Ueda

Tanka: "Beyond the glass door." Masaoka Shiki, *Japanese*. MJT, *tr.* by Makoto Ueda

Tanka: "Bliss, The." Yosano Tekkan, *Japanese*. MJT, *tr.* by Makoto Ueda

Tanka: "Bloodshot." Miyazawa Kenji, *Japanese*. MJT, *tr.* by Makoto Ueda

Tanka: "Bloom finished, The." Sasaki Yukitsuna, *Japanese*. MJT, *tr.* by Makoto Ueda

Tanka: "Bones of a fish." Fumi Saito, *Japanese*. MJT, *tr.* by Makoto Ueda

Tanka: "Boxes of sleeping pills." Nakajō Fumiko, *Japanese*. MJT, *tr.* by Makoto Ueda

Tanka: "Bulky oil lamp, A." Shaku Chōkū, *Japanese*. MJT, *tr.* by Makoto Ueda

Tanka: "But for the dew." Mori Ōgai, *Japanese*. MJT, *tr.* by Makoto Ueda

Tanka: "But for women." Akiko Yosano, *Japanese*. MJT, *tr.* by Makoto Ueda

Tanka: "By the road." Saitō Mokichi, *Japanese*. MJT, *tr.* by Makoto Ueda

Tanka: "Call to mind." Maekawa Samio, *Japanese*. MJT, *tr.* by Makoto Ueda

Tanka: "Camellias." Akiko Yosano, *Japanese*. MJT, *tr.* by Makoto Ueda

Tanka: "Casket on display, A." Tsukamoto Kunio, *Japanese*. MJT, *tr.* by Makoto Ueda

Tanka: "Casting shadows." Kondō Yoshimi, *Japanese*. MJT, *tr.* by Makoto Ueda

Tanka: "Changing." Sasaki Yukitsuna, *Japanese*. MJT, *tr.* by Makoto Ueda

Tanka: "Cherry blossoms." Tawara Machi, *Japanese*. MJT, *tr.* by Makoto Ueda

Tanka: "Cherry blossoms." Kanoko Okamoto, *Japanese*. MJT, *tr.* by Makoto Ueda

Tanka: "Cherry petals." Kanoko Okamoto, *Japanese*. MJT, *tr.* by Makoto Ueda

Tanka: "Child in my arms." Sasaki Yukitsuna, *Japanese*. MJT, *tr.* by Makoto Ueda

Tanka: "Clear spring, A." Akiko Yosano, *Japanese*. MJT, *tr.* by Makoto Ueda

Tanka: "Close by the host." Mori Ōgai, *Japanese*. MJT, *tr.* by Makoto Ueda

Tanka: "Cluster, A." Fumi Saito, *Japanese*. MJT, *tr.* by Makoto Ueda

Tanka: "Cockscomb, A." Kanoko Okamoto, *Japanese*. MJT, *tr.* by Makoto Ueda

Tanka: "Color, The." Ishikawa Takuboku, *Japanese*. MJT, *tr.* by Makoto Ueda

Tanka: "Confinement." Saitō Mokichi, *Japanese*. MJT, *tr.* by Makoto Ueda

Tanka: "Crooked fireworks." Fumi Saito, *Japanese*. MJT, *tr.* by Makoto Ueda

Tanka: "Dahlias are black." Saitō Mokichi, *Japanese*. MJT, *tr.* by Makoto Ueda

Tanka: "Dark seaweeds." Miyazawa Kenji, *Japanese*. MJT, *tr.* by Makoto Ueda

Tanka: "Day I had in mind, The." Masaoka Shiki, *Japanese*. MJT, *tr.* by Makoto Ueda

Tanka: "Day I was born, The." Maekawa Samio, *Japanese*. MJT, *tr.* by Makoto Ueda

Tanka: "Determined to try." Saitō Mokichi, *Japanese*. MJT, *tr.* by Makoto Ueda

Tanka: "Didn't a certain woman." Nakajō Fumiko, *Japanese*. MJT, *tr.* by Makoto Ueda

Tanka: "Dipped." Masaoka Shiki, *Japanese*. MJT, *tr.* by Makoto Ueda

Tanka: "Don't resemble me." Fumi Saito, *Japanese*. MJT, *tr.* by Makoto Ueda

Tanka: "Dream, A." Kondō Yoshimi, *Japanese*. MJT, *tr.* by Makoto Ueda

Tanka: "During a break." Mori Ōgai, *Japanese*. MJT, *tr.* by Makoto Ueda

Tanka: "During a fit." Kitahara Hakushū, *Japanese*. MJT, *tr.* by Makoto Ueda

Tanka: "During a trip." Sasaki Yukitsuna, *Japanese*. MJT, *tr.* by Makoto Ueda

Tanka: "Each alighted." Kitahara Hakushū, *Japanese*. MJT, *tr.* by Makoto Ueda

Tanka: "Each morning I awake." Sasaki Yukitsuna, *Japanese*. MJT, *tr.* by Makoto Ueda

Tanka: "Each shaped." Akiko Yosano, *Japanese*. MJT, *tr.* by Makoto Ueda

Tanka: "Each year." Nakajō Fumiko, *Japanese*. MJT, *tr.* by Makoto Ueda

Tanka: "Earth looks, The." Akiko Yosano, *Japanese*. MJT, *tr.* by Makoto Ueda

Tanka: "Emerging." Miyazawa Kenji, *Japanese*. MJT, *tr.* by Makoto Ueda

Tanka: "Evanescent." Akiko Yosano, *Japanese*. MJT, *tr.* by Makoto Ueda

Tanka: "Even the black gloves." Fumi Saito, *Japanese*. MJT, *tr.* by Makoto Ueda

Tanka: "Even while." Tsukamoto Kunio, *Japanese*. MJT, *tr.* by Makoto Ueda

Tanka: "Ever deeper." Fumi Saito, *Japanese*. MJT, *tr.* by Makoto Ueda

Tanka: "Ever so close." Saitō Mokichi, *Japanese*. MJT, *tr.* by Makoto Ueda

Tanka: "Except the rare time." Yosano Tekkan, *Japanese*. MJT, *tr.* by Makoto Ueda

Tanka: "Eyes, The." Nakajō Fumiko, *Japanese*. MJT, *tr.* by Makoto Ueda

Tanka: "Eyes fixed." Yosano Tekkan, *Japanese*. MJT, *tr.* by Makoto Ueda

Tanka: "Faintly white." Yosano Tekkan, *Japanese*. MJT, *tr.* by Makoto Ueda

Tanka: "Far and near." Mori Ōgai, *Japanese*. MJT, *tr.* by Makoto Ueda

Tanka: "Fearing." Ishikawa Takuboku, *Japanese*. MJT, *tr.* by Makoto Ueda

Tanka: "Fish skeleton, A." Maekawa Samio, *Japanese*. MJT, *tr.* by Makoto Ueda

Tanka: "Flower blooms, A." Kanoko Okamoto, *Japanese*. MJT, *tr.* by Makoto Ueda

Tanka: "Flowering poppies." Miya Shūji, *Japanese*. MJT, *tr.* by Makoto Ueda

Tanka: "Fly, A." Saitō Mokichi, *Japanese*. MJT, *tr.* by Makoto Ueda

Tanka: "For a moment." Maekawa Samio, *Japanese*. MJT, *tr.* by Makoto Ueda

Tanka: "For this." Nakajō Fumiko, *Japanese*. MJT, *tr.* by Makoto Ueda

Tanka: "Forgetting." Ishikawa Takuboku, *Japanese*. MJT, *tr.* by Makoto Ueda

Tanka: "Freezing my smile." Tawara Machi, *Japanese*. MJT, *tr.* by Makoto Ueda

Tanka: "Frog." Saitō Mokichi, *Japanese*. MJT, *tr.* by Makoto Ueda

Tanka: "Frolicking." Mori Ōgai, *Japanese*. MJT, *tr.* by Makoto Ueda

Tanka: "From a flour mill." Tsukamoto Kunio, *Japanese*. MJT, *tr.* by Makoto Ueda

Tanka: "From the evening darkness." Saitō Mokichi, *Japanese*. MJT, *tr.* by Makoto Ueda

Tanka: "From the moment." Tawara Machi, *Japanese*. MJT, *tr.* by Makoto Ueda

Tanka: "From the water's depth." Shaku Chōkū, *Japanese*. MJT, *tr.* by Makoto Ueda

Tanka: "From where." Saitō Mokichi, *Japanese*. MJT, *tr.* by Makoto Ueda

Tanka: "Gasoline." Kitahara Hakushū, *Japanese*. MJT, *tr.* by Makoto Ueda

Tanka: "Gazing upwards." Tawara Machi, *Japanese*. MJT, *tr.* by Makoto Ueda

Tanka: "Gleaming sliver." Kitahara Hakushū, *Japanese*. MJT, *tr.* by Makoto Ueda

Tanka: "Gloomy rain." Kondō Yoshimi, *Japanese*. MJT, *tr.* by Makoto Ueda

Tanka: "Grabbing one of." Akiko Yosano, *Japanese*. MJT, *tr.* by Makoto Ueda

Tanka: "Green leaves." Kanoko Okamoto, *Japanese*. MJT, *tr.* by Makoto Ueda

Tanka. Nikolai Stepanovich Gumilyov, *Russian*. TCRP, *tr.* by Simon Franklin

Tanka: "Hands picking a rose." Tsukamoto Kunio, *Japanese*. MJT, *tr.* by Makoto Ueda

Tanka: "Has Fate sneaked in." Ishikawa Takuboku, *Japanese*. MJT, *tr.* by Makoto Ueda

Tanka: "Having crushed." Kondō Yoshimi, *Japanese*. MJT, *tr.* by Makoto Ueda

Tanka: "Having grown up." Kondō Yoshimi, *Japanese*. MJT, *tr.* by Makoto Ueda

Tanka: "Having let flow." Kanoko Okamoto, *Japanese*. MJT, *tr.* by Makoto Ueda

Tanka: "Having lived." Toki Zenmaro, *Japanese*. MJT, *tr.* by Makoto Ueda

Tanka: "Hawkers." Masaoka Shiki, *Japanese*. MJT, *tr.* by Makoto Ueda

Tanka: "Hidden." Tsukamoto Kunio, *Japanese*. MJT, *tr.* by Makoto Ueda

Tanka: "How many people came." Kondō Yoshimi, *Japanese*. MJT, *tr.* by Makoto Ueda

Tanka: "How sad it is." Toki Zenmaro, *Japanese*. MJT, *tr.* by Makoto Ueda

Tanka: "I close my eyes." Ishikawa Takuboku, *Japanese*. MJT, *tr.* by Makoto Ueda

Tanka: "I measure." Kanoko Okamoto, *Japanese*. MJT, *tr.* by Makoto Ueda

Tanka: "I sneaked into." Kitahara Hakushū, *Japanese*. MJT, *tr.* by Makoto Ueda

Tanka: "I work." Ishikawa Takuboku, *Japanese*. MJT, *tr.* by Makoto Ueda

Tanka: "If I were to stand." Kanoko Okamoto, *Japanese*. MJT, *tr.* by Makoto Ueda

Tanka: "If only." Maekawa Samio, *Japanese*. MJT, *tr.* by Makoto Ueda

Tanka: "I'll forget I saw you." Yosano Tekkan, *Japanese*. MJT, *tr.* by Makoto Ueda

Tanka: "Illuminated." Masaoka Shiki, *Japanese*. MJT, *tr.* by Makoto Ueda

Tanka: "Imagining." Shaku Chōkū, *Japanese*. MJT, *tr.* by Makoto Ueda

Tanka: "In a grove." Tsukamoto Kunio, *Japanese*. MJT, *tr.* by Makoto Ueda

Tanka: "In a posture." Nakajō Fumiko, *Japanese*. MJT, *tr.* by Makoto Ueda

Tanka: "In my heart." Kitahara Hakushū, *Japanese*. MJT, *tr.* by Makoto Ueda

Tanka: "In my mind." Yosano Tekkan, *Japanese*. MJT, *tr.* by Makoto Ueda

Tanka: "In my possession." Fumi Saito, *Japanese*. MJT, *tr.* by Makoto Ueda

Tanka: "In search of a shore." Nakajō Fumiko, *Japanese*. MJT, *tr.* by Makoto Ueda

Tanka: "In sullen silence." Toki Zenmaro, *Japanese*. MJT, *tr.* by Makoto Ueda

Tanka: "In the blue rays." Miyazawa Kenji, *Japanese*. MJT, *tr.* by Makoto Ueda

Tanka: "In the daytime." Kitahara Hakushū, *Japanese*. MJT, *tr.* by Makoto Ueda

Tanka: "In the evening wind." Maekawa Samio, *Japanese*. MJT, *tr.* by Makoto Ueda

Tanka: "In the house." Masaoka Shiki, *Japanese*. MJT, *tr.* by Makoto Ueda

Tanka: "In the vase." Masaoka Shiki, *Japanese*. MJT, *tr.* by Makoto Ueda

Tanka: "Infinitely far." Saitō Mokichi, *Japanese*. MJT, *tr.* by Makoto Ueda

Tanka: "Innately reserved." Kanoko Okamoto, *Japanese*. MJT, *tr.* by Makoto Ueda

Tanka: "Insane thought, An." Mori Ōgai, *Japanese*. MJT, *tr.* by Makoto Ueda

Tanka: "Insect, An." Kanoko Okamoto, *Japanese*. MJT, *tr.* by Makoto Ueda

Tanka: "Into a pair of stars." Akiko Yosano, *Japanese*. MJT, *tr.* by Makoto Ueda

Tanka: "It cries and cries." Yosano Tekkan, *Japanese*. MJT, *tr.* by Makoto Ueda

Tanka: "It stands." Kanoko Okamoto, *Japanese*. MJT, *tr.* by Makoto Ueda

Tanka: "It will not be heard." Mori Ōgai, *Japanese*. MJT, *tr.* by Makoto Ueda

Tanka: "Its bloom finished." Miya Shūji, *Japanese*. MJT, *tr.* by Makoto Ueda

Tanka: "It's hazardous." Toki Zenmaro, *Japanese*. MJT, *tr.* by Makoto Ueda

Tanka: "I've swept away." Tsukamoto Kunio, *Japanese*. MJT, *tr.* by Makoto Ueda

Tanka: "Just for fun." Ishikawa Takuboku, *Japanese*. MJT, *tr.* by Makoto Ueda

Tanka: "Kidnapping." Shaku Chōkū, *Japanese*. MJT, *tr.* by Makoto Ueda

Tanka: "Knees collapsing." Nakajō Fumiko, *Japanese*. MJT, *tr.* by Makoto Ueda

Tanka: "Late at night in the kitchen." Shaku Chōkū, *Japanese*. MJT, *tr.* by Makoto Ueda

Tanka: "Late summer day." Tsukamoto Kunio, *Japanese*. MJT, *tr.* by Makoto Ueda

Tanka: "Left alone." Miyazawa Kenji, *Japanese*. MJT, *tr.* by Makoto Ueda

Tanka: "Let a poem be." Mori Ōgai, *Japanese*. MJT, *tr.* by Makoto Ueda

Tanka: "Let those grasses." Yosano Tekkan, *Japanese*. MJT, *tr.* by Makoto Ueda

Tanka: "Letter, The." Tawara Machi, *Japanese*. MJT, *tr.* by Makoto Ueda

Tanka: "Lightning." Miyazawa Kenji, *Japanese*. MJT, *tr.* by Makoto Ueda

Tanka: "Like a long." Miya Shūji, *Japanese*. MJT, *tr.* by Makoto Ueda

Tanka: "Like a white lotus." Ishikawa Takuboku, *Japanese*. MJT, *tr.* by Makoto Ueda

Tanka: "Like cracks." Miyazawa Kenji, *Japanese*. MJT, *tr.* by Makoto Ueda

Tanka: "Loneliness." Tawara Machi, *Japanese*. MJT, *tr.* by Makoto Ueda

Tanka: "Looking as though." Tawara Machi, *Japanese*. MJT, *tr.* by Makoto Ueda

Tanka: "Loud voice, A." Maekawa Samio, *Japanese*. MJT, *tr.* by Makoto Ueda

Tanka: "Magnolia." Kitahara Hakushū, *Japanese*. MJT, *tr.* by Makoto Ueda

Tanka: "Makes me writhe." Masaoka Shiki, *Japanese*. MJT, *tr.* by Makoto Ueda

Tanka: "Memories open." Maekawa Samio, *Japanese*. MJT, *tr.* by Makoto Ueda

Tanka: "Mirror in hand." Ishikawa Takuboku, *Japanese*. MJT, *tr.* by Makoto Ueda

Tanka: "Moment, The." Kondō Yoshimi, *Japanese*. MJT, *tr.* by Makoto Ueda

Tanka: "Monumental." Maekawa Samio, *Japanese*. MJT, *tr.* by Makoto Ueda

Tanka: "Moonlight, The." Sasaki Yukitsuna, *Japanese*. MJT, *tr.* by Makoto Ueda

Tanka: "Mr. Nehru." Miya Shūji, *Japanese*. MJT, *tr.* by Makoto Ueda

Tanka: "My arms." Nakajō Fumiko, *Japanese*. MJT, *tr.* by Makoto Ueda

Tanka: "My body." Miya Shūji, *Japanese*. MJT, *tr.* by Makoto Ueda

Tanka: "My heart." Tawara Machi, *Japanese*. MJT, *tr.* by Makoto Ueda

Tanka: "My mind shattered." Kanoko Okamoto, *Japanese*. MJT, *tr.* by Makoto Ueda

Tanka: "My research." Shaku Chōkū, *Japanese*. MJT, *tr.* by Makoto Ueda

Tanka: "My uncle." Kitahara Hakushū, *Japanese*. MJT, *tr.* by Makoto Ueda

Tanka: "Never have I." Mori Ōgai, *Japanese*. MJT, *tr.* by Makoto Ueda

Tanka: "New Year's temple bells." Shaku Chōkū, *Japanese*. MJT, *tr.* by Makoto Ueda

Tanka: "No news of him." Toki Zenmaro, *Japanese*. MJT, *tr.* by Makoto Ueda

Tanka: "No scar." Maekawa Samio, *Japanese*. MJT, *tr.* by Makoto Ueda

Tanka: "Nobody with me." Masaoka Shiki, *Japanese*. MJT, *tr.* by Makoto Ueda

Tanka: "Noiselessly." Yosano Tekkan, *Japanese*. MJT, *tr.* by Makoto Ueda

Tanka: "Not unlike a fish." Yosano Tekkan, *Japanese*. MJT, *tr.* by Makoto Ueda

Tanka: "Nothing." Toki Zenmaro, *Japanese*. MJT, *tr.* by Makoto Ueda

Tanka: "Nothing to be done?" Saitō Mokichi, *Japanese*. MJT, *tr.* by Makoto Ueda

Tanka: "Nowhere on the leaves." Shaku Chōkū, *Japanese*. MJT, *tr.* by Makoto Ueda

Tanka: "Ocean, The." Kondō Yoshimi, *Japanese*. MJT, *tr.* by Makoto Ueda

Tanka: "Oddly shaped." Shaku Chōkū, *Japanese*. MJT, *tr.* by Makoto Ueda

Tanka: "Often likened." Saitō Mokichi, *Japanese*. MJT, *tr.* by Makoto Ueda

Tanka: "Old Japan." Toki Zenmaro, *Japanese*. MJT, *tr.* by Makoto Ueda

Tanka: "Old soldier, An." Toki Zenmaro, *Japanese*. MJT, *tr.* by Makoto Ueda

Tanka: "On a day." Tawara Machi, *Japanese*. MJT, *tr.* by Makoto Ueda

Tanka: "On a post." Mori Ōgai, *Japanese*. MJT, *tr.* by Makoto Ueda

Tanka: "On a starry night." Maekawa Samio, *Japanese*. MJT, *tr.* by Makoto Ueda

Tanka: "On a young pine." Masaoka Shiki, *Japanese*. MJT, *tr.* by Makoto Ueda

Tanka: "On Christmas Eve." Shaku Chōkū, *Japanese*. MJT, *tr.* by Makoto Ueda

Tanka: "On occasion." Maekawa Samio, *Japanese*. MJT, *tr.* by Makoto Ueda

Tanka: "On the cloudy water." Tsukamoto Kunio, *Japanese*. MJT, *tr.* by Makoto Ueda

Tanka: "On the road." Toki Zenmaro, *Japanese*. MJT, *tr.* by Makoto Ueda

Tanka: "On the roadside." Ishikawa Takuboku, *Japanese*. MJT, *tr.* by Makoto Ueda

Tanka: "On the sandy beach." Maekawa Samio, *Japanese*. MJT, *tr.* by Makoto Ueda

Tanka: "On the snow." Tsukamoto Kunio, *Japanese*. MJT, *tr.* by Makoto Ueda

Tanka: "On the water." Tsukamoto Kunio, *Japanese*. MJT, *tr.* by Makoto Ueda

Tanka: "On the way home." Miya Shūji, *Japanese*. MJT, *tr.* by Makoto Ueda

Tanka: "One day I saw." Nakajō Fumiko, *Japanese*. MJT, *tr.* by Makoto Ueda

Tanka: "Only the green." Tawara Machi, *Japanese*. MJT, *tr. by* Makoto Ueda

Tanka: "Only when." Tsukamoto Kunio, *Japanese*. MJT, *tr. by* Makoto Ueda

Tanka: "Out of the shade." Miya Shūji, *Japanese*. MJT, *tr. by* Makoto Ueda

Tanka: "Over my." Miya Shūji, *Japanese*. MJT, *tr. by* Makoto Ueda

Tanka: "Overtaken by time." Sasaki Yukitsuna, *Japanese*. MJT, *tr. by* Makoto Ueda

Tanka: "Palm of the hand, The, / is not aware of dying." Fumi Saito, *Japanese*. MJT, *tr. by* Makoto Ueda

  ("Palm of the hand, A.") MJT, *tr. by* Makoto Ueda

Tanka: "Past the hens." Saitō Mokichi, *Japanese*. MJT, *tr. by* Makoto Ueda

Tanka: "Peacefully." Masaoka Shiki, *Japanese*. MJT, *tr. by* Makoto Ueda

Tanka: "Peony in her hair, The." Akiko Yosano, *Japanese*. MJT, *tr. by* Makoto Ueda

Tanka: "Phantom appears, A." Shaku Chōkū, *Japanese*. MJT, *tr. by* Makoto Ueda

Tanka: "Phosphorescence." Miyazawa Kenji, *Japanese*. MJT, *tr. by* Makoto Ueda

Tanka: "Plaintive, A." Sasaki Yukitsuna, *Japanese*. MJT, *tr. by* Makoto Ueda

Tanka: "Plucked, The." Miyazawa Kenji, *Japanese*. MJT, *tr. by* Makoto Ueda

Tanka: "Plucking feathers." Yosano Tekkan, *Japanese*. MJT, *tr. by* Makoto Ueda

Tanka: "Poetry." Sasaki Yukitsuna, *Japanese*. MJT, *tr. by* Makoto Ueda

Tanka: "Poppies in bloom." Yosano Tekkan, *Japanese*. MJT, *tr. by* Makoto Ueda

Tanka: "Pressing my breasts." Akiko Yosano, *Japanese*. MJT, *tr. by* Makoto Ueda

Tanka: "Red flowers." Miya Shūji, *Japanese*. MJT, *tr. by* Makoto Ueda

Tanka: "Red pepper pods." Saitō Mokichi, *Japanese*. MJT, *tr. by* Makoto Ueda

Tanka: "Red rag." Miyazawa Kenji, *Japanese*. MJT, *tr. by* Makoto Ueda

Tanka: "Reverently." Maekawa Samio, *Japanese*. MJT, *tr. by* Makoto Ueda

Tanka: "Sadly." Ishikawa Takuboku, *Japanese*. MJT, *tr. by* Makoto Ueda

Tanka: "Scattered clouds." Miyazawa Kenji, *Japanese*. MJT, *tr. by* Makoto Ueda

Tanka: "Scissors." Kondō Yoshimi, *Japanese*. MJT, *tr. by* Makoto Ueda

Tanka: "Sea inside my heart, The." Akiko Yosano, *Japanese*. MJT, *tr. by* Makoto Ueda

Tanka: "Seeds of the grass." Fumi Saito, *Japanese*. MJT, *tr. by* Makoto Ueda

Tanka: "Self-portrait, A." Saitō Mokichi, *Japanese*. MJT, *tr. by* Makoto Ueda

Tanka: "Selfish woman." Kanoko Okamoto, *Japanese*. MJT, *tr. by* Makoto Ueda

Tanka: "Sharing the gentleness." Nakajō Fumiko, *Japanese*. MJT, *tr. by* Makoto Ueda

Tanka: "Should I stroke it." Mori Ōgai, *Japanese*. MJT, *tr. by* Makoto Ueda

Tanka: "Silver greeting." Miyazawa Kenji, *Japanese*. MJT, *tr. by* Makoto Ueda

Tanka: "Since I work with those." Kondō Yoshimi, *Japanese*. MJT, *tr. by* Makoto Ueda

Tanka: "Since puberty." Sasaki Yukitsuna, *Japanese*. MJT, *tr. by* Makoto Ueda

Tanka: "Since that evening." Nakajō Fumiko, *Japanese*. MJT, *tr. by* Makoto Ueda

Tanka: "Slanted." Miya Shūji, *Japanese*. MJT, *tr. by* Makoto Ueda

Tanka: "Slowly inside me." Miya Shūji, *Japanese*. MJT, *tr. by* Makoto Ueda

Tanka: "Snake." Yosano Tekkan, *Japanese*. MJT, *tr. by* Makoto Ueda

Tanka: "Snow has fallen." Miyazawa Kenji, *Japanese*. MJT, *tr. by* Makoto Ueda

Tanka: "Snow seeping." Fumi Saito, *Japanese*. MJT, *tr. by* Makoto Ueda

Tanka: "Snowflakes." Saitō Mokichi, *Japanese*. MJT, *tr. by* Makoto Ueda

Tanka: "Soldiers on the ground." Kondō Yoshimi, *Japanese*. MJT, *tr. by* Makoto Ueda

Tanka: "Some medals." Mori Ōgai, *Japanese*. MJT, *tr. by* Makoto Ueda

Tanka: "Somehow." Ishikawa Takuboku, *Japanese*. MJT, *tr. by* Makoto Ueda

Tanka: "Somehow this impulse." Tawara Machi, *Japanese*. MJT, *tr. by* Makoto Ueda

Tanka: "Somewhere around." Shaku Chōkū, *Japanese*. MJT, *tr. by* Makoto Ueda

Tanka: "Sorrow." Ishikawa Takuboku, *Japanese*. MJT, *tr. by* Makoto Ueda

Tanka: "Spoken in response." Miya Shūji, *Japanese*. MJT, *tr. by* Makoto Ueda

Tanka: "Spoon, A." Kondō Yoshimi, *Japanese*. MJT, *tr. by* Makoto Ueda

Tanka: "Spring bird." Kitahara Hakushū, *Japanese*. MJT, *tr. by* Makoto Ueda

Tanka: "Stalks growing." Miya Shūji, *Japanese*. MJT, *tr. by* Makoto Ueda

Tanka: "Stalwartly." Tsukamoto Kunio, *Japanese*. MJT, *tr. by* Makoto Ueda

Tanka: "Standing still." Tsukamoto Kunio, *Japanese*. MJT, *tr. by* Makoto Ueda

Tanka: "Stark naked." Kanoko Okamoto, *Japanese*. MJT, *tr. by* Makoto Ueda

Tanka: "Steel pen." Miyazawa Kenji, *Japanese*. MJT, *tr. by* Makoto Ueda

Tanka: "Step by step." Mori Ōgai, *Japanese*. MJT, *tr. by* Makoto Ueda

Tanka: "Street, The." Kondō Yoshimi, *Japanese*. MJT, *tr. by* Makoto Ueda

Tanka: "Streetcar, A." Kondō Yoshimi, *Japanese*. MJT, *tr. by* Makoto Ueda

Tanka: "Strong scent, The." Kitahara Hakushū, *Japanese*. MJT, *tr. by* Makoto Ueda

Tanka: "Suddenly." Miya Shūji, *Japanese*. MJT, *tr. by* Makoto Ueda

Tanka: "Surely by now." Maekawa Samio, *Japanese*. MJT, *tr. by* Makoto Ueda

Tanka: "Sweeter than a song." Fumi Saito, *Japanese*. MJT, *tr. by* Makoto Ueda

Tanka: "Tears, tears." Toki Zenmaro, *Japanese*. MJT, *tr. by* Makoto Ueda

Tanka: "Tell them." Akiko Yosano, *Japanese*. MJT, *tr. by* Makoto Ueda

Tanka: "Ten years ago." Kanoko Okamoto, *Japanese*. MJT, *tr. by* Makoto Ueda

Tanka: "That hill." Nakajō Fumiko, *Japanese*. MJT, *tr. by* Makoto Ueda

Tanka: "Their father." Yosano Tekkan, *Japanese*. MJT, *tr. by* Makoto Ueda

Tanka: "They don't appeal to me." Kanoko Okamoto, *Japanese*. MJT, *tr. by* Makoto Ueda

Tanka: "This day in March." Tawara Machi, *Japanese*. MJT, *tr. by* Makoto Ueda

Tanka: "This huge pile." Fumi Saito, *Japanese*. MJT, *tr. by* Makoto Ueda

Tanka: "This May Day night." Tsukamoto Kunio, *Japanese*. MJT, *tr. by* Makoto Ueda

Tanka: "To do away with anger." Miya Shūji, *Japanese*. MJT, *tr. by* Makoto Ueda

Tanka: "To take a bath." Fumi Saito, *Japanese*. MJT, *tr. by* Makoto Ueda

Tanka: "To the sea, to the sea." Kanoko Okamoto, *Japanese*. MJT, *tr. by* Makoto Ueda

Tanka: "Today too." Kitahara Hakushū, *Japanese*. MJT, *tr. by* Makoto Ueda

Tanka: "Too emotional." Yosano Tekkan, *Japanese*. MJT, *tr. by* Makoto Ueda

Tanka: "Town children." Shaku Chōkū, *Japanese*. MJT, *tr. by* Makoto Ueda

Tanka: "Trailing for a while." Fumi Saito, *Japanese*. MJT, *tr. by* Makoto Ueda

Tanka: "Train speeds on, The." Shaku Chōkū, *Japanese*. MJT, *tr. by* Makoto Ueda

Tanka: "Tree with lush leaves." Masaoka Shiki, *Japanese*. MJT, *tr. by* Makoto Ueda

Tanka: "Trying to perch." Mori Ōgai, *Japanese*. MJT, *tr. by* Makoto Ueda

Tanka: "Trying to wash away." Tawara Machi, *Japanese*. MJT, *tr. by* Makoto Ueda

Tanka: "Twenty days." Kanoko Okamoto, *Japanese*. MJT, *tr. by* Makoto Ueda

Tanka: "Two chilly." Akiko Yosano, *Japanese*. MJT, *tr. by* Makoto Ueda

Tanka: "Under the blue sky." Mori Ōgai, *Japanese*. MJT, *tr. by* Makoto Ueda

Tanka: "Unlike their father." Yosano Tekkan, *Japanese*. MJT, *tr. by* Makoto Ueda

Tanka: "Unsettled." Miyazawa Kenji, *Japanese*. MJT, *tr. by* Makoto Ueda

Tanka: "'Until age thirty'." Tawara Machi, *Japanese*. MJT, *tr. by* Makoto Ueda

Tanka: "Vast wilderness." Yosano Tekkan, *Japanese*. MJT, *tr. by* Makoto Ueda

Tanka: "Warring heaven." Akiko Yosano, *Japanese*. MJT, *tr. by* Makoto Ueda

Tanka: "Water streams." Fumi Saito, *Japanese*. MJT, *tr. by* Makoto Ueda

Tanka: "'We're poor'." Toki Zenmaro, *Japanese*. MJT, *tr. by* Makoto Ueda

Tanka: "What always seemed." Ishikawa Takuboku, *Japanese*. MJT, *tr. by* Makoto Ueda

Tanka: "What on the other shore." Saitō Mokichi, *Japanese*. MJT, *tr. by* Makoto Ueda

Tanka: "When I breathe." Ishikawa Takuboku, *Japanese*. MJT, *tr. by* Makoto Ueda

Tanka: "When I think over." Fumi Saito, *Japanese.* MJT, *tr. by* Makoto Ueda

Tanka: "When neither a man." Fumi Saito, *Japanese.* MJT, *tr. by* Makoto Ueda

Tanka: "When the gardener." Maekawa Samio, *Japanese.* MJT, *tr. by* Makoto Ueda

Tanka: "When the lights go out." Nakajō Fumiko, *Japanese.* MJT, *tr. by* Makoto Ueda

Tanka: "Where." Kanoko Okamoto, *Japanese.* MJT, *tr. by* Makoto Ueda

Tanka: "Which child." Shaku Chōkū, *Japanese.* MJT, *tr. by* Makoto Ueda

Tanka: "White blossoms bloom." Akiko Yosano, *Japanese.* MJT, *tr. by* Makoto Ueda

Tanka: "White hare, A." Fumi Saito, *Japanese.* MJT, *tr. by* Makoto Ueda

Tanka: "White jet clouds." Kondō Yoshimi, *Japanese.* MJT, *tr. by* Makoto Ueda

Tanka: "White swan." Mori Ōgai, *Japanese.* MJT, *tr. by* Makoto Ueda

Tanka: "White tower, A." Akiko Yosano, *Japanese.* MJT, *tr. by* Makoto Ueda

Tanka: "Why does a room." Maekawa Samio, *Japanese.* MJT, *tr. by* Makoto Ueda

Tanka: "Wiggling out." Nakajō Fumiko, *Japanese.* MJT, *tr. by* Makoto Ueda

Tanka: "Winter day." Kitahara Hakushū, *Japanese.* MJT, *tr. by* Makoto Ueda

Tanka: "With a hangover." Sasaki Yukitsuna, *Japanese.* MJT, *tr. by* Makoto Ueda

Tanka: "With a serene look." Tawara Machi, *Japanese.* MJT, *tr. by* Makoto Ueda

Tanka: "With a thunderous crack." Nakajō Fumiko, *Japanese.* MJT, *tr. by* Makoto Ueda

Tanka: "With each quiver." Maekawa Samio, *Japanese.* MJT, *tr. by* Makoto Ueda

Tanka: "With headlights on." Kondō Yoshimi, *Japanese.* MJT, *tr. by* Makoto Ueda

Tanka: "With no flower buds." Yosano Tekkan, *Japanese.* MJT, *tr. by* Makoto Ueda

Tanka: "With red eyes." Miyazawa Kenji, *Japanese.* MJT, *tr. by* Makoto Ueda

Tanka: "With sorrow I recall." Nakajō Fumiko, *Japanese.* MJT, *tr. by* Makoto Ueda

Tanka: "With the blue." Maekawa Samio, *Japanese.* MJT, *tr. by* Makoto Ueda

Tanka: "With those who." Sasaki Yukitsuna, *Japanese.* MJT, *tr. by* Makoto Ueda

Tanka: "With warts and all." Yosano Tekkan, *Japanese.* MJT, *tr. by* Makoto Ueda

Tanka: "Without incident." Mori Ōgai, *Japanese.* MJT, *tr. by* Makoto Ueda

Tanka: "Woman." Tsukamoto Kunio, *Japanese.* MJT, *tr. by* Makoto Ueda

Tanka: "Woman, The." Tawara Machi, *Japanese.* MJT, *tr. by* Makoto Ueda

Tanka: "Wood borers." Fumi Saito, *Japanese.* MJT, *tr. by* Makoto Ueda

Tanka: "Words from." Ishikawa Takuboku, *Japanese.* MJT, *tr. by* Makoto Ueda

Tanka: "Work on the impossible." Toki Zenmaro, *Japanese.* MJT, *tr. by* Makoto Ueda

Tanka: "Writes poetry." Akiko Yosano, *Japanese.* MJT, *tr. by* Makoto Ueda

Tanka: "Writing a series." Sasaki Yukitsuna, *Japanese.* MJT, *tr. by* Makoto Ueda

Tanka: "Yellow bus, The." Nakajō Fumiko, *Japanese.* MJT, *tr. by* Makoto Ueda

Tanka: "Yolk, The." Saitō Mokichi, *Japanese.* MJT, *tr. by* Makoto Ueda

Tanka: "Young fingers." Akiko Yosano, *Japanese.* MJT, *tr. by* Makoto Ueda

Tanka: "Young maidens." Ishikawa Takuboku, *Japanese.* MJT, *tr. by* Makoto Ueda

Tanka: "Youngster, A." Sasaki Yukitsuna, *Japanese.* MJT, *tr. by* Makoto Ueda

Tanka: "Your heart." Mori Ōgai, *Japanese.* MJT, *tr. by* Makoto Ueda

Tanks. Rhyll McMaster. CBAP; NOBAu

Tanned blonde, The. The Once-over. Paul Blackburn. NeAP; PoM

Tanned young men about to dive. An Imagined Description of Myself, in Another Scene. Ory Bernstein, *Hebrew.* IP, *tr. by* Warren Bargad *and* Stanley F. Chyet

Tannhäuser. Heinrich Heine, *German.*
  Best Religion, The. TrJP, *tr. by* Emma Lazarus

Tannhauser. Newman Levy. OBAL

Tansy buttons, tansy. Letter 3. Charles Olson. PmAP *Fr.* The Maximus Poems.

Tantanoola Tiger, The. Max Harris. MoBS

Tantramar Revisited, The. Sir Charles G. D. Roberts. NOBC

Tantrum Girl Responds to Death. Michelle T. Clinton. BAP-94

Tao and Unfitness at Inistiogue on the River Nore. Thomas Kinsella. PBCIP

Tao Te Ching. Lao Tzu, *Chinese.*
  "Ancient Masters were profound and subtle, The." EnlH
  "Empty your mind of all thoughts." EnlH
  "Every being in the universe." EnlH
  "Good traveler has no fixed plans, A." EnlH
  "Some say that my teaching is nonsense." EnlH
  "Tao that can be told, The." EnlH

Tao that can be told, The. Lao Tzu. EnlH *Fr.* Tao Te Ching.

Taoism and Buddhism. Po Chü-i, *Chinese.* ChiP, *tr. by* Arthur Waley

Taoist Huang Has Died of Alcoholism, The. Shen Chou, *Chinese.* CoBLCP, *tr. by* Jonathan Chaves

Taoist Song. Hsi K'ang, *Chinese.* ChiP, *tr. by* Arthur Waley

Taos Winter. Patty L. Harjo. VoR

Tape, The. Myra Cohn Livingston. NTCP

Taped to the wall of my cell are 47 pictures: 47 black. The Idea of Ancestry. Etheridge Knight. AF; BPo; ChAP; CoAmPo; GT; ISC; NAAAL; NIP-4; NNaP; PBCAP; PoBA; RaBo

Tapered choir, at the late hour of prayer, the. Thomas, the Younger Warton. ECEV *Fr.* The Pleasures of Melancholy.

Tapestries. Colleen J. McElroy. NAAAL

Tapestry. Grace Nichols. HCP

Tapestry. Charles Simic. LCAP-2; VCAP

Tapestry Weavers, The. Anson G. Chester. BLPA

Tapping. Jayne Cortez. MoNo
  ("When i pat this floor with my tap.") ISC

Tapping at the window, wind and rain—third watch by now. (LL) Third Month, Night of the Seventeenth, Written While Drunk. Lu Yu, *Chinese.* CoBCP, *tr. by* Burton Watson

Tappster, fille another ale. *Unknown.* MiEL

Tapu. Arthur Rex Dugard Fairburn. PeNZ

Tar. Charles Kenneth Williams. VCAP

Tar paper cabin. Robert Spiess. HA

Tarantella. Hilaire Belloc. APAD; CH; EBEvV; FaBoCh; MoBrPo; OBMV; RB; UV

Tarantula, The. Reed Whittemore. CoAP

Tarantula or the Dance of Death. Anthony Hecht. CoAP

Tarantula rattling at the lily's foot, The. O Carib Isle! Hart Crane. NoAM; PFTM; PoA; VGW

Tarantulas on the Lifebuoy. Thomas Lux. LCAP-2

Tardy Epithalamium for E. and N, A. Ralph Pomeroy. GLP

"Tare-an-ages, girls, which o'yees own the child?" (LL) Pharao's Daughter. Michael Moran. BIrV; ChIV-1

Target, The. Ivor Gurney. PoFWW

Target of the hunting shepherd boys. Zebra Stallion. *Unknown, Hottentot.* PeSA

Target shudders in the layered heat, The. Technique on the Firing Line. Turner Cassity. PoA

Tarn, how delightful with thy willowed waves. Verses Written at Montauban in France, 1750. Joseph Warton. ECEV

Tarpauling Jacket. *Unknown.* OxBoLi; PeVV

Tarred road simmered in a blue haze. The reservoir was dry, The. Judgement. Ciaran Carson. PBCIP

Tarry a moment, happy feet. The Statues. Laurence Binyon. OBEV

Tarry with Me, O My Saviour. Caroline Sprague Smith. AH

Tarrying moon still drips the redness of her blood, A. Midnight. Jacob Fichman, *Hebrew.* MHP, *tr. by* Ruth Finer Mintz

Tartar horn tugs at the north wind, A. On the Frontier. Li Ho, *Chinese.* PLT, *tr. by* A. C. Graham

Tartars led in chains. The Prisoner. Po Chü-i, *Chinese.* ChiP, *tr. by* Arthur Waley

Tartars make their home on saddle horses, The. Song of the Radiant Lady, Replying to a Poem by Wang Chieh-fu. Ou-yang Hsiu, *Chinese.* SuSp, *tr. by* Irving Y. Lo

Tartarus. Oliver Wendell Holmes. NCAP

Tartary. Walter De la Mare. OxBChV

Tarts, The. Mother Goose. ReMoGo

Tartuffe. Molière, *French.* NAWM-2, *tr. by* Richard Wilbur

Tarye no lenger; toward thyn herytage. Vox Ultima Crucis. John Lydgate. OBEV

Tashkent Breaks into Bloom. "Anna Akhmatova," *Russian.* BoWoP, *tr. by* Richard McKane

Tashlich. Abba Kovner, *Hebrew.* IP, *tr. by* Warren Bargad *and* Stanley F. Chyet

Task, The. William Cowper.

Animals Enjoying Life. APo

My Pet Hare. APo

My Pet Hare. FP

    Rural Sights and Sounds. NOEC, *book* 1, *ll.* 109–210

    "Thou knowest my praise of nature most sincere." NAEL-1

    "Who loves a garden, loves a greenhouse too." OBGA

Task, The. Denise Levertov. CrSp

Task, A. Czeslaw Milosz, *Polish.* AF, *tr. by* Czeslaw Milosz

Task, The. Subhash Mukhopadhyay, *Bengali.* OMIP, *tr. by* Pritish Nandy

Task, The. Ruth Pitter. MoBrPo

Tasmania. Vivian Smith. NOBAu

Tasmanian Scenes. Louisa Meredith. NOBAu

Tassajara, 1969. Diane Di Prima. BB

Tasso's Godfrey of Bulloigne Book 4. Edward Fairfax.

    "Drearie trumpet blew a dreadfull blast, The." PBRV

Taste. Jennifer Maiden. BMAP

Taste, The. George Oppen. NNaP *Fr.* Some San Francisco Poems.

    ("Silver as / The needle's eye.") FTOS

Taste. Christopher Smart. ChIV-1; NOCV *Fr.* Hymns for the Amusement of Children.

Taste for Tomorrow. Jayanta Mahapatra. VCWP

Taste his terror on my hands. (LL) The Trout. John Montague. NoP-4

Taste now, dear Teresa, the living poison of the ivy. Carmelite. Raymond Murray, *Irish.* TIRV, *tr. by the author*

Taste of blood comes, A. Obsession. Léon Damas, *French.* NegPo, *tr. by* Ellen Conroy Kennedy

Taste of bronze drunk hot, The. (LL) Brush-Fire. U Tam'si Tchicaya, *French.* NegPo, *tr. by* Sangodare Akanji; PBMAP

Taste / of rust, The. (LL) Some Good Things to Be Said for the Iron Age. Gary Snyder. HoPM; TTTS

Taste of soul's desire, The. (LL) God Give to Men. Arna Bontemps. BPo; ColAP

Tasty 'Tanjarines' of Inhambane, The. José Craveirinha, *Portuguese.* PeSAV, *tr. by* Michael Wolfers

Tatale Swine. Kojo Laing. HBAPE

Tatale there rounding the fat woman that fried it. Tatale Swine. Kojo Laing. HBAPE

Tatar chief forced me to become his wife, A. Ts'ai Yen. WPOW *Fr.* Eighteen Verses Sung to a Tatar Reed Whistle.

Tato—Reading at the Nuyorican Poets' Cafe. Miguel Algarin. PmAP

Tattered and ragg'd, with greatcoat tied in strings. The Mole-Catcher. John Clare. EnVR

Tattered Kaddish. Adrienne Rich. ColAP

Tattered Map, The. T(tilde;a)n Đà, *Vietnamese.* AVP, *tr. by* Huỳnh Sanh Thông

Tatters. Ralph Angel. WeT

Tattle. Godfrey Turner. NOBL

Tattoo. Gregg Shapiro. UnSA

Tattoo, The. Ania Walwicz. BMAP

Tattoo, Corazon: Ritchie Valens, 1959. David Wojahn. PBCAP *Fr.* Mystery Train: A Sequence.

Tattoo'd man, The. Alan Pizzarelli. HA

Tattooed Man, The. Robert Earl Hayden. NoAM

Tattoos. Charles Wright. HCAP

Taught early that his mother's skin was the sign of error. Mr. Z. M. Carl Holman. PFE; SoSe-8

Tauhid. Askia Muhammad Touré. PoBA

Taurean reaper of the wild apple field. Tattered Kaddish. Adrienne Rich. ColAP

Tauromancy at Memphis. Diogenes Laertius, *Greek.* GrAn, *tr. by* Dudley Fitts

Tavern, The. Edwin Arlington Robinson. NCAP

Tavern at Sunset. Jonggil Kim, *Korean.* CKP, *tr. by* Jaihiun Kim

Tawny are the leaves turned but they still hold. Antique Harvesters. John Crowe Ransom. FuPo; MoAmPo; OxBA

Tawny-black sky-scurries. David Jones. OBWVE *Fr.* The Sleeping Lord.

Tax not the royal Saint with vain expense. Inside of King's College Chapel, Cambridge. Wordsworth. GTBS-P; OBNC *Fr.* Ecclesiastical Sonnets.

Taxi, The. Amy Lowell. BoWoP; LW; MoAmPo

Taxi-cab whore out at Iver, A. Limerick. Victor Gray. NOBL; PeLi

Taxi Suite. Lew Welch.

    After Anacreon. BB; NeAP; PoM

    ("When I drive cab / I am moved by strange whistles and wear a hat.") BB

Taxi to the Flame, A. Vickie Karp. WWSi

Taxidermist is sitting / before the russet breasts, A. Jean Follain, *French.* BLT, *tr. by* Czeslaw Milosz *and* Robert Hass (b. 1941)

Taxidermist's Daughter, The. Nancy Schoenberger. MoLi

Taxiing to 71 via Tijuana. Seasons Greetings, Love and Revolution. Judy Miles. PBCV

Taxis, The. Louis MacNeice. OxBTC; PNI

Taxman. George Mackay Brown. FaBoTC

Tay Bridge Disaster, The. William McGonagall.

    "Beautiful Railway Bridge of the Silv'ry Tay!" UV

Tayis Bank. *Unknown.* FaBoVe

Taylor's Arithmetic from One to Twelve. John Taylor.

    "10 Commandments, are the Law Divine." ChIV-1

Te Atairangikaahu. Kingi M. Ihaka, *Maori.* PeNZ, *tr. by* Kingi M. Ihaka

Te Deum. Charles Reznikoff. ChIV-1; TrJP

Te Deum, The. *Unknown, Latin.* AWP, *tr. by* Dryden

Te Deum. *Unknown, Latin.* OBCVT

Te Deum laudamus / O Thou Hand of Fire. (LL) Ave Maria. Hart Crane. NOBA; NoAM

Te Kaha. Rachel McAlpine. PeNZ

Te Martyrum Candidatus. Lionel Pigot Johnson. OBMV; TIRV

Te Whetu Plains. Edward Tregear. PeNZ, *tr. by* Alan Myers

Tea. Ch'u Ch'uang I, *Chinese.* OHMPC, *tr. by* Kenneth Rexroth

Tea at the Palaz of Hoon. Wallace Stevens. FaBoMo; PoA

Tea bowls, incense burning—a good feeling here! Wen Cheng-ming. CoBLCP, *tr. by* Jonathan Chaves *Fr.* The Chung-i Temple.

Tea for the Emperor arrives on a tray. Princess Parade. Sarah Gorham. FFC

Tea garden shows you how, A. Bridge. A. R. Ammons. CoAP; NAAL-2

Tea-kettle bubbled, the tea things were set, The. Poem on the Supposition of an Advertisement, A; Appearing in a Morning Paper, of the Publication of a Volume of Poems, by a Servant-Maid. Elizabeth Hands. ECWP; WoRP

Tea Party. Nancy Vieira Couto. PBCAP

Tea Party. Mary Rita Hurley. CTV

Tea party at Le Cannet, The. Bonnard; a Novel. Richard Howard. CoAP; NYBP

Tea Poems. George Mackay Brown. OxBC

Tea-rose tea-gown, etc. Ezra Pound. ColAP; MoAmPo; NOBE *Fr.* Hugh Selwyn Mauberley. (Life and Contacts). AmPP; CMoP; InPS-3; LiTM; NOBA; NoAM; TAP

Tea Shop, The. Ezra Pound. HeIP-4

Tea with the Poets. John Betjeman. PeLV

Teach me, Father, how to go. A Prayer. Edwin Markham. BoTP; CTV

Teach me I am forgotten by the dead. Ralph Waldo Emerson. PAR

Teach me, my God and King. The Elixir [*or* Elixer]. George Herbert. BoTP; ESCV; EnlH; FMP; FaBoCh; GeHe; NOSC; NoP-4

Teach me to love what I've made, and judgment. To a Milkweed. Deborah Digges. CrSp

Teach the free man how to praise. (LL) In Memory of W. B. Yeats. W. H. Auden. CMoP; EPCY; GEA; HAP; HeIP-4; HoPM; IIP; ImPo; LiTM; MeMAP; MoBrPo; NOBE; NoAM; NoP-4; OAEL-2; OxAEP-2; OxBTC; PFE; Poetr; TFi; TRP; UnPo; WeW-3

Teach Us to Mark This, God. Franz Werfel, *German.* TrJP, *tr. by* Jacob Sloan

Teach Us to Number Our Days. Rita Dove. NoAM

Teacher. Audre Lorde. MDDM

Teacher asked Paul, A. Rain. Naomi Shihab Nye. NAmP90

Teacher I Wanted to Be, The. Ingrid Wendt. IFJA

Teacher, Jimmie's toe is bleedin'. Johnny's Pet Superstition. Clara Ann Thompson. CBWP-2

Teacher of tots at Uttoxeter, A. Limerick. Kate McPower. PeLi

Teacher Taught Me, A. Anna Walters. VoR

Teachers taught her, The. Gertrude Stein. NOxBChV

Teaches the South it is not paradise. (LL) Grasse: The Olive Trees. Richard Wilbur. NAAL-2; NOBA; NYBP; NoAM

Teaching Emily Dickinson. Rachel Hadas. NMM-2

Teaching German Literature. Vincent Buckley. OBCoV

Teaching Myself to Read. Karen Fiser. IFJA

Teaching Numbers. Gary Soto. NOxBChV

Teaching Swift to Young Ladies. William Dickey. PoA

Teaching the Ape to Write Poems. James Tate. CMAP

    (Teaching the Ape to Write.) BLT

Teaching the Children. Myra Sklarew. CRP

Teahouse at Hoshioka, A. Liu E, *Chinese.* CoBLCP, *tr. by* Jonathan Chaves

Teak Forest, The. "Laurence Hope."

    For This Is Wisdom. PoLF

Team, The. Suzanne Gardinier. CBAP

Teams, The. Henry Lawson. CBAP

Teapots and Quails. Edward Lear. CBNP

Tear[e], The. Richard Crashaw. ImPo; SeCP

Tear. Thomas Kinsella. NOIV; NoP-4

Tear, The. Martin Sorescu, *Romanian*. VCWP, *tr. by* Heaney, Seamus and Joana Russell-Gebbett

Tearing and Merging of Clouds, The. Russell Edson. WeT

Tearing the hairy leeches from his throat. (LL) A Crocodile. Thomas Lovell Beddoes. APo; NOBVV; RB

Tearing Up the Tracks. Christopher Bursk. GM

Tears. Elizabeth Barrett Browning. WPE

Tears. Hyonsung Kim, *Korean*. CKP, *tr. by* Jaihiun Kim

Tears. "Owen Meredith." EBVV *Fr.* Glenaveril.

Tears. Lizette Woodworth Reese. MoAmPo

Tears. Dame Edith Sitwell. CMoP

Tears. Edward Thomas. GTBS-P; NAEL-2

Tears and Joys. Margaret Louisa Woods. LBC

Tears and love for the Gray. (LL) The Blue and the Gray. Francis Miles Finch. APN-2; BLPA; CBCWP; FaBoBe

Tears at evening?—not infrequent. Inscribed on a Plantain Leaf To Show to a Certain Person. Liu Ling-hsien, *Chinese*. CoBCP, *tr. by* Burton Watson

Tears at the Grave of Sir Albertus Morton. Sir Henry Wotton. SeCP

Tears beneath the earth, Heliodora, I give. Meleager. HePo, *tr. by* Barbara Hughes Fowler *Fr.* I'll Twine White Violets. NIP-4, *tr. by* Goldwin Smith

Tears, ere thy death, for many a one I shed. Al-Khansa, *Arabic*. AWP, *tr. by* R. A. Nicholson

Tears fall within mine heart. Il Pleut Doucement sur la Ville. Paul Verlaine, *French*. AWP, *tr. by* Ernest Dowson

Tears flow down the girl's face. Salesgirl. Henrikas Radauskas, *Lithuanian*. CEEP, *tr. by* Jonas Zdanys

Tears, Flow No More. Edward Herbert. SeCP

Tears glinting in beads. The Nightingale Path. So Chong-Ju, *Korean*. CKP, *tr. by* Jaihiun Kim

Tears have pressed white hair / to face. (LL) The Feral Pioneers. Ishmael Reed. PoBA; UnPo

Tears like a lover wept. (LL) In the Wilderness. Robert Graves. CH; ChIV-2; MoBrPo; PeECV

Tears of an Affectionate Shepherd Sick for Love, The. Richard Barnfield. *See* The Affectionate Shepherd.

Tears of Rage. "Bob Dylan." MoLi

Tears of Scotland, The. Tobias Smollett. ECEV; NOEC

Tears of the Fatherland, Anno Domini 1636. Andreas Gryphius, *German*. GePo, *tr. by* George C. Schoolfield

Tears of the World, The. Mu'tamid, King of Seville, *Arabic*. AWP, *tr. by* Dulcie L. Smith

Tears, tears. Tanka. Toki Zenmaro, *Japanese*. MJT, *tr. by* Makoto Ueda

Tears! tears! tears! / In the night, in solitude, tears. Walt Whitman. APN-1

Tears, the firebursts and the vows, The. Cracked Looking Glass. Jean Garrigue. VCAP

Tears wet her gauze kerchief, she cannot sleep. Song of the Rear Palace. Po Chü-i, *Chinese*. SuSp, *tr. by* Ronald C. Miao

Teasers, The. William Empson. OxBTC

Teasing Hsiao-te, My Son. Huang T'ing-chien, *Chinese*. SuSp, *tr. by* Michael E. Workman

Teasing Toads, The. Michael Rosen. OTCP

Technical Supplement, A. Thomas Kinsella.
    "Blade licks out and acts, A." BiHa
    "Dark hall. Great green liquid windows, A." BiHa
    "How to put it. . . without offence." BiHa
    "It is hard to beat a good meal." CIP-2
    "Point, greatly enlarged, The." BiHa
    "Veteran smiled and let us pass through, A." BiHa
    "Vital spatterings. Excess." BiHa

Technicalities for Jack Spicer. Philip Whalen. PoM

Technicians. Jean Kenward. SpW

Technique on the Firing Line. Turner Cassity. PoA

Technologies. George Starbuck. NYBP

Tecumseh. Charles Mair.
    "I love you better than I love my race." NOBC
    "There was a time on this fair continent." NOBC

Ted & marge had been married eight years. Wasp Sex Myth (Two). Anselm Hollo. PoM

Teddy Bear, Teddy Bear. *Unknown*. NTCP

Tedious tale in rhyme, but little reason, A. George Gascoigne. *See* Gascoigne's Woodmanship.

Tedious tale in rime, but little reason. / *Haud ictus sapio*. A. George Gascoigne. *See* Gascoigne's Woodmanship.

Tedium Drum, Part IV. Kevin Magee. PT *Fr.* Tedium Drum, Part IV.

Tee. Reuben Jackson. UnSA

Teel St. Trailer Court. Anne C. Bromley. CMAP

Teeth. Susan Griffin. CrSp

Teeth. Spike Milligan. OPOU

Teeth. (LL) Teeth and Gums. Mother Goose. NTCP; OxNR; ReMoGo

Teeth and Gums. Mother Goose. ReMoGo

Teeth Mother Naked at Last, The. Robert Bly.

Teeth Mother Naked at Last, The. Robert Bly. NNaP
    ("Old women watch the soldiers.") (LL) CLPP
    "But if one of those children came near that we have set / on fire." CDa

Teeth of clogs, carriage wheels, the hooves of horses. Walking in the Country outside T'ai-yüan on a Spring Day. Yang Chi, *Chinese*. CoBLCP, *tr. by* Jonathan Chaves

Teeth of flowers, hairnet of dew. I Am Going to Sleep (Suicide Poem). Alfonsina Storni, *Spanish*. BoWoP, *tr. by* Aliki *and* Willis Barnstone

Teeth on the saw. Piney Woods. Malcolm Cowley. NYBP

Teething. Tom Wayman. CDa

Teevo cheevo cheevio chee. The Woodlark. Gerard Manley Hopkins. RB

Teh. has six claims to fame: its numerous hotsprings. Sestina for the Ladies of Tehuántepec. Earle Birney. PeLV

TEHKARIHHOKEN! / Continue to listen! *Unknown*. APN-2, *tr. by* Horatio Hale *Fr.* Ancient Rites of the Condoling Council.

Teisa, a Descriptive Poem of the River Tees, Its Towns and Antiquities. Anne Wilson.
    In Praise of Drainage. ECWP

Teleg River. Teleg Song. HSü Ling, *Chinese*. ChiP, *tr. by* Arthur Waley

Teleg Song. HSü Ling, *Chinese*. ChiP, *tr. by* Arthur Waley

Telegram. Milo De Angelis, *Italian*. NeIt, *tr. by* Lawrence Venuti

Telemachus with a Transistor. Ruth Dallas. PeNZ

Teleology. May Swenson. VCAP

Telepathy. Linda Besant. IFJA

Telepathy. Thulani Davis. WeT

Telephone, The. Robert Frost. ImGa

Telephone Conversation. Wole Soyinka. NoP-4; PBMAP; TTY

Telephone Directory. Harry Crosby. SPE

Telephone line goes cold, A. The Farm on the Great Plains. William Stafford. HAP; VGW

Telephone Message, A (To Whom it May Concern). John Oxenham. NSI

Telephone poles, The. Crossing Kansas by Train. Donald Justice. AiP; NYBP

Telephone Poles. John Updike. FYAP; Poetsp

Telephone rang, The. "Korney Chukovsky," *Russian*. TCRP, *tr. by* William Jay Smith

Telephone rang / in my dream Long Distance from, The. Isabella Gardner. MoLi

Telephoning God. Gary Soto. PBCAP

Telephoning Home. Carol Ann Duffy. NBrP

Telephonist. Janet Frame. WPE

Telescope. Sydney Lea. RA

Television aerials, Chinese characters. On Roofs of Terry Street. Douglas Dunn. OxBTC

Television / radio sunday benevolent sunday. They Are Killing All the Young Men. David Henderson. PoBA

Tell a wise person, or else keep silent. The Holy Longing. Goethe, *German*. RaBo, *tr. by* Robert Bly

Tell all my mourners. Wake. Langston Hughes. OBAL; OBCoV

Tell all the Truth but tell it slant. Emily Dickinson. APN-2; AmPP; ColAP; HeIP-4; NAAL-1; NAAL-3; NALW; NAWM-2; NOBA; NoAM; NoP-4; PAR; Poetr; TAP; UnPo; WeW-3

Tell, dear Aminta, now 'tis over. Close to Aminta, on the Loss of Her Lover. Sarah Dixon. ECWP

Tell Freedom. Peter Abrahams.
    Me, Colored. PBA

Tell her I love. Poems for My Daughter. Horace Gregory. MoAmPo

Tell Her So. Mrs. Henry Linden. CBWP-4

Tell Her So. *Unknown*. PoToHe

Tell her to find her purse. (LL) The Ghost in the Martini. Anthony Hecht. NoP-4

Tell her we still expose our bottoms. Messages. Jack A. Mapanje. HBAPE

Tell him it's all a lie;. A Learned Mistress. Isobel Campbell, *Irish*. NNPT, *tr. by* Frank O'Connor

Tell Him, O Night. *Unknown*. AWP *Fr.* The Thousand and One Nights.

Tell Him So. J. A. Egerton. PWR

Tell Him So. *Unknown*. BLPA

Tell him the tale is a lie! A Learned Mistress. *Unknown*, *Irish*. OBMV, *tr. by* Frank O'Connor

Tell it to the locked-up trees. Cuckoo Song. Rudyard Kipling. NTP

Tell Me. Langston Hughes. APSN; SAmP

Tell me. Amy Lowell. *See* Venus Transiens.

Tell Me. Pamela Mordecai. PBCV

Tell me. What She Said Her Lover within Earshot. Kapilar, *Tamil.* PLW, *tr.* by A. K. Ramanujan

"Tell me a story." Bedtime Story. Lilian Moore. NTCP

Tell Me a Story. Robert Penn Warren. FuPo; MT *Fr.* Audubon.

"Tell me a story, father, please." The Natives of America. Ann Plato. BlSi

Tell me a story, Father, please do. Request Number. G. N. Sprod. AAP

Tell me a story of deep delight. (LL) Tell Me a Story. Robert Penn Warren. FuPo; MT

Tell me about the good things. How Long Has Trane Been Gone. Jayne Cortez. ISC

Tell me about the good things. How Long Has Trane Been Gone. Joe Corrie. NAAAL

Tell me about yourself they. A Word in Edgeways. Charles Tomlinson. CABP; NOBL

Tell Me Again. Nigâr Hanim, *Turkish.* PBWP, *tr.* by Tâlat S. Halman

Tell Me Again. Paul Keens-Douglas. PBCV

Tell me *Alexis* what this parting is. Dialogue. Richard Lovelace. CavPo

Tell me, before the ferryman's return. For Granny (from Hospital). J. P. Clark Bekedermo. PBMAP *Fr.* A Reed in the Tide.

Tell me, brother, what are we? The Ocean. Christopher Pearse Cranch. PAR

Tell me, draftsman of the desert. Osip Emilevich Mandelstam. TCRP, *tr.* by Bernard Meares *Fr.* Ottave.

"Tell me, good dog, whose tomb you guard so well." The Tomb of Diogenes. *Unknown, Greek.* AWP, *tr.* by John Addington Symonds

Tell me good Hobbinoll, what garres thee greete? Aprill. Edmund Spenser. NAEL-1; PoEL-1 *Fr.* The Shepheardes [*or* Shepeards *or* Shepherd's] Calender.

Tell me, good Hobbinoll, what garres thee greete? Edmund Spenser. *See* Aprill.

Tell me herdsman for the sake of Pan. Erucius of Cyzicus, *Greek.* GrAn, *tr.* by Peter Levi

Tell me if ah seeing right. Poetry Jump-Up. John Agard. NOxBChV

Tell me if I am not glad! (LL) Lines for an Old Man. T. S. Eliot. FaBoTw; RB; RaBo

Tell me, men with wisdom gifted. Hiraeth. *Unknown, Welsh.* OBWVE, *tr.* by Aneirin Talfan Davies

Tell me, my heart, how wilt thou do. Sir Arthur Gorges. NoSic *Fr.* Desportes.

Tell me, my love, since Hymen tied [*or* ty'ed]. An Hymeneal[l] Dialogue. Thomas Carew. SeCP

Tell me, my patient friends, awaiters of messages. Speech to a Crowd. Archibald MacLeish. MoAmPo

Tell me[e] no more how fair[e] she[e] is. Sonnet. Henry, Bishop of Chichester King. EnLoPo; MeLP; SeCP

Tell me no more of constancy. Against Constancy. John Wilmot, 2d Earl of Rochester. CABP; GBL; NOSC; OxAEP-1

Tell me no more of Minds embracing Minds. No Platonic [*or* Platonique] Love. William Cartwright. BeJo; EP; GBL; GEA; ImPo; NOSC; OAEL-1; PoEL-2

Tell me no secret, friend. The Burden. Francesca Yetunde Pereira. PBA

Tell me not, friend, you are unkind. Lucasta Replies to Lovelace. G. K. Chesterton. UV

Tell me not here, it needs not saying. A. E. Housman. APAD; GTBS-P; LiTM; NOBE; NoAM; OAEL-2; OBNC; OxBTC; SCV

Tell me not in idle jingle. Psalm of Marriage. Phoebe Cary. PWR

Tell me not in joyous numbers. Stephen Crane. OBAL

Tell me not in mournful numbers. Henry Wadsworth Longfellow. AH *Fr.* A Psalm of Life. APN-1; CTV; EBEvV; FaBoBe; NAAL-1; NAAL-3; OBCA; PAR; PWR; PoLF; TAP

Tell me not in mournful numbers. A Psalm of Life. Henry Wadsworth Longfellow. APN-1; CTV; EBEvV; FaBoBe; NAAL-1; NAAL-3; OBCA; PAR; PWR; PoLF; TAP

Tell me not of a face that's fair. The Resolve. Alexander Brome. NOSC; OBEV

Tell me not of joy; there's none. The Dead Sparrow. William Cartwright. CH

Tell me not of Philosophies. Apologia. Lord Alfred Bruce Douglas. ADE

Tell me not, Sweet, I am unkind. Lines Where Beauty Lingers. Franklin Pierce Adams. OBAL

Tell me not, Sweet, I am unkind[e]. Song: To Lucasta, Going to the War[re]s. Richard Lovelace. AWP; BeJo; CBLP; CaPo; ClHu; EBEvV; EnLoPo; GBL; GTBS-P; HAP; HoPM; ImPo; InPK-6; InPS-3; MeLP; NAEL-1; NIP-4; NOBE; NOSC; OAEL-1; OBEV; OBWP; OxAEP-1; OxBSP; PBMP; PoE; PoEL-3; PoRA; Poetr; SCGP; SCV; SeCP; TFi; UV; WeW-3

Tell me not what too well I know. On Catullus. Walter Savage Landor. OBEV

Tell me now in what hidden way is. Ballad[e] of Dead Ladies. François Villon, *French.* AWP; CTC; NNPT; OBVE; PoRA, *tr.* by D. G. Rossetti

'TELL me now, what should a man want'. Wang Chi, *Chinese.* ChiP; FaBoCh, *tr.* by Arthur Waley

Tell me, O[h] Muse (for thou, or none canst tell. Number, Weight, and Measure. Abraham Cowley. NOSC *Fr.* Davideis.

"Tell me, O Muse of the shifty, the man who wandered afar." Jubilee before Revolution. Andrew Lang. BXAP

Tell me, O Octopus, I begs. The Octopus. Ogden Nash. CTV; RB

Tell me, O[h] tell, what kind[e] of thing is wit. Ode: Of Wit. Abraham Cowley. BeJo; EPCY; MeLP; NAEL-1; NOSC; OAEL-1; OxAEP-1; SeCP

Tell me of thy heart's devotion. Whisper Words of Love to Me. Lizelia Augusta Jenkins Moorer. CBWP-3

Tell me, oh fate, is it decreed. James Ephriam McGirt. AAP

Tell me once, dear, how it does prove. To the Unconstant Cynthia: a Song. Sir Robert Howard *and* Dryden. NOSC

"Tell me, pray, if you may, how to make a sailor's pie?" How to Make a Sailor's Pie. Joan Aiken. NTP

Tell me, Pyrrha, what fine youth. Horace. *See* 1.5.

Tell me, shepherd, tell me, pray. Country Gods. Cometas, *Greek.* FaBoCh, *tr.* by T. F. Higham

Tell me something. Mother-in-Law. Adrienne Rich. PoPoPo

Tell Me, Tell Me. Marianne Moore. LiTM; NYBP

Tell me, tell me, Sarah Jane. Charles Causley. AYFP

Tell me, tell me, smiling child. Emily Jane Brontë. NALW

Tell me, tell me, / Unknown stranger. The Galliass. Walter De la Mare. FaBoTw

Tell me the auld, auld story. The Parrot Cry. "Hugh MacDiarmid." OxBS

Tell me the truths which you hear of our constant young lady. Difference of Opinion with Lygdamus. Ezra Pound. MeMAP *Fr.* Homage to Sextus Propertius.

Tell me, thou gentle shepherd swain. A Roundelay Between Two Shepherds. Michael Drayton. NoP-4

Tell me thou safest end of all our woe. Anne Killigrew. *See* On Death.

Tell me thou[gh] safest end of all our woe. On Death. Anne Killigrew. BoWoP; ChIV-1; KTR

Tell me, thou skilful shepherd's swain. Michael Drayton. *See* Roundelay: "Tell me, thou skilful shepherd's swain."

Tell me, thou Star, whose wings of light. The World's Wanderers. Shelley. TTTS

Tell me to what conclusion or in aid. Chaucer. OxBM *Fr.* The Wife of Bath's Prologue. FHYEP; NAEL-1; OAEL-1, *ll.* 1–862 *complete Fr.* The Canterbury Tales.

Tell me, / Was Venus more beautiful. Venus Transiens. Amy Lowell. NALW; PoA

Tell me, what is a poet's thought? A Poet's Thought. "Barry Cornwall." Ro *Fr.* English Songs.

Tell Me, What Is the Soul. Jean Valentine. BAP-96

Tell me what you're doing over here, John Gorham. John Gorham. Edwin Arlington Robinson. MoAmPo

Tell me whaur, in whit countrie. Ballat o the Leddies o Langsyne. François Villon, *French.* OBVE, *tr.* by Tom Scott

Tell me, when will bean leaves turn yellow here? (LL) Tune: Sand of Silk-washing Stream ("Layer on layer of hemp leaves, jute leaves shining"). Su Tung-p'o. CoBCP, *tr.* by Burton Watson; CoBCP

Tell me, where doth Whiteness grow. Whiteness, or Chastity. Joseph Beaumont. NOSC

Tell me where, in what country, where. Ballade. François Villon, *French.* STV, *tr.* by John Frederick Nims

Tell me where is fancy [*or* Fancie] bred. Song. Shakespeare. CH; CTC; EBEvV; GTBS-P; NAEL-1; NoSic; OAEL-1; OBEV; PoEL-2; SCGP; TFi *Fr.* The Merchant of Venice.

Tell me, where is your home? Songs of Ch'ang-kan. Ts'ui Hao, *Chinese.* CoBCP, *tr.* by Burton Watson

Tell me where thy lovely love is. Heinrich Heine. *Fr.* Heimkehr, Die. AWP, *tr.* by Ezra Pound

Tell me, why such a foul mood? Demon in Paradise. Minuchihri, *Persian.* ArPe, *tr.* by Omar S. Pound

Tell Me, Wight in the Broom. *Unknown.* NAEL-1

Tell me, woman, your parents, your name, your land. B. Calliteles. Antipater of Sidon. HePo, *tr.* by Barbara Hughes Fowler *Fr.* Epigrams.

Tell me, you anti-saints, why glass. Upon Fairford Windows. Richard Corbet. BeJo; NOSC

Tell me you Hate; and Flatter me no more. To J. G. "Ephelia." KTR; NOSC

Tell me, you years I had for my life. Remembering Brother Bob. William Stafford. IFJA

Tell me your secrets, pretty shell. Shell Secrets. *Unknown.* BoTP

Tell Our Daughters. Besmilr Brigham. CrSp

Tell the beads of the chromosomes like a rosary. George Oppen. APSN *Fr.* Route.

Tell the life of the mind, the mind creates the finite. George Oppen. APSN *Fr.* Route.

Tell them. Tanka. Akiko Yosano, *Japanese.* MJT, *tr. by* Ueda, Makoto

Tell them, because our fathers lied. (LL) Common Form. Rudyard Kipling. FaBoEE; FaBoTw; PeFWW

Tell them, I AM, Jehovah said. Christopher Smart. *Fr.* A Song to David. ImPo; NAEL-1; NOBE; OAEL-1; OBWVE; PoE; PoEL-3

Tell them in Lacedaemon [*or* Lakedaimon], passer-by. On the Army of Spartans, Who Died at Thermopylae. Simonides. FaBoEE

Tell this to ladies: how a hero man. Man without Sense of Direction. John Crowe Ransom. LiTM; MeMAP; OxBA

Tell Us, Josephine. Ron Padgett. FTOS

Tell us, streaming lady. History. James Liddy, *Irish.* CIP-2 *Fr.* Love Songs of Corca Bascinn.

Tell Us, Ye Servants of the Lord. William Staughton. AH

Tell you a story—an' it's a fac'. Jack the Giant-Killer. James Whitcomb Riley. NOxBChV

Tell you? ha! who. Maximus, to Gloucester, Letter 2. Charles Olson. NoAM *Fr.* The Maximus Poems.

Tell you I chyll. John Skelton. *Fr.* The Tunnyng [*or* Tunning] of Elynour [*or* Elinor] Rummyng [*or* Rumming]. AAS

Tell your son, my son. Message. Renata Pallottini, *Portuguese.* WPOW, *tr. by* Monique *and* Carlos Altschul

Telling. Andrew Hudgins. RA

Telling About Coyote. Simon J. Ortiz. PFTM; STP

("Old Coyote. . . / 'If he hadn't looked back'.") PFTM

Telling each other secrets. (LL) Venus's-Flytraps. Yusef Komunyakaa. FiLi; NAmP90; WeT

Telling It. Nancy Sullivan. TAP

Telling My Feelings. Yü Hsüan-chi. BoWoP, *tr. by* Geoffrey Waters

Telling of the hardships and perils of the voyage. (LL) The Magi. Ramon Guthrie. GI

Telling the Bees. John Greenleaf Whittier. APN-1; AWP; ColAP; GEA; NOBA; NoP-4; PAR; TAP

Tells me what I unto my God should be. (LL) Bishop Doane on His Dog. George Washington Doane. BLPA; FaBoBe

Telltale tit. You Worthless. *Unknown.* FaBoVe

Telluric and Magnetic. César Vallejo, *Spanish.* PFTM, *tr. by* Clayton Eshleman

Telyric. Andrei Codrescu. PmAP

Temeraire, The. Herman Melville. APN-2; GS; NCAP

Temper. Rose Fyleman. OxBChV

Temper. *Unknown.* PoToHe

Temper my spirit, O Lord. The Passionate Sword. Jean Starr Untermeyer. TrJP

Temper (1), The. George Herbert. ESCV; FSCP; GeHe; NOCV; NoP-4; PoEL-2

Temper (2), The. George Herbert. GeHe

Temperament. Robert Frost. *Fr.* Home Burial. ColAP; IMW; NAAL-2; SoSe-8; TAP; TRP

Temperament. Martial, *Latin.* AWP, *tr. by* Joseph Addison

Temperaments, The. Ezra Pound. BoLoP; MeMAP; NOBA; NoAM; OBCoV

Temperance and Virginity. Milton. *Fr.* Comus; a Masque Presented at Ludlow Castle. FHYEP; OAEL-1

Temperance Billiards Rooms, The. P. J. Kavanagh. OxBTC

Temperance Note: and Weather Prophecy. James Agee. *Fr.* Two Songs on the Economy of Abundance. MoAmPo

Temperature. Gerard Malanga. NYBP

Tempered, annealed, the hard essence of autumn metals. Needle and Thread. Pan Chao, *Chinese.* WPoS; WPOW, *tr. by* Richard Mather *and* Rob Swigart

Tempest, The. Charles Cotton. OxBoS

Tempest, The. Shakespeare. OAEL-1

Ariel's Song ("Full fathom [*or* fadom] five thy father lies"). EBEvV; NOBE; NOSC; NTP; OPOU

("Full fathom five thy father lies.") APAD; NoP-4; PoPoPo

(Sea Dirge, A.) GTBS-P

Ariel's Song: "Come unto these yellow sands." CTC; FaBoCh; NOBE

(Song: "Come unto these yellow sands.") EBEvV; PoEL-2

Ariel's Song: "Where the bee sucks, there suck I." EBEvV; NOBE

"'Be cheerful, sir:'." APAD; EnlH

"Dost thou forget." OxAEP-1

Epilogue. UV

Epilogue: "Now my charms are all o'erthrown." CTC

"Hast thou, spirit." OxAEP-1

"I do not know / One of my sex; no woman's face remember." OxBM

Magic. AWP

Sea Dirge, A. GTBS-P

("Full fathom five thy father lies.") APAD; NOP-4; PoPoPo

(Sea Dirge, A.) GTBS-P

Sea Song, A: "Master, the swabber, the boatswain and I, The." NBLV; OBCoV; PeLV

(Song.) NOBL; OxBSP

Tempest, The. William Jay Smith. MoAmPo

Tempest, The. *Unknown.* AmFP

Tempest, The. Henry Vaughan. ESCV

Tempest, The. Marya Alexandrovna Zaturenska. MoAmPo

Tempests pass through the air, as they pile up cloudbank on, The. Yearning for Winter. Karl Wilhelm Ramler, *German.* GePo, *tr. by* George C. Schoolfield

Temple, *sels.* Donne. *Fr.* La Corona. ChIV-2; ESCV; Son *Fr.* Holy Sonnets.

Temple, The. Robert Herrick. CaPo

Temple, A. Kenneth Patchen. SPE

Temple, The. Po Chü-i, *Chinese.* ChiP; OBMV, *tr. by* Arthur Waley

Temple, The. Charles Hubert Sisson. OxBTC

Temple Near Quang Tri, Not on the Map. Bruce Weigl. CDa

Temple of Artemis at Ephesos, The. Antipater of Thessalonica, *Greek.* GrAn, *tr. by* Tony Harrison

Temple of Bequeathed Love, The. Po Chü-i, *Chinese.* CoBCP, *tr. by* Burton Watson

Temple of Chastity, The. Mary Robinson. Poetr

Temple of Hsiang Yü, The. Li Shan-fu, *Chinese.* SuSp, *tr. by* Irving Y. Lo

Temple of the Animals, The. Robert Duncan. NOBA

Temple of the Ocean of Awakening. Shen Chou, *Chinese.* CoBLCP, *tr. by* Jonathan Chaves

Temple of the Orchid Fragrance Goddess. Li Ho, *Chinese.* SuSp, *tr. by* Michael Fish

Temple of Venus, The. Soame Jenyns. NOEC

Temple of Venus, The. Edmund Spenser. *Fr.* Wood Of Error. AEP

Temples of Mount T'ai greeted the sun in the east, The. Reading the Annals of Emperor Wu of the Han Dynasy. Wu Wei-yeh, *Chinese.* CoBLCP, *tr. by* Jonathan Chaves

Temples of Smoke. Yusef Komunyakaa. NAmP90

Tempora Mutantur. James Russell Lowell. HAP

Temporal. George Jonas. NOBC

Temporarily in Oxford. Anne Stevenson. NoP-4

Temporary. (LL) When Skies are Low and Days are Dark. N. M. Bodecker. AYFP; OTCP

Temporary City. Nijole Miliauskaite, *Lithuanian.* VCWP, *tr. by* Jonas Zdanys

Temporary language, A. Larry Eigner. PmAP

Tempt Me No More. C. Day Lewis. MoBrPo; OBMV; PoA *Fr.* The Magnetic Mountain.

Temptation. Nina Cassian, *Romanian.* AF; CEEP, *tr. by* Brenda Walker *and* Andrea Deletant

Temptation. Arthur Hugh Clough. PeLV *Fr.* Dipsychus [and the Spirit].

Temptation. Czeslaw Milosz, *Polish.* GI, *tr. by* Czeslaw Milosz *and* Lillian Vallee

Temptation. Aaron Shurin. PT

Temptation. Dionysios Solomos. GrIP, *tr. by* Rae Dalvin *Fr.* The Free Beseiged.

Temptation and Fall of Man, The. Caedmon. AnOE, *tr. by* C. W. Kennedy *Fr.* Genesis.

Temptation of Eve, The. Milton. EBNV *Fr.* Book IX. FHYEP; NAEL-1; NAWM-1; OAEL-1 *Fr.* Paradise Lost.

Temptation of Sir Gawain, The. *Unknown. Fr.* Sir Gawain and the Green Knight. OAEL-1, *tr. by* Brian Stone

Temptations of Saint Anthony, The. Phyllis McGinley. OxBSP

Temptations of St. Antony by His Housekeeper. Elizabeth Smither. PeNZ

Temptations still nest in it like basilisks. Dead Hand. W. S. Merwin. InPK-6

Tempter Disarmed, The. Milton. NOSC *Fr.* Book IX. FHYEP; NAEL-1; NAWM-1; OAEL-1 *Fr.* Paradise Lost.

Ten bloody years with this quill lying. Invocation. Valentin Iremonger. BIrV

Ten Commandments, The. *Unknown.* OxBChV

Ten commandments are between us. Magdalene. Marina Tsvetayeva, *Russian.* GI, *tr. by* Michael M. Naydan *and* Slava Yastremski

10 Commandments, are the Law Divine. John Taylor. ChIV-1 *Fr.* Taylor's Arithmetic from One to Twelve.

Ten Commandments, Seven Deadly Sins, and Five Wits. *Unknown.* FaBoEE

Ten cuckolds slain without confession. Ballad of Don Juan Tenorio and the Statue of the Comendador. Roy Campbell. PeSA

Ten dancers glide. Ballad of the Ten Casino Dancers. Cecília Meireles, *Portuguese*. BoWoP, tr. by James Merrill

Ten Days Leave. W. D. Snodgrass. MoAmPo; Poetsp; UnPo

Ten days of wind and rain, depressing darkness! T'ang Yin. CoBLCP, tr. by Jonathan Chaves Fr. A Rainstorm Has Dragged On for Ten Days Now, and There Is No Fire in the Kitchen. Moistening My Inkstone and Chewing on My Brush, I've Lived in Isolation Like a Monk—and Completed Eight Quatrains to Express My Feelings.

Ten Definitions of Poetry, *shorter vers.* Carl Sandburg. MoAmPo

Ten fearless Space Men orbiting in line. Space Men. Charles Connell. SpW

Ten frozen parsnips hanging in the weather. (LL) Winter Remembered. John Crowe Ransom. CBLP; HAP; MeMAP; NOBA; OxBA; UnPo; VGW

Ten Girls. Luchezar Elenkov, *Bulgarian*. CEEP, tr. by Ewald Osers

Ten heads and twenty hearts! so that this me. Perhaps. Sydney Thompson Dobell. NOBVV

Ten ii. Laurie Duggan. BMAP

Ten Lines. Emile Roumer, *French*. NegPo, tr. by Ellen Conroy Kennedy

Ten little children. Dancing on the Shore. M. M. Hutchinson. BoTP

Ten Little Christmas Trees. Rodney Bennett. BoTP

Ten Little Dicky-Birds. A. W. I. Baldwin. BoTP

Ten Little Indian Boys. M. M. Hutchinson. BoTP

Ten Little Injuns. Septimus Winner. OBAL

Ten little mice sat in a barn to spin. *Unknown*. ACTP

Ten little nigger boys went out to dine. *Unknown*. OxNR

Ten Little Rembrandts. Theodore Weiss. NoAM

Ten men will dress in white, The. The Hunters of the Deer. Dale Zieroth. NOBC

Ten Mills. Robert Frost.

  Hardship of Accounting, The. FaBoCh; OBAL

  In Divés' Dive. GI; VGW

  Span of Life, The. HoPM; LiTM; SoSe-8

  Wrights' Biplane, The. WeW-3

Ten Miscellaneous Poems Written as a Member of the Imperial Retinue on an Inspection Tour of the Frontier—We Reached Hsüan-fu and Then Returned. Yang Shih-ch'i, *Chinese*.

  "Forty *li* through Chü-yang Pass." CoBLCP, tr. by Jonathan Chaves

Ten months after Flouinel happen'd to wed Another True Maid. Matthew Prior. FaBoEE

Ten New Commandments. Robert Greacen. PeLV

Ten O'Clock Scholar, [The]. Mother Goose. OxNR; ReMoGo

Ten o'clock train to New York, The. Winter. Ruth Stone. BoWoP

10:X:57, 45 Years Since the Fall of the Ch'ing Dynasty. Philip Whalen. PoM

  (Forty-five Years Since the Fall of the Ch'ing Dynasty.) NeAP

Ten of the night is Talavera tolling. The Field of Talavera. Thomas Hardy. CMoP Fr. The Dynasts.

Ten Poems on Almond Blossoms. K'ang Hai, *Chinese*.

  "When I have chanted my new poems." CoBLCP, tr. by Jonathan Chaves

Ten Poems on the Tuan-yang Festival. Yang Chi, *Chinese*.

  Pitch-Ball. CoBLCP, tr. by Jonathan Chaves

Ten Poems Recording Things that Happened at the Ye. Liu K'o-chuang, *Chinese*.

  From "Ten Poems Recording Things that Happened at the Year's End." CoBCP, tr. by Watson, Burton (b. 1925)

Ten poems written in one month. Valerio Magrelli, *Italian*. NeIt, tr. by Dana Gioia

Ten Rules of Conduct for Individuals and Nations. Abraham Lincoln. CTV

Ten Scenes at the Hsiao Family Stone Ridge. Yang Shih-ch'i, *Chinese*. CoBLCP, tr. by Jonathan Chaves

Ten Short Poems, *fr. the Spanish of* Juan Ramón Jiminez. Juan Ramón Jiménez, *Spanish*.

  "To the bridge of love." ITG, tr. by Stephen Mitchell

Ten Songs. W. H. Auden.

  "Carry her over the water." FaBoTw; RB

  Cats and Dog. APo

  ("DOG The single creature leads a partial life.") PC

  Refugee Blues. HP; NYBP; OxAEP-2

  (Song.) NYBP

10.30 AM Mass, June 16, 1985. Paul Durcan. BiHa; CIP-2

Ten thousand almond trees by the riverbank. Song of Spring Journeying. Wang Ya, *Chinese*. SuSp, tr. by Irving Y. Lo

Ten thousand flakes about my window blow. Walter Savage Landor. FaBoEE

Ten thousand flowers in spring, the moon in autumn. Wu-Men, *Chinese*. EnlH, tr. by Stephen Mitchell

Ten thousand got drowned that never were born. (LL) Nottamun Town. *Unknown*. CBNP; OxBoLi

Ten Thousand Miles. *Unknown*. AmFP

Ten Thousand Miles Away. *Unknown*. AS

Ten thousand pains. (LL) Stormy Night in Autumn. Chu Shu-chen, *Chinese*. OHPC, tr. by Kenneth Rexroth

Ten thousand rivers of tears. Licymnios, *Greek*. InMo, tr. by Sam Hamill

Ten thousand things are heard when born. On Sound. Wei Ying-wu, *Chinese*. SuSp, tr. by Irving Y. Lo

Ten thousand things wound my heart when you're be fore my eyes. In Illness, Dismissing My Singing Girl. Ssu-k'ung Shu, *Chinese*. CoBCP, tr. by Burton Watson

Ten thousand thousand fathoms down. Thomas Love Peacock. CBNP Fr. Sir Proteus, a Satirical Ballad.

Ten thousand years. (LL) Above Pate Valley. Gary Snyder. CoAP; CoAmPo; LCAP-2; NoP-4; TRP

Ten Types of Hospital Visitor. Charles Causley. OxBC

Ten wise men standing stock-still. The Wise Ones. Bozhidar Bozhilov, *Bulgarian*. CEEP, tr. by Jascha Kessler and Aleksandar Shurbanov

Ten Years Ago. Eileen Moeller. CrSp

Ten years ago. Tanka. Kanoko Okamoto, *Japanese*. MJT, tr. by Makoto Ueda

Ten years ago, beneath the Hotel Astoria. Annus Mirabilis 1989. Elaine Feinstein. HP

Ten years ago I sat in a classroom next to my teacher. I Didn't Know. Ellen Bass. NMM-2

Ten years ago I was a visitor at the wine jar, Tune: "Song of Picking Mulberry." Song of Picking Mulberry. Ou-yang Hsiu, *Chinese*. CoBCP, tr. by Burton Watson

Ten years ago it seemed impossible. In Progress. Christina Rossetti. BoWoP; NAFL-2; WPE

Ten years ago my brother sat firm. Meeting Like This. Paul Willis. DAP 96

Ten Years and More. Miriam Waddington. NOBC

Ten years—and to my waking eye. The Terrace at Berne. Matthew Arnold. EnVR Fr. Switzerland.

Ten years / and will you be. Return to Hinton. Charles Tomlinson. CMoP

Ten years—dead and living dim and draw apart, Tune: "Song of River City." Tune: Song of River City. Su Tung-p'o, *Chinese*. CoBCP, tr. by Burton Watson

Ten years of age and intent upon a tea-brown burn. Trout Flies. Ruthven Todd. FaBoTC

Ten years of my life, spent at the window or beneath the lamp. Song of Cursive Calligraphy. Hsieh Chin, *Chinese*. CoBLCP, tr. by Jonathan Chaves

Ten Years Old. Nikki Giovanni. MBE

Ten years old with my father. Trails. Patrick Williams. PNI

Ten years older in an hour. In the Ward. Robert Lowell. NAAL-2

Ten years together without yet a cloud. Firelight. Edwin Arlington Robinson. NoAM

Tenacious, tenable. (LL) Fields of Learning. Josephine Miles. LiLi

Tenancy, The. Mary Gilmore. CBAP

Tenant at Number 9. John Blight. CBAP

Tenant sits upon his case, The. A Kreutzer Sonata. "Sasha Chorny," *Russian*. TCRP, tr. by Bernard Meares

Tenant Who Lives in Fire, The. Sandor Csoori, *Hungarian*. CEEP, tr. by Nicholas Kolumban

Tenants of an Abandoned Castle. John Dyer. APo Fr. "Grongar Hill."

Tenants of Paradise. Milton. APo Fr. Paradise Lost, IV.

Tenants of the Little Box, The. Vasco [or Vasko] Popa, *Serbo-Croatian*. HSix, tr. by Charles Simic

Tended by Faustina. Faustina, or Rock Roses. Elizabeth Bishop. FaBoMo

Tender, and averse to killing. (LL) Ode: To Miss Margaret Pulteney. Ambrose Philips. OxAEP-1; Poetr; UV

Tender Buttons. Gertrude Stein.

  Blue Coat, A. PBWP

  Colored Hats. TTTS

  Dog, A. PFTM; TTTS

  More. PBWP

  New Cup and Saucer, A. TTTS

  Nothing Elegant. PBWP

  Petticoat, A. TTTS

  Piano, A. PBWP

  Red Roses. TTTS

  Sound, A. TTTS

  Umbrella, An. TTTS

  Water Raining. PBWP

Tender each to the other, gentle. Imperialists in Retirement. Edward Lucie-Smith. PBCV

Tender fingers ran up my ankle. "Can I Tempt You to a Pond Walk?" James Schuyler. PoA

Tender-handed stroke a nettle. Written on a Window. Aaron Hill. OxBSP

Tender heart, hairy muscle. Maria Luisa Spaziani, *Italian*. NeIt, *tr. by* Beverly Allen

Tender-Heartedness. Harry Graham. CBNP; NBLV; NOxBChV; PeLV *Fr. Some Ruthless Rhymes.*

   ("But no one liked to poke up Willie.") (LL) FPC

   ("Little Willie, in the best of sashes.") FPC

Tender infant, meek and mild, The. Ballad. Samuel Johnson. CBNP; OxAEP-1

Tender mulberry leaves fill the basket-racks. Poem Written During a Dream on the Twenty-Third Day of the Intercalary [Month After The] Fourth [Month]. Ch'ien Ch'ien-i, *Chinese*. CoBLCP, *tr. by* Jonathan Chaves

Tender mulberry leaves picked so clean. Walking in the Countryside. Wang An-shih, *Chinese*. SuSp, *tr. by* Jan W. Walls

Tender, semi- / articulate flickers. For My Mother: Genevieve Jules Creeley. Robert Creeley. PoM; TRP

Tender softness, infant mild. To an Infant Expiring the Second Day of Its Birth. Mehetabel Wright. ECWP; NOEC

Tender speeches, until they feed us to the truth. (LL) Never Seek to Tell Thy Love. John Ashbery. HCAP; InPS-3

Tenderfoot, The. D. J. O'Malley. AS

Tenderly, day that I have loved, I close your eyes. Day That I Have Loved. Rupert Brooke. PoLF

Tenderly, in those times, as though she fed. Edna St. Vincent Millay. *Fr.* Sonnets from an Ungrafted Tree. NALW

Tenderness. Stephen Dunn. NIP-4

Tenderness. Aleksey Aleksandrovich Surkov, *Russian*. TCRP, *tr. by* Lubov Yakovleva

Tenderness, ache on me, and lay your neck. James Dickey. TAP *Fr.* The Zodiac.

Tenderness and resolution[!]. Reliquary. Hart Crane. PoA

Tenderness of dignity of souls, The. Peter Viereck. HoPM *Fr.* Crass Times Redeemed by Dignity of Souls.

Tenderness of love is extraordinary. The. Thanksgiving (1974). Stefan Brecht. CLPP

Tending the Graves. Jennifer Strauss. NOBAu

Tendril in the Mesh. William Everson.

   "Daughter of earth and child of the wave be appeased." NoAM

Tenebrae. Paul Celan, *German*. PoSu; VCWP, *tr. by* Michael Hamburger

Tenebrae. Austin Clarke. BIrV; CIP-2; NOIV

Tenebrae. David Gascoyne. PeECV

Tenebrae. Denise Levertov. NoP-4

Tenebræ. John Banister Tabb. APN-2

Tenebris. Angelina Weld Grimké. NAAAL; PoBA

Tenebris Interlucentem. James Elroy Flecker. MoBrPo

Tennessee. *Unknown.* AmFP

Tennessee Snow. Naomi Mitchison. WPN

Tennis. Margaret Avison. MoP

Tennis Court Oath, The. John Ashbery. NoAM; TAP; WeT

Tennyson. Alan Ansen. CoAP

Tennyson's Poems. Josephine D. Henderson Heard. CBWP-4

Tense. Brokendown Countdown. John Rice. SpW

Tense beat of the drum, The. To a Rabfak Student. Mikhail Arkadyevich Svetlov, *Russian*. TCRP, *tr. by* Daniel Weissbort

Tenson. Carenza *and* Iselda, *Provençal*. WPOW, *tr. by* Bridget Connelly *and* Doris Earnshaw

Tent Caterpillars. Susan Mitchell. WeT

Tent on the Beach: &[;The Dreamer&];. John Greenleaf Whittier. NCAP *Fr.* Tent on the Beach: &[;The Dreamer&];.

   Tent on the Beach: &[;The Dreamer&];. NCAP

Tent stitch is repeated in the blue and red, The. Oh, Nothing. John Ashbery. NAAL-2

Tent that is pitched at the base, A. War. Edgar Wallace. OBWP

Tentacled for food. In the Sea of Tears. Naomi Replansky. BrRo

Tentacles, the brazen phiz whose glare, The. Medusa. Amy Clampitt. NMM-2; VCAP

Tenth Planet, The. Alan Bold. SpW

Tenth Satire of Juvenal Imitated, The. Samuel Johnson. *See* The Vanity of Human Wishes [The Tenth Satire of Juvenal Imitated].

Tenth Satyr of Juvenal, The. Juvenal, *Latin*.

   "*Jove* grant large space of life, and length of days." OBCVT, *tr. by* Thomas Shadwell

Tenth Song. Sir Philip Sidney. *Fr.* Astrophil and Stella. AAS; SiPS

Tenth Symphony. John Ashbery. NOBA

Tents, *marquees,* and baggage-wagons. The Camp. Mary Robinson. NOBRP

Tenuous and Precarious. Stevie Smith. OxBTC

Tenzone. Ezra Pound. MeMAP; PoA *Fr.* Contemporania.

Teodoro Luna's Two Kisses. Alberto A. Ríos. PoPoPo

Tepehua Thought-Songs. *Unknown, Tepehua Indian.* STP, *tr. by* Charles Boilès

Tequila & chicken. In a Motel on Lake Erie. James Tate. LCAP-2

Terce. W. H. Auden. CMoP; PoE *Fr.* Horae Canonicae.

   ("After shaking paws with his dog / (Whose bark would tell the world that he is always kind].") GI

   ("Horae Canonicae.") GI

Terce. Donald Davie. *Fr.* Horae Canonicae. CRP

Terce. James McMichael. PoA

Terence, if I could return. To Myself, after Forty Years. Terence Hanbury White. NYBP

Terence McDiddler. *Unknown.* OxNR

Terence, this is stupid stuff. A. E. Housman. CABP; CMoP; HeIP-4; InPK-6; LiTM; MoBrPo; MoP; NAEL-2; NoAM; NoP-4; PFE; Poetr; TFi

Terentius Neo and wife. Their oval eyes. Portrait of a Married Couple. Margaret Scott. NOBAu

Teresa. Richard Wilbur. NoAM

Teresa of Avila. Elizabeth Jennings. PeECV; TOF

Terezin, the Graveyard. Bernd Jentzsch, *German*. CEEP, *tr. by* Ewald Osers

Terminal. Karl Shapiro. GM

Terminal. Martin Shea. HA

Terminal Hip. Mac Wellman.

   "Of Power, Money, Cheese, Real Estate, Conboboration, Hoohah." FTOS

Terminal Laughs. Irving Feldman. BAP-95

Terminally Ill. Anna Swirszczynska, *Polish*. PoSu, *tr. by* Czeslaw Milosz *and* Leonard Nathan (b. 1924)

Terminus. Nicholas Christopher. BAP-95

Terminus. Seamus Heaney. PoPoPo

Terminus ("It is time to be old"). Ralph Waldo Emerson. APN-1; AWP; AmPP; MeMAP; NCAP; NOBA; OxBA; PoEL-4; PoLF; SAGP; TAP

Terminus. Peter Rose. BMAP

Termite, The. Ogden Nash. KaS; OBCA

Terms of all kinds mellow with time, growing. Their Speech, Compared with Wisdom and Poetry. Robert Pinsky. NoAM; PoA *Fr.* Essay on Psychiatrists.

Terms of Appointment. Arthur Rex Dugard Fairburn. PeNZ

Ternarie of Littles, upon a Pipkin of Jellie [*or* Jelly] Sent to a Lady, A. Robert Herrick. BeJo; FaBoCh; PoEL-3

   (Littles.) BoTP

Ternissa. Walter Savage Landor. NOBE; OBNC *Fr.* The Hellenics.

   (Ternissa! You Are Fled.) PoEL-4

Ternissa! You Are Fled. Walter Savage Landor. *See* Ternissa.

Terns cried, 'Return!', The. (LL) Upon Learning That a Bird Exists Called the Turnstone. John Updike. CBNP; PeLV

Terpander. Tryphon, *Greek*. GrAn, *tr. by* Peter Jay

Terpês died among the Spartans, playing. Terpander. Tryphon, *Greek*. GrAn, *tr. by* Peter Jay

Terpsichore looks kindly on me. Korinna, *Greek*. PBWP, *tr. by* John Dillon

Terra Australis. James Philip McAuley. NOBAu

Terra Australis. Douglas Stewart. NOBAu

Terra cotta girl, The. In the Counselor's Waiting Room. Bettie M. Sellers. InPK-6

Terrace and pool of the Prince of Liang stand up in mid-sky. The Liang Terrace. Li Ho, *Chinese*. PLT, *tr. by* A. C. Graham

Terrace at Berne, The. Matthew Arnold. EnVR *Fr.* Switzerland.

Terrace in the Snow, The. Su Tung-p'o, *Chinese*. OHPC, *tr. by* Kenneth Rexroth

Terraces of Rain. David St. John. NAmP90

Terrain. A. R. Ammons. CoAmPo; VCAP

Terrapin, The. Elizabeth Smither. PeNZ

Terre, A. Wilfred Owen. LiTM; NSI; OxBTC; PeFWW; PoWW

Terre Promise. Ernest Christopher Dowson. NOBVV

Terrestrial Cuckoo, A. Frank O'Hara. CBNP

Terri. Alan Wearne. BMAP *Fr.* The Nightmarkets.

Terrible / a horse at night. Lawrence Ferlinghetti. HoPM

Terrible Beauty. Kingsley Amis. *See* Aldport (Mystery Tour).

Terrible beauty is born, A. (LL) Easter 1916. W. B. Yeats. CMoP; FaBoMo; FaBoPV; FaPoR; GEA; HAP; HeIP-4; IIP; InPS-3; LiTM; MoP; NAEL-2; NAWM-2; NIP-4; NOBE; NOIV; NoAM; NoP-4; OAEL-2; OBWP; OxAEP-2; OxBTC; PoE; PoPoPo; TFi

Terrible child-bed hast thou had, my dear, A. Shakespeare. EBEV; OxAEP-1 *Fr.* Pericles.

Terrible Door, The. Harold Monro. BoLoP; EnLoPo; FaBoTw

Terrible Infant, A. Frederick Locker-Lampson. NOxBChV; OBCoV

Terrible is my plight this night. Wolves for Company. *Unknown, Irish.* BIrV

Terrible is the price. The Price. John Davidson. EBVV

Terrible Love. John Barlas. ADE

Terrible Path, The. Brian Patten. OTCP

Terrible slowness / overtaking haste. (LL) The Tortoise. Cid Corman. InPK-6; VGW

Terrible sons of the mighty race, The. Eleazar ben Kalir, *Hebrew.* TrJP, tr. by Israel Zangwill

Terrible Thought, A. Eliezer Steinbarg, *Yiddish.* TrJP, tr. by Joseph Leftwich

Terrified / he jumps out of bed. Hearing. Miroslav Valek, *German.* CEEP, tr. by Ewald Osers

Terrifying are the attent sleek thrushes on the lawn. Thrushes. Ted Hughes. FaBoMo; TRP

Territory is Not the Map, The. Jack Spicer. CBNP

Terror. Denise Levertov. PoE

Terror. Robert Penn Warren. PoA

Terror. "Yehoash," *Yiddish.* TrJP, tr. by Isidore Goldstick

Terror and stillness and ebon-hued horror, night in its iciness. Midnight. Andreas Gryphius, *German.* GePo, tr. by George C. Schoolfield

Terror Conduction. Philip Lamantia. NeAP

Terror for fat burghers on far plains below. (LL) Rocky Acres. Robert Graves. NoAM; UnPo

Terror of Death, The. Keats.

(Terror of Death, The.) GTBS-P

Terror strikes lightly your stillness. Spider. Thomas Cole. PoA

Terrorism. Frank Stanford. FiLi

Terrorist, He Watches, The. Wislawa Szymborska, *Polish.* PoSu, tr. by Adam Czerniawski; AF, tr. by Robert A. Maguire and Magnus Jan Krynski

("Bomb, it goes off, The.") (LL) AF, tr. by Robert A. Maguire and Magnus Jan Krynski

("Bomb will go off in the bar at one twenty p.m, The.") AF, tr. by Robert A. Maguire and Magnus Jan Krynski

Terse Elegy for J.V. Cunningham. X. J. Kennedy. DiPo

Terzetto: Brixton. Bill Griffiths. NBrP

Tess. Vita Sackville-West. WPN

Tess's Lament. Thomas Hardy. FaBoTw; FaBoVe

Test, The. Ralph Waldo Emerson. OBAL

Test of Atlanta 1979, The. June Jordan. ISC

Test of Men, The. Bible, Apocrypha. TrJP *Fr.* Ecclesiasticus.

Testament. Tudor Arghezi, *Romanian.* AF, tr. by Andrei Bantas and Thomas Amherst Perry

Testament. Tudor Arghezi, *Romanian.* CEEP, tr. by Andrei Banta and Thomas Amherst Perry

Testament, The. Mikhail Yuryevich Lermontov, *Russian.* NNPT, tr. by Cornford, Frances Darwin and Esther Polianowsky Salaman

Testament of a Rebel. Breyten Breytenbach, *Afrikaans.* PeSAV, tr. by André P. Brink

Testament of Beauty, The. Robert Bridges.

Ethick. OxBTC

"Sky's unresting cloudland, that with varying play, The." EBEV

Testament of Beauty, Book III, The. Robert Bridges.

"Art is the true and happy science of the soul." GS

Testament of Cresseid, The. Robert Henryson. OxBS

Assembly of the Gods, The. PoEL-1

"I mend the fyre and beikit me about." EBEV; PoE

Testament of Mr. Andro Kennedy, The. William Dunbar. OxBS

Testimonies. Yehuda Amichai, *Hebrew.* IP, tr. by Warren Bargad and Stanley F. Chyet

Testimony, The. Kay Boyle. NMM-2

Testimony. Jane Flanders. CrSp

Testimony. Dan Pagis, *Hebrew.* HP; PoSu, tr. by Stephen Mitchell

("Without image or likeness.") (LL) HP, tr. by Stephen Mitchell

Testimony. Dan Pagis, *Hebrew.* IP, tr. by Warren Bargad and Stanley F. Chyet

Testimony. Charles Reznikoff.

Amelia was just fourteen and out of the orphan asylum. ColAP

Testimony. Carolyn M. Rodgers. BPo

Testimony in trials that never got heard. A Woman Is Talking to Death. Judy Grahn. CPO; GLP

Testimony of J. Robert Oppenheimer, The. Ai. PaTW

Testimony: The United States (1901–1910) Recitative/The South. Charles Reznikoff. FTOS

Testing-Tree, The. Stanley Kunitz. FYAP; UnPo

Tête-à-Tête. Edwin Honig. NoAM

Tête-à-Tête. May Probyn. VWP

Tête à Tête; or, Fashionable Pair: an Eclogue, The. Ann Murry. ECWP

Tetélestai. Conrad Potter Aiken. LiTM; MoAmPo

Tethered horse, A. Buson. ChAP

Tethy's Festival. Samuel Daniel.

Shadows. NOBE

("Thought must length it in the heart.") (LL) NoP-4

Tewa Song of War. *Unknown, Mayan.* PBMP, tr. by Daniel G. Brinton

Tewkesbury Road. John Masefield. BoTP

Texan Rhodes Scholar named Fred, A. Limerick. Lyndon T. Mole. PeLi

Texas. Mei-Mei Berssenbrugge. PmAP

Texas Cowboy, The. *Unknown.* AmFP

Texas Cowboy [lay down] on a barroom floor, A. The Hell-bound Train. *Unknown.* BLPA

Texas Ranger, The. Margie B. Boswell. AiP

Text, The. Gary Snyder. NAAL-2 *Fr.* Burning. NeAP; PoM *Fr.* Myths and Texts.

Text. Audrey Wurdemann. FYAP

Text Book / A case in point, the expert says;. Forensic Medicine. Gieve Patel. OMIP

Text for a Poster (2). Lee Harwood. NBrP

Text for These Distracted Times, A. Rodney Hall. CBAP

Text, Silk. Novica Tadic, *Serbo-Croatian.* HSix, tr. by Charles Simic

Thaba Bosio. S. D. R. Sutu, *Sotho.* PeSA, tr. by Dan Kunene and Jack Cope

Thahts no whurrits aht. Paroakial. Tom Leonard. FaBoTC

Thai passit in thare pilgramage. *Unknown.* OxBS *Fr.* Golagros and Gawane.

Thailand Railway. Randolph Stow. CBAP

Thair is nocht ane Winche. *Unknown.* OxBS

Thaïs. Newman Levy. PeLV

Thais, why do you call me old. Martial, *Greek.* PGA, tr. by Kenneth Rexroth

Thalaba the Destroyer. Robert Southey.

"Cold! cold! 'tis a chilly clime." NOBRP

Thalassa. Louis MacNeice. BIrV; FaBoMo; NOBE

Thalero. Angelos Sikelianos, *Greek.* GrIP, tr. by Edmund Keeley and Philip Sherrard

Thames, The. Sir John Denham. NOSC *Fr.* Cooper's Hill. BeJo; CABP; PBRV; SeCP

Thames, The. M. M. Hutchinson. BoTP

Thames nocturne of blue and gold, The. Impression Du Matin. Oscar Wilde. ADE; EBVV; MoBrPo; NAEL-2; NoAM

Thamuris Marching. Robert Browning. OAEL-2

Than all men else, than thy self only less. (LL) To Ben Jonson. Thomas Carew. BeJo; CaPo; EPCY; NAEL-1; NOSC

Than all the eastern sages knew. (LL) On the Emigration to America [and Peopling the Western Country]. Philip Freneau. ColAP; NAAL-1; NAAL-3; TAP

Than all the flourishing [or flour'shing] wreaths by laureates worn. (LL) To My Worthy Friend Master George Sands [or Sandys], on His Translation of the Psalms. Thomas Carew. BeJo; CaPo; EPCY; MeLP

Than all the gold in world that is. (LL) Freedom [or Fredome]. John Barbour. FaBoCh; OBEV; OxBS

Than any other thing! . (LL) Wishing. William Allingham. BoTP; OxBChV

Than aught, except its living years. (LL) Stanzas: "And thou art dead, as young and fair." Byron. GTBS-P; PoEL-4; Ro

Than blood in the heart. (LL) Night. Louise Bogan. NoP-4; Poetr; UnPo

Than by my threatenings[threat'nings] rest still innocent. (LL) The Apparition. Donne. ESCV; EnLoPo; FSCP; GBL; GLoP; HeIP-4; NAEL-1; NAWM-1; NOBE; NOBL; NoSic; OAEL-1; OBEV; OxBSn; PoE; SCGP; SCV; SeCP; SoSe-8; TFi

Than(by yon sunset's wintry glow). E. E. Cummings. VGW

Than calm in waters, seen[!]. (LL) To Jane: The Recollection. Shelley. GTBS-P; OBNC

Than Christ was a man. (LL) Consorting with Angels. Anne Sexton. NALW; NMM-2

Than could whole seas of craw-fish soup. (LL) To a Young Lady, with Some Lampreys. John Gay. CABP; CBLP; ECEV; NOEC; OBCoV

Than Dis, on heaps of gold fixing his look. (LL) By this Leander being near the land. Marlowe. EBEV

Than even Oxford town. (LL) The Spires of Oxford. Winifred M. Letts. PoLF; PoRA

Than ever I for him. (LL) My Name and I. Robert Graves. NYBP; NoAM

Than for a pardon that he dares admire. (LL) At Penshurst [Another]. Edmund Waller. BeJo; OAEL-1

Than go to church with oily Sue and afterwards to bed. (LL)
Correspondence between Mr. Harrison in Newcastle and Mr. Sholto
Peach Harrison in Hull. Stevie Smith. NBLV; OxBC

Than here she grants in Love's requite? Catullus. *See* Carmen 45 ("Phyllis
Corydon clutched to him").

Than, if this noble kyng. John Skelton. PBRV   *Fr.* A Replycacion.

Than *live in pleasure* far away. (LL)   Composed at the Request of a Lady,
and Descriptive of Her Feelings. Maria Gowen Brooks. APN-1; PAR

Than, Mau. John Balaban. CDa

Than never to have loved at all. (LL)   27. Tennyson. APAD; CABP;
EBEvV; FHYEP; ImPo; OAEL-2; OBNC

Than no illume at all. (LL)   Those—dying then. Emily Dickinson. APN-2;
NCAP

Than none at all. Provide, provide! (LL)   Provide, Provide. Robert Frost.
AmPP; CMoP; ChIV-1; FP; HAP; KSG; MoP; NAAL-2; NOBA; NoAM;
NoP-4; PoE; Poetr; TAP; TFi; TwCP; UnPo; WeW-3

Than on yon gable-ends o' time? (LL)   The Prows O' Reekie. Lewis
Spence. FaBoTC

Than public faces in private places. (LL)   Dedication: "Private faces in public
places." W. H. Auden. FaBoEE; PeLV

Than railroads, a soiled red-letter day. (LL)   The Sitting. Medbh
McGuckian. CABP; PNI

Than Robene Roy begouth to revell. James V, King of Scotland.   *Fr.*
Christ's Kirk on the Grene. OxBS

Than rule yon isle and be a slave. (LL)   Holyhead. September 25, 1727.
Jonathan Swift. BlrV; NOIV

Than share the city's year forlorn. (LL)   Nature. Henry David Thoreau.
AiP; FaBoBe

Than she fled through the broom. (LL)   The Broomfield Hill. *Unknown.*
ESPB; OxBB

Than smiles of other maidens are. (LL)   She is not fair to outward view.
Hartley Coleridge. GTBS-P; OBEV; OxAEP-2

Than stockit mailins. (LL)   A Poet's Welcome to His Love-Begotten
Daughter [the First Instance that Entitled Him to the Venerable
Appellation of Father]. Robert Burns. NOEC; OxBoLi; PoEL-4

Than that I lose no more for Stella's sake. (LL)   Sonnet 18: "With what
sharp checks I in myself am shent." Sir Philip Sidney. NAEL-1; NoSic

Than that it lived at all. Farewell. (LL)   Epitaph on Elizabeth, L. H. Ben
Jonson. BeJo; FaBoEE; HAP; NAEL-1; NIP-4; NOSC; NoP-4; OBEV;
PoE; Poetr; SCGP; SeCP

Than that, which one day Worms may chance refuse? (LL)   Sonnet: "My
God, where is that ancient heat towards Thee." George Herbert.
ESCV; FSCP; GeHe; NOSC; OAEL-1

Than that which you / Can do! (LL)   I, Maximus of Gloucester, to You
("Off-shore, by islands hidden in the blood"). Charles Olson. LiTM;
NOBA; NoAM; PmAP; PoM

Than the eyes of a big brown bear. (LL)   The Dancing Bear. Rachel Lyman
Field. KaS

Than the lovers. . . in the dust. . . in the cool tombs. (LL)   Cool Tombs.
Carl Sandburg. AmPP; CMoP; HAP; HeIP-4; MoAmPo; MoP; NAAL-
2; NOBA; NoAM; OxBSP; PoLF; TAP; TFi

Than the strong man in his wrath. (LL)   The Cry of the Children. Elizabeth
Barrett Browning. EBVV; OxAEP-2; VWP

Than the two hearts beating each to each! (LL)   Meeting At Night. Robert
Browning. APAD; AWP; BeJo; CABP; CBLP; EBEvV; EnVR;
FHYEP; FaBoVe; GBL; GLoP; HeIP-4; InPS-3; LoP; NAEL-2; NOBE;
NOBVV; OBEV; OBNC; OPOU; OxBSP; PFE; PeVV; PoRA; SAGP;
SCGP; SCV; SoSe-8; TFi; UnPo

Than the wind goin' over my hand. (LL)   Sea Love. Charlotte Mew. LW;
MoBrPo; OxAEP-2; OxBTC

Than this smart Misery. (LL)   Of Course—I prayed. Emily Dickinson.
APN-2; BoWoP; MoAmPo

Than those that to the earth with many tears they give. (LL)   The Dead.
Jones Very. APN-1; HAP; NOBA; NoP-4; OxBA; PAR; TAP

Than to live not perfected. (LL)   His Request to Julia. Robert Herrick.
BeJo; CaPo; CavPo; NOSC

Than to say "Abide" and yet shall not obtain. (LL)   I abide and abide and
better abide. Sir Thomas Wyatt. BoLoP; EnLoPo; SiPS

Than when sleep breathed his drowsy gale. (LL)   Stay For Me There. Henry
King. CH

Than where I loathed so much. (LL)   Discontents in Devon. Robert
Herrick. BeJo; CaPo; OxBSP

Than write such hopeless rubbish as thy worst. (LL)   A Sonnet: "Two voices
are there: one is of the deep." James Kenneth Stephen. BXAP; CABP;
EPCY; NOBL; PeLV; UV

Than you are now. (LL)   I Shall Not Care. Sara Teasdale. MoAmPo;
UnPo

Than you touch with decay. (LL)   To Death. Oliver St. John Gogarty.
FaBoEE; OBMV

Thanam o'n dhoul, do ye think I'm dead?' (LL)   Finnegan's Wake.
Unknown. BLPA; CBNP; NBLV

Thanatopsis. William Cullen Bryant. APN-1; AWP; AmPP; ColAP;
FaBoBe; NAAL-1; NAAL-3; NCAP; NOBA; OBEV; OxBA; PAR;
PWR; TAP; TFi

(So Live.) PoToHe

("Their sharpness, ere he is aware.") (LL)   CTV

Thank God. Joseph Rolnik, *Yiddish.* TrJP, *tr.* by Joseph Leftwich

Thank God, bless God, all ye who suffer not. Tears. Elizabeth Barrett
Browning. WPE

Thank God for life! *Unknown.* PoToHe

Thank God for Little Children. Frances Ellen Watkins Harper. PWR

Thank God for sleep! The Sacrament of Sleep. John Oxenham. PoLF

Thank God for sleep in the long quiet night. Morning Thanksgiving. John
Drinkwater. BoTP

Thank God, thank God, we do believe. A Christmas Carol. Christina
Rossetti. PChr

Thank God that you are still alive. To the Muse. Nadezhda Elizarovna
Maltseva, *Russian.* TCRP, *tr.* by Bernard Meares

Thank God they're all gone. Nazis. Ira Sadoff. LTA; NAmP90

Thank Goodness, the moving is over. "When the World was in Building."
Ford Madox Ford. CTC

Thank Heaven! the crisis. For Annie. Edgar Allan Poe. APN-1; AmPP;
ColAP; MeMAP; NOBA; OBEV; OxBA

Thank heav'n! I'm safely landed frae Ostend. To the Memory of Gavin
Wilson (Boot, Leg and Arm Maker). George Galloway. NOEC

Thank You. Kenneth Koch. NeAP; PoM

Thank You: A Poem in Seventeen Parts. *Unknown, Seneca Indian.* STP, *tr.*
by Richard Johnny John *and* Jerome Rothenberg

Thank You for Friends, A. Rodney Bennett. BoTP

Thank you for the booklet with the pictures of where my house / would be.
Which Letter? Arthur Vogelsang. PUP-9

Thank You for the Valentine. Diane Wakoski. HoPM

Thank you for writing and we are happy. Scatter. Paul Violi. BAP-95

Thank You, God. Nina Stiles. PoToHe

Thank You, Jesus, for this day. Marie C. Turk. CTV

Thank You, Lord. Maya Angelou. CrSp

Thank you, Mr Rason, for the Apples. E. G. Murphy. OBCoV

Thank you, my dear. Sappho, *Greek.* GrIP; PiM, *tr.* by Mary Barnard

Thank You, My Fate. Anna Swirszczynska, *Polish.* BLT, *tr.* by Czeslaw
Milosz *and* Leonard Nathan

Thank you, pretty cow, that made. The Cow. Ann Taylor. CTAV;
OxBChV

"Thank you, sir," said the cow. (LL)   The Cow and the Ass. Ann Taylor.
CTAV

Thank you. You are too. (LL)   My Erotic Double. John Ashbery. LCAP-2;
PoE; SAGP; VCAP

Thankful Acknowledgment of God's Providence, A. John Cotton. SCAP

Thankful Heart, A. Robert Herrick. *See* A Thanksgiving to God for His
House.

Thankful soil manured and winter dressed, The. Shamed by the Creature.
Mildmay Fane, 2d Earl of Westmorland. NOSC

Thanking Doctor Jen. Li K'ai-hsien, *Chinese.* CoBLCP, *tr.* by Jonathan
Chaves

Thanking My Mother for Piano Lessons. Diane Wakoski. NMM-2

Thanking Prince Chen-chi for Giving Me a Bronze Seal Engraved with
Diagrams of the Five Sacred Mountains. Hsü Chung-hsing, *Chinese.*
"This metal is engraved with Shang-style markings." CoBLCP, *tr.* by
Jonathan Chaves

Thankless for favours from on high. On a Similar Occasion for the Year
1792. William Cowper. NOCV

Thanks. *Unknown.* CTV

Thanks and a Plea to Mary. *Unknown.* MiEL

Thanks Be to God. Janie Alford. PoToHe

Thanks for Hearing. Layne Felsted. CTV

Thanks for the haggis. Could you really spare. Palladas, *Greek.* GrAn, *tr.*
by Tony Harrison

Thanks in old age—thanks ere I go. Walt Whitman. SAmP

Thanks Just the Same. *Unknown.* PoLF

Thanks, Sir, but, should it please the reverend Court. Robert Browning.
EBVVPR   *Fr.* The Ring and the Book.

Thanks to industrial Essex. Donald Davie. OxBTC

Thanks to Spring. Mary Anderson. BoTP

Thanks to the ear. Benediction. James Berry. OPOU

Thanks to the morning light. The World-Soul. Ralph Waldo Emerson.
APN-1; NCAP

Thanks to the Things. Rutger Kopland, *Dutch.* VCWP, *tr.* by James
Brockway

Thanksgibin' day am now at han'. Day befo' Thanksgibin', De. Maggie
Pogue Johnson. CBWP-4

Thanksgiving. Louise Driscoll. CTV

Thanksgiving. Steve Hassett. CDa

Thanksgiving, The. George Herbert. ESCV; GeHe

Thanksgiving. Kenneth Koch. VGW

Thanksgiving. David Abenatar Melo, *Spanish.* TrJP, *tr. by* Henry Hart Milman

Thanksgiving. Lizelia Augusta Jenkins Moorer. CBWP-3

Thanksgiving. Liz Rosenberg. PBCAP

Thanksgiving. "Yehoash," *Yiddish.* TrJP, *tr. by* Isidore Goldstick

Thanksgiving (1974). Stefan Brecht. CLPP

Thanksgiving at Snake Butte. James Welch. AiP

Thanksgiving Day. Lydia Maria Child. CTV; FPC; ImGa; NTCP; WHSW (New-England Boy's Song About Thanksgiving Day, The.) APN-1; ColAP; OBCA

Thanksgiving day, no one yet thinks of him. Who They Were. Joshua Weiner. BAP-94

Thanksgiving Dinner. Aileen Fisher. CA

Thanksgiving for a Habitat. W. H. Auden. NYBP
  For Friends Only. FP
  On Installing an American Kitchen in Lower Austria.
  Up There. OxBTC

Thanksgiving Hymn. *Unknown.* CTV, *tr. by* Theodore Baker

Thanksgiving (1956). E. E. Cummings. FaBoPV

Thanksgiving Prayer, A. Kristy Woodward. CTV

Thanksgiving to God for His House, A. Robert Herrick. BeJo; CavPo; FaBoBe; HAP; NOSC; PeECV; PoRA; SeCP; TrCP
  (Thankful Heart, A.) PoToHe

Thanksgivings, The. *Unknown, Iroquois Native American.* APN-2, *tr. by* Harriet Maxwell Converse

Thanksgivings for the Beauty of His Providence. Thomas Traherne. FaBoCh

Thar's More in the Man than Thar Is in the Land. Sidney Lanier. NOBA

Thass a funny title, Mr. Bones. April Fool's Day, or St. Mary Egypt. John Berryman. ChIV-2 *Fr.* Dream Songs.

Thassyryans king, in peas with fowle desyre. Henry Howard, Earl of Surrey. *See* Sardanapalus.

That a songster may be fed. (LL) To the Swallow. Euenus, *Greek.* OBCVT; OBVE, *tr. by* William Cowper

That a woman / begins to wear her ornaments. On Ornament. Yunsuk Hong, *Korean.* CKP, *tr. by* Jaihiun Kim

That a woman not ask a man to leave meaningful work to. Prayer for Revolutionary Love. Denise Levertov. CrSp

That after Horror—that 'twas us. Emily Dickinson. APN-2

That afternoon I had been fishing alone. A Dream of Retarded Children. Robert Bly. LoL

That alarming cry— / and before I even understand. Emily Wants to Play. Mary Jo Salter. NMM-2

That all night, eaves-high, the snow will press. Afterwards. Robert Penn Warren. *Fr.* Fall Comes in Back-Country Vermont. NYBP; VGW

That all these dyings may be life in death. (LL) Mortification. George Herbert. ESCV; FSCP; GeHe; NOSC; SeCP

That all we love is born again. (LL) Christmas at Freelands. James Stephens. TIRV; TrCP

That arches toward the other shore. (LL) Gathering the Bones Together. Gregory Orr. AmPA; Poetsp; WeT

That are impossible. (LL) To cause accord or to ag[g]re[e]. Sir Thomas Wyatt. AAS; SCGP; SiPS

That Asiatic striptease girl / who goes in for those. Automedon, *Greek.* GrAn, *tr. by* Alan Marshfield

That August afternoon the family. State Funeral. Thomas McCarthy, *Irish.* CIP-2

That August the birds kept away from the village, afraid. For the Last Time, Fire. Dennis Scott. PBCV

That axe that I hear. Buson, *Japanese.* TAL, *tr. by* Harold G. Henderson

That bears a human soul! (LL) There is no Frigate like a Book. Emily Dickinson. ChAP

That bears the zodiac. (LL) The Goose Fish. Howard Nemerov. CMoP; HeIP-4; LiTM; NIP-4; NoAM; NoP-4; PoE; Poetr

That beautiful color on the leaf. The Red Leaf. Page Sullivan. ImGa

That black forest and the fire in earnest. (LL) Gretel in Darkness. Louise Glück. AmPA; NoAM; NoP-4

That blossomed at last, red geranium, and mignonette. (LL) Red Geranium and Godly Mignonette. D. H. Lawrence. GTBS-P; NoAM

That board—you'd rave and rend them with your teeth. (LL) A Question. John Millington Synge. MoBrPo; NOIV; OBMV; OxBTC; SAGP

That boatman am I. (LL) In the Past. Trumbull Stickney. ColAP; NOBA; OxBA

That bony potbellied arrow, wing-pumping along. The Cormorant in His Element. Amy Clampitt. InPK-6; NoP-4

That brave man. (LL) The Brave Man. Wallace Stevens. PBMP; SAmP

That brave Spirit comes agen. (LL) Not Every Day Fit for Verse. Robert Herrick. BeJo; PoRA

That breathes on earth the air of paradise. (LL) Love's Justification. Michelangelo Buonarroti, *Italian.* OBVE, *tr. by* William Wordsworth

That breeze brought it. Foster Jewell. HA

That bridge from the city, that was Waimakariri. Mary Ursula Bethell. PeNZ *Fr.* By the River Ashley.

That Broad and Spreading Sweet Pear. *Unknown, Chinese.* CoBCP, *tr. by* Burton Watson

That broke up our Society upon the Stanislow. (LL) The Society Upon the Stanislaus. Bret Harte. OBAL; PaTW

That broken star. David McCord. PChr *Fr.* A Christmas Package.

That bummy smell you meet. East of the Library, Across from the Odd Fellows Building. August Kleinzahler. WWSi

That by all bodies else obscures her name. (LL) Sonnet: "Love is the peace, whereto all thoughts do strive." Greville Fulke. AAS; NoSic

That calm seems certainly safe to last tonight. (LL) On Looking Up by Chance at the Constellations. Robert Frost. CMoP; MeMAP

That can arise from aught beside. (LL) Called Proud. Walter Savage Landor. GBL; GLoP

That Can Not Be Taken Away From It. Carla Harryman. FTOS

That "cannot be done," and you'll do it. (LL) It Couldn't Be Done. E. A. Guest. BLPA; FaBoBe

That cannot long claim human entertain. Michael Drayton. *See* To the Reader of These Sonnets.

That Cassio loves her, I do well believe it. Shakespeare. OxBoV *Fr.* Othello.

That casten up full good savour. Guillaume de Lorris *and* Jean de Meun. *See* The Garden of Amour.

That Cat! Robert Fisher. PeP

That child will never lie in me, and you. The Unknown Child. Elizabeth Jennings. PBWP

That childish thoughts such joys inspire. Thomas Traherne. ESCV *Fr.* The Third Century.

That civilisation may not sink. Long-Legged Fly. W. B. Yeats. APAD; CMoP; FaBoMo; FaBoTw; InPS-3; LiTM; MoP; NAEL-2; NOBE; NoAM; NoP-4; PoE

That civilization is a transient sickness. Robinson Jeffers. *See* New Mexican Mountain.

That clock is ticking. Marie Lucille. Gwendolyn Brooks. TLR

That comes into and steadies my soul. (LL) The Pangolin. Marianne Moore. HAP; NOBA; NoAM; PBWP; Poetr

That constant Susannah. Susannah. Thulani Davis. GT

That conversation we were always on the edge. Adrienne Rich. BoWoP; NoAM *Fr.* Twenty-one Love Poems. GLP

That converse bone to bone? (LL) Sixteen Dead Men. W. B. Yeats. FaBoPV; OBWP

That cop was powerful mean. The Idiot. Dudley Randall. BPo; LTA

That corner of the earth. Aware Aware. Tram Combs. TwCP

That "Craning of the Neck." Isabella Gardner. WPE

That crazed girl improvising her music. A Crazed Girl. W. B. Yeats. InPS-3; Son

That creepycrawly traversing the stone. Close-ups of Summer. Norman MacCaig. OxBC

That crumbles in your furnaces! (LL) Armies in the Fire. Robert Louis Stevenson. EBVV; FPC

That Cypress Boat Is Drifting. *Unknown, Chinese.* CoBCP, *tr. by* Burton Watson

That Dada Strain. Jerome Rothenberg. FTOS

That dandy black-and-white gentleman doodling notes. Magpie and Pines. Louis Johnson. PeNZ

That dared attack my Chesterton. (LL) Lines to a Don. Hilaire Belloc. MoBrPo; OBSV

That dark brown rabbit, lightness in his ears. John Berryman. TwCP *Fr.* Dream Songs.

That Dark Other Mountain. Robert Francis. CRP

That Day. Anne Sexton. BoWoP; CoAmPo; SAGP

That day all the slaves were freed. Brazilian Fazenda. Patricia K. Page. FaBoWP

That day, blue white shirted. Terzetto: Brixton. Bill Griffiths. NBrP

That day I lost everything. 22.6.1941. Ondra Lysohorsky, *Lachian.* AГ, *tr. by* Ewald Osers

That day in the Interpreter's house, in one of his Significant Rooms. Christiana. Peter Redgrove. OxBC

That day, in the slipping of torsos and straining flanks. The Song. Lola Ridge. WPE

That day must come, when I shall leave my friends. Nostalgia. Vita Sackville-West. WPN

That day she threw the goose over the roof. Grandma's Man. James Welch. NoAM

That day, so innocent appeared. Picnic Remembered. Robert Penn Warren. NAAL-2

That day the challenger cracked and spread an immolating. An Explanation of the Exhibit. Rodney Jones. MoLi

That day the sails of the ship were torn. Lament for Tadhg Cronin's Children. Michael Hartnett. PBCIP; RB

That day the sunlight lay on the farms. On Heaven. Ford Madox Ford. CTC

That day the / words. John Leax. TrCP

That day they had slaughtered on the farm. Blood. Renate Wood. CMAP

That day when oats were reaped, and wheat was ripe, and barley ripening. When Oats Were Reaped. Thomas Hardy. OxBTC

That days drone elsewhere. (LL) Summer. Christina Rossetti. AYFP; CTV; PBMP

That Dear Little Cat. D'Arcy Wentworth Thompson. *See* That Little Black Cat.

That death in his windows would rise. Leah Goldberg. MHP, *tr. by* Ruth Finer Mintz *Fr.* On Blossoming.

That death might not be casual. Epilogue. Burns Singer. FaBoTw

That desire is quite over. Thinking of Love. Elizabeth Jennings. LW

That dey road no pave. The Road of the Dread. Lorna Goodison. VCWP

That did invite, but seek another place. (LL) Song: "I prithee spare me, gentle boy." Sir John Suckling. BeJo; CavPo

That dignified old woman. Mothers. Maturaipputan Ilanakanar, *Tamil*. PLW, *tr. by* A. K. Ramanujan.

That Distance Apart. Jackie Kay. NBrP

That dolphin-torn, that gong-tormented sea. (LL) Byzantium. W. B. Yeats. APAD; CMoP; EBEV; FaBoMo; HAP; InPS-3; LiTM; MoBrPo; MoP; NAEL-2; NAWM-2; NIP-4; NOBE; NoAM; NoP-4; OAEL-2; OxBTC; PoE; Poetr

That doubtful hope, that certain woe, and sure despair of health. (LL) Such[e] wayward[e] ways [*or* wais] hath love, that most[e] part[e] in discord[e]. Henry Howard, Earl of Surrey. AAS; SiPS

That doubts as fervently as it believes. (LL) Ourselves we do inter with sweet derision. Emily Dickinson. APN-2; FaBoEE

That draught whose slumber nothing can bereave. (LL) Proem: "Lo, thus, as prostrate, 'In the dust I write'." James Thomson. NOBE; OxBS

That draws all waters toward / Its live formality. (LL) Looking into History. Richard Wilbur. VCAP; VGW

That dream, her eyes like rocks studded the high. Snow on a Mountain. Dom Moraes. NoP-4

That dried-up arse, Lykainis. Antipater of Thessalonica, *Greek*. GrAn, *tr. by* Alistair Elliot

That dying is what, to live, each has to do. (LL) Curiosity. Alastair Reid. PC

That each tail should be properly placed. Mother Goose. *See* Little Bo-Peep has lost her sheep.

That eats and drinks of mealand maut. (LL) Hobie [*or* Hobbie] Noble. *Unknown*. ESPB; IBB; OxBB

That endeth the skipping and skating. Death at Suppertime. Phyllis McGinley. PBMP

That equal love knows no disparity. (LL) To Celia Pleading Want of Merit. Thomas Stanley. MeLP; NOSC

That eternal spring is hidden. Song of the Soul that Rejoices in Knowing God through Faith. Saint John of the Cross, *Spanish*. TOF, *tr. by* K. Kavanaugh *and* O. Rodrigues

That Eureka of Archimedes out of his bath. Voluptuaries and Others. Margaret Avison. MoCV

That evening all in fond discourse was spent. The Sad Lover. George Crabbe. OBNC *Fr.* Tales of the Hall.

That evening Sinda thought she heard the drums. The Dream. Robert Earl Hayden. NBV

That evening when. Akiko Yosano, *Japanese*. OHMPJ, *tr. by* Kenneth Rexroth

That ever your eyes did see. (LL) The Laily Worm and the Machrel of the Sea. *Unknown*. ESPB; OxBB; PoEL-1; SCGP

That every county in this developed state. Manifest Destiny. Pearse Hutchinson. CIP-2

That every Fool is not a Poet. (LL) Epigram from the French: "Sir, I admit your general [*or* gen'ral] Rule." Alexander Pope, *also at.* to Matthew Prior *and* to Coleridge. FaBoEE; NBLV

That Everything Moves Its Bowels. David R. Slavitt. BXAP

That evil ended. So also may this! (LL) Deor's Lament. *Unknown*, *Anglo-Saxon*. AnOE; OAEL-1, *tr. by* Charles W. Kennedy

That Exploit of Yours. Ford Madox Ford. PeFWW; PoWW

That Face. Mairtin O Direain. BiHa

That falls from the chin of the Protestant tied in the fire. (LL) The Teeth Mother Naked at Last. Robert Bly. NNaP

That fellow rides a big horse. Wang Fan-chih, *Chinese*. SuSp, *tr. by* Eugene Eoyang

That final newsreel of the war. A Welcoming Party. John Montague. PNI

That finds no object worth its constancy? (LL) To the Moon. Shelley. GTBS-P; OxAEP-2; PBMP; TTTS

That fine English poet, Donne. Limerick. Wendy Cope. PeLi

That first night in the hotel bedroom. Touching/Not Touching: My Mother. Toi Derricotte. DeD; GT

That first September day was blue and warm. The Artist on Penmaenmawr. Charles Tennyson Turner. OBNC

That fixed the tilt of the wings. (LL) Perfect. "Hugh MacDiarmid." NoP-4; RB

That flattering glass, whose smooth face wears. A Looking-Glass. Thomas Carew. CaPo

That floral apron. (LL) The Floral Apron. Marilyn Chin. LoL

That, flower of flowers, outfaces all. Meleager. *See* Heliodora's Brows.

That flower unseen, that gem of purest ray. In a Churchyard. Richard Wilbur. HeIP-4

That flowing water! That flowing water! Song of the Prophet. *Unknown*. APN-2, *tr. by* Washington Matthews *Fr.* The Mountain Chant.

That fluffy squirrel / suddenly has something human to tell me. That Moment. Ewa Lipska, *Polish*. CEEP, *tr. by* Magnus J. Krynski

That fluttering things have so distinct a shade. (LL) Le Monocle de Mon Oncle. Wallace Stevens. LiTM; MeMAP

That for annoited dullness was he made. Dryden. *See* The Crown Prince of Dullness.

That for seven *Lusters* I did never come. To the Reverend Shade of His Religious Father. Robert Herrick. CavPo; PBRV

That force is lost. Snake Eyes. Imamu Amiri Baraka. VGW

That forming on a cigarette covers the red. (LL) Morning Sun. Louis MacNeice. MoBrPo; TwCP

That fought with us upon Saint Crispin's day. (LL) Henry V before Agincourt. Shakespeare. EBEvV; FaPoR

That frantic error [*or* Frantick Errour] I adore. The Apostasy of One and But One Lady. Richard Lovelace. CaPo

That free love with bondage bound. (LL) Earth's Answer. William Blake. ChIV-1; FHYEP; InPS-3; NAEL-2; NAWM-2; NOBRP; NOEC; OAEL-2; PoE; Ro

That from the seed of men. Psalm. Peter Huchel, *German*. AF, *tr. by* Simko, Daniel

That from which these things are born. Burning the Tomato Worms. Carolyn Forché. AmPA; MDDM

That ga' me a' my will. (LL) King Henry. *Unknown*. ESPB; OxBB

That gap between the Sunday papers and lunch. Fleur Adcock. *See* Against Coupling.

That Garden of sedate Philosophy. The Garden of Epicurus. George Meredith. GaP

That ghosts are trying on her children's clothes. (LL) The Shepherd's Hut. Andrew Young. FaBoTC

That gives to her, and she to it, a grace. (LL) Faire Is My Love. Bartholomew Griffin. GBL; PoEL-2

That glitter a cold span above the sea. (LL) The Laureate. Robert Graves. BIrV; FaBoTw; OBSV

That Glove. Mary E. Tucker. CBWP-1

That God of ours, the Great Geometer. Grace to Be Said at the Supermarket. Howard Nemerov. SoSe-8

That Goddess. Iván Argüelles.
 Canto the Tenth. PT

That good, my sire, I dedicate to thee. (LL) Dedicatory Sonnet to S. T. Coleridge. Hartley Coleridge. OAEL-2; Son

That good shield I threw away. Archilochus, *Greek*. OBCVT, *tr. by* Barriss Mills

That grand and noble woman dear. Harriet Beecher Stowe's Works. Frank Barbour Coffin. AAP

That great arm-full of yellow flowers. (LL) Evadne. Hilda Doolittle. BoWoP; LW

That great stone. Clach Eanchainn. Geoffrey Fraser Dutton. FaBoTC

That Great Wingless Bird. Adrian C. Louis. UnSA

That grows, at the first touch of day, / Unendurable. (LL) First Light. Thomas Kinsella. BIrV; CMoP; PoE

That had moved the congregation so. (LL) In Church. Thomas Hardy. InPK-6; MoBrPo; SCV

That had thee here obscure. (LL) Phoebus with Admetus. George Meredith. NOBE; OBEV

That half-death. In Prague. Paul Celan, *German*. VCWP, *tr. by* Michael Hamburger

That happy and beautiful lady. (LL) The Three Cherry Trees. Walter De la Mare. CMoP; OBGa

That Harp You Play So Well. Marianne Moore. MoAmPo; PoA

That has been hurting her. (LL) Proletarian Portrait. William Carlos Williams. BLT; OBAL; SAmP; TAP

That has no face or image. (LL) Testimony. Dan Pagis, *Hebrew*. PoSu, *tr. by Stephen Mitchell*

That has not been rent. (LL) Crazy Jane Talks with the Bishop. W. B. Yeats. BoLoP; CABP; CMoP; EBEV; InPK-6; MoP; NAEL-2; NoAM; NoP-4; OAEL-2; OxAEP-2; PFE; PoE; PoPoPo; TOF; TRP

That has transfigured me. (LL) The Lamentation of the Old Pensioner. W. B. Yeats. HAP; LiLi; PeVV; TRP; WeW-3

That has yet to enter the language. (LL) Quoof. Paul Muldoon. CBNP; FaBoVe; PBCIP; PNI

That hath the power over wild beasts. (LL) Canto 47. Ezra Pound. CMoP; PoE; VGW

That haughty tyranny of thine. Love Song. Luís De León, *Spanish*. TrJP, *tr. by Thomas Walsh*

That He has raised us up forever. Amen. *Unknown. See The Seafarer.*

That he may sleep upon his hill again? (LL) Abraham Lincoln Walks at Midnight. Vachel Lindsay. AmPP; CBCWP; CMoP; MeMAP; MoAmPo; NOBA; OxBA; TAP; TFi; VGW

That he was born it cannot be denied. On a Certain Alderman. John Cunningham, *after the Greek of* Simonides. FaBoEE; OBCoV

That he was ugly we have no doubt. Socrates' Death. Michael Jackson. PeNZ

That heard me whisper. (LL) The Other Side of a Mirror. Mary Elizabeth Coleridge. SDW; VWP

That heeds no call to die. (LL) Heredity. Thomas Hardy. CTC; EBEV; RB

That her serene influence should spread. Two Loves. Richard Eberhart. CMoP

That here, obedient to their laws, we lie. (LL) Thermopylae. Simonides, *Greek*. AWP; OBVE; OBWP, *tr. by William Lisle Bowles*

That here we lie, who followed their command, (LL) For the Spartan Dead at Thermopylai (480 B.C.). Simonides, *Greek*. OBCVT, *tr. by Peter Jay*

That hid the shyest grape. (LL) Monody. Herman Melville. APN-2; NAAL-1; NAAL-3; NoP-4; OxBSP; PAR; PoE; PoEL-5; PoPoPo

That hill. Tanka. Nakajō Fumiko, *Japanese*. MJT, *tr. by Makoto Ueda*

That his daddy once tied up my garter for me! (LL) The Dark-Eyed Gentleman. Thomas Hardy. MoBrPo; NBLV; UnPo

That history is an event. Taku Skanskan. Paula Gunn Allen. HATNAP

That hobnailed goblin, the bobtailed Hob. Country Dance. Dame Edith Sitwell. MoP; NoAM

That hoe Diverne think she Marse Tyler's wife. (LL) Balance. Marilyn Nelson Waniek. FFC; NAmP90

That Holy Thing. George Macdonald. OBEV *Fr.* Paul Faber, Surgeon.

That horn chased me. Up on the Spoon. Stanley Crouch. SeSe

That hour-glass, which there ye see. The Hour-Glass. Robert Herrick. BeJo; CaPo

That houses forme within was rude and strong. The House of Richesse. Edmund Spenser. CH *Fr.* Wood Of Error. AEP

That humor now, declines for age drawes on. Thomas Churchyard. PBRV *Fr.* A Musicall Consort.

That hump of a man bunching chrysanthemums. Old Florist. Theodore Roethke. OxBSP

That hurts my pride. (LL) Tamping Ties ("Tamp 'em up solid"). *Unknown*. GM

That Hypocrite. *Unknown*. BPo

That I am as I am and so will I be. (LL) I am as I am and so will I be. Sir Thomas Wyatt. NoSic; SiPS

That I am clothed in holy robes for glory. (LL) Huswifery. Edward Taylor. ColAP; MeMAP; NAAL-1; NAAL-3; NIP-4; NOBA; NOBE; NoP-4; OxBA; SCAP; TAP; TFi

That I am mortal I know and do confess / My span of day. Star-Gazing. Ptolemy, *Greek*. GrAn, *tr. by Dudley Fitts*

That I had alighted there! (LL) Faintheart in a Railway Train. Thomas Hardy. CBLP; CTC; EnLoPo

That I had hit the Road. On the Pilgrims' Road. Andrew Young. FaBoTC

That I have come to kill him. (LL) Enemy Encounter. Padraic Fiacc. IIP, PNI

That I have lacked [*or* lakt] so long. (LL) Now must I le[a]rn[e] to live [*or* lyve] at rest. Sir Thomas Wyatt. AAS; SiPS

That I have often been in love, deep love. Ode. "Peter Pindar." NOEC

That I loved them, & that meant. Primavera. David Miller. NBrP

That I may fold it round me and in comfort lie. (LL) The Embankment (The Fantasia of a Fallen Gentleman on a Cold, Bitter Night). Thomas Ernest Hulme. APAD; EBEV; FaBoMo; GTBS-P; OPOU; OxBSP; OxBTC

That I may lose my way / And myself. (LL) Lights Out. Edward Thomas. NOBE; OxAEP-2; PoWW

That I might there present it!—Oh! to whom? (LL) The Question. Shelley. CH; GTBS-P; OBEV

That I might touch that cheek. (LL) The Living Juliet. Shakespeare. EBEvV; ImPo

That I my Best-Beloved's am; that he is mine. (LL) My Beloved Is Mine, and I Am His; He Feedeth among the Lillies. Francis Quarles. MeLP; NOBE; OBEV

That I not be a restless ghost. Margaret Mead. MDDM

That I shall never find him. (LL) The Mad Maid's Song. Robert Herrick. AWP; CH; CaPo; EnLoPo; GEA; OAEL-1; OBEV; RACG

That I shall never find my home. (LL) The Mower to the Glow-Worms [*or* Glowworms *or* Glo-Worms]. Andrew Marvell. APo; AWP; CBLP; ESCV; EnLoPo; FHYEP; FMP; FSCP; GLoP; GeHe; NAEL-1; NOBE; OAEL-1; OxBoLi; PBRV; PeLV; PoEL-2; SCGP; SeCP; TFi

That I should never be ingrate. (LL) To One That Asked Me Why I Loved J.G G. "Ephelia." KTR; NOSC; PEW

That I was christened. (LL) Perambulator Poem. David McCord. KaS; OBCA; OBCoV

That I was never blest. (LL) The Repulse. Thomas Stanley. BeJo; MeLP

That I went to warm my self in Lady Betty's Chamber. To Their Excellencies the Lords Justices of Ireland, the Humble Petition of Frances Harris, Who Must Starve, and Die a Maid if It Miscarries. Jonathan Swift. NOEC; PoEL-3

That I would not persuaded be. Service Is No Heritage. Nicholas Breton. NoSic

That if I dipped my hand the spawn would clutch it. (LL) Death of a Naturalist. Seamus Heaney. HAP; NoAM; OxBC; WeW-3

That if I stepped out of my body I would break / Into blossom. (LL) A Blessing. James Wright. ITG; InPK-6; InPS-3; NAAL-2; NOBA; NoAM; PoE; Poetr; RaBo; TRP; TwCP; VCAP; WeT

That I'm alive to tell you so. (LL) Stella's Birthday ([March 13,] 1727). Jonathan Swift. NoP-4; OAEL-1; PoE; PoEL-3; SCGP

That in black ink my love may still shine bright. (LL) Sonnet 65. Shakespeare. AWP; GTBS-P; HAP; ImPo; InPS-3; NAEL-1; NOBE; NoSic; OxAEP-1; PoRA; RaBo; SCGP; Son; TFi; UnPo

That, in rearing such a school, / Was the founder! (LL) A Fit of Rhyme [*or* Rime] against Rhyme [*or* Rime]. Ben Jonson. BeJo; OAEL-1; PoEL-2; SeCP

That in the compass of my thoughts can fall. Bible, *O.T. See* Psalm 137.

That in the manage myself takes delight. (LL) Sonnet 49: "I on my horse, and Love on me doth try." Sir Philip Sidney. NAEL-1; NoP-4; OAEL-1; PoE

That insect, without antennae, over its. The Crane. Charles Tomlinson. MoBrPo

That is a black sunrise. Shade of a Grammarian. Andrew Joron. PT

That Is All I Heard. "Yehoash," *Yiddish*. TrJP, *tr. by Isidore Goldstick*

That is all ye know on earth, and all ye need to know. (LL) Ode on a Grecian Urn. Keats. AWP; ClHu; EBEV; FaBoBe; HAP; HeIP-4; HoPM; ImPo; InPS-3; NAEL-2; NAWM-2; NIP-4; NOBE; NOBRP; OAEL-2; OBEV; OBNC; PBMP; PoE; PoEL-4; SCGP; TFi; TOF; UnPo

That is fit home for Thee! (LL) To the Cuckoo. Wordsworth. BoTP; EBEvV; GTBS-P; NOBRP; PoLF; UV

That is fluent in even the wintriest bronze. (LL) The Sense of the Sleight-of-Hand Man. Wallace Stevens. HAP; ImPo; LiTM; MoAmPo; NOBA; NoAM; PoA; TwCP; WeW-3

That is her lover lying there. Illumination. Jeffrey Wainwright. DiPo

That is her memorial. Imants Ziedonis, *Latvian*. CEEP, *tr. by Inara Cedrins*

That is how we left him / forever. Mitsuye Yamada. *See* The Club.

That is like a whisper, a bottomless howl. (LL) A Poem with a Tilde in the Title. Nina Zivancevic, *Serbo-Croatian*. CEEP; HSix, *tr. by Charles Simic*

That is most difficult. (LL) To a Friend Whose Work Has Come to Nothing. W. B. Yeats. AWP; InPK-6; LiTM; MoBrPo; OAEL-2; OBMV; OxAEP-2; PoA

That is no country for old men. The young. Sailing To Byzantium. W. B. Yeats. APAD; CABP; CMoP; ClHu; GTBS-P; GrIP; HAP; HeIP-4; HoPM; IIP; ImPo; InPK-6; InPS-3; LiTM; MoBrPo; MoP; NAEL-2; NAWM-2; NIP-4; NOBE; NoAM; NoP-4; OAEL-2; OBMV; OxBTC; PoE; PoPoPo; PoRA; RaBo; SAGP; SCGP; SoSe-8; TFi; TIRV; TOF; UnPo; WeW-3

That is reserved for his kind. (LL) The Hyænas [*or* Hyenas]. Rudyard Kipling. NAEL-2; OBSV

That is so heygh, that al ne can I telle! (LL) This Troilus [*or* Troylus], with blisse [*or* Blysse] of that supprysed [*or* supprised]. Chaucer. EBEV; PoE

That is the glebe and this is the glissando. The future is nothing. Codex. Stephen Rodefer. PmAP

That is, their authors, leave out / one thing. History Books. Thomas Lux. PUP-20

That is their quality: not mercy, not mind, not goodness, but the beauty / of God. Robinson Jeffers. *See* Birds and Fishes.

That is what they say, who were broken off from love. Muriel Rukeyser. LCAP-2 *Fr.* Eighth Elegy. Children's Elegy.

That it dide all the place aboute—. (LL) The Garden of Amour. Guillaume de Lorris *and* Jean de Meun. PoEL-1, *tr. by* Geoffrey Chaucer

That it, half spun, death may in sunder shear. Bible, *O.T. See* Psalm 55.

That it is we who are important. (LL) For a Coming Extinction. W. S. Merwin. PoPoPo

That it should come to this—that we. At the Planning Commission. Barbara Meyn. EC3

That it should end in an Albert Pick hotel. At the End of the Affair. Maxine W. Kumin. TAP

That it will never come again. Emily Dickinson. APN-2; NOBA

That Jamestown / Made long ago. (LL) American Heartbreak. Langston Hughes. AmPP; BPo; LiTM

That Journeys Are Good. Jelaluddin Rumi, *Persian*. RaBo, *tr. by* Robert Bly

That joy[e]s so ripe, so little keep[e]. (LL) To Amarantha, That She Would Dishevel[l] Her Hair[e]. Richard Lovelace. BeJo; CaPo; HoPM; NOSC; OBEV; PoE; SeCP

That June before the judge gave. Seventeen. Jonathan Holden. Poetsp

That Justice is a blind goddess. Justice. Langston Hughes. BPo

That keep him rich and orphaned and beloved? (LL) The Illiterate. William Meredith. NoP-4

That keeps the fool's conceit. (LL) O thou, that sit'st upon a throne. Christopher Smart. OxAEP-1

That kill, that kill, that kill. (LL) Elm. Sylvia Plath. NOBA; NYBP; NoAM; NoP-4; Poetr

That kindles my mother's fire! (LL) The Wife of Usher's Well. *Unknown*. AWP; AmFP; CH; EBEV; ESPB; EnSB; ImPo; NAEL-1; NOBE; NoP-4; OAEL-1; OBEV; OxAEP-1; OxBB; OxBS; OxBSn; PoEL-1; Poetr; RB; SCGP; TFi

That kingfisher jewelling upstream. Kingfisher. Norman MacCaig. NoP-4

That Kings for such a Tomb would wish to die. (LL) On Shakespear[e]. Milton. CABP; EPCY; FaBoEE; MeLP; NAEL-1; NOSC; NoP-4; PoE; PoPoPo; PoRA; SCGP

That knot in the wood if wood. The Man with the Hollow Breast. Tania Van Zyl. PeSA

That knows—it cannot see. (LL) Difference between Despair, The. Emily Dickinson. NAAL-1; NAAL-3

That labor / a face to remember in wonder. Sappho, *Greek*. OBVE, *tr. by* Guy Davenport

That lady of all gentle memories. Dante. AWP *Fr.* La Vita Nuova.

That Land (3). Stephen Sartarelli. PT

That Land (4). Stephen Sartarelli. PT

That landlike slept along the deep. (LL) On last night before we went. Tennyson. OAEL-2; PoEL-5

That lately kissed thee. (LL) To Electra. Robert Herrick. CaPo; HoPM; OBEV

That lay in the house that Jack built. (LL) The House That Jack Built. Mother Goose. BoTP; FaBoBe; LB; OxBoLi; OxNR; ReMoGo

That lead from Thirty———even to Forty-eight. (LL) Thirty-eight: Addressed to Mrs H—y. Charlotte Smith. ECWP; NALW; PEW; WPOW

That leads me from my love. (LL) White in the moon the long road lies. A. E. Housman. AWP; CMoP; GLoP; NTP

That leads me to the Lamb. (LL) Walking with God. William Cowper. ECEV; NOCV; NOEC; PeECV; PoEL-3; SCGP; TOF

That leads now when all others darken. (LL) Pole Star for This Year. Archibald MacLeish. MeMAP; OxBA

That learning, thine ambassador. Donne. *Fr.* The Litanie. PoEL-2

That leaves look[e] pale, dreading the winter's neere [*or* near]. (LL) Sonnet 97. Shakespeare. AWP; EnLoPo; GTBS-P; HeIP-4; NAEL-1; NOBE; NoSic; OAEL-1; OBEV; OxAEP-1; PoRA; SCGP; Son; TFi

That lets Him out again. (LL) Yellow Man, Purple Man. Emily Dickinson. TLR; TTTS

That lies in the house of Bedlam. (LL) Visits to St. Elizabeths. Elizabeth Bishop. CBNP; CoAP; VGW

That life may be more comfortable yet. The Choice. John Pomfret. FP

That light, reflected, but makes darkness plain. (LL) In Dispraise of the Moon. Mary Elizabeth Coleridge. CH; PEW

That, like a wounded snake, drags its slow length along. (LL) Essay on Criticism. Alexander Pope. OBCoV

That linkage of warnings sent a tremor through June. Red Poppy. Tess Gallagher. NAmP90

That literature breeds distress. (LL) Sarah Byng Who Could Not Read and Was Tossed into a Thorny Hedge by a Bull. A Cautionary Tale. Hilaire Belloc. CBNP; NoAM

That Little Black Cat. D'Arcy Wentworth Thompson. OxBChV

("And that's the best cure for a little pussy cat.") (LL) NOxBChV

(That Dear Little Cat.) NOxBChV

("Who's that's ringing at the front door bell?") CTAV

That little grey-haired lady. The Little Old Lady. Rodney Bennett. BoTP

That Little Lump of Coal. *Unknown*. AmFP

That little Negro's married and got a kid. Sister. Langston Hughes. APSN

That little pretty [*or* prettie] bleeding part. To His Savior [*or* Saviour]. The New Years [*or* yeers] Gift. Robert Herrick. ChIV-2

(That liv'd so sweetly) dead, so sweet a Grave! (LL) Music[k]'s Duel[l]. Richard Crashaw. GeHe; OAEL-1; SeCP

That lives for oneness with God? (LL) Fish cannot drown in water, A. Mechthild von Magdeburg, *German*. EnlH; WPoS, *tr. by* Jane Hirshfield

That living law, the magistrate. Donne. *Fr.* The Litanie. PoEL-2

That living there I never could look up. (LL) The Glory Trumpeter. Derek Walcott. GT; NAEL-2; NoP-4; SeSe

That long ago we drove ourselves. Twenty-One Years. Reynolds Price. BAP-96

That long fall, / when the voices stopped. The Minister's Death. Wesley McNair. AFr

That long neck of yours. Deer. No Ch'&obrev;n-my&obrev;ng, *Korean*. CKP, *tr. by* Jaihiun Kim

That Love is all there is. Emily Dickinson. NOBA

That Love is king and creed and Persian law. (LL) From Life to Love. Countee Cullen. ChIV-1; KSG

That love of mine for him had waxen wings—. The Comet. Maria Luisa Spaziani, *Italian*. NeIt, *tr. by* Beverly Allen

That love supports his reign. (LL) On a Bed of Guernsey Lilies. Christopher Smart. CABP; NOEC; PoPoPo

That love to her I cast away. (LL) Disdain Returned. Thomas Carew. CavPo; PFE

That love which once was nearest to my heart. Vetus Flamma. Robert Mezey. PoA

That Love,—whose power and sovranty we own. The Creation of My Lady. Francesco Redi, *Italian*. AWP, *tr. by* Sir Edmund Gosse

That lovely spot which thou dost see. Upon a Mole in Celia's Bosom. Thomas Carew. CBLP; CaPo

That lover of a night. Crazy Jane on God. W. B. Yeats. CMoP; EBEV; OxBTC; RACG

That Lucy's eyes surveyed. Wordsworth. *See* I traveled [*or* travell'd] among unknown men.

That maddened me, until I laughed and wept. (LL) The Barber. John Gray. ADE

That made the woods of April bright. (LL) The Yellow Violet. William Cullen Bryant. NAAL-1; NAAL-3; PoLF; TAP

That made them what they were! (LL) Transformations. Thomas Hardy. PFE; RB; TRP

That man. Night Song for Two Mystics. Paul Blackburn. NeAP

That man died in Jerusalem. Easter Dawn. Kofi Awoonor. PBMAP

That man entered through my eyes. Dream of the Forgotten Lover. Lucia Fox, *Spanish*. BoWoP, *tr. by* R. Maghan

That man over there say. Ain't I a Woman? Sojourner Truth. BlSi

That mans most Noble Passion is to Love. (LL) The Call. John Hall. MeLP; NOSC

That many friends had opened long ago. (LL) Mr Flood's Party. Edwin Arlington Robinson. AWP; AmPP; CMoP; ClHu; ColAP; EBNV; FP; HAP; HeIP-4; HoPM; LiTM; MeMAP; MoAmPo; MoP; NAAL-2; NIP-4; NOBA; NoAM; NoP-4; OxBA; PoE; PoRA; Poetr; SoSe-8; TAP; TFi; TRP; UnPo; WeW-3

That mare stood in the field. All through the Rains. Gary Snyder. CoAmPo

That may breed love's delights?. . . . (LL) The Merry Country Lad. Nicholas Breton. CH; NoSic

That me alone you lov'd, you once did say. Catullus. *See* Carmen 72.

That melancholy / fellow'll play / his handorgan. E. E. Cummings. MeMAP

That men weep hearing it, and have no choice. (LL) Ye pilgrim-folk, advancing pensively. Dante. AWP; CTC

That mendacious Old Person of Gretna. (LL) Limerick: "There was an old person of Gretna." Edward Lear. OBCoV; OxBChV

That mirror / Which makes of men a transparency. Moments of Vision. Thomas Hardy. OAEL-2

That Moment. Ted Hughes. UV *Fr.* Crow. PoE

That Moment. Ewa Lipska, *Polish*. CEEP, *tr. by* Magnus J. Krynski

That Moment. Sharon Olds. Poetr

That month. Pāri's daughters, *Tamil*. PLW, *tr. by* A. K. Ramanujan

That morn which saw me made a bride. Upon a Maid That Died the Day She Was Married. *Unknown*. PFE

That morn[e] which saw me made a Bride. Upon a Maid That Died [*or* Dyed] the Day She Was Married [*or* Marryed]. Meleager, *Greek*. AWP; OBVE, *tr. by* Robert Herrick

That morning you found your lights on. Adagio. Gerald William Barrax. GT

That mother sat beside my sister, Kei, and spoke to her before any of us. Possession: A Zuihitsu. Kimiko Hahn. BAP-96

That Mountain Far Away. *Unknown, Tewa Indian.* PBMP, *tr.* by Herbert Joseph Spinden; CA

That mountain there. Pilgrimage Song. *Unknown, Pueblo Indian.* WPE, *tr.* by Mary Austin

That mourns a man like thee. (LL) On the Death of Joseph Rodman Drake. Fitz-Greene Halleck. APN-1; BLPA; PoEL-4

That multitude of moulded hands. Jean-Joseph Rabéarivelo. *See* Cactus.

That music, remote, forlorn. (LL) The Old Summerhouse. Walter De la Mare. CMoP; GTBS-P

That must escape the knife. (LL) Autobiography of a Lungworm. Roy Fuller. MoP; NoAM; OxBC

That my Friends may weep as much as they like. (LL) An Epitaph: "I was buried near this dyke [*or* Dike]." William Blake. FaBoEE; OBCoV

That my life would be saved by the loss of my dinner?'. (LL) Patient Joe; or, The Newcastle Collier. Hannah More. ECWP; WoRP

That my old bitter heart was pierced in this black doom. A Grey Eye Weeping. Egan O'Rahilly, *Irish.* FaBoPV; OBMV, *tr.* by Frank O'Connor

That Nature Is a Heraclitean Fire and of the Comfort of the Resurrection. Gerard Manley Hopkins. EnVR; EnlH; FaBoMo; FaBoVe; GTBS-P; NoP-4; OAEL-2; PFTM; PoE; PoEL-5

That Nature wrought must unto dust be brought. (LL) A Remembrance of My Friend Mr. Thomas Morley. John Davies, of Hereford. PFE

That ne'er did wrong to thine or thee. (LL) Lovely lass o' Inverness, The. Robert Burns. GTBS-P; OBEV

That neither fame nor love might wanting be. To Sir Henry Cary. Ben Jonson. NOSC; NoP-4

That never can again be mine. Catullus. *See* Carmen 5 ("My sweetest Lesbia, let us live and love").

That never were, nor are, nor e'er shall be. (LL) Against Fruition ("Fie upon hearts that burn with mutual fire[!]"). Sir John Suckling. BeJo; CaPo

That night at Trafalgar! (LL) The Night of Trafalgar. Thomas Hardy. CH; FaBoCh; MoBrPo; OBMV

That night I think that no one slept. The Last Fight. Lewis Frank Tooker. FaBoBe

That night she felt those searching hands. Mary, Mother of Christ. Countee Cullen. PChr

That night the moon drifted over the pond. The Prediction. Mark Strand. LCAP-2; NoP-4; SPE; VCAP

That night the whole world mingled. A Certain Evening. G. K. Chesterton. OxAEP-2

That night they all gathered on the highest tower. Jovan Hristic, *Serbo-Croatian.* GI; HSix, *tr.* by Charles Simic

That night when joy began. W. H. Auden. OxBTC; SoSe-8 *Fr.* Five Songs.

That night will come. Somewhere someone will be. For My Daughter. Sharon Olds. DeD

That night will long delight us, Nealce. Petronius Arbiter, *Greek.* PGA, *tr.* by Kenneth Rexroth

That night your great guns, unawares. Channel Firing. Thomas Hardy. CABP; CMoP; EBEV; HAP; HeIP-4; ImPo; MoP; NAEL-2; NIP-4; NoAM; NoP-4; OAEL-2; OxAEP-2; OxBTC; PeECV; PeFWW; PoE; PoEL-5; PoPoPo; PoRA; PoWW; Poetr; RB; SoSe-8; TFi; UnPo

That no fair woman will, wonder not why. Carmen 69. Catullus, *Latin.* OBCVT; OBVE, *tr.* by Richard Lovelace *Fr.* Carmina.

That no one hears them among the talk and laughter. (LL) Wolves. Louis MacNeice. NoAM; OxBTC

That noble Chaucer, in those former times. Michael Drayton. EPCY *Fr.* To Henry Reynolds, of Poets and Poesy.

That none beguiled be by time's quick flowing. Love's Clock. Sir John Suckling. CaPo; NOSC; PoEL-3

That nose is out of drawing. With a gasp. Sonnet for a Picture. Swinburne. BXAP; OAEL-2; UV *Fr.* The Heptalogia.

That note comes clear, like water running clear. The Piano Tuner's Wife. Karl Shapiro. NoAM

That note you hold, narrowing and rising, shakes. For Sidney Bechet. Philip Larkin. NoP-4

That Nova was a moderate star like our good sun; it stored no doubt a. Nova. Robinson Jeffers. CMoP; HAP

That now to them dost all thy substance give. (LL) The Lost. Jones Very. APAD; APN-1; NOBA; NoP-4; PAR

That ocean you of late surveyed. To Mr. Newton [on His Return from Ramsgate]. William Cowper. NOEC

That odor in the world? (LL) Mock Orange. Louise Glück. NoAM; PoPoPo; SAGP; VCAP

That odyssey? We three left Amherst late. To My Fellow-Mariners, March, '53. Thomas Whitbread. NYBP

That of heuen they may neuer mysse! (LL) Adam Bell, Clim of the Clough, and William of Cloudesly. *Unknown.* ESPB; OxBB

That often change doth please a woman's mind. (LL) Divers[e] [*or* Dyvers] doth[e] use, as I have heard and kno[w]. Sir Thomas Wyatt. AAS; NAEL-1; SiPS; Son

That old crow-beaked hag. Agathias, *Greek.* InMo, *tr.* by Sam Hamill

That "old last act"! / And yet sometimes. Adrienne Rich. NIP-4; NOBA; TAP *Fr.* Two Songs.

That old mulemba. Geraldo Bessa Victor, *Portuguese.* PeSAV, *tr.* by Donald Burness

That Old Sauna High. Anselm Hollo. PoM

That on her lap she casts her humble Eye. On the Blessed Virgins Bashfulnesse. Richard Crashaw. HAP; OxBSP

That once this life was really mine. A Song of Life. Franz Werfel, *German.* TrJP, *tr.* by Edith Abercrombie Snow

That once which pained to think of. The Forgiven Past. Laura Riding Jackson. PBWP

That one best sleep which never wakes again. (LL) The City is of Dreadful Night. James Thomson. EBVV; PoEL-5

That one is conscious and not know why. Prospect of Release. Tom Mandel. PT *Fr.* Prospect of Release.

That one perfect word. (LL) Jack Would Speak Through the Imperfect Medium of Alice. Alice Notley. PT; PmAP

That one short hour was told. (LL) The Apparition. Stephen Phillips. LBC

That one small boy with a face like pallid cheese. Incendiary. Vernon Scannell. OxBC

That opens and bends closed those leaves. (LL) The Swan's Feet. Edith Jay Scovell. FaBoWP; OxBTC

That Orpheus Calliops sonne who stayde the running brooke. The Deaths of Orphues and Hercules. Seneca. OBVE *Fr.* Medea.

That other sun, the jealous coursing of the unrivalled blood. (LL) On the Marriage of a Virgin. Dylan Thomas. EnLoPo; OxBM

That our thought may take her immediate in its embrace. (LL) Sonnet [*or* Sonetto] 7: "Who is she that comes, makyng turn every man's eye." Guido Cavalcanti. CTC; OBVE, *tr.* by Ezra Pound

That parts fam'd Trachis from th'Euboic shore. (LL) Sonnet: Suppos'd to Be Written at Lemnos. Thomas Russell. NOBRP; NOEC

That people celebrate it by forgetting its name. (LL) At the Un-National Monument along the Canadian Border. William Stafford. HAP; HeIP-4

That people ought to be. (LL) On a Rhine Steamer. James Kenneth Stephen. FaBoA; NOBL; NOBVV; OBCoV; PeLV

That perishes at the heart' (LL) The Bitter Withy. *Unknown.* NOCV; NoP-4

That plunging mast, nailed to a whirligig gale. SOS Lifescene. Burns Singer. FaBoTC

That poet is best. Lucilius, *Greek.* InMo, *tr.* by Sam Hamill

That poets are far rarer births than kings. To Elizabeth, Countess of Rutland. Ben Jonson. BeJo; NoP-4

That poets should each other eat. (LL) To a Swallow. John Peale Bishop, *after the Greek of* Euenus. GrAn; OBVE

That points at him amazed. (LL) Full Moon and Little Frieda. Ted Hughes. NTP; OPOU; OxBC; OxBSP

That powerful swimmer / furrowing the pool. Swimmer. Mervyn Morris. HCP

That Prince, who may doe nothing but what's just. A King and No King. Robert Herrick. PBRV

That Pull from the Left. Louise Erdrich. NoAM

That pulls or shakes it from the golden tree. Marlowe. *See* By this Leander being near the land.

That quiet man with the hoe is a beast. An Inmate. Peter Kocan. NOBAu

That rabbit's foot I carried in my left pocket. Sybilline. "Ern Malley." BMAP

That raddled old queen. Tom Donnelly. PeLi

That ragged / leaking raft held. Ireland. Richard Ryan. CIP-2

That rather had to die in troth than live forsaken so. (LL) The Lady Prayeth the Return of Her Lover Abiding on the Seas. *Unknown.* GBL; OBEV

That reach through nature, moulding men. (LL) In Memoriam A.H.H. 124. Tennyson. EBVV; FHYEP; NOCV; OAEL-2; TOF

That reaches beneath the painted eaves of your home. (LL) To a Traveler. Su Tung-p'o, *Chinese.* OHPC, *tr.* by Kenneth Rexroth

That rebellious rodent called Jerry. Bill Greenwell. PeLi

That rides the glorious *Cherubim.* (LL) To Find[e] God. Robert Herrick. BeJo; NoP-4

That road / got no people. Sketches. Federico García Lorca. PFTM

That romantic star. One. Federico García Lorca. PFTM

That romps through the dark. (LL) Canis Major. Robert Frost. KaS; MoAmPo

That Room. John Montague. CIP-2

That row of icicles along the gutter. Beyond Words. Robert Frost. KaS; Spl; WeW-3

That runs his link full in your face. (LL) On Dorinda. Charles Sackville. NOSC; OBEV; OxBSP

That runs on and on at its own sweet will. (LL) Sweet Will. Philip Levine. LCAP-2; VCAP

That sail in cloudless light. Sea Grapes. Derek Walcott. TRP

That same day Jesus went out of the house and sat beside the sea. Matthew 13:1–9; That same day Jesus. Stephen Mitchell. GI *Fr.* St. Matthew.

That Saturday at eventide. (LL) The High Tide on the Coast of Lincolnshire, 1571. Jean Ingelow. EBVV; OxAEP-2

That savage trinity warily watching. (LL) Patrolling Barnegat. Walt Whitman. APN-1; OxBoS

That scalds me now—that scalds me now! (LL) I shall know why—when Time is over. Emily Dickinson. NOCV; SAmP

That scalps your naked soul. (LL) He fumbles at your Soul. Emily Dickinson. ColAP

That sculptor we knew, the passionate-eyed son of a quarryman. An Artist. Robinson Jeffers. VGW

That scything wind has cut the rich corn down. John Knox. Iain Crichton Smith. OxBS

That sea was greater than we knew. The Voyage. Edwin Muir. LiTM

That season when the leaf deserts the bole. October 1. Karl Shapiro. MoAmPo; PoA

That second time they hunted me. The Italian in England. Robert Browning. FaBoPV; OBNV

That seemd the fountaine in that sea did sayle upright. (LL) In the Bower of Bliss. Edmund Spenser. GaP

That separate rights are lost in mutual love. (LL) The Rights of Woman. Anna Laetitia Barbauld. CABP; NoP-4; PEW; Ro

That servile path thou nobly dost decline. Sir John Denham. EPCY *Fr.* To Sir Richard Fanshawe, Upon His Translation of Pastor Fido.

That shadow my likeness that goes to and fro seeking a livelihood, chattering, chaffering. Walt Whitman. APN-1

That shakes the blossoms of my hoary hair! (LL) A Little Girl Lost. William Blake. FHYEP; Ro

That shaman, owl man. The Deadly Dance. *Unknown, Aztec Indian.* STP, *tr. by* Edward Kissam

That she adored me as the most. Elegy on Any Lady by George Moore. Max Beerbohm. FaBoEE

That she appeared to say, 'I am at peace'. (LL) Very pitiful lady, very young, A. La Vita Nuova Dante. AWP; CTC

That she forgot me was the least. Emily Dickinson. CPO

That she hath gone to Heaven suddenly. Dante. CTC *Fr.* La Vita Nuova.

That she that makes me sin, awards me pain. (LL) Sonnet 151. Shakespeare. HeIP-4; OxAEP-1; PoEL-2

That she will move from mourning into morning. (LL) To My Mother. George Barker. FaBoMo; ImPo; LiTM; OxAEP-2; OxBTC; PFE; PoWW; RaBo; SAGP; Son; TwCP

That she would grow again. (LL) For My Grandmother. Countee Cullen. MoAmPo; SSLK; VGW

That Sheba led a dance. (LL) On Woman. W. B. Yeats. CMoP; ChIV-1

That shipwrackt vessel which th'Apostle bore. Upon his Majesties repairing of Pauls. Edmund Waller. PBRV

That shot Jesse James on the sly. (LL) Jesse James. *Unknown.* AS; FaBoBe; UnPo

That silent publicizer of unheard-of news. Philodemus, *Greek.* GrAn, *tr. by* William Moebius

That simple duty hath no place for fear. (LL) Abraham Davenport. John Greenleaf Whittier. AmPP; NoP-4

That since you would save none of me, I bury some of you. (LL) The Funeral[1]. Donne. AWP; BoLoP; EBEV; ESCV; EnLoPo; FSCP; HeIP-4; ImPo; MeLP; NAEL-1; NAWM-1; NoP-4; OAEL-1; OBEV; PoEL-2; PoRA; SCGP; SeCP; TFi

That situates so far. (LL) Perception of an object costs. Emily Dickinson. APN-2; NOBA

That smasher of shams, Bernard Shaw. Limerick. Frank Buckland. PeLi

That snail. Buson. ChAP

That soldier with a machinegun bolted. Two Summers in Moravia. Roger McDonald. CBAP

That some day Death who has us all for jest. Augusta Davies Webster. VWP

That son of Italy who tried to blow. Austerity of Poetry [*or* Jacopone da Todi]. Matthew Arnold. EPCY

That sort of place where you stop. Colville 1964. Kendrick Smithyman. PeNZ

That spot of blood on the drawingroom wall. The Conversation in the Drawingroom. Weldon Kees. SPE

That spring night I spent. Lady Suo, *Japanese.* OHPJ, *tr. by* Kenneth Rexroth

That sputter of rain, flipping the hedgerows. A Shower. Amy Lowell. CPO

That stad is in perplexytie. (LL) The Death of Alexander. *Unknown.* FaBoCh; OxBS

That Stalin still lives in the mausoleum. (LL) The Heirs of Stalin. Yevtushenko, *Russian.* TCRP, *tr. by* George Reavey

That stand upon the threshold of the new. (LL) Of The Last Verses in the Book. Edmund Waller. NoP-4; PoPoPo

That stand upon the threshold of the new. (LL) Old Age. Edmund Waller. NOBE; NOCV; OBEV

That star I now see. Star and Sea. William Peskett. PNI

That still my Syrinx' lips I kiss. (LL) Pan's Song. John Lyly. CBLP; NoSic; OxAEP-1; SCGP

That story. Anne Sexton. *See* Cinderella.

That story which the bold Sir Bedivere. The Passing of Arthur. Tennyson. FHYEP; NAEL-2; OBNC *Fr.* Idylls of the King.

That strange flower, the sun. Gubbinal. Wallace Stevens. NAAL-2

That Strangest is of all. (LL) The Salutation [*or* Salutations]. Thomas Traherne. ESCV; EnlH; GeHe; NOCV; NoP-4; SeCP

That street washed with violet. Last Trams. Kenneth Slessor. BMAP

That strength, which behind the tongue. Otto Orban, *Hungarian.* CEEP, *tr. by* Emery E. George

That sultry afternoon the world went strange. One Tuesday in Summer. James McAuley. BMAP

That summer I did not go crazy. To the Bone. Dorothy Allison. GLP

That summer in Culpeper, all there was to eat was white. Nineteen. Elizabeth Alexander. GT; PoPoPo

That summer it just appeared. Roller Rink. Betty Adcock. MT

That summer, the red may and the white may made. Henry Treece. NYBP

That Sunday morning, at half past ten. The Ballad of Longwood Glen. Vladimir Nabokov. NYBP

That surrounds Montecito like the echo of a scream. (LL) In Montecito. Randall Jarrell. CoAP; NYBP; VGW

That sway from mood to mood the willing mind! (LL) The Poet. William Cullen Bryant. NAAL-1; NAAL-3; NCAP; TAP

That sweet accord is seldom seen. (LL) Throughout the world, if it were sought. Sir Thomas Wyatt. NoSic; OxBSP

That teacher gave me a new name. . . again. Name Giveaway. Phillip William George. VoR

That tell us solemn secrets of ourselves. (LL) Dreams. Henry Timrod. APN-2; PAR

That terra-cotta waitress. The Villa Restaurant. Derek Walcott. WeW-3

That! that! there I was told. The Bible. Thomas Traherne. PeECV

That/ that / whose/ track is it like? *Unknown. Fr.* Poems for the Game of Silence. STP, *tr. by* Frances Densmore

That the balls of the lover are not larger than the balls of the priest. Christian Karlson Stead. PeNZ *Fr.* Quesada.

That the earth be made safer for men, and more stable. *Unknown.* APN-2, *tr. by* Frank Hamilton Cushing *Fr.* The Hardening of the World, and the First Settlement of Men.

That the German is not a Hun. (LL) The Labors of Hercules. Marianne Moore. MeMAP; OxBA

That the glass would melt in heat. The Glass of Water. Wallace Stevens. MeMAP; MoAmPo; OxBA; TAP

That the god of love—I seemed to see. (LL) Ballata: Concerning a Shepherd-Maid. Guido Cavalcanti, *Italian.* ItIP

That the high sheen of death could blot. Midsummer. James Scully. NYBP; TwCP

That the King enjoys his own again. (LL) The King Enjoys His Own Again. Martin Parker. FaBoCh; NOSC; OxBoLi; PBRV

That the Muses have no more fervent. The Person's Tale. U. A. Fanthorpe. NoP-4

That the neighborhood might be covered. Larry Eigner. PoM

That the Night Come. W. B. Yeats. PoEL-5

That the poet "does not number the streaks of the tulip." To Hugh MacDiarmid. Edwin Morgan. FaBoTw

That the proud eagle would have to wife. (LL) The Ancients of the World. Ronald Stuart Thomas. OPOU; RB

That the right man lay in the dust. (LL) After Goliath. Kingsley Amis. NOBL; OxBTC

That the risen Christ should *be* risen. (LL) Don'ts. D. H. Lawrence. LiTM; OxBoLi; PeLV

That the Science of Cartography Is Limited. Eavan Boland. NoP-4

That the war would be over before they got to you. When You Have Forgotten Sunday: The Love Story. Gwendolyn Brooks. WPOW

That the world will never be quite. Tam Cari Capitis. Louis MacNeice. FP

That then I scorn to change my state with Kings. (LL) Sonnet 29. Shakespeare. AEP; APAD; AWP; CTC; EBEV; GBL; GSo; GTBS-P; HAP; HeIP-4; ImPo; InPK-6; InPS-3; LoP; NAEL-1; NOBE; NoP-4; NoSic; OAEL-1; OBEV; OPOU; OxAEP-1; PoEL-2; PoPoPo; Poetr; SAGP; SCGP; Son; TFi; WeW-3

That there are powers above us I admit. Arthur Hugh Clough. EnVR

That there is falsehood in his looks. The Parson's Looks. Robert Burns. OxBoLi

That there should never be air. Roses. Barbara Guest. NoP-4

That therewith my song is broken. (LL) Eighth Song. Sir Philip Sidney. NoSic; PBRV

That these may be thy Praise, and my Joy too. (LL) Mount of Olives. Henry Vaughan. ESCV; GeHe

That these we take for granted. Hitchcock Blue. Lucie Brock-Broido. EOEF

That they can hardly gather one plum more. (LL) Of the Theme of Love. Margaret Lucas Cavendish. PEW

That they were born for immortality. (LL) Inside of King's College Chapel, Cambridge. Wordsworth. GTBS-P; OBNC

That thou art blamed shall not be thy defect. Sonnet 70. Shakespeare. OxAEP-1; SCGP *Fr.* Sonnets.

That Thou Art Nowhere to Be Found. George Macdonald. *Fr.* Diary of an Old Soul. TrCP

That thou find'st none. (LL) Upon the Asse That Bore Our Saviour. Richard Crashaw. ChIV-2; GeHe

That thou hast her, it is not all my grief[e]. Sonnet 42. Shakespeare. CBLP; HeIP-4; OxAEP-1 *Fr.* Sonnets.

That thou mayst fit thyself against thy fall. (LL) Church Monuments. George Herbert. ESCV; GeHe; HAP; NAEL-1; NOCV; NOSC; OAEL-1; PoE; TRP

That thou mayst injure no man, dove-like be. Prudent Simplicity. Goronwy Owen, *Latin.* FaBoEE, *tr. by* William Cowper

That thou may'st know me[e], and I'll turn my face. (LL) Good Friday [*or* Goodfriday], 1613. Riding Westward. Donne. ChIV-2; ESCV; FSCP; InPS-3; MeLP; NAEL-1; NOCV; NOSC; NoP-4; OAEL-1; PBRV; PeECV; PoE; PoEL-2; SeCP; TFi

That though thine absence starve me, I wish not thee. (LL) The Storm[e]. Donne. NoSic

That throng my hiddenness. (LL) What would I do without this world faceless incurious, *Author's own English vers. of his* "Que ferais-je sans ce monde sans visage sans questions." Samuel Beckett. NOIV; NoAM

That time / in the sun. When Sun Came to Riverwoman. Leslie Marmon Silko. VoR

That time my grandmother dragged me. The Weakness. Toi Derricotte. GT; LTA

That time of drought the embered air. Drought Year. Judith Wright. NoAM

That time of year thou may'st [*or* maist] in me behold. Sonnet 73. Shakespeare. AWP; BoLoP; CTC; ClHu; EBEV; GTBS-P; HAP; HeIP-4; HoPM; ImPo; InPK-6; InPS-3; NAEL-1; NIP-4; NOBE; NoSic; OAEL 1; OBFV; PBMP; PoE; PoEL-2; PoRA; SCGP; SoSe-8; Son; TFi; UnPo; WeW-3 *Fr.* Sonnets.

That time of year you may in me behold. The Winter Twilight, Glowing Black and Gold. Delmore Schwartz. NoAM

That time that mirth did steer my ship. Sir Thomas Wyatt. SiPS

That time / we all heard it. Paul Robeson. Gwendolyn Brooks. PoBA

That tomorrow a new walk is a new walk. (LL) Corsons Inlet. A. R. Ammons. CoAP; ColAP; MoP; NAAL-2; NOBA; NoAM; NoP-4; PoE; VCAP

That transitory moment between. A Moment Ago. David Avidan, *Hebrew.* IP, *tr. by* Warren Bargad *and* Stanley F. Chyet

That trumpet tongue which taught a nation. The Demagogue. Phyllis McGinley. FaBoEE

That tumbled meaning into wind. (LL) Snow Country Weavers. James Welch. CDW; HATNAP

That Tune. Arthur Symons. *See* A Tune.

"That turn'll get her," I said. Toujours la Politesse. Ezra Pound, *after the Chinese.* OBVE

That unhappy Old Man in a boat. (LL) Limerick: "There was an Old Man in a boat." Edward Lear. CBNP; EBEV; OBCoV

That Urinal, restored god *Plutus* eyes. The Suffering of the gods. Aristophanes, *Greek.* OBCVT, *tr. by* Thomas Randolph

That Van Gogh's ear, set free. What Is Worth Knowing? Sujata Bhatt. OMIP

That various field. (LL) Salute. James Schuyler. FYAP; NeAP

That vengeaunce I ask and cry[e]. O Cat of Carlishkind. John Skelton. *Fr.* Phyllyp Sparowe [*or* Philip Sparrow]. AAS; PoEL-1

That very day I saw that is we saw. Amir Gilbo'a, *Hebrew.* IP, *tr. by* Warren Bargad *and* Stanley F. Chyet

That very day two of them were going to a village named Emma'us. Luke: 24:13–32; That very day two of them. Eric Pankey. GI *Fr.* St. Luke.

That violence ever after would be obsolete. (LL) Your small hands, precisely equal to my own. Adrienne Rich. CPO; PoE; TRP

That Virtue but that body grant to us. (LL) Sonnet 52: "A Strife is grown between Virtue and Love." Sir Philip Sidney. NAEL-1; NoP-4

That virtuous is, when the reward's away. (LL) To Sir Henry Cary. Ben Jonson. NOSC; NoP-4

That wail! 'tis prophecy. Oh, hush! be still. The Birth Wail. Henrietta Tindal. VWP

That wan and sickly droops upon her breast! (LL) On a Discovery Made Too Late. Coleridge. GSo; Son

That wandereth lightly. (LL) Bethsabe's Song. George Peele. ChIV-1; GBL; ImPo; KSG; NOBE; NoP-4; NoSic; OxBSP; OxBoLi; PoEL-2; RB

That wants himself[e] is poor[e] indeed. (LL) The Grasshopper. Richard Lovelace. BeJo; CaPo; EBEV; FaBoPV; MeLP; NAEL-1; NOBE; NOSC; OAEL-1; OBEV; OxAEP-1; SCGP; TFi

That war should bankrupts make of merchants is no wonder. Upon the Bankruptcy of a Physician. Henricus Selyns. SCAP

That was a beautiful summer. Imants Ziedonis, *Latvian.* CEEP, *tr. by* Inara Cedrins

That was a very polite fish. Vizma Belševica, *Latvian.* CEEP, *tr. by* Inara Cedrins

That was enough. You Called Me Corazón. Sandra Cisneros. PiM

That was it. (LL) A Life. Howard Nemerov. OBCoV; PBMP

That was my very soul that stole to the lips in our kissing. The Kiss. Plato, *Greek.* STV, *tr. by* John Frederick Nims

That was not the genesis. In the Beginning. Laura Riding Jackson. KSG

That was not the summer of aspic. What Grieving Was Like. Lynn Emanuel. CMAP

That was rank folly to my head before. (LL) The Tree. Ezra Pound. CMoP; PBMP

That Was Summer. Marci Ridlon. NTCP

That was the day they killed the Son of God. The Killing. Edwin Muir. GI

That was the moment when, without. Short History of the Bourgeoisie. Hans Magnus Enzensberger, *German.* VCWP, *tr. by* Enzensberger, Hans Magnus *and* Michael Hamburger

That was the proverb. Let my mistress[e] be. Long and Lazy [*or* Lazie]. Robert Herrick. FaBoEE

That was the summer my best friend. One Season. Tony Hoagland. NAmP90

That was the year I drove around all the time. The Invention of Pittsburgh. Maggie Anderson. PBCAP

That watches and receives. (LL) The Tables Turned[: An Evening Scene, on the Same Subject]. Wordsworth. APAD; FHYEP; NAEL-2; NOBRP; OAEL-2; Ro; TOF

That Way. Anne Welsh. PeSA

That way look, my Infant, lo! The Kitten and [the] Falling Leaves. Wordsworth.

That we are here: that we can question who / we are. Presence. Philip Booth. AFr

That we can come. (LL) Jews in the Land of Israel. Yehuda Amichai, *Hebrew.* IP, *tr. by* Warren Bargad *and* Stanley F. Chyet

That We can show—Today? (LL) I asked no other thing. Emily Dickinson. APN-2; NOBA; OxBA; PBMP

That we confront. (LL) Route. George Oppen. AF; APSN

That We Head Towards. Stephany Fuller. BPo

That we know you, terrible joy. (LL) Matins. Denise Levertov. AmPP; FaBoWP; MoP; NOBA; NoAM; Poetr

That we lift, as chaff lifts, toward God. (LL) Mennonites. Julia Kasdorf. LoHo; PBCAP

That we[e] may change to evenness[e]. Donne. *Fr.* The Litanie. PoEL-2

That we may have life. My Father. Felix Mnthali. PBMAP

That we with merthe mowe safely singe. (LL) The Agincourt Carol. *Unknown.* NoP-4

That weeps. . . as thou must sing. . . / Alone, aloof. (LL) Sonnet: "Thou hast thy calling to some palace-floor." Elizabeth Barrett Browning. OxAEP-1

That went by; this may too. (LL) Deor. *Unknown, Anglo-Saxon.* EEP, *tr. by* Michael Alexander

That were not born to die. (LL) At midnight, in his guarded tent. Marco Bozzaris. Fitz-Greene Halleck. APN-1; HoPM

That what. Dream Thief. Nathaniel Mackey. GT

That when we live no more we may live ever. (LL) To My Dear and Loving Husband. Anne Bradstreet. AmPP; BoWoP; ColAP; HAP; HeIP-4; KTR; NAAL-1; NAAL-3; NIP-4; NOBA; NOCV; NOSC; NoP-4; OxBA; OxDM; OxBSP; OxWW; PEW; PiM; PoE; PoEL-3; PoLF; SAGP; SCAP; TAP; TFi; WPE; WeW-3

That where one reigns, the other shall succeed? (LL) Jealousy. Esther Johnson. LW

That which creates a happy life. A Happy Life. Mildmay Fane. BeJo; NOSC

That which has remained unlived. Astride Ivaska, *Latvian.* CEEP, *tr. by* Inara Cedrins

That which her slender waist confined. On a Girdle. Edmund Waller. AWP; BeJo; GLoP; GTBS-P; ImPo; InPK-6; NAEL-1; NOSC; NoP-4; OBEV; PoE; PoRA; SCGP; TFi

That which is, being the only answer. Question and Answer. Kathleen Jessie Raine. MoBrPo

That which is in part, finding its whole again throughout the universe. (LL) Tortoise Shout. D. H. Lawrence. LiTM; NAEL-2; PFTM

That which is marred at birth Time shall not mend. Gertrude's Prayer. Rudyard Kipling. APAD

That which mattered most could not be. (LL) After the Visit. Thomas Hardy. NOBE; OBNC

That which my fault has made me, o paint not. A Poet to a Painter. Aubrey Thomas De Vere. Son

That which then was ours, my love. Don't Ask Me for That Love Again. Faiz Ahmad Faiz, *Urdu*. VCWP, *tr. by* Agha Shahid Ali

That which to some their wishes ends present. Mary Sidney. *Fr.* Urania.

That Which We Call a Rose. Michael Dransfield. BMAP; CBAP; NOBAu

That which we call reality is that. Corals and Shells. William Bronk. APSN

That which we dare invoke to bless;. In Memoriam A.H.H. 124. Tennyson. CABP; EBVV; FHYEP; NOCV; OAEL-2; TOF *Fr.* In Memoriam A. H. H.

That while he lived never thought of death. (LL) Sonnet: "Whenas man's life, the light of human lust." Greville Fulke. NOSC; NoSic; PoEL-1

That whiskey will cook the egg. Bar. Langston Hughes. APSN

That whispers in my ear: alas, alas? (LL) Is it you standing amoung the olive trees. Mark Strand. BAP-93; NoP-4

That whistles in the wind. (LL) Lucy Gray; or, Solitude. Wordsworth. CH; GEA; NAEL-2; NOBRP; OAEL-2; OxAEP-2; OxBChV

That white cloud in its contrast. Patrizia Cavalli, *Italian*. NeIt, *tr. by* Judith Baumel

That Whitsun, I was late getting away. The Whitsun Weddings. Philip Larkin. FaBoMo; HeIP-4; MoP; NoAM; NoP-4; OxAEP-2; OxBM; OxBTC

That will not state—its sting. (LL) If you were coming in the Fall. Emily Dickinson. AmPP; CBLP; NOBA; OxBA; PoRA; SoSe-8

That Willowwood should hold her wandering!' (LL) Willowwood ("O ye, all ye that walk in Willowwood"). D. G. Rossetti. NAEL-2; OAEL-2

That Wind. Emily Jane Brontë. CH

That wink of time when I was happy still. Winter Noon. Umberto Saba, *Italian*. STV, *tr. by* John Frederick Nims

That Winter. Ruth Stone. BAP-93

That winter I stopped loving the President. A Suite for Augustus. Rita Dove.

That winter, the dead could not be buried. Leningrad Cemetery, Winter of 1941. Sharon Olds. NIP-4

That with this bright believing band. The Impercipient. Thomas Hardy. EBVV; NAEL-2

That woman still lives at her ranch. Western Civilization. James Galvin. PaTW

That woman there is almost dead. The Rat. W. H. Davies. OBWVE; OxBTC

That woman, vacuum in her mouth. The Great Nebula in Andromeda. Hugh Seidman. AmPA

That won my heart in my greener years. (LL) Green River. William Cullen Bryant. APN-1; NOBA; OxBA

That wondrous man of Cape Horn. (LL) Limerick: "There was an old man of Cape Horn." Edward Lear. CBNP; EBEV; PeLi

That would be waving and that would be crying. Waving Adieu, Adieu, Adieu. Wallace Stevens. NoP-4

That ye may love in spite of beaver hats. (LL) Modern Love. Keats. CBLP; OBNC; SCGP

That Year. Sharon Olds. NMM-2

That year no wondering shepherds came. Christmas, the Year One, A.D. Sara Henderson Hay. PoRA

That year of the cloud, when my marriage failed. River Road. Stanley Kunitz. MoP; NoAM

That year they fought in the snow. Rostov. George Sutherland Fraser. PoWW

That year we hardly slept, waking like inmates. Getting Out. Cleopatra Mathis. SoSe-8

That yellowed body of the Lord. Vladimir Iul'evich Lvov, *Russian*. TCRP, *tr. by* Sarah W. Bliumis

That you allow yourself this vast neglect of me. Sulpicia, *Latin*. OBCVT, *tr. by* Gilbert Sorrentino

That you are you, and I am me? (LL) In former days we'd both agree. Bhartrihari, *Sanskrit*. LoP, *tr. by* John Brough

That you Captain? Sure. Galway Kinnell. *Fr.* The Dead Shall Be Raised Incorruptible. NOBA; PoE

That you moulder where you played. (LL) Last Words To a Dumb Friend. Thomas Hardy. APo; FP; PC

That you two have problems. (LL) Wayman in Love. Tom Wayman. NIP-4; NOBC

That you were gane awa'. (LL) Sweet William's Ghost *or* Sweet William and May Margaret. *Unknown*. AWP; CH; ESPB

That you were once unkind befriends me now. Sonnet 120. Shakespeare. OxAEP-1 *Fr.* Sonnets.

That you'll love me when I'm old. (LL) Will You Love Me When I'm Old? *Unknown*. BLPA; FaBoBe

That your honour's petitioners (dealers in rhymes). To the Right Hon. Henry Pelham. Edward Moore. OBSV

That zephyr every year. Spring Bereaved. William Drummond, of Hawthornden. OBEV

Thatch gate works all right but I never open it. Idle Thoughts. Lu Yu, *Chinese*. CoBCP, *tr. by* Burton Watson

Thatched hut among the pines, door open near a cliff. Inscribed on a Painting. T'ang Yin, *Chinese*. CoBLCP, *tr. by* Jonathan Chaves

Thatched roof rings like heaven where mice, The. Byre. Norman MacCaig. FaBoTC

Thatcher, The. Brendan Kennelly. CIP-2

Thatcher of Thatchwood went to Thatchet a-thatching, A. *Unknown*. OxNR

That's a rich man coming. *Unknown, Tlingit Indian*. STP, *tr. by* James Koller

That's All? Anna Hajnal, *Hungarian*. CEEP; PBWP, *tr. by* Jascha Kessler

That's All. Lawrence Joseph. EOEF; PBCAP

That's All. Mother Goose. ReMoGo

That's all that I remember. (LL) Incident. Countee Cullen. BPo; ChAP; KaS; NAAAL; NAAL-2; NOxBChV; NTCP; NoAM; NoP-4; OBCA; PFE; PoBA; PoPoPo; Poetr; SSLK; VGW

That's enough of that, Mr Bones. *Some* lady you make. John Berryman. NAAL-2; VCAP *Fr.* Dream Songs.

That's genius for you. (LL) A Poem about Intelligence for My Brothers and Sisters. June Jordan. LTA

That's Jack. Jack. Charles Henry Ross. ACTP; NOxBChV; OxBChV; Spl

That's known as Lou. (LL) The Shooting of Dan McGrew. Robert W. Service. EBEvV; EBNV; FaBoBe; PoLF; PoRA; RB; UV

That's me, second from the left. Perpetuum Immobile. Bruce Dawe. CBAP

That's my last Duchess painted on the wall. My Last Duchess [Ferrara]. Robert Browning. AWP; CABP; ClHu; EBNV; EBVV; EBVVPR; EnVR; FHYEP; FaBoPV; GTBS-P; HAP; HeIP-4; HoPM; ImPo; InPK-6; InPS-3; NAEL-2; NIP-4; NOBE; NOBVV; NoP-4; OAEL-2; OBNC; OxBoV; PBMP; PFE; PeVV; PoE; PoEL-5; PoLF; PoPoPo; Poetr; SAGP; SCGP; SCV; SoSe-8; TFi; TRP

That's my topic. How complex, Alhambran arabesques of weather. How the World Works: An Essay. Albert Goldbarth. NAmP90

That's not a man in pain. A Short Lexicon of Torture in the Eighties. Edward Hirsch. VCAP

That's not even it. Recitation. Ellease Southerland. GT

That's not how to love But to drink vodka. Psalm Ajar. Tadeusz Nowak, *Polish*. CEEP, *tr. by* Leonard Kress

That's Our Lot. Moyshe-Leyb Halpern, *Yiddish*. CEEP, *tr. by* Kathryn Hellerstein

That's slowish work, Bob. What'se a-been about? Sam and Bob. William Barnes. PeVV, *tr. by* Hualing Nieh, (*Eclogue*) *Fr.* The Best Man in the Vield.

That's Success! Berton Braley. PoToHe

That's the Cape of Cats ahead. The Cats of St. Nicholas. George Seferis, *Greek*. PC, *tr. by* Edmund Keeley *and* Philip Sherrard

That's the main thing. (LL) Housewife. Anne Sexton. NALW; NMM-2

That's the only image. A Wall. Charles Simic. HCAP

That's the queer life *said the chair*. Chair, Dog, and Clock. Hilary Corke. NYBP

That's the tid i fa la truth. (LL) The Derby Ram. *Unknown*. BoTP; CBNP; NTP; OxNR; ReMoGo

That's the trouble around here. Loose Shoes. Charles Bernstein. FTOS

That's the way for Billy and me. (LL) A Boy's Song. James Hogg. BoTP; CH; CTV; FaPoR; NOxBChV; OBEV; OTCP; OxAEP-2; OxBChV

That's the way it was. (LL) Magic Words. *Unknown, Eskimo*. ImGa; PiM, *tr. by* Edward Field; RaBo; STP

That's to lay me. (LL) Cauld Lad of Hilton, The *or* The Wandering Spectre. *Unknown*. CH; FaBoCh; OxBoLi

That's what I said. (LL) The Song of the Mad Prince. Walter De la Mare. EBEV; FaBoCh; MoP; NOBE; NTP; NoAM; OxAEP-2; OxBChV

That's what I tell him. (LL) What I Tell Him. Simon J. Ortiz. ChAP

That's What It's Like. Mikhail Valentinovich Kulchitsky, *Russian*. "I love Russia." TCRP, *tr. by* Daniel Weissbort

That's what love is like. The whole river. Crossing Over. William Meredith. NoAM

That's what misery is. Poetry Is a Destructive Force. Wallace Stevens. MeMAP; OxBA; RaBo

That's what they ordered. Abishag. Shirley Kaufman. CrSp

That's what we went for, Holly and I. Carnies. Debra Allbery. PBCAP

That's What We'd Do. Mary Mapes Dodge. OBCA

That's what young women are made of. (LL) Natural History. Mother Goose. OxNR; ReMoGo; UV

That's why it has brought you to me! (LL) Fragrance comes from the scent I wear, The. *Unknown.* CoBCP, tr. by Burton Watson

That's why societies usedta throw us away/ or sell us/ or. It's Not so Good to be Born a Girl/ Sometimes. Ntozake Shange. SSLK

That's your freedom—bootleg whiskey. Two Countries. Tadeusz Borowski, *Polish.* AF, tr. by Larry Rafferty, Meryl Natchez *and* Tadeusz Pioro

That's / your son? the brother. A Man's Song, about His Daughter. *Unknown, Eskimo.* STP, tr. by Armand Schwerner

That's your third sneeze now, my good lamp. Argentarius, *Greek.* GrAn, tr. by Fleur Adcock

T'have hit the wavering form, or given this thing a name! (LL) Adam Posed. Anne Finch, Countess of Winchilsea. ChIV-1; ECWP

Thaw. Margaret Avison. FaBoWP; NOBC

Thaw. Edward Thomas. EBEV; FaBoTw; GTBS-P; MoBrPo; NTP; OxAEP-2; OxBSP; OxBTC; Spl

Thawing. Penny Harter. HA

Thawing ice the garbage blooming out of it. Matsuo Allard. HA

Theaitetos. Callimachus, *Greek.* GrAn, tr. by Peter Jay

Theare be great Prince, such as will tell you howe. Samuel Daniel. PBRV *Fr.* Epistle. To Prince Henrie].

Thease stwonen steps a-zet so true. The Stwonen Steps. William Barnes. NOBVV

Th'easie earth that covers her. Robert Herrick. *See* Upon a child.

Theater Impressions. Wislawa Szymborska, *Polish.* VCWP, tr. by Magnus J. Krynski *and* Robert A. Maguire

Theatre. Anne-Marie Albiach, *French.* MFP, tr. by Martin Sorrell

Theatre Hour. Ogden Nash. ImGa

Theatrical Venus. George Buchanan. PNI

Thebaid, The. Publius Papinius Statius, *Latin,*
 Now wretched *Oedipus,* depriv'd of Sight. OBCVT, tr. by Alexander Pope

Thebes. Honestus, *Greek.* GrAn, tr. by Peter Jay

Thebes of the Seven Gates. Sophocles. *Fr.* Antigone. NAWM-1, tr. by Robert Fagles

Th'eclipse and glory of her kind? Sir Henry Wotton. *See* On His Mistress [*or* Mistris], the Queen of Bohemia.

Thee, dear friend, a brother soothes. To Rhea. Ralph Waldo Emerson. APN-1

Thee for my recitative. To a Locomotive in Winter. Walt Whitman. AmPP; GM; InPK-6; MoAmPo; MoP; NAAL-1; NAAL-3; NCAP; NoAM; NoP-4; PoEL-5; Poetr; TAP

Thee, Menelaus, then the blessed Gods. Menelaus wounded. Homer. OBCVT, tr. by William Cowper *Fr.* The Iliad.

Thee Pompey thy past deeds by turns infest. Lucan. OBVE, tr. by Nicholas Rowe *Fr.* Pharsalia.

Thee sets a bell to swinging in my soul. Hildegarde Flanner. *Fr.* Sonnets in Quaker Language. WPE

Thee Shall I Hold. Paulinus of Nola. *See* To Ausonius.

Thee, Sovereign God, our grateful accents praise. The Te Deum. *Unknown, Latin.* AWP, tr. by Dryden

Thee the prompt waiter to a jolly toper / Hous'd in an arbour. Horace. *See* Simplicity.

Thee, Thee, Only Thee. Thomas Moore. GBL; OBNC

Thee too, Achilles, rival of the Gods. Phœnix pleads with Achilles. Homer. OBCVT, tr. by Edward, Earl of Derby *Fr.* The Iliad.

Thee too, modest tressèd maid. Moon. Henry Rowe. OBEV

Thee whilst thee dawning Aurora fro the Ocean hastned. Richard Stanyhurst. PBRV *Fr.* Virgil's Aeneid Book 4.

Thee with all mine eyes. (LL) The Lover to His Lady. Plato, *Greek.* CTC; FaBoEE; NoSic, tr. by George Turberville

Theft of fire, The. Man's worst bargain yet. Palladas, *Greek.* GrAn, tr. by Tony Harrison

Theft's hour—the bus. Late Bus (After a Series of Hold-Ups). Russell Atkins. LTA

Theh Thet Hi Can Wittes Fule-Wis. *Unknown.* HAP

Thei I singe and murthes make. *Unknown.* MiEL

Their adornment for the evening finished now, their bright skin like snow. Tune: "Spring in Jade Pavilion." Li Yü, *Chinese.* SuSp, tr. by Daniel Bryant

Their ancient, glittering eyes, are gay. (LL) Lapis Lazuli. W. B. Yeats. CABP; CMoP; EnlH; FaBoMo; FaBoTw; HeIP-4; InPS-3; LiTM; MoP; NAEL-2; NAWM-2; NOBE; NoAM; NoP-4; OAEL-2; TFi

Their Ardour kindles all the Grecian Pow'rs. Stones and Snow. Homer. OBVE, tr. by Alexander Pope *Fr.* The Iliad.

Their attendant nuns spare the tourists well. Bathing the Aged. Paul Monette. AmPA

Their auburn or black hair, curly hair. Just This. István Vas, *Hungarian.* CEEP, tr. by Jascha Kessler

Their barbarism did not assuage the grief. The Retreat of Ita Cagney. Michael Hartnett. CIP-2; PBCIP

Their bedroom window's open one flight up—. Nocturnal. Sally Ball. BAP-95

Their Behaviour. Dennis Brutus. HBAPE

Their black truck rattled up the dusty hill. The Diviners. Mary Oliver. WPE

Their bodies lined up against the walls. Waiting for Truth. Susan Griffin. GLP

Their bones in one mad dance. (LL) The Horse. Philip Levine. CoAP; VCAP

Their breath smells as sweet as the good old moonshine. (LL) Kentucky Moonshiner. *Unknown.* AS; OBAL

Their calendars are based on rice. Rice. Carol Muske. AmPA

Their cheeks were fresh and tender. Civil Song. Pier Paolo Pasolini, *Italian.* VCWP, tr. by Norman MacAfee *and* Luciano Martinengo

Their colons fed with mucus, brains with lies. Monologue. Gottfried Benn, *German.* AF, tr. by Christopher Middleton

Their Cone-like Cabins. Charles G. Ballard. VoR

Their crowns bare and dripped from their feet. (LL) November. Ted Hughes. CMoP; GTBS-P

Their departures hence and die. (LL) Upon the Loss[e] of His Mistresses. Robert Herrick. BeJo; CaPo; CavPo; NAEL-1; NOSC; PFE; PoE

Their essences of lilies and of roses. (LL) Thoughts after Ruskin. Elma Mitchell. FaBoTC

Their eyelids are drooping, no tears lie beneath. Weavers. Heinrich Heine. TrJP

Their eyes shining, grave with a perfect pleasure. (LL) The Little Dancers. Laurence Binyon. BoTP; CH; MoBrPo; OxBTC

Their faces, safe as an interior. The Middle-Aged. Adrienne Rich. HCAP; PoPoPo

Their father. Tanka. Yosano Tekkan, *Japanese.* MJT, tr. by Makoto Ueda

Their feathers were like white silk. The Birds from the Mountains. Chang Chi, *Chinese.* OHMPC, tr. by Kenneth Rexroth

Their feet on London, their heads in the grey clouds. Whit Monday. Louis MacNeice. ChIV-1; NYBP; OAEL-2; PeECV

Their fingernails and hair continue to grow. The Old. Franz Wright. LCAP-2

Their first hours wore nice costumes. Soucouyant. LeRoy Clarke. HCP

Their forces above three kilometers from our front lines. A Bottle of Suze. Pablo Picasso, *French.* PFTM, tr. by Patricia Leighten

Their garden has a silent tall stone-wall. Caserta Garden. Richard Wilbur. GaP; OBGa

Their ground they stil made good. The Greeks Like Clouds. Homer. OBVE, tr. by George Chapman *Fr.* The Iliad.

Their guilt / is not so very different from ours. Their Behaviour. Dennis Brutus. HBAPE

Their hair, pomaded, faces jaded. Sepia Fashion Show. Maya Angelou. BlSi

Their hands upon their hearts. (LL) Could man be drunk for ever. A. E. Housman. LiTM; NAEL-2; OBMV

Their hats to a queen? (LL) Queen of the Blues. Gwendolyn Brooks. NALW; SeSe

Their heels slapped their bumping mules. Merchants from Cathay. William Rose Benét. MoAmPo

Their Height in Heaven comforts not. Emily Dickinson. APN-2

Their house faces east, is protected by trees. A Storm from the East. Reed Whittemore. NYBP

Their laughter pelting down on us like trash. (LL) At the Movie: Virginia, 1956. Ellen Bryant Voigt. LTA

Their lips upon each other's lips are laid. Speechless [upon the Marriage of Two Deaf and Dumb Persons]. Philip Bourke Marston. EBVV

Their little room grew light with cries. Proper Clay. Mark Van Doren. PoRA

Their Lonely Betters. W. H. Auden. NAEL-2; NoAM; OBGa

Their minds are so frail the least squeak upsets them. Dismissing Progress and Its Progenitors. George Reavey. SPE

Their mockery brought him double force. Blind Samson. William Plomer. PeSA

Their name unknown, their praise unsung. (LL) The Minstrel Responds to Flattery. Sir Walter Scott. OBNC; OxAEP-2

Their necks and their dark heads lifted into a dawn. Loons Mating. David Wagoner. BLT

Their necks make, narrowing the sky. (LL) I Was Sleeping Where the Black Oaks Move. Louise Erdrich. NoP-4; PoPoPo

Their new landlord was a handsome man. On his rounds to collect rent she became. A Deserter. Charles Reznikoff. TRP

Their own children from death? (LL) Never again, Orpheus. Antipater of Sidon, *Greek.* GrAn; PGA, tr. by Kenneth Rexroth

Their Party, Our House. Jon Swan. NYBP

Their Patients. Robert Pinsky. NoAM *Fr.* Essay on Psychiatrists.

Their Philistinism Considered. Robert Pinsky. NoAM *Fr.* Essay on Psychiatrists.

Their ránsom, théir rescue, ánd first, fást, last friénd. (LL)   The Lantern Out of Doors. Gerard Manley Hopkins. CMoP; TrCP

Their ravish'd spirits did possess. (LL)   An Ode, upon a Question Moved, Whether Love Should Continue Forever? Edward Herbert. MeLP; NOBE; OxAEP-1; SeCP

Their relationship consisted. Jamesian. Thom Gunn. PiM

Their rugs are sodden, their heads are down. Gun Teams. Gilbert Frankau. OxBTC

Their scrape and clink together of musical coin. Some Small Shells from the Windward Islands. May Swenson. FYAP

Their sense is with their senses all mixed in. George Meredith. NAEL-2; NoP-4; OAEL-2; SCGP *Fr.* Modern Love.

Their Seriousness, with Further Comparisons. Robert Pinsky. NoAM *Fr.* Essay on Psychiatrists.

Their Sex Life. A. R. Ammons. OBCoV

Their sharpness, ere he is aware. William Cullen Bryant. *See* Thanatopsis.

Their shoulders you shook. The Preacher. Al-Mahdi, *Arabic.* TTY, *tr. by* A. J. Arberry

Their skulls were more beautiful than ours. Avebury. Dorothy Wellesley. WPN

Their spades grafted through the variably-resistant. Geoffrey Hill. PoE *Fr.* Mercian Hymns.

Their spare, fanatic sentry comes. Ants and Others. Adrien Stoutenburg. FYAP; NYBP

Their Speech, Compared with Wisdom and Poetry. Robert Pinsky. NoAM; PoA *Fr.* Essay on Psychiatrists.

Their strong foundations laid by God's right hand! (LL)   The New World. Jones Very. APN-1; PAR

Their Thing. Léon Damas, *French.* NegPo, *tr. by* Ellen Conroy Kennedy

Their Thoughts Cling to Everything They See on the Way. Allen Afterman. NOBAu

Their thoughts conversing with the sky. (LL)   Rumors from an Aeolian Harp. Henry David Thoreau. APN-1; PAR

Their throats glittering like blue sapphire. What Her Girl Friend Said to Her. Maturai Marutaṉ Iḷanākaṉār, *Tamil.* PLW, *tr. by* A. K. Ramanujan

Their time past, pulled down. Burning the Christmas Greens. William Carlos Williams. LiTM; MeMAP; MoP; NAAL-2; NOBA; NoAM

Their tongues are knives, their forks are hands and feet. Riddle. Adrian Mitchell. FaBoEE; GBL; OxBSP

Their voice that cursed. The White sky. Kondō Yoshimi, *Japanese.* MJT, *tr. by* Makoto Ueda

Their voices heard, I stumble suddenly, remembering. One More New Botched Beginning. Stephen Spender. CMoP; NYBP; NoAM

Their Wedded Love. Milton. *See* Unfallen Love.

Theirs is a gesture of sorrow, infinite and taut. Snails. E. D. Blodgett. NOBC

Theirs is the house whose windows—every pane. On the Asylum Road. Charlotte Mew. MoBrPo; VWP

Theirs is yon house that holds the parish poor. The Poor-House. George Crabbe. ECEV *Fr.* The Village.

Thekla's Song. Johann Christoph Friedrich von Schiller. AWP *Fr.* The Piccolomini.

Thelonious Monk dies. 17:II:82. David Meltzer. MoNo; SeSe

Thelonious Sphere Monk. David Henderson. MoNo

Them. Maureen Owen. BAP-94

Them always fair. (LL)   Former Beauties. Thomas Hardy. CBLP; NoAM; OBMV; OBNC

Them and [uz]. Tony Harrison. NoP-4

Them both. (LL)   To Our Blessed Lord upon the Choice of His Sepulchre. Richard Crashaw. ChIV-2; GeHe; NOSC; OAEL-1

Them ez wants, must choose. A Baker's Duzzen uv Wize Sawz. Edward Rowland Sill. FaBoBe

Them Gar'n Town People. *Unknown.* PBCV

Them old Black men. (LL)   Old Black Men Say. James A. Emanuel. MBE

Theme and Variation. Peter De Vries. NYBP

Theme and Variations. "Alta."

"Yr eyes dark and aware." NMM-2

Theme for English B. Langston Hughes. ColAP; FaBoA; HCAP; MoP; NIP-4; NOBA; NoAM; NoP-4; PoPoPo; Poetr; SSLK

Theme no poet gladly sung. Prudence. Ralph Waldo Emerson. OBAL

Theme One: The Variations. August Wilson. PoBA

Themselves, they marry, they raise their kind. (LL)   The Sheep Child. James Dickey. HCAP; MT; MoP; NOBA; NoAM; TAP; VCAP

Then. Nina Cassian, *Romanian.* CEEP, *tr. by* Laura Schiff and Virgil Nemoianu

Then. Diane Glancy. LoHo

Then. Lawrence Joseph. PBCAP

Then. Edwin Muir. CMoP; PoA; PoE

Then. Muriel Rukeyser. GLP; LCAP-2

Then a partridge-shaped cloud over dust storm, *subsel.* Canto 113. Luis Cabalquinto. NYBP *Fr.* Cantos.

Then a ploughman said, Speak to us of Work. On Work. Kahlil Gibran. PoToHe *Fr.* The Prophet.

Then after Eden. New World. Derek Walcott. OxBC

Then all the nations of birds lifted together. The Season of Phantasmal Peace. Derek Walcott. AFr; HCP; PoPoPo; VCWP

Then and Now. Paul Laurence Dunbar. PBMP

Then and Now. Frances Ellen Watkins Harper. PWR

Then and Now. Kapilar, *Tamil.* PLW, *tr. by* A. K. Ramanujan

Then and Now. James Laughlin. PmAP

Then answer no and I, and I and no. (LL)   Nothing but no and I, and I and no. Michael Drayton. GBL; PoEL-2 *Fr.* Idea.

Then are they glad because they be quiet; so he bringeth them unto their desired haven, *sel., vv. 23–30.* Bible, O.T. *See* Psalm 107.

Then, as if he would have sold. Donne. PBRV *Fr.* Satire 4.

Then, at 3 A.M. I see her bend. Intensive Care. Carol Muske. PBCAP

Then blank and gone and still, and utterly lost. (LL)   Yonnondio. Walt Whitman. NAAL-1; NAAL-3

Then, blessing all, "Go, children of my care!" The Triumph of Dullness. Alexander Pope. NOEC *Fr.* Yet, yet a moment, one dim ray of light. NAEL-1; OAEL-1; PoEL-3 *Fr.* The Dunciad.

Then bold Robin Hood to the north he would go.   Robin Hood and the Scotchman. *Unknown.* ESPB

Then both ourselves and seed at once to free. Milton. *Fr.* Book X. FHYEP *Fr.* Paradise Lost.

Then by a sunbeam [*or* sunne-beam] I will climb[e] to thee. (LL)   Mattens. George Herbert. ESCV; SCGP

Then by the bed-side, where the faded moon. Keats. PFE *Fr.* "Eve of St. Agnes."

Then call me traitor if you must. To Certain Critics. Countee Cullen. BPo

Then call your neighbours in. (LL)   Cross Patch / Draw the latch. Mother Goose. OxNR; ReMoGo

Then came fair May, the fairest maid on ground. May. Edmund Spenser. *Fr.* Wood Of Error. AEP

Then came I to the shoreless shore of silence. Prelude XXXIII. Conrad Potter Aiken. OxBA *Fr.* Preludes for Memnon; or, Preludes to Attitude.

Then came jolly Summer, being dight. Summer. Edmund Spenser. *Fr.* Wood Of Error. AEP

Then came the Autumn all in yellow clad. Autumn. Edmund Spenser. *Fr.* Wood Of Error. AEP

Then came the cry of "Call all hands on deck!" Rounding the Horn. John Masefield. MoBrPo *Fr.* Dauber.

Then came the year of fires. The Years. Catherine Davis. FFC

Then cautiously she pushed the cellar door. Edna St. Vincent Millay. *Fr.* Sonnets from an Ungrafted Tree. NALW

Then cease, like these. (LL)   A Cemetery. Emily Dickinson. CMoP; MoAmPo; OxBA

Then cherish pity, lest you drive an angel from your door. (LL)   Holy Thursday [I.] ("'Twas on a Holy Thursday, their innocent faces clean"). William Blake. CH; FHYEP; InPS-3; NAEL-2; NAWM-2; NOBE; NOBRP; NOEC; NOxBChV; NoP-4; OAEL-2; PeECV; PoE; Ro; SCV; TFi; TrCP

Then chiefly lives. (LL)   Virtue [*or* Vertue]. George Herbert. APAD; AWP; CH; ClHu; FMP; FSCP; GeHe; HAP; HeIP-4; InPS-3; MeLP; NAEL-1; NOBE; NOCV; NOSC; NoP-4; OAEL-1; OBEV; OPOU; PFE; PeECV; PoE; PoRA; SCGP; SeCP; SoSe-8; TFi

Then come, dear[e] bridegroom [*or* bridgrome], come away. (LL)   As weary pilgrim, now at rest. Anne Bradstreet. NAAL-1; NAAL-3; PoEL-3; SCAP

Then, crushed by rules, and weakened as refined. Samuel Johnson. EPCY *Fr.* Prologue Spoken by Mr[.] Garrick at the Opening of the Theatre in Drury Lane, 1747. EBEV; EPCY; NAEL-1; NOEC; OxAEP-1

Then dainty Sandys, that hath to English done. Michael Drayton. EPCY *Fr.* To Henry Reynolds, of Poets and Poesy.

Then, day by day, her broidered gown. The Earth in Spring. Judah Halevi, *Hebrew.* TrJP, *tr. by* Edward G. King

Then did he to the throng around. The Kingdom of Heaven Compared to a Grain of Mustard-Seed. Henry Vaughan. ChIV-2

Then do I thinke in deed, that better it is to be private. Sir Philip Sidney. PBRV *Fr.* The Countesse of Pembrokes Arcadia.

Then do what you can. (LL)   Do What You Can. Lawrence Joseph. PBCAP; WWSi

Then Drances, spitefull ev'n to Turnus' Name. Drances in debate. Virgil, *Latin.* OBCVT, *tr. by* Sir Richard Maitland

Then draw your curtains, and begin the dawn. (LL) Aubade: "Lark now leaves his watery [or wat'ry] nest, The." Sir William Davenant. AWP; CH; GBL; MeLP; NOBE; NOSC; OBEV; OxBSP; PoRA; TFi

Then drew near unto him all the publicans and sinners. Bible, *N.T.* NAWM-1 *Fr.* St. Luke.

Then each on a leg or thigh fastens. (LL) On Oxford. Keats. OBCoV; OxAEP-2; PeLV; SCGP

Then earthquakes, nature's agonizing pangs. James Grainger. PBCV *Fr.* The Sugar Cane.

Then, far away, the thudding of the guns. (LL) The Death-Bed. Siegfried Sassoon. AF; LiTM; NSI; PeFWW; PoFWW

Then fire burned my body to a clear shell. A Clear Shell. Frances Bellerby. FaBoWP

Then first he form'd th' immense and solid *Shield*. Vulcan Forges the Shield of Achilles. Homer, *Greek.* OBCVT; OBVE, *tr. by* Alexander Pope *Fr.* The Iliad.

Then first with locks dishevelled and bare. Barnabe Barnes. NoSic *Fr.* Parthenophil and Parthenope.

Then fled, O brethren, the wicked juba. The Ballad of Nat Turner. Robert Earl Hayden. BPo; VGW

Then flit[t] not from this heavenly boy[e]. (LL) New Heaven, New War[re]. Robert Southwell. ChIV-2; ESCV; NOBE; NoP-4

Then for a pardon that he dares admire. Edmund Waller. *See* At Penshurst [Another].

Then for / twelve years. Low Volume. Reiner Kunze, *German.* PoSu, *tr. by* Michael Hamburger

Then formd our Father Jove a third Descent. The Bronze Age. Hesiod, *Greek.* OBCVT, *tr. by* George Chapman

Then forth issued (great goddess) great Dame Nature. Dame Nature. Edmund Spenser. PoEL-1 *Fr.* Wood Of Error. AEP

Then from the bore I was forced to go. (LL) The Whummil Bore. *Unknown.* CH; ESPB

Then from the seas, the dawning gan arise. Henry Howard, Earl of Surrey. PBRV *Fr.* Virgil's Aeneid Book 4.

Then from their poverty they rose. The Ordinary Women. Wallace Stevens. OxBA

Then Frome (a nobler flood) the Muses doth implore. Michael Drayton. NOSC *Fr.* Polyolbion.

Then froze, listening for her steps. (LL) Grandma's Bureau. Robert Morgan. EOEF; WeW-3

Then gan this crafty couple to devise. The Fox and the Ape Go to Court. Edmund Spenser. NoSic *Fr.* Mother Hubbard's Tale.

Then grovelling on the bed, But shall I die. Dido's death. Virgil, *Latin.* OBCVT, *tr. by* Sir Richard Fanshawe

Then halter up this Cur that is so Curst. (LL) The Soul's Groan to Christ for Succo[u]r. Edward Taylor. NAAL-1; NAAL-3; PoEL-3

Then hate me when thou wilt; if ever, now. Sonnet 90. Shakespeare. AWP; EBEV; NOBE; NoSic; OBEV; OxAEP-1; PoEL-2 *Fr.* Sonnets.

Then have I reason to be fond of grief. Shakespeare. *See* What Answer Can I Give?

Then he began again. (LL) Cock Robin got up early. *Unknown.* ACTP; BoTP; OxNR

Then he set off and I began to follow. (LL) The Dark Wood. Dante, *Italian.* BiHa, *tr. by* Seamus Heaney

Then heavenly branches did I see arise. Petrarch. *Fr.* Visions. AWP

Then Herod, when he saw that he had been tricked by the wise men. Matthew 2:16–18. Julia Hartwig. GI *Fr.* St. Matthew.

Then hey nonny nonny, hey nonny, nonny! (LL) The Happy Heart. Thomas Dekker *and others.* CH; GTBS-P; HAP; InPS-3; NoSic; OBEV; RB; SCGP; UnPo

Then Hrothgar's minstrel rehearsed the lay. The Lay of Finn. *Unknown.* AnOE, *tr. by* Charles W. Kennedy *Fr.* Beowulf. OAEL-1, *tr. by* Charles W. Kennedy; ASW, *tr. by* Kevin Crossley-Holland

Then—I am ready to go! (LL) Tie the Strings to my Life, My Lord. Emily Dickinson. PoE; TrCP

Then I answered: Yea. (LL) Passing Away, Saith the World, Passing Away. Christina Rossetti. NoP-4; OAEL-2; OBNC; WPE *Fr.* Old and New Year Ditties.

Then I cried out upon him: Cease. Christina Rossetti. PeVV *Fr.* Despised and Rejected.

Then I said to the elegant ladies. Sappho, *Greek* BoWoP, *tr. by* Willis Barnstone

Then I saw the monkeys—mercy, how unpleasantly / they—smelt! William Makepeace Thackeray. *See* At the Zoo.

Then I Saw What the Calling Was. Muriel Rukeyser. ColAP; FaBoWP

Then I stand up on my hassock and say sing that. Pretext. Stephen Rodefer. PmAP

Then I'll Believe. B. W. Vilakazi, *Zulu.* PeSA, *tr. by* Jack Cope

Then I'll give you half a crown. (LL) Cobbler, cobbler, mend my shoe. Mother Goose. OxNR

Then in requite, sweet virgin, love me! (LL) Diaphenia like the daffadowndilly. Henry Constable. CH; GTBS-P; NOBE; PoEL-2

Then in the smoke. Andrew Crozier. NBrP *Fr.* High Zero.

Then in we went to the garden glorious. The Pastime of Pleasure. Stephen Hawes. OBGa

Then it was dusk in Illinois, the small boy. First Song. Galway Kinnell. LiLi; LiTM; NoP-4; Poetr; TwCP

Then it's a hooraw, and a hooraw. Standin' on the Walls of Zion. *Unknown.* AS

Then it's collar 'im tight. Police Station Ditties. Max Beerbohm. NOBL; PeLV; UV

Then Jesus was led up by the Spirit into the wilderness to be tempted by the devil. Matthew 4:1–11; Then Jesus was led up by the spirit. Czeslaw Milosz. GI *Fr.* St. Matthew.

Then Job answered and said. Not Flesh of Brass. Bible, *O.T.* TrJP *Fr.* Job. NAWM-1

Then Jonson came, instructed from the school. Samuel Johnson. EPCY *Fr.* Prologue Spoken by Mr[.] Garrick at the Opening of the Theatre in Drury Lane, 1747. EBEV; EPCY; NAEL-1; NOEC; OxAEP-1

Then lacked I matter. (LL) Sonnet 86. Shakespeare. CABP; NoSic; OAEL-1; OxAEP-1; SCGP; Son

Then, land!--then, England! oh, the frosty cliffs. Elizabeth Barrett Browning. NAEL-2 *Fr.* Aurora Leigh. VWP

Then Laugh. Bertha Adams Backus. BLPA; PWR; PoToHe

Then lay I lax. Circe. William Gibson. PoA

Then leave old regret. A Moral Poem. James Vincent Cunningham. VGW

Then leave the future to thy sons, / Carolina! (LL) Carolina. Henry Timrod. APN-2; CBCWP

Then Lelex rose, an old experienced man. Ovid. AWP; OBVE, *tr. by* Dryden *Fr.* Philemon and Baucis. CTC, *tr. by* Arthur Golding *Fr.* Metamorphoses.

Then let my Muse for thee this Trophy Raise. (LL) A Satyretericall Character of a Proud Upstart. John Saffin. SCAP

Then let us boast of ancestors no more. Daniel Defoe. OBSV *Fr.* The True-born Englishman.

Then listen Thebes, nurse of Semele. Euripides. OBCVT, *tr. by* Wole Soyinka *Fr.* The Bacchae.

Then live with me[e] and be my Love. (LL) The Passionate Shepherd To His Love. Marlowe. AAS; AEP; APAD; AWP; BoLoP; CABP; CBLP; CTC; ClHu; EBEvV; FaBoBe; GLoP; GTBS-P; HAP; HeIP-4; HoPM; ImPo; inPK-6; InPS-3; NAEL-1; NBLV; NIP-4; NOBE; NoP-4; NoSic; OAEL-1; OBEV; OxAEP-1; PBMP; PBRV; PFE; PoE; PoLF; PoPoPo; PoRA; Poetr; RB; SAGP; SCV; SiPS; TFi; TRP; TTTS; UV; WeW-3

Then live with me and be my love. (LL) Song: "Come, live with me and be my love." C. Day Lewis. BoLoP; NIP-4; OBMV; Poetr

Then loudly cried the bold Sir Bedivere. Tennyson. TOF *Fr.* Morte d'Arthur. EBNV; EBVVPR; FaBoBe; NIP-4; NOBVV; OAEL-2; OBNV; OxAEP-2; PoEL-5 *Fr.* Morte d'Arthur. EnVR

Then love is sin, and let me sinful be. (LL) Sonnet 14: "Alas, have I not pain enough, my friend." Sir Philip Sidney. NoP-4; NoSic; OAEL-1

Then Lytle turned with an oath—By God it's true! (LL) The Oath. Allen Tate. FaBoMo; LiTM; OxBA; VGW

Then Margery [or Marjorie] Milkduck. John Skelton. EBEV; OAEL-1; PoE *Fr.* The Tunnyng of Elynour Rummyng. AAS

Then Martha said to Jesus: "Lord, if you had been here." Christ's Promise. Bible, *N.T.* LBC *Fr.* John, 8.21.

Then might I see upon a white horse set. Sonnet 14. Edmund Spenser. ChIV-2

Then Milton rose up from the heaven of Albion ardorous! William Blake. OAEL-2 *Fr.* Milton.

Then murmured Arthur, 'Place me in the barge'. The Passing of King Arthur. Tennyson. APAD *Fr.* Morte d'Arthur. EBNV; EBVVPR; FaBoBe; NIP-4; NOBVV; OAEL-2; OBNV; OxAEP-2; PoEL-5 *Fr.* Morte d'Arthur. EnVR

Then, must it be. Elizabeth Barrett Browning. NALW *Fr.* Aurora Leigh. VWP

Then must we sleepe one ever-during night. Catullus. *See* Carmen 5 ("My sweetest Lesbia, let us live and love").

Then my old Kentucky home, good night. Stephen Collins Foster. *See* My Old Kentucky Home[, Good Night!].

Then never break your heart when Chloe dies. Alexander Pope. *See* Epistle [II,] to a Lady[: Of the Characters of Women].

Then never break your heart when Cloe dies (LL) C[h]loe. Alexander Pope. AWP; NOBE; OBSV

Then next a merry Woodsman, clad in green. The Green Dryad's Plea. Thomas Hood. *Fr.* The Plea of the Midsummer Fairies. OBNC

Then niest outspak a raucle carlin. Robert Burns. *Fr.* Love and Libery—A Cantata. NOBRP; NOEC

Then night was shaken from me. Boethius, *Latin.* MLL, *tr. by* Helen Waddell *Fr.* Consolation of Philosophy, The ("De Consolacione Philosophie").

Then no doubt it's all for the best. T. S. Eliot. OxBM *Fr.* The Cocktail Party.

Then nobody will buy. (LL) Poem by a Perfectly Furious Academician. Shirley Brooks. NOBVV; PeLV

Then one of the twelve, called Judas Iscariot. Bible, *N.T.* NAWM-1 *Fr.* St. Matthew.

Then pallid death at last will with his icy hand. Beauty's Transitoriness. Christian Hofmann von Hofmannswaldau, *German.* GePo, *tr.* by George C. Schoolfield

Then Pope, as harmony itself exact. William Cowper. EPCY *Fr.* Table Talk.

Then powdered up with *Flegme*, and *Rhume* that's salt. (LL) Nature's Cook. Margaret Lucas Cavendish. BWW

Then powdered up with phlegm, and rheum that's salt. Margaret Lucas Cavendish, Duchess of Newcastle. *See* Nature's Cook.

Then pushed her over the edge into the river. (LL) Traveling Travelling] through the dark I found a deer. William Stafford. CoAP; CoAmPo; ColAP; HeIP-4; InPK-6; LCAP-2; LiTM; NoAM; Poetr; SoSe-8; TRP; WeW-3

Then quick I seized my husband's hand while he stared at / his bride. (LL) In the Museum. Isabella Gardner. NYBP; SoSe-8

Then rising in his Rage above the Shores. River Scamander Attacks Achilles. Homer. OBVE, *tr.* by Alexander Pope *Fr.* The Iliad.

Then rose the King and moved his host by night. Tennyson. PeVV *Fr.* The Passing of Arthur. FHYEP; NAEL-2; OBNC *Fr.* Idylls of the King.

Then said Almitra, Speak to us of Love. Of Love. Kahlil Gibran. PoLF *Fr.* The Prophet.

Then said that royall Pere in sober wise. Edmund Spenser. OAEL-1 *Fr.* Wood Of Error. AEP

Then saith the timid Fay--"Oh, mighty Time!" The Fairy's Reply to Saturn. Thomas Hood. *Fr.* The Plea of the Midsummer Fairies. OBNC

Then Sang Deborah and Barak. Bible, *O.T.* *See* The Song of Deborah.

Then sang Moses and the children of Israel this song. Bible, *O.T.* OBWP *Fr.* Exodus.

Then Saturn thus: "Sweet is the merry lark." The Melodies of Time. Thomas Hood. *Fr.* The Plea of the Midsummer Fairies. OBNC

Then saw they how there hove a dusky barge. Tennyson. *See* The Passing of King Arthur.

Then scorn not the limerick either. Limerick. Robert Conquest. PeLi

Then seek your job with thankfulness and work till further orders. The Glory of the Garden. Rudyard Kipling. *Fr.* The Glory of the Garden. OBGa

Then Sense, I feare, will be a meere dull Foole. (LL) Imagination. Margaret Lucas Cavendish, Duchess of Newcastle. KTR; NOSC

Then shave myself with Uncle's full-dress sabre. (LL) Revised Notes for a Sonnet. "Edward Pygge." BXAP; OBCoV

Then sing, ye Birds, sing, sing a joyous song! Wordsworth. *Fr.* Ode: Intimations of Immortality [from Recollections of Early Childhood]. AWP; FHYEP; HAP; HeIP-4; NOBE; NOBRP; OAEL-2; OBEV; OBNC; PBMP; PoE; PoEL-4

Then sit on the lid and laugh. (LL) Then Laugh. Bertha Adams Backus. BLPA; PWR; PoToHe

Then Sohrab with his sword smote Rustum's helm. Matthew Arnold. OBWP *Fr.* Sohrab and Rustum. EBNV; OBNV

Then sprang up first the golden age, which of itself. Ovid. *See* The Golden Age.

Then sprang up first the golden age, which of itself maintained. The Golden Age. Ovid, *Latin.* NAEL-1, *tr.* by Arthur Golding *Fr.* Metamorphoses.

Then tell, O tell, how thou didst murder [or murther] me. (LL) When thou must home to shades of underground. Thomas Campion. AWP; CABP; EnLoPo; NoSic; OxAEP-1; OxBSP; PoEL-2; PoRA

Then the air was perfect. And his descent. The Parachutist. Jon Anderson. AmPo; NYBP

Then the dreadful night shall break. (LL) A Cradle Song: "Sleep, sleep, beauty bright." William Blake. OBEV; PoLF

Then, the drops were freezing on black branches of ancient ash trees. Rade Drainac. HSix, *tr.* by Charles Simic *Fr.* When the Poet Without Lying Verses in His Heart Returns to His Native Country.

Then the Ermine. Marianne Moore. PoA

Then the golden hour. Length of Moon. Arna Bontemps. LiTM

Then the knee of the wave. "Reclining Figure." Donald Hall. CoAmPo; LCAP-2

Then the long sunlight lying on the sea. The Insusceptibles. Adrienne Rich. CoAmPo; HeIP-4; Son

Then the Lord Answered ("Who is this that darkeneth counsel by words without knowledge?"). Bible, *O.T.* AWP *Fr.* Job. NAWM-1

"Knowest thou the time when the wild goates of the rocke bring forth?" OBVE

"Then the Lord answered Job out of the whirlwind, and sayd." AWP; OBVE

Then the Lord God spoke and said unto Noah. Noah's Flood. Caedmon. AnOE, *tr.* by C. W. Kennedy *Fr.* Genesis.

Then the mailman came and. 9.1.59: II. Pablo Picasso, *French.* CLPP, *tr.* by Paul Blackburn

Then the Master. Henry Wadsworth Longfellow. NAAL-1; NAAL-3 *Fr.* The Building of the Ship.

Then the mighty Lord Maxfield over the mountains fleeth. The Battle of Flodden. *Unknown.* NoSic *Fr.* Scot[t]ish Field[e].

Then the Pharisees went and took counsel how to entangle him in his talk. Matthew 22:15–22. Desanka Maksimovic. GI *Fr.* St. Matthew.

Then the Provost he uprose. William Edmonstoune Aytoun. OBWP *Fr.* Edinburgh after Flodden.

Then the son of Weohstan, stalwart in war. The Funeral Pyre. *Unknown.* AnOE, *tr.* by Charles W. Kennedy *Fr.* Beowulf. OAEL-1, *tr.* by Charles W. Kennedy; ASW, *tr.* by Kevin Crossley-Holland

Then their hearts tasted the full sadness. János Pilinszky. *See* Frankfurt.

Then Thel astonish'd view'd the Worm upon its dewy bed. William Blake. *Fr.* The Book of Thel. NAEL-2; OAEL-2; OBNC; PoE; PoEL-4

Then there is this civilising love of death, by which. Ignorance of Death. William Empson. CMoP; LiTM; NoAM

Then there shall be signs in Heaven. The Fifteen Days of Judgment. Sebastian Evans. NOBVV

Then there were those days on lower Broadway. Margaret Whiting Tearfully Sings. Eleanor Lerman. WeT

Then they paraded Pompey's urn. Jenny Mastoraki, *Modern Greek.* BoWoP; PBWP, *tr.* by Nikos Germanakos

Then thick as locusts black'ning the ground. Carnations and Butterflies. Alexander Pope. NOEC *Fr.* Yet, yet a moment, one dim ray of light. NAEL-1; OAEL-1; PoEL-3 *Fr.* The Dunciad.

Then thou alone kingdoms of hearts shouldst owe. (LL) Sonnet 70. Shakespeare. OxAEP-1; SCGP

Then, though we[e] do[e] not know, we love. (LL) Hymn: "Lord, when the wise men came from far[r]." Sidney Godolphin. BeJo; HAP; MeLP; NOBE; NOCV; NOSC; PBRV; PeECV

Then 'tis at the very best. (LL) When the wind is in the east. Mother Goose. BoTP; FaBoVe; LB; OxNR

Then, to conclude these pleasant acts. Andrew Marvell. CBNP *Fr.* Upon Appleton House [To My Lord Fairfax]. FaBoPV; GeHe; SeCP

Then to sea, boys, and let her go hang! (LL) A Sea Song: "The Master, the swabber, the boatswain and I." Shakespeare. NBLV; NOBL; OBCoV; OxBSP; PFE; PeLV

Then to the bar, all they drew near. Michael Wigglesworth. OBCA *Fr.* The Day of Doom. NAAL-1; SCAP

Then to the poor[e] she freely gives the milk[e]. (LL) Upon Sibilla. Robert Herrick. CaPo

Then to the well-trod stage amon. Mirth and Poetry. Milton. EPCY *Fr.* L'Allegro. AWP; FHYEP; GTBS-P; HAP; HoPM; ImPo; NOSC; NoP-4; OAEL-1; OBEV; PBRV; PoPoPo; TFi

Then to this maxim let us be agreed. First principles of Epicurean physics. Lucretius, *Latin.* OBCVT, *tr.* by John Nott

Then tooke they seate, and forth our passage strooke. Homer. *Fr.* Odyssey. NAWM-1, *tr.* by Robert Fitzgerald

Then Trystan and Gwalchmai went to Arthur. Trystan and Esyllt. *Unknown, Welsh.* OBWVE, *tr.* by Gwyn Jones

Then turn on the music, Marcia. Rock 'n' Roll. Lesley Frost. AiP

Then up I rose, and made no more delay. Elizabeth, Lady Culross Melvill. *Fr.* A Godly Dream. WPE

Then up three winding stairs my feet were brought. Philip Freneau. NAAL-1; NAAL-3 *Fr.* The House of Night.

Then very gently the earth grows a mane, swivels maneuvering its. Bucolic. Aimé Césaire, *French.* VCWP, *tr.* by Clayton Eshleman *and* Annette Smith

Then wake to weep. (LL) Mutability. Shelley. LaPo; NAEL-2; NoP-4; OBNC

Then was I cast from out my state. Frenzy. George Crabbe. NOBE *Fr.* Sir Eustace Grey.

Then was the dinner served, and the Minister prayed for a blessing. Arthur Hugh Clough. PeLV *Fr.* Bothie of Tober-na-Vuolich, The [A Long-Vacation Pastoral].

Then was there heard a most celestial sound. The Rivers Come to the Hall of Proteus for the Marriage of the Thames and the Medway. Edmund Spenser. *Fr.* Wood Of Error. AEP

Then watching the unposed beggars pose. Et Quid Amabo Nisi Quod Aenigma Est. Stephen Sandy. NYBP

Then we all walked under God. God. Boris Abramovich Slutsky, *Russian.* TCRP, *tr.* by J. R. Rowland

Then we stood where we could see. Vachel Lindsay. *Fr.* Bryan, Bryan, Bryan, Bryan. CMoP; MeMAP; OxBA; OxBoLi

Then wear the gold hat, if that will move her. Epitaph from *The Great Gatsby.* F. Scott Fitzgerald. OxBM *Fr.* The Great Gatsby.

Then we'll sing of Lydia Pinkham. Lydia Pinkham. *Unknown.* AS; OBCoV

Then, what do you say to the poem of Mizpah? Dialogue between Father and Daughter. Robert Browning. OBCoV

Then what have I to do with thee? (LL) To Tirzah. William Blake. FHYEP; NAEL-2; NOBE; OAEL-2; Ro

Then, what is life? I cried. (LL) The Triumph of Life. Shelley. NAEL-2; OAEL-2; PoEL-4

Then what is the answer?—Not to be deluded by dreams. The Answer. Robinson Jeffers. CMoP

Then, when I'd seen them leave the bay. And Back. Rodney Bennett. BoTP

Then why do they sneer at me? (LL) The Jew. Isaac Rosenberg. ChIV-1; MoBrPo

Then will thou go and leave me here? Valediction. Sir Robert Ayton. NOSC

Then with my white sails and bad luck. Sibyl. Robert Adamson. BMAP

Then would I make thee read, but to despight thee. (LL) There's nothing grieves me, but that age should haste. Michael Drayton. AAS; NOSC; OAEL-1

Then you will be practically unconscious without positively having / to go. (LL) Thoughts about the Person from Porlock. Stevie Smith. NAEL-2; NoAM; NoP-4

Then, when the child was gone. Empty House. Stephen Spender. NYBP; PCP

Thence forward by that painfull way they pas. Edmund Spenser. OAEL-1 *Fr.* Wood Of Error. AEP

Thence is it, as we all believe. At Cock-crow. Prudentius, *Latin.* MLL, *tr. by* Helen Waddell

Thence passing forth, they shortly do arriue. The Bower of Bliss. Edmund Spenser. OBGa *Fr.* The Bower of Bliss. PoEL-1 *Fr.* Wood Of Error. AEP

Thence passing forth, they shortly do arrive. Edmund Spenser. *See* The Bower of Bliss.

Thence to the gates cast round thine eye, and see. Martial. OBCVT, *tr. by* John Milton *Fr.* Paradise Regain'd.

Thenk, man, of min harde stundes. *Unknown.* MiEL

Thenmy of liff decayer of all kynde. Sir Thomas Wyatt. FaBoVe

Thenne wax I wounder wroth, as I well might. *Unknown.* EnVB *Fr.* Mum and the Sothsegger.

Theocritus. Oscar Wilde. NOBE

Theodor Herzl. Israel Zangwill. TrJP

Theodore and Honoria. Dryden.
　"Spectre, fiercely staring, thus reply'd, The." OxBSn

Theodore and Honoria, From [Fables Ancient and Modern from] Boccace. Dryden.
　Disdain Punished. EBNV; NOSC

Theodore Roethke Foots It. David Chapman Berry. BXAP

Theogenes sent us for Piso's pleasure—. Antipater of Thessalonica, *Greek.* GrAn, *tr. by* Alistair Elliot

Theogony. Hesiod, *Greek.*
　"As Drones, oppressive Habitants of Hives." OBCVT, *tr. by* Thomas Cooke
　Great Father Eating His Children, The. RaBo, *tr. by* Richmond Lattimore

Theology. Ted Hughes. FaBoMo; NAEL-2; NoAM; NoP-4

Theology and a Patchwork Absolute. Heather McPherson. PeNZ

Theology of Bongwi, the Baboon, The. Roy Campbell. PeSA

Theology of Jonathan Edwards, The. Phyllis McGinley. MoAmPo

Theology of Rain. Alfonsas Nyka-Niliunas, *Lithuanian.* CEEP, *tr. by* Jonas Zdanys

Theophia. Edward Benlowes.
　Pleasures of Retirement, The. NOSC

Theophilus Thistledown, the successful thistle sifter. *Unknown.* CTV; OxNR

Theories of Illusion. Maureen Seaton. PUP-20

Theory. Paul Hoover. BAP-93

Theory. David Huddle. CDa

Theory, A. Charles Simic. ChAP

Theory has it the word came first But you always. Nesting of Layer Protocols. Kit Robinson. FTOS

Theory of Climate. Geoffrey O'Brien. PT

Theory of Curve. Christopher Gilbert. LTA

Theory of the Flower, The. Michael Palmer. PT

Ther is noon oother incubus but he. Chaucer. *See* The Wife of Bath's Tale.

Ther once was this ladye from Tyre. Limerick. Tim Hopkins. PeLi

Ther was a knight, a worthy for the chaffre. Portrait of the Pornographer. G. W. Jones. BXAP

Ther was a lady fair an ear. The Kitchie-Boy. *Unknown.* ESPB

Ther[e] was also a Nonne [*or* nun], a Prioress[e]. Madame Eglantine. Chaucer. CTC; NOBE *Fr.* The General Prologue. FHYEP; NAEL-1; NAWM-1; OAEL-1; PoE *Fr.* The Canterbury Tales.

There. Rodney Bennett. BoTP

There. Philip Mead. BMAP

There Actually Stood. Roy Fuller. Son *Fr.* Mythological Sonnets.

There ain' no liars there. In My Father's House. *Unknown.* AS

There all the golden codgers lay. News for the Delphic Oracle. W. B. Yeats. CMoP; FaBoMo; LiTM; NoAM

There also stand a num'rous band. Michael Wigglesworth. ColAP *Fr.* The Day of Doom.

There also was a nun, a Prioress. Chaucer. *See* Madame Eglantine.

There always is a noise when it is dark! In the Night. James Stephens. OBMV

There ance was a may, and she lo'ed na men. Lady Grisel Baillie. *See* Werena My Heart Licht I Wad Dee.

There are abandoned corners of our Exile. The Mathmid. Hayyim Nahman Bialik, *Hebrew.* AWP, *tr. by* Maurice Samuel

There are actually people who revel. Nikolai Ivanovich Glazkov, *Russian.* TCRP, *tr. by* Daniel Weissbort

There are all kinds of men. A Thank You for Friends. Rodney Bennett. BoTP

There are always, in each of us. Emigration. Eleanor Wilner. NMM-2

There are always the poor. Soliloquy at Potsdam. Peter Porter. NOBAu

There are artifacts from every period here. A Tour of Ein Kerem. David Curzon. GI

There Are Bad Times Just around the Corner. Noël Coward. NOBL

There Are Big Waves. Eleanor Farjeon. BoTP

There Are Black. Jimmy Santiago Baca. InPS-3
　("There are black guards slamming cell gates.") LTA

There are black guards slamming cell gates. Jimmy Santiago Baca. *See* There Are Black.

There are blows in life so violent—Don't ask em! The Black Riders. César Vallejo, *Spanish.* RaBo, *tr. by* Robert Bly

There are bog-people in the foundations. The Foundations. Jennifer Maiden. BMAP

There are brightest apples on those trees. The Fertile Muck. Irving Layton. NOBC; NoAM

There are cats (not he). Joachim Du Bellay. PC, *tr. by* Felicity Bast *Fr.* Epitaph For Belaud.

There are caverns / under our feet. Shirley Kaufman. BoWoP

There are cemeteries that are lonely. Nothing but Death. Pablo Neruda, *Spanish.* SPE, *tr. by* Robert Bly

There are certain brisk people among us today. Profiteers. Jessie Pope. NSI

There are certain ladies in our land. Fortitude. Noël Coward. LBC

There are christs spiked against trees. There Is Life. Breyten Breytenbach, *Afrikaans.* VCWP, *tr. by* Breyten Breytenbach

There are days I have to pretend. First Person—1981. D. F. Brown. CDa

There are days when the dead will have nothing to do with us. Tending the Graves. Jennifer Strauss. NOBAu

There are dealers in pictures named Agnew. Tom Agnew, Bill Agnew. D. G. Rossetti. FaBoEE

There Are Different Gardens. Carl Sandburg. ImGa

There are different ways of dying without. After the Revolution. Marilyn Hacker. AmPA

There are exact arrangements. Mimikòs. Luigi Fontanella, *Italian.* NeIt, *tr. by* Michael Palma

There are fairies at the bottom of our garden! Fairies. Rose Fyleman. OxBChV

There are few of us now, soon. For Eli Jacobson. Kenneth Rexroth. RaBo

There are flowers of Zait in the garden. *Unknown, Egyptian hieroglyphics into Italian.* BoWoP; PBWP, *tr. by* Boris de Rachewiltz; *English vers. by* Ezra Pound *and* Noel Stock

There are four Graces. Beside the original three. A Statue of Bereniké. Callimachus, *Greek.* GrAn, *tr. by* Peter Jay

There are four Graces, two Aphrodites, ten Muses. *Unknown, Greek.* GrAn, *tr. by* Peter Jay

There are four men mowing down by the Isar. A Youth Mowing. D. H. Lawrence. InPK-6; MoBrPo; NoAM

There are four officers, this message says. Escape. Edmund Blunden. NSI

There are four paths. Four Paths. Nikolai Ivanovich Glazkov, *Russian.* TCRP, *tr. by* Daniel Weissbort

There are four vibrators, the world's exactest clocks. Four Quartz Crystal Clocks. Marianne Moore. AmPP; TwCP

There Are Gains for All Our Losses. Never Again. Richard Henry Stoddard. PWR

There are great puddles of blood on the world. Song in the Blood. Jacques Prévert, *French.* AF, *tr. by* Lawrence Ferlinghetti

There are hearts— stout hearts—that own no fear. The Surgeon's Knife. Eliza Cook. VWP

There are hermit souls that live withdrawn. The House by the Side of the Road. Sam Walter Foss. BLPA; FaBoBe

There are (I scarce can think it, but [I] am told). The First Satire of the Second Book of Horace [Imitated]. Alexander Pope. OAEL-1

There are in Paradise. The Shepherd Who Stayed. Theodosia Pickering Garrison. PChr

There are just so many years. Turning Pro. Ishmael Reed. SoSe-8

There are lonely cemeteries. Pablo Neruda. *See* Nothing but Death.

There are lovers who recall that. Part of the Forest. George Oppen. FTOS

There are loyal hearts, there are spirits brave. Life's Mirror. "Madeline Bridges." BLPA; FaBoBe; PWR; PoToHe

There are many and more. Many and More. Maya Angelou. LW

There are many dead in the brutish desert. First Elegy for the Dead in Cyrenaica. Hamish Henderson. OxBS (End of a Campaign.) PoWW

There are many like him there—unsymbolled heap. A Grave in Ukraine. Saul Tchernichowsky, *Hebrew.* TrJP, tr. by L. V. Snowman

There are many monsters that a glassen surface. The Octopus. James Merrill. APo; CoAP

There are many more Good Fridays. Unkept Good Fridays. Thomas Hardy. GI

There are many sounds which are neither music nor voice. The Ear. Louis MacNeice. OxBSP

There are many things. There Are Many Things I Want to Tell You. Indran Amirthanayagam. OpBo

There are many things I love to hear. Rhapsodies. Judy Turner. CTV

There Are Many Things I Want to Tell You. Indran Amirthanayagam. OpBo

There are many tonight and the rink. Skaters. Vern Rutsala. CMAP

There are many Washingtons. Which Washington? Eve Merriam. NTCP

There are many ways to die. History among the Rocks. Robert Penn Warren. CBCWP; MoAmPo *Fr.* Kentucky Mountain Farm.

There are many who say that a dog has his day. The Song of the Mischievous Dog. Dylan Thomas. OBCoV

There are many who think of Quintia in terms of beauty. Catullus. *See* De Quintia et Lesbia.

There are many winding rivers. Winding Sand. Naresh Guha, *Bengali.* OMIP, tr. by Lila Ray

There are men making death together in the wood. The Delta. Michael Dennis Browne. NYBP

There are more visionaries. Against the Transcendentalists. Muriel Spark. FaBoTC

There are nights as soft as fur on a foal. Watching Shoah in a Hotel Room in America. Adam Zagajewski, *Polish.* VCWP, tr. by Renata Gorczynski, Benjamin Ivry, *and* C. K. Williams

There are nights with no name. Léon Damas, *French.* NegPo, tr. by Ellen Conroy Kennedy

There are no accidents, or so. What Could Hold Us. Heather McHugh. NIP-4

There are no angels yet. Gabriel. Adrienne Rich. VGW

There are no crosses. A Death in the Desert. Charles Tomlinson. CABP

There are no handles upon a language. Languages. Carl Sandburg. ColAP

There are no more shopping days to Christmas. Eve. Howard Nemerov. CRP

There are no nightmares now. Only when memory settles. Seravezza. Hoyt W. Fuller. PoBA

There Are No People Song. *Navajo Oral Tradition.* TTTS

There are no roads but the frost. Old Age Compensation. James Wright. NNaP

There are no rocks. Geography: a Song. Howard Moss. OBCoV

There are no signs. The sky is entirely bland. Augury. W. H. Oliver. PeNZ

There are no simple explanations. No Simple Explanations. Jayne Cortez. GT

There are no small ones. Puritans. Elaine Equi. PmAP

There are no stars to-night. My Grandmother's Love Letters. Hart Crane. CMoP; FaBoBe; InPK-6; NOBA; NoAM; NoP-4; Poetr

There Are No Such Trees in Alpine, California. John Haines. PaTW; WeT

There are no trenches dug in the park, not yet. Nightmare at Noon. Stephen Vincent Benét. OxBA

There are no words here. The Hooded Legion. Gerald McCarthy. CDa

There are notes to lightning in my bedroom. Star Quilt. Roberta Hill Whiteman. CDW; NoAM

There are of course tho' we don't see them. Postscripts 2. Dennis Brutus. HBAPE

There are old drunks among the tenements. The Griots Who Know Brer Fox. Colleen J. McElroy. NAAAL

There are on the earth 50,000 dead whom no one mourned. Fourth Poem of a Canto of Accusation. Costa Andrade, *Portuguese.* PBMAP

There are only two things now. New Year's Eve. D. H. Lawrence. BoLoP

There are palm trees in my homeland. Antônio Gonçalves Dias. TTY, tr. by Frances Ellen Buckland *Fr.* Song of Exile.

There are people, I know, to be found. Drinking Song. James Kenneth Stephen. NOBL; PeLV

"There are people so dumb," my father said. Plain Talk. William Jay Smith. MoAmPo

There are people who know how to love. Poem of Explanations. Dahlia Ravikovitch, *Hebrew.* IP, tr. by Warren Bargad *and* Stanley F. Chyet

There are perfect illustrations. Yury Pavlovich Odarchenko, *Russian.* TCRP, tr. by Albert C. Todd.

There are, perhaps, whom passion gives a grace. The Aged Lover Discourses in the Flat Style. James Vincent Cunningham. NoAM

There are pines that are tall enough. An Elegy Is Preparing Itself. Donald Justice. CRP; HoPM

There are portraits and still-lifes. Paring the Apple. Charles Tomlinson. CMoP; OxBTC; PoE; TRP

There are quays here. Honolulu. Robert Mazzocco. WWSi

There are rapists / out there. Solea. Jessica Hagedorn. WWSi

There are records. Do not. Buying a Record. Robert Peters. BXAP

There are ribald interventions. Palinode. "Ern Malley." BMAP

There are rock-rooted ranges to dominate. Rex Ingamells. CBAP *Fr.* Memory of Hills.

There Are Roughly Zones. Robert Frost. CMoP

There are rows of bottles against the glass;. Small-town Gladys. David Campbell. BMAP

There are sea and sky about me. Midnight. Louisa Sarah Bevington. PEW

There are seeds within the tide. City. Joseph Bruchac. CDW

There are seventy times seven kinds of loving. Veterans. George Johnston. NOBC

There are sixteen lang miles, I'm sure. The Bent Sae Brown. *Unknown.* ESPB

There are so many lies in nature. Degas. Paul Monette. AmPA

There are so many things I want to say to you. My Nightingale. Boris Petrovich Kornilov, *Russian.* TCRP, tr. by Bernard Meares

There are so many things to do to-day. Every Day. Mary I. Osborn. BoTP

There are some birds in these valleys. The Decoys. W. H. Auden. CMoP; PoE

There are some days the happy ocean lies. Seascape. Stephen Spender. NoP-4

There are some hands so beautiful, so soft. The Red Cross. Mộng Tuyết, *Vietnamese.* AVP, tr. by Huỳnh Sanh Thông

There are some heights in Wessex, shaped as if by a kindly hand. Wessex Heights. Thomas Hardy. CMoP; EBVV; OAEL-2; OBNC; PoEL-5; SCGP

There Are Some Lusty Voices Singing. Geoffrey Lehmann. *Fr.* Ross's Poems. CBAP

There are some qualities—some incorporate things. Silence. Edgar Allan Poe. APN-1; ColAP; GSo; MeMAP; NCAP; NOBA; PAR

There are some questions one should know by heart. Postscript. Henri Coulette. DiPo

There are some quiet crossings in his city. Water Color. Stephen Mooney. NYBP

There are some / secrets. July 31. Norman Jordan. PoBA

There are spaces. Old Maps and New. Norman MacCaig. OxBC

There are spaces we cannot reach. Valentine. Wendy Mulford. NBrP

There are strange hells within the minds war made. Strange Hells. Ivor Gurney. OxBTC; PeFWW

There are strange things done in the midnight sun. The Cremation of Sam McGee. Robert W. Service. ChAP; NOBC; OBCoV; OBNV; PoLF; SAGP

There are strange trees in that pale field. The Forest of the Dead. James Griffyth Fairfax. NSI; PoWW

There are sunsets who whisper a good-by. Sunsets. Carl Sandburg. MoAmPo

There are the Alps. What is there to say about them? On the Fly-Leaf of Pound's Cantos. Basil Bunting. FaBoTw; NoAM; OxBTC

There are the fair-limbed nymphs o' the woods. Leigh Hunt. OBNC *Fr.* The Nymphs.

There are things best not set down in books. The Road to Patmos. John Ennis. PBCIP

There are things I don't tell her. Photo in the Locket. Jackie Kay. CPO

There are things to be said. No doubt. Cid Corman. VGW

There are things tonight I've never known. Hilo: First Night Back. Garrett Kaoru Hongo. LoL

There are things you have words for. Two Words; a Wedding. B. P. Nichol. NOBC

There are thirteen months in all the year. Robin Hood and the Three Squires. *Unknown.* EnSB

There are those fish that swim ever in the dim. Pearl Perch. John Blight. CBAP

There are those to whom place is unimportant. The Rose. Theodore Roethke. NOBA; NYBP; TRP

There are those to whom place is unimportant. The Rose. Theodore Roethke. NOBA; NYBP; TRP *Fr.* North American Sequence.

There are those who think. Prologue from "Legacy." Patricia Parker. GLP

There are thow who grow. A Knocker. Zbigniew Herbert, *Polish.* PoSu, *tr. by* Czeslaw Milosz

There are three plenties. The Fort of Ard Ruide. *Unknown.* NOIV

There are three preachers, ever preaching. The Three Preachers. Charles MacKay. EBVV

There are three ranks of men, three grades of things. Three Ranks of Men, Three Grades of Things. Nguyễn Bỉnh Khiêm, *Vietnamese.* AVP, *tr. by* Huỳnh Sanh Thông

There are three valleys where the warm sun lingers. The Long Harbour. Mary Ursula Bethell. PeNZ

There are three who await my death. *Unknown, Irish.* NOIV, *tr. by* Thomas Kinsella

There are times for dreaming. The Hours. David Diop, *French.* NegPo, *tr. by* Ellen Conroy Kennedy

There are times in life when one does the right thing. Ellen Bass. MDDM

There are times in one's life which one cannot forget. Mr. Billings of Louisville. Eugene Field. NBLV

There are times when everything I touch. Once You've Been to War. Walter McDonald. CDa

There are times when their faith in gods. Jack A. Mapanje. HBAPE *Fr.* Florrie Abraham's Witness.

There are too many poems. Cat. Kenneth Rexroth. *Fr.* A Bestiary. OBAL

There are too many waterfalls here; the crowded streams. Questions of Travel. Elizabeth Bishop. ColAP; NAAL-2; NOBA

There are truths you Americans need to be told. James Russell Lowell. OBSV *Fr.* A Fable for Critics. NAAL-1; NAAL-3

There are twelve months in all the year. Robin Hood Rescuing Three Squires. *Unknown.* ESPB; NAEL-1

There are twelve months throughout the year. September. Mary Howitt. BoTP

There are two angels, messengers of light. Peace and Love. Ella Wheeler Wilcox. PWR

There are two bends in the road, and an unexpected dip. Pont y Caniedydd. Alun Llywelyn-Williams, *Welsh.* OBWVE, *tr. by* Joseph R. Clancy

There are two births: The one when light. William Cartwright. *See* To Chloe, Who Wished Herself Young Enough for Me.

There are two extremes of love. One Night Stand. Kenward Elmslie. FTOS

There are two kinds of people on earth today. Lifting and Leaning. Ella Wheeler Wilcox. BLPA; PoToHe

There are two Mays. Emily Dickinson. NOBA

There are two men. Two Men. Andrew Lansdown. NOBAu

There are / two methods. In the Case of Lobsters. Petra von Morstein, *German.* BoWoP, *tr. by* Rosemarie Waldrop

There are two miseries in human life. Walter Savage Landor. FaBoEE

There are voices, voices. Light's dying. Birds have quit. John Berryman. CAPP-1 *Fr.* Dream Songs.

There are waste-paper baskets at the gate. (LL) High Wood. Philip Johnstone. NSI; PoFWW

There are ways to get rich: Find an old corporation. The One Day. Donald Hall. AFr

There are, who to my person pay their court. An Epistle to Dr Arbuthnot. Alexander Pope. FP *Fr.* Epistle to Dr. Arbuthnot. FHYEP; InPS-3; NoP-4; OAEL-1; OxAEP-1; PoE; PoEL-3; TFi

There are wolves in the next room waiting. The Wolves. Allen Tate. LiTM; NOBA; OxBA; PoA

There are women locked in my joints. I Walk in the History of My People. "Chrystos." UnSA

There are words like *Freedom.* Words Like Freedom. Langston Hughes. BPo

There are words that can only be said on paper. Words. Robert Finch. PoA

There are words that refuse me. Prayer. Patricia Jones. WWSi

There are youngsters now. Furniture. Phyllis Beauvais. NYBP

There arent. Untitled Requiem for Tomorrow. Conyus. PoBA

There aren't many. Inventory of Places Propitious for Love. Angel González, *Spanish.* VCWP, *tr. by* Steven Ford Brown *and* Revuelta Gutierrez

There, at no cost, on onions, rank and red. The Sallad. Virgil, *Latin.* OBCVT, *tr. by* William Cowper

There at the watershed I turned. Ba Cottage. Andrew Young. OxBSP

There be none of Beauty's daughters. Stanzas for Music. Byron. AWP; CBLP; GTBS-P; HAP; LaPo; NAEL-2; OAEL-2; PoRA

There be some sports are painful, and their labor. Shakespeare. *Fr.* The Tempest. OAEL-1

There be three Badgers on a mossy stone. The Three Badgers. "Lewis Carroll." CBNP *Fr.* Sylvie and Bruno.

There be three hundred different ways and more. Tears. "Owen Meredith." EBVV *Fr.* Glenaveril.

There be three things seeking my death. Prayer for the Speedy End of Three Great Misfortunes. *Unknown, Irish.* OBMV, *tr. by* Frank O'Connor

There be who say, in these enlightened days. Byron. EPCY *Fr.* English Bards and Scotch Reviewers.

There between the riverbank. Angel. Brad Leithauser. DiPo; FYAP

There blooms no bud in May. Walter De la Mare. MoBrPo

There blows a cold wind today, today. *Unknown.* MiEL

There by some wrinkled stones round a leafless tree. The Twelve. Allen Tate. ChIV-2

There, by the curb. Oil Slick. Judith Thurman. SSCS

There calleth me ever a marvelous horn. Home-Sickness. Justinus Kerner, *German.* AWP, *tr. by* James Clarence Mangan

There came a bird out o' a bush. Lady Isabel and the Elf-Knight. *Unknown.* ESPB

There came a Day at Summer's full. Renunciation. Emily Dickinson. APN-2; MoAmPo; NAAL-1; NAAL-3; NOBA

There came a dove, an Easter dove. My Easter Dove. Henrietta Cordelia Ray. CBWP-3

There came a ghost to Margret's door. Sweet William's Ghost *or* Sweet William and May Margaret. *Unknown.* AWP; CH; ESPB

There came a knocking at the front door. A Person from Porlock. Ronald Stuart Thomas. TOF

There came a man across the moor. Master and Guest. Mary Elizabeth Coleridge. VWP

There came a whisper from the night to me. God's Remembrance. Francis Ledwidge. TIRV

There came a Wind like a Bugle. Emily Dickinson. APN-2; CMoP; MeMAP; NAAL-1; NAAL-3; NAWM-2; NOBA; OxBA; PAR; RB; SAmP

There came an old woman from France. The Old Woman from France. *Unknown.* ReMoGo

There came from Normandy an old. The Two Lovers. Marie de France. BoWoP, *tr. by* Patricia Terry

There came gray stretches of volcanic plains. In Death Valley. Edwin Markham. APAD; APN-2; PaTW

There came this bright young thing. As for the Quince. Nuala Ni Dhomhnaill, *Irish.* BiHa; CIP-2; PBCIP, *tr. by* Paul Muldoon

There can be no songs for dead children. Kindertotenlieder. Michael Longley. CIP-2

There Ceres, distant from the powers divine. *Unknown.* OBCVT, *tr. by* Richard Hole *Fr.* Hymn to Demeter.

There chanced to be a pedlar bold. The Bold Pedlar and Robin Hood. *Unknown.* AmFP; ESPB

There chanced to meet together in an inn. Epigram. John Taylor. NOSC

There Charon stands, who rules the dreary Coast. Charon. Virgil. OBVE, *tr. by* John Dryden *Fr.* The Aeneid [*or* Eneados, *Aeneis*].

There come to me. Pause. Octavio Paz, *Spanish.* STV, *tr. by* John Frederick Nims

There comes a little space between the south. Depression in Winter. Jane Kenyon. LoL

There comes a moment in her veins. More Lovely than Antiquity. Witter Bynner. NoP-4

There comes a moment when to believe is not enough. Action. James Oppenheim. TrJP

There Comes a Time. Ella Wheeler Wilcox. PWR

There comes a time when everything is laced. The Imagination of Necessity. Andrei Codrescu. SPE

There comes an hour when begging stops. Emily Dickinson. NCAP

There comes Emerson first, whose rich words, every one. Emerson. James Russell Lowell. APN-1; AmPP; NCAP; NOBA; OxBA; PAR; TAP *Fr.* A Fable for Critics. NAAL-1; NAAL-3

There comes Poe, with his raven, like Barnaby Rudge. James Russell Lowell. OBCoV *Fr.* Poe and Longfellow. AmPP; OxBA; PAR *Fr.* A Fable for Critics. NAAL-1; NAAL-3

There comes time I call my bonny. Clinton. Sterling Plumpp. BkSV

There died a myriad. Ezra Pound. MoAmPo; NOBE; PoE; TRP *Fr.* Hugh Selwyn Mauberley. (Life and Contacts). AmPP; CMoP; InPS-3; LiTM; NOBA; NoAM; TAP

There dwelt a fair maid in the West. James Harris (The Daemon Lover). *Unknown.* ESPB

There dwelt a man in fair[e] Westmoreland [*or* Westmerland]. Johnie Armstrong. *Unknown.* ESPB; HoPM

There dwelt an old woman at Exeter. The Woman of Exeter. *Unknown.* ReMoGo

There exist rebels, strange possession joined a conspiracy and in question. Continuous Thunder. Aaron Shurin. PT

There existed a person, not a woman or a boy, being in the first part of life. The Semantic Limerick According to Dr. Johnson's Dictionary (Edition of 1765). Gavin Ewart. OBCoV

There existed an adult male person who had lived a relatively short time. The Semantic Limerick According to the Shorter Oxford English Dictionary (1933). Gavin Ewart. OBCoV

There exists no proof as. Edmund Clerihew Bentley. NOBL   *Fr.* Clerihews.

There fared a mother driven forth. The House of Christmas. G. K. Chesterton. MoBrPo

There Faunus and Sylvanus keep their courts. Sir John Denham. *Fr.* Cooper's Hill. BeJo; CABP; PBRV; SeCP

There fell red rain of spears athwart the sky. Last Judgment. John Gould Fletcher. AWP

There float away. During the rainy season. Miya Shūji, *Japanese.* MJT, *tr. by* Makoto Ueda

There flourished once a potentate. The King of Yvetot. Pierre Jean de Béranger, *French.* AWP, *tr. by* William Toynbee

There gather *Flowers* that are *newly-blowne.* (LL) 'Poet I am neither born, nor bred," A. Margaret Cavendish. KTR

There go Adem and Eve—I see. Poems from Subway to Work. Peter Orlovsky. CLPP

There go the grownups. A Lazy Thought. Eve Merriam. SSCS

There God is dwelling too. (LL) The Divine Image ("To Mercy, Pity, Peace and Love"). William Blake. APAD; BoTP; ChAP; FHYEP; NAEL-2; NOBE; NOBRP; NOEC; NoP-4; OAEL-2; OBNC; PeECV; PoE; PoEL-4; Ro

There goes the grandson, run off to the beach! The Grandson. James Scully. NYBP

There goes the Wapiti. The Wapiti. Ogden Nash. TLR

There, good night, darling! now, I fain would sleep. (LL) Crazed. Mary E. Tucker. RACG

There grew a goodly tree him faire beside. Balme. Edmund Spenser. CH *Fr.* Wood Of Error. AEP

There grew two olives, closest of the grove. Homer. OBVE, *tr. by* Pope *Fr.* Odyssey. NAWM-1, *tr. by* Robert Fitzgerald

There grows no rootless flower. The First Reader. Winfield Townley Scott. PoA

There grows one in the human brain. (LL) The Human Abstract. William Blake. FHYEP; NAEL-2; NOBRP; NOEC; OAEL-2; OxAEP-2; PoE; PoEL-4; Ro

There had been rain in the morning and a chaffinch. All Possession Is Theft. Lauris Edmond. PeNZ

There had been years of Passion—scorching, cold. And There Was a Great Calm. Thomas Hardy. CMoP; LiTM; OAEL-2

There has been. To W. C. W. M. D. Alfred Kreymborg. PoA

There has been a light snow. In a Train. Robert Bly. TTTS

There has been an accident. Reporting Back. Jo McDougall. EC2

There has been no change. Autumn. Princess Shikishi, *Japanese.* PBWP, *tr. by* Hiroaki Sato

There has to be a jail where ladies go. There Has to Be a Jail for Ladies. Thomas Merton. VGW

There have been plates but no appetite. The Museum. Wislawa Szymborska, *Polish.* PoSu, *tr. by* Magnus F. Krynski

There have been poets that in verse display. To Wordsworth. Hartley Coleridge. Son

There have been times when I have looked at life. Vision. Elizabeth N. Hauer. PoToHe

There have been times when I well might have passed and the ending have come. Thomas Hardy. OAEL-2 *Fr.* In Tenebris. NOBE

There have been times when on a city street. On City Streets. Margaret E. Bruner. PoToHe

There he is, Mars rising, a purulent red dot. For Thomas Stearns Eliot on the Occasion of His One Hundredth Birthday. Thomas Rabbitt. NAmP90

There he moved, cropping the grass at the purple canyon's lip. The Horse Thief. William Rose Benét. MoAmPo

There he stood. Lyric Poem. Semyon Isaakovich Kirsanov, *Russian.* TCRP, *tr. by* April FitzLyon

There he stood, quite suddenly. Gauguin's White Horse. Vicki Hearne. GS

There he was—having spent. "Yes, But. . . ." Theodore Weiss. TAP

There I Am Again. Lawrence Joseph. WWSi

There I could never be a boy. Poem. Frank O'Hara. NNaP

There I learned how faces fall apart. Epilogue. "Anna Andreyevna Akhmatova." *Fr.* Requiem 1935-1940. BoWoP, *tr. by* Richard McKane

There I was sitting on one leg. Daniil Kharms, *Russian.* TCRP, *tr. by* Bradley Jordan

There, I was so interested to hear about it. (LL) The Horse Show. William Carlos Williams. CMoP; FiLi; NOBA; TAP; VGW

There in Fiesole it was always fresh. Basil. Gibbons Ruark. MT

There, in some place, some time. Georgy Adamovich, *Russian.* TCRP, *tr. by* Yakov Hornstein

There, in that bed so closely curtained round. Written in a Sick Chamber. Samuel Rogers. NOBRP

There in the bracken was the ominous spoor mark. The Tantanoola Tiger. Max Harris. MoBS

There, in the corner, staring at his drink. Docker. Seamus Heaney. HeIP-4; IIP; MoP; NOIV; Poetr

There in the flower garden. *Unknown, Spanish.* BoWoP, *tr. by* Willis Barnstone

There in the fragrant pines and the cedars dusk and dim. (LL) Spring. Walt Whitman. APN-1; AWP; AmPP; CBCWP; ColAP; HAP; MeMAP; MoAmPo; NAAL-1; NAAL-3; NCAP; NOBA; NoP-4; OxBA; PAR; PoEL-5; PoPoPo; PoRA; SAmP; TAP; TFi

There in the hard light. An Irish Lake. William Robert Rodgers. BIrV

There, in the market, with Mrs. Peters. Journal of the Storm. Greg Kuzma. AmPA

There, in the very middle. Mothers. Auvaiyar, *Tamil.* PLW, *tr. by* A. K. Ramanujan

There Is. Louis Simpson. CoAmPo

There is a bar I go to when I'm in Chicago. A Story. Susan Mitchell. WWSi

There is a bareness in the images. Substance and Shadow. John Hewitt. PNI

There is a big artist named Val. D. G. Rossetti. FaBoEE; PeLi

There is a bird bath on our grass. The Bird Bath. Florence Hoatson. BoTP

There is a bird in the poplars. Metric Figure. William Carlos Williams. MoAmPo

There is a blue sky. A Song. Edward Dorn. CoAmPo

There is a boat on the lake to float on. Blarney castle. Francis Sylvester Mahony. IIP

There is a brook in the mountains. A Mountain Spring. Ch'u Ch'uang I, *Chinese.* OHMPC, *tr. by* Kenneth Rexroth

There is a camp upon a rounded hill. Soldiers in a Small Camp. Walter James Turner. NSI

There is a certain triviality in living here. The Mysterious Maps. Mark Strand. BAP-94

There is a change—and I am poor. A Complaint. Wordsworth. NOBE; PoEL-4; Ro

There is a charm in solitude that cheers. Solitude. John Clare. NOBVV; OxBSP

There is a Charm no vulgar mind can reach. On the Luxembourg Gallery. Washington Allston. APN-1

There Is a Charming Land. Adam Oehlenschläger, *Danish.* AWP, *tr. by* Robert Hillyer

There Is a City. "The Jewish Sibyl." TrJP, *tr. by* Bohn *Fr.* The Fourth Book of Sibylline Oracles.

There is a coal-black Angel. The Swamp Angel. Herman Melville. APN-2

There is a creator named God. On the Painter Val Prinsep. D. G. Rossetti. FaBoEE

There is a creature called God. Limerick. D. G. Rossetti. PeLi

There is a crying in the world. End of the World. Else Lasker-Schüler, *German.* BoWoP, *tr. by* Willis Barnstone *and* Michael Gillespie

There is a dark planet striking against us. Invisible. The Dark Planet. John Heath-Stubbs. OAEL-2

There is a dark tolling in the air. Scattering Flowers. George Hitchcock. CDa

There is a day, a dreadful day. Song—Last Day. John Clare. EnVR

There is a deep brooding. My Arkansas. Maya Angelou. BlSi; NAAAL

There is a destiny that makes us brothers. A Creed. Edwin Markham. BLPA; FaBoBe

There is a dish to hold the sea. Imagination. John Davidson. APAD; MoBrPo *Fr.* New Year's Eve.

There is a drear and lonely tract of hell. Supremacy. Edwin Arlington Robinson. APN-2; NoAM

There is a drought, the farmers have a hard time finding food. Following the Rhymes of Shao-pao Huang's Poem on Being Moved While Visiting the Farmers. Yang Shih-ch'i, *Chinese.* CoBLCP, *tr. by* Jonathan Chaves

There is a drunk on Main Avenue, slumped. Song-Maker. Anita Endrezze-Danielson. HATNAP

There is a face in the honeysuckle—eyes. The Man in the Honeysuckle. David Campbell. BMAP

There is a faculty or knack, smallish, in the mind that can turn. A. R. Ammons. NoAM. *Fr.* Sphere.

There is a fair one. The Lute Song. Kung Tzu-chen, *Chinese.* SuSp, *tr. by* An-yan Tang

"There is a fashion in this land." The Knight's Ghost. *Unknown.* ESPB

"There is a feast in your father's house." Leesome Brand. *Unknown.* ESPB

There is a fenceless garden overgrown. The Garden. Edwin Arlington Robinson. GaP

There is a fever of the spirit. Song by Mr. Cypress. Thomas Love Peacock. OAEL-2; OBNC *Fr.* Nightmare Abbey.

There is a flower, a little flower. A Field Flower. James Montgomery. BoTP *Fr.* The Daisy.

There is a flower blossoming out of season. Flower Ensnarer of Psalms. Rossana Ombres, *Italian.* BoWoP, *tr. by* I. L. Salomon

(Ensnaring Flower of Psalms.)

"There is a Flower that blooms out of season."

There is a flower that bees prefer. Purple Clover. Emily Dickinson. MoAmPo

There is a flower that blooms out of season. Ensnaring Flower of Psalms. Rossana Ombres, *Italian.* NeIt, *tr. by* Ruth Feldman

There is a flower, the Lesser Celandine. A Lesson. Wordsworth. GTBS-P

There is a fountain fill'd with blood. Praise for the Fountain Opened. William Cowper. ChIV-1; InPK-6 *Fr.* Olney Hymns.

There is a friendship that exists between. A Dog's Vigil. Margaret E. Bruner. PoToHe

There is a garden grey. Myself. Walter De la Mare. GaP

There is a Garden in her face. Thomas Campion. AAS; EBEvV; GLoP; GTBS-P; GaP; HeIP-4; ImPo; InPK-6; NAEL-1; NOSC; NoP-4; OAEL-1; PBRV; PoE; PoEL-2; Poetr; SCGP; TFi

("Till 'Cherry ripe!' themselves do cry.") (LL) GLoP; GaP; NoP-4

("Till Cherry ripe themselves doe cry.") (LL) PBRV

There is a garden where lilies. Eutopia. Francis Turner Palgrave. EBVV; OBGa

There is a garden where our hearts converse. The Promised Garden. Theo Dorgan. APAD

There is a gentle nymph not far from hence. Sabrina. Milton. *Fr.* Comus; a Masque Presented at Ludlow Castle. FHYEP; OAEL-1

There is a ghost. Ghost. Christian Morgenstern, *German.* OxBSn, *tr. by* W. D. Snodgrass

There is a girl dragging heavy. Ritual Girl. Frank Mkalawile Chipasula. HBAPE

There Is a Girl Inside. Lucille Clifton. NMM-2

There is a girl you like so you tell her. Courtship. Mark Strand. HCAP; PoPoPo

There is a god in whom I do not believe. God the Eater. Stevie Smith. BWW

There is a God that carves to each his own. (LL) Psalm 58: Si Vere Utique. Mary Sidney Herbert, Countess of Pembroke. NoP-4; PEW

There is a goddess and I know her. Her hands are not clean. Apotheosis of the Kitchen Goddess II. Teresa Noelle Roberts. CrSp

There is a golden rule in life. Do As You Would Be Done By. Matilda Caroline Edwards. PWR

There is a grape vine threatening my house. Anticipation. Sheila Richter. LoHo

There is a great amount of poetry in unconscious. Critics and Connoisseurs. Marianne Moore. AmPP; CMoP; FaBoWP; MeMAP; NOBA; NoAM; OxBA; Poetr

There is a great river this side of Stygia. The River of Rivers in Connecticut. Wallace Stevens. FaBoA; HAP; HCAP; NOBA; VGW

There Is a Green Hill Far Away. Cecil Frances Alexander. OxBChV; TIRV

There is a green spell stolen from Birmingham;. A Death at Winson Green. Francis Webb. BMAP

There is a grey thing that lives in the tree-tops. Stephen Crane. APN-2

There is a growth that hurts the child. An Age. Laura Jensen. LCAP-2

There is a hawk that is picking the birds out of our sky. Shiva. Robinson Jeffers. NOBA; NoAM; Son

There is a heigh-ho in these glowing coals. Heigh-ho on a Winter Afternoon. Donald Davie. OxBTC

There Is a High Place. Edwin Markham. AH

There is a hill and on that hill is a stone. The Heart of the World. Rabbi Nahman of Bratzlav, *Yiddish.* TrJP, *tr. by* Joseph Leftwich

There is a hill in England. Three Hills. Everard Owen. NSI

There is a hornet in the room. Buried at Springs. James Schuyler. CoAP; PoM

There is a joyful night in which we lose. When the Dumb Speak. Robert Bly. CAPP-1; NOBA

There is a kind of lace laid over the city, a lightness. The Serious Merriment of Women. Patricia Goedicke. TAP

There is a knot in the middle of my head. A Glimpse. John Wieners. FTOS

There Is a Lady ("There is a lady conquering with glances"). Walther von der Vogelweide, *German.* AWP, *tr. by* Jethro Bithell

There is a Lady sweet and kind. Thomas Ford. CBLP; CH; EBEV; EBEvV; GBL; HeIP-4; ImPo; NOBE; NOSC; OBEV

There is a lady sweet and kind. *Unknown.* NoP-4

There is a land called Lost. Two Chorale-Preludes: On Melodies by Paul Celan. Geoffrey Hill. OxBC

There Is a Land Mine Eye Hath Seen. Gurdon Robins. AH

There is a land of pure delight. A Prospect of Heaven Makes Death Easy. Isaac Watts. NOCV; NoP-4; PeECV; TOF

There is a language in a naval log. Edwin John Pratt. MoCV *Fr.* Behind the Log.

There is a Languor of the Life. Emily Dickinson. BoWoP

There is a last, solitary coach about to leave. David Vogel, *Hebrew.* HP, *tr. by* A. C. Jacobs

There is a little lightning in his eyes. Of Robert Frost. Gwendolyn Brooks. ColAP; MoP; NOBA; NoAM

There is a loneliness on city streets. Margaret E. Bruner. PoToHe

There is a lonely mountain-top. Jephthah's Daughter. "Yehoash," *Yiddish.* TrJP, *tr. by* Alter Brody

There is a magic melting pot. The Melting Pot. Dudley Randall. BPo; NBV

There is a Maker. Wizards. Alonzo Gonzales Mó, *Mayan.* STP, *tr. by* Allan F. Burns

There is a meadow. Last Light. Robert Kelly. VGW

There is a memory stays upon old. Old Ships. David Morton. CTV

There is a middleaged man, Tim Flanagan. The Middleaged Man. Louis Simpson. NNaP

There is a mole on Ahmad's cheek that draws all those who. The Mole. Al-Muntafil. RaBo, *tr. by* Robert Bly

There is a moment blind with light, split by the hum. Icarus in November. Alec Brock Stevenson. FuPo

There is a moment when they turn. The Before People. Wesley McNair. CMAP

There is a morn by men unseen. Emily Dickinson. NALW; OxBA

There is a mystery in human hearts. *Unknown.* PoToHe

There is a mystery too deep for words. Silence. John Hall Wheelock. LiTM

There is a mystic borderland that lies. Helen Field Fischer. PoToHe

There is a nation In my brawny scrotal sac. Lance Jeffers. NBV

There is a pain—so utter. Emily Dickinson. APN-2; BoWoP; NAAL-1; NCAP; NOBA

There is a painted bus. The Bus. "Peter." BoTP

There is a panther caged within my breast. The Black Panther. John Hall Wheelock. LiTM; PFE

There is a parrot imitating spring. Parsley. Rita Dove. CMAP; HCAP; LoL; NAAAL; NoAM; NoP-4; PoPoPo; VCAP

There is a path no vulture's eye hath seen. Anne Bradstreet. WPoS *Fr.* The Vanity of All Worldly Things.

There is a peaceful little community. Grazing. Mitsui Futabako, *Japanese.* WPJ, *tr. by* Kenneth Rexroth *and* Ikuko Atsumi

There is a people mighty in its youth. Tribute to America. Shelley. AiP

There is a piece of music I wanted to describe to you. Music. Caroline Halliday. NBrP

There is a place in distant seas. Richard, Archbishop Whately. NOBAu

There is a place in Montana where the grass stands up two feet. Rosebud. Jon Anderson. PaTW

There is a place that some men know. The Cross. Allen Tate. AWP; ChIV-2; MoAmPo; OxBA

There is a place where contrarieties are equally true. Vision of Beulah, The ("There is a place where contrarieties are equally true"). William Blake. OAEL-2 *Fr.* Milton.

There is a place where Contrarieties are equally True. William Blake. NOBRP *Fr.* Milton.

There is a plan far greater than the plan you know. There Is No Death. *Unknown.* BLPA

There is a pleasure in the pathless woods. The Sea. Byron. FaBoBe; ImPo; OxAEP-2; OxBoS; TFi *Fr.* The Ocean. PoEL-4 *Fr.* Childe Harold's Pilgrimage.

There is a poetaster named Wang. Han-shan, *Chinese.* SuSp, *tr. by* Eugene Eoyang

There is a poor sneak called Rossetti. On Himself. D. G. Rossetti. FaBoEE; PeLi

There is a prayer that goes Lord I am powerless. A Style of Prayer. Lynda Hull. PUP-19

There is a precise instant in time. Midway. Robert Desnos, *French.* PFTM, *tr. by* Quasha, George

There is a prison room. Tell Me, What Is the Soul. Jean Valentine. BAP-96

There is a private tension that endears. The Crack. Michael Goldman. NYBP

There is a quiet kingdom's strand. The Quiet Kingdom. Carl Busse, *German*. AWP, *tr. by* Ludwig Lewisohn

There is a quiet spirit in these woods. The Spirit of Poetry. Henry Wadsworth Longfellow. APN-1

There is a rhythm to it. Kneading Bread. Teresa Anderson. LoHo

There is a river. No End of No-Story. George Macdonald. NOBVV

There is a river clear and fair. Fragments. Catherine Maria Fanshawe. BXAP

There is a road that turning always. The Road. Edwin Muir. CMoP; ImPo; LiTM

There is a rumour. Forecast. Howard Fergus. PBCV

There is a sad carnival up the valley. Are They Dancing. Edward Dorn. NeAP; PoM

There is a schoolyard that runs. For Brothers Everywhere. Tim Seibles. NAmP90

There is a secret room. The Same Gesture. John Montague. BIrV; PNI

There is a sighing in the wood. The Silent. Jones Very. NCAP; PAR

There is / a silence. The Hole. Robert Creeley. FTOS

There is a silence where hath been no sound. Silence. Thomas Hood. CH; EBEV; GSo; NOBE; OBEV; OBNC; PoEL-4; Son

There is a singer everyone has heard. The Oven Bird. Robert Frost. APo; AWP; AmPP; GSo; HeIP-4; MeMAP; MoP; NAAL-2; NOBA; NoAM; NoP-4; OxBA; PoE; Son; TAP

There is a Smile of Love. The Smile. William Blake. RB

There is a soldier on the battlefield. *Unknown, Chinese*. BoWoP, *tr. by* Geoffrey Waters

There is a solitude like black mud! On Meditation. Robert Bly. *Fr.* Six Winter Privacy Poems. LCAP-2

There is a sphere, a secret sphere. The Inner Realm. Priscilla Jane Thompson. CBWP-2

There is a spirit, shifting around from foot to foot. (LL) Thoughts. Michael Benedikt. CoAmPo; SAGP

There is a spot where all our hopes. Home. Matilda Caroline Edwards. PWR

There is a stane in yon water. Burd Isabel and Earl Patrick. *Unknown*. ESPB

There is a stone in the air. Peru Eye, the Heart of the Lamp. Clark Coolidge. APSN

There is a strange, solemn, silent, graceless. David Ferry. FaBoA

There is a stream, I name not its name. A Highland Glen near Loch Ericht. Arthur Hugh Clough. FaBoVe *Fr.* Bothie of Tober-na-Vuolich, The [A Long-Vacation Pastoral].

There is a stream which rises. Joseph Bruchac. CDW

There is a strong wall about me to protect me. Love Song. Mary Carolyn Davies. LW

There is a Supreme God in the ethnological section. Homage to the British Museum. William Empson. CMoP; FaBoMo; LiTM; MoBrPo; PoE

There is a sway that comes soon after. To a Stranger (At the End of a Caboose). Laura Jensen. GM

There is a tall long-sided dame. Samuel Butler. OBSV *Fr.* Hudibras.

There is a temper of atmosphere which prevents rain. Five. Dennis Phillips. FTOS *Fr.* Twenty Questions.

There is a Thorn—it looks so old. The Thorn. Wordsworth. FaBoSe; Ro

There is a tide in men's affairs. Modern Moses, or "My Policy" Man. James Madison Bell. AAP

There is a timbre of voice. Echoes. Audre Lorde. NoP-4

There is a time, we know not when. The Hidden Line. Joseph Addison Alexander. BLPA

There is a tongue in every leaf. Caroline Anne Bowles. Ro *Fr.* Blackwood's Edinburgh Magazine, 13 275.

There is a train inside this iris. Iris. David St. John. GM; LCAP-2

There is a tranquil star. A Star. Federico García Lorca. PFTM

There is a tree by day. Tenebris. Angelina Weld Grimké. NAAL; PoBA

There is a tree in the orchestra. Double Bass. Sue May. NBrP

There is a tree native in Turkestan. Note on Local Flora. William Empson. EBEV; FaBoMo; OxAEP-2

There is a tribe of invisible men. The Invisible Men. Nakasuk, *Eskimo*. RaBo, *tr. by* Edward Field

There is a truce. . . . O lovers, tell. The Truce. Stella Gibbons. LW

There is a tune for which I'd offer all. A Fancy. Gérard de Nerval, *French*. FLP, *tr. by* Alistair Elliot

There is a vale which none hath seen. Rumors from an Aeolian Harp. Henry David Thoreau. APN-1; PAR

There is a very life in our despair. Byron. NOBRP *Fr.* Childe Harold's Pilgrimage Canto III. Ro *Fr.* Childe Harold's Pilgrimage.

There is a voice inside the body. A Man Lost by a River. Michael C. Blumenthal. RaBo

There is a Void, outside of Existence, which if entered into. Jerusalem; The Emanation of the Giant Albion. William Blake.

There is a wailing baby under every stone and you walk. Poem. Norman McCaig. SPE

There is a walled garden where the flowers never pale or turn dark. Paradise. Elizabeth Nancy Sargent. NYBP

There is a way of seeing that is not seeing. Trompe L'Œil. Daryl Hine. MoCV

There is a way to enter a field. Receiving the Stigmata. Rita Dove. NAAAL

There is / A welcome at the door to which no one comes? Angel Surrounded by Paysans. Wallace Stevens. HCAP; LCAP-2

There is a willow grows aslant a brook. Ophelia's Death. Shakespeare. OxAEP-1; RB *Fr.* Hamlet. NAWM-1

There is a wind where the rose was. Autumn. Walter De la Mare. OxBTC

There is a window stuffed with hay. The Hay Hotel. Oliver St. John Gogarty. BIrV

There is a wolf in me. . . fangs pointed for tearing gashes. Wilderness. Carl Sandburg. RaBo

There is a woman climbing a glass hill. Two Women. Naomi Replansky. NMM-2

There is a woman in our town. William Carlos Williams. CMoP; PoE *Fr.* Paterson.

There Is a Woman in This Town. Patricia Parker. BlSi

There is a word at heart for the next of death. Written in Exile. Kathleen Jessie Raine. TrCP; WPE

There is a Yew-tree, pride of Lorton Vale. Yew-Trees. Wordsworth. UnPo

There is a young lady, whose nose. Edward Lear. OxBChV

There is a Zone whose even Years. Emily Dickinson. APN-2; NCAP

There is always a first flinging. Variations on a Theme. Anne Wilkinson. MoCV

There is always a place for you at my table. Anne Campbell. PoToHe

There is an aggression of fact. After Jericho. Ronald Stuart Thomas. OxBC

There is an air for which I would disown. An Old Tune. Gérard de Nerval, *French*. AWP, *tr. by* Andrew Lang

There is an ancient forest, its giant trees. The Flower Pot. David Shimoni, *Hebrew*. MHP, *tr. by* Ruth Finer Mintz

There is an ancient story. My Father's Story. Priscilla Jane Thompson. CBWP-2

There is an award for this. I Was Dancing Alone in Binh Dinh Province. D. F. Brown. CDa

There is an awful quiet in the air. Prayer. Hartley Coleridge. GSo

There is an embalmer who operates. Embalmer. Rossana Ombres, *Italian*. NeIt, *tr. by* Ruth Feldman

There is an end of joy and sorrow. Ilicet. Swinburne. NOBVV

There is an evening coming in. Going. Philip Larkin. CMoP

There is an eye, there was a slit. Sabbath. John Berryman. LCAP-2 *Fr.* Dream Songs.

There Is an Hour of Peaceful Rest. William Bingham Tappan. AH

There is an I in space, I am, space. Another Day on the Pilgrimage. Peter Gizzi. BAP-95

There is an inevitability. Fable. Norman Harris. NYBP

There is an inn, a merry old inn. The Man in the Moon Stayed up To Late. J. R. R. Tolkien. OBSP

There is an old and very cruel god. Vicarious Atonement. Richard Aldington. MoBrPo

There Is an Old City. Karl Bulcke, *German*. AWP, *tr. by* Ludwig Lewisohn

There is an old he-wolf named Gambart. Limerick. D. G. Rossetti. FaBoEE; PeLi

There is another heaven and earth beyond the world of men. (LL) Conversations in the Mountains. Li Po, *Chinese*. RaBo; TAL, *tr. by* Robert Payne

There is another Loneliness. Emily Dickinson. APN-2

There is another word above this one; or outside of this one. Through the Smoke Hole. Gary Snyder. BB

There is, at times, an evening sky. Vincent Ogé. George Boyer Vashon. AAP; APN-2

There is bread and a knife on the table. . . . (LL) In the Midst of Life. Tadeusz Różewicz, *Polish*. HP

There is Bryant, as quiet, as cool, and as dignified. Bryant. James Russell Lowell. NOBA; TAP *Fr.* A Fable for Critics. NAAL-1; NAAL-3

There is but one, and that one ever. (LL) Easter ("I got me flowers to straw [or strew or strow] Thy [or the] way"). George Herbert. BoTP; CH; FHYEP; FaBoCh; NAEL-1; NOBE; OBEV

There is but one May in the year. May-Time. *Unknown*. AYFP; BoTP

There is comfort in old houses. Old Houses. Homer D'Lettuso. PoToHe

There is death enough in Europe without these. Dead Ponies. Brenda Chamberlain. OBWVE; WPE

There is delight in singing, though none hear. To Robert Browning. Walter Savage Landor. EPCY; NoP-4

There is enough. What We Know. Raymond R. Patterson. NBV

There is frost in the air. Schoenberg Op. 11. Thomas William Shapcott. *Fr.* Piano Pieces. CBAP

There is good news that spring's in the air. Spring Sentiments. Chao Yi, *Chinese.* SuSp, *tr. by* Chang Yin-nan *and* Lewis C. Walmsley

There is great mystery, Simone. Hair. Rémy de Gourmont, *French.* AWP, *tr. by* Jethro Bithell

There is Hawthorne, with genius so shrinking and rare. Hawthorne. James Russell Lowell. APN-1; AmPP; NOBA; OxBA; PAR; TAP *Fr.* A Fable for Critics. NAAL-1; NAAL-3

There is health in thy gray wing. To a Marsh Hawk in Spring. Henry David Thoreau. PoEL-4

There is in each body something splendid, I think. The Quality. Philip Schultz. NAmP90

There is in human closeness a sacred boundary. "Anna Akhmatova," *Russian.* WPOW, *tr. by* Dianne Levitin

There is in the human voice. Caught. Rodney Jones. FiLi; NAmP90

There is in this world something. The Sweetest Thing. *Unknown, Susu.* TTY, *tr. by* Ulli Beier

There is joy. Welcome Morning. Anne Sexton. CrSp

There is Law for Fire. The Seasons of Fire. Billy Marshall-Stoneking. NOBAu

There Is Life. Breyten Breytenbach, *Afrikaans.* VCWP, *tr. by* Breyten Breytenbach

There is life on other planets. Vyacheslav Kupriyanov, *Russian.* TCRP, *tr. by* Albert C. Todd

There is Lowell, who's striving Parnassus to climb. Lowell. James Russell Lowell. AmPP; NOBA; OxBA; TAP *Fr.* A Fable for Critics. NAAL-1; NAAL-3

There is moonrise under your fingernail—. Guiffre's Nightmusic. Thomas McGrath. MoNo; SeSe

There is more than glass between the snow and the huge roses. (LL) Snow. Louis MacNeice. CIP-2; CMoP; FaBoMo; LiTM; MoP; NOBE; NoAM; OPOU; OxAEP-2; OxBSP; OxBTC; PNI

There is my country under glass. At the Tourist Centre in Boston. Margaret Atwood. NoP-4; Poetr

There is naught for thee by thy haste to gain. The Created. Jones Very. APN-1; NOCV

There is neither beginning nor end to the imagination. William Carlos Williams. CLPP *Fr.* Kora in Hell.

There is never an open door to the wild beasts' home. The Uninvited. William D. Mundell. NYBP

There is no answer. We do here what we will. The Usurpers. Edwin Muir. CMoP

There is no better way to know us. A Modest Proposal. Ted Hughes. CABP

There is no bountie to be shew'd to such. Ben Jonson. PoEL-2 *Fr.* The Poetaster.

There is no break. August 8. Norman Jordan. MBE

There is no ceremony to stand on. A Lost Art. Richard Howard. BAP-94

There is no chance, no destiny, no fate. Will. Ella Wheeler Wilcox. BLPA; PoToHe

There is no chapel on the day. The Ballad of Reading Gaol. Oscar Wilde. EBVV; NoAM; TIRV *Fr.* The Ballad of Reading Gaol. CABP; OBNV; OxAEP-2

There is no clock in the forest. Timeless. Judith Nicholls. AYFP

There Is No Country. Julian Tuwim, *Polish.* TrJP, *tr. by* Watson Kirkconnell

There Is No Death. *Unknown.* BLPA

There is no death! The stars go down. John Luckey McCreery. BLPA; FaBoBe; PWR

There is no debauchery worse than thought. A Contribution on Pornography. Wislawa Szymborska, *Polish.* PoSu, *tr. by* Adam Czerniawski

There is no difference between being raped. Rape Poem. Marge Piercy. Poetsp

There is no faith in claret, and it shall. Two Gentlemen That Broke Their Promise of a Meeting. James Shirley. BeJo

There is no fire of the crackling boughs. Glenaradale. Walter Chalmers Smith. OBEV; PeVV

THERE IS NO FORM BUT SHAPE! NO LOGIC BUT. Rant Block. Michael McClure. SPE

There is no Frigate like a Book. Emily Dickinson. APN-2; ChAP; MoAmPo; OBCA; PoLF; SAmP; SoSe-8; TAP

("That bears a human soul!") (LL) ChAP

There is no god. Hi. Gregory Corso. EC3

There is no God, as I was taught in youth. John Masefield. CMoP *Fr.* Sonnets.

"There is no God," the wicked saith. Arthur Hugh Clough. CABP; NAEL-2; NOBE; NOBVV; NoP-4 *Fr.* Dipsychus [and the Spirit].

There is no great and no small. History. Ralph Waldo Emerson. APN-1

There is no great and no small. Mottoes to "History." Ralph Waldo Emerson. *Fr.* History. APN-1

There is no happy life. Love's Matrimony. William Cavendish, Duke of Newcastle. NOSC

There is no Job but cries to God and hopes. A Copy of Verses. John Wilson. SCAP

There is no joy in water apart from the sun. Song. Ralph Nixon Currey. PeSA

There Is No Joy Without Aphrodite. Mimnermus, *Greek.* GrIP, *tr. by* Richard Lattimore

There Is No Land Yet. Laura Riding Jackson. ChIV-1

There is no language but "reconstructed" imaged parentheses back into. Statistics. Barrett Watten. PmAP

There is no language for the present time. Sulking in the Seventies. Kris Hemensley. BMAP

There is no limit to the number of times. From Father to Son. Emyr Humphreys. OBWVE

There is no Lover hee or shee. A Paradox. Aurelian Townshend. SeCP

There is no more silence on the plains of the moon. Night After Bushfire. Judith Wright. OBWVE

There is no music now in all Arkansas. Variations for Two Pianos. Donald Justice. NYBP; WeT

There Is No Name So Sweet on Earth. George Washington Bethune. AH

There is no need for Pain Lord. Breyten Prays for Himself. Breyten Breytenbach, *Afrikaans.* VCWP, *tr. by* Denis Hirson

There is no needle without piercing point. Death. *Unknown.* RaBo

There is no night / when the lightning does not flash. Lady Sagami, *Japanese.* WPJ, *tr. by* Kenneth Rexroth *and* Ikuko Atsumi

There is no one among men that has not a special failing;. Madly Singing in the Mountains. Po Chü-i, *Chinese.* BLT; ChiP, *tr. by* Arthur Waley

There is no one here. Matisse: "The Red Studio." W. D. Snodgrass. GS

There is no one in this world who has time. Edith Södergran, *German.* WPoS, *tr. by* Stina Katchadourian

There is no one to share my thoughts. (LL) Alone. Chu Shu-chen, *Chinese.* OHPC, *tr. by* Kenneth Rexroth

There Is No Opera like "Lohengrin." John Wheelwright. NYBP

There is no other life. (LL) Why Log Truck Drivers Rise Earlier Than Students of Zen. Gary Snyder. LoL; NNaP

There is no outside. Moving Object. Jean Day. FTOS

There is no person lonelier. . . Than he who lies in bed. Visit the Sick. James J. Metcalfe. PoToHe

There is no place in this dark. Radiant Silhouette II. John Yau. OpBo

There is no place to hide. David Hall. CDa *Fr.* The Ambush of the Fourth Platoon.

There Is No Place to Hide. Gwendolyn MacEwen. *Fr.* The T. E. Lawrence Poems. NOBC

'There is no place to turn,' she said. The Sensualists. Theodore Roethke. EP

There is no point in work. Work. D. H. Lawrence. OBMV

There is no portrait. Robert Creeley Listens, Too. David Chapman Berry. BXAP

There is no quenching of the other thirst. Hagar. Elisabeth Eybers, *Afrikaans.* PeSA, *tr. by the author*

There is no race of men. Boethius, *Latin.* MLL, *tr. by* Helen Waddell *Fr.* Consolation of Philosophy, The ("De Consolacione Philosophie").

There is no reason for amazement: surely one always knew that cultures decay, and life's end is death. (LL) The Purse-Seine. Robinson Jeffers. CMoP; HAP; NOBA; NoAM; OxBA; PaTW; Poetr; WeW-3

There is no remedy. (LL) O death, rock me asleep. George Boleyn. SCGP; WPE

There is no remembrance of former things; neither shall there be any remembrance of things that are to come with those that shall come after. Bible, *O.T.* See Vanity of vanities, saith the Preacher, vanity of vanities; all is vanity.

There is no resting where it rots and thrives. (LL) Caserta Garden. Richard Wilbur. GaP; OBGa

There Is No Riot. Martin Carter. PBCV

There is no road here—not even a path—. Lake Baskunchak. Andrey Alekseievich Amalrik, *Russian.* TCRP, *tr. by* John Glad

There is no salvation for mankind. Ballad of a Little Lamp. René Depestre, *French.* NegPo, *tr. by* Ellen Conroy Kennedy

There is no sense that I should write a line. To Cynthia. Sir Francis Kynaston. NOSC

There is no Silence in the Earth—so silent. Emily Dickinson. FaBoEE

There is no silence upon the earth or under the earth like the silence under the sea. Silences. Edwin John Pratt. NOBC

There is no sky today. Echoes of birds. Counterparts. Stephen Dobyns. PoA

There is no smirch of sin in you, only its fires. Song of Ophelia the Survivor. Anna Wickham. WPN

There is no sound in the mirror. The Mirror. Sang Yi, *Korean*. CKP, *tr. by* Jaihiun Kim

There is no story behind it. The Butterfly. Jejuri Arun Kolatkar. AYFP

There is no thing in all the world but love. The Camel-Rider. *Unknown, Arabic*. AWP, *tr. by* Wilfrid Scawen Blunt

There is no time to ask—he knows not what. (LL) Conscious. Wilfred Owen. NSI; PoWW

There is no whispering of any friend. No Friend Like Music. Daniel Whitehead Hicky. PoToHe

There is no wind on the moon at all. Moon-wind. Ted Hughes. SpW

There Is No Word for Goodbye. Mary TallMountain. HATNAP; LoL

There is no yesterday, no today, no tomorrow. (LL) The Mind of Absolute Trust. Seng-ts'an, *Chinese*. EnlH; ITG, *tr. by* Stephen Mitchell

There is none like her, none. Tennyson. OBNC *Fr.* I have led her home, my love, my only friend. CBLP; EBVV; NAEL-2; NOBVV; PoEL-5 *Fr.* Maud [A Monodrama]. EnVR

There is none like the Boy that sold Broom, green Broom. (LL) Broom, Green Broom. *Unknown*. CH; OxBoLi; PoRA

There is none, no none but I. Sir Robert Ayton. NOSC

There Is None to Help. Chad Walsh. *Fr.* The Psalm of Christ. TrCP

There is not in the wide world a valley so sweet. The Meeting of the Waters. Thomas Moore. IIP; NOIV; OxBoLi; PoEL-4

There Is Nothin' like a Dame. Oscar, II Hammerstein. OBAL

There is nothing as sweet as independence. Independence. Adebayo Faleti, *Yoruba*. PBA, *tr. by* Bakare Gbadamosi *and* Ulli Beier

There is nothing between us. (LL) Medusa. Sylvia Plath. CAPP-1; NALW

There is nothing but water in the holy pools. How Much Is Not True. Kabir. RaBo

There is nothing left / "please. . . please." (LL) Two Vietnam Poems: (1966). Bill Knott. PBCAP

There is nothing like the cool. The Wind From Mt. Fuji. Tagami Kikusha-Ni, *Japanese*. WPJ, *tr. by* Kenneth Rexroth *and* Ikuko Atsumi

There is nothing more to say. (LL) The House on the Hill. Edwin Arlington Robinson. APN-2; GEA; MoAmPo; NAAL-2; NCAP

There is nothing new in what is said. Late Sewing. Hazel Hall. PaTW

There is nothing one man will not do to another. (LL) The Visitor. Carolyn Forché. FYAP; OPOU

There is nothing to be afraid of. Nothing at all. (LL) Brother and Sisters. Judith Wright. BMAP

There is nothing to see of America but land. Archibald MacLeish. *See* Empire Builders.

There is nought for thee by thy haste to gain. Jones Very. *See* The Created.

There is one cottage in our dale. A Sketch. Dorothy Wordsworth. Ro

There is one grief worse than any other. Daughter. Ellen Bryant Voigt. MT

There is one Mind, one omnipresent Mind. Religious Musings. Coleridge. Ro *Fr.* Religious Musings.

There is one sin: to call a green leaf grey. Ecclesiastes. G. K. Chesterton. ChIV-1; MoBrPo; OxBSP

There is one story. Simonides, *Greek*. OBCVT, *tr. by* Richmond Lattimore

There is one story and one story only. To Juan at the Winter Solstice. Robert Graves. CMoP; EBEV; FaBoMo; ImPo; LiTM; MoBrPo; MoP; NAEL-2; NoAM; NoP-4; OAEL-2; PoE; RaBo; TwCP

There is one that has a head without an eye. A Riddle. Christina Rossetti. OxBChV

There Is Only One of Everything. Margaret Atwood. NOBC

There is our herd of cars stopped. Bison Crossing Near Mt. Rushmore. May Swenson. PaTW

There is pain in my heart. Neidhart von Reuental, *German*. GePo, *tr. by* Frederick Goldin

There is pleasure in the wet, wet clay. The Lie. Rudyard Kipling. NOBL *Fr.* The Naulahka.

There is rain on the glass but it all disappears. 20-200 on 747. Heather McHugh. WeT

There is red / on the clown-lady's lips. Toulouse Lautrec. Melvin Beaunearus Tolson, *Norwegian*. PBWP, *tr. by* Nadia Christensen

There is sand where the tracks were. Tearing Up the Tracks. Christopher Bursk. GM

There is so little that is close and warm. Debris of Life and Mind. Wallace Stevens. SAmP

There is so much good in the worst. Good and Bad. Edward Wallis Hoch. CTV

There is so much good in the worst of us. Charity. *Unknown*. BLPA

There is so much of loneliness. *Unknown*. PoToHe

There is some beauty in sorrow. Placing a $2 Bet for a Man Who Will Never Go to the Horse Races Any More. Diane Wakoski. UnPo

There is some delight in bombing an Enemy. The Enemy. Dorothy, Duchess of Wellington Wellesley. WPN

There is some will talk of lords and knights. Robin Hood's Delight. *Unknown*. ESPB

There / is someone I can bear. W. S. Landor. Marianne Moore. OBAL

There is something / about sugarcane. Sugar Cane. Grace Nichols. HCP

There is something between us. Breasts. Donald Hall. OBAL

There is something I want to say. Coming Home. D. F. Brown. CDa

There is something / you want urgently. Antique Father. Carolyn Kizer. MoLi

There is sorrow enough in the natural way. The Power of the Dog. Rudyard Kipling. BLPA

There is sweet music here that softer falls. Song of the Lotus-Eaters. Tennyson. HeIP-4; ImPo; NOBE; OBEV; OBNC *Fr.* The Lotus-Eaters. EnVR; NAEL-2; OAEL-2; PoEL-5; SCGP

There is that in me.. . . I do not know what it is.. . . but I know it is in me. Walt Whitman. ColAP; PAR *Fr.* Song of Myself. ("It is eternal life.. . . it is happiness.") (LL) PAR

There is that sound like the wind. Summer. John Ashbery. NAAL-2

There is the caw of a crow. Jonathan Houghton. Edgar Lee Masters. OxBA *Fr.* Spoon River Anthology.

There is the gate or the copy of a gate. After. David Shapiro. PT

There is the loneliness of peopled places. Solitude. Babette Deutsch. LW

There is the moon, there is the sun. The Universe. Mary Britton Miller. CTV

There is the morning shuffle of traffic confined. City Walk-up, Winter 1969. Carolyn Forché. Poetr

There is the one who turns. Chiapas. Gary Soto. NoAM

There is the sack of skin, dark. After the Interrogation. Lawrence Kearney. WeT

There is the sea. Aeschylus. GrIP, *tr. by* Robert Fagles *Fr.* Agamemnon. NAWM-1, *tr. by* Robert Fagles

There is the sound of hail washed over a porthole, but. Off the Aleutian Chain. Linda Bierds. NAmP90

There is the star bloom of the moss. Forest. Jean Garrigue. LiTM; NOBA

There is the trap that catches noblest spirits, that caught—they say—God, when he walked on earth. (LL) Shine, Perishing Republic. Robinson Jeffers. CMoP; LiTM; MoP; NAAL-2; NOBA; NoAM; OxBA; PoPoPo; TAP; TFi; UnPo; VGW

There is the weight of the word. Letter to Ellen Conroy Kennedy. Edouard J. Maunick, *French*. NegPo, *tr. by* Ellen Conroy Kennedy

There is the western gate, Luke Havergal— / Luke Havergal. (LL) Luke Havergal. Edwin Arlington Robinson. APN-2; AWP; AmPP; GBL; LiTM; MeMAP; MoAmPo; NAAL-2; NOBA; NoAM; PoEL-5; TFi; UnPo

There is this cave. The Jewel. James Wright. CoAP; NAAL-2

There is this distance between me and what I see. Still Poem 9. Philip Lamantia. NeAP

There is unfeminine, (but oh, so Female). Questionnaire. Susan Saxe. GLP

There is unknown dust that is near us. Surprised by Evening. Robert Bly. VGW; WeT

There is war. (LL) Poem for the Young White Man Who Asked Me How I, An Intelligent, Well-Read Person Could Believe in the War Between Races. Lorna Dee Cervantes. PBCAP; PoPoPo; WPOW

There is weeping, as is. Far Away. Jane Miller. BAP-96

There is Whittier, whose swelling and vehement heart. Whittier. James Russell Lowell. AmPP; NOBA; OxBA *Fr.* A Fable for Critics. NAAL-1; NAAL-3

There Is Wind, There Are Matches. Gerald Stern. LCAP-2

There isn't a shadow of doubt. Limerick. *Unknown*. PeLi

There Isn't Time. Eleanor Farjeon. BoTP

There it is again. Arrival. Gerald McCarthy. CDa

"There it is!/ You play beside a death-bed like a child." Elizabeth Barrett Browning. BrRo *Fr.* Aurora Leigh. VWP

There it was, word for word. The Poem That Took the Place of a Mountain. Wallace Stevens. LCAP-2

There Lackethe Somethynge Stylle. Thomas Chatterton. OxAEP-1 *Fr.* Aella; a Tragycal Enterlude.

There lays a ship in the harbour. Our Ship She Lies in Harbour. *Unknown*. NTP

There leaft a may, an a weel-far'd may. Katharine Jaffray. *Unknown*. ESPB

There leeved a wee man at the fit o yon hill. Get Up and Bar the Door. *Unknown*. ESPB

There lie the black mountains. Twelfth Song of the Holy Young Men. *Unknown*. APN-2, *tr. by* Washington Matthews *Fr.* The Mountain Chant.

There lies a cold corpse upon the sands. Death Song. Robert Stephen Hawker. OBNC

There lies a somnolent lake. In the Past. Trumbull Stickney. ColAP; NOBA; OxBA

There lies afar behind a western hill. The Town without a Market. James Elroy Flecker. MoBrPo

There! little girl, don't cry! A Life-Lesson. James Whitcomb Riley. PoLF

There liva a laird down into Fife. The Wife Wrapt in Wether's Skin. Unknown. ESPB

There liv'd a lass in yonder dale. Katharine Jaffray. Unknown. ESPB

There livd a lord on yon sea-side. Fair Annie. Unknown. ESPB

There liv'd a man in yonder glen. Johnie Blunt. Robert Burns. OxBB

There liv'd a wife in Whistle Cockpen. Will Ye Na Can Ye Na Let Me Be. Unknown. FaBoVe

There liv'd, as Authors tell, in Days of Yore. Chaucer. OBVE Fr. The Nun's Priest's Tale. FHYEP; NAEL-1; NAWM-1; OAEL-1 Fr. The Canterbury Tales.

There lived a carl in Kellyburnbraes. Kellyburnbraes. Robert Burns. OxBB

There lived a certain man and he had three sons. . . . (LL) The Western Approaches. Howard Nemerov. ColAP; HCAP; TAP

There lived a fat old lady, in London she did dwell. The Old Lady of London. Unknown. AmFP

There lived a King, as I've been told. Sir William Schwenck Gilbert. OBCoV Fr. The Gondoliers.

There lived a king in Thule. The King in Thule. Goethe, German. STV, tr. by John Frederick Nims.

There lived a man at the foot of a hill. Get Up and Bar the Door. Unknown. EnSB

There lived a sage in days of yore. A Tragic Story. Adelbert von Chamisso, German. BoTP, tr. by Thackeray

There lived a sage in days of yore. A Tragic Story. William Makepeace Thackeray. CTV

There lived a soldier in the world. Paper Soldier. Bulat Shalvovich Okudzhava, Russian. TCRP, tr. by Albert C. Todd

There lived a wife at Usher's Well. The Wife of Usher's Well. Unknown. AWP; AmFP; CH; EBEV; ESPB; EnSB; ImPo; NAEL-1; NOBE; NoP-4; OAEL-1; OBEV; OxAEP-1; OxBB; OxBS; OxBSn; PoEL-1; Poetr; RB; SCGP; TFi

There Lived among the Untrodden Ways. Hartley Coleridge. BXAP

There lived an old man in the Kingdom of Tess. The New Vestments. Edward Lear. NOBVV

There lived an old woman at Lynn. Unknown. OxBChV

There lived in a laburnum tree. The Yellow Fairy. Charlotte Druitt Cole. BoTP

There lived in ancient Scribbletown a wise old writer-man. Puzzled. Carolyn Wells. OBCA

There lived in Gothic days, as legends tell. Edwin, The Minstrel. James Beattie. OxAEP-1

There lives a good-for-nothing cat. The Lazy Pussy. Palmer Cox. OBCA

There lives a land beside the western sea. On the South Coast of Cornwall. John Gray. NOBVV

There lives a maid down under yon brae. Katherine Jaffray. Unknown. OxBB

There lives a man in Rynie's land. Lang Johnny More. Unknown. ESPB

There lives in / my childhood street. Self Portrait 4. Tove Ditlevsen, Danish. WPOW, tr. by Ann Freeman

There lyes all this great erles gold. (LL) Young [or Younge] Andrew. Unknown. ESPB; OxBB

There may be a basement to the Atlantic. Somebody's Gone. Charles Henri Ford. SPE

There may have been a boy. The Last Train. Linda Pastan. GM

There mounts in squalls a sort of rusty mire. The Exile's Return. Robert Lowell. AmPP; OxBA

There mournful cypress grew in greatest store. The Garden of Proserpina. Edmund Spenser. Fr. Wood Of Error. AEP

There,--my blessing with you [or thee]! To Thine Own Self Be True. Shakespeare. ImPo Fr. Hamlet. NAWM-1

There, my lad, lie the Articles. Scene from a Play, Acted at Oxford, Called "Matriculation." Thomas Moore. OBSV

There never yet was honest man. Loving and Beloved. Sir John Suckling. BeJo; CaPo; CavPo; NAEL-1

There never yet was woman made. Woman's Constancy. Sir John Suckling. CaPo; CavPo

There, now and then, are found / Life-loyalties. (LL) In a Wood. Thomas Hardy. EnVR; OBNC

There on Siriu. Comet. Federico García Lorca. PFTM

There, on the darkened deathbed, dies the brain. Sonnet. John Masefield. EBEV

There on the horizon. African Poem. Agostinho Neto. PBMAP

There on the sea sails wandered. The Names of Georgian Women. Bella Akhatovna Akhmadulina, Russian. BoWoP, tr. by Stanley Noyes and Olga Carlisle

There on the sun-hot stone. The Lizard. Lydia Pender. NOxBChV

There on the top of the down. June Bracken and Heather. Tennyson. EnLoPo

There on th'extreamest Beach, and farthest Sand. Catullus. OBCVT, tr. by William Bowles Fr. The Complaint of Ariadna. Out of Catullus.

There once, on that goat island, I. Robert Penn Warren. NOBA Fr. Tiberius on Capri.

There once was a bard of Hong Kong. Limerick. Gerard Benson. OBCoV

There once was a bull named the Duke of Buccleuch. The Duke Of Buccleuch. J. A. Phelp. NOBAu

There once was a child who said: "How." A Postscript to Orwell's Animal Farm. Miadesnia. PeLi

There once was a cobbler. The Kind Mousie. Natalie Joan. BoTP

There once was a couple named Mound. Limerick. Unknown. PeLi

There Once was a Cow with a Double Udder. The Cow. Theodore Roethke. OBAL; OBCA

There once was a doctor who said. Limerick. Towanbucket. PeLi

There once was a fellow called Hyde. Limerick. E. J. Jackson. PeLi

There once was a Fellow of Trinity. Limerick. Unknown. PeLi

There once was a Fellow of Wadham / Who approved of the doings of Sodom. Limerick. Unknown. PeLi

There once was a flock of wild geese. Limerick. B. Semeonoff and C. Semeonoff. PeLi

There once was a girl from St. Paul. Limerick. Unknown. NIP-4

There once was a girl from the Congo. Limerick. George Seferis, Greek. CBNP, tr. by Hugh Haughton

There once was a judge of Assize. Limerick. Unknown. PeLi

There once was a lady called Lily. Limerick. Unknown. PeLi

There once was a lass of Shalott. Limerick. Mary Holtby. PeLi

There once was a leaf with all its lines. Robert Desnos, French. MFP, tr. by Martin Sorrell

There once was a man [or There was a young man] who said, "Damn!" Limerick. Maurice Evan Hare. NOBL; OxBoLi; PeLV; PeLi

There once was a man who said, "God." Limerick: "There once was a man who said "God." Ronald Arbuthnott Knox. NBLV; NOBL; PeLi

There once was a Marquis de Sade. De Sade. John Fuller. NBLV; PeLV

There once was a monarch of Spain. Limerick. Unknown. PeLi

There once was a painter named Scott. Limerick. D. G. Rossetti. PeLi

There once was a person of Chiswick. Limerick. J. M. Ross. PeLi

There once was a plesiosaurus. Limerick. Unknown. PeLi

There Once Was a Pithy. Florence Page Jaques. CTV; NTCP

There once was a schoolgirl named Betty. Betty. Unknown. FuFo

There once was a Scot who said: "Evil." Limerick. "H. M." PeLi

There once was a sculptor named Phidias. Limerick. Unknown. PeLi

There Once Was a Spinster of Ealing. Unknown. NIP-4

There once was a time. Unknown. NOIV

There once was a vicar of Ryhill. Limerick. Unknown. PeLi

There once was a wicked young minister. Limerick. Conrad Potter Aiken. OBAL; PeLi

There once was a Willow, and he was very old. The Willow-Man. Juliana Horatia Ewing. OxBChV

There once was a wise politician. Limerick. A. M. Sayers. PeLi

There once was a witch of Willowby Wood. The Witch of Willowby Wood. Rowena Bastin Bennett. ChAP

There once was a writer called James. Limerick. R. K. R. Thornton. PeLi

There once was an artist called Pat. Limerick. Margaret Galbreath. PeLi

There once was an eccentric of Metz. Limerick. Leslie Johnson. PeLi

There once was an eccentric old boffin. Limerick. Unknown. PeLi

There once was an Ichthyosaurus. The Ichthyosaurus. Unknown. CTV

There once was monarch called Harry. Limerick. Mary Holtby. PeLi

There once were some people called Sioux. The American Indian. Unknown. NBLV

There once were three brothers from merry Scotland. Sir Andrew Barton. Unknown. AmFP

There once were two Babes in the Wood. Limerick. Roger Woddis. PeLi

There ought to be capital punishment for cars. Thoughts on Capital Punishment. Rod McKuen. InPK-6; PFE

There our murdered brother lies. The Wake of William Orr. William Drennan. TIRV

There out of hell the Old One bellows. Lamentations of the Fallen Angels. Unknown. AnOE, tr. by Charles W. Kennedy Fr. Christ and Satan.

There piped a piper in the wood. The Magic Piper. E. L. Marsh. BoTP

There rolls the deep where grew the tree. Tennyson. HAP; NOBE; OAEL-2 Fr. In Memoriam A. H. H.

There runs a road by Merrow Down. Merrow Down. Rudyard Kipling. NOxBChV *Fr.* Just-So Stories.

There sat a happy fisherman. The Reed. Mikhail Yuryevich Lermontov, *Russian.* AWP, *tr. by* J. J. Robbins

There sat an old man on a rock. Too Late. Fitz Hugh Ludlow. PoLF

There sat down, once, a thing on Henry's heart. John Berryman. CAPP-1; HAP; HCAP; NoP-4; PoE; VCAP *Fr.* Dream Songs.

There sat two glasses filled to the brim. The Two Glasses. Ella Wheeler Wilcox. BLPA

There sate the Seniors of the Trojan Race. The Old Trojan Chiefs See Helen. Homer. OBVE, *tr. by* Alexander Pope *Fr.* The Iliad.

There, sea and sky are at a mortal war. Petronius Arbiter, *Latin.* MLL, *tr. by* Helen Waddell

There seems no reason he should've died. His hands. Dead Christ. Andrew Hudgins. RA

There set out, slowly, for a Different World. A War. Randall Jarrell. OxBSP

There shall be beds full of light odours blent. From Baudelaire. "Michael Field." ADE

There shall be no more songs. Black Power. Alvin Saxon. PoBA

There She Stands a Lovely Creature. *Unknown.* AmFP

There she took her lover to sea. Long Nook. John Wieners. FTOS

There should be no despair for you. Sympathy. Emily Jane Brontë. BWW

There should be two words, dearest, one made up. Alone. Carolyn Wells. PoToHe

There sits a fair couple courting. The Jealous Brothers. *Unknown.* AmFP

There smiled the smooth Divine, unused to wound. The Smooth Divine. Timothy Dwight. *Fr.* Here stood Hypocrisy, in sober brown. NOCV *Fr.* The Triumph of Infidelity.

There smoke, sooty smoke. *Unknown, Serbo-Croatian.* HSix, *tr. by* Charles Simic

There, spring lambs jam the sheepfold. In air. Watercolor of Grantchester Meadows. Sylvia Plath. LCAP-2; NYBP

There stands a lady on a mountain. Kiss in the Ring. *Unknown.* OxBoLi

There stands a lonely pine-tree. Song. Heinrich Heine, *German.* TrJP, *tr. by* Emma Lazarus

There stood a hill not far whose grisly top. Milton. *Fr.* Book I. FHYEP; NAEL-1; OAEL-1; OxAEP-1 *Fr.* Paradise Lost.

There stood as in the Centre of the Town. The Altar of Mercy. Publius Papinius Statius, *Latin.* OBCVT, *tr. by* William S. Lewis

There the ash-tree leaves do vall. Leaves a-Vallen. William Barnes. NOBVV

There the black river, boundary to hell. The Southern Road. Dudley Randall. GM; PoBA

There the blue-green gums are a fringe of remote disorder. Envoi. James McAuley. BMAP

There the companions of his fall, o'erwhelmed. Immortal Hate. Milton. NOBE *Fr.* Book I. FHYEP; NAEL-1; OAEL-1; OxAEP-1 *Fr.* Paradise Lost.

There the most daintie Paradise on ground. In the Bower of Bliss. Edmund Spenser. EBEV; FaBoSe; GaP *Fr.* Wood Of Error. AEP

"There the Parthenon, & there." Slides. Jennifer Maiden. CBAP

There the true Silence is, self-conscious and alone. (LL) Silence. Thomas Hood. CH; EBEV; GSo; NOBE; OBEV; OBNC; PoEL-4; Son

There the voluptuous nightingales. Shelley. *Fr.* Prometheus Unbound. NOBRP; OAEL-2

There the witches are making tea. John Greenleaf Whittier. *See* Snow-Bound [*or* Snow-Bound; a Winter Idyl].

There, there where those black spruces crowd. Ragged Island. Edna St. Vincent Millay. ColAP; NAAL-2; NoP-4

There they are. The Blackstone Rangers. Gwendolyn Brooks. NoAM; PoBA

There they are again. It's after dark. The Black Riviera. Mark Jarman. NAmP90; WeT

There they are, my fifty men and women. One Word More. Robert Browning. EnVR; PoEL-5

There they are now. Three Sentences for a Dead Swan. James Wright. NOBA

There they dismounting, drew their weapons bold. Britomart in the House of Busirane. Edmund Spenser. *Fr.* The Legend of Britomartis, or of Chastitie. NAEL-1 *Fr.* Wood Of Error. AEP

There they go. Seed Journey. Gregory Corso. VGW

There they go, down to the fatal ship. Cythera. David Ferry. DiPo; GS

There they go marching all in step so gay! Joining the Colours. Katharine Tynan. APAD

There they stand, on their ends, the fifty faggots. Fifty Faggots. Edward Thomas. MoBrPo; PeFWW; PoWW

There they were, right before my eyes: it was terrible and at the same. Fable. Eugenio de Andrade, *Portuguese.* VCWP, *tr. by* Alexis Levitin

There thou shalt find[e] my faults are thine. (LL) Judgement. George Herbert. ESCV; GeHe; SeCP

There, truly they said in this house. The Hidden People and the Star People. *Unknown.* STP, *tr. by* Barbara Tedlock *Fr.* Ceremony of Sending.

There used to be a rich old oaf. Chaucer. *See* The Miller's [*or* Milleres] Tale.

There used to be gods in everything, and now they've gone. The Companions. Howard Nemerov. NYBP

There walked on Plover's shady banks. Driving Saw-Logs on the Plover. *Unknown.* AS

There wanders many a lighted star. The North Star. John Morris-Jones, *Welsh.* OBWVE, *tr. by* Anthony Conran

There wanders through the world, a knee. The Knee. Christian Morgenstern, *German.* CBNP; RB, *tr. by* W. D. Snodgrass *and* Lore Segal

There was a bad poet named Clough. On Arthur Hugh Clough. Swinburne. FaBoEE

There was a basket of fruit between us. As It Is. Ralph Angel. WeT

There was a battle fought of late. To His Mother. John Harington. NoSic

There was a battle in the north. Geordie [An Old Ballad]. *Unknown.* ESPB; OxBB

There was a big bear. Honey Bear. Elizabeth Lang. BoTP

There was a black cross on the Italian's breast. The Italian. Mikhail Arkadyevich Svetlov, *Russian.* TCRP, *tr. by* Daniel Weissbort

There was a black girl from Pretoria. Limerick. George Seferis, *Greek.* CBNP, *tr. by* Hugh Haughton

There was a blind owl which was loved by a squirrel with a crushed head. Lovers. Russell Edson. WeT

There was a boy bedded in bracken. Carol. John Short. FaBoCh; FaBoTw

There was a boy in a village who made. Saw the Cloud Lynx. Samuel Makidemewabe, *Cree Indian.* STP, *tr. by* Howard Norman

There was a boy whose name was Jim. Jim Who Ran Away from His Nurse, and Was Eaten by a Lion. Hilaire Belloc. EBNV; NOxBChV; NoAM; OBSP; OxAEP-2; OxBChV; PeLV

There was a brave girl of Connecticut. Benjamin. Ogden Nash. PeLi

There was a bridge that Rozinante would not cross. The Bridge of Heraclitus. George Reavey. BIrV

There was a cat in Egypt, in Egypt, in Egypt. The Cat. Rose Fyleman. NOxBChV

There was a certain assistant minister. A Record of a Past Affair. Li K'ai-hsien, *Chinese.* CoBLCP, *tr. by* Jonathan Chaves

There was a Child. Courage, a Tale. Thom Gunn. GLP

There was a child went forth every day. Leaves of Grass (1855). Walt Whitman. APN-1; AWP; AmPP; ImPo; InPS-3; NAAL-1; NTP; OxBA; PBMP; SAmP; TAP

(And these become of him or her that peruses them now.) APN-1

"There was a child went forth every." CTV; PAR

(And the water plants with their graceful flat heads, all became part of him.)

(And these become of him or her that peruses them now.) PAR

There was a clever skipper, in Akron he did dwell. The Clever Skipper. *Unknown.* AmFP

There was a collection of schemers. Limerick. Basil Ransome-Davies. PeLi

There was a company of young folk living. Chaucer. *See* The Pardoner's Tale.

There was a contest. Peaches. Siv Cedering Fox. PBCAP

There Was a Crimson Clash of War. Stephen Crane. UnPo

There was a crooked man, and he went [*or* walked] a crooked mile. Mother Goose. BoTP; CBNP; FaBoBe; LB; OxBoLi; OxNR; PeLV; ReMoGo

There was a crusader of Parma. Limerick. *Unknown.* PeLi

There was a dark and awful wood. Wood. Thomas Hornsby Ferril. PoRA

There was a darkness in this man. John Gould Fletcher. *Fr.* Lincoln. MoAmPo

There was a duck egg as green as the evening sky. Ulinda. David Campbell. CBAP

There was a duke's daughter lived in York. The Cruel Mother. *Unknown.* ESPB

There was a fair maiden who lived on the shore. The Fair Maid by the Shore. *Unknown.* AmFP

There was a fair young creature who lived by the seaside. The Silvery Tide. *Unknown.* AmFP

There was a faith-healer of Deal. Limerick. *Unknown.* PeLi

There was a fat lady of Clyde. Limerick. *Unknown.* PeLi

There was a fat man of Bombay. The Man of Bombay. *Unknown.* ReMoGo

There was a fire in the night. Near the Docks. Dave Jeddie Smith. CMAP

There was a French bard who said: "Hell!" Limerick. Towanbucket. PeLi

There was a French writer named Sartre. Weldon Kees. Poetr

There was a friend of mine. The Night Whispers. Ken Smith. NBrP

There was a frost. The Frozen Greenhouse. Thomas Hardy. OBGa

There was a gallant lady all in her tender youth. Canada-I-O. *Unknown.* AmFP

There was a gallant ship, [and] a gallant ship was she. The Golden Vanity. *Unknown.* CH; ESPB; FaBoCh; PBMP

There was a gather'd stillness in the room. My Mother. William Bell Scott. GSo

There was a girl in our town. *Unknown.* OxNR

There was a gloomy lady. Not a Very Cheerful Song, I'm Afraid. Adrian Mitchell. OTCP

There was a god in each tree-stump. Second Elegy, Getic. Nichita Stanescu, *Romanian.* CEEP, *tr. by* Petru Popescu *and* Peter Jay

There was a good Canon of Durham. Limerick. William Ralph Inge. PeLi

There was a graveyard once—or cemetery. Evening Hour. Robert Penn Warren. MT

There was a great battle Saturday morning. The Battle of Argoed Llwyfain. Taliesin, *Welsh.* OBWVE, *tr. by* Anthony Conran

There was a great German Grammarian. Limerick. Thomas Thorneley. PeLi

There was a great Marxist called Lenin. Limerick. Ted Pauker. PeLi

There was a great Marxist called Lenin. Progress. Robert Conquest. OBCoV

There was a hag who kept two chambermaids. The Hag and the Slavies. Jean de La Fontaine, *French.* AWP; OBVE, *tr. by* Edward Marsh

There was a hardware shop in Main Street sold. Didn't He Ramble. James Simmons. PNI

There was a jolly beggar, and a begging he was born. The Jolly Beggar. James V, King of Scotland. OxBB

There was a jolly miller once. Isaac Bickerstaffe. EBEvV; LB; OxNR *Fr.* Love in a Village.

There was a jolly miller once. The Jolly Miller. *Unknown.* ACTP

There was a jovial beggar. The Jovial Beggar. *Unknown.* BoTP

There was a jury sat at Perth. The Earl of Errol. *Unknown.* ESPB

There was a kind lady called Gregory. Limerick. James Joyce. FaBoEE; PeLi

There was a kind of drooping bronze head. The Founder. Gerald Stern. NAmP90

There Was a King. *Unknown.* CBNP; NBLV; OxBoLi

There was a king, and a very great king. Lady Diamond. *Unknown.* ESPB

There was a king met a king. *Unknown.* OxNR

There was a knicht riding frae the east. Riddles Wisely Expounded. *Unknown.* CH; ESPB; OxBoLi

There was a knight, an he had a daughter. Erlinton. *Unknown.* ESPB

There was a knight and a lady bright. The Broomfield Hill. *Unknown.* ESPB; OxBB

There was a knight, in a summer's night. The Bonny Birdy. *Unknown.* ESPB

There was a Knight of Bethlehem. Song. Henry Neville Maughan. BoTP *Fr.* The Husband of Poverty.

There was a lady all skin and bone. The Skin-and-Bone Lady. *Unknown.* AmFP

There was a lady fair and gay. The Wife of Usher's Well. *Unknown.* ESPB

There was a lady fine and gay. Willie o [or of] Winsbury. *Unknown.* AmFP; ESPB

There was a lady lived in a hall. Two Red Roses across the Moon. William Morris. EBVV; UV

There was a lady lived in York. The Cruel Mother. *Unknown.* AmFP

There Was a Lady Loved a Swine. *Unknown.* OxNR; PFE

There was a lady of beauty rare. The Wife of Usher's Well. *Unknown.* AmFP

There was a lady of the North Country. Riddles Wisely Expounded. *Unknown.* ESPB

There was a Lass of Islington. The Fair Lass of Islington. *Unknown.* OxBB

There was a little Baby once. A Child's Christmas Carol. Christine Chaundler. BoTP

There was a little boy and a little girl. Boy and Girl. Mother Goose. OxNR; ReMoGo

There was a little boy went into a barn. *Unknown.* OxNR

There was a little dog, and he had a little tail. *Unknown.* BoTP; CTAV

There Was a Little Girl. Mother Goose, *st.* 1; *sts.* 2 *and* 3, *Unknown, at. to* Longfellow. BLPA; FaBoCh; OxBChV; OxNR; ReMoGo

There was a little girl. *Unknown.* FPC

There was a little girl, and she had a little curl. Jemima. *Unknown.* ACTP

There was a little guinea-pig. A Guinea-Pig Song. *Unknown.* OxBChV; PeP

There was a little maid, and she was afraid. *Unknown.* OxNR

There was a little man. The Little Man and Maid. *Unknown.* ACTP

There was a little man. *Unknown.* OBCoV *Fr.* Advertising Rhymes.

There was a little man and he had a little can. No More Booze. *Unknown.* AS; OBAL

There was a little man, / And he had a little gun. Sam, The Sportsman. Mother Goose. LB; OxNR; ReMoGo

There was a little man, / and he wooed a little maid. Mother Goose. OxNR; ReMoGo

There was a little one-eyed gunner. *Unknown.* OxNR

There was a little rabbit sprig. *Unknown.* BoTP

There was a little rill of water, near the den. The Coyote. Carter Revard. VoR

There was a little ship in South Amerikee. The Sweet Trinity. *Unknown.* AmFP

There was a little turtle. The Little Turtle. Vachel Lindsay. CTV; NOxBChV; NTCP; OBAL; OBCA; OBSP

There was a little woman, as I've been told. Hot Codlins. *Unknown.* ReMoGo

There was a Mad Man. *Unknown.* CBNP

There was a maid come out of Kent. A Maid of Kent. *Unknown.* CBLP; OxBoLi

There was a maid, richly arrayd. Blancheflour and Jellyflorice. *Unknown.* ESPB

There was a man a-coming from the south. Trooper and Maid. *Unknown.* AmFP

There was a man and he had nought. Mother Goose. OxNR; ReMoGo

There Was a Man and He Was Mad. *Unknown.* RB

There was a man, and his name was Dob. *Unknown.* CTAV; OxNR

There was a man, he went mad. *Unknown.* OxNR

There was a man here, Samian born, but he. Ovid. NAWM-1, *tr. by* Rolfe Humphries *Fr.* Metamorphoses.

There was a man in Arkansaw. Tuscaloosa Sam. "Orpheus C. Kerr." OBAL

There was a man in olden times. Dives and Lazarus. *Unknown.* AmFP

There was a man in our town. Man in Our Town. *Unknown.* ReMoGo

There was a man in the land of Ur. Services. Carl Rakosi. ChIV-1

There was a man in The Land of Uz whose name was Job. Job. Bible, *O.T.* NAWM-1

There was a man lived in the moon. Aiken Drum. *Unknown.* FaBoCh; OxNR

There was a man named Johnny Sands, who married Betty Hague. Johnny Sands. *Unknown.* AmFP

There was a man, now please take note. The Goat. *Unknown.* CTAV; PoLF

There was a man of double deed. *Unknown.* OxNR; RB

There was a man of Thessaly. Alexander's Song. *Unknown.* CBNP; LB; OxNR

There was a man rode through our town. *Unknown.* OxNR

There was a Man so Wise. *Unknown.* CBNP

There was a man spent seven years in hell's circles. Political. Rita Dove. FFC

There was a man who found two leaves. The Fall. Russell Edson. LCAP-2

There was a man who had no eyes. *Unknown.* OxNR

There was a man who had too many mustaches. It began with the one. The Way Things Are. Russell Edson. WeT

There was a man who married a maid. She laughed as he led her home. I Love My Love. Helen Adam. NeAP; WPOW

There was a man who never was. Dennis Lee. KaS

There was a man who studied the art of disappearing. A Parable. Li K'ai-hsien, *Chinese.* CoBLCP, *tr. by* Jonathan Chaves

There was a man who wanted to be an amateur animal. He could. The Amateur. Russell Edson. LCAP-2

There was a man who watched the river flow. The Cranes of Ibycus. Emma Lazarus. APN-2

There was a man who won a beautiful woman. The Slighted Lady. Anna Wickham. LW

There was a man who would marry his mother. The Having to Love Something Else. Russell Edson. FiLi

There was a man whose nose was long. Leonard Clark. FuFo

There Was a Man with a Tongue of Wood. Stephen Crane. MeMAP; MoAmPo *Fr.* War Is Kind.

There was a man with tongue of wood. The Tongue of Wood. *Unknown.* PFE

There was a man within our tenement. The Spritely Dead. Oscar Williams. Son *Fr.* Variations on a Theme.

"There was a marriage in Cana of Galilee. . . And both." The Bridegroom of Cana. Marjorie Lowry Christie Pickthall. TrCP

There was a monkey climbed a tree. *Unknown.* OxNR

There was a mountain, over its black roots [the deer]. Papago. CA

There was a moupit, mither mauch. The Hungry Mauchs. William Soutar. FaBoTC

There was a naughty Boy. The Naughty Boy. Keats. BoTP; CBNP; CTV; FHYEP; FaBoCh; OBCoV; OxBChV *Fr.* A Song about Myself.

There was a path. Place. Robert Creeley. LCAP-2

There was a pattering in the rafters, mother. Dialogue. James McAuley. BMAP

There was a piper had a cow. Piper and His Cow, The. Mother Goose. OxNR; ReMoGo

There was a poet whose untimely tomb. Shelley. FHYEP; TOF *Fr.* Alastor; or, The Spirit of Solitude. OAEL-2; Ro

There was a Presbyterian cat. *Unknown.* FaBoCh

There was a professor of Beaulieu. Materialism. C. E. M. Joad. PeLi

There was a queen that fell in love with a jolly sailor. The Sailor and the Shark. Paul Fort, *French.* OBMV, *tr. by* Frederick York Powell

There was a Raja, pious-minded, just. Sâvitrî; or, Love and Death. *Unknown.* TAL, *tr. by* Sir Edwin Arnold *Fr.* The Mahabharata.

There was a rash fellow called Weir. Limerick. *Unknown.* PeLi

There was a rat, for want of stairs. *Unknown.* OxNR

There was a rich lady, from London she came. A Rich Irish Lady. *Unknown.* AmFP

There was a rich lord, and lived in Forfar. Bonnie Annie. *Unknown.* ESPB

There was a rich man, who was clothed in purple and fine linen. Luke 16:19–26; "There was a rich man." Bible, O.T. Robert Frost. *Fr.* St. Luke.

There was a river under First and Main. Prairie Town. William Stafford. PFE

There was a road ran past our house. The Unexplorer. Edna St. Vincent Millay. PoA

There was a roaring in the wind all night. Resolution and Independence. Wordsworth. EBEV; FHYEP; HAP; InPS-3; NOBE; NOBRP; NOCV; NoP-4; OAEL-2; OBNC; OxAEP-2; PoEL-4; Ro; TFi

There was a roof over our heads. Alberto A. Ríos. FYAP; ImGa *Fr.* Lost on September Trail, 1967.

There was a row in the pub. After the Massacre. Musaemura Bonus Zimunya. PeSAV

There was a saviour. Dylan Thomas. ChIV-2

There was a Serpent who had to sing. The Serpent. Theodore Roethke. NOxBChV

There was a set before me a mighty hill. There Was Set Before Me a Mighty Hill. Stephen Crane. MeMAP

There was a shepherd's dochter [*or* daughter]. The Knight and Shepherd's Daughter. *Unknown.* ESPB; OxBB

There was a shepherd's son. Blow the Winds, I-Ho. *Unknown.* OxBoLi

There was a ship called *The Golden Vanitie.* The Golden Vanitie. *Unknown.* EnSB

There was a sick man of Tobago. Limerick. *Unknown.* OxBChV; PeLi

There was a small boy of Quebec. Limerick. Rudyard Kipling. PeLi

There was a song. Gerald William Barrax. GT

There was a sound of hunting in the mountains. Incident on a Front Not Far from Castel di Sangro. Harry Brown. NYBP

There was a sound of revelry by night. The Eve of Waterloo. Byron. EBEV; EBEvV; FaBoBe; FaBoCh; NOBE; OBNC; OBWP; OxAEP-2; TFi *Fr.* Childe Harold's Pilgrimage.

There was a stange student from Yale. *Unknown.* PeLi

There was a stunted handpost just on the crest. Near Lanivet, 1872. Thomas Hardy. AWP; CMoP; NoAM

There was a sudden croon of lilies. The Martyrdom of St. Theresa. Alec Derwent Hope. CBAP

There was a sunlit absence. Mossbawn Sunlight. Seamus Heaney. APAD; BIrV *Fr.* Mossbawn. CIP-2; PNI

There was a taut dryness all that summer. A Lyric Afterwards. Tom Paulin. PNI

There was a thing a full month old. *Unknown.* OxNR

There was a tide-mark on the jetty which. The Landfall. John Blight. BMAP

There was a time. To My Daughter. Keorapetse Kgositsile. GT

There was a time for discoveries. Voyage West. Archibald MacLeish. VGW

There was a time, in Esher's peaceful grove. An Heroic Epistle to Sir William Chambers. William Mason. OBGa *Fr.* An Heroic Epistle to Sir William Chambers.

There was a time in former years. She Hears The Storm. Thomas Hardy. LoP; NAEL-2

There was a time, Lesbia, when. *Carmina*, LXXII. Catullus. OBVE, *tr. by* Richard Lovelace; OxBSP, *tr. by* William Walsh *Fr.* Carmina.

There was a time, now very far away. Ballad of Immoral Earnings. Bertolt Brecht. OxBoV, *tr. by* Ralph Manheim *and* John Willett *Fr.* The Threepenny Opera.

There was a time on this fair continent. Charles Mair. NOBC *Fr.* Tecumseh.

There was a time, poor phrensied maid. To a Maniac. Amelia Alderson Opie. NOBRP

There was a time (such songs begin this way). Inflation. Charles O. Hartman. PoA

There was a time! that time the muse bewails. Verses on Hearing That an Airy and Pleasant Situation, near a Populous and Commercial Town, Was Surrounded with New Buildings. Maria Logan. ECWP

There was a time when death was terror. New Fashions. George Moses Horton. OBAL

There was a time when Eucritus and I were going. Theocritus. *See* Harvest-Home.

There was a time when fanfares. Decampment. Ernst Stadler, *German.* PeFWW, *tr. by* David McDuff

There was a time when I could. Aerin 4. Chi-ha Kim, *Korean.* CKP, *tr. by* Jaihiun Kim

There was a time, when I could feel. Palinodia. Winthrop Mackworth Praed. CBLP

There was a time when I could fly. I, Icarus. Alden Nowlan. NOxBChV

There was a time when I thought sweeter than the quiet. The Wild Man Comes to the Monastery. *Unknown.* RaBo

There was a time when I was very small. Childhood. Jens Baggesen, *Danish.* AWP, *tr. by* Longfellow

There was a time when meadow, grove and stream. Wordsworth. ImPo; NAEL-2; PBMP; SCGP; TFi; TOF; TRP *Fr.* Ode: Intimations of Immortality [from Recollections of Early Childhood]. AWP; FHYEP; HAP; HeIP-4; NOBE; NOBRP; OAEL-2; OBEV; OBNC; PBMP; PoE; PoEL-4

There was a time when the only worth. Dennis Brutus. VCWP

There was a trombonist called Herb. Limerick. Ron Rubin. PeLi

There was a troop of merry gentlemen. The Broom of Cowdenknows. *Unknown.* ESPB

There was a tumult in the city. Independence Bell—July 4, 1776. *Unknown.* BLPA; FaBoBe

There was a water dump there and regimental. Crucifix Corner. Ivor Gurney. NSI

There was a wealthy merchant / In London still did dwell. The Wars of Santa Fe. *Unknown.* AmFP

There was a weasel lived in the sun. The Gallows. Edward Thomas. GEA; InPS-3; MoBrPo; MoP; NoAM; SCGP; UnPo

There was a wee bit mousikie. Cheetie-Poussie-Cattie, O. *Unknown.* FaBoCh

There was a wee bit wifie. *Unknown.* OxNR

There was a wee lassie of Ulva. Limerick. David Fisher. PeLi

There was a whispering in my hearth. Miners. Wilfred Owen. MoBrPo; NAEL-2; NOBE; NSI; OBWVE; OxAEP-2; PeFWW

There was a wicked woman called Malady Festing. Angel Boley. Stevie Smith. EBNV

There was a widow-woman lived in far Scotland. The Wife of Usher's Well. *Unknown.* ESPB

There was a Wife from Bath, a well-appearing, *mod. vers. by* Louis Untermeyer. Chaucer. *See* Seven Pilgrims: A Wyf of Bathe.

There was a witch. Two Witches. Charles Reznikoff. OTCP

There was a witch who knitted things. Knitted Things. Karla Kuskin. KaS *Fr.* Knitted Things.

There was a woman in Ithaca. Toast. Leonard Nathan. BLT

There was a wood, a witches' wood. The Witches' Wood. Mary Elizabeth Coleridge. PBWP; VWP

There was a young artist called Saint. Limerick. *Unknown.* PeLi

There was a young belle of old Natchez. Requiem. Ogden Nash. KaS; NoP-4

There was a young boy, Jack Horner. Limerick. Fiona Pitt-Kethley. PeLi

There was a young bride named McWing. Limerick. *Unknown.* PeLi

There was a young critic of King's. Limerick. Arthur Clement Hilton. PeLi

There was a young curate called Lloyd. Limerick. Duncan Campbell McGregor. PeLi

There was a young curate of Hants. Limerick. Edmund George Valpy Knox. PeLi

There was a young curate of Kew. Limerick. *Unknown.* PeLi

There was a young curate of Salisbury. Limerick. *Unknown.* PeLi

There was a young doctor, from London he came. The Fair Damsel from London. *Unknown.* AmFP

There was a young faggot called Willy. Limerick. Kenneth Petchenik. PeLi

There was a young farmer of Leeds. *Unknown.* FuFo

There was a young fellow called Baker. Limerick. *Unknown.* PeLi

There was a young fellow called Bliss. Limerick. *Unknown.* PeLi

There was a young fellow called Cager. Limerick. *Unknown.* PeLi

There was a young fellow called Chubb. Limerick. *Unknown.* PeLi

There was a young fellow called Clyde. Limerick. *Unknown.* PeLi

There was a young fellow called Crouch. Limerick. Victor Gray. NOBL; PeLi

There was a young fellow called Hall. Limerick. *Unknown.* PeLi

There was a young fellow called Lancelot. Limerick. *Unknown.* PeLi

There was a young fellow called Price. Limerick. *Unknown.* PeLi

There was a young fellow called Shit. Limerick. Victor Gray. PeLi

There was a young fellow called Wyatt. Limerick. *Unknown.* PeLi

There was a young fellow from Tyne. Limerick. *Unknown.* PeLi

There was a young fellow named Cholmondeley. Nomenclaturik. Harry Hearson. OBCoV

There was a young fellow named Fisher. Limerick. *Unknown.* PeLi

There was a young fellow named Fonda. Limerick. Ogden Nash. PeLi

There was a young fellow named Menzies. Limerick. *Unknown.* PeLi

There was a young fellow named Skinner. Limerick. Norman Douglas. PeLi

There was a young fellow named Sydney. Limerick. Don Marquis. PeLi

There was a young fellow of Burma. Limerick. Aldous Leonard Huxley. PeLi

There was a young Fellow of Caius. Limerick. *Unknown.* NOBL

There was a young fellow of Ceuta. Limerick. *Unknown.* PeLi

There was a young Fellow of King's. Limerick. *Unknown.* NOBL

There was a young fellow of Lyme. Limerick. *Unknown.* PeLi

There was a young fellow of Perth. Limerick. *Unknown.* PeLi

There was a young fellow of Trinity. Limerick. *Unknown.* PeLi

There was a young Fellow of Wadham. Limerick. *Unknown.* NOBL

There was a young Fellow of Wadham / Who asked for a ticket to Sodom. Limerick. *Unknown.* PeLi

There was a young fellow went by. Trinity Brethren Attend. Ivor Armstrong Richards. CRP

There was a young genius of Queens'. Limerick. Arthur Clement Hilton. PeLi

There was a young girl called Bianca. Limerick. *Unknown.* PeLi

There was a young girl from a Mission. Limerick. A. H. Baynes. PeLi

There was a young girl from Uttoxeter / Who kept hens, but refused to have cocks. It a. Limerick. Alastair Chambre. PeLi

There was a young girl from Uttoxeter / Who made passing oarsmen gape through locks at her. Limerick. L. W. Bailey. PeLi

There was a young girl from Uttoxeter / Who one dreary night had a fox at her. Limerick. George Cowley. PeLi

There was a young girl from Uttoxeter / Who out on a date with two Jocks at a. Limerick. Bob Scott. PeLi

There was a young girl from Uttoxeter / Who sported a tight-fitting baroque sweater. Limerick. Stanley J. Sharpless. PeLi

There was a young girl in the choir. The Young Girl in the Choir. *Unknown.* FuFo

There was a young girl of Aberystwyth. Limerick. Swinburne. PeLi

There was a young girl of Asturias. The Young Girl of Asturias. *Unknown.* FuFo

There was a young girl of Australia. Limerick. *Unknown.* PeLi

There was a young girl of Bahari. Limerick. R. P. M. Lehmann. PeLi

There was a young girl of Cape Cod. Limerick. *Unknown.* PeLi

There was a young girl of Darjeeling. Limerick. *Unknown.* PeLi

There was a young girl of East Anglia. Limerick. Aldous Leonard Huxley. PeLi

There was a young girl of La Plata. Limerick. *Unknown.* PeLi

There was a Young Girl of Majorca. Limerick. Edward Lear. PeLi

There was a young girl of Mauritius. Limerick. Victor Gray. PeLi

There was a young girl of old Natchez. Limerick. Ogden Nash. PeLi

There was a young girl of Penzance. Limerick. *Unknown.* PeLi

There was a young girl of Shanghai. Limerick. Bertrand Arthur William Russell, 3d Earl Russell. PeLi

There was a young girl of Siam. Limerick. *Unknown.* PeLi

There was a young girl of St. Cyr. Limerick. *Unknown.* PeLi

There was a young girl of Tralee. Limerick. *Unknown.* PeLi

There was a young girl of Trebarwith. Limerick. R. J. P. Hewlson. PeLi

There was a young girl of Uttoxeter / Who noticed that men waved their cocks at her. Limerick. D. Kartun. PeLi

There was a young girl of Uttoxeter / Who worked nine to five as a choc-setter. Limerick. Stanley J. Sharpless. PeLi

There was a young girl whose frigidity. Limerick. *Unknown.* PeLi

There was a young girl with a hernia. Limerick. Heywood Broun. PeLi

There was a young goat named Billy. Billy Goat. *Unknown.* CTAV

There was a young gourmand of John's. Limerick. Arthur Clement Hilton. PeLi

There was a young Jap on a syndicate. Limerick. *Unknown.* PeLi

There was a young Japanese geisha. Limerick. Ron Rubin. PeLi

There was a young lady at court. Limerick. D. H. Cudmore. PeLi

There was a young lady called Alice. Limerick. *Unknown.* PeLi

There was a young lady called Clarice. Limerick. H. A. C. Evans. PeLi

There was a young lady called Dawes. *Unknown.* PeLi

There was a young lady called Etta. Limerick. *Unknown.* PeLi

There was a young lady called Flynn. Limerick. *Unknown.* PeLi

There was a young lady called Gloria. Limerick. *Unknown.* PeLi

There was a young lady called Harris. Limerick. Ogden Nash. PeLi

There was a young lady called Hilda. Limerick. *Unknown.* PeLi

There was a young lady called Kate. Limerick. *Unknown.* PeLi

There was a young lady called Maud. Limerick. *Unknown.* PeLi

There was a young lady called Muffet. Limerick. *Unknown.* PeLi

There was a young lady called Smith. Limerick. *Unknown.* PeLi

There was a young lady called Starky. Limerick. *Unknown.* PeLi

There was a young lady from Gloucester. Sometimes Even Parents Win. John Ciardi. NOxBChV

There was a young lady from Lynn. *Unknown.*
("She slid down through the straw and fell in.") (LL) KaS
("There was a young lady of Lynn.") CTV

There was a young lady from Pecking. Limerick. *Unknown.* PeLi

There was a young lady from Ulva. Limerick. Russell Lucas. PeLi

There was a Young lady in White. Limerick. Edward Lear. PeLi

There was a young lady named [*or* called] Bright. Limerick. Arthur Buller. NOBL; OxBoLi; PeLV; PeLi

There was a young lady named Kent. Limerick. *Unknown.* PeLi

There was a young lady named Maggie. Maggie. *Unknown.* PeP

There was a young lady named Miller. Austen Baker. PeLi

There was a young lady of Aenos. Limerick. *Unknown.* PeLi

There was a young lady of Brabant. Limerick. *Unknown.* PeLi

There was a young lady of Chichester. Limerick. *Unknown.* PeLi

There was a young lady of Chiswick. Limerick. *Unknown.* PeLi

There was a young lady of Ealing. Allan M. Laing. PeLi

There was a young lady of Ealing. Limerick. *Unknown.* PeLi

There was a young lady of Ealing / And her lover before her was kneeling. Limerick. Isaac Asimov. PeLi

There was a young lady of fashion. Limerick. *Unknown.* PeLi

There was a young lady of Florence. Limerick. *Unknown.* PeLi

There was a young lady of Graz. Limerick. George Seferis, *Greek,* CBNP, *tr. by* Peter Levi

There was a young lady of Joppa. Limerick. *Unknown.* PeLi

There was a young lady of Kew. Limerick. *Unknown.* PeLV

There was a young lady of Leicester. Limerick. Alan Clark. PeLi

There was a young lady of Limerick. Limerick. Andrew Lang. PeLi

There was a young lady of Louth. Limerick. Norman Douglas. PeLi

There was a Young Lady of Lucca. Limerick. *Unknown.* CBNP

There was a young lady of Lundy. Limerick. W. F. N. Watson. PeLi

There was a young lady of Lynn. *Unknown. See* There was a young lady from Lynn.

There was a young lady of Nantes. Limerick. S. Littman. PeLi

There Was a Young Lady of Niger. Cosmo Monkhouse. NBLV; TLR

There was a young lady of Niger. The Young Lady of Niger. *Unknown.* FPC

There was a young lady of Nîmes. Limerick. "Little Billee." PeLi

There was a Young Lady of Norway, / Who casually sat in a doorway. Limerick. Edward Lear. EBEV; PeLi

There was a young lady of Norway / Who hung by her toes in a doorway. Limerick. Swinburne. PeLi

There was a Young Lady of Parma. Limericks, I (v). Edward Lear. OBCoV

There was a young lady of Portugal. Limericks, II (iv). Edward Lear. OBCoV; OxBoLi; PeLV; PeLi

There was a young lady of Rheims. Moonshine. Walter De la Mare. OBCoV

There was a young lady of Riga. Limerick. Cosmo Monkhouse. PeLi

There was a young lady of Riga. *Unknown.* CTV

There was a young lady of Ryde, / Who ate some green apples and died. Limerick. *Unknown.* PeLi

There was a young lady of Ryde / Who was carried too far by the tide. Limerick. *Unknown.* PeLi

There was a young lady of Ryde / Whose shoe-strings were seldom untied. Limerick. Edward Lear. OxBoLi; PeLV; PeLi

There was a young lady of Rye. Limerick. *Unknown.* PeLi

There was a young lady of Slough. Limerick. *Unknown.* PeLi

There was a young lady of Spain. Limerick. *Unknown*. PeLi

There was a young lady of station. Limerick. "Lewis Carroll." PeLi

There was a young lady of Sweden. Limerick. Edward Lear. CBNP; EBEV; PeVV

There was a young lady of Tottenham. Limerick. *Unknown*. PeLi; WeW-3

There was a young lady of Trent. Limerick. *Unknown*. PeLi

There was a young lady of Twickenham. Oliver Herford. KaS

There was a young lady of Twickenham. The Young Lady of Twickenham. *Unknown*. FuFo

There was a young lady of Ulva / Who drunkenly said: 'What a hulva'. Limerick. Bill Greenwell. PeLi

There was a young lady of Ulva / Who kept a pet bee in her hand-bag. Limerick. T. Johnston. PeLi

There was a young lady of Ulva / Who said: 'I have granted a culver'. Limerick. T. Griffiths. PeLi

There was a young lady of Ulva / Who was famed far and wide for her vulva. Limerick. Gavin Ewart. PeLi

There was a young lady of Ulva / Whose boy-friend said: "Look, I will pulver." Limerick. Stanley J. Sharpless. PeLi

There was a young lady of Ulva / Whose sexual feelings were null. Va. Limerick. Barbara E. Goff. PeLi

There was a young lady of Wantage. Limerick. *Unknown*. PeLi

There was a young lady of Where? Limerick. *Unknown*. PeLi

There was a young lady of Whitby. Limerick. "Lewis Carroll." PeLi

There was a young lady. . . tut, tut! Limerick. Stanley J. Sharpless. PeLi

There was a young lady whose bonnet. Edward Lear. EBEV

There was a Young Lady whose chin. Limerick. Edward Lear. PeLi

There was a young lady whose eyes. Limerick: "There was a young lady whose eyes." Edward Lear. EBEV; NOBVV

There Was a Young Lady Whose Nose. Edward Lear. EBEV

There was a young lass of Pitlochry. Limerick. *Unknown*. PeLi

There was a young lawyer called Rex. Limerick. *Unknown*. PeLi

There was a young maid of Peru. Limerick. Isaac Asimov. PeLi

There was a young maid who said, "Why." Limerick. *Unknown*. SoSe-8

There was a young maiden from Multerry. Limerick. *Unknown*. PeLi

There was a young maiden of Devon. Limerick. *Unknown*. PeLi

There was a young man from Darjeeling. Limerick. *Unknown*. PeLi

There was a young man named Racine. Limerick. *Unknown*. PeLi

There was a young man of Australia. Limerick. *Unknown*. PeLi

There was a young man of Belgrade. Limerick. Isaac Asimov. PeLi

There was a young man of Bengal. *Unknown*. OxBoLi

There was a young man of Calcutta. Limerick. *Unknown*. PeLi

There was a young man of Cape Horn. Limerick. Swinburne. PeLi

There was a young man of Cape Race. Limerick. *Unknown*. PeLi

There was a young man of Devizes. Limerick. Archibald Marshall. PeLi

There was a young man of Devizes. The Young Man of Devizes. *Unknown*. FuFo

There was a young man of Dumfries. Limerick. *Unknown*. PeLi

There was a young man of Ghent. Limerick. *Unknown*. PeLi

There was a young man of Japan. Limerick. *Unknown*. PeLi

There was a young man of Madras. Limerick. *Unknown*. PeLi

There was a young man of Montrose. Limerick. Arnold Bennett. OxBoLi; PeLi

There was a young man of Nepal. Limerick. *Unknown*. PeLi

There was a young man of Newcastle. Limerick. Terence Melican. PeLi

There was a young man of Ostend. Limerick. E. O. Parrott. PeLi

There was a young man of Porthcawl. Limerick. A. G. Prys-Jones. PeLi

There was a young man of St John's. Limerick. *Unknown*. PeLV

There was a young man of Wood's Hole. Limerick. *Unknown*. PeLi

There was a young man so benighted. Limerick. Frances Parkinson Keyes. PeLi

There was a young man who asked, "Why." The Young Man Who Couldn't See Why. *Unknown*. FuFo

There was a young man who said: "Ayer." Limerick. *Unknown*. PeLi

There was a young man who said, Damn! Determinism. Maurice Evan Hare. OBCoV

There was a young monarch called Ed. Limerick. *Unknown*. PeLi

There was a young monk from Siberia. Limerick. *Unknown*. PeLi

There was a young outlaw named Hood. Limerick. E. O. Parrott. PeLi

There was a young peasant named Gorse. Limerick. *Unknown*. PeLi

There was a young person called Tate. Limerick. Carolyn Wells. PeLi

There was a Young Person of Ayr. Edward Lear. KaS

There was a Young Person of Kew. Limerick. Edward Lear. CBNP

There was a young person of Leigh. Limerick. Basil Ransome-Davies. PeLi

There was a young person of Smyrna. Limerick. Edward Lear. OxBoLi; PeLV

There was a young person whose history. Limericks, II (i). Edward Lear. OBCoV

There was a young plumber of Leigh. Limerick. *Unknown*. PeLi

There was a young poet of Kew. Limerick. *Unknown*. PeLi

There was a young poet of Thusis. Limerick. *Unknown*. OxBoLi; PeLi

There was a young priest of Dun Laoghaire. Limerick. *Unknown*. PeLi

There was a young princess, Snow-White. Limerick. Gerard Benson. PeLi

There was a young student called Fred. Limerick. V. R. Ormerod. PeLi

There was a young student called Jones. Limerick. *Unknown*. PeLi

There was a young student of John's. Limerick. *Unknown*. PeLi

There was a young woman, as I've heard tell. Ripperty! Kye! Ahoo! Henry Lawson. CBAP

There was a young woman called Myrtle. Limerick. *Unknown*. PeLi

There was a young woman called Starkie. Limerick: "There was a young woman called Starky." *Unknown*. NOBL

There was a young woman from Aenos. The Young Woman from Aenos. *Unknown*. OBAL

There was a young woman named Plunnery. Limerick. Edward Gorey. OBAL

There was a young woman of Dee. Limerick. *Unknown*. PeLi

There was a young woman who said. Limerick. Frances Darwin Cornford. PeLi

There was a youth[e], and a well belovd [*or* well-belovéd] youth[e]. The Bailiff's Daughter of Islington. *Unknown*. ESPB; OxBB; OxBoLi; PBMP

There was aince an auld body o' Sydney. Limerick. *Unknown*. OBCoV

There was airy music and sport at the fair. The Fair at Windgap. Austin Clarke. OxBTC

There was always the river or the train. Grandmother Watching at Her Window. W. S. Merwin. VGW

There was an a May and she lo'ed na men. Were Ne My Hearts Light I Wad Dye. Lady Grisel Baillie. KTR

There was an ancient Grecian boy. A Tiger Tale. John Bennett. OBCA

There was an ancient sage philosopher. Arms and the Man. Samuel Butler. NOSC *Fr.* Hudibras.

There was an ancient spring inside the glacier. Found. Carol Muske. AmPA

There was an archdeacon who said. Limerick. *Unknown*. OBCoV; OxBoLi

There was an Auchtergaven mouse. A Whigmaleerie. William Soutar. OxBS

There was an end to hearts and rhymes. John Hollander. EOEF

There was an Indian, who had known no change. Sonnet. Sir John Collings Squire. CH

There was an old [*or* little woman], as I've heard tell. The Old Woman and the Pedlar. Mother Goose. LB; OxNR; ReMoGo

There was an old bear that lived near a wood. The Bear and the Squirrels. Christopher Pearse Cranch. OBCA

There was an old Begum of Frome. Walter De la Mare. PeLi

There was an old Bey of Calcutta. Limerick. *Unknown*. PeLi

There was an old chap who said: "Well." W. Stewart. PeLi

There was an old codger of Broome. The Old Codger of Broome. *Unknown*. FuFo

There was an old crow. *Unknown*. OxNR

There was an old cynic who said. Limerick. Allan M. Laing. PeLi

There was an old dame from Jerusalem. Limerick. George Seferis, *Greek*. CBNP, *tr. by* Hugh Haughton

There was an old dame of Toulouse. Limerick. A. M. Sayers. PeLi

There was an old decan-/ ter. Song of the Decanter. Alfred Gibbs Campbell. AAP

There was an old Doctor called Coué. Limerick. Bob Scott. PeLi

There was an old drunk called Hieronymus. Limerick. Ron Rubin. PeLi

There was an old drunkard of Devon. Limerick. Ron Rubin. PeLi

There was an old farmer in Sussex did dwell. The Farmer's Curst Wife. *Unknown*. ESPB

There was an old farmer of Readall. Melodies. "Lewis Carroll." CBNP

There was an old fellow called Hugger. Arnold Hyde. PeLi

There was an old fellow named Hewing. Limerick. *Unknown*. PeLi

There was an old fellow of Fife. Limerick. *Unknown*. PeLi

There was an old fellow of Kaber. Limerick. Philip Larkin. OBCoV

There was an old fellow of Kaber. Limerick. Philip Larkin. OBCoV

There was an old fellow of Trinity. Limerick. Arthur Clement Hilton. PeLi

There was an old fellow of Tyre. The Old Fellow from Tyre. *Unknown*. FuFo

There was an old Fox. The Owl and the Fox. *Unknown*. BLPA

There was an old gossip called Baird. Limerick. Ogden Nash. PeLi

There was an old housewife of Staines. Limerick. E. O. Parrott. PeLi

There Was an Old Lady Named Crockett. William Jay Smith. KaS

There was an old lady of Chertsey. Limericks, II (ii). Edward Lear. OBCoV; OxBChV

There was an old lady of Harrow. An Old Lady of Harrow. *Unknown.* PeLi

There was an old lady of Leicester. Limerick. Ian T. MacKenzie. PeLi

There was an old Lady of Winchelsea. Limericks, I (ii). Edward Lear. OBCoV

There was an old madam called Rainey. Limerick. *Unknown.* PeLi

There was an old maid of Duluth. Limerick. *Unknown.* PeLi

There was an old man, / And he had a calf. *Unknown.* OxNR

There was an old man and he lived [out] in a wood. Broom, Green Broom. *Unknown.* CH; OxBoLi; PoRA

There was an old man at the foot of the hill. The Farmer's Curst Wife. *Unknown.* AmFP

There was an old man called Dupree. Limerick. "R. I." PeLi

There was an old man from Darjeeling. Old Man from Darjeeling. *Unknown.* NTCP

There was an old man from Peru. *Unknown. See* Limerick: "There was an old man of [*or* from] Peru / Who dreamt [*or* dreamed] he was eating his shoe."

There was an old man in a Barge. Edward Lear. EBEV

There was an Old Man in a boat. Limerick. Edward Lear. CBNP; EBEV; OBCoV

There was an Old Man in a tree. Limerick. Edward Lear. CABP; CBNP; NoP-4; OxBChV; PeLi; Poetr

There was an old man in a trunk. Limerick. Ogden Nash. PeLi

There was an old man in a velvet coat. Mother Goose. OxNR; ReMoGo

There was an old man named Michael Finnigin. *Unknown.* CBNP

There was an old man of Bengal. Limerick. "F. Anstey." PeLi

There was an old man of Boulogne. Limerick. *Unknown.* OxBoLi; PeLV; PeLi

There was an old man of Calcutta. Arthur. Ogden Nash. NoP-4; PeLi

There was an old man of Cape Horn. Limerick. Edward Lear. CBNP; EBEV; PeLi

There Was an Old Man of Dumbree. Edward Lear. OxBChV

There was an old man of Dunblane. Limerick. Edward Lear. EBEV

There was an old man of Dundee. Limerick. *Unknown.* PeLi

There was an old man of Ibreem. Limerick. Edward Lear. EBEV

There was an old man of Kamschatka. Limerick. Edward Lear. NOBL

There was an old man of Khartoum. Limerick. William Ralph Inge. NOBL; OxBoLi, PeLi

There was an old man of Lugano. Limerick. Victor Gray. PeLi

There was an Old Man of Nantucket. The Old Man of Nantucket. *Unknown.* PeLi

There was an old man of [*or* from] Peru / Who dreamt [*or* dreamed] he was eating his shoe. Limerick. *Unknown.* NTCP; SoSe-8

There was an old man of Peru / Who never knew what he should do. Edward Lear. EBEV

There was an old man of Peru / Who watched his wife making a stew. Edward Lear. EBEV

There was an old man of St. Bees. Sir William Schwenck Gilbert. PeLV; PeLi

There was an old man of the Cape. Limerick. Robert Louis Stevenson. PeLi

There was an old man of the coast. Limerick. Edward Lear. PeLi

There was an old man of the East. Edward Lear. EBEV

There was an old man of the West. Edward Lear. EBEV

There was an old man of Thermopylae. Limerick. Edward Lear. EBEV; NOBL; OxAEP-2; PeLi

There was an old man of Tobago. *Unknown.* CBNP; ReMoGo

There was an old man of Toulouse. Limericks, II (iii). Edward Lear. OBCoV

There was an old man of West Dumpet. Edward Lear. EBEV

There was an old man of Whitehaven. Limerick. Edward Lear. CBNP; EBEV; OxAEP-2

There was an old man on some rocks. Limerick. Edward Lear. NOBVV; PeLi

There was an old man on the Border. Limerick. Edward Lear. EBEV

There was an Old Man on whose nose. Limerick. Edward Lear. PeLi

There was an old man said, "I fear." The Shubble. Walter De la Mare. OBCoV

There was an old man who averred. Limerick. *Unknown.* PeLi

There was an Old Man who forgot. Edward Lear. NOxBChV

There was an old man who had a kite for a son. An Old Man's Son. Russell Edson. LCAP-2

There was an old man who lived in Middle Row. The Five Hens. *Unknown.* OxNR

There was an old man who [*or* that] lived in the [*or* a] wood [*or* woods]. Father Grumble. *Unknown.* AmFP

There was an old man who made his will. The Dishonest Miller. *Unknown.* AmFP

There was an old man who said: "How." Limerick. Edward Lear. OxBChV; PeLi

There was an Old Man who said, "Hush!" Limerick. Edward Lear. KaS; NOBL; OxBChV; OxBoLi; PeLV; PeLi

There was an Old Man who said: 'Well!'. Limerick. Edward Lear. PeLi

There was an old man who screamed out. Limerick. Edward Lear. CBNP; EBEV; NOBVV; OxAEP-2

There was an Old Man who supposed. Limerick. Edward Lear. NAEL-2; NOBVV; NoP-4; PeLi; Poetr

There was an old man whose despair. Limericks, II (v). Edward Lear. CBNP; OBCoV

There was an old man with a beard. John Clarke. UV

There was an Old Man with a beard. Edward Lear. CBNP; CTV; NOBL; NOxBChV; NTCP; NoP-4; OPOU; OxBChV; PeLV; PeLi; Poetr; TLR ("Have all built their nests in my beard!") (LL) NoP-4

There was an Old Man with a Beard / Who said: "I demand to be feared." Limerick. Roger Woddis. PeLi

There was an old Member called Bevan. Limerick. Barbara Leigh. PeLi

There was an old mickey called Cassidy. Limerick. Conrad Potter Aiken. PeLi

There was an old miser at [*or* of] Reading. Limerick. *Unknown.* OxBChV; PeLi

There was an old party called Pennycomequick. Mr. Pennycomequick. Phyllis M. Stone. BoTP

There was an old party of lyme. Edward Lear. OxBoLi

There was an old person of Basing. Limerick. Edward Lear. CBNP; EBEV; OBCoV; OxAEP-2; PeLi

There was an old person of Blythe. Edward Lear. EBEV

There was an old person of Bow. Limerick. Edward Lear. CBNP; EBEV; OxAEP-2

There was an Old Person of Bree. Limerick. *Unknown.* CBNP

There was an Old Person of Brigg. Limerick. Edward Lear. CBNP

There was an old person of Burton. Edward Lear. EBEV

There was an Old Person of Cadiz. Limerick. *Unknown.* CBNP

There was an old person of Cassel. Edward Lear. EBEV

There was an Old Person of Cromer. Limerick. Edward Lear. PeLi

There was an old person of Dutton. Edward Lear. EBEV

There was an Old Person of Ems. Limerick. *Unknown.* CBNP

There was an old person of Fratton. Limerick. *Unknown.* PeLi

There was an old person of Grange. Limerick. Edward Lear. CBNP

There was an old person of Gretna. Limerick. Edward Lear. OBCoV; OxBChV

There was an Old Person of Hurst. Limerick. Edward Lear. PeLi

There was an old person of Persia. Limerick. William Plomer. PeLi

There was an old person of Philae. Limerick. Edward Lear. CBNP

There was an old person of Prague. Edward Lear. EBEV

There was an old person of Rhodes. Edward Lear. EBEV

There was an old person of Skye. Edward Lear. KaS

There was an Old Person of Slough. Limerick. *Unknown.* CBNP

There was an old person of Slough. Limerick. George Robey. PeLi

There was an old pros. Zelda Chevette. PeLi

There was an old Rabbi of Ur. Dear Sir. Walter De la Mare. OBCoV

There was an old sage of New Delhi. Limerick. Joyce Parr. PeLi

There was an old Scot called McTavish. Limerick. *Unknown.* PeLi

There was an old skinflint of Hitching. Buttons. Walter De la Mare. PeLi

There Was an Old Soldier. *Unknown.* AS

There was an old soldier of Bicester. *Unknown.* OxBChV

There was an old Welshman called Morgan. Limerick. Ron Rubin. PeLi

There was an old wife and she lived all alone. The Old Wife and the Ghost. James Reeves. OTCP

There was an Old Woman. *Unknown.* CBNP; ReMoGo

There was an old woman / And nothing she had. *Unknown.* OxNR

There was an old woman and she lived in a shoe. Mother Goose. *See* There was an old woman who lived in a shoe.

There was an old woman, and what do you think? The Old Woman of Norwich. *Unknown.* ACTP

There was an old woman, and what do you think? A Strange Old Woman. Mother Goose. FaBoCh; LB; ReMoGo

There was an old woman as ugly as sin. An Old Woman. Charles Henry Ross. OxBChV

There was an old woman called Nothing-at-all. Mother Goose. OxNR

There was an old woman had three cows. *Unknown.* OxNR

There was an old woman had three sons. The Three Sons. *Unknown.* ReMoGo

There was an old woman, her name was Peg. *Unknown.* OxNR

There was an old woman in Surrey. Old Woman of Surrey. Mother Goose. OxBChV; ReMoGo

There was an old woman lived on the seashore. The Two Sisters. *Unknown.* AmFP; OxBB

There was an old woman lived under a hill. Mother Goose. LB

There was an old woman / Lived under a hill / And if she's not gone. *Unknown.* OxNR

There was an old woman / Lived under a hill / She put a mouse in a bag. Mother Goose. OxNR

There was an Old Woman named Piper. William Jay Smith. TLR

There was an old woman named Towl. Mistress Towl. *Unknown.* OxBChV

There was an old woman of Clare. The Cat's Second Song. Nancy Willard. FFC

There was an Old Woman of Gloster. Limerick. *Unknown.* PeLi

There was an old woman of Gloucester. The Old Woman of Gloucester. *Unknown.* ReMoGo

There was an old woman of Harrow. Old Woman of Harrow. *Unknown.* ReMoGo

There was an old woman of Leeds. The Old Woman of Leeds. *Unknown.* ReMoGo

There was an Old Woman of Lynn. Limerick. *Unknown.* PeLi

There was an old woman of Wales. Limerick. George Seferis, *Greek.* CBNP, *tr. by* Peter Levi

There was an old woman sat spinning. That's All. Mother Goose. OxNR; ReMoGo

There was an old woman / Sold puddings and pies. *Unknown.* OxNR

There was an old woman toss[ed] *or* tosso up in a basket [*or* blanket]. Old Woman, Old Woman. Mother Goose. LB; OxNR; ReMoGo

There was an old woman tossed up in a basket. *Unknown.* ACTP

There was an old woman / Went blackberry picking. Berries. Walter De la Mare. MoBrPo

There was an old woman who lived in a shoe. Mother Goose. FaBoBe; ImGa; LB; OxNR; ReMoGo

("And whipped them all soundly and sent them to bed.") (LL) LB

("There was an old woman and she lived in a shoe.") OxBoLi

There was an old woman / Who lived in Dundee. *Unknown.* OxNR

There was an old woman who never was wed. Ballad of an Old Woman. Frank A. Collymore. NOxBChV; NTP; PBCV

There was an orchestra—Bingo-Bango. F. Scott Fitzgerald. *See* There'd be an orchestra.

There was an owl lived in an oak, *sl. diff. vers.* The Owl in the Oak. *Unknown.* OxNR

There was an owl lived in an oak. *Unknown.* OxNR

There was an unwanted child. End, Middle, Beginning. Anne Sexton. PoE

There was ance a may, and she lo'ed na men;. Werena My Heart Licht I Wad Dee. Lady Grisel Baillie. CABP; LW

There was, as I heard it, at hall next morning. The Mere. *Unknown.* EEP, *tr. by* Michael Alexander *Fr.* Beowulf.

There was, at the end, a look of great peace on my. I Just Wanna Testify. Cornelius Eady. IFJA

There was calm rapture in the way she spoke. John Ashbery. WeT *Fr.* The New Realism.

There was Dai Puw. He was no good. On the Farm. Ronald Stuart Thomas. NoP-4; OxBTC

There was earth inside them, and. Paul Celan, *German.* PoSu, *tr. by* Michael Hamburger

There was fire & the people were yelling. running crazy. Urban Dream. Victor Hernandez Cruz. NBV

There was great beauty by the Tree. Eve. Arthur J. Bull. UnPo

There was heard a song on the chiming sea. Song of Emigration. Felicia Dorothea Hemans. VWP

There was in danger desperate delight. The Aging Poet, on a Reading Trip to Dayton, Visits the Air Force Museum and Discovers There a Plane He Once Flew. Richard Snyder. Poetsp

There was little important. An American Boyhood. Jonathan Holden. Poetsp

There was little more that summer. Harlem. Maureen Seaton. LoHo

There was movement at the station, for the word had passed around. The Man from Snowy River. Andrew Barton Paterson. CBAP

There was never a sound beside the wood but one. Mowing. Robert Frost. CMoP; ColAP; HoPM; NAAL-2; TRP; VGW

There was never nothing more me pained [*or* payned]. Sir Thomas Wyatt. AAS; GBL; SiPS

There was no bourgeoisie, the need was not for it. Bourgeoisie. Maksimilian Aleksandrovich Voloshin, *Russian.* TCRP, *tr. by* Albert C. Todd

There was no change in the summer wind. In the Flowering Season. Michael Roberts. FaBoTw

There was no / getting around it. Philosophy. Ray Catina. CDa

There was no good solution. The Polish Knot. Tomasz Jastrun, *Polish.* AF, *tr. by* Michael March *and* Jaroslaw Anders

There was no hole in the universe to fit him. Suicide. Anne Stevenson. FaBoWP

There was no magic spell. The Dream of the Cabbage Caterpillars. Libby Houston. AYFP

There was no other guarantee. Route. George Oppen. APSN *Fr.* Route.

There was no reason to expect sadness. Wen Cheng-ming. CoBLCP, *tr. by* Jonathan Chaves *Fr.* Lines Written on New Year's Day—In the Manner of Liu Hou-ts'un [Liu K'o-chuang (1187–1269)].

There was no reason whatever for the critique of pure reason to come. Love Poem #2. Yona Wollach, *Hebrew.* IP, *tr. by* Warren Bargad *and* Stanley F. Chyet

There was no respite from pain: their bodies lay fainting. Symptoms of plague in Athens. Lucretius, *Latin.* OBCVT, *tr. by* Charles Hubert Sisson

There was no road at all to that high place. The Grove. Edwin Muir. LiTM

There was no song nor shout of joy. The Ship. Sir John Collings Squire. CH

There was no way out of that forest. Forest. Judit Tóth, *Hungarian.* CEEP, *tr. by* Emery E. George

There was once a considerate crocodile. The Considerate Crocodile. Amos Russel Wells. OBCA

There was once a Filipino hombre. A Filipino Hombre. *Unknown.* AS

There was once a hog theater where hogs performed. A Performance at Hog Theater. Russell Edson. AmPA; PmAP

There was once a little animal. Similar Cases. Charlotte Perkins Stetson Gilman. PoLF

There was once a maiden who loved a cheese. Quite the Cheese. H. C. Waring. BXAP

There was once a skeleton named Flynn. Thin Flynn. *Unknown.* FuFo

There was once a swing in a walnut tree. The Walnut Tree. David McCord. OBCA

There was once a woman whose father over the years had become an ox. The Ox. Russell Edson. RaBo

There was once a young man of Oporta. Limerick. "Lewis Carroll." PeLi

There was once two Irish labouring men; to England they came over. How Paddy Stole the Rope. *Unknown.* BLPA

There was one among us who rose. Death of a Friend. Pauli Murray. PoBA

There Was One I Met [upon the Road]. Stephen Crane. MeMAP

There was one who was perfect, who had. Sometimes. P. J. Kavanagh. OxBSn

There was only one place. Chinese Food in the Fifties. Alberto Rios. PUP-20

There was set before me a mighty hill. Stephen Crane. APN-2; MeMAP *Fr.* The Black Riders [and Other Lines].

There was six jovial tradesmen, they all sat down to drinking. When Jones's Ale Was New. *Unknown.* AmFP

There was something wrong. Ode to the Cat. Pablo Neruda. PiM, *tr. by* Ken Krabbenhoft *Fr.* Ode to the Cat.

There was still the mark of an O when he got home. (LL) The Sightseers. Paul Muldoon. BiHa; CIP-2

There was such speed in her little body. Bells for John Whiteside's Daughter. John Crowe Ransom. CMoP; ColAP; FuPo; HAP; HeIP-4; HoPM; IMW; InPK-6; InPS-3; LiTM; MeMAP; MoAmPo; MoLi; MoP; NAAL-2; NIP-4; NOBA; NoAM; NoP-4; OxBA; PFE; PoE; Poetr; RB; SAGP; TAP; TFi; UnPo; VGW; WeW-3

There was that business in Siberia, in '19. The Soviet Union. John Berryman. FaBoPV

There was that fall the fall of desire. Two. Winfield Townley Scott. NYBP

There was the buffalo blowing. Composition. Peter Blue Cloud. VoR

There was the chiropodist. Plain Song. Craig Raine. TOF

There was the Dog Man again today. One Man's Family. Rosemary Catacalos. IFJA

There was the solitary palm, or scattered clumps. In Times and Places. Umberto Piersanti, *Italian.* NeIt, *tr. by* Stephen Sartarelli

There was the sonne of Ampycus of great forecasting wit. Meleager. Ovid. CTC, *tr. by* Arthur Golding *Fr.* Metamorphoses.

There was the time I got mad and hired a detective. The Laughing Place. Minnie Bruce Pratt. CPO

There was this buoyant blue balloon. The Tenth Planet. Alan Bold. SpW

There was this empty bird cage in the garden. A Sparrow's Feather. George Barker. NYBP

There was this gym-teacher. Epigram. Strato, *Greek.* GrAn, *tr. by* Teddy Hogge

There was this head had this mouth he kept shooting off. The Mouth. Ciaran Carson. PNI

There was this road. The Legs. Robert Graves. ImPo; LiTM; PeLV; RB

There was this time in Boston. The Wedding Night. Anne Sexton. PoA

There was three kings into the east. John Barleycorn [a Ballad]. Robert Burns. FaBoCh; RB

There was three ladies play'd at the ba'. The Cruel Brother. *Unknown.* AmFP; ESPB; OxBB

There was, 'tis said, and I believe, a time. Burials. George Crabbe. OAEL-1 *Fr.* The Parish Register.

There was twa sisters in a bow'r [*or* bower]. The Twa Sisters. *Unknown.* ESPB; OxBS

There was two little boys going to the school. The Twa Brothers. *Unknown.* CH; EBEV; ESPB; OxBB

There was upon the sill a pencil mark. Edna St. Vincent Millay. *Fr.* Sonnets from an Ungrafted Tree. NALW

There was. . . what?—Pale sunsets, wide expanses. Georgy Adamovich, *Russian.* TCRP, *tr. by* Yakov Hornstein

There wasn't any riot any more. (LL) An Old Woman Remembers. Sterling Brown. ISC

There wasn't much else we could do. Shooting the Dogs. Philip Hodgins. BMAP

There we go in cars, did you guess we wore sandals? A Way of Being. Barbara Guest. FTOS

There we see him, driving. The Homing Instinct. Mark Jarman. WWSi

There we was, and wanting our tea. Limerick. "P. E. A." PeLi

There went most passionately to life, impellance. Life and Impellance. William Frederick Stevenson. NOBVV

There went out in the dawning light. A Pastoral. *Unknown, Latin.* AWP, *tr. by* John Addington Symonds

There went three children down to the shore. The Black Pebble. James Reeves. OTCP

There Were an Old and Wealthy Man. *Unknown.* AmFP

There were bizarre beginnings in old lands for the making of me. Dark Blood. Margaret Abigail Walker. NALW

There were bonfires on the hillsides. Ohakune Fires. Lauris Edmond, *Maori.* PeNZ, *tr. by* Margaret Orbell

There were distinctive. Language of Love. Rae Armantrout. PmAP

There were fifteen men in green. Men in Green. David Campbell. BMAP

There were five of us within the room. I Come to Bury Caesar. Sydney Justin Harris. PoA

There were four of us about that [*or* the] bed. Shameful Death. William Morris. GTBS-P; PeVV

There were ghosts that returned to earth to hear his phrases. Large Red Man Reading. Wallace Stevens. HAP; LCAP-2

There were heaps of hoard-things in this hall underground. The Lay of the Last Survivor. *Unknown.* EEP, *tr. by* Michael Alexander *Fr.* Beowulf.

There were ladies, they lived in a bower. Mary [*or* Marie] Hamilton. *Unknown.* ESPB

There were miners from Bisbee. Tramp Miner's Song. *Unknown.* AmFP

There were never strawberries. Strawberries. Edwin Morgan. BoLoP; NoP-4

There were no antelope on the balcony. Midnight Special. Kenneth Patchen. VGW

There were no leaders, but they were first. Dog Fox Field. Les A. Murray. BMAP

There were no lines of violent diamonds, blinding light. The Madwoman in the Park. Dame Edith Sitwell. PFTM

There were no markets in Watts. Speaking with Hands. Luis J. Rodriguez. UnSA

There were no men and women then at all. Then. Edwin Muir. CMoP; PoA; PoE

There were no poems that year. For Imelda. James Simmons. PNI

There were no undesirables or girls in my set. Commander Lowell. Robert Lowell. VGW

There were once two cats of Kilkenny. The Cats of Kilkenny. *Unknown.* ChAP; PeLi; ReMoGo

There were once two young people of taste. Limerick. Monica Curtis. PeLi

There were other forms. Other Forms of Slaughter. Catherine Obianuju Acholonu. HBAPE

There were rules. On Growing Up the Darker Berry. Harriet Jacobs. ISC

There were saddened hearts in Mudville for a week or even more. Casey's Revenge. James Wilson. BLPA

There were snakes in the / tent. I Remember Haifa Being Lovely But. Lyn Lifshin. UnSA

There were so many books. she had to separate them to avoid being. Reading. Joanne Burns. BMAP

There were some dirty plates. The Last Words of My English Grandmother. William Carlos Williams. RB; RaBo; SAmP

There were some pines, a canal, a piece of sky. Landscape with Little Figures. Donald Justice. LCAP-2

There were some shepherds living in the same part of the country. Bible, *O.T.* CTV *Fr.* The Bible, Luke 2:8–20, Phillips.

There Were Some Summers. Thomas Lux. LCAP-2

There were the black flags flying. Agami Beach. Gregory Djanikian. CMAP

There were the roses, in the rain. The Act. William Carlos Williams. SAmP; VGW

There were the whales, six of them. The Stranded Whales. Geoffrey Dutton. CBAP

There were three brethren come from Spain. Three Knights from Spain. *Unknown.* CH

There were three cherry trees once. The Three Cherry Trees. Walter De la Mare. CMoP; OBGa

There were three cooks of Colebrook. *Unknown.* OxNR

There were three ghostesses. *Unknown.* CTV

There were three gipsies a-come to my door. The Wraggle Taggle Gipsies. *Unknown.* BoTP; CH

There were three in the meadow by the brook. The Code. Robert Frost. OBNV; PoA; UnPo

There were three jovial Welshmen. *Unknown.* CBNP

There were three ladies [*or* maids] lived in a bower [*or* barn]. Babylon; or, The Bonnie Banks o' Fordie. *Unknown.* AmFP; ESPB; OxBB

There were three little owls in a wood. Limerick. *Unknown.* OBCoV; PeLi

There were three ravens [*or* rauens *or* crows] sat on a tree. The Three Ravens. *Unknown.* ESPB; HeIP-4; InPK-6; NAEL-1; OAEL-1; OBEV; OxBB; PoE; PoEL-1; SCGP; TFi; UnPo

There were three sailors of Bristol city. Little Billee. William Makepeace Thackeray. FaBoCh; NOBL; OxAEP-2; OxBB

There were three sisters fair and bright. The Riddling Knight. *Unknown.* FaBoCh; PBMP; PoEL-1

There were three sisters in a hall *Unknown.* OxNR

There were three young women of Birmingham. Limericks. Cosmo Monkhouse. PFE

There were twa brethren in the North. The Twa Brothers. *Unknown.* CH; EBEV; ESPB; OxBB; OxBoV; PBMP

There were twa knights in fair Scotland. The Twa Knights. *Unknown.* ESPB

There were twa sisters [sat] in a bower [*or* bour *or* bowr]. Binnorie; or, The Two Sisters. *Unknown.* CH; EnSB; OBEV; PoE

There were two birds sat on a stone. Aristotle's Story. Mother Goose. CBNP; OxNR; ReMoGo

There were two conditions. The Pact. P. S. Rege, *Marathi.* OMIP, *tr. by* Vinay Dharwadker

There were two ghostesses. *Unknown.* FPC

There were two royal children. *Unknown, German.* GePo, *tr. by* Ingrid Waløe-Engel

There were two sisters sat in a bour. The Cruel Sister. *Unknown.* OxBB

There were two sisters, they went playing. The Twa Sisters. *Unknown.* ESPB

There were two wrens upon a tree. *Unknown.* OxNR

There, when they thought they saw in well sought Books. Sir William Davenant. PBRV *Fr.* Gondibert Book 2.

There, where a French legionnaire. In the Footsteps of Genghis Khan. Jan Barry. CDa

There, where it was, we never noticed how. The Sagging Bough. Louis Untermeyer. BXAP

There where the course is. At Galway Races. W. B. Yeats. IIP

There where the deepe did show his sandy flore, *sel. of par. by* Countess of Pembroke, Mary Sidney Herbert. Psalm 78. Bible, *O.T.* OBVE *Fr.* Psalms.

There where the Lord of all / Doth hold His hall. Bible, *O.T. See* Psalm 23.

There, where the rusty iron lies. Rooks. Charles Hamilton Sorley. MoBrPo; NSI

There, where the sun shines first. The Azalea. Coventry Patmore. GBL; GLoP *Fr.* The Unknown Eros.

There, where we still stand talking in the quad. (LL) One More New Botched Beginning. Stephen Spender. CMoP; NYBP; NoAM

There will be a rusty gun on the wall, sweetheart. A. E. F. Carl Sandburg. CMoP; MoAmPo

There will be a talking of lovely things. Michael Hartnett. PBCIP

There will be animals to teach us. Thylias Moss. NMM-2

There will be many other nights like. Listening to Sonny Rollins at the Five-Spot. Paul Blackburn. MoNo

There will be no Holyman crying out this year. Jitterbugging in the Streets. Calvin C. Hernton. PoBA

There will be no monograms on our skulls. Rebellion against the North Side. Naomi Shihab Nye. WcW-3

There will be no more cats. Mort aux Chats. Peter Porter. OxBC

There will be no speech from. No Speech from the Scaffold. Thom Gunn. OxBTC

There will be rose and rhododendron. Elegy before Death. Edna St. Vincent Millay. CMoP; LiTM; MeMAP

There, with ten Rembrandts. Ten Little Rembrandts. Theodore Weiss. NoAM

There, wrapped in his own roars, the lone airman. The Raider. William Robert Rodgers. MoBrPo

There ye gang, ye daft. The Grace of God and the Meth-Drinker. Sydney Goodsir Smith. FaBoTC

There you are. Jean-Joseph Rabéarivelo, *French*. NegPo, *tr. by* Ellen Conroy Kennedy

There you were in my dreams last night. Stepfathers. David Donnell. NOBC

There'd be an orchestra. F. Scott Fitzgerald. AiP *Fr.* Thousand-and-First Ship.
("There was an orchestra—Bingo-Bango.") OTCP

There'd be no work for tinker's hands. (LL) If "ifs" and "ans" [*or* If ifs and ands were pots and pans]. *Unknown.* FaBoBe; LB

There'd ha'e to be nae warnin'. Times ha'e changed. Prayer for a Second Flood. "Hugh MacDiarmid." EBEV

Therefore all seasons shall be sweet to thee. The Silent Icicles. Coleridge. BoTP *Fr.* Frost at Midnight. CABP; EBEV; FHYEP; HAP; NAEL-2; NOBE; NOBRP; NoP-4; OAEL-2; OBNC; PoE; PoEL-4; Poetr; Ro; TFi; TOF

Therefore do thou, stiff-set Northumberland. Imitation. Hilaire Belloc. OBCoV

Therefore I Must Tell the Truth. Torlino, *Navajo Indian.* STP, *tr. by* Washington Matthews

Therefore John read how that thou wouldst. Anna Trapnell. ChIV-2; KTR *Fr.* A Cry of a Stone.

Therefore, lest this inclement friend should maim. Frost. Vita Sackville-West. GaP

Therefore little children sing. Eugene Field. *See* Christmas Song: "Why do the bells for Christmas sing?"

Therefore myself is that one only thing. Verse III. Christina Rossetti. PEW *Fr.* The Thread of Life.

Therefore that he may raise the Lord throws down. (LL) Hymn[e] to God My God, In My Sickness[e]. Donne. EBEV; ESCV; FMP; HeIP-4; ImPo; InPS-3; MeLP; NAEL-1; NOSC; NoP-4; OAEL-1; OxAEP-1; PoE; PoEL-2; SeCP; SoSe-8; TFi; TOF

Therefore the Oxford party went off to adorn for the dinner. Bothie of Tober-na-Vuolich, The [A Long-Vacation Pastoral]. Arthur Hugh Clough.

Therefore we may singen, "Deo gracias!" *Unknown. See* Adam Lay Bound.

Therefore We Preserve Life. Shen Ch'üan, *Chinese.* TrJP, *tr. by* William C. White

Therefore, We Thank Thee, God. Reuben Grossman, *Hebrew.* TrJP, *tr. by* L. V. Snowman

Therefore, when thou wouldst pray, or dost thine alms. The Right Use of Prayer. Sir Aubrey De Vere. TIRV

Therefore, who doeth work rightful to do. *Unknown.* TAL, *tr. by* Sir Edward Arnold *Fr.* The Bhagavad-Gita.

Therefore with thee triumpheth there. The Confessors. Donne. *Fr.* The Litanie. PoEL-2

Therein was writ, how often thundering Jove. Edmund Spenser. OxBSn *Fr.* The Faerie Queene.

There'll be a day when dust flies at the bottom of the sea. Po Chü-i. SuSp, *tr. by* Irving Y. Lo *Fr.* Tune: "Ripples Sifting Sand."

There'll be no more. Finished. Kate Llewellyn. NOBAu

There'll be no time for kicking. (LL) Horse Sense. *Unknown.* BLPA; PWR

There'll be time enough to sleep. (LL) Reveille. A. E. Housman. CABP; CMoP; LiTM; MoBrPo; NoP-4; PFE; PoLF

There'll come a time when brother speaks with brother. Alcuin, *Latin.* MLL, *tr. by* Helen Waddell

There's a barrel of porter at Tammany Hall. Song. Fitz-Greene Halleck. OBAL

There's a barrel-organ caroling across a golden street. The Barrel-Organ. Alfred Noyes. MoBrPo; PoRA

There's a bird perched on my shoulder. Bird. Agnes Nemes Nagy, *Hungarian.* BoWoP; PoSu, *tr. by* Bruce Berlind

There's a bit of sky across the street. My "Patch of Blue." Mary Newland Carson. BLPA

There's a black fog hiding London. Promise. Florence Lacey. BoTP

There's a breathless hush in the Close tonight. Noel Petty. UV

There's a breathless hush in the Close tonight. Vitaï Lampada. Sir Henry John Newbolt. BLPA; EBEvV; FaPoR; NSI; OBWP; UV

There's a breathless hush on the Centre Court. Stanley J. Sharpless. UV

There's a brief spring in all of us and when it finishes. To S. T. C. on His 179th Birthday, October 12th, 1951. Maurice Carpenter. FaBoTw

There's a certain beekeeper I've fallen in love with. His hair smells. BZZZZZZZ. Amy Gerstler. PmAP

There's a certain Slant of light. Emily Dickinson. APN-2; AmPP; BoWoP; CMoP; ColAP; HAP; HeIP-4; ImGa; ImPo; LiTM; MeMAP; MoAmPo; MoP; NAAL-1; NAAL-3; NALW; NAWM-2; NCAP; NOBA; NTP; NoAM; NoP-4; OxBA; PAR; PFE; PoE; PoEL-5; PoPoPo; Poetr; RB; SAmP; SoSe-8; TFi; TOF; WPE

There's a certain young lady. A Certain Young Lady. Washington Irving. FaBoBe

There's a class of men (and women) who are always on their guard. The Men Who Come Behind. Henry Lawson. NOBAu

There's a combative artist named Whistler. Limerick. D. G. Rossetti. FaBoEE; PeLi

There's a comforting thought at the close of the day. Touching Shoulders. *Unknown.* BLPA

There's a cool in the air. Friends. Mikhail Arkadyevich Svetlov, *Russian.* TCRP, *tr. by* Daniel Weissbort

There's a cut-price whore. Pascoe Polglaze. PeLi

There's a fabulous story. The Place Where the Rainbow Ends. Paul Laurence Dunbar. PWR

There's a faerie at the bottom of my garden. My Garden. Janice Appleby Succorsa. HoPM

There's a family nobody likes to meet. The Grumble Family. *Unknown.* PWR

There's a famous seaside place called Blackpool. The Lion and Albert. Marriott Edgar. OBNV

There's a feeling that comes with the daze of joy. Undertones. George R. Sims. NOBVV

There's a fierce gray Bird, with a bending beak. John Neal. APN-1 *Fr.* The Battle of Niagara.

There's a fire / in the Architectural! The Big Fire at the Architectural College. Andrey Andreievich Voznesensky, *Russian.* CLPP, *tr. by* Anselm Hollo

There's a fortunate priest of St. Paul's. Limerick. Douglas Catley. PeLi

There's a fortune to be made in just about everything. My Great Great Etc. Uncle Patrick Henry. James Tate. CMAP; OBAL

There's a Friend for little children. Albert Midlane. OxBChV *Fr.* Above the Bright Blue Sky.

There's a game much in fashion—I think it's called Euchre. The Game of Life. John Godfrey Saxe. BLPA

There's a gathering in the village, that has never been outdone. The Country Doctor. Will M. Carleton. BLPA

There's a goblin as green. The Goblin. Jack Prelutsky. TLR

There's a god on each side. Sixth Song of the Holy Young Men. *Unknown.* APN-2, *tr. by* Washington Matthews *Fr.* The Mountain Chant.

There's a good old war-cry sounding, it hangs on every lip. Waitekauri Every Time! Edwin Edwards. PeNZ

There's a grandfather's clock in the hall, watch it closely. The. Robert Penn Warren. NoAM; NoP-4

There's a graveyard near the White House. The Unknown Soldier. Billy Rose. BLPA

There's a great big mystery. Diddie Wa Diddie. "Blind" Blake. CBNP

There's a green hollow where a river sings. The Sleeper of the Valley. Rimbaud, *French.* AWP, *tr. by* Ludwig Lewisohn

There's a grey wind wails on the clover. Numerous Celts. Sir John Collings Squire. BXAP

There's a heap o' love in the human heart. The Human Heart. Frank Carleton Nelson. PoToHe

There's a latent queer. Tim Hopkins. PeLi

There's a liddle fact of hishdory vitch few hafe oondershtand. Charles Godfrey Leland. APN-2 *Fr.* Hans Breitmann as a Politician.

There's a life awaiting on a rocky coast. It is Everywhere. Jean Toomer. GT

There's a little black train a-coming. The Little Black Train. *Unknown.* AmFP

There's / A / Little / Light. Little Light. Jim Brodey. MoNo

There's a little wet home in the trench. Canadian Song. *Unknown.* NSI

There's a lodger lives on the first floor. Cornucopia. Christopher Pearse Cranch. APN-1

There's a long-legged girl. Pickin Em Up and Layin Em Down. Maya Angelou. CBLP; NBLV

There's a man at Crewe. E. O. Parrott. PeLi

There's a man goin' 'round takin' names. The Angel of Death. *Unknown.* AmFP

There's a man, I really believe, compares with. Sappho, *Greek*. STV, *tr. by* John Frederick Nims

There's a man I really believe's in heaven. Sappho, *Greek*. WeW-3, *tr. by* John Frederick Nims

There's a man who lives in a London apartment. "So Near and Yet So Near." Lemn Sissay. NBrP

There's a man with a Nose. Nose. Ambrose Bierce. APN-2; OBAL *Fr.* The Devil's Dictionary.

There's a merry brown thrush sitting up in the [*or* a] tree. The Brown Thrush. Lucy Larcom. BoTP; OBCA

There's a mob of rumours from s. of the river. Hurricane Drummers! Self-Aid in Haggerston. Iain Sinclair. NBrP

There's a mouse house. I Wouldn't. John Ciardi. TLR

There's a neat little clock. The Clock. Mother Goose. ReMoGo

There's a notable family named Stein. Limerick. *Unknown*. NOBL

There's a one-eyed yellow idol to the north of Khatmandu. The Green Eye of the Yellow God. J. Milton Hayes. BLPA; EBEvV; EBNV

There's a patch of old snow in a corner. A Patch of Old Snow. Robert Frost. CMoP; OxBSP; WeW-3

There's a path that leads to Nowhere. The Path that Leads to Nowhere. Corinne Roosevelt Robinson. BLPA

There's a place between two stands of trees where the grass. What Kind of Times Are These. Adrienne Rich. BAP-93; LoL *Fr.* Not Somewhere Else, But Here. BAP-93

There's a place the man always say. Where? Kenneth Patchen. LiTM

There's a Portuguese person named Howell. Limerick. D. G. Rossetti. PeLi

There's a pretty fuss and bother both in country and in town. A New Song on the Birth of the Prince of Wales. John Harkness. NOBVV

There's a publishing party named Ellis. Limerick. D. G. Rossetti. PeLi

There's a puckle lairds in the auld house. The Auld House. William Soutar. OxBS

There's a puff—and so good night! (LL) Good Night. Thomas Hood. OTCP; Spl

There's a quaint little place they call Lullaby Town. Lullaby Town. John Irving Diller. BLPA

There's a race of men that don't fit in. The Men That Don't Fit In. Robert W. Service. BLPA

There's a ragged old man in the garden to-day. Mr. Scarecrow. Sheila Braine. BoTP

There's a red light on the track for Bolsum Brown. Bolsum Brown. *Unknown*. AS

There's a reid lowe in yer cheek. Sang. Robert MacLellan. OxBS

There's a Sampson lying, sleeping in the land. The Black Sampson. Josephine D. Henderson Heard. CBWP-4

There's a saucy, wild packet and a packet of fame. The *Dreadnought*. *Unknown*. AmFP

There's a seat right next to me. Brain on Ice. Michael Warr. UnSA

There's a sensitive type in Tom's River. Limerick. *Unknown*. PeLi

There's a serpent, namely, drinking. The Social Glass. Lizelia Augusta Jenkins Moorer. CBWP-3

There's a shed at the bottom of our garden. The Shed. Frank Flynn. OTCP

There's a silver house in the lovely sky. The Silver House. John Lea. BoTP

There's a Silvery Lining to Every Cloud. Matilda Caroline Edwards. PWR

There's a slow tolling bell in the dark. Limerick. Gavin Ewart. PeLi

There's a small café off the avenue. Wardour Street. Humbert Wolfe. OxBTC

There's a song of privacy that begins Go away Go away, and stills the. Olga Broumas, Jane Miller. WeT *Fr.* Black Holes, Black Stockings.

There's a sorry little scrub that is servant unto me. To Samuel, Bishop of Sens In Time of Dearth. Alcuin, *Latin*. MLL, *tr. by* Helen Waddell

There's a stench of carrion / surrounding me. (LL) From the Bridge. Claribel Alegría, *Spanish*. AF, *tr. by* Darwin Flakoll

There's a stranger inside him. Each time he wakes. What the Blue Jay Said. Frankie Paino. PuP-15

There's a three-penny Lunch on Dover Street. Eat and Walk. James Norman Hall. BLPA

There's a tiresome young man of Bay Shore. Limerick. Morris Gilbert Bishop. PeLi

There's a town called Don't-You-Worry. The Town of Don't-You-Worry. I. J. Barlett. BLPA

There's a trade you all know well. The Overlander. *Unknown*. NOBAu

There's a train that runs through Hawthorn. The Late Express. Barbara Giles. OTCP

"There's a tree in father's garden, lovelye William," says she. Lovelye William. *Unknown*. AmFP

There's a tree out in our garden which is very nice to climb. The Tree in the Garden. Christine Chandler. BoTP; OTCP

There's a very prim girl called McDrood. Limerick. *Unknown*. PeLi

There's a vile old man. Limeraiku. Ted Pauker. NOBL; PeLi

There's a volcano snow-capped in the air some twenty miles. Resort. George Oppen. FTOS

There's a wanderer, there's a wanderer, his name is Tzu-mei. Seven Songs Written while Living at T'ung-ku in 759. Tu Fu, *Chinese*. SuSp, *tr. by* Goeffrey Waters

There's a whisper down the field where the year has shot her yield. Envoi. Rudyard Kipling. OBEV

There's a whisper down the line at 11. Skimbleshanks: The Railway Cat. T. S. Eliot. NOBL

There's a woman like a dew-drop, she's so purer than the purest. Earl Mertoun's Song. Robert Browning. OBEV *Fr.* A Blot in the 'Scutcheon.

There's a wonderful family called Stein. Limerick. *Unknown*. PeLi

There's a wonderful story. The Angel's Message. Clara Ann Thompson. CBWP-2

There's a zone. No-Man's-Land. "H. d'A. B." NSI

There's all of pleasure and all of peace. A Friend of Two. Wilbur Dick Nesbit. PoLF

There's always a headscarf stooped. Glasgow 1956. Gerald Mangan. FaBoTC

There's an early memory that I carry around. My Father's Back. Edward Hirsch. VCAP

There's an emerald frog down the loo. Limerick. Ruth Silcock. PeLi

There's an Irishman, Arthur O'Shaughnessy. On the Poet, Arthur O'Shaughnessy—. D. G. Rossetti. OBCoV; PeLi

There's an ordinary woman whom the English call the 'the Queen'. The English Queen. Henry Lawson. NOBAu

There's antimony, arsenic, aluminium, selenium. The Elements. Tom Lehrer. UV

There's beauty in the azure skies. The World Is Full of Beauty. Matilda Caroline Edwards. PWR

There's been a change of more than silhouette. (LL) The Grim Sisters. Liz Lochhead. CABP; FaBoTC

There's been a Death, in the Opposite House. Emily Dickinson. APN-2; InPS-3; MeMAP; SAmP; SoSe-8

"There's been an accident," they said. Harry Graham. UV

'There's been an accident!' they said. Mr Jones. Harry Graham. PeLV *Fr.* Some Ruthless Rhymes.

There's been an eagle on a nickel. Fact. Langston Hughes. APSN; PFTM

There's blood between us, love, my love. The Convent Threshold. Christina Rossetti. NALW; NoP-4; VWP

There's blue-stemmed grass as far as I can see. Blue-Stemmed Grass. Thomas Hornsby Ferril. PaTW

There's grandfather's clock in the hall, watch it closely. The. Robert Penn Warren. *See* There's a grandfather's clock in the hall, watch it closely. The.

There's happiness in little things. *Unknown*. CTV

There's heaven above, and night by night. Johannes Agricola in Meditation. Robert Browning. TOF

There's Holmes, who is matchless among you for wit. Holmes. James Russell Lowell. NOBA *Fr.* A Fable for Critics. NAAL-1; NAAL-3

There's in my mind a woman. In Mind. Denise Levertov. NALW; NMM-2

There's Life in a Mussel; a Meditation. George Farewell. NOEC

"There's light ahead!" Hope ever cries. Hope Deferred. Clara Ann Thompson. CBWP-2

There's little coin and less devotion. (LL) The Bounty of Our Age. Henry Farley. FaBoCh; FaBoEE; NOSC

There's little joy in life for me. On the Death of Anne Brontë. Charlotte Brontë. IMW; VWP; WPE

There's lots of things I'd like to be. The Hurdy-Gurdy Man. Elizabeth Fleming. BoTP

"There's machinery in the butterfly." The Horrid Voice of Science. Vachel Lindsay. PoA

There's Many a Man Killed on the Railroad. *Unknown*. AS

There's moaning somewhere in the dark. Voice in Darkness. Richard Dehmel, *German*. AWP, *tr. by* Margarete Münsterberg

There's more in words than I can teach. Loving and Liking [Irregular Verses Addressed to A Child]. Dorothy Wordsworth. OxBChV; WoRP

There's More Pretty Girls than One. *Unknown*. AmFP

There's much afoot in heaven and earth this year. The Rainy Summer. Alice Thompson Meynell. AYFP; OxBSP; OxBTC

There's music in the old bones yet. (LL) Song for the Clatter-Bones. Frederick Robert Higgins. ChIV-1; ImPo; OBMV

There's my war club. Hunting Song. *Unknown, Chippewa Indian*. STP, *tr. by* Jerome Rothenberg

There's Nae Luck about the House. William Julius Mickle, *also at. to* Jean Adam. NOEC; OxAEP-1

(Sailor's Wife, The.) GTBS-P

There's naught but care on every hand. Robert Burns. *See* Green grow the rashes, O; / Green grow the rashes, O; / The sweetest hours that e'er I spend.

There's naught (thou say'st) but one eternal flux. The Infidel Reclaimed. Edward Young. NOEC *Fr.* Night Thoughts.

There's never enough whiskey or rain. Wishing Africa. Marilyn Bowering. NOBC

"There's no bird in a' this foreste." Johnie Cock. *Unknown.* ESPB

There's no carousing. (LL) Anacreontic. Robert Herrick. CaPo; OxBoLi

There's no comfort inside me, only a small. Beehive Cell. Richard Murphy. CIP-2

There's no dew left on the daisies and clover. Seven Times One--Exultation. Jean Ingelow. BLPA; OBNC *Fr.* Songs of Seven.

There's no Jade Emperor in the sky. *Unknown.* ChiPo

There's No Lust like to Poetry. *Unknown.* AWP, *tr. by* John Addington Symonds

There's no modesty, Todorov. To a French Structuralist. David Kirby. BLT

There's no place like home! (LL) Home, Sweet Home! John Howard Payne. APN-1; BLPA; EBEvV; FaBoBe

There's No Place to Sleep in This Bed, Tanguy. Charles Henri Ford. SPE

There's no sense making earnest out of game. Chaucer. *See* The Miller's Prologue.

There's no smoke in the chimney. The Deserted House. Mary Elizabeth Coleridge. BoTP; CH

There's no snow this Christmas. . . there was snow. Christmas 1971. Iain Crichton Smith. FaBoTC

There's no way out. In the Suburbs. Louis Simpson. TRP; WeT

There's no weather over Dikson. Nonflying Weather. Robert Ivanovich Rozhdestvensky, *Russian.* TCRP, *tr. by* Albert C. Todd

There's nobody there for to turn me out. (LL) Deep river, my home is over Jordan. *Unknown.* APN-2

There's none, that dwell about them, wish them downe. Martial. OBCVT, *tr. by* Ben Jonson *Fr.* To Penshurst.

There's not a chance now that I might recover. The Scar. John Hewitt. CIP-2; PNI

"There's not a husband whom storms don't benight." *Unknown, Greek.* GrAn, *tr. by* Peter Jay

There's not a joy the world can give like that it takes away. Stanzas for Music. Byron. GTBS-P; HAP; NOBRP

There's not a nook within this solemn Pass. The Trosachs. Wordsworth. OBEV

There's not a Shakespeare sonnet. Giving Up Smoking. Wendy Cope. APAD

There's not a tint that paints the rose. God Is Everywhere. Christina Rossetti. CTV

There's nothing grieves me, but that age should haste. Michael Drayton. AAS; NOSC; OAEL-1 *Fr.* Idea.

There's nothing happening that you hate. Leave Them Alone. Patrick Kavanagh. OxBSP

There's nothing makes a Greenland Whale. It Makes a Change. Mervyn Laurence Peake. OTCP

There's nothing now. Archilochus, *Greek.* OBCVT, *tr. by* Guy Davenport

There's nothing very beautiful and nothing very gay. Little Things. John Orrick. PoToHe

There's old Molly Hogan who cooks from a book. Stirling's Hotel. *Unknown.* AmFP

There's one Grammarian I know. Lucilius, *Greek.* GrAn, *tr. by* Peter Porter

There's one I miss. A little questioning maid. Augusta Davies Webster. VWP

There's one rides very sagely on the road. Upon the Horse and His Rider. John Bunyan. OxBSP

There's only this. Nissim Ezekiel. OMIP *Fr.* Hymns in Darkness.

There's order and law in a battleship's might. The Mystery Ships. Ronald Arthur Hopwood. NSI

There's parties ad yer meets about. Albert Chevalier. UV *Fr.* Sich a Nice Man Too!

There's pleasure, sure, in being clad in green. A Scene after Hunting at Swallowfield in Berkshire. Sneyd Davies. NOEC

There's quite enough to. Invisibility Poem: Lesbian. Ilze Mueller. LoHo

There's recompense to balm your spirit's ire. Da Silva Gives the Cue. Walter Hart Blumenthal. TrJP

There's room in [*or* on] the bus. Jittery Jim. William Jay Smith. FuFo

There's silence between one page and another. Valerio Magrelli, *Italian.* NeIt, *tr. by* Jonathan Galassi

There's snakes on the mountain. Wanderin'. *Unknown.* AS

There's snow in every street. Winter. John Millington Synge. NOIV; OBMV; OxBTC

There's snow on the fields. Christina Rossetti. BoTP

There's so much room in this world, even now. Solar Loneliness. "Strannik," *Russian.* TCRP, *tr. by* April FitzLyon

There's so much to be said on either side. Via Media Via Dolorosa. Stevie Smith. WPN

There's some are fat, and some are lean. Alicia D'Anvers. KTR *Fr.* Academia; or The Humours of the University of Oxford.

There's some really good work. The Cream Song. Apirana Ngata, *Maori.* PeNZ, *tr. by* Margaret Orbell

There's some who say she put death up her dress. Ellie Mae Leaves in a Hurry. Peter Klappert. PFE

"There's someone at the door," said gold candlestick. Green Candles. Humbert Wolfe. MoBrPo

There's Someone I Think Of. *Unknown, Chinese.* CoBCP, *tr. by* Burton Watson

There's Somethin'. Adam Small, *Afrikaans.* PeSA; PeSAV

There's something about being an Indian. Something About Being an Indian. Adrian C. Louis. UnSA

There's something in the air. The Coming of Spring. Nora Perry. PWR

"There's something in the air," he said. Two Voices. Edmund Blunden. OBWP; PeFWW

There's something that does not return, once gone. A Certain Year. Kunbae Yi, *Korean.* CKP, *tr. by* Jaihiun Kim

There's such a tiny little mouse. The Mouse. Thirza Wakley. BoTP

There's talk of a New Dawn for Blacks. The New Dawn. Mafika Pascal Gwala. PeSAV

There's teuch sauchs growin' i' the Reuch Heuch Hauch. The Sauchs in the Reuch Heuch Hauch. "Hugh MacDiarmid." NoAM

There's the field. I can see it. The Word. Neil Weiss. NYBP

There's the sea, far beyond the yellow hills. August Moon. Cesare Pavese, *Italian.* AF, *tr. by* William Arrowsmith

There's the story of me sitting in the grass in the dark. In the Dead of the Night. Norman Dubie. AmPA

There's the wonderful love of a beautiful maid. Love. *Unknown.* SoSe-8

There's three fair maids went to play at ball. The Cruel Brother. *Unknown.* AmFP

There's wheat at home where you didn't leave it? Callicteros, *Greek.* InMo, *tr. by* Sam Hamill

Theresa of Avila surely had a gold thimble. Things of This World. Anna Kamienska, *Polish.* GI, *tr. by* Curzon, David and Grazyna Drabik

Therfore that he may raise the Lord throws down. Donne. *See* Hymn[e] to God My God, In My Sickness[e].

Theris, the old man who lived by his fish traps. Leonidas, *Greek.* GrAn; PGA, *tr. by* Kenneth Rexroth

Theris the old, the waves that harvested. The Fisherman. Leonidas of Tarentum. AWP, *tr. by* Andrew Lang *Fr.* Epigrams.

Theris, thrice-old, who got his living from. Leonidas of Tarentum. HePo, *tr. by* Barbara Hughes Fowler *Fr.* Epigrams.

Theris, whose hands were cunning. Leonidas, *Greek.* GrAn; PGA, *tr. by* Kenneth Rexroth

Theris, whose hands were cunning. *Unknown, Greek.* GrAn, *tr. by* Kenneth Rexroth

Thermal Stair, The. W. S. Graham. FaBoMo

Thermopylae. Constantine P. Cavafy, *Greek.* GrIP, *tr. by* Edmund Keeley *and* Philip Sherrard

Thermopylae. Simonides, *Greek.* AWP; OBVE; OBWP, *tr. by* William Lisle Bowles

Thermopylai. Hegemon, *Greek.* GrAn, *tr. by* Peter Jay

Thermopylai. Parmenion of Macedon, *Greek.* GrAn, *tr. by* Peter Jay

Therof I have a quantyte. (LL) Chapmen. *Unknown.* FaBoVe; MiEL

Theromachos of Crete came to hang up. Leonidas of Tarentum, *Greek.* GrAn, *tr. by* Peter Levi

THESCRIBESPACKEDCAPITALSACROSSTHEPAGE. The Scribes. Suzanne Noguere. FFC

These accents seem their own defence. (LL) Some Trees. John Ashbery. CAPP-1; CoAmPo; HCAP; NAAL-2

These accents seem their own defense. John Ashbery. *See* Some Trees.

These acres, always again lost. Lost Acres. Robert Graves. NoAM

These all their care expend on outward show. Edward Young. *Fr.* Love of Fame, the Universal Passion. OBSV

These alternate nights and days, these seasons. Prologue. Archibald MacLeish. MoAmPo

These Americans I see. 13 November 1983. Lee Cataldi. BMAP

These are amazing: each. Some Trees. John Ashbery. CAPP-1; CoAmPo; ColAP; HCAP; NAAL-2

These are Aristophanes' marvellous plays. Antipater of Thessalonica, *Greek.* GrAn, *tr. by* Alistair Elliot

These are calamitous times we're living through. Modern Times. Nicanor Parra, *Spanish.* AF, *tr. by* Miller Williams

These are his due. (LL) The Relapse. Henry Vaughan. ESCV; TrCP

These are Imperial Works, and worthy Kings. (LL) Epistle IV, to Richard Boyle, Earl of Burlington. Alexander Pope. OAEL-1; PoEL-3

These are lilacs. Nijole Miliauskaite, *Lithuanian*. VCWP, *tr.* by Jonas Zdanys

These are men! the gaunt, unforesold, the vocal. Ol' Bunk's Band. William Carlos Williams. NOBA

These are my legs. I don't have to tell them, legs. Walter Jenks' Bath. William Meredith. HoPM

These are my murmur-laden shells that keep. On Some Shells Found Inland. Trumbull Stickney. APN-2; Son

These are my thoughts on realising. Anniversary. John Wain. TwCP

These, are not brayed of Tongue. (LL) Soul has Bandaged moments, The. Emily Dickinson. NALW; TRP

These Are Not Brushstrokes. Cyrus Cassells. GT

These Are Not Lost. Richard Metcalf. PoToHe

These are not roads of shining glass. My Wife. Nikolai Ivanovich Glazkov, *Russian*. TCRP, *tr.* by Daniel Weissbort

These are not words set down for the rejected. A Communication to Nancy Cunard. Kay Boyle. NMM-2

These are notes to lightning in my bedroom. Star Quilt. Roberta Hill Whiteman. CDW

These are our immortals. Looking at Models in the Sears Catalogue. Philip Dacey. CMAP

These are private words addressed to you in / public. (LL) A Dedication to My Wife. T. S. Eliot. BoLoP; OxBM

These are the absolute top of the line. Mangosteens. Daniel Hall. NoP-4

These are the arrows that kill sleep. Créide's Lament for Dínertech. *Unknown*. NOIV

These are the arrows that murder sleep. The Song of Crede. *Unknown*, *Middle Irish*. BIrV, *tr.* by Alfred Perceval Graves

These are the ashes of Timas. Sappho, *Greek* QBCVT, *tr.* by Groden, Suzy Q.

These Are the Chosen People. Robert Nathan. TrJP

These are the damned circles Dante trod. Grotesque. Frederic Manning. PeFWW

These are the days of our youth, our days of glory and honor. The Days of Our Youth. *Unknown*, *Arabic*. AWP, *tr.* by Wilfrid Scawen Blunt

These are the days when Birds come back—. Indian Summer. Emily Dickinson. APN-2; MoAmPo; NAAL-1; NAAL-3; PAR; PBMP; PFE

These are the days whose fingers. Ninth of Av. Myra Sklarew. CRP

These are the desolate, dark weeks. William Carlos Williams. MoAmPo; MoP; NOBA; OxBA

These / are the desolate, dark weeks. William Carlos Williams. *See* Are the desolate, dark weeks.

These are the dog days. Songs to Survive the Summer. Robert Hass. AmPA

These are the facts. The uncle, the elder brother, the squire. Claude to Eustace. Arthur Hugh Clough. FaBoVe *Fr.* Amours de Voyage. NOBVV

These are the fields of light, and laughing air. The Pea-Fields. Sir Charles G. D. Roberts. NOBC *Fr.* Songs of the Common Day.

These are the first citizens of contingency. Proposition. Robert Pinsky. HCAP; NoAM *Fr.* Essay on Psychiatrists.

These are the Gardens of the Desert, these. The Prairies. William Cullen Bryant. APN-1; AmPP; ColAP; NAAL-1; NAAL-3; NCAP; NOBA; OxBA; PAR; PaTW; PoEL-4; TAP

These Are the Gifts I Ask. Henry Van Dyke. FaBoBe

These are the great discoveries of my middle age. Discovering the Photograph of Lloyd, Earl, and Priscilla. Lynn Emanuel. WWSi

These are the green paths trodden by patience. The Rural Mail. John Glassco. MoCV

These are the little shoes that died. The Little Shoes That Died. Mary Gilmore. NOBAu

These are the middle years. The Middle Years. Anthony Cronin. CIP-2

These are the Nights that Beetles love. Emily Dickinson. NCAP

These are the objects, the touchable—table, refrigerator, chair. Rush Hour. Laurie Sheck. PuP-15

These are the original monies of the earth. A Cabinet of Seeds Displayed. Howard Nemerov. CRP

These are the small hours when. Epithalamion. Michael Longley. CIP-2

These are the strings of the Ægean lyre. Sunium. Trumbull Stickney. *Fr.* Sonnets from Greece. APN-1

These are the summer days, and these our walks. (LL) It is the season of the sweet wild rose. George Meredith. GBL; PoEL-5

These are the things men seek at dusk. Dusk. Helen Welshimer. PoToHe

These are the things which once possessed. True Happiness. Morris Talpalar. PoToHe

These are the times that try men's. Thomas Paine. CTV *Fr.* (American Crisis, The).

These are the voices of the pastors calling. The Old Lutheran Bells at Home. Wallace Stevens. NoAM

These are times when their faith in gods. *From* Florrie Abraham Witness, *December 1972*. Jack A. Mapanje. HBAPE

These are your lips. Vasco [*or* Vasko] Popa. PoSu, *tr.* by Anne Pennington *Fr.* Far Within Us.

"These Armageddons!" he said; and later bled. (LL) Armageddon. John Crowe Ransom. ChIV-2; MeMAP

These armored walls, and raze the citadel. (LL) The Women of Jericho. Phyllis McGinley. ChIV-1; KSG

These, as they change, Almighty Father. A Hymn on the Seasons. James Thomson. CABP *Fr.* The Seasons.

These baby chicks do not leave their mother. Paintings of Various Subjects by Fang Jih-sheng: Baby Chicks Following Their Mother. Pien Kung, *Chinese*. CoBLCP, *tr.* by Jonathan Chaves

These barrows of the century-darkened dead. Prehistoric Burials. Siegfried Sassoon. MoBrPo

These be great cities, new roofs mounting up. Alcuin, *Latin*. MLL, *tr.* by Helen Waddell

These be / Three silent things. Triad. Adelaide Crapsey. IMW; WPE

These became a part of that child who went forth every day, and who now goes, and will always go forth every day. (LL) Leaves of Grass (1855). Walt Whitman. AWP; AmPP; ImPo; InPS-3; NAAL-1; NTP; OxBA; PBMP; SAmP; TAP

These berries, which their choices, come to earth. The Aeschyleans. Bernadette Mayer. FTOS

These birds were born singing for joy. Another Song of the Same Woman, to Some Partridges, Sent to Her Alive. Florencia del Pinar, *Spanish*. BoWoP, *tr.* by Julie Allen

These Bones. T. H. Parry-Williams, *Welsh*. OBWVE, *tr.* by H. Idris Bell

These cedars don't hear. Come Into the Night Grove. Elizabeth Libbey. CMAP

These Chairs they have no words to utter. Wordsworth. Ro

These cherries are not wine-filled bowls for thirsty birds. The Flowering Cherry. Janet Frame. PeNZ

These chill pillars of fluted stone. Winter Homily on the Calton Hill. Douglas Young. OxBS

These coastal mountains are as sharp as swords. Viewing Mountains with His Reverence Hao Ch'u: To My Friends and Relatives in the Capital. Liu Tsung-yüan, *Chinese*. SuSp, *tr.* by Jan W. Walls

These conquered kings pass furiously away. End of a Year. Robert Lowell. HCAP

These country folk dancing a schottische. Country Dance. Edward Baugh. PBCV

These creatures of the languid Orient. Albery Allson Whitman. AAP *Fr.* The Octoroon.

These Damned Trees Crouch. Jim Barnes. CDW

These Days. Andrew Motion. DiPo

These Days. Charles Olson. RaBo

These Days. William Stafford. NNaP

These days are misty, insulated, mute. Louis MacNeice. CMoP *Fr.* Autumn Journal.

These days are too full fraught with diverse dangers. Alcuin, *Latin*. MLL, *tr.* by Helen Waddell

These days I get up with the birches. Days in White. Ingeborg Bachmann, *German*. BoWoP, *tr.* by Daniel Huws

These days I waken in the used light. Furious Versions. Li-Young Lee. PuP-14

These days of disinheritance, we feast. Cuisine Bourgeoise. Wallace Stevens. MeMAP

These Days the Papers in the Street. Charles Reznikoff. VGW

These days the sun could melt both gold and stone. Drought. Trần Tế Xu'o'ng, *Vietnamese*. AVP, *tr.* by Huỳnh Sanh Thông

These days, the ubiquitous db. Limerick. A. P. Cox. PeLi

These days you keep on meeting. The Seventies. Louis Johnson. PeNZ

These decibels / Are a kind of flagellation, an entity of sound. John Ashbery. PmAP *Fr.* The Skaters.

These difficulties—flamboyant tide, modest red berries. Boy Sleeping. Anne Lauterbach. PmAP

These dried-out paint brushes which fell from my lips have been removed. Sestina from the Home Gardener. Diane Wakoski. MoP

These errors loved no less than the saint loves arrows. Elegy V: [Separation of Man from God]. George Barker. FaBoTw

These evenings over the restaurants. The Stranger. Aleksandr Blok, *Russian*. TCRP, *tr.* by Jon Stallworthy *and* Peter France

These extra pounds aren't me. This Woman. Donna Trussell. IFJA

These eyes, [deare Lord], once brandons of desire. For the Magdalene. William Drummond, of Hawthornden. ChIV-2; PoEL-2

These faces are true. Back to Hometown Kingston. James Berry. PBCV

These fat cassia trees. What Her Girl Friend Said to Her. Kovatattan, *Tamil*. PLW, *tr. by* A. K. Ramanujan

These feeble sounds. Ann Yearsley. ECWP *Fr.* Remonstrance in the Platonic Shade. Flourishing on an Height.

These fell miasmic rings of mist, with ghoulish menace bound. Prejudice. Georgia Douglas Johnson. PoBA

These figures moving in my rhyme. Two Figures. N. Scott Momaday. NoP-4

These fisherfolk own just a barge. Fishermen and Cormorants. Phan Thanh Giản, *Chinese*. AVP, *tr. by* Huỳnh Sanh Thông

These five strands bear hair in a split match. Feather Bag, Stick Bag. Kim R. Stafford. CMAP

These flowers are I, poor Fanny Hurd. Voices from Things Growing in a Churchyard. Thomas Hardy. FaBoVe; OxBTC

These foreign laws of God and man. (LL) Laws of God, the Laws of Man, The. A. E. Housman. MoBrPo; NOBVV; NTP; OBSV; OxBoLi

These forty years past, our house and our domain. Tune: "Dance of the Cavalry." Li Yü, *Chinese*. SuSp, *tr. by* Daniel Bryant

These fought in any case. (LL) Ezra Pound. ColAP; HeIP-4; MoAmPo; NOBE; OBWP; PoE; PoWW; TRP; VGW *Fr.* Hugh Selwyn Mauberley. (Life and Contacts). AmPP; CMoP; InPS-3; LiTM; NOBA; NoAM; TAP

("And liars in public places.") ColAP

These fresh beauties (we can prove). Why Flowers Change Color. Robert Herrick. HAP

These gifts to Aphrodite. Callimachus. HePo *Fr.* Epigrams.

These going home at dusk. French Peasants. Monk Gibbon. TIRV

These Gothic windows, how they wear me out. The Young Glass-Stainer. Thomas Hardy. CTC

These grand and fatal movements toward death. Rearmament. Robinson Jeffers. OxBA

These Green-going-to-Yellow. Marvin Bell. FYAP

These green painted park benches are. In a Season of Unemployment. Margaret Avison. MoCV; NOBC

These have crimes accounted been[e]. (LL) Song. To Celia ("Come my Celia, let us prove"). Ben Jonson. BeJo; CBLP; OAEL-1; OBVE; OxAEP-1; SeCP; TFi

These have crimes accounted beene. Catullus. *See* Carmen 5 ("My sweetest Lesbia, let us live and love").

These hearts were woven of human joys and cares. The Dead. Rupert Brooke. CH; PeFWW; PoA; SoSe-8 *Fr.* 1914.

These hips are big hips. Homage to My Hips. Lucille Clifton. NAAAL; Poetr

These honours, Homer, had been just to thee. (LL) Mr. Pope's Welcome from Greece. John Gay. EBEV; OxAEP-1; OxBoLi; PoEL-3

These Horses Came. Ray A. Young Bear. CDW

These I have loved with passion, loved them long. Quiet Things. Grace Noll Crowell. PoLF

These I love: hidden plants that grow by the river's edge;. West Creek at Ch'u-chou. Wei Ying-wu, *Chinese*. CoBCP, *tr. by* Burton Watson

These I singing in spring collect for lovers. Walt Whitman. APN-1

These, in the day when heaven was falling. Epitaph on an Army of Mercenaries. A. E. Housman. EBEvV; NSI; NoP-4; SCGP; SoSe-8

These Indians once imitated life. The Only Bar in Dixon. James Welch. AmPA

These islands we people. Paradise. Brian Chan. HCP

These jagged passions trample. Mr and Mrs. Wendy Mulford. NBrP

These kisses are clandestine. Its Happenin / But You Dont Know Abt It. Ntozake Shange. NMM-2

These Labdanum Hours. Kathleen Fraser. PT

These labor days, when shirking hardly looks like working. Back to Town. John Hollander. NoAM

These laboratories and those picnics. In Hospital. Frank O'Hara. LCAP-2

These labouring wits, like paviours, mend our ways. Edward Young. OBSV *Fr.* Epistles to Mr. Pope.

These Lacustrine Cities. John Ashbery. CAPP-1; HCAP; PoM; UnPo

("These lacustrine cities grew out of loathing.") FTOS

These layers of piled-up skulls. The Tower of Skulls. Isaac Rosenberg. PeFWW

These Leaves. William Stafford. NNaP

These Letters—humid, sunless. The writing occurs on their walls. Michael Palmer. *See* Sun.

These light-footed, celebrated cats, created. The Tigers of Nanzen-ji. Brad Leithauser. DiPo

These lips and these eyes of the loved and the lover. Love is enough: though the World be a-waning. William Morris. GLoP

These little limbs [*or* limmes]. The Salutation [*or* Salutations]. Thomas Traherne. ESCV; EnlH; GeHe; NOCV; SeCP

These locks on doors have brought me happiness. Locks. Kenneth Koch. CoAP

These locusts by day, these crickets by night. Things of August. Wallace Stevens. PoA

These lodge in London in Lent and at other times too. The Civil Service. William Langland. NOCV *Fr.* The Vision of Piers Plowman.

These long verandahs seem to be washed clean. Wen Cheng-ming. CoBLCP, *tr. by* Jonathan Chaves *Fr.* The Chung-i Temple.

These lovely groves of fountain-trees that shake. Golden Bough. Elinor Wylie. MoAmPo; PBWP

These lover's inklings which our loves enmesh. Counsel to Unreason. Léonie Adams. PoA

These lusty plants, complete with blaring sex. Marrows. Louis Johnson. PeNZ

These market-dames, mid-aged, with lips thin-drawn. Former Beauties. Thomas Hardy. CBLP; NoAM; OBMV; OBNC *Fr.* At Casterbridge Fair.

These massed grey shadows. Mothball Fleet: Benicia, California. John Haines. WeT

These men. Tuskegee Airfield. Marilyn Nelson Waniek. GT

These men clothed their land with incorruptible. For the Spartan Dead at Plataia. Simonides, *Greek*. GrAn, *tr. by* Peter Jay

These men died with the wrong names. Dying with the Wrong Name. Sam Hamod. UnSA

These men? In their dented felt hats. The Colors of Desire. David Mura. LoL; NAmP90

These men were kings, albeit they were black. Black Majesty. Countee Cullen. PoBA; VGW

These messages are secret, the initials. Personal Column. Tom Paulin. PNI

These names like exotic diseases—*Alaria, Porphyra,.* After a Class in Seaweed. Ingrid Wendt. NMM-2

These new night. Ivory Masks in Orbit. Keorapetse Kgositsile. PoBA

These nights when the wind blows. 0°. Elizabeth Spires. DiPo

These no-man's-lands. Poem-Object. André Breton, *French*. PFTM, *tr. by* Michael Benedikt

These Obituaries of Rattlesnakes Being Eaten by the Hogs. Roger Weingarten. AmPA

These old tears in the chopping-bowl. (LL) Peeling Onions. Adrienne Rich. BoWoP; HCAP; TAP

These older towns die. Poema para los Californios Muertos. Lorna Dee Cervantes. PoPoPo

These panting damsels, dancing for their lives. The Mother's Choice. *Unknown.* OxBoLi

These pearls of thought in Persian gulfs were bred. In a Copy of Omar Khayyám. James Russell Lowell. NCAP

These people have not heard your name. In a Cathedral City. Thomas Hardy. EnLoPo; GLoP

These people, with their illegible diplomas. Metamorphoses. Howard Nemerov. HCAP

These pines, these fall oaks, these rocks. After Drinking All Night with a Friend, We Go Out in a Boat at Dawn to See Who Can Write the Best Poem. Robert Bly. WeT

These pioneers of olden days. Pioneers. Ann Harris. CTV

These plaintive verse, the posts [*or* postes] of my desire. Samuel Daniel. AAS *Fr.* To Delia.

These plum buds move one's imagination. Inscribed on a Scroll "Plum Blossoms by the Water." Huang T'ing-chien, *Chinese*. SuSp, *tr. by* Michael E. Workman

These poems, these poems. These Poems, She Said. Robert Bringhurst. NOBC

These pools that, though in forests, still reflect. Spring Pools. Robert Frost. AmPP; ColAP; NAAL-2; NOBA; NoAM; OxBA

These Purists. William Carlos Williams. OBAL

These rioteres three of which I tell. Death and the Three Revellers. Chaucer. OBNV *Fr.* The Pardoner's Tale. FHYEP; NAEL-1; NAWM-1; OAEL-1; PoE *Fr.* The Canterbury Tales.

These royall kinges, that reare up to the skye. Thomas Sackevyll in Commendation of the Worke to the Reader. Thomas, 1st Earl of Dorset Sackville. AAS

These Rumours of Hexagonal Rooms in Gone Bee City. David Eggleton. PeNZ

These scanty clothes too drab. *Unknown. Fr.* Summer. SuSp, *tr. by* Michael E. Workman *Fr.* Tzu-yeh Songs of the Four Seasons.

These seven houses have learned to face one another. On a Painting by Patient B of the Independence State Hospital for the Insane. Donald Justice. CoAP; CoAmPo; NoAM; WeT

These sheets primeval doctrines yield. On Barclay's Apology for the Quakers. Matthew Green. NOEC

These Six. Sean Lucy. CIP-2

These so, these irretrievable. (LL) Battle of the *Bonhomme Richard* and the *Serapis*. Walt Whitman. SAmP, *sect.* XXXV; ImGa, *sect.* XXXV–XXXVI; RB; UnPo, *sect.* XXXV-XXXVI; ColAP

These songs will not stand. Song: "These songs will not stand." Denis Glover. PeNZ *Fr.* Sings Harry.

These souls, my lord, assembled at the bar. The Parish Poor-Officers. Edward Ward. NOEC *Fr.* A. Journey to Hell; or, A Visit Paid to the Devil.

These spectres resting on plastic stools. Café in Warsaw. Allen Ginsberg. HAP

These Strangers, in a foreign World. Emily Dickinson. FP; SAmP

These suggestions by Asians are not taken seriously. Asian Peace Offers Rejected without Publication. Robert Bly. CAPP-1

These summer days I carry images of stone. The Phenomenology of Stones. Thomas McCarthy. PBCIP

These sweeter far than lilies are. Thanksgivings for the Beauty of His Providence. Thomas Traherne. FaBoCh

These tall lilies, color. The Lilies. Richard Emil Braun. NoAM

These tears that fall for love's sake. Gift of Love. Sowol Kim, *Korean.* CKP, *tr. by* Jaihiun Kim

These—the bright symbols of man's hope and fame. The Stars. Madison Cawein. APN-2

These the dread days which the seers have foretold. The Death of Justice. Walter Everette Hawkins. PoBA

These, these are joyes the Gods for Youth ordain. (LL) Ode 1.9. Horace, *Latin.* OBVE; OBCVT, *tr. by* John Dryden; STV, *tr. by* John Frederick Nims

These Things I Do Remember. Solomon Ephraim ben, of Lenczicz Aaron, *Hebrew.* TrJP, *tr. by* Nina Davis Salaman

These things, or not. (LL) Ease. Po Chü-i, *Chinese.* Spl, *tr. by* Arthur Waley

These Too Are Our Elders. Jack A. Mapanje. HBAPE

These tracings from a world that's dead. To Violet [with Prewar Poems]. Basil Bunting. FaBoMo; PoA

These Trees Are No Forest of Mourners. Douglas G. Jones. NOBC

These trees stand very tall under the heavens. W. D. Snodgrass. MoP

These trees that fling their leafy boughs aloft. London Trees. Beryl Netherclift. BoTP

These two meet for dinner once a week. Imaginary Translation. Marilyn Hacker. DiPo

These two tales I tell of myself and the life I led. John Hollander. VCAP *Fr.* Powers of Thirteen.

These umbered cliffs and gnarls of masonry. Rome: Building a New Street in the Ancient Quarter. Thomas Hardy. Son

These unshaped islands, on the sawyer's bench. New Zealand. James Keir Baxter. NoP-4

These verses weare made By Michaell Drayton Esquier Poett Lawreatt the night before hee dyed. Michael Drayton.
("As I therin noe others face but yours can Veiwe.") (LL) PBRV
("Soe well I love thee, as without thee I.") PBRV

These walls, so full of monument and bust. The Abbey Church at Bath. Henry Harington. FaBoEE

These weed-grown car hulks rusting in my neighbor's yard. The Window in Spring. Carl Dennis. BAP-93

These weeping Eyes, those seeing Tears. (LL) Eyes and Tears. Andrew Marvell. FSCP; GeHe

These were my friends; Tompkins, you did not know them. Survival of the Fittest, The (In Memoriam, L.C. and T.) Sir John Collings Squire. NSI

These were the sounds that dinned upon his ear. Dream of Winter. George Mackay Brown. FaBoTw

These winter days. Skeleton of Winter. Joy Harjo. LoL

These women all. Women. Heath. CTC; NoSic

These women crying in my head. The Three Emily's. Dorothy Livesay. NALW

These wonderful things. A Last World. John Ashbery. PoM

These wood-shadows, timid, patient. Philippe Jaccottet, *French.* VCWP, *tr. by* Derek Mahon

These words appall and daunt them all. Michael Wigglesworth. NAAL-3 *Fr.* The Day of Doom. NAAL-1; SCAP

These words are dedicated to those who died. Bashert. Irena Klepfisz. AF *Fr.* Bashert.

These Words, attended with a Show'r of Tears. Achilles kills Lycaon. Homer. OBCVT, *tr. by* Alexander Pope *Fr.* The Iliad.

These words spake Don Henriquez. The Last Words of Don Henriquez. Zalman Schneour, *Yiddish.* TrJP, *tr. by* Joseph Leftwich

These wreaths, Lais. Paulus Silentiarius, *Greek.* GrAn, *tr. by* Andrew Miller

Theseus: A Trilogy. Yvor Winters. NOBA

Theseus and Ariadne. Robert Graves. HAP

Thesis. Edward Dorn. NOBA

Thesis, Antithesis and Nostalgia. Alan Dugan. AFr

Thespians at Thermopylae, The. Norman Cameron. GTBS-P

Thessalian. Winifred Bryher. PoA

Thetis and the Nereids. Homer. OBCVT, *tr. by* Robert Fagles *Fr.* The Iliad.

Thetis Asks Jove to Revenge Her Son Achilles. Homer, *Greek.* OBVE, *tr. by* Dryden *Fr.* The Iliad.
("He moves into his Hall: The Pow'rs resort.") OBCVT, *tr. by* John Dryden
(Olympians.) OBCVT, *tr. by* John Dryden

They. Robert Creeley. FTOS

"They." Siegfried Sassoon. CMoP; NAEL-2; NoP-4; OBSV; OBWP

They. Ronald Stuart Thomas. OxBTC

They, after the slow building of the house. Asmodeus. Geoffrey Hill. FaBoTw

They agreed that it had been a most / *Unusual* conversation. (LL) Chocolates. Louis Simpson. InPS-3; OBCoV; OxBC

They aint no use a-telling, boy, what's for you to do. Dan Ellis's Boys. *Unknown.* AmFP

They all are riders: Spring on a two-year-old. The Seasons. Rolfe Humphries. NYBP

They all arrived, and them with generous show. The Wedding Feast. Luis de Góngora y Argote. *Fr.* The First Solitude. OBVE, *tr. by* Edward Meryon Wilson

They all came, some wore sentiments. The Other Tradition. John Ashbery. FTOS; PmAP

They all climbed up on a high board-fence. The Nine Little Goblins. James Whitcomb Riley. NOxBChV; OBCA

They all see the same movies. Powwow. W. D. Snodgrass. NYBP; SoSe-8

They all took one, and left four in. (LL) Elizabeth, Elspeth, Betsy, and Bess. Mother Goose. OxNR; ReMoGo

They all want to play Hamlet. Carl Sandburg. NOBA

They all were looking for a king. That Holy Thing. George Macdonald. OBEV *Fr.* Paul Faber, Surgeon.

"They also serve who only stand and wait." (LL) On His Blindness. Milton. APAD; AWP; CABP; ChIV-2; EBEvV; GEA; GSo; HAP; HeIP-4; ImPo; InPK-6, NAEl-1; NOBE; NOSC; NoP-4; OBEV; PBMP; PFE; PoE; PoEL-3; PoLF; PoPoPo; PoRA; Poeu, SCGP; SoSe-8; TFi; TRP; WeW-3

They amputated / Your thighs off my hips. A Pity; We Were Such a Good Invention. Yehuda Amichai, *Hebrew.* BoLoP; OxBM

They and I are civilized. (LL) Heritage. Countee Cullen. BPo; ColAP; CrDW; HeIP-4; MoAmPo; NAAAL; NAAL-2; NoAM; NoP-4; PoBA; PoPoPo; Poetr; SSLK; TTY

They answered, 'Mr Toad'. (LL) The Song of Mr Toad. Kenneth Grahame. NOBL; NOxBChV

They applaud at the periods and sigh. The Poet's Shuffle. Calvin Forbes. GT; LTA

They are a gift I have wanted again. Horses in Snow. Roberta Hill Whiteman. NoAM

They are able, with science, to measure. C Stands for Civilization. Kenneth Fearing. TrJP

They are above us. The Beautiful Strangers. James Kirkup. SpW

They are all dying. Death as History. Jay Wright. PoBA

They are all gone away. The House on the Hill. Edwin Arlington Robinson. APN-2; GEA; MoAmPo; NAAL-2; NCAP

They are all gone into the world of light! Friends Departed. Henry Vaughan. CABP; CH; ESCV; FMP; GeHe; ImPo; InPS-3; MeLP; NAEL-1; NOBE; NOCV; NOSC; NoP-4; OAEL-1; OBEV; PBRV; PeECV; PoEL-2; PoPoPo; SCGP; SeCP; TFi

They are all outline, uniformly gray. Those before Us. Robert Lowell. LCAP-2

They are as light as upper air! (LL) The Garden Seat. Thomas Hardy. GaP; HAP; RB

They are assembled, astounded, bewildered. The Last Supper. Rilke, *German.* GI, *tr. by* David Curzon and Will Alexander Washburn

They are at rest. Refrigerium. John Henry, Cardinal Newman. OBNC

They are at table. The Last Supper. Jacques Prévert, *French.* CLPP, *tr. by* Lawrence Ferlinghetti

They are bodies left unburied. Rondeau. Cheryl Clarke. FFC

They are by nature lonely things. Ideal Angels. John Robert Colombo. MoCV

They Are Coming? Josephine D. Henderson Heard. AAP; CBWP-4

They are Coming. Filippo Tommaso Marinetti. PFTM

They are cutting down the great plane-trees at the end of the gardens. The Trees Are Down. Charlotte Mew. BrRo; ChIV-2; MoBrPo; NTP; OxAEP-1; TrCP; VWP; WPE; WPOW

They are dreaming of children. Torrential. Nocturne in the Women's Prison. Maria Beneyto, *Spanish.* WPOW, *tr. by* Catherine Rodriguez-Nieto

They are extremely rare. (LL) The Frog. Hilaire Belloc. CTAV; CTV; ChAP; FaBoBe; NOxBChV; NTCP; OxBChV

They are firm, and you are tender. Breasts. Bhartṛihari, *Sanskrit*. EP, *tr. by John Brough*

They are fruit. Advent. Kathleen Norris. CrSp

They are gathering round. Concert Party. Siegfried Sassoon. NSI

They are going to some point true and unproven. (LL) Geometry. Rita Dove. CMAP; HCAP; HeIP-4; Poetr

They are heard as a choir of seven. The Pleiades. Mary Barnard. NYBP

They are holding. Crowfield. Adrian Henri. AYFP

They are in the forest. In the Forest. George Bowering. NOBC

They Are Killing All the Young Men. David Henderson. PoBA

They are lang deid, folk that I used to ken. Elegy. Robert Garioch. FaBoTC; OxBS

They are light as flakes of dandruff with scrawny legs. Crabs. Marge Piercy. NBLV

They are like figures held in some glass ball. Children Walking Home from School through Good Neighborhood. Donald Justice. DiPo; NIP-4

They are made to stand side by side. The Poor Houses. Ed Roberson. GT

They are making a crèche at the Saturday morning classes. The Crib. Robert Finch. OBCP

They are moving inwards; the circle is closing. Man Meeting Himself. Howard Sergeant. SPE

They are my secret food. The Children's Letters. Dorothy Livesay. NALW; NOBC

They are no lords, no marquesses or dukes. Shrimp. Nguyễn Văn Lạc, *Vietnamese*. AVP, *tr. by Huỳnh Sanh Thông*

They are no trophies of the sun. (LL) Praise for an Urn. Hart Crane. AWP; CMoP; HAP; LiTM; MeMAP; MoAmPo; NOBA; NoAM; OxBA; WeW-3

They are not dead, they are not dead! The Argonauts. D. H. Lawrence. GriP; NoAM

They are not here. And we, we are the Others. The Absent. Edwin Muir. NoAM

They are not long, the weeping and the laughter. Vitae Summa Brevis Spem Nos Vetat Incohare Longam. Ernest Christopher Dowson. AWP; CABP; EBVV; HAP; MoBrPo; NAEL-2; NOBE; NOBVV; NoP-4; OBEV; OxBSP; PeVV; PoRA; TFi

They are often. Lattice at "Split." Tina Darragh. FTOS

They are pounded into the earth. It Is This Way with Men. Charles Kenneth Williams. RaBo; SAGP; VCAP

They are probably married or gone by now. Friends, Outside, Night. David Keller. CMAP

They are rattling breakfast plates in basement kitchens. Morning at the Window. T. S. Eliot. AWP; PoA

They are rebuilding / the old bridge, the Nagara. Lady Ise, *Japanese*. BoWoP, *tr. by Etsuko Terasaki and Irma Brandeis*

They are rhymes rudely strung with intent less. A Dedication. Adam Lindsay Gordon. CBAP

They are running to arrive. (LL) The Rescue. Robert Creeley. CRP; VCAP

They are scattered ageless souls. How Old Are the People of the World. Charles Fort. CMAP

They are 7 in number, just 7. The Seven. *Unknown, Sumerian*. RB, *tr. by Jerome K. Rothenberg*

They are showing how we lie. In The Gallery Where the Fat Men Go. Louis Golding. PoFWW

They are slaves who fear to speak. On Freedom. James Russell Lowell. ImGa *Fr. Stanzas on Freedom.*

They are so like. Dolls. David St. John. LCAP-2

They are still so anthropologically tall here. At the Metro: Old Irrelevant Images. Jack A. Mapanje. PBMAP

They are such dear familiar feet that go. Be Patient. "George Klingle." PoToHe

They are taking us beyond Miami. The Removal. *Unknown, Seminole Indian*. STP, *tr. by Frances Densmore*

They are taller than their cars. (LL) Do It Yrself. Larry Eigner. NeAP; PoM

They are terribly white. Cyclamens. "Michael Field." NOBVV; VWP

They are the flesh we feed upon come from the depths. The Ribbon-Fish. Robert Adamson. CBAP

They are the last romantics, these candles. Candles. Sylvia Plath. NMM-2

They are the oldest living captive race. Ginkgoes in Fall. Howard Nemerov. HCAP

They Are the Same. Priscilla Jane Thompson. CBWP-2

They are the spit of virtue now. Austin Clarke. NOIV *Fr. Civil War.*

They are there just the same. The Wheels of the Trains. W. S. Merwin. GM

They are too much for me. (*fl.* 1st cent. B.C. *or* A.D. 1st cent.) Dioscorides, *Greek*. InMo, *tr. by Sam Hamill*

They are very small, my neighbors. The Minotaur Next Door. Greg Pape. PBCAP

They are waiting for me somewhere beyond Eden Rock. Eden Rock. Charles Causley. NTP; NoP-4

They are weighing the babies again on color television. Video Cuisine. Maxine W. Kumin. NoAM

They Are Wicked. Ernest Sandeen. CRP

They arrive. Sirhan Drinks His Coffee in the Cafeteria. Mahmoud Darwish, *Arabic*. VCWP, *tr. by Rana Kabbani*

They ask her. The Shower of Secret Things. Nathaniel Mackey. PmAP

They Ask: Is God, Too, Lonely? Carl Sandburg. SAGP

They ask me where I've been. Back. Wilfrid Wilson Gibson. PoFWW

They asked that man for his time. In Trying Times. Herberto Padilla, *Spanish*. AF, *tr. by Alastair Reid*

They belong here in their own quenched country. By the Boat House, Oxford. Anne Stevenson. FaBoWP

They bide their time off serpentine. Ancient Monuments. John Ormond. OBWVE

They borrowed a bed to lay His head. The Cross Was His Own. *Unknown*. BLPA

They bowed to him: "O man of God." The Prophet. "Yehoash," *Yiddish*. TrJP, *tr. by Isidore Goldstick*

They breathe with the night. The Road is Wider Than Long: An Image Diary from the Balkans, July–August 1938. Roland Penrose. SPE

They bring me gifts, they honour me. If They Honoured Me, Giving Me Their Gifts. "Michael Field." OBMV

They brought a bouquet of thistles. Thistle. Nikolai Alekseievich Zabolotsky, *Russian*. RB, *tr. by Daniel Weissbort*

They brought him in on a stretcher from the world. Grandfather. Derek Mahon. OxBC

They brought him one morning. Dimitris Tsaloumas. CBAP, *tr. by Margaret Carroll Fr. A Rhapsody of Old Men.*

They brought in the brine-crusted drift-wood. Drift-Wood. Clara Ann Thompson. CBWP-2

They brought me a quilled, yellow dahlia. Autumn. Amy Lowell. NMM-2

They brought me ambrotypes. Rutherford McDowell. Edgar Lee Masters. OxBA *Fr. Spoon River Anthology.*

They brought me here to be baptized. And Sea. Amryl Johnson. HCP

They brought me some of his clothes. The hospital gown. Aunt Ida Pieces a Quilt. Melvin Dixon. EC3

They brought the dead. Med Building. Gerald McCarthy. CDa *Fr. War Story.*

They brought thy body back to me quite dead. Luca Signorelli to His Son. Eugene Lee-Hamilton. PeVV

They built the front, upon my word. On the Building of a New Church. *Unknown*. FaBoEE

They buried him in the terrestrial globe. Sergey Sergeievich Orlov, *Russian*. TCRP, *tr. by Lubov Yakovleva*

They buried him today. My Father Today. Sam Hunt. PeNZ

They buried you in mud, in the standard issue. Armageddon: Private Gabriel Calvin Wojahn 1900–18. David Wojahn. PuP-15

They burn the radio and listen to the blues. John Tranter. NoAM *Fr. Crying in Early Infancy.*

They burn you. The Hitchhikers. Diane Wakoski. NoAM

They burnt their last witch in CONNECTICUT. Connecticut. Fitz-Greene Halleck.

They burnt their last witch in CONNECTICUT. Fitz-Greene Halleck. APN-1 *Fr. Connecticut.*

They bustle on sand beaches, day and night. Merchants. (King) Lê Thánh–tông, *Vietnamese*. AVP, *tr. by Huỳnh Sanh Thông*

They call all experience of the senses *mystic*, when the experience / is considered. Mystic. D. H. Lawrence. BLT

They call me and I go. Complaint. William Carlos Williams. SAmP

They call me Ghede. The butts. Ghede Poem. Nathaniel Mackey. PmAP

They call thee rich; I deem thee poor. Treasure. Lucilius, *Greek*. AWP, *tr. by William Cowper*

They call this "Black North." Names. Gerald Dawe. IIP; PNI

They call us aliens, we are told. On Behalf of Some Irishmen Not Followers of Tradition. "Æ." IIP

They call your mama girl. Brown Lullaby. Adam Small. PeSAV

They called her a cat. What They Said. Tanure Ojaide. HBAPE

They called it Annandale—and I was there. How Annandale Went Out. Edwin Arlington Robinson. GSo; MoAmPo; NOBA; NoAM; PFE; SoSe-8

They called my love a poor blind maid. On a Blind Girl. Baha Ad-din Zuhayr, *Arabic*. AWP, *tr. by E. H. Palmer*

They called the next panel, "New Lesbians." Robyn Selman. PUP-19

They Called Them RAF 2C's. *Unknown*. NSI

They came back from the bush-haunts. Arrivants. Musaemura Bonus Zimunya. HBAPE

They came from Persia to the sacred way. Peacocks. Walter Adolphe Roberts. PBCV

They came hurrying across the mountain highway. Monkeys on Mt. Hiei. Edith Marcombe Shiffert. WPE

They came in to the little town. We Are Going. Kath Walker. CBAP; NOBAu

They came in to the little town. We are Going. Oodgeroo of the tribe Noonuccal. BMAP

They came out of the hootch. Search and Destroy. Dale Ritterbusch. CDa

They came out of the sun undetected. The Raid. William Everson. MoP; NoAM

They came running over the perilous sands. 1945. Sir Herbert Read. OxBTC

They came, since there are certain matters, and you gentlemen have / only yourselves to blame. December 14, 1979: A Poetry Reading. Stanislaw Baranczak, *Polish.* AF, *tr.* by Magnus J. Krynski

They came that night as the. Léon Damas, *French.* NegPo, *tr.* by Ellen Conroy Kennedy

They Came This Evening. Léon Damas, *French.* TTY, *tr.* by Seth L. Wolitz

They Came to Me and Said, "There Is a Child." Muriel Rukeyser. Son *Fr.* Nine Poems for the Unborn Child.

They came to the lodge door. Wolf "Aunt." Maurice Kenny. HATNAP

They can enter the window and they will. Alien. Nancy Paddock. LoHo

They cannot speak who have no words to say. Green Hammock, White Magnolia Tree. Ruth Gilbert. PeNZ

They cannot steal, thou giv'st so much. (LL) To Saxham. Thomas Carew. BeJo; CavPo

They can't plow and harvest. Poverty on the Bank. Mei Yao Ch'en, *Chinese.* SuSp, *tr.* by Jonathan Chaves

They cared for nothing but the days and hours. The Disinherited. Charles Spear. PeNZ

"They carry on." Floodtide. Askia Muhammad Touré. PoBA

They Cast Their Nets in Galilee. William Alexander Percy. AH

They changed her name. Nechama. Shirley Kaufman. LCAP-2

They chased her and her friend through the woods. The Girl. Sharon Olds. NMM-2

They choke cities like snowstorms. Blonde White Women. Patricia Smith. GT; UnSA

They choose paths. Let Them Choose Paths. Odia Ofeimun. HBAPE; PBMAP

They chopped her down in some far wood. The Christmas Tree. John Walsh. AYFP

They chose me from my brother: 'That's the'. A Hallowe'en Pumpkin. Dorothy Aldis. AYFP

They clanged and clanged. Miron Biaoszewski. CEEP, *tr.* by Tadeusz Slawek *Fr.* They'll Paint Us.

They Clapped. Nikki Giovanni. WPOW

They climbed on sketchy ladders towards God. Cathedral Builders. John Ormond. NoP-4; PeECV

They cling to their long-standing fallacies. (LL) Limerick: "The Young things who frequent picture-palaces." Philip Heseltine. NOBL; OBCoV; PeLi

They Closed Her Eyes. Gustavo Adolfo Bécquer, *Spanish.* AWP, *tr.* by John Masefield

They come as a boon and a blessing to men. *Unknown.* OBCoV

They come as a boon and a blessing to men. The Waverly Pen. *Unknown.* OBCoV *Fr.* Advertising Rhymes.

They come as couriers of Heaven: their feet. The Three Elements. Madison Cawein. APN-2

They come down on their snowmobiles for the last time. The End of Human Reign on Bashan Hill. Bernadette Mayer. FTOS

They come from the white barrier of noon. The Diatribe of the Kite. Norman Dubie. NAmP90

They come in. Woman at Home. Vere Arnot. WPN

They come in white livery bringing the sun. The Robed Heart. Elizabeth Spires. BAP-94

They come into. Feeding the Lions. Norman Jordan. PoBA

They come into this room while the quail are crying to huddle up. Reading the Books Our Children Have Written. Dave Jeddie Smith. HCAP

They come like the ghosts of horses, shyly. The Pit Ponies. Leslie Norris. ChAP

They come not within the tall woods. To One Elect. Samuel Ichiye Hayakawa. PoA

They come, they come, with fife and drum. The Palace. Charles Stuart Calverley. EBVV

They come to resemble Buddhas. Hamburger. August Kleinzahler. PmAP

They come to you with their descriptions of your soul. Adrienne Rich. HCAP *Fr.* Shooting Script.

They come without siren-song or any ushering. To Eat To-day. Nancy Cunard. WPN

They could grow used to seeing bones. The Empire Sofa. Thomas Hornsby Ferril. PaTW

They couldn't understand why the drover cried. The Drover's Boy. Ted Egan. NOBAu

They crawled out slowly. Work-in-progress. Mahmood Jamal. NBrP

They cross from Glasgow to a black city. Settlers. Tom Paulin. IIP; PNI

They cross the frontier as their names cross your pages. The New Emigration. Kay Boyle. WPE

They cross the Suburbs. From the Suburbs. Louise Glück. FaBoWP; NALW *Fr.* Dedication to Hunger.

They crucified my Lord, an' He never said a mumbalin' word [*or* / And He never said a mumbaling word]. Crucifixion. *Unknown.* BPo; TAP

They cut back all the flowery mass / In the morning. (LL) The Lodging-House Fuchsias. Thomas Hardy. OBGa; OxBSP

They cut it in squares. Socratic. Hilda Doolittle. HoPM *Fr.* Child Poems.

They cut off his left arm / and his right arm. The National Hero. Gojko Djogo, *German.* AF, *tr.* by Michael March *and* Dušan Puvaić

They dance the world as. John Cage. APSN *Fr.* Diary: How to Improve the World (You Will Only Make Matters Worse).

They danced by the light of the moon. (LL) The Owl and the Pussy-Cat. Edward Lear. APAD; BoTP; CABP; CBNP; CTV; ChAP; EBEvV; FPC; FaBoBe; FaBoCh; GEA; GTBS-P; ITG; NBLV; NOBE; NOxBChV; NTCP; NTP; NoP-4; OBCoV; OBSP; OTCP; OxBChV; OxBM; OxBoLi; PC; PeLV; PoLF; PoRA; TFi; TLR; TTTS

They demanded in loud voices. The Rollcall of Bones. César Vallejo, *Spanish.* HSix, *tr.* by Robert Bly

They descended into hell after injustice. Miners. Branko Miljkovic, *Serbo-Croatian.* HSix, *tr.* by Charles Simic

They did not build wings for them. Irena Klepfisz. CPO

They did not come to claim you back. Helen Todd: My Birthname. Sandra McPherson. LCAP-2; LoL

They did not know. Dawn Dissolves the Monsters. Paul Éluard, *French.* AF, *tr.* by Lloyd Alexander

They did not know this face. Job. Elizabeth Sewell. ChIV-1

They did the deed of darkness. You and I Saw Hawks Exchanging the Prey. James Wright. NAAL-2; NoAM

They did their thing so well. Their Thing. Léon Damas, *French.* NegPo, *tr.* by Ellen Conroy Kennedy

They didn't get me. Alma Villanueva. UnSA

They didn't have much trouble. Teaching the Ape to Write Poems. James Tate. BLT; CMAP

They Didn't Hire Him. Gary Snyder. LCAP-2; Poetr *Fr.* Hitch Haiku. LCAP-2

They dither softly at her bedroom door. Cover Her Face. Thomas Kinsella. CIP-2

They do it with knives. Alistair Paterson. PeNZ *Fr.* The Toledo Room.

They do little interminable things. Christina. Yona Wallach, *Hebrew.* IP, *tr.* by Warren Bargad *and* Stanley F. Chyet

They do me wrong who say I come no more. Opportunity. Walter Malone. BLPA; FaBoBe; PWR

They do not care, the dying, whether it be dawn or dusk or daylight full and clear. Illi Morituri. Mary Morison Webster. PeSA

They Do Not Go Gentle. Basil T. Paquet. CDa

They do not live in the world. The Animals. Edwin Muir. CMoP; CRP; ChIV-1; EBEV; HeIP-4; KSG; MoBrPo

They do not think whom they souse with spray. (LL) Twenty-eight young men bathe by the shore. Walt Whitman. ColAP; HAP; NoP-4; PAR; SAmP

They do zay that a travellen chap. The Leane. William Barnes. EBVV

They dogged him all one afternoon. On the Way to the Mission. Duncan Campbell Scott. NOBC

They done took Cordelia. Stony Lonesome. Langston Hughes. NOBA; SAmP

They don't appeal to me. Tanka. Kanoko Okamoto, *Japanese.* MJT, *tr.* by Makoto Ueda

They don't build houses like that any more. Verandahs. Robert Francis Brissenden. CBAP; NOBAu

They don't get anywhere. The Couple Overheard. William Meredith. HoPM

They don't hold grudges. First Monday Scottsboro Alabama. Tom Weatherly. PoBA

They don't like strangers. Stoney Ridge Dance Hall. Alden Nowlan. MoCV

They Don't Speak English in Paris. Ogden Nash. OBAL

They Don't Understand a Thing. Vladimir Mayakovsky, *Russian.* TCRP, *tr.* by Bernard Meares

They don't want to stop. They can't stop. Demographics. Catherine Bowman. BAP-94

They dragged you from [the] homeland. Strong Men. Sterling Brown. BPo; CrDW; PoBA; TTY

They Dream Only of America. John Ashbery. SPE

They dressed us up in black. The Funeral. Walter De la Mare. CMoP

They drive me mad, those rosy lips, forever prattling. (*fl.* 1st cent. B.C. *or* A.D. 1st cent.) Dioscorides. HePo, *tr. by* Barbara Hughes Fowler *Fr.* Epigrams.

They drive us to Berlin. (LL) A Cartload of Shoes. Abraham Sutskever, *Yiddish.* CEEP; HP, *tr. by* David G. Roskies

They drove the thorny wood beneath my breast. At the Crossroads. Harvey Gross. PFE

They drove to the Market with ringing pockets. Hamnavoe Market. George Mackay Brown. FaBoTC

They drove us out. Exodus. Horst Bienek, *German.* AF, *tr. by* Matthew Mead

They dug his grave by lantern light. The Grave. Rudyard Kipling. NSI

They eat beans mostly, this old yellow pair. The Bean Eaters. Gwendolyn Brooks. BlSi; HAP; HeIP-4; LCAP-2; NALW; NoP-4; PoBA; PoE; PoPoPo; Poetr; TAP; TRP; TTY; WeW-3

They eat only metal oatmeal and go barefoot in the spring muds. Their women are. Pontoon. Kit Robinson. FTOS

They Eat Out. Margaret Atwood. NoAM

They enslave their children's children who make compromise with sin. (LL) Once to every man and nation comes the moment to decide. James Russell Lowell. APN-1

They expanded. McDonald's, New Hartford, NY. Valerie Worth. AiP

They exterminate poets. Bulat Shalvovich Okudzhava, *Russian.* TCRP, *tr. by* Albert C. Todd

They fastened a people to merchant ships. Edouard Glissant. NegPo, *tr. by* Ellen Conroy Kennedy *Fr.* The Indies.

They Feed They Lion. Philip Levine. LCAP-2; MoP; NNaP; NOBA; NoAM; NoP-4; VCAP

They feed they Lion and he comes. (LL) They Feed They Lion. Philip Levine. LCAP-2; MoP; NNaP; NOBA; NoAM; NoP-4; VCAP

They fell asleep but not for long, for soon. Callimachus. HePo, *tr. by* Barbara Hughes Fowler *Fr.* Hecale.

They fle[e] from me that sometime [*or* sometyme] did me se[e]k[e]. The Lover Showeth How He Is Forsaken of Such as He Sometime Enjoyed. Sir Thomas Wyatt. AAS; BoLoP; CBLP; ClHu; EnLoPo; FaBoPV; HAP; HeIP-4; HoPM; ImPo; InPK-6; InPS-3; NAEL-1; NOBE; NoSic; OAEL-1; OBEV; OxBC; PoE; PoEL-1; PoRA; SCGP; SCV; SiPS; TFi; TRP

They Flee from Me That Sometime Did Me Seek. Gavin Ewart. OxBC

They fluttered off like withered souls of men. (LL) The Pity of the Leaves. Edwin Arlington Robinson. APN-2; MoAmPo

They formed the ritual circle. A Local Man Goes to the Killing Ground. James Whitehead. MT

They fought south of the Castle. Fighting South of the Castle. *Unknown, Chinese.* AWP, *tr. by* Arthur Waley

They fought south of the ramparts. Fighting South of the Ramparts. *Unknown, Chinese.* ChiP, *tr. by* Arthur Waley

They Fought South of the Walls. Li Po, *Chinese.* SuSp, *tr. by* Joseph J. Lee

They fought south of the walls. *Unknown, Chinese.* SuSp, *tr. by* Hans H. Frankel

("Night fell, but you never came back.") (LL) CoBCP, *tr. by* Burton Watson

("They fought south of the wall.") CoBCP, *tr. by* Burton Watson

They found a taxi. He took her home. The Moral Taxi Ride. Erich Kästner, *German.* EP, *tr. by* Jerome Rothenberg

They found him in the fields and called him back to music. Bunk Johnson Blowing. Muriel Rukeyser. SeSe

They Found Him Sitting in a Chair. Horace Gregory. MoAmPo

They found in his chest a lamp of roses and a moon. Victim Number 48. Mahmoud Darwish, *Arabic.* VCWP, *tr. by* Denys Johnson-Davies

They found the path and I found the puddle. John Millington Synge. CBNP

They fuck you up, your mum and dad. This Be The Verse. Philip Larkin. NoAM; PoPoPo

They gathered shouting crowds along the road. An Old Story. Howard Nemerov. *Fr.* Epigrams. OBAL

They gave him a finger, but he took the whole hand. King Saul and I. Yehuda Amichai, *Hebrew.* PoSu, *tr. by* Assia Gutmann

They Gave Him Vinegar and Gall (Matt. 27) and Wine Mingled with Myrrh (Mark 15). Francis Quarles. NOSC

They gave it back to me / life. The Black Man's Lament. Léon Damas, *French.* NegPo, *tr. by* Ellen Conroy Kennedy

They gave its splendor to our fall. (LL) The Sumach Leaves. Jones Very. ColAP

They gave me a coat and helmet. A Soldier's Ditty. Bulat Shalvovich Okudzhava, *Russian.* TCRP, *tr. by* Deming Brown

They gave me in my kindergarten year. Now or Never. Judith Moffett. Son

They gave me the wrong name, in the first place. Her Story. Naomi Long Madgett. PoBA

They gave us the mysterious deep warehouse. The Ajax Samples. Laura Jensen. LCAP-2

They give a man a taste for death. (LL) Some can gaze and not be sick. A. E. Housman. FaBoEE; NOBVV; OBSV

They give what she has, and wind up here for the future. Very Days. Aaron Shurin. PT

They go / as shiftworkers / to the dawn. Nigel Roberts. *See* The Gull's Flight.

They go by, go by, love, the days and the hours. Teresa de Jesús, *Spanish.* WPOW, *tr. by* Maria A. Proser, Arlene Scully *and* James Scully

They got, among the bras and underpants. (LL) Bloomingdale's. Marilyn Hacker. CPO; DeD

They grabbed him in 1972. Poem for William Rummel Serving a Life Sentence in a Texas Prison for Not Fixing an Air Conditioner. Paul Fericano. EC2

They grew in beauty, side by side. The Graves of a Household. Felicia Dorothea Hemans. FaPoR; NOBRP; WPE

They grow over the Yangtze, the plum rains. Nisei: Second Generation Japanese-American. Jim Mitsui. OpBo

They guided birds and came to hear their story. Of History More Like Myth. Jean Garrigue. NYBP

They gulp jambon, they gobble down pâté. Contrasts. Đặng Thái Thuyên, *Vietnamese.* AVP, *tr. by* Huỳnh Sanh Thông

They had a happy childhood on the banks of the Hudson. Room 5600. Ernesto Cardenal, *Spanish.* CLPP, *tr. by* Cohen, Jonathan

They had a verb. I Held the Vein, But Death. Dennis Phillips. FTOS

They had agreed, walking into the delicatessen on 6th Avenue. Vintage. Robert Hass. NAmP90

They had been there a month; the water had begun to tear them apart. A Negro Soldier's Viet Nam Diary. Herbert Martin. PoBA

They had begun to whisper. Move. Lucille Clifton. NAAAL

They had changed their throats and had the throats of birds. (LL) Cuchulain Comforted. W. B. Yeats. CMoP; LiTM; OAEL-2; TOF

They had come to see the salmon lunging and leaping. The Excursion of the Speech and Hearing Class. David Wagoner. VCAP

They had dragged for hours. These Trees Are No Forest of Mourners. Douglas G. Jones. NOBC

They had faces open to whoever passed. Penniless Lovers. Eugenio de Andrade, *Portuguese.* VCWP, *tr. by* Alexis Levitin

They had gardens, they had mornings in those days! (LL) Souvenir of the Ancient World. Carlos Drummond de Andrade, *Portuguese.* ChAP; VCWP, *tr. by* Mark Strand

They had given him back to her, but not to keep. (LL) Not to Keep. Robert Frost. CMoP; OxBA; Poetr

They had hot scent across the spumy sea. Destroyers Off Jutland. Reginald McIntosh Cleveland. NSI

They had long met o' Zundays—her true love and she. The Bride-Night Fire. Thomas Hardy. EnVR

They had me laid out in a white. April Fools' Day. Yusef Komunyakaa. GT

They had never had one in the house before. Bronzeville Woman in a Red Hat. Gwendolyn Brooks. GT; NALW

They had questioned him for hours. Campaign. Ciaran Carson. BiHa; CIP-2; PNI

They had secured their beauty to the dock. The Crowd. John Masefield. OxBTC

They had stolen my soul away! (LL) Romance. Walter James Turner. APAD; CH; EBEvV; MoBrPo; NOBAu; NOBE; NOxBChV; NTP; OBMV; PoRA

They had supposed their formula was fixed. White Troops Had Their Orders but the Negroes Looked Like Men. Gwendolyn Brooks. PBMP

They had the nerve to name you Constance. Macedonius, *Greek.* InMo, *tr. by* Sam Hamill

They hanged him, I said dismissively. Dennis Brutus. VCWP

They hanged him on a clement morning, swung. Epitaph. Dennis Scott. HCP; PBCV

They hanged the King of Ai at eventide. The King of Ai. Hyam Plutzik. LiTM

They have a few amusements, presidents. *Much Ado About Nothing,* Thanksgiving, 1972. Ann Hayes. CMAP

They have been with us a long time. Telephone Poles. John Updike. FYAP; Poetsp

They have brought me a shell. Shell. Federico García Lorca, *Spanish.* CBNP

They have brought you here. The Shack Outside Boise. Vern Rutsala. CMAP

They have carried the mahogany chair and the cane rocker. Mourning Picture. Adrienne Rich. CoAP

They have cast their burden upon the Lord, and—the Lord He lays it on Martha's Sons! (LL). The Sons of Martha. Rudyard Kipling. ChIV-2

They have chiseled on my stone the words. Cassius Hueffer. Edgar Lee Masters. OxBA   *Fr.* Spoon River Anthology.

They have closed the prison where they had you. Ringing Words. Mary Kinzie. FFC

They have coarse features, their hands are deft and accustomed to a hammer and nails, to wood and iron. The Passion of Our Lord painted by an anonymous hand from the Circle of Rhenish Masters. Zbigniew Herbert, *Polish.* GI, tr. by Adam Czerniawski

They have crucified their Lord afresh. *Unknown, Latin.* MLL, *tr. by* Helen Waddell   *Fr.* Carmina Burana.

They have dreamed as young men dream. Old Black Men. Georgia Douglas Johnson. NMM-2; PoBA

They have emptied the heart of Westport. Westport House, Portrush. James Simmons. PBCIP

They have felled him to the ground. The Leader. J. P. Clark Bekedermo. PBMAP

They have fenced in the dirt road. Burial. Alice Walker. AmPA; LoHo

They have gone / into the green hill, by doors without hinges. Apples. Donald Hall. LCAP-2

They have laid the penthouse scenes away. Elegy in a Theatrical Warehouse. Kenneth Fearing. NYBP

They have left bread on the table. Bread. Gabriela Mistral, *Spanish.* WPOW, *tr. by* Allan Francovich and Kathleen Weaver

They have [or They've or Th' have] left Thee naked, Lord, O[h] that they had! On Our Crucified Lord, Naked and Bloody. Richard Crashaw. HoPM; NOSC; OAEL-1; OxBSP; SeCP; TrCP

They have lived in each other so long. The Demolition. Anne Stevenson. OxBSP

They have no graves as yet. (LL) Elegy in a Country Churchyard. G. K. Chesterton. FaPoR; MoBrPo; NSI; OBWP; OxBSP; PoFWW

They have no use for traffic lights. People on Wayward Journeys. Ofelia Zepeda. PaTW

They have no word for conscience. Carrier Indians. Ken Belford. NOBC

They have not sown, and feed on bitter fruit. (LL) A Black Man Talks of Reaping. Arna Bontemps. BPo; ColAP; NAAAL; PoBA; SSLK

They have only to look at each other to laugh. The Old Gray Couple. Archibald MacLeish. AFr

They have put my bed beside the unpainted screen. Last Poem. Po Chü-i, *Chinese.* ChiP, *tr. by* Arthur Waley

They have said evil of my dear. *Unknown. Fr.* Medieval Norman Song. AWP, *tr. by* John Addington Symonds

They have sed. Hospital/Poem. Sonia Sanchez. BPo; PoBA

They have taken my father. Gael Turnbull. NBrP

They have taken the gable from the roof of clay. Swedes. Edward Thomas. OAEL-2; RB

They have taken the maps and spread them out. Still Pond, No More Moving. Howard Moss. NYBP

They have the corner. The Women. Joseph Ceravolo. FTOS

They have the faces of / no-one. (LL) The Animals in That Country. Margaret Atwood. NALW; NoAM

They have turned, and say that I am dying. That. I Substitute for the Dead Lecturer. Imamu Amiri Baraka. PoE

They Have Turned the Church Where I Ate God. Gary Gildner. PBCAP

They have yarns / Of a skyscraper so tall they had to put hinges. Carl Sandburg. MoAmPo   *Fr.* The People, Yes.

They hear[e] and see, and sigh, and then they break[e]. (LL) Love is Love. Sir Edward Dyer. APAD; GEA; NoSic; OxBSP; RB; SCGP

They hear Thee not, O God! nor see. Ezekiel. John Greenleaf Whittier. ChIV-1

They heard the south wind sighing. The Crocuses. Frances Ellen Watkins Harper. BlSi

They heated hatchet blades over gas fires in roadside workshops and. While the Record Plays. Gyula Illyés, *Hungarian.* PFTM, *tr. by* William Jay Smith

They heaved the stone; they heaped the cairn. Aideen's Grave. Sir Samuel Ferguson. NOIV

They hire you for the silk to line their budgets. Advice from Euterpe. Carter Revard. VoR

They hold their hands over their mouths. The Poets Agree to Be Quiet by the Swamp. David Wagoner. CoAP; VGW

They hunt chameleon worlds with cameras. Adina. Harold Milton Telemaque. TTY

They hunt, the velvet tigers in the jungle. India. Walter James Turner. MoBrPo

They in the sea being burnt, they in the burnt ship drowned [or drown'd]. (LL) A Burnt Ship. Donne. EBEV; InPK-6; OBWP

They infest my life. A Plague of Telephones. Jim Wayne Miller. IFJA

They journeyed, / When the darkness of night. Ode. Ibn al-Arabi, *Arabic.* AWP, *tr. by* R. A. Nicholson

They just elected me Pope. The Poems of the Pope. Nicanor Parra, *Spanish.* VCWP, *tr. by* Edith Grossman

They just need me and maybe you. (LL) Poet-Tree. Earle Birney. APAD

They kneel on the slanting floor. The Foot-Washing. George Ella Lyon. CrSp; OxWW

They knew that they were naked, and ashamed. The Serpent. Jones Very. NCAP

They knew you once, O beautiful and wise. (LL) Bread and Music. Conrad Potter Aiken. AWP; CMoP; ImPo; LiTM; MoAmPo; NOBA; OxBA; PoRA

They laughed at one I loved. Innocence. Patrick Kavanagh. RB

They lay down by the fire and stretched. Two. Mikhail Arkadyevich Svetlov, *Russian.* TCRP, *tr. by* Daniel Weissbort

They Lay Dying Side by Side. Anna Swirszczynska, *Polish.* PoSu, *tr. by* Magnus J. Krynski and Robert A. Maguire

They lean against the cooling car, backs pressed. The Discovery of the Pacific. Thom Gunn. HeIP-4

They lean over the path. Orchids. Theodore Roethke. CMoP; ColAP; TRP

They learn in suffering what they teach in song. Shelley. *See* Julian and Maddalo; A Conversation.

They leave rice fields to travel far and wide. Grains of Rice. Phan Văn Tri, *Vietnamese.* AVP, *tr. by* Huỳnh Sanh Thông

They leave us—artists, singers, all. When London Calls. Victor James Daley. CBAP

They leave us so to the way we took. In Neglect. Robert Frost. OxBSP; VGW

They left my hands like a printer's. Blackberries. Yusef Komunyakaa. NAmP90

They left the fury of the fight. Sportsmen in Paradise. T. P. Cameron Wilson. PoFWW

They left the primrose glistening in its dew. Spring, and the Blind Children. Alfred Noyes. OxBTC

They left their Babylon bare. The Destruction of Jerusalem by the Babylonian Hordes. Isaac Rosenberg. PeFWW

They licked the platter clean. (LL) Jack Sprat could eat no fat. Mother Goose. FaBoBe; LB; OxNR; ReMoGo

They lie at rest, our blessed dead. Christina Rossetti. NOBVV

They lie in the Sunday street. The Dead. C. Day Lewis. TwCP

They lie, the men who tell for reasons of their own. Faces in the Street. Henry Lawson. CBAP

They lied, those lying traitors all. *Unknown. Fr.* Medieval Norman Song. AWP, *tr. by* John Addington Symonds

They like to come here. Pleasant sidestreets pave. The Visitors. Richard Moore. DiPo

They live alone. Neighbors. David Allan Evans. Poetsp

They live by the Lakes, an appropriate quarter. On the Lake Poets. Charles Townsend. FaBoEE

They live 'neath the curtain. Puk-Wudjies. Patrick Reginald Chalmers. BoTP

They lived out in a women's house. Stephanie Markman. BrRo   *Fr.* The Rime of the Ancient Feminist.

They locked us out without a cause—. The Glorious Strike of the Builders. *Unknown.* FaBoVe

They look at each other dully. Two Quartz Pebbles. Vasco [or Vasko] Popa. PoSu, *tr. by* Anne Pennington   *Fr.* The Quartz Pebble.

They look like big dogs badly drawn, drawn wrong. Wolves in the Zoo. Howard Nemerov. NoAM

They look / like newlyweds. Ōshima Ryōta, *Japanese.* TTTS

They look up with their pale and sunken faces. Elizabeth Barrett Browning. *Fr.* The Cry of the Children. EBVV; OxAEP-2; VWP

They looked at me all ghosts. Mellisandra. Harriet Rose. BrRo

They looked so good. The Young Fenians. Padraic Fallon. BIrV

They love indeed, who quake to say they love. (LL) Sonnet 54: "Because I breathe not love to every one." Sir Philip Sidney. CABP; ImGa; InPS-3; NoSic

They made her a grave too cold and damp. The Lake of the Dismal Swamp. Thomas Moore. BLPA

They made impudent inspection of our coast. Rex Ingamells. CBAP   *Fr.* The Great South Land.

They made me a director. The Director. Edmund George Valpy Knox. OBCoV

They Made Me Erect and Lone. Henry David Thoreau. OxBSP

They made the chamber sweet with flowers and leaves. A Pause. Christina Rossetti. VWP

They made their grim, sad faces and went out. Death of the Polar Explorers. Gabriel Gbadamosi. HBAPE

They make. Ode to Tomatoes. Francisco Alarcon. IFJA

They make a fake tiger, and hope it will seem real. The Artemisia Tiger. Chang Yü. *Fr.* Four Poems On the Ch'ung-wu Festival. CoBLCP, *tr. by* Jonathan Chaves

They make in the twining tide the motions of birds. The Bathers. W. S. Merwin. PoE

They married us when they put. Drafted. Su Wu, *Chinese.* OHMPC, *tr. by* Kenneth Rexroth

They may look on earth / and not be ashamed. Diane Di Prima. *See* April Fool Birthday Poem for Grandpa.

They May Rail at This Life. Thomas Moore. PoEL-4

They meet but with unwholesome Springs. Against Them Who Lay Unchastity to the Sex of Women. William Habington. BeJo; SeCP *Fr.* Castara.

They met him somewhere at the Polish border. Black Music. Yevgeny Borisovich Rein, *Russian.* TCRP, *tr. by* Lubov Yakovleva

They might not need me—yet they might. Emily Dickinson. PoToHe; Spl

They mock you, my country. To My Country. Ivan Alekseievich Bunin, *Russian.* TCRP, *tr. by* Simon Franklin

They more than we are what we are. Statues. Kathleen Jessie Raine. NYBP

They mount the lonely street. (LL) The Lonely Street. William Carlos Williams. PoA; TwCP

They moved like rivers in their mended stockings. The Grandmothers. Mary Oliver. WPE

They must be clean. Folding sheets. Marge Piercy. *Fr.* Six Underrated Pleasures. EC2

They must be shown as about to taste of the tree. Adam and Eve. Charles Hubert Sisson. FaBoTw

They must be verified at last. (LL) On the Death of Dean Swift. Jonathan Swift. EBEV; NOBE; NOBL; NOIV; OxAEP-1; PeLV

They must to keep their certainty accuse. The Leaders of the Crowd. W. B. Yeats. EBEV; MoBrPo; OxAEP-2

They mutilate they torment each other. A Voice. Tadeusz Rózewicz, *Polish.* BLT, *tr. by* Czeslaw Milosz

They Name Heaven. Bruce Weigl. NAmP90

They named it Aultgraat—Ugly Burn. Black Rock of Kiltearn. Andrew Young. FaBoTw; RB

They never come back, though I loved them well. Ballad of the Bird-Bride. Rosamund Marriott Watson. VWP

They never found what slowly descended, silently. Twelfth Birthday. William Stafford. CMAP

They never left / the walled garden of their arms. Waltz Poem of Those in Love and Inseparable Forever. Miguel Hernández, *Spanish.* AF, *tr. by* Timothy Baland

They never read their Hedylos, nor could. A Renaissance Drunk. George Evans. PmAP

They nicknamed me Mririda. Mririda. Mririda n'Ait Attik, *Berber into French.* WPOW, *tr. by* René Euloge; *English vers. by* Daniel Halpern *and* Paula Paley

They nod at me and I at stems. Open. Larry Eigner. NeAP

They nod, whispering, "One of ours; one of ours. Yes. Yes." (LL) The Examination. W. D. Snodgrass. CAPP-1; SAGP

They often haunt me, these substantial ghosts. The Hymn Tunes. Edward Lucie-Smith. PBCV

They only find a medicine for the itch. (LL) No Platonic [*or* Platonique] Love. William Cartwright. BeJo; GBL; ImPo; NOSC; OAEL-1; PoEL-2

They opn our mail petulantly. Wundrfulness uv th Mountees Our Secret Police, Th. Bill Bissett. NOBC

They owned their passiveness. (LL) The Subalterns. Thomas Hardy. CMoP; MoBrPo; MoP; NOBVV; NoAM; OAEL-2; Poetr

They paint yellow and red flowers. Gift Shop in Pecs. Len Roberts. PuP-16

They paper the walls of their world. The Recluses. Stuart Z. Perkoff. NeAP

They pass like a warning of snow. The Insects. Nancy Willard. LCAP-2

They pass me by like shadows, crowds on crowds. The Street. James Russell Lowell. GSo; Son

They pass too fast. Ships, and there's time for sighing. Earth Has Shrunk in the Wash. William Empson. CMoP

They pity me. / "Look at him, see." Lonely. André Spire, *French.* AWP; TrJP, *tr. by* Jethro Bithell

They played with the pebble. The Heart of the Quartz Pebble. Vasco [*or* Vasko] Popa. PoSu, *tr. by* Anne Pennington *Fr.* The Quartz Pebble.

They pointed me out on the highway, and they said. The Traveller. John Berryman. GM; PoA; VGW

They possessed nothing. The Inheritors. Gary Geddes. NOBC

"They pray for children? Let them!" cried Polyxo. Antipater of Thessalonica, *Greek.* GrAn, *tr. by* Alistair Elliot

They Pray the Best Who Pray and Watch. Edward Hopper. AH

They present light as evidence of the past. Stars. Alan Bold. SpW

They pursue space. Egypt. Wendy Mulford. NBrP

They pushed him straight against the wall. At Sunrise. Rosa Zagnoni Marinoni. PoToHe

They put him here because God came at night. Dementia Praecox. Morris Gilbert Bishop. PoA

They put Us far apart. Emily Dickinson. APN-2

They quite forgot their quarrel. (LL) Tweedledum and Tweedledee. Mother Goose. LB; NOBL; OxNR; PeLV; ReMoGo

They quiz me in the street because. To Julie. Alfred de Musset, *French.* FLP, *tr. by* Alistair Elliot

They rage and rave, caress and soothe. Waves. Xuân Quỳnh, *Vietnamese.* AVP, *tr. by* Huỳnh Sanh Thông

They Receive Instructions Against Chile. Pablo Neruda, *Spanish.* AF, *tr. by* Robert Bly *and* James Wright

They rejected life to seek the Way. Their footprints are before us. Written on a Monastery Wall. Li Shang-yin, *Chinese.* PLT, *tr. by* A. C. Graham

They Return. Jay Macpherson. NOBC; PoA *Fr.* The Way Down.

They rise, they walk again. (LL) The Heaven of Animals. James Dickey. CoAP; ColAP; HeIP-4; LiTM; MT; NAAL-2; NOBA; NoAM; PoE; TAP; TRP; VCAP

They roar / Out of the river tunnels. A Rumble. Virginia Schonborg. SSCS

They rode north. Blackie Thinks of His Brothers. Stanley Crouch. GT; PoBA

They rode upon. Ride upon the Death Chariot. Mbuyiseni Oswald Mtshali. PBMAP

They rose up in a twinkling cloud. The Stockdoves. Andrew Young. FaBoTC

They roused him with muffins--they roused him with ice. The Baker's Tale. "Lewis Carroll." EBEV; NAEL-2; OxAEP-2 *Fr.* The Hunting of the Snark. CBNP; OBNC; OBNV; PoEL-5

They sadly travelled thus, until they came. Arthur's Fight with Orgoglio and Duessa. Edmund Spenser. EBNV *Fr.* Wood Of Error. AEP

They said a while ago that the fuzz were coming to take us away. Moment of Truth. Rowley Habib. PeNZ

They said I got away in a boat. Bruce Ismay's Soliloquy. Derek Mahon. PNI

They said of my father: George was a good man. The Mystery. David Wevill. IFJA

They said, "The Master is coming." Unawares. Emma A. Lent. PoLF

They said the moon wasn't going to rise no no. August 18. Joanne Kyger. PoM

They said there was a woman in the hills. Women Are Not Gentlemen. Harley Matthews. NOBAu

They said to my grandmother: "Please do not be bitter." Bitter Fruit of the Tree. Sterling Brown. NoP-4

They said, "Wait." Well, I waited. Alabama Centennial. Naomi Long Madgett. BPo

They said we was nowhere. Chanson d'Outre Tombe. Philip Whalen. BB

They sailed away into the coloured prints. Highlanders. Iain Crichton Smith. FaBoTC

They sat by the water. The fine women. Stars Which See, Stars Which Do Not See. Marvin Bell. CMAP

They sat in even rows. Miss Clement's Second Grade. Maryfrances Cusumano Wagner. UnSA

They sat, she laughing at a quiet joke. (LL) It chanced his lips did meet her forehead cool. George Meredith. CBLP; EnVR; NOBVV

They sat there, nine women, much the same age. Apollo Takes Charge of His Muses. A. E. Stallings. BAP-94

They sate to meat, and Satyrane his chaunce. Edmund Spenser. OAEL-1 *Fr.* Wood Of Error. AEP

They saw the young girls twisting their strings, Goulburn Island. *Unknown.* NOBAu, *tr. by* Ronald M. Berndt *Fr.* Goulburn Island Song Cycle.

They saw you behind your muzzle much more clearly. To a Farmer Who Hung Five Hawks on His Barbed Wire. David Wagoner. NoAM

They say a maiden conceived. Christmas Carols. Patricia Beer. OxBC

They say a man dies. Steve Crow. HATNAP *Fr.* Songs.

They say a wife and husband, bit by bit. A Bridge instead of a Wall. *Unknown.* PoToHe

They say dogs killed you. No, Euripides. Adaios of Macedon, *Greek.* GrAn, *tr. by* Alistair Elliot

They say, God wot! On the Death of the Giraffe. Thomas Hood. FaBoEE

They say: He lives with colours. Sons. Jack Cope. PeSA

They say "he need (present) enemy (plural)." Transformations. Jack Spicer. FTOS

They say, his strange, large eyes. Father. Margit Kaffka, *Hungarian.* PBWP, *tr. by* Laura Schiff

They say I am excitable! How could. The King of Owls. Louise Erdrich. NoAM

They say I am harsh and haughty. Uncle Sam's Soliloquy. George Sands Johnson. PWR

They say Ideal beauty cannot enter. Hiram Powers' "Greek Slave." Elizabeth Barrett Browning. GS; NALW

They say, in other days. John Gray. NOBVV

They say, interpret it your own way, Christ is born. (LL) An Eclogue for Christmas. Louis MacNeice. FaBoMo; NoAM; OBMV

They say it is waiting for more, the snow. Snow Signs. Charles Tomlinson. NoAM

They say, little beast, little creator, the elders say. First Prayer for the Hottentotsgod. Breyten Breytenbach, *Afrikaans*. AF, *tr. by* Denis Hirson

They say my love is going far away. Stone Castle Music. *Unknown, Chinese*. CoBCP, *tr. by* Burton Watson

They Say My Verse Is Sad: No Wonder. A. E. Housman. NoAM

They say, old man, your horse will die. The Dead Horse. *Unknown*. AS

They say Revis found a flatrock. Mountain Bride. Robert Morgan. MT

They Say She Is Veiled. Judy Grahn. CrSp

They say "Son." Old Black Men Say. James A. Emanuel. MBE; PoBA

They say that all little girls adore their fathers / want to marry. Leslie Reese. MoLi *Fr.* My Dad Is a Magician.

They say that black people. Patricia Smith. GT

They say that Byron, though lame. Anacreontic. Austin Clarke. NOIV

They say that every idle word. Idle Words. Walter Savage Landor. OBSV

They say that Hope is happiness. Stanzas for Music. Byron. NAEL-2; OxBSP

They say that I was in my youth. Limerick. *Unknown*. PeLi

They Say That in the Unchanging Place. Hilaire Belloc. PoLF *Fr.* Dedicatory Ode.

They say that once it mirrored palace ladies. The Well of the King of Wu. Kao Ch'i, *Chinese*. CoBLCP, *tr. by* Jonathan Chaves

They say that plants don't talk, nor do. Rosalía de Castro, *Spanish*. BoWoP, *tr. by* Aliki *and* Willis Barnstone

They say that reality exists only in the spirit. Demiurge. D. H. Lawrence. GI

They say that Richard Cory owns. Richard Cory. Paul Simon. InPK-6; PFE

They say that shadow[e]s of deceased ghosts. Joshua Sylvester. Son

They say that "Time assuages." Emily Dickinson. APN-2; OxBSP

They say the experimental. Nothing. Burns Singer. OxBS

They say the first dream Adam our father had. Adam's Dream. Edwin Muir. NoP-4

They say the land is full of apes, which have. Lascelles Abercrombie. NSI *Fr.* The Sale of Saint Thomas.

They say "the lighthouse keeper's world is round." Requiem. Sam Hunt. PeNZ

They say the lion and the lizard keep. Omar Khayyám. EBEV *Fr.* The Rubáiyát of Omar Khayyám [of Naishápúr]. AWP; EBVV; FaBoBe; FaPoR; HAP; NAEL-2; PoEL-5

They say the men are. Men Are Coming Back! The. Barry Cole. OxBTC

They say the Phoenix is dying, some say dead. News of the Phoenix. Arthur James Marshall Smith. MoCV

They say the sea is cold, but the sea contains. Whales Weep Not! D. H. Lawrence. CMoP; NoAM

They say the war is over. But water still. Redeployment. Howard Nemerov. LiTM; OBWP; PoWW; TrJP

They say the world is round, and yet. Life's Scars. Ella Wheeler Wilcox. BLPA

They say there is. *Unknown, Japanese*. TAL, *tr. by* Arthur Waley

They say there is a country. Saul Tchernichovsky, *Hebrew*. MHP, *tr. by* Ruth Finer Mintz

They say there is a sweeter air. A Carriage from Sweden. Marianne Moore. HAP; LiTM; TwCP

They say there's a man on the moon. The Man on the Moon. Judy Turner. CTV

They say 'tis sinful to flirt. Sinful to Flirt. *Unknown*. AmFP

They say you have the face. Girl by the River. Federico García Lorca, *Spanish*. CBNP

They Say You're Staying in a Mountain Temple. Tu Fu, *Chinese*. CoBCP; TTTS, *tr. by* Burton Watson

They search out new regions of muteness. The Interior Prisoner. Geoffrey O'Brien. BAP-95

They see Gods wonders that are call'd. Roger Williams. SCAP

They seem hundreds of years away. Breughel. The Seed Cutters. Seamus Heaney. PNI *Fr.* Mossbawn. CIP-2; PNI

They seize the young girls of the western tribes, with their swaying. *Unknown*. NOBAu, *tr. by* Ronald M. Berndt *Fr.* Goulburn Island Song Cycle.

They sell good beer at Haslemere. West Sussex Drinking Song. Hilaire Belloc. MoBrPo

They sent him back to her. The letter came. Not to Keep. Robert Frost. CMoP; OxBA; Poetr

They serve revolving saucer eyes. The Ex-Queen Among the Astronomers. Fleur Adcock. FaBoWP; NALW; NoP-4

They served tea in the sandpile, together with. The Party. Reed Whittemore. CoAP; CoAmPo

They set out to bring Beethoven. The Bringers of Beethoven. Reiner Kunze, *German*. PoSu, *tr. by* Gordon Brotherston *and* Gisela Brotherston

They set the fish upon the table. Pesci Misti. Leonard Aaronson. FaBoTw

They set the slave free, striking off his chains. The Slave. James Oppenheim. TrJP

They severally—retard—or further / Unknown. (LL) Four Trees—upon a solitary Acre. Emily Dickinson. APN-2; PoEL-5

They shall bee upon one day. (LL) Child Waters. *Unknown*. ESPB; OxBB

They shall find him ware an' wakin', as they found him long ago! (LL) Drake's Drum. Sir Henry John Newbolt. EBEvV; FaBoCh; FaPoR; OBMV; PoRA; UV

They shall go down unto life's borderland. Sonnet to Negro Soldiers. Joseph Cotter, Sr.. PoBA

They shall have their dinner now. (LL) The Story of Fidgety Philip. Heinrich Hoffmann, *German*. ACTP

They Shall Know. Kofi Awoonor. VCWP

They shall lie there, together. (LL) The Old Churchyard of Bonchurch. Philip Bourke Marston. EBVV; OBNC

They Shall Look on Him. "Michael Field." VWP

They shall not be ashamed, but they shall speak with the enemies in the gate. (LL) Psalm 127. Bible, *O.T.* TrJP

They shall not grow old, as we that are left grow old. Those That Are Gone. Laurence Binyon. LBC

They shall not return to us, the resolute, the young. Mesopotamia. Rudyard Kipling. PoWW

They shall see Him in the crimson flush. The Pure in Heart Shall See God. Frances Ellen Watkins Harper. PWR

They shall sink under water. The Cities. "Æ." OBMV

They shared ten years as man and wife. Homecoming. Nguyễn Ý Thuần, *Vietnamese*. AVP, *tr. by* Huỳnh Sanh Thông

They shook the green leaves down. Magic Fox. James Welch. CDW; HATNAP; NoAM

They shorten tedious nights. (LL) Now winter nights enlarge. Thomas Campion. AAS; EBEV; NOSC; NTP; NoP-4; OxAEP-1; PBRV

They shorten'd the corp, and they pack'd. Cecil Frances Alexander. OxBoV

They should have slept, would have. The Lynching. Thylias Moss. GT

They shout no stranger, troublous news. Waits. Vivian Virtue. PBCV

They showed up for awhile and they died. Showing. Liam Rector. TRP

They shut me up in Prose. Emily Dickinson. APN-2; FaBoVe; InPS-3; NALW; NCAP; NOBA; NoP-4; PAR

They shut the road through the woods. The Way Through The Woods. Rudyard Kipling. CH; ChAP; EBEvV; FaBoCh; GEA; NOBE; NOxBChV; NTP; NoAM; OBEV; OBNC; OxAEP-2; OxBChV; OxBTC; SAGP; SCGP; WHSW

They sin who tell us Love can die. Love Indestructible. Robert Southey. LBC; OBNC *Fr.* The Curse of Kehama.

They Sing. Theodore Roethke. NYBP

They sing. (LL) The Second Shepherd's Play. *Unknown*. NAEL-1; OAEL-1; PoEL-1

They sing their dearest songs. During Wind and Rain. Thomas Hardy. CMoP; GTBS-P; HAP; NAEL-2; NoP-4; OAEL-2; OxBTC; PFE; PeVV; PoE; TFi; TOF; TRP

They sit and smoke on the esplanade. At a Watering-Place. Thomas Hardy. CMoP *Fr.* Satires of Circumstance in Fifteen Glimpses.

They sit in a glass egg. Dead Embryos. Judit Tóth, *Hungarian*. WPOW, *tr. by* Laura Schiff

They sit in a row. Fury of Overshoes. Anne Sexton. LCAP-2; NIP-4

They slept as they set off for the stars. Towards the Stars. Iain Crichton Smith. SpW

They slew by night. The Pentecost Castle. Geoffrey Hill. HAP

They slip on to the bus, hair piled up high. The Young Ones. Elizabeth Jennings. OxBTC

They slump in booths like rags, not even drunk. (LL) Drug Store. Karl Shapiro. CMoP; OxBA; TwCP

They sneaked into the limbo of time. Ancestral Faces. Kwesi Brew. PBA

They Sometimes Call Me. Wendy Rose. CDW

They sought it with thimbles, they sought it with care. Fit the Fifth: The Beaver's Lesson. "Lewis Carroll." *Fr.* The Hunting of the Snark. CBNP; OBNC; OBNV; PoEL-5

They sought it with thimbles, they sought it with care. Fit the Seventh: The Banker's Fate. "Lewis Carroll." *Fr.* The Hunting of the Snark. CBNP; OBNC; OBNV; PoEL-5

They sought it with thimbles, they sought it with care. Fit the Sixth: The Barrister's Dream. "Lewis Carroll." EBNV *Fr.* The Hunting of the Snark. CBNP; OBNC; OBNV; PoEL-5

They sought it with thimbles, they sought it with care. The Vanishing. "Lewis Carroll." OxAEP-2 *Fr.* The Hunting of the Snark. CBNP; OBNC; OBNV; PoEL-5

They sought the "growing tip of poetry." The Growing Tip. Mahadai Das. HCP

They sound like howling wolves from here. Song on the Way to Jail. Kakayek, *Tlingit Indian.* STP, *tr. by* James Koller

They spat on the poet. Poem of Pathos. Tadeusz Różewicz, *Polish.* FaBoPV, *tr. by* Adam Czerniawski

They speak not of torment. Flowers in the Ward. John Shaw Neilson. CBAP

They spent my life plotting against me. Possessions. Ken Smith. SPE

They spoke of the horse alive. The Horse. Philip Levine. CoAP; VCAP

They spoke the loveliest of languages. History of World Languages. D. J. Enright. OxBC

They sprint eight feet and—. Ringed Plover by a Water's Edge. Norman MacCaig. NoP-4; OxBC

They stand like penitential Augustines. Gothic Landscape. Irving Layton. TrJP

They stand there weeping in the stained daylight. Fresco: Departure for an Imperialist War. Thomas McGrath. AF

They startle dreams and compound the gloom. (LL) Composed on the Theme "Willows by the Riverside." Yü Hsüan-chi, *Chinese.* SuSp; WPOW, *tr. by* Jan W. Walls

They Starved, They Starved. Bàng Bá Lâ, *Vietnamese.* AVP, *tr. by* Huỳnh Sanh Thông

They still smell of incense, and their faces are burnt by their crossing / through the Great Dark Places. The Sleep of the Brave. Odysseas Elytis, *Greek.* AF, *tr. by* Edmund Keeley *and* Philip Sherrard

They stood—rain pelting at window, shrouded sea. In the Local Museum. Walter De la Mare. HAP

They strike mine eyes, but not my heart. (LL) Simplex Munditiis. Ben Jonson. AWP; BeJo; EBEvV; GBL; HAP; HoPM; InPS-3; NAEL-1; NOBE; NOSC; NoP-4; OAEL-1; OBEV; OxAEP-1; OxBSP; PBMP; PoE; PoPoPo; Poetr; SeCP; TFi; WeW-3

They strolled down the lane together. A Farmer's Boy. *Unknown.* CTAV; PeP

They stuck pigs in the throat. Might I not have done. Work. Gyula Illyés, *Hungarian.* RaBo, *tr. by* William Jay Smith

They suck and whisper it in mercury. The Break-up. Abraham Moses Klein. NOBC

They swore to wipe out the nomads, no thought for themselves. Song of Lung-hsi. Ch'en Tao, *Chinese.* CoBCP, *tr. by* Burton Watson

They take advantage—the soldiers need clothes. Se Aprovechan. Irving Feldman. GS

They take them out in the morning. Five Men. Zbigniew Herbert, *Polish.* PoSu, *tr. by* Czeslaw Milosz *and* Peter Dale Scott

They talk of short-lived pleasure—be it so—. Mutation. William Cullen Bryant. NCAP

They taste good to her. (LL) To a Poor Old Woman. William Carlos Williams. BLT; ColAP; MeMAP; OBAL; PiM; TAP; TTTS

They Tell Me I Am Lost. Maurice Kenny. HATNAP

They tell me: "Man." From a Talk. Yevgeny Yevtushenko, *Russian.* CLPP, *tr. by* Anselm Hollo

They tell me that Joe Turner's come and gone. Joe Turner. *Unknown.* CrDW

They tell me 'tis decided you depart. Byron. CBLP; NOBRP *Fr.* Canto the First. NAEL-2; OAEL-2; PoE *Fr.* Don Juan.

They tell us / That our skin is black. Politeness. Una Marson. PBCV

They tell you to go. And you do. (LL) Ringing the Bells. Anne Sexton. CAPP-1; HCAP; PoE; SAGP; TAP; VGW

They that go down to the sea in ships. Bible, *O.T.* CTV *Fr.* Bible O.T., Psalm 107:23–31.

They that have power to hurt, and will doe none. Sonnet 94. Shakespeare. CBLP; GTBS-P; ImPo; InPS-3; NAEL-1; NOBE; NoSic; OAEL-1; OBEV; OxAEP-1; PoE; PoEL-2; SCGP; SCV; Son; TRP *Fr.* Sonnets.

They that in play can do the thing they would. Robert Bridges. NoAM *Fr.* The Growth of Love.

They that look beyond the world, cannot be separated. William Penn. LBC

They that never had the use. An Apologie for Having Loved Before. Edmund Waller. CBLP

They That Sow at Night. Shin Shalom, *Hebrew.* MHP, *tr. by* Ruth Finer Mintz

They that wash on Monday. Mother Goose. FaBoBe; LB; NBLV ("Oh! they're sluts indeed.") (LL) LB

They think / I am stronger than I am. Naming Power. Wendy Rose. OxWW

They throw in Drummer Hodge, to rest. Drummer Hodge. Thomas Hardy. AWP; EBEV; GTBS-P; HAP; InPS-3; MoP; NAEL-2; NOBVV; NoAM; NoP-4; OBWP; OxAEP-2; PeFWW; Poetr; WeW-3

They tied my mother's legs when I was born. Years Later. Laurence David Lerner. PeSA

They toke togyder theyr counsell. *Unknown.* PeECV *Fr.* Gest of Robyn Hode. ESPB; OxBB

They told me, Francis Hinsley, they told me you were hung. Evelyn Waugh. OBCoV *Fr.* The Loved One.

They told me God came to Pius. In the Dark. Patrick Williams. PNI

They told me, Heraclitus, they told me you were dead. Brian Fore. UV

They told me, Heraclitus, they told me you were dead. Guy Hanlon. UV

They told me, Heraclitus, they told me you were dead. Heraclitus. William Johnson Cory, *par. from the Greek of* Callimachus. AWP; EBEvV; EBVV; FP; FaBoEE; FaPoR; InPK-6; NOBE; OBEV; OBNC; OxAEP-2; OxBSP; PoRA; SCGP; UV

They told me that Life could be just what I made it. Life. Nan Terrell Reed. BLPA

They told me you had been to her. Evidence Read at the Trial of the Knave of Hearts. "Lewis Carroll." CBNP; GTBS-P; NOBVV; OxBoLi; PBMP; PeLV *Fr.* Alice's Adventures in Wonderland.

They told us / Our mothers told us. Cornfields in Accra. Christine Ama Ata Aidoo. WPOW

They took a tire tool to his head. Summerfield. Jim Barnes. HATNAP, *sect.* i *Fr.* An Ex-Deputy Sheriff Remembers the Eastern Oklahoma Murderers.

They took John Henry to the steep hillside. If I Die a Railroad Man. *Unknown.* AS

They took me out. Ku Klux. Langston Hughes. BPo

They took my flock—I could care less! No more work for me. Saturn Sinking. Sándor Weöres, *Hungarian.* CEEP, *tr. by* Emery E. George

They took off / and tricolor flags came out of their assholes. Nungesser und Coli Sind Verreckt. Benjamin Péret, *French.* AF, *tr. by* Keith Hollaman

They took quickly, they took hugely. Marina Ivanovna Tsvetayeva. TCRP, *tr. by* Elaine Feinstein *Fr.* March.

They took their time to die, this dynasty. The Last of the Princes. A. K. Ramanujan. OxBC

They travelled like a blue pencil against the stars. In Praise of Antonioni. Stephen Holden. NYBP

They trod the streets and squares where now I tread. London Poets. Amy Levy. PEW

They unfold before the sky. Doors. Thérèse Plantier, *French.* BoWoP, *tr. by* Willis Barnstone *and* Elene Kolb

They wait like darkness not becoming stars. The New Pietà: For the Mothers and Children of Detroit. June Jordan. PoBA

They walk around a corner at the back of town. The War of the Roses. Michael Dransfield. BMAP

They walked beside the wave-worn beach. The Second Voice. "Lewis Carroll." *Fr.* The Three Voices. BXAP

They walked in straitened ways. The Old Ladies. Colin Ellis. OxBTC

They wanted me dead, the bastards. Yury Osipovich Dombrovsky, *Russian.* TCRP, *tr. by* Bradley Jordan

They wanted me to tell the truth. What They Wanted. Stephen Dunn. PuP-16

They was dirt-roofed, an' homely, an' ramblin', an' squat—. Cabins. Frank Bird Linderman. PaTW

They wear air. Naked in Borneo. May Swenson. NYBP

They wear big felt hats. Church Ladies. Nancy Travis. ISC

They wear white scarves and shawls. The Madwomen of the Plaza de Mayo. Eli W. Mandel. NOBC

They went to sea in a Sieve, the did. Eat Your Heart Out, Edward Lear! Roger Woddis. UV

They went to sea in a Sieve, they did. The Jumblies. Edward Lear. CABP; CBNP; CTV; EBEV; EBEvV; FaBoBe; ImPo; NAEL-2; NOxBChV; OxBChV; OxBoLi; PeLV; PeVV; PoRA; TFi; UV

They Went to the Moon Mother. *Unknown, Zuni Indian.* STP, *tr. by* Barbara Tedlock

They went with axe and rifle, when the trail was still to blaze. Western Wagons. Rosemary Benét *and* Stephen Vincent Benét. AiP; ImGa

They were a close family of giant otters. Giant Otters. Jackson Mac Low. FTOS

They were a man's words, a ballad of an old time. Ballad. James Still. MT

They Were All like Geniuses. Horace Gregory. NYBP *Fr.* The Passion of M'Phail.

They were at play, she and her cat. Femme et Chatte. Paul Verlaine, *French.* AWP; OBVE, *tr. by* Arthur Symons

They were beautiful, the old books, beautiful I tell you. The Old Books. Vernon Scannell. OxBC

They were born together, lived together. Martha and Mary. Gabriela Mistral, *Spanish*. GI, *tr. by* Dana, Doris

They were both still. Lamentations. Louise Glück. BoWoP; HCAP; VCAP

They were coming across the prairie, they were galloping hard and fast. The Cattle Thief. Emily Pauline Johnson. WPOW

They were dancing as if. Glass. Takako Uchino Lento, *Japanese*. BoWoP, *tr. by the author*

They were in an unstable condition. Kenneth Rexroth. *Fr.* The Bell. PFTM *Fr.* A Prolegomenon to a Theodicy.

They were introduced in a grave glade. The Introduction. Louis MacNeice. PNI

They were just meant as covers. My Mother Pieced Quilts. Teresa Palma Acosta. MDDM; WPOW

They were just playing, lady and cat. Paul Verlaine. *See* Femme et Chatte.

They were kings, after all. The Magi. Jeffrey Fiskin. GI

They were landing and the great thrust. The Choice. Robert Morgan. SpW

They were like fish meal. Lead. Jayne Cortez. PoBA

They were neither up nor down. (LL) Grand old Duke of York, The. *Unknown*. BoTP; LB

They were parted then at last? Winter Song. George Macdonald. NOBVV

They were sitting on the thin mattress. Wavelength. David St. John. NAmP90

They were so exceptionally well got-up for an ordinary Sunday. Love: Intimacy. Charles Kenneth Williams. CBLP

They were still young, younger than I am now. I Remember the Room Was Filled with Light. Judith Hemschemeyer. IFJA

They were the people, those who. The Broken String. *Unknown, Bushman*. PeSA, *tr. by* W. H. I. Bleek

They were, those people, a kind of solution. Constantine P. Cavafy. *See* Waiting for the Barbarians.

They were twa lovers dear. (LL) Prince Robert. *Unknown*. AmFP; ESPB; OxBB

They were. Without convenience. The Primitives Knew How Defenseless. Karen Zealand. CMAP

They were women then. Women. Alice Walker. NAAAL; NMM-2; WPOW *Fr.* In These Dissenting Times. InPS-3; PoBA

They weren't so bright, or clean, or clever. School Lesson Based on Word of Tragic Death of Entire Gillum Family. Robert Penn Warren. FuPo

They whisper of you, Nicole. Lucilius, *Greek*. InMo, *tr. by* Sam Hamill

They whispered when she passed—gave knowing looks. The Sinner. Margaret E. Bruner. PoToHe

They whisted all, with fixèd face attent. Virgil *Fr.* The Second Book of Virgil's *Aeneid*. SiPS, *tr. by* Henry Howard, Earl of Surrey *Fr.* The Aeneid [*or* Eneados, *Aeneis*].

They whisted all, with fixèd face attent. Virgil. *Fr.* The Second Book of Virgil's *Aeneid*. SiPS, *tr. by* Henry Howard, Earl of Surrey *Fr.* The Aeneid [*or* Eneados, *Aeneis*].

They who had just. Our Town. Cole Swenson. WWSi

They who in folly or mere greed. Where Are the War Poets? C. Day Lewis. FaBoMo; NoP-4; OBWP; OxBSP; OxBTC

They who prepare my evening meal below. Henry David Thoreau. APN-1

They will be telling you soon who you are. Arsenic. Howard Moss. CoAP; NYBP

They will be without arms like God. Hummingbirds. Norman Dubie. LCAP-2

They will bury that fair body and cover you. Epitaph on a Young Child. Ivor Gurney. FaBoEE

They will catch me. On Hearing the Airlines Will Use a Psychological Profile to Catch Potential Skyjackers. Stephen Dunn. AmPA

They will come for you in morning. Whispers. Roberta Hill Whiteman. CDW

They will come no more. Ezra Pound *and* Noel Stock. UV *Fr.* Mœurs Contemporaines.

They will fit, she thinks. The Marriage. Anne Stevenson. NALW

They will never die on that battlefield. Uccello. Gregory Corso. NeAP; PoM

They will perhaps. Love Poem. Norman Henry, II Pritchard. GT

They will probably come just after the New Year. The Three Magi. Stanislaw Baranczak, *Polish*. CEEP, *tr. by* Stanislaw Baranczak; GI, *tr. by* Stanislaw Baranczak *and* Clare Cavanagh

They will remaine, and so thou canst not die. Samuel Daniel. *See* When winter snows upon thy sable hairs.

They will tell the spider: Go on, you're doing good work. (LL) A. E. F. Carl Sandburg. CMoP; MoAmPo

They will tumble down from the rooftops. Judgement Day. Odia Ofeimun. HBAPE

They will wash all my kisses and fingerprints off you. Poem Ended by a Death. Fleur Adcock. NoP-4; PeNZ

They will win, I thought once. Politics. Tom Marshall. NOBC

They without message, having read. Typists. Patricia K. Page. NALW

They wondered why the fruit had been forbidden. W. H. Auden. CMoP; ChIV-1; Son *Fr.* Sonnets from China.

They won't let railways alone, those yellow flowers. Ragwort. Anne Stevenson. OPOU

They wore it walking Sunday, three small men. Spanish Blue. Herbert Morris. NYBP

They would say that she of the neck like a duiker's. On Reading an Archeological Article. Molara Ogundipe-Leslie. HBAPE

They wring their hands, their caitiff-hands. Michael Wigglesworth. NAAL-3 *Fr.* The Day of Doom. NAAL-1; SCAP

They'd eaten every one. (LL) The Walrus and the Carpenter. "Lewis Carroll." BLPA; CABP; CBNP; ChAP; EBEvV; FPC; FaBoBe; NAEL-2; NOBL; NOBVV; NoAM; OBSP; OTCP; OxAEP-2; OxBChV; PeLV; PoRA; SAGP; TFi

They'd latch the screendoors. Sunday Afternoons. Yusef Komunyakaa. NAAAL; NAmP90

They'll all get up. I know I see them. Amir Gilbo'a, *Hebrew*. IP, *tr. by* Warren Bargad *and* Stanley F. Chyet

They'll be priestin' him the morra. The Priestin' of Father John. John D. Sheridan. TIRV

They'll not exterminate you now. Georgy Vladimirovich Ivanov, *Russian*. TCRP, *tr. by* Daniel Weissbort

They'll Paint Us. Miron Biaoszewski, *Polish*.
"They clanged and clanged." CEEP, *tr. by* Tadeusz Slawek

They'll soon be flying to Mars, I hear. Progress. Samuel Hoffenstein. OBCoV

They're afraid of me. For Medgar Evers. David Ignatow. LTA

They're all gone away. (LL) Polly and Sukey. Mother Goose. LB; OxNR; ReMoGo

They're all growing green in the old countrie. (LL) Home. William Ernest Henley. MoBrPo; PoLF

They're altogether otherworldly now. Grandparents. Robert Lowell. ColAP; LiTM

They're at it again. Storm. Roger McGough. OTCP

they're bringing them home, now, too late, too early. (LL) Homecoming. Bruce Dawe. BMAP

They're changing guard at Buckingham Palace. Buckingham Palace. A. A. Milne. OxBChV

They're Dying Just the Same in Station Homesteads. Rodney Hall. *Fr.* Black Bagatelles. CBAP

They're hiding by the pebbles. Sea Fairies. Eileen Mathias. BoTP

They're in each other all along. (LL) Minute I heard my first love story, The. Jelaluddin Rumi, *Persian*. ITG, *tr. by* Coleman Barks; LoL, *tr. by* Coleman Barks

They're Leaving Memphis in Droves. *Unknown*. CrDW

They're more beautiful than the angels of heaven. Lennox Island. David McFadden. NOBC

They're nice—one would never dream of going over. A Healthy Spot. W. H. Auden. AiP

They're only boys / who used to frolic and play. Song of Becoming. Fadwa Tuqan, *Arabic*. AF, *tr. by* Naomi Shihab Nye

They're out of sorts in Sunderland. There Are Bad Times Just around the Corner. Noël Coward. NOBL

They're paltry objects when denied their roles. Staffs and Hats. *Unknown, Vietnamese*. AVP, *tr. by* Huỳnh Sanh Thông

They're putting Man-Fix on my hair. And through the window. Wanting Out. Gavin Ewart. SPE

They're richer who diminish their desires. The Truly Rich. T. Urchard. PWR

They're said to hold new-style exams this year. New-Style Examinations. Trần Tế Xu'o'ng, *Vietnamese*. AVP, *tr. by* Huỳnh Sanh Thông

They're taking down a tree at the front door. Learning by Doing. Howard Nemerov. HAP; Poetr; TwCP; WeW-3

They're waiting to be murdered. Old Couple. Charles Simic. HCAP; PoPoPo

They're with O'Leary in the grave. (LL) September 1913. W. B. Yeats. CMoP; FaBoPV; GTBS-P; HAP; MoP; NAEL-2; NoAM; PoRA

They've all grown up ugly, and nobody cares. (LL) John, Tom, and James. Charles Henry Ross. NBLV; OxBChV

They've Come. Alfonsina Storni, *Spanish*. BoWoP, *tr. by* Aliki *and* Willis Barnstone; WPOW, *tr. by* Marti Moody

They've got a brand-new organ, Sue. The New Church Organ. Will M. Carleton. PoLF

They've got the whole of death never. The Vanished. Marie-Claire Bancquart, *French*. MFP, *tr. by* Martin Sorrell

They've killed you. Martyrdom. Richard W. Thomas. PoBA

They've opened up a road in the jungle and found. 2976. Julia Uceda, *Spanish*. BoWoP, *tr. by* Willis Barnstone

They've paid the last respects in sad tobacco. Padraic O'Conaire—Gaelic Storyteller. Frederick Robert Higgins. OBMV

They've put the park bench. Notes for the Park Keeper. Peter Bland. OBGa

They've putten her into prison strang. Sir Aldingar. *Unknown.* ESPB

They've taken it apart. Three-Inch Reflector. Caroline Caddy. BMAP

Thick at the schoolgate are the ones. Soul Make A Path Through Shouting. Cyrus Cassells. GT; UnSA

Thick lids of night closed upon me, The. The Souls of the Slain. Thomas Hardy. CMoP; PoEL-5

Thick-rushing, like an ocean vast. Remembered Music. James Russell Lowell. APN-1

Thick thick the woods before my hall. Matching a Poem by Secretary Kuo. Ch'ien T'ao, *Chinese.* ChiPo, *tr. by* Burton Watson

Thick thick the woods in front of my house. Matching a Poem by Secretary Kuo. T'ao Ch'ien, *Chinese.* CoBCP, *tr. by* Burton Watson

Thicket of deadly nightshade, The. The Latvian Autumn. Johannes Bobrowski, *German.* PoSu, *tr. by* Ruth *and* Matthew Mead; CEEP, *tr. by* Ruth Mead *and* Matthew Mead

Thicket's in the thick of what, The. Scared Cows. Douglas Messerli. FTOS

Thief, The. Josephine Jacobsen. WPE

Thief, The. Stanley Kunitz. MoAmPo; VGW

Thief, The. Alden Nowlan. RaBo

Thief, The. Irene F. Pawsey. BoTP

Thief. Novica Tadic, *Serbo-Croatian.* CEEP; HSix, *tr. by* Charles Simic

Thief, and triply so!, A. Diophanes of Myrina, *Greek.* GrAn, *tr. by* Edward Lucie-Smith

Thief became the rabbi, The. The Structural Study of Myth. Jerome Rothenberg. FTOS; PoM

Thief drives to the museum in his black van, A. Girl Writing a Letter. William Carpenter. BAP-95

Thief in me is running a / round in circles, The. Zapata & the Landlord. Alfred B. Spellman. PoBA

Thieves, The. Robert Graves. BoLoP; CMoP; GTBS-P; LiTM; LoP; OAEL-2

Thieves and Whores. John Gay. ECEV *Fr.* Trivia; or, The Art of Walking the Streets of London.

Thieves, find some other house, worthy of robbing. An Unguarded House. Julianus of Egypt, *Greek.* GrAn, *tr. by* W. S. Merwin

Thigh-deep in sedge and marigolds. The Other Side. Seamus Heaney. CIP-2; PNI

Thin as a sheet his mother came to him. John Berryman. FiLi *Fr.* The Dream Songs.

Thin, Black Band, A. Sandor Csoori, *Hungarian.* VCWP, *tr. by* Len Roberts *and* Tibor Tengerdi

Thin blue smoke of our campfire, The. For the Boy Who Was Dodger Point Lookout Fifteen Years Ago. Gary Snyder. BB

Thin cypress scrapes the sky, A. Hot Day. Henrikas Radauskas, *Lithuanian.* CEEP, *tr. by* Jonas Zdanys

Thin Dog. *Unknown.* PeP

Thin Façade for Edith Sitwell, A. John Malcolm Brinnin. NYBP

Thin Flynn. *Unknown.* FuFo

Thin fox / sidled by with his stingy shadow, A. Dead Center. Ruth Whitman. NYBP

Thin gray banner, A. (LL) The Sun. Anne Sexton. NYBP; PBWP

Thin hound's body arched against the snow, The. (LL) Old Countryside. Louise Bogan. HAP; WPE

Thin in beard, and thick in purse. On Tom-o-Combe. *Unknown.* FaBoEE

Thin in the throat and the time not come for death? (LL) Unfinished History. Archibald MacLeish. NYBP; VGW

Thin leaves wave on the *wu-t'ung* tree beside the well. Lonely Night in Early Autumn. Po Chü-i, *Chinese.* TAL, *tr. by* Robert Payne

Thin lips can make a music. Redivivus. Donald Davidson. FuPo

Thin little leaves of wood fern, ribbed and toothed. Frederick Goddard Tuckerman. APN-2; TAP *Fr.* Sonnets.

Thin Mary sits there. Winter Angel. Agnes Nemes Nagy, *Hungarian.* PoSu, *tr. by* Hugh Maxton

Thin mists—thick clouds—sad all day long. Tune: "Tipsy in the Flower's Shade." Li Ch'ing-chao, *Chinese.* SuSp, *tr. by* Eugene Eoyang

Thin neon light spills on the hands in the tubs, The. Night Shift at the Fruit Cannery. Ilze Mueller. LoHo

Thin Prison, The. Leslie Norris. OTCP

Thin steel in paired lines, forever mated, cuts. North Philadelphia, Trenton, and New York. Richmond Lattimore. NYBP

Thin wet sky, that yellows at the rim, A. Marshlands. Emily Pauline Johnson. NOBC

Thin wickedly intricate, The. Dark Area. Russell Atkins. GT

Thine are all the gifts, O God! Hymn. John Greenleaf Whittier. NOxBChV

Thine elder that I am, thou must not cling. Sweeter Far than the Harp, More Gold than Gold. "Michael Field." OBMV; PeVV

Thine eyes I love, and they, as pitying me. Sonnet 132. Shakespeare. OxAEP-1 *Fr.* Sonnets.

Thine eyes shall see the light of distant skies;. To Cole, the Painter, Departing for Europe. William Cullen Bryant. APN-1; AiP; AmPP; ColAP; GEA; NAAL-1; NAAL-3; PAR; TAP

Thine eyes still shined for me, though far. Ralph Waldo Emerson. ColAP; NOBA

Thine is a strain to read amongst the hills. To the Poet Wordsworth. Felicia Dorothea Hemans. BrRo

Thine Own. Josephine D. Henderson Heard. CBWP-4

Thine own reflection in Eternity! (LL) Aspiration. Adah Isaacs Menken. AAP; CBWP-1; PAR

Thine was a brain to nature's finest mould. Charles Sumner. Henrietta Cordelia Ray. CBWP-3

Thing, The. Theodore Roethke. CMoP

Thing about a shark is—teeth, The. About the Teeth of Sharks. John Ciardi. OBCA

Thing about playing solitaire, The. Playing Solitaire. Thulani Davis. GT

Thing could barely stand. Yet taken, The. The Bull Calf. Irving Layton. InPK-6

Thing I must somehow forget. Ivor Gurney. *See* To His Love.

Thing Is to Not Let Go of the Vine, The. Ron Koertge. EC2

Thing is Violent, The. Gwendolyn MacEwen. MoCV; NOBC

Thing Itself, The. Alice Walker. NMM-2

Thing itself is in that, The. (LL) The Firebombing. James Dickey. CAPP-1; OBWP

Thing itself was rough and crudely done, The. The Knight in the Wood. John Warren. NOBVV; PeVV

Thing Language. Jack Spicer. APSN *Fr.* Language.

("Love.") (LL) FTOS

Thing Made Real, The. Ron Loewinsohn. NeAP

Thing must End. I am no boy! I am, The. Sonnet: In Time of Revolt. Rupert Brooke. OBCoV

Thing not done, The. Deutschland. Hugh Maxton. PBCIP

Thing of beauty is a joy forever, A. Endymion. Keats. CTC; EBEvV; FHYEP; ImPo; NIP-4; NOBRP; NTP; OBNC; OxAEP-2 *Fr.* Endymion: Poetic Romance.

Thing Poem. Petra von Morstein, *German.* BoWoP, *tr. by* Rosemarie Waldrop

Thing split Good Friday in two, The. Soufrière. Ellsworth McGranahan Keane. HCP; PBCV *Fr.* Volcanoe Suite.

Thing that arrests me is, The. Waking in the Dark. Adrienne Rich. FaBoWP

Thing that brought you among my people, The. Homage to John Millington Synge. Mairtin O Direain, *Irish.* NOIV, *tr. by* Thomas Kinsella

Thing that came from Outer Space, The. Never since Eden. Raymond Wilson. SpW

Thing that numbs the heart is this, The. Firm Belief. *Unknown.* PoToHe

Thing / To do / Is organize, The. Poem. Kenneth Koch. CAPP-1

Thing to do is try for that sweet skin, The. Catch What You Can. Jean Garrigue. VGW

Thing to draw with compasses, The. Circles. Harry Behn. CA

Thing we know of but we do not know, The. (LL) The Question. Frank Templeton Prince. BoLoP; GTBS-P; PeSA

Thing which fades, A. Ono no Komachi. AWP; BoWoP; PBWP, *tr. by* Arthur Waley *Fr.* Kokin Shu.

Things, The. Conrad Potter Aiken. HAP; WeW-3

Things. Donald Justice.

Stone. CRP

Things. W. S. Merwin. HAP

Things. Bob Perelman. PmAP

Things. Louis Simpson. OxBC

Things are the mind's mute looking-glass. Walter De la Mare. PoA

Things begin again. Return. Jewel C. Latimore. BlSi

Things break down in different ways. Entropic Villanelle. Thomas M. Disch. RA

Things concentrate at the edges; the pond-surface. Marginalia. Richard Wilbur. CMoP; PoA

Things Dead. Marcel Schwob, *French.* TrJP, *tr. by* William Brown Meloney

Things / do not know their collective name. Workaday Morning. Melvin Beaunearus Tolson, *Norwegian.* PBWP, *tr. by* Nadia Christensen

Things Experienced upon Withdrawal from Court. Hsieh Chin, *Chinese.* "Government wine of Peking is sweeter than honey, The." CoBLCP, *tr. by* Jonathan Chaves

Things Forbidden. *Unknown.* NoSic

Things glisten. Roof tiles rise. City. Angel González, *Spanish*. VCWP, *tr. by* Steven Ford Brown *and* Revuelta Gutierrez

Things Going out of My Life. Robert Adamson. CBAP

Things going, owing that debt. (LL) On the Debt My Mother Owed to Sears Roebuck. Edward Dorn. CoAmPo; TRP

Things Grow Up out of the Dark. Joan Dobbie. LoHo

Things harness me here. I long. Lucy's Letter. James Berry. FaBoVe; HCP

Things have their own lives here. The hall chairs. Jane Cooper. *Fr.* Dispossessions. FaBoWP

Things I Didn't Know I Loved. Nazim Hikmet, *Turkish*. AF; VCWP, *tr. by* Randy Blasing *and* Mutlu Konuk

Things I Like. Marjorie H. Greenfield. BoTP

Things I love I may not touch, The. Lines to Caste. Samuel Alfred Beadle. AAP

Things I must somehow forget. (LL) To His Love. Ivor Gurney. NAEL-2; NTP; OBWP; PeFWW; PoWW

Things I Say Are True, The. Blanca Varela, *Spanish*. BoWoP, *tr. by* Donald Yates

Things I Used to Do. *Unknown*. AS

Things I'm told, I could raise your hair, The. The Old Man's Tale. Brian Merriman. BIrV, *tr. by* David Marcus *Fr.* The Midnight Court. NOIV, *tr. by* Thomas Kinsella

Things in Each Other. Norman MacCaig. FaBoTC

Things Kept. William Dickey. NYBP

Things like littlenecks. Spring Night. Hagiwara Sakutaro, *Japanese*. PFTM, *tr. by* Hiroaki Sato

Things live there, held still in glass cases, The. Reflections on a Visit to the Burke Museum, University of Washington, Seattle. Gail Tremblay. HATNAP

Things Lovelier. Humbert Wolfe. TrJP

Things made by iron and handled by steel are born. D. H. Lawrence. Spl

Things of August. Wallace Stevens. PoA

Things of the past may only be lamented, The. Tune: "Ripples Sifting Sand." Li Yü, *Chinese*. SuSp, *tr. by* Daniel Bryant

Things of This World. Anna Kamienska, *Polish*. GI, *tr. by* Curzon, David *and* Grazyna Drabik

Things Seen. Wang Shih-chieng, *Chinese*. CoBLCP, *tr. by* Jonathan Chaves

Things Seen. Yüan Mei, *Chinese*. CoBLCP, *tr. by* Jonathan Chaves

Things Seen on Spring Days. Yüan Mei, *Chinese*. CoBLCP, *tr. by* Jonathan Chaves

Things sinister with things sublime / Alike dissolving. (LL) Going and Staying. Thomas Hardy. CMoP; NoAM

Things that are going out of my life remain, The. Things Going out of My Life. Robert Adamson. CBAP

Things That Go Bump in the Night. *Unknown*. NTCP

Things That Happen. William Stafford. NNaP

Things That Happen to You. Alonzo Gonzales Mó, *Mayan*. STP, *tr. by* Allan F. Burns

Things that make a life to please, The. A Happy Life. Martial, *Latin*. FMP; OBVE, *tr. by* Sir Richard Fanshawe

Things that make the happier life, are these, The. Ben Jonson, *ad. fr. the Latin of Martial*. FaBoEE; OBVE

Things That Matter, The. Edith Nesbit. OxBTC; VWP

Things they did together, no one knew, The. 1904. Frederick Morgan. WeW-3

Things to Come. James Reeves. OxBSP

Things to Do around a Lookout. Gary Snyder. CAPP-1; TAP

Things to Do around a Ship at Sea. Gary Snyder. CAPP-1

Things To Do in Providence. Ted Berrigan. PT

Things to draw with compasses, The. Harry Behn. *See* Circles.

Things we call women! housewife, honey, The. Hey Sweetie. Albert Goldbarth. IFJA

Things We Can Depend On. George Macdonald. CTV

Things We Dreamt We Died For. Marvin Bell. CoAP

Things we leave behind must, for those, The. The Unicorn Tapestries. William Olsen. NAmP90

Things which I have seen I now can see no more, The. (LL) There was a time when meadow, grove and stream. Wordsworth. ImPo; NAEL-2; PBMP; SCGP; TFi; TOF; TRP

Things You Gave Me. Laura Davis.
  "I look at my hands, Momma." MDDM
  "You taught me fear, Momma." MDDM

Thingumbob stands in the door, A. Sisters? Lotte Moos. NBrP

Think all but one, and me in that one Will. (LL) Sonnet 135. Shakespeare. NAEL-1; OAEL-1

"Think as I think," said a man. Stephen Crane. PFE *Fr.* The Black Riders [and Other Lines].

Think back now to that cleft. The Power Station. James Merrill. CoAmPo

THINK BLACK. (LL) Awareness. Don L. Lee. MBE

Think from how many trees. The Compost Heap. Vernon Watkins. NYBP

Think how a peacock in a forest of high trees. Peacock. D. H. Lawrence. TTTS

Think how some excellent, lean torso hugs. The Cost. Anthony Hecht. OxBC

Think how unspeakably sweet. Asclepiades, *Greek*. InMo, *tr. by* Sam Hamill

Think, in this batter'd caravanserai. Omar Khayyám. *Fr.* The Rubáiyát of Omar Khayyám [of Naishápúr]. AWP; EBVV; FaBoBe; FaPoR; HAP; NAEL-2; PoEL-5

Think it enough for me to have had thy love. (LL) On His Mistress [*or* Mistris]. Donne. BoLoP; CABP; CBLP; EBEV; ESCV; FSCP; GBL; MeLP; NAEL-1; NOBE; NoSic; OxAEP-1; PoEL-2; SCGP; SeCP

Think me not unkind and rude. The Apology. Ralph Waldo Emerson. AmPP

Think no more, lad; laugh, be jolly. A. E. Housman. CMoP

Think not, because I wonder where you fled. Another Dark Lady. Edwin Arlington Robinson. MeMAP

Think not by rigorous judgment seized. Alexander Pope. *Fr.* Three Epitaphs on John Hewet and Sarah Drew. NIP-4

Think[e] not 'cause men flattering [*or* flatt'ring] say. To A. L.; Persuasions [*or* Perswasions] to Love. Thomas Carew. CaPo; SeCP

Think not I have not heard. Menses. Edna St. Vincent Millay. NMM-2; RACG

Think not, nor for a moment let your mind. Edna St. Vincent Millay. VGW

Think not, O man that dwells herein. Upon the New Building at Appleton. Thomas Fairfax, Baron Fairfax of Cameron. NOSC

Think not of these as dead, the brave young souls. A Song of Those Who Died. Donald McDonald. PBCV

Think not this paper comes with vain pretense. Epistle from Mrs. Yonge to Her Husband. Lady Mary Wortley Montagu. NAEL-1; NALW; NoP-4

Think Not When You Gather to Zion. Eliza R. Snow. AH

Think, now: if you have found a dead bird. Advice to a Discarded Lover. Fleur Adcock. PeNZ

Think of a child who goes out. Some Notes on Courage. Susan Bartels Ludvigson. MT

Think of any of several arched. A Mathematics of Breathing. Carl Phillips. BAP-94

Think of dress in every light. Song. John Gay. OxBSP *Fr.* Achilles.

Think of him as uninjured, barely disturbed. (LL) Little Exercise. Elizabeth Bishop. CoAP; ColAP; MoAmPo; NYBP; UnPo

Think of it little, a fib. The Lie. Alfred M. Lee. AmPA

"Think of it this way," the doctor tells him. Inner Ear. T. R. Hummer. MT

Think of me as your friend, I pray. The Heart's Anchor. William Winter. PoToHe

Think of only now, and how this pencil. The Promontory Moment. May Swenson. NYBP

Think of / Stepping on shore, and finding it Heaven! Heaven. *Unknown*. PoLF

Think of sweet and chocolate. The Anniad. Gwendolyn Brooks. BlSi

Think of the shark's tiny brain. In a Museum in the Capital. William Stafford. LCAP-2

Think of the storm roaming the sky uneasily. Little Exercise. Elizabeth Bishop. CoAP; ColAP; MoAmPo; NYBP; UnPo

Think of the things that make you happy. Thinking Happiness. Robert E. Farley. PoToHe

Think of this: that under the earth. Deep Mining. Irene McKinney. PBCAP

Think of those old, enduring connections. The Family Is All There Is. Pattiann Rogers. NIP-4; PuP-14

Think of your conception, you'll soon forget. Palladas, *Greek*. GrAn; OBCVT, *tr. by* Tony Harrison

Think on thy father in the vale of years. Sophocles. OBCVT, *tr. by* Thomas Francklin *Fr.* Ajax.

Think that this world against the wind of time. Signature for Tempo. Archibald MacLeish. CRP; VGW

Think thou and act; to-morrow thou shalt die. The Choice. D. G. Rossetti. GTBS-P; OBEV *Fr.* The House of Life.

Think upon Death. Hartley Coleridge. Son

Think what you like, but. You and It. Mark Strand. NYBP

Think you I am not fiend and savage too? To the White Fiends. Claude McKay. NAAAL; PoBA

Thinke then, my soule, that death is but a groome. Contemplation of Our State in Our Deathbed. Donne. *Fr.* The Second Anniversary [*or* Anniversarie]. ESCV; SeCP *Fr.* Of the Progres[se] of the Soule; the Second Anniversarie.

Thinker, The. Berton Braley. BLPA

Thinker, The. Anthony Delius. PeSA

Thinking about the Past. Donald Justice. MT

Thinking around things that edge me into. The Crack. Clark Coolidge. PmAP

Thinking for Berky. William Stafford. MoLi

Thinking Happiness. Robert E. Farley. PoToHe

Thinking hard, hunting rhymes, humming by my lamp. Sent to Wen T'ing-yün on a Winter Night. Yü Hsüan-chi, *Chinese.* BoWoP, *tr. by* Geoffrey Waters

Thinking myself in a warm country. Six Movements on a Theme. David Ignatow. NNaP

Thinking of a Relation between the Images of Metaphors. Wallace Stevens. SAmP

Thinking of East Mountain. Li Po, *Chinese.* CoBCP; TTTS, *tr. by* Burton Watson

Thinking of her had saddened me at first. Celandine. Edward Thomas. OxBTC

Thinking of Love. Elizabeth Jennings. LW

Thinking of Mr. D. Thomas Kinsella. NoAM

Thinking of My Brother in Shantung on the Ninth Day of the Ninth Moon. Wang Wei, *Chinese.* TAL, *tr. by* Robert Payne

Thinking of My Brothers on a Moonlit Night. Tu Fu, *Chinese.* TAL, *tr. by* Robert Payne

Thinking of my father. At the Nuclear Rally. Laura Boss. UnSA

Thinking of My Father on a Bus to Baltimore. Daniel S. Simko. CEEP

Thinking of My Friends at Kou-jung Subprefecture. Yang Chi, *Chinese.* Wu Shan-yang. CoBLCP, *tr. by* Jonathan Chaves

Thinking of My Mother Who Fifteen Years Later, Has Gone East to See the Leaves. Judith Sornberger. MDDM

Thinking of My Wife. P'an Yüeh, *Chinese.* CoBCP, *tr. by* Burton Watson

Thinking of painters, musicians, poets. Orgy. Norman MacCaig. OxBC

Thinking of rain clouds that rose over the city. St. Vincent's. W. S. Merwin. VCAP

Thinking of Tents. Reed Whittemore. TAP

Thinking of "The Autumn Fields." Robert Bly. NNaP

Thinking of the Lost World. Randall Jarrell. NOBA; NoAM

Thinking of the Past. Po Chü-i, *Chinese.* ChiP, *tr. by* Arthur Waley

Thinking of the Past on an Autumn Night at Tz'u-jen Temple. Wang Shih-chieng, *Chinese.* CoBLCP, *tr. by* Jonathan Chaves

Thinking of the Way Home, a Song. Lo Yin, *Chinese.* SuSp, *tr. by* Geoffrey R. Waters

Thinking of War. Naomi Mitchison. WPN

Thinking of words that would save him, slanting. Finding Them Lost. Howard Moss. CoAP; NYBP

Thinking of you. Love Notes. Jennifer Strauss. BMAP

Thinking of you, and all that was, and all. Christina Rossetti. *Fr.* Monna Innominata. BWW

Thinking of You, Hiroshima. Betsy Sholl. PBCAP

Thinking of you, I think of the *coureurs de bois.* Coureurs de Bois. Douglas Le Pan. MoCV; NOBC

Thinking of your vocation, I am filled. To a Friend with a Religious Vocation. Elizabeth Jennings. TOF

Thinking the Alps. Michael Davidson. PmAP

Thinking to take on the power. The Wives of Mafiosi. Erica Jong. AmPA

Thinking we were safe—insanity! Story of a Hotel Room. Rosemary Tonks. APAD; LW; OxBTC

Thinks his trade is as honest as mine. (LL) The Employments of Life. John Gay. PeLV

Think'st thou that this love can stand. Ametas and Thestylis Making Hay-Ropes. Andrew Marvell. SeCP

Think'st thou to seduce me then with words that have no meaning? Thomas Campion. NAEL-1; OxAEP-1; OxBSP

Thinnest Shadow, The. John Ashbery. TTTS

Thir Lenterne Dayis Ar Luvely Lang. William Stewart. OxBS

Thir riveris and thir watteris kepit war. Charon. Virgil. OBVE, *tr. by* Gawin Douglas *Fr.* The Aeneid [*or* Eneados, *Aeneis*].

Third Avenue in Sunlight. Anthony Hecht. CoAP; VCAP

("Third Avenue in sunlight. Nature's error.") SAGP

Third Body, A. Robert Bly. LoL

Third Century, The. Thomas Traherne.

"Life of sabbaths here beneath!, A." ESCV

On News. ESCV; FMP; GeHe

("News from a foreign country came.") FMP

Recovery, The. ESCV

"Sin!/ O only fatal Woe." ESCV

"That childish thoughts such joys inspire." ESCV

Third-Class Car on a Night Train (three poems). Ōkuma Nobuyuki, *Japanese.* MJT, *tr. by* Makoto Ueda

Third Cycle of Love Poems. George Barker.

Shut the Seven Seas against Us. MoBrPo

Third Day. Thomas Traherne. ChIV-1 *Fr.* Meditations on the Six Days of the Creation.

Third day I went into the kitchen, The. Words of the Newly Wed Wife. Wang Chien, *Chinese.* CoBCP, *tr. by* Burton Watson

Third Degree. Langston Hughes. BPo

Third Dimension, The. Denise Levertov. NeAP

Third Duino Elegy, The. Rilke, *German.*

"No, we don't accomplish our love in a single year." ITG, *tr. by* Stephen Mitchell

Third Dungeness Spit Apocalypse. Nelson Bentley. PuP-16

Third Eclogue, The. Michael Drayton.

"Stay, Thames, to heare my Song, thou great and famous Flood." PoEL-2

Third Eye, The. Jay Macpherson. MoCV

Third Jungle Book, The. Ogden Nash. OxBM

Third Kind of Interior Word, The. Albert Mobilio. PT

Third Light, The. Michael Longley. PNI

Third Limick. Ogden Nash. PeLi

Third Month, Night of the Seventeenth, Written While Drunk. Lu Yu, *Chinese.* CoBCP; SuSp, *tr. by* Burton Watson

Third month, the thirtieth day. The Last Night of the Third Moon. Chia Tao, *Chinese.* CoBCP, *tr. by* Burton Watson

Third month, third day, in the air a breath of newness. Song of the Beautiful Ladies. Tu Fu, *Chinese.* CoBCP, *tr. by* Burton Watson

Third movement. Kurt Schwitters. PFTM *Fr.* Ur Sonata.

Third Ode to Persephone. Robert Kelly. *Fr.* The Book of Persephone. PoM

Third Part. Leslie Scalapino. DeD *Fr.* Floating Series.

Third Person Neuter. Heather McHugh. NAmP90

Third Psalm. Anne Sexton. NALW *Fr.* O Ye Tongues.

Third Satyre, The. Persius, *Latin.*

Argument. OBCVT, *tr. by* Barten Holyday

Third Sermon on the Warpland, The. Gwendolyn Brooks. BPo; NAAAL; SeSe

("Dust, as they say, settled, The.") (LL) NAAAL

3d Sheppard Speakes This to the Rest, The. Lady Jane Cavendish. KTR *Fr.* A Pastorall.

Third Song. T. Carmi. MHP, *tr. by* Ruth Finer Mintz *Fr.* René's Songs.

Third Song. Sir Philip Sidney. PoEL-1 *Fr.* Astrophil and Stella. AAS; SiPS

Third Voice, The. "Lewis Carroll." *Fr.* The Three Voices. BXAP

Third Wonder, The. Edwin Markham. FYAP

Third World Calling. Lawrence Ferlinghetti. BB

Third World Snapshots. John Robert Lee. PBCV

Third Ypres. Edmund Blunden. PeFWW

Thirsis a youth of the inspired train. Edmund Waller. See The Story of Phoebus and Daphne Applied, [etc.]

Thirst for green, because too long deprived, A. Vega. Lawrence Durrell. OxAEP-2

Thirst is no thing and yet it cruel can torment you. Sin. "Angelus Silesius." GePo, *tr. by* George C. Schoolfield *Fr.* The Cherubical Wanderer.

Thirstier minstrel drew in me!, A. (LL) O Blest Unfabled Incense Tree. George Darley. BIrV; FaBoCh; NOBE; OAEL-2; OBEV; OBNC

Thirsty *Earth* soaks up the *Rain,* The. Drinking. Anacreon, *Greek.* BeJo; NNPT; NOBE; OBCVT; OBEV; OBVE; OxAEP-1; PFE; SeCP, *tr. by* Abraham Cowley

Thirsty Island. Jim Tollerud. VoR

13. Edward Fitzgerald. CABP

Thirteen. Ronald Wallace. PBCAP

Thirteen faces waiting to be born. May 1970. Stephen Berg. CDa

13 November 1983. Lee Cataldi. BMAP

Thirteen Sonnets. Michael Hartnett.

Sonnet: "I saw magic on a green country road." BIrV

13 Ways of Eradicating Blackbirds. Mark DeFoe. BXAP

Thirteen Ways of Looking at a Blackbird. Wallace Stevens. CMoP; HCAP; HeIP-4; InPK-6; InPS-3; LiTM; MoP; NAAL-2; NOBA; NoAM; PoE; Poetr; RB; SAmP; TAP; TFi

("Blackbird whistling / Or just after, The.") (LL) PiM

("Cedar-limbs.") (LL) NoP-4

("In the cedar-limbs.") (LL) ChAP; ColAP; PoPoPo

Thirteen's no age at all. Thirteen is nothing. Portrait of Girl with Comic Book. Phyllis McGinley. SAGP

13th Horse Song of Frank Mitchell, The. María Sabina, *Mazatec.* PFTM, *tr. by* Jerome Rothenberg *and* David P. McAllester

13th Horse Song of Frank Mitchell (White), The. Frank Mitchell, *Navajo Indian.* STP, *tr. by* Jerome Rothenberg *and* David P. McAllester

Thirteenth Satyr of Juvenal, Imitated, The. Juvenal, *Latin*.
"Little do folks the heav'nly Powers mind." OBCVT, *tr. by* John Oldham
Thirtieth Anniversary Report of the Class of '41. Howard Nemerov. HCAP
Thirtieth of November, The. Toward the Solstice. Adrienne Rich. NAAL-2
Thirty Bob a Week. John Davidson. CABP; EBEV; EBVV; FaBoPV; FaBoTw; ImPo; NOBE; NOBVV; OAEL-2; OBNC; OxBS; OxBTC
Thirty candles and one. The Birthday. Philip Dacey. AmPA
Thirty centimes is all the money I have left. From My Parisian Diary. Mbella Sonne Dipoko. PBMAP
Thirty days hath November. Richard Grafton. MiEL
Thirty days hath September. The Months. *Unknown*. ACTP
Thirty days hath September. Mother Goose. FaBoBe; OxNR; ReMoGo
("And every fourth year, one day / more.") (LL) CTV
("And twenty-nine in each leap-year.") (LL) LB
Thirty days hath September. *Unknown*. CTV
Thirty East Forty-Second Street. Alan Davies. FTOS
Thirty-eight: Addressed to Mrs H—y. Charlotte Smith. ECWP; NALW; PEW; WPOW
.38, The. Ted Joans. PFE; WeW-3
Thirty-eighth year, The. Lucille Clifton. AmPA; OxWW
("I had not expected to be / an ordinary woman.") (LL) NMM-2
35/10. Sharon Olds. CrSp; MDDM; SAGP
34 Blues. Charlie Patton. FaBoPV
34. Chapter of the Prophet Isaiah, The. Abraham Cowley. ChIV-1
Thirty-one Camels, The. Rachel Korn, *Yiddish*. CEEP, *tr. by* Howard Schwartz
Thirty Poems of Longing for People. Chin Nung, *Chinese*.
"I get so drunk, I could be called the Earl of Dissipation!" CoBLCP, *tr. by* Jonathan Chaves
Thirty-Six Poets. Judith Baumel. WeT
Thirty-six thousand days—how long is that? Drink and Drown Your Cares. Cao Bá Quát, *Vietnamese*. AVP, *tr. by* Huỳnh Sanh Thông
Thirty-six thousand days—the human span. A Wasted Life. Nguyễn Công Trứ, *Vietnamese*. AVP, *tr. by* Huỳnh Sanh Thông
"Thirty," the doctor said, "three grains, each one." Felo de Se. Thomas Blackburn. OxBTC
Thirty-third Canto. Hans Magnus Enzensberger. PoSu *Fr.* The Sinking of the Titanic.
33. Julia Alvarez.
"He: Age doesn't matter when you're both in love." Son
("Where are the girls who were beautiful?") RA
"Mother asks what I'm put to, that means men." Son
"Thirty three is the year that Jesus Christ." Son
Thirty-three, goodbye. Happy Birthday. Frank Bidart. HCAP; VCAP
Thirty today, I saw. A Birthday Candle. Donald Justice. NYBP
32 Positions of Love, The. Paul Eluard *and* Andre Breton. PFTM, *tr. by* Marcel Jean *Fr.* The Immaculate Conception.
Thirty-two times I went forth to my life. On My Birthday. Yehuda Amichai, *Hebrew*. MHP, *tr. by* Ruth Finer Mintz
Thirty-two years since, up against the sun. Zermatt: To the Matterhorn. Thomas Hardy. OBNC
Thirty white horses upon a red hill. Teeth and Gums. Mother Goose. NTCP; OxNR; ReMoGo
Thirty years after. A Second Attempt. Thomas Hardy. CBLP
Thirty years ago. Martín Espada. UnSA
Thirty years ago: gulls keen in the blue. A Woman. Robert Pinsky. WeW-3
Thirty years ago, Marseilles lay burning in the sun, one day. Plato's Dog. John A. Scott. BMAP
Thirty years ago the young Corso in his cups. Terminal Laughs. Irving Feldman. BAP-95
Thirty Years Rising. Olena Kalytiak Davis. BAP-95
31st day of August 1914, The. Guillaume Apollinaire. *See* The Little Car.
Thirtyish, Irish, red-nosed carpenter, The. And the Scream. Stephen Berg. NAmP90
This. Adrienne Rich. FiLi
This Above All. Shakespeare. *See* To Thine Own Self Be True.
This above All Is Precious and Remarkable. John Wain. LiTM
This act reminds me, ge'men, under favour. John Byrom. *Fr.* Four Epigrams on the Naturalization Bill. NOBL
This admirable gadget, when it is. Gyroscope. Howard Nemerov. NoAM
This ae nighte [*or* ean night], this ae nighte. Lyke-Wake Dirge, The [*or* A]. *Unknown*. CH; EBEvV; EnSB; FaBoCh; HAP; HoPM; NOBE; NTP; OBEV; PeECV; PoEL-1; TFi; WeW-3
This afternoon as I sat. Elegy for Jack Bowman. Joseph Bruchac. CDW
This afternoon, at Condore Port. At Condore Port. Đào Duy Kỳ, *Vietnamese*. AVP, *tr. by* Huỳnh Sanh Thông
This afternoon I have taken the irises. The Irises. Jeanne Foster. CrSp

This afternoon I swam with a school of fish. Sea School. Barbara Howes. NYBP
This afternoon, my love, speaking to you. In Which She Satisfies a Fear with the Rhetoric of Tears. Sister Juana Inés de la Cruz. BoWoP, *tr. by* Aliki *and* Willis Barnstone
This Age. Raymond R. Patterson. NBV
This aimless drifting will conclude. Sun. Branko Miljkovic, *Serbo-Croatian*. HSix, *tr. by* Charles Simic
This Alice. Herbert Morris. PoRA
This almost bare tree is racing. November through a Giant Copper Beech. Edwin Honig. NYBP; NoAM
This alone is what I wish for you: knowledge. Demeter's Prayer to Hades. Rita Dove. NAAAL. *Fr.* Mother Love.
This altar for the Gods. *Unknown, Greek*. InMo, *tr. by* Sam Hamill
This and That. Gareth Owen. OTCP
This angel, who mediates between us. The Angel. Galway Kinnell. LCAP-2; NoAM
This animal, this sleek and beautiful ox ambling along the pleasant road. The Ox. Mary Morison Webster. PeSA
This apartment full of books could crack open. Adrienne Rich. *Fr.* Twenty-one Love Poems. GLP
This apple tree, that once was green. The Birds of Steel. W. H. Davies. NSI
This Ark is moving, not on a waste of waters. The Ark. Stanley Cook. SpW
This autumn day a noble man has died. Lamenting Noble Scholar Chu. Ni Tsan, *Chinese*. CoBLCP, *tr. by* Jonathan Chaves
This autumn, in blue prisoner's garb, hands tied behind my back. Namju Kim, *Korean*. CKP, *tr. by* Jaihiun Kim
This autumn scene is worthy of the brush. Kuan Han-ch'ing. SuSp, *tr. by* Jerome P. Seaton *Fr.* Tune: "Green Jade Flute."
This autumn the days have been hot. Sitting at Night on the Moon-viewing Terrace. Yang Wan-li, *Chinese*. SuSp, *tr. by* Jonathan Chaves
This autumn will end. Akiko Yosano, *Japanese*. OHMPJ, *tr. by* Kenneth Rexroth
This bamboo I painted a long time ago. I Once Did a Bamboo Painting for Somebody—Now He Wants Me To Do Another. I Have Written This To Answer Him. Hsü Wei, *Chinese*. CoBLCP, *tr. by* Jonathan Chaves
This bank makes welcome citizen and foreigner. Theocritus, *Greek*. GrAn, *tr. by* Anthony Holden
This Be Our Revenge. Saul Tchernichowsky, *Hebrew*. TrJP, *tr. by* Shalom Spiegel
This Be The Verse. Philip Larkin. NoAM; PoPoPo
This beast that rends me in the sight of all. Edna St. Vincent Millay. VGW
This beast which preyed on sheep. Leonidas, *Greek*. GrAn; PGA, *tr. by* Kenneth Rexroth
This beauteous form assures a piteous mind. (LL) What if this present were the world's last night? Donne. EBEV; HeIP-4; ImPo; InPS-3; MeLP; NAEL-1; NOCV; NOSC; OxAEP-1; PeECV; PoE; Son
This beauty that I see. Poem. James Schuyler. PoA
This bed thy center [*or* centre] is, these walls, thy sphere [*or* sphaere]. (LL) The Sun[ne] Rising. Donne. APAD; BoLoP; CABP; CBLP; ClHu; EBEvV; ESCV; FHYEP; FMP; FSCP; GBL; GLoP; HAP; HeIP-4; InPS-3; LoP; MeLP; NAEL-1; NIP-4; NOBE; NOSC; NoP-4; OAEL-1; PBRV; PoE; PoEL-2; PoPoPo; Poetr; SCV; SeCP; TFi; WeW-3
This began somewhere. Essay on Language. Wanda Coleman. PmAP
This biplane is the shape of human flight. The Wrights' Biplane. Robert Frost. WeW-3 *Fr.* Ten Mills.
This bird that a cat sprang loose in the house. More Joy in Heaven. Howard Nemerov. NoAM
This bird was happy once in the high trees. Boethius, *Latin*. MLL, *tr. by* Helen Waddell *Fr.* Consolation of Philosophy, The ("De Consolacione Philosophie").
This birthday card. Poem for the Birthday of Huey P. Newton. Sotère Torregian. NBV
This bit of polished marble—this. A Bit of Marble. Clinton Scollard. APN-2
This black life. Spring Rain. William Hawkins. MoCV
This black scrap from Viet Nam. Nocturn at the Institute. David McElroy. Poetsp
This Blatant Beast was finally overcome. Saint. Robert Graves. CMoP
This bleak world alone? (LL) 'Tis the Last Rose of Summer. Thomas Moore. BLPA; FaBoBe; NOIV; OxBoLi; PoEL-4
This blessing love gives again into our arms. (LL) After Making Love We Hear Footsteps. Galway Kinnell. ColAP; InPS-3; NIP-4; NoAM; NoP-4; RaBo; SAGP; VCAP
This blue-washed, old, thatched summerhouse. The Old Summerhouse. Walter De la Mare. CMoP; GTBS-P
This Body. Michael Cuddihy. CMAP

This body deemed machine—not daemon flesh. Soma. Suzanne Noguere. FFC

This body of yours, this glorious flesh. Requiem for Eduard Streltsov. Aleksandr Petrovich Tkachenko, *Russian*. TCRP, *tr. by* Bradley Jordan

This bond of the prelates I pray you revoke. Now God Stand Up for Bastards. Brian Merriman. BIrV, *tr. by* Arland Ussher *Fr.* The Midnight Court. NOIV, *tr. by* Thomas Kinsella

This bone once moved a hand. The Rune-Maker. Frederick Feirstein. RA

This Book Belongs to Susan Someone. David Clewell. NAmP90

This book by any yet unread. To My Dear Children. Anne Bradstreet. MDDM; NAAL-3

This Book is for Magda. Lew Welch. BB

This book, / made for your hands to read, your mouth to use. Marilyn Hacker. *See* Future Conditional.

This book says that his form is the same as anarchy in that it is a faculty or. Picasso and Anarchism. Leslie Scalapino. FTOS

This book was written in order to change the world. Foreword to New Numbers. Christopher Logue. OxBTC

This Bouillabaisse a noble dish is. William Makepeace Thackeray. *Fr.* The Ballad of Bouillabaisse. APAD; OBEV; OxAEP-2

This brand of soap has the same smell as once in the big. Soap Suds. Louis MacNeice. FaBoMo; NAEL-2; NOIV; NTP; SCV

This bread I break was once the oat. Dylan Thomas. ChIV-2; FaBoTw; GI; TRP

This Bridge Across. Christopher Gilbert. GT

This bright burning pyre. Elegy. Auvaiyar, *Tamil*. PLW, *tr. by* A. K. Ramanujan

This brilliant boy was stupidly drowned. In Memoriam, J.A.R., Drowned, East London. Guy Butler. PeSAV

This brown woman's voice. Nina Simone. Lance Jeffers. SeSe

This Buddha-land has iron doors, high walls. A Prison Cell. Nguyễn Văn Năng, *Vietnamese*. AVP, *tr. by* Huỳnh Sanh Thông

This burly son of a bitch. Not Just Yet. Carter Revard. VoR

This burning in the eyes, as we open doors. In Danger from the Outer World. Robert Bly. CAPP-1

This cabin, Mary, in my sight appears. Inscription. William Cowper. OBGa

This came from my counsel. On the Statue of Epaminondas in Thebes. *Unknown, Greek*. GrAn, *tr. by* Peter Levi

This cankered earth, this murrain'd patch of land. King Ethelred the Unready. Bill Greenwell. BXAP

This cat was bought upon the day. The Family Cat. Roy Fuller. OxBC

This cattle shed is Heaven now. *Unknown, Greek*. GrAn, *tr. by* Robin Skelton

This celestial seascape, with white herons got up as angels. Seascape. Elizabeth Bishop. ColAP; FaBoWP; OxBC; OxBoS

This Chauntecleer stood hye up-on his toos. Chaucer. *Fr.* The Nun's Priest's Tale. FHYEP; NAEL-1; NAWM-1; OAEL-1 *Fr.* The Canterbury Tales.

This child, exile of hope. This Child. Norman Rosten. TrJP

This child is an angel. Angel. Maxine Scates. PBCAP

This Child Is the Mother. Gloria C. Oden. BlSi

This chirping. The Sound of Birds at Noon. Dahlia Ravikovitch, *Hebrew*. VCWP, *tr. by* Chana Bloch *and* Ariel Bloch

This Christmas Day you pray me sing. For Christmas Day. Luke Wadding. TIRV, *tr. by* Thomas Kinsella

This city is made of stone, of blood, and fish. Anchorage. Joy Harjo. HATNAP; LTA; NMM-2; UnSA

This clerk-work, this first January chore. A New Diary. Dannie Abse. NoAM

This cloak of purple, Leonidas, Xerxês gives you. Imaginary Dialogue. Antiphilus, *Greek*. GrAn, *tr. by* Dudley Fitts

This clock. Clock. Valerie Worth. TLR

This clock positions each of us. The Town Clock Burning. Charles Fort. CMAP

This coloured counterfeit that thou beholdest. Sister Juana Inés de la Cruz, *Spanish*. NNPT; PBWP, *tr. by* Samuel Beckett

This Compost. Walt Whitman. AWP; MoAmPo; NAAL-1; NAAL-3; OBGa; PFTM

("Leavings from them at last.") (LL) OBGa

This concord tempers then the elements. Boethius, *Latin*. MLL, *tr. by* Helen Waddell *Fr.* Consolation of Philosophy, The ("De Consolacione Philosophie").

This Condensery: The Complete Writing of Lorine Niedecker, 1985. Lorine Niedecker.

Fancy Another Day Gone. FTOS

This Consciousness that is aware. Emily Dickinson. NAAL-1; NAAL-3; PAR

This Corruptible. Elinor Wylie. MoAmPo

This country might have. Right On: White America. Sonia Sanchez. ISC; PoBA

This country needs more noble men. This Country's Needs. Mrs. Henry Linden. CBWP-4

This Couple. C. D. Wright. CMAP

This crazy man has escaped the world. Wang Chiu-ssu. *Fr.* After Reading the Poems of Master Han Shan. CoBLCP, *tr. by* Jonathan Chaves

This creature kneeling / dusted with snow, its teeth. November. Margaret Atwood. NOBC

This cross-tree here. The Cross-tree. Robert Herrick. CavPo; ChIV-2

This crowded night my people's kindling pride. The Hour. Vivian Virtue. PBCV

. . . This Damsell was not famous for the place. Arthur Golding. PBRV *Fr.* Ovid's Metamorphoses Book 6.

This dark damnation, this hot unrainbowed rain? (LL) Reading *Paradise Lost* in Protestant Ulster 1984. Seamus Deane. BiHa; PBCIP

This darksome burn, horseback brown. Inversnaid. Gerard Manley Hopkins. CMoP; EnVR; FaBoVe; GTBS-P; ImPo; LiTM; MoBrPo; NoAM; OAEL-2; PeVV; PoRA; RB; SCGP; TFi; UnPo

This daughter watching ducks knows. Faraway Places. Walter McDonald. CDa

This dawn he rose early again. Shooting the Horses. Pamela Mordecai. PBCV

This Day Be with Me. George Macdonald. *Fr.* Diary of an Old Soul. TrCP

This day beginning to a creature gave. On Her Own Birthday. Judith Madan. ECWP

This day I saw ane endless muir. The Wire. Robert Garioch. FaBoTC

This day, I think, will be a common day. Help Me Today. Elsie Robinson. PoToHe

This day in March. Tanka. Tawara Machi, *Japanese*. MJT, *tr. by* Makoto Ueda

This day is called the Feast of Crispian. Henry V before Agincourt. Shakespeare. EBEvV; FaPoR *Fr.* King Henry V.

This day is for Israel light and rejoicing. A Sabbath of Rest. Isaac Luria, *Hebrew*. TrJP, *tr. by* Nina Davis Salaman

This day, of all our days, has done. To Penelope, January 2, 1821. Byron. FaBoEE

This day of spring is hot and gold. Spring Day. "Igor Severyanin," *Russian*. TCRP, *tr. by* Bernard Meares

This day the children of Speakthunder. In My Lifetime. James Welch. CDW

This Day, under My Hand. David Malouf. CBAP

This day, whate'er the fates decree. Stella's Birthday ([March 13,] 1727). Jonathan Swift. NoP-4; OAEL-1; PoE; PoEL-3; SCGP

This day when I lay my hope aside. Hildegarde Flanner. WPE

This day will be remembered by America's noble sons. The Battle of Bull Run. *Unknown*. AmFP

This day winding down now. Author's Prologue. Dylan Thomas. ChIV-1

This day writhes with what? The lecturer. The Ultimate Poem Is Abstract. Wallace Stevens. PoA

This day's a riddle; for the God that made. Upon the Day of Our Saviour's Nativity. Francis Quarles. NOSC

This Decoration. Hayden Carruth. NNaP

This definition poetry doth fit. Thomas Randolph. FaBoEE

This delightful young man. Heinrich Heine. *Fr.* Heimkehr, Die. AWP, *tr. by* Ezra Pound

This desert is a plateau of light. The Language of Fossils. Anita Endrezze-Danielson. HATNAP

This Dim and Ptolemaic Man. John Peale Bishop. LiTM

This dirty—little—Heart. Emily Dickinson. NCAP; PoEL-5

This divine October afternoon I would like. Pain. Alfonsina Storni, *Spanish*. WPOW, *tr. by* Merrilee Antrim

This docile one inter. Emily Dickinson. APN-2

This downhill path is easy, but there's no turning back. (LL) Amor Mundi. Christina Rossetti. NoP-4; PEW; PoEL-5; Poetr; RACG

This drawing / came / from subtle hands. On the Portrait of a Girl. Erinna, *Greek*. GrAn, *tr. by* Lenore Mayhew

This dread is like a calm. Winter Holding off the Coast of North America. N. Scott Momaday. CDW; ColAP

This dreadful, dark and dismal day. Frankie Silvers. Frances Silvers. AmFP

This dream of water—what does it harbor? I See Chile in My Rearview Mirror. Agha Shahid Ali. NoP-4

This dream the world is having about itself. Vocation. William Stafford. IFJA

This dry night nothing unusual. The War Horse. Eavan Boland. BIrV; CIP-2; PBCIP

This Durgling was a dual personage. Delivered at the Knighting of Lord Durgling by Great Bruce-Jean. Jean Toomer. GT

This dust was Timas. The Dust of Timas. Sappho, *Greek*. AWP, *tr. by* E. A. Robinson

This earth. Bill Neidjie. NOxBChV

This earth flails its environs. The Outer Layers of Nervousness. Alan Davies. FTOS

This earth gave us. California, 1852. Sharyn Jeanne Skeeter. ISC

This earth is not the steadfast place. William Vaughn Moody. *Fr.* Gloucester Moors. APN-2; NOBA; OxBA

This Earth, My Brother. Kofi Awoonor. VCWP

This earth Pythonax and his brother hides. On Two Brothers. Simonides, *Greek*. AWP, *tr. by* W. H. D. Rouse

This Easter, Arthur Winslow, less than dead. Death from Cancer. Robert Lowell. TwCP *Fr.* In Memory of Arthur Winslow.

This elderly gentleman. Hat. Tomasz Jastrun, *Polish*. AF, *tr. by* Daniel Bourne

This elemental force. Genesis. Theodore Roethke. KSG

This empty Monarch stove and rotting birch aren't much excuse. Renewal. Jonathan Johnson. BAP-96

This endless gray-roofed city, and each heart. London Despair. Frances Darwin Cornford. OBMV

This Endris Night. *Unknown*. EBEV; NOCV

This England. Shakespeare. BoTP *Fr.* King Richard II.

This England never did, nor never shall. Shakespeare. OxAEP-1 *Fr.* King John.

This Englishwoman is so refined. Stevie Smith. FaBoEE; NALW

This evening holds her breath. Winter Night. C. Day Lewis. PoA

This evening I pace chambers where I sought. In the King's Rooms. Timothy Steele. RA

This evening I prepared Wardance Soup. Wardance Soup. Phillip William George. VoR

This evening, my love, even as I spoke vainly. Sister Juana Inés de la Cruz. *Fr.* A Satirical Romance. PBWP, *tr. by* Judith Thurman

This evening stillness. Foster Jewell. HA

This evening, the sturdy Levis. Notice. Steve Kowit. BLT

This Excellent Machine. John Lehmann. OxBTC

This existence has, without the azure sphere, no reality. Quatrain. Sarmèd the Yahud, *Persian*. TrJP, *tr. by* David Shea

This exists only in my memory. Flight. Jean Starr. BAP-96

This expanse that spreads its nostrils wide. Shepherd. Avraham Shlonsky, *Hebrew*. MHP, *tr. by* Ruth Finer Mintz

This fabulous shadow only the sea keeps. (LL) At Melville's Tomb. Hart Crane. HAP; MoAmPo; MoP; NAAL-2; NoAM; NoP-4; PoA; TAP; UnPo; VGW

This face had no use for light, took none of it. Made Shine. Josephine Miles. NoAM

This fairest lady, who, as well I wot. Sonnet: Death Is Not without but within Him. Cino da Pistoia, *Italian*. AWP, *tr. by* D. G. Rossetti

This fairest one of all the stars, whose flame. Ballata: One Speaks of the Beginning of His Love. *Unknown, Italian*. AWP, *tr. by* D. G. Rossetti

This far out in the country no one is talking. Starting a Pasture. Walter McDonald. MT

This feast-day of the sun, his alter there. The Hill Summit. D. G. Rossetti. NoP-4 *Fr.* The House of Life.

This Feast of the Law. *Unknown, Hebrew*. TrJP, *tr. by* Israel Zangwill

This field-grass brushed our legs. In the Field. Richard Wilbur. NAAL-2; NYBP

This field has buried men; is browed. Pastoral. Lilian Bowes-Lyon. WPN

This field is almost white with stones. Stones. Charles Hamilton Sorley. NSI

This field of stones, he said. In a Christian Churchyard. James Thomson. NOBVV

This figure mourns that figure hanging dead. Pietá. Ann Hayes. CMAP

This final drouth of penitential tears? (LL) John Sutter. Yvor Winters. MoAmPo; MoP; NOBA; NoAM; PaTW

This first day of the year. On the Circumcision: New Year's Day. Luke Wadding. NOIV

This fisher, netted like a fish. On Naucratius, Brother of St. Basil. Gregory of Nazianzus, Saint, *Greek*. GrAn, *tr. by* Robin Skelton

This flat city shortly after dawn. Aimé Césaire. NegPo, *tr. by* Ellen Conroy Kennedy *Fr.* A Return to the Native Land.

This flattering glass, whose smooth face wears. On His Mistress Looking in a Glass. Thomas Carew. CaPo

This flesh you have loved. Kenneth Rexroth. APSN *Fr.* The Love Poems of Marichiko.

This Flock So Small. Anna Nitschmann, *German*. AH, *tr. by* Sheema Z. Buehne

This flying angel's torrent cry. Eastern Tempest. Edmund Blunden. MoBrPo

This, for my soul's peace, have I heard from Thee. *Unknown*. TAL, *tr. by* Sir Edward Arnold *Fr.* The Bhagavad-Gita.

This Form of Life Needs Sex. Allen Ginsberg. CLPP; NNaP

This formula for drawing comic rabbits made. (LL) Epitaph on an Unfortunate Artist. Robert Graves. FaBoEE; NOBL; OBCoV

This frontier post brings me sorrow. Wang Ts'an. SuSp, *tr. by* Ronald C. Miao *Fr.* Seven Poems of Lament.

This fugitive between the Earth and Sky. Prelude. Tu Fu, *Chinese*. TAL, *tr. by* Robert Payne

This furnisht Ark presents the greedy view. Francis Quarles. ESCV *Fr.* Emblems.

This Garden Being: The Hanging of Books. Clark Coolidge. FTOS

This garden does not take my eyes. The Garden. James Shirley. BeJo; GaP; NOSC; OBGa

This garden is outlandish. The Women's Jail. Miriam Waddington. NOBC

This ghoul-haunted woodland of Weir. (LL) Ulalume [or Ulalume—a Ballad]. Edgar Allan Poe. APN-1; AWP; AmPP; ImPo; MeMAP; NAAL-1; NCAP; NOBA; OxBA; TAP

This gift, her gold-hemmed saffron gown. Phalaicus, *Greek*. GrAn, *tr. by* Peter Jay

This girl all in white is my crystal of light. Epithalamium. Francis Warner. OxBM

This girl / Waits at the corner for. Girl, Boy, Flower, Bicycle. M. K. Joseph. PeNZ

This girlchild was born as usual. Barbie Doll. Marge Piercy. NIP-4; Poetr

This gives support to insects. 12th Dance—Getting Leather by Language— 21 February 1964. Jackson MacLow. PmAP

This golden head has wit in it. I live. George Meredith. NOBVV *Fr.* Modern Love.

This grandson of fishes holds inside him. Evolution from the Fish. Robert Bly. MoP; NOBA; NoAM

This great Grandmother of all creatures bred. Mutability Claims to Rule the World. Edmund Spenser. NoStc *Fr.* World Of Error. AFP

This great oppressing Ninus dead, and gone. Semiramis. Anne Bradstreet. KTR *Fr.* The Four[e] Monarchies.

This grove is too secret: one thinks of murder. The Grove beyond the Barley. Alden Nowlan. MoCV

This guy on t.v. The Electric Cop. Victor Hernandez Cruz. PoBA

This handless clock stares blindly from its tower. A Clock in the Square. Adrienne Rich. HeIP-4

This handwriting wears itself away. Valerio Magrelli, *Italian*. Nelt, *tr. by* Dana Gioia

This happened just once. Circumstances. Richard Jackson. PuP-17

This happy harmony would make them none. (LL) Sonnet. To Aurora. Sir William Alexander. GTBS-P; Son

This happy place with all delights abounds. James Thomson. UV *Fr.* On Beauty [or Beauety].

This harpie with dry red curls. Red Dust. Philip Levine. NNaP; NoAM

This has not happened before. (LL) The Hollow Thesaurus. Roger McDonald. BMAP

This has nothing. The Conjugation of the Paramecium. Muriel Rukeyser. NMM-2

This haunted heart doesn't fit. Betrayal. Léon Laleau. NegPo, *tr. by* Ellen Conroy Kennedy *Fr.* Black Music.

This he had in him that set him apart. Days of 1901. Constantine P. Cavafy, *Greek*. EP, *tr. by* Rae Dalven

This he said to american poetry. Eastward Ho! A Succession. David Bromige. FTOS

This He was then. The Carpenter. Mary Brent Whiteside. TrCP

This here is the place. This Is the Place Where. Jean Goulbourne. HCP

This Hermit good lives in that wood. Coleridge. Poetr *Fr.* The Rime of the Ancient Mariner. CABP; CH; EBEV; EBNV; FHYEP; FaBoBe; FaBoCh; HAP; HeIP-4; HoPM; ImPo; InPS-3; NOBE; NoP-4; OAEL-2; OBEV; OBNC; OBNV; OxAEP-2; OxBoS; PeECV; PoE; PoEL-4; PoPoPo; SCGP; TFi; TOF

This high-caught hooded Reason broods upon my wrist. The Falcon and the Dove. Sir Herbert Read. FaBoMo

This highest scholar in the school of sin. Sir Francis Hubert. NOSC *Fr.* The Life and Death of Edward II.

This holy night in open forum. Office Party. Phyllis McGinley. OBSV

This holy season, fit to fast and pray. Sonnet 22. Edmund Spenser. PoE *Fr.* Amoretti. AAS

This honest wife, challenged at dusk. With Her Lips Only. Robert Graves. OxBM

This horrible but superb painting. The Parable of the Blind. William Carlos Williams. LCAP-2; SAmP

This hour was set the time for heaven's descent. Twilit Revelation. Léonie Adams. MoAmPo

This Houre Her Vigill. Valentin Iremonger. CIP-2; NOIV; OxBTC

This House. Ray A. Young Bear. CDW

This is Erinna's sweet *oeuvre*, but small. Colophon to a Roll of Erinna's Poems. Asclepiades, *Greek.* GrAn, *tr. by* Lee T. Pearcy.

This is eternity. (LL) What Are Years? Marianne Moore. CMoP; MeMAP; MoAmPo; MoP; NOBA; NoAM; NoP-4; OxBA; SoSe-8

This is Flag Day. Hang Out the Flag. James Sterling Tippett. CA

This is for *Beasts,* and that for *Men* the *Spring.* (LL) The Spring. Abraham Cowley. BeJo; HAP; MeLP; OxAEP-1

This is for ntozake. Something about You. Jessica Hagedorn. PmAP

This is for the woman with one black wing. Sonnet in Primary Colors. Rita Dove. NAmP90

This is he, who, felled by foes. Worship. Ralph Waldo Emerson. APN-1

This is Hill 49, an arena for bad dreams. The Tin Woodsman. Paulette Jiles. NOBC

This is how death. Testimony. Jane Flanders. CrSp

This is how I know God exists. Christmas, Boston Nineteen Eighty Nine. Patricia Jones. WWSi

This is how it was. At the Movie: Virginia, 1956. Ellen Bryant Voigt. LTA; NoAM

This is how it's done. Rough Music. Deborah Digges. PUP-18

This is how snowflakes play about. A Finger Play for a Snowy Day. *Unknown.* BoTP

This is how they sharpen knives on a. Marina Ivanovna Tsvetayeva. PFTM *Fr.* Poem of the End.

This is idle fyno. (LL) Fara Diddle Dyno. Thomas Weelkes. CBNP; FaBoCh; OBCoV; OxBoLi; PeLV

This is in the wind. Unswerving Marine. Carl Rakosi. FTOS

THIS IS IT and so: so long. P.O.E. Lincoln Kirstein. PoWW

This is Italian. Here. The Gardens of the Villa D'Este. Anthony Hecht. ColAP; OBGa

This is joye, this is true pleasure. Verses by the Princess Elizabeth, Given to Lord Harington, of Exton, Her Preceptor. Elizabeth Queen of Bohemia. KTR

This Is Just to Say. William Carlos Williams. ChAP; HeIP-4; HoPM; InPK-6; InPS-3; KaS; NAAL-2; NIP-4; NOBA; NTP; NoAM; NoP-4; OPOU; PBMP; PoPoPo; Poetr; TAP; TRP

This is London! How d'ye like it? (LL) A Description of London. John Bancks. NOEC; OBCoV

This is made. House Cap. Bernadette Mayer. FTOS

This is Mister Beers;. Mister Beers. Hugh Lofting. FuFo

This is my cap. Inventory. Günter Eich, *German.* AF, *tr. by* David Young

This is my creed: To do some good. My Creed. Samuel Ellsworth Kiser. PoToHe

This is my curse, Pompous, I pray. Epigram. James Vincent Cunningham. HAP

This Is My Father's World. Maltbie Davenport Babcock. AH; CTV

("And earth and heaven be one.") (LL) CTV

This is my home. Husband. Popati Hiranandani, *Sindhi.* OMIP, *tr. by* Popati Hiranandani

This is my last affair. (LL) Last Affair: Bessie's Blues Song. Michael S. Harper. HCAP; LCAP-2

This is my last cry. For Stephen Dixon. Zack Gilbert. PoBA

This is my letter to the World. Emily Dickinson. APN-2; AmPP; HeIP-4; MeMAP; MoP; NAAL-1; NAAL-3; NALW; NOBA; NoAM; OxBA; OxWW; PAR; Poetr; SAmP; SCV; TAP; WPE

This is my mother's childhood home, my own. This Shade. Susanne Doyle. FFC

This is my mule, a poor long-suffering hack. Palladas, *Greek.* GrAn, *tr. by* Tony Harrison

This is my name / I have my own name. Norman Rosten. LiLi

This is my page for English B. (LL) Theme for English B. Langston Hughes. ColAP; FaBoA; HCAP; MoP; NIP-4; NOBA; NoAM; NoP-4; PoPoPo; Poetr; SSLK

This is my play's [*or* playes] last scene, here heavens appoint. Donne. EBEV; FaBoVe; MeLP; SeCP; Son *Fr.* Holy Sonnets. ESCV *Fr.* Holy Sonnets.

This is my portrait of Joanna—since the split. The Seed-Picture. Medbh McGuckian. PNI

This Is My Rock. David McCord. NTCP; TLR

This is my task: to move five cocoons. The Sleep of the Painted Ladies. Nancy Willard. LCAP-2

This is my work so. Ann Bell. FaBoVe

This is newness: every little tawdry. New Year on Dartmoor. Sylvia Plath. FaBoWP

This is no baby skin—. Brown Rosellen. FFC

This is no case of petty right or wrong. Edward Thomas. NSI; PeFWW; PoWW

This is no lif, alas, that I do lede. *Unknown.* MiEL

This is no place for Renoir's little girls. Louise Bourgeois Exhibit. Maxine W. Kumin. NMM-2

This is no poet's heaven. Colophon for Lan-t'ing Hsiu-hsi. John Peck. AmPA

This is no proper route for middle-age. Stringer's Field. Roy McFadden. PNI

This is no rune nor riddle. Hilda Doolittle. InPS-3 *Fr.* Tribute to the Angels.

("This is no rune nor symbol.") NALW

This is no white man lan'. Starvation and Blues. Edward Kamau Brathwaite. PBCV

This is none of I! (LL) The Old Woman and the Pedlar. Mother Goose. OxNR; ReMoGo

This is not a dance. Large Room with Wood Floor. Clarence Major. GT

This is not a poem but a proem. I want to be in the wide. Edward Vincent Swart. PeSAV

This is not about romance and dream. C. T. at the Five Spot. Thulani Davis. SeSe

This Is Not Death. Humbert Wolfe. MoBrPo

This is not easy to write about it involves. For All My Brothers and Sisters. Dick Lourie. CDa

This is not exactly what I mean. The World and I. Laura Riding Jackson. ColAP

This is not I. I had no body once. Naked Girl and Mirror. Judith Wright. NALW

This is not Love perhaps—Love that lays down. Not Love Perhaps. Arthur Seymour John Tessimond. APAD

This is not poetry, he said. Some Tips on Watching Birds. Deatt Hudson. NYBP

This is not sorrow, this is work: I build. The Tomb of Lt. John Learmonth, A.I.F. John Streeter Manifold. CBAP

This is not the man that women choose. Act of Love. Vernon Scannell. EP

This is not the moon. Narihira, *Japanese.* OHPJ, *tr. by* Kenneth Rexroth

This is not Turner's Venice. Desire. Lynn Emanuel. WWSi

This is not what I meant to keep. Souvenir. Naomi Long Madgett. NBV

This is not winter: where is the crisp air. California Winter. Edward Rowland Sill. APN-2

This is not yet my poem. Poem of Alienation. Antonio Jacinto, *Portuguese.* PeSAV, *tr. by* Michael Wolfers

This is not you? These phrases are not you? Prelude VI. Conrad Potter Aiken. MoAmPo *Fr.* Preludes for Memnon; or, Preludes to Attitude.

This Is of Two Worlds. Christopher Dewdney. NOBC

This is one of those Tuesdays. Temporal. George Jonas. NOBC

This is only a most piteous pretense of sleep! (LL) Beside the Bed. Charlotte Mew. BWW; MoBrPo; OxBSP; WPE

This is our lot if we live so long and labour unto the end. The Old Men. Rudyard Kipling. OBSV

This is our school. School Creed. *Unknown.* BoTP

This is Pioneer Village. The sun. Pioneer Village. Ruth Silcock. PeLi

This is plenty. This is more than enough. (LL) September Song. Geoffrey Hill. HP; NAEL-2; NoAM; NoP-4; OBWP

This is plum season, the nights. Late August. Margaret Atwood. DeD

This is prettiest of all, it is very pretty. (LL) Pretty. Stevie Smith. NAEL-2; NoAM; NoP-4

This is really the story of a / sista. The House of Desire. Sherley Anne Williams. BlSi

This is Scotch William Wallace. William Wallace. Francis Lauderdale Adams. OxBS

This is Spring for the last time. And poetry. Dust. Allen Grossman. PuP-15

This is Tarsus, one place like anyplace else. Francine's Room. Louise Erdrich. PeLi

This is that dream i wake from. Powell (Officer Charged with the beating of Rodney King). Lucille Clifton. RACG

This is Thaumareta's picture, and how well it captures. Nossis, *Greek.* GrAn, *tr. by* Sally Purcell

This is the anniversary of the day. Wedding Anniversary. Margaret E. Bruner. PoToHe

This is the arsenal. From floor to ceiling. The Arsenal at Springfield. Henry Wadsworth Longfellow. AmPP

This is the autumn and our harvest. Charles Reznikoff. *Fr.* New Year's. VGW

This is the barrow of grizzled Maronis, on which you see. Antipater of Sidon. HePo, *tr. by* Barbara Hughes Fowler *Fr.* Epigrams.

This is the beauty of being alone. Stray Animals. James Tate. NoAM

This is the black day when. The Dark Morning. Thomas Merton. PoA

This is the black sea-brute bulling through wave-wrack. Leviathan. W. S. Merwin. APo; ChIV-1; CoAmPo; MoP; NOBA; NoAM

This is the bricklayer; hear the thud. Sanctuary. Elinor Wylie. BoWoP; MoAmPo

This is the bunch of keys. This is the scar. Hans Magnus Enzensberger. *See* The Divorce.

This is the camping ground. Struggle-Road Dance. Ahmos, II Zu-Bolton. ISC

This is the chair. This is the lamp. The Lesson. C. D. Wright. CMAP

This is the Chapel: here, my son. Clifton Chapel. Sir Henry John Newbolt. OBEV

This is the chief felicity of life. Euripides. *Fr.* Medea. NAWM-1; OxBM

This is the city where men are mended. The Stones. Sylvia Plath. CAPP-1

This is the country of the Norman tower. A Warning to Conquerors. Donagh MacDonagh. IIP

This is the creature there has never been. Rilke. OBVE, *tr. by* James Blair Leishman *Fr.* Sonnets to Orpheus.

This is the cripples' hour on Seventh Avenue. Muriel Rukeyser. NoAM

This is the curse. Write. (LL) A Curse for a Nation. Elizabeth Barrett Browning. NALW; WPE; WPOW

This is the day His hour of life draws near. Allen Tate. NAAL-2; Son *Fr.* Sonnets at Christmas. HAP; LiTM; NOBA; OxBA; VGW

This is the day the circus comes. Parade. Rachel Lyman Field. OBCA *Fr.* A Circus Garland.

This is the day when the fairy kind. Friday. Sir Walter Scott. BoTP

This is the day, which down the void abysm. Shelley. FHYEP *Fr.* Prometheus Unbound. NOBRP; OAEL-2

This is the dead fiddle. Look where the wood. The Dead Fiddle. Humbert Wolfe. TrJP

This is the debt I pay. The Debt. Paul Laurence Dunbar. ColAP

This is the desk I sit at. That Day. Anne Sexton. BoWoP; CoAmPo; SAGP

This is the dust of Timias. Sappho, *Greek.* PGA, *tr. by* Kenneth Rexroth

This is the easy time, there is nothing doing. Wintering. Sylvia Plath. NALW; NMM-2

This is the end of all the songs man sings. (LL) Dregs. Ernest Christopher Dowson. OBMV; SAGP

This is the end of him, here he lies. Epitaph. Amy Levy. CABP; NOBVV; PEW; TrJP; VWP

This is the excellent foppery of the world. Shakespeare. OxBoV *Fr.* King Lear.

This is the face of him, whose quick resource. On Seeing a Little Child Spin a Coin of Alexander the Great. Charles Tennyson Turner. NOBVV

This is the farmer sowing his corn. Mother Goose. CBNP *Fr.* This is the house that Jack built.

This is the female form. Walt Whitman. EP *Fr.* Leaves of Grass (1855). APN-1

This is the festival; we will inter hope. The Tyrant. Faiz Ahmad Faiz, *Arabic.* AF, *tr. by* Naomi Lazard

This is the field where the battle did not happen. At the Un-National Monument along the Canadian Border. William Stafford. HAP; HeIP-4

This is the flat with its absence of curtains. In Residence: A Worst Case View. Sean O'Brien. OBCoV

This is the flower of the World. (LL) In Back of the Real. Allen Ginsberg. AmPP; HeIP-4

This is the forest primeval. The murmuring pines and the hemlocks. Henry Wadsworth Longfellow. APN-1; NoP-4; UV *Fr.* A Tale of Acadie. MeMAP *Fr.* Evangeline, a Tale of Acadie.

This is the form my passion takes. A Form of Passion. David McFadden. NOBC

This is the garden: colors come and go. Sonnet IV. E. E. Cummings. ChIV-1; MoAmPo

This is the gay cliff of the nineteenth century. Brooklyn Heights. John Wain. LiTM; OxBTC

This is the grave of Eusthenes the wise. Theocritus, *Greek.* GrAn, *tr. by* Anthony Holden

This is the grave of grey-haired Maronis. Antipater of Sidon, *Greek.* GrAn, *tr. by* Tony Harrison

This is the grave of Mike O'Day. On Mike O'Day. Unknown. FaBoEE

This is the green wherein a river chants. The Sleeper in the Valley. Rimbaud, *French.* OBWP, *tr. by* Robert Lowell

This is the hall of broken limbs. Guide to the Other Gallery. Dana Gioia. RA

This Is the Hay That No Man Planted. Elizabeth Jane Coatsworth. OBCA

This is the Heath of Hampstead. James Thomson. EnVR *Fr.* Sunday at Hampstead.

This is the highest learning. Turn from Self. George Macdonald. PWR

This is the horror that, night after night. Gerald Louis Gould. OxBTC

This is the hour of magic, when the Moon. The Hour of Magic. W. H. Davies. MoBrPo

This is the hour that we must mourn. Tenebrae. Austin Clarke. BIrV; CIP-2; NOIV

This is the house destroyed by Jack. The Berlin Wall Tune. Joseph Brodsky, *Russian.* AF, *tr. by* Joseph Brodsky

This is the house of Bedlam. Visits to St. Elizabeths. Elizabeth Bishop. CBNP; CoAP; VGW

This is the house that Jack built. The House That Jack Built. Mother Goose. BoTP; FaBoBe; LB; OxBoLi; OxNR; ReMoGo

"This is the farmer sowing his corn." CBNP

This is the House that Jack built. The Political House that Jack Built. William Hone. NOBRP

This is the house where Jesse White. Lowery Cot. Leonard Alfred George Strong. MoBrPo

This is the huge dream of us that we are heroes. The Flowers of Politics, I. Michael McClure. NeAP

This Is the Key. *Unknown.* CBNP; CH; FaBoCh; NTP; OTCP; OxBoLi ("This is the key of the Kingdom.") BoTP; OxNR

This is the key-ring. This is the scar. (LL) The Divorce. Hans Magnus Enzensberger, *German.* OxBM

This is the key to the playhouse. The Playhouse Key. Rachel Lyman Field. BoTP

This is the knife with a handle of horn. The House That Jack Built. *Unknown.* NBLV; OxBoLi

This is the lair of the landlady. The Landlady. Margaret Atwood. NALW

This is the land God gave to Andy Stewart. Iain Crichton Smith. FaBoTC *Fr.* The White Air of March.

This is the land of gods in exile. Sonora for Sale. Richard Shelton. PaTW

This is the landscape of the Cambrian age. Coastline. Elaine Feinstein. BrRo

This is the last hotel. Irish Hotel. David Wevill. NYBP

This is the last line I draw. Last Lines. Pamela Mordecai. HCP

This is the last stroke my toungs clock must strike. Summer's Farewell. Thomas Nashe. PoEL-2 *Fr.* Summer's Last Will and Testament.

This is the last time. Walter James Turner. *Fr.* The Seven Days of the Sun. OBMV

This is the lay of Ike. The Lay of Ike. John Berryman. LCAP-2 *Fr.* Dream Songs.

This is the letter of Hobbes the kilted and corpulent hero. Arthur Hugh Clough. FaBoPV *Fr.* Bothie of Tober-na-Vuolich, The [A Long-Vacation Pastoral].

This Is the Life. Louis MacNeice. NoAM

This is the light of the mind, cold and planetary. The Moon and the Yew Tree. Sylvia Plath. CoAP; FaBoMo; FaBoWP; NYBP; VGW; WPE; WPOW

This is the light we dream in. Negatives. Charles Wright. PoA

This is *The Making of America in Five Panels.* Empire Builders. Archibald MacLeish. GM; OxBA

This is THE MAN—all shaven and shorn. William Hone. OBCoV *Fr.* The Political House that Jack Built. NOBRP

This is the man who classified the bits. To Intellectual Detachment. Allen Tate. FuPo

This is the metre Colombian. The Metre Colombian. *Unknown.* BXAP; UV

This is the midnight—let no star. The Storm Cone. Rudyard Kipling. NoAM; OxBTC

This is the month, and this the happy morn. Milton. FaBoCh *Fr.* On the Morning of Christ's Nativity. MeLP; NOCV; NoP-4; PBRV; PoEL-3; SCGP

This is the Month, and this the happy morn. On the Morning of Christ's Nativity. Milton. GTBS-P; ImPo; MeLP; NOCV; NoP-4; PBRV; PoEL-3; SCGP

This is the month the nightingale, clod-brown. The Nightingale. John Clare. EBVV

This is the most audacious landscape. The gangster's. Alloy. Muriel Rukeyser. NoAM

This is the naked rock. Right here. From here. Lookout on a Rock on the Heights of Mount Hermon. Abba Kovner, *Hebrew.* IP, *tr. by* Warren Bargad *and* Stanley F. Chyet

This is the needle that we give. Magda Goebbels. W. D. Snodgrass. HP

This is the night mail crossing the border. The Night Mail. W. H. Auden. OxBTC

This is the one song everyone. Siren Song. Margaret Atwood. HAP; NIP-4; PoA; WeW-3 *Fr.* Songs of the Transformed.

This is the only thing as large as that. I regret I am not the physical giant. Realism. Tom Mandel. PmAP

This is the part where after a few minutes. Rapt. Irene McKinney. PBCAP

This is the place. Notes towards a Poem That Can Never Be Written. Margaret Atwood. NOBC

This is the place: be still for a while, my high-pressure steamboat! Nauvoo. Bayard Taylor. OBAL

This is the place. Even here that dauntless soul. William Blake (To Frederick Shields, on His Sketch of Blake's Work-room and Death-room, 3 Fountain Court, Strand). D. G. Rossetti. EPCY

This Is the Place to Wait. Horace Gregory. MoAmPo *Fr.* The Passion of M'Phail.

This Is the Place Where. Jean Goulbourne. HCP

This is the place / Where far from the unholy populace. In a Meadow. John Swinnerton Phillimore. OBEV

This Is the Poem I Never Meant to Write. Colleen J. McElroy. NMM-2

This is the poet and his poetry. (LL) On a Portrait of Wordsworth by B. R. Haydon. Elizabeth Barrett Browning. EPCY; HeIP-4; Ro

This is the poetry reading. Before the Poetry Reading. Louis Simpson. OxBC

This is the prettiest [*or* Prittiest] motion. To a Lady That Desired Me I Would Bear My Part with Her in a Song. Richard Lovelace. CaPo

This is the right gift for a poet. The Empress Receives the Head of a Taiping Rebel. Sarah Gorham. FFC

This is the river that had to be dammed. Pentagonia. G. E. Bates. NYBP

This is the road I tread today. The Death of Moses. *Unknown, Hebrew.* TrJP, *tr. by* Alice Lucas

This is the room where summer ends. Ararat. Peter Cooley. CMAP

This is the sadness of the sea. The Sadness of the Sea. William Carlos Williams. ColAP

This Is the Shape of the Leaf. Conrad Potter Aiken. CMoP; NOBA; OxBA *Fr.* Priapus and the Pool. (Portrait of a Girl.) MoAmPo

This is the ship of pearl, which poets feign. The Chambered Nautilus. Oliver Wendell Holmes. APN-1; APo; AmPP; ColAP; FaBoBe; HoPM; ImPo; NAAL-3; NCAP; NOBA; NoP-4; PAR; PoEL-5; PoLF; TFi *Fr.* The Autocrat of the Breakfast Table.

This is the short, sweet, sorrowful tale. A Tragedy. Doris Webb. FPC

This is the silence known, a place. Twentieth Anniversary. Betty Adcock. MT

This is the silence of astounded souls. (LL) Crossing the Water. Sylvia Plath. HCAP; RB

This is the sin against the Holy Ghost. The Unpardonable Sin. Vachel Lindsay. CMoP; ChIV-2; MeMAP

This is the skull of a hard-working man. Serapion of Alexandria, *Greek.* GrAn, *tr. by* Peter Jay

This is the solid-looking quagmire. Liberal, or Innocent by Definition. James Philip McAuley. NOBAu

This is the song of a dadaist. Chanson Dada. Tristan Tzara, *French.* PFTM, *tr. by* Rothenberg, Matthew

This is the song of Kuk-ook, the bad boy. The Song of Kuk-ook, the Bad Boy. *Eskimo Oral Tradition.* TTTS

This is the song of Mehitabel. The Song of Mehitabel. Don Marquis. OBCoV *Fr.* Archy and Mehitabel.

This is the song of the blooming trench. From the Front: The Song of the Trench, December, 1914. C. W. Blackall. NSI

This is the song of the Plane. A Song of the Air. Gordon Alchin. NSI

This is the song of those who live alone. Song. William Justema. NYBP

This is the south. I look for evidence. New Orleans. Joy Harjo. HATNAP

This is the spot where Jack Johnson. Boxing Day. Yusef Komunyakaa. ISC

This is the State above the Law. A Death-Bed. Rudyard Kipling. PoWW

This is the surest death. Mortality. Naomi Long Madgett. PoBA

This is the sweet work of Erinna, not much, of course. Asclepiades. HePo, *tr. by* Barbara Hughes Fowler *Fr.* Epigrams.

This is the tale of the man. Ticonderoga: A Legend of the West Highlands. Robert Louis Stevenson. EBNV; OBNV

This is the tale that Cassidy told. The Mornin's Mornin. Gerald Brennan. BLPA

This is the terminal: the light. At the San Francisco Airport. Yvor Winters. AiP; HeIP-4; InPK-6; NIP-4; NOBA

This is the time lean woods shall spend. Sundown. Léonie Adams. MoAmPo

This is the time of day when we in the Men's Ward. Five O'Clock Shadow. John Betjeman. PFE

This is the time of year. The Armadillo. Elizabeth Bishop. ColAP; HCAP; MoP; NAAL-2; NOBA; NYBP; NoAM; NoP-4; Poetr; TAP; VCAP; VGW

This is the time of year. William Carlos Williams. SAmP

This is the time when the fire on the hearth. At Mother's After Many Years. Vladimir Holan. CEEP

This is the tomb of great Megistias. On His Friend Megistias, Who Died at Thermopylai. Simonides, *Greek.* GrAn, *tr. by* Peter Jay

This is the true end of desire. The Ballad of the Frozen Field. Dabney Stuart. MT

This is the truth what I now tell you. The Miramichi Fire. *Unknown.* AmFP

This is the twentieth century. A First on TV. David Ignatow. RaBo

This is the twilight hour of the morning. Snail Garden. Janet Lewis. PaTW

This is the urgency: Live! The Second Sermon on the Warpland. Gwendolyn Brooks. BPo; NOBA; PoBA

This is the voice of high midsummer's heat. The Mowing. Sir Charles G. D. Roberts. NOBC

This is the way in. The words. June 1967 at Buchenwald. Alan Bold. FaBoTC

This is the way it is. We see. Ingmar Bergman's "Seventh Seal." Robert Duncan. PoE

This is the way of it, wide world over. The Way of It. Ella Wheeler Wilcox. LW

This is the way the farmers ride. *Unknown.* LB

This is the way the gentlemen ride. *Unknown.* LB

This is the way the ladies ride. Mother Goose. LB; OxNR; ReMoGo

This is the way to start a sentence about startling a sentence. Here is the. Wait. Charles Bernstein. PmAP

This is the way we make our hay. Haymaking. Alfred Percival Graves. BoTP

This is the way we wash our clothes. Wash-Day. Lilian McCrea. BoTP

This is the weather the cuckoo likes. Weathers [*or* Weather]. Thomas Hardy. ACTP; BoTP; CH; EBEvV; FaBoCh; MoBrPo; NTP; OBMV; RB

This is the week when Christmas comes. In the Week When Christmas Comes. Eleanor Farjeon. PChr

This is the Wheel of Dreams. Carriers of the Dream Wheel. N. Scott Momaday. CDW; ColAP

This is the Wiggledywasticus / Very remarkable beast. After a Visit to the Natural History Museum. Laura Elizabeth Richards. ImGa

This is the wind, the wind in a field of corn. Wind. James Fenton. NAEL-2

This is the wisdom of the ape. The Theology of Bongwi, the Baboon. Roy Campbell. PeSA

This is the world. Map. Linda Hogan. PaTW

This is the world we wanted. Gretel in Darkness. Louise Glück. AmPA; NoAM; NoP-4

This is the young man, two cars ahead. The Accident. Liz Rosenberg. PBCAP

This is thi. Tom Leonard. FaBoTC; NBrP *Fr.* Unrelated Incidents.

This Is This. Un-Now. Daniil Kharms, *Russian.* TCRP, *tr. by* Bradley Jordan

This is thy hour O Soul, thy free flight into the wordless. A Clear Midnight. Walt Whitman. HAP; NTP; OxBSP; PAR; SAmP; Spl

This is thy province, this thy wonderous way. Dryden. EPCY *Fr.* MacFlecknoe; or, A Satire [*or* Satyr] upon the True-Blue [*or* -Blew] Protestant Poet T. S. CBNP; FHYEP; HAP; OAEL-1; OBSV; OxBoLi; PeLV; Poetr; TFi

This is to say, my dear Augusta. King William's Dispatch to Queen Augusta. Coventry Patmore. FaBoEE

This is too tall, dark wave of soul. Rodin's "Gates of Hell." Jane Greer. FFC

This is true Love, by that true Cupid got. The Dance of Love. Sir John Davies. *Fr.* Orchestra; or, A Poem[e] of Da[u]ncing. NoSic; SiPS

This is what I have—this photograph from 1896. Grape Stakes. Roy Zarucchi. EC3

This is what I saw—old snow on the ground. Spring. Charles Simic. AFr

This is what it was like? God on a donkey. The Palms. David Knight. MoCV

This is what should be done by the man and woman who are wise, who. Unlimited Friendliness. Buddha, *Sanskrit.* ITG, *tr. by* Edward Conze

This is what the war ended up being about. Corporal Charles Chungtu, U. S. M. C. Bryan Alec Floyd. CDa

This Is What the Watchbird Sings, Who Perches in the Lovetree. Bruce Boyd. NeAP

This is what we really want. By Fiat of Adoration. Oscar Williams. LiTM

This is what you are to me. (LL) This Is the Shape of the Leaf. Conrad Potter Aiken. CMoP; MoAmPo; NOBA; OxBA

This is where all the stars bow down. (LL) Pibroch. Ted Hughes. FaBoMo; OAEL-2

This is where I had my sheep vision. Coleman Valley Road. Gerald Stern. BAP-93; PUP-18

This is where I once saw a deaf girl playing in a field. Deaf Girl Playing. James Tate. CMAP; LCAP-2

This is where I work. I live a little further to the east. Thirty East Forty-Second Street. Alan Davies. FTOS

This is where I would shop. At the Iga: Franklin, New Hampshire. Jane Kenyon. PuP-15

This is where stacking pays off. Patrols. D. F. Brown. CDa

This is where the People take tea. In a Chain-Store Cafeteria. Paul Grano. NOBAu

This is where the serpent lives, the bodiless. Wallace Stevens. CMoP; PoE Fr. The Auroras of Autumn.

This is where the warrior from Ibokun came. Edouard J. Maunick. NegPo, tr. by Ellen Conroy Kennedy Fr. As Far as Yoruba Land.

This is Willy Walker, and that's Tam Sim. Unknown. OxNR

This is your growing seed. Woman, rejoice. (LL) Annunciation. Primo Levi, Hebrew. AF, tr. by Ruth Feldman; GI, tr. by Ruth Feldman and Brian Swann

This is your hour—creep upon it! Herbert Kaufman. PoToHe

This island, garlanded with wild woods. Archilochus, Latin. OBVE, tr. by Guy Davenport

This Island Mopsy. Victor D. Questel. PBCV

This isn't about unrequited love. Open Windows. Marilyn Hacker. Poetr

This isn't the wind in the willows. Music in the Age of Iron. Alberto Blanco, Spanish. CLPP, tr. by Palley, Julian

This isn't what I want to write I. Amir Gilbo'a, Hebrew. IP, tr. by Warren Bargad and Stanley F. Chyet

This Italian square. Dancers at the Moy. Paul Muldoon. BIrV

This itch of scribbling has no end, no ease. The Author's Quietus. Henry Carey. FaBoVe

This? it's my Lounge Lizard look, very. Up. Bill Kushner. GLP

This jar of roses and carnations on the window-sill. Decoration. Mary Ursula Bethell. PeNZ

This Journey. Ingrid Jonker, Afrikaans. BoWoP, tr. by Jack Cope and William Plomer

This journey through another world, beyond bad dreams. Sacristans. Elizabeth Cook-Lynn. Fr. Journey. HATNAP

This keeps my hands. Bracelets. William Strode. NOSC

This kind o' sogerin' ain't a mite like our October trainin'. Letter, A ("This kind o' sogerin' ain't a mite like our October trainin' "). James Russell Lowell. OxBA Fr. The Biglow Papers.

This kiss. Mary. Lucille Clifton. CrSp

This kyng lay at Camylot upon Krystmasse. Unknown. PoE Fr. Sir Gawain and the Green Knight. OAEL-1, tr. by Brian Stone

This laboring through what is still undone. The Swan. Rilke, German. APo, tr. by Stephen Mitchell

This labour will be welcome, honoured Friend! Wordsworth. See Fair seed time had my soul, and I grew up.

This ladies' room fluorescence will not be ignored. Midnight Vapor Light Breakdown. Betsy Sholl. LTA

This lady of the West Country? (LL) An Epitaph: "Here lies one most beautiful lady." Walter De la Mare. ImPo; LiTM; MoBrPo; OBEV; RB

This Lady She Wears a Dark Green Shawl. Unknown. AmFP

This Land. Ian Mudie. NOBAu

This land is my block and my people. Song of Devotion to the Forest. David Henderson. GT

This land like a mirror turns you inward. Dark Pines under Water. Gwendolyn MacEwen. NOBC

This Land, where quarrels no disturbance wrought. Publius Papinius Statius. OBCVT, tr. by Sir Robert Howard and John Dryden Fr. The Achilleid.

This land will not always be foreign. The Winds of Orisha. Audre Lorde. NAAAL

This land's no joy. Nguyễn Chí Thiện, Vietnamese. VCWP, tr. by Huynh Sanh Thông

This landscape demands: open vowels. Campi Flegrei. Barend Toerien, Afrikaans. PeSA, tr. by the author

This last disguise, himself. (LL) The Missing Person. Donald Justice. NYBP; Poetr

This last pain for the damned the Fathers found. William Empson. CMoP; EBEV; FaBoMo; GTBS-P; LiTM; MoBrPo; NoAM; OAEL-2

This lay, a favorite of mine. Honeysuckle (Chevrefoil). Marie de France. BoWoP, tr. by Patricia Terry

This legend is told of me. Actaeon. Rayner Heppenstall. FaBoTw

This let me further add, that nature knows. Ovid. OBVE Fr. Of the Pythagorean Philosophy. OBVE, tr. by Dryden Fr. Metamorphoses.

This Life. Rita Dove. AmPA; GT

This Life a Theater. Palladas, Greek. NIP-4, tr. by Robert Bland

This life a theatre we well may call. This Life a Theater. Palladas, Greek. NIP-4, tr. by Robert Bland

This life is but a game of cards. Life's a Game. Unknown. BLPA

This life is deep and dense. Remora. James Merrill. APo

This Life is full of numbness and of balk. Sonnet 26. Christina Rossetti. Son; VWP Fr. Later Life: A Double Sonnet of Sonnets.

This life is most jolly. (LL) Song: "Blow, blow, thou winter wind." Shakespeare. AWP; CH; CTC; EBEvV; GBL; GTBS-P; ImPo; InPS-3; NAEL-1; NOBE; NoSic; OAEL-1; OBEV; OxAEP-1; PoEL-2; SCGP

This life like no other. Poem. Gregory Orr. AmPA

This life of ours would not cause you sorrow. Murasaki Shikibu, Japanese. WPJ, tr. by Kenneth Rexroth and Ikuko Atsumi

This life on earth's a poison tree. Kalidasa, Sanskrit. FP, tr. by John Brough

This life, which seems so fair. Madrigal. William Drummond, of Hawthornden. CH; GTBS-P; NOSC; OAEL-1

This life's a hollow bubble. Fin de Siècle. Edmund Vance Cooke. BLPA

This Lime-Tree Bower My Prison. Coleridge. FHYEP; FP; HeIP-4; NAEL-2; OBGa; OxAEP-2; PoE; PoEL-4; TOF

("Spirits perceive his presence.") (LL) LaPo

(This Lime-Tree Bower My Prison, A Poem Addressed to Charles Lamb of the India House, London.) Ro

This little attraction takes up no room and deals with only. The Weighing-machine. Pierre McOrlan, French. MFP, tr. by Martin Sorrell

This little book a poet. The Poet. Arseny Aleksandrovich Tarkovsky, Russian. TCRP, tr. by Peter Norman

This little bride & groom are. E. E. Cummings. AmPP

This little bunny said, "Let's play." Finger Play. Unknown. BoTP; CTAV

This little courtyard——the wind is pure. Wen Cheng-ming. CoBLCP, tr. by Jonathan Chaves Fr. The Chung-i Temple.

"This little finger on my right!" Unknown. See One, two, three, four, five / Once I caught a fish alive.

This little flag to us so dear. The Union Jack. Jeannie Kirby. BoTP

This little Grave embraces. Epitaph on the Duke of Buckingham. Unknown. PBRV

This Little House Is Sugar. Langston Hughes. NTCP

This little house swallows. Ray A. Young Bear. STP

This Little Light of Mine. Unknown. NAAAL

This little pig had a rub-a-dub. Unknown. OxNR

This little pig went to market. Mother Goose. ImGa; LB; OxNR; ReMoGo

This little Pipkin fits this little Jellie. (LL) A Ternarie of Littles, upon a Pipkin of Jellie [or Jelly] Sent to a Lady. Robert Herrick. BeJo; BoTP; FaBoCh; PoEL-3

This little residence is far from any village. Hermit Li's Herb Garden Retreat at T'ung-ch'uan. Hsü Pen, Chinese. CoBLCP, tr. by Jonathan Chaves

This little rill that, from the springs. The Rivulet. William Cullen Bryant. APN-1

This little, silent, gloomy monument. Epitaph on the Tombstone of a Child, the Last of Seven That Died Before. Aphra Behn. CABP; KTR; NOSC

This little stone, dear Sabinos. Unknown, Greek. PGA, tr. by Kenneth Rexroth

This little vault, this narrow room. Another [Epitaph on Lady Mary Villiers]. Thomas Carew. BeJo; CaPo; CavPo; OBEV; SeCP

This living hand, now warm and capable. To Fanny Brawne. Keats. BoLoP; FHYEP; HAP; InPK-6; InPS-3; NOBE; NoP-4; OAEL-2; OxBSP; PoPoPo; TRP

This loneliness. Gary Hotham. HA

This lonely figure of not much fun. Absent-Minded Professor. Howard Nemerov. Fr. Epigrams. OBAL

This lonely following in the old town. Lines for a Young Wanderer in Mexico. John Logan. PoA

This longed-for morning here is our sacrifice / to Zeus the finisher, and Artemis goddess of childbirth. Crinagoras, Greek. GrAn, tr. by Alistair Elliot

This, Lord, was an anxious brother, and. Funeral Oration for a Mouse. Alan Dugan. HAP; Poetr

This loud morning / sensed a small cry in. Third World Calling. Lawrence Ferlinghetti. BB

This Love. Imamu Amiri Baraka. See In Memory of Radio.

This love, I canna' bear it. Love's Pains. John Clare. NOBVV

This love is as good. Ancient Egyptian Oral Tradition, Egyptian. ITG, tr. by Fox, Michael V. and Robert Hass

This love / is our own mix. . . . Survival. Anne S. Perlman. CMAP

This love puts all humanity from me. Thomas Hardy. TOF Fr. She, to Him.

This loved Philology. (LL) Word made Flesh is seldom, A. Emily Dickinson. APN-2; ChIV-2; NAAL-1; NAAL-3; NALW; PAR

This lovely flower fell to seed;. For My Grandmother. Countee Cullen. MoAmPo; SSLK; VGW Fr. Four Epitaphs. PoBA

This lump of earth has left his estate. Tennyson. Fr. Maud [A Monodrama]. EnVR

"Catch not my breath, O clamorous heart." NAEL-2

This lunar beauty. W. H. Auden. MoBrPo; OBMV; OxBTC; RB

This lyfe, I see, is but a cheyre feyre. Unknown. Fr. The Cherry Fair.

This mad carnival of loving. Heinrich Heine. TrJP, tr. by Emma Lazarus Fr. To Angélique.

This makes my arm your prisoner; that, my heart. (LL) Upon a Ribbon [or Ribband]. Thomas Carew. BeJo; CaPo; NOSC; OAEL-1; PoE

This Man. G. S. Shivarudrappa, Kannada. OMIP, tr. by A. K. Ramanujan

This man charmed newcomers. Pindar. Plato, Greek. GrAn, tr. by Peter Jay

This man escaped the dirty fates. Flyer's Fall. Wallace Stevens. MeMAP; SAmP

This man has lived his life in his own fields. The Old Man of Verona. Claudian, Latin. MLL, tr. by Helen Waddell

This man in his own country prayed we know not to what Powers. Hindu Sepoy in France. Rudyard Kipling. Fr. Epitaphs of the War [1914–1918]. OBWP

This man is called Obed. His surname. Dispossessed. Evangeline Paterson. NBrP

This man is much taller than I am. Tallness. Paulette Jiles. IFJA

This man is o so. Item. E. E. Cummings. MoAmPo

'This man loved me'—then rise and trip away. (LL) Proud word you never spoke, but you will speak. Walter Savage Landor. CBLP; EnLoPo; GBL; GLoP; OBEV

This man of leisure for twenty years. Wen Cheng-ming. CoBLCP, tr. by Jonathan Chaves Fr. Improvised on Horseback to Say Good-bye to Those Who Are Seeing Me Off.

This man: this no-thing: vile: this brutish slave. Bianor, Greek. GrAn, tr. by Dudley Fitts

This Man Was Strong. C. Day Lewis. Son

This man, who his own fatherland forgets. He Is My Countryman. Antoni Slonimski, Polish. TrJP, tr. by Frances Notley

This man with my own face. (LL) The Cleaving. Li-Young Lee. NAmP90; OpBo; PnP-16

This mangled tentacle of the huge scolopendra. Antipater of Sidon, Greek. GrAn, tr. by Tony Harrison

This man's metallic; at a sudden blow. Felix Holt: The Radical. "George Eliot." LW

This marriage be wine with halvah, honey dissolving in milk. Jelaluddin Rumi, Persian. ITG, tr. by Coleman Barks

This mast, new-shaved, through whom I rive° the ropes. Choosing a Mast. Roy Campbell. FaBoTw; NoP-4; PeSA

This May Day night. Tanka. Tsukamoto Kunio, Japanese. MJT, tr. by Makoto Ueda

This meal, / unsurpassed. (LL) Soul Food. Janice Mirikitani. NMM 2; OpBo

This meal-white snow. Snow. Walter De la Mare. OxAEP-2

This Measure. Léonie Adams. MoAmPo

This melancholy people is also given. The Dogmatic Egg. Ion Barbu, Romanian. CEEP, tr. by Donald Eulert and Stefan Avadanei

This memory of my mother stays with me. Remembrance. Margaret E. Bruner. PoToHe

This menopause of mine. Bloody Pause. "Astra." BrRo

This metal is engraved with Shang-style markings. Hsü Chung-hsing. CoBLCP, tr. by Jonathan Chaves Fr. Thanking Prince Chen-chi for Giving Me a Bronze Seal Engraved with Diagrams of the Five Sacred Mountains.

This midnight breathing. A House Divided. Michael Ondaatje. MoCV

This midnight dream whispered to me. The Dream about Our Master, Shakespeare. Hyam Plutzik. RB

This might have been a place for sleep. Thistledown. Harold Monro. OxBTC

This mighty god is tall as heaven. Stone Man Peak. Chao Meng-fu. Fr. Twenty-Eight Poems Inscribed on T'ien-kuan Mountain. CoBLCP, tr. by Jonathan Chaves

This moment yearning and thoughtful sitting alone. Walt Whitman. APN-1

This month of May, one pleasant eventide. Unknown. Fr. Medieval Norman Song. AWP, tr. by John Addington Symonds

This monument will outlast. 3.30 This Monument Will Outlast (Exegi momumentum aere perennis). Horace. CTC, tr. by Ezra Pound Fr. Odes.

This morn a young squire shall be made a knight. On Knighthood. Folgore da San Geminiano, Italian. AWP, tr. by John Addington Symonds

This morn, ere yet had rung the matin peal. On a Frightful Dream. John Codrington Bampfylde. NOEC

This morn thy gallant bark, love. To the air of 'My Phillida, adieu, love!'. Mary Wollstonecraft Shelley. Ro

This Morning. Muriel Rukeyser. BoWoP; CrSp

This Morning. Charles Simic. BAP-93

This morning. The Suck. John Wieners. FTOS

This morning a cat got. Dad and the Cat and the Tree. Kit Wright. OTCP

This morning a small. La Gueule. Erin Mouré. DeD

This morning at the Luxembourg, this autumn at the Luxembourg. Luxembourg 1939. Léopold Sédar Senghor. PBMAP

This morning, between two branches of a tree. The Dependencies. Howard Nemerov. VCAP

This morning, dear mother, as soon as 'twas light. Christopher Anstey. ECEV Fr. The New Bath Guide.

This morning, flew up the lane. Lady Lost. John Crowe Ransom. NoP-4; UnPo

This morning gathering wood. Sunday Evening. Sam Hunt. PeNZ

This morning I can't seem to get out of bed. Han Yü, Chinese. CoBCP, tr. by Watson, Burton (b. 1925) Fr. Autumn Thoughts. CoBCP, tr. by Burton Watson

This morning I clipped my fingernails. Dino. Michael Lassell. GLP Fr. Times Square Poems.

This morning I fight against the silence. Against the Silences to Come. Ron Loewinsohn. PoM

This morning I heard persistent and angry blows on a carpet. In the Yard of the Policlinic. Vladimir Holan, Czech. AF, tr. by C. G. Hanzlicek and Dana Habova

This morning I wanted to bring you roses. The Roses of Saadi. Marceline Desbordes-Valmore, French. WPOW, tr. by Deirdre Lashgari

This morning I watched. Galway Kinnell. Fr. Ruins under the Stars. LCAP-2

This morning I will not. Hitomaro, Japanese. OHPJ, tr. by Kenneth Rexroth

This morning I woke / to an impatient scratching on the window. Apricot Tree. Magda Isanos, Rumanian. BoWoP, tr. by Willis Barnstone and Matei Calinescu

This morning it was cold in my office study. Sent to the Taoist Holy Man of Ch'üan-chiao. Wei Ying-wu, Chinese. CoBCP, tr. by Burton Watson

This morning / My child dances naked. Variations on a Theme. Mark Vinz. Poetsp

This morning my father looks out of the window, rubs his nose. Michael Rosen. NOxBChV

This morning of the small snow. All/ wrong. Charles Olson. NoAM Fr. Songs of Maximus. NeAP Fr. The Maximus Poems.

This morning, on the opposite shore of the river. Fire. William Carpenter. Poetsp

This morning our boat left the. Unknown, Chinese. OHMPC, tr. by Kenneth Rexroth

This morning, that dread ghost, disease, has fled. Getting Well. Ngân Giang, Vietnamese. AVP, tr. by Huỳnh Sanh Thông

This morning the air is fine for Ch'ing-ming. Yang Wei-chen. Fr. Impromptu Inspirations. CoBLCP, tr. by Jonathan Chaves

This morning the March wind is hugh, and there are many of them. Tumbleweed. Jonathan Holden. NAmP90

This morning, the memory of you. Inertia. Vivienne Finch. BrRo

This morning the sun rose over the garden wall. Human Wishes. Robert Hass. NAmP90

This morning the wind came, shaking the quince tree. Languedocienne. Marilyn Hacker. DeD

This morning, there flew up the lane. John Crowe Ransom. See Lady Lost.

This morning they are putting away the whales. Autumn. William Carpenter. Poetsp

This morning, timely rapt [or wrapt] with holy fire. On Lucy Countess[e] of Bedford. Ben Jonson. BeJo; NOSC; SeCP

This Morning Tom Child, the Painter, Died. Samuel Sewall. SCAP

This morning trampled. Paul Brown. NBrP Fr. De Rebus.

This morning view / is very plain: thou art. Our Father. James Schuyler. ChIV-2

This morning we found him. Bushed. Charles Lillard. NOBC

This morning we shall spend a few minutes. Money. Howard Nemerov. OxBC; VCAP; WeW-3

This morning, when he looked at me. Black All Day. Raymond R. Patterson. PoBA

This morning, when I had to kill. Circle of Struggle. William Pitt Root. NYBP

This morning, when I heard the crows. The Crows. David McCord. MoAmPo

This morning when I looked out the roof window. Song for the Deer and Myself to Return On. Joy Harjo. WeT

This morning with a blue flame burning. A Poem for Trapped Things. John Wieners. BB; GLP; NeAP; PmAP; PoM

This morning / with a class of girls outdoors, I saw. In a Spring Still Not Written Of. Robert Wallace. CMAP

This morning's rainbow. O. Mabson Southard. HA

This mossy [or mossie] bank they pressed [or press'd or prest]. A Pastoral[l] Dialogue. Thomas Carew. CaPo; GBL; SeCP

This motel room. Motel. William Mills. MT

This moth caught in the room tonight. Lying Awake. W. D. Snodgrass. HoPM; MoAmPo; NYBP

This motley piece to you I send. From The Spleen. Matthew Green. NoP-4 *Fr.* The Spleen.

This mound the Achaeans reared—Achilles' tomb. Epitaph on Achilles. *Unknown, Greek.* AWP, *tr.* by William M. Hardinge

This mountain's secret is the son of Euphorion of Athens. Aeschylus, *Greek.* GrAn, *tr.* by Edwin Morgan

This much I know. Bacchylides, *Greek.* InMo, *tr.* by Sam Hamill

This much, O heaven—if I should brood or rave. A Prayer in Darkness. G. K. Chesterton. MoBrPo; PoLF

This multitude of melted hands. Cactus. Jean-Joseph Rabéarivelo, *French.* NegPo, *tr.* by Ellen Conroy Kennedy

This music has lasted since the world began. The Aegean. Maria Luisa Spaziani, *Italian.* NeIt, *tr.* by Beverly Allen

This must have been a pretty garden once. (LL) Time. Mary Ursula Bethell. APAD; OBGa

"This must have been her bedroom, Mr. Choi." Counting the Children. Dana Gioia. RA

This mutilated tree gives. Rivers. Giuseppe Ungaretti, *Italian.* PeFWW, *tr.* by Jon Silkin

This my father taught. Nashoba. Jim Barnes. *Fr.* Four Things Choctaw. HATNAP

This, my hand of peace, this wound which does not heal. (LL) For My Mother. Philip Schultz. NAmP90

This nameless anxiety. in Jazz Rhythms. Janina Degutyte, *Lithuanian.* CEEP, *tr.* by M. G. Slavenas

This nation has a faithful friend. The Nation's Friend. Alfred Islay Walden. AAP

This Native Land. Thomas Osborne Davis. BoTP

This nest is none of yours, O cuckoo bird! To a Cuckoo. Phan Bội Châu, *Vietnamese.* AVP, *tr.* by Huỳnh Sanh Thông

This new and gorgeous garment, majesty. Shakespeare. OxAEP-1 *Fr.* King Henry IV, Pt. II.

This new Daks suit, greeny-brown. Metamorphosis. Peter Porter. OxBTC

This new day the eyes of children. Vail Read. AH

This new kind of metal will not suffer. Christianite. William Stafford. NoAM

This Newly Created World. *Unknown, Winnebago Indian.* AiP

This Night. N. Revathi Devi, *Telugu.* OMIP, *tr.* by V. Narayana Rao *and* A. K. Ramanujan

This night cast iron over flat land. The Unreal Song of the Old. James Koller. PoM

This night is pure and clear as thrice refinèd silver. Fountains. Sacheverell Sitwell. MoBrPo

This night of no moon. Ono no Komachi, *Japanese.* PBWP, *tr.* by Donald Keene

This night presents a play, which publick rage. Prologue to Hugh Kelly's *A Word to the Wise.* Samuel Johnson. EBEV; FaPoR; OxAEP-1

This Night Sees Ireland Desolate. Aindrais MacMarcuis, *Irish.* BIrV, *tr.* by Robin Flower

This night shall thy soul be required of thee. Scorpion. Stevie Smith. EBEV; FaBoWP; OxAEP-2; PeECV; PoE

This night, while sleep begins with heavy wings. Sonnet 38. Sir Philip Sidney. *Fr.* Astrophil and Stella. AAS; SiPS

This no wonder's of much weight. Mary Sidney, Countess of Montgomery Wroth. *Fr.* Urania.

This noiseless ball and top so round. Philocles. Leonidas of Tarentum, *Greek.* AWP, *tr.* by F. A. Wright

This, O my stomach, is a painting. American Heritage. Robert Sward. OBAL

This ocean, humiliating in its disguises. Thing Language. Jack Spicer. APSN; FTOS *Fr.* Language.

This Octopus Exploits Women. James Fenton. CBNP; NoAM

This old woman. Betsy Sholl. MDDM *Fr.* Notes From a Youngest Daughter.

This old woman follows me from room to room. Queen of the Ebony Isles. Colleen J. McElroy. NMM-2

This old world needs propping up. Windy Evening. Charles Simic. AFr

This olde man gan looke in his visage. Chaucer. *Fr.* The Pardoner's Tale. FHYEP; NAEL-1; NAWM-1; OAEL-1; PoE *Fr.* The Canterbury Tales.

This on my posy-ring I've writ. The Posy Ring. Clément Marot, *French.* AWP, *tr.* by Ford Madox Ford

This one arrived on time. Twins. Gloria Escoffery. PBCV

This one day! (LL) O Mors! Quam Amara Est Memoria Tua Homini Pacem Habenti In Substantiis Suis. Ernest Christopher Dowson. OBMV

This one for the telling of sins. And for. Vespers. Donald Davie. *Fr.* Horae Canonicae. CRP

This one lie down on grass. The Astrologer Predicts at Mary's Birth. Lucille Clifton. NALW

This one remaining rebel / is the sparrow-camel. (LL) He "Digesteth Harde Yron." Marianne Moore. CMoP; NoAM

This one request I make to him that sits the clouds above. Love and Debt Alike Troublesome. Sir John Suckling. CavPo

This one, said the sculptor, is the last of the biblical figures. David. Linda Pastan. CRP

This one was no philanthropist. For the Grave of a Peace-Loving Man. Hans Magnus Enzensberger, *German.* VCWP, *tr.* by Enzensberger, Hans Magnus and Michael Hamburger

This one was put in a jacket. Counting the Mad. Donald Justice. CoAmPo; NIP-4; NoP-4; TRP; UnPo

This One's on Me. Phyllis Gotlieb. MoCV; NOBC

This onion-dome holds all intricacies. Greenwich Observatory. Sidney Keyes. MoBrPo

This only is the witchcraft I have used:—. (LL) Her father lov'd me; oft invited me. Shakespeare. EBEV; OxAEP-1; SCV

This 'oppressed person', on £12,000 per year. On Knowing the Difference Between Prejudice, Discrimination, and Oppression. Tom Leonard. NBrP

This oriental country, year after year. A Fan from Korea. Chu Yün-ming, *Chinese.* CoBLCP, *tr.* by Jonathan Chaves

This page will be no less a riddle. John 1:14 (1969). Jorge Luis Borges, *Spanish.* GI, *tr.* by Norman Thomas Di Giovanni

This pagoda penetrates the clouds. The Pagoda of Master Chih. Wang T'ing-hsiang. *Fr.* Miscellaneous Poems on Spirit-Valley Temple. CoBLCP, *tr.* by Jonathan Chaves

This pair of skin gloves is sixty-six years old. Skins. Judith Wright. BMAP

This Pardoner had hair as yellow as wax. Chaucer. SCV *Fr.* The General Prologue. FHYEP; NAEL-1; NAWM-1; OAEL-1; PoE *Fr.* The Canterbury Tales.

This perspex model is what you might call a perfect replica. Naming of Private Parts. John Lloyd Williams. BXAP

This phalanx of pines, these demi-fountains. Martial. Thom Gunn, *Latin.* OBGa, *tr.* by Peter Porter

This picture, once, resembled thee. (LL) To Miss Charlotte Pulteney in Her Mother's Arms. Ambrose Philips. GTBS-P; LiLi; NOEC

This piece of Lydian earth holds Amyntor. Antipater of Sidon, *Greek.* GrAn, *tr.* by Tony Harrison

This pig got in the barn. *Unknown.* OxNR

This pines. This That and Then. Douglas Messerli. FTOS

This pit is Hell where through thou now must go. Elizabeth, Lady Culross Melvill. *Fr.* A Godly Dream. WPE

This Place in the Ways. Muriel Rukeyser. AiP

This place is cold. Three Poems for the Indian Steelworkers. Joseph Bruchac. CDW

This place is near Hua-yang Mountain. Yang Chi. *Fr.* Living in the Country at Kou-ch'ü in Autumn——Miscellaneous Impressions. CoBLCP, *tr.* by Jonathan Chaves

This place is the Cyprian's for she has ever the fancy. Anyte, *Greek.* GrAn, *tr.* by Ezra Pound

This place moves from me. Poem before Departure. Jean Burden. WPE

This place (quoth she) they say's enchanted. Samuel Butler. NOBL *Fr.* Hudibras.

This Place Rumor to Have Been Sodom. Robert Duncan. NOBA; NeAP; PoM

This *plat* is a true Ratatouille. Ratatouille. Gina Berkeley. PeLi

This ploughman dead in battle slept out of doors. A Private. Edward Thomas. GTBS-P; NSI; PeFWW

This Poem. Constance Urdang. PBCAP

This poem I write to teach the reader. Writing in England Now. Philip O'Connor. OxBTC

This poem is a letter to tell you that I. Transformations. Joy Harjo. HATNAP

This poem is a poem about people. Prologue to a Poem. Natan Zach, *Hebrew.* IP, *tr.* by Warren Bargad *and* Stanley F. Chyet

This poem is about the strength and sadness of potatoes. Potatoes. David Donnell. NIP-4; NOBC

This poem is concerned with language on a very plain level. Paradoxes and Oxymorons. John Ashbery. FTOS; HeIP-4; NoAM; PmAP; PoPoPo; Poetr; SAGP

This Poem Is Dedicated to Brother Andries Raditsela. Nise Malange. PeSAV

This poem is for my wife. Poem in Prose. Archibald MacLeish. MeMAP

This Poem Should Have Etc. Yona Wollach, *Hebrew.* IP, *tr.* by Warren Bargad *and* Stanley F. Chyet

This poet describes carbon paper, how it lies flat. Salad Days. Susan Musgrave. NoAM

This poet is. Meeting Mick Jagger. Robert Peters. BXAP

This pool, the quiet sky. March Evening. Leonard Alfred George Strong. MoBrPo

This Poor Man. W. J. Gruffydd, *Welsh.* OBWVE, *tr.* by Gwyn Jones

This poring over your *Grand Cyrus.* On A Romantic Lady. Mary Monck. ECWP; NOEC; RACG

This porthole overlooks a sea. Bendix. John Updike. NYBP

This prayer I make. Wordsworth. PoToHe

This prayer, O Lord, of course applies. Charles Strachey. NSI

This precarious peak commands a view. A Trip to Yüeh-lu Temple. Li Tung-yang, *Chinese.* CoBLCP, *tr.* by Jonathan Chaves

This precious priest, this goodly man, Sir John. Chaucer. *See* The Nun's Priest's Prologue.

This pretty bird, oh, how she flies and sings! Upon the Swallow. John Bunyan. OxBChV

This prince of a former dynasty. A Little Landscape by Chao Ch'ien-li. Yü Chi, *Chinese.* CoBLCP, *tr.* by Jonathan Chaves

This prophecy came by mail. Requiem for "Bird" Parker, Musician. Gregory Corso. BB

This purple cloud of grief within my heart. Old Love Butchered (Colorado Springs and Huachuca). Lance Jeffers. NBV

This pyrrhic fire the barn burned down and blew back. Complaint Against the Arsonist. Stanley Plumly. PUP-18

This quarry cries on havoc. O proud Death. Shakespeare. *Fr.* Hamlet. NAWM-1

This queen of prey (now prey to you). A Lady with a Falcon on Her Fist. Richard Lovelace. CaPo

This quest rapped at my ears broad golden doors. Meditation Twelve. Edward Taylor. KSG

This *quidam* gives that *quidam* for *one* round. Philodemus, *Greek.* GrAn, *tr.* by William Moebius

This Quiet Dust was Gentlemen and Ladies. A Cemetery. Emily Dickinson. CMoP; MoAmPo; OxBA

This quiet morning light. To Mark Anthony in Heaven. William Carlos Williams. NOBA; SAmP

This quiet mound beneath. Corporal Pym. Walter De la Mare. FaBoEE

This quiet roof, bestirred with pigeon plumes. The Graveyard by the Sea. Paul Valéry, *French.* STV, *tr.* by John Frederick Nims

This, quoth the Eskimo master. Latter-day Geography Lesson. Ronald Allison Kells Mason. PeNZ

This rage of waterangels. Rain Storm. Sasenarine Persand. HCP

This Railway Station. Allan M. Laing. UV

This ration card, once shocking pink. The Ration Card. Liz Sohappy Bahe. CDW

This red / Italian hand. For My Daughter. John Logan. CRP

This reverend shadow cast that setting sun. Upon Bishop Andrewes's [*or* Andrewes His] Picture before His Sermons. Richard Crashaw. NOSC

This ritzy vista includes the money. Love Poem. John Forbes. BMAP

This road our blithe-heart elders knew. A Lyric on the Lyric. Lizette Woodworth Reese. APN-2

This Room and Everything in It. Li-Young Lee. OpBo

This rose tree is not made to bear. Envy. Charles Lamb *and* Mary Lamb. OxBChV; WoRP

This royal throne of kings, this scepter'd isle. Shakespeare. UV *Fr.* Richard II.

This rudely sculptured porter-pot. Undying Thirst. Antipater of Sidon, *Greek.* AWP, *tr.* by Robert Bland

This Runner. Francis Webb. CBAP

This sad world we inhabit. *Unknown.* NOIV *Fr.* The Calendar of Oengus.

This said; he (begging) gather'd clouds from land. Ulysses in the Waves. Homer. *Fr.* Odyssey. NAWM-1, *tr.* by Robert Fitzgerald

This said, he reacht to take his sonne. Hector's Child and the Plume. Homer. OBVE, *tr.* by George Chapman *Fr.* The Iliad.

This said, he turned about his steed. Sidrophel, the Rosicrucian Conjurer. Samuel Butler. OxBoLi *Fr.* Hudibras.

This said, the Am'rous Youth, with both Arms stript. Consummation. Musaeus, *Greek.* OBCVT, *tr.* by *Unknown*

This said, the restles generall through the darke. Marlowe. PBRV *Fr.* Lucan's Pharsalia Book 1.

This sailor knows of wondrous lands afar. The Child and the Mariner. W. H. Davies. CH

This savage wish on certain days. Cannibal. Léon Laleau. NegPo, *tr.* by Ellen Conroy Kennedy *Fr.* Black Music.

This saying good-by on the edge of the dark. Good-by and Keep Cold. Robert Frost. CMoP

This sea horse, errant upon Sargasso weed. The Sea Horse. Ruthven Todd. APo

This sea will never die, neither will it ever grow old. Middle of the World. D. H. Lawrence. HAP; NoAM

This seems, in a world where love must take its chances. Mona Van Duyn. HAP *Fr.* Footnotes to "The Autobiography of Bertrand Russell."

This sentence have I left behind. A Nameless Epitaph. Matthew Arnold. FaBoEE

This Shade. Susanne Doyle. FFC

This shade-bestowing pear-tree, thou. The Pear-Tree. *Unknown.* AWP, *tr.* by Allen Upward *Fr.* Shi King.

This shadow at my shoulder doesn't shed. Climbing. Jennifer Maiden. BMAP; CBAP

This shall be called the laying on of hands. A Necessary Miracle. Eda Lou Walton. NYBP

This she? no, this is Diomed's Cressida. Shakespeare. OxAEP-1 *Fr.* Troilus and Cressida.

This sheepskin coat may be worn out. Wearing a Worn-Out Coat. Chin Nung, *Chinese.* CoBLCP, *tr.* by Jonathan Chaves

This ship is the ship of butchery and increase. Songs for the Cisco Kid; or, Singing: Song #2. K. Curtis Lyle. PoBA

This shirt *is* the bullet. (LL) From the Spotted Night. Ray A. Young Bear. AF

This shop in a little road I know is like a grubby sweet left. The Hairdresser's. Pierre McOrlan, *French.* MFP, *tr.* by Martin Sorrell

This short straight sword. Prelude. Ronald Allison Kells Mason. PeNZ

This silken wreath, which circles in mine arm. Upon a Ribbon [*or* Ribband]. Thomas Carew. BeJo; CaPo; NOSC; OAEL-1; PoE

This silver thing I send you for your birthday. Crinagoras, *Greek.* GrAn, *tr.* by Alistair Elliot

This silver was not carved but mesmerized. A Satyr by Diodorus. Plato the Younger, *Greek.* GrAn, *tr.* by G. R. H. Wright

This sky is to be opened. Hermetic Bird. Philip Lamantia. VGW

This slow one. (LL) Tortoise-Shell. D. H. Lawrence. CMoP; FaBoVe; NAEL-2; OAEL-2; OxAEP-2

This small. Magnet. Valerie Worth. KaS

This Smoking World. Graham Lee Hemminger *See* Tobacco ("Tobacco is a dirty word").

This Solitude of Cataracts. Wallace Stevens. LCAP-2

This song of late autumn. Autumn. Itsik Manger, *Yiddish.* TrJP, *tr.* by Ruth Whitman *and* Joseph Leftwich

This song of mine sets my soul free. Vusumzi's Song. L. T. Manyase, *Xhosa.* PeSA, *tr.* by C. M. Mcanyangwa *and* Jack Cope

This soup is cold. The Soup of Venus. James Tate. AmPA

This southern rain nourishes the mossy stones. Tu Fu. SuSp, *tr.* by William H. Nienhauser *Fr.* Rain, Four Poems.

This sparrow / who comes to sit at my window. The Sparrow. William Carlos Williams. InPS-3; LCAP-2; Poetr; VGW

This speech all Troyans did applaud; who from their traces losde. Night Piece: the Trojans outside Troy. Homer, *Greek.* OBVE, *tr.* by George Chapman *Fr.* The Iliad.

This spiritual man left the world behind. Sent To Be Inscribed on the Temple of P'u-jun (Universal Fructification) at Lou-fu Mountain. Yü Chi, *Chinese.* CoBLCP, *tr.* by Jonathan Chaves

This spoke, a huge wave tooke him by the head. Homer. OBVE, *tr.* by George Chapman *Fr.* Odyssey. NAWM-1, *tr.* by Robert Fitzgerald

This spoonful of chocolate tapioca. Thinking of the Lost World. Randall Jarrell. NOBA; NoAM

This Spring. Regina DeCormier-Shekejian. LoHo

This spring as it comes bursts up in bonfires green. The Enkindled Spring. D. H. Lawrence. NoAM

This spring rain. William J. Higginson. HA

This spring the cuckoo won't count out your years. To the Memory of a Poet. Astride Ivaska, *Latvian.* CEEP, *tr.* by Inara Cedrins

This spring, the sky is leaking. Finding Serenity. Yüan Mei, *Chinese.* ChiPo; CoBLCP, *tr.* by Jonathan Chaves

This spring, you'd swear it actually gets dark earlier. Turning Thirty. Katha Pollitt. InPS-3; LiLi

This squalid dome of soot-obscuréd glass. This Railway Station. Allan M. Laing. UV

This star is only an augury of the morning. And in the 51st Year of That Century, While My Brother Cried in the Trench, While My Enemy Glared from the Cave. Hyam Plutzik. RB

This still mountain night is not still. Earth Screaming. Esther Iverem. GT

This stone. Stone Hammer Poem. Robert Kroetsch. NOBC

This Stone. *Unknown, Greek.* AWP, *tr.* by Goldwin Smith

This stone incorporates three gods:/ the head is unmistakably goat-horned Pan's. Philodemus, *Greek.* GrAn, *tr.* by William Moebius

This stone, with not unpardonable pride. Epitaph. John Sparrow. OBCoV

This story ends with me still rowing. (LL) Rowing. Anne Sexton. BoWoP; LCAP-2

This story was told to me by another traveller. Margaret Atwood. NALW *Fr.* Circe / Mud Poems.

This story's strange, but altogether true. "R. B." SCAP

This Strange Calculation of Roots. Edouard J. Maunick, *French*. NegPo, *tr. by* Teo Savory

This strange thing must have crept. Fork. Charles Simic. AmPA; ChAP; ColAP; HCAP; LCAP-2; PoPoPo; TRP; WeW-3

This string upon my harp was best beloved. Harmonics. William Vaughn Moody. APN-2

This sudden cockerel who stood. Cock-Crow. Ralph Nixon Currey. PeSA

This Summer and Last. Thomas Hardy. OxBTC

This Summer's Sky. Bertolt Brecht, *German*. PoSu, *tr. by* Michael Hamburger

This Sun Is Hot. *Unknown*. BPo

This sun on this rubble after rain. Dennis Brutus. PBMAP

This sun was mine and yours; we shared it. Our Sun. George Seferis, *Greek*. AF, *tr. by* Edmund Keeley *and* Philip Sherrard

This sunday morning breaks blue clear, in st paul de vence. In Jimmy's Garden. Quincy Troupe. GT

This sunlight shames November where he grieves. Autumn Idleness. D. G. Rossetti. GBL; OAEL-2 *Fr.* The House of Life.

This sweete preest, this goodly man sir John. (LL) The Nun's Priest's Prologue. Chaucer. FHYEP; OAEL-1

This terrible heavy caterpillar. Miserere Nobis. Ioan Alexandru, *Romanian*. CEEP, *tr. by* Peter Jay *and* Virgil Nemoianu

This That and Then. Douglas Messerli. FTOS

This that at night keeps flashing. Little Testament. Eugenio Montale, *Italian*. PFTM, *tr. by* Cid Corman

This that I give you now. Bread. Stanley Burnshaw. TrJP

This that I swear. (LL) The Vow. Anthony Hecht. CoAmPo

This that is washed with weed and pebblestone. The Figurehead. Léonie Adams. WPE

This thatched hut, its master returned. Yang Chi. *Fr.* Living in the Country at Kou-ch'ü in Autumn——Miscellaneous Impressions. CoBLCP, *tr. by* Jonathan Chaves

This the divine Expressor did so give. Demodocus sings the fall of Troy. Homer. OBCVT, *tr. by* George Chapman *Fr.* The Odyssey.

This the house of Circe, queen of charms. Circe. John Warren. NOBVV

This the house that Jack built. The House That Jack Built. *Unknown*. FaBoBe

This, the last ornament among the peers. Hilaire Belloc. OBSV

This, the twentieth day of March. A Letter to Three Irish Poets. Michael Longley. BIrV

This then buddy is the blue routine. My Buddy. Richard Hugo. SeSe

This then is our answer under. Louis MacNeice. *See* Troll's Courtship.

This, then, is the grave of my son. The Nettles. Thomas Hardy. OxBSP

This, then, the river he had to swim. Thomas at the Wheel. Rita Dove. Poetr

This they know well: the Goddess yet abides. In Her Praise. Robert Graves. BIrV

This thin-lipped king with his helmeted head. To President Bush at the Start of the Gulf War. Robert Bly. RaBo

This, this is he; softly a while. Samson Fallen. Milton. UnPo *Fr.* Samson Agonistes. FHYEP; OAEL-1; PoEL-3

This Time. Steve Denning. CDa

This time from the top. (LL) Don't say goodbye to the Porkpie Hat that rolled. Larry Neal. GT; MoNo

This time, I mean it. A Little Tumescence. Jonathan Williams. NeAP; PoM

This time I won't permit the blue, glimpsed. Patrizia Cavalli, *Italian*. NeIt; VCWP, *tr. by* Judith Baumel

This time I'll show up. Hunting Song. *Unknown, Chippewa Indian*. STP, *tr. by* Jerome Rothenberg

This time / in the darkness. Stuntman. Lionel Kearns. MoCV

This time of pause is as though. Shag Rock. "Paul Henderson." PeNZ

This time the tomb. (LL) A Great Time. W. H. Davies. ImPo; MoBrPo

This time there was no beak. Pile of Feathers. Gerald Stern. LoL

This time they're thirteen, no longer. The Field Trip. Ellen Bryant Voigt. IFJA

This to the crown and blessing of my life. A Letter to Daphnis. Anne Finch, Countess of Winchilsea. EnLoPo; LW; NALW; NOSC; PEW

This toiling to go through something yet. The Swan. Rilke, *German*. PFE, *tr. by* M. D. Herter Norton

This Tokyo. Gary Snyder. CAPP-1; NeAP

This told, strange Teras touched her lute, and sung. The Wedding of Alcmane and Mya. George Chapman. *Fr.* Hero and Leander. AAS

This tomb Damis built for his courageous horse. Anyte. HePo, *tr. by* Barbara Hughes Fowler *Fr.* Epigrams.

This tomb, inscribed to gentle Parnell's name. Oliver Goldsmith. EPCY

This tombstone heavy with grief announces. Philetas, *Greek*. GrAn, *tr. by* Peter Jay

This, too, can bear;—I still / Am Belisarius! (LL) Belisarius. Henry Wadsworth Longfellow. APN-1; PoEL-5

This, too, I want you to know, my dear Phaedrus. To Phaedrus. Jovan Hristic, *Serbo-Croatian*. HSix, *tr. by* Charles Simic

This too is an experience of the soul. Isis Wanderer. Kathleen Jessie Raine. NALW; OxBS

This too is one of them. (LL) The Old Man's Lazy. Peter Blue Cloud. LTA

This too long wait for one who is estranged. (LL) The Wife's Complaint. *Unknown, Anglo-Saxon*. EEP, *tr. by* Michael Alexander

This, Too, Shall Pass Away. A. L. Alexander. PoToHe

This, Too, Shall [*or* Will] Pass Away. Lanta Wilson Smith. BLPA

This Tooth. Lee Bennett Hopkins. TLR

This torch, still burning in my hand. From the Greek Anthology. Crinagoras, *Greek*. PGA, *tr. by* Kenneth Rexroth

This town has docks where channel boats come sidling. Arrivals, Departures. Philip Larkin. MoBrPo

This train is bound for glory, this train. This Train. *Unknown*. AmFP; OxBoLi

This treasure is the best, of all those gifts the grain. Upon the Birth of a Young and Highly Desired Son. Christian Weise, *German*. GePo, *tr. by* George C. Schoolfield

This tree my time keeper. John Figueroa. HCP

This Troilus [*or* Troylus], with blisse [*or* Blysse] of that supprysed [*or* supprised]. Chaucer. EBEV; PoE *Fr.* Troilus and Criseyde [*or* Criseide]. EnVB

This truth-telling is well enough. Visited. Fleur Adcock. PeNZ

This tuft that thrives on saline nothingness. The Air Plant. Hart Crane. MoAmPo

This Tzu-hsia of Hsi-ho. An Inkstone Inscription for the Blind Scholar Ho Yung-kuang. Chin Nung, *Chinese*. CoBLCP, *tr. by* Jonathan Chaves

This Unimportant Morning. Lawrence Durrell. BoLoP; OxBTC

This unphilosophic sight. To a Lady's Countenance. Elinor Wylie. NALW

This urge, wrestle, resurrection of dry sticks. Cuttings. Theodore Roethke. ColAP; HCAP; LCAP-2; MoP; NAAL-2; NOBA; NoAM; OBGa; TAP; TRP; UnPo; VCAP

This used to be a dam. Damside. Margaret Atwood. LCAP-2

This vale of teargas. Unlawful Assembly. D. J. Enright. OxBTC

This valley: as if huge, dull, primordial axe. Grim Town in a Steep Valley. Thomas Lux. BAP-93

This Version of Love. Dorothy Hewett. BMAP; CBAP

This very remarkable man. On Professor Coué. Charles Cuthbert Inge. OBCoV

This voice an older friend has kept. Isaiah by Kerosene Lantern Light. Robert Harris. ChIV-1; NOBAu

This wall-paper has lines that rise. Missing My Daughter. Stephen Spender. GTBS-P

This warning, Gallus, for thy love I send. Hylas. Propertius. AWP, *tr. by* F. A. Wright *Fr.* Elegies. AWP

This was a city once, that's now a copse. Lament for Troy. Hugh, Primate of Orleans, *Latin*. MLL, *tr. by* Helen Waddell

This was a dream. (LL) In Winter in my Room. Emily Dickinson. APN-2; AmPP; MoP; NAAL-1; NAAL-3; NALW; NCAP; NOBA; NoAM; OxBA; Poetr

This was a love in which there was always. Brief Farewell. Anthony Delius. PeSA

This was a Poet—It is That. Emily Dickinson. APN-2; AmPP; NAAL-1; NAAL-3; NCAP; NOBA; PAR

This was a sweet white wildwood violet. Violet. Arthur Symons. ADE

This was a time, when only the dead. Introduction. "Anna Akhmatova," *Russian*. PFTM, *tr. by* Lenore Mayhew *and* William McNaughton

This was as far as I had got. David Wright. PeSAV *Fr.* A Peripatetic Letter to Isabella Fey.

This was her grief, that when the moon was full. The Solitary. Sylvia Lynd. WPN

This was Mr Bleaney's room. He stayed. Mr Bleaney. Philip Larkin. HoPM; InPS-3; OxBC; PoE; PoPoPo; TRP; UV

"This was Mr. Strugnell's room," she'll say. Mr. Strugnell. Wendy Cope. UV

This was my dream: I saw a Forest. Bad Dreams III. Robert Browning. OAEL-2

This was not experience. The Painted Cup. Michael Palmer. FTOS

This was not to be expected. Seaman, 1941. Molly Holden. FaBoWP

This was our first line of defense. It held. Ferniehirst Castle. Richard Hugo. NoAM

This was the brown bull of Cuailnge. The Two Bulls. *Unknown*. NOIV, *tr. by* Thomas Kinsella *Fr.* How the Bulls Were Begotten.

This was the crucifixion on the mountain. Dylan Thomas. CMoP *Fr.* A Sequence of Sonnets.

This was the hawk's way. This was the hawk. Hawk's Way. Ted Olson. HoPM

This was the moment when Before. BC:AD. U. A. Fanthorpe. OBCP

This was the surplus childhood, held as cheap! The Sunderland Children. Alice Thompson Meynell. NALW

This was the table. Its surface, its legs. The Ghost. Agnes Nemes Nagy, *Hungarian*. PoSu, tr. by Bruce Berlind

This was the wine. It stained the top of the page. Going up to Sotheby's. Muriel Spark. FaBoTC

This was the woman; what now of the man? George Meredith. EnVR; Son *Fr.* Modern Love.

This was their song, their cups among, / the evening before. Michael Wigglesworth. *See* Still was the night, serene and bright.

This water droplet, charity of the air. The Man Seeking Experience Enquires His Way of a Drop of Water. Ted Hughes. OxAEP-2

This water, sad and fearful. Slow Rain. Gabriela Mistral. PBWP, tr. by Gunda Kaiser *and* James Tipton

This watery vague how vast! This misty globe. On the Bay. Richard Watson Gilder. APN-2

This way, that way? Polar Cub. Judith Nicholls. NOxBChV

This way, this way, come and hear. Song in the Wood. John Fletcher. NOSC *Fr.* The Little French Lawyer.

This wet sack, wavering slackness. Macduff. Charles Tomlinson. OxBC

This while we are abroad. An Ode Written in the Peak[e]. Michael Drayton. NOSC

This whole land belongs to me sleeping and awake I see. Amir Gilbo'a, *Hebrew*. IP, tr. by Warren Bargad and Stanley F. Chyet

This wide, old city. (LL) An Urn for Burial. *Unknown, Tamil*. PLW, tr. by A. K. Ramanujan

This wight all mercenary projects tries. Sir Samuel Garth. *Fr.* The Dispensary. OBSV

This will really try you. Mamma! Frank Horne. BPo

This wine-press is call'd war on earth. The Wine-Press of Los. William Blake. EBEV *Fr.* Milton.

This wingtip feather from a hook-beaked eagle. Crinagoras, *Greek*. GrAn, tr. by Alistair Elliot

This winter air is keen and cold. Le Jardin des Tuileries. Oscar Wilde. GaP

This winter's morning, turning the other way. Turning. Robert Finch. MoCV

This wit was with experience bought. A Mirror for Detractors. Esther Lewis. ECWP

This Woman. Donna Trussell. IFJA

This woman is getting on her last bus. Poem for Jacqueline Hill. *Unknown*. BrRo

This woman vomiting her. Present. Sonia Sanchez. NAAAL; UnSA

This wondrous art in the human realm. To a Pyrotechnist. Chao Meng-fu, *Chinese*. CoBLCP, tr. by Jonathan Chaves

This world. Lal Ded, *Kashmiri*. WPoS, tr. by Jane Hirshfield

This World. Sarah Morgan Bryan Piatt. NCAP

This world a hunting is. Madrigal. William Drummond, of Hawthornden. OxBSP; SAGP

This world a vale of soul-making. In Cemeteries. D. J. Enright. OxBC

This world and this life are so scattered, they try me. Zu fragmentarisch ist Welt und Leben. Heinrich Heine, *German*. AWP, tr. by Charles Godfrey Leland

This World Fares as a Fancy. *Unknown*. EnVB

This world / is amazingly flat. Natalya Gorbanevskaya, *Russian*. BoWoP, tr. by Barbara Einzig

This world is gradually becoming a place. John Berryman. MoP; NOBA; NoAM; SAGP *Fr.* Dream Songs.

This World is not Conclusion. Emily Dickinson. APAD; APN-2; NAAL-1; NAAL-3; NCAP

This world lives. This World Lives Because. Ilam Peruvatuti, *Tamil*. PLW, tr. by A. K. Ramanujan

This world of ours. Sami Mansei, *Japanese*. OHMPJ, tr. by Kenneth Rexroth

This world's dead weight and cycle on your back. (LL) Night Sweat. Robert Lowell. NAAL-2; TAP; VGW

This world's just mad enough to have been made. Creation Myth on a Moebius Band. Howard Nemerov. OBCoV

This worthy lymytour, this noble Frere. The Friar's Prologue. Chaucer. PoE *Fr.* The Canterbury Tales.

This would not be the war I fought in. (LL) Newsreel. Adrienne Rich. FaBoWP; HCAP

This wrestling, as of seamen with a storm. Joseph Conrad. Malcolm Lowry. CLPP

This year again the bruise-colored oak. Seeing the Bones. Maxine W. Kumin. NoAM

This year, before it ends, holds out time as a weight to us. Eve Langley. NOBAu

This year, / I'm raising the emotional ante. These Green-going-to-Yellow. Marvin Bell. FYAP

This year, maybe, do you think I can graduate? Deferred. Langston Hughes. APSN

This year, / Next year. *Unknown*. OxNR

This year of famine, old and young suffer many strange diseases. Pien Kung. *Fr.* Mooring at K'ou-ch'üeh—Sent to Dr. Lin. CoBLCP, tr. by Jonathan Chaves

"This year she has changed greatly"—meaning you. Change. Robert Graves. OxBTC

This Year's Drive to Appomattox. Eleanor Ross Taylor. CBCWP

This Yonder Night I Sawe a Sighte. *Unknown*. MiEL

This yonge fresshe wenche, wel loking honey-swete. The Hicche-Hykeres Tale. W. F. N. Watson. BXAP

This, you were sure, whatever happened. A Pair of Shoes. Theodore Weiss. NoAM

This young boy on my hands at middle age. Teasing Hsiao-te, My Son. Huang T'ing-chien, *Chinese*. SuSp, tr. by Michael E. Workman

This young mandarin had undoubted genius. Lament for Hsieh T'iao. Shen Yüeh, *Chinese*. SuSp, tr. by Lenore Mayhew and William McNaughton

This Zone, this Breastband & girlish frock. Artemis. Perses, *Greek*. GrAn, tr. by Peter Whigham

Thise olde gentil Brito[u]ns in hir dayes. The Franklin's Prologue. Chaucer. NAEL-1; OAEL-1 *Fr.* The Canterbury Tales.

Thistle. Nikolai Alekseievich Zabolotsky, *Russian*. RB, tr. by Daniel Weissbort

Thistle and darnel and dock grew there. Nicholas Nye. Walter De la Mare. BoTP

Thistledown. Denis Glover. PeNZ *Fr.* Sings Harry.

Thistledown. James Merrill. UnPo

Thistledown. Harold Monro. OxBTC

Thistledown. Andrew Young. AYFP

Thistledown blows over the poisoned fields. The Martyred Earth. Ewart Milne. BIrV

Thistledown's flying / Though the winds are all still, The. Autumn. John Clare. EnVR; HAP; PoEL-4; WeW-3

Thistles. Ted Hughes. APAD; FaBoVe; NoAM; OxBSP; OxBTC; SoSe-8

Thistle's Characteristics, The. "Hugh MacDiarmid." FaBoTC *Fr.* A Drunk Man Looks at the Thistle.

Thistles climb the thatch. Forever, The. The Clearances. Iain Crichton Smith. FaBoTC

Tho' [or Though] conscience void of all offence. Praise. Christopher Smart. OxBChV *Fr.* Hymns for the Amusement of Children.

Tho' [or Though] Grief and Fondness in my Breast rebel. London: A Poem. Samuel Johnson. PoEL-3

Tho' I can not your cruelty constrain. Sir Thomas Wyatt. SiPS

Tho' I my party long have chose. Moderation. Christopher Smart. NOCV *Fr.* Hymns for the Amusement of Children.

Tho' ill at ease, a stranger and alone. Thoughts on Pausing at a Cottage near the Paukataug River. Sarah Kemble Knight. SCAP

Tho' I'm no Catholic. The Catholic Bells. William Carlos Williams. CMoP; NOBA; OxBA; SAmP

Tho in pale Whites my Face appear. Age. Anacreon, *Greek*. OBCVT, tr. by James Bristow

Tho' [or Thou' or Though] it were ten thousand mile! (LL) A Red, Red Rose. Robert Burns. AWP; BoLoP; CBLP; EBEvV; FaBoBe; GBL; GTBS-P; HAP; HeIP-4; HoPM; ImPo; InPK-6; NAEL-2; NIP-4; NOBE; NOBRP; NOEC; NTP; OAEL-1; OBEV; OxAEP-2; OxBS; PoEL-4; PoLF; Poetr; SCGP; TFi; UV

Tho' men say thou bring'st the Spring. (LL) The Swallow. Abraham Cowley. EBEV; OBEV; OxAEP-1

Tho' ne'er another trow me. (LL) If doughty [or daughty] deeds my lady please[s]. Robert Graham. GTBS-P; OBEV

Tho' the same death you should die. (LL) Fair Mary of Wallington. *Unknown*. ESPB; OxBB

Tho when as chearelesse night ycovered had Edmund Spenser. OAEL-1 *Fr.* Wood Of Error. AEP

Tho when they came to the sea coast, they found. Edmund Spenser. PBRV *Fr.* The Faerie Queene.

Thocht raging stormes movis us to schaik. The Reid in the Loch Sayis. *Unknown*. OxBS

Thocht that this warld be verie strange. Solace in Age. Sir Richard Maitland. OxBS

Th'o'erflowing of unbounded Wit. *etc.* (LL) Enquiry after Peace. A Fragment. Anne Finch, Countess of Winchilsea. ECWP; PoE

Tho[u]gh ye to me ne do no daliaunce. (LL) To Rosamounde. Chaucer. CBLP; EnVB; NoP-4; OAEL-1; PoE

Thole a Little. *Unknown*. *See* Wait a Little!

Thomalin, since Thirsil nothing has to leave thee. To Thomalin. Phineas Fletcher. NOSC

Thomas. Gábor Görgey, *Hungarian*. CEEP, *tr. by* Jascha Kessler

Thomas and Charlie. Peter Wild. AmPA

Thomas at the Wheel. Rita Dove. Poetr

Thomas Carlyle. Dorothy Parker. NALW *Fr.* A Pig's-Eye View of Literature.

Thomas Cromwell. *Unknown*. ESPB

Thomas Dudley, Ah! Old Must Dye. *Unknown*. SCAP

Thomas Gray's View of Nature. William Mason. EPCY; NOEC *Fr.* The English Garden.

Thomas Hardy. Walter De la Mare. NoAM

Thomas Hardy. Norman Dubie. LCAP-2

Thomas Hardy and A. E. Housman. Max Beerbohm. NBLV

Thomas Hobbes of Malmesbury thought. Limerick. Peter Alexander. PeLi

Thomas in the Fields. Lois Moyles. NYBP

Thomas Iron-Eyes. Marnie Walsh. WPOW

Thomas lay on the Huntlie bank. Thomas the Rhymer [*or* Rimer]. *Unknown*. ESPB; EnSB; FaBoCh; InPS-3; NOBE; OAEL-1; OBEV; OxBB; OxBS

Thomas Logge. Walter De la Mare. FaBoEE

Thomas MacDonagh. Francis Ledwidge. *See* Lament for Thomas MacDonagh.

Thomas o Yonderdale. *Unknown*. ESPB

Thomas Rhymer [and the Queen of Elfland]. *Unknown*. *See* Thomas the Rhymer.

Thomas Sackevyll in Commendation of the Worke to the Reader. Thomas, 1st Earl of Dorset Sackville. AAS

Thomas Stuart was a lord. Lord Thomas Stuart. *Unknown*. ESPB

Thomas the Rhymer [*or* Rimer]. *Unknown*. EnSB; FaBoCh; InPS-3; NOBE; OAEL-1; OBEV; OxBB

(True Thomas.) OxBS

(Thomas Rhymer [and the Queen of Elfland].) CH; ESPB; HAP

John Masefield Relates the Story of Tom, the Piper's Son. Louis Untermeyer. MoAmPo *Fr.* Mother Goose Up-to-Date.

Thonah! Thonah! / There is a voice above. First Song of the Thunder. *Unknown*. APN-2, *tr. by* Washington Matthews *Fr.* The Mountain Chant.

Thoreau, / grabbing on, hard. The Distances to the Friend. Jonathan Williams. NeAP

Thoreau's Fossil Lilies. Brenda Hillman. WeT

Thorn, A. *Unknown*. ReMoGo

Thorn, The. Wordsworth. FaBoSe; Ro

"High on a mountain's highest ridge."

Thorn Leaves in March. W. S. Merwin. TwCP

Thorn Merchant's Mistress, The. Yusef Komunyakaa. RACG

Thorn Vine on the Wall. *Unknown, Chinese*. CoBCP, *tr. by* Burton Watson

Thorns. Haim Guri, *Hebrew*. IP, *tr. by* Warren Bargad *and* Stanley F. Chyet

Thorow. Susan Howe. APSN; PT

Thos the damselle spake, and dyed. (LL) Mynstrelle's Songe ("O! synge untoe mie roundelaie"). Thomas Chatterton. CH; EnLoPo; HAP; ImPo; NOBE; NOEC; OBEV; OxAEP-1; SCGP

Those aeroplanes. Timetable. Günter Eich, *German*. CBNP, *tr. by* Michael Hamburger

Those animals that follow us in dream. Xochitepec. Malcolm Lowry. NOBC

Those are my best days, when I shake with fear. (LL) Devout Fits. Donne. ChIV-2; NOSC; OAEL-1; PoEL-2; Son

Those are the features, those the smiles. Lines, / Written on Seeing My Husband's Picture, painted when he was young. Anna Sawyer. ECWP; LW

Those autumns my parents slept. A Dream of Glass Bangles. Agha Shahid Ali. OpBo; WeT

Those awful words "Till death do part." Early Thoughts of Marriage. Nathaniel Cotton. OxBChV

Those Beauteous Maids. Moses ibn Ezra, *Hebrew*. TrJP, *tr. by* Solomon Solis-Cohen

Those before Us. Robert Lowell. LCAP-2

Those Being Eaten by America. Robert Bly. CoAP

Those blessèd structures, plot and rhyme. Epilogue. Robert Lowell. NoAM; NoP-4; PoPoPo; SAGP

Those boats keep rushing out to restless sea. The Sea, the World, and the Boat People. Hà Huyền Chi, *Vietnamese*. AVP, *tr. by* Huỳnh Sanh Thông

Those Boys That Ran Together. Lucille Clifton. PoBA

Those Cambridge generations, Russell's, Keynes'. On Bertrand Russell's "Portraits from Memory." Donald Davie. FaBoTw

Those camellias. Clement Hoyt. HA

Those charming eyes within whose starry sphere. On the Death of Catarina de Attayda. Luis de Camões, *Spanish*. AWP, *tr. by* R. F. Burton

Those corner winds. Martin Shea. HA

Those dabbing hens I ferociously love. Cock before Dawn. Norman MacCaig. OxBC

Those dark mountains face to face. Dark Mountains. Milton Lockyer, *Yindjibarndi*. CBAP, *tr. by* Frank Wordick

Those days we slept in a trumpet. Music for Brass. Günter Grass, *German*. AF, *tr. by* Christopher Middleton

Those days when it was all right. Letter to E. Franklin Frazier. Imamu Amiri Baraka. BPo; PoBA

Those dew-moist roses and that bushy thyme. Theocritus, *Greek*. GrAn, *tr. by* Anthony Holden

Those dreams that on the silent night intrude. On Dreams. Jonathan Swift. BIrV

Those—dying then. Emily Dickinson. APN-2; NCAP

Those eyes (dear Lord) once brandons of desire. On Mary Magdalene. William Drummond, of Hawthornden. OAEL-1

Those eyes that [*or* which] set my fancy on a fire. Conquest [*or* His Lady's Might]. Philippe Desportes. AWP; NoSic

Those famous men of old, the Ogres. Ogres and Pygmies. Robert Graves. CMoP; FaBoMo; LiTM; MoP; NoAM

Those fantastic forms, fang-sharp. City without Walls. W. H. Auden. NYBP

Those five or six young guys. Blues. Derek Walcott. GT; SeSe

Those Flapjacks of Brown's. Bert Leston Taylor. OBAL

Those folds / leak point of the exit. (LL) Environs. Larry Eigner. FTOS

Those former loves wherein our lives have run. James Agee. *Fr.* Sonnets. MoAmPo

Those forms once so well set. Forms. Tadeusz Rózewicz, *Polish*. CEEP, *tr. by* Victor Contoski

Those four black girls blown up. American History. Michael S. Harper. BPo; HCAP; NoAM; PoPoPo

Those Gambler's Blues. *Unknown*. AS

Those great rough ranters, Branns. A Simplification. Richard Wilbur. CMoP

Those great sea-horses bare their teeth and laugh at the dawn. (LL) High Talk. W. B. Yeats. CBNP; FaBoVe; RaBo

Those great sweeps of snow that stop suddenly six feet from the house. Snowbanks North of the House. Robert Bly. AiP; LCAP-2; RaBo

Those groans men use. The Mutes. Denise Levertov. NALW; NOBA

Those hands, which heav'n like to a curtain spread. Crucified. Francis Quarles. NOSC

Those hands which you so clapt [*or* clapped], go now and wring. Upon the Lines and Life of the Famous Scenic Poet, Master Shakespeare. Hugh Holland. OBWVE

Those Honours come too late. Motto to Richard Lovelace, Lucasta. Posthume Poems. Martial, *Latin*. OBCVT, *tr. by Unknown*

Those hours that with gentle work did frame. Shakespeare. AEP *Fr.* Sonnets.

Those Images. W. B. Yeats. CMoP

Those in the vegetable rain retain. Stories of Snow. Patricia K. Page. NOBC; NoP-4; PoA

Those incidental charms which first attached. Wordsworth. OAEL-2 *Fr.* School-Time. FHYEP *Fr.* The Prelude; Growth of a Poet's Mind [1850 vers.]

Those ineluctable fragments. To be up against. (LL) Miles Weeping. Michael Waters. CMAP; PuP-15

Those Last, Late Hours of Christmas Eve. Lou Ann Welte. PChr

Those lesser rivals flee. (LL) At Ithaca. Hilda Doolittle. ColAP; VGW

Those lions / had stood there. Stalingrad Theater. Mikhail Kuz'mich Lukonin, *Russian*. TCRP, *tr. by* Albert C. Todd

Those lips that Love's own hand did make. Sonnet 145. Shakespeare. Son *Fr.* Sonnets.

Those long days measured by my little feet. "George Eliot." NOBVV *Fr.* Brother and Sister. NALW

Those long uneven lines. MCMXIV. Philip Larkin. EBEV; NAEL-2; NSI; NoAM; NoP-4; OBWP; OxAEP-2

Those looks, whose beams be joy, whose motion is delight. Sonnet 77. Sir Philip Sidney. AAS; SiPS

Those lumbering horses in the steady plough. Horses. Edwin Muir. APo; CMoP; FaBoCh; OAEL-2

Those men who love the *crwth* and harp. Song and Poetry. *Unknown, Welsh*. OBWVE, *tr. by* Gwyn Jones

Those men with dollars on the mind. Gamble. Linda Hogan. HATNAP

Those mindes that wholy dote upon delight. Chorus. Lady Elizabeth Carey. KTR *Fr.* Mariam. WPE

Those moon-gilded dancers. The Gay. "Æ." OBMV

Those most assailed trees. Macrocarpas. Michael Jackson. PeNZ

Those mothers down there off the hill. Seventh Son. Ed Roberson. PoBA

Those my friendships most obtain. Contentment. Nathaniel Cotton. OxBChV

Those of Pure Origin. Roy Fuller. FaBoMo

Those of us who are there will never leave. Subject to Change. Anne Lauterbach. PT

Those old tunes take me back. I used to go. Her Dancing Days. Anna Adams. BrRo

Those Others. Ian Wedde. PeNZ

Those Paperweights with Snow Inside. Molly Peacock. RA

Those paths on the mountainside. Circumambulation of Mt. Tamalpais. Andrew Hoyem. PoA

Those people were a kind of solution. (LL) Waiting for the Barbarians. Constantine P. Cavafy, *Greek*. AF; BLT; GrIP, *tr. by* Edmund Keeley *and* Philip Sherrard

Those petty [*or* pretty] wrongs that liberty commits. Sonnet 41. Shakespeare. OxAEP-1 *Fr.* Sonnets.

Those poor, arthritically swollen knees. With Her. Czeslaw Milosz, *Polish*. GI, *tr. by* Robert Hass *and* Czeslaw Milosz

Those quaint old worn-out words! Antiques. Walter De la Mare. PoA

Those questions, sister. The Stranglehold of English Lit. Felix Mnthali. PBMAP

Those Rainy Mornings. Frank Mkalawile Chipasula. HBAPE

Those ravens black that rested. Heavy-hearted. Judah Al-Harizi, *Hebrew*. TrJP

Those reckless hosts rush to the wells. Elegy. Baruch of Worms, *Hebrew*. TrJP

Those red men you offended were my brothers. In My First Hard Springtime. James Welch. AmPA; CDW

Those rivers run from that land. Song. Robert Creeley. VGW

Those shall be renowned [*or* Renown'd] for Love. (LL) Song of Venus. Dryden. OxBoLi; PoEL-3

Those ships which left. Saigyo, *Japanese*. AWP, *tr. by* Arthur Waley

Those snooty boys in all their purple drag! Epigram. Strato, *Greek*. GrAn, *tr. by* Tony Harrison

Those speckled trout we glimpsed in a pool last year. Two Fish. Katha Pollitt. DiPo; NIP-4

Those spirits which we Animal do call. Of the Animal Spirits. Margaret Lucas Cavendish, Duchess of Newcastle. PEW

Those That Are Gone. Laurence Binyon. LBC

Those that can give, open their hands this day. A New Year's Sacrifice: To Lucinda. Thomas Carew. CaPo

Those that go searching for love. Search for Love. D. H. Lawrence. CBLP

Those times I have you when my flesh. For Eyes to Bless You. Pamela Mordecai. PBCV

Those times, recaptured in a flash. Where Have They Gone? Võ Phiến, *Vietnamese*. AVP, *tr. by* Huỳnh Sanh Thông

Those transparent Dacca gauzes. The Dacca Gauzes. Agha Shahid Ali. NoP-4

Those Troublesome Disguises. Jonathan Williams. NeAP

Those trumpeting / petals. (LL) Iris. William Carlos Williams. InPS-3; LCAP-2; WeW-3

Those two are gone who walked upright on two legs. The Leopard in Eden. Gail White. FFC

Those Two Boys. Franklin Pierce Adams. OBCoV; TrJP

Those upon whom Almighty doth intend. The Frowardness of the Elect in the Work of Conversion. Edward Taylor. SCAP *Fr.* God's Determinations [touching his Elect].

Those verses surfaced thirty years ago. Postscript, 1984. John Hewitt. BiHa

Those We Love the Best. Ella Wheeler Wilcox. PoToHe

Those were countries simple to observe, difficult. Report from a Planet. Richmond Lattimore. FYAP

Those were the days. Energy in Sweden. Kenneth Koch. NoP-4

Those were the lobsters September in Kittery. Gilbert Sorrentino. FTOS

Those who are beautiful. Robert Kelly. APSN

Those who carry grand pianos / to the tenth floor. Anna Kamienska, *Polish*. GI, *tr. by* Curzon, David and Grazyna Drabik

Those Who Died for Their Country. Ch'u Yüan. *Fr.* Nine Songs. CoBCP, *tr. by* Burton Watson

Those Who Do Not Dance. Gabriela Mistral, *Spanish*. WPoS, *tr. by* Maria Giachetti

Those who favor our plan to alter the river. Plans for Altering the River. Richard Hugo. FYAP

Those who fling off, toss head. Meeting Together of Poles & Latitudes: In Prospect. Margaret Avison. NOBC

Those who have chosen to pass the night. Violent Storm. Mark Strand. NYBP

Those who have laid the harp aside. To Wordsworth. Walter Savage Landor. OAEL-2

Those Who Lost Everything. David Diop, *French*. PBA, *tr. by* Langston Hughes

Those who love cats which do not even purr. Cats. Francis Scarfe. PeP

Those who love the most. Sara Teasdale. LW

Those who loved freedom. One Kind of Freedom Speaks. Erich Fried, *German*. AF, *tr. by* Georg Rapp

"Those who realize true wisdom." *Unknown*. EnlH *Fr.* The Bhagavad-Gita.

Those who speak know nothing. Lao Tzŭ. Po Chü-i, *Chinese*. ChiP, *tr. by* Arthur Waley

"Those who speak know nothing." The Philosophers: Lao-Tzu. Po Chü-i, *Chinese*. BLT, *tr. by* Arthur Waley

Those who the Godhead's soft Behests obey. Tibullus, *Latin*. OBCVT, *tr. by* James Grainger

Those Who Want Out. Denise Levertov. LoHo

Those who were never meant / to survive? (LL) Anchorage. Joy Harjo. NMM-2; UnSA

Those who widened the Panama Canal. Love Poem. Roque Dalton, *Spanish*. AF, *tr. by* Richard Schaaf

Those who would not accept went past. Natalya Krandievskaya, *Russian*. TCRP, *tr. by* Lubov Yakovleva

Those Who Wrestle with the Angel for Us. Brigit Pegeen Kelly. NAmP90

Those Winter Sundays. Robert Earl Hayden. APAD; ChAP; ColAP; GEA; HAP; HCAP; ISC; InPK-6; LCAP-2; MoP; NIP-4; NoAM; NoP-4; PiM; PoBA; PoPoPo; Poetr; RaBo; SAGP; SSLK; SoSe-8; TFi; UnPo; WeW-3

Those with experience look for a special kind. Going for Peaches, Fredericksburg, Texas. Naomi Shihab Nye. MT

Those years, I was a green-youthed wanderer. Arriving in Lo-yang Again. Shao Yung, *Chinese*. CoBCP, *tr. by* Burton Watson

Thou art all fair, my love; there is no spot in thee. (LL) Behold, thou art fair. Bible, O.T. OxDM; TrJP

Thou art avenged, my first-born, sleep in peace! (LL) Yussouf. James Russell Lowell. BLPA; BoTP; FaBoBe

Thou art gone to thine island home. To My Wife. John Willis Menard. AAP

Thou art indeed just, Lord, if I contend. Gerard Manley Hopkins. APAD; AWP; CMoP; EBEV; EBVV; GTBS-P; HAP; HoPM; InPK-6; LiTM; MoBrPo; NAEL-2; NOBE; NOBVV; NoAM; NoP-4; OAEL-2; PeECV; SCGP; TFi; TOF; UnPo

Thou art like night, oh sickness, deeply stilling. Thoughts During Sickness: II Sickness Like Night. Felicia Dorothea Hemans. Ro *Fr.* New Monthly Magazine, 43 329.

Thou art love's victim; and must die. Richard Crashaw. *Fr.* A Hymn to the Name and Hono[u]r of the Admirable Saint[e] T[h]eresa. NOBE; OBEV; PoEL-2

Thou art not dead, my Prote! thou art flown. To Prote. Simmias of Thebes, *Greek*. AWP, *tr. by* John Addington Symonds

Thou art not fair for all thy red and white. Thomas Campion. AAS; EnLoPo; GLoP

Thou art not near me, but I see Thine eyes. I Love Thee. Josephine D. Henderson Heard. CBWP-4

Thou art not, PENSHURST, built to envious show. To Penshurst. Ben Jonson. AWP; BeJo; CABP; NOSC; NoP-4; OAEL-1; PBRV; PoEL-2; SeCP; TFi

Thou art not so black[,] as my heart. A Jet Ring Sent. Donne. CBLP; OxBSP; PoEL-2

Thou Art, O God, the God of Might. Emily Swan Perkins. AH

Thou art, O God, the life and light. Thomas Moore. PWR

Thou art so fair, and young [*or* yong] withal [*or* withall]. Youth and Beauty. Aurelian Townshend. GBL; SeCP

Thou art the facts in ilka airt. A Stick-nest in Ygdrasil. "Hugh MacDiarmid." FaBoTC *Fr.* A Drunk Man Looks at the Thistle.

Thou Art the Sky. Rabindranath Tagore. OBMV *Fr.* Gitanjali.

Thou Art the Tree of Life. Edward Taylor. AH

Thou Art the Way. George Washington Doane. AH

Thou art the Way. "I Am the Way." Alice Thompson Meynell. NOBVV; OBMV; OxBSP

Thou art the worn memorial, Baker Street. (LL) The Metropolitan Railway. John Betjeman. EBEV; OxAEP-2; OxBTC

Thou art to all lost love the best. To the Willow-Tree. Robert Herrick. CaPo; OBEV; SCGP

Thou art too hard for me in Love. Love. George Herbert. PeECV

Thou art weary, weary, weary. A Witch's Chant. James Hogg. NOBRP

Thou as laborious, as thy master kind. Epistle to My Gardener. Nicolas Boileau-Despéaux. OBGa, *tr. by* John Ozell *Fr.* Epistle to My Gardener.

Thou, att whose feete I waste mie soule in sighes. To Mie Tirante. George Darley. Son

Thou barren waste; unprofitable strand. Winter in Lower Canada. Standish O'Grady. NOBC *Fr.* The Emigrant.

Thou bay-crowned living One that o'er the bay-crowned Dead art bowing. Felicia Hemans. Elizabeth Barrett Browning. VWP

Thou bearst the bottle, I the bag (oh Lord). The Bottle. Ralph Knevet. ChIV-2

Thou beauteous off-spring of a syre as fair. On a Sunbeam. Thomas Heyrick. NOSC

Thou Beautiful Sabbath. *Unknown, Yiddish.* TrJP, tr. by Isidore Myers

Thou bidest wall nor floor, Lord! (LL) The Hurricane. Hart Crane. CMoP; MoAmPo; OxBA; TrCP

Thou bid'st me come away. To Death. Robert Herrick. BeJo

Thou bleedest, my poor Heart! and thy distress. On a Discovery Made Too Late. Coleridge. GSo; Son *Fr.* Effusions.

Thou blind man's mark, thou fool's self-chosen snare, *Wr. considered Sonnet CIX of* Astrophil and Stella. Sir Philip Sidney. HeIP-4; ImPo; NAEL-1; NOBE; SCGP; SiPS; Son

Thou blossom bright with autumn dew. To the Fringed Gentian. William Cullen Bryant. APN-1; AWP; FaBoBe; PAR; PoLF; TAP

Thou, born to sip the lake or spring. On a Honey Bee [*or* To a Honey Bee]. Philip Freneau. TAP

Thou break'st all thy girdles, and break'st forth a god. (LL) Hymn to Comus. Ben Jonson. NOSC; OBCoV; SCGP

Thou brimming river, full, how full. Detroit River. Constance Fenimore Woolson. APN-2

Thou call'st me madman, but I call thee blockhead. (LL) To Flaxman. William Blake. FaBoEE; OxBoLi

Thou canst not die whilst any zeal abound. Samuel Daniel. NoSic; Son *Fr.* To Delia.

Thou child of Night and Silence, balmy Sleep. Sonnet 13. Anna Seward. CPO

Thou comest! all is said without a word. Sonnet. Elizabeth Barrett Browning. BWW *Fr.* Sonnets from the Portuguese.

Thou comest, Autumn, heralded by the rain. Autumn. Henry Wadsworth Longfellow. APN-1

Thou comest, much wept for: such a breeze. Tennyson. EBVV; PeECV *Fr.* In Memoriam A. H. H.

Thou cursed cock, with thy perpetual noise. On a Cock at Rochester. Sir Charles Sedley. FaBoEE; NOSC; OBCoV

Thou daughter of the royal line. The Ninth Canticle. George Wither. ChIV-1

Thou dear and mystic semblance. Lines to the Blessed Sacrament. *Unknown, Irish.* TIRV, tr. by Jeremiah J. Callanan

Thou didst delight mine eyes. Robert Bridges. MoBrPo

Thou dost loth me,—I love thee, though cause of my death. (LL) The Green Willow. *Unknown.* EBEvV; SCGP

Thou dost not heed my lay. (LL) A Mother to Her Waking Infant. Joanna Baillie. CABP; NoP-4

Thou dravest love from thee, who dravest Me. (LL) The Hound of Heaven. Francis Thompson. CABP; ChIV-2; EBEvV; EnVR; ImPo; LiTM; MoBrPo; NAEL-2; OBMV; PoEL-5; TFi

Thou dread'st and hop'st thou know'st not what. (LL) Adriani Morientis ad Animam Suam. Emperor Hadrian, *Latin.* OBCVT; OBVE; OxBSP, tr. by Matthew Prior

Thou, Earth, calm empire of a happy soul. Shelley. PeECV *Fr.* Prometheus Unbound. NOBRP; OAEL-2

Thou fair-hair'd [*or* fair-haired] angel of the evening. To the Evening Star. William Blake. CH; NAEL-2; NOEC; OAEL-2; PoE; PoLF; TFi

Thou first and worst disturber of man's rest. (LL) On a Cock at Rochester. Sir Charles Sedley. FaBoEE; NOSC; OBCoV

Thou first of human feelings, social love! London. Charles Lloyd. Ro *Fr.* Blank Verse by Charles Lloyd and Charles Lamb.

Thou flimsy, showy, melancholy weed. (LL) To the Poppy. Anna Seward. ECWP; WoRP

Thou fool profane, be silent! Epigram II. *Unknown. Fr.* Duel with Verses over a Great Man. TrJP

Thou gav'st me leave to kiss. Chop-Cherry. Robert Herrick. CavPo; EnLoPo; GLoP

Thou glorious mirror, where the Almighty's form. Byron. OxBoS *Fr.* The Ocean. PoEL-4 *Fr.* Childe Harold's Pilgrimage.

Thou Grace Divine, Encircling All. Eliza Scudder. AH

Thou Great God. *Unknown, Xhosa.* PBA, tr. by A. C. Jordan

Thou green and blooming, cool and shaded hill. The Heart on the Hill. Petrarch. AWP *Fr.* Sonnets to Laura.

Thou grimmest far o grusome tykes. To a Hedgehog. Samuel Thompson. BIrV

Thou Guide to doubt, be silent evermore. Epigram I. *Unknown. Fr.* Duel with Verses over a Great Man. TrJP

Thou hadst all passion's splendour. Emily Brontë: Du hast Diamanten. Robert Bridges. EPCY

Thou happy, happy elf! A Parental Ode to My Son, Aged Three Years and Five Months. Thomas Hood. OBCoV; PoLF

Thou has come from the old city. The Old City. Ruth Manning-Sanders. CH

Thou Has Wounded the Spirit That Loved Thee. Mrs. David Porter. BLPA

Thou hast a charmed cup, O Fame! Woman and Fame. Felicia Dorothea Hemans. VWP

Thou hast a sister by the mother's side. Shakespeare. OxAEP-1 *Fr.* Antony and Cleopatra.

Thou hast all seasons for thine ow, oh! Death. (LL) The Hour of Death. Felicia Dorothea Hemans. NOBRP; OBNC

Thou hast been wrong'd, I think old age. Old Age. Caroline Clive. VWP

Thou hast brought him a pardon from good King John. (LL) King John and the Abbot of Canterbury. *Unknown.* BoTP; EnSB

Thou hast come safe to port. Lament for Hathimoda, Abbess of Gandesheim. *Unknown, Latin.* MLL, tr. by Helen Waddell

Thou Hast Diamonds. Heinrich Heine. TrJP, tr. by Emma Lazarus *Fr.* Homeward Bound.

Thou hast filled me a golden cup. To Christina Rossetti. Dora Greenwell. VWP

Thou hast Hera's eyes, thou hast Pallas' hands. Rhodope. Rufinus, *Greek.* OBCVT, tr. by Andrew Lang

Thou hast known them all before! (LL) To My Old Schoolmaster. John Greenleaf Whittier. ColAP; NOBA

Thou hast loved and thou hast suffer'd! To a Wandering Female Singer. Felicia Dorothea Hemans. VWP

Thou hast made me, and shall thy work[e] decay? From Holy Sonnets. Donne. EBEV; MeLP; NAEL-1; NOBE; NOCV; NOSC; OxAEP-1; PoEL-2; SCGP; SeCP; Son *Fr.* Holy Sonnets. ESCV *Fr.* Holy Sonnets.

("Thou hast made me, and shall thy work decay?") GSo; NoP-4

Thou hast not left the rough-barked tree to grow. I Was Sick and in Prison. Jones Very. ColAP; NOBA

Thou hast not rais'd, Ianthe, such desire. Walter Savage Landor. GBL *Fr.* Ianthe.

Thou hast thy calling to some palace-floor. Sonnet. Elizabeth Barrett Browning. OxAEP-2; Son; VWP *Fr.* Sonnets from the Portuguese.

Thou hearest the Nightingale begin the Song of. The Lark's Song. William Blake. NOBE; OBNC *Fr.* Milton.

Thou heaven-threat'ning Rock, gentler then she! Echo to a Rock. Edward Herbert, 1st Baron Herbert of Cherbury. PoEL-2

Thou heavenly quivering beneath the deathlike above! To a Lark in War-Time. Franz Werfel, *German.* TrJP, tr. by Edith Abercrombie Snow

Thou hidden love of God, whose height. Hymn. John Wesley. ECEV; NOEC

Thou hide thy face? (LL) Speak. James Wright. HAP; NoP-4; TAP

Thou ill-formed offspring of my feeble brain. The Author to Her Book. Anne Bradstreet. APAD; AmPP; ColAP; InPK-6; NAAL-1; NAAL-3; NALW; NOBA; NoP-4; OxBA; PoE; Poetr; SCAP; TAP

Thou in the garden, I in paradise. (LL) To Amanda Walking in the Garden. N. Hookes. NOSC; OBGa

Thou inmost, ultimate. To the Body. Alice Thompson Meynell. PeVV

Thou king of terrors with thy gastly eyes. A Fig for Thee, Oh! Death. Edward Taylor. NAAL-1; NAAL-3

Thou king of wele and blisse. William Herebert. MiEL

Thou knowest my praise of nature most sincere. William Cowper. NAEL-1 *Fr.* The Sofa. *Fr.* The Task.

Thou knowest my years entire, my life. Walt Whitman. *Fr.* Prayer of Columbus. AmPP; NCAP

Thou knowest that toads and snakes and loathly worms. Shelley. PoE *Fr.* Prometheus Unbound. NOBRP; OAEL-2

Thou knowst I lov'd thee well. Martin Parker. PBRV *Fr.* Cupid's Wrongs Vindicated.

Thou know'st its use—it hides—no matter whom. (LL) Epitaph, An: "My name—my country—what are they to thee." Paulus Silentiarius, *Greek.* AWP, tr. by William Cowper

Thou know'st, my Julia, that it is thy turn. To Julia, the Flaminica Dialis, or Queen-Priest. Robert Herrick. CaPo

Thou large-brained woman and large-hearted man. To George Sand / A Desire. Elizabeth Barrett Browning. BoWoP; NAEL-2; NALW; VWP

Thou last great prophet of tautology. Dryden. *See* The Crown Prince of Dullness.

Thou leadest, O God! All's well with Thy troopers that follow. (LL) The Wild Ride. Louise Imogen Guiney. ColAP; RACG

Thou leanest to the shell of night. James Joyce. EBEV

Thou, little sandpiper, and I? (LL) The Sandpiper. Celia Laighton Thaxter. CTV; FaBoBe; OBCA; OxBChV; PWR

Thou Long Disowned, Reviled, Oppressed. Eliza Scudder. AH

Thou, Lord, Hast Been Our Sure Defense. John Hopkins. AH

Thou Lord of Hosts, Whose Guiding Hand. Octavius Brooks Frothingham. AH

Thou lovely and belovèd, thou my love. Mid-Rapture. D. G. Rossetti. FaBoBe *Fr.* The House of Life.

Thou Lovest Me. Josephine D. Henderson Heard. CBWP-4

Thou mastering me. The Wreck of the Deutschland. Gerard Manley Hopkins. CMoP; EnVR; FaBoMo; ImPo; LiTM; NOBE; NoAM; OBNC; OxAEP-2; PeECV; PoEL-5

Thou may'st love on through love's eternity. (LL) Sonnet: "If thou must love me, let it be for nought." Elizabeth Barrett Browning. BWW; CTC; GSo; HeIP-4; InPS-3; LW; OBEV; OBNC; OxAEP-2; PoToHe; SAGP; SoSe-8

Thou mighty gulf, insatiate cormorant. To Everlasting Oblivion. John Marston. NoSic; SCGP *Fr.* The Scourge of Villainy [*or* Villanie].

Thou mighty Mars, the god of soldiers brave. An Epitaph on Sir Philip Sidney. James I, King of England. Son

Thou monstrous gilt and rainbow-tinted thing. The New Organ. Josephine D. Henderson Heard. CBWP-4

Thou more than most sweet glove. The Glove. Ben Jonson. GBL *Fr.* Cynthia's Revels.

Thou must be true thyself. Be True [*or* Be True Thyself]. Horatius Bonar. CTV; FaBoBe; PWR

Thou need'st not flutter from thy half-built nest. The Robin. Jones Very. Son

Thou ne're wutt [*or* nere wilt] riddle, neighbour Jan [*or* John]. A Devonshire Song. William Strode. PoEL-2

Thou noblest monument of Albion's isle! Written at Stonehenge. Thomas, the Younger Warton. Son

Thou One in All, Thou All in One. Seth Curtis Beach. AH

Thou our health, our glory Thou. In Honour of the Holy Spirit. Hildebert, *Latin.* MLL, *tr. by* Helen Waddell

Thou, paw-paw-paw; thou, glurd; thou, spotted. Adam's Task. John Hollander. APo; NIP-4; NoP-4

Thou Pleiad of the lyric world. Adelina Patti. Adah Isaacs Menken. CBWP-1

Thou priest that art behind the screen. Ipsissimus. Eugene Lee-Hamilton. PeVV

Thou readest, but each lettered word can give. The Eye and Ear. Jones Very. APN-1

Thou retir'st to endless Rest. (LL) The Grasshopper. Abraham Cowley, *after the Greek of* Anacreon. AWP; BeJo; NOSC; OAEL-1; OBVE; OxAEP-1

Thou ridest to power, / And to endurance. (LL) Illusions. Ralph Waldo Emerson. APN-1

Thou saidst that I alone thy heart could move. Catullus. *See Carmina,* LXXII.

Thou sai'st I swore I lov'd thee best. The Variety. John Dancer. NOSC

Thou saist [*or* sayest] Love['s] dart. To Oenone. Robert Herrick. CaPo

Thou say'st [*or* sayest] my lines are hard. To My Ill Reader. Robert Herrick. CaPo

Thou say'st my lines are hard. To my ill Reader. Martial, *Latin.* OBCVT, *tr. by* Robert Herrick

Thou sculling me / Thiefth. (LL) Thorow. Susan Howe. APSN; PT

Thou Seemest Like a flower. Heinrich Heine. *See* Du bist wie eine Blume.

Thou seest me, Lucia, this year droop[e]. Crutches. Robert Herrick. CaPo

Thou shalt be judge how I do spend my time [*or* tyme]. (LL) Myn owne John poyntz sins ye delight to know. Sir Thomas Wyatt. AAS; NoSic; OBSV; OBVE; PoEL-1; SCGP; SiPS

Thou shalt die. Unknown, *Latin.* MLL, *tr. by* Helen Waddell

Thou shalt have one God only; who. The Latest Decalogue. Arthur Hugh Clough. CABP; ChIV-1; EBEV; EBVV; EBVVPR; EnVR; FaBoEE; GTBS-P; HAP; HoPM; NAEL-2; NOBE; NOBVV; NoP-4; OAEL-2; OBNC; OBSV; PBMP; PFE; PeECV; SCGP; TFi; WeW-3

Thou Shalt Not. Malka Heifetz-Tussman, *Yiddish.* AWP, *tr. by* Marcia Falk

Thou shalt not laugh in this leaf, Muse, nor they. Satire 5. Donne. OBSV *Fr.* Satires.

Thou shalt not laugh, thou shalt not romp. A Fleeting Passion. W. H. Davies. NSI

Thou shalt the mountain move; be strong in me. The Mountain. Jones Very. NCAP

Thou silent herald of Time's silent flight! To the Sun-Dial. John Quincy Adams. APN-1

Thou silver deity of secret night. Hymn to the Moon. Lady Mary Wortley Montagu. ECWP

Thou simple bird what mak'st thou here to play? Upon the Lark and the Fowler. John Bunyan. CH

Thou sleepest fast and I with woeful heart. Sir Thomas Wyatt. OxBSP

Thou sleepest where the lilies fade. Buried. Christina Rossetti. CBLP

Thou snowy farm[e] with thy five tenements! Elinda's [*or* Ellinda's] Glove. Richard Lovelace. CBLP; CaPo; NOSC

Thou sorrow, venom elfe. Upon a Spider Catching a Fly. Edward Taylor. AmPP; MeMAP; NOBA; OxBA; PeECV; PoEL-3; SCAP; TAP

Thou spark of life that wavest wings of gold. Ode to a Butterfly. Thomas Wentworth Higginson. FaBoBe

Thou still unravish'd bride of quietness. Keats. *See* Ode on a Grecian Urn.

Thou still unravished [*or* unravish'd] bride of quietness. Ode on a Grecian Urn. Keats. AWP; ClHu; EBEV; FaBoBe; HAP; HeIP-4; HoPM; ImPo; InPS-3; NAEL-2; NAWM-2; NIP-4; NOBE; NOBRP; OAEL-2; OBEV; OBNC; PBMP; PoE; PoEL-4; SCGP; TFi; TOF; UnPo

Thou strainest through the mountain fern. A Fragment. Robert Louis Stevenson. NOBVV

Thou stranger, which for Rome in Rome here seekest. Antiquitez de Rome. Joachim Du Bellay, *French.* NNPT, *tr. by* Edmund Spenser; OBVE *Fr.* Ruins of Rome.

Thou swear'st thou'lt drink no more; kind Heaven send. To Julius. Martial. FaBoEE, *tr. by* Sir Charles Sedley

Thou sweetly-smelling fresh red rose. Dialogue: Lover and Lady. Ciullo d'Alcamo, *Italian.* AWP, *tr. by* D. G. Rossetti

Thou that art by Fates degree. New Canaans Genius; Epilogus. Thomas Morton. SCAP

Thou that art wise, let wisdom minister. Sonnet: He Craves Interpreting of a Dream of His. Dante da Maiano, *Italian.* AWP, *tr. by* D. G. Rossetti

Thou that from the heavens art. Goethe. AWP *Fr.* Wanderer's Night-Songs.

Thou that loved once now loves no more. The Answer. Sir Robert Ayton. NOSC

Thou thing of years departed! The Image in Lava. Felicia Dorothea Hemans. CABP; NOBRP; VWP

Thou, to whom my name bears witness. Be Not Silent. David ben Meshullam, *Hebrew.* TrJP

Thou, to whom the World unknown. Ode to Fear. William Collins. NOEC; SCGP

Thou, too, sail on, O Ship of State! The Ship of State. Henry Wadsworth Longfellow. FaBoBe; PWR *Fr.* The Building of the Ship

Thou tryant, whom I will not name. Wedlock; a Satire. Hetty Wright. NOEC

Thou two-faced year, Mother of Change and Fate. 1492. Emma Lazarus. APN-2; PAR; WPE

Thou tyrant, whom I will not name. Wedlock, a Satire. Mehetabel Wright. ECWP

Thou visor'd, vast, unspeakable show and lesson! (LL) Broadway. Walt Whitman. NAAL-1; NAAL-3

Thou wast all that [*or* that all] to me, love. To One in Paradise. Edgar Allan Poe. AmPP; BoLoP; OBEV; OxBA; PoLF; TAP

Thou water turn'st to Wine (faire friend of Life). To Our Lord, upon the Water Made Wine. Richard Crashaw. GeHe

Thou Were My Ain Thing, An. Allan Ramsay. OxAEP-1

Thou wert the morning star among the living. To Stella. Plato, *Greek.* OBCVT, *tr. by* Shelley; EnLoPo; FaBoEE; OBVE, *tr. by* Shelley

Thou which art I, ('tis nothing to be so[e]). The Storm[e]. Donne. NoSic; OxBoS

Thou who art clothed in silk, who drawest on. Man Is a Weaver. Moses ibn Ezra, *Hebrew.* TrJP, *tr. by* Emma Lazarus

Thou who art thrown at by the great (shepherd) boys. The Zebra. *Unknown, Hottentot.* PeSAV, *tr. by* W. H. I. Bleek

Thou Who Createdst Everything. *Unknown, Middle English.* NOCV, *tr. by* Donald Davie

Thou who descendest river by river. *Unknown. See* Giraffe.

Thou who didst hang upon a barren tree. Long Barren. Christina Rossetti. PBWP; TrCP

Thou who dost all my worldly thoughts employ. Verses Written on Her Death-Bed at Bath to Her Husband in London. Mary Monk. ECWP; LW

Thou who hast slept all night upon the storm. To the Man-of-War Bird. Walt Whitman. APN-1; APo; AmPP; FaBoBe

Thou who makest thy escape from the tumult! *Unknown. See* Hyena.

Thou who wilt not love, do[e] this. Upon Some Women. Robert Herrick. BeJo; CaPo

Thou, who with all the poet's genuine rage. Richard Polwhele. NOBRP *Fr.* The Unsex'd Females.

Thou, who with firm, free step, as life arose. Lady Eleanor Butler. Anna Seward. CPO

Thou, who wouldst wear the name. The Poet. William Cullen Bryant. NAAL-1; NAAL-3; NCAP; TAP

Thou! whom Prosperity has always led. To a Querulous Acquaintance. Charlotte Smith. BWW

Thou, Whom rich and poor adore. An Offer. Arthur Guiterman. TrJP

Thou, whom the former precepts have. Superliminare. George Herbert. ESCV; NOSC; SeCP

Thou whose chaste song simplicity inspires. To Mrs. Smith, Occasioned by the First of Her Sonnets. William Hayley. Son

Thou, whose diviner soul hath caused [or caus'd] thee now. To Mr. Tilman after He Had Taken Orders. Donne. EBEV

Thou, whose exterior semblance doth belie. Wordsworth. Fr. Ode: Intimations of Immortality [from Recollections of Early Childhood]. AWP; FHYEP; HAP; HeIP-4; NOBE; NOBRP; OAEL-2; OBEV; OBNC; PBMP; PoE; PoEL-4

Thou! whose impassion'd face. The Picture of Sappho. Caroline Elizabeth Norton. VWP

Thou, whose sad heart, and weeping head lyes low. Easter-Day. Henry Vaughan. ESCV; PeECV

Thou whose spell can raise the dead. Saul. Byron. KSG

Thou, whose sweet youth and early hopes enhance. Perirrhanterium. George Herbert. ESCV

Thou, whose sweet youth and early hopes inhance. The Church-Porch. George Herbert. ESCV

"Thou wilt forget me." "Love has no such word." Spring and Autumn. William James Linton. EBVV

Thou wilt remember. Thou art not more dear. Robert Browning. OAEL-2 Fr. Pauline, mine own, bend o'er me—thy soft breast.

Thou with thy Savior art in endless bliss. (LL) In Memory of My Dear Grandchild Anne Bradstreet Who Deceased June 20, 1669, Being Three Years and Seven Months Old. Anne Bradstreet. BoWoP; NAAL-1; NAAL-3; TrCP

Thou witles wight, what meanes this mad intent. To One that Painted Eccho. Ausonius, Latin. OBCVT, tr. by George Turberville

Thou wommon boute fere. William Herebert. MiEL

Thou worshipest the shadow upon earth. (LL) A Sonnet to Heavenly Beauty. Joachim Du Bellay, French. AWP; CTC, tr. by Andrew Lang

Thou wouldst not part thy spoil. To "A Certain Rich Man." Alice Thompson Meynell. ChIV-2

Thou wretched man, whom I discover, born. Peace Discovers the Poet. George Chapman. NOSC Fr. Euthymiae Raptus; or, The Teares of Peace.

Thou wringest, with thy invisible hand, the foam. The Wind. Thomas Holley Chivers. APN-1

Thou youngest virgin-daughter of the skies. To the Pious Memory of the Accomplished [or Accomplisht] Young Lady, Mrs. Anne Killigrew, [Excellent in the Two Sister-Arts of Poesie and Painting]. Dryden. CABP; NAEL-1; OAEL-1; OBEV; PoEL-3

Thou, Zion, old and suffering. David Levi. TrJP, tr. by Mary A. Craig Fr. The Bible.

Though. (LL) Cæsura. John Ashbery. ChIV-1

Though a seeker since my birth. A Garland of Precepts. Phyllis McGinley. NBLV

Though all men should desert you. In a Late Hour. James McAuley. BMAP

Though all of you consort now underground. (LL) In Memoriam Francis Ledwidge. Seamus Heaney. CIP-2; NoAM

Though All the Fates Should Prove Unkind. Henry David Thoreau. HAP

Though all the force to hold the parts together. Being Human. Ruth Stone. IMW

Though all the lower world should ransacked be. Chapter IV. Elizabeth Singer Rowe. PEW

Though / Already / Perhaps / However. One Size Fits All: a Critical Essay. David Lehman. OBCoV

Though Amaryllis Dance in Green. Unknown. NAEL-1

Though, asked, I know not how she would resist. (LL) Two Rural Sisters. Charles Cotton. BoLoP; EnLoPo

Though at night there is the smell of morning. (LL) Neither Here nor There. William Robert Rodgers. ImPo; LiTM; MoBrPo

Though authors are a dreadful clan. I Missed His Book, but I Read His Name. John Updike. NoP-4; OBAL

Though aware of our rank and alert to obey orders. Ode: To My Pupils. W. H. Auden. MoBrPo

Though beauty be the mark of praise. An Elegy. Ben Jonson. BeJo; NoP-4; OBEV

Though buds still speak in hints. Field-Glasses. Andrew Young. GTBS-P; RB

Though by a sodaine and unfeard surprise. Under Mr. Hales Picture. Anne King. KTR

Though clasp'd and cradled in his nurse's arms. William Cowper. PoEL-3 Fr. Hope.

Though clerical errors are fun. Limerick. Unknown. PeLi

Though Clock, / To tell how night drawes hence, I've none. His Grange, or Private Wealth. Robert Herrick. BeJo; CaPo

Though countless as the Grains of Sand. Boethius. OBVE, tr. by Samuel Johnson Fr. Consolation of Philosophy, The ("De Consolacione Philosophie").

Though days do gain upon the night. The Vierzide Chairs. William Barnes. NOBVV

Though dusty wits dare scorn astrology. Sonnet 26. Sir Philip Sidney. OAEL-1; Son Fr. Astrophil and Stella. AAS; SiPS

Though Earth has full many a beautiful spot. The Land Which No Mortal May Know. Bernard Barton. PWR

Though every thing we see or hear may raise. My Observation at Sea. Mildmay Fane, 2d Earl of Westmorland. BeJo

Though faction's scorn at first did shun. John Clare. EPCY Fr. To John Keats, from His Honored Friend, William Davenant.

Though Fatherland Be Vast. Allen Eastman Cross. AH

Though forts of adamant shall ring you round. The Enemy in the Fortress. Marbod of Rennes, Latin. MLL, tr. by Helen Waddell

Though frost and snow locked [or lock'd] from mine eyes. To Saxham. Thomas Carew. BeJo

Though good things answer many good intents. Crosses. Robert Herrick. CaPo

Though he lives in the same town. What She Said. Pālaipāṭiya Peruṅkaṭuṅkō, Tamil. PLW, tr. by A. K. Ramanujan

Though he that ever kind and true. Verses Written in 1872. Robert Louis Stevenson. BLPA

Though her lips are redder than the raspberries. (LL) Berry Picking. Irving Layton. NoP-4

Though her mother told her / Not to go a-bathing. Leda and the Swan. Oliver St. John Gogarty. EBNV; HAP

Though here no towering mountain-steep. Our Island Home. Charles Timothy Brooks. APN-1

Though his plan, when he gave her a buzz. Limerick. Unknown. PeLi

Though humid summer's unfit for excursions. Unknown. Fr. Summer. SuSp, tr. by Michael E. Workman Fr. Tzu-yeh Songs of the Four Seasons.

Though I am dark. Unknown, Spanish. BoWoP, tr. by Willis Barnstone

Though I am Laila of the Persian romance. Princess Zeb-un-Nissa, Persian. BoWoP, tr. by Willis Barnstone

Though I am well-clothed, well-booted, and well-fed. Pugilist. Anna Wickham. WPN

Though I am young, and cannot tell. Death and Love. Ben Jonson. BeJo; NAEL-1; NOBE; NoP-4; PoEL-2; SeCP Fr. The Sad Shepherd.

Though I be strange, sweet friend, be thou not so. A Court Lady Addresses Her Lover. Edward, 17th Earl of Oxford De Vere. NoSic

Though I get home how late, how late! The Return. Emily Dickinson. MoAmPo

Though I had [or have] been at the doors [or doores] of death. To Sir W. A. William Drummond, of Hawthornden. PoEL-2

Though I look like you. Hand Me Down Blues. Calvin Forbes. GT

Though I must live here, and by force. To My Mistress[e] in My Absence. Thomas Carew. CaPo; NOSC

Though I regarded not. Henry Howard, Earl of Surrey. AAS; SiPS

Though I sang in my chains like the sea. (LL) Fern Hill. Dylan Thomas. CABP; CMoP; ChAP; ClHu; GEA; GTBS-P; HAP; HeIP-4; ImPo; InPK-6; InPS-3; LiTM; MoBrPo; MoP; NAEL-2; NIP-4; NOBE; NTP; NoAM; NoP-4; OAEL-2; OBWVE; OxBTC; PoE; PoLF; PoPoPo; PoRA; Poetr; SAGP; SoSe-8; TFi; TRP; TwCP

Though I should be maligned by those. Prayer for Strength. Margaret E. Bruner. PoToHe

Though I Should Seek. Henry Ustic Onderdonk. AH

Though I speak in the tongues of men or of angels: if I have no love, I am. Paul of Tarsus. ITG, tr. by Stephen Mitchell Fr. The First Letter to the Corinthians.

Though I speak with the tongues of men and angels. The Greatest of These. Bible, N.T. OAEL-1; PBMP Fr. First Corinthians.

Though I Thy Mithridates Were. James Joyce. MoP; NoAM; Poetr

Though I with strange desire. Kisses Desired. William Drummond, of Hawthornden. EnLoPo

Though I would take comfort against sorrow. The Cry of the Daughter of My People. Bible, O.T. TrJP Fr. Jeremiah.

Though I'm in Kyoto. Basho, Japanese. EnlH, tr. by John Tarrant

Though in the body she her powers do show. (LL) The Soul and the Body. Sir John Davies. CTC; NOBE; PoEL-2

Though it be cold, hard, foul, from loving man / With[h]old thee. (LL) Sepulchre. George Herbert. ESCV; MiEL

Though it may look like (Write it!) like disaster. (LL) One Art. Elizabeth Bishop. APAD; DiPo; HAP; NAAL-2; NALW; NoAM; NoP-4; PoE; PoPoPo; SAGP; SoSe-8; VCAP

Though it were ten thousand mile! Robert Burns. See A Red, Red Rose.

Though it's only a sour revenge. Dan Pagis. See Autobiography.

Though it's true we were young girls when we met. For Jan, in Bar Maria. Carolyn Kizer. VGW

Though I've a Clever Head. Unknown. HAP

Though joy is better than sorrow, joy is not great. Joy. Robinson Jeffers. CMoP

Though knowledge must be got with pain. For Scholars and Pupils. George Wither. OxBChV

Though leaves are many, the root is one. The Coming of Wisdom with Time. W. B. Yeats. FaBoEE; SoSe-8

Though loath to grieve. Ode, Inscribed to W. H. Channing. Ralph Waldo Emerson. APN-1; AmPP; ColAP; HAP; MeMAP; NAAL-1; NAAL-3; NCAP; NOBA; NoP-4; OxBA; PAR; TAP

Though logic-choppers rule the town. Tom O'Roughley. W. B. Yeats. CMoP

Though loves languish and sour. Prospect. Louis MacNeice. IIP

Though love's my daily and my nightly theme. To Emma, Extempore; Hyaena, off Gambia, June 4, 1779. Edward Thompson. NOEC

Though marriage by some folks. My Three Wives. Unknown, after Etienne Pasquier. FaBoEE

Though Mine Eye Sleep Not. Unknown. TrJP, tr. by Theodor H. Gaster Fr. The Dead Sea Scrolls.

Though most of the crewmen are whites. On Board Starship Enterprise. Unknown. PeLi

Though much a little map unfolds, more still. The River Compared to an Oratorical Sentence. Luis de Góngora y Argote. Fr. The First Solitude. OBVE, tr. by Edward Meryon Wilson

Though my eyes are dim'. (LL) An Old Song Ended. D. G. Rossetti. BoLoP; EBVV

Though My Thoughts. Francis Daniel Pastorius, German. AH, tr. by Sheema Z. Buehne

Though my wanderings are many. Suibne Geilt. NOIV

Though naked trees seem dead to sight. Hopeless Desire Soon Withers and Dies. "A. W." NoSic

Though naughty flesh will multiply. No Mean City. Patrick MacDonogh. BIrV; OxBSP

Though never claimed by us within my hearing. (LL) The Swimmers. Allen Tate. FuPo; InPS-3; MoAMPo; NOBA; NoAM

Though never in the wards of the hospital for / Disabled servicemen at Erskine. Warriors. Douglas Dunn. OxBC

Though no blossoms cluster. Mrs. Mary Furman Weston Byrd. Mary Weston Fordham. CBWP-2

Though now you are bereft and ways seem black. For One Lately Bereft. Margaret E. Bruner. PoToHe

Though of white marble and dressed straight. Crinagoras, Greek. GrAn, tr. by Alistair Elliot

Though on the day your hard blue eyes met mine. Heritage. Dorothea MacKellar. NOBAu

Though prejudice perhaps my mind befogs. I Think I Know No Finer Things than Dogs. Hally Carrington Brent. BLPA

Though regions far [or farr] divided. Aurelian Townshend. NOSC; PoEL-2

Though riders be thrown in black disgrace. Unknown, Irish. BIrV, tr. by Douglas Hyde

Though set like dough, they shall be drawn like bread. (LL) In Christ Church, Bristol, on Thomas Turner, Twice Master of the Company of Bakers. Francis, Lord Jeffrey Jeffrey. FaBoEE; NBLV; OxBoLi

Though seven times, or seventy times seven. The Women of Jericho. Phyllis McGinley. ChIV-1; KSG

Though Shakespeare asks us, "What's in a name?" Her Christening. Thomas Hood. NOBVV Fr. Miss Kilmansegg and Her Precious Leg.

Though she's the girl, I am the one who's shy. Amaru. EP, tr. by John Brough

Though short her strain nor sung with mighty boast. Erinna. Antipater of Sidon, Greek. AWP, tr. by A. J. Butler

Though silent your tongue, you can speak with your pen. (LL) How to Write a Letter. Elizabeth Turner. ACTP; OxBChV

Though Sir James (God's-a-Formula) Jeans. Limerick. R. J. P. Hewison. PeLi

Though skilled in Latin and in Greek. To a New England Poet. Philip Freneau. NAAL-1; NAAL-3

Though Tennyson, the poet king. James Madison Bell. AAP; CBCWP Fr. A Poem Entitled the Day and the War.

Though that was not what Berkeley meant at all. (LL) The Fountain. Donald Davie. GTBS-P; NoP-4; OxBTC

Though the cage fret kings, you may make free with it. (LL) The Sparrow in the Zoo. Howard Nemerov. MoP; NIP-4

Though the Clerk of the Weather insist. Pebbles. Herman Melville. NCAP

Though the cunning of the Indian and the Zulu's thirst for blood. Claflin's Alumni. Lizelia Augusta Jenkins Moorer. CBWP-3

Though the Earth Be Removed. Bible, O.T. See Psalm 46.

Though the evening comes with slow steps. The Bird. Rabindranath Tagore. SAGP

Though the Faith accommodate but Two——. Emily Dickinson. See The Sweetest Heresy received.

Though the great song return no more. The Nineteenth Century and After. W. B. Yeats. FaBoEE

Though the limerick can not be deaded. Limerick. Unknown. PeLi

Though the little clouds ran southward still, the quiet autumnal. Autumn Evening. Robinson Jeffers. ChAP

Though the mills of God grind slowly, yet they grind exceeding small. Retribution. Friedrich von Logau, German. BLPA; PoToHe, tr. by Longfellow

Though the mountain's the same warm-tinted ivory. Presence. Denise Levertov. PaTW

Though the New Teacher Is a Trifle Odd. Richard Moore. Son Fr. Word from the Hills.

Though the purity. Unknown, Japanese. OHPJ, tr. by Kenneth Rexroth

Though the road turn at last. Prisoners. Denise Levertov. NoAM; VCAP

Though the unseen may vanish, though insight fails. A Plain Song for Comadre. Richard Wilbur. NoP-4

Though the war has been over for years and nothing is / dropping out. Again. Thomas Brush. CDa

Though the willows bent down to shelter us where we played. Doll. Josephine Miles. NALW

Though the world fills with sorrow and rage. Original Mind. Nancy Paddock. LoHo

Though the world has slipped and gone. Lullaby. Dame Edith Sitwell. CMoP; LiTM; NALW

Though then I smile, and speake no words at all. (LL) To His Lovely Mistresses. Robert Herrick. CTC; CaPo; SeCP

Though there are distances between us. Desert Warfare. Michael Longley. CIP-2

Though there are wild dogs. Orpheus and Eurydice. Geoffrey Hill. TRP

Though this might take me a little time. (LL) The More Loving One. W. H. Auden. HoPM; TOF

Though this the [or thy] port and I thy servant true. Sir Thomas Wyatt. SiPS

Though thou hast passed thy summer standing, stay. Epithalamion: or, a Song. Ben Jonson. BeJo

Though thou, indeed, hast quite forgotten ruth. Ballata: Of a Continual Death in Love. Guido Cavalcanti, Italian. AWP, tr. by D. G. Rossetti

Though thou well dost wish me ill. Na Audiart. Ezra Pound. MeMAP

Though thou'rt like Judas—an apostate black. On Mackintosh. Charles Lamb. Ro Fr. Letter from Charles Lamb to Thomas Manning, 22 August 1801.

Though thousands traipse round Wordsworth's Lakeland shrine. Remains. Tony Harrison. FaBoVe

"Though three men dwell on Flannan Isle." Flannan Isle. Wilfrid Wilson Gibson. CH; PoRA

Though to good breeding she made no pretence. On a Gentleman Marrying His Cook. Colin Ellis. FaBoEE

Though to strangers' approach. Paired Lives. William Robert Rodgers. CIP-2; IIP

Though to think / Rejoiceth me. Love Song. Margot Ruddock. OBMV

Though to your life apparent stain attach. Robert Malise Bowyer Nichols. Fr. Sonnets to Aurelia. OBMV

Though Truth and Falsehood be. Donne. See Satire 3.

Though truths in manhood darkly join. Tennyson. OAEL-2 Fr. In Memoriam A. H. H.

Though 'twere ten thousand mile. Robert Burns. See A Red, Red Rose.

Though Virtue be the same when low she stands. To The Lady Lucie, Countesse of Bedford. Samuel Daniel. PBRV

Though we lived in the same lane. Answering Li Ying Who Showed Me His Poems about Summer Fishing. Yü Hsüan-chi, Chinese. BoWoP, tr. by Geoffrey Waters

Though we thought it, Doña Carolina did not die. A Dream of Husbands. Alberto A. Ríos. NoAM

Though when I lov'd thee thou wert fair. The Deposition. Thomas Stanley. CBLP

Though with no lily [or Lilie], stay with me! (LL) Cock-crowing. Henry Vaughan. ESCV; GeHe; OAEL-1; PBRV

Though ye destroy their dust. Lydia Huntley Sigourney. See Indian Names.

Though Ye Suppose. John Skelton. OxBSP

Though you are a continent and two seasons away. Cape Coast Castle Revisited. Jo Ann Hall-Evans. BlSi

Though you are sedentary always, though. Crinagoras, Greek. GrAn, tr. by Alistair Elliot

Though you are absent here, I needs must say. The Spring. Abraham Cowley. BeJo; HAP; MeLP; OxAEP-1 Fr. The Mistress.

Though you can tell me. Herman von Lingg, Japanese. OHPJ, tr. by Kenneth Rexroth

Though you do anything, he thinks no ill. (LL) Sonnet 57. Shakespeare. GTBS-P; HAP; NoSic; OBEV; PoEL-2

Though you have never possessed me. Three Moments in Paris. Mina Loy. PFTM

Though you in your hermitage. To My Father Norman Alone in the Blue Mountains. Jack Lindsay. NOBAu

Though my resolution still accuse. Epistle to Clemena, Occasioned by an Argument She Had Maintained Against the Author. Elizabeth Thomas. ECWP

Though you rule the dead, under the earth, who never smile. Julianus of Egypt, *Greek*. GrAn, *tr. by* W. S. Merwin

Though you'll forgive, I think, my sweet. Postscript to a Pettiness. Arthur Seymour John Tessimond. OxBSP

Though your dreams may seem normal and right. Limerick. J. C. B. Date. PeLi

Though your prerogative is to disdain. To His Coy Mistress. Peter Scupham. BXAP

Though your strangenesse frets my hart. Thomas Campion. AAS

Thought. Fazil Hüsnü Daglarca. CRP

Thought. Ralph Waldo Emerson. AmPP

Thought, A. Linda Hogan. CrSp

Thought, A. Mikhail Yuryevich Lermontov, *Russian*. AWP, *tr. by* Max Eastman

Thought, The. William Brighty Rands. OBEV

Thought, A. Abram Joseph Ryan. PWR

Thought, A. Robert Louis Stevenson. CTV

Thought about holy skirts—to tune of *"Wheels are growing on rose-"*. Holy Skirts. Else Von Freytag-Loringhoven. PFTM

Thought at Walden, A. Henrietta Cordelia Ray. CBWP-3

Thought beneath so slight a film, The. Emily Dickinson. AmPP; OxBA

Thought bounded / rigid edges glued. Crossing. Diane Ward. FTOS

Thought clambers up. William Carlos Williams. MeMAP *Fr.* Paterson.

Thought Eternal, The. Goethe, *German*. AWP, *tr. by* Ludwig Lewisohn

Thought flashed 'cross a kindly mind, A. A Kindly Deed. Priscilla Jane Thompson. CBWP-2

Thought-Fox, The. Ted Hughes. FaBoMo; HeIP-4; InPS-3; MoP; NTP; NYBP; NoAM; NoP-4; Poetr; SCV

Thought from Propertius, A. W. B. Yeats. OAEL-2; OxBSP

Thought from Ruddigore, A. Sir William Schwenck Gilbert. OBCoV *Fr.* Ruddigore.

Thought I heard the wind. Spring at Fort Okanogan. Ramona Wilson. VoR

Thought i'd / never grow old. Michael McClintock. HA

Thought in a Garden, A. John Hughes. ECEV

Thought in Time, A. Robert Silliman Hillyer. NYBP

Thought is deeper than all speech. Gnosis. Christopher Pearse Cranch. APN-1; ColAP; PAR

Thought is false happiness: the idea. Crude Foyer. Wallace Stevens. LiTM; MeMAP

Thought must length it in the heart. Samuel Daniel. *See* Shadows.

Thought must length it in the heart. (LL) Shadows. Samuel Daniel. NoP-4

Thought o' Mary Morison, The. (LL) Mary Morison. Robert Burns. AWP; GTBS-P; OBEV; OxBS

Thought[s] of a Briton on the Subjugation of Switzerland. Wordsworth. PBMP; UV

(England and Switzerland 1802.) GTBS-P

Thought of Death, A. Thomas Flatman. NOSC

Thought of Lake Ontario, A. Henrietta Cordelia Ray. CBWP-3

Thought of what America would be like, The. Cantico del Sole. Ezra Pound. OBAL

Thought of writing came to me today, The. W. H. Auden. NOBL *Fr.* Letter to Lord Byron.

Thought on Human Life, A. *Unknown*. OxBSP

Thought on June 26. Raymond Mazisi Kunene. PBMAP

Thought rattles along the empty railings. Respectable People. Austin Clarke. CMoP

Thought Suggested by the New Year, A. Thomas Campbell. *See* The River of Life.

Thought was / & though it had been. *Unknown*. *Fr.* Tepehua Thought-Songs. STP, *tr. by* Charles Boilès

Thought went up my mind today, A. Emily Dickinson. AmPP

Thought, with good cause thou lik'st so well the night. Sonnet 96. Sir Philip Sidney. *Fr.* Astrophil and Stella. AAS; SiPS

Thought you killed me. Letter. William Daniel Ehrhart. CDa

Thoughtful mind, when it sees a, A. The American Flag. Henry Ward Beecher. CTV

Thoughtless wits shall frequent forfeits pay, The. John Gay. ECEV *Fr.* Trivia; or, The Art of Walking the Streets of London.

Thoughts. Michael Benedikt. CoAmPo; SAGP

Thoughts. Maggie Pogue Johnson. CBWP-4

Thoughts about the Person from Porlock. Stevie Smith. NAEL-2; NoAM; NoP-4

Thoughts after Ruskin. Elma Mitchell. FaBoTC; FaBoWP

Thoughts and Recollections. Duoduo, *Chinese*.

When the People Stand Up out of the Hard Cheese. AF, *tr. by* Gregory Lee *and* John Cayley

Thoughts are broken in my memory, The. Dante. AWP *Fr.* La Vita Nuova.

Thoughts Before Dawn. John Balaban. CDa

Thoughts During an Air Raid. Stephen Spender. MoBrPo

Thoughts During Sickness: II. Sickness Like Night. Felicia Dorothea Hemans. Ro *Fr.* New Monthly Magazine, 43 329.

Thought's End. Léonie Adams. MoAmPo

Thoughts for a Cold Day. *Unknown*. BoTP

Thought's [*or* Wit's] Forge and Furnace, Mangle-Press [*or* fire-blast, meaning's press] and Screw. (LL) On Donne's Poetry. Coleridge. EPCY; NAEL-2; OAEL-2; UV

Thoughts from Sophocles. Sophocles, *Greek*. OBCVT, *tr. by* Thomas Hardy

Thoughts in a Garden. Andrew Marvell. *See* The Garden.

Thoughts in Early Autumn: Thirty Rhymes Sent to Lu-wang. P'i Jih-hsiu, *Chinese*. SuSp, *tr. by* Irving Y. Lo

Thoughts in Exile. Su Tung-p'o, *Chinese*. OHPC, *tr. by* Kenneth Rexroth

Thoughts in the Cold. Li Shang-yin, *Chinese*. CoBCP, *tr. by* Burton Watson

Thoughts of a dry brain in a dry season. (LL) Gerontion. T. S. Eliot. AmPP; CMoP; ColAP; EBEV; GTBS-P; HAP; ImPo; InPS-3; LiTM; MoP; NAAL-2; NOBA; NoAM; OAEL-2; OxAEP-2; OxBA; TAP; TFi

Thoughts of a Young Girl. John Ashbery. CoAmPo; MoLi; TAP; VGW

Thoughts of Chairman Mao. David Young. AmPA

Thoughts of Jack Kerouac—& Other Things. Peter Olds. PeNZ

Thoughts of Phena. Thomas Hardy. EBVV; NOBVV; NoP-4; OxBTC

Thoughts on Capital Punishment. Rod McKuen. InPK-6; PFE

Thoughts on Historical Sites: Wang Chao-chün. Tu Fu, *Chinese*. SuSp, *tr. by* Irving Lo

Thoughts on my sick-bed. Dorothy Wordsworth. PEW; Ro

Thoughts on One's Head. William Meredith. HAP; VCAP

Thoughts on Pausing at a Cottage near the Paukataug River. Sarah Kemble Knight. SCAP

Thoughts on the First Day of Autumn, Sent to Su Tzu-mei. Ou-yang Hsiu, *Chinese*. SuSp, *tr. by* Irving Y. Lo

Thoughts on the Sight of the Moon. Sarah Kemble Knight. SCAP

Thoughts on the Works of Providence. Phillis Wheatley. ColAP; NAAL-1; NAAL-3

Thoughts on T'ien-chin Bridge. Shao Yung, *Chinese*. CoBCP, *tr. by* Burton Watson

Thoughts Several Be. Margaret Lucas Cavendish, Duchess of Newcastle. *Fr.* A Dialogue between Melancholy and Mirth. BWW

Thoughts South of the Yangtze. Yü Hu, *Chinese*. CoBCP, *tr. by* Burton Watson

Thoughts that burned and glowed within, The. (LL) The Fire of Drift-Wood. Henry Wadsworth Longfellow. APN-1; AmPP; MeMAP; NAAL-1; NAAL-3; NCAP; NOBA; OxBA; TAP

Thoughts that do often lie too deep for tears. (LL) Ode: Intimations of Immortality [from Recollections of Early Childhood]. Wordsworth. AWP; FHYEP; GTBS-P; HAP; HeIP-4; NOBE; NOBRP; NoP-4; OAEL-2; OBEV; OBNC; PBMP; PoE; PoEL-4; PoPoPo; Ro

Thoughts that tongue can tell no word of! (LL) The Aeolian Harp. Herman Melville. AmPP; NCAP

Thoughts While Reading. Chu Hsi, *Chinese*. OHPC, *tr. by* Kenneth Rexroth

Thoughts While Studying at Hanlin Academy Sent to My Colleagues at the Chi-hsien Academy. Li Po, *Chinese*. SuSp, *tr. by* Joseph J. Lee

Thou'lt fight, if any man call Thebe whore. To Sergius. Sir Charles Sedley. FaBoEE

Thou's welcome, Wean! Mischanter fa' me. A Poet's Welcome to His Love-Begotten Daughter [the First Instance that Entitled Him to the Venerable Appellation of Father]. Robert Burns. NOEC; OxBoLi; PoEL-4

Thousand, a thousand, a thousand. A. Flavius Vopiscus. OBCVT, *tr. by* Edgar Allan Poe *Fr.* Epimanes.

Thousand-and-First Ship. F. Scott Fitzgerald.

"There'd be an orchestra." AiP

("There was an orchestra—Bingo-Bango.") OTCP

Thousand and more negro children, A. Kwela for Tomorrow. Rui Knopfli, *Portuguese*. PeSAV, *tr. by the author*

Thousand and One Nights, The. *Unknown, Arabic*.

Abu Nowas for the Barmacides. AWP

Birds. AWP

Dates. AWP

Death ("Once he will miss, twice he will miss"). AWP

Haroun Al-Rachid for Heart's-Life. AWP

Haroun's Favorite Song. AWP

Her Rival for Aziza. AWP

Inscriptions at the City of Brass. AWP

Love ("Love was before the light began"). AWP

Psalm of Battle. AWP

"Sleeper, the palm-trees drink the breathless noon." AWP

Song of the Narcissus, The. AWP

Tell Him, O Night. AWP

To Lighten My Darkness. AWP

Tumadir al-Khansa for Her Brother. AWP

  (For Her Brother.) PBWP

Wazir Dandan for Prince Sharkan, The. AWP

Thousand and Second Night, The. James Merrill. NYBP

Thousand and Three, A. Paul Verlaine, *French*. EP, *tr. by* Alistair Elliot

Thousand apples you might put in your theories. Sonnet. Bernadette Mayer. PmAP

Thousand Chinese Dinners, A. Robert Mezey.

  "From a thousand Chinese dinners, one cookie." RaBo

Thousand goblets at the farewell feast, A. To Tzu-an. Yü Hsüan-chi, *Chinese*. SuSp, *tr. by* Jan W. Walls

Thousand great resolves, as great, A. To Mutius. Elizabeth Singer. KTR

Thousand guileless sheep have bled, A. Song from the Bride of Smithfield. Sylvia Townsend Warner. MoBrPo

Thousand Hairy Savages, A. Spike Milligan. NBLV

Thousand Islands, The. Charles Sangster. NOBC *Fr.* St. Lawrence and the Saguenay.

Thousand Killed, A. Bernard Spencer. OBWP

Thousand knights have rein'd their steeds, A. Calais Sands. Matthew Arnold. EBVVPR

Thousand Martyrs I Have Made, A. Aphra Behn. NoP-4

Thousand men then came thronging together, A. Saint Called "Truth," A. William Langland. NOCV *Fr.* The Vision of Piers Plowman.

Thousand miles of pure river water, A. On the Road to Pyongyang—An Improvisation. Liu E, *Chinese*. CoBLCP, *tr. by* Jonathan Chaves

Monadnoc. Ralph Waldo Emerson.

Thousand score. (LL) To Dianeme. Robert Herrick. CaPo; FaBoBe

Thousand strands of willow at spring river's bend, A. Willow Branches. Liu Yu Hsi, *Chinese*. SuSp, *tr. by* Dell R. Hales

Thousand streets of London gray, The. The Sheep and the Goat. George Macdonald. EBVV

Thousand threads, ten-thousand strands, A. The Hundred-Fold Cord. Chang Yü. *Fr.* Four Poems On the Ch'ung-wu Festival. CoBLCP, *tr. by* Jonathan Chaves

Thousand times a day, A. (LL) Of the Birth and Bringing Up of Desire. Edward, 17th Earl of Oxford De Vere. FaBoEE; NoSic; SCGP

Thousand times I have sat in resaurant windows, A. There Is Wind, There Are Matches. Gerald Stern. LCAP-2

Thousand times you've seen that scene, A. Country Burying (1919). Robert Penn Warren. LiTM

Thousand years have passed away, A. A Call to Action. Charles Hamilton Sorley. NSI

Thousand years I was sick with darkness, A. Sun. Omer Hillel, *Hebrew*. MHP, *tr. by* Ruth Finer Mintz

Thousand years now had his breed, A. Edwin John Pratt. MoCV *Fr.* The Cachalot.

Thousand years the flesh of the wool growing, A. A Woman Knitting. Lilian Bowes-Lyon. WPN

Thousand years, with God (the Scriptures say), A. On the Life of Man. Francis Quarles. ChIV-2

Thousand years, you said, A. Lady Heguri. BoLoP, *tr. by* Geoffrey Bownas *and* Anthony Thwaite *Fr.* Manyo Shu, Part 4 of 4.

Thousands and thousands of hushed years ago. Silence. James Whitcomb Riley. GSo

Thousands have lived without love, not one without water. (LL) First Things First. W. H. Auden. CBLP; NYBP

Thousands may enter through the gates of death. (LL) An Epistle to a Lady. Mary Leapor. BWW; CABP; ECWP; NOLC

Thousands of cheers filled the chalky air. Robyn Selman. PUP-19

Thousands of flowers, thousands of petals. Yang Chi. CoBLCP, *tr. by* Jonathan Chaves *Fr.* Spring Days in My Home Town.

Thousands of images have suddenly brightened in the emptiness. Untitled. Duoduo, *Chinese*. AF, *tr. by* Gregory Lee *and* John Cayley

Thousands of miles away—the Fu-sang tree. Saying Goodbye to a Monk from Japan. Hsü Pen, *Chinese*. CoBLCP, *tr. by* Jonathan Chaves

Thousands of mountains, tens of thousands of mountains. Miscellaneous Poems Written in the Snow. Wang T'ing-hsiang, *Chinese*. CoBLCP, *tr. by* Jonathan Chaves

Thow art pretty but unconstant. Lines in the Corner of a Manuscript. *Unknown*. FaBoVe

Thrace. Peter Huchel, *German*. CEEP, *tr. by* Rich Ives

Thracian page-boy / mastered, A. Dioscorides, *Greek*. GrAn, *tr. by* Peter Whigham

Thracian Wonder, The. John Webster *and* William Rowley.

  Art Thou Gone in Haste? OxBoLi

    (Chase, The.) CH

  Love Is a Law. GBL

  "Whither shall I go." GBL

Thrash away, you'll hev to rattle. Letter, A ("Thrash away, you'll hev to rattle"). James Russell Lowell. AmPP; OxBA *Fr.* The Biglow Papers.

Thrasher in the Willow by the Lake, The. Robert Pack. ColAP

Thrashing Doves, The. Jack Kerouac. PmAP

Thraso. Samuel Rowlands. NoSic

Thraw oot your shaddaws. Moonlight among the Pines. "Hugh MacDiarmid." OAEL-2

Thrawn water? Aye, owre thrawn to be aye thrawn! By Wauchopeside. "Hugh MacDiarmid." EBEV; OxAEP-2

Thre Prestis of Peblis, The. John, of Stobo Reid.

  "In Peblis town sum tyme, as I heard tell." OxBS

Thread. Catherine Lucy Czerkawska. LW

Thread, The. Denise Levertov. CrSp

Thread, A / of meaning. Meaning light. The Dead Lady Canonized. Imamu Amiri Baraka. CAPP-1

Thread in the hand of a kind mother, The. Wanderer's Song. Meng Chiao, *Chinese*. PLT, *tr. by* A. C. Graham

Thread of Life, The. Christina Rossetti.

  Aloof. OBEV

    (Verse I.) PEW

  Verse II. PEW

  Verse III. PEW

Thread of silver marks along the sand, A. The Lost Continent. Jenny Joseph. BrRo

Thread suns / above the gray-black [*or* grey-black] wasteland [*or* wilderness]. Paul Celan, *German*. OBVE, *tr. by* Michael Hamburger ("Thread suns.") VCWP, *tr. by* Michael Hamburger

Thread the needle   thread the needle. *Unknown*. FaBoVe

Thread the nerves through the right holes. Resurrection Song. Thomas Lovell Beddoes. FaBoEE

Thread to bind the heart of man!, A. (LL) Eve-Song. Mary Gilmore. LW

Threading the Miles. Alfred Encarnacion. OpBo

Threading the palm, a web of little lines. Signs. Gjertrud Schnackenberg. InPK-6; PoA; VCAP

Threads. Stephen Sandy. BAP-95

Threads of rain weave lambent light. To the Tune "Yellow Oriole." Yang Shen, *Chinese*. CoBLCP, *tr. by* Jonathan Chaves

Threads our hands in blindness spin, The. Overruled. John Greenleaf Whittier. NCAP

Threat of loss drives us, The. Breaking the Surface. George Looney. EC3

Threaten the head that I love. (LL) The Pity of Love. W. B. Yeats. CMoP; NOBVV; PBMP

Threat'ning clouds of yesternight, The. While the Choir Sang. Priscilla Jane Thompson. CBWP-2

3. Yehuda Amichai, *Hebrew*. IP, *tr. by* Warren Bargad *and* Stanley F. Chyet

Three. Carolyn Kizer. NMM-2 *Fr.* Pro Femina.

Three a.m.—a far bell. December. Gary Snyder. InPS-3 *Fr.* Six Years.

Three Aldis, not one of them dim. Limerick. Joyce Johnson. PeLi

3 A.M. will always be the long hall. Sleep Apnea. Mark Cox. PUP-18

Three Amphigouris. Jean-Joseph Vade, *French*. CBNP

Three ancient men in Bethlehem's cave. The Mystic Magi. Robert Stephen Hawker. OBCP

Three and away. (LL) Bell horses, bell horses, what time of day? Mother Goose. BoTP; OxNR; ReMoGo

Three angels up above the street. "Bob Dylan." RaBo

Three Animals. Ron Padgett. TTTS

Three anti-depressants and one diuretic a day. Bruce Beaver. *Fr.* Letters to Live Poets. CBAP

Three Badgers, The. "Lewis Carroll." CBNP *Fr* Sylvie and Bruno.

Three Ballate. Angelo Poliziano, *Italian*. AWP, *tr. by* John Addington Symonds

Three black boys. Panther. Sam Cornish. PoBA

Three blind mice, see how they run! Mother Goose. LB; OxNR; ReMoGo

Three blocks down,k the leaves around the C & O Canal ignite. Traveling Company. Brooks Haxton. CMAP

Three bold brothers of merrie Scotland. Henry Martyn. *Unknown*. ESPB

Three Bushes, The. W. B. Yeats. EBNV

Three Butchers, The. *Unknown*. PeVV

Three Captains, The. *Unknown, French*. AWP, *tr. by* Andrew Lang

Three Cherry Trees, The. Walter De la Mare. CMoP; OBGa

Three chestnuts for morning, four at night. Tune: "Sheep on Mountain Slope." Ch'iao Chi, *Chinese*. SuSp, *tr. by* Wayne Schlepp

Three children sliding on the ice. Mother Goose. LB; NOBL; OxNR; ReMoGo

Three children sliding on the ice. *Unknown*. ACTP

Three Clerihews. Edmund Clerihew Bentley. *See* Clerihew: "Savonarola."

Three-Coloured Banner. János Pilinszky, *Hungarian*. PoSu, *tr. by* Peter Jay

Three 'coons come at his garbage. He be cross. John Berryman. LCAP-2 *Fr.* Dream Songs.

Three crests against the saffron sky. Twilight on Tweed. Andrew Lang. EBVV

Three crooked cripples went through Cripplegate. Mother Goose. OxNR

Three cups of wine a prudent man may take. The Benefits and Abuse of Alcohol. Eubulus, *Greek*. NBLV, *tr. by* Richard Cumberland

Three dark maids, I loved them when. Villancico. *Unknown, Spanish*. AWP, *tr. by* Thomas Walsh

Three darks come down together. Robert Francis. CRP; WeT

Three Dawns. Jean-Joseph Rabéarivelo, *French*. NegPo, *tr. by* Ellen Conroy Kennedy

Three days. I Starve My Belly for a Sublime Purpose. Anna Swirszczynska, *Polish*. BLT, *tr. by* Czeslaw Milosz *and* Leonard Nathan

Three days after the lightning hit it / or the beat, check this, I can play around it. Some Nets. B. P. Nichol. FTOS

Three days before he died the hospital called me. Tongues. Philip Martin. NOBAu

Three days of rain: indoors. Rainpoem. Michael Dransfield. CBAP

Three days of rest. The Sun in Capricorn. Joyce Mansour, *French*. PBWP, *tr. by* Carol Cosman

Three dead men have I loved and thou art last of the three. (LL) In the Garden at Swainston. Tennyson. OBEV; OBNC

3 Dialogues. Brandon Kershner. EC2

Three Dimensions. José Craveirinha. PBMAP

Three Dogs. E. C. Brereton. BoTP

Three Dreams at Chiang-ling. Yüan Chen, *Chinese*. SuSp, *tr. by* William H. Nienhauser

Three drunks, a leg on one quite gone, bereft. My Iambic Pentameter Lines. Robert Crawford. InPK-6

Three Easters. Alberta Turner. LCAP-2

Three Elements, The. Madison Cawein. APN-2

Three Emily's, The. Dorothy Livesay. NALW

Three Enemies, The. Christina Rossetti. TrCP

Three Epigrams. Paul Ramsey. CRP

Three Epigrams. Theodore Roethke. NBLV

"Centaur does not need a Horse, The."

Mistake, The. OBCoV

Pipling. OBCoV

Three Epigrams. Jonathan Swift. FaBoEE

(Cudgeled Husband, The.) NBLV

Three Epitaphs on John Hewet and Sarah Drew. Alexander Pope. NIP-4

Epitaph on the Stanton-Harcourt Lovers. FaBoEE

Three Evenings in a Life. Adelaide Anne Procter. VWP

Three excellent qualities in narration. Triads. *Unknown*. BIrV, *tr. by* Thomas Kinsella *Fr.* The Triads of Ireland.

Three Excerpts. André Breton. PFTM, *tr. by* Richard M. Seaver *and* Helen R. Lane *Fr.* Manifesto of Surrealism (1924).

Three-Faced, The. Robert Graves. FaBoEE

Three faces. . . / mirrored in the muddy streams of living. For Andy Goodman—Michael Schwerner—and James Chaney. Margaret Abigail Walker. BPo

Three Fates, The. Rosemary Dobson. BMAP; BoWoP

Three feet of mud in this narrow alley. Yang Chi. *Fr.* Living in a Riverside Village——Miscellaneous Impressions. CoBLCP, *tr. by* Jonathan Chaves

Three fellows were marching over the Rhine. The Hostess' Daughter. Ludwig Uhland, *German*. AWP, *tr. by* Margarete Münsterberg

Three Fishers [Went Sailing], The. Charles Kingsley. EBVV; FaPoR; PWR; PoLF

Three Floors. Stanley Kunitz. LoL

Three floors up, I fall. Living Near the Plaza of Thieves. Leslie Ullman. PBCAP

Three flutes, two oboes, English horn, violins. Guide to the Symphony. Weldon Kees. VGW

Three-fold terror of love, The; a fallen flare. The Mother of God. William Butler Yeats. ChIV-2

Three folds in cloth, yet there is but the one cloth. To the Holy Trinity. *Unknown, Irish*. NOIV, *tr. by* Thomas Kinsella

Three for Bear. Aimé Césaire, *French*. PFTM, *tr. by* Frances Densmore

Three for Children. Thom Gunn.

Aquarium, The. NOxBChV

Cannibal. NOxBChV

Three Found Poems. Laurie Duggan.

Hearts (1983). BMAP

Three Found Poems. George Hitchcock. OBAL

Three Foxes, The. A. A. Milne. OxBChV

Three Fragments. Bertolt Brecht, *German*. PFTM, *tr. by* Willett, John and Ralph Manheim

Three Friends. *Unknown, Yoruba*. BoWoP; PBA, *tr. by* Ulli Beier

Three Gates. Beth Day. BLPA

(Three Gates of Gold.) PoToHe

Three Ghostesses. *Unknown*. OBCoV; OxNR

Three Green Windows. Anne Sexton. NYBP

Three grey boys tracked us to an old house. In One Battle. Imamu Amiri Baraka. BPo

Three grey geese in a green field grazing. *Unknown*. OxNR

Three Gypsies. Shalin Hai-Jew. UnSA

Three-handed Fugue. Phyllis Gotlieb. NOBC

Three-headed hydra of family, The. Galya, Mother, and My Daughter Anna. Yevgeny Borisovich Rein, *Russian*. TCRP, *tr. by* Bernard Meares

Three Hermits, The. W. B. Yeats. CMoP

Three Hills. Everard Owen. NSI

Three Holy Kings from Morgenland. Heinrich Heine, *German*. PChr, *tr. by* Herman Eichenthal

Three hours ago he blundered up the trench. A Working Party. Siegfried Sassoon. AF; CMoP; PeFWW; PoFWW

Three hours chain-smoking words. In the Evening. Adrienne Rich. ColAP

Three hours of peace and soothing rest of brain. (LL) An Evening Lull. Walt Whitman. NAAL-1; NAAL-3

300,000,000. What Happened Here Before. Gary Snyder. NNaP

Three images of dying stick in my mind like morbid transfers. Bruce Beaver. NOBAu *Fr.* Letters to Live Poets. CBAP

Three-Inch Reflector. Caroline Caddy. BMAP

Three Inscriptions for Statues of Priapus. Virgil, *Latin*.

"It is I, lads, who look after this place." OBCVT, *tr. by* John Heath-Stubbs

Three Jolly Pigeons, The. Oliver Goldsmith. *See* Song: "Let school-masters puzzle their brain."

Three Jovial Gentlemen. Daniel Gerard Hoffman. MoBS

Three Kinds of Pleasures. Robert Bly. AiP

Three kings. Bethlehem. Marina Tsvetayeva, *Russian*. GI, *tr. by* Nina Kossman

Three Kings, The. "Rubén Dario," *Spanish*. PChr, *tr. by* Lysander Kemp

Three Kings came riding from far away. Henry Wadsworth Longfellow. ChIV-2

Three kings embark on a long journey. Starlight. Freda Downie. FaBoWP

Three kings stood before the manger. The Gifts. John Heath-Stubbs. OxBC

Three Knights from Spain. *Unknown*. CH; OxNR

("We are three brethren out of Spain.") OxNR

Three Ladies, The. Robert Creeley. NeAP

Three Ladies of London, The. Robert Wilson.

Simplicity's Song. CTC

Three limbs from the same stem of winter. A Still Life, Untitled. Karen Zealand. CMAP

Three limbs, three seasons smashed; well, one to go. John Berryman. HCAP *Fr.* Dream Songs.

Three lines of "clerk script" calligraphy. Chin Nung. CoBLCP, *tr. by* Jonathan Chaves *Fr.* Inscribed on a Lichen-Covered Wall in My Hut.

Three little chickens. A Tug-of-War. M. M. Hutchinson. BoTP

Three little children sitting on the sand. All, All a-Lonely. *Unknown*. OxBoLi

Three little ghostesses. Three Ghostesses. *Unknown*. NOxBChV; OBCoV; OxNR

Three little girls were sitting on a rail. Kate Greenaway. NOxBChV

Three little kittens [they] lost their mittens. Eliza Lee Cabot Follen. BoTP; LB; OBCA; OxNR

Three little kittens lost their mittens. Eliza Lee Cabot Follen. FPC

Three little maidens they have slain. Song. Maurice Maeterlinck, *French*. AWP, *tr. by* Jethro Bithell

Three Little Men in a Boat. Rodney Bennett. BoTP

Three little mice walked into town. Three Mice. Charlotte Druitt Cole. BoTP; CTAV

Three Little Pigs, The. Sir Alfred Scott Gatty. ACTP; BoTP; OxBChV

Three Love Poems. Norman Cameron. FaBoTw; GTBS-P

From a Woman to a Greedy Lover. FaBoEE

In the Queen's Room. OxBTC

Shepherdess. GBL; OxBS

Three lovely notes he whistled, too soft to be heard. The Unknown Bird. Edward Thomas. RB

Three lovely sisters working were. Parcæ, The; or, Three Dainty Destinies: The Armilet. Robert Herrick. CaPo

Three Magi, The. Stanislaw Baranczak, *Polish.* CEEP; GI, *tr. by* Stanislaw Baranczak *and* Clare Cavanagh

Three magnolias, identical. Yüan Mei. *Fr.* Moments of Fullfillment—— Writing Down Miscellaneous. CoBLCP, *tr. by* Jonathan Chaves

Three men came talking up the road. Night Piece. John Streeter Manifold. LiTM; MoBrPo

Three men coming down the winter hill, The. Winter Landscape. John Berryman. GS; LiTM; MoAmPo; TwCP

Three Men of Gotham. Thomas Love Peacock. FaBoCh; OBEV; OxAEP-2 *Fr.* Nightmare Abbey.

   (Wise Men of Gotham, The.) BXAP; CBNP

Three merry men, and three merry men. George Peele. NoSic *Fr.* The Old Wives' [*or* Wife's] Tale.

Three Messages. Aleksandr Blok, *Russian.*

   "Black raven in the snowy dusk." TCRP, *tr. by* Geoffrey Thurley

Three Mice. Charlotte Druitt Cole. BoTP; CTAV

Three miles extended around the fields of the homestead. Frithiof's Homestead. Esaias Tegnér. *Fr.* Frithiof's Saga. AWP, *tr. by* Longfellow

Three Mirrors, The. Edwin Muir. NoAM

Three Modes of History and Culture. Imamu Amiri Baraka. PmAP

Three Moments in Paris. Mina Loy. PFTM

Three Movements. W. B. Yeats. CMoP; FaBoEE

Three Movements and a Coda. Imamu Amiri Baraka. NAAAL

Three Musicians, The. Aubrey Beardsley. NOBVV; PeVV

"Three Observations on the Zombie Culture." Dolores Kendrick.

   26th Person, The. GT

Three O'Clock Love Song. Michael S. Harper. GT

Three Odes of Horace. Horace, *Latin.*

   Aequam Memento. OBCVT, *tr. by* Louis MacNeice

Three of us afloat in the meadow by the swing. Pirate Story. Robert Louis Stevenson. ACTP; NOxBChV

Three of us went to the top of the city. Poem from the Empire State. June Jordan. BPo

Three old hermits took the air. The Three Hermits. W. B. Yeats. CMoP

Three old ladies in an apple tree. Ballad of Old Women & of How They Are Constrained To Simulate Youth In Order To Avoid Shocking the Young. Norman Talbot. NOBAu

Three or four hours unconscious there. (LL) Milk for the Cat. Harold Monro. BoTP; FaBoBe; MoBrPo; OBMV; PC

Three Oranges. Charles Bukowski. BAP-93

Three outas from the [High] bleak Karoo. Christmas Carol. D. J. Opperman, *Afrikaans.* PeSA; PeSAV, *tr. by* Anthony Delius

Three Pagoda Dragon Pond. To the Tune "Chiu-ch'üan tzu." Wu Chen, *Chinese.* CoBLCP, *tr. by* Jonathan Chaves

Three Phases of Africa. Francis Ernest Kobina Parkes. PBA

Three pigeons down-swing. Possibilities. Peter Kane Dufault. NYBP

Three pink Hampstead intellectuals. Tea with the Poets. John Betjeman. PeLV

Three places most loved I have left. Saint Columcille. NOIV

Three Pleas. Henry Treece. PoWW

Three plum buns / To eat here at the stile. Christina Rossetti. BoTP; NTP

Three Poems. Bhartrihari, *Sanskrit.* EP, *tr. by* John Brough

Three Poems. Michelangelo Buonarroti, *Italian.* AWP, *tr. by* George Santayana

Three Poems. János Pilinszky, *Hungarian.*

   In Memoriam F.M. Dostoevsky. CEEP, *tr. by* Jascha Kessler

   Stavrogin's Farewell. CEEP, *tr. by* Jascha Kessler

   Stavrogin's Return. CEEP, *tr. by* Jascha Kessler

Three Poems. "Ping Hsin," *Chinese.*

   "Fishing boats have returned, The!" PBWP, *tr. by* Julia C. Lin

3 poems. Pomade. Aleksei Eliseievich Kruchyonykh. PFTM, *tr. by* Beth Holmgren *and* Jerome Rothenberg

Three Poems about Children. Austin Clarke. CIP-2

Three Poems About Mark Twain. Vachel Lindsay.

   When the Mississippi Flowed in Indiana. CMoP

Three Poems for the Indian Steelworkers. Joseph Bruchac. CDW

Three poems from Rediscovery (1964). Kofi Awoonor.

   Lovers' Song. PBMAP

Three Poems of the Atomic Bomb. Dame Edith Sitwell.

   Dirge for the New Sunrise. CMoP; MoBrPo

Three Poems on Ch'ang-sha. Yang Shih-ch'i, *Chinese.* CoBLCP, *tr. by* Jonathan Chaves

   Palace of Prince Ma—Now It Is a Buddhist Temple, The.

Three Poems to the tune "Lo-mei Feng." Ma Chih-yüan, *Chinese.* CoBLCP, *tr. by* Jonathan Chaves

Three Poems to the Tune "Ssu-k'uai yü." Ma Chih-yüan, *Chinese.* CoBLCP, *tr. by* Jonathan Chaves

Three poets, in three distant ages born. Lines Printed under the Engraved Portrait of Milton [In Tonson's Folio of the "Paradise Lost"]. Dryden. EPCY; InPK-6; OAEL-1; OxAEP-1

Three Portraits. George Hitchcock. VGW

Three practical farmers from back of the dale. Shepherds' Carol. Norman Nicholson. OBCP

Three Preachers, The. Charles MacKay. EBVV

Three Presidents. Robert Bly. LCAP-2

Three Puddocks, The. William Soutar. FaBoVe

Three Quatrains. Edwin Arlington Robinson. NCAP

Three Quatrains. Jelaluddin Rumi, *Persian.*

   "Let the lover be disgraceful, crazy." RaBo, *tr. by* John Moyne *and* Coleman Barks

   "Never too many fish in a swift creek." RaBo, *tr. by* John Moyne *and* Coleman Barks

   "Night full of talking that hurts, A." RaBo, *tr. by* John Moyne *and* Coleman Barks

Three Ranks of Men, Three Grades of Things. Nguyễn Bỉnh Khiêm, *Vietnamese.* AVP, *tr. by* Huỳnh Sanh Thông

Three Ravens, The. *Unknown.* AmFP; ESPB; HeIP-4; InPK-6; NAEL-1; NoP-4; OAEL-1; OBEV; OxBB; OxBSn; PFE; PoE; PoEL-1; SAGP; SCGP; TFi; UnPo

   ("Such hawkes, such hounds, and such a Leman.") (LL) OxBSn

   ("Such hawks, such hounds, and such a leman.") (LL) NoP-4; SAGP

   ("There were three Ravens sat on a tree.") NoP-4; OxBSn; PFE; SAGP

Three red foxes on my head, come down. False Youth: Autumn: Clothes of the Age. James Dickey. MT

Three regions—one long strip of hills and streams. A Sense of History. Nhu'ọ'ng Tống, *Vietnamese.* AVP, *tr. by* Huỳnh Sanh Thông

Three Riddles from *The Exeter Book.* Cynewulf. ASW; PeLV, *tr. by* Kevin Crossley-Holland *Fr.* Riddles (Exeter Book).

   ("Churning (or lovemaking): Young man made for the corner, A.") ASW, *tr. by* Kevin Crossley-Holland

Three Rioters, The. Chaucer. EBNV *Fr.* The Pardoner's Tale. FHYEP; NAEL-1; NAWM-1; OAEL-1; PoE *Fr.* The Canterbury Tales.

Three roads were shadowy and the sky over. Vanessa Vanessa. Ewart Milne. BIrV

Three Roses, The. Walter Savage Landor. NAEL-2

Three rounded flanks I loved. *Unknown.* NOIV

Three Roundels of Love Unreturned. Chaucer. *See* Merciles[s] Beaute [*or* Beautée *or* Beauty].

3 Sad Sheppards Sings This in Parts, The. Lady Jane Cavendish. KTR *Fr.* A Pastorall.

Three Sailors, The. William Makepeace Thackeray. *See* Little Billee.

Three sang of love together: one with lips. A Triad. Christina Rossetti. NAEL-2; NALW; PBWP

Three Sayings from Highlands, North Carolina. Jonathan Williams. OBAL

Three Scenes: Todmorden. Jeff Nuttall. NBrP

Three scribblers whose names end in Bert. Limerick. C. Vita-Finzi. PeLi

Three Seamstresses, The. Isaac Leibush Peretz, *Yiddish.* TrJP, *tr. by* Joseph Leftwich

Three Seasons. Francis Sparshott. NOBC

Three Self-Plagiarisms. David Avidan, *Hebrew. Fr.* Traveling in the City. IP, *tr. by* Warren Bargad *and* Stanley F. Chyet

Three Sentences for a Dead Swan. James Wright. NOBA

Three Silences. Rachel Hadas. RA

Three silences made him a single word. Sonnet. Richard Palmer Blackmur. PoA

Three Sisters. Walter De la Mare. FaBoEE

Three sisters lived downstairs. The Head of Tasso. John Skoyles. CMAP

3 : 6. "Alta."

   "One hesitates to bring a child into this world without fixing." CrSp

Three slender things that best support the. *Unknown, Irish.* IIP, *tr. by* Kuno Meyer *Fr.* The Triads of Ireland.

Three small children. West Grand Boulevard. Faye Kicknosway. IFJA

Three Small Songs for the Muse. Kathleen Norris. CrSp

Three Songs. Hart Crane. *Fr.* The Bridge. NAAL-2

   National Winter Garden. EP; InPS-3; LiTM; NAAL-2; OxBA

Three Songs. Thom Gunn.

   Baby Song. RB

Three Songs. Etheridge Knight.

I. Slim's Song. BkSV

II. Song of the Reverend Gatemouth Moore. BkSV

III. Healing Song. BkSV

Three Songs. Daniel S. Simko. CEEP

Three Songs. Rachel Wetzsteon. RA

Three Songs for the Lute. Robert Graves.

    Hedges Freaked With Snow. OxBTC

    In Her Only Way. OxBSP

Three Songs from the Haida. *Unknown.*

    Bear's Song, The. AWP, *tr. by* Constance Lindsay Skinner

    Love Song: "Beautiful is she, this woman." AWP, *tr. by* Constance Lindsay Skinner

    Song for Fine Weather. AWP, *tr. by* Constance Lindsay Skinner

Three Songs from the Temple. Don Domanski. NOBC

Three Songs of Love and Hate. Fay Zwicky.

    Stone Dolphin, The. BMAP

Three Songs of Mad Coyote. *Unknown, Nez Percé Indian.* STP, *tr. by* Herbert J. Spinden.

Three Songs of Mary. Madeleine L'Engle.

    O Simplicitas. OBCP; PChr

Three Sonnets for Iva. Marilyn Hacker. GLP

Three Sons, The. *Unknown.* ReMoGo

Three sortes of teares doe from myne eies distraine. William Alabaster. ESCV *Fr.* Divine Meditations. Son

Three sounds sum up the sense of life. Tố Hũ'u, *Vietnamese.* AVP, *tr. by* Huỳnh Sanh Thông

Three spirits came to me. April. Ezra Pound. CMoP

Three Spring Notations on Bipeds. Carl Sandburg. AWP

Three Stages. Christina Rossetti.

    Pause of Thought, A. NOBE; OBNC

Three Star Final. Conrad Potter Aiken. OxBA

Three stars, five stars rise over the hill. Confucius. *Fr.* Shao and the South. CTC, *tr. by* Ezra Pound

Three strange men came to the inn. A Lady Comes to an Inn. Elizabeth Jane Coatsworth. MoAmPo

Three straws on a staff. *Unknown.* ReMoGo

Three strings, a neck of almond, and the heart. Balalaika. Norman Dubie. AmPA

Three students sit with a pair of whores. Life. "Sasha Chorny," *Russian.* TCRP, *tr. by* Bernard Meares

Three Summers since I chose a maid. The Farmer's Bride. Charlotte Mew. BWW; BoLoP; CABP; CBLP; EBNV; FaBoWP; LW; MoBrPo; NALW; NoP-4; OxBM; OxBTC; RACG; SAGP; VWP; WPE

Three Sweatshop Women. Nanying Stella Wong. CrSp

Three that end the same way. St. Anzas VI. B. P. Nichol. FTOS

Three then came forward out of darkness, one. The Road. Conrad Potter Aiken. MoAmPo

Three Things. W. B. Yeats. OBMV

Three Things Enchanted Him. "Anna Akhmatova," *Russian.* AiP, *tr. by* Stanley Kunitz *with* Max Hayward

Three things filled this day for me. Joseph Auslander. TrJP

Three things make earth unquiet. A Servant When He Reigneth. Rudyard Kipling. ChIV-1; KSG

Three things there are more beautiful. The Beautiful. W. H. Davies. NTP

Three things there be in man's opinion dear[e]. Sonnet: "Three things there be in mans opinion dear[e]." Greville Fulke. NOCV; NOSC; NoSic; PoEL-1 *Fr.* Caelica.

Three thing[e]s there be[e] that prosper up apace. Sir Walter Ra[u]le[i]gh to His Son[ne]. Sir Walter Ralegh. InPS-3; NAEL-1; NoSic; OxBSP; PoEL-2; RB; SCGP; SiPS; Son

Three Things to Remember. William Blake. *Fr.* Auguries of Innocence. EBEV; FaBoCh; FaPoR; ImPo; OAEL-1; OBNC; OxAEP-2; OxBoLi; PeECV; PoEL-4; TFi

Three times a night it woke you. Coal Train. Jay Parini. GM

Three times down. I'm still on the mountain. (LL) Sourdough Mountain Lookout. Philip Whalen. BB

Three times he crossed our way where with me went. Old Man Pondered. John Crowe Ransom. MoAmPo

Three times round the cuckoo waltz. Cuckoo Waltz. *Unknown.* AS

Three times, sweet hawthorn, I have met thy bower. To a Bower. John Clare. GaP

Three times to the world's end I went. The Edge. Rosemary Dobson. NOBAu

Three Tiny Songs. Cid Corman.

    "I have come far to have found nothing." VGW

3 : 1. "Alta." CrSp

Three-toed sloth is the slowest creature we know, The. Fleur Adcock. OBCoV

Three turkeys fair their last have breathed. A Melancholy Lay. Marjory Fleming. FaBoCh; NBLV

Three Undated Fragments. Keats.

    "I am as brisk." CBNP

    "O grant that like to Peter I." CBNP; ChIV-2

Three Variations. Boris Pasternak, *Russian.* TrJP, *tr. by* Babette Deutsch

Three viands in three different courses served. Oyster-Crabs. Carolyn Wells. BXAP

Three virtues always grace the canine breed. The Old Hound. Huỳnh Mẫn Đạt, *Vietnamese.* AVP, *tr. by* Huỳnh Sanh Thông

Three Voices, The. "Lewis Carroll." BXAP

Three Ways to Screw Up on your Way to The Doings Three Ways. *Unknown, Seneca Indian.* STP, *tr. by* Jerome Rothenberg *and* Richard Johnny John

Three wee bit puddocks. The Three Puddocks. William Soutar. FaBoVe

Three weeks gone and the combatants gone. Vergissmeinnicht. Keith Douglas. FaBoMo; GTBS-P; InPS-3; NAEL-2; NoAM; NoP-4; OBWP; OxBTC; PoWW; RB; SoSe-8

Three weeks had past, and Richard rambles now. Delay Has Danger. George Crabbe. NOBRP

Three Wise Couples, The. Elizabeth T. Corbett. BLPA

Three wise men looked equivocally, The. The Magi. Ramon Guthrie. GI; PoE

Three wise men of Gotham. Mother Goose. CBNP; FaBoBe; OxNR; ReMoGo; Spl

    ("My tale had been longer.") (LL) LB

Three wise old women were they, were they. Elizabeth T. Corbett. BLPA; NOxBChV; OBCA; OBSP; OxBChV

Three women. Snow White. Olga Broumas. CPO

Three wonderful people called Ley. Limerick. Tim Hopkins. PeLi

Three wonderful people called Wick. Limerick. A. M. Sayers. PeLi

Three woodchoppers walk up the road. Robert Francis. TRP

Three words fall sweetly on my soul. Mother, Home, Heaven. William Goldsmith Brown. FaBoBe

Three xlvii. Laurie Duggan. BMAP

Three-year-old Archianax. Poseidippus, *Greek.* GrAn, *tr. by* Edward Lucie-Smith

Three years accounts from gamekeepers' records, an estate. Three Years in Glen Garry. Colin Simms. NBrP

Three years ago I left these city walls. Returning to Yin-ch'eng Early in the Year Ting-ch'ou (1277). Tai Piao-yüan, *Chinese.* CoBLCP, *tr. by* Jonathan Chaves

Three Years in Glen Garry. Colin Simms. NBrP

Three years she grew in sun and shower. The Education of Nature. Wordsworth. GTBS-P; HAP; PoEL-4 *Fr.* Lucy. FHYEP; NOBE; OAEL-2; OBEV; OBNC; SCGP; TFi

Three Young Rats. *Unknown.* OxBoLi; OxNR

Three youths went a-fishing. The Banished Duke of Grantham. *Unknown.* EnSB

Three/Quarters Time. Nikki Giovanni. CA

Threefold Pass, The. Ho Xuan Huong, *Vietnamese.* AVP, *tr. by* Huỳnh Sanh Thông

Threepenny Opera, The. Bertolt Brecht, *Latin.*

    Ballad of Immoral Earnings. OxBoV, *tr. by* Ralph Manheim *and* John Willett

    "Jenny Towler turned up lately." OxBoV, *tr. by* Ralph Manheim *and* John Willett

    Peachum's Morning Hymn. OxBoV, *tr. by* Ralph Manheim *and* John Willett

    "See the shark with teeth like razors." OxBoV, *tr. by* Ralph Manheim *and* John Willett

Threes. Carl Sandburg. CMoP; OxBA; PoLF

Threissa, someone's knocking at the door. The Procuress. Herodas, *Greek.* HePo, *tr. by* Barbara Hughes Fowler

Threnodia Augustalis. Dryden.

    "Sure there's a lethargy in mighty woe." IMW

Threnody: "South-wind brings, The." Ralph Waldo Emerson. APN-1

    "Was there no star that could be sent." IMW

Threnody: "Truth is a golden sunset far away." I. O. Scherzo. HoPM

Threnody: "What, what, what / What's the news from Swat?" George Thomas Lanigan. NBLV

Threshed corn lay piled like grit of ivory. The Barn. Seamus Heaney. HAP

Thresher's Labour, The. Stephen Duck.

    "Soon as the harvest hath laid bare the plains." NOEC

Threshing Machine, The. Alice Thompson Meynell. WPE

Threshold. Dean Young. NAmP90

Threshold Of The New, The. Lucretius. LBC

Thresholds of Identity. Lionel Abrahams. PeSAV

Threw me from the house, did he? King Alfred and the Peasant Woman. Anna Wickham. WPN

Thrice, and above, blest (my soul's [or soules] half[e]) art thou. Country Life: To His Brother, M. Tho: Herrick. Robert Herrick. CaPo; SeCP

Thrice Blest the Man. John Barnard. AH

Thrice-cruel maid, may Heaven frown on thee. The Elusive Maid. Abraham ibn Chasdai, *Hebrew*. TrJP, tr. by J. Chotzner

Thrice *Dido* try'd to raise her drooping Head. Release. Virgil, *Latin*. OBCVT, tr. by John Dryden

Thrice hail! proud land, whose genius boasts a Clay! The Runaway. Albery Allson Whitman. AAP   *Fr.* Not a Man and Yet a Man.

Thrice happy authors, who with little skill. A Soliloquy in the Suburbs. Charles Jenner. NOEC   *Fr.* Eclogue IV: The Poet.   AWP

Thrice he came. Malacoda. Samuel Beckett. CIP-2

Thrice the Brinded Cat Hath Mewed. Shakespeare. RB   *Fr.* Macbeth.

Thrice toss[e] these oaken ashes in the air [or ayre]. Thomas Campion. CBLP; EBEV; EnLoPo; FaBoCh; HAP; NOBE; OAEL-1; OxBSP; PoEL-2; PoRA; SCGP; TFi; WeW-3

Thrice Welcome First and Best of Days. Isaac Chanler. AH

Thrid Vertical Poetry. Roberto Juarroz, *Spanish*.
  "Lamp lit, A." VCWP, tr. by W. S. Merwin

Thrift. Cornelius Eady. CMAP; LTA

Thrift alone for meaning ceases. We Forego Mimicry. Ray DiPalma. FTOS

Thriftles thred which pampred beauty spinnes, The. A Sonet Written in Prayse of the Browne Beautie. George Gascoigne. AAS; PBRV

Thrifty Elephant, The. John Holmes. NYBP

Thro elm and maple and syringa branches. Commencement. Constance Carrier. WPE

Thro' the night Thy angels kept. A Child's Prayer. William Canton. BoTP

Throat Song: The Whirling Earth. Wendy Rose. HATNAP

Throbs the Night with Mystic Silence. Hayyim Nahman Bialik, *Hebrew*, TrJP, tr. by Bertha Beinkinstadt

Throe of Second Manassas share, The. Herman Melville. *See* The March into Virginia.

Throned, yet adoring! (LL) The Day of Judgement [or Judgment]; an Ode. Isaac Watts. ChIV-2; ECEV; HAP; NOBE; NOEC; OBEV; SCGP

Thronging the heart. Residues: Thronging the Heart. Gael Turnbull. NBrP

Throstle, The. Tennyson. ACTP

Through a crack on the right. Outhouse. Aleksandar Ristovic, *Serbo-Croatian*. HSix, tr. by Charles Simic

Through a dull tract of woe, of dread. My Birthday. George Crabbe. OxBSP

Through a Glass Eye, Lightly. Carolyn Kizer. BoWoP

Through a hospital window. In a Hospital Garden. Randall Jarrell. OBGa

Through a knotted sleeve. (LL) Shirt. Charles Simic. AFr; HCAP

Through a red prairie. (LL) The Last Quatrain of the Ballad of Emmett Till. Gwendolyn Brooks. LCAP-2; PoBA; WPE

Through a wild midnight all my mountainous past. The Monster. Henry Rago. PoA

Through all the city's streets there poured a flood. The Gathering of the Grand Army. Charlotte L. Forten Grimke. AAP

Through all the employments of life. The Employments of Life. John Gay. OxBoV; PeLV   *Fr.* The Beggar's Opera. OAEL-1

Through all the frozen winter. Smells. Kathryn Worth. AYFP

Through all the pomp of kingdoms still he shines. Homer's Gift of Fame. Homer. NOSC, tr. by George Chapman   *Fr.* The Iliad.

Through all thy various *Winter, full are found*. David Mallet. EPCY   *Fr.* To Mr. Thomson, on His Publishing the Second Edition of His Poem Called Winter.

Through All Your Abstract Reasoning. Brian Patten. FaBoTw

Through Alpine meadows soft-suffused. Stanzas from the Grande Chartreuse. Matthew Arnold. EBVV; EnVR; NAEL-2; OAEL-2; PoE; PoEL-5

Through an angled mirror. Images. Marilyn Williams. IFJA

Through and through the inspired leaves. The Book-Worms. Robert Burns. FaBoEE

Through Binoculars. Charles Tomlinson. OAEL-2

Through centuries he lived in poverty. The Good Man Has No Shape. Wallace Stevens. MeMAP

Through clouds of fire and clouds of blood. At Day's End. Hayyim Nahman Bialik, *Hebrew*. MHP, tr. by Ruth Finer Mintz

Through dangly woods the aimless. The Doze. James Reeves. CTV

Through every age, eternal God. Isaac Watts. AmFP

Through every night we hate. Mothers, Daughters. Shirley Kaufman. BoWoP; CrSp; NMM-2

Through every nook and every cranny. Granny. Spike Milligan. FuFo

Through five night watches I've stayed wide awake. Looking Far Ahead. Trần Tế Xu'o'ng, *Vietnamese*. AVP, tr. by Huỳnh Sanh Thông

Through frost and snow locked from mine eyes. To Saxham. Thomas Carew. CaPo

Through glades and glooms! Oh fair! Oh, sad! Collins. Lionel Pigot Johnson. OxAEP-2

Through gladness of this lusty May. (LL) Lusty May. *Unknown*. OBEV; OxBS

Through grass, through amber'd cornfields, our slow Stream. Meadowsweet. William Allingham. OBNC

Through grief and through danger thy smile hath cheered my way. The Irish Peasant to His Mistress. Thomas Moore. TIRV

Through heaven's vault it's cock-a-doodle-doo. Confession. Ho Xuan Huong, *Vietnamese*. AVP, tr. by Huỳnh Sanh Thông

Through high still air. (LL) Mid-August at Sourdough Mountain Lookout. Gary Snyder. ColAP; HAP; InPK-6; LoL; NoP-4; PaTW; TAP; VCAP

Through infinite immensity. (LL) I'm happiest when most away. Emily Brontë. EnVR; NAEL-2

Through lane or black archway. The Young Woman of Beare. Austin Clarke. MoP; NoAM

Through lenses the world opens. Microscope. Gwyn Thomas, *Welsh*. OBWVE, tr. by Joseph P. Clancy

Through life's dull road, so dim and dirty. On My Thirty-third Birthday. Byron. FaBoEE

Through little lands two horses drew. The Graves. Gregor Strnisa, *Slovenian*. CEEP, tr. by Michael Scammell

Through me the way is to the city of woe. The Gates of Hell. Dante. *Fr.* Inferno. NAWM-1, tr. by John Ciardi *Fr.* Divina Commedia.

Through me you enter the city of lament. Dante. *Fr.* Inferno. NAWM-1, tr. by John Ciardi *Fr.* Divina Commedia.

Through mud, fouled nuts, black grime. Removing the Plate of the Pump on the Hydraulic System of the Backhoe. Gary Snyder. LoL

Through Nurseryland. *Unknown*. BoTP; OTCP

Through pearly deeps of sky, cloud-mountains rose. Sky Picture. Henrietta Cordelia Ray. CBWP-3

Through rain falling on us no faster. Goodbye to Serpents. James Dickey. NYBP

Through random doors we wandered. Exits and Entrances. Naomi Long Madgett. BISi

Through reedy banks. The Nima. Jorge Isaacs, *Spanish*. TrJP, tr. by Alice Jane McVan

Through Ruddy Orchards. Mary Oliver. SoSe-8; WPE

Through salt marsh, grassy channel where the shark's. Tide Turning. John Frederick Nims. DiPo; FYAP

Through seas of dreams and seas of phantasies. Nirvâna. Sidney Lanier. NCAP

Through sere trees and beheaded. August Rain, after Haying. Jane Kenyon. AFr

Through smoke and falling leaves. (LL) There Are No Such Trees in Alpine, California. John Haines. PaTW; WeT

Through springtime walks, with flowers perfumed. Song. Anne Batten Cristall. ECWP

Through storm and fire and gloom, I see it stand. The Celtic Cross. Thomas D'Arcy Magee. TIRV

Through storm and wind. *Unknown*. OxNR

Through storms you reach them and from storms are free. The Enviable Isles. Herman Melville. NCAP

Through summer air. Flight. Jorge Guillén, *Spanish*. BLT, tr. by Reginald Gibbons

Through swamps and alligators I wend my weary way. On the Lakes of Ponchartrain. *Unknown*. AmFP

Through that pure *Virgin-Shrine,*. The Night. Henry Vaughan. ChIV-2; EBEV; ESCV; FSCP; GeHe; MeLP; NAEL-1; NOBE; NOCV; NoP-4; OAEL-1; OBEV; OBWVE; OxAEP-1; PoEL-2; SCGP; TFi; TOF

Through that window—all else being extinct. The Room. Conrad Potter Aiken. LiTM; MoAmPo; NOBA

Through the ample open door of the peaceful country barn. A Farm Picture. Walt Whitman. BLT; InPS-3; TRP

Through the Appalachian valleys. A Ballad of Johnny Appleseed. Helmer O. Oleson. CTV

Through the bending twigs of the coral grove. (LL) The Coral Grove. James Gates Percival. APN-1; ColAP

Through the black, rushing smoke-bursts. The Song of Callicles. Matthew Arnold. NOBE; OAEL-2; OBEV   *Fr.* Empedocles on Etna.

Through the bound cable strands, the arching path. Atlantis. Hart Crane. LiTM   *Fr.* The Bridge. NAAL-2

Through the broad bright land. (LL) The Song of the Ungirt Runners. Charles Hamilton Sorley. MoBrPo; OBEV

Through the corridor walks a blind man. The Blind Man. Yaroslav Vasilevich Smelyakov, *Russian*. TCRP, tr. by Simon Franklin

Through the cracks. Ray A. Young Bear. STP

Through the dark city. (LL) The Great Figure. William Carlos Williams. AiP; HeIP-4; InPK-6; MoP; NoAM; SAmP; TTTS

Through the dark night. Destroyers. "Klaxon." NSI

Through the Dark Sod—as Education. Emily Dickinson. NALW

Through the Dark the Dreamers Came. Earl Bowman Marlatt. AH

Through the deep litter of the years. (LL) River Road. Stanley Kunitz. MoP; NoAM

Through the deep night a magic mist led me. A Magic Mist. Owen Roe O'Sullivan, Irish. NOIV, tr. by Thomas Kinsella

Through the deep shadows of the darkening years. Paul Hamilton Hayne. APN-2

Through the downiness of the grey dawn. Your Eyes. Angelina Weld Grimké. CPO

Through the dusky purple glimmer. Anita and Giovanni. Henrietta Cordelia Ray. CBWP-3

Through the Forest Have I Gone. Shakespeare. CTC Fr. A Midsummer Night's Dream.

Through the forest the boy wends all day long. The Boy and the Flute. Bjørnstjerne Bjørnson, Norwegian. AWP, tr. by Sir Edmund Gosse

Through the great sinful streets of Naples as I past. Easter Day. Naples, 1849. Arthur Hugh Clough. EBVVPR

Through the House. Shakespeare. CTC Fr. A Midsummer Night's Dream.

Through the house what busy joy. The First Tooth. Charles Lamb and Mary Lamb. ACTP; OxBChV; WoRP

Through the imperfect glass of windows. Imperfect Air. Ralph Hawkins. NBrP

Through the lands low-lying, fast and free. A Moonlight Ride. Harriet Hamilton King. VWP

Through the lit crystal of the cup. (LL) Autumn. Roy Campbell. GTBS-P; MoBrPo; OBMV; OxBTC

Through the long death of the moon. The Death of the Moon. David Wagoner. PoA

Through the Looking-Glass. "Lewis Carroll."

Humpty Dumpty's Song. GTBS-P; OBCoV; OxBChV; OxBoLi; PeLV

(Humpty Dumpty's Recitation.) OBSP; PeVV

Jabberwocky. APAD; CABP; CBNP; CTV; ChAP; ClHu; EBEV; EBEvV; EBVV; FPC; FaBoBe; HeIP-4; HoPM; ImPo; InPK-6; InPS-3; NAEL-2; NBLV; NOBE; NOBL; NOBVV; NOxBChV; NTCP; NoAM; NoP-4; OAEL-2; OBSP; OxAEP-2; OxBChV; PFE; PeLV; PeVV; PoRA; Poetr; RB; SAGP; TFi; TRP; TTTS; UV

Walrus and the Carpenter, The. BLPA; CABP; CBNP; ChAP; EBEvV; FPC; FaBoBe; NAEL-2; NOBL; NOBVV; NoAM; OBSP; OTCP; OxAEP-2; OxBChV; PeLV; PoRA; SAGP; TFi

White Knight's Song, The. CBNP; FaBoCh; InPS-3; NAEL-2; NOBE; NOBL; NoAM; NoP-4; OAEL-2; PeLV

(Aged, Aged Man, The.) BXAP; OxBChV

(White Knight's Ballad, The.) HAP

Through the narrow aisles of pain. (LL) Solitude. Ella Wheeler Wilcox. EBEvV; PWR; PoLF; SDW

Through the night on fire with my blood. She Speaks the Morning's Filigree. Philip Lamantia. VGW

Through the open French window the warm sun. Still-Life. Elizabeth Daryush. FaBoWP; WPE; WPN

Through the open porch window. Feeling Through. Alvin Aubert. BkSV

Through the Parklands, through the Parklands. The Parklands. Stevie Smith. MoBS

Through the Porthole. Marjorie Wilson. BoTP

Through the rain forests, up a long river. The Deceptive Grin of the Gravel Porters. Gavin Ewart. FaBoMo

Through the shrubs as I can crack[e]. Doron's Jigge. Robert Greene. PoEL-2 Fr. Menaphon.

Through the slits of my eyes a perambulator passes. The Sun. Hugo Ball, German. PFTM, tr. by Christopher Middleton

Through the small holes. Cor Van den Heuvel. HA

Through the Smoke Hole. Gary Snyder. BB

Through the soft evening air enwinding all. Italian Music in Dakota. Walt Whitman. APN-2

Through the spacescope's limitless eyes. The Destroyers. Albert Rowe. SpW

Through the state of this soul. Homo Plangens. Nichita Stanescu, Romanian. CEEP, tr. by Petru Popescu and Peter Jay

Through the strait gate of passion. Paradise Re-entered. D. H. Lawrence. ChIV-2

Through the strait pass of suffering. Emily Dickinson. TOF

Through the sunny garden. Chillingham. Mary Elizabeth Coleridge. BoTP

Through the tobacco haze. Blew It. Michael Castro. SeSe

Through the vague morning, the heart preoccupied. Bombers. C. Day Lewis. CMoP

Through the viridian (and black of the burnt match). Virgo Descending. Charles Wright. ColAP; LCAP-2; TRP; WeT

Through the wall. Martin Shea. HA

. . . Through the wall, uprore. George Chapman. PBRV Fr. Homer's Iliad Book 12.

Through the white thin bone of a hare. (LL) The Collarbone [or Collar-Bone] of a Hare. W. B. Yeats. CBNP; NTP; OxAEP-2; OxBTC; RB

Through the wide, grey lit window. A Village Life. Derek Walcott. GT

Through the Window. Vladislav Felitsianovich Khodasevich, Russian. TCRP, tr. by Yakov Hornstein

Through the window I see. The Clothespin. Rhonda Bower. IFJA

Through the windy valley. Yün Shou-p'ing. CoBLCP, tr. by Jonathan Chaves Fr. Inscribed on a Painting by Shih-ku.

Through the world we safely go, Lines 1–58. William Blake. See To see a World in a Grain of Sand.

Through the world we safely go. (LL) To see a World in a Grain of Sand, Lines 1–58. William Blake. EBEvV; KaS

Through the Year. Julian S. Cutler. BLPA

Through them into the future, into night. Joseph Brodsky. See Six Years Later.

Through These Pale Cold Days. Isaac Rosenberg. TrJP

Through these ruined walls. Port Bou. Sylvia Townsend Warner. WPN

Through this toilsome world, alas! I Shall Not Pass This Way Again. Unknown. BLPA; ChAP

Through thy submitting all, to blow[e]s. Donne. Fr. The Litanie. PoEL-2

Through torrid entrances, past icy poles. To Shakespeare. Hart Crane. Son

Through tranquil years they watched the changes. Clearing for the Plough. Ernest G. Moll. NOBAu

Through Warmth and Light of Summer Skies. Austin Faricy. AH

Through water, his own waterfall. Cold Fire. George Starbuck. NYBP

Through weeds and thorns, and matted underwood. The Picture; or, The Lover's Resolution. Coleridge. Ro

Through what long heaviness, assayed in what strange fire. Carthusians. Ernest Christopher Dowson. NAEL-2

Through what obscure, half-comprehending night. Candlemas Day. Sister Mary Madeleva. AH

Through which we go / Is I. (LL) Napoleon. Walter De la Mare. FaBoCh; FaBoTw; NOBE; RB; Spl

Through wild and tangled forests. On the Mississippi. Hamlin Garland. APN-2

Through Willing Heart and Helping Hand. Frederick Lucian Hosmer. AH

Through winter-time we call on spring. The Wheel. W. B. Yeats. GTBS-P; Poetr

Through woods, Mme Une Telle, a trifle ill. Autumn Chapter in a Novel. Thom Gunn. FaBoMo; OxBTC

Through years and years. The Day We Buried Our Bully. Mbuyiseni Oswald Mtshali. PeSAV

Through You. Edwin Honig. TAP

Through your denials. (LL) Black Mother Woman. Audre Lorde. CrSp; MDDM; Poetr

Through your love words became clear. The Word "Silk." Thomas McCarthy. CIP-2

Through your own efforts learn, and Heaven helps. Advice to Students. Phùng Khắc Khoan, Vietnamese. AVP, tr. by Huỳnh Sanh Thông

Throughe a forest as I can ryde. Crow and Pie. Unknown. ESPB

Throughout a garden greene and gay. The Rose of England. Unknown. ESPB

Throughout the day our sweet bells chime. Bluebells. P. A. Ropes. BoTP

Throughout the day we are able to ban the voices. Henriëtte Roland-Holst, Dutch. PBWP, tr. by Manfred Wolf

Throughout the field I find no grain. Winter in Durnover Field. Thomas Hardy. MoBrPo

Throughout the funeral . . . even as her nails. My Mother's Face Never Moved. Anne C. Bromley. CMAP

Throughout the seventh month, rain sobs and wails. Calling All Souls. Nguyễn Du, Vietnamese. AVP, tr. by Huỳnh Sanh Thông

Throughout the whole world, experts say. Limerick. Unknown. PeLi

Throughout the world, if it were sought. Sir Thomas Wyatt. NoSic; OxBSP

Throw Away the Flowers. Elizabeth Daryush. PBWP

Throw away thy rod. Discipline. George Herbert. FHYEP; FSCP; GeHe; MeLP; NAEL-1; NOBE; NOCV; NoP-4; OBEV; OxAEP-1; PoLF

Throw away thy wrath. (LL) Discipline. George Herbert. FHYEP; FSCP; GeHe; MeLP; NAEL-1; NOBE; NOCV; NoP-4; OBEV; OxAEP-1; PoLF

Throw Hannibal on the scales, how many pounds. Hannibal ("Throw Hannibal on the scales, how many pounds"). Juvenal. OBVE, tr. by Robert Lowell Fr. Satires.

Throw him into the river. Kasenduaxtc, Tlingit Indian. STP, tr. by James Koller

Throw into the little box / A stone. The Tenants of the Little Box. Vasco [or Vasko] Popa, *Serbo-Croatian.* HSix, *tr.* by Charles Simic

Throw on rouge and powder, watch the governor pass! Tune: Sand of Silk-washing Stream ("Throw on rouge and powder, watch the governor pass!"). Su Tung-p'o. CoBCP *Fr.* Along the Road to Stone Lake.

Throw the raincoat under us! (LL) Hops. Boris Pasternak, *Russian.* LoP, *tr.* by Robert Lowell

Throw Yourself Like Seed. Miguel de Unamuno, *Spanish.* RaBo, *tr.* by Robert Bly

Throwing a ball. Sometimes I Get Distracted. Elaine Equi. BAP-95

Throwing a bomb is bad. Ethics for Everyman. Roger Woddis. NOBL

Throwing her arms around her father. Anyte, *Greek.* GrAn, *tr.* by Sally Purcell

Throwing Out at / of (Com)pare (Dis)pair, A. Tina Darragh. FTOS

Throwing Out the Flowers. Gwendolyn Brooks. ColAP *Fr.* Notes from the Childhood and the Girlhood. LCAP-2

Throwing the Beads. Sean Dunne. BiHa

Thrown from the world. (LL) Revelation in the Mother Lode. George Evans. AF; PmAP

Thrown in the moon-glade by the palm. (LL) Dirge: "Stay, Death. Not mine the Christus-wand." Herman Melville. APN-1; NCAP

Thrown off-center. Theory of Curve. Christopher Gilbert. LTA

Thru the 12 Houses of Heaven. Luis Cabalquinto. *See* Canto 113.

Thrush. George Seferis, *Greek.*

Wreck "Thrush," The. GrIP, *tr.* by Edmund Keeley and Philip Sherrard

Thrush before Dawn, A. Alice Thompson Meynell. MoBrPo; WPE

Thrush in February, The. George Meredith. OBNC

Thrush In the Trenches, A. Humbert Wolfe. NSI

Thrush is tapping a stone, A. Dawn. Gordon Bottomley. BoTP; MoBrPo

Thrush, linnet, stare and wren In Glencullen. John Millington Synge. OBMV

Thrushes. Ted Hughes. FaBoMo; TRP

Thrushes sing as the sun is going, The. Proud Songsters. Thomas Hardy. MoP

Thrush's Nest, The. John Clare. BoTP

Thrush's Song, The. *Unknown, Gaelic.* CH, *tr.* by William MacGillivray

Thrust & Parry. Greg Delanty. BiHa

Thrust and Riposte. Eugenio Montale, *Italian.* PeFWW, *tr.* by Gavin Ewart

Thrust of the dragon's tight bone, The. The Dream Feast (Three Poems). Anita Endrezze-Danielson. VoR

Thrust upon by a softly-swinging wind. (LL) The Weather-Cock Points South. Amy Lowell. CPO; NALW; NoP-4

Thrusting its armoury of hot delight. Descartes and the Stove. Charles Tomlinson. FaBoMo

Thule, The Period of Cosmography. *Unknown.* HAP

"Andalusian merchant, that returns, The." FaBoCh

Thumb. Philip Dacey. KaS

Thumb bold. *Unknown.* OxNR

Thumb he. *Unknown.* OxNR

Thumb, loose tooth of a horse. Bestiary for the Fingers of My Right Hand. Charles Simic. AmPA; LCAP-2

Thumbikin, Thumbikin, broke the barn. *Unknown.* OxNR

Thumbing Old Magazines. Gerald Vizenor. VoR

Thumbkin says, I'll dance. *Unknown.* OxNR

Thumbprint. Celeste Turner Wright. Poetsp

"Thumbs in the thumb-place." The Mitten Song. Marie Louise Allen. NTCP

Thumb's-length landscape: Snow, on a hill, A. Snow Landscape, in a Glass Globe. Jean Valentine. NMM-2

Thumbs Up. Judith Baumel. WWSi

Thumping gavel the Otterburn Ranges behind and never unravel. Otter, Redewetter. Colin Simms. NBrP

Thumping old tunes give a voice to its whereabouts. Fairground. W. H. Auden. NYBP

Thunder. Pat Therese Francis. EC2

Thunder. Yun-gi Hong, *Korean.* CKP, *tr.* by Jaihiun Kim

Thunder & the flaw of their great quarrel, The. John Berryman. VCAP *Fr.* Dream Songs.

Thunder Can Break. Christopher Okigbo. HBAPE

Thunder clouds are sweeping, shrouding. A Russian Cradle Song. David Nomberg, *Yiddish.* TrJP, *tr.* by Alter Brody

Thunder. Enter the three Witches. Shakespeare. OxBSn *Fr.* Macbeth.

Thunder God Cliff. Chao Meng-fu. *Fr.* Twenty-Eight Poems Inscribed on T'ien-kuan Mountain. CoBLCP, *tr.* by Jonathan Chaves

Thunder God rouses sleeping dragons, The. Thunder God Cliff. Chao Meng-fu. *Fr.* Twenty-Eight Poems Inscribed on T'ien-kuan Mountain. CoBLCP, *tr.* by Jonathan Chaves

Thunder has nested in the grass all night. Child Frightened by a Thunderstorm. Ted Kooser. KaS

Thunder in the Garden. William Morris. GaP

Thunder in the southern mountains, the third month of the year. Wang Chiu-ssu, *Chinese.* CoBLCP, *tr.* by Jonathan Chaves

Thunder mutters louder and more loud, The. John Clare. EnVR; NOBVV

Thunder My Brother. Malka Heifetz-Tussman, *Yiddish.* CEEP, *tr.* by Kathryn Hellerstein

Thunder. My heart trembles. Fu Hsüan, *Chinese.* OHMPC, *tr.* by Kenneth Rexroth

Thunder of the Rain God. A House in Taos. Langston Hughes. NAAAL

Thunder: Perfect Mind, The. *Unknown.*

"I was sent forth from the power." PFTM, *tr.* by George W. MacRae

"Sent from the Power." WPoS

Thunder, rain falling, falling. Inscribed on a Painting. Hsü Wei, *Chinese.* CoBLCP, *tr.* by Jonathan Chaves

Thunder roars past creeks and mountains. Picking Tea: A Ballad. Kao Ch'i, *Chinese.* SuSp, *tr.* by Irving Y. Lo

Thunder storm passing. Foster Jewell. HA

Thunder: the flesh quails, and the soul bows down. John Webster. Swinburne. *Fr.* Sonnets of English Dramatic Poets. Son

Thundering drums and cannons. Sacrifice. Christopher Okigbo. PBMAP

Thundering sea, why in savage storm did you plunge. Leonidas of Tarentum. HePo, *tr.* by Barbara Hughes Fowler *Fr.* Epigrams.

Thunderous vapours! / water-spout with lion's teeth. War. Patrice Kayo. PBMAP

Thunders over you all. (LL) Potpourri from a Surrey Garden. John Betjeman. CBLP; NOBL

Thunderstorm. Pavel Davydovich Kogan, *Russian.* TCRP, *tr.* by Daniel Weissbort

Thunderstorm, A. Archibald Lampman. NOBC

Thunderstorm. Sam Mitchell, *Aborigine.* NOBAu, *tr.* by Georg von Brandenstein

Thunderstorm in South Dakota. Kay Boyle. WPE

Thunderstorm in Town, A. Thomas Hardy. APAD; BoLoP; CBLP; EnLoPo; GBL; GLoP; OxBSP

Thurn, A. John Berryman. NOBA

Thursday. Edna St. Vincent Millay. PoA

Thursday; or, The Spell. John Gay. PoEL-3 *Fr.* The Shepherd's Week.

Thirteen bluddy years wi thim ih. Simple Simon. Tom Leonard. FaBoTC

Thus Achelous ends; his audience hear. Baucis and Philemon. Ovid, *Latin.* NOSC, *tr.* by Dryden *Fr.* Metamorphoses.

Thus Adam himself lamented loud. Milton. OAEL-1 *Fr.* Book X. FHYEP *Fr.* Paradise Lost.

Thus all is here in motion, all is life. Urban Progress. John Dyer. ECEV, *ll.* 1–20 *Fr.* The Fleece.

Thus all men's pleas the Judge with ease. Michael Wigglesworth. NAAL-3 *Fr.* The Day of Doom. NAAL-1; SCAP

Thus all that day, they spent in divers talke. Sir John Harington. PBRV *Fr.* Ariosto's Orlando Furioso Book 34.

Thus am I mine own prison. Everything. Verse II. Christina Rossetti. PEW *Fr.* The Thread of Life.

Thus at the panting Dove a Falcon flies. Hector Flees before Achilles. Homer. OBVE, *tr.* by Alexander Pope *Fr.* The Iliad.

Thus been they parted, Arthur on his way. The Cave of Despair. Edmund Spenser. OBNV *Fr.* Wood Of Error. AEP

Thus began / Outrage from lifeless things; but Discord first. Milton. NAEL-1 *Fr.* Book X. FHYEP *Fr.* Paradise Lost.

Thus being entered, they behold around. Edmund Spenser. OAEL-1 *Fr.* Wood Of Error. AEP

Thus Belial with words clothed in reason's garb. Milton. FaBoPV *Fr.* Book II. FHYEP; NAEL-1; OxAEP-1 *Fr.* Paradise Lost.

Thus briefly sketched [or sketch'd] the naked rights of man. On Mr. Paine's Rights of Man. Philip Freneau. AmPP; NAAL-1; NAAL-3

Thus by himself compelled to live each day. George Crabbe. NOBE; OBNC *Fr.* Peter Grimes. EBNV; ECEV; FHYEP; OBNV; PoEL-4; Ro *Fr.* The Borough.

Thus charg'd he; nor Argicides denied. Homer. OBVE, *tr.* by George Chapman *Fr.* Odyssey. NAWM-1, *tr.* by Robert Fitzgerald

Thus chydand with her drery desteny. Cressida's Leprosy. Robert Henryson. *Fr.* The Testament of Cresseid. OxBS

Thus could I sing and thus rejoice—but it is not so with me. (LL) Night II (Enion's Lament). William Blake. PoE; Ro

Thus critics, of less judgment than caprice. Alexander Pope. OAEL-1 *Fr.* An Essay on Criticism. NAEL-1; PoEL-3; TFi

Thus Crosslegged on Round Pillow Sat in Space. Allen Ginsberg. NNaP

Thus departed Hiawatha. (LL) Hiawatha's Photographing. "Lewis Carroll." BXAP; NOBL; PeLV

Thus did this ancient poet look. (LL) The Description of Sir Chaucer. Robert Greene. CTC; FaBoCh; NoSic; SCGP

Thus down a lone valley with cedars o'er spread. Columbia. *Unknown.* AmFP

Thus dullness, the safe opiate of the mind. On Dullness. Alexander Pope. OxBSP

Thus ebbs and flows the current of her sorrow. Lucrece's Death. Shakespeare. NoSic *Fr.* The Rape of Lucrece.

Thus ends my lay: Reluctantly I leave. Albery Allson Whitman. AAP *Fr.* Twasinta's Seminoles; Or Rape of Florida.

Thus ends my Love, but this doth grieve me most. Loves End. Edward Herbert, 1st Baron Herbert of Cherbury. SeCP

Thus Eve to Adam. Milton. *Fr.* Book IV. OAEL-1 *Fr.* Paradise Lost.

Thus every Creature, and of every Kind. Love and the Creatures. Virgil, *Latin.* EP, *tr. by* John Dryden

Thus every dream secretly and small inscribes its letters. Dreams Are Also Wounds. Breyten Breytenbach, *Afrikaans.* VCWP, *tr. by* André Brink

Thus everyone before the throne. Michael Wigglesworth. NAAL-3 *Fr.* The Day of Doom. NAAL-1; SCAP

("Moreover, there with them appear.") ColAP

("Who not at all thereon did call, / or took in vain the same.") (LL) ColAP

Thus far, O Friend! have we, though leaving much. School-Time. Wordsworth. FHYEP *Fr.* The Prelude; Growth of a Poet's Mind [1850 vers.]

Thus far was right, the rest belongs to Heav'n. (LL) Epistle to Dr. Arbuthnot. Alexander Pope. FHYEP; InPS-3; NOEC; OAEL-1; OxAEP-1; OxBoLi; PoE; PoEL-3; TFi

Thus far, with rough and all-unable pen. Epilogue. Shakespeare. CTC *Fr.* King Henry V.

Thus fareth many and many an one'. (LL) The Complaint of the Fair Armoress [or Armouress]. François Villon, *French.* AWP; CTC; OBVE, *tr. by* Algernon Charles Swinburne

Thus fell the King, who yet surviv'd the state. The Death of Priam. Virgil. OBVE, *tr. by* Sir John Denham *Fr.* The Aeneid [or Eneados, *Aeneis*].

Thus fell two Heroes; one the Pride of *Thrace.* Equity in death. Homer. OBCVT, *tr. by* Alexander Pope *Fr.* The Iliad.

Thus gamesters united in friendship are found. Packington's Pound. John Gay. *Fr.* The Beggar's Opera. OAEL-1

Thus glory hath her being! thus she stands. Glory and Enduring Fame. William Gilmore Simms. Son

Thus Harriet, rising on the stage. Harriet Simper Has Her Day. John Trumbull. *Fr.* The Progress of Dulness. AmPP

Thus hath his death raised up this soul of mine. (LL) Sonnet: "Down[e] in the depth of mine iniquity." Greville Fulke. NOSC; NoSic

Thus have I back again[e] to thy bright name. An Apologie for the Precedent Hymnes on Tereas. Richard Crashaw. ESCV

Thus have I shunned the fire for fear of burning. Shakespeare. GBL *Fr.* The Two Gentlemen of Verona.

Thus having been, that thou shouldst cease to be. (LL) To Wordsworth. Shelley. EPCY; FHYEP; NoP-4; Ro; Son

Thus having passed all peril, I was come. Happy Isle. Edmund Spenser. *Fr.* Wood Of Error. AEP

Thus he doth find of all mankind. Michael Wigglesworth. NAAL-3 *Fr.* The Day of Doom. NAAL-1; SCAP

"Thus I bestride the railing, leg o'er leg." Robert Browning. EBVVPR, *sect. IV Fr.* Red Cotton Night-Cap Country. EBVVPR

Thus I come to you. Author Unknown. William Montgomerie. OxBS

Thus I complain my grevous hevynesse. *Unknown.* MiEL

Thus I have written this poem on a jet seat in mid Heaven. (LL) Kral Majales. Allen Ginsberg. BB; PoM

Thus I / Pass [or Passe] by. Upon His Departure Hence. Robert Herrick. Poetr

Thus I resolve, and time hath taught me so. Thomas Campion. OxBSP

Thus I stand like the Turk, with his doxies around. John Gay. PeLV *Fr.* The Beggar's Opera. OAEL-1

Thus in alternate uproar and sad peace. Keats. FHYEP *Fr.* Hyperion. OAEL-2; Ro

Thus is his cheek the map of days outworn. Sonnet 68. Shakespeare. SCGP *Fr.* Sonnets.

Thus laykes this lorde by lynde-wodes eves. Gawain and the Lady of the Castle. *Unknown.* EBEV *Fr.* Sir Gawain and the Green Knight. OAEL-1, *tr. by* Brian Stone

Thus Lays of Minstrels—may they be the last! Byron. EPCY *Fr.* English Bards and Scotch Reviewers.

Thus like a Sayler by the Tempest hurl'd. Lucretius. OBCVT, *tr. by* John Dryden *Fr.* Lucretius. Book the Fifth.

Thus love, bright charlatan, besieged my heart. Vita Sackville-West. WPN

Thus man by his own strength to Heaven would soar. Dryden. NOCV *Fr.* Religio Laici.

Thus man devotes his brother and destroys. Henry Highland Garnet. CrDW

Thus, many tales *Ulysses* told his wife. Homer. OBCVT, *tr. by* George Chapman *Fr.* The Odyssey.

Thus may'st thou ever, evermore rejoice! (LL) Dejection. Coleridge. FHYEP; HeIP-4; NAEL-2; NAWM-2; NOBE; NOBRP; OAEL-2; OBNC; OxAEP-2; PoE; PoEL-4; Ro; TFi; TOF

Thus Modesty, and Spotless Innocence. Mary Mollineux. KTR *Fr.* Of Modesty.

Thus more and more the kingdoms are extended. The First Stone of the New Castle. *Unknown, Dutch.* PeSAV, *tr. by* H. C. V. Leibbrandt

Thus much he prayed, and thence away he went. Ludovico Ariosto, *Italian.* NoSic, *tr. by* Sir John Harington *Fr.* Orlando Furioso.

Thus, near the gates conferring as they drew. Ulysses and His Dog. Homer. *Fr.* Odyssey. NAWM-1, *tr. by* Robert Fitzgerald

Thus now I leave my love in fortunes. Sir Walter Ralegh. PBRV *Fr.* Fortune hath taken the away my love.

Thus o'er his art indignant Rubens reared. Rubens. Washington Allston. APN-1

Thus Passeth. *Unknown.* PFE

Thus / people, huddled in a trench. A Ballad about Friendship. Semyon Petrovich Gudzenko, *Russian.* TCRP, *tr. by* Gordon McVay

Thus piteously Love closed what he begat. A Dusty Answer. George Meredith. EBEV; EnLoPo; EnVR; GSo; GTBS-P; HAP; NOBE; NOBVV; NoP-4; OAEL-2; OBNC; OxAEP-2; PoE; PoEL-5; SCGP; Son; TFi *Fr.* Modern Love.

Thus poor thieves suffer when the greater 'scape. (LL) If he, from heaven that filched the living fire. Michael Drayton. AAS; NoP-4

Thus queth Alvred:/ 'Idelschipe and overprute, that lereth yong wif üvel thewes'. Alfred, King of England. *Fr.* The Proverbs of Alfred. PoE

Thus queth Alvred:/ 'If thu havest seorewe, ne seyethu hit than arewe' . Alfred, King of England. *Fr.* The Proverbs of Alfred. PoE

Thus queth Alvred:/ 'Ne schaltu nevere thi wif by hire wlyte cheose' . Alfred, King of England. *Fr.* The Proverbs of Alfred. PoE

Thus queth Alvred:/ 'Ne würth thu never so wod ne so wyn-drunke' . Alfred, King of England. *Fr.* The Proverbs of Alfred. PoE

Thus queth Alvred:/ 'Nevre thu, bi thine lyve, the word of thine wyve' . Alfred, King of England. *Fr.* The Proverbs of Alfred. PoE

Thus reader, by our astrologick art. Almanac Verse. *Unknown.* SCAP

Thus said The Lord in the Vault above the Cherubim. The Last Chantey. Rudyard Kipling. FaBoCh; MoBrPo

Thus said the rushing raven. A Croon on Hennacliff. Robert Stephen Hawker. NOBVV

Thus saith my Chloris bright. Giovanni Battista Guarini, *Italian.* GBL

Thus saith the great god Thoth. He Is Declared True of Word. *Unknown.* AWP *Fr.* Book of the Dead.

Thus saith the Ruler of the Skies. The Passion and Exaltation of Christ. Isaac Watts. NOCV

Thus, San Augustine's church and prison joined. Albery Allson Whitman. AAP *Fr.* Twasinta's Seminoles; Or Rape of Florida.

Thus saying, from her husband's hand her hand. The Fall. Milton. PoEL-3 *Fr.* Book IX. FHYEP; NAEL-1; NAWM-1; OAEL-1 *Fr.* Paradise Lost.

Thus saying, from her side the fatal Key. Milton. EBEV *Fr.* Book II. FHYEP; NAEL-1; OxAEP-1 *Fr.* Paradise Lost.

Thus saying rose / The monarch, and prevented all reply. Occupations of Hell. Milton. NOSC *Fr.* Book II. FHYEP; NAEL-1; OxAEP-1 *Fr.* Paradise Lost.

Thus set them *ope*. (LL) I Am the Doore. Richard Crashaw. GeHe; NAEL-1

Thus shall they lie, and wail, and cry. Michael Wigglesworth. NAAL-3 *Fr.* The Day of Doom. NAAL-1; SCAP

Thus she had lain. Africa. Maya Angelou. NIP-4

Thus should have been our travels. Over 2000 Illustrations and a Complete Concordance. Elizabeth Bishop. HCAP; LCAP-2; NAAL-2; NoAM; VCAP

Thus spake an old Chinese mandarin. Limerick. *Unknown.* PeLi

Thus Spake the Saviour. Jeremy Belknap. AH

Thus spoke the lady underneath the tree. Colonel Fantock. Dame Edith Sitwell. MoBrPo; OBMV

Thus Sung Orpheus to His Strings. *Unknown.* GBL

Thus sweetly sad of old, the *Cyclops* strove. Theocritus. OBCVT, *tr. by* Richard Duke *Fr.* The Cyclops.

Thus talking hand in hand alone they pass'd. Milton. EBEV *Fr.* Book IV. OAEL-1 *Fr.* Paradise Lost.

Thus the Mayne Glideth. Robert Browning. OBEV *Fr.* Paracelsus.

Thus the tale ended. (LL) The Skeleton in Armor [or Armour]. Henry Wadsworth Longfellow. APN-1; AWP; AmPP; CTV; FaBoBe

Thus think, then drink Tobacco. (LL) A Religious Use of [Taking] Tobacco. Robert Wisdome. OBCoV; OBEV; SCGP

Thus to *Glaucus* spake. Homer. *See* Sarpedon's Speech to Glaucus.

Thus to Glaucus spake / Divine Sarpedon, since he did not find. Sarpedon's Speech to Glaucus. Homer, *Greek.* OBVE, *tr. by* Sir John Denham *Fr.* The Iliad.

Thus, up to manhood he arose. His Manhood. George Clinton Rowe. AAP *Fr.* Toussaint L'Overture.

Thus was this place, / A happy rural seat of various view. Eden. Milton. PeECV, *ll.* 246–275 *Fr.* Book IV. OAEL-1 *Fr.* Paradise Lost.

Thus were my sympathies enlarged, and thus. Wordsworth. *Fr.* School-Time. FHYEP *Fr.* The Prelude; Growth of a Poet's Mind [1850 vers.]

Thus when the swallow, seeking prey. Song. John Gay. PoEL-3 *Fr.* The Beggar's Opera. OAEL-1

Thus while my joyless hours I lingring spend. John Phillips. *Fr.* The Splendid Shilling. BXAP; OAEL-1

Thus will despair. The Succubus. Robert Graves. EP; OAEL-2

Thus with imagin'd wing our swift scene flies. Shakespeare. EBEV; OxAEP-1 *Fr.* King Henry V.

Thus write I much, to hinder all *disgrace.* (LL) Excuse for So Much Writ upon My Verses. Margaret Lucas Cavendish, Duchess of Newcastle. KTR; PEW

Thwarted. Priscilla Jane Thompson. CBWP-2

Thy after shock, Manassas, share. (LL) The March into Virginia. Herman Melville. HAP; ImPo; NAAL-1; NCAP; PoE; TAP

Thy arms with bracelets I will deck. Homage. Gustave Kahn, *French.* TrJP, *tr. by* Jethro Bithell

Thy ax shall harm it not. (LL) Woodman, spare that tree! George Pope Morris. APN-1; BLPA; FaBoBe; PWR

Thy azure robe, I did behold, Julia's Petticoat. Robert Herrick. BeJo; CaPo; CavPo

Thy banks, O Barrow, sure must be. Written by the Barrow Side, Where She Was Sent to Wash Linen. Ellen Taylor. ECWP

Thy beauty haunts me heart and soul. The Moon. W. H. Davies. MoBrPo

Thy Best. Henry Cole. PWR

Thy blessing on the boys—for time has come. Prayer. Haim Guri, *Hebrew.* TrJP, *tr. by* Ruth H. Lask

Thy bosom is endeared with all hearts. Sonnet 31. Shakespeare. NOBE; OBEV; PoEL-2 *Fr.* Sonnets.

Thy bottle make my soul, Lord, it to hold. (LL) Thy human frame, my glorious Lord, I spy. Edward Taylor. ChIV-1; MeMAP

Thy braes were bonny, Yarrow stream. The Braes of Yarrow. John Logan. GTBS-P; SCGP

"Thy breath is far sweeter than honey." Far Sweeter than Honey. Abraham ibn Ezra, *Hebrew.* TrJP, *tr. by* Israel Abrahams

Thy Brother's Blood. Jones Very. APN-1; NOBA; PAR; PoEL-4; TAP

Thy byrth, thy beautie, nor thy brave attyre. Farewell with a Mischeife. George Gascoigne. AAS

Thy copp's, too, nam'd of Gamage, thou hast there. Ben Jonson. *Fr.* To Penshurst. AWP; BeJo; CABP; NOSC; NoP-4; OAEL-1; PBRV; PoEL-2; SeCP; TFi

Thy country, Wilberforce, with just disdain. To William Wilberforce, Esq. William Cowper. Son

Thy curate's place, thy fruitful wife. Jonathan Swift. UV *Fr.* The Parson's Case.

Thy dawn, O Ra, opens the new horizon. Adoration of the Disk by King Akhnaten and Princess Nefer Neferiu Aten. *Unknown.* AWP *Fr.* Book of the Dead.

Thy eagle-sighted prophets too. The Prophets. Donne. *Fr.* The Litanie. PoEL-2

Thy eyes and eyebrows I could spare. *Unknown.* FaBoEE

Thy fabulous provinces belong. (LL) Philomela. John Crowe Ransom. CMoP; FuPo; NAAL-2; NOBA; NoAM; OBAL; OBSV; OxBA

Thy fair smoothe words? no, no, thy fair smoothe haunches. (LL) The Author to His Wife, of a Woman's Eloquence. Sir John Harington. BoLoP; OxBM

Thy Faithful Sons. Eleazar, *Hebrew.* TrJP

Thy father all from thee, by his last will. Disinherited. Donne. FMP

Thy fingers make early flowers of. E. E. Cummings. MoAmPo; NAAL-2

Thy flattering picture, Phryne, is like thee. Phryne. Donne. FaBoEE

Thy flesh to earth, thy soul to God. General B. F. Butler. Ambrose Bierce. CBCWP

Thy flow'r afloat, goolden zummer clote! (LL) The Clote (Water-Lily). William Barnes. FaBoVe; PoEL-4

Thy forests, Windsor! and thy green retreats. Alexander Pope. NOEC; OxAEP-1 *Fr.* Windsor-Forest [*or* Windsor Forest].

Thy Forests, Windsor! and thy green retreats. Windsor-Forest [*or* Windsor Forest]. Alexander Pope.

Thy friend, whom thy deserts to thee enchain[e]. To Mr. C.B. Donne. ESCV

Thy Garden. Don Allen Johnson, *Arabic.* AWP, *tr. by* Dulcie L. Smith

Thy garden, orchard, fields. Francis Daniel Pastorius. SCAP

Thy Genius, Colebrooke, faithless to his charge. To Colebrooke Dale. Anna Seward. ECWP

Thy glass will show thee how thy beauties wear. Sonnet 77. Shakespeare. HeIP-4 *Fr.* Sonnets.

Thy Glory then I'le make my fruits and Crop. (LL) My shattred phancy stole away from mee. Edward Taylor. NOSC; SCAP

Thy God, thy life, thy Cure. (LL) Peace. Henry Vaughan. AWP; EBEV; ESCV; FMP; FSCP; FaBoCh; GeHe; HAP; NOBE; NOCV; OBEV; OxAEP-1; PoE; SCGP; TFi; TOF; TrCP; WeW-3

Thy going out, and thy income, / the Lord keeps now and aye. Bible, *O.T. See* Psalm 121.

Thy going smileth in me over. Encounter. August Stramm, *German.* PFTM, *tr. by* Jerome Rothenberg

Thy gown? Why, ay. Come, tailor, let us see't. Shakespeare. OBCoV *Fr.* The Taming of the Shrew.

Thy grace, dear Lord's my golden wrack I find. Edward Taylor. SCAP *Fr.* Preparatory Meditations Before My Approach to the Lord's Supper.

Thy heart is in the upper world, where fleet the chamois bounds. The Chamois Hunter's Love. Felicia Dorothea Hemans. VWP

Thy heart is like some icy lake. *Unknown.* OBCoV

Thy Heaven. Thomas Moore. TIRV

Thy Heifer, Friend, is hardly broak. To his Friend in Love with a young Girl. Horace, *Latin.* OBCVT, *tr. by* Thomas Creech

Thy heinous hours wait on them as their pages. (LL) Opportunity. Shakespeare. NOBE; PoEL-2

Thy hue, dear pledge, is pure and bright. To a Lock of Hair. Sir Walter Scott. GTBS-P

Thy human frame, my glorious Lord, I spy. Edward Taylor. ChIV-1; MeMAP *Fr.* Preparatory Meditations Before My Approach to the Lord's Supper.

Thy husband to a banquet goes with me. 1.4. Ovid, *Latin.* CABP; NoSic, *tr. by* Marlowe *Fr.* Elegies.

Thy image, wavering, agonizing. Osip Emilevich Mandelstam, *Russian.* TCRP, *tr. by* Bernard Meares

Thy kingdom come: yea, bid it come. Holy Family. Katharine Tynan. TIRV

Thy life be written, and not read. (LL) An Elegy Upon the Death of His Own Father. Richard Corbet. BeJo; NOSC

Thy life has touched the edges of my life. My Spirit's Complement. Henrietta Cordelia Ray. AAP; CBWP-3

Thy love thou sentest oft to me. A Contrast. James Russell Lowell. NCAP

Thy Loving Kindness, Lord, I Sing. George Barrell Cheever. AH

Thy mansion is the Christian's heart. The House of Prayer. William Cowper. ChIV-2 *Fr.* Olney Hymns.

Thy Mercies, Lord, to Heaven Reach. William Kethe. AH

Thy mercy, Lord, God now thy mercy show. Psalm 57: Miserere Mei, Deus. Mary Sidney Herbert, Countess of Pembroke. PEW

Thy mercy on Thy People, Lord! (LL) Recessional. Rudyard Kipling. AWP; BLPA; CABP; CTV; EBEvV; FaBoPV; MoBrPo; NOBE; NOBVV; NoAM; NoP-4; OBEV; OBNC; OxAEP-2; PWR; SAGP; SCGP; TFi; UV; UnPo

Thy mind[e] of neither [*or* neather] needs, in both seeing [*or* seinge] it exceeds. (LL) If Cynthia be a queen, a princess, and supreme. Sir Walter Ralegh. SiPS

Thy Mother Was like a Vine. Bible, *O.T.* TrJP *Fr.* Ezekiel.

Thy nags (the leanest things alive). Epigram. Matthew Prior. FaBoEE

Thy nature, and Thy name is Love. (LL) Wrestling Jacob. Charles Wesley. NOBE; NOCV; NOEC; OBEV; OxAEP-1; PeECV; PoEL-3; TOF

Thy nights moan into my days. Psalms of Love. Peter Baum, *German.* AWP, *tr. by* Jethro Bithell

Thy nose no man can wipe, Proclus, unless. On Proclus's Great Nose. *Unknown.* PFE

Thy place is changed; thou art the same. (LL) Sad Hesper o'er the buried sun. Tennyson. EBVV; EnVR

Thy Praise, O God, in Zion Waits. Jacob Kimball. AH

Thy praise, O Lord, will I proclaim. Palms and Myrtles. Eleazar ben Kalir, *Hebrew.* TrJP, *tr. by* Alice Lucas

Thy praise or dispraise is to me alike. To Fool or Knave. Ben Jonson. FaBoEE; NoP-2

Thy restless feet now cannot go. Christ Crucified. Richard Crashaw. OBEV

Thy sacred academ[i]e above. The Doctors. Donne. *Fr.* The Litanie. PoEL-2

Thy sacred dew: protect them with thine influence. (LL) To the Evening Star. William Blake. CH; GSo; NAEL-2; NOEC; NoP-4; OAEL-2; PoE; PoLF; TFi

Thy sacred law, O God. On God's Law. Francis Quarles. ChIV-1

Thy sheep with thee. (LL) Rom. Cap. 8 Ver. 19. Henry Vaughan. ESCV; GeHe; MeLP

Thy sins [*or* sinnes] and hairs [*or* haires] may no man equal[l] call. A Licentious Person. Donne. PeLV

Thy sleep makes ridiculous. (LL) The Humble-Bee. Ralph Waldo Emerson. APN-1; APo; MeMAP; NCAP; NOBA; OxBA

Thy sooty godhead I desire. To Vulcan. Robert Herrick. CaPo

Thy soul / Grown delicate with satieties. O Atthis. Ezra Pound. PoA

Thy soul within such silent pomp did keep. A Quiet Soul. John Oldham. OBEV

Thy stricken daughter, now, O Lord, prepares. Hymn for the Eve of the New Year. Abraham Gerondi, *Hebrew*. TrJP, *tr. by* Solomon Solis-Cohen

Thy strong arms are around me, love. Worn Out. Elizabeth Siddal. SDW

Thy summer voice, Musketaquit. Two Rivers. Ralph Waldo Emerson. APN-1; AmPP; NCAP; NOBA; OxBA; PoE

Thy sword within the scabbard keep. Momus' Song to Mars. Dryden. OxBSP *Fr.* The Secular Masque. NAEL-1; OxAEP-1; PoE; PoEL-3; SCGP

Thy tears o'erprize thy loss! Thy wife. She Was Mine. Coventry Patmore. LBC

Thy thorne without, my thorne my heart inuadeth. (LL) The Nightingale as soone as April bringeth. Sir Philip Sidney. OxAEP-1; SCGP

Thy thoughts, dear Keats, are like fresh-gathered leaves. To Keats: On Reading His Sonnet Written in Chaucer. John Hamilton Reynolds. Son

Thy throne, to Thee the rent in happiness. (LL) Meditation 42. Edward Taylor. NAAL-1; NAAL-3

Thy trivial harp will never please. Merlin I. Ralph Waldo Emerson. NCAP; OxBA; PAR *Fr.* Merlin. APN-1; AmPP; NAAL-1; NAAL-3; NOBA

Thy various works, imperial queen, we see. On Imagination. Phillis Wheatley. AmPP; BlSi; CrDW; NAAAL; OxWW

Thy voice is on the rolling air. Tennyson. EBVV; EBVVPR; FHYEP; HeIP-4; OAEL-2 *Fr.* In Memoriam A. H. H.

Thy weary feet have pressed once more thy native soil. Welcome Home. Josephine D. Henderson Heard. CBWP-4

Thy wife's pox on thee, and Bess Braughton's too. (LL) An Execration upon Vulcan. Ben Jonson. BeJo; SeCP

Thy wisdom speaks in me, and bids me dare. Shelley. OAEL-2 *Fr.* Epipsychidion.

Thy woes and weep / No more. (LL) Comfort to a Youth That Had Lost His Love. Robert Herrick. NOBE; OBEV

Thy words are compounded of sweet-smelling myrrh. Words Wherein Stinging Bees Lurk. Judah Halevi, *Hebrew*. TrJP, *tr. by* Nina Davis Salaman

Thy worldly hopes and fears have passed away. To the Memory of Keats. John Clare. EPCY

Thy worn out heart will break at last, / My Mary! (LL) To Mary. William Cowper. EnLoPo; GTBS-P; NOEC; OBEV; UV

Thy Wrath, slay Sin, and in thy Love mee bench. (LL) Was Ever Heart Like Mine? Edward Taylor. MeMAP; OxBA; PoEL-3

Thyestes. Seneca, *Latin*.

   "O yee, whome lorde of lande and waters wyde." OBVE, *tr. by* Jasper Heywood

   Senec. Traged. ex Thyeste Chor. 2. OBCVT, *tr. by* Andrew Marvell

     ("Climb at *Court* for me that will.") OBCVT; OBVE, *tr. by* Andrew Marvell

     ("Death to him 's a Strange surprise.") (LL) OBCVT, *tr. by* Andrew Marvell

     ("Let who so lyst with might mace to raygne.") OBVE, *tr. by* Jasper Heywood

     (Of the meane and sure estate.) OBCVT, *tr. by* Sir Thomas Wyatt

     ("Stond who so list upon the Slipper toppe.") OBCVT, *tr. by* Sir Thomas Wyatt

Thyme. *Unknown*. AmFP

Thyme Flowering among Rocks. Richard Wilbur. EOEF; LCAP-2

Thyrsis. Matthew Arnold. EnVR; FHYEP; NAEL-2; NOBE; NoP-4; OBEV; OBNC

   ("Our Scholar travels yet the loved hillside.") (LL) NoP-4

   "What though the music of thy rustic flute." EPCY

Thyrsis. Edward Cracroft Lefroy. AWP *Fr.* Echoes from Theocritus.

Thyrsis. Theocritus. *See* The Death of Daphnis.

Thyrsis, a youth of the inspired train. The Story of Phoebus and Daphne Applied, [etc.]. Edmund Waller. NAEL-1; NOSC

Thyrsis And Amaranta. Jean de La Fontaine, *French*. LoP, *tr. by* Alistair Elliot

Thyrsis and Milla, arm in arm together. *Unknown*. GBL

Thyrsis last Sunday was improving Amaranta's. Thyrsis And Amaranta. Jean de La Fontaine, *French*. LoP, *tr. by* Alistair Elliot

Thyrsis, sleep'st thou? Holla! Let not sorrow stay us. *Unknown*. NoSic; OxBSP

Thyself remov'd, thy power to sooth me left. (LL) On the Receipt of My Mother's Picture out of Norfolk [the Gift of My Cousin Ann Bodham]. William Cowper. NOEC; OxAEP-1

Ti-ch'ü Song Words. *Unknown, Chinese*. CoBCP, *tr. by* Burton Watson

Tiberius on Capri. Robert Penn Warren.

   "All is nothing, nothing all." NOBA

   "There once, on that goat island, I." NOBA

Tibullus, pull yourself together! Horace, *Latin*. NNPT, *tr. by* E. L. Marsh

Tibur is beautiful, too, and the orchard slopes, and the Anio. Claude to Eustace. Arthur Hugh Clough. *Fr.* Amours de Voyage. NOBVV

Tichborne's Elegy. Chidiock Tichborne. HAP; HeIP-4; InPS-3; NoP-4; NoSic; OAEL-1; PoPoPo; TFi

   ("And nowe I live, and nowe my life is donn.") (LL) PBRV

   (Elegy.) GEA

   (Elegy: "My Prime of Youth Is But a Frost of Cares.") EBEV; NOBE; SCGP; WeW-3

   ("My prime of youth is but a froste of cares.") PBRV

   (Written the Night before His Execution.) SCV

Ticket, The. John Ashbery. WeT

Tickle Rhyme, The. Ian Serraillier. NTCP; Spl

Tickled, / my thoughts wander. Celebration for My Mother. Wendy Rose. CDW

Tickling me with his whiskers. (LL) Mr. McGregor's Garden. Medbh McGuckian. CIP-2; PNI

Tickly, tickly, on your knee. *Unknown*. OxNR

Ticonderoga: A Legend of the West Highlands. Robert Louis Stevenson. EBNV; OBNV

Tiddle liddle lightum. *Unknown*. OxNR

Tiddleywinks, old man. *Unknown*. NSI

Tide be runnin' the great world over. Sea Love. Charlotte Mew. LW; MoBrPo; OxAEP-2; OxBTC

Tide gone out for good, The. The Death of Irish. Aidan Carl Mathews. PBCIP

Tide in the river, The. Eleanor Farjeon. NOxBChV; NTP

Tide rises, the tide falls, The. Henry Wadsworth Longfellow. APN-1; AmPP; ImPo; MeMAP; NOBA; OxBA; PBMP; PFE; PoE; PoPoPo; PoRA; TAP

Tide River, The. Charles Kingsley. *See* The River's Song.

Tide Turning. John Frederick Nims. DiPo; FYAP

Tidepool, A. Cor Van den Heuvel. HA

Tides, The. Paul Blackburn. PoM

Tides, The. William Cullen Bryant. TAP

Tides. John Fuller. AYFP

Tides. Helen Hunt Jackson. LW

Tides Run up the Wairau, The. Eileen Duggan. PeNZ

Tides shape the sides of the agate mountain. On Visiting My Son, Port Angeles, Washington. Duane Niatum. CDW

Tidewash. . . Memories. Lament of the Flutes. Christopher Okigbo. PBA

Tidinges I bring you, for to tell. *Unknown*. MiEL

Tie. Greg Delanty. BiHa

Tie, The. William Heyen. GM

Tie a bandage over his eyes. A Rebel. John Gould Fletcher. MoAmPo

Tie me haan up. Slave Song. David Dabydeen. PBCV

Tie one end of a rope fast over a beam. A Receipt to Cure a Love Fit. *Unknown*. NOEC

Tie the Strings to my Life, My Lord. Emily Dickinson. PoE; TrCP

Tie your own noose if you want to be. The Advice of an Efficiency Expert. Augustus Young. CIP-2

Tied to life. Giuseppe Ungaretti. *See* Vigil.

T'ien-mu Mountain Ascended in a Dream: A Farewell Song. Li Po, *Chinese*. SuSp, *tr. by* Wu-Chi Liu

T'ien-t'ai Mountain is tall. Ballad of Peach Blossom Spring. Yüan Mei, *Chinese*. CoBLCP, *tr. by* Jonathan Chaves

Tier upon tier of storied buildings, decorated pavilions. Tune: "Moth Fluttering against Lamp." Kuan Yün-shih. SuSp, *tr. by* Richard John Lynn *Fr.* Medley of Southern and Northern Tunes—Scenic Tour of West Lake.

Ties. Raymond Souster. MoCV

Tig. *Unknown*. FaBoVe

Tiger. Alec Derwent Hope, *Russian*. OxBC; RB

Tiger, The. Kuṟamakaḷ Ilaveyiṉi, *Tamil*. PLW, *tr. by* A. K. Ramanujan

Tiger. Claude McKay. BPo; CrDW

Tiger behind the bars of his cage growls, The. Peter Niblett. OTCP

Tiger Christ unsheathed his sword. For the One Who Would Take Man's Life in His Hands. Delmore Schwartz. LiTM; MoAmPo; VGW

Tiger in his strength his thirst must slake!, The. (LL) Tiger. Claude McKay. BPo; CrDW

Tiger in the tiger-pit, The. Lines for an Old Man. T. S. Eliot. FaBoTw; RB; RaBo

Tiger in the Zoo, A. Leslie Norris. OTCP

Tiger Lady. Yusef Komunyakaa. CDa

Tiger, on the other hand, is kittenish and mild, The. Hilaire Belloc. MoBrPo

Tiger shouted, "You don't mean peace, but war!," The. (LL) A Legend of Versailles. Melvin Beaunearus Tolson. NAAAL

"Tiger, strolling at my side." Triumph of Sensibility. Sylvia Townsend Warner. MoBrPo

Tiger Tale, A. John Bennett. OBCA

Tiger! Tiger! [or Tyger! Tyger!] burning bright. The Tyger. William Blake. AWP; BoTP; CH; ClHu; FaBoBe; FaBoCh; FaBoPV; FaPoR; HAP; HeIP-4; HoPM; ImPo; InPK-6; InPS-3; NAWM-2; NIP-4; NOBE; NOBRP; NOEC; NoP-4; OAEL-2; OBEV; OBNC; OPOU; PBMP; PeECV; PoE; PoEL-4; PoLF; PoRA; RB; SCGP; SCV; SoSe-8; TFi; TTTS; UnPo; WHSW. Fr. Songs of Experience.

Tigers of Nanzen-ji, The. Brad Leithauser. DiPo

Tight Corners. David Bromige.

"He thought it humanity's lot for ever to be persuading a huge rock up a mountainside." FTOS

Tight scrimmage of blankets in the dark. Ward Two. Francis Webb. CBAP

Tight-sphinctered and inhibited. Peace Delegate. Douglas Livingstone. PeSA

Tighten. Hadewijch II, *Flemish.* WPoS, tr. by Jane Hirshfield

Tightly coiled, like a snake it sits. Love. "Anna Akhmatova," *Russian.* TCRP, tr. by Daniel Weissbort

Tightness and the nilness round that space, The. From the Frontier of Writing. Seamus Heaney. CABP; PoPoPo

Tihei Mauriora I called. Sad Joke on a Marae. Apirana Taylor. PeNZ

Tiho, the Carib. Jan Carew. HCP

Til on a day. Chaucer. *See* The Tale of Sir Thopas.

Tile is loose for splendid feet, A. Stepping Out. Michael Brownstein. FTOS

Till aged Time close up mine eyes, *par. by* George Sandys. Bible, *O.T. See* Psalm 23.

Till all sweet gums and juices flow. The Prince's Progress. Christina Rossetti.

Till all their sweets are gone, and all again refuse them. (LL) Woman's Constancy. Sir John Suckling. CaPo; CavPo

Till angels wake thee, with a note like thine. (LL) An Epitaph upon the Celebrated Claudy Phillips, Musician, Who Died Very Poor. Samuel Johnson. NOEC; OxAEP-1

Till both our heads were in his aureole. (LL) Willowwood ("So sang he: and as meeting rose and rose"). D. G. Rossetti. NAEL-2; OAEL-2

Till bright as blood the peachstone showed. (LL) Peachstone. Dannie Abse. OxBC; WeW-3

Till Cherry-Ripe themselves do[e] cry. (LL) There is a Garden in her face. Thomas Campion. AAS; EBEvV; GTBS-P; HeIP-4; ImPo; InPK-6; NAEL-1; NOSC; OAEL-1; PoE; PoEL-2; Poetr; SCGP; TFi

Till Christ again turn wanderer and child. (LL) Christmas Eve under Hooker's Statue. Robert Lowell. CoAmPo

Till Christ ("Till Christ, quhome I am haldin for to lufe"). *Unknown.* OxBS *Fr.* The Gude and Godlie Ballatis.

Till Death Do Us Part. Leila Miccolis, *Portuguese.* BoWoP, tr. by Willis Barnstone *and* Nelson Cerqueira

Till dreadful[l] death do [c]ease my doleful[l] state? (LL) Pillar [or Piller] perished [or pearisht] is whe[a]rto I le[a]nt, The. Sir Thomas Wyatt, *after the Italian of* Petrarch. AAS; FaBoPV; NoSic; OBVE

Till earth restores her sons to heaven again. (LL) I Was Sick and in Prison. Jones Very. ColAP

Till Eulenspiegel. "Eduard Georgievich Bagritzky," *Russian.* TCRP, tr. by Vera Dunham

Till ev'n his beams sing, and my music[k] shine. (LL) Christmas. George Herbert. GeHe; NOSC; PeECV; TOF; TrCP

Till God calls you away. (LL) The Unquiet Grave. *Unknown.* CABP; CH; ESPB; HAP; HeIP-4; IMW; NoP-4; OAEL-1; OxBB; OxBSn; PoEL-1; RB; TFi; WeW-3

Till human voices wake us, and we drown. (LL) The Love Song of J. Alfred Prufrock. T. S. Eliot. AWP; AmPP; CMoP; ClHu; ColAP; EBEV; EBEvV; HAP; HeIP-4; HoPM; InPK-6; InPS-3; LiTM; MoAmPo; MoP; NAAL-2; NAEL-2; NAWM-2; NOBA; NOBE; NoAM; NoP-4; OAEL-2; OxAEP-2; OxBTC; PFE; PoA; PoE; PoPoPo; PoRA; Poetr; SAGP; SoSe-8; TAP; TFi; TRP; TwCP; WeW-3

Till I forget my own. (LL) To the Evening Star. Mark Akenside. OBEV; PoEL-3

Till I go to his home. (LL) Widow's Lament. *Unknown, Chinese.* ChiP, tr. by Waley, Arthur

Till I reach heaven [or heav'n] and, much more, thee. (LL) Affliction (4). George Herbert. ESCV; GeHe; NOSC

Till I shall come again, let this suffice. A Panegyric to Sir Lewis Pemberton. Robert Herrick. CaPo

Till I think the Milky Way has tumbled from the ninth height of /Heaven Heaven. (LL) Viewing the Waterfall at Mount Lu. Li Po, *Chinese.* CoBCP; TTTS, tr. by Burton Watson

Till in thy perfect love I ever live & move. (LL) In Him We Live [& Move & Have Our Being]. Jones Very. APN-1; OxBA

Till it becomes like an alien burdensome life. Constantine P. Cavafy. *See* As Much As You Can.

Till it could come no more. (LL) At the Seaside [or Sea-Side]. Robert Louis Stevenson. CTV; NTCP; OxBChV; TLR; WHSW

Till Jesus make them comprehend / His ways, his truth and light, *par. by* Christopher Smart. Bible, *O.T. See* Psalm 147.

Till life divine re-animates his dust. (LL) On the Death of the Rev. Mr. George Whitefield, 1770. Phillis Wheatley. ColAP; NAAAL; NAAL-1; NAAL-3

Till Love and Fame to nothingness do sink. (LL) The Terror of Death. Keats. AWP; CABP; EBEV; GSo; GTBS-P; HAP; HeIP-4; HoPM; ImPo; InPS-3; LaPo; NAEL-2; NIP-4; NoP-4; OAEL-2; OBEV; OBNC; PBMP; PoE; PoPoPo; PoRA; Ro; SAGP; SCGP; Son; TFi; UnPo

Till my feet, cloven too, take hold on hell? (LL) The World. Christina Rossetti. BoWoP; NALW; PEW

Till my gestures enlarged, wide over the darkening / land. (LL) Feeding Ducks. Norman MacCaig. FaBoTC

Till now the doubtful dusk reveal'd. Tennyson. GTBS-P *Fr.* By night we lingered [or linger'd] on the lawn. EBVV; EnVR; FHYEP; HAP; OAEL-2; OBNC; PeECV; PoEL-5; TOF *Fr.* In Memoriam A. H. H.

Till now your indiscretion sets us free. Eves Apologie. Emilia Lanier. BoWoP *Fr.* Salve Deus Rex Judaeorum.

Till souls and bodies both may meet. (LL) To My Mistress[e] in My Absence. Thomas Carew. CaPo; NOSC

Till St. Mungo come o'er the sea. (LL) Kemp Owyne. *Unknown.* ESPB; EnSB; OxBB

Till that her blush taught me my shame to see. (LL) Sonnet 53: "In martial sports I had my cunning tried." Sir Philip Sidney. NAEL-1; NoSic

Till that we meet again. (LL) To His Lady. Henry VIII, King of England. CTC; EBEV; NoSic

Till the day-spring breaks forth again from high. (LL) The Bird. Henry Vaughan. ESCV; GeHe; OBEV; PoE; PoEL-2

Till the good morning star. *Unknown, Greek.* GrAn, tr. by Peter Jay

Till the gossamer thread you fling catch somewhere, O my soul. (LL) Noiseless patient spider, A. Walt Whitman. BLT; ColAP; NoP-4; PAR

Till the gunpowder ran out at the heels of their boots. (LL) The Great Panjandrum [Himself]. Samuel Foote. CBNP; FaBoCh; PoLF

Till the heart-beats of hell shall be hushed by a hymn from the hunt that has harried the kernel of kings. (LL) Nephelidia. Swinburne. BXAP; EnVR; HoPM; PeVV

Till The Peonies Bloom. Yongnang Kim, *Korean.* CKP, tr. by Jaihiun Kim

Till the slow daylight pale. The Sun-Flower. Dora Greenwell. PEW; VWP; WPE

Till the white winged Reapers come! (LL) The Seed Growing Secretly. Henry Vaughan. ChIV-2; ESCV; GeHe

Till they are incandescent. (LL) Her Lips Are Copper Wire. Jean Toomer. GT

Till thy wished smile thy mother's pangs o'erpay. (LL) To a Little Invisible Being Who Is Expected Soon to Become Visible. Anna Laetitia Barbauld. ECWP; WoRP

Till twelve years' [or yeres'] age, how Christ His childhood spent. Christ[e]'s Childhood[e]. Robert Southwell. ChIV-2

Till up in the morning the sun shall rise. (LL) Moon has a face like the clock in the hall, The. Robert Louis Stevenson. NOxBChV

Till we hear the bells of dawn, it is still spring! (LL) The Last Night of the Third Moon. Chia Tao, *Chinese.* CoBCP, tr. by Burton Watson

Till we shall meet and never part. (LL) The Exequy. Henry King. BoLoP; CABP; GBL; GLoP; HAP; LoP; MeLP; NOBE; NOSC; NoP-4; OBEV; OxBM; PeECV; PoEL-2; SCGP; SeCP; TFi

Till you've earned. Mahadevi, *Kannada.* PBWP, tr. by A. K. Ramanujan

Tiller of the Soil. Avraham Shlonsky, *Hebrew.* MHP, tr. by Ruth Finer Mintz

Tillers of the earth have few idle months;. Watching the Reapers. Po Chü-i, *Chinese.* ChiP, tr. by Arthur Waley

Tilly. James Joyce. RB

Tilt. Wilt. Snow. Ralph Pomeroy. Poetsp

Tilth. Robert Graves. FaBoEE; OBSV

Tim Finnegan [or Finnigin or Finigan] liv'd in Walkin [or lived in Walker] Street. Finnegan's Wake. *Unknown.* BLPA; CBNP; NBLV

Tim tryeth truth convicting all that strive. T. Street. SCAP

Timarista and Krito. Rosanna Warren. *Fr.* Funerary Portraits. NoAM

Timber. *Unknown.* AS

Timber, The. Henry Vaughan. GeHe; OBEV; SeCP

Timbre. Ion Barbu, *Romanian.* CEEP, *tr. by* Dan Duescu

Time. Mary Ursula Bethell. APAD; FaBoWP; OBGa

Time. Robert Creeley. LCAP-2

Time. Giles, the Elder Fletcher. *Fr.* Licia.

Time. Robert Graves. LiTM

Time. George Herbert. FMP; NAEL-1

Time. Ralph Hodgson. GTBS-P

Time. Shelley. PFE; PoLF

Time. William Stafford. Son

Time after time. J. W. Hackett. HA

Time after time, afraid of the chilly spring weather. Hsü Pen. *Fr.* Five Things Sought For—In the Manner of Han Wo. CoBLCP, *tr. by* Jonathan Chaves

Time after time you're placed at the imagined. Yehuda Amichai. *Fr.* Achziv. IP, *tr. by* Warren Bargad *and* Stanley F. Chyet

Time again subdues her. (LL) Wives in the Sere. Thomas Hardy. NOBE; NOBVV

Time allowed for sleep at length elapsed, The. Thomas Cole. *Fr.* The Life of Hubert. NOEC

Time and again. Theology and a Patchwork Absolute. Heather McPherson. PeNZ

Time and again, however well we know the landscape of love. Rilke, *German.* NNPT, *tr. by* J. B. Leishman

Time and again / she had been carelessly used. Inside. Andrew Salkey. HCP

Time and again you've seen them win or lose. Nguyễn Bỉnh Khiêm, *Vietnamese.* AVP, *tr. by* Huỳnh Sanh Thông

Time and Eternity. Stephen Hawes. PoEL-1 *Fr.* The Pastime of Pleasure. OBGa

Time and Grief. William Lisle Bowles. OBEV

Time and Love, I. Shakespeare. *See* Sonnet 64.

Time and Love, II. Shakespeare. *See* Sonnet 65.

Time and Music. Janet Lewis. FFC

Time & prayer fitting, I, the god. Perses, *Greek.* GrAn, *tr. by* Peter Whigham

Time and the changing passions played them tricks. The Early Rebels. Mervyn Morris. PBCV

Time and the Garden. Yvor Winters. GaP; MoAmPo; NoAM; VGW

Time and the mortal will stand never fast. Sonnet. Luis de Camões, *Spanish.* AWP, *tr. by* Richard Garnett

Time and the weather wear away. Houses. Donald Justice. PoA; WeT

Time and the World, whose magnitude and weight. Epitaph. Robert Southey. OBNC

Time & time again the laughter after the footsteps. The Jungle. Diane Di Prima. PoM

Time be brief. Sydney Goodsir Smith. FaBoTC

Time before You, The. Medbh McGuckian. CBLP

Time between us stretches out, The. Black Winter. Frank Stewart. CDa

Time can [*or* will] say nothing but I told you so. Villanelle. W. H. Auden. MoBrPo

Time cannot break the bird's wing from the bird. To a Young Poet. Edna St. Vincent Millay. OxBSP

Time Caught in a Net. Dahlia Ravikovitch, *Hebrew.* IP, *tr. by* Warren Bargad *and* Stanley F. Chyet

Time, cruel time, come and subdue that brow. Samuel Daniel. SCGP *Fr.* To Delia.

Time does not bring relief; you all have lied. Edna St. Vincent Millay. HeIP-4; LW; SAGP

Time draws near the birth of Christ, The. Tennyson. EBVV; EBVVPR; FHYEP; NOCV; OAEL-2; PChr; SoSe-8 *Fr.* In Memoriam A. H. H.

Time drops in decay. The Moods. W. B. Yeats. CTC; EBVVPR

Time ends when vision sees its lapse in / liberty. Beata l'Alma. Sir Herbert Read. FaBoMo

Time Exposures. Muriel Rukeyser. PoA *Fr.* Night-Music.

Time flies by like a great whale. Sonnet XXXIV. Ted Berrigan. FTOS *Fr.* The Sonnets.

Time flies, hope flags, life plies a wearied wing. Christina Rossetti. *Fr.* Monna Innominata. BWW

Time flits away, time flits away, lady. Variation on Ronsard. Thomas Sturge Moore. OBMV

Time for Everything, A. Bible, *O.T. Fr.* Ecclesiastes.

("And a time to hate; a time of war, and a time / of peace.") (LL)
(Ecclesiastes 3, 1–8.)

("For everything there is a season.")

Time for rain! for your long hot dry autumn. Piano di Sorrento. Robert Browning. *Fr.* The Englishman in Italy. PoEL-5

Time for summer clothes and wine-tasting. Tune: "Six Toughies"—Written after the Roses Have Faded. Chou Pang-yen, *Chinese.* SuSp, *tr. by* James J. Y. Liu

Time goes, you say? Ah, no! The Paradox of Time. Pierre de Ronsard, *French.* AWP, *tr. by* Austin Dobson

Time has an end, they say. Hilda Doolittle. NOBA; VGW *Fr.* Good Frend.

Time has been that these wild solitudes, The. A Winter Piece. William Cullen Bryant. APN-1; AmPP; ColAP; OxBA

Time has been, when yet the muse was young, The. Byron. FHYEP *Fr.* English Bards and Scotch Reviewers.

Time has brought about great changes. Scraps of Time. Mrs. Henry Linden. CBWP-4

Time has come, the clock says time has come, The. Prelude XXVIII. Conrad Potter Aiken. OxBA *Fr.* Preludes for Memnon; or, Preludes to Attitude.

"Time has come," the Walrus, The. "Lewis Carroll." CTV

Time has come to call a halt, The. Elizabeth Bishop. *Fr.* Songs for a Colored Singer. RB

Time has come to devote myself to my hiker's stick, The. On Receiving My Letter of Termination. Yüan Hung-tao, *Chinese.* CoBLCP, *tr. by* Jonathan Chaves

Time has no spectacle more stern and strange. Lower New York. George Cabot Lodge. APN-2

Time has not quenched your beauty. Much of your bygone prime. Rufinus Domesticus. HePo, *tr. by* Barbara Hughes Fowler *Fr.* Epigrams.

Time has now gone by, The. Last Prayer. Evelyn Poole. WPN

Time has pulled up a chair, dashed. Ron Mason. Hone Tuwhare. PeNZ

Time has wrinkled your face. Voodoo. Léon Laleau. NegPo, *tr. by* Ellen Conroy Kennedy *Fr.* Black Music.

Time hath, my Lord, a wallet at his back. Ulysses Advises Achilles. Shakespeare. ImPo *Fr.* Troilus and Cressida.

Time heals not: it extends a sorrow's scope. Epigram. James Vincent Cunningham. IMW; VGW

Time I dropped your almost body down, The. The Lost Baby Poem. Lucille Clifton. BlSi; FiLi; ISC; NAAAL; WPE

Time I went to church I sat, The. Mr. Rockefeller's Hat. Helen Smith Bevington. OBAL

Time I went to see my Sister, The. Tsurayuki. *Fr.* Shui Shu. AWP, *tr. by* Arthur Waley

Time in the Rock [or, Preludes to Definition]. Conrad Potter Aiken. VGW

"Bird flying past my head said previous previous, The."
"But no, the familiar symbol, as that the."
"Mysticism, but let us have no words."
"What face she put on it, we will not discuss."
"Where we were walking in the day's light, seeing."

Time is. Alan Beam. APAD

Time is a thing. Epilogue. Stephen Spender. MoBrPo

Time is after dinner, The. Cigarettes. The Boarder. Louis Simpson. InPK-6

Time is at an end, The. Ox-Bow. Donald Davie. DiPo

Time is come I must depart, The. The Aucthour Maketh Her Wyll and Testament. Isabella Whitney. NoP-4; PEW

Time is divided into. Time Is the Mercy of Eternity. Kenneth Rexroth. VGW

Time is mainly a fiction here. There are. New Guinea Time. Louis Johnson. PeNZ

Time is my debtor for my years untold. (LL) Long Time a Child. Hartley Coleridge. GSo; LaPo; OBNC; PoEL-4; Ro; Son

Time is not remote when I, The. On the Death of Dean Swift. Jonathan Swift. EBEV; NOBE; NOBL; NOIV; OxAEP-1; PeLV *Fr.* Verses on the Death of Dr. Swift, D.S.P.D.

Time is of the essence. This is a highly skilled. Polo Grounds. Rolfe Humphries. HoPM

Time is passing now, The. The Holiday. Stevie Smith. BWW

Time is ripe and I repent, The. Oengus Céile Dé. NOIV

Time Is Swiftly Rolling On, The. Berryman Hicks. AH

Time is the feather'd thing. Jasper Mayne. OBEV

Time is the fire in which we burn. (LL) For Rhoda. Delmore Schwartz. LiTM; MoAmPo; OxBA

Time Is the Mercy of Eternity. Kenneth Rexroth. VGW

Time is the root of all this earth. Bhartrihari, *Sanskrit.* AWP, *tr. by* Paul Elmer More

Time it takes, The. Lorraine Ellis Harr. HA

Time it took he could have, The. The Invention of the Telephone. Peter Klappert. AmPA

Time I've lost in wooing, The. Thomas Moore. HoPM; NAEL-2; NOBRP; PeLV

Time like the receptions of a child's piano. The Reconciliation. Archibald MacLeish. MoAmPo

Time #2, The. Esther Iverem. WWSi

Time of Change, A. Egan O'Rahilly, *Irish*. BIrV; FaBoPV, tr. by Eavan Boland

(After the Irish of Egan O'Rahilly.) PBCIP

Time of Day. Selden Rodman. PoA

Time of day: a dim dream, probably. The Yards of Sarajevo. Richard Hugo. AF

Time of Fish Dying. Gabriela Melinescu, *Rumanian*. BoWoP, tr. by Stavros Deligiorgis

Time of fools is coming. Aleksandar Ristovic, *Serbo-Croatian*. HSix, tr. by Charles Simic

Time of grease beginneth at Midsummer day. Julians Barnes. *Fr.* Book of Hunting. WPE

Time of lamentation and curses is passing, The. Audre Lorde. CrSp *Fr.* Prologue.

Time of Man, The. Phyllis Webb. MoCV

Time of Martyrdom, The. David Diop, *French*. NegPo, tr. by Ellen Conroy Kennedy

Time of Mountains. Thomas Hornsby Ferril. PaTW

Time of naked spears, A. Death Certificate. Rui Knopfli, *Portuguese*. PeSAV, tr. by the author

Time of Turtles. Grace Perry. NOBAu

Time of Waiting. Geoffrey Dutton. CBAP

Time of Waiting in Amsterdam. Ingrid Jonker, *Afrikaans*. BoWoP, tr. by Jack Cope *and* William Plomer

Time of white violets; and on the slopes. The Convent in '45. Maria Luisa Spaziani, *Italian*. NeIt, tr. by Beverly Allen

Time on Target. William Daniel Ehrhart. CDa

Time Out. Donald Finkel. HoPM

Time Passes. Richard Percival Lister. NYBP

Time passes. Message. Yon-gyun Kim, *Korean*. CKP, tr. by Jaihiun Kim

Time passes for me in inches. On Door Jambs. Roger Bower. EC2

Time passing, and the memories of love. Time Passing, Beloved. Donald Davie. BoLoP; NoP-4

Time Passing, Beloved. Donald Davie. BoLoP; NoP-4

Time Past, A. Denise Levertov. NoAM

Time pleats dark flesh. Faces and Skulls. Jan Carew. PBCV

Time present and time past. Burnt Norton. T. S. Eliot. CMoP; LiTM; MoAmPo; NAAL-2; PoE *Fr.* Four Quartets.

Time quietly compiling us like sheaves. Seferis. Lawrence Durrell. EBEV

Time, Real and Imaginary. Coleridge. NOBE; OBEV; OxBSP; PBMP

Time Recover'd. Thomas Stanley, *after the Italian of* Girolamo Casone. OBVE

Time Reminded Me. Julia Uceda, *Spanish*. BoWoP, tr. by Willis Barnstone

Time rolls his ceaseless course. The race of yore. The Gathering. Sir Walter Scott. OBNC *Fr.* The Lady of the Lake.

Time-Servers. Judah Halevi, *Hebrew*. TrJP, tr. by Solomon Solis-Cohen

Time shall come, when free as seas or wind, The. Progress. Alexander Pope. ECEV *Fr.* Windsor-Forest [*or* Windsor Forest].

Time spirals upright this unflowing river. The Well. A. J. Seymour. PBCV

Time stands still. The Unbeseechable. Frances Darwin Cornford. MoBrPo

Time stands still, with gazing on her face! *Unknown.* EnLoPo

Time Swept Up. Vasco [*or* Vasko] Popa. PoSu, tr. by Anne Pennington *Fr.* Raw Flesh.

Time, Temperature. Jim Daniels. LTA

Time that brings [*or* bringes] all things to light. Epitaph. Thomas Morton. NOSC; SCAP

Time, that gives to music life. Time and Music. Janet Lewis. FFC

Time that is moved by little fidget wheels. Five Bells. Kenneth Slessor. BMAP; CBAP; NOBAu; PoRA

Time that's forever on his track returning. Spring Time. John Milton, *Latin*. MLL, tr. by Helen Waddell

Time the Hanlin scholar was south of the River, The. Reading the Collected Works of Li Po and Tu Fu: A Colophon. Po Chü-i, *Chinese*. SuSp, tr. by Irving Y. Lo

Time ticks away the centre of my pride. The Empty Glen. R. Crombie Saunders. OxBS

Time to be up, Marie, young sleepyhead! Pierre de Ronsard, *French*. STV, tr. by John Frederick Nims

Time to Die. Ray Garfield Dandridge. PoBA

Time to Die, The. Matilda Caroline Edwards. PWR

Time to draw the left foot back and let it. Water Eased of Its Cliffs by Falling. Alberta Turner. LCAP-2

Time to go home! James Reeves. NTP

Time to Leave. Ory Bernstein, *Hebrew*. IP, tr. by Warren Bargad *and* Stanley F. Chyet

Time to love, and a time to hate; a time of war, and a time of peace, A. (LL) A Time for Everything. Bible, *O.T.* NAWM-1; OBVE; PBMP

Time to Myself. Paulette Jiles. NOBC

Time to put off the world and go somewhere. Beggar to Beggar Cried. W. B. Yeats. CMoP; NoAM; OxAEP-2

Time to Rise. Robert Louis Stevenson. ACTP; CTV; OxBChV

Time to Talk, A. Robert Frost. FP

Time to tell you things are well, A. Snow Country Weavers. James Welch. CDW; HATNAP

Time to Tickle a Lizard, The. The Lizard. Theodore Roethke. NOxBChV

Time topples Statyllios like a doddery oak. Myrinos, *Greek*. GrAn; NNPT, tr. by Tony Harrison

Time Travel. Nick Piombino. FTOS

Time Traveler's Potlatch. Philip Lamantia. CLPP

Time wants to show you a different country. It's the one. The Gift. William Stafford. PuP-16

Time was, a [wealthy] Englishman would join. The Englishman at the Table. James Cawthorn. ECEV; NOEC *Fr.* Of Taste; an Essay.

Time was, and that was termed the time of Gold. The Olden Days. Joseph Hall. OBSV *Fr.* Virgidemiarum.

Time was away and somewhere else. Meeting Point. Louis MacNeice. CBLP; EP; PNI

Time was, ere yet in these degenerate days. Byron. EPCY; FHYEP *Fr.* English Bards and Scotch Reviewers.

Time was God judged. In the Days of Socrates. Friedrich Hölderlin, *German*. PFTM, tr. by Richard Sieburth

Time was he went for weeks without. The Elk on Mutability. John Bensko. MT

Time was I had a tender heart. Maternal Love Triumphant or Song of the Virtuous Female Spider. Ruth Pitter. WPN

Time was, I shrank from what was right. Sensitiveness. John Henry, Cardinal Newman. TrCP

Time was I was a plowman driving. Plowman. Sidney Keyes. PoRA

Time was the apple Adam ate. Original Sequence. Philip Booth. ChIV-1; KSG

Time was upon / The wing, to flie away. Upon Time. Robert Herrick. BeJo

Time was when his half million drew. Bewick Finzer. Edwin Arlington Robinson. CMoP; MeMAP; MoAmPo; NAAL-2

Time was when I was weapon and warrior. Horn. Cynewulf. AnOE, tr. by Charles W. Kennedy *Fr.* Riddles (Exeter Book).

Time was when once upon a time, such toys. Epigram. Glaukos, *Greek*. GrAn, tr. by Peter Jay

Time was, when we were sow'd, and just began. Ovid. OBCVT, tr. by John Dryden *Fr.* Of the Pythagorean Philosophy.

Time wasted and time spent. The Times. Charles Madge. OBMV

Time We Climbed Snake Mountain, The. Leslie Marmon Silko. VoR

Time! where didst thou those years inter. Recogitabo Tibi Omnes Annos Meos. William Habington. ChIV-1

Time Will Surely Come, The. Robert T. Daniel. AH

Time Wins. Benoy Majumdar, *Bengali*. OMIP, tr. by Jyotirmoy Dutta

Time with his scythe honed fine. Hay Fever. Alec Derwent Hope. NoAM

Time with your rusty scythe. The Poplars. Peter Huchel, *German*. CEEP, tr. by Rich Ives

Time, You Old Gypsy Man. Ralph Hodgson. BoTP; CH; LiTM; MoBrPo

Time, you young thief, who love to get. Max Beerbohm. UV

Time you won your town the race, The. To an Athlete Dying Young. A. E. Housman. CMoP; ChAP; HAP; HeIP-4; ImPo; InPK-6; LiTM; MoBrPo; MoP; NAEL-2; NIP-4; NoAM; NoP-4; PBMP; PFE; PoE; PoEL-5; PoRA; Poetr; SAGP; SCGP; SoSe-8; TFi; TRP; UnPo; WeW-3

Timeless. Judith Nicholls. AYFP

Timeless, Twinned. Robert Penn Warren. AFr

Timely blossom, infant fair. To Miss Charlotte Pulteney in Her Mother's Arms. Ambrose Philips. GTBS-P; LiLi; NOEC

Timepiece, A. James Merrill. HoPM

Timer. Tony Harrison. *Fr.* The School of Eloquence. NAEL-2; NoAM

Times, The. Charles Churchill.

Against Sodomy. ECEV

"Is a son born into this world of woe?" OBSV

Times, The. Charles Madge. OBMV

Times. Tom Weatherly. SeSe

Time's an hand's-breadth; 'tis a tale. John Huddlestone Wynne. OxBChV

Times are good, there's no cruel government, The. Along the River, Seeing the Home of Absconded Farmers. Kao Ch'i, *Chinese*. CoBLCP, tr. by Jonathan Chaves

Times are swiftly drawing nigh. When You and I Must Part. *Unknown.* AmFP

Times / at all. (LL) For Saundra. Nikki Giovanni. NAAAL

Time's Betrayal. Herman Melville. NCAP

Time's Changes. James Bramston. NOEC *Fr.* The Art of Politics.

Times come round again, The. To a Military Rifle, 1942. Yvor Winters. MoAmPo

Time's Dedication. Delmore Schwartz. VGW

Time's fingers bend us slowly. Crates, *Greek.* PGA, *tr. by* Kenneth Rexroth

Times followed one another. Came a morn. Aurora Leigh. Elizabeth Barrett Browning. VWP

Time's fool, but not heaven's: yet hope not for any return. Ruth Pitter. MoBrPo; OxBTC; PoRA; WPE

Times Gettin' Hard, Boys. *Unknown.* AS

Times [*or* Tymes] Go[e] By Turn[e]s. Robert Southwell. ChIV-1; NoSic; PoEL-2

Time's Hand Is Kind. Margaret E. Bruner. PoToHe

Times have changed. Anything Goes. Cole Porter. OBAL

Times have changed, there is not left to us, The. Allen Tate. PoA *Fr.* Sonnets of the Blood.

Time's Mirror. Peyton Houston. *Fr.* Sonnet Variations. Son

Time's No Grammar. Márton Kalász, *Hungarian.* CEEP, *tr. by* Jascha Kessler

Time's noblest offspring is the last. (LL) On the Prospect of Planting Arts and Learning in America. George Berkeley. AiP; FaBoA; ImPo; NOEC

Time's question only. (LL) Generation. Audre Lorde. NBV; Poetr

Times she'll sit quiet by the hearth, and times. The Woodcutter's Wife. William Rose Benét. AWP

Times Square Poems. Michael Lassell.

Dino. GLP

Going Rate, The. GLP

How to Find Love in an Instant. GLP

Stud. GLP

Times stir in me uncalendrically, chaotically. Amir Gilbo'a, *Hebrew.* IP, *tr. by* Warren Bargad *and* Stanley F. Chyet

Times wherein old Pompion was a Saint, The. New-Englands Crisis. Benjamin Tompson. SCAP

Time's Whirligig, Or, The Blue-New-Made-Gentleman Mounted. Humphrey Willis. NOSC

Time's winged chariot (poets say). To His Not-so-coy Mistress. Wynford Vaughan-Thomas. BXAP; NOBL

Timetable. Günter Eich, *German.* CBNP, *tr. by* Michael Hamburger

Timid Bunnies. Jeannie Kirby. BoTP

Timid corn-poney's heart fluttered, The. The Corn-Pone-y. Carolyn Wells. *Fr.* A Baker's Dozen of Wild Beasts. OBCA

Timid Gazelle, The. Kasmuneh, *Arabic.* TrJP

Timid grace sits trembling in her eye, A. Charles Lamb. GSo

Timid Lover. Countee Cullen. ColAP

Timidly, still half asleep, it has blossomed. The Purple Peach Tree. Su Tung-p'o, *Chinese.* OHPC, *tr. by* Kenneth Rexroth

Timokritos was bold in war. This is his grave. Anacreon, *Greek.* GrAn, *tr. by* Peter Jay

Timoleon. Herman Melville. APN-2

Timon, for you exist no more. Callimachus, *Greek.* HePo, *tr. by* Barbara Hughes Fowler. *Fr.* Epigrams.

Timon of Athens. Shakespeare.

"O blessed breeding sun! draw from the earth." OxAEP-1

"Put up thy gold: go on,—here's gold,—go on." OxAEP-1

Timon's Epitaph. AWP

"Warr'st thou 'gainst Athens?" EBEV

Timon's Villa. Alexander Pope. PoE, *ll.* 99–180 *Fr.* Epistle IV, to Richard Boyle, Earl of Burlington. OAEL-1; PoEL-3

("And Splendour borrows all her rays from Sense.") (LL) PoE

("And swear no day was ever passed so ill.") (LL) OBSV

("Who never mentions Hell to ears polite.") (LL) ECEV

Timor Mortis. *Unknown.* NoP-4

Timor Mortis conturbat me. (LL) Lament for the Makaris. William Dunbar. EBEV; EnVB; HAP; NOBE; NoP-4; OAEL-1; OBEV; OxBS; PoEL-1; SCGP

Timoshenko. Sidney Keyes. OBWP

Timothy. Timothy Steele. InPK-6; RA

Timothy Tiggs and Tomothy Toggs. Some Fishy Nonsense. Laura Elizabeth Richards. CTV

Timothy Titus took two ties. *Unknown.* OxNR

Timothy Winters. Charles Causley. PeECV; RB

Tin Frog, The. Russell Hoban. Spl

Tin Roof Blues. Sterling Brown. NAAAL

Tin shack, where my baby sleeps on his back. Everything: Eloy, Arizona, 1956. Ai. AmPA

Tin Wash Dish, The. Les A. Murray. BMAP

Tin Woodsman, The. Paulette Jiles. NOBC

Tina and Seth met in the midst of an overcrowded militarism. Histoire. Harry Mathews. NIP-4; NoP-4; PmAP

Tinder, The. Thomas Carew. CaPo

Tinder. Seamus Heaney. OxAEP-2

Tinfoil. Joyce Mansour, *French.* MFP, *tr. by* Martin Sorrell

Tingel-Tangel. Rosalind Pace. CMAP

Tingle. Getting Warm. Rae Armantrout. FTOS

Tink dere is a God in a top. *Unknown. Fr.* Work-Songs. PBCV

Tinker, / Tailor. *Unknown.* OxNR

Tinker's Wife. Patrick Kavanagh. CIP-2; InPS-3; MoP; NoAM

Tinkle of chimes, The. Tom Tico. HA

Tinkle, tinkle! The Waterfall. Frank Dempster Sherman. CTV

"Tinkle, tinkle, tinkle": 'tis the muffin-man you see. The Muffin-Man's Bell. Ann Hawkshawe. BoTP

Tinkling treble, / Rolling bass. Dream Boogie: Variation. Langston Hughes. APSN

Tint I cannot take—is best, The. Emily Dickinson. APN-2; MoAmPo

Tintern Abbey. Edward Davies. *Fr.* Chepstow: A Poem. OBWVE

Tintype of a Private in the Fifteenth Georgia Infantry. Paul Horgan. CBCWP

Tiny baby, you're ugly. King D. Kuka. VoR

Tiny bright-eye, / Slow one. D. H. Lawrence. *See* Baby Tortoise.

Tiny children. Love Song. Yityangu Ejong, *Yindjibarndi.* CBAP, *tr. by* Frank Wordick

Tiny creature moves, A. The Milk Bottle. Galway Kinnell. Poetr

Tiny Erotion, borne away / By a gnat had this to say. Lucilius, *Greek.* GrAn, *tr. by* Peter Porter

Tiny fish. Alan Pizzarelli. HA

Tiny fish enjoy themselves, The. Little Fish. D. H. Lawrence. AYFP; OxBTC; RB; Spl; TTTS

Tiny green birds skate over the surface of the room. Saturday Night in the Parthenon. Kenneth Patchen. SPE

Tiny little pine tree, still shorter than the fence, A. A Poem on a Little Pine. Hsieh Chin, *Chinese.* CoBLCP, *tr. by* Jonathan Chaves

Tiny Montgomery. "Bob Dylan." CBNP

Tiny moon as small and white as a single jasmine flower, A. A White Blossom. D. H. Lawrence. MoBrPo

Tiny new emotions, The. Poem. Tom Clark. CoAmPo

Tiny nut, a bit of tasteless betel, A. Carved on an Areca Nut. Ho Xuan Huong, *Vietnamese.* PBWP, *tr. by* Nguyen Ngoc Bich *and* Burton Raffel

Tiny petals of the mountain ash [*or* mountain-ash], The. (LL) "Upper chamber in a darkened house, An." Frederick Goddard Tuckerman. APN-2; NOBA; TAP

Tiny shoes so trim and neat. The Fairy Shoemaker. Phyllis L. Garlick. BoTP

Tiny snow of the stunningly cold black day. In the Snowfall. Gwerfyl Mechain, *Welsh.* BoWoP, *tr. by* Willis Barnstone

Tiny sun, A. In the Ashtray. Vasco Popa, *Serbian.* VCWP, *tr. by* Anne Pennington

Tío-Vivo, or the Merry-go-round. Federico García Lorca, *Spanish.* CBNP

Tip, The. Albert Goldbarth. HCAP

Tip, The. Belle Waring. PBCAP

Tip for Saturday, A. Francis Webb. BMAP

Tip their mouths open to the sky. The Small Vases from Hebron. Naomi Shihab Nye. BAP-96

Tip-Toe Tail. Dixie Willson. NTCP

Tipperary. Desmond O'Grady. BiHa

Tipperty-toes, the smallest elf. Red in Autumn. Elizabeth Gould. BoTP

Tips for Living. Leandra Garcia. CTV

Tips of the reeds silver in sunlight. A cold wind. In the Bodies of Words. May Swenson. NMM-2

Tips waves up big dipper fires. Wonderful. Ania Walwicz. BMAP

Tire tracks words lost in lost snow today. Generic Elbows. Bernadette Mayer. FTOS

Tired. Fenton Johnson. NAAAL; PoBA; PoLF; TTY

Tired and thirsty, weary of the way. After the Hunt. Detlev, Freiherr von Liliencron, *German.* AWP, *tr. by* Ludwig Lewisohn

Tired and Unhappy, You Think of Houses. Delmore Schwartz. LiTM; MoAmPo

Tired as I Can Be. *Unknown.* FaBoVe

Tired i count the ways in which it determines my life. The ISM. Wanda Coleman. PmAP

Tired legs won't climb the high road of blue clouds. Nguyễn Trãi, *Vietnamese.* AVP, *tr. by* Huỳnh Sanh Thông

Tired Memory. Coventry Patmore. EnVR *Fr.* The Unknown Eros.

Tired nature's sweet restorer, balmy Sleep! Night Thoughts. Edward Young. NOEC; OxAEP-1 *Fr.* Night Thoughts.

Tired Night, A. Tu Fu, *Chinese*. SuSp, *tr. by* Jan W. Walls

Tired of Eating Kisses. Edward Vincent Swart. PeSA

Tired of the gods and of their fires. The Ammonite. Peter Huchel, *German*. CEEP, *tr. by* Michael Hamburger

Tired of Towns. Andrew Lang. EBVV

Tired of walking in the red dust. The Retreat of Sun Ching-hsiang. Chang Yü, *Chinese*. CoBLCP, *tr. by* Jonathan Chaves

Tired swimmer in the waves of time, A. Sissinghurst. Vita Sackville-West. WPN

Tired Tim. Walter De la Mare. BoTP; NTCP

Tired with all these, for restful death I cry. Sonnet 66. Shakespeare. AWP; CTC; EBEV; FaBoPV; GTBS-P; HAP; ImPo; InPS-3; NOBE; NoSic; OAEL-1; OxAEP-1; PoEL-2; TFi; WeW-3 *Fr.* Sonnets.

Tired with books and rolling on the bed. The New River Head, a Fragment. E. Dower. NOEC

Tired with dull grief, grown old before my day. 1916 Seen from 1921. Edmund Blunden. NoP-4; PeFWW

Tired with its dogs and doves. Summer Band Concert. Vivian Smith. CBAP

Tired with too long a chase, though stout. On the Death of Squire Christopher. John Wigson. OxBSP

Tired Woman, The. Anna Wickham. MoBrPo

Tired Worker, The. Claude McKay. BPo

Tireles Sculptor, The. Henrietta Cordelia Ray. CBWP-3

Tiresias. Austin Clarke.
   "My mother wept loudly." CIP-2

Tirocinium; or, A Review of Schools. William Cowper.
   "Father, who designs his babe a priest, The." OBSV
   "To you, then, tenants of life's middle state." OBSV
   "Would you your son should be a sot or dunce." OBSV

Tirumal. Katuvan Ilaveyinanar, *Tamil*. PLW, *tr. by* A. K. Ramanujan

Tiruppavai, The. Andal.
   "I was sent forth from the power." PFTM, *tr. by* George W. MacRae
   "O sister of wealth." WPoS
   "O you who guard over." WPoS
   "We rose before dawn." WPoS

Tirzah. Jacob Cohen, *Hebrew*. MHP, *tr. by* Ruth Finer Mintz

Tirzah and the Wide World. Dahlia Ravikovitch, *Hebrew*. IP, *tr. by* Warren Bargad *and* Stanley F. Chyet

'Tis a dull sight. Old Song. Edward Fitzgerald. OBEV; OxAEP-2

'Tis a favorite project of mine. Harvey L. Carter. Poetr

'Tis a lesson you should heed. Try, Try Again. T. H. Palmer. ChAP; ImGa

'Tis a little journey. *Unknown*. PoToHe

'Tis a little thing. A Friend. Sir Thomas N. Talfourd. PoToHe

'Tis a moon-tinted primrose, with a well. Another. Thomas Lovell Beddoes. Son

'Tis a new life—thoughts move not as they did. The New Birth. Jones Very. APN-1; NCAP; NOBA; PAR

'Tis a sad land, that in one day. Death. Henry Vaughan. ChIV-1

'Tis a stern and startling thing to think. Her Death. Thomas Hood. NOBVV *Fr.* Miss Kilmansegg and Her Precious Leg.

'Tis a strange mystery, the power of words! The Power of Words. Letitia Elizabeth Landon. VWP

'Tis a strange thing, but 'tis a thing well known. Martial, *Latin*. OBCVT, *tr. by* William Hay

'Tis a time for much rejoicing. Emancipation. Priscilla Jane Thompson. CBWP-2

'Tis a world of silences. I gave a cry. Silences. Arthur William Edgar O'Shaughnessy. OBNC

'Tis advertised in Boston, New York and Buffalo. Blow Ye Winds in the Morning. *Unknown*. AmFP

'Tis affection but dissembled. Song. Sidney Godolphin. BeJo

'Tis all a Chequer-board of Nights and Days. Life's Chequer-Board. Edward Fitzgerald. LBC

'Tis all that Heav'n allows. (LL) Love And Life. John Wilmot. BoLoP; EnLoPo; GBL; HAP; NOBE; NOSC; OBEV; PoEL-3

'Tis all the way to Toe-town. Foot Soldiers. John Banister Tabb. OBAL

'Tis an act of the priest to give patience a test. Matrimony. John Williams. NOEC

'Tis an old dial, dark with many a stain. The Sundial. Austin Dobson. OBGa

'Tis bad enough in man or woman. Epigram: On Inclosures. *Unknown*. FaBoEE; OxBoLi

'Tis better to be vile then vile esteemed. Sonnet 121. Shakespeare. NoSic; OAEL-1; OxAEP-1; PoEL-2; SCGP *Fr.* Sonnets.

'Tis bitter, yet 'tis sweet. Troubled with the Itch and Rubbing with Sulphur. George Moses Horton. AAP

Tis braul I cudgel, ranters, Quakers braul. Claudius Gilbert. John Wilson. SCAP

'Tis but a night, a long and moonless night. A New Dawn. Robert Blair. LBC

'Tis but a phantom of the weary brain. Life for a Life. Mary E. Tucker. CBWP-1

'Tis charity here not to love. (LL) The Divorce. Thomas Stanley. FMP

'Tis Christmas weather, and a country house. George Meredith. NAEL-2; NOBVV *Fr.* Modern Love.

Tis clear, Great Dane, thy barque's worse than thy bite. King Canute. Stanley J. Sharpless. BXAP

'Tis customary as we part. Emily Dickinson. LW

'Tis dead night round about: Horror [*or* Horrour] doth creep[e]. The Lamp[e]. Henry Vaughan. ChIV-2; ESCV

'Tis dead of night; storms rend the troubled air. Sonnet. Mary Locke. ECWP

'Tis death! and peace, indeed, is here. Youth and Calm. Matthew Arnold. FHYEP

'Tis dreadful! The Aisle of a Temple. William Congreve. OxAEP-1

'Tis easy to be true[!] (LL) To Celia. Sir Charles Sedley. AWP; GTBS-P; NOBE; OBEV

'Tis eight o'clock,—a clear March night. The Idiot Boy. Wordsworth. NOBRP; OBNV; Ro

'Tis evening, the black snail has got on his track. Evening. John Clare. NOBVV

'Tis fine to see the Old World, and travel up and down. America for Me. Henry Van Dyke. BLPA; ChAP

'Tis folly to be wise. (LL) Ode on a Distant Prospect of Eton College. Thomas Gray. GTBS-P; ImPo; NAEL-1; NOBE; NOEC; NoP-4; OAEL-1; OxAEP-1; PoE; PoEL-3; SCGP

'Tis God shall repay: I am safer so. (LL) Patriot, The [An Old Story]. Robert Browning. FHYEP; PBMP

'Tis goodbye then to last night. Soraidh Slan Don Oidhche Areir. Niall Mor MacMuireadach, *Irish*. BIrV, *tr. by* Maire Cruise O'Brien

'Tis grown almost a danger to speak true. Epistle. To Katharine, Lady Aubigny. Ben Jonson. BeJo

'Tis hard to find in life. True Friendship. *Unknown*. *Fr.* The Panchatantra. AWP, *tr. by* Arthur Ryder

'Tis hard to say, if greater want of skill. An Essay on Criticism. Alexander Pope. OAEL-1, *ll.* 1–266 *Fr.* An Essay on Criticism. NAEL-1; PoEL-3; TFi
   ("But are not critics to their judgment too?") (LL) HAP

'Tis hard, to speake things common, properly. Horace, *Latin*. OBCVT, *tr. by* Ben Jonson

'Tis hard we should be by the men despised. Mary Lee. ECWP

'Tis his one hope: all else that round his life. Infatuation. Frederick Goddard Tuckerman. NCAP

'Tis I must learn to die. (LL) Verses Written in a Lady's Sherlock "Upon Death." Philip Dormer Stanhope. EBEV; NOEC

'Tis in every feature I would make it shine. (LL) Groves of Blarney [they look so charming], The. Richard Alfred Millikin. OBCoV

'Tis, in good truth, a most wonderful thing. Sir William Davenant. NOSC

'Tis in the spirit that attire. Elegance. Christopher Smart. NOCV *Fr.* Hymns for the Amusement of Children.

'Tis Julia's bed, and she sleeps there. (LL) Her Bed. Robert Herrick. PBRV; PFE

'Tis just the same as we had never been. (LL) Against the Fear of Death. Lucretius. AWP; OAEL-1; OBVE, *tr. by* Dryden

'Tis known, at least it should be, that throughout. Beppo; a Venetian Story. Byron. NOBL; NOBRP; OBNV; OBSV

'Tis late and cold; stir up the fire. The Dead Host's Welcome. John Fletcher. OxAEP-1 *Fr.* The Lover's Progress.

'Tis Lent, the holy time of fast and prayer. The Easter Light. Clara Ann Thompson. CBWP-2

'Tis light to love thee living, girl, when hope is full and fair. Song. Thomas Tod Stoddart. NOBRP *Fr.* Death-Wake, The; or, Lunacy.

'Tis little I— could care for Pearls. Emily Dickinson. WPoS

'Tis madness to love physic to the dead. Upon Castara's Absence. William Habington. BeJo *Fr.* Castara.

'Tis majesty to rule alone. (LL) Against Them Who Lay Unchastity to the Sex of Women. William Habington. BeJo; SeCP

'Tis Martinmass, from rig to rig. John Clare. EnVR

'Tis May, and yet the skies are overcast. Lines Written on a Very Boisterous Day in May, 1844. John Clare. OxBSP

'Tis men who say that through all hurt and pain. Love's Mourner. Augusta Davies Webster. VWP

'Tis Midnight, and the setting sun. *Unknown*. NTCP

'Tis mute, the word they went to hear on high Dodona mountain. The Oracles. A. E. Housman. HAP

'Tis near the morning watch, the dim lamp burns. The Morning Watch. Jones Very. APN-1

'Tis never or but seldom[e] known[e]. Power and Peace. Robert Herrick. CaPo

" 'Tis no sin for a man to labour in his vocation." The Ballad of Villon and Fat Madge. François Villon, *French*. OBVE, *tr. by* Swinburne

'Tis not a coat of gray or shepherd's life. To Donne. Sir Henry Wotton. NOSC; NoSic

'Tis not by brooding on delight. Marcus Curtius. Oliver St. John Gogarty. OBMV

'Tis not by guilt the onward sweep. Edward Rowland Sill. *Fr.* The Fool's Prayer. APN-2; FaBoBe; PoLF

'Tis not enough for one that is a wife. Lady Elizabeth Carey. *Fr.* Mariam. WPE

'Tis not ev'ry day that I. Not Every Day Fit for Verse. Robert Herrick. BeJo; PoRA

'Tis not for the unfeeling, the falsely refined. The Farmer of Tilsbury Vale. Wordsworth. EBEV

'Tis not how long we have to live. Anacreontic. John Thelwall. NOBRP

'Tis not how witty, nor how free. Upon Kind[e] and True Love. Aurelian Townshend. MeLP; NOSC

'Tis not I pity the flowers are about to die. Tu Fu. SuSp, *tr. by* Irving Y. Lo *Fr.* Strolling along the Riverbank, Looking for Flowers.

'Tis not on the face displayed. The Bedlamite. Thomas Mozeen. NOEC

'Tis not that Dying hurts us so. Emily Dickinson. APN-2; BoWoP

'Tis not that I am weary grown. Upon [His] Leaving His Mistress. John Wilmot, 2d Earl of Rochester. EnLoPo; GBL; NBLV; NOSC

'Tis not the gaudy stream of rosy flame. Self-Consciousness Makes All Changes Happy; Ode. Jonathan Richardson. NOEC

'Tis not to be improved. (LL) Eros. Ralph Waldo Emerson. APN-1; FaBoBe

'Tis not wealth that makes a king. Seneca. OBCVT, *tr. by* Leigh Hunt *Fr.* Part of a Chorus in Seneca's Tragedy of Thyestes.

'Tis not your faire out-side (though famous Greece). To the Queenes Most Excellent Majestie. Elizabeth Cary, Viscountess Falkland. KTR

'Tis now clear[e] day: I see a rose. The Search. Henry Vaughan. ChIV-2; ESCV; GeHe; SeCP

'Tis now since I began to dy. To Mrs. M.A. Upon Absence. Katherine Philips. CBLP; PBWP

'Tis now, since I sat[e] down before. Love's Siege. Sir John Suckling. CBLP; CaPo; PoEL-3

'Tis now the hour of mirth, the hour of love. Palace of the Gnomes. Maria Gowen Brooks. APN-1 *Fr.* Zophiël [or, the Bride of Seven].

'Tis now the raven's bleak abode. Tenants of an Abandoned Castle. John Dyer. APo *Fr.* "Grongar Hill."

'Tis of a blind beggar who a long time was blind. The Blind Beggar. *Unknown*. AmFP

'Tis of a gallant Yankee ship that flew the stripes and stars. The Yankee Man-of-War. *Unknown*. AmFP; FaBoBe

'Tis of a jolly soldier that lately came from war. The Jolly Soldier. *Unknown*. AmFP

'Tis of a lady both fair and handsome. The Servant Man. *Unknown*. AmFP

'Tis of a little drummer. The Little Drummer. Richard Henry Stoddard. AmFP

'Tis of a pedlar, a pedlar trim. The Bold Pedlar and Robin Hood. *Unknown*. AmFP

'Tis of a sad and dismal story that happened off the fatal rock. The Loss of the *New Columbia. Unknown*. AmFP

'Tis of just a cabin home. Whispering Wind. Catherine Braan Layne. PWR

'Tis of my country that I would endite. Ezra Pound. *Fr.* L'Homme Moyen Sensuel. OBSV

'Tis on October thirty-first. Hallowe'en. Lizelia Augusta Jenkins Moorer. CBWP-3

'Tis one thing to be tempted, Escalus. Shakespeare. OxBM *Fr.* Measure for Measure.

'Tis only a half truth the poet has sung. Crowded Ways of Life. Walter S. Gresham. BLPA

'Tis passed!—the sultry tyrant of the south. A Summer Evening's Meditation. Anna Laetitia Barbauld. Ro *Fr.* Poems (1773).

'Tis said, as Cupid danced [or danc't] among. How Roses Came Red. Robert Herrick. CaPo; SoSe-8

'Tis said but a name is friendship. Lines to Mrs. Isabel Peace. Mary Weston Fordham. CBWP-2

'Tis said that faith declines; believe it not;. Faith, Hope, and Charity Are the Prospects of Manhood. Leigh Hunt. ChIV-2

'Tis said the Gods lower down that chain above. George Alsop. SCAP

'Tis said there were no thought of hell. Heaven and Hell. Francis Thompson. OxBSP

'Tis so appalling—it exhilirates. Emily Dickinson. NCAP; PoE

'Tis so much joy! 'Tis so much joy! Emily Dickinson. NOCV

'Tis spring, warm glows the south. Birds' Nests. John Clare. OAEL-2; OxBSP

'Tis still observ'd, that Fame ne'er sings. Fame. Robert Herrick. FaBoEE

Tis strang. A Dialogue betwixt Man, and Nature. Margaret Lucas Cavendish, Duchess of Newcastle. PBRV

'Tis strange how much is mark'd on memory. A History of the Lyre. Letitia Elizabeth Landon. VWP

'Tis strange how my head runs on! 'tis a puzzle to understand. The City Clerk. Thomas Ashe. EBVV

'Tis strange how the newspapers honour. Limerick. Eugene Field. PeLi

'Tis strange! I saw the skies. Dreams. Thomas Traherne. FMP

'Tis strange indeed to hear us plead. Dr. Booker T. Washington to the National Negro Business League. Joseph Cotter, Sr.. AAP

'Tis strange she should confess it, though it be true. (LL) A Self[e] Accuser. Donne. FaBoEE; PeLV

'Tis strange, the Miser should his Cares employ. Epistle IV, to Richard Boyle, Earl of Burlington. Alexander Pope. OAEL-1; PoEL-3

'Tis strange to think, if we could fling aside. The Mask of Gaiety. Letitia Elizabeth Landon. VWP

'Tis summer time on Bredon. Summer Time on Bredon. Hugh Kingsmill. NOBL; UV

'Tis Sweet to Rest in Lively Hope. *Unknown*. AmFP

'Tis sweet to see the evening star appear. Byron. *Fr.* Canto the First. NAEL-2; OAEL-2; PoE *Fr.* Don Juan.

'Tis, that he has both generals in reversion. Byron. *See* The Vision of Judgment.

'Tis the cur-dog of Britain and spaniel of Spain. (LL) The Character of Sir Robert Walpole. Jonathan Swift. FaBoEE; PoE

'Tis the folks in the front that I jar. (LL) The Face. Anthony Euwer. OBAL; PeLi; PoLF

'Tis the gift to be simple, 'tis the gift to be free. Simple Gifts. *Unknown*. AH

'Tis the great art of life to manage well. Madness. John Armstrong. NOEC *Fr.* The Art of Preserving Health.

'Tis the human touch in this world that counts. The Human Touch. Spencer Michael Free. BLPA; FaBoBe; PoToHe

'Tis the Last Rose of Summer. Thomas Moore. BLPA; FaBoBe; LBC; NOIV; OxBoLi; PoEL-4

("Or give sigh for sigh.") (LL) LBC

Tis [*or* 'Tis] the middle of the night by the castle clock. Christabel. Coleridge. CH; FaBoVe; FHYEP; NAEL-2; NOBRP; OAEL-2; Ro "Beneath the lamp the lady bowed." OxBSn

'Tis the middle watch of a summer's night. The Culprit Fay. Joseph Rodman Drake. APN-1

"Tis the Octoroon ball! And the halls are alight!" Ballade des Belles Milatraisses. Rosalie Jonas. BlSi

'Tis the practice of the great. (LL) A Song: "Lying is an occupation." Laetitia Pilkington. PEW

'Tis the season when Nature awakes from her sleep. Easter; or, Spring-Time. Lizelia Augusta Jenkins Moorer. CBWP-3

'Tis the voice of the Lobster: I heard him /declare declare, *par. of* The Sluggard *by* Isaac Watts. The Lobster. "Lewis Carroll." CBNP; NOBL; OBCoV; OxBChV; PeLV; UV *Fr.* Alice's Adventures in Wonderland.

'Tis the voice of the [*or* a] sluggard; I heard him complain. The Sluggard. Isaac Watts. CH; EBEvV; ECEV; HAP; NOEC; OxBChV; OxBoLi; PoEL-3; UV

'Tis the week before Christmas and every night. For the Children or the Grown-ups? *Unknown*. OBCP

'Tis the year's [*or* yeares] midnight, and it is the day's [*or* dayes]. A Nocturnal[l] upon Saint Lucy's [*or* S. Lucies] Day, Being the Shortest Day. Donne. EBEV; ECEV; FHYEP; GBL; MeLP; NAEL-1; NOBE; NOSC; OAEL-1; OxAEP-1; PoE; PoEL-2; SCGP; SeCP; TFi

'Tis these that free the small entangled fly. Shakespeare: The Fairies' Advocate. Thomas Hood. *Fr.* The Plea of the Midsummer Fairies. OBNC

'Tis thy spirit calls thee—come away! Spirit's Song. Louisa Costello. Ro

Tis thy time to choose a lover. (LL) Ode 1.23: To Chloë ("Vitas hinnuleo"). Horace. AWP; OBVE

'Tis Timarion. Meleager, *Greek*. GrAn, *tr. by* Peter Whigham

'Tis time this heart should be unmoved. Byron. *See* On This Day I Complete My Thirty-sixth Year.

'Tis time thy prayers were said! (LL) Motley. Walter De la Mare. HoPM; PoWW

'Tis time to conclude. The Conclusion of a Letter to the Rev. Mr. C——. Mary Barber. CABP; ECWP

'Tis time to rise. *Unknown*. *See* Early to bed and early to rise.

'Tis to yourself I speak; you cannot know. Yourself. Jones Very. APN-1; NOBA; OxBA; PAR; PoEL-4; Son

'Tis true, dear[e] Ben, thy just chastizing [*or* chastising] hand. To Ben Jonson. Thomas Carew. BeJo; CaPo; EPCY; NAEL-1; NOSC

'Tis true no human eye can penetrate. Eugenio. Hugh Henry Brackenridge *and* Philip Freneau. *Fr.* The Rising Glory of America. AiP

'Tis true our life is but a long dis-ease. Song. Katherine Philips. OxBSP

'Tis true that when we trace its source, 'tis beer. (LL) Here Jack and Tom are paired with Moll and Meg. George Meredith. EnVR; PoEL-5

'Tis true—then why should I repine. In Sickness. Jonathan Swift. CABP; NOEC

'Tis true, 'tis day, what though it be? Break[e] of Day. Donne. NAEL-1; SoSe-8

'Tis true what famed Pythagoras maintained. Christopher Pitt. EPCY *Fr.* To Mr. Pope, on His Translation of Homer's Iliad.

'Tis true—yet 'tis no pity that 'tis true. James Kirke Paulding. APN-1 *Fr.* The Backwoodsman.

'Tis very hard when men forsake. Jack Hall. Thomas Hood. NOBRP

'Tis very sure God walks in mine. (LL) My Garden. Thomas Edward Brown. EBEvV; InPK-6; OBEV; OBGa; PoLF; UV

'Tis Want of Sense makes *Superfluity.* (LL) Midnight Thought, A. [*on the Death of Mrs. E. H. and Her Little Daughter*]. Elizabeth Thomas. KTR; NOSC

'Tis want of sense that makes us poor. (LL) On Leaping over the Moon. Thomas Traherne. GeHe; ImPo; NAEL-1

'Tis well, 'tis something; we may stand. Tennyson. EBVV *Fr.* In Memoriam A. H. H.

'Tis well to wake the theme of Love. Eliza Cook. VWP

'Tis well you think me truly one of those. To Keats. Leigh Hunt. Ro; Son

'Tis Winter Now. Samuel Longfellow. AH

'Tis with us perpetuall night. Catullus. *See* Carmen 5 ("My sweetest Lesbia, let us live and love").

'Tis woman that seduces all mankind! John Gay. OxBoV; PeLV *Fr.* The Beggar's Opera. OAEL-1

'Tis wretchedness too much to be cast down. Joseph in Carcere. Sir Francis Hubert. ChIV-1 *Fr.* Egypt's Favorite.

Tisiphone responds. Publius Papinius Statius, *Latin.* OBCVT, *tr. by* Alexander Pope

Tit for Tat; a Tale. John Aikin. OxBChV

Tit, tat, toe. A Baby Verse. *Unknown.* BoTP; OxNR

Titan! to whose immortal eyes, Prometheus. Byron. InPS-3; NOBE; OAEL-2; OxAEP-2; Poetr; Ro

Titanic, The. Edwin John Pratt.
Final Moments, The. NOBC

Titanic, The. *Unknown.* AmFP

Titanic, a Toast. *Unknown.* CBNP

Titanic, De. *Unknown.* AS

Titans, The. Betti Alver, *Estonian.* BoWoP, *tr. by* Willis Barnstone *and* Felix Oinas

Tithe [*or* Tythe]: To the Bride, The. Robert Herrick. CaPo

Tithonus. Tennyson. CABP; EnVR; GEA; HAP; ImPo; NAEL-2; NAWM-2; NOBE; NOBVV; NoP-4; OAEL-2; OBNC; PoE; PoEL-5; SCGP

Title divine—is mine! Emily Dickinson. APN-2; NALW; NOBA; PAR

Tittery-Irie-Aye. *Unknown.* AmFP

Titty cum tawtay. *Unknown.* OxNR

Titus and Berenice. John Heath-Stubbs. GTBS-P

Titus the brave and valorous gallant. Sir John Davies. NoSic *Fr.* Epigrams.

Titwillow. Sir William Schwenck Gilbert. *See* Ko-Ko's Song.

Tizzy Boost. Bruce Andrews.
"Appetizers'." FTOS

Tjanting. Ron Silliman.
"Not this. / What then?" PmAP
("Dig in. Wicker throne. Scratch that. Keep moving. Dressd to kill. Burgundy jumpsuit.") (LL) FTOS
("Not this.") FTOS

Tlanusi' Yi, the Leech Place. Gladys Cardiff. CDW

Tlingit Concrete Poem. Nora Dauenhauer. NIP-4

To ———: "Approaching night her mantle flings." James M. Whitfield. AAP

To ———? Richard Dehmel, *German.* AWP, *tr. by* Jethro Bithell

To ———: "Half in the dim light from the hall." W. S. Braithwaite. PoBA

To ———: "Let those with cost deck their ill-fashioned clay." Thomas Rymer. OxBSP

To. Herman Melville. NCAP

To———: "Music, when soft voices die." Shelley. AWP; CBLP; EBEvV; FHYEP; GTBS-P; HeIP-4; ImPo; NOBE; OBEV; OBNC; OxAEP-2; OxBSP; PFE; PoEL-4; Poetr; TFi

To———: "One word is too often profaned." Shelley. BoLoP; CBLP; EBEvV; GLoP; ImPo; NOBE; OBEV; OBNC; OxAEP-2; PoLF; TFi

To ———: "'Twas eve; the broadly shining sun." Edward Coote Pinkney. APN-1

To ———: "Vainly my heart had with thy sorceries striven." Sarah Helen Whitman. APN-1

To ———: "We met but in one giddy dance." Winthrop Mackworth Praed. CBLP

To. William Carlos Williams. OBAL

To A. A. A. (Akhmatova). Osip Mandelstam, *Russian.* TCRP, *tr. by* Bernard Meares

To a Beautiful Pear Tree. James Wright. HAP

To a Bed of Tulips. Robert Herrick. CaPo; GaP

To a Bicycle. *Unknown.* BXAP

To a Blockhead. Alexander Pope. *See* Another [Epigram].

To a Boon Companion. Oliver St. John Gogarty. OBMV

To a Bower. John Clare. GaP

To a Boy-Poet of the Decadence. Sir Owen Seaman. PeLV

To a Bull-Dog. Sir John Collings Squire. NSI

To a Bull Moose. Eugene O'Neill. UV

To a Butterfly. James Merrill. APo

To a Butterfly. Wordsworth. ACTP; NTP

To a Calvinist in Bali. Edna St. Vincent Millay. NoAM

To a Captious Critic. Paul Laurence Dunbar. BPo

To a Cat. Keats. FaBoCh

To a Cat. Swinburne. PC

To a Caty-did. Philip Freneau. TAP

To a Certain Civilian. Walt Whitman. CBCWP

To a Certain Most Certainly Certain Critic. David McCord. OBAL

To "A Certain Rich Man." Alice Thompson Meynell. ChIV-2

To a Chameleon. Marianne Moore. APo

To a Child. Wilfred Owen. Son

To a Child [Written in Her Album]. Wordsworth. OxBSP
(Written in the Album of a Child.) OxBChV

To a Child. Judith Wright. BMAP

To a Child Born in Time of Small War. Helen Sorrells. WPE

To a Child Dancing in the Wind. W. B. Yeats. IIP; PFE

To a Child [of] Five Years Old. Nathaniel Cotton. ECEV; OxBChV

To a Child in Death. Charlotte Mew. ChIV-2; MoBrPo

To a Child of Quality [Five Years Old, the Author Supposed Forty]. Matthew Prior. NOBE; NOEC; OBEV; PoEL-3

To a Child of Quality of Five Years Old, the Author Supposed Forty. Matthew Prior. NOEC

To a Child Running with Outstretched Arms in Canyon de Chelly. N. Scott Momaday. CDW; HATNAP

To a Child Trapped in a Barber Shop. Philip Levine. InPK-6; MoP; NOBA; NoAM; Poetr; TAP; VGW; WeT

To a Child Who Inquires. Olga Petrova. BLPA

To a Christmas Two-Year-Old. Luci Shaw. TrCP

To a Common Prostitute. Walt Whitman. MoAmPo

To a Comrade in Arms. Alun Lewis. FaBoTw; MoBrPo

To a Conscript of 1940. Sir Herbert Read. LiTM; NSI; OBWP; PoWW

To a Courtesan a Thousand Years Dead. Paul Eldridge. PoA

To a Covetous Churl. Edward May. FaBoEE

To a Cricket. William Cox Bennett. BoTP

To a Crucifix. Anna Wickham. MoBrPo

To a Cuckoo. Phan Bội Châu, *Vietnamese.* AVP, *tr. by* Huỳnh Sanh Thông

To a Cuckoo at Coolanlough. Medbh McGuckian. PBCIP

To A. D. William Ernest Henley. *See* The Blackbird.

To a Daisy. Alice Thompson Meynell. MoBrPo; Son; VWP

To a Dancer. Arthur Symons. ADE

To a Dark Girl. Gwendolyn B. Bennett. BlSi; ColAP; NAAAL; PoBA; SAGP

To a Daughter at Fourteen Forsaking the Violin. Carole Oles. WeW-3

To a Daughter Leaving Home. Linda Pastan. NIP-2

To a Daughter with Artistic Talent. Peter Meinke. Poetsp

To a Dead Dog in the River. Nguyễn Văn Lạc, *Vietnamese.* AVP, *tr. by* Huỳnh Sanh Thông

To a Dead Elephant. Douglas Livingstone. PeSA

To a:dead. / stand- / ;Still. (LL) She being Brand. E. E. Cummings. MoP; NOBA; OxBA; PeLV

To a Deaf and Dumb Little Girl. Hartley Coleridge. PoEL-4

To a Deceased Friend. Priscilla Jane Thompson. CBWP-2

To a Despondent Evening. Iftiqar Arif. NBrP

To a Discarded Fan. Nguyễn Khuyến, *Chinese.* AVP, *tr. by* Huỳnh Sanh Thông

To a Distant Friend. Wordsworth. GTBS-P

(Speak!) OBEV

To a Dog. Josephine Preston Peabody. BLPA

To a Dog Injured in the Street. William Carlos Williams. LCAP-2; LiTM; SAmP

To a Face in a Crowd. Robert Penn Warren. FuPo

To a Fair Lady Playing with a Snake. Edmund Waller. CABP; CBLP; EBEV; HoPM; NOSC; PoE

(Of a Fair Lady Playing with a Snake.) PoEL-3

To a False Friend. Thomas Hood. FP

To a Farmer Who Hung Five Hawks on His Barbed Wire. David Wagoner. NoAM

To a Fat Lady Seen from the Train. Frances Darwin Cornford. APAD; BLPA; EBEvV; FaBoWP; MoBrPo; OBMV; UV; WeW-3

To a Field Mouse. Robert Burns. *See* To a Mouse[, On Turning Her Up in Her Nest, with the Plough, November, 1785].

To a Firefly. *Unknown.* PFE

To a Fish. Leigh Hunt. NBLV; PeLV; SCGP *Fr.* The Fish, the Man, and the Spirit. HAP; NOBL; NTP; OBEV; PoEL-4

To a Flea in a Glass of Water. Desmond A. Greig. PeSA

To a Fly, Taken out of a Bowl of Punch. "Peter Pindar." NOEC

To a French Structuralist. David Kirby. BLT

To a Friend. Matthew Arnold. NAEL-2; Son

To a Friend. William Lisle Bowles. Son

To A Friend. Catullus. LBC

To a Friend. Hartley Coleridge. FP; PoLF

(Sonnet: To a Friend.) OBNC

To a Friend. Grace Stricker Dawson. BLPA

To a Friend. Joseph Rodman Drake. APN-1

To a Friend. Oliver St. John Gogarty. FP

To a Friend. Ben Jonson. BeJo

To a Friend. Amy Lowell. PoLF

To a Friend. Boris Pasternak, *Russian.* TCRP, *tr. by* Yakov Hornstein

To a Friend. Frank Stewart. EC2

To a Friend an Epigram: Of him. Martial, *Latin.* OBCVT, *tr. by* Ben Jonson

To a Friend Concerning Several Ladies. William Carlos Williams. VGW

To a Friend for Her Naked Breasts. "Eliza." KTR

To a Friend in Love during the Riots. William Parsons. NOEC

To a Friend, Inviting Him to a Meeting upon Promise. William Habington. BeJo *Fr.* Castara.

To a Friend, on Her Examination for the Doctorate in English. James Vincent Cunningham. VGW

To a Friend on her Marriage. Jane West.

"Married, poor soul! your empire's over." ECWP

To a Friend on His Marriage. Frank Templeton Prince. LiTM

To a Friend, Using the Same Rhymes of a Peom He Sent Me. Liu Ya-tzu, *Chinese.* SuSp, *tr. by* Wu-chi Liu

To a Friend Who Wouldn't Bother to Strain His Noodleboard Because Even So It Is Hard to Go Hunting When Your Rifle Is Blunt and Love Is Soft as an Old Blanket. Jacob Glatshteyn, *Yiddish.* PFTM, *tr. by* Benjamin Harshav *and* Barbara Harshav

To a Friend Whose Work Has Come to Nothing. W. B. Yeats. AWP; InPK-6; LiTM; MoBrPo; OAEL-2; OBMV; OxAEP-2; PoA

To a Friend Whose Work Has Come to Triumph. Anne Sexton. InPK-6; PFE

To a Friend with a Religious Vocation. Elizabeth Jennings. TOF

To a Friend's Child. Aliki Barnstone. BoWoP

To A Gardener. Robert Louis Stevenson. OBGa

To a Gentleman and Lady on the Death of the Lady's Brother and Sister, and a Child of the Name Avis, Aged One Year. Phillis Wheatley. BlSi

To a Gentleman, Who Desired Proper Materials for a Monody. *Unknown.* NOEC

To a Gentleman Who Disordered a Lady's Handerchief, and Immediately Cut His Thumb. Elizabeth Teft. ECWP

To a Gentleman Who Invited Me to Go A-Fishing. Elizabeth Moody. ECWP

To a Gentlewoman Objecting to Him His Grey Hairs. Robert Herrick. BeJo; CaPo

To a Giraffe. Marianne Moore. APo

To a Girl. Asclepiades, *Greek.* OBCVT, *tr. by* Andrew Lang

To a Girl. Horace. *See* Odes 1.5.

To a Girl Writing Her Father's Death. Beckian Fritz Goldberg. NAmP90

To a Golden-Haired Girl in a Louisiana Town. Vachel Lindsay. MoAmPo

To a Golden Heart, Worn round His Neck. Goethe, *German.* AWP, *tr. by* Margaret Fuller Ossoli

To a Gone Era. Irma McClaurin. BlSi

To a Goose [*or* Gosse]. Robert Southey. BXAP; NOBL; PeLV; Son

To a Gravel Walk. William Mason. OBGa

To a Guest. Vladislav Felitsianovich Khodasevich, *Russian.* TCRP, *tr. by* Michael Frayn

To A. H. James M. Whitfield. APN-2

To a Haggis. Robert Burns. FaBoVe

To a Hedgehog. Samuel Thompson. BIrV

To a Hermit in the Mountains. Hsü Pen, *Chinese.* CoBLCP, *tr. by* Jonathan Chaves

To a Hero Dead at al-Safra. Hind bint Uthatha, *Arabic.* WPOW, *tr. by* Bridget Connelly *and* Deirdre Lashgari

To a Hunchback. Ibn al-Rumi, *Arabic.* ArPe, *tr. by* Omar S. Pound

To a Jilt. Martin Donisthorpe Armstrong. FaBoEE

To A. L.; Persuasions to Love. Thomas Carew. CaPo; SeCP

To a Lady[e]. William Dunbar. EBEV; GBL; OBEV; OxBS; PeLV

To a Lady. John Gay. OBEV

To a Lady. Alexander Pope. OxBoLi *Fr.* Epistle [II,] to a Lady[: Of the Characters of Women]. NAEL-1; NOEC

To a Lady Asking Him How Long He Would Love Her. Sir George Etherege. OBEV; SAGP

To a Lady Friend. W. H. Davies. MoBrPo

To a Lady in a Garden. Edmund Waller. BeJo

To a Lady Making Love. Lady Mary Wortley Montagu. LW

To a Lady on Her Passion for Old China. John Gay. ImPo; SCGP

To a Lady on Reading Sherlock "Upon Death." Philip Dormer Stanhope. *See* Verses Written in a Lady's Sherlock "Upon Death."

To a Lady on the Death of Her Husband. Phillis Wheatley. TAP

To a Lady: She Refusing to Continue a Dispute with Me, and Leaving Me in the Argument. Matthew Prior. NoP-4

To a Lady That Desired I Would Love Her. Thomas Carew. BeJo; CBLP; CaPo; CavPo; MeLP; SCGP

("You but unlock, so we each other bless.") (LL) CavPo

To a Lady That Desired Me I Would Bear My Part with Her in a Song. Richard Lovelace. CaPo

To a Lady That Forbade to Love before Company. Sir John Suckling. CaPo

To a Lady Upon a Looking-Glass Sent. James Shirley. BeJo

To a Lady, Who Commanded Me to Send Her an Account in Verse. Mary Barber.

"How I succeed, you kindly ask." ECWP

To a Lady, Who Desired Me Not To Be in Love with Her. John Cutts. NOSC

To a Lady Who Did Sing Excellently. Edward Herbert. SeCP

To a Lady Who Sent Me a Copy of Verses at My Going to Bed. Henry King. CBLP

To a Lady, with a Guitar. Shelley. *See* With a Guitar, to Jane.

To a Lady, with a Present of a Fan. Charles Brandling. NOEC

To a Lady with Child that Asked [*or* Ask'd] an Old Shirt. Richard Lovelace. NOSC

To a Lady's Countenance. Elinor Wylie. NALW

To a Lark in War-Time. Franz Werfel, *German.* TrJP, *tr. by* Edith Abercrombie Snow

To a leg, sir, of mutton you may go. (LL) There was an old man of Tobago. *Unknown.* CBNP; ReMoGo

To a Lily. James Matthew Legaré. APN-2

To a Little Colored Boy. Priscilla Jane Thompson. CBWP-2

To a Little Girl, One Year Old, in a Ruined Fortress. Robert Penn Warren.

"Child next door is defective because the mother, The." FuPo

Colder Fire. FuPo; LiTM; MoLi

("Past paths where on their appointed occasions men climb, / and pass.") (LL) MoLi

Gull's Cry. FuPo

("White goose by palm tree, palm ragged, among stones the white oleander.")

Sirocco. FuPo

To a Little Invisible Being Who Is Expected Soon to Become Visible. Anna Laetitia Barbauld. ECWP; WoRP

To a Living Author. *Unknown.* NBLV

To a Loch Fyne Fisherman. George Campbell Hay. FaBoTC

To a Lock of Hair. Sir Walter Scott. GTBS-P

To a Locomotive in Winter. Walt Whitman. AmPP; GM; InPK-6; MoAmPo; MoP; NAAL-1; NAAL-3; NCAP; NoAM; NoP-4; PoEL-5; Poetr; TAP

To a Lofty Beauty, from Her Poor Kinsman. Hartley Coleridge. OxAEP-2

To a Louse [On Seeing One on a Lady's Bonnet at Church]. Robert Burns. APo; BLPA; FaBoVe; NAEL-2; NOBRP; NOEC; OxBS; PBMP

To a Loved One. Mary Weston Fordham. CBWP-2

To a Loved One of Other Days. Matilda Caroline Edwards. PWR

To a man eating a pear. Please Say Something. Taeko Tomioka, *Japanese.* WPOW, *tr. by* Hiroaki Sato

To a Man Who is Rob Southland. Nia Francisco. HATNAP

To a Maniac. Amelia Alderson Opie. NOBRP

To a Marsh Hawk in Spring. Henry David Thoreau. PoEL-4

To a' men living be it kend. The Rising of the Session. Robert Fergusson. OxBS

To a Military Rifle, 1942. Yvor Winters. MoAmPo

To a Milkweed. Deborah Digges. CrSp

To a Millionaire. Archibald Lampman. NOBC

To a Mosquito. William Cullen Bryant. NCAP

To a Mountain Daisy [On Turning One Down, with the Plough, in April—1786]. Robert Burns. PoLF

To a Mouse[, On Turning Her Up in Her Nest, with the Plough, November, 1785]. Robert Burns. APAD; APo; CABP; EBEvV; FaBoVe; GEA; HAP; HeIP-4; ImPo; InPS-3; NAEL-2; NOEC; NoP-4; OAEL-1; OxAEP-2; OxBS; PoE; PoLF; Ro; SCGP; TFi; UV

(To a Field Mouse.) GTBS-P

To a New-Born Child. Cosmo Monkhouse. LiLi

To a New Daughter-in-Law. *Unknown.* PoToHe

To a New England Poet. Philip Freneau. NAAL-1; NAAL-3

To a newspaper carelessly left there. *Good dog.* (LL) Dog's Death. John Updike. Poetr; Poetsp

To a Nigerian Friend. Jaihiun Kim, *Korean.* CKP, *tr. by* Jaihiun Kim

To a Nightingale. Keats. *See* Ode to a Nightingale.

To a Noisy Politician. Philip Freneau. TAP

To a Nosegay in Pancharilla's Breast. Soame Jenyns. ECEV

To a Nun. John Ormond, *after the Welsh.* EBEV; FaBoTw; NoP-4

To a Passionist. Lionel Pigot Johnson. ADE

To a Persian Cat. F. C. W. Hiley. PC

To a Pessimist. Ronald Arbuthnott Knox. OBCoV

To a Piggy Bank. Tôn Thất Diệm, *Vietnamese.* AVP, *tr. by* Huỳnh Sanh Thông

To a place of ruined stone we brought you, and sea-reaches. Sirocco. Robert Penn Warren. FuPo *Fr.* To a Little Girl, One Year Old, in a Ruined Fortress.

To a Plagiarist. Moses ibn Ezra, *Hebrew.* TrJP, *tr. by* Solomon Solis-Cohen

To a Poet. Agnes Nemes Nagy, *Hungarian.* CEEP; PoSu, *tr. by* Bruce Berlind

To a Poet a Thousand Years Hence. James Elroy Flecker. MoBrPo; PoRA

To a Poet a Thousand Years Hence. John Heath-Stubbs. OxBC

To a Poet I Knew. Jewel C. Latimore. PoBA

To a Poet, Who Would Have Me Praise Certain Bad Poets, Imitators of His and Mine. W. B. Yeats. CTC; FaBoEE

To a Political Poet. Heinrich Heine, *German.* FaBoPV, *tr. by* Tom Paulin

To a Poor Old Woman. William Carlos Williams. BLT; ColAP; MeMAP; OBAL; PiM; TAP; TTTS

To a Portrait Painter who Desired Him to Sit. Po Chü-i, *Chinese.* ChiP, *tr. by* Arthur Waley

To a Post-Office Inkwell. Christopher Darlington Morley. PoLF

To a President. Witter Bynner. OBAL

To a President. Walt Whitman. NAAL-1; NAAL-3

To a Pretty Girl. Israel Zangwill. TrJP

To a Print of Queen Victoria. James Keir Baxter. OxBC

To a Proud Beauty. "Ephelia." KTR; PEW

To a Publisher. . . Cut-out. Imamu Amiri Baraka. NeAP

To a Pyrotechnist. Chao Meng-fu, *Chinese.* CoBLCP, *tr. by* Jonathan Chaves

To a Querulous Acquaintance. Charlotte Smith. BWW

To a Rabfak Student. Mikhail Arkadyevich Svetlov, *Russian.* TCRP, *tr. by* Daniel Weissbort

To a Red-headed Do-good Waitress. Alan Dugan. Son

To a Republican. Philip Freneau. *See* On Mr. Paine's Rights of Man.

To a Republican Friend, 1848. Matthew Arnold. EBVVPR

To a Reviewer Who Admired My Book. John Ciardi. OBAL

To a River in the South. Sir Henry John Newbolt. CH

To a Sad Daughter. Michael Ondaatje. NoAM

To a Salesgirl, Weary of Artificial Holiday Trees. James Wright. NYBP

To a Scarecrow. Tần Đà, *Vietnamese.* AVP, *tr. by* Huỳnh Sanh Thông

To a School-Boy at Eton, Yes and No. Mary Savage. ECWP

To a Schoolboy. *Unknown, Serbian.* RB, *tr. by* Anne Pennington

To a Schoolmaster. Martial, *Latin.* OBCVT, *tr. by* F. A. Wright

To a Sea Eagle. "Hugh MacDiarmid." MoBrPo

To a Seagull. Gerald Griffin. TIRV

To a Seaman Dead on Land. Kay Boyle. PoA

To a Segar. Samuel Low. OBAL

To a Set of Drawing Pencils. Fay Lipshitz. IFJA

To a Shade. W. B. Yeats. NAEL-2; PoEL-5

To a Shred of Linen. Lydia Huntley Sigourney. PAR

To a Sick Friend. Hannah Wallis. ECWP

To a Single Shadow without Pity. Sam Cornish. PoBA

To a Skeleton. Anna Jane Vardhill. BLPA

To a Sky-Lark. Wordsworth.

"Up with me! up with me into the clouds!" TTTS

To a Skylark. Shelley. EBEvV; FHYEP; FaBoBe; GTBS-P; HAP; ImPo; InPS-3; NAEL-2; NOBRP; NoP-4; OAEL-2; OBEV; OBNC; OxAEP-2; PBMP; PoLF; Ro; SCGP; TFi

(Ode to a Skylark.) NOBE

To a Snail. Marianne Moore. APo; CMoP; FaBoMo; FaBoWP; MeMAP; NAAL-2; NALW; PoPoPo

To a Snowflake. Francis Thompson. MoBrPo

To a soft, oleaginous mutta. (LL) Arthur. Ogden Nash. NoP-4; PeLi

To a Solitary Disciple. William Carlos Williams. VGW

To a Squirrel. W. B. Yeats. *See* To a Squirrel at Kyle-Na-No.

To a Squirrel at Kyle-Na-No. W. B. Yeats. APo; ChAP

(To a Squirrel.) CTAV

To a Statue. Nguyễn Khuyến, *Vietnamese.* AVP, *tr. by* Huỳnh Sanh Thông

To a Steam Roller. Marianne Moore. BoWoP; CMoP; FaBoMo; MeMAP; MoAmPo; OxBA; PoPoPo; VGW

To a Stranger. Walt Whitman. APN-1; NOBA; SAmP

To a Stranger (At the End of a Caboose). Laura Jensen. GM

To a Swallow. John Peale Bishop, *after the Greek of* Euenus. GrAn; OBVE

To a Talkative Guest. Po Chü-i, *Chinese.* ChiP, *tr. by* Arthur Waley

To a Teacher of French. Donald Davie. OxBC

To a "Tenting" Boy. Charles Tennyson Turner. OBNC

To a Thesaurus. Franklin Pierce Adams. NBLV

To a Traveler. Lionel Pigot Johnson. MoBrPo

To a Traveler. Su Tung-p'o, *Chinese.* HoPM; OHPC, *tr. by* Kenneth Rexroth

To a Troubled Friend. James Wright. Son

To a Very Young Lady. Edmund Waller. SCGP; SeCP

To a Vine-clad Telegraph Pole. Louis Untermeyer. MoAmPo

To a Visiting Poet in a College Dormitory. Carolyn Kizer. PoA

To a Wandering Female Singer. Felicia Dorothea Hemans. VWP

To a Wanton. William Habington. NOSC; SeCP

To A Waterfowl. William Cullen Bryant. APN-1; APo; AWP; CH; ColAP; FaBoBe; HoPM; ImPo; NAAL-1; NAAL-3; NCAP; NOBA; NoP-4; OxBA; PAR; PWR; PoEL-4; PoLF; SoSe-8; TAP; TFi

To a Waterfowl. Donald Hall. OBAL

To a Watering Scoop. Bùi Du'o'ng Lịch, *Chinese.* AVP, *tr. by* Huỳnh Sanh Thông

To a Western Boy. Walt Whitman. APN-1

To a wild mountain, whose bare summit hides. Fragment Descriptive of the Miseries of War. Charlotte Smith. ECWP

To a woman that I knew. Her Eyes. John Crowe Ransom. LiTM; MeMAP; OBAL

To a Woman Who Wants Darkness and Time. Gerald William Barrax. PoBA

To a Wren on Calvary. Larry Levis. PuP-17

To a Young Ass. Coleridge. OxAEP-2 *Fr.* Effusions.

To a Young Beauty. W. B. Yeats. CMoP

To a Young Brother. Maria Jane Jewsbury. OxBChV

To a Young Friend. Coleridge. *See* To a Young Friend, [*on* His Proposing to Domesticate with the Author].

To a Young Friend, on His Proposing to Domesticate with the Author. Coleridge. LaPo

To a Young Girl. W. B. Yeats. EBEV

To a Young Girl Leaving the Hill Country. Arna Bontemps. GT

To a Young Heir. Samuel Johnson. *See* A Short Song of Congratulation.

To a Young Lady. William Cowper. GTBS-P

To a Young Lady That Desired a Verse of My Being Servant One Day and Mistress Another. Elizabeth Tipper. KTR; NOSC *Fr.* Pilgrim's Viaticum; or, The Destitute, But Not Forlorn.

To a Young Lady, with Some Lampreys. John Gay. CABP; CBLP; ECEV; EP; NOEC; OBCoV

To a Young Poet. Valery Yakovlevich Bryusov, *Russian.* TCRP, *tr. by* April FitzLyon

To a Young Poet. Edna St. Vincent Millay. OxBSP

To a Young Poet Who Died. John Logan. CAPP-1

To Adam, his Scribe. Chaucer. *See* To His Scribe Adam.

To Adelhard, Archbishop of Canterbury ("Brief is our life, now in the midst of the years"). Alcuin, *Latin.* MLL, *tr. by* Helen Waddell

To Adelhard, Archbishop of Canterbury ("Prince-Archbishop, Father Adelhard"). Alcuin, *Latin.* MLL, *tr. by* Helen Waddell

To Adhiambo. Gabriel Okara. PBA

(Adhiambo.) PBMAP

To after-Times thy Wit. (LL) To the Virginian Voyage. Michael Drayton. AiP; CABP; HAP; NAEL-1; NOBE; NOSC; OBEV; PBRV; PoEL-2; SCGP

To Ailsa Rock. Keats. OBNC

To air the ditty, / And to earth I. (LL) Fancy's Knell. A. E. Housman. FaBoCh; PoRA

To Alexis in Answer to his Poem against Fruition. Aphra Behn. KTR; LW; NOSC; PEW

To Algebra God is inclined. Limerick. J. C. B. Date. PeLi

To All Brothers. Sonia Sanchez. BPo

To all my length. (LL) To Earthward. Robert Frost. ImPo; MeMAP; MoAmPo; MoP; NOBA; NoAM; NoP-4; OxBA; RaBo; TAP; TRP

To All Sisters. Sonia Sanchez. PoBA

To all the humble beasts there be. Prayer for Gentleness to All Creatures. John Galsworthy. BoTP

To all the lists of Clay! (LL) Of all the Souls that stand create—. Emily Dickinson. AmPP; ITG; NAAL-1; NAAL-3; PAR

To all things light gives force; God dwells Himself in light. The Light Exists In The Fire. "Angelus Silesius." GePo, tr. by George C. Schoolfield Fr. The Cherubical Wanderer.

To all who carve their love on a picnic table. Open Letter from a Constant Reader. Mona Van Duyn. PoA

To all you ladies now at Bath. Farewell to Bath. Lady Mary Wortley Montagu. WPE

To all you ladies now at land. Song Written at Sea in the First Dutch War (1665), the Night before an Engagement. Charles Sackville. EnLoPo; NOBE; NOSC; OBEV; OBWP; OxAEP-1

To Allegra Florence in Heaven. Thomas Holley Chivers. "As an egg, when broken, never." BXAP

To allow himself to be properly held. The Man Who Closed Shop. Stephen Dunn. NIP-4

To Almystrea, on her Divine Works. Elizabeth Thomas. ECWP

To Althea, from Prison. Richard Lovelace. AWP; BLPA; BeJo; CaPo; CavPo; EBEvV; FaBoBe; GBL; GLoP; GTBS-P; HAP; ImPo; InPS-3; MeLP; NAEL-1; NOBE; NOSC; NoP-4; OBEV; PBRV; PFE; PoE; PoRA; SCGP; SeCP; TFi

To Amanda Walking in the Garden. N. Hookes. NOSC; OBGa

To Amarantha, That She Would Dishevel[l] Her Hair[e]. Richard Lovelace. BeJo; CavPo; HoPM; OBEV; SeCP

(Song: To Amarantha, That She Would Dishevel Her Hair.) CABP; CaPo; NOSC; PoE

To Amine. James Clarence Mangan. OBEV

To Amoret. Henry Vaughan. EnLoPo

To Amoret Gone from Him. Henry Vaughan. BeJo; MeLP;

To Amoret, of the Difference 'twixt Him and Other Lovers, and What True Love Is. Henry Vaughan. BeJo; FMP; SeCP

To Amoret, Walking in a Starry Evening. Henry Vaughan. BeJo; FMP

To amuse His Royal Majesty he will change water into wine. Zito the Magician. Miroslav Holub, Czech. PoSu, tr. by Ian Milner and George Theiner

To Amuse Myself. Li Po, Chinese. SuSp, tr. by Joseph J. Lee

To Amy. J. Gordon. OBAL

To an American Poet Just Dead. Richard Wilbur. HCAP; NBLV

To an Angel in the House. John Sparrow. OBCoV

To an Angry God. X. J. Kennedy. CRP

To an Artful Theatre Manager. Lorenzo Da Ponte. TrJP, tr. by John Mazzinghi Fr. Il Capriccio Dramatico.

To an Artist. Robert Burns. PBMP

To an Artist, to Take Heart. Louise Bogan. NYBP; TRP

To an Athlete Dying Young. A. E. Housman. CMoP; ChAP; HAP; HeIP-4; ImPo; InPK-6; LiTM; MoBrPo; MoP; NAEL-2; NIP-4; NoAM; NoP-4; PBMP; PFE; PoE; PoEL-5; PoRA; Poetr; SAGP; SCGP; SoSe-8; TFi; TRP; UnPo; WeW-3

To an Author. Philip Freneau. AmPP; ColAP; NOBA; OxBA

To an Author who Loved Truth More than Fame. Bessie Rayner Parkes. VWP

To an Early Primrose. Henry Kirke White. OBNC

To an Elder Poet. William Carlos Williams. PoA

To an Elderly Virgin. Mael Isu O Brolchain, Old Irish. NOIV, tr. by Thomas Kinsella

To an Enemy. Maxwell Bodenheim. TrJP

To an Expatriate Friend. Mervyn Morris. PBCV

To an Idea. David Shapiro. PT

To an Imaginary Father. Wendy Rose. CDW

To an Inconstant One. Sir Robert Ayton. OBEV

To an Indian Poet. Patty L. Harjo. VoR

To an Infant. Mary Weston Fordham. CBWP-2

To an Infant Expiring the Second Day of Its Birth. Mehetabel Wright. ECWP; NOEC

To an Isle in the Water. W. B. Yeats. AWP; TTTS

To an Oak Tree. Sir Walter Scott. OBNC Fr. Waverley.

To an Old Gentlewoman That Painted Her Face. George Turberville. OxBSP

To an Old Lady. William Empson. FaBoTw; GTBS-P; NOBE; NoAM; OxAEP-2

To an Old Philosopher in Rome. Wallace Stevens. ColAP; EnlH; MeMAP; MoP; NOBA; NoAM; Poetr

To an Old Tune. Hsin Ch'i-chi, Chinese. OHMPC, tr. by Kenneth Rexroth

To an Old Tune. Lu Kuei Meng, Chinese. OHMPC, tr. by Kenneth Rexroth

To an Unborn Infant. Isabella Kelly. ECWP

To an Unborn Pauper Child. Thomas Hardy. GTBS-P

To An Undiscerning Critic. Sir Arthur Conan Doyle. OBCoV

To and / back and forth. Robert Creeley. FTOS

To Angélique. Heinrich Heine, German.
"This mad carnival of loving." TrJP, tr. by Emma Lazarus

To Anita. Sonia Sanchez. ISC

To Ann Lear. Edward Lear. CBNP

To Anna Matilda. Robert Merry. NOBRP

To Annie. Mary E. Tucker. CBWP-1

To Another Housewife. Judith Wright. NALW

To Anthea ("Ah my Anthea! must my heart still break?"). Robert Herrick. CaPo

To Anthea ("Let's call for Hymen if agreed thou art"). Robert Herrick. EP

To Anthea ("Now is the time, when all the lights wax dim"). Robert Herrick. PoEL-3

To Anthea Lying in Bed. Robert Herrick. BeJo; SeCP

To Anthea, Who May Command Him Anything. Robert Herrick. CaPo; GTBS-P; NOBE; NOSC; OAEL-1; OBEV; SeCP

To Antonius Julus, the Son of Mark Antony, tof the Triumvirate. Horace. See 4.2: Praise of Pindar, The ("Pindarum quisquis studet aemulari").

To Any Dead Officer. Siegfried Sassoon. NSI; PoFWW

To Any M.F.H F. H. Vita Sackville-West. WPN

To Any Member of My Generation. George Barker. LiTM; Son

To any watch they keep? (LL) Neither Out Far Nor In Deep. Robert Frost. AmPP; HAP; MeMAP; MoP; NAAL-2; NOBA; NoAM; NoP-4; OxBoS; PFE; Poetr; TAP; TRP; WeW-3

To Aphrodite these wreaths. Kallirrhoê: A Dedication. Agathias, Greek. GrAn, tr. by Dudley Fitts

To Archaeanassa, on whose furrow'd brow. On Archaeanassa. Plato, Greek. AWP, tr. by Thomas Stanley

To Archbishop Lang. Unknown. OBCoV

To Archinus. Callimachus, Greek. AWP, tr. by F. A. Wright

To Ariake Kambara. Norman Rosten. NYBP

To Aristius Fuscus, see also Odes 1.22 ("Integer vitae"). Horace. OBVE Fr. Odes.

To Arno of Salzburg. Alcuin, Latin. MLL, tr. by Helen Waddell

To Artemisia.—'Tis to her we sing. Mary Leapor. PEW Fr. Essay on Friendship.

To ascend? How? Song of a Man in the Dark. "Adunis," Arabic. VCWP, tr. by Samuel Hazo

To Ashtaroth and Bel. Saul Tchernichowsky, Hebrew. TrJP, tr. by L. V. Snowman

To ask the hard question is simple. The Question. W. H. Auden. OxAEP-2

To Astarte. Unknown, Greek. GrAn, tr. by Guy Davenport

To Aunt Rose. Allen Ginsberg. CLPP; ColAP; LiTM; NAAL-2; NoAM; NoP-4; PmAP; PoE; VGW

("Aunt Rose.") (LL) NoP-4

To Aurora. Sir William Alexander, Earl of Stirling. GTBS-P Fr. Aurora. (Sonnet.)

To Ausonius. Paulinus of Nola, Latin. OBCVT, tr. by Helen Waddell

(Thee Shall I Hold.) LBC, tr. by Helen Waddell

To Autumn. William Blake. NAEL-2

To Autumn. Keats. APAD; AWP; BoTP; CABP; CH; ClHu; EBEV; EBEvV; FHYEP; HAP; HeIP-4; ImPo; InPK-6; InPS-3; LaPo; NAEL-2; NAWM-2; NIP-4; NOBE; NOBRP; NTP; NoP-4; OAEL-2; OBEV; OBNC; OxAEP-2; PBMP; PFE; PoE; PoEL-4; PoLF; PoPoPo; Poetr; RB; RaBo; Ro; SCGP; SCV; SoSe-8; TFi; TRP; UnPo; WeW-3

("For Summer has o'er-brimmed their clammy cells.") (LL) PiM

(Ode to Autumn.) GTBS-P

To 'ave a garden in fettle. Michael Hyde. BXAP

To Avisa. Henry Willoby. CBLP Fr. Willobie His Avisa.

To avoid matrimonial disasters. Limerick. Martin Fagg. PeLi

To B.C. Sir John Suckling. CaPo

To Babylon. Mother Goose. ReMoGo

("If you please, will you let the king's horses go through?") (LL) BoTP

("Will meet with a great mistake.") (LL) OxBoLi

("Yes, and back again[!].") (LL) FaBoCh

To Babylon's proud waters brought. Bible, *O.T. See* Psalm 137.

To banish the less, I find my chief relief. (LL) In Windsor Castle. Henry Howard. AAS; CABP; HAP; NOBE; NoP-4; NoSic; SCGP; SiPS

To Barba. Edward May. FaBoEE

To Bary Jade. Charles Follen Adams. OBAL

To Bayard Taylor. Sidney Lanier. NCAP

To be a birth there must be a begetting. Begetting. Dorothea Spears. PeSA

To be a giant and keep quiet about it. Trees. Howard Nemerov. Poetsp

To be a Jew in the twentieth century. Muriel Rukeyser. NALW; NMM-2; TrJP *Fr.* Letter to the Front.

To be a marionette. Marionette. Dahlia Ravikovitch, *Hebrew.* IP, *tr. by* Warren Bargad *and* Stanley F. Chyet

To be a mistress. Kiyoko Tsuda, *Japanese.* BoWoP, *tr. by* Edith Marcombe Shiffert *and* Yuki Sawa

To be a mouse. Preferably a field mouse. Or a garden mouse—. Aleksander Wat, *Polish.* AF, *tr. by* Czeslaw Milosz *and* Leonard Nathan (b. 1924)

To be a Negro in a day like this. At the Closed Gate of Justice. James David Corrothers. NAAAL

To be a nurse is. A. H. Lawrence. PoToHe

To Be a Pilgrim. Robert Conquest. OxBC

To be a Pilgrim. (LL) The Pilgrim. John Bunyan. APAD; BoTP; EBEV; EBEvV; FaPoR; NOCV; NOSC

To be a poet and not know the trade. Sanctity. Patrick Kavanagh. BIrV; NOIV; NoP-4

To be a poet—if it means to hum with winds. Sóng Hồng, *Vietnamese.* AVP, *tr. by* Huỳnh Sanh Thông

To be a poet is to be vanquished. Ars Poetica. Victor Van Vriesland, *Dutch.* TrJP, *tr. by* Adriaan J. Barnouw

To be a poet is to hum with winds. Feelings and Emotions. Xuân Diệu, *Vietnamese.* AVP, *tr. by* Huỳnh Sanh Thông

To Be a Slave of Intensity. Kabir, *Hindi.* APAD; RaBo, *tr. by* Robert Bly

To be a stranger in a strange land. Thinking of My Brother in Shantung on the Ninth Day of the Ninth Moon. Wang Wei, *Chinese.* TAL, *tr. by* Robert Payne

To be a whore, despite of grace. Madrigal. Charles Cotton. FaBoEE

To Be a Woman. Daisy Zamora, *Spanish.* IFJA, *tr. by* Margaret Randall *and* Elinor Randall

To be able To an Elder Poet. William Carlos Williams. PoA

To be able to see every side of every question. Editor Whedon. Edgar Lee Masters. CMoP; FaBoEE; NOBA; OBSV; OxBA; PoE *Fr* Spoon River Anthology.

To be alive in such an age! Today. Angela Morgan. BLPA

To be alone in a strange place in spring. The Child. Judith Wright. BMAP

To be an orphan. The Orphan. *Unknown, Chinese.* ChiP; PoA, *tr. by* Arthur Waley

To be announced. National Police Headquarters. Nicolás Guillén. PFTM, *tr. by* Vera M. Kutzinski *Fr.* The Daily Daily.

2 B BLK. Val Ferdinand. NBV

To be black Is / To be / Very-hot. (LL) But He Was Cool; or, He Even Stopped for Green Lights. Don L. Lee. BPo; MoP; PoBA

To be blessed, throat, eye and knucklebone. (LL) The Truth the Dead Know. Anne Sexton. ColAP; IMW; LCAP-2; MoAmPo; NoAM; NoP-4; PBWP; TAP; VCAP

To Be Carved on a Stone at Thoor Ballylee. W. B. Yeats. FaBoEE; IIP; NoAM; NoP-4

To be caught / out of the dullness of self by such alien thought? (LL) Down from the Country. John Blight. BMAP

To be chosen. Jeanne d'Arc. Susan Bartels Ludvigson. MT

To be delivered in the season of infinite madness. (LL) An American Memory of Africa. Kofi Awoonor. HBAPE; PBMAP

To be divorced from one's pants. (LL) French Lisette: A Ballad of Maida Vale. William Plomer. OBCoV; OxBoV

To Be Engraven on a Dial. Samuel Sewall. SCAP

To be famous is not in good taste. Boris Pasternak, *Russian.* TCRP, *tr. by* Albert C. Todd

To Be Here. Linda Gregg. AFr

To be homeless is a pride. A Jealous Man. Robert Graves. CMoP

To Be Honest, to Be Kind. Robert Louis Stevenson. PoLF *Fr.* A Christmas Sermon.

To be hot about. (LL) Weeksville Women. Elouise Loftin. ISC

To be in a place for spring and not have lived its winter. Vincent O'Sullivan. PeNZ *Fr.* Brother Jonathan, Brother Kafka.

To be in love. Gwendolyn Brooks. GT

To be in the book. To figure in the book of questions, to be part of it. Edmond Jabès. PFTM, *tr. by* Rosemarie Waldrop *Fr.* The Book of Questions.

To be: let me bash out praises—pass the tambourine. (LL) The Way We Live. Kathleen Jamie. APAD; FaBoTC

To be Long Gone. . . . (LL) Long Gone. Sterling Brown. NAAAL

To be long silent was my thought. *Unknown, German.* GePo, *tr. by* Frederick Goldin

To be lost evermore in the main. (LL) At Flores in the Azores Sir Richard Grenvile lay. Tennyson. EBEvV; EBNV; OBWP

To be merely an Indian. Charles Tomlinson. *See* Mr. Brodsky.

To be mistaken in old age and not to be afraid. Aleksey Petrovich Tsvetkov, *Russian.* TCRP, *tr. by* Albert C. Todd

To be moved comes of want, tho[ugh] want be complete. 1892-1941. Louis Zukofsky. PoA

To be my own Messiah to the. The Rows of Cold Trees. Yvor Winters. NOBA

To Be of Use. Marge Piercy. CrSp

To be or not to be, that is the question. Arthur's Anthology of English Poetry. Laurence David Lerner. PeLV

To be, or not to be, that is the question. Hamlet's Soliloquy. Shakespeare. EBEvV; HoPM; ImPo; OxAEP-1; UV *Fr.* Hamlet. NAWM-1

To be put on the train and kissed and given my ticket. Observation Car. Alec Derwent Hope. BMAP; GEA; MoP; NoAM

To Be Read above the Castle-Gate, When His Princely Highness Rode in to His Marriage Bed. Simon Dach, *German.* GePo, *tr. by* George C. Schoolfield

To Be Recited to Flossie on Her Birthday. William Carlos Williams. VGW

To be roots. In that deepest earth where no ray. Vizma Belševica, *Latvian.* CEEP, *tr. by* Inara Cedrins *and* Valters Nollendorfs

To Be Said at the Seder. Karl Wolfskehl, *German.* TrJP, *tr. by* Carol North Valhope *and* Ernst Morowitz

To Be Said Over and Over Again. György Petri, *Hungarian.* VCWP, *tr. by* Wilmer, Clive and George Gömöri

To be so held by brittleness, shapeliness. Soul Says. Jorie Graham. PoPoPo

To be spending the evening with no one. (LL) Scratch Music. C. D. Wright. CMAP; NAmP90

To be stabbed on a lonely hill. (LL) Prophets for a New Day. Margaret Abigail Walker. NAAAL

To be Sung on the Fourth of July. Wyatt Prunty. RA

To Be Sung on the Water. Louise Bogan. VGW

To be ten and skinny. Exodus. Anita Endrezze-Danielson. CDW

To be undone! (LL) With serving still. Sir Thomas Wyatt. InPK-6; NoSic; SiPS

To be untangled from these mother's bones. (LL) With Child. Genevieve Taggard. MoAmPo; NMM-2

To be up high. (LL) Get Up, Blues. James A. Emanuel. PoBA; SeSe

To be worried or teased. Jane Taylor. *See* I Like Little Pussy.

To be Young, Gifted, and Black. Weldon J. Irvine, Jr. ISC

To be your beadsman now that was your knight. (LL) A Farewell to Arms. George Peele. InPS-3; NIP-4; NOBE; NoP-4; NoSic; OBEV; OBWP; OxAEP-1; PoEL-2; PoRA; SCGP; TFi

To be your Valentine. (LL) Song: "Tomorrow is saint valentine's day." Shakespeare. CH; EBEvV; EnLoPo; NTCP; NoSic

To Beat or Not to Beat. Nina Iskrenko, *Russian.* TCRP, *tr. by* John High *and* Katya Olmsted

To beat real iron out, to work the bellows. (LL) The Forge. Seamus Heaney. NAEL-2; NoP-4; OxAEP-2

To become a man, it's little to be born. Mikhail Davidovich Lvov, *Russian.* TCRP, *tr. by* Daniel Weissbort

To become acquainted with such a self as this. *Compulsion* as the Critical Element in a Defined Perversion. Bin Ramke. WeT

To become an archer. José Garcia Villa. KaS

"To bed! To bed!" / Says Sleepy-head. Come, Let's to Bed. *Unknown.* ReMoGo

To Beethoven. Sidney Lanier. NCAP

To Begin. Fran Winant. BrRo

To begin I cut fine silk of Ch'i. Song of Regret. Pan Chieh-yû, *Chinese.* CoBCP, *tr. by* Burton Watson

To begin with he was a beautiful object. Louis MacNeice. *See* The Death of a Cat.

To begin with something not already caught. How Late Desire Looks. Katrina Roberts. BAP-95

To believe it. (LL) To a Dog Injured in the Street. William Carlos Williams. LCAP-2; LiTM; SAmP

To Belinda. Goethe, *German.* STV, *tr. by* John Frederick Nims

To Belshazzar. Byron. ChIV-1

To Ben, at the Lake. Cilla McQueen. PeNZ

To Ben Jonson. Thomas Carew. BeJo; CaPo; CavPo; EPCY; NAEL-1; NOSC

To better the condition of humanity. Our Club Work. Mrs. Henry Linden. CBWP-4

To Blossoms. Robert Herrick. BeJo; CaPo; GTBS-P; NAEL-1; NOSC; OBEV; SCGP; SeCP

To Bobby Seale. Lucille Clifton. MBE; PoBA

To brave and to know the unknown. The Unknown. John Davidson. MoBrPo

To break earth's sleep at all? (LL) Futility. Wilfred Owen. APAD; CMoP; FaBoMo; GTBS-P; MoBrPo; NAEL-2; NSI; NoAM; NoP-4; OBWP; PeFWW; RB

To break off in the middle! (LL) Sally Simpkin's Lament, [or John Jones's Kit-Cat-astrophe]. Thomas Hood. CABP; CBNP

To break the silence or your newly acquired Ming vase. Shooting for Line. Charles North. BAP-95

To Breisach, Taken by That Supremely Celebrated Hero, Bernhard, Duke of Saxony. Georg Rudolph Weckherlin, *German*. GePo, *tr. by* George C. Schoolfield

To bring forth and rear a son is my duty. A Mother's List of Duties. Ponmutiyar, *Tamil*. PLW, *tr. by* A. K. Ramanujan

To bring one chrysanthemum. Beside a Chrysanthemum. So Chong-Ju, *Korean*. VCWP, *tr. by* David R. McCann

To Bring the Dead to Life. Robert Graves. MoBrPo

To bring them to my brother King Iamye. (LL) Sir Andrew Bart[t]on. *Unknown*. AmFP; ESPB; EnSB; OxBB

To bring them to my brother King Iamye. (LL) Sir Andrew Barton. *Unknown*. ESPB; OxBB

To broaden into boundless day. (LL) By night we lingered [*or* linger'd] on the lawn. Tennyson. EBVV; EnVR; FHYEP; HAP; OAEL-2; OBNC; PeECV; PoEL-5; TOF

To Brooklyn Bridge. Hart Crane. AiP; ChIV-1; ClHu; ColAP; FaBoA; ImPo; InPS-3; KSG; LiTM; MeMAP; MoAmPo; NOBA; OxBA; PoE; PoPoPo; TFi; TRP *Fr.* The Bridge. NAAL-2

(Poem: To Brooklyn Bridge.) AmFP; AmPP; CMoP; HAP; HeIP-4; NoAM; TAP; WeW-3

To Buonaparte. *Unknown*. NOBRP

To burst into fulfillment's desolate attic. (LL) Deceptions. Philip Larkin. CMoP; GTBS-P; OxAEP-2

To burst into fulfilment's desolate attic. Philip Larkin. *See* Deceptions.

To Caelia. Richard Duke. NOSC

To Caelia. *Unknown*. FaBoEE

To call, in the harsh morning, sleep-stupid faces through the daily gate. (LL) Birmingham. Louis MacNeice. CMoP; MoBrPo; OxAEP-2

To Calliope. Robert Graves. CMoP

To calm the anxious breast, to close the streaming eye. (LL) To Sleep. Charlotte Smith. Son; WPE

To Carrey Clavel. Thomas Hardy. CBLP

To carry the child into adult life. Stevie Smith. MoP; NYBP; NoAM

To Castara, Being to Take a Journey. William Habington. NOSC

To Castara ("Do[e] not Their profane orgies hear[e].") William Habington. BeJo *Fr.* Castara.

To Castara ("Give me a heart where no impure"). William Habington. BeJo *Fr.* Castara.

To Castara, upon an Embrace. William Habington. BeJo *Fr.* Castara.

To Castara, upon Beautie. William Habington. BeJo; SeCP *Fr.* Castara.

To catch the spirit in its wayward flight. Self-Mastery. Henrietta Cordelia Ray. CBWP-3

To Cattraeth's vale in glitt'ring row. Aneirin, *Welsh*. OBVE, *tr. by* Thomas Gray *Fr.* The Gododdin.

To Catulinus That He Cannot Write Him an Epithalamium Because of the Enemy Hosts. Apollinaris Sidonius, *Latin*. MLL, *tr. by* Helen Waddell

To cause accord or to ag[g]re[e]. Sir Thomas Wyatt. AAS; SCGP; SiPS

To caves the sleeping maid. (LL) The Little Girl Lost. William Blake. FHYEP; NoBRP

To Celia. Ben Jonson. BoLoP; CBLP; EBEvV; EnLoPo; FaBoBe; GLoP; GTBS-P; ImPo; InPK-6; NOBE; OBEV; OBVE; PoLF; SAGP; SCGP

(Song) APAD; AWP; BeJo; ClHu; GBL; NAEL-1; NOSC; OAEL-1; OxAEP-1; PoE; PoEL-2; SeCP; SoSe-8; UV *See also* To The Same [Celia].

To Celia. Sir Charles Sedley. AWP; NOBE; OBEV

To Celia Pleading Want of Merit. Thomas Stanley. MeLP; NOSC

To Celia, upon Love's Ubiquity. Thomas Carew. CavPo

To Celinda. Elizabeth Singer Rowe. PEW

To Censorious Courtling. Ben Jonson. NOSC

To Certain Critics. Countee Cullen. BPo

To Charles Burney. Frances, Mme D'Arblay Burney. ECWP

To Charles Roux, of Switzerland. Nathaniel Parker Willis. APN-1

To Charlotte Cushman. Eliza Cook. VWP

To Charlotte Pulteney. Ambrose Philips. *See* To Miss Charlotte Pulteney in Her Mother's Arms.

To Charlotte von Stein. Goethe, *German*. STV, *tr. by* John Frederick Nims

To Chatterton. Keats. EPCY

To Cheer Our Minds. William Ronksley. OxBChV

To Ch'eng Fei-t'ao. Wu Chia-chi, *Chinese*. CoBLCP, *tr. by* Jonathan Chaves

To "Chick." Frank Horne. BPo *Fr.* Letters [*or* Notes] Found near a Suicide. PoBA

To Children. Lawrence McGaugh. PoBA

To Chin Nung. Cheng Hsieh, *Chinese*. CoBLCP, *tr. by* Jonathan Chaves

To Chloe, Who Wished Herself Young Enough for Me. William Cartwright. BeJo; NOSC; OxAEP-1; PoToHe

("There are two births: The one when light.") PoToHe

(To Chloe, who for His Sake Wished Herself Younger.) OBEV

To Chloris. William Drummond, of Hawthornden. OxBSP

To Chloris. Sir Charles Sedley. *See* Child and Maiden.

To Chloris, upon a Favour Received. Edmund Waller. OxBSP

To Christ. William Alabaster. NoSic

To Christ. Robert Herrick. CavPo

To Christ Our Lord. Galway Kinnell. HeIP-4; TwCP

To Christina Rossetti. "Michael Field." VWP

To Christina Rossetti. Dora Greenwell. VWP

To Christopher North. Tennyson. FaBoEE; PeLV

To circle their wagons? (LL) Why Do So Few Blacks Study Creative Writing? Cornelius Eady. GT; LTA

To civilize with graver notes our wits again. (LL) An Ode to Mr. Anthony Stafford to Hasten Him into the Country. Thomas Randolph. BeJo; NOSC

To civilize with graver notes our wits again. (LL) An Ode to Mr. [*or* Master] Anthony Stafford to Hasten Him into the Country. Thomas Randolph. NOBE; OBEV

To claim, at a dead party, to have spotted a grackle. Lying. Richard Wilbur. DiPo; HCAP; PeVV; Poetr

To clarify and allow. The Reason. Eric Pankey. GI

To Clarissa. Robert, Earl Nugent Nugent. NOEC

To clearer light, vouchsaf'd to me! (LL) Old-Testament Gospel. William Cowper. ChIV-2; TrCP

To cleave a running stream with a sword. Written in Behalf of My Wife. Li Po, *Chinese*. SuSp, *tr. by* Joseph J. Lee

To Clement Edmonds, on His *Caesar's Commentaries* Observed, and Translated. Ben Jonson. NOSC

To Clements' Ferry. Josephine D. Henderson Heard. CBWP-4

To Cleon's Eyes. Martha Sansom. ECWP

To climb and descend steps. Walker in Prague. Vitĕzslau Nezval, *Czech*. AF, *tr. by* Ewald Osers

To climb these stairs again, bearing a tray. The Kaleidoscope. Douglas Dunn. LBC

To climb[e] to thee. (LL) The Pearl. [Matt. 13:45]. George Herbert. ChIV-2; EBEV; ESCV; FHYEP; FSCP; GeHe; HAP; NOCV; NOSC; OAEL-1; PoEL-2; SeCP

To Clio, from Rome. John Dyer. NOEC

To Cloe. George, Baron Lansdowne Granville. FaBoEE; NBLV

To Cloe. Hildebrand Jacob. NOEC

To Cloe. Martial, *Latin*. AWP; NBLV, *tr. by* Thomas Moore

To Cloris. Sir Charles Sedley. BoLoP

To Close. William Carlos Williams. SAmP

To clothe the fiery thought. Poet. Ralph Waldo Emerson. OxBA; OxBSP; Spl *Fr.* Quatrains.

To Coelia. Charles Cotton. OBEV

To Cole, the Painter, Departing for Europe. William Cullen Bryant. AiP; AmPP; ColAP; GEA; TAP

(Sonnet—To an American Painter Departing for Europe.) NAAL-1; NAAL-3; PAR

To Colebrooke Dale. Anna Seward. ECWP

To Colindra. Elizabeth Thomas. LW

To Colman Returning. *Unknown*. BIrV, *tr. by* Helen Waddell

To Columbus. "Rubén Dario," *Spanish*. TTY, *tr. by* Lysander Kemp

To come a-courting *me*! (LL) The King-Fisher [*or* King-Fisher's] Song. "Lewis Carroll." CBNP; CTAV

To come back from the sweet South, to the North. Italia, Io Ti Saluto! Christina Rossetti. VWP; WPE

To come free to a city under siege. Amir Gilbo'a, *Hebrew*. IP, *tr. by* Warren Bargad *and* Stanley F. Chyet

To come vor evermwore. (LL) The Wife A-Lost. William Barnes. BoLoP; EBVV; EnLoPo; EnVR; GLoP; HAP; LBC; OBEV; OxBM; SCGP

To conclude, I announce what comes after me. So Long! Walt Whitman. PAR

To consecrate the flicker, not the flame. (LL) George Crabbe. Edwin Arlington Robinson. APN-2; CMoP; LiTM; MeMAP; MoAmPo; NAAL-2; NOBA; NoP-4; OxBA; PoEL-5; TAP

To Cordelia. Joseph Stansbury. NOBC

To covet fetters, though they golden bee. (LL) Sonnet 37: "What guile [or guyle] is this, that those her golden tresses." Edmund Spenser. NAEL-1; NoP-4; Son

To Cowper. Anne Brontë. EPCY

To creep outside and see the cops were gone. (LL) A Gesture by a Lady with an Assumed Name. James Wright. CoAmPo; LiTM

To Critic[k]s. Robert Herrick. CaPo

To cross a threshold where you await me since the poem. (LL) Further off is the measured force the word of the sea. Edouard J. Maunick, *French.* PBMAP

To crown her head, and bosom fill. (LL) The Gallery. Andrew Marvell. ESCV; MeLP; NoP-4; PoE

To Crown[e] It. Robert Herrick. CaPo

To cry or see one cry is rather embarrassing to see: between crying and. The Water of Tears. Francis Ponge, *French.* AF, *tr. by* Beth Archer

To Cupid. Joanna Baillie. LW

To cure the mind's wrong bias, Spleen. Matthew Green. ECEV *Fr.* The Spleen.

To Cynthia. Sir Francis Kynaston. CBLP; NOSC

To Cynthia, on Concealment of Her Beauty. Sir Francis Kynaston. MeLP; NOBE

To Cynthia on Her Being an Incendiary. Sir Francis Kynaston. HAP

To Cynthia, on Her Embraces. Sir Francis Kynaston. GBL

To Cyriack Skinner. Milton. GTBS-P; NoP-4; OBEV; Son

(Sonnet.) NOSC; OxAEP-1

To D———, Dead by Her Own Hand. Howard Nemerov. PoA

To Daffodils [or Daffadills]. Robert Herrick. APAD; AWP; AYFP; BeJo; CaPo; EBEvV; FaBoCh; GTBS-P; InPS-3; NOBE; NOSC; NTP; NoP-4; OBEV; OxAEP-1; PoEL-3; PoRA; SCGP; SeCP; TFi; TTTS; UnPo

To Daisies, Not to Shut So Soon[e]. Robert Herrick. BeJo; CH; CaPo; GBL; OBEV; OxBSP

To D'Annunzio: Lines from the Sea. Robert Malise Bowyer Nichols. OBMV

To Dante. Vittorio Alfieri, *Italian.* AWP, *tr. by* Lorna De' Lucchi

To Dante [or Sonnet: Guido Cavalcanti to Dante]. Guido Cavalcanti, *Italian.* AWP; OBVE, *tr. by* Shelley

To Dante. Guido Cavalcanti, *Italian.* AWP, tr. by D. G. Rossetti

To Dante (He Commends the Work of Dante's Life), *sonnet.* Giovanni Quirino, *Italian.* AWP, *tr. by* D. G. Rossetti

To Dante: He Conceives of Some Compensation in Death. Cino da Pistoia, *Italian.* AWP, tr. by D. G. Rossetti

To Dante: He Interprets Dante's Dream. Dante da Maiano, *Italian.* AWP, *tr. by* D. G. Rossetti

To Dante: He Interprets Dante's Dream. Cino da Pistoia, *Italian.* AWP, *tr. by* D. G. Rossetti

To Dante: He Mistrusts the Love of Lapo Gianni. Guido Cavalcanti, *Italian.* AWP, *tr. by* D. G. Rossetti

To Dante: He Reports, in a Feigned Vision, the Successful Issue of Lapo Gianni's Love. Guido Cavalcanti, *Italian.* AWP, *tr. by* D. G. Rossetti

To Dante in Paradise, after Fiammetta's Death. Giovanni Boccaccio. AWP *Fr.* Sonnets.

To David, about His Education. Howard Nemerov. HCAP

To David—At Six Months. Eleanor Cameron. LiLi

To-Day. Lessie M. Drown. PWR

To-day a rude brief recitative. Song for All Seas, All Ships. Walt Whitman. APN-1; CH; FaBoBe

To-Day a Shepherd. Saint, of Avila Theresa, *Spanish.* AWP, *tr. by* Arthur Symons

To-day, all day, I rode upon the Down. St. Valentine's Day. Wilfrid Scawen Blunt. EnLoPo *Fr.* The Love Sonnets of Proteus.

To-day and Thee. Walt Whitman. PFE

To-day as I went out to play. The Brown Frog. Mary K. Robinson. BoTP

To-Day I Leave Mrs. Brown's Lodgings. Sir Walter Scott. FaBoEE

To-day, I saw the catkins blow. February. Dorothy Una Ratcliffe. BoTP

To-day I went into a shop where they sell spectacles. Preparation. Amy Lowell. CPO

To-day / Is the feast day of Saint Anne. The Madwoman of Cork. Patrick Galvin. BiHa

To Day it self's too Late, the Wise liv'd Yesterday. (LL) Procrastination. Martial, *Latin.* AWP; FaBoEE; OBCVT; OBVE, *tr. by* Abraham Cowley

To-day, my friend is seventy-five;. Felix Antonius. Sir Henry John Newbolt. FP

To day old Janus opens the new yeare. A New-Yeares-Gift Sung to King Charles, 1635. Ben Jonson. SeCP

To-day the lot caved in upon me. Page from a Diary. Desmond O'Grady. NoAM

To-day there have been lovely things. Vision. May Thielgaard Watts. LW

To-day they laid him in the earth's cold colour. For Angus MacLeod. Iain Crichton Smith. OxBS

To-day we have naming of parts. Yesterday. Naming Of Parts. Henry Reed. EBEvV; HoPM; ImPo; InPS-3; MoBrPo; NOBE; OxBTC; PFE; PoRA; Poetr; RaBo; SoSe-8; TFi; UV; UnPo *Fr.* Lessons of the War. HeIP-4; OBWP

To-day's house makes to-morrow's road. The Survival. Edmund Blunden. OBEV; OBMV

To Dean-bourn, a Rude River in Devon, by Which Sometimes He Lived. Robert Herrick. BeJo; CaPo; PBRV

(Dean Bourn, a Rude River in Devon, by Which Sometimes He Lived.) CavPo

To Death. Johann Wilhelm Ludwig Gleim, *German.* GePo, *tr. by* George C. Schoolfield

To Death. Oliver St. John Gogarty. FaBoEE; OBMV

To Death. Robert Herrick. BeJo

To Death. Anne Finch, Countess of Winchilsea. NoP-4

To Death, of His Lady. François Villon, *French.* AWP, *tr. by* D. G. Rossetti

To deck her, froze into a gem. (LL) Chloris in the Snow. William Strode. NOBE; NOSC; OAEL-1; OBEV; OxBSP

To Delia. Samuel Daniel.

"And yet I cannot reprehend the flight." OBEV

Beauty, Time and Love. OBEV

(Sonnet: "Fair is my love, and cruel as she's fair.") HoPM

"But love whilst that thou mayst be loved again." NoP-4; NoSic

Half-blown Rose, The.

("Look, Delia, How we 'steem the half-blown rose.") NoP-4

(Sonnet: "Look, Delia, how we esteem the half-blown rose.")

"I must not grieve my love, whose eyes would read." OBEV

"I once may see when yeares shall wreck my wrong." AAS

"If so it hap, this of-spring of my care." AAS

"If this be love, to draw[e] a weary [or wearie] breath." AAS; GBL

("If this be love, to draw a weary breath.") GLoP; GSo

("Let others sing of knights and paladins.") CABP; GSo; NoP-4; PBRV

"None other fame mine unambitious muse." AAS

Sonnet: "Care-charmer Sleep[e], son[ne] of the sable night." PoEL-2

(45.) CABP

("Care-charmer Sleep, son of the sable Night.") CABP; GSo; NoP-4

Sonnet 33: 'When men shall find thy flower'. AEP

("When Winter snows upon thy golden hairs.") (LL) NoP-4

Sonnet: "Beauty, sweet love, is like the morning dew."

"These plaintive verse, the posts [or postes] of my desire." AAS

"Thou canst not die whilst any zeal abound." NoSic; Son

"Time, cruel time, come and subdue that brow." SCGP

"Unto the boundless Ocean of thy beauty." NoP-4

"When winter snows upon thy sable hairs." CTC; NoSic; Son

("They will remaine, and so thou canst not die.") (LL) PBRV

Why Should I Sing in Verse. Son

To Della Crusca. The Pen. Hannah Cowley. NOBRP

To Delmore Schwartz. Robert Lowell. FP

To Demeter. *Unknown, Greek.* GrIP, *tr. by* Thelma Sargent *Fr.* Homeric Hymns.

To demolish it. All Splendor on Earth. Karin Kiwus, *German.* BoWoP, *tr. by* Almut McAuley

To Dennis Brutus. Kofi Awoonor. HBAPE

To Derek Mahon. Michael Longley. *See* Letter to Derek Mahon.

To Detraction I Present my Poesie. John Marston. NoSic *Fr.* The Scourge of Villainy [or Villanie].

To Dian, Queen of Earth, and Heaven, and Hell. (LL) To Homer. Keats. EBEV; NAEL-2; NoP-4; Son

To Diana. Horace. *See* Odes 3.22: Pine Tree for Diana, The ("Montium custos nemorumque").

To Dianeme ("Dear[e], though to part it be a hell"). Robert Herrick. CaPo

To Dianeme ("Give me one kiss"). Robert Herrick. CaPo; FaBoBe

To Dianeme ("Show [or Shew] me thy feet; show [or shew] me thy legs, thy thighs"). Robert Herrick. CaPo; CavPo; NOSC

To Dianeme ("Sweet, be not proud of those two eyes"). Robert Herrick. BeJo; CaPo; GTBS-P; NOBE; NOSC; OBEV

To die and know it. This is the Black Widow, death. (LL) Mr. Edwards and the Spider. Robert Lowell. CMoP; CoAP; ColAP; FaBoMo; HeIP-4; InPS-3; LiTM; NAAL-2; NOBA; NoP-4; TFi; TwCP

To die be given us, or attain! Resignation. Matthew Arnold. FHYEP

To die, but far away. Roberto Juarroz. VCWP, *tr. by* Mary Crow *Fr.* Ninth Vertical Poetry.

To die for Man's Redemption. (LL) For Innocents' Day. Luke Wadding. NOIV; TIRV

To die like Rachel. Like Rachel. Dahlia Ravikovitch, *Hebrew*. IP, *tr. by* Warren Bargad *and* Stanley F. Chyet

To die like thirsting larks. Agony. Giuseppe Ungaretti, *Italian*. PeFWW, *tr. by* Charles Tomlinson

To die—takes just a little while. Emily Dickinson. PBMP

To die with a forlorn hope, but soon to be raised. The Survivor. Robert Graves. CMoP

To Dinah Washington. Etheridge Knight. PoBA

To dip, alas, into some unseemlier world. (LL) Old Mansion. John Crowe Ransom. FuPo; HeIP-4; MeMAP; NOBA; OxBA

To disappear. (LL) A Trip to Four or Five Towns. John Logan. CoAmPo

To Disgrace of Price. (LL) Publication—is the Auction. Emily Dickinson. APN-2; AmPP; NAAL-1; NAAL-3; NALW; NCAP; NoP-4; PAR

To Disraeli. Shirley Brooks. NOBL

To distant men, who must go there, or die. (LL) Sea-Shore. Ralph Waldo Emerson. APN-1; ColAP; OxBA

To distant service my heart is well accustomed. The Silver Spoon. Po Chü-i, *Chinese*. ChiP, *tr. by* Arthur Waley

To dive for the nimbus on the sea-floor. Nimbus. Douglas Le Pan. MoCV

To Dives. Hilaire Belloc. ChIV-2; OBSV

To do as Adam did. Beam 30, The Garden. Ronald Johnson. FTOS

To do away with anger. Tanka. Miya Shūji, *Japanese*. MJT, *tr. by* Makoto Ueda

To do celestial chores. (LL) For a Lady I Know. Countee Cullen. HeIP-4; InPK-6; MoAmPo; NIP-4; OBAL; SSLK; TAP; TRP

To do less would be nothing but dishonesty. (LL) Peter. Marianne Moore. CMoP; NAAL-2; NoP-4; OxBA

To do something very common, in my own way. (LL) A Valediction Forbidding Mourning. Adrienne Rich. NAAL-2; NoAM; NoP-4

To do the wrong'd Corinna right for thee. (LL) The Imperfect Enjoyment. John Wilmot, 2d Earl of Rochester. BoLoP

To do with ego, guilt, ambition, or even money. (LL) The Cormorant in His Element. Amy Clampitt. NoP-4

To do without what blood remained these wounds. (LL) A Terre. Wilfred Owen. LiTM; NSI; OxBTC; PeFWW; PoWW

To—do without you altogether. (LL) To Cloe. Martial, *Latin*. AWP; NBLV, *tr. by* Thomas Moore

To doat upon me ever! (LL) Love Me Not [for Comely Grace]. *Unknown*. CH; GTBS-P; ImPo; OBEV; OxBSP; PoLF

To Doctor Bale. Barnabe Googe. NoSic

To Doctor Empiric[k]. Ben Jonson. FaBoEE; NoP-4; SeCP

To Dr. F. B. on His Book of Chess[e]. Richard Lovelace. CaPo

To Dr. Moore, in Anser to a Poetical Epistle Written by Him in Wales. Helen Maria Williams. ECWP; WoRP

To Dr. Swift on His Birthday, 30th November 1721. Esther Johnson. EnLoPo

To doggerel now I turn my pen. Letter to Miss E.B. at Bath. Mary Savage. ECWP

To Don Juan Baz. Mary E. Tucker. CBWP-1

To Dorothy. Marvin Bell. VCAP

To Dorothy on Her Exclusion from the *Guinness Book of World Records*. X. J. Kennedy. Poetsp

To Dr. Jonathan Swift. Alexander Pope. OBSV *Fr.* The Dunciad.
("And the hoarse nation croaked, 'God save King Log!'.") (LL) OxAEP-1, *book* I, *ll.* 1–330
("Books and the Man I sing, the first who brings.") CBNP, *book* I, *ll.* 1–84, *first edition vers.*
("In clouded Majesty here Dullness shone.") (LL) PoE
"Here she beholds the chaos dark and deep." FHYEP

To draw no envy, Shakespeare, on thy name. To the Memory of My Beloved, the Author Mr [*or* Master] William Shakespeare[: And What He Hath Left Us]. Ben Jonson. BeJo; EPCY; HAP; HeIP-4; NOSC; NoP-4; OAEL-1; OxAEP-1; PoEL-2; PoPoPo; SeCP

To Dream Again. Shakespeare. *Fr.* The Tempest. OAEL-1

To dream of love, and, waking, to remember you. Dreams. Arthur Symons. PoA

To drift with every passion till my soul. Hélas! Oscar Wilde. ADE; GSo; MoBrPo; NAEL-2; Son; TIRV

To Drink. Jane Hirshfield. CrSp

To drink and frolic with the water-borne moon. (LL) Autumn Cove. Li Po, *Chinese*. CoBCP, *tr. by* Burton Watson

To drink, no fine wines, to eat, no fish. Li K'ai-hsien. *Fr.* Impromptu Poems. CoBLCP, *tr. by* Jonathan Chaves

To drive Paul out of any lumber camp. Paul's Wife. Robert Frost. EBNV

To dwell a weeping hermit there! Ode Written in the Beginning of the Year 1746. William Collins. AWP; CABP; GTBS-P; HAP; NAEL-1; NOBE; NOEC; NoP-4; OBEV; OxAEP-1; OxBSP; PBMP; PoE; PoEL-3; SCGP; TFi

To Dwell Together in Unity. Bible, *O.T.* *See* Psalm 133.

To E. Fitzgerald. Tennyson. FP; NOBVV; PoEL-5

To E. S. Salomon. Ambrose Bierce. CBCWP

To E.T. Robert Frost. FP

TO E. T.: 1917. Walter De la Mare. FP

To Earth. James Applewhite. PoA

To Earthward. Robert Frost. ImPo; MeMAP; MoAmPo; MoP; NOBA; NoAM; NoP-4; OxBA; RaBo; TAP; TRP

To ease his rumbling stomach our Kriton sniffs. On Kriton the Miser. Lucilius, *Greek*. GrAn, *tr. by* Dudley Fitts

To eastward ringing, to westward winging, o'er mapless miles of. When the Great Gray Ships Come In. Guy Wetmore Carryl. FaBoBe

To eat mutton cold and cut blocks with a razor. (LL) Edmund Burke. Oliver Goldsmith. FaBoEE; FaBoPV; NOEC

To eat pain like bread is a condition. Ruth Miller. *Fr.* Cycle. PeSA

To eat the world's due, by the grave and thee. (LL) Sonnet 1. Shakespeare. CTC; HeIP-4; ImPo; NoP-4

To Eat To-day. Nancy Cunard. WPN

To Edom. Heinrich Heine, *German*. TrJP

To Edward Alleyn. Ben Jonson. NOSC

To Edward FitzGerald. Robert Browning. NAEL-2; OxBSP

To Edward Thomas. Alun Lewis. PoWW

To Electra. Robert Herrick. CaPo; HoPM; OBEV

To Electra ("I'll [*or* Ile] come to thee in all those shapes"). Robert Herrick. CaPo

To Elia (unsigned). John Clare. Ro *Fr.* London Magazine, 6 151.

To Elinda. Richard Lovelace. CavPo

To Elizabeth Barrett Browning. Bessie Rayner Parkes. VWP

To Elizabeth Barrett Browning, in 1851. Dora Greenwell. VWP

To Elizabeth Barrett Browning, in 1861. Dora Greenwell. VWP

To Elizabeth, Countess of Rutland. Ben Jonson. BeJo; NoP-4

To Elsie. William Carlos Williams. CMoP; InPS-3; MeMAP; NAAL-2; NOBA; OxBA; PoE; PoPoPo

To embalm thy father's corse; What? will he die? (LL) The Perfume. Donne. ESCV; FSCP; NoSic; SeCP

To Emily Dickinson. Hart Crane. CMoP; ColAP; NIP-4; NOBA; NoAM; NoP-4; Son; TAP

To Emily Dickinson. Yvor Winters. Son

To Emma, Extempore; Hyaena, off Gambia, June 4, 1779. Edward Thompson. NOEC

To End Her Fear. John Freeman. OBMV

To English Connoisseurs. William Blake. OxBoLi

To enjoy your chrysanthemums. (LL) Stopping at a Friend's Farm. Meng Hao Jan, *Chinese*. FP, *tr. by* Innes Herdan

To Epicles. Antipater of Thessalonica, *Greek*. GrAn, *tr. by* Tony Harrison

To Evening. William Collins. *See* Ode to Evening.

To Evening. Ugo Foscolo. ItIP

To evening, but some heart did break. Tennyson. *See* One writes, that "Other friends remain."

To Everlasting Oblivion. John Marston. NoSic; SCGP *Fr.* The Scourge of Villainy [*or* Villanie].

To Every Believer. Uku Masing, *Estonian*. CEEP, *tr. by* Ivar Ivask

To every future which was not hers. (LL) New Year. Naomi Shihab Nye. LoL

To every heart which the sweet pain doth move. Dante. AWP *Fr.* La Vita Nuova.

To every hearth a little fire. A Christmas Wish. Rose Fyleman. BoTP

To every man. The Treehouse. James A. Emanuel. BPo; PoBA

To every man there openeth. The Ways. John Oxenham. PoLF

To every woman a happy ending. (LL) Barbie Doll. Marge Piercy. NIP-4; Poetr

To everything there is a season. A Time for Everything. Bible, *O.T.* NAWM-1; OBVE; PBMP *Fr.* Ecclesiastes.

To explain the nature of fishes in craft of verse. The Whale. *Unknown*. EBEV, *tr. by* Gavin Bone *Fr.* The Whale. AnOE, *tr. by* Charles Kennedy; ASW, *tr. by* Kevin Crossley-Holland *Fr.* Physiologus.

To explore the nature of rain I opened the door because inside the workings of language clear vision is impossible. Rosemarie Waldrop. PmAP *Fr.* Inserting the Mirror.

To extol[l] thee. (LL) Praise (2). George Herbert. ChIV-1; ESCV

To F——. Edgar Allan Poe. APN-1

To F. C. Mortimer Collins. NOBVV

To fail—is Infidel. (LL) Sweetest Heresy received, The. Emily Dickinson. CBLP

To fair Fidele's grassy tomb. Dirge in "Cymbeline." William Collins. CABP; NOBE; NOEC; OBEV; SCGP

To fake green strokes in water, light fidgets. Things in Each Other. Norman MacCaig. FaBoTC

To fall in love, though classically human. Advice to Colonel Valentine. Robert Graves. NYBP

To fall, like an apple, no mind. In the Emptied Rest Home. Bella Akhatovna Akhmadulina, *Russian.* BoWoP, *tr. by* Jean Valentine *and* Olga Carlisle

To Fannie. Mary E. Tucker. CBWP-1

To Fanny. Keats. BoLoP; EBEV; Son

To Fanny Brawne. Keats. NOBE

To farther this, Achitophel unites. The Malcontents. Dryden. *Fr.* Absalom and Achitophel, Pt. I. EBEvV; FHYEP; FaBoPV; HAP; NOSC; OAEL-1; PoE

To Father. Yury Kuznetsov, *Russian.* TCRP, *tr. by* Sarah W. Bliumis

To Father. Mary E. Tucker. CBWP-1

To fear himself, and love all human kind. (LL) Hymn to Intellectual Beauty. Shelley. FHYEP; HAP; HeIP-4; ImPo; NAEL-2; NOBRP; NoP-4; OAEL-2; OBNC; PoE; TOF

To feed ez they hev fed me. (LL) Letter Six—The Pious Editors' Creed. James Russell Lowell. APN-1; NCAP

To feed on that, which to disused tastes seem[e]s tough. (LL) His Picture. Donne. MeLP; OxAEP-1

To feel and speak the astounding beauty of things — earth, stone and. The Beauty of Things. Robinson Jeffers. PoA

To fertilize some other ground. (LL) Floating Island at Hawkshead. Dorothy Wordsworth. PEW; Ro

To fiddle-faddle in a minor key. (LL) Elegy: "The Cur foretells the knell of parting day." Ambrose Bierce. APN-2; OBAL

To fight aloud, is very brave. Emily Dickinson. WPE

To fill the catalogue of human woes. (LL) Ode: "I hate that drum's discordant sound." John Scott of Amwell. ECEV; NIP-4; NOEC; OxAEP-1; PeFWW

To fill the paste that's a-kneading. (LL) Ceremonies for Christmas[se]. Robert Herrick. BeJo; OBCP

To fill up half the *Orb* of Round *Eternity.* (LL) The Muse. Abraham Cowley. CABP; EPCY; PBRV

To find beyond death / Bridgeport, Ohio. (LL) In Response to a Rumor that the Oldest Whorehouse in Wheeling, West Virginia, Has Been Condemned. James Wright. CoAP; NNaP; NoAM; VCAP

To Find[e] God. Robert Herrick. BeJo; NoP-4

To find my Tom of Bedlam, ten thousand years I'll travel. *Unknown.* CBNP

To find out *death* but missest *life* at hand. (LL) Vanity [*or* Vanitie] (1). George Herbert. FMP; GeHe, NOSC; NoP-4

To find out the temperature, she tosses a cup of water into the air. Alakanak Break-Up. Mei-Mei Berssenbrugge. PmAP

To find the Western path. Morning. William Blake. FaBoCh; OAEL-2

To find they have flown away? (LL) The Wild Swans at Coole. W. B. Yeats. AYFP; CMoP; HeIP-4; InPS-3; MoBrPo; MoP; NAEL-2; NoAM; NoP-4; PoPoPo; Poetr; SCGP; SoSe-8; TFi; UnPo

To find words for this. In Western Massachusetts, Sixteen Months Sober. Joan Larkin. LoHo

To finde out *death,* but missest *life* at hand. George Herbert. *See* Vanity [*or* Vanitie] (1).

To Fine Lady Would-Be. Ben Jonson. FaBoEE; NOSC; NoP-4; OxBSP

To finish what's begun, was my intent. An Apology. Anne Bradstreet. KTR

To fit in, I lifted "Angel Baby." Fifteen. Paula Rankin. CMAP

To Flaxman. William Blake. FaBoEE; OxBoLi

To flee from memory. Emily Dickinson. FaBoEE

To fleece the Fleece from golden sheep. The Scales of the Eyes. Howard Nemerov. CMoP

To fling my arms wide. Dream Variation[s]. Langston Hughes. HAP; ISC; MBE; NAAAL; NAAL-2; NOBA; NoP-4; PoBA; SAGP; SAmP; SSLK

To float in the space between. (LL) The Idea of Ancestry. Etheridge Knight. AF; BPo; CoAmPo; ISC; NAAAL; NIP-4; NNaP; PBCAP; PoBA; RaBo

To Flood Stage Again. James Wright. NOBA

To Flossie. William Carlos Williams. SAmP

To flourish amid the incessant hell. Small Kulak Landowner. Innokenty Fiodorovich Annensky, *Russian.* TCRP, *tr. by* Lubov Yakovleva *with* Daniel Weissbort

To fly high hardly fills the belly. Cicada. Li Shang-yin, *Chinese.* SuSp, *tr. by* Eugene Eoyang *and* Irving Y. Lo

To fly off, a ripe pear in a storm. Definition of the Soul. Boris Pasternak, *Russian.* TrJP, *tr. by* Babette Deutsch

To fold the clothes. No matter who lives. I Stop Writing the Poem. Tess Gallagher. NMM-2; PiM

To fold up silks, may wrap up wit. (LL) A Fancy. Thomas Carew. BeJo; NOSC

To Fool or Knave. Ben Jonson. FaBoEE; NoP-4

To Ford Madox Ford in Heaven. William Carlos Williams. AmPP; ColAP; NOBA

To Forget Me. Theodore Weiss. CoAP

To forgive Enemies H[ayley] does pretend. On Hayley. William Blake. FaBoEE

To fork out his penny and pocket your shilling. (LL) On Communists. Ebenezer Elliot. NBLV; NOBL; NOBVV

To forsee / the man's / response--when. Floating Series 2. Leslie Scalapino. DeD *Fr.* Floating Series.

To Fortune. Robert Herrick. CavPo; OxBSP

To frame her cloudy prison for the soul! (LL) Ode: Autumn. Thomas Hood. ImPo; OAEL-2; OBEV; OBNC; OxAEP-2; PoEL-4; Ro; UnPo

To Francis Beaumont. Ben Jonson. BeJo

To Frankfort I on *Schobbas* came. The Best Religion. Heinrich Heine. TrJP, *tr. by* Emma Lazarus. *Fr.* Tannhäuser.

To Franz Kafka. Edwin Muir. FaBoTC

To free the ball the chief now turns his mind. Victory on the Last Green. Thomas Mathison. NOEC *Fr.* The Goff; an Heroi-comical Poem.

To Freedom. Agnes Nemes Nagy, *Hungarian.* PoSu, *tr. by* Bruce Berlind

To freight cars in the air. William Carlos Williams. InPK-6 *Fr.* The Descent of Winter.

To freighted ships[,] baffled in wind and blast. (LL) Stars wheel in purple, yours is not so rare. Hilda Doolittle. MoAmPo; NOBA; TAP

To fret[e] inward for losing such[e] a loss[e]. (LL) My mother's maids [*or* maydes] when they did sew [*or* sowe] and spin [*or* spynne]. Sir Thomas Wyatt. AAS; NoSic; SiPS

To Friends Who Have Also Considered Suicide. Phyllis Webb. NOBC

To friends who love you truly. (LL) The Canary. Elizabeth Turner. PeP

To fright the frost out of the grave. (LL) Death and Love. Ben Jonson. BeJo; NAEL-1; NOBE; NoP-4; PoEL-2; SeCP

To Frighten a Storm. Gladys Cardiff. CDW

To G. H. B. James Bayard Taylor. Son

To gain at harvest an eternal *Treasure.* (LL) Our Life Is Hid with Christ in God. George Herbert. ChIV-2; OAEL-1

To gallop in grand review. Red Guard. Maksimilian Aleksandrovich Voloshin, *Russian.* TCRP, *tr. by* Albert C. Todd

To gallop off to town post-haste. Friar Lubin. Clément Marot, *French.* AWP, *tr. by* Longfellow

To gather flowers Sappha went. The Apron of Flowers. Robert Herrick. CaPo

To gaze with envy on their gloomy rest. (LL) Sonnet Written in the Church-Yard at Middleton in Sussex. Charlotte Smith. CABP; ECWP; NALW; NOEC; NoP-4; PEW; WPE; WoRP

To George Sand / A Desire. Elizabeth Barrett Browning. BoWoP; NAEL-2; NALW; VWP

To George Sand: A Recognition. Elizabeth Barrett Browning. BoWoP; NAEL-2; NALW; PEW; VWP

To George Sand on her Interview with Elizabeth Barrett Browning. Isa Blagden. VWP

To Germany. Charles Hamilton Sorley. MoBrPo; NSI

To Germany. Georg Rudolph Weckherlin, *German.* GePo, *tr. by* George C. Schoolfield

To Geron. Hildebrand Jacob. NOEC

To get a fix on it. What Is Happening Now? Hubert Witheford. PeNZ

To get betimes in Boston town I rose this morning early. A Boston Ballad [1854]. Walt Whitman. OBAL

To get into it / As it lies. Shirt. Charles Simic. AFr; HCAP

To get recruits for Pain, I use. Cupid. Bernard O'Dowd. NOBAu

To Gild Refinèd Gold. Shakespeare. ImPo *Fr.* King John.

To Giovanni da Pistoia When the Author Was Painting the Vault of the Sistine Chapel, 1509. Michelangelo Buonarroti, *Italian.* ItIP
   (On the Painting of the Sistine Chapel.) NNPT, *tr. by* John Addington Symonds

To give—and forgive. Short Sermon. *Unknown, German.* CTV, *tr. by* Louis Untermeyer

To give it away, give it up, before they take it from us. Montezuma. Diane Di Prima. BB

To give me its bright plumes, they shot a jay. A Flaw. "Michael Field." VWP

To give one's life through eighty years is harder. Mary Carolyn Davies. PoToHe

To give up everything. Huck Finn at Ninety, Dying in a Chicago Boarding House Room. James Schevill. TAP

To give us comfort through the lonely dark. (LL) Douglass. Paul Laurence Dunbar. AAP; CBCWP; GSo; NAAAL; Son

To glad the heart and save from harm. (LL) The Lament of the Flowers. Jones Very. APN-1; ColAP; NOBA; OxBA

To Glaukos, and to Nereus. Lucianus, *Greek.* GrAn, *tr. by* Peter Jay

To Gluttony and Guzzling, that fastidious gourmet. Leonidas of Tarentum, *Greek*. HePo, *tr. by* Barbara Hughes Fowler   *Fr*. Epigrams.

To go away at any rate. (LL)   On Queen Caroline. *Unknown*. FaBoEE; OBCoV

To go back where we came from. (LL)   Belle Isle, 1949. Philip Levine. ColAP; SAGP; VCAP

To go in the dark with a light is to know the light.   To Know the Dark. Wendell Berry.   PFE

To go to sea in a tub. (LL)   Three Men of Gotham. Thomas Love Peacock. BXAP; CBNP; CH; FaBoCh; OBEV; OxAEP-2

To Go with Shih K'o's Painting of an Old Man Tasting Vinegar. Huang T'ing-chien, *Chinese*. CoBCP, *tr. by* Burton Watson

To God. William Blake. OAEL-2

To God ("Come to me God; but do not come"). Robert Herrick. CavPo

To God ("Do with me, God! as Thou didst deal with John"). Robert Herrick. ChIV-2

To God alone, the only donour. Francis Daniel Pastorius. SCAP

To God: an Anthem, Sung in the Chapel at White-Hall, Before the King. Robert Herrick. ChIV-1

To God Our Strength Shout Joyfully. Henry Ainsworth. AH

To God the highest glory. Song of the Angels. Lizelia Augusta Jenkins Moorer. CBWP-3

To God the Holy Ghost. Henry Constable. NoSic

To God: to illuminate all men. Beginning with Skid Road. PsalmIII. Allen Ginsberg. CAPP-1; ChIV-1

To going straight to where we are? (LL)   Our Bias. W. H. Auden. MoP; OxAEP-2; Poetr

To Grandmother on Her Going. Gail Tremblay. HATNAP

To grass, or leaf, or fruit, or wall. The Snail. Vincent Bourne, *Latin*. BoTP; CTAV; OBVE, *tr. by* William Cowper

To Greet a Letter-Carrier. William Carlos Williams. OBAL; SAmP

To greet you. You will understand. (LL)   To a Poet a Thousand Years Hence. James Elroy Flecker. MoBrPo; PoRA

To Groves. Robert Herrick. CaPo

To grow unguided at a time when none. A Tough Generation. David Gascoyne. LiTM

To H[ayley]. William Blake. FaBoEE

To H. John Wieners. FTOS

To H. C.[, Six Years Old]. Wordsworth. PoEL-4

To H.N. David Mura. UnSA

To ———: "Had I a man's fair form, then might my sighs." Keats. OxAEP-2

To hail the King of Glory. (LL)   Before the paling of the stars. Christina Rossetti. AYFP; TrCP

To Hampstead. Leigh Hunt. Ro   *Fr*. The Examiner, no. 385 316.

To hang all old strange things, let his wife beware. (LL)   Antiquary. Donne. EBEV; NOSC

To hang his pants on while he slept. (LL)   Museum Piece. Richard Wilbur. APAD; CMoP; CoAmPo; FaBoMo; InPK-6; NIP-4; TAP; TRP

To haste me hence[,] to find[e] my fortune[']s fold[e]. (LL)   Farewell to the Court. Sir Walter Ralegh. NoSic; SiPS; Son

To have been a little ill. Convalescence. Noël Coward. TTTS

To have been held down in a park. Rimbaud Having a Bath. Robert Adamson. BMAP

To have been loved once by someone—surely. When the Sun Went Down. John Ashbery. NAAL-2

To have been one. Aspects of Eve. Linda Pastan. CRP; PiM

To have it out or not? that is the question. "C. A. W." BXAP; UV

To have known him, to have loved him. Monody. Herman Melville. APN-2; NAAL-3; NoP-4; OxBSP; PAR; PoE; PoEL-5; PoPoPo

To have liv'd eminent in a degree. Upon the Death of My Ever Desired Friend Doctor Donne Dean of Pauls. Henry King. SeCP

To have / red mouth and green shanks. Moorhen. William Logan. DiPo

To have to go to bed by day? (LL)   Bed in Summer. Robert Louis Stevenson. ACTP; NBLV; OTCP; OxBChV

To Have without Holding. Marge Piercy. CrSp; NIP-4

To Haydn. Thomas Holcroft. NOEC

To heal you Hieronymus I had brought you. Bear's Blood. Ileana Malancioui, *Rumanian*. BoWoP, *tr. by* Stavros Deligiorgis

To hear a cart go jolting down the street. (LL)   The Shell. James Stephens. BoTP; CH; CMoP; MoBrPo

To hear a dripping water tap in a house. Betweens. Norman McCaig. SPE

To hear an Oriole sing. Emily Dickinson. PFE; PoEL-5

To hear Miles weep. Miles Weeping. Michael Waters. CMAP; PuP-15

To hear with eyes belongs to love's find wit. (LL)   Sonnet 23. Shakespeare. NoSic; Son

To Heaven. Robert Herrick. ChIV-2

To Heaven. Ben Jonson. BeJo; ChIV-2; HAP; NAEL-1; NOCV; NOSC; SCGP; SeCP; TRP; UnPo

To hedge us frae that black banditti, / The City Guard. (LL)   The Daft Days. Robert Fergusson. CABP

To Helen ("Helen, thy beauty is to me"). Edgar Allan Poe. APN-1; AWP; AmPP; BoLoP; CH; ClHu; ColAP; FaBoBe; GBL; GLoP; HAP; HeIP-4; HoPM; ImPo; InPS-3; LoP; MeMAP; NAAL-1; NAAL-3; NIP-4; NOBA; NOBE; NoP-4; OBEV; OxBA; PAR; PBMP; PoE; PoEL-4; PoLF; PoPoPo; PoRA; SAGP; TAP; TFi; WeW-3

("Are Holy-Land!") (LL)   GLoP; LoP; NoP-4; PoPoPo; SAGP

To Helen. Winthrop Mackworth Praed. NOBVV

To Helen in a Huff. Nathaniel Parker Willis. OBAL

To Helen of Troy (N.Y.). Peter Viereck. WeW-3

To Helen, with Crabbe's Poems: a Birthday Present. Winthrop Mackworth Praed. EPCY

To Helene. George Darley. NOBRP

To Hell and Back, with Cake. Safiya Henderson-Holmes. UnSA

To Hell with Commonsense. Patrick Kavanagh. APAD; FaBoTw

To Hell with It. Frank O'Hara. NeAP

"To hell with ye!" says she. (LL)   The Brewer's Man. Leonard Alfred George Strong. OBCoV; PeLV

To help you, you have me read. Father, You Learn to Die. Jim Handlin. EC3

To Henrietta, on Her Departure for Calais. Thomas Hood. OxBChV

To Henry Church. Wallace Stevens. ColAP   *Fr*. Notes toward a Supreme Fiction.

To Henry Constable and Henry Keir. Alexander Montgomerie. OxBS

To Henry James. Robert Louis Stevenson. OBCoV

To Henry Reynolds, of Poets and Poesy. Michael Drayton.

     "And be it said of thee." EPCY

     Chapman the Translator. EPCY

     "Grave moral Spenser after these came on." EPCY

     "Neat Marlowe, bathed in the Thepian springs." EPCY

     "Noble Sidney with this last arose, The." EPCY

     "That noble Chaucer, in those former times." EPCY

     "Then dainty Sandys, that hath to English done." EPCY

     "When after those, four ages very near." EPCY

To Henry Wright of Mobberley, Esq. on Buying the Picture of Father Malebranche. John Byrom. NOEC

To Her Dead Mate: Montana, 1966. Elizabeth Libbey. AmPA

To Her Father. Sophie Cabot Black. MoLi

To Her Father, with Some Verses. Anne Bradstreet. NAAL-3; NALW

To her friends, said the Bright one, in chatter. Limerick. Arthur Buller. PeLi

To her gardener, a lady named Liliom. Limerick. *Unknown*. PeLi

To Her in Absence; a Ship. Thomas Carew. CaPo

To her let us garlands bring. (LL)   Song: "Who is Silvia?". Shakespeare. EBEvV; FaBoBe; ImPo; NoSic; OAEL-1; OBEV; SCGP   *Fr*. The two Gentlemen of Verona.

To Her Love. Edward May. FaBoEE

To Her Lover's Complaint. Jane Barker. OxBSP

To Her of Whom They Dream. Paul Éluard, *French*. AF, *tr. by* Lloyd Alexander

To her royall highnesse the Dutchesse of Yorke. Katherine Philips. KTR

To Her Sea-faring Lover. *Unknown*. See The Lady Prayeth the Return of Her Lover Abiding on the Seas.

To herald in another year. January. Henrietta Cordelia Ray. CBWP-3

To Hero nightly, wet and rather cold. Subjectivity at Sestos. P. M. Hubbard. NYBP

To Hersa. Forceythe Willson. APN-2

To hide her ordure, claws the cat. A Quarrelsome Bishop. Walter Savage Landor. FaBoEE

To Hilda Dancing. John Bingham Morton. OBCoV

To him are opening Paradise. (LL)   Now the golden morn aloft. Thomas Gray. GTBS-P; NOEC

To Him That Was Crucified. Walt Whitman. ChIV-2

To him who in his absence from himself. Lance Jeffers. BkSV

To him who in the love of Nature holds. Thanatopsis. William Cullen Bryant. APN-1; AWP; AmPP; ColAP; FaBoBe; NAAL-1; NAAL-3; NCAP; NOBA; OBEV; OxBA; PAR; PWR; PoToHe; TAP; TFi

To Him Who Is Feared. Eleazar ben Kalir, *Hebrew*. TrJP, *tr. by* Lady Katie Magnus

To him who says he loves. Charlotte Dacre. Ro

To him with trumpets and with flutes. Sir John Davies. KSG

To Himself. Paul Fleming, *German*. GePo, *tr. by* George C. Schoolfield

To Himself. Andreas Gryphius, *German*. GePo, *tr. by* George C. Schoolfield

To Himself. Giacomo Leopardi, *Italian*. NNPT, *tr. by* John Heath-Stubbs

To His Book ("Before the Press scarce one co'd see"). Robert Herrick. OxBSP

To His Book ("Go thro forth"). Robert Herrick. CaPo

To His Book[e] ("Have I not blessed thee? Then go forth; nor fear"). Robert Herrick. CaPo

To His Book[e] ("Make haste away, and let one be"). Robert Herrick. NOSC

To His Book[e]. Martial, *Latin*. AWP; OBVE, *tr. by* Robert Herrick ("And never staine a cheeke for it.") (LL) OBCVT, *tr. by* Robert Herrick

(To his Booke.) OBCVT, *tr. by* Robert Herrick ("To read my booke the Virgin Shie.") OBCVT, *tr. by* Robert Herrick

To His Book. Leon Stokesbury. Poetr

To his book's end this last line he'd have placed. Robert Herrick. CaPo; NAEL-1

To his bride said a numbskull named Clarence. Limerick. *Unknown*. PeLi

To his Brother Hsing-chien. Po Chü-i, *Chinese*. ChiP, *tr. by* Arthur Waley

To his Brother Hsing-chien, Who was Serving in Tung-ch'uan. Po Chü-i, *Chinese*. ChiP, *tr. by* Arthur Waley

To His Chi Mistress. George Starbuck. NYBP

To His Child. William Bullokar. OxBChV

To his club-footed child said Lord Stipple. Limerick. Edward Gorey. OBCoV; PeLi

To His Conscience. Robt. Herrick. BeJo; ChIV-1; NAEL-1; NoP-4; PoEL-3

To his cottage again. (LL) The Despairing Lover. William Walsh. FaBoCh; NBLV; NOBL; OxBoLi; PeLV

To his Countrymen. James Russell Lowell. *Fr.* A Fable for Critics. NAAL-1; NAAL-3

To His Coy Love. Michael Drayton. *See* To His Coy Love, A Canzonet.

To His Coy Love, A Canzonet. Michael Drayton. NOSC; PBRV; SAGP

To His Coy Mistress. Sir Robert Ayton. NOSC

To His Coy Mistress. Edward Bird. BXAP

To His Coy Mistress. John Flood. BXAP

To His Coy Mistress, *parody*. Gerry Hamill. BXAP

To His Coy Mistress. Andrew Marvell. AWP; BoLoP; CABP; CBLP; ClHu; EBEV; EBEvV; ESCV; EnLoPo; FHYEP; FMP; FSCP; FaBoSe; GBL; GEA; GLoP; GeHe; HAP; HeIP-4; HoPM; ImPo; InPK-6; InPS-3; LoP; MeLP; NAEL-1; NIP-4; NOBE; NOSC; NoP-4; OAEL-1; OBEV; OxAEP-1; PBMP; PBRV; PFE; PoE; PoEL-2; PoLF; PoPoPo; PoRA; Poetr; SAGP; SCGP; SCV; SeCP; TFi; TRP; UV

To His Coy Mistress. Peter Scupham. BXAP

To His Coy Mistress. Stanley J. Sharpless. BXAP

To His Coy Mistress. W. J. Webster. BXAP

To His Darrest Freind. John Steward of Baldynneis. OxBS

To His Dead Body. Siegfried Sassoon. NoAM

To His Dying Brother, Master William Herrick. Robert Herrick. CaPo; CavPo; NOSC

To His Excellency General Washington. Phillis Wheatley. NAAAL; NAAL-1; NAAL-3; WPE

To His Excellency Joseph Dudley. John Saffin. SCAP

To his extreme annoyance, tempted him. (LL) On Lady Poltagrue, A Public Peril. Hilaire Belloc. MoBrPo; OBCoV; OxBoV

To his false Mistress. Ovid, *Latin*. OBCVT, *tr. by* Sir Charles Sedley

To his Father on Praising the Honest Life of the Peasant. Parvin E'tesami, *Persian*. WPOW, *tr. by* Deirdre Lashgari

To His Forsaken Mistress. Sir Robert Ayton. OBEV

(Inconstancy Reproved.) GBL

To His Friend. George Turberville. AEP; CTC

To His Friend in Elysium. Joachim Du Bellay, *French*. AWP, *tr. by* Andrew Lang

To His Friend in Love with a young Girl. Horace, *Latin*. OBCVT, *tr. by* Thomas Creech

To His Friend Master R.L., In Praise of Music and Poetry. Richard Barnfield. AAS; EPCY; Son

To His Friend, on the Untunable Times. Robert Herrick. CaPo

To His Friend P. of Courting, Traveling, Dicing, and Tennis. George Turberville. NoSic

To His Friend to Avoid Contention of Words. Robert Herrick. FP

To his genius victims fall. (LL) Namby-Pamby; or, A Panegyric on the New Versification. Henry Carey. NOEC; OBSV

To His Good Friend [*or* Freinde] Sir Anthony Cooke. Sir John Davies. *Fr.* The Gulling[e] Sonnets. Son

To His Heart. Sir Thomas Wyatt. SiPS

To His Honored Friend Thomas Stanley Esquire, Upon His Elegant Poems. James Shirley. BeJo

To His Honoured and Most Ingenious Friend Mr. Charles Cotton. Robert Herrick. CaPo; CavPo; NOSC

To His Importunate Mistress. Peter De Vries. NBLV; NIP-4

To His Importunate Mistress. Paul Griffin. UV

To His Kinsman, Master Thomas Herrick, Who Desired to Be in His Book. Robert Herrick. CaPo

To His Kinswoman, Mrs. Penelope Wheeler. Robert Herrick. CaPo

To His Lady. Sir John Davies. SiPS

To His Lady. Henry VIII, King of England. CTC; EBEV

To His Lady. Petrarch. *See* Love's Fidelity.

To His Lady Selvaggia Vergiolesi; Likening His Love to a Search for Gold, *madrigal*. Cino da Pistoia, *Italian*. AWP, *tr. by* D. G. Rossetti

To His Little Son Benedict from the Tower of London. John Hoskyns. OxBChV

(To His Son Benedict Hoskyns.) NOSC

To His Love. Ivor Gurney. NAEL-2; NTP; NoP-4; OBWP; PeFWW; PoWW

To His Love. Shakespeare. *See* Sonnet 18 *and* 106.

To His Love. *Unknown*. NoP-4

To his Love that sent him a Ring wherein was gravde, / Let Reason rule. George Turberville. PBRV

To His Love When He Had Obtained Her. Sir Walter Ralegh. NoSic

To His Lovely Mistresses. Robert Herrick. CTC; CaPo; SeCP

To His Lute. William Drummond. GSo; GTBS-P

To His Lute. Sir Thomas Wyatt. *See* The Lover Complaineth the Unkindness of His Love.

To His Maistres [*or* Mistress]. Alexander Montgomerie. GBL; OxBS

To His Mistress. Abraham Cowley. NOSC; OxAEP-1 *Fr.* Sylva.

To His Mistress. Sir Walter Ralegh. *See* Sir Walter Ralegh to the Queen.

To His Mistress. John Wilmot, 2d Earl of Rochester. OBEV

To His Mistress. James Shirley. BeJo

To His Mistress for Her True Picture. Edward Herbert. SeCP

To His Mistress Going To Bed. Donne. BoLoP; FSCP; GLoP; LoP; NoSic; OAEL-1; PBRV; PoE *Fr.* Elegies.

(Elegy XIX. To His Mistress Going to Bed.) NoP-4

(Going to Bed.) FaBoSe

(To His Mistris Going to Bed.) CBLP; OxAEP-1; SeCP

To His Mistress in Absence. Torquato Tasso, *Italian*. AWP, *tr. by* Thomas Stanley

To His Mistresses. Robert Herrick. CaPo; SeCP

To His Mother. John Harington. NoSic

To his mother's tent. (LL) Genesis XXIV. Arthur Hugh Clough. ChIV-1

To His Noble Friend, Mr Richard Lovelace, upon His Poems. Andrew Marvell. EPCY

To His Not-so-coy Mistress. Wynford Vaughan-Thomas. BXAP; NOBL

To His Pandora, from England. Alexander Craig. Son

To his Paternall Countrey. Ovid, *Latin*. OBCVT, *tr. by* Robert Herrick

To His Peculiar Friend Master Thomas Shapcott, Lawyer. Robert Herrick. NOSC

To his Queen said the circumspect Burleigh. Limerick. A. Cinna. PeLi

To his retired friend, an Invitation to Brecknock. Henry Vaughan. "Town believes thee lost, and didst thou see, The." PBRV

To His Savior The New Years Gift. Robert Herrick. ChIV-2

To His Saviour, a Child; a Present, by a Child. Robert Herrick. BeJo; ChIV-2; PeECV; SeCP; TrCP

(Child's Present, A.) OxBChV

To His Scornful Mistress. William Hammond. CBLP

To His Scribe Adam. Chaucer. NAEL-1; NoP-4

(To Adam, his Scribe.) OAEL-1

(Words unto Adam, His Own Scriveyn.) CABP

To His Servant. Horace. *See* Simplicity.

To His Sleeping Mistress. John Fletcher. *See* Song: "Oh [*or* O] fair[e] sweet face, oh [*or* O] eyes celestial bright."

To His Son. Sir Walter Ralegh. *See* Sir Walter Ra[u]le[i]gh to His Son[ne].

To His Son Benedict Hoskyns. John Hoskyns. *See* To His Little Son Benedict from the Tower of London.

To His Son Bennet. John Hoskyns. FaBoEE

To His Son [*or* Sonne], Vincent Corbet[t]. Richard Corbet. BeJo; FaBoCh; NOSC; OxAEP-1; OxBChV

To his two little girls. (LL) Star-Fix. Marilyn Nelson Waniek. LTA; NAmP90

To His Valentine. Michael Drayton. PoEL-2

To His Very Friend, Master Richard Martin. Sir John Davies. *Fr.* Dedications [*or* Orchestra]. SiPS

To His Watch. Gerard Manley Hopkins. MoBrPo

To His Watch, When He Could Not Sleep. Edward Herbert, 1st Baron Herbert of Cherbury. NOBE; PoEL-2

To His Wife. Ausonius, *Latin*. AWP, *tr. by* Terrot Reaveley Glover; OxBM, *tr. by* Helen Waddell

To His Wife. Ch'in Chia, *Chinese*. ChiP, *tr. by* Arthur Waley

To His Wife. Su Wu, *Chinese*. ChiP, *tr. by* Arthur Waley

To his Wife at Rome, when he was sick. Ovid, *Latin*. OBCVT, *tr. by* Henry Vaughan

To His Wife, for Striking Her Dog. Sir John Harington. OxBSP
To his wife said the lynx-eyed detective. Limerick. Langford Reed. PeLi
To His Young Mistress. Pierre de Ronsard, *French.* AWP, *tr. by* Andrew Lang
To hold an avalanche off. (LL) The Man With Night Sweats. Thom Gunn. CABP; PoPoPo
To Homer. Keats. EBEV; NAEL-2; NoP-4; Son
To honor the return of sparkling sun. Sonnet 15. Louise Labé, *French.* BoWoP, *tr. by* Willis Barnstone
To Honora Sneyd, *sonnet.* Anna Seward. ECWP
To honour all their deaths, who for her bleed. (LL) Sonnet 7: "When Nature made her chief work, Stella's eyes." Sir Philip Sidney. NAEL-1; NIP-4; Son
To Hope. Keats. LaPo *Fr.* Imitation of Spenser.
To house the Hag, you must doe this. Another to Bring in the Witch. Robert Herrick. BeJo
To Hsiao Shih-ying. Hsieh Chin, *Chinese.* CoBLCP, *tr. by* Jonathan Chaves
To Hsü Shih-t'ing. Hsü Wei, *Chinese.* CoBLCP, *tr. by* Jonathan Chaves
To Hugh MacDiarmid. Edwin Morgan. FaBoTw
To Hunt. William Blake. OxBoLi
To hunt the waterfalls. (LL) Louisa; After Accompanying Her on a Mountain Excursion. Wordsworth. APAD; GBL
To hurt the Negro and avoid the Jew. University. Karl Shapiro. OxBA
To I. Lavrentevaya. Natalya Gorbanevskaya, *Russian.* BoWoP, *tr. by* Daniel Weissbort
To Ianthe. Byron. *See* Dedication: To Ianthe.
To Ianthe. John Lyle Donaghy. *See* Glenarm.
To Ibn Zaidun. Wallāda, *Arabic.* WPOW, *tr. by* James Monroe *and* Deirdre Lashgari
To *Ida's* Top successful *Juno* flies. Juno seduces Jove. Homer. OBCVT, *tr. by* Alexander Pope *Fr.* The Iliad.
To ignorance revealed. (LL) Lightning is a yellow Fork, The. Emily Dickinson. InPK-6; NCAP
To indicate is to. Data. Joseph Ceravolo. PT
To Inez Milholland. Edna St. Vincent Millay. AiP; NALW; WPE
To infancy, O Lord, again I come. The Return. Thomas Traherne. GeHe
To infinity. (LL) Armchairs. Dan Pagis, *Hebrew.* IP, *tr. by* Warren Bargad *and* Stanley F. Chyet
To insist that what is true is good, no matter, no matter. George Oppen. APSN *Fr.* Route.
To Insure Survival. Simon J. Ortiz. CDW
To Intellectual Detachment. Allen Tate. FuPo
To interpose them oft, is not unwise. (LL) To Mr. Lawrence. Milton. AWP; GTBS-P; NOSC; OBEV; OxAEP-1; PBRV; PoE
To invent, and practise this one way, to annihilate all three. (LL) The Will. Donne. EBEV; ImPo; NoSic
To Ireland in the Coming Times. W. B. Yeats. NOIV; NoAM
To Iron-Founders and Others. Gordon Bottomley. OBEV; OBMV
To Isa Sleeping. Thomas Holley Chivers. APN-1
To it, O jazzmen. (LL) Jazz Fantasia. Carl Sandburg. AiP; MoAmPo; Poetr
To Italy. Giacomo Leopardi, *Italian.* AWP, *tr. by* Romilda Rendel
To J. G. "Ephelia." KTR; NOSC
To J.G. on the News of His Marriage. "Ephelia." LW
To J. H. Reynolds, Esq. Keats.
    Epistle to John Hamilton Reynolds. OBNC
    "O that our dreamings all, of sleep or wake." OAEL-2
To James. Frank Horne. BPo *Fr.* Letters [*or* Notes] Found near a Suicide. PoBA
To James Smith. Robert Burns. HoPM
To Jane ("Keen stars were twinkling, The"). Shelley. FHYEP
    (To Jane: The Keen Stars Were Twinkling.) APAD
To Jane: The Recollection. Shelley. OBNC
    (Recollection, The.) GTBS-P
    "We wandered to the pine forest." CH
To Janet. Ralph Pomeroy. NYBP
To Jann, in Her Absence. C. J. Driver. PeSA
To Jesus on His Birthday. Edna St. Vincent Millay. ChIV-2; HeIP-4; TrCP
To Jesus Villanueva, with Love. Alma Villanueva. NMM-2; UnSA
To Joan. Lucille Clifton. CrSp
To John Clare. John Clare. Son
To John Donne ("Donne, the delight of Phoebus, and each Muse"). Ben Jonson. BeJo; EPCY; NAEL-1
To John Donne ("Who shall doubt, Donne, where [*or* whe'er] I a poet be[e]"). Ben Jonson. BeJo; EPCY; NoP-4; SeCP
To Donne. Sir Henry Wotton. NoSic
    (To John Donne from Mr Henry Wotton.) NOSC

To John I ow'd great obligation. Epigram. Matthew Prior. AWP; FaBoEE; OBVE
To Keats. Leigh Hunt. Ro; Son
To Keats. Amy Lowell. Son
To John Keats, from His Honored Friend, William Davenant. John Clare. "Though faction's scorn at first did shun." EPCY
To John Keats, Poet, at Spring Time. Countee Cullen. NAAAL
To John Lamb, Esq.: Of the South-Sea House. Charles Lamb. Son
To join [*or* joyn] with them, who here confer. His Offering, with the Rest, at the Sepulcher. Robert Herrick. ChIV-2
To Josh Gibson (Legendary Slugger of the Old Negro Baseball League). George Mosby Jr. ISC
To joy, annoy, friends, foes; but 'twill not be. (LL) Of the Great and Famous . . . Sir Francis Drake, and of My Little-Little Selfe. Robert Hayman. CH; FaBoCh
To Juan at the Winter Solstice. Robert Graves. CMoP; EBEV; FaBoMo; ImPo; LiTM; MoBrPo; MoP; NAEL-2; NoAM; NoP-4; OAEL-2; PoE; RaBo; TwCP
To Judge Faolain, Dead Long Enough: A Summons. Linda McCarriston. LoL
To Judge Han Ch'o at Yang-chou. Tu Mu, *Chinese.* PLT, *tr. by* A. C. Graham
To Judith Asleep. John Ciardi. LiTM
To Julia ("How rich and pleasing thou, my Julia, art"). Robert Herrick. CaPo
To Julia ("Julia, when thy Herrick dies"). Robert Herrick. CaPo; NOSC
To Julia de Burgos. Julia De Burgos, *Spanish.* BoWoP; PBWP, *tr. by* Grace Schulman
To Julia in Shooting Togs. Sir Owen Seaman. BXAP
To Julia, the Flaminica Dialis, or Queen-Priest. Robert Herrick. CaPo
To Julia to Expedite Her Promise. John Cleveland. CBLP
To Julia under Lock and Key. Sir Owen Seaman. BXAP
To Julie. Alfred de Musset, *French.* FLP, *tr. by* Alistair Elliot
To Julius. Martial. FaBoEE, *tr. by* Sir Charles Sedley
To jump his mortal coil. (LL) Elegy on Thomas Hood. Martin Fagg. BXAP; NOBL; UV
To just such golden ones as these. (LL) O All Down within the Pretty Meadow. Kenneth Patchen. HAP; WeW-3
To justify—Despair. (LL) It was not Death, for I stood up. Emily Dickinson. APN-2; MeMAP; NAAL-1; NAAL-3; NOBA; PAR; SAmP
To justify the Dream. (LL) I reckon—when I count at all. Emily Dickinson. APN-2; MoAmPo; NIP-4; NoP-4; PAR
To K. de M. Robert Louis Stevenson. OBNC
To K. H. Thomas Edward Brown. OBNC
To Kachalov's Dog. Sergey Aleksandrovich Yesenin, *Russian.* TCRP, *tr. by* Daniel Weissbort
To Kalon. Ezra Pound. PoA
To Kate, Skating Better than Her Date. David Daiches. NYBP
To Keats: On Reading His Sonnet Written in Chaucer. John Hamilton Reynolds. Son
To Keep a True Lent. Robert Herrick. TrCP
To keep my health! Resolve. Charlotte Perkins Stetson Gilman. PoToHe
To keep our metaphysics warm. (LL) Whispers of Immortality. T. S. Eliot. CMoP; CTC; NOBA; NoAM; OBMV; OxAEP-2
To Keep the Memory of Charlotte Forten Grimké. Angelina Weld Grimké. BlSi
To keep the memory of our arms alive. (LL) To my Friend G.N. from Wrest. Thomas Carew. BeJo; CaPo
To keep things whole. (LL) Keeping Things Whole. Mark Strand. CAPP-1; CoAP; HCAP; HeIP-4; LCAP-2; PoPoPo; TAP; VCAP
To keep your marriage brimming. A Word to Husbands. Ogden Nash. OBCoV
To kill a language is to kill a people. The Frost is All Over. Pearse Hutchinson. PBCIP
To kill its enemies and cheat its friends. International Conference. Colin Ellis. FaBoEE
To kill love so as not to commit suicide. Resurrection. Sachiko Yoshihara, *Japanese.* WPJ, *tr. by* Kenneth Rexroth *and* Ikuko Atsumi
To Kiss God's Rod; Occasioned upon a Child's Sickness. Mildmay Fane. BeJo
To kiss upon thy lips a stainless fame. (LL) To George Sand / A Desire. Elizabeth Barrett Browning. BoWoP; NAEL-2; NALW; VWP
To Know All Is to Forgive All. Nixon Waterman. BLPA
To know he still is warm tho' I am cold. (LL) After Death. Christina Rossetti. GBL; NAEL-2; NALW
To know just how He suffered—would be dear. Emily Dickinson. NCAP
To Know the Dark. Wendell Berry. PFE
To know there are rhododendrons on the slopes of the Himalayas. Nearer. Judith Herzberg, *Dutch.* BoWoP, *tr. by* Shirley Kaufman

To / know whether or not art is contemporary. John Cage. APSN *Fr.* Diary: How to Improve the World (You Will Only Make Matters Worse).

To know who I am / why I came there / what and why I am and made to happen. (LL) Hôtel Transylvanie. Frank O'Hara. NeAP; PoM

To Kolya Otrada. Mikhail Kuz'mich Lukonin, *Russian.* TCRP, *tr. by* Albert C. Todd

To Krishna Haunting the Hills. Andal, *Tamil.* BoWoP, *tr. by* Willis Barnstone

To Kyris. Strato, *Greek.* GrAn, *tr. by* Teddy Hogge

To L. Julianne Perry. PoBA

To L. B. S. Winfield Townley Scott. SAGP

To L. Manlius Torquatus. Horace. *See* Odes 4.7.

To Labor. Charlotte Perkins Stetson Gilman. PoLF

To Ladies' Eyes. Thomas Moore. OxBoLi; PoEL-4

To Lady Anne Fitzpatrick, When about Five Years Old, with a Present of Shells, 1772. Horace, 4th Earl of Orford Walpole. NOEC

To Lady Wyatt. Edward Lear. CBNP

To Lake Aghmoogenegamook. The American Traveller. "Orpheus C. Kerr." OBAL

To Larr [*or* Lar]. Robert Herrick. CaPo

To laugh when Hetty is no more. (LL) Address to Her Husband. Mehetabel Wright. ECWP; LW

To Laura. Henrietta Cordelia Ray. CBWP-3

To Laura, on the French Fleet Parading before Plymouth. Ann Thomas. ECWP

To Laura Phelan: 1880-1906. Leon Stokesbury. MT

To Laurels. Robert Herrick. CaPo

To lay its fingers on the little heads. (LL) A Naming Day. Odia Ofeimun. HBAPE; PBMAP

To lay the lorn spirit, you o'er it must pray. *Unknown.* OxBSn

To lazy to be ambitious. Ryokan, *Japanese.* EnlH, *tr. by* Stephen Mitchell

To learn how to speak. Jeremy Cronin. PeSAV

To learn the scriptures is easy. Lal Ded, *Kashmiri.* WPoS, *tr. by* Jane Hirshfield

To learn the Transport by the Pain. Emily Dickinson. NOCV

To leave a light for them when they should come. (LL) The Insusceptibles. Adrienne Rich. CoAmPo; HeIP-4; Son

To leave my boots. (LL) Our Photograph[s]. Frederick Locker-Lampson. NBLV; NOBL; PeLV

To leave the earth was my wish, and no will stayed my rising. A Temple. Kenneth Patchen. SPE

To leave the world and serve God. Compiuta Donzella, *Italian.* WPOW, *tr. by* Laura Stortoni

To left and right, outside, he saw an orchard, *see also* "Without the hall, and close upon the gates" *and* "Close to the gates a spacious garden lies." Alkinoos' Garden. Homer, *Greek.* GrIP, *tr. by* Robert Fitzgerald *Fr.* Odyssey. NAWM-1, *tr. by* Robert Fitzgerald

To Leigh Hunt, Esq. Keats. Son

(Dedication: To Leigh Hunt, Esq.) OBNC

To Lesbia. Catullus. *See* Carmen 5 ("My sweetest Lesbia, let us live and love").

To Let. D. Newey-Johnson. BoTP

To let a thousand such enjoy their quiet. (LL) A Sparrow-Hawk. *Unknown.* CH; EBEV

To let me[e] live, O[h] love and hate mee too. (LL) The Prohibition. Donne. GBL; MeLP; NOSC

To let the warm Love in! (LL) Ode to Psyche. Keats. FHYEP; InPS-3; NAEL-2; NOBE; NOBRP; NoP-4; OAEL-2; OBEV; OBNC; OxAEP-2; PoE; PoEL-4; Ro; TFi; TOF

To let them dream they are not dead. (LL) Pallor. Agnes Mary Frances Robinson. VWP

To Leven Water. Tobias Smollett. OBEV

To Li Chien. Po Chü-i, *Chinese.* AWP; ChiP, *tr. by* Arthur Waley

To Li Po. 'Aisha bint Ahmad al-Qurtubiyya, *Chinese.* SuSp, *tr. by* Eugene Eoyang

To Li Po. Tu Fu, *Chinese.* TAL, *tr. by* Robert Payne

To Li Po at the Sky's End. Tu Fu, *Chinese.* ChiPo, *tr. by* Witter Bynner

To Li Po on a Spring Day. Tu Fu, *Chinese.* TAL, *tr. by* Robert Payne

To liberate my people from its yoke! (LL) Enslaved. Claude McKay. NAAAL

To Licinius. Horace. *See* Odes 2.10.

To lie down and sleep than to quarrel and fight. (LL) Two Little Kittens[, one stormy night]. *Unknown.* ACTP; OBCA; OxBChV

To lie, to push, to get / just isn't / enough. (LL) To Jesus Villanueva, with Love. Alma Villanueva. NMM-2; UnSA

To Life Eternal, I could love. (LL) Julia's Petticoat. Robert Herrick. BeJo; CaPo; CavPo

To Life I Said Yes. Chaim Grade, *Yiddish.* TrJP, *tr. by* Joseph Leftwich

To lift a leg and play the baptist. (LL) The Scribblers. Walter Savage Landor. FaBoEE; OBSV

To lift her over the threshold, and let her in at the door. (LL) The Witch. Mary Elizabeth Coleridge. BrRo; CABP; NALW; PFE; VWP; WPE

To Light. Linda Hogan. HATNAP

To light me where I soon[e] may see / How to serve you, and you trust me. (LL) To Lucasta[, from Prison]. Richard Lovelace. BeJo; CaPo

To light the dark. Litany. Elise Paschen. FFC

To light young poets' hearts. Cephalus, *Greek.* GrAn, *tr. by* W. G. Shepherd

To Lighten My Darkness. *Unknown.* AWP *Fr.* The Thousand and One Nights.

To Lindsay. Allen Ginsberg. CoAmPo

To linger till ninety, like Landor. (LL) Obit on Parnassus. F. Scott Fitzgerald. NBLV; NYBP

To Little Sister From No. 16. *Unknown.* NSI

To Liu Yü-hsi. Po Chü-i, *Chinese.* ChiP, *tr. by* Arthur Waley

To live again a butterfly. (LL) The Caterpillar. Christina Rossetti. AYFP; BoTP; CTAV; CTV; ChAP; FaBoVe; OxBChV

To live and die for thee. (LL) To Anthea, Who May Command Him Anything. Robert Herrick. CaPo; GTBS-P; NOBE; NOSC; OAEL-1; OBEV; SeCP

To live and lack the thing should rid my pain. (LL) A Complaint by Night of the Lover Not Beloved. Henry Howard, *after* Petrarch. AAS; AEP; AWP; EBEV; NAEL-1; OAEL-1; OBVE; SCGP; SiPS; Son

To live and not to be thine own. Thine Own. Josephine D. Henderson Heard. CBWP-4

To Live at the Speed of Biography. Yona Wallach, *Hebrew.* IP, *tr. by* Warren Bargad *and* Stanley F. Chyet

To Live at the Speed of Biography. Yona Wallach, *Hebrew.* IP, *tr. by* Warren Bargad *and* Stanley F. Chyet

To live because we're sure to die! (LL) To a Lady Asking Him How Long He Would Love Her. Sir George Etherege. OBEV; SAGP

To live before I sink, deeper than the diver, into the lofty depth of / sleep. (LL) Night of Sine. Léopold Sédar Senghor, *French.* PBMAP

To live by, in sunlight and moolight, until they died. (LL) Patriotic Tour and Postulate of Joy. Robert Penn Warren. AiP; NYBP

To live in court among the crew is care. To His Friend P. of Courting, Traveling, Dicing, and Tennis. George Turberville. NoSic

To live in hell, and heaven to behold. If Love In These Be Founded. Henry Constable. AAS; Son *Fr.* Diana.

To live in mankind, far, far more. . . than to live in a name. (LL) The Eagle That Is Forgotten. Vachel Lindsay. AWP; CMoP; MeMAP; MoAmPo; NOBA; OxBA

To live in Wales is to be conscious. Welsh Landscape. Ronald Stuart Thomas. FaBoMo; NoP-4

To Live Merrily, and To Trust to Good Verses. Robert Herrick. AWP; BeJo; CaPo; CavPo; NOSC; SeCP

To live more nearly as we pray. (LL) New every morning. John Keble. FaPoR; NOCV

To live with him, and sing in endles[s] morn of light[!]. (LL) At a Solemn Music[k]. Milton. EPCY; GTBS-P; HeIP-4; NOBE; OBEV; PoEL-3; SCGP

To live with thee and be thy Love. (LL) The Nimphs [*or* Nymph's] Reply to the Sheepheard [*or* Shepherd]. Sir Walter Ralegh. AAS; AEP; BoLoP; CABP; CTC; ClHu; EBEvV; GLoP; HAP; HeIP-4; HoPM; ImPo; InPK-6; InPS-3; NAEL-1; NBLV; NIP-4; NOBE; NoP-4; NoSic; OAEL-1; OBEV; PFE; PoE; PoPoPo; Poetr; RACG; RB; SCGP; SiPS; TFi; TRP; UV; WeW-3

To live within a cave—it is most good. Salve! Thomas Edward Brown. OBEV

To live without Him: lik'd it not, and di'd. (LL) Upon the Death of Sir Albert [*or* us] Morton's Wife. Sir Henry Wotton. BoLoP; EnLoPo; FaBoEE; OBEV; OxBM; PBRV; SeCP; WeW-3

To live's a gift, to dye's a debt that we. The Porch. Philip Pain. SCAP

To Lizbie Browne. Thomas Hardy. FaBoVe; NOBVV; OxAEP-2

To London once my stepps [*or* steps] I bent. London Lickpenny. *Unknown, Middle English.* OBSV

To look at the moon. (LL) Funeral Rites. Seamus Heaney. BiHa; PRCIP

To look like everyone else. (LL) Tapestry. Charles Simic. LCAP-2; VCAP

To loose three parts in four from amongst womankind. Anne Finch, Countess of Winchilsea. *See* The Circuit of Apollo.

To loosen with all ten fingers held wide and limber. Moss-Gathering. Theodore Roethke. BLT; PaTW; VGW

To Lord Byron. Keats. EPCY

To Lord Byron. Andrew Lang.

"Fashion changes! Maidens do not wear, The." EPCY

To Lord, nor Lady, nor faire England. (LL) The Fair Flower of Northumberland. *Unknown.* ESPB; OxBB

To Lord Tennyson. Sir William Watson. EPCY

To lose an oath to win a paradise? (LL) The Heavenly Rhetoric. Shakespeare. ImPo; Son

To lose it all at once. Marina Ivanovna Tsvetayeva. *Fr.* The Daughter of Jairus. BoWoP, *tr. by* Paul Schmidt

To lose three parts in four amongst womankind. (LL) The Circuit of Apollo. Anne Finch. NALW

To Love. Ovid, *Latin.*
  "O! Love! how cold, and slow to take my part!" OBCVT, *tr. by* John Wilmot

To Love and Fate an equal Sacrifice. (LL) The Exequies. Thomas Stanley. BeJo; MeLP

To love and to remember; that is good. Christina Rossetti. Son *Fr.* Later Life: A Double Sonnet of Sonnets.

To love is to die a little in the heart. Xuân Diệu, *Vietnamese.* AVP, *tr. by* Huỳnh Sanh Thông

To love me best of all. (LL) If fancy [*or* fansy] would favour. Sir Thomas Wyatt. AAS; SiPS

To love, my lord, I do[e] knight[e]'s service owe. Sir John Davies. *Fr.* The Gulling[e] Sonnets. Son

To love November, a turned joy. Late in Fall. Ramona Wilson. VoR

To love one man, he'd leave her first. (LL) Another. In Defense of Their Inconstancy [*or* Inconstancie]. A Song. Ben Jonson. BeJo; NAEL-1; SeCP

To love so much as she'll deserve. (LL) My dearest rival, lest [*or* least] our love. Sir John Suckling. BeJo; CavPo; MeLP

To love so well the world that we may believe, in the end, in God. (LL) Masts at Dawn. Robert Penn Warren. NAAL-2; NoP-4; VCAP

To love some one more dearly ev'ry day. My Task. Maude Louise Ray. PWR

To love somebody. Lady Kasa, *Japanese.* OHMPJ, *tr. by* Kenneth Rexroth

To love somebody / Who doesn't love you. Kasa no Iratsume, *Japanese.* WPOW, *tr. by* Kenneth Rexroth

To love someone / Who does not return that love. Kasa no Iratsume, *Japanese.* PBWP, *tr. by* Harold P. Wright

To love your country. Prelude. Marilyn Chin. LoL

To Lucasta ("Like to the sentinel stars, I watch all night"). Richard Lovelace. NOSC

To Lucasta. Richard Lovelace. CaPo; CavPo

To Lucasta[, from Prison]. Richard Lovelace. BeJo; CaPo; CavPo
  ("How to serve you, and you trust me.") (LL) CavPo

To *Lucasta, Going Beyond the Seas.* Richard Lovelace. *See* Song: To Lucasta, Going Beyond the Seas.

To Lucasta: Her Reserved Looks. Richard Lovelace. CaPo

To Lucasta: The Rose. Richard Lovelace. BeJo
  (Ode.) CavPo

To Lucia Playing on Her Lute, Another. Samuel Pordage. NOSC

To Lucy, Countess[e] of Bedford, with Mr. Donnes Satire's [*or* Satyres]. Ben Jonson. BeJo; EPCY; PBRV

To lull the dog across a bloodless river. (LL) Climbing. Jennifer Maiden. BMAP

To Luve Unluvit. Alexander Scott. OxBS

To luve unluvit it is ane pane. Alexander Scott. PBRV

To Lydia. Horace. *See* Odes 1.25: Ribald Romeos Less and Less Berattle ("Parcius iunctas quatiunt fenestras").

To Lysander. Aphra Behn. LW

To Lysander. Judith Madan. ECWP

To M. Denham, on His Prospective Poem. Robert Herrick. BeJo

To M. Henry Lawes, the Excellent Composer[,] of his Lyrics. Robert Herrick. CaPo

To Madam Bhen. "Ephelia." KTR

To Madame A. V. Pletneff. Karolina Pavlova, *French.* PBWP, *tr. by* Paul Schmidt

To Madame Curie. Alice Moore Dunbar-Nelson. NMM-2

To Maecenas. Horace. AWP; OBVE, *tr. by* John Dryden *Fr.* Odes.

To Mæcenas. Phillis Wheatley. NAAAL

To make a beauty, she. (LL) Child and Maiden. Sir Charles Sedley. GTBS-P; OBEV

To make a final conquest of all me. The Fair Singer. Andrew Marvell. EnLoPo; FSCP; MeLP; NOBE; NoP-4; PoEL-2; SCGP

To make a Juju of my own. A Juju of My Own. Lebert Bethune. PoBA

To make a new, and hang that by. (LL) In the Person of Womankind [A Song Apologetic]. Ben Jonson. BeJo; SeCP

To Make a Poem in Prison. Etheridge Knight. AF

To make a poet black, and bid him sing! (LL) Yet Do I Marvel. Countee Cullen. BPo; CrDW; GEA; NAAAL; NAAL-2; NoAM; PMMP; PFE; PoBA; SAGP; SSLK; Son; TAP; TTY

To make a prairie it takes a clover and one bee. Emily Dickinson. BoWoP; HeIP-4; NBLV; OBCA; OxBA

To make a resurrection there must be a death. Twin. Phyllis Haring. PeSA

To make a start. Preface. William Carlos Williams. CMoP; NOBA; NoAM *Fr.* Paterson.

To make a third she joined the former two. (LL) Lines Printed under the Engraved Portrait of Milton [In Tonson's Folio of the "Paradise Lost"]. Dryden. EPCY; InPK-6; OAEL-1; OxAEP-1

To make allowance for us all. (LL) Do we indeed desire the dead. Tennyson. EBVVPR; EnVR; OAEL-2

To Make Birds Sing. Vladimir Alekseievich Soloukhin, *Russian.* TCRP, *tr. by* Daniel Weissbort

To make me *deaf,* and mend my *sight.* (LL) Stella's Birthday, 1725. Jonathan Swift. CABP; NOEC

To make me do the thing I will, I won't. The Human Animal. Jane Mayhall. TAP

To make my grave. (LL) The Cross-tree. Robert Herrick. CavPo; ChIV-2

To make myself his wench but one half hour. (LL) In Francum. Sir John Davies. FaBoEE; OBCoV

To make peace with her own monstrous nature. (LL) Patience. Elaine Feinstein. BrRo; FaBoWP

To make quick way I'll leap o'er heavy blocks. John Dryden *and* Nahum Tate. OBSV *Fr.* Absalom and Achitophel, Pt. II.

To make some bread you must have dough. One, Two, Three—Gough! Eve Merriam. NTCP

To make that curve of the water. Curve of the Water. Hilda Morley. PmAP

To make the cherry red! (LL) Nevertheless. Marianne Moore. CMoP; MeMAP; NAAL-2; NoP-4; OxBA

To make the vapor bath. That Old Sauna High. Anselm Hollo. PoM

To make this condiment, your poet begs. A Salad. Sydney Goodsir Smith. NBLV; OBCoV

To make two rocks each others monument. (LL) The Double Rock. Henry, Bishop of Chichester King. CBLP; NOSC; SeCP

To make with you mine home. Lionel Pigot Johnson. *See* Mystic and Cavalier.

To make with you my home. (LL) Mystic and Cavalier. Lionel Pigot Johnson. MoBrPo

To make your candles last for aye. Mother Goose. OxNR; ReMoGo

To Mal Waldron and everyone and I stopped breathing. (LL) The Day Lady Died. Frank O'Hara. HCAP; LCAP-2; MoNo; MoP; NAAL-2; NOBA; NeAP; NoAM; NoP-4; PmAP; PoE; PoM; Poetr; RaBo; TRP; VCAP

To Marcus Aurelius. Zbigniew Herbert, *Polish.* VCWP, *tr. by* Miosz, Czeslaw and Peter Dale Scott

To Margo. Gavin Ewart. APAD

To Margot Heinemann. John Cornford. OBWP; OxBTC
  (Huesca.) BoLoP

To Marguerite. Matthew Arnold. CABP; EnVR; NoP-4; PoPoPo *Fr.* Switzerland.
  (To Marguerite—Continued.) GTBS-P; SoSe-8

To Maria Gisborne in England, from Italy. Shelley. NOBE *Fr.* Letter to Maria Gisborne.

To Marina. Sarah Fyge Egerton. ECWP

To Marina. Kenneth Koch. NoAM

To Mark Anthony in Heaven. William Carlos Williams. NOBA; SAmP

To market I take my own soul. Selling My Soul. Minh Đức Hoài Trinh, *Vietnamese.* AVP, *tr. by* Huỳnh Sanh Thông

To market, to market, to buy a fat pig. *Unknown.* BoTP; FaBoBe; LB; OxNR; ReMoGo

To market, to market / To buy a plum bun. Mother Goose. OxNR

To Mary. William Cowper. EnLoPo; GLoP; NOEC; UV
  (My Mary.) OBEV

To Mary. Mary E. Tucker. CBWP-1

To Mary. Charles Wolfe. OBEV
  (Song: To Mary.) OxAEP-2

To Mary: "I Sleep with Thee, and Wake with Thee." John Clare. GBL; GLoP
  (To Mary.) EnLoPo

To Mary: "It Is the Evening Hour." John Clare. BoLoP; GBL; GLoP; LBC
  (Mary.) EnLoPo

To Mary, Lady Wroth ("Madam[e], had all antiquity [*or* antiquitie] been lost"). Ben Jonson. NOSC

To Mary Unwin. William Cowper. GTBS-P; OBEV

To Marygolds. Robert Herrick. CavPo; NAEL-1

To mask a King in weeds. (LL) Poet ("To clothe the fiery thought"). Ralph Waldo Emerson. OxBA; OxBSP; Spl

To Master Davenant for Absence. Sir John Suckling. CaPo

To Match the Prince of Lang-yeh's Poem in the Old Style. Wang Seng-ta, *Chinese.* CoBCP, *tr. by* Burton Watson

To mate or man, or beast or bird. (LL) The Saxon Legend of Language. Mary Weston Fordham. AAP; CBWP-2

To Max Jacob. Rosanna Warren. DiPo

To Maystres Jane Blenner-Haiset. John Skelton. AAS *Fr.* The Garland [*or* Garlande *or* Garlands] of Laurel[l].

To Me. William Barnes. PoEL-4

To me, fair[e] Friend, you never can be old. Sonnet 104. Shakespeare. GBL; GTBS-P; HeIP-4; NoSic; OBEV; OxAEP-1; SCGP *Fr.* Sonnets.

To me he seems like a god. Sappho, *Greek.* BoWoP, *tr. by* Willis Barnstone

To me if they do. (LL) Winter Morning. Frank Flynn. AYFP; OTCP

To me, *lion* was sun on a wing. Eve Names the Animals. Susan Donnelly. Poetr

To me nothing seems as splendid nor as praiseworthy. *Unknown, German.* GePo, *tr. by* Sylvia Stevens

To me, one silly task is like another. Cassandra. Louise Bogan. HAP; MoMPo; NALW; PBWP; VGW

To me. Somewhere they are building. My Lady Carries Stones. Nick Piombino. FTOS

To me tomorrow constantly deny it. (LL) Odes 1.4. Ovid, *Latin.* CABP; NoSic, *tr. by* Marlowe

To me, whom in their lays the shepherds call. Inscription for a Grotto. Mark Akenside. NOEC; OBGa; PoEL-3

To me you are infinitely distant. Ten Lines. Emile Roumer, *French.* NegPo, *tr. by* Ellen Conroy Kennedy

To Meadows [*or* Meddowes]. Robert Herrick. AWP; CH; CaPo; NOBE; NOSC; OBEV; PBRV; PoEL-3; SeCP

To Meath of the pastures. A Drover. Padraic Colum. AWP; MoBrPo; OBMV; RB

To meet a bad lad on the African waste. The African Lion. A. E. Housman. CBNP; NOxBChV

To Meet, or Otherwise. Thomas Hardy. OBNC

To meet so enabled a Man! (LL) He preached upon "Breadth" till it argued him narrow. Emily Dickinson. AmPP; NAWM-2; NOCV

To meet the fountain of true life I run. Longing. Judah Halevi, *Hebrew.* TrJP, *tr. by* Nina Davis Salaman

To meet the Judgment Day. (LL) The Wants of Man. John Quincy Adams. APN-1; OBAL; PoLF

To Melancholy. Anne Finch, Countess of Winchilsea. WPE

To Men. Anna Wickham. MoBrPo

To Mercy, Pity, Peace and Love. The Divine Image. William Blake. APAD; BoTP; ChAP; FHYEP; NAEL-2; NOBE; NOBRP; NOEC; NoP-4; OAEL-2; OBNC; PeECV; PoE; PoEL-4; Ro *Fr.* Songs of Innocence.

To Mertill Who Desired Her to Speak to Clorinda of His Love. Elizabeth Taylor. KTR

To Mie Tirante. George Darley. Son

To Minerva. Thomas Hood. NBLV; NOBL; OxBoLi; PeLV

To Mira, On the Care of her Infant. Ann Yearsley.
"Mira, as they dear Edward's senses grow." ECWP

To Miss———. Thomas Moore. OxBSP

To Miss A[——]a M[——]a Tra[——]s; an Epistle from Scotland. Charlotte Brereton. ECWP

To Miss B. John Clare. NOBVV

To Miss Charlotte Pulteney in Her Mother's Arms. Ambrose Philips. LiLi; NOEC
(To Charlotte Pulteney.) GTBS-P

To Miss Eleanor Ambrose on the Occasion of Her Wearing an Orange Lily at a Ball in Dublin Castle on July the 12th. Philip Dormer Stanhope. EnLoPo

To Miss Kitty Phillips. Edward Lovibond. ECEV

To Miss L. F. on the Occasion of Her Departure for the Continent. Sir John Collings Squire. BXAP

To Miss Laetitia Van Lewen. Constantia Grierson. ECWP; WPE

To Miss M———, Written by Moonlight, July 18, 1782. Sir Samuel Egerton Brydges. Son

To Miss Ponsonby. Anna Seward. CPO

To mock the riddle corpses round Bapaume. (LL) Blighters. Siegfried Sassoon. CMoP; FaBoTw; MoP; NoAM; OxBSP; PoWW

To Modigliani to Prove to Him That I Am a Poet. Max Jacob, *French.* TrJP, *tr. by* Wallace Fowlie

To Monsieur de la Mothe le Vayer. Molière, *French.* AWP, *tr. by* Austin Dobson

To Morfydd. Lionel Pigot Johnson. MoBrPo; OAEL-2; OBMV

To Morning. William Blake. OxAEP-2

To-Morrow. Félix Lope de Vega Carpio, *Spanish.* AWP, *tr. by* Longfellow

To-morrow. John Masefield. MoBrPo

To-morrow, and to-morrow, and to-morrow. Shakespeare. EBEvV; ImPo *Fr.* Macbeth.
("Hang out our banners on the outward walls.") EBEV; OxAEP-1

To-morrow shall be my dancing day. My Dancing Day. *Unknown.* OxBoLi

To morrow to fresh Woods, and Pastures new. Milton. *See* Lycidas.

To-morrow we're starting for Florence. Arthur Hugh Clough. EBVVPR, canto 2, 15 *Fr.* Amours de Voyage. NOBVV

To morrow you will Live, you always cry. Martial. *See* Procrastination.

To mortal men Peace giveth these good things. Peace on Earth. Bacchylides, *Greek.* AWP, *tr. by* John Addington Symonds

To Mother. Lessie M. Drown. PWR

To Mother. Frank Horne. BPo *Fr.* Letters [*or* Notes] Found near a Suicide. PoBA

To Mother. Keorapetse Kgositsile. GT

To Mother. S. Usha, *Kannada.* OMIP, *tr. by* A. K. Ramanujan

To Mother and Steve. Mari E. Evans. BPo; PoBA

To Mother Fairie. Alice Cary. OBCA

To move over shifting borders. Eeva-Liisa Manner. PBWP *Fr.* Cambrian.

To move with the grace. Ode to Tennis. Paul Evans. NBrP

To Mr. Alexander Ross. James Beattie. OxBS

To Mr. ———, an Unlettered Poet, on Genius Unimproved. Ann Yearsley. NOEC

To Mr. Blanchard, the Celebrated Aeronaut in America. Philip Freneau. APN-1

To Mr. C., St. James's Place, London, October 22nd. Alexander Pope. OxBSP

To Mr. C.B. Donne. ESCV

To Mr. C——ge. Anna Laetitia Barbauld. *See* To Mr. S. T. Coleridge.

To Mr. Cyriack Skinner upon His Blindness. Milton. NOSC; PeECV; Son
(Sonnet.) OxAEP-1

To Mr. Gay, Who Wrote Him a Congratulatory Letter on the Finishing His House. Alexander Pope. NOEC; OBGa

To Mr. George Herbert. Donne. OBVE

To Mr. Gray. Thomas, the Younger Warton. EPCY; Son

To Mr. H. Lawes On His Airs. Milton. AWP; NoP-4
(Sonnet: To Mr. H. Lawes, on His Air[e]s.) NOSC

To Mr. Henry Lawes. Katherine Philips. NoP-4; WPE

To Mr. Henry Lawes, Who Had Then Newly Set a Song of Mine in the Year 1635. Edmund Waller. BeJo; CTC; SeCP

To Mr. Hobbes [*or* Hobs]. Abraham Cowley. BeJo
(Ode to Mr. Hobbes.) OxAEP-1

To Mr I. L ("Blessed [*or* Blesst] are your north parts, for all this long time"). Donne. SeCP

To Mr I. L ("Of that short Roll of friends writ in my heart"). Donne. FP

To Mr. Lawrence. Milton. AWP; GTBS-P; OBEV; PoE
(Sonnet.) NOSC; OxAEP-1

To Mr. Murray. Byron. Son

To Mr. Newton [on His Return from Ramsgate]. William Cowper. NOEC

To Mr Nobody. (LL) Mr Nobody. *Unknown.* CTV; ChAP

To Mr. Pope. Thomas Parnell.
"How flame the glories of Belinda's hair." EPCY

To Mr. Pope, on His Translation of Homer's Iliad. Christopher Pitt.
"'Tis true what famed Pythagoras maintained." EPCY

To Mr. Punchinello. *Unknown.* OxNR
(Mr. Punchinello.) CBNP

To Mr. R. W ("Kindly I envy thy song's [*or* songs] perfection"). Donne. ESCV

To Mr. Roland Woodward ("Like one who in [*or* who'in] her third widowhood [*or* widdowhood] doth profess[e]"). Donne. ESCV

To Mr. S. T. Coleridge. Anna Laetitia Barbauld. CABP; NOEC; NoP-4; Ro; WoRP
(To Mr. C——ge.) ECWP

To Mr Thomas Griffith at the University of Glasgow. Jane Brereton.
"You, friend, who whilom tossed the ball." ECWP

To Mr. Thomson, on His Publishing the Second Edition of His Poem Called Winter. David Mallet.
"Through all thy various *Winter, full are found.*" EPCY

To Mr. Tilman after He Had Taken Orders. Donne. EBEV

To Mr. W. B., at the Birth of His First Child. William Cartwright. BeJo

To Mr. William Long, On His Recovery from a Dangerous Illness, 1785. William Hayley. Son

To Mr. Wren, My Valentine Six Year Old. Jane Holt. ECWP

To Mrs.———, on the Death of Her Husband. Hannah Wallis. ECWP

To Mrs. B. from a Lady Who Had a Desire to See Her. *Unknown.* KTR

To Mrs. Francis-Arabella Kelly. Mary Barber. ECWP

To Mistress [*or* Maystres] Isabell Pennell. John Skelton. AAS; InPS-3; NOBE; NoSic; OBEV; OxBoLi; PoEL-1; SCGP; TTTS *Fr.* The Garland [*or* Garlande *or* Garlands] of Laurel[l].
(In Praise of Isabel Pennell.) CH

To Mrs. K———, On Her Sending Me an English Christmas Plum-Cake at Paris. Helen Maria Williams. WoRP

To Mrs K. T. (Who Asked Him Why He Was Dumb). John Cleveland. CBLP

To Mistress Katherine Bradshaw, the Lovely, That Crowned Him with Laurel. Robert Herrick. CaPo

To Mrs M. A. at Parting. Katherine Philips. CPO; FP

To Mrs. M. A. Upon Absence. Katherine Philips. CBLP; LoP

(Upon Absence.) PBWP

To Mrs. M. B. on Her Birth-Day. Alexander Pope. EnLoPo

To Mrs. Manley. Catherine Trotter. KTR

To Mrs. Manley, upon Her Tragedy Call'd The Royal Mischief. Mary Pix. KTR

To Mistress [or Maystres] Margaret Hussey. John Skelton. AAS; EBEV; EnLoPo; HoPM; InPS-3; NAEL-1; NBLV; NOBE; NoP-4; NTP; NoSic; OAEL-1; OBEV; PeLV; PoE; PoEL-1; PoRA; SCGP; SCV; TFi Fr. The Garland [or Garlande or Garlands] of Laurel[l].

(Mistress Margaret Hussey.) FaBoCh

To Mistress Margery Wentworth. John Skelton. EBEV; EnLoPo; NOBE; OAEL-1; OBEV Fr. The Garland [or Garlande or Garlands] of Laurel[l].

To Mrs. Mary Awbrey. Katherine Philips. See L'Amitie: To Mrs. M. Awbrey.

To Mrs. Norton. Frances Anne Kemble. VWP

To Mrs. Professor in Defense of My Cat's Honor and Not Only. Czeslaw Milosz, Polish. PC, tr. by Robert Hass

To Mrs. Smith, Occasioned by the First of Her Sonnets. William Hayley. Son

To Mrs Thrale [on Her Thirty-fifth Birthday]. Samuel Johnson. FaBoEE

To Mrs. W. on Her Excellent Verses. Aphra Behn. KTR

To Mrs. Will H. Low. Robert Louis Stevenson. NOBVV

To Mt. St. Helens. John Daniel. PaTW

To muddy death. . . . (LL) Ophelia's Death. Shakespeare. OxAEP-1; RB

Τὸ μέλημα τομόν. My Darling. "Michael Field." CPO

To muse on uncle Jim. (LL) Uncle Jim. Countee Cullen. GT; NAAL-2

To Music. Robert Herrick. CaPo

To Music: A Song. Robert Herrick. CaPo

To music bent is my retired mind. Thomas Campion. AAS; NOCV; PeECV

To Music, to Becalm a Sweet-sick Youth. Robert Herrick. CaPo

To Music, to Becalm His Fever. Robert Herrick. BeJo; CaPo; OBEV

To mute and to material things. Nelson, Pitt, Fox. Sir Walter Scott. OBEV Fr. Marmion.

To Mutius. Elizabeth Singer. KTR

To My Antenor, March 16, 1661/2. Katherine Philips. KTR

To My Body. Nancy Sullivan. TAP

To My Book. Ben Jonson. BeJo; FaBoVe; NAEL-1

To My Brother at St. John's College in Cambridge. Elizabeth Tollet. ECWP

To My Brother Hanson. W. S. Merwin. NAAL-2

To My Brother: Killed: Hammont Wood: October, 1918. Louise Bogan. AiP; NYBP

To My Brothers. Keats. Son

To My Cosen Mrs. Ellinor Evins. George Alsop. SCAP

To My Country. Ivan Alekseievich Bunin, Russian. TCRP, tr. by Simon Franklin

To My Country. "Rachel," Hebrew. PBWP, tr. by Diane Mintz

To My Cousin (C.R.) Marrying My Lady (A.). Thomas Carew. SeCP

To My Cousin Mary, for Mending My Tobacco Pouch. Francis Scott Key. OBAL

To My Daughter. Vadim Leonidovich Andreyev, Russian. TCRP, tr. by Belinda Brindle

To My Daughter. N. Balamani Amma, Malayalam. OMIP, tr. by N. Balamani Amma

To My Daughter. Keorapetse Kgositsile. GT

To My Daughter. James Michie. OxBSP

To My Daughter Betty. Thomas Michael Kettle. TIRV

To My Dead Brother. Clara Ann Thompson. CBWP-2

To My Dead Friend Ben: Johnson. Henry King. SeCP

To My Dead Sister. Momcilo Nastasijevic, Serbo-Croatian. HSix, tr. by Charles Simic

To My Dear and Loving Husband. Anne Bradstreet. AmPP; BoWoP; ColAP; HAP; HeIP-4; KTR; LW; NAAL-1; NAAL-3; NIP-4; NOBA; NOCV; NOSC; NoP-4; OxBA; OxBM; OxBSP; OxWW; PEW; PiM; PoE; PoEL-3; PoLF; SAGP; SCAP; TAP; TFi; WPE; WeW-3

To My Dear Children. Anne Bradstreet. NAAL-3

To My Dear Friend Mr Congreve [on His Comedy Called "The Double-Dealer"]. Dryden. EBEV; OAEL-1; OxAEP-1; PoEL-3

To my dear wife. A Last Will and Testament. John Winstanley. FaBoVe; OBSV

To my desk, books, and chair. Jane Kenyon. See Pardon.

To My Distant Beloved. Alois Jeitteles, German. TrJP, tr. by the Reverend Dr. Troutbeck

To My Dog "Blanco." Josiah Gilbert Holland. PoLF

To My Excellent Lucasia, On Our Friendship. Katherine Philips. CPO; LW; MeLP; NALW; NOSC; NoP-4; PBRV; PEW; WPE; WPOW

To My Father. John Berryman. PoPoPo

To My Father. Stewart Conn. FaBoTC

To My Father. W. S. Graham. FaBoTw

To My Father. Henrietta Cordelia Ray. AAP; BlSi; CBWP-3; Son

To My Father Norman Alone in the Blue Mountains. Jack Lindsay. NOBAu

To My Father—2. Diane Di Prima. MoLi

To My Fellow-Mariners, March, '53. Thomas Whitbread. NYBP

To My First White Hairs. Wole Soyinka. OPOU

To my firstborn land, in the south. The Firstborn Land. Ingeborg Bachmann, German. BoWoP, tr. by Daniel Huws

To My Friend. Anne Campbell. PoToHe

To My Friend. Francis Thompson. PoA

To my Friend G.N. from Wrest. Thomas Carew. BeJo; CaPo

To my Friend, Jerina. Lucille Clifton. NMM-2

To My Friend Mrs.—, on Her Holding an Argument in Favour of the Natural Equality of Both the Sexes. Clara Reeve.

"Sacred Heliconian spring, The." ECWP

To My Friends. Stephen Berg. NYBP

To My Friends. Yuly Markovich Daniel, Russian. TCRP, tr. by David Burg and Arthur Boyars

To My Friends. Nikolai Ivanovich Glazkov, Russian. TCRP, tr. by Daniel Weissbort

To my Friends. Primo Levi, Hebrew. FP, tr. by Ruth Feldman and Brian Swann

To My Friends. Johann Christoph Friedrich von Schiller, German. AWP, tr. by James Clarence Mangan

To My Friends, Who Ridiculed a Tender Leave-Taking. Matthew Arnold. EnVR Fr. Switzerland.

To My Generation. Benyamin Galai, Hebrew. TrJP, tr. by Jacob Sonntag

To My God in His Sickness. Philip Levine. NNaP

To My Grandmother, Lady-Woman. Marina Ama Omowale Maxwell. HCP

To My Heavenly Charmer. Martha Sansom. LW

To My Honoured [or Honour'd] Kinsman, John Driden [of Chesterton in the County of Huntingdon, Esquire]. Dryden.

"No porter guards the passage of your door." EBEV

To My Honoured Patron Humphery Davie. Benjamin Tompson. SCAP

To My Husband. "Eliza." KTR; LW; PBRV

To my ill Reader. Martial, Latin. CaPo; OBCVT, tr. by Robert Herrick

To My Ill-Wishers. Nikolai Ivanovich Glazkov, Russian. TCRP, tr. by Daniel Weissbort

To My Inconstant Mistress [or Mistris]. Thomas Carew. BeJo; EnLoPo; GLoP; MeLP; NOBE; SAGP; TFi

(Song.) CaPo; CavPo; GBL; NoP-4; SeCP

To My Infant Daughter. Yvor Winters. VGW

To My Ingenious and Worthy Friend William Lowndes, Esq. John Gay. OBSV

To My Ingenuous Friend, R. W. Henry Vaughan. BeJo

To My Lady. E. S. Miller. Son

To My Lady Morland at Tunbridge. Aphra Behn. CPO

To my Lady Rogers. Martial, Latin. OBCVT, tr. by Sir John Harington

To My Least Favorite Reviewer. Howard Nemerov. OBCoV

To My Lord Colrane, in Answer to His Complemental Verses Sent Me under the Name of Cleanor. Anne Killigrew. KTR

To My Lord Fairfax. Andrew Marvell. FaBoPV; GeHe; NOSC; SeCP Fr. Upon Appleton House

("From that blest bed the hero came.") OBGa

("Or innocently seems to graze.") (LL) OBGa

(Upon Appleton House, to My Lord Fairfax.) OBGa

To My Love. "The Amorous Lady." ECWP

To my love, combing her hair. Yehuda Amichai, Hebrew. PiM, tr. by Chana Bloch and Stephen Mitchell

To My Lucasia, in Defence of Declared Friendship. Katherine Philips. MeLP

To My Lyre. Eliza Cook. VWP

To My Mere English Censurer. Ben Jonson. BeJo

To My Mistress [or Mistris], I Burning in Love. Thomas Carew. SeCP

To My Mistress[e] in My Absence. Thomas Carew. CaPo; NOSC

To My Mistress Sitting by a River's Side; an Eddy. Thomas Carew. BeJo; CaPo

To My More Than Meritorious Wife. John Wilmot, 2d Earl of Rochester. OxBSP

To my most dearly-loved friend Henery Reynolds Esquire, of Poets and Poesie. Michael Drayton. *See* First Steps Up Parnassus.

To My Mother. George Barker. FaBoMo; LiTM; OxAEP-2; OxBTC; PFE; PoWW; SAGP; Son; TwCP

   (Sonnet to My Mother.) ImPo; RaBo

To My Mother. Mary Weston Fordham. CBWP-2

To My Mother. Heinrich Heine, *German.* AWP, *tr. by* Matilda Dickson

   (Sonnet to My Mother, A.) TrJP, *tr. by* Emma Lazarus

To My Mother. Frank O'Hara. FiLi

To My Mother. Edgar Allan Poe. OxBA

To My Mother. Henrietta Cordelia Ray. CBWP-3

To My Mother. Hannah Senesh, *Yiddish.* MDDM, *tr. by* Ruth Finer Mintz

To My Mother—1916. Donald S. Cox. NSI

To My Mountain. Kathleen Jessie Raine. OxBS

To My Much Esteemed Friend on Her Play Call'd Fatal-Friendship. Lady Sarah Piers. KTR

To My Muse. Agnes Mary Frances Robinson. VWP

To My Nephew, J. B. Clement Barksdale. OxBSP

To My Niece, A.M., with a New Pair of Shoes. *Unknown.* ECWP

To My Niece Dorothy, a Sleepless Baby. Dorothy Wordsworth. *See* The Cottager to Her Infant, (By My Sister.)

To My Noble Friend Master William Browne: Of the Evil Time. Michael Drayton. CABP

To My Noble Kinsman, Thomas Stanley, Esquire, on His Lyric Poems Composed by Master John Gamble. Richard Lovelace. CaPo

To My Nose. Alfred A. Forrester. BLPA

To My Old Schoolmaster. John Greenleaf Whittier. ColAP; NOBA

To My Own Face. Caroline Lindsay. VWP

To My Own Heart. Maria Jane Jewsbury. VWP

To My People. Edwin Seaver. TrJP

To my people it's as though he gave them a sacrifice. Eadwacer *Unknown, Anglo-Saxon.* WPE

To my proud foe thus, sister, humblie saye. Dido to Her Sister Anna. Virgil. OBVE, *tr. by* Henry Howard *Fr.* The Aeneid [*or* Eneados, *Aeneis*].

To my revenge and to her desperate fears. The Bubble; a Song. Robert Herrick. CaPo

To My Reverend Dear Brother, M. Samuel Stone. John Cotton. SCAP

To My Rival. "Ephelia." LW

To My Setter, Scout. Frank H. Seldon. BLPA

To My Sister. Olga Fiodorovna Berggolts, *Russian.* BoWoP, *tr. by* Daniel Weissbort

To My Sister. Wordsworth. *See* A Change in the Year.

To My Son. George Barker.

   "My darkling child the stars have obeyed." TwCP

To My Son. Margaret Johnston Grafflin. PoToHe

   (Like Mother, like Son.) BLPA

To My Son. *Unknown.* PoLF

To My Son Parker, Asleep in the Next Room. Bob Kaufman. PoBA; TwCP; VGW

To my trew love and able. *Unknown.* MiEL

To my true king I offered free from stain. A Jacobite's Epitaph. Thomas Babington Macaulay, 1st Baron Macaulay. EBEV; FaPoR; NOBE; NOBVV; OBEV; OBNC; OxAEP-2

To My Truly Valiant, Learned Friend, Who in His Book Resolved the Art Gladiatory into the Mathematics. Richard Lovelace. CaPo; PoEL-3

To my twin who lives in a cruel country. The Dual Site. Michael Hamburger. TwCP

To My Unborn Son. Cyril Morton Thorne. BLPA

To My Valentine. *Unknown.* CTV

To My Venerable Friend, the President of the Royal Academy. Washington Allston. APN-1

To My Wife. James Vincent Cunningham. SAGP; VCAP

To My Wife. Clarence Day. OxBM

To My Wife. John Willis Menard. AAP

To My Worthy and Honoured Friend, Mr George Chapman, on His Translation of Hesiod's *Works and Days.* Ben Jonson. EPCY

To My Worthy Friend Master George Sands [*or* Sandys], on His Translation of the Psalms. Thomas Carew. BeJo; CaPo; EPCY; MeLP

To My Worthy Friend, Mr. James Bayley. Nicholas Noyes. SCAP

To My Worthy Friend Mr. Peter Lely [*or* Lilly]. Richard Lovelace. CaPo; CavPo; GS; NOSC

To My Young Lover. Jane Barker. LW

To My Younger Brother. Tu Fu, *Chinese.*

   "Rumours that you lodge in a mountain temple." PLT, *tr. by* A. C. Graham

To My Youngest Kinsman, R. L. Abraham Chear. OxBChV

To Myra. Greville Fulke. *See* Myra.

To Myself. Abba Kovner, *Hebrew.* AF, *tr. by* Shirley Kaufman

To Myself. Kenneth Slessor. BMAP

To Myself, after Forty Years. Terence Hanbury White. NYBP

To Nature. Coleridge. OAEL-2

To Nature, in her shop one day, at work compounding simples. Filling an Order. John Townsend Trowbridge. OBAL

To Ned. Herman Melville. APN-2; NAAL-1; NAAL-3; NOBA; PAR; PoEL-5

To New York. Léopold Sédar Senghor, *French.* NegPo, *tr. by* Ellen Conroy Kennedy; PBA; PBMAP, *tr. by* Ulli Beier

To Nguyễn Du. Đặng Phu'o'ng, *Vietnamese.* AVP, *tr. by* Huỳnh Sanh Thông

To Night. Thomas Lovell Beddoes. Son

To Night. Shelley. AWP; FHYEP; NAEL-2; OAEL-2; OBNC; PoLF; PoRA; TFi

   (To the Night.) CH; GTBS-P

To Night. Joseph Blanco White. EBEV; GSo; OBEV; OxAEP-2; Son

To night, grave sir, both my poore house, and I. Ben Jonson. *See* Inviting a Friend to Supper.

To-night I do not come to conquer thee. Anguish. Stéphane Mallarmé, *French.* AWP, *tr. by* Arthur Symons

To-night I saw three maidens on the beach. Ibant Obscuræ. Thomas Edward Brown. OBNC

To-night is a midnight meeting, and the Earl is in the chair. George R. Sims. UV *Fr.* Two Women.

To-night retir'd the queen of heaven. To the Evening Star. Mark Akenside. OBEV; PoEL-3

To Night, the Mother of Sleep and Death. John Addington Symonds. Son

To-night the very horses springing by. Winter Evening. Archibald Lampman. NOBC

To-night the Winds Begin. Tennyson. EBVV; GTBS-P; ImPo; NOBE; OAEL-2; OBNC; PeECV; PoEL-5 *Fr.* In Memoriam A. H. H.

To-night there is no watch upon the Rhine. Claudian *See* For France.

To Nobodaddy. William Blake. OAEL-2

To Noel. Gabriela Mistral, *Spanish.* PChr, *tr. by* Doris Dana

To nothing fitter can I Thee compare. Michael Drayton. PBRV; SCGP; Son *Fr.* Idea.

To Nysus. Sir Charles Sedley. FaBoEE; OBSV

To O.E.A E. A. Claude McKay. BPo; GT

To Odelia. James Shirley. BeJo

To Oenone ("Thou saist [*or* sayest] Love[']s dart"). Robert Herrick. CaPo

To Oenone ("What conscience, say, is it in thee"). Robert Herrick. OBEV

To Old Age. Walt Whitman. Spl

To Olive. Lord Alfred Bruce Douglas. OBEV

To Olivia. Francis Thompson. MoBrPo

To One Black, and Not Very Handsome, Who Expected Commendation. Edward Herbert, 1st Baron Herbert of Cherbury. NOSC

To One Elect. Samuel Ichiye Hayakawa. PoA

To one fair Lady out of Court. The Challenge: A Court Ballad. Alexander Pope. PoEL-3

To One in Bedlam. Ernest Christopher Dowson. GSo; MoBrPo; OBMV; Son

To one in love with solitude and song. (LL) Echoes. Emma Lazarus. APN-2; GSo; PAR

To One in Paradise. Edgar Allan Poe. AmPP; BoLoP; GLoP; NCAP; OBEV; OxBA; PoLF; TAP

To one it is a piece of ground. What is a Garden? Reginald Arkell. OBGa

To one kneeling down no word came. In a Country Church. Ronald Stuart Thomas. FaBoMo; TOF

To One Married to an Old Man. Edmund Waller. FaBoEE; OxBSP; SeCP

To One Persuading a Lady to Marriage. Katherine Philips. *See* An Answer to Another Persuading a Lady to Marriage.

To one pure image of regret. (LL) We leave the well-beloved place. Tennyson. EBVV; FHYEP; PoEL-5

To One That Asked Me Why I Loved J.G G. "Ephelia." KTR; LW; NOSC; PEW

To One That Desired to Know My Mistress [*or* Mistris]. Thomas Carew. SeCP

To One that Painted Eccho. Ausonius, *Latin.* OBCVT, *tr. by* George Turberville

To one that persuades me to leave the Muses. Elizabeth Singer Rowe.

   "Forgo the charming Muses! No, in spite." PEW

To One Unequally Matched. Walter Savage Landor. CBLP

To One Who Had Censured His Public Exposition of Dante. Giovanni Boccaccio. AWP *Fr.* Sonnets.

To one who has been long in city pent. Keats. BLPA; FHYEP; FaBoBe; ImPo

To One Who Quotes and Detracts. Walter Savage Landor. FaBoEE

To One Who Said I Must Not Love. Sarah Fyge Egerton. ECWP

To One Who Sleepeth. Mary E. Tucker. CBWP-1

To One Who Waits. Katharine Lee Bates. CPO

To One Who Was with Me in the War. Siegfried Sassoon. NSI

To One Who Would Make a Confession. Wilfrid Scawen Blunt. GSo

To open himself, to *be* / the flames? (LL) Another Night in the Ruins. Galway Kinnell. AF; CoAP

To Orestes. Elizabeth Singer Rowe. PEW

To Osbert Sitwell. Cyril Connolly. OBCoV

To other eyes and ears you are a great. Bernard O'Dowd. CBAP *Fr.* The Bush.

To others / Only heaven. (LL) Luck. Langston Hughes. PiM; SAmP

To our baby that died. Yosano Tekkan, *Japanese*. MJT, *tr.* by Makoto Ueda

To Our Blessed Lady. Henry Constable. NoSic

To Our Blessed Lord upon the Choice of His Sepulchre. Richard Crashaw. GeHe; NOSC

(Upon Our Saviour's Tomb[e] Wherein Never Man Was Laid.) ChIV-2; OAEL-1

To Our Daughter. Jennifer Armitage. BrRo

To our homes, to our labours. We Must Return. Agostinho Neto, *Portuguese*. PeSAV, *tr.* by Michael Wolfers

To Our House-Dog Captain. Walter Savage Landor. PoEL-4

To our house in the street down town. (LL) Samuel Brown. Phoebe Cary. APN-2; OBAL

To Our Lord, upon the Water Made Wine. Richard Crashaw. GeHe

To our mother, maimed. American Rain. Marilyn Chin. OpBo

To our theme. The man who has stood on the Acropolis. Byron. InPS-3; OBSV *Fr.* Canto the Eleventh. NOBRP *Fr.* Don Juan.

To own nothing, but to be. Words Spoken Alone. Dannie Abse. NYBP

To Oxford. Thomas Russell. Son

To P. J. (2 Yrs Old Who Sed Write a Poem for Me in Portland, Oregon). Sonia Sanchez. MBE

(To P. J.) CA; NOxBChV

To Paint a Water Lily. Ted Hughes. CABP

To paint the summer morning. (LL) London's Summer Morning. Mary Robinson. ECWP; WoRP

To Pallas, Theris, cunning of hand, dedicated. Leonidas of Tarentum. HePo, *tr.* by Barbara Hughes Fowler *Fr.* Epigrams.

To Pallas, three girls, all of an age, skilled as the spider. Antipater of Sidon. HePo, *tr.* by Barbara Hughes Fowler *Fr.* Epigrams.

To Pan. John Fletcher. *See* The God of Sheep.

To Pan the forest-ranger, Gelo the hunter. Philip of Thessalonica, *Greek*. GrAn, *tr.* by Edwin Morgan

To Pan three brothers hung up these tools of the trade. Antipater of Sidon. HePo, *tr.* by Barbara Hughes Fowler *Fr.* Epigrams.

To Pandora. Alexander Craig. Son

To Paradise. Sylvia Plath. *See* Fever 103°.

To Paris that was once her owne though now it be not so. Ovid. OBVE, *tr.* by George Turberville *Fr.* Heroides.

To part no more forever. (LL) Still was the night, serene and bright. Michael Wigglesworth. NAAL-3

To pass all men's believing. (LL) An Immorality. Ezra Pound. CMoP; ImPo; LiTM; MoAmPo; NOBA; OBAL

To pass the hours away. (LL) Cows. James Reeves. NOxBChV

To Peace. Richard Watson Dixon. OxAEP-2

To peer into the obverse. The Psychotropic Squalls. Will Alexander. PT

To Penelope, January 2, 1821. Byron. FaBoEE

To penetrate, in the outskirts, through dark doorways. Outskirts, Afternoon. Judit Tóth, *Hungarian*. CEEP, *tr.* by Emery E. George

To Penshurst. Ben Jonson, *after the Latin of* Martial. AWP; BeJo; CABP; NOSC; NoP-4; OAEL-1; PBRV; PoEL-2; SeCP; TFi

"There's none, that dwell about them, wish them downe." OBCVT, *tr.* by Ben Jonson

To Percy Shelley. Leigh Hunt. Ro; Son

To Perilla. Robert Herrick. BeJo; CaPo; NOSC; SCGP; SeCP

To perish—of Delight. (LL) It might be lonelier. Emily Dickinson. APN-2; SAmP

To perish, or to live? (LL) 'Twas like a Maelstrom, with a notch. Emily Dickinson. APN-2; CMoP; LiTM; NCAP; PoE

To Persia's plains or Britain's sea. (LL) Odes 1.21: To Apollo and Diana ("Dianam tenerae dicite virgines"). Horace. OBVE, *tr.* by Branwell Brontë

To Pertinax Cob. Ben Jonson. BeJo

To Pete Atkin: A Letter from Paris. Clive James.

"Weather's cleared, The. We're filming at Versailles." OBSV

To Peter, Bishop of Poitiers, Who Withstood William of Aquitaine and Died in Exile. Hildebert, *Latin*. MLL, *tr.* by Helen Waddell

To Petronius Arbiter. Oliver St. John Gogarty. OBMV

To Phaedrus. Jovan Hristic, *Serbo-Croatian*. HSix, *tr.* by Charles Simic

To Philaster. Sarah Fyge Egerton. ECWP

To Phillis. Edmund Waller. SeCP

To Philomela. Benjamin Colman. SCAP

To Phryne. Owen Felltham [*or* Feltham]. NOSC

To Phyllis. Edmund Waller. BeJo

To Phyllis to Love and Live with Him. Robert Herrick. CaPo

To Phylocles, Inviting Him to Friendship. "Ephelia." KTR; NOSC; WPE

To Pi Ssu Yao. Tu Fu, *Chinese*. BLT; OHPC, *tr.* by Kenneth Rexroth

To pile like Thunder to its close. Emily Dickinson. APN-2; NCAP

To Piso, on Epicurus' Birthday. Philodemus, *Greek*. GrAn, *tr.* by William Moebius

To plant three roses for you each one only a dollar. Third Ode to Persephone. Robert Kelly. *Fr.* The Book of Persephone. PoM

To play the school games with the others. (LL) The Picnic. John Logan. CoAmPo

To play with fools, O what a fool was I! (LL) If women could be fair, and yet not fond. Edward De Vere. GTBS-P; NoSic

To Poet Edmund Waller, Occasioned for His Writing a Panegyric on Oliver Cromwell. Charles Cotton. EPCY

To Poets. George Darley. Son

To Poets. Walter Savage Landor. FaBoEE

To point a moral, or adorn a tale. (LL) Charles XII of Sweden. Samuel Johnson. NOBE; OBWP

To poll their tops that seek such change and gape for joy. (LL) Doubt of future foes exiles my present joy, The. Elizabeth I, Queen of England. CTC; NAEL-1; NALW; NoSic; PBWP; WPE

To popularize the mule, its neat exterior. The Labors of Hercules. Marianne Moore. MeMAP; OxBA

To Posthumus. Horace, *Latin*. OBCVT, *tr.* by Anna Seward

To practice for Eternity. (LL) Bearded Oaks. Robert Penn Warren. ColAP; FuPo; LiTM; MoAmPo; MoP; NAAL-2; NOBA; NoAM; NoP-4; PoA; PoE; TAP; TwCP

To Praise. Ellen Bass. CrSp

To praise the blue whale's crystal jet. The Whale, His Bulwark. Derek Walcott. OxBC; TTY

To praise thy life[,] or wail[e] thy worthy [*or* woorthie] death. Epitaph on Sir Philip Sidney. Sir Walter Ralegh. SiPS

To pray for the impossible. Of Itzig and His Dog. Dannie Abse. EC2

To pray you open your whole self. Eagle Poem. Joy Harjo. CrSp; HATNAP; WeT; WeW-3

To President Bush at the Start of the Gulf War. Robert Bly. RaBo

To prevent surprise destruction an undisclosed. Warhead Wakes. Ivor Armstrong Richards. PFE

To Priapos. *Unknown*, *Greek*. GrAn, *tr.* by Guy Davenport

To prink me up and make me higher placed. George Gascoigne. AAS; Son *Fr.* Gascoigne's Memories.

To print, or not to print—that is the question. Hamlet's Soliloquy Imitated. Richard Jago. BXAP

To print our poems the propulsive cause. Fame Makes Us Forward. Robert Herrick. CaPo

To Professor Byrd Prillerman. Maggie Pogue Johnson. CBWP-4

To profit so by Eden's blame. (LL) The Tribute. Coventry Patmore. EBEV; OBNC

To Prote. Simmias of Thebes, *Greek*. AWP, *tr.* by John Addington Symonds

To prove himself no plagiary, Moore. On J. M. S. Gent. Alexander Pope. FaBoEE

To prove that we're still here. (LL) A Dance For Ma Rainey. Al Young. NAAAL; UnSA

To pull the metal splinter from my palm. The Gift. Li-Young Lee. LoL; OpBo; RaBo; UnSA

To pull yourself up by your own roots; to eat the last meal in / your old neighborhood. (LL) Whatever it was: the grains of the glacier caked in the boot-cleats. Adrienne Rich. FaBoWP; HCAP

To Purity and Truth. *Unknown*, *Chinese*. TrJP, *tr.* by William C. White

To push my boat into the river. (LL) At the Gates. Kofi Awoonor. PBMAP; VCWP

To put off a decision. No Easy Harbour. Anne Hartigan. CIP-2

To put on shoes and be sophisticated. Ode to Language. Robert Kelly. SeSe

To put out the word, whore, thou dost me woo. To a Friend. Ben Jonson. BeJo

To Pyrrha. Horace. *See* Odes 1.5.

To Queen Elizabeth. Sir John Davies. *Fr.* Nosce Teipsum. NoSic; SiPS

To Queen Elizabeth. Mary Sidney Herbert, Countess of Pembroke. *See* To the Thrice-Sacred Queen Elizabeth.

To R. B. Gerard Manley Hopkins. CMoP; EPCY; EnVR; GTBS-P; OAEL-2; OxAEP-2

To R. Hudson. Alexander Montgomerie. OxBS

To R. K. James Kenneth Stephen. BXAP; FaBoEE; NBLV; NOBL; PeLV; UV

To rail or jest, ye know I use it not. Sir Thomas Wyatt. SiPS

To Raja Rao. Czeslaw Milosz. TOF

To range, deep-wrapt, along a heavenly height. To Bayard Taylor. Sidney Lanier. NCAP

To reach in self-defense for wigs, / Lipstick, / Sequins. (LL) The Supremes. Cornelius Eady. CMAP

To reach it. Waterfall. Anne Welsh. PeSA

To read it well: that is, to understand. (LL) To the Reader ("Pray thee, take care, that tak'st my book[e] in hand"). Ben Jonson. BeJo; NoP-4; PoE

To read my book[e], the virgin shy [or shie]. To His Book[e]. Martial, *Latin.* AWP; OBVE, *tr. by* Robert Herrick

To read on the steel-mirror of her smile. (LL) She issues radiant from her dressing-room. George Meredith. EnVR; NOBVV

To read our few poets. Ode. Hugh Maxton. PBCIP

To Redouté. John Ashbery. PoA

To Remain. Constantine P. Cavafy, *Modern Greek.* BoLoP, *tr. by* Nikos Stangos *and* Stephen Spender

To remember is not always to go back to what was. Time Reminded Me. Julia Uceda, *Spanish.* BoWoP, *tr. by* Willis Barnstone

To reply, in face of a bad season. The Ill Wind. Jay Macpherson. MoCV

To rest at noon, pale and absorbed. Eugenio Montale. ItIP

To rest my tiny back. *Unknown. See* The Squirrel.

To Restore a Dead Child. Edwin Honig.

1925. NoAM

To Retiredness. Mildmay Fane, 2d Earl of Westmorland. BeJo; NOSC

To Retirement. Luís De León, *Spanish.* TrJP, *tr. by* Thomas Walsh

To Rev. Thaddeus Saltus. Mary Weston Fordham. CBWP-2

To Rhea. Ralph Waldo Emerson. APN-1

To Richard Wagner. Sidney Lanier. APN-2; NCAP *Fr.* Street Cries.

To Richard Wright. Conrad Kent Rivers. PoBA

To riddle me that. (LL) Riddle: "The Land was white." *Unknown.* FaBoVe; OxNR

To Ride. Paul Éluard, *French.* TTTS, *tr. by* Kenneth Koch

To ride piggy-back. Slave. Langston Hughes. LiTM

To rise. Everyday History. Sandor Csoori, *Hungarian.* VCWP, *tr. by* Len Roberts

To roam the universe in length and breadth! A Hero's Will. Nguyễn Công Trú', *Vietnamese.* AVP, *tr. by* Huỳnh Sanh Thông

To Robbers furious, and to Lovers tame. Samuel Johnson, *after the Latin of* Joachim du Bellay. FaBoEE

To Robert Browning. Walter Savage Landor. EPCY; NoP-4

To Robert Fergusson. Robert Garioch. FaBoTC

To Robert Louis Stevenson. William Ernest Henley. MoBrPo

To Robert Nichols. Robert Graves. PeFWW

To Robin Redbreast. Robert Herrick. PoE

To Robinson Jeffers. Czeslaw Milosz, *Polish.* EC3, *tr. by* Czeslaw Milosz *and* Richard Lourie; PaTW

To Roosevelt. "Rubén Dario," *Spanish.* PFTM, *tr. by* Lysander Kemp

To Rosamounde. Chaucer. CBLP; EnVB; OAEL-1; PoE

(To Rosamond.) NoP-4

To Roses in the Bosom[e] of Castara. William Habington. BeJo; EnLoPo; MeLP; NOSC; OBEV; SCGP; SeCP *Fr.* Castara.

To Rufus. Catullus. *See* Carmen 69 ("That no fair woman will, wonder not why").

To run a night's distance, distances by night, nothing's easier than traveling distances. Amir Gilbo'a, *Hebrew.* IP, *tr. by* Warren Bargad *and* Stanley F. Chyet

To Russia. Vladimir Nabokov, *Russian.* TCRP, *tr. by* Vladimir Nabokov

To S.C. Robert Louis Stevenson. PeVV

To S. M., a Young African Painter, on Seeing His Works. Phillis Wheatley. BlSi; ColAP; NAAAL; NAAL-1; NAAL-3; NoP-4

To S. R. Crockett. Robert Louis Stevenson. EBVV; NOBE; OBNC; SCGP

To S. T. C. on His 179th Birthday, October 12th, 1951. Maurice Carpenter. FaBoTw

To S.V. György Petri, *Hungarian.* VCWP, *tr. by* Wilmer, Clive and George Gömöri

To safeguard man from wrongs, there nothing must. Distrust. Robert Herrick. CaPo

To Saint Margaret. Henry Constable. NoSic

To Saint Mary Magdalen ("Blessed offender [or offendour], who thyself hast [or haist] tried [or try'd]"). Henry Constable. NoSic; PoEL-2

To Saint Mary Magdalen ("Such as, retired from sight"). Henry Constable. Son

To St Mary Magdalen ("Sweete Saynt: Thow better"). Henry Constable. PBRV

To Sallie, Walking. Sterling Brown. GT

To Sally. John Quincy Adams. APN-1; AWP; OBAL

To Sally. Horace. *See* Odes 1.22.

To Samuel, Bishop of Sens In Time of Dearth. Alcuin, *Latin.* MLL, *tr. by* Helen Waddell

To Satch. Samuel Allen. ISC; PoBA; TTY

("Sometimes I feel I will *never* stop.") ISC

To save lives. (LL) Conception. Josephine Miles. APAD; ColAP

To save the [or th'] *Athenian* walls from ruin bare. (LL) When the Assault Was Intended to the City. Milton. GTBS-P; OAEL-1; OxAEP-1; SCGP; Son

To Saxham. Thomas Carew. BeJo; CaPo; CavPo

To say it once held daisies and bluebells. The Broken Bowl. James Merrill. PoA

To say the thing and having said it. Quartet. Charles Borkhuis. PT

To scare myself with my own desert places. (LL) Desert Places. Robert Frost. AFr; AmPP; CMoP; InPK-6; MoAmPo; MoP; NAAL-2; NOBA; NoAM; OxBA; PFE; PoE; RB; SoSe-8; TAP; TRP; UnPo

To School! Stevie Smith. FaBoEE

To Science. Edgar Allan Poe. *See* Sonnet—To Science.

To Scilla. Sir Charles Sedley. FaBoEE

To Scott. Winifred M. Letts. PoLF

To scug his deadly sin. (LL) Young Benjie. *Unknown.* ESPB; OxBB

To sea. Sailors' Song. Thomas Lovell Beddoes. CH; OxAEP-2 *Fr.* Death's Jest Book.

To Secretary Lu Ch'ien of Jen City. Li Po, *Chinese.* SuSp, *tr. by* Joseph J. Lee

To see a strange [or quaint] outlandish fowl. The Bounty of Our Age. Henry Farley. FaBoCh; FaBoEE; NOSC

To see a World in a Grain of Sand. Auguries of Innocence. William Blake. EBEV; FaBoCh; FaPoR; ImPo; OAEL-1; OBNC; OxAEP-2; OxBoLi; PeECV; PoEL-4; TFi

To see a World in a Grain of Sand. William Blake. EnlH; InPK-6; NTP, *ll.* 1–4 *Fr.* Auguries of Innocence. EBEV; FaBoCh; FaPoR; ImPo; OAEL-1; OBNC; OxAEP-2; OxBoLi; PeECV; PoEL-4; TFi

To see both blended in one flood. Upon the Infant Martyrs. Richard Crashaw. GeHe; NoP-4; OAEL-1

To see her is a Picture. Emily Dickinson. CPO

To see herself tonight. (LL) A Brown Girl Dead. Countee Cullen. GT; TAP

To See Long like El Greco. Yona Wallach, *Hebrew.* IP, *tr. by* Warren Bargad *and* Stanley F. Chyet

To see my father. Golden State. Frank Bidart. NoAM

To See Ol' Booker T. Maggie Pogue Johnson. CBWP-4

To see such dainty ghosts as you appear. On Meeting a Gentlewoman in the Dark. *Unknown.* FaBoEE

To see that fair lady. (LL) Edom o' Gordon. *Unknown.* ESPB; OxBB

To see that joyful day. George Gascoigne. *See* Gascoigne's Good-Morrow.

To see the abysses of the human heart. (LL) The Heart's Abysses. Walter Savage Landor. FaBoEE; OBSV

To see the cherry hung with snow. (LL) Loveliest of trees, the cherry now. A. E. Housman. AWP; ChaP; ClHu; EBEvV; FaBoBe; HAP; ImPo; InPK-6; LiTM; MoBrPo; MoP; NTP; NoAM; NoP-4; OAEL-2; OxBTC; PFE; PoE; PoLF; PoPoPo; Poetr; RB; SCGP; SoSe-8; TFi; WeW-3

To See the Cross at Christmas. Roger Cooper. TrCP

To see the land I love. (LL) Night Journey. Theodore Roethke. GM; KaS; NYBP; SAGP

To see the lark, delighted, dare. Bernard de Ventadour, *French.* STV, *tr. by* John Frederick Nims

To see them coming headstrong. In Love with the Bears. Greg Kuzma. NYBP

To see them go by drowning in the river. Eli, Eli. Judith Wright. BMAP; CBAP; GI

To see them so: fleshed, fair, erected indivisible. (LL) The Imaginary Iceberg. Elizabeth Bishop. FaBoWP; ImPo; LiTM; MoAmPo; PFE

To see these lines writ for his epitaph. (LL) Nonsense [or Nonsense]. Richard Corbet. CBNP; FaBoVe

To see what my black hen doth lay. (LL) The Black Hen. Mother Goose. LB; ReMoGo

To see what my black hen doth lay. (LL) Hickety, pickety, my black hen. Mother Goose. CTAV; FaBoBe; OxNR

To see you, as before the drink or food. (LL) So small are the flowers of Seamu. *Unknown, Egyptian hieroglyphics into Italian.* BoWoP; PBWP, *tr. by* Boris de Rachewiltz; *English vers. by* Ezra Pound *and* Noel Stock

To see you living and the fountains run. (LL) Napoli Again. Richard Hugo. AF; LCAP-2

To seek each where where man doth live. Sir Thomas Wyatt. SiPS

To seek new lechery in Death. (LL) An Epitaph on M. H. Charles Cotton. EBEV; FaBoEE

To seem the stranger lies my lot, my life. Gerard Manley Hopkins. EnVR

To Senaca Lake. James Gates Percival. BoTP

To Send Away Melancholy. Huang Tsun-hsien, *Chinese.* SuSp, *tr. by* An-yan Tang

To send me forth on a new morning, a new man. (LL) Shadows. D. H. Lawrence. LBC; OxBTC

To Send to Li Tan and Yüan Hsi. Wei Ying-wu, *Chinese.* CoBCP, *tr. by* Burton Watson

To Senna Hoy. Else Lasker-Schüler, *German.* IMW, *tr. by* Glauco Cambon

To Sergius. Sir Charles Sedley. FaBoEE

To serve her God, her Neighbour, and her Friends. (LL) A Virgin Life. Jane Barker. BWW; KTR

To serve to trust to fear. (LL) Her [*or* hir] face her [*or* hir] tongue [*or* tong] her [*or* hir] wit. Sir Arthur Gorges. LoP

To set before the king? (LL) Sing a song of sixpence. Mother Goose. FaBoBe; OxNR

To set the face, and make the heart a stone. (LL) The Unpardonable Sin. Vachel Lindsay. CMoP; ChIV-2; MeMAP

To set things right? (LL) The Earnest Liberal's Lament. Ernest Hemingway. OBAL; OBSV

To Seumas Macdonald. Chinese Poem. Iain Crichton Smith. FaBoTC

To Sextus. Martial, *Latin.* FaBoEE, *tr. by* Sir Charles Sedley

To shade and fiber, milk and memory. (LL) Lost in Translation. James Merrill. FYAP; HCAP; LCAP-2; NAAL-2; NoAM; NoP-4; VCAP

To shadows and delusions here. (LL) The Indian Burying Ground. Philip Freneau. AmPP; ColAP; HAP; NAAL-1; NAAL-3; NOBA; NoP-4; OxBA; PoEL-4; PoLF; TAP; TFi

To shaggy Pan, and all the Wood-Nymphs fair. A Shepherd's Gift. Anyte, *Greek.* AWP, *tr. by* John William Burgon

To Shakespeare. Hartley Coleridge. EPCY

To Shakespeare. Hart Crane. Son

To Shakespeare. Thomas Edwards. Son

To Shakespeare. Frances Anne Kemble. Son

To shave, or not to shave? that is the question. T. F. Dillon Crocker. BXAP

To shock-haired Pan and the nymphs who protect the cow-byres. Anyte, *Greek.* GrAn, *tr. by* John Heath-Stubbs *and* Carol A. Whiteside

To shoot, to shoot, would be my delight. A Shooting Song. William Brighty Rands. OxBChV

To shove this chair away from here. To Sit, to Stand, to Kill, to Die. Attila József, *Hungarian.* AF, *tr. by* John Batki

To Show How Humble. *Unknown.* AH

To Show My Sons. Lu Yu, *Chinese.* CoBCP, *tr. by* Burton Watson

(To Show to My Sons.) CoBCP, *tr. by* Burton Watson

To show the laboring [*or* lab'ring] bosom's deep intent. To S. M., a Young African Painter, on Seeing His Works. Phillis Wheatley. BlSi; NAAL-1; NAAL-3

To show thy little lamp: go forth, go forth! (LL) To the White Fiends. Claude McKay. NAAAL

To Show to My Sons. Lu Yu. *See* To Show My Sons.

To shred them: a narrow labor, and simply toss. Destruction of Letters. Babette Deutsch. WPE

To shun the heaven that leads men to this hell! (LL) Sonnet 129. Shakespeare. APAD; AWP; EBEV; GBL; HAP; HeIP-4; ImPo; InPS-3; NAEL-1; NIP-4; NOBE; NoSic; OAEL-1; OBEV; OxAEP-1; PBRV; PFE; PoE; PoEL-2; PoPoPo; Poetr; SCGP; SCV; Son; TFi; UnPo

To Sickness. Ben Jonson. BeJo

To Sidmouth and Castlereagh. Shelley. *See* Similes for Two Political Characters of 1819.

To Silence. Thomas Lovell Beddoes. Son

To Silence. Alice Thompson Meynell. VWP

To Simplicity. Coleridge. *Fr.* Sonnets Attempted in the Manner of Contemporary Writers. Son

To simulate the burning of the heart, the humiliation. Patrizia Cavalli, *Italian.* Nelt; VCWP, *tr. by* Judith Baumel

To sin, unshamed, to lose, unthinking. Russia. Aleksandr Blok, *Russian.* AWP, *tr. by* Babette Deutsch *and* Avrahm Yarmolinsky

To sing of wars, of captain[e]s, and of kings. The Prologue. Anne Bradstreet. BoWoP; NAAL-1; NAAL-3; NALW; NOBA; OxBA; PoE; SCAP; TAP; WPE

To sing you / one song. Pruzzian Elegy. Johannes Bobrowski, *German.* AF, *tr. by* Matthew Mead

To sin's a vice in nature, and we find. Daniel Defoe. OBSV *Fr.* More Reformation.

To Sir Francis Brian. Sir Thomas Wyatt. SiPS *Fr.* Satires.

To Sir H. W. at His Going Ambassador to Venice. Donne. MeLP

To Sir Henry Cary. Ben Jonson. NOSC; NoP-4

To Sir Henry Goodyere. Ben Jonson. NOSC

To Sir Henry Newton, upon His Re-edifying the Church of Charleton in Kent. Thomas Philipott. NOSC

To Sir Henry Vane the Younger. Milton. PBRV; Son

To Sir Henry Wotton ("Here's no more news, than virtue, I may as well"). Donne. OxAEP-1

To Sir Henry Wotton ("Sir, more than kisses, letters mingle souls"). Donne. NoSic

To Sir Horace Vere. Ben Jonson. BeJo

To Sir Hudson Lowe. Thomas Moore. OBSV

To Sir Humphry Mackworth. Thomas Yalden.

"Miner thus through perils digs his way, The." ECEV

To Sir John Wentworth, Upon His Curiosities and Courteous Entertainment at Summerly in Lovingland. Mildmay Fane. OBGa

To Sir Philip Sidney's Soul. Henry Constable. *See* On the Death of Sir Philip Sidney.

To Sir Richard Fanshawe, Upon His Translation of Pastor Fido. Sir John Denham.

"That servile path thou nobly dost decline." EPCY

To Sir Robert Wroth. Ben Jonson. BeJo

To Sir Toby. Philip Freneau. NAAL-1; NAAL-3; NoP-4; TAP

To Sir W. A. William Drummond, of Hawthornden. PoEL-2

To sit composing like a sunlit ghost. The Table. Michael Heffernan. PoA

To sit on the moon. (LL) The Witches' Ride. Karla Kuskin. NOxBChV

To sit on the veranda of a hotel in Jerusalem. Letter. Yehuda Amichai, *Hebrew.* VCWP, *tr. by* Ted Hughes *and* Yehuda Amichai

To sit people on gas-stove jets. The Mother-in-Law of the Marquis de Sade. Jennifer Maiden. NOBAu

To sit silent. Otomo no Tabito, *Japanese.* TAL, *tr. by* Arthur Waley

To Sit, to Stand, to Kill, to Die. Attila József, *Hungarian.* AF, *tr. by* John Batki

To sit upon her belly warm. Jack Frost. Fay Zwicky. BMAP

To slay the people's foe and wreak revenge. Homage to the Tru'ng queens. *Unknown, Vietnamese.* AVP, *tr. by* Huỳnh Sanh Thông

To Sleep. Giovanni Della Casa, *Italian.* AWP, *tr. by* John Addington Symonds

To Sleep. Lord Alfred Bruce Douglas. GSo

To Sleep. John Fletcher. *See* Sleep Song.

To Sleep. Keats. EBEvV; LaPo; NIP-4; OBEV; PoEL-4; Son

(Sonnet to Sleep.) NAEL-2

To Sleep. Charlotte Smith. Son; WPE

To Sleep ("Flock of sheep that leisurely pass by, A"). Wordsworth. GTBS-P

To Sleep ("Fond words have oft been spoken to thee, sleep!"). Wordsworth. Son

To Sleep ("O gentle Sleep! do they belong to thee"). Wordsworth. Son

To sleep easy all night. *Unknown.* OxNR

To sleep easy at night. Mother Goose. CTV

To sleep here, I play dead. Ia Drang Valley. Yusef Komunyakaa. MT

To Sleep I give my powers away. Tennyson. EnVR *Fr.* In Memoriam A. H. H.

To sniff at a green plum. (LL) Tune: Crimson Lips Adorned. Li Ch'ing-chao, *Chinese.* PBWP, *tr. by* C. H. Kwock *and* Vincent McHugh; BoWoP, *tr. by* Kenneth Rexroth *and* Ling Chung

Tō So-kin of Rakuyō, ancient friend, Chancellor of Gen. Exile's Letter. Li Po, *Chinese.* CTC; FaBoMo; OxBA, *tr. by* Ezra Pound

To Softness. Laurie Sheck. CrSp

To Solitude. Alice Cary. APN-2

To Some Millions Who Survive Joseph E. Mander, Sr. Sarah E. Wright. PoBA

To Some Students Caught Nodding in Class. Nguyễn Khuyến, *Vietnamese.* AVP, *tr. by* Huỳnh Sanh Thông

To Some Supposed Brothers. Essex Hemphill. GLP

(XXI.) NAAAL

To Some Young Communists from an Older Socialist. Naomi Mitchison. WPN

To Someone Who Insisted I Look up Someone. X. J. Kennedy. OBCoV

To Somes / from incarceration, Taunton State Hospital, 1972. Children of the Working Class. BB

To Song. Olga Fiodorovna Berggolts, *Russian.* BoWoP, *tr. by* Daniel Weissbort

To Soulfolk. Margaret Goss Burroughs. BlSi

To spare my sack of coals. (LL) Winter. John Millington Synge. NOIV; OBMV; OxBTC

To speak in a flat voice. Speak. James Wright. HAP; NoP-4; TAP

To speak in summer in a lecture hall. Lecture Hall. Patrick Kavanagh. FaBoTw

To speak of my influences. Jean Garrigue. LW

To Speak of Woe That Is in Marriage. Robert Lowell. MoP; NAAL-2; NoAM

To speak out clean. Telling It. Nancy Sullivan. TAP

To speak the truth, although believed too late. (LL) Upon the Saying That My Verses Were Made by Another. Anne Killigrew. PEW

To Spencer. George Turberville. NoSic

To spend uncounted years of pain. Arthur Hugh Clough. EnVR; NOBVV; OBNC; OxBSP

To Spenser. John Hamilton Reynolds. Son

To spider in our dirt-filled eyes. (LL) Osip Mandelstam. Seamus Deane. BiHa; PBCIP

To split my worship too in twain. (LL) On Stella's Birthday, 1718/1719. Jonathan Swift. CBLP; EnLoPo; IIP; InPK-6; NIP-4; NOIV; OAEL-1

To spoil the first impression. (LL) To His Saviour, a Child; a Present, by a Child. Robert Herrick. BeJo; ChIV-2; OxBChV; PeECV; SeCP; TrCP

To Spring. William Blake. BoTP; NAEL-2; NOEC; OAEL-2; OBEV; PoEL-4; PoLF; SCGP

To Spring. Charlotte Smith. BWW; WPE

To St. Augustine. "Angelus Silesius." GePo, tr. by George C. Schoolfield Fr. The Cherubical Wanderer.

To St John Baptist. Henry Constable. ChIV-2; NoSic

To St Mary Magdalen. Henry Constable. ChIV-2; NoSic

To St. Michael the Archangel. Henry Constable. ChIV-2

To St. Peter and St. Paul. Henry Constable. NoSic; Son

To stain the stiff dishonoured shroud. (LL) Sweeney Among the Nightingales. T. S. Eliot. AmPP; CMoP; FaBoMo; HAP; HeIP-4; LiTM; MoP; NAAL-2; NAEL-2; NOBA; NOBE; NoAM; NoP-4; OBMV; OxBA; PoPoPo; Poetr; TFi; WeW-3

To stand for a while, and get warm. (LL) The Satisfaction Coal Company. Rita Dove. LCAP-2; WWSi

To stand here in the wings of Europe. On a Return from Egypt. Keith Douglas. NoP-4

To stand on common ground. A Common Ground. Denise Levertov. PoM

To stand or move. (LL) A Lame Beggar. Donne. FMP; PFE

To stand up straight and tread the turning mill. A. E. Housman. OAEL-2

To stare about them, and to eat. (LL) The Cit's Country Box. Robert Lloyd. OBGa

To start again with something beautiful. Cedar Waxwing on Scarlet Firethorn. Stanley Plumly. NAmP90

To starve, or not to starve? that is the question. W. H. Ireland. BXAP

To state each horror. From the Monkey House and Other Cages. Monkey II. Irena Klepfisz. GLP

To stave off disaster, or bring the devil to heel. Tapu. Arthur Rex Dugard Fairburn. PeNZ

To stay the season of a mind. (LL) Massacre, October '66. Wole Soyinka. AF; PBMAP

To Stella. Hester Mulso. ECWP

To Stella. Plato, Greek. OBCVT; EnLoPo; FaBoEE; OBVE, tr. by Shelley (Morning and Evening Star.) AWP

To Stella. Sir Philip Sidney. See First Song.

To Stella. Jonathan Swift. NOEC

To step over the low wall that divides. To the Sea. Philip Larkin. OxBoS

To strengthen whilst one stands. (LL) Goblin Market. Christina Rossetti. CPO; EBEV; FaBoSe; NAEL-2; NALW; NOBVV; NOxBChV; OBNV; OxAEP-2; VWP

To Strephon. Sarah Dixon. ECWP

To strive, to seek, to find, and not to yield. (LL) Ulysses. Tennyson. APAD; AWP; CABP; ClHu; EBEV; EBVVPR; EnVR; FHYEP; FaPoR; HAP; HeIP-4; HoPM; ImPo; InPK-6; InPS-3; NAEL-2; NAWM-2; NIP-4; NOBE; NOBVV; NoP-4; OAEL-2; OxAEP-2; PFE; PoE; PoPoPo; PoRA; Poetr; SAGP; SCGP; SCV; SoSe-8; TFi; TRP; UnPo; WeW-3

To strongly, wrongly, vainly love thee still. (LL) Love and Death. Byron. EBEV; NOBE

To stub an oar on a rock where none should be. Basking Shark. Norman MacCaig. FaBoTC

To Stygian Forty-seventh Street below. (LL) The West Forties: Morning, Noon, and Night. Louis Edward Sissman. CoAP; NYBP

To Subprefect Chang. Wang Wei, Chinese. SuSp, tr. by Irving Y. Lo

To suffer and to die. (LL) Chorus of Angels. Cardinal Newman. NOBVV; NOCV; PoEL-5

To sulk upon my mother's breast. (LL) Infant Sorrow. William Blake. APAD; EBEvV; FHYEP; InPS-3; NAEL-2; OBNC; OxAEP-2; OxBM; OxBSP; PoEL-4; PoPoPo; RB; Ro

To Sultan Murad II. James Clarence Mangan, Turkish. NOIV

To sup with thee thou didst me home invite. The Invitation. Robert Herrick. CaPo

To survive? Joy Harjo. See Anchorage.

To sweep the dust behind the door. (LL) The Fairy Blessing. Shakespeare. CH; CTC; OxBoLi

To Sycamores. Robert Herrick. CaPo

To T. H., a Lady Resembling My Mistress. Thomas Carew. CaPo

To-ta Ti-om. Peter Blue Cloud. HATNAP

To tack to each sheep its tail. (LL) Little Bo-Peep has lost her sheep. Mother Goose. LB

To take a bath. Tanka. Fumi Saito, Japanese. MJT, tr. by Ueda, Makoto

To take a woman in your arms. It's Easy. Lee Cataldi. BMAP

To take the Cat from me. (LL) May Colven [or May Colvin]. Unknown. OxBB; PBMP

To take the only way to be forgiven. (LL) On the Benefactions in the Late Frost. Alexander Pope. NOEC; OxBSP

To take the wrong road. Little Infinite Poem. Federico García Lorca, Spanish. AF; RaBo, tr. by Robert Bly

To take us sick, that sound would not take thee? (LL) The Pursuit[e]. Henry Vaughan. GeHe; NOSC; SeCP; TrCP

To talk about trees. (LL) What Kind of Times Are These. Adrienne Rich. BAP-93; LoL

To talk alone, at the threshold, with already-gone, has-been, to-be- / announced. To be your own legend. Notebook, Two. Edmond Jabès, French. AF, tr. by Rosemarie Waldrop

To talk like Doeg, and to write like thee. (LL) Doeg, though without knowing how or why. John Dryden and Nahum Tate. FHYEP; PoEL-3

To talk to each other. (LL) Little. Dorothy Aldis. NTCP; WHSW

To Tan-Ch'iu. Li Po, Chinese. AWP, ChiP, tr. by Arthur Waley; TAL, tr. by Robert Payne

To tangled grass I cling. Spring. Marjorie Frost Fraser. ImGa

To Tarshish. Shimon Halkin, Hebrew. MHP, tr. by Ruth Finer Mintz

To taste terrain their hiers need not draw near. (LL) The Singing Bones. Randolph Stow. BMAP

To tear a heart which pants be unmoved? Byron. See Stanzas to the Po.

"To tedious Hell this body with its muddy feet in my mind!" (LL) Menses. Edna St. Vincent Millay. NMM-2; RACG

To Telembrotos. Antipater of Thessalonica, Greek. GrAn, tr. by Alistair Elliot

To tell each point he nameth with a kiss. (LL) The Sirens' Song. William Browne. GBL; NOBE; OBEV

To tell me, out of the body, out of the body travel. (LL) For Esther. Stanley Plumly. GM

To tell of Him, the Unseen God. (LL) The Silent. Jones Very. NCAP; PAR

To tell strange feats of deamons, here I am. To the Much Honoured R. F. Esq. Richard Chamberlain. SCAP

To tell the truth, each piece he read. On Hearing James W. Riley Read. Joseph Cotter, Sr. AAP

To tell the truth, I really am. The All-Night Waitress. Maura Stanton. AmPA

TO TELL their tales. Adrienne Rich. See Necessities of Life.

To tell what others were, came down? (LL) An Epicurean Ode. John Hall. CBLP; MeLP; NOSC

To tell you from the start, I have lost him whose hand and eye are gentle. He Whose Hand and Eye Are Gentle. Unknown, Welsh. OBWVE, tr. by Kenneth Hurlstone Jackson

To tender love. (LL) I Heard a Linnet Courting. Robert Bridges. LiTM; OBEV; OBMV

To Thaliarchus ("Behold yon mountains"). Odes 1.9. Horace, Latin. OBVE, tr. by Dryden Fr. Odes.

To Thaliarchus ("Thou seest the hills"). Horace. See 1.9.

To that clear majesty which in the north. To Queen Elizabeth. Sir John Davies. Fr. Nosce Teipsum. NoSic; SiPS

To that deliberate progress. (LL) Considering the Snail. Thom Gunn. LiTM; NAEL-2; TwCP

To that end, may move, in time, the stones themselves to sing. (LL) Beam 7. Ronald Johnson. APSN

To that lov'd bowl my spoon by instinct flies. (LL) The Hasty Pudding. Joel Barlow. AmPP; NAAL-3; NOBA; OBAL; OxBA; TAP

To that place day doth unyoke! (LL) Hymn to Pan. John Fletcher. NOBE; OBEV

To that sweet thief which sourly robs from me. (LL) Sonnet 35. Shakespeare. HeIP-4; ImPo; NAEL-1; NoSic; OxAFP-1; PoE; SCGP; UnPo

To the Accuser Who Is the God of This World. William Blake. See Epilogue: "Truly my Satan thou art but a dunce."

To the Age's Insanities. Marie Ponsot. VGW

To the air of 'My Phillida, adieu, love!'. Mary Wollstonecraft Shelley. Ro

To the Almighty on his radiant throne. The Hymn. Anne Finch, Countess of Winchilsea. ChIV-1 Fr. A Pindaric Poem.

To the Anxious Mother. Valente Goenha Malangatana, Portuguese. PBA, tr. by Dorothy Guedes and Philippa Rumsey; PBMAP

To the Archbishop of Tuam. *Unknown.* FaBoEE

To the Archdeacon. George Farewell. NOEC

To the Author of Agnes de Castro. Mary de la Rivière Manley. KTR

To the Author of Clarissa. Thomas Edwards. Son

To the Avon River above Stratford, Canada. James Reaney. MoCV

To the banks of the Moldau River. How They Made the Golem. John Robert Colombo. MoCV

To the banquet of the earth. Martial Sinda, *French.* NegPo, *tr. by* Ellen Conroy Kennedy

To the Barbarian. Else Lasker-Schüler, *German.* PFTM, *tr. by* Pierre Joris *and* Jerome Rothenberg

To the Bartholdi Statue. Ambrose Bierce. APN-2

To the Bat. Edith King. BoTP

To The Beloved. "Anna Akhmatova," *Russian.* LoP, *tr. by* Judith Hemschemeyer

To the Beloved. Alice Thompson Meynell. VWP

To the Best, and Most Accomplished Couple. Henry Vaughan. PeECV

To the Black Nymph. Vũ Hoàng Chu'o'ng, *Vietnamese.* AVP, *tr. by* Huỳnh Sanh Thông

To the Blacksmith with a Spade. Owen Roe O'Sullivan. IIP

To the Blessed Sacrament. Henry Constable. NoSic

To the Blessed Virgin. William Alabaster. NoSic

To the Blessed Virgin Mary. Gerald Griffin. TIRV

To the Body. Alice Thompson Meynell. PeVV

To the Body. Coventry Patmore. CABP; EnVR; OAEL-2; PoEL-5 *Fr.* The Unknown Eros.

To the Bone. Dorothy Allison. GLP

To the bone place where blood is made. Getting Down. "Chrystos." CPO

To the bridge of love. Juan Ramón Jiménez, *Spanish.* ITG, *tr. by* Stephen Mitchell *Fr.* Ten Short Poems.

To the chimney a bull's horns. Epitaph. Ljubomir Simovic, *Serbo-Croatian.* HSix, *tr. by* Charles Simic

To the Christians. Francis Lauderdale Adams. ChIV-2; OxBS

To the Christians. William Blake. *See* Epigraph.

To the City of London [*or* In Honour of the City of London]. William Dunbar. EBEV; OBEV

("Above all rivers thy river hath renown.") OPOU

To the Conference. Mrs. Henry Linden. CBWP-4

To the Countess Dowager of Huntingdon. Bathsua Pell Makin. KTR

To the Countess of Bedford ("Madam, / Reason is our soul's left hand, Faith her right"). Donne. NOSC

To the Countess of Salisbury. Donne. PeECV

To the Countesse of Bedford ("Honour is so sublime perfection"). Donne. MeLP

To the Countesse of Salisbury. Aurelian Townshend. SeCP

(Loves Victory.) MeLP

To the Critic. Michael Drayton. NOSC, *sect.* XXXI *Fr.* Idea.

To the Critics. Priscilla Pointon.

On Her Blindness. ECWP

To the Cuckoo. Michael Bruce, *rev. by* John Logan. OBEV

(Ode: To the Cuckoo.) NOEC

To the Cuckoo. Wordsworth. BoTP; EBEvV; GTBS-P; NOBRP; PoLF; UV

To the Curlew. Helen Maria Williams. WoRP

To the Daisy ("With little here to do or see"). Wordsworth. GTBS-P

To the Dandelion. James Russell Lowell.. NAAL-3

("On all these living pages of God's book.") (LL) ColAP

To the dawn. (LL) The Gull'' Flight. Nigel Roberts. NOBAu

To the Days. Adrienne Rich. BAP-93; LoL *Fr.* Not Somewhere Else, But Here. BAP-93

To the Dead. Frank Bidart. EOEF

To the Dead Cardinal of Westminster. Francis Thompson. PeVV

To the Detracter. Robert Herrick. PBRV

To the dim light and the large circle of shade. Of the Lady Pietra degli Scrovigni. Dante, *Italian.* AWP; OAEL-2; OBVE, *tr. by* D. G. Rossetti

To the Distant One. Po Chü-i, *Chinese.* TAL, *tr. by* Robert Payne

To the Divine Neighbor. Judah Leib Teller, *Yiddish.* CEEP, *tr. by* Gabriel Preil *and* Howard Schwartz

To the Driving Cloud. Henry Wadsworth Longfellow. PoEL-5

To the Eagle. Mary Weston Fordham. CBWP-2

To the Earl of Oxford, Late Lord Treasurer. Jonathan Swift, *after the Latin of* Horace. OBVE

To the Earl of Roscommon, on His Excellent Essay on Translated Verse. Dryden.

"Whether the fruitful Nile, or Tyrian shore." EPCY

To the Earl of Warwick, on the Death of Mr. Addison. Thomas Tickell. NOEC; OxAEP-1

To the East and to the West. Walt Whitman. APN-1

To the eastern grove where a spring rises. Replying to a Poem by the Monk Ling-yi at the New Spring. Liu Ch'ang-ch'ing, *Chinese.* SuSp, *tr. by* William H. Nienhauser

To the Editor of Mr. Pope's Works. Thomas Edwards. Son

To the Eminent Scholar and Meddler. Kofi Awoonor. HBAPE

To the Emperour Titus, upon his Banishing Sycophants. Martial, *Latin.* OBCVT, *tr. by* Pecke, Thomas

To the end, to the end they remain. (LL) For the Fallen. Laurence Binyon. EBEvV; NOBE; OBEV; OBWP; OxBTC; PoFWW

To the Enemies. Vladimir Holan, *Czech.* AF, *tr. by* C. G. Hanzlicek *and* Dana Habova

To the Eternal Feminine. Tristan Corbière, *French.* EP, *tr. by* Carlyle Ferren MacIntyre

To the Etruscan Poets. Richard Wilbur. OxBC

To the Evening. John Codrington Bampfylde. NOEC

To the Evening Star. Mark Akenside. PoEL-3

(Nightingale, The.) OBEV

To the Evening Star. William Blake. CH; GSo; NAEL-2; NOEC; NoP-4; OAEL-2; PoE; PoLF; TFi

To the Evening Star. Thomas Campbell. GTBS-P; OBNC

To the Excellent Mrs A. O. upon her receiving the name of Lucasia. Katherine Philips. KTR

(To the Excellent Mrs. Anne Owen.) NOSC

To the Excellent Orinda. "Philo-Philippa." KTR

To the Excellent Pattern of Beauty and Virtue, Lady Elizabeth, Countess of Ormonde. James Shirley. BeJo

To the Fair Clarinda, Who Made Love to Me, Imagin'd More Than Woman. Aphra Behn. CABP; CPO; NALW; NoP-4; PEW

To the falling London rain. (LL) London Rain. Louis MacNeice. NoP-4; Poetr

To the Family Home Awaiting Repair. A. J. Seymour. HCP

To the fancy of Arthur O'Shaughnessy. (LL) On the Poet, Arthur O'Shaughnessy—. D. G. Rossetti. OBCoV; PeLi

To the Father through the features of men's faces. (LL) What I Do Is Me. Gerard Manley Hopkins. APAD; CMoP; EBEV; EBVV; EnlH; FaBoMo; LiTM; MoBrPo; NAEL-2; NOBVV; NOCV; NoP-4; OxAEP-2; PoE; RB

To the Fifteen of Piazzale Loreto. Salvatore Quasimodo, *Italian.* AF, *tr. by* Jack Bevan

To the Filial Son, Ts'ui. Hsü Pen, *Chinese.* CoBLCP, *tr. by* Jonathan Chaves

To the Film Industry in Crisis. Frank O'Hara. CAPP-1; NOBA; OBAL

To the First of August. Ann Plato. BlSi

To the First Slave Ship. Lydia Huntley Sigourney. ColAP

To the Foot from Its Child. Pablo Neruda, *Spanish.* RB, *tr. by* Alastair Reid

To the Fortuneteller Hsüeh T'ieh-yai. Hsieh Chin, *Chinese.* CoBLCP, *tr. by* Jonathan Chaves

To the Four Courts, Please. James Stephens. BIrV; MoBrPo; UnPo

To the Fragment of a Statue of Hercules, Commonly Called the Torso. Samuel Rogers. GS

To the free skies unpent and glad and strong. (LL) To a Locomotive in Winter. Walt Whitman. AmPP; GM; InPK-6; MoAmPo; MoP; NAAL-1; NAAL-3; NCAP; NoAm; NoP-4; PoEL-5; Poetr; TAP

To the French of the Second Empire. Rimbaud. FaBoPV; OBWP, *tr. by* Robert Lowell *Fr.* Eighteen-Seventy.

To the Fringed Gentian. William Cullen Bryant. APN-1; AWP; FaBoBe; PAR; PoLF; TAP

To the garden the world anew ascending. Walt Whitman. ChIV-1; KSG

To the Gardener at Nuneham. Horace Walpole. FaBoEE

To the Generous Reader. Robert Herrick. CaPo

To the Gentlewoman of Llanarth Hall. Evan Thomas, *Welsh.* OBWVE, *tr. by* Gwyn Jones

To the ghostly garden to the laurel mute. Autumn Garden. Dino Campana, *Italian.* GaP; STV, *tr. by* John Frederick Nims

To the God of Love. Edmund George Valpy Knox. NOBL

To the gods belongs tomorrow. (LL) The Epicure ("Fill the bowl with rosie [*or* rosy] wine"). Abraham Cowley. BeJo; SeCP

To the Good Thief. Saunders Lewis, *Welsh.* OBWVE, *tr. by* Gwyn Morgan

To the Grasshopper and the Cricket. Leigh Hunt. GSo; OBNC; Son

(Grasshopper and the Cricket, The.) OxAEP-2

To the Great City of Moscow, as He Was Leaving June 25, 1636. Paul Fleming, *German.* GePo, *tr. by* George C. Schoolfield

To the Great Hard-Bop Pianists. Joel Lewis. MoNo

To the Greek Anthologists. George Rostrevor Hamilton, *after the Greek of* Satyros. FaBoEE

To the Hand. W. S. Merwin. SPE

To the Harbormaster. Frank O'Hara. CRP; CoAP; NAAL-2; PoM; VCAP

To the hard-working miner whose dangers are great. The Hard-working Miner. *Unknown.* AmFP

To the haven of the grave. Shelley. *See* Lines Written among the Euganean Hills.

To the head bobbing in the gunsight. Line. Milo De Angelis, *Italian.* NeIt, *tr. by* Lawrence Venuti

To the Heart. Tadeusz Różewicz, *Polish.* PoSu, *tr. by* Victor Contoski

To the Heavens above us. An Astrologer's Song. Rudyard Kipling. MoBrPo

To the Highland Girl of Inversneyde. Wordsworth. GTBS-P

To the Holy Goste my goodes I bequeth. *Unknown.* MiEL

To the Holy Spirit. Yvor Winters. MoAmPo; PaTW; VGW

To the Holy Trinity. *Unknown, Irish.* NOIV, *tr. by* Thomas Kinsella

To the Hon. Mrs. C——e. Jane West. ECWP

To the Honoured *Eugenia*, Commanding Me to Write to Her. "Ephelia." KTR

To the House Ghost. Paula Rankin. CMAP

To the Immortal[l] Memory [*or* Memorie] and Friendship of That Noble Pair[e], Sir Lucius Cary and Sir H. [*or* Henry] Morison. Ben Jonson. BeJo; CABP; NAEL-1; NOBE; NoP-4; NOSC; OAEL-1; PoEL-2; SeCP
  Noble Nature, The. GTBS-P
  Part of an Ode, A. OBEV

To the Infant Hampden. Written during a Sleepless Night. John Thelwall. Ro

To the Infant Martyrs. Richard Crashaw. ChIV-2; GeHe; NAEL-1; NoP-4; OxBSP

To the Innkeeper at Five Rivers, Sun Pen. Chang Yü, *Chinese.* CoBLCP, *tr. by* Jonathan Chaves

To the King. Robert Herrick. CavPo

To the King, at His Entrance into Saxham: By Master John Crofts. Thomas Carew. CaPo

To the King, on His Navy. Edmund Waller. BeJo

To the King. / Thou art the wall-stone rejected, *sels. Unknown. Fr.* Christ 1. AnOE, *tr. by* Charles W. Kennedy

To the King, upon His Com[m]ing with His Army into the West. Robert Herrick. BeJo; CaPo; CavPo

To the King, Upon His Welcome to Hampton Court. Robert Herrick. BeJo

To the King / You are the corner-stone the builders. Advent Lyrics. *Unknown, Anglo-Saxon.* ASW, *tr. by* Kevin Crossley-Holland *Fr.* Christ 1. AnOE, *tr. by* Charles W. Kennedy

To the King's Most Excellent Majesty. Phillis Wheatley. TAP

To the King's white hall. (LL) Riddle: "White bird featherless / Flew from Paradise." *Unknown.* FaBoVe; OxNR

To the Lacedemonians. Allen Tate. NAAL-2; NoAM

To the Ladies. Mary Lee, Lady Chudleigh. CABP; ECWP; GEA; NALW; NOEC; PEW; WPE; WPOW

To the Lady Anne, Countess of Dorset. Emilia Lanier.
  "To you I dedicate this work of grace." NOSC

To the Lady Arabella. Emilia Lanier. NOSC

To the Lady in the Chemisette with Black Buttons. Nathaniel Parker Willis. OBAL

To The Lady Lucie, Countesse of Bedford. Samuel Daniel. PBRV

To the Lady Margaret, Countess [*or* Countesse] of Cumberland. Samuel Daniel. NOSC

To the Lady Margaret Ley. Milton. GTBS-P; OBEV

To the Lady May. Aurelian Townshend. GBL

To the Lady Portrayed by Margaret Dumont. John Hollander. OBAL
  (For the Passing of Groucho's Pursuer.) PoA

To The Lady Radegund, With Violets. Venantius Fortunatus, *Latin.* LoP, *tr. by* Helen Waddell

To the Laggards. Joseph Bovshover, *Yiddish.* TrJP, *tr. by* Joseph Bovshover

To the Last Wedding Guest. Horace Gregory. NYBP

To the Late William Jerdan. Eliza Cook. VWP

To the Learned and Reverend Mr. Cotton Mather, on His Excellent Magnalia. Grindall Rawson. SCAP

To the legion of the lost ones, to the cohort of the damned. Gentlemen-Rankers. Rudyard Kipling. NOBVV

To the long mill's shadow. The One. Bruce Weigl. BAP-94

To the Looking-Glass world it was Alice that said. Welcome Queen Alice. "Lewis Carroll." UV *Fr.* Through the Looking-Glass.

To the Lord General[l] Cromwell[, on the Proposals of Certain Ministers at the Committee for the Propagation of the Gospel *or* May 1652]. Milton. FaBoPV; GSo; IIP; NAEL-1; NOSC; NoP-4; PBRV; PoPoPo; SCGP; Son

To the Lord Love. "Michael Field." OBMV

To the Lords of Convention 'twas Claver'se who spoke. Bonny [*or* Bonnie] Dundee. Sir Walter Scott. FaBoCh; OxBS; OxBoLi; UV *Fr.* The Doom of Devorgoil.

To the Madwoman in My Yard. Olive Senior. HCP

To the maiden. The Sea. *Unknown.* PFE

To the Maiden in the East. Henry David Thoreau. OxBA

To the Man after the Harrow. Patrick Kavanagh. CIP-2; GTBS-P

To the Man-of-War Bird. Walt Whitman. APN-1; APo; AmPP; FaBoBe

To the Marchesana of Pescara. Michelangelo Buonarroti. *See* Love's Justification.

To the Marquess of Piscat's Soul. Henry Constable. NoSic

To the Marquis of Graham on His Marriage. *Unknown.* OBSV

To the Memory of a Poet. Astride Ivaska, *Latvian.* CEEP, *tr. by* Inara Cedrins

To the Memory of G. N. Oboldueyev. Yelena Blaginina, *Russian.* TCRP, *tr. by* Vera Dunham

To the Memory of Gavin Wilson (Boot, Leg and Arm Maker). George Galloway. NOEC

To the Memory of J. Horace Kimball. "Ada." BISi

To the Memory of Keats. John Clare. EPCY

To the Memory of Mr Oldham. Dryden. AWP; EBEV; EPCY; FP; HAP; InPK-6; InPS-3; NIP-4; NOBE; NOSC; NoP-4; OAEL-1; OxAEP-1; PoE; PoEL-3; PoPoPo; Poetr; SCGP; TFi; TRP

To the Memory of My Beloved, the Author Mr William Shakespeare[: And What He Hath Left Us]. Ben Jonson. BeJo; EPCY; HAP; HeIP-4; NoP-4; NOSC; OAEL-1; OxAEP-1; PoEL-2; PoPoPo; SeCP
  "I, therefore, will begin. Soul of the age!" NOBE

To the Memory of My Dear and Ever Honored Father Thomas Dudley Esq. Who Deceased July 31, 1653, and of His Age 77. Anne Bradstreet. NAAL-1; NAAL-3

To the Memory of My Dear Daughter in Law, Mrs. Mercy Bradstreet. Anne Bradstreet. KTR

To the Memory of Sir Isaac Newton. James Thomson.
  "All—intellectual eye, our solar round." NOEC

To the Memory of the Brave Americans. Philip Freneau. AiP; AmPP; PoLF

To the Memory of the Learned and Reverend, Mr. Jonathan Mitchell. Francis Drake. SCAP

To the Men of Kent (October, 1803). Wordsworth. OBWP

To the Men Who Lose. George L. Scarborough. BLPA

To the Merchantis of Edinburgh. William Dunbar. OxBS

To the Mercy Killers. Dudley Randall. SoSe-8

To the Minister Liu. Yü Hsüan-chi, *Chinese.* BoWoP, *tr. by* Geoffrey Waters

To the moaning and the groaning of the bells. (LL) The Bells. Edgar Allan Poe. APN-1; ChAP; MeMAP; OBAL; OBCA; PoLF; TAP; TFi

To the Mock-Bird. Mary Weston Fordham. CBWP-2

To the Mocking-Bird. Richard Henry Wilde. APN-1

To the Monk Wu-hsia on the Occasion of His Editing the Lotus Sutra. Mo Shih-lung, *Chinese.* CoBLCP, *tr. by* Jonathan Chaves

To the Moon. Paul Fleming, *German.* GePo, *tr. by* George C. Schoolfield

To the Moon. Goethe, *German.* STV, *tr. by* John Frederick Nims

To the Moon. Giacomo Leopardi, *Italian.* TTTS, *tr. by* Kenneth Koch

To the Moon. Pierre de Ronsard, *French.* AWP, *tr. by* Andrew Lang

To the Moon. Shelley. GTBS-P; OxAEP-2; PBMP; TTTS

To the Moon. Charlotte Smith. BWW; Son

To the Moon. Helen Maria Williams. NoP-4

To the Moon and Back. William Plomer. OBCoV

To the mooring of starting out, that day so long ago. (LL) Soonest Mended. John Ashbery. HCAP; NAAL-2; VCAP

To the Most Beautiful Lady, the Lady Bridget Manners. Barnabe Barnes. EnLoPo

To the Most Excellent and Learned Shepherd, Colin Clout, *dedication.* William Smith. AAS; Son *Fr.* Chloris [*or* the Complaint of the Passionate Despised Shepheard].

To the Most Excellently Accomplished Mrs. Katherine Philips. Henry Vaughan. CABP

To the Most Fair and Lovely Mistress Anne Soame, Now Lady Abdie. Robert Herrick. CaPo; NOBE; NOSC

To the Most Virtuous Mistress Pot, Who Many Times Entertained Him. Robert Herrick. CaPo

To the Mothers. Ernst Toller, *German.* TrJP, *tr. by* E. Ellis Roberts

To the Mountains. Henry David Thoreau. PoEL-4

To the Much Honoured R. F. Esq. Richard Chamberlain. SCAP

To the much-tossed Ulysses, never done. Ulysses. Robert Graves. CBLP; CMoP; EP; FaBoTw; MoP; NoAM

To the Muse. Jean Adams. ECWP

To the Muse. Denise Levertov. APSN

To the Muse. Nadezhda Elizarovna Maltseva, *Russian.* TCRP, *tr. by* Bernard Meares

To the Muse. Carol Muske. PuP-17

To the Muse. Robert Louis Stevenson. EBEV

To the Muse. Philip Whalen. PoM

To the Muse. James Wright. NAAL-2; NNaP

To the Muses. William Blake. EPCY; HAP; HeIP-4; ImPo; NAEL-2; NOBE; NOEC; OAEL-2; OBEV; SCGP

(From Poetical Sketches.) NoP-4

To the Mutable Fair. Edmund Waller. BeJo; SeCP

To the Name Above Every Name, the Name of Iesus a Hymn. Richard Crashaw. *See* On the Name of Jesus.

To the New Annex to the Detroit County Jail. Richard W. Thomas. PoBA

To the New Moon. Salvatore Quasimodo, *Italian*. SpW, *tr. by* Jack Bevan

To the New Ordained. John D. Sheridan. TIRV

To the New Owner. Lucile Hargrove Reynolds. PoToHe

To the new wick / Of freedom's torch. My Thread. Dovid Hofshteyn, *Yiddish*. TrJP, *tr. by* Joseph Leftwich

To the New Year [For the Countess of Carlisle]. Thomas Carew. CaPo

To the New Year. Priscilla Jane Thompson. CBWP-2

To the New Yeere [*or* Year]. Michael Drayton. NOSC; PoEL-2

To the Newborn. Judit Tóth, *Hungarian*. WPOW, *tr. by* Laura Schiff

To the Night. Shelley. *See* To Night.

To the Nightingale. Fulbert of Chartres, *Latin*. MLL, *tr. by* Helen Waddell

To the Nightingale. Anne Finch, Countess of Winchilsea. ECWP; NALW; WPE

To the Noble Sir Francis Drake. Thomas Beedome. OxBSP

To the Noblest and Best of Ladies, the Countess of Denbigh, Perswading her to Resolution in Religion, and to render her selfe without further delay into the Communion of the Catholick Church. Richard Crashaw. GeHe; MeLP; PBRV

(Letter from Mr Crashaw to the Countess of Denbigh.) NOSC; SeCP

To the Oaks of Glencree. John Millington Synge. MoBrPo; NOIV

To the Ocean. Byron. *Fr.* The Ocean. PoEL-4 *Fr.* Childe Harold's Pilgrimage.

To the ocean now I fly. The Spirit's Epilogue. Milton. NOBE; NOSC; OBEV; OxAEP-1 *Fr.* Comus; a Masque Presented at Ludlow Castle. FHYEP; OAEL-1

To the old, long life and treasure. Song. Ben Jonson. OxBSP *Fr.* The Gypsies Metamorphosed.

To the One I Love Most. *Unknown*. *See* Lines from Love Letters.

To the One of Fictive Music. Wallace Stevens. MeMAP; MoAmPo; NoP-4

To the palaces of the Han. Wang Chao-chün. Tai Shu-lun, *Chinese*. SuSp, *tr. by* William H. Nienhauser

To the Palmetto State, in the year seventy three. Southern Work of Dr. and Mrs. L. M. Dunton. Lizelia Augusta Jenkins Moorer. CBWP-3

To the Parted One. Goethe, *German*. AWP, *tr. by* Christopher Pearse Cranch

To the Peacock of France. Marianne Moore. MeMAP

To the Pending Year. Walt Whitman. OxBSP

To the People of England, the humble Petition. The Petition of the Orangemen of Ireland. Thomas Moore. NOIV

To the People of Rome, Commiserating the Common-Wealth, in respect of the Civil Warres. Horace, *Latin*.

"Now Civill Warres a second Age consume." OBCVT, *tr. by* Sir Richard Fanshawe

To the Pianist Bill Evans. Bill Zavatsky. MoNo

To the Pious Memory of C. W. Esquire. Henry Vaughan. PeECV

To the Pious Memory of the Accomplished Young Lady, Mrs. Anne Killigrew. Dryden.

To the Pious Memory of the Accomplished [*or* Accomplisht] Young Lady, Mrs. Anne Killigrew, [Excellent in the Two Sister-Arts of Poesie and Painting]. Dryden. NAEL-1; OAEL-1; PoEL-3

(Ode to the Pious Memory of the Accomplished Young Lady, Mrs. Anne Killigrew.) OBEV

"O gracious God, how far have we." EPCY

To the placid supreme in the sweep of his reign. (LL) The Man-of-War Hawk. Herman Melville. APN-2; APo

To the pleasant Isle of Avès, to look at it once again. (LL) The Last Buccaneer. Charles Kingsley. EBEvV; EBVV; FaBoBe; PeVV

To the Po. 2 June 1819. Byron. *See* Stanzas to the Po.

To the Poet, John Dyer. Wordsworth. EPCY

To the Poet Wordsworth. Felicia Dorothea Hemans. BrRo

To the Poets. *Unknown*. PeNZ

To the Poets in New York. James Wright. NAAL-2

To the Poor. Anna Laetitia Barbauld. ECWP; NoP-4

To the Poppy. Anna Seward. ECWP; WoRP

To the Prince. Sir John Davies. *Fr.* Dedications [*or* Orchestra]. SiPS

To the Queen. Henry Stuart, Lord Darnley. OxBS

To the Queen. Anne Killigrew. KTR

To the Queen[e], Entertain[e]d at Night by the Countess[e] of Anglesey. Sir William Davenant. MeLP; NOSC

To the Queen of Bohemiah. "Eliza." KTR

To the Queen of Inconstancy, Regina Collier, in Antwerp. Katherine Philips. PEW

To the Queen of the British Government. Mrs. Henry Linden. CBWP-4

To the Queenes Most Excellent Majestie. Elizabeth Cary Falkland. KTR

To the Rats. Edward John Langford Garston. NSI

To the Reader. Richard Le Gallienne. ADE

To the Reader. Denise Levertov. AmPP; PFE; PoM; SAGP; VGW

To the Reader. Urian Oakes. SCAP

To the Reader ("Pray thee, take care, that tak'st my book[e] in hand"). Ben Jonson. BeJo; NoP-4; PoE

To the Reader of Master William Davenant's Play [*The Wits*]. Thomas Carew. CaPo

To the Reader of These Sonnets. Michael Drayton. AAS; NAEL-1; NOSC; NoP-4; Son *Fr.* Idea.

("Into these loves who but for passion looks.") NoP-4

("That cannot long one fashion entertain.") (LL) NoP-4

To the readers of our New First Unexpected. A Slap in the Face of Public Taste. D. Burliuk, Aleksandr Kruchenykh, V. Mayakovsky, *and* Viktor Khlebnikov. PFTM, *tr. by* Anna Lawton *and* Herbert Eagle *Fr.* A Slap in the Face of Public Taste.

To the Red Lory. John Shaw Neilson. NOBAu

To the Redbreast. John Codrington Bampfylde. Son

To the Retired Scholar Chang. Ni Tsan, *Chinese*. CoBLCP, *tr. by* Jonathan Chaves

To the Rev. F. D. Maurice. Tennyson. GTBS-P; NOBVV; PeECV

At Farringford.

To the Rev. [*or* Reverend] W. L. Bowles. Coleridge. Son *Fr.* Effusions.

To the Rcvd. Mr. ——— on His Drinking Sea-Water. John Winstanley. NOEC

To the Rev'd Mr. Jno. Sparhawk on the Birth of his Son. Samuel Sewall. SCAP

To the Rev. Mr. Powell. Christopher Smart. OBWVE

To the Reverend Shade of His Religious Father. Robert Herrick. CaPo; CavPo; PBRV

To the right. The Well. Padma Sachdev, *Dogri*. OMIP, *tr. by* Iqbal Masud

To the Right Hon. Henry Pelham. Edward Moore. OBSV

To the Right Honorable the Lord Windsor. Perdam Sapientiam Sapientum. William Habington. ChIV-2

To The Right Honourable Lord Byron. James Hogg.

"Nor for the crabbed state-creed, wayward wight." EPCY

To the Right Honourable Mildmay, Earl of Westmorland. Robert Herrick. BeJo

To the Right Honourable the Countesse of C. William Habington. SeCP

To the Right Honourable William, Earl of Dartmouth[, His Majesty's Principal Secretary of State for North America]. Phillis Wheatley. AmPP; CrDW; NAAAL; NALW

"No more, America, in mournful strain." WPOW

"Should you, my lord, while you pursue my song." BPo; ImGa; TTY

To the Right Worshipfull, My Singular Good Frend, Master Gabriell Harvey, Doctor of the Lawes. Edmund Spenser. NoSic *Fr.* Commendatory Sonnets.

To the Right Worshipfull, My Singular Good Friend, Master Gabriel Harvey, Doctor of the Lawes. Edmund Spenser. NoSic

To the River Duddon. Norman Nicholson. NoP-4

To the River Duddon: After-Thought. Wordsworth. *See* After-Thought.

To the River Itchin, near Winton. William Lisle Bowles. OAEL-2

(Sonnet VIII. To the River Itchin, near Winton.) Ro

To the River Otter. Coleridge. *See* Sonnet to the River Otter.

To the Rose; a Song. Robert Herrick. SeCP

To the Rose upon the Rood of Time. W. B. Yeats. ADE; NoAM

To the Royal Society. Abraham Cowley.

"Philosophy, the great and only heir." BeJo

To the Rulers. Howard Nemerov. OxBC

To the Rural Muse. John Clare.

"Muse of the fields, oft have I said farewell." EPCY

To the sagging wharf. A Summer's Dream. Elizabeth Bishop. OxBC

To the Same. Leigh Hunt. Ro

To the Same [Celia]. Ben Jonson. BeJo; NOSC; OAEL-1; SeCP *Fr.* Volpone. NAEL-1

(To Celia.) AWP

To the Same [Robert, Earl of Salisbury] [Upon the Accension of the Treasurership to Him]. Ben Jonson. NOSC

To the same purpose: he, not long before. Thomas Traherne. NoP-4

To the Same [My Dear Sister, Mrs S.]: The Tears. William Hammond. NOSC

To the scullery, and down to the back room. (LL) Ancestor. Thomas Kinsella. BIrV; NOIV; NoP-4; PBCIP; PoE

To the Sea. Philip Larkin. OxBoS

To the sea, to the sea. Tanka. Kanoko Okamoto, *Japanese.* MJT, *tr. by* Makoto Ueda

To the Second Person. John Skelton.
("O benign Jesu, my sovereign Lord and King." SCGP

To the Senegalese veterans of war. Et Cetera. Léon Damas, *French.* NegPo, *tr. by* Ellen Conroy Kennedy

To the Senses. Michael Drayton. PFE

To the Shade of Burns. Charlotte Smith. NoP-4

To the ship I carried statues. I Carried Statues. Agnes Nemes Nagy, *Hungarian.* BoWoP; PoSu, *tr. by* Bruce Berlind

To the side of the road. (LL) The Old Flame. Robert Lowell. BoLoP; CBLP; NOBA; NoAM

To the singing, to the drums. (LL) The Eagle-Feather Fan. N. Scott Momaday. NoP-4

To the Sister of Charles Lamb. Walter Savage Landor. Ro

To the sky. (LL) Draft of a Reparations Agreement. Dan Pagis, *Hebrew.* HP, *tr. by* Stephen Mitchell

To the Skylark. Wordsworth. GTBS-P

To the Snake. Denise Levertov. AmPP; LiTM; NMM-2; PoA

To the Snipe. John Clare. FaBoPV; OBNC

To the Sour[e] Reader. Robert Herrick. NBLV; NoP-4; SeCP

To the South. Maurice Thompson. CBCWP

To the south-east—three thousand leagues—. Civilization. Yüan Chieh, *Chinese.* ChiP, *tr. by* Arthur Waley

To the south there is a dragon living in a mountain pool. Tu Fu, *Chinese.* CoBCP, *tr. by* Watson, Burton (b. 1925) *Fr.* Seven Songs Written During the Ch'ien-yüan Era. CoBCP, *tr. by* Burton Watson

To the Spider. Thomas Russell. Son

To the Spirit of Keats. James Russell Lowell. Son

To the Spirits of Shakespeare and Velázquez. Sándor Weöres, *Hungarian.* CEEP, *tr. by* Emery E. George

To the Stars. Andreas Gryphius, *German.* GePo, *tr. by* George C. Schoolfield

To the State Department. Ernesto Cardenal. *See* Tahirassawichi in Washington.

To the State of Love or The Senses' Festival. John Cleveland. CBLP; EP
("Who would not die upon the spot?") (LL) EP

To the state of West Virginia. The Story of Lovers Leap. Maggie Pogue Johnson. CBWP-4

To the States, To Identify the 16th, 17th, or 18th Presidentiad. Walt Whitman. CIC; NAAL-1; NAAL-3; RaBo

To the statistical Sparta of the champs. (LL) On Hurricane Jackson. Alan Dugan. CoAP; TRP

To the Statue on the Capitol. John James Piatt. APN-2
(To the Statue on the Capitol: Looking Eastward at Dawn.) GS

To the stern God of Sea. (LL) Odes 1.5. Horace. OBCVT; AWP; EBEV; EnLoPo; OBVE; PoEL-3, *tr. by* Milton

To the still dwelling. (LL) In valleys green and still. A. E. Housman. FaBoTw; OAEL-2; SCV

To the Stone-Cutters. Robinson Jeffers. AmPP; ColAP; MoAmPo; NAAL-2; NOBA; NoP-4; OxBA; PoRA
("Honey peace in old poems, The.") (LL) NoP-4

To the Street Piano. John Davidson.
Labourer's Wife, A. EBVV

To the Sun. Saul Tchernichowsky, *Hebrew.*
"I have been to my God like the iris and the anemone." MHP, *tr. by* Ruth Finer Mintz
"I have been to my God like the iris and the anemore." MHP, *tr. by* Ruth Finer Mintz
"Images of a faded world possessed me, I cannot flee!" MHP, *tr. by* Ruth Finer Mintz
"Or the image-kingdom's idol of the past generation." MHP, *tr. by* Ruth Finer Mintz

To the Sun. *Unknown, Greek.* GriP, *tr. by* Apostolos N. Athanasskis *Fr.* The Orphic Hymns.

To the Sun-Dial. John Quincy Adams. APN-1

To the Superhuman Adelmund, When She Would Undo the Kiss Already Done. Philipp von Zesen, *German.* GePo, *tr. by* George C. Schoolfield

To the Supreme Being. Michelangelo Buonarroti, *Italian.* AWP

To The Supreme Commander, Sirian Forces. A Day on the Planet. Brian Morse. NOxBChV

To the Swallow. Euenus, *Greek.* OBCVT; OBVE, *tr. by* William Cowper

To the Swallow. Pamphilus, *Greek.* GrAn, *tr. by* Dennis Schmitz

To the temple, singing. (LL) In the Suburbs. Louis Simpson. TRP; WeT

To the Terrestrial Globe. Sir William Schwenck Gilbert. APAD; NBLV

To the Thawing Wind. Robert Frost. OxBA

To the Things That Are Immortal. Abba Kovner, *Hebrew.* IP, *tr. by* Warren Bargad *and* Stanley F. Chyet

To the Thoughtful Reader. William Meredith. NoAM

To the Thrice-Sacred Queen Elizabeth. Mary Sidney Herbert. NALW; NoP-4
(To Queen Elizabeth.) PBRV

To the thunder of bells a voice calls for blood! The Bells. Saul Tchernichowsky, *Hebrew.* MHP, *tr. by* Ruth Finer Mintz

To the Torrid Zone. Helen Maria Williams. *See* Sonnet VI. To the Torrid Zone.

To the Translator of Lucan [*or* Lucan's Pharsalia, 1614]. Sir Walter Ralegh. SiPS
(To the Translator.) PBRV

To the triple goddess of Amarynthus. Theodoridas, *Greek.* GrAn, *tr. by* John Heath-Stubbs *and* Carol A. Whiteside

To the Tune "A Floating Cloud Crosses Enchanted Mountain." Huang O, *Chinese.* BoWoP, *tr. by* Kenneth Rexroth *and* Ling Chung

To the Tune "A Hilly Garden." Li Ch'ing-chao, *Chinese.* ChiPo, *tr. by* Kenneth Rexroth *and* Ling Chung

To the Tune "Bamboo at West Lake." Shen Chou, *Chinese.* CoBLCP, *tr. by* Jonathan Chaves

To the Tune—"But I Fancy Lovely Nancy." Patrick Carey. CBLP

To the Tune "Chao-chün's Sorrow." Yang Shen, *Chinese.* CoBLCP, *tr. by* Jonathan Chaves

To the Tune "Chiang ch'eng tzu." Yang Shen, *Chinese.* CoBLCP, *tr. by* Jonathan Chaves

To the Tune "Chieh san ch'eng" ("I love the autumn moon"). Yang Shen. *Fr.* Four Poems from the Sequence "Singing of the Moon." CoBLCP, *tr. by* Jonathan Chaves

To the Tune "Chieh san ch'eng" ("I love the spring moon"). Yang Shen. *Fr.* Four Poems from the Sequence "Singing of the Moon." CoBLCP, *tr. by* Jonathan Chaves

To the Tune "Child at Play." Yang Shen, *Chinese.* CoBLCP, *tr. by* Jonathan Chaves

To the Tune, "Ch'ing-p'ing Yüeh." Yang Shen, *Chinese.* CoBLCP, *tr. by* Jonathan Chaves

To the Tune "Chiu-ch'üan tzu." Wu Chien, *Chinese.* CoBLCP, *tr. by* Jonathan Chaves

To the Tune "Flowers in the Rain." Yang Shen, *Chinese.* CoBLCP, *tr. by* Jonathan Chaves

To the Tune "Glittering Sword Hilts." Liu Yu Hsi, *Chinese.* OHMPC, *tr. by* Kenneth Rexroth

To the Tune "Heavenly Immortal" ("Waves wash off the peach blossoms"). Yang Shen, *Chinese.* CoBLCP, *tr. by* Jonathan Chaves

To the Tune "Heavenly Immortal." Yang Shen, *Chinese.* CoBLCP, *tr. by* Jonathan Chaves

To the Tune "Moon Over West River." Yang Shen, *Chinese.* CoBLCP, *tr. by* Jonathan Chaves

To the Tune "Nan-hsiang-tzu." Shen Chou, *Chinese.* CoBLCP, *tr. by* Jonathan Chaves
(Expressing My Feelings.) ChiPo, *tr. by* Jonathan Chaves

To the Tune "New Moon." Yang Shen, *Chinese.* CoBLCP, *tr. by* Jonathan Chaves

To the Tune of the Coventry Carol. Stevie Smith. FaBoTw

To the Tune—"Once I Lov'd a Maiden Fair." Patrick Carey. CBLP

To the Tune "Partridge Sky." Yang Shen, *Chinese.* CoBLCP, *tr. by* Jonathan Chaves

To the Tune, "Plum Blossoms Fall and Scatter." Li Ch'ing-chao, *Chinese.* OHPC, *tr. by* Kenneth Rexroth

To the Tune "Red Embroidered Shoes." Huang O, *Chinese.* ChiPo; PBWP; WPOW, *tr. by* Kenneth Rexroth *and* Ling Chung

To the Tune "Shui hsien-tzu." Ma Chih-yüan, *Chinese.* CoBLCP

To the Tune "Soaring Clouds." Huang O, *Chinese.* BoWoP; PBWP; WPOW, *tr. by* Kenneth Rexroth *and* Ling Chung

To the Tune "Song of the Plum Blossom at the River Town." Yang Shen, *Chinese.* CoBLCP, *tr. by* Jonathan Chaves

To the Tune "Spring at Wu Ling." Li Ch'ing-chao, *Chinese.* OHMPC, *tr. by* Kenneth Rexroth

To the Tune "Spring in Tien Is Fine." Yang Shen, *Chinese.* CoBLCP, *tr. by* Jonathan Chaves

To the Tune "Stopping My Horse to Listen." Yang Shen, *Chinese.* CoBLCP, *tr. by* Jonathan Chaves

To the Tune "The Fair Maid of Yu." Chiang Chieh, *Chinese.* OHMPC, *tr. by* Kenneth Rexroth

To the Tune "The Fall of a Little Wild Goose." Huang O, *Chinese.* WPOW, *tr. by* Kenneth Rexroth *and* Ling Chung

To the Tune "The Phoenix Hairpin." T'ang Wan, *Chinese.* WPOW, *tr. by* Kenneth Rexroth *and* Ling Chung

To the Tune "The River Is Red." Ch'iu Chin, *Chinese.* AiP; BoWoP; PBWP, *tr. by* Kenneth Rexroth *and* Ling Chung

To the Tune "The Southerner." Yang Shen, *Chinese.* CoBLCP, *tr. by* Jonathan Chaves

To the Tune "T'ien ching sha." Ma Chih-yüan, *Chinese.*
Autumn Thoughts. CoBLCP, *tr. by* Jonathan Chaves

To the Tune "Yellow Oriole" ("Threads of rain weave lambent light"). Yang Shen, *Chinese.* CoBLCP, *tr. by* Jonathan Chaves

To the Tune "Yellow Oriole" ("Willows weave spring sorrow"). Yang Shen, *Chinese.* CoBLCP, *tr. by* Jonathan Chaves

To the Tune "Yu hu-lu" ("I love the summer moon"). Yang Shen. *Fr.* Four Poems from the Sequence "Singing of the Moon." CoBLCP, *tr. by* Jonathan Chaves

To the Tune "Yu hu-lu" ("I love the winter moon"). Yang Shen. *Fr.* Four Poems from the Sequence "Singing of the Moon." CoBLCP, *tr. by* Jonathan Chaves

To the Unborn and Waiting Children. Lucille Clifton. InPK-6

To the Unconstant Cynthia: a Song. Sir Robert Howard *and* Dryden. NOSC

To the Union Savers of Cleveland. Frances Ellen Watkins Harper. AAP

To the universal question. A Prima Donna Poet Replies. Lorri Jackson. EC3

To the University. Alicia D'Anvers. KTR; NOSC *Fr.* Academia; or The Humours of the University of Oxford.

To the University of Cambridge, in New-England. Phillis Wheatley. AmPP; NAAAL; NAAL-1; NAAL-3; TAP

To the Unknown Eros. Coventry Patmore. PoEL-5 *Fr.* The Unknown Eros.

To the Unknown Warrior. G. K. Chesterton. NSI

To the Unkown Author of *Absalom and Achitophel.* Nathaniel Lee. "Take it as earnest of a faith renewed." EPCY

To the Unnamed Buddhist Nun Who Burned Herself to Death on the Night of June 3, 1966. Diane Di Prima. BB

To the Veterans of the Abraham Lincoln Brigade. Genevieve Taggard. NMM-2

To the Virgin. Maria De' Medici, *Italian.* WPoS, *tr. by* Laura Anna Stortoni *and* Mary Prentice Lillie

To the Virginian Voyage. Michael Drayton. AiP; CABP; HAP; NAEL-1; NOBE; NOSC; OBEV; PBRV; PoEL-2; SCGP

To the Virgins, to Make the Most of Time. Gavin Ewart. OBCoV

To the Virtuosos. William Shenstone. ECEV

To the Water Nymphs, Drinking at the Fountain. Robert Herrick. BeJo; CaPo; NAEL-1

To the Waters of the Chia-ling. Yüan Chen, *Chinese.* SuSp, *tr. by* William H. Nienhauser

To the Western Wind. Judah Halevi, *Hebrew.* TrJP, *tr. by* Solomon Solis-Cohen

To the Western Wind. Robert Herrick. CaPo; OBEV

To the Western World. Louis Simpson. CoAP; CoAmPo; LiTM; NOBA; PFE; TAP; TRP

To the Wheel of Progress. Mrs. Henry Linden. CBWP-4

To the White Fiends. Claude McKay. NAAAL; PoBA

To the white-mantled maidens. Korinna, *Greek.* WPOW, *tr. by* Richmond Lattimore

To the White People of America. Joshua McCarter Simpson. AAP

To the wild wild beat of a tom tom tom. Reversion. Barry O. Higgs. PeSA

To the Willow-Tree. Robert Herrick. CaPo; OBEV; SCGP

To the wind she says, "They have eaten me alive." (LL) In The Park. Gwen Harwood. BMAP; GEA

To the Wine Treasurer of the Circuit Mess. Horace Smith. UV

To the Winter Aphrodite. "Michael Field." VWP

To the Wissahiccon. Frances Anne Kemble. APN-1

To the Wooden Hermit. Han Yü, *Chinese.* SuSp, *tr. by* Kenneth O. Hanson

To the Woodville Depot. David Chapman Berry. MT

To the World [A Farewell for a Gentlewoman, Virtuous and Noble]. Ben Jonson. BeJo; SeCP

To the World: the Perfection of Love. William Habington. BeJo *Fr.* Castara.

To the Writers' Worship in Zomba. Felix Mnthali. PeSAV

To the young man I would say. I'm Older than You, Please Listen. Arthur Rex Dugard Fairburn. PeNZ

To thee, bright Castor, and thy Brother Star! Catullus. *See* The Yacht.

To Thee, Eternal Soul, Be Praise. Richard Watson Gilder. AH

To thee, fair freedom! I retire. Written at [*or* in] an Inn at Henley. William Shenstone. AWP; NOBE; NOEC; OBEV; OxAEP-1

To thee, my way in epigrams seems new. To My Mere English Censurer. Ben Jonson. BeJo

To Thee, O God. Abiel Holmes. AH

To Thee, O God, the Shepherd Kings. John Gardiner Calkins Brainard. AH

To thee obeyeth all the East as far as Ganges goes. Ovid. OBVE, *tr. by* Arthur Golding *Fr.* Metamorphoses.

To thee—rude warrior, who, we once admired. Susanna Centlivre. ECWP *Fr.* An Epistle to the King of Sweden.

To Thee the Tuneful Anthem Soars. Mather Byles. AH

To Thee, Then, Let All Beings Bend. Nathaniel Evans. AH

To thee, whose cautious step and specious air. Annabella Plumptre. ECWP; NOEC *Fr.* Ode to Moderation.

To Their Excellencies the Lords Justices of Ireland, the Humble Petition of Frances Harris, Who Must Starve, and Die a Maid if It Miscarries. Jonathan Swift. NOEC; PoEL-3

To their long home the greatest princes go. Upon a Funeral. Sir John Beaumont. NOSC

To them who crossed the flood. Inscription. Herman Melville. UnPo

To them, yes, every pane! (LL) On the Asylum Road. Charlotte Mew. VWP

To Theodora. *Unknown.* OxBChV

To Theodore. George Marion McClellan. AAP

To these bare fields, built at today's expense. (LL) Pyrography. John Ashbery. PoM; VCAP

To these whom death again did wed. An Epitaph Upon Husband and Wife Who Died and Were Buried Together. Richard Crashaw. EBEV; FaBoEE; NOBE; OBEV; OxAEP-1; OxBM; SeCP

To Thine Eternal Arms, O God. Thomas Wentworth Higginson. AH

To Thine Own Self Be True. Shakespeare. ImPo *Fr.* Hamlet. NAWM-1

To think how to unthink that thought again. (LL) Confusion. Christopher Hervey. BXAP; UV

To think of time—of all that retrospection. Walt Whitman. APN-1; ImPo; MeMAP

("To think that these are so much and so nigh to other drivers, and he there takes no interest in them.") (LL) ImPo

To think that this meaningless thing was ever a rose. Summer Is Ended. Christina Rossetti. NOBVV

To think the face we love shall ever die. Etruscan Tombs. Agnes Mary Frances Robinson. PeVV

To think to know the country and not know. A Hillside Thaw. Robert Frost. CMoP

To think what he has missed. Catullus. *See* Carmen 5 ("My sweetest Lesbia, let us live and love").

To This Book. Martin Opitz, *German.* GePo, *tr. by* George C. Schoolfield

To this corner of Grant and Vallejo. Café Trieste: San Francisco. Joseph Brodsky. EP

"To this day no one knows." Mayan Ruins. Ory Bernstein. *Fr.* Poems from Mexico. IP, *tr. by* Warren Bargad *and* Stanley F. Chyet

To this long pelt over the back of a chair. (LL) An Otter. Ted Hughes. CMoP; MoP; NoAM

To Thomalin. Phineas Fletcher. NOSC

To Thomas Palmer [on His Book "The Sprite of Trees and Herbs"]. Ben Jonson. NoSic

To Those Born Later. Bertolt Brecht, *German.* AF, *tr. by* John Willett, Ralph Manheim *and* Erich Fried

To those fair isles where crimson sunsets burn. Toussaint L'Ouverture. Henrietta Cordelia Ray. CBWP-3

To those fixed on white. People. Jean Toomer. GT

To Those of My Sisters Who Kept Their Naturals. Gwendolyn Brooks. NMM-2

To those who Dwell in Realms of day. (LL) Auguries of Innocence. William Blake. EBEV; FaBoCh; FaPoR; ImPo; OAEL-1; OBNC; OxAEP-2; OxBoLi; PeECV; PoEL-4; TFi

To Those Who Have Gone Home Tired. William Daniel Ehrhart. CDa

To those who have tried and seemingly have failed. Courage to Live. Grace Noll Crowell. PoToHe

To thrill with all the sweets of life—is living. (LL) Living. *Unknown.* BLPA; FaBoBe

To throw away the key and walk away. The Walking Tour. W. H. Auden. CMoP; MoBrPo *Fr.* Paid on Both Sides.

To throw that faint thin line upon the shore! (LL) A Dusty Answer. George Meredith. EBEV; EnLoPo; EnVR; GSo; GTBS-P; HAP; NOBE; NOBVV; NoP-4; OAEL-2; OBNC; OxAEP-2; PoE; PoEL-5; SCGP; Son; TFi

To Time. Mary Tighe. IMW

To Tirzah. William Blake. FHYEP; NAEL-2; NOBE; OAEL-1; Ro *Fr.* Songs of Experience.

To Tom Saunders on His Imprisonment. Bill Griffiths. NBrP

To touch the cup with eager lips and taste, not drain it. Living. *Unknown.* BLPA; FaBoBe

To Toussaint L'Ouverture. Wordsworth. FaBoPV; InPK-6; NOBE; OBNC; PBMP; PoRA; Ro

To transport water, stone, wood, sky. (LL) Extended Sonnet on the Death of Isaac Danziger. Meir Wieseltier, *Hebrew.* IP, *tr. by* Warren Bargad *and* Stanley F. Chyet

To travel like a bird, lightly to view. C. Day Lewis. GTBS-P *Fr.* O Dreams, O Destinations.

To tread those blest paths which before I writ. (LL) The Passionate Man[']s Pilgrimage. Sir Walter Ralegh. AAS; ChIV-2; EBEvV; NOBE; NoP-4; NoSic; OBEV; OxAEP-1; PeECV; PoE; PoEL-2; PoRA; RB; SCGP; SiPS; TFi

To treat the thing directly, Ezra Pound. A High-toned Old Fascist Gentleman. William Zaranka. BXAP

To tremble in prayer and trepidation. The Revelation. Stanley Crouch. SeSe

To true roses uplifted on the bilious tide of evening. To Redouté. John Ashbery. PoA

To Trust. Antonia Pozzi, *Italian*. PBWP, *tr. by* Lynne Lawner

To try to find my heart, it's hard enough. Wang Kuo-wei, *Chinese*. SuSp, *tr. by* Irving Y. Lo

To Tu Fu. Li Po, *Chinese*. TAL, *tr. by* Robert Payne

To turn a stone. High Noon at Los Alamos. Eleanor Wilner. NoP-4

To Turn Back. John Haines. CoAmPo; TRP

To Turn from Love. Sarah Webster Fabio. BlSi

To turn my volume o'er nor find. How to Read Me. Walter Savage Landor. NOBVV

To Two Bereaved. Thomas Ashe. NOBVV

To Tzu-an. Yü Hsüan-chi, *Chinese*. BoWoP, *tr. by* Geoffrey Waters; SuSp, *tr. by* Jan W. Walls

To Tzŭ-chih: among the 'Flowers'. Li Shang-yin, *Chinese*. PLT, *tr. by* A. C. Graham

To————. Ulalume: A Ballad. Edgar Allan Poe. *See* Ulalume [*or* Ulalume—a Ballad].

To Urania. Joseph Brodsky, *Russian*. AF, *tr. by* Joseph Brodsky

To Urania. Benjamin Colman. SCAP

To Usward. Gwendolyn B. Bennett. BlSi

To Varus. Catullus. AWP, *tr. by* Walter Savage Landor *Fr.* Carmina.
("But see not our own Load behind.") (LL) OBVE, *tr. by* Matthew Prior (*Carmina*, XXII.) OBVE, *tr. by* Matthew Prior
("Suffenus whom you know, the Witty.") OBVE, *tr. by* Matthew Prior

To veil the saintly face. Counterfable of Orpheus. Marie-Claire Bancquart, *French*. MFP, *tr. by* Martin Sorrell

To Venus. Joachim Du Bellay, *French*. FLP; LoP, *tr. by* Alistair Elliot

To Venus. Horace. AWP; OBVE *Fr.* Odes.
(IV, 1. To Venus.) OBVE

To Vernon Lee. Amy Levy. VWP

To very few, or else to none. (LL) His Content in the Country. Robert Herrick. CaPo; CavPo

To vex thy soul with these unjust alarms. To Orestes. Elizabeth Singer Rowe. PEW

To Victor Hugo of My Crow Pluto. Marianne Moore. CBNP

To Vietnam. Charlie Cobb. PoBA

To Violet [with Prewar Poems]. Basil Bunting. FaBoMo; PoA

To Violets. Robert Herrick. CaPo; OBEV; SeCP

To Virgil [*or* Vergil]. Tennyson. AWP; EBVVPR; GTBS-P; OAEL-2; PoEL-5

To [the] Virgins, to Make Much of Time. Robert Herrick. AWP; BLPA; BeJo; BoLoP; CavPo; ClHu; EBEvV; EnLoPo; GBL; GLoP; HAP; HeIP-4; ImPo; InPK-6; InPS-3; LoP; NAEL-1; NBLV; NIP-4; NOBE; NOSC; OAEL-1; OBEV; OxAEP-1; PBMP; PoE; PoEL-3; Poetr; SCGP; SCV; SeCP; SoSe-8; TFi; UV
(Counsel to Girls.) GTBS-P
(To Virgins.) CaPo
("You may forever tarry.") (LL) NoP-4; PFE; PoPoPo; SAGP

To Vittoria Colonna. Michelangelo Buonarroti, *Italian*. AWP, *tr. by* Longfellow

To Vulcan. Robert Herrick. CaPo

To W. C. W. M. D. Alfred Kreymborg. PoA

To W. L. G. on Reading His "Chosen Queen." Charlotte Forten. BlSi

To W. P. George Santayana.
"With you a part of me hath passed away." PFE

To W. R. William Ernest Henley. NOBVV

To W. S. M. Arthur W. Monroe. APN-2

To W.S.—On his Wonderful Toys. Walter Davies. NOxBChV

"To wade the sea mist, then to wade the sea." Stone Horse Shoals. Malcolm Cowley. NYBP

To wake the world this sleepy morn. (LL) Donkey, donkey, old and gray. *Unknown*. ACTP; ReMoGo

To wake up and discover. The Well-beloved. John Montague. BiHa

To Waken a Small Person. Donald Justice. NYBP

To Waken an Old Lady. William Carlos Williams. HAP; InPK-6; LiLi; SoSe-8; WeW-3

To Walk Abroad. Walking. Thomas Traherne. EBEV

To walk alone—yet wish I walked with thee. John Clare. *See* To Mary: 'It Is the Evening Hour'.

To Walk in Warm Rain. David McCord. AYFP

To walk on air. (LL) Beethoven, Opus 111. Amy Clampitt. NIP-4

To wander far from you, the centre. (LL) An Excuse of Absence. Thomas Carew. CaPo; SeCP

To waning day, to the wide round of shadow. Dante, *Italian*. STV, *tr. by* John Frederick Nims

To want to be a saint to want to be a saint to want to. Giant Steps. John Taggart. MoNo

To watch the angels fall from fire mountains. (LL) Living Apart. Maura Stanton. NAmP90

To wear the arctic fox. The Arctic Ox. Marianne Moore. NYBP

To Wed or Not to Wed. Una Marson. PBCV

To wed, or not to wed? That is the question. *Unknown*. BXAP

To weep there! (LL) The Clown's Song. Shakespeare. CTC; GBL; GTBS-P; NOBE; NoP-4; NoSic; OBEV; PoEL-2; PoRA; TFi

To weep thine ashes am I come. Lament for Aquileia Destroyed, and Never to Be Built Again. Paulinus of Aquileia, *Latin*. MLL, *tr. by* Helen Waddell

To Wei Pa, a Retired Scholar. Tu Fu, *Chinese*. OHPC, *tr. by* Kenneth Rexroth

To welcome the New-livery'd *year*. (LL) On a Bank [*or* Banck] as I Sate [*or* Sat] a-Fishing; a Description of the Spring. Sir Henry Wotton. CH; NOSC; SeCP

To Werther. Goethe. *Fr.* Trilogy of Passion. STV, *tr. by* John Frederick Nims

To western woods and lonely plains. On the Emigration to America [and Peopling the Western Country]. Philip Freneau. ColAP; NAAL-1; NAAL-3; TAP

To wet your eye withouten tear. Sir Thomas Wyatt. SiPS

To what intent or purpose was Man made. As Concerning Man. Alexander Radcliffe. NOSC; OBSV

To what purpose, April, do you return again? Spring. Edna St. Vincent Millay. BoWoP; MeMAP; MoAmPo; NoP-4; SAGP

To what serves mortal beauty—dangerous; does set danc. Gerard Manley Hopkins. EP

To What Strangers, What Welcome. James Vincent Cunningham. NoAM
Miramar Beach. PoA

To where the pale sea brooded murmuring. (LL) Constant keeping-past of shaken trees. D. G. Rossetti. PeVV, *pt.* I

To whistle and smile at the johns. (LL) As You Leave Me. Etheridge Knight. MT; NNaP

To Whistler, American. Ezra Pound. AiP; FaBoA; NAAL-2; PoA

To Whittier. Josephine D. Henderson Heard. AAP; CBWP-4

To whoever is not listening to the sea. Poet's Obligation. Pablo Neruda, *Spanish*. VCWP, *tr. by* Alastair Reid

To Whom Else? Robert Graves. FaBoMo

To whom I owe the leaping delight. A Dedication to My Wife. T. S. Eliot. BoLoP; BXBM

To Whom It May Concern. James Vincent Cunningham. FYAP

To Whom It May Concern. Adrian Mitchell. OBWP

To Whom It May Concern. Jon Stallworthy. CBLP

To whom now Pyrrha, art thou kind? Horace. *See* Odes 4.7.

To whom shall I this dancing poem send. Dedications, I: To His Very Friend, Master Richard Martin. Sir John Davies. SiPS *Fr.* Orchestra; or, A Poem[e] of Da[u]ncing. NoSic; SiPS

To whom shall I this dancing poem send. To His Very Friend, Master Richard Martin. Sir John Davies. *Fr.* Dedications [*or* Orchestra]. SiPS

To whom should I speak today? A Dispute over Suicide. *Unknown, Egyptian*. TTY, *tr. by* T. Eric Peet

To whom with healing words Adam replied. Uncloistered Virtue. Milton. NOSC *Fr.* Book IX. FHYEP; NAEL-1; NAWM-1; OAEL-1 *Fr.* Paradise Lost.

To William Camden. Ben Jonson. AWP; BeJo; NAEL-1; NOSC

To William Carlos Williams. Galway Kinnell. NoAM; Poetr

To William Drummond of Hawthornden. Mary, of Morpeth Oxlie. KTR

To William, Earl[e] of Pembroke. Ben Jonson. SeCP

To William Hayley, Esq.: In Reply to His Solicitation to Write with Him in a Literary Work. William Cowper. Son

To William Roe ("Roe (and my joy to name) th'art now, to go"). Ben Jonson. BeJo; OAEL-1

To William Roe ("When Nature bids us leave to live, 'tis late"). Ben Jonson. NOSC

To William Simpson, Ochiltree. Robert Burns. OxBS

To William (Whom We Have Missed). P. G. Wodehouse. NOBL

To William Wilberforce, Esq. William Cowper. Son

To Wordsworth. Coleridge. EPCY; FHYEP; NAEL-2; OAEL-2

To William Wordsworth from Virginia. Julia Randall. NMM-2; WPE

To William Wordsworth on His Seventy-Fifth Birthday. Hartley Coleridge. EPCY

To win the love of women one should first discover. Kenneth Koch. NNaP *Fr.* The Art of Love.

To windward midnight glowed, iridium sheen. Ice. Alan Gould. NOBAu

To Winky. Amy Lowell. PC

To winter-ground thy corse. (LL) With fairest flowers,/ Whilst summer lasts. Shakespeare. EBEV; RB

To wipe his pretty nose. (LL) I had a little husband. *Unknown.* BoTP; OxNR; ReMoGo

To wish and want and not obtain. Sir Thomas Wyatt. SiPS

To wish to climb a ladder to the loft. James Keir Baxter. PeNZ *Fr.* Autumn Testament.

To wit, the lever said. News. Lorine Niedecker. PFTM

To —. With the Following Poem, *preface to* The Palace of Art. Tennyson. EnVR; NOBRP

To witless agony. (LL) Open House. Theodore Roethke. NOBA; NoAM

To Women. Richard Hugo. NIP-4

To Women, as Far as I'm Concerned. D. H. Lawrence. InPS-3; OxBSP; RaBo

To women in contemporary voice and dislocation. Re-reading Jane. Anne Stevenson. NALW

To wood and field. (LL) Snow-Flakes. Henry Wadsworth Longfellow. APN-1; BoTP; GEA; NCAP; NOBA; NoP-4; PoEL-5; SAGP; TAP; UnPo

To Wordsworth. John Clare. OAEL-2; Son

To Wordsworth. Hartley Coleridge. Son
("When I review the course that I have run.") Ro

To Wordsworth. Walter Savage Landor. OAEL-2
"Chatting on deck was Dryden too." Ro

To Wordsworth. Shelley. EPCY; FHYEP; NoP-4; Ro; Son

To work away in art's traditional measure. Sonnet. Goethe, *German.* STV, *tr. by* John Frederick Nims

To worship / this perfection. (LL) The Gift. William Carlos Williams. ChIV-2

To wound myself upon the sharp edges of the night? (LL) The Taxi. Amy Lowell. BoWoP; LW; MoAmPo

To wrap a baby bunting in. (LL) Bye, bye, baby bunting / Daddy's gone a-hunting. *Unknown.* LB; OxNR

To wrestle with the angel—Art. (LL) Art. Herman Melville. AmPP; APN-2; ColAP; NAAL-1; NAAL-3; NCAP; NOBA; PAR

To write of Sol in his exaltation. Robert Copland. NoSic *Fr.* The High Way to the Spital House.

To write threescore: this is the second of our reign [*or* raigne]. (LL) The Anniversary [*or* Anniversarie]. Donne. BoLoP; ESCV; FHYEP; HAP; HoPM; MeLP; NOBE; NoSic; OAEL-1; OxBM; SCGP; SeCP; TFi; WeW-3

To yet more boastful visions of despair. (LL) Recalling War. Robert Graves. AF; CMoP; LiTM; NoAM; OAEL-2; OBWP; PeFWW; PoWW

To yon fause stream that, by the sea. The Mermaid. *Unknown.* CH

To You. Frank Horne. BPo *Fr.* Letters [*or* Notes] Found near a Suicide. PoBA

To You. Kenneth Koch. CAPP-1

To You. Elolongue Epanya Yondo, *French.* NegPo, *tr. by* Ellen Conroy Kennedy

To you and to me? (LL) The Bride. Bella Akhatovna Akhmadulina, *Russian.* LiLi, *tr. by* Stephen Stepanchev

To you, dere herte, variant and mutable. Unknown. MiEL

To you gave Sense, Good-humour, and a Poet. (LL) Epistle [II,] to a Lady[: Of the Characters of Women]. Alexander Pope. CABP; NAEL-1; NOEC; OAEL-1

To you I dedicate this work of grace. Emilia Lanier. NOSC *Fr.* To the Lady Anne, Countess of Dorset.

To you I'll give a coil of wire, barbed wire. Gifts as Tokens of Love. Trần Dạ Từ', *Vietnamese.* AVP, *tr. by* Huỳnh Sanh Thông

To you, Kypris, Lysidike. Asclepiades, *Greek.* GrAn, *tr. by* Alan Marshfield

To you, my friends, to you, my dear ones. Inna L'vovna Lisnyanskaya, *Russian.* TCRP, *tr. by* Albert C. Todd

To you [*or* yow], my purse [*or* purs], and to non [*or* no *or* noon] other wight. The Complaint of Chaucer to His [Empty] Purse. Chaucer. ImPo; MiEL; NAEL-1; NoP-4; OAEL-1; SCGP

To you, then, tenants of life's middle state. William Cowper. OBSV *Fr.* Tirocinium; or, A Review of Schools.

To you this fragrant oil, sweets to the sweet. A Gift. *Unknown, Greek.* GrAn, *tr. by* Guy Davenport

To you, troop so fleet. Hymn to the Winds. Joachim Du Bellay, *French.* AWP, *tr. by* Andrew Lang

To you, vague aspirations; enthusiasms. Alma Perdida. Valery Larbaud, *French.* NNPT, *tr. by* Ron Padgett *and* Bill Zavatsky

To you, whose dignitie strikes us with awe. To her royall highnesse the Dutchesse of Yorke. Katherine Philips. KTR

To your owne bents dispose you: you'le be found. Shakespeare. FaBoVe *Fr.* The Winter's Tale.

To Your Question. Duane Niatum. CDW

To Youth. Josephine D. Henderson Heard. CBWP-4

To youths, who hurry thus way. On a Painted Woman. Shelley. NBLV

To Yung-erh—Imitating a Work by Master Jade Stream. Li Tung-yang, *Chinese.* CoBLCP, *tr. by* Jonathan Chaves

To Yvor Winters, 1955. Thom Gunn. GTBS-P

To Zante. Ugo Foscolo, *Greek.* GrIP

To Zion. Judah Halevi, *Hebrew.* AWP, *tr. by* Maurice Samuel

Toad, A. Elizabeth Akers Allen. OBCA

Toad, The. Tristan Corbière, *French.* APo, *tr. by* Vernon Watkins

Toad, The. Gertrud Kolmar, *German.* APo, *tr. by* Henry A. Smith

Toad the power mower caught, A. The Death of a Toad. Richard Wilbur. CMoP; LiTM; MoP; NAAL-2; NoAM; PFE; PoA; Poetr

Toad the Tailor. Norah E. Hussey. BoTP

Toads. Philip Larkin. CMoP; NOBL; NoAM; OxAEP-2; OxBTC; PoE; Poetr; SoSe-8

Toads Revisited. Philip Larkin. CMoP; NOBL; OxAEP-2

Toadstools. Elizabeth Fleming. BoTP

Toady toady min yoself. A Digging Sing. *Unknown.* FaBoVe

Toast. Thomas McCarthy. PBCIP

Toast. Leonard Nathan. BLT

Toast to 2,000, A. Richard Percival Lister. OBCoV

Toast to the Flag, A. John Jay Daly. PoLF

Toaster, The. William Jay Smith. NOxBChV; OTCP

Tobacco. Philip Freneau. TAP

Tobacco ("Tobacco is a dirty weed"). Graham Lee Hemminger. PoLF (This Smoking World.) NBLV

Tobacco crumbs, vases and fringes. (LL) The Bean Eaters. Gwendolyn Brooks. BlSi; HAP; HeIP-4; LCAP-2; NALW; PoBA; PoE; Poetr; TAP; TRP; TTY; WeW-3

Tobacco is a dirty weed. Tobacco. Graham Lee Hemminger. NBLV; PoLF

Tobacco is a filthy weed. *Unknown.* FaBoEE

Tobacco Plant. Ivor Gurney. FP

Tobacco stains from your beautiful fingers. And I wish I did not feel like your mother, The. (LL) Rendezvous. Edna St. Vincent Millay. NALW

Tobacco Warehouse Blues. Houston A. Baker Jr. SeSe

Tobera. Jeff Tagami. OpBo

Tobias and the Angel. John Gray. NOBVV

Tobit. Bible, Apocrypha, *Greek.*
Blessed Is God. TrJP, *tr. by* D. C. Simpson

Tobroken ben the statutz hye in hevene. Envoy to Scogan. Chaucer. EnVB

Toccata of Galuppi's, A. Robert Browning. EBVV; EBVVPR; EnVR; FaBoVe; GTBS-P; HAP; NAEL-2; NOBE; NOBVV; OAEL-2; UV ("Oh Galuppi, Baldassare, this is very sad to find!") NoP-4

Today. Thomas Carlyle. PFE

Today. Thomas Carlyle. PWR

Today. Frank Crane. CTV

Today. Ethel Romig Fuller. PoToHe

Today. Langston Hughes. GLP; VGW

Today. Angela Morgan. BLPA

Today. Frank O'Hara. TTTS

Today. Sunday. Primus St. John. ISC

Today. Today We Will Not Be Invisible Nor Silent. Victoria Lena Manyarrows. UnSA

Today. Jones Very. TAP

Today a field of pumpkins. Sassafras. Barbara Guest. FTOS

Today a silver coffin guards St. Agnes'. Catacombs. István Vas, *Hungarian.* CEEP, *tr. by* Emery E. George

Today, all day, I rode upon the Down. Wilfrid Scawen Blunt. *See* St. Valentine's Day.

Today, as at my glass I stood. To Mrs. Francis-Arabella Kelly. Mary Barber. ECWP

Today as I hang out the wash I see them again, a code. The Geese. Jorie Graham. HCAP

Today as I stared, suddenly a string snapped. The Rain of Stones Is Finished. Faiz Ahmad Faiz. EC3

Today as in the past, who is the master of these rivers and mountains? Tune: "Butterflies Lingering over Flowers"—Leaving the Border. Na-lan Hsing-te, *Chinese.* SuSp, *tr. by* An-yan Tang

Today as the news from Selma and Saigon. Monet's "Waterlilies." Robert Earl Hayden. GT; Poetr

Today, as usual, the mind goes hunting for a word. Once Again the Mind. Faiz Ahmad Faiz, *Arabic.* AF, *tr. by* Naomi Lazard

Today at the edge of light. Clinton. Sterling Plumpp. BkSV *Fr.* Clinton.

Today before a goblet of wine I was shamed. Drunk Too Soon. Yüan Chen, *Chinese*. SuSp, *tr. by* Dell R. Hales

Today beneath Benignant Skies. Denis Wortman. AH

Today, dear heart, but just today. Her Answer. John Bennett. BLPA

Today even those fireflies have become. An Elegy for Mangochi Fishermen. Jack A. Mapanje. PBMAP

Today, everything takes. At the Vietnam War Memorial, Washington, D. C. Robert Dana. CDa

Today: / Hark! Heaven sings! On Christmas Day to My Heart. Clement Paman. NOSC

Today has it all, sunshine. Gwyn Williams. OBWVE *Fr.* Aspects of Now.

"Today," he said to the mirror, "the person I am inside of." Not Thinking of Himself. Jack Myers. NAmP90

Today I am a farmer in the fields. Wang Chiu-ssu. CoBLCP, *tr. by* Jonathan Chaves *Fr.* The Robber of Kuan-shan.

Today I Am a Homicide in the North of the City. Wanda Coleman. NAAAL

Today I am at home. A Few Sirens. Alice Walker. CrSp

Today / I am 24. January 3, 1970. Mae Jackson. PoBA

Today I am walking alone in a bare place. Late November in a Field. James Wright. NAAL-2; NNaP

Today I asked the money changer. Sergey Aleksandrovich Yesenin, *Russian*. TCRP, *tr. by* Geoffrey Thurley

Today I became my own secret admirer, unearthing. Self-Portrait at Eighteen. Lynn Emanuel. CMAP

Today I bring you cold chrysanthemums. Between Seasons. Li-Young Lee. TRP

Today I chopped back irises. Clearing Away. Andrew Taylor. BMAP

Today I cleared out the kitchen with Dougie so Hedley could sand the kitchen floor. A Day in the Life. Stef Pixner. BrRo

Today I don't know what to do with the Earth. Voyages. Jules Supervielle, *French*. MFP, *tr. by* Martin Sorrell

Today I found the right fruit for my prime. A Kumquat for Keats. Tony Harrison. NoP-4

Today I get this letter from you and the sun. You (III). Tom Clark. PmAP; SPE *Fr.* You.

Today I learn "tamarisk." On Returning. Brigitte Frase. LoHo

Today I learned the *coora* flower. The Coora Flower. Gwendolyn Brooks. NoP-4

Today I lost my temper. *Unknown*. CTV

Today I put on. Saint Patrick's Breastplate, *Unknown*. NOIV

Today I sat before the cliff. *Unknown, Chinese*. CoBCP, *tr. by* Burton Watson

Today I saw a picture of the cancer cells. The Cancer Cells. Richard Eberhart. HAP; LiTM

Today I saw a place no one has seen. Iron Heaven. Betti Alver. BoWoP, *tr. by* Willis Barnstone *and* Felix Oinas

Today I saw a thing of arresting poignant beauty. Snow in October. Alice Moore Dunbar-Nelson. BlSi

Today I saw a woman plowing a furrow. Sister. Gabriela Mistral, *Spanish*. BoWoP, *tr. by* Langston Hughes

Today I saw a woman wrapped in rags. At the Slackening of the Tide. James Wright. UnPo; VGW

Today I saw black men. The Men. E. Ethelbert Miller. UnSA

Today I saw the dragon-fly. Tennyson. CTAV

Today I think. Digging. Edward Thomas. GaP; MoBrPo; OxBTC

Today I think of a boy in the Transvaal. Remembering Snow. Ralph Nixon Currey. PeSA

Today I wake having swung, naked, in London. Here and There. Anne Lauterbach. PmAP

Today I woke up missing. Rising to Meet It. Chana Bloch. CrSp

Today I wrote the ending of all poems. Discreet. Maria Flook. EOEF

Today I'd like to climb the difference. Hades in Manganese. Clayton Eshleman. APSN

Today in hazy San Francisco, I face seaward. We Are Americans Now, We Live in the Tundra. Marilyn Chin. UnSA

Today in Peru, this first day of summer. Pastoral. Lawrence Raab. AmPA

Today Is a Day of Great Joy. Victor Hernandez Cruz. LoL; TTY

Today Is Armistice, a Holiday. Delmore Schwartz. TrJP

Today Is Friday. Ramon Guthrie. PoE

Today is his first day of school. The First Day of School. Tru'o'ng Anh Thuy, *Vietnamese*. AVP, *tr. by* Huỳnh Sanh Thông

Today Is Not Like They Said. Kirk Hall. NBV

Today is the anniversary of our parting. Ise Tayu, *Japanese*. WPJ, *tr. by* Kenneth Rexroth *and* Ikuko Atsumi

Today is your. April Fool Birthday Poem for Grandpa. Diane Di Prima. CLPP; UnSA

Today is your / birthday and I have tried. Diane Di Prima. *See* April Fool Birthday Poem for Grandpa.

Today it rains all over the world and we are two. Angel in the Deluge. Rosario Murillo, *Spanish*. CLPP, *tr. by* Alejandro Murguía

Today it's going to cost us twenty dollars. How Things Work. Gary Soto. NoAM

Today, lonely for my father, I saw. My Father's Wedding. Robert Bly. InPS-3; NoAM; RaBo

Today / must have been Sunday. Eden After Dark. Richard Shelton. CDa

Today my mother and sisters. They've Come. Alfonsina Storni, *Spanish*. BoWoP, *tr. by* Aliki *and* Willis Barnstone; WPOW, *tr. by* Marti Moody

Today on a sandy road. On a Recollected Road. Amir Gilbo'a, *Hebrew*. MHP, *tr. by* Ruth Finer Mintz

Today on the lip of a bowl in the backyard. The Caterpillar. Miller Williams. MT

Today ready ripe, tomorrow all too shaken. (LL) The Frailty and Hurtfulness of Beauty. Henry Howard, Earl of Surrey. AAS; EnLoPo; HoPM; SiPS

Today, recovering from influenza. The True Confession of George Barker. George Barker.

Today she parades her shape like swellings of song. Portrait of a Pregnant Woman. Bobi Jones, *Welsh*. OBWVE, *tr. by* Joseph P. Clancy

Today, should you let fall a glass it would. Tramontana at Lerici. Charles Tomlinson. GTBS-P

Today snow sparks the air like mica—the sun's. Margaret Gibson. CrSp *Fr.* Unborn Child Elegy.

Today, the angel of dread, invisible. The Angel of Dread. Miklós Radnóti, *Hungarian*. PFTM, *tr. by* Clayton Eshleman *and* Gyula Kodolanyi

Today, the angels are all writing postcards. Saying One Thing. Robert Long. NAmP90

Today, the first dead leaf in the hall. A Dead Leaf. Howard Moss. NYBP

Today the journey is ended. A Soul's Soliloquy. Wenonah Stevens Abbott. BLPA

Today the leaves cry, hanging on branches swept by wind. The Course of a Particular. Wallace Stevens. HCAP

Today, the painter tossed his brush away. The Beau Ideal. Vũ Hoàng Chu'o'ng, *Vietnamese*. AVP, *tr. by* Huỳnh Sanh Thông

Today the self-destroying anger. Bruce Beaver. *Fr.* Letters to Live Poets. CBAP

Today the sixth of june. Nigeria in the Year 1999. Catherine Obianuju Acholonu. HBAPE

Today the skies are clear and blue. Now. *Unknown*. PWR

Today the snow is drifting. Snow. Philip Levine. ColAP

Today / the west / burns down. The Coup-clock Clicks. Brian Meeks. PBCV

Today the world unwrapped itself again. Summer. Moishe Kulbak, *Yiddish*. CEEP, *tr. by* Ruth Whitman

Today,/ there came a breeze thin as the needle of a syringe. J. Kitchener Davies. OBWVE, *tr. by* Joseph P. Clancy *Fr.* The Sound of the Wind That Is Blowing.

Today there've been moments. For a Daughter Gone Away. Brendan Galvin. GM

Today! today! (LL) Glycine's Song. Coleridge. CH; OBEV

Today too. Frank K. Robinson. HA

Today too. Tanka. Kitahara Hakushū, *Japanese*. MJT, *tr. by* Makoto Ueda

Today, Tuesday, I decided to move on. Malcolm Mooney's Land. W. S. Graham. FaBoTC

Today Tutu Is Beating the Same Burru As Me. Lebert Bethune. GT

Today Was a Bad Day Like TB. "Chrystos." UnSA

Today was a day of cold spring showers. April. Howard Nemerov. *Fr.* Epigrams. OBAL

Today we have marking of folders. Yesterday. Marking of Folders. Anne Anderton. UV

Today we have naming of parts. Yesterday. Henry Reed. *See* Naming Of Parts.

Today We Will Not Be Invisible Nor Silent. Victoria Lena Manyarrows. UnSA

Today, whatever may annoy. John Kendrick Bangs. PoToHe

"Today will be the day of what we both said." (LL) West-Running Brook. Robert Frost. MoAmPo; NOBA; NoP-4

Today Will Pass. Lemn Sissay. NBrP

Today you rain on me from every corner of the sky. Sure. Naomi Shihab Nye. MT

Today you were supposed to come. I Waited for Chuang Hsüan-yüan But He Never Came. Mo Shih-lung, *Chinese*. CoBLCP, *tr. by* Jonathan Chaves

Today, your servant will give back his head. Last Words. *Unknown, Vietnamese*. AVP, *tr. by* Huỳnh Sanh Thông

Today's Meditation. Antonio Machado Ruiz, *Spanish*. AF, *tr. by* Robert Bly

Today's News. Elizabeth Alexander. ISC

Today's paper is crammed full of news: pages and pages on the Somalia. The Shape of History. Charles Henry Webb. BAP-95

Todd. Stewart Conn. FaBoTC

Toe sticking out from under the hem, The. On a Fifteenth-Century Flemish Angel. David Ray. CRP

Toe tipe. *Unknown.* OxNR

Toe, trip and go. *Unknown.* OxNR

Toe upon [*or* after] toe, a snowing flesh. Nude Descending a Staircase. X. J. Kennedy. APAD; CoAmPo; HoPM; NIP-4; OxBSP; PoA; SAGP

Toe'osh; a Laguna Coyote Story. Leslie Marmon Silko. CDW; NoAM; VoR

Together. Sarah Orne Jewett. CPO

Together. Maxine W. Kumin. BoWoP

Together. Ludwig Lewisohn. PoToHe; TrJP

Together eternity and death threaten me. Patrizia Cavalli, *Italian.* NeIt, *tr. by* Judith Baumel

Together, fourteen years older. In the Cathedral. Patricia Beer. OxBC

Together in infinite shade. Too Much Coffee. Edwin Arlington Robinson. MoAmPo

Together they stood watching on the terrace. Antony and Cleopatra. José-Maria de Heredia, *Spanish.* EP; FLP, *tr. by* Alistair Elliot

Together twists their threads, and yet draws hers the longer. (LL) A Dialogue betwixt Time and a Pilgrim[e]. Aurelian Townshend. NOBE; OAEL-1; PoEL-2; SeCP

Together we trace the child's face in the first snow. Laterna Obscura. Henrikas Nagys, *Lithuanian.* CEEP, *tr. by* Jonas Zdanys

Together with that which was spilled in battle. Servile Blood. Vasily Fyodorov, *Russian.* TCRP, *tr. by* Lubov Yakovleva

Toil. Avraham Shlonsky, *Hebrew.* MHP, *tr. by* Ruth Finer Mintz

"Toil! toil! toil!" The Wandering Jew. Eloise Bibb. CBWP-4

Toilet, The. Alexander Pope. NOBE *Fr.* The Rape of the Lock[, an Heroi-Comical Poem]. FHYEP; HAP; ImPo; OAEL-1; OBNV; PeLV; PoEL-3

Toilette, The. John Gay. ECEV

Toiling of Felix, The. Henry Van Dyke.
    Envoy: "Legend of Felix is ended, the toiling of Felix is done, The." BLPA

Token, A. Robert Creeley. VGW

Token, The. Frank Templeton Prince. FaBoTw; OxBTC

Token woman gleams like a gold molar in a toothless mouth, The. Marge Piercy. NALW

Tokens. William Barnes. PoEL-4

Toledo. Roy Campbell. MoBrPo

Toledo Room, The. Alistair Paterson.
    "They do it with knives." PeNZ

Tolerance of Crows, The. Charles Donnelly. CIP-2

Toll for the brave! On the Loss of the *Royal George.* William Cowper. EBEV; FaPoR; GTBS-P; NOBE; OxAEP-1

Toll no bell for me, dear father, dear Mother. The Changeling. Charlotte Mew. CH; NOxBChV

Toll the bell, fellow. The Red Cow Is Dead. Elwyn Brooks White. NBLV; NYBP

Tolling from St. Patrick's, The. Burial of an Irish President. Austin Clarke. BIrV

Tollund Man, The. Seamus Heaney. BIrV; CABP; CIP-2; EBEV; FaBoMo; PBCIP; PNI

Toltecs were wise, The. *Unknown.* CA

Tom. Victor D. Questel. PBCV

Tom. James Schuyler. GLP

Tom Agnew, Bill Agnew. D. G. Rossetti. FaBoEE

Tom Bone. Charles Causley. FuFo

Tom Bowling. Charles Dibdin. *See* Poor Tom.

Tom Brainless as Student and Preacher at College. John Trumbull. *Fr.* The Progress of Dulness. AmPP

Tom Brainless, at the close of last year. An Amorous Temper. John Trumbull. *Fr.* The Progress of Dulness. AmPP

Tom Brown's two little Indian boys. *Unknown.* OxNR

Tom-Cat, The. Don Marquis. PC; PoRA

Tom Child had often painted Death. This Morning Tom Child, the Painter, Died. Samuel Sewall. SCAP

Tom Deadlight. Herman Melville. APN-2; NCAP

Tom Dooley. *Unknown.* AmFP

Tom Farley. Colin Thiele. NOBAu

Tom Fool at Jamaica. Marianne Moore. NYBP

Tom—garlanded with squat and surly steel. Tom's Garland: Upon the Unemployed. Gerard Manley Hopkins. EnVR; FaBoPV; Son

Tom, He Was a Piper's Son. *Unknown.* OxNR

Tom, Jill and Bob. *Unknown.* ACTP

Tom Joanides. Lloyd Schwartz. EOEF

Tom Jones's Plum Tree. *Unknown.* AmFP

TOM never drinks: that I should much commend. Martial, *Latin.* OBCVT, *tr. by* William Hay

Tom o'Bedlam. *Unknown.* CH; EBEV; FaBoCh; OAEL-1; OxBoLi; PoRA ("And wild for to hold, though I seem tame.") (LL) NoP-4 (Loving Mad Tom.) EnSB; HAP; NOBE; NTP; WeW-3 (Tom O'Bedlam's Song.) GEA

Tom O'Roughley. W. B. Yeats. CMoP

"Tom Pearse, Tom Pearse, lend me your gray mare." Widdecombe [*or* Widdicombe] Fair. *Unknown.* CH

Tom Potts. *Unknown.* ESPB

Tom Sternhold's or Tom Sha---ll's rhymes will serve. (LL) Reason and Religion. Dryden. NOSC; OAEL-1

Tom Sucklebat, in dressing-gown, without his teeth. An Administrator. Geoffrey Grigson. FaBoEE

Tom Tell-Truth. *Unknown.* CBNP

Tom the Porter. John Byrom. NOEC

Tom Thumbkin. *Unknown.* OxNR

Tom tied a kettle to the tail of a cat. Tom, Jill and Bob. *Unknown.* ACTP

Tom-tom, c'est moi. The blue guitar. Wallace Stevens. CMoP *Fr.* The Man with the Blue Guitar.

Tom, Tom the piper's son. Mother Goose. LB; OxNR

Tom, Tom, the Piper's Son. John Crowe Ransom. *See* The Vanity of the Bright Young Men.

Tom Wedgwood Tells. Brian W. Aldiss. NOBL

Tom, Will, and Dick, and I, a jovial Crew. Theocritus. OBCVT, *tr. by* Thomas Creech *Fr.* Idyll 14.

Tom, will you let me love you in your reataurent? Litany. Carolyn Creedon. BAP-93

Tomarata. Kendrick Smithyman. PeNZ

Tomato Ketchup. *Unknown. See* On Tomato Ketchup.

Tomatoes. Stephen Dobyns. NAmP90

Tomatoes are rolling. Canning Season. Wendy Barkar. IFJA

Tomb/ A hollow hateful world. Agamemnon's Tomb. Sacheverell Sitwell. OBMV

Tomb, but his fisherman's union. (LL) Theris, the old man who lived by his fish traps. Leonidas, *Greek.* GrAn; PGA, *tr. by* Kenneth Rexroth

Tomb—just a canal-bank seat for the passer-by. (LL) Lines Written on a Seat on the Grand Canal, Dublin. Patrick Kavanagh. BIrV; CMoP; InPS-3; NOIV

Tomb of an Ancestor. Allen Curnow.
    "Oldest of us burst into tears and cried, The." PeNZ

Tomb of Crethon, The. Leonidas of Tarentum, *Greek.* AWP, *tr. by* John Hermann Merivale

Tomb of Diogenes, The. *Unknown, Greek.* AWP, *tr. by* John Addington Symonds

Tomb of Heracles, The. James McAuley. BMAP *Fr.* The Hero and the Hydra.

Tomb of Ibykos, The. *Unknown, Greek.* GrAn, *tr. by* Peter Jay

Tomb of Ilaria Giunigi, The. Edith Wharton. APN-2

Tomb of Lt. John Learmonth, A.I.F, The. John Streeter Manifold. CBAP

Tomb of the Imagination. Miguel Hernández, *Spanish.* AF, *tr. by* Tom Jones

Tomb of the Kings, The. Anne Hébert. BoWoP, *tr. by* Aliki *and* Willis Barnstone; PBWP, *tr. by* Kathleen Weaver

Tomb of the Singing Girl Ch'iung-i, The. Hsü Pen, *Chinese.* CoBLCP, *tr. by* Jonathan Chaves

Tomb on the Shore, A. Asclepiades, *Greek.* GrAn, *tr. by* Alan Marshfield

Tomb on the Thracian approaches of Olympus holds, A. On the Tomb of Orpheus. Damagetus, *Greek.* GrAn, *tr. by* John Heath-Stubbs *and* Carol A. Whiteside

Tombs, The. Latif Asad Abdullah. BAP-96

Tombs of the Hetaerae. Rilke, *German.* PFTM, *tr. by* Pierre Joris

Tombstone told when she died, The. Dylan Thomas. OxBTC

Tomcat born on railroad. Autobiography. Tom Weatherly. NBV

Tommies in the Train. D. H. Lawrence. PoWW

Tommy. Rudyard Kipling. CABP; EBEV; FaPoR; MoBrPo; NoP-4; OBWP; OxAEP-2; OxBTC; PeVV; UV

Tommy. *Unknown.* FuFo

Tommy kept a chandler's shop. *Unknown.* OxNR

Tommy O'Linn was a Scotsman born. *Unknown.* OxNR

Tommy Tibule. *Unknown.* OxNR

Tommy Tittlemouse. Mother Goose. ReMoGo

Tommy Trot, a man of law. *Unknown.* OxNR

Tommy Tucker. Mother Goose. OxNR; ReMoGo

Tommy's Dead. Sydney Thompson Dobell. PeVV

Tommy's tears and Mary's fears. Fears and Tears. *Unknown.* ReMoGo

Tomorrow. Anna Laetitia Barbauld. ECWP; PEW

Tomorrow. John Collins. GTBS-P

Tomorrow. Kenneth Fearing. CMoP

Tomorrow. Henri Michaux, *French.* PFTM, *tr.* by Armand Schwerner

Tomorrow. E. Ethelbert Miller. ISC

Tomorrow. William Olsen. NAmP90

"Tomorrow, friend, will be another day." Faith for Tomorrow. Thomas Curtis Clark. PoToHe

Tomorrow I was. Akahito, *Japanese.* OHPJ, *tr.* by Kenneth Rexroth

Tomorrow I will haul down the flag of hypocrisy. Anna Bunston DeBary. LiLi, *tr.* by Avery, Peter and John Heath-Stubbs *Fr.* The Rubáiyát.

Tomorrow I'll reform. Bits of Wisdom. Benjamin Franklin. CTV

Tomorrow is saint valentine's day. Song. Shakespeare. CH; EBEvV; EnLoPo; NTCP; NoSic *Fr.* Hamlet. NAWM-1

Tomorrow, Julia, I betimes must rise. The Perfume. Robert Herrick. CaPo

Tomorrow let loveless, let lover tomorrow make love. The Vigil of Venus. *Unknown, Latin.* GBL, *tr.* by Allen Tate

Tomorrow may be. Langston Hughes. APSN

"Tomorrow morn I'll be sixteen, and Billy Grimes the rover." Billy Grimes. *Unknown.* AmFP

Tomorrow morning I will take a shower. Valerio Magrelli, *Italian.* NeIt, *tr.* by Dana Gioia

Tomorrow shall be my dancing day. *Unknown.* See My Dancing Day.

Tomorrow, should I fail, I'll go away. Trần Tế Xu'o'ng, *Vietnamese.* AVP, *tr.* by Huỳnh Sanh Thông

Tomorrow, since I have so few. Rooster. James Tate. LCAP-2, *tr.* by Dreamy cars graze on the dewy boulevard

Tomorrow the future will be here. A Dime Found in the Snow. James Tate. WeT

Tomorrow the Heroes. Alfred B. Spellman. PoBA

Tomorrow the Past Comes. Ion Caraion, *Romanian.* AF, *tr.* by Marguerite Dorian *and* Elliott B. Urdang

Tomorrow, the twentieth, we celebrate. To Piso, on Epicurus' Birthday. Philodemus, *Greek.* GrAn, *tr.* by William Moebius

Tomorrow the wind will have fallen. Epitaph of a Sailor. Antiphilus, *Greek.* GrAn, *tr.* by Dudley Fitts

Tomorrow [*or* To morrow] to fresh woods and pastures new. (LL) Lycidas. Milton. AWP; ClHu; EBEV; EBEvV; FHYEP; GTBS-P; HAP; ImPo; InPS-2; NOBE; NOSC; OAEL-1; OBEV; OxAEP-1; PoEL-3; Poetr; SCGP; TFi; UnPo

Tomorrow we part. Tune: "Song of the Southern Country." Chu Yi-tsun, *Chinese.* SuSp, *tr.* by Irving Y Lo

Tomorrow we'll be good. Bad Blood. U Tam'si Tchicaya, *French.* NegPo, *tr.* by Ellen Conroy Kennedy

Tomorrow, We'll Dance in America. James Harms. PUP-18

Tomorrow when the farm boys find this. The Two-headed Calf. Laura Gilpin. FYAP

Tomorrow will be Monday. (LL) As Tommy Snooks and Bessy Brooks. Mother Goose. LB; OxNR; ReMoGo

Tomorrow you will live, you always cry. Procrastination. Martial, *Latin.* AWP; FaBoEE; OBVE; *tr.* by Abraham Cowley

Tomorrow / you will walk toward other evenings. History. Herberto Padilla, *Spanish.* AF, *tr.* by Alastair Reid

Tomorrows. James Merrill. OBAL

Tomorrows reactivate somnolence. Of Promises and Prophecy. Steve Chimombo. HBAPE

Tomorrow's the Fair. *Unknown.* FPC

Tom's Garland: Upon the Unemployed. Gerard Manley Hopkins. EnVR; FaBoPV; Son

Tom's sickness did his morals mend. Epigram. Matthew Prior. FaBoEE

Tone-deaf old person of Tring, A. Limerick. *Unknown.* PeLi

Tone of Voice, The. *Unknown.* PoToHe

Tongs. Mother Goose. ReMoGo

Tongue, The. Georgy Nikolaevich Obolduyev, *Russian.* TCRP, *tr.* by Vera Dunham

Tongue, The. Phillips Burrows Strong. PoToHe

Tongue (De First Instrument), De. Levi Tafari. NBrP

Tongue-Doughty Pedant. Thomas Edwards. Son

Tongue is a white water, The. (LL) Dog Creek Mainline. Charles Wright. AmPA; LCAP-2; WeT

Tongue lashing. Tonguing. Greg S. Tate. ISC

Tongue of the waves tolled in the earth's bell, The. The Want Bone. Robert Pinsky. EOEF

Tongue of Wood, The. *Unknown.* PFE

Tongue shapes and molds sound. Speech, The. Not Sense. Gail Tremblay. WeW-3

Tongue that mothered such a metaphor, The. Hogwash. Robert Francis. LCAP-2; NIP-4; TRP

Tongue-tied in Black and White. Michael S. Harper. HCAP

Tongue-tied / the bride brightens into a flower. The Bride. Tongju Yi, *Korean.* CKP, *tr.* by Jaihiun Kim

Tongues. Philip Martin. NOBAu

Tongues of the lightning Snakes flicker and twist, one to the other, The. *Aborigine Oral Tradition, Aboriginal Australian.* ITG, *tr.* by R. M., C. H. Berndt, and Robert Hass

Tongues we use for talking. Tailpiece. Max Fatchen. OTCP

Tonguing. Greg S. Tate. ISC

Tonight a blackout. Twenty years ago. Christmas Eve under Hooker's Statue. Robert Lowell. CoAmPo; OxBA

Tonight, after a rain. The Longing for Eternal Life. Liz Rosenberg. PBCAP

Tonight all the hells of young grief have opened again; the. Grief's Circle. C. S. Lewis. LBC

Tonight and forever I shall be yours so says the oleo king. Some Stories of the Beauty Wapiti. Ebbe Borregaard. NeAP

Tonight as I sleep alone. *Unknown, Japanese.* WPJ, *tr.* by Kenneth Rexroth and Ikuko Atsumi

Tonight, grave sir, both my poor[e] house and I. Inviting a Friend to Supper. Ben Jonson, *after* Martial. AWP; BeJo; FP; NOBE; NOSC; NoP-4; OAEL-1; OBCVT; OxBoLi; PeLV; PoEL-2; SeCP

Tonight / he is understanding Canada. Understanding Canada. Peter Sirr. PBCIP

Tonight he's playing the Black Orchid. Black Orchid. David Jauss. SeSe

Tonight I can write the saddest lines. Pablo Neruda, *Spanish.* LoP, *tr.* by W. S. Merwin; BoLoP

Tonight I could die as easily as the grass. In the Soul Hour. Robert Mezey. AmPA

Tonight I disentangle. Wakepick I. Kristjana Gunnars. NOBC

Tonight, I look, thunderstruck. A Note on My Son's Face. Toi Derricotte. FiLi; ISC

Tonight I looked at the pale northern sky. Back. Robert Mezey. AmPA

Tonight I think again. 3. Yehuda Amichai, *Hebrew.* IP, *tr.* by Warren Bargad *and* Stanley F. Chyet

Tonight I walked, / lost in my own meditation. For Jessica, My Daughter. Mark Strand. MoLi

Tonight I want to say something wonderful. For the Sleepwalkers. Edward Hirsch. FYAP

Tonight I watch my father's hair. Two Postures beside a Fire. James Wright. HCAP; HeIP-4

Tonight I will remember the model. When Father Decided He Did Not Love Her Anymore. Lynn Emanuel. NAmP90

Tonight, I'll pull your limbs through. The Mulatta as Penelope. Lorna Goodison. PBCV

Tonight in the cold I know most of the living are waiting. Elegy for the Nightbound. Anthony Cronin. PBCIP

Tonight in the hills there was a light. Hawktree. Dave Jeddie Smith. HCAP

Tonight I've watched. Sappho, *Greek.* OBCVT, *tr.* by Mary Barnard

Tonight my children hunch. "It Out-Herods Herod. Pray You, Avoid It." Anthony Hecht. AF; CoAP; NIP-4; NOBA; NoAM; OxBC

Tonight my mother was born. Toys, Dream. Novica Tadic, *Serbo-Croatian.* HSix, *tr.* by Charles Simic

Tonight no one takes fish. Tattered pennants. Sailing the Back River. Dave Jeddie Smith. MT

Tonight, on the deck, the lights. Two Stories. Charles Wright. FYAP; LCAP-2

Tonight our cat, Tahi, who lately lost. The Buried Stream. James Keir Baxter. OxBC

Tonight our heaven is an estuary. Pearls. Alan Gould. NOBAu

Tonight, Sally and I are making stuffed / grapeleaves. Leaves. Sam Hamod. UnSA

Tonight the Famous Psychiatrist. Louis Simpson. OxBC

Tonight, the first snow. November Song. Mark Vinz. Poetsp

Tonight the moon is high, to summon all. Elegy. William Bell. FaBoTw

Tonight the moths. Tyranny of Moths. Gerald Vizenor. VoR

Tonight the newspapers report. The Fall of Da Nang. Gerald McCarthy. CDa

Tonight the waves march. Moonlight Night: Carmel. Langston Hughes. GT

Tonight the wind gnaws. Christmas Landscape. Laurie Lee. OBCP

Tonight [*or* To-night] the winds begin to rise. To-night the Winds Begin. Tennyson. EBVV; GTBS-P; ImPo; NOBE; OAEL-2; OBNC; PeECV; PoEL-5 *Fr.* In Memoriam A. H. H.

Tonight there is no watch upon the Rhine. (LL) For France. Claudian, *Latin.* MLL, *tr.* by Helen Waddell

Tonight there's a mirror on the sidewalk. Heaven. Mark Doty. NAmP90

Tonight they need to be both host and stranger. Familiar Story. Alan Shapiro. DiPo; NIP-4

Tonight ungathered let us leave. Tennyson. EBVV; FHYEP; OAEL-2 *Fr.* In Memoriam A. H. H.

Tonight when the hoar frost falls on the wood. Christmas in the Wood. Frances Mary Frost. TrCP

Tonight / when the moon comes out. Proposition. Nicolás Guillén, *Spanish.* TTY, *tr. by* Langston Hughes

Tonight when the sea runs like a sore. Voyage to Labrador. W. S. Merwin. GS

Tonight. . . wishing. Michael McClintock. HA

Tonight with wine being poured. Jelaluddin Rumi. RaBo, *tr. by* Coleman Barks *and* John Moyne *Fr.* Four Quatrains.

Tonight, within my heart! (LL) My Little Dreams. Georgia Douglas Johnson. BlSi; NAAAL

Tonight words fall away from me like shed clothing. Last Poem. Margaret Atwood. LCAP-2

Tonite. Alan Pizzarelli. HA

Tonite I walked out of my red apartment door on East tenth street's dusk. Allen Ginsberg. HCAP *Fr.* Mugging. NoAM

Tonite, thriller was. Beware: Do Not Read This Poem. Ishmael Reed. BPo; GT; NIP-4; PoBA

Tonson: While at my House in *Fleet-street* once you lay. The Reconcilement between Jacob Tonson and Mr Congreve. An Imitation of Horace, Book III. Ode IX. Horace, *Latin.* OBCVT, *tr. by* Nicholas Rowe

Tony Get the Boys. D. L. Graham. PoBA

Tony O! Colin Francis. CH

Tony/ To be casual and have the wish to heal. The Book of Gawain. Jack Spicer. PoM *Fr.* The Holy Grail.

Tony Went to the Bodega but He Didn't Buy Anything. Martín Espada. WWSi

Tony White. Richard Murphy. BiHa

Tony's father left the family. Tony Went to the Bodega but He Didn't Buy Anything. Martín Espada. WWSi

Too Bad. Gig Ryan. NOBAu

Too Bright a Day. Norman MacCaig. GTBS-P

Too Brilliant. Po Chü-i, *Chinese.* ChiPo, *tr. by* Rewi Alley

Too Dark. Mark McCloskey. PoA

Too.' Darkly he rose, and then I slept. (LL) A True Account of Talking to the Sun at Fire Island. Frank O'Hara. HCAP; NNaP; RB; TTTS

'Too dead and dull for thee to own. (LL) To Mrs. M.A. Upon Absence. Katherine Philips. LoP

Too dearly had I bought my green and youthful years. Henry Howard, Earl of Surrey. SiPS

Too emotional. Tanka. Yosano Tekkan, *Japanese.* MJT, *tr. by* Makoto Ueda

Too foraging to blue-print or deploy! Naomi. Gwendolyn Brooks. NAAL-2

Too fragile to endure the heat of a long summer day. Sunflower. Su Shih. SuSp, *tr. by* Irving Y. Lo *Fr.* On Chao Ch'ang's Flower Paintings in Wang Po-yang's Collection.

Too frail for combat, he stands [*or* stood]. Aircraft. Rita Dove. EC3

Too frail to soar—a feeble thing. The Sparrow's Fall. Frances Ellen Watkins Harper. PWR

Too green the springing April grass. Spring in New Hampshire. Claude McKay. BPo; ChAP; CrDW

Too happy Time dissolves itself. Emily Dickinson. APN-2; NOBA

Too Late? Henry Wadsworth Longfellow. *Fr.* Morituri Salutamus.

Too Late. Fitz Hugh Ludlow. PoLF

Too Late. Philip Bourke Marston. OBNC

Too Late. Nora Perry. PoToHe

Too-Late Born, The. Archibald MacLeish. MeMAP; MoAmPo; OxBA (Silent Slain, The.) CMoP; LiTM; PeFWW

Too late for love, too late for joy. Bride Song. Christina Rossetti. OBEV; WPE *Fr.* The Prince's Progress.

Too lazy to wave the white plume fan. Summer Day in the Mountains. Li Po, *Chinese.* CoBCP, *tr. by* Burton Watson

Too Lazy to Write Poetry. Chu Yün-ming, *Chinese.* CoBLCP, *tr. by* Jonathan Chaves

Too little / has been said. The Door. Charles Tomlinson. PoA

Too little to look. Dorothy Aldis. *See* Little.

Too Long I Followed. William Drummond, of Hawthornden. Son *Fr.* Urania, or Spiritual Poems.

Too long outside your door I have shivered. The Terrible Door. Harold Monro. BoLoP; EnLoPo; FaBoTw

Too Many Daves. "Dr. Seuss." OBCA

Too Many Names. Pablo Neruda, *Spanish.* VCWP, *tr. by* Alastair Reid

Too many nights. Apology. Elizabeth Spires. FFC

Too many of the dead, some I knew well. In the Backs. Frances Darwin Cornford. BrRo

Too many splashes, too many gashes. Lone Kauri Road ("Too many splashes, too many gashes"). Allen Curnow. *Fr.* Trees, Effigies, Moving Objects. PeNZ

Too many summers out of the way of a trowel. The Lawn Roller. Robert Layzer. OBGa

Too many waves to mark two more or three. (LL) Old Woman. Iain Crichton Smith. FaBoTw; OxBTC

Too Much. Marianne Moore. CMoP *Fr.* The Jerboa. FYAP; NALW

Too Much Coffee. Edwin Arlington Robinson. MoAmPo

Too much coffee. His mind was racing. Guilt Trip. David Lehman. PUP-18

Too much good luck no less than misery. Joy May Kill. Michelangelo Buonarroti, *Italian.* AWP, *tr. by* John Addington Symonds

Too much history. The Town on the Ten Dollar Note. Laurie Duggan. BMAP

Too much of Europe, here transplanted o'er. The Columbiad. Joel Barlow. APN-1 *Fr.* The Columbiad.

Too much thought. Day-Dreamer. *Unknown, German.* CTV, *tr. by* Louis Untermeyer

Too much to drink these days, late getting up each morning. Late Rising on Spring Days. Wei Chuang, *Chinese.* CoBCP, *tr. by* Burton Watson

Too oft, I feare, thou wilt remember me. (LL) Carmen 8 ("Break off / fallen Catullus"). Catullus, *Latin.* AAS; OBCVT; OBVE, *tr. by* Thomas Campion

Too old for you as you for me. (LL) To Chloe, Who Wished Herself Young Enough for Me. William Cartwright. BeJo; NOSC; OBEV; OxAEP-1; PoToHe

Too old to carry arms and fight like the others—. Report from the Besieged City. Zbigniew Herbert, *Polish.* AF, *tr. by* John Carpenter *and* Bogdana Carpenter

Too quickly. . . And more quickly every time. (LL) The Insert. R. L. Barth. CDa

Too sad is the grief in my heart. Elegy for His Daughter Ellen. Goronwy Owen, *Welsh.* OBWVE, *tr. by* George Borrow

Too Short. Meir Wieseltier, *Hebrew.* IP, *tr. by* Warren Bargad *and* Stanley F. Chyet

Too solemn for day, too sweet for night. William Sidney Walker. OBEV

Too Soon. Francis Thompson. LBC

Too soon, alas! too soon I plunged into the world with tone and clang. Désillusion. Lady Jane Francesca Wilde. VWP

Too soon put up for the wind that blew it down. City. Michael Smith. PBCIP

Too soon! Too soon! (LL) The Pennycandystore beyond the El. Lawrence Ferlinghetti. HeIP-4; PoM; TAP

Too soon, too soon comes Death to show. Coventry Patmore. LBC

Too tart the fruit it brought! (LL) Shut Out That Moon. Thomas Hardy. CMoP; NOBE; NoAM

Too tight, it is running over. Fence Wire. James Dickey. NYBP; VGW

Too tremulously fine! (LL) The Kiss. Charlotte Dacre. CABP; NOBRP

Too-well-done. Nursery Song. Anna Wickham. NOxBChV

Too wide the earth, mine eyes no more behold thee. Written in Absence. Alcuin, *Latin.* MLL, *tr. by* Helen Waddell

Took Bladyn then his crowth, anew, and toucht. Bladyn's Song of Cloten. Charles Montague Doughty. PoEL-5 *Fr.* The Dawn in Britain.

Took his farewell journey to the Promised Land. (LL) Casey Jones. *Unknown.* AS; AmFP; OxBoLi; PeLV

Tool of Fate, The. "Yehoash," *Yiddish.* TrJP, *tr. by* Isidore Goldstick

Toolmaker / is sixty years old, The. The Toolmaker Unemployed. Martín Espada. AFr

Toolmaker Unemployed, The. Martín Espada. AFr

Toot once, strum once. Kuan Han-ch'ing. SuSp, *tr. by* Jerome P. Seaton *Fr.* Tune: "Song of Great Virtue"—Winter.

Tooth, The. Rebekah Carmichael. ECWP

Top of the World, The. Yves Bonnefoy, *French.* VCWP, *tr. by* John Naughton

Top Right Drawer. Memory Cabinet of Mrs. K. 1960. Susan Stewart. NAmP90

Topaz, and the ruby stone. (LL) Street Lanterns. Mary Elizabeth Coleridge. BoTP; PoRA

Topcliffe's horses shake. John Logan. CRP *Fr.* The Death of Southwell.

Topeka. . . Junction City. At the Train Museum. Linda Pastan. GM

Toper who spies in the distance, A. Limerick. Leslie Johnson. PeLi

Tophet. Thomas Gray. ChIV-1; FaBoEE; NOEC; OxBSP

Topics. James Merrill.

Casual Wear. NIP-4

Toplight hammered down by shadowless noon. Fire: The People. Alfred Corn. NAAL-2; VCAP *Fr.* A Call in the Midst of the Crowd.

Toppled wine-cup, A. Bits of Reminiscence. "Shu Ting," *Chinese.* VCWP, *tr. by* Carolyn Kizer

Toppling down as the sunset sky grows distant. At an Inn in Yü-kan. Liu Ch'ang-ch'ing, *Chinese.* SuSp, *tr. by* William H. Nienhauser

Topsy: Part 2. Al Young. MoNo

Topsy-Turvy Land. Phyllis M. Stone. BoTP

Topsy-turvy Land. H. E. Wilkinson. BoTP

Topsy-turvy World. William Brighty Rands. OxBChV

Torah of the Void, The. Rabbi Nahman of Bratzlav, *Hebrew.* "God, / for mercy's sake." (LL) BLT, *tr. by* Zalman Schachter

Torch, The. Theodosia Pickering Garrison. BLPA

Torch, The. Walt Whitman. SAmP

Torch of Love dispels the gloom, The. Walter Savage Landor. GLoP

Tore us down to the human. (LL) Blackbottom. Toi Derricotte. GT; LTA; NAmP90; PBCAP

Tormented with incessant pains. To Stella. Jonathan Swift. NOEC

Torn between griefs, which grief shall I lament. Sophocles. OBVE *Fr.* Women of Trachis.

Torn by screaming steel. (LL) Winter Warfare. Edgell Rickword. PoFWW

Torn feet and cursed earth. Buna. Primo Levi, *Italian.* AF, *tr. by* Ruth Feldman *and* Brian Swann

Torn hillside with its crooked hands, The. A Description of Some Confederate Soldiers. Randall Jarrell. CBCWP

Torn into light, you woke wriggling. How Much Earth. Philip Levine. NNaP

Torn Parts: the story. Fanny Howe. PT

Tornado Soup. A. K. Redwing. VoR

Tornado Survivor. Heather McHugh. EC3

Tornado Warning. Georgia Sine. CMAP

Tornados. Thylias Moss. GT

Toroddle, toroddle, toroll. (LL) Song: "Let school-masters puzzle their brain." Oliver Goldsmith. BlrV; NOIV; PoRA

Toronto Board of Trade Goes Abroad. Earle Birney. PeLV

Torque. David Rivard. PBCAP

Torrent, The. Edwin Arlington Robinson. APN-2

Torrent Cuts Off the Poet's Path, A. Antiphilus, *Greek.* GrAn, *tr. by* W. S. Merwin

Torrent / of cobalt bullets, A. Lacrimas or There Is a Need to Scream. K. Curtis Lyle. NBV; PoBA

Torrismond. Thomas Lovell Beddoes. Song: "How many times do I love thee, dear?" ImPo

Torso / Passages 18, The. Robert Duncan. PmAP

Tortoise, The. Cid Corman. InPK-6; VGW

Tortoise. Thomas Rabbitt. CMAP

Tortoise and Badger. Cheryl Clarke. FFC

Tortoise Gallantry. D. H. Lawrence. APo; CMoP; MoP

Tortoise-Shell. D. H. Lawrence. CMoP; FaBoVe; NAEL-2; OAEL-2; OxAEP-2

Tortoise Shout. D. H. Lawrence. LiTM; NAEL-2; PFTM

Torture. Margaret Atwood. PoE

Torture Chamber. Enrique Lihn, *Spanish.* VCWP, *tr. by* Mary Crow

Torture chamber is not like anything, The. Footnote to the Amnesty Report on Torture. Margaret Atwood. NoAM

Torture scene developed under a glass bell, The. Heirloom. Leonard Cohen. NOBC

Torture, that we pray it may be mild. The Beanstalk, Meditated Later. Judith Wright. NoAM

Tortured, The. May Sarton. FFC

Tortured body, lie at rest alone. Unknown Man in the Morgue. Merrill Moore. MoAmPo

Tortured mullet served the Roman's pride, The. On a Vase of Gold-Fish. Charles Tennyson Turner. NOBVV

Tory Pledges. Thomas Moore. OBSV

Tosca. Giuseppe Giacosa *and* Luigi Illica, *Italian.* "And first, a sip of wine. It comes from Spain." OxBoV, *tr. by* Edmund Tracey

Toss and turn on bamboo mat. *Unknown. Fr.* Summer. SuSp, *tr. by* Michael E. Workman *Fr.* Tzu-yeh Songs of the Four Seasons.

Toss not my soul, O Love, 'twixt hope and fear. *Unknown.* NoSic

Toss your gay heads. At April. Angelina Weld Grimké. BlSi; GT; NMM-2

Tossed [*or* Toss'd] in a troubled sea of griefs, I float. To Her in Absence; a Ship. Thomas Carew. CaPo

Tossed night between us, A. Schooner. Edward Kamau Brathwaite. PBCV

Tossed on the stormy waves of time. "I Was a Stranger and Ye Took Me In." Mary E. Tucker. CBWP-1

Tossing his mane of snows in wildest eddies and tangles. In Earliest Spring. William Dean Howells. APN-2; FaBoBe; OBEV

Total Eclipse. Michael J. Rosen. DiPo

Total failure—mdash;Master Han Shan, A. Wang Chiu-ssu. CoBLCP, *tr. by* Jonathan Chaves *Fr.* Miscellaneous Poems on Living in the Woods—In the Manner of Han Shan.

Total Influence of Outcome of the Matter: The Sun, The. Marge Piercy. *See* The Sun.

Total past felt nothing when destroyed, The. (LL) He was at Naples writing letters home. Wallace Stevens. CMoP; MeMAP; NOBA

Totalled. Peter McDonald. PNI

Totally conscious, and appropos of nothing, he comes to see me. Jelaluddin Rumi, *Persian.* EnlH, *tr. by* Coleman Barks *with* A. J. Arberry

Totem, The. Léopold Sédar Senghor, *French.* NegPo, *tr. by* Ellen Conroy Kennedy

T'other eb'ning eb'ryting was still, Oh! babe. Mister Johnson. Ben Harney. OBAL

Totting up the takings, quick Death can / reckon much faster than the businessman. Palladas, *Greek.* GrAn, *tr. by* Tony Harrison

Toucan, The. Pyke Johnson Jr. NTCP

Touch. Thom Gunn. CMoP

Touch. Kathryn Kerr. IFJA

Touch, The. James Graham, Marquess of Montrose. *Fr.* I'll Never Love Thee More. GBL; NOBE; OBEV

Touch. Octavio Paz, *Spanish.* EP, *tr. by* Charles Tomlinson; BoLoP

Touch but thy lyre, my Harry, and I hear. To M. Henry Lawes, the Excellent Composer[,] of his Lyrics. Robert Herrick. CaPo

Touch, cup / the lips. Leontius Scholasticus, *Greek.* GrAn, *tr. by* Peter Jay

Touch,—for there is a Spirit in the woods. (LL) Nutting. Wordsworth. NAEL-2; NOBRP; OAEL-2; Poetr; RB

Touch him, aye! touch him, if you dare. Samuel Bamford. NOBRP

Touch it: it won't shrink like an eyeball. A Life. Sylvia Plath. NOBA

Touch it to your cheek and it's soft. Peach. Rose Rauter. KaS

Touch Me. Stanley Kunitz. BAP-96; NoP-4

Touch of cold in the autumn night, A. Autumn. Thomas Ernest Hulme. FaBoMo; NTP

Touch of human hands—, The. Thomas Curtis Clark. PoToHe

Touch of red left on your lip, A. Out Early One Morning, I Met an Old Acquaintance. Shen Yüeh, *Chinese.* CoBCP, *tr. by* Burton Watson

Touch of the Master's Hand, The. Myra Brooks Welch. BLPA; PoToHe

Touch Thou Mine Eyes. Marion Franklin Ham. AH

Touch wood, be humble, never dare to say. Helen Foley. LW

Touché. Jessie Redmond Fauset. BlSi

Touched. Olga Broumas. NMM-2

Touching Each Other's Surfaces. Carol Jane Bangs. NIP-4

Touching Ezekiel his workman's hand. Jesus. James Philip McAuley. CBAP; ChIV-2

Touching Heartsease. Janet Sutherland. NBrP

Touching/Not Touching: My Mother. Toi Derricotte. DeD; GT

Touching Shoulders. *Unknown.* BLPA

Touching the ashes of my father. Bob Boldman. HA

Touching the tulips was a shyness. Tulips. Medbh McGuckian. PNI

Touching your goodness, I am like a man. The Illiterate. William Meredith. NoP-4; VCAP

Touchstone, The. Kalonymos ben Kalonymos, *Hebrew.* TrJP, *tr. by* J. Chotzner

Tough Captain Spud and his First Mate, Spade. Captain Spud and His First Mate, Spade. John Ciardi. OBCA

Tough Generation, A. David Gascoyne. LiTM

Tough hand closes gently on the load, The. Man Carrying Bale. Harold Monro. MoBrPo

Toughest gal I ever did see. Kissie Lee. Margaret Abigail Walker. BlSi; NALW

Toujours la Politesse. Ezra Pound, after the Chinese. OBVE

Toulouse Lautrec. Melvin Beaunearus Tolson, *Norwegian.* PBWP, *tr. by* Nadia Christensen

Tour of Duty. David Huddle. Son Nerves. CDa Words. CDa

Tour of Ein Kerem, A. David Curzon. GI

Tour to the Glaciers of Savoy, A. "Eliza." Epistle to John Walker, Esq., An. ECWP

Touring the old miles again. Baldpate Pond. E. F. Weisslitz. NYBP

Touris, white man, wipin his face. The Song of the Banana Man. Evan Jones. PBCV

Tourist came in from Orbitville, A. Southbound on the Freeway. May Swenson. ImGa; NTCP; NYBP

Tourist Country. William Stafford. NoAM

Tourist dame, A. Miss Tourist. "Lord Kitchener." PBCV

Tourist Death. Archibald MacLeish. NAAL-2

Tourist from Syracuse, The. Donald Justice. NoAM; TwCP; VCAP

Tourist, spare the avid glance. The Attic Landscape. Herman Melville. NCAP; NOBA; OBAL

Tourists. Yehuda Amichai, *Hebrew*. PoSu, *tr. by* Glenda Abramson *and* Tudor Parfitt

Tourists. Howard Moss. NYBP; NoP-4; OBCoV; PeLV

Tourists / Wonder. The Edible World. David Bromige. FTOS

Tournament of Tottenham, The. *Unknown.* OxBoLi

Tours. Charles David Wright. MT

Toussaint L'Ouverture. Henrietta Cordelia Ray. CBWP-3

Toussaint L'Overture. George Clinton Rowe.

    His Ancestry. AAP

    His Boyhood. AAP

    His Manhood. AAP

    His Prime. AAP

Toussaint, the most unhappy man of men! To Toussaint L'Ouverture. Wordsworth. FaBoPV; InPK-6; NOBE; OBNC; PBMP; PoRA; Ro

Toward a 44th Birthday. Nellie Wong. NMM-2

Toward a Poetics. Onwuchekwa Jemie. PBMAP

Toward evening, the weather turns cold. Night Rain beneath the City Walls of P'i-chou. Yang Shih-ch'i, *Chinese*. CoBLCP, *tr. by* Jonathan Chaves

Toward Guinea: For Larry Neal, 1937–1981. Houston A. Baker Jr. ISC

Toward morning, slipping the pistol under my arm. Vadim Antonov. TCRP, *tr. by* Vera Dunham *Fr.* Vindication.

Toward morning the sun strolled in the forest. Isaac. Amir Gilbo'a, *Hebrew*. MHP, *tr. by* Ruth Finer Mintz

Toward sunset, at a great height. (LL) Heart of Autumn. Robert Penn Warren. ColAP; FuPo

Toward the Corner. Laura Riding Jackson. NOxBChV

Toward the dawn. Blanche Edith Baughan. PeNZ *Fr.* Maui's Fish.

Toward the end of her life she said that the. Berthe Morisot. Anne Waldman. PmAP

Toward the end of my flight. A Dream about a Piano. Yury Davydovich Levitansky, *Russian*. TCRP, *tr. by* Sophie Lund

Toward the Greater Romance, Please Place Roses in my Skull (A Tantric Love Song). Daniela Gioseffi. DeD

Toward the laughter we no longer. To Mother. Keorapetse Kgositsile. GT

"Toward the person who has died." Dying Away. William Meredith. NoAM

Toward the Solstice. Adrienne Rich. NAAL-2

Toward Umbria. Stanley Plumly. NAmP90

Toward which all hungers leap, all pleasures pass. (LL) A Baroque Wall-Fountain in the Villa Sciarra. Richard Wilbur. AmPP; ColAP; GS; NAAL-2; NYBP; NoP-4; OBGa; Poetr; TwCP; VCAP

Toward which you lend no part! (LL) El Hombre. William Carlos Williams. CMoP; SAmP

Toward Winter. *Unknown.* NOIV

Toward world's end, through the bare / beginnings of winter. The Magi. Louise Glück. GI; PoA

Towards dawn / taxis / idle, The. Girandole. Gustaf Sobin. APSN

Towards Delhi. Kunwar Narain, *Hindi*. OMIP, *tr. by* Vinay Dahrwadker *and* Aparna Dharwadker

Towards Lillers. Ivor Gurney. NAEL-2; NoP-4

Towards nightfall when the wind. Winter Mask. Allen Tate. OxBA

Towards the altar sober-paced I went. Keats. TOF *Fr.* The Fall of Hyperion. OAEL-2

Towards the Blanched Alphabets. Gustaf Sobin. PT

Towards the end he sailed into an extraordinary mildness. Herman Melville. W. H. Auden. MeMAP; OxBA

Towards the End of a Century. E. A. Markham. NBrP

Towards the Land of the Composer. Francis Webb. BMAP

Towards the Last Spike. Edwin John Pratt.

    Gathering, The. MoCV

    Precambrian [*or* Pre-Cambrian] Shield, The. MoCV; NOBC

Towards the songs' pretended sea. (LL) Legacy. Imamu Amiri Baraka. ColAP; MoP; NOBA; NoAM; PoBA

Towards the starry sky. Takako Hashimoto, *Japanese*. WPJ, *tr. by* Kenneth Rexroth *and* Ikuko Atsumi

Towards the Stars. Iain Crichton Smith. SpW

Towards the sun, towards the south-west. D. H. Lawrence. RB *Fr.* Eagle in New Mexico.

Towards the Vanishing Point. David Lehman. PmAP

Towboat is freckled with rust. What's it doing here so far / inland?, The. Sketch in October. Tomas Tranströmer, *Swedish*. VCWP, *tr. by* Robin Fulton

Towels and nightgowns that cry / slow tears full of dirt. Pablo Neruda. *See* Walking [*or* Walkin'] Around.

Tower. Deborah Woodard. CDa

Tower, The. W. B. Yeats. CMoP; LiTM; NoAM; PoE; SCGP

Tower, no ivy, I. The wind was powerless, A. Hecuba's Testament. Rosario Castellanos, *Spanish*. STV, *tr. by* John Frederick Nims

Tower of Babel, The. Nathaniel Crouch. OxBChV

Tower of Babel, The. Joshua Sylvester. NoSic *Fr.* The Divine Weeks and Works of Guillaume de Saluste Sieur Du Bartas.

Tower of Babel, The. Laurance Wieder. ChIV-1

Tower of Brass, one would have said, A. Ode. Horace. LoP, *tr. by* Abraham Cowley *Fr.* Odes.

Tower of Famine, The. Shelley. Poetr

Tower of Refuge is our God, A! Ein feste Burg ist unser Gott. Martin Luther. CTC, *tr. by* M. Woolsey Stryker

Tower of Skulls, The. Isaac Rosenberg. PeFWW

Towering, thick, its straight trunk soars. An Old Pine. Wang An-shih, *Chinese*. SuSp, *tr. by* Jan W. Walls

Tower's reflection swims amid the waves, The. The Lake of the Returned Sword. *Unknown, Vietnamese*. AVP, *tr. by* Huỳnh Sanh Thông

Towery city and branchy between towers. Duns Scotus's Oxford. Gerard Manley Hopkins. CABP; EBEV; GTBS-P; NAEL-2; NoAM; OBMV; OxAEP-2; PeECV; PoEL-5

Town. Marie-Claire Bancquart, *French*. MFP, *tr. by* Martin Sorrell

Town again, trailing your legs and crying!, The. (LL) Wild Swans. Edna St. Vincent Millay. CMoP; MoAmPo; PBWP; UnPo

Town barberpole. Nicholas Virgilio. HA

Town believes thee lost, and didst thou see, The. Henry Vaughan. PBRV *Fr.* To his retired friend, an Invitation to Brecknock.

Town Betrayed, The. Edwin Muir. CMoP; FaBoTC

Town, / branches over the river. Kaunas 1941. Johannes Bobrowski, *German*. AF, *tr. by* Matthew Mead

Town Called Providence, Its Fate, The. Benjamin Tompson. SCAP

Town Child, The. Irene Thompson. BoTP

Town children. Tanka. Shaku Chōkū, *Japanese*. MJT, *tr. by* Makoto Ueda

Town Clerk's Views, The. John Betjeman. CMoP

Town Clock Burning, The. Charles Fort. CMAP

Town clock's face, The. Nicholas Virgilio. HA

Town does not exist, The. The Starry Night. Anne Sexton. ColAP; NoAM; PoE; VCAP

Town Dump, The. Howard Nemerov. CMoP

Town Eclogue, A. "Peter Pindar." OBCoV *Fr.* Bozzy and Piozzi.

Town Eclogues. Lady Mary Wortley Montagu. ECEV

    "Ill fates pursue me, may I never find." ECEV

Town Garden, A. Tony Lucas. OBGa

Town Hall shines farewell and the canal boat, The. On the Göta Canal, 1986. Joan Swift. PuP-14

Town History, 1917. David Huddle. PBCAP

Town I Left. Helen Sorrells. CrSp

Town I was born in was destroyed by shells, The, *see also* vers. *tr. by* A.C. Jacobs. Yehuda Amichai. PoSu, *tr. by* Yehuda Amichai *and* Ted Hughes *Fr.* Patriotic Songs.

Town is old and very steep, The. Ken. Charlotte Mew. VWP

Town is tilted toward the stream, The. A Sunday Dreamer's Guide to Yarrow, Missouri. Jim Barnes. HATNAP

Town lies in the valley, A. The Silent Town. Richard Dehmel, *German*. AWP, *tr. by* Jethro Bithell

Town might abort, A. How the Death of a City Is Never More than the Sum of the Deaths of Those Who Inhabit Its Spaces. Victor Coleman. NOBC

Town Mouse and the Country Mouse, The. Matthew Prior. BXAP

Town of Don't-You-Worry, The. I. J. Barlett. BLPA

Town of Hill, The. Donald Hall. TAP

Town of Nogood, The. W. E. Penny. BLPA

Town of Passage, The. *Unknown.* OxBoLi

Town on the Ten Dollar Note, The. Laurie Duggan. BMAP

Town or poem, I don't care how it looks. Old woman. White Center. Richard Hugo. FiLi; NAAL-2

Town Pier Parking Lot. Brendan Galvin. CMAP

Town remembers no such plenty, The. Lancashire Winter. Tony Connor. OxBTC

Town visitor's easy talk flows in an endless stream, The. To a Talkative Guest. Po Chü-i, *Chinese*. ChiP, *tr. by* Arthur Waley

Town was proud of the town's gardens, The. Flowers. D. J. Enright. OBGa

Town wasn't much, The. Jungle Warfare. Jack Spicer. APSN

Town Window, A. John Drinkwater. BoTP

Town without a Market, The. James Elroy Flecker. MoBrPo

Townshend? I knew him well, queer ways he had. Ivor Gurney. FP

Tow'rds the lofty walls of Balbi, lo! Durand of Blonden hies. Durand of Blonden. Ludwig Uhland, *German*. AWP, *tr. by* James Clarence Mangan

Towser Shall Be Tied Tonight. *Unknown.* BLPA

Toy Band, The. Sir Henry John Newbolt. BoTP

Toy Factory. Charles Simic. AF

Toy for the raking gully / shame encore there. The Crocus Turn and Gods. Joseph Ceravolo. PT *Fr.* Book III of Fits of Dawn.

Toy Horse, The. Valentin Iremonger. NOIV

Toy-maker made a toy wife and a toy child. He made a toy house and some toy years, A. Russell Edson. PmAP

Toy of the Titans. Ebenezer Elliot. Son *Fr.* The Year of Seeds.

Toys, The. Coventry Patmore. EBEV; EBVV; NOBVV; OBEV; OxAEP-2; PoToHe; SoSe-8 *Fr.* The Unknown Eros.

Toys. Carl Phillips. BAP-95

Toys. Abraham Sutskever, *Yiddish.* CEEP, *tr. by* Seymour Levitan

Toys and rose The zoo body zigzags. How Spring Comes. Alice Notley. PmAP

Toys, Dream. Novica Tadic, *Serbo-Croatian.* HSix, *tr. by* Charles Simic

Toys Talk of the World, The. Katharine Pyle. NOxBChV; OBCA

"Tra la la la—See me dance the polka." Neptune—Polka. Dame Edith Sitwell. NOBE

Tra la la la— / See me dance the polka. Polka. Dame Edith Sitwell. CBNP

Tra - ta - ta - tum! Main Street. "Demyan Bedny," *Russian.* TCRP, *tr. by* Lubov Yakovleva *with* Daniel Weissbort

Trace Elements. Chris Wallace-Crabbe. OxBSn

Tracing Back. Jane Mayhall. IFJA

Tracing of an Evening. David Shapiro. PmAP

Track. Norman Finkelstein. PT

Track. Tomas Tranströmer, *Swedish.* BLT; RB; SPE, *tr. by* Robert Bly

Track-lining Song. *Unknown.* AmFP

Track of a broad rattler, dragged over dust at dawn, The. The Catch. Brewster Ghiselin. HAP

Tracking Rabbits: Night. Jim Barnes. CDW

Tracking the Siuslaw Man. Jim Barnes. HATNAP

Tracks. John Montague. CIP-2

Tracks diverge from each other. I don't know, The. A Letter. Dan Pagis, *Hebrew.* IP, *tr. by* Warren Bargad *and* Stanley F. Chyet

Tract. William Carlos Williams. LiTM; MeMAP; MoAmPo; MoP; NOBA; NoAM; SAmP; TAP; TwCP; VGW

Tractatus. Derek Mahon. OxBSP

Tractor-driver ploughs his road as straight as a Roman's, The. Ploughing. Clive Sansom. AYFP

Tractor now is an essential, A. Horatian Variation. Leonard Bacon. NYBP

Tractor stands frozen—an agony, The. Ted Hughes. OxAEP-2

Trade. Egbert Martin. PBCV

Trade Winds. John Masefield. FaBoCh; OBMV

Trader I am to the African shore, A. Sweet Meat Has Sour Sauce. William Cowper. ECEV; NOEC; OBSV; Ro

Trader, untie the long stern-cables. Argentarius, *Greek.* GrAn, *tr. by* Fleur Adcock

Traders in Beauty and Delight. Abu Dulama, *Arabic.* ArPe, *tr. by* Omar S. Pound

Tradition, thou art for suckling children. Stephen Crane. MeMAP

Traditional Funeral Songs. *Unknown, Modern Greek.* BoWoP, *tr. by* Willis Barnstone *and* Elene Kolb

Traditional Red. Robert Huff. HoPM

Traditional Women's Song of Algeria. *Unknown, Arabic.* IMW

Traditions. Seamus Heaney. FaBoMo

Traditions of civility. (LL) The Cathedral Close. Coventry Patmore. EBVV

Traduits de la Nuit. Jean-Joseph Rabéarivelo.

"Black glassmaker, The." PBMAP

"Hide of the black cow is stretched, The." PBMAP

Trafalgar. Thomas Hardy. *See* The Night of Trafalgar.

Trafalgar. Francis Turner Palgrave. FaBoBe

Traffic flows over the bridge. (LL) The Center of Attention. Daniel Gerard Hoffman. FYAP; UnPo

Traffic Lights. Lina Kasdaglis, *Modern Greek.* BoWoP, *tr. by* Edmund *and* Mary Keeley

Trafique Is Earth's Great Atlas. George Alsop. SCAP

Tragedy. "Æ." MoBrPo

Tragedy, A. Tom Masson. OBAL

Tragedy. Jill Spargur. BLPA

Tragedy, A. Doris Webb. FPC

Tragedy is over. Blind Oedipus exits, The. Jovan Hristic, *Serbo-Croatian.* HSix, *tr. by* Charles Simic

Tragedy of a Shepherd. Mark Akenside. *See* Inscription: "Whoe'er thou art whose path, in summer lies."

Tragedy of Bricks, The. Galway Kinnell. AFr

Tragedy of Leaves, The. Charles Bukowski. HoPM

Tragedy of Valentinian, The. John Fletcher.

God Lyaeus, Ever Young. OBEV

Love's Emblems. BoLoP; NOBE; NOSC

Sleep Song. NOSC

(Song to Sleep.) OxBoLi

(To Sleep.) PoRA

Song: "Heare ye Ladies that despise." PoEL-2

Tragic Love. Walter James Turner. OBMV

Tragic Mary Queen of Scots, The. "Michael Field." EnLoPo; LW; OBMV

Tragic Mary Queen of Scots, II, The. "Michael Field." OBMV

Tragic Story, A. Adelbert von Chamisso, *German.* BoTP; CTV, *tr. by* Thackeray

Tragical Death of A, Apple Pie, The. Mother Goose.

("As you may see on t'other side.") (LL) OxNR

Tragicall Epigram, A. Sir John Harington. PBRV

Trail all your pikes, dispirit every drum. Trail All Your Pikes. Anne Finch. OPOU; WPE

Trail among the Pines, A. Lin Pu, *Chinese.* SuSp, *tr. by* Irving Y. Lo

Trail climbs in zig-zags, The. The Trail up Wu Gorge. Sun Yün-feng, *Chinese.* BoWoP; PBWP, *tr. by* Kenneth Rexroth *and* Ling Chung

Trail Crew Camp at Bear Valley. 9000 Feet. Gary Snyder. HCAP

Trail to Mexico, The. *Unknown.* AmFP; AS

Trail up Wu Gorge, The. Sun Yün-feng, *Chinese.* BoWoP; PBWP, *tr. by* Kenneth Rexroth *and* Ling Chung

Trailing for a while. Tanka. Fumi Saito, *Japanese.* MJT, *tr. by* Ueda, Makoto

Trailing her father, bearing his hand axe. Goose. Richard Emil Braun. NoAM

Trailing my stick I go down to the garden edge. Poem without a Category. Gensei, *Japanese.* EnIH, *tr. by* Burton Watson

Trails. Patrick Williams. PNI

Train, The. Mary Elizabeth Coleridge. BoTP

Train. Donald Justice. GM

Train. Helen Mackay. NSI

Train. Ken Smith. SPE

Train, The. *Unknown.* TTY, *tr. by* D. F. van der Merwe

Train: Abstraction. Genevieve Taggard. WPE

Train has come to rest and ceased its creaking, The. La Máquina a Houston. Edward Dorn. PoM

Train has just come to a stop, The. South. Blaise Cendrars, *French.* BLT, *tr. by* Monique Chefdor

Train has stopped for no apparent reason, The. En Route. Duncan Campbell Scott. NOBC

Train in the Desert—1916. Christopher Buckley. GM

Train is a-comin', oh yes. *Unknown.* CA

Train Is Off the Track, The. *Unknown.* AmFP

Train Journey. Judith Wright. NoP-4; PBWP

Train moves through the Guadarrama, The. Rainbow at Night. Antonio Machado Ruiz, *Spanish.* AF; BLT, *tr. by* Robert Bly

Train Ride. John Wheelwright. VGW

Train Rising Out of the Sea. John Ashbery. ColAP

Train Runs Late to Harlem, The. Conrad Kent Rivers. PoBA

Train she rides is sixteen coaches long. "Mystery Train" Janis Joplin Leaves Port Arthur for Points West, 1964. David Wojahn. GM; PBCAP *Fr.* Mystery Train: A Sequence.

Train shot through the dark, The. Return. Seamus Deane. BIrV; IIP; PBCIP; PNI

Train Song. Fiona Kidman. PeNZ

Train speeds on, The. Tanka. Shaku Chōkū, *Japanese.* MJT, *tr. by* Makoto Ueda

Train started to take off, The. Exile. Marta Fenyves. LoHo

Train Stops at Healy Fork, The. John Haines. BLT

Train, The! The twelve o'clock for paradise. Harold Monro. MoBrPo *Fr.* Week-End.

Train Tune. Louise Bogan. GM

Train was going downwards very slowly, The. A Dream. Evan Jones. NOBAu

Train Whistles in the Wind and Rain. Henry Carlile. PuP-17

Train whistles punctual as a clock, The. English-Speaking Persons Will Find Translations. Michael S. Glaser. UnSA

Train will come tomorrow year, The. Alan Brownjohn. OxBTC

Train Wreck, 1890: My Grandmother Lies Down with the Dead. T. R. Hummer. GM

Trained tenderly by Heaven and Earth. A Contrast. Menella Bute Smedley. VWP

Training. Herrera S. Demetrio, *Spanish.* TTY, *tr. by* Dudley Fitts

Training I received did not apply becayse. Nerves. David Huddle. CDa *Fr.* Tour of Duty. Son

Trainride, Vienna—Bonn. Margaret Atwood. LCAP-2

Trains, The. "Seumas O'Sullivan." BoTP

Trains. Hope Shepherd. BoTP

Train's french horn sighs, sheds a few tears, The. To I. Lavrentevaya. Natalya Gorbanevskaya, *Russian.* BoWoP, *tr. by* Daniel Weissbort

Trains in France. Winifred Holtby. WPN

Trains in texas grass. (LL) In Texas Grass. Quincy Troupe. GT; NAAAL

Trains Made of Stone. Ray A. Young Bear. CDW

Trains ran through the eleven, The. The Dance of the Elephants. Michael S. Harper. LCAP-2

Trainwrecked Soldiers. John Frederick Nims. GM

Trakl. Norman Dubie. NAmP90

Tram That Lost Its Way, The. Nikolai Stepanovich Gumilyov, *Russian.* TCRP, *tr. by* Yakov Hornstein

Tramontana at Lerici. Charles Tomlinson. GTBS-P

Tramp. Frank Mkalawile Chipasula. HBAPE; PeSAV

Tramp. Richard Hughes. MoBrPo

Tramp Miner's Song. *Unknown.* AmFP

Tramp, Tramp, Tramp, Keep on a-Tramping. *Unknown.* AS

Trample! trample! went the roan. The Cavalier's Escape. George Walter Thornbury. FaBoBe

Trampwoman's Tragedy, A. Thomas Hardy. NAEL-2; OBNC; OBNV

Trams. (LL) Electricity of Blossoms. Lorenzo Thomas. FTOS

Trams. Dame Edith Sitwell. NOxBChV

Tramstop swarms with schooligans, their brand, A. Election Eve, with Cat. Alex Skovron. BMAP

Tramway climbs from Merthyr to Dowlais, The. The Deluge 1939. Saunders Lewis, *Welsh.* OBWVE, *tr. by* Gwyn Morgan

Trance, The. Stephen Spender. OxBM

Trance Event. Robert Desnos, *French.* PFTM, *tr. by* Marcel Jean

Trane / must have. The Silent Prophet. Norman Jordan. NBV

Trane. / Trane. / History Love Scream Oh. Am/Trak. Imamu Amiri Baraka. PmAP

Tranquil, vacant is the river, girdled by the setting sun. A Crossing South of Li-chou. Wen T'ing-yün, *Chinese.* SuSp, *tr. by* William R. Schultz

Tranquil waters slept 'neath nature's smile, The. Noonday Thought. Henrietta Cordelia Ray. *Fr.* A Group of Musings. CBWP-3

Tranquility as his breath, his eye a camera. Observation Car and Cigar. William Stafford. LCAP-2

Tranquilized, she speaks or does not speak. Marie Ponsot. MDDM *Fr.* Nursing: Mother.

Tranquillity! thou better name. Ode to Tranquillity. Coleridge. LaPo

Transaction. A. R. Ammons. HCAP; PoA

Transcendence of God, The. Milton. *Fr.* Samson Agonistes. FHYEP; OAEL-1; PoEL-3

Transfer. Ingrid De Kok. BAP-96

Transfiguration. Djuna Barnes. SPE

Transfiguration, The. Robert Herrick. CaPo

Transfiguration. Jack Hirschman. CLPP

Transfiguration, The. Edwin Muir. ChIV-2; OxBS

Transfiguration of Beauty, The. Michelangelo Buonarroti, *Italian.* AWP, *tr. by* John Addington Symonds

Transfigurations. Joseph Donahue. PT

Transfigured Night. Ralph Gustafson. MoCV

Transformation Scene. Constance Carrier. FYAP

Transformations. Thomas Hardy. PFE; RB; TRP

Transformations. Joy Harjo. HATNAP

Transformations. Tadeusz Rózewicz, *Polish.* ChAP, *tr. by* Czeslaw Milosz

Transformations. Jack Spicer. FTOS

Transfusion. Merrill Moore. PoA

Transgressing the Real. Robert Duncan. APSN *Fr.* Passages.

Transience. John Armstrong. NOEC *Fr.* The Art of Preserving Health.

Transient Americans. Gifts. Karen Snow. FYAP

Transit. Margaret Avison. FaBoWP

Transit. Richard Wilbur. DiPo; LCAP-2; PiM

Transit Authority. Tony Sanders. BAP-95

Transition—S.M, The. Alfred Islay Walden. AAP

Transitions. Kay Keeshan Hamod. "Your mother's often gone." MDDM

Translated from the American. Sherman Alexie. UnSA

Translation. Roy Fuller. NOBE; OxBTC

Translation. Rika Lesser. PoA

Translation. Howard Nemerov. CRP

Translation by Mark Willhardt. William Dunbar. RACG

Translation From, A. Fred Levinson. AmPA

Translation from a Lost Source. Richard Caddel. NBrP

Translation from Catullus: Ad Lesbiam. Catullus. *See* Sappho.

Translation from Horace. Horace, *Latin.* OBCVT, *tr. by* Byron

Translation from Petrarch, A. Petrarch. MoBrPo, *tr. by* J. M. Synge *Fr.* Sonnets to Laura.

Translation from Petrarch. Petrarch, *Italian.* SiPS

Translation from Walter von der Vogelweide, A. Walther von der Vogelweide. MoBrPo, *tr. by* J. M. Synge

Translation of a South American Ode. Oliver Goldsmith. NOIV

Translation of Claudian's Proserpine. Claudian, *Latin.* "Ye mighty Demons, whose tremendous sway." OBCVT, *tr. by* Alfred Tennyson, 1st Baron Tennyson

Translation of Lines by Benserade. Samuel Johnson, *after the French of* Isaac Benserade. FaBoEE

Translation of "Pax Bello Potior." *Unknown, Latin.* NOBRP, *tr. by Unknown*

Translation of the 16th Ode of the 2d. Book of Horace. Horace, *Latin.* OBCVT, *tr. by* William Cowper

Translation out of Statius. To Sleep, A. Publius Papinius Statius, *Latin.* OBCVT, *tr. by* John Potenger

Translations. Adrienne Rich. WPOW

Translations from Martial. Robert Louis Stevenson. OBGa

Translations from the English. George Starbuck. VGW

Translations from the *Medea* of Euripedes ("Err shall they not, who resolute explore"). Euripides. *Fr.* Medea. NAWM-1; OxBM

Translations from the *Medea* of Euripedes ("Rites deriv'd from ancient days, The"). Euripides. *Fr.* Medea. NAWM-1; OxBM

Translator to Translated. Ezra Pound. FaBoEE

Translucent green on the wall, a dance of leaves. The Green Afternoon. Henry Rago. VGW

Translucent Mechanics, The. George Oppen. NNaP *Fr.* Some San Francisco Poems.

Translucent prophylactic, shield, interpreter. Forgetting Greek. Rachel Hadas. WeT

Transparent Life, The. Luigi Fontanella, *Italian.* NeIt, *tr. by* W. S. Di Piero

Transparent Man, The. Anthony Hecht. FYAP

Transplanting. Theodore Roethke. GaP ("Whole flower extending outward, / Stretching and reaching, The.") (LL) OBGa

Transubstantiation. Gary Geddes. NOBC

Transvestite. Lisa Zeidner. CMAP

Trap Door. Vítězslau Nezval, *Czech.* PFTM, *tr. by* Jerome Rothenberg *and* Milos Sovak

Trapped. Merle Collins. HCP

Trapped me in ice. No, not one chink is gaping. Ennui. Peter Viereck. NYBP

Trappers have collected their rabbit traps, The. Meeting Trappers on the Road in Heavy Snow. Li K'ai-hsien, *Chinese.* CoBLCP, *tr. by* Jonathan Chaves

Trapping fairies in West Virginia. Frank Gelett Burgess. OBCoV

Trashmen Shaking Hands with Hubert Humphrey at the Opening of Apache Plaza Shopping Center, Suburban Minneapolis, August 1963, The. David Wojahn. PBCAP *Fr.* Mystery Train: A Sequence.

Trauma. Brad Leithauser. InPK-6

Travail of Passion, The. W. B. Yeats. TrCP

Travel. Edna St. Vincent Millay. OBCA; PiM

Travel. Robert Louis Stevenson. CTV; FaBoCh; OTCP

Travel: After a Death. Jane Kenyon. FFC

Travel any road. The Tale of Red-Haired Motl, Mister Inspector, Rabbi Isaiah, and Commissar Blokh. Iosif Pavlovich Utkin, *Russian.* TCRP, *tr. by* Lubov Yakovleva

Travel Song. Hugo von Hofmannsthal, *German.* TrJP, *tr. by* Charles Wharton Stork

Travel was homespun, The. Distance of a City. James Berry. PBCV

Travel with grief—goodbye to joy! Nguyễn Chí Thiện, *Vietnamese.* VCWP, *tr. by* Huynh Sanh Thông

Traveler, The. Vachel Lindsay. MoAmPo

Traveler, The. Duane Niatum. HATNAP

Traveler, The. Mogwol Park, *Korean.* CKP, *tr. by* Jaihiun Kim

Traveler, The. *Unknown.* AmFP

Traveler, a traveler, Tzu-mei his name, A. Tu Fu, *Chinese.* CoBCP, *tr. by* Burton Watson *Fr.* Seven Songs Written During the Ch'ien-yüan Era.

Traveler at Night Writes His Thoughts, A. Tu Fu, *Chinese.* ChiPo; CoBCP, *tr. by* Burton Watson

Traveler, don't ridicule this farming house as too small. A Farming Family Invites the Guest to Stay Overnight. Fan Ch'eng-ta. SuSp, *tr. by* Wu-chi Liu *Fr.* Four Songs in Imitation of Wang Chien.

Traveler has come from south of the Yangtze, A. The Traveler's Moon. Po Chü-i, *Chinese.* CoBCP, *tr. by* Burton Watson

Traveler in the wilds, do not. Leonidas, *Greek*. PGA, *tr. by* Kenneth Rexroth

Traveler, I've been through a thousand changes, A. Chin Nung. CoBLCP, *tr. by* Jonathan Chaves *Fr.* On New Year's Eve of the Year Hsin-wei (1751), Drinking Alone and Sadly Chanting Poems, I Remembered My Aged Wife Who Is Living at Twisting River.

Traveler on a dusty road, A. Little and Great. Charles MacKay. PoLF

Travel[l]er; or, A Prospect of Society, The. Oliver Goldsmith.

Britain. NOEC

"My soul. . . , turn we to survey." FHYEP

On Freedom and Ambition. NOIV

"Remote, unfriended, melancholy, slow." BIrV

Traveler, rest. The time of man runs on. In Blue-Stocking Hollow. Donald Davidson. FuPo

Travel[l]er take heed for journeys undertaken in the dark of the year. October Journey. Margaret Abigail Walker. PoBA

Traveler tires of nights on the water, A. Entering the Mouth of P'eng-li Lake. Hsieh Ling-yün, *Chinese*. SuSp, *tr. by* Francis Westbrook

Traveler who wants to stay, The. Inscribed on the Wall at the Temple of the Auspicious Talisman. Tao-chi, *Chinese*. CoBLCP, *tr. by* Jonathan Chaves

Traveler will rise at midnight, The. Presented to Wang Wen-hsi. Ho Ching-ming, *Chinese*. CoBLCP, *tr. by* Jonathan Chaves

Traveler with his heavy heart, The. Ho Hsun, *Chinese*. OHMPC, *tr. by* Kenneth Rexroth

Travelers, The. Patricia Hubbell. CTV

Travelers. Josephine Miles. KaS

Travel[l]er's Curse after Misdirection[, The]. Robert Graves. CMoP; HoPM; LiTM; MoBrPo; NBLV; OBCoV; PFE

Traveler's heart has a hundred thoughts already, The. At Parting. Ho Sun, *Chinese*. CoBCP, *tr. by* Burton Watson

Traveler's homesickness, sad and lonely. Thinking of the Past on an Autumn Night at Tz'u-jen Temple. Wang Shih-chieng, *Chinese*. CoBLCP, *tr. by* Jonathan Chaves

Traveler's Moon, A [*or* The]. Po Chü-i, *Chinese*. CoBCP; SuSp, *tr. by* Chiang Yee

Travelers perhaps, / but I am not sure of finding. Nuclear Umbrella. Herberto Padilla, *Spanish*. AF, *tr. by* Alastair Reid

Traveler's Thoughts. Tu Hsün-ho, *Chinese*. CoBCP, *tr. by* Burton Watson

Traveler's thoughts stretch on forever, A. Climbing Stone Drum Mountain Above the Shores of Shang-shu. Hsieh Ling-yün, *Chinese*. SuSp, *tr. by* Francis Westbrook

Traveling along. Return to English Turn. Tom Dent. BkSV

Traveling at Break of Day. Huang Ching-jen, *Chinese*. SuSp, *tr. by* Chang Yin-nan *and* Lewis C. Walmsley

Traveling Back. Sara Hunter. LoHo

Traveling by Boat. Wang T'ing-hsiang, *Chinese*.

"At Arrow Rapids, the water splashes foam." CoBLCP, *tr. by* Jonathan Chaves

Traveling by Boat at Shun-ch'ang. Hsü Chung-hsing, *Chinese*. CoBLCP, *tr. by* Jonathan Chaves

Traveling Company. Brooks Haxton. CMAP

Traveling Early through a Snowy Valley. Yü Chi, *Chinese*. CoBLCP, *tr. by* Jonathan Chaves

Traveling for the last time. Traveling Back. Sara Hunter. LoHo

Traveling in the City. David Avidan, *Hebrew*. IP, *tr. by* Warren Bargad *and* Stanley F. Chyet

Traveling merchant west of the river, A. Tune: "Eternal Longing." *Unknown, Chinese*. SuSp, *tr. by* Hellmut Wilhelm

Traveling Onion, The. Naomi Shihab Nye. LoL; MT

Traveling sky goes landward, the blind mass, The. Headland. Brewster Ghiselin. PoA

Traveling Star. Ljubomir Simovic, *Serbo-Croatian*. HSix, *tr. by* Charles Simic

Traveling [*or* Travelling] through the dark I found a deer. William Stafford. CuAP; CoAmPo; ColAP; HAP; HeIP-4; InPK-6; LCAP-2; LiTM; NoAM; Poetr; SoSe-8; TRP; WeW-3

Traveling to Town. Duane Big Eagle. AiP

Traveling with too much baggage is not a good idea. Maria Luisa Spaziani. NeIt, *tr. by* Beverly Allen *Fr.* The Star of Free Will.

Travelled miles that day. The Poison-maker. Ian McDonald. HCP

Traveller, The. John Berryman. GM; PoA; VGW

Traveller, The. C. J. Dennis. NOBAu

Traveller, A. J. R. Rowland. CBAP

Traveller, The. Allen Tate. LiTM

TRAVELLER came from across the seas, A. Taoism and Buddhism. Po Chü-i, *Chinese*. ChiP, *tr. by* Arthur Waley

Traveller, on this ridge a leafless, barkless tree. Philip V, King of Macedon, *Greek*. GrAn, *tr. by* Edwin Morgan

Traveller take heed for journeys undertaken in the dark of the year. October Journey. Margaret Walker Alexander. GT

Traveller to Timbuktu, A. Limerick. *Unknown*. PeLi

Traveller, traveller, accept you must go back. Jules Supervielle, *French*. MFP, *tr. by* Martin Sorrell

Traveller who walks a temperate zone, A. Against Romanticism. Kingsley Amis. NoAM

Traveller, you must set out. Death in the Dawn. Wole Soyinka. PBMAP *Fr.* Idanre and Other Poems (1967).

Travellers. Arthur St. John Adcock. BoTP

Travellers came, after the long day's ride, The. The Blinkered Mind. Amy Witting. NOBAu

Traveller's Guide to Antarctica. Adrien Stoutenburg. NYBP

Travellers have seen it, uncovered. Lost City. Harold Farmer. PeSAV

Traveller's Return, The. *Unknown*. BoTP

Travellers Turning Over Borders. Basil Ransome-Davies. BXAP

Travelling. Dorothy Graddon. BoTP

Travelling, a man met a tiger, so. . . . Good Taste. Christopher Logue. OBSP

Travelling Alone. Robin Fulton. FaBoTC

Travelling Backward. Gene Baro. NYBP

Travelling eye has seen its many birds, The. Many Birds. Anne Welsh. PeSA

Travelling in the Family. Carlos Drummond de Andrade, *Portuguese*. NNPT, *tr. by* Elizabeth Bishop

Travelling in the Mountains. Tu Mu, *Chinese*. PLT, *tr. by* A. C. Graham

Travelling Northward. Tu Fu, *Chinese*. BLT; OHPC, *tr. by* Kenneth Rexroth

Travelling Out, The. Lucile Adler. NYBP

Travelling Post Office, The. Andrew Barton Paterson. CBAP; NOBAu

Travelling to Gleis-Binario. Andrew Taylor.

Goethe and Brentano. BMAP

Travelling Together. W. S. Merwin. IFJA

Travelling, / where darkness hauls the world. Tanks. Rhyll McMaster. CBAP; NOBAu

Travelogue. Amy Gerstler. WWSi

Travelogue. Peter Reading.

"Camping Provencial. Notices: (1)." PeLV

Travelogue for Exiles. Karl Shapiro. MoAmPo; TrJP

Travels in Clouds, seekes Manna, where none is. (LL) The Search. Henry Vaughan. ChIV-2; ESCV; GeHe; SeCP

Travels in the South. Simon J. Ortiz. UnSA

Travels of a Latter-Day Benjamin of Tudela. Yehuda Amichai, *Hebrew*. "I am a solitary man, not a democracy." PoSu, *tr. by* Ruth Nevo

Travels with the Band-Aid Army. Lance Henson. VoR

Travis, the Kid Was All Heart. Terry Stokes. AmPA

Travois of the Nameless. Sotère Torregian. NBV

Treacherous Death of Jesse James, The. Ann Carrel. CMAP

Treacherous rain and perilous bridge made me fear for my life. Sent to Lo-t'ien for Thinking of Me after the Rainfall. Yüan Chen, *Chinese*. SuSp, *tr. by* Angela Jung Palandri

Treacherous sea, The. (LL) Fife Tune. John Streeter Manifold. CBAP; ImPo; InPS-3; LiTM; NBLV; NOBAu

Tread back—and back, the lewd and lay. 3.1. Horace. AWP, *tr. by* Abraham Cowley; OBVE, *tr. by* Gerard Manley Hopkins *Fr.* Odes.

Tread lightly here, for here, 'tis said. An Epitaph on a Robin Redbreast. Samuel Rogers. FaBoEE

Tread lightly, she is near. Requiescat. Oscar Wilde. EBVV; MoBrPo; OBNC; PeVV; SAGP

Tread lightly, Stranger! Meleager, *Greek*. GrAn, *tr. by* Peter Whigham

Tread not the earth where lies her youthful form. Mrs. E. Cohrs Brown. Mary Weston Fordham. CBWP-2

Tread soft, for if you wake this knight alone. Epitaph on the Monument of Sir William Strode. William Strode. NOSC

Tread softly! all the earth is holy ground. Later Life: A Double Sonnet of Sonnets. Christina Rossetti. WPoS

Tread softly because you tread on my dreams. (LL) He Wishes for the Cloths of Heaven. W. B. Yeats. ADE; APAD; ChAP; MoBrPo; NoAM; OBEV

Tread softly; bid a solemn music sound. Epitaph. John Bingham Morton. FaBoEE

Treading a field I saw afar. Death on a Live Wire. Michael Baldwin. MoBS

Treadmill prisoner of that century, The. Scene with Figure. Babette Deutsch. TrJP

Treason doth never prosper [*or* Treason never prospers; what's the reason?]. Of Treason. Sir John Harington. FaBoEE; InPK-6; NOSC; NoSic; OBCoV; OxBoLi; PBRV; PFE; SoSe-8

Treason? yes, make it treason, if ye will. Warning. Alfred Gibbs Campbell. AAP

Treason's Choice. Philip Hammial. BMAP

Treasure. Lucilius, *Greek*. AWP, *tr. by* William Cowper

Treasure at the heart of the rose, The. The Rose. Gabriela Mistral, *Spanish*. WPoS, *tr. by* Langston Hughes

Treasure Holiday. William Harmon.
"I am the Gross National Product." WeT

Treasure Island. Robert Louis Stevenson.
Pirate Ditty. NOBVV

Treasure Lies In the Cornerstone, The. "Angelus Silesius." GePo, *tr. by* George C. Schoolfield   *Fr.* The Cherubical Wanderer.

Treasures. Claire Richcreek Thomas. PoToHe

Treaties. A. R. Ammons. HCAP

Treating Sheep Ailments. John Dyer. ECEV   *Fr.* The Fleece.

Treatise of the Subtle Body, A. Salamis. Lawrence Durrell. NYBP

Treaty of Human Learning, A. Greville Fulke.
"Mind of man is this world's true dimension, The." NOSC

Trebetherick. John Betjeman. CMoP

Treblinka. Michael Hamburger. HP

Tree, The. Dorothy Auchterlonie. NOBAu

Tree. (LL) Diamond Cut Diamond. Ewart Milne. PC

Tree, The. Ilya Grigoryevich Ehrenburg, *Russian*. TrJP, *tr. by* Babette Deutsch

Tree, The. John Freeman. BoTP

Tree, The. Ezra Pound. CMoP; PBMP

Tree, The. Joel Sloman. VGW

Tree, The. Cinda Thompson. CrSp

Tree, and more, / then I may sing. (LL) The Garden. Nicholas Grimald. GaP

Tree and the Chaff, The. Bible, *O.T.* *See* Psalm 1.

Tree and the Lady, The. Thomas Hardy. MoBrPo

Tree ascending there. O pure transcension, A. Rilke, Stephen Mitchell. TOF, *tr. by* James Blair Leishman   *Fr.* Sonnets to Orpheus.

Tree at my window, window tree. Robert Frost. FaBoBe; MeMAP; MoAmPo; NoAM; OxBA; TAP

Tree-blossom and May. Lament of the Red Knight. Anna Wickham. WPN

Tree by the river, The. Tree of Fire. "Adunis," *Arabic*. VCWP, *tr. by* Samuel Hazo

Tree enters and says with a bow, A. Lesson, The. Miroslav Holub, *Czech*. PoSu, *tr. by* Ian *and* Jarmila Milner

Tree grew under your hand one day, The. Lines for a Painter. Anthony Cronin. PBCIP

Tree grows old in the tree, it is summer, The. The Tree, the Lamp. Yves Bonnefoy, *French*. VCWP, *tr. by* Richard Pevear

Tree has entered my hands, The. A Girl. Ezra Pound. MoAmPo; NOxBChV

Tree in December. Melville Cane. MoAmPo

Tree in the courtyard turns color suddenly, The. Thoughts on the First Day of Autumn, Sent to Su Tzu-mei. Ou-yang Hsiu, *Chinese*. SuSp, *tr. by* Irving Y. Lo

Tree in the Garden, The. Christine Chandler. BoTP; OTCP

Tree in the wind remembered like a letter. Ivan V. Lalic. HSix, *tr. by* Charles Simic   *Fr.* Spring Liturgy for Branko Miljkovic.

Tree in the Wood, The. *Unknown*. AmFP

Tree is all alone, The. A Thought. Linda Hogan. CrSp

Tree keeps silence, The. Winter Tree. Huran Kim, *Korean*. CKP, *tr. by* Jaihiun Kim

Tree let your arms fall. No Ordinary Sun. Hone Tuwhare. PeNZ

Tree Marriage. William Meredith. GLP

Tree of Fire. "Adunis," *Arabic*. VCWP, *tr. by* Samuel Hazo

Tree of intense, The. Ode to the Watermelon. Pablo Neruda, *Spanish*. SPE, *tr. by* Robert Bly

Tree of Knowledge, The. Abraham Cowley. ChIV-1

Tree of Knowledge, The. Lizelia Augusta Jenkins Moorer. CBWP-3

Tree of knowledge was the tree of reason, The. Contraband. Denise Levertov. BLT

Tree of Liberty, The. Robert Burns. FaBoPV

Tree of roses. The water crashed headlong. Peter Levi. TOF

Tree Old Woman. Samuel Makidemewabe, *Cree Indian*. STP, *tr. by* Howard Norman

Tree Party. Louis MacNeice. OxBTC

Tree-planting Man. / Stay. (LL) Young Heroes. Gwendolyn Brooks. NAAAL

Tree rows in orchards are capable of patterns. What, The. Lyn Hejinian. FTOS   *Fr.* My Life.

Tree Sings to the Stream, The. Leah Goldberg. MHP, *tr. by* Ruth Finer Mintz   *Fr.* Songs of the Stream.

Tree still bends over the lake, The. Winter. Sheila Wingfield. EnLoPo; LW

Tree Stillness. Karen L. Mitchell. GT

Tree Telling of Orpheus, A. Denise Levertov. APSN

Tree, the close willow, swayed, The. (LL) The Visitant. Theodore Roethke. CMoP; PoE; RB; TRP; UnPo

Tree, the Lamp, The. Yves Bonnefoy, *French*. VCWP, *tr. by* Richard Pevear

Tree the tempest with a crash of wood, The. On a Tree Fallen across the Road. Robert Frost. RB

Tree toad loved a she-toad, A. Tree Toad. *Unknown*. NTCP, *ad. by* Stephanie Calmenson

Tree-topped Hill. *Unknown*. NOEC

Tree with lush leaves. Tanka. Masaoka Shiki, *Japanese*. MJT, *tr. by* Ueda, Makoto

Treefrog winks without springing. Drawings of the Song Animals. Duane Niatum. HATNAP

Treehouse, The. James A. Emanuel. BPo; PoBA

Trees. Fleur Adcock. OBGa

Trees. Sara Coleridge. ACTP; BoTP; FPC; OxBChV

Trees. Ted Hughes. NYBP

Trees. Joyce Kilmer. BLPA; ChAP; EBEvV; FPC; FaBoBe; PFE; UV

Trees, The. Bill Manhire. PeNZ

Trees. Agnes Nemes Nagy, *Hungarian*. PoSu, *tr. by* Bruce Berlind

Trees. Howard Nemerov. Poetsp

Trees and Evening Sky. N. Scott Momaday. CDW

Trees / and the wind. The Hand. Brian Fawcett. NOBC

Trees are a'ivied, the leaves they are green, The. The Bonnie Laddie's Lang a-Growin'. *Unknown*. OxBS

Trees are all bare not a leaf to be seen, The. Christmas Song. *Unknown*. NTP

Trees are ancient, thick with patterns of moss, The. Hsü Chung-hsing. CoBLCP, *tr. by* Jonathan Chaves   *Fr.* Following the Rhymes of Magistrate Liu's Poems on Entertaining Two Assistant Premiers at Pine-Snow Temple.

Trees are brilliant with flowers, The. Spring Walk to the Pavilion of Good Crops and Peace. Ou-yang Hsiu, *Chinese*. OHPC, *tr. by* Kenneth Rexroth

Trees are cages for them: water holds its breath. Stars and Planets. Norman MacCaig. OPOU; OxBSP

Trees are coming into leaf, The. Philip Larkin. NoAM; NoP-4; OPOU

Trees Are Down, The. Charlotte Mew. BrRo; ChIV-2; MoBrPo; NTP; OxAEP-2; TrCP; VWP; WPE; WPOW

Trees are in their autumn beauty, The. The Wild Swans at Coole. W. B. Yeats. AYFP; CMoP; HeIP-4; InPS-3; MoBrPo; MoP; NAEL-2; NoAM; NoP-4; PoPoPo; Poetr; SCGP; SoSe-8; TFi; UnPo

Trees are rustling outside the open window, The. Sophie Behrens. NBrP

Trees are tall, but the moon small, The. Hide and Seek. Robert Graves. KaS; NTCP

Trees are tracing in the waning haze, The. Evening. Victor Van Vriesland, *Dutch*. TrJP, *tr. by* Adriaan J. Barnouw

Trees are waving to and fro, The. Just Like This. D. A. Olney. BoTP

Trees at Night. Helene Johnson. BlSi

Trees both in hills and plaines, in plenty be. William Wood. SCAP

Trees can't tell the two of them apart, The. (LL) Field and Forest. Randall Jarrell. LCAP-2; VGW

Trees, Effigies, Moving Objects. Allen Curnow. PeNZ
Lone Kauri Road ("First time I looked seaward, westward").
Lone Kauri Road ("Too many splashes, too many gashes").

Trees full of snipers, the new kind, The. War. Lorine Niedecker. FTOS

Trees green the quiet sun. Larry Eigner. PmAP

Trees growing—right in front of my window. Pruning Trees. Po Chü-i, *Chinese*. ChiP, *tr. by* Arthur Waley

Trees have their doubts but we have ours. Ode. Paul Evans. NBrP

Trees in groves / Kine in droves. Saadi. Ralph Waldo Emerson. APN-1; MeMAP; OxBA

Trees in the Garden. D. H. Lawrence. CMoP; MoBrPo
("As the green grass glows upwards, strangers in the garden.") (LL) NoP-4
("Garden.") (LL) GaP

Trees in the Garden Rained Flowers, The. Stephen Crane. LiTM   *Fr.* War Is Kind.

Trees in the old days used to stand. Carentan O Carentan. Louis Simpson. CoAP; MoBS; NOBA; OBWP; PoE; RB; WeT

Trees inside are moving out into the forest, The. Adrienne Rich. CoAP; NOBA; WPE

Tree's leaves may be ever so good, A. Leaves Compared with Flowers. Robert Frost. NOBA

Trees like evangelists. Quick Eats. Charles Simic. PuP-17

Trees, like great jade elephants, The. John Gould Fletcher. MoAmPo *Fr.* Irradiations. MoAmPo

Trees like Tassels—hit—and swung, The. Emily Dickinson. NCAP

Trees of Life, The. Jones Very. NOBA

Trees of the elder lands, The. St. Anthony's Township. Gilbert Sheldon. CH

Trees on a Frosty Night. Mairtin O Direain, *Irish.* TIRV, *tr. by the author*

Trees So High, The. *Unknown.* OxBoLi

Trees stand clerically straight, The. The Ivanovs. Nikolai Alekseievich Zabolotsky, *Russian.* TCRP, *tr. by* Daniel Weissbort

Trees surround a wide pool, the moon casts many shadows. Night Chill. Li Shang-yin, *Chinese.* SuSp, *tr. by* Eugene Eoyang *and* Irving Y. Lo

Trees Walk Farther Away, The. Bernard Kangro, *Estonian.* CEEP, *tr. by* Ivar Ivask

Trees were forbidden me, The. Edouard J. Maunick. NegPo, *tr. by* Ellen Conroy Kennedy *Fr.* As Far as Yoruba Land.

Trees were like bubblyjocks, The. Sunny Gale. "Hugh MacDiarmid." FaBoVe

Trees were taller than the night, The. The Robber. Walter James Turner. MoBrPo

Treetalk and windsong are. Sugarfields. Barbara Mahone. PoBA

Treetops. Marvin Bell. AmPA

Treetops are shuddering. Jane Cooper. *Fr.* The Weather of Six Mornings. NYBP

Trellie. Lance Jeffers. NBV

Trellis for R, A. May Swenson. CPO

Trellis, shorn of grapes, The. Song of an Autumn Night. Chao Meng-fu, *Chinese.* CoBLCP, *tr. by* Jonathan Chaves

Tremayne. Donald Justice. MT

Trembling and sobbing. Free Fire Zone. Igor Bobrowsky. CDa

Trembling before Thine Awful Throne. Augustus Lucas Hillhouse. AH

Trembling I write my dream, and recollect. Philip Freneau. NAAL-1; NAAL-3 *Fr.* The House of Night.

Trembling November winds. Nocturnal Sounds. Kattie M. Cumbo. BlSi

Trembling old men are stamm'ring. Lines on Carmen Sylva. Emma Lazarus. TrJP

Trembling on the pulse of God. (LL) Spinster's Lullaby. Vassar Miller. NMM-2

Trembling, sand-dollar. Grunion. Wendy Rose. CDW

Trembling the spectres glide, and plaintive vent. Homer. OBVE, *tr. by* Pope *Fr.* Odyssey. NAWM-1, *tr. by* Robert Fitzgerald

Trembling with engines, gulping oil, the river. Anthony Cronin. PBCIP *Fr.* R.M.S. Titanic.

Trembling with joy. (LL) Great sea has set me in motion, The. Uvavnuk, *Eskimo.* EnlH, *tr. by* Stephen Mitchell

Tremendous Mood Swings. Burlin Barr. BAP-94

Tremendous Trifles. Rowland Howard. CTV

Tremulous word, a lingering hand, the burning, A. Taking the Night-Train. John James Piatt. APN-2

Trench Fever. Robert Swan. NSI

Trench Idyll. Richard Aldington. PeFWW

Trenches, The. Frederic Manning. NOBAu; NSI; PoWW

Trenches. Owen Rutter. NSI *Fr.* The Song of Tiadatha.

Trenches: St Eloi. Thomas Ernest Hulme. PeFWW

Trenchtown Rock. Bob Marley. PBCV

Trent, The. Michael Drayton. OBEV *Fr.* The Shepherd's Sirena. (Jovial Shepheard's Song, The.) PoEL-2

Trepidation of the Druids. Wordsworth. Son *Fr.* Ecclesiastical Sonnets.

Trespasses. Paul Zarzyski. PaTW

Tretis of the Tua Mariit Wemen and the Wedo, The. William Dunbar. OxBS

"Apon the midsummer evin, mirriest of nichtis." EnVB, *ll.* 1–149

"Bot of ane bowrd in to bed I sall yow breif yit." EBEV

Tri, tre, tre, tre, tri-tre-tre-tree! (LL) This is the way the ladies ride. Mother Goose. LB; OxNR; ReMoGo

Triad. Adelaide Crapsey. 1MW; WPE

Triad, A. Christina Rossetti. NAEL-2; NALW; PBWP

Triads. Swinburne. PBMP

Triads of Ireland, The. *Unknown, Old Irish.*

"Three slender things that best support the." IIP, *tr. by* Kuno Meyer

Triads ("Three excellent qualities in narration"). BIrV, *tr. by* Thomas Kinsella

Trial, The. Zbigniew Herbert, *Polish.* AF, *tr. by* John Carpenter *and* Bogdana Carpenter

Trial and Error. Phyllis McGinley. PeLV

Trial by Jury. Sir William Schwenck Gilbert.

When I, Good Friends, Was Called to the Bar. NAEL-2

Trials of a Tourist. Anne Tibble. NBLV

Trials that the Saviour bore have paved the golden way, The. Benefits of Sorrow. Lizelia Augusta Jenkins Moorer. CBWP-3

Triangular Legs. Sir Alan Patrick Herbert. NBLV

Tribal drum, and the rock-head of Taos mountain, remember that civilization is a transient sickness. (LL) New Mexican Mountain. Robinson Jeffers. InPS-3; MoP; NoAM

Tribal Homeland. Evangeline Paterson. NBrP

Tribal Memories. Robert Duncan. APSN; NOBA *Fr.* Passages.

Tribe surnamed the Arradas, A. His Ancestry. George Clinton Rowe. AAP *Fr.* Toussaint L'Overture.

Tribes, The. Roy Fuller. LiTM

Tribes of Ching—that's not my home. Wang Ts'an, *Chinese.* CoBCP, *tr. by* Burton Watson *Fr.* Seven Sorrows.

Tribulations of an Uneducated Poet in the 1760's, The. James Woodhouse. *Fr.* The Life and Lucubrations of Crispinus Scriblerus. NOEC

Tribunal, The. Chris Wallace-Crabbe. ChIV-2

Tribute. Eloise Bibb. CBWP-4

Tribute, The. Coventry Patmore. EBEV; OBNC *Fr.* The Angel in the House.

Tribute on the Passing of a Very Real Person. *Unknown.* PoToHe

Tribute to a Lost Steamer. Mary Weston Fordham. CBWP-2

Tribute to America. Shelley. AiP

Tribute to Capt. F. W. Dawson. Mary Weston Fordham. CBWP-2

Tribute to Matthew Arnold in a Moment of Self-Abuse, A, *limerick.* Richard Shepherd. PeLi

Tribute to Nervous. Kit Robinson. FTOS

Tribute to Robert E. Lee. Benjamin H. Hill. CTV

Tribute to the Angels. Hilda Doolittle.

"Ah (you say), this is Holy Wisdom." NALW; NoAM

"And the point in the spectrum." NALW

"And yet in some very subtle way." NALW

"Bitter, bitter jewel." NALW

"But nearer than Guardian Angel." NALW

"Every hour, every moment." NALW; NoAM

"Hermes Trismegistus." NALW

"I can not invent it." NALW

"I had been thinking of Gabriel." NALW

"I John saw. I testify." NALW

"Invisible, indivisible Spirit." BoWoP

"Not in our time, O Lord." NOBA

"Now polish the crucible." NALW

"O swiftly, re-light the flame." NALW

"O yes—you understand, I say." NALW

"Of the no need." NALW

"One of us said, how odd." NALW

"She carried a book, either to imply." NALW

"So she must have been pleased with us." NALW

"Some call that deep-deep bell." NALW

"Swiftly re-light the flame." NALW

"This is a symbol of beauty (you continue)." NALW

"This is no rune nor riddle." InPS-3

("This is no rune nor symbol.") NALW

"We have seen her." PFTM

"We have seen her/ the world over." CRP; NALW; Poetr; VGW

"'What is the jewel colour?'." NALW

"Your walls do not fall, he said." NALW

Tribute to the Bride and Groom, A. Priscilla Jane Thompson. CBWP-2

Tribute to Wyatt. Henry Howard, Earl of Surrey.

("Earth his bones, the heavens possess his ghost, The.") (LL) NoP-4

(Epitaph on Sir Thomas Wyatt.) NAEL-1

("Wyatt resteth here, that quick could never rest.") NoP-4; PeECV

Trick, The. John Mole. NOxBChV

Trick is, to live your days, The. Advice to My Son. Peter Meinke. Poetsp

Trick that everyone abhors, A. Rebecca, Who Slammed Doors for Fun and Perished Miserably. Hilaire Belloc. NOBL

Trickle drops! my blue veins leaving! Walt Whitman. APN-1; NAAL-1; NAAL-3; PAR

Trickle of sand on the grave's edge, A. Ad Infinitum. Joan Aronsten. NOBAu

Trickling. Anita Virgil. HA

Trickling, trickling / drop by tiny drop in welcome. Roadside Fountain. Momcilo Nastasijevic, *Serbo-Croatian.* HSix, *tr. by* Charles Simic

Tricks. Daniil Kharms, *Russian.* TCRP, *tr. by* Bradley Jordan

Tricks of the Trade. Gloria Escoffery. HCP

Tricks With Mirrors. Margaret Atwood. NIP-4

Trico's Song. John Lyly. NoSic *Fr.* Alexander and Campaspe. (Spring's Welcome.) OBEV

(Welcome to Spring.) NOBE

Tries a nosedive, kamikaze. Baby Random. Belle Waring. NAmP90; PBCAP

Trifle for Trafalgar Day, A. Ted Pauker. NOBL

Trifles. George Farquhar. OBCoV

Trifling song you shall hear, A. Trifles. George Farquhar. OBCoV

Trifling Women. *Unknown.* AmFP

Trilby. George Du Maurier.

  Little Work, A. FaBoBe; PoLF

Trilce. César Vallejo, *Spanish.* PFTM, tr. by Clayton Eshleman

Trilogy for X. Louis MacNeice.

  "And love hung still as crystal over the bed." CIP-2; GBL; MoBrPo

  For X. BoLoP; EnLoPo

Trilogy of Passion. Goethe, *German.* STV, tr. by John Frederick Nims

Trim the lamp; polish the lens; draw, one by one, rare. Geoffrey Hill. FaBoMo *Fr.* Mercian Hymns.

Trimming the Sails. Vassar Miller. NMM-2

Trim's Song: The Fair Kitchen-Maid. Sir Richard Steele. OxBSP *Fr.* The Funeral.

Trinidad if ah let yu. Trinidad If Ah Let You. Paul Keens-Douglas. HCP

Trinity. "Michael Field." VWP

Trinity. Amen, The. (LL) Upon a Dead Man's Head. John Skelton. AAS; HAP; SCGP

Trinity [or Trinitee] blessed, deity [or deitee] coequal. A Prayer to the Holy Trinity. Richard Stanyhurst. PoEL-2; TIRV

Trinity Brethren Attend. Ivor Armstrong Richards. CRP

Trinity Place. Phyllis McGinley. MoAmPo; OxBSP; SoSe-8

Trinity Sunday. George Herbert. OxBSP

Trio for Two Cats and a Trombone. Dame Edith Sitwell. NAEL-2; PBWP *Fr.* Façade.

Trio of Triolets, A. Gerard Manley Hopkins.

  Triolet. NOBL

Triolet. Wendy Cope. OBCoV

Triolet, A. Angelina Weld Grimké. CPO

Triolet. Gerard Manley Hopkins. NOBL *Fr.* A Trio of Triolets.

Triolet: "When first we met we did not guess." Robert Bridges. OxBSP

Triolet Against Sisters. Phyllis McGinley. KaS; OBCA

Trip Through the Mind Jail, A. Raul Salinas. FaBoA

Trip to a Mountain Village, A. Li K'ai-hsien, *Chinese.* CoBLCP, tr. by Jonathan Chaves

Trip to Berlin. Kondō Yoshimi, *Japanese.* MJT, tr. by Makoto Ueda

Trip to Four or Five Towns, A, (To James Wright). John Logan. CoAP; NNaP

  ("Gold-coloured skin of my Lebanese friends, The.") CoAmPo

Trip to Hua-yang Mountain, A. Tao-chi, *Chinese.* CoBLCP, tr. by Jonathan Chaves

Trip to Mountain West Village, A. Lu Yu, *Chinese.* CoBCP, tr. by Burton Watson

Trip to Paris and Belgium, A. D. G. Rossetti.

  Antwerp to Ghent. PeVV, sect. V

  Boulogne to Amiens and Paris. PeVV

  ("Constant keeping-past of shaken trees." PeVV, pt. I

  ("Constant keeping past of shaken trees.") EnVR

Trip to Stone Man Peak, A. Yang Wan-li, *Chinese.* SuSp, tr. by Jonathan Chaves

Trip to the Grand Banks, A. Amos Hanson. AmFP

Trip to the Village of the River of White Sand, A. Tao-chi, *Chinese.* CoBLCP, tr. by Jonathan Chaves

Trip to Yüeh-lu Temple, A. Li Tung-yang, *Chinese.* CoBLCP, tr. by Jonathan Chaves

Trip upon trenchers, and dance upon dishes. Mother Goose. NOBL; OxNR; ReMoGo

Tripart. Gayl Jones. BlSi

Triphammer Bridge. A. R. Ammons. ColAP; NAAL-2; NOBA

Triple Benison, The. Henrietta Cordelia Ray. CBWP-3

Triple Feature. Denise Levertov. NoP-4

Triple Fool[e], The. Donne. FMP; FSCP; GBL; NOSC; PBRV; SoSe-8

Triple League to Mrs Susan Dove, The. Elizabeth Thomas. KTR

Triple Overtime. Lucinda Roy. GT

Triple Trouble. Assotto Saint. GLP

Triplets for Beautiful Mistra. Nikos Karouzos, *Greek.* GrIP, tr. by Philip Sherrard

Trippers and askers surround me. Walt Whitman. ColAP; EnlH; PAR; UnPo *Fr.* Song of Myself. AmPP; MoAmPo; NAAL-3; NOBA; OxBA

Trips. Nikki Giovanni. CA

Triptych. Frank A. Collymore. PBCV

Tristan da Cunha. Roy Campbell. MoBrPo; PeSA

Tristan da Cunha. Ian D. Colvin. PeSAV

Tristan had no choice. Heinrich von Veldeke, *German.* GePo, tr. by Frederick Goldin

Tristia. Osip Emilevich Mandelstam, *Russian.*

Tristia. Osip Emilevich Mandelstam. PFTM, tr. by Bruce McClelland *Fr.* Tristia.

Tristia. PFTM, tr. by Bruce McClelland

Tristia. Ovid, *Latin.*

  "When night falls here, I think of that other night." OBCVT, tr. by David R. Slavitt

Tristium. Ovid, *Latin.*

  "And here I wish my soul died with my breath." OBVE, tr. by Henry Vaughan

  "And on this day, which poets unto thee." OBVE, tr. by Henry Vaughan

Tristram lies sick to death. Tristram's End. Laurence Binyon. OBMV

Tristram of Lyonesse. Swinburne.

  King Mark, Tristram, and Palamede. EBNV

Tristram's End. Laurence Binyon. OBMV

Tristrem and the Hunters. Thomas of Erceldoune. OxBS *Fr.* Sir Tristrem.

Trit trot to market to buy a penny doll. *Unknown.* OxNR

Triumph, The. William Gilmore Simms. Son

Triumph! How strange, how strong had triumph come. Third Ypres. Edmund Blunden. PeFWW

Triumph! My Jesus has! Triumph! His empire gained! The 15th Kühl-Psalm. Quirinus Kuhlmann, *German.* GePo, tr. by George C. Schoolfield

Triumph of Bacchus and Ariadne. Lorenzo de' Medici. CTC, tr. by Richard Aldington *Fr.* Carnival Songs.

Triumph of Charis, The. Ben Jonson. *See* Her Triumph.

Triumph of Children, The. Eve Shelnutt. CMAP

Triumph of Death, The. Shakespeare. *See* Sonnet 71.

Triumph of Dullness, The. Alexander Pope. NOEC *Fr.* Yet, yet a moment, one dim ray of light. NAEL-1; OAEL-1; PoEL-3 *Fr.* The Dunciad.

Triumph of Infidelity, The, *sels.* Timothy Dwight.

  "Here stood Hypocrisy, in sober brown." NOCV

Triumph of Life, The. Shelley. NAEL-2; NOBRP; OAEL-2; PoEL-4

  ("And answered—'Happy those for whom the fold / Of'.") (LL) NOBRP

Triumph of Love. John Hall Wheelock. MoAmPo

Triumph of Peace, The. James Shirley.

  Song to the Masquers. OxBSP

Triumph of Sensibility. Sylvia Townsend Warner. MoBrPo

Triumph of the Whale, The. Charles Lamb.

  "Io! Paean! Io! sing." OxAEP-2

Triumph of Time, The. Swinburne.

  I Will Go Back to the Great Sweet Mother. NAEL-2

Triumph of Vice, The. Alexander Pope. NOBE; OBSV *Fr.* Epilogue to the Satires, in Two Dialogues. OAEL-1

Triumph or the tomb, The. (LL) Charleston. Henry Timrod. APN-2; AmPP; CBCWP; ColAP; NOBA; OxBA; TAP

Triumphal March. T. S. Eliot. OBWP *Fr.* Coriolan.

Triumphant Demons stand, and Angels start. The Heart's Abysses. Walter Savage Landor. FaBoEE; OBSV

Triumphing chariots, statues, crowns of bay. Sonnet. William Drummond, of Hawthornden. NOSC *Fr.* Urania, or Spiritual Poems.

Triumphing over Death, and Chance, and thee O Time. (LL) On Time. Milton. ImPo; OBEV; SCGP

Triumphs of Death. Anna Hume.

  Arguement, The. KTR

Triumphs of Nature, The. Samuel Boyse. OBGa

Triumphs of Owen, The. Thomas Gray. PoEL-3

Triumphs of the Gout, The. Gilbert West.

  "Lives there on Earth to whom I am unknown." ECEV

Triumvirate, The. Elizabeth Thomas. ECWP

Triune, shaping, restless power. Sistrum. Margaret Fuller. APAD; APN-1; PAR

Trivia; or, The Art of Walking the Streets of London. John Gay.

  "Experienced men, inured to city ways." OAEL-1

  "If clothed in black you tread the busy town." ECEV

  "Let due civilities be strictly paid." OAEL-1

  Pickpockets. ECEV

  Thieves and Whores. ECEV

  "Thoughtless wits shall frequent forfeits pay, The." ECEV

  "Where Lincoln's Inn, wide space, is railed around." ECEV

  Winter Sports. ECEV

Troades. Seneca, *Latin.*

  Seneca's Troas, Act 2. Chorus. OBCVT, tr. by John Wilmot

("*Dreams, Whimsies*, and no more.") (LL) OBCVT

Trŏchĕe trĭps frŏm lŏng tŏ shŏrt. Metrical Feet. Coleridge. FHYEP; NIP-4; OxBChV; Poetr

Troika, The. Louis Simpson. NOBA

Troika, troika! The snow moon. Louis Simpson. WeT

Troilus and Cressida. Dryden.
Song from Troilus and Cressida. NoP-4
(Song.)

Troilus and Cressida. Shakespeare.
"And is it true that I must go from Troy?" OxAEP-1
"Have you seen my cousin?" OxAEP-1
"Peace, you ungracious clamours! peace, rude sounds!" OxAEP-1
"This she? no, this is Diomed's Cressida." OxAEP-1
Ulysses Advises Achilles. ImPo
"What! are my deeds forgot?" OxAEP-1
"You are for dreams and slumbers, brother priest." OxAEP-1

Troilus and Criseyde [*or* Criseide]. Chaucer. EnVB
Complaint of Troilus, The. NOBE; OBEV
Go, Little Book ("Go, litel book, go litel myn tragedy"). OAEL-1
(Chaucer's Wishes for his 'Troilus'.) EPCY
"In May, that moder is of monthes glade." EnVB
Love Unfeigned. NOBE; OBEV
Song of Troylus, The. AWP
("For hoot of cold, for cold of hoot I die.") (LL) NoP-4
("If no love is, O God, what feele I so?") NoP-4
Sorrow of Troilus, The. PoEL-1
"Swich fyn hath, lo, this Troilus for love!" NOCV
"This Troilus [*or* Troylus], with blisse [*or* Blysse] of that supprysed [*or* supprised]." EBEV; PoE
"Whan they unto the paleys were yoemen." PoE
Wooing of Criseide, The, III. PoEL-1

Trois, A. Carol Flint. EC2

Trojan Horse, The. William Drummond, of Hawthornden. PFE

Trojan Horse, The. Virgil. OAEL-1, *tr. by* Henry Howard, Earl of Surrey *Fr.* The Second Book of Virgil's *Aeneid*. SiPS, *tr. by* Henry Howard, Earl of Surrey *Fr.* The Aeneid [*or* Eneados, *Aeneis*].

Troll to her Children, The. Jane Yolen. OTCP

Trolls, The. Louis MacNeice.
Troll's Courtship. AF

Troll's Noscgay, The. Robert Graves. Son

Trombone Solo. Stoddard King. NBLV

Trompe L'Œil. Daryl Hine. MoCV

Troop home to silent grots and caves. The Mermaidens' Vesper-Hymn. George Darley. BIrV; GBL; NAEL-2; OBNC; PoEL-4 *Fr.* Syren Songs.

Troop ship, The. Isaac Rosenberg. NSI; PoWW

Troop Train. Aleksandr Petrovich Mezhirov, *Russian*. TCRP, *tr. by* Deming Brown

Troop Train. Karl Shapiro. OxBA

Trooper and Maid. *Unknown*. AmFP

Troops, The. Siegfried Sassoon. CMoP
(Prelude: The Troops.) PeFWW

Troops brought enough suffering to the people, The. On Hearing That the Sea-Barbarians Are About To Attack Hu-chou—Expressing My Feelings to Tzu-yü. Tsung Ch'en, *Chinese*. CoBLCP, *tr. by* Jonathan Chaves

Troops exulting sate in order round, The. Night Piece: the Trojans outside Troy. Homer. OBVE, *tr. by* Alexander Pope *Fr.* The Iliad.

Troopship, The. Lionel Pigot Johnson. EBVV

Troopship: Mid-Atlantic. Wilfrid Wilson Gibson. NSI

Troparion. Kassiane, *Greek*. WPoS, *tr. by* Liana Sakelliou

Trope Market. Jackson MacLow. PmAP

Trophies of pain I've gathered. whose sorrow. For H.D. Diane Di Prima. PmAP

Trophy, The. Edwin Muir. LiTM

Tropic of ice. Cape Ann; a View. John Malcolm Brinnin. NYBP

Tropic tonight, burning, filled with fast trains. At the Band Concert. John Malcolm Brinnin. PoA

Tropical Death. Grace Nichols. HCP

Tropical Fish. Christopher Vernon Hassall. PeP

Tropical Greenhouse. Dan Pagis, *Hebrew*. IP, *tr. by* Warren Bargad *and* Stanley F. Chyet

"Tropicals." René Maran, *French*. NegPo, *tr. by* Ellen Conroy Kennedy

Tropics. Ellen Bryant Voigt. WeT

Tropics in New York, The. Claude McKay. CrDW; GT; NoAM; PBMP; PFE; PoBA; TTY

Tropics vanish, and meseems that I, The. Robert Louis Stevenson. PeVV

Tropisms on John Berryman. Gerald Vizenor. VoR

Trosachs, The. Wordsworth. OBEV

Trot Along, Pony. Marion Edey *and* Dorothy Grider. CTV

Trot, and a canter, a gallop, and over, A. *Unknown*. OxNR

Troth. Michael Davidson. FTOS

Troth Between the Hill and the Stream, The. Tản Đà, *Vietnamese*. AVP, *tr. by* Huỳnh Sanh Thông

Troubadour. Peter Sirr. BiHa

Trouble. Mari E. Evans. *See* The Rebel.

Trouble. David Keppel. PoLF

Trouble. (LL) Ode: "Weep, ah weep love's losing, love's with its dwelling place." Imr el Kais, *Arabic*. AWP; TAL, *tr. by* Lady Anne Blunt *and* Wilfrid Scawen Blunt

Trouble at the Farm. Ivy O. Eastwick. BoTP

Trouble has done her good. Charity. Connie Bensley. FaBoWP

Trouble in mind, I'm blue. Richard M. Jones. NAAAL

Trouble in the "Amen Corner." Thomas Chalmers Harbaugh. BLPA

Trouble is, it's getting harder. Wild West. Mark Vinz. Poetsp

Trouble / Mellows to a golden note. (LL) Trumpet Player. Langston Hughes. NAAL-2; TTY

Trouble, not of clouds, or weeping rain, A. On the Departure of Sir Walter Scott from Abbotsford, for Naples. Wordsworth. EBEV

Trouble Oh. *Unknown*. PBCV

Trouble was too much, The. Indian Love Song. Lew Blockcolski. VoR

Trouble with a kitten is, The. The Kitten. Ogden Nash. PC

Trouble with General Sherman, The. Limerick. Basil Ransome-Davies. PeLi

Trouble with you is, The. Denunciation; or, Unfrock'd Again. Philip Whalen. NeAP

Trouble with you is, The. Love in a Warm Room in Winter. James Wright. OBAL

Troubled midnight and the noon's repose, The. (LL) La Figlia Che Piange. T. S. Eliot. CBLP; FaBoTw; GBL; HeIP-4; LoP; OxBTC; PoA; UnPo; VGW

Troubled Soldier, The. *Unknown*. AS

Troubled that you are not, as they say. George Oppen. APSN *Fr.* Route.

Troubled was a house in Ealing. The Widow's Plot; or, She Got What Was Coming to Her. William Plomer. MoP

Troubled waters, The/ are frozen fast. Murasaki Shikibu. WPJ; WPOW *Fr.* The Tale of Genji.

Troubled with the Itch and Rubbing with Sulphur. George Moses Horton. AAP

Troubles. Bozhidar Bozhilov, *Bulgarian*. CEEP, *tr. by* Jascha Kessler *and* Aleksandar Shurbanov

Troubles of the Day. William Barnes. GTBS-P

Troubles with the Soul at Morning Calisthenics. Anna Swirszczynska, *Polish*. BLT, *tr. by* Czeslaw Milosz *and* Leonard Nathan

Troubling the Water. Yusef Komunyakaa. BAP-95

Trousers of Wind. *Unknown, Amharic*. PBA; TTY, *tr. by* Sylvia Pankhurst

Trout, The. Daryl Hine. CoAP

Trout, The. John Montague. IIP; NoP-4; PBCIP; PNI; PoE

Trout Fisher. George Mackay Brown. FaBoTC; OxBC

Trout Flies. Ruthven Todd. FaBoTC

Troy. Agathias, *Greek*. GrAn; OBCVT, *tr. by* Ezra Pound

Troy. Edwin Muir. CMoP

Troy. Thomas Sackville. *Fr.* Induction to "A Mirror for Magistrates." AAS

Troy Depicted. Shakespeare. *Fr.* The Rape of Lucrece.

Truant, The. Edwin John Pratt. NOBC

Truants, The. Walter De la Mare. MoBrPo

Truce, The. Stella Gibbons. LW

Truce. Paul Muldoon. PBCIP; PNI

Truce, gentle love, a parley now I crave. Michael Drayton. NoSic *Fr.* Idea.

Truck Stop: Minnesota. Stephen Dunn. CMAP

Trucker, The. Will Dyson. NOBAu

True Account of Talking to the Sun at Fire Island, A. Frank O'Hara. HCAP; NNaP; RB; TTTS

True and earthy prayer / of salami, The. (LL) Salami. Philip Levine. NNaP; NOBA; TAP; TRP

True, and yet true that I must Stella love. (LL) Sonnet 5: "It is most true that eyes are formed to serve." Sir Philip Sidney. NAEL-1; NoSic; OAEL-1; Son

True Arab knows how to catch a fly in his hands, A. Naomi Shihab Nye. *See* Blood.

True Arab knows how to catch a fly in his hands, A. Blood. Naomi Shihab Nye. NMM-2; UnSA

True Ballad of the Great Race to Gilmore City, The. Phil Hey. Poetsp

True Beauty, The. Thomas Carew. *See* Disdain Returned.

True-blue the salmon—from his sally. No Place Like Home. Llawdden, *Welsh*. OBWVE, *tr. by* Gwyn Jones

True-born Englishman, The. Daniel Defoe.

"Breed's described, The: Now, Satire, if you can." OBSV

"In their religion they are so unev'n." OBSV

"Labouring poor, in spite of double pay, The." NOBL

"Then let us boast of ancestors no more." OBSV

"Wherever God erects a house of prayer." NOBL; OBSV

True Brahmin, in the morning meadows wet. Gardener. Ralph Waldo Emerson. OxBA *Fr.* Quatrains.

True Bride, The. Amy Gerstler. PmAP

True Confession of George Barker, The. George Barker.

"I sent a letter to my love." FaBoTw

True Dream, A. Elizabeth Barrett Browning. NALW

True ease in writing comes from Art, not Chance. An Essay on Criticism. Alexander Pope. InPK-6, *ll.* 362–383; HAP *Fr.* An Essay on Criticism. NAEL-1; PoEL-3; TFi

True Effigies of a Certain Squire: Inscribed to Clemena, The. Elizabeth Thomas. ECWP

True Encounter, The. Edna St. Vincent Millay. OxBSP

True Facts of the Case, The, *limerick*. Anthony Euwer. OBAL; PeLi

True faith discovered was, The. Wisdom. W. B. Yeats. TrCP

True faith, he claims, has the most doubt. A Modern Theologian. Paul Ramsey. *Fr.* Three Epigrams. CRP

True feelings come from my innermost heart. On a Painting "Ancient Trees and Flowing Stream." Yün Shou-p'ing, *Chinese*. CoBLCP, *tr. by* Jonathan Chaves

True Friendship. *Unknown. Fr.* The Panchatantra. AWP, *tr. by* Arthur Ryder

True Genius. Robert Lloyd. NOEC *Fr.* Shakespeare; an Epistle to David Garrick, Esq.

True genius, but true woman! dost deny. To George Sand: A Recognition. Elizabeth Barrett Browning. BoWoP; NAEL-2; NALW; PEW; VWP

True Happiness. Morris Talpalar. PoToHe

True, / he just / lets his glass / set there. (LL) Neighbor. Langston Hughes. APSN; PFTM

True Hymn, A. George Herbert. GeHe; NOCV

True Import of Present Dialogue, Black vs, The Negro. Nikki Giovanni. BPo; PoBA

True Knight [*or* True Knighthood], The. Stephen Hawes. OBEV *Fr.* The Pastime of Pleasure. OBGa

True Knowledge. William Wilkie. ECEV *Fr.* The Grasshopper and the Glowworm.

True Life Love Stories. Michael Foley.

"Ah no, ah no, they weren't all gross and slow." PNI

"*Sois sage, ô ma doleur. . .* I don't." PNI

"Sword is a cold bride. Yuk!, The." PNI

True life, natural breath; not this phantasma. (LL) The Pier-Glass. Robert Graves. CMoP; NoAM

True Line, The. Pong-u Park, *Korean*. CKP, *tr. by* Jaihiun Kim

True Love. Phoebe Cary. PoToHe

True Love, A. Nicholas Grimald. OBEV

True Love. Sir Philip Sidney. *See* The Bargain.

True Love at Last. D. H. Lawrence. PFE

True love, come O come to me. *Unknown, German*. AWP, *tr. by* Jethro Bithell

True love in every moment praises God. Mechthild von Magdeburg, *German*. WPoS, *tr. by* Jane Hirshfield

True Love in this differs from gold and clay. Shelley. FHYEP; OBNC *Fr.* Epipsychidion.

True love is sweet and true love is pleasant. William Hall. *Unknown*. AmFP

True love, true love, what have I done. In the Pines. *Unknown*. AmFP

True Lover, The. A. E. Housman. EBNV; OxBSn

True Lovers Bold, The. *Unknown*. AmFP

True lovers even in this. (LL) Never Such Love. Robert Graves. BoLoP; LoP

True Lover's Farewell, The. *Unknown*. AS

True Maid, A. Matthew Prior. EP; FaBoEE; NAEL-1; NIP-4; NOEC; PeLV

True Marriage Is True Love. William Ellery Leonard. *Fr.* Two Lives. Son

True poesy is not in words. Pastoral Poesy. John Clare. FHYEP; OAEL-2

True Protocol of Poets, The. Kapilar, *Tamil*. PLW, *tr. by* A. K. Ramanujan

True Son of God, Eternal Light. P. J. Cormican. AH

True Story Ending in False Hope, A. Pearse Hutchinson. PBCIP

True Story of the Pins. Alberto A. Ríos. NAmP90

True storyteller is a, The. *Unknown*. CA

True Tale, A. Mary Chandler. ECWP

True Tale of Robin Hood, A. *Unknown*. ESPB

True Thomas lay o'er yond grassy [*or* on Huntlie] bank. Thomas the Rhymer. *Unknown*. CH; ESPB; EnSB; FaBoCh; HAP; InPK-6; InPS-3; NOBE; OAEL-1; OBEV; OxBB; OxBS; PoE; RB; TFi

True to myself am I, and false to all. Mary Elizabeth Coleridge. VWP

True to our God, true to our native land. (LL) Lift every [*or* ev'ry] voice and sing. James Weldon Johnson. CrDW

True to the Best. Benjamin Keech. PoToHe

True to your might [*or* Truth to your mighty] winds on dusky shores. On the Death of William Edward Burghardt Du Bois by African Moonlight and Forgotten Shores. Conrad Kent Rivers. PoBA

True we are two grown men. Ed Roberson. GT

True, we must tame our rebel will. Courage. Matthew Arnold. OAEL-2

True wit is Nature to advantage dressed. Alexander Pope. HAP *Fr.* An Essay on Criticism. NAEL-1; PoEL-3; TFi

Truest Poetry Is the Most Feigning, The [*or*, Ars Poetica for Hard Times]. W. H. Auden. NYBP

Truganinny. Wendy Rose. HATNAP

Truisms, The. Louis MacNeice. IIP; NOBE; OBSV; PNI

Truly. Ingeborg Bachmann, *German*. PoSu, *tr. by* Mark Anderson

Truly alone muley. Times. Tom Weatherly. SeSe

Truly God is good to Israel. Bible, *O.T. See* Psalm 73.

Truly Great. W. H. Davies. OBMV

Truly! He goes around the whole world, the great hā' mats'a, looking for food everywhere, the great hā' mats'a, on both sides of the world. Hā' mats'a Song, La' Lasiqoala. *Unknown*. Fr. Dances and Songs of the Winter Ceremonial. APN-2, *tr. by* Franz Boas

Truly, I live in dark times! To Those Born Later. Bertolt Brecht, *German*. AF, *tr. by* John Willett, Ralph Manheim *and* Erich Fried

Truly in the east / The white bean. Song to Promote Growth. *Unknown, Navajo*. OBVE, *tr. by* Washington Matthews

Truly it was morning, and few to equal it. Levivot. Saul Tchernichovsky, *Hebrew*. MHP, *tr. by* Ruth Finer Mintz

Truly my Satan thou art but a dunce. Epilogue. William Blake. FHYEP; HAP; ImPo; OAEL-2; OBNC; OxBSP; PeECV; PoE; SCGP; WeW-3 *Fr.* The Gates of Paradise. PoEL-4

Truly my soul waiteth upon God. Bible, *O.T. See* Psalm 62.

Truly Rich, The. T. Urchard. PWR

Truly, truly, I say to you. Pier Paolo Pasolini. GI *Fr.* St. John.

Trumpet, The. Ilya Grigoryevich Ehrenburg, *Russian*. TCRP; TrJP, *tr. by* Yakov Hornstein

Trumpet, The. Robinson Jeffers.

Grass on the Cliff. PoA

Trumpet, The. Edward Thomas. MoBrPo

Trumpet, at whose voice [*or* voyce] the people came, The. (LL) The Second Anniversary [*or* Anniversarie]. Donne. ESCV; SeCP

Trumpet call and grand white stars. Christ. *Unknown, Greek*. GrAn, *tr. by* Guy Davenport

Trumpet of Liberty, The. John Taylor. NOEC

Trumpet of Liberty sounds through the World, The. *Unknown*. NOBRP

Trumpet Player. Langston Hughes. NAAL-2; TTY

Trumpeter of Fyvie, The. *Unknown*. OxBB

(Andrew Lammie.) ESPB

Trumpets. Georg Trakl, *German*. PeFWW, *tr. by* David McDuff *and* Jon Silkin

Trumpet's loud clangor, The. Fife and Drum. Dryden. *Fr.* A Song for St Cecilia's Day [1687]. AWP; FHYEP; FaBoTw; GTBS-P; HAP; ImPo; InPS-3; NOSC; OAEL-1; OBEV; OxAEP-1; PoEL-3; SCGP; TFi

Trumpet's voice, loud and authoritative, The. Reasons for Attendance. Philip Larkin. PoPoPo

Trundled from / the strangeness of the sea. The Sea-Elephant. William Carlos Williams. MeMAP; SAmP

Tru'o'ng Chi, the Lovelorn Boatman. *Unknown, Vietnamese*. AVP, *tr. by* Huỳnh Sanh Thông

Trust him not to breathe a word. (LL) Under the Lindens [*or* Lime Tree]. Walther von der Vogelweide, *German*. CTC, *tr. by* Ford Madox Ford; GePo, *tr. by* Frederick Goldin; GBL; OBVE, *tr. by* Thomas Lovell Beddoes

Trust in Me. *Unknown*. AH

Trust me, I have not earned your dear rebuke. Christina Rossetti. *Fr.* Monna Innominata. BWW

Trust me. The world is run on a shoestring. Hard Times. John Ashbery. NoAM

Trust not that thing called woman: she is worse. A Rodomontade on His Cruel Mistress. John Wilmot, 2d Earl of Rochester. OxBSP

Trust not the treason of those smiling looks. Sonnet 47. Edmund Spenser. *Fr.* Amoretti. AAS

Trust Thou Thy Love. John Ruskin. OBEV

Trust thrust first tinder kindling grown. Burnt Sienna. Norman Henry, II Pritchard. GT

"Trust us," the Voices said. (LL) The Lovely Shall Be Choosers. Robert Frost. MoAmPo; NOBA; OxBA; PoE

Trusted the servile womb to breed free men? (LL) Advice to Young Ladies. Alec Derwent Hope. NoAM; NoP-4

Trustful curator has left me alone, The. Museum of Man. Earle Birney. OxBC

Trusting you could weep. (LL) The Connoisseuse of Slugs. Sharon Olds. APAD; DeD; LW

Truth. "Æ." MoBrPo

Truth. Chaucer. AWP; NAEL-1; OAEL-1

("And Trouthe shal delivere, it is no drede.") (LL) NoP-4

("And Truthe shall deliver, it is no dread.") (LL) EnVB; MiEL; SCGP

(Balade of Bon Conseill.) EnVB; MiEL; SCGP

Truth. William Cowper.

"Man on the dubious waves of error toss'd." NOCV

Truth, The. W. H. Davies. FaBoTw

Truth. Eileen Duggan. PeNZ

Truth. Josephine D. Henderson Heard. CBWP-4

Truth, The. Randall Jarrell. FiLi; OxBC

Truth, The. Ted Joans. TTY

(Voice in the Crowd.) AmFP

Truth. Claude McKay. BPo

Truth. Howard Nemerov. HoPM; LiTM

Truth, The. Frankie Paino. NAmP90

Truth. Coventry Patmore. *See* Magna Est Veritas.

Truth. Barrie Wade. OTCP

Truth? A pebble of quartz? For once, then, something. (LL) For Once, Then, Something. Robert Frost. GEA; NOBA; NoAM

Truth About Karen, The. Kenneth Carroll. ISC

Truth about My Sister and Me, The. Anita Endrezze-Danielson. CDW

Truth about truth is elusive, The. Limerick. *Unknown.* PeLi

Truth and Consequences. Edward Baugh. PBCV

Truth and noonday light to thee, A. (LL) Duty. Ellen S. Hooper. PAR

Truth at Last. Edward Rowland Sill. APN-2

Truth Has Perished. Ulma Seligman, *Yiddish.* TrJP, *tr.* by Joseph Leftwich

Truth I do not stretch or shove, The. The Dog. Ogden Nash. Spl

Truth I pursued, as Fancy sketch'd the way. Coleridge. FaBoEE

Truth in Poetry. George Crabbe. EPCY; FHYEP *Fr.* The Village.

Truth Is, The. Linda Hogan. HATNAP; LTA; NMM-2

("Left shoe / and the right one with its white foot, The.") (LL) UnSA

Truth is a golden sunset far away. Threnody. I. O. Scherzo. HoPM

Truth is a native, naked beauty; but. Roger Williams. SCAP

Truth—is as old as God. Emily Dickinson. MoAmPo

Truth is Blind, The. David Gascoyne. SPE

Truth is, I envy them. Tornados. Thylias Moss. GT

Truth is love and love is truth. Mendacity. Alfred Edgar Coppard. OBMV

Truth is that there comes a time, The. Sad Strains of a Gay Waltz. Wallace Stevens. OxBA

Truth / like the belly of a woman turning, The. Gary Snyder. NNaP

Truth-loving Persians do not dwell upon. The Persian Version. Robert Graves. CMoP; LiTM; MoP; NOBL; NoAM; NoP-4; OBWP; WeW-3

Truth of truth was being missed. The one who was thinking, The. Pieces O'six—XVIII. Jackson Mac Low. FTOS

Truth, so far, in my book; the truth which draws. Elizabeth Barrett Browning. *Fr.* Aurora Leigh. VWP

Truth Suppressed, The. Lizeila Augusta Jenkins Moorer. CBWP-3

Truth the Dead Know, The. Anne Sexton. ColAP; IMW; LCAP-2; MoAmPo; NoAM; NoP-4; PBWP; TAP; VCAP

Truthful James to the Editor. Bret Harte. APN-2

Truth's the Best. Elizabeth Turner. OxBChV

Try Again. Eliza Cook. BoTP

Try first this figure 2. A Lesson in Handwriting. Alastair Reid. NYBP

Try hard to stay well. (LL) Going on always on and on. *Unknown, Chinese.* SuSp, *tr.* by Charles Hartman

Try our Rubber Girl-Friend (air-inflatable). Limerick. *Unknown.* PeLi

Try Smiling. *Unknown.* BLPA; PWR

Try to avoid inhaling the laden air. (LL) The Lovers of the Poor. Gwendolyn Brooks. LCAP-2; LTA; MoP; NAAAL; NAAL-2; NOBA; NoAM; Poetr; SSLK

Try to cover your shivering shoulders in rags of the oldest. Irina Ratushinskaya, *Russian.* AF, *tr.* by David McDuff

Try to see them as Monet would. The Hackeysack Players. Cynthia Huntington. NAmP90

Try Topic. Genevieve Taggard. MoAmPo

Try, Try Again. T. H. Palmer. ChAP; ImGa

Try, try again. (LL) Try, Try Again. T. H. Palmer. ChAP; ImGa

Try wading in sand. Philip Appleman. BXAP

Trying. a trying child. trying it on for size. the role. Daphne Marlatt. DeD *Fr.* Ana Historic.

Trying Again. Dahlia Ravikovitch, *Hebrew.* VCWP, *tr.* by Chana Bloch *and* Ariel Bloch

Trying for Fire. Tim Seibles. NAmP90

Trying so hard. Sunbathing. Nancy Travis. ISC

Trying to be white. (LL) The Way It Was. Lucille Clifton. NMM-2

Trying to become one with the god's. (LL) Carnival. Primus St. John. CMAP; GT

Trying to Begin. Robert Mezey. WeT

Trying to bite off her tongue. (LL) After the Fall of Saigon. Yusef Komunyakaa. AF; CDa

Trying to chop mother down is like. She Went to Stay. Robert Creeley. OBAL

Trying to fall asleep. Night Thought. Gerald Jonas. NYBP

Trying to forget him. Alexis Rotella. HA

Trying to imagine a poem of the future. The Premonition. Hyam Plutzik. WeT

Trying to make / Trouble. (LL) The Rebel. Mari E. Evans. CRP; PoBA

Trying to open locked doors with a sword, threading. Sojourn in the Whale. Marianne Moore. NALW

Trying to perch. Tanka. Mori Ōgai, *Japanese.* MJT, *tr.* by Makoto Ueda

Trying to sleep by the lake. Waiting for the End of the War. Thomas Brush. CDa

Trying to speak means flailing with. Winged Words. Rachel Hadas. FFC

Trying to Talk with a Man. Adrienne Rich. HCAP

Trying to wash away. Tanka. Tawara Machi, *Japanese.* MJT, *tr.* by Makoto Ueda

Tryst. Olga Broumas. DeD

Tryst. John Hewitt. BiHa

Tryst [*or* Trysting Place], The. William Soutar. EBEV; OxBS

(Trysting Place, The.) BoLoP

Tryst, The. John Banister Tabb. OBAL

Tryst. Sunanda Tripathy, *Oriya.* OMIP, *tr.* by Jagannath Prasad Das *and* Arlene Zide

Tryst, The. Mary E. Tucker. CBWP-1

Tryst, The. *Unknown, Welsh.* OBWVE, *tr.* by Joseph P. Clancy

Tryst in Brobdingnag, A. Adrienne Rich. NYBP

Tryst with you—I shall nurse no regret, A. To the Black Nymph. Vũ Hoàng Chu'o'ng, *Vietnamese.* AVP, *tr.* by Huỳnh Sanh Thông

Trystan and Esyllt. *Unknown, Welsh.* OBWVE, *tr.* by Gwyn Jones

Trysting, A. Richard Dehmel, *German.* AWP, *tr.* by Jethro Bithell

Trysting Bush, The. Joanna Baillie. WPE

Trysting Place, The. William Soutar. *See* The Tryst [*or* Trysting Place].

Ts'ai Chi'h. Ezra Pound. NoP-4

Tsa'lagi Council Tree. Gladys Cardiff. HATNAP

Tsar! Send out a shot! Velemir Khlebnikov. TCRP, *tr.* by Gary Kern *Fr.* Washerwoman.

Tsě' ni Gisī' n, or Song in the Rock. *Unknown. Fr.* The Night Chant. APN-2, *tr.* by Washington Matthews

Tselkov: An Interpretation. Lev Vladimir Loseff, *Russian.* TCRP, *tr.* by Walter Arndt

Tsu Mei is early dead. Chang Yu. Reading the Poems of an Absent Friend. Ou-yang Hsiu, *Chinese.* OHPC, *tr.* by Kenneth Rexroth

Tu / cson's of blackmens. Ron Welburn. NBV

Tu Do Street. Yusef Komunyakaa. LTA

Tu-lu, Tu-lu, evil waters running muddy. Tu-lu Poem. Yang Wei-chen, *Chinese.* CoBLCP, *tr.* by Jonathan Chaves

"Tu Non Se' in Terra, Si Come Tu Credi." Kathleen Jessie Raine. WPE

Tu-Whit To-Who. Shakespeare. *See* Winter.

"Tu-whitt, Tu-whitt, Tu-whoo, Tu-whoo." "Good Night," Says the Owl. Lady Erskine Crum. BoTP

Tua Mariit Wemen and the Wedo, The. William Dunbar.

Widow Has Buried Her Second Husband, The. RACG

Tubby or not tubby—there's the rub. Sir Francis Cowley Burnand. BXAP

Tube Time. Eve Merriam. TLR

Tubes. Donald Hall. LoL

Tubs of / memory. Roof Garden. James Schuyler. OBGa

Tuckanuck, I. George Cabot Lodge. APN-2

Tuckett. Bill Tuckett. Telegraph operator, Hall's Creek. Morse. Les A. Murray. NTP; NoP-4

Tudor indeed is gone and every rose. Canto 80. Ezra Pound. FaBoTw *Fr.* Cantos.

Tuesday, June 4th, 1991. Billy Collins. BAP-93

Tuesday Night Affair. Sandra Turner Bond. ISC

Tuesday; or, the Ditty. John Gay. NOEC *Fr.* The Shepherd's Week.

Tuft of Flowers, The. Robert Frost. AWP; MoAmPo; NAAL-2; OxBA

Tuft of Kelp, The. Herman Melville. APN-2; FaBoEE

Tug-of-War, A. M. M. Hutchinson. BoTP

Tug with bright streets at lonely lights like his. (LL) Flying at Night. Ted Kooser. InPK-6; PBCAP

Tugela River. William Plomer. PeSAV

Tulip. Humbert Wolfe. MoBrPo

Tulip Bed, The. William Carlos Williams. OBGa

("Reposedly.") (LL) GaP

Tulip Tree. Sacheverell Sitwell. MoBrPo

Tulips. Medbh McGuckian. PNI

Tulips and Addresses. Edward Field. NYBP; Poetsp

Tulips are too excitable, it is winter here, The. Sylvia Plath. HAP; NYBP; NoP-4; WPE; WeW-3

Tullochgorum. John Skinner. OxBS

Tully, the queen of beauty's boast. Molly Moor. George Farewell. NOEC

Tullynoe: Tête-à-Tête in the Parish Priest's Parlour. Paul Durcan. OBCoV

Tumadir al-Khansa for Her Brother. *Unknown.* AWP *Fr.* The Thousand and One Nights.

(For Her Brother.) PBWP

Tumble me down, and I will sit. To Fortune. Robert Herrick. CavPo; OxBSP

Tumbled out of heaven. The Blue Day Journey. Gwyn Jones. OBWVE

Tumbleweed. Jonathan Holden. NAmP90

Tumbling. *Unknown.* ACTP; OxBChV

Tumbling in big solitary drops. Sexual Water. Pablo Neruda, *Spanish.* PFTM, *tr.* by Clayton Eshleman

Tumbling, pausing, leaping, knocking together. Metaphysic of Snow. Donald Finkel. PoA

Tumult in a Syrian town had place, A. The Great Physician. Sadi. AWP, *tr.* by Sir Edward Arnold *Fr.* The Gulistan.

Tumult in the street!, A. *Unknown, Greek.* GrAn, *tr.* by Edward Lucie-Smith

Tumult of death, dizziness hath seized me, The. Elegy (for Himself). Moses Rimos of Majorca, *Hebrew.* TrJP, *tr.* by Israel Abrahams

Tumult of my fretted mind, The. Self-Analysis. Anna Wickham. MoBrPo

Tumult, weeping, many new ghosts. Snow Storm. Tu Fu, *Chinese.* BLT; OHPC, *tr.* by Kenneth Rexroth

Tumultuous sea, whose wrath and foam are spent. Eumares. Asclepiades, *Greek.* AWP, *tr.* by Richard Garnett

Tunbridge Wells. John Wilmot, 2d Earl of Rochester. OBSV

T'undo, or be undone. (LL) Ulysses and the Siren [*or* Syren]. Samuel Daniel. HAP; NAEL-1; NOBE; NoP-4; OBEV; OxAEP-1; PoE; PoEL-2

Tundra is a living, The. John Haines. CoAmPo

Tune. Robert Kelly. FTOS

Tune, A. Arthur Symons. BoLoP; OBNC

(That Tune.) LBC

Tune: "As in a Dream; a Song." Li Ch'ing-chao, *Chinese.* BoWoP; SuSp, *tr.* by Eugene Eoyang

Tune: "As in a Dream; a Song." Su Shih, *Chinese.* SuSp, *tr.* by Irving Y. Lo

Tune: "Autumn Waters"—Listening to Rain. Na-lan Hsing-te, *Chinese.* SuSp, *tr.* by Bruce Carpenter

Tune: "Bean Leaves Yellow." Lu Yu, *Chinese.* SuSp, *tr.* by James J. Y. Liu

Tune: "Beautiful Lady Yü, The." Chou Pang-yen, *Chinese.*

"About to leave, yet by the lamplight she lingers." SuSp, *tr.* by Irving Y. Lo

"Sparse fence, winding path, a small farmhouse." SuSp, *tr.* by Irving Y. Lo

Tune: "Beautiful Lady Yü, The." Li Yü, *Chinese.* SuSp, *tr.* by Eugene Eoyang

Tune: "Beautiful Lady Yü, The"—Spring Sorrow. Ch'en Liang, *Chinese.* SuSp, *tr.* by Hellmut Wilhelm

Tune becomes a flower, The. Georgy Vladimirovich Ivanov, *Russian.* TCRP, *tr.* by Daniel Weissbort

Tune beyond us as we are, A. Wallace Stevens. CMoP *Fr.* The Man with the Blue Guitar.

Tune: "Big String of Words, A"—The Great Wall. Na-lan Hsing-te, *Chinese.* SuSp, *tr.* by Lenore Mayhew *and* William McNaughton

Tune: "Butterflies." Kuan Yün-shih. SuSp, *tr.* by Richard John Lynn *Fr.* Medley of Southern and Northern Tunes—Scenic Tour of West Lake.

Tune: "Butterflies Lingering over Flowers" ("Back in the painted pavilion, again in late spring"). Ou-yang Hsiu, *Chinese.* SuSp, *tr.* by Eugene Eoyang

Tune: "Butterflies Lingering over Flowers." Kung Tzu-chen, *Chinese.* SuSp, *tr.* by Irving Y. Lo

Tune: "Butterflies Lingering over Flowers" ("Ruffed blue-green garden, red blossoms"). Ou-yang Hsiu, *Chinese.* SuSp, *tr.* by Jerome P. Seaton

Tune: "Butterflies Lingering over Flowers." Wang Kuo-wei, *Chinese.* SuSp, *tr.* by Ching-i Tu

Tune: "Butterflies Lingering over Flowers." Yen Chi-tao, *Chinese.* SuSp, *tr.* by An-yan Tang

Tune: "Butterflies Lingering over Flowers"—Leaving the Border. Na-lan Hsing-te, *Chinese.* SuSp, *tr.* by An-yan Tang

Tune: "Casket of Pearls, A." Li Yü, *Chinese.* SuSp, *tr.* by Daniel Bryant

Tune: "Celebration in the Eastern Plain"—Replying to a Lyric Song by the Senior Poet Ma Chih-yüan. *Unknown, Chinese.* SuSp, *tr.* by Sherwin S. S. Fu

Tune: "Charm of Nien-nu." Chiang K'uei, *Chinese.* SuSp, *tr.* by James J. Y. Liu

Tune: "Charm of Nien-nu, The." Chu Tun-ju, *Chinese.* SuSp, *tr.* by Irving Y. Lo

Tune: "Charm of Nien-nu, The." Li Ch'ing-chao, *Chinese.* SuSp, *tr.* by Eugene Eoyang

Tune: "Chilly East Wind." Kuan Yün-shih. SuSp, *tr.* by Richard John Lynn *Fr.* Medley of Southern and Northern Tunes—Scenic Tour of West Lake.

Tune: "Chrysanthemums Fresh." Liu Yung, *Chinese.* SuSp, *tr.* by James J. Y. Liu

Tune: "Clear River, a Prelude"—Lovesickness. Hsü Tsai-ssu, *Chinese.* SuSp, *tr.* by Sherwin S. S. Fu

Tune: "Coda." Kuan Yün-shih. SuSp, *tr.* by Richard John Lynn *Fr.* Medley of Southern and Northern Tunes—Scenic Tour of West Lake.

Tune: "Courtyard Full of Fragrance." Ch'in Kuan, *Chinese.* SuSp, *tr.* by James J. Y. Liu

Tune: Crimson Lips Adorned. Li Ch'ing-chao, *Chinese.* PBWP, *tr.* by C. H. Kwock *and* Vincent McHugh

("After kicking on the swing.") BoWoP, *tr.* by Kenneth Rexroth *and* Ling Chung

Tune: Crimson Lips Adorned. Li Ch'ing-chao, *Chinese.* PBWP, *tr.* by C. H. Kwock *and* Vincent McHugh

Tune: "Crows Crying at Nighit." Li Yü, *Chinese.* SuSp, *tr.* by Daniel Bryant

Tune: Crows Crying at Night. Li Yü, *Chinese.* CoBCP, *tr.* by Burton Watson

Tune: "Dance of the Cavalry." Li Yü, *Chinese.* SuSp, *tr.* by Daniel Bryant

Tune: "Decorous and Pretty." Kung Tzu-chen, *Chinese.* SuSp, *tr.* by An-yan Tang

Tune: "Decorous and Pretty"—Respectfully Offered to Circuit Inspector Kao. Liu Chih, *Chinese.* SuSp, *tr.* by Richard John Lynn

Tune: Deva-like Barbarian ("Blossoms bright, the moon dark, shadowed in thin mist"). Li Yü, *Chinese.* CoBCP, *tr.* by Burton Watson

Tune: "Deva-like Barbarian" ("Bright flowers and dim moon, enmeshed in thin drifting mist"). Li Yü, *Chinese.* SuSp, *tr.* by Daniel Bryant

Tune: Deva-like Barbarian ("On the many-leafed bedscreens, gold flickers and fades"). Wen T'ing-yün, *Chinese.* CoBCP, *tr.* by Burton Watson

Tune: Deva-like Barbarian ("People all say the southland's better"). Wei Chuang, *Chinese.* CoBCP, *tr.* by Burton Watson

Tune: "Deva-like Barbarian." *Unknown, Chinese.* SuSp, *tr.* by Hellmut Wilhelm

Tune: "Deva-like Barbarian." Wei Chuang, *Chinese.* SuSp, *tr.* by Lois M. Fusek

Tune: Deva-like Barbarian. Wen T'ing-yün, *Chinese.* CoBCP, *tr.* by Burton Watson

Tune: "Deva-like Barbarian"—Ta-po-ti. Mao Tse-tung, *Chinese.* SuSp, *tr.* by Eugene Eoyang

Tune: "Dim Fragrance"—Plum Blossoms. Chiang K'uei, *Chinese.* SuSp, *tr.* by An-yan Tang

Tune: "Distant Red Window." Chou Pang-yen, *Chinese.* SuSp, *tr.* by Irving Y. Lo

Tune: "Dreaming of the South." Wen T'ing-yün, *Chinese.* SuSp, *tr.* by William R. Schultz

Tune: Dreaming of the South. Wen T'ing-yün, *Chinese.* CoBCP, *tr.* by Burton Watson

Tune: Drunk among the Flowers. Mao Wen-hsi, *Chinese.* CoBCP, *tr.* by Burton Watson

Tune: "Echoing Heaven's Everlastingness." Li Ching, *Chinese.* SuSp, *tr.* by Daniel Bryant

Tune: "Echoing Heaven's Everlastingness." Wang Kuo-wei, *Chinese.* SuSp, *tr.* by Ching-i Tu

Tune: "Eight-beat Barbarian Tune." Sun Kuang-hsien, *Chinese.* SuSp, *tr.* by Hellmut Wilhelm

Tune: "Eight Beats of a Kan-chou Song." Liu Yung, *Chinese.* SuSp, *tr.* by James J. Y. Liu

Tune: Endless Union. Li Ch'ing-chao, *Chinese.* PBWP, *tr.* by C. H. Kwock *and* Vincent McHugh

Tune: "Eternal Longing." *Unknown, Chinese.* SuSp, *tr.* by Hellmut Wilhelm

Tune: Eternal Longing. *Unknown.* *Fr.* Four *Tz'u* from Tun-huang. CoBCP, *tr.* by Burton Watson

Tune: Flirtatious Laughter. Wei Ying-wu, *Chinese*. CoBCP, *tr. by* Burton Watson

Tune: "Flower unlike Flower." Po Chü-i, *Chinese*. SuSp, *tr. by* Eugene Eoyang

Tune for a Lonesome Fife. Donald Justice. *See* Another Song.

Tune: "Four Pieces of Jade"—Idle Leisure. Kuan Han-ch'ing, *Chinese*. SuSp, *tr. by* Jerome Seaton

Tune: "Four Pieces of Jade"—Retirement. Ma Chih-yüan, *Chinese*. SuSp, *tr. by* Sherwin S. S. Fu

Tune: "Full Moon in the Human World"—Spring Evening: Replying to a Song. *Unknown*, *Chinese*. SuSp, *tr. by* Sherwin S. S. Fu

Tune: "Full River Red." Hsin Ch'i-chi, *Chinese*. SuSp, *tr. by* Irving Y. Lo

Tune: "Full River Red"—A Four-season Song on the Hardships and Joys of Farming Life. Cheng Hsieh, *Chinese*. SuSp, *tr. by* Irving Y. Lo

Tune: "Full River Red"—A Reply to Kuo Mo-jo. Mao Tse-tung, *Chinese*. SuSp, *tr. by* Eugene Eoyang

Tune: "Gazing at the South." Li Yü, *Chinese*. SuSp, *tr. by* Daniel Bryant

Tune: Gazing at the South. Li Yü, *Chinese*. CoBCP, *tr. by* Burton Watson

Tune: "Going Up Small Pavilion." Kuan Yün-shih. SuSp, *tr. by* Richard John Lynn *Fr.* Medley of Southern and Northern Tunes—Scenic Tour of West Lake.

Tune: "Green Jade Cup." Kung Tzu-chen, *Chinese*. SuSp, *tr. by* An-yan Tang

Tune: "Green Jade Cup"—Lantern Festival. Hsin Ch'i-chi, *Chinese*. SuSp, *tr. by* Irving Y. Lo

Tune: "Green Jade Flute." Kuan Han-ch'ing, *Chinese*.

"Fear, as I see the spring go." SuSp, *tr. by* Jerome P. Seaton

"Lightly she turns back her long red sleeves." SuSp, *tr. by* Jerome P. Seaton

"This autumn scene is worthy of the brush." SuSp, *tr. by* Jerome P. Seaton

"Wind sifts through the curtain." SuSp, *tr. by* Jerome P. Seaton

Tune: "Greeting the Immortal Guest." Yün-k'an Tzu, *Chinese*. SuSp, *tr. by* Jerome P. Seaton

Tune: "Groping for Fish." Hsin Ch'i-chi, *Chinese*. SuSp, *tr. by* Irving Y. Lo

Tune: "Happy Events Approaching." Ch'in Kuan, *Chinese*. SuSp, *tr. by* James J. Y. Liu

Tune: "Happy Events Approaching." Chu Tun-ju, *Chinese*. SuSp, *tr. by* James J. Y. Liu

Tune: "Happy Events Approaching." Kuan Yün-shih. SuSp, *tr. by* Richard John Lynn *Fr.* Medley of Southern and Northern Tunes—Scenic Tour of West Lake.

Tune: "Immortal at the Magpie Bridge"—On Hearing the Cuckoo at Night. Lu Yu, *Chinese*. SuSp, *tr. by* James J. Y. Liu

Tune: "Immortal at the River." Su Shih, *Chinese*. SuSp, *tr. by* Michael E. Workman

Tune: Immortal at the River. Su Tung-p'o, *Chinese*. CoBCP

Tune: "Immortal at the River." Wang Kuo-wei, *Chinese*. SuSp, *tr. by* Ching-i Tu

Tune: "Immortal at the River"—Ascending a Little Tower at Night. Ch'en Yü-yi, *Chinese*. SuSp, *tr. by* James J. Y. Liu

Tune: "Immortal at the River"—Winter Willow. Na-lan Hsing-te, *Chinese*. SuSp, *tr. by* Irving Y. Lo

Tune: "Immortal's Auspicious Crane, An"—On Plum Blossoms. Hsin Ch'i-chi, *Chinese*. SuSp, *tr. by* Irving Y. Lo

Tune in to a raga. Assassination Raga. Lawrence Ferlinghetti. CAPP-1

Tune: "Intoxication in the East Wind." Kuan Han-ch'ing, *Chinese*.

"Grief: I've grieved as a solitary phoenix grieves." SuSp, *tr. by* Jerome P. Seaton

"Heaven in the South, earth Northward." SuSp, *tr. by* Jerome P. Seaton

Tune: "Intoxication in the East Wind" Autumn Scenery. Lu Chih, *Chinese*. SuSp, *tr. by* Sherwin S. S. Fu

Tune is cowboy, The; the words, sentimental crap. D-Y Bar. James Welch. CDW

Tune: "Jade Butterflies." Liu Yung, *Chinese*. SuSp, *tr. by* Jerome P. Seaton

Tune: "Joy All Under Heaven"—Sunset on the Western Hill. Hsü Tsai-ssu, *Chinese*. SuSp, *tr. by* Sherwin S. S. Fu

Tune: "Joy at Meeting." Li Yü, *Chinese*. SuSp, *tr. by* Eugene Eoyang

Tune: "Joy in Spring's Coming"—Seven Songs. *Unknown*, *Chinese*. SuSp, *tr. by* Wayne Schlepp

Tune: "Joy of Eternal Union"—Passing the Seven-league Shallows. Su Shih, *Chinese*. SuSp, *tr. by* Irving Y. Lo

Tune: Lotus-leaf Cup. Wei Chuang, *Chinese*. CoBCP, *tr. by* Burton Watson

Tune: "Lotus-leaf Cup." Wen T'ing-yün, *Chinese*. SuSp, *tr. by* William R. Schultz

Tune: Magnolia Blossom. Li Ch'ing-chao. PBWP, *tr. by* C. H. Kwock *and* Vincent McHugh

Tune: "Magnolia Blossoms, Abbreviated" ("From the pole of the flower vendor"). Li Ch'ing-chao, *Chinese*. SuSp, *tr. by* Eugene Eoyang

Tune: "Magnolia Blossoms, Abbreviated" ("No one invited me"). Chu Tun-ju, *Chinese*. SuSp, *tr. by* James J. Y. Liu

Tune: "Magnolia Blossoms, Slow"—Traveling on the Yangtze. Chiang Ch'un-lin, *Chinese*. SuSp, *tr. by* Bruce Carpenter

Tune: "Magpie on the Branch." Feng Yen-ssu, *Chinese*. SuSp, *tr. by* Daniel Bryant

Tune: Magpie on the Branch. *Unknown*, *Chinese*. Fr. Four *Tz'u* from Tun-huang. CoBCP, *tr. by* Burton Watson

Tune: "Manifold Little Hills." Li Ch'ing-chao, *Chinese*. SuSp, *tr. by* Eugene Eoyang

Tune: "Midnight Music." Liu Yung, *Chinese*. SuSp, *tr. by* James J. Y. Liu

Tune: "Moth Fluttering Against Lamp." Kuan Yün-shih. SuSp, *tr. by* Richard John Lynn *Fr.* Medley of Southern and Northern Tunes—Scenic Tour of West Lake.

Tune: "Moth Fluttering against Lamp." Kuan Yün-shih. SuSp, *tr. by* Richard John Lynn *Fr.* Medley of Southern and Northern Tunes—Scenic Tour of West Lake.

Tune: "Mountain Hawthorns." Wang An-shih, *Chinese*. SuSp, *tr. by* James J. Y. Liu

Tune: "Mountain Hawthorns." Yen Chi-tao, *Chinese*. SuSp, *tr. by* James J. Y. Liu

Tune of Seven Towers, The. William Morris. EnVR

Tune: "Overtures"—On Myself. Ch'iao Chi, *Chinese*. SuSp, *tr. by* Sherwin S. S. Fu

Tune: "Pacifying the Western Barbarians." Wen T'ing-yün, *Chinese*. SuSp, *tr. by* William R. Schultz

Tune: Palace of Night Revels. Chou Pang-yen, *Chinese*. CoBCP, *tr. by* Burton Watson

Tune: "Pale-golden Willows." Chiang K'uei, *Chinese*. SuSp, *tr. by* Chiang Yee

Tune: "Partridge Sky." Huang T'ing-chien, *Chinese*. SuSp, *tr. by* James J. Y. Liu

Tune: Partridge Sky. Su Tung-p'o, *Chinese*. CoBCP, *tr. by* Burton Watson

Tune: "Partridge Sky"—Parting Sorrows. Na-lan Hsing-te, *Chinese*. SuSp, *tr. by* William Golightly

Tune: "Partridge Sky"—Puppet Theater. Ku T'ai-ch'ing, *Chinese*. SuSp, *tr. by* Irving Y. Lo

Tune: "Partridge Sky"—Written at the Po-shan Monastery. Hsin Ch'i-chi, *Chinese*. SuSp, *tr. by* Irving Y. Lo

Tune: "Paying Homage at the Golden Gate." Sun Kuang-hsien, *Chinese*. SuSp, *tr. by* Hellmut Wilhelm

Tune: "Phoenix Hairpin." Lu Yu, *Chinese*. CoBCP, *tr. by* Burton Watson; SuSp, *tr. by* James J. Y. Liu

Tune: "Phoenix Hairpin"—Crab Apple. Ku T'ai-ch'ing, *Chinese*. SuSp, *tr. by* Irving Y. Lo

Tune: "Pleasure in Front of the Hall." Lu Chih, *Chinese*.

"Be a loafer / Wash off the dust of fame and gain in the vast waves." SuSp, *tr. by* Sherwin S. S. Fu

"Wine in the cup is heavy." SuSp, *tr. by* Hellmut Wilhelm

Tune: "Pleasure of Returning to the Fields: A Prelude." Huang T'ing-chien, *Chinese*. SuSp, *tr. by* James J. Y. Liu

Tune: "Pomegranate Blossoms." Kuan Yün-shih. SuSp, *tr. by* Richard John Lynn *Fr.* Medley of Southern and Northern Tunes—Scenic Tour of West Lake.

Tune: "Prelude to Allure Goddesses." Liu Yung, *Chinese*. SuSp, *tr. by* Jerome P. Seaton

Tune: "Prelude to Water Music." Su Shih, *Chinese*. SuSp, *tr. by* Eugene Eoyang

Tune: Prelude to Water Music. Su Tung-p'o, *Chinese*. CoBCP, *tr. by* Burton Watson

Tune: "Prince of Lan-ling" (*Lan-ling Wang*)—on Willows. Chou Pang-yen, *Chinese*. SuSp, *tr. by* Irving Y. Lo

Tune: "Pure Serene Music." Huang T'ing-chien, *Chinese*. SuSp, *tr. by* James J. Y. Liu

Tune: "Pure Serene Music." Li Ch'ing-chao, *Chinese*. SuSp, *tr. by* Eugene Eoyang

("And know that I'll be hard put to discover a single blossom.") (LL) CoBCP, *tr. by* Burton Watson

Tune: "Pure Serene Music." Li Yü, *Chinese*. SuSp, *tr. by* Daniel Bryant

Tune: Pure Serene Music ("Since we parted, spring half over"). Li Yü, *Chinese*. CoBCP, *tr. by* Burton Watson

Tune: "Rapt with Wine, Loudly Singing; Joy in Spring's Coming." Kuan Yün-shih, *Chinese*. SuSp, *tr. by* Richard John Lynn

Tune: "Red Embroidered Slippers"—Spring Night. *Unknown*, *Chinese*. SuSp, *tr. by* Sherwin S. S. Fu

Tune: "Remembering the Lady of Ch'in—At the Mouth of Dragon Pool." Na-lan Hsing-te, *Chinese*. SuSp, *tr. by* Lenore Mayhew *and* William McNaughton

Tune: "Remembering the Lady of Ch'in"—Loushan Pass. Mao Tse-tung, *Chinese*. SuSp, *tr. by* Eugene Eoyang

Tune: "Remembering the Prince." Na-lan Hsing-te, *Chinese*. SuSp, *tr. by* William Golightly

Tune: "Ripples Sifting Sand." Li Yü, *Chinese*. CoBCP, *tr. by* Burton Watson; SuSp, *tr. by* Daniel Bryant

Tune: "Ripples Sifting Sand." Liu Yu Hsi, *Chinese*. SuSp, *tr. by* Daniel Bryant

Tune: "Ripples Sifting Sand." Po Chü-i, *Chinese*.

"How can the tide of the river be compared to your love?" SuSp, *tr. by* Irving Y. Lo

"There'll be a day when dust flies at the bottom of the sea." SuSp, *tr. by* Irving Y. Lo

Tune: "Ripples Sifting Sand: A Song." Li Yü, *Chinese*. SuSp, *tr. by* Daniel Bryant

Tune: "Ripples Sifting Sand"—Accompanying My Husband on a Spring Outing to Stone Pavilion. Ku T'ai-ch'ing, *Chinese*. SuSp, *tr. by* Irving Y. Lo

Tune: "River Messages." Wen T'ing-yün, *Chinese*. SuSp, *tr. by* William R. Schultz

Tune: "Sailing at Night"—A Song Sequence. Ma Chih-yüan, *Chinese*. SuSp, *tr. by* Sherwin S. S. Fu

Tune: Sand of Silk-washing Stream ("Flutter flutter on clothes and cap, jujube flowers fall"). Su Tung-p'o, *Chinese*. CoBCP, *tr. by* Burton Watson

Tune: Sand of Silk-washing Stream ("Layer on layer of hemp leaves, jute leaves shining"). Su Tung-p'o, *Chinese*. CoBCP, *tr. by* Burton Watson

Tune: "Sand of Silk-washing Stream." Li Ching, *Chinese*. SuSp, *tr. by* Daniel Bryant

Tune: "Sand of Silk-washing Stream." Li Ch'ing-chao, *Chinese*.

"In the little courtyard, by the side window." SuSp, *tr. by* Eugene Eoyang

"Mild and peaceful spring glow, Cold Food Day." SuSp, *tr. by* Eugene Eoyang

Tune: Sand of Silk-washing Stream ("Soft grasses, a plain of sedge fresh with passing rain"). Su Tung-p'o, *Chinese*. CoBCP, *tr. by* Burton Watson

Tune: "Sand of Silk-washing Stream." Wang An-shih, *Chinese*. SuSp, *tr. by* James J. Y. Liu

Tune: "Sand of Silk-washing Stream." Wang Kuo-wei, *Chinese*. SuSp, *tr. by* Ching-i Tu

Tune: "Sand of Silk-washing Stream." Wei Chuang, *Chinese*. SuSp, *tr. by* Lois Fusek

Tune: "Sand of Silk-washing Stream." Wu Wei-yeh, *Chinese*. SuSp, *tr. by* Irving Y. Lo

Tune: Sand of Silk-washing Stream ("Throw on rouge and powder, watch the governor pass!"). Su Tung-p'o. CoBCP *Fr.* Along the Road to Stone Lake.

Tune: "Sheep on Mountain Slope." Ch'iao Chi, *Chinese*. SuSp, *tr. by* Wayne Schlepp

Tune: "Sheep on Mountain Slope"—Boudoir Thoughts. *Unknown*, *Chinese*. SuSp, *tr. by* Hellmut Wilhelm

Tune: "Sheep on Mountain Slope"—Lamenting the Times. Tseng Jui, *Chinese*.

"Cock's crow means profit, The." SuSp, *tr. by* Wayne Schlepp

"Great success need not be proud." SuSp, *tr. by* Wayne Schlepp

Tune: "Six Toughies"—Written after the Roses Have Faded. Chou Pang-yen, *Chinese*. SuSp, *tr. by* James J. Y. Liu

Tune: "Sky-clear Sand"—Autumn Thoughts. Ma Chih-yüan, *Chinese*. SuSp, *tr. by* Sherwin S. S. Fu

Tune: "Slow Chant." Ma Chih-yüan, *Chinese*. SuSp, *tr. by* Sherwin S. S. Fu

Tune: "Slow Chant"—Kao-tsu's Homecoming. Sui Ching-ch'en, *Chinese*. SuSp, *tr. by* Sherwin S. S. Fu

Tune: "Slow Song of Chu Ying-t'ai"—Late Spring. Hsin Ch'i-chi, *Chinese*. SuSp, *tr. by* Irving Y. Lo

Tune: "Song of a Dandy." Sun Kuang-hsien, *Chinese*. SuSp, *tr. by* Hellmut Wilhelm

Tune: "Song of Dandy"—Hunting in Autumn. Na-lan Hsing-te, *Chinese*. SuSp, *tr. by* Bruce Carpenter

Tune: "Song of Divination." Chu Yi-tsun, *Chinese*. SuSp, *tr. by* Irving Y. Lo

Tune: "Song of Divination." Su Shih, *Chinese*. SuSp, *tr. by* Eugene Eoyang

Tune: "Song of Divination"—On the Plum Tree. Lu Yu, *Chinese*. SuSp, *tr. by* James J. Y. Liu

Tune: "Song of Divination"—On the Plum Tree, after a Poem by Lu Yu. Mao Tse-tung, *Chinese*. SuSp, *tr. by* Eugene Eoyang

Tune: "Song of Divination"—Using Quotations from *Chuang-tzu*. Hsin Ch'i-chi, *Chinese*. SuSp, *tr. by* Irving Y. Lo

Tune: "Song of Flirtatious Laughter." Wei Ying-wu, *Chinese*. SuSp, *tr. by* Hellmut Wilhelm

Tune: "Song of Great Virtue"—Spring. Kuan Han-ch'ing, *Chinese*. SuSp, *tr. by* Jerome P. Seaton

Tune: "Song of Great Virtue"—Winter. Kuan Han-ch'ing, *Chinese*.

"Snow powder, flowery." SuSp, *tr. by* Jerome P. Seaton

"Toot once, strum once." SuSp, *tr. by* Jerome P. Seaton

Tune: Song of Picking Mulberry ("Evening comes with an onslaught of wind and rain"). Li Ch'ing-chao, *Chinese*. CoBCP, *tr. by* Burton Watson

Tune: "Song of Picking Mulberry." Li Ch'ing-chao, *Chinese*. SuSp, *tr. by* Eugene Eoyang

Tune: "Song of Picking Mulberry." Wang Kuo-wei, *Chinese*. SuSp, *tr. by* Ching-i Tu

Tune: "Song of Picking Mulberry" Double-Ninth Festival. Mao Tse-tung, *Chinese*. SuSp, *tr. by* Eugene Eoyang

Tune: "Song of Picking Mulberry"—Recollections of West Lake. Ou-yang Hsiu, *Chinese*. SuSp, *tr. by* Jerome P. Seaton

Tune: "Song of Plucking Cassia." Ch'iao Chi, *Chinese*. SuSp, *tr. by* Sherwin S. S. Fu

Tune: Song of River City. Su Tung-p'o, *Chinese*. CoBCP, *tr. by* Burton Watson

Tune: "Song of River City"—On a Kite. Wu Wei-yeh, *Chinese*. SuSp, *tr. by* Irving Y. Lo

Tune: "Song of River Goddess"—Moorinig My Boat at Fen-shui at Night. Huang Shu, *Chinese*. SuSp, *tr. by* James J. Y. Liu

Tune: "Song of Shou-yang." Kuan Yün-shih, *Chinese*. SuSp, *tr. by* Richard John Lynn

Tune: "Song of Shou-yang." Ma Chih-yüan, *Chinese*.

"Lovesickness— / What is the cure?" SuSp, *tr. by* Sherwin S. S. Fu

"Voice are still / The moon's bright." SuSp, *tr. by* Sherwin S. S. Fu

Tune: "Song of the Lunar Palace." Lu Chih, *Chinese*. SuSp, *tr. by* Hellmut Wilhelm

Tune: "Song of the Lunar Palace"—Sending Off Spring. Kuan Yün-shih, *Chinese*. SuSp, *tr. by* Richard John Lynn

Tune: "Song of the Southern Country." Chu Yi-tsun, *Chinese*. SuSp, *tr. by* Irving Y. Lo

Tune: "Song of the Southern Country." Li Hsün, *Chinese*. SuSp, *tr. by* Edward Schafer

Tune: "Song of the Southern Country"—Presented to a Courtesan. Hsin Ch'i-chi, *Chinese*. SuSp, *tr. by* Irving Y. Lo

Tune: "Song of the Southern Country"—Spring Thoughts at Pearl River. Chu Yi-tsun, *Chinese*. SuSp, *tr. by* Irving Y. Lo

Tune: "Song of the Wine Spring." P'an Lang, *Chinese*. SuSp, *tr. by* James J. Y. Liu

Tune: "Song of Tzu-yeh." Li Yü, *Chinese*. CoBCP, *tr. by* Burton Watson; SuSp, *tr. by* Daniel Bryant

Tune: "Southern Song, A." Li Ch'ing-chao, *Chinese*. SuSp, *tr. by* Eugene Eoyang

Tune: "Southern Song, A." Wen T'ing-yün, *Chinese*. SuSp, *tr. by* William R. Schultz

Tune: "Sparse Shadows"—Plum Blossoms. Chiang K'uei, *Chinese*. SuSp, *tr. by* An-yan Tang

Tune: "Sprig of Flowers, A"—Not Bowing to Old Age. Kuan Han-ch'ing, *Chinese*. SuSp, *tr. by* Jerome P. Seaton

Tune: "Sprig of Flowers, A"—Written for My "Ugly Studio." Chung Ssu-ch'eng, *Chinese*. SuSp, *tr. by* Sherwin S. S. Fu

Tune: "Spring at Wu-ling." Li Ch'ing-chao, *Chinese*. SuSp, *tr. by* Eugene Eoyang

Tune: "Spring in Ch'in's Garden." Hsin Ch'i-chi, *Chinese*. SuSp, *tr. by* Irving Y. Lo

Tune: "Spring in Ch'in's Garden" ("Northern landscape, / Thousand miles around covered by ice"). Mao Tse-tung, *Chinese*. SuSp, *tr. by* Eugene Eoyang

Tune: "Spring in Jade Pavilion." Li Yü, *Chinese*. SuSp, *tr. by* Daniel Bryant

Tune: "Spring in Jade Pavilion." Yen Shu, *Chinese*. SuSp, *tr. by* An-yan Tang

Tune: "Squabbling Quails." Kuan Yün-shih. SuSp, *tr. by* Richard John Lynn *Fr.* Medley of Southern and Northern Tunes—Scenic Tour of West Lake.

Tune: "Stretch of Cloud over Mount Wu, A." Li Hsün, *Chinese*. SuSp, *tr. by* Hellmut Wilhelm

Tune: "Tartar Tune of Eighteen Beats." *Unknown*, *Chinese*. SuSp, *tr. by* Sherwin S. S. Fu

Tune: "Telling of Innermost Feelings." Ku Hsiung, *Chinese*. SuSp, *tr. by* James J. Y. Liu

Tune: "Telling of Innermost Feelings." Li Ch'ing-chao, *Chinese*. SuSp, *tr. by* Eugene Eoyang

Tune: Telling of Innermost Feelings ("Long nights when he neglects me— where's he gone?"). Ku Hsiung, *Chinese*. CoBCP, *tr. by* Burton Watson

Tune: "Telling of Innermost Feelings." Lu Yu, *Chinese*. SuSp, *tr. by* James J. Y. Liu

Tune: Telling of Innermost Feelings ("Night comes and, drowsy with drink, I'm slow to shed my ornaments"). Li Ch'ing-chao, *Chinese.* CoBCP, *tr.* by Burton Watson

Tune: "Telling of Innermost Feelings." Wen T'ing-yün, *Chinese.* SuSp, *tr.* by William R. Schultz

Tune: "Telling of Innermost Feelings"—Wandering in Spring. Ch'en Tzu-lung, *Chinese.* SuSp, *tr.* by Bruce Carpenter

Tune: The Butterfly Woos the Blossoms. Li Ch'ing-chao. PBWP, *tr.* by C. H. Kwock *and* Vincent McHugh

Tune: "The Charm of Nien-nu"—Kunlun Mountains. Mao Tse-tung, *Chinese.* SuSp, *tr.* by Eugene Eoyang

Tune: The Fisherman. Li Yü, *Chinese.* CoBCP, *tr.* by Burton Watson

Tune: The Taoist Priestess. Wei Chuang, *Chinese.* CoBCP, *tr.* by Burton Watson

Tune thy music[ke] to thy heart [*or* hart]. Heart's Music. Thomas Campion. AAS; OBEV

Tune: "Tipsy in the Flower's Shade." Li Ch'ing-chao, *Chinese.* SuSp, *tr.* by Eugene Eoyang

Tune: "Treading on Grass." Ou-yang Hsiu, *Chinese.* SuSp, *tr.* by An-yan Tang

Tune: Treading on Grass. Ou-yang Hsiu, *Chinese.* CoBCP, *tr.* by Burton Watson

Tune: "Treading on Grass." Yen Shu, *Chinese.* SuSp, *tr.* by James J. Y. Liu

Tune: Ugly Rogue. Hsin Ch'i-chi, *Chinese.* CoBCP, *tr.* by Burton Watson

Tune: "Wanderings of a Youth." Liu Yung, *Chinese.* SuSp, *tr.* by Jerome P. Seaton

Tune: "Water Dragon's Chang" After Chang Chi-fu's Lyric on the Willow Catkin. Su Shih, *Chinese.* SuSp, *tr.* by James J. Y. Liu

Tune: "Water Dragon's Chant"—Loathsome Spring. Ch'en Liang, *Chinese.* SuSp, *tr.* by Hellmut Wilhelm

Tune: "Wild Geese Have Come Down; Song of Victory." *Unknown, Chinese.* SuSp, *tr.* by Sherwin S. S. Fu

Tune: "Wild Geese Have Come Down; Song of Victory"—Idle Leisure. Teng Yu-pin, *Chinese.* SuSp, *tr.* by Hellmut Wilhelm

Tune: "Willow Branches." *Unknown, Chinese.* SuSp, *tr.* by Hellmut Wilhelm

Tune: "Wu-t'ung Leaves"—Written in Jest at a Banquet. Lu Chih, *Chinese.* SuSp, *tr.* by Hellmut Wilhelm

Tuneful Hipponax rests him here. Epitaph of Hipponax. Theocritus, *Greek.* FaBoEE, *tr.* by Charles Stuart Calverley

Tuneful poet, Britain's glory. The Mutual Congratulations of the Poets Anna Seward and Hayley. Richard Porson. FaBoEE; OBSV

Tunes come to me at morning. Peace on Earth. Michael S. Harper. MoNo

Tunes fainter on winds waywarder than others. Graves Are Made to Waltz On. Peter Viereck. PoA

T'ung-ch'uan is a beautiful place. As My Way Passed Through T'ung-ch'uan, I Wished to Visit the Policy Critic of the Right, Mei, but Did Not Know Where to Find Him. Tai Piao-yüan, *Chinese.* CoBLCP, *tr.* by Jonathan Chaves

Tung-ling melons—men say that long ago. Juan Chi. CoBCP, *tr.* by Burton Watson *Fr.* Singing of Thoughts.

Tungeei, that was her native name. Captain Cook. *Aborigine Oral Tradition.* NOBAu, *tr.* by Percy Mumbulla

TUNING MYSELF BY MORNING COFFEE. May Morn. Michael McClure. SPE

Tunnel, The. Hart Crane. CMoP; MoAmPo; OxBA *Fr.* The Bridge. NAAL-2

Tunnel, The. Mark Strand. HeIP-4; TwCP

Tunny girls are lounging on its suckers, The. (LL) This Octopus Exploits Women. James Fenton. CBNP; NoAM

Tunnyng [*or* Tunning] of Elynour [*or* Elinor] Rummyng [*or* Rumming], The. John Skelton. AAS

"Then Margery [*or* Marjorie] Milkduck." EBEV; OAEL-1; PoE

Tupelo Destruction, The. *Unknown.* AmFP

Turbid current. Fumi Saito, *Japanese.* MJT, *tr.* by Ueda, Makoto

Turbulent Water, The. *Unknown, Chinese.* TAL, *tr.* by Robert Payne

Turf-Carrier [*or* Turf Carrier] on Aranmore. John Hewitt. PoRA

Turf Song. Sterling Plumpp. GT

Turf-Stacks. Louis MacNeice. LiTM; OBMV

Turkey, The. Nikolai Stepanovich Gumilyov, *Russian.* TCRP, *tr.* by Simon Franklin

Turkey in the Corn. Woody Guthrie. KaS

Turkey in the Straw. *Unknown.* AS

Turkey is dancing near the rocks, A. *Unknown, Navajo Indian.* STP, *tr.* by Jerome Rothenberg *after* David McAllester

Turkeys wade the close to catch the bees. John Clare. *Fr.* The Turkeys wade the close to catch bees. FaBoVe

Turkish Bakery, The. *Unknown, Korean.* PBWP, *tr.* by Peter H. Lee

Turkish Carpet, The. Paul Durcan. CIP-2

Turkish government allows no law, The. Greville Fulke. FaBoPV

Turkish Love Songs. *Unknown.* BoWoP, *tr.* by Reza Baraheni *and* Zahra-Soltan Shokoohtaezeh

Turkish Trench Dog, The. Geoffrey Dearmer. NSI

Turn, The. Robert Creeley. FTOS; LCAP-2

Turn (a Poem in 4 Parts). Ken Belford. NOBC

Turn again, maiden, twice slain and rotten. Hilaire Kirkland. *Fr.* Observations. PeNZ

Turn Again to Life. Mary Lee Hall. PoLF

Turn again, turn again, turn once again. Carrousel Tune. Tennessee Williams. NBLV; OBAL

Turn an earth clod. 1975. Anne Spencer. NMM-2

Turn Back, O Man. Clifford Bax. NOCV

Turn back. Turn, young lady dear. The Robber Bridegroom. Allen Tate. CBLP

Turn 'em out, knaves all three! Mother Goose. *See* Rub a dub dub.

Turn from Self. George Macdonald. PWR

Turn from that girl. I Shall Laugh Purely. Robinson Jeffers. LiTM

Turn from that road's beguiling ease; return. The Sea's Wash in the Hollow of the Heart. Denise Levertov. LW

Turn inside out turn me. Request. Tanikawa Shuntaro, *Japanese.* VCWP, *tr.* by Harold Wright

Turn inward on the brain. What the Emanation of Casey Jones Said to the Medium. Arthur James Marshall Smith. MoCV

Turn like a top, spin on your dusty axis. Instead of a Journey. Michael Hamburger. NYBP

Turn me every which way, three-cornered God. Lucky Strikes. Ron Padgett. FTOS

Turn me like a waterwheel turning a millstone. Jelaluddin Rumi, *Persian.* ITG, *tr.* by Coleman Barks

Turn Me to My Yellow Leaves. W. S. Braithwaite. NAAAL

Turn o'er thy outward man, and judge aright. The Outward Man Accused. Edward Taylor. MeMAP

Turn of noontide has begun, The. A Half-Way Pause. D. G. Rossetti. NOBVV

Turn on the prudent Ant thy heedless eyes. *ad. fr.* the Bible, Proverbs, 6, 6. Samuel Johnson. ChIV-1; KSG

Turn on the tap for straight and silver water in the sink. Seven Activities for a Young Child. Alan Brownjohn. OTCP

Turn on your left side, back to your right again. Crinagoras, *Greek.* GrAn, *tr.* by Alistair Elliot

Turn on your Side and Bear the Day to Me. George Barker. OxBTC

Turn Right Next Corner. Wichita Vortex Sutra, Part I. Allen Ginsberg. FTOS

Turn the page of stone and there. Eeva-Liisa Manner. PBWP *Fr.* Cambrian.

Turn to a golden staff. (LL) Gifts. Mary Elizabeth Coleridge. PBWP; VWP

"Turn to me in the darkness." Titus and Berenice. John Heath-Stubbs. GTBS-P

"Turn to me, sweetheart! Why do you not turn?" (LL) A Lost Jewel. Robert Graves. EnLoPo; NYBP

Turn to right, turn to left. Witches' Spells. Madeleine Edmondson. NTCP

Turn, turn, my wheel! Turn round and round. The Potter's Song. Henry Wadsworth Longfellow. PoEL-5 *Fr.* Kéramos. APN-1

Turn, turn thy beauteous face away. Song. Francis Beaumont *and* John Fletcher. NOSC; PoEL-2 *Fr.* Love's Cure.

Turn, Turn, Unhappy Souls, Return. Henry Alline. AH

"Turn, Willie Macintosh." Willie Macintosh. *Unknown.* ESPB; OxBB; OxBoLi

Turn Your Eyes Away. Ruth Stone. NAmP90

Turnabout. Linda Pastan. NIP-4

Turncoat, The. Imamu Amiri Baraka. NeAP; PoE

Turncoat, The. Priscilla Jane Thompson. CBWP-2

Turn'd to that dirt from whence he sprung. (LL) A Satirical Elegy on the Death of a Late Famous General. Jonathan Swift. HoPM; NBLV; OBSV; PFE; PoE; PoEL-3; Poetr

Turned down the gas in the hall. (LL) Death in Leamington. John Betjeman. NoP-4; OxAEP-2; RB

Turned from the "eau-forte." Ezra Pound. *Fr.* Mauberly (1920). *Fr.* Hugh Selwyn Mauberley. (Life and Contacts). AmPP; CMoP; InPS-3; LiTM; NOBA; NoAM; TAP

Turned into a weapon. (LL) The Objection to Being Stepped On. Robert Frost. NBLV; OBCoV

Turned on to the transcendent, he holds her. Going Down on America. Kelly Cherry. CMAP

Turner's Camp on the Chippewa. *Unknown.* AmFP

Turnes all the spirits of Man into desire. Greville Fulke. *See* Sonnet: "Nurse-life wheat within his green husk growing, The."

Turnest to follow it. (LL) A Pause of Thought. Christina Rossetti. NOBE; OBNC

Turning. Robert Finch. MoCV

Turning, The. Philip Levine. VGW

Turning a stone house into seven figures. Elixir. Richard Murphy. BiHa

Turning and turning in the widening gyre. The Second Coming. W. B. Yeats. APAD; BIrV; CABP; CMoP; ChIV-2; ClHu; EBEvV; FaBoMo; FaBoPV; GI; GTBS-P; HAP; HeIP-4; HoPM; ImPo; InPK-6; InPS-3; LiTM; MoBrPo; MoP; NAEL-2; NAWM-2; NIP-4; NOBE; NoAM; NoP-4; OAEL-2; OxAEP-2; OxBTC; PBMP; PoE; PoPoPo; Poetr; RaBo; SAGP; SCV; SoSe-8; TFi; TRP; UnPo

Turning Away from Lies. Robert Bly. LCAP-2

Turning back, he found no face. A Chinese Ulysses. Kazuko Shiraishi, *Japanese.* WPJ, *tr. by* Kenneth Rexroth *and* Ikuko Atsumi

Turning darkness into light. (LL) Pangur Bán. *Unknown, Gaelic.* FaBoCh; RB, *tr. by* Robin Flower

Turning Fifty. Thomas William Shapcott. BMAP

Turning, following the arrows through. The House of Madam Juju. Mieko Kanai, *Japanese.* BoWoP, *tr. by* Christopher Drake

Turning Into. Robert Duncan. CBNP

Turning into a restful roomfull. Robert Duncan. SPE

Turning into my own. Lucille Clifton. NMM-2

Turning it over, considering, like a madman. John Berryman. MoP; NoAM *Fr.* Dream Songs.

Turning mortal for thy love. (LL) The Blossom. Shakespeare. AEP; GTBS-P; OBEV

Turning my chariot I yoke my horses and go. *Unknown.* ChiP, *tr. by* Arthur Waley *Fr.* Seventeen Old Poems.

Turning of the car. Luigi Fontanella, *Italian.* NeIt, *tr. by* Michael Palma

Turning of the Year, The. Delaina Thomas. OpBo

Turning Pro. Ishmael Reed. SoSe-8

Turning, returning on world winds that know. Angel Eye of Memory. John Malcolm Brinnin. PoA

Turning round to discover that. Mevlana. Simon Pettet. PT

Turning Thirty. Katha Pollitt. InPS-3; LiLi

Turning to him, who meets me with desire. Bible, *O.T.* PBWP, *tr. by* Marcia Falk *Fr.* The Song of Songs. AWP

Turning to you, my name—. Recognized Futures. Lisa Suhair Majaj. UnSA

Turning Year, The. Su Tung-p'o, *Chinese.* OHPC, *tr. by* Kenneth Rexroth

Turnip Vendor, The. Samuel Johnson. OxNR

(Epigram.) PeLV

Turns. Tony Harrison. *Fr.* The School of Eloquence. NAEL-2; NoAM

Turns all the spirits of man into desire. (LL) Sonnet: "Nurse-life wheat within his green husk growing, The." Greville Fulke. AAS; NoP-4

Turns in the waking west and goes to sleep. (LL) The Harbor Dawn. Hart Crane. AmPP; CMoP; LiTM; MoAmPo; NOBA; NoAM; OxBA

Turns into birds again. (LL) Indian Ruins Along Rio de Flag. Greg Pape. PBCAP; PaTW

Turns into Miss T. (LL) Miss T. Walter De la Mare. FaBoBe; FuFo; NTCP

Turns on the wretched hearth the expiring brand! (LL) Truth in Poetry. George Crabbe. EPCY; FHYEP

Turnstile, The. William Barnes. CH; NOBVV

Turnstone turned rover, A. Upon Learning That a Bird Exists Called the Turnstone. John Updike. CBNP; PeLV

Turnus and the Courser, *see also* Turnus and the Wanton Courser *tr. by* Dryden. Virgil. OBVE, *tr. by* Gawin Douglas *Fr.* The Aeneid [*or* Eneados, *Aeneis*].

Turnus and the Stone. Virgil. OBVE, *tr. by* John Dryden *Fr.* The Aeneid [*or* Eneados, *Aeneis*].

Turnus and the Wanton Courser, *see also* Turnus and the Courser *tr. by* Gavin Douglas. Virgil. OBVE, *tr. by* John Dryden *Fr.* The Aeneid [*or* Eneados, *Aeneis*].

Turnus kills Pallasy. Virgil, *Latin.* OBCVT, *tr. by* John Dryden

Turnus' retreat. Virgil, *Latin.* OBCVT, *tr. by* Thomas Phaer

Turnus Summons His Allies, Aeneas Is "Perturbit wyth Gret Thochtis." Virgil. OBVE, *tr. by* Gawin Douglas *Fr.* The Aeneid [*or* Eneados, *Aeneis*].

Turnus without sword. Virgil, *Latin.* OBCVT, *tr. by* Robert Fitzgerald

Turtle. Peter Blue Cloud. HATNAP

Turtle, The. William Carlos Williams. RaBo; SAmP

Turtle, clam and crab as well, The. Covering the Subject. Richard Armour. CTV

Turtle Dove, The. Geoffrey Hill. FaBoTw

Turtle-Dove, The. *Unknown.* OxBoLi

Turtle-Doves' Nest, The. *Unknown.* BoTP

Turtle lives 'twixt plated decks, The. Ogden Nash. ImPo; NoP-4; OBAL; SoSe-8; TAP

Turtle Soup. "Lewis Carroll." *See* The Song of the Mock Turtle.

Turtle Soup. Marilyn Chin. LoL

Turtles Hatching. Mark O'Connor. NOBAu

Turtle's Song, The. *Unknown.* BPo

Tuscaloosa Sam. "Orpheus C. Kerr." OBAL

Tuscan cypresses / What is it? Cypresses. D. H. Lawrence. NAEL-2

Tuscan Life. Elizabeth Barrett Browning. *Fr.* Aurora Leigh. VWP

Tuscan Olives. Agnes Mary Frances Robinson. VWP

Tuscan, that wanderest through the realms of gloom. Dante. Henry Wadsworth Longfellow. NCAP

Tuskegee. Leslie Pinckney Hill. PFE

Tuskegee Airfield, *for the Tuskegee Airmen.* Marilyn Nelson Waniek. GT

Tuskegee Experiment. Sadiq. SeSe

Tuskegee, Tuskegee! Lance Jeffers. BkSV

Tusks that clashed in mighty brawls, The. On the Vanity of Earthly Greatness. Arthur Guiterman. APAD; BXAP; HeIP-4; HoPM; OBCA; TrJP

Tuslag. T. A. Robertson. OxBS

Tut-tut! give back the flags—how can you care. The Confederate Flags. Ambrose Bierce. CBCWP

Tutankhamen. William Dickey. Poetsp

Tutivillus, the Devil. *Unknown.* EBEV

Tutor not thyself in science: go to masters for perfection. Good Counsel. *Unknown, Turkish.* NOIV, *tr. by* James Clarence Mangan

Tutor who tooted a flute, A. Limerick. Carolyn Wells. PeLi; SoSe-8

Tutor who tooted the flute, A. *Unknown.* CTV

Tutto è Sciolto. James Joyce. OBMV

TV. John Forbes. BMAP; CBAP

TV has been showing movies of dead poets, The. Media. Howard Nemerov. PuP-16

TV Room at the Children's Hospice. Michael Ryan. NAmP90

Twa bonny [*or* bony] lads were Sandy and Jockie. Robert Burns. OxBSP

Twa Books, The. Allan Ramsay. OxBS

Twa Brothers, The. *Unknown.* CH; EBEV; ESPB; OxBB; PBMP

("And that will never be!") (LL) OxBoV

(Twin Brothers, The.) PBMP

Twa Corbies, The. *Unknown.* AWP; CH; EBEvV; ESPB; EnSB; FaBoCh; GTBS-P; HAP; InPK-6; OBEV; OxBS; PBMP; PFE; RB; SCGP; UnPo

(Two Ravens, The.) SoSe-8

Twa Knights, The. *Unknown.* ESPB

Twa Magicians, The. *Unknown.* ESPB; OxBB

(Two Magicians, The.) OAEL-1; OxBoLi

Twa Sisters, The. *Unknown.* ESPB; OxBS

Twa Sisters of Binnorie. *Unknown.* *See* Binnorie; or, The Two Sisters.

Twain that were foes, while Mary lived, are fled. His Lady's Death. Pierre de Ronsard, *French.* AWP, *tr. by* Andrew Lang

'Twas a balmy summer evening, and a goodly crowd was there. The Face upon [*or* on] the Floor. Hugh Antoine D'Arcy. BLPA; FaBoBe

'Twas a battle of States. The Battle of Gettysburg. Edgar Lee Masters. CBCWP

'Twas a busy day in the courtroom, and a curious crowd was there. The Bank Thief. J. R. Farrell. BLPA

'Twas a cloudless morn and the sun shone bright. The Cherokee. Mary Weston Fordham. CBWP-2

'Twas a comical sight that I saw by the roadside. The Song of Lies. *Unknown, Irish.* CBNP, *tr. by* Donal O'Sullivan

'Twas a dangerous cliff, as they freely confessed. A Fence or an Ambulance. Joseph Malins. BLPA

'Twas a new feeling—something more. Did Not. Thomas Moore. APAD; BoLoP; EnLoPo; GLoP; PeLV

'Twas a night of dreadful horror. The Night of Death. Frances Ellen Watkins Harper. PWR

'Twas a stylish congregation, that of Theophrastus Brown. Trouble in the "Amen Corner." Thomas Chalmers Harbaugh. BLPA

'Twas a summer evening. Robert Southey. *See* The Battle of Blenheim.

'Twas a Sunday morning, quite serene the air. City Eclogue. "W. J." NOEC

'Twas a tough task, believe it, thus to tame. Upon Dr. Davies's British Grammar. James Howell. OBWVE

'Twas all on board a ship down in a southern sea. The Golden Vanity. *Unknown.* CH; FaBoCh

'Twas all unlike your great and gracious ways. (LL) Departure. Coventry Patmore. NOBE; OBEV; OBNC

'Twas at the royal feast, for Persia won. Alexander's Feast; or, The Power of Music [*or* Musique]. Dryden. FaPoR; GTBS-P; NAEL-1; NOBE; OAEL-1; PeECV; TFi

'Twas at the silent, solemn hour. William and Margaret. David Mallet. NOEC; OxAEP-1

'Twas at the solemn hour of night. Dr. Johnson's Ghost. Elizabeth Moody. ECWP; OxBSn

'Twas August, and the fierce sun overhead. East London. Matthew Arnold. SCGP

'Twas autumn and 'round me the leaves were descending. The Banks of Champlain. *Unknown.* AmFP

'Twas battered and scarred, and the auctioneer. The Touch of the Master's Hand. Myra Brooks Welch. BLPA; PoToHe

'Twas brillig, and the slithy toves. Jabberwocky. "Lewis Carroll." APAD; CABP; CBNP; CTV; ChAP; ClHu; EBEV; EBEvV; EBVV; FPC; FaBoBe; HeIP-4; HoPM; ImPo; InPK-6; InPS-3; NAEL-2; NBLV; NOBE; NOBL; NOBVV; NOxBChV; NTCP; NoAM; NoP-4; OAEL-2; OBSP; OxAEP-2; OxBChV; PFE; PeLV; PeVV; PoRA; Poetr; RB; SAGP; TFi; TRP; TTTS; UV   *Fr.* Through the Looking-Glass.

'Twas but a single Rose. Upon a Virgin Kissing a Rose. Robert Herrick. SeCP

'Twas Christmas Eve, the month was May. A Tragedy. Tom Masson. OBAL

'Twas dead of Night, when weary Bodies close. Dido's last night. Virgil, *Latin.* OBCVT, *tr. by* John Dryden

'Twas early on a May morning. Lady Isabel. *Unknown.* ESPB

'Twas earlye, earlye in the spring. Earlye, Earlye, in the Spring. *Unknown.* AmFP

'Twas enough to make a man stare. (LL) Rub a dub dub. Mother Goose. NOBL; OxNR

'Twas eve in sunny Italy. A Tale of Italy. Eloise Bibb. CBWP-4

'Twas eve; the broadly shining sun. To ———. Edward Coote Pinkney. APN-1

'Twas evening, though not sun-set, and spring-tide. The Shepherd and the Nymph. Walter Savage Landor. OBNC   *Fr.* Gebir.

'Twas Ever Thus. Henry Sambrooke Leigh. UV

'Twas Ever Thus. *Unknown.* BXAP

'Twas ever thus from childhood's hour! Disaster. Charles Stuart Calverley. NBLV

'Twas fancy first made Celia fair. Fancy. Jonathan Smedley. OxBSP

'Twas fifty quatrains: and from unknown strands. Fifty Quatrains. "Michael Field." VWP

'Twas Fultah Fisher's boarding-house. The Ballad of Fisher's Boardinghouse. Rudyard Kipling. PoRA

'Twas going to snow—'twas snowing! Curse his luck! The Drove-Road. Wilfrid Wilson Gibson. OxBTC

'Twas here my summer paused. Emily Dickinson. APN-2

'Twas in a basement tobble d'hote. Reverie. Don Marquis. PoLF

'Twas in eighteen eleven those bards came to dine;. Leigh Hunt. EPCY   *Fr.* The Feast of the Poets.

'Twas in heaven pronounced, and 'twas muttered in hell. A Riddle. Catherine Maria Fanshawe. NOBRP

'Twas in that island summer where. He Loves and He Rides Away. Sydney Thompson Dobell. OBNC

'Twas in the days of the Revolution. Emily Geiger. *Unknown.* PoLF

'Twas in the month of August, or the middle of July. She Said the Same to Me. *Unknown.* AS

'Twas in the month of December, and in the year 1883. The Famous Tay Whale. William McGonagall. PeVV

'Twas in the moon of winter time when all the birds had fled. The Huron Carol. Jesse Edgar Middleton. OBCP

'Twas in the spring of '72. The April Fool. Eugene Field. PWR

'Twas in the town of Jacksboro in the spring [*or* year] of seventy-three. The Buffalo Skinners. *Unknown.* AS; AmFP; RB

'Twas in the year of 1898, and on the 21st of June. The Albion Battleship Calamity. William McGonagall. BXAP

'Twas just this time, last year, I died. Emily Dickinson. PoE

'Twas late, and the gay company was gone. The Declaration. Nathaniel Parker Willis. OBAL

'Twas like a Maelstrom, with a notch. Emily Dickinson. APN-2; CMoP; LiTM; NCAP; PoE

'Twas mercy brought me from my *Pagan* land. On Being Brought from Africa to America. Phillis Wheatley. ColAP; CrDW; FaBoA; ISC; NAAAL; NAAL-1; NAAL-3; NALW; NOBA; NOEC; NoP-4; TAP; TTY; WPE

'Twas midnight—every mortal eye was closed. The Helmets; a Fragment. Thomas Penrose. NOEC

Twas morning, and the Lord of day. The Lesson of the Flowers. Hafiz, *Persian.* GaP, *tr. by* E. Harriet Palmer

'Twas my pleasure to walk in the river meadows. The Midnight Court. Brian Merriman, *Modern Irish.* NOIV, *tr. by* Thomas Kinsella

'Twas night; and Flavia, to her room retired. Soliloquy of a Beauty in the Country. George Lyttelton. ECEV

'Twas not as lonesome as it might have been. The Cricket Kept the House. Edith Matilda Thomas. OBCA

'Twas not for some calm blessing to receive. Her Muffe. Richard Lovelace. PBRV

" 'Twas not so in my time," surly Grumio exclaims. Epigram. Samuel Bishop. NOEC

'Twas not the brown of chestnut boughs. Gwendoline. Bayard Taylor. BXAP

'Twas now the mid of Night, when Slumbers close. Ovid. OBCVT, *tr. by* John Dryden   *Fr.* Cinyras and Myrrha, Out of the Tenth Book of Ovid's Metamorphoses.

'Twas of a brisk young sailor, as I have heard it said. Johnny German. *Unknown.* AmFP

'Twas of a nobleman's daughter. Caroline and Her Young Sailor Bold. *Unknown.* AmFP

'Twas on a glorious summer eve. The Angel's Visit. Charlotte L. Forten Grimke. AAP

'Twas on a Holy Thursday, their innocent faces clean. Holy Thursday [I.] William Blake. CH; FHYEP; InPS-3; NAEL-2; NAWM-2; NOBE; NOBRP; NOEC; NOxBChV; NoP-4; OAEL-2; PeECV; PoE; Ro; SCV; TFi; TrCP   *Fr.* Songs of Innocence.

'Twas on a lofty vase's side. Ode on the Death of a Favourite [*or* Favorite] Cat, Drowned in a Tub [*or* Bowl] of Gold Fishes. Thomas Gray. APo; ClHu; EBEV; EBEvV; EBNV; ECEV; FHYEP; FaBoBe; GTBS-P; HoPM; InPS-3; NAEL-1; NBLV; NOBE; NOBL; NOEC; NoP-4; OAEL-1; OBCoV; OxAEP-1; PBMP; PC; PFE; PeLV; PoE; PoEL-3; PoLF; PoRA; TFi

'Twas on a Monday morning. Charlie He's My Darling. Robert Burns. CH; FaBoPV

'Twas on a Monday morning, just at the break of day. Maggie Mac. *Unknown.* AmFP

'Twas on a Monday morning, the first I saw my darling. Hanging Out the Linen Clothes. *Unknown.* AS

'Twas on a night, an evening bright. Proud Lady Margaret. *Unknown.* ESPB

'Twas on a summer noon, in Stainsford mead. My Ox Duke. John Dyer. NOEC

'Twas on a summer's day—the sixth of June. Byron. *Fr.* Canto the First. NAEL-2; OAEL-2; PoE   *Fr.* Don Juan.

'Twas on an evening fair I went to take the air. Willie's Fatal Visit. *Unknown.* ESPB

'Twas on Lake Erie's broad expanse. John Maynard. Horatio Alger Jr. BLPA; FaBoBe

'Twas on the eighth of January, just at the dawn of day. The Battle of New Orleans. *Unknown.* AmFP

'Twas on the field of Antietam where many's the soldier fell. The Battle of Antietam Creek. *Unknown.* AmFP

'Twas on the shores that round our coast. The Yarn of the *Nancy Bell.* Sir William Schwenck Gilbert. BLPA; CABP; EBEvV; EBNV; FaBoBe; FaBoCh; HoPM; NOBL; TFi; UV

Twas once in my saddle I used to be happy. Cow Boy's Lament. *Unknown.* PaTW

'Twas once *look[e] up*, 'tis now *look[e] down[e]* to Heaven. (LL) On the Blessed Virgins Bashfulnesse. Richard Crashaw. HAP; OxBSP

'Twas once upon a time, when Jenny Wren was young. When Jenny Wren Was Young. *Unknown.* ReMoGo

'Twas one October mornin'. Bigerlow. *Unknown.* AS

'Twas one of the charméd days. The Heart of All the Scene. Ralph Waldo Emerson. *Fr.* Woodnotes I ("For this present, hard"). AmPP; NOBA

'Twas only a passing thought, my love. Only a Thought. Charles MacKay. PFE; Poetr

'Twas rollog, and the minim potes. *Unknown.* UV

'Twas said of Greece two thousand years ago. Colonial Nomenclature. John Dunmore Lang. NOBAu

'Twas so, I saw thy birth: that drowsy [*or* drowsie] lake. The Shower [*or* Showre]. Henry Vaughan. ESCV; GeHe; SeCP

'Twas spring, and dawn returning breathed new-born. Idyll of the Rose. Ausonius, *Latin.* AWP, *tr. by* John Addington Symonds

'Twas Summer and the sun was mounted high. *see also* The Wanderer, *Book 1 of* The Excursion. Wordsworth. NoP-4; OAEL-2

'Twas Sunday morning, quite serene the air. A City Eclogue. "W. J." NOEC

'Twas sung of old in hut and hall. Birthday Verses Written in a Child's Album. James Russell Lowell. OxBChV

'Twas sunset's hallow'd time—and such an eve. James Kirke Paulding. APN-1   *Fr.* The Backwoodsman.

'Twas sunset's hour, the glorious day. The Exile's Reverie. Mary Weston Fordham. CBWP-2

'Twas sure a luckless planet. Out of Luck. Abraham ibn Ezra, *Hebrew.* TrJP, *tr. by* Solomon Solis-Cohen

'Twas the angel of death that to us downward flew. In Memoriam of E. B. Clark. Lizelia Augusta Jenkins Moorer. CBWP-3

'Twas the angel of Eden, to Adam he said. Dedication Day Poem. Lizelia Augusta Jenkins Moorer. CBWP-3

'Twas the dream of a God. Ireland. Dora Sigerson Shorter. IIP; OBEV; TIRV

'Twas the eve before Christmas. "Good night," had been said. Annie and Willie's Prayer. Sophia P. Snow. BLPA

'Twas the gray of early morning when the dreadful cry of "Fire!". The Milwaukee Fire. *Unknown.* AmFP

'Twas the horse thief, Andy Regan, that was hunted like a dog. Father Riley's Horse. Andrew Barton Paterson. NOBAu

T'was the night before Christmas. Up on the Moon. Nona Maiola. CTV

'Twas the night before Christmas[, when all through the house]. A Visit from St Nicholas. Clement Clarke Moore. APN-1; AiP; BLPA; CTV; ChAP; FaBoBe; NTCP; OBAL; OBCA; OBCP; OxBChV; PChr; PWR; TFi

'Twas the old flute still whistling "The Protestant Boys." (LL) The Old [*or* Ould] Orange Flute. *Unknown.* OBCoV; OxBoLi

'Twas the voice of the Wanderer, I heard her exclaim. The Wanderer. Stevie Smith. NALW

'Twas thereupon. The Arch. Herman Melville. NCAP

'Twas vanquished Britain's laurel-water! (LL) Verses Inviting Stella to Tea on the Public Fast-Day. Anna Seward. ECWP

'Twas warm—at first—like Us. Emily Dickinson. APN-2; CMoP; NAWM-2; NCAP; SoSe-8

'Twas when bright Cynthia with her silver car. A Night-Piece; or, Modern Philosophy. Christopher Smart. NOEC

'Twas when Tacita hushed the noisy world. The Dream. "Brian Bendo." NOEC

'Twas when the friendly shade of night. To Clarissa. Robert, Earl Nugent Nugent. NOEC

'Twas when the Proclamation came. Bartow Black. Timothy Thomas Fortune. AAP

'Twas When the Seas Were Roaring. John Gay. HAP *Fr.* The What D'Ye-Call-It.

'Twas when the spousal time of May. Coventry Patmore. GBL; OxAEP-2 *Fr.* The Angel in the House.

'Twas whispered in Heaven, 'twas muttered in Hell. Enigma. Catherine Maria Fanshawe. OBCoV

'Twas wond'rous, then, a bardling should be found. The Tribulations of an Uneducated Poet in the 1760's. James Woodhouse. *Fr.* The Life and Lucubrations of Crispinus Scriblerus. NOEC

Twasinta's Seminoles; Or Rape of Florida. Albery Allson Whitman.
  "'Come now, my love, the moon is on the lake;'." AAP
  "Dark rose the walls, a church and prison joined." AAP
  "Hail! home of exiles and of Seminoles!" AAP
  "Have I not seen the hills of Candahar." APN-2
  "I never was a slave—a robber took." AAP
  "Is manhood less because man's face is black?" AAP; APN-2
  "Poet hath a realm within, and throne, The." AAP
  "Thus ends my lay: Reluctantly I leave." AAP
  "Thus, San Augustine's church and prison joined." AAP
  "Upon the shells by Carribea's wave." AAP
  "We leave thee with thy guests, thou sunny maid!" AAP

Tweed and Till. *Unknown.* FaBoCh; OBEV; OxBSP
  (Says Tweed tae Till.) FaBoVe

Tweed Visited, The. William Lisle Bowles. Son

Tweedledee and Tweedledoom. Ogden Nash. OBCoV

Tweedledum and Tweedledee. Mother Goose. LB; NOBL; OxNR; PeLV; ReMoGo

Twelfth Birthday. William Stafford. CMAP

Twelfth day of Christmas, The. The Twelve Days of Christmas. *Unknown.* OxBoLi

12th Horse Song of Frank Mitchell (Blue), The. Frank Mitchell, *Navajo Indian.* APSN; AWP, *tr. by* Jerome Rothenberg

Twelfth Morning; or What You Will. Elizabeth Bishop. CBNP

Twelfth Night. Peter Scupham. OBCP

Twelfth Night. Shakespeare.
  Clown's Song, The. CTC
    (Come Away, Death.) PoRA
    (Dirge.) OBEV
    (Feste's Song.)
  "I see you what you are: you are too proud." OxAEP-1
  "Once more, Cesario." SCV
  Song: "When that I was and a little tiny boy." CH; EBEV; FaBoCh; ImPo; NOBE; NoSic; OAEL-1; PoRA; SCGP; TFi
    (Feste's Song.) PFE

(Feste's Song ("When that I was and a little tiny boy").) CBNP; NBLV; OxBoLi

(Wind and the Rain, The.)
Sweet-and-Twenty. OBEV; PoE
(Carpe Diem.) GTBS-P
("O mistress mine, where are you roaming?") AEP; APAD

12th Raga: For John Wieners. David Meltzer. *Fr.* Ragas. NeAP

Twelfth Song of the Holy Young Men. *Unknown.* APN-2, *tr. by* Washington Matthews *Fr.* The Mountain Chant.

Twelfth Song of the Thunder. *Unknown.* APN-2; AWP, *tr. by* Washington Matthews *Fr.* The Mountain Chant.

12th Dance—Getting Leather by Language—21 February 1964. Jackson MacLow. PmAP

Twelve, The. Aleksandr Blok, *Russian.* TCRP, *tr. by* Jon Stallworthy *and* Peter France
  "Black Night. / White snow." AWP, *tr. by* Babette Deutsch *and* Avrahm Yarmolinsky

Twelve. Rossana Ombres, *Italian.* NeIt, *tr. by* Ruth Feldman

Twelve, The. Allen Tate. ChIV-2

Twelve and ugly. Dresses. Kathleen Fraser. LiLi

Twelve Articles. Jonathan Swift. NBLV; OBCoV

Twelve children, twelve gray geese in starched. The Handbell Choir. Jane Flanders. PBCAP

Twelve Days of Christmas, The. *Unknown.* AmFP; OxBoLi; OxNR; PChr
  ("On the first day of Christmas.") LB

Twelve Days of Christmas, The. *Unknown.* OxBoLi

12 Gates to the City. Nikki Giovanni. PoBA

Twelve good friends. Peter and John. Elinor Wylie. MoAmPo; MoBS

Twelve herds of oxen, no less flockes of sheepe. Homer. CTC, *tr. by* George Chapman *Fr.* Odyssey. NAWM-1, *tr. by* Robert Fitzgerald

Twelve Miscellaneous Poems on the Fang Garden. Chang Yü, *Chinese.* CoBLCP, *tr. by* Jonathan Chaves

(Twelve Months, The). "Sir Gregory Gander." CTV

Twelve Months, The. *Unknown.* AYFP

Twelve months must pass ere you can yet arrive. John Wilmot, 2d Earl of Rochester. FaBoSe *Fr.* Sodom.

Twelve-noon whistle groans, The. The Tragedy of Bricks. Galway Kinnell. AFr

Twelve O'Clock. Carolyn Kizer. PuP-17

Twelve o'clock. / Along the reaches of the street. Rhapsody on a Windy Night. T. S. Eliot. CMoP; HeIP-4; InPS-3; PoE

12 O'Clock News. Elizabeth Bishop. OxBC

12 October. Myra Cohn Livingston. NTCP

Twelve Oxen, The. *Unknown.* CH

Twelve pears hanging high. Mother Goose. OxNR; ReMoGo

Twelve Songs. W. H. Auden.
  "Fish in the unruffled lakes." BoLoP; CBLP; CMoP; LoP; MoBrPo; MoP
  Roman Wall Blues. NTP
  Song: "Stop all the clocks, cut off the telephone." MoBrPo; OPOU
  Song of the Beggars. PeLV

Twelve thousand drops of laudanum a day. De Quincey in Glasgow. Edwin Morgan. FaBoTC *Fr.* Sonnets from Scotland.

Twelve turns of the rail on walls of emerald. The Walls of Emerald. Li Shang-yin, *Chinese.* PLT, *tr. by* A. C. Graham

Twelve years ago I came here. The Burn. Galway Kinnell. Poetr

Twelve years ago I made a mock. School and Schoolfellows. Winthrop Mackworth Praed. FP; OxAEP-2

Twelve years old and lovesick, bumbling. The Skokie Theatre. Edward Hirsch. IFJA

Twelve years old, my father put. Harvest Time. G. A. Watermeyer, *Afrikaans.* PeSA, *tr. by* Guy Butler, Uys Krige *and* Jack Cope

12th Horse-Song of Frank Mitchell (Blue), The. Jerome Rothenberg. FTOS

Twenties 27. Jackson MacLow. PmAP

Twenties 26. Jackson MacLow. PmAP

Twentieth Anniversary. Betty Adcock. MT

Twentieth Century. Lucian Blaga, *Romanian.* CEEP, *tr. by* Mihail Bogdan MT

Twentieth-Century Blues. Kenneth Fearing. CMoP

Twentieth year is well-nigh past, The. To Mary. William Cowper. EnLoPo; GLoP; GTBS-P; NOEC; OBEV; UV

20. Barbara Guest. PoM

21. Lawrence Ferlinghetti. CLPP

25. Lawrence Ferlinghetti. CLPP

26. Lawrence Ferlinghetti. CLPP

Twenty Below. Robert Arthur Douglas Ford. NOBC

Twenty days. Tanka. Kanoko Okamoto, *Japanese.* MJT, *tr. by* Makoto Ueda

Twenty-eight Characters Sent to Tung-ts'un on the Subject of the Poems He Burned. Cheng Hsieh, *Chinese.* CoBLCP, *tr. by* Jonathan Chaves

Twenty-Eight Lines for My Wife. Yên Ba, *Vietnamese.* AVP, *tr. by* Huỳnh Sanh Thông

Twenty-Eight Poems Inscribed on T'ien-kuan Mountain. Chao Meng-fu, *Chinese.* CoBLCP, *tr. by* Jonathan Chaves

Twenty-eight young men bathe by the shore. Walt Whitman. ColAP; HAP; NoP-4; PAR; SAmP *Fr.* Song of Myself. AmPP; MoAmPo; NAAL-3; NOBA; OxBA

Twenty-first Day of the Seventh Month. Henry Vaughan, *Chinese.* CoBLCP, *tr. by* Jonathan Chaves

Twenty-first. Night. Monday. "Anna Akhmatova," *Russian.* RaBo, *tr. by* Jane Kenyon

25 December 1960. Ingrid Jonker, *Afrikaans.* PeSA, *tr. by* Jack Cope *and* Uys Krige

25:I:68. Philip Whalen. PoM

25 Mesostics Re and Not Re Mark Tobey. John Cage. PmAP

Twenty-five people. The 26th Person. Dolores Kendrick. GT *Fr.* "Three Observations on the Zombie Culture."

Twenty-four years remind the tears of my eyes. Dylan Thomas. CMoP; OxBSP

Twenty Golden Years Ago. James Clarence Mangan. NOBVV

Twenty Grand (Saturday Night on the Block), The. Naomi Long Madgett. NBV

Twenty lines of. Susan Howe. PmAP *Fr.* Speeches at the Barriers.

Twenty little engines. James Keir Baxter. NOxBChV

Twenty lost years have stol'n their hours away. Alone in an Inn at Southampton, April the 25th, 1737. Aaron Hill. NOEC

Twenty months out of the womb. Standing in the Doorway, I Watch the Young Child Sleep. Sharon Hashimoto. OpBo

29. "Alta." CrSp

29 Poems. Louis Zukofsky.

"Blue light is the night harbor-slip." PoE

"Cars once steel and green, now old." VGW

"Not much more than being." PoE

29-77-02. Artur Miedzyrzecki, *Polish.* PoSu, *tr. by* Stanislaw Baranczak *and* Clare Cavanagh

29 Songs. Louis Zukofsky.

"In Arizona / (how many years in the mountains)." TRP

Twenty-ninth Canto. Hans Magnus Enzensberger. PoSu *Fr.* The Sinking of the Titanic.

Twenty-one Love Poems. Adrienne Rich. GLP

"Can it be growing colder when I begin." NAAL-2

"Dark lintels, the blue and foreign stones, The." NALW; NoAM

"Every peak is a crater. This is the law of volcanoes." NAAL-2; NALW; NoAM

Floating Poem, Unnumbered, The. NALW; NoAM

(Floating Poem, The.) NMM-2

"I come home from you through the early light of spring." BoWoP; CPO

"I wake up in your bed. I know I have been dreaming." CPO; NAAL-2; NoAM; TRP

"Rain on the West Side Highway." NAAL-2

"Since we're not young, weeks have to do time." CPO

"Sleeping, turning in turn like planets." TRP

"That conversation we were always on the edge." BoWoP; NoAM

"Wherever in this city, screens flicker." CPO

"Your small hands, precisely equal to my own." CPO; PoE; TRP

Twenty-one Sonnets. Christian Karlson Stead.

"Rain, and a flurry of wind shaking the pear's white blossom." PeNZ

Twenty One Times. John Taggart. PT

Twenty-One Years. Reynolds Price. BAP-96

Twenty-one Years. *Unknown.* AmFP

Twenty-one years of my life you have been. Lucille Clifton. CrSp; MDDM *Fr.* February 13, 1980.

Twenty Poems. Thomas A. Clark.

"High piled cumulus." NBrP

"In those first days." NBrP

"Under a full moon." NBrP

Twenty Poems in Imitation of Han-shan and Shih-te. Wang An-shih, *Chinese.*

"Once I was a cow, a horse." CoBCP, *tr. by* Burton Watson

Twenty Questions. Dennis Phillips.

Five. FTOS

27. Edward Fitzgerald. CABP

27 July 1830. Georgy Arkadevich Shengeli, *Russian.* TCRP, *tr. by* Daniel Weissbort

27th Dance—Walking—22 March 1964. Jackson MacLow. FTOS

Twenty-Six Nonsense Rhymes. Edward Lear. CBNP; RB

26th Person, The. Dolores Kendrick. GT *Fr.* "Three Observations on the Zombie Culture."

26th Precinct Station. Louis Simpson. EOEF

Twenty sparrows / on. Breakfast. William Carlos Williams. SAmP

Twenty-third Flight. Earle Birney. HeIP-4; OxBC

Twenty thousand crowd into the gates—. Homage to Ryszard Kapuściński. David Wojahn. BAP-95

20-200 on 747. Heather McHugh. WeT

20-200 on 737. Heather McHugh. NIP-4

22.6.1941. Ondra Lysohorsky, *Lachian.* AF, *tr. by* Ewald Osers

Twenty-two Quatrains on Receiving the Obituary Notice for my Son Shih-Chü. T'ang Hsien-tsu, *Chinese.*

"My son, you loved telling the story of Prince Nata." CoBLCP, *tr. by* Jonathan Chaves

Twenty Views of Wang-ch'uan. Wang Wei, *Chinese.* CoBCP, *tr. by* Burton Watson

Twenty-Year Marriage. Ai. BoWoP; DeD; GT; NoAM

Twenty Years Ago. A. J. Gault *and* Dill Armor Smith. BLPA

Twenty years ago today, your death changed. Speaking Through White: For My Mother. Kyoko Mori. UnSA

Twenty years and not heard from. (LL) Dream 2: Brian the Still-Hunter. Margaret Atwood. BoWoP; CrSp

Twenty years are gone. Palinode. Oliver St. John Gogarty. OBMV

Twenty Years Hence. Walter Savage Landor. GBL; NAEL-2; NOBVV

Twenty years / I tamed an ant. Aleksandr Makarov, *Russian.* TCRP, *tr. by* Albert C. Todd

Twentyseven bums give a prostitute the once. E. E. Cummings. OBAL

'Twer May, but ev'ry leaf wer dry. A Wife a-Prais'd. William Barnes. EBVV

'Twere blessed to have seen. (LL) I've seen a Dying Eye. Emily Dickinson. APN-2; AmPP; BoWoP; NAAL-3; NCAP; NOBA; PoEL-5; PoLF

'Twere well your judgments but in plays did range. Dryden. OBSV *Fr.* The Spanish Friar [*or* Fryar].

Twice. Christina Rossetti. GBL; NOBE; OBEV; OBNC; TOT; TrCP; VWP

Twice Forty moneths in wedlock I did stay. On the Death of My First and Dearest Childe, Hector Philipps. Katherine Philips. KTR

Twice I have written you that I am unhappy. A Letter to Her Father. Inib-sarri, *Akkadian.* BoWoP, *tr. by* Willis Barnstone

Twice one are two. M. M. Hutchinson. BoTP

Twice or thrice had I lovèd thee. Air[e] and Angels. Donne. CBLP; ESCV; FMP; MeLP; NAEL-1; OAEL-1; SeCP

Twice Removed. Ralph Angel. PUP-19

Twice Shy. Seamus Heaney. TwCP

Twice Times Then Is Now. Ibn Hazm al-Andalusi, *Persian.* ArPe; OBVE, *tr. by* Omar S. Pound

Twicknam [*or* Twickenham] Garden. Donne. EBEV; ESCV; EnLoPo; MeLP; PoE; PoEL-2; SCGP; SeCP

("Who's therefore true, because her truth kills me.") (LL) FMP; GaP; OBGa

Twig of willow. (LL) Counting-out Rhyme. Edna St. Vincent Millay. InPK-6; NOxBChV; Poetr; SoSe-8; TTTS

Twigs stiffen. Sense. Rae Armantrout. FTOS

Twilight. Louisa Sarah Bevington. PEW

Twilight. Paul Engle. PFE

Twilight. Louisa S. Guggenberger. NOBVV

Twilight. Heinrich Heine, *German.* AWP, *tr. by* Louis Untermeyer

Twilight. Vladislav Felitsianovich Khodasevich, *Russian.* TCRP, *tr. by* Michael Frayn

Twilight. D. H. Lawrence. OBMV

Twilight. Amy Levy. VWP

Twilight. Fujiwara No Toshinari, *Japanese.* OHMPJ, *tr. by* Kenneth Rexroth

Twilight. Cor Van den Heuvel. HA

Twilight. Anita Virgil. HA

Twilight barn was chinked with gleams; I saw, The. Foot Inspection. Siegfried Sassoon. EP

Twilight. By now the genial sea of dusk. Half Past Four, October. Anna Hajnal, *Hungarian.* BoWoP, *tr. by* Daniel Hoffman

Twilight Calm. Christina Rossetti. OBNC

Twilight comes down the mountains to. Night in the Villa by the River. Tu Fu, *Chinese.* TAL, *tr. by* Robert Payne

Twilight comes over the monastery Garden. Wang Wei, *Chinese.* OHMPC, *tr. by* Kenneth Rexroth

Twilight comes to the little farm. Hayden Carruth. NNaP

Twilight falls; I soften the dusting feathers, The. Sappho. James Wright. NoAM

Twilight glitters on the fragmented glass. Judeebug's Country. Joe Johnson. PoBA

Twilight has already descended upon a thousand trees. On the Twenty-fourth of the Third Month, in the Year Ting-wei Sailed across Lake T'ai from

Behind the Mountain. Wu Wei-yeh, *Chinese*. SuSp, *tr. by* Chang Yin-nan *and* Lewis C. Walmsley

Twilight Hour, The. Joshua McCarter Simpson. AAP

Twilight in California. Philip Dow. AmPA

Twilight in Middle March, A. Francis Ledwidge. BlrV

Twilight in the River Pavilion. Chiang Shih-ch'üan, *Chinese*. OHMPC, *tr. by* Kenneth Rexroth

Twilight in West Virginia: Six O'Clock Mine Report. Irene McKinney. PBCAP

Twilight is here, soft breezes bow the grass. In Exile. Emma Lazarus. APN-2

Twilight is sad and cloudy, The. Henry Wadsworth Longfellow. CH

Twilight is spacious, near things in it seem far. Miracles. Conrad Potter Aiken. MoAmPo

Twilight it is, and the far woods are dim, and the rooks cry. John Masefield. OxBTC

Twilight Musings. Mary Weston Fordham. CBWP-2

Twilight Night. Christina Rossetti. CBLP

Twilight of eternal day, The. (LL) 50. Tennyson. CABP; EBVV; EBVVPR; EnVR; HAP; HeIP-4; NOCV; OAEL-2; PFE; PeECV; PoEL-5; SCGP; SCV

Twilight of Vanity. Vyacheslav Kupriyanov, *Russian*. TCRP, *tr. by* Albert C. Todd

Twilight on Tweed. Andrew Lang. EBVV

Twilight on Union Street. Donald Davidson. FuPo

Twilight Polka Dots. Barbara Guest. PmAP
    ("Lake was filled with distinguished fish purchased, The.") NoP-4

Twilight Seduction. Yusef Komunyakaa. SeSe

Twilight Shadows round Me Fall, The. Ernest Edwin Ryden. AH

Twilight Time. Samuel Palmer. *See* Shoreham: Twilight Time.

Twilight turns from amethyst, The. James Joyce. PFE

Twilight was turning to darkness outside. Vladislav Felitsianovich Khodasevich, *Russian*. TCRP, *tr. by* Michael Frayn

Twilight with Xs. Dean Young. WeT

Twilights. James Wright. LCAP-2

Twilight's Last Gleaming. Arthur W. Monks. NIP-4

Twilit Revelation. Léonie Adams. MoAmPo

'Twill be all forgotten a hundred years hence. *Unknown. See* Rye Whisky.

'Twill be alovely sight. (LL) The Rain. W. H. Davies. BoTP; OxBTC

'Twill learn of things *Divine*, and first of *Thee* to sing. (LL) On the Death of Mr. Crashaw. Abraham Cowley. BeJo; EPCY; MeLP; SeCP

'Twill soon be sunrise. Down the valley waiting. Lakeward. Trumbull Stickney. APN-2

"'Twill take some getting." "Sir, I think 'twill so." Man and Dog. Edward Thomas. PeFWW

Twin. Phyllis Haring. PeSA

Twin Aces. Keith Wilson. Poetsp

Twin Brothers, The. *Unknown. See* The Twa Brothers.

Twin Hills. Vidyapati, *Sanskrit*. EP, *tr. by* Deben Bhattacharya

Twin streaks twice higher than cumulus. Vapor Trails. Gary Snyder. NAAL-2

Twine then the rays. Psycholophon. Frank Gelett Burgess. CBNP

Twined together and, as is customary. Never Such Love. Robert Graves. BoLoP; LoP

Twining her fingers through. Satyr, Cunnilinguent: To Herman Melville. Charles Martin. RA

Twinings Orange Pekoe. Judith Moffett. PoA

Twink Drives Back, in a Bad Mood, from a Party in Massachusetts. George Amabile. NYBP

Twinkle, twinkle, all the night. (LL) The Star. Jane Taylor. CABP

Twinkle, twinkle, little bat! The Mad Hatter's Song. "Lewis Carroll." CBNP; CTV; NOBL; UV   *Fr.* Alice's Adventures in Wonderland.

Twinkle, twinkle little star. Space Spot. Max Fatchen. SpW

Twinkle, twinkle, little star. The Star. Jane Taylor. ACTP; BoTP; CABP; CTV; ChAP; FPC; FaBoBe; ImGa; NOBRP; NOxBChV; NTCP; OTCP; OxBChV; OxNR; UV

Twins, The. Robert Browning. FaBoVe

Twins. Gloria Escoffery. PBCV

Twins. Robert Graves. FaBoEE; OBCoV

Twins, The. Henry Sambrooke Leigh. CTV

Twins, The. Karl Shapiro. MoAmPo; TrJP

Twins, The. James Stephens. RaBo

Twins, The. Mona Van Duyn. VCAP

Twirling. Jane Flanders. PBCAP

Twirling your blue skirts, traveling [*or* travelling] the sward. Blue Girls. John Crowe Ransom. CMoP; ColAP; FuPo; GBL; MeMAP; MoAmPo; NoAM; NoP-4; RB; TAP; VGW; WeW-3

Twirls on the tips of a carnation. The Oriental Ballerina. Rita Dove. NAAAL

Twist, The. Alfred B. Spellman. ISC

Twist about, turn about. *Unknown*. OxNR

Twist along the spine begins the form, A. A Spiral Shell. Howard Nemerov. *Fr.* Epigrams. OBAL

Twist me a crown of wind-flowers. A Crown of Windflowers. Christina Rossetti. OxBChV

Twist of cloth on the flat stones, A. Desmond O'Grady. PBCIP   *Fr.* The Dark Edge of Europe.

Twist thou and twine! in light and gloom. Featherstone's Doom. Robert Stephen Hawker. OBNC

Twisted rhombs ceased their clamour of accompaniment, The. Ezra Pound. MeMAP   *Fr.* Homage to Sextus Propertius.

Twisters. William Meissner. CMAP

Twisting, circling, the green path slants. Cheng-tao Temple. Tai Piao-yüan, *Chinese*. CoBLCP, *tr. by* Jonathan Chaves

Twisting inland. Michael McClintock. HA

Twitch nervously about. (LL) Two Postures beside a Fire. James Wright. HCAP; HeIP-4

Twitched in her belly, or he raised a fist. Figlio Maggiore. Robert Fitzgerald. NoP-4

Twitched strings, the clang of metal, beaten drums. Javanese Dancers. Arthur Symons. ADE

Twitching in the cactus. Deathwatch. Michael S. Harper. AmPA; NAAAL; PoBA

Twittingpan seized my arm, though I'd have gone. The Encounter. Edgell Rickword. OxBTC

'Twixt Carrowbrough Edge and Settlingstones. Old Skinflint. Wilfrid Wilson Gibson. OBMV

'Twixt Cup and Lip. Mark Hollis. NBLV

Twixt devil and deep sea, man hacks his caves. Arachne. William Empson. OBMV

'Twixt East and West a giant shape she grew. Sonnet on the Crimean War. William Forster. CBAP

'Twixt failure and success the point's so fine. Don't Give Up. C. C. Cameron. PoToHe   *Fr.* Success.

'Twixt handkerchief and nose. A Rub. John Banister Tabb. OBAL

Twixt nature and Pygmalion there might appear great strife. *Unknown*. OAEL-1

'Twixt optimist and pessimist. The Difference. Rowland Howard. CTV

Twixt the Girthhead and Langwoonded. The Lads of Wamphray. *Unknown*. ESPB; IBB

Twixt those twin worlds—the world of sleep, which gave. Shelley: Inscription for the Couch, Still Preserved, on which He Passed the Last NIght of His Life. D. G. Rossetti. EPCY

'Twixt Tweedledum and Tweedledee! (LL) Epigram on the Feuds between Handel and Bononcini. John Byrom. FaBoEE; NOBL; NOEC

'Twixt women's love, and men's will ever be[e]. (LL) Air[e] and Angels. Donne. CBLP; ESCV; MeLP; NAEL-1; OAEL-1; SeCP

Two. Robert Canzoneri. HoPM

Two, The. Hugo von Hofmannsthal, *German*. AWP, *tr. by* Ludwig Lewisohn

Two. Hugo von Hofmannsthal, *German*. TrJP, *tr. by* Jethro Bithell

Two. Carolyn Kizer. FFC   *Fr.* Pro Femina.
    ("Springing, full-grown, from your own head, Athena?") (LL) NMM-2

Two. Winfield Townley Scott. NYBP

Two. Mikhail Arkadyevich Svetlov, *Russian*. TCRP, *tr. by* Daniel Weissbort

Two Ajaxes Compared to Oxen, The. Homer. OBVE, *tr. by* George Chapman   *Fr.* The Iliad.

Two aldermen, three lawyers, five physicians. Of a Zealous Lady. Sir John Harington, *after the Latin of* Martial. FaBoEE

2 a.m.: moonlight. The train has stopped. Track. Tomas Tranströmer, *Swedish*. RB; SPE, *tr. by* Robert Bly

Two and Thirty Years Ago. Tennyson. *See* In the Valley of Cauteretz.

Two and two is four. Why are Fire Engines Red? *Unknown*. CBNP

2 Antemasque, The: Two Countrye Wives, the Songe. Lady Jane Cavendish. KTR   *Fr.* A Pastorall.

Two Appeals to John Harralson, Agent. *Unknown*. OBAL

Two April Mornings, The. Wordsworth. EBEV; GTBS-P; NAEL-2

Two Are Together. Geoffrey Grigson. GBL

Two Armies. Stephen Spender. OBWP; OxBTC

Two armies covered hill and plain. Music in Camp. John Reuben Thompson. BLPA; CBCWP

Two Artists, The. Constance Naden. VWP

Two Backgrounds. Edith Wharton. APN-2

Two basins, one rising from the other. Roman Fountain. Rilke, *German*. GS, *tr. by* Edward Snow

Two bees within a chrystal flowerbell rockèd. Dualisms. Tennyson. EnVR

Two Blue Swans. Elizabeth Kirschner. CMAP

Two bodies have I. *Unknown.* OxNR

Two Boys, The. Mary Lamb. Ro; WoRP

Two boys stand at the end of the full train. The Brothers: Two Saltimbanques. John Logan. LiLi

Two boys uncoached are tossing a poem together. Catch. Robert Francis. InPK-6; RaBo

Two boys, using fish heads for bait. Room for Doubt. C. G. Hanzlicek. CMAP

Two boys, whose birth beyond all question springs. Charles Churchill. OBSV *Fr.* The Prophecy of Famine.

Two Brothers, The. *Unknown.* AmFP

Two Brothers in a Field of Absence. Cynthia MacDonald. NIP-4

Two brothers we are. *Unknown.* OxNR

Two brown heads with tossing curls. Katie Lee and Willy [*or* Willie] Grey. Josie R. Hunt *and* J. H. Pixley. BLPA

Two Bulls, The. *Unknown.* NOIV, *tr. by* Thomas Kinsella *Fr.* How the Bulls Were Begotten.

Two, by themselves, each other, love and fear. Pyramus and Thisbe. Donne. FMP

Two by two in the ark of / the ache of it. (LL) Ache of Marriage, The. Denise Levertov. ITG

Two by two in the ark of / the ache of it. Denise Levertov. *See* The Ache of marriage.

Two Campers in Cloud Country. Sylvia Plath. NYBP

Two campers (King Lear and his clown?). Outward Bound. James Simmons. CIP-2

Two Canadian Landscapes. August Kleinzahler. BAP-96

Two Canadian Memorials. Rudyard Kipling. *Fr.* Epitaphs of the War [1914–1918]. OBWP

Two Captains, The. William Johnson Cory. *See* A Ballad for a Boy.

Two cars, three loos, a swimming pool. The Whiteman Blues. Lionel Abrahams. PeSAV

Two caterpillars crawling on a leaf. Immortality. Joseph Jefferson. BLPA

Two Cats / One up a tree. Diamond Cut Diamond. Ewart Milne. FaBoCh; PC

Two cats together. This and That. Gareth Owen. OTCP

Two-Cent Coal. *Unknown.* AmFP

Two Centos. William Empson. CBNP

Two Cherokee Songs of Friendship. *Unknown, Cherokee.* APN-2, *tr. by* Samuel L. Mitchill

Two Children, The. Emily Jane Brontë. PoEL-5

Two children, dressed in court costume. An Old Picture. Howard Nemerov. OxBSP

Two children in two neighbour villages. Circumstance. Tennyson. CBLP

Two children move shells from Tay Ninh. Night on the Kho Bha Dinh. Steve Denning. CDa

Two chilly. Tanka. Akiko Yosano, *Japanese.* MJT, *tr. by* Makoto Ueda

Two Chorale-Preludes: On Melodies by Paul Celan. Geoffrey Hill. OxBC

Two Christs were at Golgotha. Early Lynching. Carl Sandburg. ChIV-2; MoAmPo

Two Cities. Judit Tóth, *Hungarian.* CEEP, *tr. by* Emery E. George

Two coffees in the Español, the last. Prelude II. Conrad Potter Aiken. FYAP; NoAM *Fr.* Preludes for Memnon; or, Preludes to Attitude.

Two college sophs of Cambridge growth. Cassinus and Peter. Jonathan Swift. OAEL-1

Two Comical Folk. Mother Goose. OxNR; ReMoGo

Two converging from. The Paths. Richard Caddel. NBrP

Two Countries. Tadeusz Borowski, *Polish.* AF, *tr. by* Larry Rafferty, Meryl Natchez *and* Tadeusz Pioro

Two Countries. José Martí, *Spanish.* TTY, *tr. by* Mona Hinton

Two Couples. Debra Bruce. FFC

Two Cures for Love. Wendy Cope. OBCoV

Two dayes now in that sea he sayled has. Edmund Spenser. OxBoS *Fr.* Guyon's Voyage to the Bower of Bliss. NoSic *Fr.* Wood Of Error. AEP

Two dead divers hauled up in their bell, The. Alison Brackenbury. DiPo

Two Decisions. Vernon Watkins. OxBTC

Two Dedications. Gwendolyn Brooks. *See* The Chicago Picasso.

Chicago Picasso, The. BPo; LiTM

(Two Dedications.) NAAAL

Wall, The. PoBA

Two Deserts, The. Coventry Patmore. PFE

Two doves upon the selfsame branch. Song. Christina Rossetti. CBLP

Two Dreams, The. Giovanni Boccaccio, *Italian.* OBGa, *tr. by* Algernon Charles Swinburne

Two Drinking Songs. José Juan Tablada.

"I built my hut near where people live." AWP, *tr. by* Arthur Waley

Two Drops. Zbigniew Herbert, *Polish.* RB, *tr. by* Czeslaw Milosz

Two eaold to die. (LL) Old-Saxon Fragment. *Unknown.* CBNP; OBCoV

Two earnest young fellows named Wright. Limerick. Basil Ransome-Davies. PeLi

Two Ember Days in Alabama. Andrew Hudgins. RA

Two empires by the sea. International Hymn. George Huntington. PoLF

Two Englishmen. Douglas Stewart. CBAP

Two evils, monstrous either one apart. Winter Remembered. John Crowe Ransom. CBLP; HAP; MeMAP; NOBA; OxBA; UnPo; VGW

Two Eyes. Nhật Tiến, *Vietnamese.* AVP, *tr. by* Huỳnh Sanh Thông

Two eyes, the cathedral's spires look black. One Tourist's Cologne. Hal Colebatch. NOBAu

Two-Faced Too. *Unknown, Welsh.* OBWVE, *tr. by* Glyn Jones

Two Facts. David Huddle. IFJA

Two Families, The. Joyce L. Brisley. BoTP

Two Fawns That Didn't See the Light This Spring. Gary Snyder. HCAP

Two Figures. N. Scott Momaday. NoP-4

Two figures in deep water. Walking to Bellrock. Michael Ondaatje. NOBC

Two Figures in Dense Violet Night. Wallace Stevens. MoAmPo

Two Figures on Canvas. Gerald William Barrax. MT

Two figures there beneath the dome, walking with similar pace. St. Sophia. John Fuller. DiPo

Two Fires, The. Judith Wright. MoBrPo

Two fish. Fish Fact. Pamela Alexander. IFJA

Two Fish. Katha Pollitt. DiPo; NIP-4

Two Fish by a Willow Embankment. Hsü Wei, *Chinese.* CoBLCP, *tr. by* Jonathan Chaves

Two Fishermen. Stanley Moss. CoAP

Two Fishing Villages. Ellease Southerland. GT

Two floods I read of; water, and of wine. On the Two Great Floods. Francis Quarles. ChIV-1

Two flowers in a letter. Kenneth Rexroth. APSN *Fr.* The Love Poems of Marichiko.

Two foot-companions once in deep discourse—. The Nimmers. John Byrom. OxAEP-1

Two forms move among the dead, high sleep. The Owl in the Sarcophagus. Wallace Stevens. FaBoMo

Two forms of darkness are there. One is Night. Doubt. Mary Elizabeth Coleridge. NALW

Two Friends. David Ignatow. PBMP

Two Friends. Norman MacCaig. FP

Two Friends. Stevie Smith. WPN

Two friends at the close of summer. Why She Says No. Ellen Bryant Voigt. FaBoWP

Two friends took a trip together to Stone Man Peak. A Trip to Stone Man Peak. Yang Wan-li, *Chinese.* SuSp, *tr. by* Jonathan Chaves

Two from Israel. Dom Moraes.

"Altermann, sipping wine, reads with a look." NoP-4

2 f's/ in giraffe, The. The Giraffe. Ron Padgett. *Fr.* Three Animals. TTTS

Two Fusiliers. Robert Graves. PoFWW

Two Gardens (1969). Yona Wollach, *Hebrew.*

Preannual Poem. IP, *tr. by* Warren Bargad *and* Stanley F. Chyet

Two gardens see!—this, of enchanted flowers. Walter De la Mare. OBGa

Two Garnett brothers who run the Shell station here, The. Sweep. Rodney Jones. MT

Two gates unto the road of life there are. The Road of Life. William Morris. OBNC *Fr.* The Earthly Paradise.

Two gazed into a pool, he gazed and she. An Echo from Willow-Wood. Christina Rossetti. CABP

Two Generations. Leonard Alfred George Strong. OBMV

Two Gentlemen of Verona, The. Shakespeare.

My Thoughts Do Harbour. CTC

Silvia. OBEV

(Song.) EBEvV

"Thus have I shunned the fire for fear of burning." GBL

Two Gentlemen That Broke Their Promise of a Meeting. James Shirley. BeJo

Two German officers crossed the Rhine, parlee-voo. Hinky Dinky, Parlee-Voo. *Unknown.* AS

Two Gifts. *Unknown, Catalan.* BoWoP, *tr. by* Willis Barnstone

Two Girls. Suzanne Gardinier. BAP-96

Two girls discover. The Secret. Denise Levertov. CrSp; PBMP; Poetr

Two Glasses, The. Ella Wheeler Wilcox. BLPA

Two Graces. *Unknown.*

"Hurly, hurly, roon the table." FaBoCh

Two Grandmas. Stanley H. Barkan. UnSA

Two gray kits, The. *Unknown*. ReMoGo

Two green-webbed chairs. Children Playing Checkers at the Edge of the Forest. Adrienne Rich. LCAP-2; WeW-3

Two Gretels were exploring the forest, The. Robin Morgan. CrSp

Two half-brothers fully blind living together. How Light Is Spent. Bin Ramke. BAP-95

Two halfgrown girls hailing hallowed Easter. William Carlos Williams. MeMAP   *Fr*. Paterson.

Two hands lie still, the hairy and the white. Love for a Hand. Karl Shapiro. CoAP; NYBP

Two hands upon the breast. Now and Afterwards. Dinah Maria Mulock Craik. PoLF

Two Hangovers. James Wright. LCAP-2

Two happy lovers make one single bread. Pablo Neruda. ITG, *tr. by* Stephen Mitchell   *Fr*. Sonnet XLVIII.

Two-headed Calf, The. Laura Gilpin. FYAP

Two Hearts. Nguyễn Bính, *Vietnamese*. AVP, *tr. by* Huỳnh Sanh Thông

Two Hearts Divided. R. Williams Parry, *Welsh*. OBWVE, *tr. by* Joseph P. Clancy

Two hearts: two blades of grass I braid together. Weaving Love-Knots 2. Hsüeh T'ao. BoWoP, *tr. by* Carolyn Kizer

Two Heroes. Harriet Monroe. *See* Washington.

Two Historians. J. E. Thorold Rogers. *See* On the Historians Freeman and Stubbs.

Two hollow eyes follow a cat's crie. Mac Wellman. FTOS   *Fr*. Hollowness.

Two Hookers. A. K. Redwing. VoR

Two horses in yellow light. August. Adrienne Rich. NNaP; PBWP

Two Houses. Edward Thomas. FaBoCh

Two hummingbirds as evanescent as. Vision. Richard Eberhart. NYBP

211th Chorus. Jack Kerouac. NeAP; PmAP; PoM   *Fr*. Mexico City Blues.

Two Hundred and Nineteenth Chorus. Jack Kerouac. NeAP   *Fr*. Mexico City Blues.

230th Chorus. Jack Kerouac. NeAP   *Fr*. Mexico City Blues.

239th Chorus: "Charley Parker Looked like Buddha." Jack Kerouac. BB   *Fr*. Mexico City Blues.

Two Hundred and Twenty-Eighth Chorus. Jack Kerouac. NeAP; PmAP   *Fr*. Mexico City Blues.

225th Chorus. Jack Kerouac. NeAP   *Fr*. Mexico City Blues.

229th Chorus. Jack Kerouac. PoM   *Fr*. Mexico City Blues.

221st Chorus. Jack Kerouac. NeAP   *Fr*. Mexico City Blues.

Two hundred men and eighteen killed. James Henry. NOBVV

Two hundred miles, he had come. The Piano-Tuner. Valerie Gillies. FaBoTC

209 Canal. Richard Howard. TAP

270 The birches are worn out by mirrors. My Final Agonies. Benjamin Péret, *French*. PFTM, *tr. by* James Laughlin

225 days under grass. For Jane. Charles Bukowski. HoPM

Two in August. John Crowe Ransom. AWP; MeMAP; OxBA

Two in Bed. Abram Bunn Ross. CTV; NTCP

Two in the afternoon. The restlessness. Down the Nile. Robert Lowell. HCAP

Two in the Campagna. Robert Browning. APAD; EBEV; EBVV; EnVR; FHYEP; GTBS-P; NAEL-2; NOBE; NOBVV; NoP-4; OAEL-2; OBNC; OxAEP-2; OxBM; PoE; PoEL-5; SCGP; TFi; TOF

Two infants vis-à-vis. Bleecker Street. Jean Garrigue. TAP

Two Infinities. Edward Dowden. GSo

Two Invocations of Death. Kathleen Jessie Raine.
  "From a place I came." OxBTC

Two Irish yews, prickly green, poisonous. Gate Lodge. Richard Murphy. PBCIP

Two Japanese Prints. Pat Matsueda. EC3

Two jays came down my street. The Jays. John Heath-Stubbs. NOxBChV

Two Kinds of People. Ella Wheeler Wilcox. *See* Lifting and Leaning.

Two Kitchen Songs. Dame Edith Sitwell. CMoP

Two ladies sit in the spotless driveway. Garage Sale. Karl Shapiro. Poetsp

Two ladies to the summit of my mind. Sonnet: Of Beauty and Duty. Dante, *Italian*. AWP, *tr. by* D. G. Rossetti

Two ladies walked on the soft green grass. A Dream of Comparison. Stevie Smith. BWW

Two Laments. *Unknown, Chinese*. ChiP, *tr. by* Arthur Waley

Two large dogs. In Berlin. Ōkuma Nobuyuki, *Japanese*. MJT, *tr. by* Makoto Ueda

Two Lean Cats. Myron O'Higgins. PoBA

Two leaps the water from its race. A Mill. William Allingham. FaBoEE; OxBSP

Two Legends. Ted Hughes. *Fr*. Crow. PoE

Two legs sat upon three legs. Riddle: "Two legs sat upon three legs." Mother Goose. LB; NTCP; OxNR

Two liddle niggers all dressed in white. Raise a "Rucus" To-Night. *Unknown*. BPo; TAP

Two-line epigram is perfect, A. Step. Cyrillus, *Greek*. GrAn, *tr. by* Peter Jay

Two Lines from the Brothers Grimm. Gregory Orr. AmPA

Two Lips. Thomas Hardy. BoLoP

Two little beaks went tap! tap! tap! To Let. D. Newey-Johnson. BoTP

Two little birdies, one wintry day. The Birdies' Breakfast. *Unknown*. BoTP

Two Little Blackbirds. *Unknown*. BoTP

Two little clouds, one summer's day. The Rainbow Fairies. *Unknown*. BoTP

Two little creatures. Monkeys. Padraic Colum. OxBTC

Two little dicky-birds. Dicky-Birds. Natalie Joan. BoTP

Two little dicky birds. *Unknown*. LB; OxNR

Two little dogs / Sat by the fire. *Unknown*. OxNR

Two little elves / Were lost one night. A Fairy Dream. Dorothy Graddon. BoTP

Two little eyes to look to God. *Unknown*. CTV

Two little girls, one fair, one dark. The Lost Children. Randall Jarrell. CoAP; PBMP; TAP

Two Little Kittens. Jane Taylor. BoTP

Two Little Kittens[, one stormy night]. *Unknown*. ACTP; OBCA; OxBChV

Two Little Miss Lloyds, The. Elizabeth Turner. OxBChV

Two little princesses, The. Palace Cook's Tale. Joan Aiken. NOxBChV

Two little ships were sailing by. Upon a Christmas Morning. *Unknown*. AmFP

Two Lives. William Ellery Leonard. Son

Two lofty ships of Eng-e-land set sail. The Wild Barbaree. *Unknown*. AmFP

Two Look at Two. Robert Frost. MoAmPo

Two Lovers, The. Marie de France. BoWoP, *tr. by* Patricia Terry

Two lovers by a moss-grown spring. "George Eliot." SDW

Two Lovers on Bridge in Winter. Paula Rankin. CMAP

Two lovers to a midnight meadow came. The Amateurs of Heaven. Howard Nemerov. SoSe-8

Two Loves. Lord Alfred Bruce Douglas. ADE

Two Loves. Richard Eberhart. CMoP

Two loves I have of comfort and despair, *sl. diff. vers. also in* The Passionate Pilgrim. Sonnet 144. Shakespeare. AEP; EBEV; HeIP-4; NAEL-1; NIP-4; OAEL-1; PoEL-2; Son   *Fr*. Sonnets.

Two Lyrics. Lorenzo de' Medici, *Italian*. AWP, *tr. by* John Addington Symonds

Two Lyrics from Kilroy's Carnival: A Masque. Delmore Schwartz.
  Aria. EP

Two Magicians, The. *Unknown*. OAEL-1; OxBoLi

Two Magicians, The. *Unknown*. *See* The Twa Magicians.

Two magpies under the cypresses, The. What Birds Were There. William Everson. NoAM

Two Man a Road. *Unknown*. PBCV

Two Meetings, The. Eugene Field. PWR

Two Memorial Poems. David Avidan, *Hebrew*. IP, *tr. by* Warren Bargad *and* Stanley F. Chyet

Two Men. Andrew Lansdown. NOBAu

Two Men. Anne Waldman. IFJA

Two men appear on a tractor. Poem about the Future. Hans Magnus Enzensberger. PoSu

Two men are walking around the lake. A Walk Around the Lake. Jay Meek. CMAP

Two men lie folded in sleep. Night Sweats 2. Boyer Rickel. WeT

Two middle-aged ladies from Fordham. Limerick. *Unknown*. PeLi

Two Monkeys, The. John Gay. OBCoV

Two Months Married. Aidan Carl Mathews. PBCIP

Two More about a Crow, in the Manner of Zukofsky. *Unknown, Seneca Indian*. STP, *tr. by* Jerome Rothenberg *and* Richard Johnny John

Two Mornings. Lawrence McGaugh. PoBA

Two Mornings and Two Evenings. Elizabeth Bishop. PoA

Two Movements Which Begin at the Head and End at the Feet. Richard Caddel. NBrP

Two moving figures flow together: see. Reflection. Elisabeth Eybers, *Afrikaans*. PeSAV, *tr. by the author*

Two mules stand in front of the brick wall of a warehouse. Mule Team and Poster. Donald Justice. VCAP

Two murders this month. October. Greg Pape. AmPA

Two Musicians, The. Henrietta Cordelia Ray. CBWP-3

Two Mysteries, The. Mary Mapes Dodge. PWR; TrCP

Two nails, The. (LL) The Mirror. Michael Davitt, *Irish*. BiHa; CIP-2; PBCIP, *tr.* by Paul Muldoon

Two-natured, loving my world. The Comb and the Mirror. Elizabeth Spires. FFC

Two Neighbours, The. George Campbell Hay. OxBS

Two nights in Manchester: nothing much to do. Mr. Cooper. Anthony Thwaite. OxBTC

Two nights running I was out there. The Mummies. Maxine W. Kumin. Poetsp

Two nights yet, and daies. Landfall. Homer. OBCVT, *tr.* by George Chapman *Fr.* The Odyssey.

Two Noble Kinsmen, The. John Fletcher *and* Shakespeare.

Bridal Song, A: "Roses, their sharp spines being gone." NOBE; NOSC; NoSic

Dirge of the Three Queens. OBEV

"Hail Sovereign Queen of secrets, who hast power." PoEL-2

Two nudists of Dover. Third Limick. Ogden Nash. PeLi

Two o'clock. Explorer. Alan Brownjohn. AYFP

Two o'Clock. Katharine Pyle. *Fr.* The Wonder Clock. OBCA

Two o'clock: full moonlight, few stars. Tomas Tranströmer. *See* Track.

Two o'clock on a Saturday afternoon in November. Matinee. Susan Clements. UnSA

2 o'clock: strong moonlight, few stars. (LL) Track. Tomas Tranströmer, *Swedish*. RB; SPE, *tr.* by Robert Bly

Two, of course there are two. Death and Co. Sylvia Plath. CMoP; CoAmPo; LCAP-2

Two of far nobler shape erect and tall. Milton. PeECV, *ll.* 288–299 *Fr.* Book IV. OAEL-1 *Fr.* Paradise Lost.

Two of Them, The. Hugo von Hofmannsthal, *German*. STV, *tr.* by John Frederick Nims

Two of You, The. Czeslaw Milosz. *See* After Paradise.

Two old crows sat on a fence rail. Vachel Lindsay. OBAL

Two old dancing shoes my grandfather. Genius. Philip Levine. NoAM

Two Old Kings, The. John Byrne Leicester Warren, 3d Baron De Tabley. OBEV

Two Old Ladies. Siegfried Sassoon. OxBTC

Two or Three; a Recipe [*or* Receipt] to Make a Cuckold. Alexander Pope. BoLoP; FaBoEE

Two or three minutes—two or three hours. Minutes of Gold. *Unknown*. PoToHe

Two or three posies. Keats. CBNP

Two or three visits, and two or three bows. Two or Three; a Recipe [*or* Receipt] to Make a Cuckold. Alexander Pope. BoLoP; FaBoEE

Two pairs of mallards, tandem. Nearing Winter. Ernest Sandeen. NYBP

Two Parents, The. "Hugh MacDiarmid." FaBoTw; OxBTC

Two passive and two active—you'd imagine. Two Plus Two. Strato, *Greek*. GrAn, *tr.* by Teddy Hogge

Two Performing Elephants. D. H. Lawrence. RB

Two petals from that wild-rose tree. (LL) Memory. Thomas Bailey Aldrich. CTV; PoLF

Two Pewits. Edward Thomas. CH

Two Pictures. *Unknown*. BLPA; FaBoBe

Two Pigeons. *Unknown*. ReMoGo

Two pilgrims, broiling in the sun. Beware of Dogmas. Ebenezer Elliot. FaBoEE

Two playwrights called Beaumont and Fletcher. Limerick. Fiona Pitt-Kethley. PeLi

Two Plus Two. Strato, *Greek*. GrAn, *tr.* by Teddy Hogge

Two Poems. Aleksandr Soprovsky, *Russian*.

"Notes from the house of the dead." TCRP, *tr.* by Vladimir Lunis *and* Albert C. Todd

Two Poems. Andrey Andreievich Voznesensky, *Russian*. VCWP, *tr.* by Smith, William Jay *and* Patricia Blake

Two Poems about President Harding. James Wright. CoAP; MoP; WeT

Two Poems for Black Relocation Centers. Etheridge Knight. NNaP

Poem for Black Relocation Centers, A. NNaP

Two Poems on Insect Painting by Candidate Yin. Su Shih, *Chinese*.

On a Snail. SuSp, *tr.* by Irving Y. Lo

On A Toad. APo; SuSp, *tr.* by Irving Y. Lo

Two Poems on Night. Tu Fu, *Chinese*. SuSp, *tr.* by Jan Walls

Two Poems on the Catholic Bavarians. Edgar Bowers. CRP

Two Poems on the Eretrians Taken Prisoner by the Persians. Plato, *Greek*.

"Leaving behind for ever the thundering Aegean." GrAn, *tr.* by Peter Jay

"We are Eretrians from Euboia." GrAn, *tr.* by Peter Jay

Two Poems on the Fear of Love. Thomas R. Smith. EC2

Two Poems Presented to the Gentleman in the Office of Palace Writers Ku Yen-hsien. Lu Chi, *Chinese*.

"Off at dawn to service in the walled and storied palace." CoBCP, *tr.* by Burton Watson

Two Poems to the Tune "Chin-tzu ching" The Sutra in Gold Characters. Ma Chih-yüan, *Chinese*.

Two Poems to the Tune "Hsiao-t'iao hung." Ni Tsan, *Chinese*. CoBLCP, *tr.* by Jonathan Chaves

Two Poems to the Tune "Jen-yüeh yüan." Ni Tsan, *Chinese*. CoBLCP, *tr.* by Jonathan Chaves

Two Poems to the Tune "Po pu tuan." Ma Chih-yüan, *Chinese*. CoBLCP, *tr.* by Jonathan Chaves

Two Postures beside a Fire. James Wright. HCAP; HeIP-4

Two Prayers. Andrew Gillies. PoToHe

Two purple pigeons circle a London square. The Exiled Heart. Maurice Lindsay. OxBS

Two Pursuits. Christina Rossetti. WPE

Two Quartz Pebbles. Vasco [*or* Vasko] Popa. PoSu, *tr.* by Anne Pennington *Fr.* The Quartz Pebble.

Two Questions, The. Alice Thompson Meynell. WPE

Two Rats. *Unknown*. *See* What Became of Them?

Two Ravens, The. *Unknown*. *See* The Twa Corbies.

Two Realities. Aldous Leonard Huxley. PFE

Two Red Roses across the Moon. William Morris. EBVV; UV

Two Rivers. Ralph Waldo Emerson. APN-1; AmPP; NCAP; NOBA; OxBA; PoE

Two roads diverged in a yellow wood. The Road Not Taken. Robert Frost. APAD; AiP; AmPP; CMoP; ChAP; EBEvV; FaBoCh; HAP; HeIP-4; ImPo; LiTM; MeMAP; MoAmPo; MoP; NAAL-2; NIP-4; NTP; NoAM; NoP-4; OxBA; PFE; PoLF; PoPoPo; Poetr; SAGP; SAmP; SoSe-8; TAP; TFi; TRP; TwCP

Two Rural Sisters. Charles Cotton. BoLoP; EnLoPo *Fr.* Resolution in Four Sonnets, of a Poetical Question Put to Me by a Friend, Concerning Four Rural Sisters. PoEL-3; Son

Two Sad. William Cole. CTV

Two seas our eyes beheld—one dark, one light. From Green Mountain. William Reed Huntington. APN-2

Two Selves, The. Margaret Avison. MoP

Two separate divided silences. Severed Selves. D. G. Rossetti. BoLoP; GLoP *Fr.* The House of Life.

Two Set Out on Their Journey. Galway Kinnell. IFJA

2 : 7. "Alta."

"Loving your neighbor is all very fine when you have nice." CrSp

Two Shadows. Elizabeth Spires. DiPo

Two shall be born, the whole wide world apart. Fate. Susan Marr Spalding. BLPA; PoToHe

Two Shapes. Arthur Gregor. TAP

Two she-camels spied on a goat. Limerick. *Unknown*. PeLi

Two Sisters, The. *Aborigine Oral Tradition*. NOBAu, *tr.* by Manoowa

Two Sisters, The. *Unknown*. AmFP

(Cruel Sister, The.) OxBB

Two sisters who had no brother. Brotherless Sisters. *Unknown*, *Serbo-Croatian*. HSix, *tr.* by Charles Simic

Two snails are on their way. Song of the snails on their way to a funeral. Jacques Prévert, *French*. MFP, *tr.* by Martin Sorrell

Two Soldier's Songs. *Unknown, Chinese*. ChiP, *tr.* by Arthur Waley

Two soluble aspirins spore in this glass, their mycelia. Spilt Milk. Sarah Maguire. LW

Two songs. Louisa Sarah Bevington.

With the Tide: A Cry of Weakness. PEW

Two Songs. C. Day Lewis. HAP; NoAM; NoP-4

"I've heard them lilting at loom and belting." OBMV

Song: "Come, live with me and be my love." NIP-4; Poetr

Two Songs. Adrienne Rich.

("*Spasibo. Thanks. O.K.*") (LL) PFE

"That 'old last act'! / And yet sometimes." NIP-4; NOBA; TAP

Two Songs. Marina Tsvetayeva, *Russian*.

"Yesterday he could still look in my eyes, yet." TCRP, *tr.* by Elaine Feinstein

Two Songs About a Dead Person or a Mole—Whichever It Was. Richard Johnny John, Jerome Rothenberg, *and* Ian Tyson. PFTM *Fr.* Songs from the Society of the Mystic Animals.

Two Songs about Flowers & Where I Was Walking. *Unknown, Seneca Indian*. STP, *tr.* by Jerome Rothenberg *and* Johnny John

Two Songs from a Play. W. B. Yeats. FaBoTw; HAP; PoE, *sect.* 1; CMoP; ImPo; NOBE; OAEL-2, *sect.* 1-2 *Fr.* The Resurrection.

Two Songs from *Sweeny Agonistes*. T. S. Eliot. UnPo *Fr.* Sweeney Agonistes.

Two Songs of a Fool. W. B. Yeats. CMoP; RB

Two Songs of Peace. Yehuda Amichai, *Hebrew*. AF, *tr.* by Gutmann, Assia

Two Songs on the Economy of Abundance. James Agee. MoAmPo
Red Sea.

Two Sonnets. John Ashbery. VGW; WeT

Two Sonnets. Paul Evans.
"Mixed with age, she could foresee the future." NBrP
"Professor stood still, tall, thin, with stains, The." NBrP

Two Sonnets. Charles Hamilton Sorley. MoBrPo
"Saints have adored the lofty soul of you." NSI; PeFWW
"Such, such is Death: no triumph: no defeat." NSI; PeFWW

Two Sons. Laoiseach Mac an Bhaird. NOIV

Two Sons. Anne Sexton. PFE

Two sons are gone. Later Still. Philip Levine. ColAP

Two Souls. Marjorie Lowry Christie Pickthall. NOBC

Two spheres on meeting may so softly collide. Divided. Walter De la Mare. CBLP

Two Spirits[: An Allegory], The. Shelley. CH; OAEL-2

Two Springs. Li Ch'ing-chao, Chinese. BoWoP; OHPC, tr. by Kenneth Rexroth

Two standing women are watchtowers. A House. Libby Houston. NBrP

Two Stars, The. W. H. Davies. MoBrPo

Two statesmen met by moonlight. What the Moon Saw. Vachel Lindsay. FaBoEE; OxBSP

Two steps from my garden rail. Hayyim Nahman Bialik. Fr. Songs of the People. AWP, tr. by Maurice Samuel

Two sticks and an apple. London Bells. Unknown. OPOU

Two Stories. Charles Wright. FYAP; LCAP-2

Two stories high above Saturn St. For My Mother. Doris Brett. NOBAu

Two Strange Worlds. Francesca Yetunde Pereira. PBA

Two Streams, The. Oliver Wendell Holmes. APN-1

Two streams: one dry, one poured all night by our beds. The Interrogation. Li-Young Lee. PoPoPo

Two strong impulses: One. Jelaluddin Rumi. RaBo, tr. by Coleman Barks and John Moyne Fr. Four Quatrains.

Two Studies in Idealism: Short Survey of American and Human History. Robert Penn Warren. CBCWP

Two Summers in Moravia. Roger McDonald. CBAP

Two Surprises. R. W. McAlpine. PoLF

Two Swans, The. Thomas Hood. CH

Two sweeter babes you nare did see. Unknown. FaBoEE

Two Tales of Clumsy. Gjertrud Schnackenberg.
"When Clumsy harks the gladsome ting-a-lings." NoAM

Two tapsters traded on Thames's side. Ballad of the Two Tapsters. Vernon Watkins. MoBS

Two telephones all morning giving each other hell. Cash Positive. Peter McDonald. PNI

Two Temples. Hattie Vose Hall. BLPA

Two that could not have lived their single lives. Two in August. John Crowe Ransom. AWP; MeMAP; OxBA

Two that through windy nights kept company. The Two Neighbours. George Campbell Hay. OxBS

Two things a man's built for, killing and you-know-what. Bear Track Plantation: Shortly after Shiloh. Robert Penn Warren. Fr. Two Studies in Idealism: Short Survey of American and Human History. CBCWP

Two things crossed Main Street. Both Ways. William Stafford. CMAP

Two things I have asked of Thee. Neither Poverty nor Riches. Bible, O.T. TrJP Fr. Proverbs.

"Two things," said Kant, "fill me with breathless awe." The Third Wonder. Edwin Markham. FYAP

2976. Julia Uceda, Spanish. BoWoP, tr. by Willis Barnstone

Two Tile Beaks. Maria Amalia Fonte Boa. BoWoP, tr. by Willis Barnstone and Nelson Cerqueira

Two-toned Olds swinging sideways out of, The. Infidelity. Stanley Plumly. NAmP90

Two Tongue-Pointing (Satirical) Songs. Unknown, Aborigine. NOBAu

Two Tongues in a Tower. John Wheelwright. KSG

Two top-knots not yet plaited into one. Going to the Mountains with a Little Dancing Girl, Aged Fifteen. Po Chü-i, Chinese. ChiP, tr. by Arthur Waley

Two Tramps in Mud Time. Robert Frost. CMoP; ImPo; LiTM; MeMAP; MoAmPo; MoP; NAAL-2; NoAM; SAmP

Two Translations from Kabir. Robert Bly.
NOTL. EnlH
(Breath, The.)

Two Trees, The. W. B. Yeats. OAEL-2

Two Trinities. Kenneth Mackenzie. CBAP

Two Truths. Helen Hunt Jackson. LW

2 Variations: All About Love. Philip Whalen. NeAP

Two vases stood on the Shelf of Life. Vases. Nan Terrell Reed. BLPA

Two Vast Enjoyments Commemorated. John Danforth. SCAP

Two Vietnam Poems: (1966). Bill Knott. PBCAP
((End) of Summer (1966).) SPE
("I have work to dream.") (LL) SPE

Two Views of a Cadaver Room. Sylvia Plath. CMoP

Two Views of Two Ghost Towns. Charles Tomlinson. NoAM

Two vipers tangled into one. (LL) Similes for Two Political Characters of 1819. Shelley. FaBoPV; NAEL-2; OxBoV; RB

Two virtues ride, by stallion, by nag. The Death of Myth-making. Sylvia Plath. PoA

Two Voices. Edmund Blunden. OBWP; PeFWW

Two voices are there: one is of the deep. A Sonnet. James Kenneth Stephen. BXAP; CABP; EPCY; NOBL; PeLV; UV

Two Voices are there; one is of the sea. Thought[s] of a Briton on the Subjugation of Switzerland. Wordsworth. CABP; GTBS-P; PBMP; UV

Two Voices in a Meadow. Richard Wilbur. PBMP

Two ways I love Thee, selfishly. Rabi'a al-Adawiyya, Persian. TOF, tr. by A. J. Arberry

Two Wedding Songs. John Heath-Stubbs. NTP
"Hang flags in the airs of July."
London Birds: a Lollipop.

Two weeks across a strange sea. Katori Maru, October 1920. Jim Mitsui. OpBo; UnSA

Two went to pray? o rather say. Two Went Up into the Temple To Pray. Richard Crashaw. ChIV-2; HAP

Two Went Up into the Temple To Pray. Richard Crashaw. ChIV-2; HAP

Two were silent in a sunless church, The. Her Dilemma. Thomas Hardy. EnVR; NOBVV

Two White Horses. Unknown. AS

Two wild duck of the upland spaces. Duck. John Lyle Donaghy. BIrV

Two Wise Generals. Ted Hughes. MoBS

Two Witches. Robert Frost. CMoP
Pauper Witch of Grafton, The.
Witch of Coös, The. InPS-3; LiTM; MeMAP; MoP; NOBA; NoAM; PoE
("I stayed the night for shelter at a farm.") OxBSn
("Yes, there's something the dead are keeping back.") (LL) OxBSn

Two Witches. Charles Reznikoff. OTCP

Two Women. Naomi Replansky. NMM-2

Two Women. George R. Sims.
"To-night is a midnight meeting, and the Earl is in the chair." UV

Two Women. Tania Van Zyl. PeSA

Two Women Knitting. Mrinal Pande, Hindi. OMIP, tr. by Mrinal Pande and Arlene Zide

Two women on the lone wet strand. The Watchers. W. S. Braithwaite. NAAAL

Two women, seventies, hold hands. Day Trip. Carole Satyamurti. OPOU

Two women sit at a table by a window. Light breaks. After Twenty Years. Adrienne Rich. TRP

Two Wooden Men, The. Huy Cận, Vietnamese. AVP, tr. by Huỳnh Sanh Thông

Two wooden tubs of blue hydrangeas stand at the foot. Banal Sojourn. Wallace Stevens. GaP

Two Words; a Wedding. B. P. Nichol. NOBC

Two words from China: "Ku li"—bitter strength. Ku Li. "Robin Hyde." PeNZ

Two workmen were carrying a sheet of asbestos. Christo's. Paul Muldoon. CIP-2

Two Worlds. Matija Beckovic, Serbo-Croatian. HSix, tr. by Charles Simic

Two Worlds. Richard Watson Gilder. GS

Two worlds there are. One you think. Cleaning the Well. Fred Chappell. MT

Two X. E. E. Cummings. FaBoMo

Two-Year-Old Has Had a Motherless Week, The. Karl Shapiro. WeW-3

Two years I've been in the Eastern Capital. For Li Po. Tu Fu, Chinese. SuSp, tr. by Eugene Eoyang

Two Years Later. John Wieners. PmAP; PoM; RaBo

Two years now since I last came. Arriving at Hangchou. Yüan Mei, Chinese. CoBLCP, tr. by Jonathan Chaves

Two years now since my second marriage. Year Wu-tzu [1048], The, First Month, Night of the Twenty-sixth: A Dream. Mei Yao Ch'en, Chinese. SuSp, tr. by Jonathan Chaves

Two years thus spent in gathering knowledge. Tom Brainless as Student and Preacher at College. John Trumbull. Fr. The Progress of Dulness. AmPP

Two years we spent. The Woods. Derek Mahon. NOIV; PBCIP

Two young brunettes in the library of the husband. Roman Elegies IV. Joseph Brodsky. EP

TWO's a couple. Four on a Sidewalk. Unknown. CA

'Twould ring the bells of Heaven. The Bells of Heaven. Ralph Hodgson. BoTP; LiTM; MoBrPo; NOBE; OBEV; OxBSP

Tycoon, Poet, Saint. Abdur-Rahman Slade Hopkinson. PBCV

Tyger, The. William Blake. APAD; CTAV; ChAP; FPC; NOxBChV; NoP-4; PFE; PoPoPo *Fr.* Songs of Experience.

("And watered heaven with their tears.") (LL)

("And watered heaven with their tears.") (LL)

("And watered heaven with their tears.") (LL)

("Tyger! Tyger! burning bright.") NoP-4

Tyger [or Tiger], The, *see* The Tiger: "Tiger! tiger! burning bright." William Blake. *See* The Tyger.

Tyger, *see* The Tiger: "Tiger! tiger! burning bright." William Blake. *See* The Tyger.

Tyger! Tyger! burning bright. William Blake. *See* The Tyger.

Tying Up for the Night at Maple River Bridge. Chang Chi, *Chinese.* CoBCP, *tr. by* Burton Watson

Tyl it was noon, they stoden for to se. At the Gate. Chaucer. *Fr.* Troilus and Criseyde [or Criseide]. EnVB

Tyler scuffs oak leaves to frisk. Nothing Happened. Belle Waring. PBCAP

Tyler was no Whig at all & after his term's end. 1845. Jackson MacLow. APSN *Fr.* The Presidents of the United States of America.

Tyndarus attempting too kis a fayre lasse with a long nose. Of Tyndarus, That Frumped a Gentlewoman. *Unknown, Latin.* BIrV, *tr. by* Richard Stanyhurst

Type of the antique Rome! Rich reliquary. The Coliseum. Edgar Allan Poe. APN-1; AmPP; NOBA

Typing the Letters. John A. Scott. BMAP

Typists. Patricia K. Page. NALW

Typographical Errors. Geof Hewitt. IFJA

Tyrannic Love. Dryden.

"Ah, how sweet it is to love!" HuPM

Epilogue to *Tyrannic[k] Love.* OBCoV

Tyranny of Moths. Gerald Vizenor. VoR

Tyrant, The. Faiz Ahmad Faiz, *Arabic.* AF, *tr. by* Naomi Lazard

Tyrant in Sleep, Naught Differeth from a Common Man, A. Timothy Kendall. NoSic

Tyrant whie swel'st thou thus. Quid gloriaris? Psalm 52. Mary Sidney Herbert, Countess of Pembroke. PBRV

Tyrant, why swel'st [or swell'st] thou thus, *par. by* Countess of Pembroke, Mary Sidney Herbert. Psalm 52. Bible, *O.T.* NoSic; OBVE *Fr.* Psalms.

Tyre brought me up, who born in thee had been. Of Himself. Meleager, *Greek.* AWP, *tr. by* Richard Garnett

Tyrian dye why do you wear. To His Mistress. Abraham Cowley. NOSC; OxAEP-1 *Fr.* Sylva.

Tyson's Corner. Primus St. John. PoBA

Tywater. Richard Wilbur. CMoP; CoAmPo; LiTM; TRP

Tzar Dusan / I ask pardon. For Maria Magdalenes. Desanka Maksimovic, *Serbo-Croatian.* HSix, *tr. by* Charles Simic

Tzu-yeh Song. Li Po, *Chinese.* CoBCP, *tr. by* Burton Watson

Tzu Yeh Songs. *Unknown, Chinese.*

"All night I could not sleep." BoWoP, *tr. by* Arthur Waley

("Nights are long and I cannot sleep.") CoBCP, *tr. by* Burton Watson

"At the time when blossoms." BoWoP, *tr. by* Arthur Waley

"Cool breezes—I sleep by the open window." CoBCP, *tr. by* Burton Watson

"Fragrance comes from the scent I wear, The." CoBCP, *tr. by* Burton Watson

"Hems gathered up, sash not yet tied." CoBCP, *tr. by* Burton Watson

"I heard my love was going to Yang-chou." BoWoP, *tr. by* Arthur Waley

"I will carry my coat and not put on my belt." BoWoP, *tr. by* Arthur Waley

"In the hottest time, when all is still and windless." CoBCP, *tr. by* Burton Watson

"Out the southern gate at sundown." CoBCP, *tr. by* Burton Watson

"When ice on the pond is three feet thick." CoBCP, *tr. by* Burton Watson

Tzu-yeh Songs of the Four Seasons. *Unknown, Chinese.*

Spring. SuSp

"Before jade pavilions the new moon dims." SuSp, *tr. by* Michael E. Workman

"Bewitching the blossoms of the spring grove." SuSp, *tr. by* Ronald C. Miao

"Luminous winds flicker in the moonrise." SuSp, *tr. by* Michael E. Workman

"Plum flowers all fallen and gone." SuSp, *tr. by* Michael E. Workman

"Spring breeze stirs a springtime heart." SuSp, *tr. by* Ronald C. Miao

"Young swallows trill their new tune." SuSp, *tr. by* Michael E. Workman

Summer. SuSp, *tr. by* Michael E. Workman

U

U bet u wer. To a Poet I Knew. Jewel C. Latimore. PoBA

U feel that way sometimes. Mixed Sketches. Haki Madhbouti. BPo; TAP

U.N. Environmental Sabbath Program. *Unknown.*

"Great Spirit." FHYEP

"Great Spirit, whose dry lands thirst, help us to find." FHYEP

"We have forgotten who we are." FHYEP

"We join with the earth and with each other." FHYEP

U Name This One. Carolyn M. Rodgers. BlSi; NMM-2; PoBA

U r n / u r n / u r n. Garden Poem. Ian Hamilton Finlay. OBGa

U. S. 1946 King's X. Robert Frost. CrDW; NIP-4

U. S. Sailor with the Japanese Skull, The. Winfield Townley Scott. LiTM

U-24 Anchors off New Orleans. Turner Cassity. MT

UBI AMOR IBI OCULUS EST. (LL) Canto 90. Ezra Pound. APSN; VGW

Ubi Sunt? *Unknown.* MiEL; PoE

("Where beth they biforen us weren?") MiEL

Ubi Sunt Qui ante Nos Fuerunt? [or Contempt of the World]. *Unknown.* EBEV; HAP; NoP-4; WeW-3

("In joye withouten hende. / Amen.") (LL) NoP-4

Ubi Sunt Qui ante Nos Fuerunt? *Unknown, Latin.* WeW-3, *tr. by* George Perkins

("Where are those that were before us.") WeW-3, *tr. by* George Perkins

Ubique. Joshua Sylvester. OBEV

Ubiquity of the Need for Love, The. Ron Koertge. IFJA

Ubu Cocu. Alfred Jarry.

Chanson du Décervelage, La. CBNP, *tr. by* Cyril Connolly *and* Simon Taylor

Uccello. Gregory Corso. NeAP; PoM

Udude. Pol N Ndu. PBMAP

Ugliest little boy. The Life of Lincoln West. Gwendolyn Brooks. NoAM

Ugly Child, The. Elizabeth Jennings. NOxBChV

Ugly creatures, ugly grunting creatures. Suffering. Miroslav Holub, *Czech.* PoSu, *tr. by* Ian Milner *and* George Theiner

Ugly Girl, The. Nikolai Alekseievich Zabolotsky, *Russian.* TCRP, *tr. by* Daniel Weissbort

Ugly old man, An. No Great Matter. David Lawson. VGW

Ugolino. Dante. FaBoPV, *tr. by* Seamus Heaney *Fr.* Inferno. NAWM-1, *tr. by* John Ciardi *Fr.* Divina Commedia.

Uguisu has not come, The. Akiko Yosano, *Japanese.* OHMPJ, *tr. by* Kenneth Rexroth

Uguisu on the flowering plum, The. *Unknown, Japanese.* OHMPJ, *tr. by* Kenneth Rexroth

Uguisu sleeps in the bamboo grove, The. Kenneth Rexroth. APSN *Fr.* The Love Poems of Marichiko.

Uh nebah cross dese courts agen ess uh live un hundred yares. Lizzie and Joe in Court. Edward Cordle. PBCV

Ujamaa. Wole Soyinka. PBMAP *Fr.* The Shuttle in the Crypt.

Ukranian Pastorals. Steve Orlen. WeT

Ula Masondo's Dream. William Plomer. MoBS

Ulalume [or Ulalume—a Ballad]. Edgar Allan Poe. APN-1; AWP; AmPP; ImPo; MeMAP; NAAL-1; NOBA; OxBA; TAP

(To————. Ulalume: A Ballad.) NAAL-3

(Ulalume.) NCAP

Ulcerated tooth keeps me awake, there is. Letters from a Father. Mona Van Duyn. FYAP; NoP-4

Ulinda. David Campbell. CBAP

Ulrich von Hutten's Song. Ulrich von Hutten, *German.* GePo, *tr. by* Catherine Winkworth

Ulster. Rudyard Kipling. FaBoPV; IIP

Ulster Names. John Hewitt. BiHa

Ulster Twilight, An. Seamus Heaney. CIP 2; PBCIP

Ulster Unionist Walks the Streets of London, An. Tom Paulin. PNI

Ulsterman, An. "Lynn Doyle." TIRV

Ulstir fur fucks sake. Tom Leonard. NBrP *Fr.* Ghostie Men.

Ultima Ratio Reagan. Howard Nemerov. VGW

Ultima Ratio Regum. Stephen Spender. CMoP; ImPo; LiTM; OAEL-2; OBWP; PoWW; SAGP

("Lying under the olive tree, O world, O death?") (LL) SAGP

("Lying under the olive trees, O world, O death?") (LL) AF; NoP-4

Ultimate Antientropy, The. Theodore Weiss. NoAM

Ultimate Argument. Ion Caraion, *Romanian.* AF, *tr. by* Marguerite Dorian *and* Elliott B. Urdang

Ultimate Exile IV. Ralph Nixon Currey. PeSA

Ultimate Poem Is Abstract, The. Wallace Stevens. PoA

Ultimatum: Kid to Kid. Langston Hughes. NOxBChV

Ulumbo, a Cat. Rutger Kopland, *Dutch.* VCWP, *tr. by* James Brockway

Ulysses. Gwendolyn Brooks.
    Religion. OxWW

Ulysses. Robert Graves. CBLP; CMoP; EP; FaBoTw; MoP; NoAM

Ulysses. John Holloway. PFE

Ulysses. James Joyce.
    "Bronze by gold heard the hoofirons, steelyringing." PFTM

Ulysses. Robert Lowell. NAAL-2

Ulysses. Tennyson. APAD; AWP; CABP; ClHu; EBEV; EBVVPR; EnVR; FHYEP; FaPoR; HAP; HeIP-4; HoPM; ImPo; InPK-6; InPS-3; NAEL-2; NAWM-2; NIP-4; NOBE; NOBVV; NoP-4; OAEL-2; OxAEP-2; PFE; PoE; PoPoPo; PoRA; Poetr; SAGP; SCGP; SCV; SoSe-8; TFi; TRP; UnPo; WeW-3

Ulysses Advises Achilles. Shakespeare. ImPo *Fr.* Troilus and Cressida.

Ulysses and His Dog. Homer. *Fr.* Odyssey. NAWM-1, *tr. by* Robert Fitzgerald

Ulysses and the Siren [*or* Syren]. Samuel Daniel. HAP; NAEL-1; NOBE; NoP-4; OBEV; OxAEP-1; PoE; PoEL-2

Ulysses in the Waves. Homer. *Fr.* Odyssey. NAWM-1, *tr. by* Robert Fitzgerald

Ulysses Insults over the Cyclops. Homer. NOSC, *tr. by* George Chapman *Fr.* Odyssey. NAWM-1, *tr. by* Robert Fitzgerald

Ulysses Invokes the Dead. Homer. NOSC, *tr. by* George Chapman *Fr.* Odyssey. NAWM-1, *tr. by* Robert Fitzgerald

Ulysses Leaves the Nymph Calypso. Homer. *Fr.* Odyssey. NAWM-1, *tr. by* Robert Fitzgerald
    "Great wave drove at him with toppling crest, A." GrIP, *tr. by* Robert Fitzgerald

Ulysses' Library. David Daiches. PoA

Ulysses Reunited with Penelope. Homer. NOSC, *sect.* XXIV *Fr.* Odyssey. NAWM-1, *tr. by* Robert Fitzgerald

Umber was painting of a lion [*or* Lyon] fierce. Upon Umber: Epigram. Robert Herrick. CaPo

Umberto / Always worked hard. In the Winter. Sir Osbert Sitwell. OBGa

Umbrella, The. Ann Stanford. NYBP

Umbrella, An. Gertrude Stein. TTTS *Fr.* Tender Buttons.

Umbrella / And a raincoat, An. Conversation. Buson, *Japanese.* NTCP

Umpteen hundred and eternity. (LL) Carol for the Last Christmas Eve. Norman Nicholson. NOxBChV

Un-American Investigators. Langston Hughes. BPo

Un-American Women, The. John Tranter. BMAP

Un is okay. Zen Americana. Paula Gunn Allen. PoPoPo

Un Marin naufrageé (de Doncastre). Vers Nonsensiques. George Du Maurier. OBCoV

Un-Now. Daniil Kharms, *Russian.* TCRP, *tr. by* Bradley Jordan

Una Bhan. Tomas Mac Coisdealbhaigh, *Irish.* NOIV, *tr. by* Thomas Kinsella

Una fair, my flower of the amber tresses. Una Bhan. Tomas Mac Coisdealbhaigh, *Irish.* NOIV, *tr. by* Thomas Kinsella

Unable. Raymond Roseliep. HA

Unable, Father, Still, to Disavow. Richard Moore. Son *Fr.* Word from the Hills.

Unable to sleep / I gaze at the flowers of the bush clover. Ise Tayu, *Japanese.* WPJ, *tr. by* Kenneth Rexroth *and* Ikuko Atsumi

Unalterables. Arthur Gregor. NYBP

Unanimal mankind(and not until). (LL) When serpents bargain for the right to squirm. E. E. Cummings. MeMAP; TwCP

Unanimity Has Been Achieved, Not a Dot Less for Its Accidentalness. Bob Kaufman. NAAAL

Unanswerable Apology for the Rich, An. Mary Barber. ECWP

Unanswered. Yannis Ritsos, *Greek.* AF, *tr. by* Edmund Keeley

Unanswered yet the prayer your lips have pleaded. Pray without Ceasing. Ophelia Guyon Browning. BLPA

Unappeasable sky. Stanley Kunitz. *See* Robin Redbreast.

Unarmed Combat. Henry Reed. *Fr.* Lessons of the War. HeIP-4; OBWP

Unanswered Letter. Tess Gallagher. NIP-4

Unavoidable violence. What We Learned. Fanny Howe. FTOS

Unawakend, unwilling / to sleep or wake. (LL) Tribal Memories. Robert Duncan. APSN; NOBA

Unawakened, sweet / women. (LL) Belly Dancer. Diane Wakoski. NALW; NoAM

Unawares. Emma A. Lent. PoLF

Unawkward Singer, The. David Ferry. PFE

Unbeliever, The. Elizabeth Bishop. NAAL-2; NoAM

Unbending Prayer. René Char, *French.* AF, *tr. by* Mary Ann Caws

Unbeseechable, The. Frances Darwin Cornford. MoBrPo

Unblinding, The. Laurence Lieberman. NYBP

Unborn. John Le Gay Brereton. NOBAu

Unborn, The. Thomas Hardy. CMoP

Unborn Child, An. Derek Mahon. CABP; PNI

Unborn Child Elegy. Margaret Gibson.
    "Today snow sparks the air like mica—the sun's." CrSp

Unborn children are rowing out to the far edge of the sky, The. Cloud River. Charles Wright. MT

Unbosoming. "Michael Field." CPO; VWP

Unbounded is thy range; with varied style. The Stormy Hebrides. William Collins. NOBE *Fr.* An Ode on the Popular Superstitions of the Highlands of Scotland. NOEC; OAEL-1; OxAEP-1

Unbounded thing we know. (LL) In the Field. Richard Wilbur. NAAL-2; NYBP

Unbowel the meaning. Paul Brown. NBrP *Fr.* De Rebus.

Unbridled licentiousness with no holds barred. Reading Pornography in Old Age. Howard Nemerov. NoAM

Unbridled waters. (LL) Beasts in their major freedom / Slumber in peace tonight. Richard Wilbur. APo

Unburn the boat, rebuild the bridge. Recension Day. Duncan Forbes. APAD

Uncarved Block professes no activity, The. Inscribed on the Painting "Pleasures of the Lute by the River." Lin Hung, *Chinese.* SuSp, *tr. by* Irving Y. Lo

Uncertain Admission. Frances Bazil. LiLi

Uncertain-aged Miss Thereabouts. Smithereens. D. G. Rossetti. NOBVV

Uncertain Battle, The. David Gascoyne. PoWW

Uncertain Steps. Richard Caddel. NBrP

Uncertainty, O my delight. The Crayfish. Guillaume Apollinaire, *French.* APo, *tr. by* Roger Shattuck

Uncertainty of the Poet, The. Wendy Cope. OPOU

Uncessant minutes, whil'st you move you tell. To His Watch, When He Could Not Sleep. Edward Herbert, 1st Baron Herbert of Cherbury. NOBE; PoEL-2

Unchained Melody. Gillian Conoley. CMAP

Unchangeable, The. Shakespeare. *See* Sonnet 109.

Unchristian Jacobin whoever. Ode to a Jacobin. *Unknown.* UV

Uncircumcised, The. (LL) A Poor Christian Looks at the Ghetto. Czeslaw Milosz, *Polish.* VCWP, *tr. by* Czeslaw Milosz; HP

Uncle. Julia Kasdorf. PBCAP

Uncle. Philip Levine. NNaP

Uncle Alfred's Long Jump. Gareth Owen. OBSP

Uncle an' Aunt. William Barnes. NOBVV

Uncle Ananias. Edwin Arlington Robinson. MoAmPo; NIP-4

Uncle Bill had been there. Almost Going. David Huddle. PBCAP

Uncle Bull-Boy. June Jordan. PoBA

Uncle Devereux would blend to the one color. (LL) My Last Afternoon with Uncle Devereux Winslow. Robert Lowell. NAAL-2; NoP-4; VGW

Uncle Dog; the Poet at 9. Robert Sward. CoAP; VGW

Uncle Henry. W. H. Auden. NOBL; PeLV

Uncle Ike's Holiday. Priscilla Jane Thompson. CBWP-2

Uncle Iv Surveys His Domain from His Rocker. Jonathan Williams. NBLV; OBAL

Uncle Jim. Countee Cullen. GT; NAAL-2

Uncle Jimmie's Yarn. Priscilla Jane Thompson. CBWP-2

Uncle Remus and His Friends. Joel Chandler Harris.
    My Honey, My Love. FaBoBe

Uncle Remus: His Songs and His Sayings. Joel Chandler Harris.
    Aphorisms. CrDW
    Plantation Proverbs. CrDW

Uncle Rube on the Race Problem. Clara Ann Thompson. CBWP-2

Uncle Rube to the Young People. Clara Ann Thompson. CBWP-2

Uncle Rube's Defense. Clara Ann Thompson. CBWP-2

Uncle Sam. Kenneth Rexroth. *Fr.* A Bestiary. OBAL

Uncle Sam's Soliloquy. George Sands Johnson. PWR

Uncle Time is a ole, ole man. Dennis Scott. PBCV

Uncle Tom. Langston Hughes. SAmP

Unclean spirits cry out in the body, The. The Guest Ellen at the Supper for Street People. David Ferry. NIP-4

Unclean, unclean: my Lord, undone, all vile. Meditation 26. Edward Taylor. NAAL-1 *Fr.* Preparatory Meditations Before My Approach to the Lord's Supper.

Uncles. Nikky Finney. ISC

Uncle's First Rabbit. Lorna Dee Cervantes. NoAM

Uncloistered Virtue. Milton. NOSC *Fr.* Book IX. FHYEP; NAEL-1; NAWM-1; OAEL-1 *Fr.* Paradise Lost.

Unconcerned, The. Thomas Flatman. FaBoCh
    (Unconcerned, The: Song.) NOSC

Unconscious came a beauty. May Swenson. VCAP

Uncontrollable mystery on the bestial floor, The. (LL) The Magi. W. B. Yeats. CMoP; ChIV-2; GI; HAP; InPK-6; NoAM; OAEL-2; OxAEP-2; PChr; PoA; PoE; TRP; TrCP

Uncontrollable night, An. Fist Fight. Doug Cockrell. Poetsp

Uncool. Victoria Rathbun. EC2

Uncounted are counting, The. Report from an Unappointed Committee. William Stafford. CDa

Uncurbed in us, where fires are fanned. (LL) The Charioteer of Delphi. James Merrill. GS; GrIP

"Und now Ladies und Gentlemun, *Der Peedles!*." Fab Four Tour Deutschland: Hamburg, 1961. David Wojahn. PBCAP *Fr.* Mystery Train: A Sequence.

Undated dreams: the sea at Heringsdorf. Dreams in German. "David Martin." NOBAu

Undead, The. Richard Wilbur. CAPP-1; CoAP; CoAmPo; OxBC

Undead White European Male. Elton Glaser. BAP-95

Undefined Tenderness, An. Joel Oppenheimer. VGW

Undeodorized and radiant in rags. The First of the Month. Adrian C. Louis. NAmP90

Under. Raymond Roseliep. HA

Under. Sir John Collings Squire. FaBoTw

Under a bent when the night was deep. William Morris. PChr *Fr.* The Earthly Paradise.

Under a burning tropic sun. The Color Sergeant. James Weldon Johnson. GT

Under a ceiling high Christmas tree. Filipino Boogie. Jessica Hagedorn. UnSA

Under a Certain Little Star. Wislawa Szymborska, *Polish.* VCWP, *tr.* by Magnus J. Krynski *and* Robert A. Maguire

Under a dung-cake. Fable. D. J. Opperman, *Afrikaans.* PeSA; PeSAV, *tr.* by Jack Cope

Under a full moon. Thomas A. Clark. NBrP *Fr.* Twenty Poems.

Under a futile Torah. Both Your Mothers. Jerzy Ficowski, *Polish.* HP, *tr.* by Keith Bosley; PoSu

Under a hill. *Unknown.* OxNR

Under a hillock, in a field. The Judge. Yaroslav Vasilevich Smelyakov, *Russian.* TCRP, *tr.* by Simon Franklin *and* Albert C. Todd

Under a Lady's Picture. Edmund Waller. EnLoPo

Under a lawne, than skyes more cleare. Upon Roses. Robert Herrick. SeCP

Under a low sky. Silence. William Carlos Williams. SAmP

Under a night sky growing bright with stars. (LL) Lufthansa. John Tranter. BMAP; NOBAu

Under a sky, in a garden, there are serious women and beautiful men, were talking. Sailed. Aaron Shurin. FTOS

Under a sky studded with asterisks. On the Night in Question. Patricia Goedicke. TAP

Under a sky that never cared less. William Stafford. *See* At the Bomb Testing Site.

Under a sky the color of pea soup. The Seven of Pentacles. Marge Piercy. CrSp *Fr.* Laying Down the Tower.

Under a splintered mast. A Talisman. Marianne Moore. MoAmPo

Under a spreading chestnut tree. The Village Blacksmith. Henry Wadsworth Longfellow. APN-1; AiP; CTV; ChAP; EBEvV; FaBoBe; FaPoR; OBAL; OBCA; PAR; PWR; UV

Under a starry sky I was taking a walk. Temptation. Czeslaw Milosz, *Polish.* GI, *tr.* by Czeslaw Milosz *and* Lillian Vallee

Under a swaying. El Dorado. Richard Ryan. BIrV

Under a tent of stars a lonely man. A Romance to Night. Georg Trakl, *German.* AF, *tr.* by Simko, Daniel

Under a throne I saw a virgin sit. Greville Fulke. FaBoPV

Under a toadstool. The Elf and the Dormouse. Oliver Herford. FPC; FaBoBe

Under a tree. Among the poems I wrote with many pictures spread out before me[2]. Masaoka Shiki, *Japanese.* MJT, *tr.* by Ueda, Makoto

Under a white coverlet of snow. January. John Heath-Stubbs. OBCP

Under a Wiltshire Apple Tree. Anna Bunston DeBary. CH

Under Ben Bulben. W. B. Yeats. CMoP; HAP; IIP; LiTM; MoP; NAEL-2; NoAM; NoP-4; OxBTC

"Cast a cold eye." FaBoEE

"Irish poets, learn your trade." OxAEP-2

"Under bare Ben Bulben's head." WeW-3

Under black yews that protect them. Owls. Charles Baudelaire, *French.* APo, *tr.* by Richard Howard

Under bright city lights. Underground. Conrad Kent Rivers. SeSe

Under Cancer. John Hollander. CoAP

Under clouds, at the tag end of August. Lighting the Night Sky. Kenneth O. Hanson. FYAP

Under cracking pieces of the moon, eelpout. Spawning in Northern Minnesota. David McElroy. AmPA

Under every cathedral. The Invention of Fire. Andrew Taylor. CBAP

Under God's violent unsleeping eye. Difference. T. Harri Jones. OBWVE

Under Grand Central's tattered vault. Broadway. Mark Doty. WWSi

Under great yellow flags and banners of the ancient cold. The Shadow of Cain. Dame Edith Sitwell. OxBTC

Under her gown the girl is. The Only Daughter. Laura Riding Jackson. FuPo

Under her solemn fillet saw the scorn. (LL) Days. Ralph Waldo Emerson. APN-1; AmPP; ColAP; HAP; HeIP-4; MeMAP; NAAL-1; NAAL-3; NCAP; NOBA; NoP-4; OxBA; OxBSP; PAR; PFE; PoE; PoEL-4; TAP; TFi

Under her thin night dress? (LL) Touching/Not Touching: My Mother. Toi Derricotte. DeD

Under his Cross[e]. (LL) A Hymn[e] to God the Father. Ben Jonson. BeJo; NOSC; NoP-4; OxAEP-1; Poetr; SeCP; TrCP

Under his view the wind. The View. Howard Nemerov. NYBP

Under House Arrest. Dennis Brutus. AF

Under it a puddle of blood. Pocket Watch. Novica Tadic, *Serbo-Croatian.* HSix, *tr.* by Charles Simic

Under it out toward the island. (LL) Henry's Understanding. John Berryman. MoP; NOBA; NoAM

Under its cloak of lies. (LL) Summer Oracle. Audre Lorde. BlSi; PoBA

Under its mattresses of vines. (LL) Vacancy in the Park. Wallace Stevens. LCAP-2; SAmP

Under its spreading bankruptcy. The Splendid Bankrupt. Arthur A. Sykes. UV

Under junk heaps and stripped and burning cars. To Softness. Laurie Sheck. CrSp

Under Leafy Bowers. Judah Al-Harizi, *Hebrew.* TrJP

Under ledges. Foster Jewell. HA

Under mercury light the little pup strives. A sinister shadow ducks under the curb. Reveille. John Godfrey. FTOS

Under Milk Wood. Dylan Thomas.

Johnnie Crack and Flossie Snail. OTCP

Under Mr. Hales Picture. Anne King. KTR

Under my feet the moon. Brimming Water. Tu Fu, *Chinese.* OHPC, *tr.* by Kenneth Rexroth

Under my window. Letter in Winter. Raymond R. Patterson. PoBA

Under my window-ledge the waters race. Coole Park and Ballylee, 1931. W. B. Yeats. CMoP; GTBS-P; NOIV; NoAM; OBGa; OBMV

Under new management, Your Majesty. John Berryman. *Fr.* Eleven Addresses to the Lord. OxBC

Under other circumstances—you didn't. To a Friend. Frank Stewart. EC2

Under Sedation. Alec Derwent Hope. BMAP

Under silver wing. Crossing Nation. Allen Ginsberg. AiP

Under Sirius. W. H. Auden. FaBoMo

Under Sorrow's Sign. Gofraidh Fionn O'Dalaigh, *Irish.* BIrV, *tr.* by John Montague

Under Stars. Tess Gallagher. InPK-6

Under striped flutter of awnings, they have come. Renoir. Rosanna Warren. GS

Under thatched eaves people are quiet. Tune: "Immortal at the Magpie Bridge"—On Hearing the Cuckoo at Night. Lu Yu, *Chinese.* SuSp, *tr.* by James J. Y. Liu

Under the African lintel, Table Mountain. David Wright. PeSA *Fr.* South African Broadsheets.

Under the after-sunset sky. Two Pewits. Edward Thomas. CH

Under the almond tree. In Kensington Gardens. Arthur Symons. EnLoPo

Under the Anheuser Bush. Andrew B. Sterling. OBAL

Under the Arc de Triomphe: October 17. Marilyn Hacker. PoA

Under the arch of life, where love and death. Soul's Beauty. D. G. Rossetti. OBEV; OxAEP-2 *Fr.* The House of Life.

Under the bamboo. Sung by Wauchope and Horsfall. T. S. Eliot. *Fr.* Two Songs from *Sweeny Agonistes*. UnPo *Fr.* Sweeney Agonistes.

Under the big 500-watted lamps, in the huge sawdusted [government inspected slaughter-house]. The Slaughter-House. Alfred Hayes. ImPo; PFE

Under the blue sky. Tanka. Mori Ōgai, *Japanese.* MJT, *tr.* by Makoto Ueda

Under the boardwalk. Alan Pizzarelli. HA

Under the Boathouse. David Bottoms. MT

Under the bram bush. *Unknown.* FaBoVe

Under the bronze crown. A Baroque Wall-Fountain in the Villa Sciarra. Richard Wilbur. AmPP; ColAP; GS; NAAL-2; NYBP; NoP-4; OBGa; Poetr; TwCP; VCAP

Under the centre of the sky. Death Song. *Unknown, Ojibwa Native American.* APN-2, *tr.* by Henry Rowe Schoolcraft

Under the cold eyes, the cat eyes of those young. To Some Young Communists from an Older Socialist. Naomi Mitchison. WPN

Under the concrete benches. Weed Puller. Theodore Roethke. AmPP; HCAP; NAAL-2

Under the cone of flurried light. The Underworld. Garrett Kaoru Hongo. NAmP90; WWSi

Under the cypresses the air is still. A Life of Intimate Fleeing. Robert Kelly. FTOS

Under the death of winter's leaves he lies. Metho Drinker. Judith Wright. BMAP

Under the Drooping Willow Tree. *Unknown.* OxBoLi

Under the dry swath. Snake. Desanka Maksimovic, *Serbo-Croatian.* HSix, *tr. by* Charles Simic

Under the dusty print of hobnailed boot. Country Press. Rosemary Dobson. FaBoWP; NOBAu

Under the easy glide of water. Spell. Anuradha Mahapatra, *Bengali.* OMIP, *tr. by* Jyotirmoy Dutta *and* Carolyne Wright

Under the eaves, their back burned by the sun as hot as fire. Winter. Fan Ch'eng-ta. SuSp, *tr. by* Irving Y. Lo *Fr.* Seasonal Poems on Fields and Gardens.

Under the Edge of February. Jayne Cortez. BISi

Under the Eildon Tree. Sydney Goodsir Smith.
Slugabed. FaBoTC

Under the El on Sunday afternoon. Aside. Alan Dugan. PoA

Under the evening moon. Avedik Issahakian. ChAP

Under the Eyes. Tom Paulin. CIP-2; PNI

Under the financier's. The Jersey Marsh. David Galler. NYBP

Under the fire escape, crouched, one knee in cinders. The Desk. David Bottoms. MT; WeW-3

Under the foreign yoke, they lived in shame. Mourning a Hero. Nhu'o'ng Tống, *Vietnamese.* AVP, *tr. by* Huỳnh Sanh Thông

Under the forest, where the day is dark. The Manzanita. Yvor Winters. VGW

Under the French horns of a November afternoon. A Man in Blue. James Schuyler. FTOS; PmAP

Under the great lens of heaven, caught. Snapshot. Charles Wright. WeT

Under the green hedges, after the snow. Violets. John Moultrie. BoTP

Under the green lamp-light her letter there. Letter of a Mother. Robert Penn Warren. MoAmPo

Under the Greenwood Tree. "Hugh MacDiarmid," *after the Cretan.* OBVE

Under the greenwood tree. Song. Shakespeare. APAD; AWP; BoTP; CH; CTC; CTV; EBEvV; FaBoBe; GTBS-P; HoPM; ImPo; InPS-3; NAEL-1; NoP-4; NoSic; OAEL-1; OBEV; SCGP; TTTS; UnPo *Fr.* As You Like It.

Under the guns' noise. (LL) First Time In. Ivor Gurney. FaBoVe

Under the heaven of our holy ruler, all things turn to spring. Su Tung-p'o, *Chinese.* CoBCP, *tr. by* Burton Watson

Under the hemlocks Fancy came. On the Concord River. Henrietta Cordelia Ray. CBWP-3

Under the Hill. Richard Eberhart. PoA

Under the Hill. Daryl Hine. MoCV

Under the hills and veins of water. Last Letter to Pablo. Pat Lowther. NOBC

Under the hive-like dome the stooping haunted readers. The British Museum Reading Room. Louis MacNeice. LiTM; MoBrPo; NOBE

Under the horizontal snow. (LL) The Snow Storm. Edna St. Vincent Millay. NAAL-2; PoA

Under the house, between the road the sea-cliff. Grass on the Cliff. Robinson Jeffers. PoA *Fr.* The Trumpet.

Under the Ice. Stewart Conn. FaBoTC

Under the ice with its bouldery death's faces. The Bread Hot from the Oven. John Thompson. NOBC

Under the levys grene. (LL) My Fair Lady. *Unknown.* EnLoPo; OxBoLi; PoEL-1

Under the Light, yet under. Emily Dickinson. FaBoVe; NCAP

Under the Lindens [*or* Lime Tree]. Walther von der Vogelweide, *German.* CTC, *tr. by* Ford Madox Ford; GePo, *tr. by* Frederick Goldin; GBL; OBVE, *tr. by* Thomas Lovell Beddoes

Under the Locust Blossoms. Frederick Goddard Tuckerman. NOBA

Under the long dark boughs, like jewels red. Cherry Robbers. D. H. Lawrence. MoBrPo

Under the Long-Khánh reign when Trần held sway. The Constant Mouse. *Unknown, Vietnamese.* AVP, *tr. by* Huỳnh Sanh Thông

Under the lucent glass. In the Egyptian Museum. Janet Lewis. NYBP

Under the mattress was a day-old newspaper rolled into a scroll. Spontaneous Combustion. David Lehman. NAmP90

Under the Maud Moon. Galway Kinnell. NNaP
"Round– / cheeked girlchild comes awake, A." MoLi

Under the Microscope. Slavko Mihalic. PoSu, *tr. by* Charles Simic

Under the Mirabeau Bridge the Seine / Flows and [*or* with] our love[s]. The Mirabeau Bridge. Guillaume Apollinaire, *French.* BoLoP, *tr. by* Quentin Stevenson; OBVE, *tr. by* W. S. Merwin

Under the Mistletoe. Countee Cullen. PChr

Under the mountain, as when first I knew. Frederick Goddard Tuckerman. APN-2; HAP; TAP *Fr.* Sonnets.

Under the neon sign he stands. The Drive-In. R. S. Gwynn. RA

Under the new pond-dam. Looking Before and After. Carter Revard. HATNAP

Under the Oak Table. Colleen J. McElroy. GT

Under the oak tree, oak tree. *Unknown, Spanish.* BoWoP, *tr. by* Willis Barnstone

Under the olives, in whose night they sleep. (LL) Table-Birds. Kenneth Mackenzie. BMAP

Under the parabola of a ball. How to Kill. Keith Douglas. FaBoMo; NOBE; PoWW; RB

Under the pines I questioned the boy. Looking for a Recluse but Failing to Find Him. Chia Tao, *Chinese.* CoBCP, *tr. by* Burton Watson

Under the pink quilted covers. The Fortress. Anne Sexton. LiTM

Under the plum-blossoms are nightingales. Desolation. Amy Lowell. PoA

Under the pond, among rocks. The Dragonfly. Howard Nemerov. PoA

Under the Pondweed. *Unknown.* AWP, *tr. by* Helen Waddell *Fr.* Shi King.

Under the Pot. Robert Graves. FaBoEE

Under the quince tree. Bible, *O.T.* PBWP, *tr. by* Marcia Falk *Fr.* The Song of Songs. AWP

Under the rain's broken fingers. (LL) The Elements of San Joaquin. Gary Soto. PaTW

Under the red-and-white striped awning. The Luncheon of the Boating Party. Leon Stokesbury. MT

Under the red Korean banner. The Inupiat Christmas Pageant. Peggy Shumaker. PBCAP

Under the rock, in the sand and the gravel run. Charles Wright. *Fr.* Skins. HCAP

Under the roof and the roof's shadow turns. The Merry-go-round. Rilke, *German.* WeW-3, *tr. by* C. F. MacIntyre

Under the running tap that are not the hands of a child. (LL) Soap Suds. Louis MacNeice. FaBoMo; NAEL-2; NOIV; NTP; SCV

Under the sagging clotheslines of crepe paper. The Best Slow Dancer. David Wagoner. NoAM; VCAP

Under the scarlet-licking leaves. My Many-Coated Man. Laurie Lee. NYBP

Under the scraggy fir tree. Boris Petrovich Kornilov, *Russian.* TCRP, *tr. by* Bernard Meares

Under the separated leaves of shade. A Man Meets a Woman in the Street. Randall Jarrell. NoP-4

Under the September Peach. Robert Wallace. Son

Under the shadow of the gloomy night. Prologue. Samuel Rowlands. NOSC

Under the shuddering eyelid. Maudgalyâyana Saw Hell. Gary Snyder. *Fr.* Burning. NeAP; PoM *Fr.* Myths and Texts.

Under the sickly cressets' languid beams. Femmes Damnées. Charles Baudelaire. CPO, *tr. by* Carlyle Ferren MacIntyre *Fr.* Les Fleurs du Mal.

Under the sloped snow. As Children Together. Carolyn Forché. NoAM; OxWW

Under the slumber and winter of a silent night. In Lord Carpenter's Country. Barry O. Higgs. PeSA

Under the sovereign crests of dead volcanoes. On a Bougainvillaea Vine at the Summer Palace [*or* in Haiti]. Barbara Howes. MoAmPo; NYBP

Under the Stairs. Frank Ormsby. PBCIP

Under the stars the great wise Worm lay dead;. Fafnir. Alec Derwent Hope. BMAP

Under the sun is nothing new? To the Archdeacon. George Farewell. NOEC

Under the surface of flux and of fear there is an underground movement. Louis MacNeice. LiTM *Fr.* The Kingdom.

Under the tall black sky you look out of your body. Endless. Muriel Rukeyser. NYBP

Under the thick beams of that swirly smoking light. The Examination. W. D. Snodgrass. CAPP-1; CoAmPo; SAGP

Under the too white marmoreal Lincoln Memorial. The March 1. Robert Lowell. PoPoPo

Under the Vulture-Tree. David Bottoms. MT

Under the waning moon. Starting at Dawn. Sun Yün-feng, *Chinese.* PBWP, *tr. by* Kenneth Rexroth *and* Ling Chung

Under the Waterfall. Thomas Hardy. BoLoP; CTC; NAEL-2; NoP-4

Under the white man's menace, out of time. (LL) Outcast. Claude McKay. NAAAL

Under the white silence of the great gumtree avenue. A Finished Gentleman. Geoffrey Dutton. NOBAu

Under the wide and starry sky. Requiem. Robert Louis Stevenson. APAD; EBEvV; EBVV; FaPoR; MoBrPo; NBLV; NOBE; NOBVV; NTP; OBEV; OBNC; PoLF; PoRA; SAGP; SCGP; TFi

Under the Willow Shades. Sir William Davenant. BoLoP

Under the willow the willow. Recruiting Drive. Charles Causley. OxBTC

Under the Willows. James Russell Lowell.

    "May is a pious fraud of the almanac." APN-1

Under the wind I saw. Jean Daive, *French*. MFP, *tr. by* Martin Sorrell

Under the window, on a dusty ledge. Gardener. Mark Van Doren. GaP

Under the Window: Ouro Prêto. Elizabeth Bishop. NYBP; VCAP

Under the Woods. Edward Thomas. CH

Under the yew-tree's heavy weight. Les Hiboux. Charles Baudelaire. AWP, *tr. by* Arthur Symons

Under these words. Bi-lingual. Maria Jastrzebska. NBrP

Under this heap of stones interred lies. Upon Stephen Stoned. Sir John Suckling. ChIV-2

Under this Marble, or under this Sill. Epitaph on Himself. Alexander Pope. FaBoEE

Under this plaque I lie, the famous woman. *Unknown, Greek*. GrAn, *tr. by* Peter Jay

Under this real estate—squared street on street. Asphodel. David Malouf. CBAP

Under this stone doth lie. An Epitaph upon Thomas, Lord Fairfax. George, 2d Duke of Buckingham Villiers. NOSC

Under this stone / Lies a Reverend Drone. An Epitaph upon That Profound and Learned Casuist, the Late Ordinary of Newgate. Thomas Brown. OBSV

Under this stone, reader, survey. On Sir John Vanbrugh [Architect]. Abel Evans. FaBoEE

Under this stone there lieth at rest. An Epitaph of Sir Thomas Gravener, [Knight]. Sir Thomas Wyatt. SiPS

Under this sun voices on the radio run down. The Complete Birth if the Cool. C. D. Wright. LCAP-2

Under walls white as a birch forest the ferns of paintings grow. In an. Painter. Zbigniew Herbert, *Polish*. AF, *tr. by* John Carpenter *and* Bogdana Carpenter

Under what beechen shade, or silent oak. Sonnet; A Still Place. "Barry Cornwall." NOBRP

Under Which Lyre, a Reactionary Tract for the Times. W. H. Auden. MoBrPo; NOBL; PeLV

Under willows among the graves. Christina Rossetti. VWP

Under yonder beech-tree single on the green-sward, *Longer vers. (1878)*. Love in the Valley. George Meredith. EBVV; EnVR; NOBE; OAEL-2; OBEV

Under you, over you, on you. Ah. Robin Blaser. FTOS

Under your Milky Way. Return of the Goddess [Artemis]. Robert Graves. PoA

Underdeveloped Country, An. D. J. Enright. NOBL

Underfoot rotten boards, forest rubble, bones. Remains of an Indian Village. Alfred Wellington Purdy. NOBC

Undergone swamp ticket relative. Twenties 26. Jackson MacLow. PmAP

Underground. May Kendall. VWP

Underground. Conrad Kent Rivers. SeSe

Underground Stream, The. James Dickey. NOBA

Undergrowth's a conveyance of butterflies, The. Hope's Okay. A. R. Ammons. HCAP

Underneath a cypress shade, the Queen of Love sat mourning. *Unknown*. GBL

Underneath an old oak tree. The Raven. Coleridge. NOxBChV

Underneath my lids another eye has opened. From the Prison House. Adrienne Rich. NNaP

Underneath Oblivion. Yannis Ritsos, *Greek*. AF, *tr. by* Minas Savas

Underneath the Archers *or* What's All This about Walter's Willy? Kit Wright. OBCoV

Underneath the growing grass. The Bourne. Christina Rossetti. OBNC

Underneath the tree on some. Like They Say. Robert Creeley. BLT

Underneath the water-weeds. The Tadpole. E. E. Gould. BoTP

Underneath this greedy stone. The Epitaph of Erotion. Leigh Hunt. OBCVT

Underneath this marble stone / Lie two beauties join'd in one. Epitaph of Pyramus and Thisbe. Abraham Cowley. EnLoPo; FaBoEE

Underneath this myrtle shade. The Epicure. Abraham Cowley. OxAEP-1

Underneath this sable hearse [*or* herse]. On the Countess Dowager of Pembroke. William Browne. AWP; FaBoEE; HAP; NOBE; NOSC; NoP-4; OAEL-1; OBEV; PoEL-2; PoRA; SCGP; TFi

Underneath this wooden cross there lies. Epitaph. Karl Shapiro. *Fr.* Elegy for a Dead Soldier. HAP; LiTM; OBWP; OxBA

Undersong of terrible holy joy, An. (LL) The Old Women. George Mackay Brown. NoP-4; OxBS

Understand, he is naked in the sea. The Loved One. Joseph Hansen. NYBP

Understand that they were sitting just inside the door. The State of the Nation. Kenneth Patchen. CLPP

Understanding. H. W. Bliss. PoToHe

Understanding. Pauline E. Soroka. PoLF

Understanding. *Unknown*. PoToHe

Understanding Canada. Peter Sirr. PBCIP

Understanding Guyana. Marianne Ware. EC2

Understanding is all, my mother would tell me. Dreaming Up Mother. Robert Adamson. BMAP

Understanding must be on both sides. Relationships. Elizabeth Jennings. FP

Undertakers. Robert Johnstone. PNI

Undertaking, The. Donne. NAEL-1; NOBE

    (Undertaking or Platonic Love, The.) FSCP

Undertaking, The. Louise Glück. FaBoWP

Undertaking or Platonic Love, The. Donne. *See* The Undertaking.

Undertones. George R. Sims. NOBVV

Undertow. Langston Hughes. LiTM

Underwater eyes, an eel's. An Otter. Ted Hughes. CMoP; MoP; NoAM

Underwear. Lawrence Ferlinghetti. OBAL

Underwood. Howard Moss. TwCP

Underworld, The. Garrett Kaoru Hongo. NAmP90; WWSi

Underworld of children becomes the overworld, The. Blue Glass. Fleur Adcock. HA

Undesirable you may have been, untouchable. September Song. Geoffrey Hill. HP; NAEL-2; NoAM; NoP-4; OBWP

Undine. René Vivien. CPO

Undistinguished Visitor, The. Leo Aylen. SpW

Undo! *Unknown*. NOCV

Undo thy dore, my spuse dere! *Unknown*. MiEL

Undoing the straps. The Sewing-Box. Gabriel Gbadamosi. NBrP

Undressed. Alexis Rotella. HA

Undressing a maiden called Sue. Limerick. Brian Allgar. PeLi

Undressing Aunt Frieda. Richard Michelson. UnSA

Undue Significance a starving man attaches. Emily Dickinson. LiTM

Unduly elected body of our elders, An. Elegy for Yards, Pounds, and Gallons. David Wagoner. PoA

Undying One, The. Caroline Elizabeth Norton.

    My Childhood's Home. Ro

Undying Thirst. Antipater of Sidon, *Greek*. AWP, *tr. by* Robert Bland

Unearthly Voices. Edward Hirsch. BAP-95

Unemployed. Stephen Spender. NOBE

Unemployment. William Mills. HoPM

Unemployment in our bones, The. Derry. Seamus Deane. CIP-2; IIP

Unemployment/Monologue. June Jordan. WPOW

Unending loneliness from which others drink, The. Six Poems of Loneliness. Enrique Lihn, *Spanish*. VCWP, *tr. by* David Unger

Unending search in endless quest. P'u-Shen Sheng Man. Li Ch'ing-chao, *Chinese*. IMW, *tr. by* Duncan Mackintosh

Unequal Distribution. Samuel Hoffenstein. TrJP

Unexpected Meeting. Wislawa Szymborska, *Polish*. VCWP, *tr. by* Magnus J. Krynski *and* Robert A. Maguire

Unexpected Pleasure, An. *Unknown*. UV

Unexplorer, The. Edna St. Vincent Millay. PoA

Unfair to Men. *Unknown, Welsh*. OBWVE, *tr. by* Gwyn Jones

Unfair to Women. *Unknown, Welsh*. OBWVE, *tr. by* Gwyn Jones

Unfaithful Shepherdess, The. *Unknown*. GTBS-P

    (Faithless Shepherdess, The.) OBEV

Unfaithful Wife, The. Federico García Lorca, *Spanish*. OxBM; STV, *tr. by* John Frederick Nims

Unfallen Love. Milton. NOSC *Fr.* Book IV. OAEL-1 *Fr* Paradise Lost.

Unfathomable Sea! whose waves are years. Time. Shelley. PFE; PoLF

Unfertile Heart, The. Naomi Mitchison. WPN

Unfinished Exile. Fabio Doplicher, *Italian*. NeIt, *tr. by* Stephen Sartarelli

Unfinished History. Archibald MacLeish. NYBP; VGW

Unfinished Race, The. Norman Cameron. OxBS

Unfold, unfold! take in his light. The Revival. Henry Vaughan. NOCV; PoEL-2

Unforgiven, The. Edwin Arlington Robinson. CMoP

Unforseen, The. Amy Gerstler. DeD

Unfortunate admiral! Your poor America. To Columbus. "Rubén Dario," *Spanish*. TTY, *tr. by* Lysander Kemp

Unfortunate Coincidence. Dorothy Parker. BXAP; LW; NoP-4; PiM

Unfortunate Damsel, The. Mrs. Fleetwood Habergham. *See* The Seeds of Love.

Unfortunate lad from Madrid, An. Limerick. *Unknown.* PeLi

Unfortunate Male, The. Kalonymos ben Kalonymos. *Fr.* The Touchstone. TrJP, *tr. by* J. Chotzner

Unfortunate Miller, The. Alfred Edgar Coppard. FaBoTw

Unfortunate Miller; or, The Country Lasses Witty Invention, The. *Unknown.* OxBB

Unfortunately, he said, I have lost my manners. Some Make This Answer. Sylvia Townsend Warner. WPN

Unfriendly friendly universe. The Child Dying. Edwin Muir. FaBoTw; GTBS-P; PoWW; RB

Unfulfilled Love. Ljiljana Djurdjic, *Serbo-Croatian.* HSix, *tr. by* Charles Simic

Unfurled gull on the tide, and over the skerry, The. December Day, Hoy Sound. George Mackay Brown. OxBS

Unfurls in rain. The Newest Banana Plant Leaf. Ingrid Wendt. NMM-2

Ungag our souls!! Unstrangle our souls!! Unsmother our souls!! "Antler." CLPP *Fr.* Factory.

Ungar and Rolfe. Herman Melville. OxBA *Fr.* Clarel: A Poem and Pilgrimage in the Holy Land.

Ungathered Love. Philip Bourke Marston. OBNC

Ungod my lungs blacken. Hello Ungod. Anthony McNeill. HCP

Ungrateful Jenny. Mother Goose. OxNR

Ungreeted, and shall give its light embrace. (LL) Inscription for the Entrance to a Wood. William Cullen Bryant. APN-1; AmPP; OxBA; TAP

Unguarded House, An. Julianus of Egypt, *Greek.* GrAn, *tr. by* W. S. Merwin

Unhand me nurse! thou saucy quean! Maternal Despotism; or, The Rights of Infants. Richard Graves. NOEC

Unhappie [*or* Unhappy] Light. Madrigal. William Drummond, of Hawthornden. NOSC

Unhappy about some far off things. The Stars Go Over the Lonely Ocean. Robinson Jeffers. LiTM

Unhappy and at home. (LL) The Tollund Man. Seamus Heaney. BIrV; CABP; CIP-2; EBEV; FaBoMo; PBCIP; PNI

Unhappy Boston. Paul Revere. AiP

Unhappy country what wings you have. Even here. Eagle Valor, Chicken Mind. Robinson Jeffers. OxBA; OxBSP

Unhappy Diary Days. Gerald Vizenor. VoR

Unhappy exile, whom his fates confine, The. Charlotte Smith. BWW

Unhappy fate: that you have died. Song at Graveside. Ewald von Kleist, *German.* GePo, *tr. by* George C. Schoolfield

Unhappy Lover, The. Judah Al-Harizi, *Hebrew.* TrJP, *tr. by* J. Chotzner

Unhappy men, why do we travel so. Crinagoras, *Greek.* GrAn, *tr. by* Alistair Elliot

Unhappy merchant, Thus t'expose thy Lord. Elizabeth Middleton. KTR *Fr.* The Death and Passion of Our Lord Jesus Christ.

Unhappy people in a happy world, An. Wallace Stevens. CMoP; PoE *Fr.* The Auroras of Autumn.

Unhappy Phaeton's splendidious sire. Virgo, August. John Taylor. NOSC

Unhappy Schoolboy, The. *Unknown.* OxBChV

Unhappy sex! how hard's our fate. On Sir J—— S—— Saying in a Sarcastic Manner, My Books Would Make Me Mad; an Ode. Elizabeth Thomas. CABP; ECWP

Unhappy sight, and hath she vanished by. Sonnet 105. Sir Philip Sidney. *Fr.* Astrophil and Stella. AAS; SiPS

Unhappy summer you. This Summer and Last. Thomas Hardy. OxBTC

Unhappy they, who by their duty led. Mary Lee, Lady Chudleigh. PEW *Fr.* The Ladies Defence Or, the Bride-Woman's Counsellor Answered.

Unhappy [*or* Unhappie] Verse, the witness[e] of my unhappy state. Iambicum Trimetrum. Edmund Spenser. BoLoP; EBEV; OBEV; OxBoLi; PoEL-1

Unhappy wife. George Swede. HA

Unhappy wit, like most mistaken things. Alexander Pope. EPCY *Fr.* An Essay on Criticism. NAEL-1; PoEL-3; TFi

Unhappy woman's but a slave at large. (LL) An Essay on Woman. Mary Leapor. BWW; ECWP; NOEC

Unharvested. Robert Frost. SAmP

Unhistorical Events. Bob Kaufman. CLPP

Unholy Missions. Bob Kaufman. TTY

Unholy Sonnets. Mark Jarman. BAP-94

Unholy Spring. John Godfrey. FTOS

Unhurried as a snake I saw Time glide. On Time. Richard Hughes. MoBrPo

Unhurt like him, your Charms I'll hear. (LL) A Farewel to Worldly Joyes. Anne Killigrew. BoWoP; CABP

Unicorn, The. George Darley. OBNC; PoEL-4 *Fr.* Nepenthe.

Unicorn, The. Ion Gheorghe, *Romanian.* CEEP, *tr. by* Loring R. Taylor

Unicorn, The. Ruth Pitter. MoBrPo

Unicorn, The. Rilke, *German.*
  "Oh this is the animal that never was." TTTS, *tr. by* Stephen Mitchell

Unicorn, The. Isaac Rosenberg.
  "Sick. . . Sick. . . I will lie down and die. How." PeFWW

Unicorn and the Lady, The. Jean Garrigue. NYBP

Unicorn is supposed, The. Kenneth Rexroth. *Fr.* A Bestiary. OBAL

Unicorn stood, like a king in a dream, The. Emile Victor Rieu. OBSP

Unicorn Tapestries, The. William Olsen. NAmP90

Unicorn's hoofs, The! Dance Song. *Unknown, Chinese.* ChiP; FaBoCh, *tr. by* Arthur Waley

Unifying Principle, The. A. R. Ammons. NOBA

Unimaginative, The. Madison Cawein. APN-2

Uninscribed Monument on One of the Battlefields of the Wilderness, An. Herman Melville. CBCWP

Uninteresting specimen might still be putting out shoots, for all we know. (LL) Crazy Weather. John Ashbery. ColAP; PoE

Uninvited, The. Dorothy Livesay. NOBC; NoP-4

Uninvited, The. William D. Mundell. NYBP

Union. Emily Dickinson. FaBoA

Union Jack, The. Jeannie Kirby. BoTP

Union Man. Albert Morgan. AmFP

Union of Two, The. Haki R. Madhubuti. ISC

Unique? Adrian Rumble. SpW

Unison, A. William Carlos Williams. NOBA

Unit. Mary Elizabeth Fullerton. NOBAu

United. Paulus Silentiarius, *Greek.* AWP, *tr. by* W. H. D. Rouse

United Fruit Co, The. Pablo Neruda, *Spanish.* FaBoPV, *tr. by* Robert Bly

United States, The. Goethe, *German.* AiP; FaBoA, *tr. by* Robert Bly

United States Constitution, The. Limerick. Peter Alexander. PeLi

United States Prepare for the Permanent Revolution, The. George Hitchcock. SPE

Unity. Fazil Hüsnü Daglarca, *Turkish.* RaBo, *tr. by* Tâlat S. Halman

Universal. Ory Bernstein. *Fr.* Poems from Mexico. IP, *tr. by* Warren Bargad *and* Stanley F. Chyet

Universal Beauty. Henry Brooke.
  "While ocean thus the latent store bequeaths." ECEV

Universal Favorite, The. Carolyn Wells. NBLV

Universal Prayer [Deo Opt. Max.], The. Alexander Pope. BLPA; FaBoBe; NoP-4

Universe, The. Mary Britton Miller. CTV

Universe is Part of Ourselves, The. Robin Blaser. FTOS

Universe of the Rose. Chimako Tada, *Japanese.* VCWP, *tr. by* Kirsten Vidaeus

Universes move in me like vast ships. Evolution: A Science Fiction. Melinda Mueller. PUP-20

University. Karl Shapiro. OxBA

University Curriculum. William Price Turner. OxBS

University Examinations in Egypt. D. J. Enright. OxBTC; TwCP

University of Hunger. Martin Carter. PBCV

Unjustifiable / Shocking neglect. (LL) No Foundation. John Hollander. OBAL; OBCoV

Unjustly Punished Child. Sharon Olds. PBCAP

Unkept Good Fridays. Thomas Hardy. GI

Unkindness. George Herbert. FP; NOSC

Unknown, The. John Davidson. MoBrPo

Unknown, The. Elmer Osborn Laughlin. BLPA

Unknown, The. Denise Levertov. NAAL-2

Unknown, The. Edward Thomas. GBL

Unknown Bird, The. Edward Thomas. RB

Unknown Child, The. Elizabeth Jennings. PBWP

Unknown Citizen, The. W. H. Auden. HeIP-4; InPK-4; LiTM; MeMAP; NBLV; NIP-4; NOBL; NYBP; OBSV; PFE; PoRA; Poetr; SAGP; SoSe-8; TRP; UnPo

Unknown Color, The. Countee Cullen. OBCA

Unknown Eros, The. Coventry Patmore.
  Arbor Vitae. OBNC; PeVV
  Azalea, The. GBL; GLoP
  Departure. NOBE; OBEV; OBNC
  Farewell, A. GLoP; GTBS-P
  Legem Tuam Dilexi. PoEL-5
  Magna Est Veritas. GTBS-P; HAP; NOBE; NOBVV; OBEV; OBNC; OxBSP
  (Truth.)
  Saint Valentine's Day. OBNC
  Tired Memory. EnVR
  To the Body. CABP; EnVR; OAEL-2; PoEL-5

To the Unknown Eros. PoEL-5

Toys, The. EBEV; EBVV; NOBVV; OBEV; OxAEP-2; PoToHe; SoSe-8

Unknown faces in the street. The Turning. Philip Levine. VGW

Unknown Female Corpse. Rudyard Kipling. PoWW *Fr.* Epitaphs of the War [1914–1918]. OBWP

Unknown Girl in the Maternity Ward. Anne Sexton. MoP; NoAM

Unknown God, The. "Æ." MoBrPo

Unknown Ideal. Dora Sigerson Shorter. IIP

Unknown Land. Rex Ingamells.
"We who are called Australians have no country." NOBAu

Unknown love/ Is as bitter a thing. Lady Otomo no Sakanoé. AWP; PBWP, *tr. by* Arthur Waley *Fr.* Manyo Shu, Part 4 of 4.

("Unknown love/ is bitter.") BoWoP, *tr. by* Willis Barnstone

Unknown Man in the Morgue. Merrill Moore. MoAmPo

Unknown Master of Moulins, The. The Cardinal's Dog. John Glassco. MoCV

Unknown Soldier, The. Alun Lewis. MoBrPo

Unknown Soldier, The. Billy Rose. BLPA

Unknown Soldiers. Edgar Lee Masters. NoAM; TAP *Fr.* The New Spoon River.

Unknown to Foreign University. (LL) Zimri: "Some of their chiefs were princes of the land." Dryden. AWP; EBEV; SCV

Unknown unwanted life, The. (LL) The Orient Express. Randall Jarrell. CMoP; CoAP; NOBA; PoE

Unknown Wind, The. "Fiona Macleod." BoTP

Unlawful Assembly. D. J. Enright. OxBTC

Unlearned depths of me, The. (LL) Review from Staten Island. Gloria C. Oden. GT

Unlearning to Not Speak. Marge Piercy. CrSp

Unleash me from your hand. The Falcon to the Falconer. Jonathan Steffen. APAD

Unless, indeed, it be / Natural affinity. (LL) The Queen of Hearts. Christina Rossetti. PeVV

Unless it trembled with the strings. (LL) Preface: "Romance, who loves to nod and sing." Edgar Allan Poe. APN-1; AmPP; MeMAP; NAAL-1; NAAL-3; NCAP; OxBA; PAR

Unless light be applied to it like a poultice. The Loom. Peter Cooley. CMAP

Unless to waken so. (LL) Lines: "When youthful faith hath fled." John Gibson Lockhart. Ro

Unless we're as good as can be. (LL) The Brown Thrush. Lucy Larcom. BoTP; OBCA

Unless you can dance through a common bar. Mahsati, *Farsi.* WPOW, *tr. by* Deirdre Lashgari

Unless you can muse in a crowd all day. Elizabeth Barrett Browning. *Fr.* A Woman's Shortcomings. BLPA

Unless you remind me. Pavlov. Naomi Long Madgett. BPo

Unlike almost everything. Near the Desert Test Sites. Sherod Santos. WeT

Unlike are we, unlike, O princely Heart! Sonnet. Elizabeth Barrett Browning. BWW; CABP; EnVR; OBEV; OxAEP-2 *Fr.* Sonnets from the Portuguese.

Unlike flying or astral projection, walking through walls is a. Walking through a Wall. Louis Jenkins. RaBo

Unlike my subject now shall be my song. Philip Dormer Stanhope, 4th Earl of Chesterfield. BaEE

Unlike the hawk he has no dream of height. Sea Owl. Dave Jeddie Smith. HCAP

Unlike their father. Tanka. Yosano Tekkan, *Japanese.* MJT, *tr. by* Makoto Ueda

Unlikely Obbligato of Andersonstown. Kit Wright. OBCoV

Unlikely one will guide me; I won't know I'm being helped, An. Killarney Clary. BAP-93

Unlimited Friendliness. Buddha, *Sanskrit.* ITG, *tr. by* Edward Conze

Unloading hell behind him step by step. (LL) The Rear-Guard. Siegfried Sassoon. MoBrPo; NAEL-2; NoAM; OBWP; PoWW; SAGP

Unloading Rails. *Unknown.* AmFP

Unlocking the Doors. Jill Breckenridge. LoHo

Unloved I love, unwept I weep. Reason. Charlotte Brontë. VWP

Unlucky Nicanor, quenched by the grey and deep. Antipater of Thessalonica, *Greek.* GrAn, *tr. by* Alistair Elliot

Unmarked faces / fierce with grief. Falls Funeral. John Montague. CIP-2

Unmet at Euston in a dream. The Night City. W. S. Graham. FaBoTC

"Unmitigated England" / Came swinging down the line. Great Central Railway, Sheffield Victoria to Banbury. John Betjeman. NYBP

Unmoved by cricket song of thee or me. (LL) The Cricket. Frederick Goddard Tuckerman. APN-2; NCAP; NOBA; PAR

Unmoved by what the wind does. Sleeping with One Eye Open. Mark Strand. NYBP

Unmuzzle the broad joke. Hymeneal. Catullus. *Fr.* Carmen 61 ("Guardian of Helicon, Urania's son"). OxBM, *tr. by* Frederic Raphael *and* Kenneth McLeish *Fr.* Carmina.

Unnamable God, my essence, / my origin, my life-blood, my home, *par. by* Stephen Mitchell. Bible, *O.T. See* Psalm 19.

Unnamable God, my essence, / my origin, my life-blood, my home. (LL) Psalm 19. Bible, *O.T.* EnlH

Unnamable God, you are fathomless. Bible, *O.T. See* Psalm 104.

Unnamed Lake, The. Frederick George Scott. NOBC

Unnatural Powers. Robinson Jeffers. PBMP

Unnoticed the first of autumn as nights grow longer. The First of Autumn. Meng Hao Jan, *Chinese.* SuSp, *tr. by* Paul W. Kroll

Unnumbered suppliants crowd preferment's gate. Samuel Johnson. OBSV *Fr.* The Vanity of Human Wishes [The Tenth Satire of Juvenal Imitated]. EBEV; ECEV; NOEC; OAEL-1; OxAEP-1; PoEL-3; TFi

Unobtrusive, with deep eyes, distant. Woman in Mourning. Māris aklais, *Latvian.* CEEP, *tr. by* Inara Cedrins

Unpardonable Sin, The. Vachel Lindsay. CMoP; ChIV-2; MeMAP

Unperson from West Oceania, An. Limerick. C. Vita-Finzi. PeLi

Unpleasing to a married ear! (LL) Spring. Shakespeare. BoTP; HAP; ImPo; InPK-6; NAEL-1; NBLV; NIP-4; NOBE; NoP-4; NoSic; OAEL-1; OBEV; PoEL-2; PoRA; SCGP; TFi; UnPo

Unplumbed [*or* unplumb'd], salt, estranging sea, The. (LL) To Marguerite. Matthew Arnold. EnVR; GTBS-P; SoSe-8

Unpopular man of Cologne, An. Limerick. *Unknown.* PeLi

Unportrayable in their silk of a small fan. Tune: "Butterflies." Kuan Yün-shih. SuSp, *tr. by* Richard John Lynn *Fr.* Medley of Southern and Northern Tunes—Scenic Tour of West Lake.

Unpossessed, The. Adèle Naudé. PeSA

Unprayed-for, / And final. (LL) What Can I Tell My Bones? Theodore Roethke. AmPP; NOBA

Unpredicted, The. John Heath-Stubbs. BoLoP; OxBC

Unprofitablenes. Henry Vaughan. ESCV; FMP; GeHe; NOSC

Unpunished. Mary Elizabeth Coleridge. *See* "He Knoweth Not That the Dead Are Thine."

Unpurged images of day recede, The. Byzantium. W. B. Yeats. APAD; CMoP; EBEV; FaBoMo; HAP; InPS-3; LiTM; MoBrPo; MoP; NAEL-2; NAWM-2; NIP-4; NOBE; NoAM; NoP-4; OAEL-2; OxBTC; PoE; Poetr

Unquiet Grave, The. *Unknown.* AmFP; CABP; CH; ESPB; HAP; HeIP-4; IMW; NoP-4; OAEL-1; OxBB; OxBSn; PoEL-1; RB; TFi; WeW-3
("Wind doth blow today, my love, The.") CABP; NoP-4; OxBSn

Unquiet Grave, The. *Unknown.* EnSB

Unreal Dwelling: My Years in Volcano, The. Garrett Kaoru Hongo. UpBo

Unreal silence, An. Swallows over the Camp. Uys Krige, *Afrikaans.* PeSA, *tr. by the author and* Jack Cope

Unreal Song of the Old, The. James Koller. PoM

Unreal tall as a myth. The Bear on the Delhi Road. Earle Birney. HeIP-4; MoCV; NOBC; NYBP; NoAM; NoP-4

Unrealities, The. Johann Christoph Friedrich von Schiller, *German.* AWP, *tr. by* James Clarence Mangan

Unreasonable lenses refract the. Prairie Houses. Barbara Guest. PmMAP

Unreasonable ryche manne, An. Of unsaciable purchasers. Robert Crowley. PBRV

Unrecorded Speech. Anna Adams. BrRo

Unrelated Incidents. Tom Leonard.
"Ifyi stull / huuny / wurkt oot." FaBoTC
"Its thi lang / wij a thi / guhtr thaht hi." FaBoTC
"This is thi." FaBoTC; NBrP

Unremarkable Year, The. Roy Fuller. OxBC

Unrequited. (LL) La Dulce Culpa. Cherríe Moraga. CPO; MDDM

Unrest. Richard Watson Dixon. OBNC

Unrestricted / unrestrained / uncomprimising. Freedom Hair. Raymond Washington. NBV

Unreturning, The. Wilfred Owen. MoBrPo

Unreturning Spring, The. Laurence Binyon. NSI
("Leaf on the gray sand-path, A.") CABP

Unreturning voyage, my friends to me, The. (LL) Godspeed. John Greenleaf Whittier. GSo; Son

Unrhymed, unrhythmical, the chatter goes. At the Party. W. H. Auden. OxBSP

Unrighteous Lord of Love what law is this. Sonnet 10: 'Unrighteous Lord of Love'. Edmund Spenser. AEP; NoP-4 *Fr.* Amoretti. AAS

Unrighteous Mammon (Luke 16:9). Ernesto Cardenal, *Spanish.* GI, *tr. by* Robert Pring-Mill

Unromantic Awakening, An. Priscilla Jane Thompson. CBWP-2

Unruly hair, bare feet—busily studying books. Chu Yün-ming. *Fr.* Improvisations. CoBLCP, *tr. by* Jonathan Chaves

Unruly Horses. Vladimir Semionovich Vysotsky, *Russian.* TCRP, *tr. by* Albert C. Todd

Unsagacious Animal, An. David Gascoyne. PeLV

Unsaid. A. R. Ammons. NOBA

Unsatisfied. (LL) To the Tune "Red Embroidered Shoes." Huang O, *Chinese.* ChiPo; PBWP; WPOW, *tr. by* Kenneth Rexroth *and* Ling Chung

Unseals her earth, and lifts love in its shower. (LL) The Broken Tower. Hart Crane. AmPP; CMoP; ColAP; LiTM; MeMAP; MoAmPo; NOBA; NoAM; NoP-4; OxBA; PoPoPo; Poetr

Unseemly as a marvellous and astral renegade. Queen Anne's Lace. June Jordan. TAP

Unseen deer through seen shadows leaps through my heart, An. John Tagliabue. Poetsp

Unseen Fire. Ralph Nixon Currey. OBWP; OxBTC; PoWW

Unseen hues of immortality, The. (LL) Autumn Leaves. Jones Very. APN-1; PAR

Unseen Playmate, The. Robert Louis Stevenson. FP

Unseen, snow slides from over-laden boughs. Fire-Queen. Ruth Fainlight. PoA

Unseen Spirits. Nathaniel Parker Willis. APN-1

Unsettled. Tanka. Miyazawa Kenji, *Japanese.* MJT, *tr. by* Makoto Ueda

Unsettled, a bird lost from the flock. T'ao Ch'ien. SuSp, *tr. by* Wu-chi Liu *Fr.* Drinking Wine. CoBCP, *tr. by* Burton Watson

Unsettled again and hearing Russian spoken. Hearing Russian Spoken. Donald Davie. GTBS-P

Unsettled Motorcyclist's Vision of His Death, The. Thom Gunn. PoA

Unsettled, unhappy, near the end of April. Lamentations of the Bronze Camels. Li Ho, *Chinese.* SuSp, *tr. by* Irving Y. Lo

Unsex'd Females, The. Richard Polwhele.
   "Alas! in every aspiration bold." NOBRP
   "Thou, who with all the poet's genuine rage." NOBRP

Unsheathing of the great knife of parting, The. (LL) A Dead Child Speaks. Nelly Sachs, *German.* PoSu, *tr. by* Ruth *and* Matthew Mead; HP, *tr. by* Ruth Mead *and* Matthew Mead

Unsnapping. Gary Hotham. HA

Unspeakable. Margaret Avison. NOBC

Unspeakable sorrow!, Tune: "Gazing at the South." Tune: Gazing at the South. Li Yü, *Chinese.* CoBCP, *tr. by* Burton Watson

Unspoken. Judith Ortiz Cofer. CrSp

Unspoken World. Helen Ruggieri. LoHo

Unsquandered, sure and quiet as a root. Emily's Words. Leslie Monsour. FFC

Unstable dream[e] [*or* dreme], according [*or* accordyng] to the place. The Lover Having Dreamed Enjoying of His Love, Complaineth That the Dreame Is Not either Longer or Truer. Sir Thomas Wyatt. AAS

Unsubdued. Samuel Ellsworth Kiser. PoToHe

Unsung Heroes, The. Paul Laurence Dunbar. BPo; CBCWP

Unsuspected Fact, An. Edward Cannon. FPC

Unswerving Marine. Carl Rakosi. FTOS

"Until age thirty." Tanka. Tawara Machi, *Japanese.* MJT, *tr. by* Makoto Ueda

Until Eternity. (LL) The Bustle in a House. Emily Dickinson. HAP; HeIP-4; NAAL-1; NAAL-3; NoP-4; OxBA; PoEL-5; PoLF; SAmP

Until, gasping with appreciative racism, both together sink into the unrevealed glory of sexism. (LL) Histoire. Harry Mathews. NIP-4; PmAP

Until I asked her to please stop doing it and was astonished to. My Mother's Lips. C. K. Williams. FiLi

Until *I* fall into coma. (LL) That's enough of that, Mr Bones. *Some* lady you make. John Berryman. NAAL-2; VCAP

Until I rest by thee. (LL) The Churchyard on the Sands. John Byrne Leicester Warren, 3d Baron De Tabley. CH; GBL; OBNC

Until I Saw the Sea. Lilian Moore. AYFP; NTCP

Until I'm covered and there's only one smell, / One word. (LL) Burning Shit at An Khe. Bruce Weigl. AF; CDa

Until it alights. Lorraine Ellis Harr. HA

Until it comes to seem a boring hanger-on. (LL) As Much As You Can. Constantine P. Cavafy, *Greek.* GriP; RB, *tr. by* Edmund Keeley *and* Philip Sherrard

Until Jove let it be, no colonist. Virgil. OBCVT, *tr. by* Robert Fitzgerald *Fr.* The Georgics.

Until life goes out. *Unknown, Japanese.* OHMPJ, *tr. by* Kenneth Rexroth

Until recently there was fear. Amir Gilbo'a, *Hebrew.* IP, *tr. by* Warren Bargad *and* Stanley F. Chyet

Until Tatum passed. Standing on the Corner. Philip Levine. NNaP

Until that sun, which keeps. Trains Made of Stone. Ray A. Young Bear. CDW

Until the basket overflows with light. (LL) Song for the Sun That Disappeared behind the Rainclouds. *Hottentot Oral Tradition.* TTTS; TTY, *tr. by* Ulli Beier

Until the Desert knows. Emily Dickinson. NOBA

Until the destruction of language. (LL) Permanently. Kenneth Koch. CoAP; NoP-4; PmAP; PoA; PoM; SAGP

Until the grave increase our cold. (LL) Employment: "He that is weary, let him sit." George Herbert. FaBoVe; GeHe; SeCP

Until the meeting so mercifully ends. (LL) Indian College Blues. Adrian C. Louis. NAmP90; PaTW

Until the purple blossom is trodden in[to] the / ground. (LL) One Girl. Sappho, *Greek.* LoP; OBCVT, *tr. by* D. G. Rossetti

Until the sound of the open ocean grows and the voice. (LL) What the End Is For. Jorie Graham. NAmP90; NoP-4; PoPoPo

Until they are truly quartets. (LL) River Road Studio. Barbara Guest. PmAP; PoM

Until they come to London Bridge. (LL) St. Paul's Steeple. *Unknown.* ACTP; LB; OxNR

Until they had the lamp inside. (LL) House Fear. Robert Frost. NTP; VGW

Until they have made themselves warm, poor things! (LL) North wind doth blow, The. Mother Goose. OxNR; ReMoGo

Until They Have Stopped. Sarah E. Wright. PoBA

Until thine hands clasp girdlewise the waist of the Belov'd. Ode. Sadi, *Persian.* AWP, *tr. by* R. A. Nicholson

Until we are pure spirit at the end. (LL) Infirmity. Theodore Roethke. CoAP; NAAL-2; NYBP

Until we reach the town of Sleep. (LL) Young Night Thought. Robert Louis Stevenson. OTCP; PWR

Until ye start, as if the sea-nymphs quired! (LL) On the Sea. Keats. NoP-4; OAEL-2; OxBoS

Until yesterday I was polite and peaceful. Opinions of the New Student. Regino Pedroso, *Spanish.* TTY, *tr. by* Langston Hughes

Until you have looked at something so long. The Makings of Happiness. Ronald Wallace. PBCAP

Untimely Thought, An. Thomas Bailey Aldrich. PWR

Untitled. Georgi Borisov, *Bulgarian.* CEEP, *tr. by* Lisa Sapinkopf *and* Georgi Belev

Untitled. Duoduo, *Chinese.* AF, *tr. by* Gregory Lee *and* John Cayley

Untitled. So Chong-Ju, *Korean.* VCWP, *tr. by* David R. McCann

Untitled. Franz Wright. LCAP-2

Untitled Blues. Yusef Komunyakaa. GT; UnSA *Fr.* After a photograph by Yevgeni Yevtushenko.
   ("He knows how to steal / laughs in a place / where your skin / is your passport.") (LL) UnSA

Untitled Requiem for Tomorrow. Conyus. PoBA

Unto a heavenly course decreed. Star Morals. Friedrich Wilhelm Nietzsche, *German.* AWP, *tr. by* Ludwig Lewisohn

Unto all generations of the faithful heart. (LL) Lee in the Mountains. Donald Davidson. CBCWP; FuPo

Unto all life of mine may die [*or* dy]. (LL) The Flaming Heart. Richard Crashaw. NAEL-1; OAEL-1; PoEL-2

Unto all life of mine may die! (LL) Upon the Book and Picture of the Seraphical Saint Teresa. Richard Crashaw. HAP; NOBE; OBEV

Unto God let praise be brought. And It Came to Pass at Midnight. Yannai, *Hebrew.* TrJP

Unto Jehovah Sing Will I. Henry Ainsworth. AH

Unto my thinking, thou beheld'st all worth. To Dante. Guido Cavalcanti, *Italian.* AWP, *tr. by* D. G. Rossetti

Unto no body my woman saith she had rather a wife be. Catullus. *See* Carmen 70 ("Lesbia says she'ld rather marry me").

Unto Our God Most High We Sing. John Vance Cheney. AH

Unto that hive of beams / And garland-streams. (LL) The Star[re]. George Herbert. ESCV; PeECV

Unto the blithe and lordly fellowship. Dedication. Folgore da San Geminiano. *Fr.* Sonnets of the Months. AWP, *tr. by* D. G. Rossetti

Unto the blithe and lordly fellowship. Sonnets of the Months. Folgore da San Geminiano, *Italian.* AWP, *tr. by* D. G. Rossetti

Unto the boundless Ocean of thy beauty. Samuel Daniel. NoP-4 *Fr.* To Delia.

Unto the different dawn! (LL) There is a morn by men unseen. Emily Dickinson. NALW; OxBA

Unto the gates of hell. The Song of Esechia. John Hall. ChIV-1

Unto the Person Kind there came. Mother Doorstep. Victor James Daley. NOBAu

Unto the saints with sad complaints. Michael Wigglesworth. NAAL-3 *Fr.* The Day of Doom. NAAL-1; SCAP

Unto the silver night. Revelation. Sir Edmund William Gosse. OBEV

Unto the Upright Praise. Moses Hayyim, of Padua Luzzatto, *Hebrew.*
   Chorus: "All ye that handle harp and viol." TrJP, *tr. by* Nina Davis Salaman

Unto this place when as the Elfin Knight. The Hill of the Graces. Edmund Spenser. NOBE *Fr.* Wood Of Error. AEP

Unto this process briefly compiled. John Skelton. NoSic *Fr.* Magnificence.

Unto Thy Favor. Robert Tofte. Son *Fr.* Laura.

Unto Us a Child is Born. William Dunbar. *See* Of Christ's Nativity.

Untold want by life and land ne'er granted, The. Walt Whitman. MoAmPo

Untouched grandeur in the hinterlands. Life in the Boondocks. A. R. Ammons. HAP

Untranslatable Factual Items. E. L. T. Mesens, *French.* CBNP

Unum est Necessarium. Agnes Mary Frances Robinson. VWP

Unuttered Prayer. Josephine D. Henderson Heard. CBWP-4

Unveil thy face, O Death who art not Death. (LL) Sonnet 26: "This Life is full of numbness and of balk." Christina Rossetti. Son; VWP

Unveiling. Hilary Sametz Lloyd. MDDM

Unwanted. Edward Field. GLP; LiLi; Poetsp

Unwarmed by any sunset light. The World Transformed. John Greenleaf Whittier. *Fr.* Snow-Bound [*or* Snow-Bound; a Winter Idyl]. APN-1; AiP; AmPP; NAAL-3; NOBA; OxBA; TAP; TFi

Unwatched [*or* unwatch'd], the garden bough shall sway. Somersby, Lincolnshire; after Leaving the Refectory. Tennyson. EBVV; FHYEP; GTBS-P; OBNC; PeECV; PoEL-5; SCV *Fr.* In Memoriam A. H. H.

Unweary'd watch their list'ning Leaders keep, Th'. The Watch and the Dogs. Homer. OBVE, *tr. by* Alexander Pope *Fr.* The Iliad.

Unweathered stone beneath a rigid mane. Sonnet: To a Portrait of Hart Crane. Allen Tate. GS

Unwed Mother, An. Ho Xuan Huong, *Vietnamese.* AVP, *tr. by* Huỳnh Sanh Thông

Unwelcome. Mary Elizabeth Coleridge. CH; OBEV; OBNC; VWP; WPE

Unwelcome advice. Persius, *Latin.* OBCVT, *tr. by* Niall Rudd

Unwelcome child. The Child Compassion. Margot Ruddock. OBMV

Unwept, unhonour'd, and unsung. (LL) Caledonia. Sir Walter Scott. BLPA; EBEvV; OxBS; SoSe-8; TFi

Unwept, unhonoured, and unsung. Sir Walter Scott *See* Caledonia.

Unwilling to change their freedom for a god. (LL) Wednesday Night Prayer Meeting. Jay Wright. ISC

Unwilling to retire, tho' weary. (LL) Written in the Beginning of Mezeray's History of France. Matthew Prior. NOBE; PoEL-3

Unwind my riddle. Stephen Crane. APN-2

Unworthy, since thou hast decreed. To the Queen of Inconstancy, Regina Collier, in Antwerp. Katherine Philips. PEW

Unwounded by fate. Alabushevo. Viktor Aleksandrovich Nekipelov, *Russian.* TCRP, *tr. by* Albert C. Todd

Unwritten, The. W. S. Merwin. IFJA

Unwritten Song, The. Ford Madox Ford. BoTP

Up. Margaret Atwood. NoP-4

Up. Bill Kushner. GLP

Up. The Tables Turned[: An Evening Scene, on the Same Subject]. Wordsworth. APAD; FHYEP; NAEL-2; NOBRP; OAEL-2; Ro; TOF

Up a ladder weightless as bird legs, thinner. The Fifth Season. Reg Saner. FYAP

Up again. (LL) What Happened? John Wieners. FTOS

Up against That Wall Everywhere. Márton Kalász, *Hungarian.* CEEP, *tr. by* Jascha Kessler

Up against the Wall. David Chapman Berry. BXAP

Up ahead, I know, he felt it stirring in himself already, the glance. Orpheus and Eurydice. Jorie Graham. VCAP

Up and Down. Rachel Hadas. FiLi

Up and Down. James Merrill. GLP
Emerald, The. FiLi

Up and Down. Shakespeare. CTC *Fr.* A Midsummer Night's Dream.

Up and down the beach. The Skin Divers. George Starbuck. NYBP

Up and down the City Road. Pop Goes the Weasel! W. R. Mardale. OxNR

Up and down the lawn he walks with cycling hands. The Gardener. Craig Raine. UV

Up and swallowed Bryan's Bryaness. (LL) The Lion. Ogden Nash. TLR; WHSW

Up and up soars the Evening Star, hanging there in the sky. The Evening Star. *Aborigine Oral Tradition.* *Fr.* Moon-Bone Song [*or* Cycle]. CBAP, *tr. by* R. M. Berndt

Up and up, the Incense-burner Peak! Having Climbed to the Topmost Peak of the Incense-Burner Mountain. Po Chü-i, *Chinese.* ChiP, *tr. by* Arthur Waley

Up at a Villa—Down in the City. Robert Browning. FHYEP; GTBS-P; InPS-3; NOBE; PoRA

Up at Piccadilly oh! The Coachman. Mother Goose. OxNR; ReMoGo

Up at the prow, I wash my mouth, dripping water on my robe. Yang Chi. CoBLCP, *tr. by* Jonathan Chaves *Fr.* Miscellaneous Impressions of T'an-chou.

Up, black, striped and damasked like the chasuble. The Skunk. Seamus Heaney. NAEL-2; NoP-4; OxBC; PoE

Up, boy! arise, and saddle quick. The Message. Heinrich Heine, *German.* AWP, *tr. by* Kate Freiligrath Kroeker

"Up, down, good, bad," said. Tubes. Donald Hall. LoL

Up Early. Kit Robinson.
"Intent to consider." FTOS

Up from out of in under for? (LL) The Naughty Preposition. Morris Gilbert Bishop. NBLV; NYBP; PeLV

Up from the bronze, I saw. Roman Fountain. Louise Bogan. NoP-4; WPOW

Up from the Egg; the Confessions of a Nuthatch Avoider. Ogden Nash. PoRA

Up from the log cabin to the capitol. Edwin Markham. *Fr.* Lincoln, the Man of the People. MoAmPo

Up from the meadows rich with corn. Barbara Frietchie. John Greenleaf Whittier. APN-1; AiP; BoTP; CBCWP; CTC; ChAP; ColAP; EBNV; FaBoBe; FaPoR; NCAP; NOBA; OBAL; OBCA; PAR; PoLF; TFi

Up from the South, at break of day. Sheridan's Ride. Thomas Buchanan Read. APN-2; CBCWP; FaBoBe

Up from the trawlers in the fishdock they walk to my house. Morning Call. Richard Murphy. BiHa

Up from the valley, ten children working the fields. Woman Who Weeps. Ellen Bryant Voigt. PuP-16

Up from the Wheelbarrow. Ogden Nash. FaBoBe

Up half-known roads. (LL) The Send-Off. Wilfred Owen. MoBrPo; NSI; OBWP; OBWVE; OxBTC; PeFWW; PoWW; RB; SAGP

Up, Helsum Hairt. Alexander Scott. OxBS

Up-Hill. Christina Rossetti. *See* Uphill [*or* Up-Hill].

Up hill and down dale. *Unknown.* OxNR

Up in a dirty window in a dark room is a star. The Pilot. Russell Edson. LCAP-2

Up in Heaven. Li Ho, *Chinese.* PLT, *tr. by* A. C. Graham

Up in Mabel's Room. Kenneth Slessor. BMAP

Up in the Air. Allan Ramsay. NOEC

Up in the air and down! (LL) The Swing. Robert Louis Stevenson. CTV; ChAP; FPC; FaBoBe; LiLi; NOxBChV; NTCP; TLR

Up in the billboard, over old South Station. Manufacturing. Alan Shapiro. BAP-95

Up in the heavenly saloon. Arizona Nature Myth. James Michie. FaBoA; NOBL

Up in the hills are bank on bank of blossoming peach and plum trees. Liu Yu Hsi. SuSp, *tr. by* Daniel Bryant *Fr.* Bamboo Branch Song.

Up in the Morning Early. Robert Burns. OPOU

Up in the North. *Unknown.* OxBoLi

Up in the sky where seasons pass. Counting the Stars. Tongju Yun, *Korean.* CKP, *tr. by* Jaihiun Kim

Up into the cherry-tree. Foreign Lands. Robert Louis Stevenson. BoTP

Up into the silence the green. E. E. Cummings. TTTS

Up Johnie raise in a May morning. Johnie Cock. *Unknown.* ESPB; OxBB

Up late. Gary Hotham. HA

Up Late. Arthur Nortje. PBMAP

Up-line platform bridges a metal road, The. Ravenglass Railway Station, Cumberland. Norman Nicholson. NYBP

Up my backside a core of charcoal does its slither. I have completed my feast and. In Front of a Large Number of People. John Godfrey. FTOS

Up on the downs the red-eyed kestrels hover. John Masefield. NOBE

Up on the Moon. Nona Maiola. CTV

Up on the Spoon. Stanley Crouch. SeSe

Up on their brooms the Witches stream. The Ride-by-Nights. Walter De la Mare. ChAP

Up over the swell of hot sugar. Prometheus at Coney Island. Quentin Rowan. BAP-96

Up! quit thy bower. Joanna Baillie. NoP-4

Up Rising. Robert Duncan. APSN; NNaP *Fr.* Passages.

Up rushed a band, with compasses and scales. Philip Freneau. NAAL-1; NAAL-3 *Fr.* The House of Night.

Up stand / six. The Menage. Carl Rakosi. FTOS

Up street and down street. *Unknown.* OxNR

Up tails all! (LL) Duck''s Ditty. Kenneth Grahame. BoTP; CTAV; FPC; NOxBChV; NTCP; OTCP; OxBChV; WHSW

Up Tail[e]s All. Robert Herrick. BeJo

Up the airy mountain. The Fairies. William Allingham. CH; FPC; FaBoCh; NOBE; NOBVV; NOxBChV; OBEV; OTCP; OxBChV; TFi

Up the ash tree climbs the ivy. Upper Lambourne. John Betjeman. FaBoTw

Up the Country. Henry Lawson. CBAP

Up the crag. Weapons. Anna Wickham. MoBrPo

Up the dark avenue, leading to no end. On an Inyanga Road. Noel H. Brettell. PeSAV

Up the dusty way from Frisco town. Walk, Damn You, Walk! William De Vere. PoLF

Up the hill. Forget Me Not. Austin Clarke. CIP-2

Up the hill and down the level! The Origin of the Snake. *Unknown.* NOxBChV

Up the hill and down the level! The Origin of the Snake. *Unknown.* NOxBChV

Up the hillside beyond the road's. Glimpses. Christopher Gilbert. GT

Up the Noran Water. Shy Geordie. Helen B. Cruickshank. OxBS

Up the ravine the sun was choking with dust. Emotion on the windows from the. Saturated. Aaron Shurin. FTOS

Up the reputable walks of old established trees. The Campus on the Hill. W. D. Snodgrass. AiP; LiTM; NoAM; TAP; TwCP

Up the road. Apple Core. Clarence Major. GT

Up the street sex is sold by the piece. Limerick. *Unknown.* PeLi

Up the wooden hill. *Unknown.* OxNR

Up There. W. H. Auden. OxBTC *Fr.* Thanksgiving for a Habitat.

Up there on the mountain road, the fireworks. Blue Ridge. Ellen Bryant Voigt. NoAM

Up they go, yawning. 1915. Roger McDonald. NOBAu

Up, Timothy, up with your staff and away! The Childless Father. Wordsworth. CH

Up to Mount Olivet. William Alabaster. *Fr.* Divine Meditations. Son

Up to the bed by the window, where I be lyin'. Old Shepherd's Prayer. Charlotte Mew. MoBrPo; OxBTC; WPE

Up to the top of the haunted turf. Walter de la Mare Tells the Listener about Jack and Jill. Louis Untermeyer. MoAmPo *Fr.* Mother Goose Up-to-Date.

Up to those heights where angels rest. The Perfect Orchestra. Henrietta Cordelia Ray. CBWP-3

Up to thy summit, Lewesdon, to the brow. William Crowe. NOEC *Fr.* Lewesdon Hill.

Up, Up, Home & Away. John Forbes. NOBAu

Up, up, my drowsie [*or* drowsy] Soul[e], where thy new ear[e]. Our Companie in the Next World. Donne. *Fr.* The Second Anniversary [*or* Anniversarie]. ESCV; SeCP *Fr.* Of the Progres[se] of the Soule; the Second Anniversarie.

Up! Up! the time for sleep is past! The Expensive Wife. Judah ibn Sabbatai. TrJP *Fr.* The Gift of Judah the Woman-Hater.

Up, up! ye dames, [and] ye lasses gay! Hunting Song. Coleridge. BoTP *Fr.* Zapolya.

Up where the world grows cold. A North Pole Story. Menella Bute Smedley. OxBChV

Up with me! up with me into the clouds! Wordsworth. TTTS *Fr.* To a Sky-Lark.

Up with the sun from the sea. Tennyson. *See* Duet.

Up yonder hill, behold how sadly slow. Thomas Parnell. *Fr.* Night Piece on Death. NOEC

Up yonder on the mountain. The Shepherd's Lament. Goethe, *German.* AWP, *tr. by* Bayard Taylor

Upcheringe of the Messe, The. Luke Sheperd.
 ("Who hath not knowne or herd." PBRV

Upended, it crouches on broken limbs. Poem. Charles Tomlinson. CMoP

Upgrade, past snow-tangled bramble, past. Sila. Robert Penn Warren. NoP-4

Uphill [*or* Up-Hill]. Christina Rossetti. BLPA; CH; EBEvV; EBVV; FaBoBe; HAP; InPK-6; NAEL-2; NALW; NOBE; NTP; OAEL-2; OBEV; OBNC; PoE; PoRA; Poetr; TFi; TrCP; WPE; WeW-3
 (Up-Hill.) APAD; LBC; NoP-4; PEW; PFE; PoPoPo; SDW

Uphold Me. Karen Gershon. LW

Upkeep. Miriam Goodman. UnSA

Upland. A. R. Ammons. NOBA

Upland Shepherd, as reclined he lies, The. The Sea View. Charlotte Smith. ECWP

Upon a bed of humble clay. A Riddle. Thomas Parnell. ECEV

Upon a Black Twist, Rounding the Arm of the Countess of Carlisle. Robert Herrick. CaPo
 ("May in like chains of darkness lie.") (LL) CavPo
 (Upon a Black Twist Rounding the Arm of the Countess of Carlile.) CavPo

Upon a Braid of Hair in a Heart. Henry, Bishop of Chichester King. EnLoPo

Upon a Brook. Ku K'uang, *Chinese.* SuSp, *tr. by* Irving Y. Lo

Upon a child. Robert Herrick.
 ("Th'easie earth that covers her.") (LL) PBRV

Upon a Child That Died [*or* Dyed]. Robert Herrick. BeJo; CH; CaPo; InPK-6; NoP-4; OBEV; PFE; Poetr

Upon a Christmas Morning. *Unknown.* AmFP

Upon a cock-horse to market I'll trot. *Unknown.* OxNR

Upon a dark ball spun in time. Giraffe and Tree. Walter James Turner. CH

Upon a dark, light, gloomy, sunshine day. A Messe of Nonsense. *Unknown.* CBNP; NOSC

Upon a day, came sorrow in to me. Sonnet: On the 9th of June 1290. Dante, *Italian.* AWP, *tr. by* D. G. Rossetti

Upon a Dead Man's Head. John Skelton. HAP; SCGP
 ("*Myrres vous y.*") (LL) CABP
 (Uppon a Deedmans Hed.) AAS
 ("Youre ugly tokyn.") CABP

Upon a Dying Lady. W. B. Yeats. UnPo

Upon a Fool. John Hoskyns. FaBoEE

Upon a Funeral. Sir John Beaumont. NOSC

Upon a Girl of Seven Years Old. Alexander Pope. OxBSP

Upon a gloomy night. St John of the Cross: Songs of the Soul in Rapture. Roy Campbell. PeECV

Upon a Great Shower of Snow That Fell on May-Day, 1654. Thomas Washbourne. NOCV

Upon a House Shaken by the Land Agitation. W. B. Yeats. CMoP

Upon a lady my love is lente. *Unknown.* MiEL

Upon a little dappled nag, whose mane. William Tennant. NOBRP *Fr.* Anster Fair.

Upon a lonely desart beach. The Haunted Beach. Mary Robinson. ECWP

Upon a Maid ("Gone she is a long, long way"). Robert Herrick. CaPo

Upon a Maid[e]. Robert Herrick. CaPo; FaBoCh; FaBoEE; OxBoLi

Upon a Maid That Died [*or* Dyed] the Day She Was Married [*or* Marryed]. Meleager, *Greek.* AWP; OBVE, *tr. by* Robert Herrick
 ("Supply'd the *Epithalamie.*") (LL) OBCVT, *tr. by* Robert Herrick
 ("That Morne which saw me made a Bride.") OBCVT, *tr. by* Robert Herrick

Upon a Maid That Died the Day She Was Married. *Unknown.* PFE

Upon a Mole in Celia's Bosom. Thomas Carew. BeJo; CBLP; CaPo

Upon a Notorious Shrew. *Unknown.* FaBoEE

Upon a Rare Voice. Owen Felltham [*or* Feltham]. NOSC

Upon a Renaissance Carving. Agnes Gergely, *Hungarian.* CEEP, *tr. by* Timea K. Szell

Upon a Ribbon [*or* Ribband]. Thomas Carew. BeJo; CaPo; NOSC; OAEL-1; PoE

Upon a Rich Country Gentleman. *Unknown.* FaBoEE

Upon a Ring of Bells. John Bunyan. CH

Upon a Row of Old Books and Shoes in a Pawnbroker's Window. Suzanne Gardinier. CBAP

Upon a Sabbath-day it fell. The Eve of St. Mark. Keats. CH

Upon a Sacrament. (LL) Light exists in Spring, A. Emily Dickinson. APN-2; BoWoP; NCAP; NOBA; OxBA

Upon a simmer Sunday morn. The Holy Fair. Robert Burns. OBSV

Upon a Snail. John Bunyan. *See* Upon the [*or* a] Snail.

Upon a Spider Catching a Fly. Edward Taylor. AmPP; MeMAP; NOBA; OxBA; PeECV; PoEL-3; SCAP; TAP
 ("And thankfully, / For joy.") (LL) ColAP
 ("Thou sorrow, venom elf.") ColAP; NoP-4

Upon a sudden, as I gazing stood. Rachel Speght. *Fr.* A Dream. WPE

Upon a summer Sunday: sweet the sound. The Runaways. Mark Van Doren. PoRA

Upon a time, before the faery broods. Keats. NOBRP *Fr.* Lamia. FHYEP

Upon a tree there mounted guard. The Cock and the Fox. Jean de La Fontaine, *French.* AWP, *tr. by* Elizur Wright

Upon a tuffet of most soft and verdant moss. Little Miss Muffet. *Unknown.* BXAP

Upon a Virgin Kissing a Rose. Robert Herrick. SeCP

Upon a Wasp Chilled [*or* Child] with Cold. Edward Taylor. NAAL-1; NAAL-3; NOBA; NOCV; PoEL-3

Upon a Wheel of Cloud. (LL) Like Rain it sounded till it curved. Emily Dickinson. NCAP; RB

Upon a Young Mother of Many Children. Robert Herrick. CaPo

Upon Absence. Katherine Philips. *See* To Mrs. M.A. Upon Absence.

Upon an Ingenious Friend, Over-Vain. Thomas Fitzgerald. OxBSP

Upon an obscure night. The Obscure Night of the Soul. Saint John of the Cross. AWP; OBMV, *tr. by* Arthur Symons

Upon an old estate from ancient sires descended. The Portraits. Anna Maria Lenngren, *Swedish.* WPOW, *tr. by* C. W. Stork

Upon ane day as I did mourne full soir. Ane Godlie Dreame. Elizabeth, Lady Culross Melvill. KTR

Upon Apennine Slope. Arthur Hugh Clough. *See* Ah, That I Were Far Away.

Upon Appleton House [To My Lord Fairfax]. Andrew Marvell. FaBoPV; GeHe; SeCP
 ("And now to the abyss I pass." OAEL-1

("And now to the Abbyss I pass.") PBRV

("As *Constellations* do above.") (LL) PBRV

Garden, A. OBEV

Garden of Appleton House, The ("When in the east the morning ray"). NOBE

"Oh thou, that dear and happy isle." OxBoLi

"Then, to conclude these pleasant acts." CBNP

To My Lord Fairfax. NOSC

("From that blest bed the hero came.") OBGa

("Or innocently seems to graze.") (LL) OBGa

(Upon Appleton House, to My Lord Fairfax.) OBGa

Upon Appleton House, to My Lord Fairfax. Andrew Marvell. *See* To My Lord Fairfax.

Upon Arch-bishop Laud, Prisoner in the Tower. 1641. *Unknown.* PBRV

Upon Batt. Robert Herrick. FaBoEE

Upon Ben Johnson [*or* Jonson]. Edmund Waller. BeJo; EPCY; NOSC

Upon Ben Jo[h]nson. Robert Herrick. BeJo; CaPo; FaBoEE; NoP-4

Upon Bishop Andrewes's [*or* Andrewes His] Picture before His Sermons. Richard Crashaw. NOSC

Upon Blanche. Robert Herrick. PFE

Upon Boys Diverting Themselves in the River. Thomas Foxton. OxBChV

Upon Bunce: Epigram. Robert Herrick. CaPo

Upon Castara's Absence. William Habington. BeJo *Fr.* Castara.

Upon Castara's Departure. William Habington. NOSC

Upon Christ His Birth. Sir John Suckling. ChIV-2

Upon Christ's Nativity or Christmas. Rowland Watkyns. OBWVE

Upon Defacing of White hall. Martin Parker. *See* The King Enjoys His Own Again.

Upon Dr. Davies's British Grammar. James Howell. OBWVE

Upon Drinking in a Bowl. John Wilmot, 2d Earl of Rochester. OxBoLi (Bowl, The.) OxAEP-1

Upon Electra. Robert Herrick. BeJo

Upon Fairford Windows. Richard Corbet. BeJo; NOSC

Upon Finding Dying: An Introduction, by L. E. Sissman, Remaindered at IS. Louis Edward Sissman. NoP-4

Upon Groins: Epigram. Robert Herrick. CaPo

Upon Hearing of My Friend's Marriage Breaking Up. Dean Young. BAP-94

Upon Her Eyes. Robert Herrick. BeJo

Upon Her Feet. Robert Herrick. BeJo; CBLP; CaPo; OxBSP; PoE

Upon Her Play Being Returned to Her, Stained with Claret. Mary Leapor. ECWP

Upon her soothing breast. Emily Jane Brontë. BoWoP

Upon Her Voice. Robert Herrick. CaPo

Upon Himself ("Mop-eyed I am, as some have said"). Robert Herrick. OxBSP

Upon Himselfe Being Buried. Robert Herrick. PBRV

Upon His Departure Hence. Robert Herrick. Poetr

Upon his drinking a Bowl. Anacreon, *Greek.* OBCVT, *tr. by* John Wilmot, 2d Earl of Rochester

Upon his dull ear fell the stern command. The Black Draftee from Dixie. Carrie Williams Clifford. BlSi

Upon his frustrate and unhopeful quest. Fragment from "The Maladjusted: A Tragedy." Morris Gilbert Bishop. NBLV

Upon his Majesties repairing of Pauls. Edmund Waller. PBRV

Upon his noses strides. The Nosobame. Christian Morgenstern. CBNP

Upon His Picture. Thomas Randolph. BeJo; NOBE

Upon His Sister-in-Law, Mistress Elizabeth Herrick. Robert Herrick. CaPo

Upon His Spaniel[l] Tracie [*or* Tracy]. Robert Herrick. BeJo

Upon His Taking of Leicester. To the King. Robert Herrick. CavPo

Upon His Unconstant Mistress. Sir Robert Ayton. NOSC

Upon His Verses. Robert Herrick. NAEL-1

Upon Jack and Jill: Epigram. Robert Herrick. CaPo; NAEL-1

Upon Julia. Ernest Radford. BXAP

Upon Julia['s] Washing Herself in the River. Robert Herrick. CaPo; OBCVT

Upon Julia Weeping. Robert Herrick. PFE

Upon Julia's Arctics. Bert Leston Taylor. NBLV

Upon Julia's Arctics. Bert Leston Taylor. OBAL

Upon Julia's Breasts. Robert Herrick. CaPo

("Ravished in that fair Via Lactea.") (LL) NoP-4

Upon Julia's Clothes. Robert Herrick. APAD; AWP; BLPA; BeJo; CABP; CaPo; CavPo; ClHu; EBEV; EBEvV; EnLoPo; GBL; GLoP; GTBS-P; HAP; HeIP-4; HoPM; ImPo; InPS-3; NAEL-1; NBLV; NIP-4; NOBE; NOSC; NoP-4; OAEL-1; OBEV; OxAEP-1; OxBSP; PFE; PeLV; PoE; PoEL-3; PoPoPo; Poetr; SCGP; SeCP; TFi; TRP; TTTS; UV; WeW-3

Upon Julia's Clothes. Edmund George Valpy Knox. BXAP; UV

Upon Julia's Haire Fill'd with Dew. Robert Herrick. PBRV

Upon Julia's Petticoat. Robert Herrick. *See* Julia's Petticoat.

Upon Julia's Ribband. Robert Herrick. CaPo

Upon Julia's Voice. Robert Herrick. InPK-6; NOBE; SeCP; SoSe-8

Upon Kind[e] and True Love. Aurelian Townshend. MeLP; NOSC

Upon Lazarus His Teares. Richard Crashaw. GeHe

Upon Learning That a Bird Exists Called the Turnstone. John Updike. CBNP; PeLV

Upon learning that the mother wrote verses. Soirée. Ezra Pound. OBCoV

Upon [His] Leaving His Mistress. John Wilmot, 2d Earl of Rochester. EnLoPo; GBL; NBLV; NOSC

Upon Leaving the Parole Board Hearing. Conyus. GT; PoBA

Upon Love. The Exercise of Affection. Sir Robert Ayton. NOSC

Upon Love ("Love brought me to a silent Grove"). Robert Herrick. BeJo

Upon Love, by Way of Question and Answer. Robert Herrick. CBLP; CaPo

Upon Love Fondly Refused [*or* Refus'd] for Conscience's Sake. Thomas Randolph. BeJo; OAEL-1

Upon Lulls. Robert Herrick. CaPo

Upon M. Ben Jo[h]nson: Epigram. Robert Herrick. BeJo; CaPo

Upon Master Edmund Spenser. Francis Beaumont. FaBoEE

Upon Master Walter Montagu's Return from Travel. Thomas Carew. CaPo

Upon Mr. Hopton's Death. Henry Halswell. NOSC

Upon Mrs. Anne Bradstreet, Her Poems, Etc. John Rogers. SCAP

Upon Mistress Elizabeth Wheeler under the Name of Amarillis. Robert Herrick. CaPo

Upon Mistresse Susanna Southwell, Her Cheeks. Robert Herrick. BeJo

Upon my darling's beaming eyes. Auf meiner Herzliebsten Äugelein. Heinrich Heine, *German.* AWP, *tr. by* Richard Garnett

Upon My Dear and Loving Husband His Going into England. Anne Bradstreet. AH

Upon My Lady Carlisle's [*or* Carlile's] Walking in Hampton Court Garden. Sir John Suckling. BeJo; CABP; CaPo; CavPo; NoP-4

("Where fools with ease go in and out?") (LL) CABP

Upon my lap my sovereign sits. Lullaby. Richard Verstegan. CH; OBEV; SCGP

Upon My Lord Brohall's Wedding. Sir John Suckling. CaPo

Upon My Lord Chief Justice's Election of My Lady Anne Wentworth [*or* A.W.] for His Mistress. Thomas Carew. CaPo

Upon My Lord Winchilsea's Converting the Mount in His Garden to a Terrace. Anne Finch, Countess of Winchilsea. OBGa

Upon Nothing. John Wilmot, 2d Earl of Rochester. NOSC; OBSV; OxAEP-1; PoEL-3

("Spaniards' dispatch, Danes' wit, are mainly seen in thee.") (LL) OBCoV

Upon one day as I did mourn full sore. Elizabeth, Lady Culross Melvill. ChIV-1 *Fr.* Ane Godly Dream.

Upon One of the Maids of Honour to Queen Elizabeth. John Hoskyns. FaBoEE

Upon our anguish for each other's sake! (LL) Sonnet: "Oh, my belovèd, have you thought of this." Edna St. Vincent Millay. HeIP-4; LW

Upon Our Saviour's Tomb[e] Wherein Never Man Was Laid. Richard Crashaw. *See* To Our Blessed Lord upon the Choice of His Sepulchre.

Upon Pagget. Robert Herrick. CaPo; FaBoCh

Upon Parson Beanes. Robert Herrick. BeJo

Upon Passing the Homestead. Huang T'ing-chien, *Chinese.* SuSp, *tr. by* Michael E. Workman

Upon Paul's steeple stands a tree. St. Paul's Steeple. *Unknown.* ACTP; LB; OxNR

Upon Phillis Walking in a Morning before Sun-Rising. John Cleveland. MeLP

Upon Platonic Love: To Mistress Cicely Crofts, Maid of Honour. Sir Robert Ayton. NOSC

Upon Prue [*or* Prew], His Maid. Robert Herrick. BeJo; CaPo; NAEL-1; NoP-4

Upon Receipt of a Pound of Coffee in 1863. Mary E. Tucker. CBWP-1

Upon receiving potted peonies for a gift. Masaoka Shiki, *Japanese.* MJT, *tr. by* Makoto Ueda

Upon Rook: Epigram. Robert Herrick. CaPo

Upon Roses. Robert Herrick. SeCP

Upon Scobble [Epigram]. Robert Herrick. BeJo; CaPo; FaBoEE

Upon Seeing the Fireflies. Tu Fu, *Chinese.* SuSp, *tr. by* Wu-Chi Liu

Upon Shaving Off One's Beard. John Updike. OxBSP

Upon Showbread [*or* Shewbread]: Epigram. Robert Herrick. CaPo

Upon Sibilla. Robert Herrick. CaPo; PBRV

("Then to the poore she freely gives the milke.") (LL) PBRV

("With paste of Almonds, *Syb* her hands doth scoure;.") PBRV

Upon Sir Francis Drake's Return from His Voyage about the World, and the Queen's Meeting Him. *Unknown.* FaBoCh

Upon Sir John Lawrence's Bringing Water over the Hills [to My L. Middlesex His House at Witten]. Sir John Suckling. CaPo

Upon som honest[e] thing [*or* thyng] whil[e] that I drinke [*or* drynke]. (LL) Introduction to the Pardoner's Prologue and Tale. Chaucer. FHYEP; NAEL-1; OAEL-1; PoE

Upon Some Alterations in My Mistress, after My Departure into France. Thomas Carew. CaPo

Upon Some Women. Robert Herrick. BeJo; CaPo

Upon Stephen Stoned. Sir John Suckling. ChIV-2

Upon that God who knows what I would know. (LL) The Marrow. Theodore Roethke. NYBP; PeECV

Upon that night, when fairies light. Halloween. Robert Burns. NOBRP

Upon the Asse That Bore Our Saviour. Richard Crashaw. ChIV-2; GeHe

Upon the Author. By a Known Friend. Benjamin Woodbridge. SCAP

Upon the Bankruptcy of a Physician. Henricus Selyns. SCAP

Upon the beach are thousands of crabs; they are. Crustaceans. Roy Fuller. NoAM

Upon the Birth of a Young and Highly Desired Son. Christian Weise, *German.* GePo, *tr.* by George C. Schoolfield

Upon the Bleeding Crucifix, *later vers.* Richard Crashaw. SeCP

Upon the Body of Our Blessed Lord, Naked and Bloody. Richard Crashaw. *See* On Our Crucified Lord, Naked and Bloody.

Upon the Book and Picture of the Seraphical Saint Teresa. Richard Crashaw. NOBE; OBEV *Fr.* The Flaming Heart. CABP; NAEL-1; OAEL-1; PoEL-2

Upon the Circumcision. Milton. ChIV-2

Upon the Crucifix. William Alabaster. NoSic; PoEL-2

Upon the Curtain[e] of Lucasta's Picture [It Was Thus Wrought]. Richard Lovelace. CaPo

Upon the Day of Our Saviour's Nativity. Francis Quarles. NOSC

Upon the Death of G. B. John Cotton. SCAP

Upon the Death of Her Husband. Elizabeth Singer Rowe. ECWP

Upon the Death of His Brother Giovanni. Ugo Foscolo. ItIP

Upon the Death of His Much Esteemed Friend Mr. Jno Saffin Junr. Grindall Rawson. SCAP

Upon the Death of Mr. King Drowned in the Irish Seas. John Cleveland. *See* On the Memory of Mr. Edward King, Drowned in the Irish Seas.

Upon the Death of My Ever Desired Friend Doctor Donne Dean of Pauls. Henry, Bishop of Chichester King. SeCP

Upon the Death of Sir Albert [*or* us] Morton's Wife. Sir Henry Wotton. BoLoP; EnLoPo; FaBoEE; OBEV; OxBM; PBRV; SeCP; WeW-3

Upon the Decease of Mrs. Anne Griffin. John Fiske. SCAP

Upon the earth there are so many treasures. Earth Felicities, Heavens Allowances. Richard Steere. SCAP

Upon the ecstatic diving board the diver. Lone Bather. Abraham Moses Klein. HeIP-4

Upon the eighteenth day of June. Bonny John Seton. *Unknown.* ESPB

Upon the enigmatic, stationary world. (LL) The Face of the Horse. Nikolai Alekseievich Zabolotsky, *Russian.* RB; TCRP, *tr.* by Daniel Weissbort

Upon the Ensignes of Christes Crucifyinge. William Alabaster. *Fr.* Divine Meditations. Son

Upon the Ensigns of Christ's Crucifying. William Alabaster. NoSic

Upon the eyes, the lips, the feet. Extreme Unction. Ernest Christopher Dowson. ADE; MoBrPo; OAEL-2; OBMV; PeECV; PeVV

Upon the fifth day of November. On Mr. Pricke. *Unknown.* FaBoEE

Upon the future life we build. Timothy Thomas Fortune. AAP *Fr.* Dreams of Life.

Upon the gale she stooped her side. The Gallant Ship. Sir Walter Scott. BoTP

Upon the grass. Noontide. Henrietta Cordelia Ray. *Fr.* Idyl. CBWP-3

Upon the grass are no longer hangs the dew. Hay making. Joanna Baillie. OxAEP-2

Upon the Grave of a Beggar. Timothy Kendall. NoSic

Upon the graving of her Name upon a Tree in Barnelmes Walks. Katherine Philips. PBRV

Upon the Heavenly Scarp. Abraham Moses Klein. PoA *Fr.* The Psalter of Avram Haktani.

Upon the hills of Phrygie near a teyle there stands a tree. Baucis and Philemon. Ovid. *Fr.* Philemon and Baucis. CTC, *tr.* by Arthur Golding *Fr.* Metamorphoses.

Upon the Holy Sepulchre. Richard Crashaw. FaBoEE

Upon the Horse and His Rider. John Bunyan. OxBChV

Upon the house a crooked sign. For Sale or Rent. *Unknown.* PoToHe

Upon the Image of Death. Robert Southwell. CH; NOBE

"Before my face the picture hangs." NoSic

Upon the Infant Martyrs. Richard Crashaw. GeHe; OAEL-1

("Roses hence, or lilies rather.") (LL) NoP-4

Upon the infinite shore by the sea. The Princess. Dame Edith Sitwell. BWW *Fr.* The Sleeping Beauty.

Upon the Intimation of Love's Mortality. Jean Garrigue. NMM-2

Upon the King's Return from Flanders, 1695. Henry Hall. NOSC

Upon the Lark and the Fowler. John Bunyan. CH

Upon the level field behold. Baseball. Frank Dempster Sherman. OBCA

Upon the Lines and Life of the Famous Scenic Poet, Master Shakespeare. Hugh Holland. OBWVE

Upon the Loss[e] of His Little Finger. Thomas Randolph. BeJo; NOSC

Upon the Loss[e] of His Mistresses. Robert Herrick. BeJo; CaPo; CavPo; NAEL-1; NOSC; PFE; PoEL-2

Upon the man who's buried here. J. E. Thorold Rogers. FaBoEE

Upon [*or* up on] the mountain my Lord spoke. Every [*or* Ev'ry] Time I Feel the [*or* de] Spirit. *Unknown.* APN-2

Upon the mountain's edge with light touch resting. A Sunset. Coleridge. OxBSP

Upon the mounts of spices. (LL) The British [*or* Brittish] Church. Henry Vaughan. ESCV; PeECV

Upon the Much Lamented Death of the Right Honourable, the Lady Elizabeth Langham. Bathsua Pell Makin. KTR

Upon the Much-to Be Lamented Desease of the Reverend Mr. John Cotton. John Fiske. SCAP

Upon the New Building at Appleton. Thomas Fairfax, Baron Fairfax of Cameron. NOSC

Upon the Nipples of Julia's Breast. Robert Herrick. CaPo; NAEL-1; NOSC; PeLV

Upon the patch of earth that clings. Public Aid for Niagara Falls. Morris Gilbert Bishop. NBLV

Upon the Plymouth shore the wild rose blooms. The Wild Rose of Plymouth. Jones Very. APN-1

Upon the Poet of His Time, Ben Jonson: His Honoured Friend and Father. James Howell. NOSC

Upon the Priory Grove, His Usual Retirement. Henry Vaughan. BeJo

Upon the rivers of Babylon, there we sat and wept. Bible, *O.T. See* Psalm 137.

Upon the Same. Robert Herrick. CaPo

Upon the Saying That My Verses Were Made by Another. Anne Killigrew. CABP; KTR; NALW; PEW; WPE

("Advanc'd her height, and sparkl'd in her eye.") (LL) CABP

Upon the shells by Carribea's wave. Albery Allson Whitman. AAP *Fr.* Twasinta's Seminoles; Or Rape of Florida.

Upon the [*or* a] Snail. John Bunyan. OxBSP

("Prize which they do aim at, they procure, The.") (LL) CTAV

Upon the Springs Issuing out from the Foot of Plimouth Beach. Samuel Sewall. SCAP

Upon the Sudden Restraint of the Earl[e] of Somerset, Then Falling from Favor [*or* Favour]. Sir Henry Wotton. NOBE; NOSC; SeCP

(Earle of Somerset.) PBRV

Upon the Swallow. John Bunyan. OxBChV

Upon the threshold of the mind? (LL) O Sorrow, cruel fellowship. Tennyson. EBVVPR; EnVR; HAP; OAEL-2

Upon the Times. Mildmay Fane, 2d Earl of Westmorland. BeJo

Upon the Tomb of the Most Reverend Mr. John Cotton. Benjamin Woodbridge. SCAP

Upon the Translation of the Psalms by Sir Philip Sidney, and the Countess of Pembroke His Sister. Donne. EPCY

Upon the tree of time. A Harvest to Seduce. Melville Cane. NYBP

Upon the Troublesome Times. Robert Herrick. CaPo; CavPo

Upon the utmost corners of the warld. In Orknay. William Fowler. OxBS

Upon the Weathercock. John Bunyan. OxBChV

Upon the work of Walter Landor. Walter Savage Landor. Dorothy Parker. NALW *Fr.* A Pig's-Eye View of Literature.

Upon the Works of Ben Joson. John Oldham.

"Plain Humour, shown with her whole various face." EPCY

Upon their quivering wings. (LL) Fairyland [*or* Fairy-Land]. Edgar Allan Poe. APN-1; NAAL-1; NAAL-3

Upon this marble bust that is not I. To Inez Milholland. Edna St. Vincent Millay. AiP; NALW; WPE

Upon this place the great Gustavus died. On Gustavus Adolphus, King of Sweden. Sir Thomas Roe. FaBoEE

Upon this primrose hill. The Primrose[, Being at Montgomery Castle, upon the Hill, on Which It Is Situate]. Donne. GBL

Upon This Rock. Ruthven Todd. PoA

Upon thy Mount Lycean! (LL) Hymn to Pan. Keats. PoEL-4; Ro

Upon thy tender limbs! and so good night. (LL) To One Married to an Old Man. Edmund Waller. FaBoEE; OxBSP; SeCP

Upon Time. Robert Herrick. BeJo

Upon Umber: Epigram. Robert Herrick. CaPo

Upon Venus Putting on Mars His Armes. Leonidas of Alexandria, *Classical Greek.* SeCP, *tr.* by Richard Crashaw

Upon Vermilion Wheels. (LL) The Name—of it—is "Autumn." Emily Dickinson. InPS-3; NCAP

Upon Visiting His Lady by Moonlight. "A. W." CTC

Upon Wedlock and Death of Children. Edward Taylor. AmPP; ColAP; NAAL-1; NAAL-3

("Whether thou getst them green, or let them seed.") (LL) NoP-4

Upon what terms, with how much left unsaid. (LL) The Middle-Aged. Adrienne Rich. HCAP; PoPoPo

Upon ye Sight of My Abortive Birth. Mary Carey. KTR

Upon Your Leaving. Etheridge Knight. NNaP

Upon Your Leaving. Etheridge Knight. See Cell Song.

Upone Tabacco. Sir Robert Ayton. OxBS

Upper Broadway. Adrienne Rich. HCAP; InPS-3

Upper Canadian, The. James Reaney. NOBC

Upper Chamber, An. Frances Bannerman. OBEV

Upper chamber in a darkened house, An. "Upper chamber in a darkened house, An." Frederick Goddard Tuckerman. APN-2; NOBA; TAP Fr. Sonnets.

("Tiny petals of the mountain-ash, The.") (LL) GSo; NoP-4; PAR

Upper Family. Maxwell Bodenheim. OBAL

Upper Lambourne. John Betjeman. FaBoTw

Upper Skies, The. Robert Bridges. BoTP

Upper slopes are busy with the cricket. Elegy on the Dust. Thom Gunn. NoAM Fr. Misanthropos.

Uppon a Deedmans Hed. John Skelton. See Upon a Dead Man's Head.

Uppon the First Sight of New England, June 29, 1638. Thomas Tillam. SCAP

Upright and glorious. Do So. Denise Riley. NBrP

Uprightness. Camouflaged Troop-Ship. Amy Lowell. AiP

Upriver the wreckage of the railway trestle. The Fourth Day of the Flood. George Keithley. EC3

Uproar in Leuven, insurrection in the Sorbonne. Imitation of Monsieur Beranger. "Naum Korzhavin," Russian. TCRP, tr. by Albert C. Todd

Uprooted tree leaves, An. Group Photo from Pretoria Local on the Occasion of a Fourth Anniversary (Never Taken). Jeremy Cronin. PeSAV

Uprose the King of Men with speed. The Descent of Odin. Thomas Gray. OxAEP-1

Ups and Downs. Amy Gerstler. DeD

Upside Down. Aileen Fisher. OTCP

Upside Down Basket, The. Alan Chong Lau. UnSA

Upside-Down World, The. Hamish Hendry. BoTP

Upstairs Downstairs. Hervey Allen. PoA

Upstairs Jenny crashed her car and became a living corpse, Jake. The Charnel Ground. Allen Ginsberg. BB

Upstairs on the third floor. Bottled [New York]. Helene Johnson. BlSi; PoBA

Upstate. Simon J. Ortiz. LTA

Upstate. Derek Walcott. GT

Upstream. Carl Sandburg. MoAmPo

Upstream, against the wind, they pull hundreds of feet of rope. Song of the Boat-Pullers. Pien Kung, Chinese. CoBLCP, tr. by Jonathan Chaves

Uptown. Allen Ginsberg. TwCP

Uptown Love Poem. David St. John. WWSi

Uptown on Lenox Avenue. Prime. Langston Hughes. PoBA

Upward, and rarefy [or Rarifie] the air. (LL) The Snail [or Snayl]. Richard Lovelace. BeJo; CaPo; OAEL-1; PoEL-3

Upward in motion with wet wind. (LL) Wales Visitation. Allen Ginsberg. APSN; BB; ColAP; NNaP; NOBA; NYBP; VCAP

Upward Look, An. James Merrill. PoPoPo

Upward through crystal in a kümmel bottle. Dreamscape in Kümmel. Harold Witt. NYBP

Ur / mit / mals. Volcanic tuff. Tina Darragh. FTOS

Ur ol' Hyar lib in ur house on de hill. Ol' Doc' Hyar. James Edwin Campbell. AAP

Ur Sonata. Kurt Schwitters.

"Third movement." PFTM

Urania. Robert Andrews. NOEC

Urania, . Mary Sidney, Countess of Montgomery Wroth.

Urania. Mary Sidney, Countess of Montgomery Wroth. See Sonnet 45 and Pamphilia to Amphilanthus.

Duke's Song, The. WPE

("And friendship by her are dissolved, / suffered unspoken.") (LL) RACG

("If a clear fountain still keeping a sad course.") RACG

Sonnet 45. PEW

(Urania.) LW

Urania, or Spiritual Poems. William Drummond, of Hawthornden.

Madrigal: "Astrea in this time." NOSC

Sonnet: "Triumphing chariots, statues, crowns of bay." NOSC

Too Long I Followed. Son

Urania speaks with darkened brow. Tennyson. OAEL-2 Fr. In Memoriam A. H. H.

Urania takes her morning flight. The Adventurous Muse. Isaac Watts. NOEC

Urania: The Divine Muse. On the Death of John Dryden, Esq. Lady Sarah Piers. KTR

Uranium, with which we know. What It Could Be. Denise Levertov. PaTW

Uranne. Mary Weston Fordham. CBWP-2

Urban Convalescence, An. James Merrill. CoAP; ColAP; NAAL-2; NOBA

Urban Cowboy Hat. Maureen Owen. DeD

Urban Dream. Victor Hernandez Cruz. NBV

Urban Experience: Part One, The. Lew Blockcolski. VoR

Urban Experience: Part Two, The. Lew Blockcolski. VoR

Urban Guerrilla, An. Allen Curnow. PeNZ Fr. Moro Assassinato.

Urban Love Songs. Wing Tek Lum. OpBo

Urban, or Sylvan, or whatever name. The Passive Participle's Petition. John Byrom. ECEV

Urban Pollution. John Armstrong. ECEV; NOEC Fr. The Art of Preserving Health.

Urban Progress. John Dyer. ECEV, ll. 1–20 Fr. The Fleece.

Urceus Exit. Austin Dobson. OBEV Fr. Rose-Leaves.

Urchin, The. Konstantin Iakovlevich Vanshenkin, Russian. TCRP, tr. by Daniel Weissbort

Urchin saw a rose—a dear. Rosebud in the Heather. Goethe, German. STV, tr. by John Frederick Nims

Urchin's Dance, The. John Lyly and Thomas Ravenscroft. See By the Moon ("By the moon we sport and play").

Urdeath August Stramm, German. PFTM, tr. by Rothenberg, Jerome and Pierre Joris

Urge to wander is, The. Leaving. Rae Armantrout. FTOS

Urgent Letter, An. Hugh Maxton. PBCIP

Urgent letter that I try to write, The. Night Letter. Stanley Kunitz. AF

Urging Her of a Promise. Ben Jonson. Fr. A Celebration of Charis in Ten Lyric[k] Pieces [or Peeces]. BeJo; OxAEP-1; SeCP

Uriel. Ralph Waldo Emerson. APN-1; NAAL-1; NAAL-3; NOBA; OxBA; PAR

Uriel. William Force Stead.

How Infinite Are Thy Ways. OBMV

Uriel to his charge. Now Came Still Evening On. Milton. Fr. Book IV. OAEL-1 Fr. Paradise Lost.

Urinating Man, The. Lisa Lewis. BAP-93

Urn Burial. Ted Hughes. EBEV

Urn for Burial, An. Unknown, Tamil.

("Potter.") PLW, tr. by A. K. Ramanujan

Urns and Odours Bring Away! John Fletcher and Shakespeare. See Dirge of the Three Queens.

Ursa Major. Federico García Lorca. PFTM

Ursula. David Ray. VGW

Urumbula Song, The. Unknown, Aranda. CBAP, tr. by T. G. H. Strehlow

Us. Julius Lester. PoBA

Us Two. Nina Cassian, Romanian. PoSu, tr. by Nina Cassian

Us Two. A. A. Milne. OxBChV

Us, where love needs no speech. (LL) Ah! fair face gone from sight. Lionel Pigot Johnson. OBNC; PoEL-5

Use maketh maistry [or mast'ry], this hath been said alway. Of Use. John Heywood. FaBoEE

Use, then, my lust for whisky and for thee. The Light of Life. "Hugh MacDiarmid." CMoP

Used. Rita Dove. NAmP90

Used to be, fellows would ask if you were married. The Sweaters. Lucia Maria Perillo. UnSA

Used to hang and brush their bosoms? I feel chilly and grown old. (LL) A Toccata of Galuppi's. Robert Browning. EBVV; EBVVPR; EnVR; FaBoVe; GTBS-P; HAP; NAEL-2; NOBE; NOBVV; NoP-4; OAEL-2; UV

Used to long nights, springtime is past. In Remembrance of the Forgotten. "Lu Hsün," Chinese. SuSp, tr. by William R. Schultz

Used together: seasons, books, a piece of music. A Kind of Loss. Ingeborg Bachmann, German. AF; VCWP, tr. by Mark Anderson

Useless Day. Rosario Castellanos. WPOW, tr. by Maureen Ahern

Useless except to a collector, a rich man. (LL) Behaviour of Fish in an Egyptian Tea Garden. Keith Douglas. FaBoMo; RB

Useless Valentines / Are better. A Valentine. Jack Spicer. APSN

Useless Words. Carl Sandburg. PBMP

Uses of Poetry. Winfield Townley Scott. PoA

Ushers in a drearier day. (LL) Song. Emily Jane Brontë. AYFP; CH; FaBoCh; OxBSP; PoEL-5

Using carbon-based ink. The Gardener's Preface. Allen Fisher. NBrP

Usk. T. S. Eliot. FaBoCh; NOCV; PeECV *Fr.* Landscapes. RB

Usk, The. Charles Hubert Sisson. NOCV

Usquebaugh. Wendy Cope. UV

Usual exquisite boredom of patrols, The. Hugh Popham. OxBTC

Usurers, The. Nicolás Guillén, *Spanish.* PFTM, *tr. by* Robert Marquez

Usurp'd a Patriot's All-atoning Name. (LL) Achitophel: The Earl of Shaftsbury. Dryden. AWP; HAP; InPS-3; NOBE; NOSC; PoEL-3

Usurpers, The. Edwin Muir. CMoP

Ut pictura . . . The disconcerting lips. The Fan. Eugenio Montale, *Italian.* AF, *tr. by* William Arrowsmith

Utah. Anne Stevenson. FaBoVe

Utah Iron Horse, The. *Unknown.* AmFP

Ute Mountain. Charles Tomlinson. RB

Utilitarian View of the Monitor's Fight, A. Herman Melville. APN-2; AmPP; ColAP; NAAL-1; NAAL-3; NCAP; PAR; UnPo

Utitia' q's Song. *Unknown, Eskimo.* APN-2, *tr. by* Franz Boas

Utmost grace the Greeks could show, The. Grecian Kindness. John Wilmot, 2d Earl of Rochester. OxBSP

Utopia. Jewel C. Latimore. BPo

Utopia Anglicized. Sir William Schwenck Gilbert. OBSV *Fr.* Utopia Limited.

Utopia Limited. Sir William Schwenck Gilbert.

Utopia Anglicized. OBSV

"Utopia" The. Lee Harwood. SPE

Utrillo: "La Belle Gabrielle." Dezsö Tandori, *Hungarian.* CEEP, *tr. by* Bruce Berlind

Utter moorland, high, and wide, and flat, An. The Fork of the Road. William Renton. NOBVV

Utter Passion Uttered Utterly, An. John Todhunter. BXAP

Utter Zoo Alphabet, The. Edward Gorey. CBNP

Utterance. Donald Davidson. FuPo

Utterance. W. S. Merwin. BLT

Utterance: any continuous stretch. You Must Change Your Life. Ken Edwards. NBrP

Uttering cries that are almost human. (LL) American Poetry. Louis Simpson. FaBoA; MoP; NOBA; NoAM; TAP; WeT

Uuuuuuuuu. Dope. Imamu Amiri Baraka. APSN

V

V.A.D. (Mediterranean). Rudyard Kipling. *Fr.* Epitaphs of the War [1914–1918]. OBWP

V.A. Hospital. Anthony Petrosky. CDa

V. B. Nimble, V. B. Quick. John Updike. NYBP; NoP-4; OBCoV

V. Father Death Blues. Allen Ginsberg. CLPP *Fr.* Don't Grow Old. (Father Death Blues.)

(V from Secrets). Jessie Orton Jones.

"Sometimes I hear God's whisper in." CTV

V. Innocentia Veritas Viat Fides Circumdederunt Me Inimici Mei. Sir Thomas Wyatt. AAS

V-Letter. Karl Shapiro. NoAM; TrJP

(Love Letter.) NYBP

V. N. and C. I, The. Maggie Pogue Johnson. CBWP-4

Vacancy in the Park. Wallace Stevens. LCAP-2; SAmP

Vacancy in which, apparently, A. All is Emptiness, and I Must Spin. Thomas Kinsella. PBCIP

Vacant cornstalks rattle in the field. At the Edge of Winter. Ellen Bryant Voigt. WeT

Vacant Lot, The. Gwendolyn Brooks. NAAAL; NAAL-2; NOBA; NoAM *Fr.* A Street in Bronzeville. BPo; BlSi; FaBoWP

Vacant Lot. Dudley Randall. NoAM

Vacant Lot, A. Gibbons Ruark. PuP-15

Vacant shuttles / Weave the wind. I have no ghosts. T. S. Eliot. UV *Fr.* Gerontion. AmPP; CMoP; EBEV; GTBS-P; HAP; ImPo; InPS-3; LiTM; MoP; NAAL-2; NOBA; NoAM; OAEL-2; OxAEP-2; OxBA; TAP; TFi

Vacation. William Stafford. BLT; Poetsp

Vacation Time. Frank Hutt. BoTP

Vachel, the stars are out. To Lindsay. Allen Ginsberg. CoAmPo

Vacillation. W. B. Yeats. NoAM

"Get all the gold and silver that you can." APAD

"Must we part, Von Hügel, though much alike." OBMV

"My fiftieth year had come and gone." RaBo

Vacuum, The. Howard Nemerov. NIP-4; RB

Vacuum cleaner held over my head, A. In a Dream. David Ignatow. PoA

Vagabond, The. Robert Louis Stevenson. OxAEP-2

Vagabond, A. James Tate. NoAM

Vagabond House. Don Blanding. BLPA

Vagabonds. Langston Hughes. SAmP

Vagabonds. Marie-Madeleine, *German.* CPO, *tr. by* Lillian Faderman, Brigitte Eriksson *and* Frankie Hucklenbroich

Vagabonds, The. John Townsend Trowbridge. BLPA

Vagabond's Arising. Aina Kraujiete, *Latvian.* CEEP, *tr. by* Inara Cedrins

Vaginas of women, all the clusters. Ellen Bass. NMM-2

Vagrant whistles in the street, A. Peace! Peace! Peace! Đỗ Tấn Xuân, *Vietnamese.* AVP, *tr. by* Huỳnh Sanh Thông

Vague Lyric by G. M. Max Beerbohm. FaBoEE

Vague sea thuds against the marble cliffs, The. Time. Robert Graves. LiTM

Vaguely I hear the purple roar of the torn-down Third Avenue El. You Are Gorgeous and I'm Coming. Frank O'Hara. NeAP

Vaices That Be Gone, The. William Barnes. NOBVV

Vain Advice, The. Catherine Cockburn. LW

Vain Advice at the Year's End. James Wright. NYBP

Vain and Careless. Robert Graves. NOxBChV; NTP

Vain are those joys that erring man provides. The World Not Our Rest. Maria Frances Cecelia Cowper. ECWP

Vain Attempt. Günter Kunert, *German.* CEEP, *tr. by* Michael Hamburger

Vain, frail, short liv'd, and miserable Man. A Song of Emptiness to Fill up the Empty Pages Following. Michael Wigglesworth. SCAP

Vain Girl Jilted, The. Edith Jay Scovell. WPN

Vain old Professor of Greek, A. Limerick. Ron Rubin. PeLi

Vain Wish, A. Philip Bourke Marston. GSo

Vain World Adieu. *Unknown.* AmFP

Vainly ("Vainly / the epistles burn"). Nelly Sachs, *German.* NYBP, *tr. by* Michael Roloff

Vainly in Hell let Pluto domineer. (LL) The Character of Holland. Andrew Marvell. NOBL; PeLV

Vainly my heart had with thy sorceries striven. To ———. Sarah Helen Whitman. APN-1

Vainly / the epistles burn. Vainly. Nelly Sachs, *German.* NYBP, *tr. by* Michael Roloff

Vala; or The Four Zoas. William Blake.

Enion Replies from the Caverns of the Grave. OBNC

Enitharmon Revives with Los. OBNC

Lamentation of Enion, The. OBNC

Night II (Enion's Lament). PoE

(Enion's Lamentation.) Ro

Night VIII (The Eternal Man). PoE

Song of Enitharmon. OAEL-2

Vala, Night the Ninth Being the Last Judgment. OAEL-2

Vale from Carthage. Peter Viereck. LiTM; MoAmPo

Vale of Tear[e]s, A. Robert Southwell. NoSic

Valediction: "Before the seas again divide." Walter Adolphe Roberts. PBCV

Valediction: "Bid me not go where neither suns nor showers [show'rs]." William Cartwright. BeJo

Valediction. Sir Robert Ayton. NOSC

Valediction, A. Ernest Christopher Dowson. BoLoP

Valediction, A. Julia Randall. NMM-2

Valediction. Vita Sackville-West. WPN

Valediction: Forbidding Mourning, A. Donne. CBLP; ESCV; FHYEP; HAP; HeIP-4; HoPM; ImPo; InPS-3; MeLP; NAEL-1; NOBE; NOSC; OAEL-1; PoE; PoEL-2; Poetr; SCGP; SeCP; SoSe-8; TFi; UnPo; WeW-3

("And makes me end where I begun.") (LL) CABP; FMP; FSCP; NoP-4; PFE; PoPoPo

("And makes me end, where I begunne.") (LL) PBRV

"Our two soules therefore, which are one." UV

(Valediction Forbidding Mourning, A.) CABP; FMP; FSCP; NoP-4; PBRV; PFE; PoPoPo

Valediction Forbidding Mourning, A. Adrienne Rich. NAAL-2; NoAM; NoP-4

Valediction (Liverpool Docks), A. John Masefield. OBMV

Valediction of the Book, A. Donne. NoP-4

Valediction: Of Weeping, A. Donne. ESCV; FHYEP; FSCP; HAP; HeIP-4; InPS-3; MeLP; NAEL-1; NOSC; NoP-4; OAEL-1; PBRV; PoE; SCGP; SeCP; WeW-3

("Who e'r sighes most, is cruellest, and hasts the others death.") (LL) PBRV

("Whoe'er sighs most is cruelest, and hastes the other's death.") (LL) NoP-4

Valediction to My Contemporaries. Horace Gregory. MoAmPo

Valediction—To My Father. Eddy Van Vliet, *Flemish*. VCWP, *tr. by* John Van Tiel

Valediction to the River Duddon. Wordsworth. *See* After-Thought.

Valedictory to Standard Oil of Indiana, A. David Wagoner. NYBP

Valentine. Wendy Cope. NoP-4

Valentine. Carol Ann Duffy. APAD

Valentine, The. Mary Weston Fordham. CBWP-2

Valentine, A. Robert Graves. FuPo

Valentine. Donald Hall. NTCP

Valentine. Ernest Hemingway. OBAL

Valentine. Wendy Mulford. NBrP

Valentine. Tom Pickard. NBrP

Valentine, A. Edgar Allan Poe. NCAP

Valentine, A. Jack Spicer. APSN

Valentine, A. Priscilla Jane Thompson. CBWP-2

Valentine, A. Elizabeth Trefusis. LW *Fr.* A Valentine.
Valentine, A. LW

Valentine Browne. Egan O'Rahilly, *Irish*. NOIV, *tr. by* Thomas Kinsella

Valentine for Ben Franklin Who Drives a Truck in California, A. Diane Wakoski. NoAM

Valentine to Sherwood Anderson, A. Gertrude Stein. NoAM; PFTM

Valentine's Day. Charles Kingsley. BoTP

Valentine's Day. Kenneth May. SeSe

Valentino's Hair. Yvonne Sapia. PeVV; TRP

Valiant Love. Richard Lovelace. SeCP

Valiant's Song. John Bunyan. *See* The Pilgrim.

Valley, The. Stanley Moss. NYBP

Valley, The. Agnes Mary Frances Robinson. VWP

Valley Candle. Wallace Stevens. SAmP

Valley floors. A Collage for Richard Davis—Two Short Forms. De Leon Harrison. PoBA

Valley of Unrest, The. Edgar Allan Poe. APN-1; AmPP; NAAL-1; NAAL-3; PAR; PoEL-4

Valley Prince. Mervyn Morris. PBCV

Valley Wind, The. Lu Yün, *Chinese*. ChiP, *tr. by* Arthur Waley

Valley with a silver-grayish mist, The. A Vision. Hugo von Hofmannsthal, *German*. TrJP, *tr. by* Charles Wharton Stork

Valleys crack and burn, the exhausted plains, The. The Mahratta Ghats. Alun Lewis. OBWVE; PoWW

Valse Oubliée. John Heath-Stubbs. OxBTC

Valuable. Stevie Smith. OxBTC

"Valueless, A Duffer!" says the Sister's face. *Unknown*. NSI

Vampire, The. Rudyard Kipling. NOBVV

Van Amburgh is the man that goes with all the shows. Van Amburgh's Menagerie. *Unknown*. BLPA

Van Dieman's Land. *Unknown*. NOBAu; PeVV

Van Diemen's Land. Allen Afterman. NOBAu

Van Gogh. David Mitchell. PeNZ

Van Gogh, feeling devil-may-care. Limerick. "Pibwob." PeLi

Van Gogh would paint the landscape. In Hayden's Collage. Michael S. Harper. NAAAL

Van Winkle. Hart Crane. AmPP; MoAmPo *Fr.* Powhatan's Daughter. *Fr.* The Bridge. NAAL-2

Vandals, The. Jenny Mastoraki, *Modern Greek*. BoWoP, *tr. by* Nikos Germanakos

Vanderdecken. Douglas Livingstone. PeSAV

Vandunk's Four Humours, in Quality and Quantity. Richard Brathwaite [*or* Brathwait]. NOSC

Vane, young in yeares, but in sage counsell old. To Sir Henry Vane the Younger. Milton. PBRV; Son

Vanessa Vanessa. Ewart Milne. BIrV

Vanguard of liberty, ye Men of Kent. To the Men of Kent (October, 1803). Wordsworth. OBWP

Vanished, The. Marie-Claire Bancquart, *French*. MFP, *tr. by* Martin Sorrell

Vanished house that for an hour I knew, A. Souvenir. Edwin Arlington Robinson. NoAM

Vanished Work. Hans Magnus Enzensberger, *German*. VCWP, *tr. by* Hans Magnus Enzensberger and Michael Hamburger

Vanishes in the obscurer town. (LL) Via Crucis. Herman Melville. APN-2; NCAP

Vanishing, The. "Lewis Carroll." OxAEP-2 *Fr.* The Hunting of the Snark. CBNP; OBNC; OBNV; PoEL-5

Vanishing Lung Syndrome. Miroslav Holub, *Czech*. VCWP, *tr. by* David Young *and* Dana Hábová

Vanishing Point. Peter Cooley. AmPA

Vanishing Point, The. Peter Davison. DiPo

Vanishing Shadows. Konstantin Dmitrievich Balmont, *Russian*. TCRP, *tr. by* April FitzLyon

Vanishings, The. Stephen Dunn. BAP-93

Vanitas Vanitatum. John Webster. NOBE; OBEV *Fr.* The Devil's Law Case.
(Burial, The.) CH

Vanitas Vanitatum. Israel Zangwill. TrJP

Vanity. Birago Diop. PBMAP

Vanity. Robert Graves. GTBS-P

Vanity. Anna Wickham. FaBoTw

Vanity of All Worldly Things, The. Anne Bradstreet. ChIV-1; SCAP
"There is a path no vulture's eye hath seen." WPoS

Vanity of Existence, The. Philip Freneau. AmPP

Vanity of External Accomplishments, The. Mary Whateley. ECWP

Vanity of Human Wishes [The Tenth Satire of Juvenal Imitated], The. Samuel Johnson. EBEV; ECEV; NOEC; OAEL-1; OxAEP-1; PoEL-3; TFi
(Tenth Satire of Juvenal Imitated, The.) CABP
Charles XII of Sweden. NOBE
"Let Observation with extensive View." OBCVT; UV
Power of Prayer, The. NOBE
Scholar's Life, The. NOBE
"Unnumbered suppliants crowd preferment's gate." OBSV

Vanity of Spirit. Henry Vaughan. ESCV; GeHe; NOSC; TOF

Vanity of the Blue Girls. John Crowe Ransom. *See* Blue Girls.

Vanity of the Bright Young Men, The. John Crowe Ransom. FuPo *Fr.* Sixteen Poems in Eight Pairings.

Vanity of the World, The. Siôn Cent, *Welsh*. OBWVE, *tr. by* Joseph P. Clancy

Vanity of vanities, saith the Preacher, vanity of vanities; all is vanity. Bible, *O.T.* TrJP, *sect.* I, *ll.* 2–9; FaBoPV; NAWM-1; PBMP *Fr.* Ecclesiastes.
("There is no remembrance of former things; neither shall there be any remembrance of things that are to come with those that shall come after.") (LL) PBMP

Vanity of vanities, the Preacher saith. The One Certainty. Christina Rossetti. OBNC

Vanity [*or* Vanitie] (1). George Herbert. GeHe; NoP-4; NOSC
("To finde out *death*, but missest *life* at hand.") (LL) FSCP

Vanity, saith the preacher, vanity! The Bishop Orders His Tomb at Saint Praxed's Church. Robert Browning. CABP; EBVV; EBVVPR; EnVR; FHYEP; HAP; HeIP-4; NAEL-2; NAWM-2; NOBVV; NoP-4; OAEL-2; OBAL; PoE; Poetr; SCGP; TFi

Vanity, vanity, all is vanity. Ha! Original Sin! Ogden Nash. NBLV

Vanquished, The. Charles Eglinton. PeSA

Vanquished and weary was my soul in me. Sonnet: A Trance of Love. Cino da Pistoia. AWP, *tr. by* D. G. Rossetti

Vantage Point, The. Robert Frost. MeMAP; OxBA

Vanzetti. Charles Buckmaster. CBAP

Vapor is curling from the manhole. April in New York. Nicholas Christopher. WWSi

Vapor Trail Reflected in the Frog Pond. Galway Kinnell. AF; OBWP; VCAP; VGW
("Old watch: their / thick eyes, The.") AF

Vapor Trails. Gary Snyder. NAAL-2

Vaporetto founders in green slush, The. Gorey at the Biennale. Martin Johnston. BMAP

Vaquero. Edward Dorn. NeAP; PoM

Variable. Joshua Sylvester. NOSC

Variables of Green. Robert Graves. FaBoEE

Variation of the Song of the Moon. Shelley. *Fr.* Prometheus Unbound. NOBRP; OAEL-2

Variation on a Noel. John Ashbery. EOEF

Variation on a Theme by Rilke. Denise Levertov. CrSp

Variation on Belloc's "Fatigue." Wendy Cope. UV

Variation on Heraclitus. Louis MacNeice. MoP; NoAM

Variation on Nekrasov. "Naum Korzhavin," *Russian*. TCRP, *tr. by* Vladimir Lunis *and* Albert C. Todd

Variation on Ronsard. Thomas Sturge Moore. OBMV

Variation on the Gothic Spiral. W. S. Merwin. PoA

Variation on the Word *Sleep*. Margaret Atwood. DeD; NOBC
("I would like to be that unnoticed / and that necessary.") (LL) ITG

Variation VI. Josef Hanzlik, *German*. CEEP, *tr. by* Ewald Osers

Variations. Federico García Lorca, *Spanish*. PiM, *tr. by* Lysander Kemp

Variations. Randall Jarrell. VGW

Variations Done for Gerald Van De Wiele. Charles Olson. NOBA; NeAP; NoAM

("We salute you / season of no bungling.") (LL) NoP-4

Variations Done for Gerald Van de Wiele. Charles Olson.

"What soul / is there?" APAD

Variations for Two Pianos. Donald Justice. NYBP; WeT

Variations for Two Voices. Roberta Hill Whiteman. HATNAP

Variations of an Air. G. K. Chesterton. *See* Variations on an Air Composed on Having to Appear in a Pageant as Old King Cole.

Variations of Greek Themes. Various authors, *Greek*.

Doricha. AWP; FaBoEE; OBVE

Dust of Timas, The. AWP

"Eutychides, who wrote the songs." OBAL

Happy Man, A. AWP

Inscription by the Sea, An. AWP; FaBoEE

Lais to Aphrodite. FaBoEE

Mighty Runner, A. MeMAP; OBAL

Old Story, The. AWP

Raven, The. AWP; FaBoEE; OBAL

Variations on a Fragment by Trumbull Stickney. John Hollander. NoP-4

Variations on a Fragment by Trumbull Stickney. BAP-94

Variations on a Text by Vallejo. Donald Justice. NoAM; VCAP

Variations on a Theme. Mark Vinz. Poetsp

Variations on a Theme. Anne Wilkinson. MoCV

Variations on a Theme. Oscar Williams.

Spritely Dead, The. Son

Variations on a theme by morning. Cocoa Morning. Bob Kaufman. NBV

Variations on a Theme by William Carlos Williams. Kenneth Koch. BXAP; KaS; NBLV; NIP-4; NoAM; NoP-4; PmAP; PoM; PoPoPo

Variations on an Air: After Robert Browning. G. K. Chesterton. NOBL

(Old King Cole.) BXAP

Variations on [*or of*] an Air: After [Algernon Charles] Swinburne. G. K. Chesterton. NOBL

Variations on an Air: After W. B. Yeats. G. K. Chesterton. BXAP; NOBL

Variations on an Air Composed on Having to Appear in a Pageant as Old King Cole. G. K. Chesterton. NOBL

(Variations of an Air.)

Old King Cole ("Me clairvoyant"). BXAP; NOBL; UV

Old King Cole ("Of an old king in a story"). BXAP

Variations on Sappho. "Michael Field."

"Come, Gorgo, put the rug in place." VWP

"Maids, not to you my mind doth change." VWP

Variations on Southern Themes. Donald Justice. MT

Variations on the Word *Love*. Margaret Atwood. LW; NoAM

Varick Street. Elizabeth Bishop. AFr

Variety, The. John Dancer. NOSC

Variety Theater Manifesto, The. Filippo Tommaso Marinetti, *Italian*.

Futurism Wants to Transform the Variety Theater into a Theater of Amazement, Record-setting, and Body-madness. PFTM, *tr. by* R. W. Flint *and* Arthur A. Coppotelli

Various instants I'm not with you. Robert Johnstone. PNI *Fr.* Every Cache.

Various members of the hierarchy move, The. A Morning Letter. Robert Duncan. PoA

Various nostalgias: rock, scissor, and paper. Towards the Vanishing Point. David Lehman. PmAP

Various the roads of life; in one. Walter Savage Landor. FaBoEE

Varitalk. Weare Holbrook. NYBP

Varus, whom I chanced to meet. Carmen 10. Catullus. AWP; OBVE, *tr. by* John Hookham Frere *Fr.* Carmina.

Vary, re-vary; tune and tune again. Variable. Joshua Sylvester. NOSC

Vas en Afrique! Back to Africa! the butcher we used to / patronize in the rue Cadet market. Racists. Charles Kenneth Williams. LTA

Vase of peonies. Alexis Rotella. HA

Vases. Nan Terrell Reed. BLPA

Vashti. Frances Ellen Watkins Harper. AAP; BlSi; NALW

("But would not bow to shame.") (LL) NAAAL

Vasily Tyorkin. Aleksandr Trifonovich Tvardovsky, *Russian*.

Crossing, The. TCRP, *tr. by* April FitzLyon

Vast bedroom, The. Tracks. John Montague. CIP-2

Vast Bodies of philosophy [*or Philosophie*]. To Mr. Hobbes [*or Hobs*]. Abraham Cowley. BeJo; OxAEP-1

Vast Light. Richard Eberhart. CMoP

Vast mild melancholy splendid. Canberra in April. J. R. Rowland. NOBAu

Vast ocean of light, whose rays surround. Ocean of Light. Phineas Fletcher. NOSC

Vast oceanic movements, the flux and reflux of immeasurable tides oversweep our continent. Currents. Emma Lazarus. PAR *Fr.* By the Waters of Babylon. WPE

Vast Parnassus never knew thy face, The. To My Muse. Agnes Mary Frances Robinson. VWP

Vast wilderness. Tanka. Yosano Tekkan, *Japanese*. MJT, *tr. by* Makoto Ueda

Vasty hall of death, The. (LL) Requiescat. Matthew Arnold. AWP; EBEvV; FHYEP; NOBE; OBEV; PBMP; PoRA

Vaticide. Myron O'Higgins. PoBA

Vaudeville. Lincoln Kirstein. MoP

Vaulting Ambition. Shakespeare. *Fr.* Macbeth.

("If it were done when 'tis done, then 'twere well.") UnPo

Vaunting Oak. John Crowe Ransom. OxBA; VGW

Vedic Hymns. *Unknown, Sanskrit.*

Indra, the Supreme God. AWP

Pushan, God of Pasture. AWP

Veering and wheeling free in the open. (LL) The Harbor. Carl Sandburg. ColAP; TAP

Vega. Lawrence Durrell. OxAEP-2

Vegetable Air, The. Cathy Song. NoAM

Vegetable Destiny. Nina Cassian, *Rumanian*. PBWP, *tr. by* Michael Impey *and* Brian Swann

Vegetable Garden. Lu Yu, *Chinese*. CoBCP, *tr. by* Burton Watson

Vegetable Garden, The. Wyatt Prunty. OBGa

Vegetable Love. Marge Piercy. DeD

Vegetable Wisdom. Mark Halliday. BAP-93

Vegetables / and jewelry, right displayed. For Instance. Robert McAlmon. PoA

Vegetables are walking, The. (LL) Onion Bucket. Lorenzo Thomas. GT

Veil. Marjorie Welish. PmAP

Veil not thy mirror, sweet Amine. To Amine. James Clarence Mangan. OBEV

Veil of death hath fallen, The. To a Deceased Friend. Priscilla Jane Thompson. CBWP-2

Veil of haze protects this, A. City Afternoon. John Ashbery. HeIP-4; InPK-6; NIP-4

Veil thine eyes, O belovèd, my spouse. The Bridegroom of Cana. Marjorie Lowry Christie Pickthall. TrCP

Veil upon veil. Natura Naturans. Kathleen Jessie Raine. NYBP

Veiled, as in night. (LL) Sappho. Catullus, *Latin*. AWP, *tr. by* William Ellery Leonard

Veiled in that light amazing. The Dispraise of Absalom. *Unknown, Irish*. BIrV, *tr. by* Robin Flower

Vein and artery, though ye kill me! Ralph Waldo Emerson. *See* Mithridates.

Vein of sapphires, A. Mahadevi, *Kannada*. WPoS, *tr. by* Jane Hirshfield

Velasquez took a pliant knife. Castilian. Elinor Wylie. ColAP

Veld Eclogue: The Pioneers, A. Roy Campbell. OBSV

Velluti, the lorn heart, the sexless voice. Catullus. OBCVT, *tr. by* Leigh Hunt *Fr.* Velluti to his Revilers.

Velocity with which they write—, The. Movie Actors Scribbling Letters Very Fast in Crucial Scenes. Jean Garrigue. TAP

Velvet ground we now with pleasure tread, The. The Gardens. Abbé Jacques de Lille. OBGa

Velvet Hand, The. Phyllis McGinley. OBCoV

Velvet Shoes. Elinor Wylie. CH; MoAmPo; WHSW

Vendettas end among the gods. Alcman. OBCVT, *tr. by* Guy Davenport *Fr.* A Hymn to Artemis of the Strict Observance: For a Chorus of Spartan Girls Dressed as Doves To Sing at Dawn on the Feast of the Plow.

Vending Machine. Hans Magnus Enzensberger. PoSu

Vendors of green oranges . vendors of immaculate / ducks. Ferryman's Song at Binh Minh. Herbert Krohn. CDa

Venerable Bee, The. Abraham Moses Klein. TrJP

Venerable Mother Toothache. A Charm against the Toothache. John Heath-Stubbs. TwCP

Veneris Venefica Agrestis. Lucio Piccolo, *Italian*. OBVE, *tr. by* Charles Tomlinson

Venetia. Adah Isaacs Menken. CBWP-1

Venetian Air. Thomas Moore. OxBSP

Venetian Interior, 1889. Richard Howard. VCAP

Venetian Night, A. Hugo von Hofmannsthal, *German*. AWP, *tr. by* Ludwig Lewisohn

Venetian Nocturne. Agnes Mary Frances Robinson. VWP

Vengeful across the cold November moors. The Pity of the Leaves. Edwin Arlington Robinson. APN-2; MoAmPo

Veni Coronaberis. Geoffrey Hill. DiPo; NoP-4

Veni Creator. Alice Thompson Meynell. WPE

Veni Creator Spiritus. Charlemagne *and* Hrabanus Maurus, *par. by* Dryden. AWP; FaPoR

Venice. Henry Wadsworth Longfellow. APN-1

Venice. Herman Melville. APN-2

Venice. Arthur Symons. OxBSP

Venice Beach: Brief Song. Dorothy Barresi. SeSe

Venice Recalled. Bruce Boyd. NeAP

Venio ex Oriente. Nuala Ni Dhomhnaill. BiHa

Venom. James Dickey. PoA

Ventriloquy / is the mother tongue. Attention. Rae Armantrout. PmAP

Ventura had hair of the jungle. The Inquietude of a Particular Matter. Alberto A. Ríos. NAmP90

Venus. Federico García Lorca. PFTM

Venus, again[e] thou mov'st a war[re]. To Venus. Horace. *Fr.* Odes.

Venus and Adonis. Bartholomew Griffin. NoSic

Venus and Adonis. Shakespeare.
"At this Adonis smiles as in disdain." EBEV
Courser and the Jennet, The. NOBE
Death of Adonis, The. NoSic
"'Fondling,' she saith, "since I have hemmed thee here."" OAEL-1

Venus and Cupid. Mark Alexander Boyd. *See* Sonet: "Fra bank [*or* banc] to bank [*or* banc], fra wood [*or* wod] to wood [*or* wod] I rin."

VENUS, and young Adonis sitting by her. Venus and Adonis. Bartholomew Griffin. NoSic

Venus Attiring the Graces. William Whitehead. ECEV

Venus de Milo. Charles Marie René Leconte de Lisle, *French.* GS, *tr. by Unknown*

Venus Fly Trap, The. Readymade. John Perreault. SPE

Venus glows in the east. Work to Do Toward Town. Gary Snyder. VGW

Venus, let me never see. (LL) The Lady Who Offers Her Looking Glass to Venus. Matthew Prior, *after the Greek of* Plato. AWP; FaBoEE; NOEC; OBEV; OxBSP

Venus of Milo, The. Henrietta Cordelia Ray. CBWP-3

Venus of the Louvre. Emma Lazarus. APN-2; GS; PAR

Venus of the Salty Shell. Denis Devlin. BIrV; NOIV

Venus Pudica stands, bent. Where her hand is. The Lady at the Castle. John Hollander. NoAM

Venus, take my votive glass. The Lady Who Offers Her Looking-Glass to Venus. Matthew Prior, *after the Greek of* Plato. AWP; FaBoEE; NOEC; OBEV; OxBSP

Venus Transiens. Amy Lowell. NALW; PoA
("Tell me.") CPO

Venus's-Flytraps. Yusef Komunyakaa. FiLi; NAmP90; WeT

Venus's Looking-Glass. Christina Rossetti. NALW

Ver. Shakespeare. *See* Spring.

Verandahs. Robert Francis Brissenden. CBAP; NOBAu

Verb "To Think," The. D. J. Enright. OxBC

Verbal Gerbil. Philip Gross. PeP

Verbum caro factum est. *Unknown.* MiEL

Verdant branch was swinging here, A. So Long Ago. Morris Jacob Rosenfeld, *Yiddish.* TrJP, *tr. by* Elbert Aidline

Verge bore the remnants of his shearings, The. Grandfather's Rockery. David Woo. OpBo

Vergier. *Unknown, Provençal.* GBL, *tr. by* Ezra Pound

Vergissmeinnicht. Keith Douglas. FaBoMo; GTBS-P; InPS-3; NAEL-2; NoAM; NoP-4; OBWP; OxBTC; PoWW; RB; SoSe-8

Verifying the Dead. James Welch. CDW

Verily he is a God that judgeth the earth. (LL) Psalm 58. Bible, *O.T.* BoWoP; NAEL-1; NOCV; NoSic; WPE

Verily / The sky clears. The Sky Clears. *Unknown.* OBVE, *tr. by* Frances Densmore

Verka the Free. "Mikhail Semionovich Golodny," *Russian.* TCRP, *tr. by* Simon Franklin

Verlaine. Richard Hovey. APN-2

Verlaine. Edwin Arlington Robinson. APN-2; NAAL-2; NCAP

Vermeer. Stephen Mitchell. GI

Vermont. David Huddle. CDa

Vermont Apollinaire. William Corbett. PmAP

Vermont Ballad: Change of Season. Robert Penn Warren. ColAP

Vernal Equinox. Martin Johnston. CBAP

Vernal Equinox. Ruth Stone. MoAmPo

Verona. James Wright. NNaP

Vers de Société. Philip Larkin. FP; PeLV

Vers Negre. Richard Caddel. NBrP

Vers Nonsensiques. George Du Maurier. OBCoV

Versailles. Adrienne Rich. OBGa

Verse: "Past ruin'd Ilion." Walter Savage Landor. *See* Passed Ruin'd Ilion.

Verse: "Past ruin'd [*or* ruined] Ilion Helen lives." John Lyle Donaghy. *See* Glenarm.

Verse: "What should we know." Oliver St. John Gogarty. FaBoCh; OBMV; PoRA

Verse I. Christina Rossetti. *See* Aloof.

Verse II. Christina Rossetti. PEW *Fr.* The Thread of Life.

Verse III. Christina Rossetti. PEW *Fr.* The Thread of Life.

Verse, a breeze [']mid blossoms straying. Youth and Age. Coleridge. GTBS-P; LaPo; OBEV; OBNC; PoLF

Verse hath a middle nature: heaven keeps souls. Donne. *See* The First Anniversary [*or* Anniversarie]

Verse in Praise of Lord Henry Howard, Earl of Surrey. George Turberville. Surrey's Poetic Art. EPCY

Verse makes heroic[k] virtue live. To Mr. Henry Lawes, Who Had Then Newly Set a Song of Mine in the Year 1635. Edmund Waller. BeJo; CTC; SeCP

Verse may find him who a sermon flies, A. On the Following Work and Its Author. Jonathan Mitchell. SCAP

Verse Written in the Album of Mademoiselle. Pierre Dalcour, *French.* TTY, *tr. by* Langston Hughes

Verses: "Clean is the autumn wind." Li Po, *Chinese.* TAL, *tr. by* Robert Payne

Verses. William Henry. PeSAV

Verses: "I am monarch of troubles a host." Maria Jane Jewsbury. VWP

Verses: "I am old, sick and lonely." Su Tung-p'o, *Chinese.* TAL, *tr. by* Robert Payne

Verses. Lady Mary Wortley Montagu. *See* Verses Addressed to the Imitator of the First Satire of the Second Book of Horace: An Attack on Pope.

Verses: "Poor fellow, what is it to you." Sir Charles Hanbury Williams. OBWVE

Verses: "You who come from the old village." Wang Wei, *Chinese.* TAL, *tr. by* Robert Payne

Verses about a Nightingale and a Poet. "Eduard Georgievich Bagritzky," *Russian.* TCRP, *tr. by* Vera Dunham

Verses about the Dog's Inheritance. Nikolai Ivanovich Tryapkin, *Russian.*
"We've inherited something from our ancestors, the serfs." TCRP, *tr. by* Bradley Jordan and Katya Zubritskaya

Verses Addressed to a Friend, Just Leaving a Favourite Retirement. Samuel Henley. NOEC

Verses Addressed to the Imitator of the First Satire of the Second Book of Horace. Lady Mary Wortley Montagu.
"When God created thee, one would believe." ECWP

Verses Addressed to the Imitator of the First Satire of the Second Book of Horace: An Attack on Pope. Lady Mary Wortley Montagu. ECEV
(Verses.) CABP

Verses by the Princess Elizabeth, Given to Lord Harington, of Exton, Her Preceptor. Elizabeth, Queen of Bohemia. KTR

Verses Designed to Be Sent to Mr. Adams. Elizabeth Frances Amherst. ECWP

Verses for a First Birthday. George Barker. MoBrPo

Verses for an Album. Charles Lamb. NOBRP

Verses for Fruitwomen. Jonathan Swift. *See* Verses Made for the Women Who Cry Apples, etc.

Verses for the End of an Era. T. P., *Vietnamese.* AVP, *tr. by* Huỳnh Sanh Thông

Verses Found in Thomas Dudley's Pocket after His Death. Thomas Dudley. SCAP

Verses from the Shepherd's Hymn. Richard Crashaw. OBEV *Fr.* In the Holy Nativity of Our Lord God. GeHe; PoEL-2

Verses from the Trials of the Knave of Hearts. "Lewis Carroll." *See* Evidence Read at the Trial of the Knave of Hearts.

Verses in Baretti's Commonplace Book. Samuel Johnson. OxAEP-1

Verses Intended to Be Written below a Noble Earl's Picture. Robert Burns. HoPM

Verses Intended to Have Been Prefixed to the Novel of Emmeline, but Then Suppressed. Charlotte Smith. BWW

Verses Inviting Stella to Tea on the Public Fast-Day. Anna Seward. ECWP
("Dear Stella, 'mid the pious sorrow.") PEW
("For O! reflect, poetic daughter, / 'Twas hapless Britain's laurel-water.") (LL) PEW
(Verses / Inviting Mrs. C—to Tea on a public Fast-day During the American War.) PEW

Verses Left on a Lady's Toilet. Sarah Dixon. ECWP

Verses Made by a Catholic in Praise of Campion That Was Executed at Tyburn for Treason, As Is Made Known by the Proclamation. *Unknown.* NoSic

Verses Made for the Women Who Cry Apples, etc. Jonathan Swift. Onyons. BIrV

Verses Made Sometime Since upon. . . the Indian Squa. John Josselyn. SCAP

Verses Made the Night before He Died [or Dyed]. Sir Walter Ralegh. AAS; NoSic

(Author's Epitaph, Made By Himself, The.) NAEL-1

Verses Made the Night before His Beheading. Sir Walter Ralegh. CABP

Verses, my love! As soon could I. On the Author's Husband Desiring Her to Write Some Verses. Mary Whateley. ECWP

Verses Occasioned by the Sudden Drying Up of St. Patrick's Well. Jonathan Swift.
"Wretched Ierne! with what grief I see." OBSV

Verses of Man's Mortalitie. Simon Wastell. *See* Man's Mortality.

Verses on Blenheim. Martial, *Latin*. AWP, *tr. by* Swift

Verses on Daniel Good. *Unknown*. OxBB

Verses on Hearing That an Airy and Pleasant Situation, near a Populous and Commercial Town, Was Surrounded with New Buildings. Maria Logan. ECWP

Verses on Sir Joshua Reynolds's Painted Window at New College, Oxford. Thomas, the Younger Warton. NOEC; PoEL-3

Verses on the Death of Dr. Swift, D.S.P.D. Jonathan Swift.
"Behold the fatal day arrive!" PeLV; SCV
"Doctors tender of their fame, The." NOBL
"My female friends, whose tender hearts." NOBL
"Now Curll his shop from rubbish drains." PeLV
On the Death of Dean Swift. OxAEP-1
"Perhaps I may allow, the Dean." EPCY; NOBE; PeLV
"Suppose me dead; and then suppose." NOBE; NOEC; OxBoLi; PeLV; PoEL-3

Verses on the Prospect of Planting Arts and Learning in America. George Berkeley. *See* On the Prospect of Planting Arts and Learning in America.

Verses Put into a Lady's Prayer-Book. John Wilmot, 2d Earl of Rochester. *See* Written in a Lady's Prayer Book.

Verses Supposed to Be Written by Alexander Selkirk during His Solitary Abode on the Island of Juan Fernandez. William Cowper. EBEvV; NOEC; PoEL-3; PoLF

(Solitude of Alexander Selkirk, The.) GTBS-P

Verses to a Lady, on Her Saying She Preferred Commonalty to an Irish Peerage. Lady Sophia Burrell.
"Clock strikes five—the watchman goes, The." ECWP

Verses to Miss———. J. Wilde. NOEC

Verses to Mr. Richardson on his History of Sir Charles Grandison. Anna Williams. ECWP

Verses to my Heart's-Sister. Henrietta Cordelia Ray. AAP; CBWP-3

Verses Written at Montauban in France, 1750. Joseph Warton. ECEV

Verses Written by Mrs. Hutchinson. Lucy Hutchinson. KTR; NOSC

Verses Written during the War, 1756–1763. Thomas Osbert Mordaunt.
Sound, Sound the Clarion. EBEvV; FaBoEE; FaPoR; NOBE

Verses Written in a Garden. Lady Mary Wortley Montagu. ECWP

Verses Written in a Lady's Sherlock "Upon Death." Philip Dormer Stanhope, 4th Earl of Chesterfield. EBEV

(To a Lady on Reading Sherlock "Upon Death.") NOEC

Verses Written in a London Churchyard. Christopher Smart. CBNP

Verses Written in 1872. Robert Louis Stevenson. BLPA

Verses Written in the Chiosk [of the British Palace], at Pera, Overlooking [the City of] Constantinople. Lady Mary Wortley Montagu. ECEV; ECWP

Verses Written on Her Death-bed at Bath to Her Husband in London. Mary Monck. ECWP; LW

Verses Written on Sand. "Melech Ravitch," *Yiddish*. CEEP, *tr. by* Seymour Mayne *and* Rivka Augenfeld

Versicles on Sign-Posts. Robert Burns.
"Head pure, sinless quite of brain or soul, A." FaBoEE

Version. Dennis Scott. PBCV

Versions. Robert Kelly. *Fr.* The Book of Persephone. PoM

Versions of Love. Roy Fuller. CBLP; LiTM

Versos de Montalgo. *Unknown*. AS, *tr. by* Frank J. Dobie

Vertex, The. Yuksa Yi, *Korean*. CKP, *tr. by* Jaihiun Kim

Vertical / dead tree / with no star in its crown, A. Tadeusz Rózewicz. *See* Massacre of the Boys.

Vertical Poetry. Roberto Juarroz, *Spanish*.
"Bottom of things is neither life nor death, The." VCWP, *tr. by* W. S. Merwin

Vertigo. Tongjip Shin, *Korean*. CKP, *tr. by* Jaihiun Kim

Vertigo is my territory. Eagle. Robin Skelton. NOBC

Very apt question struck me, A. Limerick. Sydney Bernard Smith. PeLi

Very bitter weeping that ye made, The. Dante. AWP *Fr.* La Vita Nuova.

Very day one son was drowned, The. Honestus, *Greek*. GrAn, *tr. by* Robin Skelton

Very Days. Aaron Shurin. PT

Very due that being each one dwells. The Narrow Path. Norman Henry, II Pritchard. GT

Very empty cubic, blue room. No windows. No door frames. Colors. Fortunato Depero, *Italian*. PFTM, *tr. by* Victoria Nes Kirby

Very Fair My Lot. Jacob David Kamzon, *Hebrew*. TrJP, *tr. by* Sholom J. Kahn

Very few can. The Pecan, The Toucan. Robert Williams Wood. NBLV

Very few people know where they will die. A Deathplace. Louis Edward Sissman. NoP-4

Very fine conga of sweat, A. I See Chano Pozo. Jayne Cortez. MoNo; PmAP

Very fine is my valentine. A Very Valentine. Gertrude Stein. PFTM

Very first joy that Mary had, The. The Joys of Mary. *Unknown*. AmFP

Very friendly / prison, A. Tripart. Gayl Jones. BlSi

Very handsome gentleman, A. *Unknown*. BoWoP *Fr.* Shih Ching.

Very like a Whale. Ogden Nash. HAP; InPK-6; InPS-3; PoLF

Very little snail, A. What Do I See. Gertrude Stein. PFTM

Very Minor Poet Speaks, A. Isabel Valle. BLPA

Very Odd Fish, A. D'Arcy Wentworth Thompson. OxBChV

Very often when you are striving. The Would-be Critic. Mrs. Henry Linden. CBWP-4

Very old are forever, The. Ted Kooser. PBCAP

Very old are the woods. All That's Past. Walter De la Mare. NOBE; OAEL-2; OBMV; OxBTC

Very Old Man. James Henry. NOBVV

Very pitiful lady, very young, A. Dante. AWP; CTC *Fr.* La Vita Nuova.

Very Sad Conversation at Night, A. Anna Swirszczynska, *Polish*. PoSu, *tr. by* Czeslaw Milosz *and* Leonard Nathan

Very small chickens in tattered feathers. The. A Study in Aesthetics. Robert Peters. BXAP

Very small children in patched clothing, The. The Study in Aesthetics. Ezra Pound. CMoP; NOBA

Very soon the Yankee teachers. Learning to Read. Frances Ellen Watkins Harper. AAP; BlSi; NAAAL; NALW

Very True, the Linnets Sing. Autumnal Song. Walter Savage Landor. OAEL-2

Very Valentine, A. Gertrude Stein. PFTM

Vesi, the black one, the leaper who sprang. Praises of the King Dingana (Vesi). *Unknown, Zulu*. PeSA

Vesperal. Ernest Christopher Dowson. OBMV

Vespers. W. H. Auden. FaBoMo *Fr.* Horae Canonicae.

Vespers. Thomas Edward Brown. BoTP

Vespers. Donald Davie. *Fr.* Horae Canonicae. CRP

Vespers. A. A. Milne. OxBChV
"Hush! Hush! Whisper who dares!" UV

Vespers. Emile Ologoudou. PBMAP

Vespers. C. Dale Young. BAP-96

Vespers: Parousia. Louise Glück. PuP-17

Vessel with long red banners of the Prophet, A. The Plague. Nikolai Stepanovich Gumilyov, *Russian*. TCRP, *tr. by* Simon Franklin

Vestal, The. Nathalia Crane. TrJP

Vestal, The. Alexander Pope. *See* Life of a Nun.

Vestal Lady on Brattle, The. Gregory Corso. Poetr

Vestal Virgin, The. Eloise Bibb. CBWP-4

Vesta's Father. Julia Kasdorf. PBCAP

Vestiges. Basil Bunting. PFTM *Fr.* Vestiges.

Vete. Cultures. Gloria Anzaldúa. UnSA

Veteran, The. Frank S. Brown. NSI

Veteran, The. Margaret Isabel Postgate Cole. NSI

Veteran. Walter McDonald. CDa

Veteran. Lola Ridge. WPE

Veteran Greeks came home, The. The Return of the Greeks. Edwin Muir. CMoP; NoP-4; PoE

Veteran Sirens. Edwin Arlington Robinson. NOBA

Veteran smiled and let us pass through, A. Thomas Kinsella. BiHa *Fr.* A Technical Supplement.

Veterans. George Johnston. NOBC

Veterans, The. Donagh MacDonagh. CIP-2

Veterans of the Wars. Edgar Lee Masters. CBCWP

Vet's Rehabilitation. Ray Durem. PoBA

Vetus Flamma. Robert Mezey. PoA

Vex no man's secret soul--if that can be. Help. Sadi. AWP, *tr. by* Sir Edwin Arnold *Fr.* The Gulistan.

Vex th'ill-natur'd fools we cannot please. (LL) To Nysus. Sir Charles Sedley. FaBoEE; OBSV

Via Crucis. Herman Melville. APN-2; NCAP *Fr.* Clarel: A Poem and Pilgrimage in the Holy Land.

Via Margutta. Maria Luisa Spaziani, *Italian.* NeIt, *tr. by* Beverly Allen

Via Media Via Dolorosa. Stevie Smith. WPN

Viable. A. R. Ammons. TAP

Viaticum. Birago Diop, *French.* NegPo; PBMAP, *tr. by* Ellen Conroy Kennedy

Viaticum. Pao Yu, *Chinese.* OHMPC, *tr. by* Kenneth Rexroth

Viaticum. U Tam'si Tchicaya, *French.* NegPo, *tr. by* Ellen Conroy Kennedy

Vibrant naive Naabeeho women. Modern on the Surface. Nia Francisco. HATNAP

Vibration in the summer air. (LL) Midsummer. James Scully. NYBP; TwCP

Vicar, The. George Crabbe. OBSV *Fr.* The Borough.
  "But let applause be dealt in all we may." OBNC

Vicar, The. Winthrop Mackworth Praed. OBEV; OBNC; OxAEP-2; PoEL-4 *Fr.* Every-Day Characters.

Vicar of Bray, The. *Unknown.* FaBoPV; NOBE; NOBL; OBSV; OxBoLi
  ("And this is law, &c.") (LL) OBCoV

Vicar of Wakefield, The. Oliver Goldsmith.
  Elegy on the Death of a Mad Dog, An. BLPA; FaBoBe; FaBoCh; NBLV; NOEC; NOIV; OBNV; OxAEP-1; TFi
  (On the Death of a Mad Dog.) NTP
  Song: "When lovely woman stoops to folly." AWP; BoLoP; EBEvV; FHYEP; FaBoSe; NOBE; NOEC; OxAEP-1

Vicarious Atonement. Richard Aldington. MoBrPo

Vice. Anthony Hecht. OBAL

Vice longer than you wished it, marred but poignant. Catullus. *See Carmina,* XL.

Vice most obscene and unsavoury, A. Limerick. *Unknown.* NOBL; PeLV

Vice now may lift aloft her speckled head. Spoken Extempore on the Death of Mr. Pope. *Unknown.* NOEC

Vice-regal walls dominate the back street. Gym. Richard Murphy. BiHa

Vices of the Modern World. Nicanor Parra, *Spanish.* CLPP, *tr. by* Jorge Elliott

Vice's Song, The. John Pickering. NoSic *Fr.* Horestes.

Vicious Circle. Marsha Prescod. LW

Vicious winter finally yields, The. W. D. Snodgrass. MoLi *Fr.* Heart's Needle. CAPP-1

Vicissitudes of the Creator. Archibald MacLeish. MeMAP

Vickery's Mountain. Edwin Arlington Robinson. MoAmPo

Victim, The. Ellen Bryant Voigt. CrSp

Victim Number 48. Mahmoud Darwish, *Arabic.* VCWP, *tr. by* Denys Johnson-Davies

Victime to your Coldness, than your Pride, A. (LL) To J. G. "Ephelia." KTR; NOSC

Victims, The. Sharon Olds. InPS-3; SoSe-8

Victims of the demon dance. For All Unwed Mothers. Robert Fleming. ISC

Victims of the Little Box, The. Vasco [*or* Vasko] Popa, *Serbo-Croatian.* HSix, *tr. by* Charles Simic
  ("You'd be better off never waking up.") (LL) CEEP, *tr. by* Charles Simic

Victoire. Guillaume Apollinaire, *French.*
  Listen to the sea. PFTM, *tr. by* David Antin

Victor, The. C. W. Longenecker. PWR

Victor Dog, The. James Merrill. NoAM; NoP-4

Victor Garibaldi. Melvin B. Tolson. GT

Victoria Market. Francis Brabazon. NOBAu

Victoria Markets Recollected in Tranquility, The. "Furnley Maurice." NOBAu

Victoria said: "We've no quarrel." Limerick. Frank Richards. PeLi

Victoria Station. Luigi Fontanella, *Italian.* NeIt, *tr. by* Michael Palma

Victoria was bitterly short. Limerick. Cyril Mountjoy. PeLi

Victorian Family Photograph. Kit Wright. OBCoV

Victorian gent said: "This dance," A. Limerick. Frank Richards. PeLi

Victorian Grandmother. Margo Lockwood. Poetsp

Victorian Hangman Tells His Love, A. Bruce Dawe. NoAM

Victorian Idyll, A. David Wagoner. NoAM

Victorian mothers instructed their daughters, ahem. Victoria's Secret. Charles Martin. RA

Victories of Love, The. Coventry Patmore.

Victorious beauty, though your eyes. To the Countess of Salisbury. Aurelian Townshend. MeLP; SeCP

Victorious men of earth, no more. Song. James Shirley. BeJo; GTBS-P *Fr.* Cupid and Death.

Victors, The. Anthony McNeill. PBCV

Victory. Lionel Pigot Johnson. NOBVV

Victory and praise in their [*or* its] own right belong. (LL) Hymn of Apollo. Shelley. NAEL-2; OAEL-2

Victory Calypso, Lord's 1950. Egbert Moore, ("Lord Beginner"). PeLV
  (Victory Calypso.) OBCoV

Victory comes late. Emily Dickinson. APN-2; InPK-6

Victory Dance, A. Alfred Noyes. NSI; PoLF

Victory Drive, near Fort Benning, Georgia. Bin Ramke. MT

Victory in Defeat. Edwin Markham. PoLF

Victory of Samothrace, The. "Rubén Dario," *Spanish.* GS, *tr. by Unknown*

Victory on the Last Green. Thomas Mathison. NOEC *Fr.* The Goff; an Heroi-comical Poem.

Video Cuisine. Maxine W. Kumin. NoAM

Vield Path, The. William Barnes. NOBVV

Vienna in the Rain. Jay Meek. CMAP

Vierge Moderne. Edith Södergran, *Swedish.* PFTM, *tr. by* Stina Katchadourian

Vierzide Chairs, The. William Barnes. NOBVV

Vies Manquées. Edith Nesbit. VWP

Vies with this Venus her auspicious theorem? Catullus. *See* Carmen 45 ("Phyllis Corydon clutched to him").

Viet Nam Monument. Nicholas Virgilio. HA

Vietnam. Clarence Major. PoBA

Vietnam. Michael McClintock.
  "Hamburger Hill." HA

Vietnam Dream. Ron Carter. CDa

Vietnam #4. Clarence Major. NBV; PoBA

View, The. Howard Nemerov. NYBP

View, A. Beverly Quint. NYBP

View, A. Mona Van Duyn. VCAP

View, all ye eyes above, this sight which flings. Edward Taylor. NOSC *Fr.* Preparatory Meditations Before My Approach to the Lord's Supper.

View from a Cab, The. Henry Taylor. NBLV

View from an Airplane at Night, over California, The. Bruce Bawer. RA

View from an Attic Window, The, (For Francis and Barbara). Howard Nemerov. CoAP; CoAmPo

View from Cortona, A. Richard Hugo. AF

View from far: beside the gate, The. Returning Home. Yüan Mei, *Chinese.* CoBLCP, *tr. by* Jonathan Chaves

View from Skates in Berkeley, The. Quincy Troupe. UnSA

View from the Cliffs. Tu Mu, *Chinese.* OHMPC, *tr. by* Kenneth Rexroth

View from the Corner. Samuel Allen. SSLK

View from the Gorge. Ben Belitt. NYBP

View from the Window, The. Ronald Stuart Thomas. NoP-4

View it, by day, from the back. Movie House. John Updike. PeLV

View like one of Fairy-land, A. George Darley. NOBRP *Fr.* Sylvia; or, The May Queen.

View of a Pig. Ted Hughes. LiTM; OxAEP-2; OxBTC; TwCP

View of Christ's Kingdom, A. William Williams, *Welsh.*
  Marriage in Eden, The. OBWVE, *tr. by* Lewis Saunders *and* Gwyn Jones

View of Jersey, A. Edward Field. NeAP

View of my garden, A. Masaoka Shiki, *Japanese.* MJT, *tr. by* Ueda, Makoto

View of the Countryside. Wu Wei-yeh, *Chinese.* SuSp, *tr. by* Chang Yin-nan *and* Lewis C. Walmsley

View of the Library of Congress from Paul Laurence Dunbar High School, *for Doris Craig and Michael Olshausen.* Thomas Sayers Ellis. GT

View of the Town, A. In an Epistle to a Friend. Thomas Gilbert.
  Against Homosexuality. NOEC

View on Death, A. Roy W. Watson. PWR

View with a Grain of Sand. Wislawa Szymborska, *Polish.* CEEP, *tr. by* Magnus J. Krynski *and* Robert A. Maguire; BLT, *tr. by* Stanislaw Barańczak *and* Clara Cavanagh
  ("And the news inhuman.") (LL) CEEP, *tr. by* Magnus J. Krynski *and* Robert A. Maguire

Viewing Mountains with His Reverence Hao Ch'u: To My Friends and Relatives in the Capital. Liu Tsung-yüan, *Chinese.* SuSp, *tr. by* Jan W. Walls

Viewing Mr. Yü's Landscape Painting on the Wall. Wang Chi, *Chinese.* SuSp, *tr. by* Joseph J. Lee

Viewing the Ocean. Ts'ao Ts'ao, *Chinese.* CoBCP, *tr. by* Burton Watson

Viewing the Waterfall at Mount Lu. Li Po, *Chinese.* CoBCP; TTTS, *tr. by* Burton Watson
  ("Ninth height of Heaven.") (LL) ChAP
  ("Sunlight streaming on Incense Stone kindles violet.") ChAP

Views from the High Camp. W. S. Merwin. CoAmPo

Vigil. Richard Dehmel, *German*. AWP, *tr. by* Ludwig Lewisohn

Vigil. Giuseppe Ungaretti, *Italian*. PeFWW, *tr. by* Jonathan Griffin
("Entire night, An.") ItIP
("Tied to life.") (LL) ItIP
(Watch.) ItIP

Vigil of Venus, The. Pervigilium Veneris, *Latin*. GBL, *tr. by* Allen Tate; AWP, *tr. by* Thomas Stanley
"Goddesse bade the nymphs remove, The." OBVE, *tr. by* Thomas Stanley
"Love he to morrow, who lov'd never." OBVE, *tr. by* Thomas Stanley
"Over sky and land and down under the sea." OBCVT, *tr. by* Allen Tate
"*Spring*, the new, the warb'ling Spring appears, The." OBCVT, *tr. by* Thomas Parnell

Vigil strange I kept on the field one night;. Walt Whitman. APN-1; CBCWP; ColAP; HeIP-4; MeMAP; MoAmPo; NAAL-1; NAAL-3; NOBA; NoP-4; OBWP; PoE; PoPoPo; TAP

Vigilantius, or a Servant of the Lord Found Ready. Cotton Mather. SCAP

Vigils. Siegfried Sassoon. CMoP
Down the Glimmering Staircase. PoLF

Vigula divina, sorcerers call a rod. Greville Fulke. FaBoPV

(VII from Secrets). Jessie Orton Jones.
"We have tulips in our flower bed." CTV

(VIII from Secrets). Jessie Orton Jones.
"I am glad I'm who I am." CTV

Viking Terror, The. *Unknown, Old Irish*. IIP, *tr. by* Frank O'Connor

Vikings, The ("Bitter the wind tonight"). *Unknown, Irish*. BIrV, *tr. by* John Montague

Vile mouth of the exorcist, The. Lucianus, *Greek*. InMo, *tr. by* Sam Hamill

Vile snake will *always sting you*, The. (LL) Anger in its time and place. Charles Lamb *and* Mary Lamb. NOxBChV

Vile World. Simon Rae. UV

Villa D'Este. Edwin Denby. OBGa

Villa Restaurant, The. Derek Walcott. WeW-3

Village, The. George Crabbe.
"No longer truth, though shown in verse, disdain." OxAEP-1
Pauper's Funeral, The. OBNC
Poor-House, The. ECEV
Rural Life. NOBE
Truth in Poetry. EPCY; FHYEP
"Village life, and every care that reigns." NAEL-1; NOEC; OAEL-1; PoE; PoEL-4

Village, The. Marina Gashe. PBA

Village, The. Virgil, *Latin*.
"Rank weeds, that every art and care defy." OBCVT, *tr. by* George Crabbe

Village and Factory. Alexander Ilyich Bezymensky, *Russian*. TrJP, *tr. by* Babette Deutsch

Village Blacksmith, The. Henry Wadsworth Longfellow. APN-1; AiP; CTV; EBEvV; FaBoBe; FaPoR; OBAL; OBCA; PAR; PWR; UV
("Has earned a night's repose.") (LL) ChAP

Village chief made the announcement from door to door. Tune: "Slow Chant"—Kao-tsu's Homecoming. Sui Ching-ch'en, *Chinese*. SuSp, *tr. by* Sherwin S. S. Fu

Village Choir, The. *Unknown*. UV

Village Coddled in the Valley, The. George Barker. OxBSP

Village Crier, The. *Unknown, Vietnamese*. AVP, *tr. by* Huỳnh Sanh Thông

Village Curate, The. James Hurdis.
Village Fair, The. ECEV

Village for a Wedding. Jan Bolesw Ozog, *Polish*. CEEP, *tr. by* Leonard Kress

Village Life, A, (for John Robertson). Derek Walcott. GT

Village life, and every care that reigns. George Crabbe. NAEL-1; NOEC; OAEL-1; PoE; PoEL-4 *Fr.* The Village.

Village lights in the dusk. Evening Lights on the River. Chiang Shih-ch'üan, *Chinese*. OHMPC, *tr. by* Kenneth Rexroth

Village Night. Po Chü-i, *Chinese*. CoBCP, *tr. by* Burton Watson

Village Noon; Mid-Day Bells. Merrill Moore. MoAmPo

Village of the Presents, The. James McMichael. AmPA

Village Patriarch, The. Ebenezer Elliot.
"Five rivers, like the fingers of a hand." NOBRP

Village Preacher, The. Oliver Goldsmith. *Fr.* The Deserted Village. NOEC; OAEL-1; PoEL-3

Village Schoolmaster, The. Oliver Goldsmith. *Fr.* The Deserted Village. NOEC; OAEL-1; PoEL-3

Village Spa. Phyllis McGinley. OBCoV

Village, The ("Sweet was the sound, when oft at evening's close"). Oliver Goldsmith. IIP *Fr.* The Deserted Village. NOEC; OAEL-1; PoEL-3

Village! thy butcher's son, the steward now. Ebenezer Elliot. OBSV *Fr.* The Splendid Village.

Village Tudda, The. Kenneth Patchen. VGW

Village Wedding, The. Angelos Sikelianos, *Greek*. GrIP, *tr. by* Edmund Keeley *and* Philip Sherrard

Village where they ring, A. Basho, *Japanese*. TAL, *tr. by* Harold G. Henderson

Village woman brings her five-year-old son, The. Ballad of Selling a Child. Wang Chiu-ssu, *Chinese*. CoBLCP, *tr. by* Jonathan Chaves

Villagers all, this frosty tide. Carol: "Villagers all, this frosty tide." Kenneth Grahame. PChr *Fr.* The Wind in the Willows.

Villagers who gather round. Spiel of [the] Three Mountebanks. John Crowe Ransom. MoAmPo

Villain, The. W. H. Davies. MoBrPo; OxBSP; OxBTC; SAGP

Villains. Stevie Smith. OxBoV

Villancico. *Unknown, Spanish*. AWP, *tr. by* Thomas Walsh

Villanelle. William Empson. LoP; UV

Villanelle VI. Judith Barrington. FFC

Villanelle: "Every day our bodies separate." Marilyn Hacker. AmPA

Villanelle: "O winter wind, lat grievin be." Margaret Winefride Simpson. OxBS

Villanelle: "Time can [*or* will] say nothing but I told you so." W. H. Auden. MoBrPo

Villanelle. Tomas Venclova, *Lithuanian*. CEEP, *tr. by* David McDuff

Villanelle of Marguerites. Ernest Christopher Dowson. MoBrPo

Villanelle of Sunset. Ernest Christopher Dowson. ADE

Villanelle of the Poet's Road. Ernest Christopher Dowson. OBMV; UnPo

Villanelle: The Psychological Hour. Ezra Pound. CTC; NAAL-2

Villanious and Abominable Falstaff. Shakespeare. *Fr.* King Henry IV, Pt. I. NAEL-1

Villeggiature. Edith Nesbit. LW; NOBVV; PEW
(Villeggiatura.) OxBSn

Villers. Alexander Pope. *See* The Duke of Buckingham.

Villon, our sad bad glad mad brother's name? (LL) A Ballad of François Villon. Swinburne. PoEL-5; PoRA

Villon's Good-Night. William Ernest Henley. CBNP

Villon's Straight Tip to All Cross Coves. William Ernest Henley, *after* Villon. AWP; CBNP; OxAEP-2; OxBoV

Vincent Corbett, farther known. An Elegy Upon the Death of His Own Father. Richard Corbet. BeJo; NOSC

Vincent Ogé. George Boyer Vashon. AAP; APN-2

Vindication. Vadim Antonov, *Russian*.
"Toward morning, slipping the pistol under my arm." TCRP, *tr. by* Vera Dunham

Vine, The. Robert Herrick. BeJo; CaPo; CavPo; EP; NAEL-2; NoP-4

Vine and the Goat, The. Aesop, *Greek*. AWP, *tr. by* William Ellery Leonard

Vine I see, and though 'tis time to glean, A. Overripe Fruit. Kasmuneh, *Arabic*. TrJP

Vine v. Goat. Euenus, *Greek*. GrAn, *tr. by* Alistair Elliot

Vineleaf at the window, A. Sirius. Donald Revell. PT

Vines, The. John Gray. NOBVV

Vineta. Charles Spear. PeNZ

Viney, go put on de kittle, I got one o' mastah's chickens. (LL) Accountability. Paul Laurence Dunbar. APN-2; PoLF

Vineyard, The. W. S. Merwin. NNaP

Vineyard of My Beloved, The. Priscilla Jane Thompson. AAP; CBWP-2

Vintage. Robert Hass. NAmP90

Vintage to the Dungeon, The. Richard Lovelace. BeJo; CaPo

Viola's Song. Sir William Davenant. NOSC *Fr.* The Law against Lovers.

Violation, A. Richard Jackson. NAmP90

Violence. Robert Lowell. NoAM

Violence, how smoothly it came. Shadow Train. John Ashbery. LCAP-2

Violent order is disorder, and, A. Connoisseur of Chaos. Wallace Stevens. LiTM; PFTM

Violent praise the destructive rites of the hawk, The. The Beaver's Story. Vernon Watkins. NYBP

Violent Space, The. Etheridge Knight. BPo

Violent Storm. Mark Strand. NYBP

Violet. John Hollander. FYAP

Violet, The. Poor Snow. Denise Riley. NBrP

Violet. Arthur Symons. ADE

Violet, The. Jane Taylor. WoRP

Violet City: Aspects of the Transitive. Gustaf Sobin. PT

Violet in the deepest green, A. Goethe, *German*. STV, *tr. by* John Frederick Nims

Violet Twilights. Edith Södergran, *Swedish*. WPOW, *tr. by* Stina Katchadourian

Violets. John Moultrie. BoTP

Violets. P. A. Ropes. BoTP

Violets. *Unknown.* BoTP

Violets. Virginia Brady Young. HA

Violets are blue, roses are red;. The Report Card. Richard Barrows. CTV

Violets blue of the eyes divine, The. Die blauen Veilchen der Äugelein. Heinrich Heine, *German.* AWP, *tr. by* James Thomson

Violets, Daffodils. Elizabeth Jane Coatsworth. OBCA; TLR

Violin Bow and Strings. Innokenty Fiodorovich Annensky, *Russian.* TCRP, *tr. by* Lubov Yakovleva *with* Daniel Weissbort

Violin which is following me, A. Conspiracy. Jack Spicer. APSN

Violinist's shadow vanishes, The. Cadenza. Ted Hughes. CMoP; NYBP

Violins float in the sky. Europe, Late. Dan Pagis, *Hebrew.* HP, *tr. by* Stephen Mitchell

Viper, The. Hilaire Belloc. NoAM

Viper, The. Ruth Pitter. FaBoTw

Vir nullâ non donandus lauru. (LL) The Vicar. Winthrop Mackworth Praed. OBEV; OBNC; OxAEP-2; PoEL-4

Vire will wind in other shadows. Saint-Lô. Samuel Beckett. NOIV

Virgidemiarum. Joseph Hall.

   "Gentle squire would gladly entertain, A." NoSic

   "Great is the folly of a feeble brain." EBEV; FMP

   "One higher-pitched doth set his soaring thought." EPCY

   "Pardon, ye glowing ears; need will it out." NoSic

   "Sturdy ploughman doth the soldier see, The." OBSV

   "When Gullion died (who knows not Gullion?)." NoSic

   "Who doubts? The laws fell down from heaven's height." OBSV, *book* II

Virgidemiarum Book 5. Joseph Hall.

   "Hous-keping's dead, *Saturio:* wot'st thou where?" PBRV

Virgil's Aeneid Book 4. Richard Stanyhurst.

   "Thee whilst thee dawning Aurora fro the Ocean hastned." PBRV

Virgil's Aeneid Book 4. Henry Howard, Earl of Surrey.

   "Then from the seas, the dawning gan arise." PBRV

Virgils Gnat. Virgil, *Latin.*

   "Fiery Sun was mounted now on hight, The." OBCVT, *tr. by* Edmund Spenser

Virgin, The. Laura Riding Jackson. ChIV-2

Virgin Declares Her Beauties, A. Francesco da Barberini, *Italian.* AWP, *tr. by* D. G. Rossetti

Virgin is thinking of a child, The. Leonardo's Secret. Robert Bly. NNaP

Virgin Life, A. Jane Barker. KTR

   ("Since, O good Heavens! you have bestow'd on me.") BWW

Virgin Martyr, The. Ada Cambridge. NOBAu

Virgin Martyrs. John Heath-Stubbs. OxBC

Virgin Mary, The. Donne. *Fr.* The Litanie. PoEL-2

Virgin Mary, The. *Unknown, Welsh.* OBWVE, *tr. by* Joseph P. Clancy

Virgin-Mother stood at distance (there), The. Observation. Robert Herrick. ChIV-2

Virgin Mother walked barefoot, The. Begotten of the Spleen. Charles Simic. AF; LCAP-2

Virgin of the vestal kind. The Vestal Virgin. Eloise Bibb. CBWP-4

Virgin, sing the Virgin Huntress. 1.21: To Apollo and Diana ("Dianam tenerae dicite virgines"). Horace. OBVE, *tr. by* Branwell Brontë *Fr.* Odes.

Virgin Warrior, The. Gwendolyn MacEwen. FaBoWP

Virginal, A. Ezra Pound. CMoP; ColAP; MeMAP; MoAmPo; NAAL-2; NIP-4; NOBA; OxBA; Poetr; Son; TAP

Virginia. Hart Crane. *Fr.* Three Songs. NAAL-2 *Fr.* The Bridge.

Virginia. T. S. Eliot. FaBoA; InPK-6 *Fr.* Landscapes. RB

Virginia. Elouise Loftin. PoBA

Virginia Lake. James Keir Baxter. PeNZ

Virginia Portrait. Sterling Brown. GT

Virginia's Bloody Soil. *Unknown.* AmFP

Virginia's writing her diary. Bloomsbury Snapshot. Connie Bensley. OBCoV

Virgins, The. Donne. *Fr.* The Litanie. PoEL-2

Virgins, The. Derek Walcott. OxBC; SoSe-8

Virgins are like the fair flower in its lustre. What Shall I Do to Show How Much I Love Her? John Gay. *Fr.* The Beggar's Opera. OAEL-1

Virgins promis'd when I died [*or* dy'd]. An Epitaph upon a Child. Robert Herrick. FaBoEE

Virgin's Song, The. *Unknown.* NOBE

Virgins who died on the eve of marriage. Familiar Spirits. Lyall Tao Tschung Yu. OxBSn

Virgo, August. John Taylor. NOSC

Virgo Descending. Charles Wright. ColAP; LCAP-2; TRP; WeT

Virtual Particles. Frank Wilczek. NBLV

Virtual Reality. Charles Bernstein. FTOS

Virtue. Nicholas Grimald. SCGP

(Description of Virtue.) NoSic

Virtue [*or* Vertue]. George Herbert. APAD; AWP; CH; ClHu; FMP; GeHe; HAP; HeIP-4; InPS-3; MeLP; NAEL-1; NOBE; NOCV; NoP-4; NOSC; OAEL-1; OBEV; OPOU; PeECV; PFE; PoE; PoRA; SCGP; SeCP; SoSe-8; TFi

Virtue, alas, now let me take some rest. Sonnet 4. Sir Philip Sidney. *Fr.* Astrophil and Stella. AAS; SiPS

Virtue alone can never die. but lives to. Hannah Taylor. FaBoVe

Virtue conceal'd within our breast. Jonathan Swift, *after the Latin of* Horace. OBVE

Virtue, dear friends, needs no 'defense'. 1.22. Horace. OBVE, *tr. by the* Earl of Roscommon *Fr.* Odes.

Virtue dwells rarely in the bright eyed and fair. Immanuel di Roma. *Fr.* Machberoth. TrJP, *tr. by* J. Chotzner

Virtue may choose the high or low degree. The Triumph of Vice. Alexander Pope. NOBE; OBSV *Fr.* Epilogue to the Satires, in Two Dialogues. OAEL-1

Virtue of ancestors handed down. Poem in Rhyme-Prose Form. Pan Chieh-yü, *Chinese.* CoBCP, *tr. by* Burton Watson

Virtue's branches wither, virtue pines. A Priest's Song. Thomas Dekker *and others.* NoSic *Fr.* Old Fortunatus.

Virtue's Goal Is God. "Angelus Silesius." GePo, *tr. by* George C. Schoolfield *Fr.* The Cherubical Wanderer.

Virtues of an amulet / and quick surprise, The. (LL) The Warning. Robert Creeley. NeAP; NeaP; VGW

Virtues of Carnation Milk, The. *Unknown. See* Carnation Milk.

Virtues of the cane must now be sung, The. Nathaniel Weekes. *Fr.* Barbados. PBCV

Virtuoso, A. Austin Dobson. PeVV

Virtuous Wife, The. Süsskind von Trimberg, *Middle High German.* TrJP

Virtuous Woman, The. Bible, *O.T.* TrJP *Fr.* Proverbs.

Visage becomes armed, The; within, Armed Vision. N. P. van Wyk Louw, *Afrikaans.* PeSA, *tr. by* Jack Cope *and* Uys Krige

Viscount Stansgate, or Wedgwood, or Benn. Limerick. Tim Hopkins. PeLi

Viscous air, wheres' ere she fly, The. The Kingfisher. Andrew Marvell. *Fr.* Upon Appleton House [To My Lord Fairfax]. FaBoPV; GeHe; SeCP

Visible, invisible. A Jelly-Fish. Marianne Moore. APo; ChAP; OxBSP

Visibly here the tide. Wellfleet Harbor. Paul Goodman. CoAP

Vision. Delmira Augustini, *Spanish.* WPOW, *tr. by* Marti Moody

Vision, A. John Clare. EBVV; GTBS-P; NAEL-2; NOBVV; NTP; OAEL-2; OBNC; PoE

Vision. Harry Crosby. SPE

Vision. James Devaney. NOBAu

Vision. Richard Eberhart. NYBP

Vision. Elizabeth N. Hauer. PoToHe

Vision, A. Edward Herbert, 1st Baron Herbert of Cherbury. SeCP

Vision, The. Robert Herrick. CaPo; CavPo; NOSC; SCGP; SeCP

   ("*Herrick,* thou art too coorse to love.") (LL) PBRV

Vision, A. Hugo von Hofmannsthal, *German.* TrJP, *tr. by* Charles Wharton Stork

Vision. Louis Johnson. PeNZ

Vision, A. Maria Konopnicka, *Polish.* WPOW, *tr. by* Jerzy Peterkiewicz *and* Burns Singer

Vision, The. Egan O'Rahilly, *Irish.* NOIV, *tr. by* Thomas Kinsella (Reverie at Dawn.) FaBoPV, *tr. by* Frank O'Connor

Vision, The. William Taylor. NOEC

Vision, A. Ts'ao Chih, *Chinese.* ChiP, *tr. by* Arthur Waley

Vision, The. Katharine Tynan. NSI

Vision. May Thielgaard Watts. LW

Vision, A. W. B. Yeats.

   All Souls' Night. OxAEP-2

Vision. Israel Zangwill. TrJP

Vision (2). Sherman Alexie. UnSA

Vision and Prayer. Dylan Thomas. LiTM

Vision as of crowded city streets, A. Shakespeare Henry Wadsworth Longfellow. AWP

Vision at Knock. Gerry Murphy. BiHa

Vision by Sweetwater. John Crowe Ransom. CMoP; FaBoMo; MeMAP; NOBA; OxBA; RB

Vision Clear, The. J. M. Westrup. BoTP

Vision from the Blue Window. Ernesto Cardenal, *Spanish.* VCWP, *tr. by* Marc Zimmerman

Vision from the Ghetto. Raymond Washington. NBV

Vision in long filaments flows. Francis Reginald. MoCV

Vision of Beasts, A. John Heath-Stubbs. ChIV-1

Vision of Beauty, A. Ben Jonson. NOSC *Fr.* The New Inn.

   (Lovel's Song.)

Vision of Beulah, The ("There is a place where contrarieties are equally true"). William Blake. OAEL-2 *Fr.* Milton.

Vision of Beulah, The ("Thou hearest the nightingale begin the song of spring"). William Blake. *See* The Lark's Song.

Vision of Children, A. Thomas Ashe. EBVV

Vision of Christ that thou dost see, The. William Blake. ChIV-2 *Fr.* The Everlasting Gospel.

Vision of Connaught in the Thirteenth Century, A. James Clarence Mangan. NOIV

Vision of Delight, The. Ben Jonson. PoEL-2

Vision of Eve, The. Henrietta Cordelia Ray. CBWP-3

Vision of Judgment, The. Byron. OxAEP-2 *Fr.* The Vision of Judgment. OAEL-2

("'Tis, that he has both generals in reversion.") (LL) OxBSn

"At length with jostling, elbowing, and the aid." OBSV

Byron on Southey. OxBoV

"He said—(I only give the heads)—he said." EPCY

Vision of Judgment, The. OxAEP-2

("'Tis, that he has both generals in reversion.") (LL) OxBSn

Vision of MacConglinne, The. MacConglinne, *Middle Irish.* BIrV, *tr. by* John Montagu; CH, *tr. by* Kuno Meyer

Vision of Moonlight, A. Henrietta Cordelia Ray. CBWP-3

Vision of Nature, A. William Langland. PoEL-1 *Fr.* The Vision of Piers Plowman.

Vision of Noah, The. May Kendall. VWP

Vision of Piers Plowman, The. William Langland.

Age of Reason, The. NOCV

"Barones an burgeises and bondemen als." FaBoVe

Civil Service, The. NOCV

Descent into Hell, The. PoEL-1

Entertainment Industry, The. NOCV

"Envy with heavy heart asked for shrift." NAEL-1

Et Incarnatus Est. NOBE

Glutton [*or* Glutton in the Tavern], The. PoE

God's Mercy. NOCV

Good Works. NOCV

Incarnation, The. OBEV

(Incarnation, The.) PoEL-1

Poor, The. PoEL-1

Prologue. FaBoPV

Prologue: "In a summer season, when soft was the sun." EBVV; OAEL-1

(Field Full of Folk, The.) PoE

("In a summer season when the sun was mild.") NAEL-1

Saint Called "Truth," A. NOCV

Vision of Nature, A. PoEL-1

"What for feere of this ferly and of the false Jewes." EBEV

"What this mountain means, and the murky dale." OAEL-1

"Wolleward and wete-shoed went I forth after." EnVB

"Wool-chafed and wet-shoed I went forth after." NAEL-1

"Yet I courbed on my knees and cried hire of grace." EBEV

Vision of Piers Plowman, Prologue, The. William Langland.

"Barones and burgieses and bandemen als." FaBoVe

"Rectors and parish priests complained to the bishop." FaBoPV

Vision of Sin, The. Tennyson. EBVVPR; OAEL-2

Song at the Ruin'd Inn. PoEL-5

Vision of Sir Launfal, The. James Russell Lowell.

Not Only around Our Infancy. ImPo

Prelude to Part the First. APN-1

What [*or* And what] Is So Rare as a Day in June? FaBoBe; ImGa

("Climbs to a soul in grass and / flowers.") (LL) CTV

(Day in June, A.) CTV

Vision of Sunday in Heaven, A. Victor James Daley. ChIV-2

Vision of the Garden, A. James Merrill. GaP

Vision of the Graces, The. Edmund Spenser. NoSic *Fr.* Wood Of Error. AEP

Vision of the Night, The. Philip Freneau. *Fr.* The House of Night.

Vision of Truth, A. Sir John Collings Squire. NOBL

Vision of Your Body. Daisy Zamora, *Spanish.* LoL, *tr. by* Dinah Livingstone

Vision Test, The. Mona Van Duyn. FFC

Vision that appeared to me, A [*or* The]. The Vision of MacConglinne. MacConglinne, *Middle Irish.* BIrV, *tr. by* John Montagu; CH, *tr. by* Kuno Meyer

Vision to Electra, The. Robert Herrick. SeCP

Vision upon This Concei[p]t of the Faerie [*or* Faery] Queen[e], A. Sir Walter Ralegh. NAEL-1; NoSic; SCGP; Son *Fr.* Commendatory Verses to Edmund Spenser's Fairy Queen.

("And cursed the access of that celestial thief!") (LL) NoP-4

(Of Spenser's Faery Queen.) SiPS

Vision V. William Browne. NOSC *Fr.* Visions.

Visionary, The, *see also* Julian M. and A. G. Rochelle *and* The Prisoner. Emily Jane Brontë. BrRo; CH; NOBE; NOBVV; OBNC; PBWP; SCGP; SCV

Visions. William Browne.

Vision V. NOSC

Visions, The. Petrarch. AWP *Fr.* Sonnets to Laura.

Visions. Kathleen Spivack. AmPA

Visions. William Stafford. NoAM

Visions and Interpetations. Li-Young Lee. NIP-4

Visions of beauty, of light, and of love. Dreams of Beauty. Adah Isaacs Menken. CBWP-1

Visions of Bellay, The. Joachim Du Bellay, *French.*

"I saw the bird that can the sun endure." Son

"It was the time, when rest, soft sliding downe." AWP; Son

Visions of Jesus. Jerome Rothenberg. APSN

Visions of Mexico While at a Writing Symposium in Port Townsend, Washington. Lorna Dee Cervantes. NoAM

Visions of Petrarch, The. Petrarch. *See* Visions.

Visions of the Daughters of Albion. William Blake. CABP; OAEL-2

("Daughters of Albion hear her woes, and echo back her sighs, The.") (LL) Ro

("Eye sees more than the heart knows, The.") Ro

Desire and Jealousy. ECEV

"Infancy! fearless, lustful, happy, nestling for delight." OxAEP-2

Visions you never saw, The. Grandfather. Lance Henson, *Cheyenne Indian.* CDW; HATNAP, *tr. by* Lance Henson

Visit. A. R. Ammons. CoAP; TwCP

Visit, A. Sherwood Anderson. PoA

Visit. Gerald William Barrax. GT

Visit. Chitra Divakaruni. NMM-2

Visit, The. Ralph Waldo Emerson. APN-1; NOBA; PAR

Visit, The. Phillip William George. IMW; VoR

Visit, The. Mary Leapor. ECWP

Visit, A. George Ella Lyon. CrSp

Visit. Léopold Sédar Senghor. PBMAP

Visit, A. Anna Swirszczynska, *Polish.* PoSu, *tr. by* Czeslaw Milosz *and* Leonard Nathan

Visit, The. *Unknown.* ECWP

Visit, The. Ellen Bryant Voigt. WeT

Visit. James Welch. AmPA

Visit from Mr. Fox, A. *Unknown.* ChAP

("And the little ones picked the bones, O!") (LL) ChAP

("Fox set out in hungry plight, The.") ChAP

(Visit from Mr. Fox, A.) ChAP

Visit from St Nicholas, A. Clement Clarke Moore. APN-1; AiP; BLPA; CTV; ChAP; FaBoBe; NTCP; OBAL; OBCA; OBCP; OxBChV; PChr; TFi

(Night before Christmas, The.) PWR

Visit of Hope to Sydney Cove, near Botany-Bay. Erasmus Darwin. ECEV; NOEC

Visit of the Gods, The, *ad. fr. the German of* Schiller. Coleridge. OBVE

Visit the Sick. James J. Metcalfe. PoToHe

Visit to Bridge House, A. Richard Weber. BIrV

Visit to Castletown House, A. Michael Hartnett. BiHa; PBCIP

Visit to Enniskillen, A. Tadhg Dall O'Huiginn. NOIV

Visit to the Author's Paternal Seat, A. Richard Polwhele. NOEC *Fr.* The Influence of Local Attachment.

Visit to the Broken Hill Temple, A. Ch'ang Chien, *Chinese.* SuSp, *tr. by* Joseph J. Lee

Visit to the Dead, A. Norman Cameron. FaBoTC; OxBSn

Visit to the Hermit Ts'ui. Ch'ien Ch'i, *Chinese.* OHMPC, *tr. by* Kenneth Rexroth

Visit to the Monastery of Good Omen. Lu Chi, *Chinese.* OHMPC, *tr. by* Kenneth Rexroth

Visit to the Village, A. Michael Smith. PBCIP

Visitant, The. Theodore Roethke. CMoP; PoE; RB; TRP; UnPo

Visitant to our dumbly human home. The Great Moth. Robert Gittings. OxBTC

Visitation. John Dronsfield. PeSAV

Visitation, The. Elizabeth Jennings. MoBS

Visitation, The. Jan Owen. NOBAu

Visitation Rights. Heather Wishik. GLP

Visitation Rites. Jack Myers. NAmP90

Visitations. Lawrence Durrell. MoBrPo *Fr.* Eight Aspects of Melissa.

Visited. Fleur Adcock. PeNZ

Visiting a Recluse on West Mountain and Not Finding Him In. Ch'iu Wei, *Chinese*. CoBCP, *tr. by* Burton Watson

Visiting a Rural Town. Kyongnim Shin, *Korean*. CKP, *tr. by* Jaihiun Kim

Visiting an Old Friend. Đinh An, *Vietnamese*. AVP, *tr. by* Huỳnh Sanh Thông

Visiting conductor, A. A Simple Story. Gwen Harwood. FaBoWP; NOBAu

Visiting Dr Swift. Alexander Pope *and* Thomas Parnell. *See* On Riding to See Dean Swift in the Mist of the Morning.

Visiting Emily Dickinson's Grave with Robert Francis. Robert Bly. LCAP-2

Visiting Hour, The. David Wagoner. HoPM

Visiting Hour (Repatriation Hospital). Michael Dransfield. BMAP

Visiting My Gravesite: Talbott Churchyard, West Virginia. Irene McKinney. PBCAP

Visiting the Garden at Monk Wen Ko's Home. Wu Wei-yeh, *Chinese*. SuSp, *tr. by* Chang Yin-nan *and* Lewis C. Walmsley

Visiting the Hermit Cheng. Po Chü-i, *Chinese*. TAL, *tr. by* Robert Payne

Visiting the Hsi-lin Temple. Po Chü-i, *Chinese*. ChiP, *tr. by* Arthur Waley

Visiting the Oracle. Lawrence Raab. AmPA

Visiting the Temple of Accumulated Fragrance. Wang Wei, *Chinese*. CoBCP, *tr. by* Burton Watson

Visiting Tsan, Abbot of Ta-Yun. Tu Fu, *Chinese*. OHPC, *tr. by* Kenneth Rexroth

Visitor, A. "Lewis Carroll." OBCoV

Visitor, The. W. H. Davies. GBL; OBWVE

Visitor, The. Carolyn Forché. FYAP; OPOU

Visitor, A. Mary Oliver. MoLi

Visitor, The. Jack Prelutsky. OTCP

Visitor, The. Gibbons Ruark. MT

Visitor. *Unknown*. OxNR

Visitor in Marl, A. Emily Dickinson. APN-2

Visitor to Warsaw. Portrait of a Jew Old Country Style. Jerome Rothenberg. NNaP

Visitors, The. Richard Moore. DiPo

Visitors. Katha Pollitt. PuP-16

Visitors. Tu Fu, *Chinese*. BLT; OHPC, *tr. by* Kenneth Rexroth

Visitors, indignant, didactic, pronounce. Thresholds of Identity. Lionel Abrahams. PeSAV

Visitor's Parking. Anne Szumigalski. NOBC

Visits of condolence is all we get from them. Tourists. Yehuda Amichai, *Hebrew*. PoSu, *tr. by* Glenda Abramson *and* Tudor Parfitt

Visits to St. Elizabeths. Elizabeth Bishop. CBNP; CoAP; VGW

Vista. Faiz Ahmad Faiz, *Urdu*. VCWP, *tr. by* Agha Shahid Ali

Vistas between the shadowy pines were bright. Starlight Thought. Henrietta Cordelia Ray. *Fr.* A Group of Musings. CBWP-3

Vita Nuova. Stanley Kunitz. VGW

Vitae Summa Brevis Spem Nos Vetat Incohare Longam. Ernest Christopher Dowson. AWP; CABP; EBVV; HAP; NOBE; NoP-4; OBEV; OxBSP; PeVV; TFi

  (Envoy: "They are not long, the weeping and the laughter.") MoBrPo; NOBVV

  ("Our path emerges for a while, then closes / Within a dream.") (LL) CABP

Vitaï Lampada. Sir Henry John Newbolt. BLPA; EBEvV; FaPoR; NSI; OBWP; UV

Vital breath of more ethereal air, A. (LL) Haunted Houses. Henry Wadsworth Longfellow. OxBSn

Vital spark of heavenly [*or* heav'nly] flame! The Dying Christian to His Soul. Alexander Pope, *par. fr. the Latin of* Emperor Hadrian. AWP; ChIV-2; ImPo; OBEV

Vital spatterings. Excess. Thomas Kinsella. BiHa *Fr.* A Technical Supplement.

Vitality. Maria Amalia Fonte Boa, *Portuguese*. BoWoP, *tr. by* Willis Barnstone *and* Nelson Cerqueira

Vitamins and Roughage. Kenneth Rexroth. NoAM

Vitelli rides west toward Fano, the morning sun. The Death of Vitellozzo Vitelli. Irving Feldman. TwCP

Vittoria Colonna. Roy Marz. PoA

Vivaldi. Delmore Schwartz. NYBP

Vivamos, Mea Lesbia, atque Amemus. Catullus. *See* Carmen 5 ("My sweetest Lesbia, let us live and love").

Vive La Différence. Strato, *Greek*. GrAn, *tr. by* Teddy Hogge

Vive Noir! Mari E. Evans. NBV; PoBA

Vivid out of nowhere. The Other the Wings. Donald Revell. CMAP

Vivid transparence that you bring is peace, The. (LL) To Henry Church. Wallace Stevens. ColAP; NOBA

Vivre L'Orange. Hélène Cixous, *French*.

  "I urgency, I begged. *Give me your dish*, I said, icy." VCAP, *tr. by* Anne Liddle *and* Sarah Cornell

Vixen, The. John Clare. RB

Vixen woman, The. Harold Monro. OBMV *Fr.* Natural History.

Vladimir's Song. Samuel Beckett. CBNP *Fr.* Waiting for Godot.

Vlamertinghe. Edmund Blunden. NoP-4; OBWP; PeFWW

Vlaminck's Tie, the Persistent Imaginal. Michael Harlow. PeNZ

Vnhappy youth betrayd by Fate. Against the Love of Great Ones. Richard Lovelace. CBLP

Vnto all life of mine may dy. Richard Crashaw. *See* The Flaming Heart.

Vocable, as rath and bullaun, A. (LL) A New Song. Seamus Heaney. CABP; CIP-2; FaBoTw

Vocabulary. Ariel Dorfman, *Spanish*. AF, *tr. by* Ariel Dorfman *and* Edith Grossman

Vocation. Judith Herzberg, *Dutch*. WPOW, *tr. by* Manfred Wolf

Vocation. John Robert Lee. HCP

Vocation. Carol Rumens. DiPo

Vocation. William Stafford. IFJA

Voce mea ad Dominum Psalm 142. Mary Sidney Herbert, Countess of Pembroke. PBRV

Voi ch'entrate, and your life is in your hands. (LL) The Exile's Return. Robert Lowell. AmPP; OxBA

Voice, The. Thomas Hardy. APAD; BoLoP; CBLP; CMoP; EnLoPo; GBL; GTBS-P; HAP; InPS-3; LoP; MoP; NAEL-2; NoAM; NoP-4; OAEL-2; OBNC; OxAEP-2; PoE; PoEL-5; Poetr; TFi

Voice. Zbigniew Herbert, *Polish*. PoSu, *tr. by* Czeslaw Milosz

Voice. W. S. Merwin. NNaP

Voice. Albie Ollivierre. NBrP

Voice, The. Theodore Roethke. EP; VGW

Voice, A. Tadeusz Różewicz, *Polish*. BLT, *tr. by* Czeslaw Milosz

Voice, A. *Unknown*. CA

Voice, The. Edmund Wilson. NYBP

Voice and Address. Michael Palmer. FTOS; PmAP

Voice are still / The moon's bright. Ma Chih-yüan. SuSp, *tr. by* Sherwin S. S. Fu *Fr.* Tune: "Song of Shou-yang."

Voice at a Seance, A. Anthony Hecht. OxBSn

Voice, because of its austerity, will often cause dust to rise, The. Recursus. Michael Palmer. APSN

Voice by the cedar tree, A. Tennyson. *Fr.* Maud [A Monodrama]. EnVR

Voice from heaven was heard on earth, A. St. Andrew's Voyage to Mermedonia. *Unknown*. AnOE, *tr. by* Charles W. Kennedy *Fr.* Andreas.

Voice from the dark is calling me, A. Divorce. Anna Wickham. MoBrPo; NALW; SAGP

Voice from the Factories, A. Caroline Elizabeth Norton. VWP *Fr.* A Voice from the Factories.

Voice from the Invisible World, A. Goethe, *German*. AWP, *tr. by* James Clarence Mangan

Voice From the Roses, A. Maxine W. Kumin. NMM-2

Voice from the Tomb (1). Stevie Smith. PoA

Voice [Speaks] from the Well, A. George Peele. CBNP; FaBoCh; NOBE; OxBoLi *Fr.* The Old Wives' [*or* Wife's] Tale.

Voice from the Well [of Life Speaks to the Maiden], The. George Peele. NOBE; NoSic *Fr.* The Old Wives' [*or* Wife's] Tale.

(Song for the Head.) RB

Voice from under the Table, A. Richard Wilbur. AmPP; HAP; NOBA

Voice in Darkness. Richard Dehmel, *German*. AWP, *tr. by* Margarete Münsterberg

Voice in the Crowd. Ted Joans. *See* The Truth.

Voice in the Garden, A. Selima Hill. FaBoWP

Voice is calling, low and quiet, A. Spring Rain. Yongno Pyon, *Korean*. CKP, *tr. by* Jaihiun Kim

Voice is large, the man is small, The. A Frog. Friedrich von Logau, *German*. GePo, *tr. by* George C. Schoolfield

Voice of a Dissipated Woman inside a Tomb. Sor Violante do Céu, *Portuguese*. BoWoP, *tr. by* Willis Barnstone

Voice of America, 1961, The. James Liddy. CIP-2

Voice of Earth Mediums. Philip Lamantia. CLPP

Voice of God, The. Louis I. Newman. PoToHe

Voice of God Is Calling, The. John Haynes Holmes. AH

Voice of magic melody, The. My Singing Aunt. James Reeves. FuFo

Voice of my beloved, The. Bible, *O.T. See* Hark! My beloved!

Voice of my beloved! behold, he cometh leaping, The. *Unknown*. PiM *Fr.* Song of Solomon.

Voice of My White City, The. Abba Kovner, *Hebrew*. IP, *tr. by* Warren Bargad *and* Stanley F. Chyet

Voice of right amidst a world gone wrong, A. James Thomson. EPCY *Fr.* Shelley.

Voice of summer, keen and shrill. To a Cricket. William Cox Bennett. BoTP

Voice of the Ancient Bard, The. William Blake. FHYEP; Ro *Fr.* Songs of Experience.

Voice of the dead was a living voice to me, The. (LL) In the Valley of Cauteretz. Tennyson. BoLoP; LBC; NAEL-2; NOBE

Voice of the Devil, The. William Blake. *Fr.* The Marriage of Heaven and Hell. NAEL-2; NOBRP; OAEL-2

("All Bibles or sacred codes have been the causes of the following Errors.")

Voice of the glutton I heard with disdain, The. The Glutton. John Oakman. OxBChV

Voice of the last cricket, The. Splinter. Carl Sandburg. KaS; OBCA; SoSe-8; Spl

Voice of the Negro, The. Lizelia Augusta Jenkins Moorer. CBWP-3

Voice of the Studio Announcer. Archibald MacLeish. HoPM *Fr.* The Fall of the City.

Voice on the winds, A. To Morfydd. Lionel Pigot Johnson. MoBrPo; OAEL-2; OBMV

Voice out of the Sabbaths, A. Derek Walcott. WeW-3

Voice peals in this end of night, A. A Thrush before Dawn. Alice Thompson Meynell. MoBrPo; WPE

Voice said: "Follow, follow;" and I rose, A. Two Pursuits. Christina Rossetti. WPE

Voice said, "Hurl her down!,"The. The Lovely Shall Be Choosers. Robert Frost. MoAmPo; NOBA; OxBA; PoE

Voice Sings, A. Coleridge. *See* An Invocation: "Hear, sweet spirit, hear the spell."

Voice that beautifies the land, The. Twelfth Song of the Thunder. *Unknown.* APN-2; AWP, tr. by Washington Matthews *Fr.* The Mountain Chant.

Voice that breathed o'er Eden, The. Epithalamium. John Keble. NOCV

Voice that would reach you, Hunter, must speak, The. To Roosevelt. "Rubén Darío," *Spanish.* PFTM, tr. by Lysander Kemp

Voiceless, The. Oliver Wendell Holmes. APN-1 *Fr.* The Autocrat of the Breakfast Table.

Voices. Constantine P. Cavafy, *Greek.* LBC, tr. by Rae Dalven

Voices. Nora Dauenhauer. HATNAP

Voices. Walter De la Mare. UnPo

Voices. Wislawa Szymborska, *Polish.* PoSu, tr. by Magnus F. Krynski

Voices, The. Jean-Baptiste Tati-Loutard. PBMAP

Voices Answering Back: The Vampires. Lawrence Raab. AmPA

Voices are crying an unknown name in the sky. (LL) Epistle to Be Left in the Earth. Archibald MacLeish. CMoP; MoAmPo; NOBA; SAGP

Voices / are everywhere, The. Pony Farm. Laura Jensen. LCAP-2

Voices at the Window. Sir Philip Sidney. *See* Eleventh Song.

Voices from the Other World. James Merrill. TwCP; VCAP

Voices from Things Growing in a Churchyard. Thomas Hardy. FaBoVe; OxBTC

Voices moving about in the quiet house. Falling Asleep. Siegfried Sassoon. MoBrPo; OxBTC

Voices mute for ever, or since yesterday, or just stilled;. Primo Levi, *Hebrew.* AF, tr. by Ruth Feldman

Voices of the dead. They are not dead. Who hears. Ivan V. Lalic, *Serbo-Croatian.* HSix, tr. by Charles Simic

Voices of the Rain. Henrietta Cordelia Ray. CBWP-3

Voices, single row of nights. They Shall Know. Kofi Awoonor. VCWP

Void, The. Gwendolyn MacEwen. *Fr.* The T. E. Lawrence Poems. NOBC

Void inside us, The. G. M. Muktibodh, *Hindi.* OMIP, tr. by Vinay Dharwadker

Void only. "Ping Hsin." PBWP *Fr.* Multitudinous Stars.

Void that's highly embraceable, The. 225th Chorus. Jack Kerouac. NeAP *Fr.* Mexico City Blues.

Vois loude in that light to Lucifer seide, A. The Descent into Hell. William Langland. PoEL-1 *Fr.* The Vision of Piers Plowman.

Volatile Kerryman, The. Owen Roe O'Sullivan, *Irish.* BIrV, tr. by Sean O'Riada

Volatile mosquito. Meleager, *Greek.* GrAn, tr. by Peter Whigham

Volcanic tuff. Tina Darragh. FTOS

Volcanic Venus. D. H. Lawrence. InPS-3

Volcano. Ivan Van Sertima. CA; PBCV

Volcano. Derek Walcott. OxBC

Volcano is dark and suddenly thunder, The. Malcolm Lowry. CLPP

Volcanoe Suite. Ellsworth McGranahan Keane.
Soufrière. HCP; PBCV

Volcanoes. Bella Akhatovna Akhmadulina, *Russian.* PBWP, tr. by W. H. Auden

Volcanoes be in Sicily. Emily Dickinson. NALW; OxWW

Volga Towns, The. Johannes Bobrowski, *German.* PoSu, tr. by Ruth *and* Matthew Mead

Volitionist Economics. Kelvin Corcoran. NBrP

Volkswagen parked in the gap, The. Ireland. Paul Muldoon. PBCIP

Volpone. Ben Jonson. NAEL-1
"Had old Hippocrates, or Galen."
Nano's Song.
"O God, and his good angels! whither, whither." FaBoSe
Song. To Celia ("Come my Celia, let us prove"). BeJo; OAEL-1
(Carmina V [To Celia].) OBVE
(Song). PFE
("These have crimes accounted been.") (LL) AEP; FMP; NoP-4; PFE; PoPoPo
(To Celia.) FMP; OxAEP-1
To the Same [Celia]. BeJo; NOSC; OAEL-1; SeCP
(Song: To Celia.)
(To Celia.) AWP
"You that would last long, list to my song."

Voltaire at Ferney. W. H. Auden. LiTM; PoA

Volubilis, North Africa. Ralph Nixon Currey. PeSA

Volumes of books, tea and incense. Wen Cheng-ming. CoBLCP, tr. by Jonathan Chaves *Fr.* Inscribed on a Painting: Cultivating Leisure.

Voluntaries. Ralph Waldo Emerson. APN-1; CBCWP
"In an age of fops and toys." PoLF
I Can. CTV

Volunteer, The. Herbert Asquith. OBWP; OxBTC

Volunteer, The. Robert W. Service. NSI

Volunteer, The. *Unknown.* NOEC

Volunteer's Thanksgiving, The. Lucy Larcom. OBCA

Voluptuaries and Others. Margaret Avison. MoCV

Voluspo. *Unknown.* AWP, tr. by Henry Adams Bellows *Fr.* The Elder Edda.

Von Tempsky's Dance. Murray Edmond. PeNZ

Voodoo. Léon Laleau. NegPo, tr. by Ellen Conroy Kennedy *Fr.* Black Music.

Voracious, yes. But when you see it. Blue Morning Glory. Anne Pitkin. CrSp

Vorkuta. Horst Bienek, *German.* AF, tr. by Matthew Mead

Voronezh. "Anna Akhmatova," *Russian.* FaBoPV, tr. by Tom Paulin

Vorthy be the Lunn whan you se it. Mr. and Mrs. Vite's Journey. *Unknown.* NOBL

Votaries know. A Poem for Integration. Alvin Saxon. PoBA

Vote, The. Ralph Knevet. FMP; NOSC

Vote for Lunn. *Unknown.* FaBoVe

Vous frapperez Falck avec 20 per cent. (LL) The Dutch. George Canning. OxBoLi; PeLV

Vow, A. Allen Ginsberg. CLPP; OBWP
("Over Puerto Rican agony lawyers' screams in slums.") (LL) CLPP

Vow, The. Anthony Hecht. CoAmPo; InPK-6

Vow, The. Galway Kinnell. VCAP

Vow. Abba Kovner, *Hebrew.* IP, tr. by Warren Bargad *and* Stanley F. Chyet

Vow. John Updike. NYBP; PeLV

Vow for New Year's, A. Mary Carolyn Davies. PoToHe

Vow to Heavenly Venus, A. Joachim Du Bellay, *French.* AWP, tr. by Andrew Lang

Vowel. Nina Cassian, *Romanian.* AF, tr. by Brenda Walker *and* Andrea Deletant

Vowel Movements. Daryl Hine. PoA

Vowels. Rimbaud, *French.* TTTS, tr. by Kenneth Koch

Vowels of Another Language, The. Thomas M. Disch. PoA

Vows are vain. No suppliant breath. Upon Castara's Departure. William Habington. NOSC

Vox Oppressi, to the Lady Phipps. Richard Henchman. SCAP

Vox Pacifica. George Wither.
"*Sun* hath run his course through all the Signes, The." PBRV

Vox Populi. Dryden. NOBE *Fr.* The Medal [*or* Medall].

Vox Populi, Vox Dei. *Unknown.* FaBoPV
"And yet not long ago."
"I pray you, be not wroth."

Vox Ultima Crucis. John Lydgate. OBEV

"Voy wawm" said the dustman. Hymn to the Sun. Michael Roberts. FaBoCh; OxBTC

Voyage, A. W. H. Auden.
Macao. MeMAP

Voyage, The. Heinrich Heine, *German.* AWP, tr. by John Todhunter

Voyage, The. Robert Lowell.
  "We imitate, oh horror! tops and bowls." APAD
Voyage, The. Denis Florence MacCarthy. TIRV *Fr.* The Voyage of St. Brendan.
Voyage. Josephine Miles. LiTM
Voyage, The. Edwin Muir. LiTM
Voyage, The. Tennyson. OxBoS
Voyage Life is longest made at home, The. (LL) The Old Man of Verona. Claudian, *Latin.* AWP; OBCVT; OBVE, *tr. by* Abraham Cowley
Voyage of Bran, The. *Unknown, Old Irish.*
  Song of the Woman, The. TIRV
  Worship of Cromm Cruaich, The. TIRV
Voyage of Life, The. Thomas Cole.
  "As the broad mountain where the shadows flit." APN-1
Voyage of Life, The. Cynewulf. AnOE *Fr.* Christ 2.
Voyage of Maeldune, The. Tennyson. PoEL-5
Voyage of St. Brendan, The. Denis Florence MacCarthy.
  Voyage, The. TIRV
Voyage on the Thames, The. Alexander Pope. NOBE *Fr.* The Rape of the Lock[, an Heroi-Comical Poem]. FHYEP; HAP; ImPo; OAEL-1; OBNV; PeLV; PoEL-3
Voyage through death / to life upon these shores. (LL) Middle Passage. Robert Earl Hayden. BPo; ColAP; InPS-3; NAAAL; NoAM; PoBA; TRP; VCAP
Voyage to Labrador. W. S. Merwin. GS
Voyage to the Isle of Love, A. Aphra Behn.
  Dream, The. PBWP; RACG
Voyage to the Moon. Archibald MacLeish. PBMP
Voyage to Tintern Abbey, A. Sneyd Davies.
  Crooked bank still winds to something new, The. NOEC
Voyage West. Archibald MacLeish. VGW
Voyage within you, on the fabled ocean. Terra Australis. James Philip McAuley. NOBAu
Voyager's Song, The. Edward Coote Pinkney. APN-1
Voyages. Hart Crane. CMoP; MeMAP; NOBA; NoAM; TAP
  "Above the fresh ruffles of the surf." AmPP; ColAP; MoP; NAAL-2; OxBA; PoE; VGW
  "—And yet this great wink of eternity." AmPP; ColAP; HAP; ImPo; LiTM; MoAmPo; OxBA; PoE; RaBo; TRP; UnPo; VGW
  "Infinite consanguinity it bears." ColAP; OxBA
  "Meticulous, past midnight in clear rime." ColAP; NAAL-2; PoE
  "Where icy and bright dungeons lift." ColAP; HAP; MoAmPo; UnPo
  "Whose counted smile of hours and days, suppose." ColAP
Voyages. Jules Supervielle, *French.* MFP, *tr. by* Martin Sorrell
Voyeur, The. Rod McKuen. PFE
Voyeur's Dream. Barney Bush. HATNAP
Voyvodina. Ivan Gadjanski, *Serbo-Croatian.* HSix, *tr. by* Charles Simic
Voz de la Gente. Jimmy Santiago Baca. PmAP
Vuillard: "The Mother and Sister of the Artist." W. D. Snodgrass. CoAP
Vulcan come, thy hammer take. The Cup. Anacreon, *Greek.* GrIP, *tr. by* Thomas Stanley
Vulcan, contrive me such a Cup. Upon his drinking a Bowl. Anacreon, *Greek.* OBCVT; OxAEP-1; OxBoLi, *tr. by* John Wilmot
Vulcan Forges the Shield of Achilles. Homer, *Greek.* OBVE, *tr. by* Alexander Pope *Fr.* The Iliad.
  ("And bears the blazing Present through the Skies.") (LL) OBCVT, *tr. by* Pope
  (Vulcan forges the armour of Achilles.) OBCVT, *tr. by* Pope
Vulcan's Song. John Lyly. EBEV *Fr.* Sapho and Phao.
  (Song in Making of the Arrows, The.) NoSic
Vulgar Error, A. J. E. Thorold Rogers. FaBoEE
Vulgar of manner, overfed. Owed to New York. Byron Rufus Newton. BLPA; NBLV
Vulgar race of men, like herds that graze, The. Sage Philosophy. Richard Jago. ECEV *Fr.* Edge-Hill; or, The Rural Prospect Delineated and Moralised.
Vulnerary, A. Jonathan Williams. PoM
Vulture, The. Samuel Beckett. *Fr.* Echo's Bones. NoAM
Vulture, The. Aleksandr Blok, *French.* NNPT, *tr. by* Jon Stallworthy *and* Peter France
Vulture. Robinson Jeffers. NAAL-2; NOBA; NoAM; PaTW
  ("What a life after death.") (LL) SAGP
Vulture. Kenneth Rexroth. NNaP *Fr.* A Bestiary. OBAL
Vulture eats between his meals, The. Hilaire Belloc. CTAV; OxBChV
Vultures. Margaret Atwood. LCAP-2
Vultures, The. David Diop, *French.* NegPo, *tr. by* Ellen Conroy Kennedy; PBA; TTY, *tr. by* Ulli Beier; PBMAP

("At that time.") NegPo, *tr. by* Ellen Conroy Kennedy
Vultures are being spring-cleaned, The. Building Society Blues. Roger Roughton. SPE
Vultures—in the midst of war. Shaku Chōkū, *Japanese.* MJT, *tr. by* Makoto Ueda
Vultures waft circles. Remnant Ghosts at Dawn. Oliver La Grone. NBV
Vusumzi's Song. L. T. Manyase, *Xhosa.* PeSA, *tr. by* C. M. Mcanyangwa *and* Jack Cope

W

W. James Reeves. NOxBChV; NTCP
W. H. Louise Imogen Guiney. APN-2
W. H. Auden & Mantan Moreland. Al Young. LTA
W. H. *Eheu!* Coleridge. FaBoEE
W. L. M. K. Francis Reginald Scott. NOBC
W. S. Landor. Marianne Moore. OBAL
W. W. Imamu Amiri Baraka. HeIP-4; NOBA; PoBA
Wa-Sissica, the War Song. *Unknown.* APN-2 *Fr.* War Dance. APN-2, *tr. by* George Catlin
Waäit till our Sally cooms in, fur thou mun a' sights to tell. The Northern Cobbler. Tennyson. EBEV
Wabash Cannonball, The. Delmore Brothers. GM
Wad be my queen, wad be my queen. (LL) O [*or* Oh] wert thou in the cauld blast. Robert Burns. EBEV; FaBoVe; HAP; NOBE; NoP-4; OxAEP-2; OxBS; PoPoPo; SCGP
Wadasa Nakamoon, Vietnam Memorial. Ray A. Young Bear. CDa; HATNAP
Wade in the water, children. God's A-Gonna Trouble the Water. *Unknown.* NAAAL
Wade / through black jade. The Fish. Marianne Moore. AmPP; ColAP; FaBoWP; MeMAP; MoAmPo; MoP; NAAL-2; NoAM; NoP-4; OxBA; PBMP; Poetr
Wading up Brunigill's rush. October, Isle of Skye. Carter Revard. NoP-4
Waement the deid. Coronach. Alexander Scott. FaBoTC; OxBS
Waes-hael for [the] knight and [the] dame! King Arthur's Waes-hael. Robert Stephen Hawker. OBEV
Wae's me, wae's me! Cauld Lad of Hilton, The *or* The Wandering Spectre. *Unknown.* CH; FaBoCh; OxBoLi
Wafer; thin and hard and bitter pill I. To His Book. Leon Stokesbury. Poetr
Wag a leg, wag a leg. *Unknown.* OxNR
Wag ballock wag. *Unknown.* FaBoVe
Wagers. Marilyn Hacker. RA
Wages of sin is death. These words run, The. AIDS, Among Other Things. Peter Kocan. ChIV-2
Waggon-Maker, The. John Masefield. EBEV
Waggon passed with scarlet wheels, A. Two Realities. Aldous Leonard Huxley. PFE
Wagner. Rupert Brooke. FaBoTw; NOBL; PeLV
Wagon Full of Thunder. Louis Oliver. HATNAP
Wagon stopped before the house, A; she heard. Edna St. Vincent Millay. *Fr.* Sonnets from an Ungrafted Tree. NALW
Wagoner's Lad, The. *Unknown.* AmFP
Wagons, if they still ride the country roads, go empty. Autumn. Slavko Mihalic, *Croatian.* CEEP, *tr. by* Peter Kastmiler
Wagtail and Baby. Thomas Hardy. PeLV
Wah-dah do, wah-dah-do. It Don't Mean a Thing (If It Ain't Got That Swing). *Unknown.* NAAAL
Wahiawa is still. Leaving. Cathy Song. NoAM
Waif of Echo Park, The. Wanda Coleman. EC3
Waifs. Vivian Virtue. PBCV
Waiheke 1972—Rocky Bay. Christina Beer. PeNZ
Waikato-Taniwha-Rau. Vincent O'Sullivan. PeNZ
Wail, for the world's wrong! (LL) A Dirge: "Rough wind, that moanest loud." Shelley. NAFI-2; NOBE; PFE; PoRA; SAGP; SCGP
Wail of the Divorced. Mary E. Tucker. CBWP-1
Wail of the Waiter, The. Marcus Clarke. NOBAu
Wail, wail, Ah for Adonis! Lament for Adonis. Bion, *Greek.* AWP, *tr. by* John Addington Symonds
Wailing, wailing, wailing, the wind over the land and sea. Rizpah. Tennyson. PeVV; PoEL-5; RACG
Wailing wind doth not enough despair, The. Awake. Mary Elizabeth Coleridge. OBNC
Wailings of a maiden I recite, The. Wednesday; or, The Dumps. John Gay. OAEL-1 *Fr.* The Shepherd's Week.
Waillie, waillie! *Unknown.* *See* Waly, Waly ("When cockle shells turn silver bells").

Wain upon the northern steep, The. Astronomy. A. E. Housman. NoP-4; OBWP

Waist thin as the purslane creeper. Peace Poem. Velacan Maturai, *Tamil.* PLW, *tr. by* A. K. Ramanujan

Wait. Charles Bernstein. PmAP

Wait. Timothy Steele. PoA

Wait a Little! *Unknown.* NOCV

    (Thole a Little.) EnVB

Wait for Me. Robert Creeley. NOBA

Wait for me, and I'll come back. Konstantin Mikhailovich Simonov, *Russian.* TCRP, *tr. by* Lubov Yakovleva

Wait here, and I'll be back, though the hours divide. Three Star Final. Conrad Potter Aiken. OxBA

Wait, Kate! You skate at such a rate. To Kate, Skating Better than Her Date. David Daiches. NYBP

Wait Mister. Which way is home? Music Swims Back to Me. Anne Sexton. ColAP; VCAP

Wait; the great horned owls. Owls. W. D. Snodgrass. Poetsp

Wait till the darkness is deep. Wallāda, *Arabic.* WPOW, *tr. by* James Monroe *and* Deirdre Lashgari

Wait until I too hang up my carriage. Hsieh Chin. CoBLCP, *tr. by* Jonathan Chaves *Fr.* Parting from Liu Nan-chou.

Waitekauri Every Time! Edwin Edwards. PeNZ

Waiter dropped a tray of glassware and, The. Spilled. Heather McHugh. WeT

Waiter, Please. *Unknown. See* Limerick: "An Epicure, Dining at Crewe."

Waiting. John Burroughs. BLPA; FaBoBe

Waiting. Jack Cain. HA

Waiting. Jane Cooper. CrSp; NMM-2; TAP

Waiting. Robert Creeley. VGW

Waiting. John Freeman. CH

Waiting. William Ernest Henley. NAEL-2; NOBVV *Fr.* In Hospital.

Waiting. Arthur Nortje. HBAPE

Waiting. William Carlos Williams. SAmP

Waiting Both. Thomas Hardy. MoBrPo; OxBoLi; TTTS

Waiting for Audience on a Spring Night. Tu Fu, *Chinese.* OHPC, *tr. by* Kenneth Rexroth

Waiting For Breakfast, While She Brushed Her Hair. Philip Larkin. NoAM

Waiting for Death. Mordecai Gebirtig, *Yiddish.* TrJP, *tr. by* Joseph Leftwich

Waiting for Fidel. John Agard. PBCV

Waiting for Godot. Samuel Beckett.
    Vladimir's Song. CBNP

Waiting for Icarus. Muriel Rukeyser. LCAP-2; NNaP

Waiting for Lesser Duckweed: On a Proposal of Issa's. Sandra McPherson. BAP-93

Waiting for Robinson. Roberta Hill Whiteman. HATNAP

Waiting for rusted trains / silent in texas grass. Quincy Troupe. *See* In Texas Grass.

Waiting for the Barbarians. Constantine P. Cavafy, *Greek.* AF; BLT; GrIP ("They were, those people, a kind of solution.") (LL) PFTM, *tr. by* Edmund Keeley *and* Philip Sherrard

Waiting for the Bus. D. J. Enright. OxBTC

Waiting for the Cops. Martín Espada. EC2

Waiting for the East Wind. Nguyễn Đình Chiểu, *Vietnamese.* AVP, *tr. by* Huỳnh Sanh Thông

Waiting for the elevated train. Armitage Street. David Hernandez. UnSA

Waiting for the Emperor Tenji. Princess Nukada, *Japanese.* PBWP, *tr. by* Cid Corman *and* Susumu Kamaike

Waiting for the end, boys, waiting for the end. William Empson. UV *Fr.* Just a Smack at Auden. LiTM; MoBrPo; OBCoV; PeLV; UnPo

Waiting for the End of the War. Thomas Brush. CDa

Waiting for the Ferry at Inchŏn. Liu E, *Chinese.* CoBLCP, *tr. by* Jonathan Chaves

Waiting for the Fire. Philip Appleman. CDa

Waiting for the flesh that dies. (LL) The Bull. Ralph Hodgson. LiTM; MoBrPo; NSI; OBMV; OxBTC

Waiting for the Post. Dorothy Auchterlonie. CBAP

Waiting for Truth. Susan Griffin. GLP

Waiting for weeks till the last one is ready to run, they. Turtles Hatching. Mark O'Connor. NOBAu

Waiting for You to Come By. Simon J. Ortiz. CDW

Waiting, I rest in the waiting gate. The Lich Gate. Clayton Eshleman. PmAP

Waiting in Front of the Columnar High School. Karl Shapiro. HAP

Waiting, in their dark clothes, apart. (LL) An Elegy Is Preparing Itself. Donald Justice. CRP; HoPM

Waiting is the poem of waiting. On Arrival. Richard Howard. TAP

Waiting like a trap-door spider for a rookie sell-out. Baseball or the name game? Four Poems for *The St. Louis Sporting News.* Jack Spicer. PoM

Waiting-Room, The. Robin Fulton. PoA

Waiting room quiet. Gary Hotham. HA

Waiting Rooms. Howard Nemerov. PoA

Waiting to Be Fed. Ray A. Young Bear. CDW

Waiting, waiting, waiting. James Reeves. OTCP

Waiting with lowered voice. Jacques Dupin, *French.* VCWP, *tr. by* Paul Auster

Waiting with thy master's wine. (LL) Simplicity. Horace, *Latin.* OBVE, *tr. by* Gerard Manley Hopkins; AWP; InPK-6; NBLV, *tr. by* William Cowper

Waitress looks at my face, The. Truck Stop: Minnesota. Stephen Dunn. CMAP

Waitress's Kid, The. Peggy Shumaker. PBCAP

Waits, The. John Freeman. BoTP

Waits in unhope. (LL) In Ienebris. Thomas Hardy. NoAM; OAEL-2; SCGP

Wake. Langston Hughes. OBAL; OBCoV

Wake all the dead! What ho! What ho! Viola's Song. Sir William Davenant. FaBoCh; HAP; NOSC; SCGP *Fr.* The Law against Lovers.

Wake as you will, but wake in me. To Song. Olga Fiodorovna Berggolts, *Russian.* BoWoP, *tr. by* Daniel Weissbort

Wake, baillie, wake! the crafts are out. Winding-up Time. Jean Ingelow. VWP

Wake, child with the flute. Mirabai, *Hindi.* BoWoP, *tr. by* Willis Barnstone *and* Usha Nilsson

Wake, eat, and drink, evacuate, and sleep. (LL) Human Life. Matthew Prior. FaBoEE; OBCoV

Wake for Papa Montero. Nicolás Guillén, *Spanish.* PFTM, *tr. by* Langston Hughes

Wake! for the sun has driven in equal flight. The Golfer's Rubaiyat. H. W. Boynton. BXAP

Wake! for the sun, who scattered [*or* scatter'd] into flight. Omar Khayyám, *Persian. ad. by* Edward Fitzgerald. EnVR; ImPo; OBNC; TRP *Fr.* The Rubáiyát of Omar Khayyám [*of* Naishápúr]. AWP; EBVV; FaBoBe; FaPoR; HAP; NAEL-2; NoP-4; PoEL-5

Wake, Hercules, awake: but heave up thy black eye. Song. Ben Jonson. *Fr.* Pleasure Reconciled to Virtue. NAEL-1; OAEL-1

Wake, Israel, wake! Recall to-day. The Banner of the Jew. Emma Lazarus. TrJP

Wake not again the cannon's thundrous voice. Lines. Alfred Gibbs Campbell. AAP

Wake Not for the World-heard Thunder. A. E. Housman. CMoP; NoAM

Wake, now my love, awake; for it is time. Edmund Spenser. GBL *Fr.* Epithalamion: "Ye learned sisters which have oftentimes." AAS; BoLoP; CABP; FHYEP; InPS-3; NOBE; NoP-4; NoSic; OAEL-1; OBEV; OxAEP-1; PBRV; PoEL-1; PoPoPo

Wake, O my soul; awake, and raise. An Hymn. Phineas Fletcher. NOSC

Wake of William Orr, The. William Drennan. TIRV

Wake the serpent not—lest he. Fragment. Shelley. SCGP

Wake: the silver dusk returning. Reveille. A. E. Housman. CABP; CMoP; LiTM; MoBrPo; NoP-4; PFE; PoLF

Wake the Song of Jubilee. Leonard Bacon. AH

Wake up. Day calls you. Pedro Salinas, *Spanish.* NNPT, *tr. by* Willis Barnstone

Wake up, dear boy that holds the flute! Mirabai, *Hindi.* WPOW, *tr. by* Usha Nilsson

Wake up! flowers of the forest, sky-climbing birds of the prairie. Calling-One's-Own. *Ojibway Oral Tradition, Ojibway.* ITG, *tr. by* Charles Fenno Thompson *and* Robert Hass

Wake up Lord. Caribbean Woman Prayer. Grace Nichols. NBrP

Wake-up Niggers. Don L. Lee. PoBA

Wake up, wake up, darlin' Cory. Darling Cory. *Unknown.* AmFP

Wake, yes, wake (the Irish have a grimmer meaning). A Poem on Getting Up Early in the Morning (or Even Late in the Morning), When One is Old. Kay Boyle. NMM-2

Waked by the Gospel's Powerful Sound. Samson Occom. AH

Waked by the pale pink. The Genius. Archibald MacLeish. MeMAP

Wakefield Second Shepherd's Play. *Unknown. See* The Second Shepherd's Play.

Wakeful in the Township. Elizabeth Riddell. NOBAu

Wakeful they lie. (LL) Counting the Beats. Robert Graves. GBL; GTBS-P; HAP; OxAEP-2; OxBTC; WeW-3

Wakeful, vagrant, restless thing. The Power of Fancy. Philip Freneau. AmPP

Waken, lords and ladies gay. Hunting Song. Sir Walter Scott. GTBS-P; SCGP

Wakening, The. *Unknown.* OBEV

Wakening in a small room. I Remember Clifford. Philip Levine. APAD

Wakepick I. Kristjana Gunnars. NOBC

Wakes that boats make, The. The Ways. Louis Zukofsky. PoE

Waking. Hugh Maxton. BIrV; CIP-2

Waking. Katharine Pyle. OBCA

Waking, The. Theodore Roethke. APAD; AmPP; CRP; CoAP; HAP; HCAP; HeIP-4; InPK-6; InPS-3; LiTM; MoAmPo; MoP; NAAL-2; NIP-4; NOBA; NoAM; NoP-4; PFE; PoPoPo; Poetr; RaBo; TAP; TFi; TTTS; TwCP; VCAP; WeW-3

Waking. Tristan Tzara, *French.* AF, *tr. by* Mary Ann Caws

Waking alone in a multitude of loves when morning's light. On the Marriage of a Virgin. Dylan Thomas. EnLoPo; OxBM

Waking at morn, with the accustomed sigh. On the Death of His Son Vincent. Leigh Hunt. NOBVV

Waking, Child, While You Slept. Ethel Louisa Mason Anderson. WPE *Fr.* Bucolic Eclogues.

Waking Early Sunday Morning. Robert Lowell. FaBoMo; HCAP; NOBA; OxBC; VCAP

Waking from a bad dream, and thrashing out. Dream Time. Anthony Thwaite. DiPo

Waking from a Nap. Ni Tsan, *Chinese.* CoBLCP, *tr. by* Jonathan Chaves

Waking from a Nap on the Beach. May Swenson. NTCP

Waking from Sleep. Robert Bly. NOBA; NoP-4; Poetr; SPE

Waking, he found himself in a train, andante. Slow Movement. Louis MacNeice. CBLP

Waking in March. Philip Levine. PaTW

Waking in the Blue. Robert Lowell. CoAP; HCAP; MoAmPo; UnPo

Waking in the Dark. Dorothy Livesay. NOBC

Waking in the Dark. Adrienne Rich. FaBoWP

Waking is this easy. Aubade. Marilyn Chin. NIP-4

Waking Jesus sudden riding a scream like a / train. I Scream You Scream. Don McKay. NOBC

Waking, my eyes, and in the night. Petronius Arbiter, *Greek.* PGA, *tr. by* Kenneth Rexroth

Waking the Dead. Alasdair Maclean. FaBoTC

Waking this morning. This Morning. Muriel Rukeyser. BoWoP; CrSp

Waking to drizzle and the inevitable. Exmatriate. Jacqueline Lapidus. LoHo

Waking to the clatter of hot-plate kettle. The Years. John Ennis. CIP-2

Waking Up. Jerzy Harasymowicz, *Polish.* CEEP, *tr. by* Victor Contoski

Waking Up. *Unknown.* BoTP

Waking up over the candy store together. First Early Mornings Together. Robert Pinsky. CoIAP

Wakinyan. Adrian C. Louis. NAmP90

Wakonda! Talako! [deathonic] turkey gobbling in the soft-footpatch night! Spontaneous Requiem For the American Indian. Gregory Corso. BB; PoM

Walam Olum; or, Red Score [of the Lenâpé], The [*or* The Wallam Olum; The Red Score or Painted History of the Lenni Lenape]. *Unknown, Delaware (Lenape).*

"After the rushing waters had subsided the Lenape of the turtle were close together, in hollow houses, living together there." APN-2, *tr. by* Daniel Garrison Brinton

"After the Seizer there were ten chiefs, and there was much warfare south and east." OBVE, *tr. by* Daniel G. Brinton

"At first in that place, at all times, above the earth." APN-2, *tr. by* Daniel Garrison Brinton

"Great land and a wide land was the east land, A." OBVE, *tr. by* Daniel G. Brinton

"Long ago there was a mighty snake, and beings evil to men." APN-2, *tr. by* Daniel Garrison Brinton

Waldeinsamkeit. Ralph Waldo Emerson. APN-1; NOBA; PAR

Walden. William Ellery Channing. APN-1; PAR

Walden. Henry David Thoreau.

   Smoke. AWP; NoP-4; OxBA

Walden in July. Donald Junkins. NYBP

Walden Pond/ All those noxious gases rising from it. Jack Spicer. VGW *Fr.* Graphemics. VGW

Waldere 1 ("Hildegund eagerly urged him"). *Unknown, Anglo-Saxon.* ASW, *tr. by* Kevin Crossley-Holland; AnOE, *tr. by* Charles W. Kennedy

Waldere 2 ("Blade better, A"). *Unknown, Anglo-Saxon.* ASW, *tr. by* Kevin Crossley-Holland; AnOE, *tr. by* Charles W. Kennedy

Waldere addressed him, the warrior brave. Waldere 2. *Unknown, Anglo-Saxon.* AnOE, *tr. by* Charles W. Kennedy

Wales England wed; so I was bred. An Autobiography. Ernest Rhys. OBEV; OBWVE

Wales Visitation. Allen Ginsberg. APSN; BB; ColAP; NNaP; NOBA; NYBP; VCAP

Wales, which I have never seen. For My Ancestors. Rolfe Humphries. PoRA

Walk, A. Raymond Carver. GM

Walk, The. Chitra Divakaruni. PUP-19

Walk, The. Thomas Hardy. CMoP; NAEL-2; PoE; PoEL-5

Walk. Frank Horne. BPo

Walk, A. Hedwig Lachmann, *German.* TrJP, *tr. by* Jethro Bithell

Walk. Brian Merriman. BIrV, *tr. by* Brendan Behan *Fr.* The Midnight Court. NOIV, *tr. by* Thomas Kinsella

Walk, A. Rilke, *German.* RaBo, *tr. by* Robert Bly

Walk, A. Gary Snyder. NOBA

Walk, A. Nikolai Alekseievich Zabolotsky, *Russian.* RB, *tr. by* Daniel Weissbort

Walk Around the Lake, A. Jay Meek. CMAP

Walk by the Charles, A. Adrienne Rich. NYBP

Walk, Damn You, Walk! William De Vere. PoLF

Walk down the path. *Unknown.* LB

Walk east. Dawn polishes the sky. Direction. Roberta Hill Whiteman. CDW

Walk fast in snow, in frost walk slow. Winter Wise. *Unknown.* AYFP; Spl

Walk Home, The. Reed Whittemore. CoAmPo

Walk in Central Park, A. Central Park. Julian Symons. PeLV

Walk in Spring, A. K. C. Lart. BoTP

Walk in the Country, A. Su Tung-p'o. *See* Rhyming with Tzu-yu's "Treading the Green."

Walk in the Country, A. T'ang Yen-ch'ien, *Chinese.* SuSp, *tr. by* Edward H. Schafer

Walk in the Precepts. Moses ibn Ezra, *Hebrew.* TrIP, *tr. by* Solomon Solis-Cohen

Walk in Würzburg, A. William Plomer. NYBP

Walk in your sleep beyond Yeppoon. Assignation with a Somnambulist. John Streeter Manifold. CBAP

Walk into the prison, that domed citadel. My Lessons in the Jail. Miriam Waddington. MoCV

Walk on the Moon. N. Scott Momaday. CRP

Walk onto the dark stage dressed for a funeral. The Members of the Orchestra. Kevin Hart. NOBAu

Walk out into your country. Who Shall Die. James A. Randall, Jr. BPo

Walk Slowly. Adelaide Love. BLPA

Walk Through the City. Heinz Czechowski, *German.* CEEP, *tr. by* Ewald Osers

Walk to the Eastern River Bank, A. Kao Ch'i, *Chinese.* CoBLCP, *tr. by* Jonathan Chaves

Walk Together Children. *Unknown.* BPo; NAAAL

Walk warily! Remember, sister, we are. Under Sedation. Alec Derwent Hope. BMAP

Walk with de Mayor of Harlem. David Henderson. PoBA

Walk with the sun. Dream Song. Lewis Alexander. PoBA; WHSW

Walked in his garden in the cool of the evening, waited. (LL) Intimate Supper. Peter Redgrove. FaBoMo; OxBC

Walked past / the back of my head. Mescalito. Anselm Hollo. PT

Walken Hwomme at Night. William Barnes. NOBVV

Walker, a large two-hundred-fifty pound blackman. Christmas 1962. Paul Mariah. GLP

Walker in Prague. Vítězslav Nezval, *Czech.* AF, *tr. by* Ewald Osers

Walkers at Dusk. Hazel Hall. NMM-2

Walking. Temporary City. Nijole Miliauskaite, *Lithuanian.* VCWP, *tr. by* Jonas Zdanys

Walking. Thomas Traherne. EBEV

Walking a cliff with a lamb. Three Easters. Alberta Turner. LCAP-2

Walking against the Wind. Jon Stallworthy. OxBC

Walking alone in a multitude of loves when morning's light. The Marriage of a Virgin. Dylan Thomas. ChIV-2

Walking along the Hudson. Donald Petersen. CoAP

Walking among my own this windy morning. The Spring Vacation. Derek Mahon. PNI

Walking among sceptre-headed. Walking-Sticks and Paperweights and Watermarks. Marianne Moore. PoA

Walking [*or* Walkin'] Around. Pablo Neruda, *Spanish.* RaBo; SPE, *tr. by* Robert Bly

   ("It just so happens that I'm tired of being a man.") PFTM, *tr. by* Jerome Rothenberg

   ("Slow dirty tears.") (LL) VCWP, *tr. by* W. S. Merwin

   ("Towels and nightgowns that cry / slow tears full of dirt.") (LL) PFTM, *tr. by* Jerome Rothenberg

Walking around in the park. Toads Revisited. Philip Larkin. CMoP; NOBL; OxAEP-2

Walking at last by the tame little edge of the sea. Evening before Rain. Leonard Alfred George Strong. OxBTC

Walking at leisure we watch laurel flowers falling. Wang Wei, *Chinese.* TAL, *tr. by* Robert Payne

Walking at Night. Amory Hare. PoLF

Walking at Night. Philip Salom. BMAP

Walking at night on asphalt campus. Death News. Allen Ginsberg. BB; MoP

Walking beside the Kamogawa, Remembering Nansen and Fudo and Gary's Poem. Philip Whalen. BB

Walking Buddha. Barbara Guest. FTOS

Walking by map, I chose unwonted ground. On the Hall at Stowey. Charles Tomlinson. PoE

Walking by the Cliffside Dyeworks. Robert Carnevale. UnSA

Walking down Jalan Thamrin. Robert Francis Brissenden. CBAP

Walking Down the Road. Adrienne Rich. NIP-4

Walking eight hundred. Removal: Last Part. Carroll Arnett. VoR

Walking home from school one afternoon. Gjertrud Schnackenberg. WeW-3

Walking in a Meadowe Greene. *Unknown.* BoLoP

Walking in a Swamp. David Wagoner. HAP

Walking in gardens by the sides. Dylan Thomas. OBGa

Walking in late afternoon. Bruce Beaver. *Fr.* Letters to Live Poets. CBAP

Walking in the Country outside T'ai-yüan on a Spring Day. Yang Chi, *Chinese.* CoBLCP, *tr. by* Jonathan Chaves

Walking in the Countryside. Wang An-shih, *Chinese.* SuSp, *tr. by* Jan W. Walls

Walking in the Midst of Others. Michael Tarachow. EC2

Walking in the Snow. David Wagoner. Poetr

Walking into the shadows, walking alone. Lee in the Mountains. Donald Davidson. CBCWP; FuPo

Walking Late. John Montague. CIP-2

Walking north toward the point, I come on a dead seal. The Dead Seal [near McClure's Beach]. Robert Bly. NNaP

Walking often beside the waves'. Coleridge. Ronald Stuart Thomas. TOF

Walking on the Green Grass. *Unknown.* AmFP

Walking on Water. James Dickey. ChIV-2

Walking Out. Betty Adcock. MT

Walking out, I flushed some meadowlarks. The Duck Pond at Mini's Pasture, a Dozen Years Later. Philip Dow. AmPA

Walking out in the late March midnight. Thorn Leaves in March. W. S. Merwin. TwCP

Walking out of the "big E." Before the Stuff Comes Down. Gary Snyder. HeIP-4

Walking Outside the City Walls on the Day of the Cold Food Festival. Pien Kung, *Chinese.* CoBLCP, *tr. by* Jonathan Chaves

Walking Parker Home. Bob Kaufman. MoNo; NAAAL; PoBA

Walking Past Paul Blackburn's Apt. on 7th St. Diane Wakoski. TAP

Walking Road, The. Richard Hughes. OBMV

Walking Song. Ivor Gurney. NTP

Walking Song. William E. Hickson. OxBChV

Walking-Sticks and Paperweights and Watermarks. Marianne Moore. PoA

Walking swiftly with a dreadful duchess. Infelice. Stevie Smith. LW

Walking the Places I've Never Been. Yury Arabov, *Russian.* TCRP, *tr. by* John High *and* Katya Olmsted

Walking the small oval of Gibbs Pond. I Move to Random Consolations. William Heyen. AmPA

Walking the snow-crust. Anita Virgil. HA

Walking the suburbs in the afternoon. Suburban Dreams. Edwin Muir. OxBTC

Walking the town as if I owned it all. In and Out. Louis Edward Sissman. NYBP; TwCP

Walking the Wide Road. *Unknown, Chinese.* CoBCP, *tr. by* Burton Watson

Walking through a Cornfield in the Middle of Winter I Stumble over a Cow Pie and Think of the Sixties Press. Barbara Harr. BXAP

Walking through a Wall. Louis Jenkins. RaBo

Walking through twisted hollow pathways. Peter Blue Cloud. VoR

Walking to Bellrock. Michael Ondaatje. NOBC

Walking to-day by a cottage I shed tears. Scazons. C. S. Lewis. EBEV

Walking to Sleep. Richard Wilbur. NYBP; VCAP

Walking to the Mailbox. Kim R. Stafford. CMAP

Walking to the Museum. Bone Thoughts on a Dry Day: Chicago. George Starbuck. NYBP; TwCP

Walking to the Temple of Precious Light. Wen Cheng-ming, *Chinese.* CoBLCP, *tr. by* Jonathan Chaves

Walking to your place for a love feast. The Same Inside. Anna Swirszczynska, *Polish.* BLT, *tr. by* Czeslaw Milosz *and* Leonard Nathan

Walking Tour, The. W. H. Auden. CMoP; MoBrPo *Fr.* Paid on Both Sides.

Walking towards the house, the terraces. Sestina in Time of Winter. Patrick Anderson. PoA

Walking up the driftwood beach at day's end. Flood Year. Judith Wright. NoAM

Walking upstairs after breakfast. Sure. Hugo Williams. CBLP

Walking West. William Stafford. RB

Walking Westward. Christian Karlson Stead.
"Walking westward/ you have it all before you." PeNZ

Walking, when the Lake of the Air is Blue with Spring. J. S. Harry. BMAP

Walking-with-a-Cane-Pass. Rin Ishigaki, *Japanese.* WPJ, *tr. by* Kenneth Rexroth *and* Ikuko Atsumi

Walking with God. William Cowper. ECEV; NOCV; NOEC; PeECV; PoEL-3; SCGP; TOF *Fr.* Olney Hymns.

Walking with Lulu in the Wood. Naomi Lazard. NYBP

Walking with R. B. Evan Jones. PBCV

Walking with the moon. Lamenting Life. Ma Chih-yüan. *Fr.* Three Poems to the Tune "Ssu-k'uai yü." CoBLCP, *tr. by* Jonathan Chaves

Walking with the river. Bob Boldman. HA

Walking with you and another lady. A Dream of Jealousy. Seamus Heaney. NoP-4

Walking Wounded. Vernon Scannell. OBWP

Walk's end. Martin Shea. HA

"Walks in graveyards." Sunday Graveyard. Maura Stanton. CMAP

Walky-talky Jenny. *Unknown.* AS

Wall, The. Gwendolyn Brooks. PoBA *Fr.* Two Dedications.

Wall, The. William Hawkins. MoCV

Wall, The. Zbigniew Herbert, *Polish.* AF, *tr. by* John Carpenter *and* Bogdana Carpenter

Wall, The. Ismail, *Telugu.* OMIP, *tr. by* V. Narayana Rao

Wall, The. David Jones. PoA

Wall, The. Eve Merriam. TrJP

Wall. Gabriela Mistral, *Spanish.* PiM, *tr. by* Maria Giachetti

Wall, A. Charles Simic. HCAP

Wall Calendar. Dan Pagis, *Hebrew.* VCWP, *tr. by* Tsipi Keller

Wall, Cave, and Pillar Statements, after Asôka. Alan Dugan. CoAP

Wall collapses, A. Counting. Peter Everwine. IMW

Wall continues, The. Before the Actual Cold. Ray A. Young Bear. VoR

Wall-Flower, The. Henrik Arnold Thaulov Wergeland, *Norwegian.* AWP, *tr. by* Sir Edmund Gosse

Wall, no! I can't tell whar he lives. Jim Bludso of the Prairie Belle. John Milton Hay. APN-2; FaBoBe

Wall of Weeping, The. Edmond Fleg, *French.* TrJP, *tr. by* Humbert Wolfe End of Sorrow, The.
Wandering Jew Comes to the Wall, The.

Wall of woodland overlooks me, A. *Unknown. Fr.* Four Glosses. NOIV

Wall Painting by Wu Wei, A. Wang T'ing-hsiang. *Fr.* Miscellaneous Poems on Spirit-Valley Temple. CoBLCP, *tr. by* Jonathan Chaves

Wallace, The. Henry the Minstrel.
Lament for the Graham. OxBS
Schir William Wallace. OxBS

Wallace Stevens says Money is a kind of poetry. So I offer to trade him Tennes-. Money. Bob Perelman. FTOS

Wallace Stevens, what's he done? A Rouse for Stevens. Theodore Roethke. OBAL

Walled Garden. Dorothy Wellesley. OBGa

Waller, by nature for the bays designed. John Wilmot. EPCY *Fr.* An Allusion to Horace.

Waller came last, but was the first whose art. Nicolas Boileau-Despéaux. EPCY *Fr.* L'Art Poetique.

Wallet, a rawhide goatskin, a cane, A. Leonidas, *Greek.* GrAn; PGA, *tr. by* Kenneth Rexroth

Wallet stolen, so we must end our stay. A Note of Thanks. Wyatt Prunty. RA

Wallet, the hide of a goat, tough and untanned, a stick, A. Leonidas of Tarentum. HePo, *tr. by* Barbara Hughes Fowler *Fr.* Epigrams.

Wallflower to a Moonbeam. Louis Untermeyer. BXAP

Walloping Window-Blind, The. Charles Edward Carryl. NBLV; OBCA *Fr.* Davy and the Goblin.
(Nautical Ballad, A.) APN-2; OBAL

Wallowing in all kind of sin. Michael Wigglesworth. ColAP *Fr.* The Day of Doom.

Wallowing in this bloody sty. The Drunken Fisherman. Robert Lowell. AmPP; CMoP; ChIV-2; ImPo; LiTM; NOBA; OxBA; VGW

Walls. Constantine P. Cavafy, *Modern Greek.* TrJP, *tr. by* Rae Dalven

Walls. Jay Meek. CMAP

Walls are leaning. Three Songs. Daniel S. Simko. CEEP

Walls are made of rain, The. The city's walls. Cant. Imamu Amiri Baraka. NAAL-2

Walls Do Not Fall, The. Hilda Doolittle. NAAL-2

"*Amen.*" WPoS

From The Walls Do Not Fall. NoP-4

("*In the beginning / was the Word.*") (LL) AF

"In no wise is the pillar-of-fire." WPoS

"Sirius: / what mystery is this?" PBWP

"We have seen how the most amiable." BoWoP; PBWP

Walls have been shaded for so many years, The. The Soldier Walks under the Trees of the University. Randall Jarrell. OxBA

Walls. . . iridescent with eyes. The Fifth-Floor Window. Lola Ridge. WPE

Walls of Emerald, The. Li Shang-yin, *Chinese*. PLT, *tr. by* A. C. Graham

Walls of the garden, the first light, The. (LL) A Map of the Western Part of the County of Essex in England. Denise Levertov. CoAP; CoAmPo; NAAL-2

Walls of the maelstrom are painted with trees, The. Poem. Charles Madge. SPE

Walls shriek, The. Antonin Brousek. CEEP, *tr. by* Ewald Osers *Fr.* Pillars of Salt.

Walls, sun and moon dials, home from home. (LL) The West. Michael Longley. BiHa; PBCIP

Walls surrounding them they never saw, The. Donald Justice. CRP

Walnut, A. Mother Goose. ReMoGo

Walnut bark, walnut sap. Dogget Gap. *Unknown.* AmFP

Walnut Tree, The. David McCord. OBCA

Walnutry. Robert Morgan. MT

Walrus and the Carpenter, The. "Lewis Carroll." BLPA; CABP; CBNP; ChAP; EBEvV; FPC; FaBoBe; NAEL-2; NOBL; NOBVV; NoAM; OBSP; OTCP; OxAEP-2; OxBChV; PeLV; PoRA; SAGP; TFi *Fr.* Through the Looking-Glass.

Walrus stretches forth a wrinkled hand, The. The Kingfisher's Boxing Gloves. James Fenton. NoAM

Walsingham, Oh farewell! (LL) A Lament for Our Lady's Shrine at Walsingham. *Unknown.* NoP-4; NoSic; PoEL-2

Walsinghame. Sir Walter Alexander Raleigh. LoP

Walsinghame's Song. James Hogg. BXAP

Walt. Ted Hughes. NoP-4

Walt Whitman. Emanuel Carnevali. PoA

Walt Whitman. Edwin Honig. TAP

Walt Whitman. Edwin Arlington Robinson. APN-2; NCAP; OxBA

Walt Whitman. Walt Whitman. NoAM *Fr.* Song of Myself. AmPP; MoAmPo; NAAL-3; NOBA; OxBA

("I know I have the best of time and space, and was never measured and never.") ColAP

("Laughingly dash with your hair.") (LL) ColAP

Walt Whitman, a kosmos, of Manhattan the son. Walt Whitman. ColAP; NoP-4; SAmP; SCV *Fr.* Song of Myself. AmPP; MoAmPo; NAAL-3; NOBA; OxBA

Walt Whitman, an American, one of the roughs, a kosmos. Walt Whitman. PAR *Fr.* Song of Myself.

Walt Whitman at Bear Mountain. Louis Simpson. CoAmPo; LiTM; TRP

Walt Whitman Bathing. David Wagoner. BAP-95

Walt Whitman in the Civil War Hospitals. David Ignatow. WeT

Walter de la Mare Tells the Listener about Jack and Jill. Louis Untermeyer. MoAmPo *Fr.* Mother Goose Up-to-Date.

Walter Jenks' Bath. William Meredith. HoPM

Walter Lesly. *Unknown.* ESPB

Walter Parmer. Greg Williamson. RA

Walter Rawley [*or* Ralegh *or* Rawely] of the Middle Temple, in Commendation of the Steel[e] Glass[e]. Sir Walter Ralegh. *See* In Commendation of George Gascoigne's Steel Glass.

Walter Savage Landor. Dorothy Parker. NALW *Fr.* A Pig's-Eye View of Literature.

Walter Spaggot, strange old man. Peter Wesley-Smith. FuFo

Waltz, The, *sels.* Byron.

"Muse of the many-twinkling feet! whose charms." OBSV

Waltz, The. Hilary Corke. NYBP

Waltz. Dame Edith Sitwell. BWW

Waltz against the Mountains. Thomas Hornsby Ferril. VGW

Waltz Poem of Those in Love and Inseparable Forever. Miguel Hernández, *Spanish.* AF, *tr. by* Timothy Baland

Waltzer in the House, The. Stanley Kunitz. NYBP

Waltzing Matilda. Andrew Barton Paterson. CBAP

Waly, Waly [Love Be Bonny]. *Unknown.* EnSB; HAP; OBEV; OxBS; TFi

("And the green grass growing over me!") (LL) GTBS-P

(Forsaken Bride, The.) GTBS-P

(Jamie Douglas.) ESPB

Waly, Waly ("When cockle shells turn silver bells"), *with music. Unknown.* AmFP

(Waillie, waillie!) AS

Wan Chu, my adoring husband. Wan Chu's Wife in Bed. Richard Jones. NAmP90

Wan leafs shak' atour us like the snaw, The. Farewell to Dostoevski. "Hugh MacDiarmid." FaBoTC; NAEL-2 *Fr.* A Drunk Man Looks at the Thistle.

Wan / Swan. The Bereaved Swan. Stevie Smith. FaBoTw

Wanaka, mother of Clutha. The Shag. Eileen Duggan. PeNZ

Wanda's Blues. Jane Cooper. SeSe

Wanda's daddy was a railroadman, she was his little wife. Wanda's Blues. Jane Cooper. SeSe

Wander, like him, accursed through the land. (LL) Verses Addressed to the Imitator of the First Satire of the Second Book of Horace: An Attack on Pope. Lady Mary Wortley Montagu. CABP; ECEV

Wanderer, The. W. H. Auden. CMoP; MeMAP; MoP; NoAM; RB; WeW-3 (Chorus.) GTBS-P

Wanderer, The. Johannes Bobrowski, *German.* CEEP, *tr. by* Juliette Victor-Rood

Wanderer, The. Christopher John Brennan.

"When window-lamps had dwindled, then I rose." CBAP

Wanderer, The. Austin Dobson. PFE

Wanderer, The. "Andrey Platonov," *Russian.* TCRP, *tr. by* Albert C. Todd

Wanderer, The. Roland Robinson.

"I reached that waterhole, its mud designed." CBAP

Wanderer, The. Stevie Smith. NALW

Wanderer, The. *Unknown, Anglo-Saxon.* AnOE; NAWM-1; OAEL-1, *tr. by* Charles W. Kennedy

Wanderer, The ("Who liveth alone longeth for mercy"). *Unknown, Anglo-Saxon.* EEP, *tr. by* Michael Alexander

Wanderer, The. "Yehoash," *Yiddish.* TrJP, *tr. by* Isidore Goldstick

Wanderer is in love with the spring of the year, The. Song of Woe. Shen Yüeh, *Chinese.* SuSp, *tr. by* Richard B. Mather

Wanderers, The. Robert Browning. OBEV *Fr.* Paracelsus.

Wanderers, chosen of God. Chosen of God. Stefan Zweig. *Fr.* Jeremiah. TrJP, *tr. by* Eden *and* Cedar Paul

Wanderer's Night-Songs. Goethe, *German.*

"Thou that from the heavens art." AWP

Wanderer's Song, A. John Masefield. MoBrPo

Wanderer's Song. Meng Chiao, *Chinese.* PLT, *tr. by* A. C. Graham

Wanderer's Song. Arthur Symons. SAGP

Wanderers, wanderers we are. Emigrant Song. "S. Ansky," *Yiddish.* TrJP, *tr. by* Joseph Leftwich

Wanderin', *vers.* A, *with music. Unknown.* AS

Wandering above a sea of glass. Down on My Luck. Arthur Rex Dugard Fairburn. PeNZ

Wandering by the heave of the town park, wondering. On the Closing of Millom Ironworks. Norman Nicholson. FaBoTw

Wandering Curves. Keith Waldrop. PmAP

Wandering Gentleman, The. *Unknown, Chinese.* SuSp, *tr. by* Ronald C. Miao

Wandering, in autumn, the woods of boyhood. Gold Glade. Robert Penn Warren. CRP; Poetr; TRP

Wandering into dreams. A Kind of Faith. J. C. Hall. OxBSn

Wandering into Mother's bedroom. On the Fifth Anniversary of My Father's Death. Carolyn Lau. MoLi

Wandering Jack. Emile Jacot. BoTP

Wandering Jew, The. Eloise Bibb. CBWP-4

Wandering Jew Comes to the Wall, The. Edmond Fleg. *Fr.* The Wall of Weeping. TrJP, *tr. by* Humbert Wolfe

Wandering Jew once met a man, A. The Eternal Jew. Jacob Cohen, *Hebrew.* TrJP, *tr. by* I. M. Lask

Wandering late by morning seas. Shelley's Vision. Herman Melville. APN-2

Wandering on Mount Chung-nan. Meng Chiao, *Chinese.* PLT, *tr. by* A. C. Graham

Wandering oversea dreamer. Prayer after World War. Carl Sandburg. VGW

Wandering through cold streets tangled like old string. Brussels in Winter. W. H. Auden. OxBTC

Wandering traveler anxious to make the crossing, A. Crossing the Hsiang River at Night. Meng Hao Jan, *Chinese.* SuSp, *tr. by* Daniel Bryant

Wandering tribe called the Siouxs, A. Prevalent Poetry. Charles Follen Adams. PeLi

Wandering up and down one day. The Cobbler. *Unknown.* BoTP

Wanderings of Oisin, The. W. B. Yeats.
  Old Man Stirs the Fire to a Blaze, An. RB
Wand'ring in this place as a wilderness. *Unknown.* GBL
Wandsworth Common. David Bromwich. PoA
Wang Chao-chün. Li Shang-yin, *Chinese.* SuSp, *tr. by* Irving Y. Lo
Wang Chao-chün. Tai Shu-lun, *Chinese.* SuSp, *tr. by* William H. Nienhauser
Wangsun, The. Wang Yen-Shou, *Chinese.* ChiP, *tr. by* Arthur Waley
Waning Moon, The. CH; FHYEP; OxBSP
  (Moon, The.) FaBoCh; OBEV
  ("That finds no object worth its constancy?") (LL) FaBoCh; OBEV; SAGP
Waning moon looks upward; this grey night, The. Nostalgia. D. H. Lawrence. PoA
Waning Night, The. Chế Lan Viên, *Vietnamese.* AVP, *tr. by* Huỳnh Sanh Thông
Waning of the Harvest Moon, The. John Wieners. PmAP
Wanna hear something really funny? A Woman like Me. Eileen Myles. GLP
Want and winter are upon us. *Unknown. Fr.* Toward Winter. NOIV
Want Bone, The. Robert Pinsky. EOEF
Want of ♭ Want of ♮ Anne Szumigalski. FaBoWP
Want of ♭ You, The. ♮ Ivan Leonard Wright. BLPA; FaBoBe; SoSe-8
Want, predation, sleep. Mary Kinzie. FFC
Want quickens wit: Want's pupils needs must work. The Fishermen. Theocritus. AWP; OBVE, *tr. by* Charles Stuart Calverley *Fr.* Idylls.
Wanted, a Minister's Wife. *Unknown.* BLPA
Wanted / to give away pride. A Defeat. Denise Levertov. PBWP
Wanting a Mummy. Sandra McPherson. AmPA; LCAP-2
Wanting a myth for blowing up the gods. The Collective Invention. Chris Wallace-Crabbe. BMAP
Wanting children a couple once sat. Limerick. G. W. Hanney. PeLi
Wanting News. Sydney Tremayne. FaBoTC
Wanting Out. Gavin Ewart. SPE
Wanting to Die. Anne Sexton. CoAmPo; ColAP; MoP; NoAM; TAP; TRP; VCAP
Wanting to say things. My Father's Song. Simon J. Ortiz. HATNAP
Wanting to welcome the emperor. Wang Chien. SuSp, *tr. by* William H. Nienhauser *Fr.* Palace Poems.
Wanton. Silabhattarika, *Sanskrit.*
  "My husband is the same who took my maidenhead." PBWP, *tr. by* Daniel H. H. Ingalls
  ("My husband is the same man who first pierced me.") BoWoP, *tr. by* Willis Barnstone
Wanton, The. Vidya, *Sanskrit.*
  "Say, friend, if all is well still with the bowers." PBWP, *tr. by* Daniel H. H. Ingalls
Wanton herd of rakes profest, The. Horace. *See* Odes 1.25: Ribald Romeos Less and Less Berattle ("Parcius iunctas quatiunt fenestras").
Wanton laird of Young Logie, The. (LL) The Laird o' Logie. *Unknown.* CH; ESPB
Wanton troopers riding by, The. The Nymph Complaining for the Death of Her Faun [*or* Fawn]. Andrew Marvell. CH; ESCV; GeHe; HeIP-4; NAEL-1; OAEL-1; PoEL-2; RACG; SeCP
Wanton Wife of Bath, The. *Unknown.*
  "In *Bath* a wanton wife did dwell." PBRV
Wanton with long delay the gay spring leaping cometh. April, 1885. Robert Bridges. OxBSP; OxBTC
Wanton young lady of Wimley, A. Limerick. *Unknown.* PeLi
Wants. Philip Larkin. GTBS-P
Wants of Man, The. John Quincy Adams. APN-1; OBAL; PoLF
Wants to be finished waiting in the car. He ate his pear. The Alcoholic's Son at Ten. Kathleen Peirce. PBCAP
Wapentake. Henry Wadsworth Longfellow. EPCY
Wapiti, The. Ogden Nash. TLR
War. André Breton, *French.* AF, *tr. by* Mary Ann Caws *and* Jean-Pierre Cauvin
War. Michael Brownstein. FTOS
War. Đông Hồ, *Vietnamese.* AVP, *tr. by* Huỳnh Sanh Thông
War. Miguel Hernández, *Spanish.* AF; RaBo, *tr. by* Hardie St. Martin
War. Georg Heym, *German.* PeFWW, *tr. by* Patrick Bridgwater
War. S. S. Hunt. NSI
War. Max Jacob, *French.* AF, *tr. by* Michael Brownstein
War, A. Randall Jarrell. OxBSP
War. Patrice Kayo. PBMAP
War. Joseph Langland. AiP
War. Lorine Niedecker. FTOS
War. Gregory Orfalea. IFJA

War. "Georgy Avdeievich Rayevsky," *Russian.* TCRP, *tr. by* Albert C. Todd
War. Andrey Andreievich Voznesensky, *Russian.* RB, *tr. by* William Jay Smith *and* Vera Dunham
War. Edgar Wallace. OBWP
War against the Trees, The. Stanley Kunitz. HAP
War and Memory. June Jordan.
  "Daddy at the stove or sink. Large." MoLi
War-and-Peace. George Buchanan. PNI
War and Silence. Robert Bly. CAPP-1
War Bird's Burlesque, A, *with music. Unknown.* AS
War Blinded. Douglas Dunn. DiPo; OBWP
War Books. Ivor Gurney. PeFWW
War broke out in autumn at the empty border, The. Yehuda Amichai. PoSu, *tr. by* Yehuda Amichai *and* Ted Hughes *Fr.* Patriotic Songs.
War canoes were ready. Thirsty Island. Jim Tollerud. VoR
War chariots thunder, horses neigh, *the barbarians are coming.* The Barbarians Are Coming. Marilyn Chin. PUP-20
War chief danced the old way, The. At the Klamath Berry Festival. William Stafford. InPK-6
War Comes. Zalman Schneour, *Yiddish.* TrJP, *tr. by* Joseph Leftwich
War Confession. Natan Zach, *Hebrew.* IP, *tr. by* Warren Bargad *and* Stanley F. Chyet
War Dance. Miidhu, *Aborigine.* NOBAu, *tr. by* Georg von Brandenstein
War Dance. *Unknown, Iowa.* APN-2, *tr. by* George Catlin
  Approaching Dance, The.
  Eh-Ros-ka, the Warrior's Dance.
  Ha-Kon-E-Crase, the Eagle Dance.
  Wa-Sissica, the War Song.
War Down a Monkland. *Unknown.* PBCV
War drums and cymbals clash, offend the ear. Opera Actors. Phan chu Trinh, *Vietnamese.* AVP, *tr. by* Huỳnh Sanh Thông
War Elephant, The. Chế Lan Viên, *Vietnamese.* AVP, *tr. by* Huỳnh Sanh Thông
War Games. Walter McDonald. CDa
War God's Horse Song, The. *Unknown, Navajo Indian.* RB, *tr. by* Louis Watchman; TTTS
War Has Been Given a Bad Name. Bertolt Brecht, *German.* HP; NNPT; PoSu, *tr. by* John Willett
War Hope. William Hathaway. NAmP90
War Horse, The. Eavan Boland. BIrV; CIP-2; PBCIP
War Hymn. Rhigas Pheraios, *Greek.* GrIP, *tr. by* Rae Dalvin
War in a Mousetrap. Velemir Khlebnikov, *Russian.*
  "I, to make myself laugh louder and longer." TCRP, *tr. by* Gary Kern
War in Fife, The. Sydney Goodsir Smith. FaBoTC *Fr.* Armageddon in Albyn.
War in Spain has ended long ago / Aunt Rose, The. (LL) To Aunt Rose. Allen Ginsberg. CLPP; ColAP; LiTM; NAAL-2; NoAM; PmAP; PoE; VGW
War in the Air, The. Howard Nemerov. ColAP; DiPo; VCAP
War (?) in the Desert, A. *Unknown.* PeSAV
War Is Kind. Stephen Crane. LiTM; MeMAP; TAP *Fr.* War Is Kind.
  "Ah, God, the way your little finger moved." APN-2
  Candid Man, The. MoAmPo
  "Each small gleam was a voice." APN-2
  "Fast rode the knight." MeMAP; NAAL-2
  "I explain the silvered passing of a ship at night." APN-2
  "Little ink more or less!, A." APN-2; MeMAP
  "Man said to the universe, A." APN-2; AmPP; FaBoEE; LiTM; NAAL-2; OBAL; OBSV; PiM; TAP; WeW-3
  "Newspaper is a collection of half injustices, A." APN-2; AmPP; MeMAP; NAAL-2
  On the Desert. LiTM
  "Slant of sun on dull brown walls, A." LiTM; MeMAP; NAAL-2
  There Was a Man with a Tongue of Wood. MeMAP; MoAmPo
  Trees in the Garden Rained Flowers, The. LiTM
  War Is Kind. LiTM; MeMAP; TAP
  (From War is Kind.) NoP-4
  "Wayfarer / Perceiving the pathway to truth, The." APN-2; AmPP; MeMAP; MoAmPo; PFE
War is not declared any more. Every Day. Ingeborg Bachmann, *German.* BoWoP, *tr. by* Christopher Middleton; PoSu
War is the angry man waving his desperate. War-and-Peace. George Buchanan. PNI
War Lord in the Early Evening. Patricia K. Page. NoAM
War Memento (Somewhere in France 1915). Roger Hecht. CRP
War Memoir: Jazz, Don't Listen to It at Your Own Risk. Bob Kaufman. NAAAL

(O-JAZZ-O War Memoir: Jazz, Don't Listen To It At Your Own Risk.) MoNo

War of the Roses, The, *for Premier Bjelke-Petersen.* Michael Dransfield. BMAP

War of the Worlds, The. Vern Rutsala. Poetsp

War of words is done, The. Battle. John Davidson. CABP

War on the Periphery. George Johnston. NOBC

War Party. Eddy Grant. PBCV

War Photographers, The. Frank Ormsby. PNI

War Poem. Simon J. Ortiz. CDa

War Poems 1. Sang Ku, *Korean.* CKP, *tr. by* Jaihiun Kim

War Poems 7. Sang Ku, *Korean.* CKP, *tr. by* Jaihiun Kim

War Poet. Roy Fuller. *See* January 1940.

War Poet. Sidney Keyes. NoP-4; PoWW

War Poetry. John Philips. NOEC *Fr.* Blenheim.

War Rug. Natasha Waxman. IFJA

War separated, The. The Friends. Bertolt Brecht, *German.* PoSu, *tr. by* Michael Hamburger

War ships, cold tides. Yün Shou-p'ing. CoBLCP, *tr. by* Jonathan Chaves *Fr.* Seeing Off Mr. Yang on His Journey to Wu-wei Prefecture.

War shook the land where Levi dwelt. The Field of Glory. Edwin Arlington Robinson. MoAmPo

War shows what each man's country is to him. Invasion. Eileen Duggan. PeNZ

War Song, A. Bertrans de Born. *See* Song of Battle.

War Song [to Englishmen], A. William Blake. CH

War Song. John Davidson. OBNC

War Song of Dinas Vawr, The. Thomas Love Peacock. AWP; EBEvV; FaBoCh; FaPoR; HAP; NAEL-2; NOBE; NTP; OAEL-2; OxAEP-2 *Fr.* The Misfortunes of Elphin.

("And his overthrow, our chorus.") (LL) CABP; NOBRP

War Song of the Basotho, A. *Unknown.* PeSAV, *tr. by* Daniel P. Kunene

War Song of the Saracens. James Elroy Flecker. EBEvV; MoBrPo *Fr.* Hassan.

("We are they who come faster than fate: we are they who ride.") EBEvV

War Songs. Tohono O'odham, *Papago.* PaTW, *tr. by* Ruth Murray Underhill

War Songs. *Unknown, Ojibwa Native American.* APN-2, *tr. by* Henry Rowe Schoolcraft

War Songs. *Unknown, Sioux Native American.* APN-2, *tr. by* Alfred Longley Riggs

War Stories. Perry Oldham. CDa

War Story. Gerald McCarthy.
  Med Building. CDa

War Story. Jon Stallworthy. OxBC

War that we have carefully for years provoked, The. Black-out. Robinson Jeffers. LiTM

War the Source of Riches. *Unknown.* NOBRP

War-Time. William Robert Rodgers. OxBSP

War to end them all, The. Firebell for Peace. Joyce Lee. NOBAu

War Walking Near. Ray A. Young Bear. CDW

War was her life, with want and the wild air. Yorkshire Wife's Saga. Ruth Pitter. NALW

War with a thousand battles, and shaking a hundred thrones. Tennyson. *See* I hate the dreadful hollow behind the little wood.

Ward, and still in bonds, one day, A. Regeneration. Henry Vaughan. ChIV-1; ESCV; FMP; FSCP; GeHe; MeLP; NAEL-1; NoP-4; PoE

Ward has no heart, they say, but I deny it. On J. W. Ward. Samuel Rogers. FaBoEE

Ward is quiet, the mothers delivered, The. The First Day. Elizabeth Spires. PUP-20

Ward 130 in the passage on the right. 25 December 1960. Ingrid Jonker, *Afrikaans.* PeSA, *tr. by* Jack Cope *and* Uys Krige

Ward 6. Tanure Ojaide. HBAPE

Ward Two. Francis Webb. CBAP

Ward X. Lola Ridge.
  "Salvation Army lass, The." WPE

Wardance. Phillip William George. VoR

Wardance Soup. Phillip William George. VoR

Warden said to me the other day, The. Etheridge Knight. LTA; MT; NBV; PBCAP; SoSe-8

Wardour Street. Humbert Wolfe. OxBTC

Warehouse-theatre's. Martin Shea. HA

Warhead Wakes. Ivor Armstrong Richards. PFE

Warheads of mushrooms round the filter-pond. (LL) Idylls of the King. Geoffrey Hill. NoAM; PoE

Waring. Robert Browning. PoEL-5
  Assassins. OxBoV

Warlike Angels, The. Rafael Alberti, *Spanish.* AF, *tr. by* Geoffrey Connell

Warm ashes of the word, The. Cuncta Semper. Rodolfo Di Biasio, *Italian.* NeIt, *tr. by* Stephen Sartarelli

Warm hands, warm. *Unknown.* LB

Warm night fallen night. Condemned. Philippe Soupault, *French.* AF, *tr. by* Paulette Schmidt

Warm plantains and chilled light radishes. Rogers in Italy. Frank O'Hara. FTOS

Warm rain and pure wind, The. Alone in the Night. Li Ch'ing-chao, *Chinese.* OHPC, *tr. by* Kenneth Rexroth

Warm rain before dawn. Ruth Yarrow. HA

Warm rain, sunny wind start to break the chill. Li Ch'ing-chao, *Chinese.* BoWoP, *tr. by* Willis Barnstone *and* Sua Chu-chin

Warm rosebuds below, The. (LL) The World-Soul. Ralph Waldo Emerson. APN-1; NCAP

Warm shone the sun, the wind as warmly blew. Hay-Time; or, The Constant Lovers. A Pastoral. Josiah Relph. NOEC

Warm summer sun. Epitaph Placed on His Daughter's Tomb. "Mark Twain." PoLF, *ad. by* Robert Richardson

Warm sun is failing, the bleak wind is wailing, The. Autumn: A Dirge. Shelley. CH

Warm walnut seats crisscross braces. Powwow remnants. Lew Blockcolski. VoR

Warm winds crossed from the eastern coast, The. The Boss's Wife. *Unknown.* CBAP

Warme into the Armes of Death, *par. by* Richard Crashaw. Bible, *O.T. See* Psalm 23.

Warmest welcome, at an inn, The. (LL) Written at [*or in*] an Inn at Henley. William Shenstone. AWP; NOBE; NOEC; OBEV; OxAEP-1

Warming Her Pearls. Carol Ann Duffy. NoP-4

Warmth of the wind-break wall, The. Louise Herlin, *French.* MFP, *tr. by* Martin Sorrell

Warner the thinges for to obtayne. The Happy Life. Martial, *Latin.* OBCVT, *tr. by* Henry Howard, Earl of Surrey

Warning. Alfred Gibbs Campbell. AAP

Warning, The. Adelaide Crapsey. Spl; WPE
  (Cinquain: A Warning.) WeW-3

Warning, The. Robert Creeley. NeAP; TAP; VGW

Warning. Langston Hughes. PFTM

Warning. Langston Hughes. BPo

Warning. Jenny Joseph. FaBoWP; OxBTC

Warning, The. Henry Wadsworth Longfellow. APN-1; ChIV-1; NCAP; PAR

Warning. Alicia Ostriker. DeD

Warning, A. Coventry Patmore. EnLoPo

Warning. Tadeusz Rózewicz, *Polish.* PoSu, *tr. by* Magnus F. Krynski

Warning, A. *Unknown.* OxNR
  ("Robin and the redbreast, The.") CTAV

Warning against the Gypsies, A. John Langhorne. ECEV *Fr.* The Country Justice.

Warning and Reply. Emily Jane Brontë. WPE

Warning of Winter. Mary Ursula Bethell. FaBoWP; PeNZ

Warning to America, A. Philip Freneau. TAP

Warning to Children. Robert Graves. CBNP; FaBoCh; NOxBChV; NTP; NoP-4; OAEL-2

Warning to Conquerors, A. Donagh MacDonagh. IIP

Warning to One. Merrill Moore. MoAmPo

Warning to Travailers Seeking Accomodations at Mr. Devills Inn. Sarah Kemble Knight. SCAP

Warnings. Nicanor Parra, *Spanish.* AF, *tr. by* Miller Williams

Warping bandstand reminds you of the hard rage, The. Return to La Plata, Missouri. Jim Barnes. HATNAP

Warren's Address at Bunker Hill [*or* the American Soldiers]. John Pierpont. FaBoBe

Warring heaven. Tanka. Akiko Yosano, *Japanese.* MJT, *tr. by* Ueda, Makoto

Warring sighs and groans I'll wage thee. (LL) Song: "Ae fond kiss, and then we sever." Robert Burns. BoLoP; EBEvV; NAEL-2; NOBRP; NOEC; OAEL-1; OBEV; PoEL-4

Warrior. Frank Mkalawile Chipasula. PeSAV

Warrior Daughters. Colette Inez. NMM-2

Warrior / Houngan we salute you. Our Revolutions Must Be Different. Marina Ama Omowale Maxwell. HCP

Warrior is going a journey, The. Incantation. Alistair Paterson. *Fr.* Incantations for Warriors. PeNZ

Warrior Nation Trilogy. Lance Henson. ImGa; VoR

Warrior so bold and a virgin so bright. Alonzo the Brave and the Fair Imogine. Matthew Gregory Lewis. NOBRP

Warrior! whose image on thy tomb. The Effigies. Felicia Dorothea Hemans. NOBRP

Warriors. Douglas Dunn. OxBC

Warriors and chiefs! should the shaft or the sword. Song of Saul before His Last Battle. Byron. ChIV-1

Warr'st thou 'gainst Athens? Shakespeare. EBEV *Fr.* Timon of Athens.

Warru. Jack Davis. BMAP

Wars. Margaret Gibson. AFr

Wars, The. Howard Moss. VCAP

War's End. Dahlia Ravikovitch, *Hebrew.* IP, *tr. by* Warren Bargad *and* Stanley F. Chyet

Wars of Imperialism. John Foulcher. NOBAu

Wars of Santa Fe, The. *Unknown.* AmFP

Wars that are just? A simpler question: In the event. George Oppen. APSN *Fr.* Route.

Warsong of the Kwakiutl. *Kwakiutl Oral Tradition, Kwakiutl.* PaTW, *tr. by* Franz Boas

Warsong of the Kwakiutl. *Unknown.* APN-2, *tr. by* Franz Boas *Fr.* Songs of the Kwakiutl Indians.

Wartburg, 1521–22, The. Timothy Steele. RA

Wartime Dawn, A. David Gascoyne. LiTM

Warum sind denn die Rosen so blass. Heinrich Heine, *German.* AWP, *tr. by* Richard Garnett

Wary of time O it seizes the soul tonight. Easter Eve. Muriel Rukeyser. VGW

Was a bird; and the song was wordless; the singing will never be done. (LL) Everyone Sang. Siegfried Sassoon. APAD; EBEvV; GTBS-P; MoBrPo; NAEL-2; NOBE; NSI; NoAM; NoP-4; OBEV; OBWP; OPOU; OxBSP; OxBTC; TrJP

Was a child's uprooted grave. (LL) The Shell. H. M. Sarson. NSI; PoWW

Was a lying son of a bitch. (LL) The Derby Ram. *Unknown.* AmFP; OxNR

Was, at all hazards, to try to copy the Celt! (LL) The Cult of the Celtic. Anthony C. Deane. BXAP; NOBL; PeLV

Was breathing His love for a cut-away bog. (LL) The One. Patrick Kavanagh. MoBrPo; TIRV

Was broken. / He bade a warrior abandon his horse. The Battle of Maldon. *Unknown, Anglo-Saxon.* AnOE; OAEL-1, *tr. by* Charles W. Kennedy

Was faithful unto death, and shamed the Devil. (LL) Lying. Richard Wilbur. DiPo; HCAP; PeVV; Poetr

Was for 300 or maybe 400 years. (LL) Toe'osh; a Laguna Coyote Story. Leslie Marmon Silko. CDW; NoAM; VoR

Was *From Charybdis into Scylla.* (LL) The Hag and the Slavies. Jean de La Fontaine, *French.* AWP; OBVE, *tr. by* Edward Marsh

Was he a mining on the flat. He Done His Level Best. "Mark Twain." AiP

Was he married, did he try. Stevie Smith. MoP; NoAM; Poetr

Was heaven sent. (LL) Little Lyric (of Great Importance). Langston Hughes. NBLV; OBAL; OBCoV

Was here before us, knew we would come, and sees beyond us. (LL) Every peak is a crater. This is the law of volcanoes. Adrienne Rich. NAAL-2; NALW; NoAM

Was his shadow under his shield. (LL) The King of Connacht. *Unknown, Early Irish.* IIP; NNPT, *tr. by* Frank O'Connor

Was I too glib about eternal things. The Sequel. Theodore Roethke. NYBP

Was I wrong when I thought. Thought on June 26. Raymond Mazisi Kunene. PBMAP

Was, Is, and Yet-to-be. Ella Wheeler Wilcox. PoToHe

Was it a dream, or did I see it plain? Sonnet 75. Edmund Spenser. CBLP; NIP-1 *Fr.* Amoretti. AAS

Was it a dream? We sailed, I thought we sailed. A Dream. Matthew Arnold. EnVR; GBL; GTBS-P *Fr.* Switzerland.

Was it a vision, or a waking dream? I heard her voice before I saw. The Irish Fr for No. Ciaran Carson. PNI

Was it D + 10 or D + 12 we caught. Apples, Normandy, 1944. Frank Ormsby. PNI *Fr.* A Northern Spring.

Was it for this I uttered prayers. Grown-up. Edna St. Vincent Millay. NoAM

Was it he said she said or. Philip Booth. IFJA

Was it hundreds of years ago, my love. James Thomson. EnVR *Fr.* Sunday at Hampstead.

Was It Quite Like That? Suniti Namjoshi *and* Gillian Hanscombe. CPO

Was it really you all the time? Dream Sequence, Part 9. Naomi Long Madgett. BPo

Was it the proud full sail of his great verse. Sonnet 86. Shakespeare. CABP; NoSic; OAEL-1; OxAEP-1; SCGP; Son *Fr.* Sonnets.

Was it wind off the dumps. Summer Home. Seamus Heaney. PBCIP

Was it yesterday. Haiku: "Was it yesterday." Sonia Sanchez. FFC

Was it you yesterday? The Only One. Elisaveta Bagryana, *Bulgarian.* CEEP, *tr. by* Jascha Kessler *and* Aleksandar Shurbanov

Was Jesus Chaste? or did he. William Blake. ChIV-2 *Fr.* The Everlasting Gospel.

Was Jesus Humble? or did he. William Blake. ChIV-2 *Fr.* The Everlasting Gospel.

Was just that I was leaving home and my folks were growing old. (LL) Christmas at Sea. Robert Louis Stevenson. CH; EBVV; FaBoBe; PeVV

Was left all alone / Fa, le, la, la, lal, de. (LL) Aristotle's Story. Mother Goose. CBNP; OxNR; ReMoGo

Was lout, son of lout, by old lout, and was da to a lout! (LL) Blue Blood. James Stephens. MoBrPo; OBCoV; OBMV

Was made for him, to *Tyrannize* upon. (LL) The Hunting of the Hare. Margaret Lucas Cavendish, Duchess of Newcastle. BWW; FaBoVe; KTR; NOSC

Was made steward in king Henerys hall. (LL) Sir Aldingar. *Unknown.* ESPB; OxBB

Was made the Lady of the May. (LL) Phillida and Coridon. Nicholas Breton. EBEvV; NOBE; NoSic; OBEV; TTTS

Was Nature angry when she formed my clay? On Viewing Herself in a Glass. Elizabeth Teft. ECWP

Was never in Scotland hard nor sene. Christ's Kirk on the Grene. James V, King of Scotland. OxBS

Was never said in rhyme. (LL) Happy Insensibility. Keats. CH; GTBS-P; NOBE; OBEV; OBNC; PBMP

Was no more than his due who brought good news from Ghent. (LL) How They Brought the Good News from Ghent to Aix. Robert Browning. EBEvV; EBNV; FHYEP; FaBoBe; FaPoR; HoPM; NAEL-2; OBSP; PeVV; UV

Was out on the street, the word. Garland. *Unknown.* NBrP

Was Physiognomy. (LL) Spider sewed at Night, A. Emily Dickinson. NAAL-1; NAAL-3; NALW

Was pour molasses on the cat? (LL) Why did the children. Carl Sandburg. OBAL; PBMP

Was quenched by death, and broken the bruised reed. (LL) Keats. Henry Wadsworth Longfellow. Son; TAP

Was rain. (LL) Party Piece. Brian Patten. FaBoSe

Was taken and carried to Canada. (LL) Bar[']s Fight[, August 28, 1746]. Lucy Terry. BPo; BlSi; CrDW; NAAAL

Was that night on the marge of Lake Lebarge / cremated Sam McGee. Robert W. Service. *See* The Cremation of Sam McGee.

Was that sticky infusion, that rank flavor of blood, that poetry, by which I lived? (LL) The Bear. Galway Kinnell. CoAP; InPS-3; NNaP; TAP; TRP; VCAP; VGW

Was that young faithful heart! (LL) Casabianca. Felicia Dorothea Hemans. BLPA; EBEvV; EBeBe; NOBRP; VWP

Was the arrangement made between the two couples legal? Some Litanies. Michael Benedikt. CoAP; TwCP

Was the discovery of a brother walking in a storm. Torn Parts: the story. Fanny Howe. PT

Was the ethereal kind which did not stop. (LL) Wadasa Nakamoon, Vietnam Memorial. Ray A. Young Bear. CDa

Was the forgetful kingdom of death. (LL) Janet Waking. John Crowe Ransom. CMoP; ColAP; FuPo; InPK-6; MeMAP; MoAmPo; MoP; NAAL-2; NoAM; PBMP; PoE; Poetr; RB; TAP

Was the founder! Ben Jonson. *See* A Fit of Rhyme [*or* Rime] against Rhyme [*or* Rime].

Was the lady that's known as Lou. Robert W. Service. *See* The Shooting of Dan McGrew.

Was the love between them. His Lunch Bucket. Doug Cockrell. Poetsp

Was the one he kept sailing home to? (LL) Odysseus. W. S. Merwin. NoP-4

Was the only thing I had. (LL) Homecoming. Langston Hughes. SAmP; TRP

Was the silkiest day of the young year. The Day He Died. Ted Hughes. OxAEP-2

Was there another Troy for her to burn? (LL) No Second Troy. W. B. Yeats. CMoP; EnLoPo; GTBS-P; MoP; NAEL-2; NOBE; NoAM; OAEL-2; OxAEP-2; OxBTC; PoEL-5; TFi; WeW-3

Was there no star that could be sent. Ralph Waldo Emerson. IMW *Fr.* Threnody: "The South-wind brings." APN-1

Was this His coming! I had hoped to see. Ave Maria, Gratia Plena. Oscar Wilde. ChIV-2

Was this the face that launched a thousand ships? Helen. Marlowe. EBEV; EBEvV; GBL; ImPo *Fr.* Doctor Faustus. NAEL-1; OAEL-1

Was this the thing Van Horne set out / To conquer? (LL) The Precambrian [*or* Pre-Cambrian] Shield. Edwin John Pratt. MoCV; NOBC

Was told the mystic name of Love. (LL) Natura Naturans. Arthur Hugh Clough. CBLP; EnVR; HAP; NOBVV

Was two sisters loved one man. The Two Sisters. *Unknown.* AmFP

Was very kind. When she regained. The Raper from Passenack. William Carlos Williams. PFE; PoPoPo

Was, "Wae to my sister, fair Ellen." (LL) The Twa Sisters. *Unknown.* ESPB; OxBS

Was wrapped like *panettone* in Italian tinfoil. (LL) Sailing Home from Rapallo. Robert Lowell. HCAP; PoPoPo; TAP

Was you at de hall las' night. Leap Yeah Party, De. Maggie Pogue Johnson. CBWP-4

Was your / love. (LL) To Mother and Steve. Mari E. Evans. BPo; PoBA

Wash-Day. Lilian McCrea. BoTP

Wash, hands, wash. A Rhyme for Washing Hands. Rodney Bennett. BoTP

Wash man out of the earth, shear off. Eiléan Ní Chuilleanáin. BIrV; WPOW

Wash me in the water. *Unknown.* OBCoV *Fr.* Soldiers' Songs of the First World War.

Wash me on home, mama. Gary Snyder. *Fr.* Burning. NeAP; PoM *Fr.* Myths and Texts.

Wash the dishes, wipe the dishes. Mother Goose. OxNR

Washday Battles. Geoffrey Summerfield. NOxBChV

Washed ashore. Repulse Bay. Marilyn Chin. OpBo

Washed by the rain, dust and grime are laid;. Starting Early from the Ch'u-ch'êng Inn. Po Chü-i, *Chinese.* BLT; ChiP; OBVE, *tr. by* Arthur Waley

Washerwoman, The. Mary Collier. ECWP; NOEC *Fr.* The Woman's Labour; an Epistle to Mr. Stephen Duck.

Washerwoman, The. Mary Weston Fordham. CBWP-2

Washerwoman. Velemir Khlebnikov, *Russian.*

  "Tsar! Send out a shot!" TCRP, *tr. by* Gary Kern

  "We don't live in castles." TCRP, *tr. by* Gary Kern

  "Writers of the knife are we!" TCRP, *tr. by* Gary Kern

Washerwoman, The. Veronica Volkow, *Spanish.* VCWP, *tr. by* Forrest Gander

Washing-Day. Anna Laetitia Barbauld. ECWP; PEW; WoRP

Washing hanging from the lemon tree, The. The Five-Day Rain. Denise Levertov. NeAP

Washing hangs upon the line, A. Elizabeth Bishop. FaBoVe; FaBoWP *Fr.* Songs for a Colored Singer. RB

Washing Kai in the sauna. The Bath. Gary Snyder. NNaP; PmAP; TAP; VCAP

Washing My Wife's Clothes. Luân Hoán, *Vietnamese.* AVP, *tr. by* Huỳnh Sanh Thông

Washing the Coins. Douglas Dunn. FaBoPV

Washing the Dishes. Christopher Darlington Morley. PoLF

Washing-Up Song, The. Elizabeth Gould. BoTP

Washington. Lorna Dee Cervantes. *Fr.* Visions of Mexico While at a Writing Symposium in Port Townsend, Washington. NoAM

Washington. Harriet Monroe. FaBoBe *Fr.* Commemoration Ode.

Washington. Nancy Byrd Turner. CTV

Washington Heights, 1959. Michael C. Blumenthal. HCAP

Washington in Love. John Berryman. LCAP-2

Washington Monument by Night. Carl Sandburg. CMoP; ImGa

Washington, the brave, the wise. George Washington. *Unknown.* CTV

Wasn't That a Mighty Storm? *Unknown.* AmFP

Wasn't this a queer thing? I stood with your mother. A Queer Thing. Nancy Keesing. NOBAu

Wasn't this a vast world. (LL) The Three Magi. Stanislaw Baranczak, *Polish.* CEEP, *tr. by* Stanislaw Baranczak; GI, *tr. by* Stanislaw Baranczak *and* Clare Cavanagh

Wasn't this the site, asked the historian. House and Land. Allen Curnow. PeNZ

Wasn't your mother a woman? Hennamma, *Kannada.* BoWoP, *tr. by* Willis Barnstone

Wasp, The. Daryl Hine. APo; NYBP

Wasp, The. "Fiona Macleod." BoTP

Wasp, climbing the window pane. Invocation. Howard Nemerov. *Fr.* Epigrams. OBAL

Wasp Sex Myth (One). Anselm Hollo. PoM

Wasp Sex Myth (Two). Anselm Hollo. PoM

  ("'You got children, Ma'am?'' he said aloud.") (LL) LTA

Wasps, The. Homer. OBVE, *tr. by* Alexander Pope *Fr.* The Iliad.

Wasps' Nest, The. George MacBeth. OxBTC

Wassail the trees, that they may bear. Robert Herrick. PChr *Fr.* Ceremonies for Christmas[se]. BeJo; OBCP

Wassaile, The. Robert Herrick. PBRV

Wassailing Song. *Unknown.* OBCP

Waste. Harry Graham. OBCoV

Waste Land, The. T. S. Eliot. AmPP; CMoP; FaBoMo; HAP; LiTM; MoAmPo; MoP; NAAL-2; NAEL-2; NAWM-2; NOBA; NOBE; NoAM; NoP-4; OAEL-2; OxAEP-2; OxBA; OxBTC; PoE; TAP; TFi; UnPo

  (Burial of the Dead, The.) CABP

  ("You! hypocrite lecteur!—mon semblable,—mon frère!") (LL) CABP

  Death by Water. OBVE

  Game of Chess, A. SCV

  "When lovely woman stoops to folly and." UV

Waste Land Limericks. Wendy Cope. FaBoWP

Waste not, want not, is a maxim I. Rowland Howard. CTV

Waste remains, the waste remains and kills., The. (LL) Missing Dates. William Empson. CMoP; HAP; LiTM; MoBrPo; MoP; NOBE; NoAM; OAEL-2; PoE; UnPo

Wasted Day, A. Frances Darwin Cornford. MoBrPo

Wasted Day, A. Robert Fuller Murray. EBVV

Wasted flow of water hiding, A. Lonely Woman. Jayne Cortez. NBV

Wasted Life, A. Nguyễn Công Trứ, *Vietnamese.* AVP, *tr. by* Huỳnh Sanh Thông

Wasting my breath to cry hooly and fairly! (LL) Hooly and Fairly. Joanna Baillie. RACG; WoRP

Wasting Time. Opal Palmer. FaBoVe

Wastrel-Woman Poem, The. Brenda Marie Osbey. MT

Wat a joyful news, Miss Mattie. Colonization in Reverse. Louise Bennett. OBCoV; PBCV

Wat a piece of rain, Miss Kate! Wat A Rain. Valerie Bloom. PBCV

Watch, The. Frances Darwin Cornford. InPK-6; MoBrPo; OxBTC; PFE; SAGP

Watch, The. May Swenson. HAP

Watch. Giuseppe Ungaretti. *See* Vigil.

Watch a red setter stretch and sink in cloud. (LL) The Broken Home. James Merrill. ColAP; HAP; HCAP; MoP; NAAL-2; NOBA; NYBP; NoAM; NoP-4; PoPoPo

Watch and the Dogs, The. Homer. OBVE, *tr. by* Alexander Pope *Fr.* The Iliad.

Watch any day his nonchalant pauses, see. A Free One. W. H. Auden. CMoP; FaBoMo; OxAEP-2

Watch by them and bleat. (LL) Lambs at Play. Christina Rossetti. BoTP; CTAV

Watch how dem touris' like fe look. Fetchin Water. Claude McKay. PBCV

Watch: how he does it. Without a word. Disappearing Act. Laurel Blossom. MoLi

Watch it. That's the body: what goes on. The Body. William Bronk. VGW

Watch long enough, and you will see the leaf. Prelude XIX. Conrad Potter Aiken. CMoP; OxBA *Fr.* Preludes for Memnon; or, Preludes to Attitude.

Watch me rise and go. (LL) Piute Creek. Gary Snyder. CAPP-1; CoAP; CoAmPo; NAAL-2; NOBA; PaTW

Watch out for the bus. Mercado. Greg Pape. AmPA

Watch out, my dear. Praxilla, *Greek.* PBWP, *tr. by* John Dillon

Watch people stop by bodies in funeral homes. On the Symbolic Consideration of Hands and the Significance of Death. Miller Williams. InPK-6

Watch Repair. Charles Simic. NoP-4

Watch the Lights Fade. Robinson Jeffers. CMoP; NOBA

Watch these elders. They always come at night. These Too Are Our Elders. Jack A. Mapanje. HBAPE

Watch this. Judith Nicholls. SpW

Watch well the poor in this late hour. Temperance Note: and Weather Prophecy. James Agee. *Fr.* Two Songs on the Economy of Abundance. MoAmPo

Watch what you're doing. Letter to a Friend. Husein Tahmisic, *Serbian.* CEEP, *tr. by* Ewald Osers

Watch will tell the time of day, A. Mr. Coggs. Edward Verrall Lucas. BoTP; FPC

Watch Your Step—I'm Drenched. Adrian Mitchell. RB

Watch Yourself Go By. Strickland W. Gillilan. BLPA; PoToHe

  (Cure for Fault Finding, A.) PWR

Watched with the cruel watching of the stars. In Her Prison. Sarah Morgan Bryan Piatt. NCAP

Watched you / & you were turning, turning. Journey, 1966. Anselm Hollo. PmAP

Watcher, The. Edward Hirsch. PUP-18

Watcher, The. John Peck. AmPA

Watcher, The. James Stephens. MoBrPo; OBEV

Watcher, The. Ruth Stone. NYBP

Watcher, The. Clara Ann Thompson. CBWP-2

Watcher in the Wood, The. Dora Sigerson Shorter. SDW

Watchers, The. Paul Blackburn. NYBP

Watchers, The. Edmund Blunden. PoFWW

Watchers, The. W. S. Braithwaite. NAAAL

Watchers, The. Charles Spear. PeNZ

Watchful Wakeful. Amir Gilbo'a, *Hebrew.* IP, *tr. by* Warren Bargad *and* Stanley F. Chyet

Watching a Cloud. Dannie Abse. OxBC

Watching baseball. Baseball Canto. Lawrence Ferlinghetti. BB

Watching for the time of day. (LL) Clock-A-Clay [The Lady Bug]. John Clare. APo; EBEV; EBVV; EnVR; NAEL-2; NOxBChV; OAEL-2; OBNC; PoEL-4

Watching hands transplanting. Transplanting. Theodore Roethke. GaP; OBGa

Watching me / do it. (LL) Our hamster's life. Kit Wright. PeP

Watching Rushcutters' bright bayful of masts and coloured keels. Angels' Weather. Bruce Beaver. BMAP

Watching Salmon Jump. Simon J. Ortiz. CDW

Watching Shoah in a Hotel Room in America. Adam Zagajewski, *Polish.* VCWP, *tr. by* Renata Gorcyznski, Benjamin Ivry, *and* C. K. Williams

Watching Television. Robert Bly. CoAP

Watching Tennis. John Heath-Stubbs. Son

Watching the Break of thy great day. (LL) The Dawning. Henry Vaughan. GeHe; NOCV

Watching the Dance. James Merrill. NIP-4

Watching the famous eruption of the volcano on Heimaey, Iceland. The Reprieve. Hans Magnus Enzensberger. PoSu *Fr.* The Sinking of the Titanic.

Watching the moon. Lady Izumi, *Japanese.* WPoS, *tr. by* Jane Hirshfield *and* Mariko Aratani; EnIH, *tr. by* Jane Hirshfield *with* Mariko Aratani

Watching the Moon with Thoughts of Far Away. Chang Chiu-ling, *Chinese.* CoBCP, *tr. by* Burton Watson

Watching the night sky. *Unknown.* NBrP

Watching the Old Man Die. Arthur James Marshall Smith. MoCV

Watching the Reapers. Po Chü-i, *Chinese.* ChiP, *tr. by* Arthur Waley

Watching the shied core. As Bad as a Mile. Philip Larkin. InPK-6; OxBC; OxBSP

Watching the Stars. No Ch'&obrev;n-my&obrev;ng, *Korean.* CKP, *tr. by* Jaihiun Kim

Watching the Swinging. Li K'ai-hsien, *Chinese.*

"Colorful frames are erected beside the Yellow River, The." CoBLCP, *tr. by* Jonathan Chaves

Watching the Wheat-Reapers. Po Chü-i, *Chinese.* SuSp, *tr. by* Irving Lo

Watching the world disappear as if on a journey of no return. (LL) Things I Didn't Know I Loved. Nazim Hikmet, *Turkish.* AF; VCWP, *tr. by* Randy Blasing *and* Mutlu Konuk

Watching them drink shots was best. Whiskey in Whiting, Indiana. James Hazard. EC2

Watching this dawn's mnemonic of old dawning. Sestina in a Cantina. Malcolm Lowry. MoCV

Watching to see how it's done. (LL) I Stop Writing the Poem. Tess Gallagher. NMM-2; PiM

Watching TV, the Elk Bones Up on Metaphysics. John Bensko. MT

Watching Women with Children. Elaine Randell. NBrP

Watching You. Simon J. Ortiz. HATNAP

Watchmaker God. Robert Lowell. HCAP; SoSe-8

Watchmaker's Shop, The. *Unknown.* BoTP

Watchman, watchman on your height. Abraham Reisen, *Yiddish.* TrJP, *tr. by* Joseph Leftwich

Watchman, What of the Night? Bible, *O.T.* AWP *Fr.* Isaiah.

Watchman, what of the night? Charles Kingsley. EBVV

Watchman's Drum in the Streets of Officials, The. Li Ho, *Chinese.* PLT, *tr. by* A. C. Graham

Water. John R. Crossland. BoTP

Water. Ted Hughes. OxBSP

Water. Philip Larkin. FaBoMo; OxBSP; PeECV

Water. Robert Lowell. AFr; CMoP; HeIP-4; LCAP-2; NOBA; NoP-4; PoE

Water. Leslie Norris. OBWVE

Water. Gary Snyder. LCAP-2

Water. Ann Taylor. NOxBChV

Water and marble and that silentness. Venice. Arthur Symons. OxBSP

Water and nblod for thee I swete. *Unknown.* MiEL

Water and Wine, *epigram.* Friedrich von Logau, *German.* GePo, *tr. by* George C. Schoolfield

Water and Worship: An Open-Air Service on the Gatineau River. Margaret Avison. HAP

Water astonishing and difficult altogether. Water Raining. Gertrude Stein. PBWP *Fr.* Tender Buttons.

Water Babies, The. Charles Kingsley.

Little Doll, The. OxBChV

River's Song, The. ACTP

  (Tide River, The.)

Young and Old. ACTP; EBEV; FaBoBe; FaPoR; ImPo; OxAEP-2; OxBChV; PoLF

Water Bug and the Shadows, The. *Unknown, Yuman.* OBVE, *tr. by* Frances Densmore

Water bug is drawing the shadows, The. The Water Bug and the Shadows. *Unknown, Yuman.* OBVE, *tr. by* Frances Densmore

Water closing, The. Together. Maxine W. Kumin. BoWoP

Water Color. Stephen Mooney. NYBP

Water colour country. Here the hills. Tasmania. Vivian Smith. NOBAu

Water-Colour of Venice, A. Lawrence Durrell. MoBrPo

Water country's reeds and rushes, night, covered with frost, The. Farewell to a Friend. Hsüeh T'ao, *Chinese.* SuSp, *tr. by* Eric Johnson

Water doubles this world. Water Outside the Window. Nino Nikolov, *Bulgarian.* CEEP, *tr. by* Ewald Osers

Water-Drinker, The. Edward Jonson. BXAP

Water Eased of Its Cliffs by Falling. Alberta Turner. LCAP-2

Water-fall, The. Henry Vaughan. *See* The Waterfall [*or* Water-Fall].

Water, first creature of the gods. Tea Poems. George Mackay Brown. OxBC

Water flooded everywhere. Rebirth. Catriona Stamp. BrRo

Water, for anguish of the solstice:—nay. For A Venetian Pastoral By Giorgone (In the Louvre). D. G. Rossetti. GS

Water Fowl. Wordsworth. APo

Water-Front Streets. Langston Hughes. SAmP

Water gleams and mirrors this red flower, The. The Hibiscus. Nguyễn Trãi, *Vietnamese.* AVP, *tr. by* Huỳnh Sanh Thông

Water has to start, The. Coming Down to It. Malcolm Glass. BXAP

Water in a shallow container. Zuni Derivations. *Unknown, Zuni Indian.* STP, *tr. by* Dennis Tedlock

Water in my prison shatters in a prism, The. The Trout. Daryl Hine. CoAP

Water is heavy silver over stone. What Any Lover Learns. Archibald MacLeish. MeMAP

Water is in my hands / this is grief. (LL) Death of Dr. King. Sam Cornish. MBE

Water is practical. Mourning Pablo Neruda. Robert Bly. LCAP-2

Water is preeminent and gold, like a fire. Pindar. OBCVT, *tr. by* Frank J. Nisetich *Fr.* Olympian I.

Water is so clear and so calm, The. Fish Cove. Blaise Cendrars, *French.* BLT, *tr. by* Monique Chefdor

Water, is taught by thirst. Emily Dickinson. NCAP

Water Is Wide, The. *Unknown.* NTP

Water Island. Howard Moss. CoAP; NYBP; NoP-4

Water Lady, The. Thomas Hood. CH; Ro

Water-Lilies. Sara Teasdale. MoAmPo; NMM-2

Water lilies. John Wills. HA

Water lilies bloom on the Great River. Emperor Wu of Liang, *Chinese.* OHMPC, *tr. by* Kenneth Rexroth

Water lilies of summer are gone. They are no more, The. Autumn. Su Tung-p'o, *Chinese.* OHPC, *tr. by* Kenneth Rexroth

Water lily blooms, A. The Lily. Vadim Sergeievich Shefner, *Russian.* TCRP, *tr. by* Albert C. Todd

Water Maid. Christopher Okigbo. PBMAP

Water-mill, A. Antipater of Thessalonica, *Greek.* GrAn, *tr. by* Alistair Elliot

Water Mill, The. Sarah Doudney. BLPA

  (Lesson of the Water Mill, The.) PoToHe

Water Music. "Hugh MacDiarmid." FaBoTC

Water: no matter how much, there is still not enough. Fountains in the Sea. Martin Sorescu, *Romanian.* VCWP, *tr. by* Seamus Heaney *and* Joana Russell-Gebbett

Water of Tears, The. Francis Ponge, *French.* AF, *tr. by* Beth Archer

Water of the Flowery Mill (II), The. Jerome Rothenberg. FTOS

Water on a slope. Man. Archana Varma, *Hindi.* OMIP, *tr. by* Aruna Sitesh *and* Arlene Zide

Water on the white blossoms. A Daughter. Lee Upton. CMAP

Water-Ousel, The. Mary Webb. CH

Water Outside the Window. Nino Nikolov, *Bulgarian.* CEEP, *tr. by* Ewald Osers

Water Ouzel. William H. Matchett. CoAP; NYBP

Water plunges to devour us. Travel Song. Hugo von Hofmannsthal, *German.* TrJP, *tr. by* Charles Wharton Stork

Water pools. John Wills. HA

Water pulls nervously whispering satin across cool roots, cold stones. Interval. Joseph Auslander. FYAP

Water Raining. Gertrude Stein. PBWP *Fr.* Tender Buttons.

Water, rarely. Sometimes goat's milk, later cow's. Never coffee or tea. What They Drank. Campbell McGrath. WeT

Water Song. Steve Crow. HATNAP

Water Song. Solomon ibn Gabirol, *Hebrew.* TrJP, *tr.* by Israel Abrahams

Water Song. Michael S. Weaver. ISC

Water spilled on level ground. Pao Chao. SuSp, *tr.* by Irving Y. Lo *Fr.* The Weary Road.

Water sprinkler empties into parabolas, A. Tomorrow. William Olsen. NAmP90

Water still flows. Illegitimate Things. William Carlos Williams. MoAmPo

Water streams. Tanka. Fumi Saito, *Japanese.* MJT, *tr.* by Makoto Ueda

Water strider skates upon the brook, A. Plane Geometer. David McCord. NYBP

Water travels a long shot. Water Song. Steve Crow. HATNAP

Water turned to wine, The. (LL) To the Water Nymphs, Drinking at the Fountain. Robert Herrick. BeJo; CaPo; NAEL-1

Water turns / a long way down over the raw stone, The. You Are Happy. Margaret Atwood. TRP

Water under the Earth. Robert Bly. NNaP

Water understands / Civilization well, The. Ralph Waldo Emerson. AmPP; OxBSP; PoEL-4

Water was too cold for us, The. (LL) Water. Robert Lowell. AFr; CMoP; HeIP-4; LCAP-2; NOBA; NoP-4; PoE

Water washed, the water rose, The. The Fisherman. Goethe, *German.* STV, *tr.* by John Frederick Nims

Water, water I desire. The Scar[e]-Fire. Robert Herrick. HAP

Water wears away a rock. Poem. Sugwon Song, *Korean.* CKP, *tr.* by Jaihiun Kim

Water Whirligigs. D. J. Opperman, *Afrikaans.* PeSA, *tr.* by Jack Cope *and* Uys Krige

Waterbird. May Swenson. NoP-4

Waterbird goes up, A. 5 Poems. Robert Gray. CBAP

Waterbug running by the frogulp. Alan Pizzarelli. HA

Waterchew! Gregory Corso. VGW

Waterclock drips heavy. To the Tune "Song of the Plum Blossom at the River Town." Yang Shen, *Chinese.* CoBLCP, *tr.* by Jonathan Chaves

Watercolor of Grantchester Meadows. Sylvia Plath. LCAP-2; NYBP

Watercress Seller, The. Thomas Miller. OxBChV

Watered by the Strymon and great Hellespont. Antipater of Thessalonica, *Greek.* GrAn, *tr.* by Alistair Elliot

Waterfall. Seamus Heaney. HeIP-4; Poetr

Waterfall, A. Suyong Kim, *Korean.* CKP, *tr.* by Jaihiun Kim

Waterfall. Gareth Owen. Spl

Waterfall, The. Frank Dempster Sherman. CTV

Waterfall [*or* Water-Fall], The. Henry Vaughan. ESCV; GeHe; MeLP; NAEL-1; NOBE; NOCV; NOSC; OBWVE; OxAEP-1; PoEL-2

(Water-fall, The.) FMP; FSCP; PBRV

Waterfall. Anne Welsh. PeSA

Waterfall. Greg Williamson. RA

Waterfalls and Liquor ("Waterfalls sounded"). Kapilar, *Tamil.* PLW, *tr.* by A. K. Ramanujan

Waterford. Medbh McGuckian. BiHa

Waterfront Girls, The. Rufinus, *Greek.* GrAn, *tr.* by Alan Marshfield

Watergaw, The. "Hugh MacDiarmid." FaBoVe; NAEL-2

Watering place of the long-tailed stars, The. (LL) Burning Shewolf. Vasco Popa, *Serbo-Croatian.* HSix; VCWP, *tr.* by Charles Simic

Watering Rhyme, A. P. A. Ropes. BoTP

Waterlilies. Alexis Rotella. HA

Waterloo. Byron. *See* The Eve of Waterloo.

Watermelon. "Eduard Bagritzky," *Russian.* TCRP, *tr.* by Vera Dunham

Watermelon Tales. Khaled Mattawa. PUP-19

Watermelons. Charles Simic. OBAL; VCAP

Waterpot. Grace Nichols. PBCV

Waters above! eternal springs! The Showre. Henry Vaughan. SeCP

Waters are loose: from Judith and the Larb. Schoolcraft's Diary Written on the Missouri: 1830. Robert Bly. ImGa

Water's breath mingles with reflected mountains. Autumn Day, An— Leisurely Boating on West Lake. Lin Pu, *Chinese.* SuSp, *tr.* by Jonathan Chaves

Waters chased him as he fled, The. Emily Dickinson. PoEL-5

Waters deep, the waters dark, The. Casting. Howard Nemerov. OxBSP

Waters fall in rectangles, The. From My Window. Zaro Weil. AYFP

Water's flowing. Song. *Unknown, Chippewa Indian.* STP, *tr.* by Jerome Rothenberg

Waters from cold springs. Orchards in July. Zbigniew Machej, *Polish.* BLT, *tr.* by Czeslaw Milosz *and* Robert Hass

Waters hurtle through the flooded night, The. (LL) A Country Walk. Thomas Kinsella. CIP-2; CMoP

Waters of earth come and go, The. Here and Now. Philip Levine. PoA

Waters of K'un-ming Pool recalled the achievements of Han times, The. Tu Fu. SuSp, *tr.* by Wu-chi Liu *Fr.* Autumn Thoughts.

Waters of Life, The. MoBrPo

Waters of Lung-t'ou, The. HSü Ling, *Chinese.* ChiP, *tr.* by Arthur Waley

Waters of salvation. Novica Tadic. *See* Little Picture Catalogue.

Waters of Waiapu, The. Paraire Henare Tomoana, *Maori.* PeNZ, *tr.* by Margaret Orbell

Waters rippled, gleamed and fell, The. At the Cascade. Henrietta Cordelia Ray. CBWP-3

Waters saw thee, O God, The. Bible, *O.T. See* Psalm 77.

Watershed, The. Alice Thompson Meynell. VWP

Watershed. Robert Penn Warren. PoA

Waterside Village. Yün Shou-p'ing, *Chinese.* CoBLCP, *tr.* by Jonathan Chaves

Watertowers, The. W. H. Auden. OAEL-2

Waterwheels in. Ian Hamilton Finlay. KaS

Waterwings. Cathy Song. NoAM

Watteau was slightly silly to equip. L'Embarquement pour Cythère. John Streeter Manifold. CBAP

Watts. Shirley Kaufman.

  "He's learning to shoot." CrSp

Watts. Conrad Kent Rivers. PoBA

Watts. Alvin Saxon. PoBA

Watt's dream was the cream of steam engines. Limerick. Bill Greenwell. PeLi

Waulking Song: Two. Minnie Bruce Pratt. GLP

Wave approaching and the wave returning, The. Sequence. George Barker. PoA

Wave blossoms for my delight, a thousand sheets of snow, Tune: "The Fisherman." Tune: The Fisherman. Li Yü, *Chinese.* CoBCP, *tr.* by Burton Watson

Wave of coldness, A. Akiko Yosano, *Japanese.* WPOW, *tr.* by Glenn Hughes *and* Yozan T. Iwasaki

Wave over him, and whisper as they wave. (LL) *I* once was happy, when while yet a child. Charlotte Smith. PEW

Wave Symphony, The. Arthur Davison Ficke. PoA *Fr.* Four Japanese Paintings.

Wavelength. David St. John. NAmP90

Wavelets like rippling trees. The Painting, "*Mist and Rain on the Spring River,*" by Hsiao Chao. Tai Piao-yüan, *Chinese.* CoBLCP, *tr.* by Jonathan Chaves

Wavering. Denise Levertov. PmAP

Waverley. Sir Walter Scott.

  Hie Away, Hie Away. OxAEP-2

  To an Oak Tree. OBNC

Waverly Pen, The. *Unknown. Fr.* Advertising Rhymes.

Wavers a candle's shadow, at the end. (LL) Legal Fiction. William Empson. CMoP; FaBoMo; ImPo; LiTM; MoP; NoAM; NoP-4

Waves. Ralph Waldo Emerson. AmPP

Waves, The. Mary Oliver. OxBoS

Waves. *Unknown, Arabic.* ArPe, *tr.* by Omar S. Pound

Waves. Xuân Quỳnh, *Vietnamese.* AVP, *tr.* by Huỳnh Sanh Thông

Waves: applause, fathoms above, calm air. Lennie Tristano, No Wind. Jim Brodey. MoNo

Waves bluster up the bay and through the throat. A Family Photograph 1939. James Keir Baxter. OxBC

Waves claw, The. On The Beach. John Corben. Spl

Waves forever move, The. The Sisters. John Banister Tabb. APN-2

Waves Gleam in the Sunshine, The. Heinrich Heine. *Fr.* Songs to Seraphine. TrJP, *tr.* by Emma Lazarus

Waves know rocks by foam and recklessness, The. Merl. Jean Toomer. GT

Waves leap up, the wild wind blows, The. Mary Howitt. *See* The Sea-Gull.

Waves, like ridges of plow'd land, are high, The. The Sea Similized to Meadows and Pastures: the Mariners, to Shepherds: the Mast, to a May-Pole: the Fish, to Beasts. Margaret Lucas Cavendish. NoP-4

Waves now fall short, The. O. Mabson Southard. HA

Waves of brooding. (LL) My Arkansas. Maya Angelou. BlSi; NAAAL

Waves surge higher still, The. Elegy: Ise Lamenting the Death of Empress Onshi. Lady Ise, *Japanese.* BoWoP; IMW, *tr.* by Etsuko Terasaki *and* Irma Brandeis

Waves, the rough surf, swept me on the shore, The. Antipater of Thessalonica, *Greek.* GrAn, *tr.* by Alistair Elliot

Waves the short two-by-four. Painting Drunken Twilight. George Barlow. GT

Waves, the strides, the feet on which I go?, The. (LL) Tristan da Cunha. Roy Campbell. MoBrPo; PeSA

Waves want / to be wheels. Surf. Lillian Morrison. KaS; NTCP

Waves wash off the peach blossoms. To the Tune "Heavenly Immortal." Yang Shen, *Chinese.* CoBLCP, tr. by Jonathan Chaves

Waves which have kept me from reaching you, The. (LL) To the Harbormaster. Frank O'Hara. CRP; CoAP; NAAL-2; PoM; VCAP

Waving a Bough. Boris Pasternak, *Russian.* TrJP, tr. by Babette Deutsch

Waving Adieu, Adieu, Adieu. Wallace Stevens. NoP-4

Waving Good-by. Gerald Stern. MoLi

Waving Hand, A. Minnie Bruce Pratt. CPO; FiLi

Waving of the Corn, The. Sidney Lanier. APN-2

Wawking of the Fauld, The. Allan Ramsay. SCGP   *Fr.* The Gentle Shepherd.
(Peggy.) OBEV

Wax-contoured, in your face a Muse. Philodemus, *Greek.* GrAn, tr. by William Moebius

Waxwings. Robert Francis. BLT; LCAP-2; RaBo

Way, The. Robert Creeley. APAD; BoLoP; LiLi; LiTM; NeAP

Way. Tristan Tzara, *French.* NNPT, tr. by Lee Harwood

Way a crow, The. Dust of Snow. Robert Frost. CMoP; ChAP; OxBA; OxBSP; PFE; SAmP; SoSe-8; TAP; UnPo; WeW-3

Way a Ghost Dissolves, The. Richard Hugo. NAAL-2; NoAM; NoP-4

Way a tired Chippewa woman, The. Hush. David St. John. LCAP-2

Way america / loves us, The. (LL) To Some Supposed Brothers. Essex Hemphill. NAAAL

Way back in eighty-two or three. The Dreadful Fate of Naughty Nate. John Kendrick Bangs. OBCA

Way beyond the mountains and clouds. Homesickness. Kirim Kim, *Korean.* CKP, tr. by Jaihiun Kim

Way Down, The. Philip Levine. NOBA

Way Down, The. Jay Macpherson.
They Return. NOBC; PoA

Way Down, The. Ernest Sandeen. CRP

Way down Geneva. Red Boots On. Kit Wright. PeLV

Way down in the bottom. Poor Little Johnny. *Unknown.* AmFP

Way down in yonders low valley, in some lonesome place. Pretty Saro. *Unknown.* AmFP

Way down Souf whar de lillies grow. To See Ol' Booker T. Maggie Pogue Johnson. CBWP-4

Way Down South in Dixie. Song for a Dark Girl. Langston Hughes. AmPP; NAAAL; NAAL-2; NoP-4; PoBA; SAmP

Way down South in the land of cotton. Crazy Song to the Air of "Dixie." "Andy Lee." AS

Way down south where bananas. The Grasshopper and the Elephant. *Unknown.* CTV

Way down South where I was born. A Long Time Ago. *Unknown.* AmFP

Way down upon the Swanee River [or de] Swanee River [or ribber]. Old Folks at Home[, The]. Stephen Collins Foster. APN-2; FaBoBe

Way down upon the Wabash. El-a-noy. *Unknown.* AS

Way enchased with glass and beads, A. The Temple. Robert Herrick. CaPo

Way feare with thy projectes, noe false fyre, A. William Alabaster. ESCV   *Fr.* Divine Meditations. Son

Way home is close, The. Tune: "Song of the Southern Country." Li Hsün, *Chinese.* SuSp, tr. by Edward Schafer

Way I hear it, Chinese fortune cookies, The. Fortune Cookie Blues. Amy Uyematsu. LTA

Way I hear tell Aunt Jennie, The. Caledonia. Colleen J. McElroy. BlSi; NAAAL

Way I must enter, The. Lady Izumi, *Japanese.* WPoS, tr. by Jane Hirshfield *and* Mariko Aratani

Way I read a Letter's—this, The. Emily Dickinson. CBLP; InPS-3; WPE

'Way in de middle ob de air. (LL) Ezekiel Saw the Wheel. *Unknown.* APN-2

Way in is only hinted at, The. Garlic. Jeanne Foster. CrSp

Way is still clear, as if in dream, The. In the Year Chi-hai (1299), While Returning by Way of Purple Fungus Mountain at Springmouth, I Lamented for Lecture Master Chin. Tai Piao-yüan, *Chinese.* CoBLCP, tr. by Jonathan Chaves

Way It Sometimes Is, The. Henry Taylor. MT; Poetr

Way It Was, The. Lucille Clifton. NMM-2; WPE

Way Lorene and I went back, The. Need Increasing Itself by Rounds. Kathleen Peirce. PBCAP

Way love rests upon coincidence, The. On Leaving the Artists' Colony. Bruce Bawer. RA

Way of Being, A. Barbara Guest. FTOS

Way of Geometry, The. Choice. David Bromige. FTOS

Way of It, The. Ella Wheeler Wilcox. LW

Way of Life, A. Howard Nemerov. NIP-4

Way of Tet, The. Bruce Weigl. AF

Way of the World, The. William Congreve. NAEL-1
Epilogue: "After our Epilogue this crowd dismisses."
Prologue: "Of those few fools, who with ill stars are cursed."

Way out in California. The Santa Barbara Earthquake. *Unknown.* AmFP

Way Out in Idaho ("Come all you jolly railroad men"). *Unknown.* AmFP

Way Out West. Imamu Amiri Baraka. NeAP; PoBA

Way Over in the New Buryin' Groun'. *Unknown.* AS

Way she played the piano, The. October 23, 1983. June Jordan. SeSe

Way the Bird Sat, The. Ray A. Young Bear. CDW; VoR

Way the Cards Fall, The. Yusef Komunyakaa. GT

Way the incense gripped, The. Father of My Father. Lawson Fusao Inada. UnSA

Way the water goes is blink blink blink, The. Intruder in a Set Scene. Norman MacCaig. FaBoTC

Way the world is not, The. Sonnet. Bill Knott. PBCAP

Way they do, The. Loo-wit. Wendy Rose. HATNAP

Way/ they lay together, The. Peyanar. *Fr.* Seven Said by the Foster-Mother. PLW, tr. by A. K. Ramanujan

Way Things Are, The. Russell Edson. WeT

Way Things Work, The. Jorie Graham. NMM-2

Way this willow traps, The. Willow, Wishbone, Warblers. Brendan Galvin. CMAP

Way Through, The. Denise Levertov. NeAP; PoM

Way Through The Woods, The. Rudyard Kipling. CH; ChAP; EBEvV; FaBoCh; GEA; NOBE; NOxBChV; NTP; NoAM; OBEV; OBNC; OxAEP-2; OxBChV; OxBTC; SAGP; SCGP; WHSW

Way to begin is always the same, The. The Story We Know. Martha Collins. SoSe-8

Way to Fairyland, The. Eunice Close. BoTP

Way to Finish it Off, The. E. L. T. Mesens, *French.* CBNP

Way to good is never late, The. (LL) The Palmer's Ode. Robert Greene. CTC; NoSic; SCGP

Way to hump a cow is not, The. E. E. Cummings. NOBA; NoAM; OxBA

Way to Jellibolee, The. (LL) Twenty-Six Nonsense Rhymes. Edward Lear. CBNP; RB

Way to Love God, A. Robert Penn Warren. NAAL-2

Way to Make a Living, A. James Wright. NNaP

Way to the boiler was dark, The. The Return. Theodore Roethke. NAAL-2   *Fr.* The Lost Son. HAP; HCAP; LiTM; VGW

Way to the River, The. W. S. Merwin. CoAP; NYBP

Way towards each other is through our bodies, The. Jeni Couzyn. CrSp

Way up in de Hebbenly lan'. (LL) Sometimes I feel like a motherless child. *Unknown.* APN-2

'Way up in the middle o' the air. *Unknown. See* Ezekiel Saw the Wheel.

Way was long, the wind was cold, The. The Minstrel. Sir Walter Scott. OxAEP-2   *Fr.* The Lay of the Last Minstrel.

Way We Live, The. Kathleen Jamie. APAD; FaBoTC

Way which thou so well hast learn'd below, The. (LL) To the Pious Memory of the Accomplished [or Accomplisht] Young Lady, Mrs. Anne Killigrew, [Excellent in the Two Sister-Arts of Poesie and Painting]. Dryden. CABP; NAEL-1; OAEL-1; OBEV; PoEL-3

Wayfarer / Perceiving the pathway to truth, The. Stephen Crane. APN-2; AmPP; MeMAP; MoAmPo; PFE   *Fr.* War Is Kind.

Wayfarers in the Wilderness. Alexander R. Thompson. AH

Wayland knew the wanderer's fate. *Unknown. See* Deor.

Wayle whit as whalles bon, A. *Unknown.* MiEL

Wayman in Love. Tom Wayman. NIP-4; NOBC

Ways, The. John Oxenham. PoLF

Ways, The. Louis Zukofsky. PoE

Ways and the Peoples, The. Randall Jarrell. PoA

Ways and whims. DDD. Bruce Andrews. FTOS

Way's been lost for a thousand years, The. T'ao Ch'ien, *Chinese.* CoBCP, tr. by Burton Watson   *Fr.* Drinking Wine.

Ways of God to Men, The. Milton. *See* Consolation.

Wayside Station, The. Edwin Muir. FaBoTw

Wayward Son, The. Mrs. Henry Linden. CBWP-4

Wayzgoose, The. Roy Campbell.
"Attend my fable if your ears be clean." OBSV; PeSAV

Wazir Dandan for Prince Sharkan, The. *Unknown.* AWP   *Fr.* The Thousand and One Nights.

We advance! (LL) Dark Symphony. Melvin Beaunearus Tolson. ColAP; NAAAL

We all fall down. (LL) Ring-a-ring o' roses. Mother Goose. LB; OxNR; ReMoGo

We all go to the bones. Wenberi's Song. Wenberi, *Woiworung.* CBAP, tr. by A. W. Howitt

We all heard the alarm. The planes were out. The Second Dream. Jean Valentine. LCAP-2

We all know that things look strange in the night. Stranger. They look. The Never-Dead. Anna Couani. BMAP

We all know why you have come back home with no. Making Our Clowns Martyrs. Jack A. Mapanje. HBAPE

We all look on with anxious eyes. When Father Carves the Duck. Ernest Vincent Wright. NTCP; PoLF

We all place a great deal of reliance. Limerick. *Unknown*. PeLi

We all scream, most of us inside. A Screamer Discusses Methods of Screaming. James Schevill. TAP

We all sit around and watch him. (LL) Jimmy Jet and His TV Set. Shel Silverstein. OBCA; OBCoV

We all slept soundly that night. In the Dresden Gallery. Yevgeny Mikhailovich Vinokurov, *Russian*. TCRP, *tr. by* Albert C. Todd

We all wanted to go to you. Homage to Lucille, Dr. Lord-Heinstein. Marge Piercy. NMM-2

We all were watching the quiz on television. A Singular Metamorphosis. Howard Nemerov. CoAmPo

We already and first of all discern him making this thing other. David Jones. PeECV *Fr.* The Anathemata.

We always had to do our work at night. Before Action. Leon Gellert. CBAP

We always have time enough, if we. Goethe. CTV

We anchor the boat alongside a hazy island. Night on the Great River. Meng Hao Jan, *Chinese*. OHMPC, *tr. by* Kenneth Rexroth

We and They. Rudyard Kipling. NoAM *Fr.* Debits and Credits.

We approached the shore. Once more. The Oldest Place. Thomas Kinsella. PBCIP

We are a garden wall'd around. The Church the Garden of Christ. Isaac Watts. NOCV; PeECV

We are a meadow where the bees hum. Bedtime. Denise Levertov. TwCP

We Are a People. Lance Henson. VoR

We are a people who love to sing. *Unknown*. ChiPo

We are all in the dumps. *Unknown*. OxNR

We are all liars, because. Lies About Love. D. H. Lawrence. CBLP

We are all near to death. But in my friends. One Who Watches. Siegfried Sassoon. TrJP

We are all of us dreamers of dreams. Dreamer of Dreams. William Herbert Carruth. PoLF

We Are All Vultures. John Yau. PT

We are always saying. For the Obese. Paula Rankin. CMAP

We are America. The Firebombers. Anne Sexton. SAGP

We Are Americans Now, We Live in the Tundra. Marilyn Chin. UnSA

We are approaching sleep: the chestnut blossoms in the mind. Awakening. Robert Bly. CoAmPo

We are as. Soldiers. Giuseppe Ungaretti. PFTM

We are as clouds that veil the midnight moon. Mutability. Shelley. NAEL-2; OBNC

We are asleep. (LL) Dead Still. Andrey Andreievich Voznesensky, *Russian*. BoLoP; LoP, *tr. by* Richard Wilbur

We are asleep under mirrors. What do I. Before the War. Marilyn Hacker. AmPA

We are at a party that doesn't love us. Finally the party lets the mask. Below Freezing. Tomas Tranströmer, *Swedish*. VCWP, *tr. by* Robert Bly

We are betrayed by what is false within. (LL) Love's Grave. George Meredith. EnLoPo; EnVR; GBL; NOBE; OBEV; OBNC; PoEL-5; SCGP

We are born with dreams in our hearts. Immigrants in Our Own Land. Jimmy Santiago Baca. AF; UnSA

We are both from the center of the continent. Lakota Sister/Cherokee Mother. Victoria Lena Manyarrows. UnSA

We are breath of drop of rain. The Gods Wrote. Keorapetse Kgositsile. GT

We are building every day. Building. I. E. Dickenga. PWR

We are building in sorrow or joy. Building for Eternity. N. B. Sargent. BLPA

We are buried somewhere near Narva. A Mistake. Aleksandr Arkadevich Galich, *Russian*. TCRP, *tr. by* Albert C. Todd

We are burning / in our heads. A Poet Recognizing the Echo of the Voice. Diane Wakoski. NIP-4

We are calm. . . And we do not regret. Stendhal. Sergey Nikolaevich Markov, *Russian*. TCRP, *tr. by* Lubov Yakovleva

We are children of the epoch. Children of the Epoch. Wislawa Szymborska, *Polish*. AF, *tr. by* Grazyna Drabik *and* Austin Flint

We are clean for them now, as naked-clean as they are. Snake Dance. Witter Bynner. PaTW

We are comfortable on the rich grass stolen from arid beauty, and watch the sun beat on an ensemble of singers and. Sonata for the Invisible. Joy Harjo. PaTW

We are coming to the cotton fields. Song of the Freedman. *Unknown*. PBMP

We are complete [compleat]; and fate hath now. To the Excellent Mrs A. O. upon her receiving the name of Lucasia. Katherine Philips. KTR; NOSC

We are continually bored with the air. It's in the Egg. Joe Rosenblatt. NOBC

We are deadly decadent anarchists. In the Fire Lane. Thulani Davis. WWSi

We are Diana's Virgin-Train. On a Picture Painted by Herself[, Representing Two Nimphs of Diana's]. Anne Killigrew. KTR; NOSC; PEW

We are driven to odd attempts; once it would not have occurred to. Adrienne Rich. HCAP *Fr.* Shooting Script.

We are driving to the interior. (LL) Arrival at Santos. Elizabeth Bishop. FaBoWP; OxBC

We are encircled by large grieving women. Large Grieving Women. Slavko Mihalic. PoSu, *tr. by* Charles Simic

We are Eretrians from Euboia. Plato. GrAn, *tr. by* Peter Jay *Fr.* Two Poems on the Eretrians Taken Prisoner by the Persians.

We Are Four Bums. *Unknown*. AS

We are Fred Karno's army. *Unknown*. OBCoV *Fr.* Soldiers' Songs of the First World War.

We are girls of different ages. W. H. Auden. UV *Fr.* The Dog beneath the Skin. OxBTC

We are Going, for Grannie Coolwell. Oodgeroo of the tribe Noonuccal. BMAP

We Are Going. Kath Walker. CBAP; NOBAu

We are going down a long slide. Shirley Kaufman. BoWoP

We are going on a journey. The Journey. Aidan Clarke. BoTP

We Are Going to Be Here Now. Primus St. John. GT

We are going to see the rabbit. Alan Brownjohn. NOxBChV

We Are Going to Shoot at the Heart. Anna Swirszczynska, *Polish*. PoSu, *tr. by* Czeslaw Milosz *and* Leonard Nathan

We are growing old together, you and I. Old Age. Po Chü-i, *Chinese*. ChiP, *tr. by* Arthur Waley

We are heading where there is no address. Never to Meet Again. Pyong-hwa Cho, *Korean*. CKP, *tr. by* Jaihiun Kim

We are huddled in a crowd before Kolpino. Aleksandr Petrovich Mezhirov, *Russian*. TCRP, *tr. by* Deming Brown

We are in Louisiana now. Exile's Letter (Or: An Essay on Assimilation). Marilyn Chin. OpBo

We are in love's land to-day. Love at Sea. Swinburne. AWP

We are large with pity, slow and awkward. False Country of the Zoo. Jean Garrigue. LiTM

We are learning to make fire. (LL) Habitation. Margaret Atwood. BoWoP; FaBoWP; WeW-3

We are like the dead. What the Gypsy Said to Her Children. Judith Ortiz Cofer. OxWW; UnSA

We are living, we are dwelling. The Present Age. Arthur Cleveland Coxe. BLPA

We are making a good world, we are making a good day. Prayer upon Cutting down the Sacred Tree. *Unknown, Sioux Native American*. APN-2, *tr. by* John G. Bourke

We are making love. (LL) The Knowing. Sharon Olds. BAP-94

We Are Many. Pablo Neruda, *Spanish*. VCWP, *tr. by* Alastair Reid

We are men of the new world a tree prompts us to harmony. Joseph Miezan Bognini. PBMAP *Fr.* Herbe Féconde (1973).

We are near, Lord. Tenebrae. Paul Celan, *German*. PoSu; VCWP, *tr. by* Michael Hamburger

We are no other than a moving row. 68. Edward Fitzgerald. CABP

We are not come to wage a strife. The Day-Breakers [*or* Daybreakers]. Arna Bontemps. PoBA

We are not near enough to love. An Insincere Wish Addressed to a Beggar. Mary Elizabeth Coleridge. NOBVV; PEW; VWP

We are nude beneath our costumes. The Metaphysical Paintings. John Perreault. SPE

We are old friends. Hunger. Charles Simic. NNaP

We are on a primeval river in a reptilian den. Further Adventures With You. C. D. Wright. LCAP-2

We Are on Our Journey Home. *Unknown*. AH

We are one with nature O! Bird Appeal. Asa Benveniste. NBrP

We Are Passing Away. Matilda Caroline Edwards. PWR

We are reading the story of our lives. The Story of Our Lives. Mark Strand. VCAP

We Are Rising. George Clinton Rowe. AAP

We are satisfied, if you are; but why did I die? (LL) Losses. Randall Jarrell. HCAP; LCAP-2; LiTM; OxBA; PoA; SAGP; TAP; UnPo

We Are Seven. Wordsworth. BLPA; NAEL-2; NOBRP; OxBChV; Ro "I met a little cottage Girl." UV

We are shattered and battered, engulfed. *Unknown. Fr.* Toward Winter. NOIV

We are sighing, for time is flying. Class Song of '91. Eloise Bibb. CBWP-4

We are singing for the face of cisco. Songs for the Cisco Kid; or, Singing for the Face. K. Curtis Lyle. PoBA

We are slowly / undermined. Erosion. Linda Pastan. NIP-4

We are sorry to inform you. In Answer to Your Query. Naomi Lazard. NBLV

We are sorry we cannot use the enclosed. Form Rejection Letter. Philip Dacey. AmPA

We are standing under the wall. Our youth has been taken off like a. The Wall. Zbigniew Herbert, *Polish. AF, tr.* by John Carpenter *and* Bogdana Carpenter

We are stranded here against a dark blue and shaded night. Tampa Red's Contemporary Blues. K. Curtis Lyle. MoNo

We Are Such Stuff as Dreams. Petronius Arbiter, *Latin. AWP, tr.* by Howard Mumford Jones

We are talking in bed. You show me snapshots. A Family Man. Maxine W. Kumin. TAP

We are ten. My First Riot: Bronx, NYC. Safiya Henderson-Holmes. UnSA

We are the Akhail. Our youth persists. Laila Boasting. Laila Akhyaliyya, *Arabic. BoWoP, tr.* by Willis Barnstone

We are the birds always charmed by you from the top of these /belvederes belvederes. Postman Cheval. André Breton, *French. SPE, tr.* by David Gascoyne

We are the blues. Funk Lore. Imamu Amiri Baraka. UnSA

We Are the Cenotaphs. Daniel Williams. PBCV

We are the darkness in the heat of the day. Song. Dame Edith Sitwell. BWW

We are the desperate. Vagabonds. Langston Hughes. SAmP

We are the driving ones. Rilke. EnlH, *tr.* by Stephen Mitchell *Fr.* Sonnets to Orpheus.

We are the hollow men. The Hollow Men. T. S. Eliot. ImPo; InPS-3; LiTM; MoAmPo; NAAL-2; OAEL-2; OBMV; PBMP

We are the music-makers. Ode. Arthur William Edgar O'Shaughnessy. APAD; CABP; FaPoR; IIP; OBEV

We are the ones you sent to fight a war. A Relative Thing. William Daniel Ehrhart. CDa

We are the poor children, come out to see the sights. The Carol of the Poor Children. Richard Middleton. OBCP

We are the puppets of a shadow-play. Prologue: Before the Curtain. Arthur Symons. ADE

We are the stars which sing. The Song of the Stars. *Unknown, Passamaquoddy Native American.* APN-2, *tr.* by Charles Godfrey Leland

We are the Vagabonds that sleep. Ballade of the Outcasts. Stuart Merrill. APN-2

We are the writing on the wall. Dolores Kendrick. FFC

We are they who come faster than fate. War Song of the Saracens. James Elroy Flecker. MoBrPo *Fr.* Hassan.

We are they who come faster than fate: we are they who ride. James Elroy Flecker. *See* War Song of the Saracens.

We are thine, O Love, being in thee and made of thee. Hymn to Love. Lascelles Abercrombie. OBEV *Fr.* Emblems of Love.

We are things of dry hours and the involuntary plan. Kitchenette Building. Gwendolyn Brooks. BPo; FaBoWP; GT; NAAAL; NAAL-2; NoP-4; PoE; PoPoPo; Poetr; UnPo *Fr.* A Street in Bronzeville. BPo; BlSi; FaBoWP

We are this union. Epitaph. U Tam'si Tchicaya. PBMAP *Fr.* L'Arc Musical (1970).

We are three brethren out of Spain. *Unknown. See* Three Knights from Spain.

We are tied to Mars' tail. The previous days. The Captain. Blanca Varela, *Spanish.* WPOW, *tr.* by Lynne Alvarez

We are tired of your tiresome imitations of Mayakovsky. Answer to Voznesensky and Evtushenko. Frank O'Hara. LCAP-2; NNaP; PoM

We Are Transmitters. D. H. Lawrence. OxBTC

We are travelling for the sixth hour, rocks, sand, idol. The Gila Desert in Arizona. Miroslav Holub, *German.* CEEP, *tr.* by Daniel Simko

We are travelling west of Alice Springs, and Sam is at the wheel. West of Alice. W. E. Harney. NOBAu

We are truly fed up. Voice of Earth Mediums. Philip Lamantia. CLPP

We are trying to carry this timber to the building. Timber. *Unknown.* AS

We are two countries girded for the war. Foreign Affairs. Stanley Kunitz. LiTM; NYBP

We are two travelers, Roger and I. The Vagabonds. John Townsend Trowbridge. BLPA

We are unfair. We Own the Night. Imamu Amiri Baraka. CrDW; PoBA

We are upon the Scheldt. We know we move. Antwerp to Ghent. D. G. Rossetti. PeVV, *sect.* V *Fr.* A Trip to Paris and Belgium.

We are very little creatures. A E I O U. Jonathan Swift. BoTP

We are very polite to each other. Unexpected Meeting. Wislawa Szymborska, *Polish.* VCWP, *tr.* by Magnus J. Krynski *and* Robert A. Maguire

We are visitors into. Meditating on Star Light While Traveling Highway. Anita Endrezze-Danielson. HATNAP

We are waltzing now into the moonlit morning. Waltz against the Mountains. Thomas Hornsby Ferril. VGW

We Are Watching, We Are Waiting. William O. Cushing. AH

We are wed to one eternity. (LL) Invite to Eternity. John Clare. NAEL-1; NOBVV; OAEL-2; OBNC; PoEL-4

We are what suns and winds and waters make us. Regeneration. Walter Savage Landor. Ro *Fr.* Imaginary Conversations.

We are what we are, and only life surprises. (LL) Foreign Affairs. Stanley Kunitz. LiTM; NYBP

We are wolves. Wolves. Vladimir Alekseievich Soloukhin, *Russian.* TCRP, *tr.* by Daniel Weissbort

We are wrapped around each other in. What Saves Us. Bruce Weigl. NAmP90

We are, you and me. *Unknown, Japanese.* OHMPJ, *tr.* by Kenneth Rexroth

We aren't in charge, of course, and never were. Hermetic Silence. Edward Foster. PT

We artists have strange nerves! In a Hotel Writing-Room. John Cowper Powys. OxBTC

We Assume: On the Death of Our Son, Reuben Masai Harper. Michael S. Harper. AmPA; GT; LCAP-2

We ate alone in the immense dining room. The Nowhere Water. Mark Rudman. FiLi

We ate our breakfast lying on our backs. Breakfast. Wilfrid Wilson Gibson. OBMV; OxBTC

We ate our breakfast lying on our backs. Breakfast. Wilfrid Wilson Gibson. PoFWW

We athletes who, with sternest discipline. The Golden Road to Barcelona: 1992. Martin Fagg. UV

We awaken in Christ's body. Symeon, *Greek.* EnlH, *tr.* by Stephen Mitchell

We banished the tyrant-tsars. Nikolai Ivanovich Tryapkin, *Russian.* TCRP, *tr.* by Bradley Jordan

We banter / back and forth. Perfecto Flores. Jimmy Santiago Baca. TRP

We be the King's men, hale and hearty. Men Who March Away. Thomas Hardy. CH *Fr.* The Dynasts.

We Become New. Marge Piercy. TAP

We begged him to teach us Spanish. Piñon Nuts. Dixie Salazar. UnSA

We begin to move / awkwardly. (LL) Clammy cement, The. Dennis Brutus. AF

We believe without belief, beyond belief. (LL) Flyer's Fall. Wallace Stevens. MeMAP; SAmP

We ben chapmen lyght of fote. Chapmen. *Unknown.* FaBoVe; MiEL

We blk blues singers. For Walter Washington. Tom Dent. NBV

We borrowed the loan of Kerr's big ass. Kerr's Ass. Patrick Kavanagh. NOIV; RB

We both have voices inside. The Poet and the Schizophrenic. Andrew Duncan. NBrP

We both know how far we've come. (LL) Foul Line—1987. Colleen J. McElroy. LTA; NMM-2

We bought from Laotian refugees a cloth. Absorption of Rock. Maxine Hong Kingston. OpBo

We break off a branch of poplar catkins. All Year Long. *Unknown, Chinese.* OHMPC, *tr.* by Kenneth Rexroth

We Bring No Glittering Treasures. Harriet C. Phillips. AH

We broke out of our dream into a clearing. Stephano Remembers. James Simmons. PBCIP; PNI

We brought him home, I was so pleased. My New Rabbit. Elizabeth Gould. BoTP; OTCP

We brush the other, invisible moon. Sleep. Bill Knott. SPE

We brushed our hair back and our. The Last Refuge. Augustus Young. BIrV

We brushed the dirt off, held it to the light. The Coin. Edwin Morgan. FaBoTC *Fr.* Sonnets from Scotland.

We built a hut, my brother and I. The Hut. Hilda Van Stockum. CTV

We built a palace for them, made of bedrooms. R-and-R Centre: An Incident from the Vietnam War. D. J. Enright. OxBC

We built a ship upon the stairs. A Good Play. Robert Louis Stevenson. ACTP; OTCP; PWR

We Bumped Off Your Friend the Poet. Harold Norse. GLP

We burrowed night and day with tools of lead. Barbury Camp. Charles Hamilton Sorley. NSI

We bury ourselves to get high. Smoking in an Open Grave. David Bottoms. InPK-6

We but begin to hope to know, having known. Subject. Marie Ponsot. VGW

We call it a grain of sand. View with a Grain of Sand. Wislawa Szymborska, *Polish*. CEEP, *tr. by* Magnus J. Krynski *and* Robert A. Maguire; BLT, *tr. by* Stanislaw Barańczak *and* Clara Cavanagh

We Call Them Greasers. Gloria Anzaldúa. GLP

We called him "Rags." He was just a cur. Rags. Edmund Vance Cooke. BLPA

We called the statue. Niyi Osundare. HBAPE   *Fr.* Moonsongs.

We came home to the stranger. Deadly Weapon. Beatrix Gates. GLP

We came of age, and were made man and wife. Mourning for My Wife. Mei Yao Ch'en, *Chinese*. SuSp, *tr. by* Jonathan Chaves

We came to the edge. A Pretty Woman. Simon J. Ortiz. CDW

We came to the outer light down a ramp in the dark. Westland Row. Thomas Kinsella. MoP

We came to visit the cow. Freedom, New Hampshire. Galway Kinnell. LCAP-2

We came upon him sitting in the sun. The Veteran. Margaret Isabel Postgate Cole. NSI

We can always be found. Elegy: Breece D'J Pancake. Franz Wright. NAmP90

We can compose an ocean if we like. We Can Compose Ourselves. Suniti Namjoshi *and* Gillian Hanscombe. CPO

We Can Compose Ourselves. Suniti Namjoshi *and* Gillian Hanscombe. CPO

We can go by that door a dozen times. The Strong Room of the House. William Bronk. APSN

We can string out our lines. Envy. "Naum Korzhavin," *Russian*. TCRP, *tr. by* Vladimir Lunis *and* Albert C. Todd

We can tell already. Two Months Married. Aidan Carl Mathews. PBCIP

We cannot bear to roast a book. The Parental Critic. Keith Preston. NBLV

We cannot go to the country. Raleigh Was Right. William Carlos Williams. NIP-4; NoAM; Poetr; RB

We cannot know his legendary head. Archaic Torso of Apollo. Rilke, *German*. NAWM-2; RaBo, *tr. by* Stephen Mitchell

We cannot recognize a single face. (LL) The Brides Come to Yuba City. Chitra Divakaruni. OpBo; UnSA

We cannot stay their death nor stay our death. Pause. Witter Bynner. IMW

We cannot trap them in our zoos, oh, no! Dinosaurs. Carolyn Stoloff. NYBP

We cannot walk like Byron among Ayasoluk's ruined. The Pleasure of Ruins. J. D. McClatchy. PoA

We can't complain. Middle-Class Blues. Hans Magnus Enzensberger, *German*. VCWP, *tr. by* Hans Magnus Enzensberger and Michael Hamburger

We can't give them up, though. Avant Garde. Louis Dudek. *Fr.* Provincetown. MoCV

We can't help being thirsty. Jelaluddin Rumi, *Persian*. LoL, *tr. by* Coleman Barks

We can't keep it out. It keeps on filling your room. (LL) Virgo Descending. Charles Wright. ColAP; LCAP-2; TRP; WeT

We Cared for Each Other. Heinrich Heine, *German*. AWP, *tr. by* John Todhunter

We caroused. I Met This Guy Who Died. Gregory Corso. Poetsp

We caroused, we kissed, we existed once upon a time. . . . A Poem about Youth and Romanticism. "Naum Korzhavin," *Russian*. TCRP, *tr. by* Vladimir Lunis *and* Albert C. Todd

We carried you in our arms. Tears of Rage. "Bob Dylan." MoLi

We caught the tread of dancing feet. The Harlot's House. Oscar Wilde. ADE; EBVV; MoBrPo; NAEL-2; NoAM; PFE

We chanced in passing by that afternoon. The Black Cottage. Robert Frost. CBCWP; VGW

We chant and enchant. Velemir Khlebnikov, *Russian*. CBNP, *tr. by* Paul Schmidt

("Discant, descant.") (LL) NNPT, *tr. by* Paul Schmidt

We charge through the skies of disillusion. Song at the African Middle Class. Molara Ogundipe-Leslie. HBAPE; PBMAP

We climb the slopes of life with throbbing heart. Aspiration. Henrietta Cordelia Ray. CBWP-3

We climbed out of timber. On the Mountain. John Haines. BLT

We climbed the dark. We. The Island. George Woodcock. MoCV

We climbed the hill to look over our land. Our Land. Yannis Ritsos, *Greek*. GrIP, *tr. by* Edmund Keeley

We climbed through a broken window. An Old Whorehouse. Mary Oliver. CMAP

We come from a long line. For My Mother, Who Lives. Lorraine Duggin. LoHo

We come home from the movie, and you head for the TV. Saturday Night. Toi Derricotte. DeD

—We come in peace from the third planet. The First Men on Mercury. Edwin Morgan. CBNP; FaBoTC; PeLV; SpW

We come now to the space which is boy-shaped. At Sixteen. Ann Darr. DeD; LW

We come to this country. To be Sung on the Fourth of July. Wyatt Prunty. RA

We come to uncrate the newness of this world. First Things. Lucienne Desnoues, *French*. WPOW, *tr. by* Miller Williams

We come together once more, we four, in the center. Head Couples. William H. Matchett. NYBP

We conquered France, but felt our captive's charms. Alexander Pope. EPCY   *Fr.* The First Epistle of the Second Book of Horace Imitated.

We could be here. This is the valley. Small Town with One Road. Gary Soto. SoSe-8

We could count the times we went for a walk. The End of the Affair. James Simmons. PBCIP

We could have become a silence. (LL) Quick And Bitter. Yehuda Amichai, *Hebrew*. BoLoP, *tr. by* Assia Gutmann; LoP; VCWP, *tr. by* Gutmann, Assia; IP, *tr. by* Warren Bargad *and* Stanley F. Chyet

We could have crossed the road but hesitated. The Interrogation. Edwin Muir. CMoP; PoWW

We Could Have Met. Lee Cataldi. BMAP

We could not pause, while yet the noontide air. Obsequies of Stuart. John Randolph Thompson. CBCWP

We could point to the poem and say 'that map'. The Alphabet Murders. John Tranter. BMAP   *Fr.* The Alphabet Murders.

We could stand the world if it were hard all over. (LL) Across the Bay. Donald Davie. CABP; NoAM

We could wipe away a fly. The Jungle Café. Gary Soto. NoAM

We couldn't even keep the furnace lit! To Delmore Schwartz. Robert Lowell. FP

We count the broken lyres that rest. The Voiceless. Oliver Wendell Holmes. APN-1   *Fr.* The Autocrat of the Breakfast Table.

We counterfeited once for your disport. Actors. Rudyard Kipling. *Fr.* Epitaphs of the War [1914–1918]. OBWP

We crawled and cried and laughed. Autobiography. Mbella Sonne Dipoko. TTY

We crept beneath our quilts at Pilot Peak. From Land Logic. George Keithley. PaTW   *Fr.* The Donner Party.

We crept in the tall grass and slept till noon. (LL) 1916 Seen from 1921. Edmund Blunden. NoP-4

We cross many rivers, but here is no anguish; our. Arawak Prologue. Basil McFarlane. PBCV

We cross the river over dark waves. Rain on the River. Lu Yu, *Chinese*. OHMPC, *tr. by* Kenneth Rexroth

We curl into your eyes. The Female God. Isaac Rosenberg. FaBoTw

We cut grass. Santhal Poems, 1. Bishnu De, *Bengali*. OMIP, *tr. by* Samir Dasgupta *and* Stephen N. Hay

We Dance Like Ella Riffs. Carolyn M. Rodgers. PoBA; SeSe

("Again and again and oooooh.") (LL) SeSe

We dance round in a ring and suppose. The Secret Sits. Robert Frost. InPK-6

We deemed the secret lost, the spirit gone. Flaxman. Margaret Fuller. APN-1; PAR

We Delighted, My Friend. Léopold Sédar Senghor, *French*. PBA; TTY, *tr. by* Miriam Koshland

We descended the first night from Europe riding the ship's sling. Coming Back to America. James Dickey. NYBP; WeT

We did it in front of the mirror. Yehuda Amichai, *Hebrew*. BoLoP; EP, *tr. by* Harold Schimmel

We did kowtow to a blazing sun. Letter to the Immigration Officer. Jan Kemp. PeNZ

We did not flinch but gave our lives to save. Cenotaph at the Isthmos. Simonides, *Greek*. GrAn, *tr. by* Peter Jay

We did our duty. We Have Done Our Duty. Yehuda Amichai, *Hebrew*. VCWP, *tr. by* Benjamin Harshav *and* Barbara Harshav

"We did sums at school, Mummy." Halfway Street, Sidcup. Fleur Adcock. Spl

We didn't want to be white—or did we? The Struggle. Toi Derricotte. IFJA; LTA; PBCAP

We / Die soon. Gwendolyn Brooks. *See* We real cool. We.

We died in Zortman on a Sunday. The Renegade Wants Words. James Welch. CDW

We dismount; I give you wine. Seeing Someone Off. Wang Wei, *Chinese.* CoBCP, *tr. by* Burton Watson

We do assemble that a funeral. An Elegy in Memory of the Worshipful Major Thomas Leonard Esq. Samuel Danforth Jr. SCAP

We do lie beneath the grass. Dirge: "Swallow leaves her nest, The." Thomas Lovell Beddoes. NOBE; OBNC *Fr.* Death's Jest Book.

We do not care if you were. Ben Webster: "Did You Call Her Today?" Ron Welburn. SeSe

We do not play on Graves. Emily Dickinson. NIP-4; PoEL-5

We do not see them come. Scala Coeli. Kathleen Jessie Raine. NYBP

We do not wish anything to happen. Chorus. T. S. Eliot. OxBTC *Fr.* Murder in the Cathedral.

We do: the present desperate stage. The Miners' Response. Dugald Sutherland MacColl. NSI

We don't get to choose our century. Aleksandr Semionovich Kushner, *Russian.* TCRP, *tr. by* Paul Graves *and* Carol Ueland

We don't have much language for tragedy. Autumn. Thomas William Shapcott. CBAP

We don't know the ins and outs. The Wall. David Jones. PoA

We don't lack people here on the Northern coast. Amusing Our Daughters. Carolyn Kizer. VCAP; VGW

We don't live in castles. Velemir Khlebnikov. TCRP, *tr. by* Gary Kern *Fr.* Washerwoman.

We don't understand it. (LL) Poems We Can Understand. Paul Hoover. EOEF; PmAP

We don't; we take things as they are. (LL) Lying Awake. W. D. Snodgrass. HoPM; MoAmPo; NYBP

We drank the Mezcal lemonless and saltless. Drink. John L. Stanizzi. EC3

We draw our lives after ourselves in streams. The Lynx. Charles Edward Eaton. DiPo

We dream—it is good we are dreaming. Emily Dickinson. BoWoP

We dressed each other. Empress Eifuku, *Japanese.* OHMPJ; WPOW, *tr. by* Kenneth Rexroth

We Drink Farewell. Tu Mu, *Chinese.* OHMPC, *tr. by* Kenneth Rexroth

We drive between lakes just turning green. Driving through Minnesota during the Hanoi Bombings. Robert Bly. Poetr

We drove past farms, the hills terraced with sheep. Travel: After a Death. Jane Kenyon. FFC

We drove towards the city. Industrial City. Antigone Kefala. BMAP

We dug up a / grave today. August 17, 1970. Don Receveur. CDa

We eat and drink and laugh and energize. Death's Transfiguration. Israel Zangwill. TrJP

We eat / bread & stewed sausage. Taste. Jennifer Maiden. BMAP

We enter. Climbing the Chagrin River. Mary Oliver. Poetr

We entered the city at noon! High bells. The radio on. One Night Stand. Imamu Amiri Baraka. NeAP

We examine today not sacked cities, but sacked lives. The Archaeology of Divorce. Patricia Storace. FFC

We Exist. Janice Gould. UnSA

We fail, and white men call us faggots till the end of / the earth. (LL) A Poem for Black Hearts. Imamu Amiri Baraka. CAPP-1; NAAAL; PoBA; PoM

We fancied he'd share in our cause. Instead. What's In It for Me? E. A. Guest. PoToHe

We feed the chickens every day. Off We Go to Market. Gwen A. Smith. BoTP

We feel that we are greater than we know. (LL) After-Thought. Wordsworth. NOBE; OBEV; OBNC

We fell in love at "Journey for Margaret." First Love. Judith Hemschemeyer. Poetsp

We fell on the chair. Hilbert's Program. Milo De Angelis, *Italian.* NeIt, *tr. by* Lawrence Venuti

We few, we happy few, we band of brothers. Shakespeare. UnPo *Fr.* King Henry V.

We filled our ears with so much noise that. Americans in 1933–4–5–6–7–8–, Etc. Merrill Moore. FaBoA

We find in the East Indies stars there be. Of Stars. Margaret Lucas Cavendish, Duchess of Newcastle. NOSC

We finished clearing the last. Above Pate Valley. Gary Snyder. CoAP; CoAmPo; LCAP-2; NoP-4; TRP

We fish, we fish, we merrily swim. Herman Melville. CTAV; WHSW

We fished up the Atlantic Cable one day between the Barbadoes. The Cable Ship. Harry Edmund Martinson, *Swedish.* RB, *tr. by* Robert Bly

We fled from the sight inland and that night. Columbus Reaches Juana, 1492. Ralph Gustafson. NOBC

We floating Islands, living *Hebrides.* (LL) On the Memory of Mr. Edward King, Drowned in the Irish Seas. John Cleveland. HAP; OAEL-1; SeCP

We flung gravel out in arcs then cut. Before Breakup on the Chena outside Fairbanks. David McElroy. Poetsp

We follow where the Swamp Fox guides. The Swamp Fox. William Gilmore Simms. FaBoBe

We followed her unto the chamber-door. The Palace of Pleasant Regard. The Lady of the Assembly. WPE *Fr.* The Assembly of Ladies.

We followed the river to Fortune's Wheel. Douglas Oliver. NBrP *Fr.* The Infant and the Pearl.

We Forego Mimicry. Ray DiPalma. FTOS

We forget where we came from. Our Jewish. Jews in the Land of Israel. Yehuda Amichai, *Hebrew.* IP; PoSu, *tr. by* Warren Bargad *and* Stanley F. Chyet

We forgot to clear your grave, so we stood. On the Anniversary Of Your Death. Karen L. Mitchell. GT

We found a mouse in the chalk quarry today. Anne and the Field-Mouse. Ian Serraillier. NOxBChV

We found a turtle stunned by sunlight. Walking to the Mailbox. Kim R. Stafford. CMAP

We found dead animals in our sagebrush hills. Dobbin. George Bowering. NOBC

We found the little captain at the head. The Dead Foxhunter. Robert Graves. PoFWW

We four lads from Liverpool are. *Unknown.* KaS

We frolic[k], while 'tis May. (LL) Ode on the Spring. Thomas Gray. GTBS-P; NOEC

We from the black sun of fear. Chorus of the Dead. Nelly Sachs, *German.* PFTM, *tr. by* Ruth Mead *and* Matthew Mead

We fuckin never had a fuckin chance. Armed Forces Day. Steve Hassett. CDa

We gather at the ship's unlit front deck. The Mighty Tropicale Orchestra. Sean Harvey. SeSe

We gather together to ask the Lord's. Thanksgiving Hymn. *Unknown.* CTV, *tr. by* Theodore Baker

We gather where the weeping willow waves. Decoration Day. Josephine D. Henderson Heard. CBWP-4

We gave a helping hand to grass. A Helping Hand. Miroslav Holub, *Czech.* PoSu, *tr. by* George Theiner

We get no good/ By being ungenerous. Reading. Elizabeth Barrett Browning. *Fr.* Aurora Leigh. VWP

We get up at six with him and build a fire. He Considers the Birds of the Air. Karl Kirchwey. GI

We give them chocolate bars. Negotiations. Ray Catina. CDa

We give you the lake. The Lake. Barry Seiler. PT

We giving all gained all. Two Canadian Memorials. Rudyard Kipling. *Fr.* Epitaphs of the War [1914–1918]. OBWP

We Go. Karl Wolfskehl, *German.* TrJP, *tr. by* Carol North Valhope *and* Ernst Morwitz

We go, in winter's biting wind. The Diehards. Ruth Pitter. OBGa

We go no more to Calverly's. Calverly's. Edwin Arlington Robinson. NoAM

We go out in the stony midnight. Thomas McGrath. *Fr.* Letter to an Imaginary Friend, Part One. NNaP

We go out in the stony midnight. Thomas McGrath. *Fr.* Letter to an Imaginary Friend, Part Two. NNaP

We go out together into the staring town. Kenneth Patchen. MoAmPo

We go over to see the head of a woman. Balance and Beauty. Clarence Major. FTOS

We go to the Golden Palace. The Golden Palace. *Unknown, Chinese.* ChiP, *tr. by* Arthur Waley

"We gon have / mo room!" (LL) An Inconvenience. John Raven. BPo; CRP

We got a mountain on the horizon. "What Have We Got." Lemn Sissay. NBrP

We got away—for just two nights. To Be a Pilgrim. Robert Conquest. OxBC

We Got Everything We Needed Here and Aint It Something. *Unknown, Seneca Indian.* STP, *tr. by* Jerome Rothenberg *and* Richard Johnny John

We got ready and showed our home. The Scattered Congregation. Tomas Tranströmer, *Swedish.* RaBo; VCWP, *tr. by* Robert Bly

We got sunlight on the sand. There Is Nothin' like a Dame. Oscar, II Hammerstein. OBAL

We got this idea. Our Hands in the Garden. Anne Hébert, *French.* BoWoP, *tr. by* A. Poulin, Jr.

We gotta. Survival Motion: Notice. Melvin E. Brown. ISC

We grant they're thine, those beauties all. Extempore—On Being Shown a Beautiful Country Seat Belonging to Maxwell of Cardoness. Robert Burns. OBGa

We Greeks have fallen on evil. Palladas, *Greek.* PGA, *tr. by* Kenneth Rexroth

We Greet Each Other in the Side. *Unknown.* BXAP

We greet thee now open this festal morn. Greeting. Henrietta Cordelia Ray. CBWP-3

We greet you rarest White Heron of One Flight. A Greeting to Queen Elizabeth, the Rare White Heron of Single Flight. Wiremu Kingi Kerekere, *Maori.* PeNZ, *tr. by* Wiremu Kingi Kerekere

We grow accustomed to the Dark. Emily Dickinson. SAmP

We grow to the sound of the wind. Dates. *Unknown.* AWP *Fr.* The Thousand and One Nights.

We had a drinking party. Drinking with Friends amongst the Blooming Peonies. Liu Yu Hsi, *Chinese.* OHMPC, *tr. by* Kenneth Rexroth

We had a motorbike all through the war. A Motorbike. Ted Hughes. InPS-3

We had already left him. Ugolino. Dante. FaBoPV, *tr. by* Seamus Heaney *Fr.* Inferno. NAWM-1, *tr. by* John Ciardi *Fr.* Divina Commedia.

We had been in the tall grass for hours. At Midsummer. Norman Dubie. NoAM

We had been school-mates,—she and I. Imogene. Eloise Bibb. CBWP-4

We had 'em. This Time. Steve Denning. CDa

We had expected everything but revolt. Nightmare Number Three. Stephen Vincent Benét. MoAmPo

We had forgotten You, or very nearly. Christ in Flanders. Lucy Whitmell. NSI

We had gathered for the love-feast on the time appointed. Who Is My Neighbor? Josephine D. Henderson Heard. CBWP-4

We had many problems set us when Coolgardie was a camp. The Smiths. E. G. Murphy. NOBAu

We had mor than. Words. Vern Rutsala. WeW-3

We had never seen black cockatoos, though in the park. Shadow of War, 1941. Thomas William Shapcott. BMAP

We had nevertheless just been born. (LL) The Little Car. Guillaume Apollinaire, *French.* AF, *tr. by* Oliver Bernard

We had no petnames, no diminutives for you. Mary Gravely Jones. Adrienne Rich. MDDM *Fr.* Grandmothers. HCAP; NAAL-2; NoAM

We had not got half way, nor yet discerned. Theocritus. OBCVT, *tr. by* Leigh Hunt *Fr.* The Rural Journey.

We had ridden long and were still far from the inn. Sleeping on Horseback. Po Chü-i, *Chinese.* ChiP, *tr. by* Arthur Waley

We had ridden long and were still far from the inn;. Sleeping on Horseback. Po Chü-i, *Chinese.* BLT, *tr. by* Arthur Waley

We had sat up all night hearing it roar, the mere. Morning in the Islands. John Hollander. ColΛP

We had stayed up all night, my friends and I, under hanging mosque lamps. Filippo Tommaso Marinetti. PFTM *Fr.* The Manifesto of Futurism.

We had the selfsame world enlarged for each. "George Eliot." *Fr.* Brother and Sister. NALW

We had this stuff that Wayne found in the shed. Cro-Kill. Anthony Lawrence. NOBAu

We harden like trees, and like rivers are cold. (LL) The Lover; a Ballad. Lady Mary Wortley Montagu. ECWP; NAEL-1; NoP-4

We hardly had gotten the man's pants down. Richard Huelsenbeck, *German.* PFTM, *tr. by* Jerome Rothenberg

We hardly speak. The End Circulates in the Wide Space of Summer. Paul Zweig. WeT

We have a bed, and a baby too. The Laborer. Richard Dehmel, *German.* AWP, *tr. by* Jethro Bithell

We have a fiction that we live by: it is the river. Waikato-Taniwha-Rau. Vincent O'Sullivan. PeNZ

We have / a map of the universe. Wings. Miroslav Holub, *Czech.* PoSu, *tr. by* Ian Milner *and* George Theiner

We have a secret, just we three. The Secret. *Unknown.* CTV

We have a small hand with five fingers. Toil. Avraham Shlonsky, *Hebrew.* MHP, *tr. by* Ruth Finer Mintz

We have all been in rooms. Adultery. James Dickey. MT; TAP

We have all seen them circling pastures. Under the Vulture-Tree. David Bottoms. MT

We have always known that you wanted us. (LL) The Helmsman. Hilda Doolittle. CMoP; OxBA

We have amazed by our great sufferings. Pierre Jean Jouve, *French.* NNPT, *tr. by* Keith Bosley

We have an old mother that peevish is grown. The Mother Country. Benjamin Franklin. AiP

We have ascended to this paradise. The Attic. Henri Coulette. PoRA

We have bathed, where none have seen us. Bridal Song to Amala. Thomas Lovell Beddoes. GBL; NOBVV; OBNC; PoEL-4 *Fr.* Death's Jest Book.

We Have Been Believers. Margaret Abigail Walker. PoBA

We have been everywhere, suddenly. The Universe is Part of Ourselves. Robin Blaser. FTOS

We have been helping with the cake. Day before Christmas. Marchette Chute. NTCP

We Have Been Here Before. Morris Gilbert Bishop. NYBP

We have been sailing in a certain small fountain. About This Course. David Shapiro. PoA

We have been shown. Six Variations. Denise Levertov. AmPP; CoAmPo; LCAP-2

We have borne good sons to broken men. Miners' Wives. Joe Corrie. OxBS

We have climbed the mountain. Here in Katmandu. Donald Justice. CoAP; CoAmPo; HeIP-4; WeT

We have come home. Lenrie Peters. PBMAP

We have come to the edge of the woods. Jacklight. Louise Erdrich. HATNAP; WeW-3

We have come to the end of a dream. The Cities Have Fallen. Fragano Ledgister. PBCV

We have come to the jungle. Jungle. Phyllis Haring. PeSA

We have come to your shrine to worship. A Plea for Mercy. Kwesi Brew. PBA; PBMAP

We have cried in our despair. When Helen Lived. W. B. Yeats. CMoP

We have decided to make Scotland secure. Tom Leonard. NBrP *Fr.* Situations Theoretical and Contemporary.

We have disconcerted / The revolutions with our prayers. Resistance. Horst Bienek, *German.* AF, *tr. by* Matthew Mead

We Have Done Our Duty. Yehuda Amichai, *Hebrew.* VCWP, *tr. by* Benjamin Harshav *and* Barbara Harshav

We have done what we wanted. Coming to This. Mark Strand. HCAP; SAGP; VCAP

We have done with dogma and divinity. After Trinity. John Meade Falkner. OxBTC

We have erased each letter. Life As a Book That Has Been Put Down. John Ashbery. FTOS

We have faith in old proverbs full surely. Where There's a Will There's a Way. Eliza Cook. BLPA

We have for many years been bored. The Pen-guin. The Sword-fish. Robert Williams Wood. NBLV

We have forgotten how to offer alms. Nikolai Semionovich Tikhonov, *Russian.* TCRP, *tr. by* Michael Frayn

We have forgotten who we are. *Unknown.* FHYEP *Fr.* U.N. Environmental Sabbath Program.

We have gone out in boats upon the sea at night. Passage Over Water. Robert Duncan. ColAP, NOBA, NoAM

We have grown a tree of knowledge, "Worthy Claflin" is the name. The Tree of Knowledge. Lizelia Augusta Jenkins Moorer. CBWP-3

We have had the best of it. (LL) Man White, Brown Girl and All That Jazz. Gloria C. Oden. GT

We have heard no nightingales singing. Working Class. Bertram J. Warr. NOBC

We have heard of Quintia's beauty. To me she is tall, slender. Catullus. *See* De Quintia et Lesbia.

We have learned how to bear. (LL) Zone. Louise Bogan. IMW; WPE

We have lived and loved together. Charles Jefferys. BLPA; FaBoBe; PoToHe

We have lived as ectoplasm. Coda. "Ern Malley." BMAP

We have loved each other in this time twenty years. Unfinished History. Archibald MacLeish. NYBP; VGW

We have met late—it is too late to meet. A Denial. Elizabeth Barrett Browning. GBL; OBNC

We have moving over us, over head and spire. Sunday. Josephine Miles. PoA

We have no heart for the fishing—we have no hand for the oar. The Dykes. Rudyard Kipling. OBWP

We have no prairies. Bogland. Seamus Heaney. HeIP-4; NOIV; NoAM; PBCIP; PNI; PoPoPo

We have no time to stand and stare. (LL) Leisure. W. H. Davies. APAD; AWP; BoTP; CH; CTV; EBEvV; FaBoBe; LiTM; MoBrPo; NOBE; NTP; OBEV; OBMV; PoRA; TFi

We have not been happy, my Lord, we have not been too happy. Chorus. T. S. Eliot. OxBTC *Fr.* Murder in the Cathedral.

We have not forgotten you but here they have you pretend to work. Letter to a Cretan Flute-Maker. Justin Vitiello. UnSA

We have not, up to. This Is a Sad-Ass Poem for a Black Woman to Be Writing. Sherley Anne Williams. WeT

We have opened the door. The Dead Feast of the Kol-Folk. John Greenleaf Whittier. PoEL-4

We have our problems, / too, with you. (LL) High to Low. Langston Hughes. HCAP; PoPoPo

We have reached the end of pastime, for always. End of Play. Robert Graves. EBEV

We have seen her/ the world over. Hilda Doolittle. CRP; NALW;PFTM; Poetr; VGW *Fr.* Tribute to the Angels.

We have seen how the most amiable. Hilda Doolittle. BoWoP; PBWP *Fr.* The Walls Do Not Fall. NAAL-2

We have served our day. Journalists. Rudyard Kipling. *Fr.* Epitaphs of the War [1914–1918]. OBWP

We have set out from here for the sublime. Prospects. Anthony Hecht. BAP-95

We have slept in. The Message on Cape Cod. Michael S. Weaver. GT; PBCAP

We have sold our shadow. Geometrical Place. Günter Eich, *German.* AF, *tr. by* David Young

We have struck the regions wherein we are keel or reef. Zone. Louise Bogan. IMW; WPE

We have talent. People call us. To Pi Ssu Yao. Tu Fu, *Chinese.* BLT; OHPC, *tr. by* Kenneth Rexroth

We have tangled together. Growing Together. Joyce Carol Oates. CrSp

We have tested and tasted too much, lover. Advent. Patrick Kavanagh. IIP; TIRV

We have the body of a woman, an arch over the ground. It Is Not. Valerie Martinez. BAP-96

"We have the mauve or the cerise." Shop Talk. Roy Fuller. OxBC

We *have the substance, they* may keep the name! (LL) The Power of Women. Matilda Barbara Betham-Edwards. ECWP; Ro

We have to discard the past. Past. Pablo Neruda, *Spanish.* VCWP, *tr. by* Alastair Reid

We have tried words before—always in vain. The Knife. Milton Kaplan. TrJP

We have tulips in our flower bed. Jessie Orton Jones. CTV *Fr.* (VII from Secrets).

We have two arms. A Drinking Song. Trần Dạ Tù', *Vietnamese.* AVP, *tr. by* Huỳnh Sanh Thông

We have watched again. Among Hawks. Lance Henson. VoR

We have welded the towbar. The Meadow. Peter Fallon. PBCIP

We hear her in the square. At two o'clock. A Speaker in the Square. George Buchanan. PNI

We heard the thrushes by the shore and sea. In Kerry. John Millington Synge. GBL; MoBrPo

We him in glory [*or* glorie] call, The Son[ne] of Man. (LL) The Son[ne]. George Herbert. GeHe; PeECV; SeCP

We hitched up the mare and we buckled her down. Four of July. Robert Newton Peck. CA

We hold a splendid feast today. Mei Sheng *and* Fu I. *Fr.* Nineteen Old Poems of the Han. CoBCP, *tr. by* Burton Watson

We hold a splendid feast today. *Unknown, Chinese.* CoBCP, *tr. by* Burton Watson

We hold each other. We hold each other tight. (LL) On the Back of a Photograph. János Pilinszky, *Hungarian.* NNPT; PoSu, *tr. by* Peter Jay

"We hold our flat shields, we wear our jerkins of hide." Hymn to the Fallen. *Unknown, Chinese.* ChiP; OBWP, *tr. by* Arthur Waley

We hold these truths to be self-evident. Decoy. John Ashbery. PoM

We hug our little destiny again. (LL) Whatever You Say Say Nothing. Seamus Heaney. OBWP; OxBC

We hunted the wren for Robin the Bobbin. Hunting the Wren. *Unknown.* FaBoVe

We hurry on, nor passing note. Digby Mackworth Dolben. OBNC

We imitate, oh horror! tops and bowls. Robert Lowell. APAD *Fr.* The Voyage.

We in our wandering. A Song of the Open Road. *Unknown, Latin.* AWP, *tr. by* John Addington Symonds

We invite him to die. Colobus Monkey. *Unknown. Fr.* Hunter Poems of the Yoruba. RB, *tr. by* Ulli Beier

We Irish pride ourselves as patriots. Ireland. John Hewitt. CIP-2; IIP

We is gathahed hyeah, my brothahs. An Ante-Bellum Sermon. Paul Laurence Dunbar. AAP; APN-2; BPo; NAAAL

We issue from the meat of Pineapple Street. On the Island. Louis Edward Sissman. NYBP

We join with the earth and with each other. *Unknown.* FHYEP *Fr.* U.N. Environmental Sabbath Program.

We jumped in, trusting. Elevator. Naomi Shihab Nye. IFJA

We keep forgetting the gods. And if we happened to remember. Requiem on Poros. Yannis Ritsos, *Greek.* VCWP, *tr. by* Edmund Keeley

We keep our quilts in closets and do not dance. Mennonites. Julia Kasdorf. LoHo; PBCAP

We kept him an hour in the / bottom. A Cocker of Snooks. Phyllis Gotlieb. NOBC

We kiss'd again with tears. (LL) The Reconciliation. Tennyson. ImP; PoToHe; SCGP

We kissed at the barrier; and passing through. On the Departure Platform. Thomas Hardy. CBLP; NOBE; OBNC; OxBTC

We knew only that she was too pretty. The Substitute. Leslie Adrienne Miller. CMAP

We knew so much; when her beautiful eyes could lighten. Sagacity. William Rose Benét. MoAmPo

We knew thee of old. Ode to Liberty. Rudyard Kipling. GrIP

We know as we grow older. Ella Wheeler Wilcox. *See* Whatever Is—Is Best.

We know it doesn't rhyme much anymore. What Is Poetry. James Scully. FYAP

We know not what it is, dear, this sleep so deep and still. The Two Mysteries. Mary Mapes Dodge. PWR; TrCP

We know nothing whatever about Thee. (LL) O God, for as much as without Thee. Ronald Arbuthnott Knox. PeLi

We know that our master has left us for the day. (LL) Waking from Sleep. Robert Bly. NOBA; NoP-4; Poetr; SPE

We know the cities by their stones. A Postcard from Berlin. Derek Mahon. BiHa

We know the early Chaplin but before him. The Early Chaplin. Wiktor Woroszylski, *Polish.* CEEP, *tr. by* Magnus J. Krynski *and* Robert A. Maguire

We know the story. Generation. Rae Armantrout. FTOS

We know the story. The children. Remembering the Children of Auschwitz. Thomas McGrath. EC2

We know / the winter earth. November Twenty-sixth Nineteen Hundred and Sixty-three. Wendell Berry. LiTM

We know this story: how his daddy died of drink. Custom Job: Hank Williams, Jr., and the Death Car, 1958. David Wojahn. PBCAP *Fr.* Mystery Train: A Sequence.

We know what trembles on the scales. Courage. "Anna Akhmatova," *Russian.* TCRP, *tr. by* Stanley Kunitz *with* Max Hayward

We know what we mean. (LL) Be Seeing You. Vasco [*or* Vasko] Popa, *Serbian.* HP; PoSu, *tr. by* Anne Pennington

We know where deepest lies the snow. Song. Anne Brontë. PEW

We lack the courage to be where we are. Octaves. Edwin Arlington Robinson. NCAP *Fr.* Octaves.

We ladies sense it is the cuckoo builds no nest. Liberation. Ruth Stone. BoWoP

We lads in the forging-shop have unbounded strength. *Unknown.* ChiPo

We laugh and we well might weep with the Ballads of George R. Sims. (LL) The Ballad of George R. Sims. John Betjeman. OBCoV; UV

We laughed. Second Class Citizen. Jennifer Lagier. UnSA

We lay in an attic under beamed eaves. Robyn Selman. PUP-19

We lay red roses on his grave. Paul Laurence Dunbar. Robert Earl Hayden. GT; NoP-4

We lay still. Hold, Hold. T. Alan Broughton. CMAP

We learn from Horace, Homer sometimes sleep. Byron. EPCY *Fr.* Canto the Third. *Fr.* Don Juan.

We learned that you don't shoot. Statement on Our Higher Education. W. M. Ransom. CDW

We learned the Whole of Love. Emily Dickinson. APN-2

We leave each other and the habits. Gone Away. Hugo Williams. IFJA

We leave the well-beloved place. Tennyson. EBVV; FHYEP; PoEL-5 *Fr.* In Memoriam A. H. H.

We leave thee with thy guests, thou sunny maid! Albery Allson Whitman. AAP *Fr.* Twasinta's Seminoles; Or Rape of Florida.

We leave our courts to-day. Farewell to Allen University. Josephine D. Henderson Heard. CBWP-4

We left behind the painted buoy. The Voyage. Tennyson. OxBoS

We left the horses in the draw. A Season of Loss. Jim Barnes. HATNAP

We left the western island to live among strangers. The Search. John Hewitt. PNI

We left them there and went our way. (LL) You and I and Amyas. William Cornish. NOBE; NoSic

We let fire rip, we blacken the pale-gold acres. Burning Off. Geoffrey Dutton. NOBAu

We librarians went to Baja last weekend and sat in the sun. Chapter One. Stephanie Brown. BAP-93

We lie back to back. Curtains. The Suitor. Jane Kenyon. InPK-6

We lie, day creatures, overhearing night. (LL) The Sound of Night. Maxine W. Kumin. SoSe-8; WPE

We lie one against the other. Seventh Day Seventh Month. Kuan Yun She, *Chinese.* OHMPC, *tr. by* Kenneth Rexroth

We lift the curtain of the past to-day. Lincoln. Henrietta Cordelia Ray. CBWP-3

We like March—his shoes are Purple, vers. of 1878; see also *We like March.* Emily Dickinson. TTTS

We, like shades that were first conjured up. And through the Caribbean Sea. Margaret Danner. BPo

We listened to the music. Sunday Visit. Antigone Kefala. BMAP

We / little children in our shifts. Clap Your Hands for Herod. Josef Hanzlik, *Czech*. OBCP, *tr. by* Ian Milner.

We live amidst hills of desolate. South Bronx Testimonial. Sandra Maria Esteves. UnSA

We live:—dishonoured, in the shit. So what? it had to be. Iambes VIII. André Marie de Chénier, *French*. FaBoPV, *tr. by* Tom Paulin.

We live down here. Framing. Michael Davidson. FTOS

We Live in a Cage. William J. Harris. GT; PoBA

We Live in a Rickety House. Alexander McLachlan. NOBC

We live in airless space. The Tongue. Georgy Nikolaevich Obolduyev, *Russian*. TCRP, *tr. by* Vera Dunham.

We live in deeds, not years; in thoughts, not breaths. Philip James Bailey. PoToHe *Fr.* A Country Town.

We live in houses of ample weight. Edvard Munch. Charles Wright. HCAP

We live in the egg. In the Egg. Günter Grass, *German*. AF, *tr. by* Michael Hamburger *and* Christopher Middleton

We live, not feeling the country beneath us. Poem No. 286 (On Stalin). Osip Emilevich Mandelstam, *Russian*. TCRP, *tr. by* Albert C. Todd

We live on the third world from the sun. Number three. China. Bob Perelman. FTOS

We live to love—it matters not! (LL) A Cherokee Love Song. John Rollin Ridge. APN-2; PaTW

We live, while we see the sun. Pedro Calderón de la Barca. AWP *Fr.* Life Is a Dream. NAWM-1, *tr. by* Arthur Symons

We lived deep in a land of optative moods. From the Canton of Expectation. Seamus Heaney. CIP-2

We lived in language all our black selves. When the Wine Was Gone. Alvin Aubert. BkSV

We lived in strange, hostile, marvellous times. On the Book. Czeslaw Milosz, *Polish*. CEEP, *tr. by* John Carpenter *and* Bogdana Carpenter

We lived next door to the bootlegger, and were lucky. The. Autobiography. Joy Harjo. LTA

We lived one and twenty year. Upon a Notorious Shrew. *Unknown*. FaBoEE

We look at woods and say. The Finder of a Horseshoe. Osip Emilevich Mandelstam, *Russian*. TCRP, *tr. by* Bernard Meares

We looked for hours everywhere. Memory II. Vladimir Holan, *German*. CEEP, *tr. by* Bronislava Volek *and* Andrew Durkin.

We looked, we loved, and therewith instantly. Pure Death. Robert Graves. GTBS-P; LBC

We lose—because we win. Emily Dickinson. HeIP-4

We Love the Venerable House. Ralph Waldo Emerson. AH

We love thee, Ann Maria Smith. The Editor's Wooing. "Orpheus C. Kerr." OBAL

We love to squeeze bananas. Squeezes. Brian Patten. OTCP; Spl

We love to squeeze our mums. (LL) Squeezes. Brian Patten. OTCP; Spl

We love with great difficulty. Sing with Your Body. Janice Mirikitani. MDDM; WPOW

We loved as friends now twenty years and more. The Change. Henry, Bishop of Chichester King. NOSC

We loved each other and were ignorant. (LL) After Long Silence. W. B. Yeats. BoLoP; CMoP; EnLoPo; HeIP-4; HoPM; LiTM; NAEL-2; OAEL-2; OBMV; UnPo

We lying by seasand, watching yellow. Dylan Thomas. PoA

We made a mistake in this song. *Unknown, Seneca Indian*. STP, *tr. by* Jerome Rothenberg *and* Richard Johnny John

We made a model of the Solar System today. Our Solar System. Eric Finney. SpW

We made castles of grass, green halls, enormous stem-lined rooms. The Riders. Ann Stanford. WPE

We made our high bed in the low chapel. Airing the Chapel. Sylvia Kantaris. LW

We made the corn-stalk violins wail and strode the fields. Emperor Butterfly. Anna Kiss, *Magyar*. EC2, *tr. by* Nicholas Columban

We make both mead and garden gay. Daffodils. P. A. Ropes. BoTP

We make more fuss of ballads than of blueprints. Engineers' Corner. Wendy Cope. OBCoV

We make our meek adjustments. Chaplinesque. Hart Crane. CMoP; HeIP-4; LiTM; MoP; NAAL-2; NOBA; NoAM; OxBA; VGW

We make ourselves a place apart. Revelation. Robert Frost. ChIV-2

We make the world in which we live. The World We Make. Alfred Grant Walton. PoToHe

We Manage Most When We Manage Small. Linda Gregg. AmPA

We marched, and saw a company of Canadians. Canadians. Ivor Gurney. FaBoTw

We may be learning how to tell the truth. Marilyn Hacker. Son *Fr.* La Fontaine de Vaucluse.

We may live without poetry, music and art. "Owen Meredith." PoToHe

We may shut our eyes. Joys. James Russell Lowell. BoTP

We may sigh o'er the heavy burdens. The Burdens of All. Frances Ellen Watkins Harper. PWR

We mean to thrash these Prussian Pups. *Unknown*. NSI; PoWW

We meet again. Encounter. Marion Strobel. LW

We Meet in the Lives of Animals. Peter Everwine. NNaP

We meet 'neath the sounding rafter. The Revel. Bartholomew Dowling. BLPA

We meet upon the Level and we part upon the Square. The Level and the Square. Robert Morris. BLPA

We Met. Mary E. Tucker. CBWP-1

We met, a hundred of us met. The Vision. William Taylor. NOEC

We met but in one giddy dance. To ———. Winthrop Mackworth Praed. CBLP

We met for supper in your flat-bottomed boat. Dream Barker. Jean Valentine. VGW

We met, hand to hand. Twilight Night. Christina Rossetti. CBLP

We met on Charles Bridge, it was snowing. The Old Priest. Vladimir Holan, *Czech*. PoSu, *tr. by* George Theiner

We Met on Roads of Laughter. Charles Divine. FaBoBe

We met the British in the dead of winter. Meeting the British. Paul Muldoon. BiHa; CIP-2; FaBoPV; NoAM; NoP-4; PNI

We met upon a crowded street one day. Casual Meeting. Margaret E. Bruner. PoToHe

We might have died by now. Horse on a Fence. George Evans. PmAP

We might have known it always: music. An Die Musik. David Malouf. CBAP

We mind not now the merits of our kind. Marriage and Money. Sir Charles Sedley. OBSV *Fr.* The Happy Pair.

We miss a Kinsman more. Emily Dickinson. OxBSP

We more than others have the perfect right. Song of the Moderns. John Gould Fletcher. AWP

We mothers. Nelly Sachs, *German*. MDDM, *tr. by* Ruth Mead *and* Matthew Mead

We mourn to-day o'er our sister dead. Resting. Josephine D. Henderson Heard. CBWP-4

We move from one. The River. Sam Cornish. PoBA

We move in elephantine row. Express. William Allingham. NOBVV

We moved like fingers. San Francisco Poem. John Logan. NNaP

We murmur the first moonwords: / *Spasibo. Thanks. O.K.* (LL) That "old last act"! / And yet sometimes. Adrienne Rich. NIP-4; NOBA; TAP

We Must Be Free or Die. Wordsworth. *See* England, 1802 ("It is not to be thought of").

We Must Be Polite. Carl Sandburg. NOxBChV

"We Must Die Because We Have Known Them." Rilke, *German*. RaBo, *tr. by* Stephen Mitchell

We must kill our gods before they kill us. Black Trumpeter. Henry Dumas. PoBA

We must leave the handrails and the Ariadne-threads. À l'Ange Avantgardien. Francis Reginald. MoCV

We must live or die by steel. (LL) Before Disaster. Yvor Winters. PFE

We Must Look at the Harebell. "Hugh MacDiarmid." NAEL-2; NoP-4 *Fr.* In Memoriam James Joyce.

We must not quarrel, whatever we do. Her Word of Reproach. Sarah Morgan Bryan Piatt. NCAP

We must pass like smoke or live within the spirit's fire. Immortality. "Æ." AWP; OBMV; TIRV

We Must Return. Agostinho Neto, *Portuguese*. PeSAV, *tr. by* Michael Wolfers

We must see, we must know. The Slop Barrel. Philip Whalen. PmAP

We must sit down. Councils. Marge Piercy. CrSp

We need no runners here. Booze is law. Harlem, Montana. James Welch. CDW; HATNAP; PaTW; PoPoPo

We Never Close. David Clewell. NAmP90

We never half believed the stuff. James Wetherell. Edwin Arlington Robinson. MoAmPo

We Never Know. Yusef Komunyakaa. MT

We Never Said Farewell[, nor even looked]. Mary Elizabeth Coleridge. OxBSP; SAGP; WPE

We never spent time in the mountains. Interlude. Welton Smith. PoBA

We never stopped crossing borders. Luis J. Rodriguez. UnSA

We no longer control could drag us back. (LL) July in Washington. Robert Lowell. LCAP-2; NAAL-2

We now lament not, but congratulate. Donne. NOSC *Fr.* The Second Anniversary [*or* Anniversarie]. ESCV; SeCP *Fr.* Of the Progres[se] of the Soule; the Second Anniversarie.

We of Sparta fought the Argives—equal in number and arms. Chairemon, *Greek*. GrAn, *tr. by* Richard Evans

We offer you, Lord, in our strong, our sensitive hands. Offertory. John F. Deane. TIRV

We only know that in the sultry weather. England and America, 1863. Richard Monckton, 1st Baron Houghton Milnes. EBVV

We only live between. For Sheridan. Robert Lowell. HCAP

We open the street door. The Same Month They Bombed Cambodia. Amy Uyematsu. OpBo

We ought to be together, you and I. (LL) You and I. Henry Alford. BLPA; FaBoBe

We ourselves are aged. The Struggle for the Taal. Breyten Breytenbach, *Afrikaans. AF, tr. by* Denis Hirson

We outgrow love like other things. Emily Dickinson. GLoP; NOBA; SoSe-8

We owe the ancients something. You have read. Fitz-Greene Halleck. OBAL *Fr.* Fanny.

We Own the Night. Imamu Amiri Baraka. PoBA

We oxen are not only good. Leonidas of Alexandria, *Greek.* GrAn, *tr. by* Robin Skelton

We park and stare. A full sky of the stars. The Death of the Sheriff. Robert Lowell. MoAmPo

We[e] part not with the[e] at this meeting day. (LL) Sir Walter Ra[u]le[i]gh to His Son[ne]. Sir Walter Ralegh. InPS-3; NAEL-1; NoSic; OxBSP; PoEL-2; RB; SCGP; SiPS; Son

We part not with thee at this meeting day. Sir Walter Ralegh. *See* Sir Walter Ra[u]le[i]gh to His Son[ne].

We pass a stranger. He glances. The Stranger Not Ourselves. William Stafford. NNaP

We pass the flayed carcass of a cow. The Man from Changi. Graeme Hetherington. NOBAu

We Passed by Green Closes. John Clare. EnVR

We passed each other, turned and stopped for half an hour, then went our way. On the Road to the Sea. Charlotte Mew. BrRo; CPO; FaBoWP

We passed the ice of pain. The Moment. Theodore Roethke. NYBP

We passed their graves. Peace. Langston Hughes. BPo

We passed where flag and flower. Middle-Age Enthusiasms. Thomas Hardy. LiLi

We Pick Ferns, We Pick Ferns. *Unknown, Chinese.* CoBCP, *tr. by* Burton Watson

We pick off dots like runners, between. The Static. Lewis Warsh. FTOS

We pick / the bittersweet grapes. Napa, California. Ana Castillo. WPOW

We picked flints. Tinder. Seamus Heaney. OxAEP-2

We planned to shake the world together, you and I. Lamplight. May Wedderburn Cannan. NSI

We plotted our future, the young city. Here in Netanya. Meir Wieseltier, *Hebrew.* IP, *tr. by* Warren Bargad *and* Stanley F. Chyet

We Poets in Our Youth. Wordsworth. *Fr.* Resolution and Independence. EBEV; FHYEP; HAP; InPS-3; NOBE; NOBRP; NOCV; NoP-4; OAEL-2; OBNC; OxAEP-2; PoEL-4; Ro; TFi

We pointed it out to his bed-ridden eyes. Hospital. Geoffrey C. Millard. PeSA

We poor Agawams. Mr. Ward of Anagrams Thus. Nathaniel Ward. SCAP

We pour a mild drink each. Canning. Marge Piercy. *Fr.* Six Underrated Pleasures. EC2

We practice our scales. Fish Story: How Language Carries Us into the Unknown. Brigitte Frase. LoHo

We praise Love the limiter. (LL) Je T'Adore. Thomas Kinsella. MoP; NoAM

We Praise Thee, God, for Harvests Earned. John Coleman Adams. AH

We Praise Thee, If One Rescued Soul. Lydia Huntley Sigourney. AH

We pray that it will be done / In beauty / In beauty. (LL) Eagle Poem. Joy Harjo. CrSp; HATNAP; WeT; WeW-3

We pray Thee, have mercy on Zion! Prayer for Redemption. *Unknown.* TrJP

We pray to life's source, Mary. The Virgin Mary. *Unknown, Welsh.* OBWVE, *tr. by* Joseph P. Clancy

We prayse thee god. we knowelege thee lorde. Te Deum. *Unknown, Latin.* OBCVT

We prepare / the meal together. Soul Food. Janice Mirikitani. NMM-2; OpBo

We pressed our faces. The Train Stops at Healy Fork. John Haines. BLT

We promise letters and send postcards. Letter Following. Aidan Carl Mathews. PBCIP

We pulled for you when the wind was against us and the sails were low. Song of the Galley-Slaves. Rudyard Kipling. GTBS-P; HAP; NTP; PoEL-5; SCGP

We put a prop beneath the sagging bough. The Wild Cherry. Malcolm Lowry. NoP-4

We put him on the roof and we painted him blue. The Pedalling Man. Russell Hoban. NOxBChV

We put more coal on the big red fire. Father's Story. Elizabeth Madox Roberts. ImGa

We put out our hands on the window—cold. In Time of Need. William Stafford. UnPo

We raise de wheat. Song. *Unknown.* APN-2; BPo; CrDW; NAAAL; TAP

We rake the past, down to an ounce of wants. Squatter in the Foreground. Kenward Elmslie. FTOS

We ramble along up-hill through the woods. One of Our Walks. John Hollander. AFr

We ran across the meadow scabbed with cow-dung, past. Geoffrey Hill. HAP *Fr.* Mercian Hymns.

We reach the promised land. Story of Joshua. Alicia Ostriker. ChIV-1

We reach the utmost limit of the earth. Prometheus Bound. Aeschylus, *Greek.*

We Reached Out Far. Perets Markish, *Yiddish.* TrJP, *tr. by* Jacob Sonntag

We read and hear about you every day. To the Rulers. Howard Nemerov. OxBC

We Read of a People. *Unknown.* AH

We read of kings and gods that kindly took. A Cruel Mistress. Thomas Carew. CavPo

We real cool. We. Gwendolyn Brooks. CrDW; HAP; HeIP-4; HoPM; InPK-6; NAAAL; NALW; NTP; PoA; PoBA; PoE; Poetr; RaBo; SoSe-8; TAP; TFi; TRP; TTY; WeW-3

("Die soon.") (LL) KaS; LiLi; NoP-4

("Pool Players, The.") LiLi

("We / Die soon.") (LL) PoPoPo

We received thee warmly—kindly—though we knew thou wert a quiz. William Edmonstoune Aytoun *and* Sir Theodore Martin. OBCoV *Fr.* The American's Apostrophe to Boz.

We reconstruct lives in the intensive. Clan Meeting: Births and Nations: A Blood Song. Michael S. Harper. NoAM

We reden ofte and finde ywrite. Sir Orfeo. *Unknown.* EnVB

We refugees ply all trades over here. Biding Our Time. Hậu Điền, *Vietnamese.* AVP, *tr. by* Huỳnh Sanh Thông

We remember you / calling America. Poetry Concert. Michael S. Harper. TAP

We ride down the coast hwy through the rain. The Great Santa Barbara Oil Disaster OR. Conyus. AmPA; NBV

We ride them / and Tingel-Tangel / in the afternoon. John Weiners. *See* A Poem for the Insane.

We rigged up a theater behind the storehouse. Hamlet. Yevgeny Mikhailovich Vinokurov, *Russian.* TCRP, *tr. by* Daniel Weissbort

We rise from the snow where we've. Selective Service. Carolyn Forché. Poetr

We Rise on Sun Beams and Fall in the Night. Allen Ginsberg. CLPP

We rise up early and. Anna Speaks of the Childhood of Mary Her Daughter. Lucille Clifton. NALW

We roam the streets at night, lovers. Walking at Night. Philip Salom. BMAP

We rock and grunt, grunt and / shine. (LL) Song for Ishtar. Denise Levertov. MoP; NALW; NoAM; PoM

We rode at walking pace. Grenada. Mikhail Arkadyevich Svetlov, *Russian.* TCRP, *tr. by* Daniel Weissbort

We rode the canals. Boxing the Fox. Pearse Hutchinson. CIP-2

We rose before dawn. Andal. WPoS *Fr.* The Tiruppavai.

We rose to go. Sunset blazed on the windows. (LL) The Black Cottage. Robert Frost. CBCWP; VGW

We run the dangercourse. We Walk the Way of the New World. Don L. Lee. BPo; PoBA

We said: there will surely be hawthorn out. Spring Snow and Tui. Mary Ursula Bethell. PeNZ

We sail at dusk, the red moon. Night Patrol. Alan Ross. OxBoS

We sail out of season into an oyster-gray wind. Crossing the Atlantic. Anne Sexton. NoAM

We sailed in the Ark. The New Noah. "Adunis," *Arabic.* AF, *tr. by* Abdullah Al-Udhari

We salute you / season of no bungling. Charles Olson. *See* Variations Done for Gerald Van De Wiele.

We sat across the table. The Friend. Marge Piercy. CrSp; NALW; NMM-2; Poetr

We sat among Emily Dickinson's 1775 poems. Poetry Evening. Liljana Dirjan, *Yugoslav.* CEEP, *tr. by* Ewald Osers

We sat at the hut of the fisher. Twilight. Heinrich Heine, *German.* AWP, *tr. by* Louis Untermeyer

We sat before an October fire. The Necessity of Falling. William Mills. MT

We sat in the courtyard. Merida, 1969. William Matthews. EOEF

We sat together at one summer's end. Adam's Curse. W. B. Yeats. BIrV; CMoP; NAEL-2; NoAM; NoP-4; OAEL-2; PFE; WeW-3

We sat together in the trench. Trench Idyll. Richard Aldington. PeFWW

We sat, two children, warm against the wall. The Gate. Edwin Muir. CMoP; LiTM

We sat within the farm-house old. The Fire of Drift-Wood. Henry Wadsworth Longfellow. APN-1; AmPP; MeMAP; NAAL-1; NAAL-3; NCAP; NOBA; OxBA; TAP

We sate down and wept by the waters. By the Rivers of Babylon We Sat Down and Wept. Byron. ChIV-1

We saw a bloody sunset over Courtland. Remembering Nat Turner. Sterling Brown. PoBA

We saw a town by the track in Colorado. Holding the Sky. William Stafford. GM

We saw anchored worlds in a shallow stream. Lying on a Bridge. Van K. Brock. MT

We saw and woo'd each other's eyes. William Habington. *See* The Reward of Innocent Love.

We saw and wooed each others' eyes. The Reward of Innocent Love. William Habington. FMP *Fr.* Castara.

We saw death at rather close range. The Cricket. Konstantin Mikhailovich Simonov, *Russian.* TCRP, *tr. by* Lubov Yakovleva

We saw everything except that we were gay. Robyn Selman. PUP-19

We saw it all. We saw the souvenir shops, and sitting. Niagara Falls. Alan Dugan. PoA

We saw that sky. Blackness. Place of Fire. Johannes Bobrowski, *German.* PoSu; CEEP, *tr. by* Ruth Mead *and* Matthew Mead

We saw the swallows gathering in the sky. George Meredith. EnLoPo; GTBS-P; NOBE; NOBVV; OAEL-2; OBNC *Fr.* Modern Love.

We saw the water-flags in flower! (LL) The Spirit's Epochs. Coventry Patmore. EBEV; GBL; OxBSP

We saw Thee in Thy balmy nest. Verses from the Shepherd's Hymn. Richard Crashaw. OBEV *Fr.* In the Holy Nativity of Our Lord God. GeHe; PoEL-2

We say a heart breaks—like. Reginald Gibbons. IFJA

We say he is dead; ah, the word is too somber. Not Dead, but Sleeping. Clara Ann Thompson. CBWP-2

We say it for an hour, or for years. Good-By. Grace Denio Litchfield. PoToHe

We say, "It rains." An unbelievable age! Hath the Rain a Father? Jones Very. ChIV-1

We say that a loon, most graceful and dark. A Woman Gave Me a Red Star to Wear on My Headband. Jimmie Durham. HATNAP

We say the sea is lonely; better say. The Open Sea. William Meredith. CoAP; TAP; UnPo

We search the world for truth; we cull. Knowledge. John Greenleaf Whittier. PoToHe *Fr.* Miriam.

We see a forest and say. Whoever Finds a Horseshoe. Osip Emilevich Mandelstam, *Russian.* PFTM, *tr. by* Burton Raffel *and* Alla Burago

We see each living thing finally die. Sonnet 7. Louise Labé, *French.* BoWoP, *tr. by* Willis Barnstone

We see God clear and high above the town. (LL) Soul's Liberty. Anna Wickham. MoBrPo; OxBSP

We see them not—we cannot hear. Are They Not All Ministering Spirits? Robert Stephen Hawker. OxAEP-2

We send you home to a grave on Stone Tower Mountain. Weeping for Ying Yao. Wang Wei, *Chinese.* CoBCP, *tr. by* Burton Watson

We separate the fragments from the whole. (LL) Love in the Classroom. Al Zolynas. BLT; EC3; LTA

We set our sights on living, and on that alone. Ghazal. Iftiqar Arif. NBrP

We set out yesterday upon a winter drive. Alexandre Dumas. TTY *Fr.* The Lady of the Pearls.

We Settled by the Lake. F. D. Reeve. NYBP

We shall arrive, / to see, soon. (LL) Bend in the River. Simon J. Ortiz. PoPoPo

We shall bathe, my love, in an African presence. Léopold Sédar Senghor. NegPo, *tr. by* Ellen Conroy Kennedy *Fr.* Songs for Signare.

We shall be called harsh names by men unborn. Contemporary. Hortense King Flexner. PoA

"We shall cede with a brotherly embrace." The Rise of Shivaji. Zulfikar Ghose. MoBS

We shall come tomorrow morning, who were not to have her love. Emily Hardcastle, Spinster. John Crowe Ransom. CMoP; MeMAP; OxBSP

We shall die in transparent Petropolis. Osip Emilevich Mandelstam, *Russian.* PeFWW, *tr. by* David McDuff

We shall die on the battlefield. Kofi Awoonor. *See* Songs of Sorrow.

We Shall Drink to Them That Sleep. Alexander Robertson. NSI

We shall go mad no doubt and die that way. (LL) The Cool Web. Robert Graves. AWP; GTBS-P; MoP; NAEL-2; NoAM; OxBTC; PoA; Poetr; SCV

We shall have everything we want and there'll be no more dying. Ode to Joy. Frank O'Hara. GLP; NeAP; PmAP

We shall have fireworks here by this day week. (LL) Conferences, adjournments, ultimatums. Louis MacNeice. FaBoPV; OxBTC

We shall have had a good Friday. (LL) Terce. W. H. Auden. CMoP; GI; PoE

We Shall Know. *Unknown.* PWR

We shall live again. *Unknown.* STP *Fr.* Ghost-Dance Songs.

We shall not always plant [what] while others reap. From the Dark Tower. Countee Cullen. BPo; ColAP; CrDW; LiTM; NAAAL; NAAL-2; PoBA; Son

We shall not cease from exploration. T. S. Eliot. *Fr.* Little Gidding. FaBoMo; FaBoPV; FaBoTw; GTBS-P; MoP; NAEL-2; NAWM-2; NOBA; NOBE; NoAM; OAEL-2; OxAEP-2; OxBTC; PeECV; TAP; TFi *Fr.* Four Quartets.

We shall not escape Hell, my passionate. Marina Tsvetayeva, *Russian.* BoWoP, *tr. by* Elaine Feinstein *and* Angela Livingstone

We shall not ever meet them bearded in heaven. On the Death of Friends in Childhood. Donald Justice. CoAmPo; ColAP; InPK-6; LCAP-2

We shall not fall alone! (LL) Ulster. Rudyard Kipling. FaBoPV; IIP

We shall not go up against you. This Be Our Revenge. Saul Tchernichowsky, *Hebrew.* TrJP, *tr. by* Shalom Spiegel

We Shall Overcome. Breyten Breytenbach, *Afrikaans.* PeSAV, *tr. by* Ernst van Heerden

We shall overcome. *Unknown.* AH; CrDW

("We shall overcome some day.") (LL) PBMP

We shall remember the wheat stalk in the greenness of her youth. Remembrance of Beginnings of Things. Leah Goldberg, *Hebrew.* MHP, *tr. by* Ruth Finer Mintz

We Shall Return, Luanda. Ngudia Wendel. PBMAP

We shall return we will stay here. Ivar Ivask, *Estonian.* CEEP, *tr. by* Ivar Ivask

We shall sleep-out together through the dark. Ararat. Charles Tomlinson. NoP-4

We shall soon give all our attention to you. (LL) Spring Day. John Ashbery. ColAP; NOBA

We shall walk in the snow. (LL) Velvet Shoes. Elinor Wylie. CH; MoAmPo; WHSW

We shan't see Willy any more, Mamie. To a Bull-Dog. Sir John Collings Squire. NSI

We shared not one idea in thirty years. A Reformer to His Father. James Simmons. BIrV

We shipped him at the Sandwich Isles. The Whaler's Pig. Edwin James Brady. NOBAu

We should cultivate our different tastes. Cultivation. Mrs. Henry Linden. CBWP-4

We Show You That Death as a Dancer. Hamish Henderson. PoWW

We sift salt into *chapati* flour, pour oil. Making Samosas. Chitra Divakaruni. NMM-2

We sing a hymn to Artemis, for it is. Hymn to Artemis. Callimachus. HePo, *tr. by* Barbara Hughes Fowler *Fr.* Hymns.

We sirens, since we rigged up stereophonic sound. The Sirens. Gordon Challis. PeNZ

We sit at a sidewalk table. The Firebreathers at the Café Deux Magots. Miller Williams. MT

We sit at our kitchen table. The Day Before They Bombed Nagasaki. Rebecca Baggett. CrSp

We sit at the table and that is grace. November and Aunt Jemima. Thylias Moss. TRP

We sit, crookbacked, at the bar. At the Telephone Club. Henri Coulette. CoAP

We sit here, talking of Barea and Lorca. Conversation in Gibraltar 1943. Charles Causley. PoWW

We sit in the darkness. The Feeding. Lou Lipsitz. CDa

We sit indoors and talk of the cold outside. There Are Roughly Zones. Robert Frost. CMoP

We sit late, watching the dark slowly unfold. September. Ted Hughes. BoLoP

We sit on a green bench in Harrison Railroad Park. Dreams in Harrison Railroad Park. Nellie Wong. OpBo; UnSA

We sit outside. Death of Dr. King. Sam Cornish. MBE; PoBA

We sit side by side. Two Set Out on Their Journey. Galway Kinnell. IFJA

We Sit Solitary. *Unknown.* TrJP

We Sit Unhackled Drunk and Mad to Edit, *sl. diff. vers.* Malcolm Lowry. *Fr.* The Drunkards. NYBP

We sit watching the afternoon summer smell ripely. James Powell on Imagination. Larry Neal. BPo

We six pile in, the engine churning ink. Nigger Song: An Odyssey. Rita Dove. AmPA

We smell their minds like silver hammers. (LL) Jacklight. Louise Erdrich. HATNAP; WeW-3

We smiled together. Gardens. Neil Curry. OBGa

We sometimes ride, and sometimes walk. Life at Richkings. Frances, Countess of Hertford Seymour. ECWP

We sound like crying bullheads. Voices. Nora Dauenhauer. HATNAP

We sow the fertile seed and then we reap it. Evening Hymn in the Hovels. Francis Lauderdale Adams. OxBS

We speak / because / when the rain falls. Because the Dawn Breaks. Merle Collins. HCP

We speed through tunnels under the frozen ground. Subway. Susan Fawcett. CrSp

We spend our lives trying to construct sentences. Paris 1912. *Unknown.* NBrP

We spend our morning. The Memory of Elena. Carolyn Forché. LoL; NoAM

We spent all day fishing and talking. Late at Night During a Visit of Friends. Robert Bly. InPS-3

We spread torn quilts and blankets. The Picnic, an Homage to Civil Rights. Michael S. Weaver. ISC

We stand naked behind the line. On the Death of Sylvia Plath. Judith Herzberg, *Dutch.* WPOW, tr. by Manfred Wolf

We stand on the edge of wounds, hugging canned meat. Dream of Rebirth. Roberta Hill Whiteman. CDW

We stand pinned. Zocalo. Michael S. Harper. NBV

We stand together. Last Journey. John Montague. CIP-2; PBCIP; PNI

We stare and say, "Well, we have come this far." (LL) Cirque d'Hiver. Elizabeth Bishop. InPS-3

We stars, we stars. Chorus of the Stars. Nelly Sachs, *German.* PFTM, tr. by Michael Roloff

We started home, my son and I. Jaan Kaplinski, *Estonian.* BLT, tr. by Jaan Sam Hamill Kaplinski and Riina Tamm

We started our house midway through the Cultural Revolution. Building. Gary Snyder. BB

We started speaking. The Meeting. Katherine Mansfield. LW

We stayed in a resort town that Easter. In Memoriam. John Skoyles. CMAP

We stepped into the lift. The two of us, alone. Meeting in a Lift. Vladimir Holan, *Czech.* EP, tr. by Jarmila Miher and Ian Miher

We still have bards who, with aspiring head. *Unknown.* EPCY *Fr.* Common Sense: A Poem.

We stood at the back door. And the Trains Go On. Philip Levine. GM

We stood at the edge. The Jews Speak in Heaven. Gary Catalano. NOBAu

We stood by a pond that winter day. Neutral Tones. Thomas Hardy. CABP; CMoP; EBVV; EnVR; HAP; HeIP-4; InPK-6; InPS-3; MoBrPo; MoP; NAEL-2; NOBVV; NoAM; NoP-4; OAEL-2; TFi; UnPo

We stood on the rented patio. Summer Storm. Dana Gioia. RA

We stood up before day. In the Dordogne. John Peale Bishop. OBWP; PeFWW; PoWW; VGW

We stopped. Lyubomir Levchev, *Bulgarian.* CEEP, tr. by Atanas Slavov

We stripped in the first warm spring night. Belle Isle, 1949. Philip Levine. ColAP; SAGP; VCAP

We Survive! Hirsch Glick, *Yiddish.* TrJP, tr. by Ruth Rubin

We Survived Them. Anna Swirszczynska, *Polish.* AF, tr. by Czeslaw Milosz

We swam in the rain-filled gully. Rain Ditch. Pinkie Gordon Lane. ISC

We swing ungirded hips. The Song of the Ungirt Runners. Charles Hamilton Sorley. MoBrPo; OBEV

We take long trips. Jelaluddin Rumi, *Persian.* LoL, tr. by Coleman Barks

We take place in what we believe. Elephant Rock. Primus St. John. PoBA

We talk about God. Saturday Night Worship. Ann Carhart. CrSp

We talk of light things you and I in this. Father and Daughter. Sonia Sanchez. FFC; GT

We talk of old men who have forgotten their / thoughts. Errore. Pier Giorgio Di Cicco. NOBC

We talked together in the Yung-shou Temple;. The Letter. Po Chü-i, *Chinese.* ChiP, tr. by Arthur Waley

We talked [or talk'd] with open heart, and tongue. The Fountain. Wordsworth. GTBS-P; OxAEP-2

We thank Thee, Heavenly Father. Thanks to Spring. Mary Anderson. BoTP

We Thank Thee, Lord. Calvin W. Laufer. AH

We thank Thee, Lord, for quiet upland lawns. Grace and Thanksgiving. Elizabeth Gould. BoTP

We Thank You! L. E. Cox. BoTP

We, that did nothing study but the way. A Renunciation. Henry, Bishop of Chichester King. OBEV

We that have done and thought. Spilt Milk. W. B. Yeats. OxBSP

We that with like hearts love, we lovers twain. A Vow to Heavenly Venus. Joachim Du Bellay, *French.* AWP, tr. by Andrew Lang

We, the boys of Sanpete County, in obedience to the cause. The Boys of Sanpete County. *Unknown.* AmFP

We the people of the United. Preamble to the Constitution of the United States. *Unknown.* CTV

We, the rescued. Chorus of the Rescued. Nelly Sachs, *German.* PoSu; WPOW, tr. by Ruth Mead and Matthew Mead

We, the unborn. Chorus of the Unborn. Nelly Sachs, *German.* NYBP, tr. by Ruth Mead and Matthew Mead

We the White Witches are, that free. Masque of the Virtues against Love. Mary Monck. ECWP; NOEC

We think of lukewarm water, hope to get in it. (LL) Kitchenette Building. Gwendolyn Brooks. BPo; FaBoWP; GT; NAAAL; NAAL-2; NoP-4; PoE; PoPoPo; Poetr; UnPo

We think our loved ones pull us under. On the Waterfront. Michael Foley. PNI

We think so then, and we thought still! (LL) The Pelican Chorus. Edward Lear. CTAV

We think to create festivals. Poem. Antonio Machado Ruiz, *Spanish.* AWP, tr. by John Dos Passos

We thirst at first—'tis Nature's Act. Emily Dickinson. NOCV

We thought at first, this man is a king for sure. Blue Blood. James Stephens. MoBrPo; OBCoV; OBMV

We thought that Winter with his hungry pack. On the Occurrence of a Spell of Arctic Weather in May, 1858. Paul Hamilton Hayne. APN-2

We thought the grass. Photographs: A Vision of Massacre. Michael S. Harper. PoBA

We three are on the cedar-shadowed lawn. George Meredith. NOBVV *Fr.* Modern Love.

We three, being thoroughly post. A Trois. Carol Flint. EC2

We three climbed the ever-narrowing. Space Trip. James Kirkup. SpW

We Three Kings ("We three kings all orient are"). *Unknown.* FaBoVe

We Three Kings of Orient are. John Henry Hopkins, Jr. AH; APN-2; PChr

We tied branches to our helmets. Camouflaging the Chimera. Yusef Komunyakaa. WeT

We told them the myths about others. The Port. Bernadette Mayer. FTOS

We too, we too, descending once again. The Too-Late Born. Archibald MacLeish. CMoP; LiTM; MeMAP; MoAmPo; OxBA; PeFWW

—We took our work, and went, you see. Recreation. Jane Taylor. OBCoV; OxBoLi; PEW; WoRP

We took their orders and are dead. (LL) Inscription for a War. Alec Derwent Hope. BMAP; NoP-4

We tore the green tree down. Verifying the Dead. James Welch. CDW

We touched land. Not That Far. May Miller. BlSi

We traded six AK-47s. The Movie. Steve Denning. CDa

We travel like other people, but we return to nowhere. As if travelling. Mahmoud Darwish. AF, tr. by Al-Udhari, Abdullah *Fr.* Poems after Beirut.

We trust and fear, we question and believe. Our Limitations. Oliver Wendell Holmes. NCAP

We turn aside from everything. Birthday Wishes to a Minister of the Gospel. Lizelia Augusta Jenkins Moorer. CBWP-3

We two are last in Hell: what may we fear[e]. Barley-Break; or, Last in Hell. Robert Herrick. CaPo

We two boys together clinging. Walt Whitman. APN-1; FP

We two, how long we were fool'd. Walt Whitman. ITG

We two look at each other, still and hushed. The Waning Night. Chế Lan Viên, *Vietnamese.* AVP, tr. by Huỳnh Sanh Thông

We two stood simply friend-like side by side. Inapprehensiveness. Robert Browning. CBLP; NOBVV

We uncountable dread legions of Labor. Vladimir Timofeievich Kirillov, *Russian.* TCRP, tr. by Albert C. Todd

We used to gather at the high window. When Mahalia Sings. Quandra Prettyman. PoBA

We used to get intelligence reports. Time on Target. William Daniel Ehrhart. CDa

We used to picnic where the thrift. Trebetherick. John Betjeman. CMoP

We Used to Play. Don Welch. Poetsp

We used to spend the spring together. The Most Beautiful Girl in the World. Lorenz Hart. OBAL

We used to talk of so many things. Before and After Marriage. Anne Campbell. PoToHe

We used to tell each other erotic stories. Sleepless Nights. Marilyn Nelson Waniek. ISC

We wait beneath the furnace-blast. The Furnace Blast. John Greenleaf Whittier. CBCWP

We waited for an omnibus. Walking Song. William E. Hickson. OxBChV

We waited in silence for our children. Death of the Miners or, The Widows of the Earth. Raymond Mazisi Kunene, *Zulu.* PeSAV, tr. by the author

We wake and watch the sun make bright. Another Sunday Morning. Derek Mahon. CIP-2

We wake; we wake the day. Indian Singing in 20th Century America. Gail Tremblay. HATNAP; LTA

We Walk the Way of the New World. Haki Madhbouti. BPo; PoBA

We walk towards a land not of our flesh. Mahmoud Darwish, *Arabic*. VCWP, *tr. by* Rana Kabbani

We walked across a frozen river in Manchuria. Expatriates. David Woo. OpBo

We walked all that way to the water. Boyhood Winter. George Eklund. IFJA

We walked [*or* walk'd] along, while bright and red. The Two April Mornings. Wordsworth. EBEV; GTBS-P; NAEL-2

We walked and blinked at sunlight on the snow. Winter Sonnet. Linda Beatrice Brown. GT

We wander in the stifling heat. Shadow in Stone. Janice Mirikitani. OpBo

We wander now who marched before. Old Soldier. Padraic Colum. OBMV

We wandered to the pine forest. Shelley. CH *Fr.* To Jane: The Recollection. OBNC

We want what is real. We want what is real. Don't deceive us. Song of the Bald Eagle. *Unknown.* APN-2 *Fr.* Minnetare Songs.

We wanted Li Wing. Lapsus Linguae. Keith Preston. NBLV; OBAL; OBCoV

We was in the 'Blue Dragon', Sid 'Awkins and me. Homœopathy. Sir John Collings Squire. NSI

We watch through the shop-front while. Blackie, The Electric Rembrandt. Thom Gunn. PFE

We watched from the house. I Was Sleeping Where the Black Oaks Move. Louise Erdrich. HATNAP; NoP-4; PoPoPo

We watched [*or* watch'd] her breathing thro' the night. The Death-Bed. Thomas Hood. GTBS-P; NOBE; OBEV; OBNC

We watched our love burn with the lumberyard. The Lumberyard. Ruth Herschberger. WPE

We watched the deaf-mute buried. Death of a Distant In-law. Patricia Traxler. BAP-94

We watched the rain sluice down. Gift for my Mother's 90th Birthday. Maude Meehan. NMM-2

We wear the mask that grins and lies. Paul Laurence Dunbar. AAP; APN-2; CrDW; ISC; NAAAL; NIP-4; NoP-4; PBMP; PoBA; PoPoPo; SSLK; TTY; UnPo

We weave up a switchback gully & out to sloping pasture. Naive Invocation. David Rivard. NAmP90

We went north / to escape winter. Indian Song: Survival. Leslie Marmon Silko. CDW; VoR

We went off to the wake of the "whelpish youngster." Harvest of the Sea. Máire Mhac an tSaoi. PBWP

We went out, early one morning. Out Fishing. Barbara Howes. WPE

We went there on the train. *They had big barges that they towed.* Protocols. Randall Jarrell. LCAP-2; OxBC; VGW

We went there to confer. Detroit Conference of Unity and Art. Nikki Giovanni. HoPM

We went to Oldshoremore. Itinerary. Edwin Morgan. OBCoV

We went to Pumpkin Point. My Tenth Birthday. Robert Adamson. BMAP

We went to the movies every Friday and Sunday. Sweethearts. J. A. Phillips. DeD

We Went Westward o social telepathy at the. From *Spoke / Aug 19.* Hannah Weiner. FTOS

We Went Westward o social telepathy at the. Seen Words. Hannah Weiner. FTOS *Fr.* Spoke Aug 19.

We were a noisy crew; the sun in heaven. Fishing. Wordsworth. *Fr.* Introduction—Childhood and School-Time. FHYEP *Fr.* The Prelude; Growth of a Poet's Mind [1850 vers.]

We were a people taut for war; the hills. Welsh History. Ronald Stuart Thomas. OBWVE

We were a tribe, a family, a people. Scotland 1941. Edwin Muir. CABP; FaBoTC; OxBS

We were able to notice that each one in a way carried a bundle, they were. Bundles for Them. Gertrude Stein. PFTM

We were all drunk, and Acindynus was determined to keep sober. Lucianus, *Greek.* GrAn, *tr. by* Edwin Morgan

We were all sitting round the table. Christmas Dinner. Michael Rosen. OBCP

We were alone and did your life. To Children. Lawrence McGaugh. PoBA

We were apart; yet, day by day. To Marguerite. Matthew Arnold. EnVR *Fr.* Switzerland.

We were as tough as our glasses. Tyson's Corner. Primus St. John. PoBA

We were born / in the time of the first perfected machine guns;. Dialectic. Victor Serge, *Russian*. AF, *tr. by* James Brook

We were born to be gray. We went to school. The Supremes. Cornelius Eady. CMAP; LTA

We were brought up to believe. Brief Thoughts on Floods. Miroslav Holub, *Czech*. PoSu, *tr. by* Ian *and* Jarmila Milner

We were camped upon the plains near the Cimmaron. Educated Feller. *Unknown.* PaTW

We were challenged by The Dingoes—they're the pride of Squatter's Gap. A Friendly Game of Football. Edward Dyson. CBAP

We were consigned. Continuous Time. Milo De Angelis, *Italian*. NeIt, *tr. by* Lawrence Venuti

We were crowded in the cabin. Ballad of the Tempest. James Thomas Fields. FaBoBe; PoLF

We were dauntless then. Remembering Mexico, 1969. Barbara Lau. LoHo

We were enclosed. Catherine of Siena (A. K. A. Saint Catherine). WPoS, *tr. by* Suzanne, O. P. Noffke *Fr.* Prayer 20.

We were fancydancing, you see. Powwow Polaroid. Sherman Alexie. UnSA

We were finishing the fourth grade as the storm gathered. The Beginning. Vladimir Nikolaevich Sokolov, *Russian*. TCRP, *tr. by* Simon Franklin

We were forty miles from Albany. The E-ri-e. *Unknown.* AS

We were good, good and obedient. Sandor Csoori, *Hungarian*. VCWP, *tr. by* Roberts, Len *and* László Vértes

We were halfway through July. Handsome afternoon! On the Banks of the Duero. Antonio Machado Ruiz, *Spanish*. STV, *tr. by* John Frederick Nims

We were in a room that was once an attic. Amiel's Leg. Thomas Lux. CMAP

We were in love and his uncle had a farm. Geese. Mark Cox. NAmP90

We were love. Yaedi Ignatow. IFJA

We were married near the base. Happiness. Ruth Stone. NAmP90

We were nearly. Above the Pool. John Montague. NOIV

We were never invited to his house. My Rich Uncle, Whom I Only Met Three Times. Marge Piercy. UnSA

We were no good as murderers, we were clowns. (LL) Stephano Remembers. James Simmons. PBCIP; PNI

We were not even moving. No one was moving. On the Eve of Our Mutually Assured Destruction. C. D. Wright. LCAP-2

We were not here. Plato was a spider. Spinoza Was a Bee. Jaroslaw Marek Rymkiewicz, *Polish*. CBNP, *tr. by* Czeslaw Milosz

We were not likened to dogs among the Gentiles—They pity a dog. Uri Zvi Greenberg, *Hebrew*. MHP, *tr. by* Ruth Finer Mintz

We were not many—we who stood. Monterey. Charles Fenno Hoffman. FaBoBe

We were not raised to look in. You Were Never Miss Brown to Me. Sherley Anne Williams. GT

We were out in Arizona, on the Painted Desert ground. Arizona. *Unknown.* AmFP

We were playing on the green together. "Is It Nothing to You?" May Probyn. OBEV

We were riding through frozen fields in a wagon at dawn. Encounter. Czeslaw Milosz, *Polish*. ChAP; PiM, *tr. by* Czeslaw Milosz *and* Lillian Vallee

We were rumbling o'er Trumpington stones. (LL) The Country Clergyman's Trip to Cambridge. Thomas Babington Macaulay, 1st Baron Macaulay. OBSV; OxBoLi; PeLV

We were sick of seeing the liners leave. Refugees at Cobh. Sean Dunne. BiHa

We Were Sisters Weren't We. Katie Donovan. BiHa

We were situated on the approaches to a village. Tenderness. Aleksey Aleksandrovich Surkov, *Russian*. TCRP, *tr. by* Lubov Yakovleva

We were smoking some of this knockout weed when. Operation Memory. David Lehman. NAmP90

We were so poor I had to take the place of the. Charles Simic. VCAP *Fr.* The World Doesn't End.

We were the happiest pair of human kind. The Happiest Pair. George Lyttelton. LBC

We were the wrecked elect. The Fiction-Makers. Anne Stevenson. DiPo

We were then waging war against the French. The Old Vow. Trần Huiền Ân, *Vietnamese*. AVP, *tr. by* Huỳnh Sanh Thông

We were Three. Claribel Alegría, *Spanish*. AF, *tr. by* Carolyn Forché

We were three women, three men. The Sorrow of Kodio. *Unknown, Baule*. PBA, *tr. by* Miriam Koshland

We were together. Yakamochi, *Japanese*. OHPJ, *tr. by* Kenneth Rexroth

We were together in my time and at your place. In My Time, at Your Place. Yehuda Amichai, *Hebrew*. IP, *tr. by* Warren Bargad *and* Stanley F. Chyet

We were together since the War began. A Servant. Rudyard Kipling. PeFWW *Fr.* Epitaphs of the War [1914–1918]. OBWP

We were very tired, we were very merry. Recuerdo. Edna St. Vincent Millay. ChAP; ImPo; LiTM; MeMAP; NAAL-2; NoAM; OxBA; PiM; PoA; Poetr; TAP

We were waiting at the station. The Parting Kiss. Josephine D. Henderson Heard. CBWP-4

We were walking. Rice Will Grow Again. Frank A. Cross Jr. CDa

We were young, we were merry, we were very very wise. Unwelcome. Mary Elizabeth Coleridge. CH; OBEV; OBNC; VWP; WPE

We whisper in her ear, "You are not true." (LL) Epistemology. Richard Wilbur. CRP; NOBA; NoAM; OxBSP

We who also linger near the border of insanities. Near the Border of Insanities. Dannie Abse. PoA

We who are called Australians have no country. Rex Ingamells. NOBAu *Fr.* Unknown Land.

We who are here present thank the Great Spirit that we are here to praise Him. The Thanksgivings. *Unknown, Iroquois Native American.* APN-2, *tr. by* Harriet Maxwell Converse

We who are left, how shall we look again. Lament. Wilfrid Wilson Gibson. NSI; OxBTC

We who find no joy in celebrity. Rufinus Domesticus, *Greek.* InMo, *tr. by* Sam Hamill

We who had known the desert's grit and granite. Exodus. Charles Reznikoff. ChIV-1

We who have always looked with tolerant irony. A Prayer for the End of the Century. Herberto Padilla, *Spanish.* VCWP, *tr. by* Alastair Reid *and* Andrew Hurley

We who have loved, alas! may not be friends. Corinne Roosevelt Robinson. LW

We who must act as handmaidens. A Muse of Water. Carolyn Kizer. FFC; VCAP

We who play under the pines. The Song of the Rabbits outside the Tavern. Elizabeth Jane Coatsworth. OBCA; SoSe-8

We who survived the war and took to wife. Thirtieth Anniversary Report of the Class of '41. Howard Nemerov. HCAP

We who with songs beguile your pilgrimage. Prologue: "We Who with Songs Beguile Your Pilgrimage." James Elroy Flecker. FaPoR; OBMV; OxBTC; UV *Fr.* The Golden Journey to Samarkand.

We, whose lungs fill with the sweetness of day. Child of Europe. Czeslaw Milosz, *Polish.* AF, *tr. by* Jan Darowski

We will be passing the telephone booths soon. Nonplussed. Ken Bolton. BMAP

We will go no more to Shaemus, at the Nip. Shaemus. Conrad Potter Aiken. OxBA

We will go on to the end. (LL) Tortoise Gallantry. D. H. Lawrence. APo; CMoP; MoP

We will go to the wood, says Robin to Bobbin. *Unknown.* OxNR

We will grow old, and older. Robin Morgan. CrSp *Fr.* A Ceremony.

We will have to get down on all fours and eat the grasses of the cemeteries forever. Federico García Lorca. *See* Little Infinite Poem.

We will kill our love. We Are Going to Shoot at the Heart. Anna Swirszczynska, *Polish.* PoSu, *tr. by* Czeslaw Milosz *and* Leonard Nathan

We Will Live Forever. Yehuda Amichai, *Hebrew.* IP, *tr. by* Warren Bargad *and* Stanley F. Chyet

We will never meet again face to face. Yosami, the wife of Hitomaro, *Japanese.* WPJ, *tr. by* Kenneth Rexroth *and* Ikuko Atsumi

We Will Not Fear. David Diamond. AH

We will not whisper, we have found the place. Sonnet. Hilaire Belloc. MoBrPo

We will pull, we will haul, hearty, healthy, and gay. Blow the Man Down ("I'll put on my boots and I'll blow the man down"). *Unknown.* AmFP

We will return to life. Comanche Ghost Dance: An Impression. Lance Henson. VoR

We will see more passing than any. Nostalgia. Christopher Buckley. SeSe

We will sing a song. Songs from the Great Feast to the Dead. *Unknown, Eskimo.* APN-2, *tr. by* Edward William Nelson

We will take it seriously as we open our morning paper. Sonnet to Be Written from Prison. Robert Adamson. CBAP

We wish a drove of weasels transmuted into horses. Song of the Weasel. *Unknown.* APN-2 *Fr.* Minnetare Songs.

We wish not the mechanic arts to scan. Power of Women, THe. Matilda Barbara Betham-Edwards. ECWP; Ro

We wish to bury our dead. Now, a funeral. Funeral Sermon, Soweto. Wole Soyinka. VCWP

We wish you a happy May. (LL) May Day. *Unknown.* CTV

We with our Fair pitched among the feathery clover. The Individualist Speaks. Louis MacNeice. OBMV

We woke early. Names in Monterchi: To Rachel. James Wright. NNaP

We woke near midnight. Eruption: Pu'u Ō'ō. Garrett Kaoru Hongo. LoL

We Women. Edith Södergran, *Swedish.* WPOW, *tr. by* Samuel Charters

We wonder what the horoscope did show. Shakespeare. Henrietta Cordelia Ray. CBWP-3

We Wondered about the Mellow Peaches. Jack A. Mapanje. HBAPE

We wondered at the tobacco plants there in France. Tobacco Plant. Ivor Gurney. FP

We wondered what our walk should mean. Peace Walk. William Stafford. Poetsp

We won't forget the padre in a hurry. The Padre. Frank Ormsby. BiHa

We wore black arm bands, / put up a sign / in bold letters. Nellie Wong. *See* Can't Tell.

We work here together. The Pine Planters. Thomas Hardy. FaBoVe

We work, play, don't cross-reference calendars. Marilyn Hacker. VCAP *Fr.* Taking Notice.

We would awaken in a twilight gloom. Aleksandr Petrovich Mezhirov, *Russian.* TCRP, *tr. by* Deming Brown

We would climb the highest dune. With Kit, Age Seven, at the Beach. William Stafford. LiLi; RaBo

We would live merrily, merrily. (LL) The Merman. Tennyson. BoTP; UV

We would park on any quiet street. First Boyfriend. Sharon Olds. DeD

We Would See Jesus. Anna Bartlett Warner. AH

We would see jesus; earth is grand. Sir, We Would See Jesus. Frances Ellen Watkins Harper. AAP

We write them there forever. (LL) Walt Whitman. Edwin Arlington Robinson. APN-2; NCAP; OxBA

Weak is the assurance that weak flesh reposeth. Sonnet 58. Edmund Spenser. *Fr.* Amoretti. AAS

Weak man is like a broken jug, A. Lucianus, *Greek.* InMo, *tr. by* Sam Hamill

Weak Monk, The. Stevie Smith. BoWoP; FaBoTw

Weak sun. Rod Willmot. HA

Weak-winged is song. Ode Recited at the Harvard Commemoration (July 21, 1865). James Russell Lowell. APN-1; CBCWP; NOBA; OBWP

Weaker the wine, The. Su Tung-p'o, *Chinese.* OHPC, *tr. by* Kenneth Rexroth

Weakness, The. Toi Derricotte. GT; LTA

Weakness, The. Bernard O'Donoghue. NoP-4

Wealth. Ralph Waldo Emerson. APN-1

Wealth. Sadi. AWP, *tr. by* Sir Edwin Arnold *Fr.* The Gulistan.

Wealth came by water to this farmless island. Delos. Bernard Spencer. NoAM

Wealth covers sin—the poor. Epigram. Kassia, *Greek.* WPOW, *tr. by* Patrick Diehl

Wealth unto every man, I see. Worldly Wealth. Rowland Watkyns. FaBoEE

Wealthy Cit, grown old in trade, The. The Cit's Country Box. Robert Lloyd. NOEC

Weapon, The. "Hugh MacDiarmid." RB

Weapon shapely, naked, wan. The Broad-Ax. Walt Whitman. MoAmPo *Fr.* Song of the Broad-Axe. CA

Weapon that comes down as still, A. The Ballot. John Pierpont. APN-1 *Fr.* Word from a Petitioner.

Weapon that you fought with was a word, The. "He Knoweth Not That the Dead Are Thine." Mary Elizabeth Coleridge. OBNC; SAGP

Weapons. Anna Wickham. MoBrPo

Weapons Training. Bruce Dawe. OBCoV

Wear a dress. An Answer to a Man's Question, "What Can I Do About Women's Liberation?" Susan Griffin. GLP; NMM-2

Wear[e] all his beard, and none up[p]on his chin[n]. (LL) A Lady's Prayer to Cupid. Thomas Carew, *after* Giovanni Battista Guarini. CaPo; OBVE

Wear the heart like a home. Confederacy. Elise Paschen. FFC

Wear thou this fresh green garland this one day. A Garland for Advancing Years. William Bell Scott. GSo

Wearied arm, and broken sword. William Makepeace Thackeray. AiP *Fr.* Pocahontas.

Wearied, exhausted, dully sleeping. (LL) Spring in New Hampshire. Claude McKay. ChAP

Wearied of its own turning. The Burning Wheel. Aldous Leonard Huxley. ChIV-1

Wearily, drearily. In Prison. William Morris. PeVV

Wearin' o' the Green, The. *Unknown.* NOIV

Weariness. Sara Teasdale. SAGP

Weariness. Mary E. Tucker. CBWP-1

Weariness of life that has no will, The. Everyman. Siegfried Sassoon. MoBrPo

Wearing a Worn-Out Coat. Chin Nung, *Chinese.* CoBLCP, *tr. by* Jonathan Chaves

Wearing Achilles' Armour, Patroclus, along with the Myrmidons, Attacks the Trojans. Homer. OBVE, *tr. by* Christopher Logue *Fr.* The Iliad.

Wearing an overcoat in August heat. Bag Woman. Dudley Randall. NoAM

Wearing My Cap Backwards. Cheryl Clarke. NMM-2

Wearing my yellow straw hat. My Yellow Straw Hat. Lessie Jones Little. TLR

Wearing of [or Wearin' o'] the Green, The. *Unknown.* AWP; FaPoR; IIP; OxBoLi

Wearing that same black dress. The Women You Are Accustomed To. Lucille Clifton. GT

Wearing worry about money like a hair shirt. Worry about Money. Kathleen Jessie Raine. FaBoTw

Wears on his smiling face a dream of Spring. Coleridge. *See* Work Without Hope.

Weary already, weary miles to-night. A Match with the Moon. D. G. Rossetti. NOBVV

Weary Blues, The. Langston Hughes. ColAP; FaBoA; ISC; MoP; NAAAL; NOBA; NoAM; NoP-4; PoPoPo; SAmP

Weary day!—the foul Witch-Bride. (LL) The Witch-Bride. William Allingham. OxBSn

Weary, I open wide the antique pane. Poetry and the Poet. Henry Cuyler Bunner. OBAL

Weary I was, and thought to sit at rest. Elizabeth, Lady Culross Melvill. *Fr.* A Godly Dream. WPE

Weary is he, and sick of the sorrow of war. The Soldier Is Home. John Shaw Neilson. CBAP

Weary lot is thine, fair maid, A. The Rover's Adieu [or Farewell]. Sir Walter Scott. CH; EnLoPo; GTBS-P; NOBE; OBEV; OBNC *Fr.* Rokeby.

Weary men, what reap ye?—"Golden corn for the stranger." The Famine Year. Lady Jane Francesca Wilde. IIP; TIRV

Weary of myself, and sick of asking. Self-Dependence. Matthew Arnold. PBMP

Weary on ye, sad waves! On an Island. "Ethna Carbery." WPE

Weary Road, The. Lu Chao-lin, *Chinese.* SuSp, *tr.* by Robin D. S. Yates

Weary Road, The. Pao Chao, *Chinese.*
  "Have you not seen the grasses on the riverbank?" SuSp, *tr.* by Irving Y. Lo
  "Water spilled on level ground." SuSp, *tr.* by Irving Y. Lo

Weary Song to a Slow Sad Tune, A. Li Ch'ing-chao, *Chinese.* BoWoP; OHMPC, *tr.* by Kenneth Rexroth

Weary the cry of the wind is, weary the sea. Sorrow of Mydath. John Masefield. MoBrPo

Weary was when coming on a stream. Aswelay. Norman Henry, II Pritchard. PoBA

Weary way-wanderer, languid and sick at heart. The Soldier's Wife. Robert Southey. OxBSP

Weary with reading and with meditation. The Storm and Calm: Sent from Embden to M. Edw. Ma. and M. Tho. Ly. Nicholas Murford. NOSC

Weary with toil, I haste me to my bed. Sonnet 27. Shakespeare. HeIP-4; NoSic; SCGP *Fr.* Sonnets.

Weary, worn, and sorrow-laden. Storm-Beaten. Clara Ann Thompson. CBWP-2

Weary year his race now having run, The. Sonnet 62. Edmund Spenser. *Fr.* Amoretti. AAS

Weasel, by a person caught, A. The Man and the Weasel. Phaedrus, *Latin.* AWP, *tr.* by Christopher Smart

Weather, The. Gavin Ewart. OTCP

Weather. Archibald MacLeish. MoAmPo

Weather. William Meredith. NYBP; Poetr

Weather. Eve Merriam. NOxBChV; TLR
  ("Pudmuddle jump in and slide!, A.") (LL) NOxBChV

Weather. May Swenson. PaTW

Weather. *Unknown.* ACTP; ImGa; OTCP

Weather buffets our houses in armour all night. Gales. Anne Stevenson. Spl

Weather changeable at dusk and dawn, The. Written on the Lake, Returning from the Retreat at Stone Cliff. Hsieh Ling-yün, *Chinese.* CoBCP, *tr.* by Burton Watson

Weather-Cock Points South, The. Amy Lowell. CPO; NALW; NoP-4

Weather Ear. Norman Nicholson. OxBSP

Weather isn't news unless extreme, The. No News at All. Jack Butler. MT

Weather-leech of the topsail shivers, The. Tacking Ship Off Shore. Walter Mitchell. FaBoBe

Weather Newly Cleared. Wang Wei, *Chinese.* CoBCP, *tr.* by Burton Watson

Weather of Invention, The. Leslie Adrienne Miller. CMAP

Weather of Olympus, The. Robert Graves. FaBoEE; OBCoV

Weather of Six Mornings, The. Jane Cooper. NYBP

Weather of the soul, vandalized, out-at-elbow. A blight. Spared, though, The. John Ashbery. *See* Cæsura.

Weather of this winter night, my mistress, The. Childlessness. James Merrill. CoAmPo; ColAP

Weather Signs. Aratus. HePo, *tr.* by Barbara Hughes Fowler *Fr.* Phaenomena.

Weather wonderful—cannot go out in daylight. Honeymoon Postcard. Paul Durcan. OBCoV

Weathercock, The. Rose Fyleman. BoTP

Weathercock: I am puff-breasted, proud-crested. *Unknown.* EEP, *tr.* by Michael Alexander *Fr.* Riddles (Exeter Book).

Weathercock, The: "I puff my breast out, my neck swells." Cynewulf. RB, *tr.* by Geoffrey Grigson; ASW, *tr.* by Kevin Crossley-Holland *Fr.* Riddles (Exeter Book).
  ("Weathercock: My breast is puffed up and my neck is swollen.") ASW, *tr.* by Kevin Crossley-Holland

Weathered Ides Grant Young Flesh. Steve Ellis. PT

Weathered raft I saw myself. Song of the Andoumboulou: 12. Nathaniel Mackey. FTOS

Weathering. Fleur Adcock. DiPo

Weathering Out. Rita Dove. CMAP; LCAP-2; NoAM

Weathering the Depths. Alfred M. Lee. AmPA

Weathers [or Weather]. Thomas Hardy. ACTP; BoTP; CH; EBEvV; FaBoCh; MoBrPo; NTP; OBMV; RB

Weather's cleared, The. We're filming at Versailles. Clive James. OBSV *Fr.* To Pete Atkin: A Letter from Paris.

Weave garlands of roses for our hair. Anacreon, *Greek.* InMo, *tr.* by Sam Hamill

Weave like a web in the air / Divinely superfluous beauty. (LL) Divinely Superfluous Beauty. Robinson Jeffers. HeIP-4; MoAmPo

Weave the warp, and weave the woof. The Curse upon Edward. Thomas Gray. OBEV

Weaver, The. William Henry Burleigh. BLPA

Weaver, The ("I was a bachelor, I lived by myself"). *Unknown.* AS

Weaver bird built in our house, The. Kofi Awoonor. HBAPE; PBMAP

Weaver sat by the side of his loom, A. "Fanny Forester." BLPA

Weavers. Heinrich Heine. TrJP

Weavers Song, The. Thomas Deloney. PBRV

Weaving a garland long ago. Anacreon, *Greek.* InMo, *tr.* by Sam Hamill

Weaving at the Window. Wang Chien, *Chinese.* SuSp, *tr.* by William H. Nienhauser

Weaving Love-Knots. Hsüeh T'ao. BoWoP, *tr.* by Carolyn Kizer

Weaving Love-Knots 2. Hsüeh T'ao. BoWoP, *tr.* by Carolyn Kizer

Web, The. Gregory O'Donoghue. BIrV

Web, The. Theodore Weiss. CoAP

Webern. Thomas William Shapcott. *Fr.* Piano Pieces. CBAP

Webster was much possessed by death. Whispers of Immortality. T. S. Eliot. CMoP; CT; NOBA; NoAM; OBMV; OxAEP-2

We'd all had a bit too much that night when you brought out. The Sea-Cucumber. Martin Johnston. BMAP

"We'd better leave him in the sump," he said. (LL) Mending Sump. Kenneth Koch. BXAP; InPK-6; MoP; NeAP; NoAM

We'd ever so many kinds of cake. The Pirates' Tea-Party. Dorothy Una Ratcliffe. BoTP

We'd found an old Boche dug-out, and he knew. The Sentry. Wilfred Owen. EBNV; PeFWW; PoWW

We'd gained our first objective hours before. Counter-Attack. Siegfried Sassoon. MoBrPo; OxAEP-2; PeFWW; PoFWW; PoWW; SAGP

We'd launch out, but a spiral failure binds so close. John Wilkinson. NBrP

We'd rather have the iceberg than the ship. The Imaginary Iceberg. Elizabeth Bishop. FaBoWP; ImPo; LiTM; MoAmPo; PFE

Weddin' a woo a clog an' a shoe, A. Weddings. *Unknown.* FaBoVe

Wedding, The. Conrad Potter Aiken. CMoP; TAP

Wedding, A. Boris Pasternak, *Russian.*
  "Into the enormous sky flew." ITG, *tr.* by Hass, Robert and Stephen Mitchell

Wedding, A. James Tate. NoAM

Wedding, The. Pavel Nikolaevich Vasilyev. TCRP, *tr.* by David Macduff *Fr.* The Salt Riot.

Wedding. Nikolai Alekseievich Zabolotsky, *Russian.* TCRP, *tr.* by Daniel Weissbort

Wedding Anniversary. Margaret E. Bruner. PoToHe

Wedding Coat, The. Harriet Rose. BrRo

Wedding Day. Seamus Heaney. OxAEP-2

Wedding Day at Nagasaki. Rodney Hall. CBAP

Wedding Feast, The. Luis de Góngora y Argote. *Fr.* The First Solitude. OBVE, *tr.* by Edward Meryon Wilson

Wedding Feast, The. Edgar Lee Masters. ChIV-2

Wedding Gift, The. Minna Irving. BLPA

Wedding in Hanover. Lorna Goodison. GT

Wedding in the Courthouse, The. Kathleen Norris. CrSp

Wedding in the Port. Sophie Behrens. NBrP

Wedding Morn. D. H. Lawrence. MoBrPo

Wedding Night, The. Anne Sexton. PoA

Wedding night / Graciela bled lightly. Graciela. Gary Soto. NoAM

Wedding over, The. Arizona Zipper. HA

Wedding Party. Donald Hall. LCAP-2

Wedding Preparations in the Country. David St. John. LCAP-2

Wedding Reception. Melinda Goodman. GLP

Wedding Ring, The. George Crabbe. *See* The Marriage Ring.

Wedding Song. Patricia Storace. FFC

Wedding Song. *Unknown. See* My Lord Summons Me.

Wedding Song in honor of R. Solomon ben Matir. Moses ibn Ezra, *Hebrew.* "Rejoice, O youth, in the loving hind." TrJP, *tr. by* Solomon Solis-Cohen

Wedding Song: Lullaby for Sleepy Lovers. Theocritus, *English.* ITG, *tr. by* John Dryden *and* Nahum Tate

Wedding Toast, A. Richard Wilbur. ITG

Wedding Vow, The. Sharon Olds. ITG

Wedding-Wind. Philip Larkin. ITG

Weddings. *Unknown.* FaBoVe

Wedlock; a Satire. Hetty Wright. NOEC

Wedlock, a Satire. Mehetabel Wright. ECWP

Wednesbury Cocking, The. *Unknown.* EnSB

Wednesday. Marvin Bell. VCAP

Wednesday at North Hatley. Ralph Gustafson. NOBC

Wednesday in Holy Week. Christina Rossetti. *Unknown.*

Wednesday Night Prayer Meeting. Jay Wright. ISC; PoBA

Wednesday of Holy Week, 1940. Kenneth Rexroth. ChIV-1

Wednesday on a barge. Poems from Saint Pelagia Prison. Philippe Soupault, *French.* AF, *tr. by* Schmidt, Paulette

Wednesday; or, The Dumps. John Gay. OAEL-1 *Fr.* The Shepherd's Week.

Wednesdays at the bone orchard deliveries. Memo. Charles Lynch. PoBA

Wee Davie Daylicht. Robert Tennant. OxBChV

Wee Falorie Man, The. *Unknown.* FaBoVe

Wee Jamie, a canny young Scot. Limerick. Joyce Johnson. PeLi

Wee jenny wren she lays sixteen, The. *Unknown.* FaBoVe

Wee leave Creete Country; and our sayls unwrapped uphoysing. Virgil. BIrV; OBVE, *tr. by* Richard Stanyhurst *Fr.* The Aeneid [*or* Eneados, *Aeneis].*

Wee little nut lay deep in its nest, A. Among the Nuts. *Unknown.* BoTP

Wee little worm in a hickory-nut, A. James Whitcomb Riley. FPC

Wee, modest, crimson-tipped flow'r. To a Mountain Daisy [On Turning One Down, with the Plough, in April—1786]. Robert Burns. PoLF

Wee, sleeket [*or* sleekit], [, cowran], cow'rin' [*or* cowran], tim'rous beastie. To a Mouse[, On Turning Her Up in Matir. Nest, with the Plough, November, 1785]. Robert Burns. APo; CABP; EBEvV; FaBoVe; GEA; GTBS-P; HAP; HeIP-4; ImPo; InPS-3; NAEL-2; NOEC; NoP-4; OAEL-1; OxAEP-2; OxBS; PoE; PoLF; Ro; SCGP; TFi; UV

Wee Tammy Tyrie. *Unknown.* OxNR

Wee Wee Man, The. *Unknown.* CH; EBEV; ESPB; FaBoCh; OAEL-1; OxBB

Wee, wee tailor. The Oviparous Tailor. Thomas Lovell Beddoes. CBNP

Wee Willie Gray, an' his leather wallet. Robert Burns. OxBChV

Wee Willie Winkie rins [*or* runs] through the town. Willie Winkie. William Miller. LB; NOBVV; OxBChV; OxNR; ReMoGo

Weed from Catholic Europe, it took root, A. Macao. W. H. Auden. MeMAP *Fr.* A Voyage.

Weed Puller. Theodore Roethke. AmPP; HCAP; NAAL-2

Weeding. Michael Hamburger. OBGa

Weeds. J. D. McClatchy. GaP

Weeds, The. Gregory Orr. WeT

Weeds. Virgil, *Latin.* OBCVT, *tr. by* Hoblyn, Robert

Weeds grow shamelessly / on my tongue. Self-Portrait. Cecil Bodker, *Danish.* BoWoP, *tr. by* Nadia Christensen

Weedy creek, A. Making a Door. Dennis Schmitz. LCAP-2

Weedy light through the uncurtained glass, The. Hiatus. Margaret Avison. HAP

Week after our child was born, A. New Mother. Sharon Olds. CrSp

Week after week, month after month, in pain. Memorial Poem. Roy Fuller. OxBSP

Week ago I had a fire, A. All in June. W. H. Davies. OxBSP

Week-End. Harold Monro. "Train, The! The twelve o'clock for paradise." MoBrPo

Week-End by the Sea. Edgar Lee Masters. MoAmPo

Week-End Indian, The. Anita Endrezze-Danielson. VoR

Week is dealt out like a hand, The. Hope. Randall Jarrell. MoAmPo

Week of Birthdays, A. Mother Goose. *See* Birthdays.

Week on the Concord and Merrimack Rivers, A. Henry David Thoreau. Haze. Mist. AWP; AmPP; OxBA

Week-Seek. Jim Tollerud. VoR

Week Seven. Ellsworth McGranahan Keane. HCP

Week the Dirigible Came, The. Jay Meek. CMAP

Weekend Equestrian, The. Michael S. Weaver. GT

Weeksville Women. Elouise Loftin. ISC; PoBA

Weep again, come another year. (LL) Lament for Adonis. Bion, *Greek.* HePo, *tr. by* Barbara Hughes Fowler; AWP, *tr. by* John Addington Symonds

Weep, ah weep love's losing, love's with its dwelling place. Ode. Imr el Kais, *Arabic.* AWP; TAL, *tr. by* Lady Anne Blunt *and* Wilfrid Scawen Blunt *Fr.* The Mu'allaqat.

Weep, and weep long, but do not weep for me. To a Troubled Friend. James Wright. Son

Weep, Children of Israel. Thomas Moore. ChIV-1

Weep for me, friends, for now that I am hence. Tears of the World. Mu'tamid, King of Seville, *Arabic.* AWP, *tr. by* Dulcie L. Smith

Weep, Israel! your tardy meed outpour. Bar Kochba. Emma Lazarus. TrJP

Weep, Lovers, with Love's very self doth weep. Dante. AWP *Fr.* La Vita Nuova.

Weep No More. John Fletcher. CH; OBEV; OxAEP-1 *Fr.* The Queen of Corinth.

Weep no more, woful shepherds weep no more. Milton. *Fr.* Lycidas. AWP; CABP; ClHu; EBEV; EBEvV; FHYEP; GTBS-P; HAP; ImPo; InPS-3; NOBE; NOSC; NoP-4; OAEL-1; OBEV; OxAEP-1; PBRV; PFE; PoEL-3; PoPoPo; Poetr; SCGP; TFi; UnPo

Weep not because this child hath died so young. On the Death of Mistress Mary Prideaux. William Strode. NOSC

Weep not for little Leonie. Compensation. Harry Graham. CBNP; PeLV *Fr.* Some Ruthless Rhymes.

Weep[e] not, my wanton, smile upon my knee. Sephestia's Song to Her Child[e]. Robert Greene. NOBE; NTP; NoSic; OBEV; OxAEP-1; PoEL-2; SCGP *Fr.* Menaphon.

Weep not, nor backward turn your beams. A Lover, upon an Accident Necessitating His Departure, Consults with Reason. Thomas Carew. CaPo

Weep not that you no longer feel the tide. Lost Youth. Sir Roger Casement. TIRV

Weep Not To-Day. Robert Bridges. OBMV

Weep not, weep not[, / She is not dead]. Go Down Death. James Weldon Johnson. BkSV; ISC; PoBA

Weep o'er the mis'ries of a wretched maid. The Dying Prostitute; an Elegy. Thomas Holcroft. NOEC

Weep, weep for him, the Man of God. Weep, Children of Israel. Thomas Moore. ChIV-1

Weep! Weep! Weep! Tumadir al-Khansa for Her Brother. *Unknown.* AWP; PBWP *Fr.* The Thousand and One Nights.

Weep, weep, ye dwellers in the delvèd earth. Elegy on the Death of Bingo Our Trench Dog. Sir Edward De Stein. NSI

Weep, weep, ye Loves and Cupids all. Catullus, *Latin.* OBCVT, *tr. by* G. S. Davies

Weep, weep, ye woodmen! wail. Dirge. Anthony Munday. CH; CTC *Fr.* Death of Robert, Earl of Huntingdon.

Weep [*or* Weepe] with me, all you that read. Epitaph On Solomon Pavy, [Salomon *or* Salathiel Pavy], a Child of Q[ueen] El[izabeth's] Chapel. Ben Jonson. BeJo; GEA; HoPM; NAEL-1; NOBE; NOSC; OAEL-1; OBEV; PoEL-2; SCGP; SeCP; TFi; UnPo

Weep, you may weep, for you may touch them not. (LL) Greater Love. Wilfred Owen. APAD; CMoP; EnLoPo; FaBoMo; GTBS-P; ImPo; LiTM; MoBrPo; MoP; NoAM; TFi

Weep you no more, sad fountains. *Unknown.* CH; EBEV; EnLoPo; GBL; HAP; LBC; NOSC; NTP; NoP-4; NoSic; PoE; PoEL-2; TFi ("Softly, now softly lies / Sleeping.") (LL) LBC; NoP-4

Weepe for the dead, for they have lost this light. On Himselfe. Robert Herrick. FaBoEE; NOSC

Weepe O mine eyes. *Unknown.* PoEL-2

Weepe pretious Teares upon the stones. Bible, *O.T. See* Psalm 137.

Weeper, The. Richard Crashaw. FSCP *See* Saint Mary Magdalene.

Weepers, The. Rodney Jones. NAmP90

Weepers Tower in Amsterdam, The. Paul Goodman. VGW

Weepies, The. Paul Muldoon. NoAM; PNI

Weeping and Kissing. Sir Edward Sherburne. NOSC

Weeping and wakeful all the night I lie. Rhodanthe. Agathias, *Greek.* AWP, *tr. by* Andrew Lang

Weeping for Hsüeh Tzu-shu. Liu K'o-chuang, *Chinese.* CoBCP, *tr. by* Burton Watson

Weeping for the Zen Master Po-yen. Chia Tao, *Chinese*. SuSp, *tr. by* Stephen Owen

Weeping for Ying Yao. Wang Wei, *Chinese*. CoBCP, *tr. by* Burton Watson

Weeping Garden, The. Boris Pasternak, *Russian*. GaP, *tr. by* Eugene M. Kayden

Weeping Headstones of the Isaac Becketts, The. Paul Durcan. PBCIP

Weeping Melpomene assist my lays. The Fatal Dream; or, The Unhappy Favourite. Emanuel Collins. NOEC

Weeping, murmuring, complaining. A Sonnet. Oliver Goldsmith. NOIV

Weeping oaks grieve, chestnuts raise. Basil Bunting. PFTM

Weeping or smiling pearls to Celia's face. (LL) Lips and Eyes. Giovanni Battista Marino, *Italian*. OBVE; OxBSP, *tr. by* Thomas Carew

Weeping Pleiads wester, The. Sappho, *Greek*. OBCVT, *tr. by* Alfred Edward Housman

Weeping rose in her dark night of leaves, The. A Song at Morning. Dame Edith Sitwell. CMoP

Weeping Sinner, Dry Your Tears. Oliver Holden. AH

Weeping Willow, The. *Unknown*. AmFP

Weeping Woman. Denise Levertov. AF

Weeps out of western country something new. The Birth in a Narrow Room. Gwendolyn Brooks. BlSi; NoP-4

Weevily Wheat. *Unknown*. AS

Weevily Wheat. *Unknown*. AS; AmFP

Weft of leafless spray, A. November. William Dean Howells. APN-2; GaP

Wei-ch'i Chess. Li K'ai-hsien, *Chinese*. CoBLCP, *tr. by* Jonathan Chaves

Wei Wind. Confucius, *Chinese*.

Pedlar. CTC; OBVE, *tr. by* Ezra Pound

Weigh me the fire; or canst thou find. To Find[e] God. Robert Herrick. BeJo; NoP-4

Weighing-In, The. Ibn al-Rumi, *Arabic*. ArPe, *tr. by* Omar S. Pound

Weighing-machine, The. Pierre McOrlan, *French*. MFP, *tr. by* Martin Sorrell

Weighing the Baby. Ethel Lynn Beers. PoToHe

Weighing the ste[a]dfastness and state. Man. Henry Vaughan. ESCV; FMP; GeHe; MeLP; NOBE; NOCV; OBEV; PoEL-2; SCGP

Weight of stones, of thoughts. Philippe Jaccottet, *French*. VCWP, *tr. by* Derek Mahon

Weight of Sweetness, The. Li-Young Lee. RaBo

Weightless and / "smiling." (LL) In a Season of Unemployment. Margaret Avison. MoCV; NOBC

Weightless in the shower. In the Cloud Chamber. Roger Weingarten. PUP-18

Weill, gin they arena deid, it's time they were. (LL) Elegy: "They are lang deid, folk that I used to ken." Robert Garioch. FaBoTC

Wein Geist. Charles Godfrey Leland. APN-2

Weingarten Travel Blessing, The. *Unknown, German*. GePo, *tr. by* Carroll Hightower

Weir Bridge. Padraic Fallon. CIP-2

Weird Sister. In Salem. Lucille Clifton. AmPA

Wel / come back, brother. Huey. Etheridge Knight. NNaP

Wel mended tinker! sans dispute. Of John Bunyan's Life. John James. SCAP

Weland knew fully affliction and woe. Deor's Lament. *Unknown, Anglo-Saxon*. AnOE; OAEL-1, *tr. by* Charles W. Kennedy

Weland, that dauntless man, well learned to bear [or well knew about exile]. Deor. *Unknown, Anglo-Saxon*. ASW, *tr. by* Kevin Crossley-Holland

Welcome, The. Abraham Cowley. BoLoP *Fr.* The Mistress.

Welcome. David Hernandez. UnSA

Welcome Back, Mr. Knight: Love of My Life. Etheridge Knight. PBCAP; RaBo

Welcome be ye when ye go. *Unknown*. MiEL

Welcome, beautiful angels. The Horses and the Angels. Agnes Nemes Nagy, *Hungarian*. CEEP, *tr. by* Bruce Berlind

Welcome, brave gallant, with those locks so fair. A Periwig. Rowland Watkyns. NOSC

We[e]lcome! but yet no entrance, till we bless[e]. The Entertainment, or Porch-Verse, at the Marriage of Mr. Henry Northleigh [or Hen. Northly] and the Most Witty Mrs. Lettice Yard. Robert Herrick. CaPo

Welcome dear book, souls Joy, and food! The feast. H. Scriptures. Henry Vaughan. ChIV-2; ESCV

Welcome, dear dawn of summer's rising sway. May-Day. Aaron Hill. NOEC

Welcome, dear wanderer, once more! Upon Her Play Being Returned to Her, Stained with Claret. Mary Leapor. ECWP

Welcome Eumenides. Eleanor Ross Taylor. NALW

Welcome, fayre chylde, what is thy name? Dalyaunce. *Unknown*. CH

Welcome from Egypt, sir. Shakespeare. FaBoSe *Fr.* Antony and Cleopatra.

Welcome, good heart. Note I Left for Gerald Stern in an Office I Borrowed, and He Would Next, at a Summer Writers' Conference. William Matthews. PUP-18

Welcome, great Caesar, welcome now you are. To the King, Upon His Welcome to Hampton Court. Robert Herrick. BeJo

Welcome, grinned Henry, welcome fifty-one! John Berryman. TAP *Fr.* Dream Songs.

Welcome, happy Easter day! Easter Praise. Rodney Bennett. BoTP

Welcome Home. Josephine D. Henderson Heard. CBWP-4

Welcome home, driving downhill. Lament City. Thomas Lux. AmPA

Welcome home from the exhausting voyage. Sea Legs. Susan Feldman. AmPA

Welcome, little Robin. *Unknown*. BoTP

Welcome, maids of honor. To Violets. Robert Herrick. CaPo; OBEV; SeCP

Welcome me, if you will. For James Dean. Frank O'Hara. NNaP; NeAP

Welcome Morning. Anne Sexton. CrSp

Welcome, most welcome to our Vow[e]s and us. To the King, upon His Com[m]ing with His Army into the West. Robert Herrick. BeJo; CaPo; CavPo

Welcome, o Supernatural One, o Swimmer. Prayer to the Sockeye Salmon. *Unknown*. WPoS

Welcome, old friend, long-necked bottle. Argentarius, *Greek*. GrAn, *tr. by* Fleur Adcock

Welcome over the Door of an Old Inn. *Unknown*. PoToHe

"'Welcome, proud lady'." (LL) Madge Wildfire Sings. Sir Walter Scott. CABP; CH; FaBoCh; GEA; GTBS-P; HAP; NAEL-2; NOBE; NOBRP; OAEL-2; OBEV; OBNC; OxBS; PoEL-4; RACG; SCGP; TFi; UnPo

Welcome Queen Alice. "Lewis Carroll." *Fr.* Through the Looking-Glass.

Welcome, Queen Sabbath. Zalman Schneour, *Hebrew*. TrJP, *tr. by* Harry H. Fein

Welcome, stranger! glad I greet thee. To Don Juan Baz. Mary E. Tucker. CBWP-1

Welcome sweet and sacred cheer. The Banquet. George Herbert. ESCV; GeHe

Welcome sweet, and sacred feast; welcome life! The Holy Communion. Henry Vaughan. ESCV

Welcome, Sweet Rest. Michael Wigglesworth. AH

Welcome the dawn. (LL) Nightingales. Robert Bridges. CMoP; ImPo; LiTM; MoBrPo; NOBE; OAEL-2; OBEV; OBMV; OBNC; SCGP; TFi; UnPo

Welcome the Wrath. Stanley Kunitz. VGW

Welcome thou safe retreat! Solum Mihi Superest Sepulchrum. William Habington. ChIV-1; NOSC

Welcome, thrice welcome to thy native Place! Mary Gulliver to Capt. Lemuel Gulliver. John Gay *and* Alexander Pope. OAEL-1

Welcome to Hiroshima. Mary Jo Salter. DiPo; NIP-4; NMM-2; RA

Welcome to Hon. Frederick Douglass. Josephine D. Henderson Heard. CBWP-4

Welcome to May. Angelo Poliziano. ItIP

Welcome to Sack, The. Robert Herrick. BeJo; CaPo; SeCP

("Ne'r may prophetic Daphne crown my brow.") (LL) CavPo

Welcome to Spring. John Lyly. *See* Trico's Song.

Welcome to Spring. Irene Thompson. BoTP

Welcome to the party. Funny Folk. Robert Fisher. FuFo

Welcome to this my college [or colledge], and though late. To His Kinsman, Master Thomas Herrick, Who Desired to Be in His Book. Robert Herrick. CaPo

Welcome to you. Ordinance on Arrival. Naomi Lazard. BLT

Welcome to you, rich Autumn days. Rich Days. W. H. Davies. BoTP

Welcome, welcome with one voice! Opening of the Indian and Colonial Exhibition by the Queen. Tennyson. EBVVPR

Welcome, wild Northeaster! Ode to the Northeast Wind. Charles Kingsley. FaPoR; OxAEP-2

Welcome, Ye Hopeful Heirs of Heaven. Phoebe Hinsdale Brown. AH

Welcome Yule. *Unknown*. CH

Welcomed to islands over the long water. Islanders, Inlanders. Michael Mott. PoA

Welcoming Party, A. John Montague. PNI

Wele, herying and worshipe be to Crist [or Christ] that dere us [or ous] boughte. William Herebert. MiEL

Wele, thu art a waried thing. *Unknown*. MiEL

Welford Wedding, The. Elizabeth Frances Amherst. ECWP

Welkin's wind, way unhindered. The Wind. Dafydd ap Gwilym, *Welsh*. OBWVE, *tr. by* Joseph P. Clancy

Well, The. Yves Bonnefoy, *French*. VCWP, *tr. by* John Naughton

Well, The. Thomas Edward Brown. NOBVV

Well, The. Jay Macpherson. NoP-4

Well, The. Mother Goose. ReMoGo

Well, The. Nguyễn Thiên Túng, *Chinese*. AVP, *tr. by* Huỳnh Sanh Thông

Well, The. Padma Sachdev, *Dogri*. OMIP, *tr. by* Iqbal Masud

Well, The. Philip Salom. NOBAu

Well, The. A. J. Seymour. PBCV

Well, *alter ego,* Time has trudged. Why Do We Live? Israel Zangwill. TrJP

Well, as Kavanagh said, we have lived. Singing School. Seamus Heaney. InPS-3

We'll be home once more. (LL) Resurrection. Vladimir Holan, *Czech*. PoSu, *tr. by* George Theiner

We'll begin with a box, and the. Why English Is So Hard! *Unknown*. CTV

Well-beloved, The. John Montague. BiHa

Well, boy, you're off to war. The Veteran. Frank S. Brown. NSI

Well-buggered boy named Delpasse, A. Limerick. *Unknown*. PeLi

Well, cat, did you find enlightenment in the Western Paradise? The Cat. Nguyen Trai, *Vietnamese*. PC, *tr. by* Jess Williamson

Well clay it's strange at last we've come to it. The Spark's Farewell to Its Clay. Ronald Allison Kells Mason. PeNZ

We'll dance again the saraband! (LL) The Witch's Ballad. William Bell Scott. RACG

We'll dance and sing / "Noel Noel." (LL) Little tree / little silent Christmas tree. E. E. Cummings. NTCP; OBCP; PChr

Well, dear Mr. Wright, I must send you a line. To Henry Wright of Mobberley, Esq. on Buying the Picture of Father Malebranche. John Byrom. NOEC

Well, Did You Evah? Cole Porter. OBAL

Well dost thou, Love, thy solemn feast to hold. Saint Valentine's Day. Coventry Patmore. OBNC *Fr.* The Unknown Eros.

Well-dressed couple haggle, The. Knowingness. John Hughes. PNI

We'll drown the whole lot in the Rhine. (LL) We mean to thrash these Prussian Pups. *Unknown*. NSI; PoWW

Well, Froggie went a-courting and he did ride. Froggie Went a-Courting. *Unknown*. AmFP

"We'll get 'em all back," said Robert Bridges. Ezra Pound and Robert Bridges. Robert Bagg. WeT

We'll give them to the poor, says John the Red Nose. (LL) The Cutty Wren. *Unknown*. OxBoLi; UV

We'll give to idleness. (LL) A Change in the Year. Wordsworth. BoTP; OAEL-2; Ro

"We'll go home by the water," says Brian O'Linn. (LL) Brian O'Linn. *Unknown*. CBNP; FaBoVe; NBLV; OBCoV; RB

We'll go no more a-roving by the light of the moon. William Ernest Henley. MoBrPo *Fr.* Echoes.

We'll go to the meadows, where cowslips do grow. The Meadows. Ann Taylor. BoTP

Well, God is / love. Puerto Rico Song. William Carlos Williams. NYBP

Well has thou spoken and yet not taught. My Comforter. Emily Jane Brontë. VWP

We'll have a wedding at our good house. (LL) Cat came fiddling out of a barn, A. *Unknown*. CTAV

Well, Heaven be thanked my first-love failed. The County Ball. Coventry Patmore. EBVV *Fr.* The Angel in the House.

Well here again that don't apply. T. S. Eliot. FaBoVe *Fr.* Sweeney Agonistes.

Well, here I am in the *Centre Daily Times*. News Update. John Balaban. AF; CDa

Well here we are!—and don't you think we're looking quite. Address. Andrew Geddes Bain. PeSAV

We'll hoist daddy's vest. Song of the Self-Made Orphans. David Avidan, *Hebrew*. IP, *tr. by* Warren Bargad *and* Stanley F. Chyet

Well, honest John, how fare you now at home? To John Clare. John Clare. Son

Well, how are things in Heaven? I wish you'd say. To Any Dead Officer. Siegfried Sassoon. NSI; PoFWW

Well, I forget the rest. (LL) Memorabilia. Robert Browning. FHYEP; GEA; NAEL-2; NOBVV; NoP-4; OAEL-2; OBNC; PoE; PoPoPo; RB

Well I have and in fact. On Being Asked to Write a Poem Against the War in Vietnam. Hayden Carruth. CDa

Well, I may now receive, and die: my sin. Satire 4. Donne. OBSV *Fr.* Satires.

Well, I never did see it before. (LL) Our Goodman. *Unknown*. AmFP; OBAL

Well I never, did you ever. *Unknown*. FaBoCh

Well I Remember [How You Smiled]. Walter Savage Landor. *Fr.* Ianthe. (Ianthe.) HAP; OBNC

"Well, I took your advice, Doc," said Knopp. Limerick. *Unknown*. PeLi

Well, I was at the dresser. Just How It Happened. Priscilla Jane Thompson. CBWP-2

Well, I was camped out on the draw at the head of Cimarron. The Zebra Dun. *Unknown*. AmFP

Well, I went to California in the year of Seventy-six. Root Hog or Die. *Unknown*. AmFP

Well I woke up this mornin' it was Christmas Day. Adrian Henri's Talking after Christmas Blues. Adrian Henri. PeLV

Well, I would have it so. I should have known. André Marie de Chénier. *Fr.* Elegies. AWP, *tr. by* Arthur Symons

Well, if a King's a lion, at the least. Profiteers. Alexander Pope. ECEV; OBSV *Fr.* The First Epistle of the First Book of Horace Imitated.

Well; if ever I saw such another man since my mother bound my head. Mary the Cook-Maid's Letter to Dr. Sheridan. Jonathan Swift. OxBoLi; PeLV

Well, if it's a sin to like Guinness. Limerick. Cyril Ray. PeLi

Well! If the Bard was weather-wise who made. Dejection. Coleridge. FHYEP; HeIP-4; NAEL-2; NAWM-2; NOBE; NOBRP; NoP-4; OAEL-2; OBNC; OxAEP-2; PoE; PoEL-4; PoPoPo; Ro; TFi; TOF

Well, *if* you must know all the facts, I was merely reading a pamphlet. A Visitor. "Lewis Carroll." OBCoV

Well, Ignorance, the cause is yet unknown. On Learning. Elizabeth Teft. ECWP

Well! I'm goin' home. Special Rider Blues. *Unknown*. AmFP

Well, I'm in love with a feller, a feller you have seen. Common Bill. *Unknown*. AS; AmFP

Well is he born, that may behold you ever. (LL) Sonnet 8: "More than most fair [*or* fayre], full of the living fire [*or* fyre]." Edmund Spenser. PoE; Son

Well, it isn't the King, after all, my dear creature! From Miss Biddy Fudge to Miss Dorothy———. Thomas Moore. PeLV *Fr.* The Fudge Family in Paris.

Well, it was never mine. This Day, under My Hand. David Malouf. CBAP

Well, it's partly the shape of the thing. Limerick. *Unknown*. KaS; SoSe-8

Well it's six o'clock in Oakland. Oakland Blues. Ishmael Reed. NAAAL

Well, Jesus died to save me in all of my sin. The Rock Island Line. *Unknown*. AmFP

Well Langston. A Message for Langston. "Kush." NBV

Well, let's go. Basho, *Japanese*. TTTS, *tr. by* Kenneth Koch *and* Harold Henderson

Well, life has touched me, too. The Pyroxenes. James Merrill. PuP-16

Well look a-here, honey. Depot Blues. *Unknown*. AmFP

Well may I weene, faire ladies, all this while. Edmund Spenser. OAEL-1 *Fr.* Wood Of Error. AEP

Well may that kisse be sweet that's giv'n t' a sleek. Sir Richard Fanshawe. OBVE *Fr.* Il Pastor Fido.

Well may they write, that sit in parlours fine. On His Writing Verses. John Hawthorn. NOEC

Well meaning readers! you that come as friends [*or* freinds]. The Flaming Heart. Richard Crashaw. NAEL-1; OAEL-1; PoEL-2

"We'll meet no more as wont!" she said. Not as Wont. Joseph Skipsey. NOBVV

Well, Menestratus, you ask me what I think. Lucilius, *Greek*. GrAn, *tr. by* Peter Porter

Well met Neighbour. Martin Parker. "Whither away good neighbour." PBRV

"Well met, well met, my own true love." Demon [*or* Daemon] Lover. *Unknown*. AmFP; ESPB; EnSB; HAP; OAEL-1; OxBB; UnPo; WeW-3

We'll move away still further:into now. (LL) All ignorance toboggans into know. E. E. Cummings. MeMAP; NAAL-2; NOBA; OxBA

Well, never mind that now. Good night! Good night! (LL) The Sisters. Amy Lowell. NALW; NMM-2

We'll not be slow to visit Doctor Swift. (LL) On Riding to See Dean Swift in the Mist of the Morning. Alexander Pope *and* Thomas Parnell. FaBoEE; OBCoV

Well now, look at this unsightly herd. On the Yellow Footprints. Mcavoy Layne. CDa

Well Now, the Virgin. Roy Fuller. Son *Fr.* Mythological Sonnets.

We'll o'er the water and o'er the sea. O'er the Water to Charlie. Robert Burns. FaBoCh

Well of blackness, all defiling. The Contents of an Ink-bottle. Mary Elizabeth Coleridge. VWP

Well of St. Keyne, The. Robert Southey. FaBoBe

Well of the King of Wu, The. Kao Ch'i, *Chinese*. CoBLCP, *tr. by* Jonathan Chaves

Well of Vertew and Flour of Womanheid, The. *Unknown*. OxBS

Well, old spy. Award. Ray Durem. BPo; PoBA; TTY

Well, on the day I was born. Have You Anything to Say in Your Defense? César Vallejo, *Spanish*. AF, *tr. by* James Wright; RaBo

Well—one at least is safe. One shelter'd hare. My Pet Hare. William Cowper. APo; FP *Fr.* The Task.

We'll, placed in Love's triumphant chariot high. Song. William Cavendish, Duke of Newcastle. OxBSP *Fr.* The Humorous Lovers.

Well pleasing 'tis to me. Goat's-Leaf. Marie de France. PBWP, *tr. by* Aline Allard

Well, read my cheeks, and watch my eye. Lines of Life. Letitia Elizabeth Landon. NOBRP

Well, remember to do it by doing rather than by not doing. (LL) Portrait of the Artist as a Prematurely Old Man. Ogden Nash. ImPo; InPS-3; LiTM

We'll return to the little box. The Benefactors of the Little Box. Vasco [*or* Vasko] Popa, *Serbo-Croatian.* HSix, *tr. by* Charles Simic

Well rising without sound, The. William Stafford. RB

We'll roll, we'll roll the chariot along. Roll the Chariot. *Unknown.* AS

We'll run and never tire. Down in the Valley. *Unknown.* CrDW

"We'll see if it is," said Rivera. (LL) I Paint What I See. Elwyn Brooks White. NBLV; NYBP

Well-shadowed landscape, fare ye well! Farewell to Love. Sir John Suckling. CaPo; CavPo

Well, since in spight of all that Love can do. A Farewell to Love. Elizabeth Singer. KTR

Well, some may hate and some may scorn. Stanzas to————. Emily Jane Brontë. VWP; WPE

Well, sometimes it's Heaven, and sometimes it's Hell. Heaven and Hell. Willie Nelson. InPK-6

Well, son de story of my life. The Favorite Slave's Story. Priscilla Jane Thompson. AAP; CBWP-2; RACG

Well, son, I'll tell you. Mother to Son. Langston Hughes. ChAP; FiLi; ISC; NAAAL; NAAL-2; NTCP; OBCA; SAmP; TTY

We'll soon be free. *Unknown.* CrDW

We'll talk about the dead later. Nightingales. Mikhail Aleksandrovich Dudin, *Russian.* TCRP, *tr. by* Albert C. Todd

Well-tam'd Heart, A. Specifications for a Perfect Lover. Richard Crashaw. *Fr.* Wishes. To His (Supposed) Mistresse. BoLoP; EBEV; ImPo; MeLP; NOSC; OBEV; OxAEP-1; PoEL-2; SeCP

Well, Teddy, I have found you. The Lost Teddy Bear. Maggie Pogue Johnson. CBWP-4

Well-tempered, it stays straight and will not warp. Ode to the Sewing Needle. *Unknown, Vietnamese.* AVP, *tr. by* Huỳnh Sanh Thông

Well, the day of slavery back again! The Yankees Back. "The Mighty Sparrow." PBCV

Well—the links are broken. A Woman's Last Word. Adelaide Anne Procter. VWP

Well, the war is done. *Unknown, Russian.* TCRP, *tr. by* Bradley Jordan

Well then. Dirty Niggers. Jacques Roumain, *French.* NegPo, *tr. by* Ellen Conroy Kennedy

Well then; I now do plainly see. The Wish. Abraham Cowley. NOBE; NOSC; NoP-4; OBEV; OxAEP-1; PBRV *Fr.* The Mistress.

Well, then, the last day the sharks appeared. The Sharks. Denise Levertov. NeAP

Well then, the promised [*or* promis'd] hour is come at last. To My Dear Friend Mr Congreve [on His Comedy Called "The Double-Dealer"]. Dryden. EBEV; OAEL-1; OxAEP-1; PoEL-3

Well then think of your great great etc. Uncle / Patrick Henry. (LL) My Great Great Etc. Uncle Patrick Henry. James Tate. CMAP; OBAL

Well then, tomorrow! the wood exalts under the mild. Finally. Vittoria Aganoor Pompili, *Italian.* PBWP, *tr. by* Brenda Webster

Well there is in the west country, A. The Well of St. Keyne. Robert Southey. FaBoBe

Well, there you have your seasons, prodigy! Derek Walcott. PBCV *Fr.* Another Life.

Well they are gone, and here must I remain. This Lime-Tree Bower My Prison. Coleridge. FHYEP; FP; HeIP-4; LaPo; NAEL-2; OBGa; OxAEP-2; PoE; PoEL-4; Ro; TOF

Well they'd made up their minds to be everywhere because why not. The Last One. W. S. Merwin. ChAP; LCAP-2; NoAM; VGW

Well, they're quite dead, Rambuncto; thoroughly dead. Rambuncto. Margaret Widdemer. BXAP

Well, things / be / pretty bad now, Mother. Report to the Mother. Etheridge Knight. FiLi

"Well, this is where I go down to the river." Heat. Kenneth Mackenzie. BMAP; CBAP

Well, though it seems. Liddell and Scott. Thomas Hardy. OBCoV; OxBoLi; PeLV

Well, thrill. That's their story. (LL) Freely Espousing. James Schuyler. FTOS; NeAP; NoP-4

Well, to start with. Jonah and the Whale. Gareth Owen. OBSP

Well, to the matter then, there's grown of late. Old England. Anne Bradstreet. KTR *Fr.* A Dialogue between Old England and New.

We'll to the woods and gather may. Alons au bois le may cueillir. Charles, Duc d' Orléans, *French.* AWP, *tr. by* W. E. Henley

We'll to the Woods No More. A. E. Housman. OAEL-2; PoRA

Well-uh Bird, Bird, Bird, Bird is the Word. The Trashmen Shaking Hands with Hubert Humphrey at the Opening of Apache Plaza Shopping Center, Suburban Minneapolis, August 1963. David Wojahn. PBCAP *Fr.* Mystery Train: A Sequence.

"Well Uncle Ike! This beats me." Uncle Ike's Holiday. Priscilla Jane Thompson. CBWP-2

Well, Wanton Eye. Charles, Duc d' Orléans. HAP

Well water. Eight Sandbars on the Takano River. Gary Snyder. NOBA; VGW

Well Water. Randall Jarrell. InPK-6; NAAL-2; NOBA; OxBSP; VCAP; VGW

Well water, drawn from ocean depths. Island. Mai Thảo, *Vietnamese.* AVP, *tr. by* Huỳnh Sanh Thông

Well, we either do it or we don't, as the pigeon said to. Sunrise with Sea Monster. Charles North. FTOS

Well, we have come this far. Elizabeth Bishop. *See* Cirque d'Hiver.

Well—we have reached the precipice at last. On the Masquerades. Christopher Pitt. ECEV; NOEC

Well, we went down town a-shopping. The Christmas Rush. Clara Ann Thompson. CBWP-2

Well, we will do that rigid thing. Parting with Lucasia; a Song. Katherine Philips. CBLP

Well, well, I know the wise ones talk and talk. Augusta Davies Webster. BrRo *Fr.* A Castaway.

Well, well, 'tis true. Plain Dealing. Alexander Brome. NOSC

Well, well, you's cum at las'. People's Literary, De. Maggie Pogue Johnson. CBWP-4

"Well, what do you work at?" she said to me after about six. The Lion Tamer. Paul Durcan. IFJA

Well, when all is said and done. Epilogue. "Æ." MoBrPo

Well, wife, I've found the model church! I worshipped there to-day. The Model Church. John H. Yates. PWR

Well-wishing to a Place of Pleasure, A. *Unknown.* GBL

Well, World, you have kept faith with me. He Never Expected Much. Thomas Hardy. NAEL-2; NoAM; OxBTC; SCV

We'll worship Jesus / When jesus do. When We'll Worship Jesus. Imamu Amiri Baraka. APSN

Well worthy to be magnified are they. The Pilgrim Fathers. Wordsworth. AiP

Well worthy to be magnified are they. The Pilgrim Fathers. Wordsworth. AiP *Fr.* Ecclesiastical Sonnets.

Well you can tell ev'rybody. Tiny Montgomery. "Bob Dylan." CBNP

Well, you have gone now, comrades. Farewell. Ewart Alan Mackintosh. NSI

Well, you know the sun is going down. Lowdown Dirty Blues. *Unknown.* AmFP

Well You Needn't. Dave Etter. SeSe

Well, you wake up in the mornin', hear the ding dong ring. The Midnight Special. "Leadbelly." GM

"Wellcome, to the Caves of Artá!" Robert Graves. NBLV; NOBL; NYBP; PeLV

Wellfleet Harbor. Paul Goodman. CoAP

Wellfleet Whale, The. Stanley Kunitz. DiPo; NoAM

Welling water—to which I add these tears, The. (LL) The Stream. Mona Van Duyn. NMM-2; VCAP

Wellington. Charles Harpur. NOBAu

Wells up in my heart. (LL) Why, if this interval of being can be spent serenely. Rilke. EnlH; NAWM-2

Welsh Ballad, A. Edmwnd Prys, *Welsh.* OBWVE, *tr. by* Gwyn Williams

Welsh History. Ronald Stuart Thomas. OBWVE

Welsh Incident. Robert Graves. CBNP; CMoP; EBEvV; NOBE; OBSP; OxBSn; OxBTC

("'What did the mayor do?' 'I was coming to that'.") (LL) OxBSn

Welsh Landscape. Ronald Stuart Thomas. FaBoMo; NoP-4

Welsh Marches, The. A. E. Housman. FaBoTw; SCGP

Welshman in Exile Speaks, The. T. Harri Jones. OBWVE

Welshman to Any Tourist, A. Ronald Stuart Thomas. OxBC

Welt ist dumm, die Welt ist blind, Die. Heinrich Heine, *German.* AWP, *tr. by* James Thomson

Weltering London ways where children weep, The. Keats. D. G. Rossetti. EPCY

Women's Wather. T. S. Law. OxBS

W'en dey 'listed colo'ed sojers an' my 'Lias went to wah. (LL) When Dey 'Listed Colored Soldiers. Paul Laurence Dunbar. BPo; CBCWP

Wen one wife be for one man. (LL) One Wife for One Man. Frank Aig-Imoukhuede. PBMAP

Wen, wen, little wen. Against a Wen. *Unknown, Anglo-Saxon.* ASW, *tr. by* Kevin Crossley-Holland

Wenberi's Song. Wenberi, *Woiworung*. CBAP, *tr. by* A. W. Howitt

Wendell Phillips. Henrietta Cordelia Ray. CBWP-3

Wenest thou, usher, with thyn cointise. *Unknown*. MiEL

Went by; but all my grief ageän awoke. (LL) The Wind at the Door. William Barnes. EnVR; GBL; GTBS-P; LBC; OxAEP-2; PoEL-4

Went down to St. Joe's infirmary. Those Gambler's Blues. *Unknown*. AS

Went down to the yards. Long Track Blues. Sterling Brown. GM

Went forth to fight, with murderous faces. (LL) A London Fete. Coventry Patmore. EBVV; EnVR; HAP; PeVV

Went home and put a bullet through his head. (LL) Richard Cory. Edwin Arlington Robinson. APAD; APN-2; AmPP; CMoP; ChAP; ColAP; EBEvV; HAP; ImPo; InPK-6; LiTM; MeMAP; MoAmPo; NAAL-2; NCAP; NOBA; NTP; NoP-4; OxBA; PFE; PoLF; PoPoPo; PoRA; Poetr; SAGP; TAP; TFi

Went into a shoestore to buy a pair of shoes. Sale. Josephine Miles. WPE

Went on cutting bread and butter. (LL) The Sorrows of Werther. William Makepeace Thackeray. BLPA; NBLV; NOBL; NOBVV; OBCoV; PFE; PeLV

Went out last night, had a great big fight. Prove It on Me Blues. Gertrude "Ma" Rainey. NAAAL

Went to an all black school. Black and White. Michael Smith. HCP; NOxBChV

Went to dinner with her thursday. Pubescence at 39. Vickie Sears. GLP

Went up a year this evening! Emily Dickinson. HAP; WeW-3

Went with some of my students to work in the People's. Denise Levertov. CDa *Fr.* Staying Alive.

Weping haveth min wonges wet. *Unknown*. MiEL

Wer ther outher in this toun. *Unknown*. MiEL

We're a couple of swells; we stop at the best hotels. A Couple of Swells. Irving Berlin. OBCoV

We're A'[ll] Dry wi' the Drinkin' O't. *Unknown*. NOBL; OxNR

Were a tadpole and I was a fish. (LL) Evolution. Langdon Smith. BLPA; FaBoBe

"Were able to pipe, in Pluto's house I'd sing." (LL) Lament for Bion. Moschus, *Greek*. HePo, *tr. by* Barbara Hughes Fowler; AWP, *tr. by* George Chapman

Were aesthetically significant, while Elijah's were very plain. (LL) On Certain Wits. Howard Nemerov. HCAP; OxBC

We're all Americans, except the Doc. A Mad Negro Soldier Confined at Munich. Robert Lowell. FaBoMo; OxBC

We're all at home. Having Eaten Breakfast. David Chapman Berry. BXAP

Were all crying—I think it was sprats! (LL) Epicurean Reminiscences of a Sentimentalist. Thomas Hood. CBNP; PeLV

We're all in the dumps. In the Dumps. *Unknown*. CBNP

Were all our sins so empty of enjoyment. The Muted Screen of Graham Greene. Phyllis McGinley. FaBoEE

WE'RE an Africanpeople. Haki Madhbouti. MBE *Fr.* African Poems.

Were answerable to Fate alone, not Zeus. (LL) The Weather of Olympus. Robert Graves. FaBoEE; OBCoV

Were barren as this moorland hill. (LL) The Dreary Change. Sir Walter Scott. NAEL-2; OAEL-2; OBNC

Were bright and fearful presences to me. (LL) Horses. Edwin Muir. APo; CMoP; FaBoCh; OAEL-2

Were caught in bed by the dawn. (LL) We dressed each other. Empress Eifuku, *Japanese*. OHMPJ, *tr. by* Kenneth Rexroth

We're connecting. Poems for the New. Kathleen Fraser. CrSp

We're 'er Majesty's bold troubleshooter; wherever they send us we goes. Bold Troubleshooters. Peter Veale. NOBL

We're fed up with national colors! Project: Flag. Tadeusz Borowski, *Polish*. AF, *tr. by* Larry Rafferty, Meryl Natchez *and* Tadeusz Pioro

We're foot—slog—slog—slog—sloggin' over Africa. Boots. Rudyard Kipling. BLPA; FaPoR; MoBrPo

We're free and independent—Number One! Run! Run! Lu'u Văn Vong, *Vietnamese*. AVP, *tr. by* Huỳnh Sanh Thông

We're going to have a party. The Christmas Party. Adeline White. BoTP

We're going to the fair at Holstenwall. Holstenwall. Sidney Keyes. FaBoTw

Were half as silent as their pictures! (LL) Portrait of a Lady in the Exhibition of the Royal Academy. Winthrop Mackworth Praed. NOBL; PeLV; PoEL-4

Were half the power that fills the world with terror. A Message of Peace. Henry Wadsworth Longfellow. *Fr.* The Arsenal at Springfield. AmPP

Were he composer, he would surely write. Portrait of the Boy as Artist. Barbara Howes. MoAmPo

We're headed for empty–headedness. Film Noir: Train Trip Out. Lynn Emanuel. BAP-95; PUP-20

We're hoping to be arrested. Street Demonstration. Margaret Abigail Walker. BPo

Were I a king, I could command content. Poem. Edward, 17th Earl of Oxford De Vere. NTP; NoSic

Were I as base as is the lowly plain. Ubique. Joshua Sylvester. GSo; GTBS-P; NoSic; OBEV; Son

Were I employ'd a garden to contrive. The Florist's Vade-Mecum. Samuel Gilbert. OBGa *Fr.* The Florist's Vade-Mecum.

Were I idiom and. While. Bruce Andrews. FTOS

Were I in Trouble. Robert Frost. OxBSP *Fr.* Five Nocturnes.

Were I invited to a nectar feast. Sylvia. Samuel Croxall. NOEC

Were I laid on Greenland's coast. Song. John Gay. EBEvV, *sect.* I, *pt.* i; CBLP; EnLoPo; NAEL-1; NOBE; NOEC; OxBoLi; PeLV; PoEL-3 *Fr.* The Beggar's Opera. OAEL-1

Were I that wandering citizen whose city is the world. The English Graves. G. K. Chesterton. NSI

Were I the palm tree which your love returning. E Questo il Nido in Che la Mia Fenice? Alec Derwent Hope. OxBC

Were I to leave no more than a good friend. The Departure; an Elegy. Henry, Bishop of Chichester King. SeCP

Were I, who to my cost already am. A Satire [*or* Satyre] against [Reason and] Mankind. John Wilmot, 2d Earl of Rochester. NOBE; NOSC; OAEL-1; OBSV; PoEL-3; SCV

Were I (who to my cost already am). A Satire against Reason and Mankind. Grace Buchanan Sherwood. NoP-4

Were I (who to my cost already am). A Satire against Reason and Mankind. John Wilmot, 2d Earl of Rochester. CABP; SCV *Fr.* A Satire [*or* Satyre] against [Reason and] Mankind. NOSC; OAEL-1; OBSV; PoEL-3; SCV

Were it but to pleasure you. (LL) To His Mistresses. Robert Herrick. CaPo; SeCP

Were it not for making a living, which is rather a nouciance. (LL) Introspective Reflection. Ogden Nash. NBLV; OBCoV

Were it undo that is ido [*or* y-do]. He Is Far. *Unknown*. MiEL; OAEL-1

Were kicking men to death. (LL) Concert Party: Busseboom. Edmund Blunden. NSI; PoFWW

We're launched into the darkness. Night Ferry. Mark Doty. NAmP90

Were left in loneliness behind. (LL) A Winter Night. William Barnes. NOBE; OBNC

Were lost, if it were addle. (LL) A Proper New Ballad, Intitled The Fairies' Farewell. Richard Corbet. PeLV; SCGP

Were lost, if that were addle. (LL) The Fairies' Farewell. Richard Corbet. BeJo; NOSC; OxAEP-1

We're low—we're low—we're very, very low. The Song of the Low. Ernest Charles Jones. NOBVV

We're marching 'round the levee. Marching 'round the Levee. *Unknown*. AmFP

"We're married," said Eddie. The Newlyweds. John Updike. OBCoV

Were My Heart as Some Men's Are. Thomas Campion. AAS

Were Na [*or* Ne] My Heart Licht, I Wad Die. Lady Grisel Baillie. *See* Werena My Heart Licht I Wad Dee.

"We're not amused," said Victoria. Limerick. Stanley J. Sharpless. PeLi

We're not going to die. For My Daughter in Reply to a Question. David Ignatow. MoLi

We're not silent! Lord of Dreams. Abba Kovner, *Hebrew*. IP, *tr. by* Warren Bargad *and* Stanley F. Chyet

Were not the one dead, turned to their affairs. (LL) "Out, Out—." Robert Frost. ColAP; HAP; HeIP-4; NAAL-2; OxBA; PFE; Poetr; RB; SoSe-8; TRP; UnPo; VGW

We're OK. Gloria Fuertes, *Spanish*. WPOW, *tr. by* Philip Levine

We're out here, our feet in the soil, our heads craned up at the sky. Charles Wright. *Fr.* Homage to Paul Cézanne. VCAP

We're patient, prayerful, meek, resigned. (LL) Another to Urania. Benjamin Colman. ChIV-1; SCAP

"We're poor." Tanka. Toki Zenmaro, *Japanese*. MJT, *tr. by* Makoto Ueda

Were softer than her singing. Elizabeth Barrett Browning. *See* Felicia Hemans.

Were swimming in milk round the brim of a /hat hat. (LL) The Lobster. "Lewis Carroll." OxBChV

Were that woman's postcoital charms. Rufinus Domesticus, *Greek*. InMo, *tr. by* Sam Hamill

We're the hardrock men. Dynamite Song. *Unknown*. AmFP

Were there no limits to my lust. To His Importunate Mistress. Paul Griffin. UV

Were they less like themselves than what they are. (LL) Married Love. Sherod Santos. Son; WeT

Were thrilling in his heart. (LL) Young Johnstone ("Young Johnstone and the young Colnel"). *Unknown*. ESPB; OxBB

We're twenty, young—our hearts are twenty, young. The Hero of Our Times. Kiên Giang, *Vietnamese*. AVP, *tr. by* Huỳnh Sanh Thông

We're walking down Grant, through Chinatown. Playing for Time. Christopher Buckley. SeSe

Were we not fine. American Indian Art: Form and Tradition. Diane Di Prima. BB

We're wed to one eternity . (LL) An Invite to Eternity. John Clare. NAEL-2; NOBVV; OAEL-2; OBNC; Ro

We're wonderful one times one. (LL) If everything happens that can't be done. E. E. Cummings. ITG; SoSe-8; WeW-3

Were you born a wind. Song by the Brook. Sowol Kim, *Korean*. CKP, *tr. by Jaihiun Kim*

Were you ever in Quebec. Donkey Riding. *Unknown*. ACTP

Were you in love with me? Secret Love. Lyubomir Levchev, *Bulgarian*. CEEP, *tr. by Jascha Kessler and Aleksandar Shurbanov*

Were you there when they crucified my Lord? [(were you there?)]. *Unknown*. AH; APN-2; BPo; NAAAL

Were yu normal today did yu screw society. Christ I Wudint Know Normal if I Saw It When. Bill Bissett. NOBC

Werena My Heart Licht I Wad Dee. Lady Grisel Baillie. LW; OBEV ("There ance was a may, and she lo'ed na men.") OBEV (Were Na My Heart Licht, I Wad Die.) CABP

Were't aught to me I bore the canopy. Sonnet 125. Shakespeare. AEP; NoSic *Fr.* Sonnets.

Were't not enclos'd within a pale of gold. (LL) On a Seal. Plato, *Greek*. AWP; FaBoEE, *tr. by Thomas Stanley*

Wernher von Braun. Tom Lehrer. OBCoV

Wersh the wine o victorie!, An. (LL) The Mither's Lament. Sydney Goodsir Smith. FaBoTC

Werther had a love for Charlotte. The Sorrows of Werther. William Makepeace Thackeray. BLPA; NBLV; NOBL; NOBVV; OBCoV; PFE; PeLV

Wes. Boss Communication. Mari E. Evans. SeSe

We's invited down to brudder Browns. Krismas Dinnah. Maggie Pogue Johnson. CBWP-4

Wesley in Heaven. Thomas Edward Brown. OBNC

Wessex Heights. Thomas Hardy. CMoP; EBVV; OAEL-2; OBNC; PoEL-5; SCGP

West, The. Michael Longley. BiHa; PBCIP

West ascending Lotus Flower Mountain. Poem No. 19 in the Old Manner. Li Po, *Chinese*. CoBCP, *tr. by Burton Watson*

West Cliff. Chu Yi-tsun, *Chinese*. SuSp, *tr. by Chang Yin-nan and Lewis C. Walmsley*

West Coast Indian. George Clutesi. HATNAP

West Country, The. Alice Cary. APN-2

West-Country Damosel's Complaint, The. *Unknown*. ESPB

West Creek at Ch'u-chou. Wei Ying-wu, *Chinese*. CoBCP, *tr. by Burton Watson*

West Forties: Morning, Noon, and Night, The. Louis Edward Sissman. CoAP; NYBP

West Grand Boulevard. Faye Kicknosway. IFJA

West Indies, The. James Montgomery. PBCV

West Kansas full moon. Directions in Our Blood. Barney Bush. HATNAP

West Lake. Kenneth O. Hanson. CoAP

West London. Matthew Arnold. FP; GSo; SCGP; Son

West of Alice. W. E. Harney. NOBAu

West of the bridge. Waterside Village. Yün Shou-p'ing, *Chinese*. CoBLCP, *tr. by Jonathan Chaves*

West of the Sierras where. The California Phrasebook. Dennis Schmitz. AmPA

West of the village, evening rays linger on red leaves. Wu Chen. *Fr.* Paintings of Fishermen. CoBLCP, *tr. by Jonathan Chaves*

West of Your City. William Stafford. LiTM

West of your door, Blue Mountain dreams of melting. Blue Mountain. Roberta Hill Whiteman. VoR

West Paddocks. Arthur Davies. NOBAu

West Palm Beach Storm, The. *Unknown*. AmFP

West Ridge Is Menthol-Cool, The. D. L. Graham. PoBA

West River's watershed sounds beyond the sky, The. The Retired Official Yüan's High Pavilion. Tu Mu, *Chinese*. PLT, *tr. by A. C. Graham*

West-Running Brook. Robert Frost. MoAmPo; NOBA; NoP-4

West Strand Visions. James Simmons. PBCIP

West Sussex Drinking Song. Hilaire Belloc. MoBrPo

West Wall. W. S. Merwin. RaBo

West West. Bruce Andrews. FTOS

West Wind, The. John Masefield. CABP; LiTM; MoBrPo

West wind has come again to the "tower of reunay," The. Cheng Hsieh. CoBLCP, *tr. by Jonathan Chaves* *Fr.* Yangchou.

West wind slaughters the lingering heat. Once More Following the Rhymes of Pin-lao's Poem "Getting Up After Illness." Huang T'ing-chien, *Chinese*. CoBCP, *tr. by Burton Watson*

West wind strong. Loushan Pass. Mao Tse-tung, *Chinese*. ChiPo, *tr. by Kai-yu Hsu*

Wester[n] wind, when will [or wilt] thou blow. The Lover in Winter Plaineth for the Spring. *Unknown*. BoLoP; CTC; ClHu; EBEV;

EnLoPo; FaBoCh; HAP; HeIP-4; InPK-6; NAEL-1; NIP-4; NOBE; NoP-4; NoSic; OAEL-1; OBEV; OPOU; OxBSP; PFE; PoE; PoEL-1; PoPoPo; Poetr; SCGP; SoSe-8; TFi; UnPo; WeW-3

Western Approaches, The. Howard Nemerov. ColAP; HCAP; TAP

Western Capital in lawless disorder, The. Wang Ts'an. *Fr.* Seven Sorrows. CoBCP, *tr. by Burton Watson*

Western Capital is in turmoil, The. Wang Ts'an. SuSp, *tr. by Ronald C. Miao* *Fr.* Seven Poems of Lament.

Western CIV, 4 and 5. Joan Retallack. FTOS

Western Civilization. James Galvin. PaTW

Western Town. Karl Shapiro. NYBP

Western Trail Cook, 1880. Sharyn Jeanne Skeeter. ISC

Western Wagons. Rosemary Benét *and* Stephen Vincent Benét. AiP; ImGa

Western Waves of Ebbing Day, The. Sir Walter Scott. PoEL-4 *Fr.* The Lady of the Lake.

Western wind has blown but a few days, The. The Cranes. Po Chü-i, *Chinese*. ChiP; OBVE, *tr. by Arthur Waley*

Westgate-on-Sea. John Betjeman. OxBoLi

Westland Row. Thomas Kinsella. MoP

Westphalian Song. *Unknown, German*. AWP; OBVE, *tr. by Samuel Taylor Coleridge*

Westport House, Portrush. James Simmons. PBCIP

Westron wynde when wyll thou blow. *Unknown*. *See* The Lover in Winter Plaineth for the Spring.

Westward, hit a low note, for a roarer lost. A Strut for Roethke. John Berryman. NOBA

Westward Ho! Joaquin Miller. FaBoBe

Westward over Lotus Mountain. Li Po. *See* Ancient Airs.

Westward the field of the cloth of gold. A Visit. Sherwood Anderson. PoA

Wet almond-trees, in the rain. Bare Almond-Trees. D. H. Lawrence. FaBoVe

Wet Casements. John Ashbery. NAAL-2; PoM

Wet centre is bottomless, The. (LL) Bogland. Seamus Heaney. HeIP-4; NOIV; NoAM; PBCIP; PNI; PoPoPo

Wet dawn inks are doing their blue dissolve, The. Winter Trees. Sylvia Plath. HCAP; LCAP-2

Wet Day. James McAuley. BMAP

Wet Evening in April. Patrick Kavanagh. OPOU

Wet gray day, A—rain falling slowly. Morels. William Jay Smith. NYBP

Wet green velvet scums the swimming pool, A. The Frog in the Swimming Pool. Debora Greger. BAP-94

Wet Hair: If Now His Mother Should Come. Robert Penn Warren. NoAM *Fr.* Penological Study: Southern Exposure.

Wet leaf that clings to the threshold, A. (LL) Liu Ch'e. Ezra Pound. OBVE; VGW

Wet Night, A. Richard Ryan. CIP-2

Wet paint on the cheeks wings and a sudden wind. Burying Uncle Salomon. David Avidan, *Hebrew*. IP, *tr. by Warren Bargad and Stanley F. Chyet*

Wet sheet and a flowing sea, A. A Sea-Song. Allan Cunningham. BoTP; FaBoBe; FaPoR; GTBS-P; OxAEP-2

Wet, sickly/ smells of cattle yard silage fill the prairie air. Dream. Elizabeth Cook-Lynn. *Fr.* Journey. HATNAP

Wet slate roofs. Pigeons. A light. The Arrival. Daniel S. Simko. CEEP

Wet streets, black trees, a gold leaf smacked. Sonnet 4. Debra Bruce. FFC *Fr.* ("Light They Make, The").

Wet streets. It has rained drops big as silver coins. Eighteen. Maria Banus, *Rumanian*. BoWoP; LiLi, *tr. by Willis Barnstone and Matei Calinescu*

Wet Thursday. Weldon Kees. NYBP

Wet trees hung above the walks, The. The Empty House. William Dean Howells. APN-2

Wet Weather. Patricia Low. VGW

Wet weather seldom hurts the most unwise;. Signs of Rain. Virgil. APo, *tr. by John Dryden* *Fr.* The Georgics.

Wet your lungs with wine—the dogstar rises. Alcaeus, *Greek*. OBCVT, *tr. by Diane Rayor*

We've a new race to start. (LL) More of a Corpse Than a Woman. Muriel Rukeyser. NALW; NMM-2

We've all been invited up to Killisnoo. *Unknown, Tlingit Indian*. STP, *tr. by James Koller*

We've been taught for two thousand years. A Late Twentieth-Century Prayer. Ernest Sandeen. WeW-3

We've come from all four corners of the earth. International Solidarity. Phan Trọng Quảng, *Vietnamese*. AVP, *tr. by Huỳnh Sanh Thông*

We've come intil a gey queer time. Epistle to John Guthrie. Sydney Goodsir Smith. OxBS

We've drunk the boys who rushed the hills. Abdul. *Unknown*. NSI

We've formed our band and are well manned. The Californian. *Unknown.* AmFP

"We've fought before, but this is worse than rape!" Baobab Fruit Picking; or, Development in Monkey Bay. Jack A. Mapanje. PeSAV

We've fought with many men acrost the seas. Fuzzy-Wuzzy. Rudyard Kipling. MoBrPo

We've found this Scott Fitzgerald chap. Effervescence and Evanescence. Keith Preston. OBAL

We've Foxgloves in our garden. Foolish Flowers. Rupert Sargent Holland. CTV

We've got a new maid called Chrysanthemum. Limerick. *Unknown.* PeLi

We've got as far as poison-gas. (LL) Christmas: 1924. Thomas Hardy. FaBoEE; OBCP

We've heard and heard, and finally believe. The Diary. Goethe, *German.* STV, *tr. by* John Frederick Nims

We've hung David's *La Vierge et Les Saintes.* The Living Room. Gjertrud Schnackenberg. FYAP

We've inherited something from our ancestors, the serfs. Nikolai Ivanovich Tryapkin. TCRP, *tr. by* Bradley Jordan *and* Katya Zubritskaya *Fr.* Verses about the Dog's Inheritance.

We've learned where the big ones grow. Mussels. Ingrid Wendt. NMM-2

We've made a great mess of love. The Mess of Love. D. H. Lawrence. CBLP; OAEL-2

We've met in here—we know each other now. Prison Impromptu. Nguyễn Đình Kiên, *Vietnamese.* AVP, *tr. by* Huỳnh Sanh Thông

We've nothing vast to offer you, no deserts. A Welshman to Any Tourist. Ronald Stuart Thomas. OxBC

We've our business to attend Day's duties. Bending the Bow. Robert Duncan. FTOS

We've / poisoned our food, polluted our air. John Cage. APSN *Fr.* Diary: How to Improve the World (You Will Only Make Matters Worse).

We've put a fine addition on the good old church at home. The Ladies' Aid. *Unknown.* PoLF

We've reached the land of desert sweet. Dakota Land. *Unknown.* AS

We've rented a flat in Ghosh Buildings, Albert Road. The Roys. Arvind Krishna Mehrotra. OMIP

We've returned to autumn again; summer. A Word for Summer. George Seferis, *Greek.* AF, *tr. by* Edmund Keeley *and* Philip Sherrard

We've seen him before. A Charmer Turned Ascetic. Marippittiyar, *Tamil.* PLW, *tr. by* A. K. Ramanujan

We've socially-conscious biography. Limerick. *Unknown.* PeLi

We've solved the problem, the problem is solved. Bernadette Mayer. FTOS

We've sworn off nostalgia. Little Elegy for the Age. Lynne McMahon. NAmP90

We've taken our burlap sacks and entered. The Killigrew Wood. Norman Dubie. AmPA

We've traveled long together. Verses to my Heart's-Sister. Henrietta Cordelia Ray. AAP; CBWP-3

We've trod the maze of error round. Late Wisdom. George Crabbe. OBEV *Fr.* Reflections.

We've yet to cohabit. For some we simply arrive and leave parties. The Division of O'Dowd. Alan Wearne. BMAP *Fr.* The Nightmarkets.

Wexford Girl, The. *Unknown.* AmFP

Wey, Ned, man! thou luiks sae down-hearted. Susanna Blamire. ECWP

Wha cry: Owre late, owre late. (LL) The Makar. William Soutar. FaBoTC

Wha daur meddle wi' me? Little Jock Elliot. *Unknown.* IBB

Wha ebah Joe an me duz lib we likes to hab um neat. Lizzie and Joe Catch a Thief. Edward Cordle. PBCV

Wha Fe Call I'. Valerie Bloom. FaBoVe

Wha Is Perfyte. Quha Is Perfyte. Alexander Scott. OxBS

Wha kens on whatna Bethlehems. The Innumerable Christ. "Hugh MacDiarmid." EBEV; OxAEP-2; OxBS

Wha lies here? Johnny Dow [*or* Doo]. *Unknown.* FaBoEE

Wha Me Mudder Do. Grace Nichols. NOxBChV

Wha wadna be in love. Maggie Lauder. Francis Sempill. OxBS

Whale. William Rose Benét. MoAmPo

Whale. Geoffrey Dearmer. BoTP

Whale, The. Herman Melville. *Fr.* Moby Dick.

Whale, The. *Unknown.* AnOE, *tr. by* Charles Kennedy; ASW, *tr. by* Kevin Crossley-Holland *Fr.* Physiologus.
    ("Now I will sing about a kind of fish.") ASW, *tr. by* Kevin Crossley-Holland

Whale, The. *Unknown.* APo, *tr. by* Charles William Kennedy *Fr.* Physiologus.

Whale, The. *Unknown.* EBEV, *tr. by* Gavin Bone *Fr.* The Whale. AnOE, *tr. by* Charles Kennedy; ASW, *tr. by* Kevin Crossley-Holland *Fr.* Physiologus.

Whale, His Bulwark, The. Derek Walcott. OxBC; TTY

Whale hunt, The. Jacques Prévert, *French.* MFP, *tr. by* Martin Sorrell

Whale / is a room, The. In a Blind Garden. David Shapiro. ChIV-1

Whale is the greatest beast in all the ocean waste. *Unknown.* CRP, *tr. by* Richard Wilbur *Fr.* The Bestiary.

Whale on the beach, you dinosaur. Anne Sexton. AFr

Whaler's Pig, The. Edwin James Brady. NOBAu

Whaler's Rhyme. *Unknown.* NOBAu

Whales, The. Marguerite Young. WPE

Whales off Wales, The. X. J. Kennedy. OBCA

Whales Weep Not! D. H. Lawrence. CMoP; NoAM

Whales. We're going to hunt whales. The Whale hunt. Jacques Prévert, *French.* MFP, *tr. by* Martin Sorrell

Wha'll buy [my] caller herrin'? Caller Herrin'. Carolina Oliphant, Baroness Nairne. OxBS; WoRP

Whan aa sorts foregether / in Embro to the ploy. (LL) Embro to the Ploy. Robert Garioch. FaBoTC

Whan bells war rung, an mass was sung. Sweet William's Ghost. *Unknown.* CH; ESPB

Whan Cnut Cyng the Witan wold enfeoff. Beoleopard; or, The Witan's Whail. *Unknown.* CBNP; OBCoV

Whan netilles in winter bere roses rede. Impossible to Trust Women. *Unknown.* MiEL

Whan said [*or* seyd *or* seyde] was al this miracle, every man. Prologue to Sir Thopas. Chaucer. NAEL-1 *Fr.* The Canterbury Tales.

Whan that Aprille [*or* April *or* Aprill] with his[e] shoures [*or* showres] so[o]te. The General Prologue. Chaucer. CTC, *ll.* 1–37; EBEvV, *ll.* 1–78; SAGP, *ll.* 1–18, *incl. mod. vers. by* Christopher Burns; SCV, *ll.* 1–42, *incl. mod. vers. by* Nevill Coghill; TRP, *ll.* 1–18; *Fr.* The General Prologue. FHYEP; NAEL-1; NAWM-1; OAEL-1; PoE *Fr.* The Canterbury Tales.

Whan that Aprille with hise shoures soote. Aprilly. Bert Leston Taylor. OBAL

Whan that the Knight [*or* Knyght] had[de] thus his tale yto[o]ld. The Miller's Prologue. Chaucer. NAEL-1; OAEL-1 *Fr.* The Canterbury Tales.

Whan they cam' first to Yarrow. (LL) The Dowie Houms o' Yarrow. *Unknown.* ESPB; OBEV; OxBS

Whan they unto the paleys were yoemen. Chaucer. PoE *Fr.* Troilus and Criseyde [*or* Criseide]. EnVB

Whango Tree, The. *Unknown.* FPC

Whan'll we be marry'd. *Unknown.* CBLP

Whanne I this Supplicacioun. The Parting of Venus and Old Age. John Gower. PoEL-1 *Fr.* Confessio Amantis.

Whanne mine eyhnen misten. *Unknown.* MiEL

"Whar hae ye been a' day, my boy Tammy?" My Boy Tammy. Hector MacNeill. CH

Whare the braid planes in dowy murmurs wave. The Ghaists; a Kirk-yard Eclogue. Robert Fergusson. OxBS

Wharrupede thrimmered, the glottal stopped, The. Bollam's Replover, The: Farewell to Jabberwocky. Hugh Haughton. CBNP

Wharton ("Wharton! the reason and wonder of our days"). Alexander Pope. AWP *Fr.* Epistle to Sir Richard Temple.

Whas herte blod was shed for me. (LL) Worldes blisse, have good day! *Unknown.* CrSp; MiEL

What? Langston Hughes. NBLV; OBAL

What?/ a rhythm. Paul Niger. NegPo, *tr. by* Ellen Conroy Kennedy *Fr.* Initiations.

What a bankruptcy! How. Bertolt Brecht. FaBoA

What a Boy Can Do. Alberto A. Ríos. IFJA

What a charming thing's a battle! Isaac Bickerstaffe. NOEC; OBCoV *Fr.* The Recruiting Serjeant.

What a consoling poem this will be if the roadside. Shadows. Richard Jackson. SeSe

What a cost to be pure! did e'er strike your mind. Refining Fire. Lizelia Augusta Jenkins Moorer. CBWP-3

What a dainty life the milkmaid leads! Song. Thomas Nabbes. NOSC

What a fine evening is this. Song of the Boatswain of Yüeh. *Unknown, Chinese.* SuSp, *tr. by* Irving Y. Lo

What a fine hostess! Tune: "Song of the Southern Country"—Presented to a Courtesan. Hsin Ch'i-chi, *Chinese.* SuSp, *tr. by* Irving Y. Lo

What a Friend We Have in Cheeses! William Cole. OBAL

What a girl called "the dailiness of life." Well Water. Randall Jarrell. InPK-6; NAAL-2; NOBA; OxBSP; VCAP; VGW

What a grand time was the war! World War II. Langston Hughes. HCAP; PoPoPo

What a grudge I am bearing the earth. A Translation from Petrarch. Petrarch. MoBrPo, *tr. by* J. M. Synge. *Fr.* Sonnets to Laura.

What a host you are, Mancinus. Martial, *Latin.* OBVE, *tr. by* Peter Porter

What a hot day it is! for. A Terrestrial Cuckoo. Frank O'Hara. CBNP

What a kingdom you've brought me to! Fear. Devdas Chhotray, *Oriya.* OMIP, *tr. by* Jayanta Mahapatra

What a life after death. Robinson Jeffers. *See* Vulture.

What a little girl had on her mind was. Norkiko Ibaragi, *Japanese.* WPJ, *tr. by* Kenneth Rexroth *and* Ikuko Atsumi

What a Little Moonlight Can Do. Joe Heithaus. SeSe

What a lovely being is a mother! Mother. Hettye Rayburn Ramsey. PWR

"What a lovely world," said the baby chick. An Easter Chick. Thirza Wakley. BoTP

What a man, what a moon, what a fish, what a chip, what a block. Anna Couani. BMAP

What a moment of strange dreaming! Mind Flying Afar. Edgar Lee Masters. PoA

What a pox do you mean with your pride and ill-nature. A Solitary Canto to Chloris the Disdainful. John Smith. NOEC

What a proud dreamhorse pulling(smoothloomingly)through. E. E. Cummings. VGW

What a shame—the chaos of the city! Evening View from the Bell Tower at P'ing-ch'ang. T'ang Hsien-tsu, *Chinese.* CoBLCP, *tr. by* Jonathan Chaves

What a simple lot we were, but she. The Necessary Angel. Phyllis Janowitz. BAP-94

What a splish-splash that would be! (LL) If all the seas were one sea. Mother Goose. BoTP; OxNR; ReMoGo

What a spree! (LL) Picnic. Hugh Lofting. NOxBChV

What a sublime end of one's body, what an enskyment; what a life after / death death. (LL) Vulture. Robinson Jeffers. NAAL-2; NOBA; NoAM; PaTW

What a sweet little day, what a day! Yury Pavlovich Odarchenko, *Russian.* TCRP, *tr. by* Nina Kossman

What a thrill. Cut. Sylvia Plath. TAP

What a to-do to die today. *Unknown.* ACTP

What a trick. Ragout. William Zaranka. BXAP

What a wall! Play No Ball. Gerard Benson. NOxBChV

What a wonderful bird the frog are. The Frog. *Unknown.* NBLV; NOxBChV; NTCP; RB

What a word and I thought it would be. Alone. Richard Shelton. NYBP

What abou' de Law? Adam Small, *Afrikaans.* PeSAV, *tr. by* Carrol Lasker

What about his feelings—. Beginning by Value. Christopher Gilbert. GT

What about that bad short you saw last week. Black People! Imamu Amiri Baraka. BPo

What about the people who came to my father's office. The Questions. Robert Pinsky. ColAP; NAmP90; NoAM

What About You? Vladimir Mayakovsky, *Russian.* NNPT, *tr. by* Maria Enzensberger

What about You? "Edward Pygge." BXAP

What age is this? What times are now? Time's Whirligig, Or, The Blue-New-Made-Gentleman Mounted. Humphrey Willis. NOSC

What ailes Pigmalion? Is it lunacy. The Poem. Thomas Morton. SCAP

What airs in dress an' gait wad lea'e us / And ev'n Devotion! (LL) To a Louse [On Seeing One on a Lady's Bonnet at Church]. Robert Burns. BLPA; FaBoVe; NAEL-2; NOBRP; NOEC; OxBS; PBMP

What always seemed. Tanka. Ishikawa Takuboku, *Japanese.* MJT, *tr. by* Makoto Ueda

What am I after all but a child, pleas'd with the sound of my own name? repeating it over and over. Walt Whitman. OPOU

What am I? Ah, you know it. Solomon Redivivus, 1886. Constance Naden. VWP

What am I? how produced? and for what end? Know Yourself. John Arbuthnot. ECEV

What am I in the place of nourishment. A Curse on Uruk. Enheduanna, *Sumerian.* BoWoP, *tr. by* Aliki *and* Willis Barnstone

What am I? Nosing here, turning leaves over. Wodwo. Ted Hughes. CBNP; MoP; NoAM

What am I to do with my sister? Prince Yuhara. AWP, *tr. by* Arthur Waley *Fr.* Manyo Shu, Part 4 of 4.

What an elusive target. The Fights. Milton Acorn. MoCV; NOBC

What? an English sparrow sing? Did You Ever Hear an English Sparrow Sing? Bertha Johnston. BLPA

What, and how great, the Virtue and the Art. The Second Satire of the Second Book of Horace Imitated. Alexander Pope.

What and how keen and mortal soever. The Bee. Paul Valéry, *French.* APo, *tr. by* David Paul

What and where they be! (LL) If Only. Tennyson. CBLP; LBC; OxBSn; SAGP

What Answer Can I Give? Shakespeare. *Fr.* King John.
    ("*King Philip:* You are as fond of grief as your child.") LBC
    ("Then have I reason to be fond of grief.") (LL) LBC

What Any Lover Learns. Archibald MacLeish. MeMAP

What are all the hillmen wanting. The Keeper of the Midnight Gate. George Mackay Brown. OxBC

What are all those fish that lie gasping on the strand? (LL) Three Movements. W. B. Yeats. CMoP; FaBoEE

What are days for? Days. Philip Larkin. EBEV; FaBoMo; NTP; OxAEP-2; OxBC; OxBSP; PeECV; PiM; RB; TOF

What are friends? A Friend in Need Will Be Around in Five Minutes. Ogden Nash. FP

What are heavy? Sea-sand and sorrow. Christina Rossetti. FaBoEE; NTP; OxBChV; Spl

What are little boys made of? Natural History. *Unknown.* ACTP

What are little boys made of, made of? Natural History. Mother Goose. OxNR; ReMoGo; UV

What! are my deeds forgot? Shakespeare. OxAEP-1 *Fr.* Troilus and Cressida.

What are ruins to us. At Lindos. May Sarton. WPE

What are stars, but hieroglyphics of God's glory writ in lightning. Apollo. Thomas Holley Chivers. APN-1

"What are the bugles blowin' for?" said Files-on-Parade. Danny Deever. Rudyard Kipling. EBEvV; EBVV; FaPoR; GTBS-P; InPS-3; MoBrPo; NAEL-2; NOBE; NOBVV; NoAM; OxBTC; OxBoLi; PBMP; PeVV; PoLF; SCGP; SCV; TFi; UnPo

What are the islands to me. The Islands. Hilda Doolittle. MoAmPo

What are the lays of artful Addison. The Charms of Nature. Joseph Warton. *Fr.* Enthusiast, The; or, The Lover of Nature. PoEL-3

What are the Signs of Zodiac. Zodiac. Eleanor Farjeon. OTCP

What are the suburbs made of? Nursery Rhyme. Gavin Ewart. UV

What are these elations I have. The Descent of Winter. William Carlos Williams.

What are these things thou lovest? Vanity. On Her Vanity. Wilfrid Scawen Blunt. GSo

What are these women up to? They've gone and strung. The Deodand. Anthony Hecht. DiPo; NoAM

What are they doing now? I imagine Oliver. A Running Battle. Brendan Kennelly. BiHa

What are we first? First, animals; and next. 30. George Meredith. CABP; GBL; HAP; NoP-4; PoEL-5 *Fr.* Modern Love.

What are we men indeed? Grim torment's habitation. Human Misery. Andreas Gryphius, *German.* GePo, *tr. by* George C. Schoolfield

What Are We Playing At? André Chedid, *French.* BoWoP, *tr. by* Samuel Hazo *and* Mirène Ghossem

What are we to do with a heaven. Three Songs from the Temple. Don Domanski. NOBC

What are we waiting for, assembled in the forum? Waiting for the Barbarians. Constantine P. Cavafy, *Greek.* AF; BLT; GrIP; PFTM, *tr. by* Edmund Keeley *and* Philip Sherrard

What Are Years? Marianne Moore. CMoP; MeMAP; MoAmPo; MoP; NOBA; NoAM; NoP-4; OxBA; PiM; SoSe-8
    ("Soul to be strong?, The.") (LL) PiM

What are you able to build with your blocks? Block City. Robert Louis Stevenson. CTV; NOxBChV; NTCP

What Are You Doing? Edmund Vance Cooke. PWR

What are you doing away up there. Night Walk. Max Fatchen. OTCP

What are you doing here, ghost, among these urns. Father in the Railway Buffet. U. A. Fanthorpe. FaBoWP

What are you doing here in this strange world that goes on and off. Traffic Lights. Lina Kasdaglis, *Modern Greek.* BoWoP, *tr. by* Edmund *and* Mary Keeley

What are you doing, my lady, my lady. *Unknown.* OxNR

What, are you drop't? John Webster. PoEL-2 *Fr.* The White Devil.

What are you going to do with us, who have. The Pleaders. Peter Davison. NYBP

What, are you grown dull now and perplexed? Before the Court. Aleksandr Blok, *Russian.* TCRP, *tr. by* Geoffrey Thurley

What are you, Lady?—naught is here. Portrait of a Lady in the Exhibition of the Royal Academy. Winthrop Mackworth Praed. NOBL; PeLV; PoEL-4 *Fr.* Every-Day Characters.

"What are you looking at?" the farmer said. The Evening Primrose. Christopher Pearse Cranch. APN-1

What are you saving it for? Asclepiades, *Greek.* PGA, *tr. by* Kenneth Rexroth

What are you saying? Field Flowers. Louise Glück. AFr

What are you, then, my love, my friend, my father. The Quarry. Vassar Miller. WPE

What are you. . . ? they ask, in wonder. Cold Colloquy. Patrick Anderson. NOBC *Fr.* Poem on Canada.

What are you? what new device, you who hurry in such a random. The Bubble. Richard Crashaw. PBRV *Fr.* Bulla.

What art thou, love? Whence are those charms. Jacob Allestry. NOSC

What art thou, Mignon, child of mystery? Mignon. Henrietta Cordelia Ray. CBWP-3

What art thou, Spleen, which ev'ry thing dost ape? The Spleen. Anne Finch, Countess of Winchilsea. NALW; NOSC; NoP-4

What asks the Bard? He prays for naught. After Horace. Alfred Denis Godley. NOBL

What astonishing contact, old man, your hands establish with our own! Hands. Victor Serge, *Russian.* AF, *tr. by* James Brook

What authors lose, their booksellers have won. On Authors and Booksellers [*or* Publishers]. Alexander Pope. FaBoEE

"What bait do you use," said a Saint to the Devil. The Lure. John Boyle O'Reilly. TIRV

What beasts and angels practice I ignore. Little Ode. Paul Goodman. PoA

What beauteous form beneath a marble veil. On an Unfinished Statue. George Santayana. APN-2

What Became of Them? *Unknown.* BoTP; OBCA; OxBChV

(Two Rats.) CTAV

What beckoning [*or* beck'ning] ghost, along the moonlight shade. Elegy to the Memory of an Unfortunate Lady. Alexander Pope. ECEV; NOBE; NOEC; OAEL-1; OBEV; SCGP

What becomes of the girl who lives always alone? The Sorceress. Eugène Marais, *Afrikaans.* PeSA, *tr. by* Jack Cope *and* Uys Krige

What began that bustle in the village. The Birth of Moshesh. David Granmer T. Bereng, *Sotho.* PeSA; TTY, *tr. by* Dan Kunene *and* Jack Cope

What bird so sings, yet so does wail? Trico's Song. John Lyly. CH; NOBE; NoSic; OBEV; SCGP *Fr.* Alexander and Campaspe.

What Birds Were There. William Everson. NoAM

What birth is this; a poore despissed creature? Upon ye Sight of My Abortive Birth. Mary Carey. KTR

"What bluid's that on thy coat lap." Edward. *Unknown.* ESPB

What blust'ring noise now interrupts my sleep. William Drummond, of Hawthornden. NOSC *Fr.* Forth Feasting.

What bones? What bones? Stones instead. Georgia. Bin Ramke. MT

What Booker can[doth] prognosticate. The King Enjoys His Own Again. Martin Parker. FaBoCh; NOSC; OxBoLi; PBRV

What booty gave the German War? Booty from the German War. Friedrich von Logau, *German.* GePo, *tr. by* George C. Schoolfield

What Bothered Him. David Avidan. *Fr.* Samson, Our Hero. IP, *tr. by* Warren Bargad *and* Stanley F. Chyet

What bright soft thing is this? The Tear[e]. Richard Crashaw. ImPo; SeCP

What bring[s] you, sailor, home from the sea. Luck. Wilfrid Wilson Gibson. OBMV

What Brings Us Out. Naomi Shihab Nye. NAmP90

What buck last cattle lap form pits. Leaving Rattle Bar. Clark Coolidge. FTOS

What built a world may sure repair a state. (LL) To Mr. Henry Lawes. Katherine Philips. NoP-4

What bullet killed him? Dead Soldier. Nicolás Guillén, *Spanish.* TTY, *tr. by* Langston Hughes

What burlesque could, was by that genius done. Walter Harte. EPCY

What bursts in the very moment of bursting is image. On the Nature of the Iconic. Gustaf Sobin. PT

What business, or what hope brings thee to town. To Sextus. Martial, *Latin.* FaBoEE, *tr. by* Sir Charles Sedley

What can a man do that a beast cannot. In Shame and Humiliation. James Wright. CAPP-1

What can a yellow glove mean in a world of motorcars and. Yellow Glove. Naomi Shihab Nye. LoL

What can be gained by rushing these things? Aunt Janet's Museum. Kathleen Jamie. FaBoTC

What can be the matter. The Wind. Dorothy Graddon. BoTP

What can be wrong. Housewife. Susan Fromberg Schaeffer. CrSp

What Can I Do? Horace Logo Traubel. TrJP *Fr.* Chants Communal.

What can I do, I love you so much! Chu Yün-ming. *Fr.* Forest Birds (A Woman Speaks). CoBLCP, *tr. by* Jonathan Chaves

What can I do to drive away. Keats. OAEL-2

What can I give Him. My Gift. Christina Rossetti. CTV; PChr *Fr.* A Christmas Carol: "In the bleak mid-winter." ACTP; InPS-3; NOBVV; VWP

What can I give thee back, O liberal. Sonnet. Elizabeth Barrett Browning. BWW; OxAEP-2 *Fr.* Sonnets from the Portuguese.

What can I give you, my lord, my lover. The Gift. Sara Teasdale. LW

What can I say at your grave? To Father. Yury Kuznetsov, *Russian.* TCRP, *tr. by* Sarah W. Bliumis

What can I say, but that it's not easy? Rosalie Sorrels. MDDM *Fr.* Apple of My Eye.

What can I say to you? How can I now retract. Protocols. Vikram Seth. APAD

What can I send you under the earth. Traditional Funeral Songs. *Unknown, Modern Greek.* BoWoP, *tr. by* Willis Barnstone *and* Elene Kolb

What Can I Tell My Bones? Theodore Roethke. AmPP; NOBA *Fr.* Meditations of an Old Woman.

What can it be. The Caged Bird in Springtime. James Kirkup. PeP

What can lambkins do. A Chill. Christina Rossetti. BoTP

What can melt a traveler's grief? Rhyming a Friend's Poem. Yü Hsüan-chi. BoWoP, *tr. by* Geoffrey Waters

What can purge my heart. Song for Billie Holiday. Langston Hughes. MoNo

What can the cause be, when the king hath [*or* K. have] given. An Epigram. To the Household. 1630. Ben Jonson. BeJo; Son

What, can these dead bones live, whose sap is dried. The New Ezekiel. Emma Lazarus. ColAP

What can they do. The Low Road. Marge Piercy. CrSp

What can Tommy Onslow [*or* little T. O.] do? On Tom Onslow, Earl of Onslow. *Unknown.* FaBoEE

What can we say to our children? (LL) The Sad Children's Song. Grace Paley. NMM-2; SoSe-8

What can you expect. Maryam bint Abi Ya'qub al-Ansari, *Arabic.* WPOW, *tr. by* Elene Margot Kolb

What cannot be committed to memory, this can save. Photograph. Quandra Prettyman. PoBA

What Cannot Be Kept. Reginald Shepherd. GT

What care I for the leagues o sand. The Mither's Lament. Sydney Goodsir Smith. OxBS

What care I for whom she be? (LL) The Author's Resolution. George Wither. AWP; BoLoP; GTBS-P; NOBE; OBEV; OxAEP-1; SCGP

What care I how black I be? *Unknown.* OxNR

What care I, so they stand the same. Merops. Ralph Waldo Emerson. APN-1; OxBA

What care I though the world reprove. *Unknown.* NOSC

"What care I, what cares he." The Cowboy. John Antrobus. FaBoBe

What care the Dead, for Chanticleer. Emily Dickinson. APN-2

What celebration showed there be? Odes 3.28 Holiday ("Festo quid potius die"). Horace. AWP, *tr. by* Louis Untermeyer *Fr.* Odes.

What ceremony else? Shakespeare. EBEV *Fr.* Hamlet. NAWM-1

What chance / Sweet dreamlike chance. I Won't Sell His Love. Fadwa Tuqan, *Arabic.* AF, *tr. by* Mounah Aikhouri *and* Hamid Algar

What changes take place in the course of a year. The Course of a Year. George Sands Johnson. PWR

What chord did she pluck in my soul. Steve Kowit. BLT

What Church is this? Christ's Church. Who builds it? Christopher Harvey. EPCY *Fr.* The Synagogue.

What Color Is Black? Barbara Mahone. MBE

What Color Is Lonely. Carolyn M. Rodgers. BPo

What colour are they now, thy quiet waters? Evening on the Moselle. Ausonius, *Latin.* OBCVT, *tr. by* Helen Waddell

What cometh here from west to east a-wending? A Death Song. William Morris. NAEL-2

What common language to unravel? Paterson: The Falls. William Carlos Williams. ColAP

What conscience, say, is it in thee. To Oenone. Robert Herrick. OBEV

What Constellations rise with the Lion. The great Dog. Manilius Marcus, *Latin.* OBCVT, *tr. by* Thomas Creech

What Constitutes a State? Sir William Jones. BLPA

What could be done? The house was full of folks! The Inn That Missed Its Chance. Amos Russel Wells. TrCP

What Could Be Lovelier than to Hear. Elizabeth Jane Coatsworth. AYFP

What could be nicer than the spring. A Walk in Spring. K. C. Lart. BoTP

What could he know of sky and stars, or heaven's all-hidden life. The Sooth-Sayer. Sadi. AWP, *tr. by* Sir Edwin Arnold *Fr.* The Gulistan.

What Could Hold Us. Heather McHugh. NIP-4

"What could I make," Socrates might have asked. The Makers. David Galler. NYBP

What could my father do? My Father Went to Funerals. Howard Nelson. RaBo

What creature's this with his short hairs. The Character of a Roundhead. *Unknown.* FaBoPV; NOSC

What cross impetuous Planets govern me. On My Leaving London, June the 29. Sarah Fyge Egerton. KTR

What crowd is this? what have we here! we must not pass it by. Star-Gazers. Wordsworth. Poetr

What crowd is this? what have we here! we must not pass it by. Wordsworth. Poetr *Fr.* Star-Gazers. Poetr

What crowding thoughts around me wake. To Mrs. K———, On Her Sending Me an English Christmas Plum-Cake at Paris. Helen Maria Williams. WoRP

What crowds by envied power, the wish of all. Sejanus. Juvenal. OBVE, *tr. by* William Gifford *Fr.* Satires.

What cruel laws depress the female kind. Elizabeth Tollet. ECWP; NOEC *Fr.* Hypatia.

What cunning can express. Edward, 17th Earl of Oxford De Vere. NoSic

What danger is the pilgrim in. John Bunyan. EBEV *Fr.* The Pilgrim's Progress.

What dark and terrible shadow is swaying in the wind?. Easter at Christmas. Alun Lewis. PoWW

What dawn is it? Aubade. Karl Shapiro. VGW

What day did you come down from that former place. Rejoicing That the Zen Master Pao Has Arrived from Dragon Mountain. Liu Ch'ang-ch'ing, *Chinese.* CoBCP, tr. by Burton Watson

What day is it today? The way I live. Extract from a Diary. János Pilinszky, *Hungarian.* PoSu, tr. by Peter Jay

What day was it she slid. Birth of Venus. Constance Urdang. PoA

What death? John Webster. *Fr.* The Duchess of Malfi. NAEL-1

What death is worse than this? Sir Thomas Wyatt. SiPS

What demented malice, my silly Ravidus. Catullus. *See Carmina,* XL.

What desperate nightmare rapts me to this land. Legacy: My South. Dudley Randall. PoBA

What dew or what weeping. Torquato Tasso. ItIP

What dexterous thousands just within the goal. Causes of Old Age. John Armstrong. ECEV *Fr.* The Art of Preserving Health.

What did Delaware? State Quiz. *Unknown.* CTV

What did he do except lie. Banneker. Rita Dove. LCAP-2; NoAM

(What Did I Do to Be So) Black and Blue? Thomas ("Fats") Waller, Andy Razaf *and* Harry Brooks. NAAAL

What did I study in your School of Night? The School Of Night. Alec Derwent Hope. PoA

WHAT DID LEONEL RUGAMA SAY? A Report on the Protest in Front of the United States Embassy by the Pino Grande Movement. Daisy Zamora, *Spanish.* CLPP, tr. by Barbara Paschke

What did sex have to do with politics? Robyn Selman. PUP-19

What did the day bring? Letter from a Coward to a Hero. Robert Penn Warren. MoAmPo

What did the Indians call you? To the Avon River above Stratford, Canada. James Reaney. MoCV

'What did the mayor do?' 'I was coming to that'. Robert Graves. *See* Welsh Incident.

What did the Old Doctor do. 5.8.1942 / In Memory of Janusz Korczak. Jerzy Ficowski, *Polish.* HP, tr. by Keith Bosley

What did they expect of our toil and extreme. War Books. Ivor Gurney. PeFWW

What Did They Have In Mind? Nikolai Ivanovich Glazkov, *Russian.* TCRP, tr. by Daniel Weissbort

What did those girls say when you walked the strip. Words. David Huddle. CDa *Fr.* Tour of Duty. Son

What did we say to each other. Simile. N. Scott Momaday. CDW

What did you do to my father? (LL) Sam. Lucille Clifton. MoLi; UnSA

What did you hear? Advent; a Carol. Patric Dickinson. OBCP

What did you think would happen. Still-Life in the Coat Factory Office. Vickie Karp. WWSi

What difference does it make. *Unknown, Japanese.* WPJ, tr. by Kenneth Rexroth *and* Ikuko Atsumi

What different dooms our birthdays bring! Miss Kilmansegg's Birth. Thomas Hood. OBCoV; OxBoLi; PeLV *Fr.* Miss Kilmansegg and Her Precious Leg.

What dire offence from am'rous causes springs. Alexander Pope. EBNV; NOEC; Poetr *Fr.* The Rape of the Lock[, an Heroi-Comical Poem]. FHYEP; HAP; ImPo; OAEL-1; OBNV; PeLV; PoEL-3

What do a few crimes. Adultery. Alan Dugan. CAPP-1

What do caterpillars do? Caterpillars. Aileen Fisher. TLR

What do I care. Pursuit. Hilda Doolittle. WPE

"What Do I Care." Sara Teasdale. VGW

What do I expect from tomorrow's day? Vladimir Burich, *Russian.* TCRP, tr. by Albert C. Todd

What do I know of journey. David Meltzer. UnSA

What Do I See. Gertrude Stein. PFTM

What do I stare at—not the colt. The White Horse. W. H. Davies. OxBTC

What do I want with a thousand stars in broad daylight. U Tam'si Tchicaya. PBMAP *Fr.* Epitomé (1962).

What do I wish? No more than what I have. Out of Horace. James Wright. NOSC

What Do the Birds Think? Alfred Wellington Purdy. MoCV

What do the long years bring us. Retrospection. Henrietta Cordelia Ray. CBWP-3

What Do They Say. Gary Snyder. NNaP

What do they sing, the last birds. Last Songs. Galway Kinnell. VCAP

What do we do with the body, do we. As From a Quiver of Arrows. Carl Phillips. BAP-96

What do we know of what is behind us? History. Arthur Gregor. TAP

What do we plant when we plant the tree? Henry Abbey. CTV; FPC

What do we share with the past? Again for Hephaistos, the Last Time. Richard Howard. GLP

What Do Women Want? Mary Jo Salter. FFC; RA

What do you call it, bobsled champion. Twentieth-Century Blues. Kenneth Fearing. CMoP

What Do You Do When It's Spring? John Woods. CoAmPo

What do you gain, poor Thyrsis, by these tears? Theocritus, *Greek.* GrAn, *tr. by* Anthony Holden

"What do you paint, when you paint on a wall?" I Paint What I See. Elwyn Brooks White. NBLV; NYBP

What, do you plan for children now? Song for a Street-Song. Sylvia Townsend Warner. WPN

What do you say to this? The thought has just. Menander. OBCVT, *tr. by* Murray, Gilbert *Fr.* The Epitrepontes (The Arbitration).

What do you take. Prayer. Bill Manhire. PeNZ

What do you think I saw to-day. The Fairy Cobbler. A. Neil Lyons. BoTP

What do you think? Last night I saw. The Dragon. Mary Mullineaux. BoTP

What do you think of us in fuzzy endeavor. Garbageman: the Man with the Orderly Mind. Gwendolyn Brooks. CAPP-1 *Fr.* A Catch of Shy Fish.

What Do You Want? John Newlove. NOBC

What Do You Want: A Meaningful Dialogue, or a Satisfactory Talk? Ogden Nash. OBCoV

What does a bird in Cross's air. *Unknown.* NOEC *Fr.* A Collection of Hymns. . . of the Moravian Brethren.

What does a true Arab do now? (LL) Blood. Naomi Shihab Nye. EC3; NMM-2; UnSA

What does he do with them all, the old king. Elegy for Drowned Children. Bruce Dawe. BMAP; NOBAu

What Does It Matter? Noah Barker. PWR

What does it mean. Gift. Gerald William Barrax. MT

What does it take to make a day? A Day. William Leroy Stidger. PoToHe; SoSe-8

What does little birdie say? Cradle Song. Tennyson. BoTP; OxBChV; PFE *Fr.* Sea Dreams.

What does love look like? The Shape of Death. May Swenson. TAP

What does not change / is the will to change. The Kingfishers. Charles Olson. APSN; CMoP; InPS-3; NAAL-2; NOBA; NeAP; PoM; VCAP

What does not fade? The tower that long had stood. Transience. John Armstrong. NOEC *Fr.* The Art of Preserving Health.

What does she dream of, lingering all alone. Charlotte Brontë. PEW

What does she put four whistles beside heated rugs for? Random Generation of English Sentences; or, The Revenge of the Poets. William Jay Smith. OBAL

What does the bee do? / Bring home honey. Christina Rossetti. OxBChV

What does the cracker. Self. Norman Henry, II Pritchard. PoBA

What does the farmer in the spring. Spring Work at the Farm. Thirza Wakley. BoTP

What does the horse give you. Horse. Louise Glück. NALW

What does the little boy dream of? Hsieh Chin. *Fr.* What Does the Little Boy Love? CoBLCP, tr. by Jonathan Chaves

What Does the Little Boy Love? Hsieh Chin, *Chinese.* CoBLCP, tr. by Jonathan Chaves

What does the political scientist know? Artur Miedzyrzecki, *Polish.* PoSu, tr. by Stanislaw Baranczak *and* Clare Cavanagh

What does the storm say? What the trees wish. The Ways and the Peoples. Randall Jarrell. PoA

What does the veery say, at dusk in shad-thicket? Code Book Lost. Robert Penn Warren. Poetr

What doest thou here, Elijah? The Ghost of Abel. William Blake. ChIV-1

What doth this noise of thoughts within my heart. The Family [*or* Familie]. George Herbert. ESCV

What dreadful tidings to convey unto his family. (LL) Annette Myers. *Unknown.* OxBoV

What D'Ye-Call-It, The. John Gay. 'Twas When the Seas Were Roaring. HAP

What eagle can beho[u]ld her sunbright[e] eye. Sir John Davies. NoSic *Fr.* The Gulling[e] Sonnets. Son

What earthly use are these Confucian graphs? Trần Tế Xu'o'ng, *Vietnamese.* AVP, tr. by Huỳnh Sanh Thông

What ecstasies her bosom fire! To a Lady on Her Passion for Old China. John Gay. ImPo; SCGP

What else are your *Termes*. Alchemical Ingredients. Ben Jonson. *Fr.* The Alchemist. FaBoSe

What else can we do. What Are We Playing At? André Chedid, *French.* BoWoP, *tr. by* Samuel Hazo *and* Mirène Ghossem

What else could we do, for the doors were guarded. Curfew. Paul Éluard, *French. tr. by* Quentin Stevenson

What else have I to spur me into song. (LL) The Spur. W. B. Yeats. OxAEP-2; WeW-3

What else have we? We need not know. We know. The Poem of Humankind. Đông Hồ, *Vietnamese.* AVP, *tr. by* Huỳnh Sanh Thông

What else is there to do but. Twisters. William Meissner. CMAP

What Ely Was. Lynn Emanuel. PaTW

What endures? Not the arranged. Still Life. Sharan Strange. GT

What Epilogues are made, for who can tell. Epilogue. Catherine Trotter. KTR *Fr.* Queen Catharine; or, The Ruines of Love.

What ever 'tis, whose beauty here below. The Starre. Henry Vaughan. ESCV

What Every Boy Knows. "Antler." GLP

What ev'ry day thus long? fie, fie arise. Argument. Persius. OBCVT, *tr. by* Barten Holyday *Fr.* The Third Satyre.

What exactly the date was is not what was thought about is held unabated, unthought. Tedium Drum, Part IV. Kevin Magee. PT *Fr.* Tedium Drum, Part IV.

What eye doth see the heaven but doth admire. Sir John Davies. PeECV *Fr.* Orchestra; or, A Poem[e] of Da[u]ncing. NoSic; SiPS

What face, in the water. Lament. William Carlos Williams. VGW

What face she put on it, we will not discuss. Conrad Potter Aiken. *Fr.* Time in the Rock [or, Preludes to Definition]. VGW

What fainting hopes are in a lover. (LL) The Primrose. Robert Herrick. CBLP; OBEV

What fair pomp have I spied of glittering ladies. Thomas Campion. GBL; NoSic; PoEL-2; SCGP

What falls before us like snow. Moth. Lance Henson. VoR

What family has built a house beside the rapids here? Yü Chi, *Chinese.* CoBLCP, *tr. by* Jonathan Chaves

What field of all the civil wars. Andrew Marvell. *Fr.* An Horatian Ode upon Cromwell's Return from Ireland. CABP; EBEV; ESCV; FMP; GTBS-P; GeHe; HAP; IIP; InPS-3; NOBE; NOSC; OAEL-1; OBEV; OBWP; OxAEP-1; PoEL-2; SCGP; SeCP; TFi

What fills the whisper and. Hadrian's Lane. Ray DiPalma. FTOS

What flew down the chimney. Not the End of the World. Michael Ryan. NAmP90

What foes are there who could not suddenly. The Head of Medusa on a Rotella of Michelangelo da Caravaggio, in the Gallery of the Grand Duke of Tuscany. Giambattista Marino, *Italian.* GS, *tr. by* Unknown

What folly to complain. Soliloquy. Ann Yearsley. NOBRP

What for feere of this ferly and of the false Jewes. William Langland. EBEV *Fr.* The Vision of Piers Plowman.

What Frenzy Has of Late Possess'd the Brain. Sir Samuel Garth. NBLV

What Friendship is, Ardelia show. Friendship Between Ephelia and Ardelia. Anne Finch, Countess of Winchilsea. BWW; ECWP; NALW; NoP-4

What from the founder Aesop fell. The Purpose of Fable-writing. Phaedrus, *Latin.* AWP, *tr. by* Christopher Smart

What gentle ghost, besprent with April dew. An Elegy [or Elegie] on the Lady Jane Pawlet [or Paulet], [Marchioness of Winton]. Ben Jonson. SeCP

What gifts of speech a man may own. The Sincere Man. Alfred Grant Walton. PoToHe

What gifts shall we bring in worship. Nativity. Craig Powell. NOBAu

What gifts would we? Motions of the soul? The Renewal. Theodore Roethke. VGW

What Glorious Vision. Thomas Cradock. AH

What God gives, and what we take. A Grace for Children. Robert Herrick. OxBChV

What God Is. Robert Herrick. BeJo; NOSC

What God never sees. *Unknown.* OxNR

What Goes Around Comes Around, or The Proof is in the Pudding. Cheryl Clarke. CPO; FFC

What goes on in the pauses. Torture. Margaret Atwood. PoE

What golden gaine made Higginson remove. Reverend Mr, The Higginson. Edward Johnson. SCAP

What good is it to me if long ago. Sonnet 23. Louise Labé, *French.* BoWoP, *tr. by* Willis Barnstone

What grandeur makes a man seem venerable? Sonnet 21. Louise Labé, *French.* BoWoP, *tr. by* Willis Barnstone

What Grandma Knew. Edward Field. Poetsp

What great genius invented the waiting room? Waiting Rooms. Howard Nemerov. PoA

What greater torment ever could have been. Lonely Beauty. Samuel Daniel. CTC *Fr.* The Complaint of Rosamond.

What Greece, when learning flourished, only knew. Dryden. NOSC *Fr.* The Silent Woman to the University of Oxford.

What Grieving Was Like. Lynn Emanuel. CMAP

What guile [or guyle] is this, that those her golden tresses. Sonnet 37. Edmund Spenser. NAEL-1; Son *Fr.* Amoretti. AAS

What Habacuck once spake, mine eyes. Roger Williams. SCAP

What had become of the young shark? The Birth of a Shark. David Wevill. TwCP

What had November done? The Beautiful Ruined Orchard. Daniel Berrigan. FYAP

What had you been thinking about. The Tennis Court Oath. John Ashbery. NoAM; TAP; WeT

What Happened. Robert Penn Warren. *Fr.* Tale of Time. LCAP-2

What Happened? John Wieners. FTOS; PoM

What happened earlier I'm not sure of. Say You Love Me. Molly Peacock. NAmP90

What Happened Here Before. Gary Snyder. APSN; NNaP; PoM

What Happened to a Young man in a Place Where He Turned to Water. *Unknown, Apache Indian.* STP, *tr. by* Anselm Hollo

What happened to Barabbas. Speculations on the Subject of Barabbas. Zbigniew Herbert, *Polish.* GI, *tr. by* John Carpenter *and* Bogdana Carpenter

What Happened to Miss Frugle. Brian Patten. OBSP

What Happened to Professor White on Leaving the Hat Store. Ewa Lipska, *Polish.* CEEP, *tr. by* Magnus J. Krynski

What happened to the iceman after all? The Iceman. Gordon Challis. PeNZ

What Happens. Robert Long. NAmP90

What Happens. Tadeusz Rózewicz, *Polish.* AF, *tr. by* Robert A. Maguire *and* Magnus Jan Krynski

What happens afterwards, none need enquire. Conjunction. Robert Graves. LoP

What Happens in Shakzpeare. Alan Brunton. PeNZ

What happens to a dream deferred? Harlem. Langston Hughes. APSN; AiP; AmPP; CrDW; GLP; GT; HCAP; HeIP-4; InPK-6; InPS-3; LiTM; MBE; NAAAL; NIP-4; NoP-4; PBMP; PoBA; Poetr; PoPoPo; RaBo; SAmP; SSLK; SoSe-8 *Fr.* Lenox Avenue Mural. HoPM

What happens to the beautiful girls with slender hips and bright round dresses? Hamtramck: The Polish Women. Toi Derricotte. InPS-3

What happens when an old black man. Thrift. Cornelius Eady. CMAP; LTA

What happens when the dog sits on a tiger. June Jordan. BPo

What Happiness Can Equal Mine. John David. AH

What happiness you gave to me. The Yew-Tree. *Unknown, Welsh.* GBL, *tr. by* Geoffrey Grigson

What happy, secret fountain. The Dwelling-Place. Henry Vaughan. GeHe; MeLP; NOSC; PeECV

What harm have to the stars? Without My Friends the Day Is Dark. Moses ibn Ezra, *Hebrew.* TrJP, *tr. by* Solomon Solis-Cohen

What has a life must have a death. Poem in the Form of a Coffin-Puller's Song. T'ao Ch'ien, *Chinese.* CoBCP, *tr. by* Burton Watson

What has been brought to a finish. Disturbing the Sallies Forth. Clark Coolidge. FTOS

What has been particularly lacking in my life up to now is. Simplicity. Henri Michaux, *Belgian.* NNPT, *tr. by* Richard Ellmann

What has bent you. The Pine at Timber-Line. Harriet Monroe. PoA

What / has happened. Here. Robert Creeley. NOBA

What has happened in the world? Volcanic Venus. D. H. Lawrence. InPS-3

What has happened to Lulu, mother? Charles Causley. KaS; OBSP

What has poor Woman done, that she must be. Aphra Behn. WPOW *Fr.* Sir Patient Fancy.

What has that face got to do with that. In Imitation. Larry Eigner. FTOS

What Has This Bugbear Death. Lucretius. CTC; OBCVT, *tr. by* Dryden *Fr.* De Rerum Natura (On the Nature of Things).

What has want to give. Envoi. Kathleen Jessie Raine. WPE

What hast thou done to this dear friend of mine. Youth and Death. Emma Lazarus. SDW

What, hast thou run thy race? Art going down? Of the Going Down of the Sun. John Bunyan. CH

What Hath Man Wrought Exclamation Point. Morris Gilbert Bishop. NYBP

What haunts me is a farmhouse among trees. Landscape with Figures. Frank Ormsby. PBCIP

What have I done for you. England, My England. William Ernest Henley. MoBrPo; OBEV; PoLF

"What have I done?" said Christine. Limerick. *Unknown.* PeLi

"What have I earned for all that work," I said. The People. W. B. Yeats. CMoP

What have I learned but. Gary Snyder. LoL

What have I made. The Children. Constance Urdang. CoAP

What, have I thus betrayed my liberty? Sonnet 47. Sir Philip Sidney. GBL; NAEL-1; NoP-4; PoEL-1 *Fr.* Astrophil and Stella. AAS; SiPS

What have I to say to you? A Love Song: First Version, 1915. William Carlos Williams. Poetr

What have they done to Klio what have they done to our Muse. Brian Coffey. BiHa *Fr.* Advent.

What have we done to you, death. Lament for a Brother. Al-Khansa, *Arabic.* ArPe, tr. by Omar S. Pound

What have we done? What cruel passion moved thee. Dialogue after Enjoyment. Abraham Cowley. BoLoP

What Have We Got. Lemn Sissay. NBrP

What have you done with the garden that was entrusted to you? Antonio Machado Ruiz. *See* The Wind, one brilliant day, called.

What have you done with the garden that was entrusted to you? (LL) The wind, one brilliant day, called. Antonio Machado Ruiz, *Spanish.* APAD, tr. by Robert Bly

What have you got to crow about. Meleager, *Greek.* PGA, tr. by Kenneth Rexroth

What have you more than I, who crave you so? Zora Cross. *Fr.* Love Sonnets. CBAP

What have you seen on the summits, the peaks that plunge their. Charles Brasch. PeNZ *Fr.* The Estate.

"What have you there?" the great Panjandrum said. The Truant. Edwin John Pratt. NOBC

What he did with every cent. (LL) The Hardship of Accounting. Robert Frost. FaBoCh; OBAL

What he had said came back to him. Run on a Warehouse. Susan Wheeler. BAP 96

What he liked in her voice. Narcissus. Gerda Mayer. LW

What He Said ("As a little white snake"). Catti Natanar, *Tamil.* PLW, tr. by A. K. Ramanujan

What He Said ("As the deer begin to hide"). Peyanar. PLW, tr. by A. K. Ramanujan *Fr.* Nine on Happy Reunion.

What He Said ("As wild oxen bellowed"). Peyanar. PLW, tr. by A. K. Ramanujan *Fr.* Nine on Happy Reunion.

What He Said ("Because peacocks moved like you"). Peyanar. PLW, tr. by A. K. Ramanujan *Fr.* Nine on Happy Reunion.

What He Said ("Heart, knowing, The"). Allur Nanmullai, *Tamil.* PLW, tr. by A. K. Ramanujan

What He Said ("Her arms have the beauty"). Orerulavanar, *Tamil.* tr. by A. K. Ramanujan

What He Said ("In this time of rain and thunder"). Peyanar, *Tamil.* PLW, tr. by A. K. Ramanujantr. by A. K. Ramanujan *Fr.* Nine on Happy Reunion.

What He Said. Pereyin Muruvalar, *Tamil.* PLW, tr. by A. K. Ramanujan

What He Said ("My love whose bangles"). Ammuvanar, *Tamil.* PLW, tr. by A. K. Ramanujan

What He Said. Perevin Muruvalar, *Tamil.* PLW, tr. by A. K. Ramanujan

What He Said ("Red earth, The"). Peyanar. PLW, tr. by A. K. Ramanujan *Fr.* Nine on Happy Reunion.

What He Said after a Quarrel, Remembering His Wedding Night. Virruṟṟu Mūteyiṉaṉār, *Tamil.* PLW, tr. by A. K. Ramanujan

What He Said in the Desert. Otalantaiyar, *Tamil.* PLW, tr. by A. K. Ramanujan

What He Said to His Charioteer, on His Way Back. Cittalai Cattanar, *Tamil.* PLW, tr. by A. K. Ramanujan

What He Said to His Heart, Arguing against Further Ambition and Travel. Ilankiranar, *Tamil.* PLW, tr. by A. K. Ramanujan

What He[e] Suffered. Ben Jonson. *Fr.* A Celebration of Charis in Ten Lyric[k] Pieces [or Peeces]. BeJo; OxAEP-1; SeCP

What heart could have thought you? To a Snowflake. Francis Thompson. MoBrPo

What heartache—ne'er a hill! From the Flats. Sidney Lanier. APN-2; NOBA; NoP-4; OxBA

What heaven-entreated *or* heaven-besiegèd *or* heav'n-beseiged] heart is this? To the Noblest and Best of Ladies, the Countess of Denbigh, Perswading her to Resolution in Religion, and to render her selfe without further delay into the Communion of the Catholick Church. Richard Crashaw. GeHe; MeLP; PBRV

What heavy, dark delirium! Violin Bow and Strings. Innokenty Fiodorovich Annensky, *Russian.* TCRP, tr. by Lubov Yakovleva *with* Daniel Weissbort

What Hell Is. Heather McHugh. CrSp; WeT

What helps it if of love I sing. Hadewijch, *Dutch.* PBWP, tr. by Frans van Rosevelt

What Her Friend Said. Kapilar, *Tamil.* PLW, tr. by A. K. Ramanujan

What Her Friend Said Criticizing Him to Give Her Strength. Kuriyiraiyar, *Tamil.* PLW, tr. by A. K. Ramanujan

What Her Friend Said to Her, before the Rains. Kapilar, *Tamil.* PLW, tr. by A. K. Ramanujan

What Her Friend Said to Her, within the Lover's Hearing. Paranar, *Tamil.* PLW, tr. by A. K. Ramanujan

What Her Friend Said to the Foster-Mother. Kapilar, *Tamil.* PLW, tr. by A. K. Ramanujan

What Her Friend Said to the foster-mother (who is guarding her carefully). Kapilar, *Tamil.* PLW, tr. by A. K. Ramanujan

What Her Girl Friend Asked and What She Replied Regarding His Return. *Unknown, Tamil.* PLW, tr. by A. K. Ramanujan

What Her Girl Friend Said ("As the cassias blossom"). Peyanar. PLW, tr. by A. K. Ramanujan *Fr.* Nine on Happy Reunion.

What her girl friend said ("Her eyes"). Peyanar. PLW, tr. by A. K. Ramanujan *Fr.* Nine on Happy Reunion.

What her Girl Friend Said ("Saying to himself"). Peyanar. PLW, tr. by A. K. Ramanujan *Fr.* Nine on Happy Reunion.

What Her Girl Friend Said ("Your arms are beautiful again"). Peyanar. PLW, tr. by A. K. Ramanujan *Fr.* Nine on Happy Reunion.

What Her Girl Friend Said before the Elopement. Kutavayir Kirattanar, *Tamil.* PLW, tr. by A. K. Ramanujan

What Her Girl Friend Said, Consoling Her when She Was Distressed by the Town's Gossip. Uloccanar, *Tamil.* PLW, tr. by A. K. Ramanujan

What Her Girl Friend Said on Her Wedding Day. Ammuvanar, *Tamil.* PLW, tr. by A. K. Ramanujan

What Her Girl Friend Said, Seeing Her Friend Suffer in Silent Dignity over Her Husband's Infidelity. Kayamanar, *Tamil.* PLW, tr. by A. K. Ramanujan

What Her Girl Friend Said, the Lover within Earshot, behind a Fence. Uloccanar, *Tamil.* PLW, tr. by A. K. Ramanujan

What Her Girl Friend Said to her. Marutanilanakanar, *Tamil.* PLW, tr. by A. K. Ramanujan

What Her Girl Friend Said to her ("Not happy with what he has"). Pālaipāṭiya Peruṅkaṭuṅkō, *Tamil.* PLW, tr. by A. K. Ramanujan

What Her Girl Friend Said to Her ("These fat cassia trees"). Kovatattan, *Tamil.* PLW, tr. by A. K. Ramanujan

What Her Girl Friend Said to her lover on His Return. Kākkai Pāṭiṉiyār Naccelḷaiyār, *Tamil.* PLW, tr. by A. K. Ramanujan

What Her Girl Friend Said to Him ("Her soft plump shoulders"). Ammuvanar, *Tamil.* PLW, tr. by A. K. Ramanujan

What Her Girl Friend Said to Him. Kannan, *Tamil.* PLW, tr. by A. K. Ramanujan

What Her Girl Friend Said to Him. Centan Kaṇṇaṉār, *Tamil.* PLW, tr. by A. K. Ramanujan

What Her Girl Friend Said to him ("Near the salt pans"). Centan Kannanar, *Tamil.* PLW, tr. by A. K. Ramanujan

What Her Girl Friend Said to Him ("Your sands are furrowed"). Ammuvanar, *Tamil.* PLW, tr. by A. K. Ramanujan

What Her Girl Friend Said to Him (on Her Behalf) When He Came by Daylight. *Unknown, Tamil.* PLW, tr. by A. K. Ramanujan

What Her Girl Friend Said to Him, Trying to Dissuade Him from His Long Journey. *Unknown, Tamil.* PLW, tr. by A. K. Ramanujan

What Her Girl Friend Said to Him When He Wanted to Come by Day. Ammuvanar, *Tamil.* PLW, tr. by A. K. Ramanujan

What Her Girl Friend Said to the foster-mother ("If you think, mother"). Orampokiyar. PLW *Fr.* Five on the Crabs. PLW, tr. by A. K. Ramanujan

What Her Girl friend Said to the Foster-Mother ("In his fields, mother"). Orampokiyar. PLW *Fr.* Five on the Crabs. PLW, tr. by A. K. Ramanujan

What Her Girl Friend Said when He Sent a Flattering Minstrel on His Behalf. Orampokiyar, *Tamil.* PLW, tr. by A. K. Ramanujan

What Her Girl Friend Said, When the Woman Was About to Take Back Her Unfaithful Husband. Orampokiyar, *Tamil.* PLW, tr. by A. K. Ramanujan

What Her Girlfriends Said to Her. Okkur Macatti, *Tamil.* BoWoP, tr. by A. K. Ramanujan

What Her Mother Said ("If a calving cow"). *Unknown, Tamil.* PLW, tr. by A. K. Ramanujan

What Hiawatha Probably Did. *Unknown.* NBLV

What hideous noyse was that? John Webster. PoEL-2 *Fr.* The Duchess of Malfi. NAEL-1

What high rewards by little pain is won. (LL) To St Mary Magdalen. Henry Constable. ChIV-2; NoSic

What His Friend Said, Teasing the Man in Love. Milaipperun Kantan, *Tamil.* PLW, tr. by A. K. Ramanujan

What ho! my shepherds, sweet it were. A Sylvan Revel. Edward Cracroft Lefroy. AWP *Fr.* Echoes from Theocritus.

What hope is here for modern rhyme. Tennyson. EnVR *Fr.* In Memoriam A. H. H.

What hope of safety for our realm. On Sympathisers with the American Revolution. Charles Wesley. NOCV

What Horace says is. Eheu Fugaces. "Thomas Ingoldsby." FaBoEE; OxBoLi

What horrid Crime did gentle Sleep displease? A Translation out of Statius. To Sleep. Publius Papinius Statius, *Latin.* OBCVT, *tr. by* John Potenger

What horrid sin condemned the teeming Earth. On Tobacco. Charles Cotton. OBSV

What How? How now? Hath How such hearing found. On How the Cobler. *Unknown.* SCAP

What hue lies in the slit of anger. Outlines. Audre Lorde. GLP

What humour can be so rare. Sister Juana Inés de la Cruz. *Fr.* A Satirical Romance. PBWP, *tr. by* Judith Thurman

What hurrying human tides, or day or night! Broadway. Walt Whitman. NAAL-1; NAAL-3

What I choose is youse:/ baby. (LL) Coon Song. A. R. Ammons. MoP; NOBA

What I did, I won't excuse, except. The Unreal Dwelling: My Years in Volcano. Garrett Kaoru Hongo. OpBo

What I Do. Denise Riley. NBrP

What I Do Is Me. Gerard Manley Hopkins. MoBrPo

What I do to the grass, does to my thoughts and me. (LL) The Mower's Song. Andrew Marvell. CBLP; ESCV; FMP; NAEL-1; NOSC; PoEL-2; SeCP

What I don't understand is the beauty. Rothko's Yellow. Dean Young. WeT

What I expected, was. Stephen Spender. MoBrPo; NOBE; NoAM; OxAEP-2

What I fancy, I approve. No Loathsomnesse in Love. Robert Herrick. BeJo; GBL; PBMP

What I forgot to mention was the desultory. Postscript to an Elegy. Gibbons Ruark. MT

What I give that man, some other woman takes. Hopping Toad Blues. Raymond R. Patterson. SeSe

What I had now was a house too absurdly spacious for. Home Is So Sad. Ted Walker. LBC

What I "have to do" has nothing to do. Last Words. Richard Howard. DiPo *Fr.* Ithaca: The Palace at Four A.M.

What I Have to Tell You, Until Next Time. David Avidan, *Hebrew.* IP, *tr. by* Warren Bargad *and* Stanley F. Chyet

What I Have Written I Have Written. Peter Porter. BMAP; NOBAu

What I Heard at the Discount Department Store. David Budbill. RaBo; TRP

What I hope (when I hope) is that we'll. To the Dead. Frank Bidart. EOEF

What I in her am grieved to want. (LL) An Elegy: "Though beauty be the mark of praise." Ben Jonson. BeJo; NoP-4; OBEV

What I Learned from My Mother. Julia Kasdorf. PBCAP

What I Like. Alice Fulton. WeW-3

What I like about Clive. Lord Clive. Edmund Clerihew Bentley. NOBL; PeLV *Fr.* Clerihews.

What I like most is when. Crimes of Passion: The Slasher. Terry Stokes. AmPA

What I Live For. George Linnaeus Banks. BLPA; FaBoBe (Why Do I Live?) PWR; PoToHe

What I mean by too much metaphor and smile. (LL) Very like a Whale. Ogden Nash. HAP; InPK-6; InPS-3; PoLF

What I need to say to her as she reached. Feed the Mexican Back into Her. Cherríe Moraga. GLP

What I need is lots of money. Take I, 4:11:58. Philip Whalen. NeAP

What I really wanted. Aleksandr Semionovich Kushner, *Russian.* TCRP, *tr. by* Bernard Meares

What I remember about that day. Eviction. Lucille Clifton. InPS-3; NTCP

What I remember didn't happen. A Date With Robbe-Grillet. Elaine Equi. PeVV; PmAP

What I remember is the ebb and flow of sound. The Sound I Listened For. Robert Francis. AFr

What I remember of Mexico. Sunrise and Moonfall, Rosarito Beach. Campbell McGrath. WeT

What I Saw. Zbigniew Herbert, *Polish.* AF, *tr. by* John Carpenter *and* Bogdana Carpenter

What I saw was just one eye. The Bird at Dawn. Harold Monro. BoTP; MoBrPo

What I say is when I plan my future. Blue Book 18 Pages 1–4. Steve Benson. FTOS

What I shall leave thee, none can tell. To His Son [*or* Sonne], Vincent Corbet[t]. Richard Corbet. BeJo; FaBoCh; NOSC; OxAEP-1; OxBChV

What I Tell Him. Simon J. Ortiz. CDW; ChAP

What I thought was love. The Liar. Imamu Amiri Baraka. AmPP; NOBA

What I took in my hand. Son. Robert Creeley. FTOS; PoA

What I walked down to the highway. Another Sunday Morning. Carter Revard. VoR

What I wanted. In Weather. Robert Hass. AmPA

What I was doing with my white teeth exposed. The Dog. Gerald Stern. WeW-3

What I was would not work. Encounter in the Cage Country. James Dickey. CAPP-1

What I will say today. Lo Que Digo. *Unknown.* AS

What I wished you before, but harder. (LL) The Writer. Richard Wilbur. HCAP; ImGa; MoLi; NoAM; OxBC; PoPoPo; Poetr; SoSe-8

What I would not give for this century, were it only to change! Song from the Occupation Time. Ion Caraion, *Romanian .* AF, *tr. by* Marguerite Dorian *and* Elliott B. Urdang

What if a day, or a month, or a year[e]. Thomas Campion. AAS; EBEV

What if a much of a which of a wind. E. E. Cummings. ImPo; LiTM; MeMAP; MoAmPo; NAAL-2; NOBA; OxBA; PoA; PoRA; SAGP

What If God. Sharon Olds. NMM-2

What if I bade you leave. Those Images. W. B. Yeats. CMoP

What if I do go armed? she said. Arms and the Woman. Dorothea MacKellar. NOBAu

What if I should go deaf and wakeful when, old, I quit drinking? Heavenly Traveler. Chech'on Park, *Korean.* CKP, *tr. by* Jaihiun Kim

What if on a foggy night in a beachtown. Mark Jarman. *See* Questions for Ecclesiastes.

What if on a foggy night in a beachtown, a night when. Questions for Ecclesiastes. Mark Jarman. BAP-93

What if small birds are peppering the sky. It Is Winter, I Know. Merrill Moore. MoAmPo

What If Some Little Paine the Passage Have. Edmund Spenser. CH *Fr.* Wood Of Error. AEP

What if the body goes the sense. Image-Nation 3. Robin Blaser. PoM

What if the foot, ordain'd the dust to tread. Alexander Pope. FaBoPV *Fr.* An Essay on Man.

What If The Saint Must Die. John Peck. AH

What if the sun comes out. Boy Remembers in the Field. Raymond Knister. NOBC

What if the ways be stone. City Songs. Mark Van Doren. NYBP

What if there wasn't a metaphor. Stigmata. Patrick Lane. NOBC

What if this present were the world's last night? Donne. EBEV; HeIP-4; ImPo; InPS-3; MeLP; NAEL-1; NOCV; NOSC; OxAEP-1; PeECV; PoE; Son *Fr.* Holy Sonnets. ESCV

What if, with my life half over. Id. Harry Clifton. PBCIP

What in our lives is burnt. August 1914. Isaac Rosenberg. EBEV; NOBE; OBWP; OxBTC; PeFWW

What, in the Register of Doom, is writ. Bishop Orders His Tomb in St. Praxed's. Morris Gilbert Bishop. OBAL

What in the world we see. Going Home. Richard Caddel. NBrP

What interested me most about gorillas / when I first studied them. Somewhere Along the Line. "Antler." PUP-18

What invisible rat. Jean-Joseph Rabéarivelo, *French.* TTY, *tr. by* Alan Ryder; NegPo, *tr. by* Ellen Conroy Kennedy; PBMAP

What / irritation of offensively red brick is this. William Carlos Williams. MeMAP *Fr.* Paterson.

What! Irving? thrice welcome, warm heart, and fine brain. Irving. James Russell Lowell. TAP *Fr.* A Fable for Critics. NAAL-1; NAAL-3

What is a blk poem & / or what is it. Food for Thought. Val Ferdinand. NBV

What is a communist? One who hath yearnings. On Communists. Ebenezer Elliot. NBLV; NOBL; NOBVV

What is a first love worth except to prepare for a second? John Milton Hay. FaBoEE

What is a Friend? I'll tell you. A Friend. *Unknown.* PoToHe

What is a Garden? Reginald Arkell. OBGa

What is a Garden. W. S. Merwin. GaP

What is a good prince? He is the sheepdog who puts the wolves to flight. De Principe Bono et Malo. Sir Thomas More. PBRV

What is a half-truth the lobster declared. The Territory Is Not the Map. Jack Spicer. CBNP

What is a Jew in solitude? Yom Kippur 1984. Adrienne Rich. GLP; NoAM

What Is a Jewish Poem? Myra Sklarew. CRP

What is a kiss? Language Event Two. Robert Desnos, *French.* PFTM, *tr. by* Marcel Jean

What is a kiss[e]? Why this, as some approve. A Kiss[e]. Robert Herrick. CaPo

What is a locust? The Locust. *Unknown, Malagasy.* RB, *tr. by* A. Marre *and* Willard R. Trask

What is a man but a farmer. Farmer's Song at Can Tho. Herbert Krohn. CDa

What is a modern Poet's fate? The Poet's Fate. Thomas Hood. FaBoEE

What is a poet's love? The Poet's Lot. Oliver Wendell Holmes. PoEL-5

What is a sonnet? 'T is [or 'Tis] the pearly shell. The Sonnet. Richard Watson Gilder. APN-2

What is Africa to me. Heritage. Countee Cullen. BPo; ChAP; ColAP; CrDW; HeIP-4; MoAmPo; NAAAL; NAAL-2; NoAM; NoP-4; PoBA; PoPoPo; Poetr; SSLK; TTY

What is Africa to thee? The Africa Thing. Adam David Miller. NBV

What is ambition? 'Tis a glorious cheat! Ambition. Nathaniel Parker Willis. OBCA

What is ambition? 'tis unrest, defeat! Ambition. Henrietta Cordelia Ray. CBWP-3

What is an epigram? a dwarfish whole. Coleridge. FaBoEE; NIP-4

What is Beautiful. Jay Wright. GT

What is beauty, saith my sufferings, then? Marlowe. ImPo   Fr. Tamburlaine the Great.

What is beheld through glass seems glass. Prisms. Laura Riding Jackson. ColAP

What Is Beyond Us. Karen Fish. PuP-15

What Is black. Gullfish. Tom Weatherly. Fr. Cantos. PoBA

What Is Black? Mary O'Neill. NTCP

What Is Charm? Louisa Carroll Thomas. BLPA

What is failure? When the maiden. Failure. Henrietta Cordelia Ray. CBWP-3

What is fame? An empty bubble. James Grainger. PFE

"What is funny?" you ask, my child. The Anatomy of Humor. Morris Gilbert Bishop. NBLV

What is God singing in his profound. Sophocles. OBCVT, tr. by Fitts, Dudley and Robert Fitzgerald   Fr. Oedipus Tyrannus.

What Is Good? John Boyle O'Reilly. PoToHe

What is green in me. Stepping Westward. Denise Levertov. CrSp; NALW; NMM-2; Poetr; VGW

What Is Happening Now? Hubert Witheford. PeNZ

What is happening to me now that loved faces. Childhood in Jacksonville, Florida. Jane Cooper. TAP

What is he buzzing in my ears? Confessions. Robert Browning. CBLP; GTBS-P; NOBE; NOBVV; PFE

What is he, this lordling, that cometh from the fight? William Herebert. ChIV-1; MiEL

What Is Heaven? Philip James Bailey. PWR

What Is It? Marie Louise Allen. CTV

What Is It? H. E. Wilkinson. BoTP

What is it about a Great Northern boxcar. Great Northern. Dave Etter. GM

What is it, in these latter days. A Novice. Dollie Radford. SDW

What is it, inside them and undeniable. The King's Men. William Heyen. PoA

What is it men in women do require? Question Answered, The [or A]. William Blake. FaBoEE; GBL; ITG; NoP-4; OAEL-2; OxBM   Fr. Several Questions Answered.

What is it now with me. Fear of Death. John Ashbery. FaBoMo; TAP

What is it our mammas bewitches. Written for My Son, and Spoken by Him at His First Putting on Breeches. Mary Barber. CABP; ECEV; ECWP; NOEC

What is it so transforms the boulevard? Another Spirit Advances. Jules Romains, French. AWP, tr. by Joseph T. Shipley

What is it? Something sought by everyone? Different Dimensions. Ikuko Atsumi, Japanese. WPJ, tr. by Kenneth Rexroth and Ikuko Atsumi

What is it that glitters so clear and serene. Water. Ann Taylor. NOxBChV

What is it that shoots from the mountains so high. Fire. Ann Taylor. NOxBChV

What is it that winds about over the world. Air. Ann Taylor. NOxBChV

What is it that you say? (LL) Hospital for Defectives. Thomas Blackburn. GTBS-P; OxBTC

What is it that's cover'd so richly with green. Earth. Ann Taylor. NOxBChV

What is it to grow old? Growing Old. Matthew Arnold. EnVR; FHYEP; NAEL-2; NOBVV; OAEL-2; PoEL-5

What is it when a woman sleeps, her head bright. Where You Go When She Sleeps. T. R. Hummer. MT

What is it with these people-swallowing streets. All of a Sudden. Teresa de Jesús, Spanish. WPOW, tr. by Maria A. Proser, Arlene Scully and James Scully

What is it you're mumbling, old Father, my Dad? By the Exeter River. Donald Hall. MoBS

What Is Left? István Vas, Hungarian. CEEP, tr. by Emery E. George

What is Love? Mary Lamb. Ro   Fr. The Keepsake for 1829 (1828).

What is more gentle than a wind in summer? Sleep and Poetry. Keats.

What is my whole life? What? The Path Is Long. Nikolai Ivanovich Glazkov, Russian. TCRP, tr. by Daniel Weissbort

What is not rooted in static. A Bluesman's Blues. Lenard D. Moore. ISC

What is orange? Why, an orange, / Just an orange! (LL)   What is pink? A rose is pink. Christina Rossetti. OxBChV

What is our innocence. What Are Years? Marianne Moore. CMoP; MeMAP; MoAmPo; MoP; NOBA; NoAM; NoP-4; OxBA; PiM; SoSe-8

What is our life? a play of passion. On the Life of Man. Sir Walter Ralegh. EBEV; FaBoEE; NAEL-1; NOBE; NoSic; OxBSP; SCGP; SiPS; SoSe-8

What is our life on earth? Remembering Min Ch'e. Su Tung-p'o, Chinese. OHMPC, tr. by Kenneth Rexroth

What is—"Paradise." Emily Dickinson. CMoP

What is pink? A rose is pink. Christina Rossetti. ACTP; ChAP; FPC; OxBChV

What is pink? A rose is pink / By the fountain's brink. Christina Rossetti. See What is pink? A rose is pink.

What Is Poetry. John Ashbery. LCAP-2

What Is Poetry. James Scully. FYAP

What is reality? Self in 1958. Anne Sexton. HCAP

What Is Repeated, What Abides. Barbara Hendryson. CrSp

What is required? Preparing a Curriculum Vitae. Wislawa Szymborska, Polish. CEEP, tr. by Magnus J. Krynski and Robert A. Maguire

What [or And what] Is So Rare as a Day in June? James Russell Lowell. FaBoBe; ImGa   Fr. The Vision of Sir Launfal.

("Climbs to a soul in grass and / flowers.") (LL)   CTV

(Day in June, A.)   CTV

What is so strange about a tree alone in an open field? Hunting Pheasants in a Cornfield. Robert Bly. CoAmPo; TRP

What is song's eternity? Song's Eternity. John Clare. FaBoCh

What Is Terrible. Roy Fuller. PoWW

What is that general rule which tells / how long a thing will live? Holy City, City of Night. Lynda Hull. PUP-19

What is that growling! Screeching! Barking! Spring Cleaning. Phillip William George. VoR

What is the boy now, who has lost his ball. The Ball Poem. John Berryman. ChAP; CoAP; MoAmPo; NOBA; NoAM; Poetr

What is the end of great. 'Tis but to fill. Byron. OBCoV   Fr. Canto the First. NAEL-2; OAEL-2; PoE   Fr. Don Juan.

What is the evil deed I have committed? Vladimir Nabokov, Russian. TCRP, tr. by Vladimir Nabokov

What is the flower that blooms each year. The Christmas Rose. C. Day Lewis. TIRV

What is the head. Some Last Questions. W. S. Merwin. HCAP; VCAP

What is the heart of a girl? The Heart of a Girl Is a Wonderful Thing. Unknown. BLPA

"What is the jewel colour?" Hilda Doolittle. NALW   Fr. Tribute to the Angels.

What is the life. Careers. Imamu Amiri Baraka. TRP

"What is the matter, grandmother dear?" Grandma's Lost Balance. Sydney Dayre. OBCA

What is the matter with me? Unknown, Chinese. OHMPC, tr. by Kenneth Rexroth

What is the meaning of this Ideal. Walter James Turner. Fr. The Seven Days of the Sun. OBMV

What is the measure then, the magpie in the field. The Measure. Patrick Lane. NOBC

What is the metre of the dictionary? Dylan Thomas. CMoP; FaBoMo   Fr. A Sequence of Sonnets.

What is the mirror saying with its O? A Room in the Villa. William Jay Smith. NYBP

What is the misery in one that turns one with gladness. Grace Abounding. A. R. Ammons. HCAP

What is the moral? Who rides may read. The Winners. Rudyard Kipling. BLPA; FaPoR; MoBrPo   Fr. The Story of the Gadsbys.

What is the name of King Ringang's daughter? Beauty Rohtraut. Eduard Friedrich Mörike, German. AWP; OBVE, tr. by George Meredith

What is the name of this street? Osip Emilevich Mandelstam, Russian. TCRP, tr. by Bernard Meares

What is the night-bird's tune, wherewith she startles. The New Dodo: Isabrand's Song. Thomas Lovell Beddoes. CBNP

What is the old year? 'Tis a book. The Old Year. Clarence Thomas Urmy. PoToHe

What is the opposite of nuts?. Richard Wilbur. NOxBChV

What is the opposite of riot. Some Opposites. Richard Wilbur. OBCA

What is the purpose of visits to me twice since you've died? Grandmother. Grace Cavalieri. UnSA

"What is the real good?" What Is Good? John Boyle O'Reilly. PoToHe

What is the rhyme for porringer? A Difficult Rhyme. Mother Goose. OxNR; ReMoGo

What is the skill of this waking? Heard the singing. For Kay Boyle. Muriel Rukeyser. NMM-2

What is the subject? It looks like a paragraph. Prose. Bernard Welt. EOEF

What is the summer. Summer Lost. Harriet Hamilton King. VWP

What is the Sun? Wes Magee. AYFP

"What is the thing your eyes hold loveliest." The Newlyweds. Cloyd Mann Criswell. PoLF

What is the use of the rule insane. The Solution. Brian Merriman. BIrV, *tr.* by Arland Ussher *Fr.* The Midnight Court. NOIV, *tr.* by Thomas Kinsella

What is the word for "death." Flowers for Luis Bunuel. Stuart Z. Perkoff. NeAP

What is the *World*? A great *Exchange* of ware. Francis Quarles. PBRV *Fr.* Pentelogia.

What is the world, O soldiers? Napoleon. Walter De la Mare. FaBoCh; FaBoTw; NOBE; RB; Spl

What is the world? tell, Worldling (if thou know it). Mundus Qualis. Joshua Sylvester. FaBoEE

What is there hid in the heart of a rose. Song. Alfred Noyes. CH

What is there in my heart that you should sue. Lachrimae Amantis. Geoffrey Hill. NOCV *Fr.* Lachrimae; or Seven Tears Figured in Seven Passionate Pavans.

What is there left to be said? A Farewell. Arthur Rex Dugard Fairburn. PeNZ

What is there left to say? (LL) The Curse of Cromwell. W. B. Yeats. BIrV; IIP

What is there that we can do or say. A Poem. Ezekiel Mphahlele. AF

What is this flesh and blood compounded of. Allen Tate. PoA *Fr.* Sonnets of the Blood.

What is this hip yearning smooching hot. Clinton. Sterling Plumpp. BkSV *Fr.* Clinton.

What Is This Knowledge? Sir John Davies. *Fr.* Nosce Teipsum. NoSic; SiPS

What is this life if, full of care. Leisure. W. H. Davies. APAD; AWP; BoTP; CH; CTV; EBEvV; FaBoBe; LiTM; MoBrPo; NOBE; NTP; OBEV; OBMV; PoRA; TFi

What is this life, this active guest. A Solemn Meditation. William Shenstone. NOEC

What is this recompense you'd have from me? From a Woman to a Greedy Lover. Norman Cameron. FaBoEE *Fr.* Three Love Poems. FaBoTw; GTBS-P

What is this road that separates us. Way. Tristan Tzara, *French.* NNPT, *tr.* by Lee Harwood

What is this? said God. The obstinacy. Echoes. Ronald Stuart Thomas. OxAEP-2

What is this strange and uncouth thing? The Cross[e]. George Herbert. ESCV

What is this tempest. Walter James Turner. *Fr.* The Seven Days of the Sun. OBMV

What is this that I can see. Oh! Death. *Unknown.* AmFP

What is this that I have heard? Dawn Has Yet to Ripple In. Melville Cane. MoAmPo

What is this that roareth thus? Motor Bus. Alfred Denis Godley. NBLV; NOBL

What Is This Thing You Earthlings Speak Of. (LL) Cuchulainn. Michael O'Loughlin. BiHa; PBCIP

What is this wonderful thing? Brown and everywhere! Looking at a Dry Canadian Thistle Brought In from the Snow. Robert Bly. NNaP

What Is Thought but Won't Hold Still. Clark Coolidge. FTOS

What Is Time? James Marsden. PWR

"What is to be done." (LL) I went into the Maverick Bar. Gary Snyder. LoL; PaTW

What is war? J. M. Rose-Troup. NSI

What is weaker than a god? It groans hungry. Rosario Castellanos, *Spanish.* BoWoP, *tr.* by Willis Barnstone

What is wisdom: What gift of the gods. Euripides. GrIP, *tr.* by William Arrowsmith *Fr.* Bacchae.

What Is Woman? Mrs. Henry Linden. CBWP-4

What Is Worth Knowing? Sujata Bhatt. OMIP

What is wrought in the forge of the living and life. Hafiz. TAL, *tr.* by Gertrude Lowthian Bell *Fr.* Odes.

What is your feeling about the revolutionary spirit of your age. Firebrand. Harry Crosby. SPE

What is your plaster Doctor? Christmas Rhyme: North Tyrone. *Unknown.* FaBoVe

What is your substance, whereof are you made. Sonnet 53. Shakespeare. CTC; EBEV; ImPo; NoSic; OAEL-1; OBEV; OxAEP-1; SCGP *Fr.* Sonnets.

What isn't water in us must be bone. Suffering The Sea Change: All My Pretty Ones. Lucinda Roy. GT

What is't, good prying friend, you say? The Alarm. Hildebrand Jacob. NOEC

What is't you mean, that I am thus approached? The Repulse to Alcander. Sarah Fyge Egerton. ECWP

What It Could Be. Denise Levertov. PaTW

What it is all about? (LL) Civilian and Soldier. Wole Soyinka. AF; PBMAP

What It Is Like. Gerald Stern. NAmP90

What it must be like to be an angel. Parents. William Meredith. AFr; FYAP

What it showed was always the same. The Night Mirror. John Hollander. NYBP; VCAP

What It Takes. John Godfrey. FTOS

What it was, and it might serve me in a time when jests are few. (LL) A Son. Rudyard Kipling. FaBoEE; PeFWW

What It's Like Living in My Studio Late in Spring. Wen Cheng-ming, *Chinese.*
"Quiet courtyard fills with greenery, The." CoBLCP, *tr.* by Jonathan Chaves

What It's Like to Be a Black Girl (For Those of You Who Aren't). Patricia Smith. UnSA

What Jenner Said on Hearing in Elysium That Complaints Had Been Made of His Having a Statue [in Trafalgar Square]. Shirley Brooks. FaBoEE

What Jenny Knows. Jackie Kay. NOxBChV

What Johnny Told Me. John Ciardi. TLR

What joy hath yon gugel wreath of flowers that is. The Garland and the Girdle. Michelangelo Buonarroti, *Italian.* AWP, *tr.* by John Addington Symonds

What joys! what joys were thine! (LL) To the Man-of-War Bird. Walt Whitman. APN-1; APo; AmPP; FaBoBe

What jungles he swung out of into the imagination. Gorilla Gorilla. Bruce Dawe. NoAM

What, keep love in *perspective?*—that old lie. In Perspective. Robert Graves. OxBSP

What killed that kangaroo-doe, slender skeleton. River Bend. Judith Wright. BMAP

What Kin' o' Pants Does the Gambler Wear. *Unknown.* AS

What kind of a person would kill Black children? The Test of Atlanta 1979. June Jordan. ISC

What kind of Bacchus are you? By the real. Beer. Emperor Julian, *Greek.* GrAn, *tr.* by Peter Jay

What kind of beast would turn its life into words? Adrienne Rich. *Fr.* Twenty-one Love Poems. GLP

What kind of lover have you made me, mother. La Dulce Culpa. Cherríe Moraga. CPO; MDDM *Fr.* La Dolce Culpa.

What Kind of Mistress[e] He Would Have. Robert Herrick. CaPo; CavPo

What Kind of Times Are These. Adrienne Rich. BAP-93; LoL *Fr.* Not Somewhere Else, But Here.

What lack you, sir? What seek you? What will you buy? Thomas Newbery. OxBChV *Fr.* The Great Merchant, Dives Pragmaticus, Cries His Wares.

What lady would not love a shepherd swain? (LL) The Shepherd's Wife's Song. Robert Greene. HAP; NoSic; RACG

What large, dark hands are those at the window. Love On the Farm. D. H. Lawrence. CABP; CBLP; CMoP; MoBrPo; NAEL-2; NoAM; NoP-4; SAGP; SCGP

What Larkin bawled to hungry crowds. Inscription for a Headstone. Austin Clarke. BIrV; CIP-2; IIP

What led to the crassness of Custer. Limerick. Bill Greenwell. PeLi

What length of verse can serve brave *Mopsa''s* good to show? Sir Philip Sidney. *Fr.* Arcadia.

What lewd, naked and revolting shape is this? Shopping for Meat in Winter. Oscar Williams. LiTM

What linking of soul to the halcyons of the afternoon! Aegean Melancholy. Odysseus Elytis, *Greek.* VCWP, *tr.* by Edmund Keeley *and* Philip Sherrard

What lips my lips have kissed, and where, and why. Edna St. Vincent Millay. BoLoP; GEA; GSo; HeIP-4; HoPM; LoP; MeMAP; MoAmPo; NAAL-2; NIP-4; OPOU; SAGP; Son

What lissom boy among the roses. Horace, *Latin.* OBCVT, *tr.* by Douglas Keith

What little throat. The Blackbird by Belfast Lough. *Unknown, Early Irish.* IIP, *tr.* by Frank O'Connor

What lively lad most pleasured me. A Last Confession. W. B. Yeats. BoLoP; CBLP; CMoP; HAP; NIP-4; OAEL-2

What loud wave-motioned hooves awaken. The Blue Horses. James McAuley. BMAP

What Love Is. Ella Wheeler Wilcox. PWR

What love is this of thine, that cannot be. Edward Taylor. AmPP; NOCV; PoEL-3; SCAP *Fr.* Preparatory Meditations Before My Approach to the Lord's Supper.

What lovely things / Thy hand hath made. The Scribe. Walter De la Mare. CMoP; EBEvV; FaBoCh; OBMV; TrCP

What luck I can pick. Tadeusz Rózewicz, *Polish.* HP, *tr. by* Adam Czerniawski

What made the place a landscape of despair. Claus von Stauffenberg. Thom Gunn. OBWP

What made the porter stare so hard? At Devlin's Siding. Barcroft Henry Boake. CBAP

What Makes a Happy Life. Martial, *Latin.* AWP, *tr. by* Goldwin Smith

"What makes a home?" *Unknown.* PoToHe

What makes a knave a child of God. Samuel Butler. NOBL; OBSV *Fr.* Hudibras.

What makes a plenteous harvest. Virgil. AWP, *tr. by* Dryden *Fr.* Georgics.

What makes all subjects discontent. Samuel Butler. FaBoEE

What makes life worth the living. Giving and Forgiving. Thomas Grant Springer. PoToHe

What makes me disinclined. Pretences. Ibn Rashiq, *Arabic.* TTY, *tr. by* A. J. Arberry

What makes me write my dearest Freind you aske. Hester Wyat. FaBoVe

What makes my bed seem hard seeing it is soft? Elegies 1.2. Ovid. AWP, *tr. by* Marlowe, *sl. diff. vers.* *Fr.* Elegies.

What makes permeable the ghost? The Ghost. Hilary Corke. NYBP

What makes us rove that starlit corridor. Science Fiction. Kingsley Amis. NoAM

What makes your lip so strange? Thomas Middleton. *Fr.* The Changeling. PoEL-2

What man dost thou dig it for? Shakespeare. *Fr.* Hamlet. NAWM-1

What man has made of man? (LL) Lines Written in Early Spring. Wordsworth. FHYEP; GTBS-P; LaPo; NAEL-2; NOBRP; OAEL-2; PBMP; PoLF; Ro

What man is he, that boasts of fleshly might. Edmund Spenser. FHYEP *Fr.* Wood Of Error. AEP

What man is he that yearneth. Chorus. Sophocles, *Greek.* OBCVT, *tr. by* Alfred Edward Housman *Fr.* Oedipus at Colonus.

What man so wise, what earthly wit so ware. Edmund Spenser. FHYEP *Fr.* Wood Of Error. AEP

What man that sees the ever-whirling wheel. Edmund Spenser. *See* Mutability.

What marked the river's flow. "Stephany." NBV

What? Mars his sword? faire Cytherea say. Upon Venus Putting on Mars His Armes. Leonidas of Alexandria, *Classical Greek.* SeCP, *tr. by* Richard Crashaw

What masque of what old wind-withered New-Year. For Spring By Sandro Botticelli. D. G. Rossetti. GS

What matters is the renewing and long running kinship. The Union of Two. Haki R. Madhubuti. ISC

What may words say, or what may words not say. Sonnet 35. Sir Philip Sidney. *Fr.* Astrophil and Stella. AAS; SiPS

What mean these dreams, and hideous forms that rise. George the Third's Soliloquy. Philip Freneau. NOBA

What mean these loud aerial cracks I hear? *Unknown.* NOEC *Fr.* Bedlam; a Poem on His Majesty's Happy Escape from His German Dominions.

What mean these showy and these sounding signs. The Feast of Blood. Joseph Fawcett. NOEC *Fr.* The Art of War.

What mean those Amorous Curles of Jet? In Imitation of Horace. Aphra Behn. KTR; NOSC

What meanes this silence of Harvardine quils. A Supplement. Benjamin Tompson. SCAP

What meanest thou, my fortune. *Unknown.* EnLoPo

What meaneth this, that Christ an hymne did singe. William Alabaster. ESCV *Fr.* Divine Meditations. Son

What means this host of advancing. The Advance of Education. Josephine D. Henderson Heard. CBWP-4

What means this stately tablature. To My Noble Kinsman, Thomas Stanley, Esquire, on His Lyric Poems Composed by Master John Gamble. Richard Lovelace. CaPo

What means this strangeness now of late. Song. Sir Robert Ayton. NOSC

What means this vast assemblage here. Dedication Day. Maggie Pogue Johnson. CBWP-4

What means this watery canop' 'bout thy bed. On King Richard the Third, Who Lies Buried under Leicester Bridge. Sir John Suckling. CaPo

What means [*or* meaneth *or* menethe] this when I lie [*or* lye] alone. Sir Thomas Wyatt. GBL; SiPS

What meant our careful parents so to wear. Philippians 1.23. Francis Quarles. ChIV-2

What measure fate to him shall mete. Love Serviceable. Coventry Patmore. EnLoPo *Fr.* The Angel in the House.

What memory keeps fresh, frames unspoken. Small Joys. May Sarton. FFC

What men are they who haunt these fatal glooms. James Thomson. EBVV *Fr.* The City of Dreadful Night. OBNC

What Men in private whisper, never mind. Cato Uticensis. OBCVT, *tr. by* James Logan *Fr.* Cato's Moral Distichs Englished in Couplets.

What Mérida looked like the first time you were there. Things That Happen to You. Alonzo Gonzales Mó, *Mayan.* STP, *tr. by* Allan F. Burns

What Mr. Robinson Thinks. James Russell Lowell. AmPP *Fr.* The Biglow Papers.

("Gineral B. is a sensible man.") OBCoV

What more could I, a young man, want. (LL) Eating Alone. Li-Young Lee. TRP; WeW-3

What more than these I ask'd of Life I am content to have from Death. (LL) An Autobiography. Ernest Rhys. OBEV; OBWVE

What more variety of pleasures can. Everard Guilpin. PBRV *Fr.* Skialetheia Satire 5.

What more? Where is the third Calixt. Ballad of the Lords of Old Time. François Villon, *French.* AWP; PeVV, *tr. by* Swinburne

What mortal else could e'er go through it! (LL) On a Curate's Complaint of Hard Duty. Jonathan Swift. OBCoV; SCGP; TIRV

What Mother Told Me Once. Phùng Quán, *Vietnamese.* AVP, *tr. by* Huỳnh Sanh Thông

What moves that lonely man is not the boom. The Hermit. W. H. Davies. MoBrPo

What Mr. Cogito Thinks About Hell. Zbigniew Herbert, *Polish.* VCWP, *tr. by* John Carpenter *and* Bogdana Carpenter

What must a man do in this house. Blues for the Nightowl. Elton Glaser. PBCAP

What must be studied, The winter trees. Trees. Agnes Nemes Nagy, *Hungarian.* PoSu, *tr. by* Bruce Berlind

What must we do if we cannot do this. Valentine Ackland. WPN

What must we do, in a country lost already. Communist Poem, 1935. Valentine Ackland. WPN

What must you do? Writing a Curriculum Vitae. Wislawa Szymborska, *Polish.* PoSu, *tr. by* Grazyna Drabik *and* Austin Flint

What my age and climate held to view. Mark Akenside. EPCY

What my child learns of the sea. Audre Lorde. GT; PoBA

What my friend? Love this! I who have known. Walking with R. B. Evan Jones. PBCV

What mystery pervades a well! Emily Dickinson. NAAL-1; NAAL-3; NCAP

What name do I have for you? Just Walking Around. John Ashbery. NAAL-2

What nedeth these thretning wordes and wasted wynde? Sir Thomas Wyatt, *after the Italian of* Serafino. OBVE

What need I travel, since I may. Home Travel. Joseph Hall. CBLP

What need you, being come to sense. September 1913. W. B. Yeats. CMoP; FaBoPV; GTBS-P; HAP; MoP; NAEL-2; NoAM; PoRA

What needeth feignèd lovès for to seek? (LL) Love Unfeigned. Chaucer. NOBE; OBEV

What needs complaints. Comfort to a Youth That Had Lost His Love. Robert Herrick. NOBE; OBEV

What needs my Shakespeare for his honored [*or* honoured *or* honored] bones. On Shakespear[e]. Milton. CABP; EPCY; FaBoEE; MeLP; NAEL-1; NOSC; NoP-4; PoE; PoPoPo; PoRA; SCGP

What needs to be fed? On the Nature of Food. Alberta Turner. LCAP-2

What needst thou have more covering than a man? (LL) To His Mistress Going To Bed. Donne. BoLoP; CBLP; FSCP; GLoP; LoP; NoP-4; NoSic; OAEL-1; OxAEP-1; OxBM; PoE; SeCP

What, never filled? Be thy lips screwed so fast. Isaiah 66.11. Francis Quarles. ChIV-1

What new element before us unborn in nature? Is there a. Allen Ginsberg. CLPP

What new responsibilities are we hatching now. Green Ice. Vivienne Finch. BrRo

What News. Walter Savage Landor. BoLoP

What! no more favours? Not a ribbon more. To a Lady That Forbade to Love before Company. Sir John Suckling. CaPo

What no, Perdy [*or* Perdie *or* perdie][!] ye may be sure[!]. Sir Thomas Wyatt. AAS; PoEL-1

What noble courage must their hearts have fired. The Lonely Settler. Oliver, the Younger Goldsmith. NOBC *Fr.* The Rising Village.

What noise of viols is so sweet. Beggars. Francis Davidson. CH

What nonsense they talk who complain of a War. War the Source of Riches. *Unknown.* NOBRP

What now avails to gain a woman's heart. The Mortified Genius. James Graeme. NOEC

What now / what now dumb nigger damn near dead. Another Poem for Me (after Recovering from an O.D.) Etheridge Knight. NNaP

What nudity is beautiful as this. Portrait of a Machine. Louis Untermeyer. MoAmPo

What numerous votaries 'neath thy shadowy wing. To the Evening. John Codrington Bampfylde. NOEC

What num'rous lights this wretch's corpse attend. On the Funeral of a Rich Miser. *Unknown*. PFE

What nymph should I admire or trust. The Question to Lisetta. Matthew Prior. OBEV

What of her glass without her? The blank gray. Without Her. D. G. Rossetti. GBL; OBNC; PoEL-5; Son   *Fr.* The House of Life.

What of her glass without her? The blank grey. D. G. Rossetti. *See* Without Her.

What of it, that the realms of this epoch. The Animal Howl. "M. J.," *Polish.* TrJP, *tr. by* A. Glanz-Leyeles.

What of the faith and fire within us. Men Who March Away. Thomas Hardy. OBWP; PoWW

What of these verses that I write. Narcissus: To Himself. David Galler. PoA

What of this house with massive walls. The Widows' House. Sarah Orne Jewett. APN-2

"What of vile dust?" the preacher said. The Praise of Dust. G. K. Chesterton. MoBrPo

What offspring other men have got. Upon His Verses. Robert Herrick. NAEL-1

What on Earth deserves our Trust? EPITAPH. On her Son H. P. at St. Syth's Church where her body also lies Interred. Katherine Philips. CABP; KTR; NOSC; NoP-4; PBRV; PEW

What on the other shore. Tanka. Saitō Mokichi, *Japanese.* MJT, *tr. by* Makoto Ueda

What once Europa was, Nannette is now. (LL) Cupid Turned Plowman. Moschus, *Greek.* AWP, *tr. by* Matthew Prior

What one art thou, thus in torn weed yclad? Virtue. Nicholas Grimald. NoSic; SCGP

What others doth discourage and dismay. To His Coy Mistress. Sir Robert Ayton. NOSC

What ought to be admired, then? Not the children, surely. Suburban. William Dickey. WeT

What pain, to wake and miss you! Quite Forsaken. D. H. Lawrence. SCGP

What painter has not with a careless smutch. Accident in Art. Richard Hovey. APN-2

What pangs did he merit—so simple, without misdeed ? Death of a Ram. Sedulius Scottus, *Latin.* NOIV

What Pangs the tender Breast of *Dido* tore. Aeneas' firmness. Virgil, *Latin.* OBCVT, *tr. by* John Dryden

What! Parted! Not even a kiss? Limerick. "X. A. M." PeLi

What passing-bells for these who die as cattle? Anthem for Doomed Youth. Wilfred Owen. AF; APAD; CABP; CMoP; ClHu; EBEV; FaBoMo; GEA; GSo; GTBS-P; HAP; HeIP-4; HoPM; ImPo; InPK-6; InPS-3; LiTM; MoBrPo; MoP; NAEL-2; NOBE; NoAM; NoP-4; OAEL-2; OBEV; OBWP; OxBTC; PoE; PoFWW; PoPoPo; SAGP; SCV; SoSe-8; Son; TFi; WeW-3

What peer of France would let him duchess rove. French Fops. John Gay. ECEV   *Fr.* Epistle to the Right Honourable William Pulteney, Esq.

What people they were! Their boxers the strongest! Bertolt Brecht. FaBoA

What pictures now shall wanton fancy bring? On Winter. Mary Leapor. PEW

What Piggy-Wig Found. Enid Blyton. BoTP

What place have the bells come flying from? Flying Bells. Yüan Mei, *Chinese.* CoBLCP, *tr. by* Jonathan Chaves

What place, I ask her. (LL) The Sky Is Blue. David Ignatow. IFJA

What plant is not faded? Two Soldier's Songs. *Unknown, Chinese.* ChiP, *tr. by* Arthur Waley

What pleases me in my old age. Tune: "The Charm of Nien-nu." Chu Tun-ju, *Chinese.* SuSp, *tr. by* Irving Y. Lo

What pleasure can this gaudy world afford? Consideratus Considerandus. John Saffin. SCAP

What pleasure have great princes. The Quiet Life. William Byrd. NOBE; NoSic

What pleasure in such vehement commotion. Boethius, *Latin.* MLL, *tr. by* Helen Waddell   *Fr.* The Consolation of Philosophy ("De Consolacione Philosophie").

What plucky sperm invented Mrs. Gale? A New World Symphony. Kit Wright. NBLV; PeLV

What portents, from what distant region, ride. On the Ice Islands Seen Floating in the German Ocean. William Cowper. OAEL-1

What potions have I drunk of Siren tears. Sonnet 119. Shakespeare. OxAEP-1   *Fr.* Sonnets.

What Profit? Immanuel di Roma, *Hebrew.* TrJP, *tr. by* J. Chotzner

What profit to Darius of his reign? *Unknown, Latin.* MLL, *tr. by* Helen Waddell   *Fr.* Carmina Burana.

What rage is this? What furo[u]r of what kind [*or* kynd]? Sir Thomas Wyatt. AAS; EnLoPo; SiPS

What Rage, O Citizens, what fury. Lucan. OBCVT, *tr. by* Samuel Butler   *Fr.* Hudibras.

What rain! / Our sail is drenched. Mikhail Alekseievich Kuzmin, *Russian.* TCRP, *tr. by* Yakov Hornstein

What rattles in the dark? In Limbo. Richard Wilbur. AFr

What reason first imposed thee, gentle name. The Family Name. Charles Lamb. Son

What reason weaves by passion is undone. (LL) Know Thyself. Alexander Pope. ECEV; NOBE; NOEC; OAEL-1, *ll.* 1–18; TFi, *ll.* 1–42; ImPo, *ll.* 1–66; EBEvV; FHYEP; NAEL-1; PoEL-3

What regiment d'you belong to. Brothers. Giuseppe Ungaretti, *Italian.* PeFWW, *tr. by* Jonathan Griffin

What remained of our meetings? Aleksey Petrovich Tsvetkov, *Russian.* TCRP, *tr. by* Albert C. Todd

What remains of summer. The Cold. Lance Henson. CDW

What rhythm add to stillness / what applause? Diane Di Prima. *See* The Practice of Magical Evocation.

What rich profusion here. Manoah Bodman. APN-1   *Fr.* An Oration on Death.

What Riddle Asked the Sphinx. Archibald MacLeish. HoPM

What Rider Spurs Him from the Darkening East. Edna St. Vincent Millay. TrCP; WPE

What Robin Told. George Cooper. CTV

What rumour'd heavens are these. To the Unknown Eros. Coventry Patmore. PoEL-5   *Fr.* The Unknown Eros.

What ruse of vision. The Bear. N. Scott Momaday. CDW; HATNAP

What ryhthm add to stillness / what applause? (LL) The Practice of Magical Evocation. Diane Di Prima. PmAP; PoM

What sacrifice so great! A Mother's Love. Josephine D. Henderson Heard. CBWP-4

What sadness now, after our pleasure, dearest. Sad Words. René Vivien. CPO

What! Salomon! such words from you. To E. S. Salomon. Ambrose Bierce. CBCWP

What saved us? what for? (LL) From The Walls Do Not Fall. Hilda Doolittle. NoP-4; OBWP

What Saves Us. Bruce Weigl. NAmP90

What Say. John Godfrey. FTOS

What say the Bells of San Blas. The Bells of San Blas. Henry Wadsworth Longfellow. APN-1; MeMAP; OxBA; PAR

What scenes appear where-e'er I turn my view. Eloisa. Alexander Pope. *Fr.* Eloisa to Abelard. NAEL-1; PoEL-3; RACG

What Schoolmasters Say. Martin Seymour-Smith. OxBTC

What scope / is there where. The Rope. Tania Van Zyl. PeSA

What scrap is this, you thrust upon me now? The Count of Senlis at His Toilet. John Byrne Leicester Warren, 3d Baron De Tabley. PeVV

What seas what shores what grey rocks and what islands. Marina. T. S. Eliot. CABP; CMoP; FaBoMo; GTBS-P; HeIP-4; MoLi; NAEL-2; NOBE; NOCV; PoE; PoPoPo; TOF

What secret cravings of the blood. Nelly Sachs, *German.* PoSu, *tr. by* Michael Hamburger

What seemed to have bothered him the most, after it was done. False Arrest. Cornelius Eady. LTA

What seems to us for us is true. Perspective. Coventry Patmore. FaBoEE; GBL   *Fr.* The Angel in the House.

What seer is this. Ode on the Twentieth Century. Henrietta Cordelia Ray. CBWP-3

What serious students with their busied brains. Epigram LXVII: Time, the Interpreter. Hugh Crompton. NOSC

What serves for one will serve for t' other. (LL) Epitaphs [*or* Epitaph] on Two Piping-Bullfinches of Lady Ossory's, Buried under a Rose-Bush in Her Garden. Horace, 4th Earl of Orford Walpole. FaBoEE; NOEC

What shakes the eye but the invisible? The Decision. Theodore Roethke. CRP; VGW

What shall (alas) become of me? (LL) Cards and Kisses. John Lyly. CBLP; GBL; GLoP; GTBS-P; HoPM; NOBE; NoP-4; NoSic; OBEV; OxAEP-1; PBMP; PoRA; SCGP

What shall he have that killed the deer? Song: "What shall he have that kill'd the deer?" Shakespeare. NoSic   *Fr.* As You Like It.

What shall I answer for? (LL) Letter VI. W. S. Graham. FaBoTC

What shall I compare them to. Plum Blossoms on Solitary Hill. Wang An-shih, *Chinese.* SuSp, *tr. by* Jan W. Walls

What shall I do? The Fresh Green. So Chong-Ju, *Korean.* CKP, *tr. by* Jaihiun Kim

What shall I do? not to be Rich or Great. In Emulation of Mr Cowleys Poem Call'd The Motto. Mary Astell. KTR; NOSC

What shall I do this afternoon? Half Holiday. Olive Enoch. BoTP

What shall I do to be for ever known. The Motto. Abraham Cowley. BeJo; NOSC; SeCP

What Shall I Do to Show How Much I Love Her? John Gay. *Fr.* The Beggar's Opera. OAEL-1

What shall I do with all the days and hours. Frances Anne Kemble. PoToHe *Fr.* Absence.

What shall I do with my stick. The Stick. Edvard Kocbek, *Slovenian.* CEEP, *tr. by* Veno Taufer *and* Michael Scammell

What shall I do with this absurdity. The Tower. W. B. Yeats. CMoP; LiTM; NoAM; PoE; SCGP

What Shall I Give? Edward Thomas. FaBoCh; OxBChV

What shall I give my children? who are poor. Gwendolyn Brooks. BPo; PoA; WPE *Fr.* The Children of the Poor. WPE, *sect.* I, *pt.* 1-2; PoA, *sect.* I, *pt.* 1-3; NAAAL *Fr.* The Womanhood.

What shall I say, because talk I must? The Yellow Flower. William Carlos Williams. HAP

What shall I say, my Lord? With what begin? Edward Taylor. ChIV-2; HAP *Fr.* Preparatory Meditations Before My Approach to the Lord's Supper.

What shall I say to the gentlemen, mother. Landrecie. Stevie Smith. WPN

What shall I send you, my dear one, there in the underworld? The Lament. *Unknown, Greek.* GrIP, *tr. by* Margaret Alexiou

What shall I teach in the vivid afternoon. Going to School. Karl Shapiro. TrJP

What shall i wear. 104. "Alta." CrSp

What shall I your true-love tell. Messages. Francis Thompson. CH

What shall Presto do for pretty prattle. Swift. Delmore Schwartz. PoA

What shall the world do with its children? Romans Angry about the Inner World. Robert Bly. NOBA

What shall uproot a house and bring this care into his eye? (LL) October 1. Karl Shapiro. MoAmPo; PoA

What shall we add now? He is dead. Died. . . . Elizabeth Barrett Browning. NOBVV

What shall we be, sweet, you and I. These Bones. T. H. Parry-Williams, *Welsh.* OBWVE, *tr. by* H. Idris Bell

What shall we count to cool our angry pride? Count Ten. Bonaro W. Overstreet. PoToHe

What shall we do for Love these days? Epilogue. Lascelles Abercrombie. CH; MoBrPo *Fr.* Emblems of Love.

What shall we do for timber? Kilcash. *Unknown, Irish.* BIrV; IIP; OBMV, *tr. by* Frank O'Connor

What shall we do--what shall we think--what shall we say? Prelude XXIX. Conrad Potter Aiken. FaBoMo *Fr.* Preludes for Memnon; or, Preludes to Attitude.

What shall we know we don't know. Somebody Died. Robert Creeley. LCAP-2

What she and I had between us once, America. John Hollander. VCAP *Fr.* Powers of Thirteen.

What She Didn't Say. Ory Bernstein, *Hebrew.* IP, *tr. by* Warren Bargad *and* Stanley F. Chyet

What she remembers. Mother of the Groom. Seamus Heaney. OxBSP; PiM

What She Said ("And all those horses"). Kapilar, *Tamil.* PLW, *tr. by* A. K. Ramanujan

What She Said ("Are there others too"). Venkorran, *Tamil.* PLW, *tr. by* A. K. Ramanujan

What She Said ("As the lovely new flowers"). Allur Nanmullai, *Tamil.* PLW, *tr. by* A. K. Ramanujan

What She Said ("Bare root of the bean is pink, The"). Allur Nanmullai, *Tamil.* PLW, *tr. by* A. K. Ramanujan

What She Said ("Bees, six tiny legs and wings all lovely"). Orampokiyar, *Tamil.* PLW, *tr. by* A. K. Ramanujan *Fr.* Five on the Riverside Cane.

What She Said ("Bigger than earth, certainly"). Tevakulattar, *Tamil.* PLW, *tr. by* A. K. Ramanujan

What She Said ("Bird and beast"). Nannakaiyar, *Tamil.* PLW, *tr. by* A. K. Ramanujan

What She Said. Maturai Eruttalan Centamputan, *Tamil.* BoLoP, *tr. by* A. K. Ramanujan

What She Said. Ceyti Valluvan Peruncattan, *Tamil.* PLW, *tr. by* A. K. Ramanujan

What She Said ("Fishermen who go, The"). Ammuvanar, *Tamil.* PLW, *tr. by* A. K. Ramanujan

What She Said ("Forest animals walk there"). Kapilar, *Tamil.* PLW, *tr. by* A. K. Ramanujan

What She Said ("Friend, his seas swell and roar"). Ammuvanar, *Tamil.* PLW, *tr. by* A. K. Ramanujan

What She Said ("Friend, listen"). Ammuvanar, *Tamil.* PLW, *tr. by* A. K. Ramanujan

What She Said ("Green creepers planted inside the house"). Orampokiyar. PLW, *tr. by* A. K. Ramanujan *Fr.* Five on the Riverside Cane.

What She Said ("He is from those mountains"). Kapilar, *Tamil.* PLW, *tr. by* A. K. Ramanujan

What She Said ("Hovering like the heron"). Orampokiyar. PLW, *tr. by* A. K. Ramanujan *Fr.* Five on the Riverside Cane.

What She Said ("In his country"). Orampokiyar, *Tamil.* PLW, *tr. by* A. K. Ramanujan

What She Said ("In his country of cool seas, they say"). Ceyti Valluvan Peruncattan, *Tamil.* PLW, *tr. by* A. K. Ramanujan

What She Said ("In his place, mother / field-crabs cut into the pink"). Orampokiyar. PLW, *tr. by* A. K. Ramanujan *Fr.* Five on the Crabs.

What She Said ("In his place, mother, / mud-spattered spotted crabs"). Orampokiyar, *Tamil.* PLW, *tr. by* A. K. Ramanujan *Fr.* Five on the Crabs.

What She Said ("In the full river"). Orampokiyar. PLW, *tr. by* A. K. Ramanujan *Fr.* Five on the Riverside Cane.

What She Said ("In the tiny village"). Vayilanrevan, *Tamil.* PLW, *tr. by* A. K. Ramanujan

What She Said. Kollan Alici, *Tamil.* PLW, *tr. by* A. K. Ramanujan

What She Said ("Like milk"). Kollan Alici, *Tamil.* PLW, *tr. by* A. K. Ramanujan

What She Said ("Like moss on water"). Paranar, *Tamil.* PLW, *tr. by* A. K. Ramanujan

What She Said ("Like the high fanning tufts on swift horses"). Orampokiyar. PLW, *tr. by* A. K. Ramanujan *Fr.* Five on the Riverside Cane.

What She Said ("My body"). Ammuvanar, *Tamil.* PLW, *tr. by* A. K. Ramanujan

What She Said ("'O your hair,' he said"). Kapilar, *Tamil.* PLW, *tr. by* A. K. Ramanujan

What She Said. Okkur Macatti, *Tamil.* PBWP, *tr. by* A. K. Ramanujan

What She Said ("Only the dim-witted say it's evening"). Millaipperun Kantan, *Tamil.* PLW, *tr. by* A. K. Ramanujan

What She Said ("Only the thief was there, no one else"). Kapilar, *Tamil.* PLW, *tr. by* A. K. Ramanujan

What She Said ("Though he lives in the same town"). Pālaipātiya Peruṅkaṭuṅkō, *Tamil.* PLW, *tr. by* A. K. Ramanujan

What She Said ("What will happen now?"). Maturai Ilampalaciriyan Centan Kuttanar, *Tamil.* PLW, *tr. by* A. K. Ramanujan

What She Said ("When he said"). Nannakaiyar, *Tamil.* PLW, *tr. by* A. K. Ramanujan

What She Said about Her Unfaithful, Estranged Husband. Netumpalliyattan, *Tamil.* PLW, *tr. by* A. K. Ramanujan

What She Said Her Lover within Earshot. Kapilar, *Tamil.* PLW, *tr. by* A. K. Ramanujan

What She Said ("In his fields"). Orampokiyar. PLW, *tr. by* A. K. Ramanujan *Fr.* Five on the Crabs.

What She Said, Thinking of Him Crossing the Wilderness Alone. Auvaiyar, *Tamil.* *tr. by* A. K. Ramanujan

What She Said to Her Friend ("The Colors on the elephant's body"). Kapilar, *Tamil.* PLW, *tr. by* A. K. Ramanujan

What She Said to Her Friend ("You ask me to forget him"). Kapilar, *Tamil.* PLW, *tr. by* A. K. Ramanujan

What She Said to Her Girl Friend. Ammuvanar, *Tamil.* PLW, *tr. by* A. K. Ramanujan

What She Said to Her Girl Friend. Kapilar, *Tamil.* PLW, *tr. by* A. K. Ramanujan

What She Said to Her Girl Friend ("No, we will not make vows to the ever-winning goddess"). Korran, *Tamil.* PLW, *tr. by* A. K. Ramanujan

What She Said to Her Girl Friend ("O you, you wear flowers of gold"). Kapilar, *Tamil.* PLW, *tr. by* A. K. Ramanujan

What She Said to Her Girl Friend ("On the tall hill"). Paranar, *Tamil.* PLW, *tr. by* A. K. Ramanujan

What She Said to Her Girl-Friend. Venmanipputi, *Tamil.* PBWP, *tr. by* A. K. Ramanujan

What She Said to Her Girl Friend, after a Tryst at Night (Which Turned Out to Be a Fiasco). Kapilar, *Tamil.* PLW, *tr. by* A. K. Ramanujan

What She Said to Her Girl Friend, and What Her Girl Friend Said in Reply. Uruttiran, *Tamil.* PLW, *tr. by* A. K. Ramanujan

What She Said to Her Girl Friend, Her Foster-Mother within Earshot. Kapilar, *Tamil.* PLW, *tr. by* A. K. Ramanujan

What She Said to Her Girl Friend When She Returned from the Hills. Kapilar, *Tamil.* PLW, *tr. by* A. K. Ramanujan

What She Said to Him, after Meeting His Concubine. Cakalacanar, *Tamil.* PLW, *tr. by* A. K. Ramanujan

What She Wanted to Be. Ory Bernstein, *Hebrew.* IP, *tr. by* Warren Bargad *and* Stanley F. Chyet

What Shines in Winter Burns. T. R. Hummer. MT

What Ship Is This? Samuel Hauser. AH

What should be said of him cannot be said. Dante. Michelangelo Buonarroti, *Italian*. AWP, *tr. by* Longfellow

What should be the title of a king. Too, how also to include. What happened when. James Sherry. FTOS *Fr*. In Case.

What should [*or* shulde] I say[e]. Farewell: "What should I say." Sir Thomas Wyatt. GBL; NOBE; NoP-4; OBEV; PoEL-1; SiPS

What should I say. Sir Thomas Wyatt. NoSic; SCGP

What should I speak in praise of Surrey's skill. Surrey's Poetic Art. George Turberville. EPCY *Fr*. Verse in Praise of Lord Henry Howard, Earl of Surrey.

What should I tell them? Richard Wilbur. CRP *Fr*. The Mind-Reader. LCAP-2; NAAL-2; NoAM

What should one. The Picture of J. T. in a Prospect of Stone. Charles Tomlinson. NoP-4

What should we be without the sexual myth. Men Made Out of Words. Wallace Stevens. MeMAP; NOBA; OxBSP; TAP; VGW

What should we know. Verse. Oliver St. John Gogarty. FaBoCh; OBMV; PoRA

What should we see in this artifact? Incredible. A Quilt in the Bennington College Library. Dave Jeddie Smith. NAmP90

What silences we keep, year after year. Too Late. Nora Perry. PoToHe

What sin was mine, sweet, silent boy-god, Sleep. Sleep. Publius Papinius Statius, *Latin*. AWP, *tr. by* W. H. Fyfe

What since August, when the sound. Natural History. Richard Howard. TAP

What siren zooming is sounding our coming. The Exiles. W. H. Auden. OxBTC

What slender Youth bedew'd with liquid odours. The Fifth Ode of Horace. Lib. I. Milton. PBRV

What slender youth bedewed [*or* bedew'd] with liquid odours. Odes 1.5. Horace. AWP; EBEV; EnLoPo; OBVE; PoEL-3, *tr. by* Milton *Fr*. Odes.

What smoldering senses in death's sick delay. The Kiss. D. G. Rossetti. NOBVV; Son *Fr*. The House of Life.

What so beyond all madness[e] is the elf. Cupid Far Gone. Richard Lovelace. CaPo

What Soft—Cherubic Creatures. Emily Dickinson. APN-2; AmPP; HAP; MeMAP; MoAmPo; NALW; WPE

What solemn sound the ear invades. Mount Vernon. *Unknown*. AmFP

What songs should rise, how constant, how divine! (LL) Thoughts on the Works of Providence. Phillis Wheatley. ColAP; NAAL-1; NAAL-3

What soothes the angry snail? Eine Kleine Snailmusik. May Sarton. NBLV

What sort of thing is our family wealth? Reading. P'i Jih-hsiu, *Chinese*. SuSp, *tr. by* William H. Nienhauser

What soul hath struck its need of melody. Incompleteness. Henrietta Cordelia Ray. CBWP-3

What soul / isn't in default? Charles Olson. APAD *Fr*. Variations Done for Gerald Van de Wiele.

What sound awakened me, I wonder. The Deserter. A. E. Housman. OBMV

What sound awoke me? Dragon Skate. Gladys Cardiff. CDW

What sower walked over earth. Sunflower. Rolf Jacobsen, *Norwegian*. RaBo, *tr. by* Robert Bly

What spells racoon to me. Lucille Clifton. NAAAL

What sphinx of cement and aluminum bashed open their skulls. II. Allen Ginsberg. BB; CLPP; NeAP; TAP *Fr*. Howl. AmPP; LCAP-2; PoM

What spirit can lift you up, to that immortall praise. Michael Drayton. PBRV *Fr*. Poly-Olbion Song 6.

What spirit touched the faded lambrequin. The Ilex Tree. Agnes Lee. PoA

What Splendid Rays. Christian Gregor, *German*. AH

What starts as one more Monday morning class. Teaching Emily Dickinson. Rachel Hadas. NMM-2

What starts with f and ends with u-c-k? starts. The World of Expectations. Albert Goldbarth. HCAP

What stays specific in age when much else fades. Has Faded in Part But Magnificent Also Late for RC / Mirrors. Robert Grenier. PmAP

What, still alive at twenty-two. Hugh Kingsmill. BXAP; InPK-6; NBLV; NOBL; UV

What strange effects of Fortune do I prove! Frances Boothby. KTR *Fr*. The Marcelia; or, Treacherous Friend.

What strange pleasure do they get who'd / wipe whole worlds out. This Book is for Magda. Lew Welch. BB

What strange unusual prodigy is here. On the Strange Apparitions at Christ's Death. Henry Colman. ChIV-2

What stranger miracles are there? (LL) Miracles. Walt Whitman. PBMP; SAmP

What strength! what strife! what rude unrest! Westward Ho! Joaquin Miller. FaBoBe

What Strikes My Eye. Wang Shih-chieng, *Chinese*. SuSp, *tr. by* Richard John Lynn

What stripling now thee discomposes. Horace. *See* Odes 1.5.

What substance had Euridice. Kathleen Jessie Raine. NALW

What sugared termes, what all-perswading arte. What Sugared Terms. Richard Lynche. AAS; Son *Fr*. Diella.

What summer proposes is simply happiness. Tahoe in August. Robert Hass. NoP-4

What sunken splendor in the Eastern skies. To the Statue on the Capitol. John James Piatt. APN-2; GS

What sweet relief the showers to thirsty plants we see. A True Love. Nicholas Grimald. OBEV

What sweeter music[k] can we bring. A Christmas Caroll Sung to the King in the Presence at White-Hall. Robert Herrick. PChr

What taints thy shade—or doth the year decay? Addressed to a Beech Tree. Christian Carstairs. ECWP

What thanks do you get for it all? They wither. (LL) You buy some flowers for your table. Samuel Hoffenstein. OBCoV; TrJP

What that street is called—you can read it on the sign. Yelena Shwarts, *Russian*. VCWP, *tr. by* Michael Molnar

What the Birds Said. John Greenleaf Whittier. APN-1; NOBA; PAR

What the blind lost when radio. After the Revolution for Jesus the Associate Professor [*or* a Secular Man] Prepares His Final Remarks. Miller Williams. MT

What the Blue Jay Said. Frankie Paino. PuP-15

What the Bullet Sang. Bret Harte. APAD; APN-2; OBEV

What the Chairman Told Tom. Basil Bunting. NoP-4; OxBTC

What the Choir Sang about the New Bonnet. M. T. Morrison. BLPA

What the City Was Like. James Tate. WWSi

What the Concubine Said When She Heard the Wife Complain about the Concubine's Wiles. Villakaviralinar, *Tamil*. PLW, *tr. by* A. K. Ramanujan

What the day weaves. Thomas A. Clark. NBrP *Fr*. Sixteen Sonnets.

What the Devil Said. James Stephens. CMoP

What the Donkey Saw. U. A. Fanthorpe. OBCP

What the Earth Asked Me. James Wright. NYBP

What the Emanation of Casey Jones Said to the Medium. Arthur James Marshall Smith. MoCV

What the End Is For. Jorie Graham. NAmP90; NoP-4; PoPoPo

What the Engines Said. Bret Harte. ImGa

What the eye sees is a dream of sight. To the Hand. W. S. Merwin. SPE

What the Farmyard Fowl are Saying. *Unknown*. CTAV

What the Flowers Said. Jelaluddin Rumi, *Persian*. GaP, *tr. by* A. J. Arberry

What the Girl Friend Said to the Foster-Mother. Kapilar, *Tamil*. PLW, *tr. by* A. K. Ramanujan

What the goddamn hell are you talking about, boy. How I Wrote It. David Dooley. TRP

What the Gypsy Said to Her Children. Judith Ortiz Cofer. OxWW; UnSA

What the Informant Said to Franz Boas in 1920. *Unknown, Keresan Indian*. STP, *tr. by* Armand Schwerner

What the Instant Contains. Jorie Graham. BAP-93

What the king has. Ethel Romig Fuller. PoToHe

What the Light Was Like. Amy Clampitt. FaBoWP

What the Men Talk About When the Women Leave the Room. Dionisio D. Martinez. NoP-4

What the Moon Saw. Vachel Lindsay. FaBoEE; OxBSP

What the Motorcycle Said. Mona Van Duyn. NIP-4

What the music. Gustaf Sobin. PmAP

  ("In the bulb / of its / voices, are buoyant among.") (LL) PT

  ("What the music / wants is / pod and tentacle (the thing) / wiggling.") PT

What the Orderly Dog Saw. Ford Madox Ford. CTC

What the Passersby Said to the lover eloping with the girl. Uriyur Mutukorran, *Tamil*. PLW, *tr. by* A. K. Ramanujan

What the people learn our of lifting and hauling and waiting and losing. Carl Sandburg. OBAL *Fr*. The People, Yes.

What The Pool Said, On Midsummer's Day. Liz Lochhead. FaBoSe

What the Serpent Said to Adam. Archibald MacLeish. ChIV-1; MeMAP *Fr*. Songs for Eve.

What the Servants Said to Him, as He Returned Home. Maturaittamilkkuttan Katuvan Mallanar, *Tamil*. PLW, *tr. by* A. K. Ramanujan

What the Servants Said to him, as he returned home. Virrūṟṟu Mūteyiṉaṉār, *Tamil*. PLW, *tr. by* A. K. Ramanujan

What the Sonnet Is. Eugene Lee-Hamilton. GSo; HoPM; Son

What the sun burns up of it, the moon puts back. (LL) Plague of Dead Sharks. Alan Dugan. LiTM; NoAM

What the swift mind beholds at every turn. (LL) Pity me not because the light of day. Edna St. Vincent Millay. CMoP; FaBoWP; MeMAP; MoAmPo; OxBA

What the Thrush Said. Keats. EBEV

What the Thrush Says. Queenie Scott-Hopper. BoTP

What the Weather Does. *Unknown.* BoTP

What the Wind Said. Russell Hoban. AYFP

What the Women Told Me. E. Ethelbert Miller. GT

What them fellers does is ART! (LL) Art. *Unknown.* BLPA; NBLV

What Then? W. B. Yeats. CMoP

What, then, is life if love the golden is gone? What is pleasure? There Is No Joy Without Aphrodite. Mimnermus, *Greek.* GrIP, tr. by Richard Lattimore

What then should man pray for? what is't that he. Juvenal. OBCVT, *tr. by* Henry Vaughan. *Fr.* Juvenals tenth Satyre Translated.

What these can only memorize and mumble. (LL) Grandeur of Ghosts. Siegfried Sassoon. MoBrPo; OBMV

What they are doing is turning. Turn (a Poem in 4 Parts). Ken Belford. NOBC

What they conceal. (LL) Merlin I. Ralph Waldo Emerson. NCAP; OxBA; PAR

What they cut away in braids from childhood. Spacious Encounter. Tess Gallagher. NMM-2

What They Do to You in Distant Places. Marvin Bell. Poetsp

What They Drank. Campbell McGrath. WeT

What they felt then: isn't it / sweeter than every secret. Mary at Peace with the Risen Lord. Rilke, *German.* GI, *tr. by* David Curzon *and* Will Alexander Washburn

What they really say is, let them die, / and the children too. (LL) So Mexicans Are Taking Jobs from Americans. Jimmy Santiago Baca. LTA; UnSA

What They Said. Tanure Ojaide. HBAPE

What *they* think is it's the twists and turns of politics. Electra. György Petri, *Hungarian.* VCWP, *tr. by* Wilmer, Clive and George Gömöri

What they undertook to do. Gratitude to the Unknown Instructors. W. B. Yeats. EnlH

What They Wanted. Stephen Dunn. PuP-16

What thing did I love that walks the street. The Contemporary Muse. Edgell Rickword. OBSV

What thing is love? for sure love is a thing. Love. George Peele. CBLP; NOBE *Fr.* The Hunting of Cupid.

What thing is that, nor felt nor seen. A Riddle: On a Kiss. William Strode. NOSC

What thing shall be held up to woman's beauty? Woman's Beauty. Lascelles Abercrombie. MoBrPo *Fr.* Emblems of Love.

What thing / should I sing. Dove. Norma Farber. PChr

What Things Are Called. Erich Fried, *German.* AF, *tr. by* Georg Rapp

What things are steadfast? Not the birds. We Manage Most When We Manage Small. Linda Gregg. AmPA

What think you I take my pen in hand to record? Walt Whitman. APN-1

What this mountain means, and the murky dale. William Langland. OAEL-1 *Fr.* The Vision of Piers Plowman.

What tho', Valclusa, the fond Bard be fled. Sonnet to Valclusa. Thomas Russell. NOBRP

What Thomas an Buile Said in a Pub. James Stephens. MoBrPo; MoP; PoRA

(What Tomas Said in a Pub.) CMoP; NoAM

What thou lovest well remains. Ezra Pound. *See* Canto 81.

What Thou Lovest Well Remains American. Richard Hugo. NAAL-2; PaTW

What though, for showing truth to flatter'd [*or* flattered] state. Written on the Day That Mr. Leigh Hunt Left Prison. Keats. EPCY; Son

What though green leaves only witness. Wreath for a Bridal. Sylvia Plath. ITG

What though my penne wax faynt. To Maystres Jane Blenner-Haiset. John Skelton. AAS *Fr.* The Garland [*or* Garlande *or* Garlands] of Laurel[l].

What though the beauty I love and serve be cheap. François Villon. *See* The Ballad of Villon and Fat Madge.

What though the field be lost? Satan's Adjuration. Milton. *Fr.* Book I. FHYEP; NAEL-1; OAEL-1; OxAEP-1 *Fr.* Paradise Lost.

What though the music of thy rustic flute. Matthew Arnold. EPCY *Fr.* Thyrsis. EnVR; FHYEP; NAEL-2; NOBE; NoP-4; OBEV; OBNC

What though the rosebuds from my cheek. Departed Youth. Hannah Cowley. CABP; ECWP

What though they conquer us? Witter Bynner. NoP-4 *Fr.* Chinese Drawings.

What though your eyes are stars, your hair be night. To One Black, and Not Very Handsome, Who Expected Commendation. Edward Herbert, 1st Baron Herbert of Cherbury. NOSC

What thought ye to burn, when ye kindled the pyre. Epigram IV. *Unknown. Fr.* Duel with Verses over a Great Man. TrJP

What thoughts I have of you tonight, Walt Whitman[, for I]. A Supermarket in California. Allen Ginsberg. AmPP; CoAP; CoAmPo; FaBoA; HAP; HCAP; HeIP-4; InPK-6; InPS-3; LiTM; NAAL-2; NOBA; NeAP; NoAM; PBMP; PmAP; PoM; SAGP; TAP; TFi; TwCP; UnPo; WeW-3

What thoughts I have of you tonight, Walt Whitman, for I work late. A Pizza Joint in Cranston. Craig Weeden. BXAP

What time I see you passing by. *Unknown. Fr.* Popular Songs of Tuscany. AWP, *tr. by* John Addington Symonds

What time I was your one best bet. Horace. *See* 3.9: Dialogue between Horace and Lydia, A ("Donec gratus eram").

What time of night it is. Night Rain. J. P. Clark Bekederemo. PBMAP *Fr.* A Reed in the Tide.

What time the gifted lady took. George Sand. Dorothy Parker. NALW *Fr.* A Pig's-Eye View of Literature.

What time the wheat field tinges rusty brown. The Wheat Ripening. John Clare. NTP

What times are these. A Leaf, Treeless for Bertolt Brecht. Paul Celan, *French.* AF, *tr. by* Michael Hamburger

What 'tis to serve the great Utopian queen. (LL) It was in June the eight and thirtieth day. John Taylor. CBNP; NOSC

What to conceal desire, when every. Mary de la Rivière Manley. KTR *Fr.* The Royal Mischeif.

What to do with a day. The Satisfaction Coal Company. Rita Dove. LCAP-2; WWSi

What to do with salvias? In the Park. Peter Jones. OBGa

What? to have had gas, and to expect. Farewell. Ivor Gurney. FP

What to make of them, the professors. An Autumnal Sketch. August Kleinzahler. PmAP

What to say when the spider / Say when the spider what. Elegy in a Spider's Web. Laura Riding Jackson. PFTM

What Tomas Said in a Pub. James Stephens. *See* What Thomas an Buile Said in a Pub.

What tongue can her perfections tell. Sir Philip Sidney. SiPS *Fr.* Arcadia.

What torments must the virgin prove. A Song. Charlotte Lennox. ECWP

What travellers of matchlesse Venice say. An Elegie Made by Mr. Aurelian Townshend in Remembrance of the Ladie Venetia Digby. Aurelian Townshend. SeCP

What treasure greater than a friend. A Friend. Santob De Carrion. TrJP *Fr.* Proverbios Morales.

What trees are those, where the low clouds infiltrate. Side Window. John James. ImPo

What trifling coil do we poor mortals keep. Human Life. Matthew Prior. FaBoEE; OBCoV

What use has it for me—. (LL) Caterpillar. Emily Dickinson. APo; SAmP

What use to suffer in labor, give birth to children, if she. Diotimus. HePo, *tr. by* Barbara Hughes Fowler *Fr.* Epigrams.

What vaileth [*or* 'vaileth] truth [*or* trouth]? or by it to take pain [*or* payn]? Sir Thomas Wyatt. AAS

What various hindrances we meet. Exhortation to Prayer. William Cowper. NOCV *Fr.* Olney Hymns.

What Viet Nam means to me. The Long Reality. Haki R. Madhubuti. NAAAL

What virtue or what mental grace. Friendship. William Cowper.

What Voice at Moth-Hour did I hear calling. Robert Penn Warren. ColAP; DiPo; ImGa; MT

What voice is this, thou evening gale! Song. Joanna Baillie. WoRP

"What voice, what harp, are those we hear." The Minstrel. Goethe, *German.* AWP, *tr. by* James Clarence Mangan

What Was Ashore, Then. John Berryman. *Fr.* Sonnets. Son

What was he doing, the great god Pan. A Musical Instrument. Elizabeth Barrett Browning. CABP; EBEvV; EBVV; FaBoBe; NAEL-2; NoP-4; OAEL-2; OBEV; PEW; PoE; PoPoPo; Poetr; VWP; WPE

What was her beauty in our first estate. She. Richard Wilbur. AmPP; CoAmPo

What was his creed? II. N. Fifer. PoToHe *Fr.* He Lived a Life.

What was Inez supposed to do for. Rape. Jayne Cortez. GT; NMM-2; PmAP

What was it called. Custer Lives in Humbolt County. Janet Campbell Hale. VoR

What was it I wonder? The Knife. Richard Tillinghast. MT; WeT

What was it like, that country house? Country Villa. Jean Garrigue. TAP

What was it / that caught in our throats that day. The Greek Room. James W. Thompson. BPo

What was it the Engines said. What the Engines Said. Bret Harte. ImGa

What was it? What was it? Woman as Market. Muriel Rukeyser. NoAM

What was it you remember—the summer mornings. To Any Member of My Generation. George Barker. LiTM; Son

What was most striking about them. Concerning the Dead Women: The Munitions Plant Explosion: June, 1918. Elizabeth Libbey. AmPA

What was so quiet a companion. Body. Sasha Moorsom. APAD

What Was Solomon's Mind? Geoffrey Scott. OBMV

"What was that sound we heard." Why Must You Know? John Wheelwright. VGW

What was the name of that bronze-headed god / in charge of the Temple of Distraction? In the Land of the Lotus Eaters. Tony Hoagland. PUP-18

What was the name you called me? Evening Waterfall. Carl Sandburg. ImPo

What was the nub of wonder? Was it. Questions of Swimming, 1935. Peter Davison. DiPo

What Was Your Name in the States? Unknown. AS

What way does the Wind come? What way does he go? Address to a Child during a Boisterous Winter Evening. Dorothy Wordsworth. BoTP; NOxBChV; NTP; OxBChV; WoRP

What we below could not see, Winter pass. (LL) Thaw. Edward Thomas. EBEV; FaBoTw; GTBS-P; MoBrPo; NTP; OxAEP-2; OxBSP; OxBTC; Spl

What We Can. Ray A. Young Bear. VoR

What we cannot solve. Open Rebuke (Concealed Love). Tom Mandel. BAP-93

What we charge upon. Eat them for us. Song of the Gun. Unknown. APN-2 Fr. Minnetare Songs.

What we come round to. Epitaph for the Western Intelligentsia. Richard Allen. NOBAu

What we do best is breed. A Christening. Donald Davie. OxBC

What we don't forget is what we don't say. Anger Sweetened. Molly Peacock. FFC

What We Know. Raymond R. Patterson. NBV

What We Learned. Fanny Howe. FTOS

What We Teach at Claflin. Lizelia Augusta Jenkins Moorer. CBWP-3

What we think. Returning Fire. D. F. Brown. CDa

What we to-day prize and most fondly cherish. Instability. Henrietta Cordelia Ray. CBWP-3

What we want is death. The Book of During, IV. Clark Coolidge. PT Fr. The Book of During, IV.

What we, when face to face we see. Arthur Hugh Clough. ChIV-2

What weight of ancient witness can prevail. Confessio Fidei. Dryden. NOBE Fr. The Hind and the Panther.

What well-heeled knuckle-head, straight from the unisex. An Old Malediction. Anthony Hecht, after Horace. NoAM; OBCoV

What went ye out to see? a shaken reed? John. Jones Very. ChIV-2

What Were They Like? Denise Levertov. HeIP-4; NIP-4; OBWP; SAGP; VGW; WPE

What were they talking about? Ah yes, the end! Twenty-ninth Canto. Hans Magnus Enzensberger. PoSu Fr. The Sinking of the Titanic.

What were those strolling fops and dandies. By the North Sea. Aleksandr Blok, Russian. TCRP, tr. by Geoffrey Thurley

What were we playing? Was it prisoner's base? Running. Richard Wilbur. CoAP

What Were You Patching? Ruth Lisa Schechter. UnSA

What were you thinking, a child, when you lay. What Were You Thinking Dear Mother? Robert Penn Warren. Fr. Tale of Time. LCAP-2

What wert thou, Rome, unbroken, when thy ruin. Rome. Hildebert, Latin. MLL, tr. by Helen Waddell

What, what, what / What's the news from Swat? Threnody. George Thomas Lanigan. NBLV

What, why didest thou wink whan thou a wyf toke? Unknown. MiEL

What Wild Dawns There Were. Denise Levertov. NOBA; SAGP

What will be / the sacred words? Imamu Amiri Baraka. See Ka 'Ba.

What will happen now? What She Said. Maturai Ilampalaciriyan Centan Kuttanar, Tamil. PLW, tr. by A. K. Ramanujan

What will it do for him, to have internalized. A Giant Has Swallowed the Earth. Pattiann Rogers. MT

What will our father bring to us. Rondo for the Poet's Children. Jean-Joseph Rabéarivelo, French. NegPo, tr. by Ellen Conroy Kennedy

What will see us through, a certain calm. Elizabethan & Nova Scotian Music. Charles North. PmAP

What will survive of us is love. (LL) An Arundel Tomb. Philip Larkin. NoP-4; OxAEP-2; OxBM

What will they give me, when journey's done? Journey's End. Humbert Wolfe. TrJP

What will we do. Poem for Nana. June Jordan. BlSi

What will you find at the edge of the world? Landscape. Eve Merriam. KaS

What will you lack, sonny, what will you lack. Fall In. Harold Begbie. NSI

What winter floods, what showers of spring. Emily Jane Brontë. NOBVV

What wisdom and beauty his Sermon on the Mount. Gloss to Matthew V 27–28. Alec Derwent Hope. GI

What wisdom have we that by wisdom all. Relativities. Louis Untermeyer. BXAP

What witchlike spell weaves here its deep design. Anna Hempstead Branch. NALW Fr. Sonnets from a Lock Box.

What! without feeling? Don't we make pretense. Two Vast Enjoyments Commemorated. John Danforth. SCAP

What Women Are Not. Unknown. MiEL

What women wander? Among Women. Marie Ponsot. NMM-2

What wonder, Percy, that with jealous rage. To Percy Shelley. Leigh Hunt. Ro; Son

What wondrous life is this I lead! Andrew Marvell. CH Fr. The Garden, ("How vainly men themselves amaze"). AWP; HAP; InPS-3; MeLP; NIP-4; NOBE; OAEL-1; PoEL-2; PoLF; PoRA; SeCP

What Wondrous Love Is This. Alex Means. AH

What wondrous pretty things I've seen. Young Master's Account of a Puppet Show. John Marchant. OxBChV

What wond'rous projects formed the fickle fair? The Nunnery. Anna Williams. ECWP

What word have you, interpreters, of men. Of Heaven Considered as a Tomb. Wallace Stevens. PoA

What words are these have fallen from me? Tennyson. EBEV Fr. In Memoriam A. H. H.

What words have passed thy lips, Adam severe. Milton. TrCP Fr. Book IX. FHYEP; NAEL-1; NAWM-1; OAEL-1 Fr. Paradise Lost.

What works best / is the mile walk down Sleepy Hollow. Right of Way. Barry Sternlieb. GM

What would earth do without her blessed boobs. Yes, What? Robert Francis. LCAP-2

What would I do? If I Were a Queen. Christina Rossetti. NOxBChV

What Would I Do White? June Jordan. LTA; NMM-2; UnSA

What would I do with these strange tears in a cold night? Strange Tears. Liu Ya-tzu, Chinese. SuSp, tr. by Wu-chi Liu

What would I do without this world faceless incurious, Author's own English vers. of his "Que ferais-je sans ce monde sans visage sans questions." Samuel Beckett. NOIV; NoAM

What would I do without you? Eight Cows. Carol J. Pierman. CMAP

What would I give for a heart of flesh to warm me thro'. Christina Rossetti. OxBSP

What would it be like. A Sacred Grove. Fran Winant. BrRo

What would the world be, once bereft. Wildness. Gerard Manley Hopkins. Fr. Inversnaid. APAD; CMoP; EnVR; FaBoVe; GTBS-P; ImPo; LiTM; MoBrPo; NoAM; OAEL-2; PeVV; PoRA; RB; SAGP; SCGP; TFi; UnPo

What would they say to me when. Farther Away. Veronica Porumbacu, Romanian. CEEP, tr. by Dorian, Marguerite and Elliott Urdang

What would this Man? Now upward will he soar. Alexander Pope. HeIP-4 Fr. An Essay on Man.

What would we do in this world of ours. The Dreams Ahead. Edwin Carlile Litsey. PoToHe

What would you buy? (LL) Dream-Pedlary. Thomas Lovell Beddoes. BoTP; CH; FaBoBe; HAP; NOBE; OBEV; OBNC; OxAEP-2; PoEL-4

What Would You Fight For? D. H. Lawrence. OxBSP

What would you have? your gentleness shall force. Shakespeare. OxAEP-1 Fr. As You Like It.

What wourde is that that chaungeth not. Sir Thomas Wyatt. AAS

What year is this? Who can truthfully say? This Age. Raymond R. Patterson. NBV

What Yo' Gwine to [or t'] Do When Yo' [or de] Lamp Burn Down? Unknown. APN-2; BPo

What you are doing and where you are going. (LL) Letter to N.Y. Elizabeth Bishop. LiLi; TwCP

'What you are stepping westward?'—'Yea'. Stepping Westward. Wordsworth. CH; PoEL-4; Ro; SCGP

What you call me, when you call. Putting in a Word. Rosanne Wasserman. BAP-94

What You Can't See. Karen Chase. SeSe

What You Find in the Woods. James Longenbach. BAP-95

What You Goin' to Do When the Rent Comes 'Round? Andrew B. Sterling. OBAL

What you gwain to do when the meat gives out, my Baby? What Kin' o' Pants Does the Gambler Wear. Unknown. AS

What You Have Come To Expect. Stephen Dobyns. CMAP

What you have heard is true. The Colonel. Carolyn Forché. InPS-3; LoL; OBWP; SoSe-8

What You Need. Kathleen Fraser. AmPA

What you see here is a colorful illusion. She Attempts to Refute the Praises That Truth, Which She Calls Passion, Inscribed on a Portrait of the Poet. Sister Juana Inés de la Cruz, Spanish. BoWoP

"What You See Is Me." Barbara Gibbs. NYBP

What you shall find. (LL)   Advice to a Child.   Eleanor Farjeon.   AYFP;
OTCP

What You Should Know to Be a Poet.   Gary Snyder.   APSN; NNaP; PoM

What You Want Means What You Can Afford.   Cynthia Bond.   BAP-94

What you wanted to be among the bastards out there. (LL)   Death News.
Allen Ginsberg.   BB; MoP

What young Raw Muisted Beau Bred at his Glass.   Horace, *Latin*.   OBCVT,
tr. by Allan Ramsay

What your good leddy costs in coal?. . . I'll burn 'em down to port. (LL)
McAndrew's Hymn.   Rudyard Kipling.   OxBTC; PoEL-5

What your look meant then. (LL)   The Watergaw.   "Hugh MacDiarmid."
FaBoVe; NAEL-2

What Zimmer Would Be.   Paul Zimmer.   Poetsp

WhatCHU care.   Whitey, Baby.   James A. Emanuel.   NBV

What'd you get, black boy.   Mr. Roosevelt Regrets.   Pauli Murray.   PoBA

Whate'er Has Been.   Sidney Lanier.   Son

Whate'er is Born of Mortal Birth.   To Tirzah.   William Blake.   FHYEP;
NAEL-2; NOBE; OAEL-2; Ro   *Fr.* Songs of Experience.

Whate'er my darkness be.   Tenebræ.   John Banister Tabb.   APN-2

Whate'er thou art, where'er thy footsteps stray.   This, Too, Shall Pass
Away.   A. L. Alexander.   PoToHe

Whate'er thy Countrymen have done.   Written in the Beginning of Mezeray's
History of France.   Matthew Prior.   NOBE; PoEL-3

Whate'er we leave to God, God does.   Inspiration.   Henry David Thoreau.
APN-1; AmPP; ColAP; FaBoBe; NCAP; NOBA; OxBA

Whate'er you would not take again. (LL)   Our Saviour's Golden Rule.   Isaac
Watts.   NOxBChV

Whatever city or country road.   Double Elegy.   Michael S. Harper.   NoAM

Whatever constitutes.   The Act of Love.   Robert Creeley.   HAP

Whatever could have possessed you.   *Carmina*, XL.   Catullus.   OBVE, *tr. by*
Louis Zukofsky *and* Celia Zukofsky   *Fr.* Carmina.

Whatever else be lost among the years.   Eternal Values.   Grace Noll
Crowell.   PoToHe

Whatever else the turning.   That Land (4).   Stephen Sartarelli.   PT

Whatever God's divine / Decree.   To Kiss God's Rod; Occasioned upon a
Child's Sickness.   Mildmay Fane, 2d Earl of Westmorland.   BeJo

Whatever good is naturally done.   Sonnet: Of Love, in Honor of His Mistress
Becchina.   Cecco Angiolieri, da Siena, *Italian*.   AWP, *tr. by* D. G.
Rossetti

Whatever Happened?   Philip Larkin.   Son

Whatever Happened to Conway Twitty?   Tim Thorne.   BMAP

WHATEVER happened to the elephant.   Hurrah for Thunder.   Christopher
Okigbo.   HBAPE

Whatever happens with us, your body.   The Floating Poem, Unnumbered.
Adrienne Rich.   CPO; NALW; NMM-2; NoAM   *Fr.* Twenty-one Love
Poems.   GLP

Whatever he was doing, he looks up.   Not Working.   Henry Taylor.   Poetr

Whatever I find if I search will be wrong.   The Other.   Ruth Fainlight.
BrRo

Whatever I said and whatever you said.   Husband and Wife.   Arthur
Guiterman.   PoToHe

Whatever i say. (LL)   Twenty-one years of my life you have been.   Lucille
Clifton.   CrSp; MDDM

Whatever is here, it is.   Confessions of the Life Artist.   Thom Gunn.   CMoP

Whatever Is—Is Best.   Ella Wheeler Wilcox.   BLPA; PWR

("We know as we grow older.")   PoToHe

Whatever it is, it must have.   American Poetry.   Louis Simpson.   FaBoA;
MoP; NOBA; NoAM; TAP; WeT

Whatever it is, it's a passion.   Love in America.   Marianne Moore.   AiP

Whatever it was she had so fiercely fought.   The Recognition of Eve.   Karl
Shapiro.   ChIV-1   *Fr.* Adam and Eve.

Whatever it was: the grains of the glacier caked in the boot-cleats.   Adrienne
Rich.   FaBoWP; HCAP   *Fr.* Shooting Script.

Whatever she saw. (LL)   Burning the Tomato Worms.   Carolyn Forché.
MDDM; NMM-2

Whatever the bird is, is perfect in the bird.   Birds.   Judith Wright.   NoP-4

Whatever they said, those ten foot lips pouting across.   A Violation.   Richard
Jackson.   NAmP90

Whatever they wanted for their sons.   Déjà Vu.   Shirley Kaufman.   NMM-2

Whatever we do, whether we light.   Dilemma.   David Ignatow.   VGW

Whatever went wrong, that week, was more than weather.   A Hairline
Fracture.   Amy Clampitt.   NoAM

Whatever while the thought comes over me.   Dante.   AWP   *Fr.* La Vita
Nuova.

Whatever will rhyme with Summer.   Summer.   John Betjeman.   PeLi

Whatever wisdom sleep with thee. (LL)   108.   Tennyson.   CABP; EnVR;
FHYEP

Whatever you can do.   Goethe.   RaBo

Whatever you have to say, leave.   These Days.   Charles Olson.   RaBo

Whatever You Say Say Nothing.   Seamus Heaney.   OBWP; OxBC

Whatever You Want.   Angel González, *Spanish*.   VCWP, *tr. by* Steven Ford
Brown *and* Revuelta Gutierrez

Whatever your eye alights on this morning is yours.   Years of Indiscretion.
John Ashbery.   NOBA

Whatever you've given me, whiteface glass.   I don't love you.   Imamu
Amiri Baraka.   NAAAL

Whatever's good or bad or both.   Nonsense Rhyme.   Elinor Wylie.   PBMP

Whatever's merely wilful, / and not miraculous.   E. E. Cummings.   MeMAP

Whatif.   Shel Silverstein.   OTCP

What'mmmIdoin'?   slurs Lyris, feigning shock.   Martial, *Latin*.   OBCVT, *tr.
by* Tony Harrison

What's a patriot, Dad?   Lessons.   Jan Barry.   CDa

What's an old man like you doing.   Golden Age.   Mac Hammond.   EOEF

What's become of Waring.   Waring.   Robert Browning.   PoEL-5

"What's beyond making love?" A true question.   A Green Place.   Honor
Moore.   FFC

What's de Use ob Wukin in de Summer Time at All.   Maggie Pogue
Johnson.   CBWP-4

What's death, more than departure? The dead go.   To Castara, Being to Take
a Journey.   William Habington.   NOSC

What's fame? A fancied life in others' breath.   Alexander Pope.   FHYEP
Fr. An Essay on Man.

What's filling up the mirror? O, it is not I.   The Fat Man in the Mirror.
Robert Lowell.   PoA

What's Going to Happen to the Tots?   Noël Coward.   NBLV

What's Good for the Soul is Good for Sales.   Richard Wilbur.   NBLV   *Fr.*
Flippancies.

What's hallowed ground? Has earth a clod.   Hallowed Ground.   Thomas
Campbell.   BLPA

What's happened to your beautiful dress.   Orbit.   Gig Ryan.   BMAP

What's he that, in yon gilded coach elate.   A Remonstrance.   John Gerrard.
NOEC

What's heaven? A sea chest with a thousand gold / coins. (LL)
Beachcomber.   George Mackay Brown.   FaBoTC

What's in a Name?   Christina Rossetti.   FaBoVe

What's in a name? What's in a name? Fame.   Josephine D. Henderson
Heard.   CBWP-4

What's In It for Me?   E. A. Guest.   PoToHe

What's in the body you've forgotten.   Song.   Robert Creeley.   PuP-14

What's in the braine that Inck may character.   Sonnet.   Shakespeare.
PBRV   *Fr.* Sonnets.

What's in the Cupboard?   *Unknown*.   CH; OxNR

What's in there?   *Unknown*.   CH; OxNR

What's left but this to say of any war? (LL)   *Vale* from Carthage.   Peter
Viereck.   LiTM; MoAmPo

What's missing is the body, its nakedness wrapped / in marble.   Robert
Mapplethorpe's Photograph of Apollo (1988).   Mark Irwin.   PUP-19

What's Mo' Temptin' to de Palate?   Maggie Pogue Johnson.   CBWP-4

What's My Crime?   Trần Huy Liệu, *Vietnamese*.   AVP, *tr. by* Huỳnh Sanh
Thông

What's my sweetheart?—A laundress is she.   Jeannette.   Otto Julius
Bierbaum, *German*.   AWP, *tr. by* Jethro Bithell

What's My Thought Like?   Thomas Moore.   FaBoEE

What's Not in the Heart.   Abba Kovner, *Hebrew*.   AF, *tr. by* Shirley
Kaufman

What's on this May morning in the hills?   Ascension Thursday.   Saunders
Lewis, *Welsh*.   OBWVE, *tr. by* Gwyn Morgan

What's out there?   Jean Kenward.   SpW

What's poetic.   In Defence of Poetry.   Mafika Pascal Gwala.   PeSAV

What's sweeter than at the end of a summer's day.   Thanksgiving.   Kenneth
Koch.   VGW

What's That.   Anne Sexton.   LCAP-2

What's that approaching like dust like poverty.   Ballad.   Charles Simic.
LCAP-2

What's that bird, Mr Long?   Geoffrey Lehmann.   BMAP   *Fr.* Ross's Poems.

What's that shining in the leaves.   Elizabeth Bishop.   *Fr.* Songs for a
Colored Singer.   RB

What's That Smell in the Kitchen?   Marge Piercy.   NBLV; NIP-4

What's that that hirples at my side?   Heriot's Ford.   Rudyard Kipling.
PoRA   *Fr.* The Light That Failed.

What's that we see from far? the spring of Day.   A Nuptiall Song, or
Epithalamie, on Sir Clipseby Crew and His Lady.   Robert Herrick.
BeJo; CBLP; CaPo; PoEL-3; SeCP

What's that you're telling me?   The Love Charm.   *Unknown, Chippewa
Indian*.   STP, *tr. by* Jerome Rothenberg

What's the best thing in the world?   The Best Thing in the World.
Elizabeth Barrett Browning.   EBVV; NOBVV; OxBSP; SDW; VWP

What's the matter.   Dickery Dean.   Dennis Lee.   TLR

"What's the matter, old chap?" "Well, I came." Limerick. Joyce Johnson. PeLi

What's the name of this town. I Arrived in that Town, Everyone Greeted Me and I Recognized no One. When I Was Going to Read My Verses, the Devil, Hidden Behind a Tree, Called Out to Me Sarcastically and Filled My Hands with Newspaper Clippings. J. V. Foix, *Catalan.* PFTM, *tr. by* David H. Rosenthal

What's the news of the day. The Balloon. Mother Goose. OxNR

What's the Railroad to Me? Henry David Thoreau. GM; PAR; PoEL-4; TAP

What's the text today for reading. Morning. Louisa Sarah Bevington. PEW

What's the weather on about? The Weather. Gavin Ewart. OTCP

What's this? A dish for fat lips. The Shape of the Fire. Theodore Roethke. CMoP; LCAP-2; VCAP

What's this dull town to me? Robin Adair. Lady Caroline Keppel. FaBoBe

What's this that with such vigour fills my brest? Ambition. Mary Astell. KTR

What's this? What's this? (LL) The House That Fear Built: Warsaw, 1943. Jane Flanders. CrSp; PBCAP

What's to be hoped from seeing her again? Elegy. Goethe. *Fr.* Trilogy of Passion. STV, *tr. by* John Frederick Nims

What's to tell? My Talk with an Elegant Man. Kevin Walker. BAP-94

What's today?/ A Monday? Question. Martin Sorescu, *Rumanian.* CBNP, *tr. by* Michael Hamburger

What's today? / Hoops today. Litany of Time Past. Muriel Spark. FaBoTC

What's up, today, with our lovers? The Lovers Go Fly a Kite. W. D. Snodgrass. NYBP

What's worse than this past century? "Anna Akhmatova," *Russian.* BoWoP, *tr. by* Barbara Einzig

Whatsoever things are true. *Unknown.* CTV *Fr.* The Bible, Philippians 4:8.

Whatsume'er the failings on his part. Joe Gargery's Epitaph on His Father. Charles Dickens. FaBoVe *Fr.* Great Expectations.

Whaur are ye gaen sae fast, my bairn. The Baltic. Violet Jacob. FaBoTC

Whaur green abune the banks the links stretch oot. The Planticru. Robert Rendall. OxBS

Whaur yon broken brig hings owre. Song. William Soutar. FaBoTC; OxBS

Wheat. Diane Glancy. CRP

Wheat, The. Blaze Koneski, *Macedonian.* CEEP, *tr. by* Vasa D. Mihailovich

Wheat has been quickly harvested, The. Compassion for the Farmers. Li K'ai-hsien, *Chinese.* CoBLCP, *tr. by* Jonathan Chaves

Wheat is up, the barley, The. Grain for Emperor Huan. *Unknown, Chinese.* ChiPo, *tr. by* Rewi Alley

Wheat Ripening, The. John Clare. NTP

Wheatfield Under Clouded Sky. Campbell McGrath. PuP-17

("Suppose Gauguin had never seen Tahiti. Suppose the *bêche-de-mer* and.") PaTW

Wheel, The. Robert Earl Hayden. BPo

Wheel, The. Edwin Muir. NoAM

Wheel, The. Molly Peacock. RA

Wheel, The. W. B. Yeats. GTBS-P; Poetr

Wheel is the most beautiful discovery of man and the only one, The. Aimé Césaire, *French.* NegPo, *tr. by* Clayton Eshleman *and* Denis Kelly

Wheel of Fortune, The. Thom Gunn. OxBC

Wheel of the quivering Meat, The. 211th Chorus. Jack Kerouac. NeAP; PmAP; PoM *Fr.* Mexico City Blues.

Wheel Revolves, The. Kenneth Rexroth. NoAM

Wheelbarrow, The. Russell Edson. LCAP-2

Wheelchair Butterfly, The. James Tate. LCAP-2; NoAM

Wheelchairs That Kneel Down Like Elephants. Karen Fiser. IFJA

Wheels / and rails. Riding the A. May Swenson. PiM *Fr.* Riding the A.

Wheels are growing on rose-bushes. Affectionate. Else Von Freytag-Loringhoven. PFTM

Wheels hurry onward, onward, The. A Cartload of Shoes. Abraham Sutskever, *Yiddish.* CEEP; HP, *tr. by* David G. Roskies

Wheels line up, pretty right, right, The. Cattle Loading. Gordon Mackay-Warna, *Aborigine.* NOBAu, *tr. by* Georg von Brandenstein

Wheels of the Trains, The. W. S. Merwin. GM

Wheer 'asta beän saw long and meä liggin' 'ere aloän? Northern Farmer: Old Style. Tennyson. EnVR

Wheesht, wheesht, Joyce, and let me hear. "Hugh MacDiarmid." *See* Water Music.

Wheesht, wheesht, my foolish hert. "Hugh MacDiarmid." HAP; InPK-6; OxAEP-2

Whelming the dwellings of men, and the toils of the slow-/ footed oxen. Charles Kingsley. PeVV *Fr.* Andromeda.

When. "I Do Like To Be Beside the Seaside." Dame Edith Sitwell. PFTM *Fr.* Façade.

When. Tsurayuki, *Japanese.* OHMPJ, *tr. by* Kenneth Rexroth

When a Beau Goes In. Gavin Ewart. OBWP; OxBTC

When a Beautiful Woman Gets on the Jutiapa Bus. Belle Waring. NAmP90; PBCAP

When a brass sun staggers above the sky. Tramp. Richard Hughes. MoBrPo

When a Chippewa war party left the village. Fare Thee Well. *Unknown, Chippewa.* PBMP, *tr. by* Frances Densmore

When a clatter came. Sounds of the Day. Norman MacCaig. RB

When a daffadill [*or* daffodil] I see. Divination by a Daffadill [*or* Daffodil]. Robert Herrick. CaPo

When a daughter tries suicide. The Risk. Anne Sexton. BoWoP

When a disciple asked of Lu Chü how. The Sage in Unison. Harold Stewart. NOBAu

When a dream gets kicked around. (LL) Same in Blues. Langston Hughes. APSN; InPS-3; SAGP; SSLK

When a dream is born in you. A Pinch of Salt. Robert Graves. MoBrPo

When a feller hasn't got a cent. Fellowship. *Unknown.* BLPA

When a fellow loves a maiden. La Cucaracha. *Unknown.* AS

When a felon's not engaged in his employment. Policeman's Lot, A [*or* The]. Sir William Schwenck Gilbert. NOBL; PeLV *Fr.* The Pirates of Penzance.

When a feverish groom in Armenia. Limerick. Morris Gilbert Bishop. PeLi

When a friend calls to me from the road. A Time to Talk. Robert Frost. FP

When a friend dies. Marge Piercy. HeIP-4

When a friend said to Leda: "Come on." Limerick. Peter Alexander. PeLi

When a friend starts on a journey of a thousand miles. The End of the Year. Su Tung-p'o, *Chinese.* OHPC, *tr. by* Kenneth Rexroth

When a friend told a typist called Eve. Limerick. Gordon Harper. PeLi

When a green fox looks. Fox. David Campbell. CBAP

When a King Asks for a Chieftain's Daughter. Maturai Marutaṉ Iḷanākaṉār, *Tamil.* PLW, *tr. by* A. K. Ramanujan

When a man becomes tired of his life. Song, *Hamlet.* John F. Poole. BXAP

When a man can love no more. Basta! D. H. Lawrence. CBLP

When a man dies. "Anna Akhmatova," *Russian.* TCRP, *tr. by* Daniel Weissbort

When a Man has Married a Wife. William Blake. FaBoEE; OAEL-2; OxBoLi; PFE; PeLV

("Her Knees and elbows are only / glued together.") (LL) PFE

When a man hath no freedom to fight for at home. Stanzas. Byron. FaBoEE; NAEL-2; NBLV; NoP-4; OxAEP-2; PoLF; Poetr; TRP

When a man turns homeward through the moonfall. Daniel Whitehead Hicky. PoToHe

When a man's too old even to toss off, he. Limerick. Robert Conquest. PeLi

When a Negro comes in question you may watch the Southern press. The Southern Press. Lizelia Augusta Jenkins Moorer. CBWP-3

When a new world is born, the old. Rattle. Peter Blue Cloud. HATNAP

When a parasol is cooled in the crystal garden. International Chainpoem. *Unknown.* SPE

When a person cannot dispense with something. Note 25. Hyon-jong Chong, *Korean.* CKP, *tr. by* Jaihiun Kim

When a sighing begins. Chansons d'Automne. Paul Verlaine, *French.* AWP, *tr. by* Arthur Symons

When a statue turns its real gaze. After Plotinus. William Stafford. PoA

When a' the Warld had clos'd their Een. An Anacreontique on Love. Anacreon, *Greek.* OBCVT, *tr. by* Allan Ramsay

When a twister a-twisting will twist him a twist. John Wallis. OxNR

When a wax candle burns down, ashes are left behind. Cheng Hsieh. *Fr.* Mourning for My Son Jun-erh. CoBLCP, *tr. by* Jonathan Chaves

When a Woman Blue. *Unknown.* AS

When A Woman Gets Blue. Norman Jordan. ISC; NBV

When a woman gets blue. (LL) When A Woman Gets Blue. Norman Jordan. ISC; NBV

When a woman looks up at you with a twist about her eyes. The Made to Order Smile. Paul Laurence Dunbar. GT

When Abraham Lincoln was shoveled into the tombs[, he forgot them]. Cool Tombs. Carl Sandburg. AmPP; CBCWP; CMoP; ColAP; HAP; HeIP-4; MoAmPo; MoP; NAAL-2; NOBA; NoAM; OxBSP; PoLF; TAP; TFi

When Adam Day by Day. Occasional Poem. A. E. Housman. NOBL; PeLV

When Adam delf [or dalf]/ and Eve span. The Peasant's Song. *Unknown.* FaBoPV; FaBoVe

When Adam found his rib was gone. The Lady's-Maid's Song. John Hollander. LiTM; TwCP

When Adam walked in Eden young. A. E. Housman. ChIV-1

When after muchos años. Wild West Workshop Poem. Anselm Hollo. PmAP

When, after storms that woodlands rue. A Requiem[:] for Soldiers Lost in Ocean Transports. Herman Melville. APN-2; PoEL-5

When after those, four ages very near. Michael Drayton. EPCY *Fr.* To Henry Reynolds, of Poets and Poesy.

When age hath made me what I am not now. Upon His Picture. Thomas Randolph. BeJo; NOBE

When age once snows upon your heart. (LL) Cupid's Call. James Shirley. BeJo; NOSC

When air's chill north his noisome frosts shall blow. Winter. Hesiod, *Greek.* NOSC, tr. by George Chapman *Fr.* The Georgics of Heisod.

When Alcuin taught the sons of Charlemagne. The Student's Tale. Henry Wadsworth Longfellow. AmPP *Fr.* Tales of a Wayside Inn.

When Alexander Pope strolled in the city. Mr. Pope. Allen Tate. ColAP; FuPo; NOBA; NoAM; TwCP; VGW

When Alkibié married. Archilochus, *Greek.* GrAn, tr. by Guy Davenport

When all about me memories arise. For My Mother. David Diop, *French.* NegPo, tr. by Ellen Conroy Kennedy

When all Birds els[e] of their music[k] fail[e]. Money Makes the Mirth. Robert Herrick. CaPo

When all her robes are gone. (LL) Madrigal: "My Love in her attire doth show her wit." *Unknown.* BoLoP; GTBS-P; HeIP-4; ImPo; NAEL-1; NIP-4; NOBE; OBEV; OxBSP; TFi

When all is done, and my last word is said. Paul Laurence Dunbar. AAP

When all is done and said, in the end thus shall you find. The Pleasures of Thinking. Thomas Vaux. NoSic

When all is over and you march for home. Spoils. Robert Graves. HAP; NYBP; Son; WeW-3

When all is ruin once again. (LL) To Be Carved on a Stone at Thoor Ballylee. W. B. Yeats. FaBoEE; IIP; NoAM; NoP-4

When all my five and country senses see. Dylan Thomas. MoBrPo; NoAM; PoA; Son

When all / My waterfall. Her Time. Theodore Roethke. NAAL-2

When all my words were said. Enough. Digby Mackworth Dolben. EBVV

When all now dead shall reappear[e]. (LL) Poetry Perpetuates the Poet. Robert Herrick. BeJo; FaBoEE

When all of us wore smaller shoes. Ancient Lights. Austin Clarke. BIrV; CMoP

When all the days are hot and long. Swimming. Clinton Scollard. FPC

When all the others were away at Mass. Seamus Heaney. BLT; PNI *Fr.* Clearances. CIP-2; PBCIP; PNI

When all the over-work of life. The Heart Knoweth Its Own Bitterness. Christina Rossetti. VWP

When all the witches were haled to the stake and burned. King Duffus. Sylvia Townsend Warner. FaBoWP

When all the women in the transport. Pigtail. Tadeusz Rózewicz, *Polish.* HP; PoSu, tr. by Adam Czerniawski; AF, tr. by Robert A. Maguire and Magnus Jan Krynski

When all the world is young, lad. Young and Old. Charles Kingsley. ACTP; BoTP; EBEV; FaBoBe; FaPoR; ImPo; OxAEP-2; OxBChV; PoLF *Fr.* The Water Babies.

When all this All doth pass from age to age. Greville Fulke. EBEV; NoSic *Fr.* Caelica.

"When all this is over," said the swineherd. Swineherd. Eiléan Ní Chuilleanáin. BIrV; CIP-2; FaBoWP; WPOW

When all through earth and heaven dust storms rise. The Song of a Soldier's Wife. Đng Trần Côn and Phan Huy Ích (1750–1822), *Chinese.* AVP, tr. by Huỳnh Sanh Thông

When all was quiet and serene, a storm broke out at the dead. A Riot. Mrs. Henry Linden. CBWP-4

When all within is dark. From Thee to Thee. Solomon ibn Gabirol, *Hebrew,* TrJP, tr. by Israel Abrahams

When all your world of beauty's [or Beautie's] gone. (LL) To Dianeme ("Sweet, be not proud of those two eyes"). Robert Herrick. BeJo; CaPo; GTBS-P; NOBE; NOSC; OBEV

When Alysandyr Our King Was Dede. *Unknown. See* The Death of Alexander.

When an amorous youth from Atlantis. Limerick. C. Vita-Finzi. PeLi

When an archer is shooting for nothing. The Need to Win. Chuang Tzu, *Chinese.* BLT, tr. by Thomas Merton

When an obstinate fellow of Fife. Limerick. Allan M. Laing. PeLi

When and where did you first. Sexual Privacy of Women on Welfare. Pinkie Gordon Lane. BlSi

When any mortal(even the most odd). E. E. Cummings. FaBoEE

When Aphrodite saw the *Aphrodite* of Knidos. *Unknown, Greek.* GrAn, tr. by Peter Jay

When approached by a person from Porlock. Limerick. Richard Leighton Greene. PeLi

When April & dew brings primroses here. An Anecdote of Love. John Clare. NOBVV

When are the children all happy and gay? Christmas Times. Maggie Pogue Johnson. CBWP-4

When as I do record. *Unknown.* EBEV

When as in silks my Julia goes. Upon Julia's Clothes. Robert Herrick. APAD; AWP; BLPA; BeJo; CABP; CaPo; CavPo; ClHu; EBEV; EBEvV; EnLoPo; GBL; GLoP; GTBS-P; HAP; HeIP-4; HoPM; ImPo; InPS-3; NAEL-1; NBLV; NIP-4; NOBE; NOSC; NoP-4; OAEL-1; OBEV; OxAEP-1; OxBSP; PFE; PeLV; PoE; PoEL-3; PoPoPo; Poetr; SCGP; SeCP; TFi; TRP; TTTS; UV; WeW-3

When as the chill charocco blows. In Praise of Ale. Thomas Bonham. OBEV

When as the nightingale chanted her vespers. Mark Antony. John Cleveland. CBLP

When as the prince of Angels puffed with pride. To St. Michael the Archangel. Henry Constable. ChIV-2

When as the rye reach to the chin. George Peele. *See* Song: "When as [or whenas] the rye [or rie] reach to the chin."

When as the sheriff of Nottingham. Robin Hood and the Golden Arrow. *Unknown.* ESPB

When asked for a sample of his work. The Dream of Completion. Shirley Kaufman. LCAP-2

When asked her opinion. Cowboy Film. Tom Matthews. PNI

When asked, I used to say. What Zimmer Would Be. Paul Zimmer. Poetsp

When at break of day at a riverside. Piano and Drums. Gabriel Okara. NIP-4; PRA; TTY

When at Collatium this false lord arrived. [Before the Rape], Shakespeare. NoSic *Fr.* The Rape of Lucrece.

When at last he was well enough to take the sun. A Leg in a Plaster Cast. Muriel Rukeyser. MoAmPo

When / At the close of war. I Say, Mr. A. Samuel Allen. SeSe

When at the first I took my pen in hand. John Bunyan. FaBoVe *Fr.* The Author's Apology for His Book.

When Athens all the Graecian state did guide. Dryden. NOSC *Fr.* Oedipus.

When August and the sultry summer's drouth. The Valley. Agnes Mary Frances Robinson. VWP

When Aunt Insomnia came back from the planet Mars. An Evening of Home Movies. Constance Urdang. PFE

When autumn comes, my orchard trees alone. Art and Life. Agnes Mary Frances Robinson. VWP

When autumn rains flatten sycamore leaves. Rain. Gary Soto. NoAM *Fr.* The Elements of San Joaquin. PBCAP; PaTW; UnSA

When awful darkness and silence reign. The Dong with a Luminous Nose. Edward Lear. CBNP; EBNV; EBVV; NOBVV; NOxBChV; OxAEP-2; PoEL-5

When Baby's cries grew hard to bear. L'Enfant Glacé. Harry Graham. CBNP; NBLV; OBCoV; PeLV

When Bacchus first beheld the desolate. Dionysiaca. Nonnus, *Greek.* OBCVT, tr. by Elizabeth Barrett Browning *Fr.* Dionysiaca.

When beauty breaks and falls asunder. Juan's Song. Louise Bogan. NYBP; NoP-4

When beechen buds begin to swell. The Yellow Violet. William Cullen Bryant. NAAL-1; NAAL-3; PoLF; TAP

When before those eyes, my life and light. Gaspara Stampa, *Italian.* BoWoP, tr. by J. Vitiello

When Bells stop ringing—Church—begins. Emily Dickinson. APN-2

When Bibo thought fit from the world to retreat. Epigram. Matthew Prior. CBNP; FaBoEE

When Bill gives me a book, I know. The Christmas Exchange. Arthur Guiterman. CTV

When Bill was a lad he was terribly bad. Those Two Boys. Franklin Pierce Adams. OBCoV; TrJP

When Bird died, I didn't mind. Filling the Gap. Lawson Fusao Inada. MoNo; OpBo

When birds and flowers and I were happy peers. (LL) To the Dandelion. James Russell Lowell. NAAL-1

When birds break open the sky, a smell of snow. Winter Burn. Roberta Hill Whiteman. VoR

When Bishop Berkeley said "there was no matter." Canto the Eleventh. Byron. NOBRP *Fr.* Don Juan.

When Black People Are. Alfred B. Spellman. BPo; ISC; PoBA

("Borrowed breath.") (LL) ISC

When blessed Marie [or Mary] wip'd her Saviours [or Saviour's] feet. Mary [or Marie] Magdalene. George Herbert. ESCV

When bold Leander sought his distant fair. On Leander's Swimming over the Hellespont to Hero. Thomas Warton the Younger, after Martial. FaBoEE

When bored by the drone of the wedlocked pair. Sacred and Profane Love, or, There's Nothing New under the Moon Either. Peter De Vries. NBLV; OBCoV

When both hands of the town clock stood at twelve. Village Noon; Mid-Day Bells. Merrill Moore. MoAmPo

When boyhood's fire was in my blood. A Nation Once Again. Thomas Osborne Davis. IIP; NOIV

When boys played women's parts, you'd think the stage. Epilogue to "The Parson's Wedding." Thomas Killigrew. NOSC

When breezes are soft and skies are fair. Green River. William Cullen Bryant. APN-1; NOBA; OxBA

When bright Orion glitters in the skies. The Washerwoman. Mary Collier. ECWP; NOEC   Fr. The Woman's Labour; an Epistle to Mr. Stephen Duck.

When brighte Phoebus passed was the Ram. John Lydgate. EPCY   Fr. The Siege of Thebes.

When Britain first, at heaven's command. Rule, Britannia! James Thomson and David Mallet. EBEvV; FaPoR; GTBS-P; NAEL-1; NOEC; OBWP   Fr. Alfred: A Masque.

When Britain really ruled the waves. The House of Lords. Sir William Schwenck Gilbert. NAEL-2   Fr. Iolanthe.

When Bryan came to Springfield, and Altgeld gave him greeting. Vachel Lindsay.   Fr. Bryan, Bryan, Bryan, Bryan. CMoP; MeMAP; OxBA; OxBoLi

When by its magic lantern Spleen. Matthew Green. OxAEP-1   Fr. The Spleen.

When by me in the dusk my child sits down. John Berryman. ColAP   Fr. Homage to Mistress Bradstreet.

When by the labour of my 'ands. Half-Ballad of Waterval. Rudyard Kipling. PeSAV

When by thy scorn[e], O murd'ress[e] [or murderess], I am dead. The Apparition. Donne. ESCV; EnLoPo; FSCP; GBL; GLoP; HeIP-4; NAEL-1; NAWM-1; NOBE; NOBL; NoSic; OAEL-1; OBEV; OxBSn; PoE; SCGP; SCV; SeCP; SoSe-8; TFi

When by Zeus relenting the mandate was revoked. Phoebus with Admetus. George Meredith. NOBE; OBEV

When Byron's eyes were shut in death. Matthew Arnold. EPCY   Fr. Memorial Verses. CABP; NAEL-2; OAEL-2

When Caesar saw his army prone to war. Lucan. NoSic, tr. by Marlowe   Fr. Pharsalia.

When calabashes held petrol and men. Season of Omens. J. P. Clark Bekederemo. PBMAP   Fr. Casualties (1970).

"When can we have cake?" she wants to know. The Age of Reason. Mary Jo Salter. BAP-95

When Canaan did with milk and honey flow. (LL) On Death. Anne Killigrew. PEW

When cats like him submit to fate. Anne Francis. ECWP   Fr. An Elegy on a Favorite Cat.

When cats run home and light is come. The Owl. Tennyson. ACTP; BoTP; CH; CTAV; FaBoCh

When Celia frowns, I vow and swear. Verses Left on a Lady's Toilet. Sarah Dixon. ECWP

When chapman [or chapmen] billies leave the street. Tam o' Shanter. [A Tale]. Robert Burns. CABP; EBNV; ImPo; NAEL-2; NoP-4; OAEL-1; OBNV; OxBS; PeLV; Ro

When Chicken Man Came Home to Roost. Frank A. Cross Jr. CDa

When children are playing alone on the green. The Unseen Playmate. Robert Louis Stevenson. FP

When children slap their father's face. Robert Desnos. PFTM

When chill November's surly blast. Man Was Made to Mourn, a Dirge. Robert Burns. Ro

When Christ came from the shadows by the stream. Wherefore the Scars of Christ's Passion Remained in the Body of His Resurrection. Theodulf of Orleans, Latin. MLL, tr. by Helen Waddell

When Christ from Heaven comes down straightway. For the Company Underground. Francis MacNamara. NOBAu

When Christ with care and pangs of death opprest. Christs Sleeping Friends. Robert Southwell. ESCV

When civil fury first grew high. The Presbyterian Knight. Samuel Butler. EBEV; NOBE; NOSC; OxAEP-1   Fr. Hudibras.

When Cleomira disbelieves. The Force of Love. Samuel Jones. NOEC

When clerks and navvies fondle. For X. Louis MacNeice. BoLoP; EnLoPo   Fr. Trilogy for X.

When Clifford wasn't back to camp by nine. After the Wilderness. Andrew Hudgins. CBCWP

When clouds appear like rocks and towers. Unknown. OxNR

When Clumsy harks the gladsome ting-a-lings. Gjertrud Schnackenberg. NoAM   Fr. Two Tales of Clumsy.

When cockle shells turn silver bells. Waly, Waly. Unknown. AS; AmFP

When cocks curved throats for crowing. The Ballad of the Tinker's Wife. Sigerson Clifford. IIP

When, Coelia, must my old day set. To Coelia. Charles Cotton. OBEV

When confusion reigns. Confusion. Nino Nikolov, Bulgarian. CEEP, tr. by Ewald Osers

When conquering love did first my heart assail. To the Senses. Michael Drayton. PFE

When consummate the day hangs before you. Three Variations. Boris Pasternak, Russian. TrJP, tr. by Babette Deutsch

When Cousin Sam come down vrom Lon'on. Sam'el Down vrom Lon'on. William Barnes. PeVV

When Cromwell fought for power, and while he reigned. William Cowper. EPCY   Fr. Table Talk.

When Cromwell "slighted" Kenilworth. State of Preservation. Celeste Turner Wright. FFC

When Cupid once the little Thief would play. The Honey Stealer. Theocritus, Greek. OBCVT, tr. by Unknown

When Cytherea slipped her wily sash off. Antiphanes, Greek. GrAn, tr. by Edwin Morgan

When Daddy and Mum got quite plastered. Limerick. Unknown. OBCoV; PeLi

When Daddy Cums from Wuk. Maggie Pogue Johnson. CBWP-4

When daffodils begin to peer. The Pedlar's Song. Shakespeare. FaBoBe; FaBoCh; NBLV; NOBE; NoP-4; NoSic; OAEL-1; OxAEP-1; OxBSP; OxBoLi; PeLV; PoEL-2; SCGP; TFi; UV   Fr. The Winter's Tale.

When daisies pied and violets Blue. Spring. Shakespeare. HAP; ImPo; InPK-6; NAEL-1; NBLV; NIP-4; NOBE; NoP-4; NoSic; OAEL-1; OBEV; PoEL-2; PoRA; SCGP; TFi; UnPo   Fr. Love's Labour's Lost.

When Daniel Boone goes by, at night. Daniel Boone. Stephen Vincent Benét. KaS

When darkness crept and grew. Under the Hill. Richard Eberhart. PoA

When darkness settles itself. Winter Solstice. Peter Blue Cloud.   Fr. Within the Seasons. HATNAP

When day dawned with unusual light. Sudden Thaw. Andrew Young. FaBoTC; NTP

When day declining sheds a milder gleam. The Naturalist's Summer-Evening Walk. Gilbert White. NOEC

When daylight was yet sleeping under the billow. Ill Omens. Thomas Moore. PoEL-4

When de Co'n Pone's Hot. Paul Laurence Dunbar. AAP

When de Sun Shines Hot. James Ephriam McGirt. AAP

When, dearest friend, thy verse doth re-inspire. On Mr. Shirley's Poems. Thomas Stanley. BeJo

When, dearest, I but think on [or of] thee. Song. Sir John Suckling and Owen Felltham. NOSC; OBEV

When Death Came. Adam Zagajewski, Polish. VCWP, tr. by Renata Gorcyznski, Benjamin Ivry, and C. K. Williams

When Death shall close those Eyes, imperious Dame! Sappho, Greek. OBCVT, tr. by John Addison

When death shall part us from these kids. A Dialogue between Thyrsis and Dorinda. Andrew Marvell. SeCP

When Death to Either Shall Come. Robert Bridges. OBEV

When deaths cold hand shall close my eyes. Damaris, Lady Masham. KTR

When descends on the Atlantic. Seaweed. Henry Wadsworth Longfellow. APN-1; ColAP; OxBA; TAP

When despair for the world grows in me. The Peace of Wild Things. Wendell Berry. MT; SAGP; VGW

When Dey 'Listed Colored Soldiers. Paul Laurence Dunbar. BPo; CBCWP

When did I cease to be. Salute to Icheke. Okogbule Wonodi. PBMAP

When did the world begin and how? The Answers. Robert Clairmont. OTCP

When did you start your tricks. The Mosquito Knows. D. H. Lawrence. FaBoEE; OxBTC; RB

When Dido found Aeneas would not come. A Note on the Latin Gerunds. Richard Porson. FaBoEE

When Dinah's careless eye was grown too lavish. On Dinah. Francis Quarles. ChIV-1

When do I see thee most, beloved one? Lovesight. D. G. Rossetti. EBVV; GTBS-P; NAEL-2; OBNC   Fr. The House of Life.

When Dobbin and Robin, unharnessed from the plow. The Circus-Postered Barn. Elizabeth Jane Coatsworth. MoAmPo

When does it end? When does a new poem. Peter Levi. TOF

When does the soul leave the body? For My Mother. Ellen Bryant Voigt. NIP-4

When doome of Peeres and Judges fore-appointed. A Tragicall Epigram. Sir John Harington. PBRV

When Doris danced under the oak tree. Richard Eberhart. CMoP

When down the crowded aisle my wandering eyes. Eyeing the Eyes of One's Mistress. Ebenezer Jones. NOBVV

When / Dr. / Edith (Hon. D. Litt. [Leeds], Hon. D. Litt. [Durham]). A Thin Façade for Edith Sitwell. John Malcolm Brinnin. NYBP

When, dragging hideous crutches, war. A Letter to My Future Child. Trần Đức Uyên, *Vietnamese.* AVP, *tr. by* Huỳnh Sanh Thông

When dreaming [*or* foolish] kings, at odds with swift-paced time. Washington. Harriet Monroe. FaBoBe *Fr.* Commemoration Ode.

When dredful swelling seas, through boisterous windy blastes. The Felicitie of a mind imbracing vertue, that beholdeth the wretched desyres of the worlde. Lucretius, *Latin.* OBCVT, *tr. by Unknown*

When Earth slept, like a pig in the sun. Ballad of the Electric Eel. Wayne Brown. PBCV

When Earth's last picture is painted and the tubes are twisted / and dried. Rudyard Kipling. PWR; SAGP; UV

When Eastern lovers feed the fun'ral fire. Alexander Pope. *Fr.* Three Epitaphs on John Hewet and Sarah Drew. NIP-4

When Eddie had his second birthday. Eddie and the Birthday. Michael Rosen. NOxBChV

When e'er we enter life's open field. Ambition. Maggie Pogue Johnson. CBWP-4

When Egypt said, "Exterminate." Retribution. Lizelia Augusta Jenkins Moorer. CBWP-3

When Eliot died it made him seem human. New Year's Eve Poem 1965. Peter Levi. OxAEP-2

When England's multitudes observed with frowns. Bungaloid Growth. Colin Ellis. FaBoEE

When Eve did with the snake dispute. The Woman's Wish. Matthew Prior. FaBoEE

When Eve first saw the glistering day. Song with Words. James Agee. ChIV-1; MoAmPo

When Eve upon the first of men. A Reflection. Thomas Hood. FaBoEE

When even a turning to memory. Against Sadness. Natan Zach, *Hebrew.* IP, *tr. by* Warren Bargad *and* Stanley F. Chyet

When evenen sheades o' trees do hide. The Vaices That Be Gone. William Barnes. NOBVV

When evening comes. Kasa no Iratsume, *Japanese.* WPJ, *tr. by* Kenneth Rexroth *and* Ikuko Atsumi

When evening comes. Yakamochi. AWP, *tr. by* Arthur Waley *Fr.* Manyo Shu, Part 4 of 4.

When evening goes down into its jelly jelly jelly. Solo Finger Solo. Jayne Cortez. MoNo

When every one to pleasing pastime hies. Sonnet 23. Mary Sidney, Countess of Montgomery Wroth. PBRV; WPE *Fr.* Pamphilia to Amphilanthus.

When everything was over. Child Poems. Hilda Doolittle.

When Evil-Doing Comes Like Falling Rain. Bertolt Brecht, *German.* AF, *tr. by* John Willett

When faint and sad o'er Sorrow's desart wild. Monody on the Death of Chatterton. Coleridge.

When Faith and Love which parted from thee never. Sonnet: On the Religious Memorie of Mrs. Catherine Thomason My Christian Freind Deceas'd Decem. 1646. Milton. ChIV-2; OxAEP-1

When far-spent night persuades each mortal eye. Sonnet 99. Sir Philip Sidney. NoSic; PoE; Son *Fr.* Astrophil and Stella. AAS; SiPS

When Father Carves the Duck. Ernest Vincent Wright. NTCP; PoLF

When Father Decided He Did Not Love Her Anymore. Lynn Emanuel. NAmP90

When Father goes to town with me to buy my Sunday hat. When Polly Buys a Hat. E. Hill. BoTP

When father takes his spade to dig. The Robin. Laurence Alma-Tadema. BoTP

When fierce Pizarro's legions flew. The Revenge of America. Joseph Warton. ECEV

When fire and drink were a shelter. The Essence Is Not in the Living. Mairtin O Direain. BiHa, *tr. by* Douglas Sealy *and* Tomás MacSiomóin

When first Apollo got my brain with childe. The Author to His Book. George Alsop. SCAP

When first Both Gods and Men had one Times Birth. Hesiod. OBCVT, *tr. by* George Chapman *Fr.* Works and Days.

When first, descending from the moorlands. Extempore Effusion upon the Death of James Hogg. Wordsworth. EBEV; NOBE; OAEL-2; Ro; SCV

When first Diana leaves her Bed. The Progress of Beauty. Jonathan Swift. GEA; PFE

When first Eudoxos cut his lovely hair. Euphorion, *Greek.* GrAn, *tr. by* Alistair Elliot

When first, fair mistress, I did see your face. To B.C. Sir John Suckling. CaPo

When first I came here I had hope. Edward Thomas. NoAM

When first I came to Louisville, some pleasure for to find. The Lily of the West. *Unknown.* AmFP

When first I played I nearly died. New Boy's View of Rugger. Rupert Brooke. AYFP

When first I saw that dear abode. After-recollection at Sight of the Same Cottage. Dorothy Wordsworth. Ro

When first I saw true beauty, and thy joys. Mount of Olives. Henry Vaughan. ESCV; GeHe

When first I saw you in the curious street. German Prisoners. Joseph Lee. NSI

When first I took to cutlass, blunderbuss and gun. The Ballad of O'Bruadir. Frederick Robert Higgins. OBMV

When first I walked here I hobbled. The Seekonk Woods. Galway Kinnell. NoAM

When first I was courtin' sweet Rosie O'Grady. Irish Song [Rosie O'Grady]. Noël Coward. NBLV; OBCoV

When first mine eyes beheld your princely name. Owen Tudor to Queen Katherine. Michael Drayton. NoSic *Fr.* England's Heroical Epistles.

When first mine eyes did view and mark. Sir Thomas Wyatt. SiPS

When first mine infant-ear. Christendom. Thomas Traherne. PoEL-2

When first my lines [*or* verse] of heavenly [*or* heav'nly] joy[e]s made mention. Jordan (2)(II). George Herbert. CABP; ESCV; FMP; FSCP; GeHe; NAEL-1; NoSic; NoSic; OAEL-1; OBWVE; PBRV; SeCP

When first the college rolls receive his name. The Scholar's Life. Samuel Johnson. NOBE; OBSV *Fr.* The Vanity of Human Wishes [The Tenth Satire of Juvenal Imitated]. EBEV; ECEV; NOEC; OAEL-1; OxAEP-1; PoEL-3; TFi

When first the eye this forest sees. Andrew Marvell. *Fr.* Upon Appleton House [To My Lord Fairfax]. FaBoPV; GeHe; SeCP

When first the fiery-mantled sun. Ode to Winter. Thomas Campbell. GTBS-P

When first the unflowering Fern-forest. Darwinism. Agnes Mary Frances Robinson. VWP

When first the world grew dark to me. A Cross-Road Epitaph. Amy Levy. VWP

When first the year, I heard the cuckoo sing. John Gay. *Fr.* Thursday; or, The Spell. PoEL-3 *Fr.* The Shepherd's Week.

When first this canvas felt Giorgione's hand. On the Concert. Trumbull Stickney. APN-2

When first thou didst entice to thee my heart. Affliction (1). George Herbert. ESCV; FHYEP; FMP; FSCP; GeHe; MeLP; NAEL-1; NOBE; NOSC; NoP-4; SeCP

When first thou didst even from the grave. Disorder and Frailty. Henry Vaughan. ChIV-1

When first thou on me, Lord, wrought'st thy sweet print. The Ebb and Flow. Edward Taylor. AmPP; SCAP

When first thy eies unveil, give thy soul leave. Rules and Lessons. Henry Vaughan. ESCV

When first thy sweet and gracious eye. The Glance. George Herbert. ESCV

When first we met we did not guess. Triolet. Robert Bridges. OxBSP

When fishes flew and forests walked. The Donkey. G. K. Chesterton. ACTP; APo; CTAV; ChIV-3; EBEvV; FaPoR; GI; InPK-6; MoBrPo; OBEV; PFE; PoLF; RB

When fishes set umbrellas up. Christina Rossetti. VWP

When fivepence a solid meal cannot supply. The Volunteer. *Unknown.* NOEC

When flighting time is on, I go. The Birdcatcher. Ralph Hodgson. MoBrPo

When Flora Had Ourfret the Firth. Quhen Flora Had O'erfret the Firth. *Unknown.* OBEV; OxBS

When fog come creepin' over Beccles. Molly Fitton. BXAP

When for eternal worlds we steer. Vain World Adieu. *Unknown.* AmFP

When for the Thorns with which I long, too long. The Coronet. Andrew Marvell. ESCV; FHYEP; FMP; FSCP; GeHe; MeLP; NAEL-1; NOCV; NOSC; NoP-4; PBRV; PoE; SCGP; TOF

When forehead full of torments hot and red. Chercheuses de Poux, Les. Rimbaud. AWP, *tr. by* T. Sturge Moore *Fr.* Illuminations.

When formed our band, we are all well manned. California. *Unknown.* AS

'When Fortune frown'd, the feller made my fall'. Thomas Dorset Sackville. *See* Midnight ("Midnight was come, when every vital thing").

When fortune's blind goddess had shied my abode. Dick Turpin and Black Bess. *Unknown.* AmFP

When Fortune's shield protects thee, then beware. Fortune's Treachery. Judah Halevi, *Hebrew.* TrJP, *tr. by* Solomon Solis-Cohen

When forty winters shall besiege thy brow. Sonnet 2. Shakespeare. HeIP-4; ImPo; NoSic; SCGP; Son *Fr.* Sonnets.

When foxes eat the last gold grape. Escape. Elinor Wylie. ChAP; MoAmPo

When Francis preached love to the birds. Saint Francis and the Birds. Seamus Heaney. NTP; TIRV

When Francus comes to solace with his whore. In Francum. Sir John Davies. FaBoEE; OBCoV

When Franz Kafka was writing his stories they were not. Franz Kafka (I). Wiktor Woroszylski, *Polish*. CEEP, *tr. by* Magnus J. Krynski *and* Robert A. Maguire

When Freedom, from her mountain height. The American Flag. Joseph Rodman Drake. APN-1; FaBoBe

When frequent rains, and gentle show'rs descend. Nathaniel Weekes. *Fr.* Barbados. PBCV

When from afar these mountain tops I view. The Sonnet of the Mountain. Mellin de Saint-Gelais, *French*. AWP, *tr. by* Austin Dobson

When from dark error's subjugation. Nikolai Alekseyevich Nekrasov. NAWM-2, *tr. by* Juliet Soskice *Fr.* A Propos of the Wet Snow.

When from the blossoms of the noiseful day. To My Friend. Francis Thompson. PoA

When from the gates of Paradise fair Eve. The Vision of Eve. Henrietta Cordelia Ray. CBWP-3

When from the palid Sky the Sun descends. Virgil. OBCVT, *tr. by* James Thomson *Fr.* The Seasons: Winter.

When from the world, I shall be tane. To My Husband. "Eliza." KTR; LW; PBRV

When frost and dew have caused a hundred plants to wither. In Imitation of T'ao P'eng-tse. Wei Ying-wu, *Chinese*. SuSp, *tr. by* Irving Y. Lo

When frost will not suffer to dike and to hedge. December's Husbandry. Thomas Tusser. NoSic *Fr.* Five Hundred Points of Good Husbandry.

When Gabriel (no blest spirit more kind or fair). Gabriel's Appearance. Abraham Cowley. NOSC *Fr.* Davideis.

When Gaffer be dead for a month or more. Martin Fagg. BXAP

When gardens shone with flowery pride. On a Little Boy's Endeavouring to Catch a Snake. Thomas Foxton. OxBChV

When Gauguin was visiting Fiji. Limerick. Victor Gray. NOBL

When genial Spring first bears the mating thrush. Albery Allson Whitman. AAP *Fr.* The Octoroon.

When, gently raising up his drooping Head. Patroclus's Request to Achilles for his Arms. Imitated from the Beginning of the Sixteenth Iliad of Homer. Homer. OBCVT, *tr. by* Thomas Yalden *Fr.* The Iliad.

When George the Third was reigning a hundred years ago. A Ballad for a Boy. William Johnson Cory. FaPoR; OxBChV

When getting my nose in a book. A Study of Reading Habits. Philip Larkin. InPK-6; NOBL; OBCoV

When God at first made Man. The Pulley. George Herbert. AWP; ChIV-1; EBEvV; FHYEP; FMP; FSCP; GTBS-P; GeHe; HAP; HeIP-4; ImPo; InPK-6; InPS-3; NAEL-1; NOBE; NOCV; NOSC; NoP-4; OAEL-1; OBEV; OxAEP-1; PFE; SCGP; SeCP; TFi

When God created thee, one would believe. Lady Mary Wortley Montagu. ECWP *Fr.* Verses Addressed to the Imitator of the First Satire of the Second Book of Horace.

When God Descends with Men to Dwell. Hosea, I Ballou. AH

When God had finished Master Messerin. Sonnet: Of the Making of Master Messerin. Rustico Di Filippo, *Italian*. AWP, *tr. by* D. G. Rossetti

When God in the Bible makes a promise. Like Sand. Natan Zach, *Hebrew*. IP, *tr. by* Warren Bargad *and* Stanley F. Chyet

When god lets my body be. E. E. Cummings. MoAmPo; NOBA; SAGP

When God makes a great Man he intends all others to crush him. Arthur Hugh Clough. OBSV *Fr.* Amours de Voyage. NOBVV

When God scooped up a handful of dust. They Ask: Is God, Too, Lonely? Carl Sandburg. SAGP

When gods alike and mortals rose to birth. The Golden Age. Hesiod, *Greek*. OBCVT, *tr. by* Charles Elton

When gods had framed the sweet of women's face. Love and Jealousy. Robert Greene. CBLP

When God's parachute failed. Religion Back Home. William Stafford. OBAL

When gold was first discovered at Coloma, near the hill. The National Miner. *Unknown*. AmFP

When Goldie the golden eagle escaped from the Zoo. Goldie Sapiens. P. J. Kavanagh. OBCoV

When good King Arthur ruled the land. King Arthur. *Unknown*. FPC

When good King Arthur ruled this [*or* the] land. King Arthur. Mother Goose. LB; NTP; OxNR

When good St. David, as old writs record. In Honour of St. David's Day. *Unknown*. OBWVE

When Grandmamma fell off the boat. Indifference. Harry Graham. NBLV

When grapes turn. Jelaluddin Rumi, *Persian*. EnIH, *tr. by* Robert Bly

When green buds hang in the elm like dust. A. E. Housman. SAGP

When groping farms are lanterned up. A Country God. Edmund Blunden. MoBrPo

When [the] Guests First Take Their Seats. When the Guests First Take Their Seats. *Unknown*, *Chinese*. CoBCP, *tr. by* Burton Watson

When Gullion died (who knows not Gullion?). Joseph Hall. NoSic *Fr.* Virgidemiarum.

When Gwen heard at last. In Memoriam. W. J. Gruffydd, *Welsh*. OBWVE, *tr. by* R. Gerallt Jones

When,/ Halting in front of it, I look. Hitomaro. *Fr.* Shui Shu. AWP, *tr. by* Arthur Waley

When hands are joined and head bows in the dark. (LL) Penal Law. Austin Clarke. BoLoP; GTBS-P; NOIV

When, hardly moving, you decorate night's hush. The Waters of Life. Humbert Wolfe. MoBrPo

When have I known a boy. The Girl on the Land. Alice Thompson Meynell. VWP

When he breathed his last breath it was he. The Moment of My Father's Death. Sharon Olds. NAmP90; NIP-4

When he brings home a whale. Naughty Boy. Robert Creeley. HeIP-4; NOBA; NoAM

When He Came. Dorothee Sölle. "He needs you." CrSp

When he came home Mother said he looked. My Father's Martial Art. Stephen Shu Ning Liu. InPK-6

When he came out, into the world. Born Tying Knots. Samuel Makidemewabe, *Cree Indian*. STP, *tr. by* Howard Norman

When he comes home at night. Wasp Sex Myth (One). Anselm Hollo. PoM

When he comes home from work. Allegory of Death and Night. Frank Stanford. MT

When he comes up to the bedroom. Palladas, *Greek*. GrAn, *tr. by* Tony Harrison

When he died, far away, no one at the Café. Universal. Ory Bernstein. *Fr.* Poems from Mexico. IP, *tr. by* Warren Bargad *and* Stanley F. Chyet

When he first came to see me I forgot that he was dead. Memories of Her Friend Who Died. Ory Bernstein, *Hebrew*. IP, *tr. by* Warren Bargad *and* Stanley F. Chyet

When he found Laertes alone on the tidy terrace, hoeing. Laertes. Hesiod, *Greek*. OBCVT, *tr. by* Michael Longley

When he got into bed. Damon & Pythias. Robert Creeley. LCAP-2

When he got up that morning everything was different. A Journey. Edward Field. BLT

When he had made sure there were no survivors in his house. The Butchers. Homer. OBCVT, *tr. by* Michael Longley *Fr.* The Odyssey.

When he is ready he is raised and carried. The Glass King. Eavan Boland. CIP-2

When he leads [*or* lends] any poet[s] about the town. (LL) A Session[s] of the Poets. Sir John Suckling. BeJo; CaPo

When he left, the waves were flush with the railing. Thoughts in the Cold. Li Shang-yin, *Chinese*. CoBCP, *tr. by* Burton Watson

When he lies in the night away from her. The Jealous Lovers. Donald Hall. NYBP

When he planned to begin a spirit tower. King Wen's Park Divine. *Unknown*, *Chinese*. ChiPo, *tr. by* Ezra Pound

When he pressed his lips to my mouth. Steve Kowit. BLT

When he pushed his bush of black hair off his brow. Sicilian Cyclamens. D. H. Lawrence. NoAM

When he raped a young maid in a train. Limerick. *Unknown*. PeLi

When he reads. Avatars. V. Indira Bhavani, *Tamil*. OMIP, *tr. by* Martha Ann Selby

When he returned and opened his eyes and stood there, uncalled for. Honi. Dan Pagis, *Hebrew*. IP, *tr. by* Warren Bargad *and* Stanley F. Chyet

When he said. What She Said. Nannakaiyar, *Tamil*. PLW, *tr. by* A. K. Ramanujan

When he said *Mary*, she did not at once. Contemplations of Mary. Roy McFadden. PNI

When he sailed into the harbor. Korinna, *Greek*. BoWoP, *tr. by* Willis Barnstone

When he saw her. *Unknown*, *Sanskrit*. TOF, *tr. by* John Brough

When He Says So We Dance in All Directions—Wow! *Unknown*, *Seneca Indian*. STP, *tr. by* Jerome Rothenberg *and* Richard Johnny John

When he sit, he sit on what he ain't got—almost. (LL) The Frog. *Unknown*. NBLV; NOxBChV; NTCP; RB

When He Spoke to Me of Love. M. A. Mokhomo, *Sotho*. PeSA, *tr. by* Dan Kunene *and* Jack Cope

When he the nation's heart had won. The Presidents. Lizelia Augusta Jenkins Moorer. CBWP-3

When he trades in tea—it's right nearby. Song of the Merchant's Wife. Yang Shih-ch'i, *Chinese*. CoBLCP, *tr. by* Jonathan Chaves

When he walked through town, the wing-shot bird he'd hidden. The Author of American Ornithology Sketches a Bird, Now Extinct. David Wagoner. BLT

When He was barely five. The Boyhood of Christ. Saint Columbanus.
NOIV

When he was dead. (LL) The Comic Adventures of Old Mother Hubbard
and Her Dog. Sarah Catherine Martin. CBNP; FaBoBe; OxBChV;
OxNR; ReMoGo

When he was eight years old he had become. Words and Monsters. Vernon
Scannell. OxBC

When he was nine, he thought he knew. The Happy Mathematician. Anna
Wickham. WPN

When he was shot he toppled to the ground. Shot Who? Jim Lane! Merrill
Moore. MoAmPo

When he was starting out, still green. The Counterfeiter. Greg Williamson.
RA

When he was young, he broke horses. The Passion Drinker. Anita
Endrezze-Danielson. VoR

When he went down to the square, the pavilions now. Ikhnaton's Night.
Agnes Nemes Nagy, *Hungarian.* CEEP, *tr. by* Laura Schiff

When he who adores thee has left but the name. Pro Patria Mori. Thomas
Moore. GTBS-P; HoPM; OxAEP-2

When he, who is the unforgiven. The Unforgiven. Edwin Arlington
Robinson. CMoP

When he whose empire is in clouds saw Hector bent to wage. Hector
Arms. Homer. NOSC, *tr. by* George Chapman *Fr.* The Iliad.

When He Would Have His Verses Read. Robert Herrick. BeJo; CaPo;
CavPo; NOBE; NOSC; SCGP

When Heaven in mercy gives thy prayers return. Hezekiah's Display. John
Keble. ChIV-1

When Helen first saw wrinkles in her face. Walter Savage Landor.
EnLoPo *Fr.* Ianthe.

When Helen Lived. W. B. Yeats. CMoP

When Henry was a baby. Black Henry. Tejumola Ologboni. NBV

When her need for you dies. In Her Only Way. Robert Graves. OxBSP

When her need for you dies. In Her Only Way. Robert Graves. OxBSP
Fr. Three Songs for the Lute.

When *Hercules* did use to spin. The Weavers Song. Thomas Deloney.
PBRV

When Hermocrates the Miser lay in bed. Lucilius, *Greek.* GrAn, *tr. by*
Peter Porter

When Hilda does the Highland reel. To Hilda Dancing. John Bingham
Morton. OBCoV

When His Excellency Prince Norodom Chantaraingsey. Dead Soldiers.
James Fenton. AF; NoAM; NoP-4; OBWP

When his eyes took the half-sheened stillness of fish roe. Seizure. Linda
Bierds. PUP-20

When his hour for death had come. Osceola. Walt Whitman. NAAL-1;
NAAL-3

When his mouth faced my mouth, I turned aside. Amaru. EP, *tr. by* John
Brough

When hit come ter de question er de female vote. Brother Baptis' on
Woman Suffrage. Rosalie Jonas. BlSi

When holy Patrick full of grace. The White Lake. *Unknown, Irish.* TIRV,
tr. by Robin Flower

When home we return, after youth has been spending. Susanna Blamire.
ECWP

When howitzers began. Hayden Carruth. Poetsp

When I a verse shall make. His Prayer to Ben[.] Jo[h]nson. Robert
Herrick. BeJo; CaPo; NAEL-1; NOSC; NoP-4; OxBSP; PeLV

When I Admire the Greatness. Jacob Steendam, *Dutch.* AH

When I Am 19 I Was a Medic. D. F. Brown. CDa

When I am alone. The Fisherman's Wife. Amy Lowell. BoWoP

When I am alone I am happy. Waiting. William Carlos Williams. SAmP

When I am an old woman I shall wear purple. Warning. Jenny Joseph.
FaBoWP; OxBTC

When I Am Dead. George MacBeth. OxBTC

When I Am Dead. James Edward Wilson. PoLF

When I am dead, and Doctors know not why. The Damp[e]. Donne.
NOSC; SeCP

When I am dead and gone. (LL) I hoed and trenched and weeded. A. E.
Housman. LiTM; MoBrPo; UnPo; WeW-3

When I am dead and over me bright April. I Shall Not Care. Sara
Teasdale. MoAmPo; UnPo

When I am dead and thou wouldst try. *Unknown.* NOSC

When I am dead, even then. Then. Muriel Rukeyser. GLP; LCAP-2

When I am dead, I hope it may be said. On His Books. Hilaire Belloc.
FaBoEE; MoBrPo; NBLV; OxBoLi; WeW-3

When I am dead I want you to dress me. *Unknown.* OxBoLi

When I am dead, lay me down between the Yangtze. Yu Kuang-chung,
Chinese. ChiPo, *tr. by* Yu Kuang-chung

When I am dead, my dearest. Song. Christina Rossetti. APAD; AWP;
BoLoP; CABP; CH; EBEV; EBEvV; GBL; GEA; InPS-3; LBC; NAEL-
2; NOBE; NOBVV; NoP-4; OAEL-2; OBEV; OxAEP-2; PBMP; PoLF;
PoRA; Poetr; SAGP; SCV; SDW; TFi; VWP; WPE

When I am dead, withhold, I pray, your blooming legacy. Georgia Douglas
Johnson. NMM-2

When I am dead you'll find it hard. He and She. Eugene Fitch Ware.
PoLF

When I am gone. An Epitaph. Josephine D. Henderson Heard. AAP;
CBWP-4

When I am gone. (LL) The Garden by Moonlight. Amy Lowell. CPO;
NMM-2

When I am gone. Ute Mountain. Charles Tomlinson. RB

When I am grown to [a] man's estate. Looking Forward. Robert Louis
Stevenson. ACTP; NBLV; OxBChV

When I am grown up I shall go and stoop digging clams. A Girl's Song.
Unknown. APN-2, *tr. by* Franz Boas *Fr.* Songs of the Kwakiutl
Indians.

When I am hungry. Mahadevi, *Kannada.* WPoS, *tr. by* Jane Hirshfield

When I am living in the Midlands. The South Country. Hilaire Belloc.
MoBrPo; OxAEP-2

When I am lonely. Ryozan, *Japanese.* OHPJ, *tr. by* Kenneth Rexroth

When I am no one. (LL) Wish for a Young Wife. Theodore Roethke.
MoP; NAAL-2; NoAM; NoP-4; OxBSP; TAP

When I Am Old. Caroline Atherton Briggs Mason. BLPA

When I am old. Song: "When I am old." Denis Glover. PeNZ *Fr.* Sings
Harry.

When I am riding round the ring no longer. Circus-Rider to Ringmaster.
Thomas Hardy. RACG

When I am sad and weary. Celia Celia. Adrian Mitchell. FaBoEE; OPOU

When I am the sky. Cancion. Denise Levertov. NALW; PoM

When I am very earnestly digging. Pause. Mary Ursula Bethell. PeNZ

When I arrived some clansmen had already come. The Wood-Cutter.
Lupenga Mphande. HBAPE

When I ask Daddy. Ask Mummy Ask Daddy. John Agard. OTCP

When I ask or take / what I'd give. (LL) I would but I can't. *Unknown,
Greek.* FP, *tr. by* Thomas Meyer

When I ask or take / what I'd give. *Unknown.* See I would but I can't.

When I ask what things they fear. Fears of the Eighth Grade. Toi
Derricotte. GT; InPS-3

When I asked for fish in the restaurant facing the Ohio River. Carl
Sandburg. PoE *Fr.* Whiffs of the Ohio River at Cincinnati.

When I asked him about. Slave Ritual. Carolyn M. Rodgers. ISC

When I asked the very old man. Quotations. George Oppen. NNaP

When I attained enlightenment. The Testimony of J. Robert Oppenheimer.
Ai. PaTW

When i awake. I Forget. Sachiko Yoshihara, *Japanese.* WPJ, *tr. by*
Kenneth Rexroth *and* Ikuko Atsumi

When I Awoke. Raymond R. Patterson. NBV; PoBA

When I awoke before the dawn my head. Dante. See Ugolino.

When I awoke this morning. The Blue Animals. Jon Anderson. AmPA

When I awoke with cold. Coffee. James Vincent Cunningham. MoAmPo;
VGW

When I begin to see / only what I've said. Beginner's Mind. Margaret
Gibson. AFr

When I beheld the Poet blind, yet bold. On Mr Milton's "Paradise Lost."
Andrew Marvell. CABP; EPCY; FSCP; NOSC

When I behold a forrest spread. Art above Nature, to Julia. Robert
Herrick. BeJo; CABP; NOSC

When I behold Becchina in a rage. Sonnet: Of Becchina in a Rage. Cecco
Angiolieri, da Siena, *Italian.* AWP, *tr. by* D. G. Rossetti

When I behold how black, immortal ink. Silet. Ezra Pound. MoAmPo;
Son

When I behold the havoc and the spoil. Planting. George Wither. NOSC
Fr. A Collection of Emblemes, Ancient and Moderne.

When I behold the heavens as in their prime. PBWP *Fr.*
Contemplations. AmPP; NAAL-3; PoEL-3; SCAP; WPE

When I behold Thee, almost slain. His Anthem, to Christ on the Cross.
Robert Herrick. CavPo

When I behold this tickle trustles state. Petrarch. *Fr.* Visions. AWP

When I bethinke me on that speech whyleare. Edmund Spenser. NoSic;
OAEL-1 *Fr.* Wood Of Error. AEP

When I bethought me well, under the restless sun. Henry Howard, Earl of
Surrey. ChIV-1 *Fr.* A Paraphrase of Part of the Book of Ecclesiates.

When I breathe. Tanka. Ishikawa Takuboku, *Japanese.* MJT, *tr. by*
Makoto Ueda

When I built upon sand. Foundations. Leopold Staff, *Polish.* PoSu, *tr. by*
Adam Czerniawski

When I burn up without a trace. Igor Moiseievich Irtenev, *Russian*. TCRP, *tr. by* Bradley Jordan

When I burned our leaves, a wind from the dark. Looking West. William Stafford. NYBP

When I but hear her sing, I fare. Upon a Rare Voice. Owen Feltham [*or* Feltham]. NOSC

When I Buy Pictures. Marianne Moore. ColAP; OxBA

When I call to you, God. Contact. John F. Deane. TIRV

When I came back, he was gone. My Father's Leaving. Ira Sadoff. AmPA

When I Came from Colchis. W. S. Merwin. VGW

When I came to show you my summer cottage. Summer. Josephine Miles. FaBoWP; WPE

When I can hold a stone within my hand. Rumination. Richard Eberhart. LiTM

When I can read my title clear. Ninety-fifth. Isaac Watts. AmFP

When I carefully consider the curious habits of dogs. Meditatio. Ezra Pound. FaBoCh; OBAL; PBMP

When I catch sight of your fair head. Sonnet. Louise Labé. PBWP, *tr. by* Joan Keefe *and* Richard Terdiman

When I come back home, to my native village. Native Village. Chiyong Chong, *Korean*. CKP, *tr. by* Jaihiun Kim

When I come back to my father's house. Galway Kinnell. RaBo *Fr.* Memories of My Father.

When I come down to sleep death's endless night. My City. James Weldon Johnson. NAAAL

When I come to view. Silence Wager Stories. Susan Howe. FTOS

When I consider everything that grows. Sonnet 15. Shakespeare. AWP; NAEL-1; NoSic; SCGP; Son *Fr.* Sonnets.

When I consider how my light is spent. On His Blindness. Milton. APAD; AWP; CABP; ChIV-2; EBEvV; GEA; GSo; HAP; HeIP-4; ImPo; InPK-6; NAEL-1; NOBE; NOSC; NoP-4; OBEV; PBMP; PFE; PoE; PoEL-3; PoLF; PoPoPo; PoRA; Poetr; SCGP; SoSe-8; TFi; TRP; WeW-3

When I consider Life and its few years. Tears. Lizette Woodworth Reese. MoAmPo

When I consider men of golden talents. So That's Who I Remind Me Of. Ogden Nash. PoLF

When I consider the many hours spent. Lament of a Subwayite. Eugene O'Neill. UV

When I consider thy heavens, the work of thy fingers. Bible, *O.T. See* Psalm 8.

When I contemplate o'er me. The Night Serene. Luís De León, *Spanish*. TrJP, *tr. by* Thomas Walsh

When I couldn't he always discussed things. Action Would Kill It / A Gamble. Robert Adamson. BMAP; CBAP

When I crept over the hill, broken with tears. The Comforters. Dora Sigerson Shorter. CH

When I did wake this morn from sleep. Early Morn. W. H. Davies. CH

When I die, I shall be a rock. Rock. Ch'ihwan Yu, *Korean*. CKP, *tr. by* Jaihiun Kim

When I / die / I'm sure. The Rebel. Mari E. Evans. CRP; PoBA; SAGP

When I died [*or* dyed] last, and, dear [Deare], I die [*or* dye]. The Legacy [*or* Legacie]. Donne. FMP; SeCP

When I died *they* washed *me* out of the turret with a hose. (LL) The Death of the Ball Turret Gunner. Randall Jarrell. CMoP; ClHu; ColAP; HAP; HeIP-4; HoPM; InPK-6; LCAP-2; LiTM; MT; MoAmPo; NAAL-2; NIP-4; NOBA; NoAM; NoP-4; OBWP; OxBA; PoE; PoPoPo; PoWW; Poetr; RB; SAGP; SoSe-8; TAP; TFi; UnPo; VCAP; VGW

When I Do Count the Clock. Shakespeare. *See* Sonnet 12.

When I do count the clock that tells the time. Sonnet 12. Shakespeare. AWP; GSo; HeIP-4; InPS-3; NAEL-1; NoSic; OAEL-1; SCGP; Son *Fr.* Sonnets.

When I do it, I remember how it was with us. Making Love to Myself. James L. White. GLP

When I dragged the rotten log. Kenneth Rexroth. *Fr.* The Signature of All Things. NNaP

When I draw the magnificent Dutch girl. Rembrandt—Self Portrait. Gregory Corso. BB

When I drink. Contagion. James Tate. CMAP

When I drink I become / the joy of faggots. Dorothy Allison. EC2; GLP

When I drive cab. After Anacreon. Lew Welch. NeAP; PoM *Fr.* Taxi Suite.

When I drive cab / I am moved by strange whistles and wear a hat. Lew Welch. *See* After Anacreon.

When I entered the book of myths. The Book of Myths. Joy Harjo. NMM-2

When I face north a lost Cree. Returned to Say. William Stafford. CoAmPo

When I fall asleep, and even during sleep. Baudelaire. Delmore Schwartz. SAGP; TwCP; VGW

When I find that my troubles are too much. Midnight Trolleybus. Bulat Shalvovich Okudzhava, *Russian*. TCRP, *tr. by* Albert C. Todd

When I first came here I had hope. Edward Thomas. SCGP

When I first came to London, I rambled about. The Seeker. Matthew Green. ECEV

When I first learned how to write poetry. Shown to My Son Yü. Lu Yu, *Chinese*. SuSp, *tr. by* Irving Y. Lo

When I first opened my eyes. Autobiography. Janet Dubé. BrRo

When I first saw a woman after childbirth. Ishtar. Judith Wright. NALW; NoAM

When I First Saw Snow. Gregory Djanikian. CMAP; UnSA

When I found where we had crashed, in the snow. He Said. Jean Valentine. TAP

When I gathered flowers. Hitomaro, *Japanese*. OHMPJ, *tr. by* Kenneth Rexroth

When I gave my first cry. The Sea. Phạm H(cfstilde;o), *Vietnamese*. AVP, *tr. by* Huỳnh Sanh Thông

When I gaze at the sun. A Moment Please. Samuel Allen. PoBA; SSLK

When I gaze upon the sky. Reflection from Sea and Sky. Walter Savage Landor. FaBoEE

When I get home from a day's shopping in a city street. Edna's Hymn. Barry Humphries. NOBAu

When I get in Illinois. Can't You Line It? *Unknown*. NAAAL

When I get nervous, it's so hard not to. Have You Ever Faked an Orgasm? Molly Peacock. RA

When I get there, I hope they forgive me if the knot I tie is the wrong knot. (LL) Hawaii Dantesca. Charles Wright. HCAP; LCAP-2

When I Get Time. Tom Masson. BLPA

When I get to be a composer. Daybreak in Alabama. Langston Hughes. FaBoA

When I get up in the morning. Getting Up. Lilian McCrea. BoTP

When I go. After Grave Deliberation. Elizabeth Flynn. NBLV

When I go away from you. The Taxi. Amy Lowell. BoWoP; LW; MoAmPo

When I go back to earth. The Answer. Sara Teasdale. PoA

When I go[e] musing all alone. The Authors [*or* Author's] Abstract of Melancholy. Robert Burton. NOSC *Fr.* The Anatomy of Melancholy.

When I, Good Friends, Was Called to the Bar. Sir William Schwenck Gilbert. NAEL-2 *Fr.* Trial by Jury.

When I got home. Baby Lazarus. Jackie Kay. NBrP

When I got there the dead opossum looked like. Behaving Like a Jew. Gerald Stern. LoL; UnSA

When I got to the airport I rushed up to the desk. The Race. Sharon Olds. MoLi; RaBo

When I got up this mornin', I heah'd de ol' Southern whistle blow. The Southern Blues. *Unknown*. BkSV

When I got up this mornin', I heard the old Southern whistle blow. The Southern Blues. Big Bill Broonzy. GM

When I grew strong to climb. Legend. Sydney Tremayne. FaBoTC

When I grew up I went away to work. Whores. Margaret Abigail Walker. NALW

When I grow up. William Wise. ChAP

When I grow up, I plan to keep. Plans. Maxine W. Kumin. TLR

When I had firmly answered "No." The Last Ride Together (from Her Point of View). James Kenneth Stephen. BXAP; UnPo

When I had learned enough to fail every test. My Flute. Herbert Krohn. CDa

When I had met my love the twentieth time. Her Merriment. W. H. Davies. EnLoPo

When I had money, money, O! Money. W. H. Davies. OBEV; OBMV

When I had spread it all on linen cloth. The Wife's Tale. Seamus Heaney. CIP-2; SAGP

When I have a beard that's curly and weird. I'll Buy a Peacock Bird. Modwena Sedgwick. PeP

When I have a house. . . as I sometime may. Vagabond House. Don Blanding. BLPA

When I have a wife at home? (LL) Soldier, Won't You Marry Me? *Unknown*. AmFP; OxBoLi; PeLV

When I have baked white cakes. Interlude. Amy Lowell. NMM-2

When I have borne in memory what has tamed. England, 1802, V. Wordsworth. GTBS-P; OBEV

When I have chanted my new poems. K'ang Hai. CoBLCP, *tr. by* Jonathan Chaves *Fr.* Ten Poems on Almond Blossoms.

When I have crost the bar. (LL) Crossing the Bar. Tennyson. APAD; ChIV-2; ClHu; EBVV; EBVVPR; FaPoR; HeIP-4; ImPo; NAEL-2; NOBE; NOBVV; NoP-4; OAEL-2; OBEV; OBNC; OxBoS; PBMP; PWR; PeECV; PoLF; PoRA; SoSe-8; TFi; TrCP

When I have fears that I may cease to be. The Terror of Death. Keats. AWP; CABP; EBEV; GSo; GTBS-P; HAP; HeIP-4; HoPM; ImPo; InPS-

3; LaPo; NAEL-2; NIP-4; NoP-4; OAEL-2; OBEV; OBNC; PBMP; PoE; PoPoPo; PoRA; Ro; SAGP; SCGP; Son; TFi; UnPo

When I have gone. (LL) Oblivion. Ellis Ayitey Komey. PBMAP

When I have grown foolish. Peregrine's Sunday Song. Elinor Wylie. NYBP

When I have heard small talk about great men. Grandeur of Ghosts. Siegfried Sassoon. MoBrPo; OBMV

When I have lost my temper I have lost my reason, too. Temper. *Unknown.* PoToHe

When I have lost the power to feel the pang. Strangeness of Heart. Siegfried Sassoon. TrJP

When I have purged my guilt. (LL) The Palace of Art. Tennyson. EnVR; NOBRP

When I have said 'I love you' I have said. Valentine Ackland. WPN

When I have seen by Time's fell hand defac'd. Shakespeare. *See* Sonnet 64.

When I have seen by Time's fell hand defac'd [*or* defaced]. Sonnet 64. Shakespeare. AWP; EnLoPo; GTBS-P; HAP; HeIP-4; ImPo; NOBE; NoSic; OAEL-1; OxAEP-1; PoE; PoRA; SCGP; Son *Fr.* Sonnets.

When I Have Time. *Unknown.* PWR

When I hear it said of gods and great literature. Strong's Winter. Sidney Burris. BAP-96

When I hear laughter from a tavern door. Wilfrid Scawen Blunt. OBMV *Fr.* Esther [a Young Man's Tragedy].

When I hear the gravel rattling in the basket lid. In Velvet. Ann Chandonnet. EC3

When I hear the old men. A Song of Greatness. *Unknown, Chippewa Indian.* ImGa, *tr. by* Mary Austin

When I hear you. To the Pianist Bill Evans. Bill Zavatsky. MoNo

When I Heard at the Close of Day. Walt Whitman.

"Day when I rose at dawn from the bed of perfect health, refresh'd, The." ITG

When I heard at the close of the day how my name had been receiv'd with plaudits in the capitol, still it was not a happy night for me that follow'd. Walt Whitman. APN-1; AmPP; GBL; GLoP; LoP; NAAL-1; NAAL-3; NoAM; OxBA; PoE

("And that night I was / happy.") (LL) GLoP

When I Heard Dat White Man Say. Zack Gilbert. PoBA

When I heard the learn'd astronomer. Walt Whitman. AmPP; ChAP; ColAP; HAP; MoAmPo; NAAL-1; NAAL-3; NoP-4; OxBA; PAR; PBMP; PFE; PoPoPo; Poetr; SoSe-8; TAP; WeW-3

When I Held You to My Chest, You Fit. Jack Myers. AmPA

When I hit her on the head, it was good. Herbert White. Frank Bidart. AmPA

When I hoked there, I would find. Terminus. Seamus Heaney. PoPoPo

When I hug you tight at bedtime. Unspoken. Judith Ortiz Cofer. CrSp

When I in praise of babies speak. W. H. Davies. CBLP

When I Know the Power of my Black Hand. Lance Jeffers. ISC

When I languish'd, and wish'd you would something bestow. A Song by Mrs. P—. Mary Pix. KTR *Fr.* The Innocent Mistress.

When I last rade down Ettrick. (LL) Ettrick. Lady John Scott. LW

When I last wrote. Letter to a Young Father in Exile. John Logan. CAPP-1

When I lay dis body down. (LL) I know moon-rise, I know star-rise. *Unknown.* APN-2; CrDW; NAAAL; UnPo

When I lay me down to sleep. Insomnia the Gem of the Ocean. John Updike. NBLV

When I lay sick and like to die. An Elegy for Five. Richard Palmer Blackmur. PFE

When I leapt over Tower Bridge. Sir John Collings Squire. UV

When I left her door I thought / she'd try to stop me. Humiliation. Kaifi A'Zmi, *Urdu.* OMIP, *tr. by* Mumtaz Jahan

When I left my girl. Hitomaro, *Japanese.* OHPJ, *tr. by* Kenneth Rexroth

When I lie down to die. Valentin Petrovich Katayev, *Russian.* TCRP, *tr. by* Bernard Meares

When I lie down to sleep dream the Wishing Well it rings. I Am a Victim of Telephone. Allen Ginsberg. NBLV

When I lie where shades of darkness. Fare Well. Walter De la Mare. EBEvV; GTBS-P; NOBE; NoP-4; OBEV

When I lived down in Devonshire. Autobiographical Fragment. Kingsley Amis. OBCoV

When I lived in Milan the Duomo was thirty years younger. The Duomo. Maria Luisa Spaziani, *Italian.* NeIt, *tr. by* Beverly Allen

When I look at her. *Unknown, Japanese.* OHMPJ, *tr. by* Kenneth Rexroth

When I look at my elder sister now. The Elder Sister. Sharon Olds. NIP-4

When I look back and in myself behold. Age Looks Back at Youth. Thomas Vaux. NoSic

When I look forth at dawning, pool. Nature's Questioning. Thomas Hardy. EnVR; PBMP

When I look in the mirror. Hopelessness. Li Ch'ing-chao, *Chinese.* BLT, *tr. by* Kenneth Rexroth

When I look in the mirror. Hysteria. Chu Shu-chen, *Chinese.* OHPC, *tr. by* Kenneth Rexroth

When I looked into your eyes. Chinoiseries. Amy Lowell. PoRA

When I Lost Slum Life. Sipho Sepamla. PeSAV

When I love (as some have told). A Hymn to the Graces. Robert Herrick. NOSC

When I loved you, I can't but allow. Thomas Moore. EnLoPo; OxBSP

When i make love to you. For Willyce. Patricia Parker. CPO, NMM-2

When I married, I caught up. John Holmes. ImGa *Fr.* Letter to My Mother.

When I meet Gustavo and Hilda. Foreigners. Meredith Stricker. LoHo

When I meet the morning beam. The Immortal Part. A. E. Housman. MoBrPo; SCGP; SoSe-8; UnPo

When I must come to you, O my God, I pray. A Prayer to Go to Paradise with the Donkeys. Francis Jammes, *French.* RB, *tr. by* Richard Wilbur

When I open my legs to let you seek. The Return. Molly Peacock. RA

When I parted from my Good. Friedrich von Hausen, *German.* GePo, *tr. by* Frederick Goldin

When i pat this floor. Tapping. Jayne Cortez. MoNo

When I perceive your blond and graceful head. Sonnet 10. Louise Labé, *French.* PBWP, *tr. by* Joan Keefe *and* Richard Terdiman; BoWoP, *tr. by* Willis Barnstone

When I peruse the conquer'd fame of heroes and the victories of mighty generals, I do not envy the generals. Walt Whitman. APN-1; PoEL-5; SAmP

When I pick up my koto. *Unknown, Japanese.* OHMPJ, *tr. by* Kenneth Rexroth

When I play on my fiddle in Dooney. The Fiddler of Dooney. W. B. Yeats. EBVV; FaBoCh; NBLV; OxAEP-2

When I, poor Lais, with my crown. Lais to Aphrodite. Edwin Arlington Robinson, *after* Plato. FaBoEE

When I, poor Lais, with my crown. Lais to Aphrodite. Plato. FaBoEE *Fr.* Variations of Greek Themes.

When I pour sake. *Unknown, Japanese.* WPJ, *tr. by* Kenneth Rexroth *and* Ikuko Atsumi

When I put her out, once, by the garbage pail. The Geranium. Theodore Roethke. CoAP; UnPo; WeW-3

When I put myself out on a saucer. Cannibalism. Diana Chang. WPOW

When I put on my hat. When I get into my shoes again. Vow. Abba Kovner, *Hebrew.* IP, *tr. by* Warren Bargad *and* Stanley F. Chyet

When I ran, it rained. Late in the afternoon. Between the Wars. Robert Hass. VCAP

When I ran to snatch the wires off our roof. The Powerline Incarnation. Les A. Murray. CBAP

When I reached his place. It Was All Very Tidy. Robert Graves. OxBTC; RB

When I read Shakespeare I am struck with wonder. D. H. Lawrence. MoP; NoAM; OBCoV; Son

When I read the book, the biography famous. Walt Whitman. NAAL-1; NAAL-3

When I Recovered from an Illness After Returning Home To Live in Retirement, I Was Invited by My Friends to Join a Song-Lyric Club. Li K'ai-hsien, *Chinese.* CoBLCP, *tr. by* Jonathan Chaves

When I remember again. The Sparrow's Dirge. John Skelton. FaBoCh *Fr.* Phyllyp Sparowe [*or* Philip Sparrow]. AAS; PoEL-1

When I return from the land of exile and silence, / do not bring me flowers. Poem of Return. Jofre Rocha. PBMAP

When I returned from lovers' lane. The Kimono. James Merrill. ColAP

When I returned to my home town. Race. Karen Gershon. HP

When I returned to the hive I was one. The Lost Bee. Phillis Levin. RA

When I returned with drinks and nuts my friend. The Friend of the Fourth Decade. James Merrill. NYBP

When I review the course that I have run. Hartley Coleridge. *See* To Wordsworth.

When I rolled three 7's. Situation. Langston Hughes. APSN; OBAL

When I said "You have grown thin." Meeting after Separation. Marula, *Sanskrit.* BoWoP, *tr. by* Tambimuttu *and* G. V. Vaiyda

When I sailed out of Baltimore. A Child's Pet. W. H. Davies. CH; RB

When I saw my mother's head on the cold pillow. Keine Lazarovitch, 1870-1959. Irving Layton. NIP-4

When I saw that clumsy crow. Night Crow. Theodore Roethke. HoPM; InPK-6; OxBSP; VGW

When I saw that the man who stirred the fire. In the Middle of the Party. Carl Dennis. CBNP

When I saw the dark clouds, I wept. The Clouds. Mirabai, *tr. from Medieval Hindi; English version by* Robert Bly. EnlH

When I saw the dark Egyptian stain. The Moment. Sharon Olds. CrSp

When I saw the grapefruit drying, cherry [or cherries] in each centre lying. Reproof Deserved; or After the Lecture. John Betjeman. OBCoV

When I saw the woman's leg on the floor of the subway train. The Leg in the Subway. Oscar Williams. LiTM

When I saw the world had died away / the plants, the human race and all. Three Fragments. Bertolt Brecht, German. PFTM, tr. by John Willett and Ralph Manheim

When I saw your head bow, I knew I had beaten you. The Last Word. Peter Davison. InPK-6

When I say I believe that women have a soul and that its substance contains two. Lawn of Excluded Middle. Rosemarie Waldrop. FTOS

When I say something. At the lectern. Toki Zenmaro, Japanese. MJT, tr. by Makoto Ueda

When I see a couple of kids. High Windows. Philip Larkin. FaBoMo; NAEL-2; NoAM; PoPoPo

When I See Another's Pain. Mani Leib, Yiddish. TrJP, tr. by Joseph Leftwich

When I see birches bend to left and right. Birches. Robert Frost. AFr; AmPP; CMoP; FaBoVe; HeIP-4; ImGa; LiTM; MeMAP; MoAmPo; MoP; NAAL-2; NoAM; NoP-4; OxBA; PoLF; PoPoPo; PoRA; Poetr; RB; SAmP; SoSe-8; TAP; TFi; TRP

When I see blosmes springe. Unknown. MiEL

When I see buildings in a town together. Mr. Frost Goes South to Boston. Firman Houghton. UV

When I see how high it is. So Beautiful Is the Tree of Night. Pauline Hanson. TAP

When I see my mother giving away. The Power of My Mother. Sharon Olds. MDDM

When I See on Rood. Unknown. OxBSP

When I see some kid from Norway. High Wonders. Naomi Marks. BXAP

When I see the earth ornate and lovely. Veronica Gambara, Italian. PBWP, tr. by Brenda Webster

When I see the first. Yakamochi, Japanese. OHPJ, tr. by Kenneth Rexroth

When I see the lark a-moving [or stir her wings for joy]. The Lark. Bernard de Ventadour, Provençal. CTC; NNPT, tr. by Ezra Pound

When I see the lark stir her wings for joy. Can Vei La Lauzeta Mover. Bernard de Ventadour, Provençal. APSN, tr. by Paul Blackburn

When I see the searchlights splitting the moonlight. Searchlights. Kenneth Mackenzie. BMAP

When I see this end. Burn this Sari. A. Jayaprabha, Telugu. OMIP, tr. by V. Narayana Rao and A. K. Ramanujan

When I / see you / climb the walls. Pressure. Anne Waldman. PoM

When I set out for Lyonnesse. Thomas Hardy. EBVV; InPS-3; MoBrPo; RB

When I shall be without regret. Epitaph. James Vincent Cunningham. InPK-6

When I shall die. Blue Bird. Ha'un Han, Korean. CKP, tr. by Jaihiun Kim

When I show up. Song. Unknown, Chippewa Indian. STP, tr. by Jerome Rothenberg

When I sit in the Churchyard at Stoke. Limerick. A. M. Sayers. PeLi

When I sit up to bread and milk. At Breakfast. Ida M. Mills. BoTP

When I Sleep, Then I See Clearly. J. V. Foix, Catalan. PFTM, tr. by David H. Rosenthal

When I solidly do ponder. Francis Daniel Pastorius. SCAP

When I some antique jar behold. To a Lady. John Gay. OBEV

When I speak now. Volcano. Ivan Van Sertima. CA; PBCV

When I spread out my hand here today. Sitting by a Bush in Broad Daylight. Robert Frost. ChIV-1

When I stand in the center of that man's madness. Reflection by a Mailbox. Stanley Kunitz. TrJP

When I stand on the shore, I wonder where you are. Villanelle VI. Judith Barrington. FFC

When I stand with these three. The Hostages. Muriel Rukeyser. AF

When I stepped homeward to my hill. Home-coming. Léonie Adams. MoAmPo

When I still barely rose above the ground. Marina Kudimova, Russian. TCRP, tr. by Simon Franklin

When I strip, / stop walking / and drop into sleep. Anne-Marie Kegels, French. BoWoP, tr. by Willis Barnstone

When I survey [or survay] the bright. "Nox Nocti Indicat Scientiam." William Habington. BeJo; MeLP; NOBE; OBEV; SCGP Fr. Castara.

When I survey the wondrous cross. Crucifixion to the World by the Cross of Christ. Isaac Watts. AmFP; ECEV; FaPoR; NOCV; NOEC; OxAEP-1; PeECV

When I take my girl to the swimming party. The One Girl at the Boys Party. Sharon Olds. InPK-6; SAGP

When I taught you. To a Daughter Leaving Home. Linda Pastan. NIP-4

When I tell you I've waked as if in a basement. Learning a New Language. Margaret Gibson. AFr

When I think how far the onion has traveled. The Traveling Onion. Naomi Shihab Nye. LoL; MT

When I think of death. Bop Lyrics. Allen Ginsberg. OBAL

When I think of my fear. The Unblinding. Laurence Lieberman. NYBP

When I think over. Tanka. Fumi Saito, Japanese. MJT, tr. by Makoto Ueda

When I think you gone, abruptly. Black Mood. Rosalía de Castro. WeW-3

When I think you're somewhere yonder. Black Mood. Rosalía de Castro, Galician. STV, tr. by John Frederick Nims

When I thought of this Duchess affair. Limerick. Unknown. PeLi

When I through all my many poems look. To the Most Virtuous Mistress Pot, Who Many Times Entertained Him. Robert Herrick. CaPo

When I thy singing next shall heare. Againe. Robert Herrick. SeCP

When I too long have looked upon your face. Edna St. Vincent Millay. HeIP-4

When I / took my. The Watch. May Swenson. HAP

When I tread the earth, I fear to hurt the ground. Meng Chiao. SuSp, tr. by Stephen Owen Fr. Apricots Die Young.

When I try to get back to my mother. Motionless on the Dark Side of the Light. Minnie Bruce Pratt. NMM-2

When I try to say something about the birds. The Birds. Richard Jones. NAmP90

When I Vexed You. Robert Browning. OxBSP Fr. Ferishtah's Fancies.

When I visited this shrine of truth. The Pavillion-Where-the-Crane-Came. Chao Meng-fu, Chinese. CoBLCP, tr. by Jonathan Chaves

When I wake now it's below ocherous, saw-ridged. Fall River. David Rivard. PBCAP

When I wake up again, when I wake up. The Report. Jon Swan. NYBP

When I wake up in the morning. Make Believe. Gareth Owen. SpW

When I walk home through snow or slush. Winter Song. David Daiches. NYBP

When I walk the path this morning. The Homeplace. Lenard D. Moore. GT

When I was a baby. Good Luck Gold. Janet S. Wong. NOxBChV

When I was a bachelor bold and young. Bachelor Bold and Young. Unknown. AmFP

When I was a bachelor [or bach'lor or batchelor] I lived all alone [or early and young or by myself or young and gay]. The Foggy, Foggy Dew. Unknown. AS; OxBoLi; PeLV

When I was a bachelor, I lived by myself. Unknown. LB

When I was a bachelor/ I lived by myself. Mother Goose. ReMoGo

When I was a blonde I. First Corinthians at the Crossroads. Bruce Dawe. NoAM

When I was a boy. Dylan Thomas. SAGP Fr. A Child's Christmas in Wales.

When I was a boy, a relative. A Way to Make a Living. James Wright. NNaP

When I was a boy desiring the title of man. George. Dudley Randall. BPo; CoAmPo; NoAM

When I was a boy I saw the world I was in. Old-Time Childhood in Kentucky. Robert Penn Warren. AiP

When I was a boy, I used to go to bed. The Remorse for Time. Howard Nemerov. Son

When I was a child. Autobiographia Literaria. Frank O'Hara. NNaP; NOBA; TTTS

When I was a child. King: April 4, 1968. Gerald William Barrax. GT

When I was a child. The Message of the Rain. Norman H. Russell. ChAP

When I was a child. The Truth about My Sister and Me. Anita Endrezze-Danielson. CDW

When I was a child. Why Do You Write about Russia? Louis Simpson. InPS-3

When I was a child I knew red miners. Childhood. Margaret Abigail Walker. NoP-4; PBWP; PoBA; Son; WPOW

When I was a child I saw. To a Child. Judith Wright. BMAP

When I was a child I, thought. Best Society. Philip Larkin. FP

When I was a child, my father. Mattress Fire. Penny Harter. IFJA

When I was a child we played sometimes in the dark. Hide and Seek. Sara Teasdale. NMM-2

When I was a chile we used to play. Children's Rhymes. Langston Hughes. BPo; InPS-3

When I was a connoisseuse of slugs. The Connoisseuse of Slugs. Sharon Olds. APAD; DeD; LW

When I was a girl. Two Gifts. Unknown, Catalan. BoWoP, tr. by Willis Barnstone

When I was a girl I saw with the old men. You Call That a Ts'ing; a Letter. Jedediah Barrow. BXAP

When I was a good and quick little girl. Unknown, Pampa Indian. BoWoP, tr. by W. S. Merwin

When I was a greenhorn and young. Song. Charles Kingsley. NOBVV

When I was a kid. Me against the world. Charles Bukowski. BAP-94

When I was a kid I froze. The Public Mirror. Richard Katrovas. NAmP90

When I was a kid in summer. Some One Liked Me when I Was Twelve. Peter Orlovsky. GLP

When I was a lad and so was my dad. *Unknown.* OxNR

When I was a lad I served a term. The First Lord's Song. Sir William Schwenck Gilbert. PeLV *Fr.* H. M. S. Pinafore.

When I was a little boy / I had but little wit. *Unknown.* OxNR

When I was a little boy / I lived by myself. *Unknown.* BoTP; OxNR

When I was a little boy, / I washed [*or* wash'd] my / mammy's [*or* Mother's] dishes. *Unknown.* CBNP; OxNR

When I was a little boy / My mammy kept me in. *Unknown.* OxNR

When I was a little girl. Growing Up Italian. Maria Gillan. UnSA

When I was a little girl, / About seven years old. Mother Goose. OxNR; ReMoGo

When I was a little maid. The Little Maid. Anna Maria Wells. OBCA

When I was a single girl, I went dressed very fine. Oh, I Wish I Were Single Again. *Unknown.* AmFP

When I was a young girl, I used to seek pleasure. One Morning in May; or, The Young Girl Cut Down in Her Prime. *Unknown.* AmFP

When I Was a Young Maid. *Unknown.* AmFP

When I was alive, I wandered in the streets of the Capital;. Bearer's Song. Miu Hsi, *Chinese.* ChiP, *tr. by* Arthur Waley

When I was almost forty. Golden Bells. Po Chü-i, *Chinese.* BLT, ChiP, *tr. by* Arthur Waley

When I was arranging letters into words. Semyon Izrailevich Lipkin, *Russian.* TCRP, *tr. by* Albert C. Todd

When I was as high as that. A Memory. Leonard Alfred George Strong. NOBL

When I was at the party. Betty at the Party. *Unknown.* BoTP

When I was born. The Day's Ration. Ralph Waldo Emerson. APN-1

When I was born. (LL) Wonder. Thomas Traherne. CH; ESCV; GeHe; HAP; ImPo; NAEL-1; NoP-4; PoE; SeCP; TOF

When I was born in a world of sin. G. K. Chesterton on His Birth. A. E. Housman. NBLV

When I was born on Amman Hill. The Collier. Vernon Watkins. FaBoTw; OBWVE

When I was born, one of the crooked. Seven-Sided Poem. Carlos Drummond de Andrade, *Portuguese.* VCWP, *tr. by* Elizabeth Bishop

When I was born, you waited. From the Nursery. Jane Kenyon. BAP-93; LoL *Fr.* Having It Out With Melancholy. BAP-93

When I was bound apprentice, in famous Lincolnshire. The Lincolnshire Poacher. *Unknown.* CH; OxBoLi; PeLV

When I was bound for London a lady met me there. The Sheffield 'Prentice. *Unknown.* AmFP

When I was but thirteen or so. Romance. Walter James Turner. APAD; CH; EBEvV; MoBrPo; NOBAu; NOBE; NOxBChV; NTP; OBMV; PoRA

When I was christened. Perambulator Poem. David McCord. KaS; OBCA; OBCoV *Fr.* Perambulator Poems, I-VII.

When I was dead, my spirit turned. At Home. Christina Rossetti. VWP

When I was down beside the sea. At the Seaside [*or* Sea-Side]. Robert Louis Stevenson. CTV; NTCP; OxBChV; TLR; WHSW

When I was eight I listened to stories of love. Tapestries. Colleen J. McElroy. NAAAL

When I was eight, I put in the left-hand drawer. Josephine Miles. WeT

When I was eight you put me. Father's Day. Ruth Stone. NMM-2

When I was fair and young, then [*or* and] favour graced me;. Elizabeth I, Queen of England. CTC; LW; NIP-4; NTP; NoP-4; NoSic; PoRA; Poetr

When I was five I didn't know bats. Catching. Ann Carrel. CMAP

When I was five my father kidnapped me. The Gift. Mark Jarman. WeT

When I was two, we lived in Tesuque. Cherries. Joe Lamb. RaBo

When I was forced from Stella ever dear. Sonnet 87. Sir Philip Sidney. NAEL-1 *Fr.* Astrophil and Stella. AAS; SiPS

When I was four my father went to Scotland. The Truth. Randall Jarrell. FiLi; OxBC

When I Was Growing Up. Nellie Wong. OxWW; UnSA

When I was home last Christmas. Randall Jarrell. MT

When I was homee [*or* home] . Po' Boy Blues. Langston Hughes. ColAP; NAAAL

When I was in a soap box derby. The Soap Box Derby. Michael L. Kane. CTV

When I was in the garden. The Queen Bee. Mary K. Robinson. BoTP; CTAV

When I was just as far as I could walk. The Telephone. Robert Frost. ImGa

When I was little and brown. Welcome. David Hernandez. UnSA

When I was little, when. The Poplar's Shadow. May Swenson. NYBP

When I was marked for suffering, Love forswore. Sonnet. Miguel de Cervantes Saavedra, *Spanish.* AWP, *tr. by* Sir Edmund Gosse

When I was on Night Line. Ego. Philip Booth. TwCP

When I was once in Baltimore. Sheep. W. H. Davies. LiTM; MoBrPo; NTP; RB

When I was one-and-twenty. A. E. Housman. CBLP; CMoP; CTV; ChAP; EBEvV; HeIP-4; ImPo; InPK-6; LiTM; MoBrPo; NAEL-2; NoAM; PBMP; PoE; PoLF; TFi

When I was one and twenty. The Shropshire Lad's Cousin. Samuel Hoffenstein. BXAP

When I was only semen in a gland. James Keir Baxter. PeNZ *Fr.* Pig Island Letters.

When I was Saul, and sat among the cloaks. St. Paul. Thomas Merton. ChIV-2

When I Was Saved. Andrew Hudgins. PuP-17

When I was seventeen. Just How Crazy Brenda Is. Melinda Goodman. GLP

When I was seventeen, a man in the Dakar Station. Objets D'Art. Cynthia MacDonald. NMM-2

When I was sick and lay a-bed. The Land of Counterpane. Robert Louis Stevenson. CTV; ChAP; EBEV; FaBoBe; NBLV; NTCP; OxBChV; PWR; TLR; WHSW

When I was single [*or* a single girl]. I Wish I Was Single Again. *Unknown.* AS; AmFP

When I was six years old. The Chinese Checker Players. Richard Brautigan. PFE

When I was small. Clean. Ann Turner. SSCS

When I was still a child. Poem. Lesbia Harford. NOBAu

When I was ten. American Son. Mitsuye Yamada. UnSA

When I was ten my mother, having sold. The Year of the Foxes. David Malouf. NOBAu

When I was three I had a friend. Richard Edwards. LiLi; Spl

When I was three, I told a lie. The Stincher. Jackie Kay. NOxBChV

When I was three years old, my mother passed away. Cheng Hsieh. *Fr.* Seven Songs. CoBLCP, *tr. by* Jonathan Chaves

When I was told, as Delta children were. Ruby Tells All. Miller Williams. MT

When I was very young. Traveling to Town. Duane Big Eagle. AiP

When I was very young. Charles Upton. CLPP *Fr.* Panic Grass.

When I Was Well into Being Savored. Joanne Kyger. PoM

When I Was Young. Alun Llywelyn-Williams, *Welsh.* OBWVE, *tr. by* Gwyn Williams

When i was young. Sarah Pelham. FaBoVe

When I Was Young and Foolish. *Unknown.* AS

When I was young and full of faith. The Hesitating Veteran. Ambrose Bierce. CBCWP

When I was young and in my prime. T'ao Ch'ien, *Chinese.* SuSp, *tr. by* Eugene Eoyang

When I was young and in my prime, / I flourished like a vine. Thyme. *Unknown.* AmFP

When I was young and in my prime, / I thought I never could marry. Devilish Mary. *Unknown.* AmFP

When I was young and in my prime, my age twenty-two. The Lightning Flash. *Unknown.* AmFP

When I was young and used to wander. Hubert's Museum. Louis Simpson. OxBC

When I was young and wanted to see the sights. On His Queerness. Christopher Isherwood. OxBTC

When I was young, and wrote about him first. Draft for an Ancestor. George MacBeth. FaBoTC

When I was young, I did not fit into the common mold. T'ao Ch'ien. SuSp, *tr. by* Wu-chi Liu *Fr.* On Returning to My Garden and Field.

When I was young I fell in love and got but little good on't. John Clare. EnVR

When I was young I had a care. Soliloquy. Francis Ledwidge. HoPM

When I was young, I had no sense. The Fiddle. Neil Munro. BoTP

When I was young I learnt fencing. Regret. Yuan Chi, *Chinese.* ChiP, *tr. by* Arthur Waley

When I was young, I said to Sorrow. Sorrow. Aubrey Thomas De Vere. BLPA

When I was young I scribbled, boasting, on my wall. The Summing-up. Stanley Kunitz. OBAL

When I Was Young, I Stopped by a Wine Shop in Chi-men and Wrote This Poem, Inscribed It and Signed It, "Written by Lien the Eighteenth." The People of That District Have Since Taken It To Be a Poem of [the God] Lü Tung-pin! I Have Recorded It Here as an Amusement. Yü Chi, *Chinese.* CoBLCP, *tr. by* Jonathan Chaves

When I was young I us'd to wait on Massa and hand him de plate. Jim Crack Corn; or The Blue Tail Fly. *Unknown, sometimes att. to* Daniel Decatur Emmett. APN-2

When I was young, I was out of tune with the herd; Returning to the Fields. Ch'ien T'ao, *Chinese*. ChiP, *tr. by* Arthur Waley

When I was young, I went to school. The One Furrow. Ronald Stuart Thomas. HoPM; OxBC

When I was young, just starting at our game. To My Least Favorite Reviewer. Howard Nemerov. OBCoV

When I was young, not knowing the taste of grief, Tune: "Ugly Rogue." Hsin Ch'i-chi, *Chinese*. CoBCP, *tr. by* Burton Watson

When I was young on an island. Diane Hina Kahanu. IFJA

"When I was young," said Aunt to me. Other Fabrics, Other Mores! Anna Maria Lenngren, *Swedish*. PBWP, *tr. by* Nadia Christensen *and* Marianne Tiblin

When I was young, there was a song that went. For a Brother. Richard Frost. BAP-95

When I was young, throughout the hot season. Satire on Paying Calls in August. Ch'êng Hsiao, *Chinese*. ChiP, *tr. by* Arthur Waley

When I was young, unapt for use of man. Prayer yo Hymen. *Unknown*. NOSC

When I was young, with sharper sense. A Summer Commentary. Yvor Winters. LiTM

When I was young, writing was my one sport. Day Dreams. Tso Ssu, *Chinese*. ChiP, *tr. by* Arthur Waley

When I was younger. Pastoral. William Carlos Williams. AmPP; OxBA; SAmP

When I watch my two boys, Walter and Robert, at play. I Am as Happy as a Queen on Her Throne. Mrs. Henry Linden. CBWP-4

When I watch the living meet. A. E. Housman. CMoP; MoBrPo; NOBVV; NoP-4; PFE; SCGP

When I watch you. Miss Rosie. Lucille Clifton. AmPA; BlSi; NMM-2; PoBA; Poetr; TwCP

When I went into my garden, I found. Sister Bertken, *Dutch*. BoWoP, *tr. by* Willis Barnstone

When I went into my room, at mid-morning. Man and Bat. D. H. Lawrence. RB

When I Went Off to Prospect. *Unknown*. AmFP

When I went out. Akahito, *Japanese*. OHPJ, *tr. by* Kenneth Rexroth

When I Went Out. Karla Kuskin. NTCP

When I went out in. Kōkō Emperor, *Japanese*. OHPJ, *tr. by* Kenneth Rexroth

When I went out to kill myself, I caught. Saint Judas. James Wright. CoAmPo; GI; LCAP-2; NOBA; WeT

When I went to bed at night. Through the Porthole. Marjorie Wilson. BoTP

When i went to cuba in 1973 going there was still a mortal sin against. On the Question of Fans/ The Slave Quarters Are Never Air Conditioned. Hattie Gossett. EC2

When I went to that house of pleasure. And I Lounged and Lay on Their Beds. Constantine P. Cavafy, *Greek*. PFTM, *tr. by* Edmund Keeley *and* George Savidis

When I went to the circus that had pitched on the waste lot. D. H. Lawrence. CMoP; MoP

When I went with you. *Unknown, Japanese*. OHMPJ, *tr. by* Kenneth Rexroth

When I wer still a bwoy, an' mother's pride. False Friends-like. William Barnes. NOBVV

When I were just a little lad, right small. Pulling the Chain. Simon Rae. UV

When I will rise up to the heights beyond the clouds. The Path. "Valery Frantsevich Pereleshin," *Russian*. TCRP, *tr. by* Albert C. Todd

When I woke, a new snow had fallen. Robert Bly. *Fr.* Six Winter Privacy Poems. LCAP-2

When I Would Die. Josephine D. Henderson Heard. CBWP-4

When I would image her features. George Meredith. NOBVV

When I would pray and think, I think and pray. Shakespeare. FaBoSe *Fr.* Measure for Measure.

When I would sing of crooked streams and fields. The Song. Jones Very. APN-1

When I wrote of the women in their dances and wildness. The Poem as Mask. Muriel Rukeyser. CrSp; NALW

When I wrote of the women in their dances and wildness, it. Muriel Rukeyser. *See* The Poem as Mask.

When ice on the pond is three feet thick. *Unknown*. CoBCP, *tr. by* Burton Watson *Fr.* Tzu Yeh Songs.

When icicles by silver eaves. Winter Fairyland in Vermont. Francis P. Osgood. WeW-3

When icicles hang by the wall. Winter. Shakespeare. APAD; NoP-4; TRP *Fr.* Love's Labour's Lost.

When icicles hang by the wall. Winter. Shakespeare. AWP; CH; ClHu; FaBoCh; GTBS-P; HAP; ImPo; InPK-6; InPS-3; NAEL-1; NIP-4;

NOBE; NoSic; OAEL-1; OBEV; PoEL-2; PoRA; SCGP; TFi; UnPo; WeW-3 *Fr.* Love's Labour's Lost.

When I'd finished my bath. Whirlwind. Ravji Patel, *Gujarati*. OMIP, *tr. by* Hansa Jhaveri

When I'd read that long love poem. On Reading a Love Poem. Kedarnath Singh, *Hindi*. OMIP, *tr. by* Vinay Dharwadker

When idle in a poor Welsh mining valley. Rebel's Progress. Tom Earley. OBWVE

When ignorance possessed the shools. True Knowledge. William Wilkie. ECEV *Fr.* The Grasshopper and the Glowworm.

When I'm a little older. My Plan. Marchette Chute. WHSW

"When I'm alone"—the words tripped off his tongue. Siegfried Sassoon. LBC

When I'm by myself I don't know. But I. Amir Gilbo'a, *Hebrew*. IP, *tr. by* Warren Bargad *and* Stanley F. Chyet

When I'm eating this I want food. I mean what I say because. Realism. Carla Harryman. PmAP

When I'm far out in drink, your musical box. To My Daughter. James Michie. OxBSP

When I'm in bed at night. Noises in the Night. Lilian McCrea. BoTP

When I'm that far south, the old words. México. Lorna Dee Cervantes. *Fr.* Visions of Mexico While at a Writing Symposium in Port Townsend, Washington. NoAM

When in April the sweet showers fall. Chaucer. *See* The General Prologue.

When in Banaras. Lepers Cry. Peter Orlovsky. GLP

When in danger or in doubt. Sound Advice. *Unknown*. NBLV

When In Disgrace. Shakespeare. *See* Sonnet 29.

"When in disgrace° with Fortune and men's eyes." Sonnet 29. Shakespeare. AEP; APAD; AWP; CTC; EBEV; GBL; GSo; GTBS-P; HAP; HeIP-4; ImPo; InPK-6; InPS-3; LoP; NAEL-1; NOBE; NoP-4; NoSic; OAEL-1; OBEV; OPOU; OxAEP-1; PBRV; PoEL-2; PoPoPo; Poetr; SAGP; SCGP; Son; TFi; WeW-3 *Fr.* Sonnets.

When, in my effervescent youth. Who'd Be a Hero (Fictional)? Morris Gilbert Bishop. OBAL

When, in my fond embraces fast confined. To My Love. "The Amorous Lady." ECWP

When in my pilgrimage I reach. *Unknown*. ChIV-2

When in my youth I travelled. The Migration of the Grey Squirrels. William Howitt. OxBChV

When in nineteen-thirty-seven, Etta Moten, sweetheart. The Convert. Margaret Danner. BPo

When, in our turn, we show to them a Man. (LL) Christ in the Universe. Alice Thompson Meynell. VWP

When in Rome. Mari E. Evans. SoSe-8

When, in summer. A Poet's Memory Is Counsel. Kaḷḷil Āttiraiyaṉār, *Tamil*. PLW, *tr. by* A. K. Ramanujan

When, in summer. A Poet's Memory Is Counsel. Kaḷḷil Āttiraiyaṉār, *Tamil*. PLW, *tr. by* A. K. Ramanujan

When, in that final week. The Evil Days. Boris Pasternak, *Russian*. GI, *tr. by* Nina Kossman

When in the chronicle of wasted time. Sonnet 106. Shakespeare. AWP; CTC; EBEvV; EnLoPo; FaBoCh; GLoP; GTBS-P; ImPo; NAEL-1; NOBE; NoSic; OBEV; OxAEP-1; PoRA; SCGP; Son *Fr.* Sonnets.

When, in the course of human. Preamble to the Declaration of Independence. Thomas Jefferson. CTV

When in the east the morning ray. Garden of Appleton House, The ("When in the east the morning ray"). Andrew Marvell. NOBE *Fr.* Upon Appleton House [To My Lord Fairfax]. FaBoPV; GeHe; SeCP

When in the house. Telepathy. Thulani Davis. WeT

When in the mask of night there shone that cut. Landing on the Moon. May Swenson. TAP

When in the mirror of a permanent tear. Elegy: "When in the mirror of a permanent tear." Gene Derwood. ImPo; LiTM

When in the sun the hot red acres smoulder. The Zulu Girl. Roy Campbell. NoP-4; OBMV; OxAEP-2

When in your gardens entrance you provide. Of Gardens. Rene Rapin. OBGa, *tr. by* John, the Younger Evelyn *Fr.* Of Gardens.

When Indian sweat was suddenly soaked dry by the sun. Black Ore. René Depestre, *French*. NegPo, *tr. by* Ellen Conroy Kennedy

When infant Reason first exerts her sway. On Education, December 1789. Elizabeth Bentley. WoRP

When Ireland was bloody and leaderless. Limerick. Gina Berkeley. PeLi

When Isaac watched his father strain back. Abraham's Madness. Bink Noll. ChIV-1

When Israel against Philistia. David and Goliath. Nathaniel Crouch. OxBChV

When Israel came out of Egypt, *par. by* David Rosenberg. Bible, *O.T. See* Psalm 114.

When Israel, of the Lord beloved [*or* belov'd]. Rebecca's Hymn. Sir Walter Scott. ChIV-1 *Fr.* Ivanhoe.

When Israel out of Egypt came. A. E. Housman. ChIV-1

When Israel sate by Babel's stream and wept. The Lute of Afric's Tribe. Albery Allson Whitman. APN-2

When Israel was in Egypt's land. Let My People Go. *Unknown.* APN-2

When Israel went out of Egypt. Psalm 114. Bible, *O.T.* TrJP *Fr.* Psalms.

When Israel's Daughters mourn'd their past Offences. Epigram in a Maid of Honour's Prayer-Book. Alexander Pope. FaBoEE

When Israel's ruler on the royal bed. Hymn to the Supreme Being. Christopher Smart. ChIV-1

When It Comes. John Wain. PFE

When it comes. (LL) What Her Girl Friend Said, Consoling Her when She Was Distressed by the Town's Gossip. Uloccanar, *Tamil.* PLW

When it comes to Christmas time. Stopover. Sarah Kirsch, *German.* CEEP, *tr. by* Wayne Kvam

When It Happened. Hilda Schiff. HP

When it is all over. Lost Moment. Hoyt W. Fuller. PoBA

When it is finally ours, this freedom, this liberty, this beautiful. Frederick Douglass. Robert Earl Hayden. CBCWP; HCAP; ISC; NAAAL; NIP-4; PBMP; PFE; PoBA; PoPoPo; Son; TTY; VCAP

When it is not yet day. Looking for Mushrooms at Sunrise. W. S. Merwin. NOBA

When it is past—the golden moment—gone! Lost Opportunities. Henrietta Cordelia Ray. CBWP-3

When it rain five days an' de skies turned dark as night. Backwater Blues. Bessie Smith. NAAAL

When it rains I dance alone. When I Sleep, Then I See Clearly. J. V. Foix, *Catalan.* PFTM, *tr. by* David H. Rosenthal

When it was Desdemona's time to sing. English Lessons. Boris Pasternak, *Russian.* NNPT, *tr. by* Mark Rudman *and* Bohdan Boychuk

When it was evening. Matthew 27:57–61; When it was evening, there came a rich man. Rilke. GI *Fr.* St. Matthew

When it's cold and raining. Jelaluddin Rumi, *Persian.* EnlH, *tr. by* Coleman Barks *and* A. J. Arberry

When it's hot. Summer. Frank Asch. AYFP; NTCP

When it's ninety in the shade. Drive a Tractor. *Unknown.* NBLV

When it's the man I love. *Unknown, Japanese.* WPJ, *tr. by* Kenneth Rexroth *and* Ikuko Atsumi

When it's time. Listening. Aileen Fisher. NTCP

When I've finished a poem. Miserable. Hyon-jong Chong, *Korean.* CKP, *tr. by* Jaihiun Kim

When I've got the blues. *Unknown, Japanese.* WPJ, *tr. by* Kenneth Rexroth *and* Ikuko Atsumi

When J——— bawls out to the Chair for a Toast. (LL) Jinny the Just. Matthew Prior. NOBE; NOEC; OBEV; PoEL-3

When Jacob from the land of Canaan down. The Exodus from Egypt. Ezechiel of Alexandria, *Greek.* TrJP, *tr. by* E. H. Gifford

When Jael crept in to see Sisera. Limerick. Bill Greenwell. PeLi

When Jenny Wren Was Young. *Unknown.* ReMoGo

When Jesus came to Golgotha they hanged Him on a tree. Indifference. Geoffrey Anketell Studdert-Kennedy. TrCP

When Jesus commanded us to love our neighbour. Commandments. D. H. Lawrence. GI

When Jesus had thus said, he was troubled in spirit. John 13:21–30; When Jesus had thus said, he was troubled. Nina Kossman. *Fr.* St. John.

When Jesus walked upon the earth. Marion Brown Shelton. CTV

When Jesus was leaving this sin-accursed land. Whoso Gives Freely, Shall Freely Receive! Josephine D. Henderson Heard. CBWP-4

When Jill complain[e]s to Jack for want of meat[e]. Upon Jack and Jill: Epigram. Robert Herrick. CaPo; NAEL-1

When John Connu come', he come' wit' style. John Connu Rider. Andrew Salkey. NTP

When John Donne dropped to sleep all around him slept. Elegies. Hugh Maxton. PBCIP

When John Henry was a little babe. *Unknown.* AmFP; BPo

When John Henry was a little babe [*or* fellow]. *Unknown. See* John Henry was a lil [*or* little] baby.

When Johnny comes marching home again. Patrick Sarsfield Gilmore. CBCWP

When Johnson sought (as Shakespear says) that bourn. Introduction and Anecdotes. "Peter Pindar." PoEL-3 *Fr.* Bozzy and Piozzi.

When Jones's Ale Was New. *Unknown.* AmFP

When Joseph was an old man. The Cherry-Tree Carol. *Unknown.* AmFP

When *Jove* behelde how all the worlde stoode lyke a plash of raine. The Flood recedes. Ovid, *Latin.* OBCVT, *tr. by* Arthur Golding

When Judas, his betrayer. Matthew 27:3–10; When Judas, his betrayer, saw. Zbigniew Herbert. GI *Fr.* St. Matthew.

When Judas writes the history of solitude. The Sacrifice. Frank Bidart. GLP; VCAP

When Julius Fabricius, Sub-Prefect of the Weald. The Land. Rudyard Kipling. MoBrPo

When Keats was at work on *Endymion.* Limerick. Victor Gray. PeLi

When Klopstock England defied. William Blake. OAEL-2

When known, will save a double sorrow. (LL) In Sickness. Jonathan Swift. CABP; NOEC

When lads have done with labor. A. E. Housman and a Few Friends. Humbert Wolfe. BXAP; UV

When lads were home from labour. Fancy's Knell. A. E. Housman. FaBoCh; PoRA

When Lalement and de Brébeuf, brave souls. Brébeuf and His Brethren. Francis Reginald Scott. NOBC

When land is gone and money spent. *Unknown.* OxNR

When last I heard your nimble fingers play. To Lucia Playing on Her Lute, Another. Samuel Portage. NOSC

When last I saw thee, I did not thee see. Sonnet 24. Mary Sidney, Countess of Montgomery Wroth. PEW *Fr.* Pamphilia to Amphilanthus.

When last we parted, thou wert young and fair. Catherine Maria Fanshawe. LW

When, late from France, I introduced. Recipes. Julia Randall. NMM-2

When late (grave Palmer) these thy graffs [*or* grafts] and flowers. To Thomas Palmer [on His Book "The Sprite of Trees and Herbs"]. Ben Jonson. NoSic

When late I attempted your pity to move. An Expostulation. Isaac Bickerstaffe. OBCoV

When latest Autumn spreads her evening veil. Sonnet XXXII. (To Melancholy. Written on the Banks of the Arun, October 1785). Charlotte Smith. Ro

When lavish Phoebus pours out melted gold. The Pleasures of Retirement. Edward Benlowes. NOSC *Fr.* Theophia.

When Lazarus came back from the dead. Limerick. *Unknown.* PeLi

When Lazarus left his charnel-cave. Tennyson. EBVV; FHYEP; OAEL-2; PeECV; TOF *Fr.* In Memoriam A. H. H.

When Learning's Triumph o'er her barb'rous [*or* barbarous] Foes. Prologue Spoken by Mr[.] Garrick at the Opening of the Theatre in Drury Lane, 1747. Samuel Johnson. EBEV; EPCY; NAEL-1; NOEC; OxAEP-1

When leaves, in evenen winds, do vlee. Jay a-Pass'd. William Barnes. NOBVV

When leaving the primrose, bayberry dunes, seaward. The Constant. A. R. Ammons. HAP; WeW-3

When leaving with your loving in my veins. Late Light. Barbara Bellow Watson. NYBP

When legislators keep the law. Latter-Day Warnings. Oliver Wendell Holmes. NCAP

When Lesbia first I saw so heavenly fair. Lesbia. William Congreve. OxBSP

When Letty had scarce pass'd her third glad year. Letty's Globe. Charles Tennyson Turner. NOBVV; OBEV; PeVV

When life falls from us like a withered husk. (LL) Creed. Mary Ashley Townsend. BLPA; FaBoBe

When like a bud my Julia blows. To Julia under Lock and Key. Sir Owen Seaman. BXAP

When, like a running grave, time tracks you down. Dylan Thomas. OAEL-2

When like the rising day. Gerald Griffin. OBEV *Fr.* Eileen Aroon.

When lilacs last in the dooryard bloom'd. Spring. Walt Whitman. APN-1; AWP; AmPP; CBCWP; ColAP; HAP; LBC; MeMAP; MoAmPo; NAAL-1; NAAL-3; NCAP; NOBA; NoP-4; OxBA; PAR; PoEL-5; PoPoPo; PoRA; SAmP; TAP; TFi *Fr.* Memories of President Lincoln.

When Lil's husband got demobbed, I said. T. S. Eliot. *Fr.* The Waste Land. AmPP; CMoP; FaBoMo; HAP; LiTM; MoAmPo; MoP; NAAL-2; NAEL-2; NAWM-2; NOBA; NOBE; NoAM; NoP-4; OAEL-2; OxAEP-2; OxBA; OxBTC; PoE; TAP; TFi; UnPo

When little boys grown patient at last, weary. Death of Little Boys. Allen Tate. FuPo

When little Fred went to bed. Little Fred. *Unknown.* ReMoGo

When little girls begin to walk. To My Niece, A.M., with a New Pair of Shoes. *Unknown.* ECWP

When little heads weary have gone to their bed. The Plumpuppets. Christopher Darlington Morley. ChAP

When little John Hardy was four years old. John Hardy. *Unknown.* AmFP

When little matchsticks of rain bounce off drenched fields, an. The Frog. Francis Ponge, *French.* BLT, *tr. by* Beth Archer

When little people go abroad, wherever they may roam. To Henrietta, on Her Departure for Calais. Thomas Hood. OxBChV

When little things would irk me, and I grow. Morning Prayer. *Unknown.* PoToHe

When living is a pain. (LL) Love's Despair. Dryden. BoLoP; EnLoPo; GLoP; HAP; NOBE

WHEN, lo, by break of morning. *Unknown.* NoSic

When London Calls. Victor James Daley. CBAP

When Londons fatal bills were blown abroad. Marlburyes Fate. Benjamin Tompson. SCAP

When loose-strife, in flower, line. When to Slap a Woman. Paul Violi. PmAP

When, loosened from the winter's bonds. Princess Nukada. PBWP *Fr.* Manyo Shu, Part 4 of 4.

When Louis came home to the flat. Meet Me in St. Louis, Louis. Andrew B. Sterling. OBAL

When love beckons to you, follow him. The Prophet Speaks of Love. Kahlil Gibran. PFE *Fr.* The Prophet.

When love is a shimmering curtain. On Diverse Deviations. Maya Angelou. BlSi

When Love Is Done. Francis William Bourdillon.
 ("When love is done.") (LL) APAD; CTV; LBC; PFE

When love is done. (LL) When Love Is Done. Francis William Bourdillon. APAD; CTV; LBC; PFE

When *Love* is fled, and I grow old. (LL) Why I Write Not of Love. Ben Jonson. BeJo; OxBSP; PBRV

When love is ripe beyond bearing. What He Said. Perevin Muruvalar, *Tamil.* PLW, *tr. by* A. K. Ramanujan

When love is ripe beyond bearing. What He Said. Pereyin Muruvalar, *Tamil.* PLW, *tr. by* A. K. Ramanujan

When Love Meets Love. Thomas Edward Brown. UnPo

When love on time and measure makes his ground. False Love. John Lilliat. EBEV

When love was structured, so was verse—both fit. The Good Old Days. Barbara Fried. NBLV

When Love with unconfinèd wings. To Althea, from Prison. Richard Lovelace. AWP; BLPA; BeJo; CaPo; CavPo; EBEvV; FaBoBe; GBL; GLoP; GTBS-P; HAP; ImPo; InPS-3; MeLP; NAEL-1; NOBE; NOSC; NoP-4; OBEV; PBRV; PFE; PoE; PoRA; SCGP; SeCP; TFi

When lovely woman stoops to folly. Mary Demetriadis. UV

When lovely woman stoops to folly. Song. Oliver Goldsmith. AWP; BoLoP; CABP; EBEvV; FHYEP; FaBoSe; GTBS-P; HAP; ImPo; NOBE; NOEC; NoP-4; OBEV; OxAEP-1; SCGP; TFi; UnPo *Fr.* The Vicar of Wakefield.

When lovely woman stoops to folly and. T. S. Eliot. UV *Fr.* The Waste Land. AmPP; CMoP; FaBoMo; HAP; LiTM; MoAmPo; MoP; NAAL-2; NAEL-2; NAWM-2; NOBA; NOBE; NoAM; NoP-4; OAEL-2; OxAEP-2; OxBA; OxBTC; PoE; TAP; TFi; UnPo

When lovely woman wants a favour. Phoebe Cary. APN-2; FaBoBe; UV

When lovers crown their vows. (LL) The True Lover. A. E. Housman. EBNV; OxBSn

When loving is a pain. Dryden. *See* Love's Despair.

When lyart leaves bestrow the yird. Robert Burns. *Fr.* Love and Libery—A Cantata. NOBRP; NOEC

When lyart leaves bestrow the yird. Love and Libery—A Cantata. Robert Burns. NOBRP; NOEC; PoEL-4

When ma baby shouts in church. Lena Lovelace. Melvin B. Tolson. GT

When Ma Rainey. Ma Rainey. Sterling Brown. ISC; NAAAL

When Madame Bovary sat up shrieking. Fumetti. Robert Long. NAmP90

When Maggy Gangs Away. James Hogg. CABP

When Magritte died. Homage to René Magritte. George Melly. SPE

When Mahalia Sings. Quandra Prettyman. PoBA

When maidens such as Hester die. Hester. Charles Lamb. GTBS-P; OBEV

When maize stands more than ten feet high. Hey, Boys! Up Go We! *Unknown.* NOBAu

When Malindy Sings. Paul Laurence Dunbar. AAP; APN-2; ISC; NAAAL; PoBA

When mama came here as a gold panner. Jana Harris. MDDM *Fr.* When Mama Came Here as a Gold Panner.

When Mama Came Here as a Gold Panner. Jana Harris.

When man becomes more faithful to man. Communion II. U Tam'si Tchicaya, *French.* NegPo, *tr. by* Ellen Conroy Kennedy

When man first flew beyond the sky. Song In Space. Adrian Mitchell. SpW

When man walketh moon. T. Griffiths. BXAP

When many a day had come and fled. James Hogg. *See* Kilmeny.

When many years we'd been apart. Reminiscence. Wallace Irwin. NOBL

When Mary Goes Walking. Patrick Reginald Chalmers. BoTP

When Mary Rand. Uncle Alfred's Long Jump. Gareth Owen. OBSP

When Mary thro' the Garden Went. Mary Elizabeth Coleridge. BoTP

When memory's fabled daughter. Notes for a History of Poetry. David Daiches. PoA

When men a dangerous disease did 'scape. To Doctor Empiric[k]. Ben Jonson. FaBoEE; NoP-4; SeCP

When men are laid away. Inscription for a Graveyard. Yvor Winters. CRP

When men discovered freedom first. The Ash and the Oak. Louis Simpson. CoAmPo

When men shall find thy flower [*or* flow'r], thy glory, pass. Sonnet 33: 'When men shall find thy flower'. Samuel Daniel. NAEL-1; NOBE; NoSic; OBEV; SCGP; Son *Fr.* To Delia.

When men were all asleep the snow came flying. London Snow. Robert Bridges. CH; CMoP; EBEV; EBEvV; EBVV; GTBS-P; LiTM; MoBrP; MoP; NOBE; NOBVV; NoAM; OAEL-2; OBNC; OxAEP-2; OxBTC; PoEL-5; TFi

When mice with wings can wear a human face. (LL) The Bat. Theodore Roethke. ChAP; OBCA

When midnight comes a host of dogs and men. Badger. John Clare. FHYEP; HAP; NoP-4; OAEL-2; PoEL-4; PoPoPo; Poetr; SCGP

When Mike stuck a knife in Nancy. The Precinct Station. Louis Simpson. EOEF

When Milton sees his "late espoused saint." Confessional Poetry. Tony Harrison. DiPo

When mine eynen misteth. All too late. *Unknown.* EBEV; OAEL-1

When Mr. Apollinax visited the United States. Mr. Apollinax. T. S. Eliot. PoA

When Mrs Gorm (Aunt Eloise). Opportunity. Harry Graham. OBCoV; PeLV

When moiling seems at cease. According to the Mighty Working. Thomas Hardy. CMoP

When moles still had their annual general meetings. Brief Reflection on Cats Growing in Trees. Miroslav Holub. CBNP, *tr. by* Ewald Osers

When morning came. The Brother. Peter Everwine. FYAP; NNaP

When morning dawned, the Eternals rose to labour at the vintage. Revival of the Eternal Man. William Blake. Ro

When morning has come, all the chief priests and elders of the people. Bible, *N.T.* NAWM-1 *Fr.* St. Matthew.

When morning is breaking and darkness has fled. We Are Passing Away. Matilda Caroline Edwards. PWR

When Morrice views his prostrate peas. On a Fine Crop of Peas Being Spoiled by a Storm. Henry Jones. OBGa

When Moses in Horeb struck the rock. On Certain Wits. Howard Nemerov. HCAP; OxBC

When most impeach'd stands least in thy control. (LL) Sonnet 125. Shakespeare. AEP; NoSic

When Mother died. The Routine Things Around the House. Stephen Dunn. CMAP; FiLi; NAmP90

When mother divorced you, we were glad. She took it and. The Victims. Sharon Olds. InPS-3; SoSe-3

When Mother reads aloud, the past. *Unknown.* CTV; ImGa

When Mother's drinking, the door to my room. Bottled. Jill Breckenridge. LoHo

When mountain rocks and leafy trees. Nature's Lineaments. Robert Graves. FaBoTw; RB

When mountains crumble and rivers all run dry. The Line of Beauty. Arthur William Edgar O'Shaughnessy. TIRV

When Mrs. Taflan Gruffyd Lewis left Dai's flat. What about You? "Edward Pygge." BXAP

When "Music, Heavenly Maid," was *very* young. Music. Christopher Pearse Cranch. APN-1

When music, heav'nly maid, was young. The Passions; an Ode for [*or* to] Music. William Collins. GTBS-P

When my arms wrap you round I press. He Remembers Forgotten Beauty. W. B. Yeats. ADE; CTV

When my breast labors with oppressive care. A Paraphrase of the Latter part of the Sixth Chapter of St. Matthew. James Thomson. ChIV-2

When my brother hogs. Blanket Hog. Paul B. Janeczko. TLR

When my brother Tommy. Two in Bed. Abram Bunn Ross. CTV; NTCP

When my dears die, the festival-colored brightness. Gwendolyn Brooks. *Fr.* The Children of the Poor. WPE, *sect.* I, *pt.* 1-2; PoA, *sect.* I, *pt.* 1-3; NAAAL *Fr.* The Womanhood.

When my devotions could not pierce. Denial[l]. George Herbert. ESCV; FMP; FSCP; GeHe; NAEL-1; NOBE; NoP-4; OAEL-1; PBRV; PoEL-2; TOF

When My Dog Died. Freya Littledale. NTCP

When my eyes rove in search of recognition. Sentimental Education. Rachel Hadas. RA

When my father died. Between Here and Illinois. Ralph Pomeroy. Poetsp

When my father died I saw a narrow valley. Strawberries. W. S. Merwin. NoP-4

When my father dozes off beside me i become my father. Poem No. II. Sang Yi. PFTM *Fr.* Crow's-Eye View.

When my father had been dead a week. White Apples. Donald Hall. LoL; TAP

When my father wrote from the Tonkin Gulf about coyotes—. San Joaquin Valley Poems: 1969. Ed Webster. BAP-95

When my flaps peel back, I am seen. Dermis. Anthony McNeill. PBCV

When my good angel guides me to the place. Sonnet 60. Sir Philip Sidney. *Fr.* Astrophil and Stella. AAS; SiPS

When / my / grandmother / died. Sam Cornish. Poetsp

When my grandmother left the races with Mr. Hughes. Mr. Hughes. David Campbell. CBAP

When My Grandmother Said "Pussy." Carole Bernstein. UnSA

When my grandmother was dying. Sorrow. T. R. Hummer. MT

When my grave is broke up again[e]. The Relic. Donne. ESCV; FHYEP; FMP; FSCP; GBL; GEA; HAP; HeIP-4; ImPo; MeLP; NOBE; NOSC; NoP-4; OAEL-1; PoEL-2; SCGP; SeCP; TFi

When my husband. Ten Years and More. Miriam Waddington. NOBC

When my life was thrifty, thrifty. The Shearing. *Unknown, Welsh.* OBWVE, tr. by Glyn Jones

When my love becomes / All-powerful. Ono no Komachi, *Japanese.* PBWP, *tr. by* Geoffrey Bownas *and* Anthony Thwaite

When my love swears [*or* sweares] that she is made of truth, *sl. diff. vers. also in* The Passionate Pilgrim. Sonnet 138. Shakespeare. AWP; EBEV; HeIP-4; NAEL-1; NoSic; OAEL-1; OxAEP-1; PoEL-2; Poetr; SoSe-8 *Fr.* Sonnets.

When my lover touches me, what I feel in my body. Song of Obstacles. Louise Glück. LW *Fr.* Marathon.

When my mother died I was very young. The Chimney Sweeper. William Blake. CH; FHYEP; FaBoPV; HeIP-4; InPK-6; NAEL-2; NAWM-2; NOEC; OAEL-2; OxAEP-2; OxBChV; PoE; Poetr; Ro; SCGP; SoSe-8; TFi *Fr.* Songs of Innocence.

When My Poems were Lost. Raymond Mazisi Kunene, *Zulu.* PeSAV, *tr. by the author*

When my sensational moments are no more. E. E. Cummings. Son

When my sister came back from Africa. Bill's Story. Mark Doty. PuP-14

When my son comes home from the weekend trip where he. The Latest Injury. Sharon Olds. FILI

When my son was born, the moon was not bright. Meng Chiao. SuSp, *tr. by* Stephen Owen *Fr.* Apricots Die Young.

When my stepfather died in the summer. My Brother Running: V. Wesley McNair. AFr

When my words were wheat. Words. Mahmoud Darwish, *Arabic.* VCWP, *tr. by* Rana Kabbani

When my young brother was killed. War. Joseph Langland. AiP

When Narcissus died the pool of his pleasure changed. The Disciple. Oscar Wilde. OAEL-2

When Nature, at our awaking, sometimes proposes to us. The Prairie. Francis Ponge, *French.* AF, *tr. by* Beth Archer

When Nature bids us leave to live, 'tis late. To William Roe. Ben Jonson. NOSC

When Nature dreamt of making bores. Epigram: On Sir Roger Phillimore. *Unknown.* NBLV

When Nature made her chief work, Stella's eyes. Sonnet 7. Sir Philip Sidney. NAEL-1; NIP-4; Son *Fr.* Astrophil and Stella. AAS; SiPS

When nature rises on its hind legs. Mushrooms. Yury Kuznetsov, *Russian.* TCRP, *tr. by* Lubov Yakovleva

When Negro Teeth Speak. Ouologuem Yambo. PBMAP

When neither a man. Tanka. Fumi Saito, *Japanese.* MJT, *tr. by* Makato Ueda

When neither can hinder the other. (LL) Why Should a Foolish Marriage Vow. Dryden. AWP; CBLP; NAEL-1; NIP-4; OxBM

When news came that your mother'd. Kin. Michael S. Harper. LCAP-2

When next we met, she bade me turn. Apostasy. Aus of Kuraiza, *Arabic.* TrJP, *tr. by* Hartwig Hirschfeld

When night comes down on the children's eyes. At Night in the Wood. Nancy M. Hayes. BoTP

When night drifts along the streets of the city. Solitaire. Amy Lowell. MoAmPo

When night falls here, I think of that other night. Ovid. OBCVT, *tr. by* David R. Slavitt *Fr.* Tristia.

When night shadows slipped across the plain, I saw a man. A Nation Wrapped in Stone. Roberta Hill Whiteman. BoWoP; CDW

When night stirred at sea. The Planter's Daughter. Austin Clarke. CIP-2; OxBTC

When night-time bars me in. Snowdrops. Margiad Evans. OBWVE

When night's [*or* nights] black mantle could most darknes prove. Sonnet 1. Mary Sidney, Countess of Montgomery Wroth. Son *Fr.* Pamphilia to Amphilanthus.

When night's black mantle could most darkness prove. Mary Sidney, Countess of Montgomery Wroth. *See* Sonnet 1: "When night's [*or* nights] black mantle could most darknes prove."

When Noah left the Ark, the animals. The Kingfisher. John Heath-Stubbs. NOxBChV

When Noah sailed the wet and blue. Noah. Gerda Mayer. OTCP

When none cares whether it prevail or not. (LL) Magna Est Veritas. Coventry Patmore. GTBS-P; HAP; NOBE; NOBVV; OBEV; OBNC; OxBSP

When nothing is happening. How Everything Happens. May Swenson. HAP

When now the third revolving Moon appears. Marcus Aurelius Olympis Nemesianus. OBCVT, *tr. by* William Somervile *Fr.* Chace: 'Of the Litter of Whelps," The.

When Oats Were Reaped. Thomas Hardy. OxBTC

When ocean breezes blow the moon. Inscribed on the Painting, Solitary Crane, in the Collection of Jao Shih-ying. Yü Chi, *Chinese.* CoBLCP, *tr. by* Jonathan Chaves

When ocean-clouds over inland hills. Misgivings. Herman Melville. APN-2; NAAL-1; NAAL-3; NCAP; NOBA; OxBA

When o'er the wold the heedless lamb. Song. Thomas Holcroft. NOEC

When of thy loves, and happy heavenly dreams. Lines. Frances Anne Kemble. VWP

When Ol' Sis' Judy Pray. James Edwin Campbell. AAP

When on a summer dawn the birds start calling. Silence. Stefan Brecht. CLPP

When on Euphrates' banks we sate. Bible, *O.T. See* Psalm 137.

When on life's ocean first I spread my sail. On Hearing of the Intention of a Gentleman to Purchase the Poet's Freedom. George Moses Horton. AAP; APN-1; NAAAL; PAR

When on my bed the moonlight falls. Tennyson. OAEL-2; PeECV; SCGP *Fr.* In Memoriam A. H. H.

When on my sick bed I languish. A Thought of Death. Thomas Flatman. NOSC

When on my time of living I reflect. My Thirty Years. Juan Fransico Manzano, *Spanish.* TTY, *tr. by* Oliver Cobarn *and* Ursula Lehrburger

When on some balmy-breathing night of Spring. The Glow-Worm. Charlotte Smith. BWW

When on the earth had settled moral night. The Divine Mission. Alfred Gibbs Campbell. AAP

When on the high bluff discovering. From the North Saskatchewan. Eli W. Mandel. NOBC

When on the marge of evening the last blue light is broken. Louise Imogen Guiney. ColAP

When once I rose at morning. Lament for the Woodlands. *Unknown, Irish.* IIP, *tr. by* Frank O'Connor

When once the presence of a friend is gone. Songs Anthome. Lady Jane Cavendish. KTR *Fr.* A Pastorall.

When once the scourging prophet, with his cry. The Disused Temple. Norman Cameron. OxBS; OxBTC

When once the sun sinks in the west. Evening Primrose. John Clare. CH

When once they find her flower, her glory, pass. (LL) But love whilst that thou mayst be loved again. Samuel Daniel. NoP-4; NoSic

When one dreams of another. Three Dreams at Chiang-ling. Yüan Chen, *Chinese.* SuSp, *tr. by* William H. Nienhauser

When one has lived a long time alone. Galway Kinnell. LoL

When one human being is attached to another by a bond of affection that. Simone Weil. ITG, *tr. by* Stephen Mitchell *Fr.* Forms of the Implicit Love of God.

When One Loves Tensely. Don Marquis. NBLV

When one of the old, little stars doth fall from its place. Sidera Cadentia. Ford Madox Ford. OxBSP

When one or other rambles. Francis Daniel Pastorius. SCAP

When one was on the cursed tree to die. They Gave Him Vinegar and Gall (Matt. 27) and Wine Mingled with Myrrh (Mark 15). Francis Quarles. NOSC

When only the human remains. Falling from Stardom. Jonathan Holden. CMAP

When oor lads gaed ower the tap. The Kirk Bell. John, 1st Baron Tweedsmuir Buchan. NSI

When Orion straddled his apex of sky. The White Land. Roberta Hill Whiteman. HATNAP

When Orpheus sent down to the regions below. The Power of Music. Thomas Lisle. NOBL

When Oscar came to join his God. Oscar Wilde. Swinburne. PeVV

When other fair ones [*or* ladies] to the shades [*or* groves] go down. Epigram: "When other Ladies to the Shades go down." Alexander Pope. FaBoEE; OxBSP; PoEL-3

When other lips and other eyes. Self-Evident. James Robinson Planché. OBCoV

When others run to windows or out of doors. Part for the Whole. Robert Francis. PoA

When our beasts low in their stalls. Song of Shem. James Philip McAuley. ChIV-1 *Fr.* The Family of Love.

When our brother Fire was having his dog's day. Brother Fire. Louis MacNeice. AF; MoP; NOBE; NoAM

When our cars touched. Jump Cabling. Linda Pastan. InPK-6

When our children cried in the shadow of the gallows. Nathan Alterman. TrJP, *tr.* by Simon Halkin *Fr.* From All Peoples.

When our dead mother came back on the tenth. Mother, R.I.P. Barbara L. Greenberg. WeT

When our dean took a pious young spinster. Limerick. Victor Gray. NOBL; PeLi

When Our Earthly Sun Is Setting. Edwin H. Nevin. AH

When our enemies fall asleep. Ewa Lipska, *Polish.* CEEP, *tr.* by Magnus J. Krynski

When our gudeman's awa'. (LL) There's Nae Luck about the House. William Julius Mickle, *also at.* to Jean Adam. GTBS-P; NOEC; OxAEP-1

When our landlord's name was Manlove. Opening the Book. Kim R. Stafford. CMAP

When our long sun into the dark had set. Prelude. Dame Edith Sitwell. WPN

When our rude and unfashion'd words, that long. To a Lady Who Did Sing Excellently. Edward Herbert, 1st Baron Herbert of Cherbury. SeCP

When our sovereign. Builders. Dmitry Borisovich Kedrin, *Russian.* TCRP, *tr.* by Albert C. Todd

When our tears are dry on the shore. Rediscovery. Kofi Awoonor. TTY

When our two souls stand up erect and strong. Sonnet. Elizabeth Barrett Browning. BWW; BoWoP; EnVR; LW; NAEL-2; NALW; NOBE; OBEV; WPE *Fr.* Sonnets from the Portuguese.

When Our Voices Broke Off. James Seay. MT

When our wild day is wiped like a tear. Red Ridinghood. Nathan Alterman, *Hebrew.* MHP, *tr.* by Ruth Finer Mintz

When our women go crazy, they're scared there won't be. Julia Kasdorf. PBCAP

When out at Shellbrook, round by stile and tree. Shellbrook. William Barnes. OBNC

When out of bed my love doth spring. Upon Electra. Robert Herrick. BeJo

When out of the woods He came. (LL) A Ballad of Trees and the Master. Sidney Lanier. APAD; APN-2; ChIV-2; ColAP; NOBA; OxBA; PoEL-5; PoLF

When over the flowery, sharp pasture's. Flowers by the Sea. William Carlos Williams. CMoP; MoAmPo; NoAM; RB; TAP

When pails empty the last brightness. O You among Women. Frederick Robert Higgins. BIrV

When Pallas and golden-sandaled Hera saw Maeonis. Rufinus Domesticus. HePo, *tr.* by Barbara Hughes Fowler *Fr.* Epigrams.

When Parnell's Irish in the House. Wilfred Owen's Photographs. Ted Hughes. FaBoPV; OxBC

When Patty, lovely Patty, graced the crowd. Rustic Courtship. Robert Dodsley. ECEV *Fr.* Agriculture.

When Paul Bunyan was ill we sent. Willie Reader. KaS

When pavements were blown up, exposing wires[nerves]. Epilogue to a Human Drama. Stephen Spender. AF; CMoP

When pears hang green on the garden wall. NOTl. Max Beerbohm *and* William Rothenstein. UV

When Pegotty found Barkis was willing. Limerick. Douglas Catley. PeLi

When pensive on that portraiture I gaze. Sonnet on a Family Picture. Thomas Edwards. NOEC

When people call this beast to mind. The Elephant. Hilaire Belloc. BoTP

When people come with big muddy feet. Go Throw Them Out. Moyshe-Leyb Halpern, *Yiddish.* CEEP, *tr.* by Ruth Whitman

When people see the man of Cold Mountain. *Unknown, Chinese.* CoBCP, *tr.* by Burton Watson

When periwigs came first in wear. The Bald Cavalier. *Unknown.* OxBChV

When Phoebe formed a wanton smile. Sonnet. William Collins. EnLoPo; OxBSP

When Phoebus had melted the sickles of ice. Robin Hood and the Ranger. *Unknown.* ESPB

When pleasing heat, and fragrant blooms inspire. William Diaper. BXAP *Fr.* Halieutica.

When poetry walked the live, spring wood. Kingcups. Sacheverell Sitwell. MoBrPo

When poets print their works, the scribbling crew. To My Ingenious and Worthy Friend William Lowndes, Esq. John Gay. OBSV

When Polly Buys a Hat. E. Hill. BoTP

When Polly lived back in the old deep woods. Stranger. Elizabeth Madox Roberts. MoAmPo

When Poor Mary Came Wandering Home. *Unknown.* AS

When poor men to expences run. The Proud Frog. Phaedrus, *Latin.* OBCVT, *tr.* by Christopher Smart

When Pope's harmonious Muse with pleasure roves. John Gay. EPCY *Fr.* On a Miscellany of Poems.

When President John Quincy. John Quincy Adams. Rosemary Benét *and* Stephen Vincent Benét. OBCA

When—presto—turf and trees are green. Bernard de Ventadour, *French.* STV, *tr.* by John Frederick Nims

When primroses are out in Spring. Days Too Short. W. H. Davies. MoBrPo

When Prodike seemed / alone I begged for it. Prodike. Rufinus, *Greek.* GrAn, *tr.* by Alan Marshfield

When Pym last night descended into hell. On Pym. William Drummond, of Hawthornden. NOSC

When quacks with pills political would dope us. Canopus. Bert Leston Taylor. NOBL

When Radnóti wrote his last poem for his wife. For Miklos Radnóti: 1909-1944. Kate Daniels. NAmP90

When rage invades your burning breast. Sappho, *Greek.* InMo, *tr.* by Sam Hamill

When raging [*or* ragyng] love with extreme pain [*or* payne]. Consolation. Henry Howard, Earl of Surrey. AAS; EBEV; EnLoPo; NOBE; NoSic; SiPS

When ready will explode. (LL) Pan Recipe. John Agard. HCP; PBCV

When Reedisdale and Wise William. Redesdale and Wise William. *Unknown.* ESPB

When relatives came from out of town. Blackbottom. Toi Derricotte. GT; LTA; NAmP90; PBCAP; UnSA

When Reuben Pantier ran away and threw me. Dora Williams. Edgar Lee Masters. HAP *Fr.* Spoon River Anthology.

When rising from the bed of death. Joseph Addison. TOF

When rites and melodies begin. The Proof. W. H. Auden. OAEL-2 *Fr.* Five Songs.

When roaring gloom surged inward and you cried. To His Dead Body. Siegfried Sassoon. NoAM

When Robert Graves got involved. Robert Graves. Gavin Ewart. NoAM

When Robin Hood, and his merry men all. Robin Hood and the Valiant Knight. *Unknown.* ESPB

When Robin Hood and Little John. Robin Hood's Death. *Unknown.* ESPB

When Robin Hood in the green-wood livd. Robin Hood Rescuing Will Stutly. *Unknown.* ESPB

When Robin Hood was about eighteen [*or* twenty] years old. Robin Hood and Little John. *Unknown.* AmFP; ESPB

When Rooks Fly Homeward. Joseph Campbell. TIRV

When rosy plumelets tuft the larch. Tennyson. FHYEP; OBNC *Fr.* In Memoriam A. H. H.

When round your Neck his Arms he'll / throw. (LL) Elegies 1.iv: "Far from the tender Tribe of Boys remove." Tibullus, *Latin.* EP, *tr.* by Dart, John

When rule and era passed away. The Pillow. Herman Melville. APN-2 *Fr.* Clarel: A Poem and Pilgrimage in the Holy Land.

When Russian prose went into the camps. Prosaics. Boris Abramovich Slutsky, *Russian.* TCRP, *tr.* by J. R. Rowland

When Ruth was left half desolate. Ruth [or, The Influences of Nature]. Wordsworth. GTBS-P; PoEL-4

When Saint Mochua knelt to pray. The Little Pets of Saint Mochua. John Irvine. TIRV

When Sam goes back in memory. Sam. Walter De la Mare. MoBrPo

When Sanders brings feed to his chickens, some sparrows. Josephine Miles. WeT

When Sarah Pierrepont let her spirit rage. Address to the Scholars of New England. John Crowe Ransom. LiTM; MeMAP

When science starts to be interpretive. Self-Protection. D. H. Lawrence. NoP-4

When senses, which thy so[u]ldiers are. Donne. *Fr.* The Litanie. PoEL-2

When sent to certain death—we sing. Before the Attack. Semyon Petrovich Gudzenko, *Russian.* TCRP, *tr.* by Gordon McVay1

When serpents bargain for the right to squirm. E. E. Cummings. MeMAP; TwCP

When seven years were come and gane. Sweet William's Ghost. *Unknown.* ESPB

When shall I see the half-moon sink again. End of Another Home Holiday. D. H. Lawrence. EBEV; FaBoMo; OxAEP-2

When shall I see the white thorn leaves agen. The Yellowhammer. John Clare. NOBVV

When shall I tread your garden path. Dorothy Wordsworth. Ro

When Shall My Pilgrimage, Jesus My Saviour, Be Ended? Andrew Rudman, *Swedish.* AH, *tr.* by Ernest Edwin Ryden

When Shall We All Meet Again? *Unknown.* AH

When shall we be married. *Unknown.* OxNR

When shawes beene sheene, and shrads [*or* shradds] fyll [*or* full] fayre. Robin Hood and Guy of Gisborne. *Unknown.* ESPB

When she asked me to keep an eye on her things. Bewley's Oriental Café, Westmoreland Street. Paul Durcan. CIP-2

When she begins to comprehend it. (LL) To a Child of Quality [Five Years Old, the Author Supposed Forty]. Matthew Prior. NOBE; NOEC; OBEV; PoEL-3

When she came to visit me, I turned my face to the wall. Pediatrics. Carol Muske. PBCAP

When she cannot be sure. A Woman Alone. Denise Levertov. NMM-2; WPOW

When she carries food to the table and stoops down. Part of Plenty. Bernard Spencer. GBL; LiTM

When she comes home again! A thousand ways. James Whitcomb Riley. FaBoBe

When she fed the / child. The Feeding. Joel Oppenheimer. NeAP

When she gives a "psychic reading." Crepe de Chine. Tennessee Williams. NYBP

When she introduces me to her parents. Marriage. Gregory Corso. PiM *Fr.* Marriage.

When she is embraced and open to most men. (LL) Show me dear Christ. Donne. FSCP; MeLP; NAEL-1; NOSC; PeECV; PoE; Son

When she married years ago. The Italian Garden. William Carlos Williams. OBGa

When She Plays upon the Harp or Lute. Moses ibn Ezra, *Hebrew.* TrJP, *tr.* by Solomon Solis-Cohen

When she rises in the morning. Gloire de Dijon. D. H. Lawrence. CMoP; EnLoPo; GBL; GLoP; NoAM

When she sleeps, her soul, I know. Doubts. Rupert Brooke. CH

When she snoozes. Lullaby for Suzanne. Michael Stillman. TLR

When she tells him about the lump in her breast. In a Duplex Near the San Andreas Fault. Dionisio D. Martinez. NoP-4

When she was alive, now a memory. Hitomaro. *See* When she was still alive.

When She Was Born. Robert Tofte. Son *Fr.* Laura.

When She Was Here, Li Bo. Peter Williams. InPK-6

When she was little. Poem for Flora. Nikki Giovanni. BPo; CrSp; MBE; PoBA

When she was still alive. Hitomaro, *Japanese.* OHPJ, *tr.* by Kenneth Rexroth *Fr.* Manyo Shu, Part 4 of 4.

("When she was alive, now a memory.")

When she was tied to the stake. (LL) Lamkin. *Unknown.* ESPB; OxBB

When she was young and dancing. Jane Austen at the Window. Patricia Beer. FaBoWP

When shearing comes, lay down your drums. Whaler's Rhyme. *Unknown.* NOBAu

When she'is embrac'd and open to most men. Donne. *See* Show me dear Christ.

When Sherman's March was over. Iris. Herman Melville. NCAP

When she's embraced and open to most men. Donne. *See* Show me dear Christ.

When should lovers breathe their vows? Letitia Elizabeth Landon. Ro *Fr.* The Improvisatrice and Other Poems.

When silver snow decks Sylvio's cloaths [*or* clothes]. Song By an Old Shepherd. William Blake. NTP

When / Sir / Beelzebub. Sir Beelzebub. Dame Edith Sitwell. BoWoP; FaBoMo; FaBoWP; HoPM; MoBrPo; NALW; OBCoV; OxBTC *Fr.* Façade.

When Sir [*or* Sr] Joshua Reynolds died. Sir Joshua Reynolds. William Blake. FaBoEE; OxBoLi; PeLV

When Sisyphus was pushing the stone up the mountain. Sisyphus. Josephine Miles. NYBP

When skies are gentle, breezes bland. The Land. Vita Sackville-West. OBGa

When skies are low. When Skies are Low and Days are Dark. N. M. Bodecker. AYFP; OTCP

When Skies are Low and Days are Dark. N. M. Bodecker. AYFP; OTCP

When skilful traders first set up. After the Small Pox. Mary Jones. PEW

When Skyscrapers Were Invented in Chicago. Edward Hirsch. WWSi

When slaves their liberties require. Phillis's Resolution. William Walsh. OxBSP

When Slow October Changes Color. Umberto Piersanti, *Italian.* NeIt, *tr.* by Stephen Sartarelli

When smoke stood up from Ludlow. A. E. Housman. MoBrPo; SCGP

When snow lies covering the roads. Meeting. Boris Pasternak, *Russian.* FP, *tr.* by Henry Kamen

When snow like sheep lay in the fold. In Memory of Jane Fraser [*or* Frazer]. Geoffrey Hill. MoP; NAEL-2; NoAM; OxBTC

When soft Irene like a. Asclepiades, *Greek.* GrAn, *tr.* by Edward Lucie-Smith

When Sol had loosed his weary teams. Juggy's Christening. *Unknown.* NOEC

When some beloveds, 'neath whose eyelids lay. Bereavement. Elizabeth Barrett Browning. WPE

When some boys. Some Boys. Chuck Ortleb. GLP

When some great sorrow, like a mighty river. This, Too, Shall [*or* Will] Pass Away. Lanta Wilson Smith. BLPA

When someone checks into Mercy Ward. The Place They Have to Go. Ian McDonald. HCP

When someone hangs up, having said. The Business Life. David Ignatow. NNaP

When Something Happens. James A. Randall Jr. BPo; SSLK

When Songs Become Water. Martín Espada. AFr

When sorrow (using mine own fire's might). Sonnet 108. Sir Philip Sidney. *Fr.* Astrophil and Stella. AAS; SiPS

When sorrows had begirt me round. For Deliverance from a Fever. Anne Bradstreet. NAAL-1; NAAL-3; NALW

When Spanky goes. Basketball. Nikki Giovanni. NOxBChV

When Spoon River became a ganglion. Marx the Sign Painter. Edgar Lee Masters. NoAM; TAP *Fr.* The New Spoon River.

When spring doves come I'll make a stew! (LL) Little stream used to cross my land, A. Su Tung-p'o, *Chinese.* CoBCP, *tr.* by Burton Watson. CoBCP

When spring escapes. Princess Nukada, *Japanese.* WPJ, *tr.* by Kenneth Rexroth *and* Ikuko Atsumi

When stags do rut in the Plym. Alan Gibson. BXAP

When Statesmen gravely say, "We must be realistic." Statesmen. W. H. Auden. OBCoV *Fr.* Shorts [1939–1947].

When still unmarried, I recall. Beauties in White. Kiên Giang, *Vietnamese.* AVP, *tr.* by Huỳnh Sanh Thông

When storms blow loud, 't is sweet to watch at ease. Suave Mari Magno. Lucretius. AWP, *tr.* by W. H. Mallock *Fr.* De Rerum Natura (On the Nature of Things).

When suddenly I am old, and start to wear purple. (LL) Warning. Jenny Joseph. FaBoWP; OxBTC

When Sue Wears Red. Langston Hughes. NAAAL; TTY

When summer ended. Emplumada. Lorna Dee Cervantes. NoAM; PBCAP

When summer smiled, and birds on every spray. Written, Originally Extempore, on Seeing a Mad Heifer Run through the Village. Elizabeth Hands. ECWP

When summer took[toke] in hand the winter to assail. Love's Rebel. Henry Howard, Earl of Surrey. AAS; SiPS

When summer's heat hath done his part. Aestas. Joshua Sylvester. NOSC

When Sun Came to Riverwoman. Leslie Marmon Silko. VoR

When Sun Doth Rise. Roger Williams. AH

When sun goes home. Taking Turns. Norma Farber. TLR

When sun, light handed, sows this Indian water. Aubade: Lake Erie. Thomas Merton. NYBP

When Sunday came and old Katis'. Katisje's Patchwork Dress. Pauline Smith. PeSAV

When supper time is almost come. Milking Time. Elizabeth Madox Roberts. OBCA

When Susanna Jones wears red. When Sue Wears Red. Langston Hughes. NAAAL; TTY

When Susan's work was done, she'd [*or* she would] sit. Old Susan. Walter De la Mare. CMoP; MoBrPo

When swallows come I'm sick with wine. Tune: "Red Embroidered Slippers"—Spring Night. *Unknown, Chinese.* SuSp, *tr.* by Sherwin S. S. Fu

When swallows lay their eggs in snow. Fool's Song. Thomas Holcroft. CBNP; NOEC

When sweet Echo met Narcissus. Echo and Narcissus. Gerda Mayer. PeLV

When swelling buds their od'rous foliage shed. Apple-Culture. John Philips. OxAEP-1 *Fr.* Cyder.

When swimming and croquet are in full sway, dolor. Dolor. Josephine Miles. FaBoWP

When sycamore leaves were a-spreadèn. Woak Hill. William Barnes. EnVR

When Sydney and the Bush first met. Sydney and the Bush. Les A. Murray. DiPo

When tenderness. Silence. Eugenio de Andrade, *Portuguese.* VCWP, *tr.* by Alexis Levitin

When That Day Comes. Chongsam Kim, *Korean.* CKP, *tr.* by Jaihiun Kim

When that day comes, whose evening sayes I'm gone. His Sailing from Julia. Robert Herrick. PoEL-3

When that forth he doth go. (LL) Therefore John read how that thou wouldst. Anna Trapnell. ChIV-2; KTR

When that humble-headed elder, the sea, gave his wide. End of the Picnic. Francis Webb. BMAP; NOBAu

When that I was and a little tiny boy. Song. Shakespeare. CBNP; CH; EBEV; EBEvV; FaBoCh; ImPo; NBLV; NOBE; NoP-4; NoSic; OAEL-1; OxAEP-1; OxBoLi; PFE; PoEL-2; PoRA; SCGP; TFi *Fr.* Twelfth Night.

"When that my sweet son was thirty winter old." 'O, My Heart Is Woe'. *Unknown.* ChIV-2

When that repentant tears hath cleansed clear from ill. Henry Howard, Earl of Surrey. ChIV-1 *Fr.* A Paraphrase of Part of the Book of Ecclesiates.

When that rich soul[e] which to her heaven is gone. The First Anniversary [*or* Anniversarie]. Donne. NAEL-1 *Fr.* Anatomy [*or* Anatomie] of the World, An[: The First Anniversary].

When that shall fade, my verse distills your truth. (LL) Sonnet 54. Shakespeare. AWP; OBEV; PoE; SCGP

When that shall vade, by verse distils your truth. Shakespeare. *See* Sonnet 54.

When that the chill charocco blows. Thomas Bonham. *See* In Praise of Ale.

When that the fields put on their gay attire. To the Redbreast. John Codrington Bampfylde. Son

When the African Arts. At Home in Dakar. Margaret Danner. BlSi

When the air is wine and the wind is free. Song of the Queen Bee. Elwyn Brooks White. NYBP

When the alcoholic passed the crucial point. Point of No Return. Robert Graves. BIrV

When the ancients painted swans and tigers. On Seeing a Painting of Plants and Insects by Chü-ning. Mei Yao Ch'en, *Chinese.* SuSp, *tr. by* Jonathan Chaves

When the angry passion gathering in my mother's face I see. The Patter of the Shingle. *Unknown.* BLPA

When the ape. Āy: His Hill. Mutamociyar, *Tamil.* PLW, *tr. by* A. K. Ramanujan

When the Assault Was Intended to the City. Milton. GTBS-P; SCGP; Son (Sonnet.) OAEL-1; OxAEP-1

When the autumn winds go wailing. Ungathered Love. Philip Bourke Marston. OBNC

When the autumn's breezes. Mr. Edward Fordham. Mary Weston Fordham. CBWP-2

When the bare branch responds to leaf and light. Spain. Dorothy Livesay. NOBC

When the battle was over. Masses. César Vallejo. RB, *tr. by* Robert Bly *Fr.* España, Aparta de me Este Caliz.

When the bells justle in the tower. A. E. Housman. NOBVV

When the birds sang. *Unknown, Spanish.* BoWoP, *tr. by* Willis Barnstone

When the black bear is dead. Prayer to the Black Bear. *Kwakiutl Oral Tradition, Kwakiutl.* PaTW, *tr. by* Franz Boas

When the black herds of the rain were grazing. The Lost Heifer. Austin Clarke. BIrV

When the blasts of winter appear[?]. (LL) The School-Boy. William Blake. CH; FHYEP; FaBoCh; OxAEP-2

When the bleak winds of winter. Remember the Poor. Matilda Caroline Edwards. PWR

When the boat / comes in. Mother Goose. *See* Dance to your [*or* thee] daddy.

When the body becomes Your mirror. Mahadevi, *Kannada.* WPoS, *tr. by* Jane Hirshfield

When the bones are no longer curious. Overture for Bubble-Gum and Flute. Alistair Paterson. PeNZ

When the bones walk out of me. Never. George Reavey. BIrV

When the boughs of the garden hang heavy with rain. Thunder in the Garden. William Morris. GaP

When the boys came home, everything stopped. The Bird Frau. Rita Dove. CMAP

When the brain's black with demonic crisis. The Ferry Pirate. Douglas Oliver. NBrP

When the breaking wavelets pass all sparkling to the sky. Submarines. "Klaxon." NSI

When the breath of twilight blows to flame the misty skies. By the Margin of the Great Deep. "Æ." OBEV

When the breeze of a joyful dawn blew free. Recollections of The Arabian Nights. Tennyson. OBGa

When the Bright Consort first stepped out of Han palace. Song of the Radiant Lady. Wang An-shih, *Chinese.* SuSp, *tr. by* Jan W. Walls

When the bright eyes of the day. Day and Night. James Stephens. BoTP

When the British warrior queen. Boadicea: An Ode. William Cowper. FaPoR

When the bronze annals of the oak-tree close. (LL) Advice to a Prophet. Richard Wilbur. AFr; AmPP; FYAP; GEA; MoAmPo; NYBP; NoP-4; OBWP; OxBC; PoE; Poetr; TwCP; VCAP

When the buds began to burst. The Three Roses. Walter Savage Landor. NAEL-2

When the burnt flesh is finally at rest. Annotations of Auschwitz. Peter Porter. HP

When the call comes, be calm. How to Watch Your Brother Die. Michael Lassell. GLP

When the car spun from the road and your neck broke. Death and the Sun. Derek Mahon. BiHa

When the census is taken, of course. Taking the Census. Charles Robert Thatcher. NOBAu

When the census man called upon Gail. Limerick. George McWilliam. PeLi

When the century dragged, like a great wheel stuck at dead center. Robert Penn Warren. MoAmPo *Fr.* Infant Boy at Midcentury.

When the children are asleep and our old bed. Hell To Pay. Susanne Doyle. FFC

When the child's forehead full of red torments. Rimbaud. *See* Girls Looking for Lice.

When the child's forehead, pinched and tortured red. Girls Looking for Lice. Rimbaud. FLP, *tr. by* Alistair Elliot *Fr.* Illuminations.

When the chilled dough of his flesh went in an oven. Marked with D. Tony Harrison. NAEL-2 *Fr.* The School of Eloquence. NAEL-2; NoAM

When the clapper hits the bell? (LL) The Bellman's Song. *Unknown.* EBEV; SCGP

When the clouds are upon the hills. *Unknown.* OxNR

When the clouds' swoln bosoms echo back the shouts of the many and strong. Thomas Hardy. CMoP; ChIV-1; LiTM; NoAM; OxBTC *Fr.* In Tenebris. NOBE

When the cold comes. Where? When? Which? Langston Hughes. BPo

When the cold wind visits you from the corners of the earth. To Li Po. Tu Fu, *Chinese.* TAL, *tr. by* Robert Payne

When the corn's all cut and the bright stalks shine. Corn-Stalk Fiddle, THe. Paul Laurence Dunbar. AAP

When the Corsican Chief, with a view to degrade. To Buonaparte. *Unknown.* NOBRP

When the curtain of night, 'tween the dark and the light. Whistling Boy. Nixon Waterman. PoLF

When the dark months have run out. Rhyme-Prose on the Snow. Hsieh Hui-lien, *Chinese.* CoBCP, *tr. by* Burton Watson

When the dawn comes. *Unknown.* AWP, *tr. by* Arthur Waley *Fr.* Kokin Shu.

When the day darkens. The Unknown Wind. "Fiona Macleod." BoTP

When the Days Shall Grow Long. Hayyim Nahman Bialik, *Hebrew.* TrJP, *tr. by* A. M. Klein

When the deep-piled winter snow / melted on her roof. Antipater of Thessalonica, *Greek.* GrAn, *tr. by* Robin Skelton

When the dew is on the grass. *Unknown.* OxNR

When the doctor came from Chin-t'an. Weeping for Hsüeh Tzu-shu. Liu K'o-chuang, *Chinese.* CoBCP, *tr. by* Burton Watson

When the dogstar is aglow. Garden Calendar. N. M. Bodecker. TLR

When the Dumb Speak. Robert Bly. CAPP-1; NOBA

When the eager squadrons of day are faint and disbanded. The Cult of the Celtic. Anthony C. Deane. BXAP; NOBL; PeLV

When the earth was made. Red Rising. Edward Kamau Brathwaite. HCP

When the earth with spring returning buds again. To the Nightingale. Fulbert of Chartres, *Latin.* MLL, *tr. by* Helen Waddell

When the echo of the last footstep dies. Song. Eli W. Mandel. MoCV

When the enthusiasm / of our time. Before the Scales, Tomorrow. Otto René Castillo, *Spanish.* AF, *tr. by* Barbara Paschke *and* David Volpendesta

When the exposed spirit, busy in daytime. Time Exposures. Muriel Rukeyser. PoA *Fr.* Night-Music.

When the Eye of Day Is Shut. A. E. Housman. NOBVV; OAEL-2

When the Fairies. Edward Dorn. NeAP

When the Famous Black Poet speaks. Passing. Carl Phillips. PoPoPo

When the far south glittered. Pilgrimage. Austin Clarke. CIP-2; TIRV

When the farmer comes to town. The Farmer. *Unknown.* AS

When the feet of the rain tread a dance on the roofs. Gipsy-Night. Richard Hughes. OBWVE

When the female railway clerk. Nissim Ezekiel. OBCoV *Fr.* Poems in the Greek Anthology Mode.

When the fields catch flower. April. Vidame de Chartres, *French.* AWP, *tr. by* Swinburne

When the fierce north wind with his airy forces. The Day of Judgement [*or* Judgment]; an Ode. Isaac Watts. ChIV-2; ECEV; HAP; NOBE; NOEC; NoP-4; OBEV; SCGP

When the fifth month comes. Lady Ise, *Japanese.* BoWoP, *tr. by* Etsuko Terasaki *and* Irma Brandeis

When the film *Tell England* came. A Grand Night. D. J. Enright. NSI

When the first patches of snow. The Execution of Memory. Jerzy Ficowski, *Polish.* HP, *tr. by* Keith Bosley

When the Five Prominent Poets. Josephine Jacobsen. NMM-2; TAP

When the flaming lute-thronged angelic door is wide. The Travail of Passion. W. B. Yeats. TrCP

When the flower droops and the leaf wilts. Lotus. Hsü Wei, *Chinese.* SuSp, *tr. by* Irving Y. Lo

When the flowers turn to husks. Cells Breathe in the Emptiness. Galway Kinnell. PFE; VGW

When the flush of a new-born sun fell first on Eden's green and gold. The Conundrum of the Workshops. Rudyard Kipling. MoBrPo

When the Flyin' Scot. Uncle Henry. W. H. Auden. NOBL; PeLV

When the foreman whistled. Field Poem. Gary Soto. PBCAP

When the forests have been destroyed their darkness remains. The Asians Dying. W. S. Merwin. CAPP-1; CoAP; HCAP; NOBA; NYBP; PoPoPo; VCAP

When the four quarters shall. Ark Overwhelmed. Jay Macpherson. NOBC *Fr.* The Ark.

When the frost is on the punkin and the fodder's in the shock. James Whitcomb Riley. APN-2; EBEvV; FaBoBe; OBAL; PoLF

When the full moon comes. Song of the Cuban Blacks. Federico García Lorca, *Spanish.* RaBo, *tr. by* Robert Bly

When the game began between them for a jest. Stage Love. Swinburne. PoEL-5

When the gardener. Tanka. Maekawa Samio, *Japanese.* MJT, *tr. by* Makoto Ueda

When the gardener has gone this garden. In a Garden. Elizabeth Jennings. NOCV

When the gibbons howl one is sure it's dawn. Journeying by Stream: Following Chin-chu Torrent I Cross the Mountains. Hsieh Ling-yün, *Chinese.* SuSp, *tr. by* Francis Westbrook

When the god, needing something, decided to become a swan. Leda. Rilke, *German.* RaBo, *tr. by* Robert Bly

When the god of the river. Arethusa Saved. Ovid, *Latin.* OBCVT, *tr. by* Thom Gunn

When the gold fever raged I was doing very well. The Miner's Lament. *Unknown* AmFP

When the grass was closely mown. The Dumb Soldier. Robert Louis Stevenson. OxBChV

When the Great Gray Ships Come In. Guy Wetmore Carryl. FaBoBe

When the great universe hung nebulous. 'Egoisme à Deux'. Louisa Sarah Bevington. VWP

When the great universe hung nebulous. Egoisme à Deux. Louisa S. Guggenberger. NOBVV

When the great wind blew the streetlights out. Hrubín František, *Czech.* CEEP, *tr. by* Don Mager *Fr.* The City in the Full Moon.

When the green grass rose in the spring. On the Bright Side. Carter Revard. VoR

When the green lies over the earth, my dear. Angelina Weld Grimké. CPO; NAAAL

When the green woods laugh with the voice of joy. Laughing Song. William Blake. BoTP; CH; FHYEP; NAEL-2; NBLV; OxBChV; Ro *Fr.* Songs of Innocence.

When the Guests First Take Their Seats. *Unknown, Chinese.* CoBCP, *tr. by* Burton Watson

When the gunner spoke in his sleep the hut was still. The Gunner. Francis Webb. BMAP; CBAP

When the half-body dies its frightful death. Resurrection of the Right Side. Muriel Rukeyser. LCAP-2; NMM-2

When the heart's feeling. Song. Thomas Moore. OxBSP

When the heavens with stars are gleaming. For Who? Mary Weston Fordham. CBWP-2

When the herd[s] were watching. Bethlehem. William Canton. BoTP

When the high / Snows lie worn. Crows. Valerie Worth. ImGa

When the Himalayan peasant meets the he-bear in his pride. The Female of the Species. Rudyard Kipling. BLPA

When the Hindu Woman Sings Calypso. Rajandaye Ramkissoon-Chen. HCP

When the hounds of spring are on winter's traces. The Hounds of Spring. Swinburne. AWP; CTC; EBVV; EBVVPR; EnVR; FaBoBe; GTBS-P; HAP; NAEL-2; NOBE; NoP-4; OAEL-2; OBEV; PoE; SCGP; TFi; WeW-3 *Fr.* Atalanta in Calydon.

When the hysterical vision strikes. Baroque Exterior. "Ern Malley." BMAP

When the judge with his wife having sport. Limerick. *Unknown.* PeLi

When the king of the jungle first wakes up, he thinks. Sunday, Tarzan in His Hammock. Lewis Buzbee. BAP-95

When the knight had finished, no one, young or old. Chaucer. *See* The Miller's Prologue.

When the Kye Comes Hame. James Hogg. OxBS

When the lad for longing sighs. A. E. Housman. MoBrPo

When the lamp is shattered [*or* shatter'd]. Lines. Shelley. CBLP; CH; GEA; GTBS-P; ImPo; NAEL-2; OBEV; OBNC; PoEL-4

When the land lay waiting for her westward people! (LL) Empire Builders. Archibald MacLeish. OxBA

When the land of El Kanesie awakens. Animism. Birago Diop, *French.* NegPo, *tr. by* Ellen Conroy Kennedy

When the last bus leaves, moths stream toward lights. Depot in Rapid City. Roberta Hill Whiteman. BoWoP

When the last day comes. The Last Day. Kevin Hart. BMAP

When the last Flavius, drunk with fury, tore. Juvenal. OBVE, *tr. by* William Gifford *Fr.* Satires.

When the last newspaper is printed and the ink is faded and dried. Freedom in Peril. "Sagittarius." UV

When the last star breathes like a rose. Sailors. Louis Simpson. NYBP

When the leaves have fallen. The Robin in December. Stanley Cook. AYFP

When the light falls, it falls on her. Stanley Kunitz. MoAmPo

When the lights go out. Tanka. Nakajō Fumiko, *Japanese.* MJT, *tr. by* Makoto Ueda

When the little blue-bird. Let's Do It, Let's Fall in Love. Cole Porter. OBAL; PeLV; UV

When the loneliness of the tomb went down into the marketplace. Mona Sa'udi, *Arabic.* WPOW, *tr. by* Kamal Boullata

When the Lord, Almighty God, came again to His throne. (LL) A Dream of the Rood. Cynewulf, *Old English.* AnOE; OAEL-1, *tr. by* Charles W. Kennedy

When the Lord brought back those that returned to Zion. Like unto Them That Dream. Bible, *O.T.* TrJP *Fr.* Psalms.

When the Lord climbed. *Unknown, Latin.* MLL, *tr. by* Helen Waddell

When the Lord fashioned man, the Lord his God. The Mother. Catulle Mendès, *French.* TrJP, *tr. by* W. J. Robertson

When the Lord turned again the captivity of Zion, we were like them that dream. Bible, *O.T. See* Like unto Them That Dream.

When the lover. The Vow. Galway Kinnell. VCAP

When the M-16 rifle had a stoppage. Guns. Mcavoy Layne. CDa

When the man comes home he takes off his hat. A Small Light. Cathy Song. TRP

When the man in the window seat. The Experts. Jack Myers. NAmP90

When the man is busy. Revolution Is One Form of Social Change. Audre Lorde. Poetr

When the mar / when the mar / the marshymorasswamps. Tomorrow. Henri Michaux, *French.* PFTM, *tr. by* Armand Schwerner

When the master king and a starving hutted slave beneath the lash, and. On Listening to the Spirituals. Lance Jeffers. PoBA; SSLK

When the master sits at ease. Friend Cato. Anna Wickham. MoBrPo

When the Master was calling the roll. Anseo. Paul Muldoon. CIP-2; FaBoPV; PNI

When the men got happy in church. Getting Happy. Forrest Hamer. BAP-94

When the mind is at peace. Layman P'ang, *Chinese.* EnlH, *tr. by* Stephen Mitchell

When the Mint Is in the Liquor. Clarence Ousley. PoLF

When the Mississippi Flowed in Indiana. Vachel Lindsay. CMoP *Fr.* Three Poems About Mark Twain.

When the mists have rolled in splendor. We Shall Know. *Unknown.* PWR

When the mob swerved. Truth and Consequences. Edward Baugh. PBCV

When the moon appears. My Mother on an Evening in Late Summer. Mark Strand. FYAP

When the moon comes up. The Moon Rises. Federico García Lorca, *Spanish.* TTTS, *tr. by* William Bryant Logan

When the Moon is in the River of Heaven. Ou-yang Hsiu, *Chinese.* OHPC, *tr. by* Kenneth Rexroth

When the moon is on the wave. An Incantation. Byron. LaPo

When the moon shines o'er the corn. The Field Mouse. William Sharp. FPC

When the moon was full they came to the water. Moon Fishing. Lisel Mueller. CoAP

When the moored boat lifts, for its moment. In a Net of Blue and Gold. Jane Hirshfield. WeT

When the morn was shining clear. (LL) Ballad of the Tempest. James Thomas Fields. FaBoBe; PoLF

When the morning was waking over the war. Among Those Killed in the Dawn Raid Was a Man Aged a Hundred. Dylan Thomas. Son

When the mouse died at night. The Mouse. Jean Garrigue. TwCP

When the mouse died, there was a sort of pity. Death of a Whale. John Blight. BMAP; CBAP

When the movies were 35¢. Imitation of Life. Michael S. Weaver. UnSA

When the neat white. Duck. Valerie Worth. NTCP

When the new moon appears it is shouted to. Medicine Formula. *Unknown, Takelma.* SAGP, *tr. by* Edward Sapir

When the new teacher said. How the New Teacher Got Her Nickname. Brian Patten. NOxBChV

When the Night and Morning Meet. Dora Greenwell. EBVV

When the night her visions is weaving. The Harp of David. "Yehoash," *Yiddish.* TrJP, *tr. by* Alter Brody

When the nightegale singes. *Unknown.* MiEL

When the nightingale to his mate. Alba ("When the nightingale to his mate"). Ezra Pound. OBVE; VGW; WeW-3 *Fr.* Langue d'Oc.

When the noble Juyce. Cyclops and No-Man. Homer. OBCVT, *tr. by* George Chapman *Fr.* The Odyssey.

When the Norn Mother saw the Whirlwind Hour. Lincoln, the Man of the People. Edwin Markham. MoAmPo

When the old Cove Creek Dam first was started. The Song of Cove Creek Dam. *Unknown.* AmFP

When the old flaming prophet climbed the sky. On a Virtuous Young Gentlewoman That Died Suddenly. William Cartwright. HAP

When the old, long-preserved wine stands at the repast. Five Arabic Verses in Praise of Wine. *Unknown.* TrJP, *tr. by* Hartwig Hirschfeld

When the old man rubbed my back. Bear Fat. Linda Hogan. PaTW

When the Orient is lit by the great light. Vittoria Colonna, *Italian.* WPOW, *tr. by* Brenda Webster

When the other children go. The Invisible Playmate. Margaret Widdemer. CTV

When the ox was the gray enemy. People Like Us. William Matthews. APAD

When the pale moon hides and the wild wind wails. The Wolf. Georgia Roberts Durston. TLR

When the peach ripens to a rosy bloom. The Morning-Glory. Sarah Helen Whitman. ColAP

When the pencil undresses for sleep. The Pencil's Sleep. Tymoteusz Karpowicz, *Polish.* PoSu, *tr. by* Andrzej Busza *and* Bogdan Czaykowski

When the People Stand Up out of the Hard Cheese. Duoduo. AF, *tr. by* Gregory Lee *and* John Cayley *Fr.* Thoughts and Recollections.

When the pequi fruit blossomed. A Mehinaku Girl in Seclusion. Cathy Song. OpBo

When the Pilgrims. The First Thanksgiving. Jack Prelutsky. NTCP

When the pills don't work any more. Cole Porter's Son. Gerrit Henry. EOEF

When the pistol muzzle oozing blue vapour. That Moment. Ted Hughes. UV *Fr.* Crow. PoE

When the place was green with the shaky grass. Where the Lilies Used to Spring. David Gray. OxBS

When the plunging hoofs were gone. (LL) The Listeners. Walter De la Mare. AWP; CMoP; ClHu; EBEvV; HAP; HeIP-4; HoPM; ImPo; InPK-6; LiTM; MoBrPo; MoP; NOBE; NOxBChV; NTP; NoAM; NoP-4; OBEV; OBMV; OBSP; OxAEP-2; PoRA; Poetr; SoSe-8; TFi

When the pods went pop on the broom, green broom. A Runnable Stag. John Davidson. EBEvV; EBNV; FaPoR; HAP; OBEV; OxBTC

When the Poet Without Lying Verses in His Heart Returns to His Native Country. Rade Drainac, *Serbo-Croatian.*
"Then, the drops were freezing on black branches of ancient ash trees." HSix, *tr. by* Charles Simic

When the Portuguese came in. Guerillas. Seamus Deane. BiHa

When the power of Han decayed. The Lamentation. Ts'ai Yen, *Chinese.* SuSp, *tr. by* Yi-T'ung Wang

When the Present has latched its postern behind my / tremulous stay. Afterwards. Thomas Hardy. CH; CMoP; EBEV; GEA; GTBS-P; InPS-3; LiTM; MoBrPo; NOBE; NoP-4; OAEL-2; OBNC; OxAEP-2; PoEL-5; PoPoPo; TFi; TOF

When the priest made his entrance on the altar on the stroke of 10.30. 10.30 AM Mass, June 16, 1985. Paul Durcan. BiHa; CIP-2

When the prime mover of my many sighs. To Vittoria Colonna. Michelangelo Buonarroti, *Italian.* AWP, *tr. by* Longfellow

When the Prince, who was terribly smit. Limerick. Joyce Johnson. PeLi

When the proud World does most my world despise. Robert Malise Bowyer Nichols. *Fr.* Sonnets to Aurelia. OBMV

When the Pulitzers showered on some dope. Words for Hart Crane. Robert Lowell. CMoP

When the rain an the breeze an the storm an the sun. Quaco Sam. *Unknown.* FaBoVe

When the Rain Raineth. *Unknown.* RB

When the rain smell comes with the wind. (LL) Love Poem: "Rain smell comes with the wind." Leslie Marmon Silko. UnPo; VoR

When the rains began. The Prophetess. Dorothy Livesay. MoCV

When the rains came. Snail Winter. Judith C. Root. CMAP

When the Regime commanded that books with harmful knowledge. The Burning of the Books. Bertolt Brecht, *German.* PoSu, *tr. by* John Willeh

When the returning sun begins to smile. James Dance. NOEC *Fr.* Cricket; an Heroic Poem.

When the ring gleamed white and your chair hugged the edge of it. Change of Address. Kathleen Fraser. NYBP

When the ripe fruit falls. D. H. Lawrence. CMoP

When the ripe pears droop heavily. The Wasp. "Fiona Macleod." BoTP

When the river breaks loose. Tonghwan Kim, *Korean.* CKP, *tr. by* Jaihiun Kim

When the rooms are deserted. Johannes Bobrowski, *German.* PoSu, *tr. by* Ruth *and* Matthew Mead

When the rooster jumps up on the windowsill. Cuba, 1962. Ai. AmPA

When the ruff [*or* ruffe] is set elsewhere? (LL) Kisses Loath[e]some. Robert Herrick. CBLP; CaPo; CavPo; EP; OxBSP

When the ruler decided to make flourishing the region. A King's Garden World. Saba, *Arabic.* GaP, *tr. by* Wilbur Donald Newton

When the Sabbath was declining, just at twilight's mystic hour. In Memoriam. Susan Eugenia Bennett. Mary Weston Fordham. CBWP-2

When the sad ruins of that face. The Question and Answer. Thomas Beedome. NOSC

When the Saints Come Marching In. Audre Lorde. CrSp

When the sea can't bear me. The Sea. Kalju Lepik, *Estonian.* CEEP, *tr. by* Ivar Ivask

When the sea is as grey as her eyes. Soft White. Lee Harwood. SPE

When the Second World War began. Charles Reznikoff. HP *Fr.* Holocaust.

When the Secretary gave up his office. The Mountain Residence of Secretary Cheng Ching-ssu. Hsü Pen, *Chinese.* CoBLCP, *tr. by* Jonathan Chaves

When the Seed of Thy Word Is Cast. Cotton Mather. AH

When the Sex War ended with the slaughter of the Grandmothers. Song. W. H. Auden. PeLV

When the shades of night are falling, and the sun goes down. The Dustman. *Unknown.* BoTP

When the sheen on tall summer grass is pale. The Gazelles. Thomas Sturge Moore. OBMV

When the sheep are in the fauld, and the kye [*or* cows] at hame. Auld Robin Gray. Lady Anne Lindsay. CH; ECWP; GTBS-P; NOEC; OBEV; PeSAV; WPE

When the sheep are in the fauld, and the kye at hame. Auld Robin Gray. Lady Anne Lindsay. LW

When the shimmer of the moonlight now descends. The Summer Night. Friedrich Gottlieb Klopstock, *German.* GePo, *tr. by* George C. Schoolfield

When the shoals of plankton. Shooting Whales. Mark Strand. ColAP

When the shoe strings break. The Blues. Langston Hughes. TLR

When the shooting started, he crawled under. Refuge. Robert Hill Long. BAP-95

When the snake bit. Snake. Dannie Abse. NoAM

When the snow falls the flakes. The Dance. William Carlos Williams. NAAL-2

When the Snow is on the Ground. *Unknown.* ReMoGo

When the soul sought refuge in the place of rest. Self-Discipline. "Æ." MoBrPo

When the southeastern wall was first put in. The Paintings on My Wall Have Been Damaged by the Weather. T'ang Hsien-tsu, *Chinese.* CoBLCP, *tr. by* Jonathan Chaves

When the spent sun throws up its rays on cloud. Acceptance. Robert Frost. CMoP; GSo; OxBA

When the spider dropped down from the ceiling. The Grandmother Came Down to Visit Us. Joseph Bruchac. CDW

When the Spirit Spray-Paints the Sky. Sterling Plumpp. BAP-96

When the stern god. Mythic Fragment. Louise Glück. NMM-2; NoAM

When the storm passed away. Room for All. Timothy Holmes. PeSAV

When the storm thickens, when the combat burns. On General Paoli and the Corsican Struggle for Liberty. Anna Laetitia Barbauld. ECWP *Fr.* Corsica.

When the storms of life are raging. Stand by Me. *Unknown.* NAAAL

When the Students Resisted, a Minor Clash Ensued. David Knight. MoCV

When the Sultan Goes to Ispahan. Thomas Bailey Aldrich. FaBoBe

When the Summer fields are mown. Aftermath. Henry Wadsworth Longfellow. APN-1; NAAL-1; NAAL-3; NOBA; PAR; PoPoPo; TAP

When the / sun. August 2. Norman Jordan. PoBA

When the sun and the moon. Hymn to Tirumāl (Viṣṇu). Kirantaiyar, *Tamil.* PLW, *tr. by* A. K. Ramanujan

When the sun begins to throw. Skimmers. Ted Walker. NYBP

When the sun comes up we work. Ground-Thumping Song. *Unknown, Chinese.* CoBCP, *tr. by* Burton Watson

When the sun goes down and the world is still. Jock o' Dreams. Rose Fyleman. BoTP

When the sun has left the hill-top. Laurence Alma-Tadema. BoTP *Fr.* A Blessing for the Blessed.

When the sun is shining overhead. Shady Woods. E. M. Adams. BoTP

When the sun rose I was still lying in bed. Hearing the Early Oriole. Po Chü-i, *Chinese*. ChiP, *tr. by* Arthur Waley

When the Sun Shines More Years Than Fear. Janet Frame. PeNZ

When the sun shone hot the girl's arm was detected. Temperature. Gerard Malanga. NYBP

When the sun shouts and people abound. Summer Holiday. Robinson Jeffers. MoAmPo; OxBA

When the Sun Went Down. John Ashbery. NAAL-2

When the sun's whiteness closes around us. The Map. Gary Soto. NoAM

When the swans turned my sister into a swan. The Black Swan. Randall Jarrell. CMoP; PoE

When the sweet showers of April fall and shoot. Chaucer. *See* The General Prologue.

When the swift-rolling brook, swollen deep. The Storm-Wind. William Barnes. NOBE

When the sword of sixty comes nigh his head. Basil Bunting, *after the Persian of* Firdausi. OBVE

When the swordsman fell in Kurosawa's *Seven Samurai*. Heroic Simile. Robert Hass. VCAP

When the synchrotron was being built. Almagest, Last Letter to Zakarias. Siv Cedering Fox. PBCAP

When the tea is served at five o'clock. Milk for the Cat. Harold Monro. BoTP; FaBoBe; MoBrPo; OBMV; PC

When the tender bullet clearly ringing. Boris Vilde. Aleksis Rannit, *Estonian*. CEEP, *tr. by* Henry Lymann

When the tide was out. A Ship Burning and a Comet All in One Day. Richard Eberhart. NYBP

When the Tom-Tom Beats. Jacques Roumain, *French*. NegPo, *tr. by* Langston Hughes

When the towered galleys of Wang Chün came down from Yi-chou. Sorrowing for the Past at Western Pass Mountain. Liu Yu Hsi, *Chinese*. SuSp, *tr. by* Daniel Bryant

When the Tree Bares. Conrad Potter Aiken. MoAmPo

When the troubled sea swells and surrounds. Vittoria Colonna, *Italian*. PBWP, *tr. by* Brenda Webster

When the trumpet sounded, it was. The United Fruit Co. Pablo Neruda, *Spanish*. FaBoPV, *tr. by* Robert Bly

When the turuf [*or* turf] is thy tour [*or* tower]. *Unknown*. MiEL

When the universe goes up in flame. A Lament for the Willows outside the City Walls. Yün Shou-p'ing, *Chinese*. CoBLCP, *tr. by* Jonathan Chaves

When the Vacation Is Over for Good. Mark Strand. NYBP

When the village daylight dimmed. Oleg Grigorevich Chukhontsev, *Russian*. TCRP, *tr. by* Simon Franklin

When the voices of children are heard on the green. William Blake. *See* Nurse's Song ("When the voices of children are heard on the green / And laughing is heard on the hill").

When the voices of children are heard on the green / And laughing is heard on the hill. Nurse's Song. William Blake. AWP; CH; FHYEP; FaBoBe; NAEL-2; OxBChV; PeLV; SCGP *Fr.* Songs of Innocence.

When the voices of children are heard on the green / And whisperings [*or* whisprings] are in the dale. Nurse's Song. William Blake. FHYEP *Fr.* Songs of Experience.

When the wafer dissolves on my tongue, won-. Devolution. Molly Peacock. FFC

When the War Is Over. W. S. Merwin. OxBSP

When the warl's couped soon' as a peerie. Moonstruck. "Hugh MacDiarmid." NAEL-2

When the warm zummer breeze do blow over the hill. The Shep'erd Bwoy. William Barnes. EBVV

When the water fell. Flooded Mind. Norman MacCaig. OxBC

When the water's calm. Song. *Unknown*, *Chippewa Indian*. STP, *tr. by* Jerome Rothenberg

When the weather suits you not. Try Smiling. *Unknown*. BLPA; PWR

When the white flame in us is gone. Dust. Rupert Brooke. MoBrPo; OxBTC

When the white flame of verses. The Garden of Theophrastus. Peter Huchel, *German*. AF, *tr. by* Daniel Simko

When the white waters fill the spring embankments. Wild Geese on the Lake. Shen Yüeh, *Chinese*. SuSp, *tr. by* Richard B. Mather

When the white wave of a glory that is hardly I. Sinfonia Domestica. Jean Starr Untermeyer. MoAmPo

When the whole city is asleep. Tryst. Sunanda Tripathy, *Oriya*. OMIP, *tr. by* Jagannath Prasad Das *and* Arlene Zide

When the Wild Goose Finds Food He Calls His Comrades—*I Ching*. Jan Kemp. PeNZ

When the wind blows. *Unknown*. OxNR

When the wind blows loud and fearful. The Beggar Boy. Cecil Frances Alexander. OxBChV

When the wind is asleep and the weather set fair. *Unknown*. ASW, *tr. by* Kevin Crossley-Holland *Fr.* The Phoenix.

When the wind is gentle. Hsü Wei. *Fr.* A Kite. CoBLCP, *tr. by* Jonathan Chaves

When the wind is in the east. Mother Goose. BoTP; FaBoVe; LB; OxNR

When the wind is in the thrift. By the Saltings. Ted Walker. NYBP

When the wind works against us in the dark. Storm Fear. Robert Frost. CMoP; ColAP; OxBA; SAGP

When the Wine Was Gone. Alvin Aubert. BkSV

When the winter closes and the cold and the wet. Winter. Valentine Ackland. WPN

When the woods are green again. Midsummer Moon. "E. M. G. R." BoTP

When the words rustle no more. Stillness. James Elroy Flecker. CH; MoBrPo

When the Work's All Done This Fall. *Unknown*. AS

When the world ends. The Dance. Cornelius Eady. GT

When the world finally ends. Baseball. Paul Hoover. BAP-94

When the World Is Burning. Ebenezer Jones. OBEV

When the world takes over for us. Lear. William Carlos Williams. MeMAP; NAAL-2; NOBA; PoA

When the world turns completely upside down. Wild Peaches. Elinor Wylie. ColAP; FaBoWP; LiTM; LoP; NAAL-2; NALW; OxBA; WPE

When the World Was in Building. Ford Madox Ford. CTC

When the world's folk, one day of freedom. The Labourer. Iolo Goch, *Welsh*. OBWVE, *tr. by* Gwyn Williams

When the yearn redoubles itself out of nothing. Manifesto. Gloria Frym. DeD

When the years have died away'. (LL) The Poet's Song. Tennyson. EBVV; EPCY

When the yellow bird's note was almost stopped. Rejoicing at the Arrival of Chi'en Hsiung. Po Chü-i, *Chinese*. AWP; ChiP, *tr. by* Arthur Waley

When the young girls rolled into one. Patriot's Day. Steve Hassett. CDa

When the young have grown tired. For Thomas Moore. James Simmons. BiHa; PBCIP

When Thee (O holy sacrificed Lamb). To the Blessed Sacrament. Henry Constable. NoSic

When their eyes opened, it was more than morning. Making Camp. David Wagoner. VCAP

When their lordships asked Bacon. Edmund Clerihew Bentley. OBCoV *Fr.* Clerihews.

When them old hooters had plenty eating material. Hilaire Kirkland. *Fr.* Clotho, Lachesis, Atropos. PeNZ

When there are so many we shall have to mourn. In Memory of Sigmund Freud. W. H. Auden. HAP; NoAM; OAEL-2; OxBA

When there's no one about in the Quad. (LL) Limerick: "There once was a man who said "God.".". Ronald Arbuthnott Knox. NBLV; NOBL, PeLi

When these graven lines you see. A Happy Man. Carphyllides, *Greek*. AWP, *tr. by* E. A. Robinson

When these graven lines you see. A Happy Man. Carphyllides. AWP *Fr.* Variations of Greek Themes.

When these old woods were young. Under the Woods. Edward Thomas. CH

When these were past, thus gan the Titaness. Mutability. Edmund Spenser. PoEL-1 *Fr.* Wood Of Error. AEP

When Thesus with werres longe and grete. Publius Papinius Statius. OBCVT, *tr. by* Geoffrey Chaucer *Fr.* The Compleynt of feire Anelida and fals Arcite.

When they are half-undressed. (LL) The Saginaw Song. Theodore Roethke. NBLV; RB

When they ask your name. Children. Russell Edson. AmPA

When they bare the iron hand. (LL) The Martyr. Herman Melville. CBCWP; ColAP; NCAP; PoEL-5; TAP

When they brought us a pear jacket. Yury Osipovich Dombrovsky, *Russian*. TCRP, *tr. by* Bradley Jordan

When they brought you down. For Harper, Killed in Action. Walter McDonald. CDa

When they came to that blue harbour. Home. Vincent O'Sullivan. PeNZ

When they can sing no more. (LL) Coda. James Tate. AmPA; NYBP

When they confess that they have lost the penial bone. God Bless America. John Fuller. OBSV; PeLV

When they cry: / "Man overboard." Sergey Chudakov, *Russian*. TCRP, *tr. by* Albert C. Todd

When they entered through the back door. The Morning They Shot Tony Lopez, Barber and Pusher Who Went Too Far, 1958. Gary Soto. PBCAP

When they grab my leg. First Problem. Aimé Césaire, *French*. NegPo, *tr. by* Ellen Conroy Kennedy

When they had won the war. The Inner Part. Louis Simpson. PBCV; PBMP; RaBo

When they have completed its re-edification. South Parks Road. James Fenton. PeLV *Fr.* Exempla.

When they have eyes for me it's like Heaven. (LL) Malest Cornifici Tuo Catullo. Allen Ginsberg. BB; NeAP

When They Have Lost. C. Day Lewis. MoBrPo

When they [*or* Quhen thai] him fand, and gude [*or* gud] Wallace him saw. Lament for the Graham. Henry the Minstrel. OxBS   *Fr.* The Wallace.

When they in throngs a safe retirement seek. William Diaper. OBVE   *Fr.* Halieutica.

When they killed my mother it made me nervous. The State. Randall Jarrell. LiTM

When they knew what he had given them. The Fire Fetched Down. George Bradley. BAP-94

When they leave the world will be at peace. George Keithley. PuP-16

When they lowered you in the earth. Disappearance. Willis Barnstone. IMW

When they moved into the house it was winter. Gardener. Dom Moraes. OBGa

When they needed a foreign part. Partial Accounts. William Meredith. GLP

When they play like that where everyone is. *Unknown.*   *Fr.* Tepehua Thought-Songs. STP, *tr. by* Charles Boilès.

When they plow their fields. Patacara. WPoS

When they said *Carrickfergus* I could hear. The Singer's House. Seamus Heaney. EBEV; IIP

When they said the time to hide was mine. The Rabbit. Elizabeth Madox Roberts. OBCA

When they sailed out of Amsterdam. The Flying Dutchman. Ian D. Colvin. PeSAV

When they saw off Dai Evan's da. Fforestfawr. Kingsley Amis. NOBL   *Fr.* The Evans Country.

When they say Don't I know you? The Art of Disappearing. Naomi Shihab Nye. LoL

When they say to me: "Alexandria"—. Mikhail Alekseievich Kuzmin, *Russian.* TCRP, *tr. by* Yakov Hornstein

When they sd to me this. Philip Appleman. BXAP

When they sent the robot camera down. Robot Camera. Robert Johnstone. PNI

When they shot Malcolm Little down. At That Moment. Raymond R. Patterson. PoBA

When they stop poems. Today Is a Day of Great Joy. Victor Hernandez Cruz. LoL; TTY

When they stop / they, suddenly, / are gravel. (LL) Ringed Plover by a Water's Edge. Norman MacCaig. NoP-4

When they took us to the shower I saw. Death Camp. Irena Klepfisz. GLP

When they were wild. Birth. Louise Erdrich. NoP-4; PiM

When they woke me. Coming Back. Joseph Bruchac. CDW

When Thickly Beat the Storms of Life. Gurdon Robins. AH

When thin-strewn memory I look through. Miss Loo. Walter De la Mare. CMoP; OxBTC

When things go wrong, as they sometimes will. Don't Quit. *Unknown.* BLPA; PoToHe

When this appears, his rising beams presage. What Constellations rise with the Lion. The great Dog. Manilius Marcus, *Latin.* OBCVT, *tr. by* Thomas Creech

When this blasted war is over. *Unknown.* NSI

When This Cruel War Is Over. Charles Carroll Sawyer. AmFP

When this crystal shall present. To a Lady Upon a Looking-Glass Sent. James Shirley. BeJo

When this fly lived, she used to play. A Fly That Flew into My Mistress'[s] Eye. Thomas Carew. CaPo

When, this incredible thing, the principal of the junior high. Women Who Cook. Anita Skeen. GLP

When this is the thing you put on. Armor. James Dickey. CoAP

When this man, Manes, lived, he was a slave. Anyte. *See* Alive, this man was Manes, a common slave.

When this troubled life is over, hide Thou me. Hide Thou Me. *Unknown.* AmFP

When this yokel comes maundering. The Plot Against the Giant. Wallace Stevens. CMoP; OxBA; RACG; SAmP

When those renowned noble peers of Greece. Sonnet 44. Edmund Spenser. PoE   *Fr.* Amoretti. AAS

When thou and I are dead, my dear. Inseparable. Philip Bourke Marston. BoLoP

When thou art dead, and all thy wretched crew? (LL) Written on the Day That Mr. Leigh Hunt Left Prison. Keats. EPCY; Son

When thou art old there's grief enough for thee. (LL) Sephestia's Song to Her Child[e]. Robert Greene. NOBE; NTP; NoSic; OBEV; OxAEP-1; PoEL-2; SCGP

When thou dost take this sacred book into thy hand. On the Bible. Thomas Traherne. ChIV-1

When thou hast spent the ling[e]ring day in pleasure and delight. Gascoigne's [*or* Gascoygnes] Good-Night. George Gascoigne. AAS; NOCV; NoSic

When thou must home to shades of underground [*or* under ground]. Thomas Campion. AWP; CABP; EnLoPo; GLoP; LoP; NoP-4; NoSic; OxAEP-1; OxBSP; PoEL-2; PoRA

When thou, poor[e] excommunicate. To My Inconstant Mistress [*or* Mistris]. Thomas Carew. BeJo; CaPo; CavPo; EnLoPo; GBL; GLoP; MeLP; NOBE; NoP-4; OBEV; SAGP; SeCP; TFi

When thou shalt be dispos'd to set me light. Sonnet 88. Shakespeare. OxAEP-1   *Fr.* Sonnets.

When thou shalt leave this miserable life. Lucretius Paraphrased. Lucretius, *Latin.* OBCVT, *tr. by* Thomas Flatman

When thou taught'st *Cambridge*, and King *Edward* Greek. (LL) On the Detraction Which Followed upon My Writing Certain Treatises. Milton. PoE; Son

When thou the choice of Nature's wealth hast scanned. To Sir John Wentworth, Upon His Curiosities and Courteous Entertainment at Summerly in Lovingland. Mildmay Fane, 2d Earl of Westmorland. OBGa

When thou thy youth shalt view. To Phryne. Owen Felltham [*or* Feltham]. NOSC

When thou to my true-love [*or* true love] com'st. Westphalian Song. *Unknown, German.* AWP; OBVE, *tr. by* Samuel Taylor Coleridge

When Thraso meets his friend, he swears by God. Thraso. Samuel Rowlands. NoSic

When through the North a fire shall rush. Day of Judgement. Henry Vaughan. ChIV-2

When through the Universe with Horrour spread. Urania: The Divine Muse. On the Death of John Dryden, Esq. Lady Sarah Piers. KTR

When thy beauty appears. Song. Thomas Parnell. OBEV; OxAEP-1

When thy bright beams, my Lord, do strike mine eye. Edward Taylor. NAAL-1; NAAL-3   *Fr.* Preparatory Meditations Before My Approach to the Lord's Supper.

When Thy Heart with Joy O'erflowing. Theodore Chickering Williams. AH

When Thy King Is a Boy. Ed Roberson.

"You black out the sun." PoBA

When tides are wandering in or out. (LL) The Dead Knight. John Masefield. CH; GTBS-P

When time has made you wrinkled, sore and slow. A Long Way After Ronsard. James Simmons. PBCIP

When Time hath sunder'd shell from pearl. (LL) I cannot love thee as I ought. Tennyson. EBVVPR; EnVR

When time was young, and the world in infancy. The Four[e] Monarchies. Anne Bradstreet.

When to Her Lute Corinna [*or* Corrina] Sings. Thomas Campion. AAS; NAEL-1; NoP-4; NoSic; OAEL-1; PoE

When to Love's influence woman yields. A Valentine. Elizabeth Trefusis. LW   *Fr.* A Valentine.

When, to my deadly pleasure. Sir Philip Sidney. CBLP; EnLoPo; PoEL-1

When to my eyes. Midnight. Henry Vaughan. ChIV-2; ESCV

When to my lone soft bed at eve returning. Povre Ame Amoureuse. Louise Labé, *French.* AWP, *tr. by* Robert Bridges

When to Slap a Woman. Paul Violi. PmAP

When to the common rest that crowns our days. The Ages. William Cullen Bryant. APN-1

When to the flowers so beautiful. The Forget-Me-Not. *Unknown.* BoTP

When to the music of Byrd or Tallis. King's College Chapel. Charles Causley. PeECV; TOF

When to the sessions of sweet silent thought. Sonnet 30. Shakespeare. APAD; AWP; CABP; CTC; ClHu; EBEV; EBEvV; GBL; GSo; GTBS-P; HAP; HeIP-4; ImPo; InPS-3; NAEL-1; NOBE; NoP-4; NoSic; OAEL-1; OBEV; OxAEP-1; PFE; PoE; PoEL-2; PoLF; PoPoPo; PoRA; SCGP; TFi   *Fr.* Sonnets.

When Tom and Elizabeth took the farm. The Magpies. Denis Glover. NTP; PeNZ

When Tomorrow Is Too Long. Tanure Ojaide. HBAPE

When Torrid Rhymes with Forehead. Ray DiPalma. FTOS

When trembling voice brings forth that I do Stella love. (LL) Sonnet 6: "Some lovers speak, when they their Muses entertain." Sir Philip Sidney. AEP; NAEL-1; NoSic; Son

When trouble comes your soul to try. The Friend Who Just Stands By. Bertye Young Williams. PoLF; PoToHe

When trout swim down Great Ormond Street. Conrad Potter Aiken. NOBA; NoAM   *Fr.* Priapus and the Pool.

When twilight comes to Prairie. The Winning of the TV West. John T. Alexander. CTV

When Two Are Parted. Heinrich Heine, *German.* AWP, *tr. by* Louis Untermeyer

When two Evangelists shall seem to vary. On The Gospel. Francis Quarles. ChIV-2

When two lovers love each other well. Young Bearwell. *Unknown.* ESPB

When two plates of earth scrape along each other. Quake Theory. Sharon Olds. PBCAP

When two strong men stand face to face, though they come from the ends of the earth! (LL) The Ballad of East and West. Rudyard Kipling. EBNV; FaBoBe; FaPoR; OBNV

When two suns do appear. Sir Philip Sidney. SiPS   *Fr.* Arcadia.

When two who love are parted. When Two Are Parted. Heinrich Heine, *German*. AWP, tr. by Louis Untermeyer

When twofold silence was the song of love. (LL) Silent Noon. D. G. Rossetti. EnVR; GLoP; GSo; GaP; HAP; NAEL-2; NoP-4; OBNC; PoEL-5

When tyrants' crests and tombs of brass are spent. (LL) Sonnet 107. Shakespeare. AWP; CTC; EBEV; HAP; ImPo; NAEL-1; NoSic; OAEL-1; OxAEP-1; SCGP

When Ulysses braved the wine-dark sea. Making the Move. Paul Muldoon. NoAM

When under Edward or Henry the English armies. Now as Then. Anne Ridler. WPN

When upon this fabled beach. Song For a Tourist. Wayne Brown. HCP

When vain desire at last and vain regret. The One Hope. D. G. Rossetti. GSo; NAEL-2; OAEL-2 *Fr.* The House of Life.

WHEN Venus first did see. Adonis. Theocritus, *Greek*. NoSic

When Venus her Adonis found. The Death of Adonis. Philip Ayres, *after the Greek of* Theocritus. OBVE

When Venus her Adonis found. The Death of Adonis. Theocritus, *Greek*. NNPT, tr. by Philip Ayres

When Very was a celibate. Varitalk. Weare Holbrook. NYBP

When Vice triumphant holds her sov'reign sway. Byron. FHYEP *Fr.* English Bards and Scotch Reviewers.

When walnuts grew in stands like oak. Walnutry. Robert Morgan. MT

When war's red banner trailed along the sky. Robert G. Shaw. Henrietta Cordelia Ray. AAP; BlSi; CBWP-3; Son

When was it that the particles became. Wallace Stevens. PoA

When was there contract better driven by *Fate?*. On the Union. Ben Jonson. PBRV

When / Water forgets. Fire. Fazil Hüsnü Daglarca. CRP

When waves invade the yellowing wheat. Composed While under Arrest. Mikhail Yuryevich Lermontov, *Russian*. AWP, tr. by Max Eastman

When we are dead, and now no more. To My Ingenuous Friend, R. W. Henry Vaughan. BeJo

When we are dead, some Hunting-boy will pass. The Statue. Hilaire Belloc. OxAEP-2

When We Are Men. Stella Mead. BoTP

When we are old and these rejoicing veins. Edna St. Vincent Millay. VGW

When we are shadows watching over shadows. Two Shadows. Elizabeth Spires. DiPo

When we are two drunk suns. Yvonne Caroutch, *French*. BoWoP, tr. by Willis Barnstone *and* Elene Kolb

When we as strangers sought. At an Inn. Thomas Hardy. NOBVV

When we burn out the heart. The Priests. Gregor Strnisa, *Slovenian*. CEEP, tr. by Michael Scammell

When we came down from the country, we were strangers to the sea. Down from the Country. John Blight. BMAP; CBAP

When we climbed the slopes of the cutting. The Railway Children. Seamus Heaney. OPOU

When we come to that dark house. Dame Edith Sitwell. OBMV *Fr.* The Sleeping Beauty.

When we crossed the railed road. Mr. Tut's House A Recollection. Julia Fields. BkSV

When we drive in the mist to town together. Beginnings. Michael Burns. IFJA

When we enter the unknown. Our Houses. Linda Hogan. CrSp

When we fell apart in the Badlands and lay still. In the Badlands. David Wagoner. UnPo

When we first rade down Ettrick. Ettrick. Lady John Scott. LW; SoSe-8; WPE

When we for age could neither read nor write. Of The Last Verses in the Book. Edmund Waller. BeJo; EBEV; HAP; NOSC; NoP-4; PeECV; PoPoPo; SCGP; SeCP

When we fought campaigns (in the long Christmas rains). Many Sisters to Many Brothers. Rose Macaulay. NSI

When we fought the Yankees and annihilation was near. Jubilation T. Cornpone. Johnny Mercer. OBAL; OBCoV

When we go out into the fields of learning. Fields of Learning. Josephine Miles. NoAM

When we have come this long way. Anniversary Poem for the Cheyennes Who Fell at Sand Creek. Lance Henson. VoR

When we heard of a lady who. Serenades in Virginia. Andrew Hudgins. CBCWP

When we in kind embracements had agre'd [agreed]. *Unknown*. AAS; Son *Fr.* Zepheria.

When we launched life. You Tell Us What to Do. Faiz Ahmad Faiz, *Urdu*. VCWP, tr. by Agha Shahid Ali

When we lay where Budmouth Beach is. Budmouth Dears. Thomas Hardy. CH *Fr.* The Dynasts.

When we learn. It Is the Season. Josephine Jacobsen. TAP

When We Look Up. Denise Levertov. *Fr.* During the Eichmann Trial. HP

When We Looked Back. William Stafford. NYBP

When we meet them after death we will merge. Post Mortem as Angels. Barry Goldensohn. NAmP90

When we [first] moved here, pulled. An Oregon Message. William Stafford. CoAP

When we, my love, are gone to dust. A Song of Dust. John Byrne Leicester Warren, 3d Baron De Tabley. EnLoPo

When we on simple rations sup. Washing the Dishes. Christopher Darlington Morley. PoLF

When we parted with you at Geneve. An Epistle to John Walker, Esq. "Eliza." ECWP *Fr.* A Tour to the Glaciers of Savoy.

When we passed those notes to each other and laughed. Goodbye Note to Debbie Fuller: Pass It On. David Clewell. IFJA

When we played in the nursery till seven. Hello There. Brian S. Salome. BXAP

When we reach the field. Celebration: Birth of a Colt. Linda Hogan. HATNAP

When we rested between marches, I read Aristophanes. The Virgin Warrior. Gwendolyn MacEwen. FaBoWP

When we return to Russia. . . . Georgy Adamovich, *Russian*. TCRP, tr. by Yakov Hornstein

When we returned they asked us questions. More Questions. Ory Bernstein, *Hebrew*. IP, tr. by Warren Bargad *and* Stanley F. Chyet

When we saw human dignity. Easter 1984. Les A. Murray. ChIV-2

When we shuddered and took into ourselves. The Whole Story. William Stafford. NNaP

When we sigh about our trouble. Good Medicine. *Unknown*. PWR

When we speak to each other our voices are a little gruff. (LL) Beverly Hills, Chicago. Gwendolyn Brooks. Poetr; VGW

When we stand on the tops of Things. Emily Dickinson. PoE

When we start breaking up in the wet darkness. Consolations of Philosophy. Derek Mahon. BIrV; CIP-2

When we swept through farmer Nguyen's hamlet. Farmer Nguyen. William Daniel Ehrhart. NNaP

When We That Now Ha' Childern Wer Childern. William Barnes. NOBVV

When we two parted. Byron. BoLoP; CBLP; EBEvV; FHYEP; GLoP; GTBS-P; HoPM; NAEL-2; NOBE; NoP-4; OBEV; OBNC; PBMP; PoLF; PoPoPo; SCGP; TFi; UV

When we two parted. John C. Desmond. UV

When We Wake Up in the Morning. Anna Swirszczynska, *Polish*. CEEP, tr. by Magnus J. Kryński *and* Robert A. Maguire

When we were children, clasping hands. But You, My Darling, Should Have Married the Prince. Kathleen Spivack. AmPA

When we were children old Nurse used to say. The Quiet House. Charlotte Mew. BrRo; EBEV; NALW

When we were farm-boys, years ago. Recollections of "Lalla Rookh." John Townsend Trowbridge. APN-2; OBAL

When we were idlers with the loitering rills. To a Friend. Hartley Coleridge. FP; OBEV; OBNC; PoLF

When we were little childer we had a quare wee house. Grace for Light. "Moira O'Neill." TIRV

When we were silly sisters seven. Fair Mary of Wallington. *Unknown*. ESPB; OxBB

When we were small we could call anything home. Dialogue on Finding Someplace to Live. Lori Storie-Pahlitzsch. LoHo

When We Were Very Silly. John Bingham Morton.
 "Hush, hush, / Nobody cares!" UV
 "Someone asked the publisher." UV

When we would reach the anguish of the dead. Near an Old Prison. Frances Darwin Cornford. OBMV

When weary with the long day's care. Emily Jane Brontë. EnVR; VWP

When weeping noon leads on the altered day. (LL) Maquillage. Arthur Symons. ADE

When well we speak, & nothing do that's good. The Chewing [of] the Cud. Robert Herrick ChIV-1

When We'll Worship Jesus. Imamu Amiri Baraka. APSN

When wert thou born, Desire? Of the Birth and Bringing Up of Desire. Edward De Vere. FaBoEE; NoSic; SCGP

When Wesley died, the Angelic orders. Wesley in Heaven. Thomas Edward Brown. OBNC

When Westwall Downes [*or* Westwell Downs] I gan to tread. On Westwall Downes [*or* On Westwell Downs]. William Strode. NOSC; PoEL-2

When what has helped us has helped us enough. The Place of Backs. W. S. Merwin. HoPM

When what hugs stopping earth than silent is. E. E. Cummings. PoA

When, when, and whenever death closes our eyelids. Ezra Pound. MeMAP; OBMV; PoA *Fr.* Homage to Sextus Propertius.

When whispering strains do softly steal. In Commendation of Music. William Strode. OBEV

When white dew descends on the hundred grasses. Han Yü, *Chinese.* CoBCP, *tr. by* Burton Watson *Fr.* Autumn Thoughts.

When white people speak of being uptight. The Dancer. Al Young. PoBA

When, wild and high, the uproar swells. The Masses. Cornelius Mathews. APN-1 *Fr.* Poems on Man in His Various Aspects under the American Republic.

When Wild Confusion Wrecks the Air. Mather Byles. AH

When will I be home? I don't Know. Li Shang-yin, *Chinese.* OHMPC, *tr. by* Kenneth Rexroth

When will men again. The Leaping Laughers. George Barker. OBMV

When will the bell ring, and end this weariness? Last Lesson of the Afternoon. D. H. Lawrence. NoAM

When will the flowers grow there? I cannot tell. No Help. Sarah Morgan Bryan Piatt. NCAP

When will the stream be aweary of flowing. Nothing Will Die. Tennyson. PBMP

When will ye think of me, my friends? A Parting Song. Felicia Dorothea Hemans. VWP

When will you ever, Peace, wild wooddove, shy wings shut. Peace. Gerard Manley Hopkins. GTBS-P; OxBSP; TrCP

"When will you marry me, William." The West-Country Damosel's Complaint. *Unknown.* ESPB

When Willie Mae went down to the barber shop. Choosing the Blues. Angela Jackson. ISC

When willing nymphs and swains unite. The Judgement of Tiresias. Hildebrand Jacob. NOEC

When wilt Thou save the people? God Save The People. Ebenezer Elliot. BLPA; OxAEP-2

When wilt thou teach the people. D. H. Lawrence. OBSV

When Windesor walles sustain'd my wearied arme. When Windsor Walls. Henry Howard, Earl of Surrey. AAS; SiPS

When window-lamps had dwindled, then I rose. Christopher John Brennan. CBAP *Fr.* The Wanderer.

When winds are raging. Hymn. Harriet Beecher Stowe. AH; PoToHe

When winds rage and the sky is high, gibbons cry mournfully. Climbing the Heights. Tu Fu, *Chinese.* SuSp, *tr. by* Wu-Chi Liu

When winds that move not its calm surface sweep. The Ocean. Moschus, *Greek.* OBCVT, *tr. by* Shelley; AWP; OBVE, *tr. by* Shelley

When Windsor Walls. Henry Howard, Earl of Surrey. CABP
("How Each Thing Save the Lover in Spring Reviveth to Pleasure.") Son

When *Wine* has fum'd into my head. Drink. Anacreon, *Greek.* OBCVT, *tr. by* Charles Goodall

When wine runs low, it is not worth the sparing. Joshua Sylvester, *after the French of* Pierre Mathieu. FaBoEE

When winking stars at dusk peep through. Makes the Little Ones Dizzy. Samuel Hoffenstein. BXAP

When Winter fringes every bough. Henry David Thoreau. PAR

When Winter snows upon my golden hairs. Samuel Daniel. *See* Sonnet 33: 'When men shall find thy flower'.

When winter snows upon thy sable hairs. Samuel Daniel. AEP; CTC; NAEL-1; NOBE; NoSic; OBEV; SCGP; Son *Fr.* To Delia.
("They will remaine, and so thou canst not die.") (LL) PBRV
("When winter snowes upon thy sable haires.") PBRV

When winter was half over. Another Sarah. Anne Porter. KSG; TTTS

When Winter's royal robes of white. A Parting Hymn. Charlotte Forten. BlSi

When Winter's royal robes of white. A Parting Hymn. Charlotte L. Forten Grimke. NAAAL

When wise Minerva still was young. The Origin of Didactic Poetry. James Russell Lowell. PoEL-5

When wise Ulysses from his native Coast. Argus. Alexander Pope. FP

When, with a pain he desires to explain to his servitors, Baby. The Nurses. Rudyard Kipling. NoAM *Fr.* Land and Sea Tales.

When with a serious musing I behold. The Marigold. George Wither. NOSC *Fr.* A Collection of Emblemes, Ancient and Moderne.

When, with breaking heart. Anryu Suharu, *Japanese.* WPJ, *tr. by* Kenneth Rexroth *and* Ikuko Atsumi

When with eyes closed as in an opium dream. Parfum Exotique. Charles Baudelaire, *French.* AWP, *tr. by* Arthur Symons

When with May the air is sweet. Love, Whose Month Was Ever May. Ulrich von Liechtenstein, *German.* AWP, *tr. by* Jethro Bithell

When with much pains this boasted learning's got. Charles Churchill. OBSV *Fr.* The Author.

When with salt rheum and phlegm they powdered are. Margaret Lucas Cavendish, Duchess of Newcastle. *See* Nature's Cook.

When with the Virgin morning thou dost rise. Matins [*or* Mattens], or Morning Prayer. Robert Herrick. CaPo

When within my arms I hold you. Aurelia. Robert Malise Bowyer Nichols. OBMV

When without tears I looke on Christ, I see. William Alabaster. ESCV *Fr.* Divine Meditations. Son

When woods are odorous at eve. Wood Carols. Henrietta Cordelia Ray. CBWP-3

When working blackguards come to blows. Song. Ebenezer Elliot. EBEV; OxAEP-2

When world is water and all is flood, God said. Noah's Ark. Marguerite Young. WPE

When World War II was declared. Can't Tell. Nellie Wong. LTA; OpBo; UnSA

When ye hunt at the roe, then shall ye see there. Julians Barnes. *Fr.* Book of Hunting. WPE

When yet a Child, I read great *Virgil* o'er. Dream, The; An Epistle to Mr. Dryden. Elizabeth Thomas. KTR

When Yon Full Moon. W. H. Davies. MoBrPo

When you and I. When You and I Grow Up. Kate Greenaway. CTV

When you and I go down. Harold Monro. OBMV *Fr.* Midnight Lamentation. OxBTC

When You and I Grow Up. Kate Greenaway. CTV

When you and I have play'd the little hour. Reunited. Sir Gilbert Parker. OBEV

When You and I Must Part. *Unknown.* AmFP

When you and I on the Palos Verdes cliff. Shane O'Neill's Cairn. Robinson Jeffers. NOBA; NoAM

When you and I shall to our earth return. To Strephon. Sarah Dixon. ECWP

When you and my true lover meet. The Lady's Third Song. W. B. Yeats. FaBoTw

When you are called on to perform a duty. Do Your Best. Mrs. Henry Linden. CBWP-4

When you are caught breathless in an empty station. This Is the Place to Wait. Horace Gregory. MoAmPo *Fr.* The Passion of M'Phail.

When you are gone, I lie upon your bed. Suburban Wife's Song. Robert Hutchinson. NYBP

When you are old and grey and full of sleep. W. B. Yeats, *after the French of* Pierre de Ronsard. APAD; AWP; BoLoP; CMoP; CTC; ClHu; EBEvV; EBVV; GBL; GLoP; HeIP-4; LiTM; LoP; MoBrPo; MoP; NAEL-2; NAWM-2; NOBVV; NoAM; NoP-4; OBEV; OxBM; OxBTC; PiM; PoLF; SAGP; TFi

When you are standing at your hero's grave. Reconciliation. Siegfried Sassoon. NSI

When you are traveling. Ijajee's Story. Charlotte DeClue. EC2

When you are very old, at evening. Of His Lady's Old Age. Pierre de Ronsard, *French.* AWP; CTC, *tr. by* Andrew Lang

When you are walking by yourself. Kick a Little Stone. Dorothy Aldis. TLR

When you awake. The Sleeper. Sydney Clouts. PeSA

When you bared your china. Party Favour. Daniel David Moses. HATNAP

When you broke from me. Lady Izumi, *Japanese.* BoWoP, *tr. by* Willis Barnstone

When you came and you talked and you read with your. To William Carlos Williams. Galway Kinnell. NoAM; Poetr

When you came down the river to me in your rush basket. Mercy. Bruce Smith. MoLi

When you came out of your house. Remembering Althea. William Stafford. NYBP

When you came, you were like red wine and honey. Decade, [A]. Amy Lowell. CPO; MoAmPo; NALW; OxWW

When you come, as you soon must, to the streets of our city. Advice to a Prophet. Richard Wilbur. AFr; AmPP; FYAP; GEA; MoAmPo; NYBP; NoP-4; OBWP; OxBC; PoE; Poetr; TwCP; VCAP

When you come out of that. Jalapeña Gypsies. Jay Wright. NBV

When you consider the radiance, that it does not withhold. The City Limits. A. R. Ammons. HCAP; MoP; NAAL-2; NOBA; NoAM; NoP-4; PoPoPo; Poetr; VCAP

When you destroy a blade of grass. To Iron-Founders and Others. Gordon Bottomley. OBEV; OBMV

When you disappeared. For Kelly, Missing in Action. Walter McDonald. CDa

When you drink your wine, in autumn. (LL) After the Persian. Louise Bogan. NYBP; PoA

When you drive on the freeway, cars follow you. Paranoia. Michael Dennis Browne. AmPA

When you enter Chin-hua Mountain. Tsung Ch'en. CoBLCP, *tr. by* Jonathan Chaves *Fr.* Sent to Yü Te-fu upon His Receipt of an Official Commission to the Two Che's.

When you feel like saying something. The Most Vital Thing in Life. Grenville Kleiser. PoToHe; SoSe-8

When you first feel the ground under your feet. Walking in a Swamp. David Wagoner. HAP

When you first rub up against God's own skin. Ars Poetica about Ultimates. Tram Combs. TwCP

When you go away the wind clicks around to the north. W. S. Merwin. LCAP-2

When you go out at early morn. The Serving Maid. Arthur Joseph Munby. NOBVV

When you go ten miles away. Viaticum. Pao Yu, *Chinese*. OHMPC, *tr. by* Kenneth Rexroth

When you got up this morning the sun. Wind. Gary Soto. NoAM *Fr.* The Elements of San Joaquin. PBCAP; PaTW; UnSA

When you ground the lenses and the moons swam free. The Emancipators. Randall Jarrell. PoA

When you grow up, are no more children. Parent to Children. Robert Graves. OxAEP-2

When you have both. (LL) Toads. Philip Larkin. CMoP; NOBL; NoAM; OxAEP-2; OxBTC; PoE; Poetr; SoSe-8

When You Have Forgotten Sunday: The Love Story. Gwendolyn Brooks. BPo; NAAAL; WPOW

When you have me as I'm standing. Interrogation. Sophie Cabot Black. BAP-93

When you have money, buy me a ring. Whatever You Want. Angel González, *Spanish*. VCWP, *tr. by* Steven Ford Brown *and* Revuelta Gutierrez

When you have nothing more to say, just drive. The Peninsula. Seamus Heaney. IIP

When you have / once had. Self Portrait II. Tove Ditlevsen, *Danish*. IMW, *tr. by* Ann Freeman

When you have tidied all things for the night. Solitude. Harold Monro. LBC; MoBrPo

When you have wearied of the valiant spires of this country town. Oxford Canal. James Elroy Flecker. OxBTC

When you hear me singing. Rat Song. Margaret Atwood. NIP-4 *Fr.* Songs of the Transformed.

When you hint that my little lie craves negligence. Catullus. *See* Carmen 10 ("Varus, whom I chanced to meet").

When you imagine trumpet-faced musicians. Homage to Literature. Muriel Rukeyser. SeSe

When you kiss me, moths flutter in my mouth. Beija-Flor. Diane Ackerman. NIP-4

When you kissed me for the first time. The Youngest Children of an Angel. Anna Swir, *Polish*. IFJA, *tr. by* Czeslaw Milosz *and* Leonard Nathan (b. 1924)

When You Laugh. Ingrid Jonker, *Afrikaans*. WPOW, *tr. by* Elizabeth Jones

When you lay sick that spring, too weak to move. Spaces. Judy Page Heitzman. CMAP

When you lie in. Paul Celan, *German*. VCWP, *tr. by* Michael Hamburger

When you look at this memorial. Epitaph from Athens. *Unknown*, *Greek*. GrAn, *tr. by* Peter Jay

When you look before you go. Windows. Russell Hoban. AYFP

When you look down from the airplane you see lines. Field and Forest. Randall Jarrell. LCAP-2; VGW

When you look on my grave. *Unknown*. FaBoEE

When you lost touch with lovers' bare skin. Donne. James Simmons. CIP-2

When you love, or speak of it. Aphra Behn. BoWoP

When you move away, you see how much depends. Landscape, Dense with Trees. Ellen Bryant Voigt. MT

When you pick up the Tanakh and read. The Book of Ruth and Naomi. Marge Piercy. NMM-2

When you plunged. The Otter. Seamus Heaney. NoAM; PNI

When you put on the feet be sure. Dr. Potatohead Talks to Mothers. Judith Johnson Sherwin. MoP

When you reach to touch the markings. Indian Rock, Bainbridge Island, Washington. Duane Niatum. CDW

When You Read This Poem. Pinkie Gordon Lane. BlSi

When you return. If. Blaga Dimitrova, *Bulgarian*. CEEP, *tr. by* Jascha Kessler *and* Aleksandar Shurbanov

When you scuttled the ship, the shore was still in sight. Meditation of a Mariner. Dorothy Auchterlonie. CBAP

When you see a guy reach for stars in the sky. Guys and Dolls. Frank Loesser. OBAL

When you see a ragged urchin. Boys Make Men. *Unknown*. PWR

When you see me sitting quietly. On Aging. Maya Angelou. LiLi

When you see millions of the mouthless dead. Sonnet. Charles Hamilton Sorley. NSI; OBWP; PeFWW; PoFWW; PoWW

When you see my gray hair and chin. Anacreon, *Greek*. InMo, *tr. by* Sam Hamill

When you see them. Breath. Mark Strand. HCAP

When you send out invitations, don't ask me. Palladas, *Greek*. OBVE, *tr. by* Tony Harrison

When you shall see me in the toils of Time. Thomas Hardy. OxBTC *Fr.* She, to Him. EnVR

When you show me. Colors for Mama. Barbara Mahone. PoBA

When you sit happy in your own fair house. Alcuin, *Latin*. MLL, *tr. by* Helen Waddell

When you stop to consider. Dog Days. Derek Mahon. OPOU

When you suddenly. Godlike. Anselm Hollo. PmAP

When you swim in the surf off Seal Rocks, and your family. Family. Josephine Miles. FYAP; FaBoWP

When you the sun-burnt pilgrim see. Song: Good Counsel to a Young Maid. Thomas Carew. CaPo

When you think of the distances. The Distances. W. S. Merwin. NOBA

When you think of the hosts without no. Cautionary Limerick. *Unknown*. NBLV

When you think of your country. Firewing. Breyten Breytenbach, *Afrikaans*. VCWP, *tr. by* Ernst van Heerden

When you tilted toward me, arms out. After 37 Years My Mother Apologizes for My Childhood. Sharon Olds. Poetr

When you turn the corner. Final Curve. Langston Hughes. MBE

When you visit the barber. Barbershop. Martin Gardner. FPC

When you wake up from sleeping with women. Studying Horses. Robert Kelly. APSN

When you walked here. The Dumbfounding. Margaret Avison. NOBC

When you wardance, sometimes you must. Wardance. Phillip William George. VoR

When you wear a cloudy collar and a shirt that isn't white. When Your Pants Begin to Go. Henry Lawson. NOBAu

When you were. For Angela. Zack Gilbert. PoBA

When you were a holy priest. Marvellous Grass. Nuala Ni Dhomhnaill, *Irish*. PBCIP, *tr. by* Michael Hartnett

When you were a tadpole and I was a fish. Evolution. Langdon Smith. BLPA; FaBoBe

When you were alive, at least. The Dead Friend. Agnes Mary Frances Robinson. VWP

When you were born, all the poets I knew. Poem for My Sons. Minnie Bruce Pratt. FiLi; NMM-2

When you were drunk you could always whip Joe Louis. My Right Hand Don't Leave Me No More. Carter Revard. HATNAP

When you were here, ah foolish then! Arthur Symons. LBC

When you were here in wonderful Detroit. Goodbye David Tamunoemi West. Margaret Danner. BPo

When you were just a babe. Two Eyes. Nhật Tiến, *Vietnamese*. AVP, *tr. by* Huỳnh Sanh Thông

When you were not a loafer. (LL) Will you sleep forever? Korinna, *Greek*. PBWP, *tr. by* John Dillon; BoWoP, *tr. by* Willis Barnstone

When you swim there, and you, and you. Dining-Room Tea. Rupert Brooke. MoBrPo

When You Will Walk in the Field. Leah Goldberg, *Hebrew*. TrJP, *tr. by* Simon Halkin

When you woke [up] among them. After Grief. Stanley Plumly. AmPA; LCAP-2

When You Write Again. Ingrid Jonker, *Afrikaans*. PBWP, *tr. by* Jack Cope *and* William Plomer

When you wrote your letter it was April. Response. Mary Ursula Bethell. FaBoWP; PeNZ

When Young Hearts Break. Heinrich Heine, *German*. AWP, *tr. by* Louis Untermeyer

When young I scribbled, boasting, on my wall. The Summing-up. Stanley Kunitz. OBAL

When young I was awed by authority. Italics. Anselm Hollo. PmAP

When Young Ladies Get Married. *Unknown*. AmFP

When Young Melissa Sweeps. Nancy Byrd Turner. NTCP

When your capitalist boss takes his toll. Limerick. Dominic Fitzpatrick. PeLi

When Your Cheap Divorce Is Granted. "Orpheus C. Kerr." OBAL

When your client's hopping mad. The Advertising Agency Song. *Unknown*. NBLV

When your eyes gaze seaward. Golden Moonrise. W. S. Braithwaite. PoBA

When your face dawned. Yevtushenko, *Russian*. TCRP, *tr. by* Albert C. Todd

When your hour was rung at last. Rendez-vous Manqué dans la Rue Racine. John Millington Synge. BIrV

When your left arm touched my right. Exchange of Fire. Susan Musgrave. BAP-95

When your life is tumbling downhill head over heels. The New Year March: A Declaration. Yuly Markovich Daniel, *Russian*. TCRP, *tr. by* David Burg *and* Arthur Boyars

When your lips seek my lips they bring. Isolation. Arthur Symons. OxBSP

When Your Pants Begin to Go. Henry Lawson. NOBAu

When your teeth decay you cannot. I Get Up at Dawn. Lu Yu, *Chinese*. OHPC, *tr. by* Kenneth Rexroth

When you're away I sleep a lot. The Method. J. D. McClatchy. EOEF

When you're doing an escort stunt and the Huns get on your tail. You're Only a PBO. *Unknown*. NSI

When you're feeling kind of bonkers. Richard Tipping. OBCoV

When you're lying awake with a dismal headache, and repose is taboo'd by anxiety. Nightmare, [A *or* The]. Sir William Schwenck Gilbert. CBNP; NOBL; NTP; OBCoV; OxBoLi; PBMP; PeLV; PoRA *Fr.* Iolanthe.

When You're Not a Poet. Yona Wallach, *Hebrew*. IP, *tr. by* Warren Bargad *and* Stanley F. Chyet

When you're not looking. May Swenson. *See* The Hair.

When you're out in smart society. Well, Did You Evah? Cole Porter. OBAL

When you're tired and worn at the close of day. Confide In a Friend. *Unknown*. PoToHe

When youth and charms have ta'en their wanton flight. Advice to Sophronia. Mary Leapor. ECWP

When youth had led me half the race. Henry Howard, Earl of Surrey. SiPS

When Youthful Faith has Fled. John Gibson Lockhart. *See* Lines: "When youthful faith hath fled."

When youthful faith hath fled. Lines. John Gibson Lockhart. OBEV; Ro

Whenas galoshed my Julia goes. Upon Julia's Arctics. Bert Leston Taylor. OBAL

Whenas in furs my Julia goes. Upon Julia's Clothes. Edmund George Valpy Knox. BXAP; UV

Whenas in perfume Julia went. Herrick's Julia. Helen Smith Bevington. BXAP

Whenas man's life, the light of human lust. 87. Fanny [*or* Frances] Macartney Greville. CABP *Fr.* Caelica.

Whenas [*or* When as] man's life, the light of human[e] lust. Sonnet: "Whenas [*or* When as] man's life, the light of human lust." Greville Fulke. NOSC; NoSic; PoEL-1 *Fr.* Caelica.

Whenas [*or* When as] the Rye [Reach to the Chin]. Song: "When as [*or* whenas] the rye [*or* rie] reach to the chin." George Peele. CBLP; CBNP; EnLoPo; FaBoCh; FaBoVe; GBL; NOBE; NoSic; OBEV; OxBoLi; PoEL-2; TFi *Fr.* The Old Wives' [*or* Wife's] Tale.

Whenas to shoot my Julia goes. To Julia in Shooting Togs. Sir Owen Seaman. BXAP

Whenas we sat in Babylon. Bible, *O.T. See* Psalm 137.

Whence and Whither. Hayyim Nahman Bialik, *Hebrew*. TrJP, *tr. by* Helena Frank

Whence are you, learning's son? The End of Clonmacnois. *Unknown*, *Irish*. CIP-2, *tr. by* Frank O'Connor

Whence come [*or* came] ye, Cherubs? from the moon? Chanting Cherubs, The [A *Group by* Greenough]. Richard Henry Dana. APN-1

Whence come you, all of you so sorrowful? Sonnet: To Certain Ladies; When Beatrice Was Lamenting Her Father's Death. Dante, *Italian*. AWP, *tr. by* D. G. Rossetti

Whence comes those many-colored birds. The Birds of Passage. Jones Very. NCAP

Whence comest thou, Gehazi. Gehazi. Rudyard Kipling. FaBoPV

Whence did all that fury come? A Stick of Incense. W. B. Yeats. ChIV-2

Whence Had They Come? W. B. Yeats. BoLoP

Whence, hardworn drum. Tambour. István Vas, *Hungarian*. CEEP, *tr. by* Jascha Kessler

Whence let us go to. The Nicest Phantasies Are Shared. Brian Coffey. CIP-2

Whence this impatience fluttering in my breast! Urania. Robert Andrews. NOEC

Whenceness of the Which. *Unknown*. UV

Whene'er bitter foe attack thee. Advice to Hotheads. Samuel ben Elhanan Isaac, of Padua Archevolti, *Hebrew*. TrJP, *tr. by* A. B. Rhine

Whene'er I come where ladies are. Love at Large. Coventry Patmore. EBVV; NOBVV *Fr.* The Angel in the House.

Whene'er I look into your eyes. I Love But Thee. Heinrich Heine, *German*. AWP, *tr. by* Louis Untermeyer

Whene'er I take my walks abroad. Praise for Mercies Spiritual and Temporal. Isaac Watts. NOEC

Whene'er, in morning airs, I walk abroad. My Shadow's Stature. John James Piatt. APN-2

Whene'er the old exchange of profit rings. Stay My Steps in Thy Paths, That My Feet Do Not Slide. Francis Quarles. NOSC *Fr.* Emblems.

Whene'er the waist makes too much haste. A Girdle. William Strode. NOSC

Whene'er with haggard eyes I view. Rogero's Song. George Canning, George Ellis, *and* John Hookham Frere. NOEC; OBCoV; PeLV *Fr.* The Rovers.

Whenever a butterfly. A Lesson of Silence. Tymoteusz Karpowicz, *Polish*. PoSu, *tr. by* Czeslaw Milosz

Whenever a fellow called Rex. Limerick. *Unknown*. NOBL

Whenever Auntie moves around. Auntie's Skirts. Robert Louis Stevenson. WHSW

Whenever autumn comes. An Orange With the Rind Still Green. Xuân Diệu, *Vietnamese*. AVP, *tr. by* Huỳnh Sanh Thông

Whenever, Chloe, I begin. Song. Philip Dormer Stanhope. NOEC

Whenever he got in a fury, a. Limerick. *Unknown*. PeLi

Whenever he observes me purchasing. Sextus the Usurer. Martial, *Latin*. AWP, *tr. by* Kirby Flower Smith

Whenever I go by there nowadays. The Tavern. Edwin Arlington Robinson. NCAP

Whenever I have, in all humility, moved. "Furnley Maurice." NOBAu

Whenever I kissed her. Compromise. Akhtar-ul-Iman, *Urdu*. OMIP, *tr. by* C. M. Naim *and* Vinay Dharwadker

Whenever I live, like simple. Dmitry Aleksandrovich Prigov, *Russian*. TCRP, *tr. by* Albert C. Todd

Whenever I make a new poem. Lew Welch. BB

Whenever I pause. The Noise of the Village. *Unknown*, *Chippewa*. OBVE, *tr. by* Frances Densmore

Whenever I plunge my arm, like this. Under the Waterfall. Thomas Hardy. BoLoP; CTC; NAEL-2; NoP-4

Whenever I say "America." Nancy Byrd Turner. CTV

Whenever I see him. Waking in the Dark. Dorothy Livesay. NOBC

Whenever I walk to Suffern along the Erie track. The House with Nobody in It. Joyce Kilmer. BLPA; ChAP

Whenever I'm sleepless. Historiotherapy. Martin Sorescu, *Romanian*. CEEP, *tr. by* Andrei Banta

Whenever Mr. Edwards spake. The Theology of Jonathan Edwards. Phyllis McGinley. MoAmPo

Whenever Richard Cory went down town. Richard Cory. Edwin Arlington Robinson. APAD; APN-2; AmPP; CMoP; ChAP; ColAP; EBEvV; HAP; ImPo; InPK-6; LiTM; MeMAP; MoAmPo; NAAL-2; NCAP; NOBA; NTP; NoP-4; OxBA; PFE; PoLF; PoPoPo; PoRA; Poetr; SAGP; TAP; TFi

Whenever sentence is passed. Sentence. Antonin Bartusek, *German*. CEEP, *tr. by* Ewald Osers

Whenever the *moon* and *stars* are *set,*. Windy Nights. Robert Louis Stevenson. ACTP; BoTP; FPC; KaS; NTP; OTCP; OxBChV; PoRA

Whenever the wind blows / I try to question it. The Mother of Michitsuna, *Japanese*. WPJ, *tr. by* Kenneth Rexroth *and* Ikuko Atsumi

Whenever they come from Kansas. Coming from Kansas. Myra Cohn Livingston. NOxBChV

Whenever troublous hours I find. Happiness amidst Troubles. Immanuel di Roma, *Italian*. TrJP, *tr. by* J. Chotzner

Whenever war is spoken of. The Great War. Vernon Scannell. NSI; OBWP

Whenever you cannot agree. (LL) I Wish I Were [*or* Was] Single Again. *Unknown*. AS; AmFP

Whenever you drink all night you make. Martial, *Latin*. FaBoEE, *tr. by* James Michie

Whenever you see the hearse go by. Be Merry. *Unknown*. RB

Whenever you take a step. The Horizon. Kevin Hart. NOBAu

Whenever your American Way of Life is raised to the sky. America, America. K. Nisar Ahmad, *Kannada*. OMIP, *tr. by* A. K. Ramanujan

Whenne mine eynen misteith. All Too Late. *Unknown*. EBEV; OAEL-1

Whenneso will wit overstieth. *Unknown*. MiEL

Wher one would be. Sir Edward Dyer. PoEL-1

Where. Walter De la Mare. NYBP

Where? Kenneth Patchen. LiTM

Where. Tanka. Kanoko Okamoto, *Japanese*. MJT, *tr. by* Makoto Ueda

Where a bullet of sense *ought* to hit. (LL) A Pastoral Ballad by John Bull. Thomas Moore. BIrV; OBSV

Where a Roman judged a foreign people. Notre Dame. Osip Emilevich Mandelstam, *Russian*. OBVE, *tr. by* James Greene

Where a Roman Villa Stood, above Freiburg. Mary Elizabeth Coleridge. OBNC

Where a young man lands hatless from the air. (LL) "New King Arrives in His Capital by Air. . ." —Daily Newspaper. John Betjeman. NOBE; OxBoLi

Where all Manhattan that I've seen must disappear. (LL) My Sad Self. Allen Ginsberg. Poetr; UnPo; VCAP

Where all the fathers are crying: *My son is mine!*. (LL) August. Adrienne Rich. NNaP; PBWP

Where all who know may drown. (LL) The Man against the Sky. Edwin Arlington Robinson. AmPP; CMoP; OxBA

Where am I now? And what. A Song in Passing. Yvor Winters. CRP; VGW

Where am I, O awesome friend? Yitzhak Lamdan. TrJP, *tr. by* Simon Halkin *Fr.* For the Sun Declined.

Where am I, or how came I here, hath death. On Lazarus Raised From Death. Henry Colman. ChIV-2

Where among the blue clouds. Wen Cheng-ming, *Chinese.* CoBLCP, *tr. by* Jonathan Chaves

Where and to whom. Two Sons. Anne Sexton. PFE

Where angels turned into honeysuckle & poured nectar into my mouth. Backyard. Diane Di Prima. PmAP

Where are all thy beauties now, all hearts enchaining? [*or* harts enchayning?]. Thomas Campion. GBL

Where are Elmer, Herman, Bert, Tom and Charley. The Hill. Edgar Lee Masters. CMoP; ColAP; FYAP; LiTM; NOBA; NoAM; OxBA; TAP *Fr.* Spoon River Anthology.

Where are my first-born, said the brown land, sighing;. The First-born. Jack Davis. BMAP

Where are my wingèd words? Dissolved in air. Gregory of Nazianzus, Saint, *Greek.* OBCVT, *tr. by* Elizabeth Barrett Browning

Where are now, in coign or crack. Ballade of England. Louis MacNeice. NYBP

Where are our uniforms? *Unknown.* NSI

Where are the bay-leaves, Thestylis, and the charms. The Incantations. Theocritus. AWP, *tr. by* Charles Stuart Calverley *Fr.* Idylls.

Where are the birth-places of the heroes? Alpheios, *Greek.* GrAn, *tr. by* Edwin Morgan

Where are the braves, the faces like autumn fruit. Indian Reservation: Caughnawaga. Abraham Moses Klein. LiTM; NOBC; NoP-4

Where are the dear domestics, white and black. Familiar Faces, Long Departed. Robert Silliman Hillyer. NYBP

Where are the girls who were beautiful? Julia Alvarez. *See* He: Age doesn't matter when you're both in love.

Where Are the Hebrew Children? Peter Cartwright. AH

Where are the horses of the sun? The Charioteer of Delphi. James Merrill. GS; GrIP

Where Are the Men Seized in This Wind of Madness? Alda do Espírito Santo, *Portuguese.* PBMAP; TTY; WPOW, *tr. by* Alan Ryder

Where Are the Ones Who Lived Before?, *mod. English. Unknown. See* Ubi Sunt Qui ante Nos Fuerunt?

Where are the passions they essayed. Ballade of Dead Actors. William Ernest Henley. EBVV; OBMV

Where are the people as beautiful as poems. The Black Angel. Henri Coulette. CoAP; NYBP

Where are the poets, unto whom belong. Possibilities. Henry Wadsworth Longfellow. MeMAP

Where are the ribbons I tie my hair with? Ballade of Lost Objects. Phyllis McGinley. CRP; NBLV; PoRA

Where Are the War Poets? C. Day Lewis. FaBoMo; NoP-4; OBWP; OxBSP; OxBTC

Where Are the Waters of Childhood? Mark Strand. HCAP; LCAP-2; VCAP; WeW-3

Where are the women who, *entre deux guerres.* Ballad of Ladies Lost and Found. Marilyn Hacker. FFC; NMM-2; VCAP

Where are they? So the World Changes. Kofi Awoonor. VCWP

Where are they going, the crowds that pass in the street? Returning to the Port of Authority: A Picaresque. Constance Urdang. PBCAP

Where are they gone, the old familiar faces? The Old Familiar Faces. Charles Lamb. NOBRP; Ro

Where are they? I have never missed before. Leaves. "Michael Field." VWP

Where are those that were before us. *Unknown. See* Ubi Sunt Qui ante Nos Fuerunt?

Where are we. Bahamas. George Oppen. NYBP

Where are we going? where are we going. Song of Slaves in the Desert. John Greenleaf Whittier. APN-1; OxBA

Where are we to go when this is done? Sonnet. Alfred A. Duckett. PoBA

Where are you coming from, Lomey Carter. Old Christmas Morning. Roy Helton. MoAmPo

Where are you going. *Unknown.* BoTP

Where are you going? asked Manny the Mayor. Jig Tune: Not for Love. Thomas McGrath. VGW

Where Are You Going, Greatheart? John Oxenham. BLPA

Where are you going, Master mine? Whither Away? Mary Elizabeth Coleridge. CH

Where are you going [to], my pretty maid? The Milk Maid. Mother Goose. LB; OxNR; ReMoGo

Where Are You Going, My Pretty Maid. *Unknown.* NBLV

Where are you going now? Nellie Wong. IFJA

Where are you going through the streets of Rome. Roman Evening. Pier Paolo Pasolini, *Italian.* CLPP, *tr. by* Lawrence Ferlinghetti *and* Francesca Valente

Where are you going to-night, to-night. John Evereldown. Edwin Arlington Robinson. APN-2; CMoP; ColAP; MeMAP; NCAP; OxBA

Where are you going? To Scarborough Fair? Scarborough Fair. *Unknown.* OxBoLi; PeLV

Where are you going? Where aren't you going? Variation VI. Josef Hanzlik, *German.* CEEP, *tr. by* Ewald Osers

Where are you going, you little pig? The Little Piggies. Thomas Hood. BoTP

Where are you sleeping to-night, My Lad. John Oxenham. NSI

Where are your ancient waves, O river. Home-Coming. Albert Ehrenstein, *German.* TrJP, *tr. by* Babette Deutsch *and* Avrahm Yarmolinsky

Where are your fabled Doric beauty, the fringe. The Ruins of Corinth. Antipater of Sidon, *Greek.* GrAn, *tr. by* Peter Jay

Where are your heroes, my little black ones. Poem for Black Boys. Nikki Giovanni. BPo

Where are your monuments, your battles, martyrs? The Sea is History. Derek Walcott. OxBoS

Where are your oranges? The Children's Bells. Eleanor Farjeon. BoTP; CH

Where art thou, my beloved Son. Affliction of Margaret—, The. Wordsworth. GTBS-P; OxBSn; PoEL-4; RACG

Where art thou wandering, little child? The Little Maid and the Cowslips. John Clare. BoTP

Where, as a lordly dream. The Bridge. John Banister Tabb. APN-2

Where be you [*or* ye] going, you [*or* ye] Devon maid? Keats. CBLP; FHYEP

Where beeth[beth] they biforen[beforen] us weren. Ubi Sunt Qui ante Nos Fuerunt? [*or* Contempt of the World]. *Unknown.* EBEV; HAP; NoP-4; PoE; WeW-3

Where both he and I are the hunters. (LL) My Father's Wedding. Robert Bly. InPS-3; NoAM; RaBo

Where brown children are at play under pollarded willows. Trumpets. Georg Trakl, *German.* PeFWW, *tr. by* David McDuff *and* Jon Silkin

Where can I go. Captive's Song. *Unknown, Omaha Native American.* APN-2, *tr. by* Fannie Reed Giffen

Where can we buy wine? We ask. Mooring Our Boat at Tan-yang Harbor. Kao Ch'i, *Chinese.* CoBLCP, *tr. by* Jonathan Chaves

Where Cape Delgado strikes the sea. Edwin John Pratt. MoCV *Fr.* The Cachalot.

Where castles stood & grandeur died. (LL) The Flitting. John Clare. FaBoPV; OxAEP-2

Where clear air blew off the land. York Harbor Morning. George Garrett. M1

Where Coronado's men of old. Poppies of Wickenburg. Sharlot Mabridth Hall. PaTW

Where Cross the Crowded Ways of Life. Frank Mason North. AH

Where Cumbria's mountains in the north arise. James Plumptre. NOEC *Fr.* Prologue to "The Lakers; a Comic Opera."

Where death is waiting, dressed like an admiral. (LL) Nothing but Death. Pablo Neruda, *Spanish.* SPE, *tr. by* Robert Bly

Where deep in the night I hear a voice. (LL) Butcher Shop. Charles Simic. AF; AmPA; InPK-6; LCAP-2; NNaP

Where did I come from, Mother, and why? Christmas Lullaby for a New-Born Child. Yvonne Gregory. NOxBChV

Where did it roll in from, that sea of light. In Two Fields. Waldo Williams, *Welsh.* OBWVE, *tr. by* Gwyn Jones

Where did this tiger come from? Ballad of the Ferocious Tiger. Hsü Pen, *Chinese.* CoBLCP, *tr. by* Jonathan Chaves

Where did you borrow that last sigh. Song. Sir William Berkeley. OxBSP *Fr.* The Lost Lady.

Where did You Come From, Baby Dear? George Macdonald. ACTP *Fr.* At the Back of the North Wind.

(Baby, The.)

("God thought about you, and so I am here.") (LL) ACTP

Where did you come from, baby dear? Where did You Come From, Baby Dear? George Macdonald. ACTP; BLPA; OxBChV; WHSW *Fr.* At the Back of the North Wind.

Where did you get your bodies? The Dialogue. Vladimir Burich, *Russian.* TCRP, *tr. by* Katya Olmstead

Where dips the rocky highland. The Stolen Child. W. B. Yeats. CMoP; NAEL-2; NoP-4

Where Do School Days End? Josephine D. Henderson Heard. CBWP-4

Where do the gipsies come from? Sir Henry Howarth Bashford. CH

Where do the roots go? The Pit. Theodore Roethke. NAAL-2 *Fr.* The Lost Son. HAP; HCAP; LiTM; VGW

Where do we live? Variations for Two Voices. Roberta Hill Whiteman. HATNAP

Where do you go vision without me through my dreams. The Swing over the Calm Source of Our Names. Milorad Pavic, *Serbo-Croatian.* HSix, *tr. by* Charles Simic

Where do you go with your fury. Fury's Field. Cecil Bodker, *Danish*. PBWP, *tr. by* Nadia Christensen

Where do you keep your armies, O Wind God? The Storm. Nguyễn Đình Chiểu, *Vietnamese*. AVP, *tr. by* Huỳnh Sanh Thông

Where do you think I've been to-day? The Pigeon's Story. Jeannie Kirby. BoTP

Where do you think you're going, bunch of fools? Scolding Some Dunces. Ho Xuan Huong, *Vietnamese*. AVP, *tr. by* Huỳnh Sanh Thông

Where Does My Sadness Come From? Kao Ch'i, *Chinese*. CoBLCP, *tr. by* Jonathan Chaves

Where does the dragon-ox display its imposing form. Hsü Wei. *Fr.* Songs of Yen-ching. CoBLCP, *tr. by* Jonathan Chaves

Where does the stream carry my small face? The Girl Sings to the Stream. Leah Goldberg. MHP, *tr. by* Ruth Finer Mintz *Fr.* Songs of the Stream.

Where does this poem come from? Edouard J. Maunick. NegPo, *tr. by* Ellen Conroy Kennedy *Fr.* As Far as Yoruba Land.

Where does this tenderness come from? Marina Tsvetayeva, *Russian*. LoP, *tr. by* Elaine Feinstein

Where dost [*or* do'st] thou careless[e] lie. An Ode To Himself. Ben Jonson. BeJo; CABP; HAP; NOBE; NOSC; NoP-4; OxAEP-1; PBRV; PoEL-2; SCGP; SeCP

Where dost thou lie, great Nimrod of the West! Richard Henry Wilde. APN-1 *Fr.* Hesperia.

Where down the blind are driven. (LL) Eros Turannos. Edwin Arlington Robinson. CMoP; GBL; GLoP; HAP; HeIP-4; LiTM; MeMAP; MoAmPo; MoP; NAAL-2; NOBA; NoAM; NoP-4; OxBA; PoA; PoE; PoPoPo; Poetr; TAP; TFi; TRP

Where dubbed commercials / sell the tobacco and alcohol. When Songs Become Water. Martín Espada. AFr

Where dwell the lovely, wild white womenfolk. The White Women. Mary Elizabeth Coleridge. BrRo; NALW; PEW; VWP

Where-e'er My Flatt'ring Passions Rove. Isaac Watts. NOCV

Where ends our chancel in a vaulted space. The Vicar. George Crabbe. OBSV *Fr.* The Borough.

Where Engels Fears to Tread. Cyril Connolly.
 "Come on Percy, my pillion-proud, be." OBCoV
 "It was late last night when my lord came home." OBCoV
 "M is for Marx." OBCoV
 "Something is going to go, baby." OBCoV

Where England's Damon used [*or* us'd] to keep. Pastoral on the King's Death, The; [Written in 1648]. Alexander Brome. NOSC

Where e're they met, or parting place has been. (LL) Lovers How They Come and Part. Robert Herrick. GBL; OxBSP; OxBoLi; PoEL-3

Where every female delights to give her maiden to her husband. Male & Female Loves in Beulah. William Blake. OBNC *Fr.* Jerusalem; The Emanation of the Giant Albion.

Where every passion wars itself with legions. (LL) Love's Glory. Greville Fulke. PoEL-1; Son

Where fair Sabrina's wand'ring currents flow. William Somervile. NOEC *Fr.* The Bowling-Green.

Where Fire Burns. Gladys Cardiff. HATNAP

Where Fishermen Can't Swim. Matthew Sweeney. BiHa

Where folds the central lotus. William Yeats in Limbo. Sidney Keyes. MoBrPo

Where fools with ease go in and out? Sir John Suckling. *See* Upon My Lady Carlisle's [*or* Carlile's] Walking in Hampton Court Garden.

Where / from / here. 2 B BLK. Val Ferdinand. NBV

Where from the watch towers. Bay Poem. Lance Henson. VoR

Where Gallowgate meets London Road. Heraclitus at Glasgow Cross. Gerald Mangan. FaBoTC

Where gather mists and clouds, a happy world. Đào Duy Tù', *Vietnamese*. AVP, *tr. by* Huỳnh Sanh Thông

Where gentle Thames through stately channels glides. The Playhouse. Joseph Addison. ECEV

Where go the birds when the rain. Jane Heap. PoA

Where Go the Boats? Robert Louis Stevenson. CTV; FaBoBe; FaBoCh; NOxBChV; NTCP; NTP; OxBChV; TLR; WHSW

Where goats are slaughtered. Murukaṉ: His Places. Nakkiranar, *Tamil*. PLW, *tr. by* A. K. Ramanujan

Where good and evil dwell. Crickety Creek. Arkady Kutilov, *Russian*. TCRP, *tr. by* Bradley Jordan

Where had I heard this wind before. Bereft. Robert Frost. LiTM; MoAmPo; OxBA; SAGP; SoSe-8

Where hae ye been a' the day. *Unknown*. OxNR

Where has he been of race divine. Chorus of Satyrs, Driving Their Goats. Euripides. AWP *Fr.* The Cyclops.

Where has spring returned to? Tune: "Pure Serene Music." Huang T'ing-chien, *Chinese*. SuSp, *tr. by* James J. Y. Liu

Where has tenderness gone, he asked the mirror. Delirium in Vera Cruz. Malcolm Lowry. FaBoTw; NoP-4; OxBTC *Fr.* The Cantinas.

Where hast been toiling all day, sweetheart. The Child on the Judgment Seat. Elizabeth Rundle Charles. BLPA

Where hast thou been, sister? Thunder. Enter the three Witches. Shakespeare. OxBSn *Fr.* Macbeth.

Where have all the colours gone? The Darkening Garden. *Unknown*. BoTP

Where have all the flowers gone?—long time passing. Pete Seeger. NoP-4

Where have I wander'd, London, from thy haunts? Charles Lloyd. NOBRP *Fr.* Desultory Thoughts in London.

Where have these hands been. Musician. Louise Bogan. NYBP

Where Have They Gone? Võ Phiến, *Vietnamese*. AVP, *tr. by* Huỳnh Sanh Thông

Where have they led you, into what disguise. The Kingdom. Jon Swan. NYBP

Where have ye [*or* you] been all the day, / Billy Boy? *Unknown*. *See* Billy Boy.

Where have you been. Banbury Fair. Edith G. Millard. BoTP

Where have you been all the day, Billy boy, Billy boy? *Unknown*. OxNR

Where Have You Been Dear? Karla Kuskin. NTCP

Where have you been, South Wind, this May-day morning? South Wind. Siegfried Sassoon. BoTP

Where have you been this long time. Axle Song. Mairtin O Direain. BiHa

Where Have You Gone? Mari E. Evans. BPo; SAGP; TTY
 ("In another.") (LL) SAGP

Where Have You Gone, Little Boy. Patty L. Harjo. VoR

Where have you gone to, Yesterday. Yesterday. Hugh Chesterman. BoTP

Where have you hidden away. The Spiritual Canticle. Saint John of the Cross, *Spanish*. STV, *tr. by* John Frederick Nims

Where he stood and where. Jew. James A. Randall Jr. BPo

Where he was standing leaning against a statue. With a face charged with. Aleksandr Vvedensky, *Russian*. TCRP, *tr. by* Robin Milner-Gulland

Where His Lady Keeps His Heart. "A. W." CTC

Where Hurricane. LeRoy Clarke. PBCV

Where I Came From. Ruth Stone. NAmP90

Where I cling. (LL) The Last Leaf. Oliver Wendell Holmes. AmPP; FaBoBe; NAAL-1; NAAL-3; PWR; PoLF

Where I come from we have no snow. Nochebuena. Rosario Caicedo. LoHo

Where I could think of no thoroughfare. Were I in Trouble. Robert Frost. OxBSP *Fr.* Five Nocturnes.

Where I defy, and challenge, all thy utmost love. (LL) The Author Apologizes to a Lady, for His Being a Little Man. Christopher Smart. BoLoP; CBLP

Where I gaze. Tune: "Jade Butterflies." Liu Yung, *Chinese*. SuSp, *tr. by* Jerome P. Seaton

Where I go are flowers blooming. Les Planches-en-Montagnes. Michael Roberts. OBMV

Where I Live. Wesley McNair. TRP

Where I live, there are more. Scarecrows. James Kirkup. NOxBChV

Where I made one—turn down an empty Glass. (LL) Awake! for morning in the bowl of night. Omar Khayyám. EBEV; GTBS-P; PeVV, *sect.* I–XII; EBEvV; NOBVV; OxAEP-2; TAL; UV

Where I may not remove nor be removed. (LL) Sonnet 25. Shakespeare. OxAEP-1; SCGP

Where I shall need no glass. (LL) Friends Departed. Henry Vaughan. CABP; CH; ESCV; FMP; GeHe; ImPo; InPS-3; MeLP; NAEL-1; NOBE; NOCV; NOSC; NoP-4; OAEL-1; OBEV; PBRV; PeECV; PoEL-2; PoPoPo; SCGP; SeCP; TFi

Where icy and bright dungeons lift. Hart Crane. ColAP; HAP; MoAmPo; UnPo *Fr.* Voyages. CMoP; MeMAP; NOBA; NoAM; TAP

Where / if it's not too much to ask. Catullus. *See* Carmen 55.

Where if you glance behind. James Dean. Rae Desmond Jones. BMAP

Where ignorant armies clash by night. (LL) Dover Beach. Matthew Arnold. APAD; AWP; BLPA; CABP; CIHu; EBVV; EBVVPR; FaBoBe; GTBS-P; HAP; HeIP-4; HoPM; ImPo; InPK-6; InPS-3; NAEL-2; NIP-4; NOBE; NOBVV; NoP-4; OAEL-2; OBNC; OxBoS; PBMP; PFE; PeVV; PoE; PoEL-5; PoPoPo; PoRA; SAGP; SCGP; SCV; TFi; TOF

Where in blind files. Song. Eavan Boland. CIP-2; IIP

Where in the summer-warm woodlands with the sweet wind. Iphione. Thomas Caulfield Irwin. EnLoPo

Where, in what bubbly land, below. Ballade of Dead Gentlemen. C. S. Lewis. OBCoV

Where in what ever-blissfully watered gardens, upon what trees. Rilke. OBVE, *tr. by* James Blair Leishman *Fr.* Sonnets to Orpheus.

Where innocent bright-eyed daisies are. Christina Rossetti. Spl

Where is a foot worthy to walk a garden. Jelaluddin Rumi. RaBo, *tr. by* Coleman Barks *and* John Moyne *Fr.* Four Quatrains.

Where is all the bright company gone. Song. Dame Edith Sitwell. NALW

Where is all, there all should be. (LL) The Invitation. George Herbert. ChIV-1; ESCV

Where is another sweet as my sweet. The Letter. Tennyson. TTTS

Where is David?. . . Oh God's people. In Which Roosevelt Is Compared to Saul. Vachel Lindsay. ChIV-1

Where is dew? Where is sand? Where the moon? Where a star? Judith. Gertrud Kolmar, German. AF, tr. by David Kipp

Where Is He? Mother Goose. OxNR

Where is he, the wood pecker? The Woodpecker. Ni Tsan, Chinese. CoBLCP, tr. by Jonathan Chaves

Where is it now? Look, there it flies in merry sport. The Swallow's Flight. Louis Levy, Danish. TrJP, tr. by Martin S. Alwood and Sanford Kaufman

Where is it, the sad lyre which follows the quick flute? Li Shang-yin, Chinese. PLT, tr. by A. C. Graham

Where is McKinley, that respectable McKinley. Vachel Lindsay. Fr. Bryan, Bryan, Bryan, Bryan. CMoP; MeMAP; OxBA; OxBoLi

Where is my bay? Bring it, Thestylis. Where are my charms? Theocritus. See The Enchantment.

Where is my Chief, my Master, this bleak night, mavrone! O'Hussey's Ode to the Maguire. Eochadh O'Hussey, Irish. CABP; NOIV, tr. by James Clarence Mangan

Where is my country? Nellie Wong. UnSA

Where is my love. Love Lies Here. Walter De la Mare. LBC

Where is my lover and my friend? An Elegiac Ballad. Hannah Cowley. ECWP

Where is my ruined life, and where the fame. Hafiz. AWP; TAL, tr. by Gertrude Lowthian Bell Fr. Odes.

Where is neither faith nor wonder. (LL) Song with Words. James Agee. ChIV-1; MoAmPo

Where is now Elijah's God? A Martyr's Death. Menahem ben Jacob, Hebrew. TrJP

Where Is Our Holy Church? Edwin H. Wilson. AH

Where is poor Jesus gone? Jesus. Francis Lauderdale Adams. OxBS

Where is Praxiteles where. Rufinus, Greek. GrAn, tr. by Alan Marshfield

Where is that holy fire, which Verse is said. Sapho To Philaenis. Donne. RACG Fr. Elegies.

Where is that sugar, Hammond. Early Evening Quarrel. Langston Hughes. SAmP; UnPo

Where is the angel for me to wrestle? Denise Levertov. PmAP

Where is the arbiter of a thousand languages? When My Poems were Lost. Raymond Mazisi Kunene, Zulu. PeSAV, tr. by the author

Where is the bird? Rachel Blau DuPlessis. DeD Fr. Eurydice.

Where is the duke my father with his power? Shakespeare. OxAEP-1 Fr. King Richard III.

Where is the gallant race that rose. Thomas Mercer. OxBS Fr. Arthur's Seat.

Where is the grave of Sir Arthur O'Kellyn? The Knight's Tomb. Coleridge. FaBoCh; RB

Where is the hand to trace. With a Coin from Syracuse. Oliver St. John Gogarty. OBMV

Where is the home for me? The Home of Aphrodite. Euripides. AWP, tr. by Gilbert Murray Fr. Bacchae.

Where is the Jim Crow section. Merry-Go-Round. Langston Hughes. SAmP

Where is the man who has been tried and found strong and sound? A Degenerate Age. Solomon ibn Gabirol, Hebrew. TrJP, tr. by Emma Lazarus

Where is the nightingale. Hilda Doolittle. MoAmPo, sect. 2 Fr. Songs from Cyprus.

Where is the nymph, whose azure eye. Song. Thomas Moore. EnLoPo

Where is the promise of my years. Infelix. Adah Isaacs Menken. AAP; CBWP-1; PAR

Where is the star of Bethlehem? Christmas 1959 et Cetera. Gerald William Barrax. PChr

"Where is the world!" cries Young at eighty. Byron. FaBoPV Fr. Canto the Eleventh. NOBRP Fr. Don Juan.

Where is the world? not about. Merchant Marine. Josephine Miles. TAP; VGW

Where is the world we roved, Ned Bunn? To Ned. Herman Melville. APN-2; NAAL-1; NAAL-3; NOBA; PAR; PoEL-5

Where is this beautiful song being sung. Hearing a Song from My Boat. Chang Yü, Chinese. CoBLCP, tr. by Jonathan Chaves

Where is this stupendous stranger. The Nativity of Our Lord. Christopher Smart. EBEV; HAP; NOBE; NOCV; NOEC; PoEL-3; SCGP Fr. Hymns and Spiritual Songs for the Fasts and Festivals of the Church of England.

Where is your famous beauty. Antipater of Thessalonica, Greek. PGA, tr. by Kenneth Rexroth

Where Israel's tents do shine so bright. (LL) Mock on, Mock on Voltaire, Rousseau. William Blake. ChIV-1; HAP; ImPo; NAEL-2; NAWM-2; NoP-4; OAEL-2; OBNC; OxBSP; PFE; PeECV; PoE; PoEL-4; SCGP; TFi; UnPo

Where It Ends. William Bronk. APSN

Where it says snow. Errata. Charles Simic. NNaP

Where it stands in the wind. House in Spring. Wesley McNair. AFr; CMAP

Where it will break at last. (LL) The Indian Serenade. Shelley. AWP; CBLP; FaBoBe; GTBS-P; HoPM; ImPo; NAEL-2; OBEV; RaBo; TTTS

Where It's At. A. L. Hendriks. HCP

Where it's rubbed out, start there, where it's torn. Girl Tearing Up Her Face. Susan Mitchell. BAP-96

Where joy has been forgot and hope has fled. (LL) I cease not from desire till my desire. Hafiz. AWP; TAL, tr. by Gertrude Lowthian Bell

Where Knock Is Open Wide. Theodore Roethke. HAP; VGW

Where labor beckons and where peace abounds, sl. diff. vers. Aleksandr Blok. See The Scythians.

Where laurel hedges hide the coal and coke. Crematorium. John Betjeman. PoA

Where Lie All the Slain. Harry Morris. CRP

Where lies the land to which the ship would go? Mari Magno II. Arthur Hugh Clough. NTP Fr. Songs in Absence.

Where lies the Land to which yon Ship must go? Wordsworth. OBNC; PoEL-4

Where lies the truth? has man, in wisdom's creed. Wordsworth. TrCP

Where light is. To a Woman Who Wants Darkness and Time. Gerald William Barrax. PoBA

Where, like a pillow on a bed. The Ecstasy. Donne. BoLoP; CABP; CBLP; ESCV; EnLoPo; FHYEP; FMP; FSCP; GLoP; HAP; ImPo; InPS-3; LoP; MeLP; NAEL-1; NOBE; NoP-4; OAEL-1; OBEV; PoE; PoEL-2; SeCP; TFi; TOF

Where, like the prophet, thou shalt find thy God. (LL) To the Right Honourable William, Earl of Dartmouth[, His Majesty's Principal Secretary of State for North America]. Phillis Wheatley. AmPP; CrDW; NAAAL; NALW

Where Lincoln's Inn, wide space, is railed around. John Gay. ECEV Fr. Trivia; or, The Art of Walking the Streets of London.

Where lives the man that never yet did hear. Orchestra; or, A Poem[e] of Da[u]ncing. Sir John Davies. NoSic; SiPS

Where long the shadows of the wind had rolled. The Sheaves. Edwin Arlington Robinson. AWP; CMoP; HAP; ImGa; MoAmPo; MoP; NOBA; NoAM; OxBA; Poetr; SoSe-8; TAP

Where marble stood and fell. Reflection in a Green Arena. Gregory Corso. VGW

Where metalled road invades light thinning air. Sándor Weöres. OBVE Fr. The Lost Parasol.

Where might there be a refuge for me. Tell Me, Tell Me. Marianne Moore. LiTM; NYBP

Where most she works when we perceive her least. (LL) To Wordsworth. Hartley Coleridge. Ro; Son

Where Mountain Lion Lay [or Laid] Down with Deer. Leslie Marmon Silko. ImGa; Poetr; TRP; VoR; WPOW

Where music and moonlight and feeling / Are one. (LL) To Jane ("The Keen stars were twinkling"). Shelley. FHYEP

Where My Books Go. W. B. Yeats. OBEV

Where my grandfather is is in the ground. Mi Abuelo. Alberto A. Ríos. PoPoPo

Where my grandmother lived. Number Four. Doughtry Long. MBE; PoBA

Where my Sun-flower wishes to go. (LL) Ah Sun-flower. William Blake. AWP; EBEV; FHYEP; HAP; ImPo; NIP-4; NOBRP; NOEC; NoP-4; OAEL-2; OBNC; PoE; PoEL-4; PoPoPo; RB; SCGP; TFi; TOF; UnPo; WeW-3

Where Nature such dilemmas could devise. (LL) Her Dilemma. Thomas Hardy. EnVR; NOBVV

Where neither King nor shepheard want comes neare. Homer. CTC, tr. by George Chapman Fr. Odyssey. NAWM-1, tr. by Robert Fitzgerald

Where no one was was where my world was stilled. Isle of Arran. Alastair Reid. FaBoTC

Where no sad songs are sung. (LL) Big rat, big rat. Unknown, Chinese. ChiPo, tr. by Arthur Waley

Where not so long ago the breezes stirred. A Fall of Rock. William Plomer. PeSAV

Where Nothing Dwelt but Beasts of Prey. Isaac Watts. AH

Where nothing is diminished by perspective. Les A. Murray. See Equanimity.

Where Now Are the Hebrew Children? Unknown. AH

Where now / are time and space. Wind Gardens. Louis Untermeyer. BXAP

Where now these mingled ruins lie. Stanzas Occasioned by the Ruins of a Country Inn *or* On the Ruins of a Country Inn. Philip Freneau. OxBA

Where O Where Is Old Elijah. *Unknown.* AS

Where, O! where's the chain to fling. Song. Letitia Elizabeth Landon. NOBRP *Fr.* The Golden Violet.

Where of old, responsive. Echoes. John Banister Tabb. APN-2

Where, Oh Where Are the Hebrew Children? *Unknown.* BLPA

Where olive leaves are twinkling in every wind that blew. The Damsel of Peru. William Cullen Bryant. APN-1

Where on earth. The Question of Time. William Peskett. PNI

Where on the wrinkled stream the willows lean. The Water-Ousel. Mary Webb. CH

Where once my ancestors grubbed for the fern's root. Ancestors. Rowley Habib. PeNZ

Where once Three Graces stood. Callimachus, *Greek.* InMo, *tr. by* Sam Hamill

Where once we danced, where once we sang. An Ancient to Ancients. Thomas Hardy. CMoP; GTBS-P; LiTM; OxBTC; SCGP

Where one needs one's brains all the time. (LL) The Lake Isle. Ezra Pound. OBCoV; OxBSP; PoA

Where only flowers fret. Aegean. Louis Simpson. NYBP

Where or When. Philip Whalen. PoM

Where others love, and praise my Verses; still. To the Detracter. Robert Herrick. PBRV

Where oxen do low and apples do grow. Dialogue, between Crab and Gillian. Thomas D'Urfey. NOEC *Fr.* The Bath; or, The Western Lass.

Where people have dined you find refuse and tin. The Potter of Jaen. Ilya Grigoryevich Ehrenburg, *Russian.* TCRP, *tr. by* Cathy Porter

Where praise already is is the only place Grief. Rilke. RaBo, *tr. by* Robert Bly *Fr.* Sonnets to Orpheus.

Where racial memories, like snakes. Landscape of Violence. Ralph Nixon Currey. PeSA

Where run your colts at pasture? White Horses. Rudyard Kipling. PeVV

Where sea and land meet, begin there. I. Philip Nanton. HCP

Where Seed Falls. Essex Hemphill. GT

Where, selfwrung, selfstrung, sheathe-and shelterless, thóughts agáinst thoughts ín groans grínd. (LL) Spelt from Sibyl's Leaves. Gerard Manley Hopkins. CMoP; EnVR; FaBoMo; LiTM; NOBVV; OAEL-2; TOF

Where shall Celia fly for shelter. Song. Christopher Smart. EnLoPo

Where shall I gang, my ain true love? The Duke of Athole's Nurse. *Unknown.* ESPB

Where shall I have at mine own will. Sir Thomas Wyatt. SiPS

Where shall I lead the flocks to-day? Where the Flocks Shall Be Led. Adah Isaacs Menken. CBWP-1

Where Shall The Baby's Dimple Be. Josiah Gilbert Holland. BLPA

Where shall the eyes a darkness find. Huw Menai. OBWVE *Fr.* Back in the Return.

Where shall the lover rest. Fitz-Eustace's Song. Sir Walter Scott. CH; GTBS-P; NOBRP; PoEL-4 *Fr.* Marmion.

Where shall we find a Muse like thine, that can. William Cartwright. EPCY *Fr.* In the Memory of the Most Worthy Benjamin Jonson.

Where shall we go? The Hounded Lovers. William Carlos Williams. NYBP

Where shall we go? where shall we go? June Fugue. Thomas William Shapcott. NOBAu

Where she lived the close remained the best. The Way a Ghost Dissolves. Richard Hugo. NAAL-2; NoAM; NoP-4

Where she, of all the plains of Britain that doth bear. Michael Drayton. NOSC *Fr.* Polyolbion.

Where should I seat you, where. Hymn. Márton Kalász, *Hungarian.* CEEP, *tr. by* Jascha Kessler

Where silent, unrefractive whiteness lies. (LL) Stories of Snow. Patricia K. Page. NOBC; NoP-4; PoA

Where some murdered man must be. (LL) The Sea-Side Cave. Alice Cary. APN-2; ColAP

Where Somnus' temple rises from a ground. Laudanum. *Unknown.* NOEC

Where sunless rivers weep. Dream Land. Christina Rossetti. BrRo

Where Sydney Cove her lucid bosom swells. Visit of Hope to Sydney Cove, near Botany-Bay. Erasmus Darwin. ECEV; NOEC

Where tadpoles are never allowed to grow into frogs! (LL) On Being Asked to Write a Poem for 1979. Jack A. Mapanje. AF; PBMAP

Where the acorn tumbles down. The Fieldmouse. Cecil Frances Alexander. CTAV; OxBChV

Where the afternoon sun blears the city. O My Invisible Estate. Bruce Smith. Son

Where the air is full of sunlight and the flag is full of stars. (LL) America for Me. Henry Van Dyke. BLPA; ChAP

Where the bee sucks, there suck I. Ariel's Song: "Where the bee sucks, there suck I." Shakespeare. AWP; BoTP; CH; CTC; EBEvV; NAEL-1; NBLV; NOBE; NoP-4; NoSic; OBEV; OxBSP; SCGP; TFi; TTTS *Fr.* The Tempest. OAEL-1

Where the bishop groans to view him. (LL) Rich and Poor; or, Saint and Sinner. Thomas Love Peacock. NOBE; NOBL; OBSV; PeLV

Where the blood pours out the dead come to the feast. (LL) In Memoriam. Martin Johnston. BMAP; NOBAu

Where the buttercups so sweet. The Little Herd-Boy's Song. Robert Williams Buchanan. BoTP

Where the cedar leaf divides the sky. Passage. Hart Crane. CMoP; NOBA; PoE

Where the Cedars. Jacob Glatstein, *Yiddish.* TrJP, *tr. by* Joseph Leftwich

Where the city's ceaseless crowd moves on the livelong day. Sparkles from the Wheel. Walt Whitman. InPS-3; NAAL-1; NAAL-3; SAmP

Where the Corrib river chops through the Claddagh. The Last Galway Hooker. Richard Murphy. PBCIP

Where the coyote called. Foster Jewell. HA

Where the dawn has that *particular* laughter. (LL) You Also, Gaius Valerius Catullus. Archibald MacLeish. NoAM; TAP

Where the Dead Men Lie. Barcroft Henry Boake. CBAP

Where the dire Circle keeps its station. Cold Ceremony. Hannah More. ECWP *Fr.* Bas Bleu, The; or, Conversation.

Where the Flocks Shall Be Led. Adah Isaacs Menken. CBWP-1

Where the flowers and trees grow dense. Tune: "Ripples Sifting Sand"— Accompanying My Husband on a Spring Outing to Stone Pavilion. Ku T'ai-ch'ing, *Chinese.* SuSp, *tr. by* Irving Y. Lo

Where the Fu-sang tree grows. Song of Heavenly Ascent. Ts'ao Chih, *Chinese.* SuSp, *tr. by* Ronald C. Miao

Where the Great Northern plunged in. The Wreck of the Great Northern. Robert Hedin. GM

Where the Hayfields Were. Archibald MacLeish. AFr

Where the Heart Is. Ntozake Shange. GT

Where the heart reflects. (LL) Strains of Sight. Robert Duncan. CMoP; PoE

Where the Honey Speech's Hedge. Peter Cole. PT

Where the icebergs break in splinters. The Fungus Fingers. Wes Magee. SpW

Where the lighthouse breaks. (LL) Six Ten Sixty-Nine. Conyus. GT

Where the Lilies Used to Spring. David Gray. OxBS

Where the Lilies Were in Flower. Kumattur Kannanar, *Tamil.* PLW, *tr. by* A. K. Ramanujan

Where the living with effort go. The White Ship. Geoffrey Hill. OxBC

Where the lizard ran to its little prey. The Range in the Desert. Randall Jarrell. NOBA; PoWW

Where the Mississippi meets the Amazon. Ntozake Shange. ISC

Where the mob gathers, swiftly shoot along. Pickpockets. John Gay. ECEV; OAEL-1 *Fr.* Trivia; or, The Art of Walking the Streets of London.

Where the Moosatockmaguntic. The Ballad of Hiram Hover. Bayard Taylor. BXAP; OBAL

Where the mountain hare has lain. (LL) Memory. W. B. Yeats. APAD; BIrV; PoE

Where the noisy flowers are deepest, a storied building. Tune: "Water Dragon's Chant"—Loathsome Spring. Ch'en Liang, *Chinese.* SuSp, *tr. by* Hellmut Wilhelm

Where the old cow at her leisure chews her cud. (LL) Birds' Nests. John Clare. OAEL-2; OxBSP

Where the old trees reign with their forward dark. Provinces. C. D. Wright. LCAP-2

Where the Picnic Was. Thomas Hardy. OxBTC

Where the pipe ends he had fixed the long trough. Windmill At Mandanthanunguna. Pambardu, *Aborigine.* NOBAu, *tr. by* Georg von Brandenstein

Where—the place of concatenations. Nostoi. Rodolfo Di Biasio, *Italian.* NeIt, *tr. by* Stephen Sartarelli

Where the pools are bright and deep. A Boy's Song. James Hogg. BoTP; CH; CTV; FaPoR; NOxBChV; OBEV; OTCP; OxAEP-2; OxBChV

Where the quiet-coloured [*or* colored] end of evening smiles. Love among the Ruins. Robert Browning. EnVR; FHYEP; HAP; NAEL-2; NOBE; OAEL-2; OBEV; PoEL-5; SCGP

Where the racing Wairau slows, homesick for its snowshed. Cloudy Bay. Eileen Duggan. PeNZ

Where the Rainbow Ends. Robert Lowell. HCAP; MoAmPo

Where the Rainbow Ends. Richard Rive. PBA; TTY

Where the Red Lion flaring o'er the way. A Description of an Author's Bedchamber. Oliver Goldsmith. BIrV

Where the remote *Bermudas* ride. Bermudas. Andrew Marvell. APAD; AWP; CH; ESCV; FHYEP; FMP; FaBoCh; GTBS-P; GeHe; NAEL-1;

NOBE; NOCV; NOSC; NoP-4; OBEV; PBRV; PFE; PeECV; PoE; RB; SCGP; SeCP; TFi

Where the Rhine loses his majestic force. Migrating Birds. James Thomson. APo

Where the road turns to water. Cross Country. Rod Moran. NOBAu

Where the rue de la Verrerie. The St Merri district. Robert Desnos, *French.* MFP, *tr. by* Martin Sorrell

Where the sally tree went pale in every breeze. Field Work. Seamus Heaney. CBLP

Where the sea gulls sleep or indeed where they fly. The Ballet of the Fifth Year. Delmore Schwartz. OxBA; TwCP

Where the slow river. Leda. Hilda Doolittle. NAAL-2

Where the Song Went Where She Went & What Happened When They Met. *Unknown, Seneca Indian.* STP, *tr. by* Jerome Rothenberg *and* Richard Johnny John

Where the straight road had been lost sight of. Dante. *See* The Dark Wood.

Where the Sun Ends. Peter Davison. ChIV-1

Where the sun rises. Song of the Rising Sun Dance. *Unknown.* APN-2, *tr. by* Washington Matthews *Fr.* The Mountain Chant.

Where the swan drifts upon a darkening flood. (LL) Coole Park and Ballylee, 1931. W. B. Yeats. CMoP; GTBS-P; NOIV; NoAM; OBGa; OBMV

Where the thistle lifts a purple crown. Daisy. Francis Thompson. AWP; MoBrPo; OBEV; OBNC

Where the waters gently flow. The Song of the Reed Sparrow. *Unknown.* OxBChV

Where the waves break. (LL) Signature for Tempo. Archibald MacLeish. CRP; VGW

Where the Weather Suits My Clothes. John Godfrey. PmAP

Where the western zun, unclouded. Zun-zet. William Barnes. PoEL-4

Where the wheel of light is turned. Pole Star for This Year. Archibald MacLeish. MeMAP, OxBA

Where the wheel turned the water / gently shirred. (LL) The Event. Rita Dove. CMAP; NoAM

Where the wife is scouring the frying pan. Land of Little Sticks, 1945. James Tate. LCAP-2; WeT

Where the wind. Footprints on the Glacier. W. S. Merwin. MoP; NoAM

Where the wind glitters. (LL) Suddenly. Robin Blaser. FTOS

Where the wings of a sunny Dome expand. America. Herman Melville. APN-2

Where the young river, from its wild ravine. The Emigrant's Cabin. Thomas Pringle. PeSAV

Where then shall hope and fear their objects find? An Additional Poem. John Ashbery. FaBoMo

Where then shall Hope and Fear their objects find? The Power of Prayer. Samuel Johnson. NOBE *Fr.* The Vanity of Human Wishes [The Tenth Satire of Juvenal Imitated]. EBEV; ECEV; NOEC; OAEL-1; OxAEP-1; PoEL-3; TFi

Where there is neither. On Mumonkan. Toki Zenmaro, *Japanese.* MJT, *tr. by* Makoto Ueda

Where there is personal liking we go. The Hero. Marianne Moore. CMoP; NOBA; OxBA; PoA *Fr.* Part of a Novel, Part of a Poem, Part of a Play.

Where There's a Will There's a Way. Eliza Cook. BLPA

Where there's one we love to meet us! (LL) Home Is Where There Is One to Love Us. Charles Swain. BLPA; FaBoBe; PoToHe

Where there's room and bread for the poor. (LL) The Orphan Girl. *Unknown.* AS; AmFP

Where they cracked bottles merrily. (LL) The Bold Pedlar and Robin Hood. *Unknown.* AmFP; ESPB

Where they once dug for money. The Old Marlborough Road. Henry David Thoreau. PoEL-4

Where They Were. *Unknown.* AS

Where they will bury me. Temporarily in Oxford. Anne Stevenson. NoP-4

Where this is freedom: free to follow each desire. Freedom. Friedrich von Logau, *German.* GePo, *tr. by* George C. Schoolfield

Where this jolly babe was baptized. (LL) Robin Hood and Little John. *Unknown.* AmFP; ESPB

Where this train stops not even the engineer knows. Fuego. Dionisio D. Martinez. WWSi

Where thou dwellest, in what Grove. The Birds. William Blake. CH

Where, thy true treasure? Gold says, 'Not in me'. Edward Young. OAEL-1 *Fr.* Night Thoughts.

Where to? what next? (LL) The People, Yes. Carl Sandburg. MoAmPo; NOBA; NoAM; OxBA; SAGP

Where tomorrow he will try and fail his license to live. (LL) Learning Experience. Marge Piercy. NoAM; WeT

Where tongues were loud and hearts were light. The Ancre at Hamel: Afterwards. Edmund Blunden. PeFWW

Where trees are actual and take no holiday. (LL) Robinson. Weldon Kees. MoP; NYBP

Where true love is not given. (LL) Dead Love. Elizabeth Siddal. LW; NOBVV

Where, twining subtle fears with hope. Andrew Marvell. *Fr.* An Horatian Ode upon Cromwell's Return from Ireland. CABP; EBEV; ESCV; FMP; GTBS-P; GeHe; HAP; IIP; InPS-3; NOBE; NOSC; OAEL-1; OBEV; OBWP; OxAEP-1; PoEL-2; SCGP; SeCP; TFi

Where unincarnate spirits purely aspire! (LL) To George Sand: A Recognition. Elizabeth Barrett Browning. BoWoP; NAEL-2; NALW; PEW; VWP

Where Venta's Norman castle still appears. On King Arthur's Round Table, at Winchester. Thomas, the Younger Warton. Son

Where virtue's force can cause her to obey. (LL) On Fortune. Elizabeth I, Queen of England. PBWP; WPE

Where voices vanish into dream. Elected Silence. Siegfried Sassoon. MoBrPo

Where was it one first heard of the truth? The the. (LL) The Man on the Dump. Wallace Stevens. HAP; NAWM-2; NoAM

Where was you last winter, boys. The Horse Trader's Song. *Unknown.* AmFP

Where wast thou when I laid the foundations of the earth? Bible, *O.T. Fr.* Then the Lord Answered ("Who is this that darkeneth counsel by words without knowledge?"). AWP *Fr.* Job. NAWM-1

Where We Are. Julia Kasdorf. LoHo

Where we are, and at what speed: I know. The Steadying. William Heyen. BAP-96

Where we are the flowers in our clocks flare up their feathers ring the. The Great Lament of my Obscurity Three. Tristan Tzara, *French.* PFTM, *tr. by* Jerome Rothenberg

Where we had stood. Wilpena Pound. Charles Buckmaster. BMAP

Where we live, the teakettle whistles out. Now. William Stafford. NNaP

Where we made the fire. Where the Picnic Was. Thomas Hardy. OxBTC

Where we went in the boat was a long bay. The Mediterranean. Allen Tate. FaBoMo; FuPo; HAP; ImPo; LiTM; MoAmPo; VGW

Where we were walking in the day's light, seeing. Conrad Potter Aiken. *Fr.* Time in the Rock [or, Preludes to Definition]. VGW

Where were the greenhouses going. Big Wind. Theodore Roethke. AmPP; CMoP; ColAP; TRP; VGW

Where were we in that afternoon? And where. Anniversary. Richmond Lattimore. NYBP

Where were you bound for, unknown man. The Journey. Igor Bobrowsky. CDa

Where were you then? A Story. Margaret Avison. MoCV

Where? What? and turn away. (LL) A Sketch. Christina Rossetti. GTBS-P; VWP

Where When Was. Reginald Shepherd. GT

Where? When? Which? Langston Hughes. BPo

Where, where are my masters? My Masters. Sandor Csoori, *Hungarian.* VCWP, *tr. by* Len Roberts

Where, where are now the great reports. Fuimus Fumus. Joshua Sylvester. FaBoEE

Where, where but here have Pride and Truth. On Hearing That the Students of Our New University Have Joined the Agitation against Immoral Literature. W. B. Yeats. MoP; NoAM

Where will this voice go once it leaves me. Angel Atrapado VIII. John Yau. PT

Where will you and I sleep? *Wintu Oral Tradition, Wintu.* ITG, *tr. by* Dorothy Demetracopoulou *and* Robert Hass

Where Will You Be? Patricia Parker. GLP

Where will you find this year, Mary. Invitation to Mary. Mairtin O Direain, *Irish.* TIRV, *tr. by the author*

Where will your strange pilgrimage take you next? Saying Good-Bye to Feng the Hermit. Mo Shih-lung, *Chinese.* CoBLCP, *tr. by* Jonathan Chaves

Where wilt thou lead me? Speak; I'll go no further. Shakespeare. OxBSn *Fr.* Hamlet.

Where, without bloodshed, can there be. Long Feud. Louis Untermeyer. MoAmPo

Where would you look for blessing who are caught. And No Help Came. Peter Porter. BMAP

Where yon proud turrets crown the rock. The Bleeding Nun. *Unknown.* NOBRP

Where you and I will fare! (LL) Puck's Song. Rudyard Kipling. FaBoCh; OxBChV

Where you are. Peony Afternoon. So Chong-Ju, *Korean.* VCWP, *tr. by* David R. McCann

Where you are. You must let it find you. (LL) Lost. David Wagoner. PaTW

Where you do lie beneath . (LL) The Brown Girl. *Unknown*. ESPB; OxBB

Where You Go When She Sleeps. T. R. Hummer. MT

Where you going? / (Getting berries. Think I'll try a little farther.) Getting Berries. *Unknown, Bella Bella Indian*. STP, *tr. by* Franz Boas

Where you going? / (Going to get firewood.) Getting Firewood. *Unknown, Bella Bella Indian*. STP, *tr. by* Franz Boas

Where you have fallen, you stay. On the Wall of a KZ-Lager. János Pilinszky, *Hungarian*. AF; PoSu, *tr. by* Janos Csokits *and* Ted Hughes; HP, *tr. by* Ted Hughes

Where your skin / is your passport. (LL) Untitled Blues. Yusef Komunyakaa. GT

Whereas galoshed my Julia goes. Upon Julia's Arctics. Bert Leston Taylor. NBLV

Whereas, on certain boughs and sprays. The Lawyer's Invocation to Spring. Henry Howard Brownell. PoLF

Where'er I turn, art ever with me there. (LL) The Presence. Jones Very. PAR

Where'er thy navy spreads her canvas wings. To the King, on His Navy. Edmund Waller. BeJo

Where'er we tread 'tis haunted, holy ground. Byron. GrIP *Fr.* Childe Harold's Pilgrimage.

Where'er you find "the cooling western breeze." Essay on Criticism. Alexander Pope. OBCoV; PFE *Fr.* An Essay on Criticism. NAEL-1; PoEL-3; TFi

Wherefore and how I am certain, I can hardly tell; but it [*or* is so]. Arthur Hugh Clough. EBVVPR, *canto* 2, 13 *Fr.* Amours de Voyage. NOBVV

Wherefore Hidest Thou Thy Face, and Holdest Me for Thine Enemy [*or* Enemie]? Francis Quarles. MeLP; NOSC; OxAEP-1 *Fr.* Emblems.

Wherefore I marvel greatly of myself. The Flower and the Leaf. The Lady of the Arbour. OBGa

Wherefore, Lucinda, dost aspire. To Miss L. F. on the Occasion of Her Departure for the Continent. Sir John Collings Squire. BXAP

Wherefore peep'st thou, envious day? *Unknown*. GBL

Wherefore the Scars of Christ's Passion Remained in the Body of His Resurrection. Theodulf of Orleans, *Latin*. MLL, *tr. by* Helen Waddell

Wherefore this busy labor without rest? Tuskegee. Leslie Pinckney Hill. PFE

Wherefore was that cry? Shakespeare. *See* Tomorrow, and Tomorrow, and Tomorrow.

Wherein Consists the High Estate. Ebenezer Dayton. AH

Wherein he sweeter did, than had he sent her sums of gold. (LL) O NICIAS, there is no other remedy for love. Theocritus, *Greek*. NoSic

Wherein lies happiness? In that which becks. The Pleasure Thermometer. Keats. Ro

Wherein the mighty trust! (LL) The Image in Lava. Felicia Dorothea Hemans. CABP; NOBRP

Wherelings whenlings / (daughters of if but offspring of hopefear). E. E. Cummings. HAP; WeW-3

Whereon the rays of fiery / Phœbus glowed. Ovid. *See* The Golden Age.

Where's an old woman to go when the years. The Riddle. "H. E. H." PoToHe

Where's Babe Ruth, the King of Swat. The Ballad of Dead Yankees. Donald Petersen. WeT

Where's Commander All-a-Tanto? Herman Melville. PoEL-5 *Fr.* Bridegroom Dick.

Where's Ho Xuan Huong. Saigon Bar Girls, 1975. Yusef Komunyakaa. MT

Where's the peck of pickled pepper Peter Piper picked? (LL) Peter Piper picked a peck of pickled pepper[s]. Mother Goose. FaBoBe; LB; OTCP; OxNR; ReMoGo

Where's the poet? show him, show him. Keats. EPCY

Where's the public good in what you write. Palladas, *Greek*. GrAn, *tr. by* Tony Harrison

Wheresoe'er I turn mine eyes. God Everywhere. Abraham ibn Ezra, *Hebrew*. TrJP, *tr. by* D. E. de L

Wheresoe'er I turn my View. Lines on Thomas Warton's Poems. Samuel Johnson. EPCY; FaBoEE; SCGP

Whereso'er you are, my heart shall truly love you. (LL) Ubique. Joshua Sylvester. GSo; GTBS-P; NoSic; OBEV; Son

Whereto should I express. To His Lady. Henry VIII, King of England. CTC; EBEV; NoSic

Wherever God erects a house of prayer. Daniel Defoe. NOBL; OBSV *Fr.* The True-born Englishman.

Wherever I am, there's always Pooh. Us Two. A. A. Milne. OxBChV

Wherever I go (these). Poem Against the State (Of Things): 1975. June Jordan. ISC

Wherever I go to find. Pigeons. Bert Meyers. SPE

Wherever I Hang. Grace Nichols. HCP

Wherever in this city, screens flicker. Adrienne Rich. CPO *Fr.* Twenty-one Love Poems. GLP

Wherever shadow falls wherever the drowning. The Being. Hayden Carruth. PoA *Fr.* Contra Mortem.

Wherever shadow falls wherever the drowning. Contra Mortem. Hayden Carruth. PoA

Wherever that may be? (LL) Questions of Travel. Elizabeth Bishop. ColAP; NAAL-2; NOBA

Wherever we looked the land would hold us up. (LL) One Home. William Stafford. CoAP; VGW

Wherever we remove. (LL) God's Residence. Emily Dickinson. SAmP; WPoS

Wherever we turn in the storm of roses. In the Storm of Roses. Ingeborg Bachmann, *German*. AF, *tr. by* Mark Anderson

Wherever you are. A Woman with Flaxen Hair in Norfolk Heard. Robert Kelly. PmAP

Whether a dove or a seagull lighted there. Valentine Ackland. WPN

Whether at doomsday tell, ye reverend wise. Quaerè. George Farewell. NOEC; OBCoV

Whether day my spirit's yearning. The Thought Eternal. Goethe, *German*. AWP, *tr. by* Ludwig Lewisohn

Whether dinner was pleasant, with the windows lit by gunfire. No Credit. Kenneth Fearing. CMoP

Whether he hears my song or not. (LL) Mutterings Over the Crib of a Deaf Child. James Wright. LiLi

Whether his mouth be open or shut. (LL) Lines for Cuscuscaraway and Mirza Murad Ali Beg. T. S. Eliot. NBLV; NTP; OBAL; OBCoV; PeLV; UV

Whether I find thee bright with fair. Changeful Beauty. *Unknown, Greek*. EnLoPo, *tr. by* Andrew Lang

Whether I live or fail. (LL) V-Letter. Karl Shapiro. NYBP; NoAM; TrJP

Whether I see you now. *Unknown, Greek*. InMo, *tr. by* Sam Hamill

Whether I sit or lie. Ukihashi, *Japanese*. WPJ; WPOW, *tr. by* Kenneth Rexroth *and* Ikuko Atsumi

Whether it be new or old! (LL) Back and Side Go Bare, Go Bare. William Stevenson *and* John Still. HeIP-4; NAEL-1; SCGP

Whether it is from Eden's sacred plan. Hartwell Gardens. A. of Aylesbury Merrick. OBGa

Whether it rose up as a small brown bird. Questions about Poetry since Auschwitz. Tadeusz Rózewicz, *Polish*. AF, *tr. by* Robert A. Maguire *and* Magnus Jan Krynski

Whether it's sunny or not, it's sure. Poem about Morning. William Meredith. NYBP

Whether on Ida's shady brow. To the Muses. William Blake. EPCY; HAP; HeIP-4; ImPo; NAEL-2; NOBE; NOEC; NoP-4; OAEL-2; OBEV; SCGP

Whether one paints five Helens. The Ultimate Antientropy. Theodore Weiss. NoAM

Whether or Not. D. H. Lawrence. MoBrPo

Whether outside, around, or in. (LL) Fence Wire. James Dickey. NYBP; VGW

Whether that soul which now comes up to you. Hymn to the Saints, and to Marquis Hamilton[, An]. Donne. NOSC

Whether the bees have thoughts we cannot say. The Long Waters. Theodore Roethke. NYBP

Whether the bees have thoughts, we cannot say. The Long Waters. Theodore Roethke. NYBP *Fr.* North American Sequence.

Whether the fruitful Nile, or Tyrian shore. Dryden. EPCY *Fr.* To the Earl of Roscommon, on His Excellent Essay on Translated Verse.

Whether the moorings are invisible. Conversation. John Berryman. LiTM

Whether the sensitive plant, or that. Shelley. OAEL-2 *Fr.* A Sensitive Plant in a garden grew. FHYEP

Whether the third spake verity. (LL) Ballad of the Three Spectres. Ivor Gurney. PoFWW

Whether the Turkish new moon minded be. Sonnet 30. Sir Philip Sidney. NoSic; PoE *Fr.* Astrophil and Stella. AAS; SiPS

Whether the weather be fine. Weather. *Unknown*. ACTP; ImGa; OTCP

Whether the weather be fine, or whether the weather be not. *Unknown*. BoTP

Whether There Is Sorrow in the Demons. John Berryman. LiTM

Whether they work together or apart. (LL) The Tuft of Flowers. Robert Frost. AWP; MoAmPo; NAAL-2; OxBA

Whether thou getst them green, or lets them seed. (LL) Upon Wedlock and Death of Children. Edward Taylor. AmPP; ColAP; NAAL-1; NAAL-3

Whether to Ceaser he was friend or foe? Upon the Death of G. B. John Cotton. SCAP

Whether to sally and see thee, girl of my dreams. To Meet, or Otherwise. Thomas Hardy. OBNC

Whether we fall asleep under the moon. Sleep. John Haines. WeT

Whether we like it or not! (LL) Weather. *Unknown*. ACTP

Whether what we sense of this world. Metonymy as an Approach to a Real World. William Bronk. APSN; VGW

Whether White or Black be best. Verses Made Sometime Since upon. . . the Indian Squa. John Josselyn. SCAP

Whether you are a citizen or a stranger coming from elsewhere. Epitaph from Athens. *Unknown, Greek.* GrAn, *tr. by* Richmond Lattimore

Whether you say it, think it, know it. Ted Hughes. NoAM *Fr.* Stations.

Whi / te boys gone. Val Ferdinand. NBV

Which are touched in Love / must sound. (LL) Effortlessly, / Love flows from God into man. Mechthild von Magdeburg, *German.* EnlH, *tr. by* Jane Hirshfield

Which Are You? *Unknown.* PoLF

Which blamed the living man. (LL) Growing Old. Matthew Arnold. EnVR; FHYEP; NAEL-2; NOBVV; OAEL-2; PoEL-5

Which but expressions be of inward evils. (LL) In night, when colors [or colours] all to black[e] are cast. Greville Fulke. AAS; OAEL-1; Son

Which carries the feathered grass a long way down the upbeating air. (LL) I wake up in your bed. I know I have been dreaming. Adrienne Rich. CPO; NAAL-2; NoAM; TRP

Which caused [or caus'd] her thus to send thee out of door. (LL) The Author to Her Book. Anne Bradstreet. AmPP; InPK-5; NAAL-1; NAAL-3; NALW; NOBA; OxBA; PoE; Poetr; SCAP; TAP

Which child. Tanka. Shaku Chōkū, *Japanese.* MJT, *tr. by* Makoto Ueda

Which Claus of Innsbruck cast in bronze for me! (LL) My Last Duchess [Ferrara]. Robert Browning. AWP; CABP; ClHu; EBNV; EBVV; EBVVPR; EnVR; FHYEP; FaBoPV; GTBS-P; HAP; HeIP-4; HoPM; ImPo; InPK-6; InPS-3; NAEL-2; NIP-4; NOBE; NOBVV; NoP-4; OAEL-2; OBNC; OxBoV; PBMP; PFE; PeVV; PoE; PoEL-5; PoLF; PoPoPo; Poetr; SAGP; SCGP; SCV; SoSe-8; TFi; TRP

Which cover lightly, gentle earth! (LL) On My First Daughter. Ben Jonson. BeJo; EBEV; FaBoEE; HoPM; InPS-3; NAEL-1; NOBE; NOSC; NoP-4; PFE; PoE; SeCP

Which dark green oaks his noontide leisure shields. (LL) Solitude. John Clare. NOBVV; OxBSP

Which die for goodness, who have lived for crime. (LL) Sonnet 124. Shakespeare. NoSic

Which distressed all the people of Chertsey. (LL) Limericks, II (ii). Edward Lear. OBCoV; OxBChV

Which done, that Dawne, turnes then to perfect day. (LL) To Anthea Lying in Bed. Robert Herrick. BeJo; SeCP

Which dyes. George Herbert. *See* Longing.

Which Earth grants all her kind. (LL) She Hears The Storm. Thomas Hardy. LoP; NAEL-2

Which faith had dictated, and angels trod. (LL) On Exodus 3: 14: "I am that I am." Matthew Prior. ChIV-1; NOCV

Which flows not every day, but ever! (LL) Song: "When, dearest, I but think on [or of] thee." Sir John Suckling *and* Owen Feltham. NOSC; OBEV

Which from afar he bears. (LL) The Inward Morning. Henry David Thoreau. AmPP; PAR

Which goes with Bridge, and Women and Champagne. (LL) On a General Election. Hilaire Belloc. FaBoEE; NOBE; NOBL; OBSV; OxBTC; OxBoLi

Which He from Heaven doth bring[e]. (LL) New Prince, New Pomp[e]. Robert Southwell. ESCV; NOBE; NOCV; NoSic; TrCP

Which heaves but with the heaving deep. (LL) Lincolnshire Wolds and Lincolnshire Sea. Tennyson. EBEV; EBVV; EnVR; FHYEP; HeIP-4; NOBE; OBNC; PeECV; PoEL-5

Which his own lanthorn throws up from himself. (LL) To Percy Shelley. Leigh Hunt. Ro

Which hopes from thee, and thee alone, a cure! (LL) Time and Grief. William Lisle Bowles. GSo; LBC

Which I am afraid to put on. (LL) Empire of Dreams. Charles Simic. BLT; LCAP-2; VCAP

Which I wish to remark. The Heathen Pass-ee. Arthur Clement Hilton. NOBL; UV

Which I wish to remark. Plain Language from Truthful James. Bret Harte. APN-2; BLPA; CTC; EBNV; FaBoBe; NOBL; OBAL; OBCoV; PaTW; PeLV; UV

Which I wish to say is this. Gertrude Stein. NoP-4

Which is as white and hairless as an egg. (LL) Her Legs. Robert Herrick. CavPo; PFE

Which is called civilization over there. (LL) Australia. Alec Derwent Hope. BMAP; NoP-4

Which is I stood and loved you while you slept. (LL) A Poem for Emily. Miller Williams. MT; MoLi; WeW-3

Which is in me / like a hill. (LL) The Hill. Robert Creeley. CRP; RaBo; TRP

Which is not going to be wasted on me which is why I'm telling you about it. (LL) Having a Coke with You. Frank O'Hara. GLP; VCAP

Which is real. The Indigo Glass in the Grass. Wallace Stevens. PoA

Which is the cosiest voice. Gray Thrums. Clara Doty Bates. OBCA

Which is the way to Baby-land? Baby-Land. George Cooper. BoTP

Which is the way to Fairyland. The Way to Fairyland. Eunice Close. BoTP

Which is the way to London Town. *Unknown.* BoTP

Which is the way to Somewhere. Which Is the Way to Somewhere Town? Kate Greenaway. CTV

Which is, to keep that hid. (LL) The Undertaking. Donne. FSCP; NAEL-1; NOBE

Which is what. After Love. John A. Stone. MT

Which is you, old two-in-one? What the Serpent Said to Adam. Archibald MacLeish. ChIV-1; MeMAP *Fr.* Songs for Eve.

(Which is your luck.) (LL) The Ballad of Billie Potts. Robert Penn Warren. FuPo; NOBA; OxBA

Which it is not my style. Truthful James to the Editor. Bret Harte. APN-2

Which Letter? Arthur Vogelsang. PUP-19

Which Lucy's eyes surveyed! (LL) I traveled [or travell'd] among unknown men. Wordsworth. Ro

Which men who change can never know. (LL) Constancy Rewarded. Coventry Patmore. NOBVV; OxBSP

Which mighty Venus gave, and in his liver strucke the dart. Theocritus. *See* O NICIAS, there is no other remedy for love.

Which must soon come—as I cannot forget. (LL) A 14-Year-Old Convalescent Cat in the Winter. Gavin Ewart. OPOU; OxBSP

Which my God feels as blood [or bloud]; but I, as wine. (LL) The Agony [or Agonie]. George Herbert. ESCV; GeHe

Which nobody can deny. (LL) Sweet Meat Has Sour Sauce. William Cowper. ECEV; NOEC; OBSV; Ro

Which now the angels sing! (LL) It came upon the midnight clear. Edmund Hamilton Sears. AH; APN-1; PWR

Which of these statements is true? Tom Joanides. Lloyd Schwartz. EOEF

Which of thy names I take, not only bears. To Sir Horace Vere. Ben Jonson. BeJo

Which of you / is going to take my body? Song of Starvation. *Unknown, Chippewa Indian.* STP, *tr. by* Jerome Rothenberg

Which on a steeple / stands for hope. Marianne Moore. *See* The Steeple-Jack.

Which One Is Genuine? Charles Baudelaire, *French.* RaBo, *tr. by* Robert Bly

Which one? Which one? (LL) What the Serpent Said to Adam. Archibald MacLeish. ChIV-1; MeMAP

Which only breeds your beauty's overthrow. (LL) My Lady's Tears. *Unknown.* EBEV; EnLoPo; LoP; NOBE; NoSic; OBEV

Which partly assuaged his despair. (LL) Limericks, II (v). Edward Lear. CBNP; OBCoV

Which Road? William Barnes. NOBVV

Which road, which road did you take. Exaltation. Franz Werfel, *German.* TrJP, *tr. by* Edith Abercrombie Snow

Which Shall It Be? Ethel Lynn Beers. BLPA

Which teaches that all has less value than half. (LL) Bryant. James Russell Lowell. NOBA; TAP

Which the coming day will ask. (LL) Prime. W. H. Auden. CMoP; PoE

Which the same I am free to maintain. (LL) The Heathen Pass-ee. Arthur Clement Hilton. NOBL; UV

Which the same I am free to maintain. (LL) Plain Language from Truthful James. Bret Harte. APN-2; BLPA; CTC; EBNV; FaBoBe; NOBL; OBAL; OBCoV; PaTW; PeLV; UV

Which they and all the sullen world have lost. (LL) L'Amitie: To Mrs. M. Awbrey. Katherine Philips. KTR; NOSC

Which this love of yours suddenly transformed. (LL) After Paradise. Czeslaw Milosz, *Polish.* EP; ITG, *tr. by* Czeslaw Milosz *and* Robert Hass

Which thus presents and thus records true life. (LL) From Book 5. Elizabeth Barrett Browning. NALW; NoP-4; PBWP; PeVV

Which to heare, vouchsafe, O dearest dred a-while, The. (LL) The Legend of the Knight of the Red Crosse, or of Holinesse. Edmund Spenser. EPCY; FHYEP; NAEL-1; OAEL-1

Which true lovers always admire. (LL) Lord Lovel ("Lord Lovel he stood at his castle gate"). *Unknown.* AS; AmFP; BLPA; ESPB

Which turned the rock into a standing [or a pool of] water, the flint into a fountain of waters. (LL) Psalm 114. Bible, *O.T.* TrJP

Which unexpectedly / open. (LL) Aspects of Eve. Linda Pastan. PiM

Which used to lead something into somewhere. (LL) Ponder,darling,these busted statues. E. E. Cummings. CMoP; NIP-4; PoE

Which Washington? Eve Merriam. NTCP

Which waste of idle hours hath quite thrown down. (LL) Richard II. Shakespeare. GaP; OBGa

Which way he went? Rondelet. May Probyn. VWP

Which way I fly is Hell; my self am Hell. Milton. *Fr.* Book IV. OAEL-1 *Fr.* Paradise Lost.

Which we held in idea, a little handful. (LL)   The Horse Chestnut Tree. Richard Eberhart.   CMoP; LiTM; MoAmPo; PFE

Whichway.   Ron Welburn.   NBV

Whiffs of the Ohio River at Cincinnati.   Carl Sandburg.   "When I asked for fish in the restaurant facing the Ohio River."   PoE

Whigmaleerie, A.   William Soutar.   OxBS

Whig's the first letter of his odious name.   An Acrostic on Wharton.   *Unknown.*   OBSV

While.   Bruce Andrews.   FTOS

While a child I longed to be staunch in virtue.   Passing through My Shih-ning Estate.   Hsieh Ling-yün, *Chinese.*   SuSp, *tr. by* Francis Westbrook

While a cloud that floats o'er is reflected within it.   James Russell Lowell.   *See* Emerson.

While a thousand fine projects are planned ev'ry day.   A Song.   *Unknown.*   NOEC

While Adam slept, from him his Eve arose.   Epigram.   *Unknown.*   FaBoEE

While all about us peal the loud, sweet *Te Deums* of the Canterbury bells. (LL)   Madonna of the Evening Flowers.   Amy Lowell.   CPO

While all the ark's survivors lurched onto land.   Ararat.   Dan Pagis, *Hebrew.*   IP, *tr. by* Warren Bargad *and* Stanley F. Chyet

While all with silence and attention wait.   Aeneas' story.   Virgil, *Latin.*   OBCVT, *tr. by* Sir John Denham

While an intrinsic ardor prompts to write.   To the University of Cambridge, in New-England.   Phillis Wheatley.   AmPP; NAAAL; NAAL-1; NAAL-3; TAP

While an official, I never wrote lyrics.   Li K'ai-hsien.   *Fr.* When I Recovered from an Illness After Returning Home To Live in Retirement, I Was Invited by My Friends to Join a Song-Lyric Club.   CoBLCP, *tr. by* Jonathan Chaves

While apparition is the instant of illumination and of being touched.   Suicide with Squirtgun.   Tom Clark.   PmAP

While as I lived no house I had.   Upon the Grave of a Beggar.   Timothy Kendall.   NoSic

While at Prayer.   Abba Kovner, *Hebrew.*   IP, *tr. by* Warren Bargad *and* Stanley F. Chyet

While breaking the big rock.   Stone Giant.   Joseph Bruchac.   CDW

While briers an' woodbines budding green.   Epistle to J. Lapraik, an Old Scotch Bard.   Robert Burns.   Ro

While bringing Apollo the pick of the Etruscan plunder.   Simonides, *Greek.*   GrAn, *tr. by* Peter Jay

While Butler, needy wretch, was yet alive.   On the Setting Up of Mr. Butler's Monument in Westminster Abbey.   Samuel Wesley.   NBLV; NOEC; OxBSP

While by the rosebed gay you stood, and revelled in the multitude.   One among the Roses.   Edmund Blunden.   OBGa

While cheeks burn, arms open, eyes shut and lips meet! (LL)   Now.   Robert Browning.   CBLP; EP

While crickets tighten their solitary bolts.   Lace.   Dean Young.   NAmP90

While crossing a field.   In the Open.   Aleksandar Ristovic, *Serbo-Croatian.*   HSix, *tr. by* Charles Simic

While Delia shines at hurlothrumbo.   The Widow and Virgin Sisters.   William Broome.   ECEV

While driving north, lost.   I Was Looking for the University.   Clarence Major.   GT

While Dubliner leopold bloom sought solace.   Limerick.   Gerard Benson.   PeLi

While Eve waited.   The Sleep of Adam.   John Hejduk.   ChIV-1

While favour fed my hope, delight with hope was brought.   Fifth Song.   Sir Philip Sidney.   *Fr.* Astrophil and Stella.   AAS; SiPS

While gazing round this dear ramshackle one.   Other People's Glasshouses.   Ruth Pitter.   OBGa

While gentlefolks strut in their silver and satins.   Bartleme Fair.   George Alexander Stevens.   NOEC

While God is marching on. (LL)   The Battle Hymn [*or* Battle-Hymn] of the Republic.   Julia Ward Howe.   AH; APAD; APN-1; BLPA; CBCWP; CH; ColAP; EBEvV; FaBoA; FaBoBe; FaPoR; ImPo; NOBA; NOCV; NoP-4; OBWP; PAR; PWR; SAGP; SCV; TAP; TFi; WPE

While going the road to sweet Athy.   Johnny, I Hardly Knew Ye.   *Unknown.*   BIrV; IIP; OxBoLi

While greasy Joan doth keel the pot. (LL)   Winter.   Shakespeare.   APAD; AWP; CH; ClHu; FaBoCh; GTBS-P; HAP; ImPo; InPK-6; InPS-3; NAEL-1; NIP-4; NOBE; NoP-4; NoSic; OAEL-1; OBEV; PoEL-2; PoRA; SCGP; TFi; TRP; UnPo; WeW-3

While he slept, I poured salt in his ears.   Judith Recalls Holofernes.   Maura Stanton.   AmPA

While he was still speaking, Judas came, one of the twelve.   Matthew 26:47–56; While he was still speaking, Judas came.   Boris Pasternak.   GI *Fr.* St. Matthew.

While his sensible daddy goes straight into town. (LL)   To a Friend Whose Work Has Come to Triumph.   Anne Sexton.   InPK-6; PFE

While Holroyd may boast of her beautiful bottom.   On Seeing a Tapestry Chair-Bottom Beautifully Worked by His Daughter for Mrs Holroyd.   Richard Owen Cambridge.   ECEV

While Homer and Whitman roared in the pines? (LL)   Petit, the Poet.   Edgar Lee Masters.   CMoP; ColAP; MoAmPo; NOBA; NoAM; OxBA; TAP

While I am praying.   Prayer for a Thief.   Phil DuPlessis, *Afrikaans.*   PeSAV, *tr. by the author*

While I Am Young.   Silas Ballou.   AH

While i believe that what im doing depends essentially upon.   Real Estate.   David Antin.   FTOS

While I droop here. (LL)   I am a parcel of vain strivings tied.   Henry David Thoreau.   APN-1; AmPP; ColAP; NCAP; OxBA; PAR; PoEL-4; TAP

While I examine my hands. (LL)   The Leap.   James Dickey.   NIP-4; Poetr; WeT

While I fled. (LL)   Intimates.   D. H. Lawrence.   BoLoP; CBLP; NBLV; OxBSP; RaBo

While I listen to thy voice.   Edmund Waller.   BeJo

While I recline / At ease beneath.   The Cotton Boll.   Henry Timrod.   APN-2; AmPP

While I sit at the door.   Eve.   Christina Rossetti.   CH; ChIV-1; GTBS-P; NALW; NIP-4; PoEL-5; Poetr

While I slept, while I slept and the night grew colder.   Robert Francis.   KaS

While I stood here, in the open, lost in myself.   Milkweed.   James Wright.   ColAP; LCAP-2; NOBA; RaBo

While I was building neat.   It Is Dangerous to Read Newspapers.   Margaret Atwood.   CrSp; HeIP-4; OBWP

While I was walking, wondering, "Do I, don't I?"   Deaf-Mutes.   Nikolai Ivanovich Glazkov, *Russian.*   TCRP, *tr. by* Daniel Weissbort

While I watch the Christmas blaze.   The Reminder.   Thomas Hardy.   CMoP; ChAP; OBCP

While I work the fields I am not false to myself. (LL)   Moving House ("In spring and fall there are many fine days").   T'ao Ch'ien, *Chinese.*   CoBCP, *tr. by* Burton Watson

While I'm gone, white mother, kill the fattened oxen.   The White and the Black.   N. M. Khaketla, *Southern Sotho.*   PeSA, *tr. by* Jack Cope *and* Dan Kunene

While in long exile far from you I roam.   To Dr. Moore, in Anser to a Poetical Epistle Written by Him in Wales.   Helen Maria Williams.   ECWP; WoRP

While in my simple gospel creed.   Tartarus.   Oliver Wendell Holmes.   NCAP

While in the mask of night there shone that cut.   Landing on the Moon.   May Swenson.   TAP

While in the park I sing, the listning deer.   At Penshurst.   Edmund Waller.   BeJo

While, *Iris,* I at distance gaze.   A Song.   Aphra Behn.   CPO

While it keeps counting the many times we've kissed.   Catullus.   *See* Carmen 5 ("My sweetest Lesbia, let us live and love").

While It Was Raining.   Wen Cheng-ming, *Chinese.*   CoBLCP, *tr. by* Jonathan Chaves

While Jove's planet rises yonder, silent over Africa. (LL)   Home-Thoughts, from the Sea.   Robert Browning.   EBEvV; NAEL-2; SCGP

While joy gave clouds the light of stars.   The Villain.   W. H. Davies.   MoBrPo; OxBSP; OxBTC; SAGP

While ladling butter from alternate tubs.   On the Historians Freeman and Stubbs.   J. E. Thorold Rogers.   FaBoEE; OBCoV

While leanest beasts in pastures feed.   Supreme Fortune Falls Soonest.   Robert Herrick.   CaPo

While, Lydia, I was lov'd of thee.   3.9: Dialogue between Horace and Lydia, A ("Donec gratus eram").   Horace.   OBVE, *tr. by* Robert Herrick   *Fr.* Odes.

While many a merry tale, and many a song.   Samuel Johnson.   UV

While maudlin Whigs deplored [*or* deplor'd] their Cato's Fate.   On a Lady Who P-ssed [*or* P——st] at the Tragedy of Cato.   Alexander Pope.   OxBSP

While Morpheus thus doth gently lay.   Song.   Henry Killigrew.   CH

While my hair was still cut straight across my forehead.   The River-Merchant's Wife: A Letter.   Ezra Pound.   ColAP

While my hair was still cut straight across my forehead.   River Merchant's Wife, The; a Letter.   Li Po, (*sometimes at. to* Rihaku), *Chinese.*   AWP; AmPP; BoLoP; ClHu; ColAP; FYAP; GEA; GLoP; HAP; HeIP-4; InPK; InPS-3; LiLi; LoP; MeMAP; MoAmPo; MoP; NAAL-2; NIP-4; NNPT; NoAM; NOBA; NOBE; NoP-4; OBMV; OBVE; OxBA; Poetr; PoPoPo; RB; RaBo; RACG; SAGP; TAP; TFi; TRP; TTTS; TwCP; UnPo; WeW-3, *tr. by* Ezra Pound

While my mother is washing the black socks.   Terrorism.   Frank Stanford.   FiLi

While my wife at my side lies slumbering, and the wars are over long.   The Artilleryman's Vision.   Walt Whitman.   CBCWP

While neighbouring cities waste the fleeting hours.   Anna Seward.   NOEC   *Fr.* Colebrook Dale.

While Northward the hot sun was sinking o'er the trees. Psalm. Robert Bridges. FaBoTw

While now I lay me down to sleep. Robert Farren. TIRV *Fr.* Sleep.

While now upon the win' do zwell. The Bells ov Alderburnham. William Barnes. EBVV

While ocean thus the latent store bequeaths. Henry Brooke. ECEV *Fr.* Universal Beauty.

While o'er Our Guilty Land, O Lord. Samuel Davies. AH

While o'er the Deep Thy Servants Sail. George Burgess. AH

While one sere leaf, that parting autumn yields. Anna Seward. WoRP *Fr.* Sonnets.

While Over There. Charlotte Mew. *See* À Quoi Bon Dire.

While playing at the woodland's edge. The Terrible Path. Brian Patten. OTCP

While pleasure reigns unrivalled on this shore. Boston in Distress. *Unknown.* NOEC

While preaching. Now be still, and I'll begin. Chaucer. *See* The Pardoner's Prologue.

While rain, with eve in partnership. Beyond the Last Lamp. Thomas Hardy. NOBE; OBNC

While round the arméd bands. The Execution of King Charles. Andrew Marvell. PoRA

While rumbling trunks pushed down the hall upstairs. Closing the House. Jim Wayne Miller. MT

While she was talking a bear happened along, violating. The Woman at Banff. William Stafford. PFE

While shepherds watched their flocks by night. Carol. "Saki." NSI; UV

While shepherds watched their flocks by night. Nahum Tate. AmFP; NOCV; NOSC; TIRV; UV

While Sidney Bechet was. Tuskegee Experiment. Sadiq. SeSe

While sitting in my room kind Miss. Dedicated to a Young Lady Representing the Indian Race at Howard University. Alfred Islay Walden. AAP

While smoking her cigarette down to the very end. (LL) The Great Palaces of Versailles. Rita Dove. NMM-2; NoAM

While snow fell carelessly. The Crack. Denise Levertov. NALW

While snows the window-panes bedim. December. John Clare. OBCP

While snowy nightwinds, blowing bleak. Burncombe Hollow. William Barnes. OBNC

While some affect the sun, and some the shade. Robert Blair. *See* Whilst some affect the sun, and some the shade.

While some "rap" over this turmoil. The Rhetoric of Langston Hughes. Margaret Danner. BlSi

While something hummed along the river. From the Sun Itself. Roberta Hill Whiteman. HATNAP

While soon the "garden's flaunting flowers" decay. Sonnet on Reading the Poem upon the Mountain Daisy, by Mr. Burns. Helen Maria Williams. ECWP

While sorrows encompass me round. Death-Bed Song. *Unknown.* AmFP

While still young, / I didn't know I was aging. Tune: "Tartar Tune of Eighteen Beats." *Unknown, Chinese.* SuSp, *tr. by* Sherwin S. S. Fu

While stormie seas grow calme. Dido's farewell. Ovid. OBCVT, *tr. by* George Turberville *Fr.* The Heroides.

While strolling through the hills one day. Tannhauser. Newman Levy. OBAL

While summer roses all their glory yield. To the Poppy. Anna Seward. ECWP; WoRP

While sunk in deepest solitude and woe. Sorrow. Laetitia Pilkington. ECWP

While that my soul repairs to her devotion. Church Monuments. George Herbert. ESCV; GeHe; HAP; NAEL-1; NOCV; NOSC; OAEL-1; PoE; TRP

While that the sun with his beams hot. The Unfaithful Shepherdess. *Unknown.* GTBS-P; NOBE; OBEV

While the Billy Boils. David McKee Wright, *Maori.* PeNZ, *tr. by* Margaret Orbell

While the blue noon above us arches. Annihilation. Conrad Potter Aiken. GBL; GEA; MoAmPo

While the bombers, southward flocking, set Italian cities rocking. Croaked the Eagle: "Nevermore." "Sagittarius." UV

While the Choir Sang. Priscilla Jane Thompson. CBWP-2

While the Constabulary covered the mob. Summer nineteen sixty nine. Seamus Heaney. CIP-2

While the corn grows ripe and the / apples mellow. (LL) August. Celia Laighton Thaxter. CTV; ImGa

While the dead. Seminar for Backward Pupils. Günter Eich, *German.* AF, *tr. by* David Young

While the earth still turns, while the. François Villon. Bulat Shalvovich Okudzhava, *Russian.* TCRP, *tr. by* Deming Brown

While the far farewell music thins and fails. Departure. Thomas Hardy. Son

While the Great Man drives home his desire. (LL) Persephone Underground. Rita Dove. FFC; NAmP90

While the guests order. Clement Hoyt. HA

While the innocents were being massacred who says. Who Says. Julia Hartwig, *Polish.* GI, *tr. by* Stanislaw Baranczak *and* Clare Cavanagh

While the long grain is softening. Early in the Morning. Li-Young Lee. LoL

While the milder Fates consent. A Lyric to Mirth. Robert Herrick. CaPo

While the moths are coming down. (LL) Labasheedy (The Silken Bed). Nuala Ni Dhomhnaill, *Irish.* CABP

While the noon-lustre o'er the land is spread. M. J. Chapman. *Fr.* Barbadoes. PBCV

While the October air, no snow, easy to breathe. How to Get There. Frank O'Hara. NoP-4

While the people pressed upon him to hear the word of God. Luke 5:1–11; While the people pressed upon him. Czeslaw Milosz. GI *Fr.* St. Luke.

While the pulse in my neck. Desire. Leslie Ullman. NAmP90

While the Record Plays. Gyula Illyés, *Hungarian.* PFTM, *tr. by* William Jay Smith

While the river banks are quarreling. Agon. Branko Miljkovic, *Serbo-Croatian.* HSix, *tr. by* Charles Simic

While the sands o' life shall run. Robert Burns. *See* A Red, Red Rose.

While the south rains, the north. Sled Burial, Dream Ceremony. James Dickey. NoP-4

While the sun still spends his fabulous money. Kenneth Patchen. CLPP

While the sun stops, or. A Catalpa Tree on West Twelfth Street. Amy Clampitt. BAP-94

While the Tragedy's afoot. Colophon. Oliver St. John Gogarty. OBMV

While the water-wagon's ringing showers. In the Isle of Dogs. John Davidson. OBNC

While the wind upon the waters still returns. Logbook. Dan Pagis, *Hebrew.* IP, *tr. by* Warren Bargad *and* Stanley F. Chyet

While the years draw nigh when the clattering typewriter is a burden. The Evil Days. D. J. Enright. OBCoV

While these cold nights freeze me dead. (LL) Shall I come, sweet love, to thee. Thomas Campion. AAS; CBLP; EBEV; GBL; HAP; NOBE; OxAEP-1; OxBoLi; PoEL-2

While thine the victor is and free. Aphra Behn. *See* Song: Love Armed.

While thirteen moons saw smoothly run. Stanzas Subjoined to the Yearly Bill of Mortality of the Parish of All Saints, Northampton; for the Year 1787. William Cowper. NOCV

While this America settles in the mould of its vulgarity, heavily thickening to empire. Shine, Perishing Republic. Robinson Jeffers. CMoP; ColAP; LiTM; MoP; NAAL-2; NOBA; NoAM; NoP-4; OxBA; PoPoPo; TAP; TFi; UnPo; VGW

While this kind of consolation and exhortation. Surplus. Abigail Child. FTOS

While this was singing, Ovid young in love. The Ear's Delight. George Chapman. NoSic *Fr.* Ovid's Banquet of Sense.

While those disintegrated by exocet. A Shot of War. J. S. Harry. BMAP

While thou diddest love me and that neck of thine. A Dialogue in Imitation of that between Horace and Lydia. Horace, *Latin.* OBCVT

While thou hast gode and getest gode. *Unknown.* MiEL

While Thracians shal with arrowes war, Iaziges with bowe. Ovid. OBVE, *tr. by* Thomas Underdowne *Fr.* Invective against Ibis.

While through our air thy kindling course was run. The Cold Meteorite. William Reed Huntington. APN-2

While thus he spake, th'Angelic Squadron bright. Milton. SCV *Fr.* Book IV. OAEL-1 *Fr.* Paradise Lost.

While thus he thought, a monst'rous wave up-bore. Homer. OBVE, *tr. by* Pope *Fr.* Odyssey. NAWM-1, *tr. by* Robert Fitzgerald

While thus to unknown pow'rs *Cephisa* pray'd. Ovid. OBCVT, *tr. by* John Gay *Fr.* The Story of Cephisa.

While time is running away on Příkopy Street. The Clock in the Old Jewish Ghetto. Vítězslav Nezval, *Czech.* NNPT, *tr. by* Ewald Osers

While Titian was grinding rose madder. Limerick. *Unknown.* NOBL

While to you we true children of Liberty pray. The Humble Petition of the British Jacobins to their Brethren of France. *Unknown.* NOBRP

While upon the journey of life. The Mask. Patty L. Harjo. VoR

While venal crowds for worthless men engage. Elegy on the Death of Mr Sterne. Miles Peter Andrews. NOBRP

While visiting Arundel Castle. Limerick. Victor Gray. NOBL

While vulgar souls their vulgar love pursue. Cloe to Artimesa. *Unknown.* ECWP

While walking down a crowded. If I Only Was the Fellow. Will S. Adkin. BLPA

While walking in a lonely wood. The Voyeur. Rod McKuen. PFE

While we lie tumbling in the hay. (LL) The Pedlar's Song. Shakespeare. FaBoBe; FaBoCh; NBLV; NOBE; NoP-4; NoSic; OAEL-1; OxAEP; OxBSP; OxBoLi; PeLV; PoEL-2; SCGP; TFi; UV

While We Lowly Bow before Thee. Daniel C. Colesworthy. AH

While we shall be merry and sing. (LL) The Gaberlunzie Man. *Unknown.* EnSB; OxBB; OxBS

While We Slept. David Wolff. TrJP

While we slept, these formal gardens. Snowfall on a College Garden. C. Day Lewis. OBGa

While we wait. Michael McClintock. HA

While we wandered (thus it is I dream!), A. Gray Nights. Ernest Christopher Dowson. Son

While we were fearing it, it came. Emily Dickinson. MeMAP

While we were marching through Georgia. (LL) Marching through Georgia. Henry Clay Work. APN-2; CBCWP; FaPoR

While we were visiting David's grave. Despair. Denise Levertov. NNaP

While we were walking under the top. Poem. John Ashbery. SPE

While with a feeling skill I paint my hell. (LL) Sonnet 2: "Not at [the] first sight, nor with a dribbed shot." Sir Philip Sidney. NAEL-1; OAEL-1; PBRV

While with false pride, and narrow jealousy. On the Use of New and Old Words in Poetry. Anna Seward. Son

While yet Rolfe's foot in stirrup stood. The Inscription. Herman Melville. APN-2 *Fr.* Clarel: A Poem and Pilgrimage in the Holy Land.

While yet the grapes were green, thou didst refuse me. Grapes. *Unknown, Greek.* AWP, *tr.* by Alma Strettell

While yet we wait for spring, and from the dry. Robert Bridges. GSo

While you clambered up ahead. Climbing Gannett. Roberta Hill Whiteman. HATNAP

While you, great Patron of Mankind! sustain. The First Epistle of the Second Book of Horace Imitated. Alexander Pope.

While you, my lord, the rural shades admire. A Letter from Italy [to the Right Honourable Charles Lord Halifax]. Joseph Addison. NOEC

While you read / the sleepmoth begins. The Cat. William Matthews. AmPA

While you sleep off the brandy, little one. Saturday Morning. Marilyn Hacker. CPO

While you walk the water's edge. Beach Glass. Amy Clampitt. FaBoWP; NoAM; NoP-4; VCAP

While you were gone. (LL) Thank you, my dear. Sappho, *Greek.* GrIP; PiM, *tr.* by Mary Barnard

While your great-grandmother and her sons. Separate Parties. Dabney Stuart. NYBP

While your hands mold a form. Craftsmanship. Nikolai Nikolaevich Ushakov, *Russian.* TCRP, *tr.* by John Glad

While you're a white-hot youth, emit the rays. The Star System. Richard Wilbur. NBLV *Fr.* Flippancies.

While you're alive it's shameful to put yourself into. Disbelief in Yourself Is Indispensable. Yevtushenko, *Russian.* TCRP, *tr.* by Albert C. Todd

Whiles someone did chant this lovely lay, The. The Song of Bliss. Edmund Spenser. OBVE *Fr.* Wood Of Error. AEP

Whilom, as antique stories tellen us. Edmund Spenser. EPCY *Fr.* Wood Of Error. AEP

Whilom ther was dwellynge in my contree. The Friar's Tale. Chaucer. PoE *Fr.* The Canterbury Tales.

Whil'st Alexis Lay Prest [*or* Press'd]. Dryden. BoLoP; PeLV *Fr.* Marriage à la Mode.

Whilst dear Sophia plans some pictured strife. A Winter in Wales. Hester Lynch Salusbury Thrale [*later* Mrs. Piozzi]. CABP

Whilst Ec[c]ho cries [*or* cryes], "What shall become of me[e]?" Henry Constable. AAS; CBLP *Fr.* Diana.

Whilst happy I Triumphant stood. On *a* Juniper-Tree, Cut Down to Make Busks. Aphra Behn. KTR

Whilst human kind / Throughout the lands lay miserably crushed. Beyond Religion. Lucretius, *Latin.* AWP, *tr.* by William Ellery Leonard

Whilst in her prime and bloom of years. On a Female Rope-Dancer. *Unknown.* LiLi; NOEC

Whilst in This World I Stay. Philip Pain. AH

Whilst maudlin Whigs deplore their Cato's fate. Epigram. Nicholas Rowe. ECEV

Whilst my heart bleeding writes that deadlie wound. Written upon the death of the most Noble Prince Henrie. Sir Arthur Gorges. PBRV

Whilst my soul's eye beheld no light. A Dialogue betwixt God and the Soul. Sir Henry Wotton. MeLP; PeECV

Whilst on Septimius' panting Breast. Catullus. *See* Carmen 45 ("Phyllis Corydon clutched to him").

Whilst on the beach I stood, my courage fainted. Written the First Morning of the Author's Bathing at Teignmouth for the Head-Ache. Jane Cave. ECWP

Whilst some affect the sun, and some the shade. Robert Blair. NOEC *Fr.* The Grave.

Whilst the red spittle of the grape-shot sings. Rimbaud. *See* Evil.

Whilst thine the victor is, and free. (LL) Song: Love Armed. Aphra Behn. NALW; NOBE; NOSC; NoP-4; OBEV; OxAEP-1; PEW; Poetr; WPE; WeW-3

Whilst thirst of praise, and vain desire of fame. The Lady's Resolve. Lady Mary Wortley Montagu. BoWoP; ECWP; OxBSP

Whilst thou art far away, I am at peace. Siena. Lily Thicknesse. LW

Whilst thus my pen strives to eternize thee. Michael Drayton. AAS; Son *Fr.* Idea.

Whilst Titian was mixing rose madder. Limerick. *Unknown.* PeLi

Whilst what I write I do not see. Written in Juice of Lem[m]on. Abraham Cowley. CABP; SeCP *Fr.* The Mistress.

Whilst yet to prove. Farewell to Love. Donne. OAEL-1

Whilst Youth and Error led my wand'ring mind. Sonnet 5: 'Whilst Youth and Error'. Samuel Daniel. AEP *Fr.* Delia.

Whim of Time, A. Stephen Spender. MoBrPo

Whimper of Awakening Passion. Ebenezer Jones. NOBVV

Whimpers and speaks in the throat / of the Indian Princess. Elizabeth Bishop. *See* Florida.

Whins are blythesome on the knowe, The. A New Spring. Albert D. Mackie. OxBS

Whip, The. Robert Creeley. EOEF; MoP; NeAP; PoE; PoM

Whip-the-World. "Hugh MacDiarmid." FaBoVe

Whipping, The. Robert Earl Hayden. FiLi; PoBA; PoE; SSLK; SoSe-8

Whirl, snow, on the blackbird's chatter. Eager Spring. Gordon Bottomley. MoBrPo

Whirl up, sea. Oread. Hilda Doolittle. AWP; CMoP; ColAP; HeIP-4; InPS-3; MoAmPo; MoP; NAAL-2; NALW; NOBA; NoAM; OxBA; PoPoPo; Poetr; TAP

Whirl'd off at last, for speech I sought. Coventry Patmore. GBL *Fr.* The Angel in the House.

Whirled ten years beyond all bounds. Tu Mu. PLT, *tr.* by A. C. Graham *Fr.* Recalling Former Travels.

Whirling along its living freight, it came. The Locomotive. Christopher Pearse Cranch. APN-1; GM *Fr.* Seven Wonders of the World.

Whirling Round the Sun. Suzanne Noguere. FFC

Whirlpool, The. *Unknown.* PoToHe

Whirls and stands still: the moon comes: terrain. (LL) Terrain. A. R. Ammons. CoAmPo; VCAP

Whirls life within the shower of loosened hair! (LL) I play for Seasons; not Eternities! George Meredith. OBNC; SCGP

Whirlwind. Ravji Patel, *Gujarati.* OMIP, *tr.* by Hansa Jhaveri

Whirlwind. David Rokeah, *Hebrew.* MHP, *tr.* by Ruth Finer Mintz

Whirlwinds / nearly always. Fily-Dabo Sissoko, *French.* NegPo, *tr.* by Ellen Conroy Kennedy

Whirlwinds of hot autumn dust. Dust World. Adrian C. Louis. UnSA

Whirr. The invisible sponsored again by white. In the Hotel. Jorie Graham. BAP-94

Whiskers Meets Polly. Michael Stillman. TLR

Whiskey in Whiting, Indiana. James Hazard. EC2

Whiskey on your breath, The. My Papa's Waltz. Theodore Roethke. CMoP; ChAP; ClHu; ColAP; HAP; HCAP; HeIP-4; HoPM; InPK-6; InPS-3; LCAP-2; LiTM; MoP; NAAL-2; NBLV; NIP-2; NOBA; NOxBChV; NTP; NoAM; NoP-4; PBMP; PoE; PoPoPo; Poetr; RaBo; SAGP; TAP; TFi; TRP; VGW

Whisky Frisky. *Unknown.* BoTP; CTAV; FPC

Whisky Johnny. *Unknown.* AS

Whisky, Johnny, *vers.* I. *Unknown.* AmFP

Whisper, The. Eugene Gloria. OpBo

Whisper. John Banister Tabb. APN-2

Whisper flies to the empty sleeve, A. Sequel of Appomattox. Donald Davidson. CBCWP; FuPo

Whisper in odorous heights of even. (LL) Milton [Alcaics]. Tennyson. EPCY; PeECV

Whisper of yellow globes. Her Lips Are Copper Wire. Jean Toomer. GT; NoAM

Whisper Words of Love to Me. Lizelia Augusta Jenkins Moorer. CBWP-3

Whispered. Jiri Orten, *Czech.* AF, *tr.* by Lyn Coffin

Whispered, "Darling, you have saved me! curfew will not ring to-night." (LL) Curfew Must Not Ring Tonight [*or* To-Night]. Rose Hartwick Thorpe. APN-2; BLPA; FaBoBe

Whisperer, The. Mark Van Doren. MoAmPo

Whisperin' Bill. Irving Bacheller. PoLF

Whispering *Dear Warlock-Williams: Why, of course.* (LL) Vers de Société. Philip Larkin. FP; PeLV

Whispering to each handhold, "I'll be back." After Arguing against the Contention That Art Must Come from Discontent. William Stafford. NoAM

Whispering Wind. Catherine Braan Layne. PWR

Whispering worshipping. (LL) Mice in the Hay. Leslie Norris. NOxBChV

Whisperjet swings wildly, The. In Flight. Jennifer Regan. CrSp

Whispers. Roberta Hill Whiteman. CDW

Whispers of Immortality. T. S. Eliot. CMoP; CTC; NOBA; NoAM; OBMV; OxAEP-2

Whist. Eugene Fitch Ware. PoLF

Whistle, The. Charles Murray. OxBS

Whistle, and I'll Come to You, My Lad. Robert Burns. CBLP; OxAEP-2; OxBoLi

Whistle, Daughter, Whistle. *Unknown.* AmFP; OxNR; ReMoGo

Whistle howls, the wheels click along, The. (LL) "Mystery Train" Janis Joplin Leaves Port Arthur for Points West, 1964. David Wojahn. GM; PBCAP

Whistle o'er the Lave o't. Robert Burns. OxBS

Whistle of a blackbird, envious of the crackling of a fire, ends by, The. A Landscape Heard. Filippo Tommaso Marinetti. PFTM

Whistle / of the bright, The. Belfast Lough. *Unknown, Irish.* BIrV, *tr. by* John Montague

Whistle shrilled, A; the farm hands left the stack. Jack and Jill. Charles Powell. BXAP

Whistlecraft. John Hookham Frere.
    "And certainly they say, for fine behaving." OBCoV

Whistles. Dorothy Aldis. CTV

Whistles like light in leaves, O light. The Heart Flies Up, Erratic as a Kite. Delmore Schwartz. PoA

Whistling bellows of his furnace, The. Philip of Thessalonica, *Greek.* GrAn, *tr. by* Edwin Morgan

Whistling Boy. Nixon Waterman. PoLF

Whit care I for the leagues o sand. Sydney Goodsir Smith. *See* The Mither's Lament.

Whit Monday. John Hewitt. TIRV

Whit Monday. Elizaveta Kuzmina-Karavayeva, *Russian.*
    "I too have encompassed a lot: a mother thrice—." TCRP, *tr. by* Vera Dunham

Whit Monday. Louis MacNeice. ChIV-1; NYBP; OAEL-2; PeECV

White. The Colors of Night. N. Scott Momaday. PaTW

White, a shingled path. Icos. Charles Tomlinson. GTBS-P

White against a ruddy cliff you stand, chalcedony on sard. (LL) The Cameo. Edna St. Vincent Millay. FYAP; MeMAP; MoAmPo; UnPo; WPE

White Air of March, The. Iain Crichton Smith.
    "Cuillins tower, The." FaBoTC
    "Exiles have departed, The." FaBoTC
    "This is the land God gave to Andy Stewart." FaBoTC

White an' Blue. William Barnes. GBL; GTBS-P

White and blue, an outspread fan. Environs of Vanholt I. Charles Spear. PeNZ

White and curved as a shell she lies. Discoverer. James Michie. DiPo

White and red. Still Life. Francis Sullivan. CRP

White and shapeless mass—, A. (LL) The Waning Moon. Shelley. CH; FHYEP; OBEV; OxBSP

White and the Black, The. N. M. Khaketla, *Southern Sotho.* PeSA, *tr. by* Jack Cope *and* Dan Kunene

White ants, white ants and the little ribs. (LL) Snow. Charles Wright. ColAP

White Apples. Donald Hall. LoL; TAP

White as coal-ash pressed. Queen of Heaven Mausoleum. Dennis Schmitz. LCAP-2

White as her hand fair Julia threw. The Snow-Ball. Soame Jenyns. OBVE

White as I can, though not as thee. (LL) The Nymph Complaining for the Death of Her Faun [*or* Fawn]. Andrew Marvell. CH; ESCV; GeHe; HeIP-4; NAEL-1; OAEL-1; PoEL-2; RACG; SeCP

White ash amid funereal cypresses. (LL) Helen. Hilda Doolittle. BoWoP; ColAP; FaBoWP; LiTM; MoAmPo; NAAL-2; NALW; NMM-2; NOBA; NoAM; NoP-4; TAP

White bark writhed and sputtered like a fish, The. Edna St. Vincent Millay. *Fr.* Sonnets from an Ungrafted Tree. NALW

White Beach. Reginald Gibbons. BAP-96

White billows and huge waves block the river crossing. Kept Waiting in the Boat at Chiu-K'ou Ten Days by an Adverse Wind. Po Chü-i, *Chinese.* ChiP, *tr. by* Arthur Waley

White Bird, The. Rosamund Marriott Watson. VWP

White Bird, The. Wilfred Watson. MoCV

White bird featherless / Flew from Paradise. Riddle. *Unknown.* FaBoVe; OxNR

White bird of the tempest! O beautiful thing! To a Seagull. Gerald Griffin. TIRV

White Birds, The. W. B. Yeats. ADE

White birds over the grey river. Another Spring. Tu Fu, *Chinese.* BLT; OHPC, *tr. by* Kenneth Rexroth

White Blossom, A. D. H. Lawrence. MoBrPo

White blossom, white, white shell; the Nazarene. Music of Colours—White Blossom. Vernon Watkins. LiTM

White blossoms bloom. Tanka. Akiko Yosano, *Japanese.* MJT, *tr. by* Ueda, Makoto

White bones scattered. Crossing the Yellow River: June 12. Yüan Hao-wen, *Chinese.* SuSp, *tr. by* Stephen West

White Boot. Michael McClure. PuP-16

White buck come in. Anadarko John. Carroll Arnett. VoR

White butterfly, A. The Graceful Bastion. William Carlos Williams. NYBP

White carcases / of, The. Liberty. Emile Ologoudou. PBMAP

White Cat of Trenarren, The. Alfred Leslie Rowse. OxBTC; PC

White Center. Richard Hugo. FiLi; NAAL-2

White chocolate jar full of petals, The. Chez Jane. Frank O'Hara. CoAP; ColAP; NOBA; NeAP; NoAM; PoA; PoE

White Christmas. William Robert Rodgers. LiTM; MoBrPo

White chrysanthemum, The. Mitsune, *Japanese.* OHPJ, *tr. by* Kenneth Rexroth

White chrysanthemums, The. (LL) No one spoke. Ōshima Ryōta, *Japanese.* OHPJ, *tr. by* Kenneth Rexroth

White City, The. Claude McKay. BPo; CrDW; NoAM; RaBo; TAP

White Cliffs, The. Alice Duer Miller.
    English Are Frosty, The. PoLF
    I Have Loved England. PoLF

White cloud passed over the land, The. The Final Painting. Lee Harwood. SPE

White clouds are mindless, they never come to rest, The. Nesting among Clouds. Yang Chi, *Chinese.* CoBLCP, *tr. by* Jonathan Chaves

White clouds beyond the sky, The. A Mushroom Gatherer Deep in the Mountains Among the White Clouds. Hsü Wei, *Chinese.* CoBLCP, *tr. by* Jonathan Chaves

White clouds, I cannot see their end. Ch'ang-an. Ho Ching-ming. CoBLCP, *tr. by* Jonathan Chaves

White clouds, like a belt, wind around the waist of the mountains. Inscribed on a Painting. Shen Chou, *Chinese.* SuSp, *tr. by* Daniel Bryant

White clouds like a scarf enfold the the mountain's waist. Shen Chou, *Chinese.* CoBLCP, *tr. by* Jonathan Chaves

White Clover. Marvin Bell. VCAP

White clover will not ask anything. Jaan Kaplinski, *Estonian.* CEEP, *tr. by* Lehiste, Ilse

White cock in my courtyard. Elegy for a White Cock. Mei Yao Ch'en, *Chinese.* SuSp, *tr. by* Jonathan Chaves

White cock's tail / Tosses in the wind, The. Ploughing on Sunday. Wallace Stevens. RB; TTTS

White Conduit House. William Woty. NOEC

White cormorants shaped like houses stare down at you, The. Party at Hydra. Irving Layton. HeIP-4

White Crane Hill. Su Tung-p'o, *Chinese.* CoBCP, *tr. by* Burton Watson

White cup shrivels round the golden heart, The. (LL) Barren Spring. D. G. Rossetti. EBVV; IMW; NoP-4; OAEL-2; OBNC; PoEL-5

White cups white. Turkish Love Songs. *Unknown.* BoWoP, *tr. by* Reza Baraheni *and* Zahra-Soltan Shokoohtaezeh

White curtains of infinite fatigue. And the Seventh Dream Is the Dream of Isis. David Gascoyne. SPE

White dawn. Stillness. When the rippling began. A Tree Telling of Orpheus. Denise Levertov. APSN

White day, black river. The Predicter of Famine. William Carlos Williams. VGW

White Days. Reginald Shepherd. GT

White Day's Death. Hazel Hall. PaTW

White decorators interested in art. Nights of 1964-66: The Old Reliable. Marilyn Hacker. RA; VCAP

White Devil, The. John Webster.
    Dirge, A: "Call for the robin-redbreast and the wren." NOBE; OBEV ("For with his nails he'll dig them up again.") (LL) PFE
    "What, are you drop't?" PoEL-2

White Doe of Rylstone, The; or, The Fate of the Nortons. Wordsworth.
    "In trellised shed with clustering roses gay." EPCY

White Dou o Truth. The Ineffable Dou. Sydney Goodsir Smith. OxBS

White Dress, The. Marya Alexandrovna Zaturenska. MoAmPo

White dusk moved ahead of them. Image of City. Lance Henson. VoR

White Dust, The. Wilfrid Wilson Gibson. MoBrPo

White Earth. Gerald Vizenor. HATNAP

White Fields. James Stephens. OTCP

White Fisher, The. *Unknown.* ESPB

White floating clouds. Clouds like the plains come and water the earth. A Rain Song of the Quer'ränna Chai'än. *Unknown, Sia.* APN-2, *tr. by* Matilda Coxe Stevenson

White flour, earth-flesh, a cold fleece on the mountain. The Snowfall. Gwerfyl Mechain, *Welsh.* OBWVE, *tr. by* Kenneth Hurlstone Jackson

White flowers. Penny Harter. HA

White fog lifting and falling on mountain-brow. Wales Visitation. Allen Ginsberg. APSN; BB; ColAP; NNaP; NOBA; NYBP; VCAP

"White folks is white," says Uncle Jim. Uncle Jim. Countee Cullen. GT; NAAL-2

White Foolscap/Book of Cordelia. Susan Howe. PmAP

White for nothing. (LL) Lawd, Dese Colored Chillum. Ruby C. Saunders. LTA

White founts falling in the courts of the sun. Lepanto. G. K. Chesterton. EBEvV; EBNV; FaPoR; MoBrPo; OBMV; OBNV; RB

White foxes howl at mountain wind beneath the moon. Ravine on a Cold Evening. Li Ho, *Chinese.* SuSp, *tr. by* Maureen Robertson

White girl, your flesh is lilies. Morbidezza. Arthur Symons. ADE

White glare recedes to the Western hills, The. On and On for Ever. Li Ho, *Chinese.* PLT, *tr. by* A. C. Graham

White Gloves. William Plomer. PeSAV

White Goddess, The. Robert Graves. MoBrPo; NAEL-2; NoP-4; OAEL-2

White goose by palm tree, palm ragged, among stones the. Gull's Cry. Robert Penn Warren. FuPo *Fr.* To a Little Girl, One Year Old, in a Ruined Fortress.

White grief-stricken wail, The. (LL) Art Pepper. Edward Hirsch. NAmP90; SeSe

White guardians of the universe of sleep. E. E. Cummings. NYBP

White-habited, the mystic Swan. The Swan. Jay Macpherson. NoP-4

White hair fallen from my father's beard, A. (LL) Heirloom. Abraham Moses Klein. NOBC; TrJP

White hair shrouds both my temples. Blaming Sons. T'ao Ch'ien, *Chinese.* ChiPo; CoBCP, *tr. by* Burton Watson

White-haired, I walk in on my parents. David Ignatow. WeT

White-haired Lover. Karl Shapiro.

 "I swore to stab the sonnet with my pen." PoA

White-haired man, holding a fishing pole, The. Tsung Ch'en. *Fr.* Miscellaneous Words on the Lake. CoBLCP, *tr. by* Jonathan Chaves

White hairs. Jamal Isfahani, *Persian.* ArPe, *tr. by* Omar S. Pound

White hairs cover my temples. Blaming Sons. Ch'ien T'ao, *Chinese.* ChiP, *tr. by* Arthur Waley

White Hare, The. Lilian Bowes-Lyon. OxBTC

White hare, A. Tanka. Fumi Saito, *Japanese.* MJT, *tr. by* Ueda, Makoto

White Heliotrope. Arthur Symons. BoLoP; EBEV; GLoP; LoP; PeVV

White hill-side is prickled with antlers, The. Knole. Charles Hubert Sisson. NOCV

White Hope. Ishmael Reed. ISC

White Horse, The. W. H. Davies. OxBTC

White Horse, The. D. H. Lawrence. KaS; TTTS

White horse. John Wills. HA

White horse came to our farm once, A. The White Stallion / (The Runaway). Guy Owen. KaS

White Horse of Westbury, The. Charles Tennyson Turner. EBEV; PeVV

White Horsemen, with Christ their Captain: for ever He! (LL) Te Martyrum Candidatus. Lionel Pigot Johnson. OBMV; TIRV

White Horses. Rudyard Kipling. PeVV

White Horses. Irene F. Pawsey. BoTP

White horses, tails high, rise from the cedar. E Uni Que A The Hi A Tho, Father. Roberta Hill Whiteman. VoR

White-hot midday in the Snake Park, A. In the Snake Park. William Plomer. NYBP; OxBTC

White House, The. Claude McKay. AmPP; ISC; NAAAL; NIP-4; PoBA

White house in front of the park, A. Rossana Ombres, *Italian.* NeIt, *tr. by* Robert McCracken *and* Pietro Pedace

White hummocks here are rounded to a thigh. Early Summer Sea-Tryst. Frederick Thomas Bennett Macartney. CBAP

White hunter is nearly crazy, A. Gertrude Stein. PFTM

White ignorant hollow of his face, The. (LL) Father and Son. Stanley Kunitz. AF, *tr. by* Jack Bevan; MoP; Poetr; TwCP

White in the moon the long road lies. A. E. Housman. AWP; CMoP; GLoP; NTP

White Iris, A. Pauline B. Barrington. PoLF

White iris beautifies me, The. (LL) In the Carolinas. Wallace Stevens. SAmP; VGW

White is the sail and lonely. A Sail. Mikhail Yuryevich Lermontov, *Russian.* AWP, *tr. by* Max Eastman

White Island. Robert Herrick. BeJo; NOSC; NoP-4; OAEL-1; TOF

White Isle of Leuce, The. Sir Herbert Read. FaBoTw

White jet clouds. Tanka. Kondō Yoshimi, *Japanese.* MJT, *tr. by* Makoto Ueda

White Knight's Song, The. "Lewis Carroll." CBNP; FaBoCh; InPS-3; NAEL-2; NOBE; NOBL; NoAM; NoP-4; OAEL-2; PeLV *Fr.* Through the Looking-Glass.

 (Aged, Aged Man, The.) BXAP; OxBChV

 (White Knight's Ballad, The.) HAP

White Lady, The. Rosamund Marriott Watson. VWP

White Lady has asked me to dance, The. Fourth Dance Poem. Gerald William Barrax. PoBA

White Lake. James Applewhite. MT

White Lake, The. *Unknown, Irish.* TIRV, *tr. by* Robin Flower

White lambs leap. Through miles of snow. The Fire in the Snow. Vernon Watkins. LiTM

White Land, The. Roberta Hill Whiteman. HATNAP

White Lanterns. David Wojahn. NAmP90

White lather on black soap. Black Soap. Sandra McPherson. VCAP

White light, receive me your sojourner; O milky way. Elegy of the Wind. Christopher Okigbo. VCWP

White light's wet glaze on asphalt city floor. Studying the Signs. Allen Ginsberg. FTOS

White Lilies, The. Louise Glück. PoPoPo

White Lilies. Theodore Wratislaw. ADE

White Line, A. Art Lange. MoNo

White low sun, low thunderclouds; and back, A. Marina Tsvetayeva, *Russian.* AF; PeFWW, *tr. by* David McDuff *and* Jon Silkin

White man is, The. 12 Gates to the City. Nikki Giovanni. PoBA

White man is a tiger at my throat, The. Tiger. Claude McKay. BPo; CrDW

White man killed my father, The. The Time of Martyrdom. David Diop, *French.* NegPo, *tr. by* Ellen Conroy Kennedy

White Man Pressed the Locks, The. James C. Kilgore. InPK-6

White-maned, wide-throated, the heavy-shouldered children of the wind leap at the sea-cliff. Granite and Cypress. Robinson Jeffers. AmPP

White Man's Burden, The. Rudyard Kipling. FaBoPV

White man's soul, it thirsts for gain, The. The Indian's Retort. Jones Very. NCAP

White mares lashed to the sulky carriages. In Ohio. James Wright. NNaP

White mares of the moon rush along the sky, The. Night Clouds. Amy Lowell. MoAmPo

White men handed papers to my mother. Eviction. Michelle T. Clinton. ISC

White men's children spread over the earth. The Riddle. Georgia Douglas Johnson. PoBA

White metal tubes contain. Planes Landing. Jamie Grant. NOBAu

White moon gleams through scudding / Clouds, The. Sorrow. Chu Shu-chen, *Chinese.* BoWoP; OHMPC, *tr. by* Kenneth Rexroth

White moon is rising, The. The Moon Is Rising. *Unknown, Chinese.* TAL, *tr. by* Robert Payne

White moons like midnight's in the morning sun. Autumn Mushrooms. Kenneth Mackenzie. CBAP

White moth with to the closing vine, The. The Gipsy Trail. Rudyard Kipling. PoRA

White newspaper sky, A. Snow Falling. Gillian Hughes. NTP

White night, the moon an unstrung bow. Two Poems on Night. Tu Fu, *Chinese.* SuSp, *tr. by* Jan Walls

White Noise. Laurie Sheck. WWSi

White Notes. Donald Justice. LCAP-2

White nymph wandering in the woods by night, A. André Marie de Chénier. *Fr.* Elegies. AWP, *tr. by* Arthur Symons

White on White. Eugenio de Andrade, *Portuguese.*

 "Friend is sometimes desert, A." VCWP, *tr. by* Alexis Levitin

White on White. Maria Luisa Spaziani, *Italian.* NeIt, *tr. by* Beverly Allen

White one?, The. (LL) The Wings. Denise Levertov. APSN; NALW

White orchid. Raymond Roseliep. HA

White Oxen. Louis Simpson. NoAM

White Paper. V. Narayana Rao, *Telugu.* OMIP, *tr. by* V. Narayana Rao

White Pass Ski Patrol. John Logan. CAPP-1

White Peace, The. "Fiona Macleod." FaBoBe

White Peacock, The. Alice Notley. FTOS

White pearls. Pearls. Léopold Sédar Senghor, *French.* VCWP, *tr. by* Melvin Dixon

White pebbles jut from the river-stream. In the Hills. Wang Wei, *Chinese.* TAL, *tr. by* Robert Payne

White peonies blooming along the porch. Peonies at Dusk. Jane Kenyon. LoL

White People. David Henderson. PoBA

White Petticoats. Chana Bloch. CrSp

White phlox and white hydrangeas. Left Behind. Amy Lowell. CPO

"White phosphorous, white phosphorous." Overheard over S. E. Asia. Denise Levertov. BoWoP

White Phosphorus. Alice Notley. FTOS

White Pilgrim: Old Christian Cemetary, The. Brigit Pegeen Kelly. BAP-93

White Poetess. Musaemura Bonus Zimunya. PeSAV

White Port and Lemon Juice. Yusef Komunyakaa. ISC

White Rabbit, The. John Walsh. PeP

White room that I eat in and write in, The. The Shortest Day. William Dickey. IMW

White Rose, A. John Boyle O'Reilly. OBEV

White rose in red rose-garden. Swinburne. See Before the Mirror.

White Rose is a quiet horse. The Four Horses. James Reeves. TLR

White Roses. John Ashbery. TAP

White roses I tried to braid in my hair, The. Tomiko Yamakawa, Japanese. WPJ, tr. by Kenneth Rexroth and Ikuko Atsumi

White sagebrush desert, The. Noon. O Pioneers! John Peale Bishop. VGW

White Serpent. Nelly Sachs, German. BoWoP, tr. by Michael Hamburger

White Sheep. W. H. Davies. BoTP

White sheep, white sheep, on a blue hill. Riddle. Unknown. FaBoVe

White sheet on the tail-gate of a truck, A. Elegy for a Dead Soldier. Karl Shapiro. HAP; LiTM; OBWP; OxBA

White Ship, The. Geoffrey Hill. OxBC

White Ship, The. D. G. Rossetti. OBNV

White-sided flowers are thrusting up on the hillside. Hawaii Dantesca. Charles Wright. HCAP; LCAP-2

White sky, over the hemlocks bowed with snow. The Buck in the Snow. Edna St. Vincent Millay. ColAP; NALW; NoP-4

White sky, The. Kondō Yoshimi, Japanese. MJT, tr. by Makoto Ueda

White snow fills the lakeside village. Tsung Ch'en. Fr. Miscellaneous Words on the Lake. CoBLCP, tr. by Jonathan Chaves

White southern businessman needed, The. New Windows. Claudia Rankine. GT

White spider, The. Geraldine Clinton Little. HA

White Stallion / (The Runaway), The. Guy Owen. KaS

White stars falling gently. Winter Joys. Dorothy Graddon. BoTP

White Statue, The. Olive Custance. ADE

White stone lady on the grass, The. The White Lady. Rosamund Marriott Watson. VWP

White Stone Slope. Yang Shih-ch'i. CoBLCP, tr. by Jonathan Chaves Fr. The Intendant Yao Shan Has Requested Six Poems on Living in the Mountains.

White substitute teacher, A. View of the Library of Congress from Paul Laurence Dunbar High School. Thomas Sayers Ellis. GT

White Suit. Blaise Cendrars, French. NNPT, tr. by Peter Hoida

White sun. Zebra. Judith Thurman. SSCS

White Swan. A. Glanz-Leyeles, Yiddish. CEEP, tr. by Keith Bosley

White swan. Tanka. Mori Ōgai, Japanese. MJT, tr. by Makoto Ueda

White swan of cities, slumbering in thy nest. Venice. Henry Wadsworth Longfellow. APN-1

White-tailed hornet lives in a balloon, The. Robert Frost. OxBA

White temple over the gulf. Gulf. Tudor Arghezi, Romanian. CEEP, tr. by Stavros Deligiorgis

White though ye be, yet, lillies, know. How Lillies Came White. Robert Herrick. BeJo; CaPo

White Thought, The. Stevie Smith. Spl

White Tiger Years, The. Sarah Gorham. FFC Fr. Notes From a Chinese Love Manual.

White to the neck he glides and plunges. Fencing School. John Streeter Manifold. CBAP

White towelling bathrobe, The. La Toilette. Seamus Heaney. CBLP

White tower, A. Tanka. Akiko Yosano, Japanese. MJT, tr. by Ueda, Makoto

White Trash. Jim Hall. MT

White Troops Had Their Orders but the Negroes Looked Like Men. Gwendolyn Brooks. PBMP

White unicorn?, A. (LL) Black Poet, White Critic. Dudley Randall. CoAmPo

White Valentine. Winifred Welles. WPN

White Venus limpid wandering in the sky. Sonnet 5. Louise Labé, French. BoWoP, tr. by Aliki and Willis Barnstone

White violet, The. Sea Violet. Hilda Doolittle. NoP-4

White violets again and lyre orchestras. Philodemus, Greek. GrAn, tr. by William Moebius

White violets flower. Meleager, Greek. GrAn, tr. by Peter Whigham

White waters twist and turn among crumbling embankments. In the Evening, Walking in the Western Fields. Chang Yü, Chinese. CoBLCP, tr. by Jonathan Chaves

White Wedding Slippers. Anna Swirszczynska, Polish. AF, tr. by Czeslaw Milosz

White woman across the aisle from me says, "Look," The. On the Amtrak from Boston to New York City. Sherman Alexie. PoPoPo

White woman have you heard. Montgomery. Sam Cornish. MBE; PoBA; Poetsp

White Women, The. Mary Elizabeth Coleridge. BrRo; NALW; PEW; VWP

White World. Hilda Doolittle. WPoS

White world after a urine-yellow sundown. Visiting Hour (Repatriation Hospital). Michael Dransfield. BMAP

Whitecaps. Betsy Sholl. CrSp

Whitehall Stairs. Aaron Hill. NOEC

Whiteman Blues, The. Lionel Abrahams. PeSAV

Whiteness, hear me universal whiteness! Some Lines on My Mother's Illness. Yunna Petrovna Moritz, Russian. TCRP, tr. by Bernard Meares

Whiteness, or Chastity. Joseph Beaumont. NOSC

Whiter / than the crust. The Wind Sleepers. Hilda Doolittle. WPE

Whites alone upon the jury in a number of the states. Injustice of the Courts. Lizelia Augusta Jenkins Moorer. CBWP-3

Whites had taught him how to rip, The. Sam Smiley. Sterling Brown. NAAAL

Whitewash. Léon Damas, French. NegPo, tr. by Ellen Conroy Kennedy

Whitey, Baby. James A. Emanuel. NBV

Whither? Wilhelm Müller. AWP, tr. by Longfellow Fr. The Beautiful Maid of the Mill.

Whither Away? Mary Elizabeth Coleridge. CH

Whither away good neighbour. Martin Parker. PBRV Fr. Well met Neighbour.

WHITHER away so fast. Unknown. NoSic

Whither dost thou hide from the magic of my flute-call? The Snake-Charmer. Sarojini Naidu [or Nayadu]. PBWP

Whither I kneel or stand or sit in prayer. At Communion. Madeleine L'Engle. TrCP

Whither, 'midst falling dew. To A Waterfowl. William Cullen Bryant. APN-1; APo; AWP; AmPP; CH; ColAP; FaBoBe; HoPM; ImPo; NAAL-1; NAAL-3; NCAP; NOBA; NoP-4; OxBA; PAR; PWR; PoEL-4; PoLF; SoSe-8; TAP; TFi

Whither, O city, are your profits and your gilded shrines. Troy. Agathias, Greek. GrAn; OBCVT, tr. by Ezra Pound

Whither, O splendid ship, thy white sails crowding. A Passer-by. Robert Bridges. CMoP; EBEvV; ImPo; LiTM; MoBrPo; OAEL-2; OBEV; OBNC; OxBTC; SCGP

Whither, O, whither art thou fled. The Search. George Herbert. ESCV

Whither, O whither didst thou fly. The Eclipse. Henry Vaughan. OxBSP

Whither, oh! whither wilt thou wing thy way? Flight of the Spirit. Felicia Dorothea Hemans. Son

Whither? Say, whither shall I fly. The Frozen Zone; or, Julia Disdainful. Robert Herrick. CaPo; CavPo

Whither shall I go. John Webster and William Rowley. GBL Fr. The Thracian Wonder.

Whither shall I, the fair maiden, flee from Sorrow? Sorrow. Unknown, Russian. AWP, tr. by W. R. S. Ralston

Whither some great, supreme, o'er-ruling Power. The Progress of Man. George Canning and William Gifford. NOBRP

Whither, thou son of Beor, hastes thou so. On Balaam, and His Ass. Henry Colman. KSG

Whitman among the wounded, at the bedside. Reading with the Poets. Stanley Plumly. PuP-17

Whitsun Weddings, The. Philip Larkin. FaBoMo; HeIP-4; MoP; NoAM; NoP-4; OxAEP-2; OxBM; OxBTC

Whitsunday. George Herbert. GeHe

Whittier. James Russell Lowell. AmPP; NOBA; OxBA Fr. A Fable for Critics. NAAL-1; NAAL-3

Who? Florence Hoatson. BoTP

Who. Edwin Honig. TAP

Who. Who Can Be Born Black. Mari E. Evans. ISC

Who a Mother Is. Roy W. Watson. PWR

Who affirms that crystals are alive? Snow. John Davidson. FaBoTC

Who alone is Lord and God! (LL) Laus Deo! John Greenleaf Whittier. AmPP; CBCWP

Who am I? I am a lady faithful to the ways. Lady of the Ferry Inn. Gwerfyl Mechain, Welsh. BoWoP, tr. by Willis Barnstone

Who am I, Lord? Just an impostor. Elizaveta Kuzmina-Karavayeva, Russian. TCRP, tr. by Thomas E. Bird

Who am I? They often tell me. Dietrich Bonhoeffer, German. HP, tr. by Reginald H. Fuller

Who am I worthless that You spent such pains. A Prayer for the Self. John Berryman. Fr. Eleven Addresses to the Lord. OxBC

Who Among You Knows the Essence of Garlic? Garrett Kaoru Hongo. InPS-3; WeT

Who and Each. Ron Padgett. PmAP

Who are a little wise, the best fool[e]s be[e]. (LL) The Triple Fool[e]. Donne. FMP; FSCP; GBL; NOSC; PBRV; SoSe-8

Who are my friends / the sick / the weak / the poor in spirit. Nicanor Parra. GI, *tr. by* Sandra Reyes *Fr.* New Sermons and Preachings of the Christ of Elqui (1979).

Who Are My People? Rosa Zagnoni Marinoni. BLPA; PoToHe

Who are my pets. Robert Fisher. PeP

Who are these coming to the sacrifice? Keats. *Fr.* Ode on a Grecian Urn. AWP; CABP; ChAP; ClHu; EBEV; FaBoBe; HAP; HeIP-4; HoPM; ImPo; InPS-3; NAEL-2; NAWM-2; NIP-4; NOBE; NOBRP; NoP-4; OAEL-2; OBEV; OBNC; PBMP; PFE; PoE; PoEL-4; PoPoPo; Ro; SCGP; TFi; TOF; UnPo

Who are these from the strange, ineffable places. Arabia. John Meade Falkner. OxBTC

Who are these people at the bridge to meet me? They are the villagers. The Bee Meeting. Sylvia Plath. HCAP; InPS-3; NALW; Poetr; WPE

Who are these? Why sit they here in twilight? Mental Cases. Wilfred Owen. CMoP; FaBoMo; NoAM; PeFWW

Who are they. The Passengers. David Antin. NYBP

Who are they now? since the Bathurst ground. From a Republican Grave: Daniel Henry Deniehy, 1828–1865. Philip Mead. NOBAu

Who are they talking to in the big temple? The Temple. Charles Hubert Sisson. OxBTC

Who are they to be in their skin. The Subway Witnesses. Lorenzo Thomas. GT; PoBA

Who are we here? Intra-Political. Margaret Avison. MoCV

'Who are we waiting for?' '*Soup* burnt?' '. . . Eight—'. The Feckless Dinner-Party. Walter De la Mare. FP; FaBoTw

Who are you? You and I. Tennessee Williams. GLP

Who are you? and with whom do you sleep here? (LL) On a cold night I came through the cold rain. James Vincent Cunningham. HAP; TRP; VCAP

Who are you, listening to me, who are you. Poem for Half White College Students. Imamu Amiri Baraka. BPo; CAPP-1; TAP; UnPo

Who are you,little i. E. E. Cummings. NYBP

"Who are you, Sea Lady." Santorin. James Elroy Flecker. FaBoTw; OBMV

"Who are you that so strangely woke." The Princess of Scotland. Rachel Annand Taylor. FaBoTC

Who are you there that from your icy tower. The Astronomers of Mont Blanc. Edgar Bowers. PoA

Who / Are you / Who is born. Vision and Prayer. Dylan Thomas. LiTM

Who are you, whose pitiful bones. Leonidas of Tarentum, *Greek.* GrAn, *tr. by* Fleur Adcock

Who art as black as hell, as dark as night. (LL) Sonnet 147. Shakespeare. AEP; EBEV; HoPM; NAEL-1; OxAEP-1; PoEL-2

Who Art Thou, O Great Mountain. Dahlia Ravikovitch, *Hebrew.* IP, *tr. by* Warren Bargad *and* Stanley F. Chyet

Who as they walk abroad make tinkling with their feet. (LL) A Portrait. Keats. BXAP; UV

Who Be Kind To. Allen Ginsberg. NNaP

Who beat and put you out. Rufinus Domesticus, *Greek.* InMo, *tr. by* Sam Hamill

Who beckons the green ivy up. The Miracle. Walter De la Mare. UnPo

Who bought a mountain and became a hermit there? Chin Nung. CoBLCP, *tr. by* Jonathan Chaves *Fr.* I Discuss the Past and Not the Present. What Men of Today Are Worth Discussing? May the Men of the Past Not Blame Me for My Discussion of Them.

Who be describe the laws of God, and man and metre. (LL) On Peter Robinson. Francis, Lord Jeffrey. FaBoEE; NBLV; OxBoLi

Who builds a church within his heart. The Church in the Heart. Morris Abel Beer. PoToHe

Who built the canals on Mars? The Children. Iain Crichton Smith. SpW

Who But the Lord? Langston Hughes. BPo

Who by low creatures leads to heights of love. (LL) Flush or Faunus. Elizabeth Barrett Browning. FP; VWP

Who called flowers "mouths"?—these painted lips. Novas. Van K. Brock. MT

"Who called?" I said, and the words. Echo. Walter De la Mare. OBMV

Who calls? Welcome Eumenides. Eleanor Ross Taylor. NALW

Who calls her two-faced? Faces, she has three. The Three-Faced. Robert Graves. FaBoEE

Who calls? Who calls? Who? For a Mocking Voice. Eleanor Farjeon. CH

Who came whirling out of the North. Of the Scythians. Katha Pollitt. DiPo; InPS-3

Who Can Be Born Black. Mari E. Evans. ISC

Who can bear / The wail of a young orphan? Rabbi Yussel Luksh of Chelm. Jacob Glatstein, *Yiddish.* TrJP, *tr. by* Nathan Halper

Who can believe with common sense. Epigram on Fasting. Jonathan Swift. OBVE

Who can bring back the magic of that story. The Descent of the Child. Susan Langstaff Mitchell. TIRV

Who can doubt, Rice, to which eternal place. On Mr. Rice the Manciple of Christ Church in Oxford. Richard Corbet. NOSC

Who can find a virtuous woman? for her price is far above rubies. The Virtuous Woman. Bible, *O.T.* TrJP *Fr.* Proverbs.

Who can forget the attitude of mothering? Rita Dove. NAAAL *Fr.* Mother Love.

Who can grasp for the first time. New Music. Gwen Harwood. CBAP

Who can live in heart so glad. The Merry Country Lad. Nicholas Breton. CH; NoSic *Fr.* The Passionate Shepherd.

Who can remember back to the first poets. The Makers. Howard Nemerov. DiPo; FYAP

Who can say. Song. Tennyson. FaBoCh

Who can say? It is silent now. (LL) What Were They Like? Denise Levertov. HeIP-4; NIP-4; OBWP; SAGP; VGW; WPE

Who can say what the years will bring? (LL) Jade Flower Palace. Tu Fu, *Chinese.* ChiPo; OHPC, *tr. by* Kenneth Rexroth

Who can support the anguish of love? Ode. Ibn al-Arabi, *Arabic.* AWP, *tr. by* R. A. Nicholson

Who can the various city frauds recite. Thieves and Whores. John Gay. ECEV; OAEL-1 *Fr.* Trivia; or, The Art of Walking the Streets of London.

Who cannot guess God's presence out of sight. (LL) Sonnet: "Belovéd, my Belovéd, when I think." Elizabeth Barrett Browning. Son; WPE

Who cares about the filthy rich. Anacreon, *Greek.* InMo, *tr. by* Sam Hamill

Who carved Love / and placed him by. A Statue Of Eros. Zenodotus, *Greek.* GrAn, *tr. by* Peter Jay

Who claims one needs wine to dispel grief? Tune: "Autumn Waters"— Listening to Rain. Na-lan Hsing-te, *Chinese.* SuSp, *tr. by* Bruce Carpenter

Who claims your servant's wearied of the world? Still At Play. Tản Đà, *Vietnamese.* AVP, *tr. by* Huỳnh Sanh Thông

Who collects the pain. "Stephany." NBV

Who come in the night whispering. Two Girls. Suzanne Gardinier. BAP-96

Who comes? Two Tongue-Pointing (Satirical) Songs. *Unknown, Aborigine.* NOBAu

Who comes here? / A grenadier. The Grenadier. *Unknown.* OxNR

Who comes to-night? We ope the doors in vain. Henry James. Robert Louis Stevenson. OBNC

Who comfort them in darkness and in sun. (LL) Man without Sense of Direction. John Crowe Ransom. LiTM; MeMAP; OxBA

Who could dispute his choice. The Net and the Sword. Douglas Le Pan. NOBC

Who could have thought that men and women could feel. Old Paintings on Italian Walls. Kathleen Jessie Raine. NYBP

Who could help but long for the gardens of home? (LL) Spring Night in Lo-Yang—Hearing a Flute. Li Po, *Chinese.* CoBCP; TTTS, *tr. by* Burton Watson

Who could know in advance. Space. Shindo Chie, *Japanese.* WPJ, *tr. by* Kenneth Rexroth *and* Ikuko Atsumi

Who could remember cause? Both. The Victim. Ellen Bryant Voigt. CrSp

Who counts himself as nobly born. The Nobly Born. Frances Ellen Watkins Harper. PWR

Who crieth: "Woe"? who: "Alas"? The Drunkard. Bible, *O.T.* TrJP *Fr.* Proverbs.

Who crossed cold Lethe, thought it Rubicon. (LL) Fording the River. Seamus Deane. PBCIP; PNI

Who crowd the press with hourly trash. (LL) Critics. Jonathan Swift. HAP; SCV

Who dares to drop the pin destruction of our silence. Can You Change a Shilling? Toni Del Renzio. SPE

Who dat a-knockin' at the door below. What You Goin' to Do When the Rent Comes 'Round? Andrew B. Sterling. OBAL

Who died? My mother's body. My Mother's Body, My Professor, My Bower. Jean Valentine. NMM-2

Who died on the wires, and hung there, one of two. The Silent One. Ivor Gurney. NAEL-2; NoP-4; OBWP; PeFWW; PoWW *Fr.* The Silent One.

Who died? Why does the music speak such grief? A Dirge. Huy Cận, *Vietnamese.* AVP, *tr. by* Huỳnh Sanh Thông

Who dissect away the wings and the haggard heart from the dove. (LL) Letter to Alex Comfort. Dannie Abse. FaBoTw; TwCP

Who do what we are born to do. (LL) Tiger. Alec Derwent Hope, *Russian.* OxBC; RB

Who does not love the juniper tree? Juniper. Eileen Duggan. PChr

Who does not love the spring deserves no lovers. Georgian Spring. Roy Campbell. OBSV

Who does not love true poetry. Henry Clay Hall. PoToHe

Who does not sit in the seat of the scoffer. Blessed Is the Man. Marianne Moore. ChIV-1

Who does not wish ever to judge aright. The Hog, the Sheep and Goat, Carrying to a Fair. Anne Finch, Countess of Winchilsea. ECWP

Who does our hair so well. (LL) At the Hairdresser. Novica Tadic, *Serbo-Croatian*. CEEP; HSix, *tr. by* Charles Simic

Who doesn't. Tim Seibles. ISC

. . . who doesn't have the money to buy himself an island. Hôtel Fraternité. Hans Magnus Enzensberger, *German*. CLPP, *tr. by* Jerome Rothenberg

Who doeth all things well. Cecil Frances Alexander. *See* All things bright and beauteous.

Who doth desire that chaste his wife should be. Advice to the Same. Sir Philip Sidney. SiPS *Fr.* Arcadia.

Who doubts? The laws fell down from heaven's height. Joseph Hall. OBSV, *book II Fr.* Virgidemiarum.

Who Drags the Fiery Artist Down? Clarence Day. NBLV

Who dreamed [*or* dream'd] that beauty passes like a dream? The Rose of the World. W. B. Yeats. ADE; CMoP; MoBrPo; NAEL-2

Who e'r sighes most, is cruellest, and hasts the others death. Donne. *See* A Valediction: Of Weeping.

Who even dead, yet hath his mind entire! Canto 47. Ezra Pound. CMoP; PoE; VGW *Fr.* Cantos.

Who ever hath her wish, thou hast thy *Will*,. Shakespeare. *See* Sonnet 135.

Who ever knew the heavens menace so? Shakespeare. OxAEP-1 *Fr.* Julius Caesar.

Who Ever Loved, That Loved Not at First Sight? Marlowe. ImPo *Fr.* Hero and Leander. AAS

Who fears to speak of Ninety-Eight? The Memory of the Dead. John Kells Ingram. IIP

Who feasts tonight? The Fairies Feast. Charles Montague Doughty. CH

Who fed me from her gentle breast. My Mother. Ann Taylor. BLPA; OxBChV

Who findeth comfort in the stars and flowers. Envoi, L'. Thomas Lovell Beddoes. OBNC *Fr.* Death's Jest Book.

Who fired France for Mary without spot. (LL) Duns Scotus's Oxford. Gerard Manley Hopkins. CABP; EBEV; GTBS-P; NAEL-2; NoAM; OBMV; OxAEP-2; PeECV; PoEL-5

Who first reform'd our stage with justest law[e]s. An Elegy on Ben Jonson. John Cleveland. MeLP

Who first said "false as dreams?" Not one who saw. Dreams. Henry Timrod. APN-2; PAR

Who flogged you and threw you out. The Slave Girl. Rufinus, *Greek*. GrAn, *tr. by* Alan Marshfield

Who, for a single glance, gave up her life. (LL) Lot's Wife. "Anna Akhmatova," *Russian*. BoWoP; PBWP, *tr. by* Richard Wilbur

Who forced the Muse to this alliance? On Professor Drennan's Verse. Roy Campbell. GTBS-P

Who fought for Uncle Sam! (LL) The Colored Soldiers. Paul Laurence Dunbar. AAP; APN-2; CBCWP; NAAAL

Who fought their way from night to day and struggled up to God. (LL) The Unsung Heroes. Paul Laurence Dunbar. BPo; CBCWP

Who gave thee, O Beauty. Ralph Waldo Emerson. PoEL-4 *Fr.* Ode to Beauty. AmPP

Who gave thee, O Beauty. Ode to Beauty. Ralph Waldo Emerson. AmPP

Who gives him the Bath? The New Knighthood. Rudyard Kipling. UV

Who goes? On the Bus. Mitsuye Yamada. *Fr.* Camp Notes. WPOW

Who goes beyond appearance. The Spread. Spencer Selby. PT

Who goes there! hankering, gross, mystical, nude? Walt Whitman. ColAP; PAR *Fr.* Song of Myself. AmPP; MoAmPo; NAAL-3; NOBA; OxBA
("I laugh at what you call dissolution, / And I know the amplitude of time.") (LL) PAR

Who goes to join the men of Agincourt. (LL) The Volunteer. Herbert Asquith. OBWP; OxBTC

Who Goes with Fergus? W. B. Yeats. CMoP; FaBoCh; InPK-6; MoP; NAEL-2; NOBE; NOBVV; NoAM; PeVV; PoE; PoRA; TRP

Who got used to making it through murdered sons. (LL) For de Lawd. Lucille Clifton. IMW; PoBA; TAP; TwCP

Who grace, for zenith had, from which no shadowes grow. Despair. Greville Fulke. PoEL-1 *Fr.* Caelica.

Who, growing up, has never loved? Looking For Her. Tạ Hữu Thiện, *Vietnamese*. AVP, *tr. by* Huỳnh Sanh Thông

Who had always been so careful while her mistress lived. (LL) Aunt Helen. T. S. Eliot. OBAL; PoA

Who half asleep, or waking, does not hear it. The Furnace of Colors. Vernon Watkins. NYBP

Who has a face sees. Shed the Fear. Anselm Hollo. PmAP

Who has but dighted his tricks in a bed. This Is What the Watchbird Sings, Who Perches in the Lovetree. Bruce Boyd. NeAP

Who has ever stopped to think of the divinity of Lamont Cranston? In Memory of Radio. Imamu Amiri Baraka. BB; NAAAL; NAAL-2; NeAP; NoP-4; PoM; Poetr

Who has gone farthest? for I would go farther. Excelsior. Walt Whitman. SAmP

Who Has Known Heights. Mary Brent Whiteside. BLPA

Who has made all things well! Cecil Frances Alexander. *See* All things bright and beauteous.

Who has not been sleeping on an inspired day? The mind of the day sleeps us. That Can Not Be Taken Away From It. Carla Harryman. FTOS

Who has not found the Heaven—below. God's Residence. Emily Dickinson. SAmP; WPoS

Who has not seen their lover. The Avenue. Frances Darwin Cornford. LW

Who has not waked to list the busy sounds. London's Summer Morning. Mary Robinson. ECWP; WoRP

Who has not walked upon the shore. Robert Bridges. SCGP

Who Has Our Redeemer Heard. Stephen Collins Foster. AH

Who has seen the wind? / Neither I nor you. Christina Rossetti. BoTP; ChIV-2; FaBoBe; NTCP; NTP; OxBChV; TLR; WHSW
("Who has seen the wind?") ACTP; CTV; ChAP; FPC; VWP

Who has strangled the tired voice. Appeal. Noémia da Sousa, *Portuguese*. WPOW, *tr. by* Alan Ryder; TTY, *tr. by* Dorothy Guedes *and* Philippa Rumsey

Who has won for once over the world's weight. (LL) Juggler. Richard Wilbur. CMoP; LiTM; NYBP; TAP

Who hast the red pavilion of my heart? (LL) An Arab Love-Song. Francis Thompson. AWP; MoBrPo

Who Hath a Book. Wilbur Dick Nesbit. BLPA

Who hath beheld the goddess face to face. Poetry. Madison Cawein. APN-2

Who hath desired the Sea?—the sight of salt water unbounded. The Sea and the Hills. Rudyard Kipling. OxBoS; SCGP

Who hath given man speech? or what hath set therein. Swinburne. OAEL-2 *Fr.* Atalanta in Calydon.

Who hath he[a]rd of such[e] cruelty before. Sir Thomas Wyatt. AAS; SiPS

Who hath his fancy [*or* fancie] pleasèd. Song. Sir Philip Sidney. PoEL-1

Who hath his Maker's hand. (LL) Inspiration. Henry David Thoreau. APN-1; AmPP; ColAP; FaBoBe; NCAP; NOBA; OxBA

Who hath not knowne or herd. Luke Sheperd. PBRV *Fr.* The Upcheringe of the Messe.

Who hath not sent out ships to sea? The Ship That Went Down. Adah Isaacs Menken. CBWP-1

Who hath that conning by wisdam or prudence. *Unknown*. MiEL

Who have character to lose. Robert Burns. *See* Drinking Song.

Who heard the silly sailor-folk and gave them back their sea! (LL) The Last Chantey. Rudyard Kipling. FaBoCh; MoBrPo

Who Here Can Cast His Eyes Abroad. Abiel Holmes. AH

Who hired him. (LL) The Idiot. Dudley Randall. LTA

Who hung these shields here still all shiny. Antipater of Sidon, *Greek*. GrAn, *tr. by* Tony Harrison

Who hunts so late 'neath evening skies. The Soul-Hunter. Julia Ward Howe. PAR

Who I break my head against. First Claims Poem. Victor Hernandez Cruz. NBV

Who I Think You Are. Elizabeth Alexander. FFC; RA

Who, if I cried out, would hear me among the angels? The First Duino Elegy. Rilke, *German*. NAWM-2 *Fr.* Duino Elegies.

Who in each act that act have done. (LL) The Strangers. Jones Very. APN-1; OxBA

Who, in his own time, resumed the dark, the straw. (LL) The Outlaw. Seamus Heaney. MoP; OxBC

Who in one lifetime sees all causes lost. Muriel Rukeyser. NALW

Who, in such depths of misery, plunge the fair? (LL) The Natural Child. Helen Leigh. ECWP; WoRP

Who, in the brief, incredible northern spring. Let Him Return. Leona Hill. PoToHe

Who, in the dark, has cast the harbor-chain? Putting to Sea. Louise Bogan. LiTM; PoA

Who, in the garden-pony carrying skeps. Horses. Dorothy, Duchess of Wellington Wellesley. OBMV; OxBTC

Who, in the public library, one evening after rain. Public Library. Dannie Abse. OxBC

Who in the waters of this reedy lake. Diodorus Zonas, *Greek*. GrAn, *tr. by* Alistair Elliot

Who in them lov'd and sought thy face! (LL) The Book. Henry Vaughan. GeHe; PBRV

Who invited him in? What was he doing here. The Dirty Little Accuser. Norman Cameron. OxBS

Who is a friend? Who is a foe? Gripe. Lincoln Kirstein. PoWW

Who is a mother some one exclaimed? Who a Mother Is. Roy W. Watson. PWR

Who Is a Poet. Tadeusz Rózewicz, *Polish.* VCWP, tr. by Magnus J. Krynski *and* Robert A. Maguire

Who is, as if he weren't and ne'er had even come. Whoever Has Become All Divine. "Angelus Silesius." GePo, tr. by George C. Schoolfield *Fr.* The Cherubical Wanderer.

Who Is at My Window? *Unknown.* ImPo

Who is de prutties' gal you say? My Little Lize. James Martinez. PBCV

Who is divine? This bird. (LL) The Blinded Bird. Thomas Hardy. CMoP; LiTM

Who is faultless, and doesn't exist. (LL) Eve to Her Daughters. Judith Wright. NALW; NoP-4

Who is God. The Questions of Ethne Alba. *Unknown, Irish.* TIRV, tr. by James Carney

Who is it calling by the darkened river. Voices. Walter De la Mare. UnPo

Who is it hides my sandals when I'm trying to get dressed? Late for Breakfast. Mary Dawson. TLR

Who is it runs through the many-storied mansion of myth. Dwarf of Disintegration. Oscar Williams. ImPo; LiTM

Who Is It Talks of Ebony? Manmohan Ghose. OBMV

Who is it that this dark[e] night. Eleventh Song. Sir Philip Sidney. NAEL-1; NOBE; NoSic; OBEV; OxAEP-1; PoE; PoEL-1; SCGP *Fr.* Astrophil and Stella. AAS; SiPS

Who is it, then, that love deceives? (LL) Juan's Song. Louise Bogan. NYBP; NoP-4

Who is like unto thee who teachest knowledge. Hymn of Unity. *Unknown, Hebrew.* TrJP, tr. by H. M. Adler

Who Is My Brother? Pinkie Gordon Lane. BlSi

Who is my father in this world, in this house. The Irish Cliffs of Moher. Wallace Stevens. NOBA; RaBo; TOF; VGW

Who Is My Neighbor? Josephine D. Henderson Heard. CBWP-4

Who is not a stranger still. Stephany Fuller. BPo

Who is she coming, whom all gaze upon. Sonnet: A Rapture Concerning His Lady. Guido Cavalcanti, *Italian.* AWP, tr. by D. G. Rossetti

Who is she that comes, makyng turn every man's eye. Sonnet [*or* Sonetto] 7. Guido Cavalcanti. CTC; OBVE, tr. by Ezra Pound

Who is she whose-feet-go-clattering-the-hard-ground? Choice. Flavien Ranaivo, *French.* NegPo, tr. by Ellen Conroy Kennedy

Who is Silvia? What a shame. Does That Answer Your Question, Mr Shakespeare? Stanley J. Sharpless. PeLV

Who is Silvia? what is she. Silvia. Shakespeare. EBEvV; FaBoBe; ImPo; NoSic; OAEL-1; OBEV; SCGP *Fr.* The Two Gentlemen of Verona.

Who is so proud. The Performing Seal. Rachel Lyman Field. OBCA *Fr.* A Circus Garland.

Who is that BRAHMA? What that Soul of Souls. *Unknown.* TAL, tr. by Sir Edward Arnold *Fr.* The Bhagavad-Gita.

Who is that running away. C. C. Rider. Lucille Clifton. GT

Who is that soldier, hero of my heart? Tu'o'ng Phô, *Vietnamese.* AVP, tr. by Huỳnh Sanh Thông

Who is the East? Yellow Man, Purple Man. Emily Dickinson. TLR; TTTS

Who is the guest? *I* was one among *you.* The Guest. Rilke, *German.* FP, tr. by J. B. Leishman

Who is the happy warrior? Who is he. Character of the Happy Warrior. Wordsworth. FaBoBe

Who is the mighty master that can trace. To Haydn. Thomas Holcroft. NOEC

Who is the Poet? He who sings. For Adelaide. Bessie Rayner Parkes. VWP

Who is the runner in the skies. The Runner in the Skies. James Oppenheim. TrJP

Who Is the Same, Which at My Window Peepes? Edmund Spenser. *Fr.* Epithalamion: "Ye learned sisters which have oftentimes." AAS; BoLoP; CABP; FHYEP; InPS-3; NOBE; NoP-4; NoSic; OAEL-1; OBEV; OxAEP-1; PBRV; PoEL-1; PoPoPo

Who is there? Me. Marichiko, *Japanese.* APSN; OHMPJ, tr. by Kenneth Rexroth

Who is there still remembers. Late Lamented Fame of the Giant City of New York. Bertolt Brecht, tr. by Frank Jellinek *Fr.* Late Lamented Fame of the Giant City of New York.

Who is this. Peter Damian, *Latin.* MLL, tr. by Helen Waddell

Who is this? An almoner. An Almoner. "Michael Field." VWP

Who is this coming towards you. The Ghost. Iain Crichton Smith. NOxBChV

Who is this I hear?—Lo, this is I, thine heart. The Dispute of the Heart and Body of François Villon. François Villon, *French.* AWP; OBVE, tr. by Swinburne

Who is this King of glory? The Lord of hosts, he is the King of glory. Selah. (LL) Psalm 24. Bible, *O.T.* AWP; TrJP

Who is this Man / that walketh in the field. Genesis XXIV. Arthur Hugh Clough. ChIV-1

Who is this Moses? who made him, we say. A Soliloquy of One of the Spies Left in the Wilderness. Gerard Manley Hopkins. TrCP

Who is this that comes in splendour, coming from the blazing East? The Airy Christ. Stevie Smith. ChIV-2; NOCV

Who is this that darkeneth counsel by words without knowledge? Then the Lord Answered. Bible, *O.T.* AWP *Fr.* Job. NAWM-1

Who is this that howls and mutters? Who Is This Who Howls and Mutters? Stevie Smith. OxBC

Who is this whose feet. The Swan's Feet. Edith Jay Scovell. FaBoWP; OxBTC

Who is to say. Michael Palmer. BAP-93

Who is, who is the rider there. Moyshe-Leyb Halpern, *Yiddish.* TrJP, tr. by Joseph Leftwich

Who is wise?/ He who learns from everyone. The Good Man. *Unknown. Fr.* The Talmud. TrJP

Who kill'd John Keats? Keats. Byron. FaBoEE; UV

Who killed Cock [*or* poor] Robin? [*or* Here lies Cock Robin]. Mother Goose. CBNP; CTAV; OxNR; ReMoGo; UV
("Who killed poor Robin?") AmFP

Who Killed Lawless Lean? Stevie Smith. CBNP

Who killed poor Robin? Mother Goose. *See* Who killed Cock [*or* poor] Robin? [*or* Here lies Cock Robin].

"Who knocks at my door, so late in the night?" Pilgrims in Mexico. *Unknown.* OBCP

'Who knocks?' 'I, who was beautiful'. The Ghost. Walter De la Mare. CMoP; EnLoPo; LiTM; LoP; MoBrPo; NOBE; OAEL-2; OxBSn; OxBTC

Who knows? (LL) Maybe Dats Your Pwoblem Too. Jim Hall. CMAP; MT

Who knows? Years. Yon-gyun Kim, *Korean.* CKP, tr. by Jaihiun Kim

Who knows, but beasts, as they do lie. A Discourse of Beasts. Margaret Lucas Cavendish, Duchess of Newcastle. PEW

Who knows if they sing in their webs. The Ability to Make a Face Like a Spider While Singing Blues: Junior Wells. Sandra McPherson. SeSe

Who Knows Something About Women? Sylva Fischerova, *Czech and Slovak.* CEEP, tr. by Vera Orac, Stuart Friebert *and* Sylva Fischerova

Who knows / that in the depth of the ravine. Abutsu the Nun [*or* Abutsu-Ni], *Japanese.* WPJ, tr. by Kenneth Rexroth *and* Ikuko Atsumi

Who knows? This Africa so richly blest. A. L. Milner-Brown. PBA; TTY

Who knows this or that? Limits. Ralph Waldo Emerson. APN-1; OxBSP; PoEL-4

Who knows through what mysterious tensions these. The Ivory Tower. Robert Silliman Hillyer. NYBP

Who knows to live to-morrow? (LL) On Himselfe ("I fear no earthly powers"). Robert Herrick. CavPo

Who knows what fame is! Pushkin. "Anna Akhmatova," *Russian.* TCRP, tr. by Daniel Weissbort

Who knows what the moonlight means? Magic Composer. Gilbert Sorrentino. FTOS

Who knows when love has had its day. Strato, *Greek.* GrAn, tr. by Christopher Logue

Who Knows Where. Detlev, Freiherr von Liliencron, *German.* AWP, tr. by Ludwig Lewisohn

Who knows whether the sea heals or corrodes? Plague of Dead Sharks. Alan Dugan. LiTM; NoAM

Who lay in the dark thinking *Roses, Roses, Roses.* (LL) The Sleeping. Lynn Emanuel. AiP; WWSi

Who learns my lesson complete? Leaves of Grass (1855). Walt Whitman. APN-1

Who least, hath some; who most hath never all. (LL) Times [*or* Tymes] Go[e] By Turn[e]s. Robert Southwell. ChIV-1; NTP; NoSic; PoEL-2

Who Likes the Idea of Guide Cats? Gavin Ewart. NOxBChV

Who Likes the Rain? Clara Doty Bates. BoTP

Who list his wealth and ease retain. Sir Thomas Wyatt. NoSic

Who list the Romane greatnes forth to figure. Joachim Du Bellay. OBVE *Fr.* Ruins of Rome.

Who lists to see, what ever nature, arte. Edmund Spenser. PBRV *Fr.* Ruines of Rome: by Bellay.

Who lit the furnace of the mammoth's heart? The Sun. Francis Thompson. MoBrPo *Fr.* Ode to the Setting Sun.

Who live in troubled regions. (LL) Storm Warnings. Adrienne Rich. AiP; NAAL-2; NIP-4

Who lived here when the stones were green. The Philosopher. Syl Cheney-Coker. PBMAP *Fr.* The Blood in the Desert's Eyes.

Who lives where beggars rarely speed. My Mary. John Clare. NOBRP

Who liveth alone longeth for mercy. The Wanderer. *Unknown, Anglo-Saxon.* EEP, *tr. by* Michael Alexander

Who locked me. A Night in the Royal Ontario Museum. Margaret Atwood. PBWP

Who looked a great fool. *Unknown. See* A was an archer, who [*or* and] shot at a frog.

Who looked upon her awful brow. Gorgon. Ambrose Bierce. APN-2 *Fr.* The Devil's Dictionary.

Who looking back upon his troubled years. Disillusion. Bessie B. Decker. PoToHe

Who Loves a Garden. Louise Seymour Jones. BLPA

Who loves a garden, loves a greenhouse too. The Task. William Cowper. OBGa *Fr.* The Task.

Who loves beauty / veil her statues. Catullus. *See* The Death of Lesbia's Bird.

Who loves the rain. Frances Shaw. PoToHe

Who lyst his welthe and eas retayne. V. Innocentia Veritas Viat Fides Circumdederunt Me Inimici Mei. Sir Thomas Wyatt. AAS

"Who made God, daddy?" Question Time. Jack Lindsay. NOBAu

Who made honey long ago. (LL) Forefathers. Edmund Blunden. NOBE; NoP-4; OBEV; OBMV; OxBTC

Who, maiden, makes this river flow? Medicine Song of an Indian Lover. *Unknown, Ojibwa Native American.* APN-2, *tr. by* Charles Fenno Hoffman

Who make up a heaven of our misery. (LL) The Chimney Sweeper ("A Little black thing among the snow"). William Blake. EBEvV; FHYEP; NAEL-2; NAWM-2; NOEC; OAEL-2; RB; Ro

Who makes strong winds be still, gentles the sea. A Night Prayer. Alcuin, *Latin.* MLL, *tr. by* Helen Waddell

Who Maketh the Grass to Grow, *greatly abr.* Bible, *O.T. See* Psalm 147.

Who masquerades behind the winds? Moods. Leyb Kvitko, *Yiddish.* TrJP, *tr. by* Joseph Leftwich

Who may this be? Narcissus in Camden. Helen Gray Cone. BXAP

Who, mid the grasses of the field. Dante. William Cullen Bryant. APN-1

Who, minter of medallions. Reading a Medal. Terence Tiller. FaBoTw; GTBS-P

Who misreads the serious joke, the speech. The Nearsighted. Elizabeth Macklin. BAP-93

Who needs a raft that can invade the stars? Inscribed on a Painting. Yün Shou-p'ing, *Chinese.* CoBLCP, *tr. by* Jonathan Chaves

Who never held up anybody. (LL) The Shooting of John Dillinger outside the Biograph Theater July 22, 1934. David Wagoner. CoAP; FYAP; RB

Who never in his Life forgave a friend. (LL) On Hayley. William Blake. FaBoEE

Who never let each other sleep above it. (LL) I know the truth—give up all other truths! Marina Tsvetayeva, *Russian.* NNPT; WPoS, *tr. by* Elaine Feinstein; OPOU, *tr. by* Elaine Feinstein *and* Angela Livingstone

Who never mentions Hell to ears polite. Alexander Pope. *See* Timon's Villa.

Who never wept knows laughter but a jest. Compensation. E. M. Brainard. PoToHe

Who not at all thereon did call, / or took in vain the same. Michael Wigglesworth. *See* Thus everyone before the throne.

Who, now, can speak of gods. The Gods. Dennis Lee. NOBC

Who now does follow the foule Blatant Beast. Edmund Spenser. OAEL-1 *Fr.* Wood Of Error. AEP

Who now reads Cowley? if he pleases yet. Alexander Pope. EPCY *Fr.* The First Epistle of the Second Book of Horace Imitated.

Who, now, seeing Her so. Et in Arcadia Ego. W. H. Auden. CMoP

Who of little Love—know how to starve. (LL) Victory comes late. Emily Dickinson. APN-2; InPK-6

Who often found their way to pleasant meadows. Elegy for Minor Poets. Louis MacNeice. CABP; PNI

Who on yon throne of Azure sits. Retirement. Henry Vaughan. GeHe; NOSC

Who on your breast pillows his head now. A Lost Jewel. Robert Graves. EnLoPo; NYBP

Who once said all his say, when he was young! (LL) Egan O Rahilly. *Unknown, Irish.* EBEV; OBMV, *tr. by* James Stephens

Who, or why, or which, or what. The A[h]kond of Swat. Edward Lear. CBNP; FaBoCh; PeLi

Who owns these cattle, Corydon? The Herdsmen. Theocritus. AWP, *tr. by* Charles Stuart Calverley *Fr.* Idylls.

Who owns these scrawny little feet? *Death.* Examination at the Womb-Door. Ted Hughes. NAEL-2; NoP-4; OxBC

Who owns this body of mine? Starved. Laura Kasischke. FuPo

Who painted you, the non-speaker. Portrait of a Stupid Teacher of Rhetoric. *Unknown, Greek.* GrAn, *tr. by* Peter Jay

Who perished in the cause of Right. (LL) The Death of Lincoln. William Cullen Bryant. CBCWP; NAAL-1; NAAL-3; NCAP; TAP

Who plainly say, *My God, My King.* (LL) Jordan. George Herbert. FHYEP; FSCP; GeHe; HAP; InPS-3; MeLP; NAEL-1; NOCV; NOSC; NoP-4; OAEL-1; PeECV; PoE; PoEL-2; Poetr; SeCP; TFi; TrCP

Who prayed for those that did him kill! (LL) Abel's Blood. Henry Vaughan. KSG; OBWVE

Who prop, thou ask'st, in these bad days, my mind? To a Friend. Matthew Arnold. NAEL-2; Son

Who pure as light and chaste as origin has stayed. The Secret Virginity. "Angelus Silesius." GePo, *tr. by* George C. Schoolfield *Fr.* The Cherubical Wanderer.

Who puts off shift. My Naked Aunt. Archibald MacLeish. MeMAP

Who rattles in the keyhole? Questionnaire of Sleeplessness. Miodrag Pavlovic, *Serbo-Croatian.* HSix, *tr. by* Charles Simic

Who read a chapter when they rise. Charms and Knots. George Herbert. KSG

Who really lives there? (LL) At the Tourist Centre in Boston. Margaret Atwood. NoP-4; Poetr

Who really respects the earthworm. The Earthworm. Harry Edmund Martinson, *Swedish.* RB; RaBo, *tr. by* Robert Bly

Who redes this boke of imagerie. *Unknown.* MiEL

Who Reigns? Shelley. *Fr.* Prometheus Unbound. NOBRP; OAEL-2

Who represents my body in Pentagon? Who spends. Pentagon Exorcism. Allen Ginsberg. BB

Who resolves to go astray. (LL) Written in an Ovid. Matthew Prior. FaBoEE; OBCoV

Who rides at night, who rides so late? The Invisible King. Goethe, *German.* RaBo, *tr. by* Robert Bly

Who rideth through the driving rain. The King's Son. Thomas Boyd. OBMV

Who rules the world with iron rod? Tall Hat. Victor James Daley. CBAP

Who Runs America? Allen Ginsberg. FaBoA

Who said, "Peacock Pie"? The Song of the Mad Prince. Walter De la Mare. EBEV; FaBoCh; MoP; NOBE; NTP; NoAM; OxAEP-2; OxBChV

Who said to the trout. Pisces. Ronald Stuart Thomas. CABP; OxBC

Who saw the petals. The Secret Song. Margaret Wise Brown. OBCA

Who Says. Julia Hartwig, *Polish.* GI, *tr. by* Stanisław Barańczak *and* Clare Cavanagh

Who says a woman's work isn't high art? Woman's Work. Julia Alvarez. RA

Who says old age is so full of sorrow and woe? (LL) After Getting Drunk, I Scribble Songs and Poems. Lu Yu, *Chinese.* CoBCP, *tr. by* Burton Watson

Who Says That Drought Was Here? Niyi Osundare. HBAPE

Who says that sadness can be cast away for long? Tune: "Magpie on the Branch." Feng Yen-ssu, *Chinese.* SuSp, *tr. by* Daniel Bryant

Who says that the dead do not think of us? In Broad Daylight I Dream of My Dead Wife. Mei Yao Ch'en, *Chinese.* OHPC, *tr. by* Kenneth Rexroth; OxBM

Who say[e]s that fictions onl[e]y and false hair. Jordan. George Herbert. FHYEP; FSCP; GeHe; HAP; InPS-3; MeLP; NAEL-1; NOCV; NOSC; NoP-4; OAEL-1; PeECV; PoE; PoEL-2; Poetr; SeCP; TFi; TrCP

Who says that Giles and Joan at discord be? On Giles and Joan. Ben Jonson. NAEL-1; NOBL

Who says that it's by my desire. People Hide Their Love. Emperor Wu of Han, *Chinese.* ChiP, *tr. by* Arthur Waley

Who Says the River is Wide? *Unknown, Chinese.* CoBCP, *tr. by* Burton Watson

Who says you have no sheep? Herdsman's Song. *Unknown, Chinese.* ChiP, *tr. by* Arthur Waley

Who says you're like one of the dog days? Shall I Compare Thee to a Summer's Day? Howard Moss. InPK-6

Who seeks alway thine honour to preserve. (LL) Golden gift that nature did thee give, The. Henry Howard, Earl of Surrey. AAS; SiPS

Who seeks wisdom in words. Silences. David Mitchell. PeNZ

Who sees him walk the street, can scarce forbear. Marvellous Martin. Charles Harpur. CBAP

Who sees the cross at Christmas? To See the Cross at Christmas. Roger Cooper. TrCP

Who sees the curve as Robert Fludd saw it. Infield Outfield. Asa Benveniste. NBrP

Who sees, will spew; who smells, be poisoned. (LL) A Beautiful Young Nymph Going to Bed. Jonathan Swift. ECEV; NOEC

Who / SELF, / The World. Job's Epitaph. Joshua Sylvester. ChIV-1

WHo sent Jack Barrett there. (LL) The Story of Uriah. Rudyard Kipling. NOBVV; PeVV; SCV

Who shall decide, when Doctors disagree. Epistle III, to Allen Lord Bathurst. Alexander Pope.

Who Shall Deliver Me? Christina Rossetti. TOF

Who Shall Die. James A. Randall Jr. BPo

Who shall doubt, Donne, where [or whe'er] I a poet be[e]. To Donne. Ben Jonson. BeJo; EPCY; NoP-4; SeCP

Who shall have my fair [or faire or fayre] lady? My Fair Lady. *Unknown.* EnLoPo; OxBoLi; PoEL-1

Who shall I have for friends. Fujiwara No Okikaze, *Japanese.* OHMPJ, *tr. by* Kenneth Rexroth

Who shall interpret the Beloved's hair! Ode 105. Hafiz, *Persian.* EP, *tr. by* Richard Le Gallienne

Who shall invoke when we are gone. Tragic Love. Walter James Turner. OBMV

Who shall put forth on thee, / Unfathomable Sea? (LL) Time. Shelley. PoLF

Who shall speak for the people? Carl Sandburg. OxBA *Fr.* The People, Yes.

Who shall tell what did befall. Wealth. Ralph Waldo Emerson. APN-1

Who she was. Back Far Enough, Down Deep Enough. Constance Urdang. PBCAP

Who shot the snake? beat it to death on the road? In Memoriam S. L. Akintola. David Knight. MoCV

Who showed me. To Flossie. William Carlos Williams. SAmP

Who Sleeps by Day and Walks by Night. Henry David Thoreau. PoEL-4

Who smoke-snorts toasts o' My Lady Nicotine. Variations on an Air: After Robert Browning. G. K. Chesterton. BXAP; NOBL

Who so list to hount I knowe where is an hynde. Sir Thomas Wyatt. CBLP; PBRV

Who speaks the sound of an echo? Tree-Leaf Woman, *Tibetan.* WPoS, *tr. by* Miranda Shaw

Who spoke out for the dumb and the down-trodden then! (LL) Whittier. James Russell Lowell. AmPP; NOBA; OxBA

Who spurs on the road when day is done. Goethe. *See* The Erl-King.

Who stands, the crux left of the watershed. The Watertowers. W. H. Auden. OAEL-2

Who steals the common from the goose. (LL) Epigram: On Inclosures. *Unknown.* FaBoEE; OxBoLi

Who straight, *Your suit is granted*, said, and died. (LL) Redemption. George Herbert. CABP; ESCV; FMP; FSCP; GSo; GeHe; HAP; InPK-6; InPS-3; MeLP; NAEL-1; NOBE; NOCV; NOSC; NoP-4; PBRV; PeECV; PoE; PoPoPo; Poetr; SCGP; SCV; SeCP; SoSe-8; TFi; TrCP; WeW-3

Who strolls so late, for mugs a bait. French Lisette: A Ballad of Maida Vale. William Plomer. OBCoV; OxBoV

"Who stuffed that white owl?" No one spoke in the shop. The Owl-Critic. James Thomas Fields. BLPA; OBAL

Who sure intended him to stretch a rope. (LL) The Boss. James Russell Lowell. NCAP; OBAL

Who swept away my gilded fall. The Tree Sings to the Stream. Leah Goldberg. MHP, *tr. by* Ruth Finer Mintz *Fr.* Songs of the Stream.

Who take today and jerk it out of joint. Young Africans. Gwendolyn Brooks. NoAM

Who taught me betimes to love working and reading. (LL) The Sluggard. Isaac Watts. CH; EBEvV; ECEV; HAP; NOEC; OxBChV; OxBoLi; PoEL-3; UV

Who taught the bird to build her. Who Taught Them? *Unknown.* CTV

Who Taught Them? *Unknown.* CTV

"Who, tell me, shepherd, owns these rows of plants?" Cometas, *Greek.* GrAn, *tr. by* Anthony Holden

Who They Were. Joshua Weiner. BAP-94

Who think you come there? Songs of the Sioux. *Unknown, Sioux.* APN-2 *Fr.* Ghost-Dance Songs.

Who thinks of June's first rose to-day? June, 1915. Charlotte Mew. OxAEP-2

Who thought in high midsummer. Boethius, *Latin.* MLL, *tr. by* Helen Waddell *Fr.* Consolation of Philosophy, The ("De Consolacione Philosophie").

Who travels [or trauels] by the wearie wandring way. Edmund Spenser. OxAEP-1 *Fr.* Wood Of Error. AEP

Who truly longs the truth to see. Book 3, Metrum 11. Boethius, *Latin.* OBCVT, *tr. by* Sir Richard Fanshawe

Who used his masterful brush to paint this romantic beauty? T'ang Yin. *Fr.* On a Painting of a Woman Shown Half-Length. CoBLCP, *tr. by* Jonathan Chaves

Who Walks with Beauty. David Morton. BLPA; FaBoBe

Who want to love you, to love you, / love you. (LL) Conversation with a Fireman from Brooklyn. Tess Gallagher. CrSp

Who wants to think of us as five? Five keen-nosed grey-maned black-. The Sahara to America. Aleksei Eliseievich Kruchyonykh. PFTM, *tr. by* Bruce McClelland *Fr.* The Sahara to America.

Who was a man. (LL) Malcolm X. Gwendolyn Brooks. NAAAL; PoBA; TTY

Who was born, not of a virgin but a real woman. Jah Son / Another Way. Kendel Hippolyte. PBCV

Who was it came. Daniel Gerard Hoffman. CoAP

Who was it named her thus. The Chorus sing the doom of Helen. Aeschylus, *Greek.* OBCVT, *tr. by* Louis MacNeice

Who Was It, Tell Me. Heinrich Heine, *German.* TrJP, *tr. by* Richard Garnett

Who was it that took away my voice? Silence. Bella Akhatovna Akhmadulina, *Russian.* BoWoP, *tr. by* Daniel Halpern

Who was it who held me on her knee? Mother. Josephine D. Henderson Heard. CBWP-4

Who was Mary Shelley? Lorine Niedecker. APSN

Who was neither ingenious, sober, nor kind. (LL) Epitaph: "Here lies the body of Richard Hind." Francis, Lord Jeffrey Jeffrey. FaBoEE; OxBoLi

Who was responsible for the very first arms deal. Peace. Michael Longley. BiHa; CIP-2; PBCIP; PNI

Who was responsible for the very first arms deal. Peace. Tibullus, *Latin.* OBCVT, *tr. by* Michael Longley

Who / was that who. Zukofsky. Gilbert Sorrentino. FTOS

Who was this girl. Looking at Pictures to Be Put Away. Gary Snyder. NNaP

Who wd. cope in this Quick. The Web. Gregory O'Donoghue. BIrV

Who weds a sot to get his cot. Proverbial Advice on Marriage. *Unknown.* NBLV

Who weeps now anywhere in the world. Solemn Hour. Rilke, *German.* TrJP, *tr. by* C. F. MacIntyre

Who Were before Me. John Drinkwater. OBMV

Who were the builders? Question not the silence. The Nameless Doon [or Dun]. William Larminie. BIrV

Who were they out there through instruments. The Crystal Text. Clark Coolidge. PT

"Who were you, shipwrecked stranger?" Leontichos found. Callimachus, *Greek.* GrAn, *tr. by* Peter Jay

Who, when night nears, would answer for the / patterns. A Sort of Language. Burns Singer. FaBoTC

Who, who and who? The Dark Lord of Savaiki. Alistair Campbell. PeNZ

"Who—who—the bride will be?" *Unknown.* CH

Who, who will be the next man to entrust his girl to a friend? Ezra Pound. FaBoMo *Fr.* Homage to Sextus Propertius.

Who will believe me later, when I say. The Last of the Courtyard. Emily Grosholz. FFC

Who will endure. W. H. Auden. FaBoPV; OxBTC

Who will go drive with Fergus now. Who Goes with Fergus? W. B. Yeats. CMoP; FaBoCh; InPK-6; MoP; NAEL-2; NOBE; NOBVV; NoAM; PeVV; PoE; PoRA; TRP

Who will in fairest book of Nature know. Sonnet 71. Sir Philip Sidney. InPS-3; NAEL-1; NoP-4; NoSic; OAEL-1; PoE; Poetr *Fr.* Astrophil and Stella. AAS; SiPS

Who Will Know Us? Gary Soto. GM

Who Will Live in Our Houses When We Die? Michael C. Blumenthal. NoAM

Who will, may hear Sordello's story told. Sordello. Robert Browning.

Who will moan there for long? *Unknown. See* Big rat, big rat.

Who will remember, now I write? (LL) Solum Mihi Superest Sepulchrum. William Habington. ChIV-1; NOSC

Who will remember, passing through this Gate. On Passing the New Menin Gate. Siegfried Sassoon. NAEL-2; NoAM; NoP-4; OBMV; PoWW; Son

Who Will Shoe Your Pretty Little Foot? *Unknown.* AS

Who Will Show Us Any Good? Lady Jane Francesca Wilde. VWP

Who will show us where. At the Doors. "Der Nistor," *Yiddish.* TrJP, *tr. by* Joseph Leftwich

Who will take away. Spell Against Sorrow. Kathleen Jessie Raine. PBWP

Who winds the clumsy flower clock now, I wonder. Heavy Heavy Heavy. John Malcolm Brinnin. NYBP

Who, with heart in breast, could deny you love? (LL) Dear Black Head. *Unknown, Gaelic.* BIrV, *tr. by* Sir Samuel Ferguson

Who with salt tears this last farewell [or farewell] did take. (LL) Before the Birth of One of Her Children. Anne Bradstreet. BoWoP; KTR; NAAL-1; NAAL-3; NOBA; OxBM; PeECV; WPE; WPOW

Who with thy leaves shall wipe (at need). Another [To His Booke]. Robert Herrick. NOSC

Who Wot Nowe That Ys Here. *Unknown.* InPS-3

Who would be / A mermaid fair. The Mermaid. Tennyson. ACTP; BoTP

Who would be / A merman bold. The Merman. Tennyson. BoTP; UV

Who would care to pass his life away. Lotos Eating. Mortimer Collins. NOBVV

Who would enjoy just the brows of her eyes? (LL) Willow. Li Shang-yin, *Chinese*. LoP; SuSp, *tr. by* Eugene Eoyang *and* Irving Y. Lo

Who would have guessed she didn't have everything. The Leaving. Margot Fortunato. LoHo

Who would have thought it Sir, actually putting ME in a WRITING! Peter Reading. FaBoVe

Who would have thought she'd end that way? (LL) Mourning Poem for the Queen of Sunday. Robert Earl Hayden. HCAP; NAAAL; NoAM; NoP-4; PoBA; PoPoPo

Who would have thought that a disease of the ordinary world. Hsü Chung-hsing. CoBLCP, *tr. by* Jonathan Chaves *Fr.* Inquiring about the Health of Li Te-hua.

Who would here sojourn for an outstretched spell. Thoughts from Sophocles. Sophocles, *Greek*. OBCVT, *tr. by* Thomas Hardy

Who would I show it to. Elegy. W. S. Merwin. HCAP

Who Would List. *Unknown*. CTC, *tr. by* Andrew Lang *Fr.* Aucassin and Nicolette.

Who would live in others' breath? Epitaph: Iohannis Sande. Thomas Bastard. FaBoEE

Who would not be. The Laureate. William Edmonstoune Aytoun. BXAP; UV

Who would not cut the body from Head. (LL) Friend, on This Scaffold Thomas More Lies Dead. James Vincent Cunningham. CRP; InPK-6

Who would not die upon the spot? John Cleveland. *See* To the State of Love or The Senses' Festival.

Who would not laugh, if Lawrence, hired to grace. Hints from Horace. Byron.

Who would not live long. (LL) The Shield of Achilles. W. H. Auden. EBEV; FaBoMo; FaBoPV; GTBS-P; HAP; NAEL-2; NOBE; NOCV; NoAM; NoP-4; OxAEP-2; PeECV; PoA; PoE; WeW-3

Who would not weep, if Atticus were he? (LL) Atticus ("Peace to all such! but were there one whose fires"). Alexander Pope. AWP; InPK-6; NOBE; TRP

Who would not weep, if Atticus were he? (LL) Why did [*or* do] I write? what sin to me unknown. Alexander Pope. EBEV; EPCY; TOF

Who would the music be. (LL) Each More Melodious Note I Hear. Henry David Thoreau. OxBSP; PFE

Who would true Valour see. The Pilgrim. John Bunyan. APAD; BoTP; CTV; EBEV; EBEvV; FaPoR; NOCV; NOSC *Fr.* The Pilgrim's Progress.

Who would want to die defending Firestone Tire. Firestone. David Rivard. PBCAP

Who would / who could. Now Ain't That Love? Carolyn M. Rodgers. BPo

Who wouldn't want such a bed? Woman Asleep on a Banana Leaf. Katha Pollitt. InPS-3

Who writ for many. Benedicite. (LL) On Himselfe ("Weepe for the dead, for they have lost this light"). Robert Herrick. FaBoEE; NOSC

Who wrote *Who wrote Icon Basilike?*. On ["Who Wrote Icon Basilike" by Dr.] Christopher Wordsworth, Master of Trinity. Benjamin Hall Kennedy. FaBoEE; OBCoV

Whoa! but I stagger—too much wine! Argentarius, *Greek*. InMo, *tr. by* Sam Hamill

Who'd Be a Hero (Fictional)? Morris Gilbert Bishop. OBAL

Who'd believe me if. The Third Dimension. Denise Levertov. NeAP

Who'd couple with foetus, with handful of sore yell wet, with. The Whore of Kilpeck. Jeff Nuttall. NBrP

Who'd ever think that Utah would stir the world so much? Marching to Utah. *Unknown*. AmFP

Who'd Want to Be a Man? Gregory Orr. IFJA

Whoe'er has gone through London Street. A Butcher. Thomas Hood. PeLV

Whoe'er he be that to a taste aspires. James Bramston. NOEC *Fr.* The Man of Taste.

Whoe'er our stage examines, must excuse. Prologue on the Old Winchester Playhouse over the Old Butchers' Shambles. Thomas, the Younger Warton. ECEV

Whoe'er sighs most, is cruellest, and hastes the other's death. (LL) A Valediction: Of Weeping. Donne. ESCV; FHYEP; FSCP; HAP; HeIP-4; InPS-3; MeLP; NAEL-1; NOSC; OAEL-1; PoE; SCGP; SeCP; WeW-3

Whoe'er thou art whose path, in summer lies. Inscription. Mark Akenside. ECEV; NOEC

Whoever [*or* Who ever] comes to shroud me, do not harm[e]. The Funerall[1]. Donne. AWP; BoLoP; EBEV; ESCV; EnLoPo; FSCP; GLoP; HeIP-4; ImPo; MeLP; NAEL-1; NAWM-1; NoP-4; OAEL-1; OBEV; PoEL-2; PoRA; SCGP; SeCP; TFi

Whoever despises the clitoris despises the penis. The Speed of Darkness. Muriel Rukeyser. APSN; GLP; LCAP-2

Whoever feels your grip is driven mad. (LL) Chorus. Sophocles, *Greek*. PiM, *tr. by* Robert Fagles; GrIP

Whoever Finds a Horseshoe. Osip Emilevich Mandelstam, *Russian*. PFTM, *tr. by* Burton Raffel *and* Alla Burago

Whoever Has Become All Divine. "Angelus Silesius." GePo, *tr. by* George C. Schoolfield *Fr.* The Cherubical Wanderer.

Whoever has heard of St. Gingo. The New Cecilia. Thomas Lovell Beddoes. CBNP; OAEL-2

Whoever has not choked on a word. Truly. Ingeborg Bachmann, *German*. PoSu, *tr. by* Mark Anderson

Whoever hath her wish, thou hast thy Will. Sonnet 135. Shakespeare. NAEL-1; OAEL-1 *Fr.* Sonnets.

Whoever hath washed his hands of living. Courage. Sadi. AWP, *tr. by* Sir Edwin Arnold *Fr.* The Gulistan.

Whoever hurts my favor with my lady. Heinrich von Veldeke, *German*. GePo, *tr. by* Frederick Goldin

Whoever lives true life, will love true love. The Sweetness of England. Elizabeth Barrett Browning. OxAEP-2 *Fr.* Aurora Leigh. VWP

Whoever looks on life will see. James Cawthorn. ECEV *Fr.* Wit and Learning.

Whoever looks round sees Eternity there. (LL) Autumn ("The Thistledown's flying / Though the winds are all still"). John Clare. EnVR; HAP; PoEL-4; WeW-3

Whoever loves, if he do not propose. Love's Progress. Donne. OAEL-1 *Fr.* Elegies.

Whoever passes by my tomb, know. Callimachus. HePo *Fr.* Epigrams.

Whoever then are you? Whose wretched bones are these. Leonidas of Tarentum. HePo, *tr. by* Barbara Hughes Fowler *Fr.* Epigrams.

Whoever to finding fault inclines. The Cynic. St. George Tucker. OBAL

Whoever vies with Pindar's strain. Horace. *See* 4.2: Praise of Pindar, The ("Pindarum quisquis studet aemulari").

Whoever water drinks, writes wretched poetry. Water and Wine. Friedrich von Logau, *German*. GePo, *tr. by* George C. Schoolfield

Whoever weeps somewhere out in the world. Silent Hour. Rilke, *German*. AWP, *tr. by* Jessie Lemont

Whoever you are, go out into the evening. Initiation. Rilke, *German*. TrJP, *tr. by* C. F. MacIntyre

Whoever you are holding me now in hand. Walt Whitman. APN-1; NAAL-3; PoEL-5

Whole Armour of God, The. Charles Wesley. NOCV

Whole at once is bold, and regular, The. Alexander Pope. *See* Alps on Alps.

Whole church got hot and vivid, The. The Gift of Tongues. Robert Morgan. MT

Whole day long, under the walking sun, The. The Sleeping Giant. Donald Hall. NYBP; Poetsp; TwCP

Whole Duty of a Poem, The. Arthur Guiterman. PoToHe

Whole Duty of Children. Robert Louis Stevenson. CTV; NBLV; OxBChV

Whole flower extending outward, / Stretching and reaching, The. Theodore Roethke. *See* Transplanting.

Whole green sky is dying. The last tree flares, The. On a Line from Valéry. Carolyn Kizer. BAP-95; FFC

Whole heap of nickles and a whole heap of dimes, A. Shout, Little Lulu. *Unknown*. AmFP

Whole landscape drifted away to the north, The. A Window on the North. Robert Arthur Douglas Ford. MoCV

Whole lifetime assigned to me, A. Lifetime. Narayan Surve, *Marathi*. OMIP, *tr. by* Vinay Dharwadker

Whole Love. Robert Graves. ITG

Whole Mess. . . Almost, The . . Almost, The. Gregory Corso. BB

Whole New Scene, A. John Fuller. NOxBChV

Whole night long, A. Vigil. Giuseppe Ungaretti, *Italian*. PeFWW, *tr. by* Jonathan Griffin

Whole process is a lie, The. The Ivy Crown. William Carlos Williams. NAAL-2; NoAM

Whole royal family was living in one room at that time, The. The End of a Dynasty. Zbigniew Herbert, *Polish*. FaBoPV, *tr. by* Czeslaw Milosz

Whole Story, The. William Stafford. NNaP

Whole villages come. Piarco. Eric Roach. PBCV

Whole weight of history bears down, The. The Awful Mother. Susan Griffin. MDDM

Whole weight of the ocean smashes on rock, The. An Address to the Vacationers at Cape Lookout. William Stafford. NYBP

Whole white world is ours, The. White World. Hilda Doolittle. WPoS

Whole Works, The. Federico García Lorca. PFTM

Whole world now is but the minister, The. Robert Bridges. Son *Fr.* The Growth of Love.

Wholes. Larry Eigner. PmAP

Wholesome. William Meredith. TAP

Who'll Be a Witness for My Lord? *Unknown.* CrDW

Who'll buy my laces? I've laces to sell! The Lace Pedlar. Catherine A. Morin. BoTP

Who'll Help a Fairy? *Unknown.* BoTP

Who'll marry me? Cold Saturday. *Will he leave me?* With the. Questions and Answers. Diana O'Hehir. IFJA

Who'll walk the fields with us to town? Market Day. Mary Webb. CH

Whom do the stars yearn for? They blink and gleam. Yearning. Nguyễn Đình Thi, *Vietnamese.* AVP, tr. by Huỳnh Sanh Thông

Whom first we love, you know, we seldom wed. Changes. "Owen Meredith." PoLF

Whom have We next? (His syntax is. Reckoning. Fay Zwicky. NOBAu

Whom I thought I should never see more. (LL) The Bailiff's Daughter of Islington. *Unknown.* ESPB; OxBB; OxBoLi; PBMP

Whom it is eating to the bone. (LL) Childlessness. James Merrill. CoAmPo; ColAP

Whom none but Beetles—know. (LL) Of Bronze—and Blaze. Emily Dickinson. APN-2; NCAP; PAR

Whom sadder can I say? she said. (LL) The Mask. Elizabeth Barrett Browning. OBNC; VWP

Whom Shall One Teach. Bible, *O.T.* TrJP *Fr.* Isaiah.

"Whom the Gods Love die young" I used to quote. Margaret E. Bruner. PoLF

Whom the kites of Heaven solicited with sweet cries. (LL) Necrological. John Crowe Ransom. FuPo; MeMAP

Whom we have found in our beds today, today? (LL) To Any Member of My Generation. George Barker. LiTM; Son

Whom we love, whose actions. For Ronald King Our Brother. Sherley Anne Williams. WeT

Whom weave ye in. Rolfe and the Palm. Herman Melville. NCAP

Whom when I saw assembled in such wise. Virgil. PoE *Fr.* The Second Book of Virgil's *Aeneid.* SiPS, tr. by Henry Howard, Earl of Surrey *Fr.* The Aeneid [*or* Eneados, Aeneis].

Whoopee Ti Yi Yo, Git Along Little Dogies. *Unknown.* AS; ImGa ("As I walked out one morning for pleasure.") APN-2

Whoops! *Unknown.* NTCP

Whore of Kilpeck, The. Jeff Nuttall. NBrP

Whore only he could call *daughter, The.* (LL) A Castle in Lynn. Linda McCarriston. LoL; NMM-2

Whore that rides in us abides, The. *Unknown.* SCAP

Whores. Margaret Abigail Walker. NALW

Whorl inside my head buzzes, The. Terminus. Peter Rose. BMAP

Who's In. Elizabeth Fleming. BoTP

Who's in the next room?—who? Thomas Hardy. PoEL-5

Who's killed the leaves? Leaves. Ted Hughes. AYFP; OxBC

Who's most afraid of death?thou. E. E. Cummings. CMoP; PoE; VGW

Who's on first? The dust descends as. Whose Language. Charles Bernstein. PmAP

Who's that. James Kirkup. OTCP

Who's That A-Knocking? Emile Jacot. BoTP

Who's that driving a black cart. Josef Hanzlik, *German.* CEEP, tr. by Ewald Osers

Who's that knocking on the window. Innocent's Song. Charles Causley. GTBS-P; OBCP

Who's that mysterious rider. The Horseman on the Skyline. Henry Lawson. CBAP

Who's that ringing at my door bell? *Unknown.* FaBoCh; OxNR

Who's that ringing at our door-bell? That Little Black Cat. D'Arcy Wentworth Thompson. NOxBChV; OxBChV

"Who's that ringing at the front door bell?" *Unknown.* BoTP

"Who's that tickling my back?" said the wall. The Tickle Rhyme. Ian Serraillier. NTCP; Spl

Who's the Dover-based day tripper. A Trifle for Trafalgar Day. Ted Pauker. NOBL

Who's the most important man this country ever knew? Barney Google. Billy Rose. OBAL

Who's the Pretty Girl Milkin' the Cow? *Unknown.* AS

Who's therefore true, because her truth kills me[e]. (LL) Twicknam [*or* Twickenham] Garden. Donne. EBEV; ESCV; EnLoPo; MeLP; PoE; PoEL-2; SCGP; SeCP

Who's Who. W. H. Auden. MeMAP; MoBrPo; MoP; NoAM; Son

Whose accent no farewell can know. (LL) Where icy and bright dungeons lift. Hart Crane. ColAP; HAP; MoAmPo; UnPo

Whose baggage from land to land is despair. Palladas, *Greek.* GrAn, tr. by Frank Kuenstler

Whose black heart crackles to a purr. (LL) Pinetree. Agnes Nemes Nagy, *Hungarian.* CEEP; PoSu, tr. by Bruce Berlind

Whose brest hath marble beene to me. (LL) To Roses in the Bosom[e] of Castara. William Habington. BeJo; EnLoPo; MeLP; NOSC; OBEV; SCGP; SeCP

Whose broken window is a cry of art. Boy Breaking Glass. Gwendolyn Brooks. AiP; MoP; NAAL-2; NoAM; NoP-4

Whose candles light the tulip tree? Tulip Tree. Sacheverell Sitwell. MoBrPo

Whose cherry tree did young George chop? Mingled Yarns. X. J. Kennedy. OBCA

Whose cinders yet with envy they do eat. (LL) Another Tribute to Wyatt. Henry Howard, Earl of Surrey. AAS; SiPS

Whose counted smile of hours and days, suppose. Hart Crane. ColAP *Fr.* Voyages. CMoP; MeMAP; NOBA; NoAM; TAP

Whose day shall never die [*or* dy] in Night. (LL) An Epitaph Upon Husband and Wife Who Died and Were Buried Together. Richard Crashaw. EBEV; FaBoEE; NOBE; OBEV; OxAEP-1; OxBM; SeCP

Whose Doom to whom? (LL) Pit—but Heaven over it, A. Emily Dickinson. APN-2; NCAP

Whose eagle clings in sunrise to thy crest! (LL) To the Statue on the Capitol. John James Piatt. APN-2; GS

Whose eyes were sleepbound &. Wyatt's Dream. Richard Caddel. NBrP

Whose feet are so deep in the sand. (LL) Yves Tanguy. David Gascoyne. NoP-4; SPE

Whose fire from which I came, has now grown cold? (LL) One Flesh. Elizabeth Jennings. FaBoWP; LW; NoP-4; OxAEP-2; OxBTC; PBWP

Whose fish, fish. (LL) Nature's Lineaments. Robert Graves. FaBoTw; RB

Whose fruitlesse worke is broken with least wynd. (LL) *Penelope* for her *Ulisses* sake. Edmund Spenser. NoP-4; PBRV

Whose genitalia are these anyway / so sweet and lovely. Genitalia. George Tysh. PT

Whose green adventure is to run to seed. (LL) Remembering the 'Thirties. Donald Davie. FaBoPo; NoP-4; OxBTC

Whose Hand. *Unknown, Hebrew.* TrJP, tr. by Arthur Davis

Whose [*or* Who's] hat was in his hand. (LL) Ballad: "I put my hat upon my head." Samuel Johnson. CBNP; NOBL; OxAEP-1; UV

"Whose heart" "might be lost?" "Whose mask is this?" "Who has a mask." White Phosphorus. Alice Notley. FTOS

Whose is that long white box in the grove, what have they accomplished, why am I cold. (LL) The Bee Meeting. Sylvia Plath. HCAP; InPS-3; NALW; Poetr; WPE

Whose is that noble dauntless brow? Verses Intended to Be Written below a Noble Earl's Picture. Robert Burns. HoPM

Whose is the river, Excellency, whose the fish. The Geographers. Karl Shapiro. OxBA

Whose is the voice that will not let me rest? Unknown Ideal. Dora Sigerson Shorter. IIP

Whose is this horrifying face. Ecce Homo. David Gascoyne. ChIV-2; LiTM; NoP-4; OBWP; PeECV *Fr.* Miserere.

Whose Language. Charles Bernstein. PmAP

Whose laughter plays like summer lightning there. (LL) Cattle Show. "Hugh MacDiarmid." FaBoMo; HAP; MoBrPo; OBMV; OxBTC

Whose little pigs are these, these, these? *Unknown.* OxNR

Whose love is given over-well. Partial Comfort. Dorothy Parker. OBAL

Whose modest tresses were bound up for thee! (LL) To Spring. William Blake. BoTP; NAEL-2; NOEC; OAEL-2; OBEV; PoEL-4; PoLF; SCGP

Whose music is the gladness of the world. (LL) The Choir Invisible. "George Eliot." EBVV; OBNC

Whose nostrils bleed, whose life runs out from eye and / ear. (LL) The Slaughter-House. Alfred Hayes. PFE

Whose page is blanker than the raining skies. (LL) On the Edge. Philip Levine. CoAP; TAP

Whose scales turn aside the sun's sword by their polish. (LL) An Egyptian Pulled Glass Bottle in the Shape of a Fish. Marianne Moore. NALW; PBWP

Whose Scene? Ruth Stone. BoWoP

Whose senses in so evil consort, their stepdame Nature lays. Seventh Song. Sir Philip Sidney. NoP-4 *Fr.* Astrophil and Stella. AAS; SiPS

Whose shadow is less given to change than he. (LL) Upon His Picture. Thomas Randolph. BeJo; NOBE

Whose songs shall never be heard. (LL) Spectral Lovers. John Crowe Ransom. GBL; HeIP-4

Whose spittle only could restore the blind. (LL) Easter-Day. Henry Vaughan. ESCV; PeECV

Whose steadfast faith yet never moved. / Forget not this. (LL) A Supplication. Sir Thomas Wyatt. AAS; FaBoVe; GTBS-P; HAP; NAEL-1; NOBE; NoSic; OBEV; SCGP; SiPS

Whose step is the paulownia leaf that falls silently. I Do Not Know. Yong-un Han, *Korean.* CKP, tr. by Jaihiun Kim

Whose sweetheart is very drunk? Chinook Songs. *Unknown, Chinook Native American.* APN-2, tr. by Franz Boas

Whose the hand unloosed Clearista's zone. Meleager, *Greek*. GrAn, *tr. by* Peter Whigham

Whose very beard is flesh, and mouth is horn[e]. (LL) On the Card[e]s, and Dice. Sir Walter Ralegh. ChIV-2; RB; SiPS

Whose very existence / tore us down to the human. Toi Derricotte. *See* Blackbottom.

Whose wagon is perilously rapt. (LL) Santa Fe Trail. Barbara Guest. FTOS

Whose wild bad father loves you well. (LL) A Sympathy, A Welcome. John Berryman. NYBP; NoP-4

Whose Window? Alison Brackenbury. DiPo

Whose woods these are *I* think *I* know. Stopping by Woods on a Snowy Evening. Robert Frost. AmPP; CMoP; ChAP; ClHu; ColAP; FaBoCh; HAP; HeIP-4; HoPM; ImGa; ImPo; InPK-6; InPS-3; LiTM; MeMAP; MoAmPo; MoP; NAAL-2; NIP-4; NOBA; NTCP; NTP; NoAM; NoP-4; OBCA; OxBA; PFE; PoE; PoPoPo; PoRA; Poetr; RB; SAGP; SAmP; SCV; SoSe-8; TAP; TFi; TOF; TRP; TTTS

Whose work could this be, Chapman, to refine. To My Worthy and Honoured Friend, Mr George Chapman, on His Translation of Hesiod's *Works and Days*. Ben Jonson. EPCY

Whoso answers my questions. Night the Second: All or Nothing. Bayard Taylor. APN-2; BXAP *Fr.* The Echo Club.

Whoso Gives Freely, Shall Freely Receive! Josephine D. Henderson Heard. CBWP-4

Whoso in harvest mindeth to reap. To His Child. William Bullokar. OxBChV

Whoso is wise, and will observe these things, even they shall understand the lovingkindness of the Lord. (LL) Psalm 107. Bible, *O.T.* OxBoS

Whoso list to hunt, I know where is an hind. Sir Thomas Wyatt. AAS; APAD; BoLoP; CABP; EBEV; GBL; HAP; NAEL-1; NNPT; NoSic; OAEL-1; OBVE; PoE; PoEL-1; SCGP; SiPS; TFi

Whoso thou art that passest by this place. An Epitaph of Maister Win Drowned in the Sea. George Turberville. FaRoFF

Whoso walks in solitude. Ralph Waldo Emerson. *Fr.* Woodnotes II ("As sunbeams stream through liberal space"). NOBA

Whoso Would See This Song of Heavenly Choice. John Wilson. AH

Whummil Bore, The. *Unknown*. CH; ESPB

"Whu's aw thae fflag-poles ffur in Princess Street?" Heard in the Cougate. Robert Garioch. FaBoTC; OxBTC

Whut do i keer ef de white-folks do 'buse us! Uncle Rube's Defense. Clara Ann Thompson. CBWP-2

Whut you say, dah? huh, uh! chile. A Cabin Tale. Paul Laurence Dunbar. NAAAL

Why? Melba Joyce Boyd. BlSi

Why? Stephen Crane. MeMAP *Fr.* The Black Riders [and Other Lines].

Why? Wassily Kandinsky, *Russian*. TCRP, *tr. by* Albert C. Todd

Why? Myra Cohn Livingston. CA

Why all the racket, you chattering birds? Epigram. *Unknown, Greek*. GrAn, *tr. by* Thomas Meyer

Why am I a Negro? Oh, why am I black? The Slave's Lament. Massillon Coicou, *French*. NegPo, *tr. by* Ellen Conroy Kennedy

Why am I always so depressed? *Unknown, Chinese*. CoBCP, *tr. by* Burton Watson

Why am I crying after love? (LL) Spring Night. Sara Teasdale. FaBoBe; MoAmPo

Why am I not as they? (LL) Lineage. Margaret Abigail Walker. BlSi; CrSp; NALW; NMM-2; OxWW; PBWP; PoBA

Why am I so afraid. I Am Afraid of Fire. Anna Swirszczynska, *Polish*. AF, *tr. by* Czeslaw Milosz

Why and Wherefore set out one day. Metaphysics. Oliver Herford. CBNP

Why are candles brightly burning. The Christmas Tree. Lizelia Augusta Jenkins Moorer. CBWP-3

Why Are Daddies So Mean? Jane Chambers. GLP

Why are Fire Engines Red? *Unknown*. CBNP

Why are our ancestors. Ancestors. Dudley Randall. BPo

Why are saints so difficult to recognize. Sainthood. Cristoir O'Flynn. TIRV

Why are the things that have no death. Irony. Louis Untermeyer. TrJP

Why are we[e] by all creatures waited on? Donne. NOCV; PoE; PoEL-2; TrCP *Fr.* Holy Sonnets. ESCV

Why are women so energetic? Energetic Women. D. H. Lawrence. InPS-3

Why are ye wandering aye 'twixt porch and porch. Arcades Ambo. Charles Stuart Calverley. BXAP

Why are you dragged to be stoned? *Unknown. Fr.* The Talmud. TrJP

Why are you not asleep, child? Night. Georgi Djagarov, *Bulgarian*. CEEP, *tr. by* Jascha Kessler *and* Aleksandar Shurbanov

Why are you taking me this way? Where does this road go? Tell me. Unanswered. Yannis Ritsos, *Greek*. AF, *tr. by* Edmund Keeley

Why are you weeping, child of the future. Ballad of the Sad Astronaut. Judith Nicholls. SpW

Why are your eyes as big as saucers—big as saucers? Man in the Street. Robert Penn Warren. OBAL

Why art thou silent and invisible. To Nobodaddy. William Blake. OAEL-2

Why art thou silent? Is thy love a plant. To a Distant Friend. Wordsworth. GTBS-P; OBEV

Why art thou slow, thou rest of trouble, Death. Song. Philip Massinger. OxAEP-1 *Fr.* The Emperor of the East.

"Why?" Because all I haply can and do. Why I Am a Liberal. Robert Browning. Son

Why boast, O arrogant, imperious man. On Mrs. Montagu. Ann Yearsley. ECWP

Why boast we, Glaucus! our extended Reign. The Speech of Sarpedon (an Ally of the Trojans) to Glaucus. Homer. OBVE, *tr. by* Alexander Pope *Fr.* The Iliad.

Why boastest thou thyself in mischief, O mighty man? Bible, *O.T. See* Psalm 52.

Why Brownlee left, and where he went. Paul Muldoon. DiPo; NoP-4; PBCIP

Why, by an ingrained habit, deviate. With the Grain. Donald Davie. NoAM

Why call it dead, wi' life a-vled. All Still. William Barnes. NOBVV

Why came I so untimely forth. To a Very Young Lady. Edmund Waller. SCGP; SeCP

Why cannot we eat enough for a week. Envying the Pelican. Richard Weber. CIP-2

Why Can't I Leave You? Ai. AmPA

Why can't we all be like that bird? (LL) Wise old owl lived in an oak, A. Edward Hersey Richards. CTV

"Why can't you play on *that*?" (LL) Little Raindrops. Jane Euphemia Browne. BoTP; OxBChV

Why, Celia, is your spreading waist. Edward Moore. ECEV *Fr.* The Poet and His Patron. ECEV

Why cherish thus the senseless thing? That Glove. Mary E. Tucker. CBWP-1

Why Come Ye Not to Court. John Skelton.

"Such a prelate, I trow." OBSV

Why confer on us the piercing vision. To Charlotte von Stein. Goethe, *German*. STV, *tr. by* John Frederick Nims

Why, country Pan, sitting still. Anyte, *Greek*. GrAn, *tr. by* John Heath-Stubbs *and* Carol A. Whiteside

Why, cry, cry, again. (LL) A Maxim Revised. *Unknown*. BLPA; NBLV

Why Damon, why, why, why so pressing? Song. Mary Lee, Lady Chudleigh. LW

Why, Damon, with the forward day. The Dying Man in His Garden. George Sewell. GTBS-P; OBGa

Why did baby die. Christina Rossetti. VWP

Why did Hagar weep over Ishmael when he thirsted. Yitzhak Lamdan. MHP, *tr. by* Ruth Finer Mintz *Fr.* In the Khamsin.

Why did I dream of you last night? On Wakening. Philip Larkin. LBC

Why did I laugh to-night? No voice will tell. Keats. GSo

Why did [or do] I write? what sin to me unknown. Alexander Pope. EBEV; EPCY; TOF *Fr.* Epistle to Dr. Arbuthnot. FHYEP; InPS-3; NoP-4; OAEL-1; OxAEP-1; PoE; PoEL-3; TFi

Why did I wrong my judgement so. Upon His Unconstant Mistress. Sir Robert Ayton. NOSC

Why did Massenet compose *Thaïs*? Greetings from the Chateau. James Schuyler. FTOS

Why did my parents send me to the schools. Sir John Davies. ChIV-1 *Fr.* Of Human Knowledge.

Why did our blessed Savior please to break. On the Holy Scriptures. Francis Quarles. ChIV-2

Why did the children. Carl Sandburg. OBAL; PBMP *Fr.* The People, Yes.

Why did the clerk drag his fingertips. The Great Helmsman. David Woo. OpBo

WHY DID THE MAID WEEP? (LL) Why? Stephen Crane. APN-2; MeMAP; NoP-4; TAP

Why did the Maker stage such drama here? Remembering the Past in the City of the Soaring Dragon. (Lady) Thanh Quan, *Vietnamese*. AVP, *tr. by* Huỳnh Sanh Thông

Why did the sun his beams conceal. The Crucifixion. Mary Weston Fordham. CBWP-2

Why did you choose me for your wife, Joseph? Asenath. Diana Hume George. ChIV-1

Why did you come / to trouble my decline? Red Rose and a Beggar. Hilda Doolittle. APSN

Why did you come, with your enkindled eyes. Mary Webb. LW

Why did you give no hint that night. The Going. Thomas Hardy. CBLP; EBEV; LoP; NOBE; OxAEP-2; SCGP; UnPo

Why did you go. E. E. Cummings. VGW

Why did you hate to be by yourself. As to Being Alone. James Oppenheim. TrJP

Why did you kiss the girl who cried. What the Earth Asked Me. James Wright. NYBP

Why did you stay away. The Way the Cards Fall. Yusef Komunyakaa. GT

Why did your spirit. Ark Astonished. Jay Macpherson. NOBC *Fr.* The Ark.

Why didn't we think of clothes before? D. J. Enright. OBCoV *Fr.* Paradise Illustrated.

Why didst thou promise such a beauteous day. Sonnet 34. Shakespeare. HeIP-4; OxAEP-1 *Fr.* Sonnets.

Why, disease, dost thou molest. To Sickness. Ben Jonson. BeJo

Why do I curse the jazz of this hotel? The Jazz of This Hotel. Vachel Lindsay. SeSe

Why do I deny manna to another? Sather Gate Illumination. Allen Ginsberg. NeAP

Why do I draw this coole releeving ayer. Barnabe Barnes. PBRV *Fr.* Parthenophil and Parthenophe.

Why do I follow you. Sunset. Joseph Ceravolo. FTOS

Why do I hate that lone green dell? Emily Jane Brontë. VWP

Why do I languish thus, drooping and dull. Dulness[e]. George Herbert. ESCV

Why Do I Live? George Linnaeus Banks. *See* What I Live For.

Why do I love? Go ask the Glorious Sun. To One That Asked Me Why I Loved J.G G. "Ephelia." KTR; LW; NOSC; PEW

Why Do I Love You? Roy Croft. *See* Love.

"Why do I love" You, Sir? Emily Dickinson. APN-2; LW

Why do I post my love letters. Why Don't You Talk to Me? Alistair Campbell. PeNZ

Why do I think of Michael. Crazy Courage. Alma Villanueva. BAP-96

Why do I use my paper, ink, and pen. Verses Made by a Catholic in Praise of Campion That Was Executed at Tyburn for Treason, As Is Made Known by the Proclamation. *Unknown.* NoSic

Why do I write today? Apology. William Carlos Williams. OxBA; SAmP

Why do people sit in darkness as regards the Negro race? The Truth Suppressed. Lizelia Augusta Jenkins Moorer. CBWP-3

Why Do So Few Blacks Study Creative Writing? Cornelius Eady. GT; LTA

Why do the bells for Christmas ring? Christmas Song. Eugene Field. BoTP; CTV

Why do the Gentiles tumult, and the Nations, *par. by* Milton. Bible, *O.T. See* Psalm 2.

Why do the Graces now desert the Muse? Walter Savage Landor. FaBoEE

Why do the heathen rage. Psalm 2. Bible, *O.T.* NAAL-1; NAAL-3 *Fr.* Psalms.

Why do the lilies goggle their tongues at me. Grotesque. Amy Lowell. BoWoP

Why do they come? What do they seek. On a Replica of the Parthenon. Donald Davidson. FuPo

Why do those bell-tones crowd the air? London Birds: a Lollipop. John Heath-Stubbs. *Fr.* Two Wedding Songs. NTP

Why do we labor at the poem. Reasons for Music. Archibald MacLeish. MeMAP

Why Do We Live? Israel Zangwill. TrJP

Why do we love her?—that she gave us birth? This World. Sarah Morgan Bryan Piatt. NCAP

Why Do We Mourn Departing Friends? Isaac Watts. AH

Why do we return? Not in the darkened rooms. Roy Fuller. LBC *Fr.* Ghost Voice.

Why do we waste so much time in arguing? Sushi. Paul Muldoon. CABP; CIP-2

Why do you cry out, why do I like to hear you. Sound of Breaking. Conrad Potter Aiken. AWP

Why do you dig like long-clawed scavengers. Verlaine. Edwin Arlington Robinson. APN-2; NAAL-2; NCAP

Why do you dwell so long in clouds. Song to the Masquers. James Shirley. OxBSP *Fr.* The Triumph of Peace.

Why do you feel differently about a very little snail and a big one. Gertrude Stein. PFTM

Why do you frown on me, you puritans. Petronius Arbiter, *Greek.* PGA, *tr. by* Kenneth Rexroth

Why do you heave apart my stone? Gregory of Nazianzus, Saint, *Greek.* GrAn, *tr. by* Robin Skelton

Why do you hide, O dryads! when we seek. Chant for Reapers. Wilfrid Thorley. OBEV

Why do you lie with your legs ungainly huddled. The Dug-Out. Siegfried Sassoon. CH; MoBrPo; NSI; PoFWW

Why do you listen, trees? The Farm. Archibald MacLeish. AFr

Why do you play such dreary music. Radio. Frank O'Hara. PoA

Why do you rack the ore? The cornerstone alone. The Treasure Lies In the Cornerstone. "Angelus Silesius." GePo, *tr. by* George C. Schoolfield *Fr.* The Cherubical Wanderer.

Why do you rush through the field in trains. The Fat White Woman Speaks. G. K. Chesterton. OBCoV; UV

'Why do you shrink away, and start and stare?'. At the Convent Gate. Charlotte Mew. VWP

Why / do / you / sigh. Post-Coitum Tristesse: A Sonnet. Brad Leithauser. EOEF; RA

Why do you stare at the floor, Chrysilla. Irenaeus Referendarius, *Greek.* InMo, *tr. by* Sam Hamill

Why do you stare at the little box. The Judges of the Little Box. Vasco [*or* Vasko] Popa, *Serbo-Croatian.* HSix, *tr. by* Charles Simic

Why do you subdue yourself in golds and purples? The Artist. Amy Lowell. CPO

Why do you talk so much. For Robert Frost. Galway Kinnell. NOBA; VGW

"Why do / You thus devise." Susanna and the Elders. Adelaide Crapsey. WPE

Why do you visit me, white moths, so often? Georg Heym, *German.* PeFWW, *tr. by* Christopher Middleton

"Why do you wear your hair like a man?" After Dilettante Concetti. Henry Duff Traill. BXAP

Why do you wrap your wisdom in a multitude of words? I Ask My Teachers. Sister Mary Madeleva. CRP *Fr.* Concerning Death.

Why Do You Write about Russia? Louis Simpson. InPS-3

Why? doan't I pay me car-fare? A Market Basket in the Car. Thomas MacDermot. PBCV

Why does a cauliflower so much resemble a brain? Binary. Chris Wallace-Crabbe. OBCoV

Why does a room. Tanka. Maekawa Samio, *Japanese.* MJT, *tr. by* Makoto Ueda

Why does he keep bruising against me my dead father why still. Sestina with Refrain. Thomas William Shapcott. CBAP

Why Does It Snow? Laura Elizabeth Richards. NOxBChV; OBCA

Why does the night drag on and on, pitch-dark? The Long Night. Tù' Diễn Dồn, *Vietnamese.* AVP, *tr. by* Huỳnh Sanh Thông

Why does the Pygmy. The Third Jungle Book. Ogden Nash. OxBM

Why does the raven cry aloud and no eye pities her? The Lamentation of Enion. William Blake. OBNC *Fr.* Vala; or The Four Zoas.

Why does the sea burn? Why do the hills cry? Zaydee. Philip Levine. NNaP

Why does the sea moan evermore? By the Sea. Christina Rossetti. NOBVV

Why does the thin grey strand. Sorrow. D. H. Lawrence. CMoP; GTBS-P; OBMV

Why does the wind so want to be. The Wind. Elizabeth Rendall. BoTP

"Why [*or* Quhy] does [*or* dois] your brand sae [*or* so] drop wi' blude [*or* drap wi bluid]." Edward [*or* Edward, Edward]. *Unknown.* AmFP; CH; ClHu; EBEV; EBEvV; ESPB; FaPoR; HAP; HoPM; InPK-6; InPS-3; NAEL-1; NOBE; NoP-4; OBEV; OxBB; OxBS; PoEL-1; PoRA; SCGP; SoSe-8; TFi; TRP

"Why doesn't somebody buy *me* false ears?" From the Joke Shop. Roy Fuller. OxBC

Why don't I write in the language of air? Mona Sa'udi, *Arabic.* WPOW, *tr. by* Kamal Boullata

Why don't people leave off being lovable. Elemental. D. H. Lawrence. NoP-4

Why don't we rock the casket here in the moonlight? The Pale Blue Casket. Oliver Pitcher. PoBA; TTY

Why don't you / go down Old Hannah. Ol' Hannah. Doc Reese. PFTM

Why Don't You Talk to Me? Alistair Campbell. PeNZ

"Why don't you try writing something?" (LL) Teaching the Ape to Write Poems. James Tate. BLT; CMAP

Why don't you write you never. Dear Reader. Peter Meinke. Poetsp

Why dost not speak? Shakespeare. OxAEP-1 *Fr.* Coriolanus.

Why dost thou haste away, *speech of Basilius.* Madrigal. Sir Philip Sidney. NoSic; SiPS *Fr.* Arcadia.

Why dost thou hate return instead of love. Ditty. Edward Herbert, 1st Baron Herbert of Cherbury. NOSC

Why dost thou shade thy lovely face? O why. To His Mistress. John Wilmot, 2d Earl of Rochester. OBEV

Why dost thou shade thy lovely face? Oh why. Wherefore Hidest Thou Thy Face, and Holdest Me for Thine Enemy [*or* Enemie]? Francis Quarles. NOSC *Fr.* Emblems.

Why dost thou so explore. Homer. OBVE, *tr. by* George Chapman *Fr.* The Iliad.

Why dost thou sound, my dear[e] Aurelian. In Answer of an Elegiacal[l] Letter, Upon the Death of the King of Sweden [from Aurelian

Townsend, Inviting Me to Write on That Subject]. Thomas Carew. BeJo

Why each is striving, from of old. Destiny. Sir Edwin Arnold. NOBVV; OxBSP

Why English Is So Hard! *Unknown.* CTV

Why Fear to Die? Sir Philip Sidney. SiPS *Fr.* Arcadia.

Why Flowers Change Color. Robert Herrick. HAP

Why from the danger did mine eyes not start. Sonnet: Of His Pain from a New Love. Guido Cavalcanti, *Italian.* AWP, *tr. by* D. G. Rossetti

Why God Permits Evil: For Answers to This Question of Interest to Many Write Bible Answers Dept. E-7. Miller Williams. MT

Why has our poetry eschewed. Food and Drink. Louis Untermeyer. MoAmPo

Why has Spring one syllable less. What's in a Name? Christina Rossetti. FaBoVe

Why has thou not the visage of a sweetie or a cutie? Kind of an Ode to Duty. Ogden Nash. APAD

Why Hast Thou Forsaken Me? Chad Walsh. *Fr.* The Psalm of Christ. TrCP

Why hast thou nothing in thy face? Eros. Robert Bridges. CABP; CMoP; NOBE; PoEL-5

Why have crowds as magnets drawn. Why We Meet. Lizelia Augusta Jenkins Moorer. CBWP-3

Why have I locked myself inside. John Hollander. EOEF

Why have such scores of lovely, gifted girls. A Slice of Wedding Cake. Robert Graves. BoLoP; NAEL-2; NOBE; OxBTC

Why have ye no reuthe on my child? *Unknown.* MiEL

Why have you landed on Poulo Condore? On Poulo Condore. Trần Cao Vân, *Vietnamese.* AVP, *tr. by* Huỳnh Sanh Thông

Why Have You No Ruth? *Unknown.* OxBSP

Why have you risen, to stand with naked feet. With the Dawn. Thomas Caulfield Irwin. BIrV; EnLoPo

Why, having won her, do I woo? The Married Lover. Coventry Patmore. OBEV; OxAEP-2 *Fr.* The Angel in the House.

Why he turned them inside outside. (LL) The Modern Hiawatha. George A. Strong. BXAP; EBEvV; OBCoV; PeLV; UV

Why He Was There. Edwin Arlington Robinson. CMoP; NOBA

Why I Am a Liberal. Robert Browning. Son

Why I Am Not a Painter. Frank O'Hara. CoAmPo; HCAP; MoP; NOBA; NeAP; NoAM; NoP-4; PoE; PoM; PoPoPo; Poetr; VCAP

Why I Choose Black Men for My Lovers. La Loca. CLPP

Why I Didn't Go to Delphi. James Welch. CDW

Why I Don't Speak Italian. Arthur L. Clements. UnSA

Why I Like Movies. Patricia Jones. BlSi

Why I Never Answered Your Letter. Nancy Willard. CrSp

Why I Often Allude to Osiris. Ishmael Reed. GT

Why I tie about thy wrist. Bracelet. Robert Herrick. APAD; OBEV

Why I Voted the Socialist Ticket. Vachel Lindsay. MoAmPo

Why I Write Not of Love. Ben Jonson. BeJo; OxBSP; PBRV

("Some act of *Love's* bound to reherse.") PBRV

Why, if Becchina's heart were diamond. Sonnet: Of Becchina, the Shoemaker's Daughter. Cecco Angiolieri, da Siena, *Italian.* AWP, *tr. by* D. G. Rossetti

Why, if this interval of being can be spent serenely. Rilke. EnlH; NAWM-2 *Fr.* Duino Elegies.

Why in all the many races of the country where we live. Why Negroes Don't Unite. Lizelia Augusta Jenkins Moorer. CBWP-3

Why is a pump like Viscount Castlereagh? What's My Thought Like? Thomas Moore. FaBoEE

Why is everything I do in my life like a boomerang? Boomerang. John Perreault. SPE

Why Is God Love, Jack? Allen Ginsberg. CLPP; FTOS

("Because I lay my / head on pillows.") CLPP

Why is it. Lover's Meeting. Ray Mathew. CBAP

Why Is It? Lizelia Augusta Jenkins Moorer. CBWP-3

Why is it I can't sleep tonight? The Bucket. Rose Romano. UnSA

Why is it in my middle-aged dream. Black and White. Shirley Lim. UnSA

Why is it me they always sit beside. Conspiracy. Claire Bateman. CrSp

Why is it not enough, to want death's certain peace? Lamentation during His Most Painful Illness. Simon Dach, *German.* GePo, *tr. by* Ingrid Walsøe-Engel

Why is it, when I am in Rome. On Being a Woman. Dorothy Parker. PoLF

Why is my verse so barren of new pride. Sonnet 76. Shakespeare. EBEV; NoSic; OxAEP-1 *Fr.* Sonnets.

Why is the floor, Chrysilla. Irenaeus Referendarius, *Greek.* GrAn, *tr. by* W. G. Shepherd

Why is the princess so depressed. Noblesse Oblige. Celeste Turner Wright. Poetsp

Why is the snow pale blue? Irina Ratushinskaya, *Russian.* TCRP, *tr. by* Albert C. Todd

Why is the word pretty so underrated? Pretty. Stevie Smith. NAEL-2; NoAM; NoP-4; PoPoPo

Why is your forehead deep-furrowed with care? Call Me Not Back from the Echoless Shore. *Unknown.* BLPA

Why, Jack, how now? I hear strange stories. An Epistle to My Friend J. B. Robert Dodsley. NOEC

Why just now a visit. Prague. Lutz Rathenow, *German.* CEEP, *tr. by* Boria Sax

Why lean over the fire, and who is this. In the Secret House. Christopher Middleton. FaBoMo

Why, let the strucken deer go weep. Shakespeare. NoSic *Fr.* Hamlet. NAWM-1

Why linger? I must haste, or lose the Delphic bays. (LL) Corinna, from Athens, to Tanagra. Walter Savage Landor. NOBE; OBEV; OBNC

Why Linger Yet upon the Strand? Louis FitzGerald Benson. AH

Why listen, even the water is sobbing for something. The Maid's Thought. Robinson Jeffers. EP

Why Log Truck Drivers Rise Earlier Than Students of Zen. Gary Snyder. LoL; NNaP

"Why look at me like that?" Nocturne by Ben Shahn. Ronald Stuart Thomas. OxAEP-2

Why looks your Grace so heavily today? Shakespeare. OxAEP-1 *Fr.* King Richard III.

Why Lord, must something in us. Why, Lord. Mark Van Doren. AH

Why 'm i. 4 Or 5 Tadpoles. Kusano Shimpei, *Japanese.* PFTM, *tr. by* Cid Corman

Why, Madam, must I tell this idle tale? A True Tale. Mary Chandler. ECWP

Why make it doubt—it hurts it so. Emily Dickinson. NALW

Why, *Man* of *Morals,* tell me why? (LL) Drinking. Anacreon, *Greek.* BeJo; NNPT; NOBE; OBCVT; OBEV; OBVE; OxAEP-1; SeCP, *tr. by* Abraham Cowley

Why Mira Can't Go Back to Her Old House. Mirabai, *Rajasthani.* EnlH; WPoS, *tr. by* Robert Bly

("Me to climb on a jackass? Try to be serious.") (LL) WPoS, *tr. by* Robert Bly

Why mourns my beauteous friend, bereft? To Urania. Benjamin Colman. SCAP

Why muse wee thus to see the wheeles run cross. The Town Called Providence, Its Fate. Benjamin Tompson. SCAP

Why must I be hurt? Pain. Elsie Robinson. PoToHe

Why Must You Know? John Wheelwright. VGW

Why must you play chess with your friends all day? A Poem Expressing My Wife's Response to One I Sent Her. Li K'ai-hsien, *Chinese.* CoBLCP, *tr. by* Jonathan Chaves

Why must you thrust your loins. Strato, *Greek.* InMo, *tr. by* Sam Hamill

Why My Hair Is Not Gray. Picirantaiyar, *Tamil.* PLW, *tr. by* A. K. Ramanujan

Why My Mother Made Me. Sharon Olds. Poetr

Why Negroes Don't Unite. Lizelia Augusta Jenkins Moorer. CBWP-3

Why not merely the despaired of. Cascando. Samuel Beckett. NOIV

Why not? The mouths of the ginger blooms slide open. Chinoiserie. Charles Wright. AmPA

Why, O why. Grumblers. Leonard Clark. PeP

Why of the sheep do you not learn peace? An Answer to the Parson. William Blake. FaBoEE; NBLV; OxBoLi

Why only in the spring are roses borne? Lucretius. KTR, *tr. by* Lucy Hutchinson *Fr.* De Rerum Natura (On the Nature of Things).

Why puts our grand-dame [*or* Grandame] Nature on. On the Unusual Cold and Rainy [*or* Rainie] Weather in the Summer, 1648. Robert Heath. NOSC

Why reclining, interrogating? why myself and all drowsing? To the States, To Identify the 16th, 17th, or 18th Presidentiad. Walt Whitman. CTC; NAAL-1; NAAL-3; RaBo

Why rejoice in beauty? What. Reflections. Antoinette Deshoulières, *French.* PBWP, *tr. by* Yvor Winters

Why repeat? I heard you the first time. Carl Sandburg. OBAL *Fr.* The People, Yes.

Why, Rome was naked once, a bastard smudge. Humble Beginnings. Thomas Lovell Beddoes. NOBVV

Why say the idiot is not. The Locus. Cid Corman. VGW

Why seraphim like lutanists arranged. Evening without Angels. Wallace Stevens. VGW

Why She Says No. Ellen Bryant Voigt. FaBoWP

Why Should a Foolish Marriage Vow. Dryden. CBLP; NAEL-1; NIP-4; OxBM *Fr.* Marriage à la Mode.

(Song: "Why should a foolish marriage vow.") AWP

Why should I be bitter. A Woman Forsaken in Love. Saigyo. OHMPJ, *tr. by* Kenneth Rexroth *Fr.* Sixty-four Tanka.

Why should I be eaten by love. James A. Randall Jr. BPo

Why should I blame her that she filled my days. No Second Troy. W. B. Yeats. CMoP; EnLoPo; GTBS-P; MoP; NAEL-2; NOBE; NoAM; OAEL-2; OxAEP-2; OxBTC; PoEL-5; TFi; WeW-3

Why should I call Thee Lord, Who art my God? After Communion. Christina Rossetti. WPoS

Why should I confine myself. Ghetto. Guy Tirolien, *French.* NegPo, *tr. by* Ellen Conroy Kennedy

Why should I find Him here. Christ in the Clay-Pit. Jack R. Clemo. GTBS-P

Why Should I Grieve? Moses ibn Ezra, *Hebrew.* TrJP, *tr. by* Solomon Solis-Cohen

Why should I have raced my boat home from town at dusk? Returning Home at Dusk from Town, on the Fifteenth of the Seventh Month. Shen Chou, *Chinese.* SuSp, *tr. by* Irving Y. Lo

Why should I have returned? Noah's Raven. W. S. Merwin. ChIV-1; HCAP

Why should I heed their railings? What's a prude? A Marriage Prospect. William Hurrell Mallock. NOBVV

Why should I keep holiday. Compensation. Ralph Waldo Emerson. APN-1; MeMAP; TAP

Why should I let the toad work. Toads. Philip Larkin. CMoP; NOBL; NoAM; OxAEP-2; OxBTC; PoE; Poetr; SoSe-8

Why Should I Murmur. Hartley Coleridge. Son

Why should I resent. Saigyo. *See* A Woman Forsaken in Love.

Why should I say I see the things I see not. Arthur Hugh Clough. EnVR

Why should I seek for love or study it? Ribh Considers Christian Love Insufficient. W. B. Yeats. RaBo

Why Should I Sing in Verse. Samuel Daniel. Son *Fr.* To Delia.

Why Should I Wander Sadly. Süsskind von Trimberg, *Middle High German.* TrJP

Why should it be *my* dream / deferred / overlong? (LL) Tell Me. Langston Hughes. APSN; SAmP

Why should it be *my* loneliness. Tell Me. Langston Hughes. APSN; SAmP

Why should my bells, which chime thy praise, when thou. Edward Taylor. ChIV-2 *Fr.* Preparatory Meditations Before My Approach to the Lord's Supper.

Why Should the American Negro Be Proud? Maggie Pogue Johnson. CBWP-4

Why should the scribblers discompose. The Scribblers. Walter Savage Landor. OBSV

Why should this a desert be? Orlando's Rhymes. Shakespeare. CTC *Fr.* As You Like It.

Why should this flower delay so long. The Last Chrysanthemum. Thomas Hardy. CMoP

Why should this Negro insolently stride. August. Elinor Wylie. MoAmPo

Why Should Vain Mortals Tremble. Nathaniel Niles. AH

Why should we not, as well, desire death. On Death. Francis Quarles. PeECV *Fr.* Divine Fancies.

Why should we praise them, or revere. Against Seasons. Robert Mezey. NYBP

Why should you [*or* shouldst thou] swear I am forsworn. The Scrutiny [*or* Scrutinie]. Richard Lovelace. BeJo; BoLoP; CaPo; EnLoPo; GBL; MeLP; NOSC; SeCP

Why should you try to crush me? Resentment. Richard Aldington. PeFWW

Why should your face so please me. Song. Edwin Muir. OxBM

Why should your fair eyes with such sovereign grace. Michael Drayton. SCGP *Fr.* Idea.

Why sing sadly sad daughter of Pandion. To the Swallow. Pamphilus, *Greek.* GrAn, *tr. by* Dennis Schmitz

Why, sir, as to that—I did not know it was time for the. A Pique at Parting. Sarah Morgan Bryan Piatt. NCAP

Why sleeps the harp of Erin's pride? The Irish Harp: Fragment I. Sydney, Lady Morgan Owenson. Ro *Fr.* The Lay of an Irish Harp, or Metrical Fragments.

Why So Many of Them Die. Susan Wallbank. BrRo

Why so pale and wan, fond lover? Song. Sir John Suckling. APAD; AWP; BeJo; BoLoP; CaPo; CavPo; ClHu; EBEvV; EnLoPo; GLoP; GTBS-P; HAP; HeIP-4; HoPM; InPS-3; NAEL-1; NBLV; NIP-4; NOBE; NoP-4; OBEV; OxAEP-1; PBMP; PoE; PoEL-3; PoRA; SeCP; TFi; UnPo *Fr.* Aglaura.

Why solitary crow? He in his feathers. Solitary crow. Norman MacCaig. NoP-4

Why, Some of My Best Friends Are Women. Phyllis McGinley. NMM-2

Why speak not they of comrades that went under? (LL) Spring Offensive. Wilfred Owen. GTBS-P; NSI; PeFWW

Why speak of memory and death. Two Views of Two Ghost Towns. Charles Tomlinson. NoAM

Why speak of the use. Hayden Carruth. VGW

Why stand aghast. He Hath Need of Rest. Josephine D. Henderson Heard. CBWP-4

Why take time, with so little time left. About Writing Poetry. Sophie Slingeland. LoHo

Why the hell do you grumble and blame tourism. A Progressive Man's Indignation. Dimitris Tsaloumas. BMAP

Why the Old Woman Limps. Lupenga Mphande. HBAPE

Why the Resurrection Was Revealed to Women. Catharina Regina von Greiffenberg, *German.* PBWP, *tr. by* Michael Hamburger

Why, the ribs of the earth subsist frail as a breath / If but God wearieth. John Crowe Ransom. *See* Antique Harvesters.

"Why, the Southern Pacific and the / Santa Fe." *Unknown. See* Casey Jones.

Why the unbroken spiral, Virtuoso. Apple Peeler. Robert Francis. LCAP-2

Why the Wind Comes. Hirini Melbourne. PeNZ

Why, there are maidens of heroic touch. Felix Holt, the Radical. "George Eliot." LW *Fr.* Felix Holt, the Radical.

Why They Waged War. John Peale Bishop. NYBP

Why this desperation to move heaven and earth. Palladas, *Greek.* GrAn, *tr. by* Tony Harrison

Why this girl has no fear. Carmen. Victor Hernandez Cruz. PoBA

Why this man gelded Martial[l] I muse. Raderus. Donne. PeLV

Why throbs my heart when he appears? The Self-Examination. *Unknown.* ECWP

Why Time Spins Fast. Robert Browning. *Fr.* Rabbi Ben Ezra. NAEL-2; OBNC

Why Tomas Cam Was Grumpy. James Stephens. CMoP

Why vex thy soul that never nations claim thee? A Citizen of—the World. Donald McDonald. PBCV

Why wail you, pretty plover? and what is it that you fear? Happy, The Leper's Bride. Tennyson. CBLP

Why wait we for the torches' lights?, *see also* "Let us drink, and pledge the night." Let Us Drink. Alcaeus, *Greek.* AWP, *tr. by* John Hermann Merivale

Why was a radio sinful? Lord knows. But it was. The Radio under the Bed. Reed Whittemore. NYBP

Why was I born if this ends all. My Song. James Ephriam McGirt. AAP

Why was it that the thunder voice of Fate. Robert Gould Shaw. Paul Laurence Dunbar. CBCWP; PoPoPo; Son

Why We Are Late. Josephine Miles. NALW

Why We Meet. Lizelia Augusta Jenkins Moorer. CBWP-3

Why weep ye by the tide, ladie? Jock of Hazeldean. Sir Walter Scott. GTBS-P; NAEL-2; NOBRP; OxBS

Why were you born when the snow was falling? A Dirge. Christina Rossetti. EBVV; NOBVV; SCGP

Why were you not like the tree Trung Quan? What Things Are Called. Erich Fried, *German.* AF, *tr. by* Georg Rapp

Why, what a most particularly pure young man this pure young man must be. (LL) Bunthorne's Song. Sir William Schwenck Gilbert. CABP; NAEL-2; NBLV

Why, who makes much of a miracle? Miracles. Walt Whitman. PBMP; SAmP

Why Why Should I the World Be Minding. Thomas Smith. AiP

Why will Delia thus retire. A Receipt to Cure [*or* for] the Vapours. Lady Mary Wortley Montagu. ECWP; NOEC; NoP-4; PBWP; PEW; PeLV

Why will they never sleep. Ode. John Peale Bishop. LiTM

Why, William, on that old grey [*or* gray] stone. Expostulation and Reply. Wordsworth. FHYEP; NAEL-2; NOBRP; OAEL-2

Why won't Eve eat of the fruit? Eve Oh Eve. Taslima Nasrin, *Bengali.* VCWP, *tr. by* Carolyne Wright *and* Mohammad Nurul Huda

Why Would I Want. William J. Harris. PoBA

Whyles in this sorte he dyd hys tale pronounce. Virgil. OBCVT, *tr. by* Henry Howard, Earl of Surrey *Fr.* Dido's reproaches.

Whylom [*or* Whilom] ther was dwellyng[e] at Oxenford[e]. The Miller's [*or* Milleres] Tale. Geoffrey Chaucer, *Middle English.* NAEL-1; OAEL-1; OxBoLi; PeLV *Fr.* The Canterbury Tales.

Why'n't you bring me. To Greet a Letter-Carrier. William Carlos Williams. OBAL; SAmP

Why's / Wise. Imamu Amiri Baraka.

Wise 1. PFTM

Why's/Wise. Imamu Amiri Baraka.

Wise 3. FTOS

Wi' a scunner in't. (LL) Scunner. "Hugh MacDiarmid." FaBoTC; FaBoTw

Wi aw thae, hechyuch! fforeign po'entates. (LL) Heard in the Cougate. Robert Garioch. FaBoTC

Wi da lentenin days ida first o da Voar. Tuslag. T. A. Robertson. OxBS

Wi' Jock of Hazeldean. (LL) Jock of Hazeldean. Sir Walter Scott. GTBS-P; NAEL-2; NOBRP; OxBS

Wi' patchit brose and ilka pen. Lilt Your Johnnie. Unknown. BXAP

Wi' the truth of his right hand. (LL) Fause Foodrage. Unknown. ESPB; OxBB

Wich deceased of thier emocion on a past excursion day. (LL) "Wellcome, to the Caves of Artá!" Robert Graves. NBLV; NOBL; NYBP; PeLV

Wichita Vortex Sutra, Part I. Allen Ginsberg. FTOS

Wicked and the base do compass round, The. Fear Not: For They That Be With Us. Jones Very. ChIV-1

Wicked clamor, my ear grows deaf, The. Tuvia Rivner, Hebrew. MHP, tr. by Ruth Finer Mintz

Wicked Neighbor, The. "Zelda," Hebrew. WPOW, tr. by Hannah Hoffman

Wicked on the wall. (LL) Freeze-Frame. Alison Fell. NBrP

Wicked Who Would Do Me Harm, The. Unknown, Gaelic. RB, tr. by A. Carmichael

Wickedness of Peter Shannon, The. Alden Nowlan. MoCV

Wicker Basket, A. Robert Creeley. HAP; MoP; NoAM; Poetr

Wicket is the harbour and the garden is the shore, The. (LL) Pirate Story. Robert Louis Stevenson. ACTP; NOxBChV

Wickson Plums. William Corbett. PmAP

Wid my Banjo on my knee. (LL) Oh! Susanna. Stephen Collins Foster. APN-2; OBAL

Widdecombe [or Widdicombe] Fair. Unknown. CH

Wide as this night, old as this night is old and young as it is young. Lullaby. Kenneth Fearing. CMoP

Wide earth darkened so, The. (LL) Evening. James Wright. NOBA; NYBP

Wide Empty Landscape with a Death in the Foreground. N. Scott Momaday. CDW

Wide, ho? Ezra Pound, after the Chinese. OBVE

Wide is our mouth and. Need Is Our Name. Luci Shaw. TrCP

Wide Land, The. A. R. Ammons. TwCP

Wide Mizzoura, The. Unknown. AS

Wide open are the gates of Heaven. The Great Arbiter of Fate. Ch'u Yüan, Chinese. SuSp, tr. by Wu-Chi Liu

Wide Open Are Thy Loving Hands. Bernard of Clairvaux, Latin. AH, tr. by Charles P. Krauth

Wide Walls. Unknown. PoToHe

Wide was the land. Patrick Anderson. Fr. The Coming of the White Man. MoCV Fr. Poem on Canada.

Wide, Wide World, The. Rudyard Kipling. Fr. In the Neolithic Age savage warfare did I wage. NOBVV

Wide wide Yangtze, dragons in deep pools, The. The Merchant's Joy. Lu Yu, Chinese. CoBCP, tr. by Burton Watson

Widening Spell of the Leaves, The. Larry Levis. NAmP90; PBCAP

Widow, The. Walter De la Mare. LBC

Widow, A. Ted Kooser. PBCAP

Widow. Dorothy Livesay. IMW

Widow, The. Susan Bartels Ludvigson. MT

Widow, The. W. S. Merwin. NYBP; UnPo; VGW

Widow, The. Robert Southey. NOBRP; NOEC; UV

Widow and Virgin Sisters, The. William Broome. ECEV

Widow at Windsor, The. Rudyard Kipling. NAEL-2; NoAM

Widow bird sate mourning for her love, A. A Song. Shelley. BoTP; CH; GTBS-P; NOBE; OBNC; OxBSP; PoEL-4 Fr. Charles the First.

Widow (conscious that time's on the wing). Limerick. Stanley J. Sharpless. PeLi

Widow Has Buried Her Second Husband, The. William Dunbar. RACG Fr. The Tua Mariit Wemen and the Wedo.

Widow in Wintertime, A. Carolyn Kizer. IMW

Widow Speaks, The. William Dunbar. PoEL-1 Fr. The Book of the Two Married Women and the Widow.

Widow suckling / the master's field / bent over the rows, A. The Aerialist Narratives, Chapter Three. Ed Roberson. PT

Widow Teaches Poetry Writing, The. Nell Altizer. IMW

Widow, well met; whither you go today? A Contention betwixt a Wife, a Widow, and a Maid. Sir John Davies. SiPS

Widower. Bible, Apocrypha. OxBM

Widower, The. Rudyard Kipling. CBLP; LBC; OxBM

Widower, The. Royall Tyler. OBAL

Widower in the Country, The. Les A. Murray. DiPo

Widower's Courtship, The. Elizabeth Hands. WoRP

Widow's, The. Cats. Fazil Hüsnü Daglarca, Turkish. PC, tr. by Murat Nemet-Nejat

Widows. Louise Glück. NAmP90

Widows. Edgar Lee Masters. MoAmPo

Widow's Curse, The. Unknown, Irish. NOIV, tr. by Thomas Kinsella

Widows' House, The. Sarah Orne Jewett. APN-2

Widow's Hymn, A. George Wither. OBEV

Widow's Lament. Unknown, Chinese. BoWoP Fr. Shih Ching.
("Cloth-plant grew till it covered the thorn bush, The.") ChiP, tr. by Arthur Waley

Widow's Lament in Springtime, The. William Carlos Williams. CMoP; GaP; HAP; IMW; LiTM; MoP; NAAL-2; NOBA; NoAM; PoE; SAGP; SAmP; SoSe-8; TAP

Widow's Old Broom, The. Unknown. AmFP

Widow's Plot; or, She Got What Was Coming to Her, The. William Plomer. MoP

Widow's Reply to a Matchmaker, The. Nguyễn Khuyến, Vietnamese. AVP, tr. by Huỳnh Sanh Thông

Widows' Rice. Okkūr Mācāttaṉar, Tamil. PLW, tr. by A. K. Ramanujan

Widow's Song, The. Edward Coote Pinkney. APN-1

Widow's Supper. Mary Jane Moffat. IMW

Widow's Tears [or Widdowes Teares]: or, Dirge of Dorcas, The. Robert Herrick. ChIV-2

Widow's Yard, The. Isabella Gardner. Poetr

Widsith. Unknown, Anglo-Saxon.
Widsith, the Minstrel. AnOE

Width, a shining peace, under the night, A. (LL) Dead, The ("These hearts were woven"). Rupert Brooke. CH; PeFWW; PoA; SoSe-8

Width of a cube spans defensive rapture. Defensive Rapture. Barbara Guest. FTOS

Wie langsam kriechet sie dahin. Heinrich Heine, German. AWP, tr. by Richard Monckton Milnes

Wife, The. Robert Creeley. VGW

Wife, The. Denise Levertov. EP

Wife A-Lost, The. William Barnes. BoLoP; EBVV; EnLoPo; EnVR; GLoP; HAP; OBEV; OxBM; SCGP
("Since I noo mwore de zee your feace.") LBC

Wife a-Prais'd, A. William Barnes. EBVV

Wife and all. (LL) When I was a little boy / I lived by myself. Unknown. BoTP; OxNR

Wife and servant are the same. To the Ladies. Mary Lee, Lady Chudleigh. CABP; ECWP; GEA; NALW; NOEC; PEW; WPE; WPOW

Wife—at Daybreak I shall be, A. Emily Dickinson. AmPP

Wife in London, A. Thomas Hardy. NOBVV; OBWP

Wife is like a blade of grass, A. Jean-Joseph Rabéarivelo, French. NegPo, tr. by Ellen Conroy Kennedy

'Wife, land of the wave fire'. Unknown. Fr. The Saga of Gisli. OBVE, tr. by George Johnston

Wife of All Ages, The. Edith Nesbit. VWP

Wife of Bath's Prologue, The. Chaucer. FHYEP; NAEL-1; OAEL-1, ll. 1–862 complete Fr. The Canterbury Tales.
("Now wol I seye my tale, if ye wol heere.") (LL) PoEL-1
"Experience, though noon auctoritee." OxBoLi; PeLV; RACG
("Al this sentence me liketh every deel.") (LL) RACG
"If there were no authority on earth." OxBM
"Tell me to what conclusion or in aid." OxBM

Wife of Bath's Tale, The. Chaucer. FHYEP; NAEL-1; OAEL-1 Fr. The Canterbury Tales.
("In th'olde dayes of the Kyng Arthour.") OxBSn
("Ther is noon oother incubus but he.") (LL) OxBSn

Wife of Flanders, The. G. K. Chesterton. NSI

Wife of Usher's Well, The. Unknown. AWP; AmFP; CH; EBEV; ESPB; EnSB; ImPo; NAEL-1; NOBE; NoP-4; OAEL-1; OBEV; OxAEP-1; OxBB; OxBS; OxBSn; PoEL-1; Poetr; RB; SCGP; TFi

Wife Speaks, The. Mary Stanley. PeNZ

"Wife Takes a Child," The. Ellen Bryant Voigt. CrSp

Wife, there are some points on which we differ from each other. Epigram. Martial, Latin. OxBM

Wife to Husband. Fleur Adcock. PeNZ

Wife to Husband. John Harington. NoSic

Wife Waits, A. Thomas Hardy. SAGP Fr. At Casterbridge Fair.

Wife was sitting at her reel ae night, A. The Strange Visitor. Unknown. FaBoCh

Wife Who Smashed Television Gets Jail. Paul Durcan. CABP; CIP-2

Wife-Woman, The. Anne Spencer. NAAAL

Wife Wrapt [or Wrapped] in Wether's Skin, The. Unknown. AmFP; ESPB

Wife Wrapt in Wether's Skin, The. Unknown. AmFP; ESPB

Wife's Complaint, The. Unknown, Anglo-Saxon. BoLoP; EEP, tr. by Michael Alexander

Wife's Lament, The. *Unknown, Anglo-Saxon.* PBWP; PoE, *tr. by* Kemp Malone; WPE

("For him who yearning longs for his beloved.") (LL) NoP-4

("I make this song sadly about myself.") BoWoP, *tr. by* Willis Barnstone *and* Elene Kolb

("Song I sing of sorrow unceasing, A.") AnOE, *tr. by* Charles W. Kennedy

Wife's Lament. *Unknown, Anglo-Saxon.* PBWP;

Wife's Tale, The. Seamus Heaney. CIP-2; SAGP

Wife's Thoughts, The. Hsü Kan, *Chinese.* CoBCP, *tr. by* Burton Watson

Wig, rouge, honey, wax, teeth. Lucilius, *Greek.* GrAn, *tr. by* Peter Porter

Wiggling out. Tanka. Nakajō Fumiko, *Japanese.* MJT, *tr. by* Makoto Ueda

Wigs and Beards. Robert Graves. NOBL

Wiiralt Drawing in Chartres. Aleksis Rannit, *Estonian.* CEEP, *tr. by* Emery George

Wilberforce. Josephine D. Henderson Heard. CBWP-4

Wild, The. Wendell Berry. VGW

Wild, The. Joseph Warton. GaP

Wild air, world-mothering air. The Blessed Virgin Compared to the Air We Breathe. Gerard Manley Hopkins. NOBVV; PeVV

Wild and Blue. Laurie Duesing. DeD

Wild Ass. Padraic Colum. MoBrPo

Wild Asters. Ruth Stone. IMW

Wild (at Our First) Beasts Uttered Human Words. E. E. Cummings. FaBoMo; NYBP

Wild Barbaree, The. *Unknown.* AmFP

Wild Bees. James Keir Baxter. NoP-4

Wild Bill Jones. *Unknown.* AmFP

Wild bird 'bode in the tame bird's tether, The. The White Bird. Rosamund Marriott Watson. VWP

Wild bird filled the morning air, A. The Fowler. Wilfrid Wilson Gibson. NTP

Wild bird singer, sing on. Sand Creek. Charles G. Ballard. UnPo; VoR

Wild birds on the roof are bitterly complaining to man, The. Seeking Spring Beyond the city. Su Tung-p'o, *Chinese.* TAL, *tr. by* Robert Payne

Wild Boar and the Ram, The. John Gay. NOEC *Fr.* Fables.

Wild Carthage held her, Rome. A Puritan Lady. Lizette Woodworth Reese. MoAmPo

Wild Cherry, The. Malcolm Lowry. NoP-4

Wild clefting, you I sing; mountains. Night. Georg Trakl, *German.* PeFWW, *tr. by* David McDuff, Jon Silkin, *and* R. S. Furness

Wild Colloina Boy, The. *Unknown.* AmFP

Wild Common, The. D. H. Lawrence. NoAM

Wild Crab. Mary Ellen Solt. BoWoP

Wild Dog Rose, The. John Montague. BIrV; CIP-2; PBCIP; PoE

Wild Dreams of Summer What Is Your Grief. George Barker. OxBTC

Wild ducks / float with the north wind. Sun Children. Leslie Marmon Silko. VoR

Wild ducks had flown, and early this year. Astride Ivaska. CEEP, *tr. by* Inara Cedrins *Fr.* Autumn in the Cascade Mountains.

Wild-eared, / singing. (LL) Sunday Greens. Rita Dove. GT; LCAP-2

Wild-eyed team with horned and swaying heads, The. The Team. Suzanne Gardinier. CBAP

Wild Flower Man, The. Lu Yu, *Chinese.* OHPC, *tr. by* Kenneth Rexroth

Wild flowers and grass grow on. In the Mountain Village. Wang Hung Kung, *Chinese.* OHMPC, *tr. by* Kenneth Rexroth

Wild Flower's Song, The. William Blake. BoTP

Wild gander leads his flock through the cool night, The. Walt Whitman. ColAP *Fr.* Song of Myself.

Wild Garden, The. Alexander Pope. *Fr.* Awake, my St. John! leave all meaner things. NAEL-1; PoEL-3 *Fr.* An Essay on Man.

Wild gardens overlooked by night lights. Parking. Barbara Guest. FTOS; PmAP

Wild Geese, The. Wendell Berry. TRP

Wild Geese. Mary Oliver. BLT

Wild Geese. Katharine Tynan. IIP

Wild geese cry, The. Masaoka Shiki, *Japanese.* OHMPJ, *tr. by* Kenneth Rexroth

Wild Geese on the Lake. Shen Yüeh, *Chinese.* SuSp, *tr. by* Richard B. Mather

Wild geese waking in the March wind. Withdrawal Letter. Jim Carroll. PmAP

Wild Goat, The. Claude McKay. RACG

Wild goose, broken-legged on the sandbank. The Boat-pullers. Mei Yao Ch'en, *Chinese.* SuSp, *tr. by* Jonathan Chaves

Wild Goose, Wild Goose. Issa, *Japanese.* OHPJ; TTTS, *tr. by* Kenneth Rexroth

Wild Honey. Francis Webb. NOBAu

Wild Honey Suckle, The. Philip Freneau. AmPP; ColAP; NAAL-1; NAAL-3; NOBA; OxBA; PoEL-4; PoLF; TAP

Wild honey to cold cells. (LL) The Rainy Summer. Alice Thompson Meynell. AYFP

Wild Horses of Assateague Island, The. John Bensko. MT

Wild Iris, The. Louise Glück. ColAP

Wild Iron. Allen Curnow. NTP; RB

Wild Life Studies. James Fenton.

Of Bison Men. PeLV

Wild Ones[, The]. PeLV

Wild Man Comes to the Monastery, The. *Unknown.* RaBo

Wild man of Ssu-ming Mountain. Facing Wine with Memories of Lord Ho. Li Po, *Chinese.* CoBCP, *tr. by* Burton Watson

Wild midst the teeming buds of opening May. Morning, Rosamonde. Anne Batten Cristall. ECWP

Wild Mustard River, The. *Unknown.* AmFP

Wild Nature. Charles Newton. NOEC *Fr.* Stanzas.

Wild Negro Bill. *Unknown.* BPo; NAAAL

Wild Night, A. Julia Ward Howe. ColAP

Wild night bitter and vertical. Black Horseman. Branko Miljkovic, *Serbo-Croatian.* HSix, *tr. by* Charles Simic

Wild Nights—Wild Nights! Emily Dickinson. APAD; APN-2; AmPP; CBLP; HeIP-4; ITG; NAAL-1; NAAL-3; NALW; NCAP; NIP-4; NOBA; NoAM; NoP-4; OxBA; OxWW; PAR; PBWP; PoPoPo; Poetr; RaBo; SDW; TAP; WPE; WPoS

Wild Oats. Philip Larkin. InPS-3

Wild Oats. Norman MacCaig. OxBTC

Wild Old Wicked Man, The. W. B. Yeats. CMoP; RaBo

Wild Ones[, The]. James Fenton. PeLV *Fr.* Wild Life Studies.

Wild Party, The. Joseph Moncure March.

"Queenie was a blonde, and her age stood still." OBCoV

Wild patience has taken me this far, A. Integrity. Adrienne Rich. ColAP

Wild Peaches. Elinor Wylie. FaBoWP; LiTM; LoP; NAAL-2; NALW; OxBA; WPE

("And sleepy winter, like the sleep of death.") (LL) ColAP

Puritan Sonnet, IV. MoAmPo

(Puritan Sonnet.) SAGP

Wild pigeon of the leaves. Birds. *Unknown.* AWP *Fr.* The Thousand and One Nights.

Wild Ride, The, *abr.* Louise Imogen Guiney. ColAP; RACG

Wild rose bending. David Lloyd. HA

Wild Rose of Plymouth, The. Jones Very. APN-1

Wild roved the Indians once. Grand Rapids. Julia A. Moore. OBAL

Wild sea— / In the distance, A. Basho, *Japanese.* OHPJ, *tr. by* Kenneth Rexroth

Wild singing, drunken dancing. Yang Chi. *Fr.* Describing My Feelings While Living in the Spring Quarters at Chiang-ning: Four Poems to the Tune "Ching-p'ing-yeh." CoBLCP, *tr. by* Jonathan Chaves

Wild Sleeve. Marjorie Welish. FTOS

Wild Sports of the West. John Montague. CABP

Wild Strawberries. Robert Graves. FaBoCh

Wild Strawberries. Ronald Wallace. IFJA

Wild Strawberry. Maurice Kenny. HATNAP

Wild Swan, The. Johannes Bobrowski, *German.* CEEP, *tr. by* Juliette Victor-Rood

Wild Swan: "My attire is noiseless when I tread the earth." Cynewulf. AnOE, *tr. by* Charles W. Kennedy *Fr.* Riddles (Exeter Book).

Wild Swans. Edna St. Vincent Millay. CMoP; MoAmPo; PBWP; UnPo

Wild Swans at Coole, The. W. B. Yeats. AYFP; CMoP; HeIP-4; InPS-3; MoBrPo; MoP; NAEL-2; NoAM; NoP-4; PoPoPo; Poetr; SCGP; SoSe-8; TFi; UnPo

Wild Thyme. Joyce Sambrook. BoTP

Wild to be wreckage forever. (LL) Cherrylog Road. James Dickey. CoAP; ColAP; HAP; HCAP; InPS-3; MT; NAAL-2; NIP-4; NYBP; Poetr; TwCP; WeW-3

Wild Turkeys; The Dignity of the Damned. Brigit Pegeen Kelly. NAmP90

Wild Vines. Boris Pasternak. *See* Hops.

Wild water-head, what's your reason / for exalting yourself. A Torrent Cuts Off the Poet's Path. Antiphilus, *Greek.* GrAn, *tr. by* W. S. Merwin

Wild West. Mark Vinz. Poetsp

Wild West Workshop Poem. Anselm Hollo. PmAP

Wild, wild the storm, and the sea high running. Patrolling Barnegat. Walt Whitman. APN-1; OxBoS

Wild Wind. Li Meng-yang, *Chinese.* CoBLCP, *tr. by* Jonathan Chaves

Wild wind, chaotic lightning—black clouds are born. Summer Niight. *Unknown, Chinese.* SuSp, *tr. by* Edward H. Schafer

Wild winds weep, The. Mad Song. William Blake. NAEL-2; NOEC; OAEL-2; PoE; PoEL-4

Wild with All Regrets. Wilfred Owen. SCGP

"Yes, there's the orderly. He'll change the sheets." PeFWW

Wild wolves have burst through the gate. (LL) In the East. Georg Trakl, *German*. PeFWW, *tr. by* Michael Hamburger

Wild woman of the forests, The. Mirabai, *Indian*. WPoS, *tr. by* Jane Hirshfield

Wild World. Cat Stevens. UV

Wildcat was walking. *Unknown, Navajo Indian*. STP, *tr. by* Jerome Rothenberg

Wildebeest of Carmine Street, The. Edmund Pennant. EC3

Wilderness, The. Sidney Keyes.

"Red rock wilderness, The." OBWP; PoWW

Wilderness, The. Kathleen Jessie Raine. BoWoP; WPE

Wilderness. Carl Sandburg. RaBo

Wilderness. Yuksa Yi, *Korean*. CKP, *tr. by* Jaihiun Kim

Wilderness Gothic. Alfred Wellington Purdy. HeIP-4; MoCV; NOBC; NoP-4

Wilderness, The: but otherwise. Esther K. Comes to America: 1931. Jerome Rothenberg. NNaP

Wildernesse and the solitarie place shall be glad for them, The. Bible, *O.T.* OBVE *Fr.* Isaiah.

Wilderspin. Mary Elizabeth Coleridge. VWP

Wildflower. Stanley Plumly. LCAP-2

Wildflowers. Richard Howard. NoAM

Wildly-colored girl with her round belly twisted, The. In the Gallery. John Hollander. CBLP

Wildly he wandered on. Shelley. TOF *Fr.* Alastor; or, The Spirit of Solitude. OAEL-2; Ro

Wildness. Gerard Manley Hopkins. *Fr.* Inversnaid. APAD; CMoP; EnVR; FaBoVe; GTBS-P; ImPo; LiTM; MoBrPo; NoAM; OAEL-2; PeVV; PoRA; RB; SAGP; SCGP; TFi; UnPo

Wildness of haggard flights. Nocturne. Roussan Camille, *French*. TTY, *tr. by* Seth L. Wolitz

Wildness of your glances pleases me, The. Rama Kam. David Diop, *French*. NegPo, *tr. by* Ellen Conroy Kennedy

Wilfred Owen's Photographs. Ted Hughes. FaBoPV; OxBC

Wilful waste brings woeful want. *Unknown*. OxNR

Wilhelm Meister's Apprenticeship. Goethe, *German*.

Mignon. AWP, *tr. by* James Elroy Flecker; STV, *tr. by* John Frederick Nims

("Knowest thou the land where bloom the lemon trees.") AWP, *tr. by* James Elroy Flecker

Wilkes Booth came to Washington, an actor great was he. Booth Killed Lincoln. *Unknown*. AmFP

Will, The. Donne. EBEV; ImPo; NoSic

Will. Horace, *Latin*.

"O well for him whose will is strong!" OBCVT, *tr. by* Alfred Tennyson, 1st Baron Tennyson

Will. Ella Wheeler Wilcox. BLPA; PoToHe

Will a god trust in the world. (LL) Hedgehog. Paul Muldoon. BIrV; NoAM; PBCIP

Will anyone tell me what Minne is? Walther von der Vogelweide, *German*. GePo, *tr. by* Frederick Goldin

Will appear as short as one! (LL) On a Fly Drinking out of [*or* from] His Cup. William Oldys. APAD; ImPo; OBEV; OxAEP-1; SCGP

Will be a hundred years ago. (LL) Love and Age. Thomas Love Peacock. NOBVV; OBEV; OBNC

Will be changed by the love into sunshine again. (LL) Sweet Peril. George Macdonald. BLPA; FaBoBe

Will be ground by the grinders of Gambart. (LL) Limerick: "There is an old he-wolf named Gambart." D. G. Rossetti. FaBoEE; PeLi

Will be some very great person over again. James Russell Lowell. *See* Emerson.

Will betray the company I keep. (LL) The Disquieting Muses. Sylvia Plath. NALW; NMM-2

Will bury their own, don't worry. (LL) The Journey. James Wright. NoAM; PoE; WeT

Will cave in on him by and by. (LL) Renascence. Edna St. Vincent Millay. ColAP; MoAmPo

Will commit that indiscretion. Ezra Pound. *See* The Garden.

Will days, indeed, yet come in forgiveness and grace. When You Will Walk in the Field. Leah Goldberg, *Hebrew*. TrJP, *tr. by* Simon Halkin

Will dissolves, the heart becomes excited, The. Soliloquy in an Air-Raid. Roy Fuller. PoA

Will dream[e] that hope again, but else would die. (LL) The Dream[e]. Donne. CBLP; ESCV; FMP; MeLP; OAEL-1; OBEV; SeCP; TOF

Will go, and see him once before I dye. (LL) On the Numerous Accesse of the English to Waite upon the King in Holland. Katherine Philips. KTR; NOSC

Will God forever cast us off. Jesse Mercer. AmFP

Will have been undone. Quincy Troupe. *See* Boomerang: A Blatantly Political Poem.

Will he always love me? Lady Horikawa, *Japanese*. BoWoP; OHPJ, *tr. by* Kenneth Rexroth

Will He No Come Back Again? *Unknown*. OBEV

Will hear all I say and cannot say. (LL) Paula Becker to Clara Westhoff. Adrienne Rich. NAAL-2; VCAP

Will hear of as a god. (LL) How We Heard the Name. Alan Dugan. PFE

Will I! Will You Write Me a Christmas Poem? Lorine Niedecker. FTOS

Will I always be eleven. Untitled. Franz Wright. LCAP-2

Will I cease to be. Lady Izumi, *Japanese*. OHPJ, *tr. by* Kenneth Rexroth

Will I ever get it? (LL) Zizi's Lament. Gregory Corso. BB

Will i hate mirrors? Rebecca. E. Ethelbert Miller. ISC

Will in green age her hearse expect. (LL) To My Lord Fairfax. Andrew Marvell. NOSC

Will it last? he says. The Snowflake Which Is Now and Hence Forever. Archibald MacLeish. NoP-4

Will know the reason why! (LL) The Song of the Western Men. Robert Stephen Hawker. EBEvV; FaPoR; OBNC; OxAEP-2

Will lead my steps aright. (LL) To A Waterfowl. William Cullen Bryant. APN-1; APo; AWP; AmPP; CH; ColAP; FaBoBe; HoPM; ImPo; NAAL-1; NAAL-3; NCAP; NOBA; NoP-4; OxBA; PAR; PWR; PoEL-4; PoLF; SoSe-8; TAP; TFi

Will let its Keepsake—go. (LL) Single Screw of Flesh, A. Emily Dickinson. APN-2; PAR

Will linger, though enjoyed, like joy in memory yet. (LL) Stanzas Written in Dejection, near Naples [*or* —December 1818, near Naples]. Shelley. GTBS-P; NAEL-2; NAWM-2; NoP-4; PBMP; PoRA

Will live, the sinking soul to cheer! (LL) Vincent Ogé. George Boyer Vashon. AAP; APN-2

Will live with thee, or else for thee will die. (LL) 3.9: Dialogue between Horace and Lydia, A ("Donec gratus eram"). Horace. OBVE, *tr. by* Robert Herrick

Will, lost in a sea of trouble. Archilochus, *Greek*. PGA, *tr. by* Kenneth Rexroth

Will Love again awake. Muse and Poet. Robert Bridges. OBMV

Will make the Gods of humane crimes partake. (LL) I am that Dido which thou here do'st see. Ausonius, *Latin*. NoSic; OBVE, *tr. by* Sir Walter Ralegh

Will make the whole read human and exact. (LL) The Devil's Advice to Story-Tellers. Robert Graves. LiTM; MoP; NAEL-2; NoAM

Will make your glistering gold but more to shine. (LL) The Prologue: "To sing of wars, of captain[e]s, and of kings." Anne Bradstreet. BoWoP; NAAL-1; NAAL-3; NALW; NOBA; NoP-4; OxBA; PoE; SCAP; TAP; WPE

Will meet with a great mistake. Mother Goose. *See* To Babylon.

Will night already spread her wings and weave. Night-Thoughts. Solomon ibn Gabirol, *Hebrew*. TrJP, *tr. by* Emma Lazarus

Will no young British bard, no rhyme intent. Edward Davies. *Fr.* Chepstow: A Poem. OBWVE

Will not contain you. (LL) Did John's Music Kill Him? Alfred B. Spellman. NAAAL; SeSe

Will not help. (LL) This Tokyo. Gary Snyder. CAPP-1; NeAP

Will of God be done by us, The. Blessed Be the Holy Will of God. *Unknown, Irish*. TIRV, *tr. by* Douglas Hyde

Will of God we must obey, The. The Death of King Edward VII. *Unknown*. OxBoLi

Will people accept them? Tenzone. Ezra Pound. MeMAP; PoA *Fr.* Contemporania.

Will press the life-drops from the heart. (LL) The Slave Auction. Frances Ellen Watkins Harper. APN-2; BPo; ColAP; ISC; TTY

Will ripple forward and hold the train. (LL) The Rescued Year. William Stafford. ColAP; LCAP-2

Will rise and bless each future hour. (LL) Letter to Miss E. B. on Marriage. Mary Savage. ECWP; LW

Will shout "Turn back." (LL) Who will endure. W. H. Auden. FaBoPV; OxBTC

Will snarl—and man can never be alone. (LL) The Wolves. Allen Tate. LiTM; NOBA; OxBA; PoA

'Will sprawl, now that the heat of day is best. Caliban upon Setebos; or, Natural Theology in the Island. Robert Browning. AWP; EBEV; EnVR; FHYEP; NAEL-2; NOBVV; OAEL-2; OxAEP-2; PeVV

Will Stewart and John. *Unknown*. ESPB

Will still break through. (LL) My heart, thinking / "How beautiful he is." Lady Otomo no Sakanoé, *Japanese*. AWP; PBWP, *tr. by* Arthur Waley

Will tell you how he wrote, and talked, and spit. (LL) Doctor Johnson. Soame Jenyns. FaBoEE; OBSV

"Will the fire of the heart and the fire of the mind be one." (LL) Heart and Mind. Dame Edith Sitwell. LW; OxBTC; TwCP

Will the lady with locker key 43. Will You Come Out Now? Valerie Sinason. BrRo

Will the machinegunners please step forward? (LL) A Poem Some People Will Have to Understand. Imamu Amiri Baraka. GT; SAGP

Will the man who gets clean love his neighbor? Soap (II). Jerome Rothenberg. NNaP

Will the Real Me Please Stand Up? A. L. Hendriks. PBCV

Will the train never start? Train. Helen Mackay. NSI

Will the Weaver. *Unknown*. AmFP

Will the wolves lie down with the lambs and feed them? The End of Sorrow. Edmond Fleg. *Fr*. The Wall of Weeping. TrJP, *tr. by* Humbert Wolfe

Will there never come a season. To R. K. James Kenneth Stephen. BXAP; FaBoEE; NBLV; NOBL; PeLV; UV

Will there really be a "morning"? Emily Dickinson. OBCA

Will there yet come days of forgiveness and grace. Leah Goldberg, *Hebrew*. MHP, *tr. by* Ruth Finer Mintz

Will They Cry When You're Gone, You Bet. Imamu Amiri Baraka. NAAL-2

Will they have children? Will they have more children? Neighbors. James Tate. LCAP-2

Will they never fade or pass! The Farmer Remembers the Somme. Vance Palmer. NOBAu

Will they stop. Requiem. Kenneth Fearing. CMoP

Will to be tickled wants; has got the itch. *Unknown*. FaBoEE

Will to Will. Keith Waldrop. PmAP

Will waste, as this flea's death took life from thee. (LL) The Flea. Donne. APo; BoLoP; EBEV; EP; ESCV; FMP; FSCP; HoPM; ImPo; InPK-6; InPS-3; NAEL-1; NBLV; NIP-4; NoP-4; NoSic; OAEL-1; OxAEP-1; PfE; PoE; Poetr; SCV; SeCP; TFi

Will Work for Food. Stanley Plumly. PUP-20

Will Ye Na Can Ye Na Let Me Be. *Unknown*. FaBoVe

Will ye see what wonders love hath wrought? Sir Thomas Wyatt. SiPS

Will ye that I should sing. A Lady of High Degree. *Unknown, French*. AWP, *tr. by* Andrew Lang

Will Yer Write It Down for Me? Henry Lawson. CBAP

Will You Be as Hard? Douglas Hyde, *Irish*. OBMV, *tr. by* Lady Augusta Gregory

Will you buy a fine dog with a hole in his head? *Unknown*. CBNP

Will You Come? Edward Thomas. CH

Will you come a boating, my gay old hag. The Gay Old Hag. *Unknown*. BlrV

Will You Come Out Now? Valerie Sinason. BrRo

Will you come to Turvy Land. Topsy-Turvy Land. Phyllis M. Stone. BoTP

Will you find your lost dead among them? (LL) Coda. Ezra Pound. NOBA; SAGP

Will you gang wi' me, Leezie Lindsay. Leezie Lindsay. *Unknown*. FaBoCh

Will you glimmer on the sea? Moonrise. Hilda Doolittle. PoA

Will you have me? A Popular Romance. Kevin Ireland. PeNZ

Will you have us your slaves to lie to you, flatter and—leave you? (LL) Juxtaposition. Arthur Hugh Clough. CBLP; OBNC

Will you heare a tale of Robin Hood. Robin Hood and the Pedlars. *Unknown*. ESPB

Will you heare the Mode of france. The Mode of France. *Unknown*. PBRV

Will you leave me alone? I implore you! To Russia. Vladimir Nabokov, *Russian*. TCRP, *tr. by* Vladimir Nabokov

Will you leave the hills of Scotland? Highland Mary. Mary Weston Fordham. CBWP-2

Will you lend me your mare to ride but a mile? *Unknown*. OxNR

Will You Love Me When I'm Old? *Unknown*. BLPA; FaBoBe

Will you marry it, marry it, marry it. (LL) The Applicant. Sylvia Plath. NAAL-2; NOBA; PoPoPo; TwCP

Will you never let us go? (LL) Song of the Galley-Slaves. Rudyard Kipling. GTBS-P; HAP; NTP; PoEL-5; SCGP

Will you please rush down and see. To Close. William Carlos Williams. SAmP

Will you seek afar off? you surely come back at last. Walt Whitman. ChIV-1 *Fr*. Leaves of Grass (1855). APN-1

Will you sleep forever? Korinna, *Greek*. PBWP, *tr. by* John Dillon; BoWoP, *tr. by* Willis Barnstone

Will you, sometime, who have sought so long, and seek. The Finder Found. Edwin Muir. PoA

Will you speak before I am gone? Will you prove already too late? (LL) Past and present wilt—I have fill'd them, emptied them, The. Walt Whitman. ColAP; PAR

"Will you take a walk with me." The Clucking Hen. *Unknown*. BoTP

Will you turn a deaf ear. The Questioner Who Sits So Sly. W. H. Auden. OxAEP-2

"Will you walk a little faster?" said a [*or* the] whiting to a [*or* the] snail. A Lobster Quadrille. "Lewis Carroll." BoTP; CBNP; NoAM; OxAEP-2; OxBChV; UV *Fr.* Alice's Adventures in Wonderland.

"Will you walk into my parlor?" said the Spider to the Fly. The Spider and the Fly. Mary Howitt. OTCP; OxBChV; PWR; UV

Will you wear white, O my dear, O my dear? Jennie Jenkins. *Unknown*. AmFP

Will you, won't you, will you, won't you, will you / join the dance? (LL) A Lobster Quadrille. "Lewis Carroll." APAD; BoTP; CBNP; NoAM; OxAEP-2; OxBChV; UV

Will You Write Me a Christmas Poem? Lorine Niedecker. FTOS

Willesden Gree. Jimmy Pearse. UV

Willets, The. May Swenson. WPE

Willful waste brings woeful want. Mother Goose. CTV

William and Margaret. David Mallet. NOEC; OxAEP-1

William and Mary. *Unknown*. AmFP

William and Mary, / George and Anne. *Unknown*. OxNR

William Blake. James Thomson. CABP; EPCY

William Blake (To Frederick Shields, on His Sketch of Blake's Work-room and Death-room, 3 Fountain Court, Strand). D. G. Rossetti. EPCY

William Carlos Williams. Cornelius Eady. GT

William / Carlos / Williams / alive! Louis Zukofsky. PFTM *Fr.* Songs of Degrees.

William Dewy, Tranter Reuben, Farmer Ledlow late at plough. Friends Beyond. Thomas Hardy. EBVV; FaBoVe; GTBS-P; NOBVV; OBEV

William Gifford. Walter Savage Landor. FaBoEE; GTBS-P

William Hall. *Unknown*. AmFP

William I. Eleanor Farjeon. NTP

William Lisle Bowles. Byron. OBNC *Fr*. English Bards and Scotch Reviewers.

William Lloyd Garrison. Joseph Cotter, Sr.. AAP

William Lloyd Garrison. Henrietta Cordelia Ray. CBWP-3

William of Orange was always worried. Plans. Brendan Kennelly. BiHa

William Penn owned millions of. Carol Harriman. CTV

William Street. Kenneth Slessor. BMAP; CBAP

William Stukeley made his own Stonehenge. Ronald Johnson. OBGa

William the Conqueror long did reign. England's Sovereigns in Verse. *Unknown*. BLPA

William the Conqueror, ten sixty-six. *Unknown*. OxNR

William the First was the first of our kings. William I. Eleanor Farjeon. NTP

William, the wild round plums are falling. The Dressing Stations. Norman Dubie. AmPA

William Wallace. Francis Lauderdale Adams. OxBS

Wordsworth. Sidney Keyes. OxBTC

William Wordsworth (1770-1850). Gavin Ewart. NoAM

William Yeats in Limbo. Sidney Keyes. MoBrPo

Williams: An Essay. Denise Levertov. InPS-3; PmAP

Williams Avenue Zionist Church, The. Russia. William Carlos Williams. VGW

Willie. *Unknown*. AmFP

Willie and Earl Richard's Daughter, *vers*. B *and* C. *Unknown*. ESPB

Willie and Lady Margerie [*or* Maisry]. *Unknown*. ESPB; OxBB

Willie boy, Willie boy, where are you going? *Unknown*. BoTP

Willie Brew'd [*or* Brewed] a Peck o' Maut. Robert Burns. AWP; OxBS

Willie had a purple monkey climbing on a yellow stick. "Max Adeler." OBCoV

Willie Leonard; or, The Lake of Cold Finn. *Unknown*. AmFP

Willie Macintosh. *Unknown*. ESPB; OxBoLi

(Burning of Auchindown.) OxBB

Willie o Douglas Dale. *Unknown*. ESPB

Willie o [*or* of] Winsbury. *Unknown*. AmFP; ESPB

Willie poisoned Auntie's tea. Willie the Poisoner. *Unknown*. NTCP

Willie, take your little drum. Patapan. Bernard De la Monnoye, *French*. PChr

Willie the Weeper. *Unknown*. BLPA; OBAL

Willie was a widow's son. Willie and Lady Maisry. *Unknown*. ESPB

"Willie, Willie, I'll learn you a wile." Willie's Lyke-Wake. *Unknown*. ESPB

Willie Winkie. William Miller. OxBChV

("Are the children all in bed, for now it's eight o'clock?") (LL) OxNR

("But a kiss frae aff his rosy lips gi'es strength anew to me.") (LL) NOBVV

("For now it's eight o'clock *or* For it's now eight o'clock.") (LL) LB

Willie's Fatal Visit. *Unknown*. ESPB

Willie's [*or* Willie] has taen him o'er the fame. Willie's Lady. *Unknown.* ESPB

Willie's Lyke-Wake. *Unknown.* ESPB

Willing Arawak, The. Ethnocide. Howard Fergus. PBCV

Willing Graces to the Gothic pile, The. (LL) Verses on Sir Joshua Reynolds's Painted Window at New College, Oxford. Thomas, the Younger Warton. NOEC; PoEL-3

Willing it, my ailment. (LL) No Road. Philip Larkin. CBLP; EBEV; MoBrPo; OxAEP-2

Willing Mistriss, The. Aphra Behn. FaBoSe; LW *Fr.* The Dutch Lover.
("Oh! who can guess the rest?") (LL) NALW
(Willing Mistress, The.) NALW

Willobie His Avisa. Henry Willoby.
To Avisa. CBLP

Willow. Richard Watson Dixon. *See* Song: "The Feathers of the willow."

Willow. Li Shang-yin, *Chinese.* LoP; SuSp, *tr. by* Eugene Eoyang *and* Irving Y. Lo

Willow. Li Shang-yin, *Chinese.* PLT, *tr. by* A. C. Graham

Willow, The. Tu Fu, *Chinese.* OHPC, *tr. by* Kenneth Rexroth

Willow-Boughs, The. Alexander Block. BoTP

Willow Branch Song. Liu Yu Hsi, *Chinese.* SuSp, *tr. by* Daniel Bryant

Willow Branch Songs. Ch'ien Ch'ien-i, *Chinese.*
"Crescent moon hangs on the tip of the willows, A." SuSp, *tr. by* Irving Y. Lo
"Must I lament the time that's gone because I've been cast aside?" SuSp, *tr. by* Irving Y. Lo

Willow Branches. Liu Yu Hsi, *Chinese.* SuSp, *tr. by* Dell R. Hales

Willow by the Eastern Gate. *Unknown, Chinese.* CoBCP, *tr. by* Burton Watson

Willow Catkins. Hsüeh T'ao, *Chinese.* SuSp, *tr. by* Eric W. Johnson

Willow catkins beyond the garden wait for evening tides. Ch'ien Ch'ien-i. CoBLCP, *tr. by* Jonathan Chaves *Fr.* In Spring of the Year *Ping-shen.*

Willow-catkins threw off their narrow shoes. Vizma Belševica, *Latvian.* CEEP, *tr. by* Inara Cedrins

Willow catkins, white as cotton. Yang Wei-chen. *Fr.* Impromptu Inspirations. CoBLCP, *tr. by* Jonathan Chaves

Willow Eyebrows. Chao Luan-luan, *Chinese.* ChiPo, *tr. by* Kenneth Rexroth *and* Ling Chung

Willow floss in the swift wind races against the Spring Festival. Tune: "Song of River City"—On a Kite. Wu Wei-yeh, *Chinese.* SuSp, *tr. by* Irving Y. Lo

Willow leaves dancing. Eveningsong. Ramona Wilson. VoR

Willow-Man, The. Juliana Horatia Ewing. OxBChV

Willow Poem. William Carlos Williams. NAAL-2

Willow shining, The. The Knowledge of Light. Henry Rago. VGW

Willow Song. Anne Stevenson. NoP-4

Willow-tassels grow in tremors of the spring wind. Lines to Do with Youth. Witter Bynner. PoA

Willow, Wishbone, Warblers. Brendan Galvin. CMAP

Willows, The. Bret Harte. BXAP

Willows cannot hide a bright moon's sorrow. Heard on a Boat. T'an Yüan-ch'un, *Chinese.* SuSp, *tr. by* Irving Y. Lo

Willows carried a slow sound, The. Repose of Rivers. Hart Crane. AWP; CMoP; ColAP; GEA; LiTM; MeMAP; MoAmPo; NOBA; OxBA; PoE

Willows droop, The. A Winter and Spring Scene. Henry David Thoreau. NCAP

Willows of Massachusetts, The. Denise Levertov. NAAL-2

Willows outside the east gate. East Gate Willows. *Unknown, Chinese.* ChiPo, *tr. by* Rewi Alley

Willow's shadow straight up. Tune: "Prince of Lan-ling" (*Lan-ling Wang*)—on Willows. Chou Pang-yen, *Chinese.* SuSp, *tr. by* Irving Y. Lo

Willows weave spring sorrow. To the Tune "Yellow Oriole." Yang Shen, *Chinese.* CoBLCP, *tr. by* Jonathan Chaves

Willoware Cup. James Merrill. VCAP

Willowwood ("I sat with Love upon a woodside well"). D. G. Rossetti. NAEL-2; OAEL-2; PoEL-5 *Fr.* The House of Life.
("Till both our heads were in his aureole.") (LL) CABP

Willowwood ("And now love sang: but his was such a song"). D. G. Rossetti. NAEL-2; OAEL-2 *Fr.* The House of Life.

Willowwood ("O ye, all ye that walk in Willowwood"). D. G. Rossetti. NAEL-2; OAEL-2 *Fr.* The House of Life.

Willowwood ("So sang he: and as meeting rose and rose"). D. G. Rossetti. NAEL-2; OAEL-2 *Fr.* The House of Life.

Will's at the dance in the Clubroom below. A Wife Waits. Thomas Hardy. SAGP *Fr.* At Casterbridge Fair.

Will's Love, The. Besmilr Brigham. CrSp

Willy boy, Willy boy, / Where are you going? Mother Goose. OxNR; ReMoGo

Willy Drowned in Yarrow. *Unknown.* GTBS-P

Willy Lyons. James Wright. HCAP; NNaP; PoE

Willy—the moon's in a cloud—Good-night. I am going. He calls. (LL) Rizpah. Tennyson. RACG

Willy the Weeper. *Unknown.* AS

Willy Wet-Leg. D. H. Lawrence. CMoP; RB

Willy, Willy, Harry Stee. History. *Unknown.* ACTP

Willy, Willy Wilkin. Mother Goose. OxNR; ReMoGo

Willy's rare, and Willy's fair. Rare Willie Drowned in Yarrow; or, The Water o Gamrie. *Unknown.* ESPB; OxBB

Wilpena Pound. Charles Buckmaster. BMAP

Wilson and Pilcer and Snack stood before the zoo elephant. Elephants Are Different to Different People. Carl Sandburg. MoAmPo

Wilt thou forgive that sin where I begun. A Hymn to God the Father. Donne. AWP; EBEV; FMP; FSCP; HAP; InPK-6; MeLP; NAEL-1; NOBE; NOSC; OAEL-1; PeECV; PoEL-2; PoRA; SCGP; SCV; SeCP; SoSe-8; TFi; TOF

Wilt thou go with me sweet maid. An Invite to Eternity. John Clare. NAEL-2; NOBVV; OAEL-2; OBNC; Ro

Wilt thou hunt the prey for the lion? Bible, *O.T. Fr.* Then the Lord Answered ("Who is this that darkeneth counsel by words without knowledge?"). AWP *Fr.* Job. NAWM-1

Wilt thou love God, as he thee? [*or* thee!] then digest. Donne. TrCP *Fr.* Holy Sonnets. ESCV *Fr.* Holy Sonnets.

Wilt Thou not visit me? The Prayer. Jones Very. APN-1; OxBA; PAR; TrCP

Wilt thou seal up the avenues of ill? Suum Cuique. Ralph Waldo Emerson. APN-1 *Fr.* Quatrains.

Wilt thou then serve the Philistines with that gift. Milton. EBEV *Fr.* Samson Agonistes. FHYEP; OAEL-1; PoEL-3

Wilt thou use turners craft still? ye by my trouth. John Heywood. PBRV *Fr.* Epigrams.

Wiltshire Downs. Andrew Young. GTBS P; NTP; OxBTC

Wily Fox, The. Edward Davies, *Welsh.* OBWVE, *tr. by* Joseph P. Clancy

Wily Napoleon Bonaparte, The. Limerick. Douglas Catley. PeLi

Wily old writer called Maugham, A. Limerick. Martin Fagg. PeLi

Win at First and Lose at Last; or, A New Game at Cards. Laurence Price. OxBoLi

Wind, The. William Barnes. *See* The Wind at the Door.

Wind. Dionne Brand. NOxBChV

Wind, The. Thomas Holley Chivers. APN-1

Wind, The. Dafydd ap Gwilym, *Welsh.* OBWVE, *tr. by* Joseph P. Clancy

Wind. James Fenton. NAEL-2

Wind, The. Dorothy Graddon. BoTP

Wind, The. Gwendolen Haste. PaTW

Wind. Ted Hughes. NAEL-2; NoP-4; Poetr

Wind, The. Boris Pasternak, *Russian.* TCRP, *tr. by* Yakov Hornstein

Wind, The. Elizabeth Rendall. BoTP

Wind. Tim Seibles. NAmP90

Wind. Gary Soto. NoAM *Fr.* The Elements of San Joaquin. PBCAP; PaTW; UnSA

Wind, The. Robert Louis Stevenson. BoTP; CTV

Wind, The. Sara Teasdale. NMM-2

Wind, The. *Unknown.* FaBoCh; OxNR

Wind. Larry Wiggin. HA

Wind, The. Dorothy Wordsworth. *See* Address to a Child during a Boisterous Winter Evening.

Wind, 9. Subramania Bharati, *Tamil.* OMIP, *tr. by* A. K. Ramanujan

Wind, a rustle of leaves, The. The Edge of Autumn. Michael Anania. NoAM

Wind and bamboos strum and speak to each other. Meng Chiao. PLT, *tr. by* A. C. Graham *Fr.* Autumn Thoughts.

Wind and Glacier Voices. Simon J. Ortiz. HATNAP

Wind and rain see spring off. Tune: "Song of Divination"—On the Plum Tree, after a Poem by Lu Yu. Mao Tse-tung, *Chinese.* SuSp, *tr. by* Eugene Eoyang

Wind and Silver. Amy Lowell. BoWoP; HeIP-4; KaS; MoAmPo; Spl

Wind and the Bird, The. *Unknown, Bushman.* PeSA, *tr. by* W. H. I. Bleek

Wind and the Leaves, The. George Cooper. BoTP

Wind and the Moon, The. George Macdonald. NOxBChV

Wind and the Rain, The. Shakespeare. *See* Song: "When that I was and a little tiny boy."

Wind at Penistone, The. Donald Davie. LiTM

Wind at the Door, The. William Barnes. EnVR; GBL; GTBS-P; OxAEP-2; PoEL-4
(Wind, The.) LBC

Wind: "At times I resort, beyond man's discerning." Cynewulf. AnOE *Fr.* Riddles (Exeter Book).

Wind at war with wind. The Warlike Angels. Rafael Alberti, *Spanish*. AF, *tr. by* Geoffrey Connell

Wind at Your Door, The. Robert David Fitzgerald. NOBAu

Wind begun to knead the Grass, The, First Version. Emily Dickinson. NAAL-1; NAAL-3; WeW-3

Wind begun to rock the Grass, The. Emily Dickinson. APN-2; HAP; NAAL-1; NCAP; WeW-3

Wind billowing out the seat of my britches, The. Child on Top of a Greenhouse. Theodore Roethke. KaS; LCAP-2; NOxBChV; NoP-4; VGW

Wind, bird, and tree. The Words. David Wagoner. PoA

Wind / blade cutting in, The. Impressions / of Chicago; For Howlin' Wolf. Quincy Troupe. NAAAL; NBV

Wind blew, a tile fell from the roof, The. Wang An-shih. SuSp, *tr. by* Jan W. Walls *Fr.* In the Style of Han Shan and Shih Te.

Wind blew all my wedding-day, The. Wedding-Wind. Philip Larkin. ITG

Wind Blew like Water. Alice Sadongei. HATNAP

Wind Bloweth Where It Listeth, The. Countee Cullen. GT

"Wind-blown clamour of the barnacle-geese, The." (LL) Beggar to Beggar Cried. W. B. Yeats. CMoP; NoAM; OxAEP-2

Wind blows a piece of paper to my feet, The. At the Crossroads. Bill Knott. PBCAP

Wind blows, and with a little broom, The. Cathleen Sweeping. George Johnston. NOBC

Wind Blows High, The. *Unknown*. FaBoVe

Wind blows hot, The. English and foreign birds. Christmas Eve. Karl Shapiro. NYBP

Wind blows lilacs out of the east, The. Santa Fe. Joy Harjo. NAmP90; PoPoPo

Wind blows, one can smell the wild rosemary. *Unknown, Serbo-Croatian*. HSix, *tr. by* Charles Simic

Wind Blows out of the Gates of the Day, The. W. B. Yeats. RB *Fr.* The Land of Heart's Desire. (Fairy Song.) MoBrPo

Wind blows the line out from his fishing pole, The. Fisherman. Ou-yang Hsiu, *Chinese*. BLT; OHPC, *tr. by* Kenneth Rexroth

Wind blows through, The. The daughter of Minamoto no Toshitaka, *Japanese*. WPJ, *tr. by* Kenneth Rexroth *and* Ikuko Atsumi

Wind blows up the tent like a balloon, The. Crimson Tent. John Dos Passos. PoA

Wind came in for several thousand miles all night, The. On an East Wind from the Wars. Alan Dugan. AF

Wind came up out of the sea, A. Daybreak. Henry Wadsworth Longfellow. BoTP; PWR; PoLF

Wind can't blow any harder, The. Bottle Creek Blues. Sam Hunt. PeNZ

Wind-Clouds and Star-Drifts. Oliver Wendell Holmes. Sympathies. APN-1

Wind, come softly. Wind, 9. Subramania Bharati, *Tamil*. OMIP, *tr. by* A. K. Ramanujan

Wind comes from opposite poles, The. The Marriage. Mark Strand. LiLi; NoAM; SPE

Wind comes from the north, The. Suspense. D. H. Lawrence. MoBrPo

Wind comes rushing from the sea, The. One Night at Victoria Beach. Gabriel Okara. PBMAP

Wind Debates Asian Immigration, The. Peter Rose. BMAP

"Wind doth blow to-day, my love, The." The Unquiet Grave. *Unknown*. CH; ESPB; HAP; HeIP-4; IMW; OAEL-1; OxBB; PoEL-1; RB; TFi; WeW-3

Wind fills her embroidery loom with willow catkins, The. Springtime Embroidery. Yang Chi. CoBLCP, *tr. by* Jonathan Chaves *Fr.* Paintings of Ladies Engaged in Four Springtime Occupations.

Wind finds the northwest gap, fall comes. Heart of Autumn. Robert Penn Warren. ColAP; FuPo; MT; Poetr

Wind flapped loose, the wind was still, The. The Woodspurge. D. G. Rossetti. CABP; EBEV; EnVR; GEA; GTBS-P; HAP; HeIP-4; NOBE; NoP-4; OAEL-2; OBEV; OBNC; PBMP; PoEL-5; SCGP; TFi; UnPo *Fr.* The House of Life.

Wind frightens my dog, but I bathe in it, The. April Gale. Ivor Gurney. Spl

Wind From Mt. Fuji, The. Tagami Kikusha-Ni, *Japanese*. WPJ, *tr. by* Kenneth Rexroth *and* Ikuko Atsumi

Wind from off the sea says nothing new, The. The Marrow. Theodore Roethke. NYBP; PeECV

Wind from the east, oh Lapwing of the day. Hafiz. AWP; TAL, *tr. by* Gertrude Lowthian Bell *Fr.* Odes.

Wind from the northwestern quarter is lifting him high above. The Hawk's Cry in Autumn. Joseph Brodsky, *Russian*. TCRP, *tr. by* Alan Myers *and* Joseph Brodsky

Wind from the pine-trees trickles on my bare head, A. (LL) In the Mountains on a Summer Day. Li Po, *Chinese*. AWP, *tr. by* Arthur Waley

Wind Gardens. Louis Untermeyer. BXAP

Wind gathers storm clouds, The. Song of the Stormy Petrel. "Maksim Gorky," *Russian*. TCRP, *tr. by* Albert C. Todd

Wind, gigantic, wrestles the April leaves;. April Wind. Frederick Turner. RA

Wind gives way to calm. J. W. Hackett. HA

Wind has at last got into the clock, The. The Wind, the Clock, the We. Laura Riding Jackson. FaBoVe

Wind has blown the rain away and blown, A. E. E. Cummings. MoAmPo

Wind has scattered my city to the sheep, The. Ruins of the City of Hay. Randolph Stow. CBAP

Wind has stopped, The. Harumichi no Tsuraki, *Japanese*. OHPJ, *tr. by* Kenneth Rexroth

Wind has such a rainy sound, The. Christina Rossetti. TLR

Wind, I hear it sighing, The. Emily Jane Brontë. BWW

Wind in a Frolic, The. William Howitt. OxBChV ("Wind one morning sprung up from sleep, The.") NOxBChV

Wind in the Grass, The. Siegfried Emerson. BoTP

Wind in the park. Envoi: Washington Square Park. Myra Cohn Livingston. SSCS

Wind in the Tree, The. Frank Templeton Prince. OxBSP

Wind in the Trees, The. Cathy Song. OpBo

Wind in the Willows, The. Kenneth Grahame. Duck's Ditty. BoTP; CTAV; FPC; NOxBChV; NTCP; OTCP; OxBChV; WHSW

Song of Mr Toad, The. NOBL; NOxBChV

Wind in the *wu-t'ung* startles the heart, a lusty man despairs, The. Autumn Comes. Li Ho, *Chinese*. PLT, *tr. by* A. C. Graham

Wind in your hair. One Final Fling. Kemal Khojandi, *Persian*. ArPe, *tr. by* Omar S. Pound

Wind Increases, The. William Carlos Williams. NAAL-2

Wind invites wind. Chimako Tada, *Japanese*. VCWP, *tr. by* Naoshi Koriyama *and* Edward Lueders

Wind is a man and goes out from his hut, The. The Wind and the Bird. *Unknown, Bushman*. PeSA, *tr. by* W. H. I. Bleek

Wind is a shuttle made of elm-wood, The. Only the Mists are Real. Uku Masing, *Estonian*. CEEP, *tr. by* Ivar Ivask

Wind is a wolf, The. Stanley Cook. AYFP

Wind Is Blind, The. Alice Thompson Meynell. MoBrPo

Wind Is Blowing West, The. Joseph Ceravolo. TTTS

Wind is cold, The. Winter. Princess Shikishi, *Japanese*. PBWP, *tr. by* Hiroaki Sato

Wind is crisp and carries, The. Residue. Anthony McNeill. PBCV

Wind is cruel. Her clothes are worn and thin, The. Her Husband Asks Her to Buy a Bolt of Silk. Ch'en Tao, *Chinese*. OHMPC, *tr. by* Kenneth Rexroth

Wind is desolate in the fields, The. The Deserted Homestead. Loren C. Eiseley. PoA

Wind is east but the hot weather continues, The. American Letter. Archibald MacLeish. AmPP; OxBA

Wind is everything to them, The. (LL) The Marriage. Mark Strand. LiLi; NoAM; SPE

Wind is making countries, The. Homecoming. Dennis Scott. PBCV

Wind is not nigh. Zone of Death. William Everson. VGW

Wind is not right today, The. Bodega, Goodbye. Edwin Honig. NoAM

Wind is passing by, The. (LL) Who has seen the wind? / Neither I nor you. Christina Rossetti. ACTP; BoTP; CTV; ChAP; ChIV-2; FPC; FaBoBe; NTCP; NTP; OxBChV; TLR; VWP; WHSW

Wind is piercing chill, The. Battlefield. Richard Aldington. OBWP

Wind is ruffling the tawny pelt, A. A Far Cry from Africa. Derek Walcott. HeIP-4; MoP; NAEL-2; NoAM; NoP-4; PBCV; PFE; TTY; UnPo

Wind is shaking this house, The. The Storm House. Elizabeth Jennings. WPE

Wind is strong enough to move wasps, The. Desire. Alison Fell. FaBoTC

Wind is thin. *Unknown*. BoWoP, *tr. by* Willis Barnstone *Fr.* Cambridge Songs.

Wind is to the snow, The. (LL) As birds are fitted to the boughs. Louis Simpson. BoLoP; LBC

Wind is wild tonight. *Unknown*. NOIV

Wind it blew from east to west, The. Get Up and Bar the Door. *Unknown*. AmFP

Wind It Blew up the Railroad Track, The. *Unknown*. AS

Wind keen, the sky high, the gibbons wailing, The. On Climbing the Heights on the Ninth Day of the Ninth Moon. Tu Fu, *Chinese*. TAL, *tr. by* Robert Payne

Wind led me here, The. Wind Thoughts. Pinkie Gordon Lane. GT

Wind like an ocean, The. Larry Eigner. PoM

Wind may blow the snow about, The. A Country Boy in Winter. Sarah Orne Jewett. APN-2; ColAP; OBCA

Wind meets me at Penistone, The. The Wind at Penistone. Donald Davie. LiTM

Wind mutters thinly on the sagging wire. Prairie Graveyard. Anne Marriott. NOBC

Wind o' the East dark with rain. The Efficient Wife's Complaint. Confucius. CTC, tr. by Ezra Pound Fr. Airs of Pei.

Wind of dawning riffles the young furze, The. Drafts for a Quatrain. Edmund Wilson. OBAL

Wind of Death's imperishable wing?, The. (LL) Lovesight. D. G. Rossetti. EBVV; GTBS-P; NAEL-2; OBNC

Wind of January, The. Christina Rossetti. BoTP Fr. A Year's Windfalls.

Wind of old cocoa farms, The. Africa Sky. Kojo Laing. HBAPE

Wind of the West, that fans with fragrant wing. To the Western Wind. Judah Halevi, Hebrew. TrJP, tr. by Solomon Solis-Cohen

Wind on the Corn. Charles Tennyson Turner. EBVV

Wind on the Hills, The. Dora Sigerson Shorter. NOBVV

Wind, one brilliant day, called, The. Antonio Machado Ruiz, Spanish. APAD; RaBo, tr. by Robert Bly

("What have you done with the garden that was entrusted to you?") (LL) APAD, tr. by Robert Bly

Wind one morning sprang up from sleep, The. The Wind in a Frolic. William Howitt. OxBChV

Wind / only, The. Song of the Trees. Unknown, Chippewa. OBVE, tr. by Frances Densmore

Wind over the lake is mild, the moon fair, The. Written at Lakeside Residence. Chiang K'uei, Chinese. SuSp, tr. by Chiang Yee

Wind passed over my mind, A. The Image-Maker. Stanley Kunitz. AFr

Wind passes over the lake. Autumn Evening Beside the Lake. Li Ch'ing-chao, Chinese. OHPC, tr. by Kenneth Rexroth

Wind piercing, hill bare, hard to find shelter. Unknown. OBWVE, tr. by Joseph P. Clancy Fr. Winter.

Wind pours down, The. (LL) Ploughing on Sunday. Wallace Stevens. RB; TTTS

Wind rocks the car. / We sit parked by the river. Like This Together. Adrienne Rich. VGW

Wind rose cold under our robes, and straw blew loose. The Boy Shepherds' Simile. David Bottoms. MT

Wind runs free across our plains, The. For Adolf Eichmann. Primo Levi, Italian. AF, tr. by Ruth Feldman and Brian Swann

Wind rustles the bamboos, The. Yakamochi, Japanese. OHPJ, tr. by Kenneth Rexroth

Wind sall blaw for evermair, The. (LL) The Twa Corbies. Unknown. AWP; CH; EBEvV; ESPB; EnSB; FaBoCh; GTBS-P; HAP; InPK-6; OBEV; OxBS; PBMP; PFE; RB; SCGP; SoSe-8; UnPo

Wind sang to the cornfields, The. August. Eunice Fallon. BoTP

Wind Secrets. Diane Wakoski. AmPA

Wind shakes my window frames. October in the Country: [1983]. James Simmons. BiHa; CIP-2

Wind shall lull us yet, The. From the Antique. Christina Rossetti. EnLoPo

Wind sifts through the curtain. Kuan Han-ch'ing. SuSp, tr. by Jerome P. Seaton Fr. Tune: "Green Jade Flute."

Wind sighs in the reeds—autumn on the rustic shore, The. T'ang Yin. Fr. Poems Inscribed on Paintings. CoBLCP, tr. by Jonathan Chaves

Wind Sleepers, The. Hilda Doolittle. WPE

Wind Song. Carl Sandburg. MoAmPo

Wind sounds through the trees. J. W. Hackett. HA

Wind Sou'west, The. Unknown. AmFP

Wind sprang up at four o'clock, The. T. S. Eliot. ImPo

Wind sprays pale dirt into my mouth, The. The Elements of San Joaquin. Gary Soto. PBCAP; PaTW; UnSA

Wind, stirring in the dark foliage, brings, The. God's Harp. Gustav Falke, German. AWP, tr. by Ludwig Lewisohn

Wind stirs the willows, The. Songs of the Ghost Dance. Unknown, Paiute. Fr. Songs of the Paiute. APN-2 Fr. Ghost-Dance Songs.

Wind stood up, and gave a shout. James Stephens. CTV; InPK-6; KaS; MoP; NoAM

Wind subsides—a fragrance, The. Tune: "Spring at Wu-ling." Li Ch'ing-chao, Chinese. SuSp, tr. by Eugene Eoyang

Wind Suffers of Blowing, The. Laura Riding Jackson. NoP-4; RB

Wind sways the blossoms of the rock orchids, The. Listening-to-the-Rain Studio. Chu Yi-tsun, Chinese. SuSp, tr. by Chang Yin-nan and Lewis C. Walmsley

Wind sways the pines, A. Dirge in Woods. George Meredith. NAEL-2; OBEV; OBNC; PFE

Wind takes colour from the trees, The. Winds. Hugh Raymond McCrae. CBAP

Wind—tapped like a tired man, The. Emily Dickinson.

Wind—tapped like a tired Man, The. The Wind's Visit. Emily Dickinson. APN-2; FaBoVe; MeMAP; MoAmPo; TOF

Wind, That Comes on Suddenly, A. Ory Bernstein, Hebrew. IP, tr. by Warren Bargad and Stanley F. Chyet

Wind that rose, A. Emily Dickinson. RB

Wind That Shakes the Rushes, The. John Clare. PoRA

Wind that speeds the bee and plucks the bee-line. Awake! William Robert Rodgers. LiTM

Wind, the Clock, the We, The. Laura Riding Jackson. FaBoVe

Wind, the season-climate mixer. Clear and Colder. Robert Frost. OBCoV

Wind, The, / turns back. Starapple Tree. Pamela Mordecai. HCP

Wind the wind the wind blows high, The. The Wind Blows High. Unknown. FaBoVe

Wind Thoughts. Pinkie Gordon Lane. GT

Wind thrashes the maple seed-pods, The. John Ashbery. APSN Fr. The Skaters.

Wind through the box-elder trees, The. Poem Against the British. Robert Bly. CoAmPo

Wind took up the Northern Things, The. Emily Dickinson. TTTS

Wind Tossed Dragons. Hsieh Ngao, Chinese. OHMPC, tr. by Kenneth Rexroth

Wind tumbles the branches by the side of the road. Unearthly Voices. Edward Hirsch. BAP-95

Wind was a torrent of darkness among the gusty trees, The. The Highwayman. Alfred Noyes. ChAP; EBEvV; EBNV; NOxBChV; NTP; OBNV; OBSP; PoLF; SAGP

Wind was blowing over the moors, The. Charlotte Brontë. "Susan Coolidge." OBCA

Wind Was There, The. Bravig Imbs. SPE

Wind waves the lotoses in the scented palace by the water, The. For the Dancer of the King of Wu. Li Po, Chinese. TAL, tr. by Robert Payne

Wind whines and whines the shingle. On the Beach at Fontana. James Joyce. MoBrPo; OBMV; PoA; RB; RaBo

Wind whistled loud at the window-pane, The. Lullaby. William Brighty Rands. BoTP

Wind will command them with invincible sound, The. (LL) Farewell to an idea. . . The mother's face. Wallace Stevens. HCAP; PoE

Wind wilts / late flowers. Late Flowers, Wind, Sea, Sand and Fish. Bernard Kangro, Estonian. CEEP, tr. by Ivar Ivask

Wind, wind, give me back my feather. The Child on the Shore. Ursula K. Le Guin. KaS

Wind won't come to draw smiles in dream sand, The. Elegy. Yehuda Amichai, Hebrew. IP, tr. by Warren Bargad and Stanley F. Chyet

Wind writes to me, The. Faustin Charles. HCP Fr. Letters from Home. HCP

Wind writes to me, The. Letters from Home. Faustin Charles. HCP

Windharp. John Montague. CIP-2; IIP; PNI

Windhover, The. Gerard Manley Hopkins. APAD; CABP; CMoP; ClHu; EBEvV; EBVV; EnVR; GEA; GTBS-P; HAP; InPK-6; InPS-3; LiTM; MoBrPo; MoP; NAEL-2; NOBE; NOBVV; NoAM; NoP-4; OAEL-2; OBNC; OxAEP-2; PeECV; PoE; PoEL-5; PoPoPo; PoRA; Poetr; RB; SCGP; SCV; TFi; TOF; TRP; UnPo

(Windhover: To Christ Our Lord, The.) PFE

Windigo. Louise Erdrich. NoAM; PoPoPo

Windigo. Paulette Jiles. NOBC

Winding around the waters of the world. (LL) The Far Field. Theodore Roethke. ColAP; NAAL-2; NoAM

Winding creek and scattered maple groves, A. Yüan Hao-wen. SuSp, tr. by Stephen West Fr. Random Verses on Mountain Life.

Winding eastward through a wide plain. Nostalgic Urge. Chiyong Chong, Korean. CKP, tr. by Jaihiun Kim

Winding Sand. Naresh Guha, Bengali. OMIP, tr. by Lila Ray

Winding Up. Derek Walcott. NoAM

Winding-up Time. Jean Ingelow. VWP

Windless city built on decaying granite, loose ends. Thomas McGrath. Fr. Letter to an Imaginary Friend, Part Two. NNaP

Windless northern surge, the sea-gull's scream, The. The Incarnate One. Edwin Muir. PeECV

Windless summer day. George Swede. HA

Windmill, The. Edward Verrall Lucas. BoTP

Windmill At Mandanthanunguna. Pambardu, Aborigine. NOBAu, tr. by Georg von Brandenstein

Window, The. Conrad Potter Aiken. CMoP

Window, The. Dino Campana, Italian. STV, tr. by John Frederick Nims

Window, The. Raymond Carver. BLT

Window, The. Robert Creeley. FTOS; NOBA; NoAM; PmAP; TAP; VGW

Window, The. Edwin Muir. LiTM

Window, The. Nino Nikolov, Bulgarian. CEEP, tr. by Ewald Osers

Window. Carl Sandburg. PiM

Window-Blind. Denise Levertov. LCAP-2

Window cleaner's life is grand!, A. Elizabeth Fleming. BoTP

Window-Dreaming with SAS. Haim Gouri, *Hebrew*. IP, *tr. by* Warren Bargad *and* Stanley F. Chyet

Window Dressing. William Peskett. PNI

Window-Glance, The. Heinrich Heine, *German*. AWP, *tr. by* John Todhunter

Window in Spring, The. Carl Dennis. BAP-93

Window insulates me from the street, The. Maternity Gown. David Holbrook. OxBTC

Window into the ground, A. Skara Brae. Michael Longley. PBCIP

Window is nailed and boarded, The. Hallaig. Sorley MacLean. FaBoTC

Window Ledge in the Atom Age. Elwyn Brooks White. NBLV; OBAL

Window makes a frame for the sky, The. The Collection. Zhao Zhenkai, *Chinese*. VCWP, *tr. by* McDougall, Bonnie S. and Chen Maiping

Window on the east side of Chicago, or as she / climbs back up to claim herself again. Joy Harjo. *See* The Woman Hanging from the Thirteenth Floor Window.

Window on the North, A. Robert Arthur Douglas Ford. MoCV

Window pales, and by its paltry light, The. Aubade: Donna Anna to Juan, Still Asleep. Richard Howard. PoA

Window remained as before, The. The cold. Telegram. Milo De Angelis, *Italian*. Nelt, *tr. by* Lawrence Venuti

Window Sill, The. Robert Graves. EnLoPo

Window That Watched the Pru. Anne Sexton. Poetr

Window was made of ice with bears lumbering across it, The. Bad Dream. Louis MacNeice. NoAM

Window window window pane. Summer Shower. David McCord. TLR

Windows, The. George Herbert. ESCV; FMP; GeHe; MeLP; NAEL-1; NOCV; NoP-4; PFE; PeECV; PoE; SeCP; TrCP

Windows. Russell Hoban. AYFP

Windows, The. Chris Wallace-Crabbe. BMAP

Windows blurred by the same warm, slow, still rain?, The. (LL) Memo. Kenneth Fearing. CMoP; PoE

Windows. I just don't want anyone to look at me. (LL) Baby Random. Belle Waring. NAmP90; PBCAP

Windows in Providence. Aliki Barnstone. BoWoP

Window's length beyond the Pleiades, A. First Snow on an Airfield. John Ciardi. PoA

Windows of the church are bright, The. Christmas Thoughts, by a Modern Thinker. William Hurrell Mallock. NOBVV

Windows, rapturous windows! (LL) Dead Color. Charles Wright. HCAP; LCAP-2

Windows wide through day and night, The. Last Days at Teddington. Thom Gunn. OBGa

Winds. Hugh Raymond McCrae. CBAP

Winds, The. *Unknown*. ReMoGo

Winds are bleak, stars are bright. The Victoria Markets Recollected in Tranquility. "Furnley Maurice." NOBAu

Winds are dark passages among the stars, The. Turtle. Peter Blue Cloud. HATNAP

Winds' enclosure, Atlantic's premises, The. The Hebrides. Michael Longley. PBCIP

Winds had hushed at last as by command, The. The Sower. Mathilde Blind. WPE

Wind's hand, The. The Whole Works. Federico García Lorca. PFTM

Wind's in the heart of me, a fire's in my heels, A. A Wanderer's Song. John Masefield. MoBrPo

Wind's Lament, The. John Morris-Jones, *Welsh*. OBWVE, *tr. by* Anthony Conran

Winds of Africa. Dorothy S. Obi. WPOW

Winds of Change, The. Charles G. Ballard. VoR

Winds of doctrine blow both ways at once, The. Conrad Potter Aiken. VGW *Fr.* A Letter from Li Po.

Winds of Fate, The. Ella Wheeler Wilcox. BLPA

Winds of Orisha, The. Audre Lorde. NAAAL

Winds on the stems make them creak like manmade things. Stalin. Robert Lowell. HCAP

Wind's on the wold, The. Lines for a Bed at Kelmscott Manor. William Morris. CH; NTP; OBEV; PoEL-5

Winds that drift over the desert. Winds of Africa. Dorothy S. Obi. WPOW

Winds they did blow, The. The Squirrel. *Unknown*. BoTP; CTAV; OxNR

Winds through [*or* thro'] the olive trees. Long, Long Ago. *Unknown*. BoTP; PChr

Winds through the olive trees. Long, Long Ago. Katherine Parker. CTV

Wind's Visit, The. Emily Dickinson. MeMAP

Windshield Wiper. Eve Merriam. KaS

Windsor Castle. Henry Howard, Earl of Surrey.

Prisoned in Windsor, He Recounteth His Pleasure There Passed. NAEL-1

Windsor-Forest. Ausonius, *Latin*.

"Oft in her Glass the musing Shepherd spies." OBCVT, *tr. by* Alexander Pope

Windsor-Forest [*or* Windsor Forest]. Alexander Pope.

"Groves of Eden, vanished now so long, The." OAEL-1

"Here hills and vales, the woodland and the plain." ECEV

"Here too, 'tis sung, of old Diana stray'd." OxAEP-1

Hunting and Fishing. ECEV

Progress. ECEV

"Thy forests, Windsor! and thy green retreats." NOEC; OxAEP-1

Windstorm's turned the country upside down, A. Impromptu. Phan chu Trinh, *Vietnamese*. AVP, *tr. by* Huỳnh Sanh Thông

Windy Day, A. Anne Brontë. *See* Lines Composed in a Wood on a Windy Day.

Windy evening. Dark Farmhouses. Charles Simic. LCAP-2

Windy Evening. Charles Simic. AFr

Windy forest is checkered, The. Banquet at the Tso Family Manor. Tu Fu, *Chinese*. OHPC, *tr. by* Kenneth Rexroth

Windy Gap. David Campbell. NTP

Windy Nights. Rodney Bennett. KaS

Windy Nights. Robert Louis Stevenson. ACTP; BoTP; FPC; KaS; NTP; OTCP; OxBChV; PoRA

Wine. Raymond Carver. BLT

Wine. Micah Joseph Lebensohn, *Hebrew*. TrJP, *tr. by* A. M. Klein

Wine. Nikolai Nikolaevich Ushakov, *Russian*. TCRP, *tr. by* Daniel Weissbort

Wine & bath-house sensualities. *Unknown*, *Greek*. GrAn, *tr. by* Tony Harrison

Wine and cakes for gentlemen. *Unknown*. OxNR

Wine and Grief. Solomon ibn Gabirol, *Hebrew*. TrJP, *tr. by* Emma Lazarus

Wine and treacherous proposals. Hedylos, *Greek*. PGA, *tr. by* Kenneth Rexroth

Wine and Water. G. K. Chesterton. ChIV-1; MoBrPo *Fr.* The Flying Inn.

Wine and woman and song. Villanelle of the Poet's Road. Ernest Christopher Dowson. OBMV; UnPo

Wine Bowl. Hilda Doolittle. NoP-4

Wine-coloured, Homer said, wine-dark. Midnight, Lochinver. Norman MacCaig. OxBoS

Wine comes in at the mouth. A Drinking Song. W. B. Yeats. BoLoP; GLoP; LoP; OAEL-2

Wine Cup and Bright Moon. Shen Chou, *Chinese*. SuSp, *tr. by* Irving Y. Lo

Wine cup, you come here. Tune: "Spring in Ch'in's Garden." Hsin Ch'i-chi, *Chinese*. SuSp, *tr. by* Irving Y. Lo

Wine destroyed the Centaur, not just you. Philip V of Macedon. Alcaeus, *Greek*. GrAn, *tr. by* Alistair Elliot

Wine for old Adam, digging in the briars! (LL) Cana. Thomas Merton. ChIV-2; GI; TrCP

Wine in the cup is heavy. Lu Chih. SuSp, *tr. by* Hellmut Wilhelm *Fr.* Tune: "Pleasure in Front of the Hall."

Wine is drunk, the woman known, The. Gwen Harwood. LW

Wine is gone, The. Geological Hymn. Joseph Ceravolo. PmAP

Wine is love's test. Asclepiades, *Greek*. GrAn, *tr. by* Thomas Meyer

Wine it is that gives life pleasure. In Praise of Wine. *Unknown*, *Latin*. MLL, *tr. by* Helen Waddell

Wine just purchased, The. Enjoying Retirement ("The wine just purchased"). Ma Chih-yüan. *Fr.* Three Poems to the Tune "Ssu-k'uai yü." CoBLCP, *tr. by* Jonathan Chaves

Wine Menagerie, The. Hart Crane. NOBA; NoAM; OxBA; VGW

Wine of Love is music, The. James Thomson. OBEV *Fr.* Sunday up the River.

Wine of parting flowed and flowed, The. Wen Cheng-ming. CoBLCP, *tr. by* Jonathan Chaves *Fr.* Improvised on Horseback to Say Good-bye to Those Who Are Seeing Me Off.

Wine-Press of Los, The. William Blake. *Fr.* Milton.

Wine presses hard upon spring grief. Tune: "Butterflies Lingering over Flowers." Kung Tzu-chen, *Chinese*. SuSp, *tr. by* Irving Y. Lo

Wine-Songs. Moses ibn Ezra, *Hebrew*. TrJP, *tr. by* Solomon Solis-Cohen

Wine, the red coals, the flaring gas. At the Cavour. Arthur Symons. NOBVV; OxBSP

Wine, the toasts that could not be refused, The. Hedylos, *Greek*. GrAn, *tr. by* Adrian Wright

Wine, urine and ashes. Geoffrey Hill. *See* Clash of salutation. As keels thrust into shingle.

Winemaker's Beatĕtude, The. Alfred Wellington Purdy. MoCV

Wing of Separation, The. Ibn Darraj al-Andalusi, *Arabic*. AWP, *tr. by* J. B. Trend

Wing Road. Eamon Grennan. PBCIP

Wing / torn out of stone. Emblem. Roy Fisher. NBrP

Winged bull trundles to the wired perimeter, The. C. Day Lewis. OxBTC
  Fr. Flight to Italy.

Winged bulletins issued from frontier outposts. Going Out Through the
  North Gate of Chi. Pao Chao, *Chinese.* SuSp, *tr. by* Daniel Bryant

Winged in Gold. Euros Bowen, *Welsh.* OBWVE, *tr. by the author*

Wingéd lion on top of that column, The. Notes Made in the Piazza San
  Marco. May Swenson. CoAP

Winged Man. Stephen Vincent Benét. MoAmPo

Winged mimic of the woods! thou motley fool[!]. To the Mocking-Bird.
  Richard Henry Wilde. APN-1

Winged women was saying. Mary's Dream. Lucille Clifton. NALW

Winged Words. Rachel Hadas. FFC

Wingfoot Lake, Independence Day, 1964. Rita Dove. PoPoPo
  ("On her 36th birthday.") UnSA

Wings. John Godfrey. PmAP

Wings. Miroslav Holub, *Czech.* PoSu, *tr. by* Ian Milner *and* George
  Theiner

Wings, The. Denise Levertov. APSN; NALW

Wings. Maureen Seaton. FFC

Wings. *Unknown, Greek.* HePo, *tr. by* Barbara Hughes Fowler

Wings. Judith Wright. CBAP; NOBAu

Wings and Seeds. Sandra McPherson. LoL

Wings filmed, the threads of knowledge thicken. The Jam Trap. Charles
  Tomlinson. MoBrPo

Wings in the Dark. John Gray. NOBVV

Wings of a Wild Goose, The. "Chrystos." GLP

Wings of Time are black and white, The. Compensation. Ralph Waldo
  Emerson. APN-1; AmPP; NOBA; PAR

Wings outstretched, a horned owl. Signatures. Daniel Gerard Hoffman.
  VGW

Winifred Waters. William Brighty Rands. OxBChV
  ("Winifred Waters sat and sighed.") ACTP

Winifreda. *Unknown.* OBEV

Wining at the Eastern Slope tonight. Tune: "Immortal at the River." Su
  Shih, *Chinese.* SuSp, *tr. by* Michael E. Workman

Wink. Roger Gilbert-Lecomte, *French.* PFTM, *tr. by* Pierre Joris

Wink as they will. Wink most when widows wince. (LL) A High-Toned Old
  Christian Woman. Wallace Stevens. CMoP; MoP; NAAL-2; NOBA;
  NoAM; Poetr; TAP

Wink at it only with thine eyes. To the Wine Treasurer of the Circuit
  Mess. Horace Smith. UV

Winked too much and were afraid of snakes. The Monkeys. Marianne
  Moore. CMoP; MeMAP; NOBA; OxBA

Winkte. Maurice Kenny. GLP

Winner and Waster. *Unknown.*
  "Bot then kerpe the king, said, 'Kithe what ye hatten'." EnVB

Winner never quits, A. *Unknown.* CTV

Winners, The. Rudyard Kipling. BLPA; FaPoR *Fr.* The Story of the
  Gadsbys.
  (L'Envoi: "What is the moral? Who rides may read.") MoBrPo

Winning of the TV West, The. John T. Alexander. CTV

Winnings. Garrett Kaoru Hongo. OpBo; UnSA
  ("Falling night / in a brief symphony of candied light, The.") (LL) UnSA
  ("It's Gardena, late Saturday afternoon / on Vermont Avenue.") UnSA

Wino was eating soup, The. Tornado Soup. A. K. Redwing. VoR

Wintah Styles, De. Maggie Pogue Johnson. CBWP-4

Winter. Valentine Ackland. WPN

Winter. Bella Akhatovna Akhmadulina, *Russian.* BoWoP, *tr. by* Barbara
  Einzig

Winter. Rae Armantrout. FTOS

Winter. Robert Bloomfield.
  Ploughman's Horse, The. ECEV

Winter. Enid Blyton. BoTP

Winter. Ion Caraion, *Romanian.* CEEP, *tr. by* Marguerite Dorian *and* Elliott
  B. Urdang

Winter. Chang Yü. *Fr.* The Four Seasons in the Mountains. CoBLCP, *tr.
  by* Jonathan Chaves

Winter. Walter De la Mare. OAEL-2; OBMV

Winter. John Lyle Donaghy. BIrV

Winter. Fan Ch'eng-ta. SuSp, *tr. by* Irving Y. Lo *Fr.* Seasonal Poems on
  Fields and Gardens.

Winter. Hesiod, *Greek.* NOSC, *tr. by* George Chapman *Fr.* The Georgics
  of Heisod.

Winter. A. E. Housman. LBC

Winter. Richard Hughes. OBMV; OBWVE

Winter. W. D. Landor. BoTP

Winter. Mother Goose. ReMoGo

Winter. Helen G. Quigless. BkSV *Fr.* Childhood Scenes in Four Seasons.

Winter. Christina Rossetti. BoTP

Winter. Philip Salom. NOBAu

Winter. Shakespeare. GTBS-P; HAP; ImPo; NIP-4; NoP-4; OAEL-1;
  OBEV; SCGP; TFi; UnPo; WeW-3 *Fr.* Love's Labour's Lost.
  (Hiems.) FaBoCh
  (Tu-Whit To-Who.) CH

Winter. Princess Shikishi, *Japanese.* PBWP, *tr. by* Hiroaki Sato

Winter. Robert Southey. GSo

Winter. Edmund Spenser. *Fr.* Wood Of Error. AEP

Winter. Ruth Stone. BoWoP

Winter. John Millington Synge. NOIV; OBMV; OxBTC

Winter. *Unknown, Welsh.*
  "Wind piercing, hill bare, hard to find shelter." OBWVE, *tr. by* Joseph P.
  Clancy

Winter. Sheila Wingfield. EnLoPo; LW

Winter 1967. Lenard D. Moore. ISC

Winter again. John Wills. HA

Winter alleys are warm. Daddy's Friends. Esther Iverem. GT

Winter and Spring. *Unknown.* BoTP

Winter and Spring have come and gone. In Mourning for His Dead Wife.
  P'an Yüeh, *Chinese.* IMW; OHMPC, *tr. by* Kenneth Rexroth

Winter and Spring Scene, A. Henry David Thoreau. NCAP

Winter and Summer. Stephen Spender. MoBrPo

Winter and summer, whatever the weather. The Floor and the Ceiling.
  William Jay Smith. OBCP

Winter Anemones. Charles Brasch. PeNZ *Fr.* Night Cries, Wakari
  Hospital.

Winter Angel. Agnes Nemes Nagy, *Hungarian.* PoSu, *tr. by* Hugh Maxton

Winter at Tomi. Ovid, *Latin.* AWP, *tr. by* F. A. Wright

Winter Before the War, The. Walter McDonald. CDa

Winter began with. The Lake of the Woods. Richard Ryan. PBCIP

Winter being over, The. Song. Anne Collins. PEW

Winter Billet. Peter Huchel, *German.* PoSu, *tr. by* Michael Hamburger

Winter birds, The. Migration. Pinkie Gordon Lane. BlSi

Winter Bouquet. Lewis Turco. EOEF

Winter burial. Eric Amann. HA

Winter Burn. Roberta Hill Whiteman. VoR

Winter-burning in the fields. (LL) The Crows. Louise Bogan. FaBoWP;
  NALW; NMM-2

Winter by Breughel, the hill with hunters. Breughel's Winter. Rutger
  Kopland, *Dutch.* VCWP, *tr. by* James Brockway

Winter came as it does in this valley. It Was Winter. Czeslaw Milosz.
  PaTW

Winter came early this year. Full Moon that Strikes the Earth Cold. Karen
  McCosker. APAD

Winter Campaign, A. Eochaidh Ó Heóghusa. CABP

Winter Climbing, The. Andrew Greig. FaBoTC

Winter comes I walk alone, The. The Winters Spring. John Clare.
  NOBVV

Winter Coming On. Martin Bell, *after the French of* Jules Laforgue.
  FaBoMo; OBVE; OxBTC

Winter crept. Judith Nicholls. AYFP

Winter Cricket. John Heath-Stubbs. OBCP

Winter crisp and the brittleness of snow. Words for Love. Ted Berrigan.
  PmAP

Winter dawn;. Larry Gates. HA

Winter Dawn. Tu Fu, *Chinese.* BLT; OHPC, *tr. by* Kenneth Rexroth

Winter Day, A. Joanna Baillie.
  Morning. ECWP

Winter Day, A. Philip Lamantia. CLPP

Winter day. Tanka. Kitahara Hakushū, *Japanese.* MJT, *tr. by* Makoto
  Ueda

Winter day is cold and snowy, The. Aleksandr Blok, *Russian.* TCRP, *tr. by*
  Yakov Hornstein

Winter Daybreak above Vence, A. James Wright. InPS-3; LCAP-2; VCAP

Winter Days. Gareth Owen. OBCP

Winter Deepening, The. Richard Wilbur. Son

Winter Drive. James McAuley. BMAP

Winter Drive. James Philip McAuley. PoA

Winter: East Anglia. Edmund Blunden. OxBTC

Winter Eden, A. Robert Frost. GaP

Winter Encounters. Charles Tomlinson. LiTM

Winter Evening. Archibald Lampman. NOBC

Winter evening. Nicholas Virgilio. HA

Winter Evening Poem. Laura Jensen. LCAP-2

Winter evening settles down, The. Preludes. T. S. Eliot. OPOU; PFE; SAGP *Fr.* Preludes (I–IV). HeIP-4; OBMV; Poetr; TwCP; UnPo; VGW; WeW-3

Winter Fairyland in Vermont. Francis P. Osgood. WeW-3

Winter fells. Deathward. John Lyle Donaghy. BIrV

Winter Fields. John Clare. EnVR

Winter for a moment takes the mind; the snow. Prelude I. Conrad Potter Aiken. LiTM; OxBA *Fr.* Preludes for Memnon; or, Preludes to Attitude.

Winter for an Untenable Situation. Alan Dugan. PFE

Winter Galaxy. Charles Heavysege. NOBC

Winter Garden. Donald Britton. EOEF

Winter Garden. David Gascoyne. GTBS-P

Winter garden in an alder swamp, A. A Winter Eden. Robert Frost. GaP

Winter hanging over the dark well, A. The Well. Jay Macpherson. NoP-4

Winter has already shriveled—spring rushes in with / black burial steeds. Andrejs Eglitis, *Latvian.* CEEP, tr. by Inara Cedrins

Winter has at last come. Shigeyuki. *Fr.* Shui Shu. AWP, tr. by Arthur Waley

Winter has been sacked. MARCH ingorders. Roger McGough. AYFP

Winter has come; fierce is the cold;. Hot Cake. Shu Hsi, *Chinese.* ChiP, tr. by Arthur Waley

Winter has pleasures too: with Sunday sun. The Girl Cousin. Gérard de Nerval, *French.* FLP, tr. by Alistair Elliot

Winter Holding off the Coast of North America. N. Scott Momaday. CDW; ColAP

Winter Homily on the Calton Hill. Douglas Young. OxBS

Winter Hymn—to the Snow, A. Ebenezer Jones. OBNC

Winter in America. Gil Scott-Heron. ISC

Winter in Durnover Field. Thomas Hardy. MoBrPo

Winter in Étienburgh. Stephen Parker. NYBP

Winter in Lower Canada. Standish O'Grady. NOBC *Fr.* The Emigrant.

Winter in Minneapolis. Richard Ryan. PBCIP

Winter in the Fens. John Clare. EnVR

Winter in Wales, A. Hester Lynch Salusbury Thrale [*later* Mrs. Piozzi]. CABP

Winter is boring now. Cold February. Hal Summers. AYFP

Winter is cold-hearted. Summer. Christina Rossetti. AYFP; CTV; PBMP

Winter is come again. The sweet south west. January 1, 1829. Nathaniel Parker Willis. APN-1

Winter is deasie. The Auld Symie. Alan Bold. FaBoTC

Winter Is Here. "Katri Vala," *Finnish.* PBWP, tr. by Jaakko A. Ahokas

Winter is here with his grouch. Limerick. *Unknown.* PeLi

Winter is icumen [*or* icummen] in. Ancient Music. Ezra Pound. BXAP; HeIP-4; LiTM; NBLV; OBAL; OBCoV; OxBA; PBMP; PeLV; UV

Winter is passing, and the bells. Spring in the Students' Quarter. Henry Murger, *French.* AWP, tr. by Andrew Lang

Winter is setting in across Eastern Europe. The Death of a Girl in Budapest. Ch'unsu Kim, *Korean.* CKP, tr. by Jaihiun Kim

Winter is settling on the place; the sedge. Virginia Portrait. Sterling Brown. GT

Winter is the king of showmen. Winter Morning. Ogden Nash. OTCP; TLR

Winter Joys. Dorothy Graddon. BoTP

Winter Lakes, The. Wilfred Campbell. NOBC

Winter Landscape. John Berryman. GS; LiTM; MoAmPo; TwCP

Winter Landscape. Alfonsas Nyka-Niliunas, *Lithuanian.* CEEP, tr. by Jonas Zdanys

Winter Landscape. Stephen Spender. MoBrPo

Winter Lanscape—Halifax. Douglas Lochhead. NIP-4

Winter Love. Hilda Doolittle.
   "So we were together." FaBoWP

Winter Love. Elizabeth Jennings. BoLoP

Winter Mask. Allen Tate. OxBA

Winter Memories. Henry David Thoreau. AmPP; OxBA

Winter midnight. Otsuji, *Japanese.* OHMPJ, tr. by Kenneth Rexroth

Winter Moon. Langston Hughes. KaS; SAmP

Winter Moon. Maria Luisa Spaziani, *Italian.* PBWP, tr. by Lynne Lawner

Winter moon. Robert Spiess. HA

Winter Morning. Frank Flynn. AYFP; OTCP

Winter morning. Getting Up in Winter. Emperor Ch'ien Wen-Ti, *Chinese.* BLT, tr. by Kenneth Rexroth

Winter Morning. Ogden Nash. OTCP; TLR

Winter / morning. / Snowflakes. Snow Poem. Roger McGough. Spl

Winter morning sunrise, The. Rising in Winter. Hsiao Kang, *Chinese.* OHMPC, tr. by Kenneth Rexroth

Winter Morning Walk, The. William Cowper.
   "Acquaint thyself with God, if thou wouldst taste." OxAEP-1

Winter must be here, The. What We Can. Ray A. Young Bear. VoR

Winter: My Secret. Christina Rossetti. BrRo; NAEL-2; NOBVV; VWP

Winter my theme confines; whose nitry wind. Winter Sports. John Gay. ECEV; NOEC *Fr.* Trivia; or, The Art of Walking the Streets of London.

Winter Night, A. William Barnes. NOBE; OBNC

Winter Night. Louis O. Coxe. NYBP

Winter Night. C. Day Lewis. PoA

Winter Night. Boris Pasternak, *Russian.* TCRP, tr. by Yakov Hornstein

Winter Night. Po Chü-i, *Chinese.* ChiP, tr. by Arthur Waley

Winter Night. Charles Simic. HCAP

Winter Night, A. Priscilla Jane Thompson. CBWP-2

Winter Night. Wen-Ti Chien, *Chinese.* ChiP, tr. by Arthur Waley

Winter Night. John Greenleaf Whittier. *Fr.* Snow-Bound [*or* Snow-Bound; a Winter Idyl]. APN-1; AiP; AmPP; NAAL-3; NOBA; OxBA; TAP; TFi

Winter Night. Yüan Mei, *Chinese.* OHMPC, tr. by Kenneth Rexroth

Winter Night: Mount Royal. Abraham Moses Klein. NoAM

Winter Nightfall. Robert Bridges. MoBrPo; OBEV; SCGP

Winter Nightfall. Sir John Collings Squire. OxBTC

Winter Noon. Umberto Saba, *Italian.* STV, tr. by John Frederick Nims

Winter Ocean. John Updike. InPK-6; Poetr

Winter Ode to the Old Men of Lummus Park, Miami, Florida, A. Donald Justice. WeW-3

Winter of my infancy being over-past, The. Another Song. Anne Collins. KTR; PEW

Winter Offerings. Frank Ormsby. PNI

Winter Piece, A. William Cullen Bryant. APN-1; AmPP; ColAP; OxBA

Winter-Piece, A. Ambrose Philips. NOEC

Winter-Piece to a Friend Away, A. John Berryman. NOBA

Winter Poem. Nikki Giovanni. MBE; PiM

Winter Pond. Ben Belitt. NYBP

Winter rain. Penny Harter. HA

Winter Rain, The. Jones Very. NCAP

Winter Remembered. John Crowe Ransom. CBLP; HAP; MeMAP; NOBA; OxBA; UnPo; VGW

Winter Report. Ben Howard. PoA

Winter Ritual. Nichita Stanescu, *Romanian.* CEEP, tr. by Mariana Carpinisan *and* Mark Irwin

Winter Scene. Marguerite Young. WPE

Winter Sea, The. Namjo Kim, *Korean.* CKP, tr. by Jaihiun Kim

Winter shall not find me withered. Stocking Up. Sylvia Kantaris. LW

Winter Shore, The. Thomas Wade. OAEL-2

Winter Sketches. Charles Reznikoff. PoA

Winter Sky, The. So Chong-Ju, *Korean.* CKP, tr. by Jaihiun Kim

Winter Sky. So Chong-Ju, *Korean.* VCWP, tr. by David R. McCann

Winter-sky began to frown, The. Stella at Wood-Park. Jonathan Swift. BIrV

Winter snowes, all covered is the grounde, The. Alexander Barclay. PBRV *Fr.* Eclogues.

Winter Solstice. Peter Blue Cloud. *Fr.* Within the Seasons. HATNAP

Winter solstice. Pentti Saarikoski. VCWP, tr. by Herbert Lomas *Fr.* The Dance Floor on the Mountain.

Winter Solstice—for Frank. "Asphodel." BrRo

Winter Solstice Poem. Diana Scott. BrRo

Winter Song. Lucha Corpi. NMM-2

Winter Song. David Daiches. NYBP

Winter Song. George Macdonald. NOBVV

Winter Song. Elizabeth Tollet. ECWP; NOEC

Winter Sonnet. Linda Beatrice Brown. GT

Winter Sports. John Gay. ECEV *Fr.* Trivia; or, The Art of Walking the Streets of London.

Winter Storms, The. Sir William Davenant. NOSC

Winter Swan. Louise Bogan. ColAP

Winter Talent, A. Donald Davie. OAEL-2

Winter ("The wrathful winter, 'proaching on apace"). Thomas, 1st Earl of Dorset Sackville. *See* The Induction.

Winter Time [*or* Winter-Time]. Robert Louis Stevenson. ACTP; EBVV; MoBrPo; OxBChV

Winter Tree. Huran Kim, *Korean.* CKP, tr. by Jaihiun Kim

Winter Trees. Sylvia Plath. HCAP; LCAP-2

Winter trees thrown upwards. Deflowering. Mahmood Jamal. NBrP

Winter Tuesday, the city pouring fire, A. Coming Home, *Detroit,* 1968. Philip Levine. WWSi

Winter Twilight, A. Angelina Weld Grimké. NAAAL; PoBA

Winter Twilight, A. John Banister Tabb. APN-2

Winter Twilight, Glowing Black and Gold, The. Delmore Schwartz. NoAM

Winter twilight. She comes out of the lab-. Frame. Adrienne Rich. NMM-2

Winter uncovers distances, I find. The Wintry Mind. Witter Bynner. NoP-4

Winter uses all the blues there are. Blue Winter. Robert Francis. LCAP-2

Winter Verse for His Sister. William Meredith. NYBP; TAP

Winter Views Serene. George Crabbe. OBNC *Fr.* The Borough.

Winter Vision, The. Kunbae Yi, *Korean.* CKP, *tr. by* Jaihiun Kim

Winter Visit, A. Dannie Abse. NoAM

Winter [*or* Wynter] Wakeneth All [*or* Al] My Care. *Unknown.* HAP; MiEL

Winter Walking. Alfred Wellington Purdy. NoAM

Winter Warfare. Edgell Rickword. OBWP; OxBTC; PeFWW; PoFWW; PoWW

Winter will bar the swimmer soon. Swimming Chenango Lake. Charles Tomlinson. FaBoMo; MoP; NoAM

Winter Will Follow. Richard Watson Dixon. GTBS-P

Winter wind. Robert Spiess. HA

Winter Winds Cold and Blea. John Clare. GBL; OBNC

Winter Wise. *Unknown.* AYFP; Spl

Winter with the Gulf Stream. Gerard Manley Hopkins. CMoP; NoAM

Winter without Snow, A. J. D. McClatchy. FYAP

Winter Work. Peter Fallon. CIP-2; PBCIP

Wintering. Sylvia Plath. NALW

    ("Bees are flying. They taste the spring, The.") (LL) NMM-2

Winterlong, off La Manche, wind leaning. Gray stones of the gray. Flaubert in Egypt. Robert Penn Warren. NoAM

Winters at home brought wind. Once in a Lifetime, Snow. Les A. Murray. CBAP; NoP-4

Winters close, Springs open, no child stirs, The. John Berryman. NAAL-2; NoP-4 *Fr.* Homage to Mistress Bradstreet.

Winter's Cold. William Robert Rodgers. EnLoPo

Winter's coming on, The. Sanctuary. Dorothy Hewett. CBAP

Winter's Day, A. Joanna Baillie. WoRP

Winter's Song. *Unknown, Bohemian.* BoTP

Winters Spring, The. John Clare. NOBVV

Winter's Tale, A. Robert Patrick Dana. NYBP

Winter's Tale, A. D. H. Lawrence. MoBrPo

Winter's Tale, A. Sylvia Plath. FaBoA

Winter's Tale, A. Wyatt Prunty. RA

Winter's Tale, The. Shakespeare.

    "As she liv'd peerless." OxAEP-1

    Autolycus as Peddler. OAEL-1

    (Pedlar's Song, The.) CH

    Flowers of Perdita, The.

    "Give me those flowers there, Dorcas. Reverend sirs." OxAEP-1

    "Ha' not you seen, Camillo?" OxBM

    "I have said / She 's adulteress; I have said with whom." OxAEP-1

    "If you would seek us." OxAEP-1

    Pedlar's Song, The. NBLV; OxBoLi; PeLV

    (Autolycus's Song ("When daffodils begin to peer").) NOBE; OAEL-1

    (Song: "When daffodils begin to peer.") PoEL-2

    "Shepherdess--/ A fair one are you." PoE

    Song: "Jog on, jog on, the footpath way." OxBSP

    (Merry Heart, The.) BoTP

    "To your owne bents dispose you: you'le be found." FaBoVe

Winter's Tale, A. Dylan Thomas. CMoP

Winter's thunder. *Unknown.* FaBoVe; LB

Wintersong. Lawson Fusao Inada. MoNo

Wintertime nighs. Thomas Hardy. NoAM; OAEL-2; SCGP *Fr.* In Tenebris. NOBE

"Wintry Dawn." Meir Wieseltier, *Hebrew.* IP, *tr. by* Bargad, Warren and Stanley Chyet *Fr.* Wintry Dawn.

Wintry days are with us still, The. Back to the Land. Charles Larcom Graves. NSI

Wintry haw is burning out of season, The. The Haw Lantern. Seamus Heaney. NoAM; PNI

Wintry Mind, The. Witter Bynner. NoP-4

Wintry night, the hearth inhales, A. Remembering Carrigskeewaun. Michael Longley. PBCIP

Wiped out by the hugeness of the big electric crane. On All Fours. Benjamin Péret, *French.* PFTM, *tr. by* Charles Simic and Michael Benedikt

Wiping the chrome. Alan Pizzarelli. HA

Wire, The. Robert Garioch. FaBoTC

Wire. Rod Moran. NOBAu

Wire, briar, limber-lock. *Unknown.* ACTP

Wired In. Lamont B. Steptoe. UnSA

Wireless. Rodney Bennett. BoTP

Wirikota Wirikota. For the God of Peyote. *Unknown, Huichol Indian.* STP, *tr. by* Jerome Rothenberg

Wirraw init thigithir missyz. Cold, Isn't It. Tom Leonard. FaBoTC

Wisdom. William Cowper. ChIV-1 *Fr.* Olney Hymns.

Wisdom? "Laurence Hope." *See* For This Is Wisdom.

Wisdom. George Sands Johnson. PWR

Wisdom. Sara Teasdale. MoAmPo

Wisdom. W. B. Yeats. TrCP

Wisdom and Spirit of the universe! Influence of Natural Objects [in Calling Forth and Strengthening the Imagination in Boyhood and Early Youth]. Wordsworth. AWP *Fr.* Introduction—Childhood and School-Time. FHYEP *Fr.* The Prelude; Growth of a Poet's Mind [1850 vers.]

Wisdom found no place where she might dwell. Wisdom's Plight. Bible, Pseudepigrapha. *Fr.* Enoch. TrJP

Wisdom has nothing to do with age. Hy Sobiloff. VGW

Wisdom, innocently the sun rises. Ballade. Branko Miljkovic, *Serbo-Croatian.* HSix, *tr. by* Charles Simic

Wisdom is. Makeda (Queen of Sheba). WPoS

Wisdom is vain, and prophesy. (LL) The Conflict of Convictions. Herman Melville. APN-2; CBCWP; NOBA

Wisdom of AE, The. Thomas McCarthy. PBCIP

Wisdom of Merlyn, The. Wilfrid Scawen Blunt.

    "Wouldst thou be wise, O Man? At the knees of a woman begin." OBMV

Wisdom of the World, The. Siegfried Sassoon. MoBrPo

Wisdom Tooth, The. Jonathan Holden. NAmP90

Wisdom's Plight. Bible, Pseudepigrapha. *Fr.* Enoch. TrJP

Wise 1. Imamu Amiri Baraka. PFTM *Fr.* Why's / Wise.

Wise 3. Imamu Amiri Baraka. FTOS *Fr.* Why's/Wise.

Wise 5. Imamu Amiri Baraka. BB *Fr.* Wise/Whys.

Wise Child, The. Edward Lucie-Smith. PBCV

Wise emblem of our politic[k] world. The Snail [*or* Snayl]. Richard Lovelace. BeJo; CaPo; OAEL-1; PoEL-3

Wise fish digs his silver in, The. Night Catch. Heather McHugh. AmPA

Wise guys, The. Kid Stuff. Frank Horne. NOxBChV; PChr; PoBA

Wise Johnny. Edwina Fallis. CTV

Wise king dowered with blessings on his throne, The. The Trophy. Edwin Muir. LiTM

Wise may bring their learning, The. A Child's Offering. *Unknown.* CTV *Fr.* The Book of Praise for Children.

Wise Men Ask the Children the Way, The. Heinrich Heine, *German.* OBCP, *tr. by* Geoffrey Grigson

Wise men come here to shit. From a Lavatory Wall. *Unknown.* FaBoEE

Wise men in long white togas come forward during the. Inventions. Miroslav Holub, *Czech.* PoSu, *tr. by* George Theiner

Wise Men of Gotham, The. Thomas Love Peacock. *See* Three Men of Gotham.

Wise men of talent, now and in the past. A Fisherman Speaks His Mind. Nguyễn Đình Chiểu, *Vietnamese.* AVP, *tr. by* Huỳnh Sanh Thông

Wise men, you have cast me aside. *Unknown, Chinese.* CoBCP, *tr. by* Burton Watson

Wise old owl lived in an oak, A. Edward Hersey Richards. BLPA; FaBoBe; LB; OxNR

    ("Why can't we all be like that bird?") (LL) CTV

Wise Ones, The. Bozhidar Bozhilov, *Bulgarian.* CEEP, *tr. by* Jascha Kessler *and* Aleksandar Shurbanov

Wise Pallas and the immortal Muses own. (LL) Inscription for a Grotto. Mark Akenside. NOEC; OBGa; PoEL-3

Wise Rochefoucault a maxim writ. *From* The Life and Character of Dean Swift. Jonathan Swift. NOBL *Fr.* The Life and Genuine Character of Dr Swift.

Wise to have gone so early to reward. The Wazir Dandan for Prince Sharkan. *Unknown.* AWP *Fr.* The Thousand and One Nights.

Wise Triangle, A. Vasco [*or* Vasko] Popa. PoSu, *tr. by* Anne Pennington; CBNP, *tr. by* Anne Pennington *and* Charles Simic *Fr.* The Yawn of Yawns.

Wise-Unto-Hell Ecclesiast. Past Thinking of Solomon. Francis Thompson. ChIV-1

Wise up, Pablito. Each frame looks too. How to Organise a Successful Small Business. Brian Chan. HCP

Wise-Woman, The. Agnes Mary Frances Robinson. VWP

Wise/Whys. Imamu Amiri Baraka.

    Wise 5. BB

Wisely and well was it said of him, "Hang it all, he's a." Addition to Kipling's "The Dead King (Edward VII), 1910." Max Beerbohm. FaBoEE; OBCoV

Wisest men that Nature e'er could boast, The. Meditatio Tertia Decima. Francis Quarles. ChIV-1 *Fr.* Job Militant.

Wisest of all men lies buried on this spot, The. Sonnet. Daniel Casper von Lohenstein. GePo *Fr.* Arminius.

Wisest scholar of the wight most wise, The. Sonnet 25. Sir Philip Sidney. NoP-4; OAEL-1 *Fr.* Astrophil and Stella. AAS; SiPS

Wisga. Lew Blockcolski. VoR

Wish, The. Anacreon, *Greek.* OBCVT, *tr. by* Thomas Stanley

Wish, The. Mary Lee, Lady Chudleigh. LW

Wish, The. John Clare. OBGa

Wish, The. Abraham Cowley. NOBE; NOSC; NoP-4; OBEV; OxAEP-1; PBRV *Fr.* The Mistress.

Wish, A. Elizabeth Gould. BoTP

Wish. Lance Henson. CDW

Wish, A. Frances Anne Kemble. WPE

Wish, A. Laurence David Lerner. OxBTC

Wish, A. Samuel Rogers. FaPoR; GTBS-P; NOBE; OBEV; OxAEP-2

Wish, The. Thomas Stanley. AWP

Wish, A. John Millington Synge. FaBoEE

Wish. Dorothy Brown Thompson. CTV

Wish, By a Young Lady, The. Laetitia Pilkington. PEW

Wish for a Young Wife. Theodore Roethke. MoP; NAAL-2; NoAM; NoP-4; OxBSP; TAP

Wish for an Overcoat. Alfred Islay Walden. AAP

Wish Foundation, The. Carol Muske. PBCAP

Wish I was in Tennessee. Tennessee. *Unknown.* AmFP

Wish, that of the living whole, The. Tennyson. EBVV; EBVVPR; EnVR; FHYEP; HAP; OAEL-2; OBNC; TOF *Fr.* In Memoriam A. H. H.

Wish to Be Believed, The. Mona Van Duyn. PoA

Wishbone, The. Paul Muldoon. CIP-2; PBCIP

Wished Sunday's come: mirth brightens ev'ry face. White Conduit House. William Woty. NOEC

Wishes. A. C. Child. PoToHe

Wishes. Patty L. Harjo. VoR

Wishes. Philippe Jaccottet, *French.* MFP, *tr. by* Martin Sorrell

Wishes. F. Rogers. BoTP

Wishes. Robert Louis Stevenson. MoBrPo; OBEV

Wishes. *Unknown. See* Five Little Chickens.

Wishes for Her. Denis Devlin. CIP-2; NOIV

Wishes for My Son. Thomas Macdonagh. TIRV

Wishes for Sons. Lucille Clifton. NAAAL; NMM-2

Wishes for the Months. John Heath-Stubbs. AYFP

Wishes for the Supposed Mistress[e]. Richard Crashaw. *See* Wishes. To His (Supposed) Mistresse.

Wishes of an Elderly Man[, Wished at a Garden Party, June 1914]. Sir Walter Alexander Raleigh. FaBoCh; FaBoEE; NBLV; NOBL; NTP; OBCoV; PeLV

Wishes. To His (Supposed) Mistresse. Richard Crashaw. BoLoP; EBEV; ImPo; MeLP; NOSC; OBEV; OxAEP-1; PoEL-2; SeCP

(Wishes for the Supposed Mistress[e].) GTBS-P

Wishful Thinking. Michael C. Blumenthal. HCAP

Wishful Thinking Is the Master of Reality. Duoduo, *Chinese.* AF, *tr. by* Gregory Lee *and* John Cayley

Wishing. William Allingham. BoTP; OxBChV

Wishing Africa. Marilyn Bowering. NOBC

Wishing Bone Cycle, The. Jacob Nibenegenesabe, *Cree Indian.* "One time I wanted two moons." STP, *tr. by* Howard Norman

Wishing for roses, I walk through the garden. Summer Garden. "Anna Akhmatova," *Russian.* BoWoP, *tr. by* Stephen Stepanchev

Wishing Poem. *Unknown.* NTCP; OxNR

(Star Wish.) OTCP

Wishing to try retirement, I requested release from duty. Wen Cheng-ming. CoBLCP, *tr. by* Jonathan Chaves *Fr.* Improvised on Horseback to Say Good-bye to Those Who Are Seeing Me Off.

Wishing-Well, The. Wilfrid Wilson Gibson. NTP

Wisp of spring cloud, A. Tom Tico. HA

Wispy autumn clouds. Robert Spiess. HA

Wispy cuttings lie in rows, The. July in Indiana. Robert Fitzgerald. AiP; NYBP

Wisselton, wasselton, who lives here? Wassailing Song. *Unknown.* OBCP

Wistful hymn we never could remember, A. (LL) Nightingales in America. Jane Flanders. CrSp; SAGP

Wistful, / they speak of / satis- / faction, love. The People. Robert Creeley. VGW

Wistful vistas are living in objects, The. Sonnet for the Season. Art Lange. PmAP

Wiston Vault. Katherine Philips. NOSC

Wit and Learning. James Cawthorn. "Whoever looks on life will see." ECEV

"Wit was a strange unlucky child." OBCoV

Wit and Wisdom. Ambrose Philips. OxAEP-1

Wit my large eyes that needed nothing. (LL) Drinking Spree Beneath the Open Sky. Slavko Mihalic, *Croatian.* PoSu, *tr. by* Peter Kastmiler

Wit that can creep, and pride that licks the dust. (LL) Sporus. Alexander Pope. AWP; NOBE; OBSV; OxBoV; SCV

Wit, transported with enditing, A. A Tale of the Miser and the Poet. Anne Finch, Countess of Winchilsea. ECWP

Wit was a strange unlucky child. James Cawthorn. OBCoV *Fr.* Wit and Learning.

Witch. Patricia Beer. OxBC

Witch, The. Mary Elizabeth Coleridge. BrRo; CABP; NALW; PFE; VWP; WPE

Witch, The. Percy H. Ilott. BoTP

Witch, The. Thomas Middleton. Song: "In a maiden-time professed." OxBSP

Witch, The. Santal. RaBo

Witch, The. Katharine Tynan. NOBVV

Witch-Bride, The. William Allingham. NOBVV; OxBSn

Witch Doctor. Robert Earl Hayden. NoAM

Witch Doctor's Magic Flight, The. Smiler Narautjarri. NOBAu, *tr. by* Georg von Brandenstein

Witch-elms that counterchange the floor. In Memoriam. Tennyson. EBVV; OBGa; OBNC *Fr.* In Memoriam A. H. H.

Witch of Coös, The. Robert Frost. InPS-3; LiTM; MeMAP; MoP; NOBA; NoAM; PoE *Fr.* Two Witches. CMoP

("I stayed the night for shelter at a farm.") OxBSn

("Yes, there's something the dead are keeping back.") (LL) OxBSn

Witch of East Seventy-second Street, The. Morris Gilbert Bishop. NYBP

Witch of Edmonton, The. Thomas Dekker, John Ford, *and* William Rowley. "And why on me? why should the envious world." OxBSn

Witch of Fife, The. James Hogg. Ro *Fr.* The Queen's Wake.

Witch of Willowby Wood, The. Rowena Bastin Bennett. ChAP

Witch pours the libation, clouds fill the sky, The. Magic Strings. Li Ho, *Chinese.* PLT, *tr. by* A. C. Graham

Witch that came (the withered hag), The. Provide, Provide. Robert Frost. AmPP; CMoP; ChIV-1; FP; HAP; KSG; MoP; NAAL-2; NOBA; NoAM; NoP-4; PoE; Poetr; TAP; TFi; TwCP; UnPo; WeW-3

Witchcraft: New Style. Lascelles Abercrombie. MoBrPo

Witches and poets co-embrace like fate. Fatales Poetae. Henry Parrot. FaBoEE

Witches' Ballad, The. William Bell Scott. *See* The Witch's Ballad.

Witches' Blood. Alma Villanueva. NMM-2

Witches' Ride, The. Karla Kuskin. NOxBChV; TLR

Witches' Song, The. Ben Jonson. CH

Witches' Spells. Madeleine Edmondson. NTCP

Witches' Wood, The. Mary Elizabeth Coleridge. PBWP; VWP

Witchgrass. Louise Glück. AFr

Witch's Ballad, The. William Bell Scott. NOBVV; OBEV; PeVV; RACG

(Witches' Ballad, The.) CH

Witch's Chant, A. James Hogg. NOBRP

Witch's Story, The. Lawrence Raab. CMAP

With a broken hoe. (LL) Justice Denied in Massachusetts. Edna St. Vincent Millay. AiP; MoAmPo

With a clover in her hand. (LL) The Question. Frederick Goddard Tuckerman. APN-2; ColAP

With a Coin from Syracuse. Oliver St. John Gogarty. OBMV

With a decent happiness. (LL) The Rain. Robert Creeley. CoAP; CoAmPo; ColAP; PmAP; PoE; RaBo; TRP; VGW

With a dozen blows the cold betrays the pulse of time. Noonday in Immaturity. Jean-Baptiste Tati-Loutard. PBMAP *Fr.* Les Racines Congolaises (1968).

With a Fa, la, la, la, la. (LL) Song Written at Sea in the First Dutch War (1665), the Night before an Engagement. Charles, 6th Earl of Dorset Sackville. EnLoPo; NOBE; NOSC; OBEV; OBWP; OxAEP-1

With a fearful shriek, he leaped and fell across the picture— dead. (LL) The Face upon [or on] the Floor. Hugh Antoine D'Arcy. BLPA; FaBoBe

With-a-fountain's shining-shot furls. (LL) Harry Ploughman. Gerard Manley Hopkins. EnVR; FaBoMo

With a gay lady. (LL) London Bridge is broken down. Mother Goose. CBNP; CH; FaBoVe; LB; OxBoLi; OxNR; ReMoGo

With a Gift of Rings. Robert Graves. GBL

With a green scarf I blindfolded. Martin Sorescu, *Romanian.* VCWP, *tr. by* Michael Hamburger

With a Guitar, to Jane. Shelley. FHYEP; OAEL-2

("For one beloved Friend alone.") (LL) GTBS-P

(To a Lady, with a Guitar.) GTBS-P

With a half-glance upon the sky. A Character. Tennyson. EBVVPR

With a handful of weeds I weep in the slanting sun. Boudoir Lament. Yü Hsüan-chi. BoWoP, *tr. by* Geoffrey Waters

With a hangover. Tanka. Sasaki Yukitsuna, *Japanese*. MJT, *tr. by* Makoto Ueda

With a Heigho, maybe Begorrah, and certainly Fiddlededee. (LL) Irish Song [Rosie O'Grady]. Noël Coward. NBLV; OBCoV

With a hot glide up, then down, his shirts. Ironing Their Clothes. Julia Alvarez. CrSp

With a hush in their voices. Country Woman Elegy. Margaret Gibson. CrSp; MT

With a lantern that wouldn't burn. The Draft Horse. Robert Frost. CMoP; HeIP-4; HoPM; PFE; PoE; SAmP; TRP

With a large ax handle tucked in at his waist. A Woodcutter's Ax. P'i Jih-hsiu, *Chinese*. SuSp, *tr. by* William H. Nienhauser

With a Lifting of the Head. "Hugh MacDiarmid." MoBrPo

With a light frost, crouched an outrageous bird. (LL) Birdwatchers of America. Anthony Hecht. HoPM; NOBA; NoAM

With a line and hook. A Boy's Summer. Paul Laurence Dunbar. CA

With a long stirrup under fern. Craswall. Roland Mathias. OBWVE

With a louder note. (LL) Beloved person must I think, The. Akimine, *Japanese*. AWP; TAL, *tr. by* Arthur Waley

With a lucky charm around his throat. Lucilius, *Greek*. GrAn, *tr. by* Peter Porter

With a muff and a cloak and a tippet—poor Anne. (LL) On Lady Anne Hamilton. Richard Brinsley Sheridan. FaBoEE; OBCoV

With a pert moustache and a ready candid smile. The Mixer. Louis MacNeice. FP; FaBoTw

With a pint of flour and a sheet of bark. The Limejuice Tub. *Unknown*. NOBAu

With a pocketful of words and plastic tokens. Marge Piercy. *See* Song of the Fucked Duck.

With a Presentation Copy of Verses. Martin Bell. PeLV

With a pull-through and the .22. Premeditations. Geoff Page. NOBAu

With a pure colour there is little one can do. Morning Glory. Ruth Pitter. FaBoWP

With a pure note he welcomes the evening moon. The Crane. Tu Mu, *Chinese*. SuSp, *tr. by* John M. Ortinau

With a rank, Arab bloodstain. (LL) A Hand of Solo. Thomas Kinsella. CIP-2; NOIV

With a Rod No Man Alive. Walther von der Vogelweide, *German*. AWP, *tr. by* Jethro Bithell

With a serene look. Tanka. Tawara Machi, *Japanese*. MJT, *tr. by* Makoto Ueda

With a shy pity pouting in the mouth. (LL) A la Promenade. Paul Verlaine. AWP; OBVE, *tr. by* Arthur Symons

With a smiling and a charming little wife. (LL) A Shantyman's Life. *Unknown*. AS; AmFP

With a stake in his inside! (LL) Faithless Nelly Gray. Thomas Hood. BXAP; NOBL; NOBRP; UV

With a thin slice of sky on a hunk of earth. Magic. Aimé Césaire, *French*. NegPo, *tr. by* Clayton Eshleman *and* Denis Kelly

With a thousand nights' dream. Winter Sky. So Chong-Ju, *Korean*. VCWP, *tr. by* David R. McCann

With a thunderous crack. Tanka. Nakajō Fumiko, *Japanese*. MJT, *tr. by* Makoto Ueda

With a very big yawn. Mr. Beetle. Emily Hover. BoTP

With a violin in the alley grandfather and son disappeared. Beyond Melody. Nathan Alterman, *Hebrew*. MHP, *tr. by* Ruth Finer Mintz

With a wall and a ditch between us, I watched the gate-legged dromedary. The Fruit of the Tree. David Wagoner. NYBP

With a whirl of thought oppressed. The Day of Judgement. Jonathan Swift. BIrV; ChIV-1; NOBE; NOEC; OAEL-1; OBSV; SCGP

With a yellow lantern. Glow-Worms. P. A. Ropes. BoTP

With *Acme's* and *Septimius*' life. (LL) Carmen 45 ("Phyllis Corydon clutched to him"). Catullus, *Latin*. AWP; OBCVT; OBVE, *tr. by* Abraham Cowley

With afternoon tea-cakes and scones. (LL) How to Get On in Society. John Betjeman. NOBL; OBSV; OxBTC; UV

With all a woman's virtues but the pox. Alexander Pope. OBSV *Fr.* The First Satire of the Second Book of Horace [Imitated]. OAEL-1

With all its sinful doings, I must say. Italy versus England. Byron. NOBE *Fr.* Beppo; a Venetian Story. NOBL; OBNV; OBSV

With all my heart, in truth, and passion strong. The Pride of a Jew. Judah Halevi, *Hebrew*. TrJP, *tr. by* Israel Cohen

With All My Heart, Jehovah, I'll Confess. Henry Ainsworth. AH

With all my memories that could not sleep. (LL) Spleen. Ernest Christopher Dowson. ADE; APAD

With all my will, but much against my heart. A Farewell. Coventry Patmore. BoLoP; EnLoPo; GLoP; GTBS-P; NOBE; OBEV; OBNC; PoEL-5 *Fr.* The Unknown Eros.

With all the drifting race of men. Léonie Adams. *Fr.* April Mortality. MoAmPo

With all the powres my poor heart hath. Hymn in Adoration of the Blessed Sacrament. Richard Crashaw. MeLP

With all the subtle paints of Fragonard. The Flamingos. Rilke, *German*. APo, *tr. by* Stephen Mitchell

With all these loads of injuries opprest. Dryden. EBEV *Fr.* Absalom and Achitophel, Pt. I. EBEvV; FHYEP; FaBoPV; HAP; NOSC; OAEL-1; PoE

With an effort Grant swung the great block. Blocking the Pass. Charles Madge. FaBoMo

With angry brow and stately tread. The Earthquake of 1886. Josephine D. Henderson Heard. CBWP-4

With anyone to death, comes so far short. Temperament. Robert Frost. *Fr.* Home Burial. ColAP; IMW; NAAL-2; SoSe-8; TAP; TRP

With banked fire to mark the occasion. Family Evening. Daniel Huws. NYBP

With banners furled, and clarions mute. The Night-March. Herman Melville. NCAP

With Bill Pickett at the 101 Ranch. Colleen J. McElroy. WeT

With blackest moss the flower-pots [*or* flowerpots]. Mariana. Tennyson. AWP; CBLP; CH; EBVVPR; EnVR; FHYEP; InPS-3; NAEL-2; NOBE; NOBRP; OAEL-2; OBEV; OBNC; OxAEP-2; PeVV; PoE; PoEL-5; SCGP; TFi; UnPo

With blameless carriage, I lived [*or* liv'd] here. An Epitaph upon a Sober Matron. Robert Herrick. CaPo

With bleeding back, from tyrant's lash. The Fugitive. Priscilla Jane Thompson. CBWP-2

With Bolts of Melody! (LL) I would not paint—a picture. Emily Dickinson. APN-2; NAAL-1; NAAL-3; NOBA; NoP-4; TRP

With Bridget and with Nell. (LL) A Ballad[e] [upon a Wedding]. Sir John Suckling. BeJo; CaPo; EBEV; EBNV; NoP-4; OxBM; SeCP

With bridles in the evening come. (LL) At Grass. Philip Larkin. HAP; OxBTC; RB; WeW-3

With broadened nostrils to the sky upturned. Signs of Storm. James Thomson. APo

With broken tooth he clawed it. The Pleasure. David Ignatow. PFE

With broken wing they limped across the sky. Reported Missing. John Clifford Bayliss. PoWW

With bruise of lash or stone. (LL) Simon the Cyrenian Speaks. Countee Cullen. BPo; ChIV-2; HAP; MoAmPo; TTY; TrCP

With buds embalmed alive in ice. A Mile from Eden. Anne Ridler. WPN

With burning fervour. The Crystal. George Barker. LiTM; OBMV

With camel's hair I clothed my skin. Dream. Richard Watson Dixon. EBEV; NOBVV; PeVV; SCGP

With candour I confess my love. *Unknown, Egyptian hieroglyphics*. BoWoP, *tr. by* Ezra Pound *and* Noel Stock

With carrion men, groaning for burial. (LL) O, pardon me, thou bleeding piece of earth. Shakespeare. EBEvV; OxAEP-1

With cheerful mind we yield to men. Frances Gray. FaBoVe

With Child. Genevieve Taggard. MoAmPo; NMM-2

With Christ and All His Shining Train. Thomas Prince. AH

With 'Chuck, chuck, chuck, chuck!'. (LL) To Mistress [*or* Maystres] Isabell Pennell. John Skelton. AAS; CH; InPS-3; NOBE; NoSic; OBEV; OxBoLi; PoEL-1; SCGP; TTTS

With Circes let them dwell that think[e] not so. (LL) The Shepherd's Praise of Diana. Sir Walter Ralegh. NoSic; SiPS

With Circes let them dwell that thinke not so. Sir Walter Ralegh. *See* The Shepherd's Praise of Diana.

With cloud for shift / how will I hide? May Swenson. *See* Question.

With coat like any mole's, as soft and black. Mole Catcher. Edmund Blunden. OBMV

With company coming. Thanksgiving Dinner. Aileen Fisher. CA

With cords of love God often strove. Michael Wigglesworth. NAAL-3 *Fr.* The Day of Doom. NAAL-1; SCAP

With courage seek the kingdom of the dead. The Last Journey. Leonidas of Tarentum, *Greek*. AWP, *tr. by* Charles Merivale

With cousin and brother / against the stranger. (LL) Sand Nigger. Lawrence Joseph. WWSi

With curls on their brows. (LL) The Day of My Death. Pier Paolo Pasolini, *Italian*. VCWP, *tr. by* Lawrence Ferlinghetti *and* Francesca Valente

With Dad gone, Mom and I worked. Adolescence—III. Rita Dove. ISC; NoAM

With darkness and the death-hour rounding it. (LL) Sonnet: "When our two souls stand up erect and strong." Elizabeth Barrett Browning. BWW; BoWoP; EnVR; LW; NAEL-2; NALW; NOBE; OBEV; WPE

With dead shapes of heroes. The Evening. Georg Trakl, *German*. PFTM, *tr. by* Robert Firmage

With death doomed to grapple. Epitaph for William Pitt. Byron. FaBoEE

With deep affection / And recollection. The Bells of Shandon. Francis Sylvester Mahony. CH; IIP; OBEV; OxAEP-2

With delicate, mad hands, behind his sordid bars. To One in Bedlam. Ernest Christopher Dowson. GSo; MoBrPo; OBMV; Son

With Demo I fell in love, of Paphian origins. Philodemus, *Greek*. GrAn, *tr. by* William Moebius

With deportment learnt from samurai films. Glasnevin Cemetery. Michael O'Loughlin. PBCIP

With difficulty persist here and there on earth. (LL) Another Epitaph on an Army of Mercenaries. "Hugh MacDiarmid." InPK-6; MoP; NAEL-2; NSI; NoAM; NoP-4; OBWP; RB

With difficulty the ship was built. The Critics. Theodore Spencer. NYBP

With disheveled head cloths, we sit late on the bench. Summer Night at the Pond Pavillion. Chang Yü. Fr. Twelve Miscellaneous Poems on the Fang Garden. CoBLCP, *tr. by* Jonathan Chaves

With Donne, whose muse on dromedary trots. On Donne's Poetry. Coleridge. EPCY; NAEL-2; OAEL-2; PFE; UV

With double portion of his father's art. (LL) MacFlecknoe; or, A Satire [*or* Satyr] upon the True-Blue [*or* -Blew] Protestant Poet T. S. Dryden. CABP; CBNP; FHYEP; HAP; NAEL-1; NoP-4; OAEL-1; OBSV; OxAEP-1; OxBoLi; PeLV; PoE; Poetr; TFi

With dull, sea-spent eyes. (LL) Meeting-House Hill. Amy Lowell. ColAP

With each quiver. Tanka. Maekawa Samio, *Japanese*. MJT, *tr. by* Makoto Ueda

With each recurrence of this glorious morn. Composed in One of the Valleys of Westmoreland, on Easter Sunday. Wordsworth. ChIV-2

With each step upward. The Pyramid of Khufu. Khaled Mattawa. IFJA

With Earth's first Clay They did the Last Man knead. 73. Edward Fitzgerald. CABP

With elbow buried in the downy pillow. Clarimonde. Théophile Gautier. AWP Fr. Taches Jaunes, Les.

With elegies, sad songs, and mourning lays. Sextain. William Drummond, of Hawthornden. NOSC

With endless life are crown'd. Robert Herrick. See To Live Merrily, and To Trust to Good Verses.

With endless life are crowned. (LL) To Live Merrily, and To Trust to Good Verses. Robert Herrick. AWP; BeJo; CaPo; NOSC; SeCP

With envy, what the Old Man hardly feels. Wordsworth. See An Old Man [Travelling].

With Erebus deaf to prayers, in the embrace of Night. (LL) A Young Dead Woman. José-Maria de Heredia, *Spanish*. FLP; LoP, *tr. by* Alistair Elliot

With Esther. Wilfrid Scawen Blunt. OBEV Fr. Esther [a Young Man's Tragedy].

With every note / of the mountain temple. *Unknown, Japanese*. BoWoP, *tr. by* Willis Barnstone

With every rolling stone place me in the breach. Place Me in the Breach. Yehuda Karni, *Hebrew*. TrJP, *tr. by* Sholom J. Kahn

With Eyes at the Back of Our Heads. Denise Levertov. AmPP

With eyes like a lizard. (LL) Humanities Lecture. William Stafford. NNaP; NoAM

With eyes of soft humility and wonder, love, and awe. (LL) The Lark's Song. William Blake. APo; NOBE; OBNC

With fairest flowers,/ Whilst summer lasts. Shakespeare. EBEV; RB Fr. Cymbeline.

With faith I trust in Christ the Lord. Mrs. Saunder's Experience. *Unknown*. AmFP

With falling Oars they kept the time. (LL) Bermudas. Andrew Marvell. APAD; AWP; CH; ESCV; FHYEP; FMP; FaBoCh; GTBS-P; GeHe; NAEL-1; NOBE; NOCV; NOSC; NoP-4; OBEV; PBRV; PFE; PeECV; PoE; RB; SCGP; SeCP; TFi

With famin upsoaken. (LL) Wee leave Creete Country; and our sayls unwrapped uphoysing. Virgil. BIrV; OBVE, *tr. by* Richard Stanyhurst

With faults and all, not nobler, just there. (LL) Sea Canes. Derek Walcott. FP; HeIP-4

With favour and fortune fastidiously blessed [*or* blest]. The Character of Sir Robert Walpole. Jonathan Swift. FaBoEE; PoE

With fellow-angels you enjoy it now. (LL) On the Death of Mrs. Bowes. Lady Mary Wortley Montagu. LW

With fiery-lashing. Whirlwind. David Rokeah, *Hebrew*. MHP, *tr. by* Ruth Finer Mintz

With fifteen-ninety or sixteen-sixteen. On an Anniversary. John Millington Synge. FaBoEE; NOIV; OBMV

With fifty years not lived but gone, we find. The Cloak. James McAuley. BMAP

With finger rais'd he points to the prodigal pictures. (LL) My Picture-Gallery. Walt Whitman. NAAL-1; NAAL-3

With fingers weary and worn. The Song of the Shirt. Thomas Hood. EBEvV; EBVV; FaPoR

With flecked feathers and many colors. (LL) A Vision of Nature. William Langland. CTC; PoEL-1

With fleshless limbs, at rueful length, was laid. (LL) Then up three winding stairs my feet were brought. Philip Freneau. NAAL-1; NAAL-3

With focus sharp as Flemish-painted face. Dome of Sunday, The [*or* A]. Karl Shapiro. CMoP; CoAP; LiTM; MoAmPo; NoAM; OxBA

With Freedom's Seed. Aleksandr Sergeyevich Pushkin, *Russian*. TTY, *tr. by* Babette Deutsch

With gallant pomp, and beauteous pride. Ode on a Storm. *Unknown*. OxBoS

With ganial foire. Mr. Molony's Account of the Crystal Palace. William Makepeace Thackeray. PeVV

With Garments Flowing. John Clare. GBL

With glass like a bull's eye. Mrs. MacQueen (*or* The Lollie-Shop). Walter De la Mare. BoTP

With God and His Mercy. Carl Olof Rosenius. AH

With God Conversing. Gene Derwood. ImPo; LiTM

With gold unfading, WASHINGTON! be thine. (LL) To His Excellency General Washington. Phillis Wheatley. NAAAL; NAAL-1; NAAL-3; WPE

With golden reins and jade bridle, a neighing horse. Tune: "Song of a Dandy." Sun Kuang-hsien, *Chinese*. SuSp, *tr. by* Hellmut Wilhelm

With Gorgon's gear and barebill thongs and fangs. (LL) Andromeda. Gerard Manley Hopkins. EBEV; FaBoMo; OxAEP-2; SCGP

With grief and mourning I sit to spin. The Girl's Lamentation. William Allingham. TIRV

With Grotius on New-Testament yo've done. On a Sermon Preach'd Sept. the 6th, 1697. on These Words: You Have Sold Your Selves for Nought. Sarah Fyge Egerton. KTR

With guilty hope at every change of moon! (LL) Marriage. Austin Clarke. BIrV; GTBS-P

With hairs, which for the wind to play with, hung. On Lydia Distracted. Philip Ayres. EnLoPo; Son

With half a heart I wander here. In the States. Robert Louis Stevenson. AiP

With hands all reddened and sore. The Washerwoman. Mary Weston Fordham. CBWP-2

With hands and faces nicely washed. Clever Peter and the Ogress. Katharine Pyle. OBCA

With hands clasped fast, as if still he prayed. (LL) Melrose Abbey. Sir Walter Scott. OBNC; OxAEP-2

With hands tight clenched through matted hair. The Three Voices. "Lewis Carroll." BXAP

With happiness stretched [*or* stretchd] across the hills. William Blake. NAEL-2

With hate and misery / my sleeves are never dry. Lady Sagami, *Japanese*. WPJ, *tr. by* Kenneth Rexroth *and* Ikuko Atsumi

With headlights on. Tanka. Kondō Yoshimi, *Japanese*. MJT, *tr. by* Makoto Ueda

With heart at rest I climbed the citadel's. Epilogue. Charles Baudelaire, *French*. AWP, *tr. by* Arthur Symons

With hearts of poor men it is so. The Poor. Emile Verhaeren, *French*. AWP, *tr. by* Ludwig Lewisohn

With hearts revived in conceit, new land and trees they eye. Edward Johnson. Fr. Good News from New England. SCAP

With heavy groans did I approach my friends. Wine and Grief. Solomon ibn Gabirol, *Hebrew*. TrJP, *tr. by* Emma Lazarus

With Her. Czeslaw Milosz, *Polish*. GI, *tr. by* Robert Hass *and* Czeslaw Milosz

With her buskins tipped with dew. May's Invocation after a Tardy Spring. Henrietta Cordelia Ray. CBWP-3

With her head swinging like a white lily. The Anniversary of Samansa's Death. Kazuko Shiraishi, *Japanese*. WPJ, *tr. by* Kenneth Rexroth *and* Ikuko Atsumi

With her, her sister went, a warlike maid. Phineas Fletcher. NOSC Fr. The Purple Island.

With Her Lips Only. Robert Graves. OxBM

With her to leade his life. (LL) King Estmere. *Unknown*. ESPB; OBNV; OxBB

With her would I fly. (LL) To an Isle in the Water. W. B. Yeats. AWP; TTTS

With Him in New Jerusalem. (LL) O Christmas Night. Henricus Selyns, *Dutch*. AH, *tr. by* Howard Murphy, (sts. 1, 2, 4, 6)

With him ther[e] was his son[e], a young [*or* yong *or* youthful] Squier [*or* Squyer *or* Squire]. Seven Pilgrims: A Squire [*or* Squyer]. Chaucer. Fr. The General Prologue. FHYEP; NAEL-1; NAWM-1; OAEL-1; PoE Fr. The Canterbury Tales.

With his hat on the table before him. In January, 1962. Ted Kooser. Poetsp

With his head he says no. The Dunce. Jacques Prévert, *French*. MFP, *tr. by* Martin Sorrell

With his heart. Who'd Want to Be a Man? Gregory Orr. IFJA

With his kind[e] mother who partakes thy woe. Temple. Donne. *Fr.* La Corona. ChIV-2; ESCV; Son *Fr.* Holy Sonnets.

With his music. Allen Ginsberg. *See* 'Back on Times Square, Dreaming of Times Square'.

With his pale Trophees *Death* hath hung his Armes. (LL) Sonnet: "As in a duskie [*or* dusky] and tempestuous night." William Drummond, of Hawthornden. NOSC; OxAEP-1

With his tall tales and 12-string guitar? (LL) Satchmo. Melvin Beaunearus Tolson. NAAAL

With his venom. Sappho, *Greek.* GrIP, *tr. by* Mary Barnard

With his weapon a shovel. Denis Glover. PeNZ *Fr.* Arawata Bill.

With his white hair unbonneted, the stout old sheriff comes. England's Standard. Thomas Babington Macaulay, 1st Baron Macaulay. *Fr.* The Armada. FaBoCh; FaPoR

With his work, as with a glove, a man feels the universe. Open and Closed Space. Tomas Tranströmer, *Swedish.* SPE, *tr. by* Robert Bly

With honeysuckle, over-sweet, festooned. Arbor Vitae. Coventry Patmore. OBNC; PeVV *Fr.* The Unknown Eros.

With hooks delicate as the arms of stars. Crocheting. Miroslav Holub, *German.* CEEP, *tr. by* Stuart Friebert *and* Dana Hábová

With Hopeless Love. Moses ibn Ezra, *Hebrew.* TrJP, *tr. by* Solomon Solis-Cohen

With horns and [with] hounds, I waken the day. Diana's Hunting-Song. Dryden. NOBE *Fr.* The Secular Masque. NAEL-1; OxAEP-1; PoE; PoEL-3; SCGP

With how sad steps, O Moon, thou climb'st the skies! Sonnet 31. Sir Philip Sidney. AEP; AWP; BoLoP; CABP; CH; EnLoPo; GBL; GLoP; GSo; HAP; HeIP-4; InPS-3; LoP; NAEL-1; NOBE; NoSic; OBEV; OxAEP-1; PBMP; PoE; PoEL-1; PoRA; SCGP; Son; TFi; TRP *Fr.* Astrophil and Stella. AAS; SiPS

With huge impatience, he inly swelt. The House of Busyrane. Edmund Spenser. NoSic *Fr.* Wood Of Error. AEP

With human love. (LL) A Prayer for My Son. W. B. Yeats. EBEV; OxAEP-2; RaBo; TIRV

With hyacinthine curls. (LL) The Bull. William Carlos Williams. LiTM; TwCP

With hyphens, clip off endings that don't fit. Sonneteering Made Easy. S. B. Botsford. NYBP

With implements to fly away, / Passing Pomposity? (LL) Bring me the sunset in a cup. Emily Dickinson. APN-2; MoAmPo; NOCV

With innocent wide penguin eyes, three. Bird-witted. Marianne Moore. CMoP, NAAL-2

With its baby rivers and little towns, each with its abbey or its cathedral. England. Marianne Moore. MeMAP; MoAmPo

With its cloud of skirmishers in advance. An Army Corps on the March. Walt Whitman. AiP; CBCWP; InPS-3; PoLF; SAGP

With its five fingers spread. (LL) Delta. Adrienne Rich. LoL; NIP-4; PiM

With its great length of stay. (LL) Within This Book, Called Marguerite. Marjorie Welish. FTOS; PmAP

With its rat's tooth the clock. The Alarum. Sylvia Townsend Warner. MoBrPo

With Janice. Kenneth Koch. PmAP

With jewels of my elegant pain. (LL) The Race Question. Naomi Long Madgett. LTA

With joy all relics of the past I hail. Old Ruralities: A Regret. Charles Tennyson Turner. EBVV; Son

With joy Britannia sees her fav'rite goose. To the Marquis of Graham on His Marriage. *Unknown.* OBSV

With Joy erst while, (when knotty doubts arose). Upon the Much-to Be Lamented Desease of the Reverend Mr. John Cotton. John Fiske. SCAP

With joy the guardian Angel sees. Samuel's Prayer. John Keble. ChIV-1

With King Cole and his fiddlers three [!]. (LL) Old King Cole was a merry old soul. Mother Goose. FaBoBe; LB; OTCP; OxNR; ReMoGo

With Kit, Age 7, at the Beach. William Stafford. *See* With Kit, Age Seven, at the Beach.

With Kit, Age Seven, at the Beach. William Stafford. LiLi; RaBo

With last night's wine still singing in my head. Ode 487. Hafiz, *Persian.* EP, *tr. by* Richard Le Gallienne

With leaden foot Time creeps along. Absence. Richard Jago. OBEV

With Lee Remick at Midnight. Ron Padgett. WWSi

With leering looks, bullfac'd, and freckled fair. On Jacob Tonson, His Publisher. Dryden. FaBoEE; OBSV

With Life and Death I walked when Love appeared. Hymn to Colour. George Meredith. OBNC

With lifted feet, hands still. Going Down Hill on a Bicycle. Henry Charles Beeching. NOxBChV; OBEV

With lightly closed fists and arms partially rais'd. (LL) The Runner. Walt Whitman. BLT; InPK-6; InPS-3; SAmP

With lightly closed fists and arms partially raised. Walt Whitman. *See* The Runner.

With lips of flame and heart of stone. (LL) Impression Du Matin. Oscar Wilde. ADE; EBVV; MoBrPo; NAEL-2; NoAM

With little here to do or see. To the Daisy. Wordsworth. GTBS-P

With loitering step and quiet eye. In November. Archibald Lampman. NOBC

With longing I am lad. *Unknown.* MiEL

With love and longings infinite. Wordsworth. *See* The Affliction of Margaret—.

With love exceeding a simple love of the things. Melampus. George Meredith. PoEL-5

With lovers 'twas of old the fashion. To a Young Lady, with Some Lampreys. John Gay. CABP; CBLP; ECEV; EP; NOEC; OBCoV

With low thunder, with red bushes smooth. Red Rock Ceremonies. Anita Endrezze-Danielson. CDW; VoR

With lullay, lullay, like a child[e]. Lullay, Lullay, Like a Child. John Skelton. ImPo; NoSic; SCGP *Fr.* The Garland [*or* Garlande *or* Garlands] of Laurel[l].

With maggots and rotten dust and ages of repose. I lie here and plot the agony of resurrection. (LL) Antrim. Robinson Jeffers. BIrV; IIP; NOBA; VGW

With malice toward none. Second Inaugural Address. Abraham Lincoln. CTV *Fr.* Second Inaugural Address.

With Mannerly Margery Milk and Ale. (LL) Mannerly Margery Mylk and Ale. John Skelton. AAS; NAEL-1; NoP-4

With many a weary step, and many a groan. Homer. UV *Fr.* Odyssey. NAWM-1, *tr. by* Robert Fitzgerald

With marjoram [*or* margerain] gentle. To Mistress Margery Wentworth. John Skelton. EBEV; EnLoPo; NOBE; OAEL-1; OBEV *Fr.* The Garland [*or* Garlande *or* Garlands] of Laurel[l].

With Me My Lover Makes. C. Day Lewis. OBMV

With Meaning. John Weiners. BB

With Mercy for the Greedy. Anne Sexton. HCAP; TOF; VCAP

With mighty hand the Holy Lord. The Temptation and Fall of Man. Caedmon. AnOE, *tr. by* C. W. Kennedy *Fr.* Genesis.

With morning in the sky. (LL) Oh Sumptuous moment. Emily Dickinson. NAAL-1; NAAL-3

With morning tears thy mournful twilight blesses. (LL) A Letter from a Girl to Her Own Old Age. Alice Thompson Meynell. MoBrPo; VWP

With much ado you fail to tell. A Critic. Walter Savage Landor. FaBoEE

With music strong I come, with my cornets and my drums. Walt Whitman. *Fr.* Song of Myself. AmPP; MoAmPo; NAAL-3; NOBA; OxBA

With my breath I cut my way through the six forests. Lalleswari, *Kashmiri.* WPOW, *tr. by* George Grierson, *ad. by* Deirdre Lashgari

With My Crowbar Key. William Stafford. CoAmPo

With my forked branch of Lebanese cedar. The Dowser. Edwin Morgan. FaBoTC; NoP-2

With my frailty don't upbraid me. Semele to Jupiter. William Congreve. OBCoV

With my hand over my mouth. (LL) A Poem for Trapped Things. John Wieners. GLP; NeAP; PmAP; PoM

With my heart I worship. Saint Thomas Aquinas, *Latin.* MLL, *tr. by* Helen Waddell

With my large eyes which needed nothing. Slavko Mihalic. *See* Drinking Spree Beneath the Open Sky.

With my looks I am bound to look simple or fast I would rather look simple. Magna Est Veritas. Stevie Smith. OxBC

With my many illnesses I meet the spring. The First Day of Spring. Pien Kung, *Chinese.* CoBLCP, *tr. by* Jonathan Chaves

With my oldest son, I talk. Long Distance Calls. Marylee Skwirz. IFJA

With my own hands. (LL) Beneath the Shadow of the Freeway. Lorna Dee Cervantes. NMM-2; PBCAP

With my seven-fold inquisitorial eye. Submarine Tombs. Jean-Baptiste Tati-Loutard. PBMAP

With my teeth. No. Not this pig. (LL) Animals Are Passing from Our Lives. Philip Levine. CoAP; ColAP; NOBA; Poetr; RaBo; TAP; WeT

With nerves all shattered and worn. Song of the Sheet. *Unknown.* BXAP

With nets and kitchen sieves they raid the pond. The Pond. Anthony Thwaite. NYBP

With night full of spring and stars we stand. Young Girls. Raymond Souster. HeIP-4

With no flower buds. Tanka. Yosano Tekkan, *Japanese.* MJT, *tr. by* Makoto Ueda

With no money. Alan Pizzarelli. HA

With no star in its crown. (LL) Massacre of the Boys. Tadeusz Rózewicz, *Polish.* HP, *tr. by* Adam Czerniawski; AF, *tr. by* Robert A. Maguire *and* Magnus Jan Krynski

With noiseless steps good goes its way. The World. Ella Wheeler Wilcox. PWR

With north / over / the barn. (LL) Wherelings whenlings / (daughters of if but offspring of hopefear). E. E. Cummings. HAP; WeW-3

With nothing but the name of a drifter in the blue houses. (LL) Easing My Heart. Tu Mu, *Chinese*. NNPT; PLT, *tr. by* A. C. Graham

With nothing in our pockets. (LL) Song: Lift-Boy. Robert Graves. NTP; OxAEP-2

With nought to hide or to betray. L'Amitié et l'Amour. John Swanwick Drennan. BIrV

With old hours all belfry heads. Ding-Donging. Laura Riding Jackson. NoP-4

With old pleasures. (LL) The Long River. Donald Hall. CoAmPo; LCAP-2

With one arm as long as the other. (LL) Our Lady of Ardboe. Paul Muldoon. BiHa; PBCIP

With one bold stoke. The Corporal Who Killed Archimedes. Miroslav Holub, *Czech*. PoSu, *tr. by* Ian *and* Jarmila Milner

With one breath he makes the place green. On Bismillah Khan's Shehnai. Chennavira Kanavi, *Kannada*. OMIP, *tr. by* A. K. Ramanujan

With one consuming roar along the shingle. Felixstowe, or, The Last of Her Order. John Betjeman. OxBTC

With one who safeguards Gwynedd. The Stallion. Tudur Aled, *Welsh*. OBWVE, *tr. by* Joseph P. Clancy

With only his feeble lantern. Charon's Cosmology. Charles Simic. HCAP; PoPoPo

With only itself to love. (LL) Elvin's Blues. Michael S. Harper. LoL

With only night to hear them as they pass. (LL) An Exchange Of Feelings. Paul Verlaine, *French*. FLP; LoP, *tr. by* Alistair Elliot

With open ears, and with unfolded arms. (LL) Boldness[e] in Love. Thomas Carew. CaPo; CavPo

With opening and shutting wings. *Unknown. See* Song of the Fallen Deer.

With other women I beheld my love. Ballata: Of His Lady among Other Ladies. Guido Cavalcanti, *Italian*. AWP, *tr. by* D. G. Rossetti

With others / from the neighborhood. Shine. Léon Damas, *French*. NegPo, *tr. by* Ellen Conroy Kennedy

With others hast thou no will to make company. (LL) Canto 36. Ezra Pound. CTC; OBVE

With our monocles, our frayed pants. Another Planet. Boris Iulianovich Poplavsky, *Russian*. TCRP, *tr. by* Emmet Jarrett *and* Richard Lourie

With our own brown hands. (LL) What the Gypsy Said to Her Children. Judith Ortiz Cofer. OxWW; UnSA

With outward signs, as well as inward life. The First Atlantic Telegraph. Jones Very. NCAP

With oxygen simmering and morhpine peaking. Still Life. Veronica Morgan. CMAP

With Pantheist energy of will. Venice. Herman Melville. APN-2

With paste of almonds Syb her hands doth scour[e]. Upon Sibilla. Robert Herrick. CaPo

With peace, let tares and acorns be my food. (LL) The Country-Mouse. Abraham Cowley, *after the Latin of* Horace. OBVE; SeCP

With perilous stairs / Between. (LL) The Treehouse. James A. Emanuel. BPo; PoBA

With pinched cheeks hollow and wan. The Outcast. Josephine D. Henderson Heard. CBWP-4

With porcupine locks. The Katzenjammer Kids. James Reaney. MoCV

With pride they were decieved—and so to hell they went, Sections 3-24. Philip Freneau. *See* The Vision of the Night.

With proud thanksgiving, a mother for her children. For the Fallen. Laurence Binyon. EBEvV; NOBE; OBEV; OBWP; OxBTC; PoFWW

With rain. Wallace Stevens. *See* A Room on a Garden.

With red eyes. Tanka. Miyazawa Kenji, *Japanese*. MJT, *tr. by* Makoto Ueda

With reeds and bird-lime from the desert air. On a Fowler. Isidorus, *Greek*. AWP, *tr. by* William Cowper

With Reservations. Naomi Stroud Simmons. IFJA

With respect to the understanding of what is symbolized. (LL) Money. Howard Nemerov. OxBC; VCAP; WeW-3

With reverence and submission due. A Petition from the Chain Gang at Newcastle to Captain Furlong the Superintendent. Francis MacNamara. NOBAu

With rhetoric, promising nothing under the sun. (LL) Ecclesiastes. Derek Mahon. BIrV; CIP-2; ChIV-1; PNI

With right all my herte now I you grete. *Unknown*. MiEL

With rocks and stones and trees! (LL) Slumber *did* my spirit *seal*, A. Wordsworth. LaPo; NoP-4; PFE; PoPoPo; Ro

With ruder pomp, in more barbaric taste. William Gilmore Simms. APN-1 *Fr*. The City of the Silent.

With rue my heart is laden. Samuel Hoffenstein. NBLV *Fr*. The Mimic Muse.

With rue my heart is laden. A. E. Housman. AWP; CMoP; HAP; HeIP-4; HoPM; ImPo; InPK-6; LiTM; MoBrPo; NAEL-2; NoAM; NoP-4; PFE; PoE; PoPoPo; Poetr; SAGP; TFi; UnPo

With serving still. Sir Thomas Wyatt. InPK-6; NoSic; SiPS

With seven matching calfskin cases for his new suits. Home Leave. Barbara Howes. TwCP

With Ships the sea was sprinkled far and nigh. Wordsworth. SCGP

With shoes on. Going Barefoot. Judith Thurman. AYFP

With sick and famished [*or* famisht] eyes. Longing. George Herbert. ESCV; UV

With sick and famisht eyes. George Herbert. *See* Longing.

With silent Melancholy. (LL) Song: "Memory, hither come." William Blake. NAEL-2; PoEL-4

With sleep-drunken birds. Safe-Conduct. Ingeborg Bachmann, *German*. PoSu, *tr. by* Daniel Huws

With snort and pant the engine dragged. The Song of the Engine. H. Worsley-Benison. BoTP

With snow-white veil and garments as of flame. Henry Wadsworth Longfellow. *Fr*. Divina Commedia. APN-1; OxBA; TAP

With snowy light of moon I cannot you compare. Martin Opitz, *German*. GePo, *tr. by* George C. Schoolfield

With So Many Voices. Lyn Lifshin. DeD

With sober wondring, and with sweet delight. (LL) The Praise of Dancing. Sir John Davies. NOBE; PoEL-2

With solitude what sorts, that here's not wondrous rife? Michael Drayton. NOSC *Fr*. Polyolbion.

With something of angelic light. (LL) She was a Phantom of delight. Wordsworth. CTV; FaBoBe; GTBS-P; HeIP-4; ImPo; NoP-4; OAEL-2; OBEV; PBMP; PWR; PoEL-4; SCGP; TFi

With songs and honors sounding loud. Edom. Isaac Watts. AmFP

With songs of Liberty! (LL) On Liberty and Slavery. George Moses Horton. AAP; APN-1; PAR

With sorrow we number on his book. (LL) On Ben Jonson. Sidney Godolphin. BeJo; EPCY

With sorrow I recall. Tanka. Nakajō Fumiko, *Japanese*. MJT, *tr. by* Makoto Ueda

With spangles gay and candle light. The Christmas Tree. Isabel De Savitzsky. BoTP

With speculums examining / that real estate men want. Warrior Daughters. Colette Inez. NMM-2

With spices, wines, and silken stuffs. The Singer. Lizette Woodworth Reese. SDW

With stones, then drive away. (LL) Paul Laurence Dunbar. Robert Earl Hayden. GT; NoP-4

With such a sound of gently pitying laughter. (LL) My Grandmother's Love Letters. Hart Crane. CMoP; FaBoBe; InPK-6; NOBA; NoAM; NoP-4; Poetr

With such a throb does blood. Joy of Knowledge. Isidor Schneider. TrJP

With such compelling cause to grieve. Tennyson. EBVV *Fr*. In Memoriam A. H. H.

With such delights he can forget. Horace. OBCVT, *tr. by* Charles Hubert Sisson *Fr*. Epode 2.

With such rebukes mens mindes upkindled staied, and thick with preas. Turnus' retreat. Virgil, *Latin*. OBCVT, *tr. by* Thomas Phaer

With summer comes the. Haiku: The Season of Celebrity. Gavin Ewart. APAD

With sun on his back and sun on his belly. Pig. Paul Éluard, *French*. TTTS, *tr. by* Kenneth Koch

With supping cold plum [*or* pease] porridge. (LL) The Man in the moon. *Unknown*. CBNP; LB; OxBoLi; OxNR

With sweet surprise, as when one finds a flower. On Finding the Truth. Jones Very. TrCP

With sweetest milk and sugar first. The Nymph and Her Fawn. Andrew Marvell. BoTP; CTAV; FaBoCh *Fr*. The Nymph Complaining for the Death of Her Faun [*or* Fawn]. CH; ESCV; GeHe; HeIP-4; NAEL-1; OAEL-1; PoEL-2; SeCP

With tall-necked Hesperia and the Medes. A Bridge on the Sangarios. Agathias, *Greek*. GrAn, *tr. by* Guy Davenport

With tearful eye, how frequent have I seen. Mary Latter. ECWP *Fr*. Soliloquies on Temporal Indigence.

With tears of recognition never dry. (LL) A Farewell. Coventry Patmore. BoLoP; EnLoPo; GLoP; GTBS-P; NOBE; OBEV; OBNC; PoEL-5

With tears thy grief thou dost bemoan. Stanzas. Solomon ibn Gabirol, *Hebrew*. TrJP, *tr. by* Emma Lazarus

With tender back glistening. Bella Abramovna Dizhur, *Russian*. TCRP, *tr. by* Sarah W. Bliumis

With Tendrils of Poems. Michael McClure. PoM

With that delight the royal captive's brought. Richard Lovelace. *See* The Lady A. L., My Asylum [in a Great Extremity].

With that delight the royal captiv[e]'s brought. The Lady A. L., My Asylum [in a Great Extremity]. Richard Lovelace. CaPo

With that, he rais'd his tuneful voice aloud. Silenus sings. Virgil, *Latin*. OBCVT, *tr. by* Roscommon Wentworth Dillon, 4th Earl of (c.1683-1685)

With that he stripped him to the ivory skin. Amorous Neptune. Marlowe. NOBE. *Fr.* Hero and Leander. AAS

With that I saw two swans of goodly hue. Edmund Spenser. *Fr.* Prothalamion. AAS; AWP; EBEV; GTBS-P; HAP; NoP-4; NoSic; OBEV; TFi

With that low cunning, which in fools supplies. Character of a Critic. Charles Churchill. NOEC *Fr.* The Rosciad.

With that mine hand in his he took anon. The Parliament of Fowls. Chaucer. OBGa *Fr.* The Parliament of Fowls.

With that more learn'd professor, Ruhnken. (LL) Epigram on an Academic Visit to the Continent. Richard Porson. FaBoEE; OxBoLi; PeLV

With that the Wretched Child expires. (LL) Henry King, Who Chewed Bits of String, and Was Early Cut Off in Dreadful Agonies. Hilaire Belloc. FuFo; NBLV; OBCoV; OxAEP-2; PeLV

With the absolute heart of the poem of life butchered out of their own bodies good to eat a thousand years. (LL) Howl. Allen Ginsberg. MoP; NoAM; PmAP; VCAP

With the All-Highest's Son, inseperable from Him. (LL) Patmos. Friedrich Hölderlin, *German.* GrIP; OBVE, *tr. by* David Gascoyne

With the blue. Tanka. Maekawa Samio, *Japanese.* MJT, *tr. by* Makoto Ueda

With the blue-dark dome old-starred at night, green boat-lights purring over. Allen Ginsberg. *See* Galilee Shore.

With the blue-dark dome old-starred at night, green boat-lights purring over water. Galilee Shore. Allen Ginsberg. ChIV-2

With the boys busy. Philomena Andronico. William Carlos Williams. FaBoMo

With the china and tea-leaves. (LL) Modern Secrets. Shirley Lim. OPOU; UnSA

With the Dawn. Thomas Caulfield Irwin. BIrV; EnLoPo

With the door closed. (LL) Hanging Fire. Audre Lorde. NIP-4; NMM-2; NoAM; NoP-4; PoPoPo; Poetr; TRP

With the exact length and pace of his father's stride. For a Father. Anthony Cronin. FaBoTw

With the festival hour close at hand. King Kiḷḷi in Combat. Cattantaiyar, *Tamil.* PLW, *tr. by* A. K. Ramanujan

With the first gray light of dawn the remnants. Broken Off by the Music. John Yau. EOEF

With the first rains. The Girl Friend Describes the Bull Fight. Uruttiran, *Tamil.* PLW, *tr. by* A. K. Ramanujan

With the forks of flowers I eat the meat of morning. Lyric by Nine. *Unknown.* SPE

With the foul rain than rains on poverty. (LL) Lean Street. George Sutherland Fraser. FaBoTC

With the gipsies dancing round me. (LL) The Gipsy Laddie. *Unknown.* FaBoCh; OxBoLi

With the gods overthrown like that, nobody knew which way to / turn. The End of Dodona II. Yannis Ritsos, *Greek.* VCWP, *tr. by* Edmund Keeley

With the Grain. Donald Davie. NoAM

With the grave's narrowness, though not its peace. (LL) Sick Love. Robert Graves. BoLoP; CMoP; EBEV; FaBoMo; GTBS-P; HAP; NOBE; OAEL-2; OxAEP-2

With the green lamp of the spirit. Into the Glacier. John Haines. CoAP

With the Herring Fishers. "Hugh MacDiarmid." CABP; LiTM

With the it : to know that I am it. (LL) Despisals. Muriel Rukeyser. CPO; NMM-2

With the last lamp. Scott Montgomery. HA

With the last whippoorwill call of evening. Birmingham. Margaret Abigail Walker. PoBA

With the lilt of sunlight in their bones. (LL) Hymn to the Sun. Michael Roberts. FaBoCh; OxBTC

With the man behind me. Man. Ioan Alexandru, *Romanian.* CEEP, *tr. by* Andrei Banta *and* Thomas Amherst Perry

With the men of that old time? (LL) Sequel of Appomattox. Donald Davidson. CBCWP; FuPo

With the Mickey Mouse. The Girl in the Hall. John A. Stone. MT

With the music up high. Snake-Back Solo. Quincy Troupe. MoNo

With the Nice Caution of a sword between. (LL) The Antiplatonic[k]. John Cleveland. CBLP; NOSC; PBRV; SeCP

With the night half over. Philodemus, *Greek.* GrAn, *tr. by* William Moebius

With the night, my demon appears. Magdalene (I). Boris Pasternak, *Russian.* GI, *tr. by* Nina Kossman

With the old kindness, the old distinguished grace. Upon a Dying Lady. W. B. Yeats. UnPo

With the open eyes of their dead fathers. War. Andrey Andreievich Voznesensky, *Russian.* RB, *tr. by* William Jay Smith *and* Vera Dunham

With the other husks of summer. (LL) The Dragonfly. Louise Bogan. HeIP-4; Poetr

With the passion of / plain day. (LL) Star. Derek Walcott. PFE; PiM

With the Pawness, lying low, / Lying low. (LL) The Flower-fed buffaloes of the spring. Vachel Lindsay. CA; CMoP; MoAmPo; NOBA; OBCA; PoE; RB; TRP; VGW

With the persons / on the edge. (LL) Paean to Place. Lorine Niedecker. APSN; FTOS

With the Quangle Wangle Quee. (LL) The Quangle Wangle's Hat. Edward Lear. CBNP; EBEV; FPC; PeVV

With the Rain. Amir Gilbo'a, *Hebrew.* IP, *tr. by* Warren Bargad *and* Stanley F. Chyet

With the richest royalest seed. (LL) Lines on the Tombs in Westminster. Francis Beaumont. CH; FaBoCh; FaPoR; GTBS-P; HAP; NOBE; OBEV; OxAEP-1; SCGP

With [*or* Wi'] the Scotch [*or* Scots] lords at his feet. (LL) Sir Patrick Spens [*or* Spence]. *Unknown.* AWP; AmFP; BXAP; CH; ClHu; EBEV; ESPB; EnSB; FaBoCh; FaPoR; GEA; HAP; HoPM; InPK-6; InPS-3; NAEL-1; NIP-4; NOBE; NoP-4; OAEL-1; OBEV; OBSP; OxBB; OxBS; PBMP; PoE; PoEL-1; PoPoPo; RB; SCGP; TFi; UnPo; WeW-3

With the shining fields of mud. (LL) Youth and Age on Beaulieu River, Hants. John Betjeman. FaBoTw; TwCP

With the shrewd and upright man. Fool and False. *Unknown.* *Fr.* The Panchatantra. AWP, *tr. by* Arthur Ryder

With the slow smokeless burning of decay. (LL) The Wood-Pile. Robert Frost. ColAP; InPK-6; NAAL-2; NoAM; NoP-4; SAmP; VGW

With the straw of misery rotting in the steel / of cannons. (LL) Pater Noster. Jacques Prévert, *French.* CLPP, *tr. by* Lawrence Ferlinghetti

With the sweet food she makes. (LL) How doth the little busy bee. Isaac Watts. CTV; EBEvV; HoPM; OxAEP-1; UV

With the swing of his demon's tail. (LL) The Tom-Cat. Don Marquis. PC

With the swinging rainbow on his shoulder. (LL) Legend. Judith Wright. NOBAu; NTP; RB

With the thinking of winter. The Cook. Ray A. Young Bear. CDW

With the thought of the light / Of the eyes of my Annie. Edgar Allan Poe. *See* For Annie.

With the Tide: A Cry of Weakness. Louisa Sarah Bevington. PEW *Fr.* Two songs.

With the wasp at the innermost heart of a peach. A Scherzo. Dora Greenwell. NOBVV; PEW; SDW

With Thee a moment! Then what dreams have play! Desire. "Æ." OBMV; TIRV

With thee conversing I forget all time. Eve to Adam. Milton. GBL; UV *Fr.* Book IV. OAEL-1 *Fr.* Paradise Lost.

With thee, men cannot mock us in the clay. (LL) Away, Delights. Francis Beaumont *and* John Fletcher. GBL; NOBE; OBEV

With thee, sweet *Bion*, all the grace of Song. Moschus. OBCVT, *tr. by* John Oldham *Fr.* Bion. A Pastoral, in Imitation of the Greek of Moschus, bewailing the Death of the Earl of Rochester.

With their boxing-glove muzzles. Cattle. Peter Skrzynecki. CBAP

With their brains, the rugged faces / Of the rocks and stony places, *par. by* Thomas Carew. Bible, *O.T. See* Psalm 137.

With their evil eyes. Catullus. *See* Carmen 5 ("My sweetest Lesbia, let us live and love").

With their feet in the earth. Tall Trees. Eileen Mathias. BoTP

With their gifts to a difficult borning. (LL) The Manor Garden. Sylvia Plath. FaBoWP; LCAP-2

With their harsh leaves old rhododendrons fill. The Mountain Cemetery. Edgar Bowers. CoAmPo

With their lithe, long, strong legs. Bullfrog. Ted Hughes. NYBP

With their respective lions. Sea Unicorns and Land Unicorns. Marianne Moore. NALW; PFTM

With these came they who, from the bord'ring flood. Milton. OxBSn *Fr.* Paradise Lost.

With these green guests around. Who Says That Drought Was Here? Niyi Osundare. HBAPE

With these heaven-assailing spires. New York. "Æ." OBMV

With these poor offerings, a man like thee. (LL) To Leigh Hunt, Esq. Keats. OBNC; Son

With this ambiguous earth. Christ in the Universe. Alice Thompson Meynell. MoBrPo; NOBE; OxAEP-2; VWP

With this evening lake I hold discourse in the high. Above the Lake. Aleksandr Blok, *Russian.* TCRP, *tr. by* Geoffrey Thurley

With this, my derisive voice. (LL) Seven Sides and Seven Syllables. Edouard J. Maunick, *French.* NegPo; VCWP, *tr. by* Carolyn Kizer

With those who. Tanka. Sasaki Yukitsuna, *Japanese.* MJT, *tr. by* Makoto Ueda

With thoughts that please me less and less betray me. (LL) Farewell to Cupid. Greville Fulke. GBL; Son

With thy rugged, ice-girt shore. Alaska. Mary Weston Fordham. CBWP-2

With Timbrels. Bible, Apocrypha. TrJP *Fr.* Judith.

With time / and space. The Poet the Dreamer. Norman Jordan. NBV

With toilsome steps I pass through life's dull road. Addressed to ———. Lady Mary Wortley Montagu. ECWP

With tossed–aside, bruised fruit. (LL) To the Days. Adrienne Rich. BAP-93; LoL

With treble vivas and limp hedgerow flags. The Vanquished. Charles Eglington. PeSA

With trees backing them / instead of the pit's mouth. A Photo of Miners. Brendan Galvin. AFr

With trembling fingers did we weave. Tennyson. EBVV; FHYEP; OAEL-2 *Fr.* In Memoriam A. H. H.

With troubled heart and trembling hand I write. In Memory of My Dear Grandchild Anne Bradstreet Who Deceased June 20, 1669, Being Three Years and Seven Months Old. Anne Bradstreet. BoWoP; NAAL-1; NAAL-3; TrCP

With true-love showers. (LL) Ophelia's Song. Shakespeare. CH; EBEV; EBEvV; EnLoPo; GBL; NoSic; PoRA; SCGP

With trumpets clap and syphilis. (LL) Come, gaze with me upon this dome. E. E. Cummings. NoAM; OxBA

With two strange fires of equal heat possessed [*or* possest]. Love and Jealousy. Sir Philip Sidney. SiPS *Fr.* Arcadia.

With two white roses on her breasts. A Brown Girl Dead. Countee Cullen. GT; TAP

With *Usura*. Canto 45. Ezra Pound. CMoP; LiTM; MeMAP; NAAL-2; NOBA; PoE *Fr.* Cantos.

With usura hath no man a house of good stone. Canto XLV. Ezra Pound. ColAP

With vinegar / and brown paper. (LL) Jack and Gill [*or* Jill] went up the hill. Mother Goose. LB

With vision out of the reach of the field edges. The Winter Vision. Kunbae Yi, *Korean.* CKP, *tr. by* Jaihiun Kim

With visionary care. Summer Noon: 1941. Yvor Winters. ColAP

With walking sick, with curtseys lame. The Visit. Mary Leapor. ECWP

With walloping tails, the whales off Wales. The Whales off Wales. X. J. Kennedy. OBCA

With warts and all. Tanka. Yosano Tekkan, *Japanese.* MJT, *tr. by* Makoto Ueda

With water? (LL) A Statue Of Eros. Zenodotus, *Greek.* GrAn; LoP, *tr. by* Peter Jay

With water warm enough to make me. The Black and White Galaxie. Michael S. Weaver. UnSA

With what a gentle sound. September. Henrietta Cordelia Ray. CBWP-3

With what anguish of mind I remember my childhood. The Old Oaken Bucket. *Unknown.* BLPA

With what attentive courtesy he bent. The Guitarist Tunes Up. Frances Darwin Cornford. SoSe-8

With what Concern I sat and heard your Play. To My Much Esteemed Friend on Her Play Call'd Fatal-Friendship. Lady Sarah Piers. KTR

With what deep murmurs through time's silent stealth. The Waterfall [*or* Water-Fall]. Henry Vaughan. ESCV; FMP; FSCP; GeHe; MeLP; NAEL-1; NOBE; NOCV; NOSC; NoP-4; OBWVE; OxAEP-1; PBRV; PoEL-2

With what, O Codrus! is thy fancy smit? Edward Young. *Fr.* Love of Fame, the Universal Passion. OBSV

With what painful deliberation he comes down the stair. English Cocker: Old and Blind. Robert Penn Warren. APo

With what reluctance they endure restraints. Sarah Fyge Egerton. *See* The Liberty.

With what reluctance they indure restraints. (LL) The Liberty. Sarah Fyge Egerton. KTR

With what sharp checks I in myself am shent. Sonnet 18. Sir Philip Sidney. NAEL-1; NoSic *Fr.* Astrophil and Stella. AAS; SiPS

With what voice. Spider. Basho, *Japanese.* TTTS

With which we were christenèd . (LL) As Joseph Was a-Walking. *Unknown.* BoTP; PChr

With wild hair, you block out your characters. To Chin Nung. Cheng Hsieh, *Chinese.* CoBLCP, *tr. by* Jonathan Chaves

With wild surmise. Reed Whittemore. *See* The Party.

With wine and words of love and every vow. Seduced Girl. Hedylos, *Greek.* BoLoP, *tr. by* Louis Untermeyer

With wine glasses. Alexis Rotella. HA

With wings held close and slim neck bent. Swans. Leonora Speyer. FYAP

With woman's form and woman's tricks. To Miss———. Thomas Moore. OxBSP

With words too sad and strange to syllable. (LL) Two in August. John Crowe Ransom. AWP; MeMAP; OxBA

With worms eternally. (LL) To the Oaks of Glencree. John Millington Synge. MoBrPo; NOIV

With wrinkled hide and great frayed ears. Gunga. Rachel Lyman Field. OBCA *Fr.* A Circus Garland.

With yellow and purple plums. (LL) Idleness. Lu Yu, *Chinese.* OHPC; OxBM, *tr. by* Kenneth Rexroth

With yellow pears leans over. Half of Life. Friedrich Hölderlin, *German.* OBVE, *tr. by* James Blair Leishman

With you a part of me hath passed away. George Santayana. PFE *Fr.* To W. P.

With you away—despair! Quatrain. Rudaki, *Persian.* ArPe, *tr. by* Omar S. Pound

With you, fair maid. (LL) The Fair Maid of Amsterdam. *Unknown.* OxBoLi; PeLV; RB

With you first shown to me. William Barnes. EnLoPo

With you for mast and sail and flag. The Narrow Sea. Robert Graves. FaBoEE; FaBoMo

With you here at Mertu. *Unknown, Egyptian hieroglyphics into Italian.* PBWP, *tr. by* Boris de Rachewiltz; *English vers. by* Ezra Pound *and* Noel Stock

With you I have refound my name. David Diop, *French.* NegPo, *tr. by* Ellen Conroy Kennedy

With your beautiful hair and seemly. *Unknown, Greek.* PGA, *tr. by* Kenneth Rexroth

With your Death full of Flowers. (LL) IV. Allen Ginsberg. BB

With your fair eyes a charming light I see. Love, the Light-Giver [*or* To Tommaso de' Cavalieri]. Michelangelo Buonarroti, *Italian.* AWP, *tr. by* John Addington Symonds

With your name, I shall name this homeless year. Oleg Grigorevich Chukhonstev, *Russian.* TCRP, *tr. by* Simon Franklin

With your wine jars open. Farewell to Pāri's Hill. Kapilar, *Tamil.* PLW, *tr. by* A. K. Ramanujan

With youthful loss of memory, in my voiceless land. Stanzas. Viktor Korkiya, *Russian.* TCRP, *tr. by* Vera Dunham

Withal a meagre [*or* meager] man was Aaron Stark. Aaron Stark. Edwin Arlington Robinson. APN-2; MeMAP; MoAmPo; Son

Withdrawal Letter. Jim Carroll. PmAP

Withdrawn from layers of upper air, ice-blue and clear. Suburb Hilltop. Richard Moore. NYBP

Withered flowers fill the courtyard. A Sorrow in the Harem. Wang Ch'ang-ling, *Chinese.* OHMPC, *tr. by* Kenneth Rexroth

Withered grass on the plain. Tune: "Song of Dandy"—Hunting in Autumn. Na-lan Hsing-te, *Chinese.* SuSp, *tr. by* Bruce Carpenter

Withered leaves that drift in Russell Square, The. Drilling in Russell Square. Edward Richard Burton Shanks. OBMV

Withered Rose, A. "Yehoash," *Yiddish.* TrJP, *tr. by* Isidore Goldstick

Withered Tree, A. Han Yü, *Chinese.* PLT, *tr. by* A. C. Graham

Withered vines, old tree. Autumn Thoughts. Ma Chih-yüan. CoBLCP, *tr. by* Jonathan Chaves *Fr.* To the Tune "T'ien ching sha."

Withered vines, old trees, crows at dusk. Tune: "Sky-clear Sand"—Autumn Thoughts. Ma Chih-yüan, *Chinese.* SuSp, *tr. by* Sherwin S. S. Fu

Withering plum blossoms by the wayside station. Tune: "Treading on Grass." Ou-yang Hsiu, *Chinese.* SuSp, *tr. by* An-yan Tang

Within. In This Place. Robert C. Fuentes. BAP-96

Within a budding grove. Spring: The Lover and the Birds. William Allingham. OBNC

Within a copse, I met a shepherd-maid. Ballata: Concerning a Shepherd-Maid. Guido Cavalcanti, *Italian.* AWP, *tr. by* D. G. Rossetti

Within a dark and cheerless hut. The Old Saint's Prayer. Priscilla Jane Thompson. CBWP-2

Within a delicate grey ruin. The Vestal Lady on Brattle. Gregory Corso. Poetr

Within a frame, more glorious than the gem. Woman. Frances Sargent Osgood. ColAP

Within a garden all alone. Mary, The Mother of Jesus. Ada Belle Gardner. PWR

Within a greenwood sweet of myrtle savour. *Unknown, Italian.* GBL

Within a native hut, ere stirred the dawn. Nativity. Gladys May Casely Hayford. PBA; TTY

Within a thick and spreading hawthorn bush. The Thrush's Nest. John Clare. BoTP

Within an open curled Sea of Gold. A Vision. Edward Herbert, 1st Baron Herbert of Cherbury. SeCP

Within Heaven's circle I had not guessed at this. The Flight into Egypt. Peter Quennell. ImPo; LiTM

Within Her Hair. "E. C." *Fr.* Emaricdulfe. Son

Within his eyes are hung lamps of the sanctuary. The Poet. "Michael Field." ADE

Within his little parlour—but she ne'er came out again! Mary Howitt. *See* The Spider and the Fly.

Within his office, smiling. The Dove. Victor James Daley. NOBAu

Within King's College Chapel, Cambridge. Wordsworth. *See* Inside of King's College Chapel, Cambridge.

Within my casement came one night. The Dawn of Love. Henrietta Cordelia Ray. BiSi; CBWP-3

Within my Garden, rides a Bird. Emily Dickinson. AmPP

Within my head, aches the perpetual winter. Winter and Summer. Stephen Spender. MoBrPo

Within My Heart. Judah Al-Harizi, *Hebrew*. TrJP

Within my heart a stab I felt. En las Internas Entrañas. Saint, of Avila Theresa, *Spanish*. WPOW, tr. by Father Benedict Zimmerman

Within my heart for ever. (LL) Perdy [or Perdie or Perdye], I said[e] it [or yt] not. Sir Thomas Wyatt. PoEL-1; SiPS

Within my heart Love himself made Heliodora. Meleager. HePo, tr. by Barbara Hughes Fowler *Fr.* I'll Twine White Violets. NIP-4, tr. by Goldwin Smith

Within our power. (LL) In this short Life. Emily Dickinson. NTP; SAmP

Within that porch, across the way. The Cat. W. H. Davies. NOBE

Within— / The beaten pride. Uncle Tom. Langston Hughes. SAmP

Within the Casket of thy Coelick Breast. An Acrostick on Mrs. Winifret Griffin. John Saffin. SCAP

Within the circuit of this plodding life. Winter Memories. Henry David Thoreau. AmPP; ColAP; NOBA; OxBA

Within the covert of a shady grove. Love Sleeping. Plato, *Greek*. AWP; FaBoEE, tr. by Thomas Stanley

Within the dream you said. Philip Larkin. InPS-3

Within the dungeon's noxious gloom. The Cell. John Thelwall. NOEC

Within the flower there lies a seed. Spell of Creation. Kathleen Jessie Raine. FaBoCh; OxBS

Within the gentle heart Love shelters him. Of the Gentle Heart. Guido Guinicelli, *Italian*. AWP; CTC; OBVE, tr. by D. G. Rossetti

Within the Gorges there is no lack of men. Invitation to Hsiao Ch'u-shih. Po Chü-i, *Chinese*. ChiP; OBVE, tr. by Arthur Waley

Within the great grey flapping tent. The Auction Sale. Henry Reed. MoBrPo

Within the great wall's perfect round. The Window. Edwin Muir. LiTM

Within the Greenhouse Effect. Veronica Morgan. CMAP

Within the groves of Grongar Hill. (LL) Grongar Hill. John Dyer. CABP; NOEC; NoP-4; OxAEP-1; PoEL-3

Within the navel of this hideous wood. Castle. Milton. OxBSn *Fr.* Comus: a Masque Presented at Ludlow.

Within the oak a throb of pigeon wings. A Twilight in Middle March. Francis Ledwidge. BIrV

Within the palace sits a mangy king. A Game of Chess. Phan chu Trinh, *Vietnamese*. AVP, tr. by Huỳnh Sanh Thông

Within the pale blue haze above. The Storm. Coventry Patmore. EnLoPo

Within the purple graph of the Hokonuis, the dark. The Foxes. Janet Frame. WPE

Within the sand of what far river lies. Shadows of His Lady. Jacques Tahureau, *French*. AWP, tr. by Andrew Lang

Within the Seasons. Peter Blue Cloud. HATNAP

Spring Equinox. ChAP

Within the Shelter of Our Walls. Elinor Lennen. AH

Within the soul's courts is a temple fair. The Soul's Courts. Henrietta Cordelia Ray. CBWP-3

Within the space. John Kitching. SpW

Within the streams, Pausanias saith. The Last Chance. Andrew Lang. NOBVV; OxBSn

Within the thin. The Madman. S. J. Pretorius, *Afrikaans*. PeSA, tr. by Uys Krige and Jack Cope

Within the Veil. Michelle Cliff. NAAAL

Within the wires of the post, unloading the cans of garbage. Prisoners. Randall Jarrell. OxBA

Within these arms for ever swim. (LL) To My Mistress Sitting by a River's Side; an Eddy. Thomas Carew. BeJo; CaPo

Within These Doors Assembled Now. Oliver Holden. AH

Within this [or that] ample volume lies. The Book of Books. Sir Walter Scott. ChIV-1 *Fr.* The Monastery.

Within this black hive to-night. Beehive. Jean Toomer. GT; PoBA; TTY

Within This Book, Called Marguerite. Marjorie Welish. FTOS; PmAP

Within this mindless vault. Epigram. James Vincent Cunningham. RB; VGW

Within this restless, hurried, modern world. My Voice. Oscar Wilde. EBVV

Within this sober frame expect. Upon Appleton House [To My Lord Fairfax]. Andrew Marvell. FaBoPV; GeHe; SeCP

WITHIN THIS VALE. Burma-Shave Roadside Signs. *Unknown*. OBCoV *Fr.* Advertising Rhymes.

Within this vale. Burma-Shave Roadside Signs. *Unknown*. OBCoV

Within this wood, out of a rocke did rise. Petrarch. *Fr.* Visions. AWP

Within those doors, (my doors) dost hear! I *will*. (LL) Retirement. Henry Vaughan. GeHe; NOSC

Within where the wrapt machines / are praying. (LL) The Semblables. William Carlos Williams. FaBoMo; NOBA

Within your heart. Hold Fast Your Dreams. Louise Driscoll. BLPA; FaBoBe

Without a king, to see the end of time. (LL) On Mr. Paine's Rights of Man. Philip Freneau. AmPP; ColAP; NAAL-1; NAAL-3

Without a soul, a mind, a breath, or pulse. Elegy 19 (A Kiss). Pierre de Ronsard, *French*. EP; FLP, tr. by Alistair Elliot

Without a winter coat. Raising the Flag. Gerald Vizenor. VoR

Without a word. Akiko Yosano, *Japanese*. WPJ, tr. by Kenneth Rexroth and Ikuko Atsumi

Without asking, you borrowed your father's black tie. Tie. Greg Delanty. BiHa

Without Benefit of Declaration. Langston Hughes. TTY

Without Benefit of Tape. Dorothy Livesay. NOBC

Without Ceremony. Vassar Miller. MoAmPo

Without changing color. Ono no Komachi, *Japanese*. WPJ, tr. by Kenneth Rexroth and Ikuko Atsumi

Without considering whether they were fit. Elizabeth Barrett Browning. *Fr.* Aurora Leigh. VWP

Without Devotion. Marie Howe. NAmP90

Without e'er a wife? (LL) Tommy Tucker. Mother Goose. LB; OxNR; ReMoGo

Without end. The Year's end. Miya Shūji, *Japanese*. MJT, tr. by Makoto Ueda

Without ever going to college. (LL) To Hell with Commonsense. Patrick Kavanagh. APAD

Without ever having felt sorry for itself. (LL) Self-Pity. D. H. Lawrence. OxBTC; RB

Without excess no galaxies. Civilities of Lamplight. Charles Tomlinson. OxBC

Without expectation. Summer Oracle. Audre Lorde. BlSi; PoBA

Without flocks or cattle or the curved horns. A Time of Change. Egan O'Rahilly, *Irish*. BIrV; FaBoPV, tr. by Eavan Boland

Without Her. D. G. Rossetti. GBL; OBNC; PoEL-5; Son *Fr.* The House of Life.

("What of her glass without her? The blank grey.") GLoP

Without her Diadem. (LL) Sky is low—the Clouds are mean, The. Emily Dickinson. MeMAP; MoAmPo; OxBA; PBMP; PoEL-5

Without image or likeness. Dan Pagis. *See* Testimony.

Without incident. Tanka. Mori Ōgai, *Japanese*. MJT, tr. by Makoto Ueda

Without kings and warriors occasional verse fails. On Being Asked to Write a Poem for 1979. Jack A. Mapanje. AF; PBMAP

Without knowing a page / Of it / Themselves. (LL) Women. Alice Walker. NMM-2; WPOW

Without Looking. Patricia Goedicke. NMM-2

Without me you can only. Kenneth Rexroth. APSN *Fr.* The Love Poems of Marichiko.

Without My Friends the Day Is Dark. Moses ibn Ezra, *Hebrew*. TrJP, tr. by Solomon Solis-Cohen

Without my having known. The Boy Died in My Alley. Gwendolyn Brooks. NoAM

Without Name. Pauli Murray. PoBA

Without question, / Without kiss. (LL) Lethe. Hilda Doolittle. CMoP; FaBoWP; LiTM; MoAmPo; PoRA; VGW

Without relief seeking lost love. (LL) Lost Love. Robert Graves. AWP; CBLP; CH; FaBoCh; LoP; MoBrPo

Without seemliness, / without love. (LL) The Mutes. Denise Levertov. NALW; NOBA

Without so much / as trying to look. You. Carroll Arnett. VoR

Without Song. Grace Nichols. PBCV

Without support and with Support. Commentary Applied to Spiritual Things. Saint John of the Cross, *Spanish*. TOF, tr. by K. Kavanaugh and O. Rodrigues

Without that once clear aim, the path of flight. Stephen Spender. CMoP; Son

Without the hall, and close upon the gate, *see also* "Close to the gates a spacious gardes lies" *and* "To left and to right, outside, he saw an orchard." The Gardens of Alcinous. Homer. OAEL-1; OBVE, tr. by George Chapman *Fr.* Odyssey. NAWM-1, tr. by Robert Fitzgerald

Without the Herdsman. Diotimus, *Greek*. AWP, tr. by John William Burgon

Without, the lonely night is sweet with stars. Martyrdom. "Rufus Learsi." TrJP

Without—the power to die— / the low harm art. (LL) My Life Had Stood—A Loaded Gun. Emily Dickinson. APN-2; AmPP; HAP; HeIP-4; InPK-6; NAAL-1; NAAL-3; NALW; NAWM-2; NCAP; NIP-4; NoP-4; OxWW; PAR; PFTM; PoPoPo; Poetr; SAmP; TRP; WPOW; WeW-3

Without the slightest basis / for hypochondriasis. How Jack Found That Beans May Go Back on a Chap. Guy Wetmore Carryl. HoPM

Without, the sullen noises of the street! Benedictio Domini. Ernest Christopher Dowson. ADE

Without their helmets. Losers. Jonathan Holden. CMAP

Without this / what is / worth doing. Land. Carroll Arnett. VoR

Without thought, without remorse, without shame. Walls. Constantine P. Cavafy, *Modern Greek*. TrJP, *tr. by* Rae Dalven

Without warning their nest. A Call to Action. Ch'iu Chin, *Chinese*. PBWP, *tr. by* Kenneth Rexroth *and* Ling Chung

Without whose help scant do I live a day. (LL) If waker care, if sudden [*or* sodayne] pale colo[u]r. Sir Thomas Wyatt. AAS; NoSic

Without You I Am. Diana Der Hovanessian. LoHo

Withouten Time is no erthely thinge. Time and Eternity. Stephen Hawes. PoEL-1 *Fr.* The Pastime of Pleasure. OBGa

Withouten you. Little Elegy. Elinor Wylie. IMW

Witlesse gallant, a young wench that woo'd, A. Michael Drayton. AAS *Fr.* Idea.

Witness. Denise Levertov. BLT

Witness. John Montague. CIP-2

Witness. Susan Wood. EC2

Witness anew, I'm bound to pass on, A. Dan Pagis, *Hebrew*. IP, *tr. by* Warren Bargad *and* Stanley F. Chyet

Witness how it comes to pass. Epitaph in Sirmio. David Morton. PoLF

Witness the sarcophagus of non-Raphael. The Earthworker's God is Healed. Bernadette Mayer. FTOS

Witness to Death. Richmond Lattimore. VGW

Witnesses, The. X. J. Kennedy. PChr

Witnesses. W. S. Merwin. LCAP-2

Witnesses, The. Clive Sansom.
  "It was a night in winter." PChr

Wits, The. Sir John Suckling. *See* A Session[s] of the Poets.

Wit's Abuse. Anne Wharton. KTR

Wit's an unruly engine, wildly striking. The Church-Porch. George Herbert. FP *Fr.* The Church-Porch. ESCV

Wit's forge and fire-blast, meaning's press and screw. Coleridge. *See* On Donne's Poetry.

Wits, like physicians, never can agree. The Rover or The Banished Cavaliers. Aphra Behn. BWW

Wit's Pilgrimage. John, of Hereford Davies.
  Some Blaze the Precious Beauties of Their Loves. Son

Wit's queen (if what the poets sing be true). Upon a Girl of Seven Years Old. Alexander Pope. OxBSP

Wittler, hittler, or something like that. (LL) Portrait of a House Detective. Hans Magnus Enzensberger, *German*. HP, *tr. by* Michael Hamburger; PoSu

Witty as Horatius Flaccus. On Seeing Francis Jeffrey Riding on a Donkey. Sydney Smith. FaBoEE

Wives, The. Donald Hall. CoAP

Wives in the Sere. Thomas Hardy. NOBE; NOBVV

Wives of Mafiosi, The. Erica Jong. AmPA

Wizard Oil. *Unknown*. AS

Wizards. Alonzo Gonzales Mó, *Mayan*. STP, *tr. by* Allan F. Burns

Wizard's Chant, The. *Unknown, Passamaquoddy Native American*. APN-2, *tr. by* Chares Godfrey Leland *and* John Dyneley Prince

Wizard's Funeral, The. Richard Watson Dixon. NOBVV; PeVV

Wlk'n down regent street i see. Blkfern-jungal. Aileen Corpus. BMAP

Wm. Brazier. Robert Graves. NOBL

Wo, his purple an' linen, too. Dives and Laz'us. *Unknown*. TTY

Wo worth the days! The days I spent. A Few Lines to Fill up a Vacant Page. John Danforth. SCAP

Woak Hill. William Barnes. EnVR

Wobbly Rock. Lew Welch. PoM

Wo'd yee have fresh Cheese and Cream? Fresh Cheese and Cream. Robert Herrick. CBLP

Wodwo. Ted Hughes. CBNP; MoP; NoAM

Woe for the brave ship *Orient*!. The Brave Old Ship, the *Orient*. Robert Lowell. FaBoBe

Woe, having made with many fights his own. Sonnet 57. Sir Philip Sidney. *Fr.* Astrophil and Stella. AAS; SiPS

Woe Is Me! Bible, *O.T.* TrJP *Fr.* Micah.

Woe is me, my soul says, how bitter is my fate. Rachel Morpurgo, *Hebrew*. PBWP, *tr. by* Robert Alter

Woe is me, my stolen daughters! (LL) The Farewell: "Gone, gone,—sold and gone." John Greenleaf Whittier. AWP; NCAP

Woe then to the gossips! they show their evil will. Meinloh von Sevelingen, *German*. GePo, *tr. by* J. W. Thomas

Woe, this tumbleweed. A Song of Lament. Ts'ao Chih, *Chinese*. SuSp, *tr. by* Hans H. Frankel

Woe to him by this world enticed. A Child in Prison. Gofraidh Fionn O'Dalaigh. NOIV

Woe to him who slanders women. Gerald Fitzgerald, 4th Earl of Desmond. NOIV

Woe! Woe! / Hearken ye! Chant from the Iroquois Book of Rites. *Unknown, Onondaga Native American*. APN-2, *tr. by* Horatio Hale

Woe worth thee, woe worth thee, false Scottlande! Earl Bothwell. *Unknown*. ESPB

Woefully arrayed. John Skelton. ChIV-2
  ("Wofully araide.") MiEL

Woe's me! by dint of all these sighs that come. Dante. AWP *Fr.* La Vita Nuova.

Woes of the Crab, The. *Unknown*. APo *Fr.* Manyo Shu, Part 2 of 4.

Wofully araide. John Skelton. *See* Woefully arrayed.

Woggly bird sat on the whango tree, The. The Whango Tree. *Unknown*. FPC

Woke up crying the blues. A Day in the Life of a Poet. Quincy Troupe. NBV

Woke up this morning with a / limp. Poem With a Limp. Roger McGough. OBCoV

Woke up to one of those cold. Barrio Beateo. Jesse F. García. UnSA

Woken, I lay in the arms of my own warmth and listened. First Things First. W. H. Auden. CBLP; NYBP

Wol ze here a wonder thynge. Riddles Wisely Expounded. *Unknown*. ESPB

Wolcum be thu, hevene kyng. Welcome Yule. *Unknown*. CH

Wold clock's feäce is still in pleäce, The. William Barnes. FaBoVe

Wolde God that it were so. *Unknown*. MiEL

Wolf. Peter Blue Cloud. HATNAP; VoR

Wolf, The. Georgia Roberts Durston. TLR

Wolf. Kenneth Rexroth. NNaP *Fr.* A Bestiary. OBAL

wolf, A. Wolf Song. *Teton Sioux Oral Tradition, Teton Sioux*. PaTW, *tr. by* Frances Densmore

Wolf and the Dog, The. Jean de La Fontaine, *French*. OBVE, *tr. by* Elizur Wright

Wolf and the Lambs, The. Ivy O. Eastwick. BoTP

Wolf and the Stork, The. Jean de La Fontaine, *French*. OBVE, *tr. by* Marianne Moore

Wolf "Aunt." Maurice Kenny. HATNAP

Wolf-bait on the bush beside the spring, The. (LL) And change[,] with hurried hand, has swept these scenes. Frederick Goddard Tuckerman. APN-2; HAP; NOBA; TAP

Wolf-Boy. David Malouf. CBAP

"Wolf!" cried my cunning heart. The True Encounter. Edna St. Vincent Millay. OxBSP

Wolf Cub. Sergey Sergeievich Narovchatov, *Russian*. TCRP, *tr. by* Lubov Yakovleva

Wolf is still under the blanket, The. The Sounds That Arrived. Milo De Angelis, *Italian*. NeIt, *tr. by* Lawrence Venuti

Wolf Song. *Teton Sioux Oral Tradition, Teton Sioux*. PaTW, *tr. by* Frances Densmore

Wolf speaks, while chewing, The. Paul Klee, *German*. PFTM, *tr. by* Anselm Hollo

Wolf that follows, the fawn that flies, The. (LL) The Hounds of Spring. Swinburne. AWP; CTC; EBVV; EBVVPR; EnVR; FaBoBe; GTBS-P; HAP; NAEL-2; NOBE; NoP-4; OAEL-2; OBEV; PoE; SCGP; TFi; WeW-3

Wolfe Tone. Austin Clarke. CIP-2

Wolfhound. Richard Murphy. NOIV *Fr.* The Battle of Aughrim.

Wolfpen Creek. James Still. MT

Wolfram's Dirge. Thomas Lovell Beddoes. NOBE; OBEV; OxAEP-2 *Fr.* Death's Jest Book.
  (Dirge: "If Thou wilt ease Thine heart.") OBNC; PoEL-4

WOLF'S PROFILE HANGS / OVER THE THREE CROSSES, THE. From the Window of the Beverly Wilshire Hotel. Michael McClure. SPE

Wolleward and wete-shoed went I forth after. William Langland. EnVB *Fr.* The Vision of Piers Plowman.

Wolsey, or possibly my John of Gaunt. Santa Claus. Christopher Vernon Hassall. OxBTC

Wolves. Louis MacNeice. NoAM; OxBTC

Wolves. Vladimir Alekseievich Soloukhin, *Russian*. TCRP, *tr. by* Daniel Weissbort

Wolves, The. Allen Tate. LiTM; NOBA; OxBA; PoA

Wolves can outeat anyone. The Wolf and the Stork. Jean de La Fontaine, *French*. OBVE, *tr. by* Marianne Moore

Wolves for Company. *Unknown, Irish*. BIrV

Wolves in the Zoo. Howard Nemerov. NoAM

Wolves of evening will be much abroad, The. Runes for an Old Believer. Rolfe Humphries. NYBP

Wolves say to the dogs, The. J. Michael Yates. HoPM *Fr.* The Great Bear Lake Meditations.

Wolves, with men's hats on their heads. Li Po. *See* Ancient Airs.

Woman. Hira Bansode, *Marathi.* OMIP, *tr. by* Vinay Dharwadker

Woman. Eaton Stannard Barrett. TIRV

Woman. Den Sute-Jo, *Japanese.* NNPT, *tr. by* Lucien Stryk *and* Takashi Ikemoto

Woman. Fu Hsüan, *Chinese.* ChiP; ChiPo, *tr. by* Arthur Waley

Woman. Oliver Goldsmith. *See* Song: "When lovely woman stoops to folly."

Woman. Randall Jarrell. CBLP; NOBA

Woman. Rumiko Kora, *Japanese.* WPJ, *tr. by* Kenneth Rexroth *and* Ikuko Atsumi

Woman. Elouise Loftin. PoBA

Woman. Valente Goenha Malangatana, *Portuguese.* PBA; TTY, *tr. by* Dorothy Guedes *and* Philippa Rumsey; PBMAP

Woman. Milton. *Fr.* Samson Agonistes. FHYEP; OAEL-1; PoEL-3

Woman. Malangatana Ngwenya, *Portuguese.* PeSAV, *tr. by* Philippa Rumsey

Woman. Frances Sargent Osgood. ColAP

Woman, A. Robert Pinsky. WeW-3

Woman. Carl Rakosi. TAP

Woman, The. Tanka. Tawara Machi, *Japanese.* MJT, *tr. by* Makoto Ueda

Woman. Tanka. Tsukamoto Kunio, *Japanese.* MJT, *tr. by* Makoto Ueda

Woman, The. Ronald Stuart Thomas. OxBC

Woman. *Unknown.* AWP, *tr. by* H. A. Giles *Fr.* Shi King.

Woman! Elolongue Epanya Yondo, *French.* NegPo, *tr. by* Ellen Conroy Kennedy

Woman, 2. Jyotsna Milan, *Hindi.* OMIP, *tr. by* Mrinal Pande *and* Arlene Zide

Woman, a pleasing but a short-lived flow'r. An Essay on Woman. Mary Leapor. BWW; ECWP; NOEC

Woman Alone, A. Denise Levertov. NMM-2; WPOW

Woman Alone. Naomi Mitchison. WPN

Woman alone, living. From the Garden of the Women Once Fallen. Lorna Goodison. VCWP

Woman and falcons—they are easily tamed. Der von Kürenberg, *German.* GePo, *tr. by* Frederick Goldin

Woman and Fame. Felicia Dorothea Hemans. VWP

Woman and Her Dying Warrior, A. Vanparanar, *Tamil.* PLW, *tr. by* A. K. Ramanujan

Woman and the Aloe, The. Perseus Adams. PeSA

Woman and the Angel, The. Robert W. Service. ChIV-1

("'Ancient, outworn, Puritanic traditions of Right and Wrong,' The.") (LL) KSG

Woman and the boy look back at the years, The. Sestina for Jaime. Katherine Alice Power. BAP-96

Woman as gates, saying. Kollwitz, Käthe. Muriel Rukeyser. NMM-2

Woman as Market. Muriel Rukeyser. NoAM

Woman asleep. Marie-Claire Bancquart, *French.* MFP, *tr. by* Martin Sorrell

Woman Asleep on a Banana Leaf. Katha Pollitt. InPS-3

Woman at Banff, The. William Stafford. PFE

Woman at Home. Vere Arnot. WPN

Woman at Lit Window. Eamon Grennan. BLT

Woman at the Piano. Marya Alexandrovna Zaturenska. MoAmPo

Woman at the Washington Zoo, The. Randall Jarrell. CoAP; HAP; HCAP; LiTM; OxBC; TAP; TwCP; UnPo; VCAP

Woman, at the Washtub, The. Victor James Daley. NOBAu

Woman Back in the Kitchen, The. Nicholas Lloyd Ingraham. PWR

Woman begins to weep, A. (LL) Afterimages. Audre Lorde. LTA; VCAP

Woman bore me, I will rise. (LL) On the idle hill of summer. A. E. Housman. MoBrPo; NOBE; OAEL-2; OBNC; OBWP

Woman comforts a man, staring, A. Woman Alone. Naomi Mitchison. WPN

Woman coming down the snowy road, A. Grey Woman. Gladys Cardiff. CDW

Woman crossed the park and laughed, A. The Enveloping Echo. Ion Caraion, *Romanian.* AF, *tr. by* Marguerite Dorian *and* Elliott B. Urdang

Woman, don't be troublesome. Augustus Young, *Irish.* CIP-2; IIP

Woman Dragged by Welsh Corgis. Joan Retallack. FTOS

Woman drest by Age, A. Margaret Lucas Cavendish, Duchess of Newcastle. PEW

Woman fears for man, he goes. Abel's Bride. Denise Levertov. FaBoWP; NALW; VGW

Woman finally learned how to love things, so things learned, A. The Woman Who Loved Things. Cathleen Calbert. BAP-95

Woman Forsaken in Love, A. Saigyo. *Fr.* Sixty-four Tanka.

Woman Free. Elizabeth Wolstenholme-Elmy.

"Marriage, which might have been a mateship sweet." BrRo

Woman from Chianciano. Rika Lesser. FiLi

Woman from the balcony opposite, The. The Window. Nino Nikolov, *Bulgarian.* CEEP, *tr. by* Ewald Osers

Woman, Gallup, N. M. Karen Swenson. NYBP

Woman Gave Me a Red Star to Wear on My Headband, A. Jimmie Durham. HATNAP

Woman gave me butter now, A. A Present of Butter. Tadhg Dall O'Huiginn, *Irish.* BIrV, *tr. by* the Earl of Longford

Woman giving birth to herself, A. (LL) Mirror's Song. Liz Lochhead. NBrP

Woman grew, with waiting, over-quiet, A. Narrative. Elisabeth Eybers, *Afrikaans.* PeSA; PeSAV, *tr. by the author*

Woman Grows Soon Old, A. Larin Paraske, *Finnish.* PBWP, *tr. by* Jaakko A. Ahokas

Woman Hanging from the Thirteenth Floor Window, The. Joy Harjo. GLP; HATNAP; UnSA

("Window on the east side of Chicago, or as she / climbs back up to claim herself again.") (LL) UnSA

Woman has given me strength and affluence, A. Manifesto. D. H. Lawrence. CBLP

Woman I Am, The. Glen Allen. BLPA

Woman, I choose to walk here. And to draw this circle, A. (LL) Dark lintels, the blue and foreign stones, The. Adrienne Rich. NALW; NoAM

Woman I have never seen before, A. Transit. Richard Wilbur. DiPo; LCAP-2; PiM

Woman I want, The. No More than Five. Fred Levinson. AmPA

Woman in Kitchen. Eavan Boland. BiHa

Woman in Love with a Captive King, A. Nakkannaiyar, *Tamil.* PLW, *tr. by* A. K. Ramanujan

Woman in Mourning. Māris aklais, *Latvian.* CEEP, *tr. by* Inara Cedrins

Woman in my class wrote that she is sick, A. Desire. Stephen Dobyns. NAmP90

Woman in My Notebook, The. Lorna Dee Cervantes. WPOW

Woman in my shower crying, A. What Goes Around Comes Around, or The Proof is in the Pudding. Cheryl Clarke. CPO; FFC

Woman in the, The. Marge Piercy. *See* The Woman in the ordinary pudgy downcast girl.

Woman in the garden gathers lilacs, A. A. L. Hendriks. *Fr.* D'Où Venons Nous? Que Sommes Nous? Où Allons Nous. PBCV

Woman in the Mirror, The. Stefan Aug. Doinas, *Romanian.* CEEP, *tr. by* Donald Eulert *and* Stefan Avadanei

Woman in the ordinary pudgy downcast girl, The. Marge Piercy. CrSp; NMM-2

Woman in the shape of a monster, A. Planetarium. Adrienne Rich. FaBoWP; HCAP; MoP; NAAL-2; NALW; NIP-4; NOBA; NoAM; Poetr; VCAP

Woman inside an enormous sunhat, A. Close-up. Heather McPherson. PeNZ

Woman / is a problem negative. Siddhalinga Pattanshetti, *Kannada.* OMIP, *tr. by* A. K. Ramanujan

Woman is by aptitude. *Unknown.* OBWVE, *tr. by* Gwyn Williams *Fr.* Against Women.

Woman is crying like a dragon because I'm a poet, The. Clumsy Guys. Tomaz Salamun. PUP-18

Woman is perfected, The. Edge. Sylvia Plath. FaBoWP; HCAP; NAAL-2; NALW; PFE; PoE; PoPoPo; TAP; VCAP

Woman is reading a poem on the street, A. The Hug. Tess Gallagher. CrSp

Woman is singing in the valley. The shadows falling blot her out, A. Song. Gabriela Mistral, *Spanish.* WPoS, *tr. by* Langston Hughes

Woman Is Talking to Death, A. Judy Grahn. CPO; GLP

Woman is using a handkerchief, The. At the Hammersmith Palais. Alan Riddell. NOBAu

Woman Kills Sweetheart with Bowling Ball. Laura Kasischke. PUP-18

Woman Knitting, A. Lilian Bowes-Lyon. WPN

Woman lay dying on a pallet in a gateway, A. The Good Lord Saved Her. Anna Swirszczynska, *Polish.* PoSu, *tr. by* Magnus J. Krynski *and* Robert A. Maguire

Woman Lies Alone, A. Ho Xuan Huong, *Vietnamese.* AVP, *tr. by* Huỳnh Sanh Thông

Woman like Me, A. Eileen Myles. GLP

Woman living single, A. Song for Empty Cup. Hijin Park, *Korean.* CKP, *tr. by* Jaihiun Kim

Woman Looking Through a Viewmaster. C. D. Wright. LCAP-2

Woman-love can't touch my heart. *Unknown, Greek.* GrAn, *tr. by* Thomas Meyer

Woman making advances publicly, A. Judith Kazantzis. BrRo

Woman Me. Maya Angelou. BlSi; OxWW

Woman measures, A. Jean Daive, *French*. MFP, *tr. by* Martin Sorrell

Woman Meets an Old Lover, A. Denise Levertov. BLT

Woman Mourned by Daughters, A. Adrienne Rich. IMW; Poetr

Woman much missed, how you call to me, call to me. The Voice. Thomas Hardy. APAD; BoLoP; CBLP; CMoP; EnLoPo; GBL; GTBS-P; HAP; InPS-3; LoP; MoP; NAEL-2; NoAM; NoP-4; OAEL-2; OBNC; OxAEP-2; PoE; PoEL-5; Poetr; TFi

Woman named Tomorrow, The. Four Preludes on Playthings of the Wind. Carl Sandburg. CMoP; MoAmPo; NOBA

Woman Née Wu, The. Wu Chia-chi, *Chinese*. CoBLCP, *tr. by* Jonathan Chaves

Woman of Exeter, The. *Unknown*. ReMoGo

Woman of the more primitive tribes, A. Food. Josephine Jacobsen. NMM-2

Woman of Three Cows, The. *Unknown, Irish*. NOIV, *tr. by* James Clarence Mangan

Woman on the Dump, The. Elizabeth Spires. WWSi

Woman one wonderful morning, A. Europa. William Plomer. MoBS

Woman Poem. Nikki Giovanni. BlSi

Woman precedes me up the long rope, A. Climbing. Lucille Clifton. GT; LoL

Woman Pregnant, A. Blaga Dimitrova, *Bulgarian*. CEEP, *tr. by* Jascha Kessler *and* Aleksandar Shurbanov

Woman pulls the cart, The. Inscribed on the Painting, Stabbing a Tiger, by Chao Tzu-ang, in the Collection of Scholar Yang. Yang Shih-ch'i, *Chinese*. CoBLCP, *tr. by* Jonathan Chaves

Woman, rest on my brow your balsam hands. Night of Sine. Léopold Sédar Senghor, *French*. PBA

Woman riding the two mares of her thighs. The Steamboat Whistle. Archibald MacLeish. MeMAP

Woman Seed Player. Roberta Hill Whiteman. HATNAP

Woman sits on her porch. Song. Earle Thompson. HATNAP

Woman Skating. Margaret Atwood. FaBoWP

Woman / sleeps next to me on the earth, A. Night in the Forest. Galway Kinnell. TAP

Woman somewhere cries—she mourns her man, A. On Hearing a Woman Mourn Her Husband. Ho Xuan Huong, *Vietnamese*. AVP, *tr. by* Huỳnh Sanh Thông

Woman stood up in front of the table. Her sad hands, The. Miniature. Yannis Ritsos, *Greek*. VCWP, *tr. by* Edmund Keeley

Woman stops at nothing, when she wears, A. Juvenal, *Latin*. OBCVT, *tr. by* William Gifford

Woman tells me, A. A Story. Jane Hirshfield. BLT

Woman / that I knew, The. Vladimir Aleksandrovich Lugovskoy, *Russian*. TCRP, *tr. by* Gordon McVay

Woman Thing, The. Audre Lorde. BlSi; GT; NMM-2

Woman, thou shalt say to son. Mother. Dorothy, Duchess of Wellington Wellesley. WPN

Woman! thoughtless, giddy creature. The Declaimer. Henry Baker. NOEC

Woman to Child. Judith Wright. MDDM; PBWP; WPE

Woman to Her Lover, A. Christina Walsh. BrRo

Woman to Man. Ai. NoAM

Woman to Man. Judith Wright. BMAP; CBAP; NoP-4; WPE

Woman to man, they lie. In Bloemfontein. Alan Ross. BoLoP

Woman travels to Brazil for plastic, A. Tomatoes. Stephen Dobyns. NAmP90

Woman Tung. Wu Chia-chi, *Chinese*. CoBLCP, *tr. by* Jonathan Chaves

Woman Underneath, The. Robert Maitre. EP

Woman waits for me, she contains all, nothing is lacking, A. Walt Whitman. HeIP-4; NOBA; PAR

("Immortality, I plant so lovingly now.") (LL) SAGP

Woman Walking. William Carlos Williams. ColAP

Woman wants monogamy. General Review of the Sex Situation. Dorothy Parker. NAAL-2

Woman was cooking a mouse for her husband's dinner, A. Mouse Dinners. Russell Edson. SoSe-8

Woman was old and ragged and gray, The. Somebody's Mother. Mary Dow Brine. BLPA; ChAP

Woman watches her husband rubbing his nose, The. Twenty Below. Robert Arthur Douglas Ford. NOBC

Woman weak and woman mortal, through the spirit's open portal. Streets of Baltimore. *Unknown*. BLPA

Woman went into the same resturant every Tuesday night, A. Sandwiches. David Donnell. NoAM

Woman when we met on the solstice. Meet. Audre Lorde. CPO

Woman Who Could Not Live With Her Faulty Heart, The. Margaret Atwood. LCAP-2

Woman who didn't love me, The. (LL) Valentino's Hair. Yvonne Sapia. PeVV; TRP

Woman who has grown old, The. The Crows. Louise Bogan. FaBoWP; NALW; NMM-2

Woman who has nodded to me from her porch, The. Farmwife. Betsy Sholl. CrSp

Woman who looks like my mother sees a man who looks like / me, A. Four Resurrections in the Valley of the Ghosts. Yehuda Amichai, *Hebrew*. VCWP, *tr. by* Benjamin Harshav *and* Barbara Harshav

Woman Who Loved Things, The. Cathleen Calbert. BAP-95

Woman Who Loved to Cook, The. Erica Jong. TAP

Woman Who Loved Worms, The. Colette Inez. CMAP; NMM-2

Woman who loves, A. Lucille Clifton. NAAAL

Woman Who Understands, The. Everard Jack Appleton. PoLF

Woman Who Weeps. Ellen Bryant Voigt. PuP-16

Woman who writes feels too much, A. The Black Art. Anne Sexton. PoA

Woman whose arms are the bones of the poem. Aspen. Erin Mouré. DeD

Woman wired in memories, A. Adrienne Rich. NoP-4

Woman with a burning flame, A. Smothered Fires. Georgia Douglas Johnson. BlSi

Woman with a Past, A. Wilfrid Scawen Blunt. Son *Fr*. The Love Sonnets of Proteus.

Woman with broad, rough hands. Magda Portal, *Spanish*. WPOW, *tr. by* Irene Vegas-Garcia *and* Kathleen Weaver

Woman with Child, The. Freda Laughton. LiLi

Woman with Flaxen Hair in Norfolk Heard, A. Robert Kelly. PmAP

Woman with Flower. Naomi Long Madgett. GT

Woman with no face walked into the light, A. Homage to Hieronymus Bosch. Thomas MacGreevy. BIrV; SPE

Woman with the caught fox. Plea for a Captive. W. S. Merwin. NYBP; NoAM

Woman with the Wild-Grown Hair Relaxes after Another Long Day, The. Nita Penfold. CrSp

Woman, Woman, let us say these things to each other. Prelude. Conrad Potter Aiken. NYBP

Woman wore a floral apron around her neck, The. The Floral Apron. Marilyn Chin. LoL; UnSA

Woman working hard and wisely, A. Epigram. Kassia, *Greek*. WPOW, *tr. by* Patrick Diehl

Woman Writes to Her Daughter Who's Studying Overseas, A. Trinh Tiên, *Vietnamese*. AVP, *tr. by* Huỳnh Sanh Thông

Woman, you are afraid of the forest. Maria Wine, *Swedish*. PBWP, *tr. by* Nadia Christensen

Woman, you'll never credit what. The Shepherd's Tale. James Kirkup, *after the French of* Raoul Ponchon. OBCP

Womanhood, wanton, ye want. John Skelton. AAS

Womanhood, The. Gwendolyn Brooks.

Beverly Hills, Chicago. Poetr; VGW

Children of the Poor, The. WPE, *sect*. I, *pt*. 1-2; PoA, *sect*. I, *pt*. 1-3; NAAAL

("But reaching is his rule.") (LL) NAAAL

"First fight. Then fiddle. Ply the slipping string." InPK-6; NIP-4; PFE; Poetr

"What shall I give my children? who are poor." BPo; PoA; WPE

"One wants a Teller in a time like this." WPE

Rites for Cousin Vit, The. BPo; HAP; NAAAL; NoP-4; WPE; WeW-3

("'Forgive these nigguhs that know not what they do'.") (LL) SSLK

("John Cabot—out of Wilma, once a Wycliffe.") SSLK

(Riot.) SSLK

"Stand off, daughter of the dusk." NALW

Womanisers. John Press. BoLoP

Womankind. Gerald Massey. NOBVV

Woman's Answer, A. Adelaide Anne Procter. VWP

Woman's Answer, A. Henry Howard, Earl of Surrey. SiPS

Woman's Answer to "The Vampire," A. Felicia Blake. BLPA

Woman's Beauty. Lascelles Abercrombie. MoBrPo *Fr*. Emblems of Love.

Woman's Constancy. Donne. ESCV; FMP; FSCP; NBLV; NOSC; NoP-4; SAGP

Woman's Constancy. Sir John Suckling. CaPo; CavPo

Woman's deaf, and does not hear, The. (LL) On a Certain Lady at Court. Alexander Pope. NOBE; NOEC; OBEV; OxBSP; SAGP

Woman's Dream, The. Frances Horovitz. BrRo

Woman's face with Nature's own hand painted, A. Sonnet 20. Shakespeare. HeIP-4; NAEL-1; NoP-4; NoSic; OAEL-1; OxAEP-1 *Fr*. Sonnets.

Woman's Future. May Kendall. VWP

Woman's Hard Fate. *Unknown*. ECWP

Womans Labour, an epistle, The. Mary Collier. PEW

Woman's Labour; an Epistle to Mr. Stephen Duck, The. Mary Collier. Washerwoman, The. ECWP; NOEC

Woman's Last Word, A. Robert Browning. BLPA; FaBoBe; NAEL-2; RACG

Woman's Last Word, A. Adelaide Anne Procter. VWP

Woman's like the flatt'ring ocean. John Gay. PeLV *Fr.* Polly; an Opera.

Woman's Mourning Song, The. Bell Hooks. ISC

Woman's Prayer, A. Yehuda Karni, *Hebrew.* MHP, *tr. by* Ruth Finer Mintz

Woman's Question, A. Lena Lathrop, *wr. at. to* Elizabeth Barrett Browning. BLPA; PoToHe

Woman's Question, A. Adelaide Anne Procter. VWP

Woman's Room in Autumn, A. Yüan Hung-tao, *Chinese.* CoBLCP, *tr. by* Jonathan Chaves

Woman's Shortcomings, A. Elizabeth Barrett Browning. BLPA

Woman's Song, A. Colleen J. McElroy. BlSi

Woman's Song, about Men, A. *Unknown, Eskimo into French.* STP, *tr. by* Paul-Emile Victor; *English vers. by* Armand Schwerner

Woman's Sorrow, A. Ho Nansorhon, *Korean.*
"Yesterday I fancied I was young." PBWP, *tr. by* Peter H. Lee

Woman's Wish, The. Matthew Prior. FaBoEE

Woman's Work. Julia Alvarez. RA

Woman's worth to the world can never be told. Oh Woman, Blessed Woman! Mrs. Henry Linden. CBWP-4

Womb, The. Apirana Taylor. PeNZ

Wombat lives across the seas, The. Ogden Nash. CBNP

Womb's own flesh and bone—strong brotherhood, A. Nguyễn Trãi, *Vietnamese.* AVP, *tr. by* Huỳnh Sanh Thông

Women. William Cartwright. BeJo

Women, The. Cyrus Cassells. UnSA

Women, The. Joseph Ceravolo. FTOS

Women. Heath. CTC

Women. Frances Horovitz. LW

Women. Palladas, *Greek.* OBCVT, *tr. by* William Cartwright

Women. Adrienne Rich. NMM-2; TRP

Women. May Swenson. BoWoP; NALW

Women. Alice Walker. NAAAL; NMM-2; WPOW *Fr.* In These Dissenting Times. InPS-3; PoBA
("Of it / Themselves.") (LL) NAAAL

Women all / cause rue. Palladas, *Greek.* GrAn; OBCVT, *tr. by* Tony Harrison

Women all shout after me and mock, The. Palladas, *Greek.* GrAn, *tr. by* Tony Harrison

Women and Roses. Robert Browning. NAEL-2

Women Are Different. Marsha Prescod. LW

Women Are Not Gentlemen. Harley Matthews. NOBAu

Women are walking to town, The. The Rainy Season. Linda Hogan. HATNAP; TRP

Women are within her, smoking angel dust, sipping tea, The. The Administrator. Marilyn Chin. LoHo

Women, as some men say, unconstant be. Epigram. George Wither. NOSC

Women at the Corners Stand, The. Louis Golding. TrJP

Women at the Crossroad / (May Elegba Forever Guard the Right Doors). Opal Palmer Adisa. GT

Women at the Market. Angela Figueroa-Aymerich, *Spanish.* PBWP, *tr. by* Hardie St. Martin

Women at the Temple. Herodas, *Greek.* HePo, *tr. by* Barbara Hughes Fowler

Women ben full of ragerie, *in imitation of* Chaucer. Imitation of Chaucer. Alexander Pope. OBCoV

Women Beware Women. Thomas Middleton. FaBoSe
"You'll say the gentleman is somewhat simple." OxBM

Women come to sing are singing, The. A Song of Quavering. Jerome Rothenberg. FTOS

Women gather, The. Nikki Giovanni. ISC

Women / Have / A / Way / Of / Making. Beautiful Ladies. Mcavoy Layne. CDa

Women have loved before as I love now. Edna St. Vincent Millay. HeIP-4; NALW; PoA

Women have no wilderness in them. Louise Bogan. MoAmPo; NALW; NMM-2; NoAM; TwCP; VGW; WPE

Women he liked, did shovel-bearded Bob. Bob's Lane. Edward Thomas. PoE

Women I Knew, The. Lois Roma-Deeley. LoHo

Women, if we held the oxhide shield. Lament for a Warrior. *Unknown, Sotho.* PeSA, *tr. by* Dan Kunene *and* Jack Cope

Women in Dutch Painting. Eunice De Souza. OMIP

Women in Love. D. H. Lawrence.

"'I can't say it is love I have to offer—and it isn't love I want. It is something'." ITG

Women in the Polish P.O.—their clusters, The. String. Gary Gildner. CMAP

Women in Vietnam, The. Grace Paley. NMM-2

Women know how to wait here. Lines for Marking Time. Roberta Hill Whiteman. BoWoP; CDW

Women--not in / the immediate / setting, The. Floating Series 1. Leslie Scalapino. DeD *Fr.* Floating Series.

Women of Dan Dance with Swords in Their Hands to Mark the Time When They Were Warriors, The. Audre Lorde. NAAL-2; NALW; NoAM

Women of Jericho, The. Phyllis McGinley. ChIV-1; KSG

Women of Maine, The. Rush Rankin. CMAP

Women of my Color. Wanda Coleman. NMM-2

Women of my country, black and barefoot girls. Black Island. Charles Pressoir, *French.* NegPo, *tr. by* Ellen Conroy Kennedy

Women of My Land. Frankie Armstrong. BrRo

Women of Nigeria. Night in Nigeria. Ellease Southerland. GT

Women of Rubens, The. Wislawa Szymborska, *Polish.* PoSu, *tr. by* Magnus F. Krynski; VCWP, *tr. by* Magnus J. Krynski *and* Robert A. Maguire; WPOW, *tr. by* Celina Wieniewska

Women of the Future. Mary Scott. ECWP

Women of Trachis. Sophocles, *Greek.*
"Kupris bears trophies away." CTC
"Listen first, and show what you're made of." OBCVT, *tr. by* Ezra Pound
"Torn between griefs, which grief shall I lament." OBVE

Women Pleased. John Fletcher.
Song: "Oh [*or* O] fair[e] sweet face, oh [*or* O] eyes celestial[l] bright." PoEL-2
(To His Sleeping Mistress.) NOSC

Women protesting! We've seen it all before. The Home front. Aristophanes, *Greek.* OBCVT, *tr. by* Tony Harrison

Women reminded him of lilies and roses. Thoughts after Ruskin. Elma Mitchell. FaBoTC; FaBoWP

Women / should be / pedestals / moving. May Swenson. NMM-2

Women sleep, The. Broken Dreams. Hugo Williams. CBLP

Women spend the afternoon squatting on the porch. Another Life. Taslima Nasrin, *Bengali.* VCWP, *tr. by* Carolyne Wright

Women stone breakers. History Makers. George Campbell. PBCV

Women tease and scold me, The. Palladas, *Greek.* InMo, *tr. by* Sam Hamill

Women Transport Corps. *Unknown, Chinese.* WPOW, *tr. by* Kai-yu Hsu

Women were first to catch sight of him, The. The Coming of Raka. N. P. van Wyk Louw, *Afrikaans.* PeSAV, *tr. by* Guy Butler *Fr.* Raka.

Women were making clay bowls, The. What the Women Told Me. E. Ethelbert Miller. GT

Women, / What fools we are. Two Strange Worlds. Francesca Yetunde Pereira. PBA

Women Who Cook. Anita Skeen. GLP

Women Who Hate Me, The. Dorothy Allison. CPO; GLP

Women who Speak with Steak Knives. Susan Hampton. BMAP

Women, whoever wishes to know my lord. Gaspara Stampa, *Italian.* BoWoP, *tr. by* J. Vitiello

Women Wisdom. Larry Mitchell. GLP

Women with hats like the rear ends of pink ducks. To a Waterfowl. Donald Hall. OBAL

Women, women, love of women. Unknown. MiEL

Women, women, / women, women. A Fixture. May Swenson. NYBP

Women You Are Accustomed To, The. Lucille Clifton. GT

Women's Degrees. Alfred Denis Godley. NOBL

Women's Jail, The. Miriam Waddington. NOBC

Women's Locker Room. Marilyn Nelson Waniek. LTA; Poetr

Women's Marseillaise, The. F. E. M. Macaulay. BrRo

Women's Rondo. *Unknown, Aborigine.* NOBAu

Women's Room in Pennsylvania Station, The. Kate Daniels. GM

Women's Rule, *epigram.* Friedrich von Logau, *German.* GePo, *tr. by* George C. Schoolfield

Women's Songs. *Unknown, Maori.* PeNZ, *tr. by* Margaret Orbell

Won' you ring, old hammer? Hammer, Ring. *Unknown.* AmFP

Wonder, The. Rudyard Kipling. *Fr.* Epitaphs of the War [1914–1918]. OBWP

Wonder, The. Thylias Moss. ChAP

Wonder. Thomas Traherne. CH; ESCV; GeHe; HAP; ImPo; NAEL-1; NoP-4; PoE; SeCP; TOF

Wonder Bar / Wishing Well. Neon Signs. Langston Hughes. APSN

Wonder Clock, The. Katharine Pyle. OBCA

Wonder—is not precisely Knowing. Emily Dickinson. NCAP

Wonder not if I stay not here. To Master Davenant for Absence. Sir John Suckling. CaPo

Wonder of Women, or The Tragedie of Sophonisba, The. Lucan, *Latin*. "Since heaven helpes not, deepest hell weele try." OBCVT, *tr. by* John Marston

Wonder stranger ne'r was known, A. The Suffolk Miracle. *Unknown*. ESPB

Wonder that my wit cannot indite, The. (LL) Sonnet 71: "The Soverayne beauty which I doo admire." Edmund Spenser. AEP

Wonderful. Julian S. Cutler. PWR

Wonderful. Ania Walwicz. BMAP

Wonderful are thy works, as my soul overwhelmingly knoweth. The Royal Crown. Solomon ibn Gabirol, *Hebrew*. AWP, *tr. by* Israel Zangwill

Wonderful bears that walked my room all night. Bears. Adrienne Rich. NYBP

Wonderful bird is the pelican, A. Limerick. Dixon Lanier Merritt. PeLi

Wonderful Derby Ram, The. *Unknown*. BoTP *See* The Derby Ram.

Wonderful Mother, A. Pat O'Reilly. BLPA

Wonderful "One-Hoss Shay," The. Oliver Wendell Holmes. *See* The Deacon's Masterpiece

Wonderful Things. Ron Padgett. PmAP

Wonderful, this road to Cold Mountain. *Unknown, Chinese*. CoBCP, *tr. by* Burton Watson

Wonderful workings of the world: wonderful, The. Cut the Grass. A. R. Ammons. HAP; Poetr; TAP; WeW-3

Wonderful World, The. William Brighty Rands. *See* The World.

Wondering, aglow / Fourfooted, tiptoe. (LL) The Fallow Deer at the Lonely House. Thomas Hardy. AWP; CH; CMoP; OxBSP; RB; TTTS

Wondering if you haven't found someone new. (LL) Thoughts in the Cold. Li Shang-yin, *Chinese*. CoBCP, *tr. by* Burton Watson

Wonders. Lorenzo Thomas. MoNo

Wonders. *Unknown*. *See* Thule, The Period of Cosmography.

Wonders are many and none is more wonderful than man. Glengormley. Derek Mahon. CIP-2; IIP

Wonders of Nature. *Unknown*. OTCP

Wonders of Obligation. Roy Fisher. "Near Hartington." NBrP

Wonders of the Peak, The. Charles Cotton. Chatsworth. OBGa

Wond'rous crowd then 'gan aloud, A. Michael Wigglesworth. NAAL-3 *Fr.* The Day of Doom. NAAL-1; SCAP

"'Wondrous life!' cried Marvell at Appleton House." Round. Weldon Kees. CoAP

Wondrous light is filling the air, A. The Spirit of the Age. Christopher Pearse Cranch. APN-1; PAR

Wondrous the Gods, more wondrous are the Men. A Compliment to the Ladies. William Blake. BXAP; OBCoV

Wondrous the Merge. James Richard Broughton. GLP

Wondrous this masonry wasted by Fate! The Ruin. *Unknown, Anglo-Saxon*. AnOE, *tr. by* Charles W. Kennedy

Wondrous truths, which now they but conceal, The. (LL) The Origin of Man, I. Jones Very. APN-1

Won't last half an hour. (LL) A Sunshiny shower. *Unknown*. FaBoBe; LB; OxNR; ReMoGo

"Won't you look out of your window, Mrs. Gill?" The Mocking Fairy. Walter De la Mare. MoBrPo

Woo Not the World. Mu'tamid, King of Seville, *Arabic*. AWP, *tr. by* Dulcie L. Smith

Wood. Thomas Hornsby Ferril. PoRA

Wood. Novella Nikolaevna Matveyeva, *Russian*. TCRP, *tr. by* Deming Brown

Wood (and all else) by the sink. Watching Women with Children. Elaine Randell. NBrP

Wood borers. Tanka. Fumi Saito, *Japanese*. MJT, *tr. by* Makoto Ueda

Wood Carols. Henrietta Cordelia Ray. CBWP-3

Wood-chuck. *Unknown*. ImGa

Wood-Cutter, The. Lupenga Mphande. HBAPE

Wood-doves are singing along the Perkiomen, The. Thinking of a Relation between the Images of Metaphors. Wallace Stevens. SAmP

Wood Floor Dreams. Lance Henson. VoR

Wood is a good place to find, The. Walking with Lulu in the Wood. Naomi Lazard. NYBP

Wood is bare, The: a river-mist is steeping, The. Elegy. Robert Bridges. EBVV; IMW

Wood is full of shining eyes, The. The Magic Wood. Henry Treece. SPE

Wood merchant's parlour, The. Pierre McOrlan, *French*. MFP, *tr. by* Martin Sorrell

Wood of Error. Edmund Spenser. AEP *Fr.* The Faerie Queene

Wood of Flowers, The. James Stephens. BoTP

Wood of the madrone burns with a flame at once / lavender and mossy green, The. He Thanks His Woodpile. Lew Welch. BB

Wood-Pile, The. Robert Frost. ColAP; InPK-6; NAAL-2; NoAM; NoP-4; SAmP; VGW ("Out walking in the frozen swamp one gray day.") ColAP; NoP-4

Wood pile. Marlene Mountain. HA

Wood was rather old and dark, The. Little Boy Lost. Stevie Smith. FaBoTw

Wood Weasel, The. Marianne Moore. CMoP

Wood with bushes broad there was, begrown with bigtree boughs, A. Euryalus and Nisus Meet Their Deaths. Virgil. NoSic, *tr. by* Thomas Phaer *Fr.* The Aeneid [*or* Eneados, *Aeneis*].

Woodchucks. Maxine W. Kumin. HoPM; NIP-4; Poetr

Woodcutter wakes as mountain moon hangs low, The. Feelings in Nature ("Woodcutter wakes as mountain moon hangs low, The"). Ma Chih-yüan. *Fr.* Four Poems to the Tune "Ch'ing-chiang yin." CoBLCP, *tr. by* Jonathan Chaves

Woodcutter's Ax, A. P'i Jih-hsiu, *Chinese*. SuSp, *tr. by* William H. Nienhauser

Woodcutter's Wife, The. William Rose Benét. AWP

Woodcutting. Gleb Iakovlevich Gorbovsky, *Russian*. TCRP, *tr. by* Lubov Yakovleva

Woodcutting on Lost Mountain. Tess Gallagher. PaTW

Woode untoucht of old was growing there, A. The Sacred wood. Lucan, *Latin*. OBCVT, *tr. by* Thomas May

Wooden belly iron back. Riddle. *Unknown*. FaBoVe

Wooden bridge, gaunt willows. Written on the Night of the Twenty-ninth of the First Month. Yün Shou-p'ing, *Chinese*. CoBLCP, *tr. by* Jonathan Chaves

Wooden cage was wedged on the ship's prow, The. Cock at Sea. Constantine A. Trypanis. PFE

Wooden Chamber, The. Anne Hébert, *French*. WPOW, *tr. by* Birgit Swenson

Wooden Handle, The. Gojko Djogo, *Serbo-Croatian* . AF, *tr. by* Michael March *and* Dušan Puvačić

Wooden Horse Is Brought into Troy, The. Virgil. OBVE, *tr. by* Gawin Douglas *Fr.* The Acncid [*or* Eneados, *Aeneis*].

Wooden Horse then said, The. Jenny Mastoraki, *Modern Greek*. BoWoP; PBWP, *tr. by* Nikos Germanakos

Woodland Mass, The. Dafydd ap Gwilym, *Welsh*. OBWVE, *tr. by* Gwyn Williams

Woodland sprite of the rakish kind, A. A Scandal among the Flowers. Charles S. Taylor. BLPA

Woodlark, The. Gerard Manley Hopkins. RB

Woodlot, The. Amy Clampitt. HCAP

Woodman on the hill must have his rest, A. Arna Bontemps. *See* "Close Your Eyes!"

Woodman, spare that tree! George Pope Morris. APN-1; BLPA; CTV; FaBoBe; PWR ("Thy axe shall harm it not.") (LL) CTV

Woodniche. Aidan Carl Mathews. APAD

Woodnotes I ("For this present, hard"). Ralph Waldo Emerson. AmPP; NOBA "In unplowed Maine he sought the lumberers' gang." MeMAP; TAP

Woodnotes II ("As sunbeams stream through liberal space"). Ralph Waldo Emerson. NOBA "Once again the pine-tree sung." APN-1

Woodpecker, The. Ni Tsan, *Chinese*. CoBLCP, *tr. by* Jonathan Chaves

Woodpecker, The. Joyce Sambrook. BoTP

Woodpecker goes beating a little drum, The. Sleep. Charles Simic. CoAP

Woodpecker pecked out a little round hole, The. Elizabeth Madox Roberts. OBCA; TLR

Woodrow Wilson. Robinson Jeffers. FaBoPV

Woods. Jerzy Harasymowicz, *Polish*. CEEP, *tr. by* Victor Contoski

Woods. Louis MacNeice. IIP

Woods, The. Derek Mahon. NOIV; PBCIP

"Woods and the rivers are silent," The. Torquato Tasso. ItIP

Woods darken, grasses startled by wind. Lu Lun. SuSp, *tr. by* Ronald C. Miao *Fr.* Frontier Songs.

Woods decay, the woods decay and fall, The. Tithonus. Tennyson. CABP; EnVR; GEA; HAP; ImPo; NAEL-2; NAWM-2; NOBE; NOBVV; NoP-4; OAEL-2; OBNC; PoE; PoEL-5; SCGP

Woods have cast their crimson foliage, The. October. Aleksandr Sergeyevich Pushkin, *Russian*. FP, *tr. by* D. M. Thomas

Woods of Arcady are dead, The. The Song of the Happy Shepherd. W. B. Yeats. NoAM

Woods of the horizon, The. Men in the City. Alfonsina Storni, *Spanish*. PBWP, *tr. by* Rachel Benson

Woods sleep bathed in shadow, The. Evensong. Paul Gerhardt, *German*. GePo, *tr. by* Ingrid Waløe-Engel

Woods, the mountain, silent, The. On a Cold Day I Climbed Tiger Hill With Professor Ho. At the Time, the Local Prefect Had Prohibited Pleasure Excursions and Feasts, But the Mountain Was Quiet and Tranquil, So We Stayed All Day. Mo Shih-lung, *Chinese.* CoBLCP, *tr. by* Jonathan Chaves

Woodspurge, The. D. G. Rossetti. CABP; EBEV; EnVR; GEA; GTBS-P; HAP; HeIP-4; NOBE; NoP-4; OAEL-2; OBEV; OBNC; PBMP; PoEL-5; SCGP; TFi; UnPo *Fr.* The House of Life.

Woodspurge has a cup of three, The. (LL) The Woodspurge. D. G. Rossetti. CABP; EBEV; EnVR; GEA; GTBS-P; HAP; HeIP-4; NOBE; NoP-4; OAEL-2; OBEV; OBNC; PBMP; PoEL-5; SCGP; TFi; UnPo

Woodtown Manor. John Montague. PBCIP

Woodworker's Ballad. Herbert Edward Palmer. OBEV

Woody Guthrie Visited by Bob Dylan: Brooklyn State Hospital, New York, 1961. David Wojahn. PBCAP *Fr.* Mystery Train: A Sequence.

Wooed and Married and A'. Alexander Ross. OxBS

Woof of the sun, ethereal gauze. Haze. Henry David Thoreau. NCAP; TAP *Fr.* A Week on the Concord and Merrimack Rivers.

Woof reversed the the fatal shuttles weave, A. Strikers in Hyde Park. Louise Imogen Guiney. APN-2

Wooing in a Dream. Nicholas Breton. *See* A Report Song [in a Dream].

Wooing of Criseide, The, III. Chaucer. PoEL-1 *Fr.* Troilus and Criseyde [*or* Criseide]. EnVB

Wooing of Etain, The. *Unknown, Irish.* BIrV, *tr. by* John Montague

Wool-chafed and wet-shoed I went forth after. William Langland. NAEL-1 *Fr.* The Vision of Piers Plowman.

Wool Trade, The. John Dyer. *See* Urban Progress.

Woolly Words. Robert N. Feinstein. NBLV

Woolworth's. Donald Hall. OBCoV

Woosel cock so black of hue, The. Bottom's Song. Shakespeare. CTC *Fr.* A Midsummer Night's Dream.

Wooyeo Ball, The. *Unknown.* NOBAu

Word, The. Margaret Avison. MoCV

Word, The. Basil Bunting. PoA

Word, The. Mark Cox. NAmP90

Word, The. John Masefield. FP

Word, The. Stevie Smith. WPN

Word, The. Neil Weiss. NYBP

Word a Hunt, A. William Drummond, of Hawthornden. NOBE

Word Basket Woman. Gary Snyder. BB

Word-Bird knows that everybody in Britain is frightened to death of *words*, The. Gavin Ewart. PeLV

Word bites like a fish, The. Stephen Spender. NYBP

Word by Night. Charles Brasch. PeNZ

Word, defining, muzzles; the drawn line, The. Poems, Potatoes. Sylvia Plath. AFr

Word Faith means when someone sees, The. Faith. Czeslaw Milosz, *Polish.* RaBo, *tr. by* Robert Hass, Robert Pinsky *and* Renata Gorcynski

Word for Summer, A. George Seferis, *Greek.* AF, *tr. by* Edmund Keeley *and* Philip Sherrard

Word for the Hour, A. John Greenleaf Whittier. NCAP

Word from a Petitioner. John Pierpont.

Word from the Hills. Richard Moore.

    It Took TV to Civilize Our Village. Son

    Though the New Teacher Is a Trifle Odd. Son

    Unable, Father, Still, to Disavow. Son

Word goes round Repins, The. An Absolutely Ordinary Rainbow. Les A. Murray. CBAP

Word has come from the kitchen. *Unknown. See* Mary Hamilton.

Word has come to May Margerie. Jellon Grame. *Unknown.* EBEV; ESPB; OxBB

Word has come to me that she. Anacreon, *Greek.* InMo, *tr. by* Sam Hamill

Word has gane thro a' this land. The Bonny Lass of Anglesey. *Unknown.* ESPB

Word I had no one left but God. (LL) Bereft. Robert Frost. LiTM; MoAmPo; OxBA; SAGP; SoSe-8

Word in Edgeways, A. Charles Tomlinson. CABP; NOBL

Word is dead, A. Emily Dickinson. NTP; SAmP

    ("That day.") (LL) KaS

Word is fast asleep, The. Poem. Labhshankar Thacker, *Gujarati.* OMIP, *tr. by* Sitanshu Yashashchandra

Word is imitative, The. Mummer. Jack Spicer. APSN

Word is the father of the saints, The. Macumba Word. Aimé Césaire, *French.* PFTM, *tr. by* Clayton Eshleman *and* Annette Smith

Word! it cannot fail; it ever speaks, The. Jones Very. NCAP

Word Made Flesh, The. Walter James Turner. OBMV

Word made Flesh is seldom, A. Emily Dickinson. APN-2; ChIV-2; NAAL-1; NAAL-3; NALW; PAR

Word: Man, A. Washington Allston. APN-1

Word of a snail on the plate of a leaf, The? The Couriers. Sylvia Plath. LCAP-2

Word of advice about matters and things, A. Written at the White Sulphur Springs. Francis Scott Key. OBAL

Word of Encouragement, A. J. R. Pope. NBLV; NOBL

Word of God, Across the Ages. Ferdinand Q. Blanchard. AH

Word of Mouth. Ted Greenwald.

    "Open mouth open through." FTOS

Word of the Lord by night, The. Boston Hymn. Ralph Waldo Emerson. CBCWP

Word of the sun to the sky, The. Triads. Swinburne. PBMP

Word of Water, The. Edward Leslie Mayo. PoA

Word outleaps the world, and light is all. (LL) Four for Sir John Davies. Theodore Roethke. MoAmPo; NOBA; NoAM

Word over all, beautiful as the sky. Reconciliation. Walt Whitman. APN-1; HAP; MeMAP; MoAmPo; NAAL-1; NAAL-3; NoP-4; OBWP; OxBA; OxBSP; SAGP; WeW-3

Word *Plum*, The. Helen Chasin. NIP-4

Word Poem (Perhaps Worth Considering). Nikki Giovanni. PoBA

Word "Silk," The. Thomas McCarthy. CIP-2

Word sits on the kitchen counter, A. A Missed Opportunity. James Tate. IFJA

Word to Husbands, A. Ogden Nash. OBCoV

Word to New England, A. William Bradford. SCAP

Word to the violent has never been sufficient, A. "Word to the Wise Is Enough, A." Raymond R. Patterson. NBV

Word to the West End, A. Thomas Ashe. EBVV

"Word to the Wise Is Enough, A." Raymond R. Patterson. NBV

Word went forth, The. Saint Thomas Aquinas, *Latin.* MLL, *tr. by* Helen Waddell

Wordes of the Ho[o]st[e] to the Phisicien and the Pardoner, The. Chaucer. *See* Introduction to the Pardoner's Prologue and Tale.

Words. W. H. Auden. PeLV *Fr.* Shorts [1939–1947].

Words. Wayne Brown. HCP

Words. Mahmoud Darwish, *Arabic.* VCWP, *tr. by* Rana Kabbani

Words, The. Stefan Aug. Doinas, *Romanian.* CEEP, *tr. by* Peter Jay *and* Virgil Nemoianu

Words. Robert Finch. PoA

Words. Barbara Guest. FTOS

Words. Nikolai Stepanovich Gumilyov, *Russian.* TCRP, *tr. by* Simon Franklin

Words, The. Lee Harwood. SPE

Words. David Huddle. CDa *Fr.* Tour of Duty.

Words. Dan Pagis, *Hebrew.* IP, *tr. by* Warren Bargad *and* Stanley F. Chyet

Words. Sylvia Plath. APAD; CoAmPo; HCAP; NAAL-2; NALW; PoE; Poetr; VCAP

Words. William Robert Rodgers. OxBSP; PNI

Words. Vern Rutsala. WeW-3

Words. "David Samuilovich Samoylov," *Russian.* TCRP, *tr. by* Lubov Yakovleva

Words. Wislawa Szymborska, *Polish.* PoSu, *tr. by* Krystof Zarzecki

Words. *Unknown.* PoLF

Words, The. David Wagoner. PoA

Words and Legacy. Cyril Dabydeen. PBCV

Words and Monsters. Vernon Scannell. OxBC

Words and Music. Samuel Beckett.

    Song: "Age is when to a man." BIrV

Words and Music in America. Kofi Natambu. MoNo

Words and Thoughts. John Clark Pratt. CDa

Words are but leaves to the tree of mind. Samuel Alfred Beadle. AAP

Words are Doric, Doric too the man, The. Theocritus, *Greek.* GrAn, *tr. by* Anthony Holden

Words are for those with promises to keep. (LL) Their Lonely Betters. W. H. Auden. NAEL-2; NoAM; OBGa

Words are like leaves; and where they most abound. The Art of Poetry. Alexander Pope. ECEV *Fr.* An Essay on Criticism. NAEL-1; PoEL-3; TFi

Words beget Anger: Anger brings forth blows. To His Friend to Avoid Contention of Words. Robert Herrick. FP

Words cannot be wholly transparent. And that is the. George Oppen. APSN *Fr.* Route.

Words do not grow on the landscape. Jean Malley. PoA

Words, endless words I've said to serve the moment. Clytemnestra triumphant over the bodies of Agamemnon and Cassandra. Aeschylus, *Greek.* OBCVT, *tr. by* Robert Fagles

Words for Hart Crane. Robert Lowell. CMoP

Words for Jazz Perhaps. Michael Longley. SeSe

Words for Love. Ted Berrigan. PmAP

Words for My Daughter. John Balaban. RaBo

Words for My Daughter from the Asylum. Hayden Carruth. MoLi *Fr.* The Bloomingdale Papers.

Words for the Wind. Theodore Roethke. CoAP; NOBA

Words from. Tanka. Ishikawa Takuboku, *Japanese.* MJT, *tr. by* Ueda, Makoto

Words from an Old Spanish Carol. *Unknown, Spanish.* PChr, *tr. by* Ruth Sawyer

(Christmas Morn.) OBCP

Words from Confinement. Cesare Pavese, *Italian.* AF, *tr. by* William Arrowsmith

Words from Hell. David Helwig. NOBC

Words from the Goblet of Wisdom. Yüan Mei, *Chinese.* CoBLCP, *tr. by* Jonathan Chaves

Word's gane to the kitchen. Mary Hamilton. *Unknown.* ESPB; NoP-4; SCGP

Word's gone out, and now they spread the main, The. Daniel Defoe. OBWP *Fr.* The Spanish Descent.

Words have grown old inside men, The. The Words Will Resurrect. Jorge de Lima, *Portuguese.* TTY, *tr. by* John Nist

Words in Time. Archibald MacLeish. PoRA

Words keep tumbling tumbling about, Tom, The. To Tom Saunders on His Imprisonment. Bill Griffiths. NBrP

Words, Korean mums, The. (LL) Korean Mums. James Schuyler. PmAP; VCAP

Words Like Freedom. Langston Hughes. BPo

Words move, music moves, *sels.* T. S. Eliot. *Fr.* Burnt Norton. CMoP; LiTM; MoAmPo; NAAL-2; PoE *Fr.* Four Quartets.

Words of a wise man's mouth are, The. Bible, *O.T.* CTV *Fr.* The Bible, Ecclesiastes 10:12.

Words of Comfort. Đỗ Tấn Xuân, *Vietnamese* AVP, *tr. by* Huỳnh Sanh Thông

Words of Evening, The. Yves Bonnefoy, *French.* VCWP, *tr. by* Richard Pevear

Words of Old Age. Marie-Madeleine, *German.* CPO, *tr. by* Lillian Faderman, Brigitte Eriksson *and* Frankie Hucklenbroich

Words of our day, The. The Same Side of the Canoe. Alda do Espírito Santo, *Portuguese.* PBWP, *tr. by* Allan Francovich *and* Kathleen Weaver

Words of Tayko-mol. William Oandasan. HATNAP

Words of the All-Wise, The. *Unknown, Icelandic.*

"Say, dwarf, for it seems to me." OBVE, *tr. by* W. H. Auden *and* Paul B. Taylor

Words of the Newly Wed Wife. Wang Chien, *Chinese.* CoBCP, *tr. by* Burton Watson

("I sent some first for sister-in-law to try.") (LL) CoBCP, *tr. by* Burton Watson

(New Wife, The.) BLT, *tr. by* J. P. Seaton

("On the third day she went down to the kitchen.") BLT, *tr. by* J. P. Seaton

Words of the true poems give you more than poems, The. Walt Whitman. ImGa

Words, one by one. Freedom. Wimal Dissanayake. ChAP

Words Read by Lightning. Elaine Equi. WWSi

Words scoreled upon a bone. Meditation on a Bone. Alec Derwent Hope. NoAM

Words Spoken Alone. Dannie Abse. NYBP

Words Spoken by Pasternak during a Bombing. Bella Akhatovna Akhmadulina, *Russian.* BoWoP, *tr. by* Jean Valentine *and* Olga Carlisle

Words that come in smoke and go. Notes for Echo Lake 3. Michael Palmer. PmAP

Words to a Song. Agnes Nemes Nagy, *Hungarian.* BoWoP, *tr. by* Bruce Berlind

Words unto Adam, His Own Scriveyn. Chaucer. *See* To His Scribe Adam.

Words Wherein Stinging Bees Lurk. Judah Halevi, *Hebrew.* TrJP, *tr. by* Nina Davis Salaman

Words Will Resurrect, The. Jorge de Lima, *Portuguese.* TTY, *tr. by* John Nist

Words would not have come to write to you. Autumn Wind. Ruth Dallas. PeNZ *Fr.* Letter to a Chinese Poet.

Wordspinning. Olga Kirsch, *Afrikaans.* PeSA, *tr. by* Jack Cope

Wordsworth. Charlotte L. Forten Grimke. AAP

Wordsworth and His Music. Wordsworth. EPCY *Fr.* The Recluse; Home at Grasmere.

Wordsworth I love, his books are like the fields. To Wordsworth. John Clare. OAEL-2; Son

Wordsworth on Lloyd George. Mary Visick. UV

Wordsworth to the contrary notwithstanding. In Magic Words. Merrill Moore. Son

Wordsworth upon Helvellyn! Let the cloud. On a Portrait of Wordsworth by B. R. Haydon. Elizabeth Barrett Browning. EPCY; HeIP-4; Ro

Wordsworth's Grave. Matthew Arnold. *Fr.* Memorial Verses. CABP; NAEL-2; OAEL-2

Wordsworth's Grave. Sir William Watson. OBNC

Work. Andrei Codrescu. PmAP; SPE

Work. Gyula Illyés, *Hungarian.* RaBo, *tr. by* William Jay Smith

("They stuck pigs in the throat.") PFTM, *tr. by* William Jay Smith

Work. D. H. Lawrence. OBMV

Work. Aleksandr Sergeyevich Pushkin, *Russian.* AWP, *tr. by* Babette Deutsch *and* Avrahm Yarmolinsky

Work. Denise Riley. NBrP

Work. J. W. Thompson. PoToHe

Work; a Song of Triumph ("Work / Thank God for the might of it"). Angela Morgan. PoLF

Work for Small Men. Sam Walter Foss.

"Despise not any man that lives." PoToHe

Work Gangs. Carl Sandburg. GM

Work? / I don't have to work. Necessity. Langston Hughes. APSN; NOBA; RaBo

Work-in-Progress. Lawrence Ferlinghetti.

"And Pablo Neruda / that Chilean omnivore of poetry." BB

Work-in-progress. Mahmood Jamal. NBrP

Work is Progress. Bernadette Mayer. DeD

Work is a blessing, / I tell you that, I—professional sluggard! Before Breughel the Elder. Aleksander Wat, *Polish.* AF, *tr. by* Czeslaw Milosz *and* Leonard Nathan

Work it, knead it—the wax won't fall apart. Ode to the Candle. Phan chu Trinh, *Vietnamese.* AVP, *tr. by* Huỳnh Sanh Thông

Work like a sea? Wordsworth. *See* Fair seed time had my soul, and I grew up.

Work of Artifice, A. Marge Piercy. Poetsp

Work of Gardening, The. William Cowper. GaP

Work of Her that went, The. Emily Dickinson. MDDM

Work of the sun, not illusion, The. A Slogan Will Not Suffice. Kelvin Corcoran. NBrP

Work on my brain, help every faculty. Mary Pix. KTR, *act* I *Fr.* Queen Catherine.

Work on the impossible. Tanka. Toki Zenmaro, *Japanese.* MJT, *tr. by* Makoto Ueda

Work on the railroad. Roll on the Ground. *Unknown.* AmFP

Work out a perfect will. (LL) By the Statue of King Charles [*or* I] at Charing Cross. Lionel Pigot Johnson. MoBrPo; NOBE; OBEV; OBMV; OBNC; PeVV; PoEL-5

Work-Songs. *Unknown.* PBCV

Work-table, litter, books and standing lamp. Night Sweat. Robert Lowell. NAAL-2; TAP; VGW

Work / Thank God for the might of it. Work; a Song of Triumph. Angela Morgan. PoLF

Work to Do Toward Town. Gary Snyder. VGW

Work We Hate and Dreams We Love. Jimmy Santiago Baca. LoL

Work while you work. One Thing at a Time. M. A. Stodart. PoToHe

Work Without Hope. Coleridge. GSo; LaPo; NAEL-2; NOBE; OBEV; OxAEP-2; Son

(In Springtime.) BoTP

("Wears on his smiling face a dream of Spring.") (LL) BoTP

Workaday Morning. Melvin Beaunearus Tolson, *Norwegian.* PBWP, *tr. by* Nadia Christensen

Workbox, The. Thomas Hardy. InPK-6; NAEL-2; UnPo

Workday. Linda Hogan. HATNAP

Worked its filthy way out like a tongue. (LL) Welcome to Hiroshima. Mary Jo Salter. NMM-2; RA

Worker, The. Nikolai Stepanovich Gumilyov, *Russian.* TCRP, *tr. by* Simon Franklin

Worker, The. Gerald Massey. EBVV

Worker, The. Richard W. Thomas. PoBA

Worker (We Own Two Houses), The. Charles Fort. CMAP

Workers earn it. Money. Richard Armour. NBLV

Working. Maxine Scates. PBCAP

Working and Waiting. Adah Isaacs Menken. CBWP-1

Working Class. Bertram J. Warr. NOBC

Working Construction. Eric Chock. OpBo

Working late. Louis Simpson. PBCV

Working Man, The. Ellen Johnston. VWP

Working my way through life's karma. The Year *Chi-wei* (Fifteen Fifty Nine), New Year's Day. Wen Cheng-ming, *Chinese*. CoBLCP, *tr. by* Jonathan Chaves

Working on the Railway. *Unknown*. APN-2

Working out the difficult passages together. (LL) Moving House ("A Long time I've wanted to live in the southern village"). T'ao Ch'ien, *Chinese*. CoBCP, *tr. by* Burton Watson

Working Party, A. Siegfried Sassoon. AF; CMoP; PeFWW; PoFWW

"Working so many hours," said Liddell. (LL) Liddell and Scott. Thomas Hardy. OBCoV; OxBoLi; PeLV

Working Song. Buluguru, *Yaoro*. CBAP, *tr. by* E. A. Worms

Working with Mother. Myra Cohn Livingston. TLR

Working with one eye closed or heads buried. The War Photographers. Frank Ormsby. PNI

Working with Tools. A. R. Ammons. TRP

Workman plied his clumsy spade, A. Two Surprises. R. W. McAlpine. PoLF

"Workman, what will you make on the bench today?" Carpenter. George Mackay Brown. OxBC

Works and Days. Hesiod, *Greek*.

   Summer. GrIP, *tr. by* Richard Lattimore

   "When first Both Gods and Men had one Times Birth." OBCVT, *tr. by* George Chapman

Works of Art. Elizabeth Jennings. PeECV

Works of God, The. Moses ibn Ezra, *Hebrew*. TrJP, *tr. by* Solomon Solis-Cohen

Works, the days, uh, The. But Not That One. John Ashbery. LCAP-2

World, The. William Bronk. APSN

World, The. Robert Creeley. MoP; NoP-4; PmAP; VCAP

World, The. George Herbert. GeHe; NOSC

World, The. Kathleen Jessie Raine. OxBTC

World, The. William Brighty Rands. BoTP; NOxBChV; OxBChV (Wonderful World, The.) CTV

World, The. Christina Rossetti. BoWoP; NALW; PEW

World, The. Vern Rutsala. Poetsp

World, The. Henry Vaughan. *See* World, The (1).

World, The. Ella Wheeler Wilcox. PWR

World a hunting is, The. A Word a Hunt. William Drummond, of Hawthornden. NOBE

World a narrow pound, The. (LL) Solomon to Sheba. W. B. Yeats. CMoP

World and I, The. Laura Riding Jackson. ColAP

World as Garden, The. George Gascoigne. GaP

World as Meditation, The. Wallace Stevens. HeIP-4; LCAP-2

World begins at a kitchen table. No matter what, we must eat to live, The. Perhaps the World Ends Here. Joy Harjo. PaTW

World below the brine, The. Walt Whitman. APN-1; NoP-4; PBMP

World broods with warm breast and with ah! bright wings. (LL) God's Grandeur. Gerard Manley Hopkins. APAD; AWP; CABP; CMoP; ChAP; ClHu; EBVV; EnlH; GSo; HAP; ImPo; InPK-6; LiTM; MoBrPo; MoP; NAEL-2; NIP-4; NOBE; NOBVV; NoAM; NoP-4; OAEL-2; OBNC; PFE; PeVV; PoE; PoPoPo; RaBo; SCGP; SoSe-8; Son; TFi; TrCP; UnPo; WeW-3

World cheats those who cannot read, The. A Mad Poem Addressed to My Nephews and Nieces. Po Chü-i, *Chinese*. ChiP; NNPT, *tr. by* Arthur Waley

World dances with hate, The. Lamenting the Inevitable. Alicia Ostriker. UnSA

World did not force itself into my soul, it seeped into it, The. Paul-Eerik Rummo, *Estonian*. CEEP, *tr. by* Ivar Ivask

World Doesn't End, The. Charles Simic.

   "We were so poor I had to take the place of the." VCAP

World exists beyond the limits of this pane, A. Exile's Letter: After the Failed Revolution. Marilyn Chin. LoHo

World—feels Dusty, The. Emily Dickinson. MoAmPo

World goes none the lamer, The. A. E. Housman. PeVV

World has always known this one word: love, The. The Marvelous Encounter at Blue Creek. *Unknown, Vietnamese*. AVP, *tr. by* Huỳnh Sanh Thông

World / has become divided, The. Poem 143. Charles Olson. APSN; ColAP *Fr.* The Maximus Poems.

World has held great Heroes, The. The Song of Mr Toad. Kenneth Grahame. NOBL; NOxBChV *Fr.* The Wind in the Willows.

World has no such pleasing joy, The. Gaspar Pérez De Villagrá. PaTW, *tr. by* Miguel Encinias, Alfred Rodríguez, *and* Joseph P. Sánchez *Fr.* History of New Mexico.

World has room for the manly man, with the spirit of manly cheer, The. The Manly Man. *Unknown*. BLPA

World I did not wish to enter, A. A Necessitarian's Epitaph. Thomas Hardy. FaBoEE

World in gloom and splendour passes by, The. To a Millionaire. Archibald Lampman. NOBC

World in turmoil—we came south together, A. The Rebellion Over, I See Off a Friend Who Is Returning North. Ssu-k'ung Shu, *Chinese*. CoBCP, *tr. by* Burton Watson

World in Yellow, A. Marcel Duchamp, *French*. PFTM, *tr. by* Arturo Schwarz

World is, The. Denise Levertov. *See* O Taste and See.

World is a beautiful place, The. 25. Lawrence Ferlinghetti. CAPP-1; CLPP

World Is a Musician's Cliff House, The. Rodney Hall. *Fr.* Black Bagatelles. CBAP

World is all orange-round, The. The Walking Road. Richard Hughes. OBMV

World is between tips, The. The Polar Circle. Lyn Hejinian. BAP-94

World is but a sorry scene, The. Crucifixion of Our Blessed Lord. Christopher Smart. ChIV-2 *Fr.* Hymns and Spiritual Songs for the Fasts and Festivals of the Church of England.

World is charged with the grandeur of God, The. God's Grandeur. Gerard Manley Hopkins. APAD; AWP; CABP; CMoP; ChAP; ClHu; EBVV; EnlH; GSo; HAP; ImPo; InPK-6; LiTM; MoBrPo; MoP; NAEL-2; NIP-4; NOBE; NOBVV; NoAM; NoP-4; OAEL-2; OBNC; PFE; PeVV; PoE; PoPoPo; RaBo; SCGP; SoSe-8; Son; TFi; TrCP; UnPo; WeW-3

World is come upon me, I used to keep it a long way off, The. The Deserter. Stevie Smith. FaBoWP

World is dull, the world is blind, The. Die Welt ist dumm, die Welt ist blind. Heinrich Heine, *German*. AWP, *tr. by* James Thomson

World is everything that is the case, The. Tractatus. Derek Mahon. OxBSP

World Is Full of Beauty, The. Matilda Caroline Edwards. PWR

World is full of colour!, The. Colour. Adeline White. BoTP

World is full of gladness, The. Lemon Pie. E. A. Guest. OBAL

World is full of loss; bring, wind, my love, The. Song. Muriel Rukeyser. PFE

World is full of mostly invisible things, The. To David, about His Education. Howard Nemerov. HCAP

World Is Full of Remarkable Things, The. LeRoi Jones *and* Imamu Amiri Baraka. SSLK

World is full of those who love to be officials, The. Drinking Wine. Ch'ien Ch'ien-i, *Chinese*. SuSp, *tr. by* Irving Y. Lo

World is large and wide and long, The. Song of an Old Gray Wolf. *Unknown, Cheyenne Native American*. APN-2, *tr. by* Alfred Kroeber

World Is like a Woman of Folly, The. Moses ibn Ezra. *Fr.* The World's Illusion. TrJP, *tr. by* Solomon Solis-Cohen

World is made of days and, The. Aren't You Glad. Charlotte Zolotow. CTV

World is no more than the Beloved's single face, The. Asadullah Khan Ghalib, *Urdu*. EnlH, *tr. by* Jane Hirshfield

World is / not with us enough, The. O Taste and See. Denise Levertov. ChIV-1; CrSp; PBWP; TAP

World is only air / shining, granular, transparent things, The. Jan Polkowski, *Polish*. AF, *tr. by* Michael March *and* Jaroslaw Anders

World is pitiless and lewdly jeers, The. The Counsel. Roy Campbell. LBC

World is Rome, The; Carnuntum, on the Danube. Marcus Antoninus Cui Cognomen Erat Aurelius. Burns Singer. OxBS

World is several billion years of age, The. Winter Report. Ben Howard. PoA

World is so full of a number of things, The. Happy Thought. Robert Louis Stevenson. BoTP; FaBoBe; OxBChV; PWR; Spl

World is too much with us; late and soon, The. Sonnet. Wordsworth. APAD; AWP; CABP; ClHu; EBEvV; FHYEP; FaPoR; GSo; GTBS-P; HAP; HeIP-4; HoPM; ImPo; InPK-6; InPS-3; NAEL-2; NAWM-2; NOBE; NOBRP; NoP-4; OAEL-2; OBEV; OBNC; PBMP; PFE; PWR; PoE; PoEL-4; PoLF; PoPoPo; PoRA; Poetr; RaBo; Ro; SAGP; SCGP; SoSe-8; Son; TFi; TRP; WeW-3

World is Turned Upside Down, The. *Unknown*. NOSC

World is what you swim in, or dance, it is simple. The Dolphins. Carol Ann Duffy. NBrP

World is wise, for the world is old, The. Frederick William Faber. PWR

World Is with Me, The. Thomas Hood. Son

World is young today, The. A Song. Digby Mackworth Dolben. NOBVV; OBNC

World / it was long time ago that I first saw you. Remorse Came Slowly. Junko Nishi, *Japanese*. WPJ, *tr. by* Kenneth Rexroth *and* Ikuko Atsumi

World laid low, and the wind blew like a dust, The. Epigram. *Unknown, Irish*. NOIV, *tr. by* Thomas Kinsella

World Needs, the. *Unknown*. PoToHe

World Not Our Rest, The. Maria Frances Cecelia Cowper. ECWP

World of books amid a world of green, A. A Library in a Garden. Richard Le Gallienne. OBGa

World of Darkness. Robert Chatain. PoA

World of dreams, The. Philip Salom. NOBAu

World of Expectations, The. Albert Goldbarth. HCAP

World of money, promise and disease, A. (LL) The Man from Washington. James Welch. CDW; HATNAP; NoAM; PoPoPo; RaBo

World of Simon Raven, The. Peter Porter. PeLV

World on Sunday. James McAuley. BMAP

World Outside, The. Denise Levertov. CoAmPo; TRP

World outstrips us. In my day, The. Family Week at Oracle Ranch. James Merrill. BAP-94

World pursues the very track, The. The Chaunts of the Brazen Head. Winthrop Mackworth Praed. NOBRP

World-Secret. Hugo von Hofmannsthal, *German*. TrJP, *tr. by* Charles Wharton Stork

World should listen then—as I am listening now, The. (LL) To a Skylark. Shelley. EBEvV; FHYEP; FaBoBe; GTBS-P; HAP; ImPo; InPS-3; NAEL-2; NOBE; NOBRP; NoP-4; OAEL-2; OBEV; OBNC; OxAEP-2; PBMP; PoLF; Ro; SCGP; TFi

World-Soul, The. Ralph Waldo Emerson. APN-1; NCAP

World State, The. G. K. Chesterton. FP

World, that all contains, is ever moving, The. Change. Greville Fulke. NoSic *Fr.* Caelica.

World, the Devil, and Tom Paine, The. *Unknown.* AH

World, The (1). Henry Vaughan. AWP; ChIV-2; EBEV; ESCV; HAP; ImPo; NAEL-1; NOBE; NOBRP; NOVC; NOSC; OAEL-1; OxAEP-1; PeECV; PoEL-2; SCGP; SeCP; TFi; TrCP

(World, The.) FMP; FSCP; PBRV

World to Come, A. Bernard Dadié, *French*. NegPo, *tr. by* Ellen Conroy Kennedy

World Transformed, The. John Greenleaf Whittier. *Fr.* Snow-Bound [*or* Snow-Bound; a Winter Idyl]. APN-1; AiP; AmPP; NAAL-3; NOBA; OxBA; TAP; TFi

World turns mild, The; democracy, they say. Tempora Mutantur. James Russell Lowell. HAP

World under the sky, The. A Gone. Larry Eigner. NeAP

World vanishes slowly. We all study, The. The Sea Before I Start Dreaming. Branko Miljkovic, *Serbo-Croatian*. HSix, *tr. by* Charles Simic

World War II. Jeni Couzyn. PeSAV

World War II. Edward Field. GLP

World War II. Langston Hughes. HCAP; PoPoPo

World was everything that was the case?, The. James Merrill. HCAP *Fr.* Mirabell: Books of Number.

World was first a private park, The. The Fisherman. Jay Macpherson. NOBC

World was made by an Egyptian god, The. Genesis. Anghel Dumbrveanu, *Romanian*. CEEP, *tr. by* Adam J. Sorkin *and* Irina Grigorescu Pan

World We Make, The. Alfred Grant Walton. PoToHe

World will see thy picture there, The. (LL) Secrecy [*or* Secresie] Protested. Thomas Carew. CaPo; PFE; SeCP

World with all of its thought and action, The. God's Electric Power. Mrs. Henry Linden. CBWP-4

'World Without Objects Is a Sensible Emptiness," A." Richard Wilbur. CoAmPo; LiTM; MoAmPo; MoP; NAAL-2; NOBA; NoAM; PoA

World Without Peculiarity. Wallace Stevens. FiLi; HCAP

World world world world / and the face grave. Enueg II. Samuel Beckett. NoAM

World, / world you are wonderful. A Round Song. Rhyll McMaster. CBAP

Worldes bliss ne last no throwe. *Unknown.* MiEL

Worldes blisse, have good day! *Unknown.* CrSp; MiEL

Worldly Beauty. T. R. Hummer. PuP-17

Worldly matters again draw my body;. To Li Chien. Po Chü-i, *Chinese*. ChiP, *tr. by* Arthur Waley

Worldly Wealth. Rowland Watkyns. FaBoEE

Worldly wisdom of the foolish man, The. Francis Quarles. ESCV *Fr.* Emblems.

Worldman, A. Knocking Donkey Fleas off a Poet from the Southside of Chi. Haki R. Madhubuti. SeSe

World's a bubble, and the life of man, The. Life. Posidippus, *Greek*. GTBS-P; NoSic; OBCVT; OxAEP-1; PFE, *tr. by* Francis Bacon

World's a floor, whose swelling heaps retain, The. Deuteronomy 30.19. Francis Quarles. ChIV-1

World's a Floore, whose swelling heapes retaine, The. ESCV *Fr.* Emblems.

World's a garden; pleasures are the flowers, The. The Garden. Joshua Sylvester. OBGa

World's a popular disease, that reigns, The. Luke 6.25. Francis Quarles. ChIV-2

World's a stage. The trifling entrance fee, The. Hilaire Belloc. OBCoV; OxBTC

World's a stranger's room, we meet to part, The. You Gave Me Hyacinths First a Year Ago. Dorothy Hewett. BMAP

World's a theater, the earth a stage, The. The Author to His Book[e]. Thomas Heywood. NOSC *Fr.* An Apology for Actors.

World's a very happy place, The. The World's Music. "Gabriel Setoun." FaBoBe

World's a well strung fidle, mans tongue the quill, The. Nathaniel Ward. SCAP

World's an inn, The; and I her guest. On the World. Francis Quarles. HAP

World's and his HYPERION, The. (LL) In the Glorious Epiphanie of Our [*or* Ovr] Lord God[, A Hymn. Svng as by the Three Kings]. Richard Crashaw. ESCV; FSCP; PoEL-2

Worlds are breaking in my head, The. Yves Tanguy. David Gascoyne. NoP-4; SPE

Worlds are reconciled, The. (LL) A Christmas Hymn. Richard Wilbur. ChIV-2; OBCP; PChr; TrCP

World's aswirl with fun and games galore, The. The Comedy of the World. Huỳnh Thúc Kháng, *Vietnamese*. AVP, *tr. by* Huỳnh Sanh Thông

World's at an end, and we come, we come, The. (LL) Viola's Song. Sir William Davenant. FaBoCh; HAP; NOSC; SCGP

World's bright comforter, whose beamsome light, The. God's Virtue. Barnabe Barnes. NOCV *Fr.* A Divine Century of Spiritual Sonnets.

World's but theirs; but my Beloved's mine, The. Francis Quarles. *See* My Beloved Is Mine, and I Am His; He Feedeth among the Lillies.

World's deceitful, and man's life at best, The. On Mortality. Henry Colman. ChIV-1

World's disappearing, A. Read Your Fate. Charles Simic. BAP-94

World's gone forward to its latest fair, The. The Moor. Ralph Hodgson. MoBrPo

World's great age begins anew, The. Chorus. Shelley. AWP; EBEV; HAP; HeIP-4; ImPo; NAEL-2; NOBE; NoP-4; OAEL-2; OBEV; PoE; PoEL-4 *Fr.* Hellas.

World's greatest snorer, The. Be Quiet! Max Fatchen. FuFo

World's greatest tricycle rider, The. Charles Kenneth Williams. NYBP

World's Illusion, The. Moses ibn Ezra, *Hebrew*. TrJP, *tr. by* Solomon Solis-Cohen

World's Last Unnamed Poem, The. A. K. Redwing. VoR

World's light shines; shine as it will, The. But Men loved Darkness[e] Rather Than [*or* Then] Light. Richard Crashaw. ChIV-2

World's love runs thin, The. To the Tune "The Phoenix Hairpin." T'ang Wan, *Chinese*. WPOW, *tr. by* Kenneth Rexroth *and* Ling Chung

World's Music, The. "Gabriel Setoun." FaBoBe

Worlds on worlds are rolling ever. Chorus: "Worlds on worlds are rolling ever." Shelley. HeIP-4; NAEL-2 *Fr.* Hellas.

World's One Hope, The. Bertolt Brecht, *German*. AF, *tr. by* John Willett, Ralph Manheim *and* Erich Fried

World's pottage, the rat's star, The. (LL) With Mercy for the Greedy. Anne Sexton. HCAP; TOF; VCAP

World's so wide I cannot cross it, The. Fond Affection. *Unknown.* AS

World's too beautiful for human blood, The. Wound seen from afar. Philippe Jaccottet, *French*. MFP, *tr. by* Martin Sorrell

World's Wanderers, The. Shelley. TTTS

World's Way, The. Shakespeare. *See* Sonnet 66.

World's wrong, mother, The. Wyndmere, Windemere. Carol Muske. PBCAP

Worm. Bob Cobbing. NBrP

Worm artist, The. The Earth Worm. Denise Levertov. NOBA

Worm Either Way. D. H. Lawrence. NoAM

Worm Fed on the Heart of Corinth, A. Isaac Rosenberg. OAEL-2; PeFWW; PoWW

Worm unto his love, The: lo, here's fresh store. The Coffin-Worm. Ruth Pitter. MoBrPo

Worms at Heaven's Gate, The. Wallace Stevens. NoAM

Wormwood. Thomas Kinsella. CIP-2; PBCIP

Worn Out. Paul Laurence Dunbar. NAAAL

Worn Out. Elizabeth Siddal. SDW

Worn out of virtue, as the time of year. David and Bathsheba in the Public Garden. Robert Lowell. NAAL-2

Worn-out voice of the clock breaks on the hour, The. Prize for Good Conduct. Kenneth Allott. OBWP

Worn plush of the seat chafes your bare legs, The. What You Have Come To Expect. Stephen Dobyns. CMAP

Worn with life's care, love yet was love. (LL) The Marriage Ring. George Crabbe. BoLoP; EnLoPo; LBC; NOBE; OBEV; OBNC; OxBM

Worried Life Blues. *Unknown.* AmFP

Worried Skipper, The. Wallace Irwin. BLPA

Worries. *Unknown.* PoToHe

Worry about Money. Kathleen Jessie Raine. FaBoTw

Worry—is like a distant hill. *Unknown.* PoToHe

Worrying Fruit. Christina Rossetti. *Fr.* Goblin Market. CPO; EBEV; FaBoSe; NAEL-2; NALW; NOBVV; NOxBChV; OBNV; OxAEP-2; VWP

(Goblin Market.)

Worrying the carcase of an old song. (LL) Welsh Landscape. Ronald Stuart Thomas. NoP-4

Worschippe ye that loveris bene this May. Spring Song of the Birds. James I, King of Scotland. OBEV

Worsening Situation. John Ashbery. NOBA

Worship. Ralph Waldo Emerson. APN-1

Worship. John Greenleaf Whittier. ChIV-2; NOCV

Worship of Cromm Cruaich, The. *Unknown.* TIRV *Fr.* The Voyage of Bran.

Worshipping at the Great Shrine at Ise. Basho, *Japanese.* OHMPJ, tr. by Kenneth Rexroth

Worst a coat upon a coat-hanger, The. (LL) The Apparitions. W. B. Yeats. CMoP; LiTM; OxBSn; TRP

Worst Fate Bookes have, when they are once read, The. The Common Fate of Books. Margaret Lucas Cavendish, Duchess of Newcastle. PBRV

Worst side of it all, The. White Roses. John Ashbery. TAP

Worst thing about grief is the length of time during, The. If Grief Could Burn Out. Quintin McGrel Hogg Hailsham, Baron Hailsham. LBC

Worth Dying For. Christina Rossetti. *See* Meeting.

Worth keeping your foot in the door. Respectable House. Anne Stevenson. NALW

Worth of a cat and her c, The. Hywell the Good Weighs the Worth of a Cat. Felicity Bast. PC

Worth patience to regret. (LL) Before Parting. Swinburne. CBLP; EP; NOBVV

Worthless Heart, The. Immanuel di Roma, *Hebrew.* TrJP

Worthless man is a leaking wine-jar, A. Lucianus, *Greek.* GrAn, tr. by Edwin Morgan

Worthwhile. Ella Wheeler Wilcox. BLPA; EBEvV; PoToHe

Worthy art Thou, O Lord of praise! Deliverance from a Fit of Fainting. Anne Bradstreet. TAP

Worthy kyng, quhen he has seyn, The. Before Bannockburn. John Barbour. OxBS *Fr.* The Bruce.

Worthy object: Our Lord's Feet, A. (LL) Saint Mary Magdalene. Richard Crashaw. FSCV; GeHe; MeLP; OAEL-1; OBEV; SeCP

Worthy of a lover have I loved. The White Peacock. Alice Notley. FTOS

Wotton, my little Bere dwells on a hill. Ad Henricum Wottonem. Thomas Bastard. FaBoEE

Wou' ye hear of William Wallace. Gude Wallace. *Unknown.* ESPB

Would a circling surface vulture. Mahadevi, *Kannada.* BoWoP, tr. by A. K. Ramanujan

Would all did so as well as I! (LL) My mind [*or* minde *or* mynde] to me a kingdom [*or* kyngdome] is. Sir Edward Dyer, *Unknown,* wr. at. to. EBEvV; FaBoBe; ImPo; NAEL-1; NOBE; NoSic; PoEL-1; SCGP

Would-be Critic, The. Mrs. Henry Linden. CBWP-4

Would be discover'd by the Cry. (LL) The Morning Quatrains. Charles Cotton. NOSC; PeECV

Would beat anew a little while, and then no more. (LL) And Then No More. Friedrich Rückert, *German.* BIrV; BLPA, tr. by James Clarence Mangan

Would but indulgent Fortune send. The Wish. Mary Lee, Lady Chudleigh. LW

Would but some winged Angel ere too late. Omar Khayyám. *Fr.* The Rubáiyát of Omar Khayyám [of Naishápúr]. AWP; EBVV; FaBoBe; FaPoR; HAP; NAEL-2; PoEL-5

Would but the Desert of the Fountain yield. Omar Khayyám. *Fr.* The Rubáiyát of Omar Khayyám [of Naishápúr]. AWP; EBVV; FaBoBe; FaPoR; HAP; NAEL-2; PoEL-5

Would carry it away to blasphemous men. (LL) Ego Dominus Tuus. W. B. Yeats. CMoP; EPCY

Would come down, would ever come down. James Fenton. *Fr.* A German Requiem. NAEL-2; NoAM

Would congregate endlessly. (LL) Water. Philip Larkin. FaBoMo; OxBSP; PeECV

Would drop Him—Bone by Bone. (LL) There is a pain—so utter. Emily Dickinson. APN-2; BoWoP; NAAL-1; NCAP; NOBA

Would he had stayed! (LL) After he had gone the wind rose. Sylvia Townsend Warner. MoBrPo; SAGP

Would I be Shrived? John D. Swain. BLPA

Would I could cast a sail on the water. The Collarbone [*or* Collar-Bone] of a Hare. W. B. Yeats. CBNP; NTP; OxAEP-2; OxBTC; RB

Would I had loved him more! (LL) The Child's First Grief. Felicia Dorothea Hemans. BLPA; CH

Would I had seen thee dead and cold. Lady Caroline Lamb. Ro

Would I Might Go Far over Sea. Marie de France, *French.* AWP; PoRA, tr. by Arthur O'Shaughnessy

Would I might lie like this, without the pain. In Hospital. James Elroy Flecker. OxBTC

Would I were a king of children. The Child-King. Morris Wintchevsky, *Yiddish.* TrJP, tr. by Alter Brody

Would I were air that thou with heat opprest. Thomas Stanley. FaBoEE

Would I were chang'd into that golden shower. Sir Arthur Gorges. GBL

Would I were Changed. Barnabe Barnes. AAS *Fr.* Parthenophil and Parthenophe.

Would it had been the man of our wish! In the Room of the Bride-Elect. Thomas Hardy. InPK-6 *Fr.* Satires of Circumstance in Fifteen Glimpses.

Would it not be the most / prized gift that ever was! (LL) Saint Nicholas. Marianne Moore. NYBP; WPE

Would it please you if I strung my tears. The Race Question. Naomi Long Madgett. BPo; LTA

Would not have come this far. (LL) Spirits, Dancing. Arthur Gregor. NYBP; VGW

Would pause with his needle in the air. (LL) Illustrious Ancestors. Denise Levertov. AmPP; MoP; NAAL-2; NOBA; PmAP; VGW

Would pulse with all the life there was within. (LL) The Battle. Louis Simpson. InPS-3; OBWP; PBCV; PoWW

Would she have been a person. My Mother, If She Had Won Free Dance Lessons. Cornelius Eady. FiLi; ISC

Would stroke that sheep's black nose. (LL) A Child's Pet. W. H. Davies. CH; RB

Would that I streamed like water. Like Water down a Slope. Zalman Schneour, *Hebrew.* TrJP, tr. by Harry H. Fein

Would that the structure brave, the manifold music I build. Abt Vogler. Robert Browning. FHYEP; NAEL-2; OAEL-2; TOF

Would that there had never been swift ships! Callimachus. HePo *Fr.* Epigrams.

Would they swept cleaner! To a Shred of Linen. Lydia Huntley Sigourney. PAR

Would 'twere underground! (LL) Bereft. Thomas Hardy. BoLoP; NoAM

Would with Thee live, and for thee die. (LL) A Dialogue betwixt God and the Soul. Sir Henry Wotton. MeLP; PeECV

Would write a letter with / my scissors mouth. Young Woman's Neo-Aramaic Jewish Persian Blues. Jerome Rothenberg, *after Persian folk poem.* BoWoP

Would ye, with faultless judgement, learn to plan. Instructions on landscaping. Richard Jago. OBGa *Fr.* Edge-Hill.

Would you a favourite novel make. A Receipt for Writing a Novel. Mary Alcock. ECWP

Would you adopt a strong logical attitude. Synchoresis. Godfrey Turner. OBCoV

Would you be a man in fashion? *Unknown.* NOSC

Would you be an angel. Something of a Departure. Paul Muldoon. PBCIP

Would you believe, when you this Monsieur see. On English Monsieur. Ben Jonson. AEP; NBLV; NoP-4

Would you but soon return, and speak it here. (LL) A Letter to Daphnis. Anne Finch, Countess of Winchilsea. LW; PEW

Would you care for a smoke or a sherry? Mopev. UV

Would you come back if I said the earth. Nadia Tuéni, *French.* BoWoP, tr. by Willis Barnstone

Would You Have a Young Virgin? John Gay. *Fr.* The Beggar's Opera. OAEL-1

Would you have called me a nobody? (LL) Somebody being a nobody. Tennyson. FaBoEE; NOBL; OxBSP

Would you hear of an old-time [*or* old-fashioned] sea fight? Battle of the *Bonhomme Richard* and the *Serapis.* Walt Whitman. SAmP, *sect.* XXXV; ImGa, *sect.* XXXV–XXXVI; RB; UnPo, *sect.* XXXV-XXXVI *Fr.* Song of Myself. AmPP; MoAmPo; NAAL-3; NOBA; OxBA

Would you know what's soft? I dare. James Shirley. BeJo

Would you like to sin. Elinor Glyn. *Unknown.* OBCoV

Would you, my friend, in little room express. Martial, *Latin.* OBVE, tr. by Elijah Fenton

Would you prefer the examples? The pancakes? Or the words? The Male. Carla Harryman. PmAP

Would you see the little men. The Little Men. Flora Fearne. BoTP

Would You Wear My Eyes? Bob Kaufman. GT

Would you your son should be a sot or dunce. William Cowper. OBSV *Fr.* Tirocinium; or, A Review of Schools.

Wouldn't it be great to get away? Melbourne or the Bush. Philip Mead. BMAP

Wouldnt think / t look at m. Panther Man. James A. Emanuel. BPo; NBV

Wouldn't this old world be better. I Know Something Good about You. Louis C. Shimon. BLPA; PoToHe

Wouldn't you like to be a whale. Whale. Geoffrey Dearmer. BoTP

Wouldn't you like to know. Elementary. Jim Tollerud. VoR

Would'st be happy, little child. To Theodora. *Unknown.* OxBChV

Wouldst know the lark? A Listener's Guide to the Birds. Elwyn Brooks White. NYBP

Wouldst thou be wise, O Man? At the knees of a woman begin. Wilfrid Scawen Blunt. OBMV *Fr.* The Wisdom of Merlyn.

Wouldst Thou but gild my soul with Thy bright ray. (LL) When thy bright beams, my Lord, do strike mine eye. Edward Taylor. NAAL-1; NAAL-3

Wouldst thou hear what man can say. Epitaph on Elizabeth, L. H. Ben Jonson. BeJo; FaBoEE; HAP; NAEL-1; NIP-4; NOSC; NoP-4; OBEV; PoE; Poetr; SCGP; SeCP

Wound, The. Louise Glück. NoAM

Wound, A. Brendan Kennelly. BiHa

Wound-Dresser, The. Walt Whitman. APN-1; AmPP; CBCWP; ColAP; NAAL-1; NAAL-3; NOBA; OBWP; TAP

Wound seen from afar. Philippe Jaccottet, *French.* MFP, *tr. by* Martin Sorrell

Wound which the dragon had dealt him began, The. Beowulf's Death. *Unknown.* AnOE, *tr. by* Charles W. Kennedy *Fr.* Beowulf. OAEL-1, *tr. by* Charles W. Kennedy; ASW, *tr. by* Kevin Crossley-Holland

Wounded Breakfast, The. Russell Edson. LCAP-2

Wounded Cupid. Song, The. Anacreon, *Greek.* LoP, *tr. by* Robert Herrick (Wounded Cupid, The.) AWP; OBCVT; OBVE, *tr. by* Robert Herrick

Wounded Deer—leaps highest, A. Emily Dickinson. APN-2; AWP; TAP ("Lest anybody spy the blood / And 'You're hurt' exclaim!") (LL) ColAP

Wounded hands, the weary human face, The. (LL) E Tenebris. Oscar Wilde. ChIV-2; GSo; MoBrPo; NAEL-2; OxAEP-2; Son; TIRV

Wounded Hawk, The. Herbert Edward Palmer. FaBoTw

Wounded I sing, tormented I indite. Joseph's Coat. George Herbert. ChIV-1; GeHe; KSG

Wounded otter, A Michael Hartnett. PBCIP

Wounded Person, The. Walt Whitman. *Fr.* Song of Myself. AmPP; MoAmPo; NAAL-3; NOBA; OxBA

Wounded wilderness of Morris Graves, The. Lawrence Ferlinghetti. NeAP

Wounds. Michael Longley. FaBoPV; PBCIP; PNI

Wounds are terrible. The paint is old, The. The Dolls Museum in Dublin. Eavan Boland. NoP-4

Wow man I said / when you tipped my chin. Short Note on the Sparseness of the Language. Diane Di Prima. BB

Wow! wow! wow! (LL) The Duchess's Lullaby. "Lewis Carroll." CBNP; FaBoCh; NBLV; NOxBChV; UV

Woyi, The. Lew Blockcolski. VoR

Wraggle Taggle Gipsies, The. *Unknown.* BoTP; CH

Wraith-Friend, The. George Barker. OBMV

Wrap Me in Blankets of Momentary Winds. Harold Littlebird. VoR

Wrap their babies in the American flag. Immigrants. Pat Mora. UnSA

Wrap their old limbs with sombre ivy twine. (LL) November. Hartley Coleridge. LaPo

Wrap up in a blanket in cold weather and just read. Things to Do around a Lookout. Gary Snyder. CAPP-1; TAP

Wrapt in my careless cloak, as I walk to and fro. Henry Howard, Earl of Surrey. SiPS

Wrapt in the old miasmal mist. (LL) The Hippopotamus. T. S. Eliot. AWP; CBNP; HoPM; ImPo; NAEL-2; OBMV; VGW

Wrapt [*or* Wrapped] up, O Lord, in man's degeneration. Greville Fulke. NoSic *Fr.* Caelica.

Wrath of *Peleus* Son, O Muse, resound, The. The Invocation. Homer, *Greek.* OBVE; OBCVT, *tr. by* John Dryden *Fr.* The Iliad.

Wrath to Sadness. Robert Grenier. PmAP

Wrathful winter, 'proaching on apace, The. The Induction. Thomas, 1st Earl of Dorset Sackville. NoSic *Fr.* Induction to "A Mirror for Magistrates." AAS

Wreath, The. Robert Graves. BoLoP

Wreath, A. Yannis Ritsos, *Greek.* GrIP, *tr. by* Edmund Keeley

Wreath, The. Henry Vaughan. FMP

Wreath for a Bridal. Sylvia Plath. ITG

Wreath for Africa, A. Bernard Dadié, *French.* NegPo, *tr. by* Ellen Conroy Kennedy

Wreath for the Suicide Heart, A. Anthony McNeill. PBCV

Wreath of Holly, A. Joseph Cephas Holly. AAP

Wreathe violets white. Heliodora's Brows. Meleager, *Greek.* GrAn; GrIP, *tr. by* Peter Whigham

Wreathèd garland of deservèd praise, A. George Herbert. FMP; GeHe; NOSC; OAEL-1; OxBSP; Poetr; SeCP

Wreaths. Geoffrey Hill. PoA

Wreaths. Michael Longley.

Civil Servant, The. BiHa

Greengrocer, The. BiHa

Linen Workers, The. BiHa; CIP-2

Wrecche mon, why artou proud. *Unknown.* MiEL

Wreck of the Circus Train, The. Hayden Carruth. GM

Wreck of the Deutschland, The, *limerick.* David Annett. BXAP; PeLi

Wreck of the Deutschland, The. Gerard Manley Hopkins. CMoP; EnVR; FaBoMo; ImPo; LiTM; NOBE; NoAM; OBNC; OxAEP-2; PeECV; PoEL-5

"Sister, a sister calling." FaBoVe

Wreck of the Edmund Fitzgerald, The. Gordon Lightfoot. NoP-4

Wreck of the Great Northern, The. Robert Hedin. GM

Wreck of the *Hesperus,* The. Henry Wadsworth Longfellow. APN-1; BLPA; CTV; EBEvV; EBNV; FaBoBe; OBCA; OBNV; PAR

Wreck of the *Julie Plante* [*or* The *Julie Plante*], The. William Henry Drummond. BLPA; FaBoBe

Wreck of the Old 97. David Graves George. GM

Wreck of the Royal Palm, The. *Unknown.* AmFP

Wreck "Thrush," The. George Seferis. GrIP, *tr. by* Edmund Keeley *and* Philip Sherrard *Fr.* Thrush.

Wreckage Entrepreneur, The. Alice Fulton. WWSi

Wrecked Boat on the River Shore. Chiang Lu, *Chinese.* CoBCP, *tr. by* Burton Watson

Wrecked castaway. Robinson Crusoe Daniel Defoe. Maurice Sagoff. NBLV

Wrecking the Statue of Paul Bert. Thiên Thê, *Vietnamese.* AVP, *tr. by* Huỳnh Sanh Thông

Wren, The. Issa, *Japanese.* NTCP, *tr. by* R. H. Blyth

Wren, The. *Unknown.* OxBChV

Wren dropped down on my window sill, A. A Little Wren. Priscilla Jane Thompson. CBWP-2

Wrestler's Heart, The. Gary Soto. PuP-17

Wrestling. Louisa Sarah Bevington. LW; PEW

Wrestling Jacob. Charles Wesley. NOBE; NOCV; NOEC; OBEV; OxAEP-1; PeECV; PoEL-3; TOF

Wretched and foolish Jealousy [*or* Jealousie]. Against Jealousy [*or* Jealousie]. Ben Jonson. CBLP

Wretched are the poor in spirit: for what they were on earth. An Apocryphal Gospel. Jorge Luis Borges. GI, *tr. by* Norman Thomas D. Giovanni

Wretched estate of men by fortune blessed. Justice. George Chapman. NOSC *Fr.* Euthymiae Raptus; or, The Teares of Peace.

Wretched Flavia, on her couch reclined, The. Saturday: The Small-Pox. Lady Mary Wortley Montagu. BWW; ECWP; NOEC; PEW; WPE *Fr.* Six Town Eclogues.

Wretched Ierne! with what grief I see. Jonathan Swift. OBSV *Fr.* Verses Occasioned by the Sudden Drying Up of St. Patrick's Well.

Wretched Man. John Wilmot, 2d Earl of Rochester. *Fr.* A Satire [*or* Satyre] against [Reason and] Mankind. NOSC; OAEL-1; OBSV; PoEL-3; SCV

Wretched of the earth, The. I Arrive In Madrid. Al Young. GT

Wretchedness of my former years I have no need to brag, The. After Passing the Examination. Meng Chiao, *Chinese.* SuSp, *tr. by* Irving Y. Lo

Wretten by Me at the Death of My 4th Sonne and 5th Child Perigrene Payler. Mary Carey. KTR

Wretten by Me att the Same Tyme; on the Death of My 4th, & Only Child, Robert Payler. Mary Carey. KTR

Wrights' Biplane, The. Robert Frost. WeW-3 *Fr.* Ten Mills.

Wrinkled, crabbèd man they picture thee, A. Winter. Robert Southey. GSo

Wrinkled ostler, grim and thin! Song at the Ruin'd Inn. Tennyson. PoEL-5 *Fr.* The Vision of Sin. EBVVPR; OAEL-2

Wrinkles. Penny Harter. HA

Wrinkles in the taxi driver's face, The. My Father's Desk. Kate Daniels. MoLi

Wrinkles: like / valleys etched by glaciers. Riding the North Point Ferry. Wing Tek Lum. OpBo

Wrinkles on the brown face, The. The Militance of a Photograph in the Passbook of a Bantu under Detention. Michael S. Harper. VCAP

Wrists and / knees garnished with impetigo. Geoffrey Hill. *See* The Princes of Mercia were badger and raven.

Writ in my psalter. (LL) His Prayer to Ben[.] Jo[h]nson. Robert Herrick. BeJo; CaPo; NAEL-1; NOSC; NoP-4; OxBSP; OxBoLi; PeLV

Write in a lively style, as fish swim in the water. Li K'ai-hsien. *Fr.* Impromptu Poems. CoBLCP, *tr. by* Jonathan Chaves

Write it down. Write it. In ordinary ink. Starvation Camp near Jaslo. Wislawa Szymborska, *Polish.* WPOW, *tr. by* Jan Darowski

Write it in gold—a spirit of the sun. Lines Written in a Blank Leaf of the Prometheus Unbound. Thomas Lovell Beddoes. EPCY; OAEL-2

Write it. Write. In ordinary ink. Wislawa Szymborska. *See* Starvation Camp near Jaslo.

"Write me a sonnet. On the spot," said she. Sonnet Right off the Bat. Félix Lope de Vega Carpio, *Spanish*. STV, *tr. by* John Frederick Nims

Write on the giddy wind. Write on the stream as it flows. Catullus. *See* Carmen 70 ("Lesbia says she'ld rather marry me").

Write on the wind, write on the rushing waves. Catullus. *See* Carmen 70 ("Lesbia says she'ld rather marry me").

Write the poem. The Pyramids. Nick Piombino. FTOS

Write this. We have burned all their villages. Sun. Michael Palmer. APSN; FTOS

Write to Sardis, saith the Lord. Sardis. William Cowper. ChIV-2 *Fr.* Olney Hymns.

Write to thine eyes? Why, my poor pen. To Fannie. Mary E. Tucker. CBWP-1

Write! Write! Help! Help! Barnabe Barnes. Son *Fr.* Parthenophil and Parthenophe.

Write write yow Croniclers of Tyme and Fame. George Peele. PBRV *Fr.* Anglorum Feriae.

Writer, The. Richard Wilbur. HCAP; ImGa; MoLi; NoAM; OxBC; PoPoPo; Poetr; SoSe-8

Writer depersonalises his dreamwork, The. Sonnet IV. Chris Wallace-Crabbe. BMAP *Fr.* Sonnets to the Left.

Writer needs nothing but a table, A. After a Death. Edwin Morgan. FaBoTC *Fr.* Sonnets from Scotland.

Writers. Robert Lowell.

Robert Frost. MoP; NAAL-2; NoAM; Poetr; Son

Writers of the knife are we! Velemir Khlebnikov. TCRP, *tr. by* Gary Kern *Fr.* Washerwoman.

Writes poetry. Tanka. Akiko Yosano, *Japanese*. MJT, *tr. by* Makoto Ueda

Writing. William Allingham. NOBVV

Writing. Andrew Motion. DiPo

Writing. Howard Nemerov. NYBP; VCAP

Writing a Curriculum Vitae. Wislawa Szymborska, *Polish*. PoSu, *tr. by* Grazyna Drabik *and* Austin Flint

Writing a letter he said. Buffalo—Isle of Wight Power Cable. Anselm Hollo. PoM

Writing a poem. Believing in the Absurd. Harold Norse. CLPP

Writing a series. Tanka. Sasaki Yukitsuna, *Japanese*. MJT, *tr. by* Makoto Ueda

Writing again. William J. Higginson. HA

Writing Again on the Same Theme, *see also* New Thatched Hall, A. Po Chü-i, *Chinese*. CoBCP, *tr. by* Burton Watson

Writing, I crushed an insect with my nail. Interlude. Karl Shapiro. PRMP

Writing in England Now. Philip O'Connor. OxBTC

Writing in Prison. Ken Smith. NBrP

Writing in the Fire, The. Eugenijus Matuzeviius, *Lithuanian*. CEEP, *tr. by* Irene Pogoželskyte Suboczewski

Writing Letters. Rodney Bennett. BoTP

Writing My Feelings. Yüan Mei, *Chinese*. CoBLCP, *tr. by* Jonathan Chaves

Writing of poems, The. First Drift. Ron Padgett. FTOS

Writing Poetry in the Back Garden. Chao Yi, *Chinese*. SuSp, *tr. by* Chang Yin-nan *and* Lewis C. Walmsley

Writing poetry needs a mind that's nimble and free. Replying to a Poem by Li T'ien-lin. Yang Wan-li, *Chinese*. SuSp, *tr. by* Sherwin S. S. Fu

Writing these poems!/ Imagine! (LL) Autobiographia Literaria. Frank O'Hara. NNaP; NOBA; TTTS

Writing through a Text by Chris Mann. John Cage. EOEF

Writing through the Cantos. John Cage. PmAP

Writing to one man of another. Now there are 2 and. Two Men. Anne Waldman. IFJA

Writing verse on smooth paper with a new Parker pen. Fire. Amiya Chakravarty, *Bengali*. OMIP, *tr. by* Sujit Mukherjee

Written a Few Hours before the Birth of a Child. Jane Cave. ECWP

Written After Swimming from Sestos to Abydos. Byron. NAEL-2; NBLV; NoP-4

Written at [*or in*] an Inn at Henley. William Shenstone. AWP; NOBE; NOEC; OBEV; OxAEP-1

Written at Boppard on the Rhine, August 25, 1842, just before. Henry Wadsworth Longfellow. *See* Mezzo Cammin.

Written at Hsiang-kuo Temple on the Occasion of Watching Actors in the Hsing-hsiang Garden of the T'ung-t'ien-chieh Tao-ch'ang. Wang An-shih, *Chinese*. SuSp, *tr. by* Jan W. Walls

Written at Lakeside Residence. Chiang K'uei, *Chinese*. SuSp, *tr. by* Chiang Yee

Written at Mauve Garden: Pine Wind Terrace. Chu Yi-tsun, *Chinese*. SuSp, *tr. by* Chang Yin-nan *and* Lewis C. Walmsley

Written at Random. Lu Yu, *Chinese*. SuSp, *tr. by* Irving Y. Lo

Written at Sea, in the First Dutch War. Charles, 6th Earl of Dorset Sackville. *See* Song Written at Sea in the First Dutch War (1665), the Night before an Engagement.

Written at Stonehenge. Thomas, the Younger Warton. Son

Written at the End of Master Ho-ching's Collected Works. Chin Nung, *Chinese*. CoBLCP, *tr. by* Jonathan Chaves

Written at the White Sulphur Springs. Francis Scott Key. OBAL

Written Beneath a Picture. Byron. *See* Lines Written beneath a Picture.

Written beneath Hui Mountain, When Tsou Liu-yi Comes by for a Visit. Wang Shih-chieng, *Chinese*. SuSp, *tr. by* Richard John Lynn

Written by Desire of a Lady, on an Angry, Petulant Kitchen-Maid. Jane Cave. ECWP

Written by the Barrow Side, Where She Was Sent to Wash Linen. Ellen Taylor. ECWP

Written December 1790. Anna Seward. Son

Written, Directed by and Starring. James Simmons. PBCIP

Written during My Stay at White Clouds Monastery on West Lake. Su Man-shu, *Chinese*. SuSp, *tr. by* Wu-chi Liu

Written for Love of an Ascension—Coltrane. Carolyn M. Rodgers. SeSe

Written for My Neighbor. Shen Yüeh, *Chinese*. CoBCP, *tr. by* Burton Watson

Written for My Neighbor. Wang Seng-ta, *Chinese*. CoBCP, *tr. by* Burton Watson

Written for My Own Amusement. Wang An-shih, *Chinese*. CoBCP, *tr. by* Burton Watson

Written for My Son, and Spoken by Him at His First Putting on Breeches. Mary Barber. CABP; ECEV; ECWP; NOEC

Written for the Pavilion of the Drunken Old Man at Ch'u-chou. Ou-yang Hsiu, *Chinese*. CoBCP, *tr. by* Burton Watson

Written Forty Miles South of a Spreading City. Robert Bly. NNaP

Written in a Blank Leaf of Dugdale's "Monasticon." Thomas, the Younger Warton. Son

Written in a Carefree Mood. Lu Yu, *Chinese*. CoBCP, *tr. by* Burton Watson

Written in a Copy of Swift's Poems, for Wayne Burns. James Wright. NOBA

Written in a Lady's Prayer Book. John Wilmot, 2d Earl of Rochester. BoLoP

(Verses Put into a Lady's Prayer-Book.) NOSC

Written in a Sick Chamber. Samuel Rogers. NOBRP

Written in a Thunder Storm July 15th, 1841. John Clare. EnVR

Written in Absence. Alcuin, *Latin*. MLL, *tr. by* Helen Waddell

Written in an Ovid. Matthew Prior. FaBoEE; OBCoV

Written in Autumn. Thomas Cole. AiP

Written in Behalf of My Wife. Li Po, *Chinese*. SuSp, *tr. by* Joseph J. Lee

Written in Early Spring. Wordsworth. *See* Lines Written in Early Spring.

Written in Early Youth, the Time an Autumnal Evening. Coleridge. *Fr.* Effusions.

Written in Exile. Kathleen Jessie Raine. TrCP; WPE

Written in Her French Psalter. Elizabeth I, Queen of England. PBWP; PEW; WPE

("As is the inward suspicious mind.") (LL) PEW

Written in Ireland. Mary Alcock. ECWP; NOEC

Written in Jest on Elder Stonegate's Eastern Balcony. Liu Tsung-yüan, *Chinese*. SuSp, *tr. by* Jan W. Walls

Written in Juice of Lem[m]on. Abraham Cowley. SeCP *Fr.* The Mistress.

(Written in Juice of Lemon.) CABP

("Yet like them when they're burnt in sacrifice.") (LL) CABP

Written in London after a Protest Parade. Jean Garrigue. NMM-2

Written in London, September, 1802. Wordsworth. FaBoPV

(England, 1802, I.) OBEV

Written in March [While Resting on the Bridge at the Foot of Brother's Water]. Wordsworth. BoTP; NAEL-2; NTCP; PBMP; SCGP; UnPo

Written in Northampton County Asylum. John Clare. PBMP; PFE

Written in October. Charlotte Smith. NoP-4

Written in Pencil in the Sealed Railway-Car. Dan Pagis, *Hebrew*. AF, *tr. by* Stephen Mitchell

Written in Prison. John Clare. EnVR; OAEL-2

Written in the Album of a Child. Wordsworth. *See* To a Child [Written in Her Album].

Written in the Beginning of Mezeray's History of France. Matthew Prior. NOBE; PoEL-3

Written in the churchyard at Middleton in Sussex. Charlotte Smith. *See* Sonnet Written in the Church-Yard at Middleton in Sussex.

Written in the Euganean Hills, North Italy. Shelley. *See* Lines Written among the Euganean Hills.

Written in the Office Precincts. Wang T'ing-hsiang, *Chinese*. CoBLCP, *tr. by* Jonathan Chaves

Written in Unbridled Repugnance near Sioux Falls, Alabama—April 30, 1974. A. K. Redwing. VoR

Written in Water. Amy Clampitt. NMM-2

Written near a Port on a Dark Evening. Charlotte Smith. NoP-4

Written on a Gloomy Day, in Sickness. Susanna Blamire. ECWP

Written on a Leaf. *Unknown, Chinese.* BoWoP, *tr. by* Geoffrey Waters

Written on a Looking-Glass. *Unknown.* FaBoEE

Written on a Monastery Wall. Li Shang-yin, *Chinese.* PLT, *tr. by* A. C. Graham

Written on a Painting Entitled "Misty Yangtze and Folded Hills." Su Tung-p'o, *Chinese.* CoBCP, *tr. by* Burton Watson; CoBCP

Written on a Wall at Woodstock. Elizabeth I, Queen of England. PBWP; WPE

("Oh Fortune, thy wresting wavering state.") CABP; PEW

Written on a Window. Aaron Hill. OxBSP

Written on Lake View Tower. P'an Lang, *Chinese.* SuSp, *tr. by* Jonathan Chaves

Written on My Way into Exile. Han Yü, *Chinese.* CoBCP, *tr. by* Burton Watson

Written on Parting from Mr. Ying. Ts'ao Chih, *Chinese.* CoBCP, *tr. by* Burton Watson

Written on Seeing Her Two Sons at Play. Henrietta O'Neill. ECWP

Written on the Anniversary of Our Father's Death. Hartley Coleridge. Son

Written on the Banks of Wastwater During a Calm. John Wilson. LaPo

Written on the Day That Mr. Leigh Hunt Left Prison. Keats. EPCY; Son

Written on the Lake, Returning from the Retreat at Stone Cliff. Hsieh Ling-yün, *Chinese.* CoBCP, *tr. by* Burton Watson

Written on the Night of the Twenty-ninth of the First Month. Yün Shou-p'ing, *Chinese.* CoBLCP, *tr. by* Jonathan Chaves

Written on the Thirtieth Day, Ninth Month, Second Year of the Ta-li Reign [767]. Tu Fu, *Chinese.* SuSp, *tr. by* Irving Y. Lo

Written on the Wall at Chang's Hermitage. Tu Fu, *Chinese.* EOEF; EnlH; HoPM; OHPC, *tr. by* Kenneth Rexroth

Written on the Wall of Halfway Mountain Temple. Wang An-shih, *Chinese.* SuSp, *tr. by* Jan W. Walls

Written on the Wall of Pan-shan Temple. Wang An-shih, *Chinese.* CoBCP, *tr. by* Burton Watson

Written on the Walls of His Dungeon. Luís De León, *Spanish.* TrJP, *tr. by* Thomas Walsh

Written on Whitsun-Monday, 1795. Matilda Barbara Betham-Edwards. ECWP

Written, Originally Extempore, on Seeing a Mad Heifer Run through the Village. Elizabeth Hands. ECWP

Written the First Morning of the Author's Bathing at Teignmouth for the Head-Ache. Jane Cave. ECWP

Written the Night before His Execution. Chidiock Tichborne. *See* Tichborne's Elegy.

Written to a Near Neighbour in a Tempestuous Night. Henrietta, Lady Luxborough Knight. ECWP

Written upon Returning to the Mountains. Ku K'uang, *Chinese.* SuSp, *tr. by* Irving Y. Lo

Written upon the death of the most Noble Prince Henrie. Sir Arthur Gorges. PBRV

Written When Drunk. Chang Yüeh, *Chinese.* CoBCP, *tr. by* Burton Watson

Written when Governor of Soochow. Po Chü-i, *Chinese.* ChiP, *tr. by* Arthur Waley

Written While Drunk. Ch'ien T'ao, *Chinese.* ChiPo, *tr. by* Cyril Birch

Written While Lying on My Pillow in the Morning on the Twelfth Day of the Eleventh Month. Fan Ch'eng-ta, *Chinese.* SuSp, *tr. by* Wu-chi Liu

Written While Riding the Long Island Rail Road. May Swenson. GM

Written While Sick. Wen Cheng-ming, *Chinese.* CoBLCP, *tr. by* Jonathan Chaves

Written with a Diamond On Her Window at Woodstock. Elizabeth I, Queen of England. PBWP; PEW; WPE

Wrong? are they wrong? Of course they are. England's Alfred Abroad. Sir Owen Seaman. UV

Wrong! is it wrong? Well, may be. Jameson's Ride. Alfred Austin. UV

Wrong me no more. Changed, Yet Constant. Thomas Stanley. BeJo

Wrong Not, Sweete Empress of My Heart. Sir Robert Ayton. *Fr.* The Silent Lover. OBEV

Wrong Side of the Door, The. Ray DiPalma. FTOS

Wrong that are, The. Tom. Victor D. Questel. PBCV

Wrong Way Round, The. Peter Handke, *German.* CBNP, *tr. by* Michael Hamburger

Wrong Way Will Haunt You, The. Sydney Lea. RA

Wronged Lover, The. Sir Philip Sidney. SiPS *Fr.* Arcadia.

Wrongs we bear shall be redressed, The. (LL) From America. James M. Whitfield. APN-2; BPo

Wrote the clergy: "Our Dear Madame Prynne." A Hawthorne Garland. Richard Harter Fogle. OBAL

Wu land mulberry leaves grow green. Sent to My Two Little Children in the East of Lu. Li Po, *Chinese.* CoBCP, *tr. by* Burton Watson

Wu Shan-yang. Yang Chi. CoBLCP, *tr. by* Jonathan Chaves *Fr.* Thinking of My Friends at Kou-jung Subprefecture.

Wu-t'ung tree a hundred feet tall, A. Inscribed on a Painting of a Wu-t'ung Tree by Myself. Tao-chi, *Chinese.* CoBLCP, *tr. by* Jonathan Chaves

Wu Wei grew old and died. Song of the Painting "River and Mountains," by Wu Wei. Ho Ching-ming, *Chinese.* CoBLCP, *tr. by* Jonathan Chaves

Wukhand. Paul Keens-Douglas. HCP; PBCV

Wulf and Eadwacer. *Unknown.* BoWoP, *tr. by* Willis Barnstone *and* Elene Kolb

Wulf and Eadwacer. *Unknown. See* Eadwacer.

Wull ye come in early Spring. Come! William Barnes. CH

Wundrfulness uv th Mountees Our Secret Police, Th. Bill Bissett. NOBC

Wyatt resteth here, that quick could never rest. Tribute to Wyatt. Henry Howard, Earl of Surrey. EPCY; NAEL-1; NoSic

Wyatt's Dream. Richard Caddel. NBrP

Wyll and Testament. Isabella Whitney. *See* The Aucthour Maketh Her Wyll and Testament.

Wyncote, Pennsylvania: A Gloss. Thomas Kinsella. NOIV

Wyndmere, Windemere. Carol Muske. PBCAP

Wynken, Blynken, and Nod. (LL) Wynken, Blynken and Nod one night. Eugene Field. ACTP; APN-2; BLPA; BoTP; ChAP; FaBoBe; NBLV; NOxBChV; NTCP; OBAL; OBCA; OTCP; OxBChV; PoRA; TFi

Wynkyn de Worde. Edmund Clerihew Bentley. OBCoV *Fr.* Clerihews.

Wynard Sailor. Ray Mathew. CBAP

Wyse men alwaye. A Mery Gest How a Sergeaunt Wolde Lerne to Be A Frere. Sir Thomas More. AAS

Wyshe not for death, nor dreade his might. (LL) The Happy Life. Martial, *Latin.* OBCVT, *tr. by* Henry Howard, Earl of Surrey

Wyth that came Ryotte, russhynge all at ones. The Dreamer Meets Riot. John Skelton. *Fr.* The Bowge of Courte. AAS

X

"X." Jean Valentine. NMM-2

X could make a face like a fish. Theory. Paul Hoover. BAP-93

X finds gold and leaves his noose for Y. Statilius Flaccus, *Greek.* GrAn, *tr. by* Edwin Morgan

X L E B. Jack Hirschman. CLPP

X-Ray, The. Andrew Elliott. PNI

X shall stand for playmates Ten. *Unknown.* OxNR

X was a common hood. Heroes, Saints, and Neighbors. Gillian Conoley. PUP-19

X was asked. Aleksander Wat. CBNP *Fr.* Notes Written in Obory.

Xango. Edward Kamau Brathwaite. HCP

Xanthippe, singing at her lyre. Philodemus, *Greek.* InMo, *tr. by* Sam Hamill

Xanthippe's strumming, her chatter, her speaking eye, her song. Philodemus. HePo, *tr. by* Barbara Hughes Fowler *Fr.* Epigrams.

Xantippe. Amy Levy. BrRo

Xenia. Petri Gyorgy, *Hungarian.* CEEP, *tr. by* Robert Austerlitz

Xenophanes. Ralph Waldo Emerson. APN-1; NOBA

Xenophilia. Mary Kinzie. CMAP

(XII from Secrets). Jessie Orton Jones.

"Did you ever have a chipmunk for a friend?" CTV

Xkoagu, give me your heart. Prayer to the Hunting Star, Canopus. *Unknown, Bushman.* PeSA, *tr. by* W. H. I. Bleek *and* Jack Cope

Xmas for the Boys. Gavin Ewart. OBSV

Xochitepec. Malcolm Lowry. NOBC

Xunantunich. Velma Pollard. HCP *Fr.* Belize Suite. HCP

XX. P. Inman. FTOS

XXI. Essex Hemphill. *See* To Some Supposed Brothers.

(XXI from Secrets). Jessie Orton Jones.

Our Wonderful World. CTV

XXII. Essex Hemphill. NAAAL *Fr.* Conditions.

XXIV. Essex Hemphill. NAAAL *Fr.* Conditions.

Xylographer started to cross the sea, A. The Zealless Xylographer. Mary Mapes Dodge. OBAL

Y

Y-e-a-h!. Langston Hughes. *See* Dream Boogie.

Y. M. C. A, The. Mrs. Henry Linden. CBWP-4

Y por tierra hast' en tren militar. (LL) Adelita's the name of the lady, *Spanish vers. Unknown, Spanish.* AS

Ya Se Van Los Pastores. Dudley Fitts. FYAP

Yacht, The. Catullus. AWP; OBVE, *tr. by* John Hookham Frere   *Fr.* Carmina.

(Carmen 4.) AWP, *tr. by* John Hookham Frere

("Castor & Pollux / the Dioscuri.") (LL) AWP, *tr. by* John Hookham Frere

("My bean-pod boat you see here.") AWP, *tr. by* John Hookham Frere

("To thee, bright Castor, and thy Brother Star!") (LL) OBVE

Yachts, The. William Carlos Williams. AmPP; CMoP; HeIP-4; ImPo; LiTM; MeMAP; MoAmPo; MoP; NOBA; NoAM; NoP-4; OxBA; PoE; SAmP; TFi

Yachts in the harbor. Genetics. Richard Harteis. CMAP

Yachts on the Nile. Bernard Spencer. NoAM

Yahrtzeit Light, The. Lyn Lifshin. UnSA

Yahrzeit. Larry Moffi. EC3

Yak, The. Hilaire Belloc. CTAV; MoBrPo; NBLV; NOBL; NoAM; OxBChV; PeP

Yall / out there. A Chant for Young/Brothas and Sistuhs. Sonia Sanchez. BPo

Yamaha yamaha. Mysterious East. William Cole. OBAL

Yang-Se-Fu. "Yehoash," *Yiddish.* TrJP, *tr. by* Isidore Goldstick

Yangchou. Cheng Hsieh, *Chinese.*

"West wind has come again to the 'tower of makeup,' The." CoBLCP, *tr. by* Jonathan Chaves

Yangtse and Han. Tu Fu, *Chinese.* PLT, *tr. by* A. C. Graham

Yangtze River, autumn colors, The. Inscribed on the Painting, "River in Autumn." Ni Tsan, *Chinese.* CoBLCP, *tr. by* Jonathan Chaves

Yangtze rushes past the capital, The. View of the Countryside. Wu Wei-yeh, *Chinese.* SuSp, *tr. by* Chang Yin-nan *and* Lewis C. Walmsley

Yankee Doodle. Richard Shuckburg *and* Edward Bangs. AmFP; OBAL; OxBoLi; OxNR

Yankee Man-of-War, The. *Unknown.* FaBoBe

(Stately Southerner, The.) AmFP

Yankee ship came [*or* comes] down the river, A. Blow, Boys, Blow [*or* Blow, Bullies, Blow]. *Unknown.* FaBoVe

Yankees Back, The. "The Mighty Sparrow." PBCV

Yard is littered with scrap, with axles, The. Stewart Conn. FaBoTC

Yardage flows, The. Three Sweatshop Women. Nanying Stella Wong. CrSp

Yardbird's Skull. Owen Dodson. PoBA; VGW

Yardley Oak. William Cowper. NOEC

Yards of Sarajevo, The. Richard Hugo. AF

Yarn of the *Nancy Bell*, The. Sir William Schwenck Gilbert. BLPA; EBEvV; EBNV; FaBoBe; FaBoCh; HoPM; NOBL; TFi; UV

(Yarn of the "Nancy Bell," The.) CABP

Yarn Wig. Lois-Ann Yamanaka. PUP-19

Yarrow counted eight of them. July the First. Robert Currie. Poetsp

Yarrow had to learn it but he loved Young Jacob. Brothers. Robert Currie. Poetsp

Yarrow Unvisited [1803]. Wordsworth. GTBS-P; PoRA

Yarrow Visited [September, 1814]. Wordsworth. GTBS-P

Yasmin. James Elroy Flecker. *See* Hassan's Serenade.

Yawn of Yawns, The. Vasco [*or* Vasko] Popa.

Forgetful Number. HSix, *tr. by* Charles Simic

Petrified Echoes. PoSu, *tr. by* Anne Pennington

Proud Error. HSix, *tr. by* Charles Simic

Tale About a Tale, The. HSix

Wise Triangle, A. PoSu, *tr. by* Anne Pennington; CBNP, *tr. by* Anne Pennington *and* Charles Simic

Yawp! (LL) Home Sweet Home with Variations. Henry Cuyler Bunner. BXAP; OBAL

Ye Alps audacious, thro' the heavens that rise. The Hasty Pudding. Joel Barlow. AmPP; NAAL-3; NOBA; OBAL; OxBA; TAP

Ye angells bright, pluck from your wings a quill. Edward Taylor. ChIV-2; PoEL-3 *Fr.* Preparatory Meditations Before My Approach to the Lord's Supper.

Ye Anger Earth. Moses ibn Ezra. *Fr.* The World's Illusion. TrJP, *tr. by* Solomon Solis-Cohen

Ye are many—they are few. (LL) The Mask [*or* Masque] of Anarchy. Shelley. FHYEP; OBSV; OxAEP-2; RB; Ro; SCV

"Ye are the Duke of Athol's nurse." The Duke of Athole's Nurse. *Unknown.* ESPB

Ye are the spirits who preside. Joanna Baillie. ECWP *Fr.* An Address to the Muses.

Ye are the temples of the Lord. The Exhortation of a Father to His Children. Robert Smith. OxBChV

Ye ayres and windes, ye elves of hilles. Medea's Incantation. Ovid. OBVE, *tr. by* Arthur Golding *Fr.* Magic. AWP, *tr. by* Shakespeare *Fr.* Metamorphoses.

Ye banks and braes and streams around. Highland Mary. Robert Burns. AWP; GTBS-P; OBEV; SAGP

Ye banks and braes o' Bonnie Doon, *see also* "Ye flowery banks o' bonie Doon." The Banks O' Doon. Robert Burns. NOBE; NOEC

Ye beauties! O how great the sum. On a Bed of Guernsey Lilies. Christopher Smart. CABP; PoPoPo

Ye belles, and ye flirts, and ye pert little things. Song for Ranelagh. William Whitehead. ECEV

Ye blessed Creatures, I have heard the call. Wordsworth. *Fr.* Ode: Intimations of Immortality [from Recollections of Early Childhood]. AWP; FHYEP; HAP; HeIP-4; NOBE; NOBRP; OAEL-2; OBEV; OBNC; PBMP; PoE; PoEL-4

Ye[e] blushing virgins happy are. To Roses in the Bosom[e] of Castara. William Habington. BeJo; EnLoPo; MeLP; NOSC; OBEV; SCGP; SeCP *Fr.* Castara.

Ye Bruthers Dogg. Jon Anderson. NBLV

Ye buds of Brutus' land, courageous youths, now play your parts! For Soldiers. Humphrey Gifford. CH; NoSic

Ye captive souls of blindfold Cyprian's boat. My Love is Past. Thomas Watson. NoSic

Ye cats that at midnight spit love at each other. An Appeal to Cats in the Business of Love. Thomas Flatman. APAD; EnLoPo; GBL; HAP; OBCoV; PC

Ye Clerke of Ye Wethere. *Unknown.* BXAP

Ye Clouds. France. Coleridge. Ro

Ye clouds, that far above me float and pause. Coleridge. *See* France.

Ye congregation of the tribes. Psalm 58. Christopher Smart. NoP-4

Ye coop us up, and tax our bread. Caged Rats. Ebenezer Elliot. EBEV

Ye dainty nymphs, that in this blessed brook. The Lay to Eliza. Edmund Spenser. NOBE *Fr.* Aprill. NAEL-1; OBEV; PoEL-1 *Fr.* The Shepheardes [*or* Shepeards *or* Shepherd's] Calender.

Ye distant spires, ye antique towers. Ode on a Distant Prospect of Eton College. Thomas Gray. GTBS-P; ImPo; NAEL-1; NOBE; NOEC; NoP-4; OAEL-1; OxAEP-1; PoE; PoEL-3; SCGP

Ye dogg, O'Toole. Ye Bruthers Dogg. Jon Anderson. NBLV

Ye elms that wave on Malvern Hill. Malvern Hill. Herman Melville. APN-2; AmPP; CBCWP; ColAP; PAR; TAP

Ye elves of hill(s), brooks, standing lakes, and groves. Magic. Shakespeare. AWP; EBEV; OxAEP-1; SCV *Fr.* The Tempest. OAEL-1

Ye elves of hills, brooks, standing lakes, and groves. Magic. Ovid. AWP, *tr by* Shakespeare *Fr.* Metamorphoses.

Ye elves of hills, brooks, standing lakes, and groves. Shakespeare. *Fr.* The Tempest. OAEL-1

Ye flaming Powers, and winged Warrio[u]rs bright. Upon the Circumcision. Milton. ChIV-2

Ye flippering soul[e]. An Address to the Soul Occasioned by a Rain. Edward Taylor. MeMAP; NAAL-1; NAAL-3; NOBA; OxBA; PoEL-3

Ye flowery banks o' bonie Doon, *see also* "Ye banks and braes o' bonie Doon." Robert Burns. BoLoP; CH; GTBS-P; NAEL-2; NoP-4; OBEV; TFi

("And left the thorn wi' me.") (LL) OBEV

("But left the thorn wi' me.") (LL) AWP; PoEL-4; TFi; UnPo

Ye gallants of Newgate, whose fingers are nice. Newgate's Garland. John Gay. ECEV; PeLV

Ye gentlemen and ladies fair. The Hunters of Kentucky; or, Half Horse and Half Alligator. Samuel Woodworth. AS

"Ye gie corn to my horse." Clyde's Water. *Unknown.* ESPB

Ye glorious Jove-born imps how you rejoice. On the Three Children in the Fiery Furnace. Henry Colman. ChIV-1

Ye glowing seraphs, that now breathe above. Friendship in Perfection. Andrew Michael Ramsay. NOEC

Ye [*or* you] goat-herd gods, [that love the grassy mountains]. Double Sestine [*or* Sestina]. Sir Philip Sidney. HAP; ImPo; NAEL-1; NOBE; NoSic; OAEL-1; PoEL-1 *Fr.* Arcadia.

Ye golden lamps of heaven, farewell. Hymn. Philip Doddridge. ECEV

"Ye graceful peasant-girls and mountain-maids." Ballata: His Talk with Certain Peasant Girls. Franco Sacchetti, *Italian.* AWP, *tr. by* D. G. Rossetti

Ye green-robed Dryads, oft at dusky eve. Joseph Warton. ECEV, *ll.* 1–15; NOEC *Fr.* Enthusiast, The; or, The Lover of Nature. PoEL-3

Ye have been fresh and green. To Meadows [*or* Meddowes]. Robert Herrick. AWP; CH; CaPo; NOBE; NOSC; OBEV; PoEL-3; SeCP

"Ye have robbed," said he, "ye have slaughtered and made an end." He Fell among Thieves. Sir Henry John Newbolt. EBVV; FaPoR; OBEV; OBWP; OxBTC

Ye Highlands [*or* hielands] and ye Lawlands [*or* lowlands]. The Bonny Earl of Murray. *Unknown.* ESPB; NOSC; OBEV; OxBB; OxBS; SCGP

Ye holy Angels bright. Richard Baxter. NOCV *Fr.* A Psalm of Praise.

Ye humble souls that seek the Lord. Christ's Resurrection and Ascension. Philip Doddridge. NOCV

Ye know my heart, my lady dear. Sir Thomas Wyatt. SiPS

Ye know on earth and all ye need to know. (LL) Ode on a Grecian Urn. Keats. AWP; CABP; ChAP; ClHu; EBEV; FaBoBe; HAP; HeIP-4; HoPM; ImPo; InPS-3; NAEL-2; NAWM-2; NIP-4; NOBE; NOBRP; NoP-4; OAEL-2; OBEV; OBNC; PBMP; PFE; PoE; PoEL-4; PoPoPo; Ro; SCGP; TFi; TOF; UnPo

Ye ladies, walking past me piteous-eyed. Sonnet: To the Same Ladies; With Their Answer. Dante, *Italian.* AWP, *tr. by* D. G. Rossetti

Ye learned sisters which have oftentimes. Epithalamion. Edmund Spenser. AAS; BoLoP; CABP; FHYEP; InPS-3; NOBE; NoP-4; NoSic; OAEL-1; OBEV; OxAEP-1; PBRV; PoEL-1; PoPoPo

Ye living Lamps, by whose dear light. The Mower to the Glow-Worms [*or* Glowworms *or* Glo-Worms]. Andrew Marvell. APo; AWP; CBLP; ESCV; EnLoPo; FHYEP; FMP; FSCP; GLoP; GeHe; NAEL-1; NOBE; NoP-4; OAEL-1; OxBoLi; PBRV; PeLV; PoEL-2; SCGP; SeCP; TFi

Ye lords of creation, men you are called. The Lords of Creation. *Unknown.* PoLF

Ye loyal Britons, I pray draw near. The Battle of Shiloh. *Unknown.* AmFP

Ye maggots, feed on Willie's brains. Robert Burns. FaBoEE

Ye Mariners of England. Thomas Campbell. BLPA; EBEvV; FaPoR; GTBS-P; NOBE; OBEV; OBWP; OxAEP-2

Ye mariners of Spain. The Song of the Galley. *Unknown, Spanish.* AWP, *tr. by* John Gibson Lockhart

"Ye maun gang to your father, Janet." Fair Janet. *Unknown.* ESPB; OxBB

Ye may pass me by with pitying eye. Song of the Imprisoned Bird. Eliza Cook. VWP

Ye merry hearts that love to play. Win at First and Lose at Last; or, A New Game at Cards. Laurence Price. OxBoLi

Ye mighty Demons, whose tremendous sway. Claudian. OBCVT, *tr. by* Alfred Tennyson, 1st Baron Tennyson *Fr.* Translation of Claudian's Proserpine.

Ye Mongers Aye Need Masks for Cheatrie. Sydney Goodsir Smith. OxBS

Ye mountain valleys, pitifully groan! Lament for Bion. Moschus, *Greek.* AWP, *tr. by* George Chapman

Ye nymphs! if e'er your eyes were red. On the Lamented Death of Mrs. Throckmorton's Bullfinch. William Cowper. NOEC

Ye nymphs of Solyma! begin the song. Messiah: A Sacred Eclogue in Imitation of Virgil's Pollio. Alexander Pope. ChIV-1

Ye old mule, that thin[c]k your self so fair [*or* fayre]. Sir Thomas Wyatt. AAS

Ye operas, circles, I no more must view! / My toilette, patches, all the world, adieu! Lady Mary Wortley Montagu. *See* Saturday: The Small-Pox.

Ye paltry [*or* paultry] underlings of state. On the Irish Club. Jonathan Swift. OBSV

Ye Parliament of England. *Unknown.* AmFP

Ye people of Ireland, both country and city. A New Song of Wood's Halfpence. Jonathan Swift. OxBoLi

Ye people who delight in sin. The Hanging of Sam Archer. *Unknown.* AmFP

Ye pilgrim-folk, advancing pensively. Dante. AWP; CTC *Fr.* La Vita Nuova.

Ye plains, where threefold harvests press the ground. The Passage of the Mountain of St. Gothard. Georgiana Cavendish, Duchess of Devonshire. ECWP

Ye powers above and heavenly poles. On Button the Grave-Maker. *Unknown.* FaBoEE

Ye powers of truth, that bid my soul aspire. On Freedom and Ambition. Oliver Goldsmith. NOIV *Fr.* The Travel[l]er; or, A Prospect of Society.

Ye Pow'rs, o'er all the flow'ry Meads. The Fourteenth Olympick Ode. Pindar, *Greek.* OBCVT, *tr. by* Gilbert West

Ye Realms below the Skies. Hosea, II Ballou. AH

Ye saints who dwell on Europe's shore. The Handcart Song. *Unknown.* AmFP

Ye saw't floueran in my breist. The Mandrake Hert. Sydney Goodsir Smith. OxBS

Ye say they all have passed away. Indian Names. Lydia Huntley Sigourney. APN-1; ColAP; OBCA; PAR; PoLF

Ye Scattered Nations. *Unknown, Latin.* AH, *tr. by* Thomas Cradock

Ye should na shamed me here. (LL) Mary [*or* Marie] Hamilton. *Unknown.* NoP-4

Ye [*or* You] should stay longer if we durst. The Fourth Song. Francis Beaumont. NOSC *Fr.* The Masque of the Inner Temple and Gray's Inne.

Ye[e] silent shades, whose each tree here. To Groves. Robert Herrick. CaPo

Ye single folks all, that adorn this gay table. A Song for the Single Table on New Year's Day. Elizabeth Frances Amherst. ECWP

Ye smarts and belles, whose airs and arts confess. The Vanity of External Accomplishments. Mary Whateley. ECWP

Ye sons of Columbia, your attention I do crave. Fuller and Warren. Moses Whitecotton. AmFP

Ye sons of earth prepare the plough. The Sower. William Cowper. ChIV-2 *Fr.* Olney Hymns.

Ye Sorrowers. Franz Werfel. TrJP, *tr. by* Ludwig Lewisohn *Fr.* The Eternal Road.

Ye sorrowing people! who from bondage fly. The Fugitive Slaves. Jones Very. TAP

Ye stoll awaye and durst no more be seene. (LL) Admonition to Montgomerie. James I, King of England. GTBS-P; OxBS

Ye storm-winds of Autumn. Parting. Matthew Arnold. EnVR *Fr.* Switzerland.

Ye sylvan Muses, loftier strains recite. The Birth of the Squire; an Eclogue. John Gay. NAEL-1; NOEC; PoEL-3

Ye tender-hearted people, I pray you lend an ear. Samuel Allen. *Unknown.* AmFP

Ye tender young virgins attend to my lay. Perplexity: A Poem. Elizabeth Hands. WoRP

Ye that passen [*or* pasen] by the weye [*or* weiye]. *Unknown.* MiEL

Ye tradefull merchants that, with weary toile. Sonnet 15. Edmund Spenser. HeIP-4; NIP-4; OAEL-1; Son *Fr.* Amoretti. AAS

Ye true lovers bold, come listen unto me. The True Lovers Bold. *Unknown.* AmFP

Ye vales and hills whose beauty hither drew. Inscription for a Monument in Crossthwaite Curch, in the Vale of Keswick. Wordsworth. EPCY

Ye Virgin Pow'rs defend my heart. Song. Elizabeth Taylor. KTR

Ye virgins that from Cupid's tents. Isabella Whitney. PEW *Fr.* The Admonition by the Auctor to all yong Gentilwomen: And to al other Maids being in Love.

Ye walls! sole witnesses of happy sighs. Walter Savage Landor. EnLoPo *Fr.* Ianthe.

Ye Wearie Wayfarer. Adam Lindsay Gordon.
Sun and Rain and Dew from Heaven. PoLF

Ye weary, heavy laden souls. The Lonesome Dove. *Unknown.* AmFP

Ye wha are fain to hae your name. Braid Claith. Robert Fergusson. NOEC; OxBS

Ye who amid this feverish world would wear. Urban Pollution. John Armstrong. ECEV; NOEC *Fr.* The Art of Preserving Health.

Ye who intelligent the Third Heaven move. The First Canzone of the Convito. Dante, *Italian.* OBVE, *tr. by* Shelley

Ye who read in musty volumes. The Old Sac Village. Albery Allson Whitman. AAP *Fr.* Not a Man and Yet a Man.

Ye wild-eyed Muses, sing the Twins of Jove. Hymn to Castor and Pollux. *Unknown.* AWP *Fr.* Homeric Hymns.

Ye wild-eyed Muses, sing the twins of Jove. Hymn to Castor and Pollux. *Unknown, Greek.* OBCVT, *tr. by* Shelley

Yea, and a good cause why thus should I plain. From A Funeral Song, Upon the Decease of Annes His Mother. Nicholas Grimald. NoP-4

Yea, beds for all who come. (LL) Uphill [*or* Up-Hill]. Christina Rossetti. APAD; BLPA; CABP; CH; EBEvV; EBVV; FaBoBe; HAP; InPK-6; LBC; NAEL-2; NALW; NOBE; NTP; NoP-4; OAEL-2; OBEV; OBNC; PEW; PFE; PoE; PoPoPo; PoRA; Poetr; SDW; TFi; TrCP; WPE; WeW-3

Yea, gold is son of Zeus: no rust. Gold Is the Son of Zeus: Neither Moth nor Worm May Gnaw It. "Michael Field." OBMV

Yea, let me praise my lady whom I love. Sonnet: He Will Praise His Lady. Guido Guinicelli, *Italian.* AWP, *tr. by* D. G. Rossetti

Yea, the coneys are scared by the thud of hoofs. The Field of Waterloo. Thomas Hardy. CMoP; FaBoCh *Fr.* The Dynasts.

Yea, thou shalt be forgotten like spilt wine. Anactoria. Swinburne. LoP

Yea, though I'm sorry for thee. (LL) A Youth Mowing. D. H. Lawrence. InPK-6; MoBrPo; NoAM

Yeah, man, / I'll help out / with the / memorial for / Trane. Memorial for Trane. Sam Greenlee. SeSe

Yeah. / they hang you up. To All Brothers. Sonia Sanchez. BPo

Year. Milo De Angelis, *Italian.* NeIt, *tr. by* Lawrence Venuti

Year, The. Coventry Patmore. *See* Round the Year.

Year about to end, The. The Last Day of the Year. Su Tung-p'o, *Chinese.* OHPC, *tr. by* Kenneth Rexroth

Year after year. . . how many millennia of worldly affairs. The Cave of Gold Essence—in Ning-tu. T'ang Hsien-tsu, *Chinese.* CoBLCP, *tr. by* Jonathan Chaves

Year after year I have watched. Li Ch'ing-chao, *Chinese.* BoWoP; OHMPC, *tr. by* Kenneth Rexroth

Year after year in the snow, Tune: "Pure Serene Music." Li Ch'ing-chao, *Chinese.* CoBCP, *tr. by* Burton Watson; SuSp, *tr. by* Eugene Eoyang

Year after year the princess lies asleep. Parabola. Alec Derwent Hope. NOBAu; PoA

Year ago I fell in love with the functional ward, A. The Hospital. Patrick Kavanagh. BIrV; CABP; CIP-2

Year ago today by, A. By the City Gate. Ts'ui Hao, *Chinese.* OHMPC, *tr. by* Kenneth Rexroth

Year ago we walked the wood, A. Vies Manquées. Edith Nesbit. VWP

Year ago you came, A. Pietá. James McAuley. BMAP; CBAP

Year at its turn, The. The Last Day of the Year (New Year's Eve). Annette von Droste-Hülshoff, *German.* BoWoP, *tr. by* Willis Barnstone

Year away from the pigpen, and look at him, A. Variation on a Noel. John Ashbery. EOEF

Year by year on his way to the South Sea. (LL) The South. Wang Chien, *Chinese.* BLT; ChiP, *tr. by* Arthur Waley

Year Chi-wei (Fifteen Fifty Nine), New Year's Day, The. Wen Cheng-ming, *Chinese.* CoBLCP, *tr. by* Jonathan Chaves

Year dies fiercely: out of the north the beating storms, The. Year's End. William Everson. MoP; NoAM

Year 1812, The. Donald Davie, *after the Polish of* Adam Mickiewicz. OBVE; OBWP

Year has changed his mantle cold, The. Spring. Charles, Duc d' Orléans, *French.* AWP; CTC, *tr. by* Andrew Lang

Year has come to us as though out of hiding, A. Early January. W. S. Merwin. VGW

Year has run thin through the tuning room of my mind, The. A Spring Memorandum. Robert Duncan. PoA

Year Hsin-hai (Fifteen Fifty One), New Year's Eve: Keeping Watch, The. Wen Cheng-ming, *Chinese.* CoBLCP, *tr. by* Jonathan Chaves

Year I-mao (Fifteen Fifty Five), New Year's Eve, The. Wen Cheng-ming, *Chinese.* CoBLCP, *tr. by* Jonathan Chaves

Year is done, the last act of the vaudeville, The. Midnight Show. Karl Shapiro. OxBA

Year is sullen, sullen is the day, The. Sullenness. "Michael Field." VWP

Year lays down his mantle cold, The. (LL) Spring. Charles, Duc d' Orléans, *French.* AWP; CTC, *tr. by* Andrew Lang

Year 1937, The. Timur Kibirov, *Russian.* TCRP, *tr. by* Vera Dunham

Year of Our Lord two thousand one hundred and seven, The. John Heath-Stubbs. NOBL *Fr.* An Ecclesiastical Chronicle.

Year of Seeds, The. Ebenezer Elliot.

Give Not Our Blankets, Tax-Fed Squire. Son

Ralph Leech Believes. Son

Toy of the Titans. Son

Year of Sorrow, A. Aubrey Thomas De Vere.

Spring. OBNC

Year of the Bird. Brian Swann. AmPA

Year of the Foxes, The. David Malouf. NOBAu

Year of the mask of blood, my father, The. That Year. Sharon Olds. NMM-2

Year of the monkey, year of the human wave. The Way of Tet. Bruce Weigl. AF

Year of the Olive Oil, The. Charles North. FTOS

Year revolves, and I explore, The. George Crabbe. EPCY *Fr.* The Parish Register.

Year slows down. The swallows go, The. October. Clive Sansom. AYFP

Year the white women came like the plague, The. Feel Free. Natasha Tarpley. ISC

Year tips, the sun, The. Before Christmas. John Corben. AYFP

Year was as long and dark as a bed, The. Potato Thief. Pentti Saarikoski, *Finnish.* VCWP, *tr. by* Herbert Lomas

Year was the sixth of Constantine's sway, The. Constantine's Vision of the Cross. Cynewulf. *Fr.* Elene. AnOE, *tr. by* Charles W. Kennedy

Year well remembered! Happy who beheld thee! The Year 1812. Donald Davie, *after the Polish of* Adam Mickiewicz. OBVE; OBWP

Year Wu-tzu [1048], The, First Month, Night of the Twenty-sixth: A Dream. Mei Yao Ch'en, *Chinese.* SuSp, *tr. by* Jonathan Chaves

Yearbook. Milo De Angelis, *Italian.* NeIt, *tr. by* Lawrence Venuti

Yearning, A. Arapera Hineira Blank, *Maori.* PeNZ, *tr. by the author*

Yearning. Nguyễn Đình Thi, *Vietnamese.* AVP, *tr. by* Huỳnh Sanh Thông

Yearning for Winter. Karl Wilhelm Ramler, *German.* GePo, *tr. by* George C. Schoolfield

Years. Jon Anderson. AmPA

Years, The. Catherine Davis. FFC

Years, The. John Ennis. CIP-2

Years. Yon-gyun Kim, *Korean.* CKP, *tr. by* Jaihiun Kim

Years after surviving. Word Basket Woman. Gary Snyder. BB

Years ago, at a private school. An Ever-Fixed Mark. Kingsley Amis. MoP; NoAM

Years ago feasting on raw whale by the eastern sea. Third Month, Night of the Seventeenth, Written While Drunk. Lu Yu, *Chinese.* CoBCP; SuSp, *tr. by* Burton Watson

Years ago, / he began dialing your number. The Obscene Caller. Philip Dacey. AmPA

Years ago, I traveled ten thousand miles in search of honor. Tune: "Telling of Innermost Feelings." Lu Yu, *Chinese.* SuSp, *tr. by* James J. Y. Liu

Years ago I was a gardener. Writing in Prison. Ken Smith. NBrP

Years ago, to the winding banks of this lake in spring. At the Lake—Remembering My Dead Son, Yü. Pien Kung, *Chinese.* CoBLCP, *tr. by* Jonathan Chaves

Years ago, when I heard the words of my elders. T'ao Ch'ien, *Chinese.* SuSp, *tr. by* Eugene Eoyang

Years ago, when I was young. Juan Chi. CoBCP, *tr. by* Burton Watson *Fr.* Singing of Thoughts.

Years ahead, years ahead. Guy Noel Pocock. NSI

Years and scars later. Jacob. George Garrett. CRP

Years and years ago, these sounds took sides. Casting and Gathering. Seamus Heaney. NoP-4

Years and years and years ago, when I was a boy. When I was a boy. Dylan Thomas. SAGP *Fr.* A Child's Christmas in Wales.

Year's at the spring, The. Pippa's Song. Robert Browning. BLPA; BoTP; CTV; EBEvV; FHYEP; FaBoBe; ImPo; NTCP; OBEV; PoToHe; TFi; TrCP; UnPo *Fr.* Pippa Passes.

Year's Awakening, The. Thomas Hardy. CMoP; OxBTC

Years creep slowly by, Lorena. The. Lorena. H. D. L. Webster. BLPA

Year's End. William Everson. MoP; NoAM

Year's End. Ted Kooser. PBCAP

Year's end, The. Miya Shūji, *Japanese.* MJT, *tr. by* Makoto Ueda

Year's End. Ellen Bryant Voigt. NoAM

Year's End. Richard Wilbur. CoAP; HeIP-4; LiTM; NAAL-2

(At Year's End.) NYBP

Year's Ending, The. St. J. Page Yako, *Xhosa.* PeSA, *tr. by* C. M. Mcanyangwa *and* Jack Cope

Year's flowers in the grove die in a day, A. In a Day. Li Shang-yin, *Chinese.* SuSp, *tr. by* Eugene Eoyang *and* Irving Y. Lo

Years have gathered grayly, The. In a Eweleaze near Weatherbury. Thomas Hardy. EnVR

Years have gone. It is spring, The. Andrée Rexroth. Kenneth Rexroth. APSN; VGW

Years have not damaged your beauty, The. Rufinus Domesticus, *Greek.* InMo, *tr. by* Sam Hamill

Years have touched me, The. Fujiwara No Yoshifusa, *Japanese.* OHMPJ, *tr. by* Kenneth Rexroth

Years in the blood keep us naked to the bone, The. The Art of Clay. Duane Niatum. HATNAP

Years Later. Laurence David Lerner. PeSA

Years Later. Ruth Stone. BoWoP

Years later, critics would be saying. Thoreau's Fossil Lilies. Brenda Hillman. WeT

Years later, it was, after everything / got hazy in my head. Mary. Philip Appleman. GI

Years, many parti-coloured years. Walter Savage Landor. OBEV

years of a lifetime do not reach a hundred, The. *Unknown.* ChiP, *tr. by* Arthur Waley *Fr.* Seventeen Old Poems.

Years of Indiscretion. John Ashbery. NOBA

Years of manhood had not tinged, The. Charley du Bignon. Mary E. Tucker. CBWP-1

Years of my youth, years of dissipation. Sergey Aleksandrovich Yesenin, *Russian.* TCRP, *tr. by* Daniel Weissbort

Years of the modern! years of the unperform'd! Walt Whitman. NCAP

Years pass like donkeys, The. Ultimate Argument. Ion Caraion, *Romanian.* AF, *tr. by* Marguerite Dorian *and* Elliott B. Urdang

Years pass on, and overhead, The. His Prime. George Clinton Rowe. AAP *Fr.* Toussaint L'Overture.

Years pile up, but there rides with you still, The. As on a Darkling Plain. Henry Taylor. MT; Poetr

Years ride out from the world like couriers gone to a throne, The. Song of the Riders. Stephen Vincent Benét. MoAmPo *Fr.* John Brown's Body.

Years saw me still Acasto's mansion grace. An Old Cat's Dying Soliloquy. Anna Seward. ECWP; NOEC

Year's Spinning, A. Elizabeth Barrett Browning. NAEL-2

Years they come and go, The. Ad Finem. Heinrich Heine, *German.* AWP, *tr. by* Elizabeth Barrett Browning

Years they mistook me for you. Dodo. Henry Carlile. Poetsp

Years to come (empty boxcars), The. Time. William Stafford. Son

Years Vanish Like the Morning Dew. Mei Sheng, *Chinese.* IMW, *tr. by* Arthur Waley

Years will pass. Neither late nor soon, The. The Last Merchant. Wolf Ehrlich, *Russian.* TCRP, *tr. by* Daniel Weissbort

Year's Windfalls, A. Christina Rossetti.

Wind of January, The. BoTP

Years, years ago,— ere yet my dreams. The Belle of the Ball-Room. Winthrop Mackworth Praed. NOBRP *Fr.* Every-Day Characters.

Yee night, and darknes, cloudie aire. Prudentius. OBCVT, *tr. by* Alexander Huish *Fr.* Cathemerinon 2.

Yee Shall Not Misse of a Few Lines in Remembrance of Thomas Hooker. Edward Johnson. SCAP

Yeh. / Billie. For Our Lady. Sonia Sanchez. NAAAL

Yellow. De Leon Harrison. PoBA

Yellow-belly, yellow-belly, come and take a swim. *Unknown.* OxBoLi

Yellow Bird, The. James W. Thompson. PoBA

Yellow Bird Sings, The. Rabindranath Tagore. *Fr.* The Gardener. OBMV

Yellow Bittern, The. Cathal Buidhe Mac Giolla Ghunna, *Irish.* NOIV, *tr. by* Thomas Kinsella; BIrV, *tr. by* Thomas Macdonagh; CIP-2, *tr. by* Tom MacIntyre

Yellow Bittern, The. *Unknown, Irish.* CIP-2; PBCIP, *tr. by* Tom MacIntyre

Yellow blood on the dunes. Before the Pacific. Blanca Varela, *Spanish.* BoWoP, *tr. by* Willis Barnstone

Yellow/brown woman / fingers smelling always of onions. I Am Becoming My Mother. Lorna Goodison. OPOU

Yellow bus, The. Tanka. Nakajō Fumiko, *Japanese.* MJT, *tr. by* Makoto Ueda

Yellow butterflies / Over the blossoming virgin corn. Korosta Katzina Song. Koianimptiwa, *Hopi.* AWP, *tr. by* Natalie Curtis Burlin

Yellow canary trilled, A. Jealous Adam. Itsik Manger, *Yiddish.* TrJP, *tr. by* Jacob Sonntag

Yellow chirper, beaks its cage, The. (LL) In the Cage. Robert Lowell. NOBA; Son

Yellow Clover. Katharine Lee Bates. CPO

Yellow-coated pomegranate, figs like lizards' necks, A. Philip of Thessalonica, *Greek.* GrAn; OBCVT, *tr. by* Edwin Morgan

Yellow Delicious. Samuel Hazo. IFJA

Yellow Dog Blues. William Christopher Handy. NAAAL

Yellow dusk: messenger fails to appear. *Unknown, Chinese.* OBVE, *tr. by* Arthur Waley

Yellow Eyes, look at me and look for me. Let me see. Song of the White Man. *Unknown.* APN-2 *Fr.* Minnetare Songs.

Yellow Fairy, The. Charlotte Druitt Cole. BoTP

Yellow feather / of a note, A. Good Morning. Carl Rakosi. FTOS

Yellow Flower, The. William Carlos Williams. HAP

Yellow freesia arc like twining arms;. Letter: Blues. Elizabeth Alexander. RA

Yellow Glove. Naomi Shihab Nye. LoL

Yellow gold's not precious. Wang Fan-chih, *Chinese.* SuSp, *tr. by* Eugene Eoyang

Yellow Gramophone. Sheila Cussons, *Afrikaans.* PeSAV, *tr. by the author*

Yellow Hills in Back, The. Christianne Balk. IFJA

Yellow is for regret, the distal, the second hand. Charles Wright. AmPA

Yellow leaf, from the darkness, A. Brooding Grief. D. H. Lawrence. CMoP; IMW; PoE

Yellow leaves spiral down through the air. A Record of My Trip to Mount She. Yüan Hung-tao, *Chinese.* CoBLCP, *tr. by* Jonathan Chaves

Yellow Light. Garrett Kaoru Hongo. InPS-3; OpBo; WWSi; WeT

Yellow-lit Budweiser signs over oaken bars. Uptown. Allen Ginsberg. TwCP

Yellow Man, Purple Man. Emily Dickinson. TLR

Yellow november / comes swaying. Rushing. Ray A. Young Bear. CDW

Yellow-oatmeal flowers of the windmill palms. Eden. David Woo. OpBo

Yellow River, The. Nabaneeta Dev Sen, *Bengali.* OMIP, *tr. by* Nabaneeta Dev Sen

Yellow River winds along, The. Autumn Vista. Li Meng-yang, *Chinese.* CoBLCP, *tr. by* Jonathan Chaves

Yellow sand, white reeds. Crossing the Frontier. Li Meng-yang, *Chinese.* CoBLCP, *tr. by* Jonathan Chaves

Yellow Season, The. William Carlos Williams. MoAmPo

Yellow steam of Petersburg's winter, The. Petersburg. Innokenty Fiodorovich Annensky, *Russian.* TCRP, *tr. by* Lubov Yakovleva *with* Daniel Weissbort

Yellow Sunflower of Szechwan. Chang Yü, *Chinese.* SuSp, *tr. by* Irving Y. Lo

Yellow sunset splashes in the window, A. Gabriel Preil, *Yiddish.* CEEP, *tr. by* Linda Zisquit

Yellow surprise at the sun. . . . Richard Wright. *See* Between the World and Me.

Yellow the bracken. Autumn. Florence Hoatson. BoTP

Yellow Violet, The. William Cullen Bryant. NAAL-1; NAAL-3; PoLF; TAP

Yellow winds blow in from the north. Seeing Off Commander In Chief Li to Yün-chung. Li Meng-yang, *Chinese.* CoBLCP, *tr. by* Jonathan Chaves

Yellow Wolf Spirit. Ron Welburn. BAP-96

Yellowhammer, The. John Clare. NOBVV

Yellowjacket. Peter Blue Cloud. HATNAP

Yellows and creams, The. Symbols of Transformation. Ron Padgett. FTOS

Yellows cast their spells: the evening primrose. Crepuscule. Angela Shaw. BAP-96

Yeoman of the Guard. Sir William Schwenck Gilbert. Family Fool, The. NBLV

Yer glowin' gowden by the guschach. Love-Lowe. Alan Bold. FaBoTC

Yere yernes ful yerne, and yeldes never like, A. The Passage of a Year. *Unknown.* PoEL-1 *Fr.* Sir Gawain and the Green Knight. OAEL-1, *tr. by* Brian Stone

Yerokastrinos. Karen Chamberlain. APAD

Yes. Adlestrop. Edward Thomas. AYFP; CH; EBEvV; HAP; NAEL-2; NOBE; OBEV; OxBTC; UV

Yes. Brendan Kennelly. CIP-2

Yes. Muriel Rukeyser. PiM

Yes. Edward Thomas. *See* Adlestrop.

Yes a very important discovery. T. S. Eliot. OxBM *Fr.* The Cocktail Party.

Yes, and back again[!]. Mother Goose. *See* To Babylon.

Yes, and chilled with fear and despair. (LL) Judith of Bethulia. John Crowe Ransom. FYAP; FaBoMo; LiTM; MeMAP; NOBA; NoAM

Yes as alike as entirely. To My Father. W. S. Graham. FaBoTw

Yes. Autumn. The leaves yellow and red. The Answer. Stephen Berg. IMW

Yes, be like God. I wonder what I thought. Jack Spicer. NeAP *Fr.* Imaginary Elegies.

Yes! Beauty still rebels! Art, I. Alfred Noyes. OBEV

Yes, Breisach, your decrease is profit yet and prize. To Breisach, Taken by That Supremely Celebrated Hero, Bernhard, Duke of Saxony. Georg Rudolph Weckherlin, *German.* GePo, *tr. by* George C. Schoolfield

Yes, But. Rachel Hadas. NMM-2

"Yes, But. . . ." Theodore Weiss. TAP

Yes! but not his—'tis Death itself there dies. (LL) My Baptismal Birthday [or Birth-Day]. Coleridge. ChIV-2; NOCV

Yes, but we must be sure of verities. The Spring Poem. Dave Jeddie Smith. PoPoPo

Yes, contumelious fair, you scorn. The Author Apologizes to a Lady, for His Being a Little Man. Christopher Smart. BoLoP; CBLP

Yes, crazy to suppose one could describe them. Robert Pinsky. *See* Invocation: "It's crazy to think one could describe them."

Yes, do you remember an inn. Lament for Lost Lodgings. Phyllis McGinley. NYBP

Yes, ducks are valiant things. Frederick William Harvey. BoTP *Fr.* Ducks.

Yes! Ethiopia yet shall stretch. Ethiopia. Frances Ellen Watkins Harper. NAAAL

Yes, every poet is a fool. Epigram. Matthew Prior. FaBoEE

Yes, faint was my applause and cold my praise. To a Friend. Joseph Rodman Drake. APN-1

Yes, faith is a goodly anchor. After the Burial. James Russell Lowell. UnPo

Yes, farewell, farewell forever. Lady Byron's Reply to Lord Byron's "Fare Thee Well." *Unknown.* BLPA

Yes, for the multitude of people it's hard to avoid. Konstantin Konstantinovich Sluchevsky, *Russian.* TCRP, *tr. by* Albert C. Todd

Yes, from the ingrate heart, the street. The Fugitive. Alice Thompson Meynell. NOCV

Yes, gentle Time, thy gradual, healing hand. To Time. Mary Tighe. IMW

"Yes, go on! This is plain talk of plainer feelings now." John Hollander. VCAP *Fr.* Powers of Thirteen.

Yes, he said, darling, yes, of course you tried. The Appointment. Leonard Alfred George Strong. OxBTC

Yes, he's got her now. Blues. John Fuller. NOBL

Yes, his face really is so terrible. Sudden Appearance of a Monster at a Window. Lawrence Raab. BLT

Yes! hope may with my strong desire keep pace. Love's Justification. Michelangelo Buonarroti, *Italian.* OBVE, *tr. by* William Wordsworth

Yes, I am black! and radiant. Bible, *O.T.* PBWP, *tr. by* Marcia Falk *Fr.* The Song of Songs. AWP

Yes, I am in love. Mibu no Tadami, *Japanese.* OHPJ, *tr. by* Kenneth Rexroth

Yes, I believe He loved them, too. The Young Workman. Mary Dillingham Frear. TrCP

Yes, I believe in God who has created. The Spirit of Evil. Arrigo Boito. OxBoV, *tr. by* Andrew Porter *Fr.* Otello.

Yes, I caught the butterfly. Went crazy for the moment. Amir Gilbo'a, *Hebrew.* IP, *tr. by* Warren Bargad *and* Stanley F. Chyet

Yes, I did not plow, I did not sow. Aftergrowth. "Rachel," *Hebrew.* MHP, *tr. by* Ruth Finer Mintz

Yes, I do see many of us afraid of scraps. Quilt of Rights. Sandra McPherson. LoL

Yes, I have lov'd: yet often have I said. Sappho; or, The Resolve. Charlotte Dacre. NOBRP

Yes! I have seen the ancient oak. Felicia Dorothea Hemans. CTC *Fr.* The Brereton Omen.

Yes I hope that things will work out somehow. (LL) The Return of the Proconsul. Zbigniew Herbert, *Polish.* FaBoPV; PoSu, *tr. by* Czeslaw Milosz; CEEP, *tr. by* Czesw Miosz

Yes, I know, I am not your kin——. I and You. Nikolai Stepanovich Gumilyov, *Russian.* TCRP, *tr. by* Yakov Hornstein

Yes, I know: only the happy man. Bad Time for Poetry. Bertolt Brecht, *German.* PoSu, *tr. by* John Willett *and* Ralph Manheim

Yes, I only got here on my own. On My Own. Philip Levine. FYAP

Yes, I remember that pain precisely, *see also* "Ah, how well I remember that pain!" The Blood. Nina Cassian, *Romanian.* WPOW, *tr. by* Laura Schiff

Yes, I remember Willesden Gree. Willesden Gree. Jimmy Pearse. UV

Yes, I said it. Betsy Sholl. CrSp *Fr.* Job's Wife.

Yes I too have a cottage with a moss-grown roof. The Cottage Behind the Railway. Josef Hanzlik, *German.* CEEP, *tr. by* Ewald Osers

Yes, I was only sidesman here when last. Bristol and Clifton. John Betjeman. CMoP

Yes, I'd rather hear Heliodora's voice. Meleager. HePo, *tr. by* Barbara Hughes Fowler *Fr.* I'll Twine White Violets. NIP-4, *tr. by* Goldwin Smith

Yes: in the sea of life enisled. To Marguerite. Matthew Arnold. EnVR; GTBS-P; SoSe-8 *Fr* Switzerland

Yes, in the summer of 1773. Tom Wedgwood Tells. Brian W. Aldiss. NOBL

Yes, injured Woman—rise, assert thy right! The Rights of Woman. Anna Laetitia Barbauld. CABP; ECWP; NOEC; NoP-4; PEW; Ro; WoRP

Yes, it looked dark and dreary. Three Evenings in a Life. Adelaide Anne Procter. VWP

Yes, it's me. I appear thus to myself. Aleksey Petrovich Tsvetkov, *Russian.* TCRP, *tr. by* Albert C. Todd

"Yes, let me go. Yon fields are green." Request of a Dying Child. Lydia Huntley Sigourney. OBCA

Yes! let the rich deride, the proud disdain. Oliver Goldsmith. OBSV *Fr.* The Deserted Village. NOEC; OAEL-1; PoEL-3

Yes, Lizbie Browne! (LL) To Lizbie Browne. Thomas Hardy. FaBoVe; NOBVV; OxAEP-2

Yes, May and I are friends. After Church. Samuel Alfred Beadle. AAP

Yes Miss / Put up your pretty little mouth for a kiss. Admonition to the Muse. Geoffrey Taylor. FaBoEE

Yes, my darling, when life's shadows. In Memoriam. Alphonse Campbell Fordham. Mary Weston Fordham. AAP; CBWP-2

Yes! Oh yes! Salutations. Shanmuga Subbiah, *Tamil.* OMIP, *tr. by* T. K. Doraiswamy

Yes, one in a graven silence no birds breaks. (LL) Father and Son. Frederick Robert Higgins. BIrV; OBMV

Yes; or pass quick into the skies. (LL) A Fragment on Death. François Villon, *French.* CTC; PeVV, *tr. by* Swinburne

Yes, rub some soap upon your feet! A Hike on the Downs. John Betjeman. OBCoV

"Yes," said the boy, "first come the gum-tree crowds." The Boy who Dreamed the Country Night. Christopher Koch. NOBAu

Yes, so be it, though we already knew. The Sinking of the Mendi. S. E. K. Mqhayi, *Xhosa.* PeSA, *tr. by* C. M. Mcanyangwa *and* Jack Cope

Yes—somebody has lived here. The Words. Stefan Aug. Doinas, *Romanian.* CEEP, *tr. by* Peter Jay *and* Virgil Nemoianu

Yes, Southey, yes, I to the House of Prayer. A Rebuke to Robert Southey. *Unknown.* ECWP

Yes! strike again that sounding string. James M. Whitfield. NAAAL

Yes, Tadeusz Rozewicz, I too. In Praise of Old Women. Marya Fiamengo. WPOW

Yes! that fair neck, too beautiful by half. Madame d'Albert's Laugh. Clément Marot, *French.* AWP, *tr. by* Leigh Hunt

Yes, that's how I was. Judgment Day. Ronald Stuart Thomas. CRP

Yes, that's why. (LL) Reply. Reiner Kunze, *German.* PoSu, *tr. by* Ewald Osers

Yes, the Agency Can Handle That. Kenneth Fearing. WeW-3

Yes, the candidate's a dodger. The Dodger. *Unknown.* AmFP

Yes, the coneys are scared by the thud of hoofs. Thomas Hardy. *See* The Field of Waterloo.

Yes. / The North is sad. The North. Ai Ch'ing, *Chinese.* ChiPo, *tr. by* Cyril Birch

Yes, the porpoises of course, it could. The Mayan Glyphs Unread. William Bronk. APSN

Yes, the Secret Mind Whispers. Al Young. PoBA

Yes, the sun rises an angry red. New Day. Ed Ochester. CMAP

"Yes, the Town Clerk will see you." In I went. The Town Clerk's Views. John Betjeman. CMoP

Yes, there are stingy people. *Unknown, Chinese.* CoBCP, *tr. by* Burton Watson

Yes, there is holy pleasure in thine eye! Admonition to a Traveller. Wordsworth. GTBS-P

Yes, there's something the dead are keeping back. Robert Frost. *See* The Witch of Coös.

Yes, there's the orderly. He'll change the sheets. Wilfred Owen. PeFWW *Fr.* Wild with All Regrets.

Yes, these are the dog-days, Fortunatus. Under Sirius. W. H. Auden. FaBoMo

Yes, they are alive and can have those colors. A Blessing in Disguise. John Ashbery. ColAP; PoM

Yes, they begin out in a willow, I think. Crucifix in a Deathhand. Charles Bukowski. PmAP

Yes, theyll let you play. A Poem for Players. Al Young. LTA

Yes, this family portrait. Family Portrait. Carlos Drummond de Andrade, *Portuguese.* VCWP, *tr. by* Elizabeth Bishop

Yes, this is where I stand. Ballad of Hector in Hades. Edwin Muir. MoP; NOBE; NoAM

Yes, this is where she lived before she won. Interview. Sara Henderson Hay. OBCA

Yes, thou art gone! and never more. A Reminiscence. Anne Brontë. SDW; WPE

Yes; though the brine may from the desert deep. Frederick Goddard Tuckerman. HAP *Fr.* Sonnets.

"Yes, 'tis the time," I cried, "impose the chain." On the Benefactions in the Late Frost. Alexander Pope. NOEC; OxBSP

Yes, we are fighting at last, it appears. This morning, as usual. Claude to Eustace. Arthur Hugh Clough. EBVV; OxAEP-2; PeVV *Fr.* Amours de Voyage. NOBVV

Yes we did! (LL) Martin's Blues. Michael S. Harper. HCAP; PoBA

Yes, we had gone down to the shore. Songs without Words. John Ashbery. NAAL-2

Yes, we love this land together. Fatherland Song. BjØrnstjerne BjØrnson, *Norwegian.* AWP, *tr. by* William Ellery Leonard

Yes, we were looking at each other. Looking at Each Other. Muriel Rukeyser. CPO; GLP; NNaP

Yes, we were looking at each other. (LL) Looking at Each Other. Muriel Rukeyser. CPO; GLP; NNaP

Yes, we'll rally round the flag, boys, we'll rally once again. The Battle-Cry of Freedom. George Frederick Root. CBCWP; FaBoBe

Yes, What? Robert Francis. LCAP-2

Yes, yes, and there is even a photograph. Meditation on a News Item. John Updike. PeLV

Yes, yes, dear love! I am dead! Resurgam. Adah Isaacs Menken. CBWP-1

Yes, yes / it's time. My Spring Thing. Everett Hoagland. BPo

Yes yes / yeah. Brown Skin Girl. Tommy McClennan. FaBoVe

"Yes, you did, too!" Little Words. Benjamin Keech. PoToHe

Yes you have said enough for the time being. The End Is Near the Beginning. David Gascoyne. SPE

"Yes," you say, "of course at Christmas". May Sarton. CrSp *Fr.* Christmas Letter, 1970.

Yes, you will do it, silently of course. We Shall Drink to Them That Sleep. Alexander Robertson. NSI

Yes, yours, my love, is the right human face. The Confirmation. Edwin Muir. OxBM; OxBS

Yesterday. Ammuvanar. *See* What She Said to Her Girl Friend.

Yesterday. Hugh Chesterman. BoTP

Yesterday. W. S. Merwin. FYAP; LCAP-2; RaBo

Yesterday a Euclid took trees. Bright green. Breaking Green. Michael Ondaatje. NOBC

Yesterday a letter / spoke of our parting. Jane Cooper. *Fr.* The Weather of Six Mornings. NYBP

Yesterday all the past. The language of size. Spain 1937. W. H. Auden. AF; FaBoPV; NAEL-2; NoP-4; OBWP

Yesterday, as I went down to the bridge at the river. Hsü Pen. *Fr.* Five Things Sought For—In the Manner of Han Wo. CoBLCP, *tr. by* Jonathan Chaves

Yesterday at ten below. First Winter: Joy. Peggy Shumaker. PBCAP

Yesterday, at the Sessions held in Buckingham. A Case at Sessions. Walter Savage Landor. OBSV

Yesterday, dreamed He was near me. Antonio Machado Ruiz, *Spanish.* STV, tr. by John Frederick Nims

Yesterday evening I saw your corpse. Joyce Mansour, *French.* WPOW, tr. by Albert Herzing

Yesterday explorers found. Clarence Day. OBCoV *Fr.* Scenes from the Mesozoic.

Yesterday / God was / white. The Change. Matabaruka. PBCV

Yesterday he could still look in my eyes, yet. Marina Ivanovna Tsvetayeva. TCRP, tr. by Elaine Feinstein *Fr.* Two Songs.

Yesterday he was nowhere to be found. Ted Hughes. NOxBChV; NTP

Yesterday I didn't know this place. V.A. Hospital. Anthony Petrosky. CDa

Yesterday I dined with Demetrius, the boys'/ gymnastics teacher, luckiest of men. The Gymnastics Teacher. Automedon, *Greek.* GrAn, tr. by W. S. Merwin

Yesterday I fancied I was young. Ho Nansorhon. PBWP, tr. by Peter H. Lee *Fr.* A Woman's Sorrow.

Yesterday I found one left. The Survivor. Ronald Stuart Thomas. FaBoTw

Yesterday i had a wild thot. hearing james brown on the radio singing *say it.* "Alta." CrSp

Yesterday, I have always seen him. I followed him into Paris: here was the entrance. His Promise. Aaron Shurin. FTOS

Yesterday I heard that such-a-one was gone. Separation. Po Chü-i, *Chinese.* ChiP, tr. by Arthur Waley

Yesterday, / I jumped off a moving train. From My Diary. Yaroslav Vasilevich Smelyakov, *Russian.* TCRP, tr. by Simon Franklin

Yesterday I knew no lullaby. Child of Our Time. Eavan Boland. CIP-2

Yesterday I planted garlic. James Keir Baxter. PeNZ *Fr.* Jerusalem Sonnets.

Yesterday I wanted to. For Love. Robert Creeley. CoAmPo; NOBA; PmAP; VCAP

Yesterday I was / given flowers. Anthology Poem. Petra von Morstein. BoWoP, tr. by Rosemarie Waldrop

Yesterday, in a big market, I made seven thousand dollars. Back through the Looking Glass to This Side. John Ciardi. NBLV

Yesterday in drizzling rain. A Tailor Called Sorrow. Betti Alver, *Estonian.* BoWoP, tr. by Willis Barnstone and Felix Oinas

Yesterday Mrs. Friar phoned. "Mr. Ciardi." Suburban. John Ciardi. NBLV

Yesterday, Rebecca Mason. Truth's the Best. Elizabeth Turner. OxBChV

Yesterday, sitting. Just. Judith Johnson Sherwin. TAP

Yesterday / some people of this town. What She Said to Her Girl Friend. Ammuvanar, *Tamil.* PLW, tr. by A. K. Ramanujan

Yesterday the fields were only grey with scattered snow. A Winter's Tale. D. H. Lawrence. MoBrPo

Yesterday the gentle. St. Stephen's Day. Patric Dickinson. OBCP

Yesterday the House was Full of Flies. Geoffrey Summerfield. OTCP

YESTERDAY This Day's Madness did prepare. 74. Edward Fitzgerald. CABP

Yesterday was Wednesday all morning. Angel González, *Spanish.* VCWP, tr. by Steven Ford Brown and Revuelta Gutierrez

Yesterday when I'd drunk myself to bed / with water (neat). Antipater of Thessalonica, *Greek.* GrAn, tr. by Alistair Elliot

Yesterday you had a song. An Answer. Perceval Gibbon. PeSAV

Yesterday, / You were but a thought in our minds. Giovanni Azania. Don Mattera. PeSAV

Yesterday's conversation has been on my mind all day. Consolation. Dimitris Tsaloumas. BMAP

Yesterday's Illusion *or* Remembering the Thirties. Alun Llywelyn-Williams, *Welsh.* OBWVE, tr. by R. Gerallt Jones

Yet a Little While Is the Light With You. Francis Quarles. ChIV-2

Yet Ah, that Spring should vanish with the Rose! Omar Khayyám. *Fr.* The Rubáiyát of Omar Khayyám [of Naishápúr]. AWP; EBVV; FaBoBe; FaPoR; HAP; NAEL-2; PoEL-5

Yet another great truth I record in my verse. The Viper. Hilaire Belloc. NoAM

Yet Another Poem about a Dying Child. Janet Frame. PeNZ

Yet burnished by its passage, and still warm. (LL) The Harvest Bow. Seamus Heaney. BiHa; NoAM; PBCIP; PNI

Yet but Three? Shakespeare. CTC *Fr.* A Midsummer Night's Dream.

Yet C[h]loe sure was form'd without a Spot—. C[h]loe. Alexander Pope. AWP; NOBE; OBSV *Fr.* Epistle [II,] to a Lady[: Of the Characters of Women]. NAEL-1; NOEC

Yet couldn't fall out of love, not for the worst you could do. Catullus. *See* Carmen 75 ("Reason blinded by sin, Lesbia").

Yet Do I Marvel. Countee Cullen. BPo; CrDW; GEA; NAAAL; NAAL-2; NoAM; PBMP; PFE; PoBA; SAGP; SSLK; Son; TAP; TTY

Yet do not be afraid, yet give no post forlorn. To Himself. Paul Fleming, *German.* GePo, tr. by George C. Schoolfield

Yet Each Man Kills the Thing He Loves. Oscar Wilde. *Fr.* The Ballad of Reading Gaol. CABP; OBNV; OxAEP-2

Yet envies none, none are unenviable. (LL) Musketaquid. Ralph Waldo Emerson. APN-1; PAR

Yet, even 'mid merry boyhood's tricks and scapes. Frederick Goddard Tuckerman. APN-2 *Fr.* Sonnets.

Yet[t] faith still cries, Love will not[t] falsify [*or* falsely]. (LL) Sonnet 6: "My pain[e], still smothered [*or* smother'd] in my grievèd bre[a]st." Mary Sidney, Countess of Montgomery Wroth. NOSC

Yet for one rounded moment I will be. The Mortal Lease. Edith Wharton. LW

Yet Ha'e I Silence Left. "Hugh MacDiarmid." NAEL-2 *Fr.* A Drunk Man Looks at the Thistle.

Yet, hang me, but I love her dearly. Catullus. *See* Carmen 92 ("Lesbia loads me night & day with her curses").

Yet hard/ The travail is for such as bend their minds. *Unknown.* TOF, tr. by Sir Edwin Arnold *Fr.* The Bhagavad-Gita.

Yet he was there, and all my thirst. And If He Had Been Wrong for Me. Robert Duncan. RaBo

Yet here, Laertes! aboard, aboard, for shame! Shakespeare. EBEvV *Fr.* Hamlet. NAWM-1

Yet I could think, indeed, the perfect call. Arthur Hugh Clough. OBNC *Fr.* Dipsychus [and the Spirit].

Yet I courbed on my knees and cried hire of grace. William Langland. EBEV *Fr.* The Vision of Piers Plowman.

Yet I must break the chain, or seal the prisoner's woe. Emily Jane Brontë. *See* The Prisoner.

Yet if his majesty, our sovereign [*or* sovraign] Lord. Preparations. *Unknown.* CH; FaBoCh; NOBE; OBEV; PoRA; TrCP

Yet if some voice that man could trust. 35. Tennyson. CABP; OAEL-2 *Fr.* In Memoriam A. H. H.

Yet, if we look more closely, we shall find. Alexander Pope. *Fr.* An Essay on Criticism. NAEL-1; PoEL-3; TFi

Yet is day over long. (LL) Villanelle of the Poet's Road. Ernest Christopher Dowson. OBMV; UnPo

Yet is the fancy grosser than your lusts were gross? (LL) The Succubus. Robert Graves. EP; OAEL-2

Yet it was plain she struggled, and that salt. George Meredith. EnVR *Fr.* Modern Love.

Yet it's neither—you understand now? (LL) Limerick: "Said an erudite sinologue: 'How'." R. J. P. Hewison. OBCoV; PeLi

Yet let me flap this bug with gilded wings. Alexander Pope. ECEV *Fr.* Epistle to Dr. Arbuthnot. FHYEP; InPS-3; NoP-4; OAEL-1; OxAEP-1; PoE; PoEL-3; TFi

Yet like them when they'r burnt in *Sacrifice.* (LL) Written in Juice of Lem[m]on. Abraham Cowley. SeCP

Yet London, empress of the northern clime. Dryden. NAEL-1; PeECV *Fr.* Annus Mirabilis.

Yet love I best of any creature! (LL) The Complaint of Troilus. Chaucer. NOBE; OBEV

Yet love me. (LL) A Soldier. Sir John Suckling. PoE

Yet, love, mere love, is beautiful indeed. Sonnet. Elizabeth Barrett Browning. BWW; CTC; OxAEP-2 *Fr.* Sonnets from the Portuguese.

Yet matter must be gravely planned. Robert Lloyd. ECEV *Fr.* The Poetry Professors.

Yet merry it is, and quiet. (LL) The Quiet Life. William Byrd. NOBE; NoSic

Yet more of me. (LL) End of Another Home Holiday. D. H. Lawrence. EBEV; FaBoMo; OxAEP-2

Yet must I love thee, dear, and as thou art. (LL) As To His Choice of Her. Wilfrid Scawen Blunt. GSo

Yet of all that Hellas holds. Bacchylides. OBCVT, tr. by Robert Fagles *Fr.* Olympian Ode for Hiero of Syracuse (Four-Horse Chariot Race).

Yet on the other side, faine would he start. Giovanni Battista Marino. OBVE, tr. by Richard Crashaw *Fr.* The Massacre of the Innocents.

Yet once again heaven's king, and Earth's great lord. Abraham's Sacrifice of Isaac. Sir John Stradling. NOSC

Yet once an earlier David took. Goliath and David. Robert Graves. PoFWW

Yet once more, O ye Laurels and once more. Lycidas. Milton. AWP; CABP; ClHu; EBEV; EBEvV; FHYEP; GTBS-P; HAP; ImPo; InPS-3; NOBE; NOSC; NoP-4; OAEL-1; OBEV; OxAEP-1; PBRV; PFE; PoEL-3; PoPoPo; Poetr; SCGP; TFi; UnPo

Yet one more hour, then comes the night. My Drinking Song. Richard Dehmel, *German.* AWP, tr. by Ludwig Lewisohn

Yet one smile more, departing, distant sun! November. William Cullen Bryant. APN-1; GSo; Son

Yet one thing is behind. John Skelton. EPCY *Fr.* Phyllyp Sparowe [*or* Philip Sparrow]. AAS; PoEL-1

Yet Ostia boasts of her regeneration. Daniel Defoe. OBSV *Fr.* Reformation of Manners.

Yet, paying, is not paid until I die. (LL) To Her Father, with Some Verses. Anne Bradstreet. NAAL-3; NALW

Yet, Percy, not for this, should he whose eye. To the Same. Leigh Hunt. Ro

Yet, planter, let humanity prevail. Slaves. James Grainger. NOEC *Fr.* The Sugar Cane.

Yet shall my soule in silence still, *par.* by Countess of Pembroke, Mary Sidney Herbert. Psalm 62. Bible, *O.T.* PBWP *Fr.* Psalms.

Yet sighs, dear sighs, indeed true friends you are. Sonnet 95. Sir Philip Sidney. *Fr.* Astrophil and Stella. AAS; SiPS

Yet since, (O me!), a lover have I been. (LL) Sonnet 1: "When night's [*or* nights] black mantle could most darknes prove." Mary Sidney, Countess of Montgomery Wroth. CABP

Yet still I stand by tilth and filth and praise. (LL) Tilth. Robert Graves. FaBoEE; OBSV

Yet still in thought with thee I goe, *par.* by Countess of Pembroke, Mary Sidney Herbert. Bible, *O.T. See* Psalm 139.

Yet still we praise that crocus head, / April! (LL) For City Spring. Stephen Vincent Benét. BXAP; NBLV

Yet that have hearts vexed with unquiet thought. To Spenser. John Hamilton Reynolds. Son

Yet the sign is on her. (LL) The Once-over. Paul Blackburn. NeAP; PoM

Yet there belongs a Sweetnesse, softnesse too. On Sanazar's being honoured with six hundred Duckets by the Clarissimi of Venice, for composing an Elegiack Hexastick of The City. A Satyre. Richard Lovelace. PBRV

Yet there is no great problem in the world today. "Hugh MacDiarmid." OxBTC *Fr.* Lament for the Great Music.

Yet this is you. (LL) Portrait d'une Femme. Ezra Pound. CMoP; InPS-3; MeMAP; MoAmPo; MoP; NAAL-2; NOBA; NoAM; NoP-4; PFE; Poetr; TAP; TwCP

Yet this little old woman could never keep quiet. (LL) A Strange Old Woman. Mother Goose. FaBoCh; LB; ReMoGo

Yet thus insnar'd thy freedom thou may'st gain. Euphemisms of the love-blind. Lucretius, *Latin.* OBCVT, *tr.* by John Dryden

Yet-to-be-dismantled elms, the geese, The. (LL) Poem: "About the size of an old-style dollar bill." Elizabeth Bishop. FYAP; HCAP; NoAM; PoPoPo; VCAP

Yet to the wondrous St. Peter's, and yet to the solemn Rotonda. Ah, That I Were Far Away. Arthur Hugh Clough. OBNC *Fr.* Amours de Voyage. NOBVV

Yet trusting not in mine, but in His strength alone! (LL) First-Day Thoughts. John Greenleaf Whittier. APN-1; AmPP; TrCP

Yet use I not my foes, as I use Thee. (LL) Unkindness. George Herbert. FP; NOSC

Yet we were looking away! (LL) The Self-Unseeing. Thomas Hardy. EBEV; HAP; MoBrPo; NOBE; NOBVV; OBNC; OxAEP-2; RB; WeW-3

Yet what a gap in the world, the missing white frost-face of that slim yellow mountain lion! (LL) Mountain Lion. D. H. Lawrence. FaBoVe; OxBTC; RB

Yet, when I muse on what life is, I seem. Continued. Matthew Arnold. Son

Yet will I fear no evil: not even here. The Château. Henry Reed. NoP-4

Yet will I love her till I die. (LL) There is a Lady sweet and kind. Thomas Ford. CBLP; CH; EBEV; EBEvV; GBL; HeIP-4; ImPo; NOBE; NOSC; OBEV

Yet will I serve although I die therefore. (LL) Fedele's Song. Anthony Munday. HAP; SCGP

Yet, yet a moment, one dim ray of light. Alexander Pope. NAEL-1; OAEL-1; PoEL-3 *Fr.* The Dunciad.

Carnations and Butterflies. NOEC

Certain Type of Scientist Speaks, A. ECEV

Idle Pursuits. ECEV, book IV, *ll.* 565–604

"More had she spoke, but yawn'd—All nature nods." FHYEP

Reign of Chaos, The. EBEV; FaBoPV; SCV

(Triumph of Dullness [*or* Dulness], The.) NOBE

"She comes! she comes! the sable throne behold." ECEV

Triumph of Dullness, The. NOEC

Young Traveller Is Presented to the Goddess Dulness, A. NOEC

Yet you (great lady) mistress of that place. The Description of Cookham. Aemilia Bassano Lanyer. OBGa

Yeux Glauques. Ezra Pound. MoAmPo *Fr.* Hugh Selwyn Mauberley. (Life and Contacts). AmPP; CMoP; InPS-3; LiTM; NOBA; NoAM; TAP

Yevtushenko. Matija Beckovic, *Serbo-Croatian.* HSix, *tr.* by Charles Simic

Yevtushenko, Voznesensky and I. A Dream. Charles Tomlinson. OxBC

Yew-Tree, The. *Unknown, Welsh.* GBL, *tr.* by Geoffrey Grigson

Yew-Trees. Wordsworth. UnPo

Yf my deare love were but the childe of state. Shakespeare. *See* Sonnet 124.

Yf they that keepe what I you leave. Isabella Whitney. BWW *Fr.* The Manner of Her Will and What She Left to London and to All Those in It, at Her Departing. NoSic

Yggdrasill. Paul Muldoon. PBCIP

YgUDuh / ydoan / yunnuhstan. E. E. Cummings. PeLV

Yi mist yirsell so yi did. A Scream. Tom Leonard. FaBoTC

Yield, The. Gloria Frym. DeD

Yield. / No Parking. Ronald Gross. InPK-6

Yield prompt compliance to the maid's desires. Elegies, I.iv. Tibullus, *Latin.* EP, *tr.* by James Grainger

Yield to Samela. (LL) Samela. Robert Greene. GBL; NOBE; OBEV; PoEL-2

Yield to the strait allure of simple things. (LL) Poem: "Geranium, houseleek, laid in oblong beds." John Gray. ADE

Yielding clod lulls iron off to sleep. Battlefield. August Stramm, *German.* PeFWW, *tr.* by Michael Hamburger

Yillow, yillow, yillow. Metamorphosis. Wallace Stevens. InPK-6; VGW

Yippee! she is shooting in the harbor! he is jumping. Blocks. Frank O'Hara. HCAP; LCAP-2; SPE

Yir eyes ur. A Summer's Day. Tom Leonard. NBrP

"Yis, dame," quod he, "tel forth, and I wol heere." (LL) The Wife of Bath's Prologue. Chaucer. FHYEP; NAEL-1; OAEL-1, *ll.* 1–862 *complete*

Yit is God a curteis lord. *Unknown.* MiEL

Yo-ho-ho and a bottle of rum! (LL) Derelict. Young Ewing Allison. BLPA; FaBoBe

Yo soy Joaquín. Salmo: Para El. Ramon Garcia. BAP-96

Yogi, don't go away. Mirabai, *Hindi.* BoWoP, *tr.* by Willis Barnstone *and* Usha Nilsson

Yogi from far-off Beirut, A. Limerick. *Unknown.* PeLi

YOHOHEYHEYEYHEYHAHYEYEYHAHHEHYOHOHEYHEYEYHEYHAH YEYEYHAHHEHYOHOHEYHEYEYHEYHAHYEYEYHAHHEH. Two Songs About a Dead Person or a Mole—Whichever It Was. Richard Johnny John, Jerome Rothenberg, *and* Ian Tyson. PFTM *Fr.* Songs from the Society of the Mystic Animals.

Yohoweyah. When He Says So We Dance in All Directions—Wow! *Unknown, Seneca Indian.* STP, *tr.* by Jerome Rothenberg *and* Richard Johnny John

Yoke, The. Kalonymos ben Kalonymos. *Fr.* The Touchstone. TrJP, *tr.* by J. Chotzner

Yoke of Tyranny, The. Sir Philip Sidney. *See* Sonnet 47: "What, have I thus betrayed my liberty?"

Yoke Soft and Dear. John C. Kunze. AH

Yoke uneasy on the ox doth sit, The. Philip Ayres. FaBoEE

Yoko. Thom Gunn. NoAM

Yolanda and I step into the seat. Amusement. Laurie Schorr. CMAP

Yolanda Meets the Wild Boys. Jessica Hagedorn. OpBo

Yolk, The. Tanka. Saitō Mokichi, *Japanese.* MJT, *tr.* by Ueda, Makoto

Yom Kippur. Chana Bloch. CrSp

Yom Kippur. Israel Zangwill. TrJP

Yom Kippur 1984. Adrienne Rich. GLP; NoAM

Yon black man-of-war hawk that wheels in the light. The Man-of-War Hawk. Herman Melville. APN-1; APo

Yon cottager who weaves at her own door. Simple Faith. William Cowper. FHYEP

Yon is the laddie lo'ed to daunder far. Lintie in a Cage. Alice V. Stuart. OxBS

Yon Island Carrions Desperate of Their Bones. Shakespeare. RB *Fr.* King Henry V.

Yon laddie wi' the gowdan pow. A Riddle. William Soutar. OxBS

Yon rising Moon that looks for us again. Omar Khayyám. TRP *Fr.* The Rubáiyát of Omar Khayyám [of Naishápúr]. AWP; EBVV; FaBoBe; FaPoR; HAP; NAEL-2; PoEL-5

Yon silvery billows breaking on the beach. The Sonnet's Voice. Theodore Watts-Dunton. GSo

Yon spark's a poet, by my troth! The Difference. Tadhg Dall O'Huiginn, *Irish.* BIrV, *tr.* by Robin Flower

Yon strange blue city crowns a scarpèd steep. Mona Lisa. Edith Wharton. GS

Yond cawcrow's way-out. Two More about a Crow, in the Manner of Zukofsky. *Unknown, Seneca Indian.* STP, *tr.* by Jerome Rothenberg *and* Richard Johnny John

Yonder behold a little purling rill. In Praise of Drainage. Anne Wilson. ECWP *Fr.* Teisa, a Descriptive Poem of the River Tees, Its Towns and Antiquities.

Yonder come Roberta! Tell me how do you know? Midnight Special. *Unknown.* AS

Yonder come a courteous Knight. The Baffled Knight. *Unknown.* ESPB; OxBB

Yonder comes dat ole Joe Brown. Walky-talky Jenny. *Unknown.* AS

Yonder Comes My Pretty Little Girl. *Unknown.* AS

Yonder Comes the High Sheriff. *Unknown.* AS

Yonder great shadow—that blot on the passionate glare of the desert. The Dead of the Wilderness. Hayyim Nahman Bialik, *Hebrew.* AWP, *tr.* by Maurice Samuel

Yonder on the linden tree there sang a merry little bird. Dietmar von Aist [or Eist], *German*. GePo, *tr. by* J. W. Thomas

Yonder See the Morning Blink. A. E. Housman. CMoP; NOBVV

Yonder stands a pretty fair maiden. No, Sir, No. *Unknown*. AmFP

Yonder, yonder, / Yonder. (LL) The Leaden Echo and the Golden Echo. Gerard Manley Hopkins. CMoP; GTBS-P; ImPo; LiTM; MoBrPo; NOBVV; OBMV; OBNC

Yonder you weep. Jamila. Nazik Al-Mala'ika, *Arabic*. WPOW, *tr. by* Kamal Boullata

Yond's the Cardinall's window: This fortification. John Webster. PoEL-2 *Fr.* The Duchess of Malfi. NAEL-1

Yong wyf and an harvest-gos, A. *Unknown*. MiEL

Yonnondio. Walt Whitman. NAAL-1; NAAL-3

York Harbor Morning. George Garrett. MT

York: In Memoriam W. H. Auden. Joseph Brodsky. FP

York Play of the Crucifixion, The. *Unknown*. NAEL-1

Yorkshire Wife's Saga. Ruth Pitter. NALW

Yorunomado sat in. The Black Hat. Clayton Eshleman. VGW

Yoshino River. *Unknown, Japanese*. OHMPJ, *tr. by* Kenneth Rexroth

You. Carroll Arnett. VoR

You. Tom Clark.

    You (I).
    ("Between my thighs like a valentine before you have time to / wipe them.") (LL) SPE

    You (II). SPE

    You (III). SPE

    You (IV). SPE

You. Angelina Weld Grimké. CPO

You. D. H. Lawrence. NoAM

You. Poet. Sterling Plumpp. BAP-96

You. Kenneth Rexroth. HoPM *Fr.* A Bestiary. OBAL

You a gentleman and I up from the grime—. December 24 and George McBride Is Dead. Richard Hugo. HoPM

You abandon me, woman, because I am very poor. El Abandonado. *Unknown*. AS, *tr. by* Frank J. Dobie

You abandon your intent. (LL) A Jelly-Fish. Marianne Moore. APo; ChAP; OxBSP

You ain't part Indian. Wake-up Niggers. Don L. Lee. PoBA

You, all-accomplishing. Song to the Creator. Hildegard von Bingen, *German*. WPoS, *tr. by* Barbara Newman

"You almost home boy. Go on cross that sea!" (LL) My Father's Geography. Michael S. Weaver. GT; PBCAP

You Also, Gaius Valerius Catullus. Archibald MacLeish. NoAM; TAP

You also, our first great. To Whistler, American. Ezra Pound. AiP; FaBoA; NAAL-2; PoA

You always belonged here. Here. Jane Kenyon. LoL

You always know what to expect. The Country House. Louis Simpson. NOBA

You always read about it. Cinderella. Anne Sexton. HeIP-4; InPS-3; NAAL-2; SAGP

You always sang at break of day. Wolfram von Eschenbach, *German*. GePo, *tr. by* Frederick Goldin

You and I. Henry Alford. BLPA; FaBoBe

You and I. Tennessee Williams. GLP

You and I and Amyas. Latet Anguis. William Cornish. NoSic; OBEV (Knight and the Lady, The.) NOBE

You and I are like birds in a forest. Chu Yün-ming. *Fr.* Forest Birds (A Woman Speaks). CoBLCP, *tr. by* Jonathan Chaves

You and I, are we in the same story? A Battle of Wills Disguised. Marge Piercy. HeIP-4

You and I by this lamp with these. Together. Ludwig Lewisohn. PoToHe; TrJP

You and I, darling, here in the dark. Party. Cynthia Huntington. NAmP90

You and I / Have so much love. Married Love. Kuan Tao Shêng, *Chinese*. OxBM, *tr. by* Kenneth Rexroth *and* Ling Chung

You and I Saw Hawks Exchanging the Prey. James Wright. NAAL-2; NoAM

You and I will fold the sheets. Folding the Sheets. Rosemary Dobson. NOBAu *Fr.* Daily Living.

You and I will go to Finegall. *Unknown, Irish*. NOIV, *tr. by* Thomas Kinsella

You and It. Mark Strand. NYBP

You and me. *Unknown, Japanese*. WPJ, *tr. by* Kenneth Rexroth *and* Ikuko Atsumi

You and your client continue to walk. Act II - Crossing At the Tracks. Fiona Templeton. FTOS *Fr.* You: The City.

You, Andrew Marvell. Archibald MacLeish. AWP; CMoP; ColAP; FYAP; GEA; HAP; HeIP-4; HoPM; LiTM; MeMAP; MoAmPo; MoP; NAAL-2;

NOBA; NoAM; NoP-4; OxBA; PoRA; Poetr; SAGP; SoSe-8; TFi; TRP; TwCP

You appear in a tinny, nickel-and-dime light. The light of turned milk. Bitter Angel. Amy Gerstler. PmAP

You approach me carrying a book. Superballs. Tom Clark. SPE

You are. Helene Johnson. *See* Poem: "Little brown boy."

You are a bee, my flower-lovely. Argentarius, *Greek*. InMo, *tr. by* Sam Hamill

You are a friend then, as I make it out. Ben Jonson Entertains a Man from Stratford. Edwin Arlington Robinson. AmPP; MoAmPo

You Are a Jew! Delmore Schwartz. TrJP *Fr.* Genesis.

You are a landscape in the Tale of Terror. For Cora Lightbody, R.N. John Glassco. PoA

You are a lord, an earl[e], nay more, a man. To the Right Honourable Mildmay, Earl of Westmorland. Robert Herrick. BeJo

You are a stool pigeon and. Kenneth Rexroth, *after the Latin of* Martial. NNaP; PGA

You are a sunrise. To a Golden-Haired Girl in a Louisiana Town. Vachel Lindsay. MoAmPo

You are a traveller to them. Letter from Mama Dot. Frederick D'Aguiar. PBCV

You are a tried and loyal friend. To My Setter, Scout. Frank H. Seldon. BLPA

You are a tulip seen today. A Meditation for His Mistress[e]. Robert Herrick. CaPo; NOBE; NOSC; OBEV; SeCP

You are a wild look—out of an egg. Ted Hughes. NoAM, *sect.* 4 *Fr.* Stations.

You are all these people. To a Single Shadow without Pity. Sam Cornish. PoBA

You Are Alms. James W. Thompson. PoBA

You are already. Touch. Thom Gunn. CMoP

You are as faithless as a Carthaginian. A Satire on an Inconstant Lover. Jonathan Swift. CBLP

You are as fond of grief as of your child. What Answer Can I Give? Shakespeare. IMW *Fr.* King John.

You are as gold. Song. Hilda Doolittle. LiTM; MoAmPo

You are barely able to walk. But What I'm Trying to Say Mother Is. Ai. MDDM

You are beautiful and faded. A Lady. Amy Lowell. MoAmPo

You are blessëd out of measure. (LL) An Assurance. Nicholas Breton. CBLP; SCGP

You are blind like us. Your hurt no man designed. To Germany. Charles Hamilton Sorley. MoBrPo; NSI

You are bright, tremendous, wow. You (II). Tom Clark. SPE *Fr.* You.

You are clear, O rose, cut in rock. The Garden. Hilda Doolittle. NoAM

You are coming to woo me, but not as of yore. Lips That Touch Liquor. George W. Young. NBLV

You are coming toward us. Aunt Laura Moves toward the Open Grave of Her Father. Joseph De Roche. HeIP-4

You are desolate, fort of kings. *Unknown*. NOIV

You are disdainful and magnificent—. Sonnet to a Negro in Harlem. Helene Johnson. NAAAL; NIP-4; SSLK

You are drowning. How Metaphor Can Save Your Life. Myra Sklarew. CRP

You are eighty years old today, ma. To Mother. Lessie M. Drown. PWR

You are falling asleep and I sit looking at you. After Dark. Adrienne Rich. LCAP-2; LiTM; MoLi; VGW

You are flying to Dahomey, going back. Narrow Path into the Back Country. Diane Di Prima. NMM-2

You are for dreams and slumbers, brother priest. Shakespeare. OxAEP-1 *Fr.* Troilus and Cressida.

You are fortunate, dear friends, that you can tell. Vidya, *Sanskrit*. WPOW, *tr. by* Daniel Ingalls

You are from my country. Viaticum. U Tam'si Tchicaya, *French*. NegPo, *tr. by* Ellen Conroy Kennedy

You are going far away, far away from poor Jeannette. Jeannette and Jeannot. Charles Jefferys. BLPA

You Are Gorgeous and I'm Coming. Frank O'Hara. NeAP

You Are Happy. Margaret Atwood. TRP

You are here. Minor Things. Heather Ross Miller. MT

You Are Here. Carl Phillips. GT

You are here now. The Sleeping Fury. Louise Bogan. LiTM; NALW

You are holding my sister in your arms. Father and Daughter. Cathy Song. MoLi; OpBo

You are holding up a ceiling. A Marriage. Michael C. Blumenthal. PoPoPo

You are horizontal. Footpaths Cross in the Rice Field. "Lin Ling." *Unknown*. PBWP, *tr. by* Kenneth Rexroth *and* Ling Chung

You are ice and fire. Opal. Amy Lowell. NALW

You are ill and so I lead you away. Poem. Alfred Wellington Purdy. NOBC

You are impatient, says the oracle. A Reading. Virginia Hooper. PT

You are in the bush. The Bush. Victor D. Questel. HCP

You are just the kind of man. Exorcism of the Straight/Man/Demon. Aaron Shurin. GLP

You are less than one-half. The Speaker. Charles G. Ballard. VoR

You are letting her go. Cliona. Catherine Twomey. IIP

You are like a sun of the tropics. Luxury. Donald Justice. HeIP-4

You are like an everlasting friendship. Laurel O. Hoye. MDDM

You are made of almost nothing. The Dragonfly. Louise Bogan. HeIP-4; Poetr

You are mighty cute—and here is one of your bargains. (LL) A Boston Ballad [1854]. Walt Whitman. APN-1; OBAL

You are millions, we are multitude, *sl. diff. vers.* Aleksandr Blok. *See* The Scythians.

You are my friend. Lorine Niedecker. VGW

You are my mirror. May Swenson. CPO

You are my shadow in the picture. Lines for Michael in the Picture. John Logan. CAPP-1

You are my stick, my prop. Houseplant. Felicity Napier. BrRo

You are [*or* You're] not alone when you are still alone. Michael Drayton. PoEL-2 *Fr.* Idea.

You are not beautiful, exactly. To Dorothy. Marvin Bell. VCAP

You are not her darling. (LL) Birds in the high Hall-garden. Tennyson. EBVVPR; NAEL-2; PeVV

You are not here! the quaint witch Memory sees. To Maria Gisborne in England, from Italy. Shelley. NOBE *Fr.* Letter to Maria Gisborne.

You are not merry, brother. Why not laugh. The Prodigal Son. Edwin Arlington Robinson. GI; MoAmPo

You are not nearer God than we. Annunciation. Rilke, *German.* OBVE, *tr. by* James Blair Leishman

"You are not pregnant," said the man. All the Little Animals. Muriel Rukeyser. FiLi

You are not wanted. Periphery. Ruth Stone. NALW

You are now full of the fog of autumn. Nemunas. Justinas Marcinkev/ius, *Lithuanian.* CEEP, *tr. by* Irene Pogoželskyte Suboczewski

You are now / In London, that great sea. Shelley. EBEV *Fr.* Letter to Maria Gisborne.

"You are old, Father William," the young man cried. The Old Man's Comforts and How He Gained Them. Robert Southey. APAD; EBEvV; HoPM; OxBChV; UV; UnPo

"You are old," said the youth, "and your jaws are too weak." "Lewis Carroll." OxBM *Fr.* Father William. BXAP; CBNP; ChAP; HoPM; NOBL; NOBVV; OBCoV; OxBChV; PeLV; PoLF; PoRA; TFi; UV; UnPo *Fr.* Alice's Adventures in Wonderland.

You are one of those clear cold creeks. The Creek. Roland Robinson. NOBAu

You are only one of many. One of Many. Stevie Smith. OxBC

You are over there, Father Malloy. Father Malloy. Edgar Lee Masters. OxBA *Fr.* Spoon River Anthology.

You are proof that it can happen. A Tardy Epithalamium for E. and N. Ralph Pomeroy. GLP

You are punctual. (LL) Lightly stepped a yellow star. Emily Dickinson. MoAmPo; OxBA; SAmP

You are right. In dreams I might well dance. Possession. Marie Ponsot. VGW

You are right. What we call Poetry is the boat. A New Poem. Robert Duncan. FTOS; NNaP; PoM

You are sad. It is the same with me. (LL) Nocturne at Bethesda. Arna Bontemps. ChIV-2; NAAAL

You are small and intense. To a Child Running with Outstretched Arms in Canyon de Chelly. N. Scott Momaday. CDW; HATNAP

You are so small, I. Miss Cho Composes in the Cafeteria. James Tate. WeW-3

You are somewhere very close to the porch. Muse. Donald Revell. WeT

You are still the one with stone and sling. Man of My Time. Salvatore Quasimodo, *Italian.* AF, *tr. by* Jack Bevan

You are such a well-rounded sponge. Sediment. David Ignatow. NYBP

You are sucha fool / i haveta love you. Ntozake Shange. ISC

You are swooping down from heaven, pouncing upon a whole tribe. Ku´nXulaL, Thunder Bird Dance. *Unknown. Fr.* Dances and Songs of the Winter Ceremonial. *tr. by* Franz Boas

You are the baby in the barn. (LL) Nick and the Candlestick. Sylvia Plath. CoAP; FiLi; LCAP-2; NALW; PBWP; Poetr

You Are the Brave. Raymond R. Patterson. NIP-4; PoBA

You are the cause of this destruction, Lesbia. Catullus. *See* Carmen 75 ("Reason blinded by sin, Lesbia").

You are the charge of halcyons now, it may be. For the Cenotaph of a Lost Soldier. Theon, *Greek.* GrAn, *tr. by* Dudley Fitts

You are the first, and You remain the last. Another Testimony. Dan Pagis, *Hebrew.* IP, *tr. by* Warren Bargad *and* Stanley F. Chyet

You are the fish that hides. Legendary. James McAuley. BMAP

You are the grain. I Think of Housman Who Said the Poem Is a Morbid Secretion, like a Pearl. Judith Kroll. UnPo

You are the imaginary center of the universe eternity that devours. Horoscope. Rasa Livada, *Serbo-Croatian.* HSix, *tr. by* Charles Simic

You are the merry men, dwarfs of soul. The Diakka. Gerald Massey. NOBVV

You are the millions, we are multitude. The Scythians. Aleksandr Blok, *Russian.* AWP, *tr. by* Babette Deutsch *and* Avrahm Yarmolinsky

You are the most beautiful. Martial, *Greek.* PGA, *tr. by* Kenneth Rexroth

You are the notes, and we are the flute. Jelaluddin Rumi, *Persian.* EnlH, *tr. by* Robert Bly

You / are the One who put. Stars in Apple Cores. Luci Shaw. TrCP

You are the owner of one complete thought. Voice and Address. Michael Palmer. FTOS; PmAP

You are the problem I propose. The Metaphysical Amorist. James Vincent Cunningham. VGW

You are the salt of the earth. Matthew 5:13; You are the salt of the earth. Gail Holst-Warhaft. GI *Fr.* St. Matthew.

You are the town and we are the clock. Chorus. W. H. Auden. *Fr.* The Dog beneath the Skin. OxBTC

You are tired. The Midnight Tennis Match. Thomas Lux. AmPA

You are too splendid for this city street. (LL) Sonnet to a Negro in Harlem. Helene Johnson. NAAAL; NIP-4; SSLK

You are traveling to play basketball. Your team's. In Your Young Dream. Richard Hugo. InPK-6

You are wallowing in the catacombs of your anxiety. For Someone Temporizing. Thomas Erwin, *German.* CEEP, *tr. by* A. Leslie Willson

You are welcome in the secret club they have formed. (LL) What Thou Lovest Well Remains American. Richard Hugo. NAAAL-2; PaTW

You are welcome to your country, dear Antonio. The Duchess of Malfi. John Webster. NAEL-1

"You are wise, Mr. Dodgson," the young child said. Lewis Carroll. Eleanor Farjeon. OxBChV

You are with me Oregon. Oregon. Bob Kaufman. GT

You arrived that bad winter. Solstice. Gerald Dawe. PNI

You ask about the men in my past and it makes me think. Strong Pomegranate Flowers and Seeds of the Mind. Linda Gregg. PuP-16

You ask how long before I come. Still no date is set. Night Rains: to my Wife up North. Li Shang-yin, *Chinese.* PLT, *tr. by* A. C. Graham

You ask how old am I. Twice Times Then Is Now. Ibn Hazm al-Andalusi, *Persian.* ArPe; OBVE, *tr. by* Omar S. Pound

You Ask Me. Mutabaruka. PBCV

You ask me. To Madame A. V. Pletneff. Karolina Pavlova, *French.* PBWP, *tr. by* Paul Schmidt

You ask me for a poem about love. Poem Not to Be Read at Your Wedding. Beth Ann Fennelly. BAP-96

You ask me for a song, folks. Cousin Jack Song. Charley Tregonning. AmFP

You ask me, girl, why I withdraw my sword. Macedonius, *Greek.* GrAn, *tr. by* Adrian Wright

You ask me how Contempt who claims to sleep. Epigram. James Vincent Cunningham. VCAP

You ask me how it is living in exile, friend. Eavesdropper. Breyten Breytenbach, *Afrikaans.* PeSAV, *tr. by* Ernst van Heerden

You ask me my name? They got lotsa names. Madarika. Vince Gotera. OpBo

You ask me to forget him. What She Said to Her Friend. Kapilar, *Tamil.* PLW, *tr. by* A. K. Ramanujan

You ask me to sing, so I'll sing you a song. The Cranberry Song. Barney Reynolds. AmFP

You ask me what I do, and how I live? His Answer to a Friend. Robert Herrick. CavPo

You ask me what I thought about. Kenneth Rexroth. APSN; PiM *Fr.* The Love Poems of Marichiko.

You ask me what since we must part. Gifts. Juliana Horatia Ewing. LW

You ask me *What's love?*—Why, that virtue-fed vapour. Address to Lady——, Who Asked What the Passion of Love Was? Charles Morris. NOEC

You ask me / Why do I live. On the Mountain: Question and Answer. Li Po, *Chinese.* ChiPo, *tr. by* C. H. Kwock *and* Vincent McHugh

You ask the source of these transparencies. Kaleidoscope. Rachel Hadas. WeT

You ask what I have found, and far and wide I go. The Curse of Cromwell. W. B. Yeats. BIrV; IIP

You ask what place I like the best. The Kinkaiders. *Unknown.* AS

You ask when I will go back home. Ni Tsan. CoBLCP, *tr. by* Jonathan Chaves *Fr.* Following the Rhymes of Yü-chai's Poems on Autumn.

You ask which is better, whether a king or a senate rules. Neither, if, as. Quis Optimus Reipublicae Status. Sir Thomas More. PBRV

You ask why gold and velvet bind. On a New Duke. *Unknown.* FaBoEE

You ask why I make my home in the mountain forest. Li Po, *Chinese.* EnlH, *tr. by* Sam Hamill

You asked, I came. The Evil That Men Do. Queen Latifah. NAAAL

You asked me to enter the holy cloister. Banishment from Ur. Enheduanna, *Sumerian.* BoWoP, *tr. by* W. W. Hallo *and* J. J. A. van Dijk

You asked me what is the good of reading the Gospels in Greek. Readings. Czeslaw Milosz, *Polish.* GI, *tr. by* Czeslaw Milosz *and* Lillian Vallee

You asked neither for glory nor tears. Stanzas Against Forgetting. Guillaume Apollinaire, *French.* AF, *tr. by* Carolyn Forché

You asked us to hear the softest vocable of wind. Lines for Roethke Twenty Years after His Death. Duane Niatum. HATNAP

You at the Pump. Frank O'Hara. FTOS

You balanced her within a cyclone. Woman Seed Player. Roberta Hill Whiteman. HATNAP

You beastly child, I wish you had miscarried. Lightly Bound. Stevie Smith. NALW

You beat your Pate, and fancy Wit will come. Another [Epigram]. Alexander Pope. FaBoEE; NBLV; PFE

You beautious ladies, great and small. The Famous Flower of Serving-Men; or, The Lady Turn'd Serving-Man. *Unknown.* ESPB; OxBB

You became / In many acts and quiet observances. My Company. Sir Herbert Read. PoWW

You begin this way. Margaret Atwood. NOBC; NoP-4

You believed in your own story. Fairy Tales. "Shu Ting," *Chinese.* VCWP, *tr. by* Donald Finkel

You bet we'll soon forget the one that died. The One That Died. William Daniel Ehrhart. CDa

You Bet Your Life. Nancy Vieira Couto. PBCAP

You bible-sharps that thump on tubs. Villon's Good-Night. William Ernest Henley. CBNP

You bid me hold my peace. Worn Out. Paul Laurence Dunbar. NAAAL

You bid me write, Sir, I comply. Address to a Bachelor on a Delicate Occasion. Priscilla Pointon. ECWP

You bid my muse not cease to sing. Written to a Near Neighbour in a Tempestuous Night. Henrietta Knight. ECWP

You black bright stars, that shine while daylight lasteth. Thomas Morley. NoSic

You black-maned, horse-haired, long-faced creature. To the Gentlewoman of Llanarth Hall. Evan Thomas, *Welsh.* OBWVE, *tr. by* Gwyn Jones

You black out the sun. Ed Roberson. PoBA *Fr.* When Thy King Is a Boy.

You blame me that I do not write. Letter to a Friend. Jon Stallworthy. NoAM

You blessed shades, which give mee silent rest. Sonnet 30. Mary Sidney, Countess of Montgomery Wroth. KTR *Fr.* Pamphilia to Amphilanthus.

You blow on the hair of your child. Vladimir Burich, *Russian.* TCRP, *tr. by* Albert C. Todd

You both are modest. So am I. Farewell. (LL) An Epistle to Master John Selden. Ben Jonson. BeJo

You Brandenburg's support and Prussia's guarantee. On the Entrance of the Castle Bridge. Simon Dach, *German.* GePo, *tr. by* George C. Schoolfield

You brave heroic [*or* heroique] minds. To the Virginian Voyage. Michael Drayton. AiP; HAP; NAEL-1; NOBE; NOSC; OBEV; PoEL-2; SCGP

You bring the only changes to this season. For Nicholas, Born in September. Tod Perry. NYBP

You build it where you will be heard only by chance. The Cabin North of It All. James McMichael. AmPA

You build your harp frame. The Silence. Tomas Mac Siomoin, *Irish.* TIRV, *tr. by the author*

You built yourself a raven in the wind. Jean-Joseph Rabéarivelo, *French.* NegPo, *tr. by* Ellen Conroy Kennedy

You burned the dawn / with the flame of your guitar. Wake for Papa Montero. Nicolás Guillén, *Spanish.* PFTM, *tr. by* Langston Hughes

You burst into the world with smiles wide as April. Sleeping with Foxes. Roberta Hill Whiteman. CDW

You but unlock[e], we each other bless[e]. (LL) To a Lady That Desired I Would Love Her. Thomas Carew. BeJo; CBLP; CaPo; MeLP; SCGP

You buy some flowers for your table. Samuel Hoffenstein. OBCoV; TrJP *Fr.* Poems in Praise of Practically Nothing.

You call me by old names: how strange. Rhina P. Espaillat. LoHo

You Call That a Ts'ing; a Letter. Jedediah Barrow. BXAP

You call that wine? On Beer. Emperor Julian, *Greek.* PGA, *tr. by* Kenneth Rexroth

You Called Me Corazón. Sandra Cisneros. PiM

You came. And you did well to come. Sappho, *Greek.* BoWoP, *tr. by* Willis Barnstone

You came out of the thunder's belly. Ode to Santorini. Odysseus Elytis, *Greek.* GrIP, *tr. by* Edmund Keeley *and* Philip Sherrard

You came / to be / in the Month of Malcolm. Circling the Daughter. Etheridge Knight. MoLi

You came to gaze upon me. A Farewell to Arms. Aleksandr Petrovich Mezhirov, *Russian.* TCRP, *tr. by* Deming Browm

You came to it through wild country, there the sea's voice. The House in the Green Well. John Hall Wheelock. MoAmPo

You Came with Shells. June Jordan. NoAM

You can become a shaman. New Indian Medicine. Emma Lee Warrior. HATNAP

You can call me Herbie Jr. or Ashamah. Unemployment/Monologue. June Jordan. WPOW

You can cease to be babies, nor try to be men! (LL) Advice Gratis to Certain Women. Phoebe Cary. APN-2; PAR

You can come to terms with anyone. At the Cave. Artur Miedzyrzecki, *Polish.* PoSu, *tr. by* Stanislaw Baranczak *and* Clare Cavanagh

You can / die for it— / an idea. Sunrise. Mary Oliver. CrSp

You can do what you want. Deposition. Kurt Bartsch, *German.* CEEP, *tr. by* Wayne Kvam

You can explore your every desire. Antipater of Thessalonica, *Greek.* InMo, *tr. by* Sam Hamill

You can feel the muscles and veins rippling in widening and rising circles. Saying Dante Aloud. James Wright. InPK-6

You can go back in a clap of blue metal. Southbound. Betty Adcock. MT

You can hang or drown at last. (LL) A Short Song of Congratulation [*or* To a Young Heir]. Samuel Johnson. EBEV; HAP; InPK-6; InPS-3; NOBE; NOEC; OBCoV; OBSV; OxAEP-1; PFE; PeLV; PoE; PoEL-3; SCGP; TFi; UnPo

You Can Have It. Philip Levine. NoP-4; VCAP

You can hear the silence of it. David Jones. FaBoMo *Fr.* In Parenthesis.

You can lead a horse to water. *Unknown.* CTV

You can love and think, and the / "Earth cannot!" (LL) The World. William Brighty Rands. BoTP; CTV; NOxBChV; OxBChV

You can make this swooped transition on your lips. Sonnet XXXV. Ted Berrigan. FTOS *Fr.* The Sonnets.

You can see from their faces. Photographs of Pioneer Women. Ruth Dallas. PeNZ

You can see her, hair down, sipping a Coke. What a Little Moonlight Can Do. Joe Heithaus. SeSe

You can see the moon's brightness. Shih Te, *Chinese.* SuSp, *tr. by* James M. Hargett

You can see them everywhere in Cuba. Landscapes. Herberto Padilla, *Spanish.* VCWP, *tr. by* Alastair Reid *and* Andrew Hurley

You can sigh o'er the sad-eyed Armenian. An Appeal to My Countrywomen. Frances Ellen Watkins Harper. BlSi; NAAAL

You can start the Count Down, you can take a last look. Off to Outer Space Tomorrow Morning. Norman Nicholson. SpW

You can stop crying now. (LL) Do the Dead Know What Time It Is? Kenneth Patchen. HoPM; MoAmPo

You can stop me. There's Somethin'. Adam Small, *Afrikaans.* PeSA; PeSAV

You can take a dog to the keyside, but you can't push him in. The Computer's First Proverbs. Peter Finch. NBrP

You can take a tub with a rub and a scrub in a two-foot tank of tin. Pater's Bathe. Edward Abbott Parry. OxBChV

You can talk about your farms and your Chinaman's charms. The Cowboy's Life Is a Very Dreary Life. *Unknown.* AmFP

You can tell by the angle. The Londonderry Air. Nicolas Bentley. OBCoV

You cannot conquer, and be conquered. (LL) Relent, my dear yet unkind Coelia. William Percy. AAS; Son

You cannot do better than eat them yourselves. (LL) Hot cross buns! Hot-cross buns! / One a penny, two a penny. Mother Goose. BoTP; OxNR; ReMoGo

You Cannot Do This. Gwendolyn MacEwen. FaBoWP

You cannot dream. Things Lovelier. Humbert Wolfe. TrJP

You cannot ever reach to share. (LL) Stark Major. Hart Crane. FuPo; MeMAP

You cannot from the open window invade. The Crow. Rita Boumi-Pappas, *Modern Greek.* PBWP, *tr. by* Kimon Friar

You Cannot Go Down to the Spring. John Shaw Neilson. CBAP

You cannot hope. Humbert Wolfe. FaBoEE; OBCoV; OxBTC

You Cannot Lock Up the Mind. Xuân Thủy, *Vietnamese.* AVP, *tr. by* Huỳnh Sanh Thông

You cannot see mountains and valleys in the clouds. Spyglass Conversations. *Unknown, Tule Indian.* STP, *tr. by* Frances Densmore

You can't beat English lawns. Our final hope. Rolling the Lawn. William Empson. MoBrPo; OBGa

You can't count. Don't Count. Ory Bernstein, *Hebrew*. IP, *tr. by* Warren Bargad *and* Stanley F. Chyet

You can't ever imagine the Virgin Mary having vulvitis or thrush. Sonnet: Supernatural Beings. Gavin Ewart. Son

You cant grip years, Posthume. Horace, *Latin*. OBCVT, *tr. by* Basil Bunting

You can't hear it in the house. Geoffrey Lehmann. *Fr.* Ross's Poems. CBAP

You Can't Kill a Baby Twice. Dahlia Ravikovitch, *Hebrew*. VCWP, *tr. by* Chana Bloch *and* Ariel Bloch

You can't look at yourself. The Great Sadness. Federico García Lorca, *Spanish*. PFTM, *tr. by* Jerome Rothenberg

You can't say it that way any more. And "Ut Pictura Poesis" Is Her Name. John Ashbery. InPS-3; VCAP

You can't see it or hear it. Spring Breeze. Ho Hsun, *Chinese*. OHMPC, *tr. by* Kenneth Rexroth

You can't see us in spiritland, and we can't see at all. (LL) Poetry, almost blind like a camera. Jack Spicer. NeAP; PmAP

You can't spend all day staring into the sea, however. War. Michael Brownstein. FTOS

You can't tell me God would have Heaven. A Malemute Dog. Pat O'Cotter. BLPA

You can't win Love over / by crying. To Telembrotos. Antipater of Thessalonica, *Greek*. GrAn, *tr. by* Alistair Elliot

You captains brave and bold, hear our cries, hear our cries. Captain Kidd. *Unknown*. AmFP

You / catch my breath with your waking. Blues 1. Barry Wallenstein. SeSe

You cathedral, you! Pure astonishment! To Freedom. Agnes Nemes Nagy, *Hungarian*. PoSu, *tr. by* Bruce Berlind

You: caught in the net of the chosen. Patriotic Reflections. Yehuda Amichai, *Hebrew*. IP, *tr. by* Warren Bargad *and* Stanley F. Chyet

You claim his poems are garbage. Balderdash! A Poet Defended. Paul Ramsey. InPK-6

You closed the door. Poem for My Father. Toi Derricotte. MoLi; NMM-2

You closed your eyes, crossed your hands. Text, Silk. Novica Tadic, *Serbo-Croatian*. HSix, *tr. by* Charles Simic

You come forth / the color of a stone cliff. To Insure Survival. Simon J. Ortiz. CDW

You come from the line of a Cōla King. A Poet's Counsel. Kovur Kilar, *Tamil*. PLW, *tr. by* A. K. Ramanujan

You come in. Everything is where it should be. The Door Creaked Three Times. Sandor Csoori, *Hungarian*. CEEP, *tr. by* Nicholas Kolumban

You come to fetch me from my work tonight. Putting in the Seed. Robert Frost. NoAM; OxBA

You come to in the past, dark, where the fires still burn. Train Wreck, 1890: My Grandmother Lies Down with the Dead. T. R. Hummer. GM

You come to market—seeking gain, to be sure. Offered to a Man Who Sells Pines. Yü Wu-ling, *Chinese*. SuSp, *tr. by* Edward H. Schafer

You come to me. Quincy Troupe. NBV

You could be sitting now in a carrel. A Late Aubade. Richard Wilbur. Poetr; SoSe-8

You could cry / for such variety. #2, Shoes. Elizabeth Cohen. WWSi

You could draw a straight line from the heels. Man Lying on a Wall. Michael Longley. PNI

You could love here, not the lovely goat. The Milltown Union Bar. Richard Hugo. NoAM

You could sit there with the stains on your shoes. Robert Frost. *Fr.* Home Burial. ColAP; IMW; NAAL-2; SoSe-8; TAP; TRP

You could tear off a piece of road. Pilgrims. Carol J. Pierman. CMAP

You could tell that the flowers. The Shades of Grand Central. Chase Twichell. NAmP90

You couldn't bear to grow old, but we grow old. John Berryman. TAP *Fr.* Dream Songs.

You couldn't find it in the bird's weight. These Laudanum Hours. Kathleen Fraser. PT

You couldn't pack a Broadwood half a mile. The Song of the Banjo. Rudyard Kipling. FaBoCh

You coward . . . this baby that I bleed. (LL) The Abortion. Anne Sexton. LCAP-2; Poetr; VGW

You crawl around a rim. In Love with Wholes. Alberta Turner. LCAP-2

You cry, carry on in tones of pity. Philodemus, *Greek*. GrAn, *tr. by* William Moebius

You cry, waking from a nightmare. Little Sleep's-Head Sprouting Hair in the Moonlight. Galway Kinnell. InPS-3; LCAP-2

You danced a magnetic dance. So Many Feathers. Jayne Cortez. BlSi; ISC

You dare not let your eyes meet theirs. Women Are Different. Marsha Prescod. LW

You darling girls of Bagaduce, who live along the shore. The Schooner *Fred Dunbar*. Amos Hanson. AmFP

You, dead in '92 and '93. To the French of the Second Empire. Rimbaud. FaBoPV; OBWP, *tr. by* Robert Lowell *Fr.* Eighteen-Seventy.

You delude yourself. Jean-Joseph Rabéarivelo, *French*. NegPo, *tr. by* Ellen Conroy Kennedy

You did late review my lays. To Christopher North. Tennyson. FaBoEE; PeLV

You did not come. A Broken Appointment. Thomas Hardy. GBL; NAEL-2; NOBVV; NoAM

You did not see Him on the mountain of Transfiguration. To the Good Thief. Saunders Lewis, *Welsh*. OBWVE, *tr. by* Gwyn Morgan

You did not walk with me. The Walk. Thomas Hardy. CMoP; NAEL-2; PoE; PoEL-5

You didn't have to travel to become an airplane. Communication of His Thirtieth Birthday. Marvin Bell. CoAP

You die in Time, Time in Eternity. (LL) To His Watch, When He Could Not Sleep. Edward Herbert, 1st Baron Herbert of Cherbury. NOBE; PoEL-2

You died. Calvin C. Hernton. *See* Fall Down.

You died in spring, father, and now the autumn dies. American Sonnets for My Father. Daniela Gioseffi. UnSA

You died nine years ago today. February 11, 1977. Frederick Morgan. DiPo

You do look a little ill, now. Alcohol. Franz Wright. LCAP-2

You do look, my son, in a moved sort. Prospero. Shakespeare. EBEvV *Fr.* The Tempest. OAEL-1

You do not come. Ono no Komachi. *See* He does not come.

You do not come, and I wait. Fujiwara no Sadaie, *Japanese*. OHPJ, *tr. by* Kenneth Rexroth

You do not do, you do you do not do. Daddy. Sylvia Plath. BoWoP; CMoP; CoAP; ColAP; HCAP; HP; HeIP-4; InPK-6; InPS-3; LiTM; MoLi; MoP; NAAL-2; NALW; NIP-4; NMM-2; NOBA; NoAM; NoP-4; PoE; PoPoPo; Poetr; TFi; TwCP; UnPo; VCAP

You do not have to be good. Wild Geese. Mary Oliver. BLT

You do not hear me, Dad. (LL) A Child to His Sick Grandfather. Joanna Baillie. CABP; RACG

You do not limp. 194. . . . Mikhail Valentinovich Kulchitsky, *Russian*. TCRP, *tr. by* Daniel Weissbort

You do not remember the house of the customs-men. The House of the Customs-Men. Eugenio Montale. ItIP

You do not seem to realize that beauty is a liability. Roses Only. Marianne Moore. LiTM

You do understand I've waited long enough. Complaint: To the Muse. Philip Whalen. BB

You, Doctor Martin, walk. Anne Sexton. MoAmPo; NAAL-2

You don't have to believe this, I'm not asking you to. The Birth of Potchikoo. Louise Erdrich. *Fr.* Old Man Potchikoo. HATNAP

You don't have to go very far. Some Sights Sometimes Seen and Seldom Seen. William Cole. TLR

You don't have to listen to folktales. I Saw It. Ilya L'vovich Selvinsky, *Russian*. TCRP, *tr. by* Daniel Weissbort

You don't have to tell how you live each day. It's in Your Face. *Unknown*. PoLF

You don't have to understand a nightingale's song. Speech. Leopold Staff, *Polish*. PoSu, *tr. by* Adam Czerniawski

You don't know I pretend my dumb. Plea to Those Who Matter. James Welch. AmPA

You don't know or maybe you do. Dear Mama (2). Wanda Coleman. NMM-2

You Don't Know What Love Is. Raymond Carver. BXAP

You don't know who these people are, or what. Perfidia. David Lehman. NAmP90

You don't put salt on anything. The Salt. May Swenson. DeD *Fr.* Poet to Tiger. GLP

You don't see them right off. The Midwest is Full of Vibrators. Lyn Lifshin. DeD

You Don't Understand Me. Marge Piercy. NALW

You don't want madhouse and the whole thing there. (LL) Let It Go. William Empson. FaBoMo; OxBSP; OxBTC

You drank the warm breath of your turtledove. Feeding the Dove. Velemir Khlebnikov, *Russian*. TCRP, *tr. by* Gary Kern

You dreamed it. From my ground. Ark Parting. Jay Macpherson. NOBC *Fr.* The Ark.

You drink all night, and promise fairly. Martial, *Latin*. OBCVT, *tr. by* Byron

You drink from crystal. One xxxvii. Laurie Duggan. BMAP *Fr.* The Epigrams of Martial.

You drink to piss it all away. Anacreontic. R. S. Gwynn. RA

You Drive in a Circle. Ted Hughes. NYBP

You drive, the road aims for a mountain. A View. Mona Van Duyn. VCAP

You drunken / tootering / bum. The Drunkard. William Carlos Williams. PFE

You each guardian Fay shall bless. (LL) Inscription in a Beautiful Retreat Called Fairy Bower. Hannah More. ECWP; NoP-4

You earthly Souls that court a wanton flame. La Belle Confidente. Thomas Stanley. BeJo; MeLP

You Eat the Figs, So Sit Beneath the Tree. Phan Bội Châu, *Vietnamese*. AVP, *tr. by* Huỳnh Sanh Thông

You empress of the stars, the heavens' worthy crown. Spring-Joy Praising God; Praise of the Sun. Catharina Regina von Greiffenberg, *German*. WPOW, *tr. by* George C. Schoolfield

You enter the areas beyond veiled light. Sleep Watch. Lance Henson. VoR

You entered my life in a casual way. To a Friend. Grace Stricker Dawson. BLPA

You excellent women, you valiant men. Walther von der Vogelweide, *German*. GePo, *tr. by* Frederick Goldin

You expect, Puss-in-Boots. Justice. Agathias, *Greek*. GrAn; PC, *tr. by* Peter Whigham

You exquisite girl, dressed absurdly deliciously artifically. A Sweet Disorder in the Dress. Harry Hooton. NOBAu

You, Farrell O'Reilly, I feared as a boy. Farrell O'Reilly. Oliver St. John Gogarty. OxBTC

You feed us milkfish stew. Milkfish. Eugene Gloria. OpBo

You feel adequate to the demands of this position? You Will Be Hearing from Us Shortly. U. A. Fanthorpe. OBCoV

You feel no love or pity for me. Sergey Aleksandrovich Yesenin, *Russian*. TCRP, *tr. by* Daniel Weissbort

You Fight On. *Unknown*. AS

You fill me up so much. Where the Mississippi meets the Amazon. Ntozake Shange. ISC

You find it ugly, I find it lovely. (LL) William Street. Kenneth Slessor. DMAP

You find them in the darker woods. The Persistence of Nature in Our Lives. Andrew Hudgins. DiPo; WeW-3

You fit into me. Margaret Atwood. InPK-6; NALW; NoAM

You . . . flowing through selves / Toward you. (LL) Now That I Am Forever with Child. Audre Lorde. CrSp; NAAAL; NALW; PoBA; Poetr

You follow foreign ways. Two Sons. Laoiseach Mac an Bhaird. NOIV

You fool yourself and live a crazy day. Voice of a Dissipated Woman inside a Tomb. Sor Violante do Céu, *Portuguese*. BoWoP, *tr. by* Willis Barnstone

You for eternity, and have no other choice? (LL) Obit. Robert Lowell. HCAP; VCAP

You, friend, who whilom tossed the ball. Jane Brereton. ECWP *Fr. To Mr Thomas Griffith at the University of Glasgow*.

You gave m' a Mannour, *Lupus*, but I till. In Lupum. Martial, *Latin*. OBCVT, *tr. by* William Cartwright

You gave me beauty, Cytherea. Lais' Mirror. Julianus of Egypt, *Greek*. GrAn, *tr. by* Robin Skelton

You Gave Me Hyacinths First a Year Ago. Dorothy Hewett. BMAP

You gaze at me teasingly through the window. Praxilla, *Greek*. BoWoP, *tr. by* Willis Barnstone

You gentlemen, by dint of long seclusion. Byron. EPCY *Fr. Dedication: "Bob Southey! You're a poet—poet-laureate."* CTC; OAEL-2; OBSV *Fr. Don Juan*.

You gentlemen of England far and near. The Wind Sou'west. *Unknown*. AmFP

You gentlemen of England who live at home at ease. The Bay of Biscay. *Unknown*. AmFP

You get a wife, you get a house. The Cat. Ogden Nash. WHSW

You get into the tub holding *The Naked Ape*. The Dream. May Swenson. DeD *Fr. Poet to Tiger*. GLP

You give your cheeks a rosy stain. Artificial Beauty. Lucianus, *Greek*. AWP, *tr. by* William Cowper

You glow in my heart. The Bungler. Amy Lowell. LW

You go home one evening tired from work. Turtle Soup. Marilyn Chin. LoL

You go somewhere in your sleep. Nocturnal Journey. Ory Bernstein, *Hebrew*. IP, *tr. by* Warren Bargad *and* Stanley F. Chyet

You go to your church, and I'll go to mine. Your Church and Mine. Phillips H. Lord. BLPA

You gods, teach her some more humanity. (LL) A Divine Mistress. Thomas Carew. BeJo; CavPo

You gods! to fold the charmer in my arms. The Rapture. Henry Baker. NOEC

You golden freedom, both my wish and my desire. Martin Opitz, *German*. GePo, *tr. by* George C. Schoolfield

"'You got children, Ma'am?'" he said aloud. Etheridge Knight. *See* A WASP Woman Visits a Black Junkie in Prison.

You got to be scared. From Riot Rimes U.S.A. #79. Raymond R. Patterson. MBE

You Got to Cross It foh Yohself. *Unknown*. AS

"You got to pick it up." (LL) 17:II:82. David Meltzer. MoNo; SeSe

You got to walk that lonesome valley. Lonesome Valley. *Unknown*. APN-2

You gotta watch / out for the "Ol Liver." (LL) Welcome Back, Mr. Knight: Love of My Life. Etheridge Knight. PBCAP; RaBo

You govern the locks, You open life. *Unknown*. ASW *Fr. Advent Lyrics*. ASW, *tr. by* Kevin Crossley-Holland *Fr. Christ 1*. AnOE, *tr. by* Charles W. Kennedy

You grow impatient while I focus, fiddle. You Have Shown Me a Strange Image, and We Are Strange Prisoners. Jeni Couzyn. PBCAP

You grow less agile, more compliant. Exile, Representative. Breyten Breytenbach, *Afrikaans*. AF, *tr. by* Denis Hirson

You Growing. Milton Acorn. NOBC

You gulp, a frog suddenly on my dinner. You Don't Understand Me. Marge Piercy. NALW

You had two girls—Baptiste. At the Cedars. Duncan Campbell Scott. NOBC

You hailed a cab outside the nondescript. Runaways Café I. Marilyn Hacker. CPO

You happened to me. I was happened to. Nearly a Valediction. Marilyn Hacker. NMM-2

You have anti-freeze in the car, yes. Christmas Card. Ted Hughes. OBCP

You have been driving for hours. Looking for a Rest Area. Stephen Dunn. AmPA

You have been good to me, I give you this. Idolatry. Arna Bontemps. SAGP

You have been my treasure, Rose Pilgrim. Elect. Mary Ursula Bethell. PeNZ

You have been talking about. How Can I Show This Poem to Geraldine? Kitty Tsui. CPO

You have beheld a smiling Rose. The Lily in a Crystal. Robert Herrick. BeJo; NAEL-1; NOSC; PoEL-3; SCGP; SeCP

You have called at the gate of the True Vehicle. Saying Good-bye to a Singing Girl Who Has Decided to Become a Nun. Mo Shih-lung, *Chinese*. CoBLCP, *tr. by* Jonathan Chaves

You have climbed to the moon on a ladder of dead men's bones! (LL) Go Ask the Dead. Thomas McGrath. AF

You have coats and robes. You Will Die. *Unknown*. AWP, *tr. by* H. A. Giles *Fr. Shi King*.

You have come your way, I have come my way. Fronleichnam. D. H. Lawrence. GBL

You have consum'd my language, and my pen. Ovid. *Fr. De Ponto*. OBVE, *tr. by* Henry Vaughan

You have done nothing but listen to songs. Your Work. Jean-Joseph Rabéarivelo, *French*. NegPo, *tr. by* Ellen Conroy Kennedy

You have edited a thousand pages of palm-leaf manuscripts. To the Monk Wu-hsia on the Occasion of His Editing the Lotus Sutra. Mo Shih-lung, *Chinese*. CoBLCP, *tr. by* Jonathan Chaves

You have forgotten me well. (LL) When You Have Forgotten Sunday: The Love Story. Gwendolyn Brooks. BPo; NAAAL; WPOW

You have gone, oh, my friend, leaving me. Snowfall on the Seas. Hyongman Ho, *Korean*. CKP, *tr. by* Jaihiun Kim

You have heard, I suppose, of the man in the moon. The Coolie Chinee. Septimus Winner. OBAL

You have heard it said before. A Handle for the Flutist. Odia Ofeimun. HBAPE

You have heard nothing; of course I know you can have heard / nothing. Arthur Hugh Clough. EBVVPR, *canto 5, 11 Fr. Amours de Voyage*. NOBVV

You have heard that it was said. Matthew 5:27–30; You have heard that it was said. Bible, *N.T.* GI, *tr. by* Gail Holst-Warhaft. *Fr. St. Matthew*.

You have heard that it was said. Matthew 5:38–48; "You have heard that it was said, 'An eye'." Bible, *N.T.* GI, *tr. by* Jacob Glatstein. *Fr. St. Matthew*.

You have Hera's eyes Melite. Rufinus, *Greek*. GrAn, *tr. by* Alan Marshfield

You have just come in the door. The Confession. Peter Cooley. AmPA

You have netted this dawn. The Archaeology of Love. Richard Murphy. EnLoPo

You have no right to trouble me. Magic Formula. *Unknown*. CA

You have not conquered me—it is the surge. Infidelity. Louis Untermeyer. TrJP

"You have not considered the rose garden." Stavrogin's Return. János Pilinszky. CEEP, *tr. by* Jascha Kessler *Fr. Three Poems*.

You have only to wait, they will find you. Messengers. Louise Glück. ColAP; HCAP; VCAP

You have put your two hands upon me, and your mouth. Betrothed. Louise Bogan. CrSp; NMM-2

You Have Shown Me a Strange Image, and We Are Strange Prisoners. Jeni Couzyn. PBCAP

You have spoken your holy command over the city. Inanna and the City of Uruk. Enheduanna, *Sumerian.* BoWoP, *ad. by* Aliki *and* Willis Barnstone

You have stopped beating the drums. Anno Domini MCMXLVII. Salvatore Quasimodo, *Italian.* GI, *tr. by* Jack Bevan

You have / taken. Poem for a Little Boy on the Buddha's Birthday. Diane Wakoski. FiLi

You have taken back the promise. Fidelis. Adelaide Anne Procter. BLPA; FaBoBe

You have the ingredients on hand. Recipe for an Ocean in the Absence of the Sea. Richard Howard. TAP

You Have the Lovers. Leonard Cohen. NOBC

You have to act this way. (LL) How I Had to Act. Molly Peacock. FFC; NAmP90

You have to be the stronger one. The King and the Singer. Ivan V. Lalic, *Serbian.* CEEP, *tr. by* C. W. Truesdale

You have to inhabit poetry. Making Poetry. Anne Stevenson. DiPo

You have to quit talking. You have to. Quilts. Kathleen Peirce. PBCAP

You Have to Strike Back. Kate Lilley. BMAP

You have turned our land into a desolate place. Desolation. Jack Davis. BMAP

You have wished us a bonded life. (LL) A Funeral Plainsong from a Younger Woman to an Older Woman. Judy Grahn. DeD; GLP

You have your hat and coat on and she says she will be right down. The Evening Out. Ogden Nash. MoAmPo

You have your language too. The Wellfleet Whale. Stanley Kunitz. DiPo; NoAM

You have your own place to drink. Hail and beware them, when they come. (LL) A Newly Discovered "Homeric" Hymn. Charles Olson. MoP; NeAP; NoAM; PoM

You have your shadow. Your Shadow. Mark Strand. *Fr.* Elegy for My Father. HCAP; LCAP-2

You haven't finished your ape, said mother to father, who had monkey hair and blood on his whiskers. Ape. Russell Edson. PmAP; RaBo

You hear that heroic big land music? Poem. Alice Notley. PmAP

You hear the chain striking the wall. The Well. Yves Bonnefoy, *French.* VCWP, *tr. by* John Naughton

You hear them kids over there laugh this old woman? Lament for the Drowned Country. Mary Durack. NOBAu

You Hebrews are too snug in Ur. Joshua at Schechem. Charles Reznikoff. ChIV-1

You held my lotus blossom. To the Tune "Soaring Clouds." Huang O, *Chinese.* BoWoP; PBWP; WPOW, *tr. by* Kenneth Rexroth *and* Ling Chung

You held the black face of the warrior between your hands. Léopold Sédar Senghor. PBMAP

You Hide. You Hide. Edith Bruck, *Italian.* BoWoP, *tr. by* Ruth Feldman *and* Brian Swann

You hide your face. Lilith to Eve. Michelene Wandor. NBrP

You hire a cook, but she can't cook yet. Samuel Hoffenstein. OBCoV *Fr.* Poems in Praise of Practically Nothing.

You, his spark of lust, his spurt of spunk. (LL) Think of your conception, you'll soon forget. Palladas, *Greek.* GrAn; OBCVT, *tr. by* Tony Harrison

You hitched a thousand miles. August on Sourdough, a Visit from Dick Brewer. Gary Snyder. LoL

You hold a bunch of roses, Rose. Dionysius Sophistes, *Greek.* GrAn, *tr. by* Edward Lucie-Smith

You hollow-cheeked son. Baboon 2. *Unknown, Hottentot.* PeSA

You! hypocrite lecteur!—mon semblable,—mon frère! T. S. Eliot. *See* The Waste Land.

You (I). Tom Clark. SPE *Fr.* You.

You, I presume, could adroitly and gingerly. How the Women Will Stop War. Aristophanes. *Fr.* Lysistrata. NAWM-1, *tr. by* B. B. Rogers

You (II). Tom Clark. SPE *Fr.* You.

You (III). Tom Clark. SPE *Fr.* You.

You in Anger. James Reeves. OxBTC

You in evening doorways, in half-lit streets. Evening Quiet. Jovan Hristic, *Serbo-Croatian.* HSix, *tr. by* Charles Simic

You / in the night. Nelly Sachs, *German.* AF, *tr. by* Matthew Mead *and* Ruth Mead

You incongruous old woman of Smyrna! (LL) Limerick: "There was a young person of Smyrna." Edward Lear. OxBoLi; PeLV

You inquire gracefully of a man sick at heart. Separation from the Torah. Solomon ibn Gabirol, *Hebrew.* TOF, *tr. by* David Goldstein

You interest me. (LL) Note Delivered by a Female Impersonator. Heather McHugh. RACG

You intimidated me. I was thrown into hell without a trial. Denouement. Ruth Stone. BoWoP

You introduced me to my first goddess. In Memoriam Akbar Babool. Wopko Jensma. PeSAV

You invite me to a war party. War Party. Eddy Grant. PBCV

You (IV). Tom Clark. SPE *Fr.* You.

You judge a woman. To Some Supposed Brothers. Essex Hemphill. GLP; NAAAL

You just punch a hole in the son of a bitch. (LL) Carnation Milk ("Carnation milk is the best in the land"). *Unknown.* InPK-6; OBAL

You keep eating and raising a family. A Suite for Marriage. David Ignatow. NNaP

You keep me waiting in a truck. Twenty-Year Marriage. Ai. BoWoP; DeD; GT; NoAM

You killed the Dalmatian puppy. The Dogs. Michael S. Weaver. PBCAP

You Kissed Me. Josephine Slocum Hunt. BLPA; FaBoBe

You kissed me once and now I wait for more. Zodiac. Elizabeth Alexander. FFC

You knew I was coming for you, little one. Windigo. Louise Erdrich. NoAM; PoPoPo

You knew who I was. D.O.A. Tim Dlugos. EC3

You know, dear, that this vicious world. Mrs. Myrick's Lecture. Mary E. Tucker. CBWP-1

You know exactly what to do. Wendy Cope. APAD *Fr.* From June to December.

You know I have a husband. A Faithful Wife. Chang Chi, *Chinese.* OHMPC, *tr. by* Kenneth Rexroth

You know / I know. Alaskan Drinking Song. Dave Morice. EOEF

You know, I languish here. "Anna Akhmatova," *Russian.* TCRP, *tr. by* Daniel Weissbort

You know I said to Mark that I'm furious at you. The Quarrel. Diane Di Prima. NMM-2

You know it as well as the back of your hand. The Gilbert Stuart Portrait of Washington. Ted Kooser. CMAP

You know it by the northern look of the shore. North Sea off Carnoustie. Anne Stevenson. OxBoS

You know it's April by the falling-off. B Negative. X. J. Kennedy. CoAmPo

You know I've seen a lot of what the world can do. Vile World. Simon Rae. UV

You know I've seen a lot of what the world can do. Wild World. Cat Stevens. UV

You know my trouble: story. Round Midnight. Clarence Major. NAAAL

You know no more than I. (LL) So Sound You Sleep. A. E. Housman. CBLP; LBC

You know poor Mr. Dodsley has lost his wife; I believe. An Empty Heart. Samuel Johnson. LBC

You know Saint Wigbald's—yonder nunnery cell. How the Abbey of Saint Werewulf Juxta Slingsby Came by Brother Fabian's Manuscript. Sebastian Evans. PeVV

You know, she said, they made you. A Dress of Fire. Dahlia Ravikovitch, *Hebrew.* VCWP, *tr. by* Chana Bloch *and* Ariel Bloch

You know that he is going to die. The Red Dog. Laura Jensen. LCAP-2

You know that I love you, sweatheart, but every time I come around. *Unknown.* STP *Fr.* Kiowa "49" Songs.

You know that land, her lemon groves in bloom? Mignon. Goethe. STV, *tr. by* John Frederick Nims *Fr.* Wilhelm Meister's Apprenticeship.

You know the old woman. The Old Woman. Beatrix Potter. NTCP

You know the place: then. Sappho, *Greek.* PBWP, *tr. by* Mary Barnard

You know the way to heaven's door [*or* heavens doore]. (LL) Church-Music[k]. George Herbert. ESCV; GeHe; OxBSP

You know the world how big it is. Southern Africa. Nguno Wakolele. PeSAV

You know there is not much. To a Friend Concerning Several Ladies. William Carlos Williams. VGW

You know those rose sherbets. Jean Garrigue. NYBP; UnPo

You know those windless summer evenings, swollen to stasis. Cicadas. Richard Wilbur. NOBA

You know we French stormed [*or* storm'd] Ratisbon. Incident of the French Camp. Robert Browning. FaPoR; OBWP

You know we must be lonely, you and I. Souls. Paul Wertheimer, *German.* TrJP, *tr. by* Jethro Bithell

You know what it is to be born alone. Baby Tortoise. D. H. Lawrence. CMoP; PeP

You landsmen and you seamen bold. The Loss of the *Due Dispatch. Unknown.* AmFP

You Laughed and Laughed and Laughed. Gabriel Okara. PBA

You lay in the / catapults. And took aim. Stone. Luchezar Elenkov, *Bulgarian.* CEEP, *tr. by* Jascha Kessler *and* Aleksandar Shurbanov

You lay in wait. Sappho, *Greek.* BoWoP, *tr. by* Willis Barnstone

You lean on a wire fence, looking across. Somewhere along the Way. Henry Taylor. Poetr

You leaned your body in the doorway. Talkers in a Dream Doorway. Judy Grahn. GLP

You leaped from the white horses. The Distaff. Erinna, *Greek.* WPOW, *tr. by* Marylin Arthur

You learned Lear's *Nonsense Rhymes* by heart, not rote. A Plea to Boys and Girls. Robert Graves. GTBS-P; NAEL-2

You leave dead friends in. Will They Cry When You're Gone, You Bet. Imamu Amiri Baraka. NAAL-2

You left behind, Eurymedon, an infant child. Theocritus, *Greek.* GrAn, *tr. by* Anthony Holden

You left me when the weary weight of sorrow. Forgiven. Margaret Elizabeth Munson Sangster. PoToHe

You, Letting the Trees Stand as My Betrayer. Diane Wakoski. MoP

You lie now in many coffins. For Malcolm: After Mecca. Gerald William Barrax. PoBA

You lie, snail-like, on your stomach. Depression. Wendy Cope. FaBoWP

You lights, for which on earth my sight's thirst ne'er is stilled. To the Stars. Andreas Gryphius, *German.* GePo, *tr. by* George C. Schoolfield

You like it under the trees in autumn. The Motive for Metaphor. Wallace Stevens. MoAmPo

You like not that French novel? Tell me why. George Meredith. EnVR; NOBVV *Fr.* Modern Love.

You like peaches and cream. Peaches and Cream. Mudrooroo. BMAP

You like to have contests of size with people. The Contest Snake. Cheng Hsieh, *Chinese.* CoBLCP, *tr. by* Jonathan Chaves

You, little round-bellied. *Unknown, Greek.* InMo, *tr. by* Sam Hamill

You little stars that live in skies. From Caelica. Greville Fulke. NoP 4 *Fr.* Caelica.

You live here because there's no other place. So Long Solon. Jack Myers. AmPA

You live in this, and dwell in lovers' eyes. (LL) Sonnet 55. Shakespeare. AEP; AWP; CABP; CTC; EPCY; GSo; HeIP-4; ImPo; LoP; NAEL-1; NIP-4; NOBE; NoP-4; NoSic; OAEL-1; OxAEP-1; PoE; PoEL-2; PoRA; Poetr; SAGP; SCGP; Son

You Live on a Drifting Road. Robert Ivanovich Rozhdestvensky, *Russian.* TCRP, *tr. by* J. R. Rowland

You live under the microscope. Under the Microscope. Slavko Mihalic. PoSu, *tr. by* Charles Simic

You lived and moved among the best society. W. H. Auden. OBSV *Fr.* Letter to Lord Byron.

You lived, you played, you sang with a bitter grin. Epitaph for Vysotsky. Andrey Andreievich Voznesensky, *Russian.* TCRP, *tr. by* William Jay Smith

You load, focus, aim. Shooting Back. Thomas Sayers Ellis. GT

You look at me. A Drop of Dew. Shmuel Halkin, *Yiddish.* TrJP, *tr. by* Jacob Sonntag

You look at me, a hut or cage contains. Hilda Doolittle. NOCV *Fr.* Sagesse.

You look upon the air. (LL) Late. Louise Bogan. PBWP; VGW

You, love, and I. Counting the Beats. Robert Graves. GBL; GTBS-P; HAP; OxAEP-2; OxBTC; WeW-3

"You love. . . ? love. . . ? love. . . ?" all on an indrawn breath. (LL) I am to follow her. There is much grace. George Meredith. NAEL-2; NOBVV

You love me—you are sure. Emily Dickinson. CPO

You love not me? (LL) A Broken Appointment. Thomas Hardy. GBL; GLoP; NAEL-2; NOBVV; NoAM; NoP-4

You love? That's high as you shall go. The Attainment. Coventry Patmore. FaBoEE *Fr.* The Angel in the House.

You love the roses—so do I. I wish. "George Eliot." BoTP

You love us when we're heroes, home on leave. Glory of Women. Siegfried Sassoon. NAEL-2; NoP-4; OBWP; OxAEP-2; PeFWW; PoFWW

You love when all was young. Charles Kingsley. *See* Young and Old.

You loved me for a little. Midsummer. Sydney King Russell. BLPA; FaBoBe

You loved me not at all, but let it go. Edna St. Vincent Millay. VGW

You loved Menophila when you were rich. Argentarius, *Greek.* GrAn, *tr. by* Fleur Adcock

You lower my emotions, sealed in their casket. The Parting. Sara Berkeley. PBCIP

You lumbered along the stadium. My Father's First Baseball Game. Michael S. Weaver. PBCAP

You Made It Rain. Ruby C. Saunders. BlSi

You made me blue. Blue. Gerald William Barrax. *Fr.* The Old Gory. NBV

You make it in your mess-tin by the brazier's rosy gleam. A Pot of Tea. Robert W. Service. NSI; PoWW

You, Marc Chagall, should be able to tell us. The Ascensions. William Pillen. RaBo

You marched off southward with the fire of twenty. Danny. Malcolm Cowley. PoA

You Masks of the Masquerade. Gustave Kahn, *French.* TrJP, *tr. by* Jethro Bithell

You, master of delays. Killing No Murder. Sylvia Townsend Warner. MoBrPo

You may be Dirty Dinky. (LL) Dinky. Theodore Roethke. OBAL; OBCA

You may be right, divinity. Prayer. Francis Sullivan. CRP

You may be right: "How can I dare to feel?" Rejoinder to a Critic. Donald Davie. CABP; NoP-4

You may brag about your breakfast foods you eat at break of day. Sausage. E. A. Guest. OBAL

You may call, you may call. The Bad Kittens. Elizabeth Jane Coatsworth. OBCA

You may catch / a butterfly. Ars Poetica. Linda Pastan. NIP-4

You may catch all the others, but you wo——. (LL) The slithergadee has crawled out of the sea. Shel Silverstein. KaS; NBLV; NTCP; OBCoV

You may for ever tarry. (LL) To [the] Virgins, to Make Much of Time. Robert Herrick. AWP; BLPA; BeJo; BoLoP; CaPo; CavPo; ClHu; EBEvV; EnLoPo; GBL; GLoP; GTBS-P; HAP; HeIP-4; ImPo; InPK-6; InPS-3; LoP; NAEL-1; NBLV; NIP-4; NOBE; NOSC; OAEL-1; OBEV; OxAEP-1; PBMP; PoE; PoEL-3; Poetr; SCGP; SCV; SeCP; SoSe-8; TFi; UV

You may get there by candle light. (LL) To Babylon. Mother Goose. BoTP; FaBoCh; LB; NTP; OxBSP; OxNR; ReMoGo

You may give over plow, boys. Tommy's Dead. Sydney Thompson Dobell. PeVV

You May Go But This Will Bring You Back. *Unknown.* NAAAL

You may have forgot, you were drunk when you dy'd. (LL) Epigram: "When Bibo thought fit from the world to retreat." Matthew Prior. CBNP; FaBoEE

You may have seen, in road or street. The Calf. Thomas Hardy. APo

You may have sex. Disown. Rae Armantrout. FTOS

You may have troubles manifold. A Mother's Joy. Ruth Fortney Maxwell. PWR

You may leave and go to Hali-ma-fack. You May Go But This Will Bring You Back. *Unknown.* NAAAL

You may my glories and my state depose. Shakespeare. IMW *Fr.* Richard II.

You may speak of a grave in a distant land. A Reverie. Mary Weston Fordham. CBWP-2

You may talk as you please of the joys of Jamaica. The Song of the Transportationist. *Unknown.* NOBAu

You may talk o' gin and [*or* an'] beer. Gunga Din. Rudyard Kipling. EBEvV; EBVV; MoBrPo

You may then live in joy perdurably. . . . (LL) The Epitaph of Graunde [*or* La Graunde] Amoure. Stephen Hawes. EBEV; FaBoEE; NoSic; OBEV

You may want to cut them down. You may want to use a knife. Chrysanthemums. Irene McKinney. PBCAP

You may write me down in history. Still I Rise. Maya Angelou. APAD; BlSi; ISC; NAAAL

"You mean," he said, "a crocodile." (LL) The Purist. Ogden Nash. KaS; MoAmPo; NBLV; OBCA

You meaner beauties of the night. On His Mistress [*or* Mistris], the Queen of Bohemia. Sir Henry Wotton. BoLoP; CBLP; EnLoPo; FaBoCh; GBL; GLoP; GTBS-P; HAP; MeLP; NOBE; NOSC; OBEV; SCGP; SeCP; TFi

You meet your friend, your face. Selected Epigrams. Kassia, *Byzantine Greek.* PBWP, *tr. by* Patrick Diehl

You merit more; nor could [*or* cou'd] my Love do less. (LL) To My Dear Friend Mr Congreve [on His Comedy Called "The Double-Dealer"]. Dryden. EBEV; OAEL-1; OxAEP-1; PoEL-3

You midst gay crowds reside, I, hid in shades. Esther Lewis. ECWP *Fr.* A Letter to a Lady in London.

You might as well live. (LL) Résumé. Dorothy Parker. HeIP-4; InPK-6; NAAL-2; NALW; NBLV; NoP-4; OBAL; PFE; Poetr; TrJP; UV

You might ask. Battle Scene. Aricil Kilar, *Tamil.* PLW, *tr. by* A. K. Ramanujan

You might be surprised right out the window, whistling dixie on the / way. (LL) Poem for Half White College Students. Imamu Amiri Baraka. BPo; CAPP-1; TAP; UnPo

You might come here Sunday on a whim. Degrees of Gray in Philipsburg. Richard Hugo. CoAP; NAAL-2; NoAM; TRP; VCAP

You might easy know a doffer. *Unknown.* FaBoVe

You might imagine the desert as a rectangle without angles, as a. The Desert, II. Edmond Jabès, *French*. AF, *tr*. by Rosemarie Waldrop

You might suppose it easy. The Boatman. Jay Macpherson. MoCV

You, mob, / Are about to be transformed. The Mob. Mcavoy Layne. CDa

You modern wits, who call this world a star. To the Same [My Dear Sister, Mrs S.]: The Tears. William Hammond. NOSC

You, Morningtide Star, now are steady-eyed, over the east. Lying Awake. Thomas Hardy. FaBoVe

You must admit the loss of blood, brother. Missing Link. Sean Lucy. BiHa

You must agree that Rubens was a Fool. To English Connoisseurs. William Blake. OxBoLi

You must be proud, if you'll be wise. (LL) To the Ladies. Mary Lee, Lady Chudleigh. CABP; ECWP; GEA; NALW; NOEC; PEW; WPE; WPOW

You must be sad; for though it is to Heaven. To Two Bereaved. Thomas Ashe. NOBVV

You Must Change Your Life. Ken Edwards. NBrP

You must change your life fourteen times. Archaic Torsos. David Shapiro. PT

You must come back, as your grandmother did. Dandelion Greens. Jane Flanders. CrSp

"You must come here and scratch." *Unknown. See* Five Little Chickens.

You Must Have Been a Sensational Baby. Harold Norse. GLP

You must have been still sleeping, your wife there. The Sacred Hearth. David Gascoyne. FaBoTw

You must learn how to peel, man. Orange. Barbara Ferland. PBCV

You must leave here. The signs say so. Mene Mene. Ory Bernstein, *Hebrew*. IP, *tr*. by Warren Bargad *and* Stanley F. Chyet

You must live through the time when everything hurts. The Double Shame. Stephen Spender. LiTM

You must not hope to arrive. (LL) The Tourist from Syracuse. Donald Justice. NoAM; TwCP; VCAP

You must not, said the owl to the capercailzie. The End of Art. Reiner Kunze, *German*. PoSu, *tr*. by Michael Hamburger

You must not wonder, though you think it strange. For That He Looked Not upon Her. George Gascoigne. GSo; NoP-4

You must remain very much alone. Presences. Zoé Karélli, *Modern Greek*. PBWP, *tr*. by Kimon Friar

You must remember structures beyond cotton plains. If Blood Is Black Then Spirit Neglects My Unborn Son. Conrad Kent Rivers. PoBA

You must remember this when I am gone. Sanctuary. Donald Davidson. FuPo

You Must Say It. Xuân Diệu, *Vietnamese*. AVP, *tr*. by Huỳnh Sanh Thông

You must stand erect but at your ease, a posture. The Singing Lesson. David Wagoner. NoAM

You must wake and call me early, call me early, mother. Tennyson. EBEvV *Fr*. The May Queen.

You must wear them until you are dead. (LL) Limerick: "There was an archdeacon who said." *Unknown*. OBCoV; OxBoLi

You Mustn't Quit. *Unknown. See* Don't Quit.

You / my bell-clapper. Christmas Mass for a Little Atheist Jesus. Claude Maillard, *French*. BoWoP, *tr*. by Maxine W. Kumin *and* Judith Kumin

You, my Lord, have tarried long in your journey. Lord of the River Hsiang. Ch'u Yüan, *Chinese*. SuSp, *tr*. by Wu-Chi Liu

You need the untranslatable ice to watch. Appendix to the Anniad. Gwendolyn Brooks. BlSi

You neigh and whinny, seeming to invite. Macedonius, *Greek*. GrAn, *tr*. by Adrian Wright

You never can tell. (LL) Those Two Boys. Franklin Pierce Adams. OBCoV; TrJP

You Never Can Tell. Ella Wheeler Wilcox. BLPA; PoToHe

You never claimed to be someone special. She Mends an Ancient Wireless. Paul Durcan. PBCIP

You never come back. Mill-Doors. Carl Sandburg. SAGP

You never could tell what my deaf Uncle Arthur heard. And Don't Be Deaf to the Singing Beyond. Carter Revard. HATNAP

You never got to recline. For Mother on Father's Day. James Tate. FiLi

You never hear 'the People' now. The People, No. Vicki Raymond. NOBAu

You never married, never took a job—you went completely astray! Written at the End of Master Ho-ching's Collected Works. Chin Nung, *Chinese*. CoBLCP, *tr*. by Jonathan Chaves

You never touch. Akiko Yosano, *Japanese*. BoWoP; PBWP, *tr*. by Geoffrey Bownas *and* Anthony Thwaite

You, no doubt, have heard the story told of Charleston by the sea? The Crum Appointment. Lizelia Augusta Jenkins Moorer. CBWP-3

You no give me one wacky you can't pass. Dry River. *Unknown*. FaBoVe

You no sooner got out of prison. The Evening Walk. Nazim Hikmet, *Turkish*. AF, *tr*. by Randy Blasing *and* Mutlu Konuk

You noble Diggers all, stand up now, stand up now. The Digger's Song. Gerrard Winstanley. FaBoPV; NOSC

You noble fountain set in peace and joy's design. Concerning the Wolffsbrunnen near Heidelberg. Martin Opitz, *German*. GePo, *tr*. by George C. Schoolfield

You, North must go. *Unknown*. ACTP

You now solicit a few enemy thrusts. Wyndham Lewis. *Fr*. If So the Man You Are. OBSV

You nurtured grief until that leap. Waiting for Robinson. Roberta Hill Whiteman. HATNAP

You, O Tsui-Xgoa. Hymn to Tsui-Xgoa. *Unknown, Hottentot*. PeSA

You, Odysseus trainer of the wooden horse of pleasure. Odyssey or "On Absence," The. Chimako Tada, *Japanese*. VCWP, *tr*. by Naoshi Koriyama *and* Edward Lueders

You of course live in the way that is truly right. Horace. OBCVT, *tr*. by Robert Pinsky *Fr*. An Explanation of America.

You of me & / I of you, / darling, have had. Catullus. *See* Carmen 5 ("My sweetest Lesbia, let us live and love").

You of the same mind, moor-wandering near one. Largo. Paul Celan, *German*. PoSu, *tr*. by Michael Hamburger

You often went to breathe a timeless air. The Scholar. Frances Darwin Cornford. BrRo

You: on candy cameo. Me: ate dumb flash. Stage Duo. Kenward Elmslie. FTOS

You, once a belle in Shreveport. Snapshots of a Daughter-in-Law. Adrienne Rich. FaBoWP; HCAP; NAAL-2; NALW; NIP-4; NMM-2; NoAM; NoP-4; PoPoPo; Poetr; VCAP

You only come in the tormenting. Suicide. Robert Lowell. PoE

You only have to be born. Implant. Günter Kunert, *German*. CEEP, *tr*. by Michael Hamburger

You open the door after a long ride home in the dark. (LL) Refuge at the One Step Down. Belle Waring. PBCAP; SoSe

You opened the matchbox. Despair. Aleksandar Ristovic, *Serbo-Croatian*. HSix, *tr*. by Charles Simic

You ought to know Mr Mistoffelees! Mr Mistoffelees. T. S. Eliot. CBNP; NOxBChV

You ought to see my blue-eyed Sally. Stay All Night, Stay a Little Longer. *Unknown*. AmFP

You over there, young man with the guide book red-bound. Home Sweet Home with Variations. Henry Cuyler Bunner. BXAP; OBAL

"You owe me five shillings." The Bells. *Unknown*. ReMoGo

You paint the wild geese as if I could see them crying. For Contemporary Artist Pien Wei-Ch'I. Cheng Hsieh, *Chinese*. SuSp, *tr*. by Irving Y. Lo; ChiPo, *tr*. by Irving Yucheng Lo

You pass the tomb of Battus' son, well skilled. Callimachus. HePo *Fr*. Epigrams.

You pay for it, for sure, dont let nobody tell you you don. You pay. The Minute of Consciousness. Imamu Amiri Baraka. APSN

You people / of the future. Screaming My Head Off. Vladimir Mayakovsky. PFTM

You perpetuate! Roll on, reels of celluloid, as the great earth rolls on! (LL) To the Film Industry in Crisis. Frank O'Hara. CAPP-1; NOBA; OBAL

You picked up fallen stars on some clear night. The String of Pearls. Đồng Hồ, *Vietnamese*. AVP, *tr*. by Huỳnh Sanh Thông

You plant like Paul, you water like Apollos. The Rev. Nicholas Noyes to the Rev. Cotton Mather. Nicholas Noyes. SCAP

You planted life, protecting. Discords. Fabio Doplicher, *Italian*. NeIt, *tr*. by Dana Gioia

You poured down like gold, / Olympian Zeus. Parmenion of Macedon, *Greek*. GrAn, *tr*. by Peter Jay

You praise the firm restraint with which they write. On Some South African Novelists. Roy Campbell. FaBoEE; GTBS-P; InPK-6; MoBrPo; NOBL; OBCoV; OxAEP-2; OxBTC; PeLV

You pray in vain for Carrousel. (LL) The Ballad of a Barber. Aubrey Beardsley. ADE

You prayer—, you blasphemy, you. Plashes the Fountain. Paul Celan, *German*. OBVE, *tr*. by Michael Hamburger

You prisoners of New South Wales. A Convict's Tour to Hell. Francis MacNamara. NOBAu

You promise heavens free from strife. Mimnermus in Church. William Johnson Cory. NOBE; OBEV

You ramshackle Christian, awake! Peachum's Morning Hymn. Bertolt Brecht. OxBoV, *tr*. by Ralph Manheim *and* John Willett *Fr*. The Threepenny Opera.

You read the New York Times. Alfred Corning Clark. Robert Lowell. RB

You, reading over my shoulder, peering beneath. The Reader over My Shoulder. Robert Graves. NAEL-2

You recline that magnificent pair of buttocks. To Kyris. Strato, *Greek*. GrAn, *tr*. by Teddy Hogge

You recommend that the motive, in Chapter 8, should be changed. Yes, the Agency Can Handle That. Kenneth Fearing. WeW-3

You recount old tales of Thebes. Anacreon, *Greek*. InMo, tr. by Sam Hamill

You / Refuse to see. Out. Riots and Rituals. Richard W. Thomas. PoBA

You remember the big Gaston, for whom everyone predicted a bad end? Monsieur Gaston. Abraham Moses Klein. MoCV

You remember the name was Jensen. She seemed old. What Thou Lovest Well Remains American. Richard Hugo. NAAL-2; PaTW

You remember the sun of Auschwitz. The Sun of Auschwitz. Tadeusz Borowski, *Polish*. AF, tr. by Larry Rafferty, Meryl Natchez *and* Tadeusz Pioro; HP, tr. by Tadeuszt Pióro

You remove a jade pendant——to exchange for a lute. Yang Chi. *Fr.* Living in Master Fang's Garden. CoBLCP, tr. by Jonathan Chaves

You replaced the Douglas firs. You, Letting the Trees Stand as My Betrayer. Diane Wakoski. MoP

You ride dat horse. Jesus, Won't You Come B'm-By? *Unknown*. AS

You roar over the meadow and roar. Last Days. Richard Hugo. PoA

You ruthless flea, who desecrate my couch. Song of the Flea. Judah Al-Harizi, *Hebrew*. TrJP

You said, 'I will go to another land, I will go to another sea'. Constantine P. Cavafy. *See* The City.

You said: "I'll go to another country, go to another shore." The City. Constantine P. Cavafy, *Greek*. AF, tr. by Edmund Keeley

You said it went all the way. Last Words, 1968. Lance Henson. CDW

You said: My father didn't cry. Ancestral Weight. Alfonsina Storni, *Spanish*. WPOW, tr. by Marti Moody

You said, that October. December at Yase. Gary Snyder. *Fr.* Four Poems for Robin. MoP; NNaP; NOBA; NoAM

You said that your people. To Richard Wright. Conrad Kent Rivers. PoBA

You said to me: But I will be your comrade. Nudities. André Spire. AWP, tr. by Jethro Bithell

You said to me: / I shall [or would] become your comrade. Nudities. André Spire, *French*. TrJP, tr. by Stanley Burnshaw

You said you would kill it this morning. Pheasant. Sylvia Plath. RB

You sang round-dance songs. Farewell. Liz Sohappy Bahe. CDW

You sat with a bottle of beer. After the Death of an Elder Klallam. Duane Niatum. CDW

You saw a sign once: SLOW—MEN WORKING IN TREES. Slow Men Working in Trees. Anne C. Bromley. CMAP

You say, as I have often given tongue. To a Poet, Who Would Have Me Praise Certain Bad Poets, Imitators of His and Mine. W. B. Yeats. CTC; FaBoEE

You say, but with no touch of scorn. Doubt. Tennyson. NOCV *Fr.* In Memoriam A. H. H.

You say, Columbus with his argosies. Trumbull Stickney. APN-2

You say: I am sitting in a room. At a Sunlit Window. Ondra Lysohorsky, *Lachian*. AF, tr. by Ewald Osers

You say, "I will come." Lady Otomo no Sakanoé, *Japanese*. PiM, tr. by Kenneth Rexroth

You say my brow is stern and yet my smile. The Stern Brow. Walter Savage Landor. CBLP

You say my poetry. Complaint to a Court Poet. Rashidi Samarqandi, *Persian*. ArPe, tr. by Omar S. Pound

You say that I take a good deal upon myself. Monumentum Aere, Etc. Ezra Pound. NOBA

You say that you believe in Democracy for everybody. Everybody but Me. Margaret Goss Burroughs. BlSi

You say there were no people. There Are No People Song. *Navajo Oral Tradition*. TTTS

You say, to me-wards your affection's strong. Love Me Little, Love Me Long. Robert Herrick. BLPA; CBLP; CaPo; FaBoBe; SCGP

You say "Tomorrow"; a tomorrow which. Macedonius, *Greek*. GrAn, tr. by Adrian Wright

You say you are holy. Stephen Crane. MeMAP

You say you had a letter from. First Letter From Tamara A. Reiner Kunze, *German*. PoSu, tr. by Ewald Osers

You say you "live inside a full-stop." Nichita Stanescu. Brian Turner. PeNZ

You say you love; but with a voice. Stanzas. Keats. CBLP

You say you're glad I write—oh, say not so! Impromptu. Frances Anne Kemble. APN-1

You scarcely move your foot when out of nowhere spring. Voices. Wislawa Szymborska, *Polish*. PoSu, tr. by Magnus F. Krynski

You scream, waking from a nightmare. Little Sleep's-Head Sprouting Hair in the Moonlight. Galway Kinnell. LCAP-2

You sea! I resign myself to you also—I guess what you mean. Walt Whitman. OxBoS *Fr.* Song of Myself. AmPP; MoAmPo; NAAL-3; NOBA; OxBA

You see how, white with snows to the north of us. Horace. *See* 1.9.

You see, I am alive, I am alive. (LL) The Delight Song of Tsoai-Talee. N. Scott Momaday. CDW; InPK-6; PaTW

You see, my whole life. Woman Poem. Nikki Giovanni. BlSi

You see, the problem is. Blue like Death. James Welch. CDW

You see the smoke at Kapunda. Song: The Railway Train. *Unknown*. NOBAu, tr. by George Taplin

You see the worst of love, but not the best. Walter Savage Landor. GBL

You see them vanish in their speeding cars. Fugue. Howard Nemerov. TAP

You see these images. Perspective. Constance Carrier. AFr

You see these little scars? That's where my wife. Iambic Feet Considered as Honorable Scars. William Meredith. OxBSP; PoA

You see, they have no judgment. The Drowned Children. Louise Glück. HCAP; VCAP

You see this Christmas tree all silver gold? Come Christmas. David McCord. PChr

You see this dog. Flush or Faunus. Elizabeth Barrett Browning. VWP

You see this pebble-stone? It's a thing I bought. The Cock and the Bull. Charles Stuart Calverley. BXAP

You see those mothers squabbling there? In the Cemetery. Thomas Hardy. InPK-6; Son *Fr.* Satires of Circumstance in Fifteen Glimpses.

You see what I am: change me, change me! (LL) The Woman at the Washington Zoo. Randall Jarrell. CoAP; HAP; HCAP; LiTM; OxBC; TAP; TwCP; UnPo; VCAP

You see, where'er you look, on earth but vainness' hour. All Is Vanity. Andreas Gryphius, *German*. GePo, tr. by George C. Schoolfield

You seek refuge. The Gift. Greg Delanty. BiHa

You seldom talked about the Indian side. The Reservation. Susan Clements. UnSA

You send for her, you tell her to come, you get everything ready. The Impotent Lover. Automedon, *Greek*. GrAn, tr. by W. S. Merwin

You send me a letter from far, from across the sea. Poem. Valentine Ackland. WPN

You send me a photograph. Porno Love. Philip Dacey. CMAP

You send me reams of snowy paper. Leonidas of Alexandria, *Greek*. GrAn, tr. by Robin Skelton

You sent us everything from out of the under world, ghosts! who take away man's senses. A Song of the Ghost Dancer of the La' Lasiqoala. *Unknown*. *Fr.* Dances and Songs of the Winter Ceremonial. APN-2, tr. by Franz Boas

You Serve the Best Wines Always, My Dear Sir. Martial, *Latin*. InPK-6, tr. by J. V. Cunningham

You shall above all things be glad and young. E. E. Cummings. ColAP; NOBA; NoAM; OxBA

"You shall be King, dilly, dilly, when I am Queen." *Unknown*. *See* Lavender's Blue.

You shall be poor. (LL) A Woman Is Talking to Death. Judy Grahn. CPO

You shall be true to them, who are false to you. (LL) The Indifferent. Donne. BoLoP; CBLP; ESCV; NAEL-1; NAWM-1; NOSC; PBMP; SoSe-8

You shall have an apple. For Baby. *Unknown*. ReMoGo

You shall listen to all sides and filter them from yourself. (LL) Houses and rooms are full of perfumes. Walt Whitman. ColAP; PAR

You shall never remain in Thermopylae'. (LL) Limerick: "There was an old man of Thermopylae." Edward Lear. EBEV; NOBL; OxAEP-2; PeLi

You shall walk in peace! Martial Sinda, *French*. NegPo, tr. by Ellen Conroy Kennedy

You shepherds who wander this lonely mountainside. Leonidas of Tarentum, *Greek*. GrAn, tr. by Fleur Adcock

You shine in darkness, you dream under shelter. Jure Kastelan, *Croatian*. CEEP, tr. by Peter Kastmiler

You shine, my love, like a sugar maple in October. Raisin Pumpernickel. Marge Piercy. DeD

You should at times go out. Elizabeth Daryush. WPN

You should be done with blossoming by now. To a Vine-clad Telegraph Pole. Louis Untermeyer. MoAmPo

You should bid me welcome. Walther von der Vogelweide, *German*. GePo, tr. by Frederick Goldin

You should enjoy your suffering. The New Sentience. Alan Davies. FTOS

You should have many lovers. A Very Sad Conversation at Night. Anna Swirszczynska, *Polish*. PoSu, tr. by Czeslaw Milosz *and* Leonard Nathan

You should see these musical mice. New Strain. George Starbuck. TwCP

You shouldn't be afraid of the dark. Lullaby for My Dead Child. Denise Jallais, *French*. BoWoP; IMW, tr. by Maxine W. Kumin *and* Judith Kumin

You show me the poems of some woman. Translations. Adrienne Rich. WPOW

You showed your dirty face first in Detroit. To the Eminent Scholar and Meddler. Kofi Awoonor. HBAPE

You shun me, Chloë, wild and shy. Ode 1.23: To Chloë ("Vitas hinnuleo"). Horace. AWP; OBVE *Fr.* Odes.

You shut me up in a cold box and buried me. Exhumation. Elizabeth Spires. WeT

You sing a hard blues. Bulosan Listens to a Recording of Robert Johnson. Alfred Encarnacion. LTA; OpBo; UnSA

You sit at your high windows, old men. The Old Men. Alexander Javitz. TrJP

You sit in a chair, touched by nothing, feeling. In Celebration. Mark Strand. NoAM

You sit in the middle of the bed. To a Friend's Child. Aliki Barnstone. BoWoP

You slapped me. For My Torturer, Lieutenant D——. Leila Djabali, *French.* WPOW, *tr. by* Anita Barrows

You slapped my face. Short Poem. William Carlos Williams. SAmP

You sleep at the top of streets. To Waken a Small Person. Donald Justice. NYBP

You sleep here, Daphnis, on the leafy ground. Theocritus, *Greek.* GrAn, *tr. by* Anthony Holden

You sleep in a room with bluegreen curtains. In the Wake of Home. Adrienne Rich. LCAP-2

You sleep too well—too far away. TO E. T.: 1917. Walter De la Mare. FP

You smiled, you spoke, and I believed. Walter Savage Landor. BoLoP; CBLP; GBL; GLoP

You, so bravely plying reds and blues. To a Portrait Painter who Desired Him to Sit. Po Chü-i, *Chinese.* ChiP, *tr. by* Arthur Waley

You speak in a very ancient tongue. November '73. Dan Pagis, *Hebrew.* IP, *tr. by* Warren Bargad *and* Stanley F. Chyet

You speak of art. Para un Revolucionario. Lorna Dee Cervantes. Poetr

You spent all summer in cool Kabul. *Unknown, Pashto.* PBWP, *tr. by* Saduddin Shpoon

You spotted snakes [with double tongue]. Fairy Land, 2. Shakespeare. BoTP; NOBE; NoSic; OBEV; PoRA; SCGP *Fr.* A Midsummer Night's Dream.

You staged the ultimate coup de grâce. The Lundys Letter. Gerald Dawe. BiHa

You stand against the pillar. Mothers. Kavarpentu, *Tamil.* PLW, *tr. by* A. K. Ramanujan

You stand and hold the post of my small house. Auvaiyar, *Tamil.* WPOW, *tr. by* George Hart

You stand behind the old black mare. Why Can't I Leave You? Ai. AmPA

You stand beside me here, each day and every hour. Yuly Markovich Daniel, *Russian.* TCRP, *tr. by* David Burg *and* Arthur Boyars

You stand waist-high in snakes. Alice. Michael S. Harper. ISC

You start here—Cozumel—it's an island, some people. You Are Here. Carl Phillips. GT

You start it all. You are lovely. To Women. Richard Hugo. NIP-4

You stepped through. Archangel. Ai. SeSe

You still sometimes sleep. Heron. Stanley Plumly. AmPA

You stop to watch the Mandarin ducks. Urban Love Songs. Wing Tek Lum. OpBo

You strange, astonished-looking, angle-faced. The Fish, the Man, and the Spirit. Leigh Hunt. HAP; NOBL; NTP; OBEV; PoEL-4

You strange, astonished-looking, angle-faced. To a Fish. Leigh Hunt. NBLV; PeLV; SCGP *Fr.* The Fish, the Man, and the Spirit. HAP; NOBL; NTP; OBEV; PoEL-4

You, stranger, soul-mate. Grief. Siamanto, *Armenian.* AF, *tr. by* Peter Balakian *and* Nevart Yaghlian

You, stranger, who only sees us happy and free of care. Hunger. Samik, *Eskimo.* STP, *tr. by* Edward Field

You strike everything down in battle. Inanna and Ishkur. Enheduanna, *Sumerian.* BoWoP, *ad. by* W. W. Hallo *and* J. J. A. van Dijk

You strolled in the open, leisurely and alone. To the Poets in New York. James Wright. NAAL-2

You suffer as you stray and lose your heart. A Fool In Love. Xuân Diệu, *Vietnamese.* AVP, *tr. by* Huỳnh Sanh Thông

You surprise me, crow. Nigot, *Tlingit Indian.* STP, *tr. by* James Koller

You sweet soft murderess. *Unknown, German.* GePo, *tr. by* Frederick Goldin

You take and drop my hand. (LL) The Meeting. Louise Bogan. NYBP; NoAM

You take my hand and. Margaret Atwood. HAP

You take off, he takes off, we take off. Clothes. Wisława Szymborska, *Polish.* PoSu, *tr. by* Grazyna Drabik *and* Sharon Olds

You take the dollar. For One Moment. David Ignatow. NNaP

You take the rest. (LL) The Crossed Apple. Louise Bogan. HeIP-4; NALW; RACG

You talk about your harbor girls. Haul Away, My Rosy. *Unknown.* AmFP

You talk like / they don't kick. Comment on Curb. Langston Hughes. APSN *Fr.* Lenox Avenue Mural. HoPM

You taught me fear, Momma. Laura Davis. MDDM *Fr.* Things You Gave Me.

You tell me, fair one, that you ne'er can love. The Female Philosopher. Charlotte Dacre. NOBRP

You tell me not to long for you. Yosami, the wife of Hitomaro, *Japanese.* WPJ, *tr. by* Kenneth Rexroth *and* Ikuko Atsumi

You tell me that you truly love. To Him Who Says He Loves. Charlotte Dacre. Ro

You Tell Me to Sit Quiet. A. C. Jordan. PBA

You tell me you have right on your side? Familiar Oxen. Oumar Ba. PBMAP

You tell me you're promised a lover. A Letter of Advice. Winthrop Mackworth Praed. NOBL; OxBoLi; PeLV

You Tell on Yourself. *Unknown.* PoToHe

You tell them this. Interview with a Guy Named Fawkes, U.S. Army. Walter McDonald. CDa

You Tell Us What to Do. Faiz Ahmad Faiz, *Urdu.* VCWP, *tr. by* Agha Shahid Ali

You tell what you are by the friends you seek. You Tell on Yourself. *Unknown.* PoToHe

You tender virgins, fairer than the snow with which you play. Edward May, *after the Latin of* John Parkhurst. FaBoEE

You that a stranger in mid-Rome seek Rome. Rome. James Vincent Cunningham, *after the Latin of* Janus Vitalis Panormitanus. OBVE

You that alone I cared to keep. (LL) Song of a Second April. Edna St. Vincent Millay. CMoP; OxBA

You that are jealous and have a wife. *Unknown, Irish.* NOIV, *tr. by* Thomas Kinsella

You that are sprung of northern stock. To a Calvinist in Bali. Edna St. Vincent Millay. NoAM

You that are weather-wise and pretend to know. Upon a Great Shower of Snow That Fell on May-Day, 1654. Thomas Washbourne. NOCV

You, that decipher out the fate. Mourning. Andrew Marvell. FMP; SeCP

You that do search for every purling spring. Sonnet 15. Sir Philip Sidney. CABP; NAEL-1; NoSic; OAEL-1; OxAEP-1; Son *Fr.* Astrophil and Stella. AAS; SiPS

You That Have Been Often Invited. *Unknown.* AH

You that have spent the silent night. Gascoigne's Good-Morrow. George Gascoigne. AAS; CABP; NOCV; NoSic

You that in love find[e] luck[e] and [h]abunda[u]nce. Sir Thomas Wyatt. AAS; SiPS

You that Jehovah's servants are, *par. by* Countess of Pembroke, Mary Sidney Herbert. Psalm 134. Bible, *O.T.* NoSic *Fr.* Psalms.

You that know the way. Lemuel's Blessing. W. S. Merwin. CAPP-1; NYBP

You That Love England. C. Day Lewis. FaBoMo

You that love Lovers. Jelaluddin Rumi, *Persian.* ITG, *tr. by* Barks, Coleman and A. J. Arberry

You that thus wear a modest countenance. Dante. AWP *Fr.* La Vita Nuova.

You that unto your mistress' eyes. Love Deposed. Thomas Stanley. NOSC

You that with allegory's curious frame. Sonnet 28. Sir Philip Sidney. NoSic; OAEL-1 *Fr.* Astrophil and Stella. AAS; SiPS

You that would last long, list to my song. Ben Jonson. *Fr.* Volpone. NAEL-1

You, the choice minions of the proud-lipped Nine. To Poets. George Darley. Son

You: The City. Fiona Templeton.
  Act II - Crossing At the Tracks. FTOS

You, the woman; I, the man; this, the world. The Character of Love Seen as a Search for the Lost. Kenneth Patchen. CLPP; VGW

You, then, that would the comic laurels wear. Nicolas Boileau-Despréaux. EPCY, *tr. by* Sir William Soames *and* John Dryden *Fr.* L'Art Poétique.

You then vor me meade up your mind. Walken Hwomme at Night. William Barnes. NOBVV

You thieved in your need. Atman. George Campbell Hay. FaBoTC

You think Fuseli is not a Great Painter. I'm glad. To Hunt. William Blake. OxBoLi

You think I am happy. Wang Chiu-ssu. CoBLCP, *tr. by* Jonathan Chaves *Fr.* Forced Feelings.

You think I am / some strange pesticide. Bad for You. Diane Averill. CMAP

You think I am your servant but you are wrong. Table Talk. Derek Mahon. DiPo

You think I give myself to you? Giving. Nora B. Cunningham. LW

You think it horrible that lust and rage. The Spur. W. B. Yeats. OxAEP-2; WeW-3

You think that beard has made you wise. Ammianus, *Greek*. GrAn, *tr. by* Robin Skelton

You think they might come. Riding Double. Peter Wild. AmPA

You think this is some malarial dream? Vladimir Mayakovsky. TCRP, *tr. by* Bernard Meares *Fr.* The Cloud in Trousers.

You think: won't fate tap. "Georgy Avdeievich Rayevsky," *Russian*. TCRP, *tr. by* Albert C. Todd

You think you / need me. Masquerade. Carolyn M. Rodgers. BlSi

You though! Die and you'll lie dumb in the dirt; nobody care, and none. On a Lady Indifferent to Poetry. Sappho, *Greek*. STV, *tr. by* John Frederick Nims

You thought I had the strength of men. A Clever Woman. Mary Elizabeth Coleridge. BrRo; VWP

You thunder at my side. The Snoring Bedmate. *Unknown, Irish*. BIrV, *tr. by* John V. Kelleher

You thunder in my spirit as you approach again. Addressing the Comet. Ivan V. Lalic, *Serbo-Croatian*. HSix, *tr. by* Charles Simic

You tire of it, this. Self-analysis. Michael Dransfield. BMAP

You to do it, now. (LL) Thrift. Cornelius Eady. CMAP; LTA

You told me: "I am not worthy of you." Marguerite Burnat-Provins, *French*. BoWoP, *tr. by* Cassia Berman

You told me, if something is not used it is meaningless, and took my temperature. Feverish Propositions. Rosemarie Waldrop. FTOS *Fr.* The Reproduction of Profiles.

You told me it was / because of me. Lady Izumi, *Japanese*. BoWoP, *tr. by* Willis Barnstone

You told me, Maro, whilst you live. A Hinted Wish. Martial, *Latin*. AWP, *tr. by* Francis Lewis

You told me my grandfather never wept. Ancestral Weight. Alfonsina Storni, *Spanish*. WPOW, *tr. by* Marti Moody

You told me, Sir, your teeth were loose. On a Gentleman's Complaining to a Lady That He Could Not Eat Meat. *Unknown*. ECWP

You told me that I was born under a lucky star. "Ivan Venediktovich Elagin," *Russian*. TCRP, *tr. by* Helen Matveyeff

You told people I would know easily what the murdered. The Shopping-Bag Lady. Linda Gregg. AFr; WWSi

You Too. Edmund Vance Cooke. PWR

You too, Clenorides, homesickness drove. *Unknown, Greek*. GrAn, *tr. by* Tony Harrison

You too dreaming the same. (LL) Housing Shortage. Naomi Replansky. NMM-2

You too if you work hard enough. Ponce de León: A Morning Walk. Al Young. HoPM

You Too Lie down. Dennis Lee. TLR

You Too? Me Too—Why Not? Soda Pop. Robert Hollander. NIP-4

You too must die, my dear. Why do you care? The Killing of Lykaon. Homer. OBCVT, *tr. by* Robert Lowell *Fr.* The Iliad.

You too once were carried in your sleep. Childhood of a Stranger. Claire Bateman. CrSp

You took away all the oceans and all the room. Osip Emilevich Mandelstam, *Russian*. OPOU; Spl, *tr. by* Clarence Brown *and* W. S. Merwin

You took me, hostile, sullen—. Olga Fiodorovna Berggolts, *Russian*. TCRP, *tr. by* Daniel Weissbort

You took your father. The Spanish of Our Out–Loud Dreams. Martín Espada. MoLi

You toss now to the left; you toss now to the right. Crinagoras. HePo, *tr. by* Barbara Hughes Fowler *Fr.* Epigrams.

You tossed a blanket from the bed. T. S. Eliot. *Fr.* Preludes (I–IV). HeIP-4; OBMV; Poetr; TwCP; UnPo; VGW; WeW-3

You travel swiftly. Sun. Jean Kenward. SpW

You turn your back, you turn your back. To Carrey Clavel. Thomas Hardy. CBLP

You understand it? How they returned from Culloden. Culloden and After. Iain Crichton Smith. OxBS

You unseen lightning flash, you darkly radiant light. On the Ineffable Inspiration of the Holy Spirit. Catharina Regina von Greiffenberg, *German*. PBWP; WPoS, *tr. by* Michael Hamburger

You used to say, "June?" 1977: Poem for Mrs. Fannie Lou Hamer. June Jordan. NMM-2

You vanish with early tears. (LL) Tear. Thomas Kinsella. NoP-4

You vilify me, but I rise above grief. Lament after Her Husband Bishr's Murder. Al-Khirniq, *Arabic*. BoWoP, *tr. by* Willis Barnstone

You virgins that did late despair. Piping Peace. James Shirley. NOBE; PoEL-2 *Fr.* The Imposture.

You wait! Robert Frost. *See* Beyond Words.

You wait for a right moment. Sea Without Poets. Branko Miljkovic, *Serbo-Croatian*. HSix, *tr. by* Charles Simic

You wake me, / Part my thighs, and kiss me. Kenneth Rexroth. APSN *Fr.* The Love Poems of Marichiko.

You wake up filled with dread. Up. Margaret Atwood. NoP-4

You walk into the room. Ballad of a Thin Man. "Bob Dylan." CBNP

You walk on. A Door. W. S. Merwin. SPE

You walk on permafrost. Voronezh. "Anna Akhmatova," *Russian*. FaBoPV, *tr. by* Tom Paulin

You walk the streets. Self. Sharon Doubiago. NMM-2

You walked, all of a sudden, though. In Memory of Gerard Dillon. Michael Longley. BiHa; PBCIP

You walked dusty dry roads;. Southern Road. Mwatabu Okantah. SeSe

You, walking past me. Marina Tsvetayeva, *Russian*. AF, *tr. by* Mary Maddock

You wandered in the desert waste, athirst. An Oasis. Agnes Mary Frances Robinson. VWP

You want a soothing life. Traders in Beauty and Delight. Abu Dulama, *Arabic*. ArPe, *tr. by* Omar S. Pound

You want clear spectacles: your eyes are dim. The Accusation of the Inward Man. Edward Taylor. MeMAP

You want coins? Roman? Greek? Nice vase? Head of god, goddess. Ali Ben Shufti. Anthony Thwaite. OxBTC

You want help. you are sorry you are born with ears. (LL) John Coltrane: An Impartial Review. Alfred B. Spellman. PoBA; SeSe

You want the summer lightning, throw the knives. Ingeborg Bachmann, *German*. BoWoP, *tr. by* Daniel Huws

You want to integrate me into your anonymity. Black Narcissus. Gerald William Barrax. PoBA

You want to make some honey? Bee. X. J. Kennedy. OBCA; Spl

You want to tell me how it seemed. Vegetable Wisdom. Mark Halliday. BAP-93

You wanted to compare, and there. Amazon Twins. Olga Broumas. CPO

You waste the attention of your eyes. A Sad State of Freedom. Nazim Hikmet, *Turkish*. NNPT, *tr. by* Taner Baybars

You watched out for him or. Travis, the Kid Was All Heart. Terry Stokes. AmPA

You watched the slender narcissus wilt. The Elegy for Integral Domains. Norman Dubie. NAmP90

You wear, and the star running down his cheek. (LL) Swimming By Night. James Merrill. ColAP; NYBP; VGW

You wear the face. Lady Izumi, *Japanese*. BoWoP, *tr. by* Willis Barnstone

You wear the morning like your dress. Song. Hilaire Belloc. OBEV

You, weeping wide at war, weep with me now. The Coward. Eve Merriam. TrJP

You well[-]compacted groves, whose light and shade. Sonnet Made upon the Groves near Merlou Castle. Edward Herbert. NOSC

You went downstairs. The Hair. May Swenson. CPO; DeD *Fr.* Poet to Tiger. GLP

You went to the verge, you say, and came back safely. Prelude XIV. Conrad Potter Aiken. FaBoMo; TwCP *Fr.* Preludes for Memnon; or, Preludes to Attitude.

You were a girl of satin and gauze. The Wheel Revolves. Kenneth Rexroth. NoAM

You were a kind man and you died in want. (LL) Ford Madox Ford ("The lobbed ball"). Robert Lowell. OxBC; TwCP

You were a moral dandy, sir. The font. To Max Jacob. Rosanna Warren. DiPo

You were a pretty boy once, Archestratus, and. Epigram. Philip of Thessalonica, *Greek*. GrAn, *tr. by* Edith Morgan

You were a sophist. Advice. Gwendolyn B. Bennett. BlSi

You were born; must die; were loved; must love. Sonnet. Stephen Spender. MoBrPo; SoPo

You Were Broken. Giuseppe Ungaretti, *Italian*. STV, *tr. by* John Frederick Nims

You were consistently brave. Eulogy for a Hermit Crab. Pattiann Rogers. WeT

You were dying, fully conscious. Introduction to the Beyond. Blaga Dimitrova, *Bulgarian*. CEEP, *tr. by* Jascha Kessler *and* Aleksandar Shurbanov

You were dying of grief from the moment I saw you. To My Father—2. Diane Di Prima. MoLi

You were my youth, you gave to me. Dedication. N. P. van Wyk Louw, *Afrikaans*. PeSAV, *tr. by* Hugh Finn

You Were Never Miss Brown to Me. Sherley Anne Williams. GT

You were never told, Mother, how old Illya was drunk. The Czar's Last Christmas Letter: A Barn in the Urals. Norman Dubie. NoAM

You were praised, my books. Salutation the Second. Ezra Pound. NOBA; OxBA

You were reading. I was dreaming. Reading, Dreaming, Hiding. Kelly Cherry. FFC

You were separated from me Hori. The Space Invaders Machine. Pita Sharples, *Maori*. PeNZ, *tr. by the author*

You Were Shattered. Giuseppe Ungaretti. ItIP

You were tall and beautiful. First Love. Mary Dorcey. BrRo

You were the ball I was trained to keep. American Innocents, Oberlin, Ohio, 1954. Barry Goldensohn. NAmP90

You were the first to leave. K. H. Astride Ivaska, *Latvian*. CEEP, *tr. by Inara Cedrins*

You were the morning star among the living. Aster. Plato, *Greek*. GrAn, *tr. by Peter Jay*

You were the perfect one. To Mt. St. Helens. John Daniel. PaTW

You were the reason for staying. Notes to my Daughters. Shirley Kaufman. NMM-2

You were to be the centre of our dream. Nozizwe. Raymond Mazisi Kunene, *Zulu*. PeSAV, *tr. by the author*

You were wearing your Edgar Allan Poe printed cotton blouse. Kenneth Koch. AiP; CoAP; MoP; NIP-4; NNaP; NoP-4; SPE

You were writing a long poem, yes. Residue of Song. Marvin Bell. AmPA

You were young--but that was scarcely to your credit. Gerald Louis Gould. OxBTC *Fr.* Monogamy.

You weren't even a. To L. Julianne Perry. PoBA

You who are earth, and cannot rise. To the World: the Perfection of Love. William Habington. BeJo *Fr.* Castara.

You who are free, / rescue the dead. (LL) Rescue the Dead. David Ignatow. VGW; WeT

You who are still and white. Slain. T. W. H. Crosland. OBWP

You who ask where I find the courage. A Return to the Tree of Time. Vesna Parun, *Croatian*. WPOW, *tr. by Vasa D. Mihailovich and Ronald Morgan*

You who can grant, or can refuse, the pow'r. A Sea-Chaplain's Petition to the Lieutenants in the Ward-Room, for the Use of the Quarter-Gallery. "J. T." NOEC

You who come from the old village. Verses. Wang Wei, *Chinese*. TAL, *tr. by Robert Payne*

You who descend river by river. Giraffe. *Unknown, Hottentot.* PeSA

You who desired so much—in vain to ask. To Emily Dickinson. Hart Crane. CMoP; ColAP; NIP-4; NOBA; NoAM; NoP-4; Son; TAP

You Who Dog My Footsteps. Leyb Kvitko, *Yiddish*. TrJP, *tr. by Joseph Leftwich*

You who draw into yourself each depth. The Merciful Shore. Maria Luisa Spaziani, *Italian*. Nelt, *tr. by Beverly Allen*

You who / fail. Femina. Daphne Marlatt. NOBC

You who have forgotten yourself in this moving tomb. Short Revelation Concerning Death and Chaos. René Daumal, *French*. PFTM, *tr. by Pierre Joris*

You who have spoken words in the earth. Reproach to Dead Poets. Archibald MacLeish. NAAL-1

You, who inconstancy so constantly can squander. To the Moon. Paul Fleming, *German*. GePo, *tr. by George C. Schoolfield*

You, who live just for orgiastic feasts. Vladimir Mayakovsky, *Russian*. TCRP, *tr. by Bernard Meares*

You who live secure. Shemà. Primo Levi, *Italian*. AF; HP; NNPT, *tr. by Ruth Feldman and Brian Swann*

You who make your escape from the tumult. Hyena. *Unknown, Hottentot.* PeSA

You who never took. To My Ill-Wishers. Nikolai Ivanovich Glazkov, *Russian*. TCRP, *tr. by Daniel Weissbort*

You Who Occupy Our Land. Manuela Margarido, *Portuguese*. WPOW, *tr. by Allan Francovich*

You Who Sleep. Philippe Soupault, *French*. AF, *tr. by Paulette Schmidt*

You who snore with your sleeping wife so near. Tristan Corbière. OBVE, *tr. by Christopher Pilling* *Fr.* Litany of Sleep.

You who stoop, you who weep. Challenge. David Diop, *French*. NegPo, *tr. by Ellen Conroy Kennedy*

You who visit in turn. Poseidippus, *Greek*. PGA, *tr. by Kenneth Rexroth*

You who walked like a broken old dream. Negro Tramp. David Diop, *French*. NegPo, *tr. by Ellen Conroy Kennedy*

You who want. Hadewijch II, *Flemish*. WPoS, *tr. by Jane Hirshfield*

You who were darkness warmed my flesh. Woman to Child. Judith Wright. MDDM; PBWP; WPE

You who were once my friend. Alcaeus, *Greek*. InMo, *tr. by Sam Hamill*

You who will die, watch over your life; don't set sail. Epitaph for Cleonicus. Alexander of Pleuron, *Greek*. GrAn, *tr. by W. S. Merwin*

You who will find the dark fossils of paisleys. A History of Paisley. Agha Shahid Ali. PUP-20

You who would sorrow even for a token. Reciprocity. Vassar Miller. MT

You whom I could not save / Listen to me. Dedication. Czeslaw Milosz, *Polish*. AF, *tr. by Czeslaw Milosz*

You whom the kings saluted; who refused not. To the Unknown Warrior. G. K. Chesterton. NSI

You whose hands are more innocent than mine. Vesna Parun, *Croatian*. CEEP, *tr. by Peter Kastmiler*

You will ask how I came to be eavesdropping, in the first place. Confession Overheard in a Subway. Kenneth Fearing. LiTM

You will awaken me at dawn. Saga. Andrey Andreievich Voznesensky, *Russian*. TCRP, *tr. by William Jay Smith and Vera Dunham*

You will be able to see me. (LL) This Is a Photograph of Me. Margaret Atwood. NALW; NoAM; NoP-4; Poetr

You Will Be Hearing from Us Shortly. U. A. Fanthorpe. OBCoV

You will be known all over the world; you will be known all over the world, as far as the edge of the world, you great one who safely returned from the spirits. Hā' mats'a Song of the Koskimo. *Unknown. Fr.* Dances and Songs of the Winter Ceremonial. APN-2, *tr. by Franz Boas*

You will be obscured by a cloud of postures. Nadar. Richard Howard. GS

You will carry this suture. Trauma. Brad Leithauser. InPK-6

You will come into an antique town. Where I Live. Wesley McNair. TRP

You Will Die. *Unknown*. AWP, *tr. by H. A. Giles* *Fr.* Shi King.

You will find here a new representation of the universe. Horse Calligram. Guillaume Apollinaire. PFTM

You Will Forget. Chenjerai Hove. HBAPE

You will have smiled, I shall have tossed your hair. (LL) À Quoi Bon Dire. Charlotte Mew. LBC; VWP

You will have the road gate open, the front door ajar. In Memory of My Mother. Patrick Kavanagh. BIrV

You Will Know When You Get There. Allen Curnow. NoP-4; PeNZ

You will learn to speak. Colleen J. McElroy. EC2 *Fr.* Memoirs of American Speech.

You will leave house. Vagabonds. Marie-Madeleine, *German*. CPO, *tr. by Lillian Faderman, Brigitte Eriksson and Frankie Hucklenbroich*

You will need. Truganinny. Wendy Rose. HATNAP

You will not be able to stay home, brother. The Revolution Will Not Be Televised! Gil Scott-Heron. NAAAL

You will not dare to think your own thoughts. The Sentence. Yuly Markovich Daniel, *Russian*. TCRP, *tr. by David Burg and Arthur Boyars*

You will not tame this sea. The Sea and the Man. Anna Swirszczynska, *Polish*. BLT, *tr. by Czeslaw Milosz and Leonard Nathan*

You will remember the kisses, real or imagined. Resurrection. Kenneth Fearing. CMoP; PoE

You will see Coleridge, he who sits obscure. Shelley. EPCY *Fr.* Letter to Maria Gisborne.

You Will See Your Lord a-Coming. *Unknown*. AH

You wished for a love-letter, Doctor. A Love-letter. Mary E. Tucker. CBWP-1

You with the beard as red as Barbarossa's. For My Great-Grandfather: A Message Long Overdue. Maxine W. Kumin. UnSA

You with your back to the wall. (LL) Orion. Adrienne Rich. MoP; NAAL-2; NIP-4; NoAM; NoP-4; Poetr; WPE

You wonder at that Georgian terrace. Lychees. Medbh McGuckian. PBCIP

You wonder what that is, daughter. Meditation. Reiner Kunze, *German*. CEEP, *tr. by Lori Fisher*

You wonder who this is! And, why I name. On the Town's Honest Man. Ben Jonson. NOSC

You won't find them in places where society goes. Dandelions. Will D. Stanton. SoSe-8

You words, come, after me! Ingeborg Bachmann, *Hebrew*. PoSu, *tr. by Mark Anderson*

You worry me whoever you are. Badman of the Guest Professor. Ishmael Reed. BPo; SSLK

You Worthless. *Unknown*. FaBoVe

You would be hurt so night and day, / Yet love me. Sir John Suckling. *See* A Soldier.

You would have scoffed if we had told you yesterday. To a Child in Death. Charlotte Mew. ChIV-2; MoBrPo

You Would Have Understood Me. Paul Verlaine, *French*. BoLoP; MoBrPo; NOBVV, *tr. by Ernest Dowson*

You would have understood me, had you waited. Ernest Christopher Dowson. PeVV

You would hoist an old hat on the tines of a fork. A Bat on the Road. Seamus Heaney. PoE

You would not have me roar, or crow. (LL) After Galen. Oliver St. John Gogarty. FaBoEE; OBMV; PoRA

You would not recognize me. The Tourist from Syracuse. Donald Justice. NoAM; TwCP; VCAP

You would not say to children. The Folk Museum. Medbh McGuckian. CIP-2

You would shrink back / jump up. July 4, 1984: For Buck. June Jordan. NoAM

You would sleep with the moon. Alternatives. Peter Cooley. AmPA

You would think the fury of aerial bombardment. The Fury of Aerial Bombardment. Richard Eberhart. CMoP; ColAP; FYAP; FaBoMo; HeIP-4; HoPM; InPK-6; LiTM; MoP; NIP-4; NoAM; NoP-4; OBWP; PoWW; RB; TAP; TwCP; UnPo; VGW

You wouldn't be so depressed. Suggestion from a Friend. Jane Kenyon. LoL *Fr.* Having It Out With Melancholy. BAP-93

You wouldn't believe all this house has cost me. The Flitting. Medbh McGuckian. PBCIP; PNI

You wouldn't recognize her, now. Lot's Wife. Albert Goldbarth. KSG

You write with ease, to shew your breeding. Clio's Protest. Richard Brinsley Sheridan. FaBoEE

You wrote this from Beirut, two years before. Homage to Faiz Ahmed Faiz. Agha Shahid Ali. OpBo

You X-ari bush. Zebra. *Unknown, Hottentot.* PeSA

You, you caribou. Magic Words for Hunting Caribou. *Unknown, Eskimo.* STP, *tr. by* Jerome Rothenberg *and* Johnny John

You. You running across the field. Orpheus and Eurydice. Jean Valentine. FaBoWP; LCAP-2

You yourself are all the Nine. (LL) The Mutual Congratulations of the Poets Anna Seward and Hayley. Richard Porson. FaBoEE; OBSV

You yourself must be the seventh. (LL) The Seventh. Attila József, *Hungarian.* AF; NNPT, *tr. by* John Bátki

You 'Youth' has fallen from its shelf. Killed in Action. Joseph Leftwich. NSI

You'd almost think it was despair. (LL) The Combat. Edwin Muir. CMoP; FaBoTC; MoBrPo; NOBE

You'd be better off never waking up [again]. (LL) The Victims of the Little Box. Vasco Popa, *Serbo-Croatian.* HSix, *tr. by* Charles Simic

You'd better abandon all idea of feelings altogether. (LL) To Women, as Far as I'm Concerned. D. H. Lawrence. InPS-3; OxBSP; RaBo

You'd have men's hearts up from the dust. Near Perigord. Ezra Pound. FaBoMo; LiTM

You'd know the folly of being comforted. (LL) The Folly Of Being Comforted. W. B. Yeats. GBL; HeIP-4; LoP; NAEL-2; PFE

You'd like to kiss your little boy but he doesn't want to. Lady on Streetcar. Sandro Penna, *Italian.* STV, *tr. by* John Frederick Nims

You'd scarce expect one of my age. The Boy Reciter. David Everett. BLPA

You'd start at seven, and then you'd bend your back. Washing the Coins. Douglas Dunn. FaBoPV

You'd think they'd be with family. Christmas Eve. Sascha Feinstein. SeSe

You'l marvel when I tell ye o. Loudon Hill; or, Drumclog. *Unknown.* ESPB

You'll [*or* You'le] ask, perhaps, wherefore I stay. An Excuse of Absence. Thomas Carew. CaPo; SeCP

You'll be my little seven stone missionary! T. S. Eliot. *Fr.* Two Songs from *Sweeney Agonistes.* UnPo *Fr.* Sweeney Agonistes.

You'll come in. And your voice will be drowned. Football. "Nikolai Karpovich Otrada," *Russian.* TCRP, *tr. by* Daniel Weissbort

You'll ever give / Or get. (LL) For a Far-out Friend. Gary Snyder. BB; NeAP; PoM

You'll find that I'm the sort. Abner Silver's "Pu-leeze! Mr. Hemingway!" Ring Lardner. OBAL

You'll go to the plaza. Camoes and the Debt. Sophia de Mello Breyner Andresen, *Portuguese.* BoWoP, *tr. by* Willis Barnstone *and* Nelson Cerqueira

You'll make tea. Just the Two of Us. Taeko Tomioka, *Japanese.* WPOW, *tr. by* Harry *and* Lynn Guest *and* Kajima Shozo

You'll never be mentally sober. (LL) On Rachmaninoff's Birthday. Frank O'Hara. CAPP-1; PoM

You'll Never Know. Ruby Marion Wray. PWR

You'll never know how far i stand from you. (LL) Measure for Measure. Sipho Sepamla. AF; PeSAV

You'll never know *how* good you are. Auto-erotic. *Unknown.* PeLi

You'll never miss the water till your well runs dry. Joe Turner Blues. William Christopher Handy. CrDW

You'll remember Mercury. Edwin Morgan. *See* The First Men on Mercury.

You'll say the gentleman is somewhat simple. Thomas Middleton. OxBM *Fr.* Women Beware Women.

You'll see me park my car upon. The Red Light District Nurse. John Fuller *and* James Fenton. OBCoV

You'll see sometime—half. Memorandum. William Stafford. NYBP

You'll wait a long, long time for anything much. On Looking Up by Chance at the Constellations. Robert Frost. CMoP; MeMAP

Young Acacia, The. Hayyim Nahman Bialik, *Hebrew.* TrJP, *tr. by* Helena Frank

Young Africans. Gwendolyn Brooks. NoAM

Young Allan. *Unknown.* ESPB

Young and Old. Charles Kingsley. ACTP; EBEV; FaBoBe; FaPoR; ImPo; OxAEP-2; OxBChV; PoLF *Fr.* The Water Babies.

("You love when all was young.") (LL)

Young and old, rejoice. Neidhart von Reuental, *German.* GePo, *tr. by* Frederick Goldin

Young and Radiant, He Is Standing. Allen Eastman Cross. AH

Young and willing to learn (but what?) he was the boy. Razzmatazz. Gilbert Sorrentino. FTOS

Young [*or* Younge] Andrew. *Unknown.* ESPB; OxBB

Young are quick of speech, The. On Teaching the Young. Yvor Winters. NOBA; NoAM

Young attendants wrapped him in a red, The. Inpatient. Dolores Kendrick. FFC

Young Bearwell. *Unknown.* ESPB

Young Beichan. *Unknown.* AmFP; ESPB; EnSB

Young Ben he was a nice young man. Faithless Sally Brown. Thomas Hood. NOBL; OBNV

Young Benjie. *Unknown.* ESPB; OxBB

Young Birch, A. Robert Frost. SAmP

Young black girl stopped by the woods, A. Interpretation of a Poem by Frost. Thylias Moss. PuP-14

Young bride and groom of Australia, A. Limerick. *Unknown.* PeLi

Young bull, The. A Young Chieftain. Auvaiyar, *Tamil.* PLW, *tr. by* A. K. Ramanujan

Young Charlottie or, The Frozen Girl. *Unknown.* AmFP; BLPA

Young cherry trees, The. April. Linda Pastan. Poetsp

Young Chieftain, A. Auvaiyar, *Tamil.* PLW, *tr. by* A. K. Ramanujan

Young Child and His Pregnant Mother, A. Delmore Schwartz. FiLi

Young child of Diodoros's house, A. Diodoros of Sardis, *Greek.* GrAn, *tr. by* W. G. Shepherd

Young Clovis by a happy chance. On a Bashful Shepherd. "Ephelia." PEW

Young Colin Clout, a lad of peerless meed. Tuesday; or, the Ditty. John Gay. NOEC *Fr.* The Shepherd's Week.

Young composer, working that summer at an artist's colony, The. A Story about the Body. Robert Hass. NAmP90; RaBo

Young Cordwainer, The. Robert Graves. MoBS

Young Corydon [*or* Coridon] and Phyllis [*or* Phillis]. On the Happy Corydon and Phyllis. Sir Charles Sedley. BoLoP

Young Corydon (hard Fate) an humble Swain. Virgil. OBCVT, *tr. by* Thomas Creech *Fr.* The Second Eclogue.

Young couple who lived at "The Laurels," A. Limerick. W. F. N. Watson. PeLi

Young Dead Woman, A. José-Maria de Heredia, *Spanish.* FLP; LoP, *tr. by* Alistair Elliot

Young Dove, The. Moses ibn Ezra, *Hebrew.* TrJP, *tr. by* Solomon Solis-Cohen

Young Earl of Essex's Victory over the Emperor of Germany, The. *Unknown.* ESPB

Young Edward came to Emily his gold all for to show. Edwin in the Lowlands Low. *Unknown.* AmFP

Young Elvis. Cornelius Eady. CMAP

Young Endymion sleeps Endymion's sleep, The. Keats. Henry Wadsworth Longfellow. Son; TAP

Young engine-driver called Hunt, A. Limerick. Victor Gray. NOBL

Young eyes leave the volume and stray out, The. History Lesson. Mark Van Doren. NYBP

Young Fenians, The. Padraic Fallon. BIrV

Young fingers. Tanka. Akiko Yosano, *Japanese.* MJT, *tr. by* Ueda, Makoto

Young fisherboys sing like the endless sea. That's Our Lot. Moyshe-Leyb Halpern, *Yiddish.* CEEP, *tr. by* Kathryn Hellerstein

Young flirt of Ceylon, A. Ogden Nash. PeLi

Young flowers were whispering in melody. Song. Edgar Allan Poe. NOBA *Fr.* Al Aaraaf. APN-1

Young Gal's Blues. Langston Hughes. NAAL-2

Young, gifted, and black. To be Young, Gifted, and Black. Weldon J. Irvine, Jr. ISC

Young Girl. Ricarda Huch, *German.* WPOW, *tr. by* Janine Canan *and* Deirdre Lashgari

Young Girl and the Beach, The. Sophia de Mello Breyner Andresen, *Portuguese.* WPOW, *tr. by* Alexis Levitin

Young girl dancing lifts her face, The. The Dancer. Walter James Turner. NOBAu; OBMV

Young girl in remote Samarkand, A. Limerick. George Seferis, *Greek.* CBNP, *tr. by* Peter Levi

Young Girl in the Choir, The. *Unknown.* FuFo

Young girl moves like an ear of grain, A. The Young Girl and the Beach. Sophia de Mello Breyner Andresen, *Portuguese.* WPOW, *tr. by* Alexis Levitin

Young Girl of Asturias, The. *Unknown.* FuFo

Young girl of English nativity, A. Limerick. *Unknown.* PeLi

Young girl, only eleven, A. Mother-in-Law Is Cruel. Cheng Hsieh, *Chinese.* CoBLCP, *tr. by* Jonathan Chaves

Young Girl Peeling Apples. Mary Jo Salter. FFC

Young girl stood beside me, The. The Orange Tree. John Shaw Neilson. CBAP

Young girl who was no good at tennis, A. Limerick. *Unknown.* PeLi

Young Girl with a Pitcher Full of Water, A. David Wagoner. NoAM

Young Girls. Patricia K. Page. SAGP

Young Girls. Raymond Souster. HeIP-4

Young Glass-Stainer, The. Thomas Hardy. CTC

Young Harper. Valerie Gillies. FaBoTC

Young, having risen early, had gone, The. The Guardians. Geoffrey Hill. NoP-4

Young Hermes, who placed you at the starter's mark? Philip of Thessalonica, *Greek.* GrAn, *tr. by* Edwin Morgan

Young Heroes. Gwendolyn Brooks. BPo; NAAAL

Young hound howls, A. Unemployment. William Mills. HoPM

Young Housewife, The. William Carlos Williams. ColAP; HeIP-4; NAAL-2; TAP

Young Hunting. *Unknown.* ESPB; OxBB; OxBoLi

Young in Fall I said: the birds. Lorine Niedecker. VGW

Young Irish servant in Drogheda, A. Limerick. *Unknown.* PeLi

Young Japanese son was in love with a servant boy, The. Dream Data. Robert Duncan. NeAP

Young Johnny sails the sea, young Johnny sails the shore. The Green Bed. *Unknown.* AmFP

Young Johnny the miller he courted of late. The Gray Mare. *Unknown.* AmFP

Young Johnstone, *vers.* A. *Unknown.* ESPB

Young Johnstone ("Young Johnstone and the young Colnel"), *vers.* B. *Unknown.* ESPB; OxBB

Young Joseph's new coat was real nice. Limerick. Cyril Mountjoy. PeLi

Young Juan wandered by the glassy brooks. Byron. EPCY; OBCoV *Fr.* Canto the First. NAEL-2; OAEL-2; PoE *Fr.* Don Juan.

("Like Coleridge into a metaphysician.") (LL) EPCY

Young Keats, a flowering laurel on your brow. (LL) To Keats. Leigh Hunt. Ro

Young knight, what ever that dost armes professe. Edmund Spenser. FHYEP *Fr.* Wood Of Error. AEP

Young Knowledge. "Robin Hyde." PeNZ

Young lady may increase her stock, A. Cillactor, *Greek.* GrAn, *tr. by* William Moebius

Young Lady of Niger, The. *Unknown.* FPC

Young Lady of Twickenham, The. *Unknown.* FuFo

Young lady, whose life-style the malicious, A. Limerick. Gavin Ewart. PeLi

Young Lass's Soliloquy, A. Rebekah Carmichael. ECWP

Young Laundryman, The. William Carlos Williams. SAmP

YOUNG LIONEL. To what may young men best compare themselves? From Mostellaria. Plautus Titus Maccius. OBCVT, *tr. by* Thomas Heywood *Fr.* The English Traveller.

Young Lochinvar. Sir Walter Scott. *See* Lochinvar.

Young lords o' the north country, The. Lady Maisry. *Unknown.* ESPB; OxBB

Young Love. Andrew Marvell. OxAEP-1

Young Love lies sleeping. Dream-Love. Christina Rossetti. CH; HAP; PoEL-5

Young maidens. Tanka. Ishikawa Takuboku, *Japanese.* MJT, *tr. by* Ueda, Makoto

Young man, alone, on the high bridge over the Tagus, A. The High Bridge above the Tagus River at Toledo. William Carlos Williams. CTC

Young man and an aged man of late, A. On a Young Man and an Old Man. Edward May. OxBSP

Young man and I face each other, The. On The Subway. Sharon Olds. LTA

Young man and maid, pray lend attention. The Silver Dagger. *Unknown.* AmFP

Young Man and the Young Nun, The. Albert D. Mackie. OxBS

Young man by a girl was desired, A. Limerick. *Unknown.* PeLi

Young man came to me with a message from his brother, A. Leaves of Grass (1855). Walt Whitman. APN-1

Young man, hardly more, The. Gettysburg, July 1, 1863. Jane Kenyon. CBCWP

Young man / I love you and life is wonderful, The. The Spurt of Blood. Antonin Artaud, *French.* PFTM, *tr. by* Helen Weaver

Young man is a pitiful wretch, A. A Song of Parable. *Unknown, Chinese.* SuSp, *tr. by* Jan W. Walls

Young man made for the corner, A. Three Riddles from *The Exeter Book.* Cynewulf. PeLV, *tr. by* Kevin Crossley-Holland *Fr.* Riddles (Exeter Book).

Young Man Naughty's Adventure. Charlotte Brontë. VWP

Young man of alien beauty. Muireadhach Albanach O'Dalaigh. NOIV

Young Man of Devizes, The. *Unknown.* FuFo

Young man once went off to war, A. APO 96225. Larry Rottman. CDa

Young Man Thinks of Sons, The. Ronald Allison Kells Mason. PeNZ

Young Man Who Couldn't See Why, The. *Unknown.* FuFo

Young man who lived at Holme Hale, A. Limerick. Ida Thurtle. PeLi

Young Man Who Loved the Girl Who Took Care of Her Aged Father, The. Greg Kuzma. AmPA

Young man with a yellow hat. Li Ho, *Chinese.* SuSp, *tr. by* Michael Fish

Young man with passions quite gingery, A. Limerick. *Unknown.* PeLi

Young Man's Epigram on Existence, A. Thomas Hardy. MoP

Young Man's Song, A. William Bell. FaBoTw

Young Mary, loitering once her garden way. Mary and Gabriel. Rupert Brooke. ChIV-2

Young Master's Account of a Puppet Show. John Marchant. OxBChV

Young May Moon, The. Thomas Moore. OBEV; PeLV

Young men! Winifred Howard. CTV

Young men dancing, and the old. Youthful Age. Anacreon, *Greek.* AWP, *tr. by* Thomas Stanley

Young men of the world, The. Lament. Francis Stewart [*or* "Frank"] Flint. PeFWW

Young men who frequent picture palaces. Limerick. *Unknown.* PeLV

Young moon, take my leave of you yonder. Re-birth. *Unknown, Bushman.* PeSA, *tr. by* W. H. I. Bleek *and* Jack Cope

Young mouth laughs at a gift, A. Her Words. Theodore Roethke. LoP

Young Mrs. Snooks was sick of sex. Nursery Rhyme. Kenneth Burke. OBAL

Young niggers / die old. Dedication to the Final Confrontation. Lloyd M. Corbin, Jr. PoBA

Young Night Thought. Robert Louis Stevenson. OTCP; PWR

Young Noble at Night's End; a Song. Li Ho, *Chinese.* SuSp, *tr. by* Maureen Robertson

Young Oedipus learned from the Sphinx. Limerick. Basil Ransome-Davies. PeLi

Young Ones, The. Elizabeth Jennings. OxBTC

Young or old we die. Rudaki, *Persian.* ArPe, *tr. by* Omar S. Pound

Young Peggy. *Unknown.* ESPB

Young people all, attention give. Liverpool. *Unknown.* AmFP

Young people, all attention give. Mission. *Unknown.* AmFP

Young People Who Delight in Sin. *Unknown.* AmFP

Young Pilgrim Finds Refuge with the Goatherds, The. Luis de Góngora y Argote. OBVE, *tr. by* Edward Meryon Wilson *Fr.* The First Solitude.

Young Poet. Myron O'Higgins. PoBA

Young poet comes to me, A. Blind Solo. Michael S. Weaver. UnSA

Young Prince and the Young Princess, The. John Ashbery. CoAmPo

Young Prince of Tyre. "Ern Malley." BMAP

Young Reynard. George Meredith. HoPM

Young Robin of the plain, erst blithest blade. Snaith Marsh; a Yorkshire Pastoral. "Ophelia." ECWP

Young Roger came tapping at Dolly's window. Roger and Dolly. Henry Carey. CBNP; NOEC; OxNR; ReMoGo

Young Ronald. *Unknown.* ESPB

Young schizophrenic named Struther, A. Limerick. *Unknown.* OBCoV; PeLi

Young Shepherd Bathing His Feet. Peter Clarke. PBA

Young Soul. Imamu Amiri Baraka. BPo

Young Stock. Vita Sackville-West. OxBTC

Young swallows trill their new tune. *Unknown.* SuSp, *tr. by* Michael E. Workman *Fr.* Spring. SuSp *Fr.* Tzu-yeh Songs of the Four Seasons.

Young Sycamore. William Carlos Williams. TAP

Young then, / we were bored already. Epitaph. Eleanor Wilner. ChIV-1

Young things who frequent picture-palaces, The. Limerick. Philip Heseltine. NOBL; OBCoV; PeLi

Young Tommy would not go to bed. Tommy. *Unknown.* FuFo

Young Training. Lawrence McGaugh. PoBA

Young Traveller Is Presented to the Goddess Dulness, A. Alexander Pope. NOEC *Fr.* Yet, yet a moment, one dim ray of light. NAEL-1; OAEL-1; PoEL-3 *Fr.* The Dunciad.

Young Vampire, The. Nina Cassian, *Romanian.* CEEP, *tr. by* Marguerite Dorian and Elliott Urdang

Young Warrior, A. Ponmutiyar, *Tamil.* PLW, *tr. by* A. K. Ramanujan

Young Waters he did dee. (LL) Young Waters. *Unknown.* ESPB; OxBB

Young white ranchers with chew drippings, The. Rhetoric Leads to Cliché. Adrian C. Louis. NAmP90

Young Wife, A. D. H. Lawrence. MoBrPo; PBMP

Young Wife, The. Derek Walcott. DiPo

Young Wife's Lament. Brigit Pegeen Kelly. NAmP90

Young will not wear it, The. Elegy. Kutavayir Kirattanar, *Tamil*. PLW, *tr. by* A. K. Ramanujan

Young Willie stands in his stable door. Clyde's Waters. *Unknown*. OxBB

Young Woman from Aenos, The. *Unknown*. OBAL

Young Woman of Beare, The. Austin Clarke. MoP; NoAM

Young Woman Who Becomes a Bear set fire in the mountains. First Song of the Exploding Stick. *Unknown*. APN-2, *tr. by* Washington Matthews *Fr.* The Mountain Chant.

Young Woman's Neo-Aramaic Jewish Persian Blues. Jerome Rothenberg, *after Persian folk poem*. BoWoP

Young women are obsessed with beauty, The. The Clothes Pit. Douglas Dunn. OxBTC

Young women have no orifice that grips. Heterosexual Poem. Strato, *Greek*. GrAn, *tr. by* Teddy Hogge

Young women, they [*or* they'll] run like hares on the mountain. Hares on the Mountain. *Unknown*. PeLV

Young Workman, The. Mary Dillingham Frear. TrCP

Younger, / I felt the dead. Roots. Seamus Deane. PNI

Younger Poet, A. Peter Schjeldahl. PoA

Youngest Children of an Angel, The. Anna Swir, *Polish*. IFJA, *tr. by* Czeslaw Milosz *and* Leonard Nathan

Youngest Daughter, The. Cathy Song. NoAM

Youngster, A. Tanka. Sasaki Yukitsuna, *Japanese*. MJT, *tr. by* Makoto Ueda

Your absence has gone through me. Separation. W. S. Merwin. HAP; NoP-4; SAGP

Your alms are my salary. Torture Chamber. Enrique Lihn, *Spanish*. VCWP, *tr. by* Mary Crow

Your ankle wrapped in iron, yourself encased. Convict. Edward Vincent Swart. PcSAV

Your arms are beautiful again. What her Girl Friend Said. Peyanar. PLW *Fr.* Nine on Happy Reunion. PLW, *tr. by* A. K. Ramanujan

Your arms will clasp the gathered grain. The Island. Edwin Muir. OAEL-2

Your art has brought you great respect. Sent to the Painter, Lu Hsiao-feng. Li K'ai-hsien, *Chinese*. CoBLCP, *tr. by* Jonathan Chaves

Your ashen hair Shulamith [*or* Shulamite]. (LL) A Death Fugue. Paul Celan, *German*. CLPP, *tr. by* Jerome Rothenberg; HP; VCWP, *tr. by* Michael Hamburger

Your ashes will not stir, even on this high ground. In Carrowdore Churchyard. Derek Mahon. CIP-2; NoP-4; PBCIP; PNI

Your attention, ladies and gentlemen, your attention for one moment. The Pilgrim. Nicanor Parra, *Spanish*. VCWP, *tr. by* W. S. Merwin

Your Attention Please. Peter Porter. OBWP; OxBTC

Your average tourist: Fifty. 2.3. Casual Wear. James Merrill. NIP-4 *Fr.* Topics.

Your baby grows a tooth, then two. A Little Tooth. Thomas Lux. MoLi

Your baggy lyrics. To a Political Poet. Heinrich Heine, *German*. FaBoPV, *tr. by* Tom Paulin

Your bards are wearing lotuses. Nettimaiyar, *Tamil*. PLW, *tr. by* A. K. Ramanujan

Your Beauty, ripe and calm, and fresh. Lover and Philosopher. Sir William Davenant. GEA; NOBE; OBEV

Your bed's got two wrong sides. Your life's all grouse. Long Distance. Tony Harrison. NAEL-2

Your blond hair and autumn sweater. Janna. King D. Kuka. VoR

Your blood does not flow, not even a little. A Poem for Diane Wakoski. Ray A. Young Bear. CDW

Your body derns. Scunner. "Hugh MacDiarmid." FaBoTC; FaBoTw

Your body gleams like copper on the veld. The Fallen Zulu Commander. C. M. Van den Heever, *Afrikaans*. PeSA, *tr. by* Uys Krige *and* Jack Cope

Your body has moved to unstaunchable distance. N. Hugh Seidman. PoA

Your Body Is Stars. Stephen Spender. CBLP; FaBoTw

Your bookcases are crammed with manuscripts. Martial, *Latin*. OBCVT, *tr. by* Bovie, Smith Palmer

Your bosom's sweet treasures thus ever disclose! To Miss Kitty Phillips. Edward Lovibond. ECEV

Your bottoms are not purple. Horror Comic. Robert Conquest. OxBTC

Your breasts of shining black satin. The Soul of the Black Land. Guy Tirolien, *French*. NegPo, *tr. by* Ellen Conroy Kennedy

Your bum is a gorgeous basket brimming with fruits and meat. (LL) The Peasant Declares His Love. Emile Roumer, *French*. NegPo; TTY, *tr. by* John Peale Bishop

Your cheeks flat on the sand. Venus Khoury-Gata, *French*. BoWoP, *tr. by* Willis Barnstone

Your children are not your children. On Children. Kahlil Gibran. OxBM; PoToHe *Fr.* The Prophet.

Your Church and Mine. Phillips H. Lord. BLPA

Your clear eye is the one absolutely beautiful thing. Child. Sylvia Plath. HCAP; MDDM; PBWP

Your closed eyes bulge like mushrooms. Letter to Kafka. Maura Stanton. AmPA

Your clothes of snow and satin and pure blood. The Bed. Karl Shapiro. NYBP

Your comedy I've read, my friend. To a Living Author. *Unknown*. NBLV

Your correspondent must be kidding when he says. Americana IX. *Unknown*. InPS-3

YOUR coulter cuts the soil that erst was sown. A Poor Ploughman to a Gentleman for Whom He Had Taken a Little Pains. George Turberville. NoSic

Your dandelions dotting half. Grass Widows. Robert B. Shaw. CRP

Your death has come to me over hundreds of miles away. This Poem Is Dedicated to Brother Andries Raditsela. Nise Malange. PeSAV

Your death in your own car. Extended Sonnet on the Death of Isaac Danziger. Meir Wieseltier, *Hebrew*. IP, *tr. by* Warren Bargad *and* Stanley F. Chyet

Your disappointment gnaws holes. Land Donation. Thomas Erwin, *German*. CEEP, *tr. by* A. Leslie Willson

Your doctor, Lord. For Dr. and Mrs. Dresser. Margaret Avison. MoCV

Your dog, tranquil and innocent, dozes through. Adrienne Rich. *Fr.* Twenty-one Love Poems. GLP

Your door is shut against my tightened face. The White House. Claude McKay. AmPP; ISC; NAAAL; NIP-4; PoBA

Your dusky shadow at the window lingers. Morning and Evening. Antoni Slonimski, *Polish*. TrJP, *tr. by* Watson Kirkconnell

Your dying was a difficult enterprise. Lament. Thom Gunn. GLP

Your earth colored cheeks. Night Traveller. Ion Cristofor, *Romanian*. CEEP, *tr. by* Brenda Walker *and* Michaela Celea-Leach

Your *Ellen*. Frank Bidart. *See* Ellen West.

Your enemy is not the kind who wears. A Poet's Counsel. Kovur Kilar, *Tamil*. PLW, *tr. by* A. K. Ramanujan

Your European son is gone, a trench. Near Hermes. Drew Gardner. PT

Your eyen two will slay me suddenly. Merciless Beauty. Chaucer. BoLoP; EnVB; NAEL-1; SCGP *Fr.* Merciles[s] Beaute [*or* Beautée *or* Beauty]. CTC; EBEV; EnLoPo; HAP

Your Eyes. Angelina Weld Grimké. CPO

Your eyes are just. Four-Word Lines. May Swenson. GLP; WPE

Your eyes are mirth. Tom Weatherly. NBV

Your eyes are open. Carious Exposure. Gladys Cardiff. CDW

Your eyes are tonight so unusually thoughtful and sad. The Giraffe. Nikolai Stepanovich Gumilyov, *Russian*. TCRP, *tr. by* Yakov Hornstein

Your Eyes Have Their Silence. Gerald William Barrax. PoBA

Your eyes, O my beloved. Nelly Sachs, *German*. WPoS, *tr. by* Ruth and Matthew Mead

Your eyes were ever brown, the colour. On Not Being Your Lover. Medbh McGuckian. PBCIP; PNI

Your face. Mother-thought. Jaihiun Kim, *Korean*. CKP, *tr. by* Jaihiun Kim

Your face blazing above me like a sun-deity. Love, Death and the Changing of the Seasons. Marilyn Hacker.

Your face broods from my table, Suicide. John Berryman. CAPP-1; TAP *Fr.* Dream Songs.

Your face did not rot. The Lost Pilot. James Tate. CoAP; ColAP; NoAM; OBWP; TwCP; UnPo; WeT

Your face is all of silver like a halberd. Chagall's Cornflowers. Andrey Andreievich Voznesensky, *Russian*. TCRP, *tr. by* Vera Dunham *and* H. W. Tjalsma

Your face is the face of all the others. The Face of Love. Ingrid Jonker, *Afrikaans*. PeSA, *tr. by* Jack Cope

Your face scrapes my sleep tonight. Letter to be Disguised as a Gas Bill. Marge Piercy. WPE

Your face, / so pale now it is blue. Poem. David St. John. AmPA

Your face, the beauty of a time long past evokes the perfumed robes in faded hues. Léopold Sédar Senghor. NegPo, *tr. by* Ellen Conroy Kennedy *Fr.* Songs for Signare.

Your face was hidden in the leaves. A Wreath. Yannis Ritsos, *Greek*. GrIP, *tr. by* Edmund Keeley

Your faith is in what you hold. Chicago. Lola Ridge. PoA

Your father sits inside. What Hell Is. Heather McHugh. CrSp; WeT

'Your father's gone,' my bald headmaster said. The Lesson. Edward Lucie-Smith. APAD; IMW; OxBTC; TwCP

Your fine promises. Mototoshi, *Japanese*. OHPJ, *tr. by* Kenneth Rexroth

Your fingers touch me like a bird's wing. The Bird of Endless Time. James Laughlin. WeW-3

Your fires burnt my forests. The Womb. Apirana Taylor. PeNZ

Your flatteries are boring. Bassus, *Greek*. PGA, *tr.* by Kenneth Rexroth

Your foot's on my gown. After. May Probyn. VWP

Your friendship oft has made my heart to ache [*or* ake]. To H[ayley]. William Blake. FaBoEE

Your garden hut stands by the green waters. Yang Chi. *Fr.* Living in Master Fang's Garden. CoBLCP, *tr.* by Jonathan Chaves

Your ghost will walk, you lover of trees. De Gustibus. Robert Browning. FHYEP; InPS-3; SCGP

Your glories, / Matthias Bernard Braun. Kuks. Hanns Cibulka, *German*. CEEP, *tr.* by Ewald Osers

Your governor, long ago, lived in a place like this. (LL) Tune: Sand of Silk-washing Stream ("Soft grasses, a plain of sedge fresh with passing rain"). Su Tung-p'o. CoBCP, *tr.* by Burton Watson; CoBCP

Your grace, and falter on the stony path! (LL) Last Days of Alice. Allen Tate. FuPo; NAAL-2; NOBA; OxBA; UnPo

Your great mistake is to disregard the satire. The Mute Phenomena. Gérard de Nerval, *French*. NNPT, *tr.* by Derek Mahon

Your hair has turned white. Hitomaro, *Japanese*. OHPJ, *tr.* by Kenneth Rexroth

Your hair lost in the forest. Last Dawn. Octavio Paz, *Spanish*. EP, *tr.* by Eliot Weinberger

Your Hand Full of Hours. Paul Celan, *German*. OBVE, *tr.* by Michael Hamburger

Your hand in mine, we walk out. A Sword in a Cloud of Light. Kenneth Rexroth. MoLi

Your hand is heavy, Night, upon my brow. Night. Wole Soyinka. PBMAP *Fr.* Idanre and Other Poems (1967).

Your handkerchief should be blue. Love Song. *Unknown, Turkish*. BoWoP, *tr.* by Reza Baraheni *and* Zahra-Soltan Shokoohtaezeh

Your Hands. Gevorg Emin, *Armenian*. IFJA, *tr.* by Diana Der Hovanessian

Your Hands. Angelina Weld Grimké. PoBA

Your hands cracked and calloused in summer, bled. Sonnets for Stan Gage (1945–1992). Sascha Feinstein. SeSe

Your hands lie open in the long fresh grass,—. Silent Noon. D. G. Rossetti. EnVR; GLoP; GSo; GaP; HAP; NAEL-2; NoP-4; OBNC; PoEL-5 *Fr.* The House of Life.

Your hands made a tent o'er mine eyes. Whimper of Awakening Passion. Ebenezer Jones. NOBVV

Your hands, my dear, adorable. The Chilterns. Rupert Brooke. MoBrPo

Your health, Master Willow. Contrive me a bat. Tree Party. Louis MacNeice. OxBTC

Your heart. Tanka. Mori Ōgai, *Japanese*. MJT, *tr.* by Makoto Ueda

Your heart may hap to feel the pain. (LL) Ode 3. "Of late, what time the Bear turned round." Anacreon, *Greek*. NoSic

Your heart trembles in the shadows, like a face. When the Tom-Tom Beats. Jacques Roumain, *French*. NegPo, *tr.* by Langston Hughes

Your heart's a stall displaying wares. Two Hearts. Nguyễn Bính, *Vietnamese*. AVP, *tr.* by Huỳnh Sanh Thông

Your hidden loneliness, Lord. Psalm. Lucian Blaga, *Romanian*. PFTM, *tr.* by Andrei Codrescu

Your home is deep in the white clouds. The Mountain Retreat of a Recluse. Chang Yü, *Chinese*. CoBLCP, *tr.* by Jonathan Chaves

Your Honor, when my mother stood. To Judge Faolain, Dead Long Enough: A Summons. Linda McCarriston. LoL

Your house is near the southern tip of the lake. Hermit Feng's Residence on the Lake. Hsü Pen, *Chinese*. CoBLCP, *tr.* by Jonathan Chaves

Your houseplant is a delicate thing. Why So Many of Them Die. Susan Wallbank. BrRo

Your husband gave you a Ring. Lady T-rc----l's Ring. *Unknown*. NOBRP

Your husband will be with us at the treat. Ovid. *See* I.4.

"Your husband's lying here in the next bed." They Lay Dying Side by Side. Anna Swirszczynska, *Polish*. PoSu, *tr.* by Magnus J. Krynski *and* Robert A. Maguire

Your image lit in me. (LL) Epigram: "At 12 o'clock in the afternoon." Meleager, *Greek*. EP; OBCVT, *tr.* by Peter Whigham

Your infancy now a wall of memory. The Change. Ellis Ayitey Komey. PBMAP

Your innocence snuffed out. Candle. Jacob Isaac Segal, *Yiddish*. CEEP, *tr.* by Seymour Mayne

Your kind of night, David, your kind of night. Night Thoughts. Henri Coulette. FYAP

Your kindness is no kindness now. Kindness. Catherine Davis. NYBP

Your kink, Heraclea, is sucking off. Argentarius, *Greek*. GrAn, *tr.* by Fleur Adcock

Your Last Drive. Thomas Hardy. OBNC

Your laughter is light, your caress deep. Undine. René Vivien. CPO

Your laughter is like a burst pomegranate. When You Laugh. Ingrid Jonker, *Afrikaans*. WPOW, *tr.* by Elizabeth Jones

Your learn'd identities untie. An Epithalamion for Lawyers. John Donne, *English*. ITG, *tr.* by Robert Hass

Your leaves bound up compact and fair. To an Author. Philip Freneau. AmPP; ColAP; NOBA; OxBA

Your legs would be pretty, if you had legs. Portrait of a Nun. Bobi Jones, *Welsh*. OBWVE, *tr.* by Joseph P. Clancy

Your letter came.—Glutted the earth & cold. A Winter-Piece to a Friend Away. John Berryman. NOBA

Your letter came with our yesterdays tied to it. A Small Love Song. Tong-gyu Hwang, *Korean*. CKP, *tr.* by Jaihiun Kim

Your letter crossed the ocean, bringing thoughts. A Woman Writes to Her Daughter Who's Studying Overseas. Trinh Tiên, *Vietnamese*. AVP, *tr.* by Huỳnh Sanh Thông

Your life is a baby not yet born. Maria Luisa Spaziani, *Italian*. NeIt, *tr.* by Beverly Allen

Your life shall never lack a friend. (LL) Seeds of Kindness. *Unknown*. BLPA; PWR; PoToHe

Your lips were so laughing. Langston Blues. Dudley Randall. SeSe

Your little dog that barked as I came by. To His Wife, for Striking Her Dog. Sir John Harington. OxBSP

Your little hands. Samuel Hoffenstein. NBLV; OBCoV; TrJP *Fr.* Love-songs, at Once Tender and Informative.

Your little house stands in a bamboo grove. Sent in Parting to Yen Kung-su. Shen Chou, *Chinese*. CoBLCP, *tr.* by Jonathan Chaves

Your little mind! (LL) Your little hands. Samuel Hoffenstein. OBCoV

Your looks so often cast. Sir Thomas Wyatt. SiPS

Your Love fond fugitive to gain. (LL) Song: "Nothing ades to Loves fond fire." Elizabeth Wilmot, Countess of Rochester. KTR; LW

Your love is dead, lady, your love is dead. Madrigal. Ronald Stuart Thomas. BoLoP; EnLoPo

Your love lacks joy, your letter says. The Rain That Fell upon the Height. Coventry Patmore. GBL *Fr.* The Victories of Love.

Your love turned my body into water. Nur, Empress Jahan, *Persian*. BoWoP, *tr.* by Willis Barnstone

Your love's great realm, my separation measures. (LL) Written in Exile. Kathleen Jessie Raine. TrCP; WPE

Your loving Cousin. (LL) The Epistle of Deborah Dough. Mary Leapor. ECWP

Your lynx-eyes, Asia. "Anna Akhmatova," *Russian*. BoWoP, *tr.* by Stanley Kunitz *and* Max Hayward

Your man, says the Man, *will walk into the bar like this*—here his. Bloody Hand. Ciaran Carson. PBCIP

Your marvellous songs. (LL) For Thomas Moore. James Simmons. BiHa; PBCIP

Your master died from drinking too much. The Taoist Huang Has Died of Alcoholism. Shen Chou, *Chinese*. CoBLCP, *tr.* by Jonathan Chaves

Your milk was already poisoned. Childhood. Edith Bruck, *Italian*. AF, *tr.* by Ruth Feldman

Your mind and you are our Sargasso Sea. Portrait d'une Femme. Ezra Pound. CMoP; InPS-3; MeMAP; MoAmPo; MoP; NAAL-2; NOBA; NoAM; NoP-4; PFE; Poetr; TAP; TwCP

Your mind is light, soon lost for new love. (LL) The Unfaithful Shepherdess. *Unknown*. GTBS-P; NOBE; OBEV

Your mind lies open like the map of rivers. Five Birds Rise. William Hayward. NYBP

Your Miscellanies do appear. Thomas Spratt. EPCY

Your Mission. Ellen M. Huntington Gates. BLPA

Your mistress [*or* mistris], that you follow whores, still taxeth you. A Self[e] Accuser. Donne. FaBoEE; PeLV

Your morning peace still drums. Clinton. Sterling Plumpp. BkSV

Your Mother. Sam Cornish. MBE

Your mother's often gone. Kay Keeshan Hamod. MDDM *Fr.* Transitions.

Your Mouth Hit Saith. Charles D'Orleans. EnVB

Your mouth is a pomegranate. Eve to Lilith. Michelene Wandor. NBrP

"Your name is Rumplestiltskin!" cried. Rumpelstiltskin. Glyn Maxwell. OBCoV

Your name is the Wheel of Progress—a pleasant name indeed. To the Wheel of Progress. Mrs. Henry Linden. CBWP-4

Your Neighbor. H. Howard Biggar. PoToHe

Your neighbor, sir, whose roses you admire. My Neighbor's Reply. *Unknown*. PoToHe

Your nerves the nerves of a midwife / learning her trade. (LL) The Mirror in Which Two Are Seen as One. Adrienne Rich. NAAL-2; NNaP

Your nurse could only speak Italian. Sailing Home from Rapallo. Robert Lowell. FiLi; HCAP; PoPoPo; TAP

Your offspring avert their faces from you. (LL) Shemà. Primo Levi, *Italian*. AF; HP; NNPT, *tr.* by Ruth Feldman *and* Brian Swann

Your own greyhounds bark at your side. A Midnight Diner by Edward Hopper. David Ray. WeT

Your own hands are lying. (LL) Taking Off My Clothes. Carolyn Forché. AmPA; NoAM

Your Own Place. Edward Lucie-Smith. PBCV

Your parents don't like me. Farewell, Sweet Mary. *Unknown.* AmFP

Your pinks, your tulips live an hour. To the Gardener at Nuneham. Horace Walpole. FaBoEE

Your pleasure, Priapus, is the island coast. Maccius, *Greek.* GrAn, *tr. by* Peter Jay

Your Poem. Semyon Isaakovich Kirsanov, *Russian.*
"... Back then I cut off a lock." TCRP, *tr. by* Lubov Yakovleva

Your Poems at Daybreak, the Destruction of Knossos by Afternoon. Steve Ellis. PT

Your poore estates, alone. (LL) To Meadows [*or* Meddowes]. Robert Herrick. AWP; CH; CaPo; NOBE; NOSC; OBEV; PBRV; PoEL-3; SeCP

Your praises to the eternal King. (LL) For Saturday. Christopher Smart. FaBoCh; NOEC; NOxBChV; OxBChV

Your Presence. David Diop, *French.* PBA, *tr. by* Ulli Beier; PBMAP

Your punishment is just, you must confess. To a Gentleman Who Disordered a Lady's Handerchief, and Immediately Cut His Thumb. Elizabeth Teft. ECWP

Your residence on earth, a floating, nothing but a dream. Lamenting the Taoist Wei Kung-yüan. Chao Meng-fu, *Chinese.* CoBLCP, *tr. by* Jonathan Chaves

Your *rose* is *dead.* "Michael Field." VWP

Your sad tires in a mile-a. (LL) Song: "Jog on, jog on, the footpath way." Shakespeare. BoTP; FaBoCh; NoSic; OxBSP

Your sands are furrowed. What Her Girl Friend Said to Him. Ammuvanar, *Tamil.* PLW, *tr. by* A. K. Ramanujan

Your scent is in the room. Jasmine. Claude McKay. GT

Your Shadow. Mark Strand. *Fr.* Elegy for My Father. HCAP; LCAP-2

Your shining—where?—rays my wide room with gold. John Berryman. EP *Fr.* Sonnets to Chris.

Your shrunken head was bent. The Murder Trial. Perseus Adams. PeSA

Your silence is leaning toward judgement. Unanswered Letter. Tess Gallagher. NIP-4

Your silence today is a pond where drowned things live. Adrienne Rich. *Fr.* Twenty-one Love Poems. GLP

Your sister 's play'd you scorn. (LL) The Gay Goshawk [*or* Goss-Hawk]. Anna Gordon Brown. ESPB; OxBB; WPE

Your sky against my starfish I know how big. Kathleen Fraser. DeD

Your sleep is a closed almond. Iwan Goll, *German.* AF, *tr. by* Paul Zweig

Your sleep is so profound. Aurora. Timothy Steele. DiPo

Your sleep will be. Caterpillar's Lullaby. Jane Yolen. Spl

Your small hands, precisely equal to my own. Adrienne Rich. CPO; PoE; TRP *Fr.* Twenty-one Love Poems. GLP

Your smile, delicate. Woman Me. Maya Angelou. BlSi; OxWW

Your smiles are not, as other womens be. To the Lady May. Aurelian Townshend. GBL

Your smiling cheeks, burning clouds. A Poem about Fan the Fourth. Li K'ai-hsien, *Chinese.* CoBLCP, *tr. by* Jonathan Chaves

Your smiling, or the hope, the thought of it. A Simile for Her Smile. Richard Wilbur. HoPM; InPK-6; SAGP

Your son presses against me. The Apple Trees. Louise Glück. HCAP

Your soul is a sealed garden. Clair de Lune. Paul Verlaine, *French.* AWP, *tr. by* Arthur Symons

Your soul shines. Alice Walker. MT

Your sound is faultless. For Miles. Gregory Corso. MoNo

Your spouse not laboured-at nor spun. (LL) The Habit of Perfection. Gerard Manley Hopkins. ChIV-2; ImPo; MoBrPo; MoP; NoAM; OBEV; OBMV; OxAEP-2; PoRA; Poetr; RB; TFi

Your Standard's up, we fix a Conquest there. (LL) To the King, upon His Com[m]ing with His Army into the West. Robert Herrick. BeJo; CaPo; CavPo

Your stars are muscled like the lion. (LL) Baseball and Writing. Marianne Moore. BoWoP; FaBoA

Your starved and ancient Presence O Lord I wait in my room at your Mercy. (LL) The Lion for Real. Allen Ginsberg. GLP; HCAP; RB

Your steps, born of my silence here. The Footsteps. Paul Valéry, *French.* FLP; LoP, *tr. by* Alistair Elliot

Your stones I shall polish into a mirror. Jerusalem. David Rokeah, *Hebrew.* MHP, *tr. by* Ruth Finer Mintz

Your strange hair, cold light. René Vivien. CPO

Your subjects hope, dread Sire. To the King's Most Excellent Majesty. Phillis Wheatley. TAP

Your sweetness of soul was a mystery to me. Hattie Rice Rich. Adrienne Rich. *Fr.* Grandmothers. HCAP; NAAL-2; NoAM

Your tears, Niobe. Hayden Carruth. VGW

Your tears. You are not worth their merriment. (LL) Apologia Pro Poemate Meo. Wilfred Owen. LiTM; MoBrPo; NAEL-2; NSI; PeFWW; PoFWW

Your teeth are loose, your head is bald. An Admonition to Myself. Chao Meng-fu, *Chinese.* CoBLCP, *tr. by* Jonathan Chaves

Your thick metallic menstrual aroma. Mirror Poem. Rachel Blau DuPlessis. DeD

Your thighs are appletrees. Portrait of a Lady. William Carlos Williams. AmPP; CMoP; MoP; NAAL-2; NOBA; NoAM; OxBA

Your thighs your belly. Sea Flower. Mary Dorcey. BrRo

Your throat, my hunting partridge, will no longer. A Decoy Partridge. Simmias [*or* Simias] of Rhodes, *Greek.* GrAn, *tr. by* Peter Jay

Your tongue has spent the night. The Dream-Language of Fergus. Medbh McGuckian. CIP-2

Your Tongue Sparkles. "Chrystos." CPO

Your tongue thrums and moves. Kenneth Rexroth. APSN *Fr.* The Love Poems of Marichiko.

"Your touch is abrasive. My blood seethes and smarts." Occasional Verses. Marilyn Hacker. Son

Your turn came, and you chose to take it. Winter Solstice—for Frank. "Asphodel." BrRo

Your ugly token. Upon a Dead Man's Head. John Skelton. AAS; HAP; SCGP

Your vividness grants color where. To Sallie, Walking. Sterling Brown. GT

Your voice awakens. A Gong. Odia Ofeimun. PBMAP

Your voice bleeds bafflement and anger. 'Phoning. Peter Sirr. BiHa

Your voice, grief-laden, lingers in the air. On Hearing the Rail Cry. Nguyễn Khuyến, *Vietnamese.* AVP, *tr. by* Huỳnh Sanh Thông

Your voice is the color of a robin's breast. To O. E. A. Claude McKay. BPo; GT

Your voice unwrapping. Haiku. Sonia Sanchez. FFC

Your volume proves that "Nothing is worth while." To a Pessimist. Ronald Arbuthnott Knox. OBCoV

Your walk sacerdotal and slow, undulant. A Black Girl Goes By. Emile Roumer, *French.* TTY, *tr. by* Edna Worthley Underwood

Your walls do not fall, he said. Hilda Doolittle. NALW *Fr.* Tribute to the Angels.

Your way / is turning bad. *Unknown, Crow Indian.* STP, *tr. by* W. S. Merwin

Your weight sweetly upon me. Made Out of Links. Hilda Morley. PmAP

Your white house and tranquil garden, I shall leave. "Anna Akhmatova," *Russian.* TCRP, *tr. by* Daniel Weissbort

Your wicked minds requite. (LL) The Babes in the Wood ("Now ponder well, you parents dear"). *Unknown.* EnSB; OBNV; OxAEP-1

Your wife's forty-five. Gift Horse. Yusef Komunyakaa. GT

Your wisdom has been valiant, sages of Harvard. (LL) Address to the Scholars of New England. John Crowe Ransom. LiTM; MeMAP

Your wistful eyes searched each one as he passed. Stray Dog. Charlotte Mish. PoLF

Your womb is smarter than your head. Madrigal. Nicolás Guillén, *Spanish.* CLPP, *tr. by* Kenneth Rexroth

Your words are frost on speargrass. Amy Lowell. Lola Ridge. NMM-2

Your words came just when needed. Accept My Full Heart's Thanks. Ella Wheeler Wilcox. PoToHe

Your words my friend (right healthful caustics) blame. Sonnet 21. Sir Philip Sidney. NAEL-1; NoP-4; NoSic; PoE *Fr.* Astrophil and Stella. AAS; SiPS

Your Work. Jean-Joseph Rabéarivelo, *French.* NegPo, *tr. by* Ellen Conroy Kennedy

Your young breasts were gleaming. The River. Jacques Prévert, *French.* MFP, *tr. by* Martin Sorrell

You're. Sylvia Plath. FaBoTw; FaBoWP; RB

You're a better man than I am, Gunga Din! (LL) Gunga Din. Rudyard Kipling. APAD; EBEvV; EBVV; MoBrPo

You're a girl. Character. Taslima Nasrin, *Bengali.* VCWP, *tr. by* Carolyne Wright *and* Farida Sarkar

You're a grand old flag. George M. Cohan. CTV

You're a teeming truce today, my ladybug, red elytra. Unfinished Exile. Fabio Doplicher, *Italian.* Nelt, *tr. by* Stephen Sartarelli

You're clean shaven in this country. The Vegetable Air. Cathy Song. NoAM

You're excused, my father would say. As We Forgive Those. Eric Pankey. GI

You're going to be beef steers by and by. (LL) Whoopee Ti Yi Yo, Git Along Little Dogies. *Unknown.* APN-2

You're Going to Reap Just What You Sow. *Unknown.* AmFP

You're gone forever, prefect of Vĩnh -tu'ò'ng! Elegy for the Prefect of Vĩnh-tu'ò'ng. Ho Xuan Huong, *Vietnamese.* AVP, *tr. by* Huỳnh Sanh Thông

You're good for nothing, actors all! Actors. Trần Tế Xu'o'ng, *Vietnamese.* AVP, *tr. by* Huỳnh Sanh Thông

"You're good looking / for a colored man." William J. Harris. *See* A
Daddy Poem.

You're here! I hadn't dared to hope. Surprise. Macedonius, *Greek.* GrAn,
tr. by Adrian Wright

You're here. We breathe the selfsame air. Boris Pasternak, *Russian.* LoP,
tr. by J. M. Cowen

You're in love with love. Meleager, *Greek.* InMo, *tr. by* Sam Hamill

You're in the city, somewhere. I suppose if I stood. Lost Love. Dick
Allen. NIP-4

You're like a drifting log with iron nails in it. Funeral Song. Hayiaku,
Tlingit Indian. STP, *tr. by* James Koller

You're loathed by some, but then by some you're loved. Looking Forward
to Retirement. Nguyễn Công Trú, *Vietnamese.* AVP, *tr. by* Huỳnh
Sanh Thông

You're more jive than Pigmeat. Crack. Yusef Komunyakaa. WWSi

You're my friend: / I was the man the Duke spoke to. The Flight of the
Duchess. Robert Browning.

You're no king. Haim Guri, *Hebrew.* IP, *tr. by* Warren Bargad *and* Stanley
F. Chyet

You're Nothing but a Spanish Colored Kid. Felipe Luciano. PoBA

You're now transcribed, and public view. To Mr. W. B., at the Birth of His
First Child. William Cartwright. BeJo

You're Only a PBO. *Unknown.* NSI

You're right. In the Library. Michael Patrick Hearn. NTCP

You're right I brought a grain. The Sand. May Swenson. DeD *Fr.* Poet
to Tiger. GLP

You're right, Lais' smile is sweet. Paulus Silentiarius, *Greek.* PGA, *tr. by*
Kenneth Rexroth

You're saving it? What for? Asclepiades, *Greek.* GrAn, *tr. by* Alan
Marshfield

You're sleeping, Zenophila, my tender bloom. I wish. Meleager. HePo, *tr.
by* Barbara Hughes Fowler *Fr.* I'll Twine White Violets. NIP-4, *tr. by*
Goldwin Smith

You're so dumb you don't even see. Volitionist Economics. Kelvin
Corcoran. NBrP

You're so fragile. Silk and Silence. Haim Guri, *Hebrew.* IP, *tr. by* Warren
Bargad *and* Stanley F. Chyet

You're so funny! I'd give you. Kirsten. Ted Berrigan. TTTS

You're song. Jelaluddin Rumi, *Persian.* LoL, *tr. by* Coleman Barks

You're sure you heard something break. Something snap. Thrust & Parry.
Greg Delanty. BiHa

You're the Top. Cole Porter. OBAL; UnPo

You're the Top. *Unknown.* NBLV

You're thinking of children, of their. Vladimir Holan, *Czech.* PoSu, *tr. by*
Ian *and* Jarmila Milner

You're tired of this old world at last. Zone. Guillaume Apollinaire,
French. PFTM, *tr. by* Ron Padgett

Youre ugly tokyn. John Skelton. *See* Upon a Dead Man's Head.

You're walking by the tomb of Battiades. On Himself. Callimachus,
Greek. GrAn, *tr. by* Peter Jay

You're with your mother now. (LL) What I Heard at the Discount
Department Store. David Budbill. RaBo; TRP

You're wondering if I'm lonely. Song. Adrienne Rich. InPK-6; PBWP

You're wrong she says. You'll do it my way. Snobby Roberts' Message.
Ken Smith. NBrP

Yours is the face that the earth turns to me. Love-Poem. Kathleen Jessie
Raine. LW; MoBrPo

Yours is the sullen sorrow. Last Words to Miriam. D. H. Lawrence.
CBLP

Yours to absolve of ruin, or make an end. (LL) Christ Walks in This
Infernal District Too. Malcolm Lowry. NOBC

Yourself. Jones Very. APN-1; NOBA; OxBA; PAR; PoEL-4; Son

Yourself and Myself. *Unknown, Irish.* NOIV, *tr. by* Thomas Kinsella

Youth. Robert Browning. BoTP *Fr.* Saul.

Youth, A. Stephen Crane. MoAmPo *Fr.* The Black Riders [and Other
Lines].
(Content.)

Youth. Bartholomew Griffin. *See* Sonnet: "I have not spent the April of my
time."

Youth. "Laurence Hope." WeW-3

Youth. Georgia Douglas Johnson. NAAAL

Youth. Emma Lazarus. SDW

Youth. Barend Toerien, *Afrikaans.* PeSA, *tr. by the author*

Youth. Robert Wever. *See* In Youth Is Pleasure.

Youth and a maiden from Costessey, A. Limerick. S. C. Turner. PeLi

Youth and Age. Byron. *See* Stanzas for Music ("There's not a joy the
world can give like that it takes away").

Youth and Age. Coleridge. GTBS-P; LaPo; OBEV; OBNC; PoLF

Youth and Age. Richard Eberhart. AFr

Youth and Age. Mimnermus, *Greek.* AWP, *tr. by* John Addington Symonds

Youth and Age. W. B. Yeats. FaBoEE

Youth and Age on Beaulieu River, Hants. John Betjeman. FaBoTw; TwCP

Youth and Art. Robert Browning. CTC; NAEL-2; NOBVV

Youth and Beauty. Aurelian Townshend. GBL; SeCP

Youth and Calm. Matthew Arnold. FHYEP

Youth and Death. Emma Lazarus. SDW

Youth and Love. John Gay. NOBE *Fr.* The Beggar's Opera. OAEL-1

Youth and Maturity. Greville Fulke. *See* Sonnet: "Nurse-life wheat within
his green husk growing, The."

Youth, beauty, virtue, innocence. An Epitaph Upon the Lady Elizabeth,
Second Daughter to his Late Majesty. Henry Vaughan. BeJo

Youth Dreams, The. Rilke, *German.* AWP; TrJP, *tr. by* Ludwig Lewisohn

Youth gone, and beauty gone if ever there. Christina Rossetti. GBL; GSo;
OBNC; Son *Fr.* Monna Innominata. BWW

Youth in apparel that glittered, A. A Youth. Stephen Crane. APN-2;
MeMAP; MoAmPo; NAAL-2 *Fr.* The Black Riders [and Other Lines].

Youth in Arms. Harold Monro.
Carrion. NSI; PeFWW

Youth Mowing, A. D. H. Lawrence. InPK-6; MoBrPo; NoAM

Youth of a Poet, The. James Beattie. NOEC *Fr.* The Minstrel.

Youth of delight, come hither. The Voice of the Ancient Bard. William
Blake. FHYEP; Ro *Fr.* Songs of Experience.

Youth of Han-tan, The; a Song. Kao Shih, *Chinese.* SuSp, *tr. by* Joseph J.
Lee

Youth of my heart, my beloved one. Love Song to King Shu-Suen.
Kubatum, *Sumerian.* WPOW, *tr. by* Thorkild Jacobsen

Youth rambles on life's arid mount. The Progress of Poesy. Matthew
Arnold. NOBVV

Youth rode forth from his childhood's home, A. Nature's Farewell. Felicia
Dorothea Hemans. Ro

Youth Sings a Song of Rosebuds. Countee Cullen. PoLF

Youth there was, Elpenor was he nam'd, A. Homer. OBVE, *tr. by* Pope
Fr. Odyssey. NAWM-1, *tr. by* Robert Fitzgerald

Youth there was possessed of every charm, A. The Story of Inkle and
Yarico. Frances, Countess of Hertford Seymour. ECWP

Youth! Thou Wear'st to Manhood Now. Sir Walter Scott. OxBSP

Youth walks up to the white horse, The. The White Horse. D. H.
Lawrence. TTTS

Youth walks up to the white horse, to put its halter on, The. The White
Horse. D. H. Lawrence. KaS

Youth, with proud heart, pure and strong, A. The After-Glow of Pain
Clara Ann Thompson. CBWP-2

Youth with Red-gold Hair, The. Dame Edith Sitwell. FaBoTw

Youthful Age. Anacreon, *Greek.* AWP, *tr. by* Thomas Stanley

Youthful Sea, The. Tujin Park, *Korean.* CKP, *tr. by* Jaihiun Kim

Youth's Own. John Galsworthy. NSI

Youth's the season made for joys. Cotillion. John Gay. NoP-4

You've Been a Good Old Wagon, but You've Done Broke Down. Ben
Harney. OBAL

You've been asking me that question. Blue Clay. Ellease Southerland. GT

You've been torn from my life. Andromache's Lament for Hector. Homer.
OxBM *Fr.* The Iliad.

You've bolted me in prison—what's my crime? What's My Crime? Trần
Huy Liệu, *Vietnamese.* AVP, *tr. by* Huỳnh Sanh Thông

You've destroyed it everywhere in the world. Constantine P. Cavafy. *See*
The City.

You've done taken my blues and gone—. Notes on the Broadway Theatre.
Langston Hughes. SSLK

You've got nice knees. Love Song. Gavin Ewart. OxBTC

You've got to admit it's nice. (LL) Population. Mark Halliday. NAmP90;
PUP-18

You've gotten in through the transom. To a Child Trapped in a Barber
Shop. Philip Levine. InPK-6; MoP; NOBA; NoAM; Poetr; TAP;
VGW; WeT

"You've had your operation, Mrs. Brown." The Other Side. Roy Fuller.
OxBC

You've lived there long, away from the trappings of office. To a Hermit in
the Mountains. Hsü Pen, *Chinese.* CoBLCP, *tr. by* Jonathan Chaves

You've lost the kingdom. Lost. Jacob Glatstein, *Yiddish.* CEEP, *tr. by*
Ruth Whitman

You've made upon the sea. (LL) Brown Robyn's [or Robin's] Confession.
Unknown. CH; ESPB

You've moved to a house backing the outer wall. Looking for Lu Hung-
chien but Failing To Find Him. Chiao-jan, *Chinese.* CoBCP, *tr. by*
Burton Watson

You've never been in a public bath. The Bathhouse. Boris Abramovich
Slutsky, *Russian.* TCRP, *tr. by* J. R. Rowland

You've only just heard? Paid on Both Sides. W. H. Auden.

You've pluck'd [*or* plucked] a curlew, drawn a hen. On an Island. John Millington Synge. BIrV; FaBoVe; MoBrPo; OxBSP; PeVV

You've rocked at many passage rites, at drums. On African Writing. Jack A. Mapanje. HBAPE

You've seen a strawberry. Nevertheless. Marianne Moore. CMoP; MeMAP; NAAL-2; NoP-4; OxBA

You've talked to the sun and moon. Charles Wright. *Fr.* Skins. HCAP

You've Told Me, Maro. Martial, *Latin.* NIP-4, *tr. by* F. Lewis

Yow that take pleasure in yowr cruelty. Sonnet 25. Robert Sidney. PBRV

Yr eyes dark and aware. "Alta." NMM-2 *Fr.* Theme and Variations.

Yt fell abowght the Lamasse tyde. The Battle of Otterburn [*or* Oterborne]. *Unknown.* ESPB; IBB; OxBS

Yüan, Ch'ü. Ch'u Yüan, *Chinese. Fr.* Li Sao.
("I am a descendant of Emperor Kao-yang.") ChiPo, *tr. by* Burton Watson
("I will go to P'eng Hsien in the place where he dwells.") (LL) ChiPo, *tr. by* Burton Watson

Yuba City School. Chitra Divakaruni. LTA; LoHo; OpBo
("He says, / in discs, each a different color.") (LL) UnSA

Yucca clump / is blooming, The. The Yucca Moth. A. R. Ammons. NOBA

Yugoslav Cemetery. Celeste Turner Wright. WPE

Yugoslav Story. Susan Hampton. BMAP

Yuh fish fresh? Granny in de Market Place. Amryl Johnson. HCP

Yuh Lookin Good. Carolyn M. Rodgers. BPo

Yuh see all de time. Revolutionary. Michael Smith. HCP

Yule Days, The. *Unknown.* NTP

Yule Log. Robert Herrick. *See* Ceremonies for Christmas[se].

Yung Wind. Confucius, *Chinese.* CTC, *tr. by* Ezra Pound

Yussouf. James Russell Lowell. BLPA; BoTP; FaBoBe

Yves Tanguy. David Gascoyne. NoP-4; SPE

Ywis, pole hatchet, she bleared thine eye. (LL) Lullay, Lullay, Like a Child. John Skelton. ImPo; NoSic; SCGP

Z

Z is the Zenith from which we decline. Zewhyexary. Thomas M. Disch. OBCoV; RA

Z was a zany, a silly old [*or* poor harmless] fool. (LL) A was an archer, who [*or* and] shot at a frog. *Unknown.* LB; OxBChV; OxNR

Z, Y, X, and W, V. *Unknown.* OxNR

Zack Bumstead uster flosserfize. A Philosopher. Sam Walter Foss. OBAL

Zalka Peetruza. Ray Garfield Dandridge. PoBA

Zambra Dance, The. Dryden. *See* Song of the Zambra Dance.

Zang Tumb Tuuum. Filippo Tommaso Marinetti, *Italian.*
Correction of proofs + desires in speed. PFTM, *tr. by* Richard J. Pioli

Zangezi. Velemir Khlebnikov.
Plane Four. PFTM

Zangezi: R, K, L, G—. Velemir Khlebnikov, *Russian.* PFTM, *tr. by* Paul Schmidt

Zapata & the Landlord. Alfred B. Spellman. PoBA

Zapolya. Coleridge.
Glycine's Song. CH; OBEV

Zarian was saying: Florence is youth. A Water-Colour of Venice. Lawrence Durrell. MoBrPo

Zaydee. Philip Levine. NNaP

Zealless Xylographer, The. Mary Mapes Dodge. OBAL

Zealots of Yearning. David Rokeah, *Hebrew.* MHP, *tr. by* Ruth Finer Mintz; TrJP, *tr. by* I. M. Lask

Zealous Admonition to Praise. Catharina Regina von Greiffenberg, *German.* GePo, *tr. by* George C. Schoolfield

Zealous locksmith dead of late, A. On a Puritanicall Lock-Smith. William Camden. FaBoEE

Zealous Puritan, The. *Unknown.* NOSC

Zebaoth. Else Lasker-Schüler, *German.* TrJP, *tr. by* Jethro Bithell

Zebra. Judith Thurman. SSCS

Zebra, The. *Unknown, Hottentot.* PeSAV, *tr. by* W. H. I. Bleek

Zebra. *Unknown, Hottentot.* PeSA

Zebra Dun, The. *Unknown.* AmFP

Zebra Goes Wild Where the Sidewalk Ends, The. Henry Dumas. GT

Zebra Stallion. *Unknown, Hottentot.* PeSA

Zebras, The. Roy Campbell. MoBrPo

Zechariah. Bible, *O.T.*
I Return unto Zion. TrJP
Open Thy Doors, O Lebanon. AWP

Zeimbekiko ("Old man gets up turns, An"). Robin Magowan. SPE

Zeke. Leonard Alfred George Strong. MoBrPo

Zek'l Weep. *Unknown.* AS

Zella Wheeler! did I evah? The Interrupted Reproof. Priscilla Jane Thompson. CBWP-2

Zen Americana. Paula Gunn Allen. PoPoPo

Zen Buddhism and Psychoanalysis / Psychoanalysis and Zen Buddhism. Jackson MacLow. PoM

Zen mind is unperturbed by the envy of moth-browed beauties, A. Addressed to a Koto-player. Su Man-shu, *Chinese.* SuSp, *tr. by* Wu-chi Liu

Zen of Housework, The. Al Zolynas. BLT

Zenana, and Minor Poems of L.E.L., The. Letitia Elizabeth Landon. On Wordsworth's Cottage, near Grasmere Lake. Ro

Zenonis has a splendid tutor for her son—. Lucilius, *Greek.* GrAn, *tr. by* Peter Porter

ZENOPHILE! (LL) Lost! Cupid!/ One lost Cupid! Meleager, *Greek.* GrAn; OBCVT, *tr. by* Peter Whigham

Zepheria. *Unknown.*
Proud in Thy Love. Son
"When we in kind embraces had agre'd [agreed]." AAS; Son

Zephyr. Eugene Fitch Ware. PoLF

Zephyr, kindliest of winds. Dioscorides, *Greek.* GrAn, *tr. by* Peter Whigham

Zépke! Zépke! Monologue of the Crazed Mastodon. Paul Scheerbart. CBNP

Zeppelin factory, The. Rita Dove. Poetr

Zermatt: To the Matterhorn. Thomas Hardy. OBNC

0°. Elizabeth Spires. DiPo

Zero hour. Waiting yet again. James Merrill. HCAP *Fr.* The Book of Ephraim.

Zero / zero / zero / the museum of modern art. The Story of the Zeros. Victor Hernandez Cruz. PoBA

Zeugma. Christopher Reid. CBLP

Zeus, / Brazen-thunder-hurler. The Faun Sees Snow for the First Time. Richard Aldington. MoBrPo

Zeus,--by what name soe'er. Hymn to Zeus. Aeschylus. *Fr.* Agamemnon. NAWM-1, *tr. by* Robert Fagles

Zeus isn't such a raving Casanova. Palladas, *Greek.* GrAn, *tr. by* Tony Harrison

Zeus lies in Ceres' bosom. Canto 81. Ezra Pound. FaBoMo; MoP; NAAL-2; NOBA; NoAM; VGW *Fr.* Cantos.

Zeus paid Danaé in gold:/ thus I pay you. Parmenion of Macedon, *Greek.* GrAn, *tr. by* Peter Jay

Zeus was once overheard to shout at Hera. The Weather of Olympus. Robert Graves. FaBoEE; OBCoV

Zeus, whoever Zeus may be, if he. Aeschylus, *Greek.* TOF, *tr. by* Peter Levi

Zewhyexary. Thomas M. Disch. OBCoV
("Could be anything. A is unknown, A.") (LL) RA

Zhi, zhi, zhi, zhi, zhi, zhi, zhi, zhi. Battle Song. Shaka, King of the Zulus, *Zulu.* PeSAV, *tr. by* Henry Francis Fynn

Zi kholmt. (LL) A Few Words in the Mother Tongue. Irena Klepfisz. CPO; LoHo

Zig zag mothers of the gods, The. That Dada Strain. Jerome Rothenberg. FTOS

Zilver-Weed, The. William Barnes. EnVR; NOBVV

Zimbabwe. F. D. Sinclair. PeSA

Zimmer and His Turtle Sink the House. Paul Zimmer. Poetsp

Zimmer Drunk and Alone, Dreaming of Old Football Games. Paul Zimmer. PBCAP

Zimmer Imagines Heaven. Paul Zimmer. PBCAP

Zimmer in Fall. Paul Zimmer. CA

Zimmer in Grade School. Paul Zimmer. KaS; PBCAP

Zimmer's Head Thudding against the Blackboard. Paul Zimmer. PBCAP

Zimri: "In the first rank of These did Zimri stand." Dryden. *Fr.* Absalom and Achitophel, Pt. I. EBEvV; FHYEP; FaBoPV; HAP; NOSC; OAEL-1; PoE

Zimri: "Some of their chiefs were princes of the land." Dryden. AWP *Fr.* Absalom and Achitophel, Pt. I. EBEvV; FHYEP; FaBoPV; HAP; NOSC; OAEL-1; PoE

Zimri: The Duke of Buckingham. Dryden. NOBE; OBSV *Fr.* Absalom and Achitophel, Pt. I. EBEvV; FHYEP; FaBoPV; HAP; NOSC; OAEL-1; PoE
(Zimri: "Numerous host of dreaming saints succeed.") AWP

Zinnias, stout and stiff. Valerie Worth. NTCP

Zion me wan go home. *Unknown.* FaBoVe

Zion, wilt thou not ask if peace's wing. Ode to Zion. Judah Halevi, *Hebrew.* TrJP, *tr. by* Nina Davis Salaman

Zionist Marching Song. Naphtali Herz Imber, *Hebrew.* TrJP, *tr. by* Israel Zangwill

Zion's Sons and Daughters. *Unknown*. AmFP

Zippo lighter, A. Off the Back of a Lorry. Tom Paulin. PBCIP

Zirkus. Andrew Joron. PT

Zito the Magician. Miroslav Holub, *Czech*. PoSu, *tr. by* Ian Milner *and* George Theiner

Zizi's Lament. Gregory Corso. BB; NeAP; VGW

Zocalo. Michael S. Harper. NBV

Zodiac. Elizabeth Alexander. FFC

Zodiac, The. James Dickey.
   "Tenderness, ache on me, and lay your neck." TAP

Zodiac. Eleanor Farjeon. OTCP

Zodiac is changed into a sphere, The. (LL) Chosen. W. B. Yeats. BoLoP; CMoP

Zodiac Song, The. John Ruskin. NOBVV

Zoe mou, sas agapo. (LL) Maid of Athens, ere we part. Byron. EBEV; FHYEP

Zoetropes. Bill Manhire. PeNZ

Zola. Edwin Arlington Robinson. OxBA

Zolgotz. *Unknown*. AmFP

Zollverein was hardly neutral, The. One recalls. Philatelic Lessons: The German Collection. Lawrence P. Spingarn. NYBP

Zombie / Is the thing we didn't do. A Caribbean Exorcism Poem. Kendel Hippolyte. HCP

Zone. Guillaume Apollinaire, *French*. PFTM, *tr. by* Ron Padgett

Zone. Louise Bogan. IMW; WPE

Zone of Death. William Everson. VGW

Zong, A. William Barnes. BoLoP

Zonnebeke Road, The. Edmund Blunden. OBWP; PeFWW

Zoo, The. Gilbert Sorrentino. NeAP

Zoo Cages. Hải Âu Tử', *Vietnamese*. AVP, *tr. by* Huỳnh Sanh Thông

Zoo is full of cages and it lies, The. Picture Postcard of a Zoo. Oscar Williams. Son

Zoo Keeper's Wife. Sylvia Plath. EP

Zoo Manners. Eileen Mathias. BoTP

Zoom (The Commodores). Thulani Davis. ISC

Zophiël [or, the Bride of Seven]. Maria Gowen Brooks.
   Palace of the Gnomes. APN-1
   "Shade of Columbus, here thy relics rest." PAR

Zosimé was a slave in body only. Damaskius, *Greek*. GrAn, *tr. by* Peter Jay

Zouave, The. Peter Cooley. NAmP90

Zounds, gramercy, and rootity-toot! Robin Hood. Phyllis McGinley. OBSV *Fr.* Speaking of Television.

Zu fragmentarisch ist Welt und Leben. Heinrich Heine, *German*. AWP, *tr. by* Charles Godfrey Leland

Zukofsky. Gilbert Sorrentino. FTOS

Zulu Girl, The. Roy Campbell. NoP-4; OBMV; OxAEP-2

Zun-zet. William Barnes. PoEL-4

Zuni Derivations. *Unknown, Zuni Indian*. STP, *tr. by* Dennis Tedlock

Zurich Chronicle February 1916. Tristan Tzara, *French*. PFTM, *tr. by* Ralph Manheim

Zürich, the Stork Inn, *For Nelly Sachs*. Paul Celan, *French*. HP, *tr. by* Michael Hamburger

AUTHOR INDEX

Arabic, Chinese, and old-style Japanese names in the Author Index are alphabetized, following standard practice, in uninverted form. Pseudonymous names are enclosed in quotation marks.

A

"A., F. P." *See* Adams, Franklin Pierce

"A., P. E."
Limerick: "There we was, and wanting our tea."

Aal, Katharyn Machan
Leda's Sister and the Geese.

Aaron, Jonathan
Sighting, The.

Aaron, Solomon Ephraim ben, of Lenczicz (d. 1619)
These Things I Do Remember.

Aaronson, Leonard [*or* Lazarus] (b. 1894)
Homeward Journey, The.
Pesci Misti.

Abanaki Oral Tradition
Come, my beloved, let us go up the shining mountain, and sit together.

Abbey, Henry (1842–1911)
What do we plant when we plant the tree?

Abbott, Wenonah Stevens
Soul's Soliloquy, A.

Abd-ar-Rahman I
Palm Tree, The.

Abdullah, Latif Asad (b. 1956)
Tombs, The.

Abelard, Peter (1079–1142)
David's Lament for Jonathan.
Hymn for the Close of the Week.

Abercrombie, Lascelles (1881–1938)
All last night I had quiet.
Emblems of Love, *sels.*
Epitaph: "Sir, you should notice me: I am the Man."
Fear, The.
Hope and Despair.
Judith, *sels.*
Mary and the Bramble.
Sale of Saint Thomas, The, *sels.*
Stream's Song, The.
Witchcraft: New Style.

Abid ibn al-Abras (*fl.* 500–550)
Arab Chieftain to His Young Wife, An.
Lament for an Arab Encampment.

Aborigine Oral Tradition
Captain Cook.
Mapooram.
Moon-Bone Song [*or* Cycle], *sels.*
Platypus, The.
Star-Tribes, The.
Tongues of the lightning Snakes flicker and twist, one to the other, The.
Two Sisters, The.

Abrahams, Lionel (b. 1928)
Thresholds of Identity.
Whiteman Blues, The.

Abrahams, Peter (b. 1919)
Lonely Road.
Tell Freedom, *sels.*

Abrahams, William (b. 1919)
Séance.

Abse, Dannie (b. 1923)
Angels.
Brueghel in Naples.
Down the M4.

Epithalamion: "Singing, today I married my white girl."
Florida.
Footnote Extended, A.
In My Fashion.
In the Theatre.
Inscription on the Flyleaf of a Bible.
Letter to Alex Comfort.
Near the Border of Insanities.
New Diary, A.
Not Adlestrop.
Of Itzig and His Dog.
Pathology of Colours.
Peachstone.
Public Library.
Snake.
Tales of Shatz.
Watching a Cloud.
Winter Visit, A.
Words Spoken Alone.

Abu Bakr (d. 1116)
Sword, The.

Abu Dharr (d. 1208)
Oranges, The.

Abu Dhu'ayb al-Hudhali (d. 649?)
Lament for Five Sons Lost in a Plague.

Abu Dulama (d. 778)
Behold my mother!
Humorous Verse.
Traders in Beauty and Delight.

Abu Ishaq al-Ilbin (d. 1067)
Granada (1000 A.D.)

Abu Khalid, Fawziyya (b. 1955)
Mother's Inheritance.

Abu 'l-Ala al-Ma'Arri (973–1057)
Aweary Am I.

Abu Nuwas
Rake, The.

Abu Zakariya (d. 1249)
Bubbling Wine.

Abutsu the Nun [*or* Abutsu-Ni] (d. c.1282)
Diary of the Waning Moon, The, *sels.*
Who knows / that in the depth of the ravine.

Acholonu, Catherine Obianuju
Nigeria in the Year 1999.
Other Forms of Slaughter.

Ackerly, W. C.
Prayer of an Unemployed Man.

Ackerman, Diane (b. 1948)
Beija-Flor.
Lines Written in a Pittsburgh Skyscraper.
Rumored Conversation with Oneself Continues in Pittsburgh, The.
Sweep Me through Your Many-Chambered Heart.

Acklais, Maris
Dedication.
Give me your silver knife, right here.
Woman in Mourning.

Ackland, Valentine (1906–69)
Blossom into a rose as you are bidden.
Communist Poem, 1935.
Eyes of body, being blindfold by night, The.
Fanny Brawne's Letter Put Unopened In Keats's Coffin.
Instructions From England 1936.
Lonely Woman, The.
Overnight.

Poem: "You send me a letter from far, from across the sea."
What must we do if we cannot do this.
When I have said 'I love you' I have said.
Whether a dove or a seagull lighted there.
Winter.

Acorn, Milton (b. 1923)
Fights, The.
I've Tasted My Blood.
Knowing I Live in a Dark Age.
On Saint-Urbain Street.
You Growing.

Acosta, Teresa Palma
My Mother Pieced Quilts.

Acton, Helen C.
Beads of spring rain.

"Ada" (Sarah L. Forten) (1814–1898?)
Lines.
Lines: "From fair Jamaica's fertile plains."
Oh, when this earthly tenement.
To the Memory of J. Horace Kimball.

Adaios of Macedon
If you see someone beautiful / hammer it out right then.
John spared his patient labouring ox.
They say dogs killed you. No, Euripides.

"Adalis, Adelina Efimovna" (Adelina Efimovna Efron) (b. 1900)
Conversation at Midnight.

Adam, Helen (b. 1909)
I Love My Love.

Adamo, Ralph (b. 1948)
Great Escape, The.
My Answer.

Adamovich, Georgy [*or* Georgii Viktorovich] (1894–1972)
Autumn night, in a hotel, the two, An.
One of them said: "One life is much too little."
There, in some place, some time.
There was...what?—Pale sunsets, wide expanses.
When we return to Russia...

Adams, Anna (b. 1926)
Her Dancing Days.
Unrecorded Speech.

Adams, Charles Follen ("Yawcob Strauss") (1842–1918)
John Barley-Corn, My Foe.
Misplaced Sympathy.
My Infundibuliform Hat.
Prevalent Poetry.
Repartée.
To Bary Jade.

Adams, E. H.
Action Rhyme.

Adams, E. M. (b. 1919)
Haymaking.
Paddling Pool, The.
Sea, The.
Shady Woods.
Snowman, The.

Adams, Elijah
Ashland Tragedy, The.

Adams, Francis Lauderdale (1862–93)
Evening Hymn in the Hovels.
Hagar.
Jesus.

To the Christians.
William Wallace.

Adams, Franklin Pierce ("F. P. A.") (1881–1960)
Composed in the Composing Room.
Double Standard, The.
If.
Lines Where Beauty Lingers.
Rich man has his motorcar, The.
Those Two Boys.
To a Thesaurus.

Adams, H. M.
Johnny's Farm.

Adams, Henry
Buddha and Brahma.

Adams, James Barton
Cowboy's Life, The.

Adams, Jean (1710–65)
Dream, or the Type of the Rising Sun, A.
On the Phoenix.
To the Muse.

Adams, John Coleman (1849–1922)
We Praise Thee, God, for Harvests Earned.

Adams, John G. (1810–47)
Heaven Is Here.

Adams, John Quincy (1767–1848)
Send Forth, O God, Thy Light and Truth.
To Sally.
To the Sun-Dial.
Wants of Man, The.

Adams, Léonie (1899–1988)
April Mortality.
Bell Tower.
Caryatid.
Counsel to Unreason.
Country Summer.
Death and the Lady.
Early Waking.
Figurehead, The.
Ghostly Tree.
Grapes Making.
Home-coming.
Horn, The.
Kingdom of Heaven.
Light at Equinox.
Lullaby: "Hush, lullay."
Mount, The.
Night-Piece.
River in the Meadows, The.
Sundown.
This Measure.
Thought's End.
Twilit Revelation.

Adams, Nehemiah
Saints in Glory, We Together.

Adams, Perseus (b. 1933)
Murder Trial, The.
My Grandmother.
Woman and the Aloe, The.

Adams, Sarah Flower (1805–48)
Nearer, My God, to Thee.

Adamson, Robert (b. 1944)
Action Would Kill It / A Gamble.
Dead Horse Bay.
Dreaming Up Mother.
Elm Tree in Paddington, An.
Gutting the Salmon.
Home, The Spare Room, The.
My House.
My Tenth Birthday.
Passing Through Experiences.
Private, The.
Ribbon-Fish, The.
Rimbaud Having a Bath.
Sail Away.
Sibyl.
Sonnet to Be Written from Prison.
Sonnets to be Written from Prison, sels.
Things Going out of My Life.

Adcock, Arthur St. John (1864–1930)
Travellers.

Adcock, Betty (b. 1938)
Roller Rink.
Southbound.
Twentieth Anniversary.

Walking Out.

Adcock, Fleur (b. 1934)
Advice to a Discarded Lover.
Against Coupling.
Below Loughrigg.
Blue Glass.
Ex-Queen Among the Astronomers, The.
Future News.
Halfway Street, Sidcup.
Happy Ending.
Immigrant.
Message, A.
Net, The.
Night-Piece, sels.
Note on Propertius I.5.
Over the Edge.
Poem Ended by a Death.
Soho Hospital for Women, The.
Three-toed sloth is the slowest creature we
know, The.
Trees.
Visited.
Weathering.
Wife to Husband.

Addison, Joseph (1672–1719)
Account of the Greatest English Poets, An,
sels.
Campaign, The, sels.
Drummer, or the Haunted House, The, sels.
Letter from Italy [to the Right Honourable
Charles Lord Halifax], A, sels.
Ode: "How are thy servants blest, O Lord!"
Ode: "Spacious firmament on high, The."
Playhouse, The.
Song: "Oh the charming month of May!"
When rising from the bed of death.

Ade, George (1866–1944)
Il Janitoro.
Microbe's Serenade, The.
R-E-M-O-R-S-E.

"Adeler, Max" (Charles Heber Clark) (1847–1915)
Out of the Hurly-Burly.
Willie had a purple monkey climbing on a
yellow stick.

Adiga, M. Gopalakrishna (1918–92)
Do something, brother.

Adisa, Opal Palmer
Cultural Trip, A.
Discover Me.
Rainbow, The.
Women at the Crossroad / (May Elegba
Forever Guard the Right Doors).

Adkin, Will S.
If I Only Was the Fellow.

Adler, Felix (1851–1933)
Hail! the Glorious Golden City.

Adler, Friedrich
By the Waterfall.

Adler, Lucile
Travelling Out, The.

Adler, Mortimer J. (b. 1902)
Fearless, The.

Adnan, Etel (b. 1925)
Beirut-Hell Express, The, sels.

"Adunis" [or "Adonis"] ('Ali Ahmad Sa'id) (b. 1929)
Elegy for the Time at Hand.
Mirror for the Twentieth Century, A.
New Noah, The.
Passage, The.
Song of a Man in the Dark.
Tree of Fire.

"Æ" (Russell, George William) (1867–1935)
By the Margin of the Great Deep.
Cities, The.
Continuity.
Desire.
Epilogue: "Well, when all is said and done."
Exiles.
Frolic.
Gay, The.
Germinal.
Great Breath, The.
Holy Hill, A.

Immortality.
Lonely, The.
Mountain Wind, A.
New York.
On Behalf of Some Irishmen Not Followers
of Tradition.
Outcast[, The].
Pain.
Prayer: "Let us leave our island woods grown
dim and blue."
Reconciliation.
Secret, The.
Self-Discipline.
Tragedy.
Truth.
Unknown God, The.

Aengus [or Angus] the Culdee (fl. 8th cent.)
Prayer for Forgiveness, A.

Aeschylus (525–456 B.C.)
Agamemnon.
Chorus recall Helen's flight, The.
Chorus sing the doom of Helen, The.
Clytemnestra triumphant over the bodies of
Agamemnon and Cassandra.
Eumenides, The.
Libation Bearers, The.
On the Thessalians Who Fought at Marathon.
Prometheus Bound, sels.
Seven against Thebes, The, sels.
This mountain's secret is the son of
Euphorion of Athens.
Zeus, whoever Zeus may be, if he.

Aesop (6th cent. B.C.)
Ass in the Lion's Skin, The ("An ass put on
a lion's skin and went.")
Mountain in Labor, The.
Shepherd-Boy and the Wolf, The.
Swan and the Goose, The.
Vine and the Goat, The.

"Aetolus." See Alexander of Pleuron

Afer, Publius Terentius. See Terence

Afterman, Allen (b. 1941)
Pietà.
Their Thoughts Cling to Everything They See
on the Way.
Van Diemen's Land

Agard, John (b. 1949)
Ask Mummy Ask Daddy.
By all means / bless the cloth.
Don't Call Alligator Long-Mouth Till You
Cross River.
English Girl Eats Her First Mango.
Half-caste.
Listen Mr Oxford Don.
Lollipop lady.
New Shoes.
Pan Recipe.
Poetry Jump-Up.
Waiting for Fidel.

Agate, James (1877–1947)
Eumenides at Home, The.

Agathias (Agathias Scholasticus) (536–82)
Astrologer, The.
Beautiful Melite, in the throes of middle age.
Bridge on the Sangarios, A.
House in Byzantium, A.
It is not wine that makes me reel / Not juice
of grape I crave.
Justice.
Kallirrhoê: A Dedication.
Latrine in a Suburb of Smyrna, A.
Manifesto.
Not Such Your Burden.
On Lot's Wife Turned to Salt.
Partridge.
Plutarch.
Restless and discontent.
Restless and discontent / I lie awake all night
long.
Rhodanthe.
That old crow-beaked hag.
Troy.

Agee, James (1909–55)
In Heavy Mind.
Lyrics, sels.
Permit Me Voyage.

Rapid Transit.
Song with Words.
Sonnets, *sels.*
Two Songs on the Economy of Abundance, *sels.*

Agnew, Edith (b. 1897)
Let me tell to you the story.

Agnew, Joan
Freedom.
Sons of the King.

Agosin, Marjorie
Disappeared Woman I.

"Agricola" (*fl.* c.1757)
Daventry Wonder, The.

Agustini, Delmira (1886–1914)
Blindness.
From Far Away.

"Agyeya" (Sachidananda Hirananda Vatsyayan) (1911–86)
Hiroshima.

Ahmad, K. Nisar (b. 1936)
America, America.

Ai (Florence Anthony) (b. 1947)
Abortion.
Archangel.
Before You Leave.
But What I'm Trying to Say Mother Is.
Child Beater.
Country Midwife: A Day, The.
Cuba, 1962.
Disregard.
Everything: Eloy, Arizona, 1956.
Good Shepherd: Atlanta, 1981, The.
Hangman.
I Can't Get Started.
Ice.
Kid, The.
Man with the Saxophone, The.
Mexico, 1940.
Mexico, August 20, 1940.
More.
Mother's Tale, The.
Reunion with a Ghost.
Russia, 1927.
Salome.
She Didn't Even Wave.
Testimony of J. Robert Oppenheimer, The.
Twenty-Year Marriage.
Why Can't I Leave You?
Woman to Man.

Ai Ch'ing (b. 1910)
North, The.

Ái Lan Lê Liũ Huê (b. 1910)
Deathless Autumn, A.

Ai Shih-te (*fl.* c.17th cent.)
Human Mind, The.

Aichinger, Ilse (b. 1921)
Enumeration.
Glimpse from the Past.
In Which Names.

Aig-Imoukhuede, Frank (b. 1935)
One Wife for One Man.

Aiken, Conrad Potter (1889–1973)
Accomplices, The.
All Lovely Things.
And in the hanging gardens there is rain.
And in the Human Heart, *sels.*
Animula vagula blandula.
Annihilation.
At a Concert of Music.
But How It Came from Earth.
Calyx of the Oboe Breaks, The.
Dear Uncle Stranger.
Discordants, *sels.*
Doctors' Row.
Farewell Voyaging World!
Habeas Corpus Blues, The.
Hatteras Calling.
Herman Melville.
Letter from Li Po, A, *sels.*
Limerick: "It's time to make love. Douse the glim."
Limerick: "Quoth a cow in the marshes of Glynne."
Limerick: "Said a dreadfully literate cat."

Limerick: "Said Isolde to Tristan: 'How curious!'"
Limerick: "Said Old Father William: 'I'm humble.'"
Limerick: "Scion of Boston society, A."
Limerick: "Sighed a dear little shipboard divinity."
Limerick: "There once was a wicked young minister."
Limerick: "There was an old mickey called Cassidy."
Lovers, The.
Miracles.
Multitudes Turn in Darkness.
Nameless Ones, The.
Nuit Blanche: North End.
Obituary.
Prelude: "Woman, Woman, let us say these things to each other."
Preludes for Memnon; or, Preludes to Attitude, *sels.*
Priapus and the Pool, *sels.*
Punch, the Immortal Liar, *sels.*
Quarrel, The.
Road, The.
Room, The.
Sea Holly.
Senlin; a Biography, *sels.*
Shaemus.
Snowflake on asphodel, clear ice on rose.
Solitaire.
Sound of Breaking.
South End.
Summer.
Tetélestai.
Things, The.
Three Star Final.
Time in the Rock [or, Preludes to Definition], *sels.*
Wedding, The.
When the Tree Bares.
Window, The.

Aiken, Joan (b. 1924)
Do It Yourself.
How to Make a Sailor's Pie.
John's Song.
Palace Cook's Tale.
Rhyme for Night.

Aikin, John (1747–1822)
Picturesque; a Fragment.
Tit for Tat; a Tale.

Aikin, Lucy (1781–1864)
Beggar Man, The.
Swallow, that on rapid wing.

Ainger, Arthur Campbell (1841–1919)
God Is Working His Purpose Out.

Ainsworth, Henry (1571–c.1623)
Except the Lord, That He for Us Had Been.
Fire in my meditation burned.
Give ear, O heavens, to that which I declare.
How Long, Jehovah?
I Minded God.
I Spread Out unto Thee My Hands.
In the Distress upon Me.
To God Our Strength Shout Joyfully.
Unto Jehovah Sing Will I.
With All My Heart, Jehovah, I'll Confess.

Ainsworth, Ruth (b. 1908)
Good Night.

'Aisha bint Ahmad al-Qurtubiyya (*fl.* late 10th cent.)
I am a lioness.
To Li Po.

Aitken, E.
Elaine, pretending it was salt.

Akahito (Yamabé no Akahito) (d. 736?)
Black jewel like, The.
I passed by the beach.
I wish I could lend a coat. *From* Manyo Shu, Part 2 of 4.
I wish I were close.
In Waka Bay when.
Men of valor, The. *From* Manyo Shu, Part 2 of 4.
Mists rise over, The.
On Fujiyama / Under the midsummer moon.

Plum-blossom, The. *From* Manyo Shu, Part 3 of 4.
Tomorrow I was.
When I went out.

Akazome Emon (d. 1027)
I can no longer tell dream from reality.
I should not have waited.
I, who cut off my sorrows.
In my heart's depth.
It would have been better that I slept.

Akenside, Mark (1721–70)
Amoret.
Complaint, The.
For a Statue of Chaucer at Woodstock.
Hymn to Science.
Inscription for a Grotto.
Inscription: "Whoe'er thou art whose path, in summer lies."
Pleasure of Imagination, The, *sels.*
Pleasures of Imagination, The, *sels.*
To the Evening Star.
What my age and climate held to view.

Akers, Elizabeth Chase. *See* Allen, Elizabeth Akers

Akers, Ellery
Night: Volcano, California.

Äkesson, Sonja (1926–77)
Autobiography.
Ears.
Evening Walk.

Akhenaton [*or* Akhnaton] (Amenhotep IV) (d. c.1354 B.C.)
Hymn to the Sun, The.

Akhmadulina, Bella [*or* Izabella] Akhatovna (b. 1937)
Again September, like the swarm of seasons past.
At Night.
Autumn.
Blizzard.
Bride, The.
Dream, A.
Fairy Tale about Rain, A.
Fever.
Fifteen Boys, or Perhaps Even More.
Goodbye.
I Swear.
In the Emptied Rest Home.
Incantation.
Names of Georgian Women, The.
Remembrance of Yalta.
St. Bartholomew's Night.
Silence.
Sleepwalkers.
Small Aircraft.
Snowfall began its thing, The.
Sound of Rain, The.
Volcanoes.
Winter.
Words Spoken by Pasternak during a Bombing.

"Akhmatova, Anna Andreyevna" (Anna Andreyevna Gorenko) (1889–1966)
Ah—you thought I'd be the type.
Alone.
Along the hard crest of the snowdrift.
And people will think this like.
Boris Pasternak.
Courage.
Dedication.
Epigram: "Could Beatrice have written like Dante."
Everything Is Plundered[, betrayed, sold].
Grey-eyed King, The.
Guest, The.
Hands clenched under my shawl.
He loved three things [in life].
He whispers: 'I'm not sorry.
How can you look at the Neva.
I am not one of those who left the land.
I care nothing for battle odes.
I heard a voice, within me, call.
I taught myself to live simply and wisely.
I will leave your white house and tranquil garden.
I wrung my hands under my dark veil.

In the Evening.
In the Looking Glass.
Instead of a Preface.
Instead of wisdom—experience, a flat.
Introduction.
July 1914.
Land not mine, still, A.
Lord is not merciful to reapers and gardeners,
   The.
Lot's Wife.
Love.
Memory of love, you are painful!
Muse, The.
One man follows a straight path.
Pushkin.
Railings of iron.
Requiem 1935-1940, *sels.*
Requiem: "No foreign sky protected me."
Round my neck a rosary of fine beads.
Slander.
Specter, The.
Summer Garden.
Tashkent Breaks into Bloom.
There is in human closeness a sacred
   boundary.
Three Things Enchanted Him.
To The Beloved.
Twenty-first. Night. Monday.
Voronezh.
What's worse than this past century?
When a man dies.
You know, I languish here.
Your lynx-eyes, Asia.
Your white house and tranquil garden, I shall
   leave.

Akhtar-ul-Iman (b. 1915)
Compromise.

Akimine (Ki no Akimine) (*fl.* 9th cent.)
Beloved person must I think, The. *From*
   Kokin Shu

Akin, Gülten
Ellas and the Statues.

Akjartoq (*fl.* c.1920)
Old Woman's Song, An.

Al-Abbas ibn al-Ahnaf (d. 808?)
Love.

Al-Aswad, son of Ya'fur
Old Age. *From* The Mufaddaliyat.

Al-Faituri [or Al-Fituri or Al-Fayturi],
Muhammad (b. 1930)
I Am a Negro.
Knell, The.

Al-Harizi, Judah (*fl.* early 13th cent.)
Heavy-hearted.
Lightning, The.
Love Song: "Long closed door, oh open it
   again, The."
Lute, The.
Secret Kept, A.
Song of the Flea.
Song of the Pen, The.
Sun, The.
Under Leafy Bowers.
Unhappy Lover, The.
Within My Heart.

Al-Hutay'a (600?–662?)
It is new.

Al-Ifriqi al-Mutayyam (*fl.* 975)
My wife complains I pray no more.

Al-Junaid
Now I have known, O Lord.

Al-Khansa (*fl.* 7th cent.)
Elegy for Her Brother Sakhr.
In Death's Field.
Lament for a Brother.
Night, The.
On Her Brother.
On Her Brother Sakhr.
Rain to the Tribe.
Sleepless.
Tears, ere thy death, for many a one I shed.

Al-Khirniq (*fl.* 6th cent.)
Lament after Her Husband Bishr's Murder.

Al-Lajjam al-Harrani (*fl.*960)
His banquets cure most ills.

Al-Mahdi (d. 1130)
Preacher, The.

Al-Mala'ika, Nazik (b. 1923)
Jamila.

Al-Muntafil
Mole, The.

Al-Samau'al ibn Adiya (*fl.* c.550)
Are We Not the People, *sels.*
Oh, would that I knew, the day my loss is
   lamented.
Oh, Ye Censurers.

Al-Tirimmah (660?–725)
In the Heart of the Desert.
Lord of the throne.

Alabaster, William
AWAY, fear, with thy projects, no false fire.
Divine Meditations, *sels.*
Divine Sonnet, A.
Exaltatio Humanae Naturae.
Incarnatio Est Maximum Dei Donum [*or*
   Donum Dei].
Of the Reed That the Jews Set in Our
   Saviour's Hand.
On the Reed of Our Lord's Passion.
To Christ.
To the Blessed Virgin.
Upon the Crucifix.
Upon the Ensigns of Christ's Crucifying.

Alakoye, Adesanya (1943–80)
Eshu.

Alarcon, Francisco
Letter To America.
Ode to Tomatoes.

Alattur Killar
Guide to Patrons, A.

Alba, Nanina (1917–68)
Be Daedalus.
For Malcolm X.

Albanach, Muireadhach. *See* O'Dalaigh,
Muireadhach Albanach

Albanez, Franciso
One Who Is at Home, The.

Albert, Heinrich (1604–51)
Musical Pumpkin-Hut.

Alberti, Rafael (b. 1902)
Angels of the Ruins, The.
Charlie's Sad Date.
Homecoming of Love Amongst Illustrious
   Ruins.
Punishments.
Warlike Angels, The.

Albiach, Anne-Marie (b. 1937)
État, *sels.*
He accepts the circle, speech and so.
"Theatre."

Albizzi, Niccolò degli (*fl.* 13th cent.)
Prolonged Sonnet: When the Troops Were
   Returning from Milan.

Albrecht von Johannsdorf (*fl.* 1185–1209)
God's Gifts.
I discovered the sweet lovely lady.
This I know, how love begins to be.

Alcaeus [or Alkaios] (b. c.620 B.C.)
And if the wine leaves him witless.
Come tip a few with me.
Don't wait for the lamplighter.
Drinking Ode of Alcæus, A, *sels.*
Epigram: "Nicander, ooh, your leg's got
   hairs!"
Evening Song, An.
Fair Protarchus doesn't want to.
Her heart was stricken, Helen.
Hipponax.
I despise love. What weighty God.
I hate Eros. He is loathsome and will not.
I long for the call to council.
Leaving the Peloponnese.
Let Us Drink.
O frail flower.
Philip at Kynoskephalai.
Philip of Macedon.
Philip V of Macedon.
Poet has died, A.
Poverty's the worst savage crime.
So lovely . . . / so tender.

Storm, The.
Wet your lungs with wine—the dogstar rises.
You who were once my friend.

Alcayaga, Lucila Godoy. *See* **Mistral, Gabriela**

Alchin, Gordon ("Observer RFC") (d. 1947)
Song of the Air, A.

Alcman (*fl.* 7th cent. B.C.)
Alkman's Supper.
Fragment: "Mountain summits sleep, glens,
   cliffs, and caves, The."
Hymn to Artemis of the Strict Observance:
   For a Chorus of Spartan Girls Dressed as
   Doves To Sing at Dawn on the Feast of
   the Plow, A, *sels.*
Short the way, but pitiless.

Alcock, Mary (1742?–1798)
Chimney-Sweeper's Complaint, The
   ("Chimney sweeper's boy am I, A.")
Instructions, Supposed to Be Written in Paris,
   for the Mob in England.
Modern Manners.
Receipt for Writing a Novel, A.
Written in Ireland.

Alcott, Amos Bronson (1799–1888)
Sonnet 14: "Not Wordsworth's genius,
   Pestalozzi's love."
Sonnet 18: "Adventurous mariner! in whose
   gray skiff."
Sonnet 19: "Romancer, far more coy than
   that coy sex!"

Alcott, Louisa May (1832–88)
Little Kingdom I Possess, A.
Our Little Ghost.

Alcuin (c.735–804)
By these, by these same chains, O Rome.
Come, make an end of singing and of
   grieving.
Dedication to St. Michael.
Epitaph for Paulinus of Aquileia and Arno of
   Salzburg.
Epitaph for St. Amand, Bishop of Utrecht.
For His Friends.
In the Refectory.
Inscription in Monastic Refectory.
Lament for the Cuckoo.
Night Prayer, A.
On the Cross ("Adore the lifted standard of
   the Cross.")
On the Cross ("Here, dying for the world, the
   world's life hung.")
On the Killing at Lindisfarne.
One goodness ruleth by its single will.
Prayer at Night ("Fountain of light, Light,
   Source of light.")
Prayer at Night ("He lay with quiet heart in
   the stern asleep.")
Sailor rescued from his buffeting, The.
Sequence for Saint Michael.
There'll come a time when brother speaks
   with brother.
These be great cities, new roofs mounting up.
These days are too full fraught with diverse
   dangers.
To Adelhard, Archbishop of Canterbury
   ("Brief is our life, now in the midst of the
   years.")
To Adelhard, Archbishop of Canterbury
   ("Prince-Archbishop, Father Adelhard.")
To Arno of Salzburg.
To Samuel, Bishop of Sens In Time of
   Dearth.
When you sit happy in your own fair house.
Written in Absence.

Aldan, Daisy (b. 1923)
Stones: Avesbury.

Aldington, Richard (1892–1962)
After Two Years.
At the British Museum.
Battlefield.
Evening.
Faun Sees Snow for the First Time, The.
Field Manoeuvres.
Images.
In the Trenches.
Lesbia.
Possession.

Proem: "Sixty years after the fall of Troy."
Resentment.
Soliloquy 2.
Trench Idyll.
Vicarious Atonement.

Aldis, Dorothy (1896–1966)
Hallowe'en Pumpkin, A.
Hiding.
Kick a Little Stone.
Little.
Mouths.
No One Heard Him Call.
Seals all flap, The.
Whistles.

Aldiss, Brian W. (b. 1925)
Frozen Boy, The.
Tom Wedgwood Tells.

Aldrich, Henry (1647–1710)
Catch, A.

Aldrich, Thomas Bailey (1836–1907)
At a Reading.
By the Potomac.
Fannie has the sweetest foot.
Memory.
October turned my maple's leaves to gold.
Untimely Thought, An.
When the Sultan Goes to Ispahan.

Alegría, Claribel (b. 1924)
Ars Poetica.
Desire.
Documentary.
From the Bridge.
I Am Root.
Loneliness and July Ninth.
Nocturnal Visits.
Savoir Faire.
Search.
Small Country.
Summing Up.
We Were Three.

"Aleichem, Sholom" (Sholem Rabinowich) (1859–1916)
Epitaph: "Here lies a simple Jew."
Sleep, My Child.

Aleixandre, Vicente (1898–1984)
My Grandfather's Death.

Alepoudelis, Odysseus. *See* Elytis, Odysseus

Aleshkovsky, Yuz [*or* Iosif Efimovich] (b. 1929)
Comrade Stalin, you are a great scholar.

Alexander, A. L.
This, Too, Shall Pass Away.

Alexander, Alan (b. 1941)
For Raftery.
Gathering Place, The.

Alexander, Cecil Frances (1818–95)
All things bright and beauteous.
Beggar Boy, The.
Burial of Moses, The.
Crow, The.
Dreams.
Fieldmouse, The.
His Are the Thousand Sparkling Rills.
Once in Royal David's City.
There Is a Green Hill Far Away.
They shorten'd the corp, and they pack'd.

Alexander, Elizabeth
Boston Year.
Deadwood Dick.
Farewell to You.
Kevin of the N.E. Crew.
Ladders.
Letter: Blues.
Nineteen.
Ode.
Painting / (Frida Kahlo).
Passage.
Today's News.
Who I Think You Are.
Zodiac.

Alexander, John T. (b. 1940)
Winning of the TV West, The.

Alexander, Joseph Addison (1809–60)
Hidden Line, The.

Alexander, Lewis (1900–1945)
Dream Song.
Enchantment.

Negro Woman.
Nocturne Varial.

Alexander, Margaret Walker
Chicago.
Iowa Farmer.
Memory.
October Journey.
People of Unrest.

Alexander, Meena
Her Garden.

Alexander of Pleuron ("Aetolus") (b. c.315 B.C.)
Epitaph for Cleonicus.

Alexander, Pamela
At Coueron. My First Gun.
Audubon *Enfant.*
Fish Fact.

Alexander, Paul
Limerick: "Chief Stewardess on a Boeing, The."

Alexander, Peter
Limerick: "Modern composer called Cage, A."
Limerick: "Randy young girl called Miranda, A."
Limerick: "Said Marlowe: 'Bay City's a drag.'"
Limerick: "Said Wittgenstein: 'Don't be misled!'"
Limerick: "Sigmund Freud says that one who reflects."
Limerick: "Thomas Hobbes of Malmesbury thought."
Limerick: "United States Constitution, The."
Limerick: "When a friend said to Leda: 'Come on.'"

Alexander, Will (b. 1948)
Explosive Decibel Journeys.
Lightning, *sels.*
Psychotropic Squalls, The.

Alexander, William. *See* Stirling, Sir William Alexander, Earl of.

Alexandru, Ioan
Descending.
Man.
Miserere Nobis.
Prayer.

Alexie, Sherman (b. 1966)
Business of Fancydancing, The.
Capital Punishment.
Crazy Horse Speaks.
Evolution.
On the Amtrak from Boston to New York City.
Powwow Polaroid.
Reservation Love Song.
Translated from the American.
Vision (2).

Alexopoulos, Marion (b. 1948)
Night Flight.

Alfieri, Vittorio (1749–1803)
To Dante.

Alford, Henry (1810–71)
Come, ye thankful people, come.
You and I.

Alford, Janie
Thanks Be to God.

Alfred, King of England (849–99)
Proverbs of Alfred, The, *sels.*

Alfred, William (b. 1922)
Mary Lifted from the Dead.

Algarin, Miguel
At the Electronic Frontier.
Nudo de Claridad.
San Fransisco.
Tato—Reading at the Nuyorican Poets' Cafe.

Alger, Horatio, Jr. (1834–99)
John Maynard.

Ali, Agha Shahid (b. 1949)
Cracked Portraits.
Dacca Gauzes, The.
Desert Landscape.
Dream of Glass Bangles, A.
History of Paisley, A.
Homage to Faiz Ahmed Faiz.

Houses.
I See Chile in My Rearview Mirror.
In the Mountains.
Previous Occupant, The.
Snowmen.

Alici, Kollan (Velli Vītiyār?)
What She Said ("Like milk.")

Aliger, Margarita Iosifovna (1918–92)
Blue Hour, The.
I live / with a bullet in my heart.
Summer days are noticeably shortening, The.

Alkabez, Solomon Halevi (*fl.* 16th cent.)
Come, O Friend, to Greet the Bride.

Alkman (*fl.* 7th cent. B.C.)
Creatures Rest, The.

Allah, Fareedah. *See* Saunders, Ruby C.

Allard, Matsuo
Alone tonight one fish ripples the lake.
Deep in my notebook a lily pad floats away.
Icicle the moon drifting through it, An.
Passing clouds only a stand of aspens is in light.
Silence a droplet of water trickles down a stone, The.
Snow by the window paper flowers gathering dust.
Thawing ice the garbage blooming out of it.

Allbery, Debra
Assembler.
Carnies.
Offering.
Produce.

Allen, Alice E.
My Mother's Garden.

Allen, Dick (b. 1939)
Lost Love.
Short History of the Vietnam War Years, A.

Allen, Elizabeth Akers (Elizabeth Chase Akers) (1832–1911)
Endurance.
Rock Me to Sleep[, Mother].
Sea-Birds.
Toad, A.

Allen, Glen
Woman I Am, The.

Allen, Grant (1848–99)
Ballade of Evolution, A.

Allen, Hervey (1889–1949)
Upstairs Downstairs.

Allen, John Alexander (b. 1922)
Admiral, the prisoner of your giant's.

Allen, Jonathan (1749–1827)
Sinners, Will You Scorn the Message?

Allen, Lillian (b. 1951)
Belly Woman's Lament.
I Fight Back.

Allen, Lyman Whitney (1854–1930)
Coming of His Feet, The.

Allen, Marie Louise (b. 1911)
Angleworms.
Mitten Song, The.
What Is It?

Allen, Paula Gunn (b. 1939)
Catching One Clear Thought Alive.
Dear World.
Eve the fox swung.
Grandmother.
Kopis'taya.
Los Angeles, 1980.
Meditations on the Moon.
Night Vision.
Soundings.
Taku Skanskan.
Zen Americana.

Allen, Richard (1760–1831)
Epitaph for the Western Intelligentsia.
God of Bethel Heard Her Cries, The.

Allen, Samuel ("Paul Vesey") (b. 1917)
Dylan, Who Is Dead.
Harriet Tubman aka Moses.
I Say, Mr. A.
If the Stars Should Fall.
Moment Please, A.
Staircase, The.

To Satch.
View from the Corner.
Allen, William S. (1803–79)
Erie Canal, The.
Allerton, Ellen Palmer (1835–93)
Beautiful Things.
Allestry, Jacob (1653–86)
What art thou, love? Whence are those charms.
Allfrey, Phyllis Shand (b. 1915)
Child's Return, The.
Love for an Island.
Allgar, Brian
Limerick: "Undressing a maiden called Sue."
Alline, Henry (1748–84)
Christ Inviting Sinners to His Grace, *sels.*
Hard Heart of Mine.
Turn, Turn, Unhappy Souls, Return.
Allingham, William (1824–89)
Abbot of Inisfalen, The.
At Ballyshannon, Co. Donegal.
Dream, A [*or* The].
Evening, An.
Everything passes and vanishes.
Express.
Fairies, The.
Four Ducks on a Pond.
Girl's Lamentation, The.
Homeward Bound.
I walk'd in the lonesome evening.
Laurence Bloomfield in Ireland, *sels.*
Meadowsweet.
Mill, A.
No funeral gloom, my dears, when I am gone.
Riding.
Robin Redbreast.
Spring: The Lover and the Birds.
Swing Song, A.
Wishing.
Witch-Bride, The.
Writing.
Allison, Dorothy (b. 1949)
To the Bone.
When I drink I become / the joy of faggots.
Women Who Hate Me, The.
Allison, Drummond (1921–43)
Brass Horse, The.
Dedication: "Had there been peace there never had been riven."
Funeral Oration, A.
King Lot's Envoys.
No Remedy.
Allison, Young Ewing (1853–1932)
Derelict.
Allnutt, Gillian (b. 1949)
Alien.
Comfortable Words.
Allott, Kenneth (b. 1912)
Lament for a Cricket Eleven.
Prize for Good Conduct.
Statue, The.
Allpass, H. B. K. (d. 1916)
Afterwards.
Allston, Washington (1779–1843)
America to Great Britain.
Art.
Coleridge.
On a Falling Group in the Last Judgement of Michael Angelo, in the Cappella Sistina.
On Kean's Hamlet.
On Michael Angelo.
On Rembrant; Occasioned by His Picture of Jacob's Dream.
On Seeing the Picture of Æolus by Pelegrino Tibalbi, in the Institute at Bologna.
On the Group of the Three Angels Before the Tent of Abraham, by Raffaelle, in the Vatican.
On the Luxembourg Gallery.
On the Statue of an Angel, by Bienaimé, in the Possession of J.S. Copley Greene, Esq.
Rubens.
Sylphs of the Seasons, The, *sels.*
To My Venerable Friend, the President of the Royal Academy.

Word: Man, A.
Allur Nanmullai
What He Said ("Heart, knowing, The.")
What She Said ("As the lovely new flowers.")
What She Said ("Bare root of the bean is pink, The.")
Alma-Tadema, Laurence (c.1865–1940)
Bed-Time.
Blessing for the Blessed, A, *sels.*
If no one ever marries me—.
Playgrounds.
Robin, The.
Snowdrops.
Alousi, Alise
Medusa Cement.
Alpheios
Andromache's lament is still in our ears.
Where are the birth-places of the heroes?
Alqamah (*fl.* 6th cent.)
His Camel. *From* The Mufaddaliyat.
Alquit, B. (1896–1963)
Light of the World, The.
Alsop, George (c.1638–c.1680)
Author to His Book, The.
Be just (domestick monarchs) unto them.
Could'st thou (O Earth) live thus obscure, and now.
Heavens bright lamp, shine forth some of thy light.
Lines on a Purple Cap Received as a Present from My Brother.
Poor vaunting earth, gloss'd with uncertain pride.
'Tis said the Gods lower down that chain above.
To My Cosen Mrs. Ellinor Evins.
Trafique Is Earth's Great Atlas.
"Alta" (b. 1942)
Bitter Herbs.
Euch, are you having your period?
Euridice.
First Pregnancy.
I would be a fool to want more children.
Lorelei.
104.
Penus envy, they call it.
7 : 3, *sels.*
Theme and Variations, *sels.*
3 : 6, *sels.*
3 : 1.
29.
2 : 7, *sels.*
Yesterday i had a wild thot. hearing james brown on the radio singing *say it.*
Altamirano, Santiago
Eagle above Us, The.
Alterman, Nathan [*or* Natan] (1910–70)
Abandoned, The.
Beyond Melody.
From All Peoples, *sels.*
Joy of the Poor, The, *sels.*
Maid, The.
Memento of Roads.
Moon.
Red Ridinghood.
Saul.
Altizer, Nell
("Love Letters to Her Who Lives [Alas!] Away"), *sels.*
Sonnet 5: "No, I'll not, carrion, comfort you. Comfort."
Widow Teaches Poetry Writing, The.
Alvarez, Julia (b. 1950)
Bilingual Sestina.
Greg's got custody of Sally and wants.
How I Learned to Sweep.
I check my parents' house while they're abroad.
Ironing Their Clothes.
Naming the Fabrics.
33, *sels.*
Woman's Work.
Alver, Betti (b. 1906)
Children of the Wind.
Fragment.

Iron Heaven.
Iron Nerves.
Painter in the Lion Cage, The.
Stellar Hour.
Tailor Called Sorrow, A.
Titans, The.
Ama Ata Aidoo, Christine (b. 1942)
Cornfields in Accra.
Prelude: "I am the bird of the wayside."
Amabile, George (b. 1936)
Snowfall: Four Variations.
Twink Drives Back, in a Bad Mood, from a Party in Massachusetts.
Amalrik, Andrey Alekseievich (1938–80)
Lake Baskunchak.
Amann, Eric
Billboards.
Circus tent, The.
Names of the dead, The.
Night train passes, A.
Quietly dozing.
Snow falling.
Winter burial.
Amarou (*fl.* 1st? cent.)
Drunken Rose, The.
Amaru (*fl.* 5th cent.)
He marvelled at her breasts, and when he'd seen them.
Though she's the girl, I am the one who's shy.
When his mouth faced my mouth, I turned aside.
Ambapali (*fl.* 4th cent. B.C.)
Black and glossy as a bee and curled was my hair.
Ambo Oral Tradition
Five Ghost Songs, *sels.*
Ambrose, Saint (c.340–397)
Eternal, Thou.
Hymn: "Framer of the earth and sky."
O Strength and Stay upholding all creation.
Ameen, Mark (b. 1958)
Monologue of a Dying Beast.
Sonnet No. 21.
Sonnet No. 22.
Amen, Grover
Cot, The.
Amenhotep IV. *See* Akhenaton
Amergin (*fl.* before Christian era)
Amergin's Charm.
Amergin's Songs, *sels.*
Mystery, The.
Ames, Bernice (b. 1915)
Country of Water.
Amherst, Elizabeth Frances (c.1716–1779)
From a Young Woman to an Old Officer Who Courted Her.
Prize Riddle on Herself When 24, A.
Song for the Single Table on New Year's Day, A.
Verses Designed to Be Sent to Mr. Adams.
Welford Wedding, The.
Amichai [*or* Amikhai], Yehuda (b. 1924)
Achziv, *sels.*
All the generations before me.
Almost a Love Poem.
Anniversaries of War.
Appendix to the Vision of Peace, An.
Diameter of the bomb was thirty centimeters, The.
Elegy: "Wind won't come to draw smiles in dream sand, The."
Evening lies along the horizon and gives blood.
Four Resurrections in the Valley of the Ghosts.
God Has Mercy [*or* Pity] on Kindergarten Children.
Here We Loved, *sels.*
I Am a Live Man.
Ibn Gabirol.
If I forget thee, Jerusalem.
In My Time, at Your Place.
Instructions for a Waitress.
Instructions for the Waitress.

Jerusalem 1967, *sels.*
Jews in the Land of Israel.
King Saul and I.
Laments on the War Dead, *sels.*
Late in my life I come to you.
Leaves without trees.
Letter.
Like our bodies' imprint.
Little Ruth.
Look, thoughts and dreams weave over us.
Lovers in Fall.
Luxury.
Man in his life has no time to have, A.
Mayor.
My Father.
My Mother Once Told Me.
My son, in whose face there is already a sign.
Now, in the storm before the calm.
On My Birthday.
On the Day of Atonement.
Onus of Mercy, The.
Patriotic Reflections.
Patriotic Songs, *sels.*
Pity; We Were Such a Good Invention, A.
Quick And Bitter.
Song of Lies on Sabbath Eve, A.
Song of Resignation.
Songs of the Land of Zion Jerusalem, *sels.*
Summer or Its Ending.
Testimonies.
3.
To my love, combing her hair.
Tourists.
Travels of a Latter-Day Benjamin of Tudela, *sels.*
Two Songs of Peace.
We did it in front of the mirror.
We Have Done Our Duty.
We Will Live Forever.

Amiel, Barry
Death is a matter of mathematics.

"Aminado, Don" (Aminado Petrovich Shpolyansky) (1888–1957)
Honest with Oneself.

Amiri, Akhtar
I Am a Woman, *sels.*

Amirthanayagam, Indran
Elephants Are in the Yard, The.
So beautiful that couple.
There Are Many Things I Want to Tell You.

Amis, Kingsley (1922–95)
A. E. H.
After Goliath.
Against Romanticism.
Alternatives.
Autobiographical Fragment.
Beowulf.
Bookshop Idyll, A.
Dream of Fair Women, A.
Evans Country, The, *sels.*
Ever-Fixed Mark, An.
Helbatrawss, The.
Last War, The.
Mightier than the Pen.
New Approach Needed.
Note on Wyatt, A.
Nothing to Fear.
Reborn.
Science Fiction.
Shitty.
Sight Unseen.
Silent Room, The.
St. Asaph's.

Amis, Lewis R. (1856–1904)
Jehovah, God, Who Dwelt of Old.

Ammianus (*fl.* 2d cent.)
Dawn after dawn after dawn / then suddenly the Dark One.
Dawn after dawn comes on the wine.
Distaste.
Epitaph of Nearchos.
I don't refuse that kiss.
John's efforts to extract a thorn / failed miserably.
May the soil cover / your interred corpse.

Supper at Apelles'/ was a garden-butcher's work.
You think that beard has made you wise.

Ammons, Archie Randolph (b. 1926)
Apologia pro Vita Sua.
Arc Inside and Out, The.
Auto Mobile.
Bonus.
Bridge.
Cascadilla Falls.
Chasm.
City Limits, The.
Clarity.
Classic.
Cleavage.
Close-up.
Coming Right Up.
Confirmers, The.
Conserving the Magnitude of Uselessness.
Constant, The.
Coon Song.
Corsons Inlet.
Coward.
Cracking a Few Hundred Million Years.
Cut the Grass.
Easter Morning.
Eternal City, The.
First Carolina Said-Song.
Foot-Washing, The.
Garbage, *sels.*
Grace Abounding.
Gravelly Run.
Hardweed Path Going.
He Held Radical Light.
Hope's Okay.
Hymn: "I know if I find you I will have to leave the earth."
Laser.
Life in the Boondocks.
Little Thing Like That, A.
Mechanism.
Motion's Holdings.
Mountain Talk.
Needs.
Parting.
Periphery.
Pet Panther.
Play.
Prospecting.
Reflective.
Second Carolina Said-Song.
Serpent Country.
Silver.
Singing & Doubling Together.
Small Song.
So I Said I Am Ezra.
Sphere, *sels.*
Spring Coming.
Terrain.
Their Sex Life.
Transaction.
Treaties.
Triphammer Bridge.
Unifying Principle, The.
Unsaid.
Upland.
Viable.
Visit.
Wide Land, The.
Working with Tools.
Yucca Moth, The.

Ammuvanar
Six Said by the Concubines to Him.
What He Said ("My love whose bangles.")
What Her Girl Friend Said on Her Wedding Day.
What Her Girl Friend Said to Him ("Her soft plump shoulders.")
What Her Girl Friend Said to Him When He Wanted to Come by Day.
What Her Girl Friend Said to Him ("Your sands are furrowed.")
What She Said ("Fishermen who go, The.")
What She Said ("Friend, his seas swell and roar.")
What She Said ("Friend, listen.")
What She Said ("My body.")

What She Said to Her Girl Friend.

Amner, John (*fl.* c.1615)
Motet: "Stranger here, as all my fathers were, A."

"Amorous Lady, The" (*fl.* 1733–35)
Letter to My Love—All Alone, Past 12, in the Dumps, A.
On Being Charged with Writing Incorrectly.
To My Love.

Ân, Nguyễn Trung. *See* **Y Vân Tử'**

Ân, Vu'o'ng Kiều. *See* **Anh Tho'**

Anacreon Anacreontea (*fl.* 6th cent. B.C.)
Age.
All Abdéra mourned at the funeral pyre.
Anacreon's Portrait of His Mistress.
Anacreontique on Love, An.
And why.
Artemon once traveled in shadows.
Beauty.
Beneath this fragrant myrtle shade.
Come, all you painters, all you who are the best.
Count, if you can, every leaf on every tree.
Cup, The.
Dark earth drinks the sky, The.
Drink.
Drinking.
Eros cast in wax, molded into a candle, An.
Eros, playing among the roses.
Grasshopper, The.
He has few hairs, only about the ears.
If Profit offered immortality for gold.
It is lovely to walk fields of tall grass.
Love.
Mother Nature gave bulls horns.
Muses kidnapped Eros, they bound him, The.
Ode 46: "See—the young, the rosy Spring."
Ode 51: "Fly not thus my brow of snow."
Ode of Anacreon, An.
Ode of Anacreon, Paraphras'd / The Cup, An.
Odes, *sels.*
On the Grasshopper.
Only now that my hair is gray.
Paraphras'd from Anacreon.
Picture, The.
Roses (Love's delight) let's join.
Spare me the man.
Spring.
Timokritos was bold in war. This is his grave.
Upon his drinking a Bowl.
Weave garlands of roses for our hair.
Weaving a garland long ago.
When you see my gray hair and chin.
Who cares about the filthy rich.
Wish, The.
Word has come to me that she.
Wounded Cupid. Song, The.
You recount old tales of Thebes.
Youthful Age.

Anania, Michael (b. 1939)
Edge of Autumn, The.
Memorial Day.
Riversongs of Arion, The, *sels.*
Second-Hand Elegy, A.

Anaximander (b. 610 B.C.)
It is necessary that things.

Ancient Egyptian Oral Tradition
Poem to the Sun ("All the cattle are resting in the fields.")
Poem to the Sun ("Boats sail upstream and downstream alike, The.")
This love is as good.

Ancient Sumerian Oral Tradition
Courtship of Inanna and Dumuzi, The, *sels.*

Andal (*fl.* 10th cent.)
Cuckoo, noisy among the Shenbaka flowers.
O people who live in the world.
Tiruppavai, The, *sels.*
To Krishna Haunting the Hills.

Andersen, Astrid Hjertenaes (b. 1915)
Before the sun goes down.

Anderson, Barbara
Deuce: 12:23 a.m.

Anderson, Bill (b. 1928)
Letter from a Black Soldier.
Outbreak.

Anderson, Ethel Louisa Mason (1883–1958)
Afternoon in the Garden.
Bucolic Eclogues, *sels.*

Anderson, Jack (b. 1935)
Garden of Situations, A.
Invention of New Jersey, The.
Ode to Pornography.

Anderson, Jon (b. 1940)
Blue Animals, The.
In Autumn.
In Sepia.
John Clare.
Parachutist, The.
Photograph of Myself, The.
Rosebud.
Ye Bruthers Dogg.
Years.

Anderson, Laurie
Dog Show.
Red Hot.

Anderson, Maggie
Closed Mill.
Country Wisdoms.
Invention of Pittsburgh, The.
Spitting in the Leaves.

Anderson, Mary (b. 1939)
In the April Rain.
Praise the Lord for all the seasons.
Thanks to Spring.

Anderson, Maxwell (1888–1959)
Parallax.

Anderson, Patrick (1915–79)
Houses Burning; Quebec.
Poem on Canada, *sels.*
Sestina in Time of Winter.

Anderson, S. E. (b. 1943)
Junglegrave.
Sound of Afroamerican History Chapt I, The.
Sound of Afroamerican History Chapt II,
The.

Anderson, Sherwood (1876–1941)
Evening Song.
Visit, A.

Anderson, Teresa
Kneading Bread.

Anderton, Anne
Marking of Folders.

Andeyek
I know how people get treated when they
die.

Andrade, Costa (b. 1936)
Fourth Poem of a Canto of Accusation.

Andrade, Eugenio de (b. 1923)
Fable.
Music.
Penniless Lovers.
Silence.
White on White, *sels.*

Andrade, Mário de (1893–1945)
Aspiration.
Rondeau for You.

Andresen, Sophia de Mello Breyner (b. 1919)
Camoes and the Debt.
Dead Men, The.
Dionysius.
Mirrors, The.
Small Square, The.
Young Girl and the Beach, The.

Andrew, Nigel
Limerick: "In childhood it's easy to feel."

Andrew of Wyntoun (c.1350–1425)
Macbeth.

Andrews, Bruce (b. 1948)
Bomb then, bomb now—doing the breathing
arsenic job, we want.
DDD.
Gestalt me out! Slang to the point of meat-
eating, imperative ornament, dislike.
Impatient Heart, The.
Methodology.
Rich little circle south.

Species means guilt. Slave ship somatism
grease their wings wrencher.
Stalin's genius consisted of not french-
kissing.
Tizzy Dust, *sels.*
West West.
While.

Andrews, Miles Peter ("Arley") (d. 1814)
Elegy on the Death of Mr Sterne.

Andrews, Robert (b. 1766?)
Mercury; on Losing My Pocket Milton at
Luss near Ben Lomond, and Other
Mountains.
Urania.

Andrews, Tom
Cinema Vérité: The Death of Alfred, Lord
Tennyson.

Andreyev [or Andreiev], Daniil Leonidovich (1906–59)
For the Unveiling of a Memorial.
Russian Gods, The, *sels.*

Andreyev [or Andreiev], Vadim Leonidovich (1903–1976)
Deep scar engraved in the bark's dark silver,
A.
Rebecca.
To My Daughter.

Andros, Dionysius of. See Dionysius Sophistes

Aneirin (fl. 6th cent.)
Gododdin, The, *sels.*

Angel, Ralph (b. 1951)
As It Is.
Breaking and Entering.
Man in a Window.
River Has No Hair to Hold Onto, The.
Shadow Play.
Tatters.
Twice Removed.

Angell, Barbara (b. 1945)
Fox's Song.
Street Music.

Angelou, Maya (b. 1928)
Africa.
Caged Bird.
Come, And Be My Baby.
Elegy: "I lay down in my grave."
Life Doesn't Frighten Me.
Many and More.
Momma Welfare Roll.
My Arkansas.
On Aging.
On Diverse Deviations.
Phenomenal Woman.
Pickin Em Up and Layin Em Down.
Sepia Fashion Show.
Still I Rise.
Thank You, Lord.
Woman Me.

"Angelus Silesius" (Johannes Scheffler) (1624–77)
Cherubical Wanderer, The, *sels.*
God is a pure no-thing.
God, whose love and joy.
It Depends on You.

Angermayer, Frances
Conversion.

Anghelaki-Rooke, Katerina (b. 1939)
Body Is the Victory and the Defeat of
Dreams, The.
Notes on My Father, *sels.*

Angilbert (c.740–814)
Angilbert's Prayer.
Epitaph: "O King, give Angilbert thy rest."

Angira, Jared (b. 1936)
Country of the dead, The.
If.
Look in the Past, A.
Manna.
Request.

Angus, Marion (1870–1946)
Alas! Poor Queen.
Invitation.
Mary's Song.

Anh, Hà Triệu. See Hồ Dzềnh

Anh Tho' Vu'o'ng Kiều Ân (b. 1919)
Harvesting at Sunset.

Annand, James King (b. 1908)
Arctic Convoy.
Heron.
I Winna Let On.
Mavis, mavis.

Annensky, Innokenty Fiodorovich (1856–1909)
Black Spring.
It happened in Vallen-Koski.
Petersburg.
Small Kulak Landowner.
Snow.
Violin Bow and Strings.

Annett, David
Wreck of the Deutschland, The.

Ansen, Alan (b. 1922)
Fatness.
Fit of Something against Something, A.
Tennyson.

"Ansky, S." (Solomon Rappoport) (1863–1920)
Emigrant Song.
Tailor, The.

Anstey, Christopher (1724–1805)
New Bath Guide, The, *sels.*

"Anstey, F." (Thomas Anstey Guthrie) (1856–1934)
Limerick: "There was an old man of
Bengal."

Antar (fl. 6th cent.)
Poets have muddied all the little fountains,
The. *From* The Mu'allaqat
Have the poets left a single spot for a patch
to be sewn? *From* The Mu'allaqat

Anthony, Florence. See Ai

Anthony, George (1873–1950?)
Autumn Evening.

Anthony, Jim
Limerick: "Henley's a special regatta."

Antimedon [or Antomedon] (fl. c.90 B.C.–40 A.D.)
Drinking together in the evening we are
human.
Of Dronkennesse.

Antin, David (b. 1932)
David ross called up from syracuse and
wanted to know if.
Definitions for Mendy.
List of the Delusions of the Insane / What
They Are Afraid Of, A.
Passengers, The.
Private Occasion in a Public Place, A.
Real Estate.

Antipater of Sidon (fl. 2d cent. B.C.)
Already prepared in the golden chamber.
Antiodemis, Aphrodite's pet cherub, from a
baby.
Aristeides.
Bitto gives to Athena.
Epigrams, *sels.*
Erinna.
Erinna's *Distaff.*
Lysidice, I'm anxious to find out the
meaning.
My house is simple, lying beside the sea.
Never again, Orpheus.
Pindar.
Priapos of the Harbor.
Reporter of the courage of heroes.
Ruins of Corinth, The.
This is Anacreon's grave. Here lie.
This is the grave of grey-haired Maronis.
This mangled tentacle of the huge
scolopendra.
This piece of Lydian earth holds Amyntor.
Undying Thirst.
Who hung these shields here still all shiny.

Antipater of Thessalonica (fl. 1st cent. B.C. or A.D. 1st cent.)
All sea is sea. How mad it is to blame.
Am I to blame the drink or the downpour?
Deserted islands, broken sherds of land.
Don't judge men by their gravestones.
Europa (in Athens) does business / at truly
reasonable rates.
Fortune-tellers say I won't last long.
Gipsies tell me my life-line's a short one,
The.

Glykon, glory of Asia / born in Pergamum.
Gorgo, a Cretan bitch, on a deer's track.
Homer said everything beautifully, but to
   call.
I was Hermocrateia: twenty-nine / children I
   bore.
I'm not at all scared of the Pleiades setting.
In my stars there's three times ten.
In winter on her hearth lighting some coal.
It is morning, Chrysilla. Some time ago the
   clarion cock.
Italian dust covers a Libyan.
Man who first built up with good strong
   words, The.
Mentorides, please tell us who.
Neither war, nor cyclones, nor earthquakes.
Phoebus was a herdsman.
Priapus seeing Kimon with a stand.
Temple of Artemis at Ephesos, The.
That dried-up arse, Lykainis.
Theogenes sent us for Piso's pleasure—.
These are Aristophanes' marvellous plays.
"They pray for children? Let them!" cried
   Polyxo.
To Epicles.
To Telembrotos.
Unlucky Nicanor, quenched by the grey and
   deep.
Water-mill, A.
Watered by the Strymon and great
   Hellespont.
Waves, the rough surf, swept me on the
   shore, The.
When the deep-piled winter snow / melted on
   her roof.
Where is your famous beauty.
Yesterday when I'd drunk myself to bed /
   with water (neat).
You can explore your every desire.

Antiphanes (c.388–c.311 B.C.)
   Lost Bride, The.
   Man's makeshift days would flash past at the
     best.
   Piddle-paddling race of critics, rhizome-
     fanciers.
   Strange race of critics, A.
   When Cytherea slipped her wily sash off.

**Antiphilus [or Antiphilos] (fl. 1st cent. B.C.–c.1st
cent. A.D.)**
   Earthquaked, my house collapsed.
   Epitaph of a Sailor.
   Even then I said.
   Gifts to a Lady.
   Give me a mattress on the ship's poop some
     day.
   Here is the river Eurotas.
   Imaginary Dialogue.
   On Diogenes the Cynic.
   On the Death of the Ferryman, Glaucus.
   Quince Preserved through the Winter, Given
     to a Lady, A.
   Torrent Cuts Off the Poet's Path, A.

**Antistius Vetus (Gaius Antistius Vetus) (fl. A.D.
c.26)**
   Priapus the Scarecrow.

"Antler" (b. 1946)
   Factory, sels.
   Somewhere Along the Line.
   What Every Boy Knows.

Antoine, Pierre. See **Motteux, Peter Anthony**
Antokolsky, Pavel Grigoryevich (1896–1978)
   Ballad of the Wondrous Moment.
   From their journeys our dreams return.
   Hate, be a faithful prop, and find.
   Hieronymus Bosch.
   Paul the First.
   Sans Culotte.

Antoninus, Brother. See **Everson, William**
Antonov, Vadim (b. 1942)
   Vindication, sels.
Antrobus, John (b. 1933)
   Cowboy, The.
**"Anvari" (Awhad ad-Din 'Ali ibn Vahid ad-Din
Muhammad Khavarani) (1126?–1190?)**
   Hors de Combat.
Anyidoho, Kofi (b. 1947)
   Hero and Thief.

Anyte [or Anytes] (fl. 290 B.C.)
   Alive, this man was Manes, a common slave.
   And you too perished long ago, by a bush
     with matted roots.
   Big enough for an ox, the cauldron.
   Child Myro made this tomb, The.
   Children have put purple, The.
   Children have tied you, billy-goat, with
     bright, The.
   Cock, A.
   Damis set this up, to commemorate.
   Dedication: A Spear.
   Ease your weary limbs, stranger, under this
     elm—.
   Epigrams, sels.
   I am Hermes. I stand in the crossroads by a
     windy.
   I, Hermes, have been set up.
   I mourn for Antibia the virgin.
   Indeed then, it was your own courage.
   Instead of a solemn wedding and marriage-
     bed.
   Kypris keeps this spot.
   Look at the horned goat of Dionysus.
   Lounge in the shade of the luxuriant laurel's.
   On a Dolphin.
   On this her daughter's tomb.
   Shepherd's Gift, A.
   Sit down in the shade of this fine spreading
     laurel.
   This place is the Cyprian's for she has ever
     the fancy.
   Throwing her arms around her father.
   To shock-haired Pan and the nymphs who
     protect the cow-byres.
   Why, country Pan, sitting still.

Anzaldúa, Gloria (b. 1946)
   Cultures.
   Horse.
   Interface.
   We Call Them Greasers.

Apache Oral Tradition
   Now you will feel no rain.

Api
   Another Me.

Apollinaire, Guillaume (1880–1918)
   Calligram, 15 May 1915.
   Crayfish, The.
   Hat-Tomb.
   Heart, Crown, and Mirror, sels.
   Horse Calligram.
   I Imagine Angels.
   It's Raining.
   Little Car, The.
   Mirabeau Bridge, The.
   Ninth Secret Poem, The.
   On imagine les anges.
   Phantom of Clouds, A.
   Poems for Lou, sels.
   Post Card.
   Seal, The.
   Shadow.
   Sighs of the Gunner from Dakar, The.
   Stanzas Against Forgetting.
   Victoire, sels.
   Zone.

Apollinaris Sidonius (c.430–484)
   Invitation to the Dance.
   To Catulinus That He Cannot Write Him an
     Epithalamium Because of the Enemy
     Hosts.

Apollinarius
   If you insult me in my absence.
Apollonides (fl. 6 B.C.–A.D. 15)
   Beeman Cliton hews / From the flower fed
     hive.
   Cup clinks out, my friend, The.
   Lacking rich acres, thick grape-crops.
   Snow, clothing sky & mountain.
Apollonius Rhodius (222 B.C.–181 B.C.)
   Argonautica, The.
   Stealing the Golden Fleece.
Appel, Benjamin (b. 1907)
   Talker, The.
Appleman, Philip (b. 1926)
   Amurrika!
   Is There a Voice.

It is enough; time presses, we are thrifty.
La Misère.
Maples.
Mary.
More than leaves, more than flakes.
My friend, you don't understand.
Peace with Honor.
So What.
St. Matthew, sels.
Try wading in sand.
Waiting for the Fire.
When they sd to me this.

Appleton, Everard Jack (1872–1931)
   Woman Who Understands, The.
Applewhite, James (b. 1935)
   Barbecue Service.
   Bordering Manuscript.
   Marriage Portrait.
   My Grandfather's Funeral.
   Prayer for My Son.
   To Earth.
   White Lake.
Arabov, Yury [or Iurii] b. 1954
   I'm introducing it as a hunchback.
   Walking the Places I've Never Been.
Aragon, Louis (1897–1982)
   Lilacs and the Roses, The.
   Mimosas.
   Phoenix Reborn from Its Ashes, The.
   Poem to Shout in the Ruins.
Arakida Moritaké (Moritaké) (1473–1549)
   Flying Flower, A.
   Haiku: "Fallen flowers rise."
   Haiku: "Falling flower, The."
Arapaho Oral Tradition
   Ghost Dance Songs.
Aratus (fl. 3d cent. B.C.)
   Phaenomena, sels.
Arbiter, Caius Petronius. See **Petronius Arbiter**
Arbuthnot, John (1667–1735)
   Epitaph on Colonel Francis Chartres.
   Know Yourself.
**Archevolti, Samuel ben Elhanan Isaac, of
Padua (fl. 17th cent.)**
   Advice to Hotheads.
Archias
   Desire, get your bow ready / and go quietly
     after / another mark.
   "Get away from Eros!"
Archias of Byzantium (fl. c.120 B.C.)
   Not even in death can I.
   Sea Dirge.
Archias of Macedon
   Hektor of Troy.
Archilochus (c.680?–c.640? B.C.)
   Decks awash, / Mast-top dipping.
   I don't give a damn if some Thracian ape
     strut.
   Like Odysseus under the ram.
   May he lose his way on the cold sea.
   My ash spear is my barley bread.
   Sergeant to Enyalios.
   Shield, The.
   Stranded ashore from the sea.
   That good shield I threw away.
   There's nothing now.
   This island, garlanded with wild woods.
   When Alkibié married.
   Will, lost in a sea of trouble.
Arcos, René
   Dead, The.
Arendt, Erich
   Lost Bay.
   Ode I.
Aretino, Pietro (1492–1556)
   If famous Apelles with his hand of art.
Argentarius (Marcus Argentarius) (fl. c.60 B.C.)
   About Menophila's morals there are strange
     rumours.
   Aristomache loved a drink:/ The old
     chatterbox was fonder.
   Blackbird, singing on the highest branch / Of
     the oak.
   Come, Gobrys, there are other gods besides
     the Muses.

Damned bird, why have you ruined my sleep.
Dead, they'll burn you up with electricity.
Dead, you will lie under a yard of earth.
Drunk I observe the golden dance of stars.
Epigram: "Hetero-sex is best for the man of a serious turn of mind."
Her perfect naked breast.
Here lie a grasshopper and a / Cicada.
Here's to Lysidice: pour in ten ladles, boy.
I can't bear to watch your hips.
Isias my love, with your scented breath.
Look at this, golden-horned moon.
Looking and lusting is not love.
Love is not just a function of the eyes.
Melissa means honeybee; yes, you're true.
My name was Pnytagoras; I died by drowning.
Old Story, The.
Once I was reading Hesiod.
Psyllus lies here. Procuring was his trade.
Rather skinny beauty, you'll find, / is Diocleia, A.
Take off those flimsy nets, Lysidice.
That's your third sneeze now, my good lamp.
This is Callaeschrus' empty tomb.
Trader, untie the long stern-cables.
Welcome, old friend, long-necked bottle.
Whoa! but I stagger—too much wine!
You are a bee, my flower-lovely.
You loved Menophila when you were rich.
Your kink, Heraclea, is sucking off.

Arghezi, Tudor
Gulf.
Psalm.
Testament.

Argüelles, Iván (b. 1939)
That Goddess, sels.

Aridjis, Homero [or Umberto] (b. 1940)
Epitaph for a Poet.
Rain is Falling, The.

Arif, Iftiqar (b. 1943)
Ghazal.
To a Despondent Evening.

Arika, Abba. See Rab

Ariosto, Ludovico (1474–1533)
Canto XXIII, sels.
Orlando Furioso, sels.

Aristodicus of Rhodes (fl. 3d cent. B.C.)
Cricket, you'll sing no more.
On a Pet Grasshopper.

Ariston (fl. 3d cent. B.C.)
If you mice are looking for food.

Aristophanes (b. between 450 B.C. and 446 B.C., d. c.380 B.C.)
Acharnians, The, sels.
Birds, The, sels.
Clouds, The, sels.
Ecclesiazusae, The, sels.
Frogs, The, sels.
Home front, The.
Lysistrata, sels.
On the advice of Praxilla.
Peace: A Wedding Song, The.
Plutus, sels.
Son learns how to beat his father, The.
Suffering of the gods, The.

Ariwara no Yukihira (815–93)
I must leave you, but.

Arkell, Reginald (1882–1959)
What is a Garden?

"Arley." See Andrews, Miles Peter

Armantrout, Rae (b. 1947)
Attention.
Disown.
Garden, The.
Generation.
Getting Warm.
Incidence.
Language of Love.
Leaving.
Necromance.
Sense.
Winter.

Armitage, Jennifer
To Our Daughter.

Armitage, Simon (b. 1963)
Poem.

Armour, Richard (b. 1906)
Covering the Subject.
Good sportsmanship we hail, we sing.
Hiding Place.
Money.
Pachycephalosaurus.

Armstrong, Frankie
Collier Lass, The.
Month of January.
Out of the Darkness.
Women of My Land.

Armstrong, J. A.
Another Reply to "In Flanders Fields."

Armstrong, John (1709–79)
Art of Preserving Health, The, sels.
Oeconomy of Love; a Poetical Essay, The, sels.

Armstrong, Martin Donisthorpe (1882–1974)
Gold.
On a Little Bird.
To a Jilt.

Armuth, Victoria C.
Mother, A.

Arnaut Daniel (fl. c.1180–1210)
Aura Amara, L'.
Autet e bas.
Bel m'es quan lo vens m'alena.
Mot eran dous miei cossir.
Resolute desire that enters, The.

Arnett, Carroll ("Gogisgi") (b. 1927)
Anadarko John.
Drunk.
Land.
Powwow.
Removal: Last Part.
Rock Painting.
Something for Supper.
Song of the Breed.
Story of My Life, The.
You.

Arnold, Sir Edwin (1831–1904)
Destiny.
He and She.

Arnold, George (1834–65)
Beer.

Arnold, Matthew (1822–88)
Austerity of Poetry [or Jacopone da Todi].
Bacchanalia; or, The New Age, sels.
Balder Dead, sels.
Below the Surface-Stream.
Buried Life, The.
Calais Sands.
Continued.
Courage.
Dover Beach.
East London.
Empedocles on Etna, sels.
Forsaken Merman, The, sels.
Geist's Grave.
Growing Old.
"In harmony with Nature?" Restless fool.
In Utrumque Paratus.
Last Word, The.
Lines Written in Kensington Gardens, sels.
Longing.
Memorial Verses, sels.
Nameless Epitaph, A.
Obermann Once More.
Palladium.
Philomela
Poor Matthias, sels.
Progress.
Progress of Poesy, The, sels.
Quiet Work.
Requiescat.
Resignation, sels.
Rugby Chapel.
Scholar-Gipsy, The, sels.
Self-Dependence.
Shakespeare.
Sohrab and Rustum, sels.
Stanzas from the Grande Chartreuse, sels.
Strayed Reveller, The, sels.
Switzerland, sels.

Thyrsis, sels.
To a Friend.
To a Republican Friend, 1848.
West London.
Youth and Calm.

Arnot, Vere
Woman at Home.

Aronsten, Joan (b. 1914)
Ad Infinitum.

Arp, Hans [or Jean] (1887–1966)
Domestic Stones (fragment), The.
Great Unrestrained Sadist, The.
Kaspar Is Dead.
Man. The Woman, The.
Opus Nil.
People.

Arrowsmith, Pat (b. 1930)
Christmas Story (1980).
Political Activist Living Alone.

Artaud, Antonin (1896–1948)
All Writing Is Garbage.
Spurt of Blood, The.

Artemidorus (fl. 2d cent. B.C.)
Pastoral Muses once were scattered, The.

Arthur, Kevyn (b. 1942)
Gospel.
I Saw Three Ships.

Arthur, Ruth M. (1905–79)
Snowflakes.

Arvey, Verna (b. 1910)
All that I am.

Arvidson, K. O. (b. 1938)
Fish and Chips on the Merry-Go-Round.
Tall Wind, The.

"Arzhak, Nikolai." See Daniel, Yuly Markovich

Asalache, Khadambi (b. 1934)
Death of a Chief.

Asbaje, Juana Rumirez de. See Juana Inés de la Cruz, Sister

Asch, Frank (b. 1946)
Leaves.
Play.
Summer.
Sunflakes.

Asclepiades (fl. 270 B.C.)
Although she's a girl, Dorkion.
Arkheanassa.
Bitto and Nannion do not.
Colophon to a Roll of Erinna's Poems.
Dear Lamp, she swore by you.
Didyme waved an olive branch at me.
Didyme waved her wand at me.
Drink, Asklepiades.
Epigrams, sels.
Eumares.
Get drunk, my boy, don't weep, you're.
Great is a drink of snow.
I touched up sexy Hermione.
In a fit, Philaenion bit me.
It is eternally winter.
It is sweet in summer to slake.
Leave the rags, you tiny lusts.
Love has found out how to mix.
Night long and wintry / the Pleiades half set.
Nikarete's face, sweetly moistened.
On a Ring.
Once I lay down with Hermione.
Pampered Philainion stabbed me, The.
Playing once with facile.
She's black: what then? so are dead coales, but cherish.
Snow, hail and smut the sky.
Snow! Hail! Lower! Lightning! Thunder!
Stay, my tendrils, where hung.
Swearing an oath to Demeter.
Think how unspeakably sweet.
To a Girl.
To you, Kypris, Lysidike.
Tomb on the Shore, A.
What are you saving it for?
When soft Irene like a.
Wine is love's test.
You're saving it? What for?

Asclepiodotus (fl. 1st cent. B.C.)
Hear in the sea, Thetis, Memnon's alive.

Aseyev [or Aseiev], Nikolai Nikolaievich (1899–1963)
Dark Blue Hussars.
How shall I tell you.

Ashanti, Baron James (*fl.* 20th cent.)
Just Another Gig.

Ashbery, John (b. 1927)
Additional Poem, An.
And "Ut Pictura Poesis" Is Her Name.
Around the Rough and Rugged Rocks the
    Ragged Rascal Rudely Ran.
As One Put Drunk into the Packet-Boat.
As You Came from the Holy Land.
At North Farm.
Baked Alaska, *sels.*
Blessing in Disguise, A.
Boy, A.
Brute Image.
Bungalows, The.
But Not That One.
But What Is the Reader to Make of This?
Cæsura.
Cathedral Is, The.
City Afternoon.
Civilization and Its Discontents.
Crazy Weather.
Darlene's Hospital.
De Imagine Mundi.
Decoy.
Definition of Blue.
Down by the Station, Early in the Morning.
Drunken Americans.
Farm Implements and Rutabagas in a
    Landscape.
Faust.
Fear of Death.
Flow Chart, *sels.*
For John Clare.
Forties Flick.
Friends.
Glazunoviana.
Grand Abacus.
Hard Times.
He cuts down the lakes so they appear
    straight.
Hotel Lautréamont.
Houseboat Days.
How much longer will I be able to inhabit
    the divine sepulcher.
Ice-Cream Wars, The.
If the Birds Knew.
Illustration.
Instruction Manual, The.
Into the Dusk-Charged Air.
Just Walking Around.
Knocking Around.
Lament Upon the Waters, The.
Landscapeople.
Last Month.
Last World, A.
Le Livre Est sur la Table.
Leaving the Atocha Station.
Life As a Book That Has Been Put Down.
Love Poem, A.
Man of Words, A.
Many Wagons Ago.
Märchenbilder.
Meditations of a Parrot.
Melodic Trains.
Mixed Feelings.
Morning Jitters.
My Erotic Double.
Myrtle.
Never Seek to Tell Thy Love.
New Realism, The, *sels.*
Oh, Nothing.
Old Complex, The.
On Autumn Lake.
On The Empress's Mind
One Thing That Can Save America, The.
Ongoing Story, The.
Other Tradition, The.
Our Youth.
Painter, The.
Paradoxes and Oxymorons.
Picture of Little J. A. in a Prospect of
    Flowers, The.

Poem: "While we were walking under the
    top."
Pyrography.
Rain.
Rain Moving In.
Rivers and Mountains.
Saying It to Keep It from Happening.
Self-Portrait in a Convex Mirror.
Shadow Train.
Skaters, The, *sels.*
Some Trees.
Songs without Words.
Soonest Mended.
Spring Day.
Statuary.
Street Musicians.
Summer.
Syringa.
Tennis Court Oath, The.
Tenth Symphony.
These Lacustrine Cities.
They Dream Only of America.
Thinnest Shadow, The.
Thoughts of a Young Girl.
Ticket, The.
To Redouté.
Train Rising Out of the Sea.
Two Sonnets.
Variation on a Noel.
Wet Casements.
What Is Poetry.
When the Sun Went Down.
White Roses.
Worsening Situation.
Years of Indiscretion.
Young Prince and the Young Princess, The.

Ashby, Cliff (b. 1918)
Latter Day Psalms.
Stranger in This Land, A.

Ashe, Thomas (1836–89)
City Clerk, The.
Corpse-bearing.
To Two Bereaved.
Vision of Children, A.
Word to the West End, A.

Asimov, Isaac (1920–92)
Limerick: "Industrious young obstetrician,
    An."
Limerick: "'On the beach,' said John sadly,
    'there's such.'"
Limerick: "There was a young lady of Ealing
    / And her lover before her was kneeling."
Limerick: "There was a young maid of
    Peru."
Limerick: "There was a young man of
    Belgrade."

Askelon, Euenus of. *See* **Euenus**

Askew, Anne (1520–46)
Ballad Which Anne Askew[e] Made and
    Sang When She Was in Newgate, The.

"Asphodel" (Pauline Long) (b. 1921)
Full Moon in Malta.
On the Pilgrim's Way in Kent, as It Leads to
    the Coldrum Stones.
Winter Solstice—for Frank.

Asquith, Herbert (1881–1947)
Elephant, The.
Hairy Dog, The.
Ship Sails Up to Bideford, A.
Volunteer, The.

Astell, Mary (1666–1731)
Ambition.
Awake my Lute, daughters of Musick come.
In Emulation of Mr Cowleys Poem Call'd
    The Motto.

Aston, Alasdair (b. 1930)
Everything in the Garden is Lovely.

"Astra" (b. 1927)
Bloody Pause.
Daughters.
Now or Never.

"Asya" (Asya Gay)
Celan.
Deer, The.

Atherton, John (1598–1640)
Tank Town.

Atimantiyar (*fl.* 3d cent.)
Nowhere, not among the warriors at their
    festival.

Atkins, Russell (b. 1926)
Dark Area.
It's Here In The.
Lakefront, Cleveland.
Late Bus (After a Series of Hold-Ups).
Lisbon.
Narrative.
New Storefront.
Night and a Distant Church.
On the Fine Arts Garden, Cleveland.
Probability and Birds in the Yard.

Atkinson, Michael (b. 1962)
Same Trouble with Beauty You've Always
    Had, The.

Atmanam
Next Page.

Atsumi, Ikuko (b. 1940)
Different Dimensions.
Ring, The.

Attar, Samar
Return of the Dead, The, *sels.*

Āttiraiyaṉār, Kaḷḷil
Poet's Memory Is Counsel, A.

Attlee, Clement (1883–1967)
Few thought he was even a starter.

Attwood, A. A.
Farmyard, The.

Atwell, Roy (1878–1962)
Some Little Bug.

Atwood, Margaret (b. 1939)
Against Still Life.
Animals in That Country, The.
At first I was given centuries.
At the Tourist Centre in Boston.
Bored.
Circe / Mud Poems, *sels.*
Circle Game, The, *sels.*
Daguerreotype Taken in Old Age.
Damside.
Death of a Young Son by Drowning.
Disembarking at Quebec.
Dream 2: Brian the Still-Hunter.
Earth.
Eden Is a Zoo.
Elegy for the Giant Tortoises.
Eventual Proteus.
Explorers will come, The.
Five Poems for Grandmothers, *sels.*
Flowers.
Footnote to the Amnesty Report on Torture.
Game after Supper.
Habitation.
Is/Not / Not.
It Is Dangerous to Read Newspapers.
Landcrab I.
Landcrab II.
Landlady, The.
Last Poem.
Late August.
Marrying the Hangman.
More and more frequently the edges.
Morning in the Burned House.
Night in the Royal Ontario Museum, A.
Notes towards a Poem That Can Never Be
    Written.
November.
Postcard.
Procedures for Underground.
Puppet of the Wolf, The.
Resurrection.
Robber Bridegroom, The.
Settlers, The.
Solstice Poem, *sels.*
Songs of the Transformed, *sels.*
Spelling.
There Is Only One of Everything.
They Eat Out.
This Is a Photograph of Me.
Torture.
Trainride, Vienna—Bonn.
Tricks With Mirrors.
Up.
Variation on the Word *Sleep.*

Variations on the Word *Love.*
Vultures.
Woman Skating.
Woman Who Could Not Live With Her Faulty Heart, The.
You Are Happy.
You begin this way.
You fit into me.
You take my hand and.

Aubert, Alvin (b. 1930)
Baptism.
Bessie.
Bessie Smith's Funeral.
Economics.
Feeling Through.
For Mark James Robert Essex d. 1973.
How It's Done.
Opposite of Green, The.
Silence.
When the Wine Was Gone.

Auchterlonie, Dorothy (b. 1915)
Meditation of a Mariner.
Tree, The.
Waiting for the Post.

Auden, Wystan Hugh (1907–73)
A. E. Housman.
Academic Graffiti, *sels.*
Adolescence.
Aesthetic Point of View, The.
After Reading a Child's Guide to Modern Physics.
Alice is gone and I'm alone.
Always the Following Wind.
Amor Loci.
Another Time.
Anthem for St. Cecilia's Day, *sels.*
Anthem: "Let us praise our Maker, with true passion extol Him."
As I walked out one evening.
At Last the Secret Is Out.
At the Party.
Atlantis.
August 1968.
Ballad: "O what is that sound [which so thrills the ear]."
Brussels in Winter.
Bucolics, *sels.*
Calypso.
Cave of Making, The.
Chimaeras, The.
City without Walls.
Climbers, The.
Composer, The.
Consider this and in our time.
Dear, Though the Night Is Gone.
Decoys, The.
Dog beneath the Skin, The, *sels.*
Doggerel by a Senior Citizen.
Edward Lear.
Epitaph on a Tyrant.
Et in Arcadia Ego.
Exiles, The.
Fairground.
Fall of Rome, The.
First Things First.
Five Songs, *sels.*
Free One, A.
From Scars Where Kestrels Hover.
Gare du Midi.
Get There If You Can and See the Land.
Good-Bye to the Mezzogiorno.
Happy New Year, A, *sels.*
Healthy Spot, A.
Herman Melville.
History of Truth, The.
Horae Canonicae, *sels.*
Horatians, The.
I Cannot Grow.
In Memoriam: Ernst Toller.
In Memory of Sigmund Freud.
In Memory of W. B. Yeats, *sels.*
In Praise of Limestone.
It's No Use Raising a Shout.
James Honeyman was a silent child.
Journey to Iceland.
Jumbled in the Common Box.
Law like Love.

Leap Before You Look.
Letter, The.
Letter to Lord Byron, *sels.*
Limerick: "Marquis de Sade and Genet, The."
Limerick: "T. S. Eliot is quite at a loss."
Love Feast, The.
Love Letter.
Lullaby: "Din of work is subdued, The."
Lullaby: "Lay your sleeping head, my love."
Marginalia, *sels.*
May with its light behaving.
Miss Gee.
Moon Landing.
More Loving One, The.
Mundus et Infans.
Musée des Beaux Arts.
New Year Letter, *sels.*
Night Mail, The.
1929.
Novelist, The.
Now the Leaves Are Falling Fast.
Now through Night's Caressing Grip.
Ode: To My Pupils.
Ode to Terminus.
Ode to the Diencephalon.
Ode to the Medieval Poets.
On the Circuit.
On This Island.
Our Bias.
Our hunting fathers told the story.
Oxford.
Paid on Both Sides, *sels.*
Passenger Shanty.
Paysage Moralisé.
Petition.
Poem: "O who can ever praise enough."
Pora, The.
Precious Five.
"Prolific and the Devourer," The, *sels.*
Prologue: "O love, the interest itself in thoughtless heaven."
Prophets, The.
Quest, The, *sels.*
Question, The ("To ask the hard question is simple.")
Questioner Who Sits So Sly, The.
September 1, 1939.
Shield of Achilles, The.
Shorts [1927–1932], *sels.*
Shorts I, *sels.*
Silly fool, the silly fool, The.
Since.
Six Commissioned Texts, *sels.*
Song for St. Cecilia's Day.
Song: "When the Sex War ended with the slaughter of the Grandmothers."
Sonnets from China, *sels.*
Spain 1937.
St. Luke, *sels.*
Stop All the Clocks, Cut Off the Telephone.
Strings' Excitement, The.
T. S. Eliot.
Taller to-day, we remember similar evenings.
Ten Songs, *sels.*
Thanksgiving for a Habitat, *sels.*
Their Lonely Betters.
This lunar beauty.
Truest Poetry Is the Most Feigning, The [or, Ars Poetica for Hard Times].
Twelve Songs, *sels.*
Uncle Henry.
Under Sirius.
Under Which Lyre, a Reactionary Tract for the Times.
Unknown Citizen, The.
Villanelle: "Time can [or will] say nothing but I told you so."
Voltaire at Ferney.
Voyage, A, *sels.*
Wanderer, The.
Watertowers, The.
Who will endure.
Who's Who.

Augustine, Saint (354–430)
Half Of Me.
My heart was darkened over with grief, and whatever I.

Augustini, Delmira (1886–1914)
Vision.

Ault, Norman (1880–1950)
Ducks.
Pig's Tail, The.

Aus of Kuraiza (fl. 7th cent.)
Apostasy.

Auslander, Joseph (1897–1965)
Elegy: "Fled is the swiftness of all the white-footed ones."
Interval.
Sunrise Trumpets.
Three things filled this day for me.

Ausonius (Decimus Magnus Ausonius) (c.310–395)
Evening on the Moselle.
I am that Dido which thou here do'st see.
Idyll of the Rose.
Mistresse, A.
Moselle, The, *sels.*
On the Sicilian strand a hare well wrought.
Since worms and dust must be your fate.
To His Wife.
To One that Painted Eccho.
Windsor-Forest, *sels.*

Austin, Alfred (1835–1913)
Is Life Worth Living?
Jameson's Ride.
Last Night, The.

Austin, Louie. See Hunter, Albert *and* Louie Austin

Austin, Mary (1868–1934)
Grass on the Mountain, The.
Grizzly Bear
Shoshone Wedding Song.
Song of a Man About to Die in a Strange Land.
Song of the Maverick.

Austin, William
Sepulchrum Domus Mea Est.

Automedon (fl. c.6th cent. B.C.)
All the long evening.
Gymnastics Teacher, The.
Having cleaned yesterday on a goat's foot.
Impotent Lover, The.
Nicetes begins with gentle declamation.
Phoebus, accept this dinner that I bring you.
That Asiatic striptease girl / who goes in for those.

Auvaiyar (fl. between 1st and 3d cent.)
Chariot Wheel, A.
Earth's Bounty.
Elegy: "If he found a little liquor."
Elegy: "Let day, let night, come no more."
Elegy: "This bright burning pyre."
His Welcome.
Mothers.
Poet to a Dancer, A.
Shall I charge like a bull.
What She Said, Thinking of Him Crossing the Wilderness Alone.
You stand and hold the post of my small house.
Young Chieftain, A.

Ava, Frau (fl. c.1160)
I am yours, you are mine.

Avakkumova, Mariya [or Mariia] (b. 1943)
Dead man touched me with his hand, A.
Russia can't be grasped by the mind.

Avena, Thomas (b. 1959)
Cancer garden, protected by buildings, one unfinished. Still, The.

Averill, Diane
Bad for You.
Renewal.

Avery, Richard K. (b. 1934)
And the Cock Begins to Crow.

Avianus
Monkey, The.

Avicolli, Tommi (b. 1951)
Rape Poem, The.

Avidan, David (b. 1934)
Burying Uncle Salomon.
Election Speech for the Presidency of the United States of Chinamerica.

Fire the Babysitter.
Glimpse of an Open Dream.
Longterm Hatred.
Minor Mythology.
Moment Ago, A.
Practical Poems.
Prehistory.
Recurring Opportunity.
Samson, Our Hero, *sels.*
Some Futureplans.
Song of the Self-Made Orphans.
Traveling in the City, *sels.*
Two Memorial Poems.
What I Have to Tell You, Until Next Time.

Avila, Teresa of. *See* **Teresa de Cepeda Y Ahumada**

Avis, Nick
Evening star, The.
Freshly fallen snow.

Avison, Margaret (b. 1918)
Butterfly Bones; or, Sonnet against Sonnets.
Civility a Bogey.
Dumbfounding, The.
For Dr. and Mrs. Dresser.
Hiatus.
In a Season of Unemployment.
Intra-Political.
Lament: "Gizzard and some ruby inner parts, A."
Meeting Together of Poles & Latitudes: In Prospect.
Nameless One, A.
New Year's Poem.
Party, The.
Snow.
Story, A.
Stray Dog, near Ecully.
Swimmer's Moment, The.
Tennis.
Thaw.
Transit.
Two Selves, The.
Unspeakable.
Voluptuaries and Others.
Water and Worship: An Open-Air Service on the Gatineau River.
Word, The.

Awatere, Arapeta (1910–70)
Lament for Kepa Anaha Ehau.

Awoonor, Kofi (George Williams) (b. 1935)
Agosu if you go tell them.
America.
American Memory of Africa, An.
Easter Dawn.
First Circle, The.
Night of My Blood (1971), *sels.*
On Having Been an Experimental Sacred Cow for Four Years, and a Token African on Faculty.
Rediscovery.
Sea Eats the Land at Home, The.
So the World Changes.
Something has happened to me.
Song of War.
Songs of Sorrow.
They Shall Know.
This Earth, My Brother.
Three poems from Rediscovery (1964), *sels.*
To Dennis Brutus.
To the Eminent Scholar and Meddler.
Weaver bird built in our house, The.

Aworinde, Awotunde
If a Suite in Praise of the Yoruba Oracle, *sels.*

Axelrod, David B. (b. 1943)
Once in a While a Protest Poem.

Ayer, Jean
Everyday Things.

Aylen, Leo
Undistinguished Visitor, The.

Ayres, Philip (1638–1712)
Cynthia on Horseback.
Death of Adonis, The.
Describes the Place Where Cynthia Is Sporting Herself.
Epigram on Woman, An.

Ever Present.
Fly, The.
Invites His Nymph to His Cottage.
Invites Poets and Historians to Write in Cynthia's Praise.
On a Fair Beggar.
On Lydia Distracted.
Yoke uneasy on the ox doth sit, The.

Ayton [or Aytoun], Sir Robert (1570–1638)
Answer, The.
Exercise of Affection, The.
On the Prince's Death, to the King.
Posy, A: "Dear love, I am resolved with thee to live."
Rejection, The.
Song, A: On His Mistress.
Song: "What means this strangeness now of late."
Sonnet: on Loss.
Sonnet: On the River Tweed.
There is none, no none but I.
To an Inconstant One.
To His Coy Mistress.
To His Forsaken Mistress.
Upon His Unconstant Mistress.
Upon Platonic Love: To Mistress Cicely Crofts, Maid of Honour.
Upone Tabacco.
Valediction.

Aytoun, William Edmonstoune [or Edmondstoune] (1813–65)
Edinburgh after Flodden, *sels.*
Laureate, The.
Massacre of the Macpherson, The.

Aytoun, William Edmonstoune (1813–65) and Sir Theodore Martin (1816–1909)
American's Apostrophe to Boz, The, *sels.*
Royal Banquet, The.

A'yunini
Killer, The.

Azevedo, Kathleen de
Suicide, The.

A'Zmi, Kaifi (b. 1924)
Humiliation.

Azmi, Khalil-ur-Rahman (1927–78)
I and I.

B

"B., C. K."
American girl in Versailles, An.

"B., H. d'A."
Givenchy Field.
No-Man's-Land.

"B., M."
Deportation.

"B., R."
This story's strange, but altogether true.

Ba, Oumar (b. 1900?)
Drought.
Familiar Oxen.
Justice is Done.
Nobility.
Ox-Soldier, The.

Baba, Akiko (b. 1928)
In the autumn when words sound.
Punished in the moment of love.
Since I don't know my mother.

Baba Kuhi of Shiraz (948–1050)
In the market, in the cloister—only God I saw.

Babcock, Donald Campbell (b. 1885)
O God, in Whom the Flow of Days.

Babcock, Maltbie Davenport (1858–1901)
Be Strong!
School Days.
This Is My Father's World.

Baca, Jimmy Santiago (b. 1952)
Cloudy Day.
43.
Green Chile.
How We Carry Ourselves.
I Am Here.

I Applied for the Board.
Immigrants in Our Own Land.
Invasions.
It Started.
Like an Animal.
Main Character.
Mantanza to Welcome Spring.
Mu Tío Baca el Poeta de Socorro.
Oppression.
Perfecto Flores.
So Mexicans Are Taking Jobs from Americans.
There Are Black.
Voz de la Gente.
Work We Hate and Dreams We Love.

Bacchylides (b. 450 B.C.)
How white.
Keep to the one path.
Olympian Ode for Hiero of Syracuse (Four-Horse Chariot Race), *sels.*
Paean, *sels.*
Pæan of Bacchylides, On Peace, The.
Peace on Earth.
This much I know.

Bacharach, Naftali
Poem for the Sefirot as a Wheel of Light, A.

Bacheller, Irving (1859–1950)
Whisperin' Bill.

Bachmann, Ingeborg (1926–73)
Curriculum Vitae.
Days in White.
Early Noon.
Every Day.
Exile.
Firstborn Land, The.
Go, my thought, as long as a word clear enough for flight.
Great Freight, The.
In the Storm of Roses.
Invocation of the Great Bear.
Kind of Loss, A.
No Delicacies.
Out of the corpse-warm vestibule of heaven steps the sun.
Paris.
Psalm: "Be still with me, as all bells are still!"
Respite, The.
Safe-Conduct.
Settlement.
Songs from an Island.
Songs in Flight, *sels.*
Truly.
You want the summer lightning, throw the knives.
You words, come, after me!

Bachri, Sutardji Calzoum (b. 1942)
Cat.

Backus, Bertha Adams
Then Laugh.

Bacmeister, Rhoda Warner (b. 1893)
Galoshes.

Bacon, Francis (1561–1626)
Life.

Bacon, Leonard (1802–81)
Hail, Tranquil Hour of Closing Day.
Pilgrim Fathers, The.
Wake the Song of Jubilee.

Bacon, Leonard (1887–1954)
Flyfisherman in Wartime.
Horatian Variation.

Bagg, Robert (b. 1935)
Death at Pocono Lake Preserve.
Ezra Pound and Robert Bridges.
Ronald Wyn.

Baggesen, Jens (1764–1826)
Childhood.

Baggett, Rebecca
Day Before They Bombed Nagasaki, The.

"Bagritzky [or Bagritsky], Eduard Georgievich" (Eduard Georgievich Dzyubin) (1895–1934)
Black bread and a faithful wife.
He Tries out the Concords Gently.
My Honeyed Languor.
Origin.

Piece of Black Bread, A.
Smugglers.
Till Eulenspiegel.
Verses about a Nightingale and a Poet.
Watermelon.

Bagryana, Elisaveta
Old Fortress, The.
Only One, The.
River Run.

Baha Ad-din Zuhayr (d. 1258)
On a Blind Girl.

Bahe, Liz Sohappy (b. 1947)
And What of Me?
Farewell: "You sang round-dance songs."
Grandmother Sleeps.
Once Again.
Printed Words.
Ration Card, The.
Talking Designs.

Bai, Mukta (fl. 13th cent.)
I live where darkness / is not.

Baildon, Henry Bellyse (1849–1907)
Moth, A.

Bailey, Anthony (b. 1933)
Green and the Black, The.

Bailey, L. W.
Limerick: "There was a young girl from
Uttoxeter / Who made passing oarsmen
gape through locks at her."

Bailey, Philip James (1816–1902)
Country Town, A, sels.
What Is Heaven?

Baillie, Joanna (1762–1857)
Address to the Muses, An, sels.
Blackcock, The [or The Black Cock].
Child to His Sick Grandfather, A.
Disappointment, A.
Ghost of Fadon, The.
Hay making.
Hooly and Fairly.
Horse and His Rider, The.
Mother to Her Waking Infant, A.
Night Scenes of Other Times, sels.
Outlaw's Song, The.
Reverie, A
Song: "What voice is this, thou evening
gale!"
Song: Woo'd and married and a'.
Summer Day, A, sels.
Summer's Day, A.
To Cupid.
Trysting Bush, The.
Up! quit thy bower.
Winter Day, A, sels.
Winter's Day, A.

**Baillie, Lady Grisel [or Grizel or Grisell]
(1665–1746)**
Were Ne My Hearts Light I Wad Dye.
Werena My Heart Licht I Wad Dee.

Bain, Andrew Geddes (1797–1864)
Address.
Polyglot Medley.

Baird, Martha (1921–81)
Do not make things too easy.

Baker, Austen
There was a young lady named Miller.

Baker, David (b. 1954)
Snow Figure.

Baker, Donald W. (b. 1923)
Dying in Massachusetts.

Baker, Dorothy (b. 1907)
Castles in the Sand.
In the Woods.

Baker, Henry (1698–1774)
Declaimer, The.
Love's an headstrong wild desire.
Rapture, The.

Baker, Houston A., Jr. (b. 1943)
Of Walter White's Father in the Rain.
Tobacco Warehouse Blues.
Toward Guinea: For Larry Neal, 1937–1981.

Baker, Howard (b. 1905)
Ode to the Sea.

Baker, J. G.
My Trundle Bed.

Baker, Julia Aldrich
Mizpah.

**Baker, Karle Wilson ("Charlotte Wilson") (b.
1878)**
Let Me Grow Lovely.

Baker, Kathleen Leland (b. 1951)
Baby Hilary, Sir Edmund, The.
Honey Moon.

Baker, Marie Annharte (b. 1942)
Porkskin Panorama.

Baker, Thomas (b. 1871)
Steam Engine; or, The Power of the Flame,
The, sels.

Baker, Tony (b. 1954)
For Geraldine.
Poem: "First day of May Jack."
Storm clouds a smudge of damson.

Bakken, Dick
How to Eat Corn.

Balaban, John (b. 1943)
After our war, the dismembered bits.
Along the Mekong.
April 30, 1975.
Dead for Two Years, Erhart Arranges to
Meet Me in a Dream.
Dragonfish, The.
For Miss Tin in Hue.
For Mrs. Cam, Whose Name Means "Printed
Silk."
For the Missing in Action.
Graveyard at Bald Eagle Ridge.
Guard at the Binh Thuy Bridge, The.
In Celebration of Spring.
News Update.
Opening Le Ba Khon's Dictionary.
Story.
Than, Mau.
Thoughts Before Dawn.
Words for My Daughter.

Balamani Amma, N. (b. 1909)
To My Daughter.

Baldwin, A. W. I.
Ten Little Dicky-Birds.

Baldwin, James (1924–87)
Guilt, Desire and Love.
Lover's Question, A.

Baldwin, Michael (b. 1930)
Death on a Live Wire.

Baldwin, Thomas (1753–1825)
From Whence Doth This Union Arise?

Baldwin, William (fl. 1547–49)
Christ, My Beloved.
Christ to His Spouse [or The Beloved to the
Spouse].

Balfour, Lord
Best thing to give, The.

Balk, Christianne
Yellow Hills in Back, The.

Ball, Caroline Augusta (b. 1825)
Jacket of Gray, The.

Ball, Hugo (1886–1927)
Complete Sound-Poems of Hugo Ball, The.
Flight out of Time, sels.
Sun, The.

Ball, Sally
Nocturnal.

Ballard, Charles G.
During the Pageant at Medicine Lodge.
Grandma Fire.
Memo.
Now the People Have the Light.
Sand Creek.
Speaker, The.
Spirit Craft, The.
Their Cone-like Cabins.
Winds of Change, The.

Ballou, Hosea, I (1771–1852)
Dear Lord, Behold Thy Servants.
In God's Eternity.
When God Descends with Men to Dwell.

Ballou, Hosea, II (1796–1861)
Ye Realms below the Skies.

Ballou, Silas (1753–1837)
Almighty God in being was.
While I Am Young.

Balmont, Konstantin Dmitrievich (1867–1942)
I don't know the wisdom others seem to
need.
Vanishing Shadows.

Bamford, Samuel (1788–1872)
Touch him, aye! touch him, if you dare.

Bampfylde, John Codrington (1754–96)
On a Frightful Dream.
On a Wet Summer.
On Hearing That Torture Was Suppressed
throughout the Austrian Dominions.
Sonnet: "As when, to one who long hath
watched, the morn."
To the Evening.
To the Redbreast.

Bancks, John (1709–51)
Description of London, A.
Fragment, A: "In Cloe's chamber, she and I."

Bancquart, Marie-Claire (b. 1932)
Baroque.
Counterfable of Orpheus.
Curriculum vitae.
Epitaph.
Portrait of Jonah with woman.
Sea.
Town.
Vanished, The.
Woman asleep.

Bancroft, Charles (1911–69)
Tadoussac.

Bancroft, James Henry (1819–44)
Brother, Though from Yonder Sky.

Bàng Bá Lân (b. 1913)
If in a Future Life We Meet Again.
Mother, I Am Still Here With You.
They Starved, They Starved.

Bàng, Trần Văn. See Lưu Văn Vong

Bangs, Carol Jane (b. 1949)
Touching Each Other's Surfaces.

**Bangs, Edward. See Shuckburg, Richard and
Edward Bangs**

Bangs, John Kendrick (1862–1922)
Blind.
Dreadful Fate of Naughty Nate, The.
Hired Man's Way, The.
I never knew a night so black.
If I had a trunk like a big elephant.
Little Elf, The.
My Dog.
On File.
Philosophy.
Today, whatever may annoy. ·

Banim, John (1798–1842)
Soggarth Aroon.

Banker, Iowna Elizabeth
Lion Thoughts.

Banks, George Linnaeus (1821–81)
What I Live For.

Bannerman, Frances
Upper Chamber, An.

Banning, Lex (b. 1921)
And No Regrets.
Epitaph for a Scientist.
Romancero.

Bansode, Hira (b. 1939)
Woman.

Bantock, Gavin (b. 1939)
Bard.
Dirge: "Body lies under the ground."
Joy.

Banus, Maria (b. 1914)
Eighteen.
Gift Hour.
New Notebook, The.

Baraka, Imamu Amiri (LeRoi Jones) (b. 1934)
After the Ball.
Agony, An. As Now.
Alba.
All is One for Monk.
Am/Trak.
Audubon, Drafted.
Babylon Revisited.
Balboa, the Entertainer.
Ballad of the Morning Streets.

Beautiful Black Women.
Biography.
Black Art.
Black Bourgeoisie.
Black Dada Nihilismus.
Black People!
Black People: This Is Our Destiny.
Bumi.
Cant.
Careers.
Cold Term.
Contract. (For The Destruction and
    Rebuilding of Paterson), A.
Crow Jane.
Cuba Libre.
Das Kapital.
Dead Lady Canonized, The.
Dope.
Duncan Spoke of a Process.
Evil Nigger Waits for Lightnin'.
For Hettie.
For Maulana Karenga & Pharoah Sanders.
Funk Lore.
Guerrilla Handbook, A.
Hymn for Lanie Poo, sels.
I don't love you.
I Substitute for the Dead Lecturer.
In Memory of Radio.
In One Battle.
In the Tradition / (Not a White Shadow but
    Black People Will Be Victorious).
Incident.
Invention of Comics, The.
Ka 'Ba.
Kenyatta Listening to Mozart.
Last Word, The.
Leadbelly Gives an Autograph.
Legacy.
Leroy.
Letter to E. Franklin Frazier.
Liar, The.
Like Rousseau.
Look for You Yesterday, Here You Come
    Today.
Major Bowes' Diary.
Masked Angel Costume / The Sayings of
    Mantan Moreland.
Minute of Consciousness, The.
Nation Is Like Ouselves, The.
New Reality Is Better Than a New Movie!,
    A.
New World, The.
Numbers, Letters.
One Night Stand.
Ostriches and Grandmothers!
Pause of Joe, The.
Poem for Black Hearts, A.
Poem for Deep Thinkers, A.
Poem for Democrats, A.
Poem for Half White College Students.
Poem for Speculative Hipsters, A.
Poem for Willie Best, A.
Poem Some People Will Have to Understand,
    A.
Political Poem.
Politics of Rich Painters, The.
Preface to a Twenty Volume Suicide Note.
Pressures, The.
Rare Birds, The.
Return of the Native.
Sacred Chant for the Return of Black Spirit
    and Power.
Snake Eyes.
Song Form.
SOS.
State/meant.
Study Peace.
Three Modes of History and Culture.
Three Movements and a Coda.
To a Publisher. . . Cut-out.
Turncoat, The.
W. W.
Way Out West.
We Own the Night.
When We'll Worship Jesus.
Why's / Wise, sels.
Why's/Wise, sels.

Will They Cry When You're Gone, You Bet.
Wise/Whys, sels.
World Is Full of Remarkable Things, The.
Young Soul.
Baranczak, Stanislaw (b. 1946)
    December 14, 1979: A Poetry Reading.
    February 8, 1980: And No One Has Warned
        Me.
    If china, then only the kind.
    N. N. Tries to Remember the Words of a
        Prayer.
    Three Magi, The.
Barannikov, Kostya [or Kostia] (b. 1950)
    May there always be sun!
Barbauld, Anna Laetitia (1743–1825)
    Corsica, sels.
    Eighteen Hundred and Eleven.
    Life! I know not what thou art.
    Mouse's Petition, The.
    Ode to Spring.
    On a Lady's Writing.
    On the Expected General Rising of the
        French Nation.
    Poems, sels.
    Poems (1773), sels.
    Rights of Woman, The.
    To a Little Invisible Being Who Is Expected
        Soon to Become Visible.
    To Mr. S. T. Coleridge.
    To the Poor.
    Tomorrow.
    Washing-Day.
Barber, J. Delayne
    Santos and Stones.
Barber, Mary (1690?–1757)
    Conclusion of a Letter to the Rev. Mr. C—
        —, The.
    On Seeing an Officer's Widow Distracted.
    Stella and Flavia every hour.
    To a Lady, Who Commanded Me to Send
        Her an Account in Verse, sels.
    To Mrs. Francis-Arabella Kelly.
    Unanswerable Apology for the Rich, An.
    Written for My Son, and Spoken by Him at
        His First Putting on Breeches.
Barberini, Francesco da (1264–1348)
    Of Caution.
    Virgin Declares Her Beauties, A.
Barbour, John (1316?–1395)
    Bruce, The, sels.
    Buik of Alexander, The, sels.
Barbu, Ion
    Counter Play.
    Dioptric.
    Dogmatic Egg, The.
    Timbre.
Barclay, Alexander (1475–1552)
    Eclogues, sels.
Barclay, Edwin (d. 1953)
    Human Greatness.
Bardeen, Charles William (1847–1924)
    Birds' Ball, The.
Bardoloi, Nirmalprabha (b. 1933)
    Dawn.
**Barham, Richard Harris. See "Ingoldsby,
    Thomas"**
Barham, Richard Harris (1788–1845)
    Jackdaw of Rheims, The.
Baring-Gould, Sabine (1834–1906)
    Hymn: "Now the day is over."
    Onward, Christian Soldiers.
Barkan, Stanley H.
    Two Grandmas.
Barkar, Wendy
    Canning Season.
Barker, D. W.
    Limerick: "Of attractions the Sabines ain't
        stinted."
    Limerick: "One morning the Monarch said:
        'When.'"
Barker, George (b. 1913)
    Calamiterror, sels.
    Channel Crossing.
    Crystal, The.

Dog, Dog in My Manger.
Elegy V: [Separation of Man from God].
Epitaph for the Poet.
First Cycle of Love Poems, sels.
Gardens of Ravished Psyche, The.
He Comes Among.
How many apples grow on the tree?
In Memory of a Friend.
In Memory of David Archer, sels.
January jumps about.
Leaping Laughers, The.
Memorial Couplets for the Dying Ego.
My sister Clarissa spits twice if I kiss her.
News of the World II.
News of the World III.
Not in the poet is the poem or.
Oak and the Olive, The.
Ode against St. Cecilia's Day.
Pacific Sonnets, sels.
Resolution of Dependence.
Reverend Arbuthnot-Armitage-Brown, The.
Second Cycle of Love Poems, sels.
Secular Elegies, sels.
Sequence.
Song: "Now this bloody war is over."
Sonnet of Fishes.
Sonnets of the Triple-headed Manichee, sels.
Sparrow's Feather, A.
Summer Idyll.
Third Cycle of Love Poems, sels.
To Any Member of My Generation.
To My Mother.
To My Son, sels.
True Confession of George Barker, The, sels.
Turn on Your Side and Bear the Day to Me.
Verses for a First Birthday.
Village Coddled in the Valley, The.
Wild Dreams of Summer What Is Your
    Grief.
Wraith-Friend, The.
Barker, Jane (1652–1727?)
    Fidelia Arguing with Her Self on the
        Difficulty of Finding the True Religion.
    Necessity of Fate, The.
    She Begining to Study Phisick, Takes Her
        Leave of Poetry.
    To Her Lover's Complaint.
    To My Young Lover.
    Virgin Life, A.
Barker, Noah
    What Does It Matter?
Barkley, Alben (1877–1956)
    Limerick: "In New Orleans dwelt a young
        Creole."
Barks, Coleman (b. 1937)
    Becoming Milton.
    New Words, sels.
Barksdale, Clement (1609–87)
    To My Nephew, J. B.
Barlas, John (1860–1914)
    Beauty's Anadems.
    Cat-Lady, The.
    Dancing Girl, The.
    Memphian Temple, The.
    My Lady's Bath.
    Oblivion! is it not one name of death?
    Terrible Love.
Barlett, I. J.
    Town of Don't-You-Worry, The.
Barlow, George (b. 1948)
    4½ Months: Halfway Song.
    Mingus Speaks: Found Poems.
    Nook.
    Painting Drunken Twilight.
    Place Where He Arose, The.
    Salt.
Barlow, Joel (1754–1812)
    Advice to a Raven in Russia [December,
        1812].
    Along the banks where Babel's current flows.
    Columbiad, The, sels.
    Hasty Pudding, The.
    Judge Me, O God.
    O God of My Salvation, Hear.
    On the Discoveries of Captain Lewis.
    Song, A: "Fame let thy trumpet sound."

Barnard, John (1681–1770)
Nations That Long in Darkness Walked.
Thrice Blest the Man.

Barnard, Mary (b. 1909)
Pleiades, The.
Shoreline.

Barnes, Barnabe (1569–1609)
Divine Century of Spiritual Sonnets, A, *sels.*
Parthenophil and Parthenophe, *sels.*
To the Most Beautiful Lady, the Lady
Bridget Manners.

Barnes, Dick
Chuang Tzu and Hui Tzu were hundreds of
years old.

Barnes, Djuna (1892–1982)
Transfiguration.

Barnes, Jane (b. 1943)
Hot Dog Poem, The.
How to Dress Like a Femmy Dyke.
How to Dress like a Scary Dyke.

Barnes, Jim (b. 1933)
Autobiography, Chapter XLII: Three Days in
Louisville.
Autobiography, Chapter XVII: Floating the
Big Piney.
Autobiography: Last Chapter.
Bone Yard.
Camping Out on Rainy Mountain.
Captive Stone, The.
Dog Days 1978.
Ex-Deputy Sheriff Remembers the Eastern
Oklahoma Murderers, An, *sels.*
Four Things Choctaw, *sels.*
Halcyon Days.
Heartland.
La Plata, Missouri: Clear November Night.
Last Look at La Plata, Missouri.
Lying in a Yuma Saloon.
Paiute Ponies.
Return to La Plata, Missouri.
Season of Loss, A.
Sunday Dreamer's Guide to Yarrow,
Missouri, A.
Sweating It Out on Winding Stair Mountain.
These Damned Trees Crouch.
Tracking Rabbits: Night.
Tracking the Siuslaw Man.

Barnes, Jo (b. 1941)
Clinic Day.

Barnes, Julians (*fl.* 15th cent.)
Book of Hunting, *sels.*

Barnes, Kate
Mare, A.

Barnes, William (1801–86)
All Still.
Bachelor, The.
Bells ov Alderburnham, The.
Be'mi'ster.
Best Man in the Vield, The, *sels.*
Bit o' Sly Coorten, A.
Brisk Wind, A.
Burncombe Hollow.
Childhood.
Clote (Water-Lily), The.
Come!
Common a-Took In, The.
Echo, The.
Evenen in the Village.
Evening, and Maidens.
Fall, The.
False Friends-like.
Geate A-Vallen To, The.
Grammer's Shoes.
Heedless o' My Love.
In the Spring.
Jay a-Pass'd.
Jenny out from Hwome.
Leane, The.
Leaves a-Vallen.
Leeburn Mill.
Light or Sheade.
Lost Little Sister, The.
Lullaby.
Lwonesomeness.
Mater Dolorosa.
Melhill Feast.

Musings.
My Love's Guardian Angel.
My Orcha'd in Linden Lea.
Polly Be-en Upzides wi' Tom.
Railroad, The, *sels.*
Readen ov a Head-Stwone.
Rustic Childhood.
Rwose in the Dark, The.
Sam'el Down vrom Lon'on.
Seasons and Times.
Shellbrook.
Shep'erd Bwoy, The.
Shop o' Meat-Weare.
Sing Again Together.
Slow to Come, Quick a-Gone.
Sonnet: "In every dream thy lovely features
rise."
Sonnet: Leaves.
Storm-Wind, The.
Stwonen Steps, The.
To Me.
Tokens.
Troubles of the Day.
Turnstile, The.
Uncle an' Aunt.
Vaices That Be Gone, The.
Vield Path, The.
Vierzide Chairs, The.
Walken Hwomme at Night.
When We That Now Ha' Childern Wer
Childern.
Which Road?
White an' Blue.
Wife A-Lost, The.
Wife a-Prais'd, A.
Wind at the Door, The.
Winter Night, A.
With you first shown to me.
Woak Hill.
Wold clock's feäce is still in pleäce, The.
Zilver-Weed, The.
Zong, A.
Zun-zet.

Barnfield [*or* Barnefield], Richard (1574–1629)
Affectionate Shepherd, The.
Comparison of the Life of Man, A.
Cynthia, *sels.*
Ode, An: "As it fell upon a day." *From
Passionate Pilgrim.*
Sonnets, *sels.*
To His Friend Master R.L., In Praise of
Music and Poetry.

Barnstone, Aliki (b. 1956)
Mating the Goats.
To a Friend's Child.
Windows in Providence.

Barnstone, Willis (b. 1927)
Disappearance.

Baro, Gene (1924–82)
For Hani, Aged Five, That She Be Better
Able to Distinguish a Villain.
Street climbs upward steeply, The.
Travelling Backward.

Barolini, Helen
Having the Wrong Name for Mr. Wright.

Barr, Burlin
Tremendous Mood Swings.

Barr, Tina
Antique Shop.

Barras, Jonetta (b. 1950)
Peace.

Barrax, Gerald William (b. 1933)
Adagio.
Black Narcissus.
Christmas 1959 et Cetera.
Domestic Tranquility.
Efficiency Apartment.
For a Black Poet.
For Malcolm: After Mecca.
Fourth Dance Poem.
Gift.
I Had a Terror—Since September.
In the Restaurant.
King: April 4, 1968.
Old Gory, The, *sels.*
Scuba Diver Recovers the Body of a
Drowned Child, The.

Strangers Like Us: Pittsburgh, Raleigh, 1945–
1985.
There was a song.
To a Woman Who Wants Darkness and
Time.
Two Figures on Canvas.
Visit.
Your Eyes Have Their Silence.

Barreno, Maria Isabella. *See* **Three Marias,
The**

Barresi, Dorothy (*fl.* 20th cent.)
Venice Beach: Brief Song.

Barrett, Carlton. *See* **Cogil, Legon** *and* Carlton
Barrett

Barrett, Eaton Stannard (1786–1820)
Woman.

Barrington, Judith
Dirty Panes.
Villanelle VI.

Barrington, Patrick (b. 1908)
I had a duck-billed platypus when I was up
at Trinity.
I had a hippopotamus; I kept him in a shed.
Take me in your arms, Miss Moneypenny-
Wilson.

Barrington, Pauline B. (b. 1876)
White Iris, A.

Barrios, Miguel de (1625–1701)
Epitaph: "Daniel and Abigail."

Barrow, Jedediah
You Call That a Ts'ing; a Letter.

Barrows, Richard
Report Card, The.

Barry, Jan
Floating Petals.
Green Hell, Green Death.
Harvest Moon.
In the Footsteps of Genghis Khan.
Lessons.
Nights in Nha Trang.
Nun in Ninh Hoa, A.

Barry, Michael J. (1817–89)
Hymn of Freedom.

Barsotti, Charles
Limerick: "Insurance salesman named Flint,
An."

Barth, John (b. 1930)
Minstrel's Last Lay, The.

Barth, R. L.
Insert, The.
Letter from An Hoc (4), by a Seedbed.
P.O.W.s.
Postscript.

Bartlett, Elizabeth (b. 1913)
Charlotte, Her Book.
Contre Jour.
999 Call.

Barton, Bernard (1784–1849)
Land Which No Mortal May Know, The.

Barton, Joan (b. 1908)
Mistress, The.

Bartošová, Magda
And That Is Why. . . .

Bartsch, Kurt
Deposition.
Rita's husband gave Rita her walking papers.
Still Life with Cleaning Lady.

Bartusek, Antonin
Heliotropism / of branches, now darkened.
Home.
Love Song.
Royal Progress.
Sentence.
Strangled, The.

Baruch, Dorothy Walter (1899–1962)
Popcorn-Popper, The.

Baruch of Worms (*fl.* c.1200)
Elegy: "Those reckless hosts rush to the
wells."

Basheva, Miryana
Business.

Bashford, Sir Henry Howarth (1880–1961)
Where do the gipsies come from?

Bashlachov [*or* **Bashlachev**], **Aleksandr** (1960–1988)
Griboyedov's Waltz.
Basho (Matsuo Basho) (1644–94)
All That Is Left.
Ancient pool. Sound.
Around existence twine.
Autumn evening.
Beside the road.
Cool it is, and still.
Fall of night.
Finis.
First cold rain.
Friend sparrow, do not eat, I pray.
Haiku: "Lightning flashes, The!"
Haiku: "Lightning gleam, A."
Heat-lightning streak.
How cool it feels.
How rough a sea.
In the old stone pool.
It would melt.
Lightning-gleam, A.
Lightning in the clouds!
Lonely pond in age-old stillness sleeps, A.
Many, many things.
No rice—In that hour.
O cricket, from your cheery cry.
Old men, white-haired, beside the ancestral graves.
Old pond:/ frog-jump-in.
Old pond— / The sound, An.
On a withered branch.
On this road / no one will follow me.
Quick-falling dew.
Roadside thistle, eager, The.
Seventy-six Hokku, *sels.*
Some of them with staves.
Spider.
Spring moon—.
Summer grasses.
Summer grasses grow, The.
Though I'm in Kyoto.
Village where they ring, A.
Well, let's go.
Wild sea— / In the distance, A.
Worshipping at the Great Shrine at Ise.
Basho (1644–94) *and* **Shita Yaba**
Call of Two Birds, The.
Basho, Matsuo. *See* **Basho**
Bass, Ellen (b. 1947)
For Barbara, who said She Couldn't Visualize Two Women Together.
I Didn't Know.
In Celebration.
She recognizes miner's lettuce.
Tampons.
There are times in life when one does the right thing.
To Praise.
Vaginas of women, all the clusters.
Basse [*or* **Bas**], **William** (*fl.* c.1602)
Anglers Song, The, *sels.*
Bassus [*or* **Bassos**] **(Lollius Bassus) (***fl.* A.D. 1st cent.**)**
Epigrams, *sels.*
I am not going to turn into gold.
I refuse to turn into gold.
I'll never have a river of gold.
Your flatteries are boring.
Bast, Felicity
Body of the Great Cat, The.
Chang Tuan's Cats.
Chrysoberyl: The Eye of the Cat.
Empress's Cat, The.
Frost Eyebrows was the favorite cat.
Hywell the Good Weighs the Worth of a Cat.
Nebamun's Cat.
Bastard, Thomas (1566–1618)
Ad Henricum Wottonem.
De Naevo in Facie Faustinae.
De Puero Balbutiente.
Epitaph: Iohannis Sande.
In Gaetam.
Basualto, Neftalí Ricardo Reyes. *See* **Neruda, Pablo**
Bat-Miriam, Yocheved (b. 1901)
Distance Spills Itself, The.

Like this before you, just as I am.
Bateman, Claire
Beatitude.
Childhood of a Stranger.
Conspiracy.
Distances.
Bateman, Doris I.
My Rocking Chair.
Bateman, Edgar (1860–1946)
Cockney's Garden, The.
It's a Great Big Shame.
Bates, Clara Doty (1838–95)
At Grandfather's.
Gray Thrums.
Who Likes the Rain?
Bates, David (c.1810–1870)
Speak Gently.
Bates, G. E.
Pentagonia.
Bates, Katharine Lee (1859–1929)
America the Beautiful.
Despised and Rejected.
If You Could Come.
To One Who Waits.
Yellow Clover.
Bateson, Thomas
I Heard a Noise and Wishèd for a Sight.
Batterham, Eric N.
Once.
Battiss, Walter (1906–82)
Limpopo.
Baudelaire, Charles (1821–67)
Anywhere Out of the World.
Beauté, La.
Carrion, A.
Cat, The.
Cats.
Correspondences.
Damned Women.
Don Juan in Hell.
Élévation.
Epilogue: "With heart at rest I climbed the citadel's."
Exotic Scent.
Fuses I and II.
Giantess, The.
Gypsies on the Move.
Harmonie du Soir.
Head of Hair, The.
Inward Conversation.
Jewels, The.
Le Balcon.
Les Fleurs du Mal, *sels.*
Les Hiboux.
Litany to Satan.
Meditation.
Owls.
Parfum Exotique.
Peace, Be at Peace, O Thou My Heaviness.
Seven Old Men, The.
She Is Not Satisfied.
Which One Is Genuine?
Baugh, Edward (b. 1939)
Carpenter's Complaint, The.
Colour-Scheme.
Country Dance.
Getting There.
Old Talk, or West Indian History.
Truth and Consequences.
Baughan, Blanche Edith (1870–1958)
Bush Section, A, *sels.*
Maui's Fish, *sels.*
Old Place, The.
Baum, Peter (1869–1916)
Horror.
Psalms of Love.
Baumel, Judith (b. 1956)
Doing Time in Baltimore.
Thirty-Six Poets.
Thumbs Up.
Bawer, Bruce (b. 1956)
Grand Central Station, 20 December 1987.
On Leaving the Artists' Colony.
View from an Airplane at Night, over California, The.

Bax, Clifford (1886–1962)
Turn Back, O Man.
Baxter, Elizabeth
In Your Absence.
Baxter, James Keir (1926–72)
Apple Tree, The.
Autumn Testament, *sels.*
Ballad of the Stonegut Sugar Works.
Bay, The.
Buried Stream, The.
Cressida, *sels.*
Dentist's Window, A.
East Coast Journey.
Evidence at the Witch Trials.
Family Photograph 1939, A.
Firemen, The.
Five Sestinas, *sels.*
Haere Ra.
Harry Fat and Uncle Sam.
Inflammable Woman, The.
Jerusalem Sonnets, *sels.*
Mandrakes for Supper.
New Zealand.
News from a Pacified Area.
Obsequy for Dylan Thomas.
On the Death of Her Body.
Pig Island Letters, *sels.*
Private Conference of Harry Fat, The.
Rope for Harry Fat, A.
Spring-heeled Jack.
Spring Song of A Civil Servant.
To a Print of Queen Victoria.
Twenty little engines.
Virginia Lake.
Wild Bees.
Baxter, Richard (1615–91)
Now it belongs not to my care.
Psalm of Praise, A, *sels.*
"Baylebridge, William" (Charles William Blocksidge) (1883–1942)
Love Redeemed, *sels.*
Bayliss, John Clifford (b. 1919)
Apocalypse and Resurrection.
Reported Missing.
Seven Dreams.
Bayly, Thomas Haynes (1797–1839)
Mistletoe Bough, The.
Novel of High Life, A.
Out, John! out, John! what are you about, John?
Baynes, A. H.
Limerick: "So obese is my cousin from Hendon."
Limerick: "There was a young girl from a Mission."
Bazil, Frances (b. 1948)
Uncertain Admission.
Beach, Joseph Warren (b. 1880)
Dropping Your Aitches.
Horatian Ode.
Beach, Seth Curtis (1837–1925)
Mysterious Presence! Source of All.
Thou One in All, Thou All in One.
"Beachcomber." See Morton, John Bingham
Beadle, Samuel Alfred (1857–1932)
After Church.
Lines: "How I love country you have heard."
Lines to Caste.
Words are but leaves to the tree of mind.
Beam, Alan (b. 1948)
Time is.
Beardsley, Aubrey (1872–98)
Ballad of a Barber, The.
Three Musicians, The.
Beatrice [*or* **Beatritz** *or* **Beatriz**], **Countess de Die** [*or* **Dia**] **(***fl.* late 12th cent.**)**
Handsome friend, charming and kind.
I sing a song reluctantly.
Lately I've felt a grave concern.
My true love makes me happy.
Beattie, James (1735–1803)
Edwin, The Minstrel.
Epitaph, An: "Like thee I once have stemm'd the sea of life."
Minstrel, The, *sels.*

To Mr. Alexander Ross.

Beaumont, Francis (1584–1616)
Francis Beaumont's Letter from the Country to Jonson.
Letter to Ben Jonson, A.
Masque of the Inner Temple and Gray's Inne, The, *sels.*
On the Tombs in Westminster Abbey, *sels.*
Upon Master Edmund Spenser.

Beaumont, Francis (1584–1616) and John Fletcher
Captain, The, *sels.*
Knight of the Burning Pestle, The, *sels.*
Love's Cure, *sels.*
Maid's Tragedy, The, *sels.*

Beaumont, Sir John (1583–1627)
Description of Love, A.
Of My Dear Son [*or* Deare Sonne], Gervase Beaumont.
Upon a Funeral.

Beaumont, Joseph (1616–99)
Cheat, The.
Garden's quit with me: as yesterday, The.
Gentle Check, The.
Gnat, The.
Hourglass, The.
Love's Mystery.
Whiteness, or Chastity.

Beauvais, Phyllis (Phyllis Harris)
Furniture.

Beauveau, Marie-Françoise-Catherine de, Marquise de Boufflers (1711–86)
Air: Sentir avec Ardeur.

Beaver, Bruce (b. 1928)
Angels' Weather.
Déjeuner Sur l'Herbe.
Drummer, The.
Entertainer, The.
Folk Song: "O I'm off to Hullaboola where the climate's never cooler."
Letters to Live Poets, *sels.*
More than 9 Lives.
Odes and Days, *sels.*
Silo Treading.

Beck, Thomas (*fl.* 1780–1820)
Sonnet to Nothing.

Becker, Charlotte
Door-Bell, The.

Becker, Edwin (d. 1925)
Mother's Day.

Becker, Robin
Bath, The.
Gardener, The.
In Pompano Beach, Florida.
Medical Science.
Story I Like to Tell, The.

Beckett, Samuel (1906–89)
Alba.
Cascando.
Dieppe.
Echo's Bones, *sels.*
Enueg I.
Enueg II.
Gnome.
I would like my love to die.
Malacoda.
My way is in the sand flowing.
Ooftish.
Saint-Lô.
Waiting for Godot, *sels.*
What would I do without this world faceless incurious.
Words and Music, *sels.*

Beckford, "Slim" and Sam Blackwood
Johnny Tek Away Mi Wife.

Beckh, Harold (d. 1916)
Soldier's Cigarette, The.

Beckovic, Matija (b. 1939)
If I knew I'd bear myself proudly.
No one will write poetry anymore.
Two Worlds.
Yevtushenko.

Bécquer, Gustavo Adolfo (1836–70)
They Closed Her Eyes.

Beddoes, Thomas Lovell (1803–49)
Alpine Spirit's Song.
Another.
Death Sweet.
Death's Jest Book, *sels.*
Dream-Pedlary.
Fantastic Simile, A.
Humble Beginnings.
Hymn: "And many voices marshalled in one hymn."
Lake / Is a river curled and asleep like a snake, A.
Last Man, The, *sels.*
Lines Written in a Blank Leaf of the Prometheus Unbound.
New Cecilia, The.
New Dodo: Isabrand's Song, The.
Oviparous Tailor, The.
Phantom-Wooer, The.
Resurrection Song.
Second Brother, The, *sels.*
Song of the Stygian Naiades.
Sonnet: To Tartar, a Terrier Beauty.
To Night.
To Silence.
Torrismond, *sels.*

Bede, The Venerable (c.672–c.735)
Bede's Death Song.
Prayer of the Venerable Bede.
Sparrow's Flight, A.

"Bedny [*or* Bednyi], Demyan [*or* Dem'ian]" (Efim Alekseyevich Pridvorov) (1883–1945)
Main Street.

Beecher, Henry Ward
American Flag, The.

Beeching, Henry Charles (1859–1919)
First come I. My name is Jowett. *From* Balliol Rhymes.
Going Down Hill on a Bicycle.
I am featly-tripping Lee. *From* Balliol Rhymes.
Prayers.

Beeching, Henry Charles and John Bowyer Nichols
I am Branson; Nature's laws. *From* Balliol Rhymes.

Beedome, Thomas (d. 1641?)
Petition, The.
Question and Answer, The.
To the Noble Sir Francis Drake.

Beeks, Clarence King Pleasure
Parker's Mood.

Beer, Christina (b. 1945)
Fox Glove Song.
1974—The Sounds.
Waiheke 1972—Rocky Bay.

Beer-Hofmann, Richard (1866–1945)
Graf von Charolais, Der, *sels.*
Jacob's Dream, *sels.*

Beer, Morris Abel (1887?–1936)
Church in the Heart, The.

Beer, Patricia (b. 1924)
Birthday Poem from Venice.
Christmas Carols.
Christmas Eve.
Christmas Tree, The.
Creed of Mr. Nicholas Culpeper.
Dilemma.
Faithful Wife, The.
Fifth Sense, The.
Footbinding.
Gallery Shepherds.
Grave Doubts.
In a Country Museum.
In the Cathedral.
Jane Austen.
Jane Austen at the Window.
Leaping into the Gulf.
Lemmings die every year. Over the cliff.
Letter, The.
Lion Hunts.
Middle Age.
Postilion Has Been Struck by Lightning, The.
Witch.

Beerbohm, Max (1872–1956)
Addition to Kipling's "The Dead King (Edward VII), 1910."

After Hilaire Belloc.
Ballade Tragique à Double Refrain.
Brave Rover.
Chorus of a Song That Might Have Been Written by Albert Chevalier.
Elegy on Any Lady by George Moore.
Epitaph for G. B. Shaw.
In a Copy of More's (or Shaw's or Wells's or Plato's or Anybody's) Utopia.
Luncheon, A.
On the Imprint of the First English Edition of "The Works of Max Beerbohm."
Police Station Ditties.
Prayer, A: "If I popped in at Downing Street."
Same Cottage—But Another Song, of Another Season.
Savonarola ("Savonarola looks more grim today.")
Thomas Hardy and A. E. Housman.
Time, you thief, who love to get.
Vague Lyric by G. M.

Beerbohm, Max and William Rothenstein
Sonnet to the "Most Distinguished Chancellor" that Oxford Has Had.

Beers, Ethel Lynn (1827–79)
All quiet along the Potomac tonight.
Weighing the Baby.
Which Shall It Be?

Beeton, Douglas Ridley (b. 1929)
Autumn.

Beevers, John (1911–75)
Atameros.

Begay, Shonto (b. 1954)
Mother's Lace.

Begbie, Harold (1871–1929)
Fall In.

Begbie, Janet
I shouted for blood as I ran, brother.

"Beginner, Lord." See Moore, Egbert

Behan, Brendan (1923–64)
Repentance.

Behm, Richard
Message for Summer in the Suburbs, A.

Behn, Aphra (1640–89)
Abdelazer, *sels.*
And Forgive Us Our Trespasses.
Angellica's Lament.
Cabal at Nickey Nackey's, The.
Defiance, The.
Disappointment, The.
Dutch Lover, The, *sels.*
Emperor of the Moon, *sels.*
Epitaph on the Tombstone of a Child, the Last of Seven That Died Before.
In Imitation of Horace.
Letter to a Brother of the Pen in Tribulation, A.
Love's Witness.
Lucky Chance, The, *sels.*
Not to sigh and to be tender.
Oh, how the hand the lover ought to prize.
On *a* Juniper-Tree, Cut Down to Make Busks.
On Her Loving Two Equally.
On Mr. Dryden, Renegade.
On the Death of the Late Earl of Rochester.
Rover or The Banished Cavaliers, The.
Silvio's Complaint: A Song, To a Fine Scotch Tune.
Sir Patient Fancy, *sels.*
Song, A.
Song: "How strongly does my passion flow."
Thousand Martyrs I Have Made, A.
To Alexis in Answer to his Poem against Fruition.
To Lysander.
To Mrs. W. on Her Excellent Verses.
To My Lady Morland at Tunbridge.
To the Fair Clarinda, Who Made Love to Me, Imagin'd More Than Woman.
Voyage to the Isle of Love, A, *sels.*
When you love, or speak of it.

Behn, Harry (1898–1973)
Christmas Carol: "Angel told Mary, An."
Christmas Morning.

Circles.
New little boy moved in next door, A.
Behn, Robin
French Horn.
Behrens, Sophie (b. 1959)
Montecastelli Poem.
Someone Else.
Trees are rustling outside the open window, The.
Wedding in the Port.
Beissel, Henry (b. 1929)
New Wings for Icarus, *sels.*
Pans at Carnival.
Beissel, Johann Conrad (1690–1768)
Sun Now Risen, The.
Bekederemo, John Pepper Clark (b. 1935)
Abiku.
Agbor Dancer.
Casualties (1970), *sels.*
Casualties are not only those who are dead.
Death of a Lady.
Epilogue to Casualties.
Family Procession, A.
Leader, The.
New from Ethiopia and the Sudan, The.
Order of the Dead, The.
Reed in the Tide, A, *sels.*
Belford, Ken (b. 1946)
Carrier Indians.
Turn (a Poem in 4 Parts).
Belitt, Ben (b. 1911)
Late Dandelions.
Papermill Graveyard.
View from the Gorge.
Winter Pond.
Belknap, Jeremy (1744–98)
Far from Our Friends.
Thus Spake the Saviour.
"Bell, Acton." See Brontë, Anne
Bell, Ann
This is my work so.
"Bell, Currer." See Brontë, Charlotte
"Bell, Ellis." See Brontë, Emily Jane
Bell, Henry Glassford (1803–74)
Mary, Queen of Scots.
Bell, J. J. (b. 1871)
Lights, The.
Ships, The.
Bell, James Madison (1826–1902)
Anniversary Poem Entitled the Progress of Liberty, An, *sels.*
Modern Moses, or "My Policy" Man.
Poem Entitled the Day and the War, A, *sels.*
Bell, Julian (1908–37)
Redshanks, The.
Bell, Martin (1918–78)
Footnote to Enright's "Apocalypse."
Senilio Passes, Singing.
Senilio's Weather Saw.
Winter Coming On.
With a Presentation Copy of Verses.
Bell, Marvin (b. 1937)
Acceptance Speech.
Cabin in Minnesota, A.
Communication of His Thirtieth Birthday.
Drawn by Stones, by Earth, by Things That Have Been in the Fire.
Gemwood.
Here.
Hole in the Sea, The.
Impotence.
Music of the Spheres, The.
Mystery of Emily Dickinson, The.
Perfection of Dentistry, The.
Residue of Song.
Stars Which See, Stars Which Do Not See.
These Green-going-to-Yellow.
Things We Dreamt We Died For.
To Dorothy.
Treetops.
Wednesday.
What They Do to You in Distant Places.
White Clover.
Bell, William (1924–48)
Elegy: "Tonight the moon is high, to summon all."

Young Man's Song, A.
Bellamann, Henry (1882–1945)
Charleston Garden, A.
Bellamy, Dodie (b. 1951)
Letters of Mina Harker, The, *sels.*
Bellamy, Francis
Pledge of Allegiance to the Flag.
Belleau, Remy [or Remi] (1528–77)
April, pride of woodland ways.
Bellerby, Frances (1899–1975)
Clear Shell, A.
Inconclusive Evening, An.
Belloc, Joseph Hilaire Pierre (1870–1953)
Ballade of Genuine Concern.
Big Baboon, The.
Bison, The.
But how much more unfortunate are those.
Charles Augustus Fortescue.
Child, Do Not Throw This Book About.
Dedicatory Ode, *sels.*
Discovery.
Early Morning, The.
Elephant, The.
Epitaph on the Favourite Dog of a Politician.
Epitaph on the Politician Himself.
Evenlode, The.
False Heart, The.
Fatigue.
First in his pride the orient sun's display.
Four things in any land must dwell.
Franklin Hyde.
Frog, The.
Good Advice.
Ha'nacker Mill.
Henry King, Who Chewed Bits of String, and Was Early Cut Off in Dreadful Agonies.
Hippopotamus, The.
I am a sundial. Ordinary words.
I am a sundial, turned the wrong way round.
Imitation.
Is there any reward?
Jim Who Ran Away from His Nurse, and Was Eaten by a Lion.
Juliet.
Justice of the Peace, The.
Lines to a Don.
Lion, the Lion, he dwells in the waste, The.
Llama, The.
Lord Finchley tried to mend the Electric Light.
Lord Heygate had a troubled face.
Lord Hippo.
Lord Lucky.
Lord Lundy from his earliest years.
Matilda told such Dreadful Lies.
Moral Alphabet, A, *sels.*
Night, The.
Noël.
Obiter Dicta.
On a Dead Hostess.
On a General Election.
On a Puritan.
On a Sundial.
On His Books.
On Hygiene.
On Jam.
On Lady Poltagrue, A Public Peril.
On Mundane Acquaintances.
On Noman, a Guest.
Pacifist, The.
Python I should not advise, A.
Rebecca, Who Slammed Doors for Fun and Perished Miserably.
Sarah Byng Who Could Not Read and Was Tossed into a Thorny Hedge by a Bull. A Cautionary Tale.
Song: "You wear the morning like your dress."
Sonnet: "We will not whisper, we have found the place."
South Country, The.
Statesman, The.
Statue, The.
Tarantella.
This, the last ornament among the peers.
Tiger, on the other hand, is kittenish and mild, The.

To Dives.
Viper, The.
Vulture eats between his meals, The.
West Sussex Drinking Song.
World's a stage. The trifling entrance fee, The.
Yak, The.
Belševica, Vizma
Don't be oversure of your cherry-tree.
That was a very polite fish.
To be roots. In that deepest earth where no ray.
Willow-catkins threw off their narrow shoes.
Bely [or Belyi], Andrey [or Andrei] (Boris Nikolaevich Bugayev) (1880–1934)
Despair.
Dramatic Symphony, The, *sels.*
Beman, Nathan S. S. (1785–1871)
Jesus, I Come to Thee.
Bendall, Molly (fl. 20th cent.)
Conversations on the Plurality of Worlds.
"Bendo, Brian"
Dream, The.
Benedikt, Michael (b. 1937)
Divine Love.
Dossier of the Torturer.
European Shoe is constructed of grass and reed, [bound,] The.
Events by Moonlight.
Eye, The.
Fate in Incognito.
Fraudulent Days.
Grand Guignols of Love, The.
Nipplewhip, The.
Some Feelings.
Some Litanies.
Thoughts.
Benét, Rosemary and Stephen Vincent Benét
Hernando De Soto.
John Quincy Adams.
Nancy Hanks.
Peregrine White and Virginia Dare.
Western Wagons.
Benét, Stephen Vincent (1898–1943)
American Names.
Ballad of William Sycamore, The.
Daniel Boone.
For All Blasphemers.
For City Spring.
Hymn in Columbus Circle.
John Brown's Body, *sels.*
King David.
Litany for Dictatorships.
Metropolitan Nightmare.
Nightmare at Noon.
Nightmare Number Three.
1935.
Nonsense Song, A.
Rain after a Vaudeville Show.
Winged Man.
Benét, William Rose (1886–1950)
Brazen Tongue.
Eternal Masculine.
Fawn in the Snow, The.
Horse Thief, The.
Inscription for a Mirror in a Deserted Dwelling.
Jesse James was a two-gun man.
Merchants from Cathay.
Night.
Sagacity.
Whale.
Woodcutter's Wife, The.
Beneyto, Maria (b. 1925)
Nocturne in the Women's Prison.
Benford, Lawrence (b. 1946)
Beginning of a Long Poem on Why I Burned the City, The.
Benjacob, Isaac (1801–63)
Epitaph, An: "Here lies Nachshon, a man of great renown."
Benjamin, Robert Charles O'Hara (1855–1900)
Colored Heroes, Hark the Bugle.
Farmer's Soliloquy, The.
Benlowes, Edward (1603?–1676)
Theophia, *sels.*

Benn, Gottfried
Bunch of drifter sons hollered, A.
Cycle.
Fragments, / Refuse of the soul.
Little Aster.
Lovely Childhood.
Man and Woman Go Through the Cancer Ward.
Monologue.
Night Café.

Bennard, George (1873–1958)
Old Rugged Cross, The.

Bennett, Alan (b. 1934)
Place-Names of China.

Bennett, Anna Elizabeth (b. 1914)
Hush Thee, Princeling.

Bennett, Arnold (1867–1931)
Limerick: "There was a young man of Montrose."
Love Affair, A.

Bennett, Bruce (b. 1940)
Experience, The.
Leader.

Bennett, Gwendolyn B. (1902–81)
Advice.
Fantasy.
Hatred.
Heritage.
Secret.
Song: "I am weaving a song of waters."
Sonnet—2: "Some things are very dear to me—."
Sonnet: "He came in silver armor, trimmed with black."
To a Dark Girl.
To Usward.

Bennett, Henry Holcomb (1863–1924)
Flag Goes By, The.

Bennett, John (1865–1956)
Her Answer.
In a Rose Garden.
Tiger Tale, A.

Bennett, Lerone, Jr. (b. 1928)
And Was Not Improved.
Blues and Bitterness.

Bennett, Louise (b. 1919)
Back To Africa, Miss Mattie?
Colonization in Reverse.
Dutty Tough.
Excitement.
Home Sickness.
Independance wid a vengeance.
Independence Twenty-One.
Jamaica oman cunny sah!
Love Letter.

Bennett, Rodney
And Back.
Christmas-Tree Song, A.
Easter Praise.
Fluttering Leaves.
Growing River, The.
Little Brown Seed.
Little Old Lady, The.
Merry Birds.
Mister Brown.
Mistress Jenny Wren.
My Dog, Spot.
Pigeons, The.
Postman's Knock.
Rhyme for Washing Hands, A.
Robin's Song.
Ten Little Christmas Trees.
Thank You for Friends, A.
There.
Three Little Men in a Boat.
Windy Nights.
Wireless.
Writing Letters.

Bennett, Rowena Bastin (b. 1896)
Gingerbread man gave a gingery shout, The.
Smoke Animals.
Witch of Willowby Wood, The.

Bennett, William Cox (1820–95)
To a Cricket.

Bensko, John (b. 1949)
Elk on Mutability, The.

Elk Uncovers the Heavens, The.
Watching TV, the Elk Bones Up on Metaphysics.
Wild Horses of Assateague Island, The.

Bensley, Connie (b. 1929)
Bloomsbury Snapshot.
Charity.
Desires.
One's Correspondence.

Benson, Arthur Christopher (1862–1925)
Ant-Heap, The.
Land of Hope and Glory.
Phoenix, The.

Benson, Gerard
Ben Barley was a barman stout.
Cat and the Pig, The.
Leavings.
Limerick: "I'm in love with a girl from Uttoxeter."
Limerick: "'Is it thou?' 'Ay,' cries Fra Lippo Lippi."
Limerick: "There once was a bard of Hong Kong."
Limerick: "There was a young princess, Snow-White."
Limerick: "While Dubliner leopold bloom sought solace."
Play No Ball.
Probatioun Officeres Tale, The.

Benson, Louis FitzGerald (1855–1930)
O Love That Lights the Eastern Sky.
O Risen Lord upon the Throne.
O Thou Whose Feet Have Climbed Life's Hill.
Why Linger Yet upon the Strand?

Benson, Stella (1892–1933)
Frost.
Now I Have Nothing[. Even the joy of loss].

Benson, Steve
Beaten Track, The.
Beethoven's Sixth Symphony.
Blue Book 18 Pages 1–4.
Reverse Order, sels.

Bent, O. M.
Robin, The.

Bentley, Edmund Clerihew (1875–1956)
Clerihews, sels.
Savonarola ("Savonarola / Declined to wear a bowler.")

Bentley, Elizabeth (1767–1839)
On Education, December 1789.

Bentley, Nelson (d. 1990)
Third Dungeness Spit Apocalypse.

Bentley, Nicolas (1907–78)
Cecil B. De Mille.
Londonderry Air, The.
On Lady A———.

Benton, Patricia (b. 1907)
Psalm 23: "Lord is my shepherd; I shall not want, The."

Benveniste, Asa (b. 1925)
Bird Appeal.
Blue Crêpe.
Certainly Metaphysics.
End To It, An.
Infield Outfield.

Béranger, Pierre Jean de (1780–1857)
King of Yvetot, The.

Berberova, Nina Nikolaevna (b. 1901)
Eagles and butterflies (and some other things).
I remain with what was not fully said.

Berchan (fl. 8th cent.)
Fort of Rathangan, The.

Berditshev, Isaac of. See **Levi-Yitzhok of Berditchev**

Bereng, David Granmer T.
Birth of Moshesh, The.

Berenguer, Amanda
Housework.

Beresford, Ann (b. 1919)
Courtship, The.

Berg, Stephen (b. 1934)
And the Scream.
Answer, The.

Cold Cash.
Don't Forget.
Holes, The.
May 1970.
To My Friends.

Berggolts [or Bergholts], Olga Fiodorovna (1910–75)
Conversation with a Neighbor.
Friends repeat: "All means are good."
Infidelity.
My Country.
Ordeal, The.
To My Sister.
To Song.
You took me, hostile, sullen—.

Bergman, Alexander (1921–41)
Chronicler, The.
Letter.

Bergman, David (b. 1950)
Blueberry Man.

Bergner, Zekharye Khone. See **"Ravitch, Melech"**

Berkeley, George (1685–1753)
On the Prospect of Planting Arts and Learning in America.

Berkeley, Gina
Limerick: "Calculus fit to compute on, A."
Limerick: "Last Christmas, when Puss was in Boots."
Limerick: "Mr. Rochester's wife's pyromania."
Limerick: "'Princess,' said the Frog, 'Do not wince.'"
Limerick: "When Ireland was bloody and leaderless."
Ratatouille.

Berkeley, Sara (b. 1967)
Learning to Count.
Mass is over, they have gone in peace, The.
Parting, The.

Berkeley, Sir William (1606?–1677)
Lost Lady, The, sels.

Berkson, Bill (b. 1939)
Melting Milk.
Rebecca Cutlet.
Russian New Year.

Berlin, Irving
Couple of Swells, A.
God bless America.

Bernard, Artis
Snowfall.

Bernard [or Bernart] de Ventadour [or Ventadorn] (c. 1145–1180)
Can Vei La Lauzeta Mover.
Chantars No Pot Gaire Valer.
Good time of the year, The.
Joy! a heart so overflowing.
Lark, The.
Men, a word of wisdom. Give.
No Marvel Is It.
To see the lark, delighted, dare.
When—presto—turf and trees are green.

Bernard of Clairvaux (1091–1153)
Wide Open Are Thy Loving Hands.

Berners, Dame Juliana (b. 1388?)
Properties of a Good Greyhound, The.

Berni, Francesco (1495–1535)
Hair of fine silver, shaggy and twisted.

Bernstein, Carole (b. 1960)
When My Grandmother Said "Pussy."

Bernstein, Charles (Henk Marsman) (b. 1950)
Dysraphism.
From Lines of Swinburne.
Gradation.
Kiwi Bird in the Kiwi Tree, The.
Klupzy Girl, The.
Loose Shoes.
Matters of Policy.
Of Time and the Line.
Poem: "Here. Forget."
Take then these nail and boards.
Virtual Reality.
Wait.
Whose Language.

Bernstein, Ory [*or* **Ori**] **(b. 1936)**
All this is my time. No time to seek disguise.
  There'll be.
And after a Long While.
And Later by Myself.
At Woods' Edge.
Don't Count.
Games.
Her Words from the Corner.
Imagined Description of Myself, in Another
  Scene, An.
In a Park, in Siena, at Twilight.
Memories of Her Friend Who Died.
Mene Mene.
More Questions.
Nocturnal Journey.
Of All the Splendor.
Only from Afar.
Poems from Mexico, *sels.*
Season when Nothing's in Place, A.
This Is a Poem of Love.
Time to Leave.
What She Didn't Say.
What She Wanted to Be.
Wind, That Comes on Suddenly, A.

Berrigan, Daniel (b. 1921)
Beautiful Ruined Orchard, The.
Crucifix, The.
My Name.
Prayer: "I left Cornell / with half a wit; six
  mismated socks."
Rehabilitative Report: We Can Still Laugh.
Somewhere the Equation Breaks Down.

Berrigan, Ted (1934–83)
Bean Spasms.
Certain Slant of Sunlight, A.
Kirsten.
Red Shift.
Sonnets, The, *sels.*
String of Pearls.
Things To Do in Providence.
Words for Love.
See also **Waldman, Anne** *and* Ted Berrigan

Berrigan, Ted *and* **Ron Padgett**
Orange Jews.

Berry, David Chapman (b. 1947)
Alluding to the One-armed Bandit.
Cosmogony.
Dog.
Faces.
Godiva.
Having Eaten Breakfast.
In Blue.
Leaps over the Aisle of Syllogism.
On Reading Poems to a Senior Class at
  South High.
Road.
Robert Creeley Also Watches.
Robert Creeley Listens, Too.
Sun goes.
Theodore Roethke Foots It.
To the Woodville Depot.
Up against the Wall.

Berry, H. W.
Somewhere East of Suez.

Berry, James (b. 1924)
Back to Hometown Kingston.
Benediction.
Distance of a City.
Fantasy of an African Boy.
From Lucy: Holiday Reflections.
Girls Can We Educate We Dads?
Ingrown.
It's Me Man.
Lucy's Letter.
My Father.
New Speaker.
Old Man in New Country.
One.
Pods Pop and Grin.
Poem for the Wife of an Imprisoned Leader
  especially for Winnie Mandela.
Spirits of Movement.

Berry, Wendell (b. 1934)
Dance, The.
Except.
Fear of Love, The.

Grandmother, The.
Grief.
Music, A.
November Twenty-sixth Nineteen Hundred
  and Sixty-three.
Peace of Wild Things, The.
Poetry and Marriage, *sels.*
Ripening.
September 2.
Slip, The.
To Know the Dark.
Wild, The.
Wild Geese, The.

Berryman, John (1914–72)
Again, his friend's death made the man sit
  still.
Alcoholic.
Also I love him: me he's done no wrong.
American Lights, Seen from Off Abroad.
Ball Poem, The.
Black Book, The, *sels.*
Boston Common.
Cage, The.
Canto Amor.
Carpenter's Son, The.
Certainty Before Lunch.
Conversation.
Desires of Men and Women.
Dispossessed, The.
Dream Songs, *sels.*
Eleven Addresses to the Lord, *sels.*
Gislebertus' Eve.
Go, ill-sped book, and whisper to her or.
He Resigns.
Henry's Fate.
Henry's Understanding.
Homage to Mistress Bradstreet, *sels.*
I'm scared a lonely. Never see my son.
King David Dances.
Lauds.
Moon and the Night and the Men, The.
New Year's Eve.
Note to Wang Wei.
Of Suicide.
Parting as Descent.
Poet's Final Instructions, The.
Professor's Song, A.
Scholars at the Orchid Pavilion.
Song of the Tortured Girl, The.
Sonnets, *sels.*
Sonnets to Chris, *sels.*
Soviet Union, The.
Strut for Roethke, A.
Sympathy, A Welcome, A.
Thurn, A.
To My Father.
Traveller, The.
Washington in Love.
Whether There Is Sorrow in the Demons.
Winter Landscape.
Winter-Piece to a Friend Away, A.

Bersohn, Robert
Dignity of Labor, The.

Berssenbrugge, Mei-Mei (b. 1947)
Alakanak Break-Up.
Chronicle.
Constellation Quilt, The.
Experience.
Jealousy.
Spring Street Bar.
Swan, The.
Tan Tien.
Texas.

Bertken [*or* **Bertke**]**, Sister (Bertha Jacobs)
(1427–1514)**
Ditty: "I went into my garden to gather some
  herbs."
When I went into my garden, I found.

Bertolino, James
Coons, The.
Frog Voices.
Landscape, The.
On a Line by John Ashbery.

Bertrand, Aloysius (1807–1841)
Mason Abraham Knupfer is singing, trowel
  in hand, scaffolded, The.

Bertrans [*or* **Bertran** *or* **Bertrand**] **de Born** (*fl.*
12th cent.)
Perigord pres del muralh, A.
Song of Battle.

Berwick, Thurso (b. 1919)
Idleset: "Ill's the airt o the Word the day."

Besant, Linda
Telepathy.

Beshenkovskaya [*or* **Beshenkovskaia**]**, Olga (b.
1947)**
In a land whose prosperity constantly grows.
Old Russia's slavery rights. Boiler room.
Night.

Best, C. F.
Limerick: "Said a pupil of Einstein: 'It's
  rotten.'"

Best, Charles (*fl.* **c.1602**)
Sonnet of the Moon, A.

Betham-Edwards, Matilda Barbara
In a Letter to A.R.C. on Her Wishing to Be
  Called Anna.
Power of Women, The.
Written on Whitsun-Monday, 1795.

**Bethell, Mary Ursula ("Evelyn Hayes") (1874–
1945)**
By the River Ashley, *sels.*
Decoration.
Detail.
Elect.
Erica.
Long Harbour, The.
Midnight.
9th July, 1932.
Pause.
Response.
Spring Snow and Tui.
Time.
Warning of Winter.

Bethune, George Washington (1805–62)
Jesus, Shepherd of Thy Sheep.
O for the Happy Hour.
There Is No Name So Sweet on Earth.

Bethune, Lebert (b. 1937)
Blue Tanganyika.
Bwagamoyo.
For Singing In Good Mood.
Harlem Freeze Frame.
Juju of My Own, A.
Today Tutu Is Beating the Same Burru As
  Me.

Betjeman, Sir John (1906–84)
Advent 1955.
Archaeological Picnic, The.
Arrest of Oscar Wilde at the Cadogan Hotel,
  The.
Ballad of George R. Sims, The.
Beside the Seaside, *sels.*
Bristol and Clifton.
Business Girls.
Christmas.
Crematorium.
Death in Leamington.
Diary of a Church Mouse.
East Anglian Bathe.
Executive.
False Security.
Felixstowe, or, The Last of Her Order.
Five O'Clock Shadow.
Flight from Bootle, The.
Great Central Railway, Sheffield Victoria to
  Banbury.
Hike on the Downs, A.
House of Rest, *sels.*
How to Get On in Society.
Hunter Trials.
Huxley Hall.
In a Bath Teashop.
In Memory of Basil, Marquess of Dufferin
  and Ava.
In the Public Gardens.
In Westminster Abbey.
Incident in the Early Life of Ebenezer Jones,
  Poet, 1828, An.
Inevitable.
Invasion Exercise on the Poultry Farm.
Ireland with Emily.

Late-Flowering Lust.
Licorice Fields at Pontefract, The.
Limerick: "G'uggery G'uggery Nunc."
Longfellow's Visit to Venice.
Lord Cozens Hardy.
Matlock Bath.
Meditation on the A30.
Metropolitan Railway, The.
Middlesex.
Myfanwy.
"New King Arrives in His Capital by
   Air. . . "—Daily Newspaper.
NW5 and N6.
Old Friends, sels.
Old Land Dog, The.
On Seeing an Old Poet in the Café Royal.
Our padre is an old sky pilot.
Parliament Hill Fields.
Potpourri from a Surrey Garden.
Remorse.
Reproof Deserved; or After the Lecture.
Senex.
Shropshire Lad, A.
Slough.
Subaltern's Love-Song, A.
Summer.
Summoned by Bells, sels.
Sunday Afternoon Service in St. Enodoc
   Church, Cornwall.
Sunday Morning, King's Cambridge.
Tea with the Poets.
Town Clerk's Views, The.
Trebetherick.
Upper Lambourne.
Westgate-on-Sea.
Youth and Age on Beaulieu River, Hants.

Beveridge, Judith (b. 1956)
Catching Webs.
Dining Out.
Domesticity of Giraffes, The.
In the Park.

Bevington, Helen Smith (b. 1906)
Herrick's Julia.
Mrs. Trollope in America.
Mr. Rockefeller's Hat.
Nature Study, After Dufy.
Penguins in the Home.

Bevington, Louisa Sarah (1847–1895)
Afternoon.
'Dreamers?' Ah, no! else he was a dreamer.
'Egoisme à Deux.'
Measurements.
Midnight.
Morning.
One more bruised heart laid bare! one victim
   more!
Twilight.
Two songs, sels.
Wrestling.

Bewe, ------ (fl. c.1576)
I would I were Actaeon, whom Diana did
   disguise.

Bewsher, Paul (1894–1966)
Dawn Patrol, The.

Beyer, Tony (b. 1948)
Island Waters.

**Bezymensky [or Bezymenskii], Alexander Ilyich
(1898–1973)**
About a Hat.
Village and Factory.

Bharati, Subramania (1898–1921)
Wind, 9.

Bhartrihari (fl. c.500)
Breasts.
If the forest of her hair.
In former days we'd both agree.
Peace.
She who is always in my thoughts prefers.
Three Poems.
Time is the root of all this earth.

Bhatt, Sujata (b. 1956)
What Is Worth Knowing?

Bhavani, V. Indira (b. 1942)
Avatars.

**Bialik, Hayyim Nahman [or Khayim Nakhman
or Chaim Nachman] (1873–1934)**
Alone.

And If the Angel Should Ask.
At Day's End.
Beneath Thy Wing.
City of Slaughter, The.
Dance of Despair, The.
Dead of the Wilderness, The.
Death of David, The.
Graveyard, The.
I have a garden and I have a well.
If Thou Wouldst Know.
Mathmid, The.
Midnight Prayer.
Night.
Pool, The.
Prophet, Go, Flee!
Queen Sabbath.
Should I Be a Rabbi?
Songs of the People, sels.
Stars Are Lit, The.
Sunset.
Talmud Student, The.
Throbs the Night with Mystic Silence.
When the Days Shall Grow Long.
Whence and Whither.
Young Acacia, The.

Bialoszewski, Miron (b. 1922)
Ballad of Going Down to the Store, A.

Bianor (b. late 1st cent. B.C.)
House fell head-first, quietly crushing all but
   a child, The.
In the clear water by the beach.
Sardis, the old city of Gyges and Alyattes.
This man: this no-thing: vile: this brutish
   slave.

Biaoszewski, Miron
They'll Paint Us, sels.

**Bibb, Eloise (Eloise Bibb Thompson) (1878–
1927)**
Anne Boleyn.
Belshazzer's Feast.
Capt. Smith and Pocahontas.
Catharine of Arragon.
Charmion's Lament.
Class Song of '91.
Destiny.
Early spring's sweet blush, The.
Eliza in Uncle Tom's Cabin.
Expulsion of Hagar, The.
Gerarda.
Hermit, The.
Imogene.
In Memoriam Frederick Douglass.
In Memory of Arthur Clement Williams.
Judith.
Leona, dear, twelve months ago.
Lines to Mrs. M. C. Turner.
Lines to the Hon. George L. Knox.
Ode to the Sun.
Offering, An.
Sonnet: "O thou who never harbored fear."
Tale of Italy, A.
Tribute.
Vestal Virgin, The.
Wandering Jew, The.

Bibby, Cyril
Limerick: "Musical maiden from Frome, A."

Bible, Apocrypha
Baruch, sels.
Ecclesiasticus, sels.
First Maccabees, sels.
Jeremie, 17.
Judith, sels.
Steel Usurps the Forests; Silence Dethrones
   Dialogue.
Tobit, sels.
Widower.

Bible, N.T.
1 Corinthians, 15. 51, sels.
Bible, John 5:24, The, sels.
Bible, Romans 12:10,11, The, sels.
First Corinthians, sels.
First Letter to the Corinthians, The, sels.
John, 8. 21, sels.
Matthew Ten Twenty-Five– Ten Twenty-Six.
Revelation of St John The Divine, The, sels.
St. John, sels.
St. Luke, sels.

St. Mark, sels.
St. Matthew, sels.

Bible, O.T.
2 Samuel, sels.
2 Samuel, 19, sels.
"All night the cicada chirps."
Amos, sels.
Bible, Ecclesiastes 10:12, The.
Bible, Exodus 20:12, The.
Bible, Isaiah 40:31, The.
Bible, Luke 2:8–20, Phillips, The.
Bible, Matthew 6:19–21, The.
Bible, O.T., Isaiah 6:3.
Bible O.T., Matthew 5:3–10.
Bible O.T., Psalm 103:1–5, The.
Bible O.T., Psalm 107:23–31.
Bible, Proverbs 11:13, The.
Bible, Proverbs 20:11, The.
Bible, Proverbs 22:1, The.
Bible, Proverbs 3:1–4, The.
Bible, Proverbs 6:6–8, The.
Bible, Psalm 147:1,5,8,9,16–18,7,20, The.
Bible, Psalm 92:1, The.
Deuteronomy, sels.
Ecclesiastes, sels.
Exodus, sels.
Ezekiel, sels.
First Samuel, sels.
Genesis, sels.
Inscription on the Liberty Bell.
Isaiah, sels.
Jeremiah, sels.
Job, sels.
John 11:25,26.
Jonah, sels.
Judges, sels.
Lamentations, sels.
Micah, sels.
New Year, The.
Numbers, sels.
Proverbs, sels.
Psalms, sels.
Ruth, sels.
Second Samuel, sels.
Song: "I was asleep but my heart stayed
   awake."
Song of Solomon, The, sels.
Song of Songs, The, sels.
Zechariah, sels.

Bible, Pseudepigrapha
Enoch, sels.

Bickerstaffe, Isaac (c.1735–c.1812)
Expostulation, An.
Love in a Village, sels.
Recruiting Serjeant, The, sels.

**Bickersteth, Edward Henry, Bishop of Exeter
(1825–1906)**
O God, the Rock of Ages.

Bidart, Frank (b. 1939)
Another Life.
Confessional.
Elegy, sels.
Ellen West.
Golden State.
Happy Birthday.
Herbert White.
Sacrifice, The.
Self-Portrait.
To the Dead.

Bienek, Horst (b. 1930)
Exodus.
Our Ashes.
Resistance.
Vorkuta.

Bierbaum, Otto Julius (1865–1910)
Blacksmith Pain.
Jeannette.
Kindly Vision.
Oft in the Silent Night.

Bierce, Ambrose (1842–c.1914)
Confederate Flags, The.
Dead, sels.
Death of Grant, The.
Devil's Dictionary, The, sels.
Don't steal. Thou'lt never thus compete.
General B. F. Butler.

Hesitating Veteran, The.
Passing Show, The.
Statesmen, The.
To E. S. Salomon.
To the Bartholdi Statue.

Bierds, Linda
For the Sake of Retrieval.
Off the Aleutian Chain.
Seizure.
Stillness, the Dancing, The.

Big Eagle, Duane (b. 1946)
Traveling to Town.

Bigg, J. Stanyan (1825–65)
Irish Picture, An.

Biggar, H. Howard
Your Neighbor.

Biggs, Carrie
Chair That Is Filled, The.

Bilal (*fl.* c.600)
Muhammedan Call to Prayer.

Bilhana (*fl.* 11th cent.)
Black Marigolds.

Billings, William (1746–1800)
David's Lamentation.
Heavenly Vision.
Let Tyrants Shake Their Iron Rod.

Bingham, G. Clifton (1859–1913)
Love's Old Sweet Song.

Binney, Thomas (1798–1874)
Eternal Light!

Binyon, Laurence (1869–1943)
Beauty.
Belfry, The.
Burning of the Leaves, The, *sels.*
For the Fallen.
Harebell and Pansy.
House That Was, The.
Hunger.
Invocation to Youth.
Little Dancers, The.
Nothing Is Enough.
Song, A: "For mercy, courage, kindness, mirth."
Statues, The.
This Is England.
Those That Are Gone.
Tristram's End.
Unreturning Spring, The.

Bion (c.315–255 B.C.)
Dream of Venus, A.
In sleep before me *Venus* seem'd to stand.
Lament for Adonis.
Power of Love, The.

Biran, Paddy
Paddy Biran's Song.

Bird, Bessie Calhoun (b. 1906)
Proof.

Bird, Dolly (b. 1950)
Can I Say.

Bird, Edward
To His Coy Mistress.

Bird, Harold. *See* Littlebird, Harold

Birken, Sigmund von (1626–81)
Shepherd-Song ("All men may hasty-gone happiness find.")
Shepherd-Song ("I sit here at your edge, in your embankment's screen.")

Birney, Earle (b. 1904)
Anglo Saxon Street.
Bear on the Delhi Road, The.
Bushed.
Can. Hist.
Can. Lit.
Canada: Case History: 1973.
Cartagena de Indias.
Charité Espérance et Foi.
Christchurch, N. Z.
David and I that summer cut trails on the Survey.
El Greco: Espolio.
From the Hazel Bough.
Gray Woods Exploding, The.
Hot Springs.
Museum of Man.

My Love Is Young.
Poet-Tree.
Sestina for the Ladies of Tehuántepec.
Sinalóa.
Slug in Woods.
Small Faculty Stag for the Visiting Poet, A.
Toronto Board of Trade Goes Abroad.
Twenty-third Flight.

Bishop, Elizabeth (1911–79)
Anaphora.
Armadillo, The.
Arrival at Santos.
At the Fishhouses.
Bight, The.
Brazil, January 1, 1502.
Burglar of Babylon, The.
Cape Breton.
Casabianca.
Cirque d'Hiver.
Cold spring, A.
Cootchie, Miss Lula's servant, lies in marl.
Crusoe in England.
Faustina, or Rock Roses.
Filling Station.
First Death in Nova Scotia.
Fish, The.
Florida.
From Trollope's Journal.
House Guest.
Imaginary Iceberg, The.
In the Waiting Room.
Invitation to Miss Marianne Moore.
Large Bad Picture.
Letter to N.Y.
Little Exercise.
Lullaby for the Cat.
Man-Moth, The.
Manners.
Manuelzinho.
Map, The.
Monument, The.
Moose, The.
North Haven.
One Art.
Over 2000 Illustrations and a Complete Concordance.
Pink Dog.
Poem: "About the size of an old-style dollar bill."
Prodigal, The.
Questions of Travel.
Riverman, The.
Roosters.
Sandpiper.
Seascape.
Sestina: "September rain falls on the house."
Shampoo, The.
Sleeping on the Ceiling.
Some Dreams They Forgot.
Songs for a Colored Singer, *sels.*
Summer's Dream, A.
Twelfth Morning; or What You Will.
12 O'Clock News.
Two Mornings and Two Evenings.
Unbeliever, The.
Under the Window: Ouro Prêto.
Varick Street.
Visits to St. Elizabeths.

Bishop, John Peale (1892–1944)
Always, from My First Boyhood.
Ancestors, The.
Dream, The.
Hours, The.
Hunchback, The.
Hunger and Thirst.
In the Dordogne.
O Pioneers!
Ode: "Why will they never sleep."
Recollection, A.
Return, The.
Sleep Brought Me Vision.
Speaking of Poetry.
This Dim and Ptolemaic Man.
To a Swallow.
Why They Waged War.

Bishop, Morris Gilbert (1893–1973)
Adventures of Id, The.

Anatomy of Humor, The.
Bishop Orders His Tomb in St. Praxed's.
Dementia Praecox.
Diogenes.
Fragment from "The Maladjusted: A Tragedy."
Gas and Hot Air.
How to Treat Elves.
Limerick: "At spirit séances in Queen's."
Limerick: "'I have heard,' said a maid from Montclair."
Limerick Is Furtive and Mean, The.
Limerick: "Lady who rules Fort Montgomery, A."
Limerick: "One-day-old baby in Wallabout, A."
Limerick: "Pushing young man in Patchogue, A."
Limerick: "Said a fervent young lady of Hammels."
Limerick: "There's a tiresome young man of Bay Shore."
Limerick: "When a feverish groom in Armenia."
My Friend the Cuckold.
Naughty Preposition, The.
Ozymandias Revisited.
Public Aid for Niagara Falls.
Sales Talk for Annie.
Song of the Pop-Bottlers.
We Have Been Here Before.
What Hath Man Wrought Exclamation Point.
Who'd Be a Hero (Fictional)?
Witch of East Seventy-second Street, The.

Bishop, Samuel (1731–95)
Epigram. "Need from excess—excess from folly growing."
Epigram: "' 'Twas not so in my time,' surly Grumio exclaims."

Bissert, Ellen Marie (b. 1947)
Most Beautiful Woman at My Highschool Reunion, The.

Bisset, James (1762?–1832)
Ramble of the Gods through Birmingham, *sels.*

Bissett, Bill (b. 1939)
Christ I Wudint Know Normal if I Saw It When.
Dont Worry Yr Hair.
Th Wundrfulness uv th Mountees Our Secret Police.

Bitar, Walid
Kinshasa.
Looking You in the Back of the Head.

Bjørnson, Bjørnstjerne (1832–1910)
Boy and the Flute, The.
Fatherland Song.

Black, Isaac J.
Racist Psychotherapy.

Black, Jack
Awake! For Sweeney in pyjamas bright.

Black, Sophie Cabot
Interrogation.
She Drives.
To Her Father.

Blackall, C. W.
From the Front: The Song of the Trench, December, 1914.

Blackburn, Paul (1926–71)
Assistance, The.
At the Well.
Brooklyn Narcissus.
Continuity, The.
Crossing, The.
El Camino Verde.
Encounter, The.
Hot Afternoons Have Been in West 15th Street.
Invitation Standing.
Listening to Sonny Rollins at the Five-Spot.
Net of Place, The.
Night Song for Two Mystics.
Once-over, The.
Park Poem.
Phone Call to Rutherford.
Problem, The.

Selection of Heaven, The, *sels.*
17. IV. 71.
Sirventes.
Slogan, The.
Stone found me in bright sunlight, The.
Tides, The.
Watchers, The.

Blackburn, Thomas (1916–77)
Families.
Felo de Se.
Ganga.
Hospital for Defectives.
Lucky Marriage, The.
Oedipus.

Blackley, Barney
Fiery young fellow called Bryant, A.
Limerick: "Most women get married, 'tis true."

Blackmore, Sir Richard (1653–1729)
Creation, *sels.*
Possibilities, *sels.*

Blackmore, Richard Doddridge (1825–1900)
Dominus Illuminatio Mea.

Blackmur, Richard Palmer (1904–65)
Elegy for Five, An.
Resurrection.
Sonnet: "Three silences made him a single word."

Blackwood, Algernon (1869–1951)
Jack o' the Inkpot.

Blackwood, Sam. *See* Beckford, "Slim" *and* Sam Blackwood

Blaeser, Kimberly M. (fl. 20th cent.)
Certificate of Live Birth.

Blaga, Lucian (1895–1961)
Anno Domini.
Heraclitus by the Lake.
I will not crush the world's corolla of wonders.
In the Mountains.
Psalm.
Soul of the Village, The.
Twentieth Century.

Blagden, Isa (1816–1873?)
To George Sand on her Interview with Elizabeth Barrett Browning.

Blaginina, Yelena [*or* Elena] (1903–89)
To the Memory of G. N. Obolduyev.

Blair, Eric. *See* Orwell, George

Blair, Robert (1699–1746)
Grave, The, *sels.*
New Dawn, A.

Blake, "Blind" (Alphonso Higgs Blake)
Diddie Wa Diddie.

Blake, Felicia
Woman's Answer to "The Vampire," A.

Blake, Howard
Argent Solipsism.

Blake, James W. (1862–1935)
Sidewalks of New York, The.

Blake, Marie
Barter.

Blake, William (1757–1827)
America; a Prophecy, *sels.*
Angel, The.
Another [Epitaph]: "Here lies John Trot, the Friend of all mankind."
Answer to the Parson, An.
Auguries of Innocence, *sels.*
Birds, The.
Book of Thel, The, *sels.*
Book of Urizen [*or* First Book of Urizen], The.
Caverns of the Grave Ive seen, The.
Compliment to the Ladies, A.
Cradle Song, A: "Sleep, sleep, beauty bright."
Crystal Cabinet, The.
Epitaph, An: "I was buried near this dyke [*or* Dike]."
Everlasting Gospel, The, *sels.*
Gates of Paradise, The, *sels.*
Ghost of Abel, The.
Gnomic Verses, *sels.*
Grey Monk, The.

Grown old in Love from Seven till Seven times Seven.
Hebrew Nation did not write it, The.
Her whole life is an Epigram smack smooth & neatly pend.
I laid me down upon a bank.
I saw a chapel all of gold.
In a Myrtle [*or* Mirtle] Shade.
Jerusalem; The Emanation of the Giant Albion, *sels.*
Land of Dreams, The.
Long John Brown & Little Mary Bell.
Mad Song.
Marriage of Heaven and Hell, The, *sels.*
Mental Traveller, The.
Milton, *sels.*
Mr Cromek to Mr Stothard.
Mock on, Mock on Voltaire, Rousseau.
Morning.
Mr. Cromek [*or* On Cromek].
My Spectre around me night & day.
Never Pain to Tell Thy Love.
O lapwing, thou fliest around the heath.
Old maid early eer I knew, An.
On Hayley.
On Sir Joshua Reynolds.
Orator Prigg.
Prince of Love, The.
Revival of the Eternal Man.
Several Questions Answered, *sels.*
Since all the Riches of this World.
Sir Joshua Reynolds.
Smile, The.
Soft Snow.
Some people admire the work of a Fool.
Song By an Old Shepherd.
Song: "Fresh from the dewy hill, the merry year."
Song: "Memory, hither come."
Song: "My silks and fine array."
Songs of Experience, *sels.*
Songs of Innocence, *sels.*
To Autumn.
To English Connoisseurs.
To Flaxman.
To God.
To H[ayley].
To Hunt.
To Morning.
To Nobodaddy.
To Spring.
To the Evening Star.
To the Muses.
Vala; or The Four Zoas, *sels.*
Visions of the Daughters of Albion, *sels.*
War Song [to Englishmen], A.
When a Man has Married a Wife.
When Klopstock England defied.
Wild Flower's Song, The.
With happiness stretched [*or* stretchd] across the hills.

Blaker, Margaret
Pippa Passes, But I Can't Get Around This Truck.

Blamire, Susanna (1747–94)
Auld Robin Forbes.
Epistle to Her Friends at Gartmore.
I've gotten a rock, I've gotten a reel.
O Donald! ye are just the man.
O Jenny dear, lay by your pride.
Siller Croun, The.
Stoklewath; or, The Cumbrian Village, *sels.*
Wey, Ned, man! thou luiks sae down-hearted.
When home we return, after youth has been spending.
Written on a Gloomy Day, in Sickness.

Blanchard, Edward Laman (1804–45)
Ode to the Human Heart.

Blanchard, Ferdinand Q. (1876–1968)
O Child of Lowly Manger Birth.
Word of God, Across the Ages.

Blanco, Alberto (b. 1951)
Music in the Age of Iron.
Poem Seen in a Motel Fan.

Bland, Edith Nesbit. *See* Nesbit, Edith

Bland, James A. (1854–1911)
Carry me back to old Virginny.

Oh, Dem Golden Slippers!

Bland, Peter (b. 1934)
Notes for the Park Keeper.

Blandiana, Ana (b. 1942)
Couple, The.
Dance in the Rain.
From a Village.
I need only fall asleep / to return.
Links.
Song.

Blanding, Don (1894–1957)
Aloha Oe.
Vagabond House.

Blank, Arapera Hineira (b. 1932)
Yearning, A.

Blaser, Robin (b. 1925)
Ah.
Even on Sunday.
Finder, The.
4 Part Geometry Lesson, A.
Herons.
Image-Nation (the Poēsis).
Image-Nation 13 (the Telephone).
Image-Nation 3.
Poem: "And when I pay death's duty."
Poem by the Charles River.
Poem: "For years I've heard."
Ruler, The.
Suddenly.
Universe is Part of Ourselves, The.

Blaustein, Rahel. *See* "Rachel"

Blight, John (b. 1913)
Anchor, The.
Coral Reef, The.
Cormorants.
Death of a Whale.
Down from the Country.
Evolution.
Garfish.
Gate's Open, The.
Into the Ark.
Landfall, The.
Letter, The.
Mangrove.
Morgan.
Oyster-Eaters, The.
Pearl Perch.
Sun.
Tenant at Number 9.

Blind, Mathilde (1841–96)
After-Glow, The.
Ascent of Man, The, *sels.*
Beautiful Beeshareen Boy, The.
Dead abide with us! Though stark and cold, The.
Entangled.
Fantasy, A.
Love in Exile, *sels.*
On a Forsaken Lark's Nest.
Once we played at love together.
Reapers.
Russian Student's Tale, The.
Sower, The.

Blishen, Edward (b. 1920)
Abroad Thoughts.
Amid the derringers I ride.

Bliss, H. W.
Understanding.

Bliss, Philip Paul (1838–76)
"Almost persuaded," / Now to believe.

Bliss, William
Limerick: "If no Pain were, how judge we of Pleasure?"

Blitzstein, Marc (1905–64)
Cradle Will Rock, The, *sels.*

Bloch, Chana (b. 1940)
Eating Babies.
I and Thou.
Magnificat.
Primer.
Rising to Meet It.
Sacrifice, The, *sels.*
Survivors.
White Petticoats.
Yom Kippur.

Bloch, Jean-Richard (1884–1947)
Idea of a Swimmer.
Block, Alexander
Willow-Boughs, The.
Blockcolski, Lew
After the First Frost.
Flicker, The.
Flint Hills, The.
49 Stomp, The.
Indian Love Song.
Langston Hughes.
My Dream.
Peyote Vision.
Playing Pocahontas.
Powwow remnants.
Reservation Special.
Urban Experience: Part One, The.
Urban Experience: Part Two, The.
Wisga.
Woyi, The.
Blocksidge, Charles William. See "Baylebridge, William"
Blodgett, E. D. (b. 1935)
Fossil.
Snails.
Blok, Aleksandr Aleksandrovich (1880–1921)
Above the Lake.
At first she turned the whole thing to a joke.
Before the Court.
Blizzard sweeps the streets, A.
By the North Sea.
Dances of Death, sels.
Factory, The.
Girl was singing in the choir with fervor, A.
Gray Morning.
I want to live, live to distraction.
In the Dunes.
In the Restaurant.
Kite, The.
On Death.
On the Islands.
On the Railway.
Poets, The.
Red Glow in the Sky, A.
Retribution, sels.
Russia.
Scythians, The.
Sorcerer sang the spring to sleep, The.
Stranger, The.
Three Messages, sels.
Twelve, The, sels.
Vulture, The.
Winter day is cold and snowy, The.
Blokh, Raisa (1901–43)
Random talk has blown in.
Blood, Benjamin Paul (1832–1919)
Bride of the Iconoclasts, The, sels.
Late.
Bloom, Valerie (b. 1956)
Longsight Market.
Sun-a-shine, Rain-a-fall.
Wat A Rain.
Wha Fe Call I'.
Bloomfield, Robert (1766–1823)
Banks of Wye, The, sels.
Farmer's Boy, The, sels.
Shooter's Hill, sels.
Summer.
Winter, sels.
Bloomgarden [or Bloomgarten or Blumgarden], Solomon. See "Yehoash"
Blossom, Laurel
Disappearing Act.
Blount, Annabella (fl. 1700–1741)
Cure for Poetry, A.
Blount, Roy, Jr. (b. 1941)
Against Broccoli.
For the Record.
Gryll's State.
Bloze, Vytautas
Leaves have yellowed like, The.
Blue Cloud, Peter (b. 1933)
Bear: A Totem Dance As Seen by Raven.
Composition.
Crazy Horse Monument.

Death Chant.
Hawk Nailed to a Barn Door.
Oche Iron.
Old Man's Lazy, The.
Rattle.
Sweat Song.
To-ta Ti-om.
Turtle.
Walking through twisted hollow pathways.
Within the Seasons, sels.
Wolf.
Yellowjacket.
Blumenthal, Michael C. (b. 1949)
Abandoning Your Car in a Snowstorm: Rosslyn, Virginia.
Back from the Word-Processing Course, I Say to My Old Typewriter.
Blue.
Elephants Dying, The.
I Have Lived This Way for Years and Do Not Wish to Change.
Inventors.
Juliek's Violin.
Litrajure of Everyday Life, The.
Man Lost by a River, A.
Marriage, A.
Washington Heights, 1959.
Who Will Live in Our Houses When We Die?
Wishful Thinking.
Blumenthal, Walter Hart (1883–1969)
Da Silva Gives the Cue.
Blundell, G. J.
Squire Squint, shooting at a pheasant.
Blunden, Edmund Charles (1896–1974)
Almswomen.
Ancre at Hamel: Afterwards, The.
At the Great Wall of China.
Barn, The.
Come On, My Lucky Lads.
Concert Party: Busseboom.
Country God, A.
Death Mask of John Clare, The.
Departure.
Eastern Tempest.
Escape.
Forefathers.
Giant Puffball, The.
Gouzeaucourt: The Deceitful Calm.
Guard's Mistake, The.
Idlers, The.
In Festubert.
La Quinque Rue.
Late Light.
Lonely Love.
Midnight Skaters, The.
Mole Catcher.
1916 Seen from 1921.
One among the Roses.
Pike, The.
Poor Man's Pig, The.
Preparations for Victory.
Recovery, The.
Report on Experience.
Survival, The.
Third Ypres.
Two Voices.
Vlamertinghe.
Watchers, The.
Winter: East Anglia.
Zonnebeke Road, The.
Blunt, Wilfrid Scawen (1840–1922)
Esther [a Young Man's Tragedy], sels.
Gibraltar.
Honour Dishonoured.
Love Sonnets of Proteus, The, sels.
Nocturne: "Moon has gone to her rest, The."
Old Squire, The.
On Her Vanity.
Storm in Summer, A.
To One Who Would Make a Confession.
Wisdom of Merlyn, The, sels.
Bluwstein [or Blumstein], Rahel. See "Rachel"
Bly, Robert (b. 1926)
After Drinking All Night with a Friend, We Go Out in a Boat at Dawn to See Who Can Write the Best Poem.

After Long Busyness.
After the Industrial Revolution, All Things Happen at Once.
Andrew Jackson's Speech.
Anger Against Children, sels.
Asian Peace Offers Rejected without Publication.
At a March against the Vietnam War.
August Rain.
Awakening.
Busy Man Speaks, A.
Christmas Eve Service at Midnight at St. Michael's.
Come with me into those things that have felt this despair for so long.
Counting Small-Boned Bodies.
Dead Seal [near McClure's Beach], The.
Dream of Retarded Children, A.
Driving My Parents Home at Christmas.
Driving through Minnesota during the Hanoi Bombings.
Driving to Town Late to Mail a Letter.
Driving toward the Lac Qui Parle River.
Evolution from the Fish.
Executive's Death, The.
Extra Joyful Chorus for Those Who Have Read This Far, An.
For My Son Noah, Ten Years Old.
Great Society, The.
Hearing Men Shout at Night on MacDougal Street.
Hollow Tree, A.
Hunting Pheasants in a Cornfield.
Hurrying Away from the Earth.
In a Train.
In Danger from the Outer World.
In the month of May when all leaves open.
Johnson's Cabinet Watched by Ants.
Kneeling Down to Look [or Peer] into a Culvert.
Late at Night During a Visit of Friends.
Leonardo's Secret.
Listening to the Köln Concert.
Looking at a Dead Wren in My Hand.
Looking at a Dry Canadian Thistle Brought In from the Snow.
Looking at New-Fallen Snow from a Train.
Looking at Some Flowers.
Looking into a Face.
Mourning Pablo Neruda.
My Father's Wedding.
Night.
Old Boards.
Old dog bends his head listening, The.
Poem Against the British.
Poem against the Rich.
Poem in Three Parts.
Possibility of New Poetry, The.
Prodigal Son is kneeling in the husks, The.
Remembering in Oslo the Old Picture of the Magna Carta.
Romans Angry about the Inner World.
Schoolcraft's Diary Written on the Missouri: 1830.
Six Winter Privacy Poems, sels.
Sleet Storm on the Merritt Parkway.
Small Bird's Nest Made of White Reed Fiber, A.
Snowbanks North of the House.
Snowfall in the Afternoon.
Solitude Late at Night in the Woods.
Sunday in Glastonbury.
Sunset at a Lake.
Surprised by Evening.
Taking the hands of someone you love.
Teeth Mother Naked at Last, The.
Thinking of "The Autumn Fields."
Third Body, A.
Those Being Eaten by America.
Three Kinds of Pleasures.
Three Presidents.
To President bush at the Start of the Gulf War.
Turning Away from Lies.
Two Translations from Kabir, sels.
Visiting Emily Dickinson's Grave with Robert Francis.

Waking from Sleep.
War and Silence.
Watching Television.
Water under the Earth.
When the Dumb Speak.
Written Forty Miles South of a Spreading
City.
Blyth, Moira
First of all people was Adam, The.
Blyton, Carey (b. 1932)
Night Starvation or The Biter Bit.
Plug-hole Man, The.
Blyton, Enid (1897–1968)
Fairy Music.
Field-Mouse, The.
What Piggy-Wig Found.
Winter.
Boake, Barcroft Henry (1866–92)
Allegory, An.
At Devlin's Siding.
Digger's Song, The.
Where the Dead Men Lie.
Bobrowski, Johannes (1917–65)
Deserted House, The.
Elderblossom.
Kaunas 1941.
Latvian Autumn, The.
Latvian Songs.
Lithuanian Well, The.
Place of Fire.
Pruzzian Elegy.
Sanctuary.
Shadowland.
Volga Towns, The.
Wanderer, The.
When the rooms are deserted.
Wild Swan, The.
Bobrowsky, Igor
Free Fire Zone.
Journey, The.
**Bobyshev, Dmitry [or Dmitrii] Vasil'evich (b.
1936)**
Indifference— / A house.
Boccaccio, Giovanni (1313–75)
I am a young maiden, and I willingly.
Sonnets, sels.
Two Dreams, The.
Bock, Frederick (b. 1916)
Aubade: The Desert.
Big, Fat Summer—and the Lean and Hard.
Bode, Carl
Requiem: "So. They and I are back from the
outside."
Bodecker, N. M. (b. 1922)
Cats and Dogs.
First Snowflake.
Garden Calendar.
Hurry, hurry, Mary dear.
Miss Bitter.
Mr. 'Gator.
Mr. Slatter.
One Year.
Radish is / the only dish, The.
Small Rains.
Snowman Sniffles.
When Skies are Low and Days are Dark.
Bodenheim, Maxwell (1893–1954)
Advice to a Forest.
Death.
Poem: "O men, walk on the hills."
To an Enemy.
Upper Family.
Bodker, Cecil (b. 1927)
Calendar.
Fury's Field.
Self-Portrait.
Bodman, Manoah (1765–1850)
Oration on Death, An, sels.
Boe, Marilyn J.
Sunday Afternoon at the State Hospital.
**Boethius (Anicius Manlius Severinus Boethius)
(480–524)**
Boetius. Libr. 3. Metr. 6.
Book 3, Metrum 11.
Book 3, metrum 4.

Chawcer upon this fyfte meter of the second
book.
Consolation of Philosophy, The, sels.
Consolation of Philosophy, The ("De
Consolacione Philosophie"), sels.
Some Odes of the Excellent and Knowing
Severinus, Englished: Metrum 12. Lib. 3,
sels.
Bogan, Louise (1897–1970)
After the Persian.
Alchemist, The.
Betrothed.
Cartography.
Cassandra.
Come, break with time.
Crossed Apple, The.
Crows, The.
Daemon, The.
Decoration.
Didactic Piece.
Dragonfly, The.
Dream, The.
Evening in the Sanitarium.
Frightened Man, The.
Henceforth, from the mind.
Hypocrite Swift now takes an eldest
daughter.
Juan's Song.
Knowledge.
Last Hill in a Vista.
Late.
M., Singing.
Man Alone.
Masked Woman's Song.
Medusa.
Meeting, The.
Men loved wholly beyond wisdom.
Musician.
Night.
Old Countryside.
Putting to Sea.
Question in a Field.
Roman Fountain.
Several Voices Out of a Cloud.
Simple Autumnal.
Single Sonnet.
Sleeping Fury, The.
Song for the Last Act.
Spirit's Song.
Statue and Birds.
To an Artist, to Take Heart.
To Be Sung on the Water.
To My Brother: Killed: Hammont Wood:
October, 1918.
Train Tune.
Winter Swan.
Women have no wilderness in them.
Zone.
Bogen, Don
House Destroyed by Fire, The.
Last Installment, The.
Bogin, George (1920–88)
Nineteen.
Bognini, Joseph Miezan (b. 1936)
Ce Dur Appel de l'Espoir (1960), sels.
Earth and sky are infinities / Where our cries
cannot venture.
Herbe Féconde (1973), sels.
Boileau-Despéaux, Nicolas (1636–1711)
Epistle to My Gardener, sels.
Garden of Writing, The.
L'Art Poetique, sels.
Boito, Arrigo
Otello, sels.
Boker, George Henry (1823–90)
Awaking of the Poetic Faculty, The.
Blood, blood! The lines of every printed
sheet.
Brave comrade, answer! When you joined the
war.
God to Thee We Humbly Bow.
Love Is That Orbit.
Oh! craven, craven! while my brothers fall.
Sonnets: A Sequence on Profane Love, sels.
Bokov, Viktor Fiodorovich (b. 1914)
Commune for Me, The.
Salt.

Bolamba, Antoine-Roger (b. 1913)
Bonguemba.
Esanzo.
Fistful of News, A.
In a Storm.
Portrait.
Boland, Eavan (b. 1944)
Achill Woman, The.
Anna Liffey.
Black Lace Fan My Mother Gave Me, The.
Child of Our Time.
Dolls Museum in Dublin, The.
Famine Road, The.
From the Painting "Back from Market" by
Chardin.
Glass King, The.
I remember the way the big windows
washed.
In Her Own Image.
Inscriptions: "About holiday rooms there can
be."
Irish Childhood in England: 1951, An.
It's a Woman's World.
Journey, The.
Nocturne.
Ode to Suburbia.
Oral Tradition, The.
Pomegranate, The.
Song: "Where in blind files."
That the Science of Cartography Is Limited.
War Horse, The.
Woman in Kitchen.
Bold, Alan (b. 1943)
And Now.
Auld Symie, The.
Grass basks greedily in the sun.
June 1967 at Buchenwald.
Last Men on Mars.
Love-Lowe.
Malfeasance, The.
Moon.
Special Theory of Relativity, A.
Stars.
Tenth Planet, The.
Bold, Henry (1627–83)
Song: "Chloris, forbear a while."
Song: "Fire, fire."
Boldman, Bob
Day darkens.
Face wrapping a champagne glass.
Fin, A.
I end in shadow.
I hammer a nail.
I read.
In the doll's.
In the heat.
In the temple.
JANUARY FIRST.
Just past sunset.
Leaves blowing into a sentence.
Mist.
Moment in the box of jade, A.
Priest, The.
Sitting.
Touching the ashes of my father.
Walking with the river.
Boleyn, Anne (1507–36)
Defiled Is My Name Full Sore.
Boleyn, George (d. 1536)
O death, rock me asleep.
Bolger, Dermot (b. 1959)
Dublin Girl, Mountjoy, 1984.
Stardust Sequence, The, sels.
Bolles, Matthew (1769–1838)
Here, Lord, Retired, I Bow in Prayer.
Bolton, Edmund (1575?–1633?)
As to the blooming prime.
Palinode, A.
Bolton, Frank
Insult before Gift-Giving.
Bolton, Ken. See Jenkins, John and Ken Bolton.
Bolton, Ken (b. 1949)
Nonplussed.
Bolton, Sarah Knowles (1841–1916)
His Monument.
Influence.

Now.

Bona, Mary Jo (fl. 20th cent.)
Amazone.
Dream Poem.

Bonar, Horatius (1808–90)
Be True [or Be True Thyself].
Length of Days.

Boncho (Nozawa Boncho) (d. 1714)
Long, long river, The.

Boncho, Nozawa. *See* **Boncho**

Bond, Cynthia
What You Want Means What You Can
Afford.

Bond, Edward
How We See.
If Auschwitz had been in Hampshire.

Bond, Freda C.
'After the war,' they used to say, and
pictured.
Pity Wasted.

Bond, Harold
Glove, The.

Bond, Julian (b. 1940)
Look at That Gal.
Rotation.

Bond, Sandra Turner (b. 1951)
Tuesday Night Affair.

Bone, Edith (1889–1975)
On Myself.

Bone, Florence
Prayer for a Little Home, A.

Bonham, Thomas (d. 1629?)
In Praise of Ale.

Bonhoeffer, Dietrich
Who am I? They often tell me.

Bonin-Rodriguez, Paul
Steven Pudenz.

Bonitaz Nuño, Rubén (b. 1923)
Smoke.

Bonnefoy, Yves (b. 1923)
All, the Nothing, The.
De Natura Rerum.
Stone, A.
Summer Again.
Top of the World, The.
Tree, the Lamp, The.
Well, The.
Words of Evening, The.

Bontemps, Arna (1902–73)
Black Man Talks of Reaping, A.
Blight.
"Close Your Eyes!"
Day-Breakers [or Daybreakers], The.
God Give to Men.
Golgotha is a mountain, a purple mound.
Idolatry.
Length of Moon.
Miracles.
My Heart has Known its Winter.
Nocturne at Bethesda.
Nocturne of the Wharves.
Reconnaissance.
Return, The.
Southern Mansion.
To a Young Girl Leaving the Hill Country.

Booth, Philip (b. 1925)
Countershadow, The.
Crossing.
Day the Tide, The.
Deer Isle.
Ego.
First Lesson.
Game.
Hard Country.
He was fifteen. And she, Wisconsin.
Heron.
Hope.
How to See Deer.
Jake's Wharf.
Late Spring: Eastport, A.
Marin.
One Man's Wife.
Original Sequence.
Presence.

Seeing Auden Off.
Species.
Stations.
Stefansson Island.
Stove.
Supposition with Qualification.
Was it he said she said or.

Boothby, Frances (fl. c.1669)
Marcelia; or, Treacherous Friend, The, *sels.*

Borawski, Walta (b. 1947)
Cheers, Cheers for Old Cha Cha Ass
("Cheers, cheers for old Patchogue High.")
English Was Only a Second Language.
Invisible History.

Borges, Jorge Luis (1899–1986)
Afterglow.
Apocryphal Gospel, An, *sels.*
Dagger, The ("A dagger rests in a drawer.")
Everness.
Hengest Cyning.
John 1:14 (1964).
John 1:14 (1969).
Luke XXIII.
Matthew XXV:30.
Plainness.
St. John, *sels.*
St. Luke, *sels.*
St. Matthew, *sels.*

Borisov, Georgi
Untitled.

Borkhuis, Charles (b. 1947)
Inside Language.
Quartet.

Borowski, Tadeusz (1922–51)
Farewell to Maria.
Green of the distant meadows, lightly.
Night over Birkenau.
Project: Flag.
Sun of Auschwitz, The.
Two Countries.

Borregaard, Ebbe (b. 1933)
Each Found Himself at the End Of. . . .
Some Stories of the Beauty Wapiti.

Borson, Roo (b. 1952)
Flowers.
Gray Glove.
Jacaranda.
Lust.
Rain.
Talk.

Boruch, Marianne (b. 1950)
Buick.
Krakow and the Girl of Twelve.
My Son and I Go See Horses.

Bose, Buddhadeva
Frogs.

Bosley, Keith
Bird / sips water / drips music.

Bosman, Herman Charles (1905–51)
Learning Destiny.
Old I Am.
Seed.

Boss, Laura
At the Nuclear Rally.
Candy Lady, The.
My Ringless Fingers on the Steering Wheel
Tell the Story.

Bosselaar, Laure-Anne (b. 1943)
Fall.

Bossidy, John Collins (1860–1928)
Boston.
Boston Toast, A.

Bostok, Janice
Foetus kicks.
Pregnant again.

Boswell, Margie B. (1875–1952)
Texas Ranger, The.

Botsford, S. B.
Sonneteering Made Easy.

Bottomley, Gordon (b. 1874)
Dawn.
Eager Spring.
End of the World, The.
King Lear's Wife, *sels.*

Suilven and the Eagle, *sels.*
To Iron-Founders and Others.

Bottoms, David (b. 1949)
Boy Shepherds' Simile, The.
Desk, The.
Drowned, The.
In a U-Haul North of Damascus.
Sign for My Father, Who Stressed the Bunt.
Smoking in an Open Grave.
Under the Boathouse.
Under the Vulture-Tree.

Bottrall, Ronald (b. 1906)
Darkened Windows.
Icarus.
Mating Answer.

Boumi-Pappas, Rita (b. 1906)
Crow, The.

Boundzekei-Dongala, Emmanuel
Fantasy under the Moon.

Bourdillon, Francis William (1852–1921)
When Love Is Done.

Bourne, Vincent (1695–1747)
Cricket, The.
Housekeeper, The.
Silkworm, The.
Snail, The.

Bovshover, Joseph (1872–1916)
To the Laggards.

Bowden, Michael
Miller Canyon Trail No. 106.

Bowden, Samuel (1726?–1771?)
Paper Kite, The, *sels.*

**Bowen, Charles Synge Christopher Bowen,
Baron (1835–96)**
Rain it raineth all around, The.

Bowen, Euros (b. 1904)
Blackthorn.
Nettles in May.
Winged in Gold.

Bower, John Graham. *See* **"Klaxon"**

Bower, Rhonda
Clothespin, The.

Bower, Roger
On Door Jambs.

Bowering, George (b. 1938)
Dobbin.
Envies, The.
Está Muy Caliente.
Grandfather.
Grass, The.
House, The.
In the Forest.
Inside the Tulip.
Moon Shadow.
Summer Solstice, *sels.*

Bowering, Marilyn (b. 1949)
Russian Asylum.
Seeing Oloalok.
Wishing Africa.

Bowers, Edgar (b. 1924)
Adam's Song to Heaven.
Afternoon at the Beach, An.
Amor Vincit Omnia.
Astronomers of Mont Blanc, The.
Autumn Shade, *sels.*
Centaur Overheard, The.
Elegy, An: December, 1970.
Le Rêve.
Mountain Cemetery, The.
Prince, The.
Stoic: for Laura von Courten, The.
Two Poems on the Catholic Bavarians, *sels.*

Bowes-Lyon, Lilian (1895–1949)
Battlefield.
Blind Tramp, The.
Feather, The.
Leda.
Pastoral: "This field has buried men; is
browed."
Refugee, A.
White Hare, The.
Woman Knitting, A.

Bowie, Walter Russell (1882–1969)
God of the Nations.
O Holy City Seen of John.

Bowles, Caroline Anne (1786–1854)
Blackwood's Edinburgh Magazine, 13 275, *sels.*
Ellen Fitzarthur: A Metrical Tale, *sels.*
Bowles, Paul (1910–86)
Extract.
Bowles, William Lisle (1762–1854)
At Tynemouth Priory, after a Tempestuous Voyage.
Dover Cliffs.
Milton: On the Busts of Milton, in Youth and Age, *sels.*
Netley Abbey.
Sonnet: At Ostend.
Sonnet 5: "Evening, as slow thy placid shades descend."
Time and Grief.
To a Friend.
To the River Itchin, near Winton.
Tweed Visited, The.
Bowman, Catherine (b. 1957)
Demographics.
Mr. X.
Bowring, Sir John (1510–55)
God Is Love.
Boyce, Max
Ballad of Morgan the Moon, The.
Boyd, Bruce (b. 1928)
Sanctuary.
This Is What the Watchbird Sings, Who Perches in the Lovetree.
Venice Recalled.
Boyd, Elizabeth (*fl.* 1727–45)
On the Death of an Infant of Five Days Old.
Boyd, Mark Alexander (1563–1601)
Sonet: "Fra bank [*or* banc] to bank [*or* banc], fra wood [*or* wod] to wood [*or* wod] I rin."
Boyd, Melba Joyce (b. 1950)
Beer Drops.
Sunflowers and Saturdays.
Why?
"Boyd, Nancy." *See* **Millay, Edna St. Vincent**
Boyd, Thomas (1898–1935)
King's Son, The.
Boyden, Polly Chase
Mud ("Mud is very nice to feel.")
Boye, Karin (1900–1941)
Dedication, A, *sels.*
Sword, A.
Boyle, Kay (b. 1903)
Communication to Nancy Cunard, A.
For James Baldwin.
For Marianne Moore's Birthday.
Invitation in It, from American Citizen, The.
Monody to the Sound of Zithers.
New Emigration, The.
Poem for February First 1975, A.
Poem on Getting Up Early in the Morning (or Even Late in the Morning), When One is Old, A.
Spiritual for Nine Voices, The.
Testimony, The.
Thunderstorm in South Dakota.
To a Seaman Dead on Land.
Boyle, Robert. *See* **Orrery, Robert Boyle, 1st Earl of**
Boynton, H. W. (1869–1947)
Golfer's Rubaiyat, The.
Boyse, Samuel (1708–49)
On Platonic Love.
Triumphs of Nature, The, *sels.*
Bozhilov, Bozhidar (b. 1923)
Eternity.
Kentish Sestinas.
Lilies.
Troubles.
Wise Ones, The.
Brabazon, Francis
Victoria Market.
Bracken, Thomas (1843–98)
Not Understood.
Brackenbury, Alison (b. 1953)
Two dead divers hauled up in their bell, The.
Whose Window?

Brackenridge, Hugh Henry (1748–1816) *and* **Philip Freneau**
Rising Glory of America, The, *sels.*
Brackley, Lady Elizabeth. *See* **Cavendish, Lady Jane** *and* **Lady Elizabeth Brackley**
Bradbury, Ray
Switch on the Night.
Bradford, William (1589?–1657)
And Truly It Is a Most Glorious Thing.
Epitaphium Meum.
Of Boston in New England.
Word to New England, A.
Bradley, Christine E.
Skippets, the Bad One.
Bradley, George (b. 1953)
Fire Fetched Down, The.
Bradstreet, Anne (c.1612–1672)
Another.
Apology, An.
As Spring the Winter Doth Succeed.
As weary pilgrim, now at rest.
Author to Her Book, The.
Before the Birth of One of Her Children.
Contemplations, *sels.*
Deliverance from a Fit of Fainting.
Dialogue between Old England and New, A, *sels.*
Flesh and the Spirit, The.
For Deliverance from a Fever.
Four Ages of Man, The, *sels.*
Four[e] Monarchies, The, *sels.*
Four Seasons of the Year, The.
Here Follows Some Verses upon the Burning of Our House [July 10th, 1966. Copied Out of a Loose Paper].
In Honour of That High and Mighty Princess Queen Elizabeth of Happy Memory.
In Memory of My Dear Grandchild Anne Bradstreet Who Deceased June 20, 1669, Being Three Years and Seven Months Old.
In Memory of My Dear Grandchild Elizabeth Bradstreet Who Deceased August, 1665, Being a Year and Half Old.
In Reference to Her Children, 23 June, 1659 [*or* 1659].
Letter to Her Husband, Absent upon Public[k] Employment, A.
On My Dear Grandchild Simon Bradstreet, [Who Died on 16TH November, 1669, Being But A Month And One Day Old].
Prologue, The: "To sing of wars, of captain[e]s, and of kings."
To Her Father, with Some Verses.
To My Dear and Loving Husband.
To My Dear Children.
To the Memory of My Dear and Ever Honored Father Thomas Dudley Esq. Who Deceased July 31, 1653, and of His Age 77.
To the Memory of My Dear Daughter in Law, Mrs. Mercy Bradstreet.
Upon My Dear and Loving Husband His Going into England.
Vanity of All Worldly Things, The.
Bradstreet, Samuel (c.1633–1682)
Almanack for the Year of Our Lord, 1657, An.
Brady, Edwin James (1869–1925)
Whaler's Pig, The.
Brady, Nicholas. *See* **Tate, Nahum** *and* Nicholas Brady
Brainard, E. M.
Compensation.
Brainard, John Gardiner Calkins (1796–1828)
I saw two clouds at morning.
To Thee, O God, the Shepherd Kings.
Braine, Sheila
Mr. Scarecrow.
Braithwaite, William Stanley (1878–1962)
City Garden, A.
Golden Moonrise.
House of Falling Leaves, The.
In a Grave-Yard.
Quiet has a hidden sound.
Rye Bread.
Sic Vita.

To ———: "Half in the dim light from the hall."
Turn Me to My Yellow Leaves.
Watchers, The.
Braley, Berton (1882–1966)
Loyalty.
Prayer, A: "Lord, let me live like a Regular Man."
Start where you stand and never mind the past.
Success ("If you want a thing bad enough.")
That's Success!
Thinker, The.
Braley, Ephraim
Canada-I-O ("Come all ye jolly lumbermen and listen to my song.")
Bramfit, Sheila
Grandparents.
Bramston, James (1694?–1743)
Art of Politics, The, *sels.*
Man of Taste, The, *sels.*
Branch, Anna Hempstead (1875–1937)
Monk in the Kitchen, The.
Sonnets from a Lock Box, *sels.*
Brand, Dionne (b. 1953)
Epigrams to Ernesto Cardenal in Defense of Claudia, *sels.*
Military Occupations, *sels.*
Wind.
Brand, Millen (1906–80)
Lost.
Brandling, Charles (1733–1802)
To a Lady, with a Present of a Fan.
Brandreth, Gyles
Ode to a Goldfish.
Brant, Beth (b. 1941)
Her name is Helen.
Brant, LeRoy V. (b. 1890)
Green Plumes of Royal Palms.
Oh, Day of Days.
Brasch, Charles (1909–73)
Ambulando.
Estate, The, *sels.*
Home Ground, *sels.*
Life Mask.
Night Cries, Wakari Hospital, *sels.*
Shoriken.
Word by Night.
Brathwaite, Edward Kamau (b. 1930)
Ancestors.
Arrivants: A New World Trilogy, The, *sels.*
Blues.
Citadel.
Clock.
Colombe.
Harbour.
Horse Weebles.
Miss Own.
Mmenson.
Naima.
New Year Letter.
Red Rising.
Rites, *sels.*
Schooner.
Starvation and Blues.
Xango.
Brathwaite [*or* Brathwait], Richard (1588?–1673)
Vandunk's Four Humours, in Quality and Quantity.
Braun, Richard Emil (b. 1934)
Goose.
Lilies, The.
Seeking an Explanation.
Braun, Volker
New Purpose of Hadrian's Army, The.
Brautigan, Richard (1935–c.1990)
Boat, A.
Chinese Checker Players, The.
Haiku Ambulance.
Surprise.
Bray, J. J. (b. 1912)
Execution of Madame du Barry, The.
Braybrook, Patrick
Limerick: "People the Churches love best, The."

Brazelton, Ethel M. C.
Poor Lil' Brack Sheep.

Brecht, Bertolt (1898–1956)
Alabama Song.
Bad Time for Poetry.
Burning of the Books, The.
Changing the Wheel.
Children's Crusade 1939.
First Psalm (Posthumous).
Fishing-Tackle, The.
Friends, The.
From a German War Primer.
God of War, The.
I, the Survivor.
Late Lamented Fame of the Giant City of
    New York, sels.
Letter to the Actor Charles Laughton
    concerning the Work on the Play "The
    Life of Galileo."
Mary.
Mask of Evil, The.
1940.
Of Poor B.B.
One-Armed Man in the Undergrowth, The.
Solution, The.
St. Luke, sels.
This Summer's Sky.
Three Fragments.
Threepenny Opera, The, sels.
To Those Born Later.
War Has Been Given a Bad Name.
What a bankruptcy! How.
What people they were! Their boxers the
    strongest!
When Evil-Doing Comes Like Falling Rain.
World's One Hope, The.

Brecht, Stefan (b. 1924)
Sex, sels.
Silence.
Silence, 2.
Thanksgiving (1974).

Breckenridge, Jill
Bottled.
Civil Blood, sels.
General John Cabell Breckinridge.
Unlocking the Doors.

Breeze, Jean Binta (b. 1957)
Dreamer.
Lovin wasn easy all de time.
Natural High.
Riddym Ravings (The Mad Woman's Poem).

Breit, Luke
Sacramento.

"Breitman, Hans." See **Leland, Charles Godfrey**

Bremser, Ray (b. 1934)
Blood.
Poem of Holy Madness, sels.

Brennan, Christopher John (1870–1932)
Because She Would Ask Me Why I Loved
    Her.
Quest of Silence, The, sels.
Sweet silence after bells!
Wanderer, The, sels.

Brennan, Gerald
Mornin's Mornin, The.

Brennan, J. Keirn (1873–1948)
Let the Rest of the World Go By.

Brennen, Pat
Spring.

Brent, Hally Carrington (b. 1943?)
I Think I Know No Finer Things than Dogs.

Brereton, Charlotte (b. c.1720)
To Miss A[——]a M[——]a Tra[——]s; an
    Epistle from Scotland.

Brereton, E. C.
Three Dogs.

Brereton, Jane (1685–1740)
Epistle to Mrs Anne Griffiths, sels.
On Mr. Nash's Picture at Full Length.
To Mr Thomas Griffith at the University of
    Glasgow, sels.

Brereton, John Le Gay (1871–1933)
Unborn.

Breton, Andre. See **Eluard, Paul** and Andre
Breton

Breton, André (1896–1966)
Free Union.
Go For Broke.
Man and Woman Absolutely White, A.
Manifesto of Surrealism (1924), sels.
More than Suspect.
Mystery Corset, The.
On the Road to San Romano.
Poem-Object.
Postman Cheval.
Spectral Attitudes, The.
War.

Breton, Andre and **Philippe Soupault**
Magnetic Fields, The, sels.

Breton, Nicholas (1542–1626)
Assurance, An.
Chess Play, The.
Cradle Song: "Come, little babe."
Honourable Entertainment Given to the
    Queen's Majesty in Progress at Elvetham,
    1591, The, sels.
In time of yore when shepherds dwelt.
Passionate Shepherd, The, sels.
Report Song [in a Dream], A.
Service Is No Heritage.

Brett, Doris (b. 1953)
For My Mother.

Brett, Lily
I keep forgetting.
La Pathétique.
Leaving You.
My Mother's Friend.

Brettell, Noel H. (b. 1908)
African Student.
On an Inyanga Road.

Brew, Kwesi (b. 1928)
Ancestral Faces.
Lonely Traveller, The.
Plea for Mercy, A.
Search, The.

Brewster, Elizabeth (b. 1922)
Anti-Love Poems.
Death by Drowning.
Great-Aunt Rebecca.
If I Could Walk Out into the Cold Country.

Brewster, Martha (b. 1710)
Stately Structure of This Earth, The.

Breytenbach, Breyten (b. 1939)
Asylum.
Breyten Prays for Himself.
Dar es-Salaam: Harbour of Peace.
Dreams Are Also Wounds.
Eavesdropper.
Exile, Representative.
Firewing.
First Prayer for the Hottentotsgod.
Journey.
Lullaby.
Menace of the Sick.
Out There.
Sleep my little love.
Struggle for the Taal, The.
Testament of a Rebel.
There Is Life.
We Shall Overcome.

Brice, Andrew (1690–1773)
Freedom; a Poem, Written in Time of Recess
    from the Rapacious Claws of Bailiffs, sels.

Brickley, Chuck
Autumn rain—.
Deserted wharf.
Few flakes appear, A.
Outside the pub.
Puppet, The.
Sheet lightning.
Slipping in the snow.
Spring evening.
Summer evening.

Bridges, Grace Caroline
How She Operates.
Lisa's Ritual, Age 10.

**"Bridges, Madeline" (Mary Ainge De Vere) (fl.
c.1840)**
Life's Mirror.

Bridges, Robert (1844–1930)
Angel spirits of sleep.
April, 1885.
Awake, my heart, to be loved, awake, awake!
Cliff-Top, The.
Clouds Have Left the Sky, The.
Elegy on a Lady, Whom Grief for the Death
    of Her Betrothed Killed.
Elegy: "Wood is bare, The: a river-mist is
    steeping, The."
Emily Brontë: Du hast Diamanten.
Eros.
Evening darkens over, the.
First Spring Morning.
Garden in September, The.
Gay Robin Is Seen No More.
Going Home.
Growth of Love, The, sels.
I have loved flowers that fade.
I Heard a Linnet Courting.
I love all beauteous things.
I Never Shall Love the Snow Again.
I Will Not Let Thee Go.
Idle Life I Lead, The.
In autumn moonlight, when the white air
    wan.
Johannes Milton, Senex.
London Snow.
Low Barometer.
Melancholia.
Muse and Poet.
My Delight and Thy Delight.
Nightingales.
Nimium Fortunatus.
Noel; Christmas Eve, 1913.
November.
On a Dead Child.
Passer-by, A.
Pater Filio.
Philosopher to His Mistress, The.
Poor Poll.
Power of Ridicule, The, sels.
Psalm: "While Northward the hot sun was
    sinking o'er the trees."
Snow Lies Sprinkled on the Beach, The.
Spring Goeth All in White.
Storm is over, the land hushes to rest, The.
Testament of Beauty, The, sels.
Testament of Beauty, Book III, The, sels.
Thou didst delight my eyes.
Triolet: "When first we met we did not
    guess."
Upper Skies, The.
Weep Not To-Day.
When Death to Either Shall Come.
While yet we wait for spring, and from the
    dry.
Who has not walked upon the shore.
Winter Nightfall.

Brierre, Jean (b. 1909)
Harlem.

Brigham, Besmilr (b. 1923)
Tell Our Daughters.
Will's Love, The.

Brinckman, Rosemary
Fish and Bird.

Brine, Mary Dow (1816–1913)
Somebody's Mother.

Bringhurst, Robert (b. 1946)
Deuteronomy.
For the Bones of Josef Mengele, Disinterred
    June 1985.
Notes to the Reader.
These Poems, She Said ("These poems, these
    poems.")

Brinnin, John Malcolm (b. 1916)
Angel Eye of Memory.
Ascension: 1925, A View.
At the Band Concert.
Cape Ann; a View.
Heavy Heavy Heavy.
Hotel Paradiso e Commerciale.
Letter from an Island.
My Father, My Son.
Nuns at Eve.
Roethke Plain.
Skin Diving in the Virgins.

Thin Façade for Edith Sitwell, A.

Brisley, Joyce L. (b. 1896)
Two Families, The.

Brissenden, Robert Francis (b. 1928)
Verandahs.
Walking down Jalan Thamrin.

Bristol, Augusta Cooper (b. 1835)
Crime of the Ages, The.
Night.

Bristow, Paul
Limerick: "General once lived named de
Gaulle, A."

Britton, Donald
Winter Garden.

Broaddus, Andrew (1770–1848)
Help Thy Servant.

Brock-Broido, Lucie
Carrowmore.
Domestic Mysticism.
Hitchcock Blue.
Last Passenger Pigeon in the Cincinnati Zoo,
The.
Moving on in the Dark Like Loaded Boats at
Night, Though There is No Course, There
is Boundlessness.

Brock, Van K. (b. 1932)
Departure.
Lying on a Bridge.
Man in the Rain, The.
Novas.
Remembering Dresden.
Sea Birds, The.

Brod, Max (b. 1884)
Goldfish on the Writing Desk.

Brode, Anthony (b. 1923)
Breakfast with Gerard Manley Hopkins.
Calypsomania.

Brodey, Jim (b. 1942)
Lennie Tristano, No Wind.
Little Light.

Brodrick, Albert (1830–1908)
Epitaph on a Diamond Digger.
Joe's Luck.
On a Government Surveyor.
Shu' Shu' of Delgo.

**Brodsky [or Brodskii], Joseph [or Iosif]
Aleksandrovich (1940–96)**
Belfast Tune.
Berlin Wall Tune, The.
Café Trieste: San Francisco.
Eclogue IV: Winter.
Elegy.
Folk Tune.
Hawk's Cry in Autumn, The.
I Sit by the Window.
In the Lake District.
Letters from the Ming Dynasty.
May 24, 1980.
Nature Morte.
October Tune.
Odysseus to Telemachus.
Roman Elegies.
Roman Elegies IV.
Seven Strophes.
Sextet.
Sir, you are tough, and I am tough.
Six Years Later.
To Urania.
York: In Memoriam W. H. Auden.

Brody, Alter (b. 1895)
Cry of the Peoples, The.
Lamentations.

Brome, Alexander (1620–66)
Epithalamy.
On Sir G. B. his defeat.
Pastoral on the King's Death, The; [Written
in 1648].
Plain Dealing.
Prisoners, The, sels.
Resolve, The.
Riddle: "No more, no more, / We are already
pined [pin'd]."

Bromige, David (b. 1933)
Choice.
Eastward Ho! A Succession.

Edible World, The.
Lines: "Repressive desublimation."
Log.
Logical Positivist, The.
Point is not the point—, The.
Tight Corners, sels.

Bromley, Anne C.
My Mother's Face Never Moved.
Slow Men Working in Trees.
Teel St. Trailer Court.

Bromwich, David (b. 1951)
From the Righteous Man Even the Wild
Beasts Run Away.
Wandsworth Common.

Bronk, William (b. 1918)
Aspects of the World like Coral Reefs.
At Tikal.
Body, The.
Corals and Shells.
Feeling, The.
I Thought It Was Harry.
Life Supports.
March, Upstate.
Mayan Glyphs Unread, The.
Metonymy as an Approach to a Real World.
Nature of Musical Form, The.
Plainest Narrative, The.
Postcard to Send to Sumer, A.
Strong Room of the House, The.
Where It Ends.
World, The.

Brontë, Anne ("Acton Bell") (1820–49)
Arbour, The.
Captive Dove, The.
Fragment, A.
Home.
Lines Composed in a Wood on a Windy
Day.
Memory.
Night.
Reminiscence, A.
Song.
To Cowper.

Brontë, Charlotte ("Currer Bell") (1816–55)
Again I find myself alone, and ever.
Autumn day its course has run—The Autumn
evening falls, The.
Diving.
House was still—the room was still, The.
I now had only to retrace.
Is this my tomb, this humble stone.
Like wolf—and black bull or goblin hound.
Lonely Lady, The.
Nurse believed the sick man slept, The.
Obscure and little seen my way.
On the Death of Anne Brontë.
On the Death of Emily Jane Brontë.
Orphan Child, The.
Pilate's Wife's Dream.
Reason.
Retrospection, sels.
What does she dream of, lingering all alone.
Young Man Naughty's Adventure.

Brontë, Emily Jane ("Ellis Bell") (1818–48)
All hushed and still within the house.
Alone I sat; the summer day.
Anticipation.
Aye, there it is! It wakes to-night.
Come, walk with me.
D.G.C. to J.A.
Day Dream, A.
Death Scene, A.
Death, that struck when I was most
confiding.
Evening sun was sinking down, The.
F. de Samara to A. G. A.
Fair sinks the summer evening now.
Fall, leaves, fall; die, flowers, away.
Had there been falsehood in my breast.
High waving heather 'neath stormy blasts
bending.
Hope was but a timid friend.
How still, how happy! These [or Those] are
words.
I am the only being whose doom.
I know not how it falls on me.
If grief for grief can touch thee.

I'm happiest when most away.
It will not shine again.
It's over now; I've known it all.
Last Words.
Little while, a little while, A.
Long neglect has worn away.
Loud without the wind was roaring.
Love and Friendship.
Mild the mist upon the hill.
My Comforter.
Night Wind, The.
No coward soul is mine.
O come with me, thus ran the song.
O Dream, where art thou now?
O thy bright eyes must answer now.
Old Stoic, The.
Philosopher, The, sels.
Prisoner, The, sels.
Remembrance.
Self-Interrogation.
Shall Earth no more inspire thee.
She dried her tears, and they did smile.
Song.
Song: "Linnet in the rocky dells, The."
Spellbound.
Stanzas: "I'll not weep that thou art going to
leave me."
Stanzas: "Often rebuked, yet always back
returning."
Stanzas to———.
Stars.
Sun has set, and the long grass now, The.
Sympathy.
Tell me, tell me, smiling child.
That Wind.
Two Children, The.
Upon her soothing breast.
Visionary, The.
Warning and Reply.
What winter floods, what showers of spring.
When weary with the long day's care.
Why do I hate that lone green dell?
Wind, I hear it sighing, The.

Brook, Donna
School of Pain, The.

Brooke, Henry (1703?–1783)
Jack the Giant Queller; an Antique History,
sels.
Universal Beauty, sels.

Brooke, L. Leslie (1862–1940)
Johnny Crow's Garden.

Brooke, Rupert (1887–1915)
Busy Heart, The.
Chilterns, The.
Clouds.
Day That I Have Loved.
Dining-Room Tea.
Doubts.
Dust.
Fish, The.
Fragment: "Isn't ligature—or is it
ligament?—a lovely word?"
Fragment: "My lips (the inconstancy of
man!)."
Great Lover, The.
Heaven.
Hill, The.
Mary and Gabriel.
New Boy's View of Rugger.
1914, sels.
Old Vicarage, Grantchester, The.
Second Best.
Song of the Beasts (Sung, on one night, in
the cities, in the darkness), The.
Sonnet: In Time of Revolt.
Sonnet: "Oh! Death will find me, long before
I tire."
Sonnet Reversed.
Success.
Wagner.

Brookes, Peter
Limerick: "Isaac Singer (you probably
know)."

Brooks, Charles Timothy (1813–88)
Lines: Composed at the Old Temples of
Maralipoor.
Our Island Home.

Brooks, Fred Emerson (1850–1923)
Barnyard Melodies.
Foreigners at the Fair.

Brooks, Frederic
General Description of Men and Things in
Cape Town, A.

Brooks, Gwendolyn (b. 1917)
Anniad, The.
Appendix to the Anniad.
Aspect of Love, Alive in the Ice and Fire,
An.
Ballad of Edie Barrow, The.
Ballad of Rudolph Reed, The.
Bean Eaters, The.
Birth in a Narrow Room, The.
Blackstone Rangers, The.
Boy Breaking Glass.
Boy Died in My Alley, The.
Bronzeville Man with a Belt in the Back.
Bronzeville Mother Loiters in Mississippi. /
Meanwhile, a Mississippi Mother Burns
Bacon.
Bronzeville Woman in a Red Hat.
Catch of Shy Fish, A, *sels.*
Chicago *Defender* Sends a Man to Little
Rock, The.
Coora Flower, The.
Crazy Woman, The.
Cynthia in the Snow.
Egg Boiler, The.
In Honor of David Anderson Brooks, My
Father.
Jane Addams (September 6, 1860–May 21,
1935).
Jessie Mitchell's Mother.
Langston Hughes.
Last Quatrain of the Ballad of Emmett Till,
The.
Life of Lincoln West, The.
Lovely Love, A.
Lovers of the Poor, The.
Malcolm X.
Marie Lucille.
Martin Luther King, Jr.
Maxie Allen [always taught her].
Medgar Evers.
Michael Is Afraid of the Storm.
Mrs. Small went to the kitchen for her
pocketbook.
My Dreams, My Works Must Wait Till after
Hell.
Naomi.
Narcissa.
"Negro" Hero.
Notes from the Childhood and the Girlhood,
sels.
Of Robert Frost.
Old-Marrieds, The.
Old Mary.
Otto.
Paul Robeson.
Penitent Considers Another Coming of Mary,
A.
Pete at the Zoo.
Primer for Blacks.
Queen of the Blues.
Riot.
Second Sermon on the Warpland, The.
Sermon on the Warpland, The.
Speech to the Young Speech to the Progress-
Toward (Among Them Nora and Henry
III).
Still Do I Keep My Look, My Identity. . . .
Street in Bronzeville, A, *sels.*
Strong Men, riding horses. In the West.
Sundays of Satin-Legs Smith, The.
Sunset of the City, A.
Third Sermon on the Warpland, The.
To be in love.
To Those of My Sisters Who Kept Their
Naturals.
Two Dedications, *sels.*
Ulysses, *sels.*
We real cool. We.
What Shall I Give My Children?
When You Have Forgotten Sunday: The
Love Story.

White Troops Had Their Orders but the
Negroes Looked Like Men.
Womanhood, The, *sels.*
Young Africans.
Young Heroes.

Brooks, Harry. *See* **Waller, Thomas ("Fats"),
Andy Razaf** *and* **Harry Brooks**

Brooks, Jonathan Henderson (1904–45)
Muse in Late November.

Brooks, Maria Gowen (1795–1845)
Composed at the Request of a Lady, and
Descriptive of Her Feelings.
Zophiël [or, the Bride of Seven], *sels.*

Brooks, Phillips (1835–93)
Christmas Everywhere.
O little town of Bethlehem.

Brooks, Shirley (1816–74)
For A' That and A' That.
More Luck to Honest Poverty.
Poem by a Perfectly Furious Academician.
To Disraeli.
What Jenner Said on Hearing in Elysium
That Complaints Had Been Made of His
Having a Statue [in Trafalgar Square].

Brooks, William E.
Pilate Remembers.

Broome, William (1689–1745)
Rose-Bud, The.
Widow and Virgin Sisters, The.

Broonzy, Big Bill
Southern Blues, The.

Brough, Robert Barnabas (1828–60)
My Lord Tomnoddy's the son of an Earl.

**Brougham and Vaux, Henry Peter Brougham,
1st Baron (1778–1868)**
Orator's Epitaph, The.

Broughton, James Richard (b. 1913)
Feathers or Lead?
Wondrous the Merge.

Broughton, T. Alan (b. 1936)
Hold, Hold.
Lyric.
Serenade for Winds.

Broumas, Olga (b. 1949)
Amazon Twins.
Cinderella.
Eye of Heart.
Landscape with Leaves and Figure.
Landscape with Next of Kin.
Rapunzel.
She Loves.
Sleeping Beauty.
Snow White.
Touched.
Tryst.

Broumas, Olga (b. 1949) *and* **Jane Miller (b.
1925)**
Black Holes, Black Stockings, *sels.*

Broun, Heywood
Limerick: "There was a young girl with a
hernia."

Brousek, Antonin
Pillars of Salt, *sels.*

Brown, Abbie Farwell (1892–1929)
Fisherman goes out at dawn, The.
Friends.

Brown, Anna Gordon (1747–1810)
Gay Goshawk [or Goss-Hawk], The.

Brown, Arthur (1947–1982)
Assassination of Charlie Parker, The.

Brown, Beatrice Curtis (1901–74)
Jonathan Bing.

Brown, Charles Walter (1866–1934)
If I Should Die To-Night.

Brown, Christy (1932–81)
Good Friday.

Brown, D. F.
Coming Home.
Eating the Forest.
First Person—1981.
I Was Dancing Alone in Binh Dinh Province.
Illumination.
Patrols.
Returning Fire.

Still Later There Are War Stories.
When I Am 19 I Was a Medic.

Brown, Ford Madox (fl. 19th cent.)
Last of England! O'er the sea, my dear, The.

Brown, Frank S.
Veteran, The.

Brown, George Mackay (b. 1921)
Beachcomber.
Carpenter.
December Day, Hoy Sound.
Desertion of the Women and Seals, The.
Dream of Winter.
Five Voyages of Arnor, The.
Funeral of Ally Flett, The.
Haddock Fishermen.
Hamnavoe Market.
Hawk, The.
Island School.
Keeper of the Midnight Gate, The.
Kirkyard.
Old Fisherman with Guitar.
Old Women, The.
Runes from a Holy Island, *sels.*
Shroud.
Stars.
Taxman.
Tea Poems.
Trout Fisher.

Brown, Harriet
Misguided.

Brown, Harry (b. 1915)
Incident on a Front Not Far from Castel di
Sangro.

Brown, Isaac Hinton (1842–89)
Honest Deacon, The.
Only a Pin.

Brown, James (b. 1928) *and* **Alfred Ellis**
Say it loud, I'm black and I'm proud.

Brown, John (1800–1859)
Rhapsody, Written at the Lakes in
Westmorland, A.

Brown, Kate Louise (1857–1921)
Five-Fingered Maple, The.
Lady Moon is sailing, The.
Pine Music.

Brown, Lee Ann (b. 1963)
Come go with me out to the Field.
Lyric Can Snare, The.

Brown, Linda Beatrice
Green arbor that I once knew, A.
Winter Sonnet.

Brown, Maimee Lee
Created Clay.

Brown, Margaret Wise (1910–52)
Little Black Bug.
Secret Song, The.

Brown, Melvin E. (b. 1950)
Survival Motion: Notice.

Brown, Pamela (b. 1948)
I Remember Dexedrine. 1970.
Leaving.

Brown, Paul
De Rebus, *sels.*

Brown, Phoebe Hinsdale (1783–1861)
I Love to Steal Awhile Away.
Welcome, Ye Hopeful Heirs of Heaven.

Brown, Rita Mae (b. 1944)
Dancing the Shout to the True Gospel; or,
The Song Movement Sisters Don't Want
Me to Sing.
Sappho's Reply.

Brown, Rosellen
Fry says a word.
I have a neighbor.
I want to understand light years.
Storm high.
This is no baby skin—.

Brown, Spencer (b. 1909)
In an Old House.

Brown, Stephanie (b. 1961)
Chapter One.
Schadenfreude.

Brown, Sterling Allen (b. 1901)
After Winter.
Bitter Fruit of the Tree.

Cabaret.
Call Boy.
Chillen Get Shoes.
Conjured.
Crispus Attucks McCoy.
Foreclosure.
Long Gone.
Long Track Blues.
Ma Rainey.
Memphis Blues.
Odyssey of Big Boy.
Old Lem.
Old Woman Remembers, An.
Remembering Nat Turner.
Sam Smiley.
Sister Lou.
Slim Greer.
Slim in Atlanta.
Slim in Hell ("Slim Greer went to heaven.")
Southern Cop.
Southern Road.
Sporting Beasley.
Strange Legacies.
Strong Men.
Tin Roof Blues.
To Sallie, Walking.
Virginia Portrait.

Brown, Steven Ford
After the Vietnam War.

Brown, Thomas [or "Tom"] (1663–1704)
Colonels here in solemn manner meet, The.
Doctor Fell.
Epitaph upon That Profound and Learned
  Casuist, the Late Ordinary of Newgate, An.
Oaths.
Reader, beneath this turf I lie.

Brown, Thomas Edward (1830–97)
Bristol Channel, The.
Dartmoor: Sunset at Chagford.
High overhead.
I Bended unto Me.
Ibant Obscuræ.
In the Coach, *sels.*
My Garden.
Preparation.
Roman Women, *sels.*
Salve!
Sermon at Clevedon, A.
To K. H.
Vespers.
Well, The.
Wesley in Heaven.
When Love Meets Love.

Brown, Wayne (b. 1944)
Ballad of the Electric Eel.
Bind, The.
England, Autumn.
Noah.
Rilke.
Song For a Tourist.
Words.

Brown, William Goldsmith
Mother, Home, Heaven.

Browne, Francis Fisher (b. 1843)
Australian Emigrant, The, *sels.*

Browne, Isaac Hawkins (1705–60)
Foundling Hospital for Wit, The, *sels.*
Letter from a Captain in Country Quarters to
  his Corinna in Town, A.
Pipe of Tobacco, A, *sels.*

Browne, Jane Euphemia ("Aunt Effie")
Great Brown Owl, The
Little Raindrops.
Pleasant Changes.
Rooks are building on the trees, The.

**"Browne, Matthew." See Rands, William
Brighty**

Browne, Michael Dennis (b. 1940)
Delta, The.
Epithalamion/Wedding Dawn.
Hallowe'en 1971.
Iowa.
Iowa, June.
King in May, The.
Lamb.
News from the House.

Paranoia.
Peter sleep-walks.
Power Failure.
Roof of the World, The.
Talk to Me, Baby.

Browne, Moses (1704–87)
Shrimp, The, *sels.*
Survey of the Amphitheatre, A.

Browne, Sir Thomas (1605–82)
In yellow meadows I take no delight.
O for a toe, such as the funeral pyre.
Signs of Spring.

Browne, William (1591–1643)
Britannia's Pastorals, *sels.*
Britannia's Pastorals Book 2, *sels.*
Caelia, *sels.*
[Epitaph] In Obitum M.S., X Maij [*or* Maii],
  1614.
Inner Temple Masque, The, *sels.*
Love who will, for I'll love none.
On the Countess Dowager of Pembroke.
Praise of Spenser.
Song: "Choose now among this fairest
  number."
Song: "For her gait, if she be walking."
Visions, *sels.*

Browne, Sir William (1692–1774)
Epigram: "King to Oxford sent a troop of
  horse, The."

Brownell, Henry Howard (1820–72)
Burial of the Dane, The.
Lawyer's Invocation to Spring, The.
Night-Quarters.
Suspiria Noctis.

Browning, Elizabeth Barrett (1806–61)
Aurora Leigh, *sels.*
Bereavement.
Best Thing in the World, The.
Bianca Among the Nightingales.
Casa Guidi Windows, *sels.*
Cowper's Grave.
Cry of the Children, The, *sels.*
Curse for a Nation, A.
Denial, A.
Deserted Garden, The.
Died...
Face which, duly as the sun, The.
Farewells from Paradise.
Felicia Hemans.
Fifth Book.
Flush or Faunus.
Globe and Traveller, no. 6733, *sels.*
Grief.
Hiram Powers' "Greek Slave."
L.E.L.'s Last Question.
Look, The.
Lord Walter's Wife.
Man's Requirements, A.
Mask, The.
Meaning of the Look, The.
Mother and Poet.
Musical Instrument, A.
My Heart and I.
On a Portrait of Wordsworth by B. R.
  Haydon.
Part II.
Poet hath the child's sight in his breast, The.
Reward of Service.
Romance of the Swan's Nest, The.
Runaway Slave at Pilgrim's Point, The.
Sleep, The.
Song from Sylvan, A.
Sonnets from the Portuguese, *sels.*
Tears.
To George Sand / A Desire.
To George Sand: A Recognition.
True Dream, A.
Woman's Shortcomings, A, *sels.*
Year's Spinning, A.

Browning, Ophelia Guyon
Pray without Ceasing.

Browning, Robert (1812–89)
Abt Vogler.
Andrea del Sarto.
Any Wife to Any Husband.
Apparent Failure.

Appearances.
Bad Dreams.
Bad Dreams III.
Bishop Blougram's Apology, *sels.*
Bishop Orders His Tomb at Saint Praxed's
  Church, The.
Blot in the 'Scutcheon, A, *sels.*
By the Fire-Side.
Caliban upon Setebos; or, Natural Theology
  in the Island.
Childe Roland to the Dark Tower Came.
Christmas-Eve, *sels.*
Cleon the poet (from the sprinkled isles),
  sels.
Confessions.
De Gustibus, *sels.*
Dialogue between Father and Daughter.
Dîs Aliter Visum; or, Le Byron de Nos
  Jours.
Earth's Immortalities, *sels.*
Englishman in Italy, The, *sels.*
Epilogue: "At the midnight in the silence of
  the sleep-time."
Epilogue: "On the first of the Feast of
  Feasts."
Epistle Containing the Strange Medical
  Experience of Karshish, the Arab
  Physician, An.
Eurydice to Orpheus.
Eyes, Calm beside Thee (Lady, Could'st
  Thou Know!).
Face, A.
Ferishtah's Fancies, *sels.*
Flight of the Duchess, The, *sels.*
Fra Lippo Lippi, *sels.*
Garden Fancies, *sels.*
Grammarian's Funeral, A.
Guardian-Angel, The.
Heretic's Tragedy, The.
Hervé Riel.
Home-Thoughts, From Abroad.
Home-Thoughts, from the Sea.
House.
How It Strikes a Contemporary.
How They Brought the Good News from
  Ghent to Aix, *sels.*
In a Year.
In Three Days.
Inapprehensiveness.
Incident of the French Camp.
Instans Tyrannus.
Italian in England, The.
James Lee's Wife, *sels.*
Johannes Agricola in Meditation.
Laboratory, The [Ancien Régime].
Last Ride Together, The.
Life in a Love.
Light Woman, A.
Likeness, A, *sels.*
Lines on Swinburne.
Lost Leader, The.
Lost Mistress, The.
Love among the Ruins.
Love in a Life.
Lovers' Quarrel, A.
Master Hugues of Saxe-Gotha.
May and Death.
Meeting At Night.
Memorabilia.
Misconceptions.
"Moses" of Michael Angelo, The.
My Last Duchess [Ferrara].
Never the time and the place.
Now.
One Word More, *sels.*
Paracelsus, *sels.*
Parting at Morning.
Patriot, The [An Old Story].
Pauline, mine own, bend o'er me—thy soft
  breast, *sels.*
Pictor Ignotus.
Pied Piper of Hamelin, The, *sels.*
Pippa Passes, *sels.*
Pisgah-Sights. I.
Pisgah-Sights. II.
Popularity.
Porphyria's Lover.

Prologue: "Poet's age is sad: for why?, The."
Prospice.
Rabbi Ben Ezra, *sels.*
Red Cotton Night-Cap Country, *sels.*
Respectability.
Rhyme for a Child Viewing a Naked Venus
   in a Painting [of "The Judgement of
   Paris"].
Ring and the Book, The, *sels.*
Saul, *sels.*
Soliloquy of the Spanish Cloister.
Solomon and Balkis.
Sordello, *sels.*
Thamuris Marching.
To Edward FitzGerald.
Toccata of Galuppi's, A.
Twins, The.
Two in the Campagna.
Up at a Villa—Down in the City.
Waring.
Why I Am a Liberal.
Woman's Last Word, A.
Women and Roses.
Youth and Art.

Brownjohn, Alan (b. 1931)
Class Incident from Graves.
Explorer.
In a Convent Garden.
Negotiation.
Of Dancing.
Pitman's Common Sense Arithmetic, 1917,
   sels.
Seven Activities for a Young Child.
Train will come tomorrow year, The.
We are going to see the rabbit.

**"Brownjohn, John" (Charles Remington
   Talbot) (1851–91)**
School-Master and the Truants, The.

Brownlee, W. S.
Little Miss Muffet.
Said Little Boy Blue.

Brownlie, W. S.
Limerick: "Man in the Land of the
   Houyhnhnms, A."
On First Looking into Chapman's Homer.

Brownstein, Michael (b. 1943)
Glass Enclosure, The.
Jet Set Melodrama.
Last spell cast came late one afternoon in a
   brown study. I was studying my-, The.
Oracle Night, *sels.*
Paris Visitation.
Stepping Out.
War.

Bruce, Debra
("The Light They Make"), *sels.*
Two Couples.

Bruce, George (b. 1909)
My house is granite.
Singers, The.
Sumburgh Heid.

Bruce, Michael (1740–67)
Elegy: To Spring, *sels.*
To the Cuckoo.

Bruchac, Joseph (b. 1942)
Birdfoot's Grampa.
City.
Coming Back.
Elegy for Jack Bowman.
For a Winnebago Brave.
Frozen Hands.
Grandmother Came Down to Visit Us, The.
Hiking.
Let the Midnight Special.
Poem for Jan.
Prayer: "Let my words."
Second Skins—a Peyote Song.
Stone Giant.
There is a stream which rises.
Three Poems for the Indian Steelworkers.

Bruck, Edith (b. 1932)
Birth.
Childhood.
Equality, father! Your dream has come true.
Pretty soon / when people hear a quiz show
   expert.

You Hide ("You Hide.")

Brucker, H. P.
Praise Now Your God.

Bruner, Margaret E. (1886–1970?)
Angry word is like a boomerang, An.
Atonement.
Beggar, The.
Beyond the Grave.
Casual Meeting.
Clown, The.
Dog's Vigil, A.
Dreaded Task, The.
Epitaph for a Cat.
For One Lately Bereft.
For One Who Is Serene.
Gift, The.
God's ways are strange; He chastens those.
Good-by can be a happy word.
Greater Gift, The.
If Lincoln Should Return.
Lonely Dog, The.
Midwinter.
Monk and the Peasant, The.
On City Streets.
Plea for Tolerance.
Prayer for Strength.
Rebirth.
Remembrance.
Retaliation.
Selfishness.
Sinner, The.
There is a loneliness on city streets.
Time's Hand Is Kind.
Wedding Anniversary.
"Whom the Gods Love die young" I used to
   quote.

Bruno, Giordano (1548–1600)
Philosophic Flight, The.

Brunton, Alan (b. 1946)
Her voice is like some angel picking at the
   door.
I say hello to the sunshine.
Oh me / is that the ambulance chasing out of
   town?
What Happens in Shakzpeare.

Bruschetto, Lodovico. *See* Bryskett, Lodowick

Brush, Thomas
Again.
Waiting for the End of the War.

Brutus, Dennis (b. 1924)
At a Funeral.
At night.
Clammy cement, The.
Endurance.
Letters to Martha.
Nightsong: City.
Off to Philadelphia in the morning.
On the Island.
Poems About Prison.
Postscripts 2.
Prayer: "O let me soar on steadfast wing."
Robben Island Sequence.
Sand wet and cool, The.
Simple lust is all my woe, A.
Sometimes a mesh of ideas.
Sounds Begin Again, The.
Their Behaviour.
There was a time when the only worth.
They hanged him, I said dismissively.
This sun on this rubble after rain.
Under House Arrest.

Bryant, Frederick, Jr. (b. 1942)
Cathexis.

Bryant, John Frederick (1753–91)
On a Piece of Unwrought Pipeclay.

Bryant, William Cullen (1794–1878)
African Chief, The.
After a Tempest.
Ages, The.
As Shadows Cast by Cloud and Sun.
Autumn Woods.
Battle-Field, The.
Conjunction of Jupiter and Venus, The.
Constellations, The.
Crowded Street, The.
Damsel of Peru, The.

Dante.
Death of Lincoln, The.
Death of Slavery, The.
Death of the Flowers, The.
Forest Hymn, A, *sels.*
Fountain, that springest on this grassy slope.
Green River.
Hymn to the North Star.
I cannot forget with what fervid devotion.
Indian at the Burial-Place [*or* Burying-Place]
   of His Fathers, An.
Inscription for the Entrance to a Wood.
Meditation on Rhode Island Coal, A.
Midsummer.
Mighty One, before Whose Face.
Mutation.
Night Journey of a River, The.
Not Yet.
November.
O Thou Whose Own Vast Temple Stands.
October.
Oh fairest of the rural maids!
Oh mother of a mighty race.
Painted Cup, The.
Poet, The.
Prairies, The.
Rivulet, The.
Robert of Lincoln.
Summer Wind.
Thanatopsis.
Tides, The.
To a Mosquito.
To A Waterfowl.
To Cole, the Painter, Departing for Europe.
To the Fringed Gentian.
Winter Piece, A.
Yellow Violet, The.

Brydges, Sir Samuel Egerton (1762–1837)
Lines Written Immediately after Parting from
   a Lady.
On Dreams, October 15, 1782.
To Miss M———, Written by Moonlight,
   July 18, 1782.

Bryher, Winifred (b. 1894)
Blue Sleep.
Thessalian.

Bryll, Ernest (b. 1935)
In a Fever.

**Bryskett, Lodowick [*or* Lewis] (Lodovico
   Bruschetto) (1546–1612)**
Pastoral Eclogue upon the Death of Sir Philip
   Sidney Knight, A.

**Bryusov [*or* Briusov], Valery [*or* Valerii]
   Yakovlevich [*or* Iakovlevich] (1873–1924)**
O, close your pale legs!
Radiant Ranks of Seraphim.
Stonemason, stonemason, in your white
   apron.
To a Young Poet.

Bu-er, Sun (b. 1124)
Cut brambles long enough.
Late Indian summer's.

**Buchan, John, 1st Baron Tweedsmuir (1875–
   1940)**
Kirk Bell, The.
On Leave.

Buchanan, George (1506–82)
May Morning.

Buchanan, George (1904–89)
Conversations with Strangers.
I suddenly have come to love.
Jill's Death.
Lewis Mumford.
Lyle Donaghy, Poet, 1902-1949.
Revolutionary Revolution.
Song for Straphangers.
Speaker in the Square, A.
Theatrical Venus.
War-and-Peace.

Buchanan, Robert Williams (1841–1901)
Little Herd-Boy's Song, The.

Buck, Byron
Song from a Two-Desk Office.

Buckham, John Wright (1864–1945)
Hills of God, Break Forth in Singing.
O God, above the Drifting Years.

Buckland, Frank
Limerick: "That smasher of shams, Bernard
Shaw."
Buckley, Christopher (b. 1948)
Apologues of Winter Light.
Nostalgia.
Playing for Time.
Sun Spots.
Train in the Desert—1916.
Buckley, Vincent (1925–88)
Child is Revenant to the Man, The.
Ghosts, places, stories, questions.
Good Friday and the Present Crucifixion.
Man, a woman, straighten up from where, A.
No New Thing.
Origins.
Parents.
Return of a Popular Statesman.
Stroke, *sels.*
Teaching German Literature.
Buckmaster, Charles (1951–72)
End to Myth, An.
Seed.
Vanzetti.
Wilpena Pound.
Budbill, David
What I Heard at the Discount Department
Store.
Buddha (c.563–c.483 B.C.)
Unlimited Friendliness.
Buddy, Callin
Callin Buddy / Bolden.
Budenz, Julia
Poeta Fui.
Bugayev, Boris Nikolaevich. See Bely, Andrey
Bùi Công Trừng (b. 1905)
Fallen Fruit, A.
Bùi Du'o'ng Lich (1757–1827)
To a Watering Scoop.
Bùi Khải Nguyễn (*fl.* 20th cent.)
Man Who Sleeps Out in the Fields, The.
Soap Bubbles.
Bukowski, Charles (1920–94)
Black poets / young, The.
Crucifix in a Deathhand.
For Jane.
Funny Man.
I Am Dead But I Know the Dead Are Not
Like This.
Me against the world.
Mockingbird had been following the cat, The.
My Old Man.
Secret, The.
Short Order.
Startled into Life Like Fire.
Style is the answer to everything.
Three Oranges.
Tragedy of Leaves, The.
Bulcke, Karl (b. 1875)
There Is an Old City.
Bulfinch, Stephen Greenleaf (1809–70)
Hail to the Sabbath Day.
Bulkeley, Peter, the Younger (1643–91)
Like to the Grass That's Green Today.
Bull, Arthur J. (b. 1903)
Eve.
Buller, Arthur (1874–1944)
Limerick: "There was a young lady named
[*or* called] Bright."
Limerick: "To her friends, said the Bright
one, in chatter."
Bullett, Gerald (b. 1893)
Footnote to Tennyson.
Bullock, Michael (b. 1918)
Garden.
Bullokar, William (c.1520–c.1590)
To His Child.
Buluguru
Working Song.
Bumstead, Eudora S. (b. 1860)
Summer Lullaby, A.
Bunan (1602–76)
Die while you're alive.
Bungay, George W. (1818?–1892)
Creeds of the Bells.

Bunimovich, Yevgeny [*or* Evgenii] (b. 1954)
Explanatory Note.
Moscow: Summer '86.
Bunin, Ivan Alekseievich (1870–1953)
At the gates of Zion, over Kedron.
Endless downpour; misty wood.
Flax.
Flowers, and tall-stalked grasses, and a bee.
High up on a snowy peak.
It was near midnight when I entered.
Loneliness.
Stone Idol, The.
To My Country.
Bunner, Henry Cuyler (1855–96)
Behold the Deeds!
Home, *sels.*
Home, Sweet Home, with Variations.
Home, Sweet Home, with Variations, III.
One, Two, Three.
Poetry and the Poet.
Bunting, Basil (1900–1985)
Briggflatts [An Autobiography], *sels.*
Came to me— / Who?
Chomei at Toyama.
Complaint of the Morpethshire Farmer, The.
Fearful Symmetry.
Fishermen.
Gin the Goodwife Stint.
On the Fly-Leaf of Pound's Cantos.
Orotava Road, The.
To Violet [with Prewar Poems].
Vestiges, *sels.*
Weeping oaks grieve, chestnuts raise.
What the Chairman Told Tom.
When the sword of sixty comes nigh his
head.
Word, The.
Bunya no Asayasu (c. 900)
In a gust of wind the white dew.
Bunyan, John (1628–88)
Author's Apology for His Book, The, *sels.*
Of the Boy and Butterfly.
Of the Child with the Bird on the Bush.
Of the Going Down of the Sun.
Pilgrim's Progress, The, *sels.*
Upon a Ring of Bells.
Upon the Horse and His Rider.
Upon the Lark and the Fowler.
Upon the [*or* a] Snail.
Upon the Swallow.
Upon the Weathercock.
Burbank, Elevena (b. 1956)
I Danced to the Rumble of the Drum.
Burbidge, Thomas (1816–95)
She Bewitched Me.
Burden, Jean (b. 1914)
Poem before Departure.
Burdette, Robert Jones (1844–1914)
Orphan Born.
"Soldier, Rest!"
Burford, William (b. 1927)
Christmas Tree, A.
On the Apparition of Oneself.
Burge, Maureen
Diet, The.
Disillusion.
Burgess, Anthony (b. 1917)
Limerick: "Man from the *Washington Post,*
A."
Burgess, Frank Gelett (1866–1951)
Cinq Ans Après.
Leave-Taking.
Limerick: "For hours my wife says
'Goodbye.'"
Limerick: "I wish that my room had a floor."
Low Trick, A.
On Digital Extremities.
Psycholophon.
Purple Cow, The.
Table Manners.
Table Manners II.
Trapping fairies in West Virginia.
Burgess, George (1809–60)
Harvest Dawn Is Near, The.
While o'er the Deep Thy Servants Sail.

Burgon, John William (1813–88)
Pedra.
Petra, *sels.*
Burich, Vladimir b. 1932
Citizen's Way, The.
Dialogue, The.
What do I expect from tomorrow's day?
You blow on the hair of your child.
Burkard, Michael (b. 1947)
Raincoat, A.
Burke, James (1877–1958)
Missionary Hymn.
Burke, Kenneth (b. 1897)
Civil Defense.
Frigate Jones, the Pussyfooter ("Frigate Jones
was very slow and fat.")
Know Thyself.
Nursery Rhyme.
Burke, Martin
On the twelfth floor.
Rainy winter evening.
Burket, Gail Brook (b. 1905)
From Countless Hearts.
So Touch Our Hearts with Loveliness.
Burleigh, William Henry (1812–71)
Abide not in the realm of dreams.
Lead Us, O Father, in the Paths of Peace.
Weaver, The.
Burlingame, Robert
Small poems, The.
**Burliuk, D., Aleksandr Kruchenykh, V.
Mayakovsky *and* Viktor Khlebnikov**
Slap in the Face of Public Taste, A, *sels.*
**Burlyuk [*or* Burliuk], David Davidovich (1882–
1967)**
Everyone is young, young, young.
Burn, Michael
For the Common Market.
Burnand, Sir Francis Cowley (b. 1836)
Tubby or not tubby—there's the rub.
Burnat-Provins, Marguerite (1872–1952)
Fruits you give me are more savory than
others, The.
Sylvius, your hands near my mouth are
heady flowers.
You told me: "I am not worthy of you."
Burnet, Dana (b. 1888)
Road to Vagabondia, The.
Burnett, W. Hodgson (*fl.* c.1920)
My Shadow.
**Burney, Frances [*or* Fanny], Mme D'Arblay
(1752–1840)**
To Charles Burney.
Burns, Joanne (b. 1945)
How these pieces of paper: lined unlined
small large crinkled smooth.
Marble surfaces.
Reading.
Revisionism.
Burns, Michael
Beginnings.
Burns, Robert (1759–96)
Address to the Deil.
Address to the Unco Guid, or the Rigidly
Righteous.
Auld Lang Syne.
Banks O' Doon, The.
Birks of Aberfeldy, The [Composed on the
Spot].
Bonie Doon.
Bonnie Lesley.
Book-Worms, The.
Ca' the ewes [*or* yowes] to the knowes.
Cares o' love are sweeter far, The.
Charlie He's My Darling.
Come, let me take thee to my breast.
Comin' thro' the Rye.
Comin[g] thro' [*or* through] the rye, poor
body.
Cotter's Saturday Night &[;nscribed to Robert
Aiken [*or* R. A****], Esq.&];, The, *sels.*
Death and Doctor Hornbook [A True Story].
Dedication to G**** H****** Esq, A, *sels.*
De'il's [*or* Deil's] Awa wi' th' [*or* the]
Exciseman, The.

Duncan Gray cam here to woo.
Epigrams on Lord Galloway, *sels.*
Epistle to a Young Friend.
Epistle to J. Lapraik, an Old Scotch Bard.
Epitaph for James Smith.
Epitaph on a Schoolmaster.
Extempore—On Being Shown a Beautiful
   Country Seat Belonging to Maxwell of
   Cardoness.
Farewell, A [*or* The]: "It was a' for our
   rightfu' king."
First Six Verses of the Ninetieth Psalm, The.
Flow gently, sweet Afton, among thy green
   braes.
For A' That and A' That ["Is there, for
   honest poverty"].
Gardener wi' His Paidle; or, The Gardener's
   March, The.
Grace at Kirkudbright.
Green grow the rashes, O.
Green grow the rashes, O; / Green grow the
   rashes, O; / The lasses they hae wimble
   bores.
Green grow the rashes, O; / Green grow the
   rashes, O; / The sweetest hours that e'er I
   spend.
Green sleeves and tartan ties.
Halloween.
Hark, the mavis' evening sang.
Here cursing swearing Burton lies.
Highland Harry Back Again.
Highland Mary.
Holy Fair, The.
Holy Willie's Prayer.
How daur ye ca' me "Howlet-face."
Hughie Graham.
John Anderson, my jo, John, / I wonder what
   ye mean.
John Anderson my jo, John / When we were
   first acquent.
John Barleycorn [a Ballad].
Johnie Blunt.
Kellyburnbraes.
Kirk's Alarm, The.
Lo worms enjoy the seat of bliss.
Lord Galloway.
Love and Libery—A Cantata, *sels.*
Lovely lass o' Inverness, The.
Man Was Made to Mourn, a Dirge, *sels.*
Mary Morison.
Mother's Lament for the Death of Her Son,
   A.
My heart's in the Highlands, my heart is not
   here.
No more of your titled acquaintances boast.
O were my Love yon Lilac[k] fair, *sels.*
O [*or* Oh] wert thou in the cauld blast.
O'er the Water to Charlie.
Of a' the airts the wind can blaw.
On a Dog of Lord Eglinton's.
On a Noisy Polemic.
On Elphinston's Translation of Martial.
On Lord Galloway.
On Mr. Pitt's [*or* Pit's] Hair-Powder Tax.
Open the Door to Me, Oh!
Parson's Looks, The.
Patriarch, The.
Poet's Welcome to His Love-Begotten
   Daughter [the First Instance that Entitled
   Him to the Venerable Appellation of
   Father], A.
Rantin' Dog, the Daddie o't, The.
Rantin Laddie, The.
Rantin, Rovin Robin.
Red, Red Rose, A.
Scotch Drink.
Scots, wha hae wi' Wallace bled.
Silver Tassie, The.
Simmer's a pleasant time.
So vile was poor Wat, such a miscreant
   slave.
Song: "Ae fond kiss, and then we sever."
Song: "It was upon a Lammas night."
Sonnet upon Sonnets, A.
Such a Parcel of Rogues in a Nation.
Tam Glen.
Tam o' Shanter. [A Tale].

Tam Samson's Elegy.
To a Haggis.
To a Louse [On Seeing One on a Lady's
   Bonnet at Church].
To a Mountain Daisy [On Turning One
   Down, with the Plough, in April—1786].
To a Mouse[, On Turning Her Up in Her
   Nest, with the Plough, November, 1785].
To an Artist.
To James Smith.
To William Simpson, Ochiltree.
Tree of Liberty, The.
Twa bonny [*or* bony] lads were Sandy and
   Jockie.
Up in the Morning Early.
Verses Intended to Be Written below a Noble
   Earl's Picture.
Versicles on Sign-Posts, *sels.*
Wee Willie Gray, an' his leather wallet.
Whistle, and I'll Come to You, My Lad.
Whistle o'er the Lave o't.
Willie Brew'd [*or* Brewed] a Peck o' Maut.
Ye flowery banks o' bonie Doon.
Ye maggots, feed on Willie's brains.

Burnshaw, Stanley (b. 1906)
   Bread.
   End of the Flower World (A.D. 2300).
   Strange to be torn away from your embrace.
   Talmudist.

Burr, Amelia Josephine (b. 1878)
   Lynmouth Widow, A.

Burr, Gray (b. 1919)
   Sailing, Sailing.

Burrell, Lady Sophia (1750?–1802)
   Chloe and Myra, *sels.*
   Picture of a Fine Gentleman, The.
   School for Satire, The.
   Verses to a Lady, on Her Saying She
      Preferred Commonalty to an Irish Peerage,
      sels.

Burris, Sidney (b. 1953)
   Strong's Winter.

Burroughs, John (1837–1921)
   Waiting.

Burroughs, Margaret Goss (b. 1917)
   Black Pride.
   Everybody but Me.
   Only in This Way.
   To Soulfolk.

Burroughs, William S. (b. 1914)
   Cold Lost Marbles.
   My Legs Señor.

Burrowes, Elizabeth (b. 1885)
   O God, Send Men.

Bursk, Christopher (b. 1943)
   First Aid at 4 A.M.
   Lies.
   Tearing Up the Tracks.

Burstein, Abraham (b. 1893)
   Love of Hell, The.

Burt, Bates G. (1878–1948)
   O God of Youth.

Burt, Della (b. 1944)
   Little Girl's Dream World, A.
   On the Death of Lisa Lyman.
   Spirit Flowers.

Burton, Henry (1840–1930)
   Pass It On.

Burton, Robert (1577–1640)
   Anatomy of Melancholy, The, *sels.*

Bury, Charlotte (1775–1861)
   Poems on Several Occasions, *sels.*

Bush, Barney (b. 1945)
   Autumn Warrior.
   Directions in Our Blood.
   Her Voice.
   Memory Sire, The.
   Taking a Captive / 1984.
   Voyeur's Dream.

Buson (Yosa Buson) (1716–83)
   Blossoms on the pear.
   Conversation.
   Haiku: "I feel a sudden chill—."
   I go.
   No poem you send.

On the one-ton temple bell.
Over the vast field of mustard flowers.
Piercing Chill I Feel, The.
Raftsmen on their floats.
Scattering bloom, The.
Sound of a Rat, The.
Spring rain! And as yet.
Spring Scene.
Tethered horse, A.
That axe that I hear.
That snail.

Busse, Carl (b. 1872)
   In the Night of the Full Moon.
   Quiet Kingdom, The.

Butler, Guy (b. 1918)
   Cape Coloured Batman.
   Common Dawn.
   Giotto's Campanile.
   Great-great-grandmother.
   In Memoriam, J.A.R., Drowned, East
      London.
   Myths.
   Stranger to Europe, waiting release.
   Surveyor.

Butler, Jack (b. 1944)
   Afterglow.
   No News at All.
   One Reason for Stars.
   Preserves.
   Subplot.

Butler, Marylin
   Listen.

Butler, Samuel (1612–80)
   Ass will with his long ears fray, An.
   Authority is a disease, and cure.
   Convert's but a fly, that turns about, A.
   Devil was more generous than Adam, The.
   Far greater numbers have been lost by hopes.
   Great philosopher did choke, A.
   Greatest saints and sinners have been made,
      The.
   Hudibras, *sels.*
   Hypocrisy will serve as well.
   Law can take a purse in open court, The.
   Married man comes nearest to the dead, A.
   On William Prynne.
   Satire upon the Licentious Age of Charles II,
      sels.
   What makes all subjects discontent.

Butler, Samuel (1835–1902)
   O God! O Montreal!
   Prayer, A: "Searcher of souls, you who in
      heaven abide."
   Righteous Man, The.

Butler, Tony
   Limerick: "As played by the phantoms of
      Shrule."

Butler, William Allen (1825–1907)
   Nothing to Wear.

**"Buttle, Myra" (Victor William Williams
   Saunders Purcell)**
   Sweeniad, The, *sels.*

Butts, Antony
   Massenet / Never wrote a Mass in A.

Buxton, Esther W. (fl. c. 1910)
   Putting the World to Bed.

Buzbee, Lewis
   Sunday, Tarzan in His Hammock.

Buzea, Constanta (b. 1941)
   I'm Not Here / Never Was.

Buzzi, Paolo (1874–1956)
   Finger-nails.

Bye, Reed (b. 1948)
   Spring.

Byles, Mather (1706–88)
   Great God, How Frail a Thing Is Man.
   Great God, Thy Works.
   To Thee the Tuneful Anthem Soars.
   When Wild Confusion Wrecks the Air.

**Bynner, Witter ("Emanuel Morgan") (1881–
   1959)**
   Chinese Drawings, *sels.*
   Death of a Friend.
   Driftwood.
   Episode of Decay.

Grieve Not for Beauty ("Grieve not for the invisible, transported brow.")
Haskell.
Lines to Do with Youth.
More Lovely than Antiquity.
Pause.
Snake Dance.
To a President.
Wintry Mind, The.

Byrd, William (1543–1623)
Lulla, My Sweet Little Baby.
Quiet Life, The.

Byrkit, Rebecca
Only Dance There Is, The.

Byrne, David (b. 1950)
Moon Rocks, Moon in the Man.

Byrom, John (1692–1763)
Careless Content.
Epigram on the Feuds between Handel and Bononcini.
Extempore [Verses] Intended to Allay the Violence of Party-Spirit.
Four Epigrams on the Naturalization Bill, sels.
Full and True Account of a Horrid and Barbarous Robbery, A, sels.
Hymn for Christmas Day, A.
My spirit longeth for Thee.
Nimmers, The.
On Clergymen Preaching Politics.
On the Origin of Evil.
On Two Monopolists.
Passive Participle's Petition, The.
To Henry Wright of Mobberley, Esq. on Buying the Picture of Father Malebranche.
Tom the Porter.

Byron, George Gordon Noel Byron, 6th Baron (1788–1824)
Age of Bronze, The, sels.
'All Is Vanity, Saith the Preacher.'
Answer to ——'s Professions of Affection.
Beppo; a Venetian Story, sels.
Bright be the place of thy soul!
By the Rivers of Babylon We Sat Down and Wept.
Cain: A Mystery, sels.
Childe Harold's Pilgrimage, sels.
Corsair, The, sels.
Darkness.
Destruction of Sennacherib, The.
Don Juan, sels.
Elegy: "O [or Oh] snatch'd away in beauty's bloom!"
English Bards and Scotch Reviewers, sels.
Epistle from Mr Murray to Dr Polidori.
Epistle to Augusta.
Epitaph for Castlereagh, An.
Epitaph for William Pitt.
Epitaph to a Dog.
Fare thee well! and if for ever.
Giaour, The, sels.
Harp the monarch minstrel swept, The.
Hints from Horace, sels.
I saw thee weep—the big bright tear.
Incantation, An.
Jephtha's Daughter.
John Keats.
Lachin y Gair.
Lamp must be replenish'd, but even then, The, sels.
Lines on Hearing That Lady Byron Was Ill.
Lines to Mr Hodgson.
Lines Written beneath a Picture.
Love and Death.
Maid of Athens, ere we part.
Nurse's Dole in the Medea, The.
Oh! weep for those that wept by Babel's stream.
On a Carrier Who Died of Drunkenness.
On Jordan's Bank.
On My Thirty-third Birthday.
On This Day I Complete My Thirty-sixth Year.
Prisoner of Chillon, The, sels.
Prometheus.
Remember Thee! Remember Thee!
Saul.

She walks in Beauty like the night.
Sketch from Private Life, A.
So we'll go no more a-roving.
Song of Saul before His Last Battle.
Sonnet to Lake Leman.
Spirit pass'd before me: I beheld, A.
Stanzas: "And thou art dead, as young and fair."
Stanzas for Music.
Stanzas for Music ("There be none of Beauty's daughters.")
Stanzas for Music ("There's not a joy the world can give like that it takes away.")
Stanzas: "I heard thy fate without a tear."
Stanzas to the Po.
Stanzas: "When a man hath no freedom to fight for at home."
Stanzas Written on the Road between Florence and Pisa.
To Belshazzar.
To Mr. Murray.
To Penelope, January 2, 1821.
Vision of Judgment, The, sels.
Waltz, The, sels.
When we two parted.
Written After Swimming from Sestos to Abydos.

Byron, Henry James (1834–84)
Adage: "Gardener's rule applies to youth and age, The."
Rural Simplicity.

C

"C., E." (fl. c.1595)
Emaricdulfe, sels.

"C., E. F."
Limerick: "Cryptic philosopher, Kant, The."
Limerick: "I suppose I could try if I chose."

"C., I."
Battle of the Falkland Isles.

"C., J. E."
Limerick: "Old poet called Omar cried: 'Now', An."

Cable, George Washington (1844–1925)
Belle Layotte.
Criole Candjo.
Dirge of St. Malo, The.
English muskets went bim! bim!, The.
Song of Cayetano's Circus, The.

Cacamatzin (1494–1520)
My friends.

Caddel, Richard
Enchanter's Nightshade.
Going home.
Paths, The.
Translation from a Lost Source.
Two Movements Which Begin at the Head and End at the Feet.
Uncertain Steps.
Vers Negre.
Wyatt's Dream.

Caddy, Caroline (b. 1944)
Three-Inch Reflector.

Cady, Joseph
Starting 1973: What to Do Now that Peace Has Been Announced.

Caedmon (fl. c.675)
Caedmon's Hymn.
Genesis, sels.

Cage, John (1912–1992)
Diary: How to Improve the World (You Will Only Make Matters Worse), sels.
Lecture on Nothing.
25 Mesostics Re and Not Re Mark Tobey.
Writing through a Text by Chris Mann.
Writing through the Cantos.

Caicedo, Rosario
Nochebuena.

Cain, Jack
Empty elevator, An.
Empty room.
Someone's newspaper.
Waiting.

Cain, Kathleen
Lesson, The.
Returned American.

Cakalacanar
What She Said to Him, after Meeting His Concubine.

Calas, Nicolas
Columns of the Temple of Olympian Zeus.

Calbert, Cathleen
Woman Who Loved Things, The.

Calderón de la Barca, Pedro (1600–1681)
Dream Called Life, The.
Life Is a Dream, sels.

Calhoun, John
Peter Amberley.

Calisch, Edward N.. See Moise, Penina and Edward N. Calisch

Call, Wathen Mark Wilks (1817–90)
Summer Days.

Callicteros
There's wheat at home where you didn't leave it?

Callimachus (c.300–240 B.C.)
Crethis.
Does Charidas lie beneath you? If you mean.
Eileithyia, once more.
Epigrams, sels.
Galataea, sels.
"Goodbye Sun!" said the Ambracian.
Hecale, sels.
Here Saon of Akanthos, Dikon's son.
Hesiod's style and themes: the poet from Soloi.
His Son.
His twelve-year-old / son.
Hymn to Diana, sels.
Hymns, sels.
I despise neo-epic verse sagas.
Kallignotos swore to Ionis—no one.
Kallistion the wife of Kritias.
Menoitas of Lyktos.
Mousetrap, The.
On Himself.
On Pallas Bathing, from a Hymn of Callimachus.
Our guest's wound went unnoticed.
Saon of Acanthus.
Since you are dead, Timon, tell me which.
Sleep cold at someone's.
Somebody told me you were dead.
Someone spoke of your death, Herakleitos. It brought me.
Something's there, by Pan there's something hidden—.
Sopolis.
Statue of Bereniké, A.
Stranger was short: let my verse be such, The.
Theaitetos.
To Archinus.
Where once Three Graces stood.
"Who were you, shipwrecked stranger?" Leontichos found.

Calverley, Charles Stuart (1831–84)
A B C.
Arcades Ambo.
Ballad: "Auld wife sat at her ivied door, The."
Beer, sels.
Changed.
Cock and the Bull, The.
Companions.
Contentment.
Disaster.
Dover to Munich.
Flight.
Forever; 'tis a single word!
Hic Vir, Hic Est.
In the gloaming to be roaming[, where the crested waves are foaming].
Lines on Hearing the Organ.
Of Friendship.
On the Rhine.
Palace, The.
Peace.
Schoolmaster Abroad with His Son, The.

Calvert, George Henry (1803–89)
Bunker Hill.

Cambridge, Ada (1844–1926)
Fashion.
Future Verdict, The.
Virgin Martyr, The.

Cambridge, Richard Owen (1717–1802)
Fakir (a religious well known in the East), A.
On Seeing a Tapestry Chair-Bottom
   Beautifully Worked by His Daughter for
   Mrs Holroyd.

Camden, William (1551–1623)
On a Puritanicall Lock-Smith.

Cameron, C. C.
Success.

Cameron, Eleanor (b. 1912)
To David—At Six Months.

Cameron, Norman (b. 1905)
Compassionate Fool, The.
Dirty Little Accuser, The.
Disused Temple, The.
Firm of Happiness, Limited, The.
For the Fly-Leaf of a School-Book.
Forgive me, Sire, for cheating your intent.
Green, Green Is El Aghir.
She and I.
Thespians at Thermopylae, The.
Three Love Poems, sels.
Unfinished Race, The.
Visit to the Dead, A.

Camille, Roussan (1915–61)
Nocturne: "Wildness of haggard flights."

Camões [or Camõens], Luis de (1524–80)
Babylon and Sion (Goa and Lisbon).
Do This Favour For Me.
Lusiads, The, sels.
On a Shipmate, Pero Moniz, Dying at Sea.
On Revisiting Cintra after the Death of
   Catarina.
On the Death of Catarina de Attayda.
Sonnet: "Leave me, all sweet refrains my lip
   hath made."
Sonnet: "Time and the mortal will stand
   never fast."

Camp, James (b. 1923)
Female Dancer.

Camp, Pauline Frances
Rhyme of Dorothy Rose, The.

Campana, Dino (1885–1932)
Autumn Garden.
Genoa.
Window, The.

Campanella, Tomasso (1568–1639)
People is a beast of muddy brain, The.

Campbell, Alfred Gibbs (b. 1826?)
Cry "Infidel!"
Divine Mission, The.
Lines: "Wake not again the cannon's
   thundrous voice."
Song of the Decanter.
Warning.

Campbell, Alistair (b. 1925)
Bitter Harvest.
Dark Lord of Savaiki, The.
Return, The.
Sanctuary of Spirits, sels.
Why Don't You Talk to Me?

Campbell, Anne
Before and After Marriage.
Shabby Old Dad.
There is always a place for you at my table.
To My Friend.

Campbell, Calder
Ossian's Serenade.

Campbell, David (1915–79)
Anguish of Ants, The.
Ariel.
Australian Dream, The.
Duchesses.
Fox.
Hear, the bird of day.
Here, under pear-trees, on the broad
   verandahs.
Hotel Marine.
Ku-ring-gai Rock Carvings, sels.

Man in the Honeysuckle, The.
Men in Green.
Mothers and Daughters.
Mr. Hughes.
Night Sowing.
On Frosty Days.
Pallid Cuckoo.
Small-town Gladys.
Song for the Cattle.
Starting from Central Station, sels.
Ulinda.
Windy Gap.

Campbell, George (b. 1916)
History Makers.
Holy be the white head of a Negro.
In the Slums.

Campbell, Isobel (c. 1200)
Learned Mistress, A.

Campbell, James Edwin (1867–96)
Cunjah Man, De.
Mobile-Buck.
Mors et Vita.
Ol' Doc' Hyar.
Pariah, The.
'Sciplinin' Sister Brown.
Song of the Corn.
When Ol' Sis' Judy Pray.

Campbell, John (1766–1840)
I'm far from what I call my home.

Campbell, Joseph (Seosamh MacCathmhaoil)
(1881–1944)
Ad Limina.
Antiquary, The.
Blind Man at the Fair, The.
Dancer, The.
Darkness.
Every Shuiler Is Christ.
Gombeen, The.
I Am the Gilly of Christ.
I Am the Mountainy Singer.
Ideal and Reality.
O Glorious Childbearer.
Old Woman, The.
When Rooks Fly Homeward.

Campbell, Meg (b. 1937)
Journeys.
Maui.

Campbell, Roy (1902–57)
Autumn.
Ballad of Don Juan Tenorio and the Statue of
   the Comendador.
Buffel's Kop.
Choosing a Mast.
Counsel.
Driving Cattle to Casas Buenas.
Fishing Boats in Martigues.
Flaming Terrapin, The, sels.
Georgiad, The, sels.
Georgian Spring.
Golden Shower, The, sels.
Good Resolution, A.
Heartbreak Camp.
Horses on the Camargue.
Luis de Camões.
Mass at Dawn.
On Professor Drennan's Verse.
On Some South African Novelists.
On the Same.
Palm, The.
Rounding the Cape.
Secret Muse, The.
Serf, The.
Sisters, The.
St John of the Cross: Song of the Soul That
   Is Glad to Know God by Faith.
St John of the Cross: Songs of the Soul in
   Rapture.
Theology of Bongwi, the Baboon, The.
Toledo.
Tristan da Cunha.
Veld Eclogue: The Pioneers, A.
Wayzgoose, The, sels.
Zebras, The.
Zulu Girl, The.

Campbell, Thomas (1774–1844)
Battle of the Baltic.

Freedom and Love.
Hallowed Ground.
Hohenlinden.
Irish Harper and His Dog, The.
Jilted Nymph, The.
Last Man, The.
Lines on Leaving a Scene in Bavaria.
Lord Ullin's Daughter.
Maid of Neidpath, The.
Ode to Winter.
Pleasures of Hope, The, sels.
River of Life, The.
Soldier's Dream, The.
To the Evening Star.
Ye Mariners of England.

Campbell, Walter Stanley. *See* "Vestal, Stanley"

Campbell, Wilfred (William Wilfred Campbell)
(1861–1918)
How One Winter Came in the Lake Region.
Indian Summer.
Morning on the Shore.
Winter Lakes, The.

Campion, Thomas (1567–1620)
Advice to a Girl.
Are you what your faire lookes expresse?
Author of light, revive my dying spright.
Awake, awake, thou heavy sprite [or spright].
Ayres that Were Sung and Played, at
   Brougham Castle in *Westmerland*, in the
   Kings Entertainment, The, sels.
Be thou then my beauty named.
Beauty, since you so much desire.
Blame Not My Cheekes.
Breake now my heart and dye! Oh no, she
   may relent.
Come, Cheerful Day!
Fain would I wed a fair young man that
   night and day could please me.
First Love.
Follow thy fair sun unhappy shadow.
Follow your saint, follow with accents sweet.
Give beauty all her right.
Hark, All You Ladies [That Do Sleep].
Heart's Music.
Hymn in Praise of Neptune, A.
I care not for these ladies.
I must complain, yet doe enjoy my Love.
It fell on a summer's [or sommers] day.
Jack and Joan they think no ill.
Kind are her answers.
Lamentation, A.
Man of life upright, The.
Mistris [or Mistress] Since You So Much
   Desire.
My sweetest Lesbia, let us live and love.
Now winter nights enlarge.
O Come Quickly!
Observations in the Art of English Poesie,
   sels.
Secret love or two, I must confess[e], A.
Seek the Lord, and in His ways persever.
Shall I come, if I swim? wide are the waves,
   you see.
Shall I come, sweet love, to thee.
Shall I then hope when faith is fled?
Sleep, angry beauty, sleep, and fear[e] not
   me.
So quicke, so hot, so mad is thy fond sute.
Song: "O sweet delight, O more than
   human[e] bliss[e]."
There is a Garden in her face.
Think'st thou to seduce me then with words
   that have no meaning?
Thou art not fair for all thy red and white.
Though your strangenesse frets my hart.
Thrice toss[e] these oaken ashes in the air [or
   ayre].
Thus I resolve, and time hath taught me so.
To music bent is my retired mind.
Were My Heart as Some Men's Are.
What fair pomp have I spied of glittering
   ladies.
What if a day, or a month, or a year[e].
When thou must home to shades of
   underground [or under ground].

When to Her Lute Corinna [*or* Corrina]
Sings.
Where are all thy beauties now, all hearts
enchaining? [*or* harts enchayning?].

Campo, Rafael (b. 1964)
Allegory.
Aunt Toni's Heart.
Battle Hymn of the Republic, The.
El Día de los Muertos.
For J. W.

Cane, Melville (b. 1879)
Dawn Has Yet to Ripple In.
Harvest to Seduce, A.
Hymn to Night.
Tree in December.

Cangiullo, Francesco (1884–1977)
Detonation.

Cannan, May Wedderburn (1893–1973)
Lamplight.
Rouen.

Canning, George (1770–1827)
Dutch, The.
Inscription: "For one long term, or e'er her
trial came."
New Morality, *sels.*

**Canning, George (1770–1827) and John
Hookham Frere**
Friend of Humanity and the Knife Grinder,
The.

**Canning, George (1770–1827) and William
Gifford (1756–1826)**
Progress of Man, The, *sels.*

**Canning, George (1770–1827), George Ellis and
John Hookham Frere**
Rovers, The, *sels.*

Canning, Josiah D. (1816–92)
Indian Gone!, The.

Cannon, Edward
Unsuspected Fact, An.

Cannon, Hughie
Bill Bailey, Won't You Please Come Home.

Cannon, Melissa
Sisters, The.

Cannon, Noah Calwell (1796?–1850)
Ark, The.

Canton, William (1845–1926)
Bethlehem.
Child's Prayer, A.
Day-Dreams.

Canzoneri, Robert (b. 1925)
Two.

Cao Bá Quát (1809–1853)
Drink and Drown Your Cares.
Good luck, bad luck are both the Maker's
works.

Cao Tần Lê Tất Điều (b. 1942)
Booby had a little sack, The.
Five crackpots got together, talked big things.
Our friend would board the *Thu'o'ng-Tín* and
go home.

Capetanakis, Demetrios (1912–44)
Abel.
Isles of Greece, The.

Capito
Lacking grace / beauty.

Capone, Giovanna (Janet)
In Answer to Their Questions.

Caprani, Menotti Vincent (b. 1934)
Prizefighter's Prayer, The.

Caraion, Ion (1923–86)
Always, In March.
Archaic Hippocamp.
Bits of Silk.
By the Light of the Branches Outside.
Deornamentation.
Enveloping Echo, The.
Memory.
Remember.
Song from the Occupation Time.
Tomorrow the Past Comes.
Ultimate Argument.
Winter.

Carberry, H. D.
It takes a mighty fire.

**"Carbery, Ethna" (Anna Johnston MacManus)
(1866–1902)**
King of Ireland's Cairn, The.
Love-Talker, The.
On an Island.

Cardenal, Ernesto (b. 1925)
Mosquito Kingdom.
Room 5600.
St. Luke, *sels.*
Tahirassawichi in Washington.
Unrighteous Mammon (Luke 16:9).
Vision from the Blue Window.

Cardiff, Gladys (b. 1942)
Candelaria and the Sea Turtle.
Carious Exposure.
Combing.
Dragon Skate.
For His Ring and Watch on the Night Stand.
Grey Woman.
Hunting the Dugong.
Leaves like Fish.
Long Person.
Making Lists.
Swimmer.
Tlanusi' Yi, the Leech Place.
To Frighten a Storm.
Tsa'lagi Council Tree.
Where Fire Burns.

Cardona, Jacinto Jesús
Old Dream Oven, The.

Carducci, Giosuè (1835–1907)
Petrarch.
Primo Vere.
Snowfall.

Carenza (*fl.* c.1150–1350) and Iselda
Tenson.

Carew, Jan (b. 1925)
Cliffs at Manzanilla, The.
Dreamtime Lives Again, The.
Faces and Skulls.
Our Home.
Tiho, the Carib.

Carew, Thomas (1594?–1640?)
Another [On the Duke of Buckingham].
Another [Epitaph on the Lady Mary Villiers]
("Purest soul that e'er was sent, The.")
Another [Epitaph on Lady Mary Villiers]
("This little vault, this narrow room.")
Beautiful Mistress, A.
Boldness[e] in Love.
Celia Bleeding, to the Surgeon.
Comparison, The.
Complement, The.
Cruel Mistress, A.
Deposition from Love, A.
Disdain Returned, *sels.*
Divine Mistress, A.
Elegie upon the Death of the Deane of Pauls,
Dr. John Donne, An, *sels.*
Epitaph on Maria Wentworth.
Epitaph on the Lady Mary Vill[i]ers.
Eternity of Love Protested.
Excuse of Absence, An.
Fancy, A.
Fly That Flew into My Mistress'[s] Eye, A.
For a Picture Where a Queen Laments over
the Tomb of a Slain Knight.
Hymeneal[l] Dialogue, An.
Hymeneal Song on the Nuptials of the Lady
Anne Wentworth and the Lord Lovelace,
An.
In Answer of an Elegiacal[l] Letter, Upon the
Death of the King of Sweden [from
Aurelian Townsend, Inviting Me to Write
on That Subject].
Ingrateful[l] Beauty Threatened.
Lady's Prayer to Cupid, A.
Looking-Glass, A.
Lover, upon an Accident Necessitating His
Departure, Consults with Reason, A.
Love's Force.
Maria Wentworth.
Mediocrity in Love Rejected.
New Year's Sacrifice: To Lucinda, A.
On His Mistress Looking in a Glass.
On Sight of a Gentlewoman's Face in the
Water.

On the Marriage of T. K. and C. C.: The
Morning Stormy.
Pastoral[l] Dialogue, A.
Persuasions to Enjoy.
Prayer to the Wind, A.
Rapture, A.
Second Rapture, The.
Secrecy [*or* Secresie] Protested.
Song, [A]: "Ask me no more where Jove
bestows."
Song: Good Counsel to a Young Maid.
Song: Murdring Beautie.
Song: The Willing Prisoner to His Mistress.
Song: To Her Again[e], She Burning in a
Fe[a]ver.
Spring, The.
Tinder, The.
To A. L.; Persuasions [*or* Perswasions] to
Love.
To a Lady That Desired I Would Love Her.
To Ben Jonson.
To Celia, upon Love's Ubiquity.
To Her in Absence; a Ship.
To My Cousin (C.R.) Marrying My Lady
(A.).
To my Friend G.N. from Wrest.
To My Inconstant Mistress [*or* Mistris].
To My Mistress [*or* Mistris], I Burning in
Love.
To My Mistress[e] in My Absence.
To My Mistress Sitting by a River's Side; an
Eddy.
To My Worthy Friend Master George Sands
[*or* Sandys], on His Translation of the
Psalms.
To One That Desired to Know My Mistress
[*or* Mistris].
To Saxham.
To T. H., a Lady Resembling My Mistress.
To the King, at His Entrance into Saxham:
By Master John Crofts.
To the New Year [For the Countess of
Carlisle].
To the Reader of Master William Davenant's
Play [*The Wits*].
Upon a Mole in Celia's Bosom.
Upon a Ribbon [*or* Ribband].
Upon Master Walter Montagu's Return from
Travel.
Upon My Lord Chief Justice's Election of
My Lady Anne Wentworth [*or* A.W.] for
His Mistress.
Upon Some Alterations in My Mistress, after
My Departure into France.

Carey, Henry (1693?–1743)
Author's Quietus, The.
Drinking-Song, A.
Lilliputian Ode on Their Majesties'
Accession, A.
Maid's Husband, The.
Namby-Pamby.
Namby-Pamby; or, A Panegyric on the New
Versification.
Roger and Dolly.
Sally in Our Alley.

Carey, Lady Elizabeth (1589–1639)
Mariam, *sels.*

Carey, Mary (d. after 1680)
Upon ye Sight of My Abortive Birth.
Wretten by Me at the Death of My 4th
Sonne and 5th Child Perigrine Payler.
Wretten by Me att the Same Tyme; on the
Death of My 4th, & Only Child, Robert
Payler.

Carey [*or* Cary], Patrick (c.1623–1657)
Fig for the Lower House, A.
Nulla Fides.
To the Tune—"But I Fancy Lovely Nancy."
To the Tune—"Once I Lov'd a Maiden Fair."

Carhart, Ann
Saturday Night Worship.

Cariaga, Catalina (b. 1958)
Plantings.

Carkesse, James (*fl.* 1678)
His Petition to Mr. Speaker.
His Rule of Behaviour: If You Are Civil, I
Am Sober.

On the Doctors' Telling Him that till He Left off Making Verses He Was Not Fit to be Discharged.

Carleton, Will M. (1845–1912)
Country Doctor, The.
Doctor's Story, The.
New Church Organ, The.
Over the Hill to the Poor-House.

Carlile, Henry (b. 1934)
Dodo.
Listening to Beethoven on the Oregon Coast.
Spider Reeves.
Train Whistles in the Wind and Rain.

Carlisle, Andrea
Emily Dickinson's To-Do List.

Carlson, Sir Edward
Scribbled at a Cabinet Meeting.

Carlyle, Thomas (1795–1881)
Morning.
Sower's Song, The.
Today.

Carman, Bliss (William Bliss Carman) (1861–1929)
Lord of My Heart's Elation.
Low Tide on Grand Pré.
More Ancient Mariner, A.
Morning in the Hills.
Mr. Moon.
Northern Vigil, A.

Carman, Bliss (1861–1929) *and* **Richard Hovey (1864–1900)**
Earth's Lyric.

Carman, William Bliss. *See* **Carman, Bliss**

Carmi, T. (b. 1925)
René's Songs, *sels.*
She sleeps: yet is her hand awake.

Carmichael, Amy
Last Defile, The.

Carmichael, Rebekah (fl. 1790–1806)
Tooth, The.
Young Lass's Soliloquy, A.

Carnevale, Robert (fl. 20th cent.)
Walking by the Cliffside Dyeworks.

Carnevali, Emanuel (b. 1898)
Queer Things.
Walt Whitman.

Carney, Julia A. Fletcher (1823–1908)
(Little Things).

Carolan [or O'Carolan], Turlough (1670–1738)
Mabel Kelly.
Peggy Browne.

Caroutch, Yvonne (b. 1937)
Child of silence and shadow.
I come to you with the vertigoes of the source.
Limb of forests rises up, The.
Night opens like an almond.
When we are two drunk suns.

Carpenter, Maurice (b. 1911)
To S. T. C. on His 179th Birthday, October 12th, 1951.

Carpenter, William (b. 1940)
Autumn.
Fire.
Girl Writing a Letter.
Keeper, The.

Carphyllides
Happy Man, A.
Passer-by, don't blame this memorial.

Carr, Sir John (1732–1807)
Derwent; an Ode, *sels.*

Carr, Leroy (1905–1935)
How Long Blues.

Carr, Mary Jane
Castle in the Fire, The.

Carrel, Ann
Catching.
Treacherous Death of Jesse James, The.

Carrier, Constance (b. 1908)
At Tripolis.
Commencement.
Journey.
Perspective.
Pro Patria.

Prospect Before Us, The.
Transformation Scene.

Carroll, Jim (b. 1951)
Distances, The.
Heroin.
Maybe I'm Amazed.
Paregoric Babies.
Withdrawal Letter.

Carroll, Kenneth (b. 1959)
Truth About Karen, The.

"Carroll, Lewis" (Charles Lutwidge Dodgson) (1832–98)
Alice's Adventures in Wonderland, *sels.*
Brother and Sister.
Hiawatha's Photographing.
Hunting of the Snark, The, *sels.*
Limerick: "His sister named [*or* called] Lucy O'Finner."
Limerick: "There was a young lady of station."
Limerick: "There was a young lady of Whitby."
Limerick: "There was once a young man of Oporta."
Long Tale, A.
Melodies.
My Fairy.
Palace of humbug, The.
Phantasmagoria, *sels.*
Poeta Fit, Non Nascitur.
Rules and Regulations.
Sum, A.
Sylvie and Bruno, *sels.*
Sylvie and Bruno Concluded, *sels.*
Three Voices, The, *sels.*
Through the Looking-Glass, *sels.*
"Time has come," the Walrus, The.
Visitor, A.

Carroll, Paul (b. 1927)
Father.

Carruth, Hayden (b. 1921)
Ah, you beast of love.
At his last gig in horrid Amsterdam.
Bloomingdale Papers, The, *sels.*
Contra Mortem.
Emergency Haying.
Fear and Anger in the Mindless Universe.
Freedom and Discipline.
Hard Journey, A. Yes.
Insomniac Sleeps Well for Once and, The.
Late Sonnet.
Loon on Forrester's Pond, The.
Lost.
Mending the Adobe.
Mother, *sels.*
Mountain, The.
On Being Asked to Write a Poem Against the War in Vietnam.
Once more by the brook the alder leaves.
Our Tense and Wintry Minds.
Ray.
Rimrock, Where It Is.
So be it. I am.
Song: So Often, So Long I Have Thought.
Sonnet: "Cry, crow."
Summer's Early End at Hudson's Bay.
This Decoration.
Twilight comes to the little farm.
When howitzers began.
Why speak of the use.
Wreck of the Circus Train, The.
Your tears, Niobe.

Carruth, William Herbert (1859–1929)
Dreamer of Dreams.
Each in His Own Tongue.

Carryl, Charles Edward (1841–1920)
Admiral's Caravan, The, *sels.*
Davy and the Goblin, *sels.*
Sleepy Giant, The.

Carryl, Guy Wetmore (1873–1904)
Ballad: "As I was walkin' the jungle round, a-killin' of tigers an' time."
Domineering Eagle and the Inventive Bratling, The.
Embarrassing Episode of Little Miss Muffet, The.

How a Girl Was Too Reckless of Grammar [by Far].
How Jack Found That Beans May Go Back on a Chap.
Sycophantic Fox and the Gullible Raven, The.
When the Great Gray Ships Come In.

Carson, Ciaran (b. 1948)
Army.
Asylum.
Belfast Confetti.
Bloody Hand.
Bomb Disposal, The.
Campaign.
Car Cemetery, The.
Céilí.
Cocktails.
Dresden.
Hamlet.
Insular Celts, The.
Irish for No, The.
Judgement.
Knee, The.
Mouth, The.
Slate Street School.

Carson, Jo
I am asking you to come back home.

Carson, Mary Newland (b. 1934)
My "Patch of Blue."

Carson, Robert (b. 1945)
Old Sailor Looking at a Container Ship.

Carstairs, Christian (fl. 1763–86)
Addressed to a Beech Tree.
Nightingale.
On Loch Leven.
Song, A: "Farewell my Betty, and farewell my Annie."

Carter, D.
Mistress Indiarubber Duck.

Carter, Elizabeth (1717–1806)
Dialogue, A.
Ode to Wisdom.
On the Death of Mrs. Rowe.

Carter, Harvey L.
'Tis a favorite project of mine.

Carter, Jared (b. 1939)
At the Sign-Painter's.

Carter, Martin (b. 1927)
After One Year.
As New and as Old.
Being, always to arrange.
Bent.
Bitter Wood.
Childhood of a Voice.
For a Man Who Walked Sideways.
Great Dark, The.
I Come from the Nigger Yard, *sels.*
In a small city at dusk.
Mouth Is Always Muzzled, A.
Our Number.
There Is No Riot.
University of Hunger.

Carter, Ron
Vietnam Dream.

Cartier, Marie
Poem for a Chorus.

Cartwright, Peter (1785–1872)
Our Bondage It Shall End.
Where Are the Hebrew Children?

Cartwright, William (1611–43)
Beauty and Denial.
Dead Sparrow, The.
Dream Broke, A.
Falsehood.
In the Memory of the Most Worthy Benjamin Jonson, *sels.*
New Year's Gift, A.
No Platonic [*or* Platonique] Love.
On a Virtuous Young Gentlewoman That Died Suddenly.
On the Great Frost (1634).
On the Queen's Return from the Low Countries.
Song of Dalliance, A.
To Chloe, Who Wished Herself Young Enough for Me.

To Mr. W. B., at the Birth of His First Child.
Valediction: "Bid me not go where neither suns nor showers [show'rs]."
Women.
Carus, Titus Lucretius. *See* **Lucretius**
Caruthers, Mazie V.
Prayer of Any Husband.
Carver, Raymond (1939–90)
Cobweb, The.
Late Fragment.
My Daughter and Apple Pie.
No Need.
Walk, A.
Window, The.
Wine.
You Don't Know What Love Is.
Cary, Alice (1820–71)
Among the beautiful pictures.
Autumn.
Katrina on the Porch.
Kemp Owyne.
November.
Order for a Picture, An.
Sea-Side Cave, The.
To Mother Fairie.
To Solitude.
West Country, The.
Cary, Phoebe (1824–71)
Advice Gratis to Certain Women.
Day is done, and darkness, The.
Don't Give Up.
Dorothy's Dower.
Granny's House.
Jacob.
Leak in the Dike, The.
Legend of the Northland, A.
Nearer Home.
Our Heroes.
Psalm of Marriage.
Samuel Brown.
Suppose, my little lady.
True Love.
When lovely woman wants a favour.
Casalinuovo, Lucia (b. 1954)
Lizard's Tango, The.
Casement, Sir Roger (1864–1916)
Forest Thoughts.
Fragment: "He is an inharmonious note."
Lost Youth.
Casey, Peter
Merry Jovial Beggar, The.
Casey, Philip (b. 1950)
Casanova on His Deathbed.
Casey, Thomas F.
Drill, Ye Tarriers, Drill.
Cass, Stephen
Limerick: "Psychiatrist fellow from Rye, A."
Cassell, M.
Limerick: "Said Old Nick: 'Mister Lewis and me.'"
Cassells, Cyrus (b. 1957)
Courtesy, A Trenchant Grace, A.
Soul Make A Path Through Shouting.
Sung From A Hospice.
These Are Not Brushstrokes.
Women, The.
Cassian, Nina (b. 1924)
Blood, The.
Capital Punishment.
Equality.
Ghost.
Hills picking up the / moonlight like.
I left those walls.
Knowledge.
Lady of Miracles.
Like Ana.
Like Gulliver pulling a hundred ships.
Morning Exercises.
Orbits.
Ordeal.
Other Life, the.
Part of a Bird.
Performances.
Please Give This Seat to an Elderly or Disabled Person.

Puberty.
rabbit, The.
Sand.
Temptation.
Then.
Us Two.
Vegetable Destiny.
Vowel.
Young Vampire, The.
Cassity, Turner (b. 1929)
Chronology.
Epigoni Go French Line.
Flying Friendly Skies.
Gardens of Proserpine, The.
Junker-Lied.
Professionals.
Technique on the Firing Line.
U-24 Anchors off New Orleans.
Castellanos, Rosario (1925–74)
Foreign Woman.
Great fish's eyes never shut, The.
Hecuba's Testament.
Nazareth.
O cloud that wants to be the sky's arrow.
Silence Concerning an Ancient Stone.
Useless Day.
What is weaker than a god? It groans hungry.
Castillejo, Cristóbal de (1490–1550)
Some Day, Some Day.
Castillo, Ana (b. 1953)
Nani Worries about Her Father's Happiness in the Afterlife.
Napa, California.
Castillo, Otto René (1936–67)
Apolitical Intellectuals.
Before the Scales, Tomorrow.
Distances.
Casto, Robert Clayton (b. 1932)
Salt Pork, The.
Castro, Michael (b. 1945)
Blew It.
Castro, Rosalía de (1837–85)
Black Mood.
Crickets and locusts, cicadas.
How placidly shine / The river, the spring, and the sun.
I was born at birth of blossoms.
Long May.
Now all that sound of laughter, sound of singing.
Plants don't talk, people say.
They say that plants don't talk, nor do.
Catacalos, Rosemary
David Talamántez on the Last Day of Second Grade.
One Man's Family.
Catalano, Gary (b. 1947)
Australia.
Jews Speak in Heaven, The.
Cataldi, Lee (b. 1942)
Advice.
It's Easy.
13 November 1983.
We Could Have Met.
Cather, Willa Sibert (1876–1947)
Grandmither, Think Not I Forget.
Macon Prairie.
Prairie Spring.
Somewhere, sometime, in an April twilight.
Spanish Johnny.
Catherine of Siena (A. K. A. Saint Catherine) (1347–1380)
Prayer 20, *sels.*
Catina, Ray
Negotiations.
Philosophy.
Catley, Douglas
Limerick: "Boadicea often would goad."
Limerick: "Famed big-hitter in cricket, A."
Limerick: "God brought perfect man to fruition."
Limerick: "Good mechanics are all of one mind."
Limerick: "Lass of curvacious physique, A."

Limerick: "Prostitute living in London, A."
Limerick: "Scribe, to the vulgar inclined, A."
Limerick: "There's a fortunate priest of St. Paul's."
Limerick: "When Pegotty found Barkis was willing."
Limerick: "Wily Napoleon Bonaparte, The."
Catling, B. (b. 1948)
Boschlog: Being a Cartulary from The Ship of Fools.
Cato, Nancy (b. 1917)
Independence.
Cattanar, Cittalai
What He Said to his charioteer, on his way back.
Cattantaiyar
King Kiḷḷi in Combat.
Catti Natanar (b. 1940)
What He Said ("As a little white snake.")
Catullus (Gaius [*or* Caius] Valerius Catullus) (87–c.54 B.C.)
Acme and Septimius; or, The Happy Union Celebrated at the Crown and Anchor Tavern.
Attis, after Catullus 63, *sels.*
Aurelius, I'm entrusting you with all.
Carm. II.
Carmen 5 ("My sweetest Lesbia, let us live and love.")
Carmen 8 ("Break off / fallen Catullus.")
Carmina, *sels.*
Catullus, CI.
Catullus Imitated. Ep. 58.
Catullus to Lesbia.
Complaint of Ariadna. Out of Catullus, The, *sels.*
Enough, Catullus, of this silly whining.
Frae Catullus, VIII.
Kisse me, sweet: The warie lover.
Lesbia, live to love and pleasure.
Less pub than brothel, and you, the regulars.
Lines from Catullus.
Many think Quintia's beautiful. She's tall.
My deerest Mistrisse, let us live and love.
Nuptial Song of Julia and Manlius, The, *sels.*
Quintia is beautiful, many will tell you: to me.
Roman Epithalamion.
To A Friend.
Velluti to his Revilers, *sels.*
Weep, weep, ye Loves and Cupids all.
"Caudwell, Christopher" (Christopher St. John Sprigg) (1901–37)
Classic Encounter.
Progress of Poetry, The.
Caulfield, Carlota (b. 1953)
Photo That Watches, The.
Causley, Charles (b. 1917)
Angel's Song.
Apple-Tree Man, The.
Armistice Day.
At Candlemas.
At Kfar Kana.
At the British War Cemetery, Bayeux.
Autobiography.
Balaam.
Ballad for Katharine of Aragon, A.
Ballad of the Bread Man.
Betjeman, 1984.
Bible Story.
By St. Thomas Water.
Chief Petty Officer.
Colonel Fazackerley [Butterworth-Toast].
Coming from Evening Church.
Conversation in Gibraltar 1943.
Cowboy Song.
Death of a Poet.
Death of an Aircraft.
Eden Rock.
Figgie Hobbin.
For an Ex-Far East Prisoner of War.
Fox came into my garden, A.
I Am the Great Sun[, but you do not see me].
I am the song that sings the bird.
I saw a jolly hunter.

Infant Song.
Innocent's Song.
King's College Chapel.
Legend.
Loss of an Oil Tanker.
Mary's Song.
My young man's a Cornishman.
Nursery Rhyme of Innocence and Experience.
Old Mrs Thing-um-e-bob.
On Being Asked to Write a School Hymn.
On Seeing a Poet of the First World War on
    the Station at Abbeville.
On the Thirteenth Day of Christmas.
One day at a Perranporth pet-shop.
Recruiting Drive.
Sailor's Carol.
Song of Samuel Sweet, The.
Song of the Dying Gunner A.A.1.
Tell me, tell me, Sarah Jane.
Ten Types of Hospital Visitor.
Timothy Winters.
Tom Bone.
What has happened to Lulu, mother?

Cavafy, Constantine P. (1863–1933)
Alexander Jannai.
And I Lounged and Lay on Their Beds.
As Much As You Can.
Body, remember not only how much you
    were loved.
City, The.
Days of 1901.
Days of 1908.
Days of 1908.
In Despair.
Ithaka.
Nero's Deadline.
On the Street.
One Night.
One of the Jews.
Return often and take me.
Supplication.
Thermopylae.
To Remain.
Voices.
Waiting for the Barbarians.
Walls.

Cavalcanti, Guido (1250–1301)
Ballata 5: "Light do I see within my Lady's
    eyes."
Ballata: Concerning a Shepherd-Maid.
Ballata: He Reveals, in a Dialogue, His
    Increasing Love for Mandetta.
Ballata: In Exile at Sarzana.
Ballata: Of a Continual Death in Love.
Ballata: Of His Lady among Other Ladies.
Sonetto XXXV: To Guido Orlando.
Sonnet [or Sonetto] 7: "Who is she that
    comes, makyng turn every man's eye."
Sonnet: A Rapture Concerning His Lady.
Sonnet: He Compares All Things with His
    Lady, and Finds Them Wanting.
Sonnet: He Speaks of a Third Love of His.
Sonnet: Of an Ill-Favored Lady.
Sonnet: Of His Pain from a New Love.
Sonnet: Of the Eyes of a Certain Mandetta.
Sonnet: On the Detection of a False Friend.
Sonnet: To a Friend Who Does Not Pity His
    Love.
Sonnet: To His Lady Joan, of Florence.
To Dante [or Sonnet: Guido Cavalcanti to
    Dante Alighieri].
To Dante Alighieri.
To Dante Alighieri: He Mistrusts the Love of
    Lapo Gianni.
To Dante Alighieri: He Reports, in a Feigned
    Vision, the Successful Issue of Lapo
    Gianni's Love.

Cavalieri, Grace
First, The.
Grandmother.

Cavalli, Patrizia (b. 1949)
Ah, yes, to your misfortune.
And to see the city again and to see it again.
Before when you left you would always
    forget.
But first one must free oneself.
Far from kingdoms.

I have no seed to spread over the world.
I pretend to wait for you to enlarge the
    minutes.
In the shade of a metaphor.
Little of myself do I remember.
Moroccans with the carpets, The.
Now that the time seems all mine.
Of all the huntresses.
Outside, in fact, there wasn't any change.
Rain brings me back, The.
Someone told me.
That white cloud in its contrast.
This time I won't permit the blue, glimpsed.
To simulate the burning of the heart, the
    humiliation.
Together eternity and death threaten me.

Cave, Jane (c.1754–1813)
Elegy on a Maiden Name, An.
Head-Ache, The; An Ode to Health, sels.
Poem for Children, A; or, On Cruelty to the
    Irrational Creation.
Written a Few Hours before the Birth of a
    Child.
Written by Desire of a Lady, on an Angry,
    Petulant Kitchen-Maid.
Written the First Morning of the Author's
    Bathing at Teignmouth for the Head-Ache.

Cavendish, George (1499?–1561?)
Epitaph of Our Late Queen Mary, An.

Cavendish, Lady Jane (1621–1669)
Answeare to my Lady Alice Edgertons
    Songe, Of I prethy send mee back my
    Hart, An.
Pastorall, A, sels.

Cavendish, Lady Jane (1621–69) and **Lady
Elizabeth Brackley**
On My Boy Henry.
On the Death of My Deare Sister the
    Countesse of Bridgewater.

**Cavendish, Margaret Lucas. See Newcastle,
Margaret Lucas Cavendish, Duchess of**
**Cavendish, William. See Newcastle, William
Cavendish, Duke of**
Cavin, Susan (b. 1948)
Christmas with the Holy Family.
Look Away child.

Cawein, Madison (1865–1914)
Beauty.
Caverns.
Dead Cities.
Echo.
Mnemosyne.
Music.
On Reading the Life of Haroun Er Reshid.
Orgie.
Poetry.
Purple Valleys, The.
Rome.
Stars, The.
Three Elements, The.
Unimaginative, The.

Cawthorn, James (1719–61)
Of Taste; an Essay, sels.
Wit and Learning, sels.

Cecco Angiolieri, da Siena (1258–1320)
Sonnet: He Argues His Case with Death.
Sonnet: He Is Past All Help.
Sonnet: He Rails against Dante, Who Had
    Censured His Homage to Becchina.
Sonnet: He Will Not Be Too Deeply in
    Love.
Sonnet: In Absence from Becchina.
Sonnet: Of All He Would Do.
Sonnet: Of Becchina in a Rage.
Sonnet: Of Becchina, the Shoemaker's
    Daughter.
Sonnet: Of Love, in Honor of His Mistress
    Becchina.
Sonnet: Of Love in Men and Devils.
Sonnet: Of the 20th of June 1291.
Sonnet: Of Why He Is Unchanged.
Sonnet: Of Why He Would Be a Scullion.
Sonnet: To Dante Alighieri (He Writes to
    Dante, Then in Exile at Verona, Defying
    Him as No Better Than Himself).
Sonnet: To Dante Alighieri on the Last
    Sonnet of the Vita Nuova.

Cecil, Richard (fl. 20th cent.)
Richard's Blues.
"Ceiriog." See Hughes, John Ceiriog
Ceitinn, Seathrun. See Keating, Geoffrey
Celan, Paul (1920–70)
Alchemical.
All those sleep shapes, crystalline.
Aspen tree, your leaves glance white into the
    dark.
Corona.
Death Fugue, A.
Etched Away From.
Great Birthday Blaublau with Rhymework
    and Assonance.
I am the first to drink of the blue that still
    looks for its eye.
I HEAR THAT THE AXE HAS FLOWERED.
In Prague.
Irish.
Jugs, The.
Language Mesh.
Largo.
Leaf, treeless, A.
Leaf, Treeless for Bertolt Brecht, A.
Leap-Centuries.
Little night: when you.
Mandorla.
Matière de Bretagne.
Night Ray.
Nothingness, for the, The.
Plashes the Fountain.
Psalm: "No one kneads us again out of earth
    and clay."
Tenebrae.
There was earth inside them, and.
Thread suns / above the gray-black [or grey-
    black] wasteland [or wilderness].
When you lie in.
Your Hand Full of Hours.
Zürich, the Stork Inn.

**Cendrars, Blaise (Frédéric-Louis Sauser-Hall)
(1887–1961)**
Aleutian Islands.
Fish Cove.
Frisco-City.
Great Fetishes, The.
Harvest.
Prose of the Trans-Siberian and of Little
    Jeanne of France, The, sels.
South.
White Suit.

Centamputan, Maturai Eruttalan
What She Said.

Centlivre, Susanna (1669?–1723)
Epistle to the King of Sweden, An, sels.
From the Country, to Mr. Rowe in Town.

**Cephalus (Constantinus Cephalus) (fl. 10th
cent.)**
To light young poets' hearts.

Ceraman Kanaikkal Irumporai
King's Last Words, A.

Ceravolo, Joseph (1934–88)
Book III of Fits of Dawn, sels.
Celebration.
Conception.
Dangers of the Journey to the Happy Land.
Data.
Fill and Illumined.
Geological Hymn.
Ho Ho Ho Caribou.
Invisible Autumn.
Migratory Noon.
New Realism.
Spring in This World of Poor Mutts.
Spring of Work Storm.
Stolen Away.
Sunset.
Wind Is Blowing West, The.
Women, The.

Cerealius (Julius Cerealius) (fl. 1st–2d cent.)
Poet came to our games one day, A.
Poet went to the Isthmian games, A.

Cervantes, Lorna Dee (b. 1954)
Beneath the Shadow of the Freeway.
Cannery Town in August.
Colorado Blvd.

Como lo Siento.
Emplumada.
Freeway 280.
From the Bus to E. L. at Atascadero State
  Hospital.
Meeting Mescalito at Oak Hill Cemetery.
Para un Revolucionario.
Poem for the Young White Man Who Asked
  Me How I, An Intelligent, Well-Read
  Person Could Believe in the War Between
  Races.
Poema para los Californios Muertos.
Raisins are my currency.
Refugee Ship.
Uncle's First Rabbit.
Visions of Mexico While at a Writing
  Symposium in Port Townsend, Washington,
  sels.
Woman in My Notebook, The.

Cervantes Saavedra, Miguel de (1547–1616)
Sonnet: "When I was marked for suffering,
  Love forswore."

Cerveri De Girona (fl. c.14th cent.)
Iflimit iflimis haflamard foflomor meflemen
  toflomo.

Césaire, Aimé (b. 1912)
Beat It Night Dog.
Bucolic.
Different Horizon.
Ex-Voto for a Shipwreck.
First Problem.
In Memory of a Black Union Leader.
In Order to Speak.
Lagoonal Calendar.
Macumba Word.
Magic.
Miraculous Weapons, The.
Mississippi.
Notebook of a Return to the Native Land,
  sels.
On the Islands of All Winds.
Return to My Native Land, sels.
Return to the Native Land, A, sels.
State of the Union.
Three for Bear.
Wheel is the most beautiful discovery of man
  and the only one, The.

Cesaire, Aime and Rene Depestre
Discourse on Colonialism, sels.

Céu, Sor Violante do (1602?–1693)
Voice of a Dissipated Woman inside a Tomb.

Ceyti Valluvan Peruncattan
What She Said.

Chacko, Chemmanam (b. 1926)
Rice.

Chadwick, John White (1840–1904)
Abiding Love, The.

Chagy, John 1912–90
Haggai.

Chaikin, Miriam (b. 1928)
Light Another Candle.
One-Upmanship.

Chairemon (fl. c.300–c.100 B.C.)
Epitaph: "Athenagoras begot Eubulus—."
We of Sparta fought the Argives—equal in
  number and arms.

Chakrabarti, Nirendranath (b. 1924)
Amalkanti is a friend of mine.

Chakravarty, Amiya (1901–86)
Fire.

Chalkhill, John (fl. c.1600)
Coridon's Song.

Challis, Gordon (b. 1932)
Iceman, The.
Sirens, The.

Chalmers, Patrick Reginald (1872–1942)
Hay Harvest.
Puk-Wudjies.
When Mary Goes Walking.

Chamberlain, Brenda (1912–71)
Dead Ponies.
Islandman.
Lament: "My man is a bone ringèd with
  weed."
Talysarn.

Chamberlain, Karen
Yerokastrinos.

Chamberlain, Richard (1632–98)
To the Much Honoured R. F. Esq.

Chamberlayne, William (1619–89)
Pharonnida, sels.

Chambers, Jane (1937–83)
Why Are Daddies So Mean?

Chambre, Alastair
Limerick: "There was a young girl from
  Uttoxeter / Who kept hens, but refused to
  have cocks. It a."

Chamisso, Adelbert von (1781–1838)
Tragic Story, A.

Chan, Brian (b. 1942)
How to Organise a Successful Small
  Business.
Paradise.

Chan Fang-sheng (fl. c.400)
Folk-Songs.
Sailing Homeward.

Chandler, Christine
Tree in the Garden, The.

**Chandler, Ellen Louise. See Moulton, Louise
  Chandler**

Chandler, Mary (1687–1745)
My Own Epitaph.
True Tale, A.

Chandonnet, Ann
In Velvet.

Chang Chi (768–830)
Birds from the Mountains, The.
Coming at Night to a Fisherman's Hut.
Faithful Wife, A.
Night at Anchor by Maple Bridge.
Tying Up for the Night at Maple River
  Bridge.

Ch'ang Chien (fl. c.749)
Visit to the Broken Hill Temple, A.

Chang Chih-ho (c.742–c.782)
Fisherman's Songs, sels.

Chang Chiu-ling (673–740)
Since you left, my lover.
Watching the Moon with Thoughts of Far
  Away.

Chang, Diana (b. 1934)
Cannibalism.
Foreign Ways.

Chang, Edmond Yi-teh (b. 1965)
After the Storm.
Bamboo Elegy: Two.
Near-Sightedness.

Chang Heng (A.D. 78–139)
Bones of Chuang Tzu, The.
Dancers of Huai-nan, The.

Ch'ang Kuo Fan (fl. 19th cent.)
On His Thirty-Third Birthday.

Chang Tsai
Desecration of the Han Tombs, The.

Chang Yü (1333–85)
Four Poems On the Ch'ung-wu Festival, sels.
Four Seasons in the Mountains, The, sels.
Hearing a Song from My Boat.
In a Boat on the Cha River.
In a Book-Box I Found the Lost Manuscript
  of a Poem Sent to Me by the Late Kao
  [Ch'i].
In the Evening, Walking in the Western
  Fields.
Lamenting for Kao Ch'ing-ch'iu, Chi-ti.
Merchant's Joy, The.
Mountain Retreat of a Recluse, The.
Painting ("Jade cave, ten thousand flowering
  peach trees, A.")
Paintings, sels.
Pavilion for Listening to Fragrance, The.
Presented to a Lady within the Palace.
Quatrain: "At this remote village, I have no
  neighbors."
Reading the Poetry Collection of Lü Fang-
  ch'iu.
Retreat of Liu Kuo-pao, The.
Retreat of Sun Ching-hsiang, The.
Seven Poems on Living in the Mountains:
  Seeing Off, sels.

"Song of Farewell" in the Tartar Mode.
Song of the Old Oak.
Staying Overnight at T'ien-ning Ch'an
  Temple.
To the Innkeeper at Five Rivers, Sun Pen.
Twelve Miscellaneous Poems on the Fang
  Garden, sels.
Yellow Sunflower of Szechwan.

Chang Yüeh (667–730)
Written When Drunk.

Chanler, Isaac (1700–1749)
Awake My Soul, Betimes Awake.
Thrice Welcome First and Best of Days.

Channing, William Ellery (1818–1901)
Barren Moors, The.
Harbor, The.
Hymn of the Earth.
Murillo's Magdalen.
Poet's Hope, A.
Walden.

Chao, Hsu
Locust Swarm, The.

Ch'ao Li-houa [or Chao Li-hua]
Farewell: "My boat goes west, yours east."

Chao Luan-luan (fl. 8th? cent.)
Slender Fingers ("Slender, delicate, soft
  jade.")
Willow Eyebrows.

Chao Meng-fu (1254–1322)
Admonition to Myself, An.
Eulogy of the Sagely Virtue of His Imperial
  Majesty Emperor Shih-tsu, A.
Fisherman's Lyric.
In the Ancient Manner.
Inscribed on a Landscape by Mi Yüan-hui.
Inscribed on a Wall Painting of Assembled
  Immortals.
Inscribed on Sun An-chih's "Painting of
  Pines and Catalpas."
Inscribed on the Painting "Spring Dawn at
  Peach Blossom Spring" by Scholar Shang
  Te-fu.
Lamenting the Taoist Wei Kung-yüan.
Living in Retirement at Te-ch'ing.
Pavilion-Where-the-Crane-Came, The.
Poem of Prefectural Judge Yang T'ien-jui
  Righting a Wrong.
Song of an Autumn Night.
To a Pyrotechnist.
Twenty-Eight Poems Inscribed on T'ien-kuan
  Mountain, sels.

Chao Yi (1727–1814)
In Search of Solitude.
Rising Early in the Morning.
Spring Sentiments.
Strolling in the Countryside.
Writing Poetry in the Back Garden.

Chao Ying-tou (fl. 17th cent.)
Decrees of God, The.

Chapin, Edwin Hubbell (1814–80)
Hark! Hark! with Harps of Gold.
O Thou, Who Didst Ordain the Word.

Chaplin, Kathleen M.
Merry Little Men.

Chapman, Arthur (1873–1935)
Out Where the West Begins ("Out where the
  hand-clasp's a little stronger.")

Chapman, George (1559?–1634)
Bussy d'Ambois, sels.
Coronet for His Mistress Philosophy, A, sels.
Eugenia, sels.
Euthymiae Raptus; or, The Teares of Peace,
  sels.
Homer and the Brazen Head of Rumour.
Homer's Iliad Book 12, sels.
Homer's Iliad, To the Reader, sels.
Homer's Odysseys, sels.
Hymn[e] to Our Saviour on the Cross[e], A.
Masque of the Middle Temple and Lincoln's
  Inn, The, sels.
Ovid's Banquet of Sense, sels.
Shadow of Night, The.

Chapman, John Alexander (b. 1875)
Gipsy Queen.

Chapman, John Jay (1862–1933)
Lines on the Death of Bismarck.

Song: "Old Farmer Oats and his son Ned."

Chapman, M. J. (b. 1865)
African Dirge.
Barbadoes, *sels.*

Chappell, Fred (b. 1936)
Cleaning the Well.
Guess Who.
My Father Washes His Hands.
My Grandmother Washes Her Feet.
My Grandmother Washes Her Vessels.
My Mother Shoots the Breeze.
Narcissus and Echo.
Northwest Airlines.
Second Wind.
Skin Flick.

Char, René (b. 1907)
Argument.
Disdained Apparitions.
Leaves of Hypnos, *sels.*
Leaves of Hypnos No. 128.
Man flees suffocation.
Unbending Prayer.

**Charlemagne (742?–814) and Hrabanus Maurus
(*fl.* 9th cent.)**
Veni Creator Spiritus.

Charles, Dorthi (b. 1963)
Bang! the starter's gun—.
Concrete Cat.
Getting Dirty.

Charles, Elizabeth Rundle (b. 1828)
Child on the Judgment Seat, The.

Charles, Faustin (b. 1944)
Fireflies.
Letters from Home.
Omens of the Morning.
Sugar Cane.

Charles I, King of England (1600–1649)
On a Quiet Conscience.

Chartier, Alain (c.1385–c.1433)
I turn you out of doors.

Chartres, Vidame de (*fl.* 13th cent.)
April.

Chase, Joan
During the Reign of the Queen of Persia,
sels.

Chase, Karen (*fl.* 20th cent.)
What You Can't See.

Chasin, Helen (b. 1938)
City Pigeons.
Word *Plum*, The.

Chatain, Robert
World of Darkness.

Chatterton, Thomas (1752–70)
Aella; a Tragycal Enterlude, *sels.*
Bristowe Tragedie: or, The Dethe of Syr
Charles Bawdin.
Excelente Balade of Charitie, An.
If Wishing for the Mystic Joys of Love.
Methodist, The.
Ode to Miss Hoyland.
Resignation.
Sentiment.
Sunday: A Fragment Transcribed from a Ms.
in Chatterton's Handwriting.

Chattopadhyay, Shakti (b. 1933)
Forgive Me.

Châu, Lê Ngoc. See Luân Hoán

Châu, Phan Ngoc. See Nam Xuyên

Chaucer, Geoffrey (1340?–1400)
Canterbury Tale, The, *sels.*
Canterbury Tales, The, *sels.*
Complaint of Chaucer to His [Empty] Purse,
The.
Complaint unto Pity, The.
Envoy to Scogan.
Gentilesse.
Hide, Absolon, thy gilte tresses clere.
Lack of Steadfastness.
Lak of Stedfastnesse.
Legend of Good Women, The, *sels.*
Love Unfeigned, The.
Love's Garden.
Merciles[s] Beaute [*or* Beautée *or* Beauty],
sels.

Monk's Tale, The.
Parlement of Foules, The, *sels.*
Parliament of Fowls, The, *sels.*
Somtyme the world was so stedfast and
stable.
Syn I fro Love escaped am so fat.
To His Scribe Adam.
To Rosamounde.
Troilus and Criseyde [*or* Criseide], *sels.*
Truth.

Chaudhari, Bahinabai (1880–1951)
Naming of Things, The.

Chaudhari, Kirti (b. 1935)
Inertia.

Chaundler, Christine (1881–1972)
Child's Christmas Carol, A.

Chế Lan Viên Phan Ngoc Hoan (b. 1920)
Graves.
Human Skull, The.
More Thoughts on Nguyễn.
On the Way Home.
Silk Threads of Memory.
Waning Night, The.
War Elephant, The.

Chear, Abraham (d. 1668)
To My Youngest Kinsman, R. L.

Chedid, André (d. 1921)
Future and the Ancestor, The.
What Are We Playing At?

Cheek, Cris
Drawing on the Traditions, *sels.*

Cheever, George Barrell (1807–90)
Blest Be the Wondrous Grace.
Thy Loving Kindness, Lord, I Sing.

Ch'en Liang (1143–94)
Tune: "Beautiful Lady Yü, The"—Spring
Sorrow.
Tune: "Water Dragon's Chant"—Loathsome
Spring.

Ch'en Lin, Susan
Song: "I watered my horse at the Long Wall
caves."

Ch'en Shih-tao (1053–1102)
Cold Night.

Ch'en Tao (779–843)
Her Husband Asks Her to Buy a Bolt of
Silk.
Song of Lung-hsi.

Ch'en Tzu-ang (661–702)
Business men boast of their skill and
cunning.
Impressions of Things Encountered, *sels.*
Inscription on a Tree atop mount Sacrifice
(Ssu Shan) and Sent to Censor Ch'iao.
Song on Climbing the Gate Tower at Yu-
chou, A.
Song on Climbing Yu-chou Gate Tower.

Ch'en Tzu-lung (1608–47)
Ballad of the Little Cart, A.
Little cart jolting and banging through the
yellow haze of dusk, The.
Parable, A.
Tune: "Telling of Innermost Feelings"—
Wandering in Spring.

Ch'en Yü-yi (1090–1138)
Enlightment.
Journeying to Hsiang-yi.
Sitting on a Rock by Mountain Stream.
Spring Morning.
Tune: "Immortal at the River"—Ascending a
Little Tower at Night.

Chên, Yüan
Elegy, An.

Cheney-Coker, Syl
Blood in the Desert's Eyes, The, *sels.*
Hunger of the Suffering Man, The.
Letter to a Tormented Playwright.
On Being a Poet in Sierra Leone.
Outsider, The.
Poem for a Guerrilla Leader.
Poem for a Lost Lover.
Road to Exile Thinking of Vallejo, The.

Cheney, Elizabeth
Overheard in an Orchard.

Cheney, John Vance (1848–1922)
Unto Our God Most High We Sing.

Ch'ëng Hsiao (c. 220–264)
Satire on Paying Calls in August.

Cheng Hsieh (1693–1765)
Collecting Antiques.
Contest Snake, The.
For Contemporary Artist Pien Wei-Ch'I.
Girl from Ch'ang-kan is just fourteen years
old, The.
Insccribed on a Painting.
Mother-in-Law Is Cruel.
Mourning for My Son Jun-erh, *sels.*
On a Painting of a Knight-Errant.
Poem for My Wet Nurse, A.
Seven Songs, *sels.*
Small Garden, The.
Song of Surfing on the Bore.
To Chin Nung.
Tune: "Full River Red"—A Four-season Song
on the Hardships and Joys of Farming
Life.
Twenty-eight Characters Sent to Tung-ts'un
on the Subject of the Poems He Burned.
Yangchou, *sels.*

Cheng Min (b. 1924)
Student.

Chénier, André Marie de (1762–94)
Elegies, *sels.*
Iambes VIII.

Chernoff, Maxine (b. 1952)
Breasts.
How Lies Grow.
Japan, *sels.*
Lost and Found.
Man Struck Twenty Times by Lightning,
The.
Phantom Pain.

Cherry, Kelly (b. 1940)
Bride of Quietness, The.
Going Down on America.
History.
Love.
Pines without peer, The.
Raiment We Put On, The.
Reading, Dreaming, Hiding.

Chester, Anson G. (1824–1911)
Tapestry Weavers, The.

**Chesterfield, Philip Dormer Stanhope, 4th Earl
of (1694–1773)**
On Lord Ila's Improvements, near Hounslow
Heath.
On Miss Eleanor Ambrose, a Celebrated
Beauty in Dublin.
On Mr. Nash's Present of His Own Picture at
Full Length.
Song: "Whenever, Chloe, I begin."
To Miss Eleanor Ambrose on the Occasion
of Her Wearing an Orange Lily at a Ball
in Dublin Castle on July the 12th.
Unlike my subject now shall be my song.
Verses Written in a Lady's Sherlock "Upon
Death."

Chesterman, Hugh (b. 1884)
Outside.
Rhyme Sheet of Other Lands, A.
Sir Nicketty Nox.
Yesterday.

Chesterton, Frances Alice (1875–1938)
How Far Is It to Bethlehem?

Chesterton, Gilbert Keith (1874–1936)
After W. B. Yeats.
Antichrist, or the Reunion of Christendom; an
Ode.
Aristocrat, The.
Ballad of Abbreviations, A.
Ballade D'une Grande Dame.
Ballade of Suicide, A.
Certain Evening, A.
Christmas Carol: "Christ child lay on Mary's
lap, The."
Christmas Carol, A: "God rest you merry
gentlemen."
Citizenship; Form 8889512, Sub-Section Q.
Convert, The.
Donkey, The.
Ecclesiastes.
Elegy in a Country Churchyard.

English Graves, The.
Envoi: "Princess, you trapped a guileless
  Mayor."
Fat White Woman Speaks, The.
Femina Contra Mundum.
Flying Inn, The, *sels.*
For a War Memorial.
From a Spanish Cloister.
Gold Leaves.
House of Christmas, The.
Joseph.
Lepanto.
Lucasta Replies to Lovelace.
Old Song, The.
On Reading "God."
Oneness of the Philosopher with Nature, The.
Post-Recessional.
Praise of Dust, The.
Prayer in Darkness, A.
Rolling English Road, The.
Sea Replies to Byron, The.
Secret People, The.
Skeleton, The.
Song against Grocers, The.
Songs of Education, *sels.*
Sword of Surprise, The.
To the Unknown Warrior.
Variations on an Air: After Robert Browning.
Variations on [*or* of] an Air: After [Algernon
  Charles] Swinburne.
Variations on an Air: After W. B. Yeats.
Variations on an Air Composed on Having to
  Appear in a Pageant as Old King Cole,
  sels.
Wife of Flanders, The.
World State, The.

Chevalier, Albert (1860–1923)
My Old Dutch.
Sich a Nice Man Too!, *sels.*

Chevallier, C.
Limerick: "Naïve young lady of Bude, A."

Chevette, Zelda
There was an old pros.

Cheyenne Oral Tradition
Death Song of White Antelope, The.

Chhotray, Devdas (b. 1946)
Fear.

Chia Tao (779–843)
Evening View as the Snow Clears.
Last Night of the Third Moon, The.
Looking for a Recluse but Failing to Find
  Him.
Passing by a Mountain Village: Evening.
Sick cicada, unable now to fly, A.
Spending the Night at a Mountain Temple.
Weeping for the Zen Master Po-yen.

Chia Yi (201–196 B.C.)
Rhyme-Prose on the Owl.

Chiang Chieh (*fl.* 13th cent.)
To the Tune "The Fair Maid of Yu."

Chiang Ch'un-lin (1818–68)
Tune: "Magnolia Blossoms, Slow"—
  Traveling on the Yangtze.

Chiang K'uei (1155?–1235)
Tune: "Charm of Nien-nu."
Tune: "Dim Fragrance"—Plum Blossoms.
Tune: "Pale-golden Willows."
Tune: "Sparse Shadows"—Plum Blossoms.
Written at Lakeside Residence.

Chiang Lu (*fl.* 6th cent.)
Wrecked Boat on the River Shore.

Chiang Shih-ch'üan (1725–85)
Evening Lights on the River.
Twilight in the River Pavilion.

Ch'iao Chi (1280–1345)
Tune: "Overtures"—On Myself.
Tune: "Sheep on Mountain Slope."
Tune: "Song of Plucking Cassia."

Chiao-jan (730–99)
Looking for Lu Hung-chien but Failing To
  Find Him.

Chicago, Judy
And then all that has divided us will merge.

Chichibabin, Boris Alekseievich (b. 1923)
Camel.
I'll be finished, if I'll survive—.

Chicken, Edward (1698–1746)
Collier's Wedding, The, *sels.*

Ch'ien Ch'i (*fl.* 8th cent.)
Mount T'ai P'ing.
Visit to the Hermit Ts'ui.

**Ch'ien Ch'ien-i [*or* Ch'ien Ch'ien-yi] (1582–
  1664)**
Drinking Wine.
In Lamplight, Watching My Wife Preparing a
  Flower Arrangement—Playfully Inscribing
  Four Poems, *sels.*
In Spring of the Year *Ping-shen, sels.*
Miscellaneous Feelings at West Lake, *sels.*
Miscellaneous Poems Written While in Jail.
No Flowers.
On the Road to Western Hill.
Poem on Drinking Wine with the Degree-
  Holder Ku.
Poem Written During a Dream on the
  Twenty-Third Day of the Intercalary
  [Month After The] Fourth [Month].
Poems Written in Prison, *sels.*
Rebuttal of Tung-p'o's Poem on "Bathing the
  Infant," A.
Willow Branch Songs, *sels.*

Ch'ien T'ao (*fl.* early 11th cent.)
Blaming Sons.
Chill and harsh the year draws to its close;.
Flood.
I BUILT my hut in a zone of human
  habitation.
In the quiet of the morning I heard a knock
  at my door;.
LONG time ago, A.
Matching a Poem by Secretary Kuo.
Moving House.
New Corn.
Reading the Book of Hills and Seas.
Returning to the Fields.
Shady, shady the wood in front of the Hall;.
Substance, Shadow, and Spirit.
Written While Drunk.

Ch'ien Wen-Ti, Emperor (503–51)
Getting Up in Winter.
Lo-yang.

Chigetsu (Kaai Chigetsu) (1634?–1708?)
Propriety.

Chigetsu, Kaai. *See* Chigetsu

Chikako (Jusammi Chikako) (*fl.* c.1290–1316)
On this summer night.

Chikako, Jusammi. *See* Chikako

Child, A. C.
Wishes.

Child, Abigail (b. 1950)
Motive for Mayhem, A.
Squeeze.
Surplus.

Child, Lydia Maria (1802–80)
Thanksgiving Day.

Chimombo, Steve (b. 1945)
Death Song, A.
Derailment: A Delirium.
Four Ways of Dying.
Messengers, The.
Obituary.
Of Promises and Prophecy.

Chin Ch'ang-hsü (*fl.* 10th cent.)
Spring Grievance.
Spring Sorrow.

Ch'in Chia (*fl.* 2nd cent. A.D.)
Ch'in Chia's Wife's Reply.
To His Wife.

Ch'in Kuan (1049–1100)
Along the Grand Canal.
Returning from Kuang-ling.
Spring Rain.
Tune: "Courtyard Full of Fragrance."
Tune: "Happy Events Approaching."

Chin, Marilyn
Administrator, The.
Altar.
American Rain.
Aubade: "Waking is this easy."
Autumn Leaves.
Barbarian Suite.

Barbarians Are Coming, The.
Cauldron.
Composed Near the Bay Bridge (after a wild
  party).
Disorder, The.
Elegy for Chloe Nguyen.
Exile's Letter: After the Failed Revolution.
Exile's Letter (Or: An Essay on
  Assimilation).
First Lessons.
Floral Apron, The.
How I Got That Name.
Portrait of the Self as Nation, 1990–1991, A.
Prelude.
Repulse Bay.
Song of the Sad Guitar.
Turtle Soup.
We Are Americans Now, We Live in the
  Tundra.

Chin Nung (1687–1764)
Evening Scene at Twin Forests.
I Discuss the Past and Not the Present. What
  Men of Today Are Worth Discussing? May
  the Men of the Past Not Blame Me for My
  Discussion of Them, *sels.*
I Have Recently Edited My Unworthy Poems
  in Four Chapters, Copied Them Out in My
  Own Hand, and Entrusted Them to My
  Daughter to Keep. Five Miscellaneous
  Poems, *sels.*
Inkstone Inscription for the Blind Scholar Ho
  Yung-kuang, An.
Inscribed on a Lichen-Covered Wall in My
  Hut, *sels.*
Inscribed on the Wall of a Rice Cake Shop.
Mooring in the Rain at Sung-ling.
On New Year's Eve of the Year Hsin-wei
  (1751), Drinking Alone and Sadly
  Chanting Poems, I Remembered My Aged
  Wife Who Is Living at Twisting River,
  sels.
On Twisting River Is the Old Home of My
  Father. Now That My Illness Has Eased
  Up, I Have Written These Six Poems
  About the Place, *sels.*
Thirty Poems of Longing for People, *sels.*
Wearing a Worn-Out Coat.
Written at the End of Master Ho-ching's
  Collected Works.

Chine-Jo (*fl.* late 17th cent.)
Fireflies' light, The.

Chingono, Julius (b. 1949)
Epitaph, An: "Here lies Stephen Pwanya."

Chinn, Daryl Ngee
Not Translation, Not Poetry.
Skin Color from the Sun.

Chinnov, Igor Vladimirovich (b. 1909)
Sometimes, you give way to sickness.

Chino, Masako (1880–1946)
I shall hide myself / within the moon of the
  spring night.

Chipasula, Frank Mkalawile (b. 1949)
Because the Wind Remembers.
Friend, Ah You Have Changed!
Going Back Patiently.
Hanging, Zomba Central Prison, A.
Love Poem for My Country, A.
Manifesto on Ars Poetica.
My Blood Brother.
My Friendly People.
Nightsong, *sels.*
Ritual Girl.
Talking of Sharp Things.
Those Rainy Mornings.
Tramp.
Warrior.

Chiricahua Apache Oral Tradition
Song for Girls' Puberty Rites.

Chitre, Dilip (b. 1938)
My father travels on the late evening train.

Ch'iu Chin (1879–1907)
Call to Action, A.
To the Tune "The River Is Red."

Ch'iu Wei (694–789?)
Visiting a Recluse on West Mountain and
  Not Finding Him In.

Chivers, Thomas Holley (1809–58)
Apollo.
Avalon.
Call, A.
Lily Adair.
Moon of Mobile, The.
To Allegra Florence in Heaven, *sels.*
To Isa Sleeping.
Wind, The.

Chiyojo [*or* Chiyo *or* Chiyo-Ni *or* Kaga no Chiyo *or* Fukuda Chiyo-Ni] (1703–75)
After a long winter, giving / each other nothing.
Cuckoo!/ Cuckoo!
Don't dress for it.
From the mind.
Grazing.
Haiku: "Autumn's bright moon."
Haiku: "Dew of the rouge-flower, The."
Haiku: "Spring rain."
Hardly spring, with ice.
I forgot that my lips.
Morning glory!, The.
My hunter of dragonflies.
Once my parents were older.
See! The gleam.

Cho, Chi-hun (1920–68)
At Toriwon.
Falling Petals.
Nun's Dance, The.

Cho, Pyong-hwa (b. 1921)
Empty as Death.
Never to Meet Again.

Chock, Eric (b. 1950)
Bait, The.
Belt, The.
Chinese Fireworks Banned in Hawaii.
Poem for George Helm: Aloha Week 1980.
Working Construction.

Chōkū, Shaku
Imamiya Middle School.
Tanka: "After enduring."
Tanka: "Among the hundreds."
Tanka: "Arrowroot flowers."
Tanka: "Bulky oil lamp, A."
Tanka: "From the water's depth."
Tanka: "Imagining."
Tanka: "Kidnapping."
Tanka: "Late at night in the kitchen."
Tanka: "My research."
Tanka: "New Year's temple bells."
Tanka: "Nowhere on the leaves."
Tanka: "Oddly shaped."
Tanka: "On Christmas Eve."
Tanka: "Phantom appears, A."
Tanka: "Somewhere around."
Tanka: "Town children."
Tanka: "Train speeds on, The."
Tanka: "Which child."
Vultures—in the midst of war.

Cholmondeley-Pennell, Henry (1837–1915)
Night Mail North, The.

Chon, Pong-gon (1928–88)
Mischief.
Piano, The.

Ch'on, Sangbyong (b. 1930)
Namelessness.
Return to Heaven.

Chonaill, Eibhlin Dubh Ni. *See* O'Connell, Eibhlin Dubh

Chong, Chiyong (1901–5?)
Native Village.
Nostalgic Urge.
Summit, The.

Chong, Hanmo (1923–91)
Bird.
Late Autumn.
Parting.

Chong, Hyon-jong (b. 1939)
Going by far.
Miserable.
Note 25.

Chorley, Henry Fothergill (1808–72)
Brave Old Oak, The.

"Chorny [*or* Chiornyi], Sasha" (Aleksandr Mikhailovich Glikberg) (1880–1932)
Drunkard's Nocturnes, A.

Kreutzer Sonata, A.
Life.
My Love.
Stylized Donkey, A.

Chou Pang-yen (1056–1121)
Tune: "Beautiful Lady Yü, The," *sels.*
Tune: "Distant Red Window."
Tune: Palace of Night Revels.
Tune: "Prince of Lan-ling" (*Lan-ling Wang*)—on Willows.
Tune: "Six Toughies"—Written after the Roses Have Faded.

Christensen, Inger (b. 1935)
Men's Voices.

Christine de Pisan (1364–c.1430)
Alone am I, and alone I wish to be.
Christine to Her Son.
Epistle of Othea to Hector (A Lytil Bibell of Knyghthod), The, *sels.*
Fountain of tears, river of grief.
I am a widow, robed in black, alone.
I'll always dress in black and rave.
In Praise of Marriage.
Marriage is a lovely thing.

Christopher, Nicholas (b. 1951)
After Hours.
April in New York.
Far from Home.
5°.
Palm Reader, The.
Terminus.

"Chrystos" (b. c.1946)
Dream Lesbian Lover.
For Sharol Graves.
Getting Down.
I Have Not Signed a Treaty with the United States Government.
I Walk in the History of My People.
Night Visits.
Portrait of Assimilation.
Real Indian Leans Against, The.
Today Was a Bad Day Like TB.
Wings of a Wild Goose, The.
Your Tongue Sparkles.

Chu Chen Po (*fl.* 9th cent.)
Hedgehog.
Rustic temple is hidden, The.

Ch'u Ch'ing-yü (*fl.* c.826)
Gathering Lotus.
Great Wall, The.
Palace Poem.

Ch'u Ch'uang I (*fl.* 8th cent.)
Country House.
Evening in the Garden Clear after Rain.
Mountain Spring, A.
Tea.

Chu Hsi (1130–1200)
Boats Are Afloat, The.
Farm by the Lake, The.
Spring Sun.
Thoughts While Reading.

Ch'u Kuang-hsi (707–59)
Cowherd, The; a Song.
Farm Routine.
Farmer's Thoughts, A.
Streets of Ch'ang-an, The.

Chu Shu-chen (*fl.* early 12th cent.)
Alone.
Hysteria.
Lost.
Morning.
Old Anguish, The.
Plaint.
Plum Blossoms.
Sorrow.
Spring has come. I try to forget.
Spring Joy.
Stormy Night in Autumn.

Chu Tun-ju (1081?–1159?)
Tune: "Charm of Nien-nu, The."
Tune: "Happy Events Approaching."
Tune: "Magnolia Blossoms, Abbreviated" ("No one invited me.")

Chu Yi-tsun (1629–1709)
Deepening-Green Pavilion.

Inscribed on the Painting of "Garden for Retirement": Pavilion of Sincerity, on Rocky Mountain.
Listening-to-the-Rain Studio.
Majestic Valley.
Tune: "Song of Divination."
Tune: "Song of the Southern Country."
Tune: "Song of the Southern Country"— Spring Thoughts at Pearl River.
West Cliff.
Written at Mauve Garden: Pine Wind Terrace.

Chu, Yohan (1900–79)
Fireworks.
Sound of Rain, The.

Ch'u Yüan (*fl.* 4th cent. B.C.)
Great Arbiter of Fate, The.
Great Summons, The.
Lament for Ying, A.
Li Sao, *sels.*
Lord of the River Hsiang.
Nine Songs, *sels.*
Spirit of the Mountain, The.

Chu Yün-ming (1461–1527)
As I Looked at a Lake, My Thoughts Turned to a Certain Friend.
Drinking.
Fan from Korea, A.
For Several Years I Have Wanted To Grow a Garden, But Have Never Finished One. This Year It Is Already Halfway Through Summer, and This Has Made Me Despondent.
Forest Birds (A Woman Speaks), *sels.*
Improvisations, *sels.*
Landscape Painted on a Fan—Echoing a Poem by Wen Cheng-ming, A.
Late Spring—Traveling through the Mountains.
Little Landscape, A.
Making Fun of the Well at the Inn below the Mountain.
Miscellaneous Poems Written in My Studio on an Autumn Day, *sels.*
Painting of the Butterfly Dream by the Master Artist Li Tsai, A.
Poem Inscribed on a Landscape Painting, *sels.*
Remembering My Late Wife.
Shrine of General Pien, The.
Too Lazy to Write Poetry.

Chuang Tzu
Cutting up an Ox.
Man Is Born in Tao.
Need to Win, The.

Chudakov, Sergey [*or* Sergei] (b. 1936)
When they cry: / "Man overboard."

Chudleigh, Mary Lee, Lady (1656–1710)
Ladies Defence Or, the Bride-Woman's Counsellor Answered, The, *sels.*
Offering: Part One, The.
Resolve, The.
Song: "Why Damon, why, why, why so pressing?"
'Tis hard we should be by the men despised.
To the Ladies.
Wish, The.

Chukhonstev, Oleg Grigorevich (b. 1938)
Chaadayev on Basmannaya.
Elegy: "Cross between a bakehouse and a bell tower, A."
Epistle to Baron Delvig.
Farewell to Autumn.
In the Menagerie.
Parrot, The.
When the village daylight dimmed.
With your name, I shall name this homeless year.

"Chukovsky [*or* Chukovskii], Korney" (Nikolai Vasilyevich Korneichukov) (1882–1969)
Telephone rang, The.

Chung-ch'ang T'ung (179–220)
Speaking My Mind.

Ch'ung, Li
Parody of a Lover.

Chung Ssu-ch'eng (275?ND/1350?)
Tune: "Sprig of Flowers, A"—Written for My "Ugly Studio."
Chuo Wen-chün (179?–117? B.C.)
Song of Snow-white Heads.
Church, Richard (1893–1972)
Alchemist, The.
Be Frugal.
On Hearing the First Cuckoo.
Churchill, Charles (1731–64)
Author, The, *sels.*
Dedication: "Health to great Gloucester—from a man unknown."
Duellist, The, *sels.*
Ghost, The, *sels.*
Gotham, *sels.*
Night; an Epistle to Robert Lloyd, *sels.*
Prophecy of Famine, The, *sels.*
Rosciad, The, *sels.*
Times, The, *sels.*
Churchyard, Thomas (c.1520–1604)
Musicall Consort, A, *sels.*
Tale of a Friar and A Shoemaker's Wife, a.
Chute, Marchette (1909–94)
Day before Christmas.
My Dog.
My Plan.
Ciardi, John (1916–86)
About the Teeth of Sharks.
All about Boys and Girls.
Back through the Looking Glass to This Side.
Ballad of the Icondic.
Captain Spud and His First Mate, Spade.
Censorship.
Dawn of the Space Age.
Death's the Classic Look.
Elegy Just in Case.
Evil Eye, The.
Exit Line.
Faces.
First Snow on an Airfield.
Gift, The.
Goodnight.
Home Revisited: Midnight.
Homecoming—Massachusetts.
I Wouldn't.
Journal.
Man Who Sang the Sillies, The.
Mystic River.
Ode for the Burial of a Citizen.
On a Photo of Sgt. Ciardi a Year Later.
On Evolution.
On Learning to Adjust to Things.
Plea.
Sometimes Even Parents Win.
Stranger in the Pumpkin, The.
Suburban.
To a Reviewer Who Admired My Book.
To Judith Asleep.
What Johnny Told Me.
Cibber, Colley (1671–1757)
Blind Boy, The.
Cibulka, Hanns
Kremenez.
Kuks.
Mathematics.
Sky Full of Swallows.
Cillactor
Married life for a poor man.
"Sweet is the fruit," say.
Young lady may increase her stock, A.
Cinna, A.
Limerick: "Consistent disciples of Marx."
Limerick: "Did Ophelia ask Hamlet to bed?"
Limerick: "Dr. Johnson, when sober or pissed."
Limerick: "Of all God's jokes none is bluer."
Limerick: "Othello loved Desdemona."
Limerick: "Said Nelson at his most la-di-da-di."
Limerick: "Said the Queen to her favourite ghillie."
Limerick: "To his Queen said the circumspect Burleigh."
Cino da Pistoia (1270–1336)
Canzone: His Lament for Selvaggia.

Sonnet: A Trance of Love.
Sonnet: Death Is Not without but within Him.
Sonnet: Of the Grave of Selvaggia, on the Monte della Sambuca.
Sonnet: To Love, In Great Bitterness.
To Dante Alighieri: He Conceives of Some Compensation in Death.
To Dante Alighieri: He Interprets Dante's Dream.
To His Lady Selvaggia Vergiolesi; Likening His Love to a Search for Gold.
Cisneros, Sandra
Good Hot Dogs.
His Story.
Muddy Kid Comes Home.
Poet Reflects On Her Solitary Fate, The.
You Called Me Corazón.
Citèkù Ndaaya (b. 1929?)
Ndaaya's Kàsàlà, *sels.*
Cittalai Cattanar
What He Said to His Charioteer, on His Way Back.
Ciullo d'Alcamo (*fl.* c.1175)
Dialogue: Lover and Lady.
Cixous, Hélène (b. 1937)
Vivre L'Orange, *sels.*
Clairmont, Robert (b. 1902)
Answers, The.
Hero in the Land of Dough, A.
Clampitt, Amy (1920–94)
Amaranth and Moly.
Amherst.
Baroque Sunburst, A.
Beach Glass.
Beethoven, Opus 111.
Burning Child, The.
Catalpa Tree on West Twelfth Street, A.
Cormorant in His Element, The.
Cure at Porlock, A.
Dancers Exercising.
Easter Morning.
Gooseberry Fool ("The gooseberry's no doubt an oddity.")
Grasmere, *sels.*
Hairline Fracture, A.
Imago.
Kingfisher, The.
Medusa.
Meridian.
Portola Valley.
Procession at Candlemas, A.
Stacking the Straw.
Sun Underfoot Among the Sundews, The.
Syrinx.
What the Light Was Like.
Woodlot, The.
Written in Water.
Clare, John (1793–1864)
After Reading in a Letter Proposals for Building a Cottage.
Anecdote of Love, An.
Autumn ("I love the fitful gust that shakes.")
Autumn Robin, The.
Autumn ("Thistledown's flying / Though the winds are all still, The.")
Badger grunting on his woodland track, The, *sels.*
Badger ("When midnight comes a host of dogs and men.")
Ballad: The Sun Had Grown on Lessening Day.
Beanfield, The.
Birds' Lament.
Birds' Nests.
Bonny Lassie O!
Child Harold, *sels.*
Clock-A-Clay [The Lady Bug].
Country Letter.
Cowper, the poet of the fields.
Death.
Death's memories are graves.
Decay.
December.
Emmonsail's Heath in Winter.
Eternity of Nature, The.

Evening.
Evening Primrose.
Fallen Elm, The.
Farewell to the bushy clump close to the river.
Farmyard, The.
Field Path.
First Love.
Flitting, The.
Flood, The.
Fragment: "Language has not the power to speak what love indites."
Frightened Ploughman, The.
Gipsies seek wide sheltering woods again, The.
Gipsies: "Snow falls deep; the forest lies alone, The."
Grasshoppers.
Green Woodpecker's Nest, The.
Hares at Play.
Hen's Nest.
Hesperus! the day is gone.
Hymn to the Creator.
I am: yet what I am none cares or knows.
I Feel I Am[, I only know I am].
I wish I was where I would be.
Invite to Eternity.
I've Had Many an Aching Pain.
July.
June.
Lament of Swordy Well, The.
Lines Written on a Very Boisterous Day in May, 1844.
Little Maid and the Cowslips, The.
Little trotty wagtail [he went in the rain].
London Magazine, 6 151, *sels.*
Lord Byron.
Lord, hear my prayer when trouble glooms.
Lout, The: "For Sunday's play he never makes excuse."
Love's Emblem.
Loves Lives Beyond the Tomb.
Love's memories haunt my footsteps still.
Love's Pains.
Maid o' the West, The.
Married to a Soldier.
Meet Me in the Green Glen.
Milking Shed, The.
Mole-Catcher, The.
Moors, The.
Mouse's Nest.
My Early Home.
My Mary.
Nightingale, The.
No single hour can stand for naught.
Noon.
November.
O could I be as I have been.
Oh sweet is the sound o' the dove's clapping wings.
Old Year's gone away, The.
Pastoral Poesy.
Peasant Poet, The.
Pewits Nest.
Pleasant Sounds.
Ploughboy, The.
Ploughman Singing.
Poets Love Nature.
Rawk o' the autumn hangs over the woodlands, The.
Remember Dear Mary.
Sabbath Bells.
Schoolboys in Winter.
Secret, The.
Secret Love.
Shadows of Taste, *sels.*
She Tied Up Her Few Things.
Shepherd Boy, The.
Shepherd's [or Shepheards] Calendar, The, *sels.*
Signs of Winter, *sels.*
Silent Love.
Silver mist more lowly swims, The.
Solitude.
Song: "I peeled bits of straw and I got switches too."
Song: "I went my Sunday mornings round."

Song: "I would not feign a single sigh."
Song—Last Day.
Song: "Mist rauk is hanging, The."
Song—Molly Magee.
Song: "O Mary sing thy songs to me."
Song: "Soft falls the sweet evening."
Song's Eternity.
Sonnet: "Ere I had known the world and understood."
Spring Morning, A.
Stanzas: "Black absence hides upon the past."
Stanzas: "Passing of a dream, The."
Sudden Shower.
Summer Evening.
Summer Images.
Thrush's Nest, The.
Thunder mutters louder and more loud, The.
'Tis Martinmass, from rig to rig.
To a Bower.
To John Clare.
To John Keats, from His Honored Friend, William Davenant, sels.
To Mary: 'I Sleep with Thee, and Wake with Thee.'
To Mary: 'It Is the Evening Hour.'
To Miss B.
To the Memory of John Keats.
To the Rural Muse, sels.
To the Snipe.
To Wordsworth.
Turkeys wade the close to catch bees, The, sels.
Vision, A.
Vixen, The.
We Passed by Green Closes.
Wheat Ripening, The.
When I was young I fell in love and got but little good on't.
Wind That Shakes the Rushes, The.
Winter Fields.
Winter in the Fens.
Winter Winds Cold and Blea.
Winters Spring, The.
Wish, The, sels.
With Garments Flowing.
Written in a Thunder Storm July 15th, 1841.
Written in Northampton County Asylum.
Written in Prison.
Yellowhammer, The.

Clark, Alan
Limerick: "There was a young lady of Leicester."

Clark, Charles Badger, Jr. (Badger Clark) (1883–1957)
Pioneers.
Plainsmen, The.

Clark, Charles Heber. *See* **"Adeler, Max"**

Clark, J. (*fl.* c.1886)
Maxims in Rhyme for the Young.

Clark, Leonard (1905–88)
August Ends.
Fog in November, trees have no heads.
Ground Elder.
Grumblers.
Singing in the Streets.
Small Birds.
There was a man whose nose was long.

Clark, Martha Haskell
Red Geraniums.

Clark, Mary
Summer, At Home.

Clark, Thomas A. (b. 1944)
Sixteen Sonnets, sels.
Twenty Poems, sels.

Clark, Thomas Curtis (1879?–1953)
Faith for Tomorrow.
Friends.
I am still rich.
Sons of Promise.
Take time to live.
Touch of human hands—, The.

Clark, Tom (b. 1941)
Baseball and Classicism.
Daily News.
Doors.
Eyeglasses.

Going to School in France or America.
Greeks, The.
Like musical instruments.
Like musical instruments / Abandoned in a field.
Mountain Men.
Poem: "Tiny new emotions, The."
Society.
Sonnet: "Orgasm completely, The."
Statue.
Suicide with Squirtgun.
Superballs.
You, sels.

Clarke, Aidan
Journey, The.

Clarke, Austin (1896–1974)
Anacreontic.
Ancient Lights.
Burial of An Irish President.
Civil War, sels.
Envy of Poor Lovers, The.
Fair at Windgap, The.
Forget Me Not.
Her Voice Could Not Be Softer.
Inscription for a Headstone.
Intercessors.
Irish-American Dignitary.
Japanese Print.
Jest, The.
Last Republicans, The.
Lost Heifer, The.
Marriage.
Martha Blake.
Martha Blake at Fifty-one.
Mnemosyne Lay in Dust, sels.
Night and Morning.
Penal Law.
Pilgrimage.
Planter's Daughter, The.
Respectable People.
Scholar, The.
Sermon on Swift, A.
Straying Student, The.
Strong Wind, A.
Subjection of Women, The.
Tenebrae.
Three Poems about Children.
Tiresias, sels.
Wolfe Tone.
Young Woman of Beare, The.

Clarke, Cheryl (b. 1947)
14th Street was gutted in 1968.
Hair: A Narrative.
Kittatinny Tunnel in that holy place you let me hit.
Of Althea and Flaxie.
Older American, The.
Palm Leaf of Mary Magdalene.
Rondeau: "They are bodies left unburied."
San Juan: 1979.
Tortoise and Badger.
Wearing My Cap Backwards.
What Goes Around Comes Around, or The Proof is in the Pudding.

Clarke, Gillian (b. 1937)
Baby-Sitting.
Taid's Grave.

Clarke, James Freeman (1810–88)
Brother, Hast Thou Wandered Far.
Dear Friend, Whose Presence in the House.

Clarke, John
Accounting Cat, The.
Jenny hit me when we met.
Story So Far, The.
There was an old man with a beard.

Clarke, John Cooper (b. 1948)
Evidently Chicken Town.

Clarke, John Henrik (b. 1915)
Determination.
Sing Me a New Song.

Clarke, Joseph I. C. (1846–1925)
Fighting Race, The.

Clarke, LeRoy (b. 1938)
Soucouyant.
Where Hurricane.

Clarke, Macdonold (1798–1849)
In the Graveyard.

Clarke, Marcus (1846–81)
Wail of the Waiter, The.

Clarke, Pauline (b. 1921)
My name is Sluggery-wuggery.

Clarke, Peter
In Air.
Play Song.
Young Shepherd Bathing His Feet.

Clarkson, Laurence (1615–67)
Single Eye All Light, no Darkness, A, sels.

Clary, Killarney (b. 1953)
Unlikely one will guide me; I won't know I'm being helped, An.

Claudian (Claudius Claudianus) (c.370–404)
Claudian's Rufinus: or, The Court Favourite's Overthrow, sels.
De histrice. Ex Claudiano, sels.
Epitaph: "Fate to beauty still must give."
Felix, qui patriis. . . and c.: Imitated from Claudian.
For France.
Lonely Isle, The.
Old Man of Verona, The.
Punishment in Hell.
Sejanus his Fall, sels.
Translation of Claudian's Proserpine, sels.

Clausen, Jan (b. 1950)
After Touch.

Cleage, Pearl (b. 1948)
Confession.

Cleaveland, Elizabeth Hannah Jocelyn (1824–1911)
No Sects in Heaven.

Cleavland, Benjamin (1733–1811)
O Could I Find from Day to Day.

Cleghorn, Sarah Norcliffe (1876–1959)
Golf Links [lie so near The mill], The.

Cleland, William (1661?–1689)
Hallo My Fancy.

Clemens, Prudentius Aurelius. *See* **Prudentius**

Clemens, Samuel Langhorne. *See* **"Twain, Mark"**

Clementelli, Elena
Etruscan Notebook, sels.

Clements, Arthur L. (fl. 20th cent.)
Elegy.
Why I Don't Speak Italian.

Clements, Susan (fl. 20th cent)
Deer Cloud.
Matinee.
Reservation, The.
Susans.

Clemmons, Carole C. Gregory (b. 1945)
Freedom Song for the Black Woman, A.
Ghetto Lovesong—Migration.
Greater Friendship Baptist Church, The.
I'm Just a Stranger Here, Heaven Is My Home.
Love from My Father.
Love Letter.
Revelation.
Spring.

Clemo, Jack R. (b. 1916)
Burnt Bush, The.
Christ in the Clay-Pit.
Growing in Grace.
Mould of Castile.
Neither Shadow of Turning.
On the Death of Karl Barth.

Cleoboulos (d. 6th cent. B.C.)
I am the maiden in bronze set over the tomb of Midas.

Clerk, Sir John, of Penicuik (fl. 15th cent.)
Country Seat, The, sels.
Fane Wald I Luve.

Cleveland, John (1613–58)
Antiplatonic[k], The.
Elegy on Ben Jonson, An.
Epitaph on the Earl of Strafford.
Fuscara, or the Bee Errant.
Mark Antony.
On the Memory of Mr. Edward King, Drowned in the Irish Seas.

Rebel [*or* Rebell] Scot, The, *sels.*
To Julia to Expedite Her Promise.
To Mrs K. T. (Who Asked Him Why He
   Was Dumb).
To the State of Love or The Senses' Festival.
Upon Phillis Walking in a Morning before
   Sun-Rising.

Cleveland, Reginald McIntosh
Destroyers Off Jutland.

Clewell, David
Disappearing.
Goodbye Note to Debbie Fuller: Pass It On.
This Book Belongs to Susan Someone.
We Never Close.

Cliff, Michelle (b. 1946)
History of Costume, A.
Within the Veil.

Clifford, Carrie Williams (1882–1958)
Black Draftee from Dixie, The.

Clifford, George. *See* Ralegh, Sir Walter *and*
George Clifford

Clifford, John (1836–1923)
Anvil—God's Word, The.

Clifford, Sigerson (1913–85)
Ballad of the Tinker's Wife, The.

Clifton, Harry (b. 1952)
Death of Thomas Merton.
Distaff Side, The.
Eccles Street, Bloomsday, 1982.
Euclid Avenue.
Id.
Monsoon Girl.
Polly Perkins.
Seamstress, The.

Clifton, Lucille (b. 1936)
Admonitions.
Anna Speaks of the Childhood of Mary Her
   Daughter.
Astrologer Predicts at Mary's Birth, The.
At Jonestown.
At the Cemetery, Walnut Grove Plantation,
   South Carolina, 1989.
Bodies broken on, The.
C. C. Rider.
Climbing.
Coming of Kali, The.
Crazy Horse Instructs the Young Men But In
   Their Grief They Forget.
Crazy Horse Names His Daughter.
Cutting Greens.
December.
11/10 Again.
Eviction.
February 13, 1980, *sels.*
For de Lawd.
4 Daughters.
Fury.
God Send Easter.
Good Times.
Holy Night.
Homage to My Hips.
How Is He Coming Then.
I am accused of tending to the past.
I am running into a new year.
I Once Knew a Man.
If I Stand in My Window.
If mama / could see.
In Salem.
In the Inner City.
In White America.
Island Mary.
Kali.
Let There Be New Flowering.
Listen Children.
Lost Baby Poem, The.
Love Rejected.
Making of Poems, The.
Malcolm.
Mary.
Mary's Dream.
Message of Crazy Horse, The.
Miss Rosie.
Move.
My Dream About the Cows.
My Dream About the Poet.
My Mama moved among the days.
Night Vision.

Powell (Officer Charged with the beating of
   Rodney King).
Prayer.
Raising of Lazarus, The.
Sam.
Shapeshifter Poems.
She Lived.
Slave Cabin, Sotterly Plantation, Maryland,
   1989.
Song at Midnight.
Song of Mary, A.
Spring Song.
Still / it was nice.
There Is a Girl Inside.
Thirty-eighth year, The.
Those Boys That Ran Together.
To Bobby Seale.
To Joan.
To my Friend, Jerina.
To the Unborn and Waiting Children.
Turning into my own.
Way It Was, The.
What spells racoon to me.
Wishes for Sons.
Woman who loves, A.
Women You Are Accustomed To, The.

Clinton, Michelle T.
Eviction.
Tantrum Girl Responds to Death.

Clive, Caroline
Mother, The.
Old Age.

Close, Eunice
Here We Come a-Haying.
Way to Fairyland, The.

Clough, Arthur Hugh (1819–61)
Across the sea, along the shore.
Amours de Voyage, *sels.*
Bothie of Tober-na-Vuolich, The [A Long-
   Vacation Pastoral], *sels.*
Come home, come home! and where an
   home hath he.
Darkness.
Dipsychus [and the Spirit], *sels.*
Duty—that's to say, complying.
Easter Day. Naples, 1849.
Epi-Strauss-ium.
Genesis XXIV.
I dreamed a dream: I dreamt that I espied.
If to write, rewrite, and write again.
In the Great Metropolis.
Is it true, ye gods, who treat us.
Latest Decalogue, The.
Les Vaches.
Look you, my simple friend, 'tis one of
   those.
Natura Naturans.
Put forth thy leaf, thou lofty plane.
Qua Cursum Ventus.
Qui Laborat, Orat.
Say not the struggle nought [*or* naught]
   availeth.
Sic Itur.
Songs in Absence, *sels.*
Spectator ab Extra, *sels.*
Syringe cloud of aspiration, The.
That there are powers above us I admit.
To spend uncounted years of pain.
What we, when face to face we see.
Why should I say I see the things I see not.

"Clout, Colin." *See* Spenser, Edmund

Clouts, Sydney (b. 1926)
After the poem the coastline took.
Animal Kingdom.
Dawn Hippo.
Earth, Sky.
Firebowl.
Grave's Cherub, The.
Poetry Is Death Cast Out.
Prince Henry the Navigator.
Roy Kloof.
Sea and the Eagle, The.
Sleeper, The.

Clutesi, George (b. 1905)
Beast in Man, The.
Ko-Ishin-Mit Goes Fishing.
Song of the Yellow Cedar Face, A.

West Coast Indian.

Coatsworth, Elizabeth Jane (b. 1893)
And Stands There Sighing.
Bad Kittens, The.
Barn, The.
Circus-Postered Barn, The.
Daniel Webster's Horses.
Lady Comes to an Inn, A.
March.
Mouse, The.
No Shop Does the Bird Use.
Nosegay.
Old Mare, The.
On a Night of Snow.
Open Door, The.
Song of the Rabbits outside the Tavern, The.
Storm, The.
Swallows, The.
Swift things are beautiful.
This Is the Hay That No Man Planted.
Violets, Daffodils.
What Could Be Lovelier than to Hear.

Cobb, Alice S. (b. 1942)
Angela Davis.
Searching, The.

Cobb, Charlie (b. 1944)
"Containing Communism."
For Sammy Younge.
Nation.
To Vietnam.

Cobbett, William
Elegy in Newgate.

Cobbing, Bob
Alphabet of Fishes.
Beethoven Today, *sels.*
Tan tandinanan tandinane.
Worm.

Cochrane, Shirley Graves (b. 1939)
Irish Sweaters.

Cockburn, Alison Rutherford (1713–1794)
Flowers of the Forest, The.

Cockburn, Catherine (1679–1749)
Caution, The.
Vain Advice, The.

Cockrell, Doug
Field Work.
Fist Fight.
His Lunch Bucket.

Codling, Caroline
Assist me while I wander here.

Codrescu, Andrei (b. 1946)
Against Meaning.
Circle Jerk.
Grammar, A.
Imagination of Necessity, The.
Paper on Humor.
Poetry Paper.
Telyric.
Work.

Cofer, Judith Ortiz
Fever.
Unspoken.
What the Gypsy Said to Her Children.

Coffey, Brian (1905–95)
Advent, *sels.*
Cold.
Death of Hektor, The, *sels.*
Headrock.
Missouri Sequence, *sels.*
Muse, June, Related, *sels.*
Nicest Phantasies Are Shared, The.

Coffin, Frank Barbour (1870?–1951)
Ajax' Conclusion.
Harriet Beecher Stowe's Works.
Mother's Songs.

Coghill, Mary
Knowing.

Cogil, Legon *and* **Carlton Barrett**
Dem Belly Full.

Cohan, George M. (1878–1942)
Life's a Funny Proposition after All.
Over There.
You're a grand old flag.

Cohen, Elizabeth
Drive-By Shooting.
#2, Shoes.

Cohen, Jacob (b. 1881)
Eternal Jew, The.
Harp of David, The.
Surely My Soul. . . .
Tirzah.

Cohen, Leonard (b. 1934)
All There Is to Know about Adolph
    Eichmann.
Bus, The.
Elegy: "Do not look for him."
Genius, The.
Heirloom.
I Have Not Lingered in European
    Monasteries.
Killers that run, The.
Kite Is a Victim, A.
Only Tourist in Havana Turns His Thoughts
    Homeward, The.
Out of the Land of Heaven.
Suzanne takes you down to her place near
    the river.
You Have the Lovers.

Cohen, Marc (b. 1951)
Silhouette.
Sometimes in Winter.

Cohen, Robert David
Bones of Incontention, The.
Day on Kind Continent.
Storm, The.
Street of Named Houses, The.

Coicou, Massillon (1865–1908)
Lord's Prayer, The.
Slave's Lament, The.

Coignard, Gabrielle de (d. 1594)
Prayer: "Fear of death disturbs me constantly,
    The."

Cokayne, Sir Aston (1608–84)
Epitaph on a Great Sleeper.

Cokinos, Christopher
Short-Wave.

Cole, Barry (b. 1936)
Men Are Coming Back! The.

Cole, Charlotte Druitt
Christmas Eve.
Clothes-Line, The.
Dormouse, The.
Green Lady, The.
Pimpernel.
Pudding Charms.
Sun and Moon.
Three Mice.
Yellow Fairy, The.

Cole, George Douglas Howard (1889–1959)
Civil Riot, *sels.*

Cole, Henri (b. 1956)
Ascension on Fire Island.
40 Days and 40 Nights.
Prince Enters the Forest, The.

Cole, Henry (1808–82)
Thy Best.

Cole, Joanna (b. 1944)
Happy New Year, Anyway.
Hippopotamus.

Cole, Margaret Isabel Postgate (1893–1980)
Veteran, The.

Cole, Norma
Saturn.

Cole, Peter
Isaac: a Poise.
Where the Honey Speech's Hedge, *sels.*

Cole, Samuel Valentine (b. 1851)
Hammer and Anvil.

Cole, Thomas (1801–48)
Dial, The.
I saw a Cave of sable depth profound.
Lago Maggiore.
Lament of the Forest, The.
Life of Hubert, The, *sels.*
Lines Suggested by Hearing Music on the
    Boston Common at Night.
Painter, A.
Spider.
Voyage of Life, The, *sels.*
Written in Autumn.

Cole, William (b. 1919)
Back Yard, July Night.
Marriage Couplet.
Mutual Problem.
Mysterious East.
Oh, Noa, Noa!
Poor Kid.
Some Sights Sometimes Seen and Seldom
    Seen.
Two Sad.
What a Friend We Have in Cheeses!

Colebatch, Hal (b. 1947)
On the Death of Ludwig Erhard.
One Tourist's Cologne.

Coleman, Anita Scott (b. 1906)
Black Baby.

Coleman, Emily Holmes (1899–1974)
Liberator, The.

Coleman, Horace
Black Soldier Remembers, A.
Downed Black Pilot Learns How to Fly, A.
In Ca Mau.
Night Flare Drop, Tan Son Nhut.
OK Corral East Brothers in the Nam.
Poem for a "Divorced" Daughter.
Remembrance of Things Past.

Coleman, Victor (b. 1944)
Day Twenty-three.
How the Death of a City Is Never More than
    the Sum of the Deaths of Those Who
    Inhabit Its Spaces.

Coleman, Wanda (b. 1946)
African Sleeping Sickness.
American Sonnet (10).
American Sonnet (35).
At the Record Hop.
Aunt Jessie.
Be Quiet, Go Away.
Bedtime Story.
Breast Examination.
Brute Strength.
But, ruby my dear.
Coffee.
Cousin Mary.
Dear Mama (2).
Emmett Till.
Essay on Language.
ISM, The.
Mastectomy.
Today I Am a Homicide in the North of the
    City.
Waif of Echo Park, The.
Women of my Color.

Coleridge, Hartley (1796–1849)
Chaucer, *sels.*
Dedicatory Sonnet to S. T. Colerige.
Donne.
Early Death.
Full Well I Know.
He Lived amidst th' Untrodden Ways.
How Long I Sailed.
Jesus Praying.
Lines: "I have been cherish'd and forgiven."
Long Time a Child.
On the Death of Echo, A Favourite Beagle.
Poietes Apoietes.
Prayer.
She is not fair to outward view.
She was a queen of noble Nature's crowning.
Sonnets to the Seasons, *sels.*
There Lived among the Untrodden Ways.
Think upon Death.
To a Deaf and Dumb Little Girl.
To a Friend.
To a Lofty Beauty, from Her Poor Kinsman.
To Shakespeare.
To William Wordsworth on His Seventy-Fifth
    Birthday.
To Wordsworth.
Why Should I Murmur.
Written on the Anniversary of Our Father's
    Death.

Coleridge, Mary Elizabeth (1861–1907)
At a Friends' Meeting.
Awake.
Blue and White.

Broken Friendship.
'But in that Sleep of Death what Dreams
    may Come?'
Chillingham.
Clever Woman, A.
Contents of an Ink-bottle, The.
Day-dream, A.
Deserted House, The.
Devil's Funeral, The.
Doubt.
Egypt's might is tumbled down.
Fire, the lamp, and I, were alone together,
    The.
Friends—With a Difference.
From My Window.
Gifts.
Gone.
"He Knoweth Not That the Dead Are Thine."
I envy not the dead that rest.
I saw a stable low and very bare.
Impromptu.
In Dispraise of the Moon.
In London Town.
Insincere Wish Addressed to a Beggar, An.
Jealousy.
Lady of Trees, The.
L'Oiseau Bleu.
Marriage.
Master and Guest.
Moment, A.
Mortal Combat.
"My True Love Hath My Heart and I Have
    His."
Nurse's Lament, The.
Only a little shall we speak of thee.
Other Side of a Mirror, The.
Our Lady.
Poison flower that in my garden grew, The.
Punctilio.
Regina.
Shadow.
Solo.
Street Lanterns.
Train, The.
True to myself am I, and false to all.
Unwelcome.
We Never Said Farewell[, nor even looked].
When Mary thro' the Garden Went.
Where a Roman Villa Stood, above Freiburg.
White Women, The.
Whither Away?
Wilderspin.
Witch, The.
Witches' Wood, The.

Coleridge, Samuel Taylor (1772–1834)
All Seasons Shall Be Sweet.
"Angel's like a flea, The."
Answer to a Child's Question.
Apologia pro Vita Sua.
Blossoming of the Solitary Date-Tree, The.
Chamouny; the Hour Before Sunrise. A
    Hymn.
Child's Evening Prayer, A.
Christabel, *sels.*
Cologne.
Composed on a Journey Homeward; the
    Author Having Received Intelligence of the
    Birth of a Son.
Constancy to an Ideal Object.
Day-Dream, The ("If thou wert here, these
    tears were tears of light!")
Dejection.
Devil's Thoughts, The.
Dungeon, The.
Effusions, *sels.*
Egypt's might is tumbled down.
Epitaph on Himself.
Epitaph: "Stop, Christian passer-by!—Stop,
    child of God."
Fears in Solitude, *sels.*
Forbearance.
France.
Frost at Midnight, *sels.*
Fruit Plucker, The.
Good Great Man, The.
Hexameters[; Paraphrase of Psalm XLVI].
Homeric Hexameter, The.

If I had but two little wings.
Knight's Tomb, The.
Kubla Khan; or, A Vision in a Dream.
Limbo.
Lines Written in the Album at Elbingerode,
    in the Hartz Forest.
Love.
Madman and the Lethargist, The.
Metrical Feet.
Modern Critics.
Monody on the Death of Chatterton, sels.
Morning Post, no. 10,614, sels.
My Baptismal Birthday [or Birth-Day].
Ne Plus Ultra.
Nightingale, The, sels.
Ode to Tranquillity.
On Donne's First Poem.
On Donne's Poetry.
On Imitation.
On My Joyful Departure from the Same City.
Pains of Sleep, The.
Phantom.
Picture; or, The Lover's Resolution, The.
Psyche.
Raven, The.
Recollections of Love.
Reflections on Having Left a Place of
    Retirement.
Religious Musings, sels.
Remorse, sels.
Rime of the Ancient Marine, sels.
Rime of the Ancient Mariner, The, sels.
Sonnet to the River Otter.
Sonnets Attempted in the Manner of
    Contemporary Writers, sels.
Sunset, A.
This Lime-Tree Bower My Prison.
Time, Real and Imaginary.
To a Young Friend, &[;on His Proposing to
    Domesticate with the Author&];, sels.
To Nature.
To William Wordsworth.
Truth I pursued, as Fancy sketch'd the way.
Visit of the Gods, The.
W. H. Eheu!.
What is an epigram? a dwarfish whole.
Work Without Hope.
Youth and Age.
Zapolya, sels.

Coleridge, Sara (1802–52)
Blest is the tarn which towering cliffs
    o'ershade.
Father! no amaranths e'er shall wreathe my
    brow.
Garden Year, The.
Phantasmion, sels.
Storm, The.
Trees.

Coles, Don (b. 1928)
Natalya Nikolayevna Goncharov.
Photograph in a Stockholm Newspaper for
    March 13, 1910.

Colesworthy, Daniel C. (1810–93)
Be Never Discouraged.
Little word in kindness spoken, A.
While We Lowly Bow before Thee.

Collier, John (1708–76)
Pluralist and Old Soldier, The.

Collier, Mary (1690?–c.1762)
Womans Labour, an epistle, The.
Woman's Labour; an Epistle to Mr. Stephen
    Duck, The, sels.

Collier, Michael
Cave, The.
North Corridor.

Collier, Thomas Stephens (1842–93)
Cleopatra Dying.

Collins, Anne (fl. c.1653)
Another Song.
Preface to Divine Songs and Meditacions,
    The.
Song.
Song: "My straying thoughts, reduced stay."

Collins, Billy
Dead are always looking down on us, they
    say, The.

Death of Allegory, The.
Tuesday, June 4th, 1991.

Collins, Emanuel (b. 1712?)
Fatal Dream; or, The Unhappy Favourite,
    The.

Collins, John (1742?–1808)
Tomorrow.

Collins, Martha (b. 1940)
Story We Know, The.

Collins, Merle
Because the Dawn Breaks.
Callaloo.
Trapped.

Collins, Mortimer (1827–76)
If life were never bitter.
Lotos Eating.
Positivists, The.
To F. C.

Collins, William (1721–59)
Captain Molly.
Dirge in "Cymbeline."
Epistle, An, Addressed to Sir Thomas
    Hanmer, on His Edition of Shakespeares
    Works, sels.
Ode Occasioned by the Death of Mr.
    Thomson.
Ode on the Poetical Character.
Ode on the Popular Superstitions of the
    Highlands of Scotland, An, sels.
Ode to Evening.
Ode to Fear.
Ode to Simplicity.
Ode Written in the Beginning of the Year
    1746.
Passions; an Ode for [or to] Music, The.
Sonnet: "When Phoebe formed a wanton
    smile."

Collobert, Danielle (1940–1978)
III.

Collop, John (1625–1662?)
Praise of a Yellow Skin, The, or An
    Elizabeth in Gold.

Collymore, Frank A. (1893–1980)
Ballad of an Old Woman.
Monkeys.
Triptych.

Colman, Benjamin (1673–1747)
Another to Urania.
God of My Life!
Poem on Elijahs Translation, A.
Quarrel with Fortune, A.
To Philomela.
To Urania.

Colman, George, the Younger (1762–1836)
London Rurality, sels.
Maid of the Moor, The; or, The Water-
    Fiends, sels.
Miss Bailey's Ghost.
On Sir Nathaniel Wraxall the Historian.

Colman, Henry (fl. 1640)
On Balaam, and His Ass.
On Lazarus Raised From Death.
On Mortality.
On the Inscription Over the Head of Christ
    on the Cross.
On the Strange Apparitions at Christ's Death.
On the Three Children in the Fiery Furnace.

Colombo, John Robert (b. 1936)
How They Made the Golem.
Ideal Angels.

Colonna, Vittoria da, Marchesa di Pescara
(1490–1547)
As a hungry fledgling, who sees and hears.
As When Some Hungry Fledgling Hears and
    Sees.
I live on this depraved and lonely cliff.
I see in my mind, surrounding God.
Like a hungry fledgeling that watches and
    hears.
O what transparent waves, what a tranquil
    sea.
When the Orient is lit by the great light.
When the troubled sea swells and surrounds.

Colum, Padraic (1881–1972)
Book of Kells, The.
Cradle Song,A: "O men from the fields!"

Drover, A.
Fuchsia Hedges in Connacht.
Interior.
Monkeys.
No Child.
Old Soldier.
Old Woman of the Roads, The.
Plower, The.
Poor Scholar of the 'Forties, A.
River-Mates.
She Moved through the Fair.
Wild Ass.

Columbanus, Saint (fl. c.543–615)
Boat Song, A.
Boyhood of Christ, The.

Columcille [or Columba], Saint (fl. c.521–597)
Clamour of the wind making music.
Farewell to Ireland.
If I owned all of Alba.
Invocation, An: "My claw is tired of
    scribing!"
Mary mild, good maiden.
O Son of God, it would be sweet.
On some island I long to be.
Prayer to the Virgin.
Three places most loved I have left.

Columella, Lucius Junius Moderatus (fl 1st
cent. A.D.)
Autumnal Work.

Colvin, Ian D. (1877–1938)
Flying Dutchman, The.
Tristan da Cunha.

Combs, Tram (b. 1924)
Ars Poetica about Ultimates.
Aware Aware.
Just after Noon with Fierce Shears.

Cometas (fl. c.950)
Country Gods.
Phyllis, loving Demophoon.
"Who, tell me, shepherd, owns these rows of
    plants?"

Comfort, Alex (b. 1920)
Atoll in the Mind, The.
Epitaph: "One whom I knew, a student and a
    poet."
Fear of the Earth.
Hoc Est Corpus.
Letter to an American Visitor.
Lovers, The.
Song for the Heroes.
Song of Lazarus, The, sels.

Compiuta Donzella (fl. c.1205)
In the season when the world leafs and
    flowers.
To leave the world and serve God.

Comte de Lautréamont&xbd;
Maldoror, sels.

Conder, Josiah (1789–1855)
Bread of Heaven, on Thee We Feed.
Day by Day the Manna Fell.

Condon, R. D.
Limerick: "Horsewoman of charm at
    Uttoxeter, A."

Cone, Helen Gray ("Coroebus Green") (1859–
1934)
Narcissus in Camden.

Conforti, Gerard John
On the mountain slope.

Confucius (551–479 B.C.)
Airs of Pei, sels.
Chou and the South, sels.
Deer Sing, sels.
Great Digest, The, sels.
Shao and the South, sels.
Songs of Ch'en, sels.
Songs of Cheng, sels.
Songs of T'ang, sels.
Wei Wind, sels.
Yung Wind, sels.

Congreve, William (1670–1729)
Aisle of a Temple, The.
Doris.
False Though She Be [to me and love].
Hue and Cry after Fair Amoret, A.

Lesbia.
Mourning Bride, The, *sels.*
See, see, she wakes, Sabina wakes!
Semele to Jupiter.
Song: "Pious Selinda goes to prayers."
Way of the World, The, *sels.*

Conkling, Grace Hazard (b. 1878)
I will not give thee all my heart.

Conn, Stewart (b. 1936)
On Craigie Hill.
Summer Afternoon.
To My Father.
Todd.
Under the Ice.
Yard is littered with scrap, with axles, The.

Connell, Charles (b. 1910?)
Space Men.

Connolly, Cyril (1903–74)
On Geoffrey Grigson.
On Himself.
To Osbert Sitwell.
Where Engels Fears to Tread, *sels.*

Connor, T. W. (b. 1936)
She Was One of the Early Birds.

Connor, Tony (b. 1930)
Apologue.
Lancashire Winter.
Last of the Poet's Car.

Conoley, Gillian
Heroes, Saints, and Neighbors.
I'd like a little love in the wine-red
Afternoon.
Some Gangster Pain.
Unchained Melody.

Conquest, Robert (b. 1917)
Agents, The.
Appalachian Convalescence.
Bagpipes at the Biltmore.
Excerpt from a Report to the Galactic
Council.
Generalities.
Guided Missiles Experimental Range.
Horror Comic.
Lake Success.
Limerick: "My demands upon life are quite
modest."
Limerick: "Our existence would be that much
grimmer ex-."
Limerick: "Then scorn not the limerick
either."
Limerick: "When a man's too old even to
toss off, he."
Man and Woman.
Progress.
Rokeby Venus, The.
747 (London–Chicago).
To Be a Pilgrim.

Constable, Henry (1562–1613)
Diana, *sels.*
Diaphenia like the daffadowndilly.
On the Death of Sir Philip Sidney.
To God the Holy Ghost.
To Our Blessed Lady.
To Saint Margaret.
To Saint Mary Magdalen.
To Saint Mary Magdalen ("Blessed offender
[*or* offendour], who thyself hast [*or* haist]
tried [*or* try'd].")
To St John Baptist.
To St Mary Magdalen.
To St. Michael the Archangel.
To St. Peter and St. Paul.
To the Blessed Sacrament.
To the Marquess of Piscat's Soul.

Constantinus Cephalus. See Cephalus

Converse, Florence (b. 1871)
Rune of Riches, A.

Convisser, Julie
Over the Pass.

Conway, Hugh (1818–65)
Falkland at Newbury, 1643.

Conway, Jack (1887–1952)
Clothes Make the Man.

Conyus (b. 1942)
Confession to Malcolm.
Day in the Life of. . . , A.

Great Santa Barbara Oil Disaster OR, The.
He's Doing Natural Life.
I rode with Geronimo.
San Francisco County Jail Cell B-6.
Six Ten Sixty-Nine.
Untitled Requiem for Tomorrow.
Upon Leaving the Parole Board Hearing.

Coogler, J. Gordon (1865–1901)
Alas! Carolina!
Alas! for the South.
Byron.
In Memorial.
Mustacheless Bard, A.
Pretty Girl, A.

Cook, C. S.
Limerick: "Famous philosopher, Kant, The."
Limerick: "I was brought up on old
Aristotle."

Cook, Eliza (1818–89)
Idiot-Born, The.
Indian Hunter, The.
Lines / Suggested by the Song of a
Nightingale.
Mouse and the Cake, The.
My Old Straw Hat.
"No!"
Old Arm-Chair, The.
On Seeing a Bird-Catcher.
Our Father.
Sailor's Grave, The.
Song for the Workers, A.
Song of the Imprisoned Bird.
Song of the Modern Time.
Song of the Rushlight.
Song of the Ugly Maiden.
Surgeon's Knife, The.
'Tis well to wake the theme of Love.
To Charlotte Cushman.
To My Lyre.
To the Late William Jerdan.
Try Again.
Where There's a Will There's a Way.

Cook-Lynn, Elizabeth (b. 1830)
Grandfather at the Indian Health Clinic.
Journey, *sels.*
My Grandmother's Burial Ground.

Cook, Mrs. M. A. W (1806–74)
In Some Way or Other the Lord Will
Provide.

Cook, Russell Sturgis (1811–64)
Just as Thou Art.

Cook, Stanley (b. 1922)
APOLLO.
Ark, The.
Boiling an Egg.
Christmas Tree.
Flowers in Town, The.
Gathering Leaves.
Launch, The.
Robin in December, The.
Spring Flower, The.
Wind is a wolf, The.

Cooke, Edmund Vance (1866–1932)
Are You You?
Born without a Chance.
Fin de Siècle.
How Did You Die?
Pass.
Perfect Gift, The.
Plug.
Rags.
What Are You Doing?
You Too.

Cooke, Philip Pendleton (1816–50)
Florence Vane.
Orthone.

Cooke, Rose Terry (1827–92)
Arachne.
Blue-Beard's Closet.
Snow-filled Nest, The.

Coolbrith, Ina (1841–1948)
Captive of the White City.
Longing.

Cooley, Peter (b. 1940)
Alternatives.
Ararat.

Confession, The.
Elect, The.
History of Poetry, The.
Holy Family.
Loom, The.
Macular Degeneration.
Self-Portrait as Van Gogh.
Soul, The.
Vanishing Point.
Zouave, The.

Coolidge, Clark (b. 1939)
Album—A Runthru.
At Egypt, *sels.*
Book of During, IV, The, *sels.*
Brill.
Crack, The.
Crystal Text, The.
Disturbing the Sallies Forth.
Glance in White Space.
Hand Further, The.
In Nora's House with Rilke's Apollo.
Jerome in His Study.
Leaving Rattle Bar.
Manlius to Coeymans.
Noon Point.
Of What The Music to Me.
On Induction of the Hand.
Peru Eye, the Heart of the Lamp.
Rhymes with Monk.
Saturday Night.
Some Glow on the Sill.
Styro.
Tab, The.
This Garden Being: The Hanging of Books.
What is Thought but Won't Hold Still.

**"Coolidge, Susan" (Sarah Chauncey Woolsey)
(1835–1905)**
Charlotte Brontë.
Edenhall.
Measles in the Ark.
New Every Morning.

Cooper, Charles (b. 1948)
Dreams.
Rubin.

Cooper, Dennis (b. 1958)
Being Aware.
Drugs.
My Past.
No God.

Cooper, George (1838–1927)
Baby-Land.
October's Party.
Only One Mother.
What Robin Told.
Wind and the Leaves, The.

Cooper, Jane (b. 1924)
Childhood in Jacksonville, Florida.
Circle, a Square, a Triangle and a Ripple of
Water, A.
Dispossessions, *sels.*
Hotel De Dream.
In the House of the Dying.
Infusion Room, The.
Knowledge That Comes through Experience,
The.
Long, Disconsolate Lines.
March, *sels.*
Morning on the St. John's.
My young mother, her face narrow.
Poem with Capital Letters, A.
Praise.
Rent.
Waiting.
Wanda's Blues.
Weather of Six Mornings, The, *sels.*

Cooper, John Gilbert (1723–69)
Call of Aristippus, The, *sels.*

Cooper, Katherine Bradley *and* **Edith. See
"Field, Michael"**

Cooper, Roger
To See the Cross at Christmas.

Cope, Jack (b. 1913)
Flying Fish, The.
If You Come Back.
Rock Painting.
Sappho.

Sons.

Cope, Wendy (b. 1945)
At 3 A.M.
Bloody men are like bloody buses.
Budgie Finds His Voice.
Depression.
Engineers' Corner.
Exchange of Letters.
Flowers.
From June to December, *sels.*
Giving Up Smoking.
Lavatory Attendant, The.
Limerick: "If Eve hadn't eaten the apple."
Limerick: "That fine English poet, John Donne."
Lonely Hearts.
Mr. Strugnell.
Policeman's Lot, A.
Serious Concerns.
Strugnell's Bargain.
Strugnell's Rubáiyát.
Triolet.
Two Cures for Love.
Uncertainty of the Poet, The.
Usquebaugh.
Valentine.
Variation on Belloc's "Fatigue".
Waste Land Limericks.

Copeland, Benjamin (1855–1940)
Christ's Life Our Code.
Our Fathers' God.

Copenhaver, Laura S. (1868–1940)
Heralds of Christ.

Copland, Robert (fl. 1508–47)
High Way to the Spital House, The, *sels.*

Coppard, Alfred Edgar (1878–1957)
Apostate, The.
Epitaph: "Like silver dew are the tears of love."
Mendacity.
Unfortunate Miller, The.

Copping, Coral E.
Limerick: "Dad waited while Mum bought the ham."

Corben, John
After Christmas.
Before Christmas.
Harlech Castle.
In the eggs.
On The Beach.

Corbet [or Corbett], Richard (1582–1635)
Certain True Woords Spoken Concerning One Benet Corbett after Her Death.
Distracted Puritan, The.
Elegy Upon the Death of His Own Father, An.
Epitaph on Dr. Donne, Dean of Paul's, An.
Great Tom.
Her Boreale, *sels.*
Little lute, when I am gone.
Non Sequitor [or Sequitur], A.
Nonsense [or Nonsense].
On Mr. Rice the Maniple of Christ Church in Oxford.
On the Lady Arabella.
Proper New Ballad, Intitled The Fairies' Farewell, A.
To His Son [or Sonne], Vincent Corbet[t].
Upon Fairford Windows.

Corbett, E. R.
Inventor's Wife, The.

Corbett, Elizabeth T. (fl. c.1880)
Misspelled Tail, A.
Tail of the See, A.
Three Wise Couples, The.
Three wise old women were they, were they.

Corbett, Noel Marcus Francis
Sailing of the Fleet, The.

Corbett, Richard
Proper New Ballad Intituled The Faer Yes Farewell: Or God-A-Mercy Will, A.

Corbett, William (b. 1942)
Cold Lunch.
Vermont Apollinaire.
Wickson Plums.

Corbière, Edouard Joachim. *See* **Corbière, Tristan**

Corbière, Tristan (Edouard Joachim Corbière) (1845–75)
Epitaph: "Of many things adulterate."
Epitaph: "Or many things adulterate."
Litany of Sleep, *sels.*
To the Eternal Feminine.
Toad, The.

Corbin, Alice (Alice Corbin Henderson) (1881–1949)
Harvest, The.
Love at last, or if you will not.

Corbin, Lloyd M., Jr. (Djangatolum) (b. 1949)
Ali.
Ali / Is our prince.
Dedication to the Final Confrontation.

Corcoran, Kelvin (b. 1956)
Apparently in the real past tough men dazzled the illiterate tribes.
Man dances with twelve girls, A.
Nobody Thinks Hard Enough for Poetry.
Slogan Will Not Suffice, A.
Volitionist Economics.

Cordle, Edward (1857–1903)
Lizzie and Joe Catch a Thief.
Lizzie and Joe in Court.
Lizzie Discourses on the Small-Pox.

Corke, Hilary (b. 1921)
Calm Winter Sleep.
Chair, Dog, and Clock.
Choice, The.
Destroying Angel.
Ghost, The.
November Poppies.
Poem at Equinox.
Storm of Love, A.
Waltz, The.

Corkine, William
Sweet Cupid, ripen her desire.

Cormac, King of Cashel (fl. 9th cent.)
Instructions of King Cormac.

Corman, Cid (b. 1924)
Call it a louse—I'm.
Container, The.
Deceased.
Desk, The.
La Selva.
Locus, The.
There are things to be said. No doubt.
Three Tiny Songs, *sels.*
Tortoise, The.

Cormican, P. J. (1858–1945)
True Son of God, Eternal Light.

Corn, Alfred (b. 1943)
Call in the Midst of the Crowd, A, *sels.*
Contemporary Culture and the Letter "K."
Darkening Hotel Room.
Deception.
Infinity Effect at the Hôtel Soubise.
Naskeag.
Navidad, St. Nicholas Ave.
Older Man.

Cornaros, Vizentzos (16th–17th c.)
Erotocritos, *sels.*

Cornelius, Peter (1824–74)
Christmas Tree, The.

Cornford, Adam (b. 1950)
Rapture, The, *sels.*

Cornford, Frances Darwin (1886–1960)
All Souls' Night
At Night.
Autumn Morning at Cambridge.
Avenue, The.
Childhood.
Child's Dream, A.
Coast, The: Norfolk.
Country Bedroom, The.
For M.S. Singing *Fruhlingsglaube* in 1945.
Glimpse, A.
Grand Ballet.
Guitarist Tunes Up, The.
Hills, The.
In the Backs.
Inscription for a Wayside Spring.

Limerick: "How often and often I wish."
Limerick: "There was a young woman who said."
London Despair.
Near an Old Prison.
Nurse.
Ode on the Whole Duty Of Parents.
On August the Thirteenth.
Parting in Wartime.
Peasant Woman, A.
Recollection, A.
Scholar, The.
She Warns Him.
Single Woman, The.
Spring Morning.
Summer Beach.
To a Fat Lady Seen from the Train.
Unbeseechable, The.
Wasted Day, A.
Watch, The.

Cornford, John (1915–36)
Full Moon at Tierz; before the Storming of Huesca.
Letter from Aragon, A.
To Margot Heinemann.

Cornish, Sam (b. 1935)
Black Man, A.
Brother of the Streets.
Cross Over the River.
Death of Dr. King.
Fannie / lou / hamer / never / heard / of.
Frederick Douglass.
Generations 1.
Generations 2.
His Fingers Seem to Sing
Montgomery.
My brother is homemade.
One Eyed Black Man in Nebraska.
Panther.
River, The.
Sam's World ("Sam's mother has.")
To a Single Shadow without Pity.
When / my / grandmother / died.
Your Mother.

Cornish, William (c.1465–c.1523)
Latet Anguis.
Pleasure It Is.
You and I and Amyas.

"Cornwall, Barry" (Bryan Waller Proctor) (1787–1874)
Dramatic Scenes and Other Poems, *sels.*
English Songs, *sels.*
For a Fountain.
Leveller, The.
Sonnet; A Still Place.

Cornwall, Ursula
Sowing Seeds.

Corpi, Lucha (b. 1945)
Dark Romance.
Emily Dickinson.
Winter Song.

Corpus, Aileen (b. 1950)
Blkfern-jungal.

Corrie, Joe (b. 1894)
How Long Has Trane Been Gone.
Image o' God, The.
Miners' Wives.

Corrington, John William (b. 1932)
For a Woodscolt Miscarried.
On the Flesh of Christ.
Second Coming, The.

Corrothers, James David (1869–1917)
At the Closed Gate of Justice.
Indignation Dinner, An.
Me 'n' Dunbar.
Paul Laurence Dunbar.
Snapping of the Bow, The.

Corso, Gregory (b. 1930)
Birthplace Revisited.
But I Do Not Need Kindness.
Dialogue—2 Dollmakers.
Difference of Zoos, A.
Dream of a Baseball Star.
Dreamed Realization, A.
For Miles.
For Miranda.

From Another Room.
Hello.
Hi.
I Held a Shelley Manuscript.
I Met This Guy Who Died.
Love Poem for Three for Kaye & Me.
Mad Yak, The.
Marriage.
New York City—1935.
Notes after Blacking Out.
Ode to Coit Tower.
Paranoia in Crete.
Paris.
Poets Hitchhiking on the Highway.
Reflection in a Green Arena.
Rembrandt—Self Portrait.
Requiem for "Bird" Parker, Musician.
Sea Chanty.
Seed Journey.
Song: "Oh, dear! Oh, me! Oh, my!"
Spontaneous Requiem For the American
    Indian.
Uccello.
Vestal Lady on Brattle, The.
Waterchew!
Whole Mess. . . Almost, The . . Almost,
    The.
Zizi's Lament.

Cortez, Jayne (b. 1936)
For Real.
For the Poets.
Give me the Red on the Black of the Bullet
    (for Claude Reece Jr.)
Grinding Vibrato.
How Long Has Trane Been Gone.
I Am New York City.
I See Chano Pozo.
I'm A Worker.
In the Morning.
Initiation.
Lead.
Lonely Woman.
No Simple Explanations.
Orange Chiffon.
Orisha.
Phraseology.
Pray for the lovers.
Rape.
Rising, The.
Rose Solitude.
So Long.
So Many Feathers.
Solo Finger Solo.
Stockpiling of frozen trees, The.
Suppression.
Tapping.
Under the Edge of February.

Corwin, Norman (b. 1910)
On a Note of Triumph, *sels.*

Cory, David (1872–1966)
Miss You.

Cory, William Johnson (1823–92)
Ballad for a Boy, A.
Dirge: "Naiad, hid beneath the bank."
Heraclitus.
Hersilia.
Mimnermus in Church.
Poor French Sailor's Scottish Sweetheart, A.
Separation, A.

Coslett, Coslett (1834–1910)
Pole Star, The.

Cossins, A. C.
Limerick: "Modest young maiden of Rennes,
    A."

Costello, Louisa (1799–1870)
Songs of a Stranger (1825), *sels.*
Spirit's Song.

Cothi, Lewis Glyn (fl. 1447–86)
Lament for Siôn y Glyn.

Cotter, Joseph Seamon, Sr. (1895–1919)
Algernon Charles Swinburne.
And What Shall You Say?
Answer to Dunbar's "After a Visit."
Book's Creed, The.
Don't-Care Negro, The.
Dr. Booker T. Washington to the National
    Negro Business League.

Frederick Douglass.
Ned's Psalm of Life for the Negro.
On Hearing James W. Riley Read.
Sonnet to Negro Soldiers.
William Lloyd Garrison.

Cottle, Joseph (1770–1853)
Malvern Hills, *sels.*

Cotton, Charles (1630–87)
Burlesque upon the Great Frost, *sels.*
Epitaph on M. H, An.
Evening Quatrains.
Litany: "From a ruler that's a curse."
Madrigal.
Morning Quatrains, The.
On Tobacco.
Resolution in Four Sonnets, of a Poetical
    Question Put to Me by a Friend,
    Concerning Four Rural Sisters, *sels.*
Song: Montrose.
Tempest, The.
To Coelia.
To Poet Edmund Waller, Occasioned for His
    Writing a Panegyric on Oliver Cromwell.
Wonders of the Peak, The, *sels.*

Cotton, John (1584–1652)
In Saram.
Thankful Acknowledgment of God's
    Providence, A.
To My Reverend Dear Brother, M. Samuel
    Stone.

Cotton, John (fl. c.1676)
Bacon's Epitaph, Made by His Man.
Upon the Death of G. B.

Cotton, Nathaniel (1705–80)
Bee, the Ant, and the Sparrow, The.
Contentment.
Early Thoughts of Marriage.
On Lord Cobham's Garden.
To a Child [of] Five Years Old.

Couani, Anna (b. 1948)
Map of the world is felt from the inside.
    Rough around the, The.
Never-Dead, The.
Obvious, The.
What a man, what a moon, what a fish, what
    a chip, what a block.

Coulette, Henri (b. 1927)
At the Telephone Club.
Attic, The.
Black Angel, The.
Correspondence.
Family Goldschmitt, The.
Junk Shop, The.
Night Thoughts.
Postscript.
Sickness of Friends, The.

Courtney, Margaret
Be kind to thy father: for when thou were
    young.

Couto, Nancy Vieira
Living in the La Brea Tar Pits.
Lizzie.
Tea Party.
You Bet Your Life.

Couzyn, Jeni (b. 1942)
Cartography of the Subtle Heart.
Dawn.
Message of the men is linear, The.
My father's hands.
Way towards each other is through our
    bodies, The.
World War II.
You Have Shown Me a Strange Image, and
    We Are Strange Prisoners.

Coverdale, Miles (1488–1569)
Let go the whore of Babylon.
Of the Resurrection.
Song of the Virgin Mary, The.

Coward, Noël (1899–1973)
Any Part of Piggy.
Bar on the Piccola Marina, A.
Boy Actor, The.
Contours.
Convalescence.
Fortitude.
He Never Did That to Me.

Irish Song [Rosie O'Grady].
I've Been to a Marvelous Party.
Let's Do It, *sels.*
Little Ones' A. B. C, The, *sels.*
Mad Dogs and Englishmen.
Mrs Worthington, *sels.*
Room with a View, A.
Stately Homes of England, The.
There Are Bad Times Just around the Corner.
What's Going to Happen to the Tots?

Cowdery, Mae V. (b. 1910)
I Sit and Wait for Beauty.

Cowley, Abraham (1618–67)
Age.
Beauty, thou wild fantastic ape.
Cheer up, my mates, the wind does fairly
    blow.
Christ's Passion.
Chronicle; a Ballad, The.
Country-Mouse, The.
Davideis, *sels.*
Destinie.
Dialogue after Enjoyment.
Drinking.
Epicure, The.
Epicure, The ("Fill the bowl with rosie [or
    rosy] wine.")
Epicure ("Underneath this myrtle shade,
    The"), *sels.*
Epitaph of Pyramus and Thisbe.
Extasie, The.
Garden, The, *sels.*
Grasshopper, The.
Honour.
Hymn: To Light.
In Praise of Hope.
London Subverted by the Furies.
Love.
Mistress, The, *sels.*
Motto, The.
Muse, The.
My Picture.
Ode: Of Wit.
Ode upon Doctor Harvey, *sels.*
On Solitude.
On the Death of Mr. Crashaw.
On the Death of Mr. William Hervey [or
    Harvey], *sels.*
Powers of Darkness.
Resurrection, The.
Swallow, The.
Sylva, *sels.*
34. Chapter of the Prophet Isaiah, The.
To Mr. Hobbes [or Hobs].
To the Royal Society, *sels.*
Tree of Knowledge, The.

Cowley, George
Limerick: "There was a young girl from
    Uttoxeter / Who one dreary night had a
    fox at her."

Cowley, Hannah ("Anna Matilda") (1743–1809)
Blank Verse Written on the Sea Shore.
Departed Youth.
Elegiac Ballad, An.
Invocation. To Horror.
Ode to Della Crusca.
To Della Crusca. The Pen.

Cowley, Malcolm (1898–1989)
Blue Juniata, *sels.*
Danny.
Long Voyage, The.
Nocturnal Landscape.
Piney Woods.
Stone Horse Shoals.

Cowper, Maria Frances Cecelia (1726–97)
On Viewing Her Sleeping Infant.
World Not Our Rest, The.

Cowper, William (1731–1800)
Beau's Reply.
Boadicea: An Ode.
Castaway, The.
Comparison, A.
Diverting History of John Gilpin, The.
Epitaph on a Hare.
Epitaph on Dr. Johnson.
Friendship, *sels.*
Hope, *sels.*

Inscription.
Lines Written During a Period of Insanity.
Lines Written upon a Window-Shutter at
   Weston.
Negro's Complaint, The.
Nightingale and Glow-Worm, The, *sels.*
Olney Hymns, *sels.*
On a Similar Occasion for the Year 1790.
On a Similar Occasion for the Year 1792.
On a Spaniel Called Beau Killing a Young
   Bird.
On an Old Woman.
On Pruning.
On the Ice Islands Seen Floating in the
   German Ocean.
On the Lamented Death of Mrs.
   Throckmorton's Bullfinch.
On the Loss of the *Royal George.*
On the Receipt of My Mother's Picture out
   of Norfolk [the Gift of My Cousin Ann
   Bodham], *sels.*
On the Receipt of My Mother's Picture out
   of Norfolk, the Gift of My Cousin Ann
   Bodham.
Poplar Field, The.
Retirement, *sels.*
Shrubbery, The.
Simple Faith.
Squirrel, flippant, pert and full of play, The.
Stanzas Subjoined to the Yearly Bill of
   Mortality of the Parish of All Saints,
   Northampton; for the Year 1787.
Sweet Meat Has Sour Sauce.
Table Talk, *sels.*
Task, The, *sels.*
Tirocinium; or, A Review of Schools, *sels.*
To a Young Lady.
To Mary.
To Mary Unwin.
To Mr. Newton [on His Return from
   Ramsgate].
To William Hayley, Esq.: In Reply to His
   Solicitation to Write with Him in a
   Literary Work.
To William Wilberforce, Esq.
Truth, *sels.*
Verses Supposed to Be Written by Alexander
   Selkirk during His Solitary Abode on the
   Island of Juan Fernandez.
Winter Morning Walk, The, *sels.*
Work of Gardening, The.
Yardley Oak.

Cox, A. P.
Limerick: "These days, the ubiquitous db."

Cox, Donald S.
Song of the Happy Warrior, The.
To My Mother—1916.

Cox, L. E.
We Thank You!

Cox, Mark
Archaic Torso of My Uncle Phil.
Geese.
In This His Suit.
Poem for the Name Mary.
Sleep Apnea.
Word, The.

Cox, Palmer (1840–1924)
Brownies' Celebration, The.
Lazy Pussy, The.
Mouse's Lullaby, The.

Cox, Samuel K. (1823–1909)
Lord, Thou Hast Promised.

Coxe, Arthur Cleveland (1818–96)
Father, Who Mak'st Thy Suff'ring Sons.
Present Age, The.
Saviour, Sprinkle Many Nations.

Coxe, Louis O. (b. 1918)
From the Window Down.
Lake, The.
Nightsong.
Squaring the Circle.
Winter Night.

Coxon, William W.
Flash Colonial Barman, The.

Crabbe, George (1754–1832)
Birth of Flattery, The, *sels.*
Borough, The, *sels.*

Delay Has Danger.
Inebriety.
Lover's Journey, The, *sels.*
Marriage Ring, The.
Meeting.
My Birthday.
Parish Register, The, *sels.*
Patron, The, *sels.*
Procrastination.
Reflections, *sels.*
Sir Eustace Grey, *sels.*
Tales, *sels.*
Tales of the Hall, *sels.*
Village, The, *sels.*

Cradock, Thomas (1718–70)
What Glorious Vision.

Craig, Alexander (b. 1923)
To His Pandora, from England.
To Pandora.

Craig, Christine (b. 1943)
City Blues.

Craig, John (1512–1600)
O Hear My Prayer, Lord.
O Lord, That Art My God and King.

Craig, Maurice James (b. 1919)
Ballad to a Traditional Refrain.

Craik, Dinah Maria Mulock (1826–87)
Blackbird, The.
Douglas, Douglas, Tender and True.
Friendship.
God Rest You [*or* ye] Merry, Gentlemen.
Now and Afterwards.

Cranch, Christopher Pearse (1818–92)
Bear and the Squirrels, The.
Bird and the Bell, The.
Bird Language.
Cataract Isle, The.
Cornucopia.
Correspondences.
December.
Evening Primrose, The.
Gnosis.
Hours are viewless angels, The.
In the Palais Royal Garden I stood listening
   to-day.
Music.
My Old Palette.
Ocean, The.
Old Cat's Confessions, An.
Pines and the Sea, The.
Seven Wonders of the World, *sels.*
Spirit of the Age, The.

Crane, Frank
Because you care, each task will be much
   lighter.
Today.

Crane, Hart (1899–1932)
Air Plant, The.
At Melville's Tomb.
Black Tambourine.
Bridge, The, *sels.*
Broken Tower, The.
Carrier Letter.
Chaplinesque.
Circumstance, The.
Emblems of Conduct.
Enrich my resignation as I usurp those far.
For the Marriage of Faustus and Helen, *sels.*
Garden Abstract.
Hurricane, The.
Imperator Victus.
In Shadow.
Key West.
Legend.
Mango Tree, The.
My Grandmother's Love Letters.
Name for All, A.
North Labrador.
O Carib Isle!
Passage.
Phantom Bark, The.
Praise for an Urn.
Recitative.
Reliquary.
Repose of Rivers.
Royal Palm.

Sad Indian, The.
Stark Major.
To Emily Dickinson.
To Shakespeare.
Voyages, *sels.*
Wine Menagerie, The.

Crane, Nathalia (b. 1913)
Janitor's Boy, The.
Vestal, The.

Crane, Stephen (1871–1900)
Ay, workman, make me a dream.
Black Riders [and Other Lines], The, *sels.*
Impact of a dollar upon the heart, The.
Little birds of the night.
Little ink more or less!, A.
Man adrift on a slim spar, A.
Naked woman and a dead dwarf, A.
On the horizon, the peaks assembled.
Sage lectured brilliantly, The.
Tell me not in joyous numbers.
There is a grey thing that lives in the tree-
   tops.
There Was a Crimson Clash of War.
There Was One I Met [upon the Road].
There Was Set Before Me a Mighty Hill.
"Think as I think," said a man.
Tradition, thou art for suckling children.
Unwind my riddle.
War Is Kind, *sels.*
You say you are holy.

Crapsey, Adelaide (1878–1914)
Guarded Wound, The.
November Night.
Susanna and the Elders.
Triad.
Warning, The.

Crase, Douglas (b. 1944)
If I could raise rivers, I'd raise them.
Once the Sole Province.

Crashaw, Richard (1613?–1649)
And He Answered Them Nothing.
Answer for Hope.
Apologie for the Precedent Hymnes on
   Tereas, An.
Bulla, *sels.*
But Men loved Darknesse[e] Rather Than [*or*
   Then] Light.
C[h]aritas Nimia; or, The Dear[e] Bargain.
Christ Crucified.
Come See the Place Where the Lord Lay.
Death's Lecture.
Easter Day.
Ecstacy, An.
Epitaph Upon Husband and Wife Who Died
   and Were Buried Together, An.
Epithalamion.
Epithalamium: "Come, virgin tapers of pure
   wax."
Flaming Heart, The, *sels.*
Howres for the Hours of Matines, The.
Hymn in Adoration of the Blessed
   Sacrament.
Hymn to the Name and Hono[u]r of the
   Admirable Saint[e] T[h]eresa, A, *sels.*
Hymne of the Nativity, Sung by the
   Shepheards, A.
I Am the Doore.
In the Glorious Epiphanie of Our [*or* Ovr]
   Lord God[, A Hymn. Svng as by the Three
   Kings].
In the Holy Nativity of Our Lord God, *sels.*
Love's Horoscope.
Music[k]'s Duel[l].
Neither Durst Any Man From That Day Ask
   Him Any More Questions.
Ode, which Was Prefixed to a Little Prayer-
   Book Givin to a Young Gentlewoman, An.
On Marriage.
On Mary Magdalene.
On Mr. G. Herberts Booke, The Temple.
On Our Crucified Lord, Naked and Bloody.
On the Assumption.
On the Baptized Ethiopian.
On the Blessed Virgins Bashfulnesse.
On the Miracle of Loaves.
On the Miracle of Multiplied [*or* Multiplyed]
   Loaves.

On the Name of Jesus.
On the Water of Our Lord's Baptism[e].
On the Wounds of Our Crucified Lord.
Saint Mary Magdalene.
Saint Mary Magdalene or the Weeper.
Samson to His De [or a] lilah.
Tear[e], The.
To Our Blessed Lord upon the Choice of His Sepulchre.
To Our Lord, upon the Water Made Wine.
To the Infant Martyrs.
To the Noblest and Best of Ladies, the Countess of Denbigh, Perswading her to Resolution in Religion, and to render her selfe without further delay into the Communion of the Catholick Church.
Two Went Up into the Temple To Pray.
Upon Bishop Andrewes's [or Andrewes His] Picture before His Sermons.
Upon Lazarus His Teares.
Upon the Asse That Bore Our Saviour.
Upon the Bleeding Crucifix, sels.
Upon the Holy Sepulchre.
Upon the Infant Martyrs.
Weeper, The.
Wishes. To His (Supposed) Mistresse, sels.

Crates (fl. 450 B.C.)
Time's fingers bend us slowly.

Craveirinha, José (b. 1922)
Ode to a Lost Cargo in a Ship Called Save.
Poem of the Future Citizen.
Seed is in Me, The.
Tasty 'Tanjarines' of Inhambane, The.
Three Dimensions.

Crawford, Isabella Valancy (1850–87)
Battle, A.
Camp of Souls, The.
Dark Stag, The.
Said the Canoe.

Crawford, Louisa Macartney
Kathleen Mavourneen.

Crawford, Robert (b. 1959)
Herr-Knit Bunnet, The.
My Iambic Pentameter Lines.
Rain.
Scotland in the 1890s.

Crawford, Roger
Love Song of Tommo Frogley.

Crawford, Vesta Pierce (1899–1983)
Pioneer Woman.

Creedon, Carolyn (b. 1969)
Litany.

Creeley, Robert (b. 1926)
Act of Love, The.
After Lorca.
Again.
Age.
Air: "The Love of a Woman."
All That Is Lovely in Men.
America, you ode for reality!
And.
Awakening, The.
Ballad of the Despairing Husband.
Body.
Bresson's Movies.
Chasing the Bird.
City, The.
Company, The.
Counterpoint, A.
Cracks, The.
Damon & Pythias.
Death of Venus, The.
Door, The.
Edge, The.
Faces, The.
Fancy.
Fathers.
Figures, The.
Fire, The.
Flower, The.
For friendship / make a chain that holds.
For Love.
For My Mother: Genevieve Jules Creeley.
For No Clear Reason.
For W.C.W ("Rhyme is after, The.")
Gift, The.

Gift of Great Value, A.
Here.
Heroes.
Hill, The.
Hole, The.
House, The.
"I Keep to Myself Such Measures.."
I Know a Man.
If you were going to get a pet.
Immoral Proposition, The.
Innocence, The.
Invitation, The.
Invoice, The.
Just Friends.
Kind of Act Of, The.
Kore.
Language, The.
Like They Say.
Man, The.
Marriage, A.
Mazatlan: Sea.
Memory, The.
Memory Gardens.
Moon, The.
Mother's Voice.
Naughty Boy.
Oh No.
People, The.
Place.
Pool, The.
Prayer to Hermes.
Quick-Step.
Rain, The.
Rescue, The.
Rhythm, The.
River wandering down.
Self-Portrait.
She Went to Stay.
Signboard, The.
Sitting Here.
Somebody Died.
Somewhere.
Son: "What I took in my hand."
Song: "Those rivers run from that land."
Song: "What's in the body you've forgotten."
Stairway to Heaven.
Statue, The.
Talking.
They.
Three Ladies, The.
Time.
To and / back and forth.
Token, A.
Turn, The.
Wait for Me.
Waiting.
Warning, The.
Way, The.
Whip, The.
Wicker Basket, A.
Wife, The.
Window, The.
World, The.

Cresson, Abigail
Cloak of Laughter.

Crew, Louie (b. 1936)
Gay Psalm from Fort Valley, A.

Crewe, Robert Offley Ashburton Crewe-Milnes, Marquess of (1858–1945)
Harrow and Flanders.

Crinagoras (b. c.70 B.C.)
Back from the west, back from the war, Marcellus.
Dedication of a Torch.
Eartha my mother's name, now earth.
Epigrams, sels.
Epitaph on an Infant.
Forehead without scalp, dry shell without yolk of eye.
Foul sod covers a bad one here.
From the Greek Anthology.
Here are grapes ready to turn to wine.
How long in these empty thermals near the cold.
Left and right, I toss about my bed.
Linguist parrot flicked his flowery wings, The.

Lucky shepherd, if only on the hill.
On the Death of Cleopatra-Selene.
Roses used to bloom in spring.
Sailing to Italy—fitting out / commissioning—to see the friends.
This longed-for morning here is our sacrifice / to Zeus the finisher, and Artemis goddess of childbirth.
This silver thing I send you for your birthday.
This wingtip feather from a hook-beaked eagle.
Though of white marble and dressed straight.
Though you are sedentary always, though.
Turn on your left side, back to your right again.
Unhappy men, why do we travel so.

Crist, Richard
Dusty pickup, The.
She has gone.

Cristall, Anne Batten (b. c.1798)
Blind Man, The.
Evening, Gertrude.
Morning, Rosamonde.
Song: "Through springtime walks, with flowers perfumed."

Cristofor, Ion
Night Traveller.

Criswell, Cloyd Mann (b. 1908)
Newlyweds, The.

Crites, Lucile (b. 1885)
Folks and Me.

Croasdell, Ann (b. 1889)
Muffin Man, The.

Crocker, T. F. Dillon
To shave, or not to shave? that is the question.

Croft, Julian
D-Zug.
Graffiti.
Greenhalgh's Pub.

Croft, Roy (1919–77)
Love.

Croft, Sally
Blue.

Croly, George (1780?–1860)
Aestuary, An.

Crompton, Hugh (fl. 1657)
Epigram LXVII: Time, the Interpreter.
Epigram VII: Winifred.

Cronin, Anthony (b. 1925)
Apology.
Baudelaire in Brussels.
Elegy for the Nightbound.
For a Father.
Lines for a Painter.
Man Who Went Absent from the Native Literature, The.
Middle Years, The.
R.M.S. Titanic, sels.
Responsibilities.

Cronin, Jeremy (b. 1949)
Group Photo from Pretoria Local on the Occasion of a Fourth Anniversary (Never Taken).
Lullaby: "But who killed Johannes, mama?"
Motho Ke Motho Ka Batho Babang (A Person Is a Person Because of Other People).
Naval Base (Part III), The.
River That FLows through Our Land, The.
To learn how to speak.

Cronwright, Samuel Cron (1863–1936)
Song of the Wagon-whip, A.

Crosby, Fanny (Frances Jane Crosby) (1820–1915)
Blessed Assurance.
Blind but Happy.
Jesus, Keep Me Near the Cross.

Crosby, Frances Jane. See Crosby, Fanny

Crosby, Harry (1898–1929)
Firebrand.
Telephone Directory.
Vision.

Crosland, T. W. H. (1865–1924)
Slain.

Cross, Allen Eastman (1864–1942)
Gray Hills Taught Me Patience, The.
Though Fatherland Be Vast.
Young and Radiant, He Is Standing.

Cross, Jr., Frank A.
Accident, An.
Fifty Gunner, The.
Gliding Baskets.
Rice Will Grow Again.
When Chicken Man Came Home to Roost.

Cross, Mary Ann Evans Lewes. *See* **"Eliot, George"**

Cross, Zora (b. 1890)
Love Sonnets, *sels.*

Crossland, John R. (b. 1892)
Water.

Crossman, Samuel (1624?–1684)
My Song Is Love Unknown.

Croswell, William (1804–51)
Lord! Lead the Way the Saviour Went.

Crouch, Nathaniel (1632?–1725?)
David and Goliath.
Tower of Babel, The.

Crouch, Stanley (b. 1945)
Albert Ayler: Eulogy for a Decomposed
  Saxophone Player.
Blackie Thinks of His Brothers.
Chops Are Flyin.
Like a Blessing.
No New Music.
Revelation, The.
Riding Across John Lee's Finger.
Up on the Spoon.

Crow, Christine
City Park.

"Crow, Nacellai Who Sang of the." *See* **Kākkai Pātiṇiyār Naccellaiyār**

Crow, Steve (b. 1949)
El Alamein.
Louisiana.
Revival.
Songs, *sels.*
Water Song.

Crowe, William (1745–1829)
In evil hour, and with unhallow'd voice.
Lewesdon Hill, *sels.*

Crowell, Albert
Joy of Incompleteness, The.

Crowell, Grace Noll (b. 1877)
Common tasks are beautiful if we.
Courage to Live.
Definition.
Eternal Values.
I have found such joy in simple things.
I think that God is proud of those who bear.
Prayer for a Day's Walk.
Quiet Things.

Crowley, Robert
Of unsaciable purchasers.

Crowne, John (1640?–1703?)
Calisto, *sels.*

"Crowquill, Alfred." *See* **Forrester, Alfred A.**

Croxall, Samuel (1690?–1752)
Sylvia.

Crozier, Andrew (b. 1943)
High Zero, *sels.*
Humiliation in Its Disguises.
Permanent Wave.

Crozier, Lorna (b. 1948)
Last Testaments, *sels.*
Poem for Sigmund.
So this is love, a kind of sad dance.

Crsnaru, Daniela
Lions of Babylon, The.

Cruceius, Annibal
Fair Ursly, in a merry mood.

Cruickshank, Alfred (c.1880–c.1940)
Convict Song, The.
God or Mammon.
Let Us Be Frank.

Cruickshank, Helen B.
Comfort in Puirtith.
Ponnage Pool, The.

Shy Geordie.

Crum, Lady Erskine
"Good Night," Says the Owl.

Crummy, Biddy
Poem to Be Said on Hearing the Birds Sing,
  A.

"Crusca, Della." *See* **Merry, Robert**

Cruz Varela, Maria Elena (b. 1953)
Invocation.
Kaleidoscope.
Love Song for Difficult Times.

Cruz, Victor Hernandez (b. 1949)
ALONE/december/night.
Areyto.
Carmen.
Electric Cop, The.
Energy.
Essay on William Carlos Williams, An.
First Claims Poem.
Going Uptown to Visit Miriam.
Problems With Hurricanes.
Puerta Rica.
Spirits.
Story of the Zeros, The.
Today Is a Day of Great Joy.
Urban Dream.

Crystal, Catherine Nomura
Embroidery.

Csoori, Sandor (b. 1930)
Bachelor, The.
Bullet, A.
Door Creaked Three Times, The.
Everyday History.
Maybe elegies have ruined me.
My Masters.
Postponed Nightmare.
Stranger, A.
Tenant Who Lives in Fire, The.
Thin, Black Band, A.
We were good, good and obedient.

Cu', Lê Văn. *See* **Thù'a Phong**

Cuadra, Angel (b. 1931)
Brief Letter to Donald Walsh (in memoriam).
In Brief.

Cuddihy, Michael
Pendulum, The.
Steps.
This Body.

Cudmore, C. D.
Limerick: "'Active balls?' said an old man of
  Stoneham."

Cudmore, D. H.
Limerick: "Ascetic art student named Josh,
  An."
Limerick: "Ballistical student named Raffity,
  A."
Limerick: "English professor named Brooks,
  An."
Limerick: "There was a young lady at court."

Cuevish, Lucario
Before They Made Things Be Alive They
  Spoke.

Cullen, Countee (1903–46)
Black Majesty.
Brown Boy to Brown Girl.
Brown Girl Dead, A.
Christus Natus Est.
For a Mouthy Woman.
For a Poet.
For a Virgin Lady.
For Amy Lowell.
For Daughters of Magdalen.
Four Epitaphs, *sels.*
From Life to Love.
From the Dark Tower.
Fruit of the Flower.
Heritage.
Incident.
Judas Iscariot.
Leaves.
Litany of the Dark People, The.
Magnets.
Mary, Mother of Christ.
Night Rain.
Only the Polished Skeleton.

Protest.
Saturday's Child.
Scottsboro, Too, Is Worth Its Song.
Shroud of Color, The.
Simon the Cyrenian Speaks.
Song in Spite of Myself.
Tableau.
Timid Lover.
To Certain Critics.
To John Keats, Poet, at Spring Time.
Uncle Jim.
Under the Mistletoe.
Unknown Color, The.
Wind Bloweth Where It Listeth, The.
Yet Do I Marvel.
Youth Sings a Song of Rosebuds.

Cullinan, Patrick (b. 1932)
M. François le Vaillant Recalls His Travels
  to the Interior Parts of Africa.

Cully, Barbara (b. 1955)
Repressed Theme.

Cumbie, Richard
New Jersey Turnpike.

Cumbo, Kattie M. (b. 1938)
Black Sister.
Ceremony.
Domestics.
I'm a Dreamer.
Morning after. . . Love, The.
Nocturnal Sounds.

Cumming, Patricia
Caesura.
Spring.

Cummings, David
Emily's Haunted Housman.
From the Brothers Grimm to Sister Sexton to
  Mother Goose; One Transmogrification.
Sweeney, Old and Phthisic, among the
  Hippopotami.

Cummings, Edward Estlin (1894–1962)
All ignorance toboggans into know.
All in green went my love riding.
All nearness pauses, while a star can grow.
All which isn't singing is mere talking.
Always before your voice my soul.
Am was. are leaves few this. is these a or
Anyone lived in a pretty how town.
As freedom is a breakfastfood.
Being to timelessness as it's to time.
Bigness of cannon, The.
Buy me an ounce and i'll sell you a pound.
Cambridge ladies who live in furnished souls,
  The.
Come,gaze with me upon this dome.
Darling!because my blood can sing.
Faithfully tinying at twilight voice.
First of all my dreams was of, The.
For prodigal read generous.
Four III.
Gee i like to think of dead it means nearer
  because deeper firmer.
God pity me whom (god distinctly has).
Goodby Betty,don't remember me.
Great / man / is / gone, A.
Greedy the people, The.
He as O, A.
Hist / whist / little ghostthings.
How many moments must(amazing each).
I am a little church(no great cathedral).
I am so glad and very.
I carry your heart with me(i carry it in).
I like my body when it is with your.
I / never / guessed any.
I sing of Olaf glad and big.
I thank You God for most this amazing.
I was sitting in mcsoreley's.   outside it
  was New York and beauti- / fully snowing.
I will be / M o ving in the Street of her.
If everything happens that can't be done.
If i have made, my lady, intricate.
If i should sleep with a lady called death.
If in beginning twilight of winter will stand.
If there are any heavens my mother will (all
  by herself) have.
If(touched by love's own secret)we,like
  homing.
If up's the word;and a world grows greener.

If you can't eat you got to.
(Im)c-a-t(mo).
Impression.
IN) all those who got.
In heavenly realms of hellas dwelt.
In Just- / spring when the world is mud-.
In time of daffodils(who know.
It is at moments after i have dreamed.
It may not always be so; and i say.
It was a goodly co.
Item.
It's over a(see just).
L(a.
Ladies and gentlemen this little girl.
Little joe gould has lost his teeth and doesn't
   know where.
Little tree / little silent Christmas tree.
Love is a place.
Love is more thicker than forget.
Maggie and milly and molly and may.
Man who had fallen among thieves, A.
May i feel said he.
May my heart always be open to little.
Me up at does.
Mr u will not be missed.
Mouse)Won / derfully is.
My father moved through dooms of love.
My love / thy hair is one kingdom.
My specialty is living said.
My sweet old etcetera.
Next to of course god america i.
Nine birds(rising / through a gold
   moment)climb.
No man,if men are gods;but if gods must.
No Thanks, No. 70.
No time ago / or else a life.
Nobody loses all the time.
Noster was a ship of swank, The.
Notice the convulsed orange inch of moon.
Now air is air and thing is thing:no bliss.
Now comes the good rain farmers pray
   for(and).
Now does our world descend.
Now is a ship / which captain am.
O by the by / has anybody seen.
O pr / gress verily thou art m.
O sweet spontaneous.
Old age sticks / up Keep.
One Fine Day.
One X.
Out of midsummer's blazing most not night.
Pity this busy monster,manunkind.
Plato told / him.
Plato told / him:he couldn't.
Poem, or Beauty Hurts Mr. Vinal.
Politician is an arse upon, A.
Ponder,darling,these busted statues.
Portrait.
Pretty a day, A.
Purer than purest pure.
Q:dwo / we know of anything which can.
R-p-o-p-h-e-s-s-a-g-r.
Raise the shade.
Right here the other night something.
Salesman is an it that stinks excuse, A.
Season 'tis,my lovely lambs, The.
She being Brand.
Silence / .is / a / looking.
Since feeling is first.
Slightly before the middle of Congressman
   Pudd.
So shy shy shy(and with a).
Somewhere i have never travelled, gladly
   beyond.
Sonnet IV.
Space being(don't forget to
   remember)Curved.
Spring is like a perhaps hand.
Spring omnipotent goddess thou dost.
Stand with your lover on the ending earth.
Sunset.
Than(by yon sunset's wintry glow).
Thanksgiving (1956).
That melancholy / fellow'll play / his
   handorgan.
This little bride & groom are.
Thy fingers make early flowers of.

Twentyseven bums give a prostitute the once.
Two X.
Up into the silence the green.
Way to hump a cow is not, The.
What a proud dreamhorse
   pulling(smoothloomingly)through.
What if a much of a which of a wind.
Whatever's merely wilful, / and not
   miraculous.
When any mortal(even the most odd).
When god lets my body be.
When my sensational moments are no more.
When serpents bargain for the right to
   squirm.
When what hugs stopping earth than silent is.
Wherelings whenlings / (daughters of if but
   offspring of hopefear).
White guardians of the universe of sleep.
Who are you,little i.
Who's most afraid of death?thou.
Why did you go.
Wild (at Our First) Beasts Uttered Human
   Words.
Wind has blown the rain away and blown, A.
YgUDuh / ydoan / yunnuhstan.
You shall above all things be glad and
   young.

Cummins, Evelyn Atwater (b. 1891)
   I Know Not Where the Road Will Lead.
Cummins, James
   Sestina.
Cunard, Nancy
   To Eat To-day.
Cuney, Waring (1906–76)
   Death Bed, The.
   My Lord, What a Morning.
   No Images.
Cunliffe, John
   Alpha-B375-Earth Visitors'
     Guide. . . Section.
Cunningham, Allan (1784–1842)
   Gone Were but the Winter Cold.
   Hame, Hame, Hame.
   John Grumlie.
   Sea-Song, A.
Cunningham, Ed
   Limerick: "As the natives got ready to
     serve."
Cunningham, James Vincent (1911–85)
   Aged Lover Discourses in the Flat Style,
     The.
   Agnosco Veteris Vestigia Flammae.
   All in Due Time.
   Choice.
   Coffee.
   Envoi: "Hear me, whom I betrayed."
   Epigram: "After some years Bohemian came
     to this."
   Epigram: "And what is love?
     Misunderstanding, pain."
   Epigram: "Dark thoughts are my companions.
     I have wined."
   Epigram: "Dear, if unsocial privacies obsess
     me."
   Epigram: "Good Fortune, when I hailed her
     recently."
   Epigram: "Here lies my wife. Eternal peace."
   Epigram: "Here lies New Critic who would
     fox us."
   Epigram: "Homer was poor. His scholars live
     at ease."
   Epigram: "How we desire desire! Joy of
     surcease."
   Epigram: "I had gone broke, and got set to
     come back."
   Epigram: "I who by day am function of the
     light."
   Epigram: "In whose will is our peace? Thou
     happiness."
   Epigram: "Life flows to death as rivers to the
     sea."
   Epigram: "This *Humanist* Whom No Beliefs
     Constrained."
   Epigram: "This is my curse, Pompous, I
     pray."
   Epigram: "Time heals not: it extends a
     sorrow's scope."

   Epigram: "Within this mindless vault."
   Epigram: "You ask me how Contempt who
     claims to sleep."
   Epitaph: "When I shall be without regret."
   Five Epigrams, *sels.*
   For My Contemporaries.
   Friend, on This Scaffold Thomas More Lies
     Dead.
   History of Ideas.
   I married in my youth a wife.
   In innocence I said.
   Interview with Doctor Drink.
   Lady, of anonymous flesh and face.
   Meditation on Statistical Method.
   Metaphysical Amorist, The.
   Montana Pastoral.
   Moral Poem, A.
   Neaera when I'm there is adamant.
   On a cold night I came through the cold rain.
   Pope from penance purgatorial, The.
   Rome.
   Sonnet on a Still Night.
   To a Friend, on Her Examination for the
     Doctorate in English.
   To My Wife.
   To What Strangers, What Welcome, *sels.*
   To Whom It May Concern.
Cunningham, John (1729–73)
   Epigram: "Member of the modern great, A."
   Holiday Gown.
   Miller, The.
   Morning.
   On a Certain Alderman.
Cunningham, Julia (b. 1916)
   Hymn to Joy.
**Cunningham, Nora B. (late 19th/ early 20th
   cent.)**
   Giving.
**Cunninghame-Graham, Robert. See Graham,
   Robert**
Curbelo, Silvia (b. 1955)
   Listening to a White Man Play the Blues.
Curnow, Allen (b. 1911)
   Canst Thou Draw Out Leviathan with an
     Hook.
   House and Land.
   Landfall in Unknown Seas.
   Moro Assassinato, *sels.*
   Polynesia.
   Skeleton of the Great Moa in the Canterbury
     Museum, Christchurch, The.
   Small Room with Large Windows, A, *sels.*
   Spectacular Blossom.
   Tomb of an Ancestor, *sels.*
   Trees, Effigies, Moving Objects, *sels.*
   Wild Iron.
   You Will Know When You Get There.
Curran, John Philpot (1750–1817)
   Deserter, The.
Currey, Ralph Nixon (b. 1907)
   Burial Flags.
   Children Waking: Indian Hill Station.
   Cock-Crow.
   Halo.
   In Memoriam: Roy Campbell.
   Jersey Cattle.
   Landscape of Violence.
   Marrakech.
   Remembering Snow.
   Song: "There is no joy in water apart from
     the sun."
   Ultimate Exile IV.
   Unseen Fire.
   Volubilis, North Africa.
**Currie, Mary Montgomerie Currie, Baroness.
   See "Fane, Violet"**
Currie, Robert (b. 1937)
   Brothers.
   July the First.
Curry, Neil (d. 1965)
   Gardens.
Curtis, Monica
   Limerick: "There were once two young
     people of taste."
Curtis, Simon (b. 1943)
   Satie, at the End of Term.

Curzon, David (b. 1941)
Instructions to a Seed.
Proverbs 6:6.
Tour of Ein Kerem, A.
Cusack, Cyril (b. 1910)
Cross Talk.
Summer Reflection.
Cushing, James (fl. 20th cent.)
Autumn Leaves.
Every Time We Say Goodbye.
Lover Man.
Cushing, William O. (1823–1902)
We Are Watching, We Are Waiting.
Cussons, Sheila
Barn-yard, The.
1945.
Yellow Gramophone.
Cussrooee, Biddy
My Grief on the Sea.
Cust, Henry (1861–1917)
Non Nobis.
Custance, Olive (Lady Alfred Douglas)
Candle-Light.
Hyacinthus.
Masquerade, The.
Peacocks: A Mood.
Statues.
White Statue, The.
Cutler, Bruce
Doing Justice.
Cutler, Julian S.
Through the Year.
Wonderful.
Cutler, William (1812–89)
One Talent, The.
Cutting, Sewall Sylvester (1813–82)
God of the World, Thy Glories Shine.
Gracious Saviour, We Adore Thee.
Cutts, John, Baron Cutts (1661–1707)
Only tell her that I love.
To a Lady, Who Desired Me Not To Be in
Love with Her.
Cynddelw Brydydd Mawr (fl. 1155–1200)
In Praise of Owain Gwynedd.
Petition for Reconciliation.
Poem on His Death-Bed.
Cynewulf (fl. late 7th cent.)
Christ 2, sels.
Dream of the Rood, A.
Elene, sels.
Fates of the Apostles, sels.
Juliana, sels.
Riddles (Exeter Book), sels.
Cyrillus
Two-line epigram is perfect, A. Step.
Czapla, Cathy Young
Carpenter's Daughter.
Czechowski, Heinz
Walk Through the City.
Czerkawska, Catherine Lucy (b. 1950)
Thread.

D

"D., H." See Doolittle, Hilda
Da Costa, Maria Velho. See Three Marias, The
Da Ponte, Lorenzo (1749–1837)
Don Giovanni, sels.
Il Capriccio Dramatico, sels.
Da Todi, Jacopone (1228–1306)
Stabat Mater, The.
Dabydeen, Cyril (b. 1945)
Dubious Foreigner.
Fat Men, The.
Fruit of the Earth.
Husband, The.
Patriot.
Rehearsal.
Words and Legacy.
Dabydeen, David (b. 1955)
Catching Crabs.
Coolie Mother.

Coolie Odyssey.
Coolie Son.
Men and Women.
Miranda.
Slave Song.
Dacey, Florence
Farewell: "I search / for the straight path."
Dacey, Philip (b. 1939)
Birthday, The.
Form Rejection Letter.
How I Escaped from the Labyrinth.
Looking at Models in the Sears Catalogue.
Obscene Caller, The.
Porno Love.
Prisms.
Small Dark Song.
Thumb.
Dach, Simon (1605–59)
Bonds of Friendship, The.
Lamentation during His Most Painful Illness.
On the Entrance of the Castle Bridge.
To Be Read above the Castle-Gate, When
His Princely Highness Rode in to His
Marriage Bed.
**Dacre, Charlotte ("Rosa Matilda") (1782–
c.1841)**
Female Philosopher, The.
Hours of Solitude, sels.
Kiss, The.
Power of Love, The.
Sappho; or, The Resolve.
Similie.
To Him Who Says He Loves.
Dadié, Bernard (b. 1916)
Dry Your Tears, Africa!
Hands.
I Give You Thanks My God.
I thank you, Lord, for having made me
Black.
In Memoriam.
Ode to Africa.
World to Come, A.
Wreath for Africa, A.
Dafydd [or David] ab Edmwnd (fl. 1450–80)
Girl's Hair, A.
Dafydd [or David] ap Gwilym (fl. 1340–70)
Cywdd to Morvydd, The.
Girls of Llanbadarn, The.
In Morfudd's Arms.
May.
Mis Mai, sels.
Rattle Bag, The.
Ruin, The.
Seagull, The.
Wind, The.
Woodland Mass, The.
**Dafydd [or David] Bach ap Madog Wladaidd
(fl. 1340–90)**
Christmas Revel, A.
Dafydd [or David] Benfras (d. 1257)
From Exile.
Dafydd [or David] Nanmor (fl. 1450–80)
Ode to Rhys ap Maredudd of Tywyn.
Daglarca, Fazil Hüsnü (b. 1914)
Cats.
Fire.
Hollow Echo.
Thought.
Unity.
D'Aguiar, Frederick (b. 1960)
Airy Hall's Exits.
Cow Perserverance, The.
Letter from Mama Dot.
Mama Dot's Treatise.
On Duty.
Dahlberg, Edward (1900–1977)
Kansas City West Bottoms.
Đai, Lê Phu'ó'c. See Phỗ Đú'c
Daiches, David (b. 1912)
Notes for a History of Poetry.
To Kate, Skating Better than Her Date.
Ulysses' Library.
Winter Song.
Daihaku, Princess
How will you manage. From Manyo Shu,
Parts 2 of 4.

Daijiu, Nyūdo Saki no Dajō. See Kintsune
Daini no Sanmi (fl. 10th–11th cent.)
From Mt. Arima / over the bamboo plains of
Ina.
Dainty, Evelyn
Birds on the School Windowsill, The.
Daive, Jean (b. 1941)
I rise from the depths of my resemblance.
Lost in contemplation of its end.
Nomad, A.
She does not move. Takes the man's.
Space instead of furniture.
Under the wind I saw.
Woman measures, A.
Dalcour, Pierre
Verse Written in the Album of Mademoiselle.
Dale, Langham (1826–98)
Prejudice against Colour.
Dale, Peter (b. 1938)
Fragments, The, sels.
Daley, Frank (b. 1940)
Piano, The.
Daley, Victor James (1858–1905)
Dove, The.
Lachesis.
Mother Doorstep.
Tall Hat.
Vision of Sunday in Heaven, A.
When London Calls.
Woman, at the Washtub, The.
Dali, Salvador (1904–89)
Art of Picasso, The.
Great Masturbator, The.
Dallán Forgaill (fl. 6th? cent.)
Poem in Praise of Colum Cille, A.
Dallas, Sir George (1758–1833)
India Guide, The; or, Journal of a Voyage to
the East Indies in 1780, sels.
Dallas, Ruth (b. 1919)
Girl with Pitcher.
In the Giant's Castle.
Letter to a Chinese Poet, sels.
Milking before Dawn.
Photographs of Pioneer Women.
Telemachus with a Transistor.
Dalmon, Charles (b. 1872)
Early Morning Meadow Song.
Sussex Legend, A.
Dalton, Henry
Emigrant Ship, The.
Dalton, John (1709–63)
Descriptive Poem, Addressed to Two Ladies
at Their Return from Viewing the Mines,
near Whitehaven, A, sels.
Dalton, Roque
Love Poem.
My Neighbor.
Daly, John Jay (1888–1976)
Toast to the Flag, A.
Daly, Thomas Augustin (1871–1948)
Mia Carlotta.
Pennsylvania Places.
Đàm, Đỗ thi. See Tu'o'ng Phỗ
Damagetus (fl.3d cent.B.C.)
Epitaph of a Sailor.
In the name of the God of strangers, we beg
you.
On the Tomb of Orpheus.
Damas, Léon (b. 1912)
Black Man's Lament, The.
Blues.
Et Cetera.
Hiccups.
Just Like the Legend.
Obsession.
Position.
Put Down.
Reality.
S.O.S.
Sell Out.
Shine.
Sleepless Night.
So often my feeling of race.
Their Thing.

There are nights with no name.
They came that night as the.
They Came This Evening.
Whitewash.

Damaskius (*fl.* c.529)
Zosimé was a slave in body only.

D'Ambrosio, Charles (*fl.* 20th cent.)
Morning.

Dame, Enid
Lilith.
On the road to Damascus, Maryland.
Seder, The.

Damian, Peter (1007–72)
Paradise.
Who is this.

Damocharis of Kos (Damocharis Grammaticus)
(*fl.* 6th cent.)
Lead disc composed of black stuff for
marking, A.

Dana, Mary Stanley Bunce (1810–83)
O Sing to Me of Heaven.

Dana, Richard Henry (1787–1879)
Chanting Cherubs, The [A Group by
Greenough].
Daybreak.
Dying Raven, The.
Husband's and Wife's Grave, The.
Pleasure Boat, The [*or* Pleasure-Boat, The].

Dana, Robert Patrick (b. 1929)
At the Vietnam War Memorial, Washington,
D. C.
Elegy for the Duke.
Winter's Tale, A.

Dance, James (1722–74)
Cricket; an Heroic Poem, *sels.*

Dancer, John (*fl.* 1660–1707)
Variety, The.

Dandridge, Ray Garfield (1882–1930)
Time to Die.
Zalka Peetruza.

Danforth, John (1660–1730)
Few Lines to Fill up a Vacant Page, A.
Mercies of the Year, The.
On My Lord Bacon.
Poem upon the Triumphant Translation
of. . . Mrs. Anne Eliot, A.
Profit and Loss: An Elegy upon the Decease
of Mrs. Mary Gerrish.
Two Vast Enjoyments Commemorated.

Danforth, Samuel (1626–74)
Almanac Verse.
Awake yee westerne nymphs, arise and sing.

Danforth, Samuel, Jr. (1666–1727)
Ad Librum.
Elegy in Memory of the Worshipful Major
Thomas Leonard Esq, An.

Đằng Phu'o'ng
Day of Mourning at Yên-Báy, The.
To Nguyễn Du.

Đặng Thái Thuyên (1897–1931)
Contrasts.

**Đặng Tr&acircgrv;n Côn (1710–1745) *and*
Phan Huy Ich (1750–1822)**
Song of a Soldier's Wife, The.

Daniel, George (1616–57)
After a Storm, Going a Hawking.
Landscape, The.
One Desiring Me to Read, But Slept It Out,
Wakening.

Daniel, H. J. (1818–89)
My Epitaph.

Daniel, John
Moment.
To Mt. St. Helens.

Daniel, Robert T. (1773–1840)
Time Will Surely Come, The.

Daniel, Samuel (1562–1619)
Civil Wars, The, *sels.*
Cleopatra, *sels.*
Complaint of Rosamond, The, *sels.*
Delia, *sels.*
Epistle. To Prince Henrie], *sels.*
Go wailing verse, the infants of my love.
Hymen's Triumph, *sels.*

Musophilus; or, Defence of All Learning,
sels.
Ode: "Now each creature joys the other."
Tethy's Festival, *sels.*
To Delia, *sels.*
To The Lady Lucie, Countesse of Bedford.
To the Lady Margaret, Countess [*or*
Countesse] of Cumberland.
Ulysses and the Siren [*or* Syren].

**Daniel, Yuly [*or* Iuliï] Markovich ("Nikolai
Arzhak") (1925–88)**
House, A.
New Year March: A Declaration, The.
Sentence, The.
To My Friends.
You stand beside me here, each day and
every hour.

Daniells, Roy (b. 1902)
Journey.

Daniels, Jim
Day of the Two Bodies.
Time, Temperature.

Daniels, Kate (b. 1953)
Bathing.
Bus Ride.
Christmas Party.
Ethiopia.
For Miklos Radnóti: 1909-1944.
Lying Down.
My Father's Desk.
Not Singing.
Women's Room in Pennsylvania Station, The.

Danner, Margaret (b. 1915)
And through the Caribbean Sea.
At Home in Dakar.
Best Loved of Africa.
Convert, The.
Elevator Man Adheres to Form, The.
Far from Africa: Four Poems, *sels.*
Goodbye David Tamunoemi West.
Grandson Is a Hoticeberg, A.
Painted Lady, The.
Rhetoric of Langston Hughes, The.
Sadie's Playhouse.
Slave and the Iron Lace, The.
This Is an African Worm.

D'Annunzio, Gabriele (1863–1938)
Rain in the Pine Wood.

Dante Alighieri (1265–1321)
Ballata: He Will Gaze upon Beatrice.
Canzone: He Beseeches Death for the Life of
Beatrice.
Divina Comedia, *sels.*
Divina Commedia, *sels.*
First Canzone of the Convito, The.
La Vita Nuova, *sels.*
New love and the gentle heart are the same
thing.
Of the Lady Pietra degli Scrovigni.
So gentle and so virtuous she appears.
Sonnet: "Guido, I wish that you and Lapo
and I."
Sonnet: Of Beatrice de' Portinari, on All
Saints' Day.
Sonnet: Of Beauty and Duty.
Sonnet: On the 9th of June 1290.
Sonnet: To Brunetto Latini.
Sonnet: To Certain Ladies; When Beatrice
Was Lamenting Her Father's Death.
Sonnet: To Guido Cavalcanti.
Sonnet: To the Lady Pietra degli Scrovigni.
Sonnet: To the Same Ladies; With Their
Answer.
To waning day, to the wide round of shadow.

Dante da Maiano (*fl.* c.1300)
Sonnet: He Craves Interpreting of a Dream of
His.
To Dante Alighieri: He Interprets Dante
Alighieri's Dream.

D'Anvers, Alicia (1688?–1725)
Academia; or The Humours of the University
of Oxford, *sels.*

"Dao, Bei." *See* Zhenkai, Zhao

Đào Duy Kỳ (b. 1916)
At Condore Port.

Đào Duy Từ' (1572–1634)
Where gather mists and clouds, a happy
world.

D'Arcos, Joaquim Paço
Re-encounter.

D'Arcy, Hugh Antoine (1843–1925)
Face upon [*or* on] the Floor, The.

Dare, Joan
Limerick: "Cleric once heard with dismay,
A."

**"Dario, Rubén" (Félix Rubén García
Sarmiento) (1867–1916)**
Alleluya.
Far Away and Long Ago.
Three Kings, The.
To Columbus.
To Roosevelt.
Victory of Samothrace, The.

Darley, George (1795–1846)
Dove's Loneliness, The.
Elfin Pedlar, The.
Ethelstan, *sels.*
Fallen Star, The.
Labours of Idleness by Guy Penseval, The,
sels.
Lilian's Song.
Nepenthe, *sels.*
Pass of Death, The.
Rebellion of the Waters, The.
Serenade of a Loyal Martyr.
Song, A: "It is not Beauty [*or* beautie] I
demand[e]."
Sylvia; or, The May Queen, *sels.*
Syren Songs, *sels.*
To Helene.
To Mie Tirante.
To Poets.

**Darnley, Henry Stuart [*or* Stewart], Lord
(1545–67)**
Gife Langour.
To the Queen.

Darr, Ann (b. 1920)
At Sixteen.

Darragh, Tina (b. 1950)
Footnote at "Figure of Speech."
Lattice at "Split."
Lattice at/of (Com)pare (Dis)pair.
"Legion" to "Lent" for "R."
"Luteous" to "Lymph" for "F."
Sis Boom Ba.
Throwing Out at / of (Com)pare (Dis)pair, A.
Volcanic tuff.

Darring, Walter
Surprised by Me.

Daruwalla, Keki N. (b. 1937)
Of Mohenjo Daro at Oxford.

Darwin, Erasmus (1731–1802)
Botanic Garden, The, *sels.*
Poppy, The.
Visit of Hope to Sydney Cove, near Botany-
Bay.

Darwish, Mahmoud (b. 1942)
Earth Poem.
Guests on the sea: Our visit is short.
Identity Card.
On Wishes.
Poems after Beirut, *sels.*
Prison.
Psalm 2.
Sirhan Drinks His Coffee in the Cafeteria.
Steps in the Night.
Victim Number 48.
We walk towards a land not of our flesh.
Words.

Daryush, Elizabeth (1887–1976)
Anger Lay by Me All Night Long.
Children of wealth in your warm nursery.
How on Solemn Fields of Space.
If your loved one prove unworthy, why then.
Invalid Dawn.
It is pleasant to hang out.
Look, The.
Off Duty.
Still-Life.
Subalterns.
Throw Away the Flowers.

You should at times go out.

Das, Jagannath Prasad (b. 1936)
Corpse, The.

Das, Jibanananda (1899–1954)
In Camp.

Das, Kamala (b. 1934)
Hot Noon in Malabar.
House-Builders, The.
Introduction: "I don't know politics but I
know the names."

Das, Mahadai
Growing Tip, The.
Horses.
Leaf in His Ear, The.
Learner.

Dasgupta, Pranabendu (b. 1937)
Man: 1961.

Dash, Jacqueline (b. 1955)
Me Again.

Date, J. C. B.
Limerick: "Though your dreams may seem
normal and right."
Limerick: "To Algebra God is inclined."

Dậu, Nguyễn. *See* **Hậu Điền**

Dauenhauer, Nora (b. 1927)
Kelp.
Skiing on Russian Christmas.
Tlingit Concrete Poem.
Voices.

Daumal, René (1908–44)
Clavicles for a Great Poetic Game, *sels.*
Jesus before Pilate said nothing.
Persephone That Is to Say Double Issue.
Short Revelation Concerning Death and
Chaos.
St. Matthew, *sels.*

**Davenant [or D'Avenant], Sir William (1606–
68)**
Aubade: "Lark now leaves his watery [or
wat'ry] nest, The."
Christian's Reply to the Philosopher, The,
sels.
Countess of Anglesey lead Captive by the
Rebels, at the Disforresting of Pewsam,
The.
Endimion Porter and Olivia.
For the Lady Olivia Porter; a Present upon a
New Year's Day.
Gondibert, *sels.*
Gondibert Book 2, *sels.*
Law against Lovers, The, *sels.*
Lover and Philosopher.
O thou that sleep'st like pig in straw.
Soldier Going to the Field, The.
'Tis, in good truth, a most wonderful thing.
To the Queen[e], Entertain[e]d at Night by
the Countess[e] of Anglesey.
Under the Willow Shades.
Winter Storms, The.

Davenport, Robert (*fl.* 1624–40)
Sacrifice, A.

Davey, Frank (b. 1940)
She'd Say.

David ben Meshullam (*fl.* Middle Ages)
Be Not Silent.

David, John (1761–1841)
What Happiness Can Equal Mine.

Davidson, Donald (1893–1968)
Hermitage, *sels.*
Immigrant, The.
In Blue-Stocking Hollow.
Lee in the Mountains.
Lines for a Tomb.
Lines Written for Allen Tate on His Sixtieth
Anniversary.
On a Replica of the Parthenon.
Randall, my son, before you came just now.
Redivivus.
Refugees.
Sanctuary.
Sequel of Appomattox.
Twilight on Union Street.
Utterance.

Davidson, Francis (b. 1905)
Beggars.

Davidson, John (1857–1909)
Ballad of a Nun, A.
Ballad of Hell, A.
Battle.
Crystal Palace, The.
Holiday at Hampton Court.
In a Music-Hall.
In Romney Marsh.
In the Isle of Dogs.
London.
New Year's Eve, *sels.*
Northern Suburb, A.
Price, The.
Runnable Stag, A.
Snow.
Song: "Boat is chafing at our long delay,
The."
Thirty Bob a Week.
To the Street Piano, *sels.*
Unknown, The.
War Song.

Davidson, L. A.
Beyond stars.
In the dark lobby.
It is growing dark.
On my return.
Silent crowd, The.

Davidson, Lucretia (1808–25)
America.

Davidson, Michael (b. 1944?)
Century of Hands.
Dream Dream, The.
Et in Leucadia Ego.
Feeling Type and His Friends, The.
Form of Chiasmus; The Chiasmus of Forms,
The.
Framing.
Landing of Rochambeau, The.
Sensation Type and His Friends, The.
Thinking the Alps.
Troth.

Davidson, R. R.
Gravy Train, The.

Davie, Donald (1922–95)
Across the Bay.
Autumn Imagined.
Barnsley and District.
Christening, A.
Devil on Ice.
Forests of Lithuania, The, *sels.*
Fountain, The.
G. M. B.
Gardens No Emblems.
Hearing Russian Spoken.
Heigh-ho on a Winter Afternoon.
Horae Canonicae, *sels.*
In California.
Life of Service, The.
Meeting of Cultures, A.
On Bertrand Russell's "Portraits from
Memory."
Ox-Bow.
Pilate.
Priory of St Saviour, Glendalough, The.
Prose for Des Esseintes.
Rejoinder to a Critic.
Remembering the 'Thirties.
Rousseau in His Day.
Thanks to industrial Essex.
Time Passing, Beloved.
To a Teacher of French.
Wind at Penistone, The.
Winter Talent, A.
With the Grain.
Year 1812, The.

Davies, Alan (b. 1951)
Name, *sels.*
New Sentience, The.
Outer Layers of Nervousness, The.
Thirty East Forty-Second Street.

Davies, Arthur
West Paddocks.

Davies, Edward (1718–89)
Chepstow: A Poem, *sels.*
Wily Fox, The.

Davies, Frank
Limerick: "Giraffes, yes, even the strongest."

Davies, Gareth Alban (b. 1926)
Dance, The.

Davies, Gloria Evans (b. 1932)
Her Name like the Hours.

Davies, Hugh Sykes (1909–84)
Music in an Empty House.
Poem: "In the stump of the old tree, where
the heart has rotted out."
Poem: "It doesn't look like a finger it looks
like a feather of broken glass."

Davies, Idris (1905–53)
Consider Famous Men, Dai Bach.
Do You Remember 1926?
High Summer on the Mountains.
Lay Preacher Ponders, The.
Mrs. Evans Fach, You Want Butter Again.

Davies, J. Kitchener (1902–52)
Sound of the Wind That Is Blowing, The,
sels.

Davies, Sir John (1569–1626)
Contention between Four Maids Concerning
That Which Addeth Most Perfection to
That Sex.
Contention betwixt a Wife, a Widow, and a
Maid, A.
Dedications [or Orchestra], *sels.*
Epigrams, *sels.*
Faith (wench) I cannot court thy sprightly
eyes.
Gulling[e] Sonnets, The, *sels.*
In Francum.
In Fuscum.
In Librum.
Muse Reviving, The.
Nosce Teipsum, *sels.*
Of Human Knowledge, *sels.*
On a Pair of Garters.
On the Deputy of Ireland's Child.
Orchestra; or, A Poem[e] of Da[u]ncing, *sels.*
Sonnets to Philomel, *sels.*
To him with trumpets and with flutes.
To His Lady.

Davies, John, of Hereford (c.1565–1618)
Against Gaudy-Bragging-Undoughty Daccus.
Against Proud Poor Phryna.
Holy Rood, The, *sels.*
Of Kate's Baldness.
Remembrance of My Friend Mr. Thomas
Morley, A.
Scourge of Folly, The, *sels.*
Sonnet: "So shoots a star as doth my mistress
glide."
Wit's Pilgrimage, *sels.*

Davies, Mary Carolyn
Day before April, The.
Fishing Pole, The ("Fishing pole's a curious
thing, A.")
If I had known what trouble you were
bearing.
Let Me Be a Giver.
Love Song: "There is a strong wall about me
to protect me."
Man's Woman, A.
Prayer for Every Day, A.
To give one's life through eighty years is
harder.
Vow for New Year's, A.

Davies, Russell (b. 1946)
Book Review.

Davies, Samuel (1723–61)
Eternal Spirit, Source of Light.
Lord, I Am Thine.
While o'er Our Guilty Land, O Lord.

Davies, Sneyd (1709–69)
Scene after Hunting at Swallowfield in
Berkshire, A.
Voyage to Tintern Abbey, A, *sels.*

Davies, T. Glynne (b. 1926)
Caernarfon, 2 July 1969.
Old Man in a Moon Loft.
Sentences While Remembering Hiraethog.

Davies, Walter (1761–1849)
Nightfall.
To W.S.—On his Wonderful Toys.

Davies, William Henry (1871–1940)
All in June.

Ambition.
Beautiful, The.
Best Friend, The.
Bird of Paradise, The.
Birds of Steel, The.
Black Cloud, The.
Bright Day, A.
Cat, The.
Child and the Mariner, The.
Child's Pet, A.
D is for Dog.
Days Too Short.
Dog was there, outside her door, The.
Dream, A.
Dumb World, The.
Early Morn.
Elements, The.
Example, The.
Fleeting Passion, A.
Flirt, The.
Great Time, A.
Greeting, A.
Heap of Rags, The.
Her Merriment.
Her Mouth and Mine.
Hermit, The.
Hill-Side Park, The.
Hour of Magic, The.
I Am the Poet Davies, William.
Inquest, The.
Jenny Wren.
Joy and Pleasure.
Kingfisher, The.
Kitty and I.
Leaves.
Leisure.
Mind's Liberty, The.
Money.
Moon, The.
Moon and a Cloud, The.
Nailsworth Hill.
No Man's Wood.
Oh, Sweet Content.
Rain, The.
Rat, The.
Rich Days.
School's Out.
Sea, The.
Sheep.
Sluggard, The.
Songs of Joy.
Sweet Stay-at-Home.
To a Lady Friend.
Truly Great.
Truth, The.
Two Stars, The.
Villain, The.
Visitor, The.
When I in praise of babies speak.
When Yon Full Moon.
White Horse, The.
White Sheep.

Davis, Abijah (1763–1817)
Blest Is the Man Whose Tender Breast.

Davis, Andra
From Him.

Davis, Catherine (b. 1924)
Belongings.
Kindness.
Out of Work, Out of Touch, Out of Sorts.
Years, The.

Davis, Daniel Webster (1862–1913)
Aunt Chloe's Lullaby.
I Can Trust.
Linin' ub De Hymns, De.
Miss Liza's Banjer.
My Childhood's Happy Days.
Negro Meets to Pray, The.
Nigger's Got to Go, De.

Davis, Dick (b. 1945)
Childhood of a Spy.
6 A.M. Thoughts.

Davis, Frank Marshall (b. 1905)
Arthur Ridgewood, M.D.
Flowers of Darkness.
Four Glimpses of Night.
Giles Johnson, Ph.D.

I Sing No New Songs.
Jazz Band.
Robert Whitmore.
Snapshots of the Cotton South.

Davis, Harold Lenoir (1896–1960)
Stalks of Wild Hay.

Davis, Jack (b. 1917)
Day Flight.
Desolation.
First-born, The.
One Hundred and Fifty Years.
Warru.

Davis, Laura
Things You Gave Me, *sels.*

Davis, Lloyd
Bob Hosey Is Dead.

Davis, Olena Kalytiak
Thirty Years Rising.

Davis, Ozora Stearns (1866–1931)
At Length There Dawns the Glorious Day.

Davis, Robert H. (b. 1954)
At the Door of the Native Studies Director.
Black Buoy.
Raven is Two-Faced.
Raven Tells Stories.

Davis, Thadious M. (b. 1944)
Asante Sana, Te Te.
Double Take at Relais de L'Espadon.
"Honeysuckle Was the Saddest Odor of All, I Think."
It's All the Same.
Remembering Fannie Lou Hamer.

Davis, Thomas Osborne (1814–45)
Girl I Left behind Me, The.
Lament for the Death of Eoghan Ruadh O'Neill.
Nation Once Again, A.
This Native Land.

Davis, Thulani
Boppin' is Safer than Grindin'.
C. T. at the Five Spot.
C.T.'s variation.
Desire 1.
Expandable Language.
In the Fire Lane.
Playing Solitaire.
Rogue and Jar: 4/27/77.
Susannah.
Telepathy.
Zoom (The Commodores).

Davis, William Virgil
January.

Davison, Edward (b. 1898)
Conscientious Objector.
In This Dark House.
Minesweeper Sunk, A.
Nocturne: "Be thou at peace this night."
Owl, The.

Davison, Peter (b. 1928)
Bed Time.
Cross Cut.
Equinox 1980.
Last Word, The.
Lunch at the Coq d'Or.
Money Cry, The.
Motley.
Pleaders, The.
Questions of Swimming, 1935.
Star Watcher, The.
Vanishing Point, The.
Where the Sun Ends.

Davison, Walter (1581–c.1608)
Ode: "At her fair hands how have I grace entreated."

Davitt, Michael (b. 1950)
Counterfeiter, The.
In Memory of Elizabeth Kearney, Blasket-Islander.
Mirror, The.
Old People.
Shortening the Road.

Davys, Mary (1674–1732)
Modern Poet, The, *sels.*

Dawe, Bruce (b. 1930)
Abandonment of Autos.
Americanized.

At Shagger's funeral there wasn't much to say.
Beatitudes.
Copy-writer's Dream, The.
Dogs in the Morning Light.
Drifters.
Elegy for Drowned Children.
Family Man, The.
First Corinthians at the Crossroads.
Going.
Gorilla Gorilla.
Happiness Is the Art of Being Broken.
Homecoming.
Homo Suburbiensis.
Morning Becomes Electric.
Not-so-good Earth, The.
On the Death of Ronald Ryan.
Perpetuum Immobile.
Renewal Notice.
Suburban Lovers.
Victorian Hangman Tells His Love, A.
Weapons Training.

Dawe, Gerald (b. 1952)
Likelihood of Snow, The/ The Danger of Fire.
Lundys Letter, The.
Names.
Question of Covenants, A.
Seamen's Mission.
Sheltering Places.
Solstice.

Dawson, Grace Stricker (b. 1891)
To a Friend.

Dawson, Mary
Late for Breakfast.

Dawson, William James (1854–1928)
House of Pride, The.

Day, Beth
Three Gates.

Day, Clarence (1874–1935)
Egg, The.
Might and Right.
Scenes from the Mesozoic, *sels.*
To My Wife.
Who Drags the Fiery Artist Down?

Day, Dorothea (1897–1980)
My Captain.

Day, James William
Rowan County Crew, The.

Day, Jean
From momentary work, a wrench, to just fall forward.
Moving Object.

Day, Jeffery (1896–1918)
Call of the Air, The.
Dawn.
North Sea.
On the Wings of the Morning.

Day, John (1574–1640)
Prayer: "Grant that no Hobgoblins fright me."

Day Lewis, Cecil (1904–72)
Album, The.
Almost Human.
As One Who Wanders into Old Workings.
At Lemmons.
Birthday Poem for Thomas Hardy.
Bombers.
Can the Mole Take.
Chiefly to Mind Appears.
Christmas Rose, The.
Come Up, Methuselah.
Committee, The.
Conflict, The.
Consider These, for We Have Condemned Them.
Dead, The.
Departure in the Dark.
Desire is a witch.
Do Not Expect Again a Phoenix Hour.
Emily Brontë.
Failure, A.
Few Things Can More Inflame.
Flight to Italy, *sels.*
From Feathers to Iron, *sels.*
Happy View, A.

It Is Becoming Now to Declare My
   Allegiance.
"Let Us Now Praise Famous Men."
Magnetic Mountain, The, *sels.*
Maple and Sumach.
Meeting the first time for many years.
My Mother's Sister.
Nabara, The.
Newsreel.
Now I have come to reason.
O Dreams, O Destinations, *sels.*
Oh Dreams, Oh Destinations, *sels.*
Overtures to Death, *sels.*
Poem for an Anniversary.
Reconciliation.
Remembering Con Markievicz.
Requiem for the Living, *sels.*
Rest from Loving and Be Living.
Sheepdog Trials in Hyde Park.
Snowfall on a College Garden.
Stand-To, The.
Sun Came Out in April, The.
This Man Was Strong.
Two Songs.
When They Have Lost.
Where Are the War Poets?
Winter Night.
With Me My Lover Makes.
You That Love England.
Dayre, Sydney (*fl.* 1881)
Grandma's Lost Balance.
Lesson for Mamma, A.
Morning Compliments.
Dayton, Ebenezer (*fl.* mid–18th cent.)
Wherein Consists the High Estate.
De Angelis, Milo (b. 1951)
And Then the Water.
Continuous Time.
Finite Intuition.
Hilbert's Program.
In the Lungs.
Line.
Narrator, The.
Now she is unadorned.
On the Way to Mind.
Protect Me, My Talisman.
Rowing in Familiar January.
Sounds That Arrived, The.
Telegram.
Year.
Yearbook.
De, Bishnu (b. 1909)
Santhal Poems, 1.
De Brun, Padraig (1889–1960)
Calvary.
Is It Not You, Lord!
De Burgos, Julia (1914–53)
Nothing.
Poem to My Death.
To Julia de Burgos.
De Carrion, Santob [*or* Shem-Tob] (*fl.* 14th
cent.)
Proverbios Morales, *sels.*
Resignation.
Self-Defense.
De Carvalho, Ruy Duarte (b. 1941)
I Come from a South.
De Casseres, Benjamin (1873–1945)
Moth-Terror.
De [*or* Du] **Guillet, Pernette** (c.1520–1545)
Chanson.
Epigram: "As the body denies the means to
   look."
Non Que Je Veuille Ôter la Liberté.
De Hearn, Nellie
Shut-In, The.
de Jesús, Teresa
Curfew.
Flag of Chile, The.
Proverbs.
De Kok, Ingrid (b. 1951)
Transfer.
De la Mare, Walter ("Walter Ramal") (1873–
1956)
Alas, Alack!
All but blind.

All That's Past.
Alone.
Antiques.
Arrogance.
As Lucy went a-walking one morning cold
   and fine.
At Ease.
At the Keyhole.
Autumn.
Ballad of Christmas, A.
Bards, The.
Berries.
Brueghel's Winter.
Bunches of Grapes.
Buttons.
Corporal Pym.
Crazed.
Cupboard, The.
Dear Sir.
Divided.
Echo.
Epitaph, An: "Here lies a most beautiful
   lady."
Faint Music.
Fare Well.
Feckless Dinner-Party, The.
Five Eyes.
Fly, The.
Funeral, The.
Galliass, The.
Ghost, The.
Good-bye.
Hare, A.
Hi!
Hi! handsome hunting man.
Holly, The.
Ice.
Immanent.
In the Dock.
In the Garden.
In the Local Museum.
Iron.
Jim Jay.
John Mouldy.
Kiph.
Last Chapter, The.
Listeners, The.
Love Lies Here.
Lucy.
Martha.
Me.
Miracle, The.
Miss Loo.
Miss T.
Mocking Fairy, The.
Moonlight.
Moonshine.
Motley.
Mrs. MacQueen (*or* The Lollie-Shop).
Myself.
Napoleon.
Ned Vaughan.
Nicholas Nye.
Nod.
Nostalgia.
Old Men, The.
Old Shellover.
Old Summerhouse, The.
Old Susan.
Owl, The.
Peace.
Please to Remember.
Pooh!
Portrait, A.
Railway Junction, The.
Rainbow, The.
Reserved.
Revenant, The.
Ride-by-Nights, The.
Robin, A.
Sam.
Santa Claus.
Scarecrow, The.
Scholars.
Scribe, The.
Shubble, The.
Silver.

Silver Penny, The.
Sleeper, The.
Slim cunning hands at rest, and cozening
   eyes.
Snow.
Solitude.
Some One.
Someone came knocking.
Song of Finis, The.
Song of the Mad Prince, The.
Song of the Shadows, The.
"Sooeep!"
Spotted Flycatcher, The.
Stone, The.
Storm, The.
Stranger, The.
Summer Evening.
Sunk Lyonesse.
Supper.
Susannah Prout.
Tartary.
There blooms no bud in May.
There was an old Begum of Frome.
Things are the mind's mute looking-glass.
Thomas Hardy.
Thomas Logge.
Three Cherry Trees, The.
Three Sisters.
Tired Tim.
TO E. T.: 1917.
Truants, The.
Two gardens see!—this, of enchanted
   flowers.
Voices.
Where.
Widow, The.
Winter.
De la Monnoye, Bernard
Patapan.
De la Tierra, Tatiana (b. 1961)
De Ambiente.
De Ledrede, Richard (*fl.* 19th cent.)
Festival of the Nativity, The.
De León, Luís (1528–91)
Life of the Blessed, The.
Love Song: "That haughty tyranny of thine."
Night Serene, The.
To Retirement.
Written on the Walls of His Dungeon.
De Lille, Abbé Jacques
Gardens, The, *sels.*
De' Medici, Maria (1573–1642)
(To the Virgin).
De Mello Breyner, Sophia (b. 1919)
Beach.
Day of sea in the sky, made.
Flute, The.
I feel the dead in the cold of violets.
Muse teach me the song.
Small Square, The.
De Morgan, Augustus (1806–71)
Great Fleas [have little fleas upon their backs
   to / bite 'em].
De Regnier, Henri (b. 1864)
Je ne veux de personne aupres de ma
   tristesse.
Night.
De Roche, Joseph (b. 1938)
Aunt Laura Moves toward the Open Grave of
   Her Father.
Blond.
De Savitzsky, Isabel
Christmas Tree, The.
De Stein, Sir Edward (1887–1965)
Chloe.
Elegy on the Death of Bingo Our Trench
   Dog.
**De Tabley, John Byrne Leicester Warren, 3d
Baron** (1835–95)
Churchyard on the Sands, The.
Circe.
Count of Senlis at His Toilet, The.
Knight in the Wood, The.
Nuptial Song.
Philoctetes.
Pilgrim Cranes, The.

Power of Interval, The.
Song of Dust, A.
Song of Faith Forsworn, A.
Sonnet: "Record is nothing, and the hero great."
Study of a Spider, The.
Two Old Kings, The.

De Veaux, Alexis (b. 1948)
Sisters, The.

De Vere, Sir Aubrey (1788–1846)
Children Band, The.
Right Use of Prayer, The.
Rock of Cashel, The.

De Vere, Aubrey Thomas (1814–1902)
Autumnal Ode.
Correggio's Cupolas at Parma.
Dominica Pentecostes.
Feast of the Most Holy Trinity.
In Ruin Reconciled.
Poet to a Painter, A.
Serenade: "Softly, O midnight Hours!"
Song: Little Black Rose, The.
Sorrow.
Year of Sorrow, A, sels.

De Vere, Edward, 17th Earl of Oxford (1550–1604)
Court lady Addresses Her Lover, A.
If women could be fair, and yet not fond.
Labouring man, that tills the fertile soil, The.
Lively lark stretched forth her wing, The.
Of the Birth and Bringing Up of Desire.
Poem: "Were I a king, I could command content."
SITTING alone upon my thought, in melancholy mood.
What cunning can express.

De Vere, William (1844–1904)
Walk, Damn You, Walk!

De Viau, Theophile (1591–1626)
Sleep.

De Villagrá, Gaspar Pérez
History of New Mexico, sels.

De Vries, Peter (b. 1910)
Bacchanal.
Christmas Family Reunion.
Loveliest of Pies.
Mirror.
Poets have their ear to the ground more than most people.
Psychiatrist.
Sacred and Profane Love, or, There's Nothing New under the Moon Either.
Theme and Variation.
To His Importunate Mistress.

De Vries, Rachel
On Alabama Ave., Paterson, NJ, 1954.

Dean, Debi Kang
In the Way Back.

Deane, Anthony C. (1870–1946)
Cult of the Celtic, The.
Ode: "I sing a song of sixpence, and of rye."

Deane, John F. (b. 1943)
Contact.
Offertory.
On a dark night.

Deane, Seamus (b. 1940)
Brethren, The.
Burial, A.
Derry.
Fording the River.
Guerillas.
History Lessons.
Northern Ireland: Two Comments.
Osip Mandelstam.
Power Cut.
Reading *Paradise Lost* in Protestant Ulster 1984.
Return.
Roots.
Scholar I.
Scholar II.
Schooling, A.

Deanovich, Connie
Connie Deanovich.
National Assessment.

Road Block: Sante Fe, New Mexico.

Dearmer, Geoffrey (b. 1893)
Turkish Trench Dog, The.
Whale.

DeBary, Anna Bunston (b. 1869)
Rubáiyát, The, sels.
Snowdrop, The.
Under a Wiltshire Apple Tree.

Decker, Bessie B.
Disillusion.

DeClue, Charlotte
Ijajee's Story.

DeCormier-Shekejian, Regina
Left Eye of Odin, The.
This Spring.

Ded, Lal (fl. 16th cent.)
At the end of a crazy-moon night.
Coursing in emptiness.
I drag a boat over the ocean.
I searched for my Self.
I was passionate.
Impermanence.
On the way to God the difficulties.
Soul, like the moon, The.
This world.
To learn the scriptures is easy.

Dederick, Robert (b. 1919)
Karoo Town.
Robben Island.

Deems, Charles F. (1820–93)
I Shall Not Want: In Deserts Wild.

Defoe, Daniel (1660–1731)
More Reformation, sels.
Reformation of Manners, sels.
Spanish Descent, The, sels.
True-born Englishman, The, sels.

DeFoe, Mark
13 Ways of Eradicating Blackbirds.

DeFrees, Madeline (b. 1919)
Letter to an Absent Son.

Degen, Iosif Lazarevich. See Degen, Yona

Degen, Yona [or Iona] (Iosif Lazarevich Degen) b. 1925
My comrade is in the final agony before death.

Degutyte, Janina
Etude in Glass.
In Jazz Rhythms.

Dehmel, Richard (1863–1920)
Before the Storm.
Harvest Song.
Laborer, The.
My Drinking Song.
Silent Town, The.
To ———?
Trysting, A.
Vigil.
Voice in Darkness.

Dehn, Paul (1912–76)
Alternative Endings to an Unwritten Ballad.
Armistice.
At the Dark Hour.
Game of Consequences, A.
Leaden Treasury of English Verse, A, sels.
Potted Swan, sels.
Rhymes for a Modern Nursery, sels.
St. Aubin d'Aubigne.

Dei-Anang, Michael (b. 1909)
My Africa.

DeJong, David Cornel (1905–67)
On the Twenty-fifth of July.

Dekker, Thomas
Art thou poore yet hast thou golden Slumbers.

Dekker, Thomas (1572?–1632?) and others
Folly's Song.
Old Fortunatus, sels.
Pleasant Comedy of Patient Grissell [or Grissel or Grissill], The, sels.
Portrait, A.
Shoemaker's Holiday, The, sels.
Sun's Darling, The, sels.

Dekker, Thomas, John Ford and William Rowley
Witch of Edmonton, The, sels.

Del Giudice, Paula
Rules to Live By.

Del Medigo, Joseph Solomon (1591–1655)
Epigram: "If men be judged wise."

Del Renzio, Toni
Can You Change a Shilling?

Delaney, W. W.. See "Lee, Andy"

Delanty, Greg (b. 1958)
Gift, The.
Thrust & Parry.
Tie.

Delany, Clarissa Scott (1901–27)
Solace.

DeLeeuw, Adele
Auction Sale—Household Furnishings.

Delius, Anthony (b. 1916)
Brief Farewell.
Deaf-and-Dumb School.
Distance.
Footnote.
Gamblers, The.
Intuition.
Lady Anne Bathing.
Shadow, killer of doves.
Thinker, The.

Della Casa, Giovanni (1503–56)
To Sleep.

Delle Colonne, Guido (fl. 13th cent.)
Canzone: To Love and to His Lady.

Delmore Brothers
Wabash Cannonball, The.

Delone, Vadim Nikolaevich (1947–83)
Ballad of Fate.

Deloney, Thomas (1543–1600)
Destruction of Jerusalem, The, sels.
Long have I lov'd this bonny Lasse.
Princely Ditty in Praise of the English Rose, A.
Weavers Song, The.

Dementyev [or Dement'ev], Andrey Dmitrievich b. 1928
As long as we feel another's pain.
It's all over...

Dementyev [or Dement'ev], Nikolai Ivanovich (1907–35)
Mother, The.

Demetriadis, Mary
When lovely woman stoops to folly.

Demetrio, Herrera S. (b. 1902)
Training.

Demodocus (fl. 4th? cent. B.C.)
All the Cilicians are bad.
Nasty snake once bit a Cappadocian, A.

Dempster, Roland Tombekai (1910–65)
Africa's Plea.
Is This Africa.

Den Sute-Jo (1633–98)
On the road through the clouds.
Snowy morning, A.
Woman.

Denby, Edwin (b. 1903)
Villa D'Este.

Denham, Sir John (1615–69)
Cooper's Hill, sels.
Had Cowley ne'er spoke, Killigrew ne'er writ.
On Mr. Abraham Cowley, His Death and Burial amongst the Ancient Poets.
Preface to *The Progress of Learning.*
Song, A: "Morpheus, the humble god, that dwells."
Song, A: "Somnus, the humble god, that dwells."
To Sir Richard Fanshawe, Upon His Translation of Pastor Fido, sels.

Denney, Reuel (b. 1915)
Fixer of Midnight.

Denning, Steve
Fire Support Burk.
Kim-San.
Movie, The.
Night on the Kho Bha Dinh.
This Time.

Dennis, C. J. (1876–1938)
Martyred Democrat, The.
Traveller, The.
Dennis, Carl
In the Middle of the Party.
Loss.
Miracle, The.
Nuts and Raisins.
Window in Spring, The.
Dennis, Nigel (b. 1912)
Maltese Goat.
Dent, Tom (b. 1932)
Dream Orpheum Balcony.
For Cool Papa Bell.
For Lil Louis.
For Walter Washington.
Ray Charles at Mississippi State.
Return to English Turn.
Denwood, Jonathan (1869–1933)
Bleeberrying.
Depero, Fortunato (1892–1960)
Colors.
Depestre, Rene. *See* **Cesaire, Aime** *and* Rene
Depestre
Depestre, René (b. 1926)
Ballad of a Little Lamp.
Black Ore.
Epiphanies of the Voodoo Gods, *sels.*
"Der Nistor" (Pinhas Kahanovitch) (1884–1956)
At the Doors.
Der von Kürenberg (1150–75)
"Late at night I stood on a battlement."
Morning star goes under cover, The.
Woman and falcons—they are easily tamed.
Derricotte, Toi (b. 1941)
Allen Ginsberg.
Blackbottom.
Boy at the Paterson Falls.
Christmas Eve: My Mother Dressing.
Fears of the Eighth Grade.
Feeding, The.
Friendship, The.
Good Old Dog, The.
Hamtramck: The Polish Women.
In an Urban School.
Minks, The.
Note on my Son's Face, A.
On Stopping Late in the Afternoon for
Steamed Dumplings.
On the Turning Up of Unidentified Black
Female Corpses.
Poem for My Father.
Promise, The.
St. Peter Claver.
Saturday Night.
Struggle, The.
Touching/Not Touching: My Mother.
Weakness, The.
Derwood, Gene
After Reading St. John the Divine.
Elegy: "When in the mirror of a permanent
tear."
Rides.
With God Conversing.
Desbordes-Valmore, Marceline (1786–1859)
Roses of Sa'adi, The.
Deshoulières, Antoinette (1637–94)
Reflections.
**Desmond, Gerald Fitzgerald, 4th Earl of
(Gearold Iarla Mac Gearailt) (d. 1398)**
Against Blame of Woman.
Woe to him who slanders women.
Desmond, John C.
When we two parted.
Desnos, Robert (1900–1945)
Ars Poetica.
Cuckoo.
Epitaph: "I lived in those times. For a
thousand years."
Hour farther witch art in Heaven.
If, like winds semaphored by a rose.
I've dreamed such dreams of you that you're
losing / your reality.
Language Event Two.
Letter to Youki.

Like.
Midway.
Night Watchman of Pont-au-Change, The.
St Merri district, The.
There once was a leaf with all its lines.
Trance Event.
When children slap their father's face.
Desnoues, Lucienne (b. 1921)
First Things.
Desportes, Philippe (1545–1606)
Conquest [*or* His Lady's Might].
Desprez, Frank
Lasca.
Detsinyi, Ludwig. *See* "**Martin, David**"
Deutsch, Babette (1895–1982)
Barges on the Hudson.
Destruction of Letters.
Earliness at the Cape.
Fireworks.
Homage to the Philosopher.
Late Reflections.
Memory.
No Moon, No Star.
Paradigm.
Poem, The: "Painter of Dante's awful ferry-
ride, The."
Scene with Figure.
Solitude.
Stranger than the Worst.
Tak for Sidst.
Dev Sen, Nabaneeta (b. 1938)
Yellow River, The.
Devaney, James (b. 1890)
Vision.
Devi, N. Revathi
This Night.
Devlin, Denis (1908–59)
Ank'hor Vat.
Anteroom: Geneva.
Ascension.
Daphne Stillorgan.
Encounter.
Heavenly Foreigner, The, *sels.*
Lancet, The.
Little Elegy.
Lough Derg.
Memoirs of a Turcoman Diplomat, *sels.*
Renewal by Her Element.
Venus of the Salty Shell.
Wishes for Her.
**Devonshire, Georgiana Cavendish, Duchess of
(1757–1806)**
Passage of the Mountain of St. Gothard, The.
Dewdney, Christopher (b. 1951)
Concordat Proviso Ascendant, *sels.*
Grid Erectile.
Out of Control; the Quarry.
Spring Trances in the Control Emerald Night,
sels.
This Is of Two Worlds.
Dharker, Imtiaz (b. 1954)
Purdah, 1.
Dharmakirti
Proof.
Dharmaraj, Ramola
Full of rain, the word.
Dharwadker, Vinay (b. 1954)
New Delhi, 1974.
Dhasal, Namdeo (b. 1949)
Stone-masons, My Father, and Me.
"Dhoomil" (Sudama Pandeya) (1935–75)
City, Evening, and an Old Man: Me, The.
Dhu 'l-Nún
I die, and yet not dies in me.
Dhu'l-Rumma (696?–736?)
Of all garments.
Di Biasio, Rodolfo (b. 1937)
Cuncta Semper.
Nostoi.
Poem of the Dawn and the Night.
Snow Poem.
Di Cicco, Pier Giorgio (b. 1949)
Errore.
Flying Deeper into the Century.

Head Is a Paltry Matter, The.
Male Rage Poem.
Di Filippo, Rustico (1200?–1270)
Sonnet: Of the Making of Master Messerin.
Di Michele, Mary (b. 1949)
Moon and the Salt Flats, The.
Di Montorio, Antonio (1404–77)
El Ropero.
Di Piero, W. S. (b. 1945)
Ice Plant in Bloom.
Near Damascus.
San Antonio de Padua.
Di Prima, Diane (b. 1934)
Abyss.
American Indian Art: Form and Tradition.
April Fool Birthday Poem for Grandpa.
Backyard.
Brief Wyoming Meditation.
Death Poems in September.
Death Sunyata Chant: A Rite for Passing
Over.
For H.D.
For the Dead Lecturer.
Fragmented Address to the FBI.
Goodbye Nkrumah.
I Ching.
I Fail as a Dharma Teacher.
In Memory of My First Chapatis.
Jungle, The.
Letter to Jeanne (at Tassajara).
Loba, *sels.*
Loba Addresses the Goddess, The / or The
Poet as Priestess Addresses the Loba-
Goddess.
Montezuma.
Narrow Path into the Back Country.
Notes on the Art of Memory.
On Sitting Down to Write, I Decide Instead
to Go to Fred Herko's Concert.
Paracelsus.
Poem in Praise of My Husband (Taos).
Practice of Magical Evocation, The.
Quarrel, The.
Revolutionary Letter #1.
Short Note on the Sparseness of the
Language.
Song For Baby-O, Unborn.
Tassajara, 1969.
To My Father—2.
To the Unnamed Buddhist Nun Who Burned
Herself to Death on the Night of June 3,
1966.
Diamond, David (b. 1915)
We Will Not Fear.
Diamond, Lucy
Eskimo Baby, An.
Greenland Winter, A.
Kayak Song, A.
Diaper, William (1686?–1717)
Brent; a Poem to Thomas Palmer Esq, *sels.*
Halieutica, *sels.*
Dibdin, Charles (1745–1814)
Anchorsmiths, The.
Captain Wattle and Miss Roe.
Jolly Young Waterman, The.
Lady's Diary, The.
Poor Tom.
Popular Functionary, A.
Dickenga, I. E.
Building.
Dickens, Charles (1812–90)
Fine Old English Gentleman; New Version,
The.
Great Expectations, *sels.*
Dickey, James (b. 1923)
Adultery.
After the Night Hunt.
Armor.
Birth, A.
Bread.
Buckdancer's Choice.
Bums, on waking.
Cherrylog Road.
Coming Back to America.
Common Grave, A.
Dog Sleeping on My Feet, A.

Driver, The.
Dusk of Horses, The.
Encounter in the Cage Country.
Falling.
False Youth: Autumn: Clothes of the Age.
Fence Wire.
Firebombing, The.
Folk Singer of the Thirties, A.
For the First Manned Moon Orbit, *sels.*
For the Nightly Ascent of the Hunter Orion
   over a Forest Clearing.
Gamecock.
Goodbye to Serpents.
Heaven of Animals, The.
Hedge Life.
Hospital Window, The.
Hunting Civil War Relics at Nimblewill
   Creek.
Ice Skin, The.
In the Marble Quarry.
In the Mountain Tent.
Inside the River.
Landfall, The.
Leap, The.
Lifeguard, The.
Madness.
Magus, The.
Movement of Fish, The.
Night Bird.
On the Coosawattee, *sels.*
Performance, The.
Power and Light.
Pursuit from Under.
Reincarnation (I) ["Still, passed through the
   spokes of an old wheel, on and around"].
Reincarnation (II).
Screened Porch in the Country, A.
Shark's Parlor, The.
Sheep Child, The.
Slave Quarters.
Sled Burial, Dream Ceremony.
Springer Mountain.
Strength of Fields, The.
Sun.
Underground Stream, The.
Venom.
Walking on Water.
Zodiac, The, *sels.*

Dickey, R. P. (b. 1936)
   Materialism.

Dickey, William (b. 1928)
   Arrival of the Titanic, The.
   Canonical Hours.
   Happiness.
   January White Sale.
   Poet's Farewell to His Teeth, The.
   Shortest Day, The.
   So full of sleep are those who lose the way.
   Suburban.
   Teaching Swift to Young Ladies.
   Things Kept.
   Tutankhamen.

Dickinson, Emily (1830–86)
   Abraham to kill him.
   Admirations—and Contempts—of time, The.
   Afraid! Of whom am I afraid?
   After a hundred years.
   After great pain a formal feeling comes—.
   Ah, Necromancy Sweet!
   Ah, Teneriffe!
   Alter! When the Hills do—.
   Altered look about the hills, An.
   Although I put away his life.
   Ample make this Bed.
   Apparently with no surprise.
   "Arcturus" is his other name.
   Are Friends Delight or Pain?
   As if some little Arctic flower.
   As imperceptibly as Grief.
   At Half past Three, a single Bird.
   At least—to pray—is left—is left.
   Auctioneer of Parting, The.
   Banish Air from Air.
   Bat is dun with wrinkled Wings, The.
   Be Mine the Doom.
   Beauty be not caused—It Is.
   Because I could not stop for Death.

Because you are going.
Bee, The.
Bee his burnished Carriage, A.
Bee is not afraid of me, The.
Bees are Black, with Gilt Surcingles—.
Before I got my eye put out.
Before you thought of Spring.
Behind Me—dips Eternity.
Belshazzar had a Letter.
Besides the autumn poets sing.
Better—than Music! For I—who heard it.
Between the form of Life and Life.
Bible is an antique Volume, The.
Bird came down the Walk[—A], A.
Blazing in Gold and quenching in Purple.
Bloom—is Result—to meet a Flower.
Bone that has no Marrow, The.
Brain—is wider than the Sky, The.
Brain, within its Groove, The.
Bring me the sunset in a cup.
Bustle in a House, The.
Butterfly upon the Sky, The.
By a departing light.
Called Back.
Cat.
Caterpillar.
Cemetery, A.
Clock stopped, A.
Clock strikes one that just struck two, The.
Clover's simple Flame, The.
Color, Caste, Denomination.
Color of the Grave is Green, The.
Come show thy Durham Breast.
Come slowly—Eden!
Consulting summer's clock.
Could I but ride indefinite.
Could mortal lip divine.
Crumbling is not an instant's Act.
Dare you see a Soul *at the White Heat?*.
Dear March, Come in.
Death is a Dialogue between.
Death is the supple Suitor.
Delight is as the flight.
Despair's advantage is achieved.
Did Our Best Moment last.
Did the Harebell loose her girdle.
Difference between Despair, The.
Distance that the dead have gone, The.
Do People moulder equally.
Drama's Vitallest Expression is the Common
   Day.
Dropped into the Ether Acre.
Drowning is not so pitiful.
Drunkard cannot meet a Cork, A.
Dying Tiger—moaned for Drink, A.
Earth has many keys, The.
Eden is that old-fashioned House.
Elijah's Wagon knew no thill.
Ended, ere it begun.
Essential oils—are wrung.
Evening.
Except the Heaven had come so near.
Experiment escorts us last.
Exultation is the going.
Faded Boy—in sallow Clothes, A.
"Faith" is a fine invention.
Faith—is the Pierless Bridge.
Fame is a bee.
Fame is a fickle food.
Far from Love the Heavenly Father.
Farthest Thunder that I heard, The.
Finding is the first Act.
First Day's Night had come, The.
For each ecstatic instant.
Four Trees—upon a solitary Acre.
Frigid and sweet Her parting Face.
Further in Summer than the Birds.
Fuzzy fellow, without feet, A.
Gentian weaves her fringes, The.
Glass was the Street—in tinsel Peril.
Glee—The great storm is over.
Go not too near a House of Rose.
Go slow, my soul, to feed thyself.
God is a distant—stately Lover.
God is indeed a jealous God.
God's Residence.
Good Morning—Midnight.

Great Streets of silence led away.
He ate and drank the precious Words.
He fumbles at your Soul.
He preached upon "Breadth" till it argued
   him narrow.
He put the Belt around my life.
He scanned it—staggered.
He showed me hights I never saw.
He touched me, so I live to know.
Heart asks Pleasure—*first*, The.
Heart! We [*or* Heart, we] will forget him!
"Heaven"—is what I cannot reach!
"Heavenly Father"—take to thee.
Her breast is fit for pearls.
Her—'last Poems.'
Her Losses make our Gains ashamed.
Her sweet Weight on my Heart a Night.
His Feet are shod with Gauze.
His Mansion in the Pool.
"Hope" is the thing with feathers.
How brittle are the Piers.
How happy is the little Stone.
How many times these low feet staggered.
How noteless Men, and Pleiads, stand.
How the old Mountains drip with Sunset.
How the Waters closed above Him.
Hummingbird, A.
I am afraid to own a Body.
I am alive—I guess.
I asked no other thing.
I can wade Grief.
I cannot dance upon my Toes.
I cannot live with You.
I could bring You Jewels—had I a mind to.
I died for Beauty—but was scarce.
I dreaded that first Robin, so.
I dwell in Possibility.
I felt a cleavage in my mind.
I felt a Funeral in my Brain.
I found the words to every thought.
I gave myself to Him—.
I got so I could take his name.
I had been hungry, all the Years.
I had no time to hate, because.
I had not minded—Walls.
I have never seen volcanoes.
I have no Life but this.
I heard a Fly buzz—when I died[—died].
I know some lonely Houses off the Road.
I know that He exists.
I laughed a crumbling laugh.
I like a look of Agony.
I like to see it lap the Miles.
I many times thought Peace had come.
I measure every Grief I meet.
I met a King this afternoon!
I never hear the word "escape."
I never lost as much but twice.
I never saw a Moor.
I reason, Earth is short.
I reckon—when I count at all.
I saw no Way. The Heavens were stitched.
I shall keep singing!
I shall know why—when Time is over.
I should have been too glad, I see.
I should not dare to leave my friend.
I showed her Hights she never saw.
I started Early—Took my Dog.
I stepped from Plank to Plank.
I suppose the time will come.
I taste a liquor never brewed.
I think I was enchanted.
I think that the Root of the Wind is Water.
I think the Hemlock likes to stand.
I took my Power in my Hand.
I took one Draught of Life.
I watched the Moon around the House.
I would not paint—a picture.
I Years had been from Home.
If anybody's friend be dead.
If I can stop one Heart from breaking.
If I may have it, when it's dead.
If you were coming in the Fall.
I'll tell you how the Sun rose.
I'm ceded—I've stopped being Theirs.
I'm Nobody! Who are you?
I'm sorry for the Dead—Today.

I'm "wife"—I've finished that.
Immortal is an ample word.
In this short Life.
In Winter in my Room.
Indian Summer.
Infinite a sudden Guest, The.
It always felt to me—a wrong.
It ceased to hurt me, though so slow.
It dropped so low—in my Regard.
It is an honorable Thought.
It might be lonelier.
It sounded as if the Streets were running.
It was a quiet way—.
It was not Death, for I stood up.
It would have starved a Gnat.
It would never be Common—more—I said.
It's easy to invent a Life.
It's like the Light.
It's such a little thing to weep.
I've known a Heaven, like a Tent.
I've seen a Dying Eye.
Just as He spoke it from his Hands.
Lad of Athens, faithful be.
Lady feeds Her little Bird, The.
Last Night that She lived, The.
Let me not thirst with this Hock at my Lip.
Letter to Bee.
Light exists in Spring, A.
Lightly stepped a yellow star.
Lightning is a yellow Fork, The.
Like Eyes that looked on Wastes.
Like Rain it sounded till it curved.
Little Dog that wags his tail, A.
Little East of Jordan, A.
Little Madness in the Spring, A.
Loss of something ever felt I, A.
Love a Life can show Below, The.
Love—is anterior to Life.
Love—is that later Thing than Death.
Love—thou art high.
Man may make a Remark, A.
Martyr Poets—did not tell, The.
Me—come! My dazzled face.
Me from Myself—to banish.
Mine—by the Right of the White Election!
Mine Enemy is growing old
Missing All—prevented Me, The.
Moon, The.
Moon upon her fluent Route, The.
More than the Grave is closed to me.
Morns are meeker than they were, The.
Mountains grow—unnoticed, The.
Much Madness is divinest Sense.
Murmur of a Bee, The.
Murmuring of Bees, has ceased, The.
Musicians wrestle everywhere.
My Cocoon tightens—Colors tease.
My friend must be a Bird.
"My husband"—women say—.
My Life Had Stood—A Loaded Gun.
My nosegays are for Captives.
My period had come for Prayer.
My Portion is Defeat—today.
My Triumph lasted till the Drums.
Name—of it—is "Autumn," The.
Narrow Fellow in the Grass, A.
Nature assigns the Sun.
Nature—sometimes sears a Sapling.
Nature—the Gentlest Mother is.
Nearest Dream recedes—unrealized, The.
New feet within my garden go—.
No Passenger was known to flee.
No Rack can torture me.
None can experience stint.
Not any higher stands the Grave.
Not at Home to Callers.
Not "Revelation" 'tis, that waits.
Now I knew I lost her.
Of all the Souls that stand create—.
Of all the Sounds despatched abroad.
Of Bronze—and Blaze.
Of Course—I prayed.
Of God we ask one favor.
Of nearness to her sundered Things.
Of Paul and Silas it is said.
Oh give it Motion—deck it sweet.
Oh Sumptuous moment.

On a Columnar Self.
One crown that no one seeks.
One Crucifixion is recorded—only.
One dignity delays for all.
One need not be a Chamber—to be Haunted.
One of the ones that Midas touched.
One who could repeat the Summer day, The.
Only News I know, The.
Opinion is a flitting thing.
Our journey had advanced.
Our lives are Swiss.
Ourselves we do inter with sweet derision.
Ourselves were wed one summer—dear.
Outer—from the Inner, The.
Over the fence.
Pain—expands the Time.
Pain—has an Element of Blank.
Papa above!
Parting.
Pass to thy Rendezvous of Light.
Pedigree of Honey, The.
Perception of an object costs.
Pit—but Heaven over it, A.
Poets light but Lamps, The.
Prayer is the little implement.
Precious—moldering pleasure—'tis, A.
Presentiment—is that long Shadow—on the
    Lawn.
Prison gets to be a friend, A.
Props assist the House, The.
Province of the Saved, The.
Publication—is the Auction.
Purple Clover.
Rat is the conciscst Tenant, The.
Read—Sweet—how others—strove.
Rearrange a "Wife's" affection!
"Remember me" implored the Thief!
Remorse—is Memory—awake.
Renunciation.
Renunciation—is a piercing Virtue.
Reportless Subjects, to the Quick.
Return, The.
Riddle we can guess, The.
Robin is a Gabriel, The.
Saddest noise, the sweetest noise, The.
Safe in their Alabaster Chambers.
Satisfaction—is the Agent.
Savior! I've no one else to tell.
Severer Service of myself.
Shade upon the mind there passes, A.
She dealt her pretty words like Blades.
She rose to His Requirement—dropt.
Show is not the Show, The.
Single Screw of Flesh, A.
Sky is low—the Clouds are mean, The.
Snow, The.
So proud she was to die.
Soft Sea washed around the House, A.
Softened by Time's consummate plush.
Solemn thing—it was—I said, A.
Some keep the Sabbath going to Church.
Some one prepared this mighty show.
Some things that fly there be.
Somehow myself survived the Night.
Soul has Bandaged moments, The.
Soul selects her own Society—The The.
Soul that hath a Guest, The.
Soul's distinct connection, The.
Soul's Superior instants, The.
Sown in dishonor!
Spider holds a Silver Ball, The.
Spider sewed at Night, A.
Spirit lasts, but in what mode, The.
Split the Lark—and you'll find the Music.
Spring is the Period.
Stimulus beyond the Grave, The.
Struck, was I, not yet by Lightning.
Success is counted sweetest.
Sun and Fog contested, The.
Sun kept setting—setting—still, The.
Surgeons must be very careful.
Suspense.
Sweet Mountains—Ye tell Me no lie.
Sweetest Heresy received, The.
Tell all the Truth but tell it slant.
That after Horror—that 'twas us.
That it will never come again.

That Love is all there is.
That she forgot me was the least.
Their Height in Heaven comforts not.
There are two Mays.
There came a Wind like a Bugle.
There comes an hour when begging stops.
There is a Languor of the Life.
There is a morn by men unseen.
There is a pain—so utter.
There is a Zone whose even Years.
There is another Loneliness.
There is no Frigate like a Book.
There is no Silence in the Earth—so silent.
There's a certain Slant of light.
There's been a Death, in the Opposite House.
These are the Nights that Beetles love.
These Strangers, in a foreign World.
They might not need me—yet they might.
They put Us far apart.
They say that "Time assuages."
They shut me up in Prose.
This Consciousness that is aware.
This dirty—little—Heart.
This docile one inter.
This is my letter to the World.
This was a Poet—It is That.
This World is not Conclusion.
Those—dying then.
Thought beneath so slight a film, The.
Thought went up my mind today, A.
Through the Dark Sod—as Education.
Through the strait pass of suffering.
Tie the Strings to my Life, My Lord.
Tint I cannot take—is best, The.
'Tis customary as we part.
'Tis little I— could care for Pearls.
'Tis not that Dying hurts us so.
'Tis so appalling—it exhilarates.
'Tis so much joy! 'Tis so much joy!
Title divine—is mine!
To die—takes just a little while.
To fight aloud, is very brave.
To flee from memory.
To hear an Oriole sing.
To know just how He suffered—would be
    dear.
To learn the Transport by the Pain.
To make a prairie it takes a clover and one
    bee.
To pile like Thunder to its close.
To see her is a Picture.
Too happy Time dissolves itself.
Trees like Tassels—hit—and swung, The.
Truth—is as old as God.
'Twas here my summer paused.
'Twas just this time, last year, I died.
'Twas like a Maelstrom, with a notch.
'Twas warm—at first—like Us.
Under the Light, yet under.
Undue Significance a starving man attaches.
Union.
Until the Desert knows.
Victory comes late.
Visitor in Marl, A.
Volcanoes be in Sicily.
Water, is taught by thirst.
Waters chased him as he fled, The.
Way I read a Letter's—this, The.
We do not play on Graves.
We dream—it is good we are dreaming.
We grow accustomed to the Dark.
We learned the Whole of Love.
We like March—his shoes are Purple.
We lose—because we win.
We miss a Kinsman more.
We outgrow love like other things.
We thirst at first—'tis Nature's Act.
Went up a year this evening!
What care the Dead, for Chanticleer.
What is—"Paradise."
What mystery pervades a well!
What Soft—Cherubic Creatures.
When Bells stop ringing—Church—begins.
When we stand on the tops of Things.
While we were fearing it, it came.
"Why do I love" You, Sir?
Why make it doubt—it hurts it so.

Wife—at Daybreak I shall be, A.
Wild Nights—Wild Nights!
Will there really be a "morning"?
Wind begun to knead the Grass, The.
Wind begun to rock the Grass, The.
Wind—tapped like a tired man, The.
Wind that rose, A.
Wind took up the Northern Things, The.
Wind's Visit, The.
Within my Garden, rides a Bird.
Wonder—is not precisely Knowing.
Word is dead, A.
Word made Flesh is seldom, A.
Work of Her that went, The.
World—feels Dusty, The.
Wounded Deer—leaps highest, A.
Yellow Man, Purple Man.
You love me—you are sure.

Dickinson, Patric (b. 1914)
Advent; a Carol.
St. Stephen's Day.

Dickinson, Peter (b. 1927)
Moses and the Princess.

Dickson, Samuel Henry (1798–1872)
Song—Written at the North.

Diên Nghi
Her Story.

Dietmar von Aist [or Eist] (fl. 12th cent.)
Bird Was Singing, A.
Gay summer's bliss, good-bye!
How can I hope a wise heart to attain.
Lady Stood, A.
Lady stood alone, A.
Parting at Morning.
Yonder on the linden tree there sang a merry
little bird.

Dietz, Mrs. William H.
Gentle Jesus meek and mild.
Help us to do the things we should.

Điều, Lê Tất. See Cao Tần

Digby, John (1580–1655)
Grieve not, dear love, although we often part.
One Night Away from Day.
Sooner or Later.

Digges, Deborah
Rock, Scissors, Paper.
Rough Music.
To a Milkweed.

Dillard, Richard H. W. (b. 1937)
Meditation for a Pickle Suite.
Mullins Farm, The.

Diller, John Irving
Lullaby Town.

Dillon, George (b. 1906)
Hard Lovers, The.

Dimitrova, Blaga (b. 1922)
Child and Sea.
If.
Introduction to the Beyond.
Steady.
Woman Pregnant, A.

Dimoski, Slave Gorgo
Rest.
Revenge.

Đinh An
Visiting an Old Friend.

Dinka Oral Tradition
Magnificent Bull, The.

Diodoros of Sardis
Young child of Diodoros's house, A.

Diodorus Zonas (b. 125? B.C.)
Come tawny bees.
For Demeter winnowing, for the Hours who
haunt the furrows.
From the field's plane tree.
Pan Asks about Daphnis.
Pomegranate just splitting, a peach just furry,
A.
Spare the mother of acorns, man. Cut down
some paliurus.
Who in the waters of this reedy lake.

Diogenes Laertius (fl. A.D. 3d cent.)
Nor, by God, shall we neglect.
Tauromancy at Memphis.

Dionysius Sophistes (Dionysius of Andros)
No wonder I slipped, being soaked.
You hold a bunch of roses, Rose.

Diop, Birago (b. 1906)
Animism.
Ball.
Breaths.
Desert.
Diptych.
Kassak.
Omen.
Spirits.
Vanity.
Viaticum.

Diop, David (1927–60)
Africa my Africa.
Challenge.
For a Black Child.
For My Mother.
He Who Has Lost All.
Hours, The.
Listen, comrades of the flaming centuries.
Negro Tramp.
Rama Kam.
Renegade, The.
Suffer, Poor Negro!
Those Who Lost Everything.
Time of Martyrdom, The.
Vultures, The.
With you I have refound my name.
Your Presence.

Diophanes of Myrina
Thief, and triply so!, A.

Dioscorides (fl. 3d cent. B.C.)
Epigrams, sels.
First fruits from her fruitful bed, The.
Hiero's former Nurse.
My downfall: those pink articulate lips.
They are too much for me.
Thracian page-boy / mastered, A.
Zephyr, kindliest of winds.

Diotimus (fl. c.250 B.C.)
Cold Pastoral.
Epigrams, sels.
Homing at dusk—the snow falls on them—
cattle.
Without the Herdsman.

DiPalma, Ray (b. 1943)
Annotations Tropes and Lacunae of the Itoku
Master.
Bed, The.
Each moment is surrounded.
Empire Smoke, Forgeries, Salient and The
Ritz.
Fragment.
Hadrian's Lane.
Memory's wedge / makes a valley.
Motion of the Cypher.
Pink maniac, A.
Poem for Claude.
Poem: "In danger of which."
Prerogative of Lieder, The.
Rebus Tact.
Rumor's rooster / halloos the distorted.
Sheaf Mark.
Table, The.
We Forego Mimicry.
When Torrid Rhymes with Forehead.
Wrong Side of the Door, The.

DiPasquale, Emanuel (b. 1943)
Rain.

Dipoko, Mbella Sonne (b. 1936)
Autobiography.
Exile.
From My Parisian Diary.
Our Life.
Pain.
Poem of Villeneuve St Georges, A.

Dirjan, Liljana
Poetry Evening.

Disch, Thomas M. [or "Tom"] (b.1940)
Abecedary.
Argument Resumed; Or, Up Through Tribeca,
The.
Ballade of the New God.

Bookmark, A.
Cardinal Detoxes: A Play in One Act, The.
Clouds, The.
Convalescing in London.
Cow of Our Time, A.
Crumbling Infrastructure, The.
Entropic Villanelle.
Garage Sale as a Spiritual Exercise, The.
Homage to the Carracci.
In Praise of New York.
La, La, La!
Poems: "I think that I shall never read."
Rapist's Villanelle, The.
Vowels of Another Language, The.
Zewhyexary.

Dischell, Stuart (fl. 20th cent.)
Chamber, The.

Dissanayake, Wimal (b. 1939)
Freedom.

Ditlevsen, Tove (1918–76)
Morning.
Old Folk, The.
Self Portrait 4.
Self Portrait II.

Divakaruni, Chitra (b. 1956)
Brides Come to Yuba City, The.
Childhood.
Indian Movie, New Jersey.
Indigo.
Making Samosas.
Outside Pisa.
Restroom.
Visit.
Walk, The.
Yuba City School.

Divine, Charles (1889–1949)
We Met on Roads of Laughter.

Dix, William Chatterton (1837–98)
As with Gladness Men of Old.

Dixon, Henry (1675–1760)
Description of a Good Boy, The.

Dixon, Melvin
Aunt Ida Pieces a Quilt.
Place, Places.

Dixon, Richard Watson (1833–1900)
Both Less and More.
By the Sea.
Dawning.
Dream.
Judgment of the May, The.
Love's Consolation, sels.
Ode: The Spirit Wooed.
Song: "Feathers of the willow, The."
To Peace.
Unrest.
Winter Will Follow.
Wizard's Funeral, The.

Dixon, Sarah (fl. 1716–45)
Close to Aminta, on the Loss of Her Lover.
Lines Occasioned by the Burning of Some
Letters.
Request of Alexis, The.
Returned Heart, The.
Slattern, The.
To Strephon.
Verses Left on a Lady's Toilet.

Dizhur, Bella Abramovna b. 1903
With tender back glistening.

Djabali, Leila (b. 1933)
For My Torturer, Lieutenant D——.

Djagarov, Georgi
Autumn.
Night.

Djangatolum. See Corbin, Lloyd M., Jr.

Djanikian, Gregory (b. 1949)
Agami Beach.
How I Learned English.
In the Elementary School Choir.
When I First Saw Snow.

Djogo, Gojko (b. 1940)
Black Sheep, The.
National Hero, The.
Wooden Handle, The.

Djurberaui
All You Others, Eat.

Djurdjic, Ljiljana (b. 1946)
Blue Frog Kisses My Sweetheart.
I carry my black sheep back to her herd.
Lucifer has bad habits.
Unfulfilled Love.

D'Lettuso, Homer
Old Houses.

Dlugos, Tim (d. 1991)
D.O.A.
Healing the World from Battery Park.

Do Espirito Santo, Aldo (b. 1926)
Where Are the Men Seized in this Wind of
Madness?

Đỗ Tấn Xuân
Peace! Peace!
Words of Comfort.

Doak, Katherine
Before I slept, I saw the nebula.

Doane, George Washington (1799–1858)
Bishop Doane on His Dog.
Evening Contemplation.
Fling Out the Banner!
Life Sculpture.
Once More, O Lord.
Thou Art the Way.

Doane, William Croswell (1832–1913)
Ancient of Days, who sittest throned in glory.
Modern Baby, The.
Preacher's Mistake, The.

Dobbie, Joan (b. 1946)
My First Memory, Switzerland, Circa 1947.
Things Grow Up out of the Dark.

Dobell, Sydney Thompson (1824–74)
Balder, sels.
Desolate.
He Loves and He Rides Away.
"How's My Boy?"
Nuptial Eve, A, sels.
Orphan's Song, The.
Perhaps.
Tommy's Dead.

Dobler, Patricia
His Depression.
1920 Photo.

**Dobson, Austin (Henry Austin Dobson) (1840–
1921)**
Ars Victrix, sels.
Ballad of 'Beau Brocade,' The.
Ballade of the Armada, A.
Before Sedan.
Dora versus Rose.
Fame and Friendship.
Garden Song, A.
In After Days.
Incognita.
Ladies of St. James's, The.
Rose-Leaves, sels.
Sundial, The.
Virtuoso, A.
Wanderer, The.

Dobson, Henry Austin. See Dobson, Austin

Dobson, John (fl. c.1746)
Robin; a Pastoral Elegy.

Dobson, Rosemary (b. 1920)
Being Called For.
Bystander, The.
Child with a Cockatoo.
Country Press.
Daily Living, sels.
Edge, The.
Eutychus.
Fever, The.
In a Café.
Three Fates, The.

Dobyns, Stephen (b. 1941)
Black Dog, Red Dog.
Counterparts.
Delicate, Plummeting Bodies, The.
Desire.
Favorite Iraqi Soldier.
Freight Cars.
General Matthei Drives Home through
Santiago.
Gun, The.
Shaving.

Tomatoes.
What You Have Come To Expect.

Dock, Christopher (d. 1771)
O Children, Would You Cherish?

Dodd, Wayne (b. 1930)
Letter.
Like Deer Our Bodies.
Of His Life.
Of Rain and Air.
Outside My Cabin.

Doddridge, Philip (1702–51)
Christ's Resurrection and Ascension.
Hymn: "Ye golden lamps of heaven,
farewell."
Meditations on the Sepulchre in the Garden.

Dodge, Mary Mapes (1831–1905)
Letters at School, The.
Mayor of Scuttleton burned his nose, The.
Poor Crow!
That's What We'd Do.
Two Mysteries, The.
Zealless Xylographer, The.

Dodgson, Charles Lutwidge. See "Carroll,
Lewis"

Dodsley, Robert (1703–64)
Agriculture, sels.
Epistle to My Friend J. B, An.
Progress of Love, The.
Song: "Man's a poor deluded bubble."
Stolen Kiss, The.

Dodson, Owen (1914–83)
Black Mother Praying.
Confession Stone, The.
I Break the Sky.
Mary Passed This Morning.
Poems for My Brother Kenneth, sels.
Yardbird's Skull.

Dogen (1200–1253)
On Non-dependence of Mind.
On the Treasury of the True Dharma Eye.

Doinas, Stefan Aug.
Ascent, The.
Man with Exploded Eyes, The.
Moment of Parting.
Pythia.
Woman in the Mirror, The.
Words, The.

Dolben, Digby Mackworth (1848–67)
Enough.
He Would Have His Lady Sing.
Sea Song, A.
Song, A: "World is young today, The."
We hurry on, nor passing note.

**Dolmatovsky [or Dolmatovskii], Yevgeny [or
Evgenii] Aronovich b. 1915**
Hero.

Domanski, Don (b. 1950)
Deadsong.
Three Songs from the Temple.

**Dombrovsky [or Dombrovskii], Yury [or Iurii]
Osipovich (1909–78)**
I'm at the bottom again. The baron's there.
They named me dead, the bastards.
When they brought us a pear jacket.

Domin, Hilde (b. 1912)
Birthdays.

Domino, Ruth (b. 1908)
Sparrow in the Dust, A.

Donaghy, John Lyle (b. 1902)
Deathward.
Duck.
Glenarm.
Portrait.
Winter.

Donahue, Joseph (b. 1954)
Desire's green / and gold corona / in the
wavering branch.
Opiate Phobia.
Transfigurations.

Donald, Christine M. (b. 1950)
Eye for an Eye, An.
I Expect You Think This Huge Dark Coat.

Donatus, Saint (829–76)
Land Called Scotia, The.

Đông Hồ Lâm Tấn Phác (1906–1969)
Buying a Dress for My Love.
Poem of Humankind, The.
River, The.
String of Pearls, The.
War.

Dongala, Emmanuel (b. 1941)
Fantasy under the Moon.

Donnchadh Mor O'Dala (d. 1244)
At Saint Patrick's Purgatory.

Donne, John (1572–1631)
Air[e] and Angels.
Anatomy [or Anatomie] of the World, An[:
The First Anniversary], sels.
And now good morrow to our waking souls.
Anniversary [or Anniversarie], The.
Antiquary.
Apparition, The.
Bait[e], The.
Blossom [or Blossome], The.
Bracelet, The.
Break[e] of Day.
Bridegroom comes, she sits on the stove,
The.
Broken Heart, The.
Burnt Ship, A.
Calm[e], The.
Canonization, The.
Computation, The.
Damp[e], The.
Dark an' stormy may come de wedder.
Disinherited.
Dream[e], The.
Ecstasy, The.
Elegies, sels.
Epithalamion for Lawyers, An.
Epithalamion Made at Lincoln's Inn [or
Lincolnes Inne].
Expiration, The.
Farewell to Love.
Fever, A.
Flea, The.
Funeral[l], The.
God grant thee thine own wish, and grant
thee mine.
Good Friday [or Goodfriday], 1613. Riding
Westward.
Good-Morrow, The.
Good[-]Morrow, The.
Hero and Leander.
Holy Sonnets, sels.
Hymn[e] to Christ, at the Author's Last
Going into Germany, A, sels.
Hymn[e] to God My God, In My Sickness[e].
Hymn to God the Father, A.
Hymn to the Saints, and to Marquis
Hamilton[, An].
Hymne to Christ, at the Author's Last Going
into Germany, A.
Indifferent, The.
Jet Ring Sent, A.
Klockius so deeply hath sworn[e], ne'er more
to come.
Lame Beggar, A.
Lamentations of Jeremy, for the Most Part
According to Tremeullius, sels.
Lecture upon the Shadow, A.
Legacy [or Legacie], The.
Licentious Person, A.
Litanie, The, sels.
Lovers' Infiniteness[e].
Love's Alchemy [or Alchemie].
Love's Deity [or Deitie].
Love's Growth.
Message, The.
Negative Love.
Nocturnal[l] upon Saint Lucy's [or S. Lucies]
Day, Being the Shortest Day, A.
Of the Progres[se] of the Soule; the Second
Anniversarie, sels.
Our Love Hath No Decay.
Paradox, The.
Phryne.
Primrose[, Being at Montgomery Castle, upon
the Hill, on Which It Is Situate], The.
Progress[e] of the Soul[e], The, sels.
Prohibition, The.

Pyramus and Thisbe.
Raderus.
Relic, The.
Resurrection, Imperfect.
Satire 4, *sels.*
Satires, *sels.*
Self[e] Accuser, A.
Slowly, slowly.
Song: "Go and catch a falling star."
Song: "Sweetest love, I do not go[e]."
Storm[e], The, *sels.*
Sun[ne] Rising, The.
To Mr I. L ("Blessed [*or* Blesst] are your north parts, for all this long time.")
To Mr I. L ("Of that short Roll of friends writ in my heart.")
To Mr. R. W ("Kindly I envy thy song's [*or* songs] perfection.")
To Mr. Roland Woodward ("Like one who in [*or* who'in] her third widowhood [*or* widdowhood] doth profess[e].")
To Mr. Tilman after He Had Taken Orders.
To Mr. C.B.
To Mr. George Herbert.
To Sir H. W. at His Going Ambassador to Venice.
To Sir Henry Wotton ("Here's no more news, than virtue, I may as well.")
To Sir Henry Wotton ("Sir, more than kisses, letters mingle souls.")
To the Countess of Bedford ("Madam, / Reason is our soul's left hand, Faith her right.")
To the Countess of Salisbury.
To the Countesse of Bedford ("Honour is so sublime perfection.")
Triple Fool[e], The.
Twicknam [*or* Twickenham] Garden.
Undertaking, The.
Upon the Translation of the Psalms by Sir Philip Sidney, and the Countess of Pembroke His Sister.
Valediction, A: Forbidding Mourning.
Valediction: Forbidding Mourning, A, *sels.*
Valediction of the Book, A.
Valediction: Of Weeping, A.
Will, The.
Woman's Constancy.

Donnell, David (b. 1939)
Canadian Prairies View of Literature, The.
Lakes.
Potatoes.
Sandwiches.
Stepfathers.

Donnelly, Charles (1914–37)
Flowering Bars, The.
Poem: "Between rebellion as a private study and the public."
Tolerance of Crows, The.

Donnelly, Dorothy (b. 1903)
Blue Flag.
Girandole.

Donnelly, Susan (b. 1939)
Eve Names the Animals.

Donnelly, Tom (d. 1976)
Myself When Young.
That raddled old queen.

Donovan, Katie (b. 1962)
First Autumn Night.
We Were Sisters Weren't We.

Doob, Jeannette
My Mother's Blue Vase.

Dooley, David (b. 1947)
How I Wrote It.

Dooley, Ebon (b. 1942)
Easter Bunny Blues or All I Want for Xmas Is the Loop, The.
Prophet's Warning or Shoot to Kill, The.
Query.

Dooley, Maura (b. 1957)
At Les Deux Magots.
No, Go On.

Doolittle, Hilda ("H. D.") (1886–1961)
Acon.
Adonis.
At Baia.

At Ithaca.
Birds in Snow.
Centaur Song.
Child Poems, *sels.*
Circe.
Epigram: "Golden one is gone from the banquets, The."
Erige Cor Tuum ad Me in Caelum.
Eurydice, *sels.*
Evadne.
Evening.
Flowering of the Rod, The, *sels.*
Fragment 113: "Not honey, / not the plunder of the bee."
Fragment 36: "I know not what to do."
Garden.
Gift, The.
Good Frend, *sels.*
Halcyon, *sels.*
Helen.
Helen in Egypt, *sels.*
Helmsman, The.
Hermes of the Ways.
Hippolytus Temporizes.
Holy Satyr.
Hymen, *sels.*
In Time of Gold.
Islands, The.
Lais.
Leda.
Let Zeus Record, *sels.*
Lethe.
Moonrise.
Mysteries Remain, The.
Orchard.
Oread.
Pear Tree.
Pool, The.
Pursuit.
Red Rose and a Beggar.
Sagesse, *sels.*
Sea Poppies.
Sea Rose.
Sea Violet.
Sheltered Garden.
Shrine, The.
Sigil, *sels.*
Song: "You are as gold."
Songs from Cyprus, *sels.*
Tribute to the Angels, *sels.*
Walls Do Not Fall, The, *sels.*
White World.
Wind Sleepers, The.
Wine Bowl.
Winter Love, *sels.*

Doplicher, Fabio (b. 1938)
Asymmetry of the Universe.
Discords.
Interludes.
Unfinished Exile.

Dor, Moshe (b. 1932)
Before sleep Baba arranges extra.

Dorcey, Mary (b. 1950)
First Love.
Sea Flower.

Dorfman, Ariel (b. 1942)
I Just Missed the Bus and I'll Be Late for Work.
Last Waltz in Santiago.
Vocabulary.

Dorgan, Theo (b. 1953)
Promised Garden, The.

Doria, Prinzivalle (*fl.* 12th cent.)
Canzone: Of His Love, with the Figure of a Sudden Storm.

D'Orleans, Charles
Not long ago I hied me apace.
Oft in my thought full busily have I sought.
Smiling mouth and laughing eyen° gray, The.
Your mouth hit saith me "Bas me, bas me, sweet."

Dorn, Edward (b. 1929)
Air of June Sings, The.
Are They Dancing.
Biggest Killing, The.
For the New Union Dead in Alabama.

From Gloucester Out.
Geranium.
Gunslinger, *sels.*
Hide of My Mother, The.
Home on the Range, February 1962.
La Máquina a Houston.
Los Mineros.
Morning to Remember, A; or, E Pluribus Unum.
Mourning Letter, March 29 1963.
On the Debt My Mother Owed to Sears Roebuck.
Oxford, *sels.*
Rick of Green Wood, The.
Song, A.
Song, The: "So light no one noticed."
Thesis.
Vaquero.
When the Fairies.

Dorney, Elizabeth
Chemistry of Character, The.

Dornin, Christopher L.
In a Building Named for a Governor.

Dorr, Julia Caroline Ripley (1825–1913)
Legend of the Organ-Builder, The.
Not Mine.

Dorset, Catherine Ann (1750–1817)
Peacock "At Home," The.

Dorsey, Thomas A. (1899–1993)
Take My Hand, Precious Lord.

Dos Passos, John (1896–1970)
Crimson Tent.

Doten, Elizabeth ("Lizzie") (b. 1829)
In a Hundred Years.

Doty, Mark (b. 1953)
Adonis Theater.
Almost Blue.
Bill's Story.
Broadway.
Difference.
Harbor Lights.
Heaven.
Night Ferry.

Doubiago, Sharon
Father.
From the Waitress Papers.
Mother, *sels.*
Self.
Signal Hill.
South America Mi Hija, *sels.*

Double-face
If there is someone above.

Doudney, Sarah (1843?–1926)
Christian's "Good-Night," The.
Sweet Surprises.
Water Mill, The.

Doughty, Charles Montague (1843–1926)
Dawn in Britain, The, *sels.*
Fairies Feast, The.

Douglas, Lady Alfred. *See* **Custance, Olive**

Douglas, Lord Alfred Bruce (1870–1945)
Apologia.
Dead Poet, The.
Green River, The.
Impression de Nuit; London.
Ode to My Soul.
Rejected.
To Olive.
To Sleep.
Two Loves.

Douglas, Gawin [*or* Gavin] (1474?–1522)
King Hart, *sels.*
Palace [*or* Palice] of Honor [*or* Honour], The, *sels.*

Douglas, Keith (1920–44)
Aristocrats.
Behaviour of Fish in an Egyptian Tea Garden.
Cairo Jag.
Deceased, The.
Desert Flowers.
Enfidaville.
Gallantry.
How to Kill.
Knife, The.

Marvel, The.
Offensive, The.
On a Return from Egypt.
Russians.
Simplify Me When I'm Dead.
Soissons.
Vergissmeinnicht.

"Douglas, Marian" (Annie Douglas Green Robinson) (1842–1913)
Ant-Hills.
Good Thanksgiving, A.
Snow-Man, The.

Douglas, Norman
Limerick: "There was a young fellow named Skinner."
Limerick: "There was a young lady of Louth."

Douglas, William (1672–1748)
Annie Laurie.

Douglass, Frederick (c.1817–1895)
Middle Passage.
Narrative of the Life of Frederick Douglass, an American Slave, *sels.*

Dove, Olive
Dragon has come, A.
Snowing. Snowing. Snowing.

Dove, Rita (b. 1952)
Adolescence—I.
Adolescence—II.
Adolescence—III.
After Reading *Mickey in the Night Kitchen* for the Third Time Before Bed.
Aircraft.
Alfonzo Prepares to Go Over the Top.
Anti-Father.
Arrow.
Banneker.
Beauty and the Beast.
Bird Frau, The.
Bistro Styx, The.
Blown apart by loss, she let herself go.
Cameos.
Canary.
Courtship.
David Walker (1785–1830).
Daystar.
Dusting.
Elevator Man, 1949.
Event, The.
Fifth Grade Autobiography.
First Book, The.
Fish in the Stone, The.
Flash Cards.
Genie's Prayer Under the Kitchen Sink.
Geometry.
Great Palaces of Versailles, The.
Hill of Beans, A.
History.
Horse and Tree.
House Slave, The.
Island Women of Paris, The.
Lady Freedom Among Us.
Lint.
Listen to the sound of my horn. . . .
Lost Brilliance.
Mother Love, *sels.*
Motherhood.
Nigger Song: An Odyssey.
Nightmare.
Ö.
Oriental Ballerina, The.
Parsley.
Pastoral.
Persephone, Falling.
Persephone Underground.
Political.
Receiving the Stigmata.
Roast Possum.
Satisfaction Coal Company, The.
Secret Garden, The.
Sightseeing.
Small Town.
Sonnet in Primary Colors.
Suite for Augustus, A, *sels.*
Sunday Greens.
Taking in Wash.
Teach Us to Number Our Days.

This Life.
Thomas at the Wheel.
Used.
Weathering Out.
Wingfoot Lake.
Zeppelin factory, The.

Dow, Philip (b. 1937)
Air.
Dried Fruit.
Drunk Last Night with Friends, I Go to Work Anyway.
Duck Pond at Mini's Pasture, a Dozen Years Later, The.
Life, The.
Skunk, The.
Suite for Celery and Blind Date.
Twilight in California.

Dowden, Edward (1843–1913)
Burdens.
In the Cathedral Close.
Leonardo's "Mona Lisa."
Two Infinities.

Dower, E. (fl. c.1738)
New River Head, a Fragment, The.

Dowland, John (1562–1626)
Come away, come, sweet love.
Dear, if you change, I'll never choose again.
Fine knacks for ladies, cheape choise brave and new.

Dowling, Bartholomew (1823?–1863)
Revel, The.

Downar, Joan
From the Bramble Hedge.

Downie, Freda
Great-Grandfather.
Her Garden.
Miss Grant.
Starlight.

Dowriche, Anne (fl. 1589–96)
French Historie, The, *sels.*

Dowson, Ernest Christopher (1867–1900)
Autumnal.
Benedictio Domini.
Breton Afternoon.
Carthusians.
De Amore, *sels.*
Dregs.
Epigram: "Because I am idolatrous and have besought."
Exchanges.
Exile.
Extreme Unction.
Flos Lunae.
Garden of Shadow, The.
Gray Nights.
Last Word, A.
Non Sum Qualis Eram Bonae sub Regno Cynara[e].
Nuns of the Perpetual Adoration.
O Mors! Quam Amara Est Memoria Tua Homini Pacem Habenti In Substantiis Suis.
Passing of Tennyson, The.
Spleen.
Terre Promise.
To One in Bedlam.
Valediction, A.
Vesperal.
Villanelle of Marguerites.
Villanelle of Sunset.
Villanelle of the Poet's Road.
Vitae Summa Brevis Spem Nos Vetat Incohare Longam.
You would have understood me, had you waited.

Doyle, Sir Arthur Conan
To An Undiscerning Critic.

Doyle, Sir Francis Hastings (1810–88)
Private of the Buffs; or, The British Soldier in China.

Doyle, Kirby (1810–88)
Strange.

"Doyle, Lynn" (Leslie Alexander Montgomery) (1873–1961)
Ulsterman, An.

Doyle, Susanne
Hell To Pay.

Some Girls.
This Shade.

Drainac, Rade (1899–1943)
Classic Verses.
Landscape.
Leaf.
My hunger is infinite and my hands always empty.
Opus III, *sels.*
When the Poet Without Lying Verses in His Heart Returns to His Native Country, *sels.*

Drake, Francis (b. 1650, d. after 1668)
To the Memory of the Learned and Reverend, Mr. Jonathan Mitchell.

Drake, Joseph Rodman. *See* **Halleck, Fitz-Greene** *and* **Joseph Rodman Drake**

Drake, Joseph Rodman (1795–1820)
American Flag, The.
Bronx.
Culprit Fay, The.
Mocking-Bird, The.
National Painting, The.
Niagara.
To a Friend.

Dransfield, Michael (1948–73)
Bum's Rush.
Day at a Time.
Endsight.
Epiderm.
Fix.
Flying.
Geography, *sels.*
Loft.
Memoirs of a Velvet Urinal.
Minstrel.
Pas de Deux for Lovers.
Pioneer Lane.
Portrait of the Artist as an Old Man.
Rainpoem.
Self-analysis.
Strange Bird, A.
That Which We Call a Rose.
Visiting Hour (Repatriation Hospital).
War of the Roses, The.

Draycott, Jane
Search.

Drayson, Phyllis
Blackbird, The.
Hide and Seek.

Drayton, Michael (1563–1631)
Agincourt.
As love and I, late harbour'd in one inn.
Cryer, The.
Cupid, I hate thee, which I'd have thee know.
David and Goliath, *sels.*
England's Heroical Epistles, *sels.*
First Steps Up Parnassus.
Heart, The.
His Defence Against the Idle Critic.
Idea, *sels.*
Idea's Mirrour, *sels.*
Moone-Calfe, The, *sels.*
Moses His Birth and Miracles, *sels.*
Most Excellent Song Which Was Solomon's, The, *sels.*
Muses' Elysium [or Elizium], *sels.*
Muses' Elysium X, The, *sels.*
Noah's Flood, *sels.*
Ode Written in the Peak[e], An.
Other Song of the Faithful, for the Mercies of God, An
Pigwiggen.
Poly-Olbion.
Poly-Olbion Song 6, *sels.*
Polyolbion, *sels.*
Roundelay Between Two Shepherds, A.
Sacrifice to Apollo, The.
Shepherd's Garland, The, *sels.*
Shepherd's Sirena, The, *sels.*
Skeltoniad, A.
Song of Jonah in the Whale's Belly, The.
Song of the Faithful, A.
These verses weare made By Michaell Drayton Esquier Poett Lawreatt the night before hee dyed.

Third Eclogue, The, *sels.*
To Henry Reynolds, of Poets and Poesy, *sels.*
To His Coy Love, A Canzonet.
To His Valentine.
To My Noble Friend Master William
   Browne: Of the Evil Time.
To the New Yeere [*or* Year].
To the Senses.
To the Virginian Voyage.

Drennan, John Swanwick [*or* Swanick] (1809–93)
Epigram: "Golden casket I designed, A."
Epigram: "Love signed the contract blithe
   and leal."
L'Amitié et l'Amour.
On the Telescopic Moon.

Drennan, William (1754–1820)
Wake of William Orr, The.

Drevniok, Betty
Deep snow.
Snow at dusk.

"Drinan, Adam." *See* **MacLeod, Joseph Gordon**

Drinkwater, John (1882–1937)
Birthright.
Cottage Song.
Deer.
Invocation: "As pools beneath stone arches
   take."
Moonlit Apples.
Morning Thanksgiving.
Reciprocity.
Sun, The.
Sunrise on Rydal Water.
Town Window, A.
Who Were before Me.

Driscoll, Louise (b. 1875)
Hold Fast Your Dreams.
Marigolds.
My garden is a pleasant place.
Thanksgiving.

Driver, C. J. (b. 1941)
Ballad of Hunters, A.
Birthdays.
In Solitary Confinement, Sea Point Police
   Cells.
Letter to Breyten Breytenbach from Hong
   Kong.
To Jann, in Her Absence.

Drofenko, Sergey [*or* Sergei] (1937–71)
Sketches from History.

Dromgoole, Will Allen (1865–1943)
Building the Bridge.
Old Ladies.

Dronsfield, John (1900–1951)
Visitation.

Droste-Hülshoff, Annette von (1797–1848)
In the Grass.
Last Day of the Year (New Year's Eve),
   The.
On the Tower.

Drown, Lessie M.
To-Day.
To Mother.

Druce, Robert (1929–)
Apropos of Garden Statuary: A Disquisition
   upon a Minor Genre.

Druk, Vladimir (b. 1957)
Communal Krakovyak.
Drukascripts.

Drummond de Andrade, Carlos (1902–87)
Dead in Frock Coats, THe.
Dirty Hand, The.
Family Portrait.
In the middle of the road there was a stone.
Looking for Poetry.
Motionless Faces.
Residue.
Seven-Sided Poem.
Souvenir of the Ancient World.
Travelling in the Family.

Drummond, William Henry (1854–1907)
Log Jam, The.
Madrigal.
Wreck of the *Julie Plante* [*or* The *Julie
Plante*], The.

Drummond, William, of Hawthornden (1585–1649)
Against the king, sir, now why would ye
   fight?
Book, The.
Change Should Breed Change.
Content and Resolute.
Doth then the world go thus, doth all thus
   move?
For a Lady's Summons of Non-Entry.
For the Baptiste.
For the Magdalene.
Forth Feasting, *sels.*
Hymn of the Fairest Fair, The, *sels.*
I know that all beneath the moon decays.
If of the dead save good nought should be
   said.
Invocation: "Pheobus, arise! / And paint the
   sable skies."
Iöas' Epitaph.
Kisses Desired.
Madrigal: "Beauty [*or* Beautie], and the life,
   The."
Madrigal: "Daedal of my death, A."
Madrigal: "Like the Idalian Queen[e]."
Madrigal: "My thoughts hold mortal[l] strife."
Madrigal: "This life, which seems so fair."
Madrigal: "This world a hunting is."
Madrigal: "Unhappie [*or* Unhappy] Light."
Of Phyllis.
On Mary Magdalene.
On Pym.
Redeem Time Past.
Regrat.
Saint John Baptist.
Sanquhar, whom this earth could scarce
   contain.
Sextain: "Sith gone is my delight and only
   pleasure."
Sextain: "With elegies, sad songs, and
   mourning lays."
Sonet to Sleepe.
Sonnet: "Alexis, here she stayed; among
   these pines."
Sonnet: "As in a duskie [*or* dusky] and
   tempestuous night."
Sonnet: "Slide soft, fair forth, and make a
   crystal plain."
Spring Bereaved.
Spring Bereaved 2.
Statue of Medusa, The.
Stolen Pleasure.
To Chloris.
To His Lute.
To Sir W. A..
Trojan Horse, The.
Urania, or Spiritual Poems, *sels.*
Word a Hunt, A.

Drunina, Yuliya [*or* Iuliia] Vladimirovna (1924–91)
In all ages, always, everywhere, and
   everywhere.
So many times I've seen hand-to-hand
   combat.

Dryden, John (1631–1700)
Absalom and Achitophel, Pt. I, *sels.*
Alexander's Feast; or, The Power of Music
   [*or* Musique].
Amboyna; or, The Cruelties of the Dutch to
   the English Merchants, *sels.*
Amphitryon, *sels.*
Annus Mirabilis, *sels.*
Aureng-Zebe, *sels.*
Character of a Good Parson, The.
Cleomenes, *sels.*
Conquest of Granada, The, *sels.*
Cymon and Iphigenia, *sels.*
Evening's Love, An, *sels.*
Happy the man, and happy he alone.
Hind and the Panther, The, *sels.*
Indian Emperor, The, *sels.*
King Arthur, *sels.*
Lines Printed under the Engraved Portrait of
   Milton [In Tonson's Folio of the "Paradise
   Lost"].
Love Triumphant, *sels.*
MacFlecknoe; or, A Satire [*or* Satyr] upon

the True-Blue [*or* -Blew] Protestant Poet
   T. S, *sels.*
Marriage à la Mode, *sels.*
Medal [*or* Medall], The, *sels.*
Oedipus, *sels.*
On Jacob Tonson, His Publisher.
Religio Laici, *sels.*
Secret Love; or, The Maiden Queen, *sels.*
Secular Masque, The, *sels.*
Silent Woman to the University of Oxford,
   The, *sels.*
Song for St Cecilia's Day [1687], A, *sels.*
Song: "SYLVIA the fair, in the bloom of
   fifteen."
Song to a Fair Young Lady, Going Out of
   the Town in the Spring.
Spanish Friar [*or* Fryar], The, *sels.*
State of Innocence, The, *sels.*
Theodore and Honoria, *sels.*
Theodore and Honoria, From [Fables Ancient
   and Modern from] Boccace, *sels.*
Threnodia Augustalis, *sels.*
To My Dear Friend Mr Congreve [on His
   Comedy Called "The Double-Dealer"].
To My Honoured [*or* Honour'd] Kinsman,
   John Driden [of Chesterton in the County
   of Huntingdon, Esquire], *sels.*
To the Earl of Roscommon, on His Excellent
   Essay on Translated Verse, *sels.*
To the Memory of Mr Oldham.
To the Pious Memory of the Accomplished
   [*or* Accomplisht] Young Lady, Mrs. Anne
   Killigrew, [Excellent in the Two Sister-
   Arts of Poesie and Painting].
Troilus and Cressida, *sels.*
Tyrannic Love, *sels.*
See also **Howard, Sir Robert** *and* **John
Dryden**

Dryden, John (1631–1700) *and* **Nahum Tate**
Absalom and Achitophel, Pt. II, *sels.*

Du Bellay, Joachim (1522–60)
Epitaph For Belaud, *sels.*
Heureux Qui, comme Ulysse, A Fait un Beau
   Voyage.
Hymn to the Winds.
I Saw the Bird That Dares Behold the Sun.
It Was the Time.
Regrets, *sels.*
Rome.
Ruins of Rome, *sels.*
Sonnet to Heavenly Beauty, A.
To His Friend in Elysium.
To Venus.
Visions of Bellay, The, *sels.*
Vow to Heavenly Venus, A.

Du Bois, Dorothea (1728–74)
Song: "Scholar first my Love implor'd, A."

Du Maurier, George (1834–96)
Music.
Trilby, *sels.*
Vers Nonsensiques.

Du Tử' Lê Lê Cu' Phách
Dawn of a New Humankind, The.

Dubé, Janet
Autobiography.
So to Tell the Truth.

Dube, Oswald Basize (b. 1957)
He Was a Man of Jokes outside Office.

Dubie, Norman (b. 1945)
Apocrypha of Jacques Derrida, The.
At Midsummer.
Balalaika.
Czar's Last Christmas Letter: A Barn in the
   Urals, The.
Diatribe of the Kite, The.
Dressing Stations, The.
Elegy for Integral Domains, The.
Elegy for Wright & Hugo.
Elizabeth's War with the Christmas Bear.
February; the Boy Breughel.
Fox Who Watched for the Midnight Sun,
   The.
Funeral, The.
Ganges, The.
Hummingbirds.
In the Dead of the Night.

Killigrew Wood, The.
Lamentations.
Obscure, The.
Pastoral: "It all happened so fast. Fenya was
  in the straight chair."
Radio Sky.
Thomas Hardy.
Trakl.

Dubois, Lady Dorothea (1728–74)
Song: "Scholar first my love implored, A."

**DuBois, William Edward Burghardt (1868–
1963)**
Song of the Smoke, The.

Duchamp, Marcel (1887–1968)
Cast Shadows.
Deferment.
Electricity Breadthwise.
1914 Box, The.
Speculations.
SURcenSURE.
World in Yellow, A.

Duché, Jacob (1738–98)
Chilled by the Blasts of Adverse Fate.
Great Lord of All, Whose Work of Love.

Duck, Stephen (1705–56)
On Richmond Park, sels.
Thresher's Labour, The, sels.

Duckett, Alfred A. (b. 1918)
Sonnet: "Where are we to go when this is
  done?"

**Duclaux, Mme. See Robinson, Agnes Mary
Frances**

Dudek, Louis (b. 1918)
Atlantis, sels.
Coming Suddenly to the Sea.
Dead, The.
García Lorca.
Provincetown, sels.

Dudin, Mikhail Aleksandrovich (b. 1916)
Nightingales.

Dudley, Michael
At the backyard fence.
Home late.
Lulling me to sleep.
Menstrual cramps.

Dudley, Thomas (1576–1653)
Verses Found in Thomas Dudley's Pocket
  after His Death.

Dudley, William E. (b. 1887)
City, Lord, Where Thy Dear Life, The.

Duerden, Richard (b. 1927)
Dance with Banderillas.
Moon Is to Blood.
Musica No. 3.

Duesing, Laurie
Blossoming.
Reprieve.
Send Pictures, You Said...
Wild and Blue.

Dufault, Peter Kane (b. 1923)
Black Jess.
Burden.
Driving Home.
First Night, A.
In an Old Orchard.
Letter for Allhallows, A.
Mud Dauber Wasp, The.
On Aesthetics, More or Less.
Owl.
Possibilities.

**Dufferin, Helen Selina Blackwood, Countess of
(1807–67)**
Charming Woman, The.
Countess of Dufferin, The.
Mother's Lament, The.

Duffield, George, Jr. (1818–88)
Stand Up! Stand Up for Jesus.

Duffy, Carol Ann (b. 1955)
Dolphins, The.
Foreign.
In Your Mind.
Oppenheim's Cup and Saucer.
Plainsong.
Politico.
Prayer.

Telephoning Home.
Valentine.
Warming Her Pearls.

Duffy, Maureen (b. 1933)
I am beset with a dream of fair woman.
Semi-Skilled Lover.

Dugan, Alan (b. 1923)
Adultery.
Against a Sickness: To the Female Double
  Principle God.
Against the Text "Art Is Immortal."
American against Solitude.
Aside.
Elegy: "I know but will not tell."
Fabrication of Ancestors.
From Heraclitus.
Funeral Oration for a Mouse.
Glad at the Cold (1955).
How We Heard the Name.
Internal Migration: On Being on Tour.
Last Statement for a Last Oracle.
Let Heroes Account to Love.
Love Song: I and Thou.
Memorial Service for the Invasion Beach
  Where the Vacation in the Flesh Is Over.
Memories of Verdun.
Mirror Perilous, The.
Niagara Falls.
Not to Choose.
Note: The Sea Grinds Things Up.
On a Seven-Day Diary.
On an East Wind from the Wars.
On Being a Householder.
On Hurricane Jackson.
On Trading Time for Life by Work
On Trees.
Plague of Dead Sharks.
Portrait from the Infantry.
Prayer: "God, I need a job because I need
  money."
Prison Song.
Stutterer.
Thesis, Antithesis and Nostalgia.
To a Red-headed Do-good Waitress.
Wall, Cave, and Pillar Statements, after
  Asôka.
Winter for an Untenable Situation.

Dugan, Michael (b. 1947)
Herbaceous Plodd.

Duggan, Eileen (1894–1972)
Ballad of the Bushman.
Cloudy Bay.
Invasion.
Juniper.
Prophecy.
Rosa Luxembourg.
Shag, The.
Tides Run up the Wairau, The.
Truth.

Duggan, Laurie (b. 1949)
Ash Range, The, sels.
Dogs, sels.
Eight xx.
Epigrams of Martial, The, sels.
Qantas Bags.
Ten ii.
Three Found Poems, sels.
Three xlvii.
Town on the Ten Dollar Note, The.

Duggin, Lorraine
For My Mother, Who Lives.
Learning My Father's Language.

Duhamel, Denise (b. 1961)
Bulimia.
Feminism.

Duke, Richard (1658–1711)
Song, A.
To Caelia.

Duke, William (1757–1840)
Hail Our Incarnate God!

Dumaine, Christine
Second Language.

Dumas, Alexandre (1802–70)
Lady of the Pearls, The, sels.

Dumas, Edmund (d. 1884)
Our School Now Closes Out.

Dumas, Henry (1935–68)
America.
Black Star Line.
Black Trumpeter.
Buffalo.
Concentration Camp Blues.
Island within Island.
Knees of a Natural Man.
Knock on Wood.
Root Song.
Zebra Goes Wild Where the Sidewalk Ends,
  The.

Dumbrveanu, Anghel
Genesis.
Seeds of Flight.

Dunbar, Jennie
A-Hunting.

Dunbar-Nelson, Alice Moore (1875–1935)
April is on the way!
I sit and sew—a useless task it seems.
Music! Lilting, soft and languorous.
Proletariat Speaks, The.
Snow in October.
Sonnet: "I had no thought of violets of late."
To Madame Curie.

Dunbar, Paul Laurence (1872–1906)
Accountability.
Ante-Bellum Sermon, An.
Black Samson of Brandywine.
Boy's Summer, A.
Cabin Tale, A.
Colored Soldiers, The.
Common Things.
Companion's Progress, A.
Compensation
Corn-Stalk Fiddle, THe.
Dawn.
Deacon Jones' Grievance.
Death Song[, A].
Debt, The.
Dinah Kneading Dough.
Douglass.
Ere sleep comes down to soothe the weary
  eyes.
Frederick Douglass.
Harriet Beecher Stowe.
Haunted Oak, The.
Her Thought and His.
Howdy, Honey, Howdy!
In the Morning.
Little brown baby wif spa'klin' eyes.
Lover's Lane.
Made to Order Smile, The.
Misapprehension.
Mystery, The.
Negro Love Song, A.
Not they who soar, but they who plod.
Ode to Ethiopia.
Old Cabin, The.
Paradox, The.
Philosophy.
Place Where the Rainbow Ends, The.
Poet, The.
Robert Gould Shaw.
Ships That Pass in the Night.
Signs of the Times.
Slow Through the Dark.
Soliloquy of a Turkey.
Song of Summer.
Spiritual, A.
Summer in the South.
Summer's Night, A.
Sympathy.
Then and Now.
To a Captious Critic.
Unsung Heroes, The.
We wear the mask that grins and lies.
When all is done, and my last word is said.
When de Co'n Pone's Hot.
When Dey 'Listed Colored Soldiers.
When Malindy Sings.
Worn Out.

Dunbar, Robert (d. 1866)
Caraguin, The, sels.
Cruise, The, sels.

Dunbar, William (c.1465–c.1530)
All Erdly Joy Returns in Pane.

Amendis to the Telyouris and Sowtaris for the Turnament Maid on Thame, The.
Ane Ballat of Our Lady, *sels.*
Ballad of Kynd Kittok, The.
Book of the Two Married Women and the Widow, The, *sels.*
Dance of the Sevin Deidly Synnis, The.
Golden [*or* Goldyn] Targe, The, *sels.*
In Prais of Wemen.
In Praise of Women.
In secreit place, this hyndir [*or* hindir] nycht [*or* nicht].
Lament for the Makaris.
Magryme, The.
Meditatioun in Wyntir.
Of Christ's Nativity.
On the Resurrection of Christ.
Petition of the Gray Horse, Auld Dunbar, The.
Quod Dunbar to Kennedy.
Remonstrance to the King.
Testament of Mr. Andro Kennedy, The.
To a Lady[e].
To the City of London [*or* In Honour of the City of London].
To the Merchantis of Edinburgh.
Translation by Mark Willhardt.
Tretis of the Tua Mariit Wemen and the Wedo, The, *sels.*
Tua Mariit Wemen and the Wedo, The, *sels.*

Duncan, Andrew (b. 1956)
In the Red Grove.
Poet and the Schizophrenic, The.

Duncan, Robert (b. 1919)
Achilles' Song.
African Elegy, An.
After a Passage in Baudelaire.
Among my friends love is a great sorrow.
And If He Had Been Wrong for Me.
Ark for Lawrence Durrell, An.
Ballad of Mrs. Noah, The.
Bending the Bow.
Childhood's Retreat.
Chords Passages 14.
Close.
Coming out of the house to die.
Correspondences.
Dance, The.
Dancing Concerning a Form of Women, A.
Dante, *sels.*
Dream Data.
Drinking Fountain, The.
Eyesight II.
Food for Fire, Food for Thought.
Fourth Song the Night Nurse Sang.
Glimpse, A.
Homage and Lament for Ezra Pound in Captivity.
Ingmar Bergman's "Seventh Seal."
Interlude, An.
Letting the beat go.
Morning Letter, A.
My mother would be a falconress.
New Poem, A.
Night Scenes.
Often I Am Permitted to Return to a Meadow.
Owl Is an Only Bird of Poetry, An.
Part-Sequence for Change, A.
Passage Over Water.
Passages, *sels.*
Passages 37.
Persephone.
Poem Beginning with a Line by Pindar, A.
Poems from the Margins of Thom Gunn's Moly, *sels.*
Poetry, a Natural Thing.
Presence of the Dance / The Resolution of the Music, The.
Question, The.
Returning to Roots of First Feeling.
Rites of Participation, *sels.*
Roots and Branches.
Shelley's "Arethusa" Set to New Measures.
Sleep is a Deep and Many Voiced Flood.
Song of the Borderguard, The.
Songs of an Other.

Spring Memorandum, A.
Strains of Sight.
Structure of Rime XVIII.
Structure of Rime XXIII.
Styx.
Temple of the Animals, The.
This Place Rumord to Have Been Sodom.
Torso / Passages 18, The.
Turning Into.
Turning into a restful roomfull.

Dunkerley, William Arthur. *See* **Oxenham, John**

Dunkin, William (1709?–1765)
Epistle to Robert Nugent, Esq. with a Picture of Doctor Swift in Old Age, An, *sels.*

Dunn, Douglas (b. 1942)
After the War.
Clothes Pit, The.
Dream of Judgement, A.
Elegies, *sels.*
Elegy for the Lost Parish.
Emblems.
Estuarial Republic, The.
France.
Gardeners.
Glasgow Schoolboys, Running Backwards.
Green Breeks.
House Next Door, The.
In the Grounds.
Kaleidoscope, The.
Musical Orchard, The.
On Roofs of Terry Street.
Patricians, The.
Remembering Lunch.
Removal from Terry Street, A.
Supreme Death.
War Blinded.
Warriors.
Washing the Coins.

Dunn, Gwen
Journey Back to Christmas.

Dunn, Max (b. 1895)
O, where were we before time was.

Dunn, Stephen (b. 1939)
At the Smithville Methodist Church.
Dancing with God.
Day and Night Handball.
Happiness.
He/She.
Let's See If I Have It Right.
Looking for a Rest Area.
Man Who Closed Shop, The.
On Hearing the Airlines Will Use a Psychological Profile to Catch Potential Skyjackers.
Routine Things Around the House, The.
Something Like Happiness.
Tenderness.
Truck Stop: Minnesota.
Vanishings, The.
What They Wanted.

Dunn, Stephen P. (b. 1928)
Men Talk.

Dunne, Sean (b. 1956)
Refugees at Cobh.
Throwing the Beads.

Duoduo (b. 1951)
At Parting.
Looking out from death you will always see.
Thoughts and Recollections, *sels.*
Untitled.
Wishful Thinking Is the Master of Reality.

Du'o'ng Bá Trac (1884–1944)
Prison Life.

Dupin, Jacques (b. 1927)
Mineral Kingdom.
Songs of Rescue, *sels.*
Waiting with lowered voice.

DuPlessis, Phil (b. 1944)
Prayer for a Thief.

DuPlessis, Rachel Blau
Eurydice, *sels.*
Mirror Poem.

Dupuy, J. (d. 1964)
Michael Met a Duck.

Durack, Mary (b. 1913)
Lament for the Drowned Country.

Durand, Oswald (1840–1906)
Black Man's Son, The.
Francie-the-Possessed.

Durant, Mrs. Kenneth. *See* **Taggard, Genevieve**

Durcan, Paul (b. 1944)
Around the corner from Francis Bacon.
Backside to the Wind.
Bewley's Oriental Café, Westmoreland Street.
Birth of a Coachman.
Divorce Referendum, Ireland, 1986, The.
Going Home to Mayo, Winter, 1949.
Hat Factory, The.
Honeymoon Postcard.
Ireland 1972.
Irish Hierarchy Bans Colour Photography.
Jewish Bride, The.
Kilfenora Teaboy, The.
Lion Tamer, The.
Micheál Mac Liammóir.
Pietà's Over—and, now, my dear, droll, husband, The.
She Mends an Ancient Wireless.
Sister Agnes Writes to Her Beloved Mother.
10.30 AM Mass, June 16, 1985.
Tullynoe: Tête-à-Tête in the Parish Priest's Parlour.
Turkish Carpet, The.
Weeping Headstones of the Isaac Becketts, The.
Wife Who Smashed Television Gets Jail.

Durem, Ray (1915–63)
Award.
Friends.
I Know I'm Not Sufficiently Obscure.
Problem in Social Geometry—the Inverted Square!
Vet's Rehabilitation.

D'Urfey [*or* Durfey], Thomas (1653–1723)
Bath; or, The Western Lass, The, *sels.*
Chloe Divine.
Fisherman's Song, The.
Fool's Preferment, A, *sels.*

Durham, Jimmie (b. 1940)
Columbus Day.
Justiniano Lamé Has Been Killed.
Middle.
Woman Gave Me a Red Star to Wear on My Headband, A.

Duris (*fl.* c.3d cent. B.C.)
Ephesos.

Durrell, Lawrence (b. 1912)
Acropolis.
Ballad of the Good Lord Nelson, A.
Ballad of the Oedipus Complex.
Death of General Uncebunke, The; a Biography in Little, *sels.*
Delos.
Eight Aspects of Melissa, *sels.*
In Arcadia.
In Crisis.
In the Garden: Villa Cleobolus.
Lesbos.
Mythology.
Nemea.
On First Looking into Loeb's Horace.
On Seeming to Presume.
Paphos.
Poggio.
Salamis.
Sarajevo.
Seferis.
Stoic.
Strip-tease.
Swans.
This Unimportant Morning.
Vega.
Water-Colour of Venice, A.

Durston, Georgia Roberts
Hippopotamus, The.
Wolf, The.

Dutton, Geoffrey (b. 1922)
Burning Off.
Finished Gentleman, A.
Fish Shop Windows.

Stranded Whales, The.
Time of Waiting.

Dutton, Geoffrey Fraser (b. 1924)
Clach Eanchainn.
Street.

Dwight, Timothy (1752–1817)
As down a lone valley with cedars
o'erspread.
I Love Thy Kingdom, Lord.
Shall Man, O God of Light.
Sing to the Lord Most High.
Triumph of Infidelity, The, *sels.*

Dybek, Stuart (b. 1942)
Brass Knuckles.
Cherry.
My Father's Fights.
My Neighborhood.

Dyer, Sir Edward. *See* Greville, Fulke, 1st
Baron Brooke *and* Sir Edward Dyer

Dyer, Sir Edward (c.1540–1607)
I would it were not as it is.
Love is Love.
My mind [*or* minde *or* mynde] to me a
kingdom [*or* kyngdome] is.
PROMETHEUS, when first from heaven high.
Wher one would be.

Dyer, George (1755–1841)
In deep distress, I cried to God.

Dyer, John (1699–1758)
Country Walk, The, *sels.*
Fleece, The, *sels.*
Grongar Hill, *sels.*
My Ox Duke.
To Clio, from Rome.

Dyer, Lady Catherine (*fl.* c.1641)
Sir William Dyer, Knight, *sels.*

"Dylan, Bob" (Robert Zimmerman) (b. 1941)
Ballad of a Thin Man.
Blowin' in the Wind.
Boots of Spanish Leather.
Don't ya tell Henry.
It's Alright, Ma (I'm Only Bleeding).
Quinn the Eskimo.
Tears of Rage.
Three angels up above the street.
Tiny Montgomery.

Dyment, Clifford (1914–70)
As a boy with a richness of needs I
wandered.
Fox.
Sanctuary.

Dyson, Edward (1865–1931)
Friendly Game of Football, A.
Old Whim Horse, The.

Dyson, Will (1880–1938)
Trucker, The.

Dzyubin, Eduard Georgievich. *See* "Bagritzky,
Eduard Georgievich"

E

"E." *See* Fullerton, Mary Elizabeth

Eady, Cornelius (b. 1954)
Dance, The.
False Arrest.
Hank Mobley's.
I Just Wanna Testify.
January.
Jazz Dancer.
My Mother, If She Had Won Free Dance
Lessons.
My Mother is a God Fearing Woman.
Romare Bearden Retrospective at the
Brooklyn Museum.
Sherbet.
Song.
Success.
Supremes, The.
Thrift.
Why Do So Few Blacks Study Creative
Writing?
William Carlos Williams.
Young Elvis.

"Eagle, Solomon." *See* Squire, Sir John
Collings

Earley, Jaci (b. 1939)
One Thousand Nine Hundred and Sixty-Eight
Winters.

Earley, Tom (b. 1911)
Rebel's Progress.

"Eastaway, Edward." *See* Thomas, Edward

Eastburn, James Wallis (1797–1819)
O Holy, Holy, Holy, Lord.

Eastman, Max (1883–1969)
Animal.
Rainy Song.

Eastwick, Ivy O.
At Sunset.
Cherry Tree.
Feather for My Cap, A.
Larch Wood Secrets.
Lucy Lavender.
Miller, Miller.
Morning.
Pretty Maid Marion.
Scarf, The.
Trouble at the Farm.
Wolf and the Lambs, The.

Eaton, Anthony (b. 1943)
Dove Apologizes to His God for Being
Caught by a Cat, The.

Eaton, Charles Edward (b. 1916)
Lynx, The.

Eberhart, Richard (b. 1904)
Analogue of Unity in Multeity.
Brotherhood of Men, *sels.*
Cancer Cells, The.
Concord Cats.
Dam Neck, Virginia.
Flux.
For a Lamb.
Fury of Aerial Bombardment, The.
Garden God, The.
Groundhog, The.
Half-bent Man.
Hard Structure of the World, The.
Hardy Perennial.
Horse Chestnut Tree, The.
Human Being Is a Lonely Creature, The.
I walked over the grave of Henry James.
I went to see Irving Babbitt.
If I could only live at the pitch that is near
madness.
In a hard intellectual light / I will kill all
delight.
Loon Call, A.
Marrakech.
Matin Pandemoniums, The.
New England Bachelor, A.
New Hampshire, February.
On a Squirrel Crossing the Road in Autumn,
in New England.
On Shooting Particles beyond the World.
Plain Song Talk.
Rainscapes, Hydrangeas, Roses, and Singing
Birds.
Roc, The.
Rumination.
Sea Burial from the Cruiser *Reve.*
Sea-Hawk.
Seals, Terns, Time.
Ship Burning and a Comet All in One Day,
A.
Soul Longs to Return Whence It Came, The.
Spider expects the cold of winter, The.
Spite Fence.
Two Loves.
Under the Hill.
Vast Light.
Vision.
When Doris danced under the oak tree.
Youth and Age.

Echeruo, Michael (b. 1937)
Man and God Distinguished.
Melting Pot.

Eddy, Mary Baker (1821–1910)
O'er Waiting Harp-Strings of the Mind.
Shepherd, Show Me How to Go.

Eddy, Zachary (1815–91)
Floods Swell around Me, Angry, Appalling.
Jesus, Enthroned and Glorified.

Eden, Helen Parry (b. 1885)
Four-Paws.

Edey, Marion and **Dorothy Grider**
Trot Along, Pony.

Edgar, Marriott (1880–1951)
Lion and Albert, The.

Edman, Irwin (1896–1954)
La Donna E Perpetuum Mobile.
Peace.

Edmond, Lauris (b. 1924)
All Possession Is Theft.
Difficult Adjustment, A.
Ghosts II.
Jardin des Colombières.
Latter Day Lysistrata.
Ohakune Fires.
Sums, The.

Edmond, Murray (b. 1949)
House.
Sprig of Karo, A.
Von Tempsky's Dance.

Edmonds, Paul (1915–58)
Little Tommy Tiddler.

Edmondson, Madeleine
Witches' Spells.

Edson, C. L.
Ravin's of Piute Poet Poe.

Edson, Russell (b. 1935)
Amateur, The.
Ape.
Automobile, The.
Bringing a Dead Man Back into Life.
Childhood of an Equestrian, The.
Children.
Conjugal.
Cottage in the Wood, A.
Counting Sheep.
Darwin Descending.
Death of an Angel, The.
Fall, The.
Feeding the Dog.
Floor is something we must fight against.
Whilst seemingly, The.
Having to Love Something Else, The.
In All the Days of My Childhood.
In the Forest.
Journey through the Moonlight, A.
Large thing comes in, A.
Long Picnic, The.
Lovers.
Mouse Dinners.
Old Man's Son, An.
Optical Prodigal, The.
Ox, The.
Performance at Hog Theater, A.
Pilot, The.
Rat's Legs, The.
Retirement of the Elephant, The.
Tearing and Merging of Clouds, The.
Toy-maker made a toy wife and a toy child.
He made a toy house and some toy years,
A.
Way Things Are, The.
Wheelbarrow, The.
Wounded Breakfast, The.

Edwards, Amelia Blandford (1831–91)
Give Me Three Grains of Corn, Mother.

Edwards, Edwin
Waitekauri Every Time!

Edwards, Ken (b. 1950)
Firmament Doth Shake, The.
Geraniums, South London.
You Must Change Your Life.

Edwards, Matilda Caroline
Church Walking with the World, The.
Do As You Would Be Done By.
Home.
I Love the Night.
Remember the Poor.
There's a Silvery Lining to Every Cloud.
Time to Die, The.
To a Loved One of Other Days.

We Are Passing Away.
World Is Full of Beauty, The.

Edwards, Richard (1523–66)
Amantium Irae Amoris Redintegratio.
Blue Room, The.
Rain, The.
Recollections of an Old Spook.
When I was three I had a friend.

Edwards, Thomas (1699–1757)
Sonnet on a Family Picture.
To Shakespeare.
To the Author of Clarissa.
To the Editor of Mr. Pope's Works.
Tongue-Doughty Pedant.

Eedes, Richard (1555–1604)
No Love, to Love of Man and Wife.

"Effie, Aunt." *See* Browne, Jane Euphemia

Efron, Adelina Efimovna. *See* **"Adalis, Adelina Efimovna"**

Egan, Ted
Drover's Boy, The.

Egerton, J. A. (b. 1935)
Tell Him So.

Egerton, Sarah Fyge (1670–1723)
Emulation, The.
Female Advocate Or, An Answer to a Late
Satyr*, The, *sels.*
Liberty, The.
On a Sermon Preach'd Sept. the 6th, 1697.
on These Words: You Have Sold Your
Selves for Nought.
On My Leaving London, June the 29.
On My Wedding Day.
Repulse to Alcander, The.
To Marina.
To One Who Said I Must Not Love.
To Philaster.

Eggleton, David (b. 1953)
Painting Mount Taranaki.
These Rumours of Hexagonal Rooms in
Gone Bee City.

Eglington, Charles (b. 1918)
Arrival and Departure.
Buffalo.
Lourenço Marques.
Lowveld, The.
Vanquished, The.

Eglitis, Andrejs
I see how the grasping fingers of lovers do
not let go, till.
In a Naples Bar.
Winter has already shriveled—spring rushes
in with / black burial steeds.

**Ehrenburg [or Erenburg], Ilya Grigoryevich
(1891–1967)**
I lived obscurely and uncertainly.
January 1939.
Potter of Jaen, The.
"Reconnaissance in force"—just three brief
words.
Retribution.
Sons of Our Sons, The.
Tree, The.
Trumpet, The.

Ehrenstein, Albert (1884–1950)
Ares.
Home-Coming.
Homer.
Poet and War, The.
Suffering.

Ehrhart, William Daniel
Blizzard of Sixty-Six, The.
Confirmation, A.
Farmer Nguyen.
Guerrilla War.
Hunting.
Invasion of Grenada, The.
Letter.
Making the Children Behave.
Night Patrol.
One That Died, The.
Relative Thing, A.
". . . the light that cannot fade. . . ."
Time on Target.
To Those Who Have Gone Home Tired.

Ehrlich [or Erlikh], Wolf (1902–37)
Last Merchant, The.
Louse.

Ehrmann, Max (1872–1945)
Away.
Hate and the Love of the World, The.
I ponder on life.
If You Made Gentler the Churlish World.
Mother.
Prayer, A: "Let me do my work each day."

Eich, Günter (1907–72)
Geometrical Place.
Inventory.
Old Postcards.
Seminar for Backward Pupils.
Timetable.

Eichendorff, Joseph, Freiherr von (1788–1857)
On My Child's Death.

Eifuku, Empress (1271–1342)
We dressed each other.

Eigner, Larry (b. 1927)
All Intents.
B.
Back to it.
Bare trees / alternate, The.
Dark swimmers, The.
Do It Yrself.
Don't go.
Elysee.
Environs.
Fete, A.
Flake diamond of / the sea.
Fleche.
For Sleep.
From the sustaining air.
Gone, A.
How it comes about.
I have felt it as they've said.
If you weep, I think that.
In Imitation.
It Sounded.
Keep Me Still, for I Do Not Want to Dream.
Letter for Duncan.
Live / , bird which.
Noise Grimaced.
Open.
Open Air Where.
Passages.
Temporary language, A.
That the neighborhood might be covered.
Trees green   the quiet sun.
Wholes.
Wind like an ocean, The.

Eikei (*fl.* late 10th cent.)
Autumn has come / To the lonely cottage.

Eimers, Nancy
Another Kimono.
History of Navigation, A.
Night Without Stars, A.
No Friends of the Heart.

Eiseley, Loren C. (1907–77)
And as for Man.
Deserted Homestead, The.

Eisenhuth, Christoph
Night in the Village.

Eisner, Aleksey [or Aleksei] (1908–84)
Autumn nears. The branches yellow.

Ejong, Yityangu (d. *before* 1981)
Love Song: "Tiny children."

Ekelof, Gunnar
Absentia Animi.
For night comes.
Greece.
Hangman / what will you do with my arms?
If you ask me where I am.
Like ankle-rings, this music.

Eklund, George
Boyhood Winter.
Dressing My Daughter.

Ela, David H. (1831–1907)
Chosen Three, on Mountain Height, The.

**"Elagin, Ivan Venediktovich" (Ivan
Venediktovich Matveyev) (1918–87)**
Amnesty.
Come now, my friend, you must not say.

Has my life been a failure? I wonder—.
I know that a gangster will not murder me.
I like these foreign shores and I have never.
You told me that I was born under a lucky
star.

Elder, Anne (1918–76)
Carried Away.
Farmer Goes Beserk.
One Foot in the Door.
School Cadets.

Eldridge, Paul (b. 1888)
To a Courtesan a Thousand Years Dead.

Eleanora Fagan. *See&xit;* Holiday, Billie

Eleazar (*fl.* Middle Ages)
Thy Faithful Sons.

Elenkov, Luchezar
Amphora / as an emotion.
Poet.
Sauna.
Stone.
Ten Girls.

**Elijah ben Menahem Hazaken, of LeMans (*fl.*
11th cent.)**
Precepts He Gave His Folk.

**"Eliot, George" (Mary Ann [or Marian] Evans
Lewes Cross) (1727–1805)**
Armgart, *sels.*
At Set of Sun.
Brother and Sister, *sels.*
Choir Invisible, The.
Death of Moses, The.
Felix Holt, the Radical, *sels.*
How Lisa Loved the King, *sels.*
Roses.
Two lovers by a moss-grown spring.

Eliot, Thomas Stearns (1888–1965)
Animula.
Ash Wednesday [or Ash-Wednesday], *sels.*
Aunt Helen.
Boston Evening Transcript, The.
Bustopher Jones: The Cat About Town.
Cat Morgan Introduces Himself.
Choruses from "The Rock," *sels.*
Cocktail Party, The, *sels.*
Coriolan, *sels.*
Cousin Nancy.
Dedication to My Wife, A.
Eyes that last I saw in tears.
Five-Finger Exercises, *sels.*
Four Quartets, *sels.*
Gerontion.
Growltiger's Last Stand.
Gus: The Theatre Cat.
Hippopotamus, The.
Hollow Men, The.
Journey of the Magi.
La Figlia Che Piange.
Landscapes, *sels.*
Lines for an Old Man.
Love Song of J. Alfred Prufrock, The, *sels.*
Macavity: The Mystery Cat.
Marina.
Mr. Apollinax.
Mr Mistoffelees.
Morning at the Window.
Murder in the Cathedral, *sels.*
Naming of Cats is a difficult matter.
Portrait of a Lady.
Preludes (I–IV), *sels.*
Rhapsody on a Windy Night.
Rum Tum Tugger is a Curious Cat.
Skimbleshanks: The Railway Cat.
Song for Simeon, A.
Song of the Jellicles, The.
St. Luke, *sels.*
St. Matthew, *sels.*
Sweeney Agonistes, *sels.*
Sweeney Among the Nightingales.
Sweeney Erect.
Waste Land, The, *sels.*
Whispers of Immortality.
Wind sprang up at four o'clock, The.

"Eliza" (*fl.* 18th cent.)
Dart, The.
Lover, The.
To a Friend for Her Naked Breasts.

To My Husband.
To the Queen of Bohemiah.
Tour to the Glaciers of Savoy, A, *sels.*

Elizabeth I, Queen of England (1533–1603)
Ah silly pugg wert thou so sore afraid.
Doubt of future foes exiles my present joy,
   The.
On Fortune.
On Monsieur's Departure.
When I was fair and young, then [*or* and]
   favour graced me;.
Written in Her French Psalter.
Written on a Wall at Woodstock.
Written with a Diamond On Her Window at
   Woodstock.

Elizabeth of York, Queen (1465–1503)
My heart is set upon a lusty pin.

Elizabeth, Queen of Bohemia (1596–1660)
Verses by the Princess Elizabeth, Given to
   Lord Harington, of Exton, Her Preceptor.

Ellerton, John (1826–93)
Day Thou Gavest, Lord, Is Ended, The.

Ellerton, John Lodge (1801–73)
Now the Laborer's Task Is O'er.

Elliot, Alistair (b. 1932)
House-Rules I: Reading.

Elliot, Ebenezer (1781–1849)
Battle Song.
Beware of Dogmas.
Caged Rats.
Child, is thy father dead?
Drone *v.* Worker.
Epigram: "'Prepare to meet the King of
   Terrors,' cried."
God Save the People.
Here lies the man who stripp'd Sin bare.
How Different!
In these days, every mother's son or
   daughter.
John. In the sound of that rebellious word.
On a Rose in December.
On Communists.
Paddy, I have but stol'n your living.
Plaint.
Poet *vs.* Parson.
Song: "Donought would have everything."
Song: "When working blackguards come to
   blows."
Splendid Village, The, *sels.*
Spring.
Village Patriarch, The, *sels.*
Year of Seeds, The, *sels.*

Elliot, Jane [*or* Jean] (1727–1805)
Flowers of the Forest, The.

Elliott, Andrew (b. 1961)
Angel.
Here Today.
Love Poem, The.
Stay Behind, The.
X-Ray, The.

Elliott, F. Ann
Pictures.
Snow, The.

Elliott, Harley (b. 1940)
For Farmers.

Ellis, Alfred. *See* **Brown, James** and Alfred Ellis
Ellis, Colin (1895–1969)
Adder's Epigrams.
Bungaloid Growth.
Epitaph, An: "He worshipped at the altar of
   Romance."
International Conference.
Modern World, The.
New Vicar of Bray, The.
Old Ladies, The.
On a Gentleman Marrying His Cook.

Ellis, Edwin John
Himself, *sels.*

Ellis, George. *See* **"Gander, Sir Gregory"**; *also*
   Canning, George, George Ellis and **John**
   Hookham Frere

Ellis, Harold (*fl.* 1851)
Limerick: "O sage of the stage, Shaw of
   Shaws!"

Ellis, John (1698–1791)
Sarah Hazard's Love Letter.

Ellis, Pat Mayne
"Scientists find universe awash in tiny
   diamonds."

Ellis, Robert (1812–75)
Hour of Sleep, The.

Ellis, Steve (b. 1952)
Weathered Ides Grant Young Flesh.
Your Poems at Daybreak, the Destruction of
   Knossos by Afternoon.

Ellis, Thomas Sayers
Kiss in the Dark, A.
Shooting Back.
View of the Library of Congress from Paul
   Laurence Dunbar High School.

Ellis, Vivian Locke
At Common Dawn.

Ellsworth, Erastus Wolcott (b. 1822)
Mayflower, The.

"Elmo" (*fl.* c.1902?)
Our Ernest.

Elmslie, Kenward
Amazon Club.
Big Bar.
Duo-Tang.
Feathered Dances.
Fruit.
Island Celebration.
Japanese City.
Marbled Chuckle in the Savannahs.
One Night Stand.
Picnic.
Squatter in the Foreground.
Stage Duo.

Elmusa, Sharif
Little Piece of Sky, A.

Elovic, Barbara
Brooklyn Bound.

Éluard, Paul (Eugène Grindel) (1895–1952)
Curfew.
Dawn Dissolves the Monsters.
Invention, The.
Lady Love.
Liberty, *sels.*
Lover, secretly behind your smile.
Meetings.
Nazi Song.
November 1936.
Pig.
To Her of Whom They Dream.
To Ride.

Eluard, Paul *and* **Andre Breton**
Immaculate Conception, The, *sels.*

Elwell, F. E.
Courtesy is a quality of soul / refinement
   impossible to purchase.
Important Words.
Politeness is to do and say.

Elwood, Thomas
Prayer, A: "O that mine eyes might closed
   be."

Elytis, Odysseus (Odysseus Alepoudelis) (1911–91)
Aegean Melancholy.
Anniversary.
Autopsy, The.
Axion Esti, *sels.*
March toward the Front, The.
Ode to Santorini.
Orientations, *sels.*
Origin of Landscape or the End of Mercy,
   The.
Siblings, The, *sels.*
Sleep of the Brave, The.

Emanuel, James A.
Black Man, 13th Floor.
Church Burning: Mississippi.
Emmett Till.
For "Mr. Dudley," a Black Spy.
Get Up, Blues.
Negritude.
Negro, The.
Nightmare.
Old Black Men Say.
Panther Man.
Treehouse, The.

Whitey, Baby.

Emanuel, Lynn
Blond Bombshell.
Desire.
Dig, The.
Discovering the Photograph of Lloyd, Earl,
   and Priscilla.
Film Noir: Train Trip Out.
Frying Trout While Drunk.
Inspiration.
Of Your Father's Indiscretions and the Train
   to California.
On Waking after Dreaming of Raoul.
Patient.
Self-Portrait at Eighteen.
Silence. She Is Six Years Old.
Sleeping, The.
What Ely Was.
What Grieving Was Like.
When Father Decided He Did Not Love Her
   Anymore.

Embiricos, Andreas (1901–1975)
Caryatids, The.

Embury, Emma Catherine (1806–63)
Pilgrim, The.

Emerson, Ralph Waldo (1803–82)
Alphonso of Castile.
Apology, The.
Art.
Astræa.
Awed I behold once more.
Bacchus.
Blight.
Boston Hymn.
Brahma.
Character.
Chartist's Complaint, The.
Circles.
Compensation ("Why should I keep
   holiday.")
Compensation ("Wings of Time are black and
   white, The.")
Concord Hymn.
Days.
Day's Ration, The.
Dear brother, would you know the life.
Each and All.
Eros.
Experience.
Fable: "Mountain and the squirrel, The."
Flower Chorus.
Forbearance.
Forerunners.
Freedom.
Give all to love;.
Good-bye, proud world! I'm going home.
Grace.
Guy.
Hamatreya.
Harp, The.
History, *sels.*
Humble-Bee, The.
Illusions.
In my garden three ways meet.
Initial, Dæmonic, and Celestial Love, *sels.*
Intellect.
Letters.
Limits.
Love, *sels.*
Maia.
Manners are the happy way of doing things.
Merlin, *sels.*
Merops.
Mithridates.
Monadnoc, *sels.*
Motto to "The Poet."
Music.
Musketaquid.
Nature [1836].
Nemesis.
Nominalist and Realist.
Ode, Inscribed to W. H. Channing.
Ode to Beauty, *sels.*
Parks and Ponds.
Past, The.
Patient Pan, The.
Problem, The, *sels.*

Prudence.
Quatrains, *sels.*
Rhodora, The [On Being Asked Whence Is the Flower].
Saadi.
Sea-Shore.
Snow-Storm, The.
Solution.
Song of Nature.
Sphinx is drowsy, The.
Spiritual Laws.
Spring Prayer.
Sursum Corda.
Teach me I am forgotten by the dead.
Terminus ("It is time to be old.")
Test, The.
Thine eyes still shined for me, though far.
Thought.
Threnody: "South-wind brings, The," *sels.*
To Rhea.
Two Rivers.
Uriel.
Visit, The.
Voluntaries, *sels.*
Waldeinsamkeit.
Water understands / Civilization well, The.
Waves.
We Love the Venerable House.
Wealth.
Woodnotes I ("For this present, hard"), *sels.*
Woodnotes II ("As sunbeams stream through liberal space"), *sels.*
World-Soul, The.
Worship.
Xenophanes.

Emerson, Siegfried
Wind in the Grass, The.

Emin, Gevorg (b. 1919)
In the orchard at twilight.
Your Hands.

Emmett, Daniel Decatur (1815–1904)
Boatman's Dance ("Ober de mountains, slick as an eel.")
Dixie [*or* Dixie's Land].

Empson, William (1906–84)
Arachne.
Aubade: "Hours before dawn we were woken by the quake."
Bacchus, *sels.*
Beautiful Train, The.
Camping Out.
Death of the King's Canary, The, *sels.*
Dissatisfaction with Metaphysics.
Earth Has Shrunk in the Wash.
Homage to the British Museum.
Ignorance of Death.
Invitation To Juno.
Just a Smack at Auden.
Legal Fiction.
Let It Go.
Missing Dates.
Mother, saying Anne good night.
Note on Local Flora.
Poem about a Ball in the Nineteenth Century.
Reflection from Rochester.
Rolling the Lawn.
Scales, The.
Sea Voyage.
Sonnet: "Not wrongly moved by this dismaying scene."
Success.
Teasers, The.
This last pain for the damned the Fathers found.
To an Old Lady.
Two Centos.
Villanelle.

Encarnacion, Alfred (b. 1958)
Bulosan Listens to a Recording of Robert Johnson.
Seattle, Autumn, 1933.
Threading the Miles.

Endersby, J.
Limerick: "Few people could hope to compare."

Endrezze-Danielson, Anita (b. 1952)
Birdwatching at Fan Lake.

Canto Llano.
Dream Feast (Three Poems), The.
Eclipse.
Exodus.
Girl Who Loved the Sky, The.
Hansel, Gretel and Ruby Redlips.
In the Flight of the Blue Heron: To Montezuma.
Language of Fossils, The.
Learning the Spells; a Diptych.
Manifest Destiny.
Meditating on Star Light While Traveling Highway.
Notes from an Analyst's Couch.
November Harvest.
Passion Drinker, The.
Raven/Moon.
Red Rock Ceremonies.
Return of the Wolves.
Reviewing Past Lives while Leaf-Burning.
Song-Maker.
Stripper, The.
Sunset at Twin Lake.
Truth about My Sister and Me, The.
Week-End Indian, The.

Engle, Paul (b. 1908)
Ending, The.
Lord of Each Soul.
Moving In.
Portrait of a King's Mistress, Nude.
Twilight.

English, Maurice (b. 1909)
Form Was the World.

English, Thomas Dunn (1819–1902)
Ben Bolt.

English, William (1710?–1778)
Cashel of Munster.

Engman, John
Another Word for Blue.
Atlantis.
Mushroom Clouds.
One Minute of Night Sky.
Staff.

Engonopoulos, Nikos (1910–1985)
On Boetian Roads.

Enheduanna (fl. c.2300 B.C.)
Antiphonal Hymn in Praise of Inanna.
Appeal to the Moongod Nanna-Suen to Throw Out Lugalanne.
Banishment from Ur.
Condemning the Moongod Nanna.
Crimes of Lugalanne.
Curse on Uruk, A.
Final Prayer.
Hymn to Inanna, The, *sels.*
Inanna and An.
Inanna and Ebih.
Inanna and Enlil.
Inanna and Ishkur.
Inanna and the Anunna.
Inanna and the City of Uruk.
Inanna and the Divine Essences.
Inanna Exalted, *sels.*
Restoration of Enheduanna to Her Former Station, The.

Ennis, John (b. 1944)
Alice of Daphne, 1799.
Coyne's.
Drink of Spring, A.
Meeting at a Salesyard.
Road to Patmos, The.
Years, The.

Ennius, Quintus (239–169 B.C.)
Andromache Captive, *sels.*

Enoch, Olive
Bluebells.
Half Holiday.
Laughter.

Enomoto Seifu-Jo (1731–1814)
Everyone is asleep.

Enright, Dennis Joseph (b. 1920)
Anecdote from William IV Street.
Apocalypse.
Better Be Kind to Them Now.
Buy One Now.
Child's Guide to Welfare, A.

Development.
Egyptian Cat, The.
Evil Days, The.
Flowers.
Grand Night, A.
Guest.
History of World Languages.
In Cemeteries.
Kyoto Garden, A.
Laughing Hyena, after [*or* by] Hokusai, The.
Lucifer Broods.
Midstream.
Monuments of Hiroshima, The.
No Offence.
Old field is sad, The.
Paradise Illustrated, *sels.*
Poet Wondering What He Is Up To.
Posterity was always a great reader.
R-and-R Centre: An Incident from the Vietnam War.
Royalties.
Since Then.
Underdeveloped Country, An.
University Examinations in Egypt.
Unlawful Assembly.
Verb "To Think," The.
Waiting for the Bus.

Enright, Nick
John Keats rose at dawn.

Enslin, Theodore (b. 1925)
Fire Poem, The.

Enzensberger, Hans Magnus (b. 1929)
At Thirty-three.
Divorce, The.
For a Senior College Textbook.
For the Grave of a Peace-Loving Man.
Holiday, The.
Hôtel Fraternité.
Karl Heinrich Marx.
Last Will and Testament.
Middle-Class Blues.
Poem about the Future.
Poison, The.
Portrait of a House Detective.
Short History of the Bourgeoisie.
Sinking of the Titanic, The, *sels.*
Song for Those Who Know.
Vanished World.
Vending Machine.

"Ephelia" (Joan Philips) (fl. c.1679)
First Farewell to J.G G.
In the Person of a Lady, to Bajazet, Her Unconstant Gallant.
Love's First Approach.
Maidenhead.
On a Bashful Shepherd.
Pair-Royal of Coxcombs, The, *sels.*
To a Proud Beauty.
To J. G.
To J.G. on the News of His Marriage.
To Madam Bhen.
To My Rival.
To One That Asked Me Why I Loved J.G G.
To Phylocles, Inviting Him to Friendship.
To the Honoured *Eugenia*, Commanding Me to Write to Her.

Epshtein, Mikhail Semionovich. *See* "Golodny, **Mikhail Semionovich**"

Epstein, Daniel Mark (b. 1948)
Homage to Mallarmé, *sels.*
Old Times.

Equena
Before he died.

Equi, Elaine (b. 1953)
Bouquet of Objects, A.
Breakfast with Jerome.
Date with Robbe-Grillet, A.
In a Monotonous Dream.
Ode to Chicago.
Puritans.
Sometimes I Get Distracted.
Words Read by Lightning.

Eratosthenes (fl. 6th cent.)
Bacchus, receive my offering, not.
Meditation, Followed by Excellent Advice.

Erdrich, Louise (b. 1954)
Birth.

Butcher's Wife, The.
Captivity.
Dear John Wayne.
Family Reunion.
Francine's Room.
I Was Sleeping Where the Black Oaks Move.
Indian Boarding School: The Runaways.
Jacklight.
King of Owls, The.
Lady in the Pink Mustang, The.
Love Medicine, A.
Night Sky.
Old Man Potchikoo, *sels.*
Owls.
Shelter.
Strange People, The.
That Pull from the Left.
Windigo.

Erhardt, Amelia
Amelia Erhardt.

Erickson, C. L.
Light in the Window, The.

Erinna (*fl.* **3d cent. B.C.**)
Baucis.
Distaff, The.
Epigrams, *sels.*
Epitaph on a Betrothed Girl.
On the Portrait of a Girl.

Eristi-Aya (c.1790–1745 B.C.)
Letter to Her Mother, A.

"Ern Malley" (1918–43)
Baroque Exterior.
Boult to Marina.
Coda.
Colloquy with John Keats.
Culture as Exhibit.
Documentary Film.
Dürer: Innsbruck, 1495.
Egyptian Register.
Night Piece.
Palinode.
Perspective Lovesong.
Petit Testament.
Sonnets for the Novachord.
Sweet William.
Sybilline.
Young Prince of Tyre.

Ernst, John F. (*fl.* **late 18th cent.**)
O Jesus Christ, True Light of God.

Ernst, Max (1891–1976)
Hundred Headless Woman, The, *sels.*

Erskine, John (1879–1951)
Kings and Stars.
Shepherd Speaks, The.

Erskine, Thomas Erskine, 1st Baron (1750–1823)
James Alan Park / Came naked stark.
On Scott's Poem "The Field of Waterloo."
On Tom Moore's Translation of Anacreon.

Erucius [or Erycius] of Cyzicus (*fl.* **c.30 B.C.**)
Even though he lies underground.
Glaukon and Korydon, mountain herdsmen.
How massively, with what a fine stiff rise.
I am Athenian, that was my city.
I, the priest of Rhea, long-haired.
Kleson's goat snorted all night through the dark.
May supple-footed theatre-growing ivy.
Tell me herdsman for the sake of Pan.

Erwin, Thomas
For Someone Temporizing.
Land Donation.
Playing for Keeps.

Escoffery, Gloria (b. 1923)
After the Fall.
Farewell to a Jovial Friend.
Mother Jackson Murders the Moon.
No Man's Land.
Tricks of the Trade.
Twins.

Esdaile, Arundell James Kennedy (1880–1956)
On a War-worker, 1916.

Eshleman, Clayton (b. 1935)
Black Hat, The.
Deeds Done and Suffered by Light.

Foo to the Infinite.
Hades in Manganese.
Lich Gate, The.
Notes on a Visit to Le Tuc d'Audoubert.
Placements I.

Eskimo Oral Tradition
Magic Words.
Song of Kuk-ook, the Bad Boy, The.

Esolen, Tony
Northwestern Mathematics.

Espada, Martín (b. 1955)
Bully.
Coca-Cola and Coco Frio.
Dándole la mano a Mongo.
Jorge the Church Janitor Finally Quits.
Latin Night at the Pawnshop.
Majeski Plays the Saxophone.
Mi Vida: Wings of Fright.
Mrs. Baez Serves Coffee on the Third Floor.
Music of Astronomy, The.
Niggerlips was the high school name / for me.
Rednecks.
Savior Is Abducted in Puerto Rico, The.
Secret of the Legal Secretary's Cigarette Smoke, The.
Shaking Hands with Mongo.
Sleeping on the Bus.
Spanish of Our Out–Loud Dreams, The.
Thirty years ago.
Tony Went to the Bodega but He Didn't Buy Anything.
Toolmaker Unemployed, The.
Waiting for the Cops.
When Songs Become Water.

Espaillat, Rhina P. (b. 1932)
Metrics.
You call me by old names: how strange.

Espírito Santo, Alda do (b. 1926)
Same Side of the Canoe, The.
Where Are the Men Seized in This Wind of Madness?

Espy, Willard R. (b. 1910)
My TV came down with a chill.

Essex, Robert Devereux, 2d Earl of (1567–1601)
Change thy minde since she doth change.
Happy were he could finish forth his fare.

Esson, Louis (Thomas Louis Buvelot Esson) (1879–1943)
Shearer's Wife, The.

Esson, Thomas Louis Buvelot. See **Esson, Louis**

Esteves, Sandra Maria
South Bronx Testimonial.

E'tesami, Parvin (1910–41)
To His Father on Praising the Honest Life of the Peasant.

Etherege, Sir George. See **Walsh, William** and Sir George Etherege

Etherege, Sir George (1653–91)
Comical Revenge, The, *sels.*
To a Lady Asking Him How Long He Would Love Her.

Etter, Dave (b. 1928)
Great Northern.
Monk's Dream.
Riding the Rock Island Through Kansas.
Romp.
Stuffy Turkey.
Well You Needn't.

Eubulus (*fl.* **4th cent.**)
Benefits and Abuse of Alcohol, The.

Euenus (Euenus the Grammarian, Euenus of Askelon, Euenus of Paros) (*fl.* **5th cent. B.C.**)
B kw rm.
If hate is painful and if love's a pain.
To the Swallow.
Vine v. Goat.

Euodos
Echo:/ mimic, / last sip.

Euphorion (b. c.276 B.C.)
Not the wild olive, not the fatal stones.
When first Eudoxos cut his lovely hair.

Euripides (485–406 B.C.)
Agamemnon struggles to avert the sacrifice of his daughter Iphigeneia].

Alcestis, *sels.*
Bacchae, *sels.*
Bellerophon, *sels.*
Cyclops, The, *sels.*
Hecuba, *sels.*
Heracles, *sels.*
Hippolytus, *sels.*
Ion, *sels.*
Iphigeneia at Aulis, *sels.*
Iphigenia [*or* Iphigeneia] in Aulis, *sels.*
Maenads on Cithaeron, The.
Medea, *sels.*
Phoenician Women, The, *sels.*
Suppliant Women, The, *sels.*

Euwer, Anthony (1877–1955)
Limeratomy, The, *sels.*
Limerick: "Ankle's chief end is exposiery, The."
True Facts of the Case, The.

Evald, Johannes (1743–81)
King Christian.

Evans, Abbie Huston (b. 1881)
Fundament Is Shifted, The.
On the Curve-Edge.

Evans, Abel (1679–1737)
Author's Epitaph, Written by Himself, An.
Keep the commandments, Trapp, and go no further.
On Sir John Vanbrugh [Architect].

Evans, David Allan (b. 1940)
Bullfrogs.
Neighbors.
Retired Farmer.
Story of Lava, The.

Evans, Evan (1731–88)
Hall of Ifor Hael, The.

Evans, George (b. 1948)
Eye Blade.
Horse on a Fence.
Renaissance Drunk, A.
Revelation in the Mother Lode.

Evans, H. A. C.
Limerick: "There was a young lady called Clarice."

Evans, Humphrey (b. 1914)
And Again.

Evans, Margiad (1909–58)
Rain.
Resurrection.
Snowdrops.

Evans, Mari E. (b. 1923)
And the Old Women Gathered.
Black Jam for Dr. Negro.
Boss Communication.
Daufuskie.
How Will You Call Me, Brother.
I Am a Black Woman.
If there be sorrow.
Into Blackness Softly.
Marrow of My Bone.
Rebel, The.
Spectrum.
Status Symbol.
To Mother and Steve.
Vive Noir!
When in Rome.
Where Have You Gone?
Who Can Be Born Black.

Evans, Mike (b. 1941)
Mushrooms grew / Overnight.

Evans, Nathaniel (1742–67)
To Thee, Then, Let All Beings Bend.

Evans, Paul
Infamous Doctrine.
Ode to Tennis.
Ode: "Trees have their doubts but we have ours."
Sofa Book, The, *sels.*
Two Sonnets, *sels.*

Evans, Sebastian (1830–1909)
Fifteen Days of Judgment, The.
How the Abbey of Saint Werewulf Juxta Slingsby Came by Brother Fabian's Manuscript.
Seven Fiddlers, The.

Evelyn, Mary (1665–85)
Mundus Muliebris.
Everaerts, Jan Nicolai. *See* **Johannes Secundus**
"Everage, Edna." *See* **Humphries, Barry**
Everard, Harrison
Holloe Menn, The.
Everett, David (1794–1865)
Boy Reciter, The.
Everhard, Jim (b. 1946)
Curing Homosexuality.
Eversley, Mary
Just to Be Needed.
Everson, Ronald G. (b. 1903)
Cold-Weather Love.
Injured Maple.
Laprairie Hunger Strike.
Letter from Underground.
Old Snapshot.
One-Night Expensive Hotel.
Pauper Woodland.
Stranded in My Ontario.
Everson, William (Brother Antoninus) (b. 1912)
Advent.
Canticle to the Waterbirds, A.
Flight in the Desert, The.
Kingfisher Flat.
Making of the Cross, The.
Man-Fate, The.
Narrows of Birth, The.
Poet Is Dead, The.
Raid, The.
Runoff.
South Coast, The.
Tendril in the Mesh, *sels.*
What Birds Were There.
Year's End.
Zone of Death.
Everwine, Peter (b. 1930)
Brother, The.
Burden of Decision, The.
Clearing, The.
Counting.
Distance.
Drinking Cold Water.
From the Meadow.
Going.
In the End.
Learning to Speak.
Marsh, New Year's Day, The.
Night.
Perhaps It's as You Say.
Routes.
Someone Knocks.
We Meet in the Lives of Animals.
"Evoe." *See* **Knox, Edmund George Valpy**
Ewart, Gavin (b. 1916)
Black Box, The.
Bofors A. A. Gun, The.
Charles Augustus Milverton.
Christmas Message, A.
Clarissa Harlowe Poem, The.
Creation Myth Haiku.
Deceptive Grin of the Gravel Porters, The.
Dell, The.
Dialogue between the Head and Heart, A.
Ella Mi Fu Rapita!
Ending.
Exeter Riddle, An.
Fiction: A Message.
Fiction: The House Party.
14-Year-Old Convalescent Cat in the Winter, A.
From V. C. (a Gentleman of Verona).
Great Women Composers, The.
Haiku: After The Orgies.
Haiku: The Season of Celebrity.
Hymn to Proust.
It's Hard to Dislike Ewart.
Jubilate Matteo.
Larkin Automatic Car Wash, The.
Lifelines.
Limerick: "Life is sad and so slow and so cold."
Limerick: "There was a young lady of Ulva / Who was famed far and wide for her vulva."

Limerick: "There's a slow tolling bell in the dark."
Limerick: "Young lady, whose life-style the malicious, A."
Lines: "Other day I was loving a sweet little fruitpie-and-cream, The."
Love Song: "You've got nice knees."
Lovesleep, The.
Miss Twye.
New Poet Arrives, A.
North American Haiku.
Not Wavell but Browning.
Nursery Rhyme.
Office Friendships.
Officers' Mess.
Old Husband Suspects Adultery, An.
On the Tercentenary of Milton's Death.
One for the Anthologies.
Owl Writes a Detective Story, The.
Pastoral: "Dominic Francis Xavier Brotherton-Chancery."
Poets.
Prayer: "Lord I am not entirely selfish."
Psychoanalysis.
Robert Graves.
Semantic Limerick According to Dr. Johnson's Dictionary (Edition of 1765), The.
Semantic Limerick According to the Shorter Oxford English Dictionary (1933), The.
Short Time.
Sonnet: Equality of the Sexes.
Sonnet: Supernatural Beings.
They Flee from Me That Sometime Did Me Seek.
To Margo.
To the Virgins, to Make the Most of Time.
Wanting Out.
Weather, The.
When a Beau Goes In.
Who Likes the Idea of Guide Cats?
William Wordsworth (1770–1850).
Word-Bird knows that everybody in Britain is frightened to death of *words,* The.
Xmas for the Boys.
Ewer, W. N. (1885–1977)
Five Souls.
How odd / Of God.
Ewing, Juliana Horatia (1841–85)
Bluebells.
Burial of the Linnet, The.
Dolls' Wash, The.
Friend in the Garden, A.
Garden Lore.
Gifts.
Little Kings and Queens of the May.
Willow-Man, The.
Eybers, Elisabeth (b. 1915)
Confrontation with an Artist.
Hagar.
Narrative.
Reflection.
Röntgen Photograph.
Sleep-Walking Child.
Snail.
Ezechiel of Alexandria (*fl.* 2d cent. B.C.)
Exodus from Egypt, The.
Ezekiel, Nissim (b. 1924)
Goodbye Party for Miss Pushpa T. S.
Hymns in Darkness, *sels.*
Patriot, The.
Poems in the Greek Anthology Mode, *sels.*
Songs for Nandu Bhende, *sels.*
Ezobi, Joseph (*fl.* 12th cent.)
Silver Bowl, The, *sels.*

F

Faber, Frederick William (1814–63)
Eternal Years, The.
Right Must Win, The.
World is wise, for the world is old, The.
Fabio, Sarah Webster (1928–79)
All Day We've Longed for Night.
Back into the Garden.

Black Man's Feast.
Evil Is No Black Thing.
For Louis Armstrong, A Ju-Ju.
To Turn from Love.
Facos, James (b. 1924)
Fable.
Fagg, Martin
Burialle of the Dede.
Elegy on Thomas Hood.
Golden Road to Barcelona: 1992, The.
Limerick: "Dickensian borough of Coketown, The."
Limerick: "Quirky old gent, name of Freud, A."
Limerick: "Salopian student of Greek, A."
Limerick: "To avoid matrimonial disasters."
Limerick: "Wily old writer called Maugham, A."
Mrs Nightingale.
When Gaffer be dead for a month or more.
Fainlight, Harry
Bride, A.
Fainlight, Ruth (b. 1931)
Another Full Moon.
Archive Film Material.
Fire-Queen.
Future is timid and wayward, The.
Handbag.
Other, The.
Spring in the City.
Stubborn.
"Fair, C. A." (b. 1923)
Chinese Poems: Arthur Waley.
Fairbridge, Kingsley (1885–1924)
Magwere, Who Waits Wondering.
South African Exhibition, 1907.
Fairburn, Arthur Rex Dugard (1904–57)
Album Leaves, *sels.*
Beggar to Burgher.
Cave, The.
Diogenes.
Down on My Luck.
Farewell, A: "What is there left to be said?"
Full Fathom Five.
I'm Older than You, Please Listen.
Naked Girl Swimming, A.
Tapu.
Terms of Appointment.
Fairfax, Edward
Tasso's Godfrey of Bulloigne Book 4, *sels.*
Fairfax, James Griffyth (1886–1976)
Forest of the Dead, The.
Fairfax of Cameron, Thomas Fairfax, Baron (1612–71)
On the Fatal Day January 30, 1648.
Shortness of Life.
Upon the New Building at Appleton.
Faiz, Faiz Ahmad (1911–84)
Don't Ask Me for That Love Again.
Fragrant Hands.
No Sign of Blood.
Once Again the Mind.
Prison Daybreak, A.
Prison Evening, A.
Rain of Stones Is Finished, The.
So Bring the Order for My Execution.
Tyrant, The.
Vista.
You Tell Us What to Do.
Falckner, Justus (1672–1723)
Rise, Ye Children.
Falconar, Maria (b. 1771?)
Prefatory Epistle, A.
Falconer, E. J.
Cradle Song at Bethlehem.
Doves.
Elephant is like a wall, The.
Little Finger Game, A.
Marketing.
Falconer, William (1732–69)
Shipwreck, The, *sels.*
Faleti, Adebayo
Independence.
Falke, Gustav (1853–1916)
God's Harp.
Strand-Thistle.

Falkland, Elizabeth Cary, Viscountess (d. 1639)
To the Queenes Most Excellent Majestie.
Falkner, John Meade (1858–1922)
After Trinity.
Arabia.
Christmas Day; the Family Sitting.
Fallis, Edwina
Wise Johnny.
Fallon, Eunice
August.
Fallon, Padraic (1905–74)
Assumption.
Dardanelles 1916.
For Paddy Mac.
Head, The.
Hedge Schoolmaster, A.
Kiltartan Legend.
Lakshmi.
Mater Dei.
Odysseus.
Painting of My Father.
Pot Shot.
Weir Bridge.
Young Fenians, The.
Fallon, Peter (b. 1951)
Airs and Graces.
Herd, The.
Himself.
Meadow, The.
Moons.
My Care.
Spring Song.
Winter Work.
Fan Ch'eng-ta (1126–93)
Consoling the Yü Farmers.
Four Songs in Imitation of Wang Chien, sels.
Seasonal Poems on Fields and Gardens, sels.
Written While Lying on My Pillow in the
Morning on the Twelfth Day of the
Eleventh Month.
Fan Yun (451–505)
Farewell to Shen Yueh.
Fandel, John (b. 1925)
Indians
**Fane, Mildmay. See Westmorland, Mildmay
Fane, 2d Earl of**
**"Fane, Violet" (Mary Montgomerie Currie,
Baroness Currie)**
In an Irish Churchyard.
Siren, The.
Fanning, Roger (b. 1962)
Shoelace.
Fanshawe, Catherine Maria (1765–1834)
Enigma.
Fragments.
Riddle, A: "'Twas in heaven pronounced, and
'twas muttered in hell."
When last we parted, thou wert young and
fair.
Fanshawe, Sir Richard (1608–66)
Il Pastor Fido, sels.
Fanthorpe, U. A. (b. 1929)
At the Ferry.
BC:AD.
Father in the Railway Buffet.
Nativities.
Not my best side, I'm afraid.
Our Dog Chasing Swifts.
Person's Tale, The.
Reindeer Report.
Relief of Myopia, The.
Resuscitation Team.
What the Donkey Saw.
You Will Be Hearing from Us Shortly.
Farber, Norma (1909–84)
Bow down, mountain, to hear the gladness
issuing.
Dove.
For a Quick Exit.
Hog at the Manger.
How They Brought the Good News by Sea.
Jubilate Herbis.
Ladybug's Christmas.
Manhattan Lullaby.
Spider.

Taking Turns.
Farewell, George (fl. c.1733)
Adieu to My Landlady, An.
Country Man, The, sels.
Molly Moor.
Privy-Love for My Landlady.
Quaerè.
There's Life in a Mussel; a Meditation.
To the Archdeacon.
Faricy, Austin (b. 1911)
Through Warmth and Light of Summer
Skies.
Farid-uddin Attar (1119–1202)
Conference of the Birds, The, sels.
Farjeon, Eleanor (1881–1965)
Advice to a Child.
Bedtime.
Blackfriars.
Cats sleep / Anywhere.
Children's Bells, The.
Children's Carol, The.
Down! Down!
First Gathering.
Flower-Seller, The ("Flower-seller's fat,
The.")
For a Mocking Voice.
For Snow.
Good Night.
Holly and Mistletoe.
In the Week When Christmas Comes.
Jenny White and Johnny Black.
Keeping Christmas.
Lewis Carroll.
Light the Lamps Up, Lamplighter!
Mistress Malone.
Mistress Peck-Pigeon.
Ned.
Night Will Never Stay, The.
Over the garden wall.
Tailor.
There Are Big Waves.
There Isn't Time.
Tide in the river, The.
William I.
Zodiac.
Farley, Henry (fl. c.1621)
Bounty of Our Age, The.
Farley, Robert E.
Thinking Happiness.
Farmer, Harold (b. 1943)
Lost City.
"Farningham, Marianne" (Mary Ann Hearn)
Last Hymn, The.
Farnsworth, Robert (b. 1929)
Coloring Book.
Farquhar, George (1678–1707)
Song, A.
Trifles.
Farrar, John Chipman (1896–1976)
Chanticleer.
Comparison, A.
Farrell, J. R.
Bank Thief, The.
**Farren, Robert (Roibéard O'Faracháin) (b.
1909)**
Immolation.
Lineage.
Sleep, sels.
Stable Straw.
Farrokhzad, Forugh (1935–67)
Born Again.
I'm Sad.
In the land of dwarfs.
O Realm Bejewelled.
On Earth.
Once More.
Someone like No One Else.
Fatchen, Max (b. 1920)
Be Quiet!
Hullo, Inside.
I often meet a monster.
It's a Bit Rich.
'Jump over the moon?' the cow declared.
Night Walk.
Oh Erica, Not Again!

Space Spot.
Tailpiece.
Fauset, Jessie Redmond (1888–1961)
Oblivion.
Oriflamme.
Touché.
Fawcett, Brian (b. 1944)
Hand, The.
Fawcett, Joseph (1758?–1804)
Art of War, The, sels.
Fawcett, Susan
Subway.
Fawkes, Francis (1720–77)
Elegy on the Death of Dobbin, the
Butterwoman's Horse, An.
Fay, John
Limerick: "Hopeful old fellow called
Rousseau, A."
Fazio degli Uberti (1326–60)
Canzone: His Portrait of His Lady, Angiola
of Verona.
Of England, and of Its Marvels.
Fazli, Nida (b. 1940)
Page from the New Diary, A.
Fearing, Kenneth (1902–61)
American Rhapsody.
Any Man's Advice to His Son.
C Stands for Civilization.
Confession Overheard in a Subway.
Cultural Notes.
Dirge: "1-2-3 was the number he played but
today the number came 3-2-1."
Elegy in a Theatrical Warehouse.
Evening Song.
Green Light.
Love, 20 Cents the First Quarter Mile.
Lullaby: "Wide as this night, old as this
night is old and young as it is young."
Memo.
Minnie and Mrs. Hoyne.
No Credit.
Obituary.
Operative No. 174 Resigns.
Pact.
Pay-off.
People vs. the People, The.
Portrait.
Readings, Forecasts, Personal Guidance.
Requiem: "Will they stop."
Resurrection.
Tomorrow.
Twentieth-Century Blues.
Yes, the Agency Can Handle That.
Fearne, Flora
Little Men, The.
Feaver, Vicki
Coat.
Feinman, Alvin (b. 1929)
November Sunday Morning.
Feinstein, Elaine (b. 1930)
Annus Mirabilis 1989.
Calliope in the Labour Ward.
Coastline.
June.
Lais, courtesan of Corinth, why has.
Magic Apple Tree, The.
Medium, The.
Patience.
Feinstein, Martin (1892–1934)
Burning Bush.
Feinstein, Robert N. (b. 1915)
Woolly Words.
Feinstein, Sascha
Christmas Eve.
Sonnets for Stan Gage (1945–1992).
Feiritear, Piaras (1600–1653)
Lay your weapons down, young lady.
Feirstein, Frederick (b. 1940)
Mark Stern.
Mark Stern Wakes Up.
Rune-Maker, The.
Feldman, Irving (b. 1928)
All of Us Here, sels.
Death of Vitellozzo Vitelli, The.

Double, The.
Dream, The.
Family History.
Little Lullaby.
Old Men, The.
Scene of a Summer Morning.
Se Aprovechan.
Terminal Laughs.

Feldman, Susan (b. 1950)
How the Invalids Make Love.
Intruder.
Lamentations of an Au Pair Girl.
Sea Legs.

Fell, Alison (b. 1944)
And Again.
August 6, 1945.
Desire.
Freeze-Frame.
Medusa on Skyros.
Pushing Forty.
Significant Fevers.

Felltham, Owen. *See* **Suckling, Sir John** *and* Owen Felltham

Felltham [or Feltham], Owen (c.1602–1668)
On a Hopeful Youth.
On the Duke of Buckingham, Slain by Felton, the 23rd August, 1628.
To Phryne.
Upon a Rare Voice.

Felsted, Layne
Thanks for Hearing.

Fêng Mêng-lung (c. 1590–1646)
Love-Poem.

Feng Yen-ssu (903–60)
Tune: "Magpie on the Branch."

Fennelly, Beth Ann (b. 1971)
Poem Not to Be Read at Your Wedding.

Fenollosa, Ernest Francisco (1853–1900)
East and West, *sels.*
Ode on Reincarnation, *sels.*

Fenton, Elijah (1683–1730)
Olivia's lewd, but looks devout.

Fenton, James (b. 1949)
Cambodia.
Dead Soldiers.
Exempla, *sels.*
German Requiem, A, *sels.*
God, A Poem.
In Paris with You.
Kingfisher's Boxing Gloves, The.
Lines for Translation into Any Language.
Lollipops of the Pomeranian Baroque.
Nothing.
This Octopus Exploits Women.
Wild Life Studies, *sels.*
Wind.

Fenton, James *and* **John Fuller**
Born too soon.
Poem against Catholics.
Red Light District Nurse, The.

Fenyves, Marta
Exile.

Ferdinand, Val
Blues (in Two Parts), The.
Food for Thought.
2 B BLK.
Whi / te boys gone.

Fergus, Howard (b. 1937)
Ethnocide.
Forecast.
Lament for Maurice Bishop.

Ferguson, James (1842–c.1910)
Auld Daddy Darkness creeps frae his hole.

Ferguson, Sir Samuel (1810–86)
Aideen's Grave.
At the Polo-Ground.
Burial of King Cormac, The.
Fairy Thorn, The.
Lament for the Death of Thomas Davis.

Fergusson, Robert (1750–74)
Braid Claith.
Daft Days, The.
Drinking Song.
Epigram on a Lawyer's Desiring One of the Tribe to Look with Respect to a Gibbet.

Ghaists; a Kirk-yard Eclogue, The.
Hallow-Fair.
Leith Races, *sels.*
Rising of the Session, The.
Sow of Feeling, The.

Fericano, Paul
Poem for William Rummel Serving a Life Sentence in a Texas Prison for Not Fixing an Air Conditioner.

Ferland, Barbara (b. 1919)
Ave Maria.
Expect No Turbulence.
Orange.

Ferlinghetti, Lawrence (b. 1919)
After the Cries of the Birds.
Assassination Raga.
Away above a harborful.
Baseball Canto.
Christ Climbed Down / from His bare Tree.
Constantly risking absurdity.
Cro-Magnons carried stones for books.
DaDa would have liked a day like this one.
Dark Portrait, A.
Dog trots freely in the street, The.
Don't let that horse / eat that violin.
Frightened / by the sound of my own voice.
He is one of the prophets come back.
In Golden Gate Park that day.
In Goya's greatest scenes we seem to see.
Ladakh Buddhess Biker.
Lost Parents.
Monet's Lilies Shuddering.
One Thousand Fearful Words for Fidel Castro.
Oral Messages, *sels.*
Pennycandystore beyond the El, The.
People getting divorced.
Pictures of a Gone World, *sels.*
Poet's eye obscenely seeing, The.
Pound at Spoleto.
Retired Ballerinas, Central Park West.
River Still To Be Found, A.
Sandinista Avioncitos.
Sarolla's women in their picture hats.
Sea and Ourselves at Cape Ann, The.
Sometime during eternity / some guys show up.
Starting from San Francisco.
Terrible / a horse at night.
Third World Calling.
Underwear.
Work-in-Progress, *sels.*
Wounded wilderness of Morris Graves.

Fernández, Abraham
If You Happy Would Be.

Fernandez, Renaldo
Legacy of a Brother.

Ferrarelli, Rina
Emigrant/Immigrant ("From the people.")
Emigrant/Immigrant ("Slight accent, A.")

Ferré, Rosario (b. 1940)
I Hear You've Let Go.

Ferril, Thomas Hornsby (b. 1896)
Always Begin Where You Are.
Blue-Stemmed Grass.
Empire Sofa, The.
Morning Star.
Time of Mountains.
Waltz against the Mountains.
Wood.

Ferriter, Pierce (*fl.* c.1653)
Lay Your Arms Aside.

Ferry, David (b. 1924)
Adam's Dream.
Anasazi drink from underground rivers, The.
Cythera.
Embarkation for Cythera, The.
Guest Ellen at the Supper for Street People, The.
He stands against what looks like the other side.
My Parents En Route.
Photographs from a Book: Six Poems, *sels.*

Picture of Eakins and a couple of other people, A.
Plate 134. By Eakins. 'A cowboy in the West.'
Rereading Old Writing.
Soldier, The.
There is a strange, solemn, silent, graceless.
Unawkward Singer, The.

Fet [*or* Foeth], Afanasi Afanasievich (1820–92)
Morning Song.

Fetherling, Doug (b. 1949)
Elijah Speaking.
Explorers as Seen by the Natives.

Fiacc, Padraic (b. 1924)
British Connection, The.
Enemy Encounter.
First Movement.
Gloss.
Goodbye to Brigid / An Agnus Dei.
Haemorrhage.
Intimate Letter 1973.
Introit.
Poet, The.
Saint Coleman's Song for Flight/ An Ite Missa Est.
Soldiers.

Fiamengo, Marya (b. 1926)
In Praise of Old Women.

Fiawoo, F. K.
Soliloquy on Death.

Fichman, Jacob [*or*Jakov] (1881–1958)
Abishag.
Afternoon Light.
In the Old City.
Midnight.

Ficke, Arthur Davison (1883–1945)
Four Japanese Paintings, *sels.*
Perspective of Co-ordination.

Ficowski, Jerzy
Girl of Six from the Ghetto Begging in Smolna Street in 1942, A.
Assumption of Miriam from the Street in the Winter of 1942, The, *sels.*
Both Your Mothers.
Cogito Ergo.
Execution of Memory, The.
5.8.1942 / In Memory of Janusz Korczak*.
I did not manage to save.
I would like just to be silent.
Ovid Twice Exiled.
Pawiak 1943.
Seven Words, The.

Fiedler, Leslie A. (b. 1917)
No Ghost Is True.

Field, Barron (1786–1846)
Kangaroo, Kangaroo!

Field, Edward (b. 1924)
Both My Grandmothers ("Both my grandmas came from far away.")
Bride of Frankenstein, The.
Curse of the Cat Woman.
Event, An.
Floor Is Dirty, The.
Icarus.
Journey, A.
Lower East Side: The George Bernstein Story.
Mae West.
Plant Poem.
Tulips and Addresses.
Unwanted.
View of Jersey, A.
What Grandma Knew.
World War II.

Field, Eugene (1850–95)
Angel's Visit, The.
April Fool, The.
Bachelor Hall.
Christmas Song: "Why do the bells for Christmas ring?"
Dinkey-Bird, The.
Duel, The.
Fly-Away Horse, The.
Jest 'fore Christmas.
Johnny's Team.

Limerick: "'Tis strange how the newspapers
   honour."
Little Boy Blue.
Little Peach, The.
Mr. Billings of Louisville.
Norse Lullaby.
Piazza Tragedy, A.
Red.
Rock-a-by Lady, The.
Sioux, The.
Sugar-Plum Tree, The.
Two Meetings, The.
Wynken, Blynken and Nod one night.

**"Field, Michael" (Katherine Bradley and Edith
Cooper)**
After Mass.
After Soufrière.
Ah, Eros doth not always smite.
Almoner, An.
Already to mine eyelids' shore.
And on My Eyes Dark Sleep by Night.
Aridity.
As two fair vessels side by side.
Beloved, my glory in thee is not ceased.
Beloved, now I love God first.
Bury Her at Even.
Caput Tuum Ut Carmelus.
Constancy.
Cyclamens.
Dance of Death, A.
Descent from the Cross.
Dying Viper, A.
Ebbtide at Sundown.
Elsewhere.
Embalmment.
Eros.
Fellowship.
Fifty Quatrains.
Flaw, A.
From Baudelaire.
Girl, A.
Goad, The.
Gold Is the Son of Zeus: Neither Moth nor
   Worm May Gnaw It.
Gray mob-cap and a girl's, A.
I love you my life—'tis so I love you.
I sing thee with the stock-dove's throat.
If They Honoured Me, Giving Me Their
   Gifts.
La Gioconda.
Leaves.
Life Plastic.
Lo, my loved is dying, and the call.
Love rises up some days.
Loved, on a sudden thou didst come to me.
Lovers, fresh plighting lovers in our age.
Macrinus against Trees.
Methinks my love to thee doth grow.
Mummy Invokes his Soul, The.
My Darling.
My lady has a lovely rite.
Nests in Elms.
Nightfall.
Noon.
O Wind, thou hast thy kingdom in the trees.
Palimpsest, A.
Penetration.
Picture, A.
Poet, The.
Portrait, A.
Prologue.
Second Thoughts.
She is singing to Thee, Domine!.
So jealous of your beauty.
Sometimes I do despatch my heart.
Sullenness.
Sweet-Briar in Rose.
Sweeter Far than the Harp, More Gold than
   Gold.
They Shall Look on Him.
To Christina Rossetti.
To the Lord Love.
To the Winter Aphrodite.
Tragic Mary Queen of Scots, The.
Tragic Mary Queen of Scots, II, The.
Trinity.
Unbosoming.

Variations on Sappho, sels.
Your rose is dead,.

Field, Rachel Lyman (1894–1942)
Circus Garland, A, sels.
Dancing Bear, The.
Fourth of July.
General Store.
Gypsies.
Manhattan Lullaby.
Merry-Go-Round.
Playhouse Key, The.
Skyscrapers.
Some People.
Something told the wild geese.
Summer Morning, A.

Fielding, Henry (1707–54)
Don Quixote in England, sels.

Fields, Dorothy
Fine romance! with no kisses!, A.

Fields, James Thomas (1817–81)
Alarmed Skipper, The.
Ballad of the Tempest.
Jupiter and Ten.
Owl-Critic, The.

Fields, Julia (b. 1938)
Aardvark.
Alabama.
Citizen.
Jolly fat widows, The.
Mr. Tut's House A Recollection.
Poems: Birmingham 1962–1964, sels.

Fifer, H. N.
He Lived a Life, sels.

Figueroa-Aymerich, Angela (1902–84)
Women at the Market.

Figueroa, John (b. 1920)
At Home the Green Remains.
Birth Is.
Epitaph: "Old man is gone, The."
Portrait of a Woman (and a Man).
This tree my time keeper.

Fiksman, David Mironovich. See "Knut, Dovid"

Filicaia, Vincenzo da (1642–1707)
Italy.

**Finch, Anne. See Winchilsea, Anne Finch,
Countess of**

Finch, Anne (b. 1908)
Essay on Marriage, sels.

Finch, Annie (b. 1956)
Dickinson.
For Grizzel McNaught (1709–1792).
Reply From His Coy Mistress, A.
Sapphics for Patience.

Finch, Francis Miles (1827–1907)
Blue and the Gray, The.

Finch, Peter (b. 1947)
Computer's First Proverbs, The.
Customize the Grass.
Passion Shaved beneath the Grain-Silo.

Finch, Robert (b. 1900)
Aria Senza da Capo.
Collective Portrait, The.
Crib, The.
Last Visit.
Room.
Silverthorn Bush.
Turning.
Words.

Finch, Vivienne
Green Ice.
Inertia.

Fincke, Gary
Era of the Vari-Vue, The.

Finkel, Donald (b. 1929)
Flagpole Sitter, The.
Gesture.
Hands.
Hunting Song.
In the Clearing.
Joyful Noise, A.
Letter to My Daughter at the End of Her
   Second Year.
Metaphysic of Snow.
Spring Song.

Time Out.

Finkelstein, Norman (b. 1954)
Track, sels.

Finlay, Ian Hamilton (b. 1925)
Garden Poem.
Great frog race.
lackblockblackb.
Waterwheels in.

Finney, Eric
Our Solar System.
Supposing.

Finney, Nikky (b. 1957)
Uncles.

Finnigan, Joan (b. 1925)
May Day Rounds: Renfrew County, sels.

Finnin, Olive Mary (b. 1906)
Man from Strathbogie, The.

Firdausi (Abul Kasim Mansur) (940–1020)
Alas for Youth.
Shahnamah, The, sels.

Fischer, Helen Field (b. 1940)
New Leaf, A [or The].
There is a mystic borderland that lies.

Fischerova, Sylva
Who Knows Something About Women?

Fiser, Karen
Teaching Myself to Read.
Wheelchairs That Kneel Down Like
   Elephants.

Fish, Karen
What Is Beyond Us.

Fishback, Margaret (b. 1904)
Complacent Cliff-Dweller, The.
Sitting Pretty.

Fisher, Aileen (b. 1906)
After a Bath.
Benjamin Jones Goes Swimming.
Cat in the Snow.
Caterpillars.
Fair Exchange.
Houses are faces.
Listening.
Moles.
Mouse Dinner.
On Mother's Day.
Sandpile Town.
Snowy Benches.
Thanksgiving Dinner.
Upside Down.

Fisher, Aileen and Olive Rabe
Pioneers.

Fisher, Allen (b. 1944)
Birdland.
Gardener's Preface, The.

Fisher, David (1794–1886)
Limerick: "There was a wee lassie of Ulva."

Fisher, K.
Story of the Corn.

Fisher, Mahlon Leonard (b. 1874)
In Cool, Green Haunts.

Fisher, Robert (b. 1943)
Funny Folk.
Incredible Henry McHugh, The.
O Goldfish!
That Cat!
Who are my pets.

Fisher, Roy (b. 1930)
As he came near death things grew shallower
   for us.
Emblem.
Entertainment of War, The.
On the open side, look out.
Paraphrases.
Wonders of Obligation, sels.

Fisher, Salih Michael (b. 1956)
Assumption about the Harlem Brown Baby.

Fishman, Charles
Death March.

Fiske, John (1892–1901)
Upon the Decease of Mrs. Anne Griffin.
Upon the Much-to Be Lamented Desease of
   the Reverend Mr. John Cotton.

Fiskin, Jeffrey
Magi, The.

Fitch, Eleazar Thompson (1791–1871)
By Vows of Love Together Bound.
Lord, at This Closing Hour.

Fitger, Arthur (1840–1900)
Evening Prayer.

Fitton, Molly
When fog come creepin' over Beccles.

Fitts, Dudley (1903–68)
Southwest Passage.
Ya Se Van Los Pastores.

Fitzgerald, Edward (1809–83)
Life's Chequer-Board.
19.
Old Song.
Rubáiyát of Omar Khayyám of Naishápúr,
  The.
Some We Loved.

**Fitzgerald, F. Scott (Francis Scott Key
  Fitzgerald) (1896–1940)**
Great Gatsby, The, *sels.*
Obit on Parnassus.
Thousand-and-First Ship, *sels.*

Fitzgerald, Mary Scott
Rendezvous.

**Fitzgerald, Pierce (Piaras Mac Gearailt) (1709–
  91)**
Answer to Thomas Barry, An.

Fitzgerald, Robert (1910–85)
Cobb Would Have Caught It.
Entreaty.
Errantry.
Figlio Maggiore.
History.
Imprisoned, The.
Jesu, Joy of Man's Desiring.
July in Indiana.
Metaphysical.
Metaphysician.
Midsummer.
Mise en Scène.
Queens, The.
Shore of Life, The.
Song for September.
Souls Lake.

Fitzgerald, Robert David (1902–87)
Bog and Candle.
Copernicus.
Edge.
Essay on Memory, *sels.*
Face of the Waters, The.
Favour.
Grace before Meat.
1918-1941.
Wind at Your Door, The.

Fitzgerald, Thomas (1695?–1752)
Upon an Ingenious Friend, Over-Vain.

Fitzgerald, Zelda Sayre (1900–1948)
I Do Love My Charlie So.
Over the Top with Pershing.

Fitzpatrick, Conal (b. 1951)
Discovering Lasseter.

Fitzpatrick, Dominic
Limerick: "When your capitalist boss takes
  his toll."

Flaccus, Aulus Persius. *See* **Persius**

Flaccus, Gaius Valerius. *See* **Valerius Flaccus,
  Gaius**

Flaccus, Quintus Horatius. *See* **Horace**

Flaccus, Statilius (*fl.* **1st cent. B.C.)**
Bowlegged, pinchered sand-digger.
Flaccus gave me, the silver lamp.
Just as he gets a beard.
X finds gold and leaves his noose for Y.

Flaischlen, Cäsar (1864–1920)
Most Quietly at Times.

Flanders, Jane (b. 1940)
Big Cars.
Dandelion Greens.
Handbell Choir, The.
House That Fear Built: Warsaw, 1943, The.
Nightingales in America.
Other Lives of the Romantics.
Planting Onions.
Testimony.

Twirling.

Flanders, Michael (1922–75)
Have Some Madeira, M'dear?

Flanner, Hildegarde (1899–1987)
Hawk Is a Woman.
Let Us Believe.
Memo.
Sonnets in Quaker Language, *sels.*
Swift Love, Sweet Motor.
This day when I lay my hope aside.

Flatman, Thomas (1637–88)
Appeal to Cats in the Business of Love, An.
Batchelor's Song, The.
Nudus Redibo.
On Marriage.
Sad Day, The.
Thought of Death, A.
Unconcerned, The.

Flavell [*or* Lavell], Thomas (b. 1906)
County of Mayo, The.

Flavius Claudius Julianus. *See* **Julian, Emperor**

Flecker, James Elroy (1884–1915)
Ballad of Hampstead Heath, The.
Ballad of the Londoner.
God Save the King.
Golden Journey to Samarkand, The, *sels.*
Hassan, *sels.*
In Hospital.
No Coward's Song.
Old Ships, The.
Oxford Canal.
Parrot, The.
Rioupéroux.
Santorin.
Stillness.
Tenebris Interlucentem.
To a Poet a Thousand Years Hence.
Town without a Market, The.

Flecknoe, Richard (1600–1678)
Ant, The.
Invocation of Silence.
On the Death of Our Lord.

Fleg, Edmond (1874–1964)
Wall of Weeping, The, *sels.*

Fleischman, Paul (b. 1952)
Fireflies.

Fleming, Elizabeth
Balloon Seller, The.
Fires.
Hedgehog and His Coat, The.
Hurdy-Gurdy Man, The.
If I Were a Pig.
In the Mirror.
Lavender Bush, The.
Old Mrs. Jarvis.
Patchwork Quilt, The.
Secret, The.
Toadstools.
Who's In.
Window cleaner's life is grand!, A.

Fleming, Marjory (1803–11)
Melancholy Lay, A.
Sonnet, A: "O lovely O most charming pug."

Fleming, Paul (1609–40)
Concerning Himself.
Devotion.
How He Should Like to Be Kissed.
It is in vain, the sorrow.
To Himself.
To the Great City of Moscow, as He Was
  Leaving June 25, 1636.
To the Moon.

Fleming, Robert (b. 1950)
For All Unwed Mothers.

Fletcher, Curley W.
High-loping Cowboy, The.

Fletcher, Giles, the Elder (c.1549–1611)
Licia, *sels.*

Fletcher, Giles, the Younger (1585–1623)
Christs Victorie, and Triumph in Heaven, and
  Earth, over, and after death, *sels.*
Christ's Victory and Triumph, *sels.*

Fletcher, John (1579–1625)
Beggar's Bush, *sels.*
Chances, The, *sels.*

Elder Brother, The, *sels.*
Faithful Shepherdess, The, *sels.*
Fletcher's Lament for his Friend.
Little French Lawyer, The, *sels.*
Lover's Progress, The, *sels.*
Mad Lover, The, *sels.*
Nice Valor, The, *sels.*
Spanish Curate, The, *sels.*
Take, oh, take those lips away.
Tragedy of Valentinian, The, *sels.*
Women Pleased, *sels.*
See also **Beaumont, Francis** and **John
  Fletcher**

Fletcher, John (1579–1625) *and others*
Bloody Brother, The, *sels.*
Maid in the Mill, The, *sels.*
Queen of Corinth, The, *sels.*

Fletcher, John (1564–1616) *and* **William
  Shakespeare**
King Henry VIII, *sels.*
Two Noble Kinsmen, The, *sels.*

Fletcher, John Gould (1886–1950)
Before Olympus.
Green Symphony.
Irradiations, *sels.*
Last Frontier, The.
Last Judgment.
Lincoln.
London Nightfall.
Monadnock, The.
Rebel, A.
Skaters, The.
Song of the Moderns.

Fletcher, Louisa
Land of Beginning Again, The.

Fletcher, Phineas (1580–1650)
Against a Rich Man Despising Poverty.
Divine Wooer, The, *sels.*
Hymn: "Drop, drop, slow tears."
Hymn, An: "Wake, O my soul; awake, and
  raise."
Locusts, or Appolyonists, The, *sels.*
Ocean of Light.
Purple Island, The, *sels.*
To Thomalin.

Flexner, Hortense King (b. 1885)
Contemporary.

Flint, Annie Johnson (1866–1931)
At the Place of the Sea.

Flint, Carol
Trois, A.

Flint, Francis Stewart [*or* "Frank"] (1885–1960)
Eau-Forte.
Hats.
Lament: "Young men of the world, The."

Flint, James (1779–1885)
In Pleasant Lands Have Fallen the Lines.

Flood, John
To His Coy Mistress.

Flook, Maria (b. 1952)
Continental Divide, The.
Discreet.

Florian, Douglas (b. 1950)
First things first.
Send my spinach.

Florsheim, Stewart (fl. 20th cent.)
Jewish Singles Event, The.

Floyd, Bryan Alec
Captain James Leson, U. S. M. C.
Corporal Charles Chungtu, U. S. M. C.
Corporal Kevin Spina, U. S. M. C.
Lance Corporal Purdue Grace, U. S. M. C.
Private First Class Brooks Morgenstein, U. S.
  M. C.
Private Ian Godwin, U. S. M. C.
Private Jack Smith, U. S. M. C.
Sergeant Brandon Just, U. S. M. C.

**Flynn, Desiré (Sheila Desiré Savory Rodd) (b.
  1917)**
Collector, The.
From the Rain Forest.

Flynn, Elizabeth (1890–1964)
After Grave Deliberation.

Flynn, Frank
Clothes on the Washing Line.
Shed, The.

Winter Morning.

Flynn, M. P.
Decision.
Down in the field.
Sandlot Days.

Foerster, Richard
Life Drawing.

Fogarty, Lionel (b. 1958)
No Grudge.
Remember Something Like This.

Fogel, Aaron (b. 1947)
Printer's Error, The.

Fogel, Alice B. (b. 1954)
Necessity, The.

Fogel, Ephim G. (1920–1992)
Shipment to Maidanek.

Fogel, Ephraim
Shipment to Maidanek.

Fogle, Richard Harter (b. 1911)
Hawthorne Garland, A.

Foix, J. V. (1893–1987)
I Arrived in that Town, Everyone Greeted Me and I Recognized no One. When I Was Going to Read My Verses, the Devil, Hidden Behind a Tree, Called Out to Me Sarcastically and Filled My Hands with Newspaper Clippings.
When I Sleep, Then I See Clearly.

Folcachiero de' Folcachieri (fl. c.1175)
Canzone: He Speaks of His Condition through Love.

Foley, Helen (1896–1937)
Touch wood, be humble, never dare to say.

Foley, James William (1874–1939)
Drop a Pebble in the Water.
Song of Summer Days.

Foley, Michael (b. 1947)
Brothers and Sisters.
Lucky Eugene.
Middle Manager in Paradise, The.
On the Waterfront.
Provincial Adolescence, A.
True Life Love Stories, sels.

Folger, Peleg (1734–89)
Praise ye the Lord, O celebrate his fame.

Follain, Jean (1903–71)
Black Meat.
Buying.
Face the Animal.
Mirror, A.
Music of Spheres.
School and Nature.
Taxidermist is sitting / before the russet breasts, A.

Follen, Eliza Lee Cabot (1787–1860)
Good Moolly Cow, The.
Lord, Deliver, Thou Canst Save.
Oh! Look at the Moon.
Three little kittens [they] lost their mittens.

Fontanella, Luigi (b. 1943)
After the Party.
Father-Sequence.
For Emma.
I'm on a straight path with the sun gone down.
Image of the frozen lake, The.
In the nighttime someone in my place.
It's a slow warmth I find once more.
Mimikòs.
Sleeplessness.
Transparent Life, The.
Turning of the car.
Victoria Station.

Fonte Boa, Maria Amalia
Two Tile Beaks.
Vitality.

Foot, P. W. R.
Limerick: "Cried the maid: 'You must marry me, Hume!'"
Limerick: "Philosopher Berkeley once said, The."

Foote, Samuel (1720–77)
Great Panjandrum [Himself], The.

Forbes, Calvin (b. 1945)
Dark Mirror.
Europe / Is endowed with the first move.

Gabriel's Blues.
Hand Me Down Blues.
Home.
Lullaby for Ann-Lucian.
My Father's House.
Picture of a Man.
Poet's Shuffle, The.
Potlicker Blues.
Potter's Wheel, The.
Reading Walt Whitman.

Forbes, Duncan (b. 1947)
Politics of Envy.
Recension Day.

Forbes, John (b. 1950)
Age of Plastic, The.
Angel.
Death, an Ode.
Four Heads & How to Do Them.
Love Poem.
Malta.
Monkey's Pride.
Speed, a Pastoral.
TV.
Up, Up, Home & Away.

Forché, Carolyn (b. 1950)
As Children Together.
Burning the Tomato Worms, sels.
City Walk-up, Winter 1969.
Colonel, The.
Elegy.
Island, The.
Kalaloch.
Memory of Elena, The.
Morning Baking, The.
On Returning to Detroit.
Reunion.
Selective Service.
Taking Off My Clothes.
Visitor, The.

Ford, Charles Henri (b. 1913)
Bad Habit, The.
Desire to be in Two Places at Once, The.
January wraps up the wound of his arm.
Overturned Lake, The.
Plaint.
Somebody's Gone.
There's No Place to Sleep in This Bed, Tanguy.

Ford, Ford Madox (Ford Madox Hueffer) (1873–1939)
Antwerp, sels.
Old Houses of Flanders, The.
On Heaven.
Sanctuary, The.
Sidera Cadentia.
That Exploit of Yours.
Unwritten Song, The.
What the Orderly Dog Saw.
"When the World Was in Building."

Ford, John (1586–1640?)
Broken Heart, The, sels.
Lover's Melancholy, The, sels.
See also **Dekker, Thomas, John Ford, and William Rowley**

Ford, Mary A.
Hundred Years from Now, A.

Ford, Robert Arthur Douglas (b. 1915)
Back to Dublin.
Earthquake.
Revenge of the Hunted.
Sakhara.
Twenty Below.
Window on the North, A.

Ford, Simon (1619?–1699)
London's Resurrection, sels.

Ford-Smith, Honor (b. 1951)
Aux Leon...Women.
Lala: The Dressmaker.

Ford, Thomas (1580–1648)
There is a Lady sweet and kind.

Ford, William (fl. 20th cent.)
Of Miles Davis.

Fordham, Mary Weston (fl. c.1897)
Alaska.
Atlanta Exposition Ode.

Bells of St. Michael.
"By the Rivers of Babylon."
Cherokee, The.
Chicago Exposition Ode.
Christ Child, The.
Coming Woman, The.
Creation.
Crucifixion, The.
Death of a Grandparent. Mrs. Jennette Bonneau.
Dedicated to the Right Rev'd D. A. Payne.
Dying Girl, The.
Exile's Reverie, The.
For Who?
Grafted Bud, The.
Highland Mary.
In Memoriam. Alphonse Campbell Fordham.
In Memoriam. Susan Eugenia Bennett.
June.
Lines to———.
Lines to Florence.
Lines to Mrs. Isabel Peace.
Magnolia.
Maiden and River.
Marriage.
Mother's Recall.
Mr. Edward Fordham.
Mrs. E. Cohrs Brown.
Mrs. Louise B. Weston.
Mrs. Mary Furman Weston Byrd.
Mrs. Rebecca Weston.
Nativity, The.
Nestle-down Cottage.
October.
Ode to Peace.
On Parting with a Friend.
Passing of the Old Year.
Past, The.
Pen, The.
Queenie.
Rally Song.
Requiem: "O, insatiable monster! Could'st thou not."
Rev. Samuel Weston.
Reverie, A.
Saxon Legend of Language, The.
Serenade: "Sleep, love sleep."
Shipwreck.
Snow Storm, The.
Snowdrop, The.
Song to Erin.
Sonnet to My First Born.
Stars and Stripes.
Sunset.
To a Loved One.
To an Infant.
To My Mother.
To Rev. Thaddeus Saltus.
To the Eagle.
To the Mock-Bird.
Tribute to a Lost Steamer.
Tribute to Capt. F. W. Dawson.
Twilight Musings.
Uranne.
Valentine, The.
Washerwoman, The.

Fore, Brian
They told me, Heraclitus, they told me you were dead.

Foresman, Rebecca
How to Forget.

"Forester, Fanny" (Emily Chubbuck Judson) (1817–54)
Weaver sat by the side of his loom, A.

Forrest, Frederick (fl. c.1766)
St. Anthony and His Pig; a Cantata.

Forrest-Thomson, Veronica (1947–75)
Strike.

Forrester, Alfred A. ("Alfred Crowquill") (1804–92)
To My Nose.

Forster, Edward Morgan (1879–1970)
I strove with none for none was worth my strife.

Forster, William (1818–82)
Devil and the Governor, The, sels.
Love Has Eyes.

Poor of London, The.
Sonnet on the Crimean War.

Forsyth, Sarah
My Christmas; Mum's Christmas.

Fort, Charles
For Martin Luther King.
How Old Are the People of the World.
Town Clock Burning, The.
Worker (We Own Two Houses), The.

Fort, Paul (1872–1960)
Ballade: "Pretty maid she died, she died, in love-bed as she lay, The."
Pan and the Cherries.
Sailor and the Shark, The.

Forten, Charlotte (1839–1914)
Parting Hymn, A.
Poem: "In the earnest path of duty."
To W. L. G. on Reading His "Chosen Queen."

Forten, Sarah L.. See "Ada"

Fortunato, Margot
Leaving, The.

Fortune, Timothy Thomas (1856–1928)
Bartow Black.
Byron's Oak at Newstead Abbey.
Dreams of Life, sels.
Edgar Allan Poe.

Foscolo, Ugo (1778–1827)
To Evening.
To Zante.
Upon the Death of His Brother Giovanni.

Fosdick, Harry Emerson (1878–1969)
Prince of Peace His Banner Spreads, The.

Foss, Sam Walter (1858–1911)
Calf-Path, The.
Coming American, The, sels.
House by the Side of the Road, The.
Husband and Heathen.
Man from the Crowd, The.
Philosopher, A.
Work for Small Men, sels.

Foster, David (b. 1944)
Fleeing Atalanta, The, sels.

Foster, Edward (b. 1948)
Hermetic Silence.
In Your Words.
Marriage of True Minds, The.
Morning.
Poetry and Joy.

Foster, Jeanne
Garlic.
Irises, The.
Lynn.
Moving.

Foster, Michael
Recruiting Song.

Foster, Stephen Collins (1826–84)
Gwine to Run All Night; or, De Camptown Races.
Jeanie with the Light Brown Hair.
My Old Kentucky Home[, Good Night!].
Oh! Susanna.
Old Folks at Home[, The].
Who Has Our Redeemer Heard.

Foulcher, John (b. 1952)
After the Flood.
Wars of Imperialism.

Foulkes, William H. (1877–1961)
Take Thou Our Minds, Dear Lord.

Fowler, Alastair
Catacomb Suburb.
Relative.

Fowler, Andrew (1760–1850)
Awake, My Soul! In Grateful Songs.
O Gracious Jesus, Blessed Lord!

Fowler, Laurence (b. 1892)
Gather Ye Rosebuds.

Fowler, Russell T.
In Blanco County.

Fowler, William (1560–1612)
In Orknay.

Fox, Gail (b. 1942)
It Is Her Cousin's Death.
Portrait.

She Lay Wrapped.

Fox, Lucia (b. 1930)
Dream of the Forgotten Lover.

Fox, Ruth (b. 1895)
Another Kind of Burning.

Fox, Siv Cedering (b. 1939)
Almagest, Last Letter to Zakarias.
Grandmother.
In the evening.
Miss Pimberton Of.
Peaches.

Foxton, Thomas (c.1695–1740)
On a Little Boy's Endeavouring to Catch a Snake.
Upon Boys Diverting Themselves in the River.

Fraire, Isabel (b. 1936)
If night takes the form of a whale and.

Frame, Janet (b. 1925)
Christmas and Death.
Clown, The.
Flowering Cherry, The.
Foxes, The.
Letter.
Place, The.
Telephonist.
When the Sun Shines More Years Than Fear.
Yet Another Poem about a Dying Child.

France, Ruth. See "Henderson, Paul"

Frances, Emmanuel [or Immanuel] ben David (1618–c.1703)
Price of Begging, The.

Frances, Jacob ben David (1615–77)
Song of Hate.

Francescato, Martha Paley (b. 1934)
Parody.
Semen.

Francis, Anne (1738–1800)
Elegy on a Favorite Cat, An, sels.

Francis, Colin (b. 1906)
Tony O!

Francis, Errol (b. 1956)
Fragments of the Green Island, sels.
Rotogravure.

Francis of Assisi, Saint (1181–1226)
Cantica: Our Lord Christ: Of Order.
Canticle of Living Creatures.
Canticle of the Sun.
Cantico del Sole.
Prayer of St. Francis of Assisi for Peace.

Francis, Pat Therese
Thunder.

Francis, Robert (b. 1901)
Apple Peeler.
Base Stealer, The.
Blood stains how to remove from cotton.
Blue Jay [or Bluejay].
Blue Winter.
Bouquets.
Boy Riding Forward Backward.
By Night.
Catch.
Cold and the colors of cold: mineral, shell.
Come Out into the Sun.
Coming and Going.
Cypresses.
December.
Dog-Day Night.
Epitaphs, sels.
Exclusive Blue.
Fair and Unfair.
Fall.
Hogwash.
Hound, The.
Identity.
Juniper.
Like Ghosts of Eagles.
Mouse whose name is Time, The.
Mr. Eliot's Day.
Night Train.
Part for the Whole.
Pitcher.
Reading of the Psalm, The.
Sheep.
Silent Poem.

Sound I Listened For, The.
Squash in Blossom.
Swimmer.
That Dark Other Mountain.
Three darks come down together.
Three woodchoppers walk up the road.
Waxwings.
While I slept, while I slept and the night grew colder.
Yes, What?

Francis Xavier, Saint (1506–52)
Hymn.

Francisco, Nia (b. 1952)
Kayenta Times Yet Dreaming On.
Modern on the Surface.
Roots of Blue Bells.
To a Man Who is Rob Southland.

Francisco, Prince Ioann Shakhovskoy, Archbishop of San. See "Strannik"

Franco, Veronica (1546–91)
No more words! To the field, to arms.

Frank, Florence Kiper (b. 1890)
Jewish Conscript, The.

Frankau, Gilbert (1884–1952)
Deserter, The.
Eyes in the Air.
Gun Teams.
Headquarters.

Franklin, Benjamin (1706–90)
Bits of Wisdom.
Jack and Roger.
Mother Country, The.

Franklin, Michael
Scarecrow stood in a field one day, A.

František, Hrubín (1910–1971)
City in the Full Moon, The, sels.
Honeycomb of Bees, The.

Franzen, John (b. 1904)
O God of Stars and Distant Space.

Frase, Brigitte
Fish Story: How Language Carries Us into the Unknown.
Homegoing.
On Returning.
Put a Woman into the Memory Box.

Fraser, C. Lovat (1890–1921)
Robin's Song, The.

Fraser, George Sutherland (1915–80)
Christmas Letter Home.
Home Town Elegy.
Lament: "In a dismal air; a light of breaking summer."
Lean Street.
Letter to Anne Ridler.
Rostov.

Fraser, Kath (b. 1947)
Song: "I love you, Mrs. Acorn. Would your husband mind."

Fraser, Kathleen (b. 1937)
Because you aren't here to be what I can't think of I need most.
Boot, wet sand and more white along the borders defining a trail of lush / chemicals we adhere to.
Casa de Pollos.
Change of Address.
Dresses.
Flowers.
Frammenti Romani.
History of my feeling for you (or is it the way you change), The.
How Tuesday Began.
Poem in Which My Legs Are Accepted.
Poems for the New.
Re:searches (Fragments, after Anakreon, for Emily Dickinson).
These Labdanum Hours.
What You Need.
Your sky against my starfish I know how big.

Fraser, Marjorie Frost
Spring.

Frear, Mary Dillingham (b. 1810)
Young Workman, The.

Free, Spencer Michael (b. 1856)
Human Touch, The.

Freedman, William (b. 1937)
Family, The.
Freeman, Arthur (b. 1938)
Cell of Himself, The.
Naples Again.
Freeman, Carol [or Carole] (b. 1941)
Christmas Morning I.
Do Not Think.
I Saw Them Lynch.
Freeman, Enoch W. (1798–1835)
Hither We Come, Our Dearest Lord.
Freeman, James (1759–1835)
Lord of the Worlds Below!
Freeman, Jan
Autumn Sequence, sels.
Freeman, John (1880–1929)
Asylum.
Crowns, The.
Hounds, The.
To End Her Fear.
Tree, The.
Waiting.
Waits, The.
Freeman, Mary Eleanor Wilkins (1852–1930)
Blue-eyed Mary.
Marm Grayson's Guests.
Ostrich is a Silly Bird, The.
Pretty Ambition, A.
Freeman, Robert (1878–1940)
Braving the Wilds All Unexplored with music.
Freer, Ulli (b. 1947)
Take the Toys from the Boys.
Freeth, John (1731?–1808)
Botany Bay.
Bunker's Hill, or the Soldier's Lamentation.
Cottager's Complaint, on the Intended Bill for Enclosing Sutton-Coldfield, The.
Frémont, John Charles (1813–90)
On Recrossing the Rocky Mountains after Many Years.
French, William Percy (1854–1920)
Mountains of Mourne, The.
Queen's After-Dinner Speech, The.
Freneau, Philip (1752–1832)
Adventures of Simon Swaugum, a Village Merchant, The.
American Soldier, The.
Beauties of Santa Cruz, The, sels.
British Prison Ship, The, sels.
By Babel's Streams with music.
Columbus to Ferdinand.
George the Third's Soliloquy.
House of Night, The, sels.
Hurricane, The.
Indian Burying Ground, The.
Indian Convert, The.
Indian Student; or, Force of Nature, The.
Literary Importation.
On a Honey Bee [or To a Honey Bee].
On Mr. Paine's Rights of Man.
On Observing a Large Red-Streak Apple.
On the Civilization of the Western Aboriginal Country.
On the Conflagrations at Washington.
On the Emigration to America [and Peopling the Western Country].
On the Great Western Canal of the State of New York.
On the Religion of Nature.
On the Uniformity and Perfection of Nature.
Power of Fancy, The.
Stanzas Occasioned by the Ruins of a Country Inn or On the Ruins of a Country Inn.
To a Caty-did.
To a New England Poet.
To a Noisy Politician.
To an Author.
To Mr. Blanchard, the Celebrated Aeronaut in America.
To Sir Toby.
To the Memory of the Brave Americans.
Tobacco.
Vanity of Existence, The.
Warning to America, A.

Wild Honey Suckle, The.
See also **Brackenridge, Hugh Henry,** and **Philip Freneau**
Frere, John Hookham. See **Canning, George** and **John Hookham Frere; Canning, George, George Ellis,** and **John Hookham Frere**
Frere, John Hookham (1769–1846)
Boy and the Parrot, The.
Fable, A.
Fable of the Piece of Glass and the Piece of Ice, The.
Prospectus and Specimen of an Intended National Work by William and Robert Whistlecraft...Relating to King Arthur and His Round Table, sels.
Whistlecraft, sels.
Fried, Barbara (b. 1924)
Good Old Days, The.
Fried, Erich (b. 1921)
Exile.
Measures Taken, The.
My Girlfriends.
One Kind of Freedom Speaks.
What Things Are Called.
Friedmann, Pavel
Butterfly, The.
Friedrich von Hausen (d. 1190)
Help! How Minne has deserted me.
I think sometimes about.
My heart and my body want to separate.
She may not accuse me.
When I parted from my Good.
Friend, Robert (b. 1913)
Letter to P.
Frink, A. L.
Rose Still Grows beyond the Wall, The.
Fritsch, H. S.
How Old Are You?
Froissart, Jean (c.1337–1410?)
Rondel: "Love, love, what wilt thou with this heart of mine?"
Frost, Carol
Apple Rind.
Frost, Frances Mary (1905–59)
Christmas in the Wood.
Snow-Stars.
Frost, Lesley (1899–1983)
Rock 'n' Roll.
Frost, Richard (b. 1929)
For a Brother.
Frost, Robert (1874–1963)
Acceptance.
Acquainted with the Night.
After Apple-Picking.
Aim Was Song, The.
America Is Hard to See.
Answer, An.
Armful, The.
At Woodward's Gardens.
August.
Away!
Axe-Helve, The.
Bear puts both arms around the tree above her, The.
Bearer of evil tidings, The.
Bereft.
Beyond Words.
Birches.
Black Cottage, The.
Boundless Moment, A.
Brook in the City, A.
Brown's Descent; or, The Willy-Nilly.
Canis Major.
Choose Something like a Star.
Clear and Colder.
Code, The.
Come In.
Considerable Speck, A.
Cow in Apple Time, The.
Death of the Hired Man, The.
Demiurge's Laugh, The.
Departmental.
Desert Places.
Design.

Directive.
Draft Horse, The.
Drumlin Woodchuck, A.
Dust of Snow.
Egg and the Machine, The.
Ends.
Fire and Ice.
Fireflies in the Garden.
Five Nocturnes, sels.
Flower-Boat, The.
For Allan, Who Wanted to See How I Wrote a Poem.
For Once, Then, Something.
Forgive, O Lord, my little jokes on Thee.
Fountain, a Bottle, a Donkey's Ears and Some Books, A.
From Plane to Plane.
Gathering Leaves.
Gift Outright, The.
Girl's Garden, A.
Good-by and Keep Cold.
Happiness Makes Up in Height for What It Lacks in Length.
Hill Wife, The, sels.
Hillside Thaw, A.
Home Burial, sels.
I Shall Say What Inordinate Love Is.
In Hardwood Groves.
In Neglect.
In White.
In winter in the woods alone.
Investment, The.
It takes all sorts of in- and outdoor schooling.
John L. Sullivan Enters Heaven.
Last Word of a Bluebird, The.
Leaf-Treader, A.
Leaves Compared with Flowers.
Lesson for Today, The.
Limerick: "For Travelers Going Sidereal."
Line-Gang, The.
Line-Storm Song, A.
Lockless Door, The.
Lost in Heaven.
Love and a Question.
Lovely Shall Be Choosers, The.
Lucretius versus the Lake Poets.
Master Speed, The.
Meeting and Passing.
Mending Wall.
Middleness of the Road, The.
Minor Bird, A.
Mood Apart, A.
Most of It, The.
Mowing.
My November Guest.
Need of Being Versed in Country Things, The.
Neither Out Far Nor In Deep.
Never Again Would Birds' Song Be The Same.
New Hampshire, sels.
Not to Keep.
Nothing Gold Can Stay.
Objection to Being Stepped On, The.
Old Man's Winter Night, An.
On a Tree Fallen across the Road.
On Looking Up by Chance at the Constellations.
On the Heart's Beginning to Cloud the Mind.
Once by the Pacific.
Onset, The.
"Out, Out—."
Oven Bird, The.
Pan with Us.
Pasture, The.
Patch of Old Snow, A.
Paul's Wife.
Peaceful Shepherd, The.
Pod of the Milkweed.
Prayer in Spring, A.
Pride of Ancestry.
Provide, Provide.
Putting in the Seed.
Range-finding.
Reluctance.
Revelation.

Road Not Taken, The.
Rose Family, The.
Runaway, The.
Sand Dunes.
Secret Sits, The.
Semi-Revolution, A.
Servant to Servants, A.
Silken Tent, The.
Sitting by a Bush in Broad Daylight.
Sound of Trees, The.
Spring Pools.
St. Luke, *sels.*
Stopping by Woods on a Snowy Evening.
Storm Fear.
Strong Are Saying Nothing, The.
Subverted Flower, The.
Telephone, The.
Ten Mills, *sels.*
There Are Roughly Zones.
Time to Talk, A.
To E.T.
To Earthward.
To the Thawing Wind.
Tree at my window, window tree.
Tuft of Flowers, The.
Two Look at Two.
Two Tramps in Mud Time.
Two Witches, *sels.*
U. S. 1946 King's X.
Unharvested.
Vantage Point, The.
West-Running Brook.
White-tailed hornet lives in a balloon, The.
Winter Eden, A.
Wood-Pile, The.
Young Birch, A.

Frothingham, Nathaniel Langdon (1793–1870)
O God Whose Presence Glows in All.

Frothingham, Octavius Brooks (1822–95)
Thou Lord of Hosts, Whose Guiding Hand.

Frug, Simeon Grigoryevich (1860–1916)
Sail Peacefully Home.
Talmud, The.

Frym, Gloria (b. 1947)
Manifesto.
Yield, The.

Fu Hsien (239–294)
Ruinous Rains.

Fu Hsüan (d. 278)
Gentle Wind [fans the calm night], A.
Thunder. My heart trembles.
Woman.

Fuentes, Robert C. (b. 1958)
In This Place.

Fuertes, Gloria (b. 1920)
Autobiography.
Birds Nest in My Arms, The.
Climbing.
Human Geography.
I Write Poems.
Interior Landscape.
Love Which Frees.
We're OK.

Fujiwara no Atsutada (d. 961?)
I think of the days.

Fujiwara no Go-Kanesuke (*fl.* 10th cent.)
River Izumi, The.

Fujiwara no Go-Kyōgoku (*fl.* late 12th cent.)
Cricket cries, The.

Fujiwara no Kiyosuke (d. 1177)
I may live on until.

Fujiwara no Masatsune (1170–1221)
From Yoshino / Mountain the autumn.

Fujiwara no Michinobu (973–95)
In the dawn, although I know.

Fujiwara no Sadaie (1162–1242)
You do not come, and I wait.

Fujiwara no Sadayori (*fl.* 11th cent.)
As the mists rise in the dawn.

Fujiwara No Toshinari
In all the world.

Fukao, Sumako (1893–1974)
Bright House.

Fukui, Hisako (b. 1929)
Now is the time.

Fukunaka, Tomoko (b. 1928)
It's Not the Same.

Fulbert of Chartres (c.975–1028)
Abbot John, in stature small, The.
To the Nightingale.

Fuller, Ethel Romig
Today.
What the king has.

Fuller, Hoyt W. (b. 1928)
Lost Moment.
Seravezza.

Fuller, John (b. 1937)
Alex at the Barber's.
Blues.
Butterfly, The.
De Sade.
Fox-Trot, *sels.*
God Bless America.
Linda, Linda, slender and pretty.
Sonata.
St. Sophia.
Statue, The.
Tides.
Whole New Scene, A.
See also **Fenton, James** *and* **John Fuller**

Fuller, Margaret (1810–50)
Flaxman.
Freedom and Truth.
Jesus a Child His Course Begun.
Sistrum.

Fuller, Margaret Witter (1872–1954)
Memoirs, I, *sels.*

Fuller, Roy (b. 1912)
Autobiography of a Lungworm.
Autumn 1942.
Christmas Day.
Consolations of Art.
Coptic Socks.
Crustaceans.
Day, The.
Death.
Dedicatory Epistle, with a Book of 1949.
During a Bombardmant by V-Weapons.
Edmond Halley.
Family Cat, The.
Faust's Servant.
From the Joke Shop.
Ghost Voice, *sels.*
Good-bye for a Long Time.
Hittites, The.
Image, The.
In Africa.
January 1940.
Limerick: "How varied the family Sen!"
Love and Murder.
Memorial Poem.
Metamorphoses.
Middle of a War, The.
Mythological Sonnets, *sels.*
Other Side, The.
Outside the Supermarket.
Peculiar Christmas, A.
Preserving.
Reading in the Night.
Shop Talk.
Soliloquy in an Air-Raid.
Sonnet: "Crumbled rock of London is
   dripping under, The."
Spring 1943.
Spring 1942.
Those of Pure Origin.
Translation.
Tribes, The.
Unremarkable Year, The.
Versions of Love.
What Is Terrible.

Fuller, Stephany (b. 1947)
In the Silence.
Let Me Be Held When the Longing Comes.
My Love When This Is Past.
That We Head Towards.
Who is not a stranger still.

Fullerton, Mary Elizabeth ("E.") (1868–1946)
Farmer, The.
Man's [a] Sliding Mood, A.
Martyr.

Ninety.
Poetry.
St. John, *sels.*
Stupidity.
Unit.

Fulton, Alice (b. 1952)
A.M.: The Hopeful Monster.
Cherry Bombs.
Everyone Knows the World Is Ending.
My Diamond Stud.
News of the Occluded Cyclone.
Powers of Congress.
Priming Is a Negligee, The.
Risk Management.
Self-Storage.
What I Like.
Wreckage Entrepreneur, The.

Fulton, Robin (b. 1937)
Museums and Journeys.
Remembering an Island.
Remembering Walls.
Resolutions.
Stopping by Shadows.
Travelling Alone.
Waiting-Room, The.

Fumi Saito (b. 1909)
Tanka: "Bones of a fish."
Tanka: "Cluster, A."
Tanka: "Crooked fireworks."
Tanka: "Don't resemble me."
Tanka: "Even the black gloves."
Tanka: "Ever deeper."
Tanka: "In my possession."
Tanka: "Palm of the hand, The, / is not
   aware of dying "
Tanka: "Seeds of the grass."
Tanka: "Snow seeping."
Tanka: "Sweeter than a song."
Tanka: "This huge pile."
Tanka: "To take a bath."
Tanka: "Trailing for a while."
Tanka: "Water streams."
Tanka: "When I think over."
Tanka: "When neither a man."
Tanka: "White hare, A."
Tanka: "Wood borers."
Turbid current.

Fumiko, Nakajō
Tanka: "Although blooming."
Tanka: "As the surgical knife."
Tanka: "Boxes of sleeping pills."
Tanka: "Didn't a certain woman."
Tanka: "Each year."
Tanka: "Eyes, The."
Tanka: "For this."
Tanka: "In a posture."
Tanka: "In search of a shore."
Tanka: "Knees collapsing."
Tanka: "My arms."
Tanka: "One day I saw."
Tanka: "Sharing the gentleness."
Tanka: "Since that evening."
Tanka: "That hill."
Tanka: "When the lights go out."
Tanka: "Wiggling out."
Tanka: "With a thunderous crack."
Tanka: "With sorrow I recall."
Tanka: "Yellow bus, The."

Funk, Allison
After Dark.

Funk, Wilfred John (1883–1965)
Hospital.
Rest in Peace.

Furness, William Henry (1802–96)
Evening Hymn.
In the Morning I Will Pray.

Furse, Margaret Cecilia
Lamp Flower, The.

Fyleman, Rose (1877–1957)
Balloon Man, The.
Cat, The.
Christmas Wish, A.
Conversation.
Donkey, The.
Fairies.
Fairy Flute, The.

Fairy Went a-Marketing, A.
Frog, The.
Goblin lives in our house, in our house, in
  our house, A.
Good Morning.
I Don't Like Beetles.
Jock o' Dreams.
(Mice).
Mrs. Brown.
Pretty Lady.
Primrose Hill.
Punch and Judy.
Solo with Chorus.
Temper.
Weathercock, The.
Fynn, Henry Francis (Mbuyazi) (1803–61)
  Adieu, to Fortune.
**Fyodorov [or Fiodorov], Vasily [or Vasilii
  Dmitrievich] (1918–84)**
  Servile Blood.

G

"G., E. O."
  My Church ("My church has but one
    temple.")
Gaba, Ntsikana (1780–1821)
  Great Hymm.
  Great Hymm.
Gabai, Ilya Iankelevich (1935–73)
  For the Last Time on My Native Estate...
Gabriel, Charles H. (1856–1932)
  My Evening Prayer.
Gadjanski, Ivan (b. 1937)
  Voyvodina.
**Gaetulicus (Gnaeus Cornelius Lentulus
  Gaetulicus) (fl. A.D. c.26)**
  Here, by the seashore, there lies /
    Archilochus.
Gaffarel, Jacques
  Celestial Alphabet Event.
Gaius Valerius Catullus. *See* Catullus
Galai, Benyamin [or Benjamin] (b. 1921)
  Canaan, oh Canaan!
  Of Those Who Go, Not to Return.
  To My Generation.
**Galanskov, Yury [or Iurii] Timofeievich (1939–
  72)**
  Night is dark, The.
Galassi, Jonathan (b. 1949)
  Our Wives.
Galbreath, Margaret
  Limerick: "There once was an artist called
    Pat."
Gale, Norman (b. 1862)
  Country Faith, The.
Gal'ed, Zerubavel
  Chickory.
Galguera, Robin Boody
  Alloy.
  Second Childhood.
Galich, Aleksandr Arkadevich (1919–77)
  Mistake, A.
  Prospectors' Little Waltz, The.
Galindo, David Escobar (b. 1943)
  Short Story, A.
Gallagher, Joseph (b. 1929)
  John J. Curtis.
Gallagher, Katherine (b. 1935)
  Girl's Head, A.
Gallagher, Tess (b. 1943)
  After the Chinese.
  Black Silk.
  Breasts.
  Conversation with a Fireman from Brooklyn.
  Deaf Poem.
  Each Bird Walking.
  Horse in the drugstore / wants to be admired,
    The.
  Hug, The.
  I Stop Writing the Poem.
  Instructions to the Double.
  Kidnap[p]er.

Not There.
Now That I Am Never Alone.
On Your Own.
One kiss.
Red Poppy.
Spacious Encounter.
Stepping Outside.
Strange Thanksgiving.
Sudden Journey.
Unaswered Letter.
Under Stars.
Woodcutting on Lost Mountain.
Gallaudet, Thomas H. (1787–1851)
  Jesus, in Sickness and in Pain.
Galler, David (b. 1929)
  Jersey Marsh, The.
  Makers, The.
  Narcissus: To Himself.
Galloway, George (b. 1755)
  To the Memory of Gavin Wilson (Boot, Leg
    and Arm Maker).
Galsworthy, John (1867–1933)
  Limerick: "Angry young husband called
    Bicket, An."
  Peace in the World.
  Prayer, The.
  Prayer for Gentleness to All Creatures.
  So Might It Be.
  Youth's Own.
**Galt, John (1779–1839) and "Christopher
  North"**
  Canadian Boat Song.
Galvin, Brendan (b. 1938)
  Chickadee.
  For a Daughter Gone Away.
  Great Blue.
  Green Evening, A.
  Listening to September.
  Old Trip by Dream Train, The.
  Photo of Miners, A.
  Pitch Pines.
  Seals in the Inner Harbor.
  Town Pier Parking Lot.
  Willow, Wishbone, Warblers.
Galvin, James (b. 1951)
  Independence Day, 1956: A Fairy Tale.
  Western Civilization.
Galvin, Patrick (b. 1927)
  Madwoman of Cork, The.
  My Father Spoke with Swans.
  Plaisir d'Amour.
Gambara, Veronica (1485–1550)
  When I see the earth ornate and lovely.
Gambold, John (1711–71)
  Mystery of Life, The.
Gammons, Susan E.
  Just One Day.
Gander, Forrest (b. 1956)
  Table Laid with Horrors, A.
"Gander, Sir Gregory" (George Ellis)
  (The Twelve Months).
Gangnus, Aleksandr Rudolfovich (1910–72)
  Firing back at my heavy heart.
Gangopadhyay, Sunil (b. 1934)
  Calcutta and I.
Gannett, William Channing (1840–1923)
  From Heart to Heart.
  He Hides within the Lily.
Ganse, Hervey Doddridge (1822–91)
  Lord, I Know Thy Grace Is nigh Me.
García, Jesse F. (fl. 20th cent.)
  Barrio Beateo.
  I Ain't Going to Hurry No More.
Garcia, Leandra
  Tips for Living.
García Lorca, Federico (1895–1936)
  At the Poorhouse.
  Ballad of Black Grief.
  Below.
  Casida of Sobbing.
  Comet.
  Corridor.
  Faithless Wife, The.
  Girl by the River.

Great Sadness, The.
Guitar.
In a Corner of the Sky.
Lament for Ignacio Sánchez Mejías.
Little Infinite Poem.
Little Mute Boy, The.
Memory.
Mister Lizard is Crying.
Moon Rises, The.
New York.
Ode for Walt Whitman.
One.
Poem of Solitude at Columbia University.
Preciosa and the Wind.
Prelude.
Quarrel, The.
Rundown Church (Ballad of the First World
  War).
Serenata.
Shell.
Silly Song.
Six Strings, The.
Sketches.
Sleepwalkers' Ballad.
Song of the Cuban Blacks.
Star, A.
Swath.
Tío-Vivo, or the Merry-go-round.
Unfaithful Wife, The.
Ursa Major.
Variations.
Venus.
Whole Works, The.
Garcia, Ramon
  Salmo: Para El.
Gardiner, Allen F. (1794–1851)
  Natal Hunters, The.
Gardinier, Suzanne (b. 1961)
  Agricultural Show, Flemington, Victoria, The.
  On a Grey-haired Old Lady Knitting at an
    Orchestral Concert.
  Supremer Sacrifice, The.
  Team, The.
  Two Girls.
  Upon a Row of Old Books and Shoes in a
    Pawnbroker's Window.
Gardner, Ada Belle (d. 1949)
  Mary, The Mother of Jesus.
Gardner, Carl (b. 1931)
  Dead Man Dragged from the Sea, The.
  Reflections.
Gardner, Carolyn
  If you ever come to our house.
Gardner, Drew (b. 1968)
  Fire Music.
  Near Hermes.
Gardner, Edmund (1752?–1798)
  Sonnet Written in Tintern Abbey,
    Monmouthshire.
Gardner, Isabella (1915–81)
  Cock-a-Hoop.
  In the Museum.
  Loud Song, Mother, A.
  Nightmare.
  Telephone rang / in my dream Long Distance
    from, The.
  That "Craning of the Neck."
  Widow's Yard, The.
Gardner, John (1933–82)
  Feat of Gardening, The, *sels.*
Gardner, Martin (b. 1914)
  Barbershop.
"Gardons, S. S." *See* Snodgrass, William
  DeWitt
Garioch, Robert (Robert Sutherland) (1909–81)
  At Robert Fergusson's Grave[, October
    1962].
  Campidoglio.
  Did Ye See Me?
  Elegy: "They are lang deid, folk that I used
    to ken."
  Embro to the Ploy.
  Fair Cop, A.
  Glisk of the Great.
  Heard in the Cougate.
  I Was Fair Beat.

In Princes Street Gairdens.
Judgment Day.
Merulius Lacrymans.
On Seein an Aik-Tree Sprent Wi Galls.
Property.
Sanct Christopher II ("Sanct Christopher's a
　muckle sanct and strang.")
To Robert Fergusson.
Wire, The.

Garland, Hamlin (1860–1940)
Boyish sleep.
Dakota Wheat-Field, A.
Fighting Fire.
Goin' Back T'morrer.
Gold-Seekers, The.
Horses Chawin' Hay.
In August.
Indian Summer.
On the Mississippi.
Plowing: A Memory.
Prairie Fires.

Garlick, Phyllis L.
Fairy Feet.
Fairy Shoemaker, The.
Lullaby, lullaby.

Garman, Douglas (fl. 1920–30)
Ode on the Death of Haig's Horse, sels.

Garner, Alan (b. 1934)
Summer Solstice.

Garnet, Henry Highland (1817–82)
Bound on a voyage of awful length.
Down let the shrine of Moloch sink.
Hear ye not how, from all high points of
　Time.
Proud Nimrod first the bloody chase began.
Thus man devotes his brother and destroys.

Garnett, Richard (1835–1906)
Fading-Leaf and Fallen-Leaf.

Garnett, Ruth (b. 1954)
Dealing Scraps.

Garrett, George (b. 1929)
Bubbles.
Buzzard.
Giant Killer.
In the Hospital.
Jacob.
Luck's Shining Child.
Magi, The.
Revival.
Romantic.
York Harbor Morning.

Garrick, David (1716–79)
Epitaph on Laurence Sterne.
Friend Col and I, both full of whim.
Heart of Oak.
Jupiter and Mercury.
On a Certain Lord Giving Some Thousand
　Pounds for a House.
On Oliver Goldsmith.
On Sir John Hill, M. D., Playwright.

Garrigue, Jean (1914–72)
After Reading "The Country of the Pointed
　Firs."
Amsterdam.
Amsterdam Letter.
Bleecker Street.
Catch What You Can.
Cortège for Colette.
Country Villa.
Cracked Looking Glass.
Epitaph for My Cat.
False Country of the Zoo.
Forest.
From Venice was that afternoon.
Mouse, The.
Movie Actors Scribbling Letters Very Fast in
　Crucial Scenes.
Now Snow Descends.
Of History More Like Myth.
Old Haven.
On the Legends of a Dancer.
Primer of Plato.
Remember That Country.
Shore.
Song for "Buvez les Vins du Postillion"—
　Advt.

Stranger, The.
To speak of my influences.
Unicorn and the Lady, The.
Upon the Intimation of Love's Mortality.
Written in London after a Protest Parade.
You know those rose sherbets.

Garrison, Theodosia Pickering (1874–1944)
Closed Door, The.
Ilicet.
Shepherd Who Stayed, The.
Torch, The.

Garrison, William Lloyd (1805–79)
Freedom for the Mind.

Garstin, Crosbie (1887–1930)
Chemin Des Dames.
Nocturne: "Red flame flowers bloom and die,
　The."

**Garston, Edward John Langford ("E. J. L.")
(b. 1893)**
To the Rats.

Garth, Sir Samuel (1661–1719)
Dispensary, The, sels.
What Frenzy Has of Late Possess'd the
　Brain.

Garvey, Marcus (1887–1940)
Centenary's Day.
Keep Cool.

Gascoigne, George (1539–77)
Adventures of Master F. I, The, sels.
And every yeare a worlde my will did
　deeme.
Arraignment of a Lover, The.
Before mine eye to feede my greedy will.
Councell Given to Master Bartholmew
　Withipoll.
De Profundis, sels.
Divorce of a Lover, The ("Divorce me nowe
　good death.")
Farewell with a Mischeife.
For That He Looked Not upon Her.
For why? the gaines doth seldome quitte the
　charge.
Fruits of War, The, sels.
Gascoigne's Good-Morrow.
Gascoigne's [or Gascoygnes] Good-Night.
Gascoigne's Memories, sels.
Gascoigne's Woodmanship.
Gloze Upon This Text, Dominus iis opus
　habet, A.
Green Knight's Farewell to Fancy, The.
I Could Not though I Would.
Lullaby [or Lullabie] of a Lover, The.
Magnum Vectigal Parsimonia.
Praise of Philip Sparrow, The, sels.
Sonet Written in Prayse of the Browne
　Beautie, A.
Steele Glas, The.
Straunge [or Strange] Passion of a Lover, A.
To prinke me up and make me higher plaste.
World as Garden, The.

Gascoyne, David
And the Seventh Dream Is the Dream of Isis.
Cage, The.
Cubical Domes, The.
De Profundis.
Elegy: "Friend, whose unnatural early death."
End Is Near the Beginning, The.
Eve.
Landscape.
Miserere, sels.
Orpheus in the Underworld.
Rex Mundi.
Sacred Hearth, The.
Salvador Dali.
Tenebrae.
Tough Generation, A.
Truth is Blind, The.
Uncertain Battle, The.
Unsagacious Animal, An.
Wartime Dawn, A.
Winter Garden.
Yves Tanguy.

Gashe, Marina
Village, The.

Gaspar, Frank (b. 1946)
Kapital.

Gasztold, Carmen Bernos de
Noah's Prayer.
Prayer of the Cat, The.
Prayer of the Donkey, The.

Gates, Beatrix (b. 1949)
Deadly Weapon.

Gates, Ellen M. Huntington (1835–1920)
Sleep Sweet.
Your Mission.

Gates, Larry
At the river-bend.
Crow flies off, The.
Killdeer, The.
Lights are going out, The.
On the jewelweed.
Rowing.
Silent Buddha, The.
Winter dawn;.

Gatsos, Nikos (b. 1914)
Amorgos, sels.

Gatty, Sir Alfred Scott (1847–1918)
Three Little Pigs, The.

Gault, A. J. (1818–1903) and Dill Armor Smith
Twenty Years Ago.

Gauradas
Dear Echo, do me a favour; it's somewhat
　. . . Some what?

Gautier, Théophile (1811–72)
Art.
Her Toys.
Posthumous Coquetry.
Taches Jaunes, Les, sels.

Gaxe
I wonder what eagle did to him.

Gay, Asya. See "Asya"

Gay, John (1685–1732)
Achilles, sels.
Acis and Galatea, sels.
Beggar's Opera, The, sels.
Birth of the Squire; an Eclogue, The.
Cotillion.
Damon and Cupid.
Epistle to the Right Honourable William
　Pulteney, Esq, sels.
Fable XXI: The Rat-catcher and Cats.
Fables, sels.
I'm like a skiff on the ocean tost.
Molly Mog [or The Fair Maid of the Inn].
Mr. Pope's Welcome from Greece.
My Own Epitaph.
New Song of New Similies , A.
Newgate's Garland.
Ode for the New Year, An.
On a Miscellany of Poems, sels.
Polly; an Opera, sels.
She who hath felt a real pain.
Shepherd's Week, The, sels.
Sweet William's Farewell to Black-Eyed [or
　Black-Ey'd] Susan.
To a Lady.
To a Lady on Her Passion for Old China.
To a Young Lady, with Some Lampreys.
To My Ingenious and Worthy Friend William
　Lowndes, Esq.
Toilette, The.
Trivia; or, The Art of Walking the Streets of
　London, sels.
Two Monkeys, The.
What D'Ye-Call-It, The, sels.

Gay, John and Alexander Pope
Mary Gulliver to Capt. Lemuel Gulliver.

Gbadamosi, Gabriel (b. 1961)
Death of the Polar Explorers.
Flying Home.
No Blacks, No Irish, sels.
Padraic's Point.
Reading, The.
Sango, sels.
Sewing-Box, The.

**Gearailt, Gearold Iarla Mac. See Desmond,
　Gerald Fitzgerald, 4th Earl of**

Gearailt, Piaras Mac. See Fitzgerald, Pierce

Gebirtig, Mordecai (1877–1942)
Waiting for Death.

Geda, Sigitas
  God's Family.
  I walked out into Lithuania.
  Repentance: The Devil's Blossom.
  Sebastian's Lament, 1943.
  Steep eyes of wooden gods.
Geddes, Alexander (1737–1802)
  Epistle to the President of the Scottish
    Society of Antiquaries: On Being Chosen a
    Correspondent Member.
Geddes, Gary (b. 1940)
  Inheritors, The.
  Transubstantiation.
Geier, Joan Austin
  On Your Twenty-First Birthday.
Geiger, Timothy
  Insomnia.
Geisel, Theodore Seuss. See "Seuss, Dr."
Gellert, Leon (b. 1892)
  Before Action.
  Emu makes, though prone to fret, The.
  House-Mates.
Gensei (1623–68)
  Poem without a Category.
Gentry, Jane
  Aunt Lucy.
Geoghegan, J. B. (1815–89)
  Down in a Coal Mine.
George, David Graves
  Wreck of the Old 97.
George, Diana Hume b. 1948
  Asenath.
George, Glenda (b. 1951)
  Quasi Quasi . . . as If Repeated.
George, Phillip [or "Phil"] William
  America's Wounded Knee.
  Favorite Grandson Braid.
  First Grade.
  Moon of Huckleberries.
  Morning Vigil.
  Name Giveaway.
  Prelude to Memorial Song: 100 Years Later.
  Spokane Falls.
  Spring Cleaning.
  Spruce.
  Sunflower Moccasins.
  Visit, The.
  Wardance.
  Wardance Soup.
George, Stefan (1868–1933)
  Invocation and Prelude.
  Jahr der Seele, Das, sels.
  Lord of the Isle, The.
  Rapture.
  Stanzas Concerning Love.
Georges, Esther Valck
  Alley Cat.
Gerard, Gertrude
  In Arabia.
Gergely, Agnes (b. 1933)
  Auden in Old Age.
  Crazed Man in Concentration Camp.
  Encelado and the Facts.
  Gnosis.
  Magdalene.
  Silences.
  Upon a Renaissance Carving.
Gerhardt, Paul (1607–76)
  Evensong.
  Go out in this dear summertide.
  O sacred head, now wounded.
Gerondi, Abraham (fl. 13th cent.)
  Hymn for the Eve of the New Year.
Gerrard, John (fl. c.1769)
  Remonstrance, A.
Gershon, Karen (b. 1923)
  At a Reception.
  Experiments with God.
  I Was Not There.
  Race.
  Uphold Me.
Gershwin, Ira (1896–1983)
  Babbitt and the Bromide, The.
  Blah, Blah, Blah.

  Embraceable You.
  I Got Rhythm.
  It Ain't Neccessarily So.
  'S Wonderful.
Gerstler, Amy (b. 1956)
  Bitter Angel.
  BZZZZZZZ.
  Marriage.
  Travelogue.
  True Bride, The.
  Unforseen, The.
  Ups and Downs.
Getsi, Lucia Cordell
  Oradour-sur-Glane. Silence.
Ghalib, Asadullah Khan (1797–1869)
  Colors of tulips and roses are not the same,
    The.
  Even at prayer, our eyes look inward.
  For the raindrop, joy is in entering the river.
  Let the ascetics sing of the garden of
    Paradise.
  World is no more than the Beloved's single
    face, The.
Gheorghe, Ion
  Cathedral Stones.
  Moonlit nights on the Atlantic Ocean!
  Unicorn, The.
Ghiselin, Brewster (b. 1903)
  Catch, The.
  Credo.
  Headland.
  Rattler, Alert.
Ghose, Manmohan (1869–1924)
  Who Is It Talks of Ebony?
Ghose, Zulfikar (b. 1935)
  Rise of Shivaji, The.
Giacosa, Giuseppe and Luigi Illica
  Tosca, sels.
Gibbon, Monk (b. 1896)
  French Peasants.
  Poetry of Gerard Manley Hopkins, The.
  Prayer of the Arab Physician, The.
Gibbon, Perceval (1878–1926)
  Answer, An.
  Mooimeisjes.
Gibbons, Orlando (1583–1625)
  Silver swan, who living had no note, The.
Gibbons, Reginald (b. 1947)
  American Trains.
  Hoppy.
  We say a heart breaks—like.
  White Beach.
Gibbons, Stella (b. 1902)
  Continuity.
  Truce, The.
Gibbs, Barbara
  "What You See Is Me."
Gibbs, C. Armstrong
  Limerick: "Serious young lady from Welwyn,
    A."
Gibbs, Margaret E.
  On the Banisters.
  Song of the Bath, The.
Gibran, Kahlil (1883–1931)
  Prophet, The, sels.
Gibson, Alan (1856–1922)
  When stags do rut in the Plym.
Gibson, Douglas
  January.
Gibson, Margaret (b. 1944)
  Beginner's Mind.
  Country Woman Elegy.
  Invisible Work.
  Learning a New Language.
  Long Walks in the Afternoon.
  October Elegy.
  Onion, The.
  Unborn Child Elegy, sels.
  Wars.
Gibson, Walker (b. 1919)
  Advice to Travelers.
  Blues for an Old Blue.
  Essay on Lunch.

Gibson, Wilfrid Wilson (1878–1962)
  All Being Well.
  Ambulance Train.
  Back.
  Breakfast.
  Conscript, The.
  Drove-Road, The.
  Flannan Isle.
  Fowler, The.
  Geraniums.
  Henry Turnbull.
  Ice, The.
  Lament: "We who are left, how shall we
    look again."
  Long Tom.
  Luck.
  Michael's Song.
  Old Skinflint.
  Parrot, The.
  Parrots, The.
  Prelude: "As one, at midnight, wakened by
    the call."
  Question, The.
  Retreat.
  Sight.
  Stone, The.
  Troopship: Mid-Atlantic.
  White Dust, The.
  Wishing-Well, The.
Gibson, William (1826–87)
  Circe.
Gidlow, Elsa (b. 1898)
  Chains of Fire, sels.
Gifford, Fannie Stearns (b. 1884)
  Songs of Conn the Fool, The, sels.
Gifford, Humphrey [or Humfrey] (fl. c.1580)
  For Soldiers.
  In the Praise of Music.
Gifford, William. See Canning, George and
  William Gifford
Gifford, William (1756–1826)
  Baviad, The, sels.
Gilbart, Thomas (fl. c.1583)
  Declaration of the Death of John Lewes, A.
Gilbert, Bernard (b. 1882)
  If The War Keeps On.
Gilbert, Celia (b. 1932)
  Circles.
  Midwives, The.
Gilbert, Christopher (b. 1950)
  Beginning by Example, sels.
  Beginning by Value.
  Directions, The.
  Glimpses.
  Kite-Flying.
  Now.
  Pushing.
  Theory of Curve.
  This Bridge Across.
Gilbert, Jack (b. 1925)
  Abnormal Is Not Courage, The.
  Meaning Well.
Gilbert, James Stanley (1855–1906)
  Beyond the Chagres.
Gilbert-Lecomte, Roger (1907–43)
  Preface or The Drama of Absence in an
    Eternal Heart.
  Son of the Bone Speaks, The.
  Wink.
Gilbert, Ruth (b. 1917)
  Green Hammock, White Magnolia Tree.
  Leah, sels.
Gilbert, Samuel (d. 1692?)
  Florist's Vade-Mecum, The, sels.
Gilbert, Sandra M. (b. 1936)
  After a Death.
  Dream Kitchen, The.
  Elegy: "Pages of history open, The."
  Fog Dream, The.
  Ladies' Home Journal, The.
  Mafioso.
  Parachutist's Wife, The.
Gilbert, Thomas (1713?–1747)
  View of the Town, A. In an Epistle to a
    Friend, sels.

Gilbert, Sir William Schwenck (1836–1911)
Captain Reece.
Etiquette.
Ferdinando and Elvira; or, The Gentle
    Pieman.
Gondoliers, The, *sels.*
H. M. S. Pinafore, *sels.*
Iolanthe, *sels.*
Mikado, The, *sels.*
Patience, *sels.*
Pirates of Penzance, The, *sels.*
Rival Curates, The.
Ruddigore, *sels.*
Story of Prince Agib, The.
There was an old man of St. Bees.
Thought from Ruddigore, *A.*
To the Terrestrial Globe.
Trial by Jury, *sels.*
Utopia Limited, *sels.*
Yarn of the *Nancy Bell,* The.
Yeoman of the Guard, *sels.*

Gilbert, Zack (b. 1925)
For Angela.
For Stephen Dixon.
My Own Hallelujahs.
When I Heard Dat White Man Say.

Gilbo'a, Amir (b. 1917)
Against the Wind.
Ancient Song.
Back and forth. As in a swing. When there's.
Birth.
Circle of Weeping, The.
City defenseless by day one sees desolation,
    A.
Death in Spring, A.
Ends of Things were heard no more, The.
Evening of the Whirlwind.
From All Sides Laughter Shall Strike Them.
Gazelle I send you to the wolves not in the
    wood they're.
Havdala.
I guess it will come suddenly. And every.
I looked outside. Pools of water.
I love this sunlight cold in spaces transparent
    turning blue.
I pray from the heart a prayerbook.
I press pen to paper like a pistol to the
    temple.
I wanted to write the lips of sleepers.
If they show me a stone and I say stone they
    will say stone.
I'll grab hold of a butt of dream.
In a night hour this is how the things are
    written. And now night.
In Darkness.
Isaac.
I've Come to the Simplest Words.
Kingdom of Silence.
Morning-Selah.
Moses.
My city mine. No more can I.
My left hand's like after a vow. It hurts. I'm
    trying to dream again.
My Soul Wanders About.
Of late from time to time there's risen.
On a Recollected Road.
Our Dreams.
Rain Falls and Floods.
Song of Blue and Red, A.
Song Yet Song.
That very day I saw that is we saw.
They'll all get up. I know I see them.
This isn't what I want to write I.
This whole land belongs to me sleeping and
    awake I see.
Times stir in me uncalendrically, chaotically.
To come free to a city under siege.
To run a night's distance, distances by night,
    nothing's easier than traveling distances.
Until recently there was fear.
Watchful Wakeful.
When I'm by myself I don't know. But I.
With the Rain.
Yes, I caught the butterfly. Went crazy for
    the moment.

Gilder, Richard Watson (1844–1909)
Failure and Success.

God of the strong, God of the weak.
Hour in a Studio, An.
New Day, The, *sels.*
On the Bay.
Sonnet, The.
To Thee, Eternal Soul, Be Praise.
Two Worlds.

Gildner, Gary (b. 1938)
Cabbage in Polish is kapusta—ka*poos*ta.
Digging for Indians.
First Practice.
High-Class Bananas, The.
House on Buder Street, The.
Letter to a Substitute Teacher.
Life of the Wolf, The.
Meeting the Reincarnation Analyst.
My Father after Work.
Nails.
Poems.
Primarily We Miss Ourselves As Children.
Runner, The.
String.
They Have Turned the Church Where I Ate
    God.

Giles, Barbara
Late Express, The.
Mrs. Lorris, Who Died of Being Clean.

Giles, Joseph (fl. late 18th cent.)
Leasowes: Or, A Poetical Description of the
    Late Mr. Shenstone's Rural Retirement,
    The, *sels.*

Gilkey, James G. (1889–1964)
O God, in Whose Great Purpose.
Outside the Holy City.

Gill, Gagan (b. 1959)
Girl's desire moves among her bangles, The.

Gill, Julia (1820–82)
Christ and the Little Ones.

Gillan, Maria
Arturo.
Ebba Dawson: Mardel Rest Home, Haskell,
    New Jersey.
Growing Up Italian.
In memory we are walking.
My Daughter at 14: Christmas Dance, 1981.
Public School No. 18: Paterson, New Jersey.

Gillies, Andrew (1870–1942)
Two Prayers.

Gillies, Valerie (b. 1948)
Ericstane Brooch, The.
Fellow Passenger.
Piano-Tuner, The.
Young Harper.

Gilligan, Angie (b. 1950)
Bathsheba in mourning.
Household Dilemma.
Mortgage.

Gillilan, Pamela
Alien at the Zoo.
Alien goes Shopping.

Gillilan, Strickland W. (1869–1954)
"Are You There?"
Be hopeful, friend, when clouds are dark and
    days are.
Finnigin to Flannigan.
Need of Loving.
On the Antiquity of Microbes.
Reading Mother, The.
Watch Yourself Go By.

Gillington, Mary C. (1892–1902)
Dead March, A.

Gillom, Arthur L.
I want you when the shades of eve are
    falling.

Gilman, Caroline (1794–1888)
Anna Playing in a Graveyard.
Boat, The.
Dead Sister, The.

Gilman, Charlotte Perkins Stetson (1860–1935)
Resolve.
Similar Cases.
To Labor.

Gilman, Samuel (1791–1858)
O God, Accept the Sacred Hour.

Gilmore, Brian G. (b. 1962)
Bow to Allah.

Gilmore, Joseph Henry (1834–1918)
He Leadeth Me.

Gilmore, Mary (1865–1902)
Eve-Song.
Fourteen Men.
Harvesters, The.
Heritage.
Little Shoes That Died, The.
Myall in Prison, The.
Nationality.
Saturday Tub, The.
Tenancy, The.

Gilmore, Patrick Sarsfield ("Louis Lambert") (1829–92)
When Johnny comes marching home again.

Gilpin, Laura (b. 1950)
Two-headed Calf, The.

"Ginger." *See* Irwin, Wallace

Ginger, Aleksandr Samsonovich (1897–1965)
Name, A.

Ginsberg, Allen (1926-97)
After Lalon.
After Yeats.
America I've given you all and now I'm
    nothing.
American Change.
At Apollinaire's Grave.
'Back on Times Square, Dreaming of Times
    Square.'
Bayonne Turnpike to Tuscarora.
Blue Angel, The.
Bop Lyrics.
Café in Warsaw.
Caw caw caw crows shriek in the white sun
    over grave stones.
Chances "R."
Change: *Kyoto-Tokyo Express,* The.
Charnel Ground, The.
Continuation of a Long Poem of These
    States, *sels.*
Crossing Nation.
Death News.
Death to Van Gogh's Ear!
Describe: The Rain on Dasaswamedh Ghat.
Don't Grow Old, *sels.*
Dream Record: June 8 1955.
Easter Sunday.
Elegy for Neal Cassady.
End, The.
First Party at Ken Kesey's with Hell's
    Angels.
Footnote to Howl.
Friday the Thirteenth.
Galilee Shore.
Green Automobile, The.
Haunting Poe's Baltimore.
Homework.
Howl, *sels.*
Hymmnn.
I Am a Victim of Telephone.
In Back of the Real.
Kaddish.
Kral Majales.
Last Night in Calcutta.
Lion for Real, The.
Malest Cornifici Tuo Catullo.
Memory Gardens.
Message.
Mugging, *sels.*
My Alba.
My Sad Self.
On Burroughs' Work.
On Neal's Ashes.
Pentagon Exorcism.
Please master can I touch your cheek.
Poem Rocket.
Prophecy, A.
PsalmIII: "To God: to illuminate all men.
    Beginning with Skid Road."
Pull my daisy.
Salutations to Fernando Pessoa.
Sather Gate Illumination.
Shrouded Stranger, The.
Siesta in Xbalba, *sels.*
Strange New Cottage in Berkeley, A.
Studying the Signs.
Sunflower Sutra.

Supermarket in California, A.
Sweet Levinsky in the night.
This Form of Life Needs Sex.
Thus Crosslegged on Round Pillow Sat in
  Space.
To Aunt Rose.
To Lindsay.
Uptown.
Vow, A.
Wales Visitation.
We Rise on Sun Beams and Fall in the
  Night.
What new element before us unborn in
  nature? Is there a.
Who Be Kind To.
Who Runs America?
Why Is God Love, Jack?
Wichita Vortex Sutra, Part I.
Ginsberg, Louis (1896–1976)
Biography of an Agnostic.
Clocks.
Hounds of the Soul, The.
Hymn to Evil.
Prices.
Roots.
Song: "I know that any weed can tell."
Soon at Last My Sighs and Moans.
Gio, The Lady (*fl.* **12th cent.**)
Sprouting grass waiting for spring, The.
Gioia, Dana (b. 1950)
California Hills in August.
Counting the Children.
Country Wife, The.
Guide to the Other Gallery.
In Cheever Country.
Lives of the Great Composers.
Maze Without a Minotaur.
My Confessional Sestina.
Next Poem, The.
Prayer.
Summer Storm.
Sunday News, The.
Giorno, John (b. 1936)
Life Is a Killer.
Scum & Slime.
Gioseffi, Daniela
American Sonnets for My Father.
Bicentennial Anti-Poem for Italian-American
  Women.
Some Slippery Afternoon.
Toward the Greater Romance, Please Place
  Roses in my Skull (A Tantric Love Song).
Giovanni, Nikki (b. 1943)
Adulthood.
Alabama Poem.
Basketball.
Beautiful Black Men.
Concerning One Responsible Negro with Too
  Much Power.
December of My Springs, The.
Detroit Conference of Unity and Art.
Dreams.
Ego Tripping [(There May Be a Reason
  Why)].
For Saundra.
Funeral of Martin Luther King, Jr, The.
Genie in the Jar, The.
Kidnap Poem.
Knoxville, Tennessee.
Legacies.
Life I Led, The.
Master Charge Blues.
Mothers.
Mother's Habits.
My Poem.
Nikki-Rosa.
Poem for Aretha.
Poem for Black Boys.
Poem for Flora.
Poem (for Langston Hughes), A.
Poem For My Nephew.
Poem for Unwed Mothers.
Poem of Angela Yvonne Davis.
Seduction.
Springtime.
Stars.
Ten Years Old.

They Clapped.
Three/Quarters Time.
Trips.
True Import of Present Dialogue, Black vs,
  The Negro.
12 Gates to the City.
Winter Poem.
Woman Poem.
Women gather, The.
Word Poem (Perhaps Worth Considering).
**Gippius, Zinaida Nikolayevna [or Nikolaevna]
  (1869–1945)**
Little Demon, The.
She is shameless, despicable, vile.
Girard, Antoine *and* **Sieur de Saint-Amant**
Grave of Marmousette, The.
Giscombe, C. S. (b. 1950)
All (Facts, Stories, Chance).
"In" Sequence, *sels.*
Look Ahead—Look South, *sels.*
(1980).
(1978, Remembering 1962).
(1962 At the Edge of Town).
(The Recent Past).
Gittings, Robert (b. 1911)
Great Moth, The.
Given, Thomas
Poetical Epistle tae Cullybackey Auld
  Nummer.
Song for February, A.
Gizzi, Peter
Another Day on the Pilgrimage.
Gladden, Washington (1836–1918)
O Lord of Life.
O Master, Let Me Walk with Thee.
Gladding, Jody
Asparagus.
Gladwin, Herman (b. 1906)
Dear Miss.
Glancy, Diane
At the Pauwels.
Christopher.
First Reader Santee Training School, 1873,
  The.
Johnna at the Windmill.
Kemo Sabe.
Rahab.
Raid on a Cheyenne Village.
Then.
Wheat.
Glanz-Leyeles, Aaron. See Leyeles, A.
Glaser, Elton
Blues for the Nightowl.
Cheap Replicas of the Eiffel Tower.
Confluences at San Francisco.
Coroner.
Revelation: The Movie.
Undead White European Male.
Glaser, Michael S.
Changing Address Books.
English-Speaking Persons Will Find
  Translations.
Preparations for Seder.
Glass, Malcolm (b. 1936)
Boy; or, Son of Rip-off, The.
Coming Down to It.
Glassco, John (1909–81)
Brummell at Calais.
Cardinal's Dog, The.
Day when it will not matter, The.
Entailed Farm, The.
For Cora Lightbody, R N.
One Last Word.
Quebec Farmhouse.
Rural Mail, The.
Glatshteyn, Jacob (1896–1971)
To a Friend Who Wouldn't Bother to Strain
  His Noodleboard Because Even So It Is
  Hard to Go Hunting When Your Rifle Is
  Blunt and Love Is Soft as an Old Blanket.
Glatstein [or Glatsteyn], Jacob (1896–1971)
Back to the Ghetto.
Bratzlav Rabbi to His Scribe, The.
How much Christian, so to speak, can I get?
I still remember the half-lit meaning.

If you should be surprised, Nathan.
Lost.
Rabbi Yussel Luksh of Chelm.
Ruth.
St. Matthew, *sels.*
Where the Cedars.
Glaukos
Epigram: "Time was when once upon a time,
  such toys."
Inscription by the Sea, An. *From* Variations
  of Greek Themes.
No, not earth, nor a stone slab.
Pan and the Nymphs.
Glaze, Andrew (b. 1920)
Outlanders, The.
Glazkov, Nikolai Ivanovich (b. 1918)
Bast shoe idly on the road, A.
Boyarina Morozova, The.
Conversation of a Private and the Virgin.
Deaf-Mutes.
Declaration.
Four Paths.
I strolled around the zoo.
Introduction to a Poem.
Khikhimora.
My Wife.
Path Is Long, The.
Poetograd.
Prayer: "Lord, stand up for the Soviets."
Races will disappear.
Raven, The.
Simple Man, A.
Subject for a Story.
Tale of the Cyclopses, The.
There are actually people who revel.
To My Friends.
To My Ill-Wishers.
What Did They Have In Mind?
Gleason, Madeline (b. 1913)
Once and Upon.
Gleim, Johann Wilhelm Ludwig (1719–1803)
Anacreon, my teacher.
To Death.
Glenn, Mel (b. 1943)
José Cruz.
Glick, Hirsch [or Glik, Hirsh] (1922–44)
We Survive!
**Glikberg, Aleksandr Mikhailovich. See
  "Chorny, Sasha"**
Glissant, Edouard (b. 1928)
Indies, The, *sels.*
Gloria, Eugene (b. 1957)
In Language.
Milkfish.
Whisper, The.
Glover, Denis (1912–80)
All of These.
Arawata Bill, *sels.*
Brightness.
Home Thoughts.
Magpies, The.
Old Jason, the Argonaut, The.
Printers.
Sings Harry, *sels.*
Glover, Jean
O'er the Muir Amang the Heather.
Glover, R. W.
It Isn't the Town, It's You.
Glover, Richard (1712–85)
Admiral Hosier's Ghost.
Glück, Louise (b. 1943)
All Hallows.
Amazons.
Apple Trees, The.
Brown Circle.
Celestial Music.
Cottonmouth Country.
Daisies.
Dedication to Hunger, *sels.*
Departure.
Descending Figure.
Drowned Children, The.
Elms.
Field Flowers.
First Memory.

For Jane Myers.
For My Mother.
Garden, The.
Gift, The.
Gratitude.
Gretel in Darkness.
Hesitate to Call.
Horse.
Hyacinth.
Illuminations.
Labor Day.
Lamentations.
Lullaby: "My mother's an expert at one thing."
Magi, The.
Marathon, *sels.*
Messengers.
Metamorphosis, *sels.*
Mock Orange.
Mount Ararat.
Mountain, The.
My Neighbor in the Mirror.
Mythic Fragment.
Nativity Poem.
Night Piece.
Palais des Arts.
Paradise.
Phenomenal Survivals of Death in Nantucket.
Poem: "In the early evening, as now, a man is bending."
Pomegranate.
Pond, The.
Racer's Widow, The.
Red Poppy, The.
School Children, The.
St. Luke, *sels.*
Undertaking, The.
Vespers: Parousia.
White Lilies, The.
Widows.
Wild Iris, The.
Witchgrass.
Wound, The.

Glycon
Everything's laughter / everything dust.
Nothing but laughter, nothing.

Gnanakoothan (b. 1938)
Tamil, it's true, is the breath of my life.

Godden, James
Lost.

Godeschalk (805–69)
Sequaire.

Godfrey, John (b. 1945)
Air.
Bath.
In Front of a Large Number of People.
My Mother, Life.
One or More Together.
Our Lady.
Radiant dog on doublecross, and I.
Reveille.
Show Me a Rose.
So Let's Look at It Another Way.
Unholy Spring.
What It Takes.
What Say.
Where the Weather Suits My Clothes.
Wings.

Godley, Alfred Denis (1856–1925)
After Horace.
Motor Bus.
Women's Degrees.

Godley, Elizabeth
Ninety-Nine.
Ragged Robin.

Godolphin, Sidney (1610–43)
Chloris, it is not thy disdain.
Constancy[e].
Elegy on D. D.
Elegy on John Donne, *sels.*
Hymn: "Lord, when the wise men came from far[r]."
No more unto my thoughts appear.
On Ben Jonson.
Song: "Chloris, it is not thy disdaine."
Song: "Noe more unto my thoughts appeare."

Song: "Or love me less, or love me more."
Song: "'Tis affection but dissembled."

Godsey, Edwin S.
I Hope I Don't Have You Next Semester, But.

Godwin, A. (*fl.* 15th cent.)
Song for My Lady.

Goedicke, Patricia (b. 1931)
After the Second Operation.
Coin of the Realm.
Daily the Ocean between Us.
In the Ocean.
In the Waiting Room.
Lucky.
On the Night in Question.
One More Time.
Serious Merriment of Women, The.
Without Looking.

Goethe, Johann Wolfgang von (1749–1832)
Anacreon's Grave.
Death of a Fly.
Diary, The.
Ecstatic Longing.
Erl-King, The.
Faust, *sels.*
Fisherman, The.
Found.
Holy Longing, The.
Hunter's Song at Nightfall, The.
Ill Humor.
Invisible King, The.
Irish Lamentation, An.
King in Thule, The.
King of Thulé, The.
Lay of the Captive Count, The.
May Song.
Meeting, the Departure, The.
Minstrel, The.
Nature and Art.
Permanence in Change.
Prometheus.
Roman Elegy Ia.
Rose, The.
Rosebud in the Heather.
Shepherd's Lament, The.
Song of the Traveler at Evening.
Sonnet: "To work away in art's traditional measure."
Symbolum.
Thought Eternal, The.
To a Golden Heart, Worn round His Neck.
To Belinda.
To Charlotte von Stein.
To the Moon.
To the Parted One.
Trilogy of Passion, *sels.*
United States, The.
Violet in the deepest green, A.
Voice from the Invisible World, A.
Wanderer's Night-Songs, *sels.*
We always have time enough, if we.
Whatever you can do.
Wilhelm Meister's Apprenticeship, *sels.*

Goff, Barbara E.
Limerick: "There was a young lady of Ulva / Whose sexual feelings were null. Va."

Goffstein, M. B. (b. 1940)
On This Day.

Gogan, Cothrai (b. 1926)
Mountain Drive.
Prayer of a Pagan Woman.

Gogarty, Oliver St. John (1878–1957)
After Galen.
Airman's Breastplate, The.
Anachronism.
Colophon.
Conquest, The.
Death May Be Very Gentle.
Dedication: "Tall unpopular men."
Farrell O'Reilly.
Hay Hotel, The.
Image-Maker, The.
Leda and the Swan.
Marcus Curtius.
Non Dolet.
On First Looking into Krafft-Ebing's

Psychopathosexualis [*or* Psychopathia Sexualis].
On the Use of Jayshus.
Palinode.
Per Iter Tenebricosum.
Plum Tree by the House, The.
Portrait with Background.
Ringsend.
To a Boon Companion.
To a Friend.
To Death.
To Petronius Arbiter.
Verse: "What should we know."
With a Coin from Syracuse.

"Gogisgi." See Arnett, Carroll

Gold, Artie (b. 1947)
I Don't Have the Energy.
Life.

Goldbarth, Albert (b. 1948)
Family Grove.
Hey Sweetie.
History of Civilization, A.
How the World Works: An Essay.
Letter, A.
Life is Happy.
Lot's Wife.
Nile, The.
Still Life, Symbolic of Lines, A.
Tip, The.
World of Expectations, The.

Goldberg, Beckian Fritz
Being Pharaoh.
In the Badlands of Desire.
In the Middle of Things, Begin.
Monsoon.
Possibilities, The.
To a Girl Writing Her Father's Death.

Goldberg, Israel. See "Learsi, Rufus"

Goldberg, Leah (1911–70)
Dialogue.
My Mother's House, *sels.*
Nameless Journey, *sels.*
Observation of a Bee.
Of Myself.
On Blossoming, *sels.*
On this day they break bread.
Our Backs are to the Cypress.
Prodigal Son, The.
Remembrance of Beginnings of Things.
Songs of the Stream, *sels.*
Symposium, The, *sels.*
When You Will Walk in the Field.
Will there yet come days of forgiveness and grace.

Goldensohn, Barry (b. 1937)
American Innocents, Oberlin, Ohio, 1954.
Honeymoon.
Marrano, The.
Post Mortem as Angels.

Golding, Arthur
Ovid's Metamorphoses Book 6, *sels.*

Golding, Louis (b. 1895)
I shall slough my self as a snake its skin.
In The Gallery Where the Fat Men Go.
Is It Because of Some Dear Grace.
Jack.
Judaeus Errans.
O Bird, So Lovely.
Quarries in Syracuse.
Women at the Corners Stand, The.

Goldman, Michael (b. 1936)
Crack, The.

Goldsmith, Oliver (1730?–1774)
Captivity, The, *sels.*
Description of an Author's Bedchamber, A.
Deserted Village, The, *sels.*
Double Transformation, The.
Epilogue to "The Sister," *sels.*
Retaliation, *sels.*
She Stoops to Conquer, *sels.*
Sonnet, A: "Weeping, murmuring, complaining."
This tomb, inscribed to gentle Parnell's name.
Translation of a South American Ode.
Travel[l]er; or, A Prospect of Society, The, *sels.*

Vicar of Wakefield, The, *sels.*

Goldsmith, Oliver, the Younger (1794–1861)
Rising Village, The, *sels.*

Goldstein, Lawrence
Permissive Entry: A Sermon on Fame.

Goldsworthy, Peter (b. 1951)
Act six begins.
After Babel.

Golffing, Francis C. (b. 1910)
Higher Empiricism, The.

Goll, Claire (1891–1977)
Prayer: "In the bright bay of your morning,
O God."

Goll, Iwan [*or* Yvan] (1891–1950)
John Landless Leads the Caravan.
Lackawanna Elegy.
Last river leaves for desolation, The.
Pear-Tree, The.
Requiem for the Dead of Europe, *sels.*
Song for a Jewess.
Your sleep is a closed almond.

"Golodny [*or* Golodnyi], Mikhail Semionovich" (Mikhail Semionovich Epshtein) (1903–49)
Judge Gorba.
Stallion, The.
Verka the Free.

Gomez, Antonio Enriquez (d. 1662)
Elegy: "I die for Your holy word without
regret."

Gomez de Avellaneda, Gertrudis (1814–73)
On Leaving.
On Leaving Cuba, Her Native Land.

Gomez, Jewelle (b. 1948)
My Chakabuku Mama.

Gonçalves Dias, Antônio (1823–64)
Song of Exile, *sels.*

Gondlevsky [*or* Gondlevskii], Sergey [*or* Sergei] (b. 1952)
May God grant me the memory to recall my
life.

Góngora y Argote, Luis de (1561–1627)
First Solitude, The, *sels.*
Let Me Go Warm.
Rosemary Spray, The.

Gonzales, Alonzo
Chipmunk can't drag it along.
Chipmunk was standing.
Mole makes his pole redhot.

Gonzáles Martínez, Enrique (1871–1952)
Last Journey.

Gonzales, Ray
Praise the Tortilla, Praise the Menudo, Praise
the Chorizo.

Gonzales, Rebecca
South Texas Summer Rain.

González, Angel
Before I could call myself Ángel González.
City.
Diatribe Against the Dead.
Future, The.
Inventory of Places Propitious for Love.
Whatever You Want.
Yesterday was Wednesday all morning.

Gonzalez, Anson (b. 1936)
First Friday bell shatters the morning.
Gasparillo Remembered.
Little Rosebud Girl.

Goode, Kate Tucker
Failure.

Goodge, W. T. (1862–1909)
Bad Break!, A.
Federation.
How We Drove the Trotter.

Goodison, Lorna (b. 1947)
Always homing now soul toward light.
Birth Stone.
For Don Drummond.
From the Garden of the Women Once Fallen.
Gleanings.
Guinea Woman.
I Am Becoming My Mother.
Jamaica 1980.
Keith Jarrett—Rainmaker.
Kenscoff.

Mulatta as Penelope, The.
On Becoming a Tiger.
Road of the Dread, The.
Songs of the Fruits and Sweets of Childhood.
Wedding in Hanover.

Goodman, Melinda (b. 1957)
Just How Crazy Brenda Is.
Wedding Reception.

Goodman, Miriam (fl. 20th cent.)
Upkeep.

Goodman, Mitchell (b. 1923)
Coming and Going.
Man and Wife.

Goodman, Paul (1911–72)
April 1962.
Classical Quatrain, A.
"Dreams Are the Royal Road to the
Unconscious."
I planned to have a border of lavender.
Little Ode.
Long Lines.
Long Lines: Youth and Age.
Lordly Hudson, The.
My Daughter Very Ill.
Saint Harmony my patroness.
Sonnet 21: "I start awake at night afraid of
death."
Sprayed with strong poison.
Stanzas: "I thought I woke: the midnight
sun."
Weepers Tower in Amsterdam, The.
Wellfleet Harbor.

Goodrich, Samuel Griswold ("Peter Parley") (1783?–1860)
Higglety, Pigglety, Pop!

Goodwill, E. S.
Here is a beetle as black as my hat.

Googe, Barnabe (1540–94)
Coming Homeward out of Spain.
Epitaph of the Death of Nicholas Grimald,
An.
Fly, The.
Goyng towardes Spayne.
Of Money.
Out of Sight, Out of Mind.
To Doctor Bale.

Gorbanevskaya [*or* Gorbanyevskaya *or* Gorbanevskaia], Natalya [*or* Natal'ia] (b. 1936)
And there is nothing at all—neither fear.
And where am I from? From an anecdote.
Here, as in a painting, yellow noon burns [*or*
noon burns yellow].
In my own twentieth century.
Like a human born of Anders's army.
Love, love! What nonsense it is.
Not because of you, not because of me, just
that.
Sukhanovo.
This world / is amazingly flat.
To I. Lavrentevaya.

Gorbovsky [*or* Gorbovskii], Gleb Iakovlevich b. 1931
Woodcutting.

Gordon, Adam Lindsay (1833–70)
Dedication, A: "They are rhymes rudely
strung with intent less."
Hippodromania; or, Whiffs from the Pipe,
sels.
How We Beat the Favourite.
Question not, but live and labor.
Sick Stockrider, The.
Ye Wearie Wayfarer, *sels.*

Gordon, J. (1865–1901)
To Amy.

Gordon, Judah Leib (1830–92)
Simhat Torah.

Gore-Booth, Eva (1872–1926)
Heretic's Pilgrimage, A.

Gorenko, Anna Andreyevna. See "Akhmatova, Anna Andreyevna"

Gorey, Edward (b. 1925)
Limerick.
Limerick: "As tourists inspected the apse."
Limerick: "Babe, with a cry brief and dismal,
The."

Limerick: "Dowager Duchess of Spout, The."
Limerick: "Each night father fills me with
dread."
Limerick: "From the bathing machine came a
din."
Limerick: "Headstrong young lady of Ealing,
A."
Limerick: "Incautious young woman named
Venn, An."
Limerick: "Lady, who signs herself 'Vexed,'
A."
Limerick: "Some Harvard men, stalwart and
hairy."
Limerick: "There was a young woman named
Plunnery."
Limerick: "To his club-footed child said Lord
Stipple."
Listing Attic, The, *sels.*
Utter Zoo Alphabet, The.

Gorges, Sir Arthur (1577–1625)
Desportes, *sels.*
Henceforth I will not set my love.
Her [*or* hir] face her [*or* hir] tongue [*or*
tong] her [*or* hir] wit.
She that holds me under the laws of love.
Would I were chang'd into that golden
shower.
Written upon the death of the most Noble
Prince Henrie.

Görgey, Gabór (b. 1929)
Folkway.
Fragments of Ten Poems.
Thomas.

Gorham, Sarah
Empress Receives the Head of a Taiping
Rebel, The.
Notes From a Chinese Love Manual, *sels.*
Princess Parade.

"Gorky [*or* Gorkii], Maksim" (Aleksey Maksimovich Peshkov) (1868–1936)
Song of the Stormy Petrel.

Gorman, Leroy
Beyond the laughing billboard girl.
Billboard girl.
Down the billboard girl's bare belly.
For the smell.
Her long paper legs.
I hear her sew.
I shut down the lawnmower.
Loud wind.
My family asleep.
One AM.

Gormley, Queen of Ireland (fl. 13th cent.)
Gormley's Laments, *sels.*

Gorton, Samuel (c.1592–1677)
Serpent with a voyce, so slie and fine, The.

Gosse, Sir Edmund William (1849–1928)
Lying in the Grass.
On Yes Tor.
Revelation.

Gossett, Hattie
On the Question of Fans/ The Slave Quarters
Are Never Air Conditioned.

Gotera, Vince (b. 1952)
Dance of the Letters.
Gambling.
Madarika.

Gotlieb, Phyllis (b. 1926)
Cocker of Snooks, A.
Death's Head.
Late Gothic.
This One's on Me.
Three-handed Fugue.

Goto, Miyoko (b. 1898)
Gay colors flow.
I listen to the pulse of a life / different from
mine.

Gottheil, Gustav (1827–1903)
Come, O Sabbath Day.

Götz, Johann Nikolaus (1721–81)
First Rondeau: After a French Poet of the
Fourteenth Century.
Second Rondeau.

Goulbourne, Jean
One Acre.
This Is the Place Where.

Gould, Alan (b. 1949)
Demolisher.
Galaxies.
Ice.
Observed Observer, The.
Pearls.

Gould, E. E.
Tadpole, The.

Gould, Elizabeth (b. 1904)
Grace and Thanksgiving.
Midsummer Night.
Mincemeat.
Mistress Comfort.
My New Rabbit.
Red in Autumn.
Shining Things.
Slumber in Spring.
Such a Blustery Day!
Washing-Up Song, The.
Wish, A.

Gould, Gerald Louis (1885–1936)
Child's Song.
Monogamy, *sels.*
This is the horror that, night after night.

Gould, Hannah Flagg (1789–1865)
Day of God! Thou Blessed Day.
Dying Child's Request, The.
Frost looked forth, one still, clear night, The.
Spider, The.

Gould, Janice (b. 1949)
We Exist.

Gouri, Haim. *See* **Guri, Haim**

Gourmont, Rémy de (1858–1915)
Hair.

Gowar, Mick (b. 1951)
Annabell and the Witches.
Christmas Thank You's.
Rat Trap.

Gower, John (1325–1408)
Confessio Amantis, *sels.*

Gozzano, Guido (1883–1916)
Most Beautiful, The.

Grabill, James ("Jim")
Ars Poetica.

Grachova [*or* Grachiova], Nina (b. 1971)
Of what use to me are the nights full of
wine.

Graddon, Dorothy
Fairy Dream, A.
North Wind, The.
Travelling.
Wind, The.
Winter Joys.

Grade, Chaim (b. 1910)
At night and in the wind and the rain.
Sodom.
To Life I Said Yes.

Graeme, James (1721–66)
Mortified Genius, The.

Grafflin, Margaret Johnston
To My Son.

Grafton, Richard (d. 1527)
Thirty days hath November.

Graham, A. M.
Aconite, The.

Graham, D. L. (1944–70)
Soul.
Tony Get the Boys.
West Ridge Is Menthol-Cool, The.

Graham, Harry ("Col. D. Streamer") (1874–1936)
Aunt Eliza.
Battue of Berlin, The, *sels.*
Breakfast.
Cockney of the North, The.
Gourmand, The.
Grandpapa.
Indifference.
L'Enfant Glacé.
Lord Gorbals.
Opportunity.
Some Ruthless Rhymes, *sels.*
"There's been an accident," they said.
Waste.

Graham, Jorie (b. 1951)
At Luca Signorelli's Resurrection of the
Body.
For My Father Looking for My Uncle.
From the New World.
Geese, The.
In the Hotel.
Mind.
My Garden, My Daylight.
Of Forced Sightes and Trusty Ferefulness.
Opulence.
Orpheus and Eurydice.
Over and Over Stitch.
Salmon.
San Sepolcro.
Soul Says.
Way Things Work, The.
What the End Is For.
What the Instant Contains.

Graham, Joyce Anstruther Maxtone. *See*
"Struther, Jan"

Graham, Matthew (*fl.* **20th cent.)**
After the War; When Coltrane Only Wanted
to Play Dance Tunes.

Graham, Robert (Robert Cunninghame-Graham) (1735–99)
If doughty [*or* daughty] deeds my lady
please[s].

Graham, Virginia (b. 1912)
Disillusionment.
Ein Complaint.

Graham, William Sydney (1918–86)
Baldy Bane.
Beast in the Space, The.
Children of Greenock, The.
Constructed Space, The.
Dark Dialogues, The, *sels.*
Johann Joachim Quantz's Five Lessons.
Letter II.
Letter V.
Letter VI.
Listen. Put on Morning.
Lying Dear, The.
Malcolm Mooney's Land.
Many without Elegy.
Night City, The.
Stepping Stones, The.
Thermal Stair, The.
To My Father.

Grahame, Kenneth (1859–1932)
Wind in the Willows, The, *sels.*

Grahn, Judy (b. 1940)
Common Woman, The, *sels.*
Confrontations with the Devil in the Form of
Love, *sels.*
Edward the Dyke and Other Poems, *sels.*
Funeral Plainsong from a Younger Woman to
an Older Woman, A.
Helen you Always Were / The Factory, *sels.*
History of Lesbianism, A.
Paris and Helen.
Spider Webster's Declaration: He Is Singing
the End of the World Again.
Talkers in a Dream Doorway.
They Say She Is Veiled.
Woman Is Talking to Death, A.

Grainger, James (1724–67)
Bryan and Pereene.
Solitude: An Ode.
Sugar Cane, The, *sels.*
What is fame? An empty bubble.

**Grammaticus, Damocharis. See Damocharis of
Kos**

Granade, John A. (c.1770–1807)
Come All Ye Mourning Pilgrims.
Sweet Rivers of Redeeming Love.

Grandmaster Flash *and* the Furious Five
Message, The.

Grandsen, K. W. (b. 1925)
Interview, An.

Grano, Paul (b. 1894)
Headlined in Heaven.
In a Chain-Store Cafeteria.

Grant, Eddy (b. 1948)
War Party.

Grant, Jamie (b.1949)
Auditor Thinks about Female Nature, An.
Planes Landing.

Grant, Richard E. (b. 1949)
Broken Heart, Broken Machine.

**Granville [*or* Grenville], George, Baron
Lansdowne (1666–1735)**
Cloe ("Bright as the day, and like the
morning fair.")
Impatient with Desire.
Love is begot by fancy, bred.
Our King returned, and banished peace
restored.
To Cloe.

Grass, Günter (b. 1927)
Gasco.
In the Egg.
Music for Brass.
Saturn.

Grave, John (*fl.* **mid–17th cent.)**
If Thou Wilt Hear.

Graves, Alfred Percival (1846–1931)
Haymaking.
Irish Lullaby.

Graves, Charles Larcom (1856–1944)
Back to the Land.
Flapper, The.

Graves, John Woodcock (1795–1886)
John Peel.

Graves, Richard (1715–1804)
Maternal Despotism; or, The Rights of
Infants.

Graves, Robert Ranke (1895–1985)
Advice to Colonel Valentine.
Allansford Pursuit, The.
Allie, call the birds in.
Ambrosia of Dionysus and Semele, The.
Angry Samson.
At First Sight.
Beach, The.
Beauty in trouble flees to the good angel.
Birth of a Great Man.
Blue-Fly, The.
Broken Girth, The.
By this exchange of eyes, this encirclement.
Call it a good marriage—.
Carol of Patience.
Cat Goddesses.
Certain Mercies.
Change.
Clearing, The.
Conjunction.
Cool Web, The.
Corner Knot, The.
Counting the Beats.
Cry Faugh!
Damocles.
Dead Cow Farm.
Dead Foxhunter, The.
Death Grapple, The.
Death Room, The.
Devil's Advice to Story-Tellers, The.
Down, Wanton, Down!
Down, wanton, down! Have you no shame.
1805.
End of Play.
Epitaph on an Unfortunate Artist.
Escape.
Eugenist, The.
Face in the Mirror, The.
Fallen Tower of Siloam, The.
Flying Crooked.
For the Rain It Raineth Every Day.
Forced Music, The.
Foreboding, The.
Friday Night.
From the Embassy.
Frosty Night, A.
Full Moon.
Gardener.
General Elliott, The.
Gift of Sight.
Glutton, The.
Goliath and David.
Grotesques.
Hag-Ridden.

Henry and Mary.
Hide and Seek.
I Wonder What It Feels Like to Be Drowned?
I'd Love to Be a Fairy's Child.
In Broken Images.
In Her Only Way.
In Her Praise.
In Perspective.
In Procession.
In the Beginning Was a Word.
In the Wilderness.
In time all undertakings are made good.
Interruption.
It Was All Very Tidy.
It's a Queer Time.
Jealous Man, A.
Lament for Pasiphaë.
Land of Whipperginny, The.
Laureate, The.
Leda.
Legs, The.
Lollocks.
Lost Acres.
Lost Jewel, A.
Lost Love.
Lost World, A.
Love Story, A.
Love without hope, as when the young bird-catcher.
Lovers in Winter.
Metaphor, The.
Mirror mirror tell me.
My Name and I.
Naked and the Nude, The.
Narrow Sea, The.
Nature's Lineaments.
Neglectful Edward.
Never Such Love.
Not at Home.
Ogres and Pygmies.
On Dwelling.
On Portents.
One Hard Look.
Ouzo Unclouded.
Parent to Children.
Persian Version, The.
Pier-Glass, The.
Pinch of Salt, A.
Plea to Boys and Girls, A.
Poets' Corner.
Point of No Return.
Portrait, The.
Problems Of Gender.
Pure Death.
Queen Mother to New Queen.
Quiet Glades of Eden, The.
Read Me, Please!
Reader over My Shoulder, The.
Recalling War.
Reproach to Julia.
Return of the Goddess [Artemis].
Richard Roe and John Doe.
Rocky Acres.
Saint.
Sea Horse, The.
Sergeant-Major Money.
Sharp Ridge, The.
She is no liar, yet she will wash away.
She tells her love while half asleep.
Sick Love.
Slice of Wedding Cake, A.
Song: How Can I Care?
Song: Lift-Boy.
Song of Blodeuwedd, The.
Spoils.
Star-Talk.
Straw, The.
Succubus, The.
Surgical Ward: Men.
Survivor, The.
Symptoms Of Love.
Theseus and Ariadne.
Thieves, The.
Three-Faced, The.
Three Songs for the Lute, *sels.*
Tilth.

Time.
To Bring the Dead to Life.
To Calliope.
To Juan at the Winter Solstice.
To Robert Nichols.
To Whom Else?
Travel[l]er's Curse after Misdirection[, The].
Troll's Nosegay, The.
Twins.
Two Fusiliers.
Ulysses.
Under the Pot.
Vain and Careless.
Valentine, A.
Vanity.
Variables of Green.
Warning to Children.
Weather of Olympus, The.
"Wellcome, to the Caves of Artá!"
Welsh Incident.
White Goddess, The.
Whole Love.
Wigs and Beards.
Wild Strawberries.
Window Sill, The.
With a Gift of Rings.
With Her Lips Only.
Wm. Brazier.
Wreath, The.
Young Cordwainer, The.

Gray, Sir Alexander (1882–1968)
On a Cat, Ageing.
Scotland.
Sir Halewyn.

Gray, Cecil (b. 1923)
Funeral Service.
Misses Norman lived on Marine Square, The.

Gray, David (1838–61)
Golden Wedding, The.
In the Shadows, *sels.*
My Epitaph.
Sonnet: "October's gold is dim—the forests rot."
Where the Lilies Used to Spring.

Gray, Frances
With cheerful mind we yield to men.

Gray, John (1866–1934)
Barber, The.
Battledore.
Crucifix, A.
Femmes Damnées.
Flying Fish, The.
Le Voyage À Cythère.
Les Demoiselles de Sauve.
Mishka [is poet among the beasts].
Night Nurse Goes Her Round, The.
On A Picture.
On the South Coast of Cornwall.
Parsifal Imitated from the French of Paul Verlaine.
Poem: "Geranium, houseleek, laid in oblong beds."
Spleen.
They say, in other days.
Tobias and the Angel.
Vines, The.
Wings in the Dark.

Gray, Robert (b. 1945)
Curriculum Vitae.
Dusk, The.
5 Poems.
Flames and Dangling Wire.
Journey: the North Coast.

Gray, Stephen (b. 1941)
Apollo Café.
Girl with Doves.
Girl with Long Dark Hair.
Hottentot Venus.

Gray, Thomas (1716–71)
Bard, The [A Pindaric Ode], *sels.*
Curse upon Edward, The.
Death of Hoel, The.
Descent of Odin, The.
Elegy Written in a Country Churchyard, *sels.*
Epitaph on Dr. Keene.
Epitaph on Dr. Keene's Wife.

Hymn to Adversity.
Ode on a Distant Prospect of Eton College.
Ode on the Death of a Favourite [or Favorite] Cat, Drowned in a Tub [or Bowl] of Gold Fishes.
Ode on the Pleasure Arising from Vicissitude, *sels.*
Ode on the Spring.
On Dr. Keene, Bishop of Chester.
On Lord Holland's Seat near Margate, Kent.
Progress of Poesy, The.
Sonnet [on the Death of Mr. Richard West].
Tophet.
Triumphs of Owen, The.

Gray, Victor (b. 1926)
"All the World's a Stage."
Limerick: "Charlotte Brontë said, 'Wow, sister! *What* a man!'"
Limerick: "Example of Kant's sterling wit, An."
Limerick: "First chap to fuck little Sophie, The."
Limerick: "I was thrilled when I went to the Zoo."
Limerick: "It's a pity that Casabianca."
Limerick: "Meanwhile, back home at the ranch."
Limerick: "Oedipus said to the Sphinx."
Limerick: "Old East End worker called Jock, An."
Limerick: "One midnight, old D. G. Rossetti."
Limerick: "One morning old Wilfrid Scawen Blunt."
Limerick: "Postmaster-General cried: 'Arsehole!', The."
Limerick: "Rebuke by the Bishop of London, A."
Limerick: "Said a famous old writer called Fender."
Limerick: "Said a gloomy young fellow called Fart."
Limerick: "Said Arnold to Arthur Hugh Clough."
Limerick: "Said Tennyson: 'Yes, *Locksley Hall*'s.'"
Limerick: "Said the famous philosopher, Russell."
Limerick: "Sir John Shagbag (Conservative, Nore)."
Limerick: "Taxi-cab whore out at Iver, A."
Limerick: "There was a young fellow called Crouch."
Limerick: "There was a young fellow called Shit."
Limerick: "There was a young girl of Mauritius."
Limerick: "There was an old man of Lugano."
Limerick: "When Gauguin was visiting Fiji."
Limerick: "When Keats was at work on *Endymion*."
Limerick: "When our dean took a pious young spinster."
Limerick: "While visiting Arundel Castle."
Limerick: "Young engine-driver called Hunt, A."

Gray, William B. (1891–1977)
She Is More to Be Pitied than Censured.

Greacen, Robert (b. 1920)
Bird flew tangent-wise to the open window, A.
Captain Fox sits reading metaphysics.
Carnival at the River.
Father and Son.
St Andrew's Day, blind November fumbling.
Summer Day, A.
Ten New Commandments.

"Green, Coroebus." *See* **Cone, Helen Gray**

Green, F. Pratt (b. 1903)
Old Couple, The.

Green, Jane
Songs of Divorce.

Green, Joseph (1706–80)
Permit Us, Lord, to Consecrate.

Green, Matthew (1696–1737)
On Barclay's Apology for the Quakers.

Seeker, The.
Spleen, The, *sels.*

Green, Melissa (b. 1954)
More than novelty crooked its finger—silent, austere.

Greenaway, Kate (1846–1901)
Five Sisters.
Happy Child, A.
School is over.
Three little girls were sitting on a rail.
When You and I Grow Up.
Which Is the Way to Somewhere Town?

Greenberg, Alvin
Freight Train, Freight Train.

Greenberg, Barbara L. (b. 1932)
Mother, R.I.P.

Greenberg, Uri Zvi (1896–81)
At Your Feet, Jerusalem.
By the Waters of the Sava.
In the covenant's radiance that moment had come.
Jerusalem, *sels.*
Lord! You saved me from Ur-Germany as I fled.
Naming Souls.
Penny for you, philosophers of eternity, A.
We were not likened to dogs among the Gentiles—They pity a dog.

Greene, Albert Gorton (1802–68)
Old Grimes.

Greene, Alice (1858–1920)
Four roads lead out of the town.

Greene, Carl H. (b. 1945)
Excuse, The.
Realist, The.
Something Old, Something New.

Greene, Richard Leighton (1904–83)
Limerick: "When approached by a person from Porlock."
Song to Imogen [in Basic English].

Greene, Robert (1558?–1592)
Description of the Shepherd and His Wife, The.
Farewell to Folly, *sels.*
Greene's Farewell to Folly, *sels.*
Greene's Groatsworth of Wit, *sels.*
Greene's Mourning Garment, *sels.*
Greene's Vision, *sels.*
Ideals.
Love and Jealousy.
Menaphon, *sels.*
Never Too Late, *sels.*
Night Visitor, A.
Palmer, The.
Pandosto, *sels.*
Perimedes [*or* Perimedes, the Blacksmith], *sels.*

Greenfield, Eloise (b. 1929)
Moochie ("Moochie likes to keep on playing.")

Greenfield, Freddie (b. 1929)
Oh God Forbid.

Greenfield, Marjorie H.
Things I Like.

Greenlee, Sam (*fl.* 20th cent.)
Memorial for Trane.

Greenwald, Ted (b. 1942)
And, Hinges.
I hear a step. A step.
Licorice Chronicles, *sels.*
Privets Come into Season at High Tide.
Word of Mouth, *sels.*

Greenwell, Bill
Christopher Robin Changes Guard with Dylan Thomas.
King Ethelred the Unready.
Limerick: "By Loch Ness they can toss, like confetti."
Limerick: "Filthy young fellow called Lawrence, A."
Limerick: "For his Campbell's Soup screen-prints, society's."
Limerick: "Glib little beer-buff from Troon, A."

Limerick: "In Genesis, Adam's the winner."
Limerick: "No, listen, there's this albatross."
Limerick: "Pop's tops!"
Limerick: "Reason we're asked to endure, The."
Limerick: "Shelley's death—was it really his wish."
Limerick: "There was a young lady of Ulva / Who drunkenly said: 'What a hulva.'"
Limerick: "Watt's dream was the cream of steam engines."
Limerick: "What led to the crassness of Custer."
Limerick: "When Jael crept in to see Sisera."
That rebellious rodent called Jerry.

Greenwell, Dora (1812–82)
Broken Chain, The.
Christina.
Content, content! within a quiet room.
Demeter and Cora.
Fidelity Rewarded.
Picture, A.
Saturday Review, The.
Scherzo, A.
Sun-Flower, The.
To Christina Rossetti.
To Elizabeth Barrett Browning, in 1851.
To Elizabeth Barrett Browning, in 1861.
When the Night and Morning Meet.

Greer, Jane
Rodin's "Gates of Hell."

Greger, Debora (b. 1949)
Air-Conditioned Air.
Frog in the Swimming Pool, The.
Garden, The.
Lives of the Saints, *sels.*
Of.
Patches of Sky.
Piranesi in L.A.

Gregerson, Linda (b. 1950)
Salt.

Gregg, Linda (b. 1942)
Adult.
Beckett Kit, The.
Copperhead, The.
Dark Thing Inside the Day, A.
Esta.
Girl I Call Alma, The.
Gnostics on Trial.
Lies and Longing.
Lilith.
My Father and God.
Night Music.
Not Saying Much.
Shopping-Bag Lady, The.
Sigismundo.
Strong Pomegranate Flowers and Seeds of the Mind.
To Be Here.
We Manage Most When We Manage Small.

Gregor, Arthur (b. 1923)
Enough! Let this season end.
History.
Irreconcilables.
Late Last Night.
Likeness, The.
Lyric: "Embodiment of what, The."
Poem: "So many pigeons at Columbus."
Spirits, Dancing.
Sunbather in Late October, A.
Two Shapes.
Unalterables.

Gregor, Christian (1723–89)
What Splendid Rays.

Gregory, Horace (1898–1982)
Chinese Garden, The.
Chorus for Survival, *sels.*
Death and Empedocles 444 B.C.
Elegy and Flame.
For You, My Son.
Longface Mahoney Discusses Heaven.
On a Celtic Mask by Henry Moore.
Passion of M'Phail, The, *sels.*
Poems for My Daughter.

Postman's Bell Is Answered Everywhere, The.
Rehearsal, The.
They Found Him Sitting in a Chair.
To the Last Wedding Guest.
Valediction to My Contemporaries.

Gregory, Leona
Silence, an Eloquent Applause.

Gregory, Mrs. Horace. *See* Zaturenska, Marya Alexandrovna

Gregory of Nazianzus, Saint (c.330–390)
Leave my tomb. Employ your pick.
On Naucratius, Brother of St. Basil.
Where are my wingèd words? Dissolved in air.
Why do you heave apart my stone?

Gregory the Great, Saint (540–604)
Behold, the Shade of Night Is Now Receding.

Gregory, Yvonne (b. 1919)
Christmas Lullaby for a New-Born Child.

Greiffenberg, Catharina Regina von (1633–94)
Concerning the Fruit-bringing Autumn Season.
On the Fruit-Providing Autumn Season.
On the Ineffable Inspiration of the Holy Spirit.
On the Sweet Comfort Brought by Grace, *sels.*
Spring Joy Praising God.
Spring-Joy Praising God; Praise of the Sun.
Why the Resurrection Was Revealed to Women.
Zealous Admonition to Praise.

Greig, Andrew
In the Tool-shed.
Maid and I, The.
Winter Climbing, The.

Greig, Desmond A. (b. 1926)
On a Scooter.
To a Flea in a Glass of Water.

Gréki, Anna (1931–67)
Before Your Waking.
Future is for tomorrow, The.

Grenfell, Joyce (1910–79)
First To Go, The.
Stately as a Galleon.

Grenfell, Julian (1888–1915)
Into Battle.
Prayer for Those on the Staff.

Grenier, Robert (b. 1941)
Crow.
Has Faded in Part But Magnificent Also Late for RC / Mirrors.
Oakland, *sels.*
Phantom Anthems, *sels.*
Sunday Morning.
Wrath to Sadness.

Grennan, Eamon (b. 1941)
Conjunctions.
Facts of Life, Ballymoney.
Incident.
Lizards in Sardinia.
Men Roofing.
Soul Music: The Derry Air.
Sunday Morning Through Binoculars.
Wing Road.
Woman at Lit Window.

Grenville, R. H.
Praise is a quiet and a gracious thing.

Gresham, Walter S.
Crowded Ways of Life.

Greville, Fanny [*or* Frances] Macartney (c. 1727–1789)
Miss F[——]ny M[——]t[——]y to Miss P[——]ly B[——]s.
Prayer for Indifference, A, *sels.*

Greville, Fulke, 1st Baron Brooke (1554–1628)
Caelica, *sels.*
Epitaph on Sir Philip Sidney.
Mustapha, *sels.*
Treaty of Human Learning, A, *sels.*
Turkish government allows no law, The.
Under a throne I saw a virgin sit.
Vigula divina, sorcerers call a rod.

Grew, Gwendolyn
Burning the Letters.
Grey of Fallodon, Pamela Grey, Viscountess (1852–1933)
Echo.
Grider, Dorothy. See **Edey, Marion** and Dorothy Grider
Grier, Eldon (b. 1917)
I Am Almost Asleep.
Kissing Natalia.
More Than Most People.
Mountain Town—Mexico.
My Winter Past.
On the Subject of Waves.
Sensible Is the Label.
Grierson, Constantia (1706?–1732)
To Miss Laetitia Van Lewen.
Grieve, Christopher Murray. See **"MacDiarmid, Hugh"**
Griffin, Bartholomew (d. 1602)
Fidessa, More Chaste than Kind[e], sels.
Venus and Adonis.
Griffin, Gerald (1803–40)
Eileen Aroon, sels.
Hy-Brasail—the Isle of the Blest.
Song: "Place in thy memory, dearest, A."
To a Seagull.
To the Blessed Virgin Mary.
Griffin, Paul
Limerick: "I once had a cat called Maria."
New Tarantella.
To His Importunate Mistress.
Griffin, "Sin-Killer"
Man of Calvary, The, sels.
Griffin, Susan (b. 1943)
Answer to a Man's Question, "What Can I Do About Women's Liberation?," An.
Awful Mother, The.
Bad Mother, The.
I like to think of Harriet Tubman.
I Wake Thinking of Myself as a Man.
Love Should Grow Up like a Wild Iris in the Fields.
Miracle.
Rebecca, sweet-one, little-one.
Song My.
Song of the Woman with Her Parts Coming Out, The.
Stories and Poems.
Sunday Morning.
Teeth.
Waiting for Truth.
Griffith, Llewelyn Wyn (1890–1977)
Barren Tree, The, sels.
Silver Jubilee.
Griffiths, Ann (1776–1805)
His left hand, in heat of noonday.
Lo, between the Myrtles Standing.
Griffiths, Bill (b. 1948)
After Stroke.
Animal.
Compass Poem.
For P—Celtic: found text from Machen.
Into Prison.
Terzetto: Brixton.
To Tom Saunders on His Imprisonment.
Griffiths, T.
La Belle Dame sans Merci.
Limerick: "Is there really a new Mr. Nixon."
Limerick: "There was a young lady of Ulva / Who said: 'I have granted a culver'."
On First Looking into Chapman's Homer.
When man walketh moon.
Grigson, Geoffrey (b. 1905)
Above the High.
Administrator, An.
Before a Fall.
Bibliotheca Bodleiana.
Burials.
By the Road.
Critics and Poets.
End of the Affair.
In the Spring Garden.
Landscape Gardeners, The.
May Trees in a Storm.

On a Lover of Books.
On the Relinquishment of a Title.
Professionals, The.
Two Are Together.
Grimald, Nicholas (1519–62)
Funeral Song, Upon the Decease of Annes His Mother, A, sels.
Garden, The.
True Love, A.
Virtue.
Grimberg, Faina (b. 1951)
For a long time I haven't seen such a young face.
Grimké, Angelina Weld (1880–1958)
At April.
Black Finger, The.
Brown Girl.
Butterflies, white butterflies, in the sunshine.
Caprichosa.
For the Candle Light.
Garden Seat, The.
Mona Lisa, A.
Naughty Nan.
Tenebris.
To Keep the Memory of Charlotte Forten Grimké.
Triolet, A.
When the green lies over the earth, my dear.
Winter Twilight, A.
You.
Your Eyes.
Your Hands.
Grimke, Charlotte L. Forten (1837–1914)
Angel's Visit, The.
Charles Sumner.
Gathering of the Grand Army, The.
Parting Hymn, A.
Wordsworth.
Grimmelshausen, Hans Jakob Christoffel von (1621–76)
Come, balm of night, oh nightingale.
Grindal, Edmund (1519–83)
Give Peace in These Our Days, O Lord.
Grindel, Eugène. See **Éluard, Paul**
Griswold, Alexander V. (1766–1843)
Holy Father, Great Creator.
Groch, Eric
Friend to Birds.
Grogan, Sabina (fl. 20th cent.)
Elizabeth, Listening.
Grosholz, Emily
Back Trouble.
Eden.
Last of the Courtyard, The.
Legacies.
Life of a Salesman.
Old Fisherman, The.
On the Ferry, Toward Patras.
Outer Banks, The.
Remembering the Ardèche.
Gross, Harvey (b. 1922)
At the Crossroads.
Gross, Philip (b. 1952)
Son and Heir.
Verbal Gerbil.
Gross, Ronald (b. 1935)
Yield. / No Parking.
Grossman, Allen (b. 1932)
Dust.
Great Work Farm Elegy.
Grossman, Reuben (1905–74)
Therefore, We Thank Thee, God.
Gruber, Abraham L.
My Neighbor's Roses.
Gruber, Johann A. (1694–1763)
Love That's Pure, Itself Disdaining.
Gruffudd ab yr Ynad Coch (fl. c.1280)
Lament for Llywelyn ap Gruffudd.
Gruffydd, Owen (1643–1730)
Men That Once Were, The, sels.
Gruffydd, W. J. (1881–1954)
Gwladys Rhys.
In Memoriam.
This Poor Man.

Grundtvig, Nicolai Frederik Severin (1783–1872)
I Know a Flower So Fair and Fine.
Grunthal, Ivar
All great men were ground to powder.
And thus a monologue keeps flowing.
Constant starburst showers us, A.
I broke the second part of the First Commandment.
Gryphius, Andreas (1616–64)
All Is Vanity.
Evening.
Human Misery.
Midnight.
On the Birth of Jesus.
Solitude.
Tears of the Fatherland, Anno Domini 1636.
To Himself.
To the Stars.
Gu Cheng (b. 1956)
Ark.
Discovery.
Epigraph: "In the sea of life."
Forever Parted: Graveyard.
Generation, A.
Guarini, Giovanni Battista (1537–1612)
Claim to Love.
Spring.
Thus saith my Chloris bright.
Gubanov, Leonid (1946–83)
Palette of Grief.
Gudzenko, Semyon [or Semion] Petrovich (1922–53)
Ballad about Friendship, A.
Before the Attack.
I fought on foot in every quarter.
Not from old age our death will come.
Guérin, Charles (1873–1904)
Partings.
Guernsey, Bruce (b. 1944)
Louis B. Russell.
Guerzo di Montecanti (fl. 13th cent.)
He Is Out of Heart with His Time.
Guest, Barbara (b. 1920)
Bleat.
Defensive Rapture.
Direction.
Emphasis Falls on Reality, An.
Geese Blood.
Green Revolutions.
Heavy violets there is no way.
If So.
Luminous, The.
Nebraska.
Otranto.
Parachutes, My Love, Could Carry Us Higher.
Parade's End.
Piazzas.
Poem: "Disturbing to have a person."
Prairie Houses.
Red Lilies.
River Road Studio.
Roses.
Santa Fe Trail.
Sassafras.
Sunday Evening.
20.
Twilight Polka Dots.
Walking Buddha.
Way of Being, A.
Wild gardens overlooked by night lights. Parking.
Words.
Guest, Edgar Albert (1881–1959)
Becoming a Dad.
Equipment.
Friend's Greeting, A.
Home.
It Couldn't Be Done.
Kindly Neighbor, The.
Lemon Pie.
Lord, Make a Regular Man out of Me.
Myself.
Out Fishin'.
Sausage.

What's In It for Me?

Guggenberger, Louisa S. (b. 1945)
Afternoon.
"Am I to Lose You?"
Egoisme à Deux.
Love and Language.
Twilight.

Guha, Naresh (b. 1924)
Winding Sand.

Guidacci, Margherita (b. 1921)
All Saints' Day, *sels.*
At night the wallpaper shakes.

Guillaume de Lorris (c.1215–c.1278) *and* **Jean de Meun (d. 1305)**
Romance [*or* Romaunt] of the Rose, The, *sels.*

Guillaume de Poitiers (d. c. 1240)
Behold, the Meads.

Guillén, Jorge (1893–1984)
Flight.

Guillén, Nicolás (b. 1904)
Daily Daily, The, *sels.*
Dead Soldier.
Don't Know No English.
Guadalupe, W.I.
Madrigal.
Moon.
Proposition.
Sensemayá.
Sightseers in a Courtyard.
Usurers, The.
Wake for Papa Montero.

Guilpin, Everard (b. 1572?)
Skialetheia Satire 5, *sels.*

Guiney, Louise Imogen (1861–1920)
At a Symphony.
Fog.
In the Reading-Room of the Brtish Museum.
Knight Errant, The.
Lights of London, The.
Open, Time, and let him pass.
Salutation, A.
Strikers in Hyde Park.
Sunday Chimes in the City.
W. H.
When on the marge of evening the last blue light is broken.
Wild Ride, The.

Guinicelli, Guido (*fl.* 13th cent.)
He Perceives His Rashness in Love, but Has No Choice.
Of the Gentle Heart.
Sonnet: He Will Praise His Lady.
Sonnet: Of Moderation and Tolerance.

Guiterman, Arthur (1871–1943)
Alibi.
Ancient History.
Anthologistics.
Bears.
Brief Essay on Man.
Christmas Exchange, The.
Consolation.
Everything in Its Place.
Habits of the Hippopotamus.
Heredity.
Husband and Wife.
Little Lost Pup.
Local Note.
Mavrone.
Of Certain Irish Fairies.
Of Courtesy.
Of Giving.
Offer, An.
On the Vanity of Earthly Greatness.
Sea-Chill.
Song of Hate for Eels.
Strictly Germ-proof.
Whole Duty of a Poem, The.

Gullans, Charles (b. 1929)
Satyr.

Gumilyov [*or* Gumiliov *or* Gumilev], Nikolai Stepanovich (1886–1921)
Captains, *sels.*
Giraffe, The, *sels.*
I and You.
I, who could have been the best of poems.

Memory.
No flowers will live in my room.
Plague, The.
Progeny of Cain, The.
Sixth Sense, The.
Tanka.
Tram That Lost Its Way, The.
Turkey, The.
Words.
Worker, The.

Gunn, Thom (b. 1929)
Allegory of the Wolf Boy, The.
Apartment Cats.
As Expected.
Autobiography.
Autumn Chapter in a Novel.
Bed, The.
Black Jackets.
Blackie, The Electric Rembrandt.
Breakfast.
Breaking Ground, *sels.*
Butcher's Son, The.
Byrnies, The.
Carnal Knowledge.
Cherry Tree, The.
Claus von Stauffenberg.
Confessions of the Life Artist.
Considering the Snail.
Courage, a Tale.
Discovery of the Pacific, The.
Donahue's Sister.
Elegy on the Dust.
Expression.
Faustus Triumphant.
Feel of Hands, The.
Fever.
For Signs.
From the Highest Camp.
From the Wave.
Garden of the Gods, The.
High Fidelity.
Idea of trust, or, The.
In Santa Maria del Popolo.
In the Tank.
Innocence.
Iron Landscapes (and the Statue of Liberty).
Jamesian.
Jesus and His Mother.
Lament: "Your dying was a difficult enterprise."
Last Days at Teddington.
Last Man, The.
Lines for a Book.
Man With Night Sweats, The.
Map of the City, A.
Martial.
Messenger, The.
Mirror for Poets, A.
Misanthropos, *sels.*
Missing, The.
Modes of Pleasure.
Moly.
Monster, The.
My Sad Captains.
No Speech from the Scaffold.
On the Move.
Pope's Carnations Knew Him.
Road Map, The.
St. Martin and the Beggar.
Street Song.
Tamer and Hawk.
Three for Children, *sels.*
Three Songs, *sels.*
To Yvor Winters, 1955.
Touch.
Unsettled Motorcyclist's Vision of His Death, The.
Wheel of Fortune, The.
Yoko.

Gunnars, Kristjana (b. 1948)
Changeling VIII.
Wakepick I.

Günther, Johann Christian (1695–1723)
Consolation Aria.
Departure Aria.

Guobin, Huang
My poem is a bridge, silent, lonely;.

Guri [*or* Gouri], Haim [*or* Chaim *or* Khayim] (b. 1923)
Age Is Ended, An.
Album.
And of all that was theirs only the letters were left.
And This Happened.
And this happened in Prague many years ago.
At the Train Station.
But We Shall Bloom.
Dance.
Flame and wood and blackened stones like these.
Heritage.
His Mother.
Holiday's End.
I live now in an ancient book.
I pray you, forgive me in the stillness of your shoes swollen on these sands.
If a flame has fallen among the cedars.
I'll be an amulet, I'll be good news.
In the Amorite City.
It seems to me I'm watching over walls.
Jericho.
Mistake.
My Samsons.
Northern Romance.
Odysseus.
Of the Azazmeh Too.
Pictures of Jews.
Pictures of the Jews.
Piraeus.
Piyyut for Rosh Hashana.
Piyyut for the New Year.
Prayer: "Thy blessing on the boys for time has come."
Requiescat.
Silent Words, The.
Silk and Silence.
Thorns.
Window-Dreaming with SAS.
You're No King.

Gurney, Dorothy Frances (1858–1932)
Lord God Planted a Garden, The.

Gurney, Ivor (1890–1937)
After War.
April Gale.
Ballad of the Three Spectres.
Bohemians, The.
Butchers and Tombs.
Canadians.
Companion—North-East Dug-Out.
Crucifix Corner.
December 30th.
Epitaph on a Young Child.
Escape, The.
Farewell.
Felling a Tree.
First Time In.
Generations.
High Hills, The.
I saw French once—he was South Africa cavalry—.
If I walked straight slap.
It Is Near Toussaints'.
La Gorgue.
Love Song: "Out of the blackthorn hedges."
Moments.
On the Night.
Requiem: "Pour out your light, O stars."
Sea-Marge.
Silent One, The, *sels.*
Songs I had are withered, The.
Strange Hells.
Target, The.
To His Love.
Tobacco Plant.
Towards Lillers.
Townshend? I knew him well, queer ways he had.
Walking Song.
War Books.

Gurr, Robin
Creation.

Gustafson, Ralph (b. 1909)
Armorial.

Columbus Reaches Juana, 1492.
In the Yukon.
Mothy Monologue.
My Love Eats an Apple.
Of Green Steps and Laundry.
Swans of Vadstena, The.
Transfigured Night.
Wednesday at North Hatley.

Guthrie, Ramon (1896–1973)
Homage to Paul Delvaux.
Magi, The.
Today Is Friday.

Guthrie, Thomas Anstey. *See* **"Anstey, F."**

Guthrie, Woody (1912–67)
Turkey in the Corn.

Gutteridge, Bernard (b. 1916)
Enemy Dead, The.
In September 1939.
Man into a Churchyard.
Shillong.

Guxnawu
Song for the Richest Woman in Wrangell.

Gwala, Mafika Pascal (b. 1946)
In Defence of Poetry.
My house is bugged.
New Dawn, The.

"Gwenallt." *See* **Jones, David Gwenallt**

Gwerfyl Mechain (c.1460–c.1500)
Hostess of the Ferry Inn, The.
Snowfall, The.

Gwynn, R. S. (b. 1948)
Among Philistines.
Anacreontic.
Approaching a Significant Birthday, He
  Peruses The Norton Anthology of Poetry.
Body Bags.
Classroom at the Mall, The.
Drive-In, The.
1916.
Release.
Snow White and the Seven Deadly Sins.

Gwynn, Stephen Lucius (1864–1950)
On One Dying in a Convent.

Gyorgy, Petri
Xenia.

H

"H., C. G."
Power of Innocence, The.

"H——, Captain" (*fl.* c.1716)
Imitation of Martial, Book II Ep, An 105.

"H., H." *See* **Jackson, Helen Hunt**

"H., H. E."
Riddle, The.

"H., M. C. D."
Hymn for Airmen.

Hà Huyền Chi Đặng Trí Hoàn (b. 1935)
Sea, the World, and the Boat People, The.

Haaff, Katherine Maurine
Good thoughts are the threads.

Haas, Rosamond
Autumn evening.
Building the dollhouse.
Moon at the window.
Rain mixed with sleet.

Haavikko, Paavo (b. 1931)
Darkness, *sels.*
Short Year, The, *sels.*

Habergham, Mrs. Fleetwood
Seeds of Love, The.

Habib, Rowley (Nga Pitiroirangi) (b. 1935)
Ancestors.
Moment of Truth.

Habington, William (1605–54)
Castara, *sels.*
Cogitabo Pro Peccato Meo.
Cupio Dissolvi.
Perdam Sapientiam Sapientum.
Queen of Aragon, The, *sels.*
Recogitabo Tibi Omnes Annos Meos.
Solum Mihi Superest Sepulchrum.
To a Wanton.

To Castara, Being to Take a Journey.
To the Right Honourable the Countesse of C.
Upon Castara's Departure.

Hacker, Marilyn (b. 1942)
After the Revolution.
Against Silence.
Almost Aubade.
Aube Provençale.
Ballad of Ladies Lost and Found.
Before the War.
Cancer Winter.
Canzone: "Consider the three functions of the
  tongue."
Canzone: "No better lost than any other
  woman."
Coda, *sels.*
Days of 1992.
Dusk: July.
Eight Days in April.
Elevens.
Elysian Fields.
February 25.
Feeling and Form.
Fifteen to Eighteen.
Hang-Glider's Daughter, The.
Imaginary Translation.
La Fontaine de Vaucluse, *sels.*
Languedocienne.
Letter from the Alpes-Maritimes.
Love, Death and the Changing of the
  Seasons, *sels.*
Mother II.
Muses, The.
Mythology.
Nearly a Valediction.
Nights of 1964-66: The Old Reliable.
Nights of 1964–1966: The Old Reliable.
1973.
Occasional Verses.
Open Windows.
Part of a True Story.
Presentation Piece.
Rondeau after a Transatlantic Telephone Call.
Runaways Café I.
Runaways Café II.
Rune of the Finland Woman.
Saturday Morning.
Sonnet for Iva.
Taking Notice, *sels.*
Three Sonnets for Iva.
Under the Arc de Triomphe: October 17.
Villanelle: "Every day our bodies separate."
Wagers.

Hackett, J. W.
Bitter morning, A.
Deep within the stream.
Fleeing sandpipers, The.
Half of the minnows.
Long line of web, A.
Moon fades into dawn.
Old spider web, An.
Searching on the wind.
Stillness of dawn, The.
Time after time.
Wind gives way to calm.
Wind sounds through the trees.

Hadas, Rachel (b. 1948)
Codex Minor.
Forgetting Greek.
House Beside the Sea, The.
Journey Out.
Kaleidoscope.
Lair, The.
Mars and Venus.
Moments of Summer.
Pass it on, II.
Red Hat, The.
Sentimental Education.
Teaching Emily Dickinson.
Three Silences.
Up and Down.
Winged Words.
Yes, But.

Hadewijch (*fl.* 13th cent.)
Ah yes, when love allows.
All Things Confine.
Had I been mindful of my high descent.

Knowing Love in Herself.
Love has seven names.
Love has subjugated me.
Love's Constancy.
Love's Maturity.
Madness of love, The.
What helps it if of love I sing.

Hadewijch II (*fl.* 13 cent.)
All things.
If I desire something, I know it not.
Tighten.
You who want.

**Hadrian, Emperor (Publius Aelius Hadrianus)
  (A.D. 76–138)**
Adriani Morientis ad Animam Suam.
Animula, vagula, blandula: The Emperor
  Hadrian to his soul.
Hadrian's Address to His Soul When Dying,
  sels.
My little wandring sportful Soule.
My soul, my pleasant soul and witty.

Hafiz (d. 1389)
Lesson of the Flowers, The.
Lips of the one I love are my perpetual
  pleasure, The.
Love's hidden pearl is shining yet.
Mortal never won to view thee.
My soul is the veil of his love.
Ode 105.
Ode 147: "Beauty alone will not account for
  her."
Ode 173: "All the long night we talked of
  your long hair."
Ode 44: "Last night, as half asleep I
  dreaming lay."
Ode 487: "With last night's wine still singing
  in my head."
Odes, *sels.*
Persian Song of Hafiz, A.

Hafsa bint al-Hajj (d. 1184)
Shall I come there, or you here?

Hagedorn, Friedrich von (1708–54)
Anacreon.

Hagedorn, Hermann (1882–1964)
Mother.

Hagedorn, Jessica Tarahata (b. 1949)
Filipino Boogie.
Latin Music in New York.
Listen.
Natural Death.
Smokey's Getting Old.
Solea.
Something about You.
Song for My Father.
Yolanda Meets the Wild Boys.

Hagiwara Sakutaro (1886–1942)
Chair.
Lover of Love.
So Terrifyingly Melancholy.
Spring Night.

Hahn, Kimiko (b. 1955)
Hula Skirt, 1959, The.
Possession: A Zuihitsu.

Hải Âu Tử (*fl.* 20th cent.)
Zoo Cages.

Hai-Jew, Shalin (*fl.* 20th cent.)
Kinged.
Three Gypsies.

Hải, Nguyễn Hoàng. *See* **Nguyễn Tất Nhiên**

Haicéad, Pádraigín (c.1600–1654)
On Hearing It Has Been Ordered in the
  Chapterhouse of Ireland That the Friars
  Make No More Songs or Verses.

Haida
Song for Smooth Waters.

"Haida Charlie"
How is it all gonna turn out.

**Hailsham, Quintin McGrel Hogg Hailsham,
  Baron (b. 1907)**
If Grief Could Burn Out.

Haines, John (b. 1924)
And When the Green Man Comes.
Awakening.

Choosing a Stone.
Cloud Factory, The.
Dürer's Vision.
Eye in the Rock, The.
Field of the Caribou, The.
Flight, The.
Foreboding.
House of the Injured, The.
If the Owl Calls Again.
Into the Glacier.
Mothball Fleet: Benicia, California.
On the Mountain.
Poem Like a Grenade, A.
Sleep.
Snowbound City, The.
There Are No Such Trees in Alpine,
    California.
To Turn Back.
Train Stops at Healy Fork, The.
Tundra is a living, The.

Hairston, William [*or* Will] (b. 1928)
Alabama Bus.

Hajnal, Anna (b. 1907)
After all, what have I become?
Fear.
Felled Plane Tree, The.
Half Past Four, October.
Jaguar is Getting Ready, The.
That's All?

Hakutsu (*fl.* c.704)
O pine-tree standing. *From* Manyo Shu, Part
    3 of 4.

**Haldane, John Burdon Sanderson (J. B. S.
    Haldane) (1892–1964)**
Cancer's a Funny Thing.

Hale, Edward Everett (1822–1909)
Lend a Hand.
Look Up *or* Lend a Hand.

Hale, Janet Campbell (b. 1947)
Aaron Nicholas, Almost Ten.
Cinque.
Custer Lives in Humbolt County.
Desmet, Idaho, March 1969.
On a Catholic Childhood.
On Death and Love.
Salad La Raza.
Six Feet Under.

Hale, Robert Beverly (1901–85)
Big Nasturtiums, The.

Hale, Sarah Josepha Buell (1788–1879)
Mary's Lamb [*or* Mary and Her Lamb].
Mole and the Eagle, The.
Our Father in Heaven.

Halevi, Judah (1085–1140)
Awake, My Fair.
Dove of rarest worth, A.
Earth in Spring, The.
Fortune's Treachery.
God, Whom Shall I Compare to Thee?
Grey Hair, The.
He cometh, O bliss!
Heal Me, My God.
Hymn for Atonement Day.
Immortal Israel.
Israel's Duration.
Jerusalem.
Letter to His Friend Isaac, A.
Longing.
Longing for Jerusalem.
Lord, Where Shall I Find Thee?
Love Song: "Let my sweet song be pleasing
    unto Thee."
Love Song: "See'st thou o'er my shoulders
    falling."
Marriage Song.
Meditation on Communion with God.
Mirror, The.
My Heart Is in the East.
My Sweetheart's Dainty Lips.
Ode to Zion.
On Parting with Moses ibn Ezra.
Ophra.
Parting.
Pride of a Jew, The.

Sabbath, My Love.
Song of Loneliness.
Time-Servers.
To the Western Wind.
To Zion.
Words Wherein Stinging Bees Lurk.

Halkin, Shimon (b. 1898)
Before your wonders I stand, my world.
Here is much burning anger, mighty hate.
Reward.
Seventy-five are my abyssed forests.
To Tarshish.

Halkin, Shmuel (1897–1960)
Drop of Dew, A.

Hall, Amanda Benjamin (b. 1890)
It Seems That God Bestowed Somehow.
Limerick: "King Richard, in one of his
    rages."

Hall, Daniel (b. 1952)
Love-Letter-Burning.
Mangosteens.

Hall, David
Ambush of the Fourth Platoon, The, *sels.*
Disgrace.
How is it the stomach knows first.

Hall, Donald (b. 1928)
Airstrip in Essex, 1960, An.
Alligator Bride, The.
Another Elegy.
Apples.
Blue Wing, The.
Brain Cells, The.
Breasts.
By the Exeter River.
Christ Church Meadows, [Oxford].
Christmas Eve in Whitneyville, 1955.
Clown, The.
Exile.
Farm, The.
Foundations of American Industry, The.
Funeral, The.
Gold.
Grace, A.
Granite and Grass.
Henyard Round, The.
Je Suis une Table.
Jealous Lovers, The.
Long River, The.
Mr. Wakeville on Interstate 90.
Mount Kearsarge.
My son, my executioner.
Names of Horses.
New Hampshire.
O Cheese.
Old Pilot, The.
One Day, The.
Ox Cart Man.
Peaches.
Pluvia.
Poet at Twenty, A.
Professor Gratt.
Raisin, The.
"Reclining Figure."
Ruminant pillows! Gregarious soft boulders!
Scream, The.
Second Stanza for Dr. Johnson, A.
Shudder [, The].
Sister on the Tracks, A.
Six Poets in Search of a Lawyer.
Sleeping Giant, The.
Small Fig Tree, A.
St. Matthew, *sels.*
Sudden Things.
T. R.
To a Waterfowl.
Town of Hill, The.
Tubes.
Valentine.
Wedding Party.
White Apples.
Wives, The.
Woolworth's.

Hall-Evans, Jo Ann (b. 1934)
Cape Coast Castle Revisted.
Seduction.

Hall, Hattie Vose
Two Temples.

Hall, Hazel (1886–1924)
For a Broken Needle.
Instruction.
Late Sewing.
Listening Macaws, The.
Walkers at Dusk.
White Day's Death.

Hall, Henry (d. 1713)
Upon the King's Return from Flanders, 1695.

Hall, Henry Clay
Who does not love true poetry.

Hall, J. C. (b. 1920)
Kind of Faith, A.

Hall, James Baker (b. 1935)
Stafford in Kansas.

Hall, James Norman (1887–1951)
Eat and Walk.

Hall, Jim (b. 1947)
Figure a Poem Makes, The.
Maybe Dats Your Pwoblem Too.
Preposterous.
Reel World, The.
Reign of Terror.
White Trash.

Hall, John (1529–66)
Job. I.
Numeri XIII.
Praise of Faith, The.
Praise of Godly Love Out of 1 John. 4, The.
Proverb, XXX.
Song of Esechia, The.

Hall, John (1627–56)
Call, The.
Epicurean Ode, An.
On an Hour[e]-Glass[e].
Pastoral[l] Hymn[e], A.
Song: "Distil not poison in mine ears."

Hall, John (b. 1945)
Even as the wandering traveler doth stray.

Hall, Joseph (1574–1656)
Coxcomb, The.
Home Travel.
Satire VIII.
Virgidemiarum, *sels.*
Virgidemiarum Book 5, *sels.*

Hall, Judith
St. Peregrinus' Cancer.

Hall, Kirk (b. 1944)
Blackgoldblueswoman.
Today Is Not Like They Said.

Hall, Mary Lee
Turn Again to Life.

Hall, Rodney (b. 1935)
Black Bagatelles, *sels.*
Journey.
Mistress Macintosh.
Owner of My Face, The, *sels.*
Text for These Distracted Times, A.
Wedding Day at Nagasaki.

Hall, Sharlot Mabridth (1870–1943)
Boot Hill.
Poppies of Wickenburg.

Hallack, Cecily
Divine Office of the Kitchen, The.

Halleck, Fitz-Greene (1790–1867)
Alnwick Castle.
Connecticut, *sels.*
Fanny, *sels.*
Field of the Grounded Arms, The.
Marco Bozzaris, *sels.*
On the Death of Joseph Rodman Drake.
Red Jacket.
Song: "There's a barrel of porter at
    Tammany Hall."

**Halleck, Fitz-Greene *and* Joseph Rodman
    Drake**
Croaker Papers, The, *sels.*

Halley, Anne (b. 1929)
Against Dark's Harm.
Housewife's Letter: To Mary.
I'd Rather See than be One, but.

Halliday, Caroline (b. 1947)
Music.
Ode to My Daugther's Plimsolls and the
    Mess in Her Room.

Halliday, Mark
Population.
Reality U.S.A.
Seventh Avenue.
Vegetable Wisdom.

Halloran, Laurence Hynes (1766–1831)
Animal Magnetism; the Pseudo-Philosopher Baffled.

Halpern, Daniel (b. 1945)
Argument.
Arriving.
Dance, The.
Early Death, An.
Ethnic Life, The.
Fish.
Landing, The.
Naming the Unborn.
Street Fire.
Summer, 1970.

Halpern, Moyshe-Leyb [or Moishe-Leib or -Leyb] (1886–1932)
Gingilee.
Go Throw Them Out.
My Portrait.
Restless as a Wolf.
That's Our Lot.
Who is, who is the rider there.

Halsall, Martyn
Return to Ararat.

Halswell, Henry (fl. 1656)
Upon Mr. Hopton's Death.

Ham, Judy F.
Exiles.

Ham, Marion Franklin (1867–1956)
As Tranquil Streams.
O Thou Whose Gracious Presence Shone.
Touch Thou Mine Eyes.

Hamburger, Michael (b. 1924)
Between the Lines.
Dual Site, The.
Garden, Wilderness.
Instead of a Journey.
Memory.
Treblinka.
Weeding.

Hame'iri, Avigdor (1890–1970)
Passover in Jerusalem.
Purity.

Hamer, Forrest
Getting Happy.

Hamill, Gerry (b. 1919)
It was far in the night and the bairnies grat.
Limerick: "Fat-tailed Dwarf Lemur, in bed, A."
Limerick: "Gamekeeper of Lady Chatterley, The."
Limerick: "'If you're aristocratic,' said Nietzsche."
Limerick: "Left-wing young lady from Wick, A."
Limerick: "Said Tebbitt: 'I don't understand 'em.'"
Song of the GPO, A.
To His Coy Mistress.

Hamill, Janet (b. 1945)
Open Window.

Hamilton, Bobb (b. 1928)
Poem to a Nigger Cop.

Hamilton, Cicely (1872–1952)
March of the Women, The.

Hamilton, Elizabeth (1758–1816)
My Ain Fireside.

Hamilton, George Rostrevor ("George Rostrevor") (1888–1967)
Don's Holiday.
Exchange.
Exile.
No Occupation.
Old Ox, The.
Schoolmaster.
To the Greek Anthologists.

Hamilton, Horace (b. 1911)
Before Dawn.

Hamilton, John (b. 1947)
Cold Blows the Wind.

Hamilton, M. Eliza
For My Father's Mother Who Has Alzheimer's.

Hamilton, Robert Browning
Along the Road.

Hammerstein, Oscar, II (1895–1960)
Kansas City.
Money Isn't Everything!
There Is Nothin' like a Dame.

Hammial, Philip (b. 1937)
Automobiles of the Asylum.
Jane.
Petit Guignol.
Russians Breathing.
Sadie.
Treason's Choice.

Hammon, Jupiter (1720?–1806?)
Address to Miss Phillis Wheatley, An, *sels.*
Evening Thought, An [: Salvation by Christ with Penetential Cries].

Hammond, Mac (b. 1926)
Golden Age.
In Memory of V. R. Lang.

Hammond, William (b. 1614?)
Delay, whose parents Phlegm and Slumber are.
On the Infrequency of Celia's Letters.
On the Same [Death of My Dear Brother, Mr. H.S., Drowned]: The Boat.
To His Scornful Mistress.
To the Same [My Dear Sister, Mrs S.]: The Tears.

Hamod, Kay Keeshan
Transitions *sels.*

Hamod, Sam
After the Funeral of Assam Hamady.
Dying with the Wrong Name.
Leaves.
Moving, *sels.*

Hampton, Susan (b. 1949)
Crafty Butcher, The.
Fire station's delight, The.
In Andrea's Garden.
Women who Speak with Steak Knives.
Yugoslav Story

Han-ch'ing. *See* **Kuan Han-ch'ing**

Han, Ha'un (1919–75)
Blue Bird.
Oaten Pipe.

Han-shan (c.700–c.780)
Clambering up the Cold Mountain path.
Cold Mountain Poem No. 158.
Cold Mountain Poems.
From my father and mother I inherited land enough.
In an Abandoned Garden.
Man lives his life in a dust bowl.
My father and mother left me a good living.
Parrots dwell in the west country.
Swine gobble dead men's flesh.
There is a poetaster named Wang.

Han Wo (fl. c.902)
Sent to a Ch'an Master.

Han, Yong-un (1879–1944)
Ferryboat and the Traveler, The.
I Do Not Know.
Silence of Love, The.

Han Yü (786–824)
Amongst the Cliffs.
Autumn Thoughts, *sels.*
Demoted I Arrive at Lan-t'ien Pass and Show This Poem to My Brother's Grandson Han Hsiang.
Don't shoo the morning flies away.
Evening: for Chang Chi and Chou K'uang.
Flowering Plums.
Girl from Flower Mountain, The.
Girl of Mt. Hua, The.
Mornings the sparrow twitters seeking food.
Occasional Poem ("Ancient annals strewn left and right.")
Officer at the Rapids, The.
Poem on Losing One's Teeth.
Pond in a Bowl, The.
Pond in a Jardiniere, A, *sels.*

Sentiments at Autumn.
South Mountains, The, *sels.*
Southern Mountains.
To the Wooden Hermit.
Withered Tree, A.
Written on My Way into Exile.

Hanaford, Phoebe A. (1829–1921)
Cast Thy Bread upon the Waters.

Hanagid, Samuel (993–1056)
Prison, The.

Handke, Peter (b. 1942)
Wrong Way Round, The.

Handlin, Jim
Cold winter morning.
Father, You Learn to Die.
Full autumn moon, A.
Sunset.

Hands, Elizabeth (fl. c.1789)
Favourite Swain, The.
Lob's Courtship.
On an Unsociable Family.
Perplexity: A Poem.
Poem on the Supposition of an Advertisement, A; Appearing in a Morning Paper, of the Publication of a Volume of Poems, by a Servant-Maid.
Poem on the Supposition of the Book Having Been Published and Read, A.
Widower's Courtship, The.
Written, Originally Extempore, on Seeing a Mad Heifer Run through the Village.

Handy, M. P.
Only a Little Thing.

Handy, William Christopher (1873–1958)
Beale Street Blues.
Joe Turner Blues.
St. Louis Blues.
Yellow Dog Blues.

Hanh, Huỳ. *See* **Huỳnh Thúc Kháng**

Hanim, Leylâ (d. 1847)
Let's get going.

Hanim, Nigâr (1862–1918)
Tell Me Again.

Hankey, Katherine
I Love to Tell the Story.

Hanlon, Gail (b. 1952)
Plainsong.

Hanlon, Guy
They told me, Heraclitus, they told me you were dead.

Hann, Isaac (1690–1778)
After Reading the Life of Mrs. Catherine Stubbs in Isaac Ambrose's "War with the Devils."

Hanney, G. W.
Limerick: "Wanting children a couple once sat."

Hans, Marcie
Hurt.

Hanscombe, Gillian. *See* **Namjoshi, Suniti** *and* **Gillian Hanscombe**

Hansen, Chadwick (b. 1926)
Creator of Infinities.

Hansen, Joseph
Dakota: Five Times Six.
Loved One, The.

Hanson, Amos
Schooner *Fred Dunbar*, The.
Trip to the Grand Banks, A.

Hanson, Kenneth O. (b. 1922)
Before the Storm.
Lighting the Night Sky.
Take It from Me.
West Lake.

Hanson, Pauline (b. 1917)
And I Am Old to Know.
From Creature to Ghost.
So Beautiful Is the Tree of Night.

Hanzlicek, C. G.
C.G. Hanzlicek.
In the Dark Again.
Last Trains, The.
Room for Doubt.

Hanzlik, Josef (b. 1938)
Clap Your Hands for Herod.
Cottage Behind the Railway, The.
Variation VI.
Who's that driving a black cart.

Harasymowicz, Jerzy (b. 1933)
Green Lowland of Pianos, A.
Old Age.
Waking Up.
Woods.

Harata Tangikuku (fl. c.1860–1875)
Invalid's Song.

Harbaugh, Henry
Aloe Plant, The.
Jesus, I Live to Thee.

Harbaugh, Thomas Chalmers (1817–67)
Trouble in the "Amen Corner."

Hard, Walter
Medical Aid.

Harding, Samuel (fl. 1640)
Noblest bodies are but gilded clay.

Hardison, O. B., Jr. (b. 1928)
Marina.
Small Talk in a Garden.
Stella Maris.

Hardt, Ernst (1876–1947)
Specter, The.

Hardwick, Natalie (b. c.1975)
Other Side, The.

Hardy, Elizabeth Clark (1794–1854)
Some Time at Eve.

Hardy, Thomas (1840–1928)
According to the Mighty Working.
After A Journey.
After the Visit.
Afternoon Service at Mellstock.
Afterwards.
Ah, are you digging on my grave.
Ancient to Ancients, An.
And There Was a Great Calm.
Anniversary, An.
At an Inn.
At Casterbridge Fair, sels.
At Castle Boterel.
August Midnight, An.
Bags of Meat.
Beeny Cliff.
Bereft.
Beyond the Last Lamp.
Birds at Winter Nightfall.
Blinded Bird, The.
Bride-Night Fire, The.
Broken Appointment, A.
Burghers, The.
Calf, The.
Cardinal Bembo's Epitaph on Raphael.
Channel Firing.
Choirmaster's Burial, The.
Christmas Ghost-Story, A.
Christmas: 1924.
Church Romance, A.
Circus-Rider to Ringmaster.
Colonel's Soliloquy, The.
Comet at Yell'ham, The.
Commonplace Day, A.
Contretemps, The.
Convergence of the Twain, The.
Country Wedding, The.
Curtains now are drawn, The.
Dark-Eyed Gentleman, The.
Darkling Thrush, The.
Departure.
Domicilium.
Dream Question, A.
Drizzling Easter Morning, A.
Drummer Hodge.
During Wind and Rain.
Dynasts, The, sels.
Echo-Elf Answers, The.
Embarcation.
Epitaph for George Moore.
Epitaph: "I never cared for Life: Life cared
  for me."
Epitaph on a Pessimist.
Exeunt Omnes.
Faintheart in a Railway Train.

Fallow Deer at the Lonely House, The.
First or Last.
First Sight of Her and After.
Five Students, The.
For Life I had never cared greatly.
Friends Beyond.
Frozen Greenhouse, The.
Garden Seat, The.
George Meredith (1828-1909).
Going, The.
Going and Staying.
Great Things.
Hap.
Harbour Bridge, The.
Haunter, The.
He Abjures Love.
He Never Expected Much.
Her Dilemma.
Heredity.
His Immortality.
House of Hospitalities, The.
I am the one whom ringdoves see.
I found her out there.
I look into my glass.
I looked up from my writing.
I need not go.
I said to Love.
I say, "I'll seek her side."
If it's ever spring again.
If you had known.
Impercipient, The.
In a Cathedral City.
In a Eweleaze near Weatherbury.
In a Wood.
In Death Divided.
In Front of the Landscape.
In Tenebris, sels.
In the Night She Came.
In the Servants' Quarters.
In the vaulted way, where the passage turned.
In Time of "The Breaking of Nations."
Lacking Sense, The.
Last Chrysanthemum, The.
Last Leaf, The.
Last Words To a Dumb Friend.
Lausanne: In Gibbon's Old Garden: 11–12
  p.m.
Let me enjoy the earth no less.
Levelled Churchyard, The.
Liddell and Scott.
Lines to a Movement in Mozart's E-Flat
  Symphony.
Lodging-House Fuchsias, The.
Long Plighted.
Lying Awake.
Man He Killed, The.
Men Who March Away.
Middle-Age Enthusiasms.
Midnight on the Great Western.
Moments of Vision.
Mongrel, The.
Mound, The.
Mute Opinion.
My spirit will not haunt the mound.
Nature's Questioning.
Near Lanivet, 1872.
Necessitarian's Epitaph, A.
Nettles, The.
Neutral Tones.
New Toy, The.
New Year's Eve.
Newcomer's Wife, The.
Often when warring for he wist not what.
Old Furniture.
On a Midsummer Eve.
On an Invitation to the United States.
On Sturminster Foot-Bridge.
On the Departure Platform.
On the Portrait of a Woman About to Be
  Hanged.
Once at Swanage.
One We Knew.
Oxen, The.
Paying Calls.
Peace-Offering, The.
Phantom Horsewoman, The.
Pine Planters, The.

Pink Frock, The.
Pity of It, The.
Placid Man's Epitaph, A.
Poet, A.
Postponement.
Proud Songsters.
Rain on a Grave.
Reminder, The.
Respectable Burgher, The.
Roman road runs straight and bare, The.
Rome: Building a New Street in the Ancient
  Quarter.
Ruined Maid, The.
Sapphic Fragment.
Satires of Circumstance in Fifteen Glimpses,
  sels.
Schreckhorn, The.
Second Attempt, A.
Self-Unseeing, The.
Selfsame Song, The.
She Hears The Storm.
She, to Him, sels.
Shelley's Skylark.
Shut Out That Moon.
Singer Asleep, A (Algernon Charles
  Swinburne), sels.
Snow in the Suburbs.
Souls of the Slain, The.
Strange House, The.
Subalterns, The.
Sunshade, The.
Superseded, The.
Tess's Lament.
This Summer and Last.
Thoughts of Phena.
Thunderstorm in Town, A.
To an Unborn Pauper Child.
To Carrey Clavel.
To Lizbie Browne.
To Meet, or Otherwise.
Trampwoman's Tragedy, A.
Transformations.
Tree and the Lady, The.
Two Lips.
Unborn, The.
Under the Waterfall.
Unkept Good Fridays.
Voice, The.
Voices from Things Growing in a
  Churchyard.
Wagtail and Baby.
Waiting Both.
Walk, The.
Weathers [or Weather].
Wessex Heights.
When I set out for Lyonnesse.
When Oats Were Reaped.
Where the Picnic Was.
Who's in the next room?—who?
Wife in London, A.
Winter in Durnover Field.
Wives in the Sere.
Workbox, The.
Year's Awakening, The.
Young Glass-Stainer, The.
Young Man's Epigram on Existence, A.
Your Last Drive.
Zermatt: To the Matterhorn.

Hare, Amory (1885–1946)
Walking at Night.

Hare, Maurice Evan (1886–1967)
Alfred de Musset.
Determinism.
Limerick: "There once was a man [or There
  was a young man] who said, 'Damn!'"

Hare, Patrick (b. 1936)
Deceit in the Park.

Haresnape, Geoffrey (b. 1939)
African Tramp, The.

Harford, Lesbia (1891–1927)
Beauty and Terror.
Experience.
Poem: "I'm like all lovers, wanting love to
  be."
Poem: "Sometimes I wish that I were Helen-
  fair."
Poem: "When I was still a child."

Hargreaves, William (1881–1941)
Burlington Bertie from Bow.
Haring, Phyllis (b. 1919)
Earth Asks and Receives Rain, The.
Foetus.
Forbidden, The.
Jungle.
Overture to Strangers.
Twin.
Harington, Henry (1727–1816)
Abbey Church at Bath, The.
Harington [or Harrington], Sir John (1561–1612)
Against an Old Lecher.
Ariosto's Orlando Furioso Book 34, sels.
Author, of His Own Fortune, The.
Author to His Wife, of a Woman's Eloquence, The.
Fair, Rich, and Young.
Groome of the Chambers religion in King Henry the eights time, A.
Of a Zealous Lady.
Of an Heroical Answer of a Great Roman Lady to Her Husband.
Of honest Theft. To my good friend Master Samuel Daniel.
Of Treason.
To His Wife, for Striking Her Dog.
Tragicall Epigram, A.
Harington, John (fl. c.1550)
Husband to Wife.
Life is long that loathsomely doth last, The.
Of the Wars in Ireland.
Sir John Raynsford's Confession.
Sonnet Written upon My Lord Admiral Seymour, A.
To His Mother.
Wife to Husband.
Harington, Lucy, Countess of Bedford (d. 1627)
Elegy: "Death be not proud, thy hand gave not this blow."
Harjo, Joy (b. 1951)
Anchorage.
Autobiography.
Bird.
Blue Elliptic.
Book of Myths, The.
Eagle Poem.
Early morning woman.
For Alva Benson, and for Those Who Have Learned to Speak.
For Anna Mae Aquash Whose Spirit Is Present Here and in the Dappled Stars.
Grace.
Healing Animal.
I Give You Back.
Legacy.
New Orleans.
Perhaps the World Ends Here.
Petroglyph.
Remember the sky that you were born under.
Resurrection.
Santa Fe.
She Had Some Horses.
Skeleton of Winter.
Sonata for the Invisible.
Song for the Deer and Myself to Return On.
Strange Fruit.
Transformations.
Woman Hanging from the Thirteenth Floor Window, The.
Harjo, Patty L. ("Ya-Ka-Nes") (b. 1947)
Death.
Mask, The.
Taos Winter.
To an Indian Poet.
Where Have You Gone, Little Boy.
Wishes.
Harkness, John
New Song on the Birth of the Prince of Wales, A.
Harlow, Michael (b. 1937)
Poem Then, for Love, sels.
Vlaminck's Tie, the Persistent Imaginal.
Harmer, David
Space Explorer's Story, The.

Harmon, William (b. 1938)
Bureaucratic Limerick ("Bureau of Labor Statistics, The.")
Dawn Horse, The.
Invoice No. 13, A Masque of Resignation.
Legion: Civic Choruses, sels.
Treasure Holiday, sels.
Harms, James
Breakfast on the Patio.
Explaining the Evening News to Corbyn.
My Androgynous Years.
Tomorrow, We'll Dance in America.
Harney, Ben (1872–1938)
Mister Johnson.
You've Been a Good Old Wagon, but You've Done Broke Down.
Harney, W. E. (1895–1903)
West of Alice.
Harper, Frances Ellen Watkins (1825–1911)
Appeal to My Countrywomen, An.
Aunt Chloe's Politics.
Bible Defence of Slavery.
Burdens of All, The.
Bury Me in a Free Land.
Crocuses, The.
Deliverance.
Double Standard, A.
Eliza Harris.
Ethiopia.
Free Labor.
Go Work in My Vineyard.
God Bless Our Native Land.
Grain of Sand, A.
He "Had Not Where to Lay His Head."
Learning to Read.
Let the Light Enter!
Lines: "At the Portals of the Future."
Mission of the Flowers, The.
Moses: A Story of the Nile, sels.
Night of Death, The.
Nobly Born, The.
Nothing and Something.
Present Age, The.
Pure in Heart Shall See God, The.
Refiner's Gold, The.
Renewal of Strength
Save the Boys.
She's Free!
Sir, We Would See Jesus.
Slave Auction, The.
Slave Mother, The.
Songs for the People.
Sparrow's Fall, The.
Thank God for Little Children.
Then and Now.
To the Union Savers of Cleveland.
Vashti.
Harper, Gordon
Limerick: "When a friend told a typist called Eve."
Harper, Michael S. (b. 1938)
Alice.
Alone.
American History.
Bandstand.
Barricades.
"Bird Lives": Charles Parker [in St. Louis].
Blue Ruth: America.
Breaded Meat, Breaded Hands.
Br'er Sterling and the Rocker.
Clan Meeting: Births and Nations: A Blood Song.
Come Back Blues.
Dance of the Elephants, The.
Dear John, Dear Coltrane.
Deathwatch.
Debridement.
Double Elegy.
Drive In, The.
Driving the Big Chrysler across the Country of My Birth.
Effendi.
Elvin's Blues.
Eve (Rachel).
Families Album, The.
Fireplace, The.
For Bud.

Ghost of Soul-making, The.
Goin' to the Territory.
Grandfather.
Guerrilla-Cong, The.
Here Where Coltrane Is.
High Modes: Vision as Ritual: Confirmation.
History as Apple Tree.
Homage to the New World.
In Hayden's Collage.
Jazz Station.
Kin.
Landfill.
Last Affair: Bessie's Blues Song.
Lecturing on the Theme of Motherhood.
Makin' Jump Shots.
Mama's Report.
Martin's Blues.
Militance of a Photograph in the Passbook of a Bantu under Detention, The.
Mother Speaks: The Algiers Motel Incident, Detroit, A.
Narrative of the Life and Times of John Coltrane: Played by Himself, A.
Newletter from My Mother.
Nightmare Begins Responsibility.
Peace on Earth.
Photographs: A Vision of Massacre.
Poetry Concert.
Reuben, Reuben.
Sandra: At the Beaver Trap.
Song: I Want a Witness.
Three O'Clock Love Song.
Tongue-tied in Black and White.
We Assume: On the Death of Our Son, Reuben Masai Harper.
Zocalo.
Harpur, Charles (1813–68)
Basket Of Summer Fruit, A.
Bush Justice.
Coast View, A, sels.
Creek of the Four Graves, The, sels.
Flight of Wild Ducks, A.
Marvellous Martin.
Wellington.
Harr, Barbara (b. 1937)
Walking through a Cornfield in the Middle of Winter I Stumble over a Cow Pie and Think of the Sixties Press.
Harr, Lorraine Ellis
After the snowfall.
Hot summer wind, A.
Indian summer.
Late snowfall;.
On the old scarecrow.
Pale dawn moon, A.
Sparkler goes out, The.
Time it takes, The.
Until it alights.
Harries, Neil
Dog-watch.
Harrigan, Edward [or "Ned"] (1845–1911)
My Dad's Dinner Pail.
Harriman, Carol
William Penn owned millions of.
Harrington, James (1611–77)
Inconstancy.
Harris, Ann
Pioneers.
Harris, Benjamin (c.1640–1720)
Account of the Cruelty of the Papists, An.
God save the King, that King that sav'd the land.
Of the French Kings Nativity.
Harris, Claire (b. 1937)
Framed.
Policeman Cleared in Jaywalking Case.
Harris, Jana (b. 1947)
When Mama Came Here as a Gold Panner, sels.
Harris, Joel Chandler (1848–1908)
Uncle Remus and His Friends, sels.
Uncle Remus: His Songs and His Sayings, sels.
Harris, June Brown
Home to me is laughter.

Harris, Marie
Physics One.
Harris, Max (b. 1921)
Martin Buber in the Pub.
Message from a Cross.
Tantanoola Tiger, The.
Harris, Norman (b. 1918)
Fable: "There is an inevitability."
Harris, Peter (b. 1955)
Some Songs Women Sing.
Harris, Phyllis. *See* **Beauvais, Phyllis**
Harris, Robert (b. 1951)
Ambition, The.
Call, The.
Isaiah by Kerosene Lantern Light.
Literary Excellence.
Riding Over Belmore Park.
Sydney.
Harris, Sydney Justin (1917–86)
I Come to Bury Caesar.
Harris, William J. (b. 1942)
Daddy Poem, A.
For Bill Hawkins, a Black Militant.
Grandfather Poem, A.
Historic Moment, An.
My baby / loves flowers.
Practical Concerns.
Rib Sandwich.
Samantha Is My Negro Cat.
We Live in a Cage.
Why Would I Want.
Harris, Wilson (b. 1921)
Charcoal.
Laocoön.
Harrison, De Leon (b. 1941)
Collage for Richard Davis—Two Short
Forms, A.
Room, The.
Seed of Nimrod, The.
Some Days / Out Walking Above.
Yellow.
Harrison, Florence (b. 1884)
Faerie Fair, The.
Summer Day, A.
Harrison, Gregory (b. 1928)
Alone in the Grange.
Playground, The.
Harrison, James [*or* Jim] (b. 1937)
After the Anonymous Swedish.
Helen.
Leda's Version.
Locations.
Lullaby for a Daughter.
Penelope.
Poem: "Form is the woods: the beast."
Returning at Night.
Sketch for a Job Application Blank.
Sound.
Suite to Fathers.
Harrison, Tony (b. 1937)
Breaking the Chain.
Call of Nature, The.
Confessional Poetry.
Durham.
Hands, The.
Heartless Art, The.
"I've done my bits of mindless aggro too."
Kumquat for John Keats, A.
Long Distance.
Queen's English, The.
Remains.
School of Eloquence, The, *sels.*
Study.
Them and [uz].
Harrison, William (1685–1713)
In Praise of Laudanum.
Harrod, Lois Marie
Fitting Room.
"Harry, Blind." *See* **Henry the Minstrel**
Harry, J. S. (b. 1939)
Honesty-Stones.
Poem Films Itself, The.
Shot of War, A.
Walking, when the Lake of the Air is Blue
with Spring.

Harryman, Carla
Allegory.
Magic (or Rousseau).
Male, The.
Matter.
Mothering.
My Story.
Realism.
That Can Not Be Taken Away From It.
Hart, Elizabeth Anna (1822–88)
Mother Tabbyskins.
Hart, Henry (b. 1954)
Prisoner of Camau, The.
Hart, Kevin (b. 1954)
Flemington Racecourse.
Horizon, The.
Last Day, The.
Members of the Orchestra, The.
Story, The.
Hart, Lorenz (1895–1943)
Blue Room, The.
I Wish I Were in Love Again.
Lady Is a Tramp, The.
Manhattan.
Most Beautiful Girl in the World, The.
Mountain Greenery.
Hart-Smith, William (b. 1911)
Boomerang.
Golden Pheasant. Mating Pair.
Inca Tupac Upanqui, The.
Nullarbor.
Harte, Bret (Francis Bret Harte) (1836–1902)
Ballad of the Emeu, The.
California Madrigal.
Chicago.
Colenso Rhymes for Orthodox Children.
Dow's Flat.
Further Language from Truthful James.
Her Letter.
John Burns of Gettysburg.
Miss Edith's Modest Request.
Mrs. Judge Jenkins[; Being the Only Genuine
Sequel to "Maud Muller"].
Plain Language from Truthful James.
Schemmelfennig.
Second Review of the Grand Army, A.
Society Upon the Stanislaus, The.
Stage-Driver's Story, The.
Tale of a Pony, The.
Truthful James to the Editor.
What the Bullet Sang.
What the Engines Said.
Willows, The.
Harte, Walter (1709–74)
Enchanted Region; or, Mistaken Pleasures,
The.
Essay on Satire, Particularly on The Dunciad,
An, *sels.*
Mock-Epic Satire.
What burlesque could, was by that genius
done.
Harteis, Richard (b. 1946)
Genetics.
Grace of Animals, The.
Hermit's Curse, The.
Mirage.
Star Trek III.
Harter, Penny
Bitter tea.
Broken bowl.
Cat's whiskers, The.
Clouds.
Grandmother's mirror.
In the mirror.
Mattress Fire.
On the padlock.
Only letting in the cat.
Pine needles.
Snowflakes.
Thawing.
White flowers.
Winter rain.
Wrinkles.
Hartigan, Anne (b. 1932)
Advent.
Brazen Image.

No Easy Harbour.
Salt.
St. Bridget's Cross.
**Hartigan, Patrick Joseph ("John O'Brien")
(1879–1952)**
Field of the Cloth of Gold, The.
Hartman, Charles O. (b. 1949)
Inflation.
Hartman, Mary R.
Life's made up of little things.
Hartmann von Aue (1170–1215)
I go, with your good grace, lords and
kinsmen.
I said I would always live for her.
None Is Happy.
Often a friend will greet me thus.
Hartnett, Michael (b. 1941)
All that is left and definite.
All the death-room needs.
All the same, it would make you laugh.
Death of an Irishwoman.
Domestic Scene.
Enamoured of the miniscule / of the careful
and compact.
Farewell to English, A, *sels.*
For My Grandmother, Bridget Halpin.
I have exhausted the delighted range.
I have heard them knock / on my dimension.
I think sometimes / of the fingernail slotted.
Lament for Tadhg Cronin's Children.
Last Vision of Eoghan Rua Ó Súilleabháin,
The.
Notes on My Contemporaries, *sels.*
Pity the man who English lacks.
Possibility That Has Been Overlooked Is the
Future, The.
Purge, The, *sels.*
Retreat of Ita Cagney, The.
Small Farm, A.
There will be a talking of lovely things.
Thirteen Sonnets, *sels.*
Visit to Castletown House, A.
Wounded otter, The.
Hartsough, Lewis (1828–1919)
Come, Friends and Neighbors, Come.
Let Me Go Where Saints Are Going.
Hartwig, Julia (b. 1921)
Above Us.
St. Matthew, *sels.*
Who Says.
Harumichi no Tsuraki (*fl.* 10th cent.)
Wind has stopped, The.
Harvey, Christopher (1597–1663)
Church Festivals.
Synagogue, The, *sels.*
Harvey, Frederick William (1888–1957)
Ducks, *sels.*
November.
Harvey, Sean
Mighty Tropicale Orchestra, The.
Harwood, Gwen (b. 1920)
At the Sea's Edge.
Carnal Knowledge.
Clair de Lune.
Death has no features of his own.
Father and Child.
Homage to Ferd. Holthausen.
Hospital Evening.
In the Bistro.
In The Park.
Lion's Bride, The.
Mid-Channel.
Mother who gave me life.
New Music.
Night Thoughts: Baby & Demon.
Nightfall.
Panther and Peacock.
Prize-giving.
Sea Anemones, The.
Second Life of Lazarus, The.
Simple Story, A.
Suburban Sonnet.
Wine is drunk, the woman known, The.
Harwood, Lee (b. 1939)
Animal Days.
As your eyes are blue.

Final Painting, The.
Soft White.
Text for a Poster (2).
"Utopia" The.
Words, The.

Hasford, Gustav
Bedtime Story.

Hashimoto, Sharon (b. 1953)
Eleven A.M. on My Day Off, My Sister
Phones Desperate for a Babysitter.
Mirror of Matsuyama, The.
Standing in the Doorway, I Watch the Young
Child Sleep.

Hashimoto, Takako (1899–1963)
Towards the starry sky.

Haskell, Dennis (b. 1947)
Call, The.

Haskell, Jefferson (b. 1807)
My Latest Sun Is Sinking Fast.

Hasluck, Nicholas (b. 1942)
Islands which have.
Rottnest Island, sels.

Hass, Robert (b. 1941)
Against Botticelli.
Bashō, A Departure.
Between the Wars.
Concerning the Afterlife, the Indians of
Central California Had Only the Dimmest
Notions.
Fall.
Heroic Simile.
House.
Human Wishes.
Image, The.
In Weather.
Late Spring.
Meditation at Lagunitas.
Misery and Splendor.
Palo Alto.
Privilege of Being.
Return of Robinson Jeffers, The.
Song: "Afternoon cooking in the fall sun."
Songs to Survive the Summer.
Spring Rain.
Story about the Body, A.
Tahoe in August.
Vintage.

Hassall, Christopher Vernon (1912–64)
Santa Claus.
Tropical Fish.

Hassett, Steve
Armed Forces Day.
Christmas.
Mother's Day.
Patriot's Day.
Thanksgiving.

Haste, Gwendolen (1889–1979)
Montana Wives, sels.
Wind, The.

Hastings, Beatrice (1879–1943)
Mind Pictures.

Hastings, Thomas (1784–1872)
Hail to the Brightness of Zion's Glad
Morning.
Jesus, Merciful and Mild!
Now Be the Gospel Banner.
Now from Labor and from Care.

Hatfield, Edwin Francis (1807–83)
Hallelujah! Praise the Lord.

Hathaway, James B.
Congressman Visits the Grade School, The.

Hathaway, William (b. 1944)
My Words.
Poem in Response to Doom, A.
War Hope.

Hatshepsut (d. 1468 B.C.)
Obelisk Inscriptions, sels.

Hatsui Shizue (b. 1900)
Scattered petals gather on the road.
Silently / time passes.

Hatton, Joseph (1840–1907?)
Christmas Bills.

Hatton, R. (fl. 1631)
Epithalamium: "Hymen hath together tied."

Hatun, Mihri (d. 1504)
At one glance / I loved you.

Hậu Đề;n Nguyễn Dậu
Biding Our Time.

Hauer, Elizabeth N.
Vision.

Hauge, Olav H.
Across the Swamp.
I stand here, do you understand.

Haughton, Hugh (b. 1948)
Bollam's Replover, The: Farewell to
Jabberwocky.
Homard à Igor Stravinsky: Vernacular
Variations.

Hauser, Samuel (1833–1914)
What Ship Is This?

Havergal, Frances Ridley (1836–79)
Just when Thou wilt, O Master, call!

"Havhesp, Dewi." See **Roberts, David**

Hawaiian Oral Tradition
Here all seeking is over.

Hawes, Stephen (1474–1523)
Pastime of Pleasure, The, sels.

Hawker, Robert Stephen (1804–75)
Aishah Schechinah.
Are They Not All Ministering Spirits?
Butterfly, The.
Cornish Emigrant's Song, The.
Croon on Hennacliff, A.
Death Song.
Featherstone's Doom.
King Arthur's Waes-hael.
Legend of the Hive, A.
Mystic Magi, The.
Poor Man and His Parish Church, The.
Quest of the Sangraal, The, sels.
Song of the Western Men, The.

Hawkins, Desmond
Night Raid.

Hawkins, Ralph
Birds.
Cattle.
Imperfect Air.

Hawkins, Walter Everette (b. 1886)
Death of Justice, The.
Spade Is Just a Spade, A.

Hawkins, William (b. 1940)
New Light, A.
Spring Rain.
Wall, The.

Hawkshawe [or Hawkshaw], Ann
Moonlight, The.
Muffin-Man's Bell, The.
Old Kitchen Clock, The.

Hawley, Beatrice (1944?–1985)
Bad Mother, The.
Evening.

Hawling, Francis (fl. c.1727–c.1751)
Signal; or, A Satire against Modesty, The,
sels.

Hawthorn, John (fl. c.1779)
Journey and Observations of a Countryman,
The, sels.
On His Writing Verses.

"Hawthorne, Alice." See **Winner, Septimus**

Hawthorne, Hildegarde (1871?–1952)
Song, A: "Sing me a sweet, low song of
night."

Hawthorne, Nathaniel (1804–64)
I Left My Low amd Humble Home.
Ocean has its silent caves, The.
Oh could I raise the darken'd veil.
Oh, Man can seek the downward glance.

Haxton, Brooks (b. 1950)
Auspice.
Traveling Company.

Hay, Clarence Leonard (1884–1969)
Down and Out.

"Hay, Elijah." See **Seiffert, Marjorie Allen**

Hay, George Campbell (1915–84)
Atman.
Bizerta.
Flooer o the Gean.

Song: "Day will rise and the sun from
eastward."
Sonnet: "Beckie, my luve!—What is't, ye
twa-faced tod?"
To a Loch Fyne Fisherman.
Two Neighbours, The.

Hay, John (b. 1915)
Defend Us, Lord, from Every Ill.

Hay, John Milton (1838–1905)
Enchanted Shirt, The.
Good Luck and Bad ("Good luck is the
gayest of all gay girls.")
Jim Bludso of the Prairie Belle.
Little Breeches.
Pledge at Spunky Point, The.
What is a first love worth except to prepare
for a second?

Hay, Sara Henderson (1906–87)
Christmas, the Year One, A.D.
Interview.

Hayakawa, Samuel Ichiye (b. 1906)
To One Elect.

Hayashi, Fumiko (1904–51)
Lord Buddha, The.

Hayati, Bibi (d. 1853)
Before there was a trace of this world of
men.
Is this darkness the night of Power, or the
black falling of your hair?

Hayden, Robert Earl (1913–80)
[American Journal].
Aunt Jemima of the Ocean Waves.
Bahá'u'lláh in the Garden of Ridwan.
Ballad of Nat Turner, The.
Ballad of Remembrance, A.
Ballad of Sue Ellen Westerfield, The.
Bone-Flower Elegy.
Broken Dark, The.
Diver, The.
Double Feature.
Dream, The.
El-Hajj Malik El-Shabazz.
For a Young Artist.
Frederick Douglass.
Full Moon.
Homage to the Empress of the Blues.
In the Mourning Time.
Incense of the Lucky Virgin.
Inference of Mexico, An, sels.
Letter from Phillis Wheatley, A.
Locus.
Middle Passage.
Monet's "Waterlilies."
Mourning Poem for the Queen of Sunday.
'Mystery Boy' Looks for Kin in Nashville.
Names.
Night-Blooming Cereus, The.
Night, Death, Mississippi.
O Daedalus, Fly Away Home.
On Lookout Mountain.
Paul Laurence Dunbar.
Perseus.
Plague of Starlings, A.
Road in Kentucky, A.
Runagate Runagate.
Soledad.
Sphinx.
Stars, sels.
Summertime and the Living.
Tattooed Man, The.
Those Winter Sundays.
Wheel, The.
Whipping, The.
Witch Doctor.

Hayes, Alfred (1911–85)
Angel, The.
Epistle to the Gentiles.
Joe Hill.
Nice Part of Town, A.
Slaughter-House, The.

Hayes, Ann
Much Ado About Nothing, Thanksgiving,
1972.
Pietá.

Hayes, Daniel (fl. 18th cent.)
Poem Dedicated to Mrs. Blennerhasset, the

Only Female Member of the Limerick Hell
   Fire Club, A.
Hayes, Donald Jeffrey (b. 1904)
   Appoggiatura.
"Hayes, Evelyn." *See* **Bethell, Mary Ursula**
Hayes, J. Milton (1884–1940)
   Green Eye of the Yellow God, The.
Hayes, Nancy M.
   At Night in the Wood.
   Shiny Little House, The.
Hayford, Gladys May Casely (Aquah Laluah)
   (1904–50)
   Nativity.
   Shadow of Darkness.
Hayford, James (b. 1913)
   Mason's Trick.
Hayiaku
   Funeral Song.
Hayley, William (1745–1820)
   Essay on Epic Poetry, An, *sels.*
   To Mr. William Long, On His Recovery
     from a Dangerous Illness, 1785.
   To Mrs. Smith, Occasioned by the First of
     Her Sonnets.
Hayman, Jane
   Murdered Girl Is Found on a Bridge, The.
Hayman, Robert (1579?–1631?)
   Of the Great and Famous. . . Sir Francis
     Drake, and of My Little-Little Selfe.
   Owen's Epigrams, *sels.*
   Pleasant Life in Newfoundland, The.
Hayne, Paul Hamilton (1830–86)
   Charlotte Brontë.
   October.
   On the Occurrence of a Spell of Arctic
     Weather in May, 1858.
   Rose and the Thorn, The.
Haynes, Carol (b. 1897)
   Any Wife or Husband.
Haynes, David (b. 1957)
   Mediatrix.
Hays, Hoffman Reynolds (1904–80)
   Case, The.
   For One Who Died Young.
   January.
   Manhattan.
   Sacred Children, The.
Hays, Will S. (1837–1909)
   O'Grady's Goat.
Hayward, Charles W. (1866–1950)
   King George V.
Hayward, William (b. 1906)
   Five Birds Rise.
Hazard, James
   Whiskey in Whiting, Indiana.
Hazo, Samuel (b. 1928)
   Battle News.
   Yellow Delicious.
Head, Gwen
   Night Sweats.
Head, Sir Henry (1861–1940)
   Destroyers.
Headly, Henry (1765–88)
   Invocation to Melancholy, An, *sels.*
Heaney, Seamus (b. 1939)
   Alphabets.
   Anahorish.
   Ash Plant, The.
   At a Potato Digging.
   Barn, The.
   Bat on the Road, A.
   Blackberry-Picking.
   Bog Queen.
   Bogland.
   Broagh.
   Cana Revisited.
   Casting and Gathering.
   Casualty.
   Clearances, *sels.*
   Death of a Naturalist.
   Digging.
   Docker.
   Dream of Jealousy, A.
   Drink of Water, A.

Exposure, *sels.*
Field Work.
Follower.
Forge, The.
From the Canton of Expectation.
From the Frontier of Writing.
Funeral Rites.
Girls Bathing, Galway 1965.
Guttural Muse, The.
Harvest Bow, The.
Haw Lantern, The.
Hazel Stick for Catherine Ann, A.
In Memoriam Francis Ledwidge.
Iron Spike.
La Toilette.
Limbo.
Mid-Term Break.
Mossbawn, *sels.*
Mother of the Groom.
Mud Vision, The.
New Song, A.
North.
Other Side, The.
Otter, The.
Outlaw, The.
Oysters.
Peacock's Feather, A.
Peninsula, The.
Poor Women in a City Church.
Postcard from North Antrim, A.
Punishment.
Railway Children, The.
Requiem for the Croppies.
Rite of Spring.
Saint Francis and the Birds.
Scaffolding.
Schoolbag, The.
Ship of Death, A.
Singer's House, The.
Singing School.
Skunk, The.
Sloe Gin.
Song: "Rowan like a lip-sticked girl, A."
Station Island, *sels.*
Strand at Lough Beg, The.
Summer Home.
Summer nineteen sixty nine.
Sweeney Praises the Trees.
Sweeney Redivivus, *sels.*
Terminus.
Tinder.
Tollund Man, The.
Traditions.
Twice Shy.
Ulster Twilight, An.
Waterfall.
Wedding Day.
Whatever You Say Say Nothing.
Wife's Tale, The.
Heap, Jane (d. 1964)
   Where go the birds when the rain.
Heard, Josephine D. Henderson (b. 1861)
   Admiration.
   Advance of Education, The.
   Assurance.
   Bereft.
   Birth of Jesus, The.
   Birth of Time, The.
   Bishop James A. Shorter.
   Black Sampson, The.
   City by the Sea, The.
   Day after Conference, The.
   December.
   Deception.
   Decoration Day.
   Do You Think?
   Doxology.
   Earthquake of 1886, The.
   Easter Morn.
   Epitaph, An: "When I am gone."
   Eternity.
   Fame.
   Farewell to Allen University.
   Forgetfulness!
   General Robert Smalls.
   Happy Heart, A.
   He Comes Not To-night.

He Hath Need of Rest.
Heart-Hungry.
Hope Thou in God.
Hope! Thou vain, delusive maiden.
I Love Thee.
I Will Look Up.
In Memory of James M. Rathel.
Judge Not.
Love Letters.
Matin Hymn.
Message to a Loved One Dead, A.
Morn.
Mother.
Mother's Love, A.
Music.
My Canary.
My Grace Is Sufficient.
My Husband's Birthday.
My Mocking Bird.
National Cemetery, Beaufort, South Carolina,
   The.
New Organ, The.
Night.
On Genessarett.
Out in the Desert.
Outcast, The.
Parting, The.
Parting Kiss, The.
Quarrel, The.
Quarto Centennial, The.
Question, The.
Resting.
Retrospect.
Rev. Andrew Brown, over the Hill to Rest.
Rt. Rev. Richard Allen.
Sabbath Bells.
Slumbering Passion.
Solace.
Sunshine after Cloud.
Tennyson's Poems.
They Are Coming?
Thine Own.
Thou Lovest Me.
To Clements' Ferry.
To Whittier.
To Youth.
Truth.
Unuttered Prayer.
Welcome Home.
Welcome to Hon. Frederick Douglass.
When I Would Die.
Where Do School Days End?
Who Is My Neighbor?
Whoso Gives Freely, Shall Freely Receive!
Wilberforce.
Hearn, Mary Ann. *See* **"Farningham,**
   Marianne"
Hearn, Michael Patrick
   At Dawn.
   In the Library.
Hearne, Betsy
   Commuters.
Hearne, Thomas (1678–1735)
   On the Tack.
Hearne, Vicki (b. 1946)
   Gauguin's White Horse.
   Riding a Nervous Horse.
Hearson, Harry (*fl.* c.1940)
   Nomenclaturik.
Heath, ------ (*fl.* c.1500)
   Women.
Heath, Robert (b. 1931)
   On Clarastella walking in Her Garden.
   On the Unusual Cold and Rainy [*or* Rainie]
     Weather in the Summer, 1648.
   Seeing Her Dancing.
Heath-Stubbs, John (b. 1918)
   Artorius, *sels.*
   Ballad of Don and Dave and Di, The.
   Beggar's Serenade.
   Carol for Advent.
   Charm against the Toothache, A.
   Dark Planet, The.
   December: Prayer to St. Nicholas.
   Ecclesiastical Chronicle, An, *sels.*
   Epitaph: "Mr. Heath-Stubbs as you must
     understand."

February.
Footnote to Belloc's "Tarantella."
Gifts, The.
History of the Flood, The.
January.
Jays, The.
July.
Kingfisher, The.
Lady's Complaint, The.
Mozart.
Not Being Oedipus.
One thinks of *one* as a pronoun employed
    principally.
Poet of Bray, The.
Preliminary Poem.
Send for Lord Timothy.
Simcox was one of several rather
    uninteresting.
Titus and Berenice.
To a Poet a Thousand Years Hence.
Two Wedding Songs, *sels.*
Unpredicted, The.
Valse Oubliée.
Virgin Martyrs.
Vision of Beasts, A.
Watching Tennis.
Winter Cricket.
Wishes for the Months.

Heavysege, Charles (1816–76)
Dead, The.
Winter Galaxy.

Heber, Reginald (1783–1826)
By Cool Siloam's Shady Rill.
From Greenland's Icy Mountains.

Hébert, Anne (b. 1916)
Alchemy of Day, The.
Bread Is Born.
Crown of Happiness.
Great Fountains, The.
Life in the Castle.
Offended, The.
Our Hands in the Garden.
Skinny Girl, The.
Spring over the City.
Tomb of the Kings, The.
Wooden Chamber, The.

Hecht, Anthony (b. 1923)
Alceste in the Wilderness.
At the Frick.
Avarice.
Birdwatchers of America.
Book of Yolek, The.
Clair de Lune.
Cost, The.
Death the Painter.
Deodand, The.
Double Sonnet.
Dover Bitch, The.
End of the Weekend, The.
Feast of Stephen, The.
Firmness.
From the Grove Press.
Gardens of the Villa D'Este, The.
Ghost in the Martini, The.
Giant Tortoise.
Gift of Song, The.
Going the Rounds; a Sort of Love Poem.
Goliardic Song.
Hill, A.
Improvisations on Aesop.
"It Out-Herods Herod. Pray You, Avoid It."
Japan.
Jason.
La Condition Botanique.
Letter, A.
Lizards and Snakes.
Lot of Night Music, A.
Man Who Married Magdalene, The.
Meditation.
'More Light! More Light!'
Mysteries of Caesar, The.
Naming the Animals.
Old Malediction, An.
Paradise Lost, Book V: An Epitome.
Peripeteia.
Pig.
Prospects.

Samuel Sewall.
Sestina d'Inverno.
Still Life.
Tarantula or the Dance of Death.
Third Avenue in Sunlight.
Transparent Man, The.
Vice.
Voice at a Seance, A.
Vow, The.

Hecht, Roger (b. 1926)
War Memento (Somewhere in France 1915).

Hedge, Frederic Henry (1805–90)
Sovereign and Transforming Grace.

Hedin, Robert
Wreck of the Great Northern, The.

Hedylos (*fl.* 270? B.C.)
Dedication to Aphrodite, A.
From dawn to dark, and back from dark to
    dawn.
Let's drink up: with wine, what original.
Musical Wine-Jar, A.
Our prize fish is done!
Seduced Girl.
Wine and treacherous proposals.
Wine, the toasts that could not be refused,
    The.

Heffernan, Michael (b. 1942)
Message, The.
Naked War.
Putting On My Shoes I Hear the Floor Cry
    Out beneath Me.
Reading Aquinas.
Sunday Service.
Table, The.

Heffernan, William (b. 1937)
Kathaleen Ny-Houlahan [*or* Kathleen-Ni-
    Houlahan].

Hegemon (*fl.* c.370 B.C.)
Thermopylai.

Hegesippus (*fl.* 300 B.C.)
Hang that day with black, that night, sinister,
    moonless.

Heginbothom, Ottiwell (1744–68)
Great God, let all my tuneful pow'rs.

Heguri, Lady (*fl.* 8th cent.)
Thousand years, you said, A. *From* Manyo
    Shu, Part 4 of 4.

Heidbreder, Robert
Copycat, copycat / Shadow's a copycat!

Heide, Florence Parry (b. 1919)
Rocks.

Heifetz-Tussman, Malka (b. 1896)
Mount Gilboa.
Thou Shalt Not.
Thunder My Brother.

Heikel, Karen Alice. *See* "Vala, Katri"

Heine, Heinrich (1797–1856)
Ad Finem.
Anno 1829.
Auf meiner Herzliebsten Äugelein.
Azra, The.
Coffin, The.
Dear Maiden.
Die blauen Veilchen der Äugelein.
Die Lotusblume ängstigt.
Ein Fichtenbaum steht einsam.
Enfant perdu.
Es fällt ein Stern herunter.
Es Stehen Unbeweglich.
Farewell: "Linden blossomed, the nightingale
    sang, The."
Fresco-Sonnets to Christian Scthe.
Hebrew Melodies, *sels.*
Heimkehr, Die, *sels.*
Homeward Bound, *sels.*
I Love But Thee.
I Met by Chance.
I Wept as I Lay Dreaming.
Ich Weiss Nicht Was Soll es Bedeuten.
If, Jerusalem, I Ever Should Forget Thee.
I'm Black and Blue.
Im Traum sah ich ein Männchen klein und
    putzig.
Lassie, What Mair Wad You Hae?
Looking Back.

Lorelei.
Love's Résumé.
Mädchen mit dem rothen Mündchen.
Maiden Lies in Her Chamber, A.
Mein Herz, Mein Herz Ist Traurig.
Mein Kind, wir waren Kinder.
Mein Liebchen, wir sassen zusammen.
Memory, A.
Message, The.
Mir träumte von einem Königskind.
Mir träumte wieder der alte Traum.
Mond ist aufgegangen, Der.
Morning After, The.
My Songs Are Poisoned ("My songs, they
    say, are poisoned.")
New Jewish Hospital at Hamburg, The.
North Sea, The, *sels.*
Oh Lovely Fishermaiden.
Princess Sabbath.
Proem: "Out of my own great woe."
Rose, die Lilie, die Taube, die Sonne, Die.
Sag', wo ist dein schönes Liebchen.
Sea Hath Its Pearls, The.
Shepherd Boy, The.
Solomon.
Song: "There stands a lonely pine-tree."
Songs to Seraphine, *sels.*
Sonnet to My Mother, A.
Storm, The.
Tannhäuser, *sels.*
Three Holy Kings from Morgenland.
To a Political Poet.
To Angélique, *sels.*
To Edom.
To My Mother.
Twilight.
Voyage, The.
Warum sind denn die Rosen so blass.
We Cared for Each Other.
Weavers.
Welt ist dumm, die Welt ist blind, Die.
When Two Are Parted.
When Young Hearts Break.
Who Was It, Tell Me.
Wie langsam kriechet sie dahin.
Window-Glance, The.
Wise Men Ask the Children the Way, The.
Zu fragmentarisch lst Welt und Leben.

Heinrich von Morungen (d. 1222)
Alas, shall I not see again.
I believe there is no one alive who weeps for
    my sorrow.
I heard on the meadow.
It has gone with me as with a child.
Legacy, The.
Many a man gets bewitched by the elves.

Heinrich von Rugge (*fl.* 12th cent.)
He That Loves a Rosy Cheek.

Heinrich von Veldeke (1140?–1210?)
In April when the flowers spring.
Tristan had no choice.
Whoever hurts my favor with my lady.

Heinze, Helga Marie
Late Flowers.
Storm.

Heissenbüttel, Helmut
Homesick.

Heithaus, Joe (*fl.* 20th cent.)
What a Little Moonlight Can Do.

Heitzman, Judy Page
March.
Spaces.

Hejduk, John
Sleep of Adam, The.

Hejinian, Lyn (b. 1941)
Cell, The, *sels.*
Guard, The, *sels.*
Mask of Anger, A.
My Life, *sels.*
Oxota: A Short Russian Novel, *sels.*
Person, The, *sels.*
Polar Circle, The.

Heller, Binem (b. 1943)
Pesach Has Come to the Ghetto Again.

Helton, Roy (b. 1886)
Lonesome Water.
Old Christmas Morning.

Helwig, David (b. 1938)
  Considerations.
  Dead Weasel, A.
  Drunken Poem.
  For Edward Hicks.
  Lot.
  Words from Hell.
Hemans, Felicia Dorothea (1793–1835)
  Agony in the Garden, The.
  Brereton Omen, The, *sels.*
  Casabianca.
  Chamois Hunter's Love, The.
  Child's First Grief, The.
  Corinne at the Capitol.
  Dreaming Child, The.
  Effigies, The.
  England's Dead.
  Evening Prayer, at a Girls' School.
  Flight of the Spirit.
  Grave of a Poetess, The.
  Graves of a Household, The.
  Homes of England, The.
  Hour of Death, The.
  Image in Lava, The.
  Indian Woman's Death-Song, The.
  Landing of the Pilgrim Fathers [in New
    England], The.
  Last Song of Sappho, The.
  Lost Pleiad, The.
  Magic Glass, The.
  Mirror in the Deserted Hall, The.
  Mozart's Requiem.
  Nature's Farewell.
  New Monthly Magazine, 43 329, *sels.*
  Night-Blooming Flowers.
  Parting Song, A.
  Properzia Rossi.
  Sabbath Sonnet.
  Second Sight.
  Siege of Valencia, The, *sels.*
  Song of Emigration.
  Songs of the Affections, with Other Poems,
    sels.
  Stranger's heart! Oh! wound it not!, The.
  To a Wandering Female Singer.
  To the Poet Wordsworth.
  Woman and Fame.
Hemensley, Kris (b. 1946)
  Mile from Poetry, A, *sels.*
  Sulking in the Seventies.
Hemingway, Ernest (1899–1961)
  Champs d'Honneur.
  Chapter Heading.
  Earnest Liberal's Lament, The.
  Neo-Thomist Poem.
  Valentine.
Hemminger, Graham Lee (1896–1949)
  Tobacco ("Tobacco is a dirty weed.")
Hemp, Christine E.
  Living Lean.
Hemphill, Essex (1957–95)
  Conditions, *sels.*
  Cordon Negro.
  Family Jewels.
  Homocide.
  Isn't It Funny?
  Soft Targets.
  To Some Supposed Brothers.
  Where Seed Falls.
Hemphrey, Malcolm
  Lanes in Summer.
Hempseed, Isabell
  Rufty and Tufty.
Hemschemeyer, Judith (b. 1935)
  First Love.
  Giving birth in Greek.
  I Remember the Room Was Filled with
    Light.
  My grandmother had bones as delicate.
  My Mother's Death.
  Painters, The.
Henchman, Richard (c.1655–1725)
  In Consort to Wednesday, Jan. 1st. 1701.
  Vox Oppressi, to the Lady Phipps.
Henderson, Alice Corbin. *See* **Corbin, Alice**
Henderson, David (b. 1943)
  Alvin Cash/Keep on Dancin'.

  Coltrane Memorial, A.
  Do Nothing Till You Hear from Me.
  Elvin Jones Gretsch Freak.
  Horizon Blues.
  Keep on Pushing.
  Lee Morgan.
  Louisiana Weekly #4, The.
  Song of Devotion to the Forest.
  Sonny rollins seeking.
  Thelonious Sphere Monk.
  They Are Killing All the Young Men.
  Walk with de Mayor of Harlem.
  White People.
Henderson, E. H.
  March Wind, The.
Henderson, Hamish (b. 1919)
  End of a Campaign.
  First Elegy for the Dead in Cyrenaica.
  Flyting o' Life and Daith, The.
  Seven Good Germans.
  We Show You That Death as a Dancer.
"Henderson, Paul" (Ruth France) (1913–67)
  Shag Rock.
Henderson-Holmes, Safiya (b. 1952)
  Battle, Over and Over Again, The.
  Failure of an Invention.
  Friendly Town #1.
  Friendly Town #3.
  Goodhousekeeping #17.
  My First Riot: Bronx, NYC.
  To Hell and Back, with Cake.
Hendriks, A. L. (b. 1922)
  Boundary.
  Cirrhosis.
  D'Où Venons Nous? Que Sommes Nous? Où
    Allons Nous, *sels.*
  Hot Summer Sunday.
  Jamaican Small Gal.
  Migrant, The.
  Recollections of the Sun.
  Where It's At.
  Will the Real Me Please Stand Up?
Hendry, Hamish (*fl.* c.1897)
  Silver Bells.
  Silver Road, The.
  Upside-Down World, The.
Hendry, J. F. (b. 1912)
  Constant North, The.
Hendryson, Barbara
  Prayer for a Tenspeed Heart.
  What Is Repeated, What Abides.
Henjō Abbot
  If the winds of heaven.
Henley, Samuel (1740–1815)
  Verses Addressed to a Friend, Just Leaving a
    Favourite Retirement.
Henley, William Ernest (1849–1903)
  All in a Garden Green.
  Ballade Made in the Hot Weather.
  Ballade of Dead Actors.
  Bowl of Roses, A.
  Easy is the triolet.
  Echoes, *sels.*
  England, My England.
  From a Window in Princes Street.
  Home.
  In Hospital, *sels.*
  Moral, The.
  Out of Tune.
  Rondel: "Beside the idle summer sea."
  Since Those We Love and Those We Hate.
  Street Scene.
  To Robert Louis Stevenson.
  To W. R.
  Villon's Good-Night.
  Villon's Straight Tip to All Cross Coves.
Hennamma (*fl.* late 17th cent.)
  Wasn't your mother a woman?
Hennell, Thomas (1903–45)
  Mermaiden, A.
  Queen Anne's Musicians.
  Shepherd and Shepherdess.
Henri, Adrian (b. 1932)
  Adrian Henri's Talking after Christmas Blues.
  Crowfield.

  Early Spring.
  Mrs. Albion You've Got a Lovely Daughter.
Henry, Gerrit (b. 1950)
  Cole Porter's Son.
Henry, James (1798–1876)
  Another and another and another.
  My Stearine Candles.
  Old Man.
  Once on a time a thousand different men.
  Out of the Frying Pan into the Fire.
  "Pain, who made thee?" thus I said once.
  Two hundred men and eighteen killed.
  Very Old Man.
Henry, Patrick
  Is life so dear, or peace so sweet.
**Henry the Minstrel ("Blind Harry") (*fl.* c.1470–
c.1492)**
  Wallace, The, *sels.*
Henry VIII, King of England (1491–1547)
  Pastime with good company.
  To His Lady.
Henry, William
  Verses.
Henryson, Robert (c.1425–c.1506)
  Preiching of the Swallow, The.
  Robin [*or* Robene] and Makyne.
  Taill of the Foxe, That Begylit the Wolf, in
    the Schadow of the Mone, The.
  Tale of the Upland Mouse and the Burgess
    Mouse, The.
  Testament of Cresseid, The, *sels.*
Henson, David
  Last Atlantean, The.
Henson, Lance (b. 1944)
  Among Hawks.
  Anniversary Poem for the Cheyennes Who
    Fell at Sand Creek.
  At Chadwicks Bar and Grill.
  Bay Poem.
  Between Rivers and Seas.
  Buffalo Blood.
  Cold, The.
  Comanche Ghost Dance: An Impression.
  Coyote Fragments.
  Crazy Horse: The Last Morning.
  Curtain.
  Dawn in January.
  Day Song.
  Epitaph: Snake River.
  Flock.
  Grandfather.
  I Am Singing the Cold Rain.
  Image of City.
  Last Words, 1968.
  Moon at Three A.M.
  Moth.
  Near Twelve Mile Point.
  North of my grandfathers house.
  Old Man Told Me.
  Old Story.
  Other.
  Our Smoke Has Gone Four Ways.
  Poem for Carroll, Descendant of Chiefs.
  Rain.
  Scattered Leaves.
  Sitting Alone in Tulsa Three A.M.
  Sleep Watch.
  Solitary.
  Splitting Wood Near Morris, Oklahoma on
    Robbie and Lesa McMurtry's Farm.
  Sundown at Darlington 1878.
  Travels with the Band-Aid Army.
  Warrior Nation Trilogy.
  We Are a People.
  Wish.
  Wood Floor Dreams.
Heóghusa, Eochaidh Ó
  On Maguire's Winter Campaign.
  Winter Campaign, A.
Hepburn, Mrs. Patrick. *See* **Wickham, Anna**
Hepburn, Thomas Nicoll. *See* **"Setoun, Gabriel"**
Heppenstall, Rayner (1911–81)
  Actaeon.
Heraclitus of Halicarnassus (*fl.* c.240 B.C.)
  By Heraclides.

Soil is freshly dug, the half-faded wreaths of leaves, The.

Herbert, Sir Alan Patrick (1890–1971)
After the Battle.
Cookers, The: A Song of the Transport.
Dead-Mule Tree: A Song of Wisdom.
General inspecting the trenches, The.
German Graves, The.
I Like Them Fluffy.
Less Nonsense.
Lines for a Worthy Person Who Has Drifted by Accident into a Chelsea Revel.
Saturday Night.
Triangular Legs.

Herbert, Audrey
After the Battle.
Beaucourt Revisited.
Limerick: "All his life, Mr. George Bernard Shaw."

Herbert, Cicely (b. 1937)
Everything changes. We plant.

Herbert, E.
Balloon Man, The.

Herbert, George (1593–1633)
Aaron.
Affliction (1).
Affliction (3).
Affliction (4).
Affliction: "Kill me not every [or ev'ry] day."
Agony [or Agonie], The.
Altar, The.
Ana(Mary-Army)gram.
Answer, The.
Antiphon: "Let all the world in ev'ry corner sing / My God and King."
Artillery [or Artillerie].
Bag, The.
Banquet, The.
Bitter-Sweet.
British Church, The.
Bunch of Grapes, The.
Charms and Knots.
Christmas.
Church-Floor[e], The.
Church-Lock and Key.
Church Militant, The, sels.
Church Monuments.
Church-Music[k].
Church-Porch, The, sels.
Clasping of Hands.
Collar, The.
Complaining.
Confession.
Conscience.
Courage.
Cross[e], The.
Dawning, The.
Death, thou wast once an uncouth hideous thing.
Decay.
Denial[l].
Dialogue, A.
Discipline.
Divinity.
Doomsday.
Dulness[e].
Easter ("I got me flowers to straw [or strew or strow] Thy [or the] way.")
Easter ("Rise heart; thy Lord is risen. Sing his praise.")
Easter-Wings.
Elixir [or Elixer], The.
Employment: "He that is weary, let him sit."
Employment (1).
Evensong [or Even-Song].
Family [or Familie], The.
Flower, The.
Forerunners, The.
Frailty.
Glance, The.
Good Friday.
Grace.
Grieve Not the Holy Spirit, etc.
H[oly] Communion, The.
H. Scriptures, The ("Oh Book! infinite sweetnesse! let my heart.")

H. Scriptures, The ("Oh that I knew how all thy lights combine.")
Heaven.
Holy Baptism (1).
Holy Baptism (2).
Hope.
Humility.
Invitation, The.
JESU is in my heart, his sacred name.
Jordan.
Jordan (2)(II): "When first my lines [or verse] of heavenly [or heav'nly] joy[e]s made mention."
Joseph's Coat.
Judge not the preacher; for He is thy Judge.
Judgement.
Justice.
L'Envoy.
Life.
Longing.
Love.
Love bade me welcome[: yet my soul drew back].
Love-Joy.
Love (1).
Love ("Thou art too hard for me in Love.")
Love (2).
Man.
Mary [or Marie] Magdalene.
Mattens.
Memoriae Matris Sacrum, sels.
Misery [or Miserie].
Mortification.
Obedience.
Odour. 2. Cor. 2, The.
Our Life Is Hid with Christ in God.
Paradise.
Parody [or Parodie], A.
Peace.
Pearl. [Matth. 13.45 or Matt. 13:45], The.
Perirrhanterium.
Perseverance.
Pilgrimage, The.
Posy [or Posie], The.
Praise (2).
Prayer (I).
Priesthood, The.
Pulley, The.
Quidditie [or Quiddity], The.
Quip, The.
Redemption.
Reprisal[l], The.
Rose, The.
Sacrifice, The.
Search, The.
Sepulchre.
Sighs and Groans [or Grones].
Sin: "O that I could a sin once see!"
Sin (1).
Sin's Round.
Sion.
Size, The.
Son[ne], The.
Sonnet: "My God, where is that ancient heat towards Thee."
Sonnet: "Sure Lord, there is enough in thee to dry."
Star[re], The.
Storm, The.
Sunday.
Superliminare.
Temper (1), The.
Temper (2), The.
Thanksgiving, The.
Time.
Trinity Sunday.
True Hymn, A.
Unkindness.
Vanity [or Vanitie] (1).
Virtue [or Vertue].
Whitsunday.
Windows, The.
World, The.
Wreathèd garland of deservèd praise, A.

Herbert, Mary Sidney. See **Pembroke, Mary Sidney Herbert, Countess of**

Herbert, William. See **Pembroke, William Herbert, Earl of**

Herbert, Zbigniew (b. 1924)
Abandoned, The.
Apollo and Marsyas.
At the Gate of the Valley.
Biology Teacher.
Damastes (Also Known As Procrustes) Speaks.
Devil, A.
Drawer.
Elegy of Fortinbras.
End of a Dynasty, The.
Fathers of a Star, The.
Five Men.
From Mythology.
Hakeldama.
Hen is the best example of what living constantly with humans, The.
I would like to describe the simplest emotion.
Knocker, A.
Longobards, The.
Meditations of Mr. Cogito on Redemption.
Mother.
Mr. Cogito Meditates on Suffering.
Mr. Cogito Tells about the Temptation of Spinoza.
Naked Town, A.
Our Fear.
Painter.
Pan Cogito on Virtue.
Pan Cogito's Thoughts on Hell.
Passion of Our Lord painted by an anonymous hand from the Circle of Rhenish Masters, The.
Power of Taste, The.
Remembering My Father.
Report from the Besieged City.
Return of the Proconsul, The.
Rosy Ear.
Sense of Identity.
Speculations on the Subject of Barabbas.
St. Matthew, sels.
To Marcus Aurelius.
Trial, The
Two Drops.
Voice.
Wall, The.
What I Saw.
What Mr. Cogito Thinks About Hell.

Herbert of Cherbury, Edward Herbert, 1st Baron (1583–1648)
Another [Madrigal].
Breaking from under that thy cloudy veil.
Description, A.
Ditty: "If you refuse me once, and think again."
Ditty: "Why dost thou hate return instead of love."
Echo to a Rock.
Elegy for Dr. Donne, sels.
Elegy over a Tomb.
Epitaph. Caecil. Boulstr.
In a Glass-Window for Inconstancy.
Inconstancy's the Greatest of Sins.
Kissing.
La Gialletta Gallante, or the Sunburned Exotic Beauty.
Loves End.
Madrigal: "How should I love my best?"
Now that the April of your youth adorns.
Ode, upon a Question Moved, Whether Love Should Continue Forever? An.
One Another's Mystery.
Parted Souls.
Platonic Love.
Sinner's Lament, A.
Sonnet: "Innumerable Beauties, thou white haire."
Sonnet Made upon the Groves near Merlou [or Merlow] Castle.
Sonnet of Black Beauty.
Tears, Flow No More.
To a Lady Who Did Sing Excellently.
To His Mistress for Her True Picture.

To His Watch, When He Could Not Sleep.
To One Black, and Not Very Handsome,
    Who Expected Commendation.
Vision, A.

Herbertson, Agnes Grozier (1800–1881)
    Little Betty Blue.

Herder, Johann Gottfried von (1744–1803)
    Esthonian Bridal Song.
    Sir Olaf.

Herebert, William (c.1270–c.1333)
    Biseth you in this ilke lif.
    Com, Shuppere, Holy Gost, ofsech oure
        thoughtes.
    Crist, buyere of alle icoren.
    Herodes, thou wikked foe, wharof is thy
        dredinge?
    Heyl, Levedy, see-sterre bright.
    Holy moder, that bere Crist.
    Holy Wroughte of sterres bright.
    Jesu our raunsoun.
    Thou king of wele and blisse.
    Thou wommon boute fere.
    Wele, herying and worshipe be to Crist [or
        Christ] that dere us [or ous] boughte.
    What is he, this lordling, that cometh from
        the fight?

Heredia, José-Maria de (1842–1905)
    Antony and Cleopatra.
    Flute; a Pastoral, The.
    Laborer, The.
    Young Dead Woman, A.

Herford, Oliver (1863–1935)
    Bunny Romance, A.
    Crocodile once dropped a line, A.
    Elf and the Dormouse, The.
    Eve.
    Fall of J. W. Beane, The.
    I heard a bird sing.
    Metaphysics.
    Musical Lion, The.
    Platypus, The.
    Smile of the Goat has a meaning that few,
        The.
    Smile of the Walrus is wild and distraught,
        The.
    Snail's Dream, The.
    There was a young lady of Twickenham.

Herlin, Louise (b. 1925)
    Echo of fireplace on the dividing wall, An.
    Gull inch-perfect over water, the busy crane,
        The.
    Light brush of dawn, A.
    Morning space expands the building's.
    Red round sun, The.
    Sky has recovered its haze-blue tints, The.
    So many traces, fragile monuments.
    Warmth of the wind-break wall, The.

"Hermes, Paul." *See* **Thayer, William Roscoe**

Hermocreon (fl. 3d? cent. B.C.)
    Inscription on a Statue.
    Nymphs of the surface, whom Hermokreon
        gave.

Hernandez, B. Vincent
    Sunday morning.

Hernandez, David (fl. 20th cent.)
    Armitage Street.
    Martin and My Father.
    Pigeons are the spiks of Birdland.
    Welcome.

Hernández, Miguel (1910–42)
    I go on in the dark, lit from within; does day
        exist?
    July 18, 1936–July 18, 1938.
    Lullaby of the Onion.
    Tomb of the Imagination.
    Waltz Poem of Those in Love and
        Inseparable Forever.
    War.

Hernton, Calvin C. (b. 1932)
    D Blues.
    Distant Drum, The.
    Fall Down.
    Jitterbugging in the Streets.
    Long Blues, The.
    Patient: Rockland County Sanitarium, The.
    Poem.

Herodas (fl. 3d cent. B.C.)
    Friends in Private.
    Procuress, The.
    Schoolmaster, The.
    Women at the Temple.

Herodicus (fl. 2d cent. B.C.)
    Out of Hellas if you please, Aristarchean
        pedants.

Herrera, Juan Felipe
    Mission Street Manifesto.

Herrick, Robert (1591–1674)
    Againe.
    All Things Decay and Die.
    Amber Bead, The.
    Ambition ("In man, ambition is the
        common'st thing.")
    Anacreontic.
    Anacreontic[k] Verse.
    Another [To His Booke].
    Another Charme for Stables.
    Another Charme (variant).
    Another ("Let the superstitious wife.")
    Another to Bring in the Witch.
    Apparition of His Mistress[e] Calling Him to
        Elizium [or Elysium], The.
    Apron of Flowers, The.
    Argument of His Book, The.
    Art above Nature, to Julia.
    Ass[e], The.
    Bad Season Makes the Poet Sad, The.
    Barley-Break; or, Last in Hell.
    Beggar to Mab, the Fairy [or Fairie] Queen,
        The.
    Bell-Man, The.
    Bellman, The.
    Body is the Soul's [or Soules] poor[e] house,
        or home, The.
    Bracelet.
    Bubble; a Song, The.
    Calling, and Correcting.
    Canticle to Apollo, A.
    Captived Bee; or, The Little Filcher, The.
    Ceremonies for Candlemas[se] Eve.
    Ceremonies for Christmas[se], sels.
    Ceremony upon Candlemas Eve.
    Charme, or an Allay for Love, A.
    Charmes.
    Cheat of Cupid; or, The Ungentle Guest,
        The.
    Cherry-ripe.
    Chewing [of] the Cud, The.
    Chop-Cherry.
    Christmas Caroll Sung to the King in the
        Presence at White-Hall, A, sels.
    Christ's Sadness.
    Clothes Do But Cheat and Cozen [or
        Cousen] Us.
    Comfort to a Youth That Had Lost His Love.
    Coming of Good Luck, The.
    Conjuration, to Electra, A.
    Corinna's Going A-Maying.
    Country Life: To His Brother, M. Tho:
        Herrick.
    Country Life, to the Honored Mr. Endymion
        Porter[, Groome of the Bed-Chamber to
        His Maj.], The.
    Cross-tree, The.
    Crosses.
    Cruell Maid, The.
    Cruelties.
    Crutches.
    Curse. A Song, The.
    Custard, The.
    Definition of Beauty, The.
    Delight in Disorder.
    Dirge of Jephthah's Daughter, The.
    Discontents in Devon.
    Distrust ("To safeguard man from wrongs,
        there nothing must.")
    Divination by a Daffadill [or Daffodil].
    Dream[e]s.
    End of His Work, The.
    Entertainment, or Porch-Verse, at the
        Marriage of Mr. Henry Northleigh [or Hen.
        Northly] and the Most Witty Mrs. Lettice
        Yard, The.
    Epitaph upon a Child, An.

    Epitaph upon a Sober Matron, An.
    Epitaph upon a Virgin, An.
    Epithalamy to Sir Thomas Southwell and His
        Lady, An.
    Eternity.
    Eye, The.
    Fair[e] Days; or, Dawn[e]s Deceitful[l].
    Fairy Temple; or, Oberon's Chapel, The.
    Fame.
    Fame Makes Us Forward.
    Farewell Frost; or, Welcome the Spring.
    Four Sweet Months, The.
    Four[e] Things Make Us Happy Here.
    Fresh Cheese and Cream.
    Frolic[k], A.
    Frozen Zone; or, Julia Disdainful, The.
    Funeral[l] Rites of the Rose, The.
    God to Be First Served.
    God's Mercy.
    Good Friday: Rex Tragicus; or, Christ Going
        to His Cross[e].
    Good-Night, or Blessing, The.
    Grace for a Child.
    Grace for Children, A.
    Hag, The ("Hag is astride, The.")
    Hag, The ("Staff[e] is now greased [or
        greas'd], The.")
    Her Bed.
    Her Legs.
    His Age, Dedicated to His Peculiar Friend,
        Master John Wickes, under the Name of
        Posthumus.
    His Answer to a Friend.
    His Anthem, to Christ on the Cross.
    His Cavalier.
    His Content In the Country.
    His Creed.
    His Desire.
    His Farewell [or Fare-well] to Sack.
    His Grange, or Private Wealth.
    His Hope or Sheet-Anchor.
    His Last Request to Julia.
    His Litany to the Holy Spirit.
    His Offering, with the Rest, at the Sepulcher.
    His Own Epitaph.
    His Poetry His Pillar.
    His Prayer for Absolution.
    His Prayer to Ben Jonson.
    His Request to Julia.
    His Return to London.
    His Sailing from Julia.
    His Saviour['] Words, Going to the Cross[e].
    His Tears to Thamesis [or Thamasis].
    His Winding-Sheet.
    Hock-Cart, or Harvest Home, The.
    Hour-Glass, The.
    How Lillies Came White.
    How Marigolds Came Yellow.
    How Roses Came Red.
    How Violets Came Blue.
    Hymn to the Graces, A.
    Hymne to Love, An.
    Ill Government.
    Impossibilities to His Friend.
    In the Dark None Dainty.
    Invitation, The.
    Julia's Petticoat.
    King and No King, A.
    Kiss[e], A.
    Kisses Loath[e]some.
    Kissing and bussing differ both in this.
    Life is the body's [or Bodies] light, which
        once declining.
    Lily in a Crystal, The.
    Lips Tongueless[e].
    Long and Lazy [or Lazie].
    Love Me Little, Love Me Long.
    Love Palpable.
    Love What It Is.
    Lovers How They Come and Part.
    Lyric[k] for Legacies.
    Lyric to Mirth, A.
    Mad Maid's Song, The.
    Man's Dying-Place Uncertain.
    Matins [or Mattens], or Morning Prayer.
    May-pole is up, The.
    Maypole is up, The.

Meditation for His Mistress[e], A.
Moderation.
Money Gets the Mastery [*or* Masterie].
Money Makes the Mirth.
Mount of the Muses, The.
Music, thou soul of heaven, care-charming spell.
My Ben!
Neutrality Loathsome.
New-Year's [*or* New-Yeares] Gift Sent to Sir Simeon Steward, A.
Night-Piece, to Julia, The.
No Coming to God without Christ.
No Difference in the Dark [*or* i'th'dark].
No Loathsomnesse in Love.
No Lock against Lechery.
Not Every Day Fit for Verse.
Not To Love.
Nothing New.
Nuptiall Song, or Epithalamie, on Sir Clipseby Crew and His Lady, A.
Oberon's Feast.
Oberon's Palace.
Observation ("Virgin-Mother stood at distance (there), The.")
Ode for Ben Jonson, An.
Ode to Master Endymion Porter, upon His Brother's Death, An.
On Himself.
On Himselfe ("I fear no earthly powers.")
On Himselfe ("I will no longer kiss.")
On Himselfe ("I'll [*or* Il'e] write no more of Love; but now repent.")
On Himselfe ("Let me not live, if I not love.")
On Himselfe ("Weepe for the dead, for they have lost this light.")
Orpheus he went (as poets tell).
Panegyric to Sir Lewis Pemberton, A.
Parcæ, The; or, Three Dainty Destinies: The Armilet.
Perfume, The.
Peter-penny, The.
Pillar of Fame, The.
Plaudite, or End of Life, The.
Poet Loves a Mistress, but Not to Marry, The.
Poetry Perpetuates the Poet.
Posting to Printing.
Power and Peace.
Power in the People, The.
Present Time Best Pleaseth, The.
Primrose, The.
Putrefaction is the end.
Rainbow; or Curious Covenant, The.
Request to the Graces, An.
Right Hand, The.
Ring Presented to Julia, A.
Salutation.
Scar[e]-Fire, The.
Seest thou those diamonds which she wears.
Sho[o]e Tying, The.
Silken Snake, The.
Single Life Most Secure.
Spell, The.
Steam in Sacrifice.
Supreme Fortune Falls Soonest.
Temple, The.
Ternarie of Littles, upon a Pipkin of Jellie [*or* Jelly] Sent to a Lady, A.
Thanksgiving to God for His House, A.
Tithe [*or* Tythe]: To the Bride, The.
To a Bed of Tulips.
To a Gentlewoman Objecting to Him His Grey Hairs.
To Anthea ("Ah my Anthea! must my heart still break?")
To Anthea ("Let's call for Hymen if agreed thou art.")
To Anthea Lying in Bed.
To Anthea ("Now is the time, when all the lights wax dim.")
To Anthea, Who May Command Him Anything.
To Blossoms.
To Christ.
To Critic[k]s.

To Crown[e] It.
To Daffodils [*or* Daffadills].
To Daisies, Not to Shut So Soon[e].
To Dean-bourn, a Rude River in Devon, by Which Sometimes He Lived.
To Death.
To Dianeme ("Dear[e], though to part it be a hell.")
To Dianeme ("Give me one kiss.")
To Dianeme ("Show [*or* Shew] me thy feet; show [*or* shew] me thy legs, thy thighs.")
To Dianeme ("Sweet, be not proud of those two eyes.")
To Electra.
To Electra ("I'll [*or* Ile] come to thee in all those shapes.")
To Find[e] God.
To Fortune.
To God: an Anthem, Sung in the Chapel at White-Hall, Before the King.
To God ("Come to me God; but do not come.")
To God ("Do with me, God! as Thou didst deal with John.")
To Groves.
To Heaven.
To His Book.
To His Book ("Before the Press scarce one co'd see.")
To His Book[e] ("Have I not blessed thee? Then go forth; nor fear.")
To His Book[e] ("Make haste away, and let one be.")
To his book's end this last line he'd have placed
To His Conscience.
To His Dying Brother, Master William Herrick.
To His Friend, on the Untunable Times.
To His Friend to Avoid Contention of Words.
To His Honoured and Most Ingenious Friend Mr. Charles Cotton.
To His Kinsman, Master Thomas Herrick, Who Desired to Be in His Book.
To His Kinswoman, Mrs. Penelope Wheeler.
To His Lovely Mistresses.
To His Mistresses.
To His Peculiar Friend Master Thomas Shapcott, Lawyer.
To His Savior [*or* Saviour]. The New Years [*or* yeers] Gift.
To His Saviour, a Child; a Present, by a Child.
To Julia ("How rich and pleasing thou, my Julia, art.")
To Julia ("Julia, when thy Herrick dies.")
To Julia, the Flaminica Dialis, or Queen-Priest.
To Keep a True Lent.
To Larr [*or* Lar].
To Laurels.
To Live Merrily, and To Trust to Good Verses.
To M. Denham, on His Prospective Poem.
To M. Henry Lawes, the Excellent Composer[,] of his Lyrics.
To Marygolds.
To Meadows [*or* Meddowes].
To Mistress Katherine Bradshaw, the Lovely, That Crowned Him with Laurel.
To Music.
To Music: A Song.
To Music, to Becalm a Sweet-sick Youth.
To Music, to Becalm His Fever, *sels.*
To My Ill Reader.
To Oenone ("Thou saist [*or* sayest] Love[']s dart.")
To Oenone ("What conscience, say, is it in thee.")
To Perilla.
To Phyllis to Love and Live with Him.
To Robin Redbreast.
To Sycamores.
To the Detracter.
To the Generous Reader.
To the King.

To the King, upon His Com[m]ing with His Army into the West.
To the King, Upon His Welcome to Hampton Court.
To the Most Fair and Lovely Mistress Anne Soame, Now Lady Abdie.
To the Most Virtuous Mistress Pot, Who Many Times Entertained Him.
To the Reverend Shade of His Religious Father.
To the Right Honourable Mildmay, Earl of Westmorland.
To the Rose; a Song.
To the Sour[e] Reader.
To the Water Nymphs, Drinking at the Fountain.
To the Western Wind.
To the Willow-Tree.
To Violets.
To Virgins.
To [the] Virgins, to Make Much of Time.
To Vulcan.
Transfiguration, The.
Up Tail[e]s All.
Upon a Black Twist, Rounding the Arm of the Countess of Carlisle.
Upon a child.
Upon a Child That Died [*or* Dyed].
Upon a Maid[e].
Upon a Maid ("Gone she is a long, long way.")
Upon a Virgin Kissing a Rose.
Upon a Young Mother of Many Children.
Upon Batt.
Upon Ben Jo[h]nson.
Upon Blanche.
Upon Bunce: Epigram.
Upon Electra.
Upon Groins: Epigram.
Upon Her Eyes.
Upon Her Feet.
Upon Her Voice.
Upon Himself ("Mop-eyed I am, as some have said.")
Upon Himselfe Being Buried.
Upon His Departure Hence.
Upon His Sister-in-Law, Mistress Elizabeth Herrick.
Upon His Spaniel[l] Tracie [*or* Tracy].
Upon His Verses.
Upon Jack and Jill: Epigram.
Upon Julia['s] Washing Herself in the River.
Upon Julia Weeping.
Upon Julia's Breasts.
Upon Julia's Clothes.
Upon Julia's Haire Fill'd with Dew.
Upon Julia's Ribband.
Upon Julia's Voice.
Upon Love, by Way of Question and Answer.
Upon Love ("Love brought me to a silent Grove.")
Upon Lulls.
Upon M. Ben Jo[h]nson: Epigram.
Upon Mistress Elizabeth Wheeler under the Name of Amarillis.
Upon Mistresse Susanna Southwell, Her Cheeks.
Upon Pagget.
Upon Parson Beanes.
Upon Prue [*or* Prew], His Maid.
Upon Rook: Epigram.
Upon Roses.
Upon Scobble [Epigram].
Upon Showbread [*or* Shewbread]: Epigram.
Upon Sibilla.
Upon Some Women.
Upon the Loss[e] of His Mistresses.
Upon the Nipples of Julia's Breast.
Upon the Same.
Upon the Troublesome Times.
Upon Time.
Upon Umber: Epigram.
Vine, The.
Vision, The.
Vision to Electra, The.
Wassaile, The.

Welcome to Sack, The.
What God Is.
What Kind of Mistress[e] He Would Have.
When He Would Have His Verses Read.
White Island.
Why Flowers Change Color.
Widow's Tears [or Widdowes Teares]: or,
  Dirge of Dorcas, The.
Wounded Cupid, The.

Herschberger, Ruth (b. 1917)
Huron, The.
Lumberyard, The.

Herschell, William M. (1873–1939)
Kid Has Gone to the Colors, The.

Hershenson, Miriam
Husbands and Wives.

Hervey, Christopher (fl. mid–18th cent.)
Confusion.

Herzberg, Judith (b. 1934)
Nearer.
On the Death of Sylvia Plath.
Reunion.
Vocation.

Herzing, Albert
Small Boy, Dreaming, A.

Heseltine, Philip
Limerick: "Young things who frequent
  picture-palaces, The."

Hesiod (fl. c.700 B.C.)
Against sloth.
Anatomy of Winter, The.
Bronze Age, The.
Georgics of Heisod, The, sels.
Golden Age, The.
Iron Age, The.
Laertes.
Theogony, sels.
Works and Days, sels.

Hesketh, Phoebe (b. 1909)
Boy with Kite.
Death of a Gardener.
Love's Advocate.

Hesse, Hermann (1877–1962)
Night.
Spring Song.

Hessey, Vera
Frog and the Bird, The.

Hester, M. L. (b. 1947)
Lightning Rod Salesman, The.

Hetherington, Graeme (b. 1937)
Man from Changi, The.

Hewett, Dorothy (b. 1923)
Anniversary.
In Moncur Street.
Moon-Man.
Sanctuary.
Summer Solstice, sels.
This Version of Love.
You Gave Me Hyacinths First a Year Ago.

Hewison, R. J. P.
Genius.
Limerick: "Said an erudite sinologue:
  'How.'"
Limerick: "There was a young girl of
  Trebarwith."
Limerick: "Though Sir James (God's-a-
  Formula) Jeans."

Hewitt, Geof (b. 1943)
Typographical Errors.

Hewitt, John (1907–87)
Because I paced my thought by the natural
  world.
Calling on Peadar O'Donnell at Dungloe.
Father's Death, A.
From a Museum Man's Album.
From the Tibetan.
Frontier, The.
Glens, The.
I write for my own kind.
Ireland.
Irishman in Coventry, An.
King's Horses, The.
Local Poet, A.
O country people, you of the hill farms.
Once alien here my fathers built their house.

Postscript, 1984.
Ram's Horn, The.
Rome Sunday[,] June 1960.
Saint Stephen's Day.
Scar, The.
Search, The.
Sonnets for Roberta (1954), sels.
Substance and Shadow.
Tryst.
Turf-Carrier [or Turf Carrier] on Aranmore.
Ulster Names.
Whit Monday.

Hey, Phil
True Ballad of the Great Race to Gilmore
  City, The.

Heyen, William (b. 1940)
Dog Sacrifice at Lake Ronkonkoma.
I Move to Random Consolations.
King's Men, The.
Passover: the Injections.
Riddle: "From Belsen a crate of gold teeth."
Snapper, The.
Spirit of Wrath, The.
Steadying, The.
Tie, The.

Heym, Georg
War.
Why do you visit me, white moths, so often?

Heyrick, Thomas (1649–94)
On a Sunbeam.
On an Indian Tomineois, the Least of Birds.

Heyward, DuBose (1885–1940)
Equinox.
Jasbo Brown.

Heywood, John (c.1497–1580)
Ballad on the Marriage of Philip and Mary,
  A, sels.
Epygrams, sels.
Of Use.
On Botching.
Praise of His Lady, A.
Quiet Neighbour, A.

Heywood, Thomas (1575?–1650)
Apology for Actors, An, sels.
Epitaph, An: "I was, I am not; smiled, that
  since did weep."
Hierarchie of the Blessed Angells, sels.
Jupiter and Ganimede.
Rape of Lucrece, The, sels.

Hibernicus Exul (fl. 8th–9th cent.)
O Christ, receive these souls in thy Mother's
  house.

Hicks, Berryman (1778–1839)
Time Is Swiftly Rolling On, The.

Hickson, William E. (1803–70)
Walking Song.

Hicky, Daniel Whitehead (b. 1902)
No Friend Like Music.
When a man turns homeward through the
  moonfall.

Hidalgo, José (b. 1934)
No.

Hiebert, Paul Gerhardt (b. 1892)
Farmer and the Farmer's Wife, The.

Hiểu, Nguyễn Khắc. See Tản Đà

Higgins, Brian (1930–65)
Analogy.
Baedeker for Metaphysicians.
Corrupt Man in the French Pub, The.
Genesis.

Higgins, Frederick Robert (1896–1941)
Ballad of O'Bruadir, The.
Captain Noah.
Chinese Winter.
Father and Son.
Little Clan, The.
O You among Women.
Old Jockey, The.
Padraic O'Conaire—Gaelic Storyteller.
Song for the Clatter-Bones.

Higginson, Thomas Wentworth (1823–1911)
Ode to a Butterfly.
Past Is Dark with Sin and Shame, The.
To Thine Eternal Arms, O God.

Higginson, William J.
Before the descent.
Ducks land, The.
Evening star.
High tide.
Holding the water.
I look up.
Interstices.
More intricate.
Robin listens, A.
Summer moon.
This spring rain.
Writing again.

Higgs, Barry O. (b. 1943)
Deaf is like.
In Lord Carpenter's Country.
Night Shore.
Parson's Pleasure.
Reversion.

High, John (b. 1957)
Lives of Thomas—Episodes and Prayers,
  The, sels.

Highet, Gilbert (1906–78)
Homage.

Higo, Aig (b. 1929)
Hidesong.
Ritual Murder.

Hikmet, Nazim (1902–63)
Angina Pectoris.
Cucumber, The.
Evening Walk, The.
Letters from a Man in Solitary.
Letters from Chankiri Prison.
Sad State of Freedom, A.
Since I was thrown inside.
Things I Didn't Know I Loved.

Hilberry, Conrad (b. 1928)
Body and mind, we used to think, were two.
Spoon.

Hildebert (1056–1133)
Christian Rome.
For Whitsuntide.
In Honour of the Holy Spirit.
Mood of Vichy, The.
Nor God, nor man, the image thou dost see.
On the Death of Henry the Lion.
Prayer to God the Father.
Rome.
Shepherd cheerfully, The.
Songs you sent me I have read, The.
To Peter, Bishop of Poitiers, Who Withstood
  William of Aquitaine and Died in Exile.

Hildegard von Bingen (1098–1197)
Alleluia-verse for the Virgin.
Antiphon for Divine Wisdom.
Antiphon for the Angels.
Antiphon for the Holy Spirit.
Holy Spirit, / giving life to all life.
I am the one whose praise.
I am the one whose praise echoes on high.
Like the honeycomb dropping honey.
Now in the people.
O crimson blood.
Song to the Creator.
Soul is kissed by God, The.

Hiley, F. C. W. (fl. 19th cent.)
To a Persian Cat.

Hill, Aaron (1685–1750)
Alone in an Inn at Southampton, April the
  25th, 1737.
Garden Window, The.
May-Day.
Modesty.
On a Lady, Preached into the Colic, by One
  of Her Lovers.
Whitehall Stairs.
Written on a Window.

Hill, Benjamin H.
Tribute to Robert E. Lee.

Hill, E.
When Polly Buys a Hat.

Hill, Geoffrey (b. 1932)
Apology for the Revival of Christian
  Architecture in England, An, sels.
Asmodeus.
Canticle for Good Friday.

Christmas Trees.
Distant Fury of Battle, The.
"Domaine Public."
Four Poems Regarding the Endurance of
Poets, *sels.*
Funeral Music, *sels.*
Genesis.
Guardians, The.
Hymns to Our Lady of Chartres, *sels.*
Imaginative Life, The.
In Memory of Jane Fraser [*or* Frazer].
In Piam Memoriam.
Lachrimae Amantis.
Lachrimae; or Seven Tears Figured in Seven
Passionate Pavans, *sels.*
Mercian Hymns, *sels.*
Merlin.
Mystery of the Charity of Charles Péguy,
The, *sels.*
Orpheus and Eurydice.
Ovid in the Third Reich.
Pentecost Castle, The.
Picture of a Nativity.
Pre-Raphaelite Notebook, A.
Requiem for the Plantagenet Kings.
September Song.
Short History of British India, A.
Song from Armenia, A.
Turtle Dove, The.
Two Chorale-Preludes: On Melodies by Paul
Celan.
Veni Coronaberis.
White Ship, The.
Wreaths.
Hill, Joe (1879–1914)
Preacher and the Slave, The.
Hill, Leona
Let Him Return.
Hill, Leslie Pinckney (1880–1960)
So Quietly.
Tuskegee.
Hill, Roberta. *See* **Whiteman, Roberta Hill**
Hill, Selima (b. 1945)
Below Hekla.
Crossing the Desert in a Pram.
Looking for Camels.
Ram, The.
Voice in the Garden, A.
Hille, Peter (1854–1904)
Beauty.
Maiden, The.
Hillel, Omer (b. 1926)
Sun.
Hillhouse, Augustus Lucas (1792–1859)
Trembling before Thine Awful Throne.
Hillman, Brenda (b. c.1945)
At a Motel.
Cleave and *Cleave.*
Mighty Forms.
Quartz Tractate.
Thoreau's Fossil Lilies.
Hillyer, Robert Silliman (1895–1961)
As One Who Bears beneath His Neighbor's
Roof.
Assassination, The.
Eternal Return, The.
Familiar Faces, Long Departed.
Ivory Tower, The.
Letter to Robert Frost, A.
Lullaby: "Long canoe, The."
Moo!
Nocturne.
Over Bright Summer Seas.
Pastoral: "So soft in the hemlock wood."
Prothalamion, *sels.*
Thought in Time, A.
Hilton, Arthur Clement (1851–77)
Ding Dong.
Heathen Pass-ee, The.
Limerick: "There was a young critic of
King's."
Limerick: "There was a young genius of
Queens'."
Limerick: "There was a young gourmand of
John's."
Limerick: "There was an old fellow of
Trinity."

Octopus.
Hilton, David (b. 1938)
Finding a Chet Baker Album in the
Dimestore 2-for-$1 Pile.
Hilton, John (d. 1657)
Madrigal: "My mistress frowns when she
should play."
Hind bint Utba (fl. early 7th cent.)
Fury against the Moslems at Uhud.
Tambourine song for Soldiers Going into
Battle.
Hind bint Uthatha (fl. early 7th cent.)
To a Hero Dead at al-Safra.
Hindley, Charles (d. 1893)
Mother Shipton's Prophecies.
Hine, Daryl (b. 1936)
Bewilderment at the Entrance of the Fat Boy
into Eden, A.
Côte de Liesse.
Destruction of Sodom, The.
Double-Goer, The.
Fabulary Satire IV.
Here is another poem in a picture.
Letting Go.
March, *sels.*
Plain Fare.
Point Grey.
Riddle: "Invisible, chimerical."
Si Monumentum Requiris.
Survivors, The.
Trompe L'Œil.
Trout, The.
Under the Hill.
Vowel Movements.
Wasp, The.
Hines, Nellie Womack
Home!
Hines, P. R.
My Garden.
Hinh, Nguyễn thi. *See* **Thanh Quan, (Lady)**
Hinkson, Katharine Tynan. *See* **Tynan,
Katharine**
Hinsley, Clarissa
My Newts.
Hioki no Ko-okima
On the shore of Nawa. *From* Manyo Shu,
Part 3 of 4.
Hiott, Lynda
Tale of Mushrooms.
Hippius, Zinaida (1869–1945)
Grey Frock, A.
L'Imprévisibilité.
Hippolyte, Kendel (b. 1952)
Air between Us (for an Expatriate), The.
Caribbean Exorcism Poem, A.
Jah Son / Another Way.
Reggae Cat (for Boston Jack).
Revo Lyric.
Hiranandani, Popati (b. 1924)
Husband.
Hirsch, Edward (b. 1950)
After the Last Practice.
Art Pepper.
Fast Break.
For the New World.
For the Sleepwalkers.
Man on a Fire Escape.
My Father's Back.
Short Lexicon of Torture in the Eighties, A.
Skokie Theatre, The.
Unearthly Voices.
Watcher, The.
When Skyscrapers Were Invented in Chicago.
Hirschman, Jack (b. 1933)
Headlands.
Transfiguration.
X L E B.
Hirshbein, Peretz (b. 1880)
Captive.
I Shall Weep.
Stars Fade.
Hirshfield, Jane
For the Women of Poland: December 1981.
In a Net of Blue and Gold.

Justice without Passion.
Of Gravity & Angels.
Story, A.
To Drink.
Hisho. *See* **Ryojin Hisho**
Hitchcock, George
Figures in a Ruined Ballroom.
May All Earth Be Clothed in Light.
One Whose Reproach I Cannot Evade, The.
Scattering Flowers.
Song of Expectancy.
Three Found Poems.
Three Portraits.
United States Prepare for the Permanent
Revolution, The.
**Hitomaro (Kakinomoto no Hitomaro) (fl. 7th–
8th cent.)**
Bay of Tsunu, The.
Colored leaves, The.
For my sister's sake. *From* Manyo Shu, Part
1 of 4.
Gossip grows like weeds.
I sit at home.
In the empty mountains.
In the sea of ivy clothed Iwami. *From*
Manyo Shu, Part 2 of 4.
May the men who are born. *From* Manyo
Shu, Part 2 of 4.
My girl is waiting for me.
My thoughts are with a boat.
O boy cutting grass. *From* Manyo Shu, Part
3 of 4.
On the Eastern horizon.
On the moor of Kasuga. *From* Manyo Shu,
Part 3 of 4.
On the shingle.
Pheasant of the mountain, The.
Plovers cry, The.
Strange old man, A.
This morning I will not.
When, / Halting in front of it, I look. *From*
Shui Shu.
When I gathered flowers.
When I left my girl.
When she was still alive. *From* Manyo Shu,
Part 4 of 4.
Your hair has turned white.
Hittan of Tayyi
Hamasah, *sels.*
Ho Ch'e Ch'ang (659–744)
Homecoming.
Ho Chi Minh (1890–1969)
Song of a Cotton Yarn, The.
Ho Ching-ming (1483–1521)
Alone I stand, facing the flowers' shade.
Ballad of the Government Granary Clerk.
Ballad of Yi River.
Bamboo Branch Song.
Ch'ang-an.
Ch'en-hsi County.
Fish in a Painting.
Night of the Fourteenth.
Presented to Wang Wen-hsi.
Rainy Night.
Seeing Off Han Ju-ch'ing as He Returns to
the Land Within the Passes.
Song of the Painting "River and Mountains,"
by Wu Wei.
Hồ Dzềnh Hà Triệu Anh (b. 1919)
Shilly-Shally.
Ho Hsun (d. 527)
Spring Breeze.
Traveler with his heavy heart, The.
Ho Hyongman (b. 1945)
For the Poor.
Snowfall on the Seas.
Ho Nansorhon (1563–1603)
Woman's Sorrow, A, *sels.*
Ho Sun (d. 518)
At Parting.
Hồ Văn Hảo (b. 1917)
Revolutionary Youth.
Ho Xuan Huong (fl. late 18th cent.)
Bonze Got Stung By a Bee, The.
Buddhist Priest, A.

Cake-That-Drifts-in-Water, The.
Carved on an Areca Nut.
Confession.
Elegy for the Prefect of Vĩnh-tu'ò'ng.
Funny Grotto, The.
Girl Caught Napping By Day, A.
Girl Without a Sex, The.
Jackfruit, The.
Man-and-Wife Mountain, The.
Ode to the Fan.
On Being a Concubine.
On Hearing a Woman Mourn Her Husband.
On Picking Flowers.
Poking Fun At a Bonze.
Scolding Some Dunces.
Shrine of Ts'en Yi-tung, The.
Snail.
Swinging.
Threefold Pass, The.
Unwed Mother, An.
Woman Lies Alone, A.

Hoagland, Everett (b. 1942)
Anti-Semanticist, The.
Big Zeb Johnson.
Gorée ten miles offshore beckons.
It's a Terrible Thing!
Love Child—a Black Aesthetic.
My Spring Thing.

Hoagland, Tony
In the Land of the Lotus Eaters.
One Season.
Poem for Men Only.
Question, The.
Sweet Rain.

Hoàn, Đặng Trí. *See* **Hà Huyền Chi**
Hoan, Phan Ngọc. *See* **Chế Lan Viên**
Hoàng Trinh (*fl.* 20th cent.)
Forty.

Hoare, Florence
Pedlar Jim.

Hoare, Prince (1755–1834)
Arethusa, The.

Hoatson, Florence
Autumn.
Bird Bath, The.
Who?

Hoban, Russell (b. 1925)
Egg Thoughts.
Friendly Cinnamon Bun, The.
Jigsaw Puzzle.
October Tuesday.
Old Man Ocean, how do you pound.
Pedalling Man, The.
Small, Smaller.
Summer goes, summer goes.
Tin Frog, The.
What the Wind Said.
Windows.

Hoberman, Mary Ann (b. 1930)
Bugs, *sels.*
Folk Who Live in Backward Town, The.
Let's dress up in grown-up clothes.

Hobsbaum, Philip (b. 1932)
Lesson in Love, A.

Hoccleve [*or* Occleve], Thomas (1370?–1450?)
De Regimine Principum, *sels.*
Hoccleve's Complaint, *sels.*
Regement of Princes, *sels.*

Hoch, Edward Wallis
Good and Bad.

Hochman, Sandra (b. 1936)
Couple, The.
Goldfish Wife, The.

Hodes, Aubrey (b. 1927)
Jew Walks in Westminster Abbey, A.

Hodge, Arthur J. (*fl.* late 19th cent.)
Five Were Foolish.

Hodgins, Philip (b. 1959)
Death Who.
Making Hay.
Self-Pity.
Shooting the Dogs.

Hodgkinson, T.
Sand of Palestine, The.

Hodgson, A. B. L.
In Memoriam.

Hodgson, Ralph (1871–1962)
After.
Bells of Heaven, The.
Birdcatcher, The.
Bull, The.
Eve, with her basket, was.
Flying Scrolls, *sels.*
Ghoul Care.
Gipsy Girl, The.
Great Auk's ghost rose on one leg, The.
Hammers, The.
House across the Way, The.
Hymn to Moloch.
Late, Last Rook, The.
Moor, The.
Mystery, The.
Reason Has Moons.
Silver Wedding.
Song of Honor [*or* Honour], The.
Stupidity Street.
Time.
Time, You Old Gypsy Man.

Hodgson, William Noel (1893–1916)
Back to Rest.
Before Action.
England to Her Sons.
Glimpse.

Hodza, Aaron (1924–83)
Slighted Wife, The.

Hoffenstein, Samuel (1890–1947)
As the Crow Flies, Let Him Fly, *sels.*
Babies Haven't Any Hair.
Birdie McReynolds.
Dry.
I'm fond of doctors and drivers of hacks.
Invocation, *sels.*
Invocation: "Come, lovely Muse, desert for me."
Love-Songs, at Once Tender and Informative.
Lullaby: "Sleep, my little baby, sleep."
Makes the Little Ones Dizzy.
Mimic Muse, The, *sels.*
Miss Millay Says Something Too.
Mr. Vachel Lindsay Discovers Radio.
Poems in Praise of Practically Nothing, *sels.*
Progress.
Sheep.
Shropshire Lad's Cousin, The.
Songs about Life and Brighter Things Yet, *sels.*
Songs of Fairly Utter Despair, *sels.*
Unequal Distribution.

Hoffman, Balthasar (1686–1775)
Be Glorified Eternally.

Hoffman, Charles Fenno (1806–88)
Monterey.

Hoffman, Daniel Gerard (b. 1923)
As I Was Going to Saint Ives.
Center of Attention, The.
È, the Feasting Florentines.
Exploration.
Lines Written near Linton, on Exmoor.
Seals in Penobscot Bay, The.
Signatures.
Special Train, A.
Three Jovial Gentlemen.
Who was it came.

Hoffman, O. S.
Five best doctors anywhere, The.

Hoffman, Sydney
Limerick: "No Portuguese Lady is Nautical."

Hoffmann, Heinrich (1809–94)
Story of Augustus Who Would Not Have Any Soup, The.
Story of Fidgety Philip, The.
Story of Johnny Head-in-Air, The.

Hoffmann, Roald
Deceptively Like a Solid.

Hofmann, Michael (b. 1957)
First Night.

Hofmannsthal, Hugo von (1874–1929)
Ballad of the Outer Life.
Emperor of China Speaks, The.
Many Indeed Must Perish in the Keel.
Ship's Cook, a Captive Sings, The.
Stanzas on Mutability.

Travel Song.
Two, The.
Two of Them, The.
Venetian Night, A.
Vision, A.
World-Secret.

Hofmannswaldau, Christian Hofmann von
Beauty's Transitoriness.
Description of Perfect Beauty.
He Loves in Vain.
So sweet, so golden.

Hofshteyn [*or* Hofstein], Dovid [*or* David] (1889–1952)
My Thread.

Hogan, Linda (b. 1947)
Bear Fat.
Celebration: Birth of a Colt.
Daybreak.
Eclipse II.
Friday Night.
Gamble.
Heritage.
Lost Girls, The.
Man in the Moon.
Map.
New Apartment.
Our Houses.
Rainy Season, The.
Seeing through the Sun.
Thought, A.
To Light.
Truth Is, The.
Workday.

Hogan, Michael (b. 1943)
Spring

Hogg, James ("The Ettrick Shepherd") (1770–1835)
Boy's Song, A.
Flying Tailor, The.
Isabelle.
James Rigg.
Lock the door, Lariston, lion of Liddesdale.
McLean's Welcome.
Queen's Wake, The, *sels.*
To The Right Honourable Lord Byron, *sels.*
Walsinghame's Song.
When Maggy Gangs Away.
When the Kye Comes Hame.
Witch's Chant, A.

Hogg, Robert (b. 1942)
Little Falls.

Hoggra, Robert
Poem: "In its going down, the moon."

Holan, Vladimir (1905–80)
At Mother's After Many Years.
Between the idea and the word.
But.
Cave of Words, The.
Chicken, The.
Children at Christmas in 1945.
Epoch.
Glimpsed from the train, which takes shadow for truth.
How to live? How be simple and literal?
In the Yard of the Policlinic.
Meeting in a Lift.
Memory II.
Mother.
Old Priest, The.
Reminiscence.
Resurrection.
To the Enemies.
You're thinking of children, of their.

Holbrook, David (b. 1923)
Drought.
Maternity Gown.

Holbrook, Weare
Varitalk.

Holcroft, Thomas (1745–1809)
Dying Prostitute, The; an Elegy.
Fool's Song.
Gaffer Gray.
On Shakespeare and Voltaire.
Seasons, The.
Song: "When o'er the wold the heedless lamb."

To Haydn.

Holden, Jonathan (b. 1941)
Against Paradise.
Alone is delicious.
American Boyhood, An.
Dancing School.
Falling from Stardom.
Liberace.
Losers.
Seventeen.
Tumbleweed.
Wisdom Tooth, The.

Holden, Molly (b. 1927)
Giant Decorative Dahlias.
Photograph of Haymaker, 1890.
Seaman, 1941.

Holden, Oliver (1765–1844)
How Sweet Is the Language of Love.
Weeping Sinner, Dry Your Tears.
Within These Doors Assembled Now.

Holden, Stephen (b. 1939)
In Praise of Antonioni.

Holder, C. S.
King's Wood, The.

Hölderlin, Friedrich (1770–1843)
Bread and Wine, *sels.*
Half of Life.
In the Days of Socrates.
Patmos.
Ripe, Being Plunged into Fire.

"Holiday, Billie" (Eleanora Fagan) (1915–1959)
Fine and Mellow.

Holland, Hugh (1569–1635)
Epitaph on Prince Henry.
Upon the Lines and Life of the Famous
Scenic Poet, Master William Shakespeare.

Holland, Josiah Gilbert (1819–81)
God, Give Us Men!
Marble Prophecy, The, *sels.*
To My Dog "Blanco."
Where Shall the Baby's Dimple Be.

Holland, Norah M. (1876–1925)
Little Dog-Angel, A.

Holland, Sir Richard (c.1420–c.1485)
Buke of the Howlat, The, *sels.*

Holland, Rupert Sargent
Foolish Flowers.

Hollander, John (b. 1929)
Adam's Task.
Angler's Story, The.
Appearance and Reality.
Back to Town.
Breadth. Circle. Desert. Monarch. Month.
Wisdom.
Curse, The.
Danish Wit.
Effet de Neige.
Garden, The.
Great Bear, The.
Grounds of Winter.
Hall of Ocean Life.
Helicon.
Heliogabalus.
Historical Reflections.
In the Gallery.
Lady at the Castle, The.
Lady's-Maid's Song, The.
Last Words.
Late Fourth, A.
Lion Named Passion, A.
Mad Potter, The.
Morning in the Islands.
Movie-Going.
Night Mirror, The.
Ninth of July, The.
No Foundation.
Old-Fashioned Song, An.
Old Guitar, The.
One of Our Walks.
Powers of Thirteen, *sels.*
Russian Soul II, The.
Some Walks with You.
State of Nature, A.
Sunday Evenings.
Swan and Shadow.
There was an end to hearts and rhymes.

To the Lady Portrayed by Margaret Dumont.
Under Cancer.
Variations on a Fragment by Trumbull
Stickney.
Violet.
Why have I locked myself inside.

Hollander, Martha
Central Park.

Hollander, Robert (b. 1933)
You Too? Me Too—Why Not? Soda Pop.

Hollenbeck, Peter
Anorexia.

Höllerer, Walter
Held back, like a bow drawn tight.

Hollis, Mark (b. 1908)
Careless Talk.
'Twixt Cup and Lip.

Hollo, Anselm (b. 1934)
Amazing Grace.
Buffalo—Isle of Wight Power Cable.
Discovery of LSD a True Story, The.
Dream of Instant Total Representation, The.
Godlike.
Italics.
Journey, 1966.
Le Jazz Hot.
Mescalito.
On the occasion of becoming an echo.
Rain.
Shed the Fear.
That Old Sauna High.
Wasp Sex Myth (One).
Wasp Sex Myth (Two).
Wild West Workshop Poem.

Holloway, Geoffrey
Grown-ups.

Holloway, John (b. 1920)
Ulysses.

Holloway, Lucy Ariel Williams (b. 1905)
Northboun'.

Holloway, Stanley (1890–1982)
Old Sam.

Holly, Joseph Cephas (1825–55)
Our family tree is in the sear.
Patriot's Lament, The.
This Is a Fatherland to Me.
Wreath of Holly, A.

Holm, Bill
Advice.

Holman, Felice (b. 1919)
City Dump, The.
I Can Fly.
Supermarket.

Holman, Jesse L. (1783–1842)
Lord, in Thy Presence Here.

Holman, M. Carl (b. 1919)
And on This Shore.
Mr. Z.
Notes for a Movie Script.
Picnic: the Liberated.

Holmes, Abiel (1763–1837)
To Thee, O God.
Who Here Can Cast His Eyes Abroad.

Holmes, Georgiana Klingle. See "Klingle, George"

Holmes, Janet
Against the Literal.
Love of the Flesh, The.

Holmes, John (1904–62)
Boy Reading.
Evening Meal in the Twentieth Century.
Good Night! Good Night!
Herself listening to herself, having no name.
Letter to My Mother, *sels.*
Map of My Country, A.
Metaphor for My Son.
Misery is a good thing if misery is spread.
Peace Is the Mind's Old Wilderness.
Somerset Dam for Supper, The.
Thrifty Elephant, The.

Holmes, John Haynes (1879–1964)
God of the Nations, Near and Far.
O'er Continent and Ocean.
Voice of God Is Calling, The.

Holmes, Oliver Wendell (1809–94)
Angel of Peace, Thou Hast Wandered Too
Long.
At the "Atlantic" Dinner, December 15,
1874.
Autocrat of the Breakfast Table, The, *sels.*
Cacoëthes Scribendi.
Daily Trials.
Dorothy Q.
Flaneur, The.
Height of the Ridiculous, The.
Iris, Her Book.
Last Leaf, The.
Latter-Day Warnings.
Limerick: "Reverend Henry Ward Beecher,
The."
Many Things.
My aunt! my dear unmarried aunt!
Nearing the Snow-Line.
Ode for a Social Meeting.
Old Ironsides.
Old Man Dreams, The.
Our Father! While Our Hearts Unlearn.
Our Limitations.
Parody on "A Psalm of Life," A.
Ploughman, The.
Poem for the Meeting of the American
Medical Association, A.
Poet's Lot, The.
Prelude to a Volume Printed in Raised
Letters for the Blind.
Professor at the Breakfast Table, The, *sels.*
Prologue.
Sea Dialogue, A.
Tartarus.
Two Streams, The.
Wind-Clouds and Star-Drifts, *sels.*

Holmes, R. Ernest (b. 1943)
Little girl's heart must be wide and, A.

Holmes, Ruth
No Thoroughfare.

Holmes, Timothy (b. 1936)
Deep.
Room for All.

Holmes, W. F.
Old Brown Horse, The.

Holmes, W. K.
Dream Ship, The.

Holst-Warhaft, Gail
In the end is the body—what we know.
Old Men of Athens, The.
St. John, *sels.*
St. Matthew, *sels.*

Holt, Christian
Dear heavenly Father.

Holt, Jane (fl. 1701–17)
To Mr. Wren, My Valentine Six Year Old.

Holtby, Mary
Answer to a Kind Enquiry.
Dawn Chorus.
Limerick: "Said Mars when entangled with
Venus."
Limerick: "There once was a lass of Shalott."
Limerick: "There once was monarch called
Harry."
Sister Swallow to Swinburne.

Holtby, Winifred (1898–1935)
Beauty the Lover's Gift?
Boats in the Bay.
For the Ghost of Elinor Wylie.
Man who hated the spring was cold and
narrow, The.
Resurrection.
Trains in France.

Hölty, Ludwig Heinrich Christoph (1748–76)
Harvest Song.

Holub, Miroslav (b. 1923)
Achilles and the Tortoise.
Biodrama.
Boy's Head, A.
Brief Reflection on Cats Growing in Trees.
Brief Reflection on Charlemagne.
Brief Thoughts on cats Growing on Trees.
Brief Thoughts on Cracks.
Brief Thoughts on Floods.
Bullfight.

Corporal Who Killed Archimedes, The.
Crocheting.
Death in the Evening.
Experimental Animals.
Fairy Tale.
Fly, The.
Forest, The.
Franklin Bridge in Philadelphia, The.
Garden of Old People, The.
Gila Desert in Arizona, The.
Great and Strong.
Helping Hand, A.
History Lesson, A.
How to Paint a Perfect Christmas.
Immanuel Kant.
In the Miscroscope.
Interferon.
Inventions.
Jewish Cemetery at Olsany, Kafka's Grave,
    April, Sunny Weather, The.
Lesson, The.
Man Cursing the Sea.
Napoleon.
On the Origin of the Contrary.
One-Way Conversation About Radio City
    Music Hall, A.
Silence.
Suffering.
Swans in Flight.
Vanishing Lung Syndrome.
Wings.
Zito the Magician.

Holyday, Barten (1593–1661)
Bogs, purgatory, wolves and ease, by fame.
Clay, sand, and rock, seem of a diff'rent
    birth.
Pride cannot see itself by mid-day light.

Holz, Arno (1863–1929)
Buddha.
Leave-Taking, A.
Phantasus, *sels.*
Roses Red.

"Home, Cecil." *See* **Webster, Augusta Davies**

Homer (*fl.* before 700 B.C.)
Battle of the Frogs and Mice, The, *sels.*
Iliad, The, *sels.*
Odyssey, *sels.*

Hone, William (1780–1838)
Political House that Jack Built, The, *sels.*

Honestus (*fl.* A.D. 40)
I would never marry a young girl or an old
    woman.
Thebes.
Very day one son was drowned, The.

Hồng Chu'o'ng (b. 1921)
It's Me, Your Son.

Hong, Yun-gi (b. 1933)
Maple Leaves.
Thunder.

Hong, Yunsuk (b. 1925)
On Ornament.
Spring Fever.

Hongo, Garrett Kaoru (b. 1951)
Eruption: Pu'u Ō'ō.
Four Chinatown Figures.
Hilo: First Night Back.
Hongo Store 29 Miles Volcano Hilo, Hawaii,
    The.
Legend, The.
Mendocino Rose.
O-Bon: Dance for the Dead.
Pier, The.
Redness: Thinking it Through.
Something Whispered in the *Shakuhachi.*
Stay with Me.
Underworld, The.
Unreal Dwelling: My Years in Volcano, The.
Who Among You Knows the Essence of
    Garlic?
Winnings.
Yellow Light.

Honig, Edwin (b. 1919)
Being Somebody.
Bodega, Goodbye.
November through a Giant Copper Beech.
Now, My Usefullness Over.

Tête-à-Tête.
Through You.
To Restore a Dead Child, *sels.*
Walt Whitman.
Who.

Hood, Thomas (1799–1845)
Ballad: Time of Roses.
Bed-time.
Bridge of Sighs, The.
Butcher, A.
Choosing Their Names.
Death-Bed, The.
Domestic Asides; or, Truth in Parentheses.
Domestic Poems, *sels.*
Dream Fairy, The.
Dust to Dust.
Epicurean Reminiscences of a Sentimentalist.
Fair Ines.
Faithless Nelly Gray.
Faithless Sally Brown.
False Poets and True.
First Attempt in Rhyme, A.
Flying Visit, A.
Friendly Address, A.
Good Night.
Haunted House, The, *sels.*
I remember, I remember.
Irish Schoolmaster, The.
Jack Hall.
Lament of Toby the Learned Pig, The.
Little Piggies, The.
Love.
Miss Kilmansegg and Her Precious Leg, *sels.*
No sun—no moon!
Nocturnal Sketch, A.
Ode: Autumn.
Ode on a Distant Prospect of Clapham
    Academy.
On the Death of the Giraffe.
Our Village—by a Villager.
Parental Ode to My Son, Aged Three Years
    and Five Months, A.
Plea of the Midsummer Fairies, The, *sels.*
Poet's Fate, The.
Poor dear dead have been laid out in vain,
    The.
Public Dinner, A.
Reflection, A.
Ruth.
Sally Simpkin's Lament, [*or* John Jones's
    Kit-Cat-astrophe].
Sea of Death, The.
Silence.
Song.
Song of the Shirt, The.
Sonnet: "It is not death, that sometime in a
    sigh."
Sonnet to Vauxhall.
Sonnet Written in Keats's *Endymion.*
To a False Friend.
To Henrietta, on Her Departure for Calais.
To Minerva.
Two Swans, The.
Water Lady, The.
World Is with Me, The.

Hood, Thomas [*or* "Tom"], Jr. (1835–74)
Ballad of the Basking Shark, The.
Confounded Nonsense.
Ravings.

Hoofdakker, Rudi van den. *See* **Kopland,
Rutger**

Hook, Theodore (1788–1841)
Cautionary Verses to Youth of Both Sexes.

Hookes, N. (1628–1712)
To Amanda Walking in the Garden.

Hooks, Bell (b. 1952)
Body Inside the Soul, The.
Woman's Mourning Song, The.

Hoole, Barbara
Poems, *sels.*

Hooper, Ellen S. (1812–48)
Better a sin which purposed wrong to none.
Duty.
Heart, heart, lie still.

Hooper, Peter (b. 1919)
Pencilled by the Rain.

Hooper, Virginia (b. 1955)
Argument for Resurrection.
Deep Season.
Drawing Room Drama.
Lost in the Galleries.
Reading, A.
Seven Doors Away.

Hooton, Harry (1908–61)
Sweet Disorder in the Dress, A.

Hoover, Herbert
Boy has two jobs, A.

Hoover, Paul (b. 1946)
Baseball.
Desire.
Heart's Ease.
Poems We Can Understand.
Theory.

Hope, Alec Derwent (b. 1907)
Advice to Young Ladies.
Australia.
Bed, The.
Beware of Ruins.
Beyond Phigalia.
Blason, A.
Bounce to Pope.
Brides, The.
Commination, A.
Death of the Bird, The.
Double Looking Glass, The.
Dunciad Minor, *sels.*
E Questo il Nido in Che la Mia Fenice?
Easter Hymn.
Fafnir.
Faustus.
Female Principle, The.
Flower Poem.
Gateway, The.
Gloss to Matthew V 27–28.
Hay Fever.
House of God, The.
Imperial Adam, naked in the dew.
Inscription for a War.
Lingam and the Yoni, The.
Lot and His Daughters I.
Lot and His Daughters II.
Martyrdom of St. Theresa, The.
Massacre of the Innocents.
Meditation on a Bone.
Möbius Strip-Tease.
Moschus Moschiferus.
Observation Car.
On an Engraving by Casserius.
Parabola.
Paradise Saved.
Prometheus Unbound.
Return of Persephone, The.
School Of Night, The.
St. Luke, *sels.*
Tiger.
Under Sedation.

Hope, Allan. *See* **Mutabaruka**

Hope, Christopher (b. 1944)
Flight of the White South Africans, The.
Lines on a Boer War Pin-up Girl Seen in the
    Falcon Hotel, Bude.

**"Hope, Laurence" (Adela Florence Cory
Nicolson) (1815–1904)**
Kashmiri Song.
Request.
Teak Forest, The, *sels.*
Youth.

Hope, T.
Death Again.

Hopi Oral Tradition
Song of Creation.

Hopkins, Ellice
Life in Death.

Hopkins, Gerard Manley (1844–89)
Andromeda.
At the Wedding March.
Binsey Poplars (Felled 1879).
Blessed Virgin Compared to the Air We
    Breathe, The.
Bugler's First Communion, The.
Caged Skylark, The.
Candle Indoors, The.

Hopkins

Carrion Comfort.
Child Is Father to the Man, The.
Cuckoo, The.
Duns Scotus's Oxford.
Felix Randal the farrier,° O is he dead then? my duty / all ended.
Fragments, sels.
God's Grandeur.
Habit of Perfection, The.
Hailstorm in May.
Handsome Heart, The.
Harry Ploughman.
Heaven-Haven.
Hurrahing in Harvest.
I wake and feel the fell of dark, not day.
In Honour of St. Alphonsus Rodriguez.
In the Valley of the Elwy.
Inversnaid.
It was a hard thing to undo this knot.
Lantern Out of Doors, The.
Leaden Echo and the Golden Echo, The.
May Magnificat, The.
Moonless darkness stands between.
Moonrise.
Mrs. Hopley, on Seeing Her Children Say Goodnight to Their Father.
My own heart let me more have pity on; let.
Not of All My Eyes See.
Peace.
Pied Beauty.
Rainbow, The.
Sea and the Skylark, The.
Seven Epigrams, sels.
She schools the flighty pupils of her eyes.
Soliloquy of One of the Spies Left in the Wilderness, A.
Sonnet: "No worst, there is none. Pitched past pitch of grief."
Sonnet: "Patience, hard thing! the hard thing but to pray."
Sonnet: "Shepherd's brow, fronting forked lightning, owns, The."
Spelt from Sibyl's Leaves.
Spring.
Spring and Fall.
Starlight Night, The.
Summer Malison, The.
That Nature Is a Heraclitean Fire and of the Comfort of the Resurrection.
Thou art indeed just, Lord, if I contend.
To His Watch.
To R. B.
To seem the stranger lies my lot, my life.
To what serves mortal beauty—dangerous; does set danc.
Tom's Garland: Upon the Unemployed.
Trio of Triolets, A, sels.
What I Do Is Me.
Windhover, The.
Winter with the Gulf Stream.
Woodlark, The.
Wreck of the Deutschland, The, sels.

Hopkins, John (c.1520–1570)
Thou, Lord, Hast Been Our Sure Defense.

Hopkins, John Henry, Jr. (1810–91)
Alleluia! Christ is risen today.
God of Our Fathers, Bless This Our Land.
We Three Kings of Orient are.

Hopkins, Josiah (1786–1862)
O Turn Ye, O Turn Ye.

Hopkins, Lee Bennett (b. 1938)
Flash.
This Tooth.

Hopkins, Tim (1859–1936)
Do Not Go Gentle ("Do not go gentle into Death's esteemed vale.")
Limerick: "She was caught, a young girl of Uttoxeter."
Limerick: "Ther once was this ladye from Tyre."
Limerick: "Three wonderful people called Ley."
Limerick: "Viscount Stansgate, or Wedgwood, or Benn."
There's a latent queer.

Hopkinson, Abdur-Rahman Slade (b. 1934)
Chord, The.
December 1974: a Lament.
Madwoman of Papine, The.
Origami.
Tycoon, Poet, Saint.

Hopkinson, Francis (1737–91)
Arise and see the glorious sun.
At Length the Busy Day Is Done.
Battle of the Kegs, The.

Hopkinson, Joseph (1770–1842)
Hail, Columbia.

Hoppe, Anna (1889–1941)
Precious Child, So Sweetly Sleeping.

Hopper, Edward (1818–88)
Jesus Saviour, Pilot Me.
They Pray the Best Who Pray and Watch.

Hopwood, Ronald Arthur (1868–1949)
Mystery Ships, The.

Horace (Quintus Horatius Flaccus) (65–8 B.C.)
Ad Ministram.
Art of Cookery, In Imitation of Horace's Art of Poetry. To Dr. Lister, The, sels.
Art of Poetry, The, sels.
Ask not ungainly askings of the end.
Being half foxt he praiseth Bacchus.
Boy, I hate their empty shows.
Candidate, The, sels.
Conclusion. After the Manner of Horace, ad librum suum, The.
Conservation.
Dialogue in Imitation of that between Horace and Lydia, A.
Diffugere nives, redeunt iam gramina campis.
18th Ode 1st Book, translated or rather Imitated.
8th Ode of Book I. of Horace imitated in the Cumberland Manner and Dialect, The.
Epistle: To Elizabeth, Countess of Rutland.
Epistles, sels.
Epode 2, sels.
Epodes, sels.
Explanation of America, An, sels.
First Epistle of the Second Book of Horace, Imitated, The, sels.
First Ode of the Fourth Book of Horace, The.
First Satire of the Second Book of Horace, Imitated: To Mr. Fortescue, The, sels.
Fourteenth Ode of the Second Book of Horace, The.
Good bailiff of my farm, that snug domain.
Harlequin-Horace, The, sels.
Hints from Horace, sels.
Horat. Carm. lib. 4. Ode 13.
If, O Maecenas, versed in lore antique.
Imitation of Horace. Book I, Satyr IX, Written in June, 1681, An, sels.
Imitation of the Seventeenth Epistle of the First Book of Horace. Address'd to Dr. S[wi]ft, An, sels.
Imitation of the Sixth Satire of the Second Book of Horace, An, sels.
Mark of success in this painful discrimination, A.
Need for consistency, The.
Ne'er fash your thumb what gods decree.
New Buildings.
Nunc est bibendum, Cleopatra's Death.
Ode of Horace, not exactly copyed, but rudely imitated, An, sels.
Odes, sels.
People's fury cannot move, The.
Reconcilement between Jacob Tonson and Mr Congreve. An Imitation of Horace, Book III. Ode IX, The.
Remember, when blinde Fortune knits her brow.
Satires, The, sels.
Simplicity.
Snow's on the fellside, look! How deep.
Soracte.
Such is the worlde, who beares the swey.
Three Odes of Horace, sels.
Tibullus, pull yourself together!
'Tis hard, to speake things common, properly.
To his Friend in Love with a young Girl.
To Posthumus.
To the People of Rome, Commiserating the Common-Wealth, in respect of the Civil Warres, sels.
Translation from Horace.
Translation of the 16th Ode of the 2d. Book of Horace.
What lissom boy among the roses.
What young Raw Muisted Beau Bred at his Glass.
Will, sels.
You cant grip years, Posthume.

Horan, Robert (b. 1922)
By Hallucination Visited.
Farewell to Narcissus.

Horder, John (b. 1936)
Sick image of my father fades, The.

Horgan, Paul (b. 1903)
Now Evening Puts Amen to Day.
Tintype of a Private in the Fifteenth Georgia Infantry.

Horikawa, Lady (fl. 12th cent.)
How can one e'er be sure. From Hyaku-Nin-Isshu.
How long will it last?
Will he always love me?

Horn, Edward Newman (b. 1903)
Pussycat sits on a chair.

Horne, Frank (b. 1899)
Kid Stuff.
Letters [or Notes] Found near a Suicide, sels.
Mamma!
On Seeing Two Brown Boys in a Catholic Church.
Patience. . . patience.
Resurrection.
Walk.

Horne, Richard Henry [or Hengist] (1803–84)
Plough, The.

Horovitz, Frances (1938–83)
Do you not know that I need to touch you.
In Painswick Churchyard.
Irthing Valley.
Loving You.
Messenger, The.
Moon.
Night-Piece.
Rain—Birdoswald.
Woman's Dream, The.
Women.

Horta, Maria Teresa (b. 1937)
Saved.
Swimming Pool.
See also **Three Marias, The.**

Horton, George Moses (1797?–1883?)
Acrostics.
Creditor to His Proud Debtor, The.
Division of an Estate.
Early Affection.
General Grant—the Hero of the War.
George Moses Horton, Myself.
Imploring to Be Resigned at Death.
Lover's Farewell, The.
New Fashions.
On Hearing of the Intention of a Gentleman to Purchase the Poet's Freedom.
On Liberty and Slavery.
On Summer.
Praise of Creation.
Slave's Complaint, The.
Snaps for Dinner, Snaps for Breakfast, and Snaps for Supper.
Troubled with the Itch and Rubbing with Sulphur.

Hosack, William (1808–83)
Isle of Streams, or, the Jamaica Hermit, The, sels.

Hoshi, Saigyo. See Saigyo

Hoshino, Tatsuko (b. 1903)
O brightness / of peony's buds.

Hosking, Arthur Nicholas (b. 1874)
Land of the Free.

Hoskins, Gary
Homework, homework.

Hoskins, Katherine (b. 1909)
Baucis and Philemon.
Côte d'Azur.

Hoskyns [or Hoskins], John (1566–1638)
Bellows Maker of Oxford, The.
Epitaph, An: On a Man for Doing Nothing.
Epitaph on Sir Walter Pye.
Epitaph on the Fart in the Parliament House.
Here lies the man that madly slain.
His Own Epitaph, When He Was Sick.
Of the Loss of Time.
On a Contentious Companion.
On a Whore.
On One That Lived Ingloriously.
Present in Abscence.
To His Little Son Benedict from the Tower
　of London.
To His Son Bennet.
Upon a Fool.
Upon One of the Maids of Honour to Queen
　Elizabeth.

Hosmer, Frederick Lucian (1840–1929)
From Age to Age They Gather.
Hear, Hear, O Ye Nations.
O Beautiful, My Country.
O Day of Light and Gladness.
Through Willing Heart and Helping Hand.

Hospital, Carolina
Freedom.
Mother Tongue, The.

Hoss, E. Embree (1849–1919)
O God, Great Father, Lord, and King.

Hotchkiss, Joanne
My Grandfather.

Hotham, Gary
Coffee.
Distant thunder.
Every night.
Fog.
Home early.
Letting.
Library book, The.
Morning fog.
Morning quiet.
My wife still asleep.
Night comes.
On the ceiling.
Quietly.
Stalled car.
Sun and moon.
Sunset dying.
This loneliness.
Unsnapping.
Up late.
Waiting room quiet.

Hottentot Oral Tradition
Song for the Sun That Disappeared behind
　the Rainclouds.

Hough, Graham (b. 1908)
Age of Innocence.

Houghton, Firman
Mr. Frost Goes South to Boston.

Housman, Alfred Edward (1859–1936)
African Lion, The.
Along the field as we came by.
As I Gird on for Fighting.
As into the Garden Elizabeth Ran.
As through the wild green hills of Wyre.
Astronomy.
Aunts and Nieces or Time and Space.
Be still, my soul, be still; the arms you bear
　are brittle.
Because I liked you better.
Bredon Hill.
Carpenter's Son, The.
Could man be drunk for ever.
Crossing alone the nighted ferry.
Deserter, The.
Easter Hymn.
Eight O'Clock.
1887.
Elephant, or the Force of Habit, The.
Epitaph on an Army of Mercenaries.
Fairies break their dances, The.
Fancy's Knell.
Far in a western brookland.
Farewell to barn and stack and tree.
For My Funeral.
Fragment of a Greek Tragedy.

Fragment of an English Opera.
From far, from eve and morning.
G. K. Chesterton on His Birth.
Grenadier.
Half-way, for one commandment broken.
"Hallelujah!" was the only observation.
Harlem.
He would not stay for me; and who can
　wonder?
Hell Gate.
Her strong enchantments failing.
Here dead lie we because we did not choose.
Ho, everyone that thirsteth.
I Counsel You Beware.
I did not lose my heart in summer's even.
I hoed and trenched and weeded.
If it chance your eye offend you.
Immortal Part, The.
In midnights of November.
In the morning, in the morning.
In valleys green and still.
Infant Innocence.
Inhuman Henry.
Is my team ploughing.
Isle of Portland, The.
It nods and curtseys and recovers.
Jack and Jill.
Lads in their hundreds to Ludlow come in
　for the fair, The.
Lancer.
Land of Lost Content, The.
Laws of God, the Laws of Man, The.
Loitering with a vacant eye.
Look not in my eyes, for fear.
Loveliest of trees, the cherry now.
March.
Mark 16:19–20; So then the Lord Jesus,
　after.
Mill-stream, now that noises cease, The.
My dreams are of a field afar.
New Mistress, The.
Night Is Freezing Fast, The.
Now Dreary Dawns the Eastern Light.
Now hollow fires burn out to black.
O Have You Caught the Tiger?
Occasional Poem.
Oh see how thick the goldcup flowers.
Oh, when I was in love with you.
Oh who is that young sinner with the
　handcuffs on his wrists?
Olive in its orchard, The.
On moonlit heath and lonesome bank.
On the idle hill of summer.
On Wenlock Edge the wood's in trouble.
Oracles, The.
Others, I am not the first.
Parta Quies.
Pope, The.
Purple William or The Liar's Doom.
Rain, it streams on stone and hillock, The.
Rainy Pleiads Wester, The.
Recruit, The.
Reveille.
Shades of night were falling fast, The.
Shake hands, we shall never be friends, all's
　over.
Sigh that heaves the grasses, The.
Sinner's Rue.
Sloe was lost in flower, The.
So Sound You Sleep.
Soldier from the Wars Returning.
Some can gaze and not be sick.
Stars have not dealt me the worst they could
　do, The.
Stars, I Have Seen Them Fall.
Tell me not here, it needs not saying.
Terence, this is stupid stuff.
They Say My Verse Is Sad: No Wonder.
Think no more, lad; laugh, be jolly.
To an Athlete Dying Young.
To stand up straight and tread the turning
　mill.
True Lover, The.
Wake Not for the World-heard Thunder.
We'll to the Woods No More.
Welsh Marches, The.
When Adam walked in Eden young.

When green buds hang in the elm like dust.
When I was one-and-twenty.
When I watch the living meet.
When Israel out of Egypt came.
When smoke stood up from Ludlow.
When the bells justle in the tower.
When the Eye of Day Is Shut.
When the lad for longing sighs.
White in the moon the long road lies.
Winter.
With rue my heart is laden.
World goes none the lamer, The.
Yonder See the Morning Blink.

Houston, Libby (b. 1941)
Dream of the Cabbage Caterpillars, The.
House, A.
Judging Lear.
Old Woman and the Sandwiches, The.
Scales.
Story of Canobie Dick, The.

Houston, Peyton (1910–94)
Sonnet Variations, *sels.*

Hovanessian, Diana Der
At Mt. Auburn Cemetery.
Radio Yerevan.
Without You I Am.

Hove, Chenjerai
Child's Parliment.
Country Life.
Lost Bird.
Migratory Bird ("One day he perched on a
　tree with dew.")
Other Syllabus, The.
Red Hills of Home.
You Will Forget.

**Hovell-Thurlow, Edward, 2d Baron Thurlow
(1781–1829)**
May! queen of blossoms.

Hover, Emily
Mr. Beetle.

Hovey, Richard (1864–1900)
Accident in Art.
At Sea.
Barney McGee.
Eleazar Wheelock.
Evening on the Potomac.
Mocking-Bird, The.
Sea Gypsy, The.
Song by the Shore, A.
Verlaine.

Hovey, Richard. See also **Carman, Bliss** and
Richard Hovey

Howard, Anne, Duchess of Arundel (1557–1630)
Good Shepherd's Sorrow for the Death of
　His Beloved Son, The.

Howard, Ben (b. 1944)
Winter Report.

Howard, Dorothy S. (b. 1921)
Birkett's Eagle.

Howard, Frances Minturn
Sampler from Haworth.

Howard-Jones, Stuart (1904–74)
Hibernia.

Howard, Leonard (1699?–1764)
Humours of the King's Bench Prison, a
　Ballad, The.

Howard, Richard (b. 1929)
Again for Hephaistos, the Last Time.
Agreement with Sir Charles Sedley.
Among the Missing.
At the Monument to Pierre Louÿs.
Aubade: Donna Anna to Juan, Still Asleep.
Author of *Christine*, The.
Bonnard; a Novel.
Compulsive Qualifications, *sels.*
Crepuscular.
Far Cry after a Close Call, A.
Giovanni da Fiesole on the Sublime.
Ithaca: The Palace at Four A.M, *sels.*
Landed: A Valentine.
Lost Art, A.
Nadar.
Natural History.
Nikolaus Mardruz to his Master Ferdinand,
　Count of Tyrol, 1565.

1915: A Pre-Raphaelite Ending, London.
On Arrival.
Oystering.
Recipe for an Ocean in the Absence of the
  Sea.
Secular Games.
Seeing Cousin Phyllis Off.
209 Canal.
Venetian Interior, 1889.
Wildflowers.

Howard, Sir Robert (1626–98) *and* **John Dryden**
To the Unconstant Cynthia: a Song.

Howard, Rowland
Difference, The.
Tremendous Trifles.
Waste not, want not, is a maxim I.

Howard, Vanessa
Monument in Black.

Howard, Winifred (d. 1909)
Young men!

Howarth, B. L.
Brown paper worn next to the skin.

Howe, Fanny (b. 1940)
First Chance Twice.
From a donkey, excuse me, one lesson is
  given.
"O'clock," *sels.*
Scattered Light.
Seeking Out His face in a Cup.
Torn Parts: the story.
What We Learned.

Howe, George
Sun-Witch to the Sun, The.

Howe, Julia Ward (1819–1910)
Battle Hymn of the Republic, The.
In the beauty of the lilies Christ.
Kosmos.
Mother's Day Proclamation of 1870.
My Last Dance.
Robert E. Lee.
Soul-Hunter, The.
Wild Night, A.

Howe, Marie (b. 1950)
Death, the Last Visit.
How Many Times.
Part of Eve's Discussion.
Split, The.
Without Devotion.

Howe, Solomon (1750–1835)
Our Kind Creator.

Howe, Susan (b. 1937)
Defenestration of Prague, *sels.*
He plodded away through drifts of i / ce.
Secret History of the Dividing Line, *sels.*
Silence Wager Stories.
Speeches at the Barriers, *sels.*
Thorow.
White Foolscap/Book of Cordelia, *sels.*

Howell, Christopher
Liberty and Ten Years of Return.
Memories of Mess Duty and the War.
Reminder to the Current President, A.

Howell, James (1594–1666)
Elegy upon His Tomb in Herndon-Hill
  Church, Erected by His Wife, Who Speaks,
  An.
Upon Dr. Davies's British Grammar.
Upon the Poet of His Time, Ben Jonson: His
  Honoured Friend and Father.

Howell, Thomas (c.1568–1581)
Acre of performance is worth a, An.

Howells, William Dean (1837–1920)
Empty House, The.
Forlorn.
In Earliest Spring.
November.
Robin and the Cows, The.
Royal Portraits, The.

Howes, Barbara (b. 1914)
Blue Garden, The.
Chimera.
Danaë.
Death of a Vermont Farm Woman.
Early Supper.

Flight.
Home Leave.
Letter from the Caribbean, A.
Mistral.
On a Bougainvillaea Vine at the Summer
  Palace [*or* in Haiti].
On Galveston Beach.
Out Fishing.
Portrait of the Boy as Artist.
Returning to Store Bay.
Rune for C, A.
Sea School.
2nd Wind.

Howitt, Mary (1799–1888)
Buttercups and Daisies.
Cry of the Animals, The.
Dying Child, The.
Hummingbird, The.
Sale of the Pet Lamb, The.
Sea-Gull, The.
September.
Spider and the Fly, The.
Spring Song, A.
Squirrel, The.

Howitt, William (1792–1879)
Migration of the Grey Squirrels, The.
Wind in a Frolic, The.

Hoye, Laurel O.
You are like an everlasting friendship.

Hoyem, Andrew (b. 1935)
Circumambulation of Mt. Tamalpais.

Hoyt, Clement
Down from the bridge rail.
Hair, in my comb's teeth.
Hallowe'en mask, A.
In that empty house.
In that lightning flash.
Leaves moil in the yard.
Pretty matron, The.
Those camellias.
While the guests order.

Hoyt, Helen (b. 1887)
Memory.

Hristic, Jovan (b. 1933)
Barbarians.
Evening Quiet.
In a dark hour (there are more and more of
  them now).
In the big library scholars sit and read books.
Sentimental Voyage Around My Room, A.
That night they all gathered on the highest
  tower.
To Phaedrus.
Tragedy is over. Blind Oedipus exits, The.

Hroswitha von Gandersheim (c.935–1005)
In Praise of Virginity.
Paphnutius, *sels.*

Hsi-chün (fl. c.105 B.C.)
Lament of Hsi-chün.

Hsi K'ang (c.223–262)
Sent to the Hsiu-ts'ai on His Entry into the
  Army.
Taoist Song.

Hsiang Chi (232–202 B.C.) (Hsiang Yü)
Song of Kai-hsia.

Hsiang Ssu (fl. 9th cent.)
Ailing Japanese Monk, The.

Hsiao Kang
Flying Petals.
Rising in Winter.

Hsiao-Wei, Liu
For My Wife.

Hsiao Yen
Spring Song of Tzu-yeh, A.

Hsiao-yün-shih-hai-ya.&xbd; *See* **Kuan Yün-shih**

Hsieh Chin (1369–1415)
In Grief, Lamenting for My Elder Brother
  Ts'ang-ch, *sels.*
Inscribed on a Painting of Dragons by Ch'en
  So-weng.
Parting from Liu Nan-chou, *sels.*
Playful Poem on a Chicken Egg, A.
Poem on a Little Pine, A.
Sandal Mountain.

Song of Cursive Calligraphy.
Things Experienced upon Withdrawal from
  Court, *sels.*
To Hsiao Shih-ying.
To the Fortuneteller Hsüeh T'ieh-yai.
What Does the Little Boy Love?, *sels.*

Hsieh Hui-lien (397–433)
Fulling Cloth for Clothes.
Rhyme-Prose on the Snow.

Hsieh Ling-yün (385–433)
By T'ing Yang Waterfall.
Climbing a Solitary Islet in the River.
Climbing Stone Drum Mountain Above the
  Shores of Shang-shu.
Climbing the Tower by the Pond.
Entering the Mouth of P'eng-li Lake.
Exchange of Poems by Tung-yang Stream,
  An, *sels.*
Journeying by Stream: Following Chin-chu
  Torrent I Cross the Mountains.
Leaving West Archery Hall at Dusk.
Passing through My Shih-ning Estate.
Passing White Banks Pavilion.
Replying to a Poem from My Cousin Hui-
  lien.
Spending the Night on Stone Gate Mountain.
Written on the Lake, Returning from the
  Retreat at Stone Cliff.

Hsieh Ngao (fl. 13th cent.)
Wind Tossed Dragons.

Hsieh Shang (308–57)
Song of the Thoroughfare.

Hsieh T'iao (464–99)
In a Provincial Capital Sick in Bed.
Jade Steps Plaint.
Song of the Men of Chin-ling.

Hsin Ch'i-chi (1140–1207)
To an Old Tune.
Tune: "Full River Red."
Tune: "Green Jade Cup"—Lantern Festival.
Tune: "Groping for Fish."
Tune: "Immortal's Auspicious Crane, An"—
  On Plum Blossoms.
Tune: "Partridge Sky"—Written at the Po-
  shan Monastery.
Tune: "Slow Song of Chu Ying-t'ai"—Late
  Spring.
Tune: "Song of Divination"Using Quotations
  from *Chuang-tzu.*
Tune: "Song of the Southern Country"—
  Presented to a Courtesan.
Tune: "Spring in Ch'in's Garden."
Tune: Ugly Rogue.

Hsü Chün-ch'ien (fl. 6th cent.)
Beginning of Spring—A Stroll with My
  Wife.
Sitting Out New Year With My Wife.
Sitting Up with My Wife on New Year's
  Eve.

Hsü Chung-hsing (1517–78)
At Dawn, Climbing the Heavenly Pillar Peak
  of Mysterious Mountain, *sels.*
Cane of Ch'iung Bamboo, The.
Following the Rhymes of Magistrate Liu's
  Poems on Entertaining Two Assistant
  Premiers at Pine-Snow Temple, *sels.*
Inquiring about the Health of Li Te-hua, *sels.*
Song of Catching Tigers, *sels.*
Thanking Prince Chen-chi for Giving Me a
  Bronze Seal Engraved with Diagrams of
  the Five Sacred Mountains, *sels.*
Traveling by Boat at Shun-ch'ang.

Hsü Kan (171–217)
Boudoir Thoughts, *sels.*
Wife's Thoughts, The.

HSü Ling (507–583)
Teleg Song.
Waters of Lung-t'ou, The.

Hsü Pen (1335–80)
Ballad of the Ferocious Tiger.
Ballad of the Merchant.
Deserted Estate at South Garden, The.
Five Things Sought For—In the Manner of
  Han Wo, *sels.*
Following the Rhymes of Kao Chi-ti's Poem:
  "We Had Planned to Travel to Cloud Cliff
  But Couldn't Because of Rain."

Hermit Feng's Residence on the Lake.
Hermit Li's Herb Garden Retreat at T'ung-ch'uan.
In Harmony with Kao "The Second" Ch'i's Poem "On Hearing a P'i-p'a Played Next Door."
Leisurely Stroll, A, *sels.*
Mountain Residence of Secretary Cheng Ching-ssu, The.
Poem on Buddha's Begging Bowl—For Hui-ku, His Holiness Ming, A.
Saying Goodbye to a Monk from Japan.
To a Hermit in the Mountains.
To the Filial Son, Ts'ui.
Tomb of the Singing Girl Ch'iung-i, The.

Hsü Tsai-ssu (*fl.* c.1300)
Tune: "Clear River, a Prelude"—Lovesickness.
Tune: "Joy All Under Heaven"—Sunset on the Western Hill.

Hsü Wei (1521–93)
Abandoning the Plans of Visiting West Lake.
Buddhist Monk Cut and Burned His Own Flesh to Make The Rains Stop—A Man From His Native Place Asked Me to Write a Poem to Send to Him, A.
Colossal:/ Like towers and pavilions from the flat plain.
From Chekiang I Went to Hsin-an and Climbed Even-with-the-Clouds Mountain. On the Way Back There Were Many Beautiful Sights at the Inns Where I Stayed and Yet I Could Not Write One Word of Poetry. When I Got Back to the Main Road I Wrote These Four Lines to Make Fun of Myself.
I Once Did a Bamboo Painting for Somebody—Now He Wants Me To Do Another. I Have Written This To Answer Him.
I Tried to Exchange Two Painting for Some Grain But Failed.
Inscribed on a Painting.
Inscribed on a Painting of Windy Bamboo, to Be Presented to Tzu-kan.
Inscribed on Paintings for the People of Hangchow, *sels.*
Kite, A, *sels.*
Lotus.
Mushroom Gatherer Deep in the Mountains Among the White Clouds, A.
On the Road Through the Wu-i Mountains—Making Fun of Chia-tse for Falling Off His Horse.
Painting of People Strolling through a Pine Forest, A.
Returning from the Seventy-Two Mountains.
Songs of Yen-ching, *sels.*
To Hsü Shih-t'ing.
Two Fish by a Willow Embankment.

Hs'üan-Chi, Y'ü
On a Visit to Ch'ung Chen Taoist Temple.

Hsüan-ying. *See* Su Man-shu

Hsüeh T'ao (768–831)
Autumn Spring.
Farewell to a Friend.
Moon, The.
Spring-gazing Song.
Weaving Love-Knots.
Weaving Love-Knots 2.
Willow Catkins.

Huang Ching-jen (1749–83)
Mixed Emotions.
Questing-for-Spring Arbor.
Sentiments on New Year's Eve in the Year Kuei-ssu.
Traveling at Break of Day.

Huang E (1498–1569)
Pearl-teardrops roll and gather.

Huang O [*or* Huang Ho] (1498–1569)
Farewell to a Southern Melody, A.
To the Tune "A Floating Cloud Crosses Enchanted Mountain."
To the Tune "Red Embroidered Shoes."
To the Tune "Soaring Clouds."
To the Tune "The Fall of a Little Wild Goose."

Huang Shu (1131–91)
Tune: "Song of River Goddess"—Moorinig My Boat at Fen-shui at Night.

Huang Su-ju. *See* "Pai Wei"

Huang T'ing-chien (1045–1105)
Buffalo Boy.
Clear Bright.
Climbing K'uai Pavilion.
Following the Rhymes of Chang Hsün, in My Study in Late Spring.
Following the Rhymes of Fellow Graduate P'ei Chung-mou.
Following the Rhymes of Wang An-shih's Poem "Inscribed on the Wall of the Temple of Western Great Unity."
In My Study in Monastery, Rising after a Nap, *sels.*
Inscribed on a Scroll "Plum Blossoms by the Water."
Living in Exile at Ch'ien-nan.
On a Painting of Ants and Butterflies.
Once More Following the Rhymes of Pin-lao's Poem "Getting Up After Illness."
Out in the Snow, Spending the Night at the New Stockade, Extremely Depressed.
Passing Hung-fu Monastery with Yüan-ming: Inscribed in Jest.
Song of the Clear River.
Teasing Hsiao-te, My Son.
To Go with Shih K'o's Painting of an Old Man Tasting Vinegar.
Tune: "Partridge Sky."
Tune: "Pleasure of Returning to the Fields: A Prelude."
Tune: "Pure Serene Music."
Upon Passing the Homestead.

Huang Tsun-hsien (1848–1905)
Recuperating in Chang Villa.
Sent in Lieu of a Letter to Shih-wu, Lan-ku, and Other Friends.
Spending the Night in an Inn at Swatow and Writing about My Feelings, Sent to Liang Shih-wu.
To Send Away Melancholy.

Hubbard, P. M. (1910–80)
Subjectivity at Sestos.

Hubbell, Patricia (b. 1928)
Owl of the Greenwood.
Shadows.
Streetcleaner's Lament, The.
Travelers, The.

Hubert, Sir Francis (1568 *or* 1569–1629)
Egypt's Favorite, *sels.*
Life and Death of Edward II, The, *sels.*

Huch, Ricarda (1864–1947)
Arrival in Hell.
Death Seed.
Music stirs me, for you.
Young Girl.

Huchel, Peter (1903–81)
Ammonite, The.
Eastern River.
Garden of Theophrastus, The.
In the rush odour of Danish meadows.
King Lear.
Landscape Beyond Warsaw.
Meeting.
Melpomene.
On the Way.
Poplars, The.
Psalm.
Roads.
Spindle, The.
Thrace.
Winter Billet.

Huddle, David (b. 1942)
Almost Going.
Bac Ha.
Cousin.
Delivering the Times, 1952-1944.
Gregory's House.
Holes Commence Falling.
Miss Florence Jackson.
My Daddy, Whenever He Went Some Place.
Theory.
Tour of Duty, *sels.*

Town History, 1917.
Two Facts.
Vermont.

Hudgins, Andrew (b. 1951)
After the Wilderness.
Around the campfire we sang hymns.
At Chancellorsville.
Burial Detail.
Dead Christ.
Elegy for My Father, Who Is Not Dead.
Hereafter, The.
Persistence of Nature in Our Lives, The.
Praying Drunk.
Saints and Strangers.
Serenades in Virginia.
Seventeen.
Soldier on the Marsh, A.
Southern Crescent Was on time, The.
Telling, The.
Two Ember Days in Alabama.
When I Was Saved.

Hudson, Deatt
Some Tips on Watching Birds.

Huê, Lê Liễu. *See* Ái Lan

Huệ, Trần Sĩ. *See* Trần Huiền Ân

Hueffer, Ford Madox. *See* Ford, Ford Madox

Huelsenbeck, Richard (1892–1974)
We hardly had gotten the man's pants down.

Huelsenbeck, Richard (1892–1974), **Marcel Janko,** *and* **Tristan Tzara**
L'amiral cherche une maison à louer.

Huff, Robert (b. 1924)
Course, The.
Traditional Red.

Huffstickler, Albert
Lament for an Old Woman.

Huggins, Horatio Nelson (1830–95)
Hiroona, *sels.*

Hugh, Primate of Orleans (1094–1160)
Lament for Troy.

Hughes, Cyril
Limerick: "Remember when you are bemusing."

Hughes, Dorothy (b. 1910)
Age of Sheen, The.

Hughes, Gillian
Snow Falling.

Hughes, Jabez
As years advance, the abated soul, in most.

Hughes, James D.
My Son.

Hughes, John (1677–1720)
Thought in a Garden, A.

Hughes, John (b. 1962)
Dog Day Lesson.
Knowingness.
Respect for Law and Order, A.

Hughes, John Ceiriog ("Ceiriog") (1832–87)
Epilogue to Alun Mabon.
Mountain Stream, The.

Hughes, Langston (1902–67)
Advice.
Afro-American Fragment.
American Heartbreak.
Angola Question Mark.
April Rain Song.
As Befits a Man.
As I Grew Older.
Aunt Sue's Stories.
Backlash Blues, The.
Bad Luck Card.
Bad Man.
Bad Morning.
Ballad of the Girl Whose Name Is Mud.
Ballad of the Landlord.
Ballad of the Man Who's Gone.
Bar.
Be-Bop Boys.
Blue Monday.
Blues, The.
Blues at Dawn.
Boogie: 1 A.M.
Brass Spittoons.
Café: 3 A.M.

Carol of the Brown King.
Catch.
Children's Rhymes.
Chord.
Christ in Alabama.
City.
Croon.
Cross.
Cultural Exchange.
Danse Africaine.
Daybreak in Alabama.
Dead in There.
Death in Yorkville.
Deferred.
Dinner Guest: Me.
Down and Out.
Dream Boogie.
Dream Boogie: Variation.
Dream Variation[s].
Drum.
Dust Bowl.
Early Evening Quarrel.
Easy Boogie.
Ennui.
Esthete in Harlem.
Fact.
Feet O' Jesus.
50–50.
Final Curve.
Fire.
Flatted Fifths.
Florida Road Workers.
Frederick Douglass: 1817-1895.
Freedom Train.
Freedom will not come.
Gal's Cry for a Dying Lover.
Gauge.
Genius Child.
Go Slow.
Gypsy Man.
Hard Daddy.
Harlem Sweeties.
Heaven, Heaven, Heaven Is the Place.
High to Low.
Homecoming.
Homesick Blues.
Hope.
House in Taos, A.
I, Too, Sing America.
Impasse.
In time of silver rain.
Island.
Jam Session.
Jazz Band in a Parisian Cabaret.
Jazzonia.
Jim Crow Car.
Juke Box Love Song.
Junior Addict.
Justice.
Ku Klux.
Lament over Love.
Lenox Avenue Mural, *sels.*
Let America Be America Again.
Letter.
Letter to the Academy.
Life Is Fine.
Lincoln Monument: Washington.
Little Lyric (of Great Importance).
Little Old Letter.
Little Song.
Lord has a child, The.
Lover's Return.
Luck.
Madam and Her Madam.
Madam and the Census Man.
Madam and the Minister.
Madam and the Rent Man.
Madam and the Wrong Visitor.
Madam's Calling Cards.
Madam's Past History.
Madrid—1937.
Mama and Daughter.
Me and the Mule.
Merry-Go-Round.
Militant.
Miss Blues'es Child.
Moonlight Night: Carmel.

Morning After.
Mother to Son.
Motto.
Mulatto.
My People.
Necessity.
Negro Servant.
Negro Speaks of Rivers, The.
Neighbor.
Neon Signs.
Night funeral / In Harlem.
Nightmare Boogie.
Notes on the Broadway Theatre.
October 16[: The Raid].
Old Walt Whitman.
Parade.
Passing.
Peace.
Pennsylvania Station in New York, The.
Personal.
Piggy-back.
Po' Boy Blues.
Poem: "I loved my friend."
Porter.
Preference.
Prime.
Projection.
Question.
Question and Answer.
Red Silk Stockings.
Request.
Sailor.
Saturday Night.
Sea Calm.
Seascape.
Share-Croppers.
Shepherd's Song at Christmas.
Sister.
Situation.
Slave.
So *long* / is in the song.
Song for a Dark Girl.
Song for Billie Holiday.
Special Bulletin.
Stars.
Still Here.
Stony Lonesome.
Strange Hurt.
Subway Rush Hour.
Suicide's Note.
Sun Song.
Sweet Words on Race.
Sylvester's Dying Bed.
Tambourines! / Tambourines! / Tambourines.
Tell Me.
Theme for English B.
Third Degree.
This Little House Is Sugar.
Today.
Tomorrow may be.
Trumpet Player.
Ultimatum: Kid to Kid.
Un-American Investigators.
Uncle Tom.
Undertow.
Vagabonds.
Wake.
Warning.
Water-Front Streets.
Weary Blues, The.
What?
When Sue Wears Red.
Where? When? Which?
Who But the Lord?
Winter Moon.
Without Benefit of Declaration.
Words Like Freedom.
World War II.
Young Gal's Blues.

Hughes, Pegatha
  Handful of Pebbles, Mouthful of Stones.

Hughes, Richard (1900–1976)
  Burial of the Spirit of a Young Poet.
  Felo de Se.
  Gipsy-Night.
  Glaucopis.
  Image, The.

Invocation to the Muse.
Lover's Reply to Good Advice.
Old Cat Care.
On Time.
Ruin, The.
Sermon, The.
Tramp.
Walking Road, The.
Winter.

Hughes, Ted (b. 1930)
  After Lorca.
  Amulet.
  Bear, The.
  Bull Moses, The.
  Bullfrog.
  Cadenza.
  Cat and Mouse.
  Childish Prank, A.
  Christmas Card.
  Cleopatra to the Asp.
  Crow, *sels.*
  Crow's First Lesson.
  Crow's Theology.
  Day He Died, The.
  Dove, A.
  Esther's Tomcat.
  Examination at the Womb-Door.
  Famous Poet.
  Fern.
  Full Moon and Little Frieda.
  God, A.
  Harvest Moon, The.
  Hawk Roosting.
  Heptonstall.
  Heptonstall Old Church.
  Her Husband.
  Horses, The.
  Howling of Wolves, The.
  I see a bear.
  Jaguar, The.
  Kreutzer Sonata.
  Lake, The.
  Leaves.
  Lupercalia.
  Man Seeking Experience Enquires His Way
    of a Drop of Water, The.
  Minstrel's Song.
  Modest Proposal, A.
  Moon-Hops.
  Moon-transport.
  Moon-wind.
  Motorbike, A.
  My Brother Bert.
  My Uncle Dan's an inventor, you may think.
  New Year's [or Year] Song.
  November.
  October robin kept, An.
  Old Age Gets Up.
  Orf.
  Orts, *sels.*
  Otter, An.
  Pibroch.
  Pike, three inches long, perfect.
  Ravens.
  Relic.
  River.
  River in March, The.
  Roe-Deer.
  Roger the Dog.
  Rooks love excitement. When I walked in
    under the rookery.
  Root, Stem, Leaf, *sels.*
  Second Glance at a Jaguar.
  September.
  Seven Sorrows, The.
  Six Young Men.
  Skylarks, *sels.*
  Snowdrop.
  Song of a Rat.
  St. Matthew, *sels.*
  Stations, *sels.*
  Stealing Trout.
  Still-Life.
  Theology.
  Thistles.
  Thought-Fox, The.
  Thrushes.

To Paint a Water Lily.
Tractor stands frozen—an agony, The.
Trees.
Two Wise Generals.
Urn Burial.
View of a Pig.
Walt.
Water.
Wilfred Owen's Photographs.
Wind.
Wodwo.
Yesterday he was nowhere to be found.
You Drive in a Circle.

Hugo, Richard (1923–82)
Brief History.
Death of the Kapowsin Tavern.
December 24 and George McBride Is Dead.
Degrees of Gray in Philipsburg.
Elegy: "I expected him to look dead in the casket."
Ferniehirst Castle.
Freaks at Spurgin Road Field, The.
Graves at Elkhorn.
Hilltop, The.
In Your Bad Dream.
In Your Young Dream.
Lady in Kicking Horse Reservoir, The.
Last Days.
Letter to Bell from Missoula.
Letter to Levertov from Butte.
Letter to Logan from Milltown.
Letter to Reed from Lolo.
Letter to Scanlon from Whitehall.
Letter to Wagoner from Port Townsend.
Letter to Welch from Browning.
Map of Montana in Italy, A.
Milltown Union Bar, The.
Montana Ranch Abandoned.
My Buddy.
Napoli Again.
Open Country.
Places and Ways to Live.
Plans for Altering the River.
River Now, The.
Salt Water Story.
Skykomish River Running.
To Women.
View from Cortona, A.
Way a Ghost Dissolves, The.
What Thou Lovest Well Remains American.
White Center.
Yards of Sarajevo, The.

Hugo, Victor (1802–85)
At dawn tomorrow, time of whitening fields.
Be like the bird, who.
Feuilles d'Automne, sels.
Genesis of Butterflies, The.
Good night! Good night! / Far flies the light.
Grave and the Rose, The.
Jeanne was on bread and water in a dark room.
More Strong Than Time.
Poor Children, The.
Russia 1812.
She had no shoes on, she had freed her hair.

Huidobro, Vincente (1893–1948)
Altazor, sels.
Ars Poetica.
Cow Boy.
Express.

Hull, Akasha (Gloria) (b. 1944)
Another Rhythm.

Hull, Lynda
Address.
Combat Zone/War Stories.
Dartmouth Women's Prison, 1992.
Fiat Lux.
Frugal Repasts.
Holy City, City of Night.
Hospice.
Jail, Flames—Jersey, 1971.
Letter, The.
Lost Fugue for Chet.
Love Song During Riot with Many Voices.
Ornithology.
Shore Leave.
Style of Prayer, A.

Hulme, Keri (b. 1947)
He Hola.

Hulme, Thomas Ernest (1883–1917)
Above the Dock.
Autumn.
Conversion.
Embankment (The Fantasia of a Fallen Gentleman on a Cold, Bitter Night), The.
Image.
Trenches: St Eloi.

Hume, Alexander (c.1556–1609)
Of Gods Omnipotencie.
Of the Day Estivall, sels.
Summer's Day, A.

Hume, Anna (fl. 17th cent.)
Triumphs of Death, sels.

Hume, Tobias (d. 1645)
No Other Choice.

Hummer, T. R. (b. 1950)
Apocatastasis Foretold in the Shape of a Canvas of Smoke.
Beating, The.
Ideal, The.
Inner Ear.
Poem in the Shape of a Saxophone.
Rural Carrier Stops to Kill a Nine-Foot Cottonmouth, The.
Sorrow.
Train Wreck, 1890: My Grandmother Lies Down with the Dead.
What Shines in Winter Burns.
Where You Go When She Sleeps.
Worldly Beauty.

Hummer, Terry
Austerity in Vermont.
Heart Attack in the Country, A.
Mississippi 1955 Confessional.
Spring Comes to Mid-Ohio in a Holy Shower of Stars.

Humphreys, Emyr (b. 1919)
Apple Tree and a Pig, An.
From Father to Son.

Humphries, Barry ("Edna Everage") (b. 1934)
Edna's Alphabet.
Edna's Hymn.

Humphries, Rolfe (1894–1969)
Aria.
Dafydd ap Gwilym Resents the Winter.
For My Ancestors.
Heresy for a Class-Room.
Offering of the Heart Tapestry from Arras, XV Century, The.
Polo Grounds.
Runes for an Old Believer.
Seasons, The.
Summer Landscape; or, The Dragon's Teeth, The.

Hunt, Josephine Slocum
You Kissed Me.

Hunt, Josie R. and J. H. Pixley
Katie Lee and Willy [or Willie] Grey.

Hunt, Leigh (1784–1859)
Abou Ben Adhem (may his tribe increase!).
Christmas.
Epitaph of Erotion, The.
Examiner, no. 385 316, The, sels.
Faith, Hope, and Charity Are the Prospects of Manhood.
Feast of the Poets, The, sels.
Fish, the Man, and the Spirit, The, sels.
Morning Chronicle, 2 436, sels.
Nile, The.
Nymphs, The, sels.
On Receiving a Crown of Ivy from the Same.
On the Death of His Son Vincent.
Rondeau.
Rondeau: Jenny Kiss'd [or Kissed] Me.
Song of the Grass, The.
Story of Rimini, The, sels.
To John Keats.
To Percy Shelley.
To the Grasshopper and the Cricket.
To the Same.

Hunt, S. S. ("Bernard Moore")
War.

Hunt, Sam (b. 1946)
At Castor Bay.
Birth of a Son.
Bottle Creek Blues.
Maintrunk Country Roadsong.
My Father Scything.
My Father Today.
Porirua Friday Night.
Requiem: "They say 'the lighthouse keeper's world is round.'"
Sunday Evening.

Hunter, Albert (1897–1984) and Louie Austin (1897–1972)
Down-Hearted Blues.

Hunter, Anne (1742–1841)
North American Death Song.
Pastoral Song, A.

Hunter, Sara
Traveling Back.

Hunter, William (1811–77)
"Go Bring Me," Said the Dying Fair.
Joyfully, Joyfully Onward I Move.

Hunter, William Elijah (1839–1913)
Monologue in a Rand Hospital.

Huntington, Cynthia
Breaking.
Hackeysack Players, The.
Party.
Rhapsody.

Huntington, George (1825–1904)
International Hymn.

Huntington, William Reed (1838–1909)
Cold Meteorite, The.
From Green Mountain.
Lowlands.

Hurdis, James (1763–1801)
Adriano; or, The First of June, sels.
Favourite Village, The, sels.
Village Curate, The, sels.

Hurley, Mary Rita
Limerick: "Old Indian chief, Running B'ar, An."
Tea Party.

Hurley, Maureen
Invisible Boundaries.

Hurston, Zora Neale
Faith hasn't got no eyes, but she long-legged.

Huss, Avraham (b. 1924)
Command, The.
Green Refrain, The.

Hussey, Anne
Ezra Pound's Eye.
Saturday Night.

Hussey, Dyneley (1893–1972)
Kingfisher, The.

Hussey, Norah E.
I Spy.
My Garden.
Toad the Tailor.

Hutcheon, Lessel
Flight to Flanders, The.

Hutchinson, Abby (1829–92)
Kind Words Can Never Die.

Hutchinson, Lucy (b. 1620, d. after 1675)
Verses Written by Mrs. Hutchinson.

Hutchinson, M. M. (b. 1904)
Dancing on the Shore.
Harvest.
Making Tens.
My New Umbrella.
Ten Little Indian Boys.
Thames, The.
Tug-of-War, A.
Twice one are two.

Hutchinson, Pearse (b. 1927)
Amhrán na mBréag.
Be born a saint; or keep.
Boxing the Fox.
Bright after Dark.
Fleadh Cheoil.
Frost is All Over, The.
Gaeltacht.
Look, No Hands.
Malaga.

I

Manifest Destiny.
True Story Ending in False Hope, A.

Hutchinson, Robert (b. 1924)
Suburban Wife's Song.

Hutt, Frank (b. 1869)
Vacation Time.

Hutten, Ulrich von (1488–1523)
Ulrich von Hutten's Song.

Hutton, Virgil (b. 1931)
Dusk over the lake.
Moving shadows, The.

Huws, Daniel (b. 1932)
Family Evening.
Goodbye to Regal.

Huxley, Aldous Leonard (1894–1963)
Antic Hay, sels.
Burning Wheel, The.
Fifth Philosopher's Song.
First Philosopher's Song.
Limerick: "There was a young fellow of
Burma."
Limerick: "There was a young girl of East
Anglia."
Second Philosopher's Song.
September.
Two Realities.

Huy Cận (b. 1919)
Body, The.
Dirge, A: "Who died? Why does the music
speak such grief?"
Talking With the Pyramid.
Two Wooden Men, The.

Huỳnh Mẫn Đạt (1807–83)
Old Hound, The.
Old Whore Becomes a Nun, The.

Huỳnh Phú Sổ (d. 1947?)
Bread.

Huỳnh Thúc Kháng (Huỳ Hanh) (1876–1947)
Comedy of the World, The.
Farewell Song, A.

Hwang Chin-i (c.1500–1544)
Blue hill is my desire, The.
I cut in two / A long November night.
Mountains are steadfast but the mountain
streams.

Hwang, Kumch'an (b. 1918)
Candlelight.
Prayer.

Hwang, Tong-gyu (b. 1938)
Small Love Song, A.
Smaller Love Song, A.

Hybrias The Cretan ((fl. c. 200)
Song of Hybrias the Cretan.

Hyde, Abby Bradley (1799–1872)
And canst thou, sinner slight.
Dear Saviour, If These Lambs Should Stray.

Hyde, Arnold
There was an old fellow called Hugger.

Hyde, Douglas (1860–1944)
Cold, Sharp Lamentation.
He Meditates on the Life of a Rich Man.
Will You Be as Hard?

Hyde, Michael (b. 1908)
To 'ave a garden in fettle.

**"Hyde, Robin" (Iris Gulver Wilkinson) (1906–
39)**
Beaches, The, sels.
Deserted Village, The.
Houses, The, sels.
Ku Li.
Last Ones, The.
Pihsien Road.
Young Knowledge.

Hyde, William deWitt (1858–1917)
Creation's Lord, We Give Thee Thanks.

Hyland, Gary
Fet Walks Melody Home.

Hywel ab Owain Gwynedd (d. 1170)
Exultation.
Poet's Loves, The.

I, Fu. See **Mei Sheng** and Fu I

"I, Mary." See **Osborn, Mary I.**

"I., R."
Limerick: "There was an old man called
Dupree."

Ibaragi, Norkiko (b. 1926)
Dialogue.
What a little girl had on her mind was.

Ibarbourou, Juana de (1897–1979)
Assignation, The.
Life-Hook.
Strong Bond, The.

Ibbetson, Julius Caesar (1759–1817)
O mortal man, that lives by bread.

Ibn Abithur, Joseph
Sanctification.

Ibn al-Arabi (1165–1240)
My heart is capable of every form.
Ode: "They journeyed, / When the darkness
of night."
Ode: "Who can support the anguish of love?"
Oh, her beauty—the tender maid! Its
brilliance gives light.

Ibn al-Rumi (836–96)
Compromise, The.
Slow Giving.
To a Hunchback.
Weighing-In, The.

Ibn-Chasdai, Abraham (fl. c.1250)
Advice to Bores.
Elusive Maid, The.
Meek and the Proud, The.
Poor Scholar, The.

Ibn Darraj al-Andalusi (fl. 11th cent.)
Wing of Separation, The.

Ibn-Ezra, Abraham (1092–1167)
Ages of Man, The.
Far Sweeter than Honey.
Freedom.
God Everywhere.
God Supreme.
Law, The.
Living God, The.
Out of Luck.
Song of Chess, The.

Ibn Hazm al-Andalusi (994–1064)
Separation by Death.
Twice Times Then Is Now.

Ibn Kolthum
Pour Us Wine. From The Mu'allaqat

Ibn Rashiq (d. 1064)
Pretences.

Ibn Zaydun (1003–71)
Cordova.

Ibnu 'l-Farid (c.1181–1235)
Let passion's swelling tide my senses drown!

Ibrahim, Abdullah
Africa, Music and Show Business.

Ibsen, Henrik (1828–1906)
In the Orchard.

Ibycus (fl. 564 B.C.–561 B.C.)
In Spring, quince trees.
In the Spring the quince and the.

Icaza, Francisco A. de (1863–1925)
Responding Voice.

Ích, Phan Huy. See **Đặng Trần Côn** and Phan
Huy Ích

Ichijitsu, Ōkura
Snow falls and falls, The.

Idley, Peter (d. 1473?)
Covetousness.
Sources of Good Counsel.

Ietaka (Fujiwara no Ietaka) (1158–1237)
Old Scent of the Plum Tree.

Ignatow, David (b. 1914)
Absolutely.
Against the Evidence.
All Quiet.
Allegory, An.
And the Same Words.
Bagel, The.

Brooding.
Business Life, The.
Dialogue, A.
Dilemma.
Dog barks and is for the moment a dog
heard, The.
Dream, The.
Each Day.
East Bronx.
Elegy: "I must wait for a stranger to knock
on my door."
Europe and America.
Figures of the Human.
First on TV, A.
Fisherwoman, The.
For Medgar Evers.
For My Daughter in Reply to a Question.
For One Moment.
Get the Gasworks.
Harold.
He Puts Me to Rest.
I see a truck mowing down a parade.
In a Dream.
In the Dark.
Journey, The.
Kaddish.
Last night I spoke to a dead woman with
green face.
Lunchtime.
Mother, how wrinkled and old must you
become.
Mystique.
News Report.
Night at an Airport.
No Theory.
Notes for a Lecture.
Park.
Pleasure, The.
Professional, The.
Promenade.
Refuse Man, The.
Rescue the Dead.
Ritual Three.
Sediment.
Self-employed.
Signal, The.
Simultaneously, five thousand miles apart.
Six Movements on a Theme.
Sky Is Blue, The.
Suite for Marriage, A.
Sunday at the State Hospital.
Two Friends.
Walt Whitman in the Civil War Hospitals.
White-haired, I walk in on my parents.

Ignatow, Yaedi
Androgeny is the universe.
We were love.

Ihaka, Kingi M. (b. 1921)
Te Atairangikaahu.

Ilam Peruvaluti
This World Lives Because.

Ilanakanar, Maturai Marutan
What Her Girl Friend Said to Her.
When a King Asks for a Chieftain's
Daughter.

Ilanakanar, Maturaiputan
Mothers.

Ilankiranar
What He Said to His Heart, Arguing against
Further Ambition and Travel.

Ilantiraiyan, Tontaiman
Great Wagon, The.

Ilaveyini, Kuramakal
Tiger, The.

Illica, Luigi. See **Giacosa, Giuseppe** and **Luigi
Illica**

Illyés, Gyula (b. 1902)
Deep Dusk.
Logbook of a Lost Caravan.
Part of a Novel.
Sour-Cherry Trees.
While the Record Plays.
Work.

Ilott, Percy H.
Witch, The.

Image, Selwyn (1849–1930)
Meditation for Christmas, A.

Imaizumi Sogetsu-Ni (d. 1804)
How beautiful the Buddhist statues.

Iman, Yusef
Love Your Enemy.

Imber, Naphtali Herz (1856–1909)
Hatikvah—a Song of Hope.
Zionist Marching Song.

Imbs, Bravig (1904–46)
Sleep.
Wind Was There, The.

Imlah, Mick (b. 1956)
Clio's.
Goldilocks.

Immanuel di Roma (c.1270–1330)
Elegy: "Floods of tears well from my deepest heart, The."
Happiness amidst Troubles.
Love has never read the Ave Maria.
Machberoth, sels.
My Sweet Gazelle!
On the Wall.
Paradise.
What Profit?
Worthless Heart, The.

Imr el [or ul] Kais (520–65)
Ode: "Weep, ah weep love's losing, love's with its dwelling place." From The Mu'allaqat

Imre, Flora
So, then, the soul craves an earthly body.

Inada, Lawson Fusao (b. 1938)
Blue Gene.
Blues for Dan Morin.
Concentration Constellation.
Father of My Father.
Filling the Gap.
From Our Album.
Great Bassist, The.
Kicking the Habit.
Plucking Out a Rhythm.
Projected Scenario of a Performance to Be Given Before the UN.
Wintersong.

Inez, Colette (b. 1931)
Absolving You.
Apothegms and Counsels.
Instructions for the Erection of a Statue to Myself in Central Park.
Old Lady Across the Hall Has Gone to Live Behind the Door, The.
Slumnight.
Warrior Daughters.
Woman Who Loved Worms, The.

Infante, Guillermo Cabrera (b. 1929)
I Want-a-name-'ere La Guantanamera.

Ingalls, John James (1833–1900)
Opportunity.

Ingamells, Rex (1913–55)
Great South Land, The, sels.
Memory of Hills, sels.
Unknown Land, sels.

Inge, Charles Cuthbert (b. 1868)
Limerick: "Certain young gourmet of Crediton, A."
On Professor Coué.

Inge, William Ralph (1860–1954)
Limerick: "There was a good Canon of Durham."
Limerick: "There was an old man of Khartoum."

Ingelow, Jean (1820–97)
About the Fairies.
Cold and Quiet.
Divided.
Echo and the Ferry.
For Exmoor.
High Tide on the Coast of Lincolnshire, 1571, The.
Little babe, while burns the west.
Long White Seam, The.
One Morning, Oh, So Early!
Songs of Seven, sels.
Story, A.

Winding-up Time.

"Ingoldsby, Thomas" (Richard Harris Barham) (1788–1845)
Eheu Fugaces.
Ingoldsby Legends, The, sels.
Lines Left at Mr Theodore Hook's House in June, 1834.
Not a sous had he got,—not a guinea or note.

Ingraham, Nicholas Lloyd
She Would Have Roses.
Woman Back in the Kitchen, The.

Ingram, Anne, Viscountess Irwin (c.1696–1764)
Castle Howard, the Seat of the Rt. Hon. Charles, Earl of Carlisle, sels.
Epistle to Pope Occasioned by His Characters of Women, An, sels.

Ingram, John Kells (1823–1907)
Memory of the Dead, The.

Inib-sarri (c.1790–1745 B.C.)
Letter to Her Father, A.

Inman, P.
Centered.
Colloam.
Dust Bowl, sels.
Subtracted Words.
XX.

Inman, Will (b. 1923)
108 Tales of a Po 'Buckra, sels.

Innes, Guy (1882–1953)
'It's three No Trumps,' the soldier said.

Inoue, Michiko (fl. mid 20th cent.)
Get Angry, Compass.

Instone, R. B. S.
Limerick: "How Socratic is Somerset Maugham!"

Iolo Goch (c.1320–c.1398)
Labourer, The.

Ion of Chios (b. c.490 B.C.)
Don't leave me.

Irby, Ken (b. 1936)
Heredom.
January 1965, Looking on.
Sequence.

Ireland, Kevin (b. 1933)
My First Forty Years.
Popular Romance, A.

Ireland, W. H.
To starve, or not to starve? that is the question.

Iremonger, Valentin (b. 1918)
Descending.
Dog, The.
Hector.
Icarus.
Invocation: "Ten bloody years with this quill lying."
This Houre Her Vigill.
Toy Horse, The.

Irenaeus Referendarius (fl c.6th cent.)
Eyes filled with speaking fire.
O supercilious delicious Rhodope.
Why do you stare at the floor, Chrysilla.
Why is the floor, Chrysilla.

"Ironquill." See Ware, Eugene Fitch

Irtenev, Igor Moiseievich (b. 1947)
Camelia.
Ditchdigger, The.
When I burn up without a trace.

Irumporai, Ceraman Kanikkal
King's Last Words, A.

Irvine, John (1903–64)
Invocation to Saint Bride.
Little Pets of Saint Mochua, The.
Saint Colm-Cille and the Cairn of Farewell.
Saint Fiacre.

Irvine, Weldon J., Jr. (b. 1943)
To be Young, Gifted, and Black.

Irving, Minna (b. 1872)
Marching Still.
Wedding Gift, The.

Irving, Washington (1783–1859)
Certain Young Lady, A.

Irwin, Mark
Robert Mapplethorpe's Photograph of Apollo (1988).

Irwin, Thomas Caulfield (1823–83)
Iphione.
Swift, sels.
With the Dawn.

Irwin, Wallace ("Ginger"; "Hashimura Togo") (1876–1959)
Constant Cannibal Maiden, The.
Reminiscence.
Worried Skipper, The.

Isaac ben Abun, Simeon ben, of Mainz (fl. c.1020)
All the Hosts of Heaven speak the mighty word.
I Come to Supplicate.

Isaac ben Samuel of Dampière (fl. c.1175)
His Hand Shall Cover Us.

Isaacs, Jorge (1837–95)
Nima, The.

Isakovsky [or Isakovskii], Mikhail Vasilevich (1900–1973)
Enemy had burned his cottage home, The.

Isanos, Magda (1916–44)
Apricot Tree.

Ise, Lady (d. 939)
As the first spring mists appear.
Because we suspected / the pillow would say "I know."
Correspondence: / when I have sad thoughts.
Elegy: Ise Lamenting the Death of Empress Onshi.
Even in dreams.
Even in my dreams / I must no longer meet you.
Flower of waves, A.
Hanging from the branches of a green / willow tree.
If I consider / My body like the fields.
If it is you, there / in the light boat on the pond.
Is it your command.
Like a ravaged sea / this bed.
Near a Waterfall at Ryumon.
News of the palace.
Not even in dreams / Can I meet him anymore.
On Seeing the Field Being Singed.
Seeing the Plum Blossoms by the River.
Seeing the Returning Geese.
Shall I come to see.
Since "the pillow knows all."
They are rebuilding / the old bridge, the Nagara.
When the fifth month comes.

Ise Tayu (fl. 11th cent.)
Clear water of the imperial pond, The.
Farmer's clothes are soaked through and never dried, The.
I thought the chrysanthemum bloomed in autumn.
In Nara, the ancient capital.
It is already so late at night.
Only the waning morning moon / visits my garden.
Today is the anniversary of our parting.
Unable to sleep / I gaze at the flowers of the bush clover.

Iselda. See Carenza and Iselda

Isherwood, Christopher (1904–86)
Common Cormorant [or Shag], The.
On His Queerness.

Ishigaki, Rin (b. 1920)
Clams.
Cocoon.
Shellfish.
Walking-with-a-Cane-Pass.

Ishikawa Takuboku (1885–1920)
Tanka: "Accidentally."
Tanka: "As if in water."
Tanka: "Beastly face."
Tanka: "Color, The."
Tanka: "Fearing."
Tanka: "Forgetting."

Ishkhan

Tanka: "Has Fate sneaked in."
Tanka: "I close my eyes."
Tanka: "I work."
Tanka: "Just for fun."
Tanka: "Like a white lotus."
Tanka: "Mirror in hand."
Tanka: "On the roadside."
Tanka: "Sadly."
Tanka: "Somehow."
Tanka: "Sorrow."
Tanka: "What always seemed."
Tanka: "When I breathe."
Tanka: "Words from."
Tanka: "Young maidens."

Ishkhan, Moushegh (b. 1913)
Armenian Language Is the Home of the
Armenian, The.

Isidorus (d. 450?)
My name is Eteocles. The sea seduced me
from my farm.
Now Endymion dedicates / his cold bed's
failure to the moon.
On a Fowler.

Iskander, Fazil Abdulovich (b. 1929)
Devil and the Shepherd, The.
Overtired branches are fragile.

Iskrenko, Nina (b. 1951)
Polystylistics is when a knight from the
Middle Ages.
To Beat or Not to Beat.

Isler, Elizabeth
Little Things, The.

Ismail (b. 1928)
Wall, The.

Issa (Kobayashi Issa) (1763–1827)
Bird in the cage, The.
Cat, The.
Don't worry, spiders.
Flying out from.
From the bough / floating down river.
In my life / As in the twilight.
In the cherry blossom's shade.
Man pulling radishes, The.
Mosquito at my ear.
No mother! No father!
One person.
Only one guy and.
Wild Goose, Wild Goose.
Wren, The.

Issa, Kobayashi. See **Issa**

Issahakian, Avedik (1875–1957)
Climb Mount Fuji.
Don't kill that fly!
Even with insects—.
For you fleas too.
Mosquito at my ear—.
Under the evening moon.

Issaia, Nana (b. 1934)
Dream.
Sacrifice.

Ita, Saint (480–570)
Jesukin.

Italicus, Tiberius Catius Asconius Silius. See
Silius Italicus

Itwaru, Arnold H. (b. 1942)
And in this carnival you offer me.
Body Rites.

**Ivanov, Georgy [or Georgii] Vladimirovich
(1894–1958)**
Boiling up over the years.
Covered with a glory that had lost its luster.
Even the graves are not tended in Russia.
Fog. The road I usually wander down.
I imagine everything wrapped in a beatific
mist.
I walk and think of various things.
If you want to live, then live...
People? What do I care about people?
Spring said nothing to me—it couldn't.
They'll not exterminate you now.
Tune becomes a flower, The.

Ivanov, Vyacheslav Ivanovich (1866–1949)
Holy Rose, The.
Russian Mind, The.

Ivanova, Iraida Gustavovna Geinike. See
Odoyevtseva, Irina

Ivask, Ivar
And then I told about the red soil of
Oklahoma.
Foliage foliage.
I am the shepherd of the heavenly flock.
We shall return we will stay here.

Ivask, Yury [or Iurii] (1907–86)
Ode for the Dancing Khlysty.
Shall we forget the shiver.

Ivaska, Astride
Autumn in the Cascade Mountains, sels.
For My Godmother.
K. H.
That which has remained unlived.
To the Memory of a Poet.

Iverem, Esther
Daddy's Friends.
Earth Screaming.
Keeper.
Murmur.
Time #2, The.

Iverson, Lucille
Outrage.

Iwaszkiewicz, Jaroslaw (b. 1894)
How Does the Negative Look. . . .
Pope in Ancona, The.

Izen, Hirose
As the late night passes.

Izumi, Lady (Izumi Shikibu) (c.974–c.1030)
After the Death of Her Daughter in Child-
birth.
Although the wind.
Another cruel letter today.
As I dig for wild orchids.
As the rains of spring.
At the Sutra Chanting of Her Dead Daughter.
Come quickly—as soon as.
Cricket Heard.
From darkness / I go onto the road / of
darkness.
From that first night.
Here in this world / I won't live.
I cannot say,
I go out of darkness / Onto a road of
darkness.
I left my hills.
I picked an azalea.
I wish you would come.
If you have no time.
If you love me.
In the Autumn, on Retreat at a Mountain
Temple.
In the dusk the path.
It is the time of rain and snow.
Lying here alone.
Never could I think / Our love a worldly
commonplace.
On nights when hail / falls noisily.
On this winter night.
Orange leaves are gone.
Out of the darkness / on a dark path.
Pillow that knows all, The.
Recklessly / I cast myself away.
Since that night / I cannot know myself.
Someone else / looked at the sky.
Watching the moon.
Way I must enter, The.
When you broke from me.
Will I cease to be.
You told me it was / because of me.
You wear the face.

J

"J., L."
Day at the Farm, A.

"J., L. E."
Limerick: "Conception, an Archbishop said,
The."

"J., M."
Animal Howl, The.
Funeral, The.

Song of a Jewish Boy.

"J., W."
City Eclogue, A.

Jabès, Edmond (b. 1912)
Beginning of the Book, The.
Book, The.
Book of Questions, The, sels.
Desert, The.
Desert, II, The.
Notebook, Two.

Jaccottet, Philippe (b. 1925)
Dawn.
Daybreak / mingles blood.
Distances.
Don't worry, you'll get there! You're close.
Fruit.
Glimpses.
I rise with an effort and look out.
Letter of the 26th June.
Reason.
Right at the end of night.
Serenity.
Swifts.
These wood-shadows, timid, patient.
Weight of stones, of thoughts.
Wishes.
Wound seen from afar.

Jacinto, Antonio (b. 1924)
Letter from a Contract Worker.
Monangamba.
Poem of Alienation.

Jackowska, Nicki (b. 1942)
Family Outing—a Celebration.
Insect Kitchen, The.
Meeting, The.
Sisters, The.

Jackson, Angela (b. 1951)
Billie in Silk.
Choosing the Blues.
Love of Travellers, The.
Make/n My Music.
Ohnedaruth.

Jackson, David (b. 1931)
Grandmother Jackson.

Jackson, E. J.
Limerick: "There once was a fellow called
Hyde."

**Jackson, Helen Hunt ("H. H."; "Saxe Holm")
(1830–85)**
Cheyenne Mountain.
Crossed Threads.
Dreams.
Grab-Bag.
In Time of Famine.
Last Words.
My Lighthouses.
October.
October's Bright Blue Weather.
Poppies on the Wheat.
September [Days Are Here].
Tides.
Two Truths.

Jackson, Laura Riding (1901–91)
All things that wake enjoy the sun.
Dimensions.
Ding-Donging.
Elegy in a Spider's Web.
Forgiven Past, The.
Forgotten Girlhood, sels.
Head Itself.
Helen's Burning.
In the Beginning.
Lullaby, The.
Makeshift.
Nothing so far but moonlight.
Only Daughter, The.
Poet's Corner, The.
Prisms.
Sad Boy, The.
Starved.
Summary for Alastor.
Take hands. / There is no love now.
There Is No Land Yet.
Toward the Corner.
Virgin, The.
Wind Suffers of Blowing, The.

Wind, the Clock, the We, The.
World and I, The.

Jackson, Leroy F.
Fun.
Grandpa dropped his glasses once.

Jackson, Lorri
Prima Donna Poet Replies, A.

Jackson, Mae (b. 1946)
Blues Today, The.
For Some Poets.
I Remember ("I remember / January, / 1968.")
January 3, 1970.
Reincarnation.

Jackson, Michael (b. 1940)
Macrocarpas.
Mask-Maker.
Moths, The.
Red Flag, The.
Return from Luluabourg.
Socrates' Death.

Jackson, Reuben (b. 1956)
After the Dance.
Albert james was black long before me.
Big Chill Variations.
For Thurman Thomas.
Jamal's Lamentation.
Lady's Way.
Lonely Affair, A.
1973.
Sunday Brunch.
Tee.

Jackson, Richard
Angels of 1912 and 1972, The.
Circumstances.
Homeric.
Shadows.
Violation, A.

Jacob, Hildebrand (1693–1739)
Alarm, The.
Here Delia's buried at fourscore.
Judgement of Tiresias, The.
Swain, give o'er your fond pretension.
To Cloe.
To Geron.

Jacob, Max (1876–1944)
Cock and the Pearl, The, *sels.*
Horrible Today, The.
In Search of the Traitor.
Moon Poem.
1914.
To Modigliani to Prove to Him That I Am a Poet.
War.

Jacob, Violet (1863–1946)
Baltic, The.
Jock, to the First Army.
Last o' the Tinkler, The.
Pride.
Tam i' the Kirk.

Jacobs, Bertha. *See* **Bertken, Sister**

Jacobs, Harriet (b. 1951)
It is not just.
On Growing Up the Darker Berry.

Jacobs, Henry Eyster (1844–1932)
Lord Jesus Christ, We Humbly Pray.

Jacobs, Henry S. (1827–93)
How Goodly Is Thy House.

Jacobs, Leland B. (b. 1907)
Subway train, the / subway train, The.

Jacobsen, Josephine (b. 1908)
Bush.
Destinations.
Food.
Hourglass.
It Is the Season.
Limbo Dancer, The.
Matadors, The.
Motion, The.
Only Alice.
Primer, The.
Rainy Night at the Writers' Colony.
Reindeer and Engine.
Sea Fog, The.
Shade-Seller, The.

Sisters, The.
Thief, The.
When the Five Prominent Poets.

Jacobsen, Rolf (b. 1907)
Catacombs in San Callisto, The.
Cobalt.
Express train 1256 races alongside hidden, remote villages. House.
Green Light.
Guardian Angel.
Rubber.
Sunflower.

Jacopo da Lentino (*fl.* 13th cent.)
Canzonetta: He Will Neither Boast nor Lament to His Lady.
Canzonetta: Of His Lady, and of His Making Her Likeness.
Of His Lady in Heaven.
Sonnet: Of His Lady's Face.

Jacot, Emile
Jack Tar.
Wandering Jack.
Who's That A-Knocking?

Jafri, Ali Sardar (b. 1913)
Morsel.

Jago, Richard (1715–81)
Absence.
Edge-Hill; or, The Rural Prospect Delineated and Moralised, *sels.*
Hamlet's Soliloquy Imitated.

Jahan, Nur, Empress (d. 1646)
Moon of Id came, The.
Your love turned my body into water.

Jahin, Salah
Quatrains.

Jakuren (d. 1202)
Hanging raindrops, The.

Jallais, Denise
Lullaby for My Dead Child.

Jamal Isfahani (d. 1192)
White hairs.

Jamal, Mahmood (b. 1948)
Deflowering.
Work-in-progress.

James, Alice Archer Sewall ("James") (b. c.1870?)
Graffiti.

James, Allston
Honor (1969).

James, Clive (b. 1939)
Book of my enemy has been remaindered, The.
Johnny Weissmuller Dead in Acapulco.
To Pete Atkin: A Letter from Paris, *sels.*

James, David (b. 1955)
Blind Man Who Sells Brushes, The.
Harvest.
Love of Water Faucets, The.

James, Elmore (1918–1963)
Sunnyland.

James I, King of England (1566–1625)
Admonition to Montgomerie.
Epitaph on Sir Philip Sidney, An.
Lady Cicely Wemyss.
Sonnet on Sir William Alexander's Harsh Verses after the English Fashion, A.

James I, King of Scotland (1394–1437)
Kingis Quair, The, *sels.*
Spring Song of the Birds.

James, John (1633–1729)
Of John Bunyan's Life.
On the Decease of the Religious and Honourable Jno Haynes Esqr.

James, John (1633–1729) *and* **Robert Wedderburn**
Balulalow.

James, John (b. 1939)
After Christopher Wood.
Cambridge.
For the Safety of Lovers.
On Leaving the Footpath.
Side Window.

Sister Midnight.

James, Nicholas (*fl.* c.1742)
Complaints of Poverty, The, *sels.*

James, Sibyl
Inner Mongolia—The Grasslands.
Short Wave In Shanghai.

James, Thomas (1593?–1635?)
Lines on His Companions Who Died in the Northern Seas.

James, Thomas (1946–73)
Hunting for Blueberries.
Letter to a Mute.
Letters to a Stranger.
Mummy of a Lady Named Jemutesonekh XXI Dynasty.
Reasons.

James V, King of Scotland (1513–42)
Christ's Kirk on the Grene, *sels.*
Jolly Beggar, The.

James, William (1842–1910)
Hogamous, higamous.

Jami, Nuru'ddin Abdu 'R-Rahman (1414–92)
Even from earthly love thy face avert not.

Jamie, Kathleen (b. 1962)
Aunt Janet's Museum.
Black Spiders.
Way We Live, The.

Jamieson, Robert Alan
De.

Jamíl (660?–701)
Salsabíl.

Jamison, Barbara
Ask This of a Mother Whose Daughter Has Been Tortured.

Jammes, Francis (1868–1938)
Amsterdam.
Child Reads an Almanac, The ("The child reads on; her basket of eggs stands by.")
Five Sorrowful Mysteries, The.
Little Donkey, The.
Love.
Prayer to Go to Paradise with the Asses.
Prayer to Go to Paradise with the Donkeys, A.

Jana Bai (*fl.* 14th cent.)
Cast off all shame.
She was my staff and I am blind.

Janeczko, Paul B. (b. 1945)
Blanket Hog.
How to Hug Your Three-Year-Old Daughter.

Janevski, Slavko
Song of the Eternal Sailor, The.

Janeway, Cill
Rose.

Janko, Marcel. *See* **Huelsenbeck, Richard, Marcel Janko,** *and* **Tristan Tzara**

Janosco, Beatrice
Garden Hose, The.

Janowitz, Phyllis (b. 1940)
Change.
Necessary Angel, The.
Reach.

Japanese Oral Tradition
Butterfly Wine.

Jaques, Florence Page (1890–1972)
There Once Was a Puffin.

Jarmain, John
Embarkation, 1942.

Jarman, Mark (b. 1955)
Black Riviera, The.
Cavafy in Redondo.
Children are hiding among the raspberry canes, The.
Desire of Water, The.
Gift, The.
Grid.
Homing Instinct, The.
Los Angeles.
Mirror, The.
Questions for Ecclesiastes.
Shrine and the Burning Wheel, The.
Supremes, The.
Unholy Sonnets.

Jarrell, Randall (1914–65)
Aging.
Augsburg Adoration, The.
Author to the Reader, The.
Bats.
Bird of Night, The.
Black Swan, The.
Blind Sheep, The.
Burning the Letters.
Camp in the Prussian Forest, A.
Chipmunk's Day, The.
Cinderella.
Come to the Stone.
Country Life, A.
Dead Wingman, The.
Death of the Ball Turret Gunner, The.
Description of Some Confederate Soldiers, A.
Eighth Air Force.
Elementary Scene, The.
Emancipators, The.
Field and Forest.
Field Hospital, A.
For an Emigrant.
Front, A.
Game at Salzburg, A.
Girl in a Library, A.
Happy Cat, The.
Hope.
House in the Wood, The.
Hunt in the Black Forest, A.
In a Hospital Garden.
In Montecito.
In Nature There Is Neither Right nor Left nor
   Wrong.
In the Camp There Was One Alive.
Islands, The.
Jews at Haifa.
Jonah.
Knight, Death, and the Devil, The.
Lonely Man, The.
Losses.
Lost Children, The.
Lullaby, A: "For wars his life and half a
   world away."
Man Meets a Woman in the Street, A.
Märchen, The.
Mockingbird, The.
Nestus Gurley.
Next Day.
90 North.
On the Railway Platform.
Orient Express, The.
Pilot from the Carrier, A.
Pilots, Man Your Planes.
Player Piano, The.
Prisoners.
Protocols.
Range in the Desert, The.
Refugees, The.
Second Air Force.
Seele im Raum.
Sick Child, A.
Sick Nought, The.
Sleeping Beauty: Variation of the Prince,
   The.
Snow-Leopard, The.
Soldier Walks under the Trees of the
   University, The.
Soul, A.
State, The.
Thinking of the Lost World.
Truth, The.
Variations.
War, A.
Ways and the Peoples, The.
Well Water.
When I was home last Christmas.
Woman.
Woman at the Washington Zoo, The.
Jarry, Alfred (1873–1907)
Passion of Jesus Considered as an Uphill
   Race, The.
Ubu Cocu, *sels.*
Jastrun, Tomasz (b. 1950)
Hat.
Polish Knot, The.
Scrap.

Seed, The.
Jastrzebska, Maria
Bi-lingual.
My Illness and Other Animals.
Jauss, David (b. 1951)
After the End of the World.
Black Orchid.
Javitz, Alexander
Old Men, The.
Jayadeva (*fl.* 12th cent.)
Gita Govinda, The, *sels.*
Jayaprabha, A. (b. 1957)
Burn this Sari.
Jean de Meun. *See* **Guillaume de Lorris** *and*
Jean de Meun
Jebeleanu, Eugen
Hannibal.
Jeffers, Lance (1919–85)
Flesh of the Young Men Is Burning, The.
Grief Streams Down My Chest.
How High the Moon.
I do not know the power of my hand.
My Blackness Is the Beauty of This Land.
Nina Simone.
Old Love Butchered (Colorado Springs and
   Huachuca).
On Listening to the Spirituals.
There is a nation in my brawny scrotal sac.
To him who in his absence from himself.
Trellie.
Tuskegee, Tuskegee!
When I Know the Power of my Black Hand.
Jeffers, Robinson (1887–1962)
Age in Prospect.
Answer, The.
Ante Mortem.
Antrim.
Apology for Bad Dreams.
Artist, An.
Ascent to the Sierras.
Autumn Evening.
Ave Caesar.
Beaks of Eagles, The.
Beauty of Things, The.
Birds.
Birds and Fishes.
Birth-Dues.
Black-out.
Bloody Sire, The.
Boats in a Fog.
But I Am Growing Old and Indolent.
Carmel Point.
Cassandra.
Clouds of Evening.
Coast-Road, The.
Compensation.
Continent's End.
Credo.
Cremation.
Crumbs or the Loaf.
Deer Lay Down Their Bones, The.
Divinely Superfluous Beauty.
Eagle Valor, Chicken Mind.
Evening Ebb.
Eye, The.
Fawn's Foster-Mother.
Fire on the Hills.
Gale in April.
Granite and Cypress.
Gray Weather.
Haunted Country.
Hurt Hawks.
I Shall Laugh Purely.
Inquisitors, The.
Joy.
Life from the Lifeless.
Love the Wild Swan.
Maid's Thought, The.
May-June, 1940.
New Mexican Mountain.
Night.
Noon.
Nova.
November Surf.
Original Sin.
Pelicans.

Phenomena.
Place for No Story, The.
Post Mortem.
Prescription of Painful Ends.
Promise of Peace.
Purse-Seine, The.
Rearmament.
Rock and Hawk.
Science.
Self-Criticism in February.
Shane O'Neill's Cairn.
Shine, Perishing Republic.
Shine, Republic.
Shiva.
Stars Go Over the Lonely Ocean, The.
Still the mind smiles at its own rebellions.
Summer Holiday.
To the Stone-Cutters.
Trumpet, The, *sels.*
Unnatural Powers.
Vulture.
Watch the Lights Fade.
Woodrow Wilson.
Jefferson, Blind Lemon
Easy Rider Blues.
Jefferson, Joseph (1829–1905)
Immortality.
Jefferson, Thomas
Preamble to the Declaration of Independence.
Jefferys [*or* Jeffries], Charles
Jeannette and Jeannot.
Jeannot's Answer.
We have lived and loved together.
Jeffrey, Francis, Lord Jeffrey (1773–1850)
Epitaph: "Here lies the body of Richard
   Hind."
In Christ Church, Bristol, on Thomas Turner,
   Twice Master of the Company of Bakers.
On Peter Robinson.
Jeffrey, William (1896–1946)
On Glaister's Hill, *sels.*
Stones in Jordan's stream, The.
Jeitteles, Alois (1794–1858)
To My Distant Beloved.
Jeitteles, Benedict (1762–1813)
Epitaph for a Judge.
Jekyll, Joseph (1752–1837)
See, one physician, like a sculler, plies.
Jemie, Onwuchekwa (b. 1940)
Iroko.
Toward a Poetics.
Jemmat, Catherine (*fl.* 1750–66)
Rural Lass, The.
Jenkins, Christina (b. 1962)
Sunday Morning.
Jenkins, John (b. 1949) *and* **Ken Bolton (b.**
1949)
In Ferrara.
Jenkins, Louis (b. 1942)
Appointed Rounds.
Confessional Poem.
Football.
In a Tavern.
Library.
Walking through a Wall.
Jenks, Orville
Dying Mine Brakeman, The.
Jenks, Tudor (1857–1922)
Accommodating Lion, An.
Hard to Bear.
Jenner, Charles (1736–74)
Eclogue IV: The Poet, *sels.*
Jenner, Edward (1749–1823)
Signs of Rain.
Jenner, Henry L.
My Savior, hear my prayer.
Jennings, Elizabeth (b. 1926)
Afterthought.
Animals' Arrival, The.
Answers.
At Night.
Counterpart, The.
Delay.
First Love.

Fountain.
Fragment for the Dark.
Friendship.
Her Garden.
In a Garden.
In the Night.
Interrogator, The.
Letter to Peter Levi, A.
My animals are made of wool and glass.
My Grandmother.
Not in the Guide-Books.
One Flesh.
Relationships.
Song at the Beginning of Autumn.
Song for a Birth or a Death.
Sonnets of Michelangelo, The, *sels.*
Storm House, The.
Teresa of Avila.
Thinking of Love.
To a Friend with a Religious Vocation.
Ugly Child, The.
Unknown Child, The.
Visitation, The.
Winter Love.
Works of Art.
Young Ones, The.

Jennings, Humphrey (1907–50)
Prose Poem.

Jennings, Kate
Couples.
Just the Two of Us.

Jensen, Laura (b. 1948)
Adoration of the Anchor.
After I Have Voted.
Age, An.
Ajax Samples, The.
As the Window Darkens.
Candles Draw Well after All, The.
Cloud Parade, The.
House Is an Enigma.
Household.
In the Hospital.
Indian.
Kitchen.
Kite.
Pony Farm.
Red Dog, The.
Sleep in the Heat.
Talking to the Mule.
To a Stranger (At the End of a Caboose).
Winter Evening Poem.

Jensma, Wopko (b. 1939)
In Memoriam Akbar Babool.
In Memoriam Ben Zwane.

Jentzsch, Bernd
Dead Father, The.
Terezin, the Graveyard.

Jenyns, Soame (1704–87)
Art of Dancing, The, *sels.*
Choice, The.
Doctor Johnson.
Epistle Written in the Country to the Right
  Honourable the Lord Lovelace, An, *sels.*
Epitaph on Dr Samuel Johnson.
Modern Fine Gentleman, The, *sels.*
Modern Fine Lady, The, *sels.*
Snow-Ball, The.
Temple of Venus, The.
To a Nosegay in Pancharilla's Breast.

"Jerry, Bongo" (Robin Small) (b. 1948)
Mabrak.

Jesús, Teresa de
All of a Sudden.
They go by, go by, love, the days and the
  hours.

Jewell, Foster
Cliff dweller ruins.
Disturbing some brush.
Fall wind in pinyons.
Finding this cavern.
Last screech owl cry.
Mountain shadow.
Nearing the mountain.
Some unknown sound.
Somewhere behind me.
That breeze brought it.

This evening stillness.
Thunder storm passing.
Under ledges.
Where the coyote called.

Jewett, Ellen A.
Sermon in a Stocking.

Jewett, Sarah Orne (1849–1909)
At Home from Church.
Caged Bird, A.
Country Boy in Winter, A.
Together.
Widows' House, The.

"Jewish Sibyl, The"
Fourth Book of Sibylline Oracles, The, *sels.*

Jewsbury, Maria Jane (1800–1833)
Farewell to the Muse, A.
My heart's in the kitchen, my heart is not
  here.
Partings.
Summer Eve's Vision, A.
To a Young Brother.
To My Own Heart.
Verses: "I am monarch of troubles a host."

Jiles, Paulette (b. 1933)
Paper Matches.
Tallness.
Time to Myself.
Tin Woodsman, The.
Windigo.

Jiménez, Juan Ramón (1881–1958)
Green was the maiden, green, green!
I am not I.
I unpetalled you, like a rose.
Lamb Was Bleating Softly, The.
Ten Short Poems, *sels.*

Jito, Empress (645–702)
Even a flaming fire can be snatched. *From*
  Manyo Shu, Part 1 of 4.
On the Death of the Emperor Temmu.
Spring is passing and.
Stars pass, The.
Sudden Appearance of Cherry Blossoms, The.
  From Manyo Shu, Part 3 of 4.

Joachim, Paulin (b. 1931)
Burial.

Joad, C. E. M. (1891–1953)
Materialism.

Joan, Natalie
Dicky-Birds.
Kind Mousie, The.

Joans, Ted (b. 1928)
Black People.
Its Curtains.
Protective Grigri, The.
Scenery.
.38, The.
Truth, The.

Johannes Barbucollas (*fl.* c.551)
Don't halt your voyage, sailor, nor drop sail.

Johannes Secundus (Jan Nicolai Everaerts)
Basia, *sels.*

John, Gwen (1876–1939)
Child's Winter Evening, A.

John of Damascus, Saint (c.700–c.760)
Day of Resurrection, The.

John of the Cross, Saint (1542–91)
Christmas Ballad.
Commentary Applied to Spiritual Things.
Coplas about the Soul Which Suffers with
  Impatience to See God, *sels.*
Dark Night, The.
More Stanzas Applied to Spiritual Things.
O Flame of Living Love.
Obscure Night of the Soul, The.
Song of the Soul That Knows God by Faith.
Song of the Soul that Rejoices in Knowing
  God through Faith.
Spiritual Canticle, The.
Stanzas Concerning an Ecstasy Experienced
  in High Contemplation.
Stanzas of the Soul that Suffers with Longing
  to See God.

John Paul II, Pope. *See* Wojtyla, Karol

**John, Richard Johnny, Jerome Rothenberg, and
Ian Tyson**
Songs from the Society of the Mystic
  Animals, *sels.*

Johnson, Amryl (b. 1939)
And Sea.
Conqueror of a Forbidden Landscape.
Gifts.
Granny in de Market Place.
Identikit, The.

Johnson, Ann
Grandma.

Johnson, Burges (1877–1963)
Soap, the Oppressor.

Johnson, Don Allen ("Mustafa") (b. 1942)
Fountain, The.
Home Game.
I Traveled with Them.
Thy Garden.

Johnson, Edward (1598–1672)
Among These Troopes of Christs Souldiers,
  Came. . . . Mr. Roger Harlackenden.
Good News from New England, *sels.*
Mr. Eliot Pastor of the Church of Christ at
  Roxbury.
Mr. Thomas Shepeard.
Oh King of Saints, how great's thy work, say
  we.
Onely the Reverend Grave and Godly Mr.
  Buckly Remaines.
Reverend Mr, The. Higginson.
Yee Shall Not Misse of a Few Lines in
  Remembrance of Thomas Hooker.

**Johnson, Emily Pauline ("Tekahionwake")
(1886–1913)**
Cattle Thief, The.
Marshlands.
Ojistoh.

Johnson, Esther ("Stella") (1681–1728)
If It Be True.
Jealousy.
To Dr. Swift on His Birthday, 30th
  November 1721.

Johnson, Fenton (1886–1958)
Aunt Jane Allen.
Lonely Mother, The.
My God in Heaven said to me.
Scarlet Woman, The.
Singing Hallelujia.
Song of the Whirlwind.
Tired.

Johnson, Fred (b. 1940)
Arabesque.
Fire, Hair, Meat and Bone.

Johnson, George Sands (1894?–1951?)
Beyond the Beaten Way.
By the Pasture Bars.
Christmas Rhyme, A.
Course of a Year, The.
Deacon Brown's Conclusion.
I Am Growing Old.
If We Try.
Old Rustic Mill, The.
Uncle Sam's Soliloquy.
Wisdom.

Johnson, Georgia Douglas (1886–1966)
Common Dust.
Credo.
Escape.
Heart of a woman [goes forth with the
  dawn], The.
I Want to Die While You Love Me.
Interracial.
Lost Illusions.
My Little Dreams.
Old Black Men.
Prejudice.
Riddle, The.
Smothered Fires.
Suppliant, The.
When I am dead, withhold, I pray, your
  blooming legacy.
Youth.

Johnson, Helene (1907–95)
Bottled [New York].

Invocation: "Let me be buried in the rain."
Magalu.
Poem: "Little brown boy."
Remember not the promises we made.
Road, The.
Sonnet to a Negro in Harlem.
Summer Matures.
Trees at Night.

Johnson, James Weldon (1871–1938)
Before a Painting.
Brothers.
Color Sergeant, The.
Creation, The, *sels.*
Fifty Years.
Girl of fifteen.
Glory of the Day Was in Her Face, The.
Go Down Death.
Judgment Day, The.
Lift every [*or* ev'ry] voice and sing.
Listen, Lord—[a Prayer].
Mother Night.
My City.
O Black and unknown bards of long ago.
Sence You Went Away.

Johnson, Joe (b. 1940)
If I Ride This Train.
Judeebug's Country.

Johnson, Jonathan (b. 1967)
Renewal.

Johnson, Joyce
Bat that blocks at close of play, The.
Limerick: "Both Keats and Boccaccio tell a."
Limerick: "Exposing his plate to the air."
Limerick: "Old Woman who lived in the Shoe, The."
Limerick: "Simple living was clearly the nub."
Limerick: "Three Aldis, not one of them dim."
Limerick: "Wee Jamie, a canny young Scot."
Limerick: "'What's the matter, old chap?' 'Well, I came.'"
Limerick: "When the Prince, who was terribly smit."

Johnson, Leslie
Limerick: "Don't think it will fall to your lot."
Limerick: "If you feel that you're right on your beam ends."
Limerick: "My purpose was purely corrective."
Limerick: "Sardines seem to get out of hand."
Limerick: "There once was an eccentric of Metz."
Limerick: "Toper who spies in the distance, A."
Paradise Lost, Book IV, lines 639—654.

Johnson, Linton Kwesi (b. 1952)
Bass Culture.
Beacon of Hope.
Great Insohreckshan, Di.
Reggae fi Dada.

Johnson, Lionel Pigot (1867–1902)
Age of a Dream, The.
By the Statue of King Charles [*or* I] at Charing Cross.
Church of a Dream, The.
Collins.
Dark Angel, with thine aching lust.
Dead.
Decadent's Lyric, A.
Destroyer of a Soul, The.
In Honorem Doriani Creatorisque Eius.
In Honour of Dorian and his Creator.
In Memory, *sels.*
Lambeth Lyric.
Mystic and Cavalier.
Nihilism.
Oxford.
Precept of Silence, The.
Roman Stage, The.
Saint Columba.
Stranger, A.
Te Martyrum Candidatus.
To a Passionist.
To a Traveler.

To Morfydd.
Troopship, The.
Victory.

Johnson, Louis (b. 1924)
Bread and a Pension.
Death of the Bosun's Mate.
Here Together Met.
Magpie and Pines.
Marrows.
New Guinea Time.
Seventies, The.
Tahiti.
Vision.

Johnson, Maggie Pogue (b. 1949)
Ambition.
As We Sow We Shall Reap.
Christmas Times.
Dat Mule ob Brudder Wright's.
Day befo' Thanksgibin', De.
Dedicated to Dr. W. H. Sheppard.
Dedication Day.
Dream, A.
I Wish I Was a Grown Up Man.
James Hugo Johnston.
Krismas Dinnah.
Leap Yeah Party, De.
Lost Teddy Bear, The.
Meal Time.
Men Folks ob Today, De.
Negro Has a Chance, The.
Old Maid's Soliloquy.
People's Literary, De.
Poet of Our Race.
Sister Johnson's Speech.
Sometimes.
Story of Lovers Leap, The.
Strawberry, The.
Superstitions.
Thoughts.
To Professor Byrd Prillerman.
To See Ol' Booker T.
V. N. and C. I, The.
What's de Use ob Wukin in de Summer Time at All.
What's Mo' Temptin' to de Palate?
When Daddy Cums from Wuk.
Why Should the American Negro Be Proud?
Wintah Styles, De.

Johnson, Margaret (b. 1926)
Day Dreams, or Ten Years Old.

Johnson, Norman M.
Hob the Elf.

Johnson, Pyke, Jr. (1889–1969?)
Toucan, The.

Johnson, Robert (c.1898–1937)
Hellhound on My Trail.
Love in Vain.

Johnson, Ronald (b. 1935)
Ark, *sels.*
Ark 34, Spire on the Death of L.Z.
Ark 44, The Rod of Aaron.
Beam 30, The Garden.
Letters to Walt Whitman, *sels.*
William Stukeley made his own Stonehenge.

Johnson, Samuel (1709–84)
Anacreon's Dove.
Ballad: "Put my hat upon my head."
Ballad: "I therefore pray thee, Renny dear."
Ballad: "If the man who turnips cries."
Ballad: "Tender infant, meek and mild, The."
Comets and Princes.
Do They Return?
Empty Heart, An.
Epitaph on William Hogarth, An.
Epitaph upon the Celebrated Claudy Phillips, Musician, Who Died Very Poor, An.
I am Cassander come down from the Sky.
Idyll: "Hermit hoar, in solemn cell."
If the man who Turneps cries.
Lines on Thomas Warton's Poems.
London: A Poem.
London: A Poem in Imitation of the Third Satire of Juvenal, *sels.*
On the Death of Dr [*or* Mr] Robert Levet [a Practiser in Physic].
ad. fr. the Bible, Proverbs, 6, 6.

Prologue Spoken by Mr[.] Garrick at the Opening of the Theatre in Drury Lane, 1747, *sels.*
Prologue to Garrick's *Lethe.*
Prologue to Hugh Kelly's *A Word to the Wise.*
Short Song of Congratulation [*or* To a Young Heir], A.
Song Composed for Fanny Burney, A.
To Mrs Thrale [on Her Thirty-fifth Birthday].
To Robbers furious, and to Lovers tame.
Translation of Lines by Benserade.
Turnip Vendor, The.
Vanity of Human Wishes [The Tenth Satire of Juvenal Imitated], The, *sels.*
Verses in Baretti's Commonplace Book.
While many a merry tale, and many a song.

Johnson, Samuel (1822–82)
Father, in Thy Mysterious Presence Kneeling.
I Bless Thee, Lord, for Sorrows Sent.
Life of Ages, Richly Poured.

Johnson, Siddie Joe (1906–77)
Midnight in Bonnie's Stall.

Johnston, Bertha
Did You Ever Hear an English Sparrow Sing?

Johnston, Ellen (1835–1873)
Address to Nature on its Cruelty, An.
Lines: To a Young Gentleman of Surpassing Beauty.
Lines to Ellen, the Factory Girl.
Mother's Love, A.
Nelly's Lament for the Pirnhouse Cat.
Working Man, The.

Johnston, George (b. 1913)
Bliss.
Bulge, The.
Cathleen Sweeping.
Indoors.
Music on the Water.
Noctambule.
O Earth, Turn!
Veterans.
War on the Periphery.

Johnston, Martin (b. 1947)
Airport.
Directions for Dreamfishing.
Gorey at the Biennale.
In Memoriam.
In Transit: A Sonnet Square, *sels.*
Quantum.
Sea-Cucumber, The.
Vernal Equinox.

Johnston, T.
Limerick: "There was a young lady of Ulva / Who kept a pet bee in her hand-bag."

Johnstone, Philip
High Wood.

Johnstone, Robert (b. 1951)
Eden Says No.
Every Cache, *sels.*
Fruit of Knowledge, The.
New Incidents in the Life of Shelley, *sels.*
Robot Camera.
Undertakers.

Jolobe, J. J. R. (1902–76)
Making of a Servant, The.

Jonas, George (b. 1935)
For the Record.
Four Stanzas Written in Anxiety.
Portrait: The Freedom Fighter.
Temporal.

Jonas, Gerald (b. 1935)
Night Thought.

Jonas, Rosalie (1861?–1953)
Ballade des Belles Milatraisses.
Brother Baptis' on Woman Suffrage.

Jonas, Samuel Alroy
Lines on the Back of a Confederate Note.

Jones, Alice
Foot, The.

Jones, Bobi (b. 1929)
Portrait of a Nun.
Portrait of a Pregnant Woman.
Portrait of an Engine Driver.

Spring at Nant Dywelan.

Jones, David (1895–1974)
A, a, a, Domine Deus.
Anathemata, The, *sels.*
In Parenthesis, *sels.*
Mabinog's Liturgy, *sels.*
Sleeping Lord, The, *sels.*
Wall, The.

Jones, David Gwenallt ("Gwenallt") (1899–1968)
Cymru.
Earth, The.
Old Woman, An.
Rhydcymerau.

Jones, Douglas G. (b. 1929)
Beautiful Creatures Brief as These.
For Spring.
From Sex, This Sea.
I Thought There Were Limits.
On a Picture of Your House.
Perishing Bird, The.
River; North of Guelph, The.
Soliloquy to Absent Friends.
Summer Is a Poem by Ovid.
These Trees Are No Forest of Mourners.

Jones, Ebenezer (1820–60)
Development of Idiotcy, A.
Eyeing the Eyes of One's Mistress.
High Summer.
When the World Is Burning.
Whimper of Awakening Passion.
Winter Hymn—to the Snow, A.

Jones, Elijah
How Big Was Alexander?

Jones, Ellis (1884–1948?)
Eaves.

Jones, Ernest Charles (*fl.* c.1852)
Song of the Low, The.

Jones, Evan (b. 1927)
Dream, A.
Genesis.
Lament of the Banana Man, The.
November 1956.
Point, I imagine, is, The.
Song of the Banana Man, The.
Study in Blue.
Walking with R. B.

Jones, G. W. (b. 1931?)
Portrait of the Pornographer.

Jones, Gayl (b. 1949)
Journal, *sels.*
Many Die Here.
Satori.
Tripart.

Jones, Glyn (b. 1905)
Again.
Esyllt.
Profile of Rose.

Jones, Gwilym R. (b. 1903)
Psalm to the Creatures.

Jones, Gwyn (b. 1951)
Blue Day Journey, The.

Jones, Henry
On a Fine Crop of Peas Being Spoiled by a
   Storm.

Jones, Jacquie (b. 1965)
Drugs.

Jones, Jessie Orton
Secrets, *sels.*

Jones, LeRoi. *See* **Baraka, Imamu Amiri**

Jones, Louise Seymour
Who Loves a Garden.

Jones, M. Keel
Election Reflection.

Jones, Mary (d. 1778)
After the Small Pox.
Epistle from Fern Hill.
Epistle to Lady Bowyer, An.
Lass of the Hill, The.
Soliloquy on an Empty Purse.
Stella's Epitaph.

Jones, Patricia (b. 1951)
Christmas, Boston Nineteen Eighty Nine.
Day of the Dead.

I Done Got So Thirsty That My Mouth
   Waters at the Thought of Rain.
Prayer.
Song: "I have so little sorrow."
Why I Like Movies.

Jones, Peter (b. 1929)
In the Formal Garden.
In the Park.

Jones, Rae Desmond (b. 1941)
Age.
Front Window, The.
James Dean.
Shakti.

Jones, Richard
Bell, The.
Birds, The.
Certain People.
Hearing Aid, The.
Leaving Town after the Funeral.
Mechanic, The.
Wan Chu's Wife in Bed.

Jones, Richard M. (c. 1889–1945)
Trouble in mind, I'm blue.

Jones, Rodney (b. 1950)
Blasphemy, A.
Caught.
Contempt.
Explanation of the Exhibit, An.
First Birth, The.
Grand Projection.
Mosquito, The.
Mule.
Progress Alley.
Romance of the Poor.
Sweep.
Weepers, The.

Jones, Roger
Revelations, First Time.

Jones, Samuel (d. 1732)
Force of Love, The.
Ploughman, in Imitation of Milton, The.
Poverty, in Imitation of Milton.

Jones, T. Gwynn (1871–1944)
Argoed.

Jones, T. Harri (1921–65)
Difference.
Welshman in Exile Speaks, The.

Jones, Thomas Samuel, Jr. (1882–1932)
As in a Rose-Jar.

Jones, Sir William (1746–94)
Epigram: "On parent knees, a naked new-
   born child."
Hymn to Indra, A.
Hymn to Na'ra'yena, A.
Hymn to Su'rya, A.
What Constitutes a State?

Jones, William Basil Tickell
Match me such marvel save in college port.

Jong, Erica (b. 1941)
Aging.
Alcestis on the Poetry Circuit.
Buddha in the Womb, The.
Castration of the Pen.
Climbing You.
Colder.
How You Get Born.
Man under the Bed, The.
Parable of the Four-Poster.
Seventeen Warnings in Search of a Feminist
   Poem.
Wives of Mafiosi, The.
Woman Who Loved to Cook, The.

Jonker, Ingrid (1933–65)
Begin Summer.
Bitterberry daybreak.
Child Who Was Shot Dead by Soldiers at
   Nyanga, The.
Dog.
Don't sleep, look!
Face of Love, The.
I Am with Those.
I Don't Want Any More Visitors.
I Drift in the Wind.
Journey round the World.
Lost City.

Pregnant Woman.
This Journey.
Time of Waiting in Amsterdam.
25 December 1960.
When You Laugh.
When You Write Again.

Jonson, Ben (1572–1637)
Against Jealousy [*or* Jealousie].
Alchemist, The, *sels.*
And must I sing? What subject shall I
   choose?
Another. In Defense of Their Inconstancy, A
   Song.
Celebration of Charis in Ten Lyric[k] Pieces
   [*or* Peeces], A, *sels.*
Cocklorrel woulds needs have the devil his
   guest.
Cynthia's Revels, *sels.*
Devil Is an Ass, The, *sels.*
Doing a filthy pleasure is, and short.
Dream[e], The.
Elegy [*or* Elegie], An: "Let me be what I
   am, as Virgil cold."
Elegy [*or* Elegie] on the Lady Jane Pawlet,
   [Marchioness of Winton], An, *sels.*
Elegy, An: "Though beauty be the mark of
   praise."
Epicoene; or, The Silent Woman, *sels.*
Epigram. To the Household. 1630, An.
Epigram. To the Small-Pox, An.
Epistle Answering to One That Asked to Be
   Sealed of the Tribe of Ben, An.
Epistle to Elizabeth, Countess of Rutland.
Epistle. To Katharine, Lady Aubigny.
Epistle to Master John Selden, An, *sels.*
Epitaph on Elizabeth, L. H.
Epitaph on Master Philip Gray, An.
Epitaph on Master Vincent Corbet[t], An.
Epitaph On Solomon Pavy, [Salomon *or*
   Salathiel Pavy], a Child of Q[ueen]
   El[izabeth's] Chapel.
Epithalamion; or, a Song.
Epode: "Not to know vice at all, and keep[e]
   true state."
Eupheme, *sels.*
Every Man in His Humour, *sels.*
Execration upon Vulcan, An.
Fair friend, 'tis true, your beauties move.
Fit of Rhyme [*or* Rime] against Rhyme [*or*
   Rime], A.
Gypsies Metamorphosed, The, *sels.*
Hour-Glass [*or* Houre-Glasse], The.
Hour Glass, The ("Consider this small dust,
   here in the glass.")
Hymn[e] on the Nativity of My Saviour, A.
Hymn[e] to God the Father, A.
In the Person of Womankind [A Song
   Apologetic].
Inviting a Friend to Supper.
Little Shrub Growing By, A.
Masque of Christmas, The.
Masque of Queens, The, *sels.*
Mind of the Frontispiece to a Book, The.
Musical Strife; in a Pastoral Dialogue, The.
My Picture Left in Scotland.
New Inn, The, *sels.*
New-Yeares-Gift Sung to King Charles, 1635,
   A.
New years [*or* yeares], expect new gifts:
   sister, your harp[e].
Now, bride and bridegroom, help to sing.
Nymph's Passion, A.
Oberon, the Fairy Prince, *sels.*
Ode, An: "High-spirited friend, / I send not
   balms, nor corsives to your wound."
Ode to Himself.
Ode. To Sir William Sydney, on His
   Birthday.
On Court-Worm[e].
On Don Surly.
On English Monsieur.
On Giles and Joan.
On Groin.
On Gut.
On Lieutenant Shift.
On Lucy Countess[e] of Bedford.
On Margaret Ratcliffe.

On My First Daughter.
On My First Son [or Sonne].
On Playwright ("Playwright convict of public
wrongs to men.")
On Poet-Ape.
On Something, That Walks [or Walkes]
Somewhere.
On Spies.
On the Famous Voyage, sels.
On the Town's Honest Man.
On the Union.
Pleasure Reconciled to Virtue, sels.
Poetaster, The, sels.
Return of Astraea, The.
Sad Shepherd, The, sels.
Song, A: "Oh do[e] not wanton with those
eyes."
Song. That Women Are But Men's Shadows.
Sonnet to the Noble Lady, the Lady Mary
Wroth, A.
Things that make the happier life, are these,
The.
To a Friend.
To Celia.
To Censorious Courtling.
To Clement Edmonds, on His Caesar's
Commentaries Observed, and Translated.
To Doctor Empiric[k].
To Edward Alleyn.
To Elizabeth, Countess of Rutland.
To Fine Lady Would-Be.
To Fool or Knave.
To Francis Beaumont.
To Heaven.
To John Donne ("Donne, the delight of
Phoebus, and each Muse.")
To John Donne ("Who shall doubt, Donne,
where [or whe'er] I a poet be[e].")
To Lucy, Countess[e] of Bedford, with Mr.
Donnes Satire's [or Satyres].
To Mary, Lady Wroth ("Madam[e], had all
antiquity [or antiquitie] been lost.")
To My Book.
To My Mere English Censurer.
To My Worthy and Honoured Friend, Mr
George Chapman, on His Translation of
Hesiod's Works and Days.
To Penshurst, sels.
To Pertinax Cob.
To Sickness.
To Sir Henry Cary.
To Sir Henry Goodyere.
To Sir Horace Vere.
To Sir Robert Wroth.
To the Immortal[l] Memory and Friendship
of That Noble Pair[e], Sir Lucius Cary and
Sir H. Morison, sels.
To the Memory of My Beloved, the Author
Mr [or Master] William Shakespeare[: And
What He Hath Left Us], sels.
To the Reader ("Pray thee, take care, that
tak'st my book[e] in hand.")
To the Same [Robert, Earl of Salisbury]
[Upon the Accension of the Treasurership
to Him].
To the World [A Farewell for a
Gentlewoman, Virtuous and Noble].
To Thomas Palmer [on His Book "The Sprite
of Trees and Herbs"].
To William Camden.
To William, Earl[e] of Pembroke.
To William Roe ("Roe (and my joy to name)
th'art now, to go.")
To William Roe ("When Nature bids us leave
to live, 'tis late.")
Vision of Delight, The, sels.
Volpone, sels.
Why I Write Not of Love.
Witches' Song, The.

Jonson, Edward
Water-Drinker, The.

Jordan, A. C. (1906–64)
You Tell Me to Sit Quiet.

Jordan, Charlie
Keep It Clean.

Jordan, Franklin E.
I love America where truth can be shouted
from the housetops.

Jordan, John (b. 1930)
Lolek.

Jordan, June (b. 1936)
All the world moved next to me strange.
Cameo No. II.
Case in Point.
Clock on Hancock Street.
DeLiza Spend the Day in the City ("DeLiza
drive the car to fetch, Alexis.")
Female and the Silence of a Man, The.
For My Mother.
Getting Down to Get Over.
Grand Army Plaza.
I Must Become a Menace to My Enemies.
If You Saw a Negro Lady.
In Memoriam: Martin Luther King, Jr.
Intifada.
July 4, 1984: For Buck.
My Sadness Sits around Me.
New Pietà: For the Mothers and Children of
Detroit, The.
1977: Poem for Mrs. Fannie Lou Hamer.
Nobody Riding the Roads Today.
Notes on the Peanut.
October 23, 1983.
Okay "Negroes."
Onesided Dialog.
Poem about Intelligence for My Brothers and
Sisters, A.
Poem About My Rights.
Poem Against the State (Of Things): 1975.
Poem for Guatemala.
Poem for My Family: Hazel Griffin and
Victor Hernandez Cruz.
Poem for Nana.
Poem for South AFrican Women.
Poem from the Empire State.
Poem to My Sister, Ethel Ennis, Who Sang
"The Star-spangled Banner" at the Second
Inauguration of Richard Milhous Nixon.
Queen Anne's Lace.
Reception, The.
Roman Poem Number Nine.
Second Poem from Nicaragua Libre: War
Zone.
Snow, The.
Some people despise me be- / cause I have a
Venus mound.
Speculations on the Present through the Prism
of the Past.
Sunflower Sonnet Number One.
Sunflower Sonnet Number Two.
Test of Atlanta 1979, The.
Uncle Bull-Boy.
Unemployment/Monologue.
War and Memory, sels.
What happens when the dog sits on a tiger.
What Would I Do White?
You Came with Shells.

Jordan, Norman (b. 1938)
August 2.
August 8.
Be You.
Black Warrior.
Feeding the Lions.
I have seen them trying.
July 27.
July 31.
Poet the Dreamer, The.
Silent Prophet, The.
When A Woman Gets Blue.

Jordan, Thomas (1612?–1685)
Careless Gallant, The.

Joron, Andrew
Baring the Device.
Birdsongs are aging, The.
Shade of a Grammarian.
Zirkus.

Jortin, John (1698–1770)
Epitaph of Felis, The.

Joseph, Allison (fl. 20th cent.)
Junior High Dance.
My Father's Heroes.

Joseph, Jenny (b. 1932)
Back to Base.
Dog body and cat mind, The.
Lost Continent, The.
Rose in the Afternoon.
Warning.

Joseph, Lawrence (b. 1948)
Curriculum Vitae.
Do What You Can.
In the Age of Postcapitalism.
Mama Remembers.
Sand Nigger.
That's All.
Then.
There I Am Again.

Joseph, M. K. (1914–81)
Distilled Water.
Epilogue to a Poetry Reading.
Girl, Boy, Flower, Bicycle.
Mercury Bay Eclogue.

Joshi, Umashankar (b. 1911)
Passing through Rajasthan.

Joso. See **Naito Joso**

Josselyn, John (1630–75)
And the bitter storm augments; the wild
winds wage.
Description of a New England Spring.
Verses Made Sometime Since upon. . . the
Indian Squa.

Jouve, Pierre Jean (1887–1976)
We have amazed by our great sufferings.

Joyce, James (1882–1941)
Advertisement for Finnegans Wake, An.
All day I hear the noise of waters.
Ballad of Joking Jesus, The.
Blurb for Anna Livia Plurabelle, A.
Ecce Puer.
Finnegans Wake, sels.
Flood.
Flower Given to My Daughter, A.
Gas from a Burner, sels.
Holy Office, The.
I hear an army charging upon the land.
Limerick: "There was a kind lady called
Gregory."
My dove, my beautiful one.
Nightpiece.
On the Beach at Fontana.
Post Ulixem Scriptum.
Right Heart in the Wrong Place, The.
Sleep now, O sleep now.
Thou leanest to the shell of night.
Though I Thy Mithridates Were.
Tilly.
Tutto è Sciolto.
Twilight turns from amethyst, The.
Ulysses, sels.

Joyce, Jane Wilson
Crazy Quilt.

Joyce, William
My Daughter's Pundalunda.

József, Attila (1905–37)
Attila József.
Freight trains are pulling in.
Seventh, The.
To Sit, to Stand, to Kill, to Die.

Juan Chi (210–63)
Poems Expressing My Feelings, sels.
Singing of Thoughts, sels.

Juan II, of Castile (1405–54)
Cancion: "O love, I never, never thought."

**Juana Inés de la Cruz, Sister (Juana Rumirez
de Asbaje) (1651–95)**
Fifth Villancico, in Alternating Voices,
Written for the Feast of the Nativity in
Puebla, 1689, The, sels.
First Dream, sels.
First Villancico, Written for the Nativity of
Our Lord, Puebla, 1689, The, sels.
Green Enravishment of Human Life.
Happy Easter, my Lady.
I can't hold you and I can't leave you.
In Which She Satisfies a Fear with the
Rhetoric of Tears.
My Divine Lysi.
Satirical Romance, A, sels.

She Attempts to Refute the Praises That
Truth, Which She Calls Passion, Inscribed
on a Portrait of the Poet.
She Proves the Inconsistency of the Desires
and Criticism of Men Who Accuse Women
of What They Themselves Cause.
Stay, shade of my shy treasure! Oh, remain.
This coloured counterfeit that thou beholdest.

Juarroz, Roberto (b. 1925)
Any movement kills something.
Eleventh Vertical Poetry, *sels.*
Fifth Vertical Poetry, *sels.*
Ninth Vertical Poetry, *sels.*
Seventh Vertical Poetry, *sels.*
Sixth Vertical Poetry, *sels.*
Thrid Vertical Poetry, *sels.*
Vertical Poetry, *sels.*

"Judah" (*fl.*** Middle Ages)**
Fragrant Thy Memories.

Judah, Daniel ben (*fl.*** c.1350)**
Living God O magnify and bless, The.

Judah ibn Sabbatai (*fl.*** 12th cent.)**
Gift of Judah the Woman-Hater, The, *sels.*

Judah ibn Tibbon (1120–1190?)
Father's Testament, A.

Judson, Adoniram (1788–1850)
Come Holy Spirit, Dove Divine.
Our Father, God.

Judson, Emily Chubbuck. *See* **"Forester, Fanny"**

Judson, Sarah (1803–45)
Proclaim the Lofty Praise.

Juhász, Ferenc (b. 1928)
Birth of the Foal.

Julian, Emperor (Flavius Claudius Julianus; "Julian the Apostate") (332–63)
Beer.
On Beer.

Julian [*or***Juliana] of Norwich (1343–1443)**
God wants to be thought of.
I understood that.

"Julian the Apostate." *See* **Julian, Emperor**

Julian, V. M.
Mr. Squirrel.

Julianus of Egypt (*fl.*** 5th cent.)**
Anastasia, the Graces blossom and you were
their flower.
'Drink was the end of you, Anacreon.'
Epitaph in Dialogue on the Sceptic
Philosopher Pyrrho.
I kept singing this, and I will call it out from
the grave.
Julianus Sees a Bronze Statue of Icarus in a
Public Bath.
Julianus Sees a Magistrate's Axe.
Julianus Sees the Chair of the Sophist
Craterus.
Lais' Mirror.
On a Young Wife.
Though you rule the dead, under the earth,
who never smile.
Unguarded House, An.

Julius Cerealius. *See* **Cerealius**

Julius Polyaenus
Although your ears must be plentifully
occupied.
Hope is what skims time always from our
lives.

Juljan. *See* **Tuwim, Julian**

Junkins, Donald (b. 1931)
Walden in July.

Jussawalla, Adil (b. 1940)
Sea Breeze, Bombay.

Justema, William (b. 1904)
Song: "This is the song of those who live
alone."

Justice, Donald (b. 1925)
About My Poems.
American Scenes (1904).
Anonymous Drawing.
Another Song.
Assassination, The.
Beyond the Hunting Woods.
Birthday Candle, A.

Bus Stop.
But That Is Another Story.
Childhood.
Children Walking Home from School through
Good Neighborhood.
Counting the Mad.
Crossing Kansas by Train.
Dancer's Life, A.
Dreams of Water.
Elegy Is Preparing Itself, An.
Evening of the Mind, The.
First Death.
Heart, let us this once reason together.
Here in Katmandu.
Houses.
In Bertram's Garden.
In Memory of the Unknown Poet, Robert
Boardman Vaughn.
Incident in a Rose Garden.
Invitation to a Ghost.
Landscape with Little Figures.
Lethargy.
Love's Stratagems.
Luxury.
Man Closing Up, The.
Memo from the Desk of X.
Men at forty / Learn to close softly.
Missing Person, The.
Mrs. Snow.
Mule Team and Poster.
Nostalgia and Complaint of the Grandparents.
Ode to a Dressmaker's Dummy.
On a Painting by Patient B of the
Independence State Hospital for the Insane.
On the Death of Friends in Childhood.
Poem to Be Read at 3 A.M.
Poet at Seven, The.
Psalm and Lament.
Sadness, An Improvisation.
Snowfall, The.
Sonatina in Yellow.
Suicides, The.
Tales from a Family Album.
Things, *sels.*
Thinking about the Past.
To Waken a Small Person.
Tourist from Syracuse, The.
Train.
Tremayne.
Variations for Two Pianos.
Variations on a Text by Vallejo.
Variations on Southern Themes.
Walls surrounding them they never saw, The.
White Notes.
Winter Ode to the Old Men of Lummus
Park, Miami, Florida, A.

**Juvenal (Decimus Junius Juvenalis) (c.50–c.130
A.D.)**
Client, the patron, the age, The.
Corruption of manners, The.
Favourite's fall, The.
Fortune a Goddess is to Fools alone.
Juvenals tenth Satyre Translated, *sels.*
London, *sels.*
Part of Juvenal's Sixth Satire, Modernized in
Burlesque Verse, *sels.*
Satires, *sels.*
Tenth Satyr of Juvenal, The, *sels.*
Thirteenth Satyr of Juvenal, Imitated, The,
sels.
Vanity of Human Wishes, The, *sels.*
Woman stops at nothing, when she wears, A.

Juvencus, Gaius Vettius Aquilinus (*fl.*** c.330)**
Naught in the world keeps an immortal stay.

K

Kabir (c.1488–1512)
Between the conscious and the unconscious,
the mind has put up a swing.
Flute of interior time is played whether we
hear it or not, The.
Guest is inside you, and also inside me, The.
Hopeful Spiritual Athlete, The.
How Much Is Not True.
I have been thinking of the difference
between water.

Inside this clay jar there are meadows and
groves and the One who made them.
Knowing nothing shuts the iron gates; the
new love opens them.
My friend, this body is His lute. He tightens
the strings and plays its songs.
Simple Purification, The.
Swan, tell my your old story.
To Be a Slave of Intensity.

Kaccipettu Nannakaiyar (*fl.*** 3d cent.)**
My lover capable of terrible lies.

Kaffka, Margit (1880–1918)
Father.

Kafka, Franz (1883–1924)
Before the Law stands a doorkeeper.

Kagank
It's only whiskey that makes you pity me.

Kageyama, Claire (*fl.*** 20th cent.)**
Mama.

Kahanovitch, Pinhas. *See* **"Der Nistor"**

Kahanu, Diane Hina
When I was young on an island.

Kahclamet, Philip
Crier, The.

Kahn, Gustave (1886–1941)
Homage.
Makin' Whoopee.
Pilgrim from the East, The.
Song: "O lovely April, rich and bright."
You Masks of the Masquerade.

Kakayek
Song on the Way to Jail.

**Kākkai Pāṭiniyār Naccellaiyār ("Nacellai Who
Sang of the Crow")**
King's Double Nature, A.
Mothers.
What Her Girl Friend Said to Her Lover on
His Return.

Kalász, Márton (b. 1934)
Hymn: "Where should I seat you, where."
Impromptu.
Legacy.
Maiden.
Time's No Grammar.
Up against That Wall Everywhere.

Kalidasa (*fl.*** c.500)**
Salutation to the Dawn.
Seasons, The.
This life on earth's a poison tree.

Kalir, Eleazar ben (*fl.*** 7th–8th cent.)**
O Hark to the Herald.
Palms and Myrtles.
Prayer for Dew.
Prophet Jeremiah and the Personification of
Israel, The.
Terrible sons of the mighty race, The.
To Him Who Is Feared.

Kallman, Chester (1921–75)
Dead Center.
Romance, A.

Kalonymos ben Judah (*fl.*** c.1160)**
Although tormented and ill-treated.

Kalonymos ben Kalonymos (1286–c.1328)
Touchstone, The, *sels.*

Kalonymos ben Moses of Lucca (*fl.*** c.950)**
His sovereignty is o'er my gathered throng.
Sovereignty, His.

Kalvos, Andreas (1792–1869)
Altar of the Fatherland, The.

Kāmakkaṇṇiyār, Veṛipātiya
Leaf in Love and War, A.

Kamatari (Fujiwara no Kamatari) (614–69)
Hey! Ho! Hurrah!

Kamatari, Fujiwara no. *See* **Kamatari**

Kambala
KYE HO! Wonderful!

Kambar, Chandrashekhar (b. 1938)
Pond Named Ganga, A.

Kamienska, Anna (1920–86)
Annunciation.
On the Cross.
Prayer That Will Be Answered, A.
Saint Martha.
St. Luke, *sels.*

St. Matthew, *sels.*
Things of This World.
Those who carry grand pianos / to the tenth
floor.
Kamzon, Jacob David
Very Fair My Lot.
Kanai, Mieko (b. 1947)
House of Madam Juju, The.
In the Town With Cat-/ Shaped Maze.
Kanavi, Chennavira (b. 1928)
On Bismillah Khan's Shehnai.
Kandel, Lenore (b. 1932)
First they slaughtered the angels.
Spring 61.
Kandinsky [*or* Kandinskii], Wassily (1866–1944)
Chalk and Soot.
Sounds.
Why?
Kane, Michael L.
Soap Box Derby, The.
Kane, Paul
Disciples Asleep at Gethsemane.
Kaneko, Lonny
Bailey Gatzert: The First Grade, 1945.
Kaneko Mitsuharu (1895–1975)
Opposition.
**Kanemasa (Minamoto Kanemasa) (*fl.* 12th
cent.)**
Awaji Island—.
Guardian of the gate.
Kanemasa, Minamoto. *See* **Kanemasa**
Kanemori (*fl.* 10th cent.)
Although I hide it.
In the mountain village.
K'ang Hai (1475–1541)
Dreaming of Master Chung-lu.
Listening to the Rain.
Sitting by Myself.
Ten Poems on Almond Blossoms, *sels.*
Kang, Un-gyo (b. 1945)
Grass Leaves.
Rotation (1).
Kangro, Bernard
Late Flowers, Wind, Sea, Sand and Fish.
Old Age.
Trees Walk Farther Away, The.
Kanié, Anoma
All That You Have Given Me, Africa.
Kaniyan Punkunran
Every Town a Home Town.
Kannan
What Her Girl Friend Said to Him.
Kaṇṇaṉār, Centaṉ
What Her Girl Friend Said to Him.
What Her Girl Friend Said to him ("Near the
salt pans.")
Kantan, Millaipperun
What His Friend Said, teasing the man in
love.
What She Said ("Only the dim-witted say it's
evening.")
Kantaris, Sylvia (b. 1936)
Airing the Chapel.
Awakening to Snow.
Body Language.
Not-loving.
Stocking Up.
Kao Ch'i (1336–74)
Along the River, Seeing the Home of
Absconded Farmers.
Ballad of a Ferocious Tiger.
Ballad of the Deserted Mansion.
Ballad of the Neighborhood Shaman.
Cold Spring.
Going Out to the Country on a Boat Trip,
Sheltering from Rain Beneath a Tree.
In the Mountains, Parting from Master Ning
as I Return to West Bank.
Lament of a Soldier's Wife.
Lying at Leisure during Rain.
Mooring Our Boat at Tan-yang Harbor.
Moss below the Stairs.
Nodding Off.
Old Cowboy, The.

On a Painting by Hsia Kuei Entitled
"Returning in Wind and Snow to a Village
Home."
On a Painting of the Radiant Emperor's
Night Revels by Candlelight.
Passing By the Battlefield at Feng-k'ou.
Picking Tea: A Ballad.
Returning to Lotus Village.
Seeing Flowers I Remember My Late
Daughter, Shu.
Seeking out Hermit Hu.
Silkworm Song of Torchlit Fields.
Song of the Duck Hunters.
Song of the Man of Green Hill, The.
Spring Day—Remembering Living on the
River, A.
Sunflower.
Walk to the Eastern River Bank, A.
Well of the King of Wu, The.
Where Does My Sadness Come From?
Kao Shih (702?–765)
Song of Yen.
Youth of Han-tan, The; a Song.
Kapilar
Farewell to Pāri's Hill.
His Hill.
Kāri Sober.
Memory of the Hill, A.
Pāri! Pāri! they cry.
Pāri's Green Land, Remembered.
Pāri's Hill Is Partial to Dancers.
Then and Now.
True Protocol of Poets, The.
Waterfalls and Liquor ("Waterfalls sounded.")
What Her Friend Said.
What Her Friend Said to Her, before the
Rains.
What Her Friend Said to the Foster-Mother.
What Her Friend Said to the foster-mother
(who is guarding her carefully).
What She Said ("And all those horses.")
What She Said ("Forest animals walk there.")
What She Said ("He is from those
mountains.")
What She Said Her Lover within Earshot.
What She Said ("'O your hair,' he said.")
What She Said ("Only the thief was there, no
one else.")
What She Said to Her Friend ("Colors on the
elephant's body, The.")
What She Said to Her Friend ("You ask me
to forget him.")
What She Said to Her Girl Friend.
What She Said to Her Girl Friend, after a
Tryst at Night (Which Turned Out to Be a
Fiasco).
What She Said to Her Girl Friend, Her
Foster-Mother within Earshot.
What She Said to Her Girl Friend ("O you,
you wear flowers of gold.")
What She Said to Her Girl Friend When She
Returned from the Hills.
What the Girl Friend Said to the Foster-
Mother.
Kapitonos
No charm.
Kaplan, Milton (b. 1910)
Knife, The.
Kaplinski, Jaan (b. 1941)
I UNDERSTOOD I UNDERSTOOD.
In spring during spring.
Like a black hedgehog.
My wife and children were waiting for ice
cream.
We started home, my son and I.
White clover will not ask anything.
Kappiyarrukkappiyanar
Harvest of War.
Karandikar, Vinda (b. 1918)
Knot, The.
Karélli, Zoé (b. 1901)
Presences.
Kariara, Jonathan (b. 1935)
Leopard lives in a Muu tree, A.
Karibo, Minji
Superstition.

Kariuki, Joseph E. (b. 1931)
New Life.
Karni, Yehuda (1884–1949)
Place Me in the Breach.
Put me into the breach with every rolling
stone.
Woman's Prayer, A.
Karouzos, Nikos (1926–90)
Triplets for Beautiful Mistra.
Karp, Vickie
Consequences of Waking, The.
Still-Life in the Coat Factory Office.
Taxi to the Flame, The.
Karpowicz, Tymoteusz (b. 1921)
Artistic Copy.
Dog Which Barked Itself Out, The.
From Bosch's Hill.
From the Skein of the Straight Line.
Hunting.
Lesson of Silence, A.
On Opening an Old House.
Pencil's Sleep, The.
Rifle, The.
Silence is sucking the earth dry.
Karr, Mary
Post-Larkin Triste.
Kartun, D.
Limerick: "There was a young girl of
Uttoxeter / Who noticed that men waved
their cocks at her."
Kasa, Lady (*fl.* mid–8th cent.)
I dreamed I held / A sword against my flesh.
I love and fear him.
To love somebody.
Kasa no Iratsume (*fl.* 8th cent.)
Evening comes and sorrow crowds my mind.
Gods of heaven are irrational, The.
I dreamed I held / A sword against my flesh.
I love and fear him.
To love somebody / Who doesn't love you.
To love someone / Who does not return that
love.
When evening comes.
Kaschnitz, Marie Luise (1901–74)
Humility.
Resurrection.
Kasdaglis, Lina (b. 1928)
Traffic Lights.
Kasdorf, Julia
Dying with Amish Uncles.
Green Market, New York.
Leftover Blessings.
Mennonites.
Uncle.
Vesta's Father.
What I Learned from My Mother.
When our women go crazy, they're scared
there won't be.
Where We Are.
Kasenduaxtc
Throw him into the river.
Kasischke, Laura
Woman Kills Sweetheart with Bowling Ball.
Kasmuneh (*fl.* 12th–13th cent.)
Overripe Fruit.
Timid Gazelle, The.
Kassia [*or* Kassiane] (b. 804?)
Epigram: "Poverty? wealth? seek neither."
Epigram: "Wealth covers sin—the poor."
Epigram: "Woman working hard and wisely,
A."
Lord, this woman who fell into many sins.
Selected Epigrams.
Sticheron for Matins, Wednesday of Holy
Week.
Troparion.
Kastelan, Jure
As if it resembled your hair.
Blood and the Storm.
Corpse in the House.
Parting.
You shine in darkness, you dream under
shelter.
Kästner, Erich (1899–1924)
Moral Taxi Ride, The.

Kataiyaṅ Kaṇṇaṉār
In Praise of a Cremation Ground.
Katayev [or Kataev], Valentin Petrovich (1897–1986)
Distrust the pomp of Caesar.
For a long time, not a year, not two.
When I lie down to die.
Katda
My wife went away, left me.
Katene-Horvath, Hera (b. 1912)
In Days Gone By.
Kates, J.
No altarpiece includes the painter.
Katrovas, Richard (b. 1953)
Beating, The.
Black English.
Dog and a Boy, A.
My Friends the Pigeons.
Public Mirror, The.
Sky.
Katuvan Ilaveyinanar
Tirumal.
Katz, Bobbi (b. 1933)
Recipe.
Spring is when.
Katzin, Olga. *See* "Sagittarius"
Kaufman, Bob (b. 1925)
African Dream.
Afterwards, They Shall Dance.
Battle Report.
Blues Note.
Cocoa Morning.
Falling.
Geneology.
Grandfather Was Queer, Too.
Heavy Water Blues.
I Have Folded My Sorrows.
I, Too, Know What I Am Not.
Jail Poems.
Mingus.
Oregon.
Patriotic Ode on the Fourteenth Anniversary of the Persecution of Charlie Chaplin.
Private Sadness.
To My Son Parker, Asleep in the Next Room.
Unanimity Has Been Achieved, Not a Dot Less for Its Accidentalness.
Unhistorical Events.
Unholy Missions.
Untitled.
Walking Parker Home.
War Memoir: Jazz, Don't Listen to It at Your Own Risk.
Would You Wear My Eyes?
Kaufman, David Samuilovich. *See* "Samoylov, David Samuilovich"
Kaufman, Herbert
This is your hour—creep upon it!
Kaufman, Shirley (b. 1923)
Abishag.
Always She Moves from Me.
Apples.
Beetle on the Shasta Daylight.
Déjà Vu.
Dream of Completion, The.
His Wife.
I Hear You.
I see bodies in the morning kneel.
Looking at Henry Moore's Elephant Skull Etchings in Jerusalem during the War.
Mothers, Daughters.
Nechama.
Next Year, in Jerusalem.
Notes to my Daughters.
There are caverns / under our feet.
Watts, *sels.*
We are going down a long slide.
Kaune, Gayle
Case Study.
Kavanagh, P. J. (b. 1931)
Goldie Sapiens.
Praying.
Sometimes.
Temperance Billiards Rooms, The.

Kavanagh, Patrick (1905–69)
Advent.
Art McCooey.
Canal Bank Walk.
Christmas Childhood, A, *sels.*
Come Dance with Kitty Stobling.
Dear Folks.
Epic.
Father Mat, *sels.*
Gold Watch.
Great Hunger, The, *sels.*
Hospital, The.
I Had a Future.
I May Reap.
If ever you go to Dublin town.
In Memory of My Mother.
Inniskeen Road: July Evening.
Innocence.
Intimate Parnassus.
Is.
Kerr's Ass.
Leave Them Alone.
Lecture Hall.
Lines Written on a Seat on the Grand Canal, Dublin.
Long Garden, The.
Memory of my Father.
October.
On Looking into E. V. Rieu's Homer.
One, The.
Peace.
Ploughman.
Question to Life.
Sanctity.
Self-slaved, The.
Shancoduff.
Spraying the Potatoes.
Stony Grey Soil.
Tinker's Wife.
To Hell with Commonsense.
To the Man after the Harrow.
Wet Evening in April.
Kavarpentu
Mothers.
Kawai Chigetsu-Ni (1632–1736)
Cats making love in the temple.
Grasshoppers / Chirping in the sleeves.
"Kay"
Christmas Verse, A.
Kay, Jackie (b. 1961)
Baby Lazarus.
Dressing Up.
English Cousin Comes to Scotland.
He Told Us He Wanted a Black Coffin.
Mother Poem (two), The.
Mummy and Donor and Deirdre.
Photo in the Locket.
Stincher, The.
That Distance Apart.
What Jenny Knows.
Kayamanar
What Her Girl Friend Said, Seeing Her Friend Suffer in Silent Dignity over Her Husband's Infidelity.
Kaye/Kantrowitz, Melanie
Jerusalem Shadow.
Kayo, Patrice
Song of the Initiate.
War.
Kazakova, Rimma Fiodorovna (b. 1932)
I am growing calmer.
"Kazanova, Kid." *See* Stack, Philip
Kazantzakis, Nikos (1883–1957)
Odyssey: A Modern Sequel, The, *sels.*
Kazantzis, Judith
Arachne.
Frightened Flier Goes North, The.
In Memory, 1978.
Woman making advances publicly, A.
Kazarnovsky [or Kazarnovskii], Yury [or Iurii] (1904–56)
Chinese Laundry.
Kazin, Vasily [or Vasilii] Vasilevich (1898–1981)
Accordionist, The.
Keach, Benjamin (d. 1704)
How Glorious Are the Morning Stars.

Keane, Ellsworth McGranahan ("Shake" Keane) (b. 1927)
Coming Back.
Once the wind.
Volcanoe Suite, *sels.*
Week Seven.
Kearney, Lawrence
After the Interrogation.
Kearns, Lionel (b. 1937)
Environment.
Foreign Aid.
Stuntman.
Keary, E. (*fl.* 1857–88)
Old Age.
Keate, George (1729–97)
Burlesque Ode, on the Author's Clearing a New House of Some Workmen, A, *sels.*
Keating, Geoffrey (Seathrum Ceitinn) (b. 1570)
At the news from Fal's high plain I cannot sleep.
Keen Thyself, Poor Wight.
Mourn for Yourself.
O lady full of guile.
Keats, John (1795–1821)
Addressed to Haydon.
All These Are Vile.
Bright star[, would I were stedfast as thou art—].
Dawlish Fair.
Dream, after Reading Dante's Episode of Paolo and Francesca, A.
Endymion, *sels.*
Endymion: Poetic Romance, *sels.*
Epistle to George Keats, *sels.*
Eve of St Agnes, The.
Eve of St. Mark, The.
"Eve of St. Agnes," The, *sels.*
Faery Song.
Fall of Hyperion, The, *sels.*
Fancy.
Fragment: "I am as brisk."
Fragment: "O grant that like to Peter I."
Fragment of an Ode to Maia Written on May Day, 1818.
Happy Insensibility.
Happy is England! I could be content.
How many bards gild the lapses of time!
Human Seasons, The.
Hyperion, *sels.*
I Had a Dove [and the Sweet Dove Died], *sels.*
I stood tip-toe upon a little hill, *sels.*
Imitation of Spenser, *sels.*
In drear-nighted December.
Keen, fitful gusts are whispering here and there.
La Belle Dame Sans Merci.
Lamia, *sels.*
Lines on the Mermaid Tavern.
Meg Merrilies [or Merrilees].
Modern Love.
Nebuchadnezzar's Dream.
Ode: "Bards of passion and of mirth."
Ode on a Grecian Urn.
Ode on Indolence.
Ode on Melancholy.
Ode to a Nightingale, *sels.*
Ode to Psyche.
On First Looking into Chapman's Homer.
On Oxford.
On Seeing the Elgin Marbles.
On Sitting Down to Read "King Lear" Once Again.
On the Grasshopper and [the] Cricket.
On the Sea.
On the Sonnet.
Palpitating snake, A.
Pensive they sit, and roll their languid eyes.
Pleasure Thermometer, The.
Portrait, A.
Robin Hood.
Sharing Eve's Apple.
Sleep and Poetry, *sels.*
Song: "oh, blush not so, oh, blush not so."
Song about Myself, A, *sels.*
Song: "I Had a Dove and the Sweet Dove Died."

Song of Spring.
Sonnet: "After dark vapours have oppress'd our plains."
Spenser! a jealous honourer of thine.
Stanzas: "You say you love; but with a voice."
Swarms of minnows show their little heads.
Terror of Death, The.
Three Undated Fragments, *sels.*
To a Cat.
To Ailsa Rock.
To Autumn.
To Chatterton.
To Fanny.
To Fanny Brawne.
To ———: "Had I a man's fair form, then might my sighs."
To Homer.
To J. H. Reynolds, Esq, *sels.*
To Leigh Hunt, Esq.
To Lord Byron.
To My Brothers.
To one who has been long in city pent.
To Sleep.
Two or three posies.
What can I do to drive away.
What the Thrush Said.
Where be you [*or* ye] going, you [*or* ye] Devon maid?
Where's the poet? show him, show him.
Why did I laugh to-night? No voice will tell.
Written on the Day That Mr. Leigh Hunt Left Prison.

Keble, John (1792–1866)
Balaam.
Epithalamium: "Voice that breathed o'er Eden, The."
Fill High the Bowl.
Forest Leaves in Autumn, *sels.*
Hezekiah's Display.
New every morning.
Samuel's Prayer.
See Lucifer like lightning fall.

Kedrin, Dmitry [*or* Dmitrii] Borisovich (1907–45)
Builders.

Keech, Benjamin
Discovery.
Little Words.
Love Is Kind.
True to the Best.

Keegan, John (1809–49)
Irish Reaper's Harvest Hymn.

Keens-Douglas, Paul (b. 1942)
Tell Me Again.
Trinidad If Ah Let You.
Wukhand.

Kees, Weldon (1914–55)
Aspects of Robinson.
Beach in August, The.
Colloquy.
Coming of the Plague, The.
Conversation in the Drawingroom, The.
For My Daughter.
Guide to the Symphony.
Heat in the Room, The.
Henry James at Newport.
January.
La Vita Nuova.
1926.
Robinson.
Robinson at Home.
Round: "'Wondrous life!' cried Marvell at Appleton House.'"
Small Prayer.
There was a French writer named Sartre.
Wet Thursday.

Keeshig-Tobias, Lenore
I grew up on the reserve.
Mother with Child.

Keesing, Nancy (b. 1923)
Queer Thing, A.
Reverie of a Mum.

Kefala, Antigone
Freedom fighter, she said, A.
Industrial City.

Party, The.
Saturday Night.
Sunday Visit.

Kegels, Anne-Marie (b. 1912)
I write to make you suffer.
Nocturnal Heart.
When I strip, / stop walking / and drop into sleep.

Keith, Joseph Joel
Definitions.

Keithley, George (b. 1935)
Donner Party, The, *sels.*
Fourth Day of the Flood, The.
When they leave the world will be at peace.

Kelen, S. K. (b. 1956)
First Circle, The.
Gods Ash Their Cigarettes, The.
Rabbit Shoeshine.

Keller, David
Friends, Outside, Night.
In the Middle of the Journey.
Mussels.

Kellman, Anthony (b. 1958)
Bajan.
King, The.

Kelly, Aileen
Given flesh returns nothing but bread, The.

Kelly, Brigit Pegeen
All Wild Animals Were Once Called Deer.
Courting the Famous Figures at the Grotto of Improbable Thought.
Leaving, The.
Of Royal Issue.
Silver Lake.
Southern Review, The, *sels.*
Those Who Wrestle with the Angel for Us.
White Pilgrim: Old Christian Cemetary, The.
Wild Turkeys; The Dignity of the Damned.
Young Wife's Lament.

Kelly, Isabella (c.1759–1857)
To an Unborn Infant.

Kelly, Robert (b. 1934)
Bittersweet growing up the red wall.
Book of Persephone, The, *sels.*
Coming.
In June was a jar had.
Last Light.
Life of Intimate Fleeing, A.
Looking.
Loom, The, *sels.*
Mapping.
Newark.
Ode to Language.
Poem for Easter.
Rainmakers, The.
Recessional.
Sound, The.
Studying Horses.
Those who are beautiful.
Tune.
Woman with Flaxen Hair in Norfolk Heard, A.

Kelly, Roy (b. 1949)
Death, Don't Be Boring.
Ode to a Nightingale.

Kelpius, Johannes (1673?–1708)
I Love My Jesus Quite Alone.

Kelso, Ian
Busy Old Fool.

Kemal Khojandi (d. 1401?)
One Final Fling.

Kemble, Frances Anne [*or* "Fanny"] (1809–93)
Absence, *sels.*
Faith.
Farewell to Italy.
Impromptu.
Lines.
Petition, A.
Sonnet: "If there were any power in human love."
To Mrs. Norton.
To Shakespeare.
To the Wissahiccon.
Wish, A.

Kemp, Jan (b. 1949)
Letter to the Immigration Officer.
Poem: "Puriri moth's wing, A."
"When the Wild Goose Finds Food He Calls His Comrades"—*I Ching.*

Kempis, Thomas À
Imitation of Christ, The, *sels.*

Ken, Thomas (1637–1711)
Evening Hymn, An.
Glory to Thee, My God, This Night.
Morning Hymn.

Kendall, Henry Clarence (1839–82)
Bell-Birds.
Beyond Kerguelen.
Christmas Creek.
Last of His Tribe, The.
Mooni.
Orara.

Kendall, May (1861–1943)
Education's Martyr.
Ether Insatiable.
Failures.
Fossil, A.
Lay of the Trilobite, The.
Legend of the Crossing-Sweeper.
Lower Life, The.
Philanthropist and the Jelly-fish, The.
Pure Hypothesis, A.
Underground.
Vision of Noah, The.
Woman's Future.

Kendall, Timothy (*fl.* 1577)
Desire of Dominion.
Difference Between a King and a Tyrant, The.
Of a Good Prince and an Evil.
Tyrant in Sleep, Naught Differeth from a Common Man, A.
Upon the Grave of a Beggar.

Kendrick, Dolores (b. 1927)
Alone for a Week.
Gethsemane A. D.
Inpatient.
Note to the Ophthalmologist.
Sidney, Looking for her Mother.
Solo: The Good Blues.
"Three Observations on the Zombie Culture," *sels.*
We are the writing on the wall.

Kennedy, Benjamin Hall (1804–89)
Bad luck to this marching.
On ["Who Wrote Icon Basilike" by Dr.] Christopher Wordsworth, Master of Trinity.

Kennedy, Gerta
Chesapeake.

Kennedy, James (1793–1827)
Exile's Reveries, The, *sels.*

Kennedy, Walter (c.1460–c.1508)
Honour with Age.

Kennedy, X. J. (b. 1929)
Artificer.
At a Low Mass for Two Hot-Rodders.
B Negative.
Bee.
Brats.
Cross Ties.
Down in Dallas, down in Dallas.
Driving Cross-Country.
Emily Dickinson in Southern California.
Epitaph for a Postal Clerk.
First Confession.
Golgotha.
Hangover Mass.
Help!
Hummingbird.
In a Prominent Bar in Secaucus [One Day].
Japanese Beetles.
Joshua.
Keep a hand on your dream.
Last Child.
Last Lines.
Last Lines on a Wrestler.
Lighting a Fire.
Little Elegy.
Loose Woman.
Mingled Yarns.

Mother's Nerves.
Nothing in Heaven Functions as It Ought.
Nude Descending a Staircase.
On a Child Who Lived One Minute.
One winter night in August.
Terse Elegy for J.V. Cunningham.
To an Angry God.
To Dorothy on Her Exclusion from the
   Guinness Book of World Records.
To Someone Who Insisted I Look up
   Someone.
Whales off Wales, The.
Witnesses, The.

Kennelly, Brendan (b. 1936)
Bread.
Dream of a Black Fox.
Horse's Head, The.
In the Sea.
Island, The.
Limerick Train, The.
Master.
My Dark Fathers.
Pilgrim, The.
Plans.
Position of Praise, The.
Proof.
Running Battle, A.
Swimmer, The.
Thatcher, The.
Wound, A.
Yes.

Kenney, Richard (b. 1948)
Apples on Champlain.
Aubade: "Cold snap. Five o'clock."
Encantadas, The, *sels.*
Hours of the Day, The, *sels.*
La Brea.
Light.
Perfect Disc of the Moon, The.
Plume.
Sawmill.

Kenny, Maurice (b. 1929)
December.
First Rule.
Legacy.
Molly.
O Wendy, Arthur.
Reverberation.
Strawberrying.
Sweetgrass.
They Tell Me I Am Lost.
Wild Strawberry.
Winkte.
Wolf "Aunt."

Kenny, Nick
Patty-Poem.

Kenrei Mon-in Ukyo no Daibu (*fl.* 12th cent.)
I was sure I would never get lost / in the
   tangled roads of love.
Leaves of the bush clover rustle in the wind,
   The.
My heart, like my clothing / is saturated with
   your fragrance.

Kenward, Jean
Composition, The.
E. T.
Moon.
Planets.
Sun.
Technicians.
What's out there?

Kenyon, Jane (1947–95)
At the Iga: Franklin, New Hampshire.
August Rain, after Haying.
Back from the City.
Bat, The.
Briefly It Enters, and Briefly Speaks.
Coats.
Depression in Winter.
February: Thinking of Flowers.
Finding a Long Gray Hair.
From Room to Room.
Gettysburg, July 1, 1863.
Having It Out With Melancholy, *sels.*
Here.
Let Evening Come.
November Calf.

Otherwise.
Peonies at Dusk.
Pharaoh.
Portrait of a Figure near Water.
Potato.
Reading Aloud to My Father.
Suitor, The.
Travel: After a Death.

Kenyon, John (1784–1856)
Champagne Rosée.

Kenzheyev [or Kenzheiev], Bakhyt (b. 1950)
Poets have often noticed.

Keppel, David (1849?–1939)
Trouble.

Keppel, Lady Caroline
Robin Adair.

Ker, L. (*fl.* c.1787)
Death of the Gods; an Ode Written in
   Imitation of Pindar, The.

Kerekere, Wiremu Kingi (b. 1923)
Greeting to Queen Elizabeth, the Rare White
   Heron of Single Flight, A.

Kerner, Justinus (1786–1862)
Home-Sickness.

Kerouac, Jack (John Kerouac) (1922–1969)
Arms folded.
Birds singing.
Buddha.
Flies.
How to Meditate.
Hymn.
In my medicine cabinet.
Mexican Loneliness.
Mexico City Blues, *sels.*
Missing a kick.
My Gang.
Poem.
Scripture of the Golden Eternity, The, *sels.*
Sea Shroud, The.
Straining at the padlock.
Thrashing Doves, The.

Kerr, Kathryn
Touch.

"Kerr, Orpheus C." (Robert Henry Newell) (1836–1901)
American Traveller, The.
Columbia's Agony.
Dear Father, Look Up..
Editor's Wooing, The.
Neutral British Gentleman, The.
O, Be Not Too Hasty, My Dearest.
Rejected "National Hymns," The, *sels.*
Tuscaloosa Sam.
When Your Cheap Divorce Is Granted.

Kershner, Brandon
3 Dialogues, *sels.*

Kessler, Milton (b. 1930)
Secret Love.

Kessler, Miriam
All their names were Vincent, Ernie, Paul.
Eli, Eli.

Kethe, William (*fl.* 16th cent.)
Old Hundredth.
Such as in God the Lord Do Trust.
Thy Mercies, Lord, to Heaven Reach.

Kettle, Thomas Michael (1880–1917)
To My Daughter Betty.

Key, Francis Scott (1779–1843)
Star-Spangled Banner, The.
To My Cousin Mary, for Mending My
   Tobacco Pouch.
Written at the White Sulphur Springs.

Keyes, Frances Parkinson
Limerick: "There was a young man so
   benighted."

Keyes, Sidney (1923–43)
Advice for a Journey.
Death and the Plowman.
Early Spring.
Elegy: "April again, and it is a year again."
Europe's Prisoners.
Expected Guest, The.
Foreign Gate, The, *sels.*
Gardener, The.
Grail, The.

Greenwich Observatory.
Holstenwall.
Neutrality.
Plowman.
Timoshenko.
War Poet.
Wilderness, The, *sels.*
William Wordsworth.
William Yeats in Limbo.

Keyser, Gustave
In the wake.
Rainy summer night.

Kgositsile, Keorapetse (b. 1938)
Acknowledgement.
Air, I hear, The.
For Art Blakey and the Jazz Messengers.
For Eusi, Ayi Kwei and Gwen Brooks.
Gods Wrote, The.
Ivory Masks in Orbit.
My Name Is Afrika.
Origins.
Present is a Dangerous Place to Live, The,
   sels.
Song for Ilva Mackay and Mongane.
Spirits Unchained.
To Mother.
To My Daughter.

Khải, Phan Đình. *See* Lê Đừ̛c Tho

Khaketla, Bennett Makalo (b. 1913)
Lesotho.

Khaketla, N. M. (b. 1918)
White and the Black, The.

Khan, Akhlaq Mohammad. *See* "Shahryar"

Khan, Fath Ali. *See* Saba

Kharms, Daniil (1905–42)
Beginning of a Beautiful Day (A Symphony),
   The.
Each Tuesday above a roadway.
Event on the Street, An.
From "The Blue Notebook" No. 12.
Khaldeyev, Naldeyev, and Peppermaldeyev.
Railroad Happening, A.
See the house took flight.
Symphony No. 2.
There I was sitting on one leg.
Tricks.
Un-Now.

Khavarani, Awhad ad-Din 'Ali ibn Vahid ad-Din Muhammad. *See* "Anvari"

Khlebnikov, Oleg (b. 1956)
Miracle Workers, *sels.*

Khlebnikov, Velemir [or Viktor Vladimirovich] (1885–1922)
Bo-be-o-bee sang the mouth.
Feeding the Dove.
Four Poems.
Good World, *sels.*
I need but little! A crust of bread.
Incantation by Laughter.
It has the unassuming face of a burnt-out
   candle.
Lone Performer, The.
Manifesto of the Presidents of the Terrestrial
   Globe.
Night Before the Soviets, The, *sels.*
Night in the Trench, A, *sels.*
Once again, once again.
Persons, people, and the years.
Stop Fooling.
Suppose I make a timepiece of humanity.
War in a Mousetrap, *sels.*
Washerwoman, *sels.*
We chant and enchant.
Zangezi, *sels.*
Zangezi: R, K, L, G—.
See also Burliuk, D., Aleksandr
   Kruchenykh, V. Mayakovsky, *and* Viktor
   Khlebnikov

Khodasevich, Vladislav Felitsianovich (1886–1939)
Amidst a smoking desolation.
Ballad: "Oh, quietly mad I'd like to be."
In Front of the Mirror.
Monkey.
Monument, The.
Plainsong.

Shape ships to seek some shining shore.
Through the Window.
To a Guest.
Twilight.
Twilight was turning to darkness outside.
Kholin, Igor (b. 1929)
Recently in Sokol.
Khoury-Gata, Venus (b. 1937)
Autumn made colors burn, The.
Your cheeks flat on the sand.
Khu, Đặng Xuân. *See* **Sóng Hồng**
Ki [or Kii], Lady (fl. 8th cent.)
I know the reputation / of the idle ways.
Ki no Tomonori (fl. early 10th cent.)
In the eternal / Light of the spring day.
Ki no Tsurayuki (882–946)
No, the human heart.
Out in the marsh reeds.
Ki No Washika, Lady (fl. 8th cent.)
No.
Kibirov, Timur (b. 1955)
Year 1937, The.
Kibkarjuk
Song of the Rejected Woman.
Kicknosway, Faye (b. 1936)
Mr. Muscle-On.
West Grand Boulevard.
Kidman, Fiona (b. 1940)
Guy Fawkes '58.
Train Song.
Kie Tapu
Song by a Woman Accused of Adultery.
Kiên Giang (Tru'o'ng Khuông Trinh) (b. 1929)
Beauties in White.
Hero of Our Times, The.
Kikaku (1661–1707)
Above the boat.
bantam rooster, A.
Kilār, Ālattūr
Guide to Patrons, A.
Kilār, Aricil (b. 1943)
Battle Scene.
Kilar, Kovur
Poet's Counsel, A ("You come from the line of a Cōla King.")
Poet's Counsel, A ("Your enemy is not the kind who wears.")
Kilgore, James C. (b. 1928)
White Man Pressed the Locks, The.
Killigrew, Anne (1660–85)
Alexandreis.
Farewell to Worldly Joyes, A ("Farewell to unsubstantial joyes.")
On a Picture Painted by Herself[, Representing Two Nimphs of Diana's].
On Death.
Pastoral Dialogue.
To My Lord Colrane, in Answer to His Complemental Verses Sent Me under the Name of Cleanor.
To the Queen.
Upon the Saying That My Verses Were Made by Another.
Killigrew, Henry (1613–1700)
Song: "While Morpheus thus doth gently lay."
Killigrew, Thomas (1612–83)
Epilogue to "The Parson's Wedding."
Kilmer, Joyce (1886–1918)
House with Nobody in It, The.
Roofs.
Trees.
Kilmer, Nicholas (b. 1941)
Petrarch, *sels.*
Kilner, Dorothy (1755–1836)
Henry's Secret.
Kiḻr, Peruṅkuṉṟūr
Parade, A.
Kim, Chi-ha (b. 1941)
Aerin 4.
Aerin I.
Bird.
Kim, Chongsam (1921–84)
Bird, A.
Salt Sea, The.

When That Day Comes.
Kim, Ch'unsu (b. 1922)
Death of a Girl in Budapest, The.
Kim, Huran (b. 1934)
Fish Cooking.
Winter Tree.
Kim, Hyonsung (1913–76)
Absolute Solitude, The.
Prayer in Autumn.
Tears.
Kim, Jaihiun (b. 1934)
Law of Fall, The.
Mother-thought.
To a Nigerian Friend.
Kim, Jonggil (b. 1926)
Christmas.
Tavern at Sunset.
Kim, Kirim (b. 1909)
Homesickness.
Sea and the Butterfly, The.
Spring.
Kim, Kwanggun (b. 1912)
Gaslight.
Lyricism of an Autumn Day.
Snowy Night.
Kim, Kwangnim (b. 1929)
Conflict.
Lord's Day, The.
Kim, Kwangsop (1905–77)
Dove in Songbukdong, The.
Pathos.
Kim, Kyudong (b. 1923)
Home.
Mother's Letter from the North.
Kim, Myung Mi (b. 1957)
Bounty, II, The.
Kim, Namjo (b. 1927)
Heart's Flag.
Music.
My baby has no name yet.
Winter Sea, The.
Kim, Namju (b. 1946)
Spring Comes to the Hills and Fields.
This autumn, in blue prisoner's garb, hands tied behind my back.
Kim, Sowol (1902–34)
Azaleas, The.
Flowers in the Mountains.
Gift of Love.
Song by the Brook.
Kim, Suyong (1921–69)
Grass lies flattened.
Waterfall, A.
Kim, Tonghwan (b. 1901)
Boatsong of the Sungari, The.
When the river breaks loose.
Kim, Tongmyong (1901–66)
Banana Plant, The.
My mind is a lake.
Kim, Yangshik (b. 1931)
Elegy: "Because of you I have lived."
Grass Flower.
Kim, Yojong (b. 1933)
Labyrinth.
Sea of Lemon, The.
Kim, Yon-gyun (b. 1942)
Message.
Years.
Kim, Yongnang (1903–50)
May.
Till The Peonies Bloom.
Kim, Yongt'ae (b. 1936)
Hotel North.
Landscape I.
Kimball, Jacob (1761–1826)
Thy Praise, O God, in Zion Waits.
King, Anne (b. 1621?)
Inscription on Monument of Dorothy, Lady Hubert.
Under Mr. Hales Picture.
King, Ben (Benjamin Franklin King) (1857–99)
Cultured Girl Again, The.
Hair-Tonic Bottle, The.
If I Should Die Tonight.

Mermaid, The.
Pessimist, The.
Sum of Life, The.
King, Benjamin Franklin. *See* **King, Ben**
King, Dorothy (b. 1914?)
Billy Boy.
Gipsy Man.
Jenny and Johnny.
King, E. L. M. (1870–1962)
Cobwebs.
King, Edith (b. 1878)
Duck, The.
Evening Song.
Hedgehog is a little beast, The.
Pebbles.
Rabbit, The.
To the Bat.
King, Francis (b. 1923)
Séance.
King, Harriet Hamilton (1840–1920)
Dream Maiden, A.
Moonlight Ride, A.
Summer Lost.
King, Helen
If we give love and sympathy.
King, Henry, Bishop of Chichester (1592–1669)
Change, The.
Contemplation upon Flowers, A.
Departure; an Elegy, The.
Double Rock, The.
Elegy upon S[ir] W[alter] R[aleigh], An.
Exequy, The, *sels.*
Forfeiture, A.
Renunciation, A.
Sic Vita.
Silence: A Sonnet.
Sonnet: "Go, thou that vainly dost mine eyes invite."
Sonnet: "Tell me[e] no more how fair[e] she[e] is."
Surrender, The.
To a Lady Who Sent Me a Copy of Verses at My Going to Bed.
To My Dead Friend Ben: Johnson.
Upon a Braid of Hair in a Heart.
Upon the Death of My Ever Desired Friend Doctor Donne Dean of Pauls.
King, Jane (b. 1952)
Clichés for an Unfaithful Husband.
Hymn: "For you I would put on embroidered robes."
Moments.
King, Jenny
I Enter by the Darkened Door.
King, Jill
Grief Plucked Me Out of Sleep.
King Pleasure. *See* **Beeks, Clarence**
King, Stoddard (1889–1933)
Breakfast Song in Time of Diet.
Crime at Its Best.
Difference, The.
Hearth and Home.
Idyll: "He was a selfish shellfish."
Trombone Solo.
King, William (1662–1712)
Art of Cookery, The, *sels.*
Beggar Woman, The.
Kingsley, Charles (1819–75)
Airly Beacon, Airly Beacon.
Alton Locke, *sels.*
Andromeda, *sels.*
Farewell, A: "My fairest child, I have no song to give you."
Farewell, To C. E. G, A.
Invitation, The.
Last Buccaneer, The.
Ode to the Northeast Wind.
Song: "When I was a greenhorn and young."
Three Fishers [Went Sailing], The.
Valentine's Day.
"Watchman, what of the night?"
Water Babies, The, *sels.*
Kingsley, Henry (1830–76)
At Glastonbury.

Kingsmill, Hugh (1889–1949)
Summer Time on Bredon.
What, still alive at twenty–two.
Kingston, Jeremy (b. 1931)
Distances.
Kingston, Maxine Hong
Absorption of Rock.
Restaurant.
Kinnell, Galway (b. 1927)
After Making Love We Hear Footsteps.
Angel, The.
Another Night in the Ruins.
Avenue Bearing the Initial of Christ into the
New World, The, *sels.*
Bear, The.
Blackberry Eating.
Braemar.
Burn, The.
Burning.
Cells Breathe in the Emptiness.
Correspondence School Instructor Says
Goodbye to His Poetry Students, The.
Crying only a little bit.
Daybreak.
Dead Shall Be Raised Incorruptible, The,
sels.
Deconstruction of Emily Dickinson, The.
Duck-chasing.
Farm Picture.
First Song.
Flower Herding on Mount Monadnock.
For Robert Frost.
Fossils, The.
Freedom, New Hampshire.
Getting the Mail.
Hcn Flower, The.
In a Parlor Containing a Table.
In Fields of Summer.
La Bagarède.
Lackawanna.
Last Gods.
Last Hiding Places of Snow, The.
Last Songs.
Lastness.
Little Sleep's-Head Sprouting Hair in the
Moonlight.
Man on the Hotel Room Bed, The.
Man Splitting Wood in the Daybreak, The.
Memories of My Father, *sels.*
Middle of the Way, *sels.*
Milk Bottle, The.
Night in the Forest.
On the Oregon Coast.
Path among the Stones, The.
Porcupine, The.
Reply to the Provinces.
River That Is East, The.
Room, The.
Ruins under the Stars, *sels.*
Saint Francis and the Sow.
Seekonk Woods, The.
Shroud, The.
Spindrift.
Supper after the Last, The.
To Christ Our Lord.
To William Carlos Williams.
Tragedy of Bricks, The.
Two Set Out on Their Journey.
Under the Maud Moon.
Vapor Trail Reflected in the Frog Pond.
Vow, The.
When one has lived a long time alone.
Kinsella, John (b. 1963)
Chess Piece Cornered.
Orpheus.
Sick Woman.
Kinsella, Thomas (b. 1929)
All is Emptiness, and I Must Spin.
Ancestor.
Another September.
Artists' Letters.
At the Crossroads.
Baggot Street Deserta.
Ballydavid Pier.
Carol: "Garden and gardener He made."
Chrysalides.
Clarence Mangan.

Country Walk, A.
Cover Her Face.
Death Bed.
Dispossessed, The.
Downstream.
Endymion.
Finistére.
First Light.
Folk Wisdom.
Furnace, The.
Hand of Solo, A.
Hen Woman.
His Father's Hands.
In the Ringwood.
Je T'Adore.
Lady of Quality, A.
Mask of Love.
Messenger, The, *sels.*
Mirror in February.
Model School, Inchicore.
Nightwalker, *sels.*
Nuchal, a Fragment.
Oldest Place, The.
Ritual of Departure.
Route of the Táin, The.
Scylla and Charybdis.
Secret Garden, The.
Songs of the Psyche, *sels.*
Tao and Unfitness at Inistiogue on the River
Nore.
Tear.
Technical Supplement, A, *sels.*
Thinking of Mr. D.
Westland Row.
Wormwood.
Wyncote, Pennsylvania: A Gloss.
Kintsune (*fl.* 13th cent.)
Flowers whirl away, The.
Kinzie, Mary
Among mosquitoes.
Boy.
But her arm—damp, small.
Canicula.
Glinting like water.
Heat-heavy creatures.
Impromptu.
In air hard as sand.
Orchard dying, The.
Ringing Words.
Sound Waves.
Sun and Moon.
Want, predation, sleep.
Xenophilia.
Kipling, Rudyard (1865–1936)
American Spirit speaks, The.
Arithmetic on the Frontier.
Astrologer's Song, An.
At His Execution.
Ballad of East and West, The.
Ballad of Fisher's Boardinghouse, The.
Bill 'Awkins.
Boots.
Bridge-Guard in the Karroo.
Chant-Pagan.
City of Sleep, The.
Conundrum of the Workshops, The.
Cuckoo Song.
Dane-Geld.
Danny Deever.
Death-Bed, A.
Debits and Credits, *sels.*
Derelict, The.
Dykes, The.
'Eathen in 'is blindness bows down to wood
an' stone, The.
Eddi's Service.
En-Dor.
Envoi: "There's a whisper down the field
where the year has shot her yield."
Epitaphs of the War [1914–1918], *sels.*
Evarra and His Gods.
Female of the Species, The.
Flight of the Bucket, The.
For all we have and are.
For to Admire.
Ford o' Kabul River.
Fuzzy-Wuzzy.

Galley-Slave, The.
Gallio's Song.
Gehazi.
Gentlemen-Rankers.
Gertrude's Prayer.
Gethsemane [1914–18].
Gipsy Trail, The.
Glory of the Garden, The, *sels.*
Gods of the Copybook Headings, The.
Grave, The.
Gunga Din.
Half-Ballad of Waterval.
His Apologies.
Hyænas [*or* Hyenas], The.
If.
If you can keep your head when all [about
you].
In the Neolithic Age savage warfare did I
wage, The.
Just-So Stories, *sels.*
Kim, *sels.*
King, The.
La Nuit Blanche.
Ladies, The.
Land, The.
Land and Sea Tales, *sels.*
Last Chantey, The.
Life's Handicap, *sels.*
Light That Failed, The, *sels.*
Limerick: "There was a small boy of
Quebec."
Looking Glass, The.
Loot, *sels.*
Lovers' Litany, The.
Mandalay.
McAndrew's Hymn.
Mesopotamia.
Municipal.
My Boy Jack.
My Rival.
Naaman's Song.
Nativity, A.
Naulahka, The, *sels.*
Neighbours.
New Knighthood, The.
Ode to Liberty.
Old Men, The.
Power of the Dog, The.
Puck of Pook's Hill, *sels.*
Rabbi's Song, The.
Rebirth.
Recall, The.
Recessional.
Return, The.
Sacrifice of Er-Heb, The.
St. Helena Lullaby, A.
Sea and the Hills, The.
Sergeant's Weddin', The.
Servant When He Reigneth, A.
Sestina of the Tramp-Royal.
Shillin' a Day.
Song of the Banjo, The.
Song of the Galley-Slaves.
Sons of Martha, The.
Storm Cone, The.
Story of the Gadsbys, The, *sels.*
Story of Uriah, The.
Supplication of the Black Aberdeen.
Tommy.
Ulster.
Vampire, The.
Way Through The Woods, The.
When Earth's last picture is painted and the
tubes are twisted / and dried.
White Horses.
White Man's Burden, The.
Widow at Windsor, The.
Widower, The.
Kirantaiyar
Hymn to Tirumāl (Viṣṇu).
Kirattanar, Kutavayir
What Her Girl Friend Said before the
elopement.
Young will not wear it, The.
Kirby, David (b. 1944)
To a French Structuralist.

Kirby, Jeannie
  Aeroplane, The.
  Child's Morning Prayer, A.
  I wonder why the grass is green.
  Pigeon's Story, The.
  Proud Little Spruce Fir.
  Timid Bunnies.
  Union Jack, The.
Kircher, Pamela
  Looking at the Sea.
Kirchwey, Karl (b. 1956)
  Ambulance.
  He Considers the Birds of the Air.
  Natural History.
  Rogue Hydrant, August.
  Sonogram.
  St. Matthew, *sels.*
Kirilenko-Voloshin, Maksimilian. *See* **Voloshin, Maksimilian Aleksandrovich**
Kirillov, Vladimir Timofeievich (1890–1943)
  We uncountable dread legions of Labor.
Kirkland, Hilaire (1941–75)
  Clotho, Lachesis, Atropos, *sels.*
  Observations, *sels.*
Kirkpatrick, Patricia
  For a Woman Murdered While Running at
    Land's End, October 1979.
Kirkup, James (b. 1923)
  Astronaut, The.
  Baby's Drinking Song.
  Beautiful Strangers, The.
  Caged Bird in Springtime, The.
  Correct Compassion, A.
  Earth Tremor in Lugano.
  My Thing from Outer Space.
  Old Gramophone Records.
  Questions and Answers (a ballad).
  Scarecrows.
  Shepherd's Tale, The.
  Space Trip.
  Who's that.
**Kirsanov, Semyon [*or* Semion] Isaakovich
  (1906/ND/72)**
  Lyric Poem.
  New Heart, The.
  Your Poem, *sels.*
Kirsch, Olga (b. 1924)
  Blockhouse.
  Wordspinning.
Kirsch, Sarah (b. 1935)
  Air already smells like snow, my lover, The.
  Dandelions for Chains ("Dandelions meet me
    wherever I am.")
  Date.
  Don Juan is coming in the morning.
  Drinking Vodka.
  Legend of Lilja.
  Mail.
  Pictures.
  Sad Day in Berlin.
  Seven Skins.
  Stopover.
Kirschner, Elizabeth
  Blueness of Stars, The.
  Fall of Light, The.
  Two Blue Swans.
Kirstein, Lincoln (b. 1907)
  Double Date.
  Fall In.
  Foresight.
  Gripe.
  P.O.E.
  Rank.
  Vaudeville.
Kiser, Samuel Ellsworth (1862–1942)
  Bargain Sale, A.
  Fighter, The.
  My Creed.
  Unsubdued.
Kiss, Anna (b. 1939)
  Emperor Butterfly.
Kitahara Hakushū (1885–1942)
  At a hospital in Tokyo during the summer of
    1911.
  Tanka: "After letting my wife."

  Tanka: "After lunch."
  Tanka: "Ailing child, An."
  Tanka: "Almost invisible."
  Tanka: "Autumn bellflower."
  Tanka: "During a fit."
  Tanka: "Each alighted."
  Tanka: "Gasoline."
  Tanka: "Gleaming sliver."
  Tanka: "I sneaked into."
  Tanka: "In my heart."
  Tanka: "In the daytime."
  Tanka: "Magnolia."
  Tanka: "My uncle."
  Tanka: "Spring bird."
  Tanka: "Strong scent, The."
  Tanka: "Today too."
  Tanka: "Winter day."
"Kitchener, Lord" (b. 1922)
  Miss Tourist.
Kitching, John
  I know where I'm going.
  If he cried, he cried in private.
  My Gerbil.
  No need to scan the skies.
  Planets turn in stately dance, The.
  Space Captain.
  Swirling world stands still, The.
  Within the space.
Kiwus, Karin (b. 1942)
  All Splendor on Earth.
Kiyoko Tsuda (b. 1920)
  To be a mistress.
Kiyowara Fukuyabu (c.900–930)
  River-Fog.
Kizer, Carolyn (b. 1925)
  Afternoon Happiness.
  Amusing Our Daughters.
  Antique Father.
  Bitch.
  Blessing, The.
  Columns and Caryatids.
  Copulating Gods, The.
  Food of Love.
  For Jan, in Bar Maria.
  Great Blue Heron, The.
  Hera, Hung from the Sky.
  Intruder, The.
  Lines to Accompany Flowers for Eve.
  Muse of Water, A.
  On a Line from Valéry.
  One to Nothing.
  Pro Femina, *sels.*
  Race Relations.
  Running Away from Home, *sels.*
  Semele Recycled.
  Skein, The.
  Summer near the River.
  Through a Glass Eye, Lightly.
  To a Visiting Poet in a College Dormitory.
  Twelve O'Clock.
  Widow in Wintertime, A.
Klaj, Johann (1616–56)
  Oh golden life, waken! Fortunate night!
  Stroll-Joy.
Klappert, Peter (b. 1942)
  Ellie Mae Leaves in a Hurry.
  For the Poet Who Said Poets Are Struck by
    Lightning Only Two or Three Times.
  Invention of the Telephone, The.
  Lord's Chameleons, The.
  Poem for L. C.
Klauber, Edgar
  On Buying a Dog.
"Klaxon" (John Graham Bower) (1886–1940)
  Destroyers.
  Submarines.
Klee, Paul (1879–1940)
  Friend, A.
  Happy one, who is almost / an idiot, The.
  Master knows what he want, The.
  Poem.
  Wolf speaks, while chewing, The.
Klein, Abraham Moses (1909–72)
  Autobiographical.
  Baal Shem Tov.
  Ballad of the Days of the Messiah.

  Biography.
  Break-up, The.
  For the Sisters of the Hôtel Dieu.
  Haggadah.
  Heirloom.
  In re Solomon Warshawer.
  Indian Reservation: Caughnawaga.
  Lone Bather.
  Monsieur Gaston.
  Montreal.
  Political Meeting.
  Portrait of the Poet as Landscape.
  Psalter of Avram Haktani, The, *sels.*
  Rabbi Yom-Tob of Mayence Petitions His
    God.
  Rev Owl.
  Rocking Chair, The.
  Venerable Bee, The.
  Winter Night: Mount Royal.
Klein, Robin
  Amanda!
Kleinzahler, August (b. 1949)
  Autumnal Sketch, An.
  Case in Point, A.
  East of the Library, Across from the Odd
    Fellows Building.
  Ebenezer Californicus.
  Hamburger.
  Like cities, like storms.
  Love Poem.
  Lunatic of Lindley Meadow, The.
  Poetics.
  San Francisco/New York.
  Spleen.
  Two Canadian Landscapes.
Kleiser, Grenville (1868–1953)
  Most Vital Thing in Life, The.
Kleist, Ewald von (1715–59)
  Song at Graveside.
Klemm, Wilhelm
  Clearing-Station.
Klepfisz, Irena (b. 1941)
  About My Father.
  Bashert, *sels.*
  Death Camp.
  Dinosaurs and Larger Issues.
  Few Words in the Mother Tongue, A.
  From the Monkey House and Other Cages:
    Monkey II.
  My Mother's Sabbath Days.
  Perspectives on the Second World War.
  They did not build wings for them.
Klimentov, Andrei Platonovich. *See* **"Platonov,
  Andrey"**
"Klingle, George" (Georgiana Klingle Holmes)
  Be Patient.
Klingsor, Tristan (1874–1966)
  Song of the Cat, The.
"Klip-Klip." *See* **Rutter, Owen**
Kloefkorn, William
  On the Road.
Klopstock, Friedrich Gottlieb (1724–1803)
  Early Graves, The.
  Fredensborg.
  Lake of Zurich, The.
  Rose Wreaths, The.
  Summer Night, The.
**Klyuyev [*or* Kliuev], Nikolai Alekseievich
  (1884–1937)**
  Lenin, *sels.*
Knapp, Shepherd (1873–1946)
  Lord God of Hosts.
  Not Only Where God's Free Winds Blow.
Knevet, Ralph (1601–72)
  Bottle, The.
  Contrition.
  Habitation, The.
  Harp, The.
  Navigation.
  Vote, The.
Knibbs, Henry Herbert (1874–1945)
  Out There Somewhere.
Knight, David (b. 1926)
  Chief of the West, Darkling, The.
  In Memoriam S. L. Akintola.

Palms, The.
"When the Students Resisted, a Minor Clash Ensued."

Knight, Etheridge (1933–91)
Another Poem for Me (after Recovering from an O.D.)
As You Leave Me.
Belly Song.
Cell Song.
Circling the Daughter.
Crazy pigeon strutting outside my cell.
Dark Prophecy: I Sing of Shine.
Feeling Fucked/Up Up.
For Black Poets Who Think of Suicide.
For Freckle-Faced Gerald.
For Langston Hughes.
Green Grass and Yellow Balloons.
Haiku: "Eastern guard tower."
Hard Rock Returns to Prison from the Hospital for the Criminal Insane.
He sees through stone.
Huey.
Idea of Ancestry, The.
It was a funky deal.
My life, the quality of which.
On the Yard.
On Watching Politicians Perform at Martin Luther King's Funeral.
Poem for Myself (Or Blues for a Mississippi Black Boy), A.
Poem of Attrition, A.
Poem to Galway Kinnell, A.
Portrait of Malcolm X.
Report to the Mother.
Sun came, Miss Brooks—, The.
Three Songs, *sels.*
To Dinah Washington.
To Make a Poem in Prison.
Two Poems for Black Relocation Centers, *sels.*
Upon Your Leaving.
Violent Space, The.
Warden said to me the other day, The.
WASP Woman Visits a Black Junkie in Prison, A.
Welcome Back, Mr. Knight: Love of My Life.

Knight, Henrietta, Lady Luxborough (1699–1756)
Bullfinch in Town, The.
Written to a Near Neighbour in a Tempestuous Night.

Knight, Henry Coggswell (1789–1835)
Lunar Stanzas.

Knight, Richard Payne (1750–1824)
Landscape, The, *sels.*

Knight, Sarah Kemble (1666–1727)
Pleasant Delusion of a Sumpteous Citty.
Resentments Composed because of the Clamor of Town Topers Outside My Apartment.
Thoughts on Pausing at a Cottage near the Paukataug River.
Thoughts on the Sight of the Moon.
Warning to Travailers Seeking Accomodations at Mr. Devills Inn.

Knister, Raymond (1899–1932)
Boy Remembers in the Field.
February's Forgotten Mitts.
Row of Stalls, A, *sels.*

Knopfli, Rui (b. 1932)
Death Certificate.
Kwela for Tomorrow.

Knott, Bill
Ant Dodger.
At the Crossroads.
Death.
Feeding the Sun.
Funny Poem.
Goodbye.
Hair Poem.
Poem: "After your death."
Poem: "At your light side trees shy."
(Poem) (Chicago) (The Were-Age).
Poem: "Only response, The."
Shorts / Excerpts ("I keep a TV monitor on my chest.")

Sleep.
Sonnet: "Way the world is not, The."
Two Vietnam Poems: (1966).

Knowles, Frederic Lawrence (1869–1905)
Grief and Joy, *sels.*

Knowles, James D. (1798–1838)
O God, though Countless Worlds of Light.

Knowles, Suzanne (b. 1911)
Fox Dancing.
Tails and Heads.

Knox, Caroline
Rune, A.

Knox, Edmund George Valpy ("Evoe") (1881–1971)
Director, The.
Last Bus, The.
Limerick: "There was a young curate of Hants."
To the God of Love.
Upon Julia's Clothes.

Knox, J. Mason (b. 1872)
Co-operation.

Knox, Ronald Arbuthnott (1888–1957)
Anglican curate in want, An.
Limerick: "Evangelical vicar in want."
Limerick: "There once was a man who said 'God'."
O God, for as much as without Thee.
To a Pessimist.

Knox, William (1789–1825)
Oh! why should the spirit of mortal be proud?

"Knut, Dovid" (David Mironovich Fiksman) (1900–1955)
I remember a dim evening in Kishinyov [*or* Kishinev].
I was walking along the Sea of Galilee.

Ko, Un (b. 1933)
Chongno Street.
Sky, The.

Kocan, Peter (b. 1947)
AIDS, Among Other Things.
Bill.
Cows graze across the hill.
Inmate, An.
Mutineer's Ballad, The.
Sleepers, The.

Kocbek, Edvard (1904–81)
Dialectics.
Game, The.
Hands.
Longing for Jail, A.
Stick, The.

Koch, Christopher (b. 1932)
Boy who Dreamed the Country Night, The.
Shelly Beach.

Koch, Kenneth (b. 1925)
Alive for an Instant.
Art of Love, The, *sels.*
Circus, The.
Days and Nights, *sels.*
Down at the docks.
Energy in Sweden.
Fresh Air, *sels.*
Geography.
Girl and Baby Florist Sidewalk Pram Nineteen Seventy Something.
In Love with You.
Locks.
Mending Sump.
One Train May Hide Another.
Permanently.
Poem for My Twentieth Birthday.
Poem of the Forty-eight States, A.
Poem: "Thing / To do / Is organize, The."
Schoolyard in April.
Sleeping with Women.
Taking a Walk with You.
Talking to Patrizia.
Thank You.
Thanksgiving.
To Marina.
To You.
Variations on a Theme by William Carlos Williams.

With Janice.
You were wearing your Edgar Allan Poe printed cotton blouse.

Kochetkov, Aleksandr (1900–1953)
Ballad About a Smoke-Filled Railway Carriage.

Koehn, Adam (b. 1974)
Divorce.

Koertge, Ron (b. 1940)
Thing Is to Not Let Go of the Vine, The.
Ubiquity of the Need for Love, The.

Koestenbaum, Phyllis (b. 1930)
Harriet Feigenbaum is a Sculptor.
Sonnet 37: "I'd decided I initiate most."

Koestenbaum, Wayne
1975.

Koethe, John (b. 1945)
Falling Water.
Mission Bay.
Substitute for Time, The.

Kogan, Pavel Davydovich (1918–42)
Star.
Thunderstorm.

Koianimptiwa
Korosta Katzina Song.

Kojijū (1121–1201)
On the Spirit of the Heart as Moon-Disk.

Kōka, Stewardess of the Empress. *See* **Stewardess of the Empress Kōka.**

Kōkō Emperor (fl. 9th cent.)
When I went out in.

Kolatkar, Jejuri Arun (b. 1932)
Alphabet, The.
Butterfly, The.
Old woman grabs, An.

Kollan Alici
What She Said.

Kollar, Sybil
Late Arrivals.
Sunday Matinee.

Koller, James (b. 1936)
I Have Cut an Eagle.
O Dirty Bird Yr Gizzard's Too Big & Full of Sand.
Some Magic.
Unreal Song of the Old, The.

Kolmar, Gertrud (1894–1943?)
Judith.
Out of the Darkness.
Paris.
Sacrifice, The.
Toad, The.

Komey, Ellis Ayitey (1927–72)
Change, The.
Oblivion.

Komunyakaa, Yusef (b. 1947)
After a photograph by Yevgeni Yevtushenko, *sels.*
After the Fall of Saigon.
April Fools' Day.
Back Then.
Banking Potatoes.
Birds on a Powerline.
Blackberries.
Boat People.
Boxing Day.
Break from the Bush, A.
Cage Walker, The.
Camouflaging the Chimera.
Crack.
Dead at Quang Tri, The.
Elegy for Thelonious.
"Everybody's Reading Li Po" Silkscreened on a Purple T-Shirt.
Facing It.
February in Sydney.
Gift Horse.
Ia Drang Valley.
Imhotep.
Instructions for Building Straw Huts.
Landscape for the Disappeared.
My Father's Love Letters [*or* Loveletters].
Nude Study.
Report from the Skull's Diorama.
Saigon Bar Girls, 1975.

Salt.
Slam, Dunk, and Hook.
Smokehouse, The.
Somewhere Near Phu Bai.
Speed Ball.
Starlight Scope Myopia.
Sunday Afternoons.
Temples of Smoke.
Thorn Merchant's Mistress, The.
Tiger Lady.
Troubling the Water.
Tu Do Street.
Twilight Seduction.
Venus's-Flytraps.
Way the Cards Fall, The.
We Never Know.
White Port and Lemon Juice.
Kondo, Tadashi
Autumn light.
Koneski, Blaze
Wheat, The.
Konopnicka, Maria (1842–1910)
Vision, A.
Kooser, Ted (b. 1939)
Abandoned Farmhouse.
Afterlife, The.
At the End of the Weekend.
At the Office Early.
Camera.
Central.
Child Frightened by a Thunderstorm.
City Limits.
Country School.
Finding, A.
Flying at Night.
Genuine Poem, Found on a Blackboard in a
Bowling Alley in Story City, Iowa.
Gilbert Stuart Portrait of Washington, The.
How to Make Rhubarb Wine.
In January, 1962.
Late Lights in Minnesota.
Onion Woman, The.
Selecting a Reader.
Self-Portrait at Thirty-Nine.
Shooting a Farmhouse.
Very old are forever, The.
Widow, A.
Year's End.
Kopelke, Kendra (b. 1957)
Eager Street.
**Kopland, Rutger (Rudi van den Hoofdakker)
(b. 1934)**
Breughel's Winter.
Johnson Brothers Ltd.
Natzweiler.
Thanks to the Things.
Ulumbo, a Cat.
Kora, Rumiko (b. 1932)
Woman.
Korinna [or Corinna] (fl. c.500? B.C.)
Although I was her pupil, / even I reproach
Myrtis.
I blame Myrtis.
I come tonight to sing you songs.
I disapprove even of eloquent / Myrtis.
I Korinna am here to sing the courage.
Kithairon sang of cunning Kronos.
Terpsichore looks kindly on me.
To the white-mantled maidens.
When he sailed into the harbor.
Will you sleep forever?
Korkiya [or Korkiia], Viktor b. 1948
Stanzas: "With youthful loss of memory, in
my voiceless land."
Korn, Rachel [or Rokhl] (1898–1982)
Keep Hidden from Me ("Keep from me all
that I might comprehend!")
Put Your Word to My Lips.
Thirty-one Camels, The.
Korneichukov, Nikolai Vasilyevich. See
"Chukovsky, Korney"
Kornilov, Boris Petrovich (1907–38)
Continuation of Life.
Drawer of My Writing Desk, The.
High Seas on the Caspian.
My Nightingale.

Under the scraggy fir tree.
Kornilov, Vladimir Nikolaevich (b. 1928)
Announcer, The.
Johnny.
Poorer than X.
Sky, The.
Snow.
Koroneu
Funeral Eva.
Korran
What She Said to Her Girl Friend ("No, we
will not make vows to the ever-winning
goddess.")
**Korvin-Piotrovsky, Vladimir L'vovich (1891–
1966)**
Farewell, Captain. In bygone days.
**"Korzhavin, Naum" (Naum Moiseievich
Mandel) (b. 1925)**
Envy.
For certain, I did not live thus in this world.
How difficult to live without you!
I could be in Paris or Vienna.
I was never an ascetic.
Imitation of Monsieur Beranger.
Leningrad.
Or did I really fall out of love with my
country?—.
Poem about Youth and Romanticism, A.
Variation on Nekrasov.
Kosovic, Ante (1882–1958)
Ah Dalmatia, if only I could send word of
your dear sons.
Kossman, Nina
Judas' Reproach.
Pilate's Wife.
St. John, sels.
Kostakis, Peter
Circle with a Hole in the Middle, The.
Fire Parcel.
Kostelanetz, Richard (b. 1940)
Concentric.
Disintegration.
Kovatattan
What Her Girl Friend Said to Her ("These fat
cassia trees.")
Kovner, Abba (b. 1918)
Between mountains coils a city. Wind.
Dimmed Observation.
Dinosaurs wept angry tears.
Front Page.
Hour's Late, The.
How Many Poems Were Lost.
I Don't Know if Mount Zion would
recognize itself.
Lookout on a Rock on the Heights of Mount
Hermon.
Lord of Dreams.
'My Little Sister', sels.
My Sister.
Of All My Loves.
On My Words.
Poem: Alte Zachen.
Scientists Are Mistaken, The.
Sun-Watchers.
Tashlich.
To Myself.
To the Things That Are Immortal.
Voice of My White City, The.
Vow.
What's Not in the Heart.
While at Prayer.
Kovur Kilar
Poet's Counsel, A ("You come from the line
of a Cola king.")
Poet's Counsel, A ("Your enemy is not the
kind who wears.")
Kowit, Steve (b. 1938)
Cosmetics do no good.
In the morning.
Lurid Confessions.
Notice.
What chord did she pluck in my soul.
When he pressed his lips to my mouth.
Koziol, Urszula (b. 1935)
Alarum.

Kramer, Lotte
Red Cross telegram, The.
Shoemaker's Wife, The.
**Krandievskaya [or Krandievskaia], Natalya [or
Natal'ia] (1888–1963)**
Those who would not accept went past.
Krasnikov, Gennady (b. 1951)
Come on, Mama, we'll slake the lime.
Kraujiete, Aina
City Girls.
In Chalk Rooms.
Vagabond's Arising.
Kraus, Karl (1874–1936)
Express Train.
On the Threshold.
Kremer, Pem
Epiphany.
Kretzmer, Herbert
Limerick: "Kinky young girl from Uttoxeter,
A."
Kreymborg, Alfred (1883–1966)
To W. C. W. M. D.
Krichevsky [or Krichevskii], Ilya (1963–91)
Exhausted from depression.
Refugees.
Kriebel, Casper (fl. mid–18th cent.)
Now Sleep My Little Child So Dear.
Krige, Uys (b. 1910)
Distant View.
Encounter.
Farm Gate.
Soldier, The.
Swallows over the Camp.
Taking of the Koppie, The.
Kriloff, Ivan Andreevich (1768–1844)
Peasant and the Sheep, The.
Krishnamurti, M. (b. 1912)
Spirit's Odyssey, The.
Krmpotic, Vesna (b. 1932)
December Forest, A.
Kroetsch, Robert (b. 1927)
Stone Hammer Poem.
Krohn, Herbert
Can Tho, favela of crowing cocks.
Farmer's Song at Can Tho.
Ferryman's Song at Binh Minh.
My Flute.
Kroll, Judith (b. 1943)
Dick and Jane.
I Think of Housman Who Said the Poem Is a
Morbid Secretion, like a Pearl.
Not Thinking of America.
Sestina: "Is this the object."
Kruchenykh, Aleksandr. See Burliuk, D.,
Aleksandr Kruchenykh, V. Mayakovsky,
and Viktor Khlebnikov
**Kruchyonykh [or Kruchionykh or
Kruchenykh], Aleksei Eliseievich (1886–
1968)**
At midnight I noticed on my sheet a.
Battle of India and Europe.
Declaration of the Word as Such.
Heights.
Pomade, sels.
Sahara to America, The, sels.
Krustev, Ivan
Nostalgia for Titian.
Krynicki, Ryszard (b. 1943)
By entering the grand lottery.
I Can't Help You.
Krysl, Marilyn
Grandmother.
**Kryukova [or Kriukova], Yelena [or Elena] (b.
1956)**
Song of Songs.
Kshetrayya (fl. 17th cent.)
Dancing-Girl's Song.
Ku Hsiung (fl. c.928)
Tune: "Telling of Innermost Feelings."
Tune: Telling of Innermost Feelings ("Long
nights when he neglects me—where's he
gone?")
Ku K'uang (725?–c.814)
On the River.
Sonny grows up in Fukien.

Upon a Brook.
Written upon Returning to the Mountains.

Ku Sang (b. 1919)
Shame.
War Poems 1.
War Poems 7.

Ku T'ai-ch'ing (1799–1876?)
Tune: "Partridge Sky"—Puppet Theater.
Tune: "Phoenix Hairpin"—Crab Apple.
Tune: "Ripples Sifting Sand"—Accompanying
My Husband on a Spring Outing to Stone
Pavilion.

Kuan Han-ch'ing (Han-ch'ing) (c.1220–c.1300)
Tune: "Four Pieces of Jade"—Idle Leisure.
Tune: "Green Jade Flute," sels.
Tune: "Intoxication in the East Wind," sels.
Tune: "Song of Great Virtue"—Spring.
Tune: "Song of Great Virtue"—Winter, sels.
Tune: "Sprig of Flowers, A"—Not Bowing to
Old Age.

Kuan Tao Shêng (1262–1319)
Married Love.

Kuan Yun She (fl. 13th cent.)
Sending Off Spring.
Seventh Day Seventh Month.

Kuan Yün-shih (Hsiao-yün-shih-hai-ya) (1286–1324)
Medley of Southern and Northern Tunes—
Scenic Tour of West Lake, sels.
Tune: "Rapt with Wine, Loudly Singing; Joy
in Spring's Coming."
Tune: "Song of Shou-yang."
Tune: "Song of the Lunar Palace"—Sending
Off Spring.

Kubatum (fl. c.2038 B.C.)
Love Song to King Shu-Suen.

**Kublanovsky [or Kublanovskii], Yury [or Iurii]
Mikhailovich (b. 1947)**
He who gave weight to the wind.
My Russia, mine!

Kuder, Blanche Bane
Blue Bowl, The.

Kudimova, Marina (b. 1953)
Outing, The.
When I still barely rose above the ground.

Kuhlmann, Quirinus (1651–89)
15th Kühl-Psalm, The.
From deepest need cry out, oh hungered
heart!

Kujo, Takeko (1887–1928)
I do not consider myself worth counting.

Kuka, King D.
Evening.
February Morning.
Gallery of My Heart.
Jackie.
Janna.
My Friend the Wind.
My Song.
Tiny baby, you're ugly.

Kukai (774–835)
Singing Image of Fire.

Kulbak, Moishe (1896–1940)
Summer.

**Kulchitsky [or Kulchitskii], Mikhail
Valentinovich (1919–43)**
Dreamer, visionary, green-eyed sluggard!
Mayakovsky.
194...
That's What It's Like, sels.

Kumar, Sati (b. 1938)
Come Back, Alexander.

Kumattur Kannanar
Where the Lilies Were in Flower.

Kumbirai, Joseph (1922–86)
Dawn.

Kumin, Maxine W. (b. 1925)
After Love.
At the End of the Affair.
Chain, The.
Credo.
Despair.
Envelope, The.
Excrement Poem, The.

Family Man, A.
For My Great-Grandfather: A Message Long
Overdue.
Fräulein Reads Instructive Rhymes.
Getting the Message.
Height of the Season, The.
Hermit Has a Visitor, The.
Hermit Wakes to Bird Sounds, The.
How It Is.
In the Absence of Bliss.
In the Root Cellar.
Journey, The.
Living Alone with Jesus—.
Louise Bourgeois Exhibit.
Making the Jam without You.
Masochist, The.
May 10th.
Morning Swim.
Mummies, The.
My Father's Neckties.
Noted in The New York Times.
Nuns of Childhood: Two Views, The.
Plans.
Presence, The.
Prothalamion.
Rendezvous, The.
Retrieval System, The.
Saga.
Seeing the Bones.
Sound of Night, The.
Spree.
Together.
Video Cuisine.
Voice From the Roses, A.
Woodchucks.

Kunene, Raymond Mazisi (b. 1930)
"Advice" to a Young Poet.
Death of the Miners or, The Widows of the
Earth.
Echoes, The.
Elegy.
Meeting with Vilakazi, the Great Zulu Poet,
A.
Nozizwe.
Thought on June 26.
When My Poems were Lost.

Kunert, Günter (B. 1929)
Every Day.
Implant.
News from Behind the Seven Hills.
Realization.
Vain Attempt.

Kung Tzu-chen (1792–1841)
Lute Song, The.
Miscellanies of the Year Chi-hai.
My neighbor's child cries in the middle of
the night.
Tune: "Butterflies Lingering over Flowers."
Tune: "Decorous and Pretty."
Tune: "Green Jade Cup."

Kung, Wang Hung (fl. 20th cent.)
In the Mountain Village.

Kunio, Tsukamoto
Tanka: "After death."
Tanka: "All the way."
Tanka: "As night falls."
Tanka: "Because the folks."
Tanka: "Casket on display, A."
Tanka: "Even while."
Tanka: "From a flour mill."
Tanka: "Hands picking a rose."
Tanka: "Hidden."
Tanka: "In a grove."
Tanka: "I've swept away."
Tanka: "Late summer day."
Tanka: "On the cloudy water."
Tanka: "On the snow."
Tanka: "On the water."
Tanka: "Only when."
Tanka: "Stalwartly."
Tanka: "Standing still."
Tanka: "This May Day night."
Tanka: "Woman."

Kunitz, Stanley Jasspon (b. 1905)
Abduction, The.
After the Last Dynasty.
Approach to Thebes, The.

Benediction.
Catch, The.
Chariot.
Choice of Weapons, A.
End of Summer.
Father and Son.
For the Word Is Flesh.
Foreign Affairs.
Goose Pond's imaginable snows.
He runs among the wise men: He.
Illumination, The.
Image-Maker, The.
Intimations of Mortality.
Knot, The.
Last Picnic, The.
Night Letter.
Old Cracked Tune, An.
Passing Through.
Portrait, The.
Prophecy on Lethe.
Quinnapoxet.
Reflection by a Mailbox.
River Road.
Robin Redbreast.
Round, The, sels.
Science of the Night, The.
She wept, she railed, she spurned the meat.
Snakes of September, The.
Summing-up, The.
Testing-Tree, The.
Thief, The.
Three Floors.
Touch Me.
Vita Nuova.
Waltzer in the House, The.
War against the Trees, The.
Welcome the Wrath.
Wellfleet Whale, The.
When the light falls, it falls on her.

**Kunjufu, Johari Amini; Johari M.. See
Latimore, Jewel C.**

**Kunyayev [or Kuniaev], Stanislav Iurievich (b.
1932)**
It's hard to understand how one can leave.

Kunze, John C. (c.1745–1807)
Yoke Soft and Dear.

Kunze, Reiner (b. 1933)
Aerial, The.
Almost a Spring Poem.
Brief Curriculum.
Bringers of Beethoven, The.
Diary Page 69.
End of ARt, The.
First Letter From Tamara A.
Hymn To a Woman Under Interrogation.
Kind of Hope, A.
Low Volume.
Meditation.
Need for Censorship, The.
Refuge Even Beyond Refuge.
Reply.
Return from the Convention.

Kuo Mo-jo (1892–1978)
Impressions of Shanghai.

Kuo P'o (276–324)
Poem on the Wandering Immortal.

Kuppner, Frank (b. 1952)
Passing Through Doorways.

**Kupriyanov [or Kuprianov], Vyacheslav (b.
1939)**
Epidemic / of freedom, An.
There is life on other planets.
Twilight of Vanity.

Kuriyiraiyar
What Her Friend Said Criticizing Him to
Give Her Strength.

Kuroda, Saburoh (1919–80)
Afternoon 3.

Kurup, G. Shankara
Master Carpenter, The.

Kusano Shimpei (b. 1903)
Birthday Party.
4 Or 5 Tadpoles.
Skylarks and Fuji.

Kusatao (1901–83)
Cat, The.

"Kush"
Message for Langston, A.

Kushner, Aleksandr Semionovich (b. 1936)
And if you sleep, and if the sheets are clean.
Envelope looks so peculiar, The.
He who doesn't dance still dances.
No better fate is given than to die in Rome.
Remembering Love.
We don't get to choose our century.
What I really wanted.

Kushner, Bill (b. 1931)
Up.

Kushner, Dale M. (fl. 20th cent.)
Grandma in the Shower.

Kushniroff, Aaron (1891–1952)
Die My Shriek.

"Kusikov, Aleksandr Borisovich" (Aleksandr Borisovich Kusikyan) (1896–1977)
Mountain Forest.

Kusikyan, Aleksandr Borisovich. See "Kusikov, Aleksandr Borisovich"

Kuskin, Karla (b. 1932)
Catherine said "I think I'll bake."
I woke up this morning.
Knitted Things, sels.
Question, The.
Rose on My Cake, The.
When I Went Out.
Where Have You Been Dear?
Witches' Ride, The.

Kutavayir Kirattanar
Elegy: "Young will not wear it, The."
What Her Girl Friend Said before the Elopement.

Kuthaiyir (663?–723?)
At Her Grave.

Kutilov, Arkady (1925–88)
Crickety Creek.

Kuzma, Greg (b. 1944)
Dump, The.
In Love with the Bears.
Journal of the Storm.
Monster, The.
Pelican, The.
Poetry.
Sometimes.
Young Man Who Loved the Girl Who Took Care of Her Aged Father, The.

Kuzmin, Mikhail Alekseievich (1875–1936)
If they say: "you must suffer both torture and burning"—.
What rain! / Our sail is drenched.
When they say to me: "Alexandria"—.

Kuzmina-Karavayeva, Elizaveta (Mother Maria or Mat' Mariia) (1891–1945)
And copper and worn my farthing.
Even in repentance there is pleasure.
Everything has been checked. My inventory is ready.
I still kept thinking that I was rich.
Whit Monday, sels.
Who am I, Lord? Just an impostor.

Kuzminsky [or Kuzminskii], Konstantin Konstantinovich (b. 1940)
I'm cold. I'm destitute and absurd.

Kuznetsov, Yury [or Iurii] (b. 1941)
Atomic Fairy Tale.
Mushrooms.
Should I see a cloud high up in the sky.
To Father.

Kvitko [or Kwitko], Leyb [or Leib] (1893–1952)
Moods.
You Who Dog My Footsteps.

Kwakiutl Oral Tradition
Healing Prayer to the Salmon-Berry Vines.
Prayer to the Black Bear.
Prayer to the Sockeye Salmon.
Warsong of the Kwakiutl.

Kwiatek, Joellen
"Nearer God, Nearer Realite."

Kwon, Ilsong (b. 1933)
Apocalypse, The.
Rapture.

Kydios
Beware. There are fawns.

Kyei, Kojo Gyinaye (b. c.1930)
African in Louisiana.
Talking Drums, The.

Kyger, Joanne (b. 1934)
And with March a Decade in Bolinas.
August 18.
Caption for a Miniature.
Destruction.
Don't Hope to Gain by What Has Preceded.
Every day I burn a stick of incense.
I Have No Strength for Mine.
It's been a long time.
Maze, The.
My Father Died This Spring.
News bulletin from Keith Lampe.
Of All Things for You to Go Away Mad.
Pan as the Son of Penelope.
Philip Whalen's Hat.
Pigs for Circe in May, The.
When I Was Well into Being Savored.

Kynaston, Sir Francis (1587–1642)
To Cynthia.
To Cynthia, on Concealment of Her Beauty.
To Cynthia on Her Being an Incendiary.
To Cynthia, on Her Embraces.

L

"L., E. J." See Garston, Edward John Langford

"L., L. E." See Landon, Letitia Elizabeth

La Coste, Marie (c.1840–c.1909)
Somebody's Darling.

La Follette, Melvin Walker (b. 1930)
Didactic Sonnet.

La Fontaine, Jean de (1621–95)
Aesop's Fable of the Frogs.
Cat Changed to a Woman, The.
Cock and the Fox, The.
Crow and the Fox, The.
Donkey and the Lapdog, The.
Eagle and the Beetle, The.
Fox and the Crow, The.
Hag and the Slavies, The.
Love and Folly.
Man and His Image, The.
Rat and the Elephant, The.
Saddled Ass, The.
Thyrsis And Amaranta.
Wolf and the Dog, The.
Wolf and the Stork, The.

La Grone, Oliver (b. 1906)
Lines to the Black Oak.
Remnant Ghosts at Dawn.
Suncoming.

La Loca
Why I Choose Black Men for My Lovers.

Labé, Louise (1524–66)
Povre Ame Amoureuse.
Sonnet 1: "Not Ulysses, no, nor any other man."
Sonnet 2: "O handsome chestnut eyes, evasive gaze."
Sonnet 3: "O interminable desires, O futile hope."
Sonnet 4: "From that first flash when awful Love took flame."
Sonnet 5: "White Venus limpid wandering in the sky."
Sonnet 6: "Coming of that limpid star is twice, The."
Sonnet 7: "We see each living thing finally die."
Sonnet 8: "I live, I die, I burn myself and drown."
Sonnet 10: "When I perceive your blond and graceful head."
Sonnet 11: "O eyes clear with beauty, O tender gaze."
Sonnet 12: "Lute, companion of my calamity."
Sonnet 13: "If I could linger on his lovely chest."
Sonnet XIV.
Sonnet 15: "To honor the return of sparkling sun."
Sonnet XVI: "After an age when thunderbolts and hail."
Sonnet 17: "I flee the city, temples, and each place."
Sonnet 18: "Kiss me again, re-kiss and kiss me whole."
Sonnet XIX: "After having slain very many beasts."
Sonnet XX.
Sonnet 21: "What grandeur makes a man seem venerable?"
Sonnet 22: "O blazing Sun, how happy you are there."
Elegy 23: "How does it help me if, with flawless art."
Sonnet 23: "What good is it to me if long ago."
Sonnet 24: "Don't blame me, ladies, if I've loved. No sneers."
Sonnet 9: "As soon as I lie down in my soft bed."
Sonnet: "As long as I continue weeping."
Sonnet: "Seer foretold that I would love one day, A."
Sonnet: "When I catch sight of your fair head."

Labriola, Gina
Orgy (That Is, Vegetable Market, at Sarno).

Labrunie, Gérard. See Nerval, Gérard de

Lacaussade, Auguste (1817–97)
Salaziennes, Les, sels.

Lacey, Florence (d. 1945)
Promise.

Lachmann, Hedwig (1870–1918)
Home-Sickness.
Walk, A.

Lacina, Melody
Red Cross Lessons at City Park Pool.

Lady of the Arbour, The (fl. c.1450)
Flower and the Leaf, The, sels.

Lady of the Assembly, The (fl. late 15th cent.)
Assembly of Ladies, The, sels.

Laederach, Monique (b. 1938)
Penelope, sels.

Laforgue, Jules (1860–87)
For the Book of Love.
Solo by Moonlight.

Lagier, Jennifer (fl. 20th cent.)
Second Class Citizen.

Lagrone, Oliver (fl. 20th cent.)
I Heard the Byrd.

"Laider." See Mac Coisdealbhaigh, Tomas

Laila Akhyaliyya (fl. late 7th cent.)
Camel.
Laila Boasting.
Lamenting Tauba.

Laing, Alexander Kinnan (b. 1903)
Original Sin.

Laing, Allan M. (b. 1887)
Grace for Ice-Cream, A.
Limerick: "It's a nightmare that horrifies hakes."
Limerick: "Said a medical student, unmanned."
Limerick: "There was an old cynic who said."
Limerick: "When an obstinate fellow of Fife."
New Jerusalem, The.
There was a young lady of Ealing.
This Railway Station.

Laing, Dilys Bennett (1906–60)
Eros Out of the Sea.
Lines on the Sea.

Laing, Kojo
Africa Sky.
Godhorse.
Huge car with the sad voice, The.
I am the freshly dead husband.
Many Worlds Are Walked Once.
One Hundred Lines for the Coast.
Race on Gathering Bites.
Same Corpse, The.
Senior Lady Sells Garden Eggs.
Tatale Swine.

Laing, Ronald David (b. 1927)
If she did not love you, she would not be.
Laird, Christopher (b. 1946)
Sea at Evening, The.
Lake, Dr. Tony
Facing Change.
Lake, Paul
Blue Jay.
Crime and Punishment.
In Rough Weather.
Introduction to Poetry.
Lakides, Lucy
Armed Forces.
Lakshminkara (fl. 8th cent.)
Lay your head on a block of butter and chop.
Lal Ded (fl. 16th cent.)
I drag a boat over the ocean.
Laleau, Léon (b. 1892)
Black Music, sels.
Lalic, Ivan V. (b. 1931)
Addressing the Comet.
Broadcast.
First Actor to Hamlet.
Inscribed in the Silver of the Sea.
Insomnia.
King and the Singer, The.
Love in July.
Raven's Monologue.
Roll Call of Mirrors.
Spring Liturgy for Branko Miljkovic, sels.
Voices of the dead. They are not dead. Who hears.
Lalleswari (fl. late 14th cent.)
Good repute is water carried in a sieve.
I set forth hopeful—cotton-blossom Lal.
With my breath I cut my way through the six forests.
Laluah, Aquah. See Hayford, Gladys May Casely
Lâm thị Mỹ Dạ (b. 1949)
Like Leaves.
Lamantia, Philip (b. 1927)
Hermetic Bird.
Man Is in Pain.
Morning Light Song.
Romantic Movement, The.
She Speaks the Morning's Filigree.
Still Poem 9.
Terror Conduction.
Time Traveler's Potlatch.
Voice of Earth Mediums.
Winter Day, A.
Lamartine, Alphonse Marie Louis de (1790–1869)
Cedars of Lebanon, The.
Lamb, Charles (1775–1834)
As When a Child.
David in the Cave of Adullam.
Family Name, The.
Farewell to Tobacco, A.
Free Thoughts on Several Eminent Composers.
Going or Gone.
Hester.
Hypochondriacus.
Letter from Charles Lamb to Thomas Manning, 22 August 1801, sels.
Methinks How Dainty Sweet It Were.
Nonsense Verses.
Old Familiar Faces, The.
On an Infant Dying as Soon as Born.
Salome.
"Timid grace sits trembling in her eye, A."
To John Lamb, Esq.: Of the South-Sea House.
Triumph of the Whale, The, sels.
Verses for an Album.
Lamb, Charles (1775–1834) and Mary Lamb (1764–1847)
Anger in its time and place.
Boy and the Snake, The.
Choosing a Name.
Cleanliness.
Envy.
First Tooth, The.

Going into Breeches.
Lamb, Elizabeth Searle
Broken kite, sprawled.
Far back under a ledge.
Far shore, The.
Leaving all the morning glories closed.
Lizard inching, A.
Old album, The.
Pausing.
Shimmering beneath the glaze.
Still. . . some echo.
Lamb, Joe
Cherries.
Lamb, Lady Caroline (1785–1828)
Fugitive Pieces and Reminiscences of Lord Byron with Some Original Poetry, Letters and Recollections of Lady Caroline Lamb, ed. I. Nathan, sels.
New Canto, A.
Would I had seen thee dead and cold.
Lamb, Mary (1764–1847)
Helen.
Keepsake for 1829 (1828), The, sels.
Parental Recollections.
Two Boys, The.
See also **Lamb, Charles** and **Mary Lamb.**
"Lambert, Louis." See Gilmore, Patrick Sarsfield
Lamdan, Yitzhak (1899–1954)
Feigned Courage.
For the Sun Declined, sels.
In the Khamsin, sels.
Israel.
Lamkin, Kurtis
Golden Season.
Lampadius, Sabina (fl. ca. 377)
As a symbol.
Lampman, Archibald (1861–99)
City of the End of Things, The.
Heat.
In November.
Thunderstorm, A.
To a Millionaire.
Winter Evening.
Lamport, Felicia (b. 1916)
Eggomania.
Mother, Mother, Are You All There?
Poll Star.
Lancaster, Osbert (b. 1908)
Afternoons with Baedeker, sels.
Lancaster, Sarah
Come on, my fellow pilgrims, come.
Landon, Letitia [or Laetitia] Elizabeth ("L. E. L.") (1802–38)
Child Screening a Dove from a Hawk, A.
Dying Child, The.
Enchanted Island, The.
Farewell!
Fragments, sels.
Gifts Misused.
Girl at Her Devotions, A.
Golden Violet, The, sels.
History of the Lyre, A.
Improvisatrice and Other Poems, The, sels.
Lady, thy face is very beautiful.
Life and Literary Remains of L.E.L., sels.
Lines of Life.
Lines Written Under a Picture of a Girl Burning a Love-Letter.
Marriage Vow, The.
Mask of Gaiety, The.
New Monthly Magazine, 44 286–8, sels.
Poor, The.
Power of Words, The.
Revenge.
Small Miseries.
Song.
Stern Truth.
Zenana, and Minor Poems of L.E.L, The, sels.
Landor, W. D.
Winter.
Landor, Walter Savage (1775–1864)
Above all gifts we most should prize.
Age.

Alas! 'tis very sad to hear.
Alciphron and Leucippe.
Art thou afraid the adorer's prayer.
Autumnal Song.
Before a Saint's Picture.
Bourbons.
Called Proud.
Case at Sessions, A.
Citation and Examination of William Shakespeare, The, sels.
Cowley's Style.
Critic, A.
Darling Shell, where hast thou been.
Death of the Day.
Death Stands above Me[, whispering low].
Defiance.
Distribution of Honours for Literature.
Does it become a girl so wise.
Dragon-Fly, The.
Duke of York's Statue, The.
Dull Is My Verse.
Epigrams must be curt, nor seem.
Exhausted now her sighs, and dry her tears.
Faesulan Idyll.
For an Epitaph at Fiesole.
Foreign Ruler, A.
Gardener, The.
Gebir, sels.
Georges, The.
"God scatters beauty as he scatters flowers."
Graceful Acacia.
Had We Two Met.
Have I, this moment, led thee from the beach.
Heart's Abysses, The.
Hellenics, The, sels.
Here lies Landor.
How often, when life's summer day.
How to Read Me.
Ianthe, sels.
Idle Words.
Imaginary Conversations, sels.
Interlude.
Ireland never was contented.
Is it no dream that I am he.
Izaac Walton, Cotton, and William Oldways.
Keats.
La Promessa Sposa.
Last Fruit Off an Old Tree, The, sels.
Lately Our Poets [loitered in green lanes].
Listen, mad girl! for giving ear.
Love and Age.
Love ran with me, then walk'd, then sate.
Loves who many years held all my mind, The.
Memory.
Mimnermus Incert.
Mother, I Cannot Mind My Wheel.
Neither in idleness consume thy days.
No charm can stay, no medicine can assuage.
No, thou hast never griev'd but I griev'd too.
O fond, but fickle and untrue.
O friends! who have accompanied thus far.
O Friendship! Friendship! the shell of Aphrodite.
On Catullus.
On Himself.
On Man.
On Seeing a Hair of Lucretia Borgia.
On the Heights.
On the smooth brow and clustering hair.
Our youth was happy: why repine.
Perfidious, The.
Pericles and Aspasia, sels.
Pigmies and Cranes.
Place where soon I think to lie, The.
Plays.
Poem: "I cannot tell, not I, why she."
Poet! I like not mealy fruit; give me.
Progress of Evening.
Pyrrha! your smiles are gleams of sun.
Quarrelsome Bishop, A.
Reflection from Sea and Sky.
Reproof of Thanks.
Retired this hour from wondering crowds.
Rose Aylmer.
Scentless laurel a broad leaf displays, The.

Scribblers, The.
Sensible Girl's Reply to Moore's, A.
Shakespeare, *sels.*
Silent, you say, I'm grown of late.
Stern Brow, The.
Ten thousand flakes about my window blow.
There are two miseries in human life.
Three Roses, The.
To One Unequally Matched.
To One Who Quotes and Detracts.
To Our House-Dog Captain.
To Poets.
To Robert Browning.
To the Sister of Charles Lamb.
To Wordsworth.
Torch of Love dispels the gloom, The.
Twenty Years Hence.
Various the roads of life; in one.
What News.
Why do the Graces now desert the Muse?
William Gifford.
Years, many parti-coloured years.
You see the worst of love, but not the best.
You smiled, you spoke, and I believed.

Lane, Patrick (b. 1939)
At the Edge of the Jungle.
If.
Measure, The.
Passing into Storm.
Stigmata.

Lane, Pinkie Gordon (b. 1937)
Girl at the Window.
Lake Murry.
Midnight Song.
Migration.
Nocturne: "Listening for the sound."
On Being Head of the English Department.
Rain Ditch.
Sexual Privacy of Women on Welfare.
Spring.
When You Read This Poem.
Who Is My Brother?
Wind Thoughts.

Lang, Andrew (1844–1912)
Brahma.
Epistle to Mr. Alexander Pope, *sels.*
Jubilee before Revolution.
Last Chance, The.
Limerick: "There was a young lady of Limerick."
Odyssey, The.
On the Death of Lord Tennyson.
Tired of Towns.
To Lord Byron, *sels.*
Twilight on Tweed.

Lang, Doug
Depression, The.

Lang, Elizabeth (b. 1957)
Honey Bear.

Lang, John Dunmore (1799–1878)
Colonial Nomenclature.

Lang, V. R. (1924–56)
Suicide, The.

Lange, Art (b. 1952)
Fine Line, A.
Mbizo.
Perugia.
Sonnet for the Season.
White Line, A.

Langfield, June Mercer
Full fathom five thy father lies.

Langford, G. W.
Speak gently; it is better far.

Langfur, Charlene
Report from Another Country.

Langhorne, John (1735–79)
Country Justice, The, *sels.*
Studley Park.

Langland, Joseph (b. 1917)
Crane.
Fall of Icarus: Brueghel.
Hunters in the Snow: Brueghel.
Sacrifice of a Red Squirrel.
Sea-Change: For Harold, A.
War.

Langland, William (1330–1400)
Vision of Piers Plowman, The, *sels.*
Vision of Piers Plowman, Prologue, The, *sels.*

Langley, Eve (b. 1908)
Native Born.
This year, before it ends, holds out time as a weight to us.

Langton, Stephen (d. 1228)
Hymn to the Holy Spirit.
O Holy Ghost.

Langworthy, Yolande
Drifting Sands and a Caravan.

Lanier [*or* Lanyer], Emilia [*or* Aemelia] (1569–1645)
Description of Cooke-ham, The.
Salve Deus Rex Judaeorum, *sels.*
To the Lady Anne, Countess of Dorset, *sels.*
To the Lady Arabella.

Lanier, H. Glenn
O Christ of Bethlehem.

Lanier, Sidney (1842–81)
Ballad of Trees and the Master, A.
Clover.
Dying Words of Stonewall Jackson, The.
Evening Song.
From the Flats.
Hymns of the Marshes, *sels.*
Laus Mariae.
Marsh Song—at Sunset.
Marshes of Glynn, The.
Mocking Bird, The.
My Springs.
Nirvâna.
Raven Days, The.
Resurrection.
Revenge of Hamish, The.
Song for "The Jacquerie."
Song of the Chattahoochee.
Stirrup-Cup, The.
Street Cries, *sels.*
Struggle.
Symphony, The.
Thar's More in the Man than Thar Is in the Land.
To Bayard Taylor.
To Beethoven.
Waving of the Corn, The.
Whate'er Has Been.

Lanigan, George Thomas (1845–86)
Threnody: "What, what, what / What's the news from Swat?"

Lanjewar, Jyoti (b. 1950)
I Never Saw You.

Lankesh, P. (b. 1935)
Mother.

Lansdown, Andrew (b. 1954)
Behind the Veil.
Golgotha.
Mercy.
Two Men.

Lansing, Gerrit
Gold in the Mud, The.

Lanusse, Armand (1812–67)
Epigram: "'Do you not wish to renounce the Devil?'"

Lanyer, Aemilia Bassano (1569–1645)
Description of Cooke-ham, The.
Description of Cookham, The.
Salve Deus Rex Judæorum, *sels.*

Lao Tzu (c.604–531 B.C.)
All things pass.
Tao Te Ching, *sels.*

Lapidus, Jacqueline (b. 1941)
Exmatriate.

Larbaud, Valery (1881–1957)
Alma Perdida.
Images.

Larcom, Lucy (1824–93)
Brown Thrush, The.
Dumpy Ducky.
In the Tree-Top.
Spring Whistles.
Volunteer's Thanksgiving, The.

Lardner, Ring (1885–1933)
Abner Silver's "Pu-leeze! Mr. Hemingway!"

Hail to Thee, Blithe Owl.
Hardly a Man Is Now Alive.
Parodies of Cole Porter's "Night and Day."
Quiescent, a Person Sits Heart and Soul.

Larkin, Joan (b. 1939)
Clifton.
Genealogy.
In Western Massachusetts, Sixteen Months Sober.
Rape.
Rhyme of My Inheritance.

Larkin, Mary Ann (b. 1945)
Dance Half Done, The.
House of Broughton Street, The.
Immigrant Daughter's Song.
Riding on a Streetcar with My Father.

Larkin, Philip (1922–85)
Age.
Ambulances.
Annus Mirabilis.
Arrivals, Departures.
Arundel Tomb, An.
As Bad as a Mile.
At Grass.
Aubade: "I work all day, and get half-drunk at night."
Best Society.
Broadcast.
Card-Players, The.
Church Going.
Coming.
Cut grass lies frail.
Days.
Deceptions.
Dedicated, The.
Dublinesque.
Explosion, The.
Faith Healing.
Fiction and the Reading Public.
First Sight.
For Sidney Bechet.
Forget What Did.
Going.
Going, Going.
Here.
High Windows.
Homage to a Government.
Home is so sad. It stays as it was left.
I Remember, I Remember.
If grief could burn out.
If, My Darling.
Is it for now or for always.
Lines on a Young Lady's Photograph Album.
Livings, *sels.*
Maiden Name.
Mr Bleaney.
Myxomatosis.
Naturally the Foundation Will Bear Your Expenses.
Next, Please.
Night-Music.
MCMXIV.
No Road.
North Ship, The.
Nothing to Be Said.
On Wakening.
Places, Loved Ones.
Poetry of Departures, *sels.*
Posterity.
Reasons for Attendance.
Sad Steps.
Self's the Man.
So through that unripe day you bore your head.
Spring.
Study of Reading Habits, A.
Sunny Prestatyn.
Take One Home for the Kiddies.
Talking in bed ought to be easiest.
This Be The Verse.
To the Sea.
Toads.
Toads Revisited.
Trees are coming into leaf, The.
Vers de Société.

Waiting For Breakfast, While She Brushed Her Hair.
Wants.
Water.
Wedding-Wind.
Whatever Happened?
Whitsun Weddings, The.
Wild Oats.
Within the dream you said.

Larminie, William (1885–1930)
Nameless Doon [or Dun], The.

Lart, K. C.
Walk in Spring, A.

Lasker-Schüler, Else (1876–1945)
Abraham and Isaac.
Always in the parting year.
Chronica.
End of the World.
Georg Trakl.
George Grosz.
Hagar and Ishmael.
Homesick.
I Have a Blue Piano.
I Know That I Must Die Soon.
Jacob and Esau.
Jacob ("Jacob: a bull among his herd.")
Love-Song.
Love Song: "Come to me in the night—we shall sleep closely together [or Let us sleep entwined]."
Love's Flight.
My Love-Song.
My People.
Reconciliation.
Rock Crumbles, The.
To Senna Hoy.
To The Barbarian.
Zebaoth.

Lassell, Michael (b. 1947)
How to Watch Your Brother Die.
Times Square Poems, sels.

Lathbury, Mary Artemisia ("Aunt Mary") (1841–1913)
Break Thou the Bread of Life.
Day Is Dying in the West.
Song of Hope.

Lathrop, Lena
Woman's Question, A.

Lathrop, Walter (d. 1903)
Here Is a Toast That I Want to Drink.

Latifah, Queen
Evil That Men Do, The.

Latimer, Bette Darcie (b. 1927)
For William Edward Burghardt Du Bois on His Eightieth Birthday.

Latimore, Jewel C. (Johari Amini; Johari M. Kunjufu) (b. 1935)
Ceremony.
Positives.
Promise, The.
Return.
Saint Malcolm.
Signals.
To a Poet I Knew.
Utopia.

Latta, Ruth
Hand reaches up, A.

Latter, Mary (1722?–1777)
Soliloquies on Temporal Indigence, sels.

Lattimore, Richmond (1906–84)
Anniversary.
Bathtubs.
December Fragments.
Game Resumed.
Krankenhaus of Leutkirch, The.
Max Schmitt in a Single Scull.
North Philadelphia, Trenton, and New York.
Note on the L and N.
Remorse.
Report from a Planet.
Rise and Shine.
RMS Lusitania.
Shadowgraphs, The.
Witness to Death.

Lau, Alan Chong
My Ship Does Not Need a Helmsman.

Upside Down Basket, The.

Lau, Barbara
Remembering Mexico, 1969.

Lau, Carolyn
On the Fifth Anniversary of My Father's Death.

Laufer, Calvin W. (1874–1938)
We Thank Thee, Lord.

Laughlin, Elmer Osborn (b. 1867)
Unknown, The.

Laughlin, James (b. 1914)
Bird of Endless Time, The.
Inn at Kirchstetten, The.
Kind-, The.
Mountain Afterglow, The.
Rhyme.
Step on His Head.
Swarming Bees, The.
Then and Now.

Laughton, Freda (b. 1907)
Woman with Child, The.

Lauterbach, Anne (b. 1942)
Boy Sleeping.
Clamor.
For Example (1): Stepping Out.
For Example (5): Song of the Already Sung.
Here and There.
Mimetic.
Platonic Subject.
Psyche's Dream.
Subject to Change.

Laux, Dorianne
Children's Train, The.
China.
Ghosts.

Lavant, Christine (b. 1915)
Buy Us a Little Grain.
Do Not Ask.

Lavater, Louis (1867–1953)
Barrier, The.

Lavrin, Aleksandr (b. 1952)
As I remember, barracks still stand.

Lavrov, Leonid (1906–43)
Notes on the Impossible, sels.

Law, T. S. (b. 1910)
Wemen's Wather.

Lawes, Henry (1596–1662)
Table of Contents.

Lawless, Emily (1845–1913)
After Aughrim.

Lawrence, A. H.
To be a nurse is.

Lawrence, Anthony (b. 1957)
Cro-Kill.
Fencing.
Robert Penn Warren's book.

Lawrence, David Herbert (1885–1930)
All Soul''s Day.
American Eagle, The.
Andraitx—Pomegranate Flowers.
Argonauts, The.
Aware.
Baby Tortoise.
Bare Almond-Trees.
Bare Fig-trees.
Basta!
Bat.
Bavarian Gentians.
Body of God, The.
Bride, The.
Brooding Grief.
Butterfly, the wind blows sea-ward[, strong beyond the garden wall!].
Cherry Robbers.
Collier's Wife, The.
Commandments.
Cypresses.
Death Is Not Evil, Evil Is Mechanical.
Demiurge.
Desire.
Desire Is Dead.
Doe at Evening, A.
Don Juan.
Don'ts.
Drained Cup, The.

Eagle in New Mexico, sels.
Elemental.
Elephant Is Slow to Mate, The.
Eloi, Eloi, Lama Sabachthani?
End of Another Home Holiday.
Energetic Women.
English are so nice, The.
Enkindled Spring, The.
Evening Land, The.
Fatality.
Fate and the Younger Generation.
Fidelity and love are two different things, like a flower and a gem.
Figs.
Flowers and Men ("Flowers achieve their own floweriness and its's a miracle.")
Food of the north tastes too much of the fat of the pig, The.
Fronleichnam.
Gazelle calf, O my children, The.
Giorno dei Morti.
Gloire de Dijon.
Glory is of the sun, too, and the sun of suns.
Go deeper than love, for the soul has greater depths.
Gods! The Gods!, The.
Grasshopper Is a Burden.
Green.
"Gross, Coarse, Hideous" (Police Description of My Pictures).
Hands of God, The.
Healing.
Hibiscus and Salvia Flowers.
Hills, The.
History.
How beastly the bourgeois is.
Humming-Bird.
Hymn to Priapus.
I Am in a Novel.
I Am like a Rose.
In Trouble and Shame.
Innocent England.
Intimates.
It's no good, the women are in eruption.
Kangaroo.
Kisses in the Train.
Last Lesson of the Afternoon.
Last Words to Miriam.
Let There Be Light!
Lies About Love.
Lightning.
Little Fish.
Lizard ran out on a rock and looked up, listening, A.
Lord Tennyson and Lord Melchett.
Lord's Prayer.
Love On the Farm.
Love Thy Neighbour.
Lui et Elle.
Man and Bat.
Man of Tyre went down to the sea, The.
Manifesto.
Maximus.
Medlars and Sorb-Apples.
Men in New Mexico.
Mess of Love, The.
Middle of the World.
Moonrise.
Morning Work.
Mosquito Knows, The.
Mountain Lion.
My name is Jesus, I am Mary's son.
My way is not thy way, and thine is not mine.
Mystic.
New Heaven and Earth.
New Year's Eve.
Nostalgia.
O! start a revolution, somebody!
On the Balcony.
Paradise Re-entered.
Passing Visit to Helen.
Pax.
Peacock.
Piano, The.
Proper Pride.
Quetzalcoatl Looks Down on Mexico.

Quite Forsaken.
Race and Battle.
Rainbow, The.
Red Geranium and Godly Mignonette.
Release.
Retort to Jesus.
River Roses.
Root of Our Evil, The.
Sea-weed sways and sways and swirls.
Search for Love.
Self-Pity.
Self-Protection.
Service of All the Dead.
Shadows.
Ship of Death, The.
Sicilian Cyclamens.
Snake came to my water-trough, A, sels.
Song of a Man Who Has Come Through.
Song of a Man Who Is Loved.
Sorrow.
Spray.
Spring Morning.
St. Matthew, sels.
Stand up, but not for Jesus!
Storm in the Black Forest.
Suburbs on a Hazy Day.
Suspense.
Swan.
Tabernacle.
Things made by iron and handled by steel
 are born.
To Women, as Far as I'm Concerned.
Tommies in the Train.
Tortoise Gallantry.
Tortoise-Shell.
Tortoise Shout.
Trees in the Garden.
True Love at Last.
Twilight.
Two Performing Elephants.
Volcanic Venus.
We Are Transmitters.
Wedding Morn.
Whales Weep Not!
What Would You Fight For?
When I read Shakespeare I am struck with
 wonder.
When I went to the circus that had pitched
 on the waste lot.
When the ripe fruit falls.
When wilt thou teach the people.
Whether or Not.
White Blossom, A.
White Horse, The.
Wild Common, The.
Willy Wet-Leg.
Winter's Tale, A.
Women in Love, sels.
Work.
Worm Either Way.
You.
Young Wife, A.
Youth Mowing, A.

Lawson, David (b. 1940)
 No Great Matter.
Lawson, Henry (1867–1922)
 English Queen, The.
 Faces in the Street.
 Horseman on the Skyline, The.
 Men Who Come Behind, The.
 Ned's Delicate Way.
 Ripperty! Kye! Ahoo!
 Teams, The.
 Up the Country.
 When Your Pants Begin to Go.
 Will Yer Write It Down for Me?
Lawson, Mrs. David. See Ridge, Lola
Lax, Robert (b. 1915)
 Morning Stars, The.
Layamon (fl. c.1200)
 Brut, The, sels.
Layman P'ang (740–808)
 My daily affairs are quite ordinary.
 When the mind is at peace.
Layne, Catherine Braan
 Whispering Wind.

Layne, Mcavoy
 Beautiful Ladies.
 Collect Call.
 Gettin' Straight.
 Guns.
 Intersection in the Sky.
 Mob, The.
 On Hats and Things.
 On the Yellow Footprints.
Layton, Irving (b. 1912)
 Berry Picking.
 Birth of Tragedy, The.
 Bull Calf, The.
 Butterfly on Rock.
 Cain.
 Cold Green Element, The.
 Day Aviva Came to Paris, The.
 Fertile Muck, The.
 For Mao Tse-tung; a Meditation on Flies and
  Kings.
 For Musia's Grandchildren.
 From Colony to Nation.
 Gothic Landscape.
 Grand Finale.
 Improved Binoculars, The.
 Keine Lazarovitch, 1870-1959.
 Party at Hydra.
 Tall Man Executes a Jig, A.
Layzer, Robert (b. 1931)
 Lawn Roller, The.
Lazard, Naomi
 In Answer to Your Query.
 Ordinance on Arrival.
 Walking with Lulu in the Wood.
Lazarus, Emma (1849–87)
 Age and Death.
 Banner of the Jew, The.
 Bar Kochba.
 By the Waters of Babylon, sels.
 City Visions.
 Cranes of Ibycus, The.
 Echoes.
 Elixir, The.
 1492.
 Gifts.
 In Exile.
 Kindle the Taper.
 Lines on Carmen Sylva.
 Long Island Sound.
 New Colossus, The.
 New Ezekiel, The.
 Phantasies, sels.
 South, The.
 Venus of the Louvre.
 Youth.
 Youth and Death.
Le Bel, Natasha (b. 1977)
 Boxing the Female.
 Foot Fire Burn Dance.
Lê Đù'c Tho (Phan Đình Khải) (b. 1911)
 Fighter's Thoughts of Spring, A.
Le Fanu, Joseph Sheridan (1814–73)
 Beatrice, sels.
Le Gallienne, Richard (1866–1947)
 Ballad of London, A.
 Beauty Accurst.
 Décadent to His Soul, The.
 I meant to do my work today.
 Library in a Garden, A.
 Melton Mowbray Pork Pie, A.
 Song: "She's somewhere in the sunlight
  strong."
 Sunset in the City.
 To the Reader.
Le Guin, Ursula K. (b. 1929)
 Child on the Shore, The.
Lễ, Nguyễn Thú'. See Thể Lữ'
Le Pan, Douglas (b. 1914)
 Country without a Mythology, A.
 Coureurs de Bois.
 Incident, An.
 Net and the Sword, The.
 Nimbus.
Le Sueur, Meridel (b. 1900)
 Budded with Child.

Lê Thánh–tông, King (1442–97)
 Conduct of Kings, The.
 King's Portrait, A.
 Merchants.
Lea, John
 Silver House, The.
Lea, Sydney
 At the Flyfisher's Shack.
 Clouded Evening, Late September.
 Feud, The.
 Insomnia: The Distances.
 Museum.
 Prayer for the Little City.
 Telescope.
 Wrong Way Will Haunt You, The.
"Leadbelly" (Huddie Ledbetter)
 Midnight Special, The.
 Take this hammer, (huh!) carry it to the
  captain, (huh!).
Leaf, Ebba M.
 Dear Mother.
 Her Son.
Leapor, Mary (1722–46)
 Advice to Sophronia.
 Crumble Hall, sels.
 Epistle of Deborah Dough, The.
 Epistle to a Lady, An.
 Epistle to Artemisia, sels.
 Essay on Friendship, sels.
 Essay on Woman, An.
 Headache, The.
 Man the Monarch.
 Mira to Octavia.
 Mira's Picture, a Pastoral, sels.
 Mira's Will.
 On Winter.
 Proserpine's Ragout.
 Sacrifice: An Epistle to Celia, The.
 Soto, a Character.
 Strephon to Celia.
 Upon Her Play Being Returned to Her,
  Stained with Claret.
 Visit, The.
Lear, Edward (1812–88)
 A[h]kond of Swat, The.
 Alphabet, An.
 Calico Pie.
 Cold Are the Crabs.
 Courtship of the Yonghy-Bonghy-Bo, The.
 Daddy Long-legs and the Fly, The.
 Dong with a Luminous Nose, The.
 Duck and the Kangaroo, The.
 Incidents in the Life of My Uncle Arly.
 Jumblies, The.
 Le Hibou et la Poussiquette.
 Limerick.
 Limerick: "There was a Young Girl of
  Majorca."
 Limerick: "There was a Young Lady of
  Norway, / Who casually sat in a doorway."
 Limerick: "There was a young lady of Ryde /
  Whose shoe-strings were seldom untied."
 Limerick: "There was a young lady of
  Sweden."
 Limerick: "There was a Young Lady whose
  chin."
 Limerick: "There was a young lady whose
  eyes."
 Limerick: "There was a Young Person of
  Kew."
 Limerick: "There was a young person of
  Smyrna."
 Limerick: "There was an Old Man in a
  boat."
 Limerick: "There was an Old Man in a tree."
 Limerick: "There was an old man of Cape
  Horn."
 Limerick: "There was an old man of
  Dunblane."
 Limerick: "There was an old man of
  Ibreem."
 Limerick: "There was an old man of
  Kamschatka."
 Limerick: "There was an old man of the
  coast."
 Limerick: "There was an old man of
  Thermopylae."

Limerick: "There was an old man of
    Whitehaven."
Limerick: "There was an old man on some
    rocks."
Limerick: "There was an old man on the
    Border."
Limerick: "There was an Old Man on whose
    nose."
Limerick: "There was an old man who said:
    'How.'"
Limerick: "There was an Old Man who said,
    'Hush!'"
Limerick: "There was an Old Man who said:
    'Well!'"
Limerick: "There was an old man who
    screamed out."
Limerick: "There was an Old Man who
    supposed."
Limerick: "There was an old person of
    Basing."
Limerick: "There was an old person of
    Bow."
Limerick: "There was an Old Person of
    Brigg."
Limerick: "There was an Old Person of
    Cromer."
Limerick: "There was an old person of
    Grange."
Limerick: "There was an old person of
    Gretna."
Limerick: "There was an Old Person of
    Hurst."
Limerick: "There was an old person of
    Philae."
Limericks, I (ii).
Limericks, I (v).
Limericks, II (i).
Limericks, II (ii).
Limericks, II (iii).
Limericks, II (iv).
Limericks, II (v).
Mr. and Mrs. Spikky Sparrow.
New Vestments, The.
Nutcrackers and the Sugar-Tongs, The.
O dear! How disgusting is life!
Our mother was the pussy-cat, our father was
    the owl.
Pelican Chorus, The.
Pobble Who Has No Toes, The.
Quangle Wangle's Hat, The.
Scroobious Pip went out one day, The.
Self-Portrait of the Laureate of Nonsense.
Teapots and Quails.
(The Owl and the Pussy-Cat).
There is a young lady, whose nose.
There was a young lady whose bonnet.
There Was a Young Lady Whose Nose.
There was a Young Person of Ayr.
There was an old man in a Barge.
There Was an Old Man of Dumbree.
There was an old man of Peru / Who never
    knew what he should do.
There was an old man of Peru / Who
    watched his wife making a stew.
There was an old man of the East.
There was an old man of the West.
There was an old man of West Dumpet.
There was an Old Man who forgot.
There was an Old Man with a beard.
There was an old party of lyme.
There was an old person of Blythe.
There was an old person of Burton.
There was an old person of Cassel.
There was an old person of Dutton.
There was an old person of Prague.
There was an old person of Rhodes.
There was an old person of Skye.
To Ann Lear.
To Lady Wyatt.
Twenty-Six Nonsense Rhymes.

Learmont, John (*fl.* c.1791)
    Address to the Plebeians, An, *sels.*

"Learsi, Rufus" (Israel Goldberg) (1887–1938)
    Martyrdom.

Leax, John
    Fire Burns Low, The.
    Her Seventeenth Winter.

Incarnation Poem.
That day the / words.

Lebensohn, Micah Joseph (1828–52)
    Wine.

Lebovitz, Richard
    HANDSAWWWWWWWWWWWWWWWWWW.

**Leconte de Lisle, Charles Marie René (1818–
94)**
    Hialmar Speaks to the Raven.
    Palanquin, The.
    Venus de Milo.

Lecount, David E.
    Bridge toll-booth—, The.

Ledbetter, Huddie. *See* "Leadbelly"

Ledgister, Fragano (b. 1956)
    Cities Have Fallen, The.
    On Parade.

Ledwidge, Francis (1891–1917)
    Ardan Mór.
    Fear, A.
    God's Remembrance.
    June.
    Lament for the Poets: 1916.
    Lament for Thomas MacDonagh.
    My Mother.
    Soliloquy.
    Twilight in Middle March, A.

Lee, Agnes (1868–1939)
    Ilex Tree, The.
    Motherhood.

Lee, Alfred M. [*or* "Al"] (b. 1932)
    Among Sharks.
    Far Side of Introspection, The.
    Karl Marx.
    Lie, The.
    Poem for the Year Twenty Twenty.
    Weathering the Depths.

"Lee, Andy" (W. W. Delaney)
    Crazy Song to the Air of "Dixie."

Lee, Bert. *See* Weston, R. P. *and* Bert Lee

Lee, Brian (b. 1935)
    Bad Dog.
    In the Green Shade.
    Rain.

Lee, Dennis (b. 1939)
    Billy Batter.
    Civil Elegies, *sels.*
    Coat, The.
    Coming of Teddy Bears, The.
    Dickery Dean.
    Gods, The.
    I Eat Kids Yum Yum!
    Last Cry of the Damp Fly, The.
    Skyscraper, skyscraper.
    There was a man who never was.
    You Too Lie down.

Lee, Don. L.. *See* Madhubuti, Haki R.

Lee, J. H.
    Limerick: "Man from Maputo and so on, A."

Lee, Jang-hi (1902–28)
    Spring is a Cat, The.

Lee, John Robert (b. 1948)
    Kite.
    Lusca.
    Mango.
    Return.
    Third World Snapshots.
    Vocation.

Lee, Joseph (1862–1937?)
    German Prisoners.

Lee, Joyce (b. 1913)
    Firebell for Peace.
    My Father's Country.

Lee, Laurie (b. 1914)
    Boy in Ice.
    Christmas Landscape.
    Edge of Day, The.
    Field of Autumn.
    Home From Abroad.
    Invasion Summer.
    Milkmaid.
    Moment of War, A.
    My Many-Coated Man.
    Sunken Evening [in Trafalgar Square].

Lee, Li-Young (b. 1957)
    Between Seasons.
    City in Which I Love You, The.
    Cleaving, The.
    Early in the Morning.
    Eating Alone.
    Final Thing, A.
    From blossoms comes.
    Furious Versions.
    Gift, The.
    Here I Am.
    I Ask My Mother to Sing.
    Interrogation, The.
    Irises.
    Mnemonic.
    Persimmons.
    Story, A.
    This Room and Everything in It.
    Visions and Interpetations.
    Weight of Sweetness, The.

Lee, Nathaniel (1653–93)
    Nathaniel Lee to Sir Roger L'Estrange.
    To the Unkown Author of *Absalom and
    Achitophel, sels.*

Lee-Hamilton, Eugene (1845–1907)
    Among the Firs.
    Henry I to the Sea.
    Idle Charon.
    Imaginary Sonnets, *sels.*
    Ipsissimus.
    Luca Signorelli to His Son.
    Noon's Dream-Song.
    Sunken Gold.
    What the Sonnet Is.

Lees, Joseph (1748–1824)
    Jone o' Grinfilt.

Lefroy, Edward Cracroft (1855–91)
    Echoes from Theocritus, *sels.*

Leftwich, Joseph (1892–1983)
    Killed in Action.
    Tailor, The.

Legaré, James Matthew (1823–59)
    Tallulah.
    To a Lily.

Léger, Alexis Saint-Léger. *See* "Perse, St.-John"

Lehman, David (b. 1948)
    Amnesia.
    Arrival at Kennedy.
    Difference Between Pepsi and Coke, The.
    Enigma Variations.
    Fear.
    First Offense.
    For David Shapiro.
    Guilt Trip.
    Heaven.
    Moment of Truth, The.
    One Size Fits All: a Critical Essay.
    Operation Memory.
    Perfidia.
    Spontaneous Combustion.
    Towards the Vanishing Point.

Lehmann, Geoffrey (b. 1940)
    Night Flower.
    Pigs, The.
    Poem for Maurice O'Shea, A.
    Pope Alexander VI.
    Roses, *sels.*
    Ross's Poems, *sels.*
    Saving the Harvest.
    Song for Past Midnight.

Lehmann, John (1907–87)
    Ballad of Banners (1944), The.
    No Easy Answer.
    This Excellent Machine.

Lehmann, R. P. M.
    Limerick: "There was a young girl of
    Bahari."

Lehrer, Tom (b. 1928)
    Alma.
    Elements, The.
    Wernher von Braun.

Lei-Lanilau, Carolyn (b. 1946)
    Kolohe or Communication.

Leib [*or* Leyb], Mani (1883–1953)
    Door and Window Bolted Fast.
    Hush, hush, do not speak.

In little hands she holds an open book.
Psalmodist.
When I See Another's Pain.

Leigh, Barbara
Limerick: "There was an old Member called Bevan."

Leigh, F.. See Murray, L. *and* F. Leigh

Leigh, Helen (*fl.* 1788, d. c.1795)
Lady and the Doctor, The.
Natural Child, The.

Leigh, Henry Sambrooke (1837–83)
Only Seven.
Rhymes (?).
'Twas Ever Thus.
Twins, The.

Leigh, Richard (1649?–1728)
Greatness in Little.
On a Fair Lady, Looking in the Glass.

Leighton, Robert (1611–84)
Bunch of Larks, The.

Leipoldt, C. Louis (1880–1947)
Banded Cobra, The.
On My Old Ramkiekie.
Oom Gert's Story.

Leiser, Joseph (b. 1873)
Kol Nidra.

Leithauser, Brad (b. 1953)
Angel.
Buried Graves, The.
Ghost of a Ghost, The.
Haunted, The.
In a Japanese Moss Garden.
In Minako Wada's House.
Old Bachelor Brother.
Post-Coitum Tristesse: A Sonnet.
Tigers of Nanzen-ji, The.
Trauma.

Leland, Charles Godfrey ("Hans Breitman") (1824–1903)
Ballad by Hans Breitmann.
Ballad: "Der noble Ritter Hugo."
Breitmann in Paris.
Breitmann in Politics, *sels.*
Hans Breitmann as a Politician, *sels.*
Hans Breitmann's Party [*or* Barty].
Wein Geist.

Leland, John (1554?–1600)
Day Is Past and Gone, The.
Now Behold the Saviour Pleading.

Len
Limerick: "Said the Chinese philosopher, Lin."

L'Engle, Madeleine (b. 1918)
At Communion.
Three Songs of Mary, *sels.*

Lenier, Sue (b. 1957)
Finale.

Lennen, Elinor
Within the Shelter of Our Walls.

Lenngren, Anna Maria (1754–1817)
Other Fabrics, Other Mores!
Portraits, The.

Lennon, John (1940–80)
Fat Budgie, The.

Lennox, Charlotte (1729?–1804)
Art of Coquetry, The, *sels.*
Song, A: "What torments must the virgin prove."

Lenski, Lois (1893–1974)
Sing a Song of People.

Lent, Emma A.
Unawares.

Lenton, Mrs. Babington. See Pope, Jessie

Leonard, Priscilla
Happiness is like a crystal.

Leonard, Tom (b. 1944)
Cold, Isn't It.
Fathers and Sons.
Feed Ma Lamz.
Ghostie Men, *sels.*
Good Style.
Jist Ti Let Yi No.
Miracle of the Burd and the Fishes, The.
On Knowing the Difference Between Prejudice, Discrimination, and Oppression.

Paroakial.
Poetry.
Scream, A.
Simple Simon.
Situations Theoretical and Contemporary, *sels.*
Six Glasgow Poems.
Summer's Day, A.
Unrelated Incidents, *sels.*

Leonard, William Ellery (1876–1944)
Two Lives, *sels.*

Leong, Russell (b. 1950)
Aerogrammes.

Leonidas of Alexandria (d. 450 B.C.)
Menodotis.
Upon Venus Putting on Mars His Armes.
We oxen are not only good.
You send me reams of snowy paper.

Leonidas of Tarentum (c.290–c.220 B.C.)
Ambrosia, brought safe.
Antiginides' two daughters, Melo.
Atthis hung up the belt with the pompoms.
By themselves in the twilight.
Cleitagoras.
Cold water falling out of the split rock.
Don't waste yourself, dragging out the life of a vagrant.
Eileithyia, brought safe.
Epigrams, *sels.*
Eros taught Pratalidas his adolescent beauty.
Eurotas said to the goddess of love.
Evening and morning old Platthis kept.
Far from Italy, far from my native Tarentum.
For that goatfucker, goatfooted.
Give me one small smothering of earth.
Go softly past the graveyard where.
Good hunting, rabbit-catcher and bird-catcher.
His poor mother gives Mikythos'.
I am the tomb of Tellen, I contain.
"I'm like a vine supported on a stick."
Last Journey, The.
Night and mist, what bones you have eaten.
Nymphs of water, daughters of Doros.
Philocles.
Philokles offers his bouncing.
Pity poor Philinos—young.
Remember Euboulos [*or* Eubolus], who lived and died sober?
Sheep-folds, holy spring of the Nymphs.
Silver Eros the ankle bracelet, The.
Silver Love, an anklet, A.
Sōsos the cattleman slew the lion.
Spring on the Coast.
Staff and slippers hang here, Kypris, A.
Sudden strong squalls from the sou'-west.
Sun whirls an axle on fire, The.
Theris, the old man who lived by his fish traps.
Theris, whose hands were cunning.
Theromachos of Crete came to hang up.
This beast which preyed on sheep.
Tomb of Crethon, The.
Traveler in the wilds, do not.
Wallet, a rawhide goatskin, a cane, A.
Who are you, whose pitiful bones.
You shepherds who wander this lonely mountainside.

Leonovich, Vladimir (b. 1937)
I have to write a page.

Leontius Scholasticus [*or* Leontius Referendarius] (*fl.* 6th cent.)
My little cup, go now and taste.
Orpheus, dying, not all Music died.
Touch, cup / the lips.

Leopardi, Giacomo (1798–1837)
Calm after the Storm, The.
Infinite, The.
Infinito, L'.
Saturday Night in the Village.
Sè Stesso, A.
To Himself.
To Italy.
To the Moon.

Lepik, Kalju
Curse.
Let Me Hold Your Hand.

Nobody talks earth's language.
Sea, The.

Lerman, Eleanor
Evenings in the Sea.
Margaret Whiting Tearfully Sings.

Lermontov, Mikhail Yuryevich (1814–41)
Composed While under Arrest.
Daemon, The, *sels.*
Dagger.
Mountain, The.
Reed, The.
Sail, A.
Testament, The.
Thought, A.

Lerner, Laurence David (b. 1925)
All Day and All October.
Arthur's Anthology of English Poetry.
14 July 1956.
Poet at Fifty, The.
Raspberries.
St. Enda.
Wish, A.
Years Later.

Leslie, Kenneth (1892–1974)
By Stubborn Stars, *sels.*
Halibut Cove Harvest.

Leslie, Sir Shane (1886–1971)
Forest Song.
Holy Cross.
Saint Patrick.

Lesoro, E. A. S. (b. 1929)
Muscovy Drake, The.

Lesser, Rika (b. 1953)
Degli Sposi.
Translation.
Woman from Chianciano.

Lester, Julius (b. 1939)
In the Time of Revolution, *sels.*
On the Birth of My Son, Malcolm Coltrane.
Us.

L'Estrange, Sir Roger (1616–1704)
Mr L'Estrange's Verses in the Prison at Lynn.

Leto, Denise Nico (*fl.* 20th cent.)
For Talking.
Mary Morelle Show, The.

Letters, Francis
Inglorious Milton, The.

Letts, Winifred M. (1882–1971)
Boys.
Elfin People Fill the Tubes, The.
Harbour, The.
Irish Skies.
Pensioners.
Spires of Oxford, The.
Spring, the Travelling Man.
To Scott.

Leuty, Helen
Apple Harvest.
Night, The.
Poplars.

Levchev, Lyubomir
Abandoned Churches.
Appassionato.
Capriccio 9.
Carmen, or the Made-Up Girl.
Confession and Salute to the Fire.
Last night I was coming back home alone.
Secret Love.
We stopped.

Leveridge, Lilian (1879–1953)
Cry from the Canadian Hills, A.

Levertov, Denise (b. 1923)
Abel's Bride.
About Marriage.
Ache of marriage, The.
Acolyte, The.
Adam's Complaint.
Advent 1966.
Art.
At the Edge.
Bedtime.
Beginners.
Beyond the End.
Brass Tacks.

By Rail through the Earthly Paradise, Perhaps Bedfordshire.
Caedmon.
Cancion: "When I am the sky."
Cat as Cat, The.
Christmas 1944.
Claritas.
Closed World, The.
Clouds as I see them, rising, The.
Come into animal presence.
Common Ground, A.
Contraband.
Crack, The.
Dead Butterfly, The.
Defeat, A.
Despair.
Divorcing.
Dog of Art, The.
Don't You Hear that Whistle Blowin'.
Dragonfly-Mother, The.
During the Eichmann Trial, sels.
Earliest Spring.
Earth Worm, The.
Else a great Prince in prison lies.
Embroidery (I), An.
Eros at Temple Stream.
Everything That Acts Is Actual.
Eye Mask.
February Evening in New York.
Five-Day Rain, The.
Fountain, The.
Fragrance of Life, Odor of Death.
Gathered at the River.
Goddess, The.
Goethe's Blues.
Good Dream, The.
Goodbye to Tolerance.
Grace-Note, The.
Gulf, The.
Gypsy's Window, The.
Hands, The.
Hymn to Eros.
Hypocrite women, how seldom we speak.
I Learned That Her Name Was Proverb.
Illustration [—a Footnote], The.
Illustrious Ancestors.
In California During the Gulf War.
In Mind.
In Thai Binh (Peace) Province.
Innocent, The.
Intrusion.
Invocation: "Silent, about-to-be-parted-from house."
Jacob's Ladder, The.
Last Night's Dream.
Leaving Forever.
Life at War.
Like Loving Chekhov.
Living.
Long Way Round, The.
Losing Track.
Mad Song.
Malice of Innocence, The.
Map of the Western Part of the County of Essex in England, A.
Mass for the Day of St. Thomas Didymus, sels.
Matins.
Merritt Parkway.
Mutes, The.
Note to Olga (1966), A.
O Taste and See.
Obsessions.
October.
Old Adam, The.
Olga Poems.
One A.M.
Open Secret.
Overheard.
Overheard over S. E. Asia.
Overland to the Islands.
Partial Resemblance.
People at Night.
Pilots, The.
Pleasures.
Prayer for Revolutionary Love.
Presence.

Prisoners.
Psalm Concerning the Castle.
Quarry Pool, The.
Quest, The.
Recognition, The.
Relearning the Alphabet.
Runes, The.
Scenes from the Life of the Peppertrees.
Sea's Wash in the Hollow of the Heart, The.
Secret, The.
Seeing for a Moment.
Settling.
Sharks, The.
She and the Muse.
Six Variations, sels.
Son, The.
Song for Ishtar.
Springtime, The.
Staying Alive, sels.
Stepping Westward.
Sunday Afternoon.
Suspended.
Task, The.
Tenebrae.
Terror.
Third Dimension, The.
Those Who Want Out.
Thread, The.
Time Past, A.
To the Muse.
To the Reader.
To the Snake.
Tree Telling of Orpheus, A.
Triple Feature.
Unknown, The.
Variation on a Theme by Rilke.
Wavering.
Way Through, The.
Weeping Woman.
What It Could Be.
What Were They Like?
What Wild Dawns There Were.
Where is the angel for me to wrestle?
Wife, The.
Williams: An Essay.
Willows of Massachusetts, The.
Window-Blind.
Wings, The.
With Eyes at the Back of Our Heads.
Witness.
Woman Alone, A.
Woman Meets an Old Lover, A.
World Outside, The.

Levi, David (1816–98)
Bible, The, sels.

Levi, Peter (b. 1931)
I imagine where God has never been.
In stone settlements when the moon is stone.
Life Is a Platform, sels.
New Year's Eve Poem 1965.
Pancakes for the Queen of Babylon, sels.
Tree of roses. The water crashed headlong.
When does it end? When does a new poem.

Levi, Primo (1919–87)
Annunciation.
Buna.
For Adolf Eichmann.
Reveille.
Shemà.
Survivor, The.
To my Friends.
Voices mute for ever, or since yesterday, or just stilled;.

Levi-Yitzhok [or Levi-Isaac] of Berditchev (Isaac of Berditshev) (1740–1809)
Kaddish.

Levien, Michael (b. 1927)
In the Falling Deer's Mouth.

Levin, Bernard
Limerick: "Earnest young leftie named Tariq."
Limerick: "Prince Charles in his Welsh principality."

Levin, Konstantin (1924–84)
Artillery was burying us.

Levin, Phillis (b. 1954)
Citizens and Sky.

Dark Horse.
Lost Bee, The.
Meeting of Friends, A.
Night Coach.
Planting Roses.
Shadow Returns, The.

Levine, Mark (b. 1965)
Capitalism.

Levine, Philip (b. 1928)
Above It All.
And the Trains Go On.
Angel Butcher.
Animals Are Passing from Our Lives.
At the Fillmore.
Autumn.
Baby Villon.
Belief.
Belle Isle, 1949.
Blasting from Heaven.
Buying and Selling.
Cemetery at Academy, California, The.
Clouds.
Coming Home, Detroit, 1968.
Cutting Edge, The.
Death of Saul, The.
Distant Winter, The.
Fox, The.
Gangrene.
Genius.
Heaven.
Here and Now.
Horse, The.
How Much Earth.
I Remember Clifford.
In the New Sun.
Keep Talking.
Later Still.
Life Ahead, The.
Lost Angel, The.
Mad Day in March.
Midget, The.
Milkweed.
1933.
Old Testament, The.
On My Own.
On the Edge.
Ordinary Morning, An.
Poem Circling Hamtramck, Michigan, All Night in Search of You, The.
Rain Downriver.
Red Dust.
Reply, The.
Salami.
Sierra Kid, sels.
Simple Truth, The.
Sleepless Night, A.
Snails.
Snow.
Soloing.
Standing on the Corner.
Survivor, The.
Sweet Will.
They Feed They Lion.
To a Child Trapped in a Barber Shop.
To My God in His Sickness.
Turning, The.
Uncle.
Waking in March.
Way Down, The.
You Can Have It.
Zaydee.

Levinson, Fred (b. 1936)
No More than Five.
Poem against Rats, A.
Poem: "Country / was back in the hands of the patriots, The."
Sharks in Shallow Water.
Translation From, A.

Levis, Larry (b. 1946)
Bat Angels.
Cocoon, The.
Fish.
For Zbigniew Herbert, Summer, 1971, Los Angeles.
Linnets.
Magnolia.
Poem You Asked For, The.

Story.
To a Wren on Calvary.
Widening Spell of the Leaves, The.
Levitansky [*or* **Levitanskii**], **Yury** [*or* **Iurii**]
Davydovich (b. 1922)
Dream about a Piano, A.
Levy, Amy (1861–89)
Ballad of Religion and Marriage, A.
Birch-Tree at Loschwitz, The.
Cross-Road Epitaph, A.
Epitaph: "This is the end of him, here he
lies."
Felo de Se.
In the Mile End Road.
London Plane-Tree, A.
London Poets.
Magdalen.
March Day in London, A.
Minor Poet, A.
Old House, The.
On the Threshold.
Reminiscence, A.
Sequel to 'A Reminiscence," The.
Straw in the street where I pass to-day.
To Vernon Lee.
Twilight.
Xantippe.
Levy, Louis (1875–1940)
Swallow's Flight, The.
Levy, Newman (1888–1966)
Rigoletto.
Tannhauser.
Thaïs.
Lewis, Alun (1915–44)
All day it has rained, and we on the edge of
the moors.
Autumn, 1939.
Christmas Holiday.
Dawn on the East Coast.
Easter at Christmas.
Goodbye.
In Hospital: Poona (1).
Infantry.
Jungle, The.
Mahratta Ghats, The.
Peasants, The.
Post-Script: for Gweno.
Sentry, The.
Song (On Seeing Dead Bodies Floating Off
the Cape).
To a Comrade in Arms.
To Edward Thomas.
Unknown Soldier, The.
Lewis, Angelo (b. 1950)
America Bleeds.
Clear.
Lewis, Clive Staples (1898–1963)
Apologist's Evening Prayer, The.
Ballade of Dead Gentlemen.
Epigrams and Epitaphs, *sels.*
Epitaph, An: "Erected by her sorrowing
brothers."
Evensong.
Evolutionary Hymn.
Grief's Circle.
Impression, An.
Joys Once Shared.
Late Passenger, The.
Love's as Warm as Tears.
Naked Seed, The.
Nativity, The.
On a Vulgar Error.
Pilgrim's Problem.
Prayer: "Master, they say that when I seem."
Scazons.
Sequence, The.
Sonnet: "Bible says Sennacherib's campaign
was spoiled, The."
Stephen to Lazarus.
Lewis, Diane Q.
Ruth.
**Lewis, Dominic Bevan Wyndham ("Timothy
Shy") (1891–1969)**
Downland Crisis, A, *sels.*
If So the Man You Are, *sels.*
Lost Chord, The.

Pastoral: "'Lumpish trollop, The !'"
Sapphics.
Shot at Random, A.
Lewis, Emily
My Dog.
Lewis, Esther (*fl.* 1747–89)
Advice to a Young Lady Lately Married.
Letter to a Lady in London, A, *sels.*
Mirror for Detractors, A.
Lewis, Howell Elvet [*or* **Elfed**] **(1860–1953)**
Life's Morning.
Lewis, J. Patrick (b. 1942)
How to Tell a Camel.
Stories.
Lewis, Janet (b. 1889)
April Hill, The.
At Carmel Highlands.
Country Burial.
Fossil, 1975.
Girl Help.
Grandmother Remembers, A.
In the Egyptian Museum.
Lullaby: "Lulee, lullay."
Lullaby: "Lullee, lullay."
Remembered Morning.
Snail Garden.
Time and Music.
Lewis, Joel
To The Great Hard-Bop Pianists.
Lewis, Lisa (b. 1956)
Bridget.
My Students.
Urinating Man, The.
**Lewis, Matthew Gregory ("Monk" Lewis)
(1775–1818)**
Alonzo the Brave and the Fair Imogine.
Lewis, Michael
August.
Lewis, Naomi
Footprint on the Air, A.
Lewis, Percy Wyndham (1882–1957)
One-Way Song, *sels.*
Song of the Militant Romance, The.
Lewis, Richard
Journey from Patapsko to Annapolis, A, *sels.*
Lewis, Robert
If you had a friend strong, simple, true.
Lewis, Saunders (b. 1893)
Ascension Thursday.
Deluge 1939, The.
Mary Magdalene.
Pine, The.
To the Good Thief.
Lewisohn, Ludwig (1882–1955)
Heinrich Heine.
Together.
Leybourne, George (1842?–1884)
Man on the Flying Trapeze, The.
Leyden, John (1775–1811)
Lay of the Ettercap, The.
Leyeles, A. (Aaron Glanz-Leyeles) (1889–1966)
Castles.
Madison Square.
White Swan.
Leyvik, H.
Open up, gate.
L'Hermite, Tristan
Jealousy.
Li Ching (916–61)
Tune: "Echoing Heaven's Everlastingness."
Tune: "Sand of Silk-washing Stream."
Li Ch'ing-chao (1084–1151)
Alone in the Night.
As in a Dream.
Autumn Evening Beside the Lake.
Clear Bright.
Day of Cold Food, The.
"Fisherman's Honor," The.
Hopelessness.
I let the incense grow cold.
Last night thin rain, gusty wind.
Light mist, then dense fog.
Melting in thin mist and heavy clouds.
Mist.

Poem to the Tune of "Tsui hua yin."
Poem to the Tune of "Yi chian mei."
P'u-Shen Sheng Man.
Quail Sky.
Rattan bed, paper netting. I wake from
morning sleep.
Red lotus incense fades on / the jewelled
curtain.
Sky links cloud waves, links dawn fog.
To the Tune "A Hilly Garden."
To the Tune, "Plum Blossoms Fall and
Scatter."
To the Tune "Spring at Wu Ling."
Tune: "As in a Dream; a Song."
Tune: "Charm of Nien-nu, The."
Tune: Crimson Lips Adorned.
Tune: Endless Union.
Tune: Magnolia Blossom.
Tune: "Magnolia Blossoms, Abbreviated"
("From the pole of the flower vendor.")
Tune: "Manifold Little Hills."
Tune: "Pure Serene Music."
Tune: "Sand of Silk-washing Stream," *sels.*
Tune: "Song of Picking Mulberry."
Tune: Song of Picking Mulberry ("Evening
comes with an onslaught of wind and
rain.")
Tune: "Southern Song, A."
Tune: "Spring at Wu-ling."
Tune: "Telling of Innermost Feelings."
Tune: Telling of Innermost Feelings ("Night
comes and, drowsy with drink, I'm slow to
shed my /ornaments ornaments.")
Tune: The Butterfly Woos the Blossoms.
Tune: "Tipsy in the Flower's Shade."
Two Springs.
Warm rain, sunny wind start to break the
chill.
Weary Song to a Slow Sad Tune, A.
Year after year I have watched.
Li Chü (fl. mid 20th cent.)
Harvesting Wheat for the Public Share.
Li Ho (799–817)
About Horse, *sels.*
Arrowhead from the Ancient Battlefield of
Ch'ang-p'ing, An.
At Ch'ang-ku, Reading: To Show to My Man
Pa.
Autumn Comes.
Bring in the Wine.
Bronze Immortal Takes Leave of Han, A.
Ch'ang-ku.
Criticisms, *sels.*
Dawn in Stone City.
Don't Go Out of the Door.
Dream of Heaven, A.
For the Examination at Ho-nan-fu: Songs of
the Twelve Months, *sels.*
Girl Combs Her Hair, A.
Grave of Little Su, The.
High Dike.
In Protest.
King of Ch'in Drinks Wine, The.
Lamentations of the Bronze Camels.
Liang Terrace, The.
Magic Strings.
Musing, *sels.*
My Man Pa Replies.
New Bamboo in the North Garden at Ch'ang-
ku.
Northern Cold, The.
Northland in Cold, The.
On and On for Ever.
On the Frontier.
Piece for Magic Strings, A.
Ravine on a Cold Evening.
Sing Loud.
Song of the Sacred Strings.
Temple of the Orchid Fragrance Goddess.
Up in Heaven.
Watchman's Drum in the Streets of Officials,
The.
Young man with a yellow hat.
Young Noble at Night's End; a Song.
Li Hsün (855?–930?)
Tune: "Song of the Southern Country."
Tune: "Stretch of Cloud over Mount Wu, A."

Li K'ai-hsien (1502–68)
Commiserating with the Poor.
Compassion for the Farmers.
Describing My Feelings upon Encountering Snow, *sels.*
Drunk, Climbing to the Peak of Iron Tomb on Wei Mountain.
Early Summer: At the Riverside, Seeing Off Li Chiu-ho as He Returns to Yeh with the Books I Lent Him, *sels.*
Earthquake, *sels.*
Gazing at Ch'ang-po Mountain.
Impromptu Poems, *sels.*
In the Second Month of Summer, Taking My Family to the Villages East of the City.
Meeting Trappers on the Road in Heavy Snow.
Night of the First Full Moon, The.
Night of the Seventeenth, The.
On My Birthday—Sick.
On Snow, *sels.*
On the Cold Food Festival, Entertaining at the Southern Estate—the Guests Were Li Chiu-ho, Ma Nan-yeh, Wei Tung-kao, Li Hu-ch'uan, Huang K'ung-ts'un, Li Lung-t'ang, and Hu Hu-shan.
Parable, A.
Pleasures among the Fields during the Four Seasons, *sels.*
Poem about Fan the Fourth, A.
Poem Expressing My Wife's Response to One I Sent Her, A.
Prosperous Villager, The.
Record of a Past Affair, A.
Recording a Weird Happening.
Sent to the Master Physician, "Almond Orchard" Shih.
Sent to the Painter, Lu Hsiao-feng.
Songs of the Frontier, *sels.*
Staying Overnight on the Banks of Embroidered River.
Thanking Doctor Jen.
Trip to a Mountain Village, A.
Watching the Swinging, *sels.*
Wei-ch'i Chess.
When I Recovered from an Illness After Returning Home To Live in Retirement, I Was Invited by My Friends to Join a Song-Lyric Club, *sels.*

Li Ling
Parting from Su Wu.

Li Meng-yang (1413–1529)
Autumn Vista.
Crossing the Frontier.
Mooring at Hsia-k'ou at Night.
Oriole at Dawn, An.
Seeing Off Commander In Chief Li to Yün-chung.
Song of Lin Liang's Painting "Two Horned Falcons."
Spring Vista from the Tower of Illuminated Distance.
Wild Wind.

Li P'in (*fl.* late 9th cent.)
Crossing Han River.

Li Po (701–62)
Ancient Air.
Ancient Airs.
At Su Terrace Viewing the Past.
At Yellow Crane Tower Taking Leave of Meng Hao-jan.
Autumn Cove.
Awakening from Drunkenness on a Spring Day.
Birds have vanished into the sky, The.
Boating Song.
Bring the Wine!
Calling on a Taoist Priest in Tai-t'ien Mountain but Failing to See Him.
Clearing at Dawn.
Climbing Phoenix Terrace at Chin-ling.
Conversations in the Mountains.
Drinking Alone beneath the Moon, *sels.*
Drinking Alone in Moonlight.
Drinking Alone in the Moonlight.
Drinking Alone under Moonlight.
Exile's Letter.

Facing Wine with Memories of Lord Ho, *sels.*
Fighting on the South Frontier.
For the Dancer of the King of Wu.
Girl of Yueh, The.
Girls of Yueh, The.
In Imitation of Ancient Songs.
In Reply When Lesser Officials of Chung-tu Brought a Pot of Wine and Two Fish to My Inn as Gifts.
In the Mountains on a Summer Day.
In Yüeh Viewing the Past.
Jade Stairs Resentment.
Jewel Stairs' Grievance, The.
Lament of the Frontier Guard.
Listening to a Monk from Shu Playing the Lute.
Moon over Mountain Pass.
Moon over the Mountain Pass, The.
Night with a Friend, A.
On Climbing the Phoenix Tower at Chinling.
On the Mountain: Question and Answer.
On the river, every day these heavy rains.
One set on the highway to sing.
Poem by the Bridge at Ten-shin.
Poem No. 19 in the Old Manner.
Presented to Wang Lun.
River Merchant's Wife, The; a Letter.
Road to Shu Is Hard, The.
Saying Farewell to a Friend.
Seeing a Friend Off.
Seeing Meng Hao-jan Off to Kuang-ling.
Self-abandonment.
Sent to My Two Little Children in the East of Lu.
Separation on the River Kiang.
Sitting Alone in Ching-t'ing Mountain.
Song of a Dream Visit to T'ien-mu.
Song of Hsiang-yang.
Song of War, A.
Songs of Ch'iu-p'u, *sels.*
Spring Night in Lo-Yang—Hearing a Flute.
Still Night Thoughts.
Summer Day in the Mountains.
Summit Temple, The.
Taking Leave of a Friend.
They Fought South of the Walls.
Thinking of East Mountain.
Thoughts While Studying at Hanlin Academy Sent to My Colleagues at the Chi-hsien Academy.
T'ien-mu Mountain Ascended in a Dream: A Farewell Song.
To Amuse Myself.
To Secretary Lu Ch'ien of Jen City.
To Tan-Ch'iu.
To Tu Fu.
Tzu-yeh Song.
Verses: "Clean is the autumn wind."
Viewing the Waterfall at Mount Lu.
Written in Behalf of My Wife.
You ask why I make my home in the mountain forest.

Li Shan-fu (*fl.* c.874)
My Detacted Villa.
Temple of Hsiang Yü, The.

Li Shang-yin (812–58)
About Geese.
At eight stealing a mirror glance.
Bite back passion. Spring now sets.
Boudoir Feelings.
Candle casts dark shadows, The.
Cicada.
"Coming" is an empty word, "going" leaves no trace.
Coming was an empty promise, you have gone, and left no footprint.
Crooked Lady.
Day after day spring's glory vies with the glorious sun.
Double curtains hang deep in the room of Never Grieve.
East wind sighs, the fine rains come, The.
Evening comes. My mind is troubled.
Exile.
Fallen Flowers.
First Month: at Ch'ung-jang House.

For ever hard to meet, and as hard to part.
For Lotus Flower.
Her beauty is hidden by a cloudy screen.
Hibiscus Flowers.
I Wake Up Alone.
In a Day.
Lady in the Moon, The, *sels.*
Last night's planets and stars, last night's wind.
Last night's stars, last night's winds.
Little Peach Blossoms in the Garden.
Ma-wei.
Night Chill.
Night Rains: to my Wife up North.
Old harem is quiet and deserted, The.
Patterned Lute, The.
Peonies.
Phoenix tail on scented silk, flimsy layer on layer.
Poem for My Little Boy.
Richly painted zither, for no reason, has fifty strings, The.
Spring Rain.
Thoughts in the Cold.
To Tzŭ-chih: among the 'Flowers.'
Walls of Emerald, The.
Wang Chao-chün.
When will I be home? I don't Know.
Where is it, the sad lyre which follows the quick flute?
Willow.
Written on a Monastery Wall.

Li Shen (772–846)
Pitying the Farmer.

Li Tung (*fl.* 9th cent.)
For the Monk San-tsang on His Return to the Western Regions.

Li Tung-yang (1447–1511)
Following the Rhymes of Yang T'ing-ho's Poem, "On the Road Back, Accompanying the Imperial Retinue on a Visit to the Tombs of Former Emperors."
Inscribed on the Painting "Meaning of a Poem by Wang Wei."
Long Handscroll of Bamboo by Wang Meng-tuan, The.
Song of the Painting "Catching Fish."
To Yung-erh—Imitating a Work by Master Jade Stream.
Trip to Yüeh-lu Temple, A.

Li Yi (c.749–c.829)
At Night atop Shou-hsiang Citadel, Hearing Tartar Flutes.
Looking in a Mirror the Day before the Advent of Autumn.

Li Yü (937–78)
One scull in the spring wind, one leaf of a boat.
Tune: "Beautiful Lady Yü, The."
Tune: "Casket of Pearls, A."
Tune: "Crows Crying at Nihgit."
Tune: Crows Crying at Night.
Tune: "Dance of the Cavalry."
Tune: Deva-like Barbarian ("Blossoms bright, the moon dark, shadowed in thin mist.")
Tune: "Deva-like Barbarian" ("Bright flowers and dim moon, enmeshed in thin drifting mist.")
Tune: Gazing at the South.
Tune: "Joy at Meeting."
Tune: "Pure Serene Music."
Tune: Pure Serene Music ("Since we parted, spring half over.")
Tune: Ripples Sifting Sand.
Tune: "Ripples Sifting Sand: A Song."
Tune: Song of Tzu-yeh.
Tune: "Spring in Jade Pavilion."
Tune: The Fisherman.

Liagarang
Snails.

Libbey, Elizabeth (b. 1947)
Before the Mountain.
Come Into the Night Grove.
Concerning the Dead Women: The Munitions Plant Explosion: June, 1918.
Juana Bautista Lucero, Circa 1926, to Her Photographer.

Marceline, to Her Husband.
Spring And.
To Her Dead Mate: Montana, 1966.

Libera, Sharon Mayer
Mother, I may do violence to you.

Lichtenstein, Alfred (1889–1914)
Leaving for the Front.

Licymnios (*fl.* c.5th cent. B.C.)
Hypnos, seeing how.
Ten thousand rivers of tears.

Liddy, James (b. 1934)
Donagh MacDonagh.
Epithalamion I–IV, *sels.*
History.
Love Songs of Corca Bascinn, *sels.*
Paean to Eve's Apple.
Strand Hotel, Rosslare, The.
Voice of America, 1961, The.

Lieberman, Elias (1883–1969)
I Am an American.
Sholom Aleichem.

Lieberman, Laurence (b. 1935)
Coral Reef, The.
Unblinding, The.

Liechtenstein, Ulrich von (*fl.* 13th cent.)
Love, Whose Month Was Ever May.

Liessin, Abraham (b. 1872)
Spring Nocturne.

Lifshin, Lyn (b. 1944)
After the Anti-Semitic Calls on a Local Talk
Station.
Being Jewish in a Small Town.
Fitzi in the Yearbook.
I Remember Haifa Being Lovely But.
Midwest is Full of Vibrators, The.
Penthouse Playboy.
With So Many Voices.
Yahrtzeit Light, The.

Lightfoot, Gordon (b. 1938)
Wreck of the Edmund Fitzgerald, The.

Lihn, Enrique (1929–1988)
Cemetery in Punta Arenas.
Dark Room, The.
Favorite Little Shrine, A.
Goodnight, Achilles.
Of all despondencies, death-despair must be
the worst.
Six Poems of Loneliness.
Torture Chamber.

Liliencron, Detlev, Freiherr von (1844–1909)
After the Hunt.
Autumn.
Who Knows Where.

Lillard, Charles (b. 1944)
Bushed.
Lobo.

Lilley, Kate (b. 1960)
Sewing Lesson, The.
You Have to Strike Back.

Lilliard, R. W.
America's Answer.

Lilliat, John (c.1550–c.1599)
False Love.

Lim, Shirley (b. 1944)
Black and White.
Father from Asia.
I defy you Wallace Stevens.
Lost Name Woman.
Modern Secrets.
Starlight Haven.

Lim-Wilson, Fatima (fl. 20th cent.)
Inventing the Filipino.

Lima, Jorge de (1893–1953)
Distribution of Poetry.
Enormous Hand, The.
Papa John.
Poem of any Virgin.
Words Will Resurrect, The.

**"Limonov, Eduard Veniaminovich" (Eduard
Veniaminovich Savenko) (b. 1943)**
I would hold another person in my thoughts.

Lin Hung (*fl.* c.1383)
Drinking Wine.
Inscribed on the Painting "Pleasures of the
Lute by the River."

Sailing at Night on Flowing-sand River.
Saying Farewell to Magistrate Ch'en Ta-yu.

Lin Pu (967–1028)
Autumn Day, An—Leisurely Boating on
West Lake.
Trail among the Pines, A.

Lincoln, Abraham (1809–65)
Gettysburg Address, The.
I Am Not Bound to Win.
Memory.
Second Inaugural Address, *sels.*
Ten Rules of Conduct for Individuals and
Nations.

Lincoln, Mary W. (1818–82)
Kings of France.

Lindbergh, Anne Morrow (b. 1906)
Even.

Linden, Mrs. Henry (b. 1859)
All We Ask Is Justice.
As Women of Our Race.
Bird Song, The.
Brave Man and Brave Woman.
Church Bells, The.
Count Your Blessings.
Cultivation.
Do Your Best.
Encouragement.
Fall Is Here, The.
For the Good of the Pythian Order.
God's Electric Power.
Golden Jubilee of Wilberforce.
Gossip.
Household of Ruth, The.
I Am as Happy as a Queen on Her Throne.
Last Day of the Year; or, New Year's Eve,
The.
Let Us Strive to Do Something.
Life's Golden Sunset.
Lonely World.
Man Is What He Wills to Be.
Marriage Vow.
May.
Missionary, The.
New Year's Morning; or, the First Day of
the Year.
October Is Here.
Oh Woman, Blessed Woman!
Orphan Girl, An.
Our Club Work.
Our Noble Booker T. Washington.
Parting Lovers, The.
Paul Laurence Dunbar.
Pay Your Debts.
Prospect of the Future, The.
Riot, A.
Scraps of Time.
Silent Night, The.
Sun of Our Existence, The.
Tell Her So.
This Country's Needs ("This country needs
more noble men.")
To the Conference.
To the Queen of the British Government.
To the Wheel of Progress.
Wayward Son, The.
What Is Woman?
Would-be Critic, The.
Y. M. C. A., The.

Linderman, Frank Bird
Cabins.

Lindh, Stewart
Settler.

Lindon, J. A. (b. 1914)
Limerick issued from Lear, The.
Limerick: "Mr. Alan Jay Lerner (with by-
play)."
My Garden.

Lindsay, Caroline (1844–1912)
Love or Fame.
To My Own Face.

Lindsay [*or* Lyndsay], Sir David (c.1490–c.1555)
Ane Satire [*or* Satyre] of the Three [*or*
Thrie] Estaitis, *sels.*
Dreme, The, *sels.*
Historie of Squyer William Meldrum, The,
sels.

Monarche, The, *sels.*

Lindsay, Jack (b. 1900)
Angry Dusk.
Question Time.
To My Father Norman Alone in the Blue
Mountains.

Lindsay, Lady Anne (1750–1825)
Auld Robin Gray.

Lindsay, Maurice (b. 1918)
Exiled Heart, The.
Hurlygush.
Love's Anniversaries.

Lindsay, Nicholas Vachel (1879–1931)
Abraham Lincoln Walks at Midnight.
Apple-Barrel of Johnny Appleseed, The.
At Mass.
Booker Washington Trilogy, The, *sels.*
Broncho That Would Not Be Broken, The.
Bryan, Bryan, Bryan, Bryan, *sels.*
Chinese Nightingale, The.
Congo, The.
Dove of New Snow, The.
Eagle That Is Forgotten, The.
Factory windows are always broken.
Flower-fed buffaloes of the spring, The.
General William Booth Enters into Heaven.
Ghosts of the Buffaloes, The.
Horrid Voice of Science, The.
I heard Immanuel singing.
In Which Roosevelt Is Compared to Saul.
Jazz of This Hotel, The.
King of Yellow Butterflies, The.
Leaden-eyed, The.
Little Turtle, The.
Moon's the North Wind's cooky, The.
Mysterious Cat, The.
Nancy Hanks, Mother of Abraham Lincoln.
Net to Snare the Moonlight, A.
Pontoon-Bridge Miracle, The.
Rain.
Spider and the Ghost of the Fly, The.
Statue of Old Andrew Jackson, The.
Three Poems about Mark Twain, *sels.*
To a Golden-Haired Girl in a Louisiana
Town.
Traveler, The.
Two old crows sat on a fence rail.
Unpardonable Sin, The.
What the Moon Saw.
Why I Voted the Socialist Ticket.

Lindsay, Sarah
Property of Density, The.

Lingg, Herman von (1820–1905)
Though you can tell me.

Link, Lenore M.
Holding Hands.

Linton, William James (*fl.* c.1851)
Epicurean.
Spring and Autumn.

Lion-Face, Dakini
KYE HO! Wonderful!

Lipkin, Jean (b. 1926)
Father.
Pre Domina.

**Lipkin, Semyon [*or* Semion] Izrailevich (b.
1911)**
Conjunction.
He who appointed weight to the wind.
In the Desert.
When I was arranging letters into words.

Lipshitz, Fay (b. 1941)
To a Set of Drawing Pencils.

Lipsitz, Lou (b. 1938)
Bedtime Story.
Feeding, The.
Prospect Beach.
Skinny / poem, / all / your / ribs.

Lipska, Ewa (b. 1945)
If there is a God.
That Moment.
What Happened to Professor White on
Leaving the Hat Store.
When our enemies fall asleep.

Lipton, James (b. 1946)
Misericordia!

Lisboa, Henriqueta
Minor Elegy.
Lisella, Julia
Song of the Third Generation.
Lisle, Thomas (1709–67)
Power of Music, The.
Lisnyanskaya [or Lisnianskaia], Inna L'vovna (b. 1928)
To you, my friends, to you, my dear ones.
List, Amedie Eva
Mon that wist for raine, The.
Lister, Elizabeth H.
Limerick: "Don't thee think, Zurrr, I be zo amazin'."
Limerick: "I consider I really am through."
Lister, Richard Percival (b. 1914)
Bone China.
Lament of an Idle Demon.
Mind Reborn in Streatham Common, A.
Revolutionaries, The.
Tale of Jorkyns and Gertie; or, Vice Rewarded, The.
Time Passes.
Toast to 2,000, A.
Litchfield, Grace Denio (1849–1946)
Good-By.
Litsey, Edwin Carlile
Dreams Ahead, The.
"Little Billee"
Limerick: "Devil, who plays a deep part, The."
Limerick: "Devil's no longer a myth, The."
Limerick: "Said an elderly Bishop called Greville."
Limerick: "There was a young lady of Nîmes."
Little, Geraldine Clinton
Fallen horse.
Now ice-covered.
White spider, The.
Little, Janet (1759–1813)
Given to a Lady Who Asked Me to Write a Poem.
Little, Lessie Jones
My Yellow Straw Hat.
Littlebird, Harold (Harold Bird) (b. 1951)
Alone is the hunter.
Coming Home in March.
Could I Say I Touched You.
For Drum Hadley.
For the Girls 'cause They Know.
For Tom Numkena, Hopi/Spokane.
Gaa-a-Muna, a Mountain Flower.
Hummingbird.
If You Can Hear My Hooves.
In a Double Rainbow.
Mother / Deer / Lady.
Oh but It Was Good.
Old Moke.
Pennsylvania Winter Indian 1974.
Wrap Me in Blankets of Momentary Winds.
LittleCoon. See &bd;Oliver, Louis
Littledale, Freya
When My Dog Died.
Littlefield, Milton S. (1864–1934)
O Son of Man, Thou Madest Known.
Littleton, Edward (1698?–1734)
Spider, The.
Littman, Jeffery
Limerick: "O Great Queen Whom I idolize."
Littman, S.
Limerick: "There was a young lady of Nantes."
Litvinoff, Emanuel (b. 1915)
If I Forget Thee.
Liu, Bea
Mother.
Liu Ch'ang-ch'ing (710?–785?)
At an Inn in Yü-kan.
Encountering a Snowstorm, I Stay with the Recluse of Mount Hibiscus.
Listening to the Washblock in the Moonlight.
Rejoicing That the Zen Master Pao Has Arrived from Dragon Mountain.

Replying to a Poem by the Monk Ling-yi at the New Spring.
Saying Goodby to the Monk Ling-ch'e.
Sent to the Taoist of Dragon Mountain, Hsü Fa-leng.
Snow on Lotus Mountain.
Liu Cheng (d. 217)
Poem without a Category.
Liu Chih (c.1280–c.1335)
Tune: "Decorous and Pretty"—Respectfully Offered to Circuit Inspector Kao.
Liu Chün (430–64)
In Imitation of Hsü Kan ("Since you went away.")
Liu E (1857–1909)
Boiling Falls.
House of Red Leaves, The.
I remember when we made our first promises of love.
New Year's Eve.
On the Fifteenth Day of the Eighth Month: Watching a Rainstorm from a Tower in Seoul, sels.
On the Night of the Sixteenth of the Eighth Month: Watching the Moon from the Deck of the Ship, Aimo-maru in the Black Water Sea.
On the Road to Pyongyang—An Improvisation.
On the Twenty-fourth: Improvisations, sels.
Pleasures of Shinbashi.
Poem on Falling Leaves.
Poems for Yukiko of Tamba, sels.
Teahouse at Hoshioka, A.
Waiting for the Ferry at Inchŏn.
Liu Hsün's Wife
Curtain of the Wedding Bed, The.
Liu K'o-chuang (1187–1269)
Leaving the City.
Ten Poems Recording Things that Happened at the Ye, sels.
Weeping for Hsüeh Tzu-shu.
Liu Ling-hsien (fl. 6th cent.)
Inscribed on a Plantain Leaf To Show to a Certain Person.
Liu Pang (256–195 B.C.)
Song of the Great Wind.
Liu, Stephen Shu Ning (b. 1930)
My Father's Martial Art.
Liu Tsung-yüan (773–819)
Arriving at North Pond by Stupid Brook on a Morning Walk after the Rain.
Drinking at Night in the Western Pavilion of the Fa-hua Temple.
Farmers, sels.
Feeling Old Age.
Meditation Hall.
On Covering the Bones of Chang Chin, the Hired Man.
Poem to Send to Friends in the Capital, A.
River Snow.
Viewing Mountains with His Reverence Hao Ch'u: To My Friends and Relatives in the Capital.
Written in Jest on Elder Stonegate's Eastern Balcony.
Liu Ya-tzu (1887–1958)
Dragons and snakes tangle in my dream; they can hardly recoil.
Filled with Emotions on the Moon-ferrying Bridge at Arashiyama.
For Guests after Their Visit.
Miscellaneous Poems on Lake Biwa, sels.
On Hearing the News of the Japanese Surrender.
On the Second Day of the Fifth Month—Written after Drink.
Overjoyed at Soviet Russia's Entry into the War.
Strange Tears.
To a Friend, Using the Same Rhymes of a Poem He Sent Me.
Liu Yu Hsi (772–842)
Bamboo Branch Song.
Chin-ling.

Coming Again to Heng-yang, I Mourn for Liu Tsung-yüan.
Drinking with Friends amongst the Blooming Peonies.
Looking at My Knife-hilt Ring, a Song.
Song of Spring Replying to a Poem by Po Chü-yi, a.
Sorrowing for the Past at Western Pass Mountain.
To the Tune "Glittering Sword Hilts."
Tune: "Ripples Sifting Sand."
Willow Branch Song.
Willow Branches.
Liu Yung (fl. c.1034)
Tune: "Chrysanthemums Fresh."
Tune: "Eight Beats of a Kan-chou Song."
Tune: "Jade Butterflies."
Tune: "Midnight Music."
Tune: "Prelude to Allure Goddesses."
Tune: "Wanderings of a Youth."
Livada, Rasa (b. 1948)
Horoscope.
Livesay, Dorothy (b. 1909)
Children's Letters, The.
Eve.
Fantasia.
Green Rain.
Leader, The.
Prophetess, The.
Spain.
Three Emily's, The.
Uninvited, The.
Waking in the Dark.
Widow.
Without Benefit of Tape.
Livingston, Myra Cohn (1926–96)
Car Wash.
Coming from Kansas.
Cried a man on the Salisbury Plain.
Dark, The.
Doll.
Envoi: Washington Square Park.
Father.
4-Way Stop.
Invitation.
Lazy Witch.
Lemonade Stand.
Night / creeps in, The.
Poor.
74th Street.
Swimming Pool.
Tape, The.
12 October.
Why?
Working with Mother.
Livingstone, Douglas (b. 1932)
Bad Run at King's Rest.
Bateleur.
Evasion, An.
Lake Morning in Autumn.
On Clouds.
One Time.
Peace Delegate.
Piece of Earth, A.
Sleep of My Lions, The.
Sunstrike.
To a Dead Elephant.
Vanderdecken.
"Lizzie." See **Doten, Elizabeth**
Llawdden (fl. c.1460)
No Place Like Home.
Llewellyn, Kate (b. 1940)
Colonel.
Finished.
Lloyd, Charles (1775–1839)
Blank Verse by Charles Lloyd and Charles Lamb, sels.
Desultory Thoughts in London, sels.
Lloyd, David (1597–1633)
At the bottom.
Duck feathers.
Longest night, The.
Moonlit sleet.
Over dried grass.
Quietly shaping.
Wild rose bending.

Lloyd, Evan (1734–76)
Methodist, The, *sels.*
Powers of the Pen, The, *sels.*

Lloyd, Hilary Sametz
Unveiling.

Lloyd, Robert (1733–64)
Actor, The, *sels.*
Cit's Country Box, The.
Familiar Epistle to J. B. Esq, A, *sels.*
On Rhyme, *sels.*
Poetry Professors, The, *sels.*
Shakespeare; an Epistle to David Garrick,
Esq, *sels.*

Lluellyn [or Lluelyn], Martin (1616–82)
Epithalamium: To Mistress M. A.

Llwyd, Huw (c.1568–1630)
Fox's Counsel, The.

Llwyd, Morgan (1619–59)
Summer, The, *sels.*

Llywelyn ab y Moel (d. 1440)
Battle of Waun Gaseg, The.

Llywelyn Goch ap Meurig Hen (*fl.* 1360–90)
Lament for Lleucu Llwyd.

Llywelyn-Williams, Alun (b. 1913)
In Berlin, August 1945: Lehrte Bahnhof.
Pont y Caniedydd.
When I Was Young.
Yesterday's Illusion *or* Remembering the
Thirties.

Lo Fu (b. 1928)
Song of the Cricket.

Lo Yin (833–909)
Book burning Pit, The.
Sent to the Ch'an Master Wu-hsiang.
Thinking of the Way Home, a Song.

Lochhead, Douglas (b. 1922)
Winter Lanscape—Halifax.

Lochhead, Liz (b. 1947)
Abortion, An.
Dreaming Frankenstein.
Furies, The, *sels.*
Grim Sisters, The.
Heartbreak Hotel.
Hickie, The.
Mirror's Song.
My Mother's Suitors.
Neckties.
Riddle-Me-Ree.
What The Pool Said, On Midsummer's Day.

Locke, Anne Vaughan (c. 1530–c. 1590)
Sin and despair have so possess'd my heart.
So foul is sin and loathsome in thy sight.

Locke, Mary (*fl.* 1786–1816)
Sonnet: "I hate the Spring in parti-coloured
vest."
Sonnet: "'Tis dead of night; storms rend the
troubled air."

Locker-Lampson, Frederick (1821–95)
Mr. Placid's Flirtation.
My Life Is a———.
Old Oak Tree at Hatfield Broadoak, The.
Our Photograph[s].
Terrible Infant, A.

Lockhart, John Gibson (1794–1854)
Lines: "When youthful faith hath fled."

Lockwood, Margo (b. 1939)
December Eclipse.
Victorian Grandmother.

Lockyer, Milton
Dark Mountains.

Loden, Rachel
My Night with Philip Larkin.

Lodge, George Cabot
Fall.
Lower New York.
On an Æolian Harp.
Pastoral: "Slopes of the sun and vine, and
thou dark stream."
Strong saturation of sea! O widely flown.
Tuckanuck, I.

Lodge, Thomas (1558?–1625)
Animal Weather-Forecasting.
Phyllis, *sels.*
Robert, Second Duke of Normandy, *sels.*

Rosalynde; or Euphues' Golden Legacy, *sels.*
Scillaes Metamorphosis, *sels.*
Shepherd's Sorrow, Being Disdained in Love,
The.

Loesser, Frank (1910–69)
Guys and Dolls.

Loewinsohn, Ron (b. 1937)
Against the Silences to Come.
Insomniac Poem.
Mrs. Loewinsohn etc.
My Sons.
Pastoral: "Death. / The death of a million."
Stillness of the Poem, The.
Thing Made Real, The.

Loftin, Elouise (b. 1950)
Virginia.
Weeksville Women.
Woman.

Lofting, Hugh (1886–1947)
Mister Beers.
Picnic.

Logan, John (1748–88)
Braes of Yarrow, The.
Love Poem.
To a Young Poet Who Died.

Logan, John (1923–1971?)
Brothers: Two Saltimbanques, The.
Century Piece for Poor Heine, A.
Cycle for Mother Cabrini, A, *sels.*
Death of Southwell, The, *sels.*
For My Daughter.
Letter to a Young Father in Exile.
Lines for a Young Wanderer in Mexico.
Lines for Michael in the Picture.
Lines on His Birthday.
Lines to His Son on Reaching Adolescence.
Picnic, The.
Rescue, The.
San Francisco Poem.
Saturday Afternoon at the Movies.
Short Life of the Hermit, A, *sels.*
Spring of the Thief.
Trip to Four or Five Towns, A.
White Pass Ski Patrol.

Logan, Maria (*fl.* c.1793)
Verses on Hearing That an Airy and Pleasant
Situation, near a Populous and Commercial
Town, Was Surrounded with New
Buildings.

Logan, Robert
On a Prize Crucifix by a Student Sculptor.

Logan, William (b. 1950)
Moorhen.
New York.

Logau, Friedrich von (1604–55)
A.E.I.O.U.
Birth is Death, Death is Birth.
Booty from the German War.
Divine Revenge.
Drunkenness.
Faith.
Fools and Wise Men.
Freedom.
French Dress.
Frog, A.
German Language, The.
Old Nobility, The.
One Faith and No Faith.
Our Naughty Time.
Physicians' Fortune, The.
Powerful Servants.
Retribution.
Soul and Body.
Water and Wine.
Women's Rule.

Logghe, Joan
Marriage.

Logue, Christopher (b. 1926)
Epitaph: "I am old."
Foreword to New Numbers.
Friday. Wet Dusk.
Good Taste.
I shall vote Labour because.
London Airport.

Logue, Mary
Sweet Oranges.

Lohenstein, Daniel Casper von (1635–83)
Arminius, *sels.*
Her Eyes.
Night Thoughts Concerning a Dream.

Lohmann, Jeanne
Lady on a Bus.
Nothing So Wise.

Loines, Russell Hillard (1874–1922)
On a Magazine Sonnet.

Lok, Henry (c.1553–1608)
Sundry Christian Passions Contained in Two
Hundred, *sels.*

**Lokhvitskaia, Nadezhda Aleksandrovna. *See*
"Teffi"**

Lomax, Marion (b. 1953)
Other Woman, The.

Lomax, Pearl Cleage (b. 1948)
Glimpse.

Long, Doughtry ("Doc Long")
Black Love Black Hope.
Ginger Bread Mama.
Negro Dreams.
Number Four.
One Time Henry Dreamed the Number.

Long, Pauline. *See* "Asphodel"

Long, Peter (*fl.* 19th cent.)
Remember Thy Creator Now.

Long, Robert (b. 1954)
Found and Lost.
Fumetti.
Goodbye.
Have a Nice Day.
Saying One Thing.
What Happens.

Long, Robert Hill (b. 1952)
Refuge.

Longenbach, James
What You Find in the Woods.

Longenecker, C. W.
Victor, The.

Longfellow, Henry Wadsworth (1807–82)
Aftermath.
Afternoon in February.
Arrow and the Song, The.
Arsenal at Springfield, The, *sels.*
Autumn.
Belisarius.
Bells of San Blas, The.
Blind Bartimaeus at the gates.
Bridge, The.
Builders, The.
Building of the Ship, The.
Chaucer.
Children's Hour, The.
Christmas Bells.
Christmas Carols.
Couplet: February 24, 1847.
Cross of Snow, The.
Cumberland, The.
Curfew.
Dante.
Day is done, and the darkness, The.
Daybreak.
Divina Commedia, *sels.*
Elegiac Verse, *sels.*
(Evangeline), *sels.*
Evangeline, a Tale of Acadie, *sels.*
Evening Star, The.
Excelsior.
Fire of Drift-Wood, The.
Fragment: December 18, 1847.
From My Arm-Chair.
Galley of Count Arnaldos, The.
Golden Mile-Stone, The.
Harvest Moon, The.
Haunted Houses.
Hawthorne.
Holiest of all holidays are those, The.
Hymn to the Night.
In the Churchyard at Cambridge.
It Is Not Always May.
Jewish Cemetery at Newport, The.
Keats.
Kéramos, *sels.*
Killed at the Ford.

Legend of Rabbi Ben Levi, The.
Little Moon, The.
Meeting, The.
Mezzo Cammin.
Milton.
Morituri Salutamus, *sels.*
My Cathedral.
My Lost Youth.
Nature.
Night.
Nuremberg.
Old Clock on the Stairs, The.
Poets, The.
Poet's Calendar, The.
Possibilities.
Psalm of Life, A, *sels.*
Rain in Summer.
Rainy Day, The.
Rhyme of Sir Christopher, The.
Ropewalk, The.
Sand of the Desert in an Hour-Glass.
Seaweed.
Shakespeare.
Skeleton in Armor [*or* Armour], The.
Slave's Dream, The.
Snow-Flakes.
Song of Hiawatha, The, *sels.*
Song of the Bird, The.
Sound of the Sea, The.
Spanish Student, The, *sels.*
Spirit of Poetry, The.
Sunset.
Tales of a Wayside Inn, *sels.*
Three Kings came riding from far away.
Tide rises, the tide falls, The.
To the Driving Cloud.
Twilight is sad and cloudy, The.
Venice.
Village Blacksmith, The.
Wapentake.
Warning, The.
Wreck of the *Hesperus*, The.

Longfellow, Samuel (1819–92)
Again as evening's shadow falls.
Holy Spirit, Truth Divine.
O Life That Maketh All Things New.
'Tis Winter Now.

Longley, Michael (b. 1939)
Amish Rug, An.
Ash Keys.
Caravan.
Company.
Desert Warfare.
Detour.
Emily Dickinson.
Epithalamion: "These are the small hours when."
Fleance.
Freeze-up annexes the sea even, The.
Frozen Rain.
Ghetto.
Gorse Fires.
Hebrides, The.
In Memoriam.
In Memory of Gerard Dillon.
Kindertotenlieder.
Leaving Inishmore.
Letter to Derek Mahon.
Letter to Three Irish Poets, A.
Light Behind the Rain.
Linen Industry, The.
Man Lying on a Wall.
No Continuing City.
On Slieve Gullion 'men and mountain meet.'
Peace.
Persephone.
Remembering Carrigskeewaun.
Rune.
Skara Brae.
Strand, The.
Sulpicia.
Swans Mating.
Third Light, The.
West, The.
Words for Jazz Perhaps.
Wounds.
Wreaths, *sels.*

Lönnrot, Elias (1802–84)
Kalevala, The, *sels.*
Lonzano, Menahem ben Judah (d. after 1608)
Gentleman, The.
Loomis, Charles Battell (1861–1911)
Jack and Jill.
O-U-G-H.
Looney, George
Breaking the Surface.
Lopate, Phillip
Once a long time ago, you remember.
Lope de Vega Carpio, Félix (1562–1635)
At Dawn the Virgin Is Born.
Little Carol of the Virgin, A.
Song of the Virgin Mother, A.
Sonnet Right off the Bat.
To-Morrow.
Lopez-Penha, Abraham Z. (b. 1870)
Dusk.
López Velarde, Ramón (1888–1921)
Malefic Return, The.
My Cousin Agueda [*or* Agatha].
Lord, Everett W. (1871–1965)
Legend of the Admen, The.
Lord, Phillips H. (1902?–1975)
Your Church and Mine.
Lorde, Audre (1934–92)
Afterimages.
And What About the Children.
Beams.
Between Ourselves.
Black Mother Woman.
Chain.
Child Shall Lead, A.
Coal.
Coniagui women, The.
Conversations in Crisis.
Dahomey.
Echoes.
Ethiopia for Tifa.
Evening News, The.
Father Son and Holy Ghost.
Father, the Year Is Fallen.
Fishing the White Water.
For the Record.
From the House of Yemanjá.
Generation.
Hanging Fire.
Harriet there was always somebody calling us crazy.
Learning to Write.
Litany for Survival, A.
Love, Maybe.
Love Poem.
Meet.
Movement Song.
Naturally.
New York City 1970.
Night-Blooming Jasmine, The.
Now That I Am Forever with Child.
October, *sels.*
On a Night of the Full Moon.
Outlines.
Paperweight.
Political Relations.
Power.
Prologue, *sels.*
Question of Climate, A.
Revolution Is One Form of Social Change.
Rite of Passage.
Rock Thrown into the Water Does Not Fear the Cold, A.
Sisters in Arms.
Song for a Thin Sister.
Story Books on a Kitchen Table, *sels.*
Suffer the Children.
Summer Oracle.
Teacher.
What my child learns of the sea.
When the Saints Come Marching In.
Winds of Orisha, The.
Woman Thing, The.
Women of Dan Dance with Swords in Their Hands to Mark the Time When They Were Warriors, The.
Loseff [*or* Losev], Lev Vladimir (b. 1937)
Reading Milosz.

Tselkov: An Interpretation.
Lotaryov, Igor' Vasilievich. *See* "Severyanin, Igor"
"Lothrop, Amy." *See* Warner, Anna Bartlett
Lothrop, Harriett Mulford (1844–1921)
Little Brown Seed, The.
Louis, Adrian C. (b. 1846)
Couch Fantasy.
Dust World.
First of the Month, The.
Indian College Blues.
Practicing Death Songs.
Rhetoric Leads to Cliché.
Something About Being an Indian.
That Great Wingless Bird.
Wakinyan.
Lourie, Dick (b. 1931)
For All My Brothers and Sisters.
Louw, N. P. van Wyk (b. 1906)
Armed Vision.
At Dawn the Light Will Come.
Ballad of the Drinker in His Pub.
Dedication.
From the Ballad of Evil.
Gods Are Mighty, The.
Little Chisel, The.
Oh the Inconstant.
Oh wide and sad land, alone.
Raka, *sels.*
Love, Adelaide (b. 1890)
Walk Slowly.
Love, Monifa Atungaye (b. 1955)
Initiation.
Lovelace, Richard (1618–58)
Advice to My Best Brother, Colonel Francis Lovelace.
Against the Love of Great Ones.
Anniversary on the Hymeneals of My Noble Kinsman, Thomas Stanley, Esquire, An.
Another ("As I beheld a winters evening air.")
Another ("Centaur, siren [*or* syren], I forgo[e], The.")
Ant, The.
Apostasy of One and But One Lady, The.
Black Patch on Lucasta's Face, A.
Cupid Far Gone.
Dialogue.
Dual, The.
Elinda's [*or* Ellinda's] Glove.
Fair Beggar, The.
Falcon, The.
Fly about a Glass[e] of Burnt Claret, A.
Fly Caught in a Cobweb, A.
Fool much bit by fleas put out the light, A.
Grasshopper, The.
Gratiana Dancing [*or* Daucing] and [*or* &] Singing.
Her Muffe.
In Allusion to the French Song.
La Bella Bona-Roba.
La Bourbon, A.
Lady A. L., My Asylum [in a Great Extremity], The.
Lady with a Falcon on Her Fist, A.
Loose Saraband, A ("Nay, prethee [*or* prithee] dear, draw nigher.")
Love Enthroned.
Love Made in the First Age[: To Chloris].
Lucasta Laughing.
Lucasta's Fan[ne], with a Looking-Glass[e] in It.
Lucasta's World.
Mock Charon, A.
Mock Song, A.
Night! loathed [*or* loathèd] jailor of the locked-up [*or* lock'd up] sun.
On Sanazar's being honoured with six hundred Duckets by the Clarissimi of Venice, for composing an Elegiack Hexastick of The City. A Satyre.
Orpheus to Beasts.
Orpheus to Woods.
Painture [*or* Peinture].
Scrutiny [*or* Scrutinie], The.
Snail [*or* Snayl], The.

Song: "If to be absent were to be."
Song: "In mine one [or own] monument I lie
   [or lye]."
Song: "Strive not, vain Lover, to be fine."
Song: To Lucasta, Going to the War[re]s.
Sonnet: "Depose your finger of that Ring."
To a Lady That Desired Me I Would Bear
   My Part with Her in a Song.
To a Lady with Child that Asked [or Ask'd]
   an Old Shirt.
To Althea, from Prison.
To Amarantha, That She Would Dishevel[l]
   Her Hair[e].
To Dr. F. B. on His Book of Chess[e].
To Elinda.
To Lucasta.
To Lucasta: Her Reserved Looks.
To Lucasta ("Like to the sentinel stars, I
   watch all night.")
To Lucasta: The Rose.
To My Noble Kinsman, Thomas Stanley,
   Esquire, on His Lyric Poems Composed by
   Master John Gamble.
To My Truly Valiant, Learned Friend, Who
   in His Book Resolved the Art Gladiatory
   into the Mathematics.
To My Worthy Friend Mr. Peter Lely [or
   Lilly].
Upon the Curtain[e] of Lucasta's Picture [It
   Was Thus Wrought].
Valiant Love.
Vintage to the Dungeon, The.

Loveman, Robert (1864–1923)
   (April Rain).

Lovibond, Edward (1724–75)
   To Miss Kitty Phillips.

Loving, Pierre (1893–1950)
   Black Horse Rider, The.

Low, Patricia (b. 1932)
   First Day of the Hunting Moon, The.
   Wet Weather.

Low, Samuel (b. 1765)
   To a Segar.

Lowbury, Edward (b. 1913)
   Huntsman, The.
   Swan.

Lowe, C. M. (b. 1930)
   Hay-Time.

Lowe, Robert, Viscount Sherbrooke (1811–92)
   Songs of the Squatters.

Lowell, Amy (1874–1925)
   April.
   Artist, The.
   Autumn.
   Behind a Wall.
   Bullion.
   Bungler, The.
   Camouflaged Troop-Ship.
   Carrefour.
   Chinoiseries.
   Cyclists, The.
   Decade, [A].
   Desolation.
   Dreams in War Time, sels.
   Eleanora Duse, sels.
   Epitaph on a Young Poet Who Died before
     Having Achieved Success.
   Falling Snow.
   Fisherman's Wife, The.
   Free Fantasia on Japanese Themes.
   Frimaire.
   From One Who Stays.
   Garden by Moonlight, The.
   Grotesque.
   Hoar-Frost.
   Hora Stellatrix.
   Interlude.
   Katydids.
   Lady, A.
   Left Behind.
   Letter, The.
   Lilacs.
   Madonna of the Evening Flowers.
   Meeting-House Hill.
   Music.
   Night Clouds.

Opal.
Painted Ceiling, The.
Patterns.
Petals.
Preparation.
Proportion.
Sea Shell.
Shower, A.
Sisters, The.
Solitaire.
Sprig of Rosemary, A.
Summer Rain.
Taxi, The.
To a Friend.
To John Keats.
To Winky.
Venus Transiens.
Weather-Cock Points South, The.
Wind and Silver.

Lowell, James Russell (1819–91)
   After the Burial.
   Auspex.
   Bibliolaters, sels.
   Biglow Papers, The, sels.
   Birthday Verses Written in a Child's Album.
   Boss, The.
   Contrast, A.
   Darkened Mind, The.
   Fable for Critics, A, sels.
   First Snowfall [or Snow-Fall], The.
   Fitz Adam's Story.
   Fountain, The.
   His Throne Is with the Outcast.
   Hob Gobbling's Song.
   In a Copy of Omar Khayyám.
   In an Album.
   Joys.
   Memoriae Positum R. G. Shaw.
   Misconception, A.
   My Love.
   Ode Recited at the Harvard Commemoration
     (July 21, 1865), sels.
   Oriental Apologue, An.
   Origin of Didactic Poetry, The.
   Present Crisis, The, sels.
   Remembered Music.
   Science and Poetry.
   Sixty-Eighth Birthday.
   Sonnet.
   Stanzas on Freedom, sels.
   Street, The.
   Tempora Mutantur.
   To the Dandelion, sels.
   To the Spirit of Keats.
   Under the Willows, sels.
   Vision of Sir Launfal, The, sels.
   Yussouf.

Lowell, Maria White (1821–53)
   Opium Fantasy, An.
   Rouen, Place de la Pucelle.

Lowell, Robert (1917–77)
   After the Convention.
   After the Surprising Conversions.
   Alfred Corning Clark.
   As a Plane Tree by the Water.
   At the Indian Killer's Grave.
   Between the Porch and the Altar, sels.
   Beyond the Alps.
   Book of Wisdom, The.
   Central Park.
   Children of Light.
   Child's Song.
   Christmas Eve under Hooker's Statue.
   Colloquy in Black Rock.
   Commander Lowell.
   David and Bathsheba in the Public Garden.
   Dead in Europe, The.
   Death and the Bridge.
   Death of the Sheriff, The.
   Dolphin.
   Down the Nile.
   Drunken Fisherman, The.
   End of a Year.
   Epilogue: "Those blessèd structures, plot and
     rhyme."
   Exile's Return, The.
   Eye and Tooth.

Ezra Pound.
Fall 1961.
Falling Asleep over the Aeneid.
Fat Man in the Mirror, The.
Fishnet.
For George Santayana.
For John Berryman.
For Sale.
For Sheridan.
For the Union Dead.
Ford Madox Ford ("Lobbed ball plops, then
   dribbles to the cup, The.")
Ford Madox Ford ("Taking Ford's dictation
   on Samuel Butler.")
Fourth of July in Maine.
Frederick Kuh, Manx Cat.
George III.
Ghost is someone: death has left a hole, A.
Grandparents.
Harriet.
Hawthorne.
History has to live with what was here.
Holy Innocents, The.
Home after Three Months Away.
Identification in Belfast (I.R.A. Bombing).
In Memory of Arthur Winslow, sels.
In the Cage.
In the Ward.
It Did.
July in Washington.
Katherine's Dream.
Lady Ralegh's Lament.
Last Things, Black Pines at 4 a.m.
Lesson, The.
Mad Negro Soldier Confined at Munich, A.
Man And Wife.
March 1, The.
March 1, The.
Memories of West Street and Lepke.
Mexico, sels.
Mr. Edwards and the Spider.
Mouth of the Hudson, The.
My Last Afternoon with Uncle Devereux
   Winslow.
Near the Ocean.
Neo-Classical Urn, The.
New Year's Day.
Night Sweat.
Nihilist as Hero, The.
Notice.
Obit.
Old Flame, The.
Opposite House, The.
Public Garden, The.
Quaker Graveyard in Nantucket, The.
Reading Myself.
Robespierre and Mozart as Stage.
Sailing Home from Rapallo.
Saint-Just 1767-93 ("Saint-Just: his name
   seems stolen from the Missal.")
Salem.
Shako, The.
Shifting Colors.
Skunk Hour.
Soft Wood.
Stalin.
Suicide.
T. S. Eliot.
Those before Us.
To Delmore Schwartz.
To Speak of Woe That Is in Marriage.
Ulysses.
Violence.
Voyage, The, sels.
Waking Early Sunday Morning.
Waking in the Blue.
Watchmaker God.
Water.
Where the Rainbow Ends.
Words for Hart Crane.
Writers, sels.

Lowell, Robert Traill Spence (1816–91)
   Brave Old Ship, the Orient, The.

Lowery, Mike (b. 1941)
   Nam.
   Smell of Old Newspapers Is Always Stronger
     after Sleeping in the Sun, The.

Stroke.

Lowry, Malcolm (1909–57)
After Publication of Under the Volcano.
Cantinas, The, *sels.*
Christ Walks in This Infernal District Too.
Death of a Oaxaquenian.
Drunkards, The, *sels.*
Epitaph: "Malcolm Lowry."
Eye-Opener.
For *Under the Volcano.*
He Liked the Dead.
Joseph Conrad.
Roar of the Sea and the Darkness, The, *sels.*
Salmon Drowns Eagle.
Sestina in a Cantina.
Strange Type.
Volcano is dark and suddenly thunder, The.
Wild Cherry, The.
Xochitepec.

Lowry, Robert (1862–99)
Beautiful River.

Lowther, Pat (1935–75)
Last Letter to Pablo.
Stone Diary, A.

Loy, Mina (1882–1966)
Love Songs.
Lunar Baedeker.
Three Moments in Paris.

Lu Chao-lin (c.641–680)
Lotuses on the Crooked Pond.
Mount Wu Is High.
Weary Road, The.

Lu Chi (261–303)
She Thinks of Her Beloved.
Two Poems Presented to the Gentleman in
the Office of Palace Writers Ku Yen-hsien,
sels.
Visit to the Monastery of Good Omen.

Lu Chih (1246?–1309?)
Tune: "Intoxication in the East Wind"
Autumn Scenery.
Tune: "Pleasure in Front of the Hall," *sels.*
Tune: "Song of the Lunar Palace."
Tune: "*Wu-t'ung* Leaves"—Written in Jest at
a Banquet.

"Lu Hsün" (Chou Shu-jen) (1881–1936)
Call to Arms.
Hesitation.
In Remembrance of the Forgotten.
Lamenting Yang Ch'uan.
Self-mockery.
Sending Off O.E. Who Brought an Orchid
Home to Japan.

Lu Kuei Meng (d. c.881)
Fisherman on a Southern Stream.
Lone Wild Goose, A.
Replying to Hsi-mei's "Thoughts in Early
Autumn."
To an Old Tune.

Lu Lun (*fl.* c.770)
Frontier Songs, *sels.*

Lu T'ung ("Yu-ch'uan-tzu") (d. 835)
Eclipse of the Moon, The.

Lu Yu (1125–1210)
After Getting Drunk, I Scribble Songs and
Poems.
Autumn Thoughts.
Autumn Thoughts ("Mornings up before the
rooster calls.")
Autumn Thoughts ("Sumac showing faint
traces of red.")
Blue Rapids.
Boating in Autumn.
Border Mountain Moon.
Evening in the Village.
Farm Families, *sels.*
Feeling Sorry for Myself.
Harp Song.
Herd-Boy, A.
How I Sailed on the Lake till I Came to the
Eastern Stream.
I Get Up at Dawn.
I Had Occasion to Tell a Visitor about an
Old Trip I Took.
I Walk Out into the Country at Night.
Idle Thoughts.

Idleness.
Impressions.
In a Boat on a Summer Evening.
In a Boat on a Summer Evening, I Heard the
Cry of a Water Bird.
In a Dream.
In a Dream I Traveled among Ten Thousand
Acres of Lotuses.
In the Country.
Inscribed on My Grass-script Calligraphy
Written While Drunk.
Insomnia.
It Has Snowed Repeatedly and We Can
Count On a Good Crop of Wheat and
Barley.
Lazy.
Leaving the Monastery Early in the Morning.
Long Sigh.
Merchant's Joy, The.
My Village Home.
Night Thoughts.
Occasional Poem, A.
Pedlar of Spells, The.
Phoenix Hairpins.
Rain Cleared and the Breeze and Sunshine
Are Superb as I Stroll Outside the Gate,
The.
Rain on the River.
Sailing on the Lake to the Ching River.
Sending Tzu-lung Off to a Post in Chi-chou.
Shown to My Son Yü.
Sitting Outdoors.
Sitting Up at Night.
Sounds of Autumn.
Stone on the Hilltop, The.
Third Month, Night of the Seventeenth,
Written While Drunk.
To Show My Sons.
Trip to Mountain West Village, A.
Tune: "Bean Leaves Yellow."
Tune: "Immortal at the Magpie Bridge."
Tune: "Immortal at the Magpie Bridge"—On
Hearing the Cuckoo at Night.
Tune: "Phoenix Hairpin."
Tune: "Song of Divination"—On the Plum
Tree.
Tune: "Telling of Innermost Feelings."
Vegetable Garden.
Wild Flower Man, The.
Written at Random.
Written in a Carefree Mood.

Lu Yün (262–303)
For Ku Yen-hsien, A Poem for Him to Give
to His Wife.
Peacock flew, far off to the south-east; A.
Valley Wind, The.

Luân Hoán (Lê Ngoc Châu (b. 1941)
Washing My Wife's Clothes.

Lucan (Marcus Annaeus Lucanus) (A.D. 39–65)
All great things crush themselves.
Cato at his wedding.
Cato in the desert.
Civile Wares betweene the Howses of
Lancaster and Yorke, The, *sels.*
False One, The, *sels.*
Hudibras, *sels.*
Pharsalia, *sels.*
Pompey compared with Caesar.
Pompey's death and apotheosis.
Sacred wood, The.
Shame, no Statist.
Wonder of Women, or The Tragedie of
Sophonisba, The, *sels.*

Lucas, Alice (1852–1935)
Prayer before Sleep.

Lucas, Edward Verrall (1868–1938)
Mr. Coggs.
O England, Country of My Heart's Desire.
Pekinese / Adore their ease, The.
Windmill, The.

Lucas, Frank Lawrence (1894–1967)
Spain, 1809.

Lucas, Russell
Bishop's hand on a widow's breast, A.
Limerick: "There was a young lady from
Ulva."

Lucas, St. John (1879–1934)
Curate Thinks You Have No Soul, The.

Lucas, Tony (b. 1941)
Town Garden, A.

Luciano, Felipe
You're Nothing but a Spanish Colored Kid.

Lucianus [*or* Lucian] (b. c.125, d. after 180)
Artificial Beauty.
Beard-wagging stick-waving beggarman
Cynic, A.
Calimachus.
Do tell me, Hermes, what was it like when
the soul.
Enjoy your fortune as if you were about to
die.
For Glaukos, for the Nereids.
For mortals, mortal things. And all things
leave us.
I am Priapus. I was put here according to
custom.
I was Kallimachos, age five.
If you really imagine wisdom grows with a
beard.
On an Infant.
Poor painter captures, The.
To Glaukos, and to Nereus.
Vile mouth of the exorcist, The.
We were all drunk, and Acindynus was
determined to keep sober.
Weak man is like a broken jug, A.
Worthless man is a leaking wine-jar, A.

Lucie-Smith, Edward (b. 1933)
Hymn Tunes, The.
Imperialists in Retirement.
Lesson, The.
Poet in Winter.
Wise Child, The.
Your Own Place.

Lucilius (*fl.* 1st cent. A.D.)
Apollophanes married for an alibi.
As a poet put it once, an ant / may seem 'a
monstrous elephant.'
As thin little Proclus was fanning the fire.
Asclepiades the Miser was horrified.
Aulus / is childless.
Bad actors love to play great villains.
Cleombrotus the bruiser.
Crown your Bacchus with lettuce leaves, not
ivy.
Diophon, seeing / another man.
Doubly unfortunate are those who dwell in
Hell—.
Eutychides the thief was in a rare.
Eutychides, who wrote the songs. *From*
Variations of Greek Themes.
Eutychos was prolific as a painter.
Eutychus the painter / Fathered twenty sons.
Final adventure of Skinny Marcus—.
Further adventure of Skinny Marcus—.
Gently, so as not to rouse / His skinny girl.
Here I am launching my Second Book of
Epigrams—.
Hermogenes is rather short.
HIS GRATEFUL OPPONENTS SET UP THIS
STATUE OF APIS THE BOXER.
I'm round at Heliodorus' place—.
It's said you take a long time over a bath.
Lazy Marcus once dreamed.
Lean Gaius, who was thinner than a straw.
Lifted by a little breeze.
Light-fingered Dio takes after the God of
Thieves.
Lysimachus' cushion caught Antiochus' eye.
Marcus in the armed hoplites' race.
Mean old Hermon.
My Dad was worried about his brother.
Of a covetous Niggard, and a needie Mouse.
Olympicus, the welter-weight.
Olympikos, with your ugly face.
On an Old Woman.
On Kriton the Miser.
Orator Flaccus can commit solecisms.
Poor Calpurnius, the most Schweikian soldier
in the land.
Recent earthquake, A.
Some say you dye your hair, Nikylla.
That poet is best.

There's one Grammarian I know.
They whisper of you, Nicole.
Tiny Erotion, borne away / By a gnat had this to say.
Treasure.
Well, Menestratus, you ask me what I think.
When Hermocrates the Miser lay in bed.
Wig, rouge, honey, wax, teeth.
With a lucky charm around his throat.
Zenonis has a splendid tutor for her son—.

Lucretius (Titus Lucretius Carus) (94–55 B.C.)
Against the Fear of Death, *sels.*
Beyond Religion.
De Rerum Natura (On the Nature of Things), *sels.*
Dissolution of the world proovd from the mortality of every part, The.
Epicurus praised.
Euphemisms of the love-blind.
Felicitie of a mind imbracing vertue, that beholdeth the wretched desyres of the worlde, The.
First principles of Epicurean physics.
Gods, by right of Nature, must possess, The.
How They Communicate.
Lucretius. Book the Fifth, *sels.*
Lucretius Paraphrased.
Poem Sacred to the Memory of Sir Isaac Newton, A, *sels.*
Posture, The.
Symptoms of plague in Athens.
Threshold Of The New, The.

Lucy, Sean (b. 1931)
Friday Evening.
Longshore Intellectual.
Missing Link.
Senior Members.
Supervising Examinations.
These Six.

Ludlow, Fitz Hugh (1836–90)
Socrates Snooks.
Too Late.

Ludvigson, Susan Bartels (b. 1942)
Jeanne d'Arc.
Man Arrested in Hacking Death Tells Police He Mistook Mother-in-Law for Raccoon.
Punishment, The.
Some Notes on Courage.
Widow, The.

Lugovskoy [*or* Lugovskoi], Vladimir Aleksandrovich (1901–57)
Bandit, The.
Bear, The.
Woman / that I knew, The.

Lui Chi (1311–75)
Poet Thinks, A.

Lukonin, Mikhail Kuz'mich (1918–76)
My Friends.
Stalingrad Theater.
To Kolya Otrada.

Lum, Wing Tek
Backup, The.
Chinese Hot Pot.
Going Home.
On M. Butterfly.
Picture of my Mother's Family, A.
Riding the North Point Ferry.
Urban Love Songs.

Lummis, Charles Fletcher (1859–1928)
Poe-'em of Passion, A.

Lumumba, Patrice Emery (1926–51)
Dawn in the Heart of Africa.

Lupellus
Limerick: "Solipsist with triplets said: 'Though,' A."

Luria, Isaac (1534–72)
Sabbath of Rest, A.

Luswat
Shaman Song.

Luther, Martin (1483–1546)
Cradle Hymn.
Ein feste Burg ist unser Gott.
From depths of woe I cry to you.
From heaven above to earth I come.
From Heaven High I Come to You.

In the bonds of Death He lay.
In the very midst of life.
Mighty Fortress Is Our God, A.

Luttrell, Henry (1765?–1851)
Letter to Julia, in Rhyme, *sels.*
O death, thy certainty is such.
On a Man Run Over by an Omnibus.

Lu'u Văn Vong (Trần Văn Bảng) (fl. 20th cent.)
Paradise.
Run! Run!

Lux, Thomas (b. 1946)
Amiel's Leg.
Barn Fire.
Farmers.
Flying Noises.
Gold on Mule.
Grim Town in a Steep Valley.
History and Abstraction.
History Books.
If You See This Man.
Lament City.
Little Tooth, A.
Midnight Tennis Match, The.
Milkman and His Son, The.
My Grandmother's Funeral.
Night above the Town.
Solo Native.
Tarantulas on the Lifebuoy.
There Were Some Summers.
This Is a Poem for the Fathers and for Michael Ryan.

Luzzatto, Isaac (fl. 16th cent.)
Death, Thou Hast Seized Me.

Luzzatto, Moses Hayyim, of Padua (1707–47)
Unto the Upright Praise, *sels.*

Lvov, Mikhail Davidovich (1916–87)
To become a man, it's little to be born.

Lvov, Vladimir Iul'evich (1926–61)
That yellowed body of the Lord.

Ly Ngoc Kieu (Dieu Nhan) (1041–1113)
Birth, old age.

Lý Thu'ò'ng Kiệt (1019–1105)
Southern emperor rules the Southern land, The.

Lyall, Sir Alfred Comyn (1835–1911)
Studies at Delhi, 1876, *sels.*

Lydgate, John (1370?–1451?)
Balade Simple.
Boy Serving at Table, The.
Complaint of the Black Knight, The, *sels.*
Court of Sapience, *sels.*
Henry before Agincourt: October 25, 1415.
Lover's New Year's Gift, A.
Siege of Thebes, The, *sels.*
Vox Ultima Crucis.

Lydston, Donna R.
Family, The.

Lyle, K. Curtis (b.1944)
Lacrimas or There Is a Need to Scream.
Sometimes I Go to Camarillo and Sit in the Lounge.
Songs for the Cisco Kid; or, Singing for the Face.
Songs for the Cisco Kid; or, Singing: Song #2.
Tampa Red's Contemporary Blues.

Lyles, Peggy
Doe's leap, A.
Moon.
Summer night.
Summer stillness.

Lyly, John (1553–1606)
Alexander and Campaspe, *sels.*
Endimion, *sels.*
Midas, *sels.*
Mother Bombie, *sels.*
Sapho and Phao, *sels.*

Lyly, John and Thomas Ravenscroft
Mayde's Metamorphosis, The, *sels.*

Lynch, Charles (b. 1943)
If We Cannot Live People as People.
Memo.

Lynch, Thomas Toke (1818–71)
Lift Up Your Heads, Rejoice!

Lynche, Richard (fl. 1596–1601)
Diella, *sels.*

Lynd, Sylvia (1888–1952)
Beauty and the Beast.
Solitary, The.

Lynde, Benjamin (1666–1745)
Lines Descriptive of Thomson's Island.

Lyon, George Ella (b. 1949)
Archaeology.
Birth.
Foot-Washing, The.
Inventing Sin.
Salvation.
Visit, A.

Lyon, P. H. B. (b. 1893)
Envoi: "Earth puts her colours by."

Lyons, A. Neil (1880–1940)
Fairy Cobbler, The.

Lyons, John C. M. (b. 1959)
Island Muse.
Lure of the Cascadura.
"Skin Skin, Yuh Na Know Meh."

Lysaght, Sidney Royce
Deserted Home, A.

Lysohorsky, Ondra (1909–89)
At a Sunlit Window.
Ballad of Jan Palach, Student and Heretic.
22.6.1941.

Lyte, Henry Francis (1793–1847)
Abide with me[; fast falls the eventide].

Lytle, William Haines (1826–63)
Antony and Cleopatra.

Lyttelton, George (1709–73)
Happiest Pair, The.
Soliloquy of a Beauty in the Country.

Lytton, Edward Robert Bulwer-Lytton, 1st Earl of. *See* "Meredith, Owen"

M

"M." (fl. c.1776)
On the Frequent Review of the Troops.

"M., H."
Limerick: "There once was a Scot who said: 'Evil.'"

M–rt–n, B–ll (fl. c.1726)
Humble Wish, The.

"M., X. A."
Limerick: "What! Parted! Not even a kiss?"

"Ma." *See* Rainey, Gertrude "Ma"

Ma Chih-yüan (1260?–1334?)
Four Poems to the Tune "Ch'ing-chiang yin," *sels.*
Three Poems to the tune "Lo-mei Feng," *sels.*
Three Poems to the Tune "Ssu-k'uai yü," *sels.*
To the Tune "Shui hsien-tzu."
To the Tune "T'ien ching sha," *sels.*
Tune: "Four Pieces of Jade"—Retirement.
Tune: "Sailing at Night"—A Song Sequence.
Tune: "Sky-clear Sand"—Autumn Thoughts.
Tune: "Slow Chant."
Tune: "Song of Shou-yang," *sels.*
Two Poems to the Tune "Chin-tzu ching"
The Sutra in Gold Characters, *sels.*
Two Poems to the Tune "Po pu tuan," *sels.*

Mabuza, Lindiwe
Summer nineteen seventy.

Mac an Bhaird, Geoffrey Mac Briain (fl. c.1600)
Morning Prayer.

Mac an Bhaird, Laoiseach (fl. late 16th cent.)
Fond greeting, hillock there, A.
Two Sons.

Mac Coisdealbhaigh, Tomas ("Laider") (fl. mid–17th cent.)
Una Bhan.

Mac Con Brettan, Bláthmac (fl. 8th cent.)
Poem to Mary, A, *sels.*

Mac Con Midhe, Giolla Brighde (fl. mid–13th cent.)
Defence of Poetry, A.

Mac Cuarta, Seamas Dall (1650–1733)
Houses of Corr an Chait are cold, The.

Mac Giolla Ghunna, Cathal Buidhe (c.1680–1756)
Yellow Bittern, The.

Mac Low, Jackson (b. 1922)
Almost Casanova Electricity.
1st Dance—Making Things New—6 February 1964.
Giant Otters.
Giant Philosophical Otters.
Lack of Balance but not Fatal, A.
Mani-Mani Gatha.
Pieces O'six—XVIII.
Pieces O'six—XXIV.
7th Light Poem: For John Cage—17 June 1962.
27th Dance—Walking—22 March 1964.

Mac Siomoin, Tomas (b. 1938)
Silence, The.

Mac Thiên Tích (d. 1780)
Morning Bell at Tiêu Monastery, The.

MacAndrew, Rachel
Pony, The.
Robin Hood.

Macarthur, Bessie J. B. (b. 1889)
Nocht o' Mortal Sicht.

Macartney, Frederick Thomas Bennett (1887–1980)
Early Summer Sea-Tryst.
Kyrielle: Party Politics.
No Less than Prisoners.

Macaulay, F. E. M. (fl. c.1904)
Women's Marseillaise, The.

Macaulay, Rose (1881–1958)
Many Sisters to Many Brothers.

Macaulay, Thomas Babington Macaulay, 1st Baron (1800–1859)
Armada, The, sels.
Battle of Naseby, The.
Country Clergyman's Trip to Cambridge, The.
Dies Iræ.
Jacobite's Epitaph, A.
Lays of Ancient Rome, sels.
Radical War Song, A.

MacBeth [or Macbeth], George (1932–92)
Bedtime Story.
Draft for an Ancestor.
Five-Minute Orlando Macbeth, The.
Killing, The.
Land-Mine, The.
Miner's Helmet, The.
Ode to English Food, An.
Orange Poem, The.
Orlando Commercial, The.
Political Orlando, The.
Renewal, The.
Return, The.
Rumanian of Maria Banus, The, sels.
Scissor-Man.
Snowdrops.
Star, A.
Wasps' Nest, The.
When I Am Dead.

MacCaig, Norman (b. 1910)
After His Death.
Aspects.
Aunt Julia.
Basking Shark.
Beach Talk.
Blue Tit on a String of Peanuts.
By Achmelvich Bridge.
Byre.
Celtic Cross.
Close-ups of Summer.
Cock before Dawn.
Crofter's Kitchen, Evening.
Drifter.
Drowned, The.
Ego.
Explicit Snow.
Feeding Ducks.
Fetching Cows.
Flooded Mind.
Golden Calf.

Gone Are the Days.
Half-Built Boat in a Hayfield.
In My Mind.
Interruption to a Journey.
Intruder in a Set Scene.
July Evening.
Kingfisher.
Loch Sionascaig.
Looking Down on Glen Canisp.
Midnight, Lochinver.
Milne's Bar.
Moorings.
Movements.
No Interims in History.
Nude in a Fountain.
Old Edinburgh.
Old Maps and New.
Orgy.
Porpoises.
Praise of a Collie.
Ringed Plover by a Water's Edge.
Sheep Dipping.
Shore Road, The.
Sleet.
Solitary crow.
Sounds of the Day.
Spate in Winter Midnight.
Stars and Planets.
Summer Farm.
Things in Each Other.
Too Bright a Day.
Two Friends.
Wild Oats.

MacCarthy, Denis Florence (1817–82)
Paschal Fire, The.
Pillar Towers of Ireland, The.
Voyage of St. Brendan, The, sels.

MacCathmhaoil, Seosamh. See Campbell, Joseph

Maccius
I swore, love, by your / dominion, to rest.
Philistion's a hard bitch:/ in her book "penniless lover."
Your pleasure, Priapus, is the island coast.

MacColl, Dugald Sutherland (1859–1948)
Miners' Response, The.

MacConglinne (fl. 12th cent.)
Vision of MacConglinne, The.

MacDermot, Thomas (1870–1933)
Cuba.
Market Basket in the Car, A.
San Gloria, sels.

"MacDiarmid, Hugh" (Christopher Murray Grieve) (1892–1978)
Another Epitaph on an Army of Mercenaries.
At My Father's Grave.
Bagpipe Music.
Bonnie Broukit Bairn, The.
British Leftish Poetry, 1930-40.
By Wauchopeside.
Cattle Show.
Cloudburst and Soaring Moon.
Cophetua.
Crowdieknowe.
Crystals like Blood.
Dead Liebknecht, The.
Drunk Man Looks at the Thistle, A, sels.
Eemis-Stane, The.
Empty Vessel.
Ex Vermibus.
Facing the Chair.
Farmer's Death.
First Hymn to Lenin.
Fleggit Bride, The.
Glen of Silence, The.
Glog-Hole, The.
Great Wheel, The.
Harry Semen.
Ho, my little sparrow! For well I know.
I heard Christ sing quhile roond him dar.
In Memoriam James Joyce, sels.
In the Children's Hospital.
In the Pantry.
Innumerable Christ, The.
Lament for the Great Music, sels.
Light of Life, The.
Lourd on my hert as winter lies.

Love.
Moonlight among the Pines.
Moonstruck.
O wha's the bride that carries the bunch.
Old Wife in High Spirits.
On a Raised Beach.
On the Ocean Floor.
On the Oxford Book of Victorian Verse.
One of the Principal Causes of War.
Parley of Beasts.
Parrot Cry, The.
Perfect.
Prayer for a Second Flood.
Reflections in a Slum.
Robber, The.
Royal Stag, The.
Sauchs in the Reuch Heuch Hauch, The.
Scotland small? Out multiform, our infinite Scotland small?
Scunner.
Second Hymn to Lenin, sels.
Sic Transit Gloria Scotia.
Skeleton of the Future, The.
Spanish War, The.
Storm-Cock's Song, The.
Sunny Gale.
To a Sea Eagle.
Two Parents, The.
Under the Greenwood Tree.
Water Music, sels.
Watergaw, The.
Weapon, The.
Wheesht, wheesht, my foolish hert.
Whip-the-World.
With a Lifting of the Head.
With the Herring Fishers.

MacDonagh, Donagh (1912–68)
Ballade which Villon Made.
Charles Donnelly, sels.
Dublin Made Me.
Going to Mass Last Sunday.
Hungry Grass, The.
Just an Old Sweet Song.
Prothalamium.
Veterans, The.
Warning to Conquerors, A.

Macdonagh, Thomas (1878–1916)
John-John.
Lifting of the Cloud, The.
Man Upright, The.
Wishes for My Son.

Macdonald, Andrew (1755?–1790)
Lover's Leap; a Tale, The.

MacDonald, Cynthia (b. 1932)
Celebrating the Freak.
Inheritance.
Instruction from Bly.
Lady Pitcher, The.
Late Mother, The.
Objets D'Art.
Two Brothers in a Field of Absence.

Macdonald, George (1824–1905)
At the Back of the North Wind, sels.
Baby-Sermon, A.
Better Things.
Christmas Prayer, A.
Diary of an Old Soul, sels.
Here lie I, Martin Elginbrodde.
Hurt of Love, The.
Mammon Marriage.
No End of No-Story.
Paul Faber, Surgeon, sels.
Professor Noctutus.
Shall the Dead Praise Thee?
Sheep and the Goat, The.
Shortest and Sweetest of Songs, The.
Sweet Peril.
Things We Can Depend On.
Turn from Self.
Wind and the Moon, The.
Winter Song.

MacDonogh, Patrick (1902–61)
Escape to Love, sels.
No Mean City.
Now the Holy Lamp of Love.
She Walked Unaware.

Mace, Frances Laughton (1836–99)
Only Waiting.

Macedonius (fl. c.6th cent.)
Be patient, Morning Star, with Love; though close.
Beauty kissed your mouth, and gave the petals.
Because you will not hear it.
Dedication, A: "Anchored now to Neptune's temple floor, I."
Earth and Goddess of Birth.
Every year men harvest grapes, not seeing.
I dreamt I held the laughter-loving girl.
Praise memory and forgetfulness!
She who shook and swayed among the chorus.
They had the nerve to name you Constance.
You ask me, girl, why I withdraw my sword.
You neigh and whinny, seeming to invite.
You say "Tomorrow"; a tomorrow which.
You're here! I hadn't dared to hope. Surprise.

MacEwen, Gwendolyn (b. 1941)
Arcanum One.
Breakfast for Barbarians, A.
Caravan, The.
Dark Pines under Water.
Discovery, The.
Manzini; Escape Artist.
Open Secrets.
Sea Things.
T. E. Lawrence Poems, The, sels.
Thing is Violent, The.
Virgin Warrior, The.
You Cannot Do This.

MacEwen, Pearl Forbes
Kite, The.
My Little Dog.

MacFayden, H. R. (b. 1877)
Lone Wild Fowl, The.

MacGabhrain, Aodh. See **MacGowran, Hugh**

MacGill-Eain, Somhairle. See **MacLean, Sorley**

MacGill, Patrick (b. 1890)
Matey.
Star-shell holds the sky beyond, A.

Macgillivray, Pittendrigh (1856–1938)
Return, The.

MacGowran, Hugh (Aodh MacGabhrain) (fl. c.1720)
Description of an Irish Feast, The.
O'Rourke's Feast.

Macgoye, Marjorie Oludhe
August the First; Court Martial. The Mother Speaks.
August the First: The Shadow. Patel Speaks.
August the First: The Watchman Speaks.
For Miriam.
Mathenge.
Omera.

MacGreevy [or McGreevy], Thomas (1894–1967)
Aodh Ruadh O'Domhnaill.
De Civitate Hominum.
Homage to Hieronymus Bosch.
Homage to Jack Yeats.
Homage to Marcel Proust.
Nocturne of the Self-evident Presence.
Recessional.

Machado de Assis, Joaquim Maria (1839–1908)
Blue Fly.

Machado Ruiz, Antonio (1875–1939)
Between living and dreaming.
Come sing with me in chorus: it's nothing, all we know.
Coplas.
Dream Below the Sun, The, sels.
Ephemeral Past, The.
Here's another Spaniard! Welcome!
In our souls everything.
Lament of the Virtues and Verses on Account of the Death of Don Guido.
Last night, as I was sleeping.
Look, our Spaniard's yawning.
Lord, you have ripped away from me what I loved most.
Meditation for this Day.
Moral Proverbs and Folk Songs, sels.

On the Banks of the Duero.
Parables, I.
Poem: "Figures in the fields against the sky!"
Poem: "Frail sound of a tunic trailing, A."
Poem: "Naked is the earth."
Poem: "We think to create festivals."
Portrait.
Rainbow at Night.
Spanish Folk Songs, sels.
Summer Night.
Today's Meditation.
Wind, one brilliant day, called, The.
Yesterday, dreamed He was near me.

Machej, Zbigniew (b. 1958)
Orchards in July.

Machi, Tawara
Tanka: "All the more."
Tanka: "Although."
Tanka: "Arriving."
Tanka: "As though to let loose."
Tanka: "Cherry blossoms."
Tanka: "Freezing my smile."
Tanka: "From the moment."
Tanka: "Gazing upwards."
Tanka: "Letter, The."
Tanka: "Loneliness."
Tanka: "Looking as though."
Tanka: "My heart."
Tanka: "On a day."
Tanka: "Only the green."
Tanka: "Somehow this impulse."
Tanka: "This day in March."
Tanka: "Trying to wash away."
Tanka: "'Until age thirty.'"
Tanka: "With a serene look."
Tanka: "Woman, The."

Machiavelli, Niccolò (1469–1527)
Opportunity.

MacIntyre, Tom (b. 1933)
Drumlin Prayer.
On Sweet Killen Hill.
Yellow Bittern, The.

Mack, Alexander (1679–1735)
I Am the Lord.

Mack, L. V. (b. 1947)
Biafra.
Death Songs.

Mackail, John William
Positivists ever talk in s-/Uch an epic style as Dawkins. From Balliol Rhymes.

Mackail, John William and Cecil Arthur Spring-Rice
On the Hon. George Nathaniel Curzon, Commoner of Balliol. From Balliol Rhymes.

MacKay, Charles (1814–89)
Little and Great.
Louise on the Door-Step.
Mowers: An Anticipation of the Cholera, 1848, The.
Only a Thought.
Poor Man's Sunday Walk, The.
Ship, The.
Three Preachers, The.

Mackay, Helen
Train.

Mackay-Warna, Gordon
Cattle Loading.

MacKaye, Percy (1875–1956)
After Tempest.

MacKellar, Dorothea (b. 1885)
Arms and the Woman
Fancy Dress.
Heritage.

Mackellar, Thomas
At the door of Mercy Sighing.

MacKenzie, Ian T.
Limerick: "There was an old lady of Leicester."

Mackenzie, Kenneth (1913–55)
Autumn Mushrooms.
Caesura.
Children go, The.
Door swung open, The.
Earth Buried.

Fool, The.
Ginger-flowers.
God! How I Long for You.
Heat.
Hospital—Retrospections, The.
Searchlights.
Shall then another do what I have done.
Sick Men Sleeping.
Table-Birds.
Two Trinities.

Mackey, Mary (b. 1945)
Kama Sutra of Kindness: Position No. 2, The.

Mackey, Nathaniel (b. 1947)
Alphabet of Ahtt.
Capricorn Rising.
Dream Thief.
Falso Brilhante.
Ghede Poem.
John Coltrane Arrived with An Egyptian Lady.
Kiche Manitou.
Memphite Recension.
Phantom Light of All Our Day, The.
Shower of Secret Things, The.
Slipped Quadrant.
Song of the Andoumboulou.
Song of the Andoumboulou: 12.
Song of the Andoumboulou: 6.
Song of the Andoumboulou: 7.

MacKie, Alastair (b. 1925)
Back-Green Odyssey, sels.

Mackie, Albert D. (b. 1904)
New Spring, A.
Young Man and the Young Nun, The.

Mackintosh, Ewart Alan (1893–1917)
Cha Till Maccruimein (Departure of the 4th Camerons).
Farewell: "Well, you have gone now, comrades."
In Memoriam[, Private D. Sutherland].

Mackintosh, Newton (fl. c.1900)
Lucy Lake.

Macklin, Elizabeth (b. 1952)
Nearsighted, The.

Maclaurin, John, Lord Dreghorn (1734–96)
Elegy: "Nor Hammond's love nor Shenstone's was sincere."

Maclean, Alasdair (b. 1926)
Death of an Old Woman.
Home Thoughts from Home.
Rain, The.
Waking the Dead.

MacLean, Sorley (Somhairle MacGill-Eain) (b. 1911)
Black boat, perfect Greek.
Calvary.
Clan MacLean, The.
Cry of Europe, The.
Death Valley.
Going Westwards.
Hallaig.
Heroes.
Highland Woman, A.
My een are nae on Calvary.

MacLeish, Archibald (1892–1983)
Aeterna Poetae Memoria.
American Letter.
Ars Poetica.
Brave New World.
Burying Ground by the Ties.
Conquistador, sels.
Corporate Entity.
Critical Observations.
Eleven.
Empire Builders.
End of the World, The.
Epistle to Be Left in the Earth.
Epistle to the Rapalloan.
Ezry.
Fall of the City, The, sels.
Farm, The.
Genius, The.
Grazing Locomotives.
Hypocrite Auteur.
Immortal Autumn.

Immortal Helix.
Invocation to the Social Muse.
L'An Trentiesme de Mon Eage.
Lines for an Interment.
Long Hot Summer.
Memorial Rain.
Mother Goose's Garland.
My Naked Aunt.
Not Marble nor the Gilded Monuments.
Old Gray Couple, The.
Panic, *sels.*
Poem in Prose.
Poet Speaks from the Visitors' Gallery, A.
Pole Star for This Year.
Pony Rock.
Prologue: "These alternate nights and days, these seasons."
Reasons for Music.
Reconciliation, The.
Reproach to Dead Poets.
Seafarer.
Signature for Tempo.
Snowflake Which Is Now and Hence Forever, The.
Songs for Eve, *sels.*
Speech to a Crowd.
Speech to Those Who Say Comrade.
Starved Lovers.
Steamboat Whistle, The.
Too-Late Born, The.
Tourist Death.
Unfinished History.
Vicissitudes of the Creator.
Voyage to the Moon.
Voyage West.
Weather.
What Any Lover Learns.
What Riddle Asked the Sphinx.
Where the Hayfields Were.
Words in Time.
You Also, Gaius Valerius Catullus.
You, Andrew Marvell.

MacLellan, Robert (b. 1907)
Sang.

"Macleod, Fiona" (William Sharp) (1855–1908)
Bells of Youth, The.
Invocation of Peace, *sels.*
Moon-Child, The.
Unknown Wind, The.
Wasp, The.
White Peace, The.

MacLeod, Joseph Gordon ("Adam Drinan") (b. 1903)
Men of the Rocks, *sels.*

MacLeod, Mairi (1569–1674?)
Complaint about Exile, A.

MacLow, Jackson (b. 1922)
Antic Quatrains.
59th Light Poem: for La Monte Young and Marian Zazeela—6 November 1982.
1st Dance—Making Things New—6 February 1964.
Presidents of the United States of America, The, *sels.*
2nd Light Poem: For Diane Wakoski.
6th Dance—Doing Things With Pencils—17-18 February 1964.
Trope Market.
12th Dance—Getting Leather by Language—21 February 1964.
Twenties 27.
Twenties 26.
Zen Buddhism and Psychoanalysis / Psychoanalysis and Zen Buddhism.

MacManus, Anna Johnston. *See* "Carbery, Ethna"

MacMarcuis, Aindrais
This Night Sees Ireland Desolate.

MacMuireadach, Niall Mor
Soraidh Slan Don Oidhche Areir.

Macnab, Roy (b. 1923)
El Alamein Revisited.
Majuba Hill.
River used to store up in its mouth, The.
Road to Bologna, The.
Seven of the Clock.

MacNamara, Francis (b. 1811?)
Convict's Tour to Hell, A.
For the Company Underground.
Petition from the Chain Gang at Newcastle to Captain Furlong the Superintendent, A.

MacNamee, Giolla Brighde (*fl.* late 13th cent.)
Childless.

MacNeice, Louis (1907–63)
Alcohol.
Apple Blossom.
August.
Autobiography.
Autumn Journal, *sels.*
Autumn Sequel, *sels.*
Bad Dream.
Bagpipe Music.
Ballade of England.
Bar-Room Matins.
Belfast.
Birmingham.
Brandy Glass, The.
British Museum Reading Room, The.
Brother Fire.
Carrickfergus.
Charon.
Christmas Shopping.
Circe.
Closing Album, The, *sels.*
Coda.
Cradle Song: "Clock's untiring fingers wind the wool of darkness, The."
Dark Age Glosses, *sels.*
Death of a Cat, The, *sels.*
Ear, The.
Eclogue for Christmas, An.
Elegy for Minor Poets.
Entered in the Minutes, *sels.*
Entirely.
Figure of Eight.
Glass Falling.
Goodbye to London.
Grey Ones, The.
House on a Cliff.
Il Piccolo Rifiuto.
In Lieu.
Individualist Speaks, The.
Introduction, The.
Invocation: "Dolphin plunge, fountain play."
Jehu.
June Thunder.
Kingdom, The, *sels.*
Leaving Barra.
Libertine, The.
London Rain.
Meeting Point.
Mixer, The.
Morning Sun.
Museums offer us, running from among the buses.
Nature Morte.
Nature Notes, *sels.*
Nostalgia.
Novelettes, *sels.*
Nuts in May.
Old Story, The.
Perdita.
Perseus.
Pet Shop.
Prayer Before Birth.
Precursors.
Prognosis.
Prospect.
Sense of Smell, The.
Slow Movement.
Snow.
Soap Suds.
Spring Voices.
Springboard, The.
Star-Gazer.
Streets of Laredo, The.
Sunday Morning.
Sunlight on the garden, The.
Tam Cari Capitis.
Taxis, The.
Thalassa.
This Is the Life.
Tree Party.

Trilogy for X, *sels.*
Trolls, The, *sels.*
Truisms, The.
Turf-Stacks.
Variation on Heraclitus.
Whit Monday.
Wolves.
Woods.

MacNeill, Hector (1746–1818)
My Boy Tammy.

Macoubrie, John (1925–83)
Boethius at Cavalzero.

Macpherson, James ("Ossian") (1736–96)
Fragments of Ancient Poetry, Collected in the Highlands of Scotland, *sels.*

Macpherson, Jay (b. 1931)
Ark, The, *sels.*
Beauty of Job's Daughters, The.
Boatman, The.
Fisherman, The.
Garden of the Sexes, The.
Garden shut, a fountain sealed, A.
Go Take the World.
Hail Wedded Love!
Ill Wind, The.
Leviathan.
Lost Soul, A.
Martyrs, The.
Swan, The.
Third Eye, The.
Way Down, The, *sels.*
Well, The.

MacSweeney, Barry (b. 1948)
Blackbird: Elegy for William Gordon Calvert.

Macuilxochitl (b. c.1435)
Battle Song.

MacWard, Owen Roe (d. 1849) *and* **Hugh O'Donnell**
Dark Rosaleen.

Macy, Arthur (1842–1904)
Peppery Man was cross and thin, The.

Madan, Judith (1702–81)
Abelard to Eloisa.
Ode Composed on Sleep, An.
On Her Own Birthday.
To Lysander.

Madden, F. A. V.
I put my hat upon my head.

Maddox, Everette
Breakfast.
Great Man's Death: An Anecdote, The.
1941.

Madeleva, Sister Mary (b. 1887)
Candlemas Day.
Concerning Death, *sels.*
From an Afternoon Caller.
O / Holy / Wood.
Of Mary, *sels.*

Madge, Charles (b. 1912)
At War.
Birds of Tin, The.
Blocking the Pass.
Fortune.
Landscape I.
Loss.
Lusty Juventus.
Monument, A.
On One Condition.
Poem: "Walls of the maelstrom are painted with trees, The."
Solar Creation.
Times, The.

Madgett, Naomi Long (Naomi Long Witherspoon) (b. 1923)
Alabama Centennial.
Black Woman.
Brothers at the Bar.
Deacon Morgan.
Dream Sequence, Part 9.
Echoes.
Exits and Entrances.
Her Story.
Images.
Midway.
Mortality.

New Day.
Nomen.
Offspring.
Pavlov.
Plea for My Heart's Sake.
Quest.
Race Question, The.
Sally: Twelfth Street.
Simple.
Souvenir.
Star Journey.
Twenty Grand (Saturday Night on the Block),
   The.
Woman with Flower.

Madhubuti, Haki R. (Don. L. Lee) (b. 1942)
African Poems, *sels.*
After Her Man Had Left Her for the Sixth
   Time That Year / (An Uncommon
   Occurrence).
America calling.
Assassination.
Awareness.
Back Again, Home.
Big Momma.
Black woman Poems, *sels.*
But He was Cool; or, He Even Stopped for
   Green Lights.
Change is Not Always Progress.
Change-Up.
Communication in Whi-te.
Don't Cry, Scream.
Empty Warriors.
Judy-One.
Knocking Donkey Fleas off a Poet from the
   Southside of Chi.
Loneliness, A.
Long Reality, The.
Malcolm Spoke / Who Listened?
Man Thinking about Woman.
Men and Birth: the Unexplainable.
Mixed Sketches.
My brothers i will not tell you.
One Sided Shoot-Out.
Poem for a Poet, A.
Poem Looking for a Reader, A.
Poem to Complement Other Poems, A.
Poet: What Ever Happened to Luther?
Positives for Sterling Plumpp.
Primitive, The.
React for Action.
Self-Hatred of Don L. Lee, The.
Union of Two, The.
Wake-up Niggers.
We Walk the Way of the New World.

Madigan, Rick (fl. 20th cent.)
Curtis Fuller.
Stereo Time with Booker Little.

Madison, Dolley (1768–1849)
Lafayette.

Maeterlinck, Maurice (1862–1949)
Last Words, The.
Song: "Three little maidens they have slain."

Magee, John Gillespie, Jr. (1922–41)
High Flight.

Magee, Kevin (b. 1957)
Instrumentum Vocale.
Tedium Drum, Part IV, *sels.*

Magee, Michael (b. 1946)
It Is the Stars That Govern Us.

Magee, Thomas D'Arcy (fl. c.1848)
Celtic Cross, The.
Celts, The.

Magee, Wes (b. 1939)
Are You Ready?
British Garden, A.
Epitaphs for some Space Beasts.
Fungus Fingers, The.
Giant Rocket.
Gran's Green Parrot.
How to Reach the Sun. . . on a Piece of
   Paper.
What is the Sun?

Mager, Don (b. 1942)
Letters from a Married Man, *sels.*

Maginn, William (1793–1842)
Rime of the Auncient Waggonere, The.

Magowan, Robin (b. 1936)
Days of 1956.
Paros. A day mild as morning's milk.
Susan.
Zeimbekiko.
Zeimbekiko ("Old man gets up turns, An.")

Magrelli, Valerio (fl. c.1957)
Each photographed face.
Especially in weeping.
Every evening, bent over the bright.
I have finally learned.
I have from you this red.
I have often imagined that glances.
I look for a way of writing.
I love uncertain gestures.
I sit, in treatment, at the movies, devoted.
If I must dial a number to call you.
If you melt some lead.
In summer, like the theaters, I close up.
In the evening when the light is dim.
Pen slides, The.
Side by side after the meal.
Ten poems written in one month.
There's silence between one page and
   another.
This handwriting wears itself away.
Tomorrow morning I will take a shower.

Maguire, Sarah (b. 1957)
Fall, The.
Perfect Timing.
Spilt Milk.

Mahadevi (Mahadeviyakka) (fl. 12th cent.)
I do not call it his sign.
It was like a stream.
Like a silkworm weaving.
Like an elephant.
Like / treasure hidden in the ground.
O brothers, why do you talk.
(On Her Decision to Stop Wearing Clothes).
Other men are thorn.
People, / male and female.
Riding the blue sapphire mountains.
So long as this breath fills your nostrils.
Till you've earned.
Vein of sapphires, A.
When I am hungry.
When the body becomes Your mirror.
Would a circling surface vulture.

Mahapatra, Anuradha (b. 1956)
Spell.

Mahapatra, Jayanta (b. 1928)
Ash.
Main Temple Street, Puri.
Monsoon Day Fable, A.
October Morning, An.
Rain of Rites, A.
Sanskrit.
Summer Poem, A.
Taste for Tomorrow.

Mahapatra, Sitakant (b. 1937)
Election, The.

Mahlmann, Siegfried August (1771–1826)
Allah gives light in darkness.

Mahon, Derek (b. 1941)
Achill.
Afterlives, *sels.*
Another Sunday Morning.
Antarctica.
Banished Gods, The.
Bruce Ismay's Soliloquy.
Chinese Restaurant in Portrush, The.
Consolations of Philosophy.
Courtyards in Delft.
Dark Country, A.
Death and the Sun.
Dejection.
Derry Morning.
Disused Shed in Co. Wexford, A.
Dog Days.
Ecclesiastes.
Everything Is Going to Be All Right.
Ford Manor.
Garage in Co. Cork, A.
Girls in Their Seasons.
Girls on the Bridge.
Glengormley.

Globe in North Carolina, The.
Grandfather.
I Am Raftery ("I am Raftery, hesitant and
   confused.")
In Carrowdore Churchyard.
Kinsale.
Last of the Fire Kings, The.
Lives.
Matthew V. 29-30.
My Wicked Uncle.
Poem Beginning with a Line by Cavafy.
Postcard from Berlin, A.
Refusal to Mourn, A.
St. Eustace.
Snow Party, The.
Spring Vacation, The.
Table Talk.
Tractatus.
Unborn Child, An.
Woods, The.

Mahone, Barbara (b. 1944)
Colors for Mama.
Poem for Positive Thinkers, A.
Sugarfields.
What Color Is Black?

**Mahony, Francis Sylvester ("Father Prout")
(1805–66)**
Bells of Shandon, The.
Blarney castle.

Mahsati (fl. 12th cent.)
Better to live as a rogue and a bum.
Gone are the games we played all night.
Good-looking, I'll never stoop for you.
I knew like a song your vows weren't strong.
Unless you can dance through a common bar.

Mai Thảo (Nguyễn Đăng Quý) (b. 1927)
Coaxing My Illness.
Island.

Maiden, Jennifer (b. 1949)
Air.
Anorexia.
Climbing.
Dew.
Foundations, The.
Green Side, The.
In the Gloaming.
Language.
Mother-in-Law of the Marquis de Sade, The.
New.
Slides.
Taste.

Mailer, Norman (b. 1923)
Devils.
Eternities.

Maillard, Claude
Christmas Mass for a Little Atheist Jesus.

Mainwaring, M. G.
Gothic columns of petrified motion.

Maiola, Nona
Up on the Moon.

Mair, Charles (1838–1927)
Last Bison, The, *sels.*
Tecumseh, *sels.*

Maitland, Sir Richard (1496–1586)
Solace in Age.

Maitre, Robert
Woman Underneath, The.

Majaj, Lisa Suhair (fl. 20th cent.)
Recognized Futures.

Majer, Hugo
On my winter walk.
Spring / slips / silent / snowdrops.

Major, Clarence (b. 1936)
Apple Core.
Balance and Beauty.
Beaulieu.
Blind Old Woman.
Design, The.
Giant Red Woman.
I Was Looking for the University.
Inside Diameter.
Isolate.
Large Room with Wood Floor.
Lost in the Desert.
My Seasonal Body, My Ears.

On Trying to Imagine the Kiwi Pregnant.
On Watching a Caterpillar Become a
    Butterfly.
Round Midnight.
Self World.
Swallow the Lake.
Vietnam.
Vietnam #4.

Major, Elizabeth (*fl.* c.1656)
    Honey on the Rod, *sels.*

Majumdar, Benoy (b. 1934)
    Time Wins.

Makabo, Calvin (d. 1943)
    Desert Conflict.

Makarov [or Makarov-Krotkov], Aleksandr (b. 1959)
    Life lasts the course of a kiss.
    Twenty years / I tamed an ant.

Makeda (Queen of Sheba) (fl. 1000 B.C.)
    I fell.
    Wisdom is.

Makhfi Zibu'n-Nisa (1639–1703)
    Beauty of the Friend it was that taught me,
        The.

Makidemewabe, Samuel
    Born Tying Knots.
    Saw the Cloud Lynx.
    Tree Old Woman.

Makin, Bathsua Pell (*fl.* 17th cent.)
    To the Countess Dowager of Huntingdon.
    Upon the Much Lamented Death of the Right
        Honourable, the Lady Elizabeth Langham.

Maksimovic, Desanka (*fl.* c.1898)
    Bloody Fable.
    Darkness was born in the forest. I found it
        there.
    For All Mary Magdalenes.
    For Maria Magdalenes.
    For the Barren Woman.
    Snake.
    St. Matthew, *sels.*

Malam, Charles (b. 1906)
    Steam Shovel.

Malancioui, Ileana (b. 1940)
    Bear's Blood.

Malanga, Gerard (b. 1943)
    Temperature.

Malangatana, Valente Goenha (b. 1936)
    To the Anxious Mother.
    Woman.

Malange, Nise (b. 1960)
    This Poem Is Dedicated to Brother Andries
        Raditsela.

Malé, Belkis Cuza (b. 1942)
    My Mother's Homeland.

Malik de Coteau, Delano Abdul (b. 1940)
    Motto Vision 1971.
    Oui Papa.

Malinowitz, Michael (b. 1951)
    Glose.

Malins, Joseph (1844–1926)
    Fence or an Ambulance, A.

Mallalieu, Herbert B. (b. 1914)
    Empedocles on Etna.
    Epilogue: "Phoenix on the hot sirocco's
        breath."

Mallarmé, Stéphane (1842–98)
    Album Leaf.
    Anguish.
    Another Fan.
    Après-midi d'un Faune, L', *sels.*
    Breeze from the Sea.
    Glazier, The.
    Lace curtain self-destructs, A.
    L'Après-Midi d'un Faune.
    Le Livre, *sels.*
    Sea-Wind.
    Sigh.

Mallet, David. *See* **Thomson, James** *and* David
    Mallet

Mallet, David (1705–65)
    Of Verbal Criticism, *sels.*
    To Mr. Thomson, on His Publishing the
        Second Edition of His Poem Called
        Winter, *sels.*

William and Margaret.

**"Malley, Ern" (James McAuley *and* Harold
    Stewart) (1917–76)**
    Dürer; Innsbruck, 1495.

Malley, Jean
    Words do not grow on the landscape.

Malloch, Douglas (1877–1938)
    Ain't It [*or* It's] Fine Today.
    Be the Best of Whatever You Are.

Mallock, William Hurrell (1849–1923)
    Brussels and Oxford.
    Christmas Thoughts, by a Modern Thinker.
    Marriage Prospect, A.
    Softly the Evening.

"Malone, Carroll." *See* **McBurney, William B.**

Malone, Walter (1866–1915)
    Opportunity.

Malouf, David (b. 1934)
    Asphodel.
    Bicycle.
    Die Musik, An.
    Early Discoveries.
    For Two Children.
    Guide to the Perplexed.
    Judas Touch, The.
    Snow.
    This Day, under My Hand.
    Wolf-Boy.
    Year of the Foxes, The.

Malroux, Claire (b. 1935)
    Every morning the curtain rises.
    Fingers probe.
    In October.
    Octet Before Winter.

Maltseva, Nadezhda Elizarovna (b. 1950)
    To the Muse.

Manaka, Matsemela (b. 1956)
    Pula, *sels.*

Manchán, Saint (d. 665)
    Manchán's Prayer.

Mandel, Eli W. (b. 1922)
    Envoi: "My country is not a country."
    Four Songs from the Book of Samuel.
    From the North Saskatchewan.
    Houdini.
    Madwomen of the Plaza de Mayo, The.
    Minotaur Poems, *sels.*
    On the 25th Anniversary of the Liberation of
        Auschwitz.
    Song: "When the echo of the last footstep
        dies."

Mandel, Naum Moiseievich. *See* **"Korzhavin,
    Naum"**

Mandel, Tom (b. 1942)
    Jews in Hell.
    Open Rebuke (Concealed Love).
    Prospect of Release, *sels.*
    Realism.
    Say Ja.
    Shade, The.

Mandelbaum, Harriet
    Deus "Sex" Machina.

**Mandelstam [or Mandelshtam], Osip Emilevich
    (1892–1938)**
    Ariosto.
    Batyushkov.
    Body was given to me—what to do with it,
        A.
    Bread is poisoned and the air's drunk dry,
        The.
    By denying me the seas, the right to run and
        fly.
    Charlie Chaplin Poem, The.
    Enough of snivelling! Shove our papers in
        the desk.
    Finder of a Horseshoe, The.
    For the resounding valor of milennia to
        come.
    I drink to military asters, to all that I'm
        censured about.
    I must read only children's books.
    I Was Washing Outside in the Darkness.
    I'll chase through the gypsy camp of dark
        streets.
    I'll tell you bluntly.

Last night I tell you, I do not lie.
[Last Poems].
Leningrad.
Mounds of Human Heads Are Wandering
    into the Distance.
Not yet dead, not yet alone.
Notre Dame.
O how much I would like—.
Ottave, *sels.*
Petersburg Strophes.
Petropolis.
Phaedra.
Poem No. 286 (On Stalin).
Shy speechless sound, The.
Silentium.
Skillful mistress of guilty glances.
Stalin Epigram, The.
Stanzas, *sels.*
Still far from patriarch or sage.
Thy image, wavering, agonizing.
To A. A. A. (Akhmatova).
Tristia, *sels.*
What is the name of this street?
Whoever Finds a Horseshoe.
You took away all the oceans and all the
    room.

Mandeville, Bernard (1670–1733)
    On Honour.

Mangan, Gerald (b. 1951)
    Glasgow 1956.
    Heraclitus at Glasgow Cross.
    Nights in Black Valley.

Mangan, James Clarence (1803–49)
    Gone in the Wind.
    Hymn for Pentecost.
    Karamanian Exile, The.
    Nameless One, The.
    Rest Only in the Grave.
    Siberia.
    Song from the Coptic, A.
    To Amine.
    To Sultan Murad II.
    Twenty Golden Years Ago.
    Vision of Connaught in the Thirteenth
        Century, A.

Mangan, Kathy
    Above the Tree Line.

Manger, Itsik [or Itzik or Itzig] (1901–69)
    Adam and Eve.
    Autumn.
    I Am the Autumn.
    Jealous Adam.
    Mother Sarah's Lullaby ("Mother Sarah rocks
        the cradle.")
    Rachel Goes to the Well for Water ("Rachel
        stands by the mirror and plaits.")

Mangoaela, Z. D. (1883–1963)
    Boast of Masopha.

Manhire, Bill (b. 1946)
    Children.
    Contemplation of the Heavens.
    Late Victorian Girl, The.
    On Originality.
    Prayer: "What do you take."
    Selenologist, The.
    Trees, The.
    Zoetropes.

Manifold, John Streeter (1915–85)
    Assignation with a Somnambulist.
    Defensive Position.
    Deserter, The.
    Fencing School.
    Fife Tune.
    Garcia Lorca Murdered in Granada.
    Griesly Wife, The.
    L'Embarquement pour Cythère.
    Makhno's Philosophers.
    Making Contact.
    Night Piece.
    Sirens, The.
    Tomb of Lt. John Learmonth, A.I.F., The.

Manilius, Marcus ((fl. c. 1st cent. A.D.)
    Astronomica, The, *sels.*
    What Constellations rise with the Lion. The
        great Dog.

Manley, Mary de la Rivière (1663–1724)
    Lost Lover, The, *sels.*

Royal Mischeif, The, *sels.*
Song: "Ah, Dangerous Swain, tell me no more."
To the Author of Agnes de Castro.

Manley, Frank
Dead Letters.

Mann, Chris (b. 1948)
Comrades Marathon, The.
Poet's Progress, The.

Manner, Eeva-Liisa (b. 1921)
Cambrian, *sels.*
Lunar Games, The.

Manning, Frederic (1882–1935)
Face (Guillemont), The.
Grotesque.
Leaves.
Trenches, The.

Manning-Sanders, Ruth (b. 1895)
Come Wary One.
Old City, The.

Mannyng [or Manning], Robert (1288–1338)
Handling Sin, *sels.*
Praise of Women.

Mansei. *See* **Sami Mansei**

Mansel, William Lort (1753–1820)
Sun's Perpendicular Rays, The.

Mansfield, Katherine (Kathleen Beauchamp Murry) (1888–1923)
Meeting, The.
Secret Flowers.

Mansour, Joyce (b. 1928)
Anti-mnemonic self-vaccination.
Beyond the breakers.
Embrace the Blade.
From an ass to an analyst and back.
Gently stroke a wound.
Last night I saw your corpse.
North Express.
Regulation equipment.
Seated on her bed legs spread open.
Sun in Capricorn, The.
Tinfoil.
Yesterday evening I saw your corpse.

Mansur, Abul Kasim. *See* **Firdausi**

Manwell, Juana. *See* **Owl Woman**

Manyarrows, Victoria Lena
Lakota Sister / Cherokee Mother.
Today We Will Not Be Invisible Nor Silent.

Manyase, L. T. (b. 1915)
Mother Crab and Her Family, The.
Vusumzi's Song.

Manzano, Juan Fransico (1797–1854)
My Thirty Years.

Mao Tse-tung [or Mao Zedong] (1893–1976)
Long March, The.
Loushan Pass.
Midstream.
"Spring in Ch'in's Garden" ("Alone I stand in autumn cold.")
Tune: "Deva-like Barbarian"—Ta-po-ti.
Tune: "Full River Red"—A Reply to Kuo Mo-jo.
Tune: "Remembering the Lady of Ch'in"—Loushan Pass.
Tune: "Song of Divination"—On the Plum Tree, after a Poem by Lu Yu.
Tune: "Song of Picking Mulberry" Double-Ninth Festival.
Tune: "Spring in Ch'in's Garden" ("Northern landscape, / Thousand miles around covered by ice.")
Tune: "The Charm of Nien-nu"—Kunlun Mountains.

Mao Wen-hsi (fl. c.930)
Tune: Drunk among the Flowers.

Mapanje, Jack A.
After Wiriyamu Village Massacre by Protuguese.
Another Fools' Day Touches Down: Shush.
At the Metro: Old Irrelevant Images.
Baobab Fruit Picking; or, Development in Monkey Bay.
Before Chilembwe Tree.
Cheerful Girls at Smiller's Bar, The.
Elegy for Mangochi Fishermen, An.

Florrie Abraham Witness.
Glory Be to Chingwe's Hole.
Making Our Clowns Martyrs.
Messages.
On African Writing.
On Being Asked to Write a Poem for 1979.
On His Royal Blindness Paramount Chief Kwangala.
Steve Biko is Dead.
These Too Are Our Elders.
We Wondered about the Mellow Peaches.

Mar, Laureen (b. 1953)
My Mother, Who Came from China, Where She Never Saw Snow.

Mar, Yekhi'el [or Yehiel] (1921–69)
Handfuls of Wind.

Marais, Eugène (1871–1936)
Dance of the Rain, The.
Deep River.
Heart-of-the-Daybreak.
Here We have No Firm Dwelling-Place.
Radio Cradle-song.
Sorceress, The.

Maran, René (1887–1960)
Human Soul.
Silence.
"Tropicals."

Marbod of Rennes (1035–1123)
Enemy in the Fortress, The.
Epitaph for Bruno of Angers.
Hymn of the Magdalen.
I give you no greeting, Geoffrey.
Meditation among Trees.
Now must I mend my manners.
Of the Resurrection of the Body.
Prayer to God the Father.

Marcabrun (fl. 12th cent.)
At the Fountain.

Marcela de Carpio de San Felix, Sister (fl. 16th cent.)
Amor Mysticus.

March, Ausiàs (1397?–1459)
As someone on his back for months of illness.
Day's in dread of losing her bright features, The.
Know what I'm like? Some captain moors his ship.
Let others hail the holidays with laughter.
Much as a man who takes delight in dreaming.
Not so with me as with the little page.
Out scouting for sound counsels? How to prosper?

March, Joseph Moncure (1899–1977)
Wild Party, The, *sels.*

Marchant, John (fl. c.1751)
Little Miss and Her Parrot.
Young Master's Account of a Puppet Show.

Marchbank, Isobel
Sinn Fein: Ourselves Alone.

Marchenko, Nikolai Nikolaevich. *See* **"Morshen, Nikolai Nikolaevich"**

Marcinkeviius, Justinas
Father's Winter.
Landscape With Apparition.
Nemunas.

Marckant, John (fl. 16th cent.)
O Lord, Turn Not Away Thy Face.

Mardale, W. R. (fl. c.1853)
Pop Goes the Weasel!

Mardhekar, B. S. (1909–56)
Forest of yellow bamboo trees, The.

Margarido, Manuela (b. 1926)
You Who Occupy Our Land.

Margolis, Gary (b. 1945)
For the Woman at the Fast-Food Fish Place Who Called Me Pig.

Marguerite de Navarre (1492–1549)
Autant En Emporte le Vent.
Smell of death is so powerful, The.

"Maria, Laura." *See* **Robinson, Mary**

Mariah, Paul (b. 1937)
Christmas 1962.
Quarry/Rock.

Marianus (fl. c.500–c.600)
In this bath Cypris once was bathed by Love, her son.

Marias, Eugène
Desert Lark, The.

Marichiko
Every morning.
I cannot forget.
I hold your head tight.
I wish I could be.
Who is there? Me.

Marie de France (c.1155–1189)
Chartivel, *sels.*
Goat's-Leaf.
Honeysuckle (Chevrefoil).
Lay of the Honeysuckle, The.
Nightingale, The.
Two Lovers, The.
Would I Might Go Far over Sea.

Marie-Madeleine, Baroness von Puttkamer (fl. 19th cent.)
Crucifixa.
Sappho.
Vagabonds.
Words of Old Age.

Marinetti, Filippo Tommaso (1876–1944)
Landscape Heard, A.
Manifesto of Futurism, The, *sels.*
They are Coming.
Variety Theater Manifesto, The, *sels.*
Zang Tumb Tuuum, *sels.*

Marino, Giambattista [or Giovanni Battista] (1569–1625)
Beautiful Slave, The.
Fading Beauty.
Head of Medusa on a Rotella of Michelangelo da Caravaggio, in the Gallery of the Grand Duke of Tuscany, The.
Lips and Eyes.
Massacre of the Innocents, The, *sels.*
Out of the Italain.

Marinoni, Rosa Zagnoni (1888?–1970)
At Sunrise.
For a New Home.
Who Are My People?

Marippittiyur
Charmer Turned Ascetic, A.
Hunter Once, Now an Ascetic, A.

Mark, Rickman
Snow in Town.

Markham, E. A. (b. 1939)
Don't Talk to Me about Bread.
Grandfather's Sermon and Michael Smith.
Her story.
Late Return.
Old Thought for a New Couple, An.
Rewrite.
Towards the End of a Century.

Markham, Edwin (1852–1940)
After Reading Shakspere.
Avengers, The.
Creed, A.
Forgotten Man, The.
How the Great Guest Came.
In Death Valley.
Leaf from the Devil's Jest-Book, A.
Lincoln, the Man of the People, *sels.*
Man with the Hoe, The.
Outwitted.
Prayer, A: "Teach me, Father, how to go."
Preparedness.
Right Kind of People, The.
There Is a High Place.
Third Wonder, The.
Victory in Defeat.

Markham, Gervase (1568–1637)
Fragment, A: "I walked [or walk'd] along a stream for pureness rare."

Markish, Perets [or Peretz] (1895–1952)
We Reached Out Far.

Markman, Stephanie
And / mother why did you tell me.
Rime of the Ancient Feminist, The, *sels.*

Markov, Sergey [or Sergei] Nikolaevich (1906–79)
Stendhal.

Marks, Leo (b. 1920)
Code Poem for the French Resistance.
Marks, Naomi
Come Live with Me.
High Wonders.
Marks, S. J. (b. 1939)
How can I tell you.
Marlatt, Daphne (b. 1942)
Ana Historic, *sels.*
Femina.
Steveston, *sels.*
Marlatt, Earl Bowman (1892–1976)
Spirit of Life, in This New Dawn.
Through the Dark the Dreamers Came.
Marley, Bob (1945–89)
Trenchtown Rock.
Marlowe, Christopher (1564–93)
Doctor Faustus, *sels.*
Elegies.
Hero and Leander, *sels.*
Lucan's Pharsalia Book 1, *sels.*
Ovids Elegies Book 1, *sels.*
Passionate Shepherd [*or* Sheepheard] To His
Love, The.
Tamburlaine the Great, *sels.*
"Marnia" (1968–92)
Accoutrement.
I must be able to protect you.
I want to love you very much.
Maro, Publius Vergilius. See Virgil
Marot, Clément (1495–1544)
Friar Lubin.
Love-Lesson, A.
Madame d'Albert's Laugh.
Posy Ring, The.
**Marquis, Don (Donald Robert Perry Marquis)
(1878–1937)**
Archy and Mehitabel, *sels.*
Certain Maxims of Archy.
Limerick: "It needn't have ribaldry's taint."
Limerick: "There was a young fellow named
Sydney."
Noah an' Jonah an' Cap'n John Smith.
Only Thy Dust.
Reverie.
Tom-Cat, The.
When One Loves Tensely.
**Marquis, Donald Robert Perry. See Marquis,
Don**
Marriot, John (1893–1977)
On John Donne's Book of Poems.
Marriott, Anne (b. 1913)
As You Come In.
Beaver Pond.
Prairie Graveyard.
Marsden, James (1908–73)
What Is Time?
Marsh, David
Mice.
Marsh, E. L.
Magic Piper, The.
Marshall, Archibald (1866–1934)
Limerick: "There was a young man of
Devizes."
Marshall, Edward (b. 1932)
Leave the Word Alone.
Marshall, Jack (b. 1937)
Hitchhiker.
Sesame.
Marshall, Tom (b. 1938)
Interior Monologue 666.
Politics.
Summer.
Marshall-Stoneking, Billy (b. 1947)
On the Death of Muriel Rukeyser.
Passage.
Picture Postcard.
Seasons of Fire, The.
Marsman, Henk. See Bernstein, Charles
Marson, Una (1905–65)
Brown Baby Blues.
Gettin de Spirit.
Kinky Hair Blues.
Politeness.

Repose.
To Wed or Not to Wed.
Marston, John (1575–1634)
Malcontent, The, *sels.*
Metamorphosis of Pigmalions Image, The,
sels.
Metamorphosis of Pygmalion's Image, The,
sels.
Satires, *sels.*
Scourge of Villainy [*or* Villanie], The, *sels.*
Scourge of Villanie, The, *sels.*
Marston, Philip Bourke (1850–87)
After.
Inseparable.
Love's Music.
Not Thou but I.
Old Churchyard of Bonchurch, The.
Speechless [upon the Marriage of Two Deaf
and Dumb Persons].
Too Late.
Ungathered Love.
Vain Wish, A.
Martí, José (1853–95)
Simple Verses, *sels.*
Two Countries.
**Martial (Marcus Valerius Martialis) (c.40–
c.104)**
Ad Flaccum.
Ad Sabellum.
Allusion to Martial, An.
Antipathy.
As *Lesbias* Sparrow, *Tricksy* wanton is.
Bee's Burial, A.
Believe me, sir, I'd love to spend whole days.
Bought Locks.
Certain Dinner For Thirty, A.
Country Pleasures.
Critics.
Dasius, chucker-out / at the Turkish Baths.
De Cœnatione Micae.
De Gellia.
De Hortis Julii Martialis.
De Libro suo.
De M. Antonio.
Don't pay any attention.
Either get out of the [my] house or conform
to my tastes, woman.
Epigram 34: "Lesbia, why are your amours."
Epigram: "Milo's from home; and, Milo
being gone."
Epigram: "Wife, there are some points on
which we differ from each other."
Epitaph for Erotion.
Erotion.
Erotion rests here, in the.
For every letter drink a glass.
Garland of roses, whether you come.
Happy Life, The.
Hinted Wish, A.
How he would drinke his Wine.
I do not love you, Dr. *Fell.*
I muse not that your Dog turds oft doth eate.
I often bow; your hat you never stir.
I send you a lock of hair.
If memory serves, we've shared together.
If you and I, Julius, old friend.
In Lesbiam.
In Lupum.
In Ponticum.
Inviting a Friend to Supper.
Kindest thing of all is to comply, The.
Laid with papyrus to catch fire.
Last night, after five pints of wine.
Lentinus! thou dost nought but fume, and
fret.
Little country box you boast, A.
Lycoris darling, once I burned for you.
Martial's Favourites.
Monsieur Naso, verolè, A.
Motto to Richard Lovelace, Lucasta.
Posthume Poems.
My Lord, th' Indictment do's not run.
Near Neighbors.
Near the Vipsanian columns where the
aqueduct.
Old Man's Case, The.
On the Death of a Young and Favorite Slave.

Out of an Epigram of Martial.
Paradise Regain'd, *sels.*
Parret, The.
Post-Obits and the Poets.
Procrastination.
Roman Presents.
Roman Thank-You Letter, A.
Sextus the Usurer.
Since your marriage you have lost the look.
Song from Poetaster, or The Arraignment.
Swan her sweetest Notes sings as she dies,
The.
Temperament.
Thais, why do you call me old.
'Tis a strange thing, but 'tis a thing well
known.
To a Friend an Epigram: Of him.
To a Schoolmaster.
To Cloe.
To His Book[e].
To Julius.
To my ill Reader.
To my Lady Rogers.
To Penshurst, *sels.*
To Sextus.
To the Emperour Titus, upon his Banishing
Sycophants.
Tom never drinks: that I should much
commend.
Verses on Blenheim.
What a host you are, Mancinus.
What Makes a Happy Life.
What'mmmIdoin'? slurs Lyris, feigning
shock.
Whenever you drink all night you make.
Would you, my friend, in little room express.
You are the most beautiful.
You drink all night, and promise fairly.
You Serve the Best Wines Always, My Dear
Sir.
Your bookcases are crammed with
manuscripts.
You've Told Me, Maro.
Martin, Angus (b. 1952)
Forest.
Malcolm MacKerral.
Martin, Charles (b. 1942)
E. S. L.
Easter Sunday, 1985.
Leaving Buffalo.
Metaphor of Grass in California.
Satyr, Cunnilinguent: To Herman Melville.
Sharks at the New York Aquarium.
Speech Against Stone.
Victoria's Secret.
Martin, Chuck
Size Is Relative.
"Martin, David" (Ludwig Detsinyi) (b. 1915)
Dreams in German.
Martin, Dorothy McGrath
(On the Merry, Merry-Go-Round).
Martin, Egbert (1859–87)
National Anthem.
Trade.
Martin, Herbert (b. 1933)
Antigone I.
Antigone VI.
Lines: "Singularly and in pairs the decade
has been ripped by bullets."
Negro Soldier's Viet Nam Diary, A.
Martin, John
God's Dark.
Martin, Philip (b. 1931)
Tongues.
Martin, Sarah Catherine (1768–1826)
Comic Adventures of Old Mother Hubbard
and Her Dog, The.
**Martin, Theodore. See Aytoun, William
Edmonstoune** *and* **Sir Theodore Martin
(1816–1909)**
Martin, William
Apple Orchard in the Spring, An.
Martinez, Dionisio D.
Avant-Dernières Pensées.
Fuego.
In a Duplex Near the San Andreas Fault.

Necessary Story.
What the Men Talk About When the Women Leave the Room, *sels.*

Martinez, James (c.1860–c.1945)
Dis Time No Stan' Like befo' Time.
My Little Lize.

Martinez, Valerie (b. 1961)
It Is Not.

Martinson, Harry Edmund (b. 1904)
Cable Ship, The.
Cotton.
Dusk in the Country.
Earthworm, The.
On the Congo.

Marty, Sid (b. 1944)
In the Dome Car of the "Canadian."

Martynov, Leonid Nikolaevich (1905–80)
Be kind / Be iron—.
Daedalus.
Idlers.
It seems to me I'm resurrected.
Lord of Nature.
River Silence, The.
Seashore, The.
Sunflower.

Marula (*fl.* c.1156)
Meeting after Separation.

Marutanilanakanar
Hunchback and the Dwarf, The.
What Her Girl Friend Said to her.

Marvell, Andrew (1621–78)
Ametas and Thestylis Making Hay-Ropes.
Bermudas.
Character of Holland, The, *sels.*
Clorinda and Damon.
Coronet, The.
Damon the Mower.
Definition Of Love, The.
Dialogue Between The Resolved Soul and Created Pleasure, A.
Dialogue between the Soul and [the] Body, A.
Dialogue between Thyrsis and Dorinda, A.
Epitaph upon —, An.
Execution of King Charles, The.
Eyes and Tears.
Fair Singer, The.
First Anniversary of the Government under O.C, The, *sels.*
Gallery, The.
Garden, The.
Garden, The ("How vainly men themselves amaze"), *sels.*
Horatian Ode upon Cromwell's Return from Ireland, An, *sels.*
Last Instructions to a Painter, The, *sels.*
Match, The.
Mourning.
Mower Against Gardens, The.
Mower to the Glow-Worms [*or* Glowworms *or* Glo-Worms], The.
Mower's Song, The.
Nymph Complaining for the Death of Her Faun [*or* Fawn], The, *sels.*
On Mr Milton's "Paradise Lost."
Picture of Little T. C. in a Prospect of Flowers, The.
see also Ros.
To His Coy Mistress.
To His Noble Friend, Mr Richard Lovelace, upon His Poems.
Upon Appleton House [To My Lord Fairfax], *sels.*
Young Love.

"Mary, Aunt." See Lathbury, Mary Artemisia

Maryam bint Abi Ya'qub al-Ansari (*fl.* early 11th cent.)
What can you expect.

Marz, Roy (b. 1911)
Vittoria Colonna.

Masaoka Shiki (1867–1902)
All the hot night.
Among the poems I wrote with many pictures spread out before me[2].
During a trip.
During an illness.

First of May[3], The.
Fresh from the Void.
Frozen in the ice.
Having molded clay in the shape of my ailing form.
I can see the stones.
My room.
On the eve of death.
Shitting in the winter turnip field.
Spring night.
Tanka: "Beyond the glass door."
Tanka: "Day I had in mind, The."
Tanka: "Dipped."
Tanka: "Hawkers."
Tanka: "Illuminated."
Tanka: "In the house."
Tanka: "In the vase."
Tanka: "Makes me writhe."
Tanka: "Nobody with me."
Tanka: "On a young pine."
Tanka: "Peacefully."
Tanka: "Tree with lush leaves."
Upon receiving potted peonies for a gift.
View of my garden, A.
Wild geese cry, The.

Mase, Sidney Warren
It's Simply Great.

Masefield, John (1878–1967)
Being her friend, I do not care, not I.
Biography, *sels.*
C. L. M.
Captain Stratton's Fancy.
Cardigan Bay.
Cargoes.
Consecration, A.
Crowd, The.
Dauber, *sels.*
Dead Knight, The.
Epilogue: "I have seen flowers come in stony places."
Fellow Mortal, A.
Her heart is always doing lovely things.
Laugh and Be Merry.
Lemmings, The.
Lollingdon Downs, *sels.*
No man takes the farm.
On Eastnor Knoll.
On Growing Old.
Partridges.
Passing Strange, The.
Port of Holy Peter.
Port of Many Ships.
Posted.
Reynard the Fox, *sels.*
Roadways.
Rose of the World, The.
Sea Change.
Sea-Fever.
Sonnet: "There, on the darkened deathbed, dies the brain."
Sonnets, *sels.*
Sorrow of Mydath.
Tewkesbury Road.
To-morrow.
Trade Winds.
Twilight it is, and the far woods are dim, and the rooks cry.
Up on the downs the red-eyed kestrels hover.
Valediction (Liverpool Docks), A.
Waggon-Maker, The.
Wanderer's Song, A.
West Wind, The.
Word, The.

Masham, Damaris, Lady (1659–1708)
When deaths cold hand shall close my eyes.

Masing, Uku
For Polka.
Only the Mists are Real.
To Every Believer.

Masini, Donna
Nightscape.

Mason, Caroline Atherton Briggs (1823–90)
When I Am Old.

Mason, Herbert
Gilgamesh, *sels.*

Mason, Ronald Allison Kells (1905–71)
Be Swift O Sun.

Body of John.
Ecce Homunculus.
Footnote to John II: 4.
Judas Iscariot / sat in the upper.
Latter-day Geography Lesson.
Old Memories of Earth.
On the Swag.
Prelude: "This short straight sword."
Sonnet of Brotherhood.
Spark's Farewell to Its Clay, The.
Young Man Thinks of Sons, The.

Mason, Walt (1862–1939)
Football.

Mason, William (1725–97)
Against Formal Gardens.
English Garden, The, *sels.*
Heroic Epistle to Sir William Chambers, An, *sels.*
Ode to Memory, *sels.*
To a Gravel Walk.

Massey, Gerald (1828–1907)
All's Right with the World.
As proper mode of quenching legal lust.
Desolate.
Diakka, The.
O, Lay Thy Hand in Mine, Dear!
Womankind.
Worker, The.

Massinger, Philip (1583–1640)
Emperor of the East, The, *sels.*
Men May Talk of Country-Christmasses.

Masson, Tom (Thomas Lansing Masson) (1866–1934)
Enough.
He Took Her.
My Poker Girl.
Tragedy, A.
When I Get Time.

Master, Thomas
Cat and the Lute, The.

Masters, Edgar Lee (1869–1950)
Battle of Gettysburg, The.
Business Reverses.
Fiddler Jones.
Gettysburg.
In Memory of Bryan Lathrop.
Jennie McGrew.
Keats to Fanny Brawne.
Lost Orchard, The.
Margaret Fuller Slack.
Mind Flying Afar.
New Spoon River, The, *sels.*
Silence.
Spoon River Anthology, *sels.*
Supplication.
Veterans of the Wars.
Wedding Feast, The.
Week-End by the Sea.
Widows.

Masters, Marcia Lee (b. 1910)
At My Mother's Bedside.

Mastin, Florence Ripley (b. 1896)
From the Telephone.

Mastoraki, Jenny (b. 1949)
Crusaders knew the Holy Places, The.
Death of a Warrior, The.
Prometheus.
Then they paraded Pompey's urn.
Vandals, The.
Wooden Horse then said, The.

Mat' Mariia. *See* Kuzmina-Karavayeva, Elizaveta

Matabaruka
Change, The.

Mataira, Katerina Te Hei Koko (b. 1932)
Restoring the Ancestral House.

Mataka, Laini (b. 1949)
Next Door.
Ornithology.

Matchett, William H. (b. 1923)
Head Couples.
Water Ouzel.

Matevski, Mateja
Bells.
Rains, *sels.*

Mathams, Walter J.
Jesus, friend of little children.
Mathema, N. C. G. (b. 1949)
Maze of Blood, A.
Mather, Cotton (1663–1728)
Epitaph: "Dummer the shepherd sacrific'd."
Eternal God, How They're Increased.
Go then, my dove, but now no longer mine.
I Lift My Eyes Up to the Hills.
My Heart, How Very Hard It's Grown.
O Glorious Christ of God; I live.
Vigilantius, or a Servant of the Lord Found Ready.
When the Seed of Thy Word Is Cast.
Mather, Joseph (1737–1804)
File-Hewer's Lamentation, The.
God save great Thomas Paine.
Mathew, Ray (b. 1929)
Good Thing, A.
Lover's Meeting.
One Day.
Poem in Time of Winter.
Seeing St. James's.
Wynyard Sailor.
Mathews, Aidan Carl (b. 1956)
At the Wailing Wall.
Caedmon.
Death of Irish, The.
Descartes at Daybreak.
Letter Following.
Library, The.
Minding Ruth.
Persons Unknown.
Severances.
Spectrum.
Two Months Married.
Woodniche.
Mathews, Cornelius (1817–89)
Poems on Man in His Various Aspects under the American Republic, sels.
Mathews, Esther
Song: "I can't be talkin' of love, dear."
Mathews, Harry (b. 1930)
Aboard a Boat at Night, Drinking with My Wife.
At Night, Hearing Someone Singing in the House Next Door.
Back from Green Dragon, Presented to Hsieh Shih-chih.
Condition of Desire.
Dappled Horse, The.
Histoire.
Lunar Eclipse.
Marrying Again.
My Neighbor to the South, the Office Clerk Hsiao, Came in the Evening to Say Good-bye.
Offering for the Cat, An.
Out and Back on the Fifteenth Night of the First Month.
Sad Birds, The.
Sad Remembrance.
Sharing Lodging with Hsieh Shih-hou.
Shih-hou Pointed Out to Me that from Ancient Times There Had Never Been a Poem on the Subject of Lice.
Mathias, Eileen
All in Red.
Go Out.
In the Wood.
Just Jumbo.
Little Things.
My Hut.
Sea Fairies.
Tall Trees.
Zoo Manners.
Mathias, Roland (b. 1915)
Craswall.
Departure in Middle Age.
God Is.
Mathis, Cleopatra (b. 1942)
Elegy for the Other.
Getting Out.
Seven Months.
Mathison, Thomas (d. 1754)
Goff; an Heroi-comical Poem, The, sels.

"Matilda, Anna." See **Cowley, Hannah**
"Matilda, Rosa." See **Dacre, Charlotte**
Matshoba, Mtutuzeli (b. 1950)
Mantatee Horde, The.
Matsueda, Pat
Two Japanese Prints.
Matsumoto Koyu-Ni (fl. late 18th cent.)
At Ichiyiama / Boating on Lake Nio.
Mattawa, Khaled (fl. 20th cent.)
Pyramid of Khufu, The.
Watermelon Tales.
Mattera, Don (b. 1935)
Day They Came for Our House, The.
Giovanni Azania.
Matthews, Harley (b. 1889)
Women Are Not Gentlemen.
Matthews, Jack (b. 1889)
Cheerleaders, The.
Gravity's the villain in this piece—.
Paradigm of a Hero.
People in These Houses, The.
Matthews, Marc (b. 1937)
Come Come.
Guyana not Ghana.
Realarro.
Matthews, Tom (b. 1945)
Cowboy Film.
Even the whales now.
Happy Arabia.
Private But Sulphurous.
Robert Sat.
Matthews, William (b. 1942)
Buddy Bolden Cylinder, The.
Cat, The.
Directions.
Dream, The.
In Memory of the Utah Stars.
Merida, 1969.
Mingus at the Showplace.
Mood Indigo.
My Father's Body.
Note I Left for Gerald Stern in an Office I Borrowed, and He Would Next, at a Summer Writers' Conference.
Oh Yes.
People Like Us.
Praise.
Psychopathology of Everyday Life, The.
Maturai Ilampalaciriyan Centan Kuttanar
What She Said ("What will happen now?")
Maturaittamilkkuttan Katuvan Mallanar
What the Servants Said to Him, as He Returned Home.
Matuzeviius, Eugenijus
Writing in the Fire, The.
Matveyev, Ivan Venediktovich. See "Elagin, Ivan Venediktovich"
Matveyeva [or Matveieva], Novella Nikolaevna (b. 1934)
Dream.
Eggplants Have Pins and Needles, The.
Hymn to the Pepper.
I, he says, am not a warrior.
Laughter of a Faun, The.
Lighthouse.
Procurers.
Robert Frost.
Wood.
Maughan, Henry Neville
Husband of Poverty, The, sels.
Maunick, Edouard J. (b. 1931)
As Far as Yoruba Land, sels.
Les Manèges de la Mer (1964), sels.
Letter to Ellen Conroy Kennedy.
Seven Sides and Seven Syllables.
This Strange Calculation of Roots.
Maura, Sister (b. 1915)
Creation of Light, The.
Each Day.
"Maurice, Furnley" (Frank Wilmot) (1881–1942)
Echoes of wheels and singing lashes.
Victoria Markets Recollected in Tranquility, The.

Whenever I have, in all humility, moved.
Maurice, Thomas (1754–1824)
Epistle to the Right Hon. Charles James Fox, An, sels.
Richmond Hill, sels.
Maurus, Hrabanus. See Charlemagne and Hrabanus Maurus
Mavilis, Lorenzo (1860–1912)
Olive Tree.
Maxton, Hugh (b. 1947)
At the Protestant Museum.
Cernunnos.
Deutschland.
Elegies.
Ode.
Urgent Letter, An.
Waking.
Maxwell, Glyn (b. 1962)
Rumplestiltskin.
Maxwell-Hall, Agnes (b. 1894)
Jamaica Market.
Maxwell, James Clerk (1831–79)
Rigid Body Sings.
Maxwell, Marina Ama Omowale (b. 1934)
Our Revolutions Must Be Different.
To My Grandmother, Lady-Woman.
Maxwell, Ruth Fortney
Mother's Joy, A.
May, Edward (fl. c.1633)
Five Things White.
On a Young Man and an Old Man.
To a Covetous Churl.
To Barba.
To Her Love.
You tender virgins, fairer than the snow with which you play.
May, Julia Harris (1833–1912)
If we could know.
May, Kenneth (fl. 20th cent.)
Valentine's Day.
May, Sue (b. 1955)
Double Bass.
House.
Mildmay Grove.
Mayakovsky [or Maiakovskii], Vladimir Vladimirovich (1893–1930)
At the Top of My Voice.
But Could You?
Can't Stand It.
Cloud in Trousers, The, sels.
For a Violin, Somewhat Nervously.
How I Became a Dog.
I know the force of words, I know their clarion call.
In Re Conferences.
It's already past one. You'll have gone to bed.
Last Statement.
Listen.
Listen, / if stars are lit.
Mayakovsky's Suicide Note.
Now listen! / If the stars shine.
Ode on the Revolution.
On Being Kind to Horses.
On Trash.
Our March.
Past one o'clock. You must have gone to bed.
Pro Eto, sels.
Screaming My Head Off.
They Don't Understand a Thing.
What About You?
You, who live just for orgiastic feasts.
See also **Burliuk, D., Aleksandr Kruchenykh, V. Mayakovsky, and Viktor Khlebnikov.**
Mayer, Bernadette (b. 1945)
Aeschyleans, The.
Birthday Sonnet for Grace.
Boats.
Carlton Fisk is My Ideal.
Earthworker's God is Healed, The.
End of Human Reign on Bashan Hill, The.
First turn to me after a shower.
Garden, The.

Gay full story is authentic verve fabulous jay gull stork.
Generic Elbows.
House Cap.
It moves across and over / across the ground.
Midwinter Day, *sels.*
Port, The.
Sonnet: "Beauty of songs your absence I should not show."
Sonnet: Kamikaze: "Dawn and night of fighting, lovers like actual wars."
Sonnet: "Thousand apples you might put in your theories."
We've solved the problem, the problem is solved.
Work in Progress.

Mayer, Gerda (b. 1927)
April Poem.
Ballad: "Knight went down to the river's rim, A."
Bilberries.
Count Carrots.
Crunch, The.
Dandelions.
Drip Drip or Not Bloody Likely.
Echo and Narcissus.
529 1983.
Narcissus.
Noah.
Old Mrs. Lazibones.
Poor Mrs. Prior.
Song: "Does the policeman sleep with his boots on."

Mayer, Hansjörg (b. 1943)
Oil.

Mayhall, Jane (b. 1921)
City Sparrow.
For the Market.
Human Animal, The.
Marshes, The.
Tracing Back.

Mayne, Jasper (1604–72)
Time is the feather'd thing.

Mayne, John (1759–1836)
Logan Braes.

Mayne, Seymour (b. 1944)
Before Passover.
Roots.

Mayo, Edward Leslie (b. 1904)
Diver, The.
El Greco.
Word of Water, The.

Mayröcker, Friederike (b. 1924)
Patron of Flawless Serpent Beauty.

Mazur, Gail (b. 1937)
Family Plot, October.
Fracture Santa Monica.
Lilacs on Brattle Street.
May, Home after a Year Away.
Phonic.
Spring Planting.

Mazzocco, Robert (b. 1932)
Honolulu.
Muertes.
PBS.

M'Baye, Annette (b. 1927)
Silhouette.

Mbuyazi. *See* Fynn, Henry Francis

McAlmon, Robert (1896–1956)
For Instance.
Frost in the Corn, The.

McAlpine, R. W.
Two Surprises.

McAlpine, Rachel (b. 1940)
Bird-Woman.
Te Kaha.

McAuley, James (b. 1935)
Because.
Blue Horses, The.
Cloak, The.
Dialogue.
Envoi.
Gnostic Prelude.
Hero and the Hydra, The, *sels.*
In a Late Hour.

Keep the season: let the hive.
Late Winter.
Legendary.
Nocturne.
One Tuesday in Summer.
Pietá.
Released on Parole.
Seven Days of Creation, The, *sels.*
Wet Day.
Winter Drive.
World on Sunday.

McAuley, James Philip (1917–76)
Art of Poetry, An.
Because.
Convalescence.
Family of Love, The, *sels.*
In the Huon Valley.
In the Twentieth Century.
Jesus.
Letter to John Dryden, A, *sels.*
Liberal, or Innocent by Definition.
Merry-go-round.
New Guinea.
Pietà.
Terra Australis.
Winter Drive.

McBain, Katie
I Want to Be Your Daughter Now, *sels.*

McBride, Mekeel (b. 1950)
Going Under of the Evening Land, The.
Loneliness.
Red Letters.

McBurney, William B. ("Carroll Malone") (d. 1892?)
Croppy Boy, The.

McCabe, Angela (b. 1951)
Back.
Blind Adolphus.
Bloom Street.
From Lois in London.
Inside History.

McCabe, Victoria (b. 1948)
For Starters.

McCaffery, Steve (b. 1947)
Evoba, *sels.*
Little Hans.
Panopticon, *sels.*

McCaffrey, Phillip
Apprehension.

McCaig, Norman (b. 1910)
Betweens.
Poem: "There is a wailing baby under every stone you walk."

McCarriston, Linda
Billy.
Castle in Lynn, A.
Healing the Mare.
Hotel Nights with My Mother.
Revision.
To Judge Faolain, Dead Long Enough: A Summons.

McCarthy, Eugene (1916–1970?)
Kilroy is gone.
Right of Way.

McCarthy, Gerald
Arrival.
Fall of Da Nang, The.
Finding the Way Back.
Hooded Legion, The.
Sound of Guns, The.
War Story, *sels.*

McCarthy, Justin Huntly (1860–1936)
If I Were King.

McCarthy, T. L.
Limerick: "Immaculate Sir Walter Raleigh, The."
Limerick: "Mrs. Whitehouse, mixed bathing at Deal."

McCarthy, Thomas (b. 1954)
Claud Cockburn.
Dying Synagogue at South Terrace, The.
Emigration Trains, The.
Feeding Ground.
November in Boston.
Party Shrine.

Phenomenology of Stones, The.
Poet of the Mountains, The.
Quatrain without Sparrows, Helpful Bells or Hope.
Question Time.
Shopkeepers at the Party Meeting.
Sorrow Garden, The.
State Funeral.
Toast.
Wisdom of AE, The.
Word "Silk," The.

McClatchy, J. D. (b. 1945)
At a Reading.
Capriccio of Roman Ruins and Sculpture with Figures, A.
Dragonfly.
Found Parable.
Grasshopper.
Method, The.
My Mammogram.
Pleasure of Ruins, The.
Snake.
Weeds.
Winter without Snow, A.

McClaurin, Irma (b. 1945)
I, Woman.
Mask, The.
To a Gone Era.

McClellan, George Marion (b. 1860)
Daybreak.
Feet of Judas, The.
Hydromel and Rue.
January Dandelion, A.
Lines to Mount Glen.
Love is a flame that burns with sacred fire.
September Night, A.
Sun went down in beauty, The.
To Theodore.

McClennan, Tommy
Brown Skin Girl.

McClintock, Michael
Across the sands.
Bluebird alights, The.
Broken window, A.
Dead cat.
Drizzling rain, A.
First melt, The.
Glimmering morning.
Grasshopper, A.
Hearing.
Here's a guy.
Hungry / without money—.
I eat alone.
Letting my tongue.
Long summer day.
Look it's clear.
Merry-go-round, The.
Overtaken.
Peering out.
Poppy, A.
Pushing.
Rowing downstream.
Sat down.
She leaves.
Side-canyon, A.
Single tulip!, A.
Small girl, A.
Thought i'd / never grow old.
Tonight. . . wishing.
Twisting inland.
Vietnam, *sels.*
While we wait.

McCloskey, Mark (b. 1938)
Too Dark.

McClure, Michael (b. 1932)
Aelf-Scin, the shining scimmer the gleam, the shining, The.
Breech, The.
Canticle.
Dark Brown, *sels.*
Flowers of Politics, I, The.
Flowers of Politics, II, The.
For Artaud.
For Monk.
For the Death of 100 Whales.
From the Window of the Beverly Wilshire Hotel.

Ghost Tantras, *sels.*
Hymn to Saint Geryon.
Hymn to St. Geryon, *sels.*
Jazz at the Intergalactic Nightclub.
Mad Sonnet 1.
Mad Sonnet: Fame.
Mad Sonnet: Grace.
May Morn.
Moiré.
Ode for Soft Voice.
Ode to Jackson Pollock.
Peyote Poem, *sels.*
Rant Block.
Reading Frank O'Hara in a Mexican
    Rainstorm.
Rug, The.
Senate Hearings.
Song: "Platinum fur and brass revolver
    shine."
White Boot.
With Tendrils of Poems.

McCombs, Davis
River and Under the River, The.

McCord, David (b. 1897)
Ascot Waistcoat.
Axolotl / looks a littl, The.
Baccalaureate.
Blesséd Lord, What It Is to Be Young.
Books Fall Open.
Christmas Package, A, *sels.*
Cocoon.
Come Christmas.
Crickets.
Crows.
Epitaph on a Waiter.
Every Time I Climb a Tree.
Father and I in the Woods.
Five Chants.
Gloss.
Glowworm.
History of Education.
Mantis.
Mr. Bidery's Spidery Garden.
Perambulator Poems, I-VII, *sels.*
Pickety Fence, The.
Plane Geometer.
Singular Indeed.
Song of the Train.
Summer Shower.
This Is My Rock.
To a Certain Most Certainly Certain Critic.
To Walk in Warm Rain.
Walnut Tree, The.

McCosker, Karen (b. 1948)
Full Moon that Strikes the Earth Cold.

McCrae, Hugh Raymond (1876–1958)
Mimshi Maiden, The.
Song of the Rain.
Winds.

McCrae, John (1872–1918)
In Flanders Fields the poppies blow.

McCrea, Lilian
Boots and Shoes.
Getting Up.
My Toys.
Noises in the Night.
Pussy-Cat and Puppy-Dog.
Rain.
Wash-Day.

McCreery, John Luckey (1835–1906)
There is no death! The stars go down.

McCuaig, Ronald (b. 1908)
Au Tombeau de Mon Père.
Betty by the Sea.
Recitative: "Farmer's son is good and mad,"
    The.

McCullers, Carson
Slumber Party.

McDaniel, Jeffrey
Following Her to Sleep.

McDonald, Donald (b. c.1915)
Breakfast in Bed (Influenza in War-time).
Citizen of—the World, A.
Song of Those Who Died, A.

McDonald, Dorothy Nell
Birthday Wish, A.

McDonald, Ellie (b. 1937)
Itherness.

McDonald, Ian (b. 1933)
Life/Death.
Place They Have to Go, The.
Poison-maker, The.

McDonald, Nan (1921–73)
Burragorang.
Hatters, The.

McDonald, Peter (b. 1962)
Cash Positive.
Christmas.
Pleasures of the Imagination.
Sunday in Great Tew.
Totalled.

McDonald, Roger (b. 1941)
Apis Mellifica.
Bachelor Farmer.
Blizzard, The.
Components.
Flights.
Hollow Thesaurus, The.
Incident in Transylvania.
1915.
Two Summers in Moravia.

McDonald, S. P.
Casey—Twenty Years Later.

McDonald, Walter (b. 1934)
Caliban in Blue.
Children of Saigon, The.
Christmas Bells, Saigon.
Faraway Places.
For Harper, Killed in Action.
For Kelly, Missing in Action.
Hauling Over Wolf Creek Pass in Winter.
Interview with a Guy Named Fawkes, U.S.
    Army.
Last Still Days in a Bunker, The.
Never in My Life.
Once You've Been to War.
Pee Wee Coach, The.
Retired Pilot to Himself, The.
Rocket Attack.
Starting a Pasture.
Veteran.
War Games.
Winter Before the War, The.

McDougall, Jo
Reporting Back.

McElroy, Colleen J. (b. 1935)
Caledonia.
Dreams of Johnson Grass.
For Want of a Male a Shoe Was Lost.
Foul Line—1987.
From Homegrown: An Asian-American
    Anthology of Writers.
Ghost-Who-Walks, The.
Gra'ma was a little bit of a thing.
Griots Who Know Brer Fox, The.
Horoscope.
Illusion.
In My Mother's Room.
Learning to Swim at Forty-Five.
Looking for a Country under Its Original
    Name.
Memoirs of American Speech, *sels.*
Pike Street Bus.
Queen of the Ebony Isles.
Ruth.
Tapestries.
This Is the Poem I Never Meant to Write.
Under the Oak Table.
With Bill Pickett at the 101 Ranch.
Woman's Song, A.

McElroy, David (b. 1941)
Before Breakup on the Chena outside
    Fairbanks.
Dragging in Winter.
Making It Simple December 8, 1969.
Nocturn at the Institute.
Ode to a Dead Dodge.
Report from the Correspondent They Fired.
Spawning in Northern Minnesota.

McFadden, David (b. 1940)
Form of Passion, A.
House Plants.

Lennox Island.

McFadden, Roy (b. 1921)
Contemplations of Mary.
Epithalamium: "So you are married, girl. It
    makes me sad."
First Letter to an Irish Novelist.
For the Record.
Grand Central Hotel, The.
March.
Memories of Chinatown, *sels.*
My Mother's Young Sister.
Stringer's Field.

McFarlane, Basil (b. 1922)
Arawak Prologue.

McFarlane, J. E. Clare (1894–1962)
On National Vanity.

McGaugh, Lawrence (b. 1940)
To Children.
Two Mornings.
Young Training.

McGinley, Phyllis (1905–78)
About Children.
Adversary, The.
All around the Town, *sels.*
Ballade of Lost Objects.
Choice of Weapons, A.
City Christmas.
Conquerors, The.
Daniel at Breakfast.
Day after Sunday, The.
Death at Suppertime.
Demagogue, The.
Evening Musicale.
Garland of Precepts, A.
Giveaway, The.
How to Start a War.
I Know a Village, *sels.*
Independent, The.
Journey toward Evening.
Lament for Lost Lodgings.
Last Year's Discussion: The Nobel Russian.
Midcentury Love Letter.
Muted Screen of Graham Greene, The.
Notes for a Southern Road Map.
Ode to the End of Summer.
Office Party.
Old Beauty, The.
Portrait of Girl with Comic Book.
Public Journal.
Publisher's Party.
Reflections at Dawn.
Spanish Lions, The.
Speaking of Television, *sels.*
Spectator's Guide to Contemporary Art, *sels.*
Temptations of Saint Anthony, The.
Theology of Jonathan Edwards, The.
Trial and Error.
Trinity Place.
Triolet Against Sisters.
Velvet Hand, The.
Village Spa.
Why, Some of My Best Friends Are Women.
Women of Jericho, The.

McGirt, James Ephriam (1874–1930)
Born like the pines to sing.
Century Prayer, The.
Memory of Lincoln and the Yankees.
My Song.
Nothing to Do.
Tell me, oh fate, is it decreed.
When de Sun Shines Hot.

McGonagall, William (1825–1902)
Albion Battleship Calamity, The.
Famous Tay Whale, The.
Hen It Is a Noble Beast, The.
Tay Bridge Disaster, The, *sels.*

McGough, Robert
Fight of the Year, The.

McGough, Roger (b. 1937)
Bully night / I do not like.
Cousin Nell.
Cousin Reggie.
First Day at School.
40—   Love.
Goodbat Nightman.
Harum Scarum.

He Who Owns the Whistle Rules the World.
If Life's a Lousy Picture, Why Not Leave
before the End.
Italic.
Just Another Autumn Day.
Kleptomaniac, The.
Leader, The.
Let me die a youngman's death.
MARCH ingorders.
May.
My Cat and I.
Newly Pressed Suit, The.
Noah's Ark.
P.C. Plod versus the Dale St. Dog Strangler.
Phew.
Poem for a Dead Poet.
Poem With a Limp.
Potato clock, a potato clock, A.
Prayer to Saint Grobianus.
Snow Poem.
Snowman, The.
Snowman in a field.
Square Dance, A.
Storm.
Summer with Monika, *sels.*
Survivor.

McGrath, Campbell
Dialectical Poem #1.
James Wright, Richard Hugo, the Vanishing
Forests of the Pacific Northwest.
Sunrise and Moonfall, Rosarito Beach.
What They Drank.
Wheatfield Under Clouded Sky.

McGrath, John (b. 1935)
Song.

McGrath, Thomas (1916–90)
Black Train, The.
Blues for Warren.
Bread of this World; Praises III, The.
Coal Fire in Winter, A.
Death for the Dark Stranger.
End of the Line, The.
End of the world: it was given to me to see
it, The.
Epitaph: "Again, traveller, you have come a
long way led by that star."
Fresco: Departure for an Imperialist War.
Go Ask the Dead.
Guiffre's Nightmusic.
Jig Tune: Not for Love.
Letter for Marian, A.
Letter to an Imaginary Friend, *sels.*
Letter to an Imaginary Friend, Part One, *sels.*
Letter to an Imaginary Friend, Part Two, *sels.*
Long Way Outside Yellowstone, A.
Nocturne Militaire.
Ode for the American Dead in Asia.
Offering.
Reading the Names of the Vietnam War
Dead.
Remembering the Children of Auschwitz.
Song: "Lovers in ladies' magazines."

McGreevy, Thomas. *See* **MacGreevy, Thomas**

McGregor, Duncan Campbell
Limerick: "There was a young curate called
Lloyd."

McGuckian, Medbh (b. 1950)
Aphrodisiac, The.
Coleridge.
Collusion.
Dream-Language of Fergus, The.
Flitting, The.
Flower Master, The.
Folk Museum, The.
Gateposts.
Laurentia.
Little House, Big House.
Lychees.
Mast Year, The.
Mr. McGregor's Garden.
On Ballycastle Beach.
On Not Being Your Lover.
Orchid House, The.
Presence, The.
Sea or Sky?
Seed-Picture, The.
Sitting, The.

Sofa, The.
Time before You, The.
To a Cuckoo at Coolanlough.
Tulips.
Waterford.

McGuire, Jack
Streets of Forbes, The.

McHugh, Heather (b. 1948)
And What Do You Get.
Corps d'Esprit.
Earthmoving Malediction.
I Knew I'd Sing.
In Light of Time.
Inflation.
Night Catch.
Note Delivered by a Female Impersonator.
Oven Loves the TV Set, The.
Place Where Things Got.
Spilled.
Take Care.
Third Person Neuter.
Tornado Survivor.
20-200 on 747.
20-200 on 737.
What Could Hold Us.
What Hell Is.

McKay, Claude (1889–1948)
Africa.
After the Winter.
America.
Baptism.
Enslaved.
Fetchin Water.
Flame-Heart.
Harlem Dancer, The.
Harlem Shadows.
I Know My Soul.
If we must die—let it not be like hogs.
In Bondage.
Jasmine.
Lynching, The.
My Mother.
Negro's Tragedy, The.
North and South.
Outcast.
Pagan Isms, The.
St. Isaac's Church, Petrograd.
Spring in New Hampshire.
Subway Wind.
Tiger.
Tired Worker, The.
To O.E.A E. A.
To the White Fiends.
Tropics in New York, The.
Truth.
White City, The.
White House, The.
Wild Goat, The.

McKay, Don (b. 1942)
Barbed Wire Fence Meditates upon the
Goldfinch, A.
I Scream You Scream.
March Snow.

McKay, Lois Weakley
Night.

McKean, James (fl. 20th cent.)
After Listening to Jack Teagarden. . . .

McKinney, Irene
Chrysanthemums.
Dance, The.
Deep Mining.
Rapt.
Sunday Morning, 1950.
Twilight in West Virginia: Six O'Clock Mine
Report.
Visiting My Gravesite: Talbott Churchyard,
West Virginia.

McKinney, Laurence (b. 1944)
Oboe.

McKinnon, Barry (b. 1944)
Bushed.
North, The.

McKuen, Rod (b. 1933)
Thoughts on Capital Punishment.
Voyeur, The.

McLachlan, Alexander (1818–40)
Emigrant, The, *sels.*

We Live in a Rickety House.

McLaughlin, Kathy
Suicide Pond.

McLeod, Irene (b. 1891)
Lone Dog.

McMahon, Lynne
Ann Lee.
Barbie's Ferrari.
Convalescence.
Devolution of the Nude.
Hopkins and Whitman.
Little Elegy for the Age.

McManus, Frank R.
Limerick: "Precede us, O Lord, with Thy
Grace."

McManus, James (b. 1951)
Spike Logic.

McMaster, Rhyll (b. 1947)
Back Steps Lookout.
Clockface.
Mutton Bird Man.
Profiles of My Father.
Round Song, A.
Tanks.

McMichael, James (b. 1939)
Cabin North of It All, The.
Great Garret, or 100 Wheels, The.
Inland Lighthouse, The.
Lutra, the Fisher.
Person She Is, The, *sels.*
Terce.
Village of the Presents, The.

McMullen, Anna (b. 1904)
By the River.

McMullen, Richard E.
It happens working.

McNair, Wesley (b. 1941)
Before People, The.
House in Spring.
Hunt Walking.
Mina Bell's Cows.
Minister's Death, The.
My Brother Inside the Revolving Doors.
My Brother Running: V.
Where I Live.

McNaughton, Anne
Balls.
Jelly Piece Song, The.

McNeill, Anthony (fl. c.1941)
Dermis.
Don.
Hello Ungod.
Residue.
Saint Ras.
Straight Seeking.
Victors, The.
Wreath for the Suicide Heart, A.

McNeill, Louise
Hill Daughter.

McOrlan, Pierre (1882–1970)
Accessories shop, The.
Battery woman.
Hairdresser's, The.
Horse butcher, The.
Modern circus, The.
Produce from the colonies.
Weighing-machine, The.
Wood merchant's parlour, The.

McPherson, Heather (b. 1942)
Close-up.
Have You Heard of Artemisia?
Theology and a Patchwork Absolute.

McPherson, Sandra (b. 1943)
Ability to Make a Face Like a Spider While
Singing Blues: Junior Wells, The.
At the Grave of Hazel Hall.
Bittern, The.
Black Soap.
Children.
Coconut for Katerina, A.
Edge Effect.
Elegies for the Hot Season.
For Elizabeth Bishop.
Games.
Gnawing the Breast.

Helen Todd: My Birthname.
His Body.
Marlow and Nancy.
Microscope in Winter, The.
Museum of the Second Creation, The.
1943.
Page.
Peter Rabbit.
Phlox Diffusa: A Poem for My Fiftieth
    Birthday.
Pregnancy.
Quilt of Rights.
Resigning from a Job in a Defense Industry.
Seaweeds.
Sentience.
Sisters.
Some Metaphysics of Junior Wells.
Streamers.
Suspension: Junior Wells on a Small Stage in
    a Converted Barn.
Waiting for Lesser Duckweed: On a Proposal
    of Issa's.
Wanting a Mummy.
Wings and Seeds.

McPower, Kate
    Limerick: "Teacher of tots at Uttoxeter, A."

McQueen, Cilla (b. 1949)
    Studio Poem.
    To Ben, at the Lake.

McTair, Roger (b. 1943)
    Guerrillas.
    Politics Kaiso.

McTurk, Michael (1843–1915)
    Deh 'Pon Um Again.
    Query.

McWatt, Mark
    Boat Builder, The.
    Lady Northcote.
    Man in the House, A.
    Stone.

McWilliam, George
    Limerick: "When the census man called upon
    Gail."

Mead, Margaret (1901–78)
    Misericordia.
    That I not be a restless ghost.

Mead, Philip (b. 1953)
    Cinema Point.
    From a Republican Grave: Daniel Henry
    Deniehy, 1828–1865.
    Man and the Tree, The.
    Melbourne or the Bush.
    There.

Mead, Stella (d. 1981)
    Last Gate, The.
    When We Are Men.

Means, Alex (1801–83)
    What Wondrous Love Is This.

Mearns, Hughes (1875–1965)
    Antigonish.
    Perfect Reactionary, The.

Mechain, Gwerfyl (c.1460–1500)
    In the Snowfall.
    Lady of the Ferry Inn.

Mechthild von Magdeburg (1210–94)
    Desert Has Many Teachings, The.
    Effortlessly, / Love flows from God into
    man.
    Fish cannot drown in water, A.
    God Speaks to the Soul.
    God's Absence.
    How God Answers the Soul.
    How God Comes to the Soul.
    How the Soul Speaks to God.
    I cannot dance, O Lord.
    Love Flows from God.
    Of all that God has shown me.
    True love in every moment praises God.

Medici, Lorenzo de' (1449–92)
    Carnival Songs, *sels.*
    Two Lyrics, *sels.*

Medicine-Tail
    He was there / Old Man Coyote.

Meehan, Maude
    Gift for my Mother's 90th Birthday.
    Is There Life after Feminism.

Small Wings, *sels.*

Meek, Jay
    Vienna in the Rain.
    Walk Around the Lake, A.
    Walls.
    Week the Dirigible Came, The.

Meeks, Brian (b. 1953)
    Coup-clock Clicks, The.
    Las' Rights.

Meenakshi, R. (b. 1944)
    If Hot Flowers Come to the Street.

Mehri (1404–47)
    Coming Across.

Mehrotra, Arvind Krishna (b. 1947)
    Roys, The.

Mei Sheng (*fl.* 1st cent. B.C.) *and* Fu I
    Nineteen Old Poems of the Han, *sels.*

Mei Sheng (*fl.* 1st cent. B.C.)
    Years Vanish Like the Morning Dew.

Mei Yao Ch'en (1002–60)
    Aboard a Boat at Night, Drinking with My
    Wife.
    At Night, Hearing Someone Singing in the
    House Next Door.
    Back from Green Dragon.
    Boat-pullers, The.
    Borrowing Rice from Ju-hui.
    Chiang Lin-chi Treats Me to Mudfish.
    Crescent moon shines, The.
    Dappled Horse, The.
    Dream at Night, A.
    Eating Shepherd's-purse.
    Elegy for a White Cock.
    Excuse for Not Returning the Visit of a
    Friend, An.
    Fish Peddler.
    Friend Advises Me to Stop Drinking, A.
    I Remember the Blue River.
    I Remember the River at Wu Sung.
    In Broad Daylight I Dream of My Dead
    Wife.
    Little Village, A.
    Lunar Eclipse.
    Marrying Again.
    Meeting the Herdsmen.
    Melon Girl.
    Mourning for My Wife.
    My Neighbor to the South, the Office Clerk
    Hsiao, Came in the Evening to Say Good-
    bye.
    Next Door.
    Offering for the Cat, An.
    On Hearing that Holders of the *Chin-shih*
    Degree Are Dealing in Tea.
    On Seeing a Painting of Plants and Insects
    by Chü-ning.
    On the Death of a New Born Child.
    On the Death of His Wife.
    On the Night of the Fifteenth Day of the
    First Month I Go Out and Return.
    On the Thirteenth Day of the Eleventh Month
    I Went to the Granary for the First Time
    since My Illness.
    Out and Back on the Fifteenth Night of the
    First Month.
    Poverty on the Bank.
    Sad Remembrance.
    Second Marriage.
    Sharing Lodging with Hsieh Shih-hou.
    Shih-hou Pointed Out to Me That from
    Ancient Times There Had Never Been a
    Poem on the Subject of Li.
    Solitary Falcon above the Buddha Hall of the
    Monastery of universal Purity, A.
    Sorrow.
    Swarming Mosquitoes.
    Year Wu-tzu [1048], The, First Month, Night
    of the Twenty-sixth: A Dream.

**Meidhre, Brian MacGiolla. See Merriman,
Brian**

**Meigs, Mildred Plew (Mildred Plew Merryman)
(d. 1944)**
    Abraham Lincoln.
    Pirate Don Durk of Dowdee, The.
    Shepherd Left Behind, The.

Meilyr Brydydd (*fl.* 1100–1137)
    Poem on His Death-Bed.

Meinke, Peter
    Advice to My Son.
    Atomic Pantoum.
    Dear Reader.
    Death of the Pilot Whales, The.
    Elegy for a Diver.
    Helen.
    Poet, Trying to Surprise God, The.
    Sonnet on the Death of the Man Who
    Invented Plastic Roses.
    Supermarket.
    This is a poem to my son Peter.
    To a Daughter with Artistic Talent.

Meinloh von Sevelingen (*fl.* c.1170)
    My eyes have seen and chosen for me a
    handsome youth.
    Woe then to the gossips! They show their
    evil will.

Meïr of Rothenburg (1215–53)
    Burning of the Law, The.

Meireles, Cecília (1901–64)
    Ballad of the Ten Casino Dancers.
    Dead Horse, The.
    Pyrargyrite Metal, 9.
    Roosters Will Crow, The.
    Song: "I placed my dream in a boat."

Meissner, William [*or* "Bill"]
    After Going Off the Road During the
    Snowstorm.
    Twisters.

Melbourne, Hirini (b. 1949)
    Tamaki of a Hundred Lovers.
    Why the Wind Comes.

Meleager (*fl.* 1st cent. B.C.)
    All that he is . . . does . . . is attractive.
    Asclepias who loves to love.
    Burn not too oft who flutters at thy flame.
    Busy with love, the bumble bee.
    By Cypris, Cupid!
    By Timo's locks.
    Cicala stoned with dew.
    Clearista.
    Counts itself lucky.
    Cupid at Venus' breast.
    Dorcas, be off! & tell her this.
    Down through the earth as a last gift.
    Epigram: "And now I, Meleager, am among
    them."
    Epigram: "As honey in wine / wine, honey."
    Epigram: "At 12 o'clock in the afternoon."
    Epigram: "Breath of my life, The—no less."
    Epigram: "I was thirsty."
    Epigram: "It is true that I held Thero fair."
    Eyes / flatterers of Soul.
    Foresworn now the love-vows!
    Garland for Heliodora, A.
    Goat-foot Pan has quit his flocks.
    Heliodora's Brows.
    I swear by desire.
    I'll Twine White Violets, *sels.*
    In heart's space hath Eros.
    In the Spring.
    Inconstant Dawn, thou tak'st thy time.
    Little Love-God, The.
    Lost! Cupid!/ One lost Cupid!
    Lost Desire.
    Love at the Door.
    Love cast!
    Love in silence shall.
    Love like a heavy wave.
    Love's night and a lamp.
    More than Apollo's golden lyre.
    Mother of gods.
    Night and Night's longing.
    O Gentle Ships.
    Of Himself.
    Of His Death.
    Petals fall from Heliodora's image, The.
    Pour this wine.
    Regions of Tyre are noted, The.
    *She's gone! Call Rape! Call Robbers!
    Violence!.*
    Something in my soul.
    Soul counsels flight.
    Sounds of love are needles in my ears, The.
    Spring.
    Sweetly hath Dorcas of Lycaenis learnt.

'Tis Timarion.
Tread lightly, Stranger!
Upon a Maid That Died [*or* Dyed] the Day
   She Was Married [*or* Marryed].
Volatile mosquito.
What have you got to crow about.
White violets flower.
Whose the hand unloosed Clearista's zone.
You're in love with love.

Meléndez, Jesús Papoleto
Oye Mundo/Sometimes.

Melican, Terence
Limerick: "There was a young man of
   Newcastle."

Melinescu, Gabriela (b. 1942)
Birth.
Time of Fish Dying.

Melly, George (b. 1926)
Homage to René Magritte.

Melo, David Abenatar (b. 1550)
Thanksgiving.

Melo Neto, João Cabral de (b. 1920)
Daily Space.
Education by stone: through lessons, An.
Emptiness of man is not like, The.
End of the World, The.
Knife All Blade, A.
Landscape of the Capibaribe River.

Meltzer, David (b. 1937)
18:VI:82.
Eyes, the Blood, The.
Prayerwheel: 2.
Ragas, *sels.*
Revelations.
17:II:82.
What do I know of journey.

Melvill, Elizabeth, Lady Culross (*fl.* c.1603)
Ane Godlie Dreame.
Ane Godly Dream, *sels.*
Godly Dream, A, *sels.*
Sonnet sent to Blackness to Mr. John
   Welsch, by the Lady Culross, A.

Melville, Herman (1819–91)
Aeolian Harp, The.
After the Pleasure Party.
America.
Apparition, The.
Arch, The.
Archipelago, The.
Art.
Attic Landscape, The.
Ball's Bluff.
Battle Summers, The.
Bench of Boors, The.
Berg, The.
Billy Budd, Foretopman, *sels.*
Blue-Bird, The.
Bridegroom Dick, *sels.*
By the Jordan.
Camoëns.
Chipmunk, The.
Clarel: A Poem and Pilgrimage in the Holy
   Land, *sels.*
College Colonel, The.
Coming Storm, The.
Commemorative of a Naval Victory.
Conflict of Convictions, The.
Dirge for McPherson, A.
Enthusiast, The.
Enviable Isles, The.
Far Off-Shore.
Formerly a Slave.
Fragments of a Lost Gnostic Poem of the
   Twelfth [*or* 12th] Century.
Fruit and Flower Painter.
Greek Architecture.
Guide and Guard.
Haglets, The.
Healed of My Hurt.
Herba Santa.
House-Top, The.
Immolated.
In a Bye-Canal.
In a Church of Padua.
In a Garret.
In the Desert.

In the Pauper's Turnip-Field.
In the Prison Pen.
Inscription: "To them who crossed the flood."
Iris.
Island, The.
John Marr, *sels.*
Little Good Fellows, The.
Lover and the Syringa-Bush, The.
Maldive Shark, The.
Malvern Hill.
Man-of-War Hawk, The.
March into Virginia, The.
Martyr, The.
Memorial on the Slain at Chickamauga.
Misgivings.
Moby Dick, *sels.*
Monody.
New Ancient of Days, The.
Night-March, The.
Old Age in His Ailing.
Parthenon, The.
Pebbles.
Pontoosuc.
Portent, The.
Ravaged Villa, The.
Requiem[:] for Soldiers Lost in Ocean
   Transports, A.
Return of the Sire de Nesle *A.D. 16*, The.
Rolfe and the Palm.
Rosary Beads.
Rose Farmer, The.
Rose Window.
Rusty Man, The.
Shelley's Vision.
Sheridan at Cedar Creek.
Shiloh [A Requiem].
Song from *Mardi.*
Spirit appeared to me, and said, A.
Stonewall Jackson.
Swamp Angel, The.
Temeraire, The.
Time's Betrayal.
Timoleon.
To.
To Ned.
Tom Deadlight.
Tuft of Kelp, The.
Uninscribed Monument on One of the
   Battlefields of the Wilderness, An.
Utilitarian View of the Monitor's Fight, A.
Venice.
We fish, we fish, we merrily swim.

Melville, Pauline
Homeland.
Honor Maria, I see you.
Stonebridge Park Estate.

Menahem ben Jacob (d. 1203)
Harvesting of the Roses, The.
Martyr's Death, A.

**Menahem ben Makhir of Ratisbon (*fl.* 11th
cent.)**
How Sweet Thy Precious Gift of Rest.

Menai, Huw (1887–1961)
Back in the Return, *sels.*

Menander (342–290 B.C.)
Epitrepontes (The Arbitration), The, *sels.*
On Epicurus and Themistokles.

Menard, John Willis (1838–93)
Good-bye! Off for Kansas.
Negro's Lament, The.
To My Wife.

Menashe, Samuel (b. 1925)
Annunciation, The.

Mendelssohn, Felix
Every Day.

Mendelssohn, Moses (1728–86)
Self-Portrait.

Mendès, Catulle (1841–1909)
I Go by Road.
Mother, The.

Mendes, Moses (d. 1758)
Chaplet, The, *sels.*
On the Death of a Lady's Owl.

Mendes Zapata, Santiago
Story of the Eaters, A.

Meng Chiao (751–814)
After Passing the Examination.
Apricots Die Young, *sels.*
Autumn Meditations, *sels.*
Autumn Thoughts, *sels.*
Ballad of Ching Mountain.
Complaint of a Neglected Wife.
Excursion to the Dragon Pool Temple on
   Chung-nan, An.
Expressing My Feelings.
Failing the Examination.
Impromptu.
Lament for Lu Yin.
Laments of the Gorges, *sels.*
On Failing the Examination.
On Mount Ching.
Sadness of the Gorges, *sels.*
Seeing Off Master Tan.
Song of the Old Man of the Hills.
Stones Where the Haft Rotted, The.
Stopping on a Journey at the East Water
   Pavilion at Lo-ch'eng.
Wanderer's Song.
Wandering on Mount Chung-nan.

Meng Hao Jan (689–740)
Crossing the Hsiang River at Night.
First of Autumn, The.
Night on the Great River.
On the Street of Lo-yang.
Parting from Wang Wei.
Passing the Night on a River in Chien-te.
Paying a Visit to Monk Yung's Cloister.
Returning by Night to Lu-Men.
Seeking Hsin E in the Western Hills.
Spending the Night at the Hillside Lodge of
   Master Yeh and Waiting for My Friend
   Ting.
Starting Early from Yü-p'u Deep.
Stopping at a Friend's Farm.

Menken, Adah Isaacs (1839?–1868)
Adelina Patti.
Answer Me.
Aspiration.
Autograph on the Soul, The.
Battle of the Stars.
Dreams of Beauty.
Drifts That Bar My Door.
Dying.
Fragment: "Cold chain of life presseth
   heavily on me tonight, The."
Genius is power.
Hear, O Israel! and plead my cause against
   the ungodly nation.
Hemlock in the Furrows.
In Vain.
Infelix.
Into the Depths.
Judith.
Karazah to Karl.
Memory, A.
Miserimus.
My Heritage.
Myself.
One Year Ago.
Pro Patria.
Release, The.
Resurgam.
Sale of Souls.
Saved.
Ship That Went Down, The.
Venetia.
Where the Flocks Shall Be Led.
Working and Waiting.

Menzies, G. K. (1869–1954)
General, The.

Mercer, Jesse (1769–1841)
Will God forever cast us off.

Mercer, Johnny (1909–76)
Glow-Worm, The.
I'm an Old Cowhand.
Jubilation T. Cornpone.

Mercer, Thomas (*fl.* c.1770)
Arthur's Seat, *sels.*

Meredith, George (1828–1909)
Ballad of Past Meridian, A.
Dirge in Woods.
Garden of Epicurus, The.

Hymn to Colour.
King Harald's Trance.
Love in the Valley.
Lucifer in Starlight.
Melampus.
Modern Love, *sels.*
Nuptials of Attila, The, *sels.*
Orchard and the Heath, The.
Phoebus with Admetus.
Thrush in February, The.
When I would image her features.
Young Reynard.

Meredith, Louisa (1812–95)
Tasmanian Scenes.

"Meredith, Owen" (Edward Robert Bulwer-Lytton, 1st Earl of Lytton) (1831–91)
Aux Italiens.
Changes.
Glenaveril, *sels.*
Last Wish, The.
We may live without poetry, music and art.

Meredith, William (b. 1919)
Accidents of Birth.
Bachelor.
Battle Problem.
Botanical Trope, A.
Cheer, The.
Consequences, *sels.*
Country Stars.
Couple Overheard, The.
Crossing Over.
Dying Away.
Effort at Speech.
For Guillaume Apollinaire.
His Plans for Old Age.
Iambic Feet Considered as Honorable Scars.
Ideogram.
Illiterate, The.
Jain Bird Hospital in Delhi, The.
Korean Woman Seated by a Wall, A.
Last Things.
Major Work, A.
Old Field Mowed, An.
On Falling Asleep by Firelight.
Open Sea, The.
Parents.
Partial Accounts.
Poem about Morning.
Preponderance, The.
Recollection of Bellagio.
Rhode Island.
Ritual Mouse, A.
Thoughts on One's Head.
To the Thoughtful Reader.
Tree Marriage.
Walter Jenks' Bath.
Weather.
Wholesome.
Winter Verse for His Sister.

Meredith, William Tuckey (b. 1839)
Farragut, Farragut / Old Heart of Oak.

Merezhkovsky [*or* Merezhkovskii], Dmitry [*or* Dmitrii] Sergeievich (1866–1941)
She Loves Me, She Loves Me Not.

Meriluoto, Aila (b. 1924)
Still.

Merkel, Bob
Owls.

Merriam, Eve (b. 1916)
Catch a Little Rhyme.
Counting-out Rhyme.
Coward, The.
How to Eat a Poem.
Landscape.
Lazy Thought, A.
Lullaby "Purple."
One, Two, Three—Gough!
Restricted.
Sing a Song of Subways.
Spell of Weather, A.
Tube Time.
Wall, The.
Weather.
Which Washington?
Windshield Wiper.

Merriam, Lillie Fuller
At the Door.

Merrick of Aylesbury, A.
Hartwell Gardens.

Merrill, Boynton, Jr. (b. 1925)
Fossil, The.
Mite, The.
Mule, The.

Merrill, Christopher
Because the Dead Sea released its hostages—the taste for salt, a rudder and a sail.

Merrill, James (1926–95)
About the Phoenix.
After Greece.
Angel.
Annie Hill's Grave.
Between Us.
Black Mesa, The.
Body.
Book of Ephraim, The, *sels.*
Broken Bowl, The.
Broken Home, The.
Changing Light at Sandover, The, *sels.*
Charioteer of Delphi, The.
Charles on Fire.
Childlessness.
Coda: The Higher Keys, *sels.*
Country of a Thousand Years of Peace, The.
Current, The.
Days of 1941 and '44.
Days of 1964.
Family Week at Oracle Ranch.
Foliage of Vision.
Friend of the Fourth Decade, The.
Furnished Room, The.
Getting Through.
Grand Canyon, The.
Green Eye, The.
Hotel de l'Univers et Portugal.
In Nine Sleep Valley, *sels.*
In the Dark.
Kimono, The.
Kite Poem.
Laboratory Poem.
Last Words.
Losing the Marbles.
Mad Scene, The.
Maisie.
Manos Karastefanís.
Matinees.
Mirabell: Books of Number, *sels.*
Mirror.
Octopus, The.
Parrot Fish, The.
Pier: Under Pisces, The.
Power Station, The.
Preface to the Memoirs, A.
Pyroxenes, The.
Remora.
Renewal, A.
Scenes of Childhood.
Scripts for the Pageant, *sels.*
Snapshot of Adam.
Swimming By Night.
Syrinx.
Thistledown.
Thousand and Second Night, The.
Timepiece, A.
To a Butterfly.
Tomorrows.
Topics, *sels.*
Up and Down.
Upward Look, An.
Urban Convalescence, An.
Victor Dog, The.
Vision of the Garden, A.
Voices from the Other World.
Watching the Dance.
Willowware Cup.

Merrill, Stuart (1863–1915)
Ballade of the Chinese Lover.
Ballade of the Outcasts.

Merrill, William Pierson (1867–1954)
Not Alone for Mighty Empire.
Rise Up, O Men of God.

Merriman [*or* Merryman], Brian [*or* Bryan] (Brian MacGiolla Meidhre) (1747–1805)
Midnight Court, The, *sels.*

Merritt, Dixon Lanier (1879–1972)
Limerick: "Wonderful bird is the pelican, A."

Merry, Robert ("Della Crusca") (1755–98)
Adieu and Recall to Love, The.
Laurel of Liberty. A Poem, The, *sels.*
Madness.
Sir Roland; a Fragment.
To Anna Matilda.

Merryman, Mildred Plew. *See* Meigs, Mildred Plew

Mersar
Allace! So Sobir Is the Micht.

Merson, Billy (1881–1947)
Spaniard That Blighted My Life, The.

Merton, Thomas (1915–68)
Aubade: Lake Erie.
Cana.
Dark Morning, The.
Elegy for Ernest Hemingway, An.
Elegy for the Monastery Barn.
Evening Prayer.
Lent in a Year of War.
Reader, The.
Responsory, 1948, A.
St. Malachy.
St. Paul.
There Has to Be a Jail for Ladies.

Merwin, William Stanley (b. 1927)
Animals, The.
Another Year Come.
Approaches, The.
Asians Dying, The.
Ballad of John Cable and Three Gentlemen.
Ballade of Sayings.
Bathers, The.
Birds Waking.
Black Jewel, The.
Black Plateau, The.
Bones, The.
Bread.
Broken, The.
Burning Mountain.
Burning the Cat.
Burnt Child, The.
Caesar.
Carol of the Three Kings.
Daybreak.
Dead Hand.
Departure's Girl-friend.
Diggers, The.
Distances, The.
Divinities.
Door, A.
Drunk in the Furnace, The.
Dusk in Winter.
Early January.
Elegy: "Who would I show it to."
Evening.
Exercise.
February.
Fields, The.
Finding a Teacher.
Fly.
Footprints on the Glacier.
For a Coming Extinction.
For the Anniversary of My Death.
Glass.
Grandfather in the Old Men's Home.
Grandmother Watching at Her Window.
Hearing.
Herds, The.
Highway, The.
Home for Thanksgiving.
I Live up Here.
In the Winter of My Thirty-eighth Year.
Initiate, The.
Judgment of Paris, The.
Lament for the Makers.
Last One, The.
Lemuel's Blessing.
Letter.
Leviathan.
Looking for Mushrooms at Sunrise.
Losing a Language.
Low Fields and Light.
Moths, The.
Mountain, The.

Native, The.
Night of the Shirts, The.
Night Singing.
Noah's Raven.
Odysseus.
Old Boast, The.
Old Room, The.
One of the Lives.
Peasant.
Piper, The.
Place of Backs, The.
Plea for a Captive.
"Portland" Going Out, The.
"Prodigal Son," The, *sels.*
Rain Travel.
Resolution.
River of Bees, The.
Room, The.
Sapphire, The.
Separation.
Sire.
Small Woman on Swallow Street.
Snowfall.
Some Last Questions.
Song of Man Chipping an Arrowhead.
Song of Three Smiles.
St. Vincent's.
Stranger, The.
Strawberries.
Sunset after Rain.
Surf-casting.
Things.
Thorn Leaves in March.
To My Brother Hanson.
To the Hand.
Travelling Together.
Unwritten, The.
Utterance.
Variation on the Gothic Spiral.
Views from the High Camp.
Vineyard, The.
Voice.
Voyage to Labrador.
Way to the River, The.
West Wall.
What is a Garden.
Wheels of the Trains, The.
When I Came from Colchis.
When the War Is Over.
When you go away the wind clicks around to
    the north.
Widow, The.
Witnesses.
Yesterday.

Mesens, E. L. T.
Arid Husband, The.
Untranslatable Factual Items.
Way to Finish it Off, The.

Messerli, Douglas (b. 1947)
Actually Swallowed.
Along Without: A Fiction in Film for Poetry,
    sels.
Angry with China.
Annunciation, The.
Closure.
Essay on Concrete, An.
From Hear to Air.
Going to Sea.
Harrowing.
Scared Cows.
This That and Then.

Metastasio, Pietro (1698–1782)
Age of Gold.

Metcalf, Richard
These Are Not Lost.

Metcalfe, James J.
Visit the Sick.

Mew, Charlotte (1870–1928)
À Quoi Bon Dire.
Absence.
Afternoon Tea.
Again.
At the Convent Gate.
Beside the Bed.
Call, The.
Cenotaph, The.
Changeling, The.

Domus Caedet Arborem.
Fame.
Farmer's Bride, The.
Forest road, The.
Here Lies a Prisoner.
I Have Been Through the Gates.
I So Liked Spring.
In Nunhead Cemetery.
In the Fields.
June, 1915.
Ken.
Madeleine in Church.
Monsieur Qui Passe.
My heart is lame with running after yours so
    fast.
Ne Me Tangito.
Not for that city of the level sun.
Old Shepherd's Prayer.
On the Asylum Road.
On the Road to the Sea.
Pedlar, The.
Quiet House, The.
Rambling Sailor, The.
Rooms.
Saturday Market, *sels.*
Sea Love.
Shade-Catchers, The.
Smile, Death.
Song: "Love, love today, my dear."
To a Child in Death.
Trees Are Down, The.

Mey, Mildred T.
Quiet Days.

Meyers, Bert (1928–79)
Daybreak.
Pigeons.
Suburban Dusk.

Meyers, Linda Curtis
Apple-Eater, The.

Meyn, Barbara
At the Planning Commission.

**Meynell, Alice Thompson (Mrs. Wilfrid
Meynell) (1847–1922)**
After a Parting.
At Night.
Beyond Knowledge.
Chimes.
Christ in the Universe.
Cradle-Song at Twilight.
Easter Night.
Father of Women, A [Ad Sororem E. B.].
Fugitive, The.
General Communion, A.
Girl on the Land, The.
"I Am the Way."
In Portugal, 1912.
In Sleep.
Lady Poverty was fair, The.
Launch, The.
Letter from a Girl to Her Own Old Age, A.
Maternity.
Modern Mother, The.
November Blue.
October Redbreast, The.
Parentage.
Parted.
Rainy Summer, The.
Renouncement.
Roaring Frost, The.
Shattered Lute, A.
Shepherdress, The.
Singers to Come.
Song of Derivations, A.
Song of the Night at Daybreak.
Study, A.
Summer in England, 1914.
Sunderland Children, The.
Threshing Machine, The.
Thrush before Dawn, A.
To "A Certain Rich Man."
To a Daisy.
To Silence.
To the Beloved.
To the Body.
Two Questions, The.
Veni Creator.
Watershed, The.

Wind Is Blind, The.

Meynell, Viola (1886–1956)
Frozen Ocean, The.
Sympathy.

Mezey, Robert (b. 1935)
Against Seasons.
Back.
Confession, A.
Couplets, XX.
Funeral Home, The.
How Much Longer?
If I Should Die Before I Wake.
In the Soul Hour.
Night on Clinton.
Stream Flowing, The.
Street Scene.
Thousand Chinese Dinners, A, *sels.*
Trying to Begin.
Vetus Flamma.

Mezhirov, Aleksandr Petrovich (b. 1923)
Ballad about the Circus.
Farewell to Arms, A.
From the War.
I can usually feel at home in rooms.
Ice of Ladoga, The.
Lines about a Little Boy.
Loneliness chases me.
Man lives in the wide world, A.
Troop Train.
We are huddled in a crowd before Kolpino.
We would awaken in a twilight gloom.

Mhac an tSaoi, Máire (b. 1922)
Harvest of the Sea.

Mhlongo, Swidi-Nonkamfela (b. 1948)
His Praises.

Miadesnia
Postscript to Orwell's *Animal Farm*, A.

Mibu no Tadami (*fl.* 10th cent.)
Since I left her.
Yes, I am in love.

Miccolis, Leila (b. 1947)
I wanted to see you, / thighs showing.
Till Death Do Us Part.

Michael of Kildare, Friar (*fl.* 14th cent.)
Swet Jesus.

Michael, Ras
Preface: "I stood watching / I the parade of
    floats."

Michaux, Henri (1899–1984)
Simplicity.
Slices of Knowledge, *sels.*
Tomorrow.

Michelangelo Buonarroti (1474–1564)
Celestial Love.
Dante.
Doom of Beauty, The.
Garland and the Girdle, The.
I see in your handsome face, my Lord.
Joy May Kill.
Love, the Light-Giver [*or* To Tommaso de'
    Cavalieri].
Love's Entreaty.
Love's Justification.
On the Brink of Death.
Prayer for Purification, A.
Three Poems, *sels.*
To Giovanni da Pistoia When the Author
    Was Painting the Vault of the Sistine
    Chapel, 1509.
To the Supreme Being.
To Vittoria Colonna.
Transfiguration of Beauty, The.

Michelson, Max
Bird, The.
Hymn to Night, A.

Michelson, Richard
Undressing Aunt Frieda.

Michie, James (b. 1927)
Arizona Nature Myth.
Discoverer.
Dooley Is a Traitor.
Ghost of an Education, The.
Nine Times.
To My Daughter.

Michinobu (Fujiwara no Michinobo)
Day will soon be gone, The. *From* Hyaku-Nin-Isshu.

Michitsuna, the Mother of (*fl.* late 10th cent.)
Have you any idea.
Is our love over?
Sighing, sleeping alone all night.
Whenever the wind blows / I try to question it.

Mickle, William Julius (1735–88)
Cumnor Hall.
There's Nae Luck about the House.

Middleton, Christopher (b. 1926)
Adelaide's Dream.
Edward Lear in February.
In Some Seer's Cloud Car.
In the Secret House.
News from Norwood.
Oystercatchers.

Middleton, Elizabeth (b. 1619?)
Death and Passion of Our Lord Jesus Christ, The, *sels.*
S—uche Is the Love I beare thy Honest Hart.

Middleton, Jesse Edgar (b. 1872)
Huron Carol, The.

Middleton, Richard (1882–1911)
Carol of the Poor Children, The.

Middleton, Thomas (1580–1627)
Changeling, The.
Melancholy.
Witch, The, *sels.*
Women Beware Women, *sels.*

Midlane, Albert (1825–1909)
Above the Bright Blue Sky, *sels.*

Miedzyrzecki, Artur (b. 1922)
At the Cave.
At Work.
Can You Imagine.
End of the Game.
Golden Age, The.
Penguins.
29-77-02.
What does the political scientist know?

"Mighty Chalkdust, The" (b. 1940)
Brain Drain.

"Mighty Sparrow, The" (Francisco Slinger) (b. 1935)
Get to Hell Outa Here.
Yankees Back, The.

Miguel de Guevara (1585–1646)
Raise me up, Lord, who am fallen down.

Mihalic, Slavko (b. 1928)
Approaching Storm.
Atlantis.
Autumn.
Drinking Spree Beneath the Open Sky.
Elegy: "From the old settlements only the writings."
Exile's Return, The.
I cannot say the name of the city.
Large Grieving Women.
Maestro, extinguish the candle, serious times have come.
Man Who Decided, The.
Metamorphosis.
Morning Roar of the City, The.
On the Carpet, Staring at Myself.
Screams in the Dark.
Second-Class Citizen.
Under the Microscope.

Miidhu
War Dance.

Mikata Shami [*or* Mikata no Sami] (Yamada Mikata) (*fl.* late 7th cent.)
Bound up it always.

Mikata, Yamada. *See* **Mikata Shami**

Milaipperun Kantan
What His Friend Said, Teasing the Man in Love.
What She Said ("Only the dim-witted say it's evening.")

Milan, Jyotsna (b. 1941)
Woman, 2.

Miles, George Henry (1824–71)
Said the Rose.

Miles, Josephine (1911–85)
Album.
As Difference Blends into Identity.
Beach Party Given by T. Shaughnessy for the Sisters.
Belief.
Bibliographer.
Bounty.
Bureau 2.
Campaign, The.
Care.
Civilian.
Conception.
Concert.
Day the Winds, The.
Dear Frank, Here is a poem.
Doctor Who Sits at the Bedside of a Rat, The.
Doll.
Dolor.
Dream.
Entrepreneur chicken shed his tail feathers, surplus, The.
Family.
Fields of Learning.
Find.
Forecast.
Gypsy.
In the town where every man is king.
Made Shine.
Maxim.
Merchant Marine.
Monkey.
None.
Oedipus.
Officers.
On Inhabiting an Orange.
Parent.
Preliminary to Classroom Lecture.
Reason.
Ride.
Sale.
Savages, The.
Sisyphus.
So Graven.
Sorrow.
Summer.
Sunday.
Tally.
Travelers.
Voyage.
When I was eight, I put in the left-hand drawer.
When Sanders brings feed to his chickens, some sparrows.
Why We Are Late.

Miles, Judy
Seasons Greetings, Love and Revolution.

Miles, Susan (Ursula Roberts) (b. 1887)
Hares, The.
He Sports by Himself.
Microcosmos.
Plumbers.

Miliauskaite, Nijole (b. 1950)
In the damp places.
On winter nights, when my grandmother.
Temporary City.
These are lilacs.

Miljkovic, Branko (1934–60)
Agon.
Ballade: "Wisdom, innocently the sun rises."
Black Horseman.
Everyone Will Write Poetry.
In Praise of Plants, *sels.*
Miners.
Sea Before I Start Dreaming, The.
Sea Without Poets.
Shepherd's Flute.
Sleepers.
Sun.

Millard, Edith G.
Banbury Fair.

Millard, Geoffrey C. (b. 1931)
Hospital.

Millay, Edna St. Vincent ("Nancy Boyd") (1892–1950)
Above these cares my spirit in calm abiding.

Afternoon on a Hill.
Ancient Gesture, An.
And you as well must die, belovèd dust.
Apostrophe to Man.
Armenonville.
Ashes of Life.
At least, my dear.
Autumn.
Ballad of the Harp-Weaver, The.
Bean-Stalk, The.
Buck in the Snow, The.
Cameo, The.
Childhood Is the Kingdom Where Nobody Dies.
Conscientious Objector.
Counting-out Rhyme.
Courage that my mother had, The.
Departure.
Dirge Without Music.
Elegy before Death.
Epitaph for the Race of Man, *sels.*
Euclid alone has looked on Beauty bare.
Even in the moment of our earliest kiss.
Exiled.
Fatal Interview, *sels.*
First Fig.
Fitting, The.
From a Train Window.
From a Very Little Sphinx.
God's World.
Grown-up.
Hardy Garden, The.
Hearing your words, and not a word among them.
I, being born a woman and distressed.
I do but ask that you be always fair.
I dreamed I moved among the Elysian fields.
I know I am but summer to your heart.
I Shall Forget You Presently, My Dear.
I shall go back again to the bleak shore.
I think I should have loved you presently.
I too beneath your moon, almighty Sex.
I will put Chaos into fourteen lines.
If I should learn, in some quite casual way.
If in the years to come you should recall.
In the Grave No Flower.
It is the fashion now to wave aside.
Justice Denied in Massachusetts.
Lament: "Listen, children: / Your father is dead."
Love is not all: it is not meat nor drink..
Love is not all: it is not meat or drink.
Love me no more, now let the god depart.
Loving you less than life, a little less.
Make bright the arrows.
Memorial to D. C, *sels.*
Menses.
Modern Declaration.
Moriturus.
My most distinguished guest and learnèd friend.
Never May the Fruit Be Plucked.
Night is my sister, and how deep in love.
Not in a silver casket cool with pearls.
Not with libations, but with shouts and laughter.
O God, I Cried, No Dark Disguise.
Oh, Oh, you will be sorry for that word!
Oh, sleep forever in the Latmian cave.
On Hearing a Symphony of Beethoven.
On the wide heath at evening overtaken.
Only until this cigarette is ended.
Passer Mortuus Est.
Pear Tree, The.
Philosopher, The.
Pity me not because the light of day.
Poet and His Book, The.
Portrait to a Neighbour.
Ragged Island.
Recuerdo.
Renascence, *sels.*
Rendezvous.
Return, The.
Second Fig.
Since of no creature living the last breath.
Snow Storm, The.
Song of a Second April.

Sonnet: "Oh, my belovèd, have you thought
  of this."
Sonnet to Gath.
Sonnets from an Ungrafted Tree, *sels.*
Spring.
Spring in the Garden.
Strawberry Shrub, old-fashioned, quaint as
  quinces.
Think not, nor for a moment let your mind.
This beast that rends me in the sight of all.
Thursday.
Time does not bring relief; you all have lied.
To a Calvinist in Bali.
To a Young Poet.
To Inez Milholland.
To Jesus on His Birthday.
Travel.
True Encounter, The.
Unexplorer, The.
What lips my lips have kissed, and where,
  and why.
What Rider Spurs Him from the Darkening
  East.
When I too long have looked upon your face.
When we are old and these rejoicing veins.
Wild Swans.
Women have loved before as I love now.
You loved me not at all, but let it go.

Miller, Adam David (b. 1922)
Africa Thing, The.
Crack in the Wall Holds Flowers.
Hungry Black Child, The.
Mulch.
Pruning, The.

Miller, Alice Duer (1874–1942)
White Cliffs, The, *sels.*

Miller, Cincinnatus Heine. *See* **Miller, Joaquin**

Miller, David
Primavera.

Miller, E. Ethelbert (b. 1950)
Another Love Affair/Another Poem.
Dressed Up.
Jasmine.
Men, The.
Mississippi.
Rebecca.
She is flat on her back.
Tomorrow.
What the Women Told Me.

Miller, E. K.
My Father's Garden.

Miller, E. S. (b. 1904)
To My Lady.

Miller, Heather Ross (b. 1939)
Girl, Prince, Lizard.
Minor Things.

Miller, Jane (b. 1925)
Countryside.
Far Away.
See also **Broumas, Olga** and **Jane Miller.**

Miller, Jim Wayne (b. 1936)
Closing the House.
Hanging Burley.
Hungry Dead, The.
Plague of Telephones, A.
Squirrel Stand.

**Miller, Joaquin (Cincinnatus Heine [*or* Hiner]
  Miller) (1841–1913)**
Africa.
At Our Golden Gate.
Byron, *sels.*
Columbus.
Defense of the Alamo, The.
For Those Who Fail.
In Père La Chaise.
Pilgrims of the Plains.
Sierras.
Westward Ho!

Miller, Leslie Adrienne
My Students Catch Me Dancing.
Substitute, The.
Weather of Invention, The.

Miller, Madeleine Sweeny (b. 1890)
How Far to Bethlehem?

Miller, Mary Britton (1883–1975)
Cat.

Universe, The.

Miller, May (b. 1918)
Closing, A.
Gift from Kenya.
Not That Far.
Scream, The.

Miller, Peter (b. 1920)
Capture of Edwin Alonzo Boyd, The.
Prevention of Stacy Miller, The.

Miller, Russell
Limerick: "'If you dream,' said the eminent
  Freud."

Miller, Ruth (b. 1919)
Aspects of Love, *sels.*
Birds.
Cycle, *sels.*
It Is Better to Be Together.
Long Since Last.
Mantis.
Penguin on the Beach.
Plankton.
Sterkfontein.

Miller, Stephen Paul
I Was on a Golf Course the Day John Cage
  Died of a Stroke.

Miller, Thomas (1807–74)
Evening.
Watercress Seller, The.

Miller, Vassar (b. 1924)
Adam's Footprint.
Aubade: "I press against the emptiness."
Beat Poem by an Academic Poet.
Beside a Deathbed.
Bird in the Hand, A.
Bout with Burning.
Christmas Mourning.
Defense Rests.
Dirge in Jazz Time.
Final Hunger, The.
How far is it to you by foot?
Judas.
Light Reading.
Love's Bitten Tongue, *sels.*
Mourning, A.
On Approaching My Birthday.
Prayer to my Muse.
Quarry, The.
Reciprocity.
Remembering Aunt Helen.
Slump.
Spinster's Lullaby.
Subterfuge.
Trimming the Sails.
Without Ceremony.

Miller, William (1810–72)
Willie Winkie.

Milligan, Spike (b. 1918)
Bad Report—Good Manners.
Christmas 1970.
Granny.
Limerick: "Man who was asked out to
  dinner, A."
My sister Laura's bigger than me.
Teeth.
Thousand Hairy Savages, A.

Millikin, Richard Alfred (1764–1815)
Groves of Blarney [they look so charming],
  The.

Mills, Ida M.
At Breakfast.
In Days Gone By.

Mills, William (b. 1935)
Motel.
Necessity of Falling, The.
Pity.
Rituals along the Arkansas.
Unemployment.

Mills, William G.
Arise, O glorious Zion.

Milne, Alan Alexander (1882–1956)
Bad Sir Brian Botany.
Buckingham Palace.
Disobedience.
From a Full Heart.
Gold Braid.

Happiness.
Hoppity.
King's Breakfast, The.
More It Snows, The.
Puppy and I.
Three Foxes, The.
Us Two.
Vespers.

Milne, Ewart (b. 1903)
Diamond Cut Diamond.
Martyred Earth, The.
Vanessa Vanessa.

Milner, B. E.
Christmas Night.

Milner-Brown, A. L.
Who knows? This Africa so richly blest.

**Milnes, Richard Monckton, 1st Baron
  Houghton (1809–85)**
England and America, 1863.
Good Night and Good Morning.
Lady Moon, Lady Moon, where are you
  roving?
Men of Old, The.
Sir Walter Scott at the Tomb of the Stuarts
  in St. Peter's.

Milosz, Czeslaw (b. 1911)
Abundant Catch (Luke 5:4–10).
After Paradise.
And yet the books will be there on the
  shelves, separate beings.
Bypassing rue Descartes.
Cafe.
Campo dei Fiori.
Child of Europe.
Dedication: "You whom I could not save /
  Listen to me."
Encounter.
Esse.
Faith.
Felicitous Life, A.
Garden of Earthly Delights, The, *sels.*
Incantation.
It Was Winter.
My Faithful Mother Tongue.
On Angels.
On the Book.
On the Other Side.
Poor Christian Looks at the Ghetto, A.
Proof.
Readings.
Screens will be set there.
"Six Lectures in Verse," *sels.*
St. Luke, *sels.*
St. Mark, *sels.*
St. Matthew, *sels.*
Sun, The.
Task, A.
Temptation.
To Mrs. Professor in Defense of My Cat's
  Honor and Not Only.
To Raja Rao.
To Robinson Jeffers.
With Her*.

Milosz, O. V. de L. (1877–1939)
Bridge, The.
Strophes.

Milton, John (1608–74)
Arcades, *sels.*
At a Solemn Music[k], *sels.*
Comus: a Masque Presented at Ludlow, *sels.*
Comus; a Masque Presented at Ludlow
  Castle, *sels.*
Fifth Ode of Horace. Lib. I, The.
Il Penseroso, *sels.*
Lady That in the Prime.
L'Allegro, *sels.*
Lament for Damon.
Lycidas, *sels.*
O Nightingale, that on yon bloomy Spray.
On His Blindness.
On His Deceased Wife.
On Shakespear[e].
On the Detraction Which Followed upon My
  Writing Certain Treatises.
On the Late Massacre [*or* Massacher] in
  Piedmont [*or* Piemont].

On the Lord Gen[eral] Fairfax at the Siege of Colchester.
On the Morning of Christ's Nativity, *sels.*
On the New Forcers of Conscience Under the Long Parliament.
On the University Carrier Who Sick'n'd [*or* Sickened] in the Time of His Vacancy [, Being Forbid to go to London, by Reason of the Plague].
On Time.
Paradise Lost, *sels.*
Paradise Lost, IV, *sels.*
Praise the Lord.
Samson Agonistes, *sels.*
Song: on [*or* of] May Morning.
Sonnet: "How soon hath Time the suttle [*or* subtle] theef [*or* thief] of youth."
Sonnet: On the Religious Memorie of Mrs. Catherine Thomason My Christian Freind Decea'd Decem. 1646.
Spring Song.
Spring Time.
Star That Bids the Shepherd Fold, The.
To Cyriack Skinner.
To Mr. Lawrence.
To Mr. Cyriack Skinner upon His Blindness.
To Mr. H. Lawes On His Airs.
To Sir Henry Vane the Younger.
To the Lady Margaret Ley.
To the Lord General[l] Cromwell[, on the Proposals of Certain Ministers at the Committee for the Propagation of the Gospel *or* May 1652].
Upon the Circumcision.
When the Assault Was Intended to the City.
Mimnermus (c.650–c.590 B.C.)
There Is No Joy Without Aphrodite.
Youth and Age.
Minamoto no Morotada (*fl.* 12th cent.)
In the mountain village.
Minamoto no Tōru (d. 949)
Like Michinoku.
Minamoto no Toshitaka, the daughter of (*fl.* 12th cent.)
For the sake of a night of a little sleep.
Wind blows through, The.
Minamoto no Tsunenobu (*fl.* late 11th cent.)
In the evening / The rice leaves in the garden.
Ming, T'ao T'ung. See T'ao Hung Ching
Minh Đức Hoài Trinh (Võ thi Hoài Trinh) (b. 1930)
Selling My Soul.
Minhinnick, Robert (b. 1952)
Grandfather in the Garden.
"Minsky, Nicolai Maksimovich" (Nicolai Maksimovich Vilenkin)
Immortality.
Minty, Judith (b. 1937)
Look to the Back of the Hand.
Minuchihri (d. 1041?)
Demon in Paradise.
I send you my verses.
Recantation.
Mirabai [*or* Mira Bai] (1498–1547)
All I Was Doing Was Breathing.
At the Holi festival of color.
Clouds, The.
Friend, don't be angry.
Friend, how can I meet my lord?
Hari helps his people.
Hari, look at me a while.
Heat of Midnight Tears, The.
I can't break with the Dark One.
I don't sleep. All night.
I was going to the river for water.
It's True I Went to the Market.
Keep me as your servant, O Girdhar.
Let me see you.
Love has stained my body.
Mira is dancing with bells tied on her ankles.
My eyes are thirsty.
My love is in my house.
O friend, understand: the body.
O friends, I am mad.
O friends on this Path.

O King, I know you gave me poison.
O my friends.
Rana, I know you gave me poison.
Rana, why do you treat me as your enemy?
Song of the flute, O sister, is madness, The.
Wake, child with the flute.
Wake up, dear boy that holds the flute!
Why Mira Can't Go Back to Her Old House.
Wild woman of the forests, The.
Yogi, don't go away.
Mirikitani, Janice
Breaking Tradition.
Doreen had a round face.
Fisherman, The.
Jade.
Shadow in Stone.
Sing with Your Body.
Soul Food.
Suicide Note.
Mische John, Elizabeth
Racial Memories.
Mish, Charlotte
Stray Dog.
Mishkovsky, Zelda. See "Zelda"
Mishler, Richard M.
Ceremony.
Mishra, Soubhagya Kumar (b. 1941)
Robinson Crusoe.
Mistral, Frédéric (1830–1914)
Leaf-picking, The.
Mirèio, *sels.*
Mistral, Gabriela (Lucila Godoy Alcayaga) (1889–1957)
Bread.
Death Sonnet I.
Drops of Gall.
Dusk.
Everything Is Round.
Martha and Mary.
Midnight.
Prayer, *sels.*
Rose, The.
Sister.
Sleep Close to Me.
Slow Rain.
Song.
Those Who Do Not Dance.
To Noel.
Wall.
Mitcalfe, Barry (b. 1930)
Lamentation on Ninety-Mile Beach.
Mitcham, Judson
Explanations.
Knowledge of Water, A.
Mitchell, Adrian (b. 1937)
Accountant in His Bath, The.
Autobahnmotorwayautoroute.
Beggar shouts his martial wares, The.
Calypso's Song to Ulysses.
Celia Celia.
Dumb Insolence.
Fifteen Million Plastic Bags.
From Rich Uneasy America to My Friend Christopher Logue.
Giving Potatoes.
Goodbye.
Icarus Schmicarus.
Nature Poem.
Not a Very Cheerful Song, I'm Afraid.
Nothingmas Day.
Oxford Hysteria of English Poetry, The.
Private Transport.
Quite Apart from the Holy Ghost.
Remember Suez?
Riddle: "Their tongues are knives, their forks are hands and feet."
Song In Space.
Speck Speaks, A.
To Whom It May Concern.
Watch Your Step—I'm Drenched.
Mitchell, Cyprus R.
Soul of Jesus Is Restless, The.
Mitchell, David (b. 1940)
At Pakiri Beach.
My Lai / Remuera / Ponsonby.
Silences.

Van Gogh.
Mitchell, Elma (b. 1919)
Thoughts after Ruskin.
Mitchell, Frank (b. 1912)
13th Horse Song of Frank Mitchell (White), The.
12th Horse Song of Frank Mitchell (Blue), The.
Mitchell, G. M.
Nurse, The.
Mitchell, John (1880–1951)
Reply to "In Flanders Fields."
Mitchell, Jonathan (1624–68)
On the Following Work and Its Author.
Mitchell, Karen L. (b. 1955)
Black Patent Leather Shoes.
Monster, The.
Night Rain.
On the Anniversary Of Your Death.
Tree Stillness.
Mitchell, Larry (b. 1938)
Faggots and their friends now live in Ramrod, The.
Men love papers, The. They love to sign them, file them and.
Men spread disease among the faggots, one of the things they, The.
Sons and Fathers.
Women Wisdom.
Mitchell, Lorna
Hermaphrodite's Song, The.
Mitchell, Lucy Sprague (1878–1967)
House of the mouse, The.
Mitchell, Matthew (b. 1928)
Printing Jenny
Mitchell, Mrs. James Herbert. See Strobel, Marion
Mitchell, Nora
Locker Room, The.
Mitchell, Sam
Thunderstorm.
Mitchell, Stephen (b. 1943)
Annunciation, The.
Good Samaritan et Al, The.
Parable of the Sower, The.
St. Luke, *sels.*
St. Matthew, *sels.*
Vermeer.
Mitchell, Susan (b. 1944)
Dead, The.
Face, The.
Feeding the ducks at the Howard Johnson Motel.
Girl Tearing Up Her Face.
Havana Birth.
Maps.
Once, Driving West of Billings, Montana.
Rapture.
Story, A.
Tent Caterpillars.
Mitchell, Susan Langstaff (1866–1926)
Descent of the Child, The.
Immortality.
Mitchell, Susanna Valentine
Of Earthly Love.
Mitchell, Walter (1826–1908)
Tacking Ship Off Shore.
Mitchison, Naomi (b. 1897)
Dick and Colin at the Salmon Nets.
Hartmanswillerkopf.
Midsummer Apple Tree, The.
My True Love Hath My Heart.
Old Love and New Love.
Tennessee Snow.
Thinking of War.
To Some Young Communists from an Older Socialist.
Unfertile Heart, The.
Woman Alone.
Mitford, Mary Russell (1787–1855)
Song: "Fairest things are those which live, The."
Mitsuhashi, Takajo (1899–1972)
Hair ornament of the sun, The.
O bird's singing!

Mitsui Futabako (b. 1919)
Grazing.
Mitsui, Jim (b. 1940)
At Bon Odori.
Because of My Father's Job.
Destination: Tule Lake Relocation Center,
May 20, 1942.
Katori Maru, October 1920.
Nisei: Second Generation Japanese-American.
Photograph of a Child, Japanese-American
Evacuation, Bainbridge Island, Washington,
March 30, 1942.
Picture of a Japanese Farmer, Woodland,
California, May 20, 1942.
Mitsune (Oshikochi no Mitsune) (fl. c.900)
Ceaseless snow.
Since I heard. *From* Kokin Shu
White chrysanthemum, The.
Miu Hsi (186–245)
Bearer's Song.
Poem in the Form of a Coffin-Puller's Song.
Miyazawa Kenji (1896–1933)
Daydreaming on the Trail.
Pictures of the Floating World.
River in Hell (two poems).
Siwashing it out once in Siuslaw Forest.
Snow on Saddle Mountain, The.
Spring and the Ashura.
Tanka: "At dawn."
Tanka: "At last."
Tanka: "Bloodshot."
Tanka: "Dark seaweeds."
Tanka: "Emerging."
Tanka: "In the blue rays."
Tanka: "Left alone."
Tanka: "Lightning."
Tanka: "Like cracks."
Tanka: "Phosphorescence."
Tanka: "Plucked, The."
Tanka: "Red rag."
Tanka: "Scattered clouds."
Tanka: "Silver greeting."
Tanka: "Snow has fallen."
Tanka: "Steel pen."
Tanka: "Unsettled."
Tanka: "With red eyes."
Mizejewski, Linda
Anaerobics: Elaine Powers, Wheeling, West
Virginia.
Parents Sleeping.
Mnasalces (fl. 3d cent. B.C.)
Aristocrateia, / You've crossed the dark
stream.
Broad-acred Ascra bore me.
Epigrams, *sels.*
I, wretched Virtue, sit.
My fighting days are done.
No longer, cricket, sitting.
Promachus hangs here.
Setting their country free.
Mnotoza, Zim (b. 1961)
Still There's No Trace.
Mnthali, Felix (b. 1933)
Celebration, The.
My Father.
Neocolonialism.
Sizeline.
Stranglehold of English Lit, The.
To the Writers' Worship in Zomba.
Mó, Alonzo Gonzales
Conversations in Mayan.
How Just One Poor Man Lives.
Things That Happen to You.
Wizards.
Mo Shih-lung (c.1539–1587)
Drinking Wine.
Flower Shadows.
Friend Comes to Visit on a Summer Night,
A.
Gathering Lotus with Singing Girls.
I Waited for Chuang Hsüan-yüan But He
Never Came.
I Went to Gold Mountain to Visit a Ch'an
Master But He Was Not at Home.
Meditation Rock, The.
On a Cold Day I Climbed Tiger Hill With
Professor Ho. At the Time, the Local

Prefect Had Prohibited Pleasure Excursions
and Feasts, But the Mountain Was Quiet
and Tranquil, So We Stayed All Day.
Saying Good-bye to a Singing Girl Who Has
Decided to Become a Nun.
Saying Good-Bye to Feng the Hermit.
Staying Overnight at Blue Cloud Temple.
To the Monk Wu-hsia on the Occasion of
His Editing the Lotus Sutra.
**Moberley, Lucy Gertrude (L. G. Moberley) (b.
1860)**
Commandeered.
Mobilio, Albert (b. 1955)
Step One.
Step Seven.
Third Kind of Interior Word, The.
Mocikiranar
Not Rice, Not Water.
Modena, Leone da (1571–1648)
Epitaph: "Implacable angel / Has shot his
dart, The."
Modisane, Bloke (1923–86)
Black Blues.
Blue Black.
Lonely.
Moeller, Eileen
Domestic Poem.
Ten Years Ago.
Moerman, Ernst
Louis Armstrong.
Moffat, Mary Jane
In This New Year.
Passing of Sorrow, The.
Widow's Supper.
Moffett, Judith (b. 1942)
Diehard.
Now or Never.
Twinings Orange Pekoe.
Moffi, Larry
Putting an End to the War Stories.
Yahrzeit.
Mohodahi (fl. between c.700 and c.1050)
On the holy day of your going out to war.
Moiro
Hail, forest nymphs, daughters of the river.
Now you lie—a grape-offering.
**Moise, Penina (1797–1880) and Edward N.
Calisch**
God Supreme! To Thee We Pray.
Mokhomo, M. A.
When He Spoke to Me of Love.
Moldaw, Carol (b. 1956)
64 Panoramic Way.
Mole, John
Jack-in-the-Box is faithful.
Penny Toys, *sels.*
Taking the Plunge.
Trick, The.
Mole, Lyndon T.
Limerick: "Texan Rhodes Scholar named
Fred, A."
Molière (Jean Baptiste Poquelin) (1622–73)
Tartuffe.
To Monsieur de la Mothe le Vayer.
Moll, Ernest G. (b. 1900)
Beware the cuckoo, though she bring.
Bush Speaks, The.
Clearing for the Plough.
Mollineux, Mary (1651–95)
Epistle, An: "Is Friends fled, or Love grown
cold?"
Of Modesty, *sels.*
Solitude.
**Molodovsky [or Molodowsky], Kadya (1894–
1975)**
God of Mercy.
Prayers: I.
Song of the Sabbath.
Molony, Linda (b. 1960)
Cat Washing.
Momaday, N. Scott (b. 1934)
Angle of Geese.
Bear, The.
Burning, The.

But Then and There the Sun Bore Down.
Carriers of the Dream Wheel.
Colors of Night, The.
Delight Song of Tsoai-Talee, The.
Eagle-Feather Fan, The.
Earth and I Gave You Turquoise.
Forms of the Earth at Abiquiu.
Four Notions of Love and Marriage.
Gift, The.
Gourd Dancer, The.
Headwaters.
North Dakota, North Light.
Pit Viper.
Plainview: 3.
Rainy Mountain Cemetery.
Simile.
Story of a Well-made Shield, The.
To a Child Running with Outstretched Arms
in Canyon de Chelly.
Trees and Evening Sky.
Two Figures.
Walk on the Moon.
Wide Empty Landscape with a Death in the
Foreground.
Winter Holding off the Coast of North
America.
Mombert, Alfred (b. 1872)
Along the Strand.
Idyl: "And my young sweetheart sat at board
with me."
Sleeping They Bear Me.
Momoi, Beverly Acuff
Portrait.
Quickness of Fear, The.
Monar, Rooplall (b. 1947)
Judgement Day.
Koker.
Monck, Mary (1678–1715)
Masque of the Virtues against Love.
On A Romantic Lady.
Verses Written on Her Death-bed at Bath to
Her Husband in London.
**Moncrieff, Charles Kenneth Michael Scott
(1889–1930)**
Au Champ d'Honneur.
Monette, Paul (1945–95)
Bathing the Aged.
Brother of the Mount of Olives.
Degas.
Into the Dark.
Money-Coutts, Francis Burdett (1852–1923)
On A Wife.
Mộng Tuyết (Lâm Thái Úc (b. 1918)
Red Cross, The.
"Monk." See Lewis, Matthew Gregory
Monk, Geraldine (b. 1952)
Beneath the Radar—for the RAF and All
Low Flying Aircraft.
His hands old edging out of time.
Make-Up.
Poem for August—or for My Birthday.
Spring Bank.
Monk, Mary (1677?–1715)
Fire Us with Ice, Burn Us with Snow.
Verses Written on Her Death-Bed at Bath to
Her Husband in London.
Monkhouse, Cosmo (1840–1901)
Any Soul to Any Body.
Limerick: "There was a young lady of Riga."
Limericks.
There Was a Young Lady of Niger.
To a New-Born Child.
Monks, Arthur W.
Twilight's Last Gleaming.
Monro, Harold (1879–1932)
Bird at Dawn, The.
Bitter Sanctuary.
Cat's Meat.
Children of Love.
City-Storm.
Dog.
Every Thing.
Fresh Air, The.
Hearthstone.
Hurrier, The.

Living.
Man Carrying Bale.
Midnight Lamentation, *sels.*
Milk for the Cat.
Natural History, *sels.*
Nightingale near the House, The.
One Blackbird.
Overheard on a Saltmarsh.
Solitude.
Strange Meetings, *sels.*
Street Fight.
Terrible Door, The.
Thistledown.
Week-End, *sels.*
Youth in Arms, *sels.*

Monroe, Arthur W.
To W. S. M.

Monroe, Bill
In the Pines.

Monroe, Harriet (1861–1936)
Commemoration Ode, *sels.*
Farewell: "Good-bye!—no [*or* nay] do not grieve that it is over."
In High Places.
Pine at Timber-Line, The.

Monsour, Leslie
Dream of Dying, A.
Emily's Words.
Sweeping.

Montagu, Lady Mary Wortley (1689–1762)
Addressed to ———.
Answer to a Love-Letter in Verse, An.
Be plain in dress and sober in your diet.
Between your sheets you soundly sleep.
Epistle from Mrs. Yonge to Her Husband.
Epistle: "How happy you who varied joys pursue."
Epitaph: "Here lie John Hughes and Sarah Drew."
Epitaph: "Here lies John Hughes and Sarah Drew."
Farewell to Bath.
Hymn to the Moon.
Lady's Resolve, The.
Lover, The; a Ballad.
Man in Love, A.
On the Death of Mrs. Bowes.
Receipt to Cure [*or* for] the Vapours, A.
Six Town Eclogues, *sels.*
To a Lady Making Love.
Town Eclogues, *sels.*
Verses Addressed to the Imitator of the First Satire of the Second Book of Horace, *sels.*
Verses Addressed to the Imitator of the First Satire of the Second Book of Horace: An Attack on Pope.
Verses Written in a Garden.
Verses Written in the Chiosk [of the British Palace], at Pera, Overlooking [the City of] Constantinople.

Montague, John (b. 1929)
Above the Pool.
All Legendary Obstacles lay between.
Answer, The.
At Last.
Bright Day, A.
Cage, The.
Cassandra's Answer.
Cave of Night, The, *sels.*
Deer Park.
Dowager.
Drink of Milk, A.
Falls Funeral.
Flowering Absence, A.
Grafted Tongue, A.
Hearth Song.
Herbert Street Revisited.
Hero's Portion.
King & Queen.
Lament for the O'Neills.
Last Journey.
Leaping Fire, The, *sels.*
Like dolmens round my childhood, the old people.
Locket, The.
Lost Tradition, A.
Mother Cat, The.

Mount Eagle.
Old Mythologies.
Point, The.
Process.
Same Gesture, The.
She Cries.
Silver Flask, The.
That Room.
Tracks.
Trout, The.
Walking Late.
Welcoming Party, A.
Well-beloved, The.
Wild Dog Rose, The.
Wild Sports of the West.
Windharp.
Witness.
Woodtown Manor.

Montale, Eugenio (1896–1981)
Day and Night.
Eel, The.
Eel, the North Sea siren, The.
Eel, the siren, The.
Fan, The.
House of the Customs-Men, The.
Late in the Night.
Lemon Trees, The.
Little Testament.
Personae Separatae.
Precautions.
Storm splattering the tough magnolia, The.
Thrust and Riposte.
To rest at noon, pale and absorbed.

Montgomerie, Alexander (1540?–1610?)
Away Vane World.
Description of Tyme, A.
Night Is Near [*or* Neir] Gone, The.
Remembers thou in Æsope of a taill.
Solsequium, The.
To Henry Constable and Henry Keir.
To His Maistres [*or* Mistress].
To R. Hudson.

Montgomerie, William (b. 1904)
Author Unknown.
Edge of the War (1939–), The.
Elegy for William Soutar.
Epitaph: "My brother is skull and skeleton now."
Glasgow Street.
Kinfauns Castle, *sels.*

Montgomery, James (1771–1854)
Brahmin, The, *sels.*
Daisy, The, *sels.*
Nativity.
West Indies, The, *sels.*

Montgomery, Leslie Alexander. *See* "Doyle, Lynn"

Montgomery, Niall
Eyewash.

Montgomery, Scott
Crying.
Evening lecture.
Her silence at dinner.
Moonrise white cat eating the cardinal.
With the last lamp.

Montgomery, U. M.
Grey Brother.

Montoya, José (b. 1932)
Faces at the First Farmworkers Constitutional Convention, *sels.*

Montrose, James Graham, Marquess of (1612–50)
His Metrical Prayer.
His Metrical Vow.
I'll Never Love Thee More, *sels.*

Montross, Percy
Oh, My Darling Clementine.

"Monty Python"
All things dull and ugly.

Moody, Elizabeth (d. 1814)
Dr. Johnson's Ghost.
Housewife's Prayer on the Morning Preceding a Fete, The.
Sappho Burns Her Books and Cultivates the Culinary Arts.

To a Gentleman Who Invited Me to Go A-Fishing.

Moody, Minnie Hite
Say This of Horses.

Moody, William Vaughn (1869–1910)
Bracelet of Grass, The.
Departure, The.
Fire-Bringer, The, *sels.*
Gloucester Moors, *sels.*
Harmonics.
Ode in Time of Hesitation, An, *sels.*
On a Soldier Fallen in the Philippines.

Moon, Chung-hee (b. 1947)
Flock of Birds, A.
Poem at Forty.

Moon, Toksu (b. 1927)
Ode to Fallen Leaves.
Signpost.
Song for Grass Leaf.

Mooney, Stephen (b. 1937)
Water Color.

Moor, George
Eternale Footeman's Tale, The.

Moore, Alan (b. 1960)
Girls' School.

"Moore, Bernard." *See* Hunt, S. S.

Moore, Clement Clarke (1779–1863)
Lord of Life, All Praise Excelling.
Visit from St Nicholas, A.

Moore, Edward (1712–57)
Nun, The.
Poet and His Patron, The, *sels.*
Song 3: "As Phyllis the gay, at the break of the day."
To the Right Hon. Henry Pelham.

Moore, Egbert ("Lord Beginner")
Victory Calypso, Lord's 1950.

Moore, Honor (b. 1945)
First Time: 1950.
Green Place, A.
Memoir.

Moore, James
For You.
One Reason I Went to Prison.

Moore, John Travers (b. 1908)
Astronauts.
Springburst.

Moore, Julia A. (1847–1920)
Ashtabula Disaster, The.
Grand Rapids.
Little Libbie.
Sketch of Lord Byron's Life.

Moore, Lenard D. (b. 1958)
Again.
Bluesman's Blues, A.
Eternal Landscape, The.
Farther and farther.
From the Field.
Homeplace, The.
Indian Girl.
Silent deer the sound of a waterfall.
Stars.
Summer noon.
Winter 1967.

Moore, Lilian (b. 1909)
Bedtime Story.
In the Fog.
Listen! / Listen to the witch!
No One.
Pigeons are cityfolk.
Sometimes.
Spectacular.
Until I Saw the Sea.

Moore, Marianne Craig (1887–1972)
Animals Sick of the Plague, The.
Arctic Ox, The.
At Rest in the Blast.
Baseball and Writing.
Bird-witted.
Black Earth.
Blessed Is the Man.
Buffalo, The.
Carriage from Sweden, A.
Charity Overcoming Envy.
Critics and Connoisseurs.

Dream.
Egyptian Pulled Glass Bottle in the Shape of a Fish, An.
England.
Enough.
Face, A.
Fish, The.
Fish wade / through black jade, The.
Four Quartz Crystal Clocks.
Glory.
Granite and Steel.
Grave, A.
He "Digesteth Harde Yron."
His Shield.
Hometown Piece for Messrs. Alston and Reese.
I May, I Might, I Must.
In Distrust of Merits.
In the Days of Prismatic Color.
In the Public Garden.
In This Age of Hard Trying, Nonchalance Is Good and.
Jelly-Fish, A.
Jerboa, The, sels.
Keeping Their World Large.
Labors of Hercules, The.
Leonardo Da Vinci's.
Love in America.
Marriage.
Mind, Intractable Thing, The.
Mind Is an Enchanting Thing, The.
Monkeys, The.
Monkeys winked too much and were afraid of snakes, The.
Nevertheless.
Nevertheless you've seen a strawberry.
New York.
Nine Nectarines and Other Porcelain.
No Swan So Fine.
O To Be A Dragon.
Old Amusement Park.
Pangolin, The.
Paper Nautilus, The.
Part of a Novel, Part of a Poem, Part of a Play, sels.
Past Is the Present, The.
Peter.
Pigeons.
Pigeons are city folk.
Poetry.
Roses Only.
Saint Nicholas.
Sea Unicorns and Land Unicorns.
Silence.
Snakes, Mongooses, Snake-Charmers and the Like.
Sojourn in the Whale.
Spenser's Ireland.
St. Valentine.
Student, The.
Talisman, A.
Tell Me, Tell Me.
That Harp You Play So Well.
Then the Ermine.
To a Chameleon.
To a Giraffe.
To a Snail.
To a Steam Roller.
To the Peacock of France.
To Victor Hugo of My Crow Pluto.
Tom Fool at Jamaica.
W. S. Landor.
Walking-Sticks and Paperweights and Watermarks.
What Are Years?
When I Buy Pictures.
Wood Weasel, The.

Moore, Merrill (1903–57)
Americans in 1933–4–5–6–7–8–, Etc.
And to the Young Men.
Book of How, The.
Cumae.
Fable.
How She Resolved to Act.
In Magic Words.
It Is Winter, I Know.
Literature: The God, Its Ritual.

Noise That Time Makes, The.
Old Men and Old Women Going Home on the Street Car.
Pandora and the Moon.
Shot Who? Jim Lane!
Transfusion.
Unknown Man in the Morgue.
Village Noon; Mid-Day Bells.
Warning to One.

Moore, Nicholas (b. 1918)
Fivesucked the features of my girl by glory.
Island and the Cattle, The.
Patient, The.
Song: "Little onion lay by the fireplace, A."

Moore, Richard (b. 1927)
Suburb Hilltop.
Visitors, The.
Word from the Hills, sels.

Moore, Rosalie (b. 1910)
Catalogue, sels.

Moore, Thomas (1779–1852)
Announcement of a New Grand Acceleration Company for the Promotion of the Speed of Literature.
Argument, An.
Believe me, if all those endearing young charms.
Cherries; a Parable, The.
Copy of an Intercepted Despatch from His Excellency Don Strepitoso Diabolo.
Dear Harp of My Country.
Did Not.
Duke is the lad to frighten a lass, The.
Echo.
Echoes.
Epitaph on Robert Southey.
Epitaph on Tuft-Hunter.
Fudge Family in Paris, The, sels.
Fum and Hum, the Two Birds of Royalty.
Go where glory waits thee.
Harp That Once through Tara's Halls, The.
How Oft Has the Banshee Cried.
I Saw from the Beach.
I Wish I Was by That Dim Lake.
Ill Omens.
In the morning of life, when its cares are unknown.
Irish Antiquities.
Irish Peasant to His Mistress, The.
Journey Onwards, The.
Kiss, The.
Lake of the Dismal Swamp, The.
Lalla Rookh, sels.
Long, Long Be My Heart with Such Memories Filled.
Meeting of the Waters, The.
Minstrel Boy, The.
Nonsense.
Odes to Nea, sels.
Oft in the stilly night.
Oh! blame not the bard, if he fly to the bowers.
Oh! where's the slave so lowly.
Pastoral Ballad by John Bull, A.
Petition of the Orangemen of Ireland, The.
Poetical Works of the Late Thomas Little Esq, The, sels.
Pro Patria Mori.
Rhymes on the Road, sels.
Scene from a Play, Acted at Oxford, Called "Matriculation."
She Is Far from the Land.
Song of Fionnuala, The.
Song: "When the heart's feeling."
Song: "Where is the nymph, whose azure eye."
Sound the Loud timbrel o'er Egypt's dark sea!
Sweet Innisfallen.
Take Back the Virgin Page.
Thee, Thee, Only Thee.
They May Rail at This Life.
Thou art, O God, the life and light.
Thy Heaven.
Time I've lost in wooing, The.
'Tis the Last Rose of Summer.
To Ladies' Eyes.

To Miss———.
To Sir Hudson Lowe.
Tory Pledges.
Venetian Air.
Weep, Children of Israel.
What's My Thought Like?
When I loved you, I can't but allow.
Young May Moon, The.

Moore, Thomas Sturge (1870–1944)
Beautiful Meals.
Daughter of Admetus, A.
Duet, A.
Dying Swan, The.
Event, The.
Gazelles, The.
Kindness.
Lubber Breeze.
On Harting Down.
Response to Rimbaud's Later Manner.
Sent from Egypt with a Fair Robe of Tissue to a Sicilian Vinedresser.
Variation on Ronsard.

Moorer, Lizelia Augusta Jenkins (fl. c. 1907)
Accompanying a Gift ("From thy patient, who while here.")
Accompanying a Gift ("One whose love will never end.")
Africa.
Benefits of Sorrow.
Bible, The.
Birthday Wishes to a Husband.
Birthday Wishes to a Minister of the Gospel.
Birthday Wishes to a Physician.
Christmas Eve.
Christmas Tree, The.
Circle, The.
Claflin's Alumni.
Crum Appointment, The.
Dedication Day Poem.
Dialogue, A.
Door of Hope, The.
Duty, or Truth at Work.
Easter; or, Spring-Time.
Emancipation Day.
Eutawville Lynching, The.
Hallowe'en.
Immortality.
In Memoriam of E. B. Clark.
Injustice of the Courts.
Jim Crow Cars.
Legal Mouse, A.
Lela's Charms.
Lines to a Graduate.
Loyalty to the Flag.
Lynching.
Misunderstood.
Mountain Tops.
Must Be Freed.
Negro Ballot, The.
Negro Heroines.
Negro Schools, The.
Notable Dinner, A.
Peonage System, The.
Pharaohs of Today, The.
Prejudice.
Presidents, The.
Price of Disrespect, The.
Refining Fire.
Retribution.
Russia's Resentment.
Social Glass, The.
Social Life, The.
Song of the Angels.
Southern Press, The.
Southern Pulpit, The.
Southern Work of Dr. and Mrs. L. M. Dunton.
Sympathy.
Thanksgiving.
Tree of Knowledge, The.
Truth Suppressed, The.
Voice of the Negro, The.
What We Teach at Claflin.
Whisper Words of Love to Me.
Why Is It?
Why Negroes Don't Unite.
Why We Meet.

Moorsom, Sasha (1932–93)
Body.
Company of the Birds, The.
Don't be literary, darling, don't be literary.
Jewels In My Hand.

Moos, Lotte
Black Shawl, The.
Sisters?
Spendthrifts.

Mopev
Would you care for a smoke or a sherry?

Mor, Amus
Coming of John, The.

Mora, Pat
Cortez's Horse.
Depression Days.
Elena.
Gentle Communion.
Immigrants.
La Migra.
Mangos y limones.
Señora X No More.
Sonrisas.

Moraes, Dom (b. 1938)
Babur.
Gardener.
Kanheri Caves.
Santa Claus.
Snow on a Mountain.
Two from Israel, *sels.*

Moraga, Cherríe (b. 1952)
Feed the Mexican Back into Her.
For the Color of My Mother.
For You, Mamá.
Half-Breed.
La Dolce Culpa, *sels.*
Later, she met Joyce.
Loving in the War Years.

Moran, Michael ("Zozimus")
Pharao's Daughter.

Moran, Rod (b. 1952)
Cross Country.
Wire.

Mordaunt, Charles, Earl of Peterborough (1658–1735)
I Said to My Heart.

Mordaunt, Thomas Osbert (1730–1809)
Verses Written during the War, 1756–1763, *sels.*

Mordecai ben Isaac (*fl.* 13th–14th cent.)
Fair Thou Art.
Rock of My Salvation.

Mordecai, Pamela (b. 1942)
Easy Life.
For Eyes to Bless You.
Last Lines.
Shooting the Horses.
Starapple Tree.
Tell Me.

More, Hannah (1745–1833)
Bas Bleu; Or, Conversation, The, *sels.*
Bas Bleu, The; or, Conversation, *sels.*
Gin-Shop, The; A Peep into Prison, *sels.*
Hackney Coachman, The; Or, The Way to Get a Good Fare.
Inscription in a Beautiful Retreat Called Fairy Bower.
Patient Joe; or, The Newcastle Collier.
Riot; or, Half a Loaf Is Better than No Bread, The.
Search after Happiness, The, *sels.*
Sensibility; a Poetical Epistle, *sels.*
Slave Trade, The, *sels.*
Slavery.
Slavery, a Poem, *sels.*
Sorrows of Yamba, or the Negro Woman's Lamentation, The.

More, Henry (1614–87)
Psychozoia, or, the Life of the Soul, *sels.*

More, Sir Thomas (Saint Thomas More) (1478–1535)
Child's Song.
De Principe Bono et Malo.
Mery Gest How a Sergeaunt Wolde Lerne to Be A Frere, A.

Mine high estate, power and auctority.
Minstrel Boy to the war is gone, The.
Pageant Verses.
Quis Optimus Reipublicae Status.
Rueful Lamentation on the Death of Queen Elizabeth, A.

Morejón, Nancy (b. 1944)
Central Park Some People (3 P.M.)
Reason for Poetry, The.

Moreland, Wayne (b. 1948)
Sunday Morning.

Moreton, J. B. (*fl.* 18th cent.)
Ballad: "Altho' a slave me is born and bred."

Morgan, Albert (b. 1908)
Union Man.

Morgan, Angela (1874–1957)
Choice.
God the Artist.
Today.
Work; a Song of Triumph ("Work / Thank God for the might of it.")

Morgan-Browne, L. E.
Purple, White and Green, The.

Morgan, Edwin (b. 1920)
Cinquevalli is falling, falling.
Computer's First Christmas Card, The.
Dowser, The.
First Men on Mercury, The.
Glasgow Sonnets.
Itinerary.
King Billy.
Loch Ness Monster's Song, The.
My Greenhouse.
Second Life, The.
Siesta of a Hungarian Snake.
Sonnets from Scotland, *sels.*
Spacepoem 3: Off Course.
Starlings in George Square, The.
Strawberries.
To Hugh MacDiarmid.

"Morgan, Emanuel." See Bynner, Witter

Morgan, Frederick (b. 1922)
February 11, 1977.
I Saw My Darling.
1904.

Morgan, Robert (b. 1944)
Bellrope.
Choice, The.
Death Crown.
Ghosts in the Carpet.
Gift of Tongues, The.
Grandma's Bureau.
Hay Scuttle.
Hollow, The.
Honey.
Mountain Bride.
Passenger Pigeons.
Stretching.
Walnutry.

Morgan, Robin (b. 1941)
Ceremony, A, *sels.*
Damn you, lady, get out of my blood for good.
Hallowing of Hell, The, *sels.*
Heirloom.
Invisible woman in the asylum corridor, The.
Network of the Imaginary Mother, The, *sels.*
On the Watergate Women.
Pedestrian Woman, The.
Phobiphilia.
Two Gretels were exploring the forest, The.

Morgan, Veronica
Still Life.
Within the Greenhouse Effect.

Morganfield, McKinley. See Waters, Muddy

Morganwg, Iolo. See Williams, Edward

Morgenstern, Christian (1871–1914)
Delayed Action.
Fish's Nightsong.
Ghost.
Great Lalula, The.
Hen, The.
Knee, The.
Korf's Clock.
Midnightmouse, The.

Moonsheep stands on the huge lawn, The.
Nosobame, The.
Palmstroem in Animal Costume.
Pearl-hen counts; one, two, three, four, The.
Police Inquiry, The.

Mori, Kyoko
Speaking Through White: For My Mother.

Mori Ōgai (1862–1922)
In Nara (two poems).
Tanka: "But for the dew."
Tanka: "Close by the host."
Tanka: "During a break."
Tanka: "Far and near."
Tanka: "Frolicking."
Tanka: "Insane thought, An."
Tanka: "It will not be heard."
Tanka: "Let a poem be."
Tanka: "Never have I."
Tanka: "On a post."
Tanka: "Should I stroke it."
Tanka: "Some medals."
Tanka: "Step by step."
Tanka: "Trying to perch."
Tanka: "Under the blue sky."
Tanka: "White swan."
Tanka: "Without incident."
Tanka: "Your heart."

Moriarty, Laura (b. 1952)
Rondeaux: "Each page a day."

Morice, Dave (b. 1946)
Alaskan Drinking Song.

Mörike [*or* Möricke], Eduard Friedrich (1804–75)
Beauty Rohtraut.
Prisoner, The.

Morin, Catherine A.
High June.
Lace Pedlar, The.

Morin, Maud
Bachelors' Buttons.
Shower and Sunshine.

Moritaké. See Arakida Moritaké

Moritz, A. F. (b. 1947)
April Fool's Day, Mount Pleasant Cemetary.

Moritz [*or* Morits], Yunna Petrovna [*or* Iunna Pinkhusovna] (b. 1937)
Autumn.
Baltic Summer.
In Memory of Titian Tabidze.
In that town I was twenty. Snow there lay.
Some Lines on My Mother's Illness.

Morley, Christopher Darlington (1890–1957)
Animal crackers, and cocoa to drink.
Dial Call.
Elegy Written in a Country Coal-Bin.
Forever Ambrosia.
Gospel of Mr. Pepys, The.
In Honour of Taffy Topaz.
Pennsylvania Deutsch.
Plumpuppets, The.
Public Beach (Long Island Sound).
Song for a Little House.
To a Post-Office Inkwell.
Washing the Dishes.

Morley, Hilda (b. 1916)
Curve of the Water.
Epidaurus: / you loved it.
For Elaine de Kooning.
Lizard's heart throbs, The.
Made Out of Links.
Parents.
Rondanini Pieta, The.

Morley, I. D. M.
Limerick: "Far beyond all the girls of Pirelli."

Morley, Thomas
Sing we and chant it.
You black bright stars, that shine while daylight lasteth.

Moronelli da Fiorenza, Pier (*fl.* 13th cent.)
Canzonetta: A Bitter Song to His Lady.

Morpurgo, Rachel [*or* Rahel] (1790–1871)
Song: "Ah, vale of woe, of gloom and darkness moulded."
Sonnet: "My soul surcharged with grief now loud complains."

Woe is me, my soul says, how bitter is my
fate.

Morris, Betty (b. 1948)
Limerick: "Poet from Cheltenham Spa, A."

Morris, Charles (1745–1838)
Address to Lady———, Who Asked What
the Passion of Love Was?
Country and Town.

Morris, George Pope (1802–64)
Main-Truck; or, A Leap for Life, The.
Woodman, spare that tree!

Morris, Harry (b. 1924)
Because Thou Did'st Give.
Maine Lake at Night.
Where Lie All the Slain.

Morris, Herbert (b. 1928)
Road, The.
Spanish Blue.
This Alice.

Morris, John N. (b. 1931)
Mirror, The.

Morris-Jones, John (1864–1929)
North Star, The.
"Old age never comes alone"—it brings
sighs.
Wind's Lament, The.

Morris, Lewis (1701–65)
Poem of the Frost and Snow.

Morris, Mervyn (b. 1937)
Day my father died, The.
Early Rebels, The.
Family Pictures.
For Consciousness.
Give T'anks.
House-Slave, The.
Joseph of Arimathaea.
One, Two.
Peace-Time.
Pilate.
Pre-Carnival Party.
Swimmer.
To an Expatriate Friend.
Valley Prince.

Morris, Robert (1818?–1888)
Level and the Square, The.

Morris, Thomas (1732–1806?)
Sapphics: At the Mohawk-Castle, Canada.

Morris, William (1834–96)
Another for the Briar Rose.
Death Song, A.
Defense of Guenevere, The.
Earthly Paradise, The, *sels.*
End of May, The.
For the Briar Rose.
Golden Wings, *sels.*
Haystack in the Floods, The.
Hollow Land, The, *sels.*
In Prison.
Judgement of God, The.
Life and Death of Jason, The, *sels.*
Lines for a Bed at Kelmscott Manor.
Love Is Enough, *sels.*
Message of the March Wind, The.
Near Avalon.
Pomona.
Riding Together.
Shameful Death.
Story of Sigurd the Volsung, The, *sels.*
Summer Dawn.
Thunder in the Garden.
Tune of Seven Towers, The.
Two Red Roses across the Moon.

Morrison, Blake
Ballad of the Yorkshire Ripper, The, *sels.*

Morrison, Lillian (b. 1917)
Rural Recreation.
Sidewalk Racer Or, On the Skateboard, The.
Surf.

Morrison, M. T.
What the Choir Sang about the New Bonnet.

Morrison, Mary
Nobody Knows but Mother.

Morse, Brian
Day on the Planet, A.

Morse, Carl (b. 1934)
Dream of the Artfairy.
Fairy Straighttalk.
Scenes of Childhood.

Morse, Samuel French (b. 1916)
Song in the Cold Season.

**"Morshen, Nikolai Nikolaevich" (Nikolai
Nikolaevich Marchenko) (b. 1917)**
He lived so little: only forty years.

Morstein, Petra von (b. 1941)
Anthology Poem.
For one who says he feels.
In the Case of Lobsters.
Justice.
Nineteen Sixty Eight.
Thing Poem.

Morton, David (1886–1957)
Epitaph in Sirmio.
Old Ships.
Who Walks with Beauty.

**Morton, John Bingham ("Beachcomber")
(1893–1979)**
Another Canto.
Dancing Cabman, The.
Epitaph: "Glassblower lies here at rest, A."
Epitaph: "Tread softly; bid a solemn music
sound."
John Percy / Said to his nursy.
Let poets praise the softer winds of spring.
On Sir Henry Ferrett, M.P.
Spring in London.
To Hilda Dancing.
When We Were Very Silly, *sels.*

Morton, Thomas (1764–1838)
Carmen Elegiacum.
Epitaph: "Time that brings [or bringes] all
things to light."
New Canaans Genius; Epilogus.
New English Canaan; Prologue.
Poem: "I sing th' adventures of mine worthy
wights."
Poem, The: "Rise Oedipus, and if thou canst
unfold."
Poem, The: "What ailes Pigmalion? Is it
lunacy."
Song, The: "Drink and be merry, merry,
merry boys."
Song: "Drinke and be merry, merry, merry
boyes."

Morton, W. C.
Dafney's Lamentation.

Morus, Huw (1622–1709)
In Praise of a Girl.

Mosby, Jr., George
To Josh Gibson (Legendary Slugger of the
Old Negro Baseball League).

Moschus (fl. 3d cent. B.C.)
Bion. A Pastoral, in Imitation of the Greek of
Moschus, bewailing the Death of the Earl
of Rochester, *sels.*
Cupid Turned Plowman.
Europa.
Idyll 1.
Lament for Bion.
Ocean, The.
Pan, Echo, and the Satyr.

Moser, Leo
Limerick: "Quadratic function, ambitious, A."

Moses, Daniel David (b. 1952)
Corn, The.
Party Favour.
Report on Her Remains.
Some Grand River Blues.

Moses ibn Ezra (c.1070–1138)
Beautiful Is the Loved One.
Beauty of the Stars, The.
Book of Tarshish, The, *sels.*
Dying Wife to Her Husband, A.
Elegy: "In pain she bore the son who her
embrace."
Elegy: "My thoughts impelled me to the
resting-place."
End of Man Is Death, The.
Garden of Song, The.
God That Doest Wondrously.
Hot Flame of My Grief, The.

I Went Out into the Garden.
Man Is a Weaver.
Men Are Children of This World.
My Love is Like a Myrtle.
On My Sorrowful Life.
Sources of My Being, The.
Splendor of Thine Eyes, The.
Strange Love.
Those Beauteous Maids.
To a Plagiarist.
Walk in the Precepts.
Wedding Song in honor of R. Solomon ben
Matir, *sels.*
When She Plays upon the Harp or Lute.
Why Should I Grieve?
Wine-Songs, *sels.*
With Hopeless Love.
Without My Friends the Day Is Dark.
Works of God, The.
World's Illusion, The, *sels.*
Young Dove, The.

Moses, William Robert (b. 1911)
Boy at Target Practice; a Contemplation.
Dark and Dark.
Night Wind in Fall.

Moss, Howard (b. 1922)
Arsenic.
At the Algonquin.
Burning Love Letters.
Cats and Dogs.
Crossing the Park.
Dead Leaf, A.
Einstein's Bathrobe.
Elegy for My Father.
Elegy for My Sister.
Finding Them Lost.
Front Street.
Game of Chance, A.
Geography: a Song.
Gift to Be Simple, The.
Great Spaces.
Hand, The.
King Midas.
Lie, The.
Long Island Springs.
Meeting, The.
Ménage à Trois.
Morning Glory.
Movies for the Home.
Persistence of Song, The.
Piano Practice.
Pruned Tree, The.
Roof Garden, The.
Rules of Sleep.
Shall I Compare Thee to a Summer's Day?
Still Pond, No More Moving.
Tourists.
Underwood.
Wars, The.
Water Island.

Moss, Stanley (b. 1935)
For Margaret.
God Poem.
Hangman's Love Song, The.
Sailing from the United States.
Squall.
Two Fishermen.
Valley, The.

Moss, Thomas (1740?–1803)
Beggar, The.

Moss, Thylias (b. 1954)
Anointing, An.
Botanical Fanaticism.
Dennis's Sky Leopard.
Fisher Street.
Interpretation of a Poem by Frost.
Lessons from a Mirror.
Lunchcounter Freedom.
Lynching, The.
November and Aunt Jemima.
Owl In Daytime, The.
Party to which Wolves are Invited, The.
Raising a Humid Flag.
Sunrise Comes to Second Avenue.
There will be animals to teach us.
Tornados.
Wonder, The.

Mother Goose (*fl.* 17th–18th cent.)
Aristotle's Story.
As I was going along, long, long.
As I was going to St. Ives.
As I was going up Pippen Hill.
As Tommy Snooks and Bessy Brooks.
At the siege of Belle Isle.
Awake, arise, / Pull out your eyes.
Baa, baa, black sheep, have you any wool?
Baby, baby, naughty baby.
Baby's Dance, The.
Balloon, The.
Bandy Legs.
Barber, barber, shave a pig.
Bat, bat, come under my hat.
Bell horses, bell horses, what time of day?
Bessy Bell and Mary Gray.
Betty Blue.
Betty Pringle's Pig.
Birthdays.
Black Hen, The.
Black I am and much admired.
Bless you, bless you, burnie-bee [*or* bonnie-bee].
Blind man, blind man.
Blow the fire, blacksmith.
Blow, wind, blow! and go, mill, go!
Bob Robin.
Bobby Shaftoe's [*or* Shafto's] gone to sea.
Bonny Cravet, The.
Bow-wow, says the dog.
Boy and Girl.
Boy and the Sparrow.
Boys and girls come out to play.
Buttons, a farthing a pair.
By the Fire.
Bye, baby bunting.
Caesar's Song.
Candle, A.
Carrion crow sat upon [*or* on] an oak, The [*or* A].
Catch.
Chimney, A.
Christmas comes but once a year.
Clock, The.
Coachman, The.
Cobbler, cobbler, mend my shoe.
Cock-a-doodle-doo! / My dame has lost her shoe.
Cock doth crow / To let you know, The.
Come, butter, come.
Come dance a jig.
Come, let's to bed.
Cross Patch / Draw the latch.
Curly Locks [!] Curly Locks [!] wilt thou be mine?
Curr dhoo, curr dhoo.
Cushy cow bonny, let down thy milk.
Daffadowndilly.
Dame Trot and her cat.
Dance a baby diddy.
Dance, Thumbkin, dance.
Dance to your [*or* thee] daddy.
Dapple-gray.
Dickery [*or* dickory], dickery [*or* dickory], dare.
Diddle, diddle, dumpling, my son John.
Diddlety, diddlety, dumpty.
Difficult Rhyme, A.
Ding, dong, bell, / Pussy's in the well.
Dingty diddlety.
Doctor Faustus was a good man.
Doctor Foster went to Gloucester [*or* Glo'ster].
Dove and the Wren, The.
Ducks and Drakes.
Elizabeth, Elspeth, Betsy, and Bess.
Every lady in this land.
For every evil under the sun.
For want of a nail[, the shoe was lost].
Forehead, Eyes, Cheeks, Nose, Mouth, and Chin.
Formed long ago, yet made today.
Georgie Porgie, pudding and pie.
Girl in the lane, The.
God made the bees.
Good Advice.

Goosey, goosey, gander[, where *or* whither shall I wander? shall I wander?].
Handy Pandy, Jack-a-Dandy.
Hark, hark, the dogs do bark.
Hart he loves the high wood, The.
Hector Protector was dressed all in green.
Hickety, pickety, my black hen.
Hickory, dickory, dock.
Hie, hie, says Anthony.
High Diddle Diddle.
Higher than a house, / Higher than a tree.
Hot cross buns! Hot-cross buns! / One a penny, two a penny.
Hot Pease Man, The.
House That Jack Built, The.
How many days has my baby to play?
Humpty Dumpty sat on a wall.
Hush-a-bye, baby[, on the tree-top].
I had a little hobby horse, it was well shod.
I have a little sister, they call her Peep-Peep.
I love sixpence, jolly [*or* pretty] little sixpence.
I saw a ship a-sailing.
I saw three ships come sailing by.
I would, if I could.
If all the seas were one sea.
If all the world were apple-pie.
If I had [*or* I'd] as much money as I could spend.
If wishes were horses.
I'll tell you a story / About Jack a Nory.
In marble walls [*or* halls] as white as milk.
Intery, mintery, cutery corn.
Is John Smith within?
Jack and Gill [*or* Jill] went up the hill.
Jack and His Fiddle.
Jack be nimble.
Jack Sprat could eat no fat.
Jenny Wren.
Jerry Hall, / He is so small.
John Cook had a little grey mare.
Johnny shall have a new bonnet.
King Arthur.
King of France, the king of France / with forty thousand men, The.
Ladybird, Ladybird fly away home.
Leg over leg.
Lion and the unicorn, The.
Little Bird, The.
Little Bo-Peep has lost her sheep.
Little Boy Blue, come blow [up] your horn[!].
Little girl, little girl, / Where have you been?
Little Jack Horner/ Sat in a corner.
Little Jumping Joan.
Little King Pippin.
Little maid, pretty maid, / Whither goest thou?
Little Miss Muffet / Sat on a tuffet.
Little Moppet, The.
Little Polly Flinders.
London Bridge is broken down.
Long-tailed pig, A.
Lucy Locket lost her pocket.
Man in the wilderness asked [of] me [*or* said to me], The [*or* A].
March, march, head erect.
Margery Mutton-pie.
Mary, Mary, quite contrary.
Master and Man.
Merchants of London, The.
Milk Maid, The.
Mr. Frog Went a-Courting.
My father he died, but I can't tell you how.
My Kitten.
My maid Mary, / She minds the dairy.
Natural History.
Niddle Noddle.
North wind doth blow, The.
Nut Tree, A.
Old King Cole was a merry old soul.
Old Mother Goose.
Old Mother Twitchett had [*or* has] but one eye.
Old Woman and the Pedlar, The.
Old Woman of Surrey.
Old Woman, Old Woman.

One misty, moisty morning.
One to Ten.
One, two, / Buckle my shoe.
One, two, three, four, / Mary at the cottage door.
Other Little Tune, T'.
Pancake Day.
Pat-a-cake, pat-a-cake, baker's man.
Pease porridge [*or* pudding] hot.
Peter Piper picked a peck of pickled pepper[s].
Peter White will ne'er go right.
Piper and His Cow, THe.
Pit, pat, well-a-day.
Plum Pudding, A.
Polly and Sukey.
Poor old Robinson Crusoe!
Pretty John Watts.
Pumpkin-Eater, The.
Pussy-Cat, Pussy-Cat,/ where have you been?
Pussycat.
Quarrle, The.
Rain, rain, go to Spain.
Riddle me, riddle me ree.
Riddle: "Two legs sat upon three legs."
Ride a cock-horse [*or* a-cock horse] to Banbury Cross, / To see a fine lady upon a white horse.
Ride away, ride away / Johnny shall ride.
Ring-a-ring o' roses.
Robert Barnes, or [my] fellow fine.
Robert Rowley rolled a round roll round.
Robin-a-bobin.
Robin and Richard / Were two pretty men.
Robin Hood, Robin Hood, / Is in the mickle wood.
Rock-a-bye, baby, thy cradle is green.
Rub a dub dub.
Sam, the Sportsman.
Saturday, Sunday.
See-saw, Margery Daw, / Jack[y] shall have a new master.
See-saw, Margery Daw, / The old hen flew over the malt house.
See-saw, sacradown [*or* Sacaradown].
See, see, what shall I see?
Shall We Go A-Shearing?
Shoeing.
Sieve, A.
Simple Simon met a pieman.
Sing a song of sixpence.
Sing, sing, / What shall I sing?
Six little mice sat down to spin;.
Smiling girls, rosy boys.
Snail, The.
Solomon Grundy.
Sow came in with the saddle, The.
Speak when you're spoken to, / Come for one call.
Spring is showery, flowery, bowery;.
Strange Old Woman, A.
Sulky Sue.
Sunshine.
Taffy was a Welshman, Taffy was a thief.
Tarts, The.
Teeth and Gums.
Ten O'Clock Scholar, [The].
That's All.
There was a crooked man, and he went [*or* walked] a crooked mile.
There Was a Little Girl.
There was a little man, / and he wooed a little maid.
There was a man and he had nought.
There was a piper had a cow.
There was an old man in a velvet coat.
There was an old woman called Nothing-at-all.
There was an old woman lived under a hill.
There was an old woman / Lived under a hill / She put a mouse in a bag.
There was an old woman who lived in a shoe.
They that wash on Monday.
Thirty days hath September.
This is the house that Jack built, *sels.*
This is the way the ladies ride.

This little pig went to market.
Three blind mice, see how they run!
Three children sliding on the ice.
Three crooked cripples went through
  Cripplegate.
Three wise men of Gotham.
To Babylon.
To make your candles last for aye.
To market, to market / To buy a plum bun.
To sleep easy at night.
Tom, Tom the piper's son.
Tommy Tittlemouse.
Tommy Tucker.
Tongs.
Tragical Death of A, Apple Pie, The.
Trip upon trenchers, and dance upon dishes.
Tweedledum and Tweedledee.
Twelve pears hanging high.
Two Comical Folk.
Ungrateful Jenny.
Walnut, A.
Wash the dishes, wipe the dishes.
Well, The.
When I was a bachelor/ I lived by myself.
When I was a little girl, / About seven years
  old.
When the wind is in the east.
Where Is He?
Who killed Cock [or poor] Robin? [or Here
  lies Cock Robin].
Willful waste brings woeful want.
Willy boy, Willy boy, / Where are you
  going?
Willy, Willy Wilkin.
Winter.

Mother Maria. *See* **Kuzmina-Karavayeva,**
Elizaveta

Motherwell, William (1797–1935)
I've plucked the berry from the bush, the
  brown nut from the tree.

Mothibi, Chief
Speech.

Motion, Andrew (b. 1952)
These Days.
Writing.

Mototoshi (Fujiwara no Mototoshi) (1056–1142)
Your fine promises.

Motoyoshi Prince (*fl.* late 9th cent.)
I am unhappy. / I do not care what happens.

Mott, Michael (b. 1930)
Islanders, Inlanders.

Motteux, Peter Anthony (Pierre Antoine)
(1660–1718)
Song, A: "Slaves to London, I'll deceive
  you."

Mottram, Eric
Brief Novel (3).
Peace Project (5).
Smell of canyon rain storm.

Moulton, Louise Chandler (Ellen Louise
Chandler) (1835–1908)
At End.
Shall I complain because the feast is o'er.

Moultrie, John (1799–1874)
Fairy Maimounè, The.
Forget Thee?
Violets.

Mounsey, Messenger (1693–1788)
Here lie my old bones: my vexation now
  ends.

Mountain, Marlene
After your visit.
At dusk hot water from the hose.
Beneath / leaf mold.
C o y O t e.
Empty mailbox.
End of the cold spell.
Faded flowers of the bed sheets autumn
  night.
Frog.
Gosling following its neck to the bug.
He leans on the gate going staying.
Hoot.
In her old voice the mountains.
In / the / woods.
K k k k k.

Krĭk'ĭt.
My neighbor's rooster hops the stick i throw.
Old towel folding it again autumn evening.
On this cold.
One fly everywhere the heat.
Pick-up truck.
Pig and i spring rain.
Quiet day, A.
Rain.
Seed catalog in the mailbox cold drizzle.
Smoke from a neighbor's chimney loneliness.
Sn wfl k s.
Summer night clothes whirling in a dryer.
Wood pile.

Mountjoy, Cyril
Limerick: "Gay soccer spectator from Wix,
  A."
Limerick: "Psychic researcher's elation, A."
Limerick: "Slow-footed stockman called
  Beales, A."
Limerick: "Victoria was bitterly short."
Limerick: "Young Joseph's new coat was real
  nice."

Mouré, Erin
Aspen.
La Gueule.
She Touched Me.

Moyer, Linda Lancione
Listen.

Moyles, Lois
Report from California.
Tale Told by a Head, A.
Thomas in the Fields.

Mozart, Wolfgang Amadeus (1756–91)
Kanonentext.

Mozeen, Thomas (d. 1768)
Bedlamite, The.
Kilruddery Hunt, The.

Mozley, Abigail (b. 1947)
Summer I taught English to the French, The.

Mphahlele, Ezekiel (b. 1919)
Exile in Nigeria.
Homeward Bound.
Poem, A: "What is there that we can do or
  say."

Mphande, Lupenga (b. 1947)
Why the Old Woman Limps.
Wood-Cutter, The.

Mpondo, Simon (b. 1935?)
Season of the rains, The.

Mqhayi, S. E. K. (1875–1945)
Black Army, The.
Pleiades, The.
Sinking of the Mendi, The.

Mririda n'Ait Attik
Azouou! Evening Breeze! What a perfect
  name!
God Hasn't Made Room.
Like Smoke.
Mririda.

Msham, Mwana Kupona (c.1810–1860)
Poem to Her Daughter, *sels.*

Mtshali, Mbuyiseni Oswald (b. 1940)
Birth of Shaka, The.
Day We Buried Our Bully, The.
Farewell to My Scooter.
Inside My Zulu Hut.
Removal of Our Village, KwaBhanya, The.
Ride upon the Death Chariot.

Mu Hua (*fl.* c.300)
Rhyme-Prose on the Sea.

Mudie, Ian (1911–76)
This Land.

Mudrooroo (b. 1939)
Hide and Seek.
Peaches and Cream.
Song Cycle of Jacky, The, *sels.*

Mueller, Ilze
Another Time Track.
Invisibility Poem: Lesbian.
Night Shift at the Fruit Cannery.

Mueller, Jenny
Allegory.

Mueller, Lisel (b. 1924)
Commuter.
Historical Museum, Manitoulin Island.

Lonesome Dream, The.
Mermaid, The.
Monet Refuses the Operation.
Moon Fishing.
Palindrome.
Reading the Brothers Grimm to Jenny.

Mueller, Melinda
Evolution: A Science Fiction.

Mühlenberg, William Augustus (1796–1877)
I Would Not Live Alway.
Like Noah's Weary Dove.
Saviour, Who Thy Flock Art Feeding.

Muir, Edwin (1887–1959)
Abraham.
Absent, The.
Adam's Dream.
Animals, The.
Annunciation, The.
Ballad of Hector in Hades.
Ballad of the Flood.
Brothers, The.
Castle, The.
Child Dying, The.
Childhood.
Combat, The.
Confirmation, The.
Difficult Land, The.
Face, The.
Fathers, The.
Finder Found, The.
For Ann Scott-Moncrieff.
Gate, The.
Good Man in Hell, The.
Good Town, The.
Grove, The.
Horses.
Horses, The ("Barely a twelvemonth after.")
Human Fold, The.
In Love For Long.
Incarnate One, The.
Interrogation, The.
Island, The.
Killing, The.
Labyrinth, The.
Love's Remorse.
Mary Stuart.
Merlin.
Myth, The.
Mythical Journey, The.
Oedipus.
One foot in Eden still, I stand.
Refugees, The.
Return, The ("Doors flapped open in Ulysses'
  house.")
Return of the Greeks, The.
Rider Victory, The.
Ring, The.
Road, The.
Robert the Bruce.
Scotland 1941.
Scotland's Winter.
Song: "Why should your face so please me."
Suburban Dreams.
Then.
Three Mirrors, The.
To Franz Kafka.
Town Betrayed, The.
Transfiguration, The.
Trophy, The.
Troy.
Usurpers, The.
Voyage, The.
Wayside Station, The.
Wheel, The.
Window, The.

Mukhopadhyay, Subhash (b. 1919)
Task, The.

Mukhopadhyay, Vijaya (b. 1937)
Monday.

Mukta Bai (*fl.* 13th cent.)
Although he has no form.

Muktibodh, G. M. (1917–64)
Void inside us, The.

Muldoon, Paul (b. 1951)
Aisling.
Anseo.

Avenue, The.
Bearded Woman, by Ribera, The.
Big House, The.
Briefcase, The.
Brock.
Centaurs, The.
Christo's.
Clonfeacle.
Cuba.
Dancers at the Moy.
Field Hospital, The.
Gathering Mushrooms.
Glad Eye, The.
Hedgehog.
Ireland.
Lass of Aughrim, The.
Ma.
Making the Move.
Meeting the British.
Milkweed and Monarch.
Mixed Marriage, The.
Our Lady of Ardboe.
Quoof.
Right Arm, The.
Sightseers, The.
Soap-Pig, The.
Something of a Departure.
Sushi.
Truce.
Weepies, The.
Why Brownlee left, and where he went.
Wishbone, The.
Yggdrasill.
Mulford, Wendy
Egypt.
Goodbye to the Bay of Naples.
Green Chateau, The.
In a Hot Country.
Mr and Mrs.
Moon, The.
Valentine.
Mullen, F.
I took him by the arm and said.
Let Observation, shuddering the While.
Mullen, Harryette
Dance She Does, The.
Jump City.
Momma Sayings.
Muse and Drudge, sels.
Roadmap.
Saturday Afternoon, When Chores Are Done.
Müller, Wilhelm (1794–1827)
Beautiful Maid of the Mill, The, sels.
Mullineaux, Mary
Dragon, The.
Mullins, Brighde
At the Lakehouse.
Mulso, Hester (1727–1801)
To Stella.
Mumford, Lewis (1895–1990)
Consolation in War.
Munby, Arthur Joseph (1828–1910)
One Way of Looking at It.
Post Mortem.
Serving Maid, The.
Munday, Anthony (1553–1633)
Death of Robert, Earl of Huntingdon, sels.
Fedele and Fortunio, sels.
Primaleon of Greece, sels.
Mundell, William D. (b. 1913)
Uninvited, The.
Muneyuki (Minamoto no Muneyuki) (b. 939)
I can feel the loneliness.
Mungoshi, Charles (b. 1947)
Dotito is our brother.
Letter to a Son, A.
Munib-ur-Rahman (b. 1924)
Tall Buildings.
Munivar, Parancoti
Sacred Marriage of Shiva and Parvati, The,
sels.
Munkittrick, Richard Kendall (1853–1911)
Molasses River.
Old King Cabbage.
Redingote and the Vamoose, The.

Song of the Owl, The.
Munro, Hector Hugh. See "Saki"
Munro, Neil (1864–1930)
Fiddle, The.
Fingal's Weeping.
Macleod's Lament.
Mura, David
Argument: on 1942, An.
Colors of Desire, The.
Gardens We Have Left.
Grandfather and Grandmother in Love.
Grandfather-in-law.
Hibakusha's Letter (1955), The.
Huy Nguyen: Brothers, Drowning Cries.
Letters from Poston Relocation Camp (1942–
45).
Listening.
Natives, The.
Nisei Picnic: From an Album, A.
Recognitions.
To H.N.
Murakami Kijo
Against far off snow mountains.
Murasaki Shikibu (974–1031)
From the North send a message.
I feel of others' affairs / as though they
were.
Someone passes.
Tale of Genji, The, sels.
This life of ours would not cause you
sorrow.
Muratori, Fred
Sensible Qualities.
Mure, Sir William (1594–1657)
Cry of Blood, and of a Broken Covenant,
The, sels.
Murford, Nicholas (fl. 1647–52)
Storm and Calm: Sent from Embden to M.
Edw. Ma. and M. Tho. Ly, The.
Murger, Henry (1822–61)
Old Loves.
Spring in the Students' Quarter.
Murillo, Rosario
Angel in the Deluge.
Conversation in Front of a Helicopter.
Murphy, E. G. (1867–1939)
Smiths, The.
Thank you, Mr Rason, for the Apples.
Murphy, Frank
Paper Clip, Historian, Coathanger.
Murphy, Gerry (b. 1952)
Small Fat Boy Walking Backwards, A.
Vision at Knock.
Murphy, Richard (b. 1927)
Archaeology of Love, The.
Battle of Aughrim, The, sels.
Beehive Cell.
Elixir.
Epitaph on a Fir-Tree.
Gate Lodge.
Girl at the Seaside.
Gym.
High Island.
Last Galway Hooker, The.
Little Hunger.
Morning Call.
Nest in a Wall, A.
Pat Cloherty's Version of The Maisie.
Philosopher and the Birds, The.
Poet on the Island, The.
Reading Lesson, The.
Roof-Tree.
Sailing to an Island.
Seals at High Island.
Tony White.
Murray, Charles (1864–1941)
Whistle, The.
Murray, Joan (b. 1945)
Madonna vs. Child.
Murray, John (1741–1815)
Hark! 'Tis the Saviour of Mankind.
Murray, L. and F. Leigh
Charlie Piecan.
Murray, Les A. (b. 1938)
Absolutely Ordinary Rainbow, An.
Broad Bean Sermon, The.

Bulahdelah—Taree Holiday Song Cycle, The,
sels.
Dog Fox Field.
Drugs of War, The.
Easter 1984.
Equanimity.
Greenhouse Vanity, The.
Hearing Impairment.
Lament for the Country Soldiers.
Louvres.
Mitchells, The.
Morse.
Names of the Humble, The.
Noonday Axeman.
Once in a Lifetime, Snow.
Portrait of the Autist as a New World Driver.
Powerline Incarnation, The.
Quality of Sprawl, The.
Smell of Coal Smoke, The.
Sydney and the Bush.
Sydney Highrise Variations, The, sels.
Tin Wash Dish, The.
Widower in the Country, The.
Murray, Michele (1934–74)
Dance Poem, sels.
Poem of Two, sels.
Poem to My Grandmother in Her Death.
Murray, Patrick J. (b. 1911)
God's Little Angel.
Murray, Paul (b. 1947)
Rain.
Murray, Pauli (b. 1910)
Conquest.
Dark Testament.
Death of a Friend.
For Mack C. Parker.
Harlem Riot, 1943.
Inquietude.
Mr. Roosevelt Regrets.
Redemption.
Returning Spring.
Song: "Because I know deep in my own
heart."
Without Name.
Murray, Raymond (b. 1938)
Carmelite.
Murray, Robert Fuller (1863–94)
Wasted Day, The.
Murray, Rona (b. 1924)
Lizard, The.
Murry, Ann (b. c.1755, d. after 1816)
Familiar Epistle, A.
Tête à Tête; or, Fashionable Pair: an Eclogue,
The.
Murry, Kathleen Beauchamp. See **Mansfield,
Katherine**
Murthy, Janaki Srinivas. See "Vaidehi"
Muruvalar, Pereyin
He has held.
What He Said.
Mus, David
Joy of Cooking, The, sels.
Musaeus (?late 5th cent. A.D.)
Consummation.
Courtship.
Hero and Leander, sels.
Musgrave, Susan (b. 1951)
Burial of the Dog.
Exchange of Fire.
I Am Not a Conspiracy Everything Is Not
Paranoid.
Judas Goat, The.
Returning to the Town Where We Used to
Live.
Salad Days.
Muske, Carol (b. 1945)
August, Los Angeles, Lullaby.
Child with Six Fingers.
Eulogy, The.
Field Trip.
Found.
Hyena.
Intensive Care.
Little L.A. Villanelle.
Painter's Daughter, The.

Pediatrics.
Rice.
Swansong.
To the Muse.
Wish Foundation, The.
Wyndmere, Windemere.
Muslih-Din. *See* **Sadi**
Musset, Alfred de (1810–57)
Juana.
Souvenir.
To Julie.
"Mustafa." *See* **Johnson, Don Allen**
Mutabaruka (Allan Hope) (b. 1952)
Free Up de Lan, White Man.
Revolutionary Poets.
You Ask Me.
Mu'tamid, King of Seville (1040–95)
Tears of the World.
Woo Not the World.
Mutamociyar
Āy: A Gift of Elephants.
Āy: His Hill.
Mutanabbi (915–65)
Shame kept my tears away.
Mutswairo, Solomon (b. 1924)
My Birds.
Mutukorran, Uriyur
What the Passersby Said to the lover eloping
with the girl.
Muuse, 'Abdillaahi
Elder's Reproof to his Wife, An.
Muzahim al-Ugaili (fl. 700)
Earth outside, The.
Mycall, John (d. 1833)
Our States, O Lord.
Myers, Garry Cleveland
Dear God.
Talking to God.
Myers, Jack (b. 1941)
Apprentice Painter, The.
Experts, The.
Have a Nice Day.
Jake Addresses the World from the Garden.
Mirror for the Barnyard.
Not Thinking of Himself.
So Long Solon.
Visitation Rites.
When I Held You to My Chest, You Fit.
Myers, Walter Dean (b. 1937)
Summer.
Myles, Eileen (b. 1949)
December 9th.
Maxfield Parrish.
New England Wind.
Sadness of Leaving, The.
Woman like Me, A.
Mylonas, Eva (b. 1936)
Holidays.
Myrinos
"L" may stand for fifty, Lais.
Time topples Statyllios like a doddery oak.
Mystic, Rabi'a the. *See* **Rabi'a al-Adawiyya**

N

Na-lan Hsing-te (Nara Singde) (1655–85)
Tune: "Autumn Waters"—Listening to Rain.
Tune: "Big String of Words A"—The Great
Wall.
Tune: "Butterflies Lingering over Flowers"—
Leaving the Border.
Tune: "Immortal at the River"—Winter
Willow.
Tune: "Partridge Sky"—Parting Sorrows.
Tune: "Remembering the Lady of Ch'in—At
the Mouth of Dragon Pool."
Tune: "Remembering the Prince."
Tune: "Song of Dandy"—Hunting in
Autumn.
Nabbes, Thomas (1605?–1641)
Song, The: "Beauty no more the subject be."
Song: "What a dainty life the milkmaid
leads!"

**Nabokov, Vladimir Vladimirovich (Vladimir
Sirin) (1899–1977)**
Ballad of Longwood Glen, The.
Evening of Russian Poetry, An.
Execution, The.
Fame.
Lines Written in Oregon.
Literary Dinner, A.
Ode to a Model.
On Discovering a Butterfly.
Room a dying poet took, The.
To Russia.
What is the evil deed I have committed?
Nadaud, Gustave (1820–93)
Carcassonne.
Naden, Constance (1858–1889)
Love Versus Learning.
Love's Mirror.
Moonlight and Gas.
Natural Selection.
Pantheist's Song of Immortality, The.
Pessimist's Vision, The.
Poet and Botanist.
Scientific Wooing.
Sister of Mercy, The.
Solomon Redivivus, 1886.
Two Artists, The.
Nadir, Moishe (Yitzhok Reis) (1885–1943)
Adjectives.
Nadson, Semion Yakovlevich (1862–87)
Brother, The.
Nagase, Kiyoko (b. 1906)
Mother.
Nagy, Agnes Nemes (b. 1922)
Between.
Bird.
Figtrees.
Four-Light Window, A.
Geyser, The.
Ghost, The.
Horses and the Angels, The.
I Carried Statues.
Ikhnaton's Night.
Lazarus.
Like one who brought news from far.
Pinetree.
Scene, The.
Simile.
Sincerity.
Storm.
To a Poet.
To Freedom.
Trees.
Winter Angel.
Words to a Song.
Nagys, Henrikas
Hallesches Tor: Communion.
Laterna Obscura.
Poem.
**Nahman [or Nachman] of Bratzlav, Rabbi
(1770–1811)**
Annul Wars.
Heart of the World, The.
Torah of the Void, The, *sels.*
Nahuatl Oral Tradition
Elegy.
Song for the Festival of Tlaloc, the Rain
God.
Nahum (fl. c.1300)
Spring Song.
Naidu [or Nayadu], Sarojini (1879–1949)
Hindu Cradle Song.
Snake-Charmer, The.
Naiman, Adeline
Jennie Lubell is In a Nursing Home in
Provincetown, *sels.*
**Nairne, Carolina Oliphant, Baroness (1766–
1845)**
Caller Herrin'.
Laird o' Cockpen, he's proud an' he's great,
The.
Land o' the Leal, The.
Naisby, T. H. (1931–89)
Reflections on Hillsborough in Memoriam.
Naito Joso (Joso) (1662–1704)
Autumn cicada, The.

Fields and mountains.
I've just come up.
Najara, Israel (1555–1628)
God of the World.
Loved of My Soul.
Nakamura, Chio (b. 1913)
Diary without Dates, A.
Nakamura, Teijo (b. 1900)
Season of changing clothes, The.
Nakasuk
Great Farter, The.
Invisible Men, The.
Magic Words to Feel Better.
Nakatsukasa
If it were not for the voice. *From Shui Shu.*
Nakkannaiyar (fl. between 1st and 3d cent.)
Woman in Love with a Captive King, A.
Nakkiranar
Murukaṉ: His Places.
Murukaṉ, the Red One.
Nalungiaq
Heaven and Hell.
Nam, Nguyễn. *See* **Viên Linh**
Nam Trân Nguyễn Học Sỹ (1907–67)
Against Tunes in a Minor Key.
Beauty and the Poet.
Nam Xuyên (Phan Ngọc Châu) (b. 1909)
Bamboo hedgerow cut a dark-green swath,
The.
Namatianus (4th cent. A.D.)
Roma.
Namjoshi, Suniti (b. 1941)
Caliban's Journal.
From the Travels of Gulliver.
Namjoshi, Suniti and Gillian Hanscombe
Because of India, before and after.
In that particular temple.
Was It Quite Like That?
We Can Compose Ourselves.
Nankivell, Austin Threlfall
Off Coronel.
Nannakaiyar
What She Said ("Bird and beast.")
What She Said ("When he said.")
Nannestad, Elizabeth (b. 1943)
Portrait of a Lady.
Queen of the River.
Nanton, Philip (b. 1947)
I.
Naone, Dana (b. 1949)
Girl with the Green Skirt.
I make all the poetic pauses.
Long Distance.
Presence, The.
Sleep.
Napier, Felicity
Houseplant.
Nara. *See* **Narayana Rao, V.**
Narain, Kunwar (b. 1927)
Towards Delhi.
Narasimhaswami, K. S. (b. 1915)
Consolation to Empty Pitchers.
Narayana Rao, V. (Nara) (b. 1932)
White Paper.
Narbut, Vladimir Ivanovich (1888–1944)
October.
Narihira (Ariwara no Narihira) (825–80)
Even in the age.
I have always known / That at last I would.
This is not the moon.
**Narovchatov, Sergey [or Sergei] Sergeievich
(1919–81)**
Wolf Cub.
Nash, Ogden (1902–71)
Adventures of Isabel.
Anatomy of Happiness, The.
Ant has made himself illustrious, The.
Arthur.
Benjamin.
Canary, The.
Cat, The.
City, The.
Columbus.

Come On In, the Senility Is Fine.
Cook called McMurray, A.
Cow is of the bovine ilk, The.
Curl Up and Diet.
Did Someone Say "Babies"?
Dog, The.
Duck, The.
Eel, The.
Emmet is an ant (archaic), The.
England Expects.
Evening Out, The.
Exit, Pursued by a Bear.
Experiment Degustatory.
Family Court.
First Limick.
Fly, The.
Friend in Need Will Be Around in Five
  Minutes, A.
Genealogical Reflection.
Germ, The.
Golly, How Truth Will Out.
Grackle's voice is less than mellow.
Grandpa Is Ashamed.
Ha! Original Sin!
I Can't Have a Martini, Dear, but You Take
  One, or, Are You Going to Sit There
  Guzzling All Night?
I Never Even Suggested It.
Ill Met by Zenith.
Introspective Reflection.
Invocation: "Senator Smoot (Republican,
  Ut.)"
Kind of an Ode to Duty.
Kitten, The.
Lady from near Rising Sun, A.
Lama, The.
Limerick: "Careless explorer named Blake,
  A."
Limerick: "Crusader's wife slipped from the
  garrison, A."
Limerick: "Cute secretary, none cuter, A."
Limerick: "Elderly bride of Port Jervis, An."
Limerick: "Jolly young fellow from Yuma,
  A."
Limerick: "Lama of Outer Mongolia, A."
Limerick: "Novelist of the Absurd, A."
Limerick: "Old Danish jester named Yorick,
  An."
Limerick: "There was a young fellow named
  Fonda."
Limerick: "There was a young girl of old
  Natchez."
Limerick: "There was a young lady called
  Harris."
Limerick: "There was an old gossip called
  Baird."
Limerick: "There was an old man in a
  trunk."
Lines to a World-famous Poet Who Failed to
  Complete a World-famous Poem; or, Come
  Clean, Mr. Guest!
Lines Written to Console Those Ladies
  Distressed by the Lines 'Men Never Make
  Passes, etc.'
Lion, The.
Love Under the Republicans (Or Democrats).
Man Can Complain, Can't He?, A.
Mermaid, The.
Mr. Artesian's Conscientiousness.
Morning Prayer.
New Nutcracker Suite, The, sels.
Notes for the Chart in 306.
Octopus, The.
Oh to Be Odd!
Old Men.
One from One Leaves Two, sels.
Panther is like a leopard, The.
Parent, The.
Parsnip, children, I repeat, The.
Peekaboo, I Almost See You.
Perfect Husband, The.
Pig, if I am not mistaken, The.
Portrait of the Artist as a Prematurely Old
  Man.
Private Dining Room, The.
Purist, The.
Reflection on Babies.

Reflection on Ingenuity.
Reflections on Ice-breaking.
Reprise.
Requiem: "There was a young belle of old
  Natchez."
Rhinoceros, The.
Riding on a Railroad Train.
Samson Agonistes.
Say About Seven or Seven-Fifteen.
Sea-Gull, The.
Seven Spiritual Ages of Mrs. Marmaduke
  Moore, The.
Shrimp who sought his lady shrimp, A.
So That's Who I Remind Me Of.
Song of the Open Road.
Song to Be Sung by the Father of Infant
  Female Children.
Strange Case of Mr. Ormantude's Bride, The.
Sweet Dreams.
Taboo to Boot.
Tale of Custard the Dragon, The.
Termite, The.
Theatre Hour.
They Don't Speak English in Paris.
Third Jungle Book, The.
Third Limick.
Turtle lives 'twixt plated decks, The.
Tweedledee and Tweedledoom.
Up from the Egg; the Confessions of a
  Nuthatch Avoider.
Up from the Wheelbarrow.
Very like a Whale.
Wapiti, The.
What Do You Want: A Meaningful Dialogue,
  or a Satisfactory Talk?
Winter Morning.
Wombat lives across the seas, The.
Word to Husbands, A.
Young flirt of Ceylon, A.

Nashe [or Nash], Thomas (1567–1601)
  Choise of valentines, The.
  Summer's Last Will and Testament, sels.
Naso, Publius Ovidius. See **Ovid**
Nasrin, Taslima (b. 1962)
  Another Life.
  At the Back of Progress. . . .
  Border.
  Character.
  Eve Oh Eve.
Nastasijevic, Momcilo (1894–1938)
  Burial.
  Deaf Things, sels.
  Gray Moment.
  Roadside Fountain.
  Still Trees.
  String, The.
  To My Dead Sister.
Natambu, Kofi
  Funky Butt Legacy Song (An Epic in
    Progress), The.
  Words and Music in America.
Nathan, Leonard (b. 1924)
  Answer of Sorts, An.
  At the Well.
  Bladder Song.
  Body Count.
  Breathing Exercises.
  Day the Perfect Speakers Left, The.
  Election, The.
  Hole.
  Just Looking, Thank You.
  Letter.
  So you aren't Tolstoy or Saint Francis.
  Toast.
Nathan, Robert (1894–1985)
  Christian, Be Up.
  Mountaineer, The.
  Now Blue October.
  Sonnet: "Because my grief seems quiet and
    apart."
  These Are the Chosen People.
Naudé, Adèle (b. 1910)
  Africa.
  From a Venetian Sequence.
  Idiot, The.
  Portrait.

Unpossessed, The.
Navajo Oral Tradition
  Ground-Squirrel Song.
  Night Chant, The.
  There Are No People Song.
Naylor, James Ball (1860–1945)
  Authorship.
"Nayo." See **Watkins, Nayo-Barbara**
Ndebele, Njabulo S. (b. 1948)
  Revolution of the Aged, The.
Ndlovu, Thembinkosi
  Elegy for the Dead of Soweto.
Ndu, Pol N (1940–78)
  Evacuation.
  Udude.
Neal, John (1793–1876)
  Battle of Niagara, The, sels.
Neal, Larry (b. 1937)
  Don't say goodbye to the Porkpie Hat that
    rolled.
  Harlem Gallery: From the Inside.
  James Powell on Imagination.
  Lady's Days.
  Malcolm X—an Autobiography.
  Middle Passage and After, The.
Neale, John Mason (1818–66)
  Hymn for Easter Morn.
  Oh, Give Us Back the Days of Old!
Needell, Claire (b. 1965)
  Reaches the Body, sels.
Negri, Ada (1870–1945)
  Make way! From the Noisy ceilings of
    workshops.
Neidhart von Reuental (fl. 13th cent.)
  On the Mountain.
  "Sing, my golden cock, I'll give thee grain!"
  Summer, now we must live without your
    sweet weather.
  There is pain in my heart.
  "Young and old, rejoice."
Neidjie, Bill (fl. 1987)
  This earth.
Neihardt, John Gneisenau (1881–1973)
  Song of Jed Smith, The, sels.
  Song of the Indian Wars, The, sels.
Neilson, John Shaw (1872–1942)
  Crane Is My Neighbor, The.
  Flowers in the Ward.
  In the Street.
  May.
  Orange Tree, The.
  Schoolgirls Hastening.
  Soldier Is Home, The.
  Sundowner, The.
  Take Down the Fiddle, Karl!
  To the Red Lory.
  You Cannot Go Down to the Spring.
Nekipelov, Viktor Aleksandrovich (1928–89)
  Alabushevo.
Nekrasov, Nikolai Alekseyevich (1821–77)
  Capitals Are Rocked, The.
  Propos of the Wet Snow, A, sels.
Nekrasova, Ksenya [or Kseniia] (1912–58)
  Blind Man, The.
  Rublyov XVth Century.
  Street perturbs my mind somehow, The.
Nelson, Crawdad
  How We Make Lumber Out of Trees.
Nelson, David (1793–1844)
  My Days are Gliding Swiftly By.
Nelson, Eric (1944–85)
  Kitchens.
Nelson, Frank Carleton
  Human Heart, The.
Nelson, Howard
  My Father Went to Funerals.
Nelson, Lynn. See **Waniek, Marilyn Nelson**
Nelson, Willie (b. 1933)
  Heaven and Hell.
Nemerov, Howard (b. 1920)
  Amateurs of Heaven, The.
  Angel and Stone.
  At a Country Hotel.

Author to His Body on Their Fifteenth
Birthday, 29.ii.80, The.
Backward Look, The.
Because You Asked about the Line between
Prose and Poetry.
Blue Suburban.
Blue Swallows, The.
Boom!
Boy with Book of Knowledge.
Brainstorm.
Brief Journey West, The.
Cabinet of Seeds Displayed, A.
Carol: "Now is the world withdrawn all."
Casting.
Companions, The.
Creation Myth on a Moebius Band.
Death of God, The.
Dependencies, The.
Dial Tone, The.
Dialogue.
Dragonfly, The.
Dying Garden, The.
Easter.
Elegy for a Nature Poet.
Epigrams, sels.
Eve.
Extract from Memoirs.
Fable of the War, A.
Fall Again, The.
Fugue.
Ginkgoes in Fall.
Gnomes, sels.
"Good-bye," said the river, "I'm going
downstream."
Goose Fish, The.
Grace to Be Said at the Supermarket.
Gyroscope.
Historical Judas, The.
History of a Literary Movement.
Holding the Mirror Up to Nature.
I Only Am Escaped Alone to Tell Thee.
Icehouse in Summer, The.
Insomnia I.
Learning by Doing.
Learning the Trees.
Life, A.
Life Cycle of Common Man.
Lobsters.
Lot Later.
Low-Level Cross-Country.
Makers, The.
Manners.
Mapmaker on His Art, The.
Marriage of Heaven and Earth, The.
May Day Dancing, The.
Media.
Metamorphoses.
Models.
Money.
More Joy in Heaven.
Mousemeal.
Mud Turtle, The.
Murder of William Remington, The.
Mystery Story.
Negro Cemetery Next to a White One, A.
Nicodemus.
Night Operations, Coastal Command RAF.
Old Picture, An.
On Being Asked for a Peace Poem.
On Certain Wits.
Ozymandias II.
Phoenix comes of flame and dust, The.
Picture, A.
Primer of the Daily Round, A.
Reading Pornography in Old Age.
Redeployment.
Reflexions on the Seizure of the Suez, and
on a Proposal to Line the Banks of That
Canal with Billboard Advertisements.
Remorse for Time, The.
Salt Garden, The.
Santa Claus.
Scales of the Eyes, The.
September, the First Day of School.
Sigmund Freud.
Singular Metamorphosis, A.
Snowflakes.

Speculation.
Spell before Winter, A.
St. John, sels.
Statues in the Public Gardens, The.
Storm Windows.
Style.
Sunday at the End of Summer.
Sweeper of Ways, The.
Thirtieth Anniversary Report of the Class of
'41.
To D———, Dead by Her Own Hand.
To David, about His Education.
To My Least Favorite Reviewer.
To the Rulers.
Town Dump, The.
Translation.
Trees.
Truth.
Ultima Ratio Reagan.
Vacuum, The.
View, The.
View from an Attic Window, The.
Waiting Rooms.
War in the Air, The.
Way of Life, A.
Western Approaches, The.
Wolves in the Zoo.
Writing.

**Nemesianus, Marcus Aurelius Olympis (c. 3rd
cent. A.D.)**
Chace: 'Of the Litter of Whelps," The, sels.

Nerber, John (1915?–1968)
Castaway.

**Neruda, Pablo (Neftalí Ricardo Reyes Basualto)
(1904–73)**
America, I do not call your name without
hope.
Body of a woman, white hills, white thighs.
Burial in the East.
Cat's Dream.
Dictators, The.
Drunk as drunk on turpentine.
Elephant, sels.
Funeral in the East.
Girl lithe and tawny, the sun that forms.
Heights of Macchu Picchu, The, sels.
In my sky at twilight you are like a cloud.
Letter to Miguel Otero Silva, in Caracas.
Melancholy inside Families.
Nothing but Death.
Ode to My Socks.
Ode to the Cat.
Ode to the Watermelon.
Past.
Poem.
Poetry.
Poet's Obligation.
Sexual Water.
Sonnet XII, sels.
Sonnet XVII.
Sonnet XLVIII, sels.
They Receive Instructions Against Chile.
To the Foot from Its Child.
Tonight I can write the saddest lines.
Too Many Names.
United Fruit Co, The.
Walking [or Walkin'] Around.
We Are Many.

Nerval, Gérard de (Gérard Labrunie) (1808–55)
Fancy, A.
Girl Cousin, The.
Grandmother, The.
Mute Phenomena, The.
Old Tune, An.

Nesbit, Edith (Edith Nesbit Bland) (1858–1924)
Among His Books.
Appeal.
At Parting.
Child's Song in Spring.
Claim, The.
Dead to the Living, The.
Goose-Girl, The.
Gray Folk, The.
Great Industrial Centre, A.
Haunted.
Husband of To-Day, The.
Kiss, The.

Love's Guerdons.
Morning Song.
Song: "Oh, baby, baby, baby dear."
Things That Matter, The.
Vies Manquées.
Villeggiature.
Wife of All Ages, The.

Nesbit, Wilbur Dick (1871–1927)
All to Myself.
Friend of Two, A.
Who Hath a Book.

Netherclift, Beryl (b. 1911)
London Trees.

Neto, Agostinho (1922–79)
African Poem.
Farewell at the Moment of Parting.
Grieved lands of Africa, The.
We Must Return.

Nettimaiyar
Your bards are wearing lotuses.

Netumpalliyattan
What She Said about Her Unfaithful,
Estranged Husband.

Nevin, Edwin H. (1814–89)
Happy, Saviour, Would I Be.
When Our Earthly Sun Is Setting.

Newbery, Thomas (fl. c.1563)
Great Merchant, Dives Pragmaticus, Cries His
Wares, The, sels.

Newbolt, Sir Henry John (1862–1938)
Admirals All.
Cities Drowned.
Clifton Chapel.
Commemoration.
Drake's Drum.
Felix Antonius.
From Generation to Generation.
Gillespie.
He Fell among Thieves.
Master and Man.
Messmates.
Moonset.
Rilloby-Rill.
Song: "Flowers that in thy garden rise, The."
To a River in the South.
Toy Band, The.
Vitaï Lampada.

**Newcastle, Margaret Lucas Cavendish, Duchess
of (1623?–1673)**
Claspe, The.
Common Fate of Books, The.
Convent of Pleasure, The, sels.
Courting the Faerie Queen.
Dialogue between Melancholy and Mirth, A,
sels.
Dialogue betwixt Man, and Nature, A.
Dialogue betwixt the Body and the Mind, A.
Discourse of Beasts, A.
Discourse of Melancholy, A.
Dissert, A.
Excuse for So Much Writ upon My Verses.
Fort or Castle of Hope, The, sels.
Her Descending Down.
Hunting of the Hare, The.
Imagination.
Landscape, A.
Love, how thou'rt tired out with rhyme!
Mirth and Melancholy.
Nature's Cook.
O do not grieve, Dear Heart, nor shed a tear.
Of Many Worlds in This World.
Of Stars.
Of the Animal Spirits.
Of the Theme of Love.
'Poet I am neither born, nor bred," A.
Poetresses Hasty Resolution, The.
Poetresses Petition, The.
Sea Similized to Meadows and Pastures: the
Mariners, to Shepherds: the Mast, to a
May-Pole: the Fish, to Beasts, The.
Soul and Body.
Soul's Garment, The.
Woman drest by Age, A.

**Newcastle, William Cavendish, Duke of (1592–
1676)**
Humorous Lovers, The, sels.
Love's Epitaph.

Love's Matrimony.
Love's Sun.
Newell, Robert Henry. *See* **"Kerr, Orpheus C."**
Newey-Johnson, D.
To Let.
Newlove, John (b. 1938)
America.
Double-headed Snake, The.
Pride, The.
Samuel Hearne in Wintertime.
What Do You Want?
Newman, John Henry, Cardinal (1801–90)
Dream of Gerontius, The, *sels.*
Pillar of the Cloud, The.
Refrigerium.
Sensitiveness.
Newman, Lesléa (b. 1955)
Poem for My Grandmother's Grandmother.
Newman, Louis I. (b. 1895)
Voice of God, The.
Newman, Michael (b. 1846)
Negative Passage.
Newsome, Mary Effie Lee (1885–1979)
Morning Light.
Newth, Rebecca
I had gone out to check on new lambs.
Newton, Byron Rufus (1861–1938)
Owed to New York.
Newton, Charles (b. 1776?)
Stanzas, *sels.*
Newton, John (1725–1807)
Glorious Things of Thee Are Spoken.
Name of Jesus, The, *sels.*
Nezahualcoyotl (1402–72)
Flower Songs.
Nezval, Vitězslau (1900–58)
City With Towers.
Clock in the Old Jewish Ghetto, The.
Lilac by the Museum on St. Wenceslas
   Square, The.
Moon over Prague.
Prague in the Midday Sun.
Trap Door.
Walker in Prague.
Ng Shao (fl. 6th cent.)
New Wife, The.
Ngân Giang (fl. 20th cent.)
Getting Well.
Ngani, A. Z.
Praises of King George VI.
Ngata, Apirana (1874–1945)
Cream Song, The.
Ngatho, Stella (b. 1953)
Footpath.
Ngawai, Tuini (1910–65)
Great King.
News, The.
Ngunaitponi (David Unaipon) (1873–1967)
Song of Hungarrda, The.
Nguyễn Bính
Girl Next Door, The.
Two Hearts.
Nguyễn Bỉnh Khiêm (1491–1585)
Before the world of power you'll fold your
   arms.
Clouds float through dreams, are nowhere to
   be seen.
Men jostle and men fight with labored
   breath.
My hair has thinned, my teeth have worn
   away.
On Reading the Buddha's Scriptures.
Rich look grand, the poor seem cheap and
   mean, The.
Self-Reflection.
Three Ranks of Men, Three Grades of
   Things.
Time and again you've seen them win or
   lose.
Nguyễn Chí Thiện (b. 1933)
All Come to Me.
Jungle night—it rains and rains, roofs leak,
   A.
Model children of the regime, The.

My poetry is no poetry, no.
Party left me in the wilds, The.
Sundry Notes, *sels.*
This land's no joy.
Travel with grief—goodbye to joy!
Nguyễn Công Trú' (1778–1858)
Hero's Will, A.
Looking Forward to Retirement.
Ode to All Flowers.
Officialdom.
Scholars and soldiers marshaled in two files!
Wasted Life, A.
Nguyễn Đ&inh Chiểu (1822–88)
Blind Poet Looks at the World Outside, A.
Elegy for Tru'o'ng Định.
Fisherman Speaks His Mind, A.
Fleeing From Bandits.
Loyal Horse, The.
Storm, The.
Waiting for the East Wind.
Nguyễn Đình Kiên (d. 1942)
Back In Prison.
Prison Impromptu.
Nguyễn Đình Thi (b. 1924)
Yearning.
Nguyễn Du (1765–1820)
Calling All Souls.
Nguyễn Duy Nhuệ (b. 1948)
Bamboos of Vietnam.
Nguyễn Gia Thiều (1741–98)
Song of Sorrow Inside the Royal Harem, A.
Nguyễn Hữ'u Chu (fl. 20th cent.)
Neither Fish Nor Fowl.
Nguyễn Hữ'u Huân (d. 1875)
Carrying a Canguc Around the Neck
Nguyễn Khuyến (1835–1909)
At an Exposition.
Comedian Gets a Curtain Lecture, The.
French National Holiday, The.
Old Age.
On Hearing the Rail Cry.
Scholar-Laureate in Retirement, A.
Self-Portrayal.
To a Discarded Fan.
To a Statue.
To Some Students Caught Nodding in Class.
Widow's Reply to a Matchmaker, The.
Nguyễn Ngọc Thuận (fl. 20th cent.)
Prisoner's Funeral, A.
Nguyễn Nhu'ọ'c Pháp (1914–38)
In a Garret.
**Nguyễn Tất Nhiên (Nguyễn Hoàng Hải) (1952–
92)**
Folk Songs For Today.
Nguyễn Thiên Túng (fl. 15th cent.)
Well, The.
Nguyễn Trãi (1380–1442)
Among the great, no smooth and open world.
Ask to be put in charge of streams and hills!
Both favor and disgrace you have full
   known.
For years you wallowed in the scholar's
   world.
He tends the tree who wants to eat the fruit.
Hibiscus, The.
How blessed is a middle rank in life!
Old Banyan Tree, The.
Round shape water takes inside the gourd, A.
Tired legs won't climb the high road of blue
   clouds.
Womb's own flesh and bone—strong
   brotherhood, A.
Nguyễn Văn Lạc (1842–1915)
Shrimp.
To a Dead Dog in the River.
Nguyễn Văn Năng (1902–68)
I Shall Not Die.
Prison Cell, A.
Nguyễn Ý Thuần (b. 1953)
Homecoming.
Nhạ, Nguyễn Quang. *See* **Tô Giang Tử'**
Nhan, Dieu. *See* **Ly Ngoc Kieu**
Nhật Tiến (b. 1936)
Two Eyes.

Nho'n, Đoan Thế. *See* **Võ Phiến**
Nhu'ọ'ng Tống Hoàng Phạm Trân (1897–1948)
Mourning a Hero.
Sense of History, A.
Ní Chuilleanáin, Eiléan (b. 1942)
Dead Fly.
Letter to Pearse Hutchinson.
Old Roads.
Rose-Geranium, The, *sels.*
Site of Ambush, *sels.*
Swineherd.
Wash man out of the earth, shear off.
Ní Dhomhnaill, Nuala (b. 1952)
As for the Quince.
Aubade: "It's all the same to morning what it
   dawns on."
Bond, The.
Broken Doll, The.
Feeding a Child.
I cannot lie here anymore.
Labasheedy (The Silken Bed).
Leaba Shíoda.
Marvellous Grass.
Parthenogenesis.
Poem for Melissa.
Race, The.
Shannon Estuary Welcoming the Fish, The.
Venio ex Oriente.
Ní Tsan (1301–74)
Following the Rhymes of the Six Poems
   "Thinking of the Past at Ku-Su and
   Ch'ien-t'ang."
Following the Rhymes of Yü-chai's Poems
   on Autumn, *sels.*
Inscribed on a Painting.
Inscribed on a Painting by Myself.
Inscribed on the Painting, "River in Autumn."
Lamenting Noble Scholar Chu.
Man in Hangchou Spread Word that I Had
   Died. Chen-chü Heard of This and Was
   Upset, So I Have Written This To Send
   Him, A.
On the Fifteenth Day of the Ninth Month of
   the Year Kuei-mao of the Chih-cheng
   Period (Oct. 22, 1363), I Painted This to
   Send to the Summoned Scholar, Sheng-po,
   and Inscribed This Poem on It.
On the Twentieth Day.
Painting "Solitary Fisherman by a Spring
   River" The.
To the Retired Scholar Chang.
Two Poems to the Tune "Hsiao-t'iao hung,"
   sels.
Two Poems to the Tune "Jen-yüeh yüan,"
   sels.
Waking from a Nap.
Woodpecker, The.
Niatum, Duane (b. 1938)
After the Death of an Elder Klallam.
Apology.
Art of Clay, The.
Ascending Red Cedar Moon.
Chief Leschi of the Nisqually.
Crow's Way.
Drawings of the Song Animals.
Elegy for Chief Sealth.
First Spring.
Homage to Chagall.
Indian Rock, Bainbridge Island, Washington.
Lines for Roethke Twenty Years after His
   Death.
Maggie.
No One Remembers Abandoning the Village
   of White Fir.
Novelty Shop, The.
Old Woman Awaiting the Greyhound Bus.
On Hearing the Marsh Bird's Water Cry.
On Leaving Baltimore.
On Visiting My Son, Port Angeles,
   Washington.
Pieces.
Reality of Autumn, The.
Slow Dancer That No One Hears but You.
Snowy Owl near Ocean Shores ("Snowy owl,
   storm cast from the arctic tundra.")
To Your Question.
Traveler, The.

Nibenegenesabe, Jacob
  Wishing Bone Cycle, The, *sels.*
Niblett, Peter
  Tiger behind the bars of his cage growls,
    The.
Nicaenetus (*fl. 3d cent. B.C.*)
  Not in the city, Philoterus.
  Speaks Bito's tomb to whomsoever reads.
Nicarchus of Alexandria (*fl. A.D. 1st cent.*)
  Agelaus was kind to Acestorides.
  All great events have harbingers.
  Another doctor story. Our G.P., Marcus.
  Diodorus the hunchback / Went to Socles the
    quack.
  Have you heard the latest miser story.
  I like a lot of woman, full grown.
  I like a woman built on ample lines.
  If blocked, a fart can kill a man.
  It's true I will die. So what do I care.
  Law should have ear-plugs, not bandaged
    eyes, The.
  Listen! The night-raven's song.
  Little Diodoros is so skinny.
  Mighty Runner, A. *From* Variations of Greek
    Themes.
  Nicole may have been a beauty long ago.
  Niconoë has just inched past her prime.
  No man's forever fully satisfied.
  One deaf man went to law with.
  Path of glory leads but to the grave, The.
  Phido the miser's crying.
  Raven, The. *From* Variations of Greek
    Themes.
  Single stench two winds have parted, A.
  Sweet Nicarete, who served Athene's shuttle.
  Take note who stoop.
Nichol, B. P. (*b. 1944*)
  Ferry Me Across.
  Gorg, a Detective Story.
  Monotones.
  Scraptures: 7th Sequence.
  Some Nets.
  St. Anzas IX.
  St. Anzas VI.
  Two Words; a Wedding.
Nicholl, Louise Townsend (*1890–1981*)
  Cigar Smoke, Sunday, after Dinner.
  Cruse, The.
Nicholls, Judith
  Andromeda.
  Ballad of the Sad Astronaut.
  Cat.
  Dog.
  Earthrise.
  Earthset.
  Journey.
  Mary Celeste.
  Moonscape.
  Polar Cub.
  Season Song.
  Space-Shuttle.
  Storytime.
  Timeless.
  Watch this.
  Winter crept.
Nichols, Carrie May
  Boomerang, The.
Nichols, Grace (*b. 1950*)
  Caribbean Woman Prayer.
  Configurations.
  Epilogue: "I have crossed an ocean."
  I am the rain.
  Like a Beacon.
  Old Magic.
  Sky.
  Sugar Cane.
  Tapestry.
  Tropical Death.
  Waterpot.
  Wha Me Mudder Do.
  Wherever I Hang.
  Without Song.
Nichols, John Bowyer. *See* Beeching, Henry
  Charles *and* John Bowyer Nichols
Nichols, Kevin
  Feast of Stephen, The.

Nichols, Robert Malise Bowyer (*1893–1944*)
  Aurelia.
  Comrades: an Episode.
  Don Juan's Address to the Sunset.
  Fisbo, *sels.*
  Flower of Flame, The, *sels.*
  Get-Away, *sels.*
  Harlot's Catch.
  Moon behind High Tranquil Leaves, The.
  Noon.
  Sonnets to Aurelia, *sels.*
  Sprig of Lime, The.
  To D'Annunzio: Lines from the Sea.
Nicholson, John (*1790–1843*)
  On a Calm Summer's Night.
Nicholson, L.
  Bubbles.
Nicholson, Norman (*1914–87*)
  Blackberry, The.
  Caedmon.
  Carol for the Last Christmas Eve.
  Carol: "Mary laid her Child among."
  Cleator Moor.
  Cowper's Tame Hare.
  For Hokey and Henrietta.
  Halley's Comet.
  Michaelmas.
  Off to Outer Space Tomorrow Morning.
  On the Closing of Millom Ironworks.
  Ravenglass Railway Station, Cumberland.
  Rockferns.
  Shepherds' Carol.
  Song at Night.
  To the River Duddon.
  Weather Ear.
Nicias (*c.470–413 B.C.*)
  Fountain at the Tomb, The.
  I, Hermes, guard Cyllene's wooded slopes.
  Spring blossoms, honey-bee, in the colours
    you parade.
Nicol, Abioseh (*b. 1924*)
  African Easter.
  Meaning of Africa, The.
Nicolson, Adela Florence Cory. *See* "Hope,
  Laurence"
Nicolson, Veronica
  Limerick: "I once took my girl to Southend."
Niedecker, Lorine (*b. 1903*)
  As praiseworthy / the power of breathing.
  Darwin.
  Element Mother, The.
  For best work.
  Grandfather / advised me.
  I married.
  In the great snowfall before the bomb.
  Lake Superior.
  Margaret Fuller.
  Museum Man! / I wish he'd take Pa's
    spitbox!, The.
  My mother saw the green tree toad.
  News.
  Nursery Rhyme.
  Old man who seined.
  Paean to Place.
  Poems at the Porthole.
  Smile / to see the lake.
  So he said / on radio.
  Subliminal.
  This Condensery: The Complete Writing of
    Lorine Niedecker, 1985, *sels.*
  War.
  Who was Mary Shelley?
  Will You Write Me a Christmas Poem?
  You are my friend.
  Young in Fall I said: the birds.
Niemoller, Pastor (*1892–1984*)
  First they came for the Jews.
Nietzsche, Friedrich Wilhelm (*1844–1900*)
  Solitary, The.
  Star Morals.
Niger, Paul (*1917–62*)
  Initiations, *sels.*
Nightingale, Madeleine (*b. 1879*)
  Apple Rhyme, The.
  Caravan, The.
  Scissor-Man, The.

Nigot
  You surprise me, crow.
Nikitin, Ivan Savvich (*1824–77*)
  Night in a Village, A.
Nikolayeva [*or* Nikolaeva], Olesya [*or* Olesia]
  (*b. 1955*)
  Seven Beginnings.
Nikolov, Lyubomir
  Axes lie next to the river, The.
  What the Servants Said to him, as he
    returned home.
Nikolov, Nino
  Confusion.
  Don't Move Away.
  Water Outside the Window.
  Window, The.
Niles, John Jacob (*1892–1980*)
  In All the Magic of Christmas-Tide.
Niles, Nathaniel (*1741–1828*)
  Why Should Vain Mortals Tremble.
Nimatullah [*or* Ni'matu'llah], Seid [*or* Sayyid]
  (*d. 1431*)
  Song of Seyd [*or* Seid] Nimetollah of
    Kuhistan.
Nims, Bonnie
  On a Cold Autumn Day.
Nims, John Frederick (*b. 1913*)
  Agamemnon before Troy.
  Clock without Hands.
  Conclusion: "If what began (look far and
    wide) will end."
  Contemplation.
  Freight.
  Love and Death.
  Love Poem: "My clumsiest dear, whose
    hands shipwreck vases."
  Parting: 1940.
  Philosopher.
  Tide Turning.
  Trainwrecked Soldiers.
"Nirala" (Suryakant Tripathi) (*1896–1961*)
  Betrayal, The.
Nishi, Junko (*fl. mid 20th cent.*)
  Remorse Came Slowly.
  Revolution.
Nitschmann, Anna (*1715–60*)
  This Flock So Small.
Nizami Arudi (*fl. 1110*)
  Calling the Doctor (1000 A.D.)
No Ch'ŏn-myŏng (*1913–57*)
  Behind Prison Bars.
  Cricket.
  Deer.
  Watching the Stars.
Noailles, Anna de (*1876–1933*)
  Image.
  Poem on Azure.
Nobuyuki, Ōkuma
  And Then.
  Ashtray (two poems).
  Even Invisible Things (two poems).
  Fiery Declarations (two poems).
  Humans Bought and Sold (two poems).
  In Berlin.
  Labor Day[1] (four poems).
  Returning from Abroad.
  Stone Buddha (two poems).
  Third-Class Car on a Night Train (three
    poems).
Noel, Henry (*d. 1597*) *and* **William Strode**
  On His Mistress.
"Nogar, Rui" (*b. 1933*)
  Poem of the Conscripted Warrior.
Noguere, Suzanne (*b. 1947*)
  Barney Bigard.
  Pervigilium Veneris.
  Scribes, The.
  Secret, The.
  Soma.
  Whirling Round the Sun.
Noho-mai-te-Rangi (*fl. c.18th cent.*)
  Song for Te Hauapu.
Noin (*988?–1050*)
  After the storm / On Mount Mimuro.
  As I approach / The mountain village.

Nokan, Charles (b. 1937)
My head is immense.

Noll, Bink (b. 1927)
Abraham's Madness.

Nomberg, David
Russian Cradle Song, A.

Nonnus (fl. 5th cent.)
Dionysiaca, sels.

Noonuccal, Oodgeroo. See **Walker, Kath**

Nordbrandt, Henrik
China Observed Through Greek Rain in Turkish Coffee.
No matter where we go, we always arrive too late.
Our love is like Byzantium.
Sailing.
Streets.

Norman, Peter
I could have been Lord Dacre or a balalaika-maker.

Norman, Rosemary (b. 1946)
Cabbage.
My Son and I.

Norris, Alfred (b. 1914)
Humble Heart, A.

Norris, Anne
Limerick: "Rose gives a tremulous glance, The."

Norris, John (1657–1711)
Meditation, The.
My Estate.

Norris, John W. (b. 1893)
Give Peace, O God, the Nations Cry.

Norris, Kathleen (b. 1947)
Advent.
Lilith and the Doctor.
Memorandum / The Accountant's Notebook.
Moon of the First Communion.
Mrs. Schneider in Church.
Poem about Faith, A.
Sky Is Full of Blue and Full of the Mind of God, The.
Stomach.
Three Small Songs for the Muse.
Wedding in the Courthouse, The.

Norris, Leslie (b. 1921)
Ballad of Billy Rose, The.
Cage Bird and Sky Bird.
Camels, the Kings' Camel, The.
Elegy for Lyn James.
Merlin and the Snake's Egg.
Mice in the Hay.
Pit Ponies, The.
Quiet-eyed Cattle, The.
Shepherd's Dog, The.
Stable Cat, The.
Thin Prison, The.
Tiger in the Zoo, A.
Water.

Norse, Harold (b. 1926)
Believing in the Absurd.
Business of poetry, The.
Colosseum.
I Would Not Recommend Love.
I'm Not a Man.
Picasso Visits Braque.
We Bumped Off Your Friend the Poet.
You Must Have Been a Sensational Baby.

North, Charles (b. 1941)
Air and Angels.
Elizabethan & Nova Scotian Music.
Few Facts about Me, A.
From the French.
Hospital.
Leap Year.
Little Cape Cod Landscape.
Note to Tony Towle (After WS), A.
Shooting for Line.
Sunrise with Sea Monster.
Year of the Olive Oil, The.

"North, Christopher." See **Wilson, John;** also **Galt, John** and **"Christopher North"**

North, Dudley, 3d Baron North (1581–1666)
Air: "So full of courtly reverence."
Platonic is a pretty name.

North, E.
Out of Doors.

North, Frank Mason (1850–1935)
Where Cross the Crowded Ways of Life.

Nortje, Arthur (1942–73)
Asseverations.
At Lansdowne Bridge.
At Rest from the Grim Place.
Autopsy.
Cosmos in London.
Immigrant.
Letter from Pretoria Central Prison.
Native's Letter.
Newcombe at the Croydon Gallery.
Up Late.
Waiting.

Norton, Andrews (1786–1853)
My God, I Thank Thee.

Norton, Caroline Elizabeth (1808–76)
Arab's Farewell to His Horse, The.
As when from dreams awaking.
Bingen on the Rhine.
Dreams.
I do not love thee!—no! I do not love thee!
Marriage and Love, sels.
Obscurity of Woman's Worth.
Picture of Sappho, The.
Sonnet 7: "Like an enfranchised bird, who wildly springs."
Undying One, The, sels.
Voice from the Factories, A, sels.

Norton, John (1651–1716)
Funeral Elegy Upon that Pattern and Patron of Virtue, A.

Norwalk, Tadeusz (b. 1930)
Psalm of Love.

Norworth, Jack (1879–1959)
Take Me Out to the Ball Game.

Nossis (fl. c.290 B.C.)
Laugh aloud, then pass by, with a kind.
Let us go into the temple.
Let us go to the temple.
Melinna herself! It is—see how kindly.
Most honoured Hera, who descends from heaven.
Nothing is sweeter than love.
Nothing is sweeter than love, all other blessings.
This is Thaumareta's picture, and how well it captures.

Notley, Alice (b. 1945)
Alice Ordered Me to be Made.
Beginning with a stain, as the universe did perhaps.
California Girlhood, A.
Désamère.
How Spring Comes.
Jack Would Speak Through the Imperfect Medium of Alice.
One of the Longest Times.
Poem: "You hear that heroic big land music?"
White Peacock, The.
White Phosphorus.

Novikov, Denis Gennad'evich (b. 1967)
On my right hand I'll seat one of my loves.

Nowak, Tadeusz (b. 1930)
Psalm Ajar.
Psalm of the Field.
Psalm To Cheer Up.

Nowlan, Alden (1933–83)
Beginning.
Bull Moose, The.
For Jean Vincent d'Abbadie, Baron St.-Castin.
God Sour the Milk of the Knacking Wench.
Grove beyond the Barley, The.
I, Icarus.
In the Operating Room.
Mother and Son.
Only when my heart freezes.
Rites of Manhood, The.
Stoney Ridge Dance Hall.
Suppose This Moment Some Stupendous Question.
Thief, The.

Wickedness of Peter Shannon, The.

Noyes, Alfred (1880–1958)
Art, I.
Art, II.
Barrel-Organ, The.
Butterfly Garden, The.
Cure, The.
Daddy Fell into the Pond.
Flower of Old Japan, The, sels.
He did not come in the dawning. He did not come at noon.
Highwayman, The.
Kilmeny.
New Duckling, The.
Salute from the Fleet, A, sels.
Sherwood in the twilight, is Robin Hood awake?
Song: "What is there hid in the heart of a rose."
Spring, and the Blind Children.
Victory Dance, A.

Noyes, Nicholas (1647–1717)
Consolatory Poem Dedicated unto Mr. Cotton Mather, A.
Præfatory Poem to the Little Book, Entituled, Christianus per Ignem, A.
Prefatory Poem, on. . . Magnalia Christi Americana.
Rev. Nicholas Noyes to the Rev. Cotton Mather, The.
To My Worthy Friend, Mr. James Bayley.

Nugent, Robert, Earl Nugent (1709–88)
Epigram: "I loved thee beautiful and kind."
Epigram: "My heart still hovering round about you."
Epigram: "Since first you knew my am'rous smart."
To Clarissa.

Nukada, Princess (fl. late 7th cent.)
As we pass through the field of purple herbs.
At Nigitazu we wait for the moon.
Does that bird.
Longing for you.
Waiting for the Emperor Tenji.
When, loosened from the winter's bonds. From Manyo Shu, Part 4 of 4.
When spring escapes.

Nurton, C.
My Doggie.

Nuttall, Jeff
Dub Eleven.
Three Scenes: Todmorden.
Whore of Kilpeck, The.

Nuur, Faarah (d. 1930)
Limits of Submission, The.

Nweke, Chuba
Moon Song.

Nye, Naomi Shihab (b. 1952)
Art of Disappearing, The.
Blood.
Elevator.
Famous.
Going for Peaches, Fredericksburg, Texas.
Hello.
House Made of Rain, The.
Hugging the Jukebox.
Man Who Makes Brooms, The.
My Father and the Figtree.
New Year.
Nobody's newspaper tells what the Costa Ricans did.
Rain.
Rebellion against the North Side.
Small Vases from Hebron, The.
Streets.
Sure.
Traveling Onion, The.
What Brings Us Out.
Yellow Glove.

Nyka-Niliunas, Alfonsas
Before Dawn.
Lied.
March.
Theology of Rain.
Winter Landscape.

Nystrom, Debra (b. 1954)
Prairie Wind.

O

"O., G. S."
　　Engine Driver, The.

O Brolchain, Mael Isu (*fl.* **c.1086**)
　　I give Thee thanks, my King.
　　My sins in their completeness.
　　To an Elderly Virgin.

O Dalaigh, Lochlann Og (*fl.* **mid–16th cent.**)
　　In Praise of Three Young Men.

O Direain, Mairtin (**1910–88**)
　　Axle Song.
　　Berkeley.
　　Essence Is Not in the Living, The.
　　Homage to John Millington Synge.
　　Invitation to Mary.
　　That Face.
　　Trees on a Frosty Night.

O Domhnaill, Maghnas (**d. 1563**)
　　Famished end to my tale this night, A.
　　Heart made full of thought, A.
　　Love, I think, is a disease.

O Heigeartaigh, Padraig (**1871–1936**)
　　My sorrow, Donncha, my thousand-cherished.

O Riordain, Sean (**1917–77**)
　　Claustrophobia.
　　Death was at hand.
　　Freedom.
　　Ice Cold.
　　Moths, The.
　　My Mother's Burying.

Oakes, Urian (**1631–81**)
　　Elegie upon The Death of the
　　　Reverend. . . Mr. Thomas Shepard, An,
　　　sels.
　　To the Reader.

Oakman, John (**1748?–1793**)
　　Glutton, The.

Oandasan, William (**b. 1947**)
　　Acoma.
　　Grandmothers Land.
　　Song of Ancient Ways, The.
　　Words of Tayko-mol.

Oates, Joyce Carol (**b. 1938**)
　　Growing Together.
　　How Delicately.
　　Suicide, The.

Obeyd-i-Zàkànì
　　Gorby and the Rats.

Obi, Dorothy S.
　　Winds of Africa.

Obolduyev [*or* **Obolduev**]**, Georgy** [*or* **Georgii**]
　　Nikolaevich (**1898–1954**)
　　Rod, The.
　　Tongue, The.

O'Brien, Edward Joseph Harrington (**1890–**
　　1941)
　　Her Fairness, Wedded to a Star.

O'Brien, Fitz-James (**1828–62**)
　　Ghost, The.

O'Brien, Geoffrey (**b. 1948**)
　　Interior Prisoner, The.
　　Ornamental Syllable.
　　Prophetic Child, The.
　　Scroll.
　　Theory of Climate.

"O'Brien, John." *See* **Hartigan, Patrick Joseph**

O'Brien, Sean (**b. 1952**)
　　In Residence: A Worst Case View.

O'Bruadair, David [*or* **Daibhi**] (**c.1625–1698**)
　　Adoramus Te, Christe.
　　Change, The.
　　Eire.
　　For the Family of Cuchonnacht O Dalaigh.
　　New Style, The.
　　O it's best to be a total boor.
　　O'Bruadair.
　　Shrewish, barren, bony, nosy servant, A.

"Observer RFC." *See* **Alchin, Gordon**

O'Byrne, Cathal (**1883–1957**)
　　Donegal Hush Song, A.

Occom, Samson (**1723–92**)
　　Waked by the Gospel's Powerful Sound.

Ochester, Ed (**b. 1939**)
　　Canaries in Uncle Arthur's Basement, The.
　　Gift, The.
　　In the Library.
　　New Day.
　　Oh, By the Way.
　　110 Year Old House.
　　Penn Central Station at Beacon, N.Y, The.
　　Relatives, The.

O'Coileain, Sean (**1754–1816**)
　　Lament for Timoleague.

O'Connell, Eibhlin Dubh (**Eibhlin Dubh Ni**
　　Chonaill) (**b. 1743**)
　　Lament for Art O Laoghaire, The, *sels.*

O'Connor, Frank (**Michael Francis O'Donovan**)
　　(**1903–66**)
　　Angry Poet, The.

O'Connor, Mark (**b. 1945**)
　　Fire.
　　Sun-Hunters, The.
　　Turtles Hatching.

O'Connor, Patrick (**b. 1899**)
　　Exiles.
　　Lights of Dublin, The.
　　My prayer is that I have friends.

O'Connor, Philip (**b. 1916**)
　　Fag-End.
　　Poems.
　　Raspberry in the Pudding, The.
　　Writing in England Now.

O'Cotter, Pat
　　Malemute Dog, A.

O'Dalaigh, Gofraidh Fionn (**d. 1387**)
　　Child in Prison, A.
　　Under Sorrow's Sign.

O'Dalaigh, Muireadhach Albanach
　　(**Muireadhach Albanach**) (**c.1180–1220**)
　　Invocation: "Last night my soul departed."
　　Mighty Mary, hear me.
　　My body's self deserts me now.
　　On the Death of His Wife.
　　On the Gift of a Knife.
　　Young man of alien beauty.

Odarchenko, Yury [*or* **Iurii**] **Pavlovich** (**1903–**
　　60)
　　And you, Vanya.
　　Bears became cucumbers.
　　Cap, a sword, flowers, A.
　　On Red Square, on the chopping block.
　　There are perfect illustrations.
　　What a sweet little day, what a day!

Oden, Gloria C. (**b. 1923**)
　　Bible Study.
　　Carousel, The.
　　Man White, Brown Girl and All That Jazz.
　　Private Letter to Brazil, A.
　　Review from Staten Island.
　　Riven Quarry, The.
　　This Child Is the Mother.

O'Donnell, George Marion
　　Semmes in the Garden.

O'Donnell, Hugh. *See* **MacWard, Owen Roe,**
　　and **Hugh O'Donnell**

O'Donoghue, Bernard (**b. 1945**)
　　Apparition, The.
　　Weakness, The.

O'Donoghue, Gregory (**b. 1951**)
　　Web, The.

O'Donovan, Michael Francis. *See* **O'Connor,**
　　Frank

O'Donovan Rossa, Mary (**1845–c.1900**)
　　Returned Picture, The.

O'Dowd, Bernard (**1866–1953**)
　　Australia.
　　Bush, The, *sels.*
　　Cupid.

Odoyevtseva [*or* **Odoevtseva**]**, Irina** (**Iraida**
　　Gustavovna Geinike Ivanova) (**1901–90**)
　　Ground Glass.

Ōe no Chisato (*fl.* **9th cent.**)
　　As I watch the moon.

Oehlenschläger, Adam (**1779–1850**)
　　There Is a Charming Land.

Oengus Céile Dé (*fl.* **late 10th cent.**)
　　Time is ripe and I repent, The.

Oerke, Andrew
　　Sun is the blind eyes of statues gilded, The.

O'Faracháin, Roibéard. *See* **Farren, Robert**

Ofeimun, Odia
　　Beyond Fear.
　　Gong, A.
　　Handle for the Flutist, A.
　　How Can I Sing.
　　Judgement Day.
　　Let Them Choose Paths.
　　Naming Day, A.
　　Poet Lied, The.
　　Prologue: "I have come down."

O'Flynn, Cristoir (**b. 1927**)
　　God?
　　Sainthood.

Og MacWard, Fearghal (*fl.* **early 17th cent.**)
　　Flight of the Earls, The, 1607, *sels.*

Ogarev, Nikolay Platonovich (**1813–79**)
　　Road, The.

O'Gillan, Angus (*fl.* **14th cent.**)
　　Dead at Clonmacnois, The.

Ogilvy, Eliza (**1822–1912**)
　　Grannie's Birthday.
　　Natal Address to My Child, March 19th
　　　1844, A.
　　Newly Dead and Newly Born.

O'Gnive [*or* **O'Gnimh**]**, Fearflatha** (*fl.* **c.1562**)
　　After the Flight of the Earls.
　　Downfall of the Gael, The.
　　Passing of the Poets, The.

O'Gorman, Ned (**b. 1929**)
　　Kiss, The.

O'Grady, Desmond (**b. 1935**)
　　Berlin Metro.
　　Dark Edge of Europe, The, *sels.*
　　Dying Gaul, The.
　　Finn's Wishes.
　　Great Horse Fair, The.
　　Hellas, *sels.*
　　Homecoming.
　　If I Went Away.
　　In the Greenwood, *sels.*
　　Lines in a Roman Schoolbook, *sels.*
　　Page from a Diary.
　　Poet in Old Age Fishing at Evening, The.
　　Professor Kelleher and the Charles River.
　　Purpose.
　　Reading the Unpublished Manuscripts of
　　　Louis MacNeice at Kinsale Harbour.
　　Tipperary.

O'Grady, Standish (*fl.* **c.1793–c.1841**)
　　Emigrant, The, *sels.*

Ogundipe-Leslie, Molara
　　On Reading an Archeological Article.
　　Song at the African Middle Class.

O'Hara, Frank (**1926–66**)
　　Abortion, An.
　　Answer to Voznesensky and Evtushenko.
　　Autobiographia Literaria.
　　Ave Maria.
　　Blocks.
　　Captains Courageous.
　　Chez Jane.
　　Cornkind.
　　Day Lady Died, The.
　　Easter.
　　For James Dean.
　　Having a Coke with You.
　　Homosexuality.
　　Hôtel Transylvanie.
　　How poecile and endearing is the Porch.
　　How to Get There.
　　Hunter, The.
　　Image of Leda, An.
　　In Favor of One's Time.
　　In Hospital.
　　In Memory of My Feelings.
　　Interior (With Jane).
　　Les Étiquettes Jaunes.
　　Les Luths.
　　Life on Earth, *sels.*
　　Madrid.
　　Mary Desti's Ass.
　　Meditations in an Emergency.
　　My Heart.

1951.
Ode: "Idea of justice may be precious, An."
Ode: Salute to the French Negro Poets.
Ode to Joy.
Ode to Michael Goldberg's Birth and Other
    Births, sels.
Ode to Tanaquil Leclercq: "Smiling through
    my own memories of painful excitement
    your wide eyes."
On Rachmaninoff's Birthday.
Personal Poem.
Poem: "At night Chinamen jump."
Poem: "Eager note on my door said 'Call
    me', The."
Poem: "Hate is only one of many responses."
Poem: "I don't know as I get what D.H.
    Lawrence is driving at."
Poem: "'Instant coffee with slightly sour
    cream.'"
Poem: "Khrushchev is coming on the right
    day!"
Poem: "Lana Turner has collapsed!"
Poem: "O solo mio, hot diggety, nix 'I
    wather think I can.'"
Poem: "There I could never be a boy."
Poetry.
Princess Elizabeth of Bohemia, as Perdita.
Radio.
Rhapsody.
Rogers in Italy.
Sleeping on the Wing.
Song: "Did you see me walking by the Buick
    Repairs?"
Step Away from Them, A.
Steps.
Summer Breezes.
Terrestrial Cuckoo, A.
To Hell with It.
To My Mother.
To the Film Industry in Crisis.
To the Harbormaster.
Today.
True Account of Talking to the Sun at Fire
    Island, A.
Why I Am Not a Painter.
You Are Gorgeous and I'm Coming.
You at the Pump.

O'Hara, Theodore (1820–67)
Bivouac of the Dead, The.

O'Hare, Felix
Shoofly, The.

O'Heffernan, Mahon (fl. early 17th cent.)
I ask, who will buy a poem?
My Son, Forsake Your Art.

O'Hehir, Diana
Questions and Answers.

O'Higgins, Brian (1882–1935)
Mountain Altar, The.

O'Higgins, Myron (b. 1918)
Two Lean Cats.
Vaticide.
Young Poet.

O'Huiginn, Tadhg Dall (1550–91)
Difference, The.
Present of Butter, A.
Satire on the O'Haras, A.
Visit to Enniskillen, A.

O'Huiginn, Tadhg Og (d. 1448)
Lament for Fearghal Ruadh.

**O'Hussey [or O'Heughusa], Eochadh [or
Eochy] (d. 1612)**
Change in Style, A.
Mag Uidhir's Winter Campaign.
O'Hussey's Ode to the Maguire.

Ojaide, Tanure
Launching Our Community Developement
    Fund.
Ward 6.
What They Said.
When Tomorrow Is Too Long.

Ojenke. See Saxon, Alvin

Ojibway Oral Tradition
Calling-One's-Own.

Okai, Atukwei (b. 1941)
999 Smiles.

Okamoto, Kanoko (1889–1939)
All day long having / buried himself.
Tanka: "As I gaze upon."
Tanka: "Cherry blossoms."
Tanka: "Cherry petals."
Tanka: "Cockscomb, A."
Tanka: "Flower blooms, A."
Tanka: "Green leaves."
Tanka: "Having let flow."
Tanka: "I measure."
Tanka: "If I were to stand."
Tanka: "Innately reserved."
Tanka: "Insect, An."
Tanka: "It stands."
Tanka: "My mind shattered."
Tanka: "Selfish woman."
Tanka: "Stark naked."
Tanka: "Ten years ago."
Tanka: "They don't appeal to me."
Tanka: "To the sea, to the sea."
Tanka: "Twenty days."
Tanka: "Where."

O'Kane, T. C. (b. 1830)
My Mother's Prayer.

Okantah, Mwatabu (fl. 20th cent.)
Afreeka Brass.
Southern Road.

Okara, Gabriel (b. 1921)
Call of the River Nun, The.
Mystic Drum, The.
Once upon a Time.
One Night at Victoria Beach.
Piano and Drums.
Snowflakes Sail Gently Down, The.
Spirit of the Wind.
To Adhiambo.
You Laughed and Laughed and Laughed.

O'Keefe [or O'Keeffe], John (1747–1833)
Air: "Flaxen-headed cow-boy, as simple as
    may be, A."
Amo, Amas.
I Want a Tenant; a Satire.

O'Keeffe, Adelaide (1776–1855)
Beasts and Birds.
Kite, The.

Okigbo, Christopher (1932–67)
Come Thunder.
Distances, sels.
Distances (1964), sels.
Elegy for Alto.
Elegy for Slit-Drum.
Elegy of the Wind.
Heavensgate (1961), sels.
Hurrah for Thunder.
Lament of the Drums (1964), sels.
Lament of the Flutes.
Limits (1962), sels.
Sacrifice.
Thunder Can Break.
Water Maid.

Okikaze, Fujiwara No
Who shall I have for friends.

Okita, Dwight
In Response to Executive Order 9066: All
    Americans of Japanese Descent Must
    Report to Relocation Centers.
Nice Thing About Counting Stars, The.
Notes for a Poem on Being Asian American.

Okkūr Mācāttaṉar
Widows' Rice.

Okkur Macatti (fl. between 1st and 3d cent.)
What Her Girlfriends Said to Her.
What She Said.

Okopenko, Andreas (b. 1930)
Interview with Herr Limerick.

Oku, Princess (661–701)
How will you cross the autumn mountain
    alone?

Okudzhava, Bulat Shalvovich (b. 1924)
As a child I came upon a grasshopper.
As I Sat in the Armchair of the Tsar.
Everything here is curtained in darkness.
François Villon.
I don't believe in God and fate.
I have never soared, never soared.
I need to worship someone.

In the City Park.
Midnight Trolleybus.
Paper Soldier.
Reflections Near the House Where Titian
    Tabidze Lived.
Soldier's Ditty, A.
They exterminate poets.

Okura. See Yamanoé no Okura

Oldham, John (1653–83)
Cup, The.
Quiet Soul, A.
Satire, A, sels.
Satires, sels.
Satyr, A, sels.
Upon the Works of Ben Joson, sels.

Oldham, Perry
Noon.
War Stories.

Olds, Peter (b. 1944)
My Mother Spinning.
Psycho.
Thoughts of Jack Kerouac—& Other Things.

Olds, Sharon (b. 1942)
After 37 Years My Mother Apologizes for
    My Childhood.
Armor.
Cambridge Elegy.
Connoisseuse of Slugs, The.
Dead Body Itself, The.
Death of Marilyn Monroe, The.
Eggs.
Elder Sister, The.
First Boyfriend.
First Love.
First Sex.
For My Daughter.
Girl, The.
Glass, The.
Greed and Aggression.
Guild, The.
I Go Back to May 1937.
In the Hospital Near the End.
Indictment of Senior Officers.
Knowing, The.
Language of the Brag, The.
Last Acts.
Latest Injury, The.
Leningrad Cemetery, Winter of 1941.
May 1968.
Moment, The.
Moment of My Father's Death, The.
Monarchs.
Mother, The.
New Mother.
On The Subway.
One Girl at the Boys Party, The.
Pajamas.
Power of My Mother, The.
Pull, The.
Quake Theory.
Quest, The.
Race, The.
Rites of Passage.
Satan Says.
Saturn.
Seventh Birthday of the First Child.
Sex without Love.
Sign of Saturn, The.
Sisters of Sexual Treasure, The.
Size and Sheer Will.
Solitary.
Station.
Summer Solstice, New York City.
That Moment.
That Year.
35/10.
Unjustly Punished Child.
Victims, The.
Wedding Vow, The.
What If God.
Why My Mother Made Me.

Oldys, William (1687–1761)
On a Fly Drinking out of [or from] His Cup.
On Himself.

Oles, Carole (b. 1939)
To a Daughter at Fourteen Forsaking the
    Violin.

Oleson, Helmer O.
Ballad of Johnny Appleseed, A.
Oleynikov, Nikolai Makarovich ("Makar Svirepy") (1891–1942)
Beetle, The.
Olitski, Leib (1894–1975)
My Song to the Jewish People.
Oliver, Douglas (b. 1937)
Ferry Pirate, The.
Infant and the Pearl, The, *sels.*
Oracle of the Drawned, The.
Snowdonia at a Distance.
Oliver, Louis (LittleCoon) (b. 1904)
Empty Kettle.
Horned Snake, The.
Wagon Full of Thunder.
Oliver, Mary (b. 1935)
At Blackwater Pond the tossed waters have settled.
Bats.
Blossom.
Climbing the Chagrin River.
Diviners, The.
Ghosts.
Grandmothers, The.
In Blackwater Woods.
In the Pinewoods, Crows and Owl.
Journey, The.
Kingfisher rises out of the black wave, The.
Landscape.
Lightning.
Little Owl Who Lives in the Orchard.
May, and among the miles of leafing.
Old Whorehouse, An.
Poem for My Father's Ghost.
Poppies send up their, The.
Rabbit, The.
Rain in Ohio.
Sleeping in the Forest.
Some Questions You Might Ask.
Strawberry Moon.
Sunrise.
Through Ruddy Orchards.
Visitor, A.
Waves, The.
Wild Geese.
Oliver, W. H. (b. 1925)
Augury.
Counter-Revolution.
Parihaka.
Ollivierre, Albie (b. 1961)
Talk War.
Voice.
Olney, D. A.
Just Like This.
Olofsson, Tommy (b. 1950)
Autobiography.
Ologboni, Tejumola ("Rockie D. Taylor") (b. 1945)
Black Henry.
Changed Mind (or the Day I Woke Up).
I Wonta Thank Ya.
Ologoudou, Emile (b. 1935)
Liberty.
Vespers.
O'Loughlin, Michael (b. 1958)
Cuchulainn.
Elegy for the Unknown Soldier.
Glasnevin Cemetery.
Irish Requiem, An.
Posthumous.
Shards, The, *sels.*
Olsen, Donald D.
Auction; Saturday 2:00.
Olsen, William
Dead Monkey, The.
Oasis Motel, The.
Storm Chasers, The.
Tomorrow.
Unicorn Tapestries, The.
Olson, Charles (1910–70)
Across Space and Time.
Anecdotes of the Late War.
As the dead prey upon us.
Chain of memory is resurrection   I am a vain man, The.

Death of Europe, The.
Distances, The.
In cold hell, in thicket, how.
Kingfishers, The.
La Chute.
La Préface.
Librarian, The.
Lordly and Isolate Satyrs, The.
Maximus Poems, The, *sels.*
Merce of Egypt.
Moon Is the Number 18, The.
Newly Discovered "Homeric" Hymn, A.
Perfume / of flowers! A haw, The.
Praises, The.
Ring of, The.
Song of Ullikummi, The.
These Days.
Variations Done for Gerald Van De Wiele.
Olson, Elder (1909–92)
Ballad of the Scarecrow Christ.
Childe Roland, etc.
In Defense of Superficiality.
Plot Improbable, Character Unsympathetic.
Reflections on Mirrors.
Olson, Ernst W. (1870–1958)
God of Peace, in Peace Preserve Us.
Olson, Ted (b. 1899)
Hawk's Way.
Om Ui-Gil (*fl.* 17th cent.)
Sitting at Night.
O'Malley, D. J.
Tenderfoot, The.
Omar ben Abi Rabi'a (d. 720)
Damsel, The.
Omar Khayyám (d. 1123)
Rubáiyát of Omar Khayyám [of Naishápúr], The, *sels.*
Ombres, Rossana (b. 1931)
Ballad of Noah's Daughter.
Embalmer.
Ensnaring Flower of Psalms.
Excursion to Ravenna of A Young Girl with Her Parents, *sels.*
Flower Ensnarer of Psalms.
Meadow Bug.
Strange Adventure.
Twelve.
White house in front of the park, A.
Ome Shushiki (1668–1725)
Be careful! Be careful!
O'Meallain, Fear Dorcha (*fl.* c.1650)
Exodus to Connacht.
O'Mealy, Bob (b. 1948)
I was jus.
It aint no.
Onakatomi Yoshinobu (921–91)
Deer on pine mountain, The.
Deer which lives, The. *From Shui Shu.*
Ondaatje, Michael (b. 1943)
Biography.
Breaking Green.
Burning Hills.
Cinnamon Peeler, The.
Elizabeth.
House Divided, A.
Inner Tube.
Letters and Other Worlds.
Light.
Notes for the Legend of Salad Woman.
Rock Bottom, *sels.*
To a Sad Daughter.
Walking to Bellrock.
Onderdonk, Henry Ustic (1789–1858)
On Zion and on Lebanon.
Spirit in Our Hearts, The.
Though I Should Seek.
O'Neal, John
Shades of Pharoah Sanders Blues for My Baby.
O'Neill, Eugene (1888–1953)
Lament of a Subwayite.
To a Bull Moose.
O'Neill, Henrietta (1758–93)
Ode to the Poppy.
Written on Seeing Her Two Sons at Play.

O'Neill, Mary
My fingers are antennae.
Sound of Water.
What Is Black?
"O'Neill, Moira" (Nesta Higginson Skrine) (1870–1955)
Corrymeela.
Grace for Light.
Her Sister.
O'Neill, Rose Cecil (1874–1944)
Dream of Sappho, A.
I made a house of houselessness.
Lee.
Master-Mistress, The.
Sister, The.
Ono no Komachi (834–80)
Although I come to you constantly.
As certain as color.
Cicadas sing, The.
Color of the flowers / has faded, The.
Colors of the flowers fade, The.
Doesn't he realize / that I am not.
Doesn't he realize / that I am not / like the swaying kelp.
Following the roads.
He does not come.
I fell asleep thinking of him.
If it were real / Perhaps I'd understand it.
Imperceptible / It withers in the world.
In the daytime.
No moon, no chance to meet.
Since I've felt this pain.
So lonely am I.
This night of no moon.
When my love becomes / All-powerful.
Without changing color.
Ono no Takamura (802–52)
Did I ever think. *From* Kokin Shu
Ono no Yoshiki (d. 902)
My love / Is like the grasses.
Onuora Oku (Orlando Wong) (b. 1950)
Last Night.
Pressure Drop.
Reflection in Red.
Oodgeroo of the tribe Noonuccal (1920–93)
Dawn Wail for the Dead.
Last of His Tribe.
No more boomerang.
Song: "Life is ours in vain."
We are Going.
O'odham, Tohono Owl Woman
Healing Songs.
War Songs.
"Ophelia" (*fl.* mid–18th cent.)
Snaith Marsh; a Yorkshire Pastoral.
Opie, Amelia Alderson (1769–1853)
Poems, *sels.*
To a Maniac.
Opitz, Martin (1597–1639)
Ah Dearest, let us haste us.
Concerning the Wolffsbrunnen near Heidelberg.
I'll lay this halfway me, which we the body name.
To This Book.
With snowy light of moon I cannot you compare.
You golden freedom, both my wish and my desire.
Opoku, Andrew Amankwa (b. 1912)
River Afram.
Oppen, George (b. 1908)
Animula.
Bahamas.
Book of Job and a Draft of a Poem to Praise the Paths of the Living, The.
Daedalus: The Dirge.
Discrete Series 1929–1933.
Eclogue: "Men talking, The."
Exodus.
Five Poems about Poetry, *sels.*
Forms of Love, The.
From a Photograph.
Gold on Oak Leaves.
Latitude, Longitude.
Little Pin: Fragment, The.

Myself I Sing.
Occurrences, The.
Of Being Numerous, *sels.*
Part of the Forest.
Population.
Power, the Enchanted World, *sels.*
Psalm: "In the small beauty of the forest."
Quotations.
Resort.
Route, *sels.*
Sara in Her Father's Arms.
Some San Francisco Poems, *sels.*
Survival: Infantry.

Oppenheim, James (1882–1932)
Action.
As to Being Alone.
Future, The.
Handful of Dust, A.
Hebrews.
Runner in the Skies, The.
Slave, The.

Oppenheimer, Joel (b. 1930)
Bath, The.
Blue Funk.
Bus Trip, The.
Father Poem.
Feeding, The.
Innocent Breasts, The.
Leave It to Me Blues.
Love Bit, The.
Mare Nostrum.
Mother Poem.
Poem in Defense of Children.
Undefined Tenderness, An.

Opperman, D. J. (b. 1914)
Christmas Carol: "Three outas from the [High] bleak Karoo."
Fable of the Speckled Cow.
Fable: "Under a dung-cake."
Water Whirligigs.

Oppian (*fl* 3rd cent)
Great Chain of Being, The.
Halieutica, *sels.*
Prayer, A.

O'Rahilly [*or* O'Reilly], Egan (1670–1726)
Brightest of the Bright, The.
Brightness most bright I beheld on the way, forlorn.
Brightness of brightness lonely met me where I wandered.
Drenching night drags on: no sleep or snore, The.
Grey Eye Weeping, A.
Inis Fal.
Lament for Banba.
Last Lines.
More Power.
No help I'll call till I'm put in the narrow coffin.
Time of Change, A.
Valentine Browne.
Vision, The.

Orampokiyar
Five on the Crabs, *sels.*
Five on the Riverside Cane, *sels.*
What Her Girl Friend Said when He Sent a Flattering Minstrel on His Behalf.
What Her Girl Friend Said, When the Woman Was About to Take Back Her Unfaithful Husband.
What She Said ("In his country.")

Orban, Otto (b. 1936)
Certain Years.
Gypsy Christmas.
Peace Pillar.
Requiem: "He tossed a life preserver to the young castaway in '55."
Snowfall in Boston.
Summer on the Lake, A.
That strength, which behind the tongue.

O'Reilly, John Boyle (1844–90)
Builder's Lesson, A.
Cry of the Dreamer, The.
Infinite, The.
Lure, The.
What Is Good?

White Rose, A.
O'Reilly, Pat (b. 1947)
Wonderful Mother, A.
Orerulavanar
Relations.
What He Said ("Her arms have the beauty.")
Oresick, Peter
Passion and Woe in Marriage: A Ukrainian Love Story, The.
"Orestes" (*fl.* c.1796)
Sonnet to Opium; Celebrating Its Virtues, A.
Orfalea, Gregory
War.
"Orinda." *See* Philips, Katherine
O'Riordan, Conor (1874–1948)
Hymn to the Virgin Mary.
Orléans, Charles, Duc d' (1391–1465)
Alons au bois le may cueillir.
Dieu Qu'il la Fait.
Go, Sad Complaint.
Honure, joy, helthe, and plesaunce.
My Gostly Fader, I Me Confesse.
Rondel: "Strengthen, my Love, this castle of my heart."
Smiling Mouth and Laughing Eyen Grey, The.
Spring.
Well, Wanton Eye.
Orlen, Steve [*or* Stephen] (b. 1942)
Aga Khan, The.
Big Friend of the Stones.
Biplane, The.
Ukranian Pastorals.
Orlov, Sergey [*or* Sergei] Sergeievich (1921–77)
They buried him in the terrestrial globe.
Orlovitz, Gil (1918–55)
Art of the Sonnet, *sels.*
Orlovsky, Peter (b. 1933)
Collaboration: Letter to Charlie Chaplin.
Dick Tracy's yellow Hat and Blacksuit.
Dream May 18, 1958.
I Dream of St. Francis.
Lepers Cry.
Poems from Subway to Work.
Second Poem.
Snail Poem.
Some One Liked Me when I Was Twelve.
Ormerod, V. R.
Limerick: "In dealing with time it is found."
Limerick: "Night's bible-black darkness prevails."
Limerick: "There was a young student called Fred."
Ormond, John (b. 1923)
Ancient Monuments.
At His Father's Grave.
Cathedral Builders.
Lament for a Leg.
To a Nun.
Ormsby, Eric (b. 1941)
My Mother in Old Age.
Origins.
Skunk cabbage with its smug and opulent smell, The.
Starfish.
Ormsby, Frank (b. 1947)
At the Jaffé Memorial Fountain, Botanic Gardens.
Day in August, A.
Home.
Interim.
Landscape with Figures.
My careful life says: "No surrender."
Northern Spring, A, *sels.*
Ornaments.
Padre, The.
Spot the Ball.
Survivors.
Under the Stairs.
War Photographers, The.
Winter Offerings.
Orozco, Olga (b. 1920)
Sphinxes Inclined to Be.
Orpingalik
Alcheringa Definitions.
In a Time of Sickness.

Songs are thoughts, sung out with the breath when people are moved by great forces and ordinary speech no longer suffices.
Orr, Bob (b. 1949)
Here.
Parable.
Orr, Elaine
In This Motherless Geography.
Orr, Gregory (b. 1947)
Adolescence.
All morning the dream lingers.
Doll, The.
Elegy: "Not only doesn't the Ohio."
Gathering the Bones Together.
Mother, The.
Nicole at Thirteen.
Parable, A.
Poem: "This life like no other."
Sweater, The.
Two Lines from the Brothers Grimm.
Weeds, The.
Who'd Want to Be a Man?
Orrery, Robert Boyle, 1st Earl of (1621–79)
On Christmas Day.
Orrick, John
Little Things.
Orten, Jiri
Last Poem, The.
Whispered.
Ortiz de Montellano, Ana Luisa
Space Between, The.
Ortiz, Simon J. (b. 1941)
Bend in the River.
Bony.
Canyon de Chelly.
Creation.
Dry Root in a Wash.
Forming Child Poems.
Four Bird Songs.
My Father's Song.
Pretty Woman, A.
Returned from California.
San Diego Poem, A.
Serenity in Stones, The.
Spreading Wings on Wind.
Story of How a Wall Stands, A.
Survival This Way.
Telling About Coyote.
To Insure Survival.
Travels in the South.
Upstate.
Waiting for You to Come By.
War Poem.
Watching Salmon Jump.
Watching You.
What I Tell Him.
Wind and Glacier Voices.
Ortleb, Chuck (b. 1950)
Metaphor as Illness.
Militerotics.
On Finding Out that the One You Slept with the Night Before Was Murdered the Next Day.
Some Boys.
Orwell, George (Eric Blair) (1903–50)
As One Non-Combatant to Another.
Dressed man and a naked man, A.
Italian soldier shook my hand, The.
Osadebay, Dennis C. (b. 1911)
African Trader's Complaint, The.
Osaki, Mark (b. 1952)
Amnesiac.
Osbey, Brenda Marie (b. 1951)
In These Houses of Swift Easy Women.
Portrait.
Wastrel-Woman Poem, The.
Osborn, Mary I. ("Mary I")
Christmas.
Every Day.
My Playmate.
Swing, The.
Osborn, Selleck (c.1782–1826)
Modest Wit, A.
Osborne, Louis Shreve (b. 1923)
Riding Down from Bangor.

Osgood, Frances Sargent (1811–50)
Ah! woman still.
Ellen Learning to Walk.
Forgive and Forget.
He bade me "Be Happy," he whisper'd
   "Forget me;."
Woman.

Osgood, Francis P. (b. 1910)
Winter Fairyland in Vermont.

Osgood, Kate Putnam (1841–1910)
Driving Home the Cows.

O'Shaughnessy, Arthur William Edgar (1844–81)
Line of Beauty, The.
Ode: "We are the music-makers."
Silences.
Song: "I made another garden, yea."
Song: "I went to her who loveth me no
   more."

Osherow, Jacqueline
Late Night Tête-à-Tête with a Moon in
   Transit.

Ōshima Ryōta (1718–87)
And Then.
No one spoke.
They look / like newlyweds.

"Ossian." *See* Macpherson, James

Ostriker, Alicia (b. 1937)
Anxiety about Dying.
Eighth and the Thirteenth, The.
Everywoman Her Own Theology.
Exchange, The.
Greedy Baby / sucking the sweet tit.
Happy birthday, a gray day like the first
   one—.
I Brood about Some Concepts, for Example.
In the Twenty-Fifth Year of Marriage, It
   Goes On.
Lamenting the Inevitable.
Leaf Pile, The.
Meditation in Seven Days, A.
Minor Van Gogh (He Speaks), A.
Propaganda Poem: Maybe for Some Young
   Mamas.
Story of Joshua.
Warning.

O'Sullivan, Maggie (b. 1951)
Busk, Pierce.
Lottery & Requiem.

**O'Sullivan, Owen Roe (Eoghan Rua O
Suilleabhain) (1748–84)**
His Request.
Magic Mist, A.
Seamus, Light-hearted and Loving Friend of
   My Brea, *sels.*
To the Blacksmith with a Spade.
Volatile Kerryman, The.

"O'Sullivan, Seumas" (James Starkey) (1879–1958)
In North Great George's Street.
Lamplighter, The.
Piper, A [*or* The].
Starling Lake, The.
Trains, The.

**O'Sullivan, Teig Gaelach (Tadhg Gaelach O
Suilleabhain) (1715–99)**
Poem to the Heart of Jesus, A.

O'Sullivan, Vincent (b. 1937)
Brother Jonathan, Brother Kafka, *sels.*
Dogknotting in Quezaltenango.
Don't Knock the Rawleigh's Man.
Elegy for a Schoolmate.
Home.
Look Sheila Seeing You've Asked Me.
Still Shines When You Think of It.
Waikato-Taniwha-Rau.

Osundare, Niyi (b. 1947)
Excursion.
Eyeful Glances.
Goree.
I Sing of Change.
Moonsongs, *sels.*
Our Earth Will Not Die.
Sand Seer, The.
Who Says That Drought Was Here?

Oswald von Wolkenstein (1377–1445)
O Margie, Marge, dear Margaret.

Otalantaiyar
Six on the Desert Ways.
What He Said in the Desert.

Otomo no Sakanoé, Lady (c.728–746)
Do not smile to yourself.
Dress that my brother has put on is thin,
   The. *From* Manyo Shu, Part 1 of 4.
I gave the jewel away to its owner.
I swore not to love you.
It is other people who have separated.
My brother has on / a thin robe.
My heart, thinking / "How beautiful he is."
My love hurts me because you cannot know.
Orange tree, The.
Sent from the Capital to Her Elder Daughter.
Unknown love / Is as bitter a thing. *From*
   Manyo Shu, Part 4 of 4.
You say, "I will come."

Otomo no Tabito (Tabito) (665–731)
Better get drunk and cry.
To sit silent.

**"Otrada, Nikolai Karpovich" (Nikolai
Karpovich Turochkin) (1918–40)**
Football.

Otsuji (1881–1920)
Winter midnight.

Otsup, Georgii Avdeievich. *See* "Rayevsky,
Georgy Avdeievich"

Otto, Heinrich (*fl.* 18th cent.)
Lord, Dear God! to Thy Attending.

Otway, Thomas (1652–85)
Enchantment, The.

Ou-yang Hsiu (1007–72)
Answer to Ting Yuan Ch'en, An.
Calligraphy Practice.
Cicada, The.
Distant Mountains.
East Wind.
Fisherman.
Green Jade Plum Trees in Spring.
In the Evening I Walk by the River.
Inscribed on the Arbor of the Old Drunkard
   (Tsui-weng-t'ing) at Ch'u-chou.
Old Age.
Old fisherman spends his night beneath the
   western cliffs.
Reading the Poems of an Absent Friend.
Song of "Hand-in-Hand," A.
Song of Liang Chou.
Song of "Night After Night," A.
Song of Picking Mulberry ("Ten years ago I
   was a visitor at the wine jar.")
Song of Spring at West Lake, A, Sent to
   Circuit Officer Hsieh.
Song of the Radiant Lady, Replying to a
   Poem by Wang Chieh-fu.
Spring Day on West Lake.
Spring Walk to the Pavilion of Good Crops
   and Peace.
Thoughts on the First Day of Autumn, Sent
   to Su Tzu-mei.
Tune: "Butterflies Lingering over Flowers"
   ("Back in the painted pavilion, again in
   late spring.")
Tune: "Butterflies Lingering over Flowers"
   ("Ruffed blue-green garden, red
   blossoms.")
Tune: "Song of Picking Mulberry"—
   Recollections of West Lake.
Tune: Treading on Grass.
When the Moon is in the River of Heaven.
Written for the Pavilion of the Drunken Old
   Man at Ch'u-chou.

Ouloguem, Yambo (b. 1940)
Dear Husband.

Ousley, Clarence (1863–1948)
When the Mint Is in the Liquor.

Outram, George (1805–51)
Annuity, The.
On Hearing a Lady Praise a Certain Rev.
   Doctor's Eyes.

Overbury, E. J.
Springtime brings on the shearing, The.

Overstreet, Bonaro W. (b. 1902)
Count Ten.

Overton, Ron
Blues in "C."

Ovid (Publius Ovidius Naso) (43 B.C.–A.D. 17)
Amores, *sels.*
Arethusa Saved.
Art of Love, The, *sels.*
Baucis and Philemon, Imitated, From the
   Eighth Book of Ovid's Metamorphose,
   sels.
Cadmus sows teeth.
Catiline his Conspiracy, *sels.*
Cinyras and Myrrha, Out of the Tenth Book
   of Ovid's Metamorphoses, *sels.*
Constant Penelope sends to thee, careless
   Ulysses.
De Ponto, *sels.*
Defensive measures.
Echo.
Elegies, *sels.*
Elegies 2.i.
Elegy 9b: "If I heard a voice from heaven
   say 'Live without.'"
Fasti (Roman Feast-Days), *sels.*
Flood recedes, The.
Heroides, *sels.*
Ibis, *sels.*
Invective against Ibis, *sels.*
Io recovers her shape.
Medea rejuvenates Aeson.
Medea's invocation.
Metamorphoses, *sels.*
Narcissus on the grassy Verdure lies.
Of the Pythagorean Philosophy, *sels.*
Ovids Walnut-Tree transplanted, *sels.*
Pygmalion and the Statue, *sels.*
Rape of Lucrece, The.
Remedies for Love, The, *sels.*
Story of Cephisa, The, *sels.*
To his false Mistress.
To his Paternall Countrey.
To his Wife at Rome, when he was sick.
To Love, *sels.*
Tristia, *sels.*
Tristium, *sels.*
Winter at Tomi.

Owen, Everard
Three Hills.

Owen, Gareth (b. 1922)
Gathering in the Days.
Half asleep.
Jonah and the Whale.
Make Believe.
Message Understood.
Owl and the astronaut sailed through space,
   The.
Shed in Space.
Space Shot.
This and That.
Uncle Alfred's Long Jump.
Waterfall.
Winter Days.

Owen, Goronwy (1723–69)
Elegy for His Daughter Ellen.
Invitation, The.
Prudent Simplicity.

Owen, Guy (1925?–1981)
Epitaph for a Beatnik Poet.
Epitaph for a Meat-Packer.
White Stallion / (The Runaway), The.

Owen, Jan
Visitation, The.

Owen, Maureen (b. 1943)
African Sunday.
All That Glitters.
Amelia Earhart Series, *sels.*
For Emily (Dickinson).
Narcolepsy.
Them.
Urban Cowboy Hat.

Owen, R. C.
Limerick: "Said philosopher-physicist Jeans."

Owen, Wilfred (1893–1918)
Anthem for Doomed Youth.
Apologia Pro Poemate Meo.

Arms and the Boy.
At a Calvary near the Ancre.
Chances, The.
Conscious.
Dead-Beat, The.
Disabled.
Dulce Et Decorum Est.
End, The.
Exposure.
Fragment: "I saw his round mouth's crimson deepen as it fell."
From My Diary, July 1914.
Futility.
Greater Love.
Hospital Barge at Cérisy.
Insensibility.
It was a navy boy, so prim, so trim.
Mental Cases.
Miners.
Next War, The.
On Seeing a Piece of Our Artillery Brought into Action.
Parable of the Old Man and the Young, The.
Roads also have their wistful rest, The.
Send-Off, The.
Sentry, The.
Shadwell Stair.
Show, The.
Smile, Smile, Smile.
Sonnet, to a Child.
Spring Offensive.
Strange Meeting.
Terre, A.
To a Child.
Unreturning, The.
Wild with All Regrets.

Owens, Grace W.
Oh, who can make a flower?

Owens, Rochelle (b. 1936)
Devils Clowns and Women.

Owenson, Sydney, Lady Morgan (1783?–1859)
Joy a fix'd state—a tenure, not a start!
Kate Kearney.
Lay of an Irish Harp, or Metrical Fragments, The, *sels.*

Owl Woman (Juana Manwell) (fl. c.1880)
Songs for the Four Parts of the Night.

Oxenham, John (William Arthur Dunkerley) (1861–1941)
Art thou lonely, O my brother?
Burdened Ass, The.
Everymaid.
Sacrament of Sleep, The.
Telephone Message, A (To Whom it May Concern).
Ways, The.
Where Are You Going, Greatheart?
Where are you sleeping to-night, My Lad.

Oxlie, Mary, of Morpeth (fl. c.1656)
To William Drummond of Hawthornden.

Ozog, Jan Bolesw
Song of the Field.
Village for a Wedding.

P

P., T.
Verses for the End of an Era.

Pace, Rosalind
This Is English and I Am Speaking It No Matter What.
Tingel-Tangel.

Pacheco, Andrew
I hear but my brain doesn't get the.

Pacheco, José Emilio (b. 1939)
Boundaries.
On the Fragile Labyrinth.
Song to Be Written on a Wave.

Pack, Richardson (1682–1728)
Epistle from a Half-Pay Officer in the Country to His Friend in London, An.

Pack, Robert (b. 1929)
Boat, The.
Frog Prince, The.

Proton Decay.
Raking Leaves.
Thrasher in the Willow by the Lake, The.

Pacosz, Christina
Seed Is the Light of the Earth, The.

Paddock, Nancy
Alien.
Epiphany.
Original Mind.
Silos, The.

Padeshah Khatun (fl. 14th cent.)
Sovereign Queen.

Padgaonkar, Mangesh (b. 1929)
Salaam, / to everyone, salaam.

Padgett, Ron (b. 1942)
Advice to Young Writers.
After the Broken Arm.
Big Bluejay Composition.
Chocolate Milk.
December.
Detach, Invading.
Early Triangles.
First Drift.
Louisiana Perch.
Lucky Strikes.
Nothing in that drawer.
see also Poema del City 2.
Poema del City 2.
Sandwich Man, The.
Something or Other.
Strawberries in Mexico.
Symbols of Transformation.
Tell Us, Josephine.
Three Animals, *sels.*
Who and Each
With Lee Remick at Midnight.
Wonderful Things.
See also **Berrigan, Ted** *and* **Ron Padgett.**

Padilla, Herberto (b. 1932)
Daily Habits.
Discourse on Method, The.
Fountain, a house of stone, A.
History.
In Trying Times.
Landscapes.
Man on the Edge.
Nuclear Umbrella.
Prayer for the End of the Century, A.
Self-Portrait of the Other.
Sometimes I plunge into the ocean, for a long time.
Song of the Juggler.

Page, G. K.
Kaleidoscope.

Page, Geoff (b. 1940)
Country Nun.
Elegist, The.
Grit.
In Dante's Hell.
Inscription at Villers-Bretonneux.
Jerry's Plains, 1848.
Late Night Radio.
Premeditations.
Road Show.
Smalltown Memorials.

Page, Patricia K. (b. 1916)
After Rain.
Arras.
Brazilian Fazenda.
Deaf-Mute in the Pear Tree.
Element.
Evening Dance of the Grey Flies.
Images of Angels.
Man with One Small Hand.
Permanent Tourists, The.
Photos of a Salt Mine.
Puppets.
Schizophrenic.
Snowman, The.
Stenographers, The.
Stories of Snow.
Suffering.
T-Bar.
Typists.
War Lord in the Early Evening.
Young Girls.

Pagis, Dan (b. 1930)
Acrobatics.
Another Testimony.
Ararat.
Armchairs.
Autobiography.
Biped is quite a strange creature, The.
Conversation.
Decline of an Empire.
Draft of a Reparations Agreement.
End of the Questionnaire.
Epilogue to Robinson Crusoe.
Europe, Late.
Final Exam.
Footprints.
Honi.
Houses.
I Was Before I Was, who now.
In the Laboratory.
Instructions for Crossing the Border.
Last Ones, The.
Lesson in Observation, A.
Letter, A.
Limits of Physics, The.
Logbook.
Needless Return.
November '73.
Outside the Line.
Pages of an Album.
Photo at the Bridge.
Picture Postcard from Our Youth.
Plans.
Roll Call, The.
Roll-Call In the Concentration Camp.
Scrawled in Pencil in a Sealed Car.
Siege.
Souvenir, The.
Story, The.
Testimony.
Tropical Greenhouse.
Wall Calendar.
Witness anew, I'm bound to pass on, A.
Words.
Written in Pencil in the Sealed Railway-Car.

"Pai Wei" (HuangSu-ju) (b. 1902)
Madrid.

Pain, Barry (1864–1928)
Army of the Dead, The.
Ride a Cock Horse.

Pain, D. W.
Limerick: "Modern young curate called Hyde, A."

Pain, Philip (d. 1668?)
Meditation 8.
Meditation 10.
Meditation 62.
Meditations for July 19, 1666.
Meditations for July 25, 1666.
Meditations for July 26, 1666, *sels.*
Meditations for August 1, 1666.
Porch, The.
Whilst in This World I Stay.

Paine, Albert Bigelow (1861–1937)
Cooky-Nut Trees, The.
Dancing Bear, The.
Mis' Smith.

Paine, Thomas (1737–1809)
(The American Crisis), *sels.*

Paino, Frankie
Horse Latitudes.
Truth, The.
What the Blue Jay Said.

Painter, Charlotte
Elegy for Jack Moffat.

Palagyi, Louis (b. 1866)
Aimless.

Palaipatiya Perunkatunko
What Her Girl Friend Said to Her.
What She Said.

Palamas, Costis (1859–1943)
Life Immovable, *sels.*

Palazzeschi, Aldo (1885–1974)
Nuns Go Walking.
Stranger, The.

Paley, Grace (b. 1922)
In Aix.

Love.
On Mother's Day.
People in My Family.
Quarrel.
Sad Children's Song, The.
Women in Vietnam, The.

Palgrave, Francis Turner (1824–97)
Eutopia.
Linnet in November, The.
Trafalgar.

Palinskaite, Violeta
Silence.

Palladas [or Pallades] (360–430)
Blacksmith's quite a logical man, The.
Born crying, and after crying, die.
Born naked. Buried naked. So why fuss?
By what right do they call Zeus a lover?
Cuckolded husbands have no certain sign.
Death feeds us up, keeps an eye on our
weight.
Don't fash yourself, man! Don't complain.
Drink to drown my sorrows and restart, A.
Each new daybreak we are born again.
Fate didn't hustle Gessius to his death.
God rot the guts and the guts' indulgences.
God's philosophical and so can wait.
Grammar commences with a five line curse.
Grammarian's daughter, The.
He, cursed with an ugly wife.
Hope! Fortune! Je m'en fous!
"I know all," you say; of incompleteness, you
have enough.
I was promised a horse but what I got
instead.
Ignorant man does well to shut his trap, The.
Ignorant of all logic and all law.
It's no great step for a poor man to the
grave.
Just look at them, the shameless well-to-do.
Let this life of worry.
Life's a performance. Either join in.
Life's an ocean crossing where winds howl.
Lifetime's teaching grammar come to this, A.
Loving the rituals that keep men close.
Lyf So Short, The.
Man stole fire, and Zeus created flame.
Maurus.
Meditation.
Mein Breast, mein Corset und mein Legs.
Mere ants and gnats and trivia with stings.
Monks.
Murderer & Sarapis, The.
Poor devil that I am, being so attacked.
Poor little donkey! It's no joke.
Racing, reckoning fingers flick.
Sad and great evil is the expectation of
death, A.
So, Mister Moneybags, you're loaded? So?
Thanks for the haggis. Could you really
spare.
Theft of fire, The. Man's worst bargain yet.
Think of your conception, you'll soon forget.
This is all the life there is.
This is my mule, a poor long-suffering hack.
This Life a Theater.
Totting up the takings, quick Death can /
reckon much faster than the businessman.
We Greeks have fallen on evil.
When he comes up to the bedroom.
When you send out invitations, don't ask me.
Where's the public good in what you write.
Whose baggage from land to land is despair.
Why this desperation to move heaven and
earth.
Women.
Women all / cause rue.
Women all shout after me and mock, The.
Women tease and scold me, The.
Zeus isn't such a raving Casanova.

Pallottini, Renata
Message.

Palma, Michael (fl. 20th cent.)
Coming of Age.

Palmer, E. Harriet (1840–82)
Parterre, The.

Palmer, Herbert Edward (b. 1880)
Aunt Zillah Speaks.

Ishmael.
Rock Pilgrim.
Woodworker's Ballad.
Wounded Hawk, The.

Palmer, John F. (b. c.1870)
Band Played On, The.

Palmer, John Williamson (1825–1906)
Stonewall Jackson's Way.

Palmer, Michael (b. 1943)
Baudelaire Series, *sels.*
Dearest Reader.
Eighth Sky.
Erolog.
Fifth Prose.
Letters to Zanzotto, *sels.*
Notes for Echo Lake 2.
Notes for Echo Lake 3.
O you in that little bark.
Of this cloth doll which.
Or maybe this / is the sacred.
Painted Cup, The.
Project of Linear Inquiry, The.
Recursus.
Sun.
Theory of the Flower, The.
Voice and Address.
Who is to say.

Palmer, Opal (b. 1954)
Wasting Time.

Palmer, Ray (1808–87)
Jesus, These Eyes Have Never Seen.
Lord, My Weak Thought in Vain Would
Climb.
My Faith Looks Up to Thee.

Palmer, Samuel (1805–81)
Shoreham: Twilight Time.

Palmer, T. H. (1782–1861)
Try, Try Again.

Palmer, Vance (1885–1959)
Farmer Remembers the Somme, The.
Snake, The.

Palquera, Shem-Tob ben Joseph (1225–90)
Adapt thyself to time and circumstance.
Mouth and the Ears, The.

Paman, Clement (fl. c.1660)
On Christmas Day to My Heart.

Pambardu
Windmill At Mandanthanunguna.

Pamphilus
To the Swallow.

Pan Chao (A.D. 48–117?)
Needle and Thread.

Pan Chieh-yû (fl.c.48–46 B.C.)
Poem in Rhyme-Prose Form.
Present from the Emperor's New Concubine,
A.
Song of Regret.

P'an Lang (d. 1009)
Tune: "Song of the Wine Spring."
Written on Lake View Tower.

P'an Yüeh (d. 300)
In Mourning for His Dead Wife.
Lamenting the Dead.
Rhyme-Prose on the Idle Life.
Thinking of My Wife.

Panchenko, Nikolai Vasil'evich (b. 1928)
Ballad of the Shot Heart.

Pande, Mrinal (b. 1946)
Two Women Knitting.

Pandeya, Sudama. *See* "Dhoomil"

Paniker, K. Ayyappa (b. 1930)
Itch, The.

Pankey, Eric (b. 1959)
As We Forgive Those.
Confession of Cleopas, The.
Reason, The.
St. Luke, *sels.*

Pant, Sumitranandan (1900–77)
Almora Spring.

Pāṇtiyaṇc Aṛivutai Nampi
Children.

"Pantycelyn." *See* Williams, William

Pao Chao (414–66)
Going Out Through the North Gate of Chi.
Imitating the Old Poems.

In Imitation of Ancient-style Poetry.
In Imitation of "The King of Huai-nan."
Presented as a Farewell to Secretary Fu.
Rhyme-Prose on the Desolate City.
Weary Road, The, *sels.*

Pao-chen, Liu. *See* "Tan Ying"

Pao Yu (fl. 5th cent.)
Viaticum.

Papago
There was a mountain, over its black roots
[the deer].

Papaionnou, Yannis (1913–1972)
Nights I stay awake without hope.

Papaleo, Joseph (fl. 20th cent.)
American Dream: First Report.

Pape, Greg (b. 1947)
Birds of Detroit.
Dinner on the Miami River.
For Rosa Yen, Who Lived Here.
In Line at the Supermarket.
Indian Ruins Along Rio de Flag.
La Llorona.
Making a Great Space Small.
Mercado.
Minotaur Next Door, The.
October.
Storm Pattern.
Street Music.

Paquet, Basil T.
Basket Case.
Easter '68.
Graves Registration.
Group Shot.
In a Plantation.
It Is Monsoon at Last.
Morning—A Death.
Mourning the Death, by Hemorrhage, of a
Child from Honai.
Night Dust-off.
They Do Not Go Gentle.

Paramore, Edward E., Jr. (1895–1956)
Ballad of Yukon Jake, The.

Paranar
What Her Friend Said to Her, within the
Lover's Hearing.
What She Said ("Like moss on water.")
What She Said to Her Girl Friend ("On the
tall hill.")

Paraske, Larin (1833–1904)
My Little Love Lies on the Ground.
Sad Is the Seagull.
Woman Grows Soon Old, A.

Pari, Daughter of
That Month.

Parini, Jay (b. 1948)
Coal Train.

Pāri's daughters&xbd;
That month.

Park, Chaesam (b. 1933)
Flute Holes.
Landscape, A.

Park, Chech'on (b. 1945)
Changtzu 33.
Distrust.
Heavenly Traveler.

Park, Hijin (b. 1931)
Ode to Merciful Bodhisattva.
Song for Empty Cup.

Park, Mogwol (1919–78)
April.
Love.
Lowering the Coffin.
Traveler, The.

Park, Namsu (b. 1918)
Birds.
Hands.

Park, Pong-u (1934–90)
True Line, The.

Park, Roswell (1807–69)
Jesus Spreads His Banner o'er Us.

Park, Song-yong (b. 1934)
Fruit Tree.
Opium Poppy, The.

Park, Tujin (b. 1916)
Before Thy Love.
Hymn to the Graveyard.
Sun, The.
Youthful Sea, The.

Park, Yongch'ol (1904–38)
Departing Boat, The.

Parker, C. J.
Old soak from Stoke, An.

Parker, Dorothy (1893–1967)
Bohemia.
Certain Lady, A.
De Profundis.
Experience.
Flaw in Paganism, The.
General Review of the Sex Situation.
Godmother.
Indian Summer.
Inventory.
Little Old Lady in Lavender Silk, The.
On Being a Woman.
One Perfect Rose.
Partial Comfort.
Pictures in the Smoke.
Pig's-Eye View of Literature, A, *sels.*
Prophetic Soul.
Sanctuary.
Some Beautiful Letters, *sels.*
Song of One of the Girls.
Symptom.
Unfortunate Coincidence.

Parker, Edwin Pond (1836–1925)
Master, No Offering.

Parker, Sir Gilbert (1862–1932)
Reunited.

Parker, Henry Adams
Apple Blossoms.

Parker, Katherine
Long, Long Ago.

Parker, Martin (c.1600–c.1656)
Cupid's Wrongs Vindicated, *sels.*
King Enjoys His Own Again, The.
Well met Neighbour, *sels.*

Parker, Patricia (b. 1944)
For Willyce.
From the Cavities of Bones.
I Followed a Path.
Love Isn't.
My Brother.
My lady ain't no lady.
Prologue from "Legacy."
There Is a Woman in This Town.
Where Will You Be?

Parker, Stephen (b. 1939?)
Winter in Étienburgh.

Parker, Theodore (1810–60)
Higher Good, The.

Parkerson, Michelle (b. 1953)
Statistic.

Parkes, Bessie Rayner (1829–1925)
For Adelaide.
Summer Sketches, *sels.*
To an Author who Loved Truth More than Fame.
To Elizabeth Barrett Browning.

Parkes, Francis Ernest Kobina (b. 1932)
Apocalypse.
Blind Steersmen.
Three Phases of Africa.

"Parley, Peter." See Goodrich, Samuel Griswold

Parmenion of Macedon
For a little gold, Zeus bought Danae.
Gutsy bugs grabbed grub from me till disgusted, The.
Protection of a cheap coat suffices, The.
Statue of Nemesis at Rhamnus, The.
Thermopylai.
You poured down like gold, / Olympian Zeus.
Zeus paid Danaé in gold:/ thus I pay you.

Parmenter-Newell, Catherine
Dream House.

Parnell, Fanny (1854–83)
After Death.

Parnell, Thomas. *See* **Pope, Alexander** *and* Thomas Parnell

Parnell, Thomas (1679–1718)
Elegy, to an Old Beauty, An.
Essay on the Different Styles of Poetry, The, *sels.*
Hezekiah, *sels.*
Hymn to Contentment, A.
Night Piece on Death, *sels.*
On Bishop Burnet's Being Set on Fire in His Closet.
Riddle, A: "Upon a bed of humble clay."
Song: "When thy beauty appears."
To Mr. Pope, *sels.*

Parone, Edward
Morning Track, The.

Paros, Euenus of. See Euenus

Parr, Joyce
Limerick: "There was an old sage of New Delhi."

Parra, Nicanor (b. 1914)
Anti-Lazarus, The.
Discourse of the Good Thief, The.
Inflation.
Letters from the Poet Who Sleeps in a Chair.
Lord's Prayer.
Manifesto, *sels.*
Man's mother is very sick, A.
Modern Times.
New Sermons and Preachings of the Christ of Elqui (1979), *sels.*
Pilgrim, The.
Poems of the Pope, The.
Sentences.
Tablets, The.
Vices of the Modern World.
Warnings.

Parrhasios (fl. 5th cent. B.C.)
Herakles.
I tell you (you needn't believe it).

Parrish, Elsie
Essie Parrish in New York.

Parrish, John (fl. c.1793)
Democratic Barber; or, Country Gentleman's Surprise, The.

Parrot, Henry (fl. 1600–1626)
Fatales Poetae.
On a Poet.

Parrott, E. O.
Limerick: "Bashful young fellow of Brighton, A."
Limerick: "Brickie who had a fine tool, A."
Limerick: "Carpenter living in Crewe, A."
Limerick: "Couturier from Haverford West, A."
Limerick: "I spotted these daffs by the lake."
Limerick: "O, I yearn to go back to the Cam!"
Limerick: "Said a girl in green Mansfield Park."
Limerick: "Shepherd who lived up in Gwent, A."
Limerick: "There was a young man of Ostend."
Limerick: "There was a young outlaw named Hood."
Limerick: "There was an old housewife of Staines."
More Bagpipe Music.
There's a man at Crewe.

Parry, David Fisher (b. 1908?)
Miniver Cheevy, Jr..

Parry, Edward Abbott (1803–1943)
I Would Like You for a Comrade.
Jam Fish, The.
Ode on a Grecian Urn.
Pater's Bathe.
Round about the cauldron go!

Parry, Joseph (1841–1903)
New Friends and Old Friends.

Parry, R. Williams (1884–1956)
Branwen's Starling.
Fox, The.
Miraculous Dawn.
Old Boatman of Death's River, The.

On a Soldier Killed in the Great War.
Two Hearts Divided.

Parry-Williams, T. H. (1887–1975)
Christmas Carol: "Close to a quarter of a century since then."
Llyn y Gadair.
These Bones.

Parshchikov, Aleksey [or Aleksei] Ivanovich (b. 1954)
Prelude, Spoken to My Work Tools.

Parsons, Clere (1908–31)
Different.
Introduction: "I bespeak words."

Parsons, William (1758?–1828)
To a Friend in Love during the Riots.

Parthasarathy, Rajagopal (b. 1934)
Speaking of Places.

Partridge, Frances (b. 1900)
My Days Go On.

Parulekar, Rajani (b. 1945)
Birthmarks.

Parun, Vesna (b. 1922)
Ballad of the Deceived Flowers.
Let's Get the Coachman Drunk.
Mother of Man.
Open Door.
Return to the Tree of Time, A.
Sleeping Youth.
You whose hands are more innocent than mine.

Pascal, Paul (b. 1925)
Tact.

Paschen, Elise
Confederacy.
Litany.

Pasman, Heinz
Black Hairs, The.

Pasolini, Pier Paolo (1922–75)
Civil Song.
Day of My Death, The.
Lines from the Testament.
Part of a Letter to the Codignola Boy.
Prayer to My Mother.
Roman Evening.
Sex, consolation for misery!
Southern Dawn.
St. John, *sels.*

Passerat, Jean (1534–1602)
Love in May.
Song: "Shephard loveth thow me vell?"

Pastan, Linda (b. 1932)
After Reading Nelly Sachs.
April.
Ars Poetica.
Aspects of Eve.
At Home.
At the Train Museum.
Because the night you asked me.
Camellias.
David.
Duet for One Voice.
Elegy.
Erosion.
Ethics.
Five Stages of Grief, The.
Grammar Lesson.
Hat Lady, The.
Imperfect Paradise, The.
Jump Cabling.
Last Train, The.
Letter to a Son at Exam Time.
Love Poem.
Marks.
Notes from the Delivery Room.
Passover.
Returning.
September.
To a Daughter Leaving Home.
Turnabout.

Pasternak, Boris Leonidovich (1890–1960)
Autumn.
Cape Mootch.
Christmas Star.
Darling, it's frightening! When a poet loves.
Definition of the Soul.

Devotion is a heavy cross.
English Lessons.
Evil Days, The.
Feasts, The.
February. Get your ink and weep.
Fresco Come to Life.
Fresh Paint.
From Superstition.
Garden of Gethsemane, The.
Hamlet.
Hamlet in Russia, A Soliloquy.
Highest Sickness, The.
Hops.
In the Breeze.
In The Wood.
Magdalene (I).
Marburg.
Mary Magdalene (I).
May It Be.
Meeting.
Miracle, The.
Night.
O had I known that it ends like this.
On Early Trains.
Piano, trembling, makes the lips grow dry,
The.
Poem, A, *sels.*
Poem: "So they begin. With two years gone."
Snow is falling, snow is falling.
St. Mark, *sels.*
St. Matthew, *sels.*
Three Variations.
To a Friend.
To be famous is not in good taste.
Waving a Bough.
Wedding, A, *sels.*
Weeping Garden, The.
Wind, The.
Winter Night.
You're here. We breathe the selfsame air.

Pastorius, Francis Daniel (1651–1720)
As often as some where before my feet.
Delight in books from evening.
Epigram: "At ten a clock, when I the fire
rake."
Extract the quint-essence.
Great God, Preserver of All Things.
I have a pretty little flow'r.
If Any Be Pleased to Walk into My Poor
Garden.
If thou wouldest roses scent.
Learn, lads and lasses, of my garden.
Most weeds, whilst young.
On His Garden Book.
Penance, A.
Though My Thoughts.
Thy garden, orchard, fields.
To God alone, the only donour.
When I solidly do ponder.
When one or other rambles.

Patacara (fl. 6th cent. B.C.)
When they plow their fields.

Patchen, Kenneth (1911–72)
All the Roary Night.
Animal I wanted, The.
Because His Sister Saw Shakespeare in the
Moon.
Because It's Good to Keep Things Straight.
Biography of Southern Rain.
Body Beside the Ties, The.
Character of Love Seen as a Search for the
Lost, The.
Constant Bridegrooms, The.
Deer and the Snake, The.
Do the Dead Know What Time It Is?
Easy Decision, An.
Eight Early Poems, *sels.*
Empty Dwelling Places.
From my high love I look at that poor world
there.
I have lighted the candles, Mary.
In Judgment of the Leaf.
In Memory of Kathleen.
In the footsteps of the walking air.
Like a Mourningless Child.
Lions of fire, The.
Magical Mouse, The.

Midnight Special.
Mirru.
Moon, Sun, Sleep, Birds, Live.
Naked Land, The.
Nice Day for a Lynching.
O All Down within the Pretty Meadow.
O my love / The pretty towns.
O now the drenched land wakes.
O terrible is the highest thing.
Origin of Baseball, The.
Pastoral: "Dove walks with sticky feet, The."
Saturday Night in the Parthenon.
'Sea is Awash with Roses, The.'
State of the Nation, The.
Street Corner College.
Temple, A.
Village Tudda, The.
We go out together into the staring town.
Where?
While the sun still spends his fabulous
money.

Patel, Essop (b. 1943)
Haanetjie's Morning Dialogue.

Patel, Gieve (b. 1940)
Forensic Medicine.

Patel, Ravji (1939–68)
Whirlwind.

Pater, Walter (1839–94)
Mona Lisa.

Paterson, Alistair (b. 1929)
Incantations for Warriors, *sels.*
Overture for Bubble-Gum and Flute.
Toledo Room, The, *sels.*

Paterson, Andrea
Because I Could Not Dump.

Paterson, Andrew Barton (1864–1941)
Father Riley's Horse.
Man from Snowy River, The.
Old Australian Ways.
Road to Hogan's Gap, The.
Travelling Post Office, The.
Waltzing Matilda.

Paterson, Evangeline
Dispossessed.
In a South African Museum.
Tribal Homeland.

Patil, Chandrashekhar (b. 1939)
Freak.

Patmore, Coventry Kersey Dighton (1823–96)
Angel in the House, The, *sels.*
Barren Shore, The.
Evening Scene, An.
Flesh-Fly and the Bee, The.
From the small life that loves with tooth and
nail.
Girl of All Periods: An Idyll, The.
How fair a flower is sown.
King William's Dispatch to Queen Augusta.
London Fete, A.
Night and Sleep.
Parting.
Rosy Bosom'd Hours, The.
Round the Year.
Save by the Old Road none attain the new.
Science, the agile ape, may well.
She Was Mine.
Storm, The.
Too soon, too soon comes Death to show.
Two Deserts, The.
Unknown Eros, The, *sels.*
Victories of Love, The, *sels.*
Warning, A.

Paton, Alan (1903–88)
I Have Approached.
Prison House, The.

Patrick, Bishop (d. 1084)
Invocation: "Almighty God, who fillest the
recesses of the heavens."

Patrick, Luther (b. 1895)
Sleepin' at the Foot o' the Bed.

Patrick, Saint (fl. c.5th cent.)
St Patrick's Breastplate.
Saint Patrick's Breastplate; or, The Deer's
Cry.

Pattanshetti, Siddhalinga (b. 1939)
Woman / is a problem negative.

Patten, Brian (b. 1946)
After Frost.
Bee's Last Journey to the Rose, The.
Complacent Tortoise, The.
Earth-ling, The.
Frogologist, The.
How the New Teacher Got Her Nickname.
I Don't Believe in Human-tales.
Lion and the Echo, The.
Mum won't let me keep a rabbit.
Ode on Celestial Music.
Party Piece.
Portrait of a Young Girl Raped at a Suburban
Party.
Squeezes.
Terrible Path, The.
Through All Your Abstract Reasoning.
What Happened to Miss Frugle.

Patterson, Raymond R. (b. 1929)
At That Moment.
Birmingham 1963.
Black All Day.
Black Power.
From Riot Rimes U.S.A. #78.
From Riot Rimes U.S.A. #79.
Glory, Glory. . . .
Harlem Suite.
Hopping Toad Blues.
I've Got a Home in That Rock.
Letter in Winter.
Night-Piece.
Schwerner, Chaney, Goodman.
Sundown Blues.
Surplus Blues.
This Age.
What We Know.
When I Awoke.
"Word to the Wise Is Enough, A."
You Are the Brave.

Pattison, William (1706–27)
Ad Coelum.

Patton, Charlie (1887–1934)
34 Blues.

Pau-Llosa, Ricardo
Frutas.
Ganaderia.
Island of Mirrors, The.
Ostiones Y Cangrejos Moros.

Pauker, Ted (b. 1917)
Garland for a Propagandist.
Grouchy Good Night to the Academic Year,
A.
Limeraiku.
Limerick: "There was a great Marxist called
Lenin."
Trifle for Trafalgar Day, A.

"Paul, John." *See* **Webb, Charles Henry**

Paul, Louis (1901–70)
Cynical Portraits.

Paul the Deacon (c.720–800)
Epitaph for His Niece, Sophia.
He Intercedes with Charlemagne for His
Brother in Exile.

Paulding, James Kirke (1779–1860)
Backwoodsman, The, *sels.*

Paulin, Tom (b. 1949)
Anastasia McLaughlin.
And Where Do You Stand on the National
Question.
Black Bread.
Cadaver Politic.
Desertmartin.
Impossible Pictures, The.
In the Lost Province.
Lyric Afterwards, A.
Manichean Geography I.
Of Difference Does It Make.
Off the Back of a Lorry.
Other Voice, The.
Personal Column.
Presbyterian Study.
Settlers.
Still Century.
Surveillances.
Ulster Unionist Walks the Streets of London,
An.

Under the Eyes.

Paulinus of Aquileia (c.726–802)
Lament for Aquileia Destroyed, and Never to be Built Again.

Paulinus of Nola (353–431)
St. Paulinus to his Wife Therasia, *sels.*
To Ausonius.

Paulus [or Paulos] Silentiarius (*fl.* c.560)
And now you comb and braid your hair.
Bitten by a rabid dog, a man sees.
Choicer than all / flush of youth.
Come, give me kisses, Rhodope.
Description of Hagia Sophia.
Dont' tell me I'm getting gray.
Epigram: "Kissing Hippomenes, I crave."
Epitaph, An: "My name—my country—what are they to thee."
Epitaph: Atticus.
Epitaph: Chryseomallus the Mime.
Epitaph: "Here I— / What does."
Epitaph to Let, An.
Eros has changed his quiver.
Even clothed in wrinkles, dear Philinna.
For whom now will you comb your hair in lover's fashion?
Giving her mother's / zealous eye.
Gold cut the knot of otherwise.
Goodbye: I bite the word back.
How many stolen glances can we trade.
I believe the grief of Tantalus in Hell.
I saw them, caught them in the act.
In Peterborough Churchyard.
Locked in Hippomenes' kisses.
Man (they say), A.
Mild, of sweet / countenance.
On a Bath-House in which Both Men and Women Bathe.
On a High House in Byzantium.
Our kisses / Rhodope.
Our kisses / Rhodope / let us steal.
Sappho kisses softly.
Set foot once beyond Nilotic Meroë.
She has not come.
She lay all night beside me.
She plucked one thread.
Slip off that gown.
Sober man, I'll take the wine, A.
Soft are Sappho's kisses.
Take off your clothes, my love!
These wreaths, Lais.
United.
You're right, Lais' smile is sweet.

Pavese, Cesare (1908–50)
August Moon.
Grappa in September.
Words from Confinement.

Pavic, Milorad (b. 1929)
Flying Temple.
Great Serbian Migration 1690.
Holy Mass For Relja Krilatica, *sels.*
Swing over the Calm Source of Our Names, The.

Pavlova, Karolina (1807–93)
To Madame A. V. Pletneff.

Pavlovic, Miodrag
Morning Inscription.
Questionnaire of Sleeplessness.

Pawar, Daya (b. 1935)
Buddha, The.

Pawsey, Irene F.
Bramble Jam.
Browny Bee.
Browny Hen, The.
Egg for Easter, An.
Eggs for Breakfast.
Found in the Woods.
Greedy Little Pig, The.
Haytime.
June.
Thief, The.
White Horses.

Payne, Basil (b. 1928)
Lines in Memory of My Father.

Payne, Daniel Alexander (1811–93)
Pleasures, The, *sels.*

Payne, John Howard (1791–1852)
Clari, the Maid of Milan, *sels.*

Paz, Octavio (b. 1914)
Along Galeana Street.
Brotherhood.
Counterparts.
Doomed Garden, A.
Engaged.
Exclamation.
Friendship.
Girl.
Here.
Hymn Among the Ruins.
I Speak of the City.
Key of Water, The.
Landscape.
Last Dawn.
Pause.
Small Variation.
Solo for Two Voices.
Stanzas for an Imaginary Garden.
Touch.

Peabody, Josephine Preston (1874–1922)
To a Dog.

Peabody, Richard
Burning the Dolls.

Peacock, Molly (b. 1947)
Anger Sweetened.
Buffalo.
Chriseaster.
Desire.
Devolution.
Don't think governments end the world. The blast.
Dream Come True.
Good Girl.
Have You Ever Faked an Orgasm?
How I Come to You.
How I Had to Act.
Our Room.
Return, The.
Say You Love Me.
She Lays ("She lays each beautifully mooned finger.")
Smell.
So, When I Swim to the Shore.
Spell, The.
Surge, The.
Those Paperweights with Snow Inside.
Wheel, The.

Peacock, Thomas Love (1785–1866)
Andonis, My Daughter.
Border Ballad, A.
Crotchet Castle, *sels.*
Earth Song.
Fear.
For the Children.
Ghosts, The.
Grave of Love, The.
Gryll Grange, *sels.*
In Respect of the Elderly.
In the days of old.
Maid Marian.
Margaret Love Peacock, for Her Tombstone, 1826.
Melincourt, *sels.*
Misfortunes of Elphin, The, *sels.*
Newark Abbey.
Nightmare Abbey, *sels.*
Rhododaphne, *sels.*
Rich and Poor; or, Saint and Sinner.
Sir Proteus, a Satirical Ballad, *sels.*
Six Eagles.

Peacocke, M. R. (b. 1930)
Railway Allotments.

Peake, Mervyn Laurence (1911–68)
Conceit.
Frivolous Cake, The.
I cannot give the reasons.
It Makes a Change.
My Uncle Paul of Pimlico.
O here it is! And there it is!
Sensitive, Seldom and Sad.

Pearce, Norman V.
Blind.

Pearl, Robert
Mourning Song.

Pearse, Jimmy
As he stood in their shop, Mr. Boosey.
Willesden Gree.

Pearse, Padraic (1880–1916)
Fool, The.
I am Ireland.
Ideal.
Mother, The.
Prayer to Mother Mary.
Renunciation.

Pearson, Mrs.. *See* Sharpe, Richard Scrafton *and* Mrs. Pearson

Peck, John (b. 1941)
Cider and Vesalius.
Colophon for Lan-t'ing Hsiu-hsi.
Here Is a Song.
Ringers, The.
Spring Festival on the River, The.
Watcher, The.
What If the Saint Must Die.

Peck, Robert Newton
Four of July.

Peck, Samuel Minturn (b. 1854)
Kiss in the Rain, A.

Pedroso, Regino
Opinions of the New Student.

Peele, George (1559–96)
Anglorum Feriae, *sels.*
Arraignment of Paris, The, *sels.*
Hunting of Cupid, The, *sels.*
Love of King David and Fair Bethsabe, *sels.*
Old Wives' [or Wife's] Tale, The, *sels.*
Polyhymnia, *sels.*

Peeradina, Saleem (b. 1944)
Sisters.

Peirce, Kathleen
Alcoholic's Son at Ten, The.
Divided Touch, Divided Color.
Farmers.
Near Burning.
Need Increasing Itself by Rounds.
Quilts.

Peire Vidal (c.1175–1205)
Song of Breath.

Peiyu, Gong. *See* "Shu Ting"

Pelham, Sarah
When i was young.

Pembroke, Mary Sidney Herbert, Countess of (1562–1621)
If Ever Hapless Woman Had a Cause.
Laudate Dominum.
O Lord, Thou Hast Searched and Known Me.
Psalm 57: Miserere Mei, Deus.
Psalm 58: Si Vere Utique.
Psalm 84: "How lovely is thy dwelling."
Psalm 89 Misericordias, *sels.*
Psalm 92: Bonum Est Confiteri.
Psalm 100: "O all you lands, the treasures of your joy."
Quid gloriaris? Psalm 52.
To the Thrice-Sacred Queen Elizabeth.
Voce mea ad Dominum Psalm 142.

Pembroke, William Herbert, Earl of (1580–1630)
Disdain Me Still.
Song: "Soules joy, now I am gone."

Pender, Lydia
Lizard, The.

Penfold, Merimeri (b. 1824)
Land Laws, The.
Tamaki of a Hundred Lovers.

Penfold, Nita
Woman with the Wild-Grown Hair Relaxes after Another Long Day, The.

Penkethman, John (*fl.* c.1630)
Schoolmaster's Precepts, A.
Some Boys.

Penn, William
They that love beyond the world, cannot be separated.

Penna, Sandro (1906–77)
Lady on Streetcar.

Pennant, Edmund (b. 1917)
Wildebeest of Carmine Street, The.

Pennecuik, Alexander (d. 1730)
Marriage betwixt Scrape, Monarch of the Maunders, and Blobberlips, Queen of the Gypsies, A, *sels.*

Penny, Anne (1731–84)
Odes Sung in Commemoration of the Marine Society, *sels.*

Penny, Rob (b. 1940)
And We Conquered.
Be Cool, Baby.
I Remember How She Sang.
Real People Loves One Another, The.

Penny, W. E.
Town of Nogood, The.

Penrose, Roland (1900–1984)
Road Is Wider than Long, The, *sels.*

Penrose, Thomas (1742–79)
Helmets; a Fragment, The.

Penstone, M. M.
Praise to God for things we see.

Pepler, H. D. C. (1878–1951)
Concerning Dragons.

Percival, James Gates (1795–1856)
Coral Grove, The.
May.
To Senaca Lake.

Percy, William (1575–1648)
Coelia, *sels.*

Percy, William Alexander (1885–1942)
They Cast Their Nets in Galilee.

Pereira, Francesca Yetunde (b. 1933)
Burden, The.
Mother Dark.
Paradox, The.
Two Strange Worlds.

"Pereleshin, Valery Frantsevich" (Valerii Frantsevich Salatko-Petrishche) (b. 1913)
In the final hour, dear.
Path, The.

Perelman, Bob (b. 1947)
Broken Mirror, The.
China.
Chronic Meanings.
Cliff Notes.
Let's Say.
Marginalization of Poetry, The.
Money.
Seduced by Analogy.
Things.

Péret, Benjamin (1899–1959)
Hymn of the Patriotic War Veterans.
Joan of Arc.
Little Song of the Maimed.
Making Feet and Hands.
My Final Agonies.
Nungesser und Coli Sind Verreckt.
On All Fours.
Staircase with a Hundred Steps, The.

Peretz [or Perets], Isaac Leibush [or Yitskhok Leybush] (1852?–1915)
All through the stranger's wood I strolled.
Believe not that the world is for naught, made.
Eternal Sabbath.
Hope and Faith.
In the Silent Night.
Little People.
Three Seamstresses, The.

Perevin Muruvalar
Elegy: "He has held."
What He Said.

Perillo, Lucia Maria (b. 1958)
Skin.
Sweaters, The.

Perkins, Emily Swan (1866–1941)
Thou Art, O God, the God of Might.

Perkins, Silas H.
Common Road, The.

Perkoff, Stuart Z. (1930–74)
Feasts of Death, Feasts of Love.
Flowers for Luis Bunuel.
Recluses, The.

Perlberg, Mark (b. 1929)
Hiroshige.

Perlman, Anne S.
At Fifty in the Crystal-Dead Eye of the Center.
Family Reunion.
Summer Adjustments.
Survival.

Perreault, John (b. 1937)
Boomerang.
Metaphysical Paintings, The.
Readymade.
Shoe.

Perrine, Laurence (b. 1915)
Janus.

Perronet, Edward (1725–92)
All hail the Power of Jesus' name!

Perry, Grace (b. 1927)
Time of Turtles.

Perry, Julianne (b. 1952)
No Dawns.
To L.

Perry, Nora (1831–76)
Coming of Spring, The.
"Next year, next year," we say.
Too Late.

Perry, Tod (b. 1931)
For Nicholas, Born in September.

Persand, Sasenarine
Rain Storm.

"Perse, St.-John" (Alexis Saint-Léger Léger) (1887–1975)
Anabasis, *sels.*
Exile, *sels.*

Perses (*fl.* 316 B.C.)
Artemis.
Death came before Marriage, Philaenion.
Lucina, Care.
Mnasylla, the daughter you lament.
Time & prayer fitting, I, the god.

Persius (Aulus Persius Flaccus) (A.D. 34–62)
Bitter end, A.
First Satyr of Aulus Persius Flaccus. In Dialogue betwixt the Poet and His Friend, or Monitor, The, *sels.*
One Thousand Seven Hundred and Thirty Eight. A Dialogue Something like Horace, *sels.*
Prologue of Persius, The.
Satires, *sels.*
Third Satyre, The, *sels.*
Unwelcome advice.

Peruncattan, Ceyti Valluvan
What She Said ("In his country of cool seas, they say.")

Peruncittiranar
Bard's Family, A.

Peruṅkaṭuṅkō, Pālaipāṭiya
What Her Girl Friend Said to her ("Not happy with what he has.")
What She Said ("Though he lives in the same town.")

Perunkunrur Kilar
Parade, A.

Peruvatuti, Ilam
This World Lives Because.

Peseroff, Joyce
Adolescent.
Bluebird.
Dog in the Lifeboat, A.
Hardness Scale, The.

Peshkov, Aleksey Maksimovich. *See* "Gorky, Maksim"

Peskett, William (b. 1952)
Bottles in the Zoological Museum.
From Belfast to Suffolk.
Inheritors, The.
Question of Time, The.
Star and Sea.
Window Dressing.

Pessoa, Fernando (1888–1935)
Ascent of Vasco da Gama, The.
Blighter that is at the end of the sea, The.
If, after I die they should want to write my biography.
In the terrible night, natural substance of all nights.

Maritime Ode, *sels.*
Oblique Rain, *sels.*
Portuguese Sea, The.
She brings the surprise of being.
"Startling Reality of Things," The.

Petchenik, Kenneth
Limerick: "There was a young faggot called Willy."

"Peter"
Bus, The.
Saint Wears a Halo, The.
Speed Track, The.

Peters, Lenrie (b. 1932)
After They Put Down Their Overalls.
Home Coming.
I am asking about the way ahead.
Isatou died.
One long jump.
Parachute Men say.
Song: "Clawed green-eyed."
We have come home.

Peters, Robert (b. 1924)
Blessing a Bride and Groom; a Wedding Night Poem.
Buying a Record.
Crazy Bill to the Bishop.
Darkling Chicken, The.
Feathered Friends.
Final Soliloquy on a Randy Rooster (in a Key of Yellow).
I, Lessimus, of Salt Lake City.
Meeting Mick Jagger.
Melon-Slaughterer; or, A Sick Man's Praise for a Well Woman.
Reflecting on the Aging-Process.
Study in Aesthetics, A.

Petersen, Donald (b. 1928)
Ballad of Dead Yankees, The.
Walking along the Hudson.

Peterson, Henry (1818–91)
Ode for Decoration Day, *sels.*

Peterson, Nancy
Search, The.

Peterson, Peter (b. 1926)
On First Looking into Chapman's Homer II.

Peterson, Ruth Delong (b. 1606)
Midwest Town.

Petrarch (Francesco Petrarca) (1304–74)
Alone and pensive, the most deserted fields.
Bicause I have the still kept fro lyes and blame.
Ever mine [*or* myn] hap[pe] is slack and slo[w] in coming [*or* commyng].
How oft have I, my dear [*or* dere] and cruel[l] foe.
My Galley.
Now that the sky and earth and wind are still.
Sonnets to Laura, *sels.*
Translation from Petrarch.
Visions, *sels.*
Whoso list to hunt, I know where is a hind.

Petri, György (b. 1913)
By an Unknown Poet from Eastern Europe, 1955.
Christmas 1956.
Electra.
Gratitude.
Morning Coffee.
Night Song of the Personal Shadow.
Once again.
To Be Said Over and Over Again.
To S.V.

Petrie, Paul (b. 1936)
Church of San Antonio de la Florida, The.
Dream, The.
Enigma Variations, The.
Murderer, The.
Not Seeing Is Believing.
Old Pro's Lament, The.
Phases of Darkness, The.

Petröczi, Kata Szidónia (1662–1708)
Swift Floods.

Petronius Arbiter (Caius Petronius Arbiter) (d. A.D. 66)
Catiline his Conspiracy, *sels.*

Encouragement to Exile.
Fornication is a filthy business.
Fragment of Petronius, A.
Fragment of Petronius, Paraphras'd, A.
Good God, what a night that was.
I had just gone to bed.
Malady of Love Is Nerves, The.
Man in the middle of the street.
Out of Petronius.
Satyricon, *sels.*
Short and dirty, is all the fun of it.
That night will long delight us, Nealce.
There, sea and sky are at a mortal war.
Waking, my eyes, and in the night.
We Are Such Stuff as Dreams.
Why do you frown on me, you puritans.

Petrosky, Anthony (b. 1948)
Jurgis Petrakas, the Workers' Angel,
Organizes the First Miners' Strike in
Exeter, Pennsylvania.
V.A. Hospital.

Petrov, Aleksandar
Poetry in a Glass Cube.
Poetry in an empty dress.
Poetry in the Underground Passage.
Poetry Visits an Old Lady.

Petrova, Olga (1884–1977)
To a Child Who Inquires.

Pettet, Simon (b. 1953)
Annul.
Echo.
Mevlana.
Rose Garland Sonnet.

Pettingell, Phoebe
Ode on Zero.

Pettit, Michael
Driving Lesson.
Legless Boy Climbing In and Out of Chair.
Pavlov's Dog.
Self-Portrait Approaching Promontory, Utah.
Sparrow of Espanola.

Petty, Noel
Great Poll-Tax Victory of '88, The.
It was in the Spring of 1825.
There's a breathless hush in the Close
tonight.

Pewhairangi, Kumeroa Ngoingoi (b. 1922)
Do Not Turn Away.
I Sit Here.

Peyanar
Nine on Happy Reunion, *sels.*
Seven Said by the Foster-Mother, *sels.*

Peynetsa, Andrew
Boy and the Deer, The.

Pfeiffer, Emily Jane (1827–90)
Any Husband to Many a Wife.
Lost Light, The.
Out of the Night, *sels.*
Peace to the odalisque, the facile slave.
Song of Winter, A.

Phác, Lâm Tấn. *See* **Đông Hồ**

Phách, Lê Cư'. *See* **Du Tử' Lê**

Phaedrus (fl. c.8 A.D.)
Aesop at Play.
Dog in the River, The.
Fox and the Grapes, The.
Man and the Weasel, The.
Proud Frog, The.
Purpose of Fable-writing, The.

Phalaicus (fl. c.300 B.C.)
This gift, her gold-hemmed saffron gown.

Phạm Hổ (b. 1926)
Hand, The.
Sea, The.
Tall Trees.

Phạm Quý Thích (1760–1825)
Summer Drought.

Phan Bội Châu Phan Văn San (1867–1940)
Alarm Clock, The.
Character.
Epitaph for My Dog.
Human Nature.
In a Canton Jail.
Mourning Nguyễn Thái Học and Nguyễn Thị
Giang.

My Shadow and I.
Rights.
To a Cuckoo.
You Eat the Figs, So Sit Beneath the Tree.

Phan chu Trinh (1872–1926)
Breaking Rocks on Poulo Condore.
Dogs in the Loft.
Game of Chess, A.
Impromptu.
Ode to the Candle.
Opera Actors.

Phan Thanh Giản (1796–1867)
Fishermen and Cormorants.

Phan Trong Quảng
Independence Day.
International Solidarity.
Ricksha Man's Impromptu, A.

Phan Văn Hy
Ricksha man does quite a simple job, The.

Phan Văn Tri (1830–1910)
Grains of Rice.
Mosquito, you are blessed with all nice
things!
Opera Actors.
Rice Mill, The.

Phanias
By Themis & the wine that made me tipsy.
Here Lysis set an empty tomb.
It's a sign of the times when even barbers.
Stick he used to tap out feet, The.

Phelp, J. A.
Duke Of Buccleuch, The.

Phelps, Sylvanus D. (1816–95)
Saviour, Thy Dying Love.

Pheraios, Rhigas (1759–98)
War Hymn.

Philetas (b. c.320 B.C.)
Past fifty and cloyed at last.
This tombstone heavy with grief announces.

Philip, John (b. 1927)
Manly Ferry.

Philip, Marlene (b. 1947)
Oliver Twist.
Salmon Courage.

Philip of Thessalonica (fl. A.D. 1st cent.)
Bronze warship-beaks, old voyage-avid
weapons.
Epigram: "You were a pretty boy once,
Archestratus, and."
His anchor, seaweed-probing, boat-securing.
I, a ship, built on the profits / from my
master's amorous trade.
I am a plane-tree. I was sound and strong
when the blasts.
Long farewell to all you universe-swivelling
optics, A.
Look at these most wretched remains of a
man.
Moment ago the shrill flute whistled in the
bridal chamber, A.
Old Nico brought wreaths to the tomb of
Melite.
Queen of black-earth Egypt, divine Isis.
Sky will extinguish its stars, and the sun,
The.
Sosicles the farmer dedicated these sheaves.
Stranger, beware! This terrible tomb.
To Pan the forest-ranger, Gelo the hunter.
Whistling bellows of his furnace, The.
Yellow-coated pomegranate, figs like lizards'
necks, A.
Young Hermes, who placed you at the
starter's mark?

Philip V, King of Macedon (238–179 B.C.)
Traveller, on this ridge a leafless, barkless
tree.

Philipott, Thomas (c.1616–1682)
To Sir Henry Newton, upon His Re-edifying
the Church of Charleton in Kent.

Philips, Ambrose (1675–1749)
Happy Swain, The.
Ode: To Miss Margaret Pulteney.
To Miss Charlotte Pulteney in Her Mother's
Arms.
Winter-Piece, A.

Wit and Wisdom.

Philips, David
If you hear rustling in the straw.

Philips, Joan. *See* "**Ephelia**"

Philips, John (1676–1704)
Blenheim, *sels.*
Cyder, *sels.*

Philips, Katherine ("Orinda") (1631–64)
Against Love.
Answer to Another Persuading a Lady to
Marriage, An.
Corneille's Pompey, *sels.*
EPITAPH. On her Son H. P. at St. Syth's
Church where her body also lies Interred.
Friendship, *sels.*
Friendship in Emblem, or the Seal, to my
Dearest Lucasia.
Friendship in Embleme, or the Seal. To my
dearest Lucasia.
Friendship's Mystery, To My Dearest
Lucasia.
L'Amitie: To Mrs. M. Awbrey.
Lucasia, Rosania and Orinda Parting at a
Fountain, July 1663.
Marry state affords but little Ease, A.
No blooming youth shall ever make me err.
On Rosania's Apostasy, and Lucasia's
Friendship.
On the 3. of September, 1651.
On the Death of My First and Dearest
Childe, Hector Philipps.
On the Death of the Queen of Bohemia.
On the Numerous Accesse of the English to
Waite upon the King in Holland.
On the Welsh Language.
Orinda to Lucasia.
Parting with Lucasia; a Song.
Sea-Voyage from Tenby to Bristol, A.
Song: "'Tis true our life is but a long dis-
ease."
To her royall highnesse the Dutchesse of
Yorke.
To Mr. Henry Lawes.
To Mrs M. A. at Parting.
To Mrs. M.A. Upon Absence.
To My Antenor, March 16, 1661/2.
To My Excellent Lucasia, On Our Friendship.
To My Lucasia, in Defence of Declared
Friendship.
To the Excellent Mrs A. O. upon her
receiving the name of Lucasia.
To the Queen of Inconstancy, Regina Collier,
in Antwerp.
Upon the graving of her Name upon a Tree
in Barnelmes Walks.
Wiston Vault.

Phillimore, John Swinnerton (1873–1926)
In a Meadow.

Phillips, Adora
Photograph & Story in *The Press*: The
Mother Whose Children Burned to Death.
Summer My Mother Fell in Love and
Wanted to Leave My Father, The.

Phillips, Carl (b. 1959)
Africa Says.
As From a Quiver of Arrows.
Mathematics of Breathing, A.
Passing.
Reach, The.
Sunday.
Toys.
You Are Here.

Phillips, David (1922–88)
Limerick: "Heart of O'Leary, S.J., The."

Phillips, Dennis (b. 1951)
Etudes, *sels.*
Exile, *sels.*
I Held the Vein, But Death.
Means, *sels.*
On Entries Emptiness.
Twenty Questions, *sels.*

Phillips, Harriet C. (1806–84)
We Bring No Glittering Treasures.

Phillips, J. A.
Sweethearts.

Phillips, John (1676–1709)
Splendid Shilling, The, *sels.*

Phillips, Pauline
Limerick: "I've combed out my beard and I've found."

Phillips, Robert (b. 1938)
Running on Empty.

Phillips, Stephen (1864–1915)
Apparition, The.

Phillpotts, Eden (b. 1862)
Badgers, The.
Houses, The.
Man's Days.
Miniature.

"Philo-Philippa" (*fl.* c.1667)
To the Excellent Orinda.

Philodemus (c.110–c.30 B.C.)
Antikrates knew the stars.
Apologies, dear Aphrodite. I.
Cypris who puts the sea to rest.
Death has torn ten years from us.
Double-horned, nocturnal Moon.
Epigrams, *sels.*
Hello. Hello. What's your name?
—"Hello there."—*Hello there yourself.*
Herakles' rebuttal was too much.
Here it's rose-time again, chick-peas in season.
"I know, fair lady, how to love the lover well."
I, who used to score five, even nine times.
In the middle of the night.
Naked warmth of you is still, The.
Oh feet, oh legs, oh thighs / that formed the deathrow.
Once I was in love. Who's been exempted?
Philainion is short and.
Roses are already here.
Seven plus thirty years are gone.
Sixty sun-decked years Charito has gotten to.
Small thing and moreover black is she, A.
Strumming and patter / the meaningful glances, The.
That silent publicizer of unheard-of news.
This *quidam* gives that *quidam* for *one* round.
This stone incorporates three gods:/ the head is unmistakably goat-horned Pan's.
To Piso, on Epicurus' Birthday.
Wax-contoured, in your face a Muse.
White violets again and lyre orchestras.
With Demo I fell in love, of Paphian origins.
With the night half over.
Xanthippe, singing at her lyre.
You cry, carry on in tones of pity.

Philpot, William (1823–89)
Maritae Suae.

Phipson, Thomas (1815–76)
Press, The.

Phổ Đức (Lê Phưố'c Đai) (b. 1939)
Buffalo Boy On a Field of Corpses, The.

Phocylides (*fl.* 6th cent. B.C.)
On the Problem of Choosing a Wife.

Phùng Khắc Khoan (1528–1613)
Advice to Students.

Phùng Quán (1932–1995)
What Mother Told Me Once.

Phylip, Siôn (d. 1620)
Seagull, The.

Phylip, William (d. 1670)
Farewell to Hendre Fechan.

P'i Jih-hsiu (c.833–883)
Impromptu on a Hangover.
Lament for the People of Lung.
Lament of a Woman Acorn-gatherer.
Mosquitoes.
On a Crab.
Reading.
Song of a Farmer.
Thoughts in Early Autumn: Thirty Rhymes Sent to Lu-wang.
Woodcutter's Ax, A.

Piatt, John James (1835–1917)
Farther.
Fires in Illinois.

My Shadow's Stature.
Taking the Night-Train.
To the Statue on the Capitol.

Piatt, Sarah Morgan Bryan (1836–1919)
Answering A Child.
Army of Occupation.
Doubt, A.
Giving Back the Flower.
Her Word of Reproach.
If I had made the world—ah me!
In A Queen's Domain.
In Her Prison.
Lesson in a Picture, A.
No Help.
Palace-Burner, The.
Pique at Parting, A.
Sad Spring-Song.
Stone For A Statue.
This World.

"Pibwob"
Limerick: "Van Gogh, feeling devil-may-care."

Picabia, Francis (1879–1953)
Eunuch Unique, *sels.*
Spermal Chimney.

Picasso, Pablo (1881–1973)
Bottle of Suze, A.
9.1.59: II.
9.1.59: VI.
Poems: "Hasten on your childhood to the hour when white in."

Piccolo, Lucio (1903–69)
Veneris Venefica Agrestis.

Pichamurti, N. (1900–78)
National Bird.

Picirantaiyar
Why My Hair Is Not Gray.

Pickard, Tom (b. 1946)
Dawn Raid on an Orchard.
Detente.
Gypsy Music in Krakow.
Rape.
Recipe: Pastime for the Unemployed.
Valentine.

Pickering [*or* Pikerying], John (b. 1567)
Horestes, *sels.*

Pickthall, Marjorie Lowry Christie (1883–1922)
Bridegroom of Cana, The.
Child's Song of Christmas, A.
Père Lalement.
Quiet.
Resurgam.
Two Souls.

Pien Kung (1476–1532)
At the Lake—Remembering My Dead Son, Yü.
First Day of Spring, The.
Inscribed on an Album Leaf Painted by Dr. Lin.
Mooring at K'ou-ch'üeh—Sent to Dr. Lin, *sels.*
New Year's Day—Following the Rhymes of Inspector Luan-chiang.
On Hearing That San-p'ing's Newly Brewed Chrysanthemum Wine Is Ready to Drink—Investigating with a Poem.
On the Sixteenth Day I Visit the Temple Again.
Paintings, *sels.*
Paintings of Various Subjects by Fang Jih-sheng: Baby Chicks Following Their Mother.
Song of the Boat-Pullers.
Song of the Transport Workers—Seeing Off Fang Wen-yü on His Way to His Post as Inspector of Transportation.
Song of the Woodcutter of the Sea.
Walking Outside the City Walls on the Day of the Cold Food Festival.

Pierce, Adams Franklin
In Fourteen Hundred and Ninety-.

Piercy, Marge (b. 1936)
Apron Strings.
Attack of the Squash People.
Barbie Doll.
Battle of Wills Disguised, A.

Book of Ruth and Naomi, The.
Cast Off, The.
Councils.
Crabs.
Cyclist, The.
Death of the small commune, The.
For the Young Who Want To.
Friend, The.
Gracious Goodness.
Hand Games.
Hello Up There.
Homage to Lucille, Dr. Lord-Heinstein.
Just Anger, A.
Kid on Her Way, A.
Landed Fish.
Last Scene in the First Act.
Laying Down the Tower, *sels.*
Learning Experience.
Letter to be Disguised as a Gas Bill.
Low Road, The.
Moon Is Always Female, The.
My Mother's Body, *sels.*
My Mother's Novel, *sels.*
My Rich Uncle, Whom I Only Met Three Times.
Noon of the Sunbather.
Peaceable Kingdom, The.
Postcard from the Garden.
Quiet Fog, The.
Raisin Pumpernickel.
Rape Poem.
Sabbath of Mutual Respect, The.
Sand Roads, *sels.*
Secretary Chant, The.
September Afternoon at Four O'Clock.
Six Underrated Pleasures, *sels.*
Something to Look Forward To.
Song of the Fucked Duck.
Spring Offensive of the Snail, The.
To Be of Use.
To Have without Holding.
Token woman gleams like a gold molar in a toothless mouth, The.
Unlearning to Not Speak.
Vegetable Love.
We Become New.
What's That Smell in the Kitchen?
When a friend dies.
Woman in the ordinary pudgy downcast girl, The.
Work of Artifice, A.
You Don't Understand Me.

Pierman, Carol J.
Eight Cows.
How We Learned about Friction.
Pilgrims.

Pierpont, John (1785–1866)
Airs of Palestine, *sels.*
Fourth of July, The.
Fugitive Slave's Apostrophe to the North Star, The.
Warren's Address at Bunker Hill [*or* to the American Soldiers].
Word from a Petitioner, *sels.*

Piers, Lady Sarah (d. 1720)
To My Much Esteemed Friend on Her Play Call'd Fatal-Friendship.
Urania: The Divine Muse. On the Death of John Dryden, Esq.

Piersanti, Umberto (b. 1941)
In Times and Places.
Second Image Sequence.
When Slow October Changes Color.

Pietri, Pedro Juan (b. 1940)
Old Buildings, The.

Pike, Cecily E.
Jack Frost.

Pilinszky, János (b. 1921)
Afterword.
Apocrypha.
Celebration of Nadir.
Desert of Love, The.
Extract from a Diary.
Fable: "Once upon a time / there was a lonely wolf."
Fragment from the Golden Age.
Frankfurt.

French Prisoner, The.
Hangman's Room, The.
Harbach 1944.
Monstrance.
On the Back of a Photograph.
On the Wall of a KZ-Lager.
One Fine Day.
Paraphrase.
Passion of Ravensbrück.
Scaffold in Winter.
Stone Wall and Celebration.
Three-Coloured Banner.
Three Poems, *sels.*

Pilkington, Laetitia (1712?–1750)
Dol and Roger.
Fair and Softly goes far or, The Wary
   Physician.
Memory, a Poem.
Song, A.
Song, A: "Lying is an occupation."
Song, A: "Strephon, your breach of faith and
   trust."
Sorrow.
Wish, By a Young Lady, The.

Pillen [*or* Pillin], William (1910–85)
Ascensions, The.

Pilling, Christopher (b. 1936)
Adoration of the Magi, The.

Pima Oral Tradition
Datura Hunting Song.

Pinar, Florencia del (b. c.1460)
Another Song of the Same Woman, to Some
   Partridges, Sent to Her Alive.

Pindar (c.518–c.438 B.C.)
Afterlife in Elysium.
Athens.
First Nemeæn Ode of Pindar, The, *sels.*
First Olympionique of Pindar. To Hiero of
   Syracuse, victorious in the Horse-race, The,
   sels.
For Asopichus of Orchomenus: Winner in the
   Stade Run.
Fourteenth Olympick Ode, The.
Olympian I, *sels.*
Pindar on the Eclipse of the Sun.
Progress of Poesy, The, *sels.*
Second Olympique Ode of Pindar, The, *sels.*

"Pindar, Peter" (John Wolcot) (1738–1819)
Apple Dumplings and a King, The.
Bozzy and Piozzi, *sels.*
Epigram: "Midas, they say, possessed the art
   of old."
Hymn to the Guillotine.
Instructions to a Celebrated Laureat, *sels.*
Ode: "That I have often been in love, deep
   love."
Ode to a Country Hoyden.
On a Stone Thrown at a Very Great Man,
   But Which Missed Him.
Resignation; an Ode to the Journeyman
   Shoemakers, *sels.*
Royal Tour, The.
Royal Tour, and Weymouth Amusements,
   The, *sels.*
Sorrows of Sunday; an Elegy, The, *sels.*
To a Fly, Taken out of a Bowl of Punch.

"Ping Hsin" (Hsieh Wang-ying) (b. 1900)
Deliverance.
Multitudinous Stars, *sels.*
Orphan beat of my heart, The.
Spring Waters, *sels.*
Stars, The, *sels.*
Three Poems, *sels.*

Ping, Wang (b. 1957)
Of Flesh and Spirit.
Song of Calling Souls.

Pinkerton, Helen
On Dorothea Lange's Photograph "Migrant
   Mother" (1936).
On Vermeer's "Young Woman with a Water
   Jug" (1658) in the Metropolitan Museum.

Pinkney, Edward Coote [*or* Coate] (1802–28)
Health, A.
Italy.
On Parting.
Serenade: "Look out upon the stars, my
   love."

To ———: "'Twas eve; the broadly shining
   sun."
Voyager's Song, The.
Widow's Song, The.

Pinsky, Robert (b. 1940)
Dante's Inferno, Canto XXXIV (The Final
   Canto).
Doctor Frolic.
Dying.
Essay on Psychiatrists, *sels.*
Explanation of America, An, *sels.*
Figured Wheel, The.
First Early Mornings Together.
Ginza Samba.
Hearts, The.
Living, The.
Long Branch Song, A.
Memorial.
New Saddhus, The.
Physical Comparison with Professors and
   Others.
Poem about People.
Questions, The.
Ralegh's Prizes.
Shirt.
Song of Reasons.
Street, The.
Want Bone, The.
Woman, A.

Pinto, Jasmine
I had a pet lizard called Albert.

Pinto, Vivian de Sola (1895–1969)
At Piccadilly Circus.

Pinytos (*fl.* A.D. 1st cent.)
Epitaph: Sappho.

Piombino, Nick (b. 1942)
Frozen Witness, The.
My Lady Carries Stones.
Pyramids, The.
Time Travel.

Piontek, Heinz
In the Woods.

Piper, Linda (b. 1949)
Missionaries in the Jungle.
Sweet Ethel.

Piron, Alexis (1689–1773)
Here lies Piron—a man of no position.

Pise, Constantine (1801–66)
Let the Deep Organ Swell.

Pitcher, Oliver (b. 1923)
Pale Blue Casket, The.
Salute.

Pitchford, Kenneth (b. 1930)
Lobotomy.
104 Boulevard Saint-Germain.
Queen, The.
Surgery.

Pitiroirangi, Nga. See Habib, Rowley

Pitkin, Anne
Blue Morning Glory.

Pitman, Hassall
Limerick: "Cynical sage with a kink, A."

Pitt, Christopher (1699–1748)
Fable of the Young Man and His Cat, The.
On the Masquerades.
To Mr. Pope, on His Translation of Homer's
   Iliad, *sels.*

Pitt-Kethley, Fiona
God made the sex-shop keeper.
Limerick: "Platinum blonde, Goldilocks, A."
Limerick: "There was a young boy, Jack
   Horner."
Limerick: "Two playwrights called Beaumont
   and Fletcher."

Pitter, Ruth (b. 1897)
But for Lust.
Coffin-Worm, The.
Diehards, The.
Digdog.
Dun-Colour [*or* Dun-Color].
Eternal Image, The.
Hen under Bay-Tree, The.
Irish Patriarch, The.
Lost Tribe, The.
Maternal Love Triumphant or Song of the
   Virtuous Female Spider.

Military Harpist, The.
Morning Glory.
1938.
Old, childless, husbandless, bereaved, alone.
Old Nelly's Birthday.
Old Woman Speaks of the Moon, An.
Other People's Glasshouses.
Portrait of a Gentleman.
Sparrow's Skull, The.
Swan Bathing, The.
Task, The.
Time's fool, but not heaven's: yet hope not
   for any return.
Unicorn, The.
Viper, The.
Yorkshire Wife's Saga.

Pix, Mary (1666–c.1709)
Deceiver Deceived, The, *sels.*
Innocent Mistress, The, *sels.*
Queen Catherine, *sels.*
Spanish Wives, The, *sels.*
To Mrs. Manley, upon Her Tragedy Call'd
   The Royal Mischief.

**Pixley, J. H.. See Hunt, Josie R. and J. H.
Pixley**

Pixner, Stef (b. 1945)
Day in the Life, A.

Pizzarelli, Alan
Bearded lady, The.
Bending back.
Bright awning is cranked, A.
Brim-shadow, The.
BuzzZ.
Driving.
Drop of ocean.
Fat lady, The.
Flinging the frisbee.
Fwap!
Girl / loosens her bra, The.
Just before dawn.
Just before the storm.
Late in the evening.
Meteor.
Moving van zooms, A.
On the merry-go-round.
Opening the mailbox.
Piece of buttered popcorn, A.
Scarecrow.
Shade springs open, The.
Snow falls from trees.
Spark, A.
Stranger passing, A.
Sun brightens.
Tattoo'd man, The.
Tiny fish.
Tonite.
Under the boardwalk.
Waterbug running by the frogulp.
Wiping the chrome.
With no money.

"Placido" (1809–44)
Farewell to My Mother.
Prayer to God.

Plaiwon
Limerick: "I once knew a spinster of
   Staines."

Planché, James Robinson (1796–1880)
Ching a Ring.
Love, You've Been a Villain.
Self-Evident.

Plantier, Thérèse (b. 1911)
Doors.
Overdue Balance Sheet.

Plarr, Victor Gustave (1863–1929)
Epitaphium Citharistriae.
Of Change of Opinions.
Shadows.

Plath, Sylvia (1932–63)
All the Dead Dears.
Amnesiac.
Among the Narcissi.
Appearance, An.
Applicant, The.
Ariel.
Arrival of the Bee Box, The.
Balloons.

Barren Woman.
Bed Book, The, *sels.*
Bee Meeting, The.
Black Rook in Rainy Weather.
Blackberrying.
Candles.
Child.
Colossus, The.
Couriers, The.
Crossing the Water.
Cut.
Daddy.
Death and Co.
Death of Myth-making, The.
Disquieting Muses, The.
Edge.
Elm.
Event.
Fever 103°.
Flute Notes from a Reedy Pond.
Frog Autumn.
Getting There.
Green Rock, Winthrop Bay.
Gulliver.
Hanging Man, The.
I Am Vertical.
Kindness glides about my house.
Lady Lazarus.
Last Words.
Life, A.
Love Letter.
Magi.
Manor Garden, The.
Mary's Song.
Medallion.
Medusa.
Metamorphosis.
Metaphors.
Mirror.
Moon and the Yew Tree, The.
Morning Song.
Mushrooms.
Mussel Hunter at Rock Harbor.
Mystic.
New Year on Dartmoor.
Nick and the Candlestick.
Night Dances, The.
Night Shift.
Night Walk.
Paralytic.
Parliament Hill Fields.
Pheasant.
Poems, Potatoes.
Point Shirley.
Poppies in July.
Poppies in October.
Rival, The.
Sheep in Fog.
Sleep in the Mojave Desert.
Snakecharmer.
Spinster.
Stars over the Dordogne.
Stings.
Stones, The.
Swarm, The.
Tulips are too excitable, it is winter here,
  The.
Two Campers in Cloud Country.
Two Views of a Cadaver Room.
Watercolor of Grantchester Meadows.
Winter Trees.
Wintering.
Winter's Tale, A.
Words.
Wreath for a Bridal.
You're.
Zoo Keeper's Wife.

Plato (*fl.* **492–347 B.C.**)
Alexis.
Apple, The.
Aristophanes.
Aster.
Dion.
Farewell: "Far from the deep roar of the
  Aegean main."
Kiss, The.
Kissing Helena, together.

Lais to Aphrodite. *From* Variations of Greek
  Themes.
Love Sleeping.
Lover to His Lady, The.
On a Seal.
On Alexis.
On Archaeanassa.
Pan Piping.
Pindar.
Sappho.
Sit down under the high crown.
Sokrates to Agathon.
Sokrates to his Lover.
Sokrates to Xanthippé.
To Stella.
Two Poems on the Eretrians Taken Prisoner
  by the Persians, *sels.*

Plato, Ann (b. **1920**)
Advice to Young Ladies.
Natives of America, The.
Reflections, Written on Visiting the Grave of
  a Venerated Friend.
To the First of August.

Plato the Younger (*fl.* **1st–2d cent.**)
Life brings everything, time's length can
  shift.
Satyr by Diodorus, A.

**"Platonov, Andrey" (Andrei Platonovich
  Klimentov) (1899–1951)**
Wanderer, The.

Platt, Anna M.
Crocuses.

Plautus Titus Maccius (c.250–184 B.C.)
English Traveller, The, *sels.*
Newe enterlued for chyldren to playe named
  Jacke Jugeler, A, *sels.*

Plenty-hawk
If all of me is still there.

Plisetsky [*or* **Plisetskii**]**, German Borisovich** (b.
  1931)
Papers have been sold. In them it's all made
  clear, The.
Pipe, The.

Plomer, William (**1903–73**)
Atheling Grange; or, The Apotheosis of Lotte
  Nussbaum.
Azure, or green, or purple when the sun.
Bamboo.
Blind Samson.
Devil-Dancers, The.
Europa.
Fall of Rock, A.
Father and Son: 1939.
French Lisette: A Ballad of Maida Vale.
Headline History.
In the Snake Park.
Levantine, A.
Limerick: "There was an old person of
  Persia."
Mews Flat Mona.
Murder on the Downs, The.
Namaqualand after Rain.
Playboy of the Demi-World[: 1938], The.
Prisoner, The.
Right-of-Way: 1865, A.
Scorpion, The.
Seven Rainy Months.
To the Moon and Back.
Tugela River.
Ula Masondo's Dream.
Walk in Würzburg, A.
White Gloves.
Widow's Plot; or, She Got What Was
  Coming to Her, The.

Plowman, Max
Dead Soldiers, The.

Plumly, Stanley (b. **1939**)
After Grief.
After Whistler.
Birthday.
Cedar Waxwing on Scarlet Firethorn.
Complaint Against the Arsonist.
For Esther.
Fungo.
Giraffe.
Hedgerows.

Heron.
Infidelity.
Iron Lung, The.
My Mother's Feet.
Out-of-the-Body Travel.
Peppergrass.
Reading with the Poets.
Toward Umbria.
Wildflower.
Will Work for Food.

Plumpp, Sterling (b. **1940**)
Another mule kicking.
Beyond the Nigger.
Clinton, *sels.*
Half Black, Half Blacker.
I Told Jesus.
Living Truth, The.
Poems are not places.
Poet.
Remembered.
Turf Song.
When the Spirit Spray-Paints the Sky.

Plumptre, Annabella (**1761–1838**))
Ode to Moderation, *sels.*

Plumptre, James (**1770–1832**)
Prologue to "The Lakers; a Comic Opera,"
  sels.

Plunkett, Joseph Mary (**1887–1916**)
I Saw the Sun at Midnight, Rising Red.
I See His Blood upon the Rose.
Saint Augustine.
Spark, The.
Stars Sang in God's Garden, The.

Plutzik, Hyam (**1912–62**)
And in the 51st Year of That Century, While
  My Brother Cried in the Trench, While
  My Enemy Glared from the Cave.
Dream about Our Master, William
  Shakespeare, A.
I Am Disquieted When I See Many Hills.
Jim Desterland.
King of Ai, The.
Mythos of Samuel Huntsman, The.
Of Objects Considered as Fortresses in a
  Baleful Place.
Premonition, The.

Plymell, Charles
San Fransisco Ward.

Po Chü-i (**772–842**)
Aboard a Boat, Reading Yüan Chen's Poems.
After Collecting the Autumn Taxes.
After Eating.
After Getting Drunk, Becoming Sober in the
  Night.
After Passing the Examination.
Alarm at First Entering the Yang-tze Gorges.
Arriving at Hsün-yang.
At the End of Spring.
Bamboo by Li Ch'e Yun's Window, The.
Beginning of Summer, The.
Being on Duty all Night in the Palace and
  Dreaming of the Hsien-yu Temple.
Being Visited by a Friend During Illness.
Better Come Drink Wine with Me, *sels.*
Bitter Cold, Living in the Village.
Buying Flowers.
Children.
Chrysanthemums in the Eastern Garden, The.
Chu Ch'ên Village.
Chuang Tzu, The Monist.
Climbing the Ling-Ying Terrace and Looking
  North.
Climbing the Terrace of Kuan-yin and
  Looking at the City of Ch'ang-an.
Cranes, The.
Crow Cries at Night, The.
Dream of Mountaineering, A.
Dreaming of Yüan Chên.
Dreaming that I Went with Li and Yü to
  Visit Yüan Chên.
Drunk, Facing Crimson Leaves.
Early Levée, An.
Ease.
Eating Bamboo-Shoots.
Escorting Candidates to the Examination
  Hall.

Evening View at River Pavilion, Inviting
Guest.
Everlasting Sorrow, The, *sels.*
Feelings Wakened by a Mirror.
Fifteenth Volume, The.
Fishing in the Wei River.
Five-string[1], The.
Flower, A.
Flower Market, The.
Getting Up Early on a Spring Morning.
Going Alone to Spend a Night at the Hsien-
Yu Temple.
Going to the Mountains with a Little Dancing
Girl, Aged Fifteen.
Golden Bells.
Good-bye to the People of Hangchow.
Grand Houses at Lo-yang, The.
Grass on Ancient Plain, a Song of Farewell.
Half in the Family, Half Out.
Half-recluse, The.
Harp, The.
Hat Given to the Poet by Li Chien, The.
Having Climbed to the Topmost Peak of the
Incense-Burner Mountain.
Hearing the Early Oriole.
Hermit and Politician.
Idle Droning.
Illness.
Illness and idleness give me much leisure.
Immeasurable pain!
In Early Summer Lodging in a Temple to
Enjoy the Moonlight.
Invitation to Hsiao Ch'u-shih.
Kept Waiting in the Boat at Chiu-K'ou Ten
Days by an Adverse Wind.
Lao Tzŭ.
Last Poem.
Lazy Man's Song.
Letter, The.
Liao-ling[, sheer patterned silk—what is it
like?].
Light Furs, Fat Horses.
Lodging with the Old Man of the Stream.
Lonely Night in Early Autumn.
Looking in the Lake.
Losing a Slave-Girl.
Lotus-gatherer's Song.
Mad Poem Addressed to My Nephews and
Nieces, A.
Madly Singing in the Mountains.
My servant wakes me: 'Master, it is broad
day.'
New Thatched Hall, A.
New thatched hall, five spans by three, A.
Night Snow.
Old Age.
Old charcoal seller, An.
Old Lute, The.
Old Man of Hsin-feng witih the Broken Arm,
The.
Old Man with the Broken Arm, The.
On a Box Containing his Own Works.
On a Moonlit Night, Sent to my Brothers and
Sisters.
On an Ancient Tomb East of the Village.
On Being Removed from Hsün-yang and Sent
to Chung-chou.
On Being Sixty.
On Board Ship: Reading Yüan Chên's
Poems.
On Hearing Someone Sing a Poem by Yüan
Chên.
On his Baldness.
On the Way to Hangchow: Anchored on the
River at Night.
Painting Bamboo, a Song.
Parrot.
Parting from the Winter Stove.
Passing T'ien-mên Street in Ch'ang-an and
Seeing a Distant View of Chung-nan
Mountains.
Philosophers: Lao-Tzu, The.
Pine Sounds.
Pine-trees in the Courtyard, The.
Planting Bamboos.
Planting Flowers on the Eastern
Embankment.

Poem on the Wall, The.
Poems in Depression, at Wei Village.
Pouring Out My Feelings after Parting from
Yüan Chen.
Prisoner, The.
Pruning Trees.
P'u—Hua Fei Hua.
Question Addressed to Liu Shih-chiu, A.
Quiet House in Ch'ang-lo Ward, A.
Rain.
Reading the Collected Works of Li Po and
Tu Fu: A Colophon.
Realizing the Futility of Life.
Red Cockatoo, The.
Red embroidered carpet.
Rejoicing at the Arrival of Chi'en Hsiung.
Releasing a Migrant 'Yen' (Wild Goose).
Remembering Golden Bells.
Resignation.
Rising Late, and Playing with A-ts'ui, Aged
Two.
Seeing Hsia Chan off by River.
Sentimental Poem.
Separation.
Sick Leave.
Silver Spoon, The.
Since I lay ill, how long has passed?
Sitting at Night.
Sleeping on Horseback.
Song of the Lute.
Song of the pines.
Song of the Rear Palace.
Spring River, The.
Starting Early from the Ch'u-ch'êng Inn.
Stopping the Night at Jung-yang.
Taoism and Buddhism.
Temple, The.
Temple of Bequeathed Love, The.
Thinking of the Past.
To a Portrait Painter who Desired Him to Sit.
To a Talkative Guest.
To his Brother Hsing-chien.
To his Brother Hsing-chien, Who was
Serving in Tung-ch'uan.
To Li Chien.
To Liu Yü-hsi.
To the Distant One.
Too Brilliant.
Traveler's Moon, The.
Tune: "Flower unlike Flower."
Tune: "Ripples Sifting Sand," *sels.*
Village Night.
Visiting the Hermit Cheng.
Visiting the Hsi-lin Temple.
Watching the Reapers.
Watching the Wheat-Reapers.
Winter Night.
Writing Again on the Same Theme.
Written when Governor of Soochow.

Pocock, Guy Noel (1880–1955)
Years ahead, years ahead.

Poe, Edgar Allan (1809–49)
Al Aaraaf, *sels.*
"Alone."
Annabel Lee.
Bells, The.
City in the Sea, The.
Coliseum, The.
Conqueror Worm, The.
Dream-Land [*or* Dreamland].
Dream within A Dream, A, *sels.*
Dreams, *sels.*
Eldorado.
Enigma, An.
Fairyland [*or* Fairy-Land].
For Annie.
Happiest day—the happiest hour, The.
Haunted Palace, The.
Israfel.
Lake: To———, The.
Lenore.
Preface: "Romance, who loves to nod and
sing."
Raven, The.
Silence.
Sleeper, The.
Sonnet—To Science.

Stanzas.
Stanzas: "How often we forget all time, when
lone."
To F——.
To Helen ("Helen, thy beauty is to me.")
To My Mother.
To One in Paradise.
Ulalume [*or* Ulalume—a Ballad].
Valentine, A.
Valley of Unrest, The.

Pointon, Priscilla (c.1740–1801)
Address to a Bachelor on a Delicate
Occasion.
Letter to a Sister, Giving an Account of the
Author's Wedding-Day, *sels.*
To the Critics, *sels.*

Polglaze, Pascoe
There's a cut-price whore.

Polite, Frank (b. 1934)
Imitations Based on the American.
Mine.

Politian. *See* **Poliziano, Angelo**

Polito, Robert
Animal Mimicry.

**Poliziano, Angelo [*or* Andrea] (Politian) (1454–
94)**
She Finds Herself in a Garden.
Three Ballate, *sels.*
Welcome to May.

Polkowski, Jan (b. 1953)
I Don't Know That Man.
Noli Me Tangere.
World is only air / shining, granular,
transparent things, The.

Pollak, Felix (b. 1909)
Dream, The.

Pollard, Velma (b. 1937)
Belize Suite.
Su Su.

Pollitt, Katha (b. 1949)
Of the Scythians.
Onion.
Small Comfort.
Turning Thirty.
Two Fish.
Visitors.
Woman Asleep on a Banana Leaf.

Polwhele, Richard (1760–1838)
Influence of Local Attachment, The, *sels.*
Unsex'd Females, The, *sels.*

Pomeroy, Ralph (b. 1926)
Between Here and Illinois.
High Wind at the Battery.
Snow.
Tardy Epithalamium for E. and N, A.
To Janet.

Pomfret, John (1767–1802)
Choice, The.
No Barren Leaves.

Pommy-Vega, Janine (b. 1942)
Ah certainty of love in the hand.
Here before the sunrise blue and in this
solitude.

Pompeius (d. A.D. 33)
Even if I am only more dust.
Lais, who was a lovely flower.

**Pompili [*or* Pompilj], Vittoria Aganoor (1855–
1910)**
Fear.
Finally.

Ponciano, Angelo de
Empties Coming Back.

Pond, Lily
Ovulation.

Ponge, Francis (1899–1988)
Delights of the Door, The.
Frog, The.
Oyster, the size of an average pebble, is of
more rugged appearance, The.
Prairie, The.
Silent World Is Our Only Homeland, The.
Sun as a Spinning Top (I), The.
Water of Tears, The.

Ponika, Kohine Whakarua (b. 1920)
Call Together.
Song of Yearning, A.

Ponmutiyar
Mother's List of Duties, A.
Young Warrior, A.
Ponsot, Marie (b. 1922)
Among Women.
Analogue.
Communion of Saints: The Poor Bastard
under the Bridge.
La Une, A.
"Love is not Love."
Matins and Lauds.
Multipara: Gravida 5.
Nursing: Mother, *sels.*
Old Mama Saturday.
Possession.
Residual Paralysis.
Rockefeller the Center.
Subject.
To the Age's Insanities.
"Pontiff"
Rime of the Gentle Pacifist, The.
Poole, Evelyn
Last Prayer.
Poole, John F. (1786?–1872)
Song, *Hamlet.*
Popa, Vasco [or Vasko] (b. 1922)
Admirers of the Little Box, The.
Benefactors of the Little Box, The.
Besieged Serenity, *sels.*
Blackbird's Field, The, *sels.*
Burning Shewolf.
Craftsmen of the Little Box, The.
Enemies of the Little Box, The.
Eyes of a Wolf.
Far Within Us, *sels.*
Games, *sels.*
Heaven's Ring.
In the Ashtray.
Judges of the Little Box, The.
Last News about the Little Box.
Little box grows [gets] her first teeth, The.
Other World, The.
Owners of the Little Box, The.
Prisoners of the Little Box, The.
Quartz Pebble, The, *sels.*
Raw Flesh, *sels.*
St Sava's Spring, *sels.*
Story of a Story, The.
Tenants of the Little Box, The.
Victims of the Little Box, The.
Yawn of Yawns, The, *sels.*
Pope, Alexander (1688–1744)
Alley; an Imitation of Spenser, The.
Another [Epigram].
Argus.
Challenge: A Court Ballad, The.
Cibber! write all thy verses upon glasses.
Dunciad, The, *sels.*
Dying Christian to His Soul, The.
Elegy to the Memory of an Unfortunate
Lady, *sels.*
Eloisa to Abelard, *sels.*
Epigram Engraved on the Collar of a Dog
Given [or Which I Gave] to His Royal
Highness.
Epigram from the French: "Sir, I admit your
general [or gen'ral] Rule."
Epigram in a Maid of Honour's Prayer-Book.
Epigram on One Who Made Long Epitaphs.
Epigram: "When other Ladies to the Shades
go down."
Epilogue to the Satires, in Two Dialogues,
sels.
Epistle I, to Sir Richard Temple, Lord
Cobham, *sels.*
Epistle III, to Allen Lord Bathurst, *sels.*
Epistle IV, to Richard Boyle, Earl of
Burlington, *sels.*
Epistle [II,] to a Lady[: Of the Characters of
Women].
Epistle to Dr. Arbuthnot, *sels.*
Epistle to Lord Burlington, *sels.*
Epistle to Miss [or Miss Teresa] Blount, on
Her Leaving the Town after the
Coronation.
Epistle to Sir Richard Temple, *sels.*
Epitaph for One Who Would Not Be Buried

in Westminster Abbey ("Heroes, and
Kings! your distance keep.")
Epitaph on Himself.
Epitaph on James Moore Smythe.
Epitaph: "See here, nice Death, to please his
palate."
Essay on Criticism, An.
Essay on Man, An, *sels.*
Farewell to London in the Year 1715, A.
First Epistle of the First Book of Horace
Imitated, The, *sels.*
First Epistle of the Second Book of Horace
Imitated, The, *sels.*
First Satire of the Second Book of Horace
[Imitated], The, *sels.*
Garden, The.
Gulliver in Lilliput.
Happy Life of a Country Parson, The.
Hymn Written in Windsor Forest, A.
Imitation of Chaucer.
Impromptu.
Inscriptio.
Intended for Sir Isaac Newton.
Lord Coningsby's Epitaph.
Messiah: A Sacred Eclogue in Imitation of
Virgil's Pollio.
Ode on Solitude.
Odyssey, *sels.*
On a Certain Lady at Court.
On a Lady Who P-ssed [or P———st] at the
Tragedy of Cato.
On Authors and Booksellers [or Publishers].
On Dennis.
On Dullness.
On J. M. S. Gent.
On Poets.
On the Benefactions in the Late Frost.
On the Candidates for the Laurel.
On the Erection of Shakespeare's Statue in
Westminster Abbey.
Quoth Cibber to Pope, tho' in verse you
foreclose.
Rape of the Lock[, an Heroi-Comical Poem],
The, *sels.*
Second Epistle of the Second Book of
Horace Imitated, The, *sels.*
Second Satire of the Second Book of Horace
Imitated, The, *sels.*
Three Epitaphs on John Hewet and Sarah
Drew, *sels.*
To Mr. Gay, Who Wrote Him a
Congratulatory Letter on the Finishing His
House.
To Mrs. M. B. on Her Birth-Day.
To Mr. C., St. James's Place, London,
October 22nd.
Two or Three; a Recipe [or Receipt] to Make
a Cuckold.
Universal Prayer [Deo Opt. Max.], The.
Upon a Girl of Seven Years Old.
Windsor-Forest [or Windsor Forest], *sels.*
See also **Gay, John** *and* **Alexander Pope.**
Pope, Alexander (1688–1744) *and* **Thomas
Parnell**
On Riding to See Dean Swift in the Mist of
the Morning.
Pope, J. R. (1909–91)
Word of Encouragement, A.
Pope, Jessie (Mrs. Babington Lenton) (d. 1941)
Profiteers.
Pope, Walter (c.1636–1714)
Old Man's Wish, The.
Popham, Hugh (b. 1920)
Usual exquisite boredom of patrols, The.
**Poplavsky [or Poplavskii], Boris Iulianovich
(1903–35)**
Another Planet.
Popov, Aleksandr Iakovlevich. *See* **"Yashin,
Aleksandr Iakovlevich"**
Poquelin, Jean Baptiste. *See* **Molière**
Pordage, Samuel (1633–c.1691)
To Lucia Playing on Her Lute, Another.
Porete, Marguerite
Beloved, what do you want of me?
Porson, Richard (1759–1808)
Bathos, The.

Epigram on an Academic Visit to the
Continent.
Here lies a Doctor of Divinity.
Mutual Congratulations of the Poets Anna
Seward and Hayley, The.
Note on the Latin Gerunds, A.
Porson on German Scholarship.
Porta, Antonio (b. 1935)
Age of unhappiness has arrived, or is it, The.
I'm walking out on Rome.
Portal, Magda (b. 1901)
Film Vermouth: Six o'Clock Show.
Shores of anguish.
Woman with broad, rough hands.
Porter, Adrian
Perfect Child, The.
Porter, Anne (b. 1911)
Another Sarah.
Oaks and Squirrels.
Porter, Cole (1891–1964)
Always True to You in My Fashion, *sels.*
Anything Goes.
Brush Up Your Shakespeare.
Friendship.
I'm a Gigolo.
Let's Do It, Let's Fall in Love.
My Heart Belongs to Daddy.
Night and Day.
Nobody's Chasing Me.
Old-Fashioned Garden, An.
Well, Did You Evah?
You're the Top, *sels.*
Porter, Dorothy (b. 1954)
Lollies Noir.
P. M. T.
Porter, Fairfield (1907–75)
Island in the Evening, The.
Porter, Hal (b. 1917)
Four Winds.
Hobart Town, Van Diemen's Land (11th
June, 1837).
In a Bed-Sitter.
Porter, Mrs. David
Thou Has Wounded the Spirit That Loved
Thee.
Porter, Peter (b. 1929)
Affair of the Heart.
And No Help Came.
Angel in Blythburgh Church, An.
Annotations of Auschwitz.
Australian Garden, An.
Consumer's Report, A.
Cost of Seriousness, The.
Don't Be Afraid, I Am With You.
Easiest Room in Hell, The.
Exequy, An.
Gertrude Stein at Snails Bay.
Happening at Sordid Creek.
'In the New World Happiness is Allowed.'
Japanese Jokes.
King of the Cats is Dead, The.
Last of England, The.
May, 1945.
Metamorphosis.
Mort aux Chats.
Nine Points of the Law, *sels.*
Non Piangere, Liù.
On First Looking into Chapman's Hesiod.
On This Day I Complete My Fortieth Year.
Sanitized Sonnets, The, *sels.*
Sex and the Over Forties.
Soliloquy at Potsdam.
St Cecilia's Day Epigram.
Sydney Cove, 1788.
Talking to You Afterwards.
What I Have Written I Have Written.
World of Simon Raven, The.
Your Attention Please.
Porumbacu, Veronica (1921–77)
Anesthesia.
Farther Away.
From what once was, from the crazy nights.
Of Autumn.
Pupil, The.
Poseidippus (fl. c.270 B.C.)
Don't tell lies with your tears.

Doricha.
Doricha, your soft bones are.
Here in this rough trench lies.
If Pythias has a customer.
If someone's with her.
On sea and land alike.
Three-year-old Archianax.
World's a bubble, and the life of man, The.
You who visit in turn.

Posey, Alexander L.
Autumn.
July.
Midsummer.
Nightfall.
Song of the Oktahutchee.

Posner, David (1938–85)
Birds, The.
Campus, The.
On a Recent Protest against Social
   Conditions.

Poster, Carol (b. 1956)
Robert Bly Finds Something in New Jersey.
Synthesizing Several Abstruse Concepts with
   an Experience.

Potamkin, Harry Alan (1900–1933)
Cargoes of the Radanites.

Potos, Andrea
Depending on the Light.

Potter, Beatrix (1866–1943)
Old Woman, The.

Potts, Paul (b. 1911)
For My Father.
Muse to an Unknown Poet, The.

Poulsson, Emilie (1853–1939)
Judging by Appearances.

Pound, Ezra (1885–1972)
Alba ("As cool as the pale wet leaves.")
Alchemist, The.
Ancient Music.
Ancient Wisdom, Rather Cosmic.
And the days are not full enough.
And Thus in Nineveh.
April.
Ballad for Gloom.
Ballad of the Goodly Fere.
Ballatetta.
Bathtub [or Bath Tub], The.
Beautiful Toilet, The.
Cantico del Sole.
Canto 32.
Canto 49.
Canto 51.
Canto XLV.
Cantos, sels.
Cino.
Coda.
Coming of War, The; Actaeon.
Commission.
Contemporania, sels.
Dance Figure.
De Aegypto.
Doria.
Epilogue: "O chansons foregoing."
Faun, The.
Fine fish to net.
For an officer / in the old Capital, fox fur.
For deep deer-copse beneath Mount Han.
Fragmenti.
Full be the year, abundant be the grain.
Garden, The.
Girl, A.
Greek Epigram.
Green robe, green robe, lined with yellow.
Heaven conserve thy course in quietness.
"Hid! Hid!" the fish-hawk saith.
Homage to Sextus Propertius, sels.
Hugh Selwyn Mauberley. (Life and Contacts),
   sels.
I dreamt that I was God Himself.
Immorality, An.
In A Station of the Metro.
Ité.
Know then: / Toward summer when the sun
   is in Hyades.
Lake Isle, The.
Langue d'Oc, sels.

L'Art, 1910.
Les Millwin.
L'Homme Moyen Sensuel, sels.
Lies a dead deer on younder plain.
Liu Ch'e.
Locusts a-wing, multiply.
Lustra, sels.
Meditatio.
Monumentum Aere, Etc.
Mr. Housman's Message.
Na Audiart.
Near 'Perigord.
O Atthis.
Pact, A.
Papyrus.
Phyllidula.
Pick a fern, pick a fern, ferns are high.
Pine boat a-shift.
Pisan Canto 124, sels.
Portrait d'une Femme.
Profiteer, The.
Provincia Deserta.
Reflection and Advice.
Return, The.
River-Merchant's Wife: A Letter, The.
Salutation.
Salutation the Second.
Seafarer, The.
Sestina: Altaforte.
Silet.
Soirée.
Song of the Bowmen of Shu.
South-Folk in Cold Country.
Study in Aesthetics, The.
Tame Cat.
Tea Shop, The.
Temperaments, The.
To Kalon.
To Whistler, American.
Toujours la Politesse.
Translator to Translated.
Tree, The.
Ts'ai Chi'h.
Villanelle: The Psychological Hour.
Virginal, A.
Wide, ho?

Pound, Ezra (1885–1972) *and* **Noel Stock**
Mœurs Contemporaines, sels.
Poems of Alfred Venison, the Poet of
   Titchfield Street, The, sels.

Powell, Anthony (b. 1905)
Caledonia.

Powell, Charles
Jack and Jill.

Powell, Craig (b. 1941)
Nativity.

Powell, Jim (b. 1951)
It was fever that made the world.

Powell, Sidney Walter (1878–1952)
Gallipoli, sels.

Power, Katherine Alice (b. 1949)
Sestina for Jaime.

Powers, Horatio Nelson (1826–90)
New Year, The.

Powys, John Cowper (1872–1963)
In a Hotel Writing-Room.
Nunc Dimittis.
Ridge, The, sels.

Pozdnyayev [or Pozdniaev], Mikhail (b. 1953)
Remembrance of Five Loaves.

**Pozhenyan [or Pozhenian], Grigory [or
Grigorii] Mikhailovich (b. 1922)**
Cities.
Clear fall afternoon beckons, A.
Poet and Tsar.

Pozzi, Antonia (1912–38)
To Trust.

Prabhu, Allama
For the Lord of Caves.

Praed, Winthrop Mackworth (1802–39)
Arrivals at a Watering-Place.
Beauty and Her Visitors.
Chancery Morals.
Chaunt of the Brazen Head, The, sels.
Chaunts of the Brazen Head, The.

County Ball, The, sels.
Every-Day Characters, sels.
Goodnight to the Season!
Letter of Advice, A.
Lines Written for a Blank Page of "The
   Keepsake."
Palinodia.
Royal Education.
School and Schoolfellows.
Stanzas to the Speaker Asleep.
Talented Man, The.
To Helen.
To Helen, with Crabbe's Poems: a Birthday
   Present.
To ———: "We met but in one giddy
   dance."

Prager, Marie-Francoise (b. 1925?)
I'll act out a weird dream.

Prassinos, Gisèle (b. 1920)
Conversation, A.
Hair Tonic.

Pratt, Claire
Fog has settled, The.

Pratt, Edwin John (1882–1964)
Behind the Log, sels.
Brébeuf and His Brethren, sels.
Cachalot, The, sels.
Come Not the Seasons Here.
From Stone to Steel ("From stone to bronze,
   from bronze to steel.")
Prize Cat, The.
Ritual, The.
Shark, The.
Silences.
Titanic, The, sels.
Towards the Last Spike, sels.
Truant, The.

Pratt, John Clark
Words and Thoughts.

Pratt, Marjory Bates
Not a breath of air.

Pratt, Minnie Bruce (b. 1946)
All the Women Caught in Flaring Light.
Child Taken from the Mother, The.
Laughing Place, The.
Motionless on the Dark Side of the Light.
Place Lost and Gone, the Place Found, The.
Poem for my Sons.
Waulking Song: Two.
Waving Hand, A.

Pratt, Samuel Jackson (1749–1814)
Cottage Pictures, sels.

Praxilla (fl. c.450 B.C.)
Adonis, Dying.
Lovely girl, you look at me through the
   window.
Most beautiful of things I leave is sunlight.
Peeking in through.
Watch out, my dear.
You gaze at me teasingly through the
   window.

Prayton, Michael
Muses Elizium, The, sels.

Preil, Gabriel (b. 1910)
How to Read the First Line.
Lines on the Rambam.
Memory of Autumns at Springtime.
Yellow sunset splashes in the window, A.

Prelutsky, Jack (b. 1940)
Bring on the clowns!
First Thanksgiving, The.
Ghoul, The.
Goblin, The.
Harvey Always Wins.
Homework! Oh, homework!
It's Halloween.
Man on the Flying Trapeze, The.
Mother Goblin's Lullaby.
Pancake Collector, The.
Skeleton Parade.
Spaghetti Nut, The.
Visitor, The.

Prentiss, Elizabeth Payson (1818–78)
Kitty.
More Love to Thee, O Christ.

Prescod, Marsha
Vicious Circle.
Women Are Different.
Prescot, Kenrick (1702–79)
Balsham Bells.
Press, J. E.
Limerick: "Lord, since it's hard to explain."
Press, John (b. 1920)
African Christmas.
Farewell: "Smell of death was in the air, The."
Womanisers.
Pressoir, Charles (b. 1910)
Black Island.
Country Graveyard.
Preston, James (b. 1951)
Sunfish Races.
Preston, Keith (1884–1927)
Complete Cynic, The.
Effervescence and Evanescence.
Lapsus Linguae.
Parental Critic, The.
Probably.
Preston, Margaret Junkin (1820–77)
Grave in Hollywood Cemetery, Richmond, A.
Ready.
Prestwich, Edmond (fl. 1651)
How to Choose a Mistress.
Pretorius, S. J.
Madman, The.
Prettyman, Quandra (b. 1933)
Mood, The.
Photograph.
Still Life: Lady with Birds.
When Mahalia Sings.
Prévert, Jacques (1900–1977)
Alicante.
August Bank Holiday.
Barbara.
Barbara remember.
Discourse on Peace, The.
Dunce, The.
Familial.
First paint a cage.
I'm the way I am.
Inventory.
Last Supper, The.
Message, The.
Pater Noster.
Quartier Libre.
River, The.
Song in the Blood.
Song of the snails on their way to a funeral.
Whale hunt, The.
Prewett, Frank (1893–1962)
I Shall Take You in Rough Weather.
If I Love You.
Pack, The.
Plea for Peace.
Red-Man, The.
Preygel [or Preigel'], Sofiya [or Sofiia] Iul'evna (1904–86)
Hospital, The.
Price, Jonathan (1931–85)
Considered Reply to a Child, A.
Forked Radish, A.
Price, Laurence (fl. 1625–1680?)
Maidens of London's Brave Adventures, Or, a Boon Voyage Intended for the Sea, The.
Win at First and Lose at Last; or, A New Game at Cards.
Price, Reynolds (b. 1933)
Twenty-One Years.
Price, Sandra
Edge, The.
Price, W. H. G.
Limerick: "Said a Marxist who stood on the pier."
Pridvorov, Efim Alekseyevich. See "Bedny, Demyan"
Prigov, Dmitry [or Dmitrii] Aleksandrovich (b. 1940)
People are on the one side understandable.
Whenever I live, like simple.

Primrose, Lady Diana (fl. c.1630)
Chain of Pearl, A, sels.
Prince, Frank Templeton (b. 1912)
Babiaantje, The.
Memoirs in Oxford, sels.
Old Age of Michelangelo, The.
Question, The.
Soldiers Bathing.
To a Friend on His Marriage.
Token, The.
Wind in the Tree, The.
Prince, Thomas (1687–1758)
Give Ear, O God, to My Loud Cry.
O Lord, Bow Down Thine Ear.
With Christ and All His Shining Train.
Pringle, Thomas (1789–1834)
Caffer Commando, The.
Emigrant's Cabin, The.
Ghona Widow's Lullaby, The.
Prior, Matthew (1664–1721)
Alma; or, The Progress of the Mind, sels.
Another True Maid.
Better Answer to Cloe [or Chloe] Jealous, A.
Chameleon, The.
Chaste Florimel.
Democritus and Heraclitus.
Dutch Proverb, A.
Earning a Dinner.
English Ballad, on the Taking of Namur by the King of Great Britain, 1695, An.
Enigma.
Epigram: "Thy nags (the leanest things alive)."
Epigram: "To John I ow'd great obligation."
Epigram: "Tom's sickness did his morals mend."
Epigram: "When Bibo thought fit from the world to retreat."
Epigram: "Yes, every poet is a fool."
Epitaph, An: "Interred [or Interr'd] beneath this marble stone."
Epitaph: "Meek Francis lies here, friend, without stop or stay."
Fable, A: "In Æsop's tales an honest wretch we find."
Fatal Love.
For My Own Monument.
Hans Carvel, Impotent and Old.
Human Life.
In Imitation of Anacreon.
Insatiable Priest, The.
Jinny the Just.
Lady Who Offers Her Looking-Glass to Venus, The.
Les Estreines.
Letter to the Honourable Lady Miss Margaret Cavendish Holles-Harley, A.
Mercury and Cupid.
Nonpareil.
Ode, An: "Merchant, to secure his treasure, The."
On Exodus 3: 14: "I am that I am."
On Himself.
On My Birthday, July 21.
Orange, The.
Paraphrase from the French, A.
Phillis's Age.
Pleasure: The Second Book of Solomon on the Vanity of the World, sels.
Question to Lisetta, The.
Quid Sit Futurum Cras Fuge Quaerere.
Reasonable Affliction, A.
Remedy Worse than the Disease, The.
Simile, A.
Solomon on the Vanity of the World, sels.
To a Child of Quality [Five Years Old, the Author Supposed Forty].
To a Child of Quality of Five Years Old, the Author Supposed Forty.
To a Lady: She Refusing to Continue a Dispute with Me, and Leaving Me in the Argument.
Town Mouse and the Country Mouse, The.
True Maid, A.
Woman's Wish, The.
Written in an Ovid.

Written in the Beginning of Mezeray's History of France.
Prismanova, Anna Semionovna (1898–1960)
Siren.
Pritam, Amrita (b. 1919)
Annunciation, The.
Creative Process, The.
Daily Wages.
Pritchard, Norman Henry, II
Aswelay.
Burnt Sienna.
Cassandra and Friend.
Cloak, The.
Gyre's Galax.
Landscape with Nymphs and Satyrs.
Love Poem.
Narrow Path, The.
Paysagesque.
Self.
Signs, The.
Springtime.
Probyn, May
After.
Anniversaries.
As the Flower of the Grass.
Ballade of Lovers.
Barcarolle.
Before.
Blossom.
Changes.
China Maniacs.
End of the Journey, The.
Frustrated.
"Is It Nothing to You?"
Kyrielle.
Lai.
Love in Mayfair.
Masquerading.
Model, The.
More than They that Watch for the Morning.
Rondelet: "Say what you please."
Rondelet: "Which way he went?"
Song Out of Season, A.
Tête-à-Tête.
Procter, Adelaide Anne (1825–64)
Envy.
Fidelis.
Homeless.
Legend of Provence, A.
Lost Chord, A.
Love Token, A.
My Journal.
Philip and Mildred.
Three Evenings in a Life.
Woman's Answer, A.
Woman's Last Word, A.
Woman's Question, A.
Proctor, Bryan Waller. See "Cornwall, Barry"
Proctor, Thomas (fl. c.1578)
Respice Finem.
Prokofiev, Aleksandr Andreievich (1900–1971)
Betrothed, The.
Prokosch, Frederic (b. 1908)
Conspirators, The.
Gothic Dusk, The.
Propertius (Sextus Propertius) (c.54 B.C.–A.D. c.2)
Elegies, sels.
Ghosts do exist; death does not finish everything.
Homage to Sextus Propertius, sels.
Proust, Marcel (1871–1922)
My True Love Hath My Heart.
"Prout, Father." See Mahony, Francis Sylvester
Prudentius (Prudentius Aurelius Clemens) (348–c.410)
At Cock-crow.
Cathemerinon 2, sels.
Come from the confines of the sunset world.
Easter Eve.
For the Kindling of the Light on Easter Eve.
Funeral Hymn upon the Obsequies of a Friend, A, sels.
Funerall Hymne out of Prudentius, A, sels.
Hymn Before Sleep.
Hymn for Morning.

On the Morning of Christ's Nativity, *sels.*

Prunty, Wyatt
Elderly Lady Crossing on Green.
Ferris Wheel, The.
Insomnia.
Note of Thanks, A.
Reading Before We Read, Horoscope and Weather.
To be Sung on the Fourth of July.
Vegetable Garden, The.
Winter's Tale, A.

Prys, Edmwnd (1544–1623)
Welsh Ballad, A.

Prys, Thomas (c.1564–1639)
Poem to Show the Trouble That Befell Him When He Was at Sea, A.

Prys-Jones, A. G. (b. 1888)
Day Which Endures Not, A.
Limerick: "Artist who lived in St. Ives, An."
Limerick: "There was a young man of Porthcawl."
Saint Govan.

Ptolemy (Claudius Ptolemaeus) (*fl.* 121–51)
From the Greek.
Star-Gazing.

Public Enemy
Don't believe the hype.
Party for your Right to Fight.

Publius Papinius Statius. *See* **Statius, Publius Papinius**

Publius Terentius Afer. *See* **Terence**

Pudjipangu
Aeroplane.

Pudney, John (1909–77)
For Johnny.
Missing.
On Seeing My Birthplace from a Jet Aircraft.
Stiles.

Pugh, Sheenagh (b. 1950)
Craft I left in was called Esau, The.
'Do you think we'll ever get to see Earth, sir?'
Sometimes things don't go, after all.

Pugliesi, Giacomino (*fl.* 13th cent.)
Canzone: Of His Dead Lady.
Canzonetta: Of His Lady in Absence.

Pullen, Eugene Henry (1832–99)
"Now I Lay Me Down to Sleep."

Pulsford, Doris
Limerick: "Budding young playwright named Coward, A."

Punkanuttiraiyar
Mothers.

Purcell, Victor William Williams Saunders. *See* **"Buttle, Myra"**

Purdy, Alfred Wellington (b. 1919)
Alive or Not.
Blue City, The.
Cariboo Horses, The.
Country North of Belleville, The.
Dead Poet, The.
Dead Seal.
Evergreen Cemetery.
Lament for the Dorsets.
Madwoman on the Train, The.
Night Song for a Woman.
Poem: "You are ill and so I lead you away."
Remains of an Indian Village.
Spinning.
What Do the Birds Think?
Wilderness Gothic.
Winemaker's Beat-étude, The.
Winter Walking.

Purohit, Swami (1882–1936?)
I Know That I Am a Great Sinner.
Miracle Indeed, A.
Shall I Do This.

Pushkin, Aleksandr Sergeyevich (1799–1851)
Autumn.
I loved you.
I Loved You Once.
Message to Siberia.
No, never think, my dear, that in my heart I treasure.

October.
Prophet, The.
With Freedom's Seed.
Work.

Putnam, Howard Phelps (Phelps Putnam) (1874–1948)
Ballad of a Strange Thing.
Hasbrouck and the Rose.

Puttenham, George (1529–90)
Her Majestie resembled to the crowned piller.
Ye must read upward.
Partheniades, *sels.*

Pye, Henry James (1745–1813)
Aerophorion, *sels.*

"Pygge, Edward" (b. 1938)
Crow Resting.
Notes for a Revised Sonnet.
Notes for a Sonnet.
Occam's Razor Starts in Massachusetts.
Revised Notes for a Sonnet.
Robert Lowell's Notebook, *sels.*
Shantih shantih shantih.
What about You?

Pyke, B. K.
Blacksmith.

Pyle, Katharine (1863–1938)
August.
Circus Parade, The.
Clever Peter and the Ogress.
Toys Talk of the World, The.
Waking.
Wonder Clock, The, *sels.*

Pyon, Yongno (1898–1961)
Non-gae.
Spring Rain.

Pyrlaeus, Johann C. (1713–85)
Jesu, Come on Board.

Q

"Q." *See* **Quiller-Couch, Sir Arthur Thomas**

Qabula, Alfred Temba (b. 1942)
Migrant's Lament: A Song.

Qaisi, Aziz (b. 1945)
Outside the Furnace.

Qaqatcguk
I keep dreaming I'm dead.

Qorratu'l-Ayn (1814–52)
He the Beloved, *sels.*

Quarles, Francis (1592–1644)
Are all such off'rings, as are crusht, and bruis'd.
Argalus and Parthenia, *sels.*
Be Sad, My Heart.
Behold this needle; when the *Arctick* stone.
Best-Beloved, The.
Born in Winter.
Crucified.
David's Epitaph on Jonathan.
Deuteronomy 30.19.
Divine Fancies, *sels.*
Emblems, *sels.*
Epigram: "My soul, sit thou a patient looker-on."
Galatians 6.14.
Isaiah 66.11.
Job Militant, *sels.*
Luke 6.25.
Matthew 9.12.
Meditatio Septima.
My soul, what's lighter than a feather? Wind.
Nahum 2.10.
Of Common Devotion.
Of St Stephen.
On a Feast.
On Balaam's Ass.
On Change of Weathers.
On Dinah.
On God's Law.
On Jacob's Purchase.
On Judas Iscariot.
On Saul and David.
On the Babel-Builders.
On the Cuckoo.

On The Gospel.
On the Holy Scriptures.
On the Life of Man.
On the Ploughman [*or* Plough-Man].
On the Two Great Floods.
On the World.
On Those That Deserve It.
On Zacchaeus [*or* Zacheus].
On Zacheus [*or* Zacchaeus].
Pentelogia, *sels.*
Philippians 1.23.
They Gave Him Vinegar and Gall (Matt. 27) and Wine Mingled with Myrrh (Mark 15).
Upon the Day of Our Saviour's Nativity.
Yet a Little While Is the Light With You.

Quasimodo, Salvatore (1901–68)
Ancient Winter.
Anno Domini MCMXLVII.
Antico Inverno.
Auschwitz.
Man of My Time.
19 January 1944.
To the Fifteen of Piazzale Loreto.
To the New Moon.

Queneau, Raymond (1903–76)
If You Imagine.

Quennell, Peter (b. 1905)
Divers, The.
Flight into Egypt, The.
Leviathan, *sels.*
Procne.

Questel, Victor D. (1949–82)
Bush, The.
Judge Dreadword.
Near Mourning Ground.
This Island Mopsy.
Tom.

Quevedo y Villegas, Francisco de (1580–1645)
Sonnet: Death Warnings.

Quickenden, Beatrice (1902–67)
Hail, oh hail to the king who does in glory reign.

Quigless, Helen G. (b. 1944)
Childhood Scenes in Four Seasons, *sels.*
Evening.
Moving.

Quiller-Couch, Sir Arthur Thomas ("Q") (1863–1944)
Doom Ferry.
Harbour of Fowey, The.
Lady Jane.
Planted Heel, The.
Sage Counsel.

Quillet, Claude (1602–61)
Callipaedia; or, The Art of Getting Beautiful Children, *sels.*

Quillinan, Edward (1791–1851)
Hour Glass, The.

Quinn, Roderic (1867–1949)
Fisher, The.

Quinones, Lolly (1934–79)
February.

Quint, Beverly
View, A.

Quirino, Giovanni (*fl.* c.1300)
To Dante Alighieri (He Commends the Work of Dante's Life).

Quý, Nguyễn Đăng. *See* **Mai Thảo**

R

"R., E. M. G."
Midsummer Moon.

Raab, Lawrence (b. 1946)
Assassin's Fatal Error, The.
Attack of the Crab Monsters.
For You.
Magic Problems.
On the Island.
Pastoral: "Today in Peru, this first day of summer."
Room, The.
Sudden Appearance of a Monster at a Window.

Visiting the Oracle.
Voices Answering Back: The Vampires.
Witch's Story, The.

Rab (Abba Arika) (*fl.* 3d cent.)
Kingdom of God, The.

Rabbitt, Thomas (b. 1943)
Bernadette Murphy, 1943-1955.
Blue Lights.
Coon Hunt.
For Thomas Stearns Eliot on the Occasion of
His One Hundredth Birthday.
For Those Who Will Live Forever.
Gargoyle.
My Father's Watch.
Old Sipsey Valley Road, The.
Over All.
Power of Faith, The.
Tortoise.

Rabe, Olive. *See* **Fisher, Aileen** *and* **Olive Rabe**

Rabéarivelo [*or* **Rebéarivelo**]**, Jean-Joseph**
(1901–37)
Cactus.
Close by, to the north, there were two
oranges.
Here is.
Here She Stands.
Imaginary tremolo.
May I come in? May I come in?
One day some young poet.
Reading.
Rondo for the Poet's Children.
Slowly / like a crippled cow.
There you are.
Three Dawns.
Traduits de la Nuit, *sels.*
What invisible rat.
Wife is like a blade of grass, A.
You built yourself a tower in the wind.
You delude yourself.
Your Work.

Rabelais, François (c.1494–1553)
Antidoted Fanfreluches: or, a Galimatia of
Extravagant Conceits Found in an Ancient
Monument, The.

Rabémanganjara, Jacques (b. 1913)
Lamba, *sels.*
Lament: "Blue, so blue that eye of sky."
Song: "Isle!/ Island of the syllables of
flame!"

Rabi'a al-Adawiyya (Rabi'a the Mystic) (712–
801)
I am fully qualified to work as a doorkeeper,
and for this reason.
My Lord / if I worship Thee from fear of
Hell.
O my Lord.
O my Lord, if I worship you from fear of
Hell.
O my Lord, the stars glitter and eyes of men
are closed.
Stars are shining / the eyes of men are
closed.
Two ways I love Thee, selfishly.

Rabi'a bint Isma'il of Syria (d. 755)
Sufi Quatrain.

Rabi'a of Balkh (*fl.* 10th cent.)
My wish for you / that God should make
your love.

Rabinowich, Sholem. *See* **"Aleichem, Sholom"**

"Rachel" [*or* **"Rahel"**] **(Rahel Blumstein** [*or*
Blaustein *or* **Bluwstein**]) (1890–1931)
Aftergrowth.
Barren.
Dawn.
Here on Earth.
His Wife.
Jonathan.
Kinnereth.
Only of myself I knew how to tell.
To My Country.

Racine, Jean (1639–99)
My time's too short, your highness. It was I.
Phaedra.

Radauskas, Henrikas
Arrow in the Sky.
Harbor.

Hot Day.
Salesgirl.
Star, Sun, Moon.

Radcliffe, Alexander (*fl.* 1669–96)
As Concerning Man.

Radcliffe, Ann (1764–1823)
Mysteries of Udolpho, The, *sels.*
Night.
Song of a Spirit.
Sonnet: "Now the bat circles on the breeze of
eve."
Stanzas: "How smooth that lake expands its
ample breast!"

Radford, Dollie (Mrs. Ernest Radford) (b.
1858)
Novice, A.
Soliloquy of a Maiden Aunt.

Radford, Ernest (b. 1853)
Upon Julia.

Radnóti, Miklós (1909–44)
Angel of Dread, The.
Clouded Sky.
Forced March.
Letter to My Wife.
Peace, Horror.
Picture Postcards.
Postcard (Found on His body after He Was
Killed by the Nazis).
Seventh Eclogue.

Rae, Simon (b. 1952)
Pulling the Chain.
Vile World.

Raftery [*or* **Raifteiri**]**, Anthony** [*or* **Antoine**]
(1784–1835)
I Am Raftery [*or* Raferty].
I am Raifteiri, the poet, full of courage and
love.
Lass from Bally-na-Lee, The.

Rago, Henry (1915–69)
Childhood Painting Lesson.
Coming of Dusk upon a Village in Haiti,
The.
Green Afternoon, The.
Knowledge of Light, The.
Monster, The.
Summer Countries, The.

"Raimar, Freimund." *See* **Rückert, Friedrich**

Raine, Craig (b. 1944)
Attempt at Jealousy, An.
City Gent.
Dandelions.
Gardener, The.
In Modern Dress.
Martian Sends a Postcard Home, A.
Nature Study.
Onion, Memory, The.
Plain Song.
Sexual Couplets.

Raine, Kathleen Jessie (b. 1908)
Air.
Beinn Naomh, *sels.*
By the River Eden.
Daisies of Florence.
Envoi: "Take of me what is not my own."
Envoi: "What has want to give."
Eudaimon.
Heirloom.
Human Form Divine, The.
Images.
In Time.
Instrument, The.
Isis Wanderer
Kore in Hades.
Lachesis.
Last Things.
Love-Poem: "Yours is the face that the earth
turns to me."
Message from Home.
Natura Naturans.
Old Paintings on Italian Walls.
On its way I see.
Puer Aeternus.
Pythoness, The.
Question and Answer.
Rose.
Scala Coeli.

Spell Against Sorrow.
Spell of Creation.
Statues.
To My Mountain.
"Tu Non Se' in Terra, Si Come Tu Credi."
Two Invocations of Death, *sels.*
What substance had Euridice.
Wilderness, The.
World, The.
Worry about Money.
Written in Exile.

Rainey, Gertrude "Ma" ("Ma" Rainey) (1886–
1939)
Prove It on Me Blues.
See See Rider, see what you done done!

Rajasekhara (c. 7th cent.)
Moonlight.

Rajeevan, Savithri (b. 1955)
Pair of Glasses, A.

Rakosi, Carl (b. 1903)
Exercises in Scriptural Writing, *sels.*
Florida.
Fluteplayers from Finmarken.
Founding of New Hampshire, The.
Good Morning.
In a Warm Bath.
Israel.
January of a Gnat, The.
Journey Away, A.
Lord, What is Man?
Medium IV: Sights, The.
Memoirs, The.
Menage, The.
Origins.
Paraguay.
Services.
Unswerving Marine.
Woman.

Rakovszky, Zsuzsa
Difficulties of Falling Asleep.

Ralegh, Sir Walter (1552?–1618)
Advice, The.
'As ye came from the holy land.'
As you came from the holy land.
Commendatory Verses to Edmund Spenser's
Fairy Queen, *sels.*
Concei[p]t begotten by the eyes.
Epitaph on Sir Philip Sidney.
Epitaph on the Earl of Leicester [*or*
Leceister].
Excuse, The.
Farewell to False Love, A.
Farewell to the Court.
Fortune hath taken away my love.
Fortune hath taken the away my love, *sels.*
His Petition to Queen Anne of Denmark
(1618).
If Cynthia be a queen, a princess, and
supreme.
In Commendation of George Gascoigne's
Steel Glass.
Lie, The.
Like to a hermit[e] poor[e][,] in place
obscure.
Likes to a hermit poor in place obscure.
Love and Time.
Love Indestructible.
My Body in the Walls Captived.
My thoughts are winged with hopes.
Nature, that washed her hands in milk.
Nimphs [*or* Nymph's] Reply to the
Sheepheard [*or* Shepherd], The.
Ocean's Love to Cynthia, The, *sels.*
On the Card[e]s, and Dice.
On the Life of Man.
On the Snuff of a Candle.
Passionate Man['ˌ]s Pilgrimage, The.
Poem Put into My Lady Laiton's Pocket, A.
Shepherd's Praise of Diana, The.
Silent Lover, The, *sels.*
Sir Walter Ra[u]le[i]gh to His Son[ne].
Sir Walter Ralegh to the Queen.
Sweet Unsure.
To His Love When He Had Obtained Her.
To the Translator of Lucan [*or* Lucan's
Pharsalia, 1614].

Verses Made the Night before He Died [*or* Dyed].

Verses Made the Night before His Beheading.

Ralegh, Sir Walter (1552?–1618) *and* **George Clifford**

Another of the Same. *From* Commendatory Verses to Edmund Spenser's Fairy Queen.

Raleigh, Sir Walter Alexander (1861–1922)

Lines Suggested by an Edition of Blake's Poems.

Nymph's Reply to the Shepherd, The.

Walsinghame.

Wishes of an Elderly Man[, Wished at a Garden Party, June 1914].

"Ramal, Walter." *See* **De la Mare, Walter**

Ramanujan, A. K. (b. 1929)

At Forty.

Breaded Fish.

Elements of Composition.

Hindoo: He Doesn't Hurt a Fly or a Spider Either, The.

In the Zoo.

Last of the Princes, The.

Love Poem for a Wife, 2.

Pleasure.

Self-Portrait.

Small-scale Reflections on a Great House.

Snakes.

Some Indian Uses of History on a Rainy Day.

Some People.

Ramke, Bin (b. 1947)

Buchenwald.

Compulsion as the Critical Element in a Defined Perversion.

Georgia.

How Light Is Spent.

Nostalgia.

Victory Drive, near Fort Benning, Georgia.

Ramkissoon-Chen, Rajandaye

Father.

When the Hindu Woman Sings Calypso.

Ramler, Karl Wilhelm (1725–98)

Yearning for Winter.

Ramsay, Allan (1686–1758)

Carle He Came o'er the Croft, The.

Epigram: "Lasses, like nuts at bottom brown."

Gentle Shepherd, The, *sels.*

Lass of Patie's Mill, The.

Lass with a Lump of Land.

Ode to Mr. F— [*or* Mr. Forbes].

Poet's Wish; an Ode, The.

Polwart on the Green.

Thou Were My Ain Thing, An.

Twa Books, The.

Up in the Air.

Ramsay, Andrew Michael (1686–1743)

Friendship in Perfection.

Ramsey, Hettye Rayburn

Home and Mother.

Mother.

Ramsey, Jarold (b. 1937)

Hand-Shadows.

Ontogeny.

Tally Stick, The.

Ramsey, Paul (b. 1924)

Angels take approaches, The. Some enter by root.

Hours, The.

Images for the Gospel of Christ.

On Words and Concepts and Things.

Poet Defended, A.

Three Epigrams, *sels.*

Ranaivo, Flavien (b. 1914)

Carry me.

Choice.

Distress.

Humped Ox, The.

Love Song: "Do not love me, my friend."

Old Merina Theme.

Song of a Common Lover.

Song of a Young Girl.

Ranasinghe, Anne

Holocaust 1944.

Randall, Belle (b. 1940)

City Hall.

Hundred Ways of Playing Solitaire, A, *sels.*

Playing at Cards.

Randall, Dudley (b. 1914)

Abu / 's a stone black revolutionary.

Analysands.

Ancestors.

Bag Woman.

Ballad of Birmingham.

Black Poet, White Critic.

Blackberry Sweet.

Booker T. and W. E. B.

Different Image, A.

George.

Hail, Dionysos.

Idiot, The.

Intellectuals, The.

Langston Blues.

Legacy: My South.

Melting Pot, The.

Memorial Wreath.

Old Witherington.

On Getting a Natural.

Pacific Epitaphs.

Poet Is Not a Jukebox, A.

Primitives.

Profile on the Pillow, The.

Rite, The.

Roses and Revolutions.

Southern Road, The.

Souvenirs.

To the Mercy Killers.

Vacant Lot.

Randall, Jr., James A., (b. 1938)

Don't Ask Me Who I Am.

Execution.

Jew.

When Something Happens.

Who Shall Die.

Why should I be eaten by love.

Randall, James Ryder (1839–1908)

My Maryland.

Randall, Julia (b. 1923)

Adam Says See, *sels.*

Miracles.

Recipes.

Rockland.

To William Wordsworth from Virginia.

Valediction, A.

Randell, Elaine (b. 1951)

Watching Women with Children.

Randolph, Innes (1837–87)

Rebel, The.

Randolph, Thomas (1605–35)

Answer to Mr. Ben Jonson's Ode, to Persuade Him Not to Leave the Stage, An.

Conceited Pedlar, The, *sels.*

Devout Lover, A.

Elegy, An: "Love, give me leave to serve thee, and be wise."

Gratulatory to Mr. Ben Johnson for His Adopting of Him to Be His Son, A.

In Praise of Women in General.

Mask for Lydia, A.

Milkmaid's Epithalamium, The.

Ode to Mr. [*or* Master] Anthony Stafford to Hasten Him into the Country, An.

On a Maid of Honour Seen by a Scholar in Somerset Garden.

On Grafting.

On Sir Robert Cotton the Antiquary.

On the Death of a Nightingale.

Phyllis.

Poet, The.

Song, A: "Music, thou queen of souls, get up and string."

This definition poetry doth fit.

Upon His Picture.

Upon Love Fondly Refused [*or* Refus'd] for Conscience's Sake.

Upon the Loss[e] of His Little Finger.

Rands, William Brighty ("Matthew Browne") (1823–80)

Cat of Cats, The.

Dream of a Boy Who Lived at Nine Elms, The.

Dream of a Girl Who Lived at Sevenoaks, The.

Gipsy Jane.

Godfrey Gordon Gustavus Gore&mdash.

Lullaby: "Wind whistled loud at the window-pane, The."

Pedlar's Caravan, The.

Shooting Song, A.

Stalky Jack.

Thought, The.

Topsy-turvy World.

Winifred Waters.

World, The.

Rankin, Jennifer (1941–79)

Forever the Snake.

Love Affair 36.

Man is following me, A.

Old Circles.

Old Currawong.

Sea and Other Stories, The.

Sea-bundle.

Tale.

Rankin, Jeremiah Eames (1828–1904)

God Be with You till We Meet Again.

Laboring and Heavy Laden.

Rankin, Paula (b. 1945)

Bedtime Story.

Fifteen.

For the Obese.

Hot Bath in an Old Hotel.

Middle Age.

To the House Ghost.

Two Lovers on Bridge in Winter.

Rankin, Rush

Women of Maine, The.

Rankine, Claudia

Eden.

Man. His Bowl. His Raspberries, The.

New Windows.

Rankins, William (*fl.* 1588–1601)

Satyrus Peregrinans, *sels.*

Rannit, Aleksis

Boris Vilde.

Jaan Oks.

So I See You Still.

Wiiralt Drawing in Chartres.

Ransetsu (Hattori Ransetsu) (1653–1708)

Deep in the night.

Fields and mountains turn.

One plum blossom blooms.

Ransetsu, Hattori. *See* **Ransetsu**

Ransford, R. W.

She Found Me Roots.

Ransom, Cherra S.

Lot's Wife.

Ransom, John Crowe (1888–1974)

Address to the Scholars of New England.

Amphibious Crocodile.

Antique Harvesters.

Armageddon.

Bells for John Whiteside's Daughter.

Blackberry Winter ("If the lady hath any loveliness, let it die.")

Blue Girls.

Captain Carpenter rose up in his prime.

Dead Boy.

Dog.

Emily Hardcastle, Spinster.

Equilibrists, The.

First Travels of Max.

Good Ships.

Her Eyes.

Inland City.

Janet Waking.

Judith of Bethulia.

Lady Lost.

Little Boy Blue.

Man without Sense of Direction.

Miss Euphemia.

Necrological.

Old Man Playing with Children.

Old Man Pondered.

Old Mansion.

Our Two Worthies.

Painted Head.

Painting: A Head.

Parting, without a Sequel.
Persistent Explorer.
Philomela.
Piazza Piece.
Sixteen Poems in Eight Pairings, *sels.*
Somewhere Is Such a Kingdom.
Spectral Lovers.
Spiel of [the] Three Mountebanks.
Survey of Literature.
Tall Girl, The.
Two in August.
Vaunting Oak.
Vision by Sweetwater.
Winter Remembered.

Ransom, W. M. (b. 1945)
Catechism, 1958.
Critter.
Grandpa's .45.
Indian Summer: Montana, 1956.
Message from Ohanapecosh Glacier.
On the Morning of the Third Night above
    Nisqually.
Statement on Our Higher Education.

Ransome-Davies, Basil
Limerick: "Cassandra declining to follow."
Limerick: "Finding God's taboos totalitarian."
Limerick: "Is it really so very unthinkable."
Limerick: "Said Plato: 'The things that we
    feel.'"
Limerick: "There was a collection of
    schemers."
Limerick: "There was a young person of
    Leigh."
Limerick: "Trouble with General Sherman,
    The."
Limerick: "Two earnest young fellows named
    Wright."
Limerick: "Young Oedipus learned from the
    Sphinx."
Raymond Chandler: The Big Sleep.
Travellers Turning Over Borders.

Rao, B. R. Lakshman
Green Snake.

Rao, Bhanuji (b. 1926)
Fish.

Raphael, Lennox (b. 1940)
Mike 65.

Rapin, Rene (1621–87)
Of Gardens, *sels.*
Of Roses and Hyacinths.

Rappoport, Solomon. *See* "Ansky, S."

Rashidi Samarqandi (*fl.* 1100)
Complaint to a Court Poet.

Ratcliffe, Dorothy Una (1892–1967)
February.
Pirates' Tea-Party, The.

Ratcliffe, Stephen
Beginning in the light as heard, wheel on
    stone.
Space in the light said to be where one /
    comes from, *sels.*

Rathbun, Victoria
Uncool.

Rathenow, Lutz
After David Samuilow.
No Picture.
Prague.

Rathkey, W. A.
Limerick: "G. B. Shaw wrote to Yeats:
    'P'raps it's mad of me.'"

Ratti, John (b. 1933)
Division.

Rattigan, Terence
Limerick: "'I would doubt,' said the Bishop
    of Balham."

**Ratushinskaya [*or* Ratushinskaia], Irina (b.
1954)**
But only not to think about the journey.
No, I'm not afraid: after a year.
Try to cover your shivering shoulders in rags
    of the oldest.
Why is the snow pale blue?

Raut, Paresh Chandra (b. 1936)
Snake.

Rauter, Rose
Peach.

Raven, John (b. 1936)
Assailant.
Inconvenience, An.
Roach / came struttin, A.

Ravenel, Beatrice Witte (1870–1956)
Alligator, The.

Ravenscroft, Edward (c.1643–1707)
In Derision of a Country Life.

Ravenscroft, Thomas. *See* **Lyly, John** *and*
Thomas Ravenscroft

Ravenscroft, Thomas (c.1592–c.1635)
Belmans Song, A.
Hawking for the Partridge.
Hey ho, what shall I say?
Madrigal: "My mistress is as fair as fine."
Sing we now merily.

Ravikovitch [*or* Ravikovich], Dahlia (b. 1936)
Blue West, The.
Dear Mickey.
Dress of Fire, A.
Everlasting Forests, The.
Hills of Salt.
Hovering at a Low Altitude.
How Hong Kong Was Destroyed.
Human Qualities.
King over Israel.
Like Rachel.
Man of Mystery.
Marionette.
On the Road at Night There Stands the Man.
Poem of Explanations.
Portrait.
Private View, A.
Requiem after Seventeen Years
Sinking Rising.
Sound of Birds at Noon, The.
Surely You Remember.
Time Caught in a Net.
Tirzah and the Wide World.
Trying Again.
War's End.
Who Art Thou, O Great Mountain.
You Can't Kill a Baby Twice.

**"Ravitch, Melech" (Zekharye Khone Bergner)
(1893–1976)**
Verses Written on Sand.

Rawlinson, Gloria (b. 1918)
Islands Where I Was Born, The.
Simple Matter, A.

Raworth, Tom (b. 1938)
Collapsible.
Cross Divide.
Empty Pain-Killer Bottles, The.
Horse Power.
Hot Day at the Races.
My Face Is My Own, I Thought.
Nothing.
South America.

Rawson, Grindall (1659–1715)
To the Learned and Reverend Mr. Cotton
    Mather, on His Excellent Magnalia.
Upon the Death of His Much Esteemed
    Friend Mr. Jno Saffin Junr.

Ray, Cyril
Limerick: "At last I've seduced the *au pair.*"
Limerick: "I was sitting there, taking my
    ease."
Limerick: "Not that it always transpired."
Limerick: "Well, if it's a sin to like
    Guinness."

Ray, David (b. 1932)
At the Washing of My Son.
Card-Players, The.
Eskimo Girl, The.
Greens.
In the Third Month.
Midnight Diner by Edward Hopper, A.
On a Fifteenth-Century Flemish Angel.
On the Photograph "Yarn Mill," by Lewis W.
    Hine.
Ursula.

Ray, Henrietta Cordelia (1861?–1916)
After the Storm.
Afterglow, The.
Ambition.
Among the Berkshire Hills.

Anita and Giovanni.
Antigone and Oedipus.
April.
Aspiration.
At Christmas-Tide.
At Nature's Shrine.
At Sunset.
At the Cascade.
August.
Awakening.
Beethoven.
Boat Song.
Broken Heart.
Charity.
Charles Sumner.
Chateaux en Espagne.
Cloud Fantasy.
Cloud Song.
Coming of Spring, The.
Compensation.
Cuckoo Song.
Dante.
Dawn of Love, The.
Dawn's Carol.
December.
Dream of Elfland, A.
Dream within a Song, A.
Easter Carol.
Echo Reverie.
Echo's Complaint.
Emerson.
Enchanted Shell, The.
Evening Prayer.
Fading Skiff, The.
Failure.
Fancy and Imagination.
February.
Fisherman's Story, The.
Fragment, A: "Our fancies are but joys all
    unexprest."
Full Vision.
God's Ways, Not Our Ways.
Greeting.
Group of Musings, A, *sels.*
Hermit and the Soul, The.
Hidden Essence.
Hour's Glory, The.
Hymn to the Thousand Islands.
Ideal, An.
Idyl, *sels.*
Idyl of Spring, An.
In Memoriam Frederick Douglass.
In Memoriam Paul Laurence Dunbar.
Incompleteness.
Instability.
Invocation to the Muse.
January.
July.
June.
Life.
Life's Boundary.
Limitations.
Lincoln.
Lines Written on a Farewell View of the
    Franconia Mountains at Twilight.
Listening Nydia.
Little Fay's Thanksgiving.
Longfellow.
Lost Opportunities.
Love's Vista.
Maid of Ehrenthal, The.
March.
May.
May's Invocation after a Tardy Spring.
Messengers, The.
Mignon.
Mildred's Doves.
Milton.
Mist Maiden, The.
Musidora's Vision.
My Easter Dove.
My Spirit's Complement.
Nature's Minor Chords.
Nature's Uplifting.
Niobe.
November.
O Restless Heart, Be Still!

Ocean Musing, An.
October.
Ode on the Twentieth Century.
On a Nook Called Fairyland.
On the Concord River.
On the Picture of a Child.
On the rapids of the St. Lawrence.
Our Task.
Pastoral: "Annette came through the meadows."
Perfect Orchestra, The.
Picture, A.
Poet's Ideal, The.
Poet's Ministrants, The.
Prayer: "O Christ, who in Gethsemane."
Quebec.
Quest of the Ideal, The.
Questioning.
Raphael.
Recompensed?
Repose.
Retrospection.
Reunited.
Reverie.
Rhyme of the Antique Forest.
Robert G. Shaw.
Sculptor's Vision, The.
Sea Cadences.
Self-Mastery.
September.
Shadow and Sunrise.
Shakespeare.
Siren Bird, The.
Sky Picture.
Snow Song.
Song: "O sweet, sad, singing river."
Soul Incense.
Soul's Courts, The.
Star Song.
Sunset Picture.
Thought at Walden, A.
Thought of Lake Ontario, A.
Tireles Sculptor, The.
To Laura.
To My Father.
To My Mother.
Toussaint L'Ouverture.
Triple Benison, The.
Two Musicians, The.
Venus of Milo, The.
Verses to my Heart's-Sister.
Vision of Eve, The.
Vision of Moonlight, A.
Voices of the Rain.
Wendell Phillips.
William Lloyd Garrison.
Wood Carols.

Ray, Maude Louise
My Task.

"Rayevsky [or Raevskii], Georgy [or Georgii] Avdeievich" (Georgii Avdeievich Otsup) (1897–1962)
O, he who flashed above the moon afar.
War.
You think: won't fate tap.

Raymond, Vicki (b. 1949)
Extinguish, one by one.
People, No, The.
Reculver Bay.

Razaf, Andy. See Waller, Thomas ("Fats"), Andy Razaf and Harry Brooks

Read, Sir Herbert (1893–1968)
Beata l'Alma.
Cranach.
End of a War, The.
Falcon and the Dove, The.
Garden Party.
Happy Warrior, The.
Mutations of the Phoenix, sels.
My Company.
My men go wearily.
1945.
Short Poem for Armistice Day, A.
Sic et Non.
Summer Rain.
To a Conscript of 1940.
White Isle of Leuce, The.

Read, Thomas Buchanan (1822–72)
Sheridan's Ride.

Read, Vail (b. 1909)
This new day the eyes of children.

Reader, Willie
When Paul Bunyan was ill we sent.

Reading, Peter (b. 1946)
Ballad: "I'll tell you a story / concerning John and Joan."
Correspondence.
Travelogue, sels.
Who would have thought it Sir, actually putting ME in a WRITING!

Reaney, James (b. 1926)
Granny Crack.
Katzenjammer Kids, The.
Le Tombeau de Pierre Falcon.
Lost Child, The.
School Globe, The.
Suit of Nettles, A, sels.
To the Avon River above Stratford, Canada.
Upper Canadian, The.

Reason, Charles Lewis (1818–93)
Freedom, sels.
Spirit Voice, The; or Liberty Call to the Disfranchised (State of New York).

Reavey, George (1907–76)
Bridge of Heraclitus, The.
Dismissing Progress and Its Progenitors.
How many fires.
Never.

Rebelo, Jorge
Poem.
Poem for a Militant.

Receveur, Don
August 17, 1970.
Doper's Dream.
Eagle in the Land of Oz.
Night Fear.

Rector, Liam (b. 1949)
Showing.

Redgrove, Peter (b. 1932)
Christiana.
Corposant.
Curiosity-Shop, The.
Designer sits, head in hand, The.
Dog Prospectus.
For No Good Reason.
Ghostly Father, The.
Idea of Entropy at Maenporth Beach, The.
Intimate Supper.
Light Hotel.
Million, The.
Minerals of Cornwall, Stones of Cornwall.
Negotium Perambulans.
Red Indian Corpse.
Required of You This Night.
Secretary, The.
Serious Readers.

Redi, Francesco (1626–98)
Bacchus in Tuscany, sels.
Creation of My Lady, The.

Redmond, Eugene B. (b. 1937)
Dance Bodies #1.
Definition of Nature.
Distance.
Gods in Vietnam.
Love Necessitates.
My tongue paints a path of fire.
Parapoetics.
Poetic Reflections Enroute To, and During, The Funeral and Burial of Henry Dumas, Poet.
Spearo's Blues (or: Ode to a Grecian Yearn).

Redwing, A. K. (b. 1948)
Agent of Love.
Blue Jeaned Rock Queen in Search of Happiness on a Blind Thursday at 1/3 Speed and Crying, A.
Chrome Babies Eating Chocolate Snowmen in the Moonlight.
Cosmic Eye.
Hoofer, The.
Lost Mohican Visits Hell's Kitchen, A.
Sitting Bull's Will versus the Sioux Treaty of 1868 and Monty Hall.

Tornado Soup.
Two Hookers.
World's Last Unnamed Poem, The.
Written in Unbridled Repugnance near Sioux Falls, Alabama—April 30, 1974.

Reed, Henry (1914–86)
Auction Sale, The.
Chard Whitlow.
Château, The.
Lessons of the War, sels.
Sailor's Harbor.

Reed, Ishmael (b. 1938)
Badman of the Guest Professor.
Beware: Do Not Read This Poem.
Black Cock, The.
Black Power Poem.
Catechism of d Neoamerican Hoodoo Church.
Chattanooga.
Dualism.
Feral Pioneers, The.
Gangster's Death, The.
I Am a Cowboy in the Boat of Ra.
Instructions to a Princess.
Jacket Notes.
Lake Bud.
Oakland Blues.
Poem for Two Daughters.
Poetry Makes Rhythm in Philosophy.
Railroad Bill, a conjure man.
Rain Rain on the Splintered Girl.
Reactionary Poet, The.
Sermonette.
Turning Pro.
White Hope.
Why I Often Allude to Osiris.

Reed, J. D. (b. 1940)
Lost Silvertip.
Reports Come In, The.

Reed, Langford (1889–1954)
Limerick: "Consider the lowering Lynx."
Limerick: "Goddess capricious is Fame, A."
Limerick: "Indolent vicar of Bray, An."
Limerick: "Patriot living at Ewell, A."
Limerick: "Said a fair-headed maiden of Klondike."
Limerick: "Said a foolish young lady of Wales."
Limerick: "To his wife said the lynx-eyed detective."

Reed, Mary Davis
One Year to Live.

Reed, Nan Terrell (b. 1886)
Life.
Vases.

Rees, John Machreth
Merioneth.

Reese, Doc
Ol' Hannah.

Reese, Leslie (b. 1961)
My Dad Is a Magician, sels.

Reese, Lizette Woodworth (1856–1935)
April in Town.
Blackberry Blossoms.
Christmas Folk-Song, A.
Death's Guerdon.
Flower of Mullein, A.
In Time of Grief.
Lavender Woman, The.
Little Song of Life, A.
Love, Weeping, Laid This Song.
Lydia Is Gone This Many a Year.
Lyric on the Lyric, A.
One Night.
Ownership.
Puritan Lady, A.
Singer, The.
Spicewood.
Spring Ecstasy.
Street Scene, A.
Tears.

Reeve, Clara (1729–1807)
Character, A.
New Cantata, A.
To My Friend Mrs.——, on Her Holding an Argument in Favour of the Natural Equality of Both the Sexes, sels.

Reeve, F. D. (b. 1928)
Alcoholic.
Falls, The.
Hope.
We Settled by the Lake.

Reeves, James (1909–78)
Animals' Houses.
Black Pebble, The.
Cows.
Double Autumn, The.
Doze, The.
Four Horses, The.
Giant Thunder[, striding home].
Grasshopper and the Bird, The.
Horn, The.
If Pigs Could Fly.
Little Brother, The.
Mr Kartoffel's a whimsical man.
Mr. Tom Narrow.
My Singing Aunt.
Noah was an Admiral.
Old Wife and the Ghost, The.
Others.
Sea is a hungry dog, The.
Slowly the tide creeps up the sand.
Spells.
Stone Gentleman, The.
Things to Come.
Time to go home!
W.
Waiting, waiting, waiting.
You in Anger.

Reeves, W. James
W.

Reeves, William Pember (1857–1932)
Passing of the Forest, The.

Regan, J. M. (b. 1947)
Partial Luetic History of an Individual at Risk.

Regan, Jennifer
In Flight.

Rege, P. S. (1910–78)
Pact, The.

Rege, Sadanand (1923–82)
Old Leaves from the Chinese Earth.

Reginald, Francis
À l'Ange Avantgardien.
Cloth of Gold.
Lass in Wonderland, A.
Vision in long filaments flows.

Reid, Alastair (b. 1926)
Calenture.
Curiosity.
Daedalus.
Figures on the Frieze, The.
Geneva.
Ghosts.
Glass Town, The.
Isle of Arran.
James Bottle's Year.
Lesson for Beautiful Women, A.
Lesson in Handwriting, A.
Me to You.
Pigeons.
Scotland.
Small Sad Song.
Spell for Sleeping, A.

Reid, Christopher (b. 1949)
At the Wrong Door.
Gardeners, The.
Howl, Howl.
Memres of Alfred Stoker, sels.
Perversion, A.
Zeugma.

Reid, John, of Stobo (c.1430–1505)
Thre Prestis of Peblis, The, sels.

Rein, Yevgeny [or Evgenii] Borisovich (b. 1935)
Black Music.
Calendar of the Air.
Galya, Mother, and My Daughter Anna.
Glimpsed through a Lens.

Reinmar der Alte (fl. 1185–1205)
Messenger, hear what I say.
No one needs to ask.

Reinmar von Hagenau (fl. 12th cent.)
As on the Heather.

Childish Game, A.

Reinmar von Zweter (fl. 13th cent.)
I Came a-Riding.

Reis, Yitzhok. See Nadir, Moishe

Reisen, Abraham (1876–1953)
Burn Out Burn Quick.
Healing.
Watchman, watchman on your height.

Reiss, James (b. 1941)
Breathers, The.
Green Tree, The.
Habla Usted Español?
On Hot Days.
Slight Confusion, A.

Reiter, Thomas
Rights of Way.

Reitz, F. W. (1844–1934)
Proclamation, or Paper Bomb, The.

Relph, Josiah (1712–43)
Hay-Time; or, The Constant Lovers. A Pastoral.

Rendall, Elizabeth
Wind, The.

Rendall, Robert (1898–1967)
Angle of Vision.
Planticru, The.
Shore Tullye.

Renton, William
After Nightfall.
Crescent Moon.
Foal, The.
Fork of the Road, The.
Moon and Candle-light.
Shadow of Himself, The.

Repetto, Vittoria
6th grade—our lady of pompeii.

Replansky, Naomi (b. 1918)
Housing Shortage.
I Met My Solitude[. We two stood glaring].
In the Sea of Tears.
Two Women.

Resnikoff, Alexander
Bad and Good.

Retallack, Joan (b. 1941)
Biographia Literaria.
Here's Looking at You Francis Bacon.
Japanese Presentation I and II.
Not a Cage.
Secret Life of Gilbert Bond, The.
Western CIV, 4 and 5.
Woman Dragged by Welsh Corgis.

Revard, Carter (b. 1931)
Advice from Euterpe.
And Don't Be Deaf to the Singing Beyond.
Another Sunday Morning.
Birch Canoe.
"But Still in Israel's Paths They Shine."
Coming of Age in the County Jail.
Coyote, The.
Discovery of the New World.
Driving in Oklahoma.
ESP.
Getting Across.
Home Movies.
In Kansas.
January 15 as a National Holiday.
Looking Before and After.
My Right Hand Don't Leave Me No More.
North of Santa Monica.
Not Just Yet.
October, Isle of Skye.
On the Bright Side.
Support Your Local Police Dog.

Revell, Donald
Hotel Sander, The.
Muse.
New Dark Ages.
Other the Wings, The.
Sirius.
Survey.

Reverdy, Pierre (1889–1960)
Flower Market.
For the Moment.
Inn.
Secret.

Squares.

Revere, Paul (1735–1818)
Unhappy Boston.

Revett, Eldred (b. c.1635)
Ode: Hastening His Friend into the Country.

Rexroth, Kenneth (1905–82)
Andrée Rexroth, sels.
Bad Old Days, The.
Bestiary, A, sels.
City of the Moon, The, sels.
Dawn in a tree of birds, A.
Delia Rexroth.
Fact.
Fifty.
Fish Peddler and Cobbler.
For a Masseuse and Prostitute.
For Eli Jacobson.
Further Advantages of Learning.
Here is Klito's little shack.
I have sworn ten thousand times.
I Lais, once an arrow.
I used to tell you, "Frances, we grow old."
Letter to William Carlos Williams, A.
Lights in the Sky are Stars, The, sels.
Living Pearl, A.
Long lifetime, A.
Love Poems of Marichiko, The, sels.
Lute Music.
Lyell's Hypothesis Again.
Lysidike dedicates.
Naked out of the dark we came.
Observations in a Cornish Teashop.
On the Eve of the Plebiscite.
Only Years.
Prolegomenon to a Theodicy, A, sels.
Proust's Madeleine.
Signature of All Things, The.
Song for a Dancer.
Strength through Joy.
Sword in a Cloud of Light, A.
Time Is the Mercy of Eternity.
Vitamins and Roughage.
Wednesday of Holy Week, 1940.
Wheel Revolves, The.
You are a stool pigeon and.

Reynolds, Barney
Cranberry Song, The.

Reynolds, Elizabeth Gardner
Little Black Dog, The.

Reynolds, Henry (fl. 1628)
Black Maid to the Fair Boy, The.

Reynolds, John (fl. 17th cent.)
Death's Vision, sels.
Nosegay, A.

Reynolds, John Hamilton (1796–1852)
Peter Bell.
To Keats: On Reading His Sonnet Written in Chaucer.
To Spenser.

Reynolds, Lucile Hargrove
To the New Owner.

Reznikoff, Charles (1894–1976)
About an excavation.
Babylon: 539 B.C.E.
By the Well of Living and Seeing, sels.
Children.
David.
Day of Atonement.
Deserter, A.
Exodus.
Five Groups of Verse, sels.
Hebrew of your poets, Zion, The.
Holocaust, sels.
House-wreckers have left the door and a staircase, The.
I do not believe that David killed Goliath.
I Will Go into the Ghetto.
I Will Write Songs against You.
If there is a scheme.
Israel II.
Isreal I.
Jews in Babylonia, sels.
Joshua at Schechem.
Lamps Are Burning, The.
Let other people come as streams.
Mass Graves, sels.

Massacres, *sels.*
New Year's, *sels.*
Te Deum.
Testimony, *sels.*
Testimony: The United States (1901–1910)
   Recitative/The South.
These Days the Papers in the Street.
Two Witches.
Winter Sketches.

Rhianus (*fl.* **3d cent. B.C.**)
Archinos, this retsina bottle contains.

Rhodenbaugh, Suzanne
Civil War, The.

Rhodes, Anthony (b. 1916)
Repetition.

Rhodes, Hugh (*fl.* **c.1550**)
Rising in the Morning.

Rhodes, Margaret G.
Best of All, The.
Carol Singers, The.

Rhys, Ernest (1859–1946)
Autobiography, An.

Rhys, Jean (1890–1979)
Obeah Night.

Ribback, Alan
Ar(chibald')s Poetica.

Ribemont-Dessaignes, Georges (b. 1884)
Artichokes.
Sliding Trombone.

Rice, Grantland (1880–1954)
Alumnus Football.

Rice, Helen Steiner
God, Are You There?
He Was One of Us.
It's Me Again, God.
Legend of the raindrop, The.
Prayer for the Young and Lovely, A.

Rice, John
Brokendown Countdown.
I am. . . Star Counting.
Man and Height.
On some other planet.
Rockets and quasars.
Sky Seasons.
Sun stuff, star fluff.

Rice, Stan (b. 1942)
Incanto, *sels.*
Look! she is dead: no cover can cover her:
   look.
Singing Death.

Rich, Adrienne (b. 1929)
Abnegation.
After Dark.
After Twenty Years.
Afterwake, The.
At a Bach Concert.
Attention.
August.
Aunt Jennifer's tigers prance across a screen.
Autumn Sequence.
Bears.
Blood-Sister.
Burning of Paper instead of Children, The.
Charleston in the Eighteen-Sixties.
Children Playing Checkers at the Edge of the
   Forest.
Clock in the Square, A.
Contradictions: Tracking Poems, *sels.*
Culture and Anarchy.
Dark woman, head bent, listening for
   something, A.
Delta.
Design in Living Colors.
Dialogue.
Diving into the Wreck.
Eastern War Time, *sels.*
Epilogue for a Masque of Purcell.
Face to Face.
Final Notations.
5:30 A.M.
Focus.
For an Album.
For the Dead.
For the Record.
Frame.

From a Survivor.
From an Old House in America.
From the Prison House.
Gabriel.
Grandmothers, *sels.*
Hunger.
I Am in Danger—Sir—.
I Dream I'm the Death of Orpheus.
In a Classroom.
In the Evening.
In the Wake of Home.
In those years, people will say, we lost track.
Insomniacs, The.
Insusceptibles, The.
Integrity.
Jerusalem.
Like This Together.
Living in Sin.
Living Memory.
Loser, The.
Love in the Museum.
Lucifer in the Train.
Merced.
Middle-Aged, The.
Mirror in Which Two Are Seen as One, The.
Mother-in-Law.
Mourning Picture.
Necessities of Life.
Ninth Symphony of Beethoven Understood at
   Last as a Sexual Message, The.
North American Time, *sels.*
Not Somewhere Else, But Here, *sels.*
Origins and History of Consciousness.
Orion.
Paula Becker to Clara Westhoff.
Peeling Onions.
Phantasia for Elvira Shatayev.
Phenomenology of Anger, The.
Planetarium.
Power.
Primary Ground, A.
Prospective Immigrants Please Note.
Re-forming the Crystal.
Readings of History.
Roofwalker, The.
Shooting Script, *sels.*
Snapshots of a Daughter-in-Law.
Song: "You're wondering if I'm lonely."
Storm Warnings.
Stranger, The.
Survivors, The.
Tattered Kaddish.
This.
Toward the Solstice.
Translations.
Trees inside are moving out into the forest,
   The.
Trying to Talk with a Man.
Tryst in Brobdingnag, A.
Twenty-one Love Poems, *sels.*
Two Songs, *sels.*
Upper Broadway.
Valediction Forbidding Mourning, A.
Versailles.
Waking in the Dark.
Walk by the Charles, A.
Walking Down the Road.
Woman Mourned by Daughters, A.
Woman wired in memories, A.
Women.
Yom Kippur 1984.

Rich, Moss
Limerick: "I wonder how King Arthur felt."
Limerick: "It is clear that Napoleon's
   Queen."
Opera Teacher neemed Enna, An.

Richardowlands. *See* **Verstegan, Richard**

Richards, Edward Hersey (b. 1874)
Wise old owl lived in an oak, A.

Richards, Frank
Limerick: "Boastful young fellow of Neath,
   A."
Limerick: "'Come now,' said Bell, 'this is
   choice.'"
Limerick: "From the elephant paddock one
   day."

Limerick: "George Stephenson said: 'These
   repairs.'"
Limerick: "George Washington said to his
   dad."
Limerick: "Goliath was known for ferocity."
Limerick: "Great-grandfather at Waterloo."
Limerick: "In Pinter's new play that's now
   running."
Limerick: "Keeper who worked at the zoo,
   A."
Limerick: "Monkey exclaimed with great
   glee, A."
Limerick: "'No more mistresses,' King
   Edward said."
Limerick: "Poor Ophelia sighed: 'I deplore.'"
Limerick: "Ronald Reagan screamed out in
   dismay."
Limerick: "Rupert Murdoch, with glee,
   shouted: 'What.'"
Limerick: "Said a boastful young student
   from Hayes."
Limerick: "Said Freud: 'I've discovered the
   Id.'"
Limerick: "Said Paisley: 'I've given up
   hope.'"
Limerick: "Said the vet as he looked at my
   pet."
Limerick: "Said Wellington: 'What's the
   location.'"
Limerick: "Said Wilbur Wright, 'Oh, this is
   grand.'"
Limerick: "Victoria said: 'We've no
   quarrel.'"
Limerick: "Victorian gent said: 'This dance,'
   A."

Richards, George (c.1755–1814)
Almighty spake, and Gabriel sped, Th'.
Long as the Darkening Cloud Abode.

Richards, Ivor Armstrong (1893–1974)
End of a Course.
Nothing at All.
Trinity Brethren Attend.
Warhead Wakes.

Richards, Laura Elizabeth (1850–1943)
After a Visit to the Natural History Museum.
Alibazan.
Antonio, Antonio.
(Bibbily Boo and Wollypotump).
Eletelephony.
Kindness to Animals.
King of the Hobbledygoblins, The.
Mermaidens, The.
Monkeys and the Crocodile, The.
Mouse, The.
Mrs. Snipkin and Mrs. Wobblechin.
My Uncle Jehoshaphat.
Nicholas Ned.
Old Joe Jones and his old dog Bones.
Owl and the Eel and the Warming-Pan, The.
Poor unfortunate Hottentot, A.
Punkydoodle and Jollapin.
Some Fishy Nonsense.
Why Does It Snow?

Richards, Michael (b. 1915)
After Christmas.
Christmas Spider, The.

Richardson, Anthony
Song to Hymen: 1942.

Richardson, Dorothy M. (1873–1957)
Message.

Richardson, Frederic
Pantry Ghosts, The.

Richardson, James
As If Ending.

Richardson, Jonathan (1667?–1745)
On My Late Dear Wife.
Self-Consciousness Makes All Changes
   Happy; Ode.

Richardson, Justin (b. 1889)
O to scuttle from the battle and to settle on
   an atoll far from brutal mortal neath a
   wattle portal!
Retort Perfect, The.

Richardson, Mamie A. (*fl* **1920s**)
Sonnet: "I still shall smile and go my
   careless way."

Richter, C. F. (1676–1711)
My Soul before Thee Prostrate Lies.
Richter, Milan
Light?
Richter, Sheila
Anticipation.
Rickel, Boyer
Night Sweats 2.
Poem to Begin the Second Decade of AIDS.
Rickword, Edgell (1898–1982)
Cascade, The.
Contemporary Muse, The.
Cosmogony.
Encounter, The.
Handmaid of Religion, The.
Moonrise Over Battlefield.
Soldier Addresses his Body, The.
Winter Warfare.
Riddell, Alan (1927–77)
At the Hammersmith Palais.
Riddell, Elizabeth (b. 1909)
Children March, The.
Letter, The.
Soldier in the Park, The.
Suburban Song.
Wakeful in the Township.
Ridge, John Rollin (1827–67)
California, *sels.*
Cherokee Love Song, A.
Mount Shasta.
Rainy Season in California, The.
Stolen White Girl, The.
Ridge, Lola (Mrs. David Lawson) (1873–1941)
Amy Lowell.
Chicago.
Dream, The.
Electrocution.
Fifth-Floor Window, The.
Ghetto, The, *sels.*
Réveille.
Saint's Bridge.
Song, The: "That day, in the slipping of torsos and straining flanks."
Spring wind on the Bowery, A.
Veteran.
Ward X, *sels.*
Ridler, Anne (b. 1912)
At Christmas.
At Parting.
Backgrounds to Italian Paintings: Fifteenth Century.
Bathing Song.
Choosing a Name.
Christmas and Common Birth.
Crab is in again, his monthly house, The.
For a Child Expected.
Lumber of Spring.
Mile from Eden, A.
Nothing Is Lost.
Now as Then.
Now Phillipa Is Gone.
On a Picture by Michele Da Verona, of Arion as a Boy Riding upon a Dolphin.
Prayer in a Pestilent Time.
River God's Song.
Ridley, George
Cushie Butterfield.
Ridlon, Marci (b. 1942)
Fernando ("Fernando has a basketball.")
That Was Summer.
Rieu, Emile Victor (1887–1972)
Lost Cat, The.
Unicorn stood, like a king in a dream, The.
Rifat, Oktay
Stars.
Rihaku. *See* Li Po
Riley, Denise (b. 1948)
Affections Must Not.
Do So.
Housing.
It Really Is the Heart.
Poor Snow.
What I Do.
Work.

Riley, James Whitcomb (1849–1916)
Back to Griggsby's Station.
Country Pathway, A.
Craqueodoom.
Days Gone By, The.
Diners in the Kitchen, The.
Eternity.
Extremes.
Few of the Bird-Family, A.
Good-by er Howdy-do.
He Is Not Dead.
Hired Man's Faith in Children, The.
Jack the Giant-Killer.
King of Oo-Rinktum-Jing, The.
Life-Lesson, A.
Little Orphant Annie's come to our house to stay.
Nine Little Goblins, The.
Nonsense Rhyme, A.
Old Sweetheart of Mine, An.
Old Swimmin'-Hole, The.
Out of the Hitherwhere.
Raggedy Man, The.
Rose in October, A.
Sea-Song from the Shore, A.
Silence.
Wee little worm in a hickory-nut, A.
When she comes home again! A thousand ways.
When the frost is on the punkin and the fodder's in the shock.
Riley, Peter
Ospita.
Rilke, Rainer Maria (1875–1926)
Abishag.
Ah, not to be cut off.
Annunciation.
Annunciation over the Shepherds, *sels.*
Archaic Torso of Apollo.
Autumn.
Autumn Day.
Black Cat.
Buddha in Glory.
Death.
Departure of the Prodigal Son*, The.
Dove that ventured outside, flying far from the dovecote.
Duino Elegies, *sels.*
Flamingos, The.
For, Lord, the Crowded Cities Be.
From a Childhood.
Gazelle, The.
Going Blind.
Guest, The.
I live my life in growing orbits.
Initiation.
Joseph's Suspicion.
Just as the winged energy of delight.
Lament: "Oh, everything is far."
Last Evening.
Last Supper, The.
Leda.
Letters, *sels.*
Letters to a Young Poet, *sels.*
Love Song, *sels.*
Man Watching, The.
Mary at Peace with the Risen Lord.
Mary's Visitation.
Merry-go-round, The.
On the Death of Countess Luise Schwerin.
On the Marriage at Cana.
Panther, The.
Parks, The, *sels.*
Pietà.
Prayer of the Maidens to Mary.
Presaging.
Roman Fountain.
Rose, Oh Pure Contradiction.
Rose, oh pure contradiction, joy.
Second Duino Elegy, The, *sels.*
Seventh Duino Elegy, The, *sels.*
Silent Hour.
Solemn Hour.
Solitary, The.
Solitude is like rain.
Sometimes a man stands up during supper.

Song of Love, The.
Sonnets to Orpheus, *sels.*
Sonnets to Orpheus I, 12, The.
St. John, *sels.*
St. Luke, *sels.*
St. Matthew, *sels.*
Stranger, The.
Swan, The.
Third Duino Elegy, The, *sels.*
Time and again, however well we know the landscape of love.
Tombs of the Hetaerae.
Unicorn, The, *sels.*
Walk, A.
"We Must Die Because We Have Known Them."
Youth Dreams, The.
Rimbaud, Arthur (1854–91)
Eighteen-Seventy, *sels.*
Farewell: "Autumn already!—But why regret an eternal sun if we are embarked on."
Hunger.
Illuminations, *sels.*
Sensation.
Sleeper in the Valley, The.
Sleeper of the Valley, The.
Song of the Highest Tower.
Stolen Heart, The.
Vowels.
Rimos of Majorca, Moses (1406–30)
Elegy (for Himself).
Rinckhart [or Rinkhart], Martin (1586–1649)
Now thank we all our God.
Ríos, Alberto A. (b. c 1952)
At Kino Viejo, Mexico.
Chinese Food in the Fifties.
Domingo Limón.
Dream of Husbands, A.
I Held His Name.
Incident at Imuris.
Inquietude of a Particular Matter, The.
Island of the Three Marias.
La Sequia.
Language of Great-Aunts, The.
Lost on Septemter Trail, 1967, *sels.*
Madre Sofía.
Man Then Suddenly Stops Moving, A.
Man Who Became Old, The.
Mi Abuelo.
Nani.
Teodoro Luna's Two Kisses.
True Story of the Pins.
What a Boy Can Do.
Rist, Johann (1607–67)
Eternity, Thou Thunderous Word, *sels.*
She Boasts of Her Constancy.
Ristovic, Aleksandar (b. 1933)
About Death and Other Things.
Dead Leaves.
Despair.
Flirting with a Pig.
Gingerbread Heart.
Law, The.
Maids.
Monastic Outhouse.
Old Motif.
Out in the Open.
Outhouse.
Time of fools is coming.
Ritchie, Elisavietta (b. 1932)
Sorting Laundry.
Ritsos, Yannis (b. 1909)
After the Defeat.
Afternoon is all fallen plaster, black stones, dry thorns, The.
Audible and Inaudible.
Distant, The.
End of Dodona II, The.
Epitaphios, *sels.*
Marpessa's Choice.
Miniature.
Missing, The.
Not Even Mythology.
Our Land.
Penelope's Despair.
Requiem on Poros.

Return.
Search.
Unanswered.
Underneath Oblivion.
Wreath, A.

Rittenhouse, Jessie Belle (Mrs. Clinton Scollard) (1869–1948)
My Wage.

Ritterbusch, Dale
Search and Destroy.

Rivard, David
Baby Vallejo.
Change My Evil Ways.
Earth to Tell of the Beasts.
Fall River.
Firestone.
How It Will Always Seem.
Later History.
Naive Invocation.
1966.
One Too Many Mornings.
Summons.
Torque.

Rive, Richard (b. 1931)
Where the Rainbow Ends.

Rivers, Conrad Kent (1933–68)
Death of a Negro Poet, The.
Four Sheets to the Wind and a One-Way Ticket to France.
If Blood Is Black Then Spirit Neglects My Unborn Son.
In Defense of Black Poets.
Mourning Letter from Paris, A.
On the Death of William Edward Burghardt Du Bois by African Moonlight and Forgotten Shores.
Prelude: "Night and the hood."
Still Voice of Harlem, The.
To Richard Wright.
Train Runs Late to Harlem, The.
Underground.
Watts.

Rivner, Tuvia (b. 1924)
Fire in the Stone, The.
Lullaby: "Nocturnal, my panther, has eyes that spark, The."
Sunflower.
Wicked clamor, my ear grows deaf, The.

Roach, Eric (1915–74)
At Guaracara Park.
Love Overgrows a Rock.
Piarco.

Robbins, Howard Chandler (1876–1952)
And have the bright immensities.
Put Forth, O God, Thy Spirit's Might.
Sabbath Day Was By, The.

Roberson, Ed (b. 1939)
Aerialist Narratives, Chapter Three, The.
Blue Horses.
Eclipse.
Four Lines of a Black Love Letter Between Teachers.
If the Black Frog Will Not Ring.
Mayday.
Othello Jones Dresses for Dinner.
Poll.
Poor Houses, The.
Seventh Son.
Sonnet.
True we are two grown men.
When Thy King Is a Boy, sels.

Roberts, Cecil Edric Mornington (b. 1894)
Prayer for a Pilot.

Roberts, Sir Charles G. D. (1860–1943)
Mowing, The.
Potato Harvest, The.
Skater, The.
Songs of the Common Day, sels.
Tantramar Revisited, The.

Roberts, Daniel C. (1841–1907)
God of Our Fathers, Whose Almighty Hand.

Roberts, David ("Dewi Havhesp") (1831–84)
Beloved, The.

Roberts, Dorothy (b. 1907)
Cold.
Dazzle.

Roberts, Elizabeth Madox (1886–1941)
Christmas Morning.
Cold Fear.
Father's Story.
Firefly.
Hens, The.
Milking Time.
Mr. Wells.
Orpheus.
People, The.
Rabbit, The.
Sky, The.
Stranger.
Woodpecker pecked out a little round hole, The.

Roberts, G. D. (1860–1943)
Burnt Lands.
Marsyas.
Night Sky, The.
Old Morgan.

Roberts, Katrina
How Late Desire Looks.

Roberts, Len
Gift Shop in Pecs.

Roberts, Mary M. (1877–1959)
Little Pudding.

Roberts, Michael (1902–48)
H. M. S. Hero.
Hymn to the Sun.
In the Flowering Season.
Les Planches-en-Montagnes.
Midnight.
St. Gervais.
St. Ursanne.

Roberts, Michele (b. 1949)
Demeter Grieving.
Madwoman at Rodmell.
Magnificat.
Out of Chaos Out of Order Out.
Rite de Passage.
Sibyl's Song, The.

Roberts, Nigel (b. 1941)
After / the Moratorium Reading.
Gull'' Flight, The.
Max Factor Pink.
Mona Lisa Tea Towel, The.
Nigger and Some Poofters, A.

Roberts, Teresa Noelle
Apotheosis of the Kitchen Goddess II.

Roberts, Theodore Goodridge (1877–1953)
Blue Heron, The.

Roberts, Ursula. See **Miles, Susan**

Roberts, Walter Adolphe (1886–1962)
Maroon Girl, The.
On a Monument to Martí.
Peacocks.
Valediction: "Before the seas again divide."

Robertson, Alexander (d. 1916)
We Shall Drink to Them That Sleep.

Robertson, Edith Anne (b. 1883)
Deean Tractorman, Clear, The.
Deean Tractorman, Deleerit, The.

Robertson, James Logie (1846–1922)
Discovery of America, The.
Schule Laddie's Lament on the Lateness o' the Season, A.

Robertson, T. A. (b. 1909)
Tuslag.

Robey, George (1869–1954)
Limerick: "There was an old person of Slough."

Robins, Gurdon (1813–83)
There Is a Land Mine Eye Hath Seen.
When Thickly Beat the Storms of Life.

Robinson, Agnes Mary Frances (Mme Duclaux) (1857–1944)
Art and Life.
Aubade Triste.
Celia's Home-Coming.
Darwinism.
Dead Friend, The.
Etruscan Tombs.
Idea, The.
Love, Death, and Art.
Neurasthenia.

Oasis, An.
Orchard at Avignon, An.
Pallor.
Personality.
Posies.
Scape-Goat, The.
Search for Apollo, A.
Sibyl, The.
Song: "Oh for the wings of a dove."
Stornelli and Strambotti.
To My Muse.
Tuscan Olives.
Unum est Necessarium.
Valley, The.
Venetian Nocturne.
Wise-Woman, The.

Robinson, Annie Douglas Green. See **"Douglas, Marian"**

Robinson, Charles (1818–94)
Had I but strength enough, and time.

Robinson, Corinne Roosevelt (1861–1933)
Path that Leads to Nowhere, The.
We who have loved, alas! may not be friends.

Robinson, Edwin Arlington (1869–1935)
Aaron Stark.
Another Dark Lady.
As It Looked Then.
Ballade of Broken Flutes.
Ben Jonson Entertains a Man from Stratford.
Bewick Finzer.
Boston.
Calvary.
Calverly's.
Captain Craig, sels.
Cassandra.
Charles Carville's Eyes.
Children of the Night, The.
Clavering.
Clerks, The.
Cliff Klingenhagen had me in to dine.
Companion, The.
Credo.
Dark hills at evening in the west.
Eros Turannos.
Eutychides.
Exit.
Field of Glory, The.
Firelight.
Flammonde.
Fleming Helphenstine.
For a Dead Lady.
Garden, The.
George Crabbe.
Gift of God, The.
Haunted House.
Hillcrest.
House on the Hill, The.
How Annandale Went Out.
"If the Lord Would Make windows in Heaven."
Inscription by the Sea, An.
Isaac and Archibald were two old men.
James Wetherell.
John Evereldown.
John Gorham.
Karma.
Lais to Aphrodite.
L'Envoi.
Lost Anchors.
Luke Havergal.
Man against the Sky, The.
Many Are Called.
Master, The.
Mighty Runner, A.
Miller's wife had waited long, The.
Miniver Cheevy, child of scorn.
Mr Flood's Party.
New England.
New Tenants, The.
Octaves, sels.
Old Story, An.
Pity of the Leaves, The.
Poem for Max Nordau, A.
Prodigal Son, The.
Raven, The.
Recalled.

Reuben Bright.
Reunion.
Richard Cory.
Sheaves, The.
Sonnet: "Master and the slave go hand in hand, The."
Sonnet: "Oh for a poet—for a beacon bright."
Souvenir.
St. Luke, *sels.*
St. Matthew, *sels.*
Story of the Ashes and the Flame, The.
Supremacy.
Tact.
Tavern, The.
Three Quatrains.
Too Much Coffee.
Torrent, The.
Uncle Ananias.
Unforgiven, The.
Verlaine.
Veteran Sirens.
Vickery's Mountain.
Walt Whitman.
Why He Was There.
Zola.

Robinson, Elizabeth (b. 1961)
Mortar.
New Language, The.

Robinson, Elsie (1883–1956)
Beauty as a Shield.
Help Me Today.
Pain.

Robinson, Frank K.
Brief day ending.
Down rippling, The.
Today too.

Robinson, Grant P.
I Fights Mit Sigel!

Robinson, Kit (b. 1949)
First Thing.
Nesting of Layer Protocols.
Nursery Rhyme.
On the Corner.
Pontoon.
Severance.
Tribute to Nervous.
Up Early, *sels.*

Robinson, Martha
Stanzas Written between Dover and Calais, in July, 1792.

Robinson, Mary ("Laura Maria") (1758–1800)
Birth-Day, The.
Camp, The.
Canzonet.
Haunted Beach, The.
January, 1795.
London's Summer Morning.
Mrs Robinson to the Poet Coleridge.
Modern Female Fashions.
Modern Male Fashions.
Stanzas: "In this vain, busy world, where the good and the gay."
Temple of Chastity, The.

Robinson, Mary K. (b. 1857)
Brown Frog, The.
Dandelion Puff, The.
Queen Bee, The.

Robinson, Roland (b. 1912)
Cradle, The.
Creek, The.
Deep Well, *sels.*
Jarrangulli.
Wanderer, The, *sels.*

Robinson, Wey
Horse & Rider.

Robson, Jeremy (b. 1939)
Blues for the Lonely*.

Rocha, Jofre (b. 1941)
Poem of Return.

Roche, Paul (b. 1927)
Brick, The.

Rochester, Elizabeth Wilmot, Countess of (d. 1681)
Song: "Cloris misfortunes that can be exprest."

Song: "Nothing ades to Loves fond fire."

Rochester, John Wilmot, 2d Earl of (1647–80)
Against Constancy.
Allusion to Horace, An, *sels.*
Constancy.
Description of Maidenhead, A.
Disabled Debauchee, The.
Epitaph on Charles II.
Fall, The.
Grecian Kindness.
Imperfect Enjoyment, The.
Impromptu on Charles II.
Letter from Artemisia in the Town, to Chloe [*or* Cloe], in the Country, A.
Love And Life.
Mistress, The: A Song.
Platonic Lady, The.
Poet, whoe'er thou art, God damn thee.
Ramble in St. James's Park, A.
Rochester Extempore.
Rochester to the Post Boy.
Rodomontade on His Cruel Mistress, A.
Satire [*or* Satyre] against [Reason and] Mankind, A, *sels.*
Satire on Charles II, A.
Sodom, *sels.*
Song: "Absent from thee, I languish still."
Song: "Fair Chloris in a pigsty lay."
Song: "Give me leave to rail at you."
Song: "Leave this gaudy gilded stage."
Song: "Love a woman? You're [*or* Y'are] an ass."
Song of a Young Lady to Her Ancient Lover, A.
To His Mistress.
To My No More Than Meritorious Wife.
Tunbridge Wells.
Upon Drinking in a Bowl.
Upon [His] Leaving His Mistress.
Upon Nothing.
Written in a Lady's Prayer Book.

Rock, Madeleine Caron
He Is the Lonely Greatness.

Rodd, Sheila Desiré Savory. *See* **Flynn, Desiré**

Rodefer, Stephen (b. 1940)
Codex.
Plane Debris, *sels.*
Pretext.

Rodgers, Carolyn M. (b. 1942)
Breakthrough.
Feminism.
For H. W. Fuller.
For Sistuhs Wearin' Straight Hair.
Group Therapy.
It Is Deep.
Jesus Was Crucified or: It Must Be Deep.
Masquerade.
Me, in Kulu Se and Karma.
Newark, for Now (68).
Now Ain't That Love?
One.
Poem for Some Black Women.
Poem No. 1.
Portrait.
Slave Ritual.
Some Me of Beauty.
Testimony.
U Name This One.
We Dance Like Ella Riffs.
What Color Is Lonely.
Written for Love of an Ascension—Coltrane.
Yuh Lookin Good.

Rodgers, William Robert (1909–69)
Awake!
Beagles.
Carol: "Deep in the fading leaves of night."
Directions to a Rebel.
Field Day.
Home Thoughts from Abroad.
Irish Lake, An.
Lent.
Life's Circumnavigators.
Lovers, The.
Neither Here nor There.
Net, The.
Paired Lives.
Party, The.

Raider, The.
Resurrection: An Easter Sequence, *sels.*
Scapegoat.
Sing, Brothers, Sing!
Snow.
Stormy Night.
Swan, The.
War-Time.
White Christmas.
Winter's Cold.
Words.

Roditi, Edouard (b. 1910)
Aurora Borealis.
Hand.
Night Prayer of Glückel of Hameln, The.
Seance.

Rodman, Selden (b. 1909)
Time of Day.

Rodney, Janet (b. 1941)
Anywoman's Lyric, *sels.*

Rodriguez, Judith (b. 1936)
About this Woman.
At the Nature-Strip.
Eskimo Occasion.
Handloom, The.
How Come the Truck-Loads?
In-flight Note.
Lifetime Devoted to Literature, A.
Mahogany Ship, The.
Nasturtium Scanned.
New York Sonnet.
Nu-plastik Fanfare Red.
Rebeca in a Mirror.

Rodriguez, Luis J.
Always Running.
Fire.
Heavy blue veins streaked across my mother's legs, some of them bunched up into dark lumps at her ankles.
Speaking with Hands.
String Bean.
We never stopped crossing borders.

Rodriguez, Magdalena de
June 10.

Rodriguez, W. R.
Accordian Player, The.

Roe, Barbara
Into concrete mixer throw.

Roe, Sir Thomas (1581–1644)
On Gustavus Adolphus, King of Sweden.

Roethke, Theodore (1908–63)
Academic.
Bat, The.
Big Wind.
Bound.
Bring the Day!
Carnations.
Ceiling, The.
Child on Top of a Greenhouse.
Chums, The.
Coming of the Cold, The.
Cow, The.
Cuttings ("Sticks-in-a-drowse droop over sugary loam.")
Cuttings ("This urge, wrestle, resurrection of dry sticks.")
Decision, The.
Dinky.
Dolor.
Donkey, The.
Dream, The.
Duet.
Elegy for Jane.
Far Field, The.
Field of Light, A.
Follies of Adam, The.
For An Amorous Lady.
Four for Sir John Davies, *sels.*
Frau Bauman, Frau Schmidt, and Frau Schwartze.
Genesis.
Geranium, The.
Give Way, Ye Gates.
Heard in a Violent Ward.
Her Longing.
Her Reticence.

Her Time.
Her Words.
Hippo, The.
I knew a woman, lovely in her bones.
In a Dark Time, *sels.*
In Evening Air.
Infirmity.
Journey to the Interior.
Judge Not.
Kitty-Cat Bird, he sat on a fence, The.
Lady and the Bear, The.
Light Listened.
Lizard, The.
Long live the weeds that overwhelm.
Long Waters, The.
Lost Son, The, *sels.*
Marrow, The.
Meadow Mouse, The.
Meditation at Oyster River.
Meditations of an Old Woman, *sels.*
Minimal, The.
Moment, The.
Monotony Song, The.
Moss-Gathering.
My Papa's Waltz.
Night Crow.
Night Journey.
North American Sequence, *sels.*
Old Florist.
Open House.
Orchids.
Partner, The.
Praise to the End!, *sels.*
Prayer: "If I must of my Senses lose."
Reckoning, The.
Renewal, The.
Reply, The.
Right Thing, The.
Root Cellar.
Rose, The.
Rouse for Stevens, A.
Running Lightly over Spongy Ground.
Saginaw Song, The.
Second Shadow.
Sensualists, The.
Sequel, The.
Serpent, The.
Shape of the Fire, The.
She.
Sloth, The.
Slug.
Snake.
Song for the Squeeze-Box.
St. Matthew, *sels.*
Supper with Lindsay.
Swan, The.
They Sing.
Thing, The.
Three Epigrams, *sels.*
Transplanting.
Visitant, The.
Voice, The.
Waking, The.
Weed Puller.
Where Knock Is Open Wide.
Wish for a Young Wife.
Words for the Wind.
Rogers, Del Marie
Desert.
Late, Watching Television.
Rogers, Elymas Payson (1815–61)
Poem on the Fugitive Slave Law, A, *sels.*
Repeal of the Missouri Compromise
Considered, The, *sels.*
Rogers, F.
Wishes.
Rogers, George (1805–46)
As gentle dews distill.
Rogers, John (1630–84)
Upon Mrs. Anne Bradstreet, Her Poems, Etc.
Rogers, Pattiann (b. 1940)
Abundance and Satisfaction.
Achieving Perspective.
Concepts and Their Bodies (The Boy in the
Field Alone).
Discovering Your Subject.
Doomsayers, The.

Elinor Frost's Marble-Topped Kneading
Table.
Eulogy for a Hermit Crab.
Family Is All There Is, The.
Finding the Tattooed Lady in the Garden.
Geocentric.
Giant Has Swallowed the Earth, A.
Good Heavens.
Hummingbird: a Seduction, The.
Next Story, The.
Objects of Immortality, The.
Possible Salvation of Continuous Motion,
The.
Power of Toads, The.
Suppose Your Father Was a Redbird.
Rogers, Robert Cameron (1862–1912)
Health at the Ford, A.
Rosary, The.
Rogers, Samuel (1763–1855)
Boy of Egremond, The.
Captivity.
Epitaph on a Robin Redbreast, An.
Ginevra.
Human Life, *sels.*
Italy, *sels.*
On J. W. Ward.
Sleeping Beauty, The.
To the Fragment of a Statue of Hercules,
Commonly Called the Torso.
Wish, A.
Written in a Sick Chamber.
Rogetsu, Ishii
Roasting chestnuts.
Rokeah [*or* Rokeakh], David (b. 1916)
Beyond Imagination.
Hands full of sun are in spring's longing for
you.
Jerusalem.
Negev.
Open-Eyed Angel.
Solar Years.
Whirlwind.
Zealots of Yearning.
Roland-Holst, Henriëtte (1869–1952)
Concerning the Awakening of My Soul.
I Looked for a Sounding-Board.
Mother of Fishermen.
Small Paths.
Throughout the day we are able to ban the
voices.
Roland, Patrick
Spring Burning.
Rolfe, Edwin (1909–54)
No Man Knows War.
Song: "Keep the dream alive and growing
always."
Rolland, John (c.1530–c.1580)
Seven Seages, The, *sels.*
Rolle of Hampole, Richard (1300–1349)
Ghostly Gladness.
Song of the Love of Jesus, A, *sels.*
Rolleston, Thomas William Hazen (1857–1920)
Dead at Clonmacnois, The.
Rollings, Alane (b. 1950)
Light Years and the Love Lost in the
Oleanders.
Rolls, Eric (b. 1923)
Bamboo.
Dog Fight.
Rain Forest.
Rolnik, Joseph (1879–1955)
Thank God.
Roma-Deeley, Lois
Women I Knew, The.
Romaine, Harry (*fl.* c.1895)
Ad Coelum.
Romains, Jules (b. 1885)
Another Spirit Advances.
Romanelli, Samuele (1757–1814)
From Battle Clamour.
Love.
Romanes, George John (1848–94)
Simple Nature.
Romano, Emily
August heat.

Romano, Jennie
Old Houses.
Romano, Rose (fl. 20th cent.)
Bucket, The.
But My Blood.
So I Lost My Temper.
Romero, Leo
If Marilyn Monroe.
Romero, Nidia Sanabria de (b. 1928)
New Suit, The.
Ronald, C. J.
In Memoriam J.H.H.
Ronksley, William (*fl.* c.1712)
To Cheer Our Minds.
Ronsard, Pierre de (1524–85)
And lightly, like the flowers.
Corinna In Vendome.
Deadly Kisses.
Elegy 19 (A Kiss): "Without a soul, a mind,
a breath, or pulse."
Fragment of a Sonnet.
His Lady's Death.
His Lady's Tomb.
Of His Lady's Old Age.
On His Lady's Waking.
Paradox of Time, The.
Revenge, The.
Rose, The.
Roses.
Sonnet For Helen.
Time to be up, Marie, young sleepyhead!
To His Young Mistress.
To the Moon.
Rooney, John Jerome (1866–1934)
Men behind the Guns, The.
Root, George Frederick (1820–95)
Battle Cry [*or* Battle-Cry] of Freedom, The.
Root, Judith C.
Naming the Shells.
Small Differences.
Snail Winter.
Root, William Pitt (b. 1941)
Circle of Struggle.
Estrangements.
Ropes, P. A.
Before Spring.
Bluebells.
Daffodils.
Disappointed Shrimper, The.
Dust.
Glow-Worms.
I Will Keep Christmas.
If I were oh, so very small.
In February.
Poppies.
Violets.
Watering Rhyme, A.
**"Ropshin, V." (Boris Viktorovich Savinkov)
(1879–1925)**
Guillotine's / Sharp blade?, The.
Roscoe, William (1823–59)
Butterfly's Ball [and the Grasshopper's
Feast], The.
**Roscommon, Wentworth Dillon, 4th Earl of
(c.1633–1685)**
Essay on Translated Verse, An, *sels.*
Rose, Billy (1899–1966)
Barney Google.
Does the Spearmint Lose Its Flavor on the
Bedpost Overnight?
Unknown Soldier, The.
Rose, Sir George (1782–1873)
Forensic Jocularities.
Rose, Harriet
Mellisandra.
Succubus, The.
Wedding Coat, The.
Rose, Margaret (b. 1920)
Autumn Song.
Butterfly, The.
Little Bird's Song, A.
Little Fir Tree, The.
Magic Whistle, The.
November is a spinner.

Rose, Peter (b. 1955)
Anglo-Saxon Comedy.
Terminus.
Wind Debates Asian Immigration, The.
Rose, Wendy (b. 1948)
Alaskan Fragments June 1981—Summer
Solstice.
America.
Celebration for My Mother.
Comparison of Hands One Day Late Summer
El Sobrante.
Day They Cleaned Up the Border El
Salvador, February, 1981, The.
Epitaph: "Roots of mankind are tangled in
my hair, The."
For My People.
For Steph.
For Walter Lowenfels.
Grunion.
I Expected My Skin and My Blood to Ripen.
If I Am Too Brown or Too White for You.
Leaving Port Authority for the St. Regis
Rezz.
Loo-wit.
Naayawva Taawi.
Naming Power.
Oh father, now that I have touched.
Oh My People I Remember.
Poem to a Redskin.
Robert.
Saint Patrick's Day, 1973.
Self Dirge.
Six Nations Museum Onchiota, New York—
January.
Story Keeper.
They Sometimes Call Me.
Throat Song: The Whirling Earth.
To an Imaginary Father.
Truganinny.
Rose-Troup, J. M.
What is war?
Roseliep, Raymond (1917–83)
After Beethoven.
After Tosca.
Banker, The.
Birthcry!
Black hen, The.
Blind man's, The.
Blues are the big thing.
Brushing my sins.
Buttoning his fly.
Campfire Extinguished.
Cat, The.
Child.
Flea . .
He removes his glove.
In white tulips.
Morning-Glory, The.
On the apple.
Ordering my tombstone.
Pacing.
Piano practice.
Rain.
Sailor, The.
Seance.
Sistine Chapel.
Sky.
Unable.
Under.
White orchid.
Rosen, Kenneth (b. 1940)
Abstinence.
Act, An.
Castrato.
Confab.
Girls.
Rosen, Michael (b. 1940)
Aldrin Collins and Armstrong.
Chivvy.
Christmas Dinner.
Eddie and the Birthday.
From the winter wind.
Giant Jojo.
Here is the News.
Here is the News from space.
Humpty Dumpty went to the moon.
One, Two, Three.

Teasing Toads, The.
This morning my father looks out of the
window, rubs his nose.
Rosen, Michael and Susanna Steele
Humpty Dumpty.
Rosen, Michael J. (b. 1954)
Night Before His Parents' First Trip to
Europe His Mother Writes a Letter "To
Our Children," The.
Total Eclipse.
Rosenbaum, Benjamin (b. 1897?)
O Pity Our Small Size.
Rosenberg, David (b. 1943)
Isaiah: Chapter 66.
Job Speaks, sels.
Rosenberg, Harold (1906–78)
Epos.
Rosenberg, Isaac (1890–1918)
Amulet, The, sels.
August 1914.
Beauty.
Break of Day in the Trenches.
Burning of the Temple, The.
Chagrin.
Daughters of War.
Dead Heroes, The.
Dead Man's Dump, sels.
Destruction of Jerusalem by the Babylonian
Hordes, The.
Expression.
Female God, The.
Garden of Joy, The.
Girl to Soldier on Leave.
I Am the Blood.
Immortals, The.
Jew, The.
Louse Hunting.
Love and Lust.
Marching.
Mirror, The.
Moses, sels.
On Receiving News of the War.
One Lost, The.
Returning, We Hear the Larks.
Soldier: Twentieth Century.
Spiritual Isolation.
Spring.
Spring 1916.
Through These Pale Cold Days.
Tower of Skulls, The.
Troop ship, The.
Unicorn, The, sels.
Worm Fed on the Heart of Corinth, A.
Rosenberg, Liz (b. 1955)
Accident, The.
City Baseball.
In the End We Are All Light.
Longing for Eternal Life, The.
Poem of my Heart, The.
Prose Poems, sels.
Story of My Life, The.
Suburban Childhood, A.
Thanksgiving.
Rosenberg, Sydell
In the laundermat.
Library closing—.
Rosenblatt, Joe (b. 1933)
Ant Trap, The.
Cat.
Fish.
Ichthycide.
It's in the Egg.
Metamorpho I.
Of Dandelions & Tourists.
Saphire (Metamorpho's Chick).
Rosenfeld, Morris Jacob (1862–1923)
Another While.
Cry from the Ghetto, A.
Jewish May, The.
My Camping Ground.
Simchas Torah.
So Long Ago.
Rosenhane, Gustav (1619–84)
Sonnet: "And then I sat me down, and gave
the rein."
Sonnet: "Deep in a vale where rocks on
every side."

Rosenius, Carl Olof (1816–68)
With God and His Mercy.
Ross, Abram Bunn (b. 1866)
Two in Bed.
Ross, Alan (b. 1922)
Antwerp: Musée Des Beaux-Arts.
Cricket at Oxford.
Destroyers in the Arctic.
Epilogue: " 'O where are you going?' said
reader to rider.") (Five Songs.
In Bloemfontein.
Mess Deck.
Night Patrol.
Off Brighton Pier.
Stanley Matthews.
Ross, Alexander (1699–1784)
Wooed and Married and A'.
Ross, Charles Henry (c.1842–1897)
Jack.
John, Tom, and James.
Old Woman, An.
Ross, Charles Sarsfield
Old Mothers.
Ross, David (1896–1975)
On Apples.
Ross, J. M.
Limerick: "There once was a person of
Chiswick."
Ross, W. W. Eustace (1894–1966)
Creek, shining, The.
Diver, The.
Fish dripping, A.
If / ice shall melt.
On Angels.
Snake Trying, The.
Rossetti, Christina Georgina (1830–94)
Advent.
After Communion.
After Death.
Amen.
Amor Mundi.
Apple Gathering, An.
Ash Wednesday.
At Home.
Autumn.
Baby lies so fast asleep.
Bed of Forget-Me-Nots, A.
Before the paling of the stars.
Behold a Shaking, sels.
Better Resurrection, A.
Birthday, A.
Bitter for Sweet.
Bourne, The.
Bread and milk for breakfast.
Bruised Reed Shall He Not Break, A.
Buried.
By the Sea.
Cardinal Newman.
Caterpillar, The.
Chill, A.
Chilly Night, A.
Christmas Carol, A: "In the bleak mid-
winter," sels.
Christmas Carol, A: "Thank God, thank God,
we do believe."
City Mouse and the Garden Mouse, The.
Cobwebs.
Comparisons.
Convent Threshold, The, sels.
Cousin Kate.
Crown of Windflowers, A.
Dead before Death.
Despised and Rejected, sels.
Dirge, A: "Why were you born when the
snow was falling?"
Don't look for the flaws as you go.
Dream Land.
Dream-Love.
Dumb Friend, A.
Easter Monday.
Echo.
Echo from Willow-Wood, An.
End, An.
Endure Hardness.
Enrica, 1865.
Eve.

Ferry me across the water, / Do, boatman, do.
First Spring Day, The.
Flint.
Fly away, fly away over the sea.
Frisky lamb / And a frisky child, A.
Frog's Fate, A.
From Sunset to Star Rise.
From the Antique.
Goblin Market, *sels.*
God Is Everywhere.
Good Friday.
Green Cornfield, A.
Grown and Flown.
Handy Mole who plied no shovel, A.
Heart Knoweth Its Own Bitterness, The.
Hope and Joy.
Hoping Against Hope.
Hopping frog, hop here and be seen.
Horses of the sea, / Rear a foaming crest, The.
Hurt no living thing; / Ladybird, nor butterfly.
I caught a little ladybird / That flies far away.
I do not look for love that is a dream.
I dug and dug amongst the snow.
If a pig wore a wig.
If I Were a Queen.
If Only.
In An Artist's Studio.
In Progress.
Iniquity of the Fathers upon the Children, The.
Introspective.
Is the moon tired? she looks so pale.
Italia, Io Ti Saluto!
Kindness is a language which the.
"Kookoorookoo! kookoorookoo!" / Crows the cock before the morn.
L.E.L E. L.
Lambs at Play.
Last Rites.
Later Life: A Double Sonnet of Sonnets, *sels.*
Let's Be Merry.
Life's Parallels, A.
Long Barren.
Lord Jesus, who would think that I am Thine?
Love from The North.
Love Me - I Love You.
Lowest Place, The.
Luscious and Sorrowful.
Marvel of marvels, if I myself shall behold.
Maude Clare.
May.
May-Time.
Meeting.
Memory.
Mirage.
Mix a pancake, / Stir a pancake.
Monna Innominata, *sels.*
My Dream.
No, Thank You, John.
Noble Sisters.
O Lady Moon, your horns point toward the east.
O sailor, come ashore, / What have you brought for me?
October.
October Garden, An.
Old and New Year Ditties, *sels.*
Old-World Thicket, An.
On Keats, 18 January, 1948 (Eve of St Agnes).
On the Wing.
One Certainty, The.
Passing and Glassing.
Pause, A.
Pin has a head, but has no hair, A.
Poor Ghost, The.
Postman, The.
Prince's Progress, The, *sels.*
Promises like Pie-Crust.
Pussy cat, Pussy cat.
Pussy has a whiskered face.
Queen of Hearts, The.

Rainbow, The.
Reflection.
Remember me when I am gone away.
Rest.
Riddle, A: "There is one that has a head without an eye."
Royal Princess, A.
St. Peter once: "Lord, dost Thou wash my feet?"
Sappho.
Seldom "can't."
Shut Out.
Sing-Song, *sels.*
Sketch, A.
Sleeping at last, the trouble and tumult over.
Soeur Louise de la Miséricorde (1674).
Somewhere or other there must surely be.
Song: "Oh roses for the flush of youth."
Song: "She sat and sang alway."
Song: "Two doves upon the selfsame branch."
Song: "When I am dead, my dearest."
Soul, A.
Spring.
Spring Fancies, *sels.*
Study AA Soul), A.
Summer.
Summer Is Ended.
Summer Wish, A.
Symbols.
There's snow on the fields.
They lie at rest, our blessed dead.
Thread of Life, The, *sels.*
Three Enemies, The.
Three plum buns / To eat here at the stile.
Three Stages, *sels.*
Triad, A.
Twice.
Twilight Calm.
Twilight Night.
Two Pursuits.
Under willows among the graves.
Uphill [*or* Up-Hill].
Venus's Looking-Glass.
Wednesday in Holy Week.
What are heavy? Sea-sand and sorrow.
What does the bee do? / Bring home honey.
What is pink? A rose is pink.
What would I give for a heart of flesh to warm me thro'.
What's in a Name?
When fishes set umbrellas up.
Where innocent bright-eyed daisies are.
Who has seen the wind? / Neither I nor you.
Who Shall Deliver Me?
Why did baby die.
Wind has such a rainy sound, The.
Winter.
Winter: My Secret.
World, The.
Year's Windfalls, A, *sels.*

Rossetti, Dante Gabriel (1828–82)
Aspecta Medusa.
Blessed damozel leaned out, The.
Chimes.
Choice, The.
Even So.
For A Venetian Pastoral By Giorgone (In the Louvre).
For "Our Lady of the Rocks."
For Spring By Sandro Botticelli.
For "The Wine of Circe" by Edward Burne-Jones.
Fragment, A: "'I saw the Sibly at Cumæ.'"
Half-Way Pause, A.
House of Life, The, *sels.*
Jenny.
John Keats.
Limerick: "There is a creature called God."
Limerick: "There is an old he-wolf named Gambart."
Limerick: "There once was a painter named Scott."
Limerick: "There's a combative artist named Whistler."
Limerick: "There's a Portuguese person named Howell."

Limerick: "There's a publishing party named Ellis."
London to Folkestone.
Match with the Moon, A.
Memory.
My Sister's Sleep.
Old Song Ended, An.
On Himself.
On Refusal of Aid between Nations.
On Robert Buchanan, Who Attacked Him under the Pseudonym of "Thomas Maitland."
On the Painter Val Prinsep.
On the Poet, Arthur O'Shaughnessy—.
Orchard-Pit, The.
Percy Bysshe Shelley: Inscription for the Couch, Still Preserved, on which He Passed the Last NIght of His Life.
"Retro Me, Sathana."
Rose Mary, *sels.*
Smithereens.
Stratton Water.
Sudden Light.
There is a big artist named Val.
Tom Agnew, Bill Agnew.
Trip to Paris and Belgium, A, *sels.*
White Ship, The.
William Blake (To Frederick Shields, on His Sketch of Blake's Work-room and Death-room, 3 Fountain Court, Strand).

Rossi, Azariah di (1513–78)
Epitaph: "From out the stormy sea unto the shore."

Rosten, Norman (1914–95)
Aesthetic.
Black boy, the night hides you.
Out of Our Shame.
This Child ("This child, exile of hope").
This is my name / I have my own name.
To Ariake Kambara.

"Rostrevor, George." See Hamilton, George Rostrevor

Rotella, Alexis
After he leaves.
After the full moon.
Against his coat.
Asparagus I bite off their heads.
At the edge.
Barefoot through clover.
Breakfast alone.
Butterfly lands on Park Place, A.
Clutching a fist of hair.
Discussing divorce.
During our argument.
Everyone talking at once.
From green to grey.
From her neon window.
From the window.
His footsteps in the room.
Holding his gaze.
In his wedding band watching the clouds pass.
In the garbage bin.
In the guest room.
In the Queen Anne's lace a toad.
Late August.
Leading him in.
Left to the wind.
Lying in the wet grass.
Not speaking.
Only I laugh.
Opening his.
Phone call.
Rainbow, A.
StarrynightIenteryourmirror.
Surrendering to a rain-washed stone.
Swans stir of his breath against my hair.
Trying to forget him.
Undressed.
Vase of peonies.
Waterlilies.
With wine glasses.

Roth, Hal
Argument ended.
Evening star.
Her black negligee.
Her eyes still closed.

Rothenberg, Jerome (b. 1931)
Aleph Poem.
At the Castle.
Beadle's Testimony, The.
Cokboy, *sels.*
Corkby, Part Two.
Crazy Dog Events.
Dos Geshray (The Scream).
Esther K. Comes to America: 1931.
48 Words for a Woman's Dance Song.
Hunger.
Numerology.
Others Hunters in the North the Cree, The.
Poem in Yellow after Tristan Tzara, A.
Poland / 1931 "The Wedding."
Portrait of a Jew Old Country Style.
Portrait of Myself with Arshile Gorky and
    Gertrude Stein.
Praises of the Bantu Kings (1–10).
Realtheater Piece Two.
Seneca Journal 1: "A Poem of Beavers."
Seven Hells of Jigoku Zoshi, The, *sels.*
Soap (II).
Song of Quavering, A.
Structural Study of Myth, The.
That Dada Strain.
12th Horse-Song of Frank Mitchell (Blue),
    The.
Visions of Jesus.
Water of the Flowery Mill (II), The.
Young Woman's Neo-Aramaic Jewish Persian
    Blues.
See also **John, Richard Johnny, Jerome
    Rothenberg,** *and* **Ian Tyson.**
Rothenstein, William. *See* **Beerbohm, Max** *and*
    William Rothenstein.
Rottman, Larry
APO 96225.
Roughton, Roger
Building Society Blues.
Soluble Noughts and Crosses; or, California,
    Here I Come.
Roumain, Jacques (1907–44)
Dirty Niggers.
Ebony Wood, *sels.*
Guinea.
New Negro Sermon.
When the Tom-Tom Beats.
Roumer, Emile (b. 1903)
Black Girl Goes By, A.
Peasant Declares His Love, The.
Ten Lines.
Rous, Francis (1579–c.1658)
Help, Lord, because the Godly Man.
I to the Hills Will Lift Mine Eyes.
Rowan, Quentin (b. 1976)
Prometheus at Coney Island.
Rowbotham, David (b. 1934)
Bus-Stop on the Somme, The.
Cliff, The.
Mullabinda.
Nebuchadnezzar's Kingdom-Come.
Prey to Prey.
Rowe, Albert (b. 1915)
Destroyers, The.
Space Settlement.
Rowe, Elizabeth Singer (1674–1737)
Chapter IV.
Chapter V.
Expostulation, The.
Hymn: "In vain the dusky night retires."
Laplander's Song to His Mistress, A.
Paraphrase on the Canticles, A, *sels.*
To Celinda.
To one that persuades me to leave the
    Muses, *sels.*
To Orestes.
Upon the Death of Her Husband.
Rowe, George Clinton (1853–1903)
God Speed.
Mrs. Francis Ellen Harper.
Reason Why, The.
Toussaint L'Overture, *sels.*
We Are Rising.
Rowe, Henry (1754–1819)
Moon.

Sun.
Rowe, James Wilton (1865–1933)
Lake Chemo.
Rowe, Nicholas (1674–1718)
Epigram: "Whilst maudlin Whigs deplore
    their Cato's fate."
Rowland, J. R. (b. 1925)
Canberra in April.
London.
Traveller, A.
Rowlands, Samuel (1570?–1630?)
Boreas.
Epigram 29: "Gentlewoman of the dealing
    trade, A."
Melancholy Conceit, *sels.*
Prologue: "Under the shadow of the gloomy
    night."
Sir Revel.
Thraso.
Rowlandson, Thomas (1756–1827)
Epitaph on a Willing Girl.
Rowley, William. *See* **Dekker, Thomas, John
    Ford** *and* **William Rowley; Webster, John**
    and **William Rowley**
Rowse, Alfred Leslie (b. 1903)
White Cat of Trenarren, The.
Rowswell, Albert K.
Should You Go First.
Roy, Lucinda
Bread Man, The.
Ride, The.
Suffering The Sea Change: All My Pretty
    Ones.
Triple Overtime.
Royle, Edwin Milton (1862–1942)
Doan't You Be What You Ain't.
Rózewicz, Tadeusz (b. 1921)
Busy with Many Jobs.
Draft for a Contemporary Love Poem.
Draft of a Modern Love Poem.
Fight With An Angel.
Forms.
Homework Assignment on the Subject of
    Angels.
I Build.
I see madmen who.
In the Midst of Life.
Lament: "I turn to you high priests."
Larva, The.
Massacre of the Boys.
Memory of a Dream From the Year 1963.
Moment.
Pigtail.
Poem of Pathos.
Posthumous Rehabilitation.
Proofs.
Questions about Poetry since Auschwitz.
Return, The.
Roots.
She Looked At the Sun.
Survivor, The.
Talent.
To the Heart.
Transformations.
Voice, A.
Warning.
What Happens.
What luck I can pick.
Who Is a Poet.
**Rozhdestvensky [*or* Rozhdestvenskii], Robert
    Ivanovich (b. 1932)**
Nonflying Weather.
You Live on a Drifting Road.
Ruark, Gibbons (b. 1941)
Basil.
For a Suicide, a Little Early Morning Music.
Lament: "One sore thing is the way."
Larkin.
Lost Letter to James Wright, with Thanks for
    a Map of Fano.
Muse's Answer, The.
Postscript to an Elegy.
Rose Growing into the House, The.
Sleeping Out with My Father.
Vacant Lot, A.
Visitor, The.

Rubadiri, James David (b. 1930)
African Thunderstorm, An.
Stanley Meets Mutesa.
Rubin, Larry (b. 1930)
Brother-in-Law, The.
Dinner at the Mongoloid's.
Houses of Emily Dickinson, The.
Manual, The.
Rubin, Ron
Limerick: "I'm getting deep lines on my
    forehead."
Limerick: "'I'm glad pigs can't fly,' said
    young Sellers."
Limerick: "There was a trombonist called
    Herb."
Limerick: "There was a young Japanese
    geisha."
Limerick: "There was an old drunk called
    Hieronymus."
Limerick: "There was an old drunkard of
    Devon."
Limerick: "There was an old Welshman
    called Morgan."
Limerick: "Vain old Professor of Greek, A."
Rubisova, Yelena [*or* Elena] (b. 1910)
Humility is the eye of the needle.
Rubtsov, Nikolai Mikhailovich (1936–71)
Farewell Song.
Good Filya.
Rucker, Trish
Swallow Creek.
Swallows of Capistrano, The.
**Rückert, Friedrich ("Freimund Raimar")
    (1788–1866)**
And Then No More.
Barbarossa.
Ride round the Parapet, The.
Rudaki (870?–c.940)
Came to me— / Who?
Quatrain: "With you away—despair!"
Young or old we die.
Ruddock, Margot
Autumn, Crystal Eye.
Child Compassion, The.
I Take Thee Life.
Love Song: "Though to think / Rejoiceth
    me."
O Holy Water.
Spirit, Silken Thread.
Take Away.
Rudman, Andrew (d. 1708)
When Shall My Pilgrimage, Jesus My
    Saviour, Be Ended?
Rudman, Mark (b. 1948)
Nowhere Water, The.
Rudnik, Raphael (b. 1933)
Dream.
Lady in the Barbershop, The.
Penny Trumpet.
Ruff, "Whistling Bill"
Delia Holmes ("Delia, Delia, why didn't you
    run?")
Ruffilli, Paolo (b. 1949)
Malaria.
Ruffin, Paul (b. 1941)
Hotel Fire: New Orleans.
Rufinus (*fl.* between 150 *and* 400)
Amymone.
Did I not say we grow old.
Europa's kiss / even if.
Her eyes are gold.
Here Rhodoklea / is a garland.
I do not enjoy.
I hate an easy woman.
I have armoured my feelings.
If girls were nice.
In Spite.
Lay neither the scrawny.
Leaving the Boys Behind.
Let us wash each other's body.
Letter from Ephesos.
Melissias denies she's in love.
Pallas and / golden-shoed Hera.
Prodike.
Rhodope.

Rhodope is so stuck up / because of her beauty.
Rhodope, Melite and Rhodoklea / contested.
Silvertoed virgin, A.
Slave Girl, The.
So it's hullo now.
Waterfront Girls, The.
Where is Praxiteles where.
You have Hera's eyes Melite.

Rufinus Domesticus (*fl.* c.550)
Ah, Melissa, where's your famous golden beauty.
Epigrams, *sels.*
Europa kisses sweetly.
Her foot sparkled like silver.
How can any man throw out.
How could I have known.
I wove this garland, Rodokleia.
Kiss from her! Her mouth, coming even close to your own, how, A.
Lover's Posy, The.
We who find no joy in celebrity.
Were that woman's postcoital charms.
Who beat you and put you out.
Years have not damaged your beauty, The.

Ruggieri, Helen
Forked Tongue.
Ohio Is the Iroquois Word for Beautiful.
Unspoken World.

Ruiz, Juan, Archpriest of Hita (*fl.* c.1343)
Praise of Little Women.

Ruiz, Judy
Gifts.

Rukeyser, Muriel (1913–80)
Ajanta.
All the Little Animals.
Alloy.
Along history, forever.
Ballad of Orange and Grape.
Believing in those inexorable laws.
Birth of Venus, The.
Boy with His Hair Cut Short.
Boys of These Men Full Speed.
Breaking Open.
Bunk Johnson Blowing.
Burning the Dreams.
Campaign.
Ceiling Unlimited.
Children, the Sandbar, That Summer.
Columbus.
Conjugation of the Paramecium, The.
Cries From Chiapas.
Dam, The.
Darkness Music.
Death and the Dancer.
Despisals.
Don Baty, the Draft Resister.
Easter Eve.
Effort at Speech between Two People.
Eighth Elegy. Children's Elegy, *sels.*
Endless.
Eyes of Night-Time.
Fields Where We Slept.
For Kay Boyle.
Gauley Bridge.
George Robinson: Blues.
He Had a Quality of Growth.
Holy Family.
Homage to Literature.
Hostages, The.
In the Underworld.
Iris.
Käthe Kollwitz.
Kollwitz, Käthe.
Leg in a Plaster Cast, A.
Letter to the Front, *sels.*
Looking at Each Other.
Madboy's Song.
Meeting, The.
More of a Corpse Than a Woman.
Motive.
Myth.
Night Feeding.
Night-Music.
Nine Poems for the Unborn Child, *sels.*
Nuns in the Wind.
Paper Anniversary.

Place at Albert Bay, The.
Poem as Mask, The.
Poem: "I lived in the first century of world wars."
Poem Out of Childhood.
Power of Suicide, The.
Question, The.
Rational Man.
Reading Time : 1 Minute 26 Seconds.
Resurrection of the Right Side.
Rondel: "Now that I am fifty-six."
St. Roach.
Sand-Quarry with Moving Figures.
Song IV: The Calling-Up.
Song: "World is full of loss; bring, wind, my love, The."
Soul and Body of John Brown, The.
Speaking Tree, The.
Speed of Darkness, The.
Then.
Then I Saw What the Calling Was.
This is the cripples' hour on Seventh Avenue.
This Morning.
This Place in the Ways.
Waiting for Icarus.
Who in one lifetime sees all causes lost.
Woman as Market.
Yes, *sels.*

Rumaker, Michael (b. 1932)
Fairies Are Dancing All Over the World, The.

Rumble, Adrian
Black Hole.
Close Encounter, A.
Eagle has Landed, The.
Unique?

Rumens, Carol (b. 1944)
Double Bed.
Easter Garland, An.
Geography Lesson.
In the Cloud of Unknowing.
Limerick: "Ancient biologist, Heine, An."
Vocation.

Rumi, Jelaluddin [*or* Jalal al-Din] (1207–73)
All day and night, music.
Beauty That All Night Long, A.
Core of masculinity does not derive from being male, The.
Daylight, full of small dancing particles.
Dīvāni Shamsi Tabrīz, *sels.*
Do you think I know what I'm doing?
Don't grieve. Anything you lose comes round.
Drunkards are rolling in slowly, The.
Four Quatrains, *sels.*
Friend remarks to the Prophet, "Why is it," A.
Has anyone seen the boy who used to come here?
Human shape is a ghost, The.
I am your mother, your mother's mother.
I died as mineral and became a plant.
I, you, he, she, we.
If there be any lover in the world, O Moslems, 'tis I.
Keep walking, though there's no place to get to.
Light you give off, The.
Little by little, wean yourself.
Lo, for I to myself am unknown, now in God's name what must I do?
Minute I heard my first love story, The.
Morning: a polished knifeblade.
Names.
New Rule, The.
Out beyond ideas of wrongdoing and rightdoing.
Outside, the freezing desert night.
Praise to the emptiness that blanks out existence. Existence.
Quatrain: "I cry:/ but you want comforting."
Say Yes Quickly.
Someone Digging in the Ground.
Song of the spheres in their revolutions, The.
Strange Business.

That Journeys Are Good.
This marriage be wine with halvah, honey dissolving in milk.
Three Quatrains, *sels.*
Totally conscious, and appropos of nothing, he comes to see me.
Turn me like a waterwheel turning a millstone.
We can't help being thirsty.
We take long trips.
What the Flowers Said.
When grapes turn.
When it's cold and raining.
You are the notes, and we are the flute.
You that love Lovers.
You're song.

Rummo, Paul-Eerik
Again again again again again.
Here you grew up. On a land which is flat.
Sky bends over the earth, The.
World did not force itself into my soul, it seeped into it, The.

Runcie, John (1864–1939)
Slumber Song of the Gardens, A.

Rushin, Kate (b. 1951)
Bridge Poem, The.

Rushing, Jimmy (1903–1972)
Good Morning, Blues.
Sent for You Yesterday.

Rushton, Edward (1756–1814)
Human Debasement; a Fragment.

Ruskin, John (1817–1900)
La Madonna dell' Acqua.
Trust Thou Thy Love.
Zodiac Song, The.

Russell, Bertrand Arthur William Russell, 3d Earl (1872–1970/)
Limerick: "There was a young girl of Shanghai."

Russell, G. J.
It Might Have Been Worse.

Russell, George William. See "Æ"

Russell, Irwin (1853–99)
Christmas Night in the Quarters, *sels.*

Russell, Norman H. (b. 1921)
Message of the Rain, The.

Russell, Sanders
Poem: "I keep feeling all space as my image."

Russell, Sydney King (b. 1897)
Midsummer.

Russell, Thomas (1762–88)
Names and Order of the Books of the Old Testament, The.
Sonnet: Suppos'd to Be Written at Lemnos.
Sonnet to Valclusa.
To Oxford.
To the Spider.

Rutilius (*fl.* c.416)
Roma.

Rutsala, Vern (b. 1934)
American Dream.
Bodies.
Late at Night.
Lovers in Summer.
Shack Outside Boise, The.
Silence, The.
Skaters.
War of the Worlds, The.
Words.
World, The.

Rutter, Joseph (*fl.* 1635)
Epithalamium: "Hymen, god of marriage bed."

Rutter, Owen ("Klip-Klip") (1889–1944)
Song of Tiadatha, The, *sels.*

Ryan, Abram Joseph (Father Ryan) (1839–86)
Better than Gold ("Better than grandeur, better than gold.")
Lines: "Gather the sacred dust."
Sword of Robert Lee, The.
Thought, A.

Ryan, Father. See **Ryan, Abram Joseph**

Ryan, Gig (b. 1956)
Cruising.
Elegy for 6 So Far.

If I Had a Gun.
In the Purple Bar.
Ode to My Car.
Orbit.
Too Bad.

Ryan, John C. (b. c.1960)
Pawntickets.

Ryan, Kay
Outsider Art.

Ryan, Michael (b. 1946)
Barren Poem.
Letter from an Institution: III.
Not the End of the World.
Prothalamion.
Speaking.
Switchblade.
This Is a Poem for the Dead.
TV Room at the Children's Hospice.

Ryan, Richard (b. 1949)
At the End.
Deafness.
El Dorado.
Father of Famine.
From My Lai the Thunder Went West.
Ireland.
Lake of the Woods, The.
O, Saw Ye the Lass.
Wet Night, A.
Winter in Minneapolis.

Ryashentsev [or Riashentsev], Yury [or Iurii] (b. 1931)
April in Town.

Ryden, Ernest Edwin (1886–1981)
Twilight Shadows round Me Fall, The.

Rye, Anthony
Redbreast smoulders in the waste of snow, The.

Ryman, James (fl. late 15th cent.)
Farewele Advent; Cristemas [or Christemas] is cum [or cumen].

Rymer, Thomas (1641–1713)
To ———: "Let those with cost deck their ill-fashioned clay."

Rymkiewicz, Jaroslaw Marek (b. 1934)
Spinoza Was a Bee.

Ryojin Hisho (Hisho) (fl. c.1179?)
May the man who gained my trust yet did not come.

Ryokan (1758–1831)
First days of spring—the sky.
In all ten directions of the universe.
To lazy to be ambitious.

Ryozan (fl. 10th cent.)
When I am lonely.

Ryuichi, Tamura (b. 1923)
Every Morning After Killing Thousands of Angels.
Human House.
My Imperialism.
October Poem.
Standing Coffin.

S

Sa Nguyên
Dress of Hà-Đông silk, The.

Saarikoski, Pentti (b. 1937)
Dance Floor on the Mountain, The, *sels.*
Invitation to the Dance, *sels.*
Potato Thief.
Revolution.

Saba (Fath Ali Khan) (fl. early 19th cent.)
King's Garden World, A.

Saba, Umberto (1883–1957)
Winter Noon.

Sabina, María (b. 1894)
Chants, The, *sels.*
Midnight Velada, The, *sels.*
Shaman.
13th Horse Song of Frank Mitchell, The.

Sacchetti, Franco (1335–1400?)
Ballata: His Talk with Certain Peasant Girls.
Catch: On a Wet Day.

Sachdev, Padma (b. 1940)
Well, The.

Sachs, Hans (1494–1576)
Fair Melody: To Be Sung by Good Christians, A.

Sachs, Nelly (1891–1969)
Above the rocking heads of the mothers.
Already embraced by the arm of heavenly solace.
Awakening— / Voices of birds.
But look / but look.
But Perhaps [God needs the longing, wherever else should it dwell].
Chorus of the Dead.
Chorus of the Rescued.
Chorus of the Stars.
Chorus of the Unborn.
Dead Child Speaks, A.
How long have we forgotten how to listen!
If I only knew.
In flight in escape.
In the blue distance.
In the evening your vision widens.
Landscape of Screams.
Last one / to die here, The.
Line Like.
O my mother.
O sister, / where do you pitch your tent?
O the Chimneys.
O the night of the weeping children!
Oblivion! Skin.
Rushing at Times Like Flames.
Someone.
Vainly ("Vainly / the epistles burn.")
We mothers.
What secret cravings of the blood.
White Serpent.
You / in the night.
Your eyes, O my beloved.

Sackville, Charles, 6th Earl of Dorset (1688–1706)
On Dorinda.
On Mr. Edward Howard, upon His British Princes.
Song Written at Sea in the First Dutch War (1665), the Night before an Engagement.

Sackville, Thomas, 1st Earl of Dorset (1536–1608)
Induction to "A Mirror for Magistrates," *sels.*
Thomas Sackevyll in Commendation of the Worke to the Reader.

Sackville-West, Victoria [or Vita] Mary (1892–1962)
Absence.
Beechwoods at Knole.
Bull, The.
Craftsmen.
Dream, A.
Extract from Solitude, *sels.*
Frost.
Full Moon.
Garden, The.
Greater cats with golden eyes, The.
Land, The.
Nostalgia.
On the Lake.
Out with a Gun.
Persia.
Pruning in March.
Rose, The.
September 1939.
Sissinghurst.
Sometimes When Night.
Spinster.
Tess.
Thus love, bright charlatan, besieged my heart.
To Any M.F.H F. H.
Valediction.
Young Stock.

Sadi [or Saadi or Sa'di] (Muslih [or Musliud] -Din) (1184–1291)
Gulistan, The, *sels.*
Ode: "Until thine hands clasp girdlewise the waist of the Belov'd."

Sadiq
Tuskegee Experiment.

Sadoff, Ira (b. 1945)
At the Half-Note Café.
Bath, The.
Civil Rights.
Concise History of the World, A.
Fifties, The.
My Father's Leaving.
Nazis.
Poem after Apollinaire.

Sadoleto, Jacopo (1477–1547)
Poem of Jacobus Sadoletus on the Statue of Laocoon, The.

Sadongei, Alice (b. 1959)
After Seeing Paintings in a Small Book by T. C. Cannon (1946-1978).
Don't forget when the sticks are ready for picking.
For Carlos Charles Bucillio.
Poems Come to Me in the Night.
Wind Blew like Water.

Sáenz, Benjamin Alire
Resurrections.

Saffarzadeh, Tahereh (b. 1939)
Birthplace.

Saffin, John (1626–1700)
Acrostick on Mrs. Elizabeth Hull, An.
Acrostick on Mrs. Winifret Griffin, An.
Brief Elegie on My Dear Son John, A.
Consideratus Considerandus.
Elegie on the Deploreable Departure of the Honered and Truely Religious Chieftain John Hull, An.
Lamentation on My Dear Son Simon, A.
One Presenting a Rare Book to Madame Hull.
Satyretericall Charracter of a Proud Upstart, A.
Sweetly (my Dearest) I left thee asleep.
To His Excellency Joseph Dudley.

Saffoti, Carol Lee
Espresso.

Safiya bint Musafir (fl. early 7th cent.)
At the Badr Trench.

Sagami, Lady (fl. c.1000)
In the gathering dew.
There is no night / when the lightning does not flash.
With hate and misery / my sleeves are never dry.

"Sagittarius" (Olga Katzin) (b. 1896)
Come into the Army, Maud.
Croaked the Eagle: "Nevermore."
Freedom in Peril.
Limerick: "Rather extreme vegetarian, A."
Nerves.
Passionate Profiteer to His Love, The.
Servant of the House.
Stalin Moy Golubchik.

Sagoff, Maurice
Preface Shrink Lit: Elements of Style.
Robinson Crusoe Daniel Defoe.

Sahay, Raghuvir (1929–90)
Our Hindi is a widower's new wife.

Sa'id, 'Ali Ahmad. See "Adunis"

Saigyo (Saigyo Hoshi) (1118–90)
Although I do not know.
In my boat that goes.
Like those boats which are returning.
Mingling my prayer.
My heart emptied.
Since I am convinced.
Sixty-four Tanka, *sels.*
Startled / By a single scream.
Those ships which left.

Sail, Lawrence (b. 1942)
Christmas Night.

Sainsbury, Ian
I put my hat upon my head.
Loveliest of Counties, Shropshire Now.

Saint-Amant, Sieur de. See Girard, Antoine *and* Sieur de Saint-Amant

Saint, Assotto (b. 1957)
Triple Trouble.

Saint-Gelais, Mellin de (1491–1558)
Sonnet of the Mountain, The.

St. John, Bruce (1923–91)
Bajan Litany.
Subtlety.

St. John, David (b. 1949)
Avenues, The.
Dolls.
For Lerida.
Hush.
I know the moon is troubling.
Iris.
Leap of Faith.
Meridian.
My friend, a man I love as wholly.
Poem: "Your face, / so pale now it is blue."
Quote Me Wrong Again and I'll Slit the
     Throat of Your Pet Iguana.
Slow Dance.
Terraces of Rain.
Uptown Love Poem.
Wavelength.
Wedding Preparations in the Country.

St. John, Primus (b. 1939)
Benign Neglect / Mississippi, 1970.
Carnival.
Elephant Rock.
Lynching and Burning.
Morning Star, The.
Ocean of the Streams of Story.
Pearle's Poem.
Reading a Story to My Child.
Song.
Sunday.
Tyson's Corner.
We Are Going to Be Here Now.

Saitō Mokichi (1882–1953)
Tanka: "All that past life."
Tanka: "Aspiration."
Tanka: "By the road."
Tanka: "Confinement."
Tanka: "Dahlias are black."
Tanka: "Determined to try."
Tanka: "Ever so close."
Tanka: "Fly, A."
Tanka: "Frog."
Tanka: "From the evening darkness."
Tanka: "From where."
Tanka: "Infinitely far."
Tanka: "Nothing to be done?"
Tanka: "Often likened."
Tanka: "Past the hens."
Tanka: "Red pepper pods."
Tanka: "Self-portrait, A."
Tanka: "Snowflakes."
Tanka: "What on the other shore."
Tanka: "Yolk, The."

Sakanoe No Korenori
In the dawn.

"Saki" (Hector Hugh Munro) (1870–1916)
Carol: "While shepherds watched their flocks
     by night."

Salaam, Kalamu ya (b. 1947)
Our World Is Less Full Now That Mr. Fuller
     Is Gone.

Salamah, son of Jandal (*fl.* 6th cent.)
Gone Is Youth. *From* The Mufaddaliyat.

Salamun, Tomaz (b. 1941)
Clumsy Guys.
Homage to a Hat and Uncle Guido and Eliot.
Jonah.

Salatko-Petrishche, Valerii Frantsevich. *See*
     "Pereleshin, Valery Frantsevich"

Salazar, Dixie (*fl.* 20th cent.)
Piñon Nuts.
Taking It Back.

Saldaña, Diego de (*fl.* 15th cent.)
Eyes So Tristful.

Salimon, Vladimir (b. 1952)
Food-Factory Kitchen.
Salute, Friends!

Salinas, Luis Omar (b. 1937)
I Go Dreaming Roads in My Youth.

Salinas, Pedro (1892–1951)
Wake up. Day calls you.

Salinas, Raul
Trip Through the Mind Jail, A.

Salis, Gunars
Bomb Victim in the Cathedral Speaks to a
     Child, A.
Song.

Salis-Seewis, Johann Gaudenz von (1763–1834)
Song of the Silent Land.

Salkey, Andrew (b. 1943)
Away.
Clearsightedness.
Dry River Bed.
Inside.
John Connu Rider.
Postcard from Mexico, 16.X.1973.
Remember Haiti, Cuba, Vietnam.
Song for England, A.
Soufrière.

Salom, Philip (b. 1950)
Ghazal on signs of Love and Occupation.
Walking at Night.
Well, The.
Winter.
World of dreams, The.

Salome, Brian S.
Hello There.

Salsbury, Nate (b. 1888)
Apex.

Salter, Mary Jo (b. 1954)
Age of Reason, The.
Chernobyl.
Emily Wants to Play.
England.
Frost at Midnight.
Rebirth of Venus, The.
Refrain.
Summer 1983.
Welcome to Hiroshima.
What Do Women Want?
Young Girl Peeling Apples.

Salzman, Eric
Double Dactyls.

Samain, Albert (1858–1900)
Pannyra of the Golden Heel.

Sambrook, Joyce
Wild Thyme.
Woodpecker, The.

Sami Mansei (Mansei) (*fl.* 8th cent.)
This world of ours.

Samik
Hunger.

Samio, Maekawa
Tanka: "Because my room."
Tanka: "Call to mind."
Tanka: "Day I was born, The."
Tanka: "Fish skeleton, A."
Tanka: "For a moment."
Tanka: "If only."
Tanka: "In the evening wind."
Tanka: "Loud voice, A."
Tanka: "Memories open."
Tanka: "Monumental."
Tanka: "No scar."
Tanka: "On a starry night."
Tanka: "On occasion."
Tanka: "On the sandy beach."
Tanka: "Reverently."
Tanka: "Surely by now."
Tanka: "When the gardener."
Tanka: "Why does a room."
Tanka: "With each quiver."
Tanka: "With the blue."

"Samoylov [or Samoilov], David Samuilovich"
     (David Samuilovich Kaufman) (1920–1990)
Ballad about the German Censor, The.
Death of Ivan, The.
Forties, fateful forties, The.
Ivan and the Serf.
Old Derzhavin.
Pestel, the Poet, and Anna.
Poem not flowery but bare, A.
Words.

Sampson, Dennis (*fl.* 20th cent.)
Anaconda, The.

Sampter, Jessie E. (b. 1883–1938)
Kadia the Young Mother Speaks.
Promised Land, The.

Summer Sabbath.

Samuel Ha-Nagid (993–1055)
I Look Up to the Sky.
Proverbs.

San Garde, Evelina
Giant's Cake, A.

San Geminiano [or Gimignano], Folgore da (*fl.*
     13th cent.)
On Knighthood.
Sonnet: Of Virtue.
Sonnets of the Months, *sels.*
Sonnets of the Months: Conclusion.
Sonnets of the Months: September.

San, Phan Văn. *See* **Phan Bội Châu**

Sanchez, Sonia (b. 1935)
Answer to Yo / Question.
Anthem, An.
Black Magic.
Blues.
Chant for Young/Brothas and Sistuhs, A.
Definition for Blk/Children.
Father and Daughter.
For Our Lady.
Haiku.
Haiku: "Was it yesterday."
Haiku: "Your voice unwrapping."
Homecoming.
Hospital/Poem.
July.
Liberation / Poem.
Listenen to Big Black at S. F. State.
Memorial.
Nigger.
Norma.
Now Poem. For Us.
On Watching a World Series Game.
Personal Letter No. 3.
Poem at Thirty.
Poem for Etheridge.
Poem for my Brother, A.
Poem for My Father, A.
Poem for my Most Intelligent 10:30 AM
     Class/Fall 1985, A.
Poem: "Look at me 8th."
Prelude to Nothing.
Present.
Right On: White America.
Song No. 2: "I say. all you young girls
     waiting to live."
Song No. 3: "Cain't nobody tell me any
     different."
Summary.
Summer Words of [*or* for] a Sistuh [*or*
     Sister] Addict.
To All Brothers.
To All Sisters.
To Anita.
To P. J.
To P. J. (2 Yrs Old Who Sed Write a Poem
     for Me in Portland, Oregon).

Sandall, Harold C.
Song: "Love that is hoarded, moulds at last."

Sandburg, Carl (1878–1967)
A. E. F.
Alice Corbin is gone.
Aprons of Silence.
At a Window.
Auctioneer.
Balloon Faces.
Bas-Relief.
Be Ready.
Blue Island Intersection.
Broadway.
Broken-Face Gargoyles.
Buffalo Dusk.
Bundles.
Buttons.
Caboose Thoughts.
Chicago.
Child of the Romans.
Choose.
Cool Tombs.
Crapshooters.
Death Snips Proud Men.
Early Copper.
Early Lynching.
Elephants Are Different to Different People.

Evening Waterfall.
Falltime.
Fish Crier.
Flash Crimson.
Fog comes / on little cat feet, The.
For You.
Four Preludes on Playthings of the Wind.
Gargoyle.
Gone.
Grass.
Halsted Street Car.
Happiness.
Harbor, The.
Horses and Men in the Rain.
I am the people—the mob—the crowd—the
   mass.
Ice Handler.
In Tall Grass.
Jack was a swarthy, swaggering son-of-a-gun.
Jazz Fantasia.
Joy.
Languages.
Lawyers Know Too Much, The.
Limited.
Lines Written for Gene Kelly to Dance To.
Little girl, be careful what you say.
Little girl saw her first troop parade and
   asked, "What are those?," The.
Long Shadow of Lincoln: A Litany, The.
Losers.
Lost.
Love in Labrador.
Mag.
Man in the street is fed, The.
Milk white moon, put the cows to sleep.
Mill-Doors.
Mist Forms.
Moist Moon People.
Nocturne in a Deserted Brickyard.
Old Timers.
On a Flimmering Floom You Shall Ride.
One Modern Poet.
Osawatomie.
People Who Must.
People, Yes, The, *sels.*
Poetry is any page from a sketchbook of
   outlines of a.
Population Drifts.
Prairie Waters by Night.
Prayer after World War.
Prayers of Steel.
Precious Moments.
Primer Lesson.
Psalm of Those Who Go Forth before
   Daylight.
River Roads.
Sandhill People.
Sea-wash never ends, The.
Shirt.
Shovel Man, The.
Sins of Kalamazoo are neither scarlet nor
   crimson, The.
Skyscraper.
Smoke and Steel, *sels.*
Soiled Dove.
Soup.
Southern Pacific.
Splinter.
Stars are too many to count, The.
Sunset from Omaha Hotel Window.
Sunsets.
Ten Definitions of Poetry.
There Are Different Gardens.
They all want to play Hamlet.
They Ask: Is God, Too, Lonely?
Three Spring Notations on Bipeds.
Threes.
Upstream.
Useless Words.
Washington Monument by Night.
We Must Be Polite.
Whiffs of the Ohio River at Cincinnati, *sels.*
Wilderness.
Wind Song.
Window.
Work Gangs.

Sandeen, Ernest (b. 1908)
   Late Twentieth-Century Prayer, A.
   Nearing Winter.
   Plaint of Flowers, A.
   Poète Manqué.
   They Are Wicked.
   Way Down, The.

Sanders, Donald T. (b. 1944)
   Poem for Shane on Her Brother's Birthday.

Sanders, Edward (b. 1939)
   Cutting Prow, The.
   Fugs, The.
   Holy Was Demeter Walking th' Corn
     Furrow.
   Leaves of heaven, The.
   Pindar's Revenge.

Sanders, Tony
   Transit Authority.

Sandstrom, Flora
   Stately Lady, The.

Sandy, Stephen (b. 1934)
   Declension.
   Et Quid Amabo Nisi Quod Aenigma Est.
   Hunter's Moon.
   Threads.

Sandys, Edwin (1561–1629)
   In pilgrim life our rest.

Sandys, George (c.1577–1644)
   Bounty of Jehovah Praise, The.
   Judah in exile wanders.
   O Blest Estate, Blest from Above.
   Paraphrase Upon Job, A, *sels.*

Saner, Reg (b. 1931)
   Fifth Season, The.

Sanesada (Fujiwara no Sanesada) (1139–91)
   Cuckoo calls. / When I look there is only, A.

Sanesada, Fujiwara no. *See* Sanesada

Sangster, Charles (1822–93)
   Sonnets Written in the Orillia Woods, *sels.*
   St. Lawrence and the Saguenay, *sels.*

Sangster, Margaret Elizabeth (b. 1894)
   Bit of the Book in the morning, A.
   Blind Man, The.
   In Gratitude for Friends.
   Prayer for Faith, A.

**Sangster, Margaret Elizabeth Munson (1838–
1912)**
   Forgiven.
   Oh, face to face with trouble.
   Our Own.
   Patience with the Living.
   Sin of Omission, The.

Sanjō Emperor (fl. 11th cent.)
   Involuntary, / I may live on.

**Sannazaro, Jacopo (Actius Sincerus
Sannazarius) (1458–1530)**
   Like to these unme[a]surable mountains [*or*
     mountayns].

Sanpu (1647–1732)
   May rains!

Sansom, Clive (1910–81)
   Dustman, The.
   Flotilla.
   Innkeeper's Wife, The.
   Me—Pirate.
   Milkman, The.
   October.
   Ploughing.
   Postman, The.
   Snowflakes.
   Witnesses, The, *sels.*

Sansom, Martha (1690–1736)
   Clio, *sels.*
   Invitation from a Country Cottage, The.
   It was not that I lost direction.
   Song: "Foolish eyes, thy streams give over."
   To Cleon's Eyes.
   To My Heavenly Charmer.

Sant, Andrew (b. 1950)
   Homage to the Canal People.
   Soundwaves.

Sant' Angelo, Bartolomeo di (fl. 13th cent.)
   Sonnet: He Jests Concerning His Poverty.

Sant, Indira (b. 1914)
   Household Fires.

Santal
   Witch, The.

Sant'Ana, Gloria de
   African Day.

Santayana, George (1863–1952)
   Before a Statue of Achilles.
   Cape Cod.
   Echo.
   I Would I Might Forget That I Am I.
   Minuet on Reaching the Age of Fifty, A.
   Ode V: "Of thee the Northman by his
     beachèd galley."
   On a Piece of Tapestry.
   On an Unfinished Statue.
   Sonnets, *sels.*
   To W. P., *sels.*

Santob de Carrion (fl. 14th cent.)
   Consejos y Documentos al Rey Dom Pedro,
     sels.

Santos, Sherod (b. 1949)
   Air Base at Châteauroux, France, The.
   Childhood.
   Death.
   Inspiration.
   Late November.
   Married Love.
   Near the Desert Test Sites.
   Nineteen Fifty-five.
   Sheltering Ground, The, *sels.*

Sanuki, Lady (fl. early 13th cent.)
   Like a great rock, far out at sea. *From*
     Hyaku-Nin-Isshu.

Sapgir, Genrik Veniaminovich (b. 1928)
   Fearless One.

Sapia, Yvonne (b. 1946)
   Grandmother, a Caribbean Indian, Described
     by My Father.
   Valentino's Hair.

Sappho (fl. c.612 B.C.)
   About the cool water.
   All the stars turn away their faces.
   All the while, believe me, I prayed.
   Alone.
   Andromache's Wedding.
   Andromeda / forgot.
   As the full moon slowly rose.
   At last, on delicate feet.
   Bridal Songs: "Happy bridegroom! / Now
     your wedding has come true."
   Come, holy tortoise shell.
   Come out of Crete / and find me here.
   Come to me from Crete to this holy temple.
   Cool Retreat, A.
   Don Juan, *sels.*
   Don't ask me what to wear.
   Doricha. *From* Variations of Greek Themes.
   Dust of Timas, The.
   Epithalamium, *sels.*
   Eros seizes and shakes my very soul.
   Eternal Aphrodite.
   Evening Star who gathers everything.
   Farewell to Anactoria.
   Forever Dead.
   Frae the Aiolic o Psappho.
   Full Moon.
   Glow and beauty of the stars, The.
   He is almost a god, a man beside you.
   He is more than a hero.
   Here are fine gifts, children.
   Here lies the dust of Timas.
   Hermes came to me in a dream. I said.
   Hesperos, you bring home all the bright
     dawn disperses.
   High on the upper, outermost bough.
   Honestly I wish I were dead!
   Honestly I'd as soon be dead!
   Hymn to Venus, An.
   I could not hope / to touch the sky.
   I fell in love with you, Atthis.
   I have no embroidered headband.
   I hear that Andromeda.
   I longed to.
   I love / love's delicacy.
   If my nipples were to drip milk.

If you had lusted after something noble or decent.
In gold sandals.
It would be wrong for us. It is not right.
Leave Krete and come to this holy temple.
Leaving Crete, come visit again our temple.
Like a mountain whirlwind.
Like a sweet apple reddening on the high.
Like the very gods in my sight is he.
Love—bittersweet, irrepressible.
Love, like a mountain-wind upon an oak.
Marriage of Hector and Andromache, The.
Moon Has Set, The.
Moon has veil'd her Silver Light, The.
Mother darling, I cannot work the loom.
Muse of the Golden Throne.
Must be some girl from the villages.
My Atthis, although our dear Anaktoria.
My lovely friends.
My mother always said.
Now in my / heart I / see clearly.
O dream from the blackness.
O Gongyla, my darling rose.
Ode to Anactoria.
Ode to Aphrodite.
On a Lady Indifferent to Poetry.
On your dazzling throne, Aphrodite.
On your throne, a marvel of art, immortal.
One Girl.
Pain penetrates.
Peer of the gods is that man, who.
People do gossip.
Percussion, salt and honey.
Pleiades disappear, The.
Pleiads now no more are seen, The.
Round about Me.
Sapho's Ode out of Longinus.
Sapphic Fragment.
Sapphics.
"Sappho, if you do not come out."
Silent on the subject of vengeance.
Some prefer a glory of horsemen; warships.
Some say cavalry and others claim.
Some say nothing on earth excels in beauty.
Some there are who say that the fairest thing seen.
Someday you will be dead.
Someone, I tell you, / will remember us.
Song for the Goddess of Love.
Stars around the luminous moon—how soon they.
Thank you, my dear.
That labor / a face to remember in wonder.
Then I said to the elegant ladies.
There's a man, I really believe, compares with.
There's a man I really believe's in heaven.
These are the ashes of Timas.
This is the dust of Timias.
To me he seems like a god.
Tonight I've watched.
Weeping Pleiads wester, The.
When Death shall close those Eyes, imperious Dame!
When rage invades your burning breast.
With his venom.
You came. And you did well to come.
You know the place: then.
You lay in wait.

Sargant, Edmund Beale
Cuckoo Wood, The.

Sargent, Elizabeth Nancy (b. 1934)
Break, The.
Child of the season of adventure, child of the heart.
Paradise.

Sargent, Epes (1813–80)
Life on the Ocean Wave, A.
Planet Jupiter, The.
Rockall.
Sea-Breeze at Matanzas, The.

Sargent, N. B.
Building for Eternity.

Sarmèd the Yahud (*fl.* 17th cent.)
Quatrain: "Sarmèd, whom they intoxicated from the cup of love."

Quatrain: "This existence has, without the azure sphere, no reality."

Sarmiento, Félix Rubén García. *See* **"Dario, Rubén"**

"Sarnicol." *See* **Thomas, Thomas Jacob**

Sarson, H. M.
Lovely Things.
Road to Town, The.
Shell, The.

Sartarelli, Stephen (b. 1954)
Early Spring, An.
Phantasmatikon.
That Land (3).
That Land (4).

Sarton, May (1914–95)
After a Train Journey.
All Souls.
At Lindos.
Autumn Sonnets, The, *sels.*
Christmas Letter, 1970, *sels.*
Easter, 1968.
Eine Kleine Snailmusik.
Fruit of Loneliness.
Gestalt at Sixty, *sels.*
I Must Away.
In Time Like Air.
Late Autumn.
Letter from Chicago.
Muse as Medusa, The.
My Sisters, O My Sisters.
Now I become myself. It's taken.
Nursery Rhyme.
Of Grief, *sels.*
Prothalamion for an Autumn Wedding.
Small Joys.
Snow Light, The.
Tortured, The.

Sarumaru (*fl.* 9th cent.)
Deep in the mountain.

Sassoon, Siegfried (1886–1967)
Aftermath.
Ancient History.
At Daybreak.
At the Grave of Henry Vaughan.
Attack.
Babylon that was beautiful is Nothing now.
Base Details.
Blighters.
Blues at Lord's, The.
Brevities.
Child's Prayer, A.
Christ and the Soldier.
Concert Party.
Conclusion: "Image dance of change, An."
Counter-Attack.
Daybreak in a Garden.
Death-Bed, The.
December Stillness.
Does It Matter?[—losing your legs?].
Dreamers.
Dug-Out, The.
Elected Silence.
Everyman.
Everyone Sang.
Falling Asleep.
Fathers, The.
Fight to a Finish.
Foot Inspection.
General, The.
Glory of Women.
Grandeur of Ghosts.
Haunted.
Hero, The.
I Shall Find You.
In Barracks.
In Heytesbury Wood.
In Me, Past, Present, Future Meet.
"In the Pink."
Invocation: "Come down from heaven to meet me when my breath."
Lamentations.
Limitations.
Memorial Tablet.
Morning Glory.
Night on the Conroy.
On Passing the New Menin Gate.
One-legged Man, The.

One Who Watches.
Picture-Show.
Post-Mortem, A.
Power and the Glory, The.
Prehistoric Burials.
Presences Perfected.
Rank stench of those bodies haunts me still, The.
Rear-Guard, The.
Reconciliation.
Redeemer, The.
Repression of War Experience.
South Wind.
Sporting Acquaintances.
Stand-to: Good Friday Morning.
Strangeness of Heart.
Stretcher Case.
Suicide in [the] Trenches.
"They."
To Any Dead Officer.
To His Dead Body.
To One Who Was with Me in the War.
Troops, The.
Two Old Ladies.
Vigils, *sels.*
"When I'm alone"—the words tripped off his tongue.
Wisdom of the World, The.
Working Party, A.

Satchidanandan, K. (b. 1946)
Genesis.

Sato, Hiroaki
In your panties.

Satyamurti, Carole (b. 1939)
Day Trip.
Reflections.

Satyrus (2d cent. B.C)
Echo, tongueless, sings her sweet.

Sa'udi, Mona (b. 1945)
How do I enter the silence of stones.
When the loneliness of the tomb went down into the marketplace.
Why don't I write in the language of air?

Saunders, Lesley
Mothers of Sons.

Saunders, Mary Wright
Remembering Day.

Saunders, R. Crombie (b. 1914)
Empty Glen, The.
Ressaif My Saul.

Saunders, Ruby C. (Fareedah Allah)
Cinderella.
Funky Football.
Generation Gap, The.
Hush Honey.
Lawd, Dese Colored Chillum.
You Made It Rain.

Sauser-Hall, Frédéric-Louis. *See* **Cendrars, Blaise**

Savage, Derek S. (b. 1917)
Fall of Leaves.

Savage, Mary (*fl.* 1763–77)
Disaster, The.
Letter to Miss E.B. at Bath.
Letter to Miss E.B. on Marriage, *sels.*
To a School-Boy at Eton, Yes and No.

Savage, Richard (1698–c.1743)
Authors of the Town, The, *sels.*
Bastard, The, *sels.*
Progress of a Divine, The, *sels.*

Savard, Jeannine
Carnival Figure of Guatemalan Clay, A.
Daughter's Brooch, The.
Descent of Fire, The.
Fall, The.

Savenko, Eduard Veniaminovich. *See* **"Limonov, Eduard Veniaminovich"**

Savinkov, Boris Viktorovich. *See* **"Ropshin, V."**

Sawyer, Anna (*fl.* 1794–1801)
Lines, / Written on Seeing My Husband's Picture, painted when he was young: "Those are the features, those the smiles."
Sunday Schools.

Sawyer, Charles Carroll (1887–1979)
When This Cruel War Is Over.

Sawyer, Ruth (b. 1880)
Feast o' Saint [or St.] Stephen, The.
Saxe, John Godfrey (1816–87)
Blind Men and the Elephant, The.
Early Rising.
Game of Life, The.
News, Indeed!—pray do you call it news, The.
Rhyme of the Rail[s].
Story of Life, The.
Saxe, Susan (b. 1949)
Questionnaire.
Saxena, Sarveshwar Dayal (1927–84)
Black panther is sleeping on the crags, The.
Saxon, Alvin (Ojenke)
Black Power.
Poem for Integration, A.
Watts.
Sayers, A. M.
It Always Seems.
Limerick: "I admire your felicitous phrasing."
Limerick: "There once was a wise politician."
Limerick: "There was an old dame of Toulouse."
Limerick: "Three wonderful people called Wick."
Limerick: "When I sit in the Churchyard at Stoke."
Prithee, let no raindrop fall.
Sayers, Dorothy Leigh (1893–1957)
Devil to Pay, The, *sels.*
Sayles, James M. (b. 1948)
Star of the Evening.
Sayres, Cortlandt W. (b. 1927)
Bankrupt.
Scalapino, Leslie (b. 1948)
Considering How Exaggerated Music Is.
Crowd and Not Evening Or Light, *sels.*
Floating Series, *sels.*
Flush / a Play.
Hmmmm, *sels.*
Or a Play.
Picasso and Anarchism.
Scannell, Vernon (b. 1922)
Act of Love.
Any Complaints?
Apple-raid, The.
Autumn.
Cat.
Dead Dog.
Discriminator, The.
Five Domestic Interiors.
Great War, The.
Hide and Seek.
Incendiary.
Jailbird.
"Moth has got into it, The."
Old Books, The.
Poem on Bread.
Poetry Reading.
Popular Mythologies.
Protest Poem.
Six Reasons for Drinking.
Walking Wounded.
Words and Monsters.
Scarborough, George L.
To the Men Who Lose.
Scarfe, Francis (b. 1911)
Cats.
Grotto, The.
Kitchen Poem.
Merry Window, The.
Ode in Honour.
Scates, Maxine
Angel.
Angel's Flight.
Floor Plans.
Going to Mass after Fifteen Years.
1956.
Working.
Scève, Maurice
Délie.
Schacht, Marshall (b. 1905)
Not to Forget Miss Dickinson.
Schaefer, Sister M. Cherubim (b. 1886)
Rejoice, Let Alleluias Ring.

Schaeffer, Susan Fromberg (b. 1941)
Housewife.
Schafer, John C.
Battle Lines.
Schaukal, Richard
Images.
Schechter, Ruth Lisa (1927–89)
What Were You Patching?
Scheele, Roy (b. 1942)
Gap in the Cedar, The.
Scheerbart, Paul (1863–1915)
Monologue of the Crazed Mastodon.
Scheffauer, Ethel Talbot
Limerick: "Mr Lear, I'm the Akond of Swat."
Scheffler, Johannes. *See* "Angelus Silesius"
Schelling, Andrew (b. 1953)
Isha Upanishad.
Run My Hand Under.
Scherzo, I. O.
Threnody: "Truth is a golden sunset far away."
Schevill, James (b. 1920)
Freud: Dying London, He Recalls the Smoke of His Cigar Beginning to Sing.
Green Frog at Roadstead, Wisconsin.
Huck Finn at Ninety, Dying in a Chicago Boarding House Room.
London Pavement Artist.
Screamer Discusses Methods of Screaming, A.
Schick, Eleanor
Last summer.
Schiff, Hilda
Discovery.
German Frontier at Basel: 1942 and 1992, The.
When It Happened.
Schiller, Johann Christoph Friedrich von (1759–1805)
Maid of Orleans, The.
Piccolomini, The, *sels.*
To My Friends.
Unrealities, The.
Schimelpfenig, Mary Jo
Geography of Lunch, A.
Schirmer, David (1623–83)
He Loves.
Schjeldahl, Peter (b. 1942)
Younger Poet, A.
Schloss, David
Poem: "I had never heard of the whiteness."
Schmitz, Dennis (b. 1937)
Bird-Watching.
California Phrasebook, The.
Chicago: Near West-Side Renewal.
Goodwill, Inc.
Ladder: Roger Vail's Photo of a Rockface in the Carrara (Italy) Marble Quarries, The.
Letter to Ron Silliman on the Back of a Map of the Solar System, A.
Making a Door.
Making Chicago.
Mile Hill.
Mole, The.
Name of Our Country, The.
Picture of Okinawa, A.
Poke-Pole Fishing.
Queen of Heaven Mausoleum.
Star & Garter Theater.
String.
Schnack, Anton
Nocturnal Landscape.
Schnackenberg, Gjertrud (b. 1953)
Angels Grieving over the Dead Christ.
Darwin in 1881.
Living Room, The.
Nightfishing.
Paperweight, The.
Signs.
Supernatural Love.
Two Tales of Clumsy, *sels.*
Walking home from school one afternoon.
Schneider, Isidor (1896–1977)
Insects.
Joy of Knowledge.

Schneour, Zalman (b. 1887)
Besieged.
Cherries.
Forsaken.
Fruited Month, The.
Last Words of Don Henriquez, The.
Like Water down a Slope.
Middle Ages draw near. Do you hear, sensitive man, do you feel, The.
Poppies.
Road, The.
Song of the Snow.
War Comes.
Welcome, Queen Sabbath.
Schneurson, Zelda. *See* "Zelda"
Schoenberger, Nancy (b. 1950)
Taxidermist's Daughter, The.
Scholasticus, Agathias. *See* Agathias
Schomberg, Ralph (1714–92)
Judgment of Paris, The, *sels.*
Schonborg, Virginia (b. 1913)
Rumble, A.
Schorr, Laurie
Amusement.
Schreiber, Ron (b. 1934)
Alarming New Development, An.
House Is Old, The.
Schreiner, Olive (1855–1920)
Cry of South Africa, The.
Schroeder, Peter (b. 1928)
All Human Things.
Schubert, David (1913–46)
Successful Summer, A.
Schulman, Grace
Burial of a Fisherman in Hydra.
For That Day Only.
Present Perfect, The.
Schultz, Philip (b. 1945)
Answering Machine, The.
For My Father.
For My Mother.
I'm Not Complaining.
My Guardian Angel Stein.
Ode.
Pumpernickel.
Quality, The.
Schuyler, James (1923–91)
Buried at Springs.
Can I Tempt You to a Pond Walk?
Crocus Night.
Crystal Lithium, The.
Earth's Holocaust.
Elizabethans Called It Dying, The.
Father or Son.
February.
Freely Espousing.
Grand Duo.
Greetings from the Chateau.
Growing Dark.
Head, A.
I Think.
Korean Mums.
Let's All Hear It for Mildred Bailey!
Letter to a Friend: Who Is Nancy Daum?
Man in Blue, The.
Master of the Golden Glow, The.
Our Father.
Poem: "This beauty that I see."
Roof Garden.
Royals.
Salute.
Self-Pity Is a Kind of Lying, Too.
Shimmer.
Sleep.
Song: "I'm about to go shopping."
Spring.
Stone Knife, A.
Sunday.
Tom.
Schwartz, Delmore (1913–66)
Abraham.
All of us always turning away for solace.
Ballet of the Fifth Year, The.
Baudelaire.
Beautiful American Word, Sure, The.

Dark and Falling Summer, The.
Do the Others Speak of Me Mockingly,
Maliciously?
Dog Named Ego, the Snowflakes as Kisses,
A.
Dogs Are Shakespearean, Children Are
Strangers.
During December's Death.
For the One Who Would Take Man's Life in
His Hands.
Genesis, sels.
Heart Flies Up, Erratic as a Kite, The.
I Am a Book I neither Wrote nor Read.
I Am Cherry Alive[; the little girl sang].
I Did Not Know the Truth of Growing Trees.
In the Naked Bed, in Plato's Cave.
Jacob.
Little Morning Music, A.
Look, in the Labyrinth of Memory.
Mind Is an Ancient and Famous Capital, The
("The mind is a city like London.")
O Child, Do Not Fear the Dark and Sleep's
Dark Possession.
Passionate Shepherd to His Love, The.
Poem: "Old man in the crystal morning after
snow."
Prothalamion.
Repetitive Heart, The, sels.
Sarah.
Self Unsatisfied Runs Everywhere, The.
Sequel, The.
Shenandoah, sels.
Small Score, A.
Socrates' Ghost Must Haunt Me Now.
Sonnet on Famous and Familiar Sonnets and
Experiences.
Starlight like Intuition Pierced the Twelve.
Swift.
Time's Dedication.
Tired and Unhappy, You Think of Houses.
Today Is Armistice, a Holiday.
Two Lyrics from Kilroy's Carnival: A
Masque, sels.
Vivaldi.
Winter Twilight, Glowing Black and Gold,
The.
Young Child and His Pregnant Mother, A.

Schwartz, Leonard (b. 1963)
Exiles: Ends.
Monuments to the Not Yet Lived.

Schwartz, Lloyd (b. 1941)
Pornography.
Self-Portrait.
78's.
Tom Joanides.

Schwarz, Sibylla (1621–38)
Sonnet: "If love is chaste, what bears
adultery?"

Schwerner, Armand
Tablet V.

Schwitters, Kurt (1887–1948)
Anna Blossom Has Wheels.
Desire.
Murder Machine 43.
Ur Sonata, sels.

Schwob, Marcel (1867–1905)
Actions.
Moments.
Things Dead.

Scollard, Clinton (1860–1932)
As I came down from Lebanon.
Bit of Marble, A.
Swimming.

Scollard, Mrs. Clinton. See **Rittenhouse, Jessie
Belle**

Scott, Alexander (1525?–1584)
Bequest of His Heart, A.
Coronach.
Lament of the Master of Erskine.
Letter to Robert Fergusson.
My Heart Is High Above.
Of May.
Quha Is Perfyte.
Rondel of Luve [or Love], A.
To Luve Unluvit.
To luve unluvit it is ane pane.

Up, Helsum Hairt.

Scott, Alexander (b. 1920)
Calvinist Sang.
Coronach.
Scotched, sels.

Scott, Bob
Limerick: "Sky's are a pitiful lot, The."
Limerick: "There was a young girl from
Uttoxeter / Who out on a date with two
Jocks at a."
Limerick: "There was an old Doctor called
Coué."

Scott, Dennis (1939–91)
Apocalypse Dub.
Dreadwalk.
Epitaph: "They hanged him on a clement
morning, swung."
For the Last Time, Fire.
Grampa.
Homecoming.
Marrysong.
Mouth.
Uncle Time is a ole, ole man.
Version.

Scott, Diana (b. 1947)
Lucy Taking Birth.
Prayer for the Little Daughter between Death
and Burial.
Winter Solstice Poem.

Scott, Duncan Campbell (1862–1947)
At Gull Lake; August, 1810.
At the Cedars.
En Route.
Forsaken, The.
On the Way to the Mission.

Scott, Elizabeth (1708–76)
Now Let Our Hearts Their Glory Wake.
See How the Rising Sun.

Scott, Francis Reginald (1899–1985)
Bangkok.
Brébeuf and His Brethren.
Canadian Authors Meet, The.
Lakeshore.
Laurentian Shield.
Night Club.
W. L. M. K.

Scott, Frederick George (1861–1944)
Unnamed Lake, The.

Scott, Geoffrey (1884–1924)
All Our Joy Is Enough.
Frutta di Mare.
Skaian Gate, The, sels.
What Was Solomon's Mind?

Scott-Heron, Gil (b. 1949)
Revolution Will Not Be Televised!, The.
Winter in America.

Scott-Hopper, Queenie
Amy Elizabeth Ermyntrude Annie.
My Party.
What the Thrush Says.

Scott, John A. (b. 1948)
Changing Room.
Helen Paints a Room (1984).
Plato's Dog.
Typing the Letters.

Scott, Lady John (1810–1900)
Ettrick.

Scott, Margaret (b. 1934)
Portrait of a Married Couple.

Scott, Mary (1752?–1793)
Women of the Future.

Scott of Amwell, John (1730–83)
Ode: "I hate that drum's discordant sound."
Ode: Written After Reading Some Modern
Love-Verses.

Scott, Peter Dale (b. 1929)
Argenteuil County.
Loon's Egg, The.

Scott, Robert Balgarnie Young (1899–1987)
O Day of God, Draw Nigh.

Scott, Tom (b. 1918)
Mankind Toun, The.
Real Muse, The.

Scott, W. N. (b. 1923)
Bundaberg Rum.

Scott, Sir Walter (1771–1832)
Antiquary, The, sels.
Bride of Lammermoor, The, sels.
Datur Hora Quieti.
Doom of Devorgoil, The, sels.
Dreary Change, The.
Eve of Saint John, The.
Fire, with well-dried logs supplied, The.
Friday.
Gallant Ship, The.
Guy Mannering, sels.
Heart of Midlothian, The, sels.
Hour with thee! When earliest day, An.
Hunting Song.
Ivanhoe, sels.
Jock of Hazeldean.
Lady of the Lake, The, sels.
Lay of the Last Minstrel, The, sels.
Lullaby of an Infant Chief.
MacGregor's Gathering.
Maid of Neidpath, The.
Marmion, sels.
Monastery, The, sels.
Old Mortality, sels.
On Having Piles.
Peveril of the Peak, sels.
Pibroch of Donuil Dhu.
Pirate, The, sels.
Quentin Durward, sels.
Rokeby, sels.
To a Lock of Hair.
To-Day I Leave Mrs. Brown's Lodgings.
Waverley, sels.
Youth! Thou Wear'st to Manhood Now.

Scott, William Bell (1812–90)
Death.
Garland for Advancing Years, A.
Music.
My Mother.
Rhyme of the Sun-Dial, A.
Witch's Ballad, The.

Scott, Winfield Townley (1910–68)
Annual Legend.
First Reader, The.
Five for the Grace of Man.
Mistress Severin.
Mr. Whittier.
O Lyric Love.
Swedish Angel.
To L. B. S.
Two.
U. S. Sailor with the Japanese Skull, The.
Uses of Poetry.

Scovel, Myra
Silence, The.

Scovell, Edith Jay (b. 1907)
After Midsummer.
Alone.
Betrothal, A.
Boy Fishing, The.
City Worker, The.
Death from Cancer.
First Year, The, sels.
Flowers.
In a Wood.
Love's Immaturity.
Poor Mother, The.
Stranger, A.
Suicide, The.
Swan's Feet, The.
Vain Girl Jilted, The.

Scriven, R. C.
Cricketer.
Marrog, The.

Scudder, Eliza (1821–96)
Thou Grace Divine, Encircling All.
Thou Long Disowned, Reviled, Oppressed.

Scully, James (b. 1937)
Crew Practice on Lake Bled, in Jugoslavia.
Fantasy of Little Waters, A.
Glass Blower, The.
Grandson, The.
Late Spring, A.
Midsummer.
What Is Poetry.

Scully, W. C. (1855–1943)
'Nkongane.

Scupham, Peter (b. 1933)
House of Geraniums, A.
To His Coy Mistress.
Twelfth Night.

Scythinus (5th cent. B.C.)
And now you're ready who while she was
here.

Seager, Francis (fl. c.1550)
Prayer to Be Said When Thou Goest to Bed,
A.

Seager, Millicent
Birds' Nests.

Seagrave, Artis (fl. 18th cent.)
Let All Created Things.

Seale, Jane Epton
Nape.

Seaman, E. William (b. 1927)
Double Dactyls.

Seaman, Sir Owen (1861–1936)
Ballad of a Bun, A.
Birthday Ode to Mr. Alfred Austin, A.
England Expects?
England's Alfred Abroad.
Nocturne at Danieli's, A.
Plea for Trigamy, A.
Sitting Bard, The.
To a Boy-Poet of the Decadence.
To Julia in Shooting Togs.
To Julia under Lock and Key.

Sears, Edmund Hamilton (1810–76)
Calm, on the Listening Ear of Night.
It came upon the midnight clear.

Sears, Vickie
Pubescence at 39.

Seaton, Maureen
Christmas in the Midwest.
Fear of Shoplifting.
Fear of Subways.
Grief.
Harlem.
Theories of Illusion.
Wings.

Seaver, Edwin (b. 1900)
To My People.

Seaver, George (1890–1976)
Communion Hymn.

Seay, James (b. 1939)
Ballet of Happiness, The.
Clouds over Islands.
It All Comes Together Outside the Restroom
in Hogansville.
Let Not Your Hart Be Truble.
Options.
When Our Voices Broke Off.

Sedgwick, Henry Dwight (1861–1957?)
Leo to His Mistress.

Sedgwick, Modwena
I'll Buy a Peacock Bird.

Sedley, Sir Charles (1639–1701)
Happy Pair, The, sels.
Mulberry Garden, The, sels.
On a Cock at Rochester.
On Fruition.
On the Happy Corydon and Phyllis.
Out of French.
See! Hymen comes; how his torch blazes!
Song: "Hears not my Phillis how the birds."
Song: Love Still Has Something of the Sea.
Song: "Phillis is my only joy."
To Celia.
To Cloris.
To Nysus.
To Scilla.
To Sergius.

Sedulius Scottus (d. 858)
Apologia pro Vita Sua.
Death of a Ram.
Defeat of the Norsemen, The, sels.
Nunc Viridant Segetes.
Request for Meat and Drink.

Seeger, Alan (1888–1916)
Rendezvous, The.

Seeger, Pete
Where have all the flowers gone?—long time
passing.

Seferis, George (1900–1971)
Cats of St. Nicholas, The.
Last Day, The.
Last Stop.
Les Anges Sont Blancs.
Limerick: "There once was a girl from the
Congo."
Limerick: "There was a black girl from
Pretoria."
Limerick: "There was a young lady of Graz."
Limerick: "There was an old dame from
Jerusalem."
Limerick: "There was an old woman of
Wales."
Limerick: "Young girl in remote Samarkand,
A."
Mathios Paskalis among the Roses.
Memory II.
Mythistorima, sels.
Our Sun.
Poplar Leaf, The.
Thrush, sels.
Word for Summer, A.

Segal, Jacob Isaac
Candle.
Rest.

Segalen, Victor (1878–1919)
Mongol Libation.

Segers, Michael
In the eggshell after the chick has hatched.

Segooa, Demetrius
Praises of the Train.

Sei Shonagon (fl. 10th cent.)
Since our relations / are like the crumbling.

Seibert, T. Lawrence
Casey Jones.

Seibles, Tim
For Brothers Everywhere.
Trying for Fire.
Who doesn't.
Wind.

Seidel, Frederick (b. 1936)
Dimpled Cloud, A.
Pol Pot.

Seidman, Hugh (b. 1946)
Drop the Wires.
Great Nebula in Andromeda, The.
Icon.
Making of Color, The.
Modes of Vallejo Street, San Diego, Los
Angeles, The, sels.
N.
Science as Art.
Tale of Genji.

Seifert, Jaroslav (1901–86)
Candlestick, The.
Fingerprints.
Garland on the Wrist, A.
It was afternoon or later.
Never Again.

Seiffert, Marjorie Allen ("Elijah Hay")
Cubist Portrait.

Seiler, Barry (b. 1946)
Digging in the Streets of Gold.
Lake, The.

Selby, Spencer (b. 1945)
Spread, The.

Seldon, Frank H.
To My Setter, Scout.

Selerie, Gavin
Exit on Feedback.

Seligman, Ulma (fl. 16th–17th cent.)
Truth Has Perished.

**Sellar, W. C.. See Yeatman, R. J. and W. C.
Sellar**

Sellers, Bettie M. (b. 1926)
In the Counselor's Waiting Room.

Selman, Robyn
And so I went forth, exhilarated.
And so I went forth in uniform.
Avec Amour.
I befriended Mike with the good hash pipe.
I licked and kissed her in a bathroom stall.
I thought the gesture was only about me.

Ill-equipped bride-to-be, I left home, An.
Minds I admired, the strong-bodied, The.
Next came Bob, but before him I had Phil.
Old man waves to me through iron bars, The.
One of us had to be the first to lead.
They called the next panel, "New Lesbians."
Thousands of cheers filled the chalky air.
We lay in an attic under beamed eaves.
We saw everything except that we were gay.
What did sex have to do with politics?

Seltzer, George R. (1902–74)
Come, All Ye People.

**Selvinsky [or Sel'vinskii], Ilya [or Karl]
L'vovich (1899–1968)**
I Saw It.
Mighty Ocean, The.
Portrait of My Mother.
Reader of Poetry, The.
Sebastopol.

Selyns, Henricus (1636–1701)
Epitaph for Peter Stuyvesant.
O Christmas Night.
Of Scolding Wives and the Third Day Ague.
On Maids and Cats.
On Mercenary and Unjust Bailiffs.
Reasons for and against Marrying Widows.
Upon the Bankruptcy of a Physician.

Semeonoff, B. and C. Semeonoff
Limerick: "There once was a flock of wild
geese."

Sempill, Francis (1616–82)
Maggie Lauder.

Sempill, Robert (c.1595–c.1665)
Life and Death of [Habbie Simson] the Piper
of Kilbarchan, The.

Seneca (4 B.C.–A.D. 65)
Hercules Furens, sels.
Hercules Oetaeus, sels.
Hippolytus, sels.
Medea, sels.
O barbarous Corsica, locked in by crags.
Oedipus, sels.
Part of a Chorus in Seneca's Tragedy of
Thyestes, sels.
Power of love over gods them selves, The.
Thyestes, sels.
Troades, sels.

Senesh, Hannah (1921–44)
Blessed Match, The.
One—Two—Three.
To My Mother.

Seng-ts'an (d. 606)
Mind of Absolute Trust, The.

Senghor, Léopold Sédar (b. 1906)
"African Image Is Not An Image by
Equation. . . , The."
Be not amazed beloved, if sometimes my
song grows dark.
Before night comes I think of you and for
you before I fall.
Black Woman.
Blues.
French Garden.
I am alone in the plains.
I know not when it was, I still confuse
childhood and Eden.
I Want to Say Your Name.
I will pronounce your name, Naëtt, I will
declaim you, Naëtt!
In Memoriam.
Joal.
Kaya-Magan am I! the first person.
Luxembourg 1939.
Man and Beast.
Midnight Elegy.
Negro Mask.
Night of Sine.
Ode for Three Koras and Balaphong, sels.
On the Appeal from the Race of Sheba: II.
Paris in the Snow.
Pearls.
Prayer for Peace, sels.
Prayer to the Masks.
Return of the Prodigal Son, sels.
Song of the Initiate.
Songs for a Three-String Guitar.

Songs for Signare, sels.
Speech and Image: An African Tradition of
the Surreal.
Taga for Mbaye Dyôb.
To New York.
Totem, The.
Visit.
We Delighted, My Friend.
You held the black face of the warrior
between your hands.
Senior, Olive (b. 1943)
Ancestral Poem.
Birdshooting season the men.
Children's Hospital.
Epitaph: "Last year the child died."
Hill Country.
Searching for Grandfather.
To the Madwoman in My Yard.
Sepamla, Sipho (b. 1932)
Civilization Aha.
I Remember Sharpeville.
If you still have bacon and eggs for
breakfast.
Law that says, The.
Measure for Measure.
Odyssey, The.
On Judgement Day.
Silence: 2.
Talk to the Peach Tree.
When I Lost Slum Life.
Serapion of Alexandria (c.200–150 B.C.)
This is the skull of a hard-working man.
Serge, Victor (1890–1947)
Asphyxiated Man, The.
Constellation of Dead Brothers.
Dialectic.
Hands.
Sergeant, Howard (b. 1914)
Inundation, The.
Man Meeting Himself.
Serote, Mongane Wally (b. 1944)
Another Alexandra.
Breezing Dawn of the New Day, The.
Death Survey.
Growing, The.
Hell, Well, Heaven.
Ofay-Watcher Looks Back.
Poem, A: "Gasp sounded, The."
Serraillier, Ian (b. 1912)
After Ever Happily [or , The Princess and
the Woodcutter].
Anne and the Field-Mouse.
Mouse in the Wainscot, The.
Old Sussex Road, The.
Tickle Rhyme, The.
Servasius, Sulpicius Lupercus (4th cent. A.D.)
Rivers level granite mountains.
Service, Robert W. (1874–1958)
Cremation of Sam McGee, The.
Going Home.
Grand-Père.
Inspiration.
Men That Don't Fit In, The.
My Madonna.
Pot of Tea, A.
Shooting of Dan McGrew, The.
Spell of the Yukon, The.
Volunteer, The.
Woman and the Angel, The.
Seth, Vikram (b. 1952)
All you who sleep tonight.
Doctor's Journal Entry for August 6, 1945,
A.
God's Love.
Golden Gate, The, sels.
Protocols.
"Setoun, Gabriel" (Thomas Nicoll Hepburn)
Jack Frost.
Romance.
World's Music, The.
"Seuss, Dr." (Theodore Seuss Geisel) (b. 1904)
Too Many Daves.
**"Severyanin [or Severianin], Igor" (Igor'
Vasilievich Lotaryov) (1887–1941)**
Epilogue: "I, the genius Severyanin."
Lilac ice cream! Lilac ice cream!

Minor Elegy, A.
Prologue: "Mirra Lokhvitskaia's ashes are
now entombed."
Russian Woman.
Same Old Way, The.
Spring Day.
Sewall, Samuel (1652–1730)
Once More, Our God, Vouchsafe to Shine!
This Morning Tom Child, the Painter, Died.
To Be Engraven on a Dial.
To the Rev'd Mr. Jno. Sparhawk on the Birth
of his Son.
Upon the Springs Issuing out from the Foot
of Plimouth Beach.
Seward, Anna (1742–1809)
Colebrook Dale, sels.
December Morning.
Elegy.
Eyam.
Invocation, To the Genius of Slumber
Written Oct. 1787.
Lady Eleanor Butler.
Lake, The; Or, Modern Improvement in
Landscape.
Old Cat's Dying Soliloquy, An.
On Catania and Syracuse Swallowed Up by
an Earthquake, from the Italian of Filicaja.
On the Use of New and Old Words in
Poetry.
Sonnet 12.
Sonnet 13.
Sonnet 19.
Sonnet 31.
Sonnet 32.
Sonnet: "From a rived tree, that stands beside
the grave."
Sonnet: Ingratitude.
Sonnet: "Stranger, when o'er yon slant, warm
field no cloud."
Sonnets, sels.
Speech of the Nymph.
To Colebrooke Dale.
To Honora Sneyd.
To Miss Ponsonby.
To the Poppy.
Verses Inviting Stella to Tea on the Public
Fast-Day.
Written December 1790.
Sewell, Elizabeth (b. 1919)
Job.
Sewell, George (1688–1726)
Dying Man in His Garden, The.
Sexton, Anne (1928–74)
Abortion, The.
After Auschwitz.
All My Pretty Ones.
And One for My Dame.
Big heart.
Black Art, The.
Child Bearers, The.
Cinderella.
Consorting with Angels.
Crossing the Atlantic.
Death of the Fathers, The, sels.
Earth, The.
End, Middle, Beginning.
Farmer's Wife, The.
Firebombers, The.
Flee on Your Donkey.
For God While Sleeping.
For My Lover, Returning to His Wife.
Fortress, The.
From the Garden.
Funnel.
Fury of Flowers and Worms, The.
Fury of Overshoes.
Hansel and Gretel.
Her Kind.
Housewife.
I Remember.
I'm dreaming the My Lai soldier again.
In Celebration of My Uterus.
In the Deep Museum.
January 1st.
Jesus Dies.
Lament: "Someone is dead."

Letter Written on a Ferry While Crossing
Long Island Sound.
Little Girl, My String Bean, My Lovely
Woman.
Lobster.
Moss of His Skin, The.
Mr. Mine.
Music Swims Back to Me.
No So. Not So.
Noon Walk on the Asylum Lawn.
Nude Swim, The.
O Ye Tongues, sels.
Obsessive Combination of Ontological
Inscape, Trickery and Love, An.
Pain for a Daughter.
Ringing the Bells.
Risk, The.
Road Back, The.
Room of My Life, The.
Rowing.
Self in 1958.
Sixth Psalm.
Snow White and the Seven Dwarfs.
Some Foreign Letters.
Somewhere in Africa.
Starry Night, The.
Sun, The.
Sylvia's Death.
That Day.
Three Green Windows.
To a Friend Whose Work Has Come to
Triumph.
Truth the Dead Know, The.
Two Sons.
Unknown Girl in the Maternity Ward.
Wanting to Die.
Wedding Night, The.
Welcome Morning.
Whale on the beach, you dinosaur.
What's That.
Window That Watched the Pru.
With Mercy for the Greedy.
You, Doctor Martin, walk.
Seymour, A. J. (1914–89)
Drums / Then again drums.
First of August.
For Christopher Columbus, sels.
Millionaire.
My Aim.
Name Poem.
Slaves / Humming in the twilight by the
shanty door.
To the Family Home Awaiting Repair.
Well, The.
**Seymour, Frances, Countess of Hertford (1699–
1754)**
Life at Richkings.
Story of Inkle and Yarico, The.
**Seymour, Sir Thomas (Baron Seymour of
Sudeley) (1508?–1549)**
FORGETTING God.
Seymour-Smith, Martin (b. 1928)
He Came to Visit Me.
What Schoolmasters Say.
Shafarman, Gail
Russia 1914/Bolinas 1988.
Shahid (Roosevelt Williamson) (b. 1951)
Letters Come to Prison.
**"Shahryar" (Akhlaq Mohammad Khan) (b.
1936)**
Still Life.
Shaka, King of the Zulus (1787–1828)
Battle Song.
"Shake." See Keane, Ellsworth McGranahan
Shakely, Lauren (b. 1948)
Definition.
**Shakespeare, William (1564–1616). See also
Fletcher, John and William Shakespeare**
All's Well That Ends Well, sels.
Antony and Cleopatra, sels.
As You Like It, sels.
Comedy of Errors, The, sels.
Coriolanus, sels.
Cymbeline, sels.
Epitaph on Himself.
Even as the sun with purple-colour'd face.

Hamlet, *sels.*
Henry IV, *sels.*
Henry VI (skeleton), *sels.*
Julius Caesar, *sels.*
King Henry IV, Pt. I, *sels.*
King Henry IV, Pt. II, *sels.*
King Henry V, *sels.*
King Henry VI, Pt. I, *sels.*
King Henry VI, Pt. III, *sels.*
King John, *sels.*
King Lear, *sels.*
King Richard II, *sels.*
King Richard III, *sels.*
Love's Labour's Lost, *sels.*
Macbeth, *sels.*
Madrigal, A: "Crabbed age and youth cannot live together." *From* Passionate Pilgrim.
Measure for Measure, *sels.*
Merchant of Venice, The, *sels.*
Midsummer Night's Dream, A, *sels.*
Much Ado about Nothing, *sels.*
Othello, *sels.*
Pericles, *sels.*
Phoenix and the Turtle, The.
Rape of Lucrece, The, *sels.*
Richard II, *sels.*
Richard III, *sels.*
Romeo and Juliet, *sels.*
Sonnets, *sels.*
Taming of the Shrew, The, *sels.*
Tempest, The, *sels.*
(The Merchant of Venice), *sels.*
Timon of Athens, *sels.*
Troilus and Cressida, *sels.*
Twelfth Night, *sels.*
Two Gentlemen of Verona, The, *sels.*
Venus and Adonis, *sels.*
Winter's Tale, The, *sels.*

Shalamov, Varlam Tikhonovich (1907–82)
Pegasus.

Shalom, Shin (b. 1904)
All Is Not So Simple.
At evening when flicker.
Drink wonder, my heart, drink in the wonder.
Guard me, Oh God, from hating man my brother.
In the world's heart burns a torch of fire.
Stoker, The.
Suddenly we will wake from sleep at night.
They That Sow at Night.

Shange, Ntozake (b. 1948)
About Atlanta.
Advice.
Ancestral Messengers/Composition 13.
Bocas: A Daughter's Geography.
Dream of Pairing.
Elegance in the extreme.
For Colored Girls Who Have Considered Suicide When the Rainbow Is Enuf, *sels.*
Frank Albert and Viola Benzena Owens.
I live in music.
Its Happenin / But You Dont Know Abt It.
It's Not so Good to be Born a Girl/ Sometimes.
My father is a retired magician.
Nappy Edges.
Nappy Edges (A Cross Country Sojourn).
Oh, I'm 10 Months Pregnant.
Okra to greens.
Rite-ing.
Somebody almost walked off wid alla my stuff.
Tango.
Where the Heart Is.
Where the Mississippi meets the Amazon.
You are sucha fool / i haveta love you.

Shanks, Edward Richard Burton (1892–1953)
Boats at Night.
Drilling in Russell Square.
Going In to Dinner.
Halt, The.
High Germany.
Sleeping Heroes.

Shannon, Monica (d. 1965?)
Only My Opinion.

Shao Yung (1011–77)
Arriving in Lo-yang Again.

Song of Delight.
Song on Being Too Lazy to Get Up.
Thoughts on T'ien-chin Bridge.

Shaoxuan, Cui
Black hair and red cheeks: for how long?

Shapcott, Thomas William (b. 1935)
Autumn.
Bicycle Rider, The.
Blue Paisley Shirt, The.
City of Home is reached only in dreams, The.
Flying Fox.
June Fugue.
Litanies of Julia Pastrana (1832-1860), The.
Near the School for Handicapped Children.
Piano Pieces, *sels.*
Post Operative.
Sestina with Refrain.
Shadow of War, 1941.
Turning Fifty.

Shapiro, Alan (b. 1952)
Familiar Story.
Letter said you had to speak to me, The.
Manufacturing.

Shapiro, David (b. 1947)
About This Course.
After.
Archaic Torsos.
Book of Glass, A.
Canticle.
Commentary Text Commentary Text Commentary Text.
Counter-Example, The.
Dead Will Not Praise You, The.
For the Evening Land.
House (Blown Apart).
In a Blind Garden.
Lateness.
Lord I sleep and I sleep.
Realistic Bar and Grill, A.
Sentences.
Taking a Look.
To an Idea.
Tracing of an Evening.

Shapiro, Gregg
Tattoo.

Shapiro, Harvey (b. 1924)
After the love-making.
Feast of the Ram's Horn.
For W C W.
Happiness of 6 A.M.
Heart, The.
Hello There!
Montauk Highway.
Mountain, Fire, Thornbush.
National Cold Storage Company contains, The.
Provincetown, Mass.

Shapiro, Karl (b. 1913)
Adam and Eve, *sels.*
All tropic places smell of mold.
Alphabet, The.
Aubade: "What dawn is it?"
Auto Wreck.
Bed, The.
Boy-Man.
Buick.
California Winter.
Calling the Child.
Christmas Eve.
Conscientious Objector, The.
Cut Flower, A.
D. C.
Dirty word hops in the cage of the mind like the Pondicherry vulture, The.
Dome of Sunday, The [*or* A].
Drug Store.
Elegy for a Dead Soldier, *sels.*
Elegy for Two Banjos.
First Time, The.
Fly, The.
Garage Sale.
Geographers, The.
Girls Working in Banks.
Going to School.
Haircut.
Hollywood.

Hospital.
In India.
Intellectual, The.
Interlude.
Jew at Christmas Eve, The.
Leg, The.
Love for a Hand.
Lower the Standard: That's My Motto.
Manhole Covers.
Midnight Show.
My grandmother moves to my mind in context of sorrow.
Necropolis.
Nigger.
Nostalgia.
October 1.
Phenomenon, The.
Piano Tuner's Wife, The.
Poet.
Poets of Hell, The.
Progress of Faust, The.
Puritan, The.
Quintana lay in the shallow grave of coral.
Scyros.
Six Religious Lyrics, *sels.*
Southerner, The.
Terminal.
Travelogue for Exiles.
Troop Train.
Twins, The.
Two-Year-Old Has a Motherless Week, The.
University.
V-Letter.
Waiting in Front of the Columnar High School.
Western Town.
White-haired Lover, *sels.*

Sharah, Jemal (b. 1969)
Package for Another World.
Parting Roundel.

Sharkey, Michael (b. 1946)
Greenwood's.
Hots, The.

Sharma, B. C. Ramachandra
American Tourist.

Sharp, William. *See* "Macleod, Fiona"

Sharp, William
Field Mouse, The.

Sharpe, R. L.
Bag of Tools, A.

Sharpe, Richard Scrafton (c.1775–1852) *and* Mrs. Pearson
Country Mouse and the City Mouse, The.

Sharples, Pita (b. 1941)
Haka: The Blossoming.
Space Invaders Machine, The.

Sharpless, Stanley J. (b. 1910)
Better a day in Oxbridge.
Chaucer: The Wogan's Tale.
Costa Geriatrica.
Does That Answer Your Question, Mr Shakespeare?
"Go to the Ant."
Hamlet.
In Praise of Cocoa, Cupid's Nightcap.
King Canute.
Limerick: "Albert Einstein's the man we must credit."
Limerick: "April. Bad month. Visit spa."
Limerick: "Archimedes, the early truth-seeker."
Limerick: "In Illyria, the love-sick Orsino."
Limerick: "Let the eugenist reach for his gun!"
Limerick: "Marconi, whose ardour was tireless."
Limerick: "Monsieur Gauguin? 'E's gone to Tahiti."
Limerick: "Ninety summers—and never a platitude."
Limerick: "Said a herring one day to a sole."
Limerick: "Said Orville to Wilbur 'Hold tight!'"
Limerick: "Smile on the famed Mona Lisa, The."

Limerick: "There was a young girl from Uttoxeter / Who sported a tight-fitting baroque sweater."
Limerick: "There was a young girl of Uttoxeter / Who worked nine to five as a choc-setter."
Limerick: "There was a young lady of Ulva / Whose boy-friend said: 'Look, I will pulver.'"
Limerick: "There was a young lady . . . tut, tut!"
Limerick: "'We're not amused,' said Victoria."
Limerick: "Widow (conscious that time's on the wing)."
Low Church.
Moment of Eschatological Doubt, A.
Paradise Lost as a Haiku.
Pied Beauty.
Sonnet: "How do I hate you? Let me count the ways."
Summonee's Tale, The.
There's a breathless hush on the Centre Court.
To His Coy Mistress.

Shaw, Angela (b. 1967)
Courtesan.
Crepuscule.

Shaw, Arthur
Limerick: "Certain young pate who was addle, A."
Limerick: "Chap was so pose that was adi, A."
Limerick: "In gonia once which was Pata."
Limerick: "Nice pot of gold that was mari, A "

Shaw, Charles (b. 1892)
Search, The.

Shaw, Dunstan
Retrospection.

Shaw, Frances
Who loves the rain.

Shaw, Joan Fern
Cow.

Shaw, Knowles
Handwriting on the Wall, The.

Shaw, Luci (b. 1928)
Craftsman.
For They Shall See God.
Getting Inside the Miracle.
Groundhog is, at best, a simple soul, The.
Man Cannot Name Himself.
Need Is Our Name.
Stars in Apple Cores.
To a Christmas Two-Year-Old.

Shaw, Robert B. (b. 1916)
Gargoyle.
Grass Widows.

Shaw, Robert B. (b. 1947)
Shut In.

Shaw, Stanley
Christopher Smart.

Shchapova, Yelena [or Elena] Sergeievna, Countess de Carli (b. 1950)
Smells.

Shchipachov [or Shchipachiov], Stepan Petrovich (1899–1980)
Blue spaces do not see themselves, The.
Little Birch Tree, The.

Shchirovsky [or Shchirovskii], Vladimir (1909–41)
Dance of the Soul.
I don't enclose the universe in my grasp.
I really don't want to die now.

Shea, Martin
Bolted space.
Caught shoplifting.
Held it.
Long night, The.
Moving.
Red-flashing lights.
Sparrows sunning.
Terminal.
Those corner winds.
Through the wall.

Walk's end.
Warehouse-theatre's.

Sheck, Laurie (b. 1953)
Mannequins.
Return, The.
Rush Hour.
To Softness.
White Noise.

Shefatiah, Amittai ben (*fl.* c.900)
Hymn of Weeping.

Sheffield, John, Duke of Buckingham and Normandy (1648–1721)
On Mr. Hobbs, and His Writings.
On One Who Died Discovering Her Kindness.
Reconcilement, The.

Shefner, Vadim Sergeievich (b. 1915)
Forest Fire.
Lily, The.

Sheikh, Ghulam Mohammed (b. 1937)
Jaisalmer, 1.

Sheldon, Gilbert (1598–1677)
St. Anthony's Township.

Shelley, Mary Wollstonecraft (1797–1851)
Oh listen while I sing to thee.
On Reading Wordsworth's Lines on Peele Castle.
Stanzas: "Oh, come to me in dreams, my love!"
To the air of 'My Phillida, adieu, love!'

Shelley, Percy Bysshe (1792–1822)
Adonais; An Elegy on the Death of John Keats, *sels.*
Alastor; or, The Spirit of Solitude, *sels.*
Autumn: A Dirge.
Aziola, The.
Charles the First, *sels.*
Cloud, The.
Dirge, A: "Rough wind, that moanest loud."
England in 1819.
Epipsychidion, *sels.*
Feelings of a Republican on the Fall of Bonaparte.
Fragment: "Wake the serpent not—lest he."
From the Arabic: An Imitation.
Hate-Song, A.
Hellas, *sels.*
Hymn of Apollo.
Hymn of Pan.
Hymn to Intellectual Beauty.
I fear thy kisses, gentle maiden.
Indian Serenade, The.
Invitation, The.
Julian and Maddalo; A Conversation.
Lament, A: "O world! O life! O time!"
Letter to Maria Gisborne, *sels.*
Lines to a Reviewer.
Lines: "When the lamp is shattered [or shatter'd]."
Lines Written among the Euganean Hills.
Lines Written in the Bay of Lerici.
Love's Philosophy.
Mask [or Masque] of Anarchy, The, *sels.*
Mont Blanc.
Mutability.
Ode to Liberty, *sels.*
Ode to the West Wind.
On a Faded Violet.
On a Painted Woman.
On Fanny Godwin.
On Keats.
On the Medusa of Leonardo da Vinci in the Florentine Gallery.
Ozymandias [of Egypt].
Peter Bell the Third, *sels.*
Prometheus Unbound, *sels.*
Question, The.
Question, The ("I dream'd that, as I wander'd by the way.")
Revolt of Islam, The, *sels.*
Rose Leaves, When The Rose is Dead, *sels.*
Sensitive Plant in a garden grew, A, *sels.*
Similes for Two Political Characters of 1819.
Song: "Rarely, rarely, comest thou."
Song to the Men of England.
Sonnet: "Lift not the painted veil which those who live."

Sonnet to Byron.
Stanzas—April, 1814.
Stanzas to Edward Williams.
Stanzas Written in Dejection, near Naples [or —December 1818, near Naples].
Summer and Winter.
Time.
To a Skylark.
To Jane ("Keen stars were twinkling, The.")
To Jane: The Recollection, *sels.*
To————: "Music, when soft voices die."
To Night.
To————: "One word is too often profaned."
To the Moon.
To Wordsworth.
Tower of Famine, The.
Tribute to America.
Triumph of Life, The.
Two Spirits[: An Allegory], The.
Waning Moon, The.
With a Guitar, to Jane.
World's Wanderers, The.

Shelnutt, Eve
At the Mass Graveyard.
Family.
Memory.
O Hero.
Triumph of Children, The.

Shelton, Marion Brown
When Jesus walked upon the earth.

Shelton, Richard (b. 1933)
Alone.
Because the Moon Comes.
Certain Choices.
Connais Tu le Pays?
Eden After Dark.
Job the Father.
Letter to a Dead Father.
On Lake Pend Oreille.
Prophets, The.
Requiem for Sonora.
Sonora for Sale.

Shelton, Thomas Russell
Patches.

Shen Chou (1427–1509)
Bamboo Villa, The.
Consoling Wu Te-cheng on the Death of His Son.
Drinking at Night with Yen Kung-mou.
Inscribed on a Painting.
Inscribed on the Fan of a Wealthy Old Man.
Lady Picking Flowers, A.
Moon in a Winecup, The.
On the Fifteenth Day of the Seventh Month I Came Home Late from the City.
Painting of Peach Blossom Spring, A.
Paying a Sick-call to Yao Ts'un-tao in the Rain.
Reading in the Autumn.
Returning Home at Dusk from Town, on the Fifteenth of the Seventh Month.
Sent in Parting to Yen Kung-su.
Stone Bridge, The, *sels.*
Taoist Huang Has Died of Alcoholism, The.
Temple of the Ocean of Awakening.
To the Tune "Bamboo at West Lake."
To the Tune "Nan-hsiang-tzu."
White clouds like a scarf enfold the the mountain's waist.
Wine Cup and Bright Moon.

Shen Ch'üan (*fl.* 17th cent.)
Therefore We Preserve Life.

Shen Yüeh (441–513)
Farewell to Fan Yun at An Ch'eng.
Fishing Rod, The.
Four Recollections.
Fragrant Tree, The.
Hand in Hand; a Song.
I Say Goodby to Fan An-ch'eng.
Lament for Hsieh T'iao.
Out Early One Morning, I Met an Old Acquaintance.
Response to Wang Ssu-yüan's Poem on the Moon, A.
Six Poems on Remembering, *sels.*
Song of Woe.

Shengeli
Spending the Night in the Eastern Park.
Wild Geese on the Lake.
Written for My Neighbor.

Shengeli, Georgy [or Georgii] Arkadevich (1894–1956)
Derzhavin.
27 July 1830.

Shenstone, William (1714–63)
Elegy 11: "Ah me, my friend! it will not, will not last!"
Hint from Voiture.
Lines Written on a Window at The Leasowes.
On the Clerk of a Country Parish.
School-Mistress, The.
Solemn Meditation, A.
To the Virtuosos.
Written at [or in] an Inn at Henley.

Shepard, Ollie (1897–1984)
It's a Low Down Dirty Shame.

Sheperd, Luke (fl. 1548)
Upcheringe of the Messe, The, sels.

Shepherd, Sir Fleetwood (1634–98)
Epitaph on the Duke of Grafton.

Shepherd, Hope
Trains.

Shepherd, Nathaniel Graham (1835–69)
Calling the Roll.

Shepherd, Reginald (b. 1963)
Brotherhood.
Lucky One, The.
Skin Trade.
What Cannot Be Kept.
Where When Was.
White Days.

Shepherd, Richard
Tribute to Matthew Arnold in a Moment of Self-Abuse, A.

"Shepherd, The Ettrick." See Hogg, James

Shepherd, William (1768–1847)
Ode on Lord Macartney's Embassy to China.

Sheppard, Robert (b. 1955)
Letter from the Blackstock Road, sels.
Materialization of Soap 1947, The.

Sherburne, Sir Edward (1618–1702)
And She Washed His Feet with Her Tear[e]s, and Wiped Them with the Hairs of Her Head.
Dream, The.
Weeping and Kissing.

Sheridan, Helen Selina (1807–67)
Charming Woman, The.

Sheridan, John D. (1903–80)
Joe's No Saint.
Priestin' of Father John, The.
To the New Ordained.

Sheridan, Richard Brinsley (1751–1816)
Clio's Protest.
Duenna, The, sels.
Geranium, The.
Lines by a Lady on the Loss of her Trunk.
On Lady Anne Hamilton.
School for Scandal, The, sels.

Sherlock, Philip (b. 1902)
Beauty Too of Twisted Trees, A.
Dinner Party 1940.
Jamaican Fisherman.
Pocomania.

Sherman, Charlotte Watson (b. 1958)
Roots.

Sherman, Frank Dempster (1860–1916)
Baseball.
Blossoms.
Daisies.
Kite, A.
Waterfall, The.

Sherry, James (b. 1946)
Free Radicals.
Hazardous Waste.
In Case, sels.
Lepidoptery.
Pay Cash Only.
Radiant.
She'll be comin' 'round the mountain when the shell sometimes is empty.

Shershenevich, Vadim Gabrielevich (1893–1942)
Plot with Bitterness.

Sherwin, Judith Johnson (b. 1936)
Dr. Potatohead Talks to Mothers.
Gentle Heart, A: Two.
Goddess.
Just.
Light Woman's Song, The.
Rhyme for the Child as a Wet Dog.

Sherwood, Grace Buchanan (b. 1883)
Disabled Debauchee, The.
Love and Life.
Satire against Reason and Mankind, A.
Song of a Young Lady to Her Ancient Lover, A.

Sherwood, Kate Brownlee (1841–1914)
Albert Sidney Johnston.

Sherwood, Margaret (1864–1955)
In Memoriam—Leo: A Yellow Cat.

Sherwood, Robert E. (1896–1955)
Old Hokum Buncombe, The.

Shibafune, Onoe No
In the spring ravine.

Shiffert, Edith Marcombe (b. 1916)
Manners.
Monkeys on Mt. Hiei.
Shadow of a Branch, The.

Shiffrin, Nancy
For My Neverborn.

Shigeyuki (Minamoto no Shigeyuki) (d. 1000)
Winter has at last come. From Shui Shu.

Shih Te (fl. c.8th? cent.)
Far, faraway, steep mountain paths.
I laugh at my failing strength in old age.
Since apes are still able to learn.
You can see the moon's brightness.

Shikibu, Izumi. See Izumi, Lady

Shikishi, Princess (d. 1201)
Autumn.
Blossoms have fallen, The.
I slept in the past / that will never come back.
Life, like a thread piercing through jewels.
Spring.
Winter.

Shimon, Louis C.
I Know Something Good about You.

Shimoni, David (1886–1957)
At times spirit surges up from bodies' prison.
Flower Pot, The.
Gleaning.

Shin, Kyongnim (b. 1936)
Reed had been weeping, The.
Visiting a Rural Town.

Shin, Sokch'o (1909–76)
Catapulting a Stone.
Flute.
Gong Dance, The.

Shin, Sokchong (1907–74)
From your eyes.
If you call / I will come to you.
It is Not Time Yet to Light the Candle.

Shin, Tong-yop (1930–69)
Land of Flowering Azaleas, The.

Shin, Tongjip (b. 1924)
Shoe, A.
Vertigo.

Shinder, Jason (b. 1955)
Prayer.

Shindo Chie (b. 1920)
Space.

Shinkawa, Kazue (b. 1929)
Event Which Makes No News, An.

Shipman, Thomas (1632–80)
Frost, 1654, The: To Mr. W.L., sels.
Kiss, The 1656. To Mrs. C.
Resolute Courtier, The.

Shiraishi, Kazuko (b. 1931)
Anniversary of Samansa's Death, The.
Chinese Ulysses, A.
I Fire at the Face of the Country Where I Was Born.
Man Root, The.
Phallic Root.

Phallus.

Shirley, James (1596–1666)
Contention of Ajax and Ulysses, The, sels.
Cupid and Death, sels.
Cupid's Call.
Fie on Love.
Garden, The.
Good-night.
Imposture, The, sels.
Love for Enjoying.
Lover that Durst Not Speak to His M[istress], A.
Love's Hue and Cry.
On the Duke of Buckingham.
To a Lady Upon a Looking-Glass Sent.
To His Honored Friend Thomas Stanley Esquire, Upon His Elegant Poems.
To His Mistress.
To Odelia.
To the Excellent Pattern of Beauty and Virtue, Lady Elizabeth, Countess of Ormonde.
Triumph of Peace, The, sels.
Two Gentlemen That Broke Their Promise of a Meeting.
Would you know what's soft? I dare.

Shirome (fl. 10th cent.)
If I were only sure.

Shivarudrappa, G. S. (b. 1926)
This Man.

Shizuka (fl. 12th cent.)
How I long for the man who climbed Mt. Yoshino.

Shkapskaya [or Shkapskaia], Maria [or Mariia] Mikhailovna (1891–1952)
My body had no entrance, and the black.

Shklyarevsky [or Shkliarevskii], Igor (b. 1938)
My younger brother is stronger than me.

Shlonsky, Avraham (1900–1973)
Grape-gathering.
Jezrael.
Morning in My City.
Prayer: "Forgive me, you whom they cast in a name."
Shepherd.
Tiller of the Soil.
Toil.

Shoaf, Diann Blakely (fl. 20th cent.)
Birmingham, 1962.
Solo, New Orleans.

Shoku, Princess
I would that even now. From Hyaku-Nin-Isshu.

Sholl, Betsy
Catechism.
Dawn.
Distinct Call of the Alligator, The.
Farmwife.
Girl Named Spring, A.
Hospital State, The.
Job's Wife, sels.
Midnight Vapor Light Breakdown.
Notes From a Youngest Daughter, sels.
Outside the Depot.
Riding Hood.
Small Patch of Ice, A.
Soup Kitchen.
Spring Fragments, sels.
Thinking of You, Hiroshima.
Whitecaps.

Shomer, Enid
Passive Resistance

Shore, Jane (b. 1947)
Astronomer's Journal, An.
High Holy Days.

Short, John (b. 1911)
Carol: "There was a boy bedded in bracken."

Shorter, Dora Sigerson (1866–1918)
Comforters, The.
Ireland.
Mother, The.
Mountain Maid, The.
Skeleton in the Cupboard, The.
Unknown Ideal.
Watcher in the Wood, The.

Wind on the Hills, The.

Shpolyansky, Aminado Petrovich. *See*
"Aminado, Don"

**Shteiger, Anatoly [*or* Anatoli] Sergeievich
(1907–44)**
No one waits down below, as when we were
young.

Shu Hsi (c. 265–306)
Hot Cake.

Shu-jen, Chou. *See* "Lu Hsün"

"Shu Ting" (Gong Peiyu) (b. 1952)
Assembly Line.
Bits of Reminiscence.
Fairy Tales.
Gifts.
Longing.
Maple Leaf.
Missing You.
Perhaps our cares.
Perhaps these thoughts of ours.
Singing Flower, The.

Shuckburg, Richard *and* **Edward Bangs**
Yankee Doodle.

Shūji, Miya
During the rainy season.
Tanka: "After rainfall."
Tanka: "As if it came."
Tanka: "At a corner."
Tanka: "Flowering poppies."
Tanka: "Its bloom finished."
Tanka: "Like a long."
Tanka: "Mr. Nehru."
Tanka: "My body."
Tanka: "On the way home."
Tanka: "Out of the shade."
Tanka: "Over my."
Tanka: "Red flowers."
Tanka: "Slanted."
Tanka: "Slowly inside me."
Tanka: "Spoken in response."
Tanka: "Stalks growing."
Tanka: "Suddenly."
Tanka: "To do away with anger."
Year's end, The.

Shulman, Max (b. 1919)
Honest Abe Lincoln.

Shumaker, Peggy (b. 1952)
Bush Navigator: The Last Morning of Hands.
Circle of Totems, The.
First Winter: Joy.
Inupiat Christmas Pageant, The.
Waitress's Kid, The.

Shune (*fl.* c.1160–c.1180)
All during a night.

**Shunzei, &bi;The daughter of&xbi; (1171?–
1252?)**
As the season changes.
How can I blame the cherry blossoms.
It is unreasonable to ask my tears.

Shuraikh
Distich.

Shurin, Aaron (b. 1947)
Agora.
Blue Shade.
City of Men.
Continuous Thunder.
Exorcism of the Straight/Man/Demon.
Forward or Back.
His Promise.
Material's Daughter.
Sailed.
Saturated.
Temptation.
Very Days.

Shurtleff, Ernest W. (1862–1917)
Lead On, O King Eternal.

Shuttle, Penelope (b. 1947)
Early Pregnancy.
Expectant Mother.
Gone Is the Sleepgiver.
Locale.
Maritimes.
Old Man, The.
Passion, *sels.*

**Shwarts [*or* Shvarts], Yelena [*or* Elena] (b.
1948)**
Beast Flower.
Elegies on the Cardinal Points.
Elegy on an X-ray Photo of My Skull.
Remembrance of Strange Hospitality.
What that street is called—you can read it on
the sign.

"Shy, Timothy." *See* **Lewis, Dominic Bevan
Wyndham**

Siamanto (1878–1915)
Dance, The.
Grief.

Siddal, Elizabeth (1834–62)
At Last.
Dead Love.
Lust of the Eyes, The.
Silent Wood, A.
Worn Out.

Sidgwick, Frank (b. 1903)
Cheerful Chilterns, The.

Sidgwick, Henry
Strenuous Life, The.

Sidney, Sir Philip (1554–86)
Absence.
Arcadia, *sels.*
Astrophil and Stella, *sels.*
Countesse of Pembrokes Arcadia, The, *sels.*
Dirge: "Ring out your bells [*or* belles], let
mourning shows [*or* shewes] be spread."
Farewell, A.
In wonted walkes.
Lady My Treasure.
Like as the dove which seeled-up doth fly.
Lord, the Lord my shepherd is, The.
Love Me, O Love.
Nightingale as soone as Aprill bringeth, The.
Psalms, *sels.*
Sleep, baby mine, Desire; nurse Beauty
singeth.
Song: "No, no, no, no, I cannot hate my
foe."
Song: "O fair! O sweet! when I do look on
thee."
Song: "Who hath his fancy [*or* fancie]
pleasèd."
Splendidis longum valedico nugis.
Thou blind man's mark, thou fool's self-
chosen snare.
When, to my deadly pleasure.

Sidney, Robert (1563–1626)
Ah dearest limbs, my life's best joy and stay.
Alas, why say you I am rich? when I.
Forsaken woods, trees with sharp storms
opressed.
Songe 17: "Sun is set, and masked night,
The."
Sonnet 25: "Yow that take pleasure in yowr
cruelty."

Siegel, Robert (b. 1839)
Ego.

Sigerson, George (1839–1925)
My Own Cáilin Donn.

Sigourney, Lydia Huntley (1791–1865)
Blessed Comforter Divine.
God Save the Plough.
Indian Names.
Laborers of Christ! Arise.
Onward, Onward, Men of Heaven.
Request of a Dying Child.
Stars, The.
To a Shred of Linen.
To the First Slave Ship.
We Praise Thee, If One Rescued Soul.

Sikelianos, Angelos [*or* Anghelos] (1884–1951)
Rehearsing for Death.
Return, The.
Thalero.
Village Wedding, The.

Silabhattarika (*fl.* before 11th cent.)
He who stole my virginity / is the same man.
Wanton, *sels.*

Silcock, Ruth
Limerick: "Hibiscus is flaming and frillier."
Limerick: "In the rain in a yard in
Cessnock."

Limerick: "Land of blue skies, and sunlight,
A."
Limerick: "There's an emerald frog down the
loo."
Pioneer Village.

**Silius Italicus, Tiberius Catius Asconius (c.25–
c.101 A.D.)**
Punica, The, *sels.*

Silkin, Jon (b. 1930)
Death of a Son.
Lilies of the Valley.
Space in the Air, A.

Silko, Leslie Marmon (b. 1948)
Alaskan Mountain Poem #1.
Deer Song.
Four Mountain Wolves.
Hawk and Snake.
Horses at Valley Store.
In Cold Storm Light.
Indian Song: Survival.
Invention of White People, The.
It Was a Long Time Before.
Long Time Ago.
Love Poem: "Rain smell comes with the
wind."
Poem for Ben Barney.
Poem for Myself and Mei: Abortion.
Prayer to the Pacific.
Preparations.
Slim Man Canyon.
Sun Children.
Time We Climbed Snake Mountain, The.
Toe'osh; a Laguna Coyote Story.
When Sun Came to Riverwoman.
Where Mountain Lion Lay [*or* Laid] Down
with Deer.

Sill, Edward Rowland (1841–87)
Baker's Duzzen uv Wize Sawz, A.
California Winter.
Fool's Prayer, The, *sels.*
Opportunity.
Truth at Last.

Sillè, Nicasius de (b. 1610)
God Set Us Here.

Silliman, Ron (b. 1946)
Hidden, *sels.*
Paradise, *sels.*
Tjanting, *sels.*

Sillitoe, Alan (b. 1928)
Optics.
Picture of Loot.
Synagogue in Prague.

"Silurist." *See* **Vaughan, Henry**

Silveira, Onésima (b. 1936)
Different Poem, A.

Silvers, Frances
Frankie Silvers.

Silverstein, Shel [*or* Shelley] (b. 1932)
Clarence Lee from Tennessee.
Dirtiest Man in the World, The.
Friendship.
Hug o' War.
Jimmy Jet and His TV Set.
Lazy People, The.
Listen to the MUSTN'TS, child.
Longmobile.
Nobody loves me.
One Inch Tall.
Rock 'N' Roll Band.
Sarah Cynthia Sylvia Stout Would Not Take
the Garbage Out.
Sick.
Slithergadee has crawled out of the sea, The.
Whatif.

Simcox, George Augustus (1841–1905)
Love's Votary.

Simic, Charles (b. 1938)
Against Whatever It Is That's Encroaching.
Ancient Autumn.
Animal Acts.
Ballad: "What's that approaching like dust
like poverty."
Begotten of the Spleen.
Bestiary for the Fingers of My Right Hand.
Bird calls me, A.
Book Full of Pictures, A.

Breasts.
Brooms.
Butcher Shop.
Charon's Cosmology.
Classic Ballroom Dances.
Clouds Gathering.
Cold, The.
Concerning My Neighbors, the Hittites.
Crepuscule with Nellie.
Dark Farmhouses.
Elementary Cosmogony.
Empire of Dreams.
Errata.
Eyes Fastened with Pins.
Fear passes from man to man.
Fork.
Great Infirmities.
Grocery.
Harsh Climate.
Hearing Steps.
Hunger.
Inner Man, The.
Lesson, The.
Marvels of the City, The.
My Shoes.
Nothing.
Old Couple.
Old Mountain Road.
Pastoral: "I came to a field."
Poem: "Every morning I forget how it is."
Poem without a Title.
Prodigy.
Promises of Leniency and Forgiveness.
Psalm: "Old ones to the side."
Quick Eats.
Read Your Fate.
Shelley.
Shirt.
Sleep.
Spoon, The.
Spoons with Realistic Dead Flies on Them.
Spring.
Stone.
Story, The.
Strictly for Posterity.
Summer Morning.
Tapestry.
Theory, A.
This Morning.
Toy Factory.
Wall, A.
Watch Repair.
Watermelons.
Windy Evening.
Winter Night.
World Doesn't End, The, *sels.*

Simko, Daniel S.
Arrival, The.
Coming Home.
Jewish Cemetery in Prague, The.
Thinking of My Father on a Bus to
   Baltimore.
Three Songs.

Simmerman, Jim (b. 1952)
Child's Grave, Hale County, Alabama.

Simmias [or Simias] of Rhodes (*fl.* c.300 B.C.)
At the Tomb of Sophokles.
Decoy Partridge, A.

Simmias of Thebes (*fl.* 5th cent. B.C.)
To Prote.

Simmons, James (b. 1933)
After Eden.
Archæologist, The.
Birthday Poem, A.
Cavalier Lyric.
Claudy.
Didn't He Ramble.
Eden.
End of the Affair, The.
Experience.
Fear Test: Integrity of Heroes.
For Imelda.
For Thomas Moore.
From the Irish.
Goodbye, Sally.
Honeymoon, The.
In the Wilderness.

Influence of Natural Objects, The.
John Donne.
Join me in celebrating.
Long Way After Ronsard, A.
Lullaby for Rachael.
October in the Country: [1983].
One of the Boys.
Outward Bound.
Playing with Fire.
Pleasant Joys of Brotherhood, The.
Reformer to His Father, A.
Rogation Day: Portrush.
Stephano Remembers.
West Strand Visions.
Westport House, Portrush.
Written, Directed by and Starring.

Simmons, Naomi Stroud
With Reservations.

Simms, Colin
ARCS above OXUS.
Otter, Redewetter.
St Kilda-Wren, 1957.
Three Years in Glen Garry.

Simms, William Gilmore (1806–72)
By the Swanannoa.
City of the Silent, The, *sels.*
Glory and Enduring Fame.
Lost Pleiad, The.
New Moon, The.
Swamp Fox, The.
Triumph, The.

Simon, Leslie
Bernice Got Next to Isis.
Hattie Went to Market.
Nellie Gives into Blanche.

Simon, Paul (b. 1942)
Richard Cory.
Sound of Silence, The.

Simone dall' Antela (*fl.* c.1300)
Prolonged Sonnet: In the Last Days of the
   Emperor Henry VII.

Simonides (c.556–468 B.C.)
Because of these men's courage, no smoke
   rose.
Cenotaph at the Isthmos.
Drinker, glutton supreme.
Flux.
For the Athenian Dead at Plataia.
For the Spartan Dead at Plataia.
For the Spartan Dead at Thermopylai (480
   B.C.)
Great light was born in Athens when, A.
Here lies Anacreon.
I Brotachos of Gortyn lie here. This.
No alien dust covers your tomb.
On a Hound.
On His Friend Megistias, Who Died at
   Thermopylai.
On the Army of Spartans, Who Died at
   Thermopylae.
On Theodoros.
On Two Brothers.
Stone of Megakles who's dead, The.
Stranger, when you come to / Lakedaimon.
There is one story.
Thermopylae.
While bringing Apollo the pick of the
   Etruscan plunder.

Simonov, Konstantin Mikhailovich (1915–79)
Blind Man, The.
By the Campfire.
Cricket, The.
Lieutenant, The.
Remember, Alyosha, the roads of Smolensk.
Wait for me, and I'll come back.

Simons, Mary Crescenzo
Return to Mankiller Flats, Oklahoma.

Simovic, Ljubomir (b. 1935)
Breakfast.
Crucifixion.
Curses.
Epitaph: "To the chimney a bull's horns."
Epitaphs from Karansko Cemetery.
Notation in Gold.
One Evening.
Traveling Star.

Simpson, Joshua McCarter (1820–76)
Away to Canada.
First of August in Jamaica, The.
"No, Master, Never!"
Old Liberia Is Not the Place for Me.
To the White People of America.
Twilight Hour, The.

Simpson, Louis (b. 1923)
Aegean.
After Midnight.
American Poetry.
Arm in Arm.
As birds are fitted to the boughs.
Ash and the Oak, The.
Back in the States.
Battle, The.
Before the Poetry Reading.
Boarder, The.
Carentan O Carentan.
Chocolates.
Climate of Paradise, The.
Constant Lover, The.
Country House, The.
Custom of the World, The.
Doubting.
Dream of Governors, A.
Dvonya.
Early in the Morning.
Fine Day for Straw Hats, A.
Friend of the Family, A.
Goodnight, The.
Green Shepherd, The.
Heroes, The.
Hot Night on Water Street.
Hubert's Museum.
I dreamed that in a city dark as Paris.
In California.
In the Suburbs.
Inner Part, The.
Isidor.
It Was the Last of the Parades.
Jamaica.
Landscape with Barns.
Laurel Tree, The.
Legend of Success, The Salesman's Story,
   The.
Man Who Married Magdalene, The.
Memories of a Lost War.
Middleaged Man, The.
Morning Light, The.
Music in Venice.
My father in the night commanding No.
New Lines for Cuscuscaraway and Mirza
   Murad Ali Beg.
Night in Odessa, A.
On the lawn at the villa.
Outward.
Physical Universe.
Precinct Station, The.
Redwoods, The.
Riders Held Back, The.
Runner, The.
Sailors.
Son of the Romanovs, A.
Squeal.
Story About Chicken Soup, A.
Stumpfoot on 42nd Street.
Suddenly.
Summer Storm.
Sway.
Tailor's Wedding, The.
There Is.
Things.
To the Western World.
Tonight the Famous Psychiatrist.
Troika, The.
Troika, troika! The snow moon.
26th Precinct Station.
Walt Whitman at Bear Mountain.
White Oxen.
Why Do You Write about Russia?
Working late.

Simpson, Margaret Winefride (1893–1939)
Villanelle: "O winter wind, lat grievin be."

Simpson, Ronald Albert (b. 1929)
All Friends Together.
Antarctica.

Diver.
Lake.
Sims, George R. (1847–1922)
Christmas Day in the Workhouse.
Garden Song, A.
'Ostler Joe.
Two Women, *sels.*
Undertones.
Sinason, Valerie (b. 1946)
In the Beginning.
Renaming, The.
Will You Come Out Now?
Sinclair, F. D. (b. 1921)
Zimbabwe.
Sinclair, Iain
Bull Called Remorse, A.
German Bite.
Hurricane Drummers! Self-Aid in Haggerston.
Painting with a knife the Invader.
Star-breath descends. line.
Sinclair, Keith (b. 1922)
Bomb Is Made, The.
Memorial to a Missionary.
Sonnet from Below the Age Gap.
Sinda, Martial (b. c.1930)
To the banquet of the earth.
You shall walk in peace!
Sine, Georgia
Tornado Warning.
Singde, Nara. *See* Na-lan Hsing-te
Singer, Burns (James Burns Singer) (1928–64)
Birdsong.
Epilogue: "That death might not be casual."
For Josef Herman.
Marcus Antoninus Cui Cognomen Erat Aurelius.
Nothing.
Peterhead in May.
Sort of Language, A.
SOS Lifescene.
Still and All.
Singer, Elizabeth (1674–1737)
Cant. 5.6 &c.
Farewel to Love, A.
Pindarick, to the Athenian Society, A.
To Mutius.
Singer, James Burns. *See* **Singer, Burns**
Singh, Kedarnath (b. 1934)
On Reading a Love Poem.
Singh, Shamsher Bahadur (1911–93)
On the Slope of this Hill.
Singleton, John (fl. c.1767)
General Description of the West Indian Islands, A, *sels.*
Sinha, Kabita (b. 1931)
Diamond of Character, The.
Siôn Cent (fl. 1400–1430)
Vanity of the World, The.
Sirin, Vladimir. *See* **Nabokov, Vladimir Vladimirovich**
Sirr, Peter (b. 1960)
Beginnings.
Collector's Marginalia, The.
Guide to Holland, A.
'Phoning.
Troubadour.
Understanding Canada.
Sissay, Lemn (b. 1967)
"So Near and Yet So Near."
Today Will Pass.
"What Have We Got."
Sissman, Louis Edward (b. 1928)
Big Rock-Candy Mountain, The.
Cockaigne: A Dream.
Day in the City, A.
Deathplace, A.
December 27, 1966.
Disappearance in West Cedar Street, A.
Dying: An Introduction.
Elegy: E. W.
In and Out.
On the Island.
Sweeney to Mrs. Porter in the Spring.
Upon Finding Dying: An Introduction, by L. E. Sissman, Remaindered at IS.

West Forties: Morning, Noon, and Night, The.
Sissoko, Fily-Dabo (1900–1964)
Bombax Tree, The.
Brush Fire.
Dawn in the Valley.
Grandmother.
Like a Flower.
Meeting Bida.
Whirlwinds / nearly always.
Sisson, Charles Hubert (b. 1914)
Adam and Eve.
and B, A.
At First.
Black Rocks.
Carmen Saeculare.
Cato.
Cranmer was person of this parish.
Easter.
Family Fortunes.
In Autumn.
Knole.
Letter to John Donne, A.
Marcus Aurelius.
Money.
Nature of Man, The.
Over the Wall: Berlin, May 1975.
Queen of Lydia, The.
Temple, The.
Usk, The.
Sitwell, Dame Edith (1887–1964)
Ass-Face.
Aubade: "Jane, Jane, / Tall as a crane."
Bat, The.
Bells of Grey Crystal.
Bird's Song, A.
Cat, The.
Colonel Fantock.
Country Dance.
Dark Song.
Drum; the Narrative of the Demon of Tedworth, The.
Elegy for Dylan Thomas.
En Famille.
Evening.
Extract from Romance, *sels.*
Façade, *sels.*
Gardener Janus Catches a Naiad.
Gold Coast Customs, *sels.*
Green Song.
Hambone and the Heart, The.
Heart and Mind.
How Many Heavens.
Interlude.
King of China's Daughter, The.
Lament of Edward Blastock, The.
Lullaby: "Though the world has slipped and gone."
Madam Mouse Trots.
Madwoman in the Park, The.
Most Lovely Shade.
Neptune—Polka.
Panope.
Poet Laments the Coming of Old Age, The.
Polka.
Prelude.
Said King Pompey, the emperor's ape.
Scotch Rhapsody.
Serenade: Any Man to Any Woman.
Shadow of Cain, The.
Sleeping Beauty, The, *sels.*
Solo for Ear-Trumpet.
Song at Morning, A.
Song: "Now that Fate is dead and gone."
Song: "We are the darkness in the heat of the day."
Song: "Where is all the bright company gone."
Spinning Song.
Still falls the Rain—.
Street Song.
Swans, The.
Switchback.
Tears.
Three Poems of the Atomic Bomb, *sels.*
Trams.
Two Kitchen Songs.

Waltz.
Youth with Red-gold Hair, The.
Sitwell, Sir Osbert (1892–1969)
Elegy for Mr. Goodbeare.
English Beach Memory: Mr. Thuddock.
Fountains ("Proud fountains, wave your plumes.")
How Shall We Rise to Greet the Dawn?, *sels.*
In the Potting Shed.
In the Winter.
Judas and the Profiteer.
Maxixe.
Mrs. Busk.
Next War, The.
On the Coast of Coromandel.
Sitwell, Sacheverell (1897–1988)
Agamemnon's Tomb, *sels.*
Fountains ("This night is pure and clear as thrice refinèd silver.")
Kingcups.
"Psittachus Eois Imitatrix Ales ab Indis."
Red-Gold Rain, The.
River God, The.
Tulip Tree.
Sizemore, George
Drill Man Blues.
Skeat, Walter William (1835–1912)
Clerk Ther Was of Cauntebrigge Also, A.
Skeen, Anita (b. 1946)
Women Who Cook.
Skeeter, Sharyn Jeanne (b. 1945)
California, 1852.
Midwest, Midcentury.
Western Trail Cook, 1880.
Skelton, John (1460?–1529)
Auncient Acquaintance, Madam, The.
Bouge of Court, The, *sels.*
Bowge of Courte, The.
Colin Clout, *sels.*
Collyn Clout, *sels.*
Elinour Rumming, *sels.*
Garland [or Garlande or Garlands] of Laurel[l], The, *sels.*
Gup, Scot!
How the Doughty Duke of Albany like a Coward Knight Ran Away Shamefully, *sels.*
Knowledge, Acquaintance.
Lawde and Prayse Made for Our Sovereigne Lord the Kyng, A, *sels.*
Magnificence, *sels.*
Manner of the World Nowadays, The, *sels.*
Mannerly Margery Mylk and Ale.
Now sing we, as we were wont.
Philip Sparrow.
Phillip Sparow, *sels.*
Phyllyp Sparowe [or Philip Sparrow], *sels.*
Prayer to the Father of [or in] Heaven, A.
Replycacion, A, *sels.*
Speak [or Speke], Parrot, *sels.*
Though Ye Suppose.
To the Second Person, *sels.*
Tunnyng [or Tunning] of Elynour [or Elinor] Rummyng [or Rumming], The, *sels.*
Upon a Dead Man's Head.
Why Come Ye Not to Court, *sels.*
Woefully arrayed.
Womanhod, wanton, ye want.
Skelton, Robin (b. 1925)
Ballad of a Mine, A.
Eagle.
Lakeside Incident.
Skinner, Jeffrey
Ballad of the Swimming Angel.
Earth Angel.
For Stuart Porter, Who Asked for a Poem That Would Not Depress Him Further.
Late Afternoon, Late in the Twentieth Century.
Objects in Mirror are Closer Than They Appear.
Restoration.
Rolling in Clover.
Silk Robe.
Starling Migration, The.

Skinner, John (1721–1807)
Tullochgorum.

Skinner, Knute (b. 1929)
Cold Irish Earth, The.

Skipsey, Joseph (fl. c.1892)
"Get up!" the caller calls, "Get up!"
Hey Robin.
Mother Wept.
Not as Wont.

Skirrow, Desmond (1924–76)
Ode on a Grecian Urn Summarized.

Skirving, Adam (1719–1803)
Johnnie Cope.

Sklarew, Myra (1934–1987?)
Holocaust.
How Metaphor Can Save Your Life.
Instructions for Elijah.
Ninth of Av.
Speech Warts.
Teaching the Children.
What Is a Jewish Poem?

Skovron, Alex (b. 1948)
Election Eve, with Cat.

Skoyles, John (b. 1949)
Good Cheer.
Head of Tasso, The.
In Memoriam.

Skrine, Nesta Higginson. *See* "O'Neill, Moira"

Skrzynecki, Peter (b. 1945)
Cattle.
Feliks Skrzynecki.
Hunting Rabbits.

Skwirz, Marylee
Long Distance Calls.

Skythinos (c.90 B.C.–A.D. 50)
Epigram: "Great woe, fire & war come on me."

Sladen, Douglas Brook Wheelton (1856–1947)
Summer Christmas in Australia, A.

Slater, Francis Carey (1876–1958)
Songless Land, The.
Stars in Sand.

Slavitt, David R. (b. 1935)
Broads.
Dead Bird.
Griefs of Women, The.
That Everything Moves Its Bowels.

Slessor, Kenneth (1901–71)
All-night Taxi Stand, The.
Beach Burial.
Bushranger, A.
Choker's Lane.
Country Towns.
Five Bells.
Fixed Ideas.
Last Trams.
Metempsychosis.
Night-Ride, The.
North Country.
Nuremberg.
Out of Time, *sels.*
Polarities.
Sleep.
South Country.
To Myself.
Up in Mabel's Room.
William Street.

Slingeland, Sophie
About Writing Poetry.
Babouchka.

Slinger, Francisco. *See* "Mighty Sparrow, The"

Sloan, Mary Margaret (b. 1946)
Eccentricity of the Middle Ground.

Sloman, Joel (b. 1943)
In a Remote Cloister Bordering the Empyrean.
Tree, The.

Slomkowska, Lusia
Alphabet by the Pool on a Sunday Afternoon, The.

Slonimski, Antoni (1895–1976)
All.
Elegy: "No more, no more Jewish townships in Poland."

He Is My Countryman.
London Spring.
Morning and Evening.
Remembrance.

Sluchevsky [*or* Sluchevskii], Konstantin Konstantinovich (1837–1904)
I told her: the sidewalks are muddy.
Nothing but anniversaries, anniversaries...
Yes, for the multitude of people it's hard to avoid.

Slutsky [*or* Slutskii], Boris Abramovich (1919–86)
Bathhouse, The.
Boss, The.
Burnt.
Clerks.
Filled with the final weariness.
God.
Horses in the Sea.
Hospital.
How They Killed My Grandmother.
Pit of Cologne, The.
Prosaics.

Small, Adam (b. 1936)
Brown Lullaby.
Second Coming.
There's Somethin'.
What abou' de Law?

Small, Jonathan
Eating the Elephant Whole.
Pig-Sticking Season, The.

Small, Robin. *See* "Jerry, Bongo"

Smart, Christopher (1722–71)
Author Apologizes to a Lady, for His Being a Little Man, The.
Hymn to the Supreme Being, *sels.*
Hymns and Spiritual Songs for the Fasts and Festivals of the Church of England, *sels.*
Hymns for the Amusement of Children, *sels.*
Jubilate Agno, *sels.*
Morning Hymn, A.
Morning-Piece; or, An Hymn for the Hay-Makers, A.
Night-Piece; or, Modern Philosophy, A.
On a Bed of Guernsey Lilies.
Psalm 58.
Song to David, A, *sels.*
"Song to David, A," *sels.*
Song: "Where shall Celia fly for shelter."
To the Rev. Mr. Powell.
Verses Written in a London Churchyard.

Smedley, Jonathan (1671–1729)
Fancy.

Smedley, Menella Bute (1820–77)
Cavour.
Contrast, A.
Face from the Past, A.
Irish Fairy lost her way, An.
North Pole Story, A.
Sorrowful Sea-Gull, The.

Smeeton, John P.
Jack Frost in the Garden.

Smelyakov [*or* Smeliakov], Yaroslav [*or* Iaroslav] Vasilevich (1912–72)
Blind Man, The.
Dancing, phosphorescent drops.
Earth.
From My Diary.
Judge, The.
Locomotives' graveyard, The.
Lovely Leda.
Manon Lescaut.
Menshikov.
Monument, The.
Peter and Aleksey.
Portrait.
Should I ever fall ill.

Smiler Narautjarri
Witch Doctor's Magic Flight, The.

Smiley, Joseph Bert (1864–1903)
St. Peter at the Gate.

Smith, Alexander (1830–67)
Boy's Poem, A, *sels.*

Smith, Anna Deavere
Fires in the Mirror, *sels.*

Smith, Arabella Eugenia (d. 1916)
If I Should Die Tonight.

Smith, Arthur James Marshall (1902–80)
Ballade un Peu Banale.
Brigadier.
Common Man, The.
Dead stare out of empty sockets, The.
Lonely Land, The.
News of the Phoenix.
Political Intelligence.
Resurrection of Arp.
Watching the Old Man Die.
What the Emanation of Casey Jones Said to the Medium.

Smith, Bertha Wilcox
Mister Snow Man.

Smith, Bessie (1895–1937)
Backwater Blues.
Black Mountain Blues.
Empty Bed Blues.
In the House Blues.

Smith, Bruce (b. 1949)
American Lunch.
In My Father's House, *sels.*
Laundry.
Mercy.
O My Invisible Estate.

Smith, Caroline Sprague (1827–88)
Tarry with Me, O My Saviour.

Smith, Charlotte (1749–1806)
Beachy Head, *sels.*
Captive Escaped in the Wilds of America. Addressed to the Hon. Mrs. O'Neill, The.
Dead Beggar, an Elegy Addressed to a Lady, The.
Fragment Descriptive of the Miseries of War.
Glow-Worm, The.
Invitation to the Bee.
Montalbert, *sels.*
Nepenthe.
Ode to Death.
On Being Cautioned against Walking on an Headland Overlooking the Sea, because It Was Frequented by a Lunatic.
On the Aphorism "L'Amitié est l'Amour sans Ailes."
On the Departure of the Nightingale.
Partial Muse, has from my earliest hours, The.
Sea View, The.
Sonnet XXXII. (To Melancholy. Written on the Banks of the Arun, October 1785).
Sonnet V. To the South Downs: "Ah, hills beloved!—where once, an happy child."
Sonnet Written at the Close of Spring [*or* Elegiac Sonnet].
Sonnet Written in the Church-Yard at Middleton in Sussex.
Stanzas: "Ah! think'st thou, Laura, then, that wealth."
Thirty-eight: Addressed to Mrs H—y.
To a Querulous Acquaintance.
To Sleep.
To Spring.
To the Moon.
To the Shade of Burns.
Unhappy exile, whom his fates confine, The.
Verses Intended to Have Been Prefixed to the Novel of Emmeline, but Then Suppressed.
Written in October.
Written near a Port on a Dark Evening.

Smith, Cicely Fox-
Admiral Dugout.

Smith, Dave Jeddie (b. 1942)
Antipastoral Memory of One Summer, An.
August, on the Rented Farm.
Bats.
Championship Fight.
Cleaning a Fish.
Cuba Night.
Cumberland Station.
Desks.
Dome Poem.
Elegy in an Abandoned Boatyard.
Fisherman's Whore, The.
Hawktree.

Hole, Where Once in Passion We Swam.
Lake Drummond Dream.
Looking for the Melungeon.
March Storm, Poquoson, Virginia, 1963.
Mending Crab Pots.
Near the Docks.
On a Field Trip at Fredericksburg.
Pink Slip at Tool & Dye.
Pulling a Pig's Tail.
Quilt in the Bennington College Library, A.
Rain Forest.
Reading the Books Our Children Have
  Written.
Roundhouse Voices, The.
Sailing the Back River.
Sea Owl.
Smithfield Ham.
Snapshot of a Crab-Picker among Barrels
  Spilling Over, Apparently at the End of
  Her Shift.
Spring Poem, The.

Smith, Dill Armor. *See* **Gault, A. J.** *and* **Dill
Armor Smith**

Smith, Elizabeth Oakes (1806–93)
Ode to Sappho.

Smith, Eunice (*fl.* late 18th cent.)
Dear Brethren, Are Your Harps in Tune?
Dear Happy Souls.

Smith, Florence (1845–71)
Song: "How pleasant it is that always."

Smith, Francis J. (b. 1920)
First Prelude.

Smith, Gary
Penitential Cries of Jupiter Hammond, The.

Smith, George (1713–76)
Country Lovers; or, Isaac and Marget Going
  to Town, on a Summer's Morning, The.

Smith, Gwen A.
Off We Go to Market.

Smith, Harry Bache (1860–1936)
My Angeline.

Smith, Horace [*or* Horatio] (1779–1849)
Bit of Colour, A.
Evening; an Elegy.
Macbeth.
To the Wine Treasurer of the Circuit Mess.

Smith, Horace (1779–1849) *and* **James Smith
(1775–1839)**
Cui Bono?

Smith, Iain Crichton (b. 1928)
By the Sea, *sels.*
Children, The.
Chinese Poem.
Christmas 1971.
Clearances, The.
Culloden and After.
For Angus MacLeod.
For My Mother.
Gaelic Songs.
Gaelic Stories.
Ghost, The.
Glass of Water, The.
Highlanders.
How Often I Feel Like You.
In the late evening.
John Knox.
Law and the Grace, The.
Life, A, *sels.*
Listen, I have flown through darkness
  towards joy.
Milk jugs, cups.
None is the same as another.
Nose went away by itself, The.
Old Woman.
Poem in March.
Retired.
Shall Gaelic Die?
Strangers.
Towards the Stars.
White Air of March, The, *sels.*

Smith, James (1775–1839)
Playhouse Musings.
See also **Smith, Horace** *and* **James Smith**

Smith, Jessie Welborn
Sew a Pocket.

Smith, John (1580–1631)
In the Due Honor of the Author Master
  Robert Norton.
John Smith of His Friend Master John
  Taylor.
Sea Marke.

Smith, John (1662–1717)
Solitary Canto to Chloris the Disdainful, A.

Smith, John (b. 1934)
Have You Heard the Sun Singing?

Smith, Jordan (b. 1954)
Mandolin.

Smith, Kay (b. 1911)
Annunciation.
Footnote to the Lord's Prayer, *sels.*

Smith, Ken (b. 1938)
Encounter at St. Martin's.
Jack's Postcards.
Living with the Boss.
Night Whispers, The.
Possessions.
Snobby Roberts' Message.
Train.
Writing in Prison.

Smith, Langdon (1858–1908)
Evolution.

Smith, Lanta Wilson
This, Too, Shall [*or* Will] Pass Away.

Smith, Laurence
Christmas Tree.
Skeleton House.

Smith, Margoret
Cataract.

Smith, May Riley (1842–1927)
If We Knew.
Last Dance, The.
My Life Is a Bowl.
Sometime, when all life's lessons have been
  learned.

Smith, Michael (1954–83)
Asleep in the City.
Black and White.
Black Bud.
Chimes.
City.
Dis-ya dutty, a we create it.
Fall.
From the Chinese.
Go Blow Fire, A.
I an I Alone; or Goliath.
In Prison.
Mitching.
Revolutionary.
Stopping to Take Notes.
Visit to the Village, A.

Smith, Pamela
Poor old lady, she swallowed a fly.

Smith, Patricia (b. 1955)
Annie Pearl Smith Discovers Moonlight.
Biting Back.
Blonde White Women.
Dylan, Two Days.
Sweet Daddy.
They say that black people.
What It's Like to Be a Black Girl (For Those
  of You Who Aren't).

Smith, Pauline (1882–1959)
Katisje's Patchwork Dress.

Smith, R. T. (b. 1904)
Making the Snowshoes.

Smith, Ray (b. 1915)
Apple, The.

Smith, Robert (d. 1555)
Exhortation of a Father to His Children, The.

Smith, Samuel Francis (1808–95)
America.
As flows the rapid river.
Down to the Sacred Wave.
Morning Light Is Breaking, The.
Softly Fades the Twilight Ray.

Smith, Samuel J. (1771–1835)
Arise, my soul! With rapture rise!

Smith, Stevie (1902–71)
Admire Cranmer!
After-Thought, The.

Airy Christ, The.
Angel Boley.
Anger's Freeing Power.
Animula, Vagula, Blandula.
Autumn.
Away, melancholy, / Away with it, let it go.
Bag-Snatching in Dublin.
Ballet of the Twelve Dancing Princesses,
  The.
Be Off!
Bereaved Swan, The.
Bog-Face.
Broken Friendship, The.
But Murderous.
Celts, The.
Childe Rolandine.
Commuted Sentence, The.
Conventionalist, The.
Conviction IV.
Correspondence between Mr. Harrison in
  Newcastle and Mr. Sholto Peach Harrison
  in Hull.
Dear Female Heart, I am sorry for you.
Death Sentence, The.
Dedicated Dancing Bull and the Water Maid,
  The, *sels.*
Deserter, The.
Distractions and the Human Crowd.
Dream of Comparison, A.
Drugs made Pauline vague.
Edmonton, thy cemetery.
Emily Writes Such a Good Letter.
Exeat.
Fairy Story.
Freddy.
Frog Prince, The.
Galloping Cat, The.
God the Eater.
Goodnight.
Grange, The.
Great Unaffected Vampires and the Moon.
Heavenly City, The.
Holiday, The.
House of Mercy, A.
How cruel is the story of Eve.
Human Affection.
I forgive you, Maria.
I Remember.
I rode with my darling in the dark wood at
  night.
In my dreams I am always saying goodbye
  and riding away.
In the Night.
Infelice.
Is it wise.
Jungle Husband, The.
Lads of the village, we read in the lay, The.
Lady "Rogue" Singleton.
Landrecie.
Le Revenant.
Lightly Bound.
Little Boy Lost.
Lord Barrenstock and Epicene.
Love me, Love me, I cried to the rocks and
  the trees.
Magna Est Veritas.
Major Macroo.
Man is a spirit. This the poor flesh knows.
Marriage I Think.
Mrs Simpkins never had very much to do.
Mother, among the dustbins and the manure.
Mother love is a mighty benefaction.
Murderer, The.
My Cats.
My Hat.
My Muse sits forlorn.
My Tortoise.
New Age, The.
No Categories!
None of the other birds seem to like it.
Not Waving But Drowning.
Octopus, The.
On the Death of a German Philosopher.
One of Many.
Our Bog is dood, our Bog is dood.
Papa Love Baby.
Parklands, The.

Persian, The.
Pleasures of friendship are exquisite, The.
Portrait, A.
Pretty.
Private Means is dead.
Quand on n'a pas ce que l'on aime, il faut aimer ce que l'on a—.
Revenge, Timotheus cries, and in that shout.
Reversionary.
Rise from Your Bed of Languor.
River God, The.
Salon d'Automne.
Satin-clad, with many a pearl.
Scorpion.
Sigh no more ladies nor gentlemen at all.
Singing Cat, The.
Souvenir de Monsieur Poop.
Sterilization.
Sunt Leones.
Tenuous and Precarious.
This Englishwoman is so refined.
Thoughts about the Person from Porlock.
To carry the child into adult life.
To School!
To the Tune of the Coventry Carol.
Two Friends.
Valuable.
Via Media Via Dolorosa.
Villains.
Voice from the Tomb (1).
Wanderer, The.
Was he married, did he try.
Weak Monk, The.
White Thought, The.
Who Is This Who Howls and Mutters?
Who Killed Lawless Lean?
Word, The.

Smith, Sydney (1771–1845)
On Seeing Francis Jeffrey Riding on a Donkey.

Smith, Sydney Bernard
Deadly Seven, The.
Limerick: "Angst, poetry, urbanized fret."
Limerick: "I haven't a clue where I've been."
Limerick: "Sign your name in the book. It's just ink."
Limerick: "Very apt question struck me, A."

Smith, Sydney Goodsir (1915–75)
Aa my life, my leman said.
Armageddon in Albyn, *sels.*
Bishop Blomfield's First Charge to His Clergy.
Cokkils.
Deevil's Waltz, The.
Epistle to John Guthrie.
Gangrel Rymour and the Pairdon of Sanct Anne, The, *sels.*
Grace of God and the Meth-Drinker, The.
Ineffable Dou, The.
Leander Stormbound.
Mandrake Hert, The.
Mither's Lament, The.
Omens.
Salad, A.
Time be brief.
Under the Eildon Tree, *sels.*
Ye Mongers Aye Need Masks for Cheatrie.

Smith, Thomas (1883–1969)
Why Why Should I the World Be Minding.

Smith, Thomas R.
Two Poems on the Fear of Love.

Smith, Vivian (b. 1933)
At an Exhibition of Historical Paintings, Hobart.
Early Arrival: Sydney.
Fishermen, Drowned beyond the West Coast.
Reflections.
Summer Band Concert.
Tasmania.

Smith, Walter Chalmers (1824–1908)
Glenaradale.

Smith, Welton
Beast Section, The.
Interlude.
Malcolm.
Nigga Section, The.

Strategies.
Smith, William (*fl.* c.1596)
Chloris [*or* the Complaint of the Passionate Despised Shepheard], *sels.*

Smith, William Jay (b. 1918)
Abruptly all the palm trees rose like parasols.
American Primitive.
Around My Room.
Bachelor's-Buttons.
Big Gumbo.
Brooklyn Bridge, Brooklyn Bridge.
Cats are not at all like people.
Closing of the Rodeo, The.
Crocodile wept bitter tears, The.
Dachshunds ("The dachshund leads a quiet life.")
Floor and the Ceiling, The.
Independence Day.
Jittery Jim.
Journey to the Interior.
Lovers, The.
Moon.
Morels.
Nightwood.
Park in Milan, The.
Pavane for the Nursery, A.
Persian Miniature.
Plain Talk.
Polar Bear never makes his bed, The.
Quail in Autumn.
Random Generation of English Sentences; or, The Revenge of the Poets.
Rear Vision.
Room in the Villa, A.
Said Dorothy Hughes to Helen Hocking.
Tempest, The.
There Was an Old Lady Named Crockett.
There was an Old Woman named Piper.
Toaster, The.

Smither, Elizabeth (b. 1941)
Best Cowboy Movie, The.
Casanova's Ankle ("Casanova was turned by an ankle.")
City Girl in the Country.
Temptations of St. Antony by His Housekeeper.
Terrapin, The.

Smithyman, Kendrick (b. 1922)
Circus at the Barber's Shop.
Colville 1964.
Hint for the Incomplete Angler.
Tomarata.

Smolensky [*or* Smolenskii], Vladimir Aleksandrovich (1901–61)
No matter how I shout—there's no reply.

Smollett, Tobias (1721–71)
Tears of Scotland, The.
To Leven Water.

Smukler, Linda (b. 1954)
Shower, The.

Smyth, Paul (b. 1944)
Frame for the Angels, A, *sels.*

Snapp, Thomas
Actor, The.

Sneak, Hymie
Limerick: "Lad of the brainier kind, A."

Sneeden, Ralph (*fl.* 20th cent.)
Coltrane and My Father.

Snider, P. M.
Communion.

Snodgrass, C. A.
Poem for Christmas, A.

Snodgrass, William DeWitt ("S. S. Gardons") (b. 1926)
After experience taught me that all the ordinary.
Albert Speer.
April Inventory.
Campus on the Hill, The.
Examination, The.
Flat One, A.
He fed them generously who were his flocks.
Heart's Needle, *sels.*
Leaving the Motel.
Lobsters in the Window.

Locked House, A.
Lovers Go Fly a Kite, The.
Lying Awake.
Magda Goebbels ("This is the needle that we give.")
Magic Flute, The.
Matisse: "The Red Studio."
Mementos, 1.
Men's Room in the College Chapel, The.
Monet: 'Les Nymphéas.'
Mutability.
No Use.
Old Apple Trees.
Operation, The.
Owls.
Powwow.
Snow Songs.
Song: "Sweet beast, I have gone prowling."
Ten Days Leave.
These trees stand very tall under the heavens.
Vuillard: "The Mother and Sister of the Artist."

Snow, A. H. (b. 1910)
Gardener.

Snow, Carol
Mask Series.

Snow, Eliza R. (1804–87)
Song of the Desert.
Think Not When You Gather to Zion.

Snow, Karen (b. 1823)
Gifts.

Snow, Sophia P. (1745–86)
Annie and Willie's Prayer.

Snyder, Gary (b. 1930)
Above Pate Valley.
After Work.
All the Spirit Powers Went to Their Dancing Place.
All through the Rains.
As for Poets.
August on Sourdough, a Visit from Dick Brewer.
August Was Foggy.
Avocado.
Axe Handles.
Bath, The.
Bedrock.
Before the Stuff Comes Down.
Building.
Burning Island.
Burning the small dead.
By Frazier Creek Falls.
Cartagena.
Changing Diapers.
Circumambulating Arunachala.
Dead by the Side of the Road, The.
Dragonfly / Dead on the snow.
Eight Sandbars on the Takano River.
Elwha River, The.
Fire in the Hole.
For a Far-out Friend.
For a Stone Girl at Sanchi.
For John Chappell.
For Nothing.
For the Boy Who Was Dodger Point Lookout Fifteen Years Ago.
Four Poems for Robin, *sels.*
Front Lines.
Geese Gone Beyond.
Getting in the Wood.
Grand Entry, The.
Hay for the Horses.
Heifer Clambers Up, A.
Hitch Haiku, *sels.*
Hop, Skip, and Jump.
How Do You Shape an Axe Handle?
How Poetry Comes to Me.
I went into the Maverick Bar.
It.
Kyoto Born in Spring Song.
L M F B R.
Late October Camping in the Sawtooths.
Long Hair.
Looking at Pictures to Be Put Away.
Manichaeans, The.
Meeting the Mountains.
Mid-August at Sourdough Mountain Lookout.

Milton by Firelight.
Mother Earth: Her Whales.
Mountains and Rivers without End: The Market, *sels.*
My home was at Cold Mountain from the start.
Myths and Texts, *sels.*
Nansen.
No Shoes No Shirt No Service.
Old dutch woman would spend half a day, The.
Old Woman Nature.
Out West.
Path to Han-shan's place is laughable, The.
Pine Tree Tops.
Piute Creek.
Praise for Sick Women.
Prayer for the Great Family.
Removing the Plate of the Pump on the Hydraulic System of the Backhoe.
Right in the Trail.
Ripples on the surface of the water.
Riprap.
Six Years, *sels.*
Sixth-Month Song in the Foothills.
Some Good Things to Be Said for the Iron Age.
Song of the Taste.
Things to Do around a Lookout.
Things to Do around a Ship at Sea.
This Tokyo.
Through the Smoke Hole.
Trail Crew Camp at Bear Valley. 9000 Feet.
Truth / like the belly of a woman turning, The.
Two Fawns That Didn't See the Light This Spring.
Vapor Trails.
Walk, A.
Water.
What Do They Say.
What Happened Here Before.
What have I learned but.
What You Should Know to Be a Poet.
Why Log Truck Drivers Rise Earlier Than Students of Zen.
Word Basket Woman.
Work to Do Toward Town.

Snyder, Richard (b. 1905)
Aging Poet, on a Reading Trip to Dayton, Visits the Air Force Museum and Discovers There a Plane He Once Flew, The.
Blue Sparks in Dark Closets.
Chicago, Summer Past.
Mongoloid Child Handling Shells on the Beach, A.

So Chong-Ju (b. 1915)
Beside a Chrysanthemum.
Beside the Chrysanthemum.
Flower-Patterned Snake.
Fresh Green, The.
If I Became a Stone.
Looking at Mt. Mudung.
Nightingale Path, The.
Peony Afternoon.
Sneeze, A.
Untitled.
Winter Sky.

Sobiloff, Hy (1912–70)
Child's Sight, The.
Snake's Destiny, The.
Wisdom has nothing to do with age.

Sobin, Gustaf (b. 1935)
Eleven Rock Poems.
Girandole.
Irises.
Notes on Sound, Speech, Speech-Crystals and the Celestial Echo.
On the Nature of the Iconic.
Out of the Identical.
Premises.
Towards the Blanched Alphabets.
Violet City: Aspects of the Transitive.
What the music.

Södergran, Edith (1892–1923)
Decision, A.

Forest Lake.
Hell.
Homecoming.
Hope.
I saw a tree that was greater than all the others.
Instinct.
On Foot I Had to Walk Through the Solar Systems.
Pain.
Question.
There is no one in this world who has time.
Vierge Moderne.
Violet Twilights.
We Women.

Sokolov, Vladimir Nikolaevich (b. 1928)
Artist has to be enslaved, An.
Beginning, The.
Everything as in a good old-fashioned novel.
Garland, The.
Recollections of the Cross.
Snow's white pencil outlining the buildings...

Soldati, Joseph A.
Surroundings.

Solheim, James
Cambrian Night.

Sölle, Dorothee
He gave answers to questions they didn't ask.
I don't as they put it believe in god.
When He Came, *sels.*

Sologub, Fyodor [or Fiodor] Kuz'mich (1863–1927)
Amphora, The.
Austere the Music of My Songs.
Devil's Swing, The.

Solomon ibn Gabirol (1021–58)
Almighty! what is man?
Before I Was Born.
Defiance.
Degenerate Age, A.
From Thee to Thee.
His Illness.
In Praise of Wisdom.
In the Morning I Look for You.
Invitation.
Meditations.
Morning Song.
Night, and the heavens beam serene with peace.
Night-Thoughts.
O Soul, with Storms Beset.
Royal Crown, The, *sels.*
Separation from the Torah.
Song of the Wind and the Rain.
Stanzas: "With tears thy grief thou dost bemoan."
Water Song.
Wine and Grief.

Solomon, Marvin (b. 1933)
Cages.

Solomos, Dionysios (1798–1857)
Free Beseiged, The, *sels.*

Soloukhin, Vladimir Alekseievich (b. 1924)
Lost Songs.
To Make Birds Sing.
Wolves.

Solovyov [or Solov'iov], Vladimir Sergeievich (1853–1900)
Panmongolism! The word's barbaric.

Solt, Mary Ellen
Forsythia.
Marriage.
Moonshot Sonnet.
Rain Down.
Wild Crab.

Somervile [or Somerville], William (1675–1742)
Bowling-Green, The, *sels.*
Chase, The, *sels.*
Hobbinol, *sels.*
Hudibras and Milton Reconciled.
Inquisitive Bridegroom, The.

Sondheim, Stephen (b. 1930)
Gee, Officer Krupke.

Soné
Blessed are they who sow but do not reap.

Sone Yoshitada (fl. late 10th cent.)
Lower leaves of the trees, The.

Song, Cathy (b. 1955)
Beauty and Sadness.
Easter: Wahiawa, 1959.
Father and Daughter.
Girl Powdering Her Neck.
Heaven.
Leaving.
Lost Sister.
Mehinaku Girl in Seclusion, A.
Out of Our Hands.
Picture Bride.
Small Light, A.
Vegetable Air, The.
Waterwings.
Wind in the Trees, The.
Youngest Daughter, The.

Sóng Hồng (Đặng Xuân Khu) (1907–1988)
To be a poet—if it means to hum with winds.

Song, Sugwon (b. 1940)
Cuckoo on Mt. Chiri, The.
Poem: "Water wears away a rock."

Sontonga, Enoch (c.1860–1904)
Lord, bless Africa.

Sophocles (c.495–c.406 B.C.)
Ajax, *sels.*
Antigone, *sels.*
'Antigone," The, *sels.*
Chorus sing of the doom of Thebes' royal family, The.
Chorus sing of the laws of the gods, The.
Electra, *sels.*
Elektra's Keening.
Ocdipus at Colonus, *sels.*
Oedipus the King [or Oedipus Rex], *sels.*
Oedipus Tyrannus, *sels.*
Speech of Ajax.
Thoughts from Sophocles.
Women of Trachis, *sels.*

Šopov, Aco
Poem.

Soprovsky [or Soprovskii], Aleksandr (1953–90)
Two Poems, *sels.*

Sorby, Angela
Museum Piece.

Sorescu, Martin (b. 1936)
Adam paced the footpaths of paradise in a.
Carbon Paper.
Carnival.
Chess.
Fountains in the Sea.
Fresco.
Historiotherapy.
Map.
Perseverance.
Precautions.
Question.
Reading Matter.
Segment, A.
Shakespeare created the world in seven days.
Start.
Tear, The.
With a green scarf I blindfolded.

Sorley, Charles Hamilton (1895–1915)
All the Hills and Vales Along.
Barbury Camp.
Call to Action, A.
Expectans Expectavi.
Hundred thousand million mites we go, A.
Rooks.
Song of the Ungirt Runners, The.
Sonnet: "When you see millions of the mouthless dead."
Stones.
To Germany.
Two Sonnets, *sels.*

Sornberger, Judith
Place to begin is not your death, The.
Thinking of My Mother Who Fifteen Years Later, Has Gone East to See the Leaves.

Soroka, Pauline E.
Understanding.

Sorrells, Helen (b. 1908)
From a Correct Address in a Suburb of a Major City.

Mountain Corral.
To a Child Born in Time of Small War.
Town I Left.

Sorrels, Rosalie
Apple of My Eye, *sels.*

Sorrentino, Gilbert (b. 1929)
Classic Case, A.
Good Night!
Handbook of Versification.
Land of Cotton.
Magic Composer.
Oranges Returned, The.
Razzmatazz.
September in Kittery.
Zoo, The.
Zukofsky.

Sosei (*fl.* **9th cent.**)
She said she would come.

Sosnora, Viktor Aleksandrovich (b. 1936)
Do you envy, my comrades-in-arms.

Sotheby, William (1757–1833)
Netley Abbey; Midnight.

Soto, Gary (b. 1952)
After Tonight.
Behind Grandma's House.
Black Hair.
Braly Street.
Brown Girl, Blonde Okie.
Chiapas.
Drought, The.
Elements of San Joaquin, The, *sels.*
Fair Trade.
Field Poem.
Graciela.
Harvest.
History.
Hoeing.
How Things Work.
Jungle Café, The.
Making Money: Drought Year in Minkler,
　California.
Map, The.
Mexicans Begin Jogging.
Morning They Shot Tony Lopez, Barber and
　Pusher Who Went Too Far, 1958, The.
Not Knowing.
Oranges.
Small Town with One Road.
Soup, The.
Sun.
Tale of Sunlight, The.
Teaching Numbers.
Telephoning God.
Who Will Know Us?
Wrestler's Heart, The.

Soupault, Philippe. *See* **Breton, Andre** *and*
Philippe Soupault

Soupault, Philippe (b. 1897)
Comrade.
Condemned.
Life-Saving Medal.
One o'Clock.
Poems from Saint Pelagia Prison.
Route.
Sporting Goods.
Sunday.
You Who Sleep.

Sousa, John Philip (1854–1932)
Feast of the Monkeys, The.
Have You Seen the Lady?

Sousa, Noémia da (b. 1927)
Appeal.
Poem of João, The.

Souster, Raymond (b. 1921)
Choosing Coffins.
Flight of the Roller Coaster.
Hunter, The.
Ladybug.
Lagoons, Hanlan's Point.
Man Who Finds That His Son Has Become a
　Thief, The.
May fifteenth.
On the Rouge.
Six-Quart Basket, The.
Ties.
Young Girls.

Soutar, William (1898–1943)
Auld House, The.
Auld Sang.
Guns, The.
Hungry Mauchs, The.
Makar, The.
Permanence of the Young Men, The.
Riddle, A: "Yon laddie wi' the gowdan
　pow."
Room, The.
Scotland.
Song: "Whaur yon broken brig hings owre;."
Summer is by.
Supper.
Three Puddocks, The.
Tryst [*or* Trysting Place], The.
Whigmaleerie, A.

Southard, O. Mabson
Across the still lake.
At the window, sleet.
By mist.
Down to dark leaf-mold.
Gleaming—sunken stones.
Hushed, the lake-shore's pines.
In the garden pool.
In the sea, sunset.
Mirrored by the spring.
Now the leaves are still.
Old rooster crows, The.
On a leaf, a leaf.
On the top fence-rail.
One breaker crashes.
Patter of rain, A.
Perching bolt upright.
Snow-laden bushes
Steadily it snows.
Still sunlit, one tree.
This morning's rainbow.
Waves now fall short, The.

Southerland, Ellease
Blue Clay.
Night in Nigeria.
Pale Ant.
Recitation.
Two Fishing Villages.

Southern Bushmen Oral Tradition
Day we die, The.

Southerne, Thomas (1660–1746)
Song: "Pursuing beauty, men descry."

Southey, Robert (1774–1843)
Battle of Blenheim, The.
Bishop Hatto.
Cataract of Lodore, The, *sels.*
Curse of Kehama, The, *sels.*
Devil, The.
Ebb Tide, The.
Epitaph: "Time and the World, whose
　magnitude and weight."
Go, Valentine.
Inchcape Rock, The.
Joan of Arc, *sels.*
Monthly Magazine, 4 287, *sels.*
Morning Post, no. 9198, *sels.*
Ode to a Pig while His Nose Was Being
　Bored.
Old Man's Comforts and How He Gained
　Them, The.
Poems, *sels.*
Scholar, The.
Soldier's Wife, The.
Sweet Spenser, sweetest bard; yet not more
　sweet.
Thalaba the Destroyer, *sels.*
To a Goose [*or* Gosse].
Well of St. Keyne, The.
Widow, The.
Winter.

Southwell, Robert (1561?–1595)
At Fotheringay.
At Home in Heaven.
Burning Babe, The.
Child[e] My Choice [*or* Choyse], A
Christ[e]'s Childhood[e].
Christs Sleeping Friends.
Content and Ri[t]ch[e], *sels.*
David's Peccavi.
Ensamples of Our Savior.

Look[e] Home.
Loss[e] in Delay[e].
Man's Civil[l] War[re].
Marie [*or* Mary] Magdalens Complaint at
　Christs Death.
New Heaven, New War[re].
New Prince, New Pomp[e].
Of the Blessed Sacrament of the Altar.
Seek[e] Flowers of Heaven.
Sinnes Heavie Loade.
Times [*or* Tymes] Go[e] By Turn[e]s.
Upon the Image of Death, *sels.*
Vale of Tear[e]s, A.

Southwick, Marcia
Brothers.
Child, Invisible Fire.
Horse on the Wall.
Rain's Marriage, The.
Ruins, The.
Sun Speaks, The.

Souza, Eunice De (b. 1940)
De Souza Prabhu.
Women in Dutch Painting.

Soyinka, Wole (b. 1934)
Abiku.
After the Deluge.
Apologia (Nkomati).
Civilian and Soldier.
Fado Singer.
Funeral Sermon, Soweto.
Harvest of Hate.
He escape the lynch days. He survives.
Huge with Time, a wombfruit lanced.
Hunchback of Dugbe, The.
I think it rains.
Idanre and Other Poems (1967), *sels.*
Massacre, October '66.
"No!" He Said.
Rust and silence fill the thatch.
Shuttle in the Crypt, The, *sels.*
Telephone Conversation.
To My First White Hairs.

Spacks, Barry (b. 1931)
Emblem of Two Foxes, An.
Freshmen.
October.

Spalding, Susan Marr (*fl.* **19th cent.**)
Fate.

Spargur, Jill
Tragedy.

Spark, Muriel (b. 1918)
Against the Transcendentalists.
Canaan.
Elegy in a Kensington Churchyard.
Faith and Works.
Going up to Sotheby's.
Kensington Gardens.
Litany of Time Past.
She Wolf, The.

Sparrow, John (1906–92)
Apology and Explanation.
Epitaph: "This stone, with not unpardonable
　pride."
To an Angel in the House.

Sparshott, Francis (b. 1926)
Entanglement.
Improperia.
Naming of the Beasts, The.
Paysage Choisi.
Reply to the Committed Intellectual.
Three Seasons.

Spaziani, Maria Luisa (b. 1924)
Aegean, The.
Comet, The.
Convent in '45, The.
Destiny.
Duomo, The.
Figurehead, The.
Grain of sand, the beginning of the desert,
　The.
If it were a sea, this immense wind.
Journey in the Orient.
Merciful Shore, The.
Pure Dust.
Rome has a thousand fountains, and in May
　they sing.

Star of Free Will, The, *sels.*
Tender heart, hairy muscle.
Via Margutta.
White on White.
Winter Moon.
Your life is a baby not yet born.

Spear, Charles (b. 1910)
At a Danse Macabre.
Disinherited, The.
Environs of Vanholt I.
Memoriter.
Remark.
Vineta.
Watchers, The.

Spear, Roberta (b. 1948)
August/Fresno 1973.
Bat, The.
Bringing Flowers.
Chestnuts for Verdi.
Sale of Smoke, A.

Spears, Dorothea (b. 1901)
Begetting.

Spee, Friedrich (1591–1635)
Spouse of Jesus Laments Her Heart's Flame, The.

Speer, Laurel
Mama Rosanna's Last Bead-Clack.

Speers, Edith (b. 1949)
Australorp.

Speght, Rachel (b. 1597)
Dream, A, *sels.*
Dreame, The, *sels.*

Spellman, Alfred B. (b. 1934)
Did John's Music Kill Him?
For My Unborn and Wretched Children.
In Orangeburg My Brothers Did.
John Coltrane: An Impartial Review.
Tomorrow the Heroes.
Twist, The.
When Black People Are.
Zapata & the Landlord.

Spence, Lewis (1874–1955)
Carse, The.
Great Tay of the Waves.
Prows O' Reekie, The.
Stown Bairn, The.

Spence, Michael
Lost People, The.

Spencer, Anne (1882–1975)
At the Carnival.
Before the Feast of Shushan.
Creed.
Dunbar.
Lady, Lady, I saw your face.
Letter to My Sister.
1975.
Substitution.
Wife-Woman, The.

Spencer, Bernard (1909–63)
Blue Arm.
Boat Poem.
Castanets.
Delos.
Egyptian Dancer at Shubra.
Olive Trees.
Part of Plenty.
Rendezvous, The.
Spring Wind, A.
Thousand Killed, A.
Yachts on the Nile.

Spencer, James Harvey (1870–1950)
For You.

Spencer, Theodore (1902–49)
Californians, The.
Circle, A.
Critics, The.
Day was a year at first, The.
Return.

Spencer, William Robert (1770–1834)
Beth Gêlert; or, The Grave of the Greyhound.

Spender, Stephen (1909–95)
Acts passed beyond the boundary of mere wishing.

After They Have Tired of the Brilliance of Cities.
Air Raid Across the Bay at Plymouth.
Auden at Milwaukee.
Auf dem Wasser zu Singen.
Awaking.
Barn, The.
Beethoven's Death Mask.
Daybreak.
Double Shame, The.
Elementary School Classroom in a Slum, An.
Empty House.
Epilogue: "Time is a thing."
Epilogue to a Human Drama.
Express, The.
Farewell in a Dream.
Funeral, The.
History and Reality.
"I" Can Never Be a Great Man, An.
I think continually of those who were truly great.
Icarus.
Ice.
In railway halls, on pavements near the traffic.
Judas Iscariot.
Landscape near an Aerodrome, The.
Marginal Field, The.
Marston, dropping it in the grate, broke his pipe.
Mask.
Memento.
Missing My Daughter.
New Year.
Not palaces, an era's crown.
One More New Botched Beginning.
Polar Exploration.
Port Bou.
Prisoners, The.
Pylons, The.
Rejoice in the Abyss.
Rolled over on Europe: the sharp dew frozen to stars.
Room above the Square, The.
Rough.
Seascape.
Shapes of Death, The.
Song: "Stranger, you who hide my love."
Sonnet: "You were born; must die; were loved; must love."
Statistics.
Stopwatch and an Ordnance Map, A.
Thoughts During an Air Raid.
Trance, The.
Two Armies.
Ultima Ratio Regum.
Unemployed.
What I expected, was.
Whim of Time, A.
Winter and Summer.
Winter Landscape.
Without that once clear aim, the path of flight.
Word bites like a fish, The.
Your Body Is Stars.

Spenser, Edmund ("Colin Clout") (1552?–1599)
Amorette, *sels.*
Amoretti, *sels.*
Astrophel, *sels.*
Colin Clout's Come Home Again, *sels.*
Commendatory Sonnets, *sels.*
Daphnaïda, *sels.*
Epithalamion, *sels.*
Epithalamion: "Ye learned sisters which have oftentimes," *sels.*
Faerie Queene, The, *sels.*
Fowre Hymnes, *sels.*
Hymn[e] of Heavenly Beauty [*or* Beautie], An, *sels.*
Iambicum Trimetrum.
Mother Hubberd's Tale, *sels.*
Penelope for her *Ulisses* sake.
Prothalamion, *sels.*
Ruines of Rome: by Bellay, *sels.*
Ruines of Time, The.
Shepheardes [*or* Shepeards *or* Shepherd's] Calender, The, *sels.*

Shepherd's Calendar, 'June', The, *sels.*
Sonnet 12: "I saw an ugly beast come from the sea."
Sonnet 13: "I saw a woman sitting on a beast."
Sonnet 14: "Then might I see upon a white horse set."
Sonnet 15: "I saw new Earth, new Heaven, said Saint John."
Sonnet 73: 'Being my self captived here.'
To the Right Worshipfull, My Singular Good Friend, Master Gabriel Harvey, Doctor of the Lawes.

"Speranza." *See* **Wilde, Lady Jane Francesca**

Speyer, Leonora (1872–1956)
Swans.

Spicer, Jack (b. 1925)
Army Beach with Trumpets.
Book of Galahad, The.
Book of Music, A.
Cantata.
Cardplayers, The.
Conspiracy.
Duet for a Chair and a Table.
Five Words for Joe Dunn on His 22nd Birthday.
Fort Wayne.
Four Poems for *The St. Louis Sporting News.*
Ghost Song.
Good Friday: For Lack of an Orchestra.
Graphemics, *sels.*
Hisperica Famina.
Holy Grail, The, *sels.*
Imaginary Elegies, *sels.*
Imaginary Elegies, I IV.
Improvisations on a Sentence by Poe.
Jungle Warfare.
Lament for the Makers: "No call upon anyone but the timber drifting in the waves."
Language, *sels.*
Love Poems, *sels.*
Morphemics.
Mummer.
Orfeo.
Phonemics.
Song for Bird and Myself.
Song of a Prisoner.
Territory is Not the Map, The.
Transformations.
Valentine, A.

Spiess, Robert
Asparagus bed.
Becoming dusk,—.
Blue jays in the pines.
Chain saw stops, The.
Dirt road, A.
Dry, summer day.
Lean-to of tin.
Light river wind, A.
Long wedge of geese, A.
Marsh marigold.
Muttering thunder.
Ostrich fern on shore.
Patches of snow.
Shooting the rapids!
Tar paper cabin.
Winter moon.
Winter wind.
Wispy autumn clouds.

Spingarn, Lawrence P. (b. 1917)
Philatelic Lessons: The German Collection.

Spire, André (1886–1968)
Abishag.
Duster, dust away, my friend.
Hear, O Israel! / Will you never tire of repeating in your prayers.
It Was Not You.
Lonely.
Nativité.
Now You're Content.
Nudities.
Spring.

Spires, Elizabeth (b. 1952)
Apology.

Beds, The.
Comb and the Mirror, The.
Courtesan with Fan.
Exhumation.
First Day, The.
Globe.
Good Friday. Driving Weekend.
Interrogations of the Sparrow.
Mutoscope.
Robed Heart, The.
Sunday Afternoon at Fulham Palace.
Two Shadows.
Woman on the Dump, The.
0°.

Spivack, Kathleen (b. 1938)
But You, My Darling, Should Have Married
    the Prince.
Child's Visit to the Biology Lab, A.
Dido: Swarming.
Dust.
Judgment, The.
Love U.S.A.
March 1st.
Private Pain in Time of Trouble.
Visions.

Spofford, Harriet Prescott (1835–1921)
Fossil Raindrops, The.

Spooner, Lawrence
Looking-Glass for Smokers, A, *sels.*

Spratt, Thomas (1635–1713)
On His Mistress Drown'd.
Your Miscellanies do appear.

Sprigg, Christopher St. John. *See* "Caudwell,
Christopher"

Spring-Rice, Cecil Arthur. *See* Mackail, John
William *and* Cecil Arthur Spring-Rice

Spring-Rice, Cecil Arthur (1858–1918)
Day.
I am the Dean of Christ Church, Sir. *From
    Balliol Rhymes*
I vow to thee, my country, all earthly things
    above.

Springer, Thomas Grant
Giving and Forgiving.
Harmony.

Sprod, G. N.
Request Number.

**Squire, Sir John Collings ("Solomon Eagle")
(1884–1950)**
Ballade of the Poetic Life.
"Break, Break, Break."
Celtic Lyric, The.
Country Wooing, *sels.*
Dilemma, The.
Doris and Philemon, *sels.*
Homœopathy.
If Gray Had Had to Write His Elegy in the
    Cemetery of Spoon River Instead of in
    That of Stoke Poges.
Interior.
It did not last; the Devil howling Ho.
My Father's Cot, *sels.*
Numerous Celts.
Passing of Arthur, The.
She Dwelt among the Untrodden Ways.
Ship, The.
Sonnet: "There was an Indian, who had
    known no change."
Stockyard, The.
Survival of the Fittest, The (In Memoriam,
    L.C. and T.)
Swallow, The, *sels.*
To a Bull-Dog.
To Miss L. F. on the Occasion of Her
    Departure for the Continent.
Under.
Vision of Truth, A.
When I leapt over Tower Bridge.
Winter Nightfall.

Sri Sri (1910–83)
Some People Laugh, Some People Cry, *sels.*

Ssu-k'ung Shu (740–790?)

Exhorting Myself.
In Heaven.
In Illness, Dismissing My Singing Girl.
In the Country.
In the Mountains.
Occasional Poem, An.
Oxhead Temple.
Rebellion Over, I See Off a Friend Who Is
    Returning North, The.

Stack, Philip ("Kid Kazanova") (1900?–1948)
Admonition.

Stadler, Ernst
Decampment.

Staff, Leopold (1878–1957)
Duckweed.
Foundations.
Kingdom.
Portrait.
Speech.

Stafford, Kim R.
Feather Bag, Stick Bag.
Opening the Book.
Proposal.
Walking to the Mailbox.

Stafford, William (1914–93)
Accountability.
Address to the Vacationers at Cape Lookout,
    An.
After Arguing against the Contention That
    Art Must Come from Discontent.
After Plotinus.
Allegiances.
Among Strangers.
Animal That Drank Up Sound, The.
Ask Me.
At Cove on the Crooked River ("At Cove at
    our camp in the open canyon.")
At the Bomb Testing Site.
At the Edge of Town.
At the Klamath Berry Festival.
At the Playground.
At the Un-National Monument along the
    Canadian Border.
Baby Ten Months Old Looks at the Public
    Domain, A.
Bess.
Bi-Focal.
Both Ways.
Bring the North.
Broken Home.
Ceremony.
Christianite.
Day You Are Reading This, The.
Epitaph Ending in And, The.
Escape, The.
Farm on the Great Plains, The.
First Grade.
For Alexis Christa von Hartmann: Proved
    Not Guilty.
Gift, The.
Holding the Sky.
Humanities Lecture.
In a Museum in the Capital.
In the Deep Channel.
In Time of Need.
Indian Cave Jerry Ramsey Found, The.
Late at Night.
Looking West.
Lost in the Centuries.
Maybe Alone on My Bike.
Memorandum.
Moles.
Moment, The.
Monday.
Montana Eclogue.
Monuments for a Friendly Girl at a Tenth
    Grade Party.
Near.
Notice What This Poem Is Not Doing.
Now.
Observation Car and Cigar.
One Home.
One of the Years.
Oregon Message, An.
Peace Walk.

People of the South Wind.
Prairie Town.
Preservation.
Priest Lake.
Religion Back Home.
Remembering Althea.
Remembering Brother Bob.
Report from an Unappointed Committee.
Report to Crazy Horse.
Rescued Year, The.
Returned to Say.
Ritual to Read to Each Other, A.
Runaway Teen.
School Days.
Serving with Gideon.
Shepherd.
Sound from the Earth, A.
Stared Story, A.
Story, A.
Story That Could Be True, A.
Stranger Not Ourselves, The.
Strangers.
Strokes.
Survey, A.
These Days.
These Leaves.
Things That Happen.
Thinking for Berky.
Time.
Tourist Country.
Traveling [*or* Travelling] through the dark I
    found a deer.
Twelfth Birthday.
Vacation.
Visions.
Vocation.
Walking West.
Well rising without sound, The.
West of Your City.
When We Looked Back.
Whole Story, The.
With Kit, Age Seven, at the Beach.
With My Crowbar Key.
Woman at Banff, The.

Stagnelius, Erik Johann (1793–1823)
Memory.

Stallings, A. E.
Apollo Takes Charge of His Muses.

Stallworthy, Jon (b. 1935)
Again.
Almond Tree, The.
At Half Past Three in the Afternoon.
Beginning of the End, The.
Letter from Berlin, A.
Letter to a Friend.
Miss Lavender.
Mother Tongue.
Poem about Poems about Vietnam, A.
Pour Commencer.
Question of Form and Content, A.
Sindhi Woman.
Source, The.
To Whom It May Concern.
Walking against the Wind.
War Story.

Stamp, Catriona (b. 1950)
Rebirth.

Stampa, Gaspara (c.1523–1554)
All the planets in heaven, all the stars.
At dawn of the day the Creator.
Deeply repentant of my sinful ways.
Holy angels, in envy I cast no sigh.
Hunger.
I am now so weary with waiting.
If I could believe that death.
Often I compare my lord to heaven.
Often when alone I liken my lord / to the
    cosmos.
Stars have given me a hard fate, The.
When before those eyes, my life and light
Women, whoever wishes to know my lord.

Standing, Sue
Cellar Door, *sels.*

Standish, Celia
New Year's Days.

Stanescu, Nichita
Adolescents on the Sea.
Engagement.
Evocation.
Homo Plangens.
Marina.
Second Elegy, Getic.
Song.
Winter Ritual.
Stanfield, Leontine
Little Cat Angel, The.
Stanford, Ann (1916–87)
Beating, The.
Covenant of Grace, The, *sels.*
Fathers, The.
Night of Souls.
Riders, The.
Umbrella, The.
Stanford, Frank (1948–78)
Allegory of Death and Night.
Between Love and Death.
Intruder, The.
Inventory.
Island Funeral.
Place on a Grave.
Terrorism.
Stanizzi, John L.
Drink.
Stanley, John
Limerick: "Bells from the steeple resound, The."
Limerick: "Fact of the matter is, Jack, The."
Limerick: "Miranda, remember that Inn?"
Stanley, Mary (1919–80)
Put Off Constricting Day.
Sestina: "Body of my love is a familiar country, The."
Wife Speaks, The.
Stanley, Thomas (1625–78)
All Things Drink.
Beauty.
Bracelet, The.
Celia Singing.
Changed, Yet Constant.
Cold Kiss, The.
Combat, The.
Deposition, The.
Divorce, The.
Exequies, The.
Expectation.
Glowworm, The.
Grasshopper thrice-happy! who.
La Belle Confidente.
Love Deposed.
Love's Innocence.
Magnet, The.
Ode XV.
Old I Am.
On a Violet in Her Breast.
On Mr. Shirley's Poems.
On S. John the Baptist.
Paraphrase Upon Part of the CXXXIX Psalm, A.
Pythagoric letter, two ways spread, The.
Quickness.
Relapse, The.
Repulse, The.
Self-Deceaver, The.
Snow-Ball, The.
Song: "Fool, take up thy shaft again."
Song: "I prithee let my heart alone."
Speaking and Kissing.
Swallow, The.
Time Recover'd.
To Celia Pleading Want of Merit.
Wish, The.
Would I were air that thou with heat opprest.
Stanley-Wrench, Margaret (1917–1974)
Hinterland.
Newdigate Prize Poem 1937, The, *sels.*
Storm, The.
Stansbury, Joseph (1740–1809)
To Cordelia.
Stansbury, Mary Anna Phinney
How He Saved St. Michael's.
Stanton, Frank Lebby (1857–1927)
Keep a-Goin'.

Stanton, Henry T. (1886–1954)
Moneyless Men, The.
Stanton, Maura (b. 1946)
All-Night Waitress, The.
Ballad of the Magic Glasses.
Biography.
Childhood.
Comfort.
Extracts: From the Journal of Elisa Lynch.
Grocery Store, The.
Judith Recalls Holofernes.
Letter to Kafka.
Living Apart.
Portrait by Bronzino, A.
Shoplifters.
Sunday Graveyard.
Stanton, Will D. (b. 1918)
Dandelions.
Stanyhurst, Richard (1547–1613)
Prayer to the Holy Trinity, A.
Virgil's Aeneid Book 4, *sels.*
Starbird, Kaye (b. 1916)
Hound, The.
Starbuck, George (b. 1931)
Bone Thoughts on a Dry Day: Chicago.
Chip.
Cold Fire.
Communication to the City Fathers of Boston.
High Renaissance.
Margaret Are You Drug.
Monarch of the Sea.
New Strain.
Of Late.
On First Looking in on Blodgett's Keats's "Chapman's Homer."
Out in the Cold.
Pit Viper.
Poems from a First Year in Boston, *sels.*
Said.
Said / Agatha Christie to.
Skin Divers, The.
Sonnet with a Different Letter at the End of Every Line.
Spell against Spelling, The.
Starry Night, The.
Technologies.
To His Chi Mistress.
Translations from the English.
Starkey, James. *See* **"O'Sullivan, Seumas"**
Starr, Jean (b. 1935)
Flight.
Statius, Publius Papinius (A.D. c.61–96)
Achilleid, The, *sels.*
Altar of Mercy, The.
Compleynt of feire Anelida and fals Arcite, The, *sels.*
Forest felled, A.
Moment of battle, The.
Silvae, *sels.*
Sleep.
Thebaid, The, *sels.*
Tisiphone responds.
Translation out of Statius. To Sleep, A.
Staughton, William (1770–1829)
Tell Us, Ye Servants of the Lord.
Stead, Christian Karlson (b. 1932)
April Notebook.
Clodian Songbook, *sels.*
Quesada, *sels.*
Twenty-one Sonnets, *sels.*
Walking Westward, *sels.*
Stead, William Force (b. 1884)
I Closed My Eyes To-Day and Saw.
Uriel, *sels.*
Stedman, Edmund Clarence (1833–1908)
Ballad of Lager Bier, The.
Prelude to *An American Anthology.*
Steegmuller, Francis (b. 1906)
Le Hibou et la Poussiquette.
Steel, M. (1879–1952)
Little Lucy Lester.
Steele, Frank (b. 1935)
Country Greeting.
Greener Grass.

Markings.
Steele, Peter (b. 1939)
Cana.
Marking Time.
Steele, Sir Richard (1672–1729)
Funeral, The, *sels.*
Steele, Susanna. *See* **Rosen, Michael** *and* Susanna Steele
Steele, Timothy (b. 1948)
At Will Robers Beach.
Aubade, An.
Aurora.
Devotional Sonnet, A.
Epitaph: "Here lies Sir Tact, a diplomatic fellow."
Eros.
In the King's Rooms.
Joseph.
Library, The.
One Morning.
Rural Colloquy with a Painter.
Sheets, The.
Timothy.
Wait.
Wartburg, 1521–22, The.
Steendam, Jacob (1616–72)
Oh, Sing to God.
When I Admire the Greatness.
Steere, Richard (1643–1721)
Earth Felicities, Heavens Allowances.
Monumental Memorial of Marine Mercy, A.
On a Sea-Storm nigh the Coast.
Poem upon the Caelestial Embassy, A.
Stefanile, Felix (b. 1920)
How I Changed My Name, Felice.
Stefanovich, Nikolai (1912–79)
For all of us destiny is undivided.
Steffen, Jonathan (b. 1958)
Falcon to the Falconer, The.
Stein, Deborah (b. 1977)
Heat.
Stein, Dona Luongo
Searching for Schüpfen.
Stein, Gertrude (1874–1946)
Bundles for Them.
Cézanne.
Four Saints in Three Acts, *sels.*
George Hugnet.
I Am Rose [my eyes are blue].
I think very well of Susan but I do not know her name.
Identity A Poem.
In This Way.
It is not a range of a mountain.
Kneeling.
Leave, A.
Let us describe how they went. It was a very windy night and the road.
Lifting Belly, *sels.*
On Her Way.
Patriarchal Poetry, *sels.*
Portraits and Repetition, *sels.*
Sacred.
Scenes from the Door.
Stanzas in Meditation, *sels.*
Suppose an Eyes.
Susie Asado.
Teachers taught her, The.
Tender Buttons, *sels.*
Valentine to Sherwood Anderson, A.
Very Valentine, A.
What Do I See.
Which I wish to say is this.
White hunter is nearly crazy, A.
Why do you feel differently about a very little snail and a big one.
Stein, Julia
Grand Tradition of Western Culture, The.
Stein, Rose M. (d. 1938)
Lines to Mother.
Steinbarg, Eliezer (1880–1932)
Terrible Thought, A.

Steinberg, Jakov [*or* **Jacob**] **(1887–1947)**
Heart, The.
Steinbergh, Judith W. (b. 1943)
Letting the Parakeet Fly.
Steinmar (*fl.* late 13th cent.)
Farmhand lay all hidden, A.
Since she gives so little pay.
"Stella." *See* **Johnson, Esther**
Stennett, Samuel (1728–95)
Promised Land, The.
Stephanou, Lydia (b. 1922)
"Case of Assault," A.
"Stephany"
I have spent my life.
It is again.
Moving deep.
What marked the river's flow.
Who collects the pain.
Stephen, James Kenneth (1859–92)
After the Golden Wedding, *sels.*
Drinking Song.
England and America, *sels.*
Grievance, A.
In the Backs.
Last Ride Together (from Her Point of
View), The.
Malines.
Remonstrance, A.
Sincere Flattery of R. B.
Sincere Flattery of W. W. (Americanus).
Sonnet, A: "Two voices are there: one is of
the deep."
To R. K.
Stephens, Brunton (1835–1902)
Gentle Anarchist, The.
Stephens, Harry
Night-herding Song[, A].
Stephens, James (1880–1950)
Blue Blood.
Cage, The.
Christmas at Freelands.
Crest Jewel, The.
Daisies, The.
Danny Murphy.
Dark Wings.
Day and Night.
Deirdre.
Donnybrook.
Evening.
Fifteen Acres, The.
Glass of Beer, A.
Goat Paths, The.
Good and bad and right and wrong.
Hate.
In the Night.
In the Poppy Field.
In Waste Places.
Lake, The.
Little things, that run, and quail.
Main-Deep, The.
Night, The.
Odell.
Outcast, The.
Red-haired Man's Wife, The.
Rivals, The.
Seumas Beg.
Shell, The.
Snare, The.
Sweet Apple.
To the Four Courts, Please.
Twins, The.
Watcher, The.
What the Devil Said.
What Thomas an Buile Said in a Pub.
White Fields.
Why Tomas Cam Was Grumpy.
Wind stood up, and gave a shout.
Wood of Flowers, The.
Stephens, Michael (b. 1946)
After Asia.
Stephenson, John (1808–86)
If angels sung a Savior's birth.
Steptoe, Lamont B. (b. 1949)
Election Time.
O' yes.
Such a Boat of Land.

Wired In.
Sterling, Andrew B. (1874–1955)
Meet Me in St. Louis, Louis.
Under the Anheuser Bush.
What You Goin' to Do When the Rent
Comes 'Round?
Stern, Anatol (1899–1968)
Europa.
Stern, Gerald (b. c.1925)
Behaving Like a Jew.
Bite, The.
Bull-roarer, The.
Coleman Valley Road.
Cow Worship.
Dancing, The.
Dog, The.
Expulsion, The.
Faces I Love, The.
Founder, The.
I Hate My Moaning.
I Remember Galileo.
I Would Call It Derangement.
Kissing Stieglitz Goodbye.
Morning Harvest.
Nice Mountain.
Nobody else living knows that song as well
as I do.
On the Far Edge of Kilmer.
Peddler's Village.
Pile of Feathers.
Power of Maples, The.
Romance.
Romania, Romania.
There Is Wind, There Are Matches.
Waving Good-by.
What It Is Like.
Sternberg, Jacob (b. 1890)
Little birds in a row.
Sternhold, Thomas (c.1500–1549)
I Lift My Heart to Thee.
Lord Descended from Above, The.
My Shepherd Is the Living Lord.
Sternlieb, Barry (b. 1947)
Right of Way.
Stevens, Cat
Wild World.
Stevens, George Alexander (1710–84)
Bartleme Fair.
Repentance.
Simple Pastoral, A.
Stevens, George W. (1866–1926)
Organist, The.
Stevens, Michael
Carp, The.
Stevens, Wallace (1879–1955)
American Sublime, The.
Anecdote of the Jar.
Angel Surrounded by Paysans.
Anglais Mort à Florence.
Annual Gaiety.
Arrival at the Waldorf.
Asides on the Oboe.
Auroras of Autumn, The, *sels.*
Banal Sojourn.
Bantams in Pine-Woods.
Beginning, The.
Bouquet of Belle Scavoir.
Brave Man, The.
Candle a Saint, The.
Comedian as the Letter C, The.
Connoisseur of Chaos.
Continual Conversation with a Silent Man.
Contrary Theses (I).
Course of a Particular, The.
Credences of Summer.
Crude Foyer.
Cuisine Bourgeoise.
Curtains in the House of the Metaphysician,
The.
Dance of the Macabre Mice.
Death of a Soldier, The.
Debris of Life and Mind.
Depression before Spring.
Disillusionment of Ten O'Clock.
Domination of Black ("At night, by the
fire.")

Dry Loaf.
Dwarf, The.
Earthy Anecdote.
Emperor of Ice-Cream, The.
Esthétique du Mal, *sels.*
Evening without Angels.
Extract from Addresses to the Academy of
Fine Ideas, An.
Farewell to Florida.
Final Soliloquy of the Interior Paramour.
Flyer's Fall.
Gallant Château.
Girl in a Nightgown.
Glass of Water, The.
God is Good. It Is a Beautiful Night.
Good Man Has No Shape, The.
Gray Stones and Gray Pigeons.
Gubbinal.
Hibiscus on the Sleeping Shores.
High poetry and low.
High-Toned Old Christian Woman, A.
Holiday in Reality.
Homunculus et la Belle Étoile.
House was quiet and the world was calm,
The.
I feel an apparition.
Idea of Order at Key West, The.
Idiom of the Hero.
In the Carolinas.
Indigo Glass in the Grass, The.
Irish Cliffs of Moher, The.
John Smith and his son, John Smith.
Large Red Man Reading.
Le Monocle de Mon Oncle.
Less and Less Human, O Savage Spirit.
Life Is Motion.
Lunar Paraphrase.
Man on the Dump, The.
Man with the Blue Guitar, The, *sels.*
Martial Cadenza.
Men Made Out of Words.
Metamorphosis.
Metaphor as Degeneration.
Mrs. Alfred Uruguay.
Motive for Metaphor, The.
No Possum, No Sop, No Taters.
Nomad Exquisite.
Not Ideas about the Thing but the Thing
Itself.
Notes toward a Supreme Fiction, *sels.*
Nuances of a Theme by Williams.
Of Heaven Considered as a Tomb.
Of Mere Being.
Of Modern Poetry.
Of the Manner of Addressing Clouds.
Old Lutheran Bells at Home, The.
On the Adequacy of Landscape.
Ordinary Women, The.
Owl in the Sarcophagus, The.
Paltry Nude Starts on a Spring Voyage, The.
Peter Quince at the Clavier.
Plain Sense of Things, The.
Planet on the Table, The.
Pleasures of Merely Circulating, The.
Plot Against the Giant, The.
Ploughing on Sunday.
Poem That Took the Place of a Mountain,
The.
Poems of Our Climate, The.
Poetry Is a Destructive Force.
Postcard from the Volcano, A.
Prejudice against the Past, The.
Primitive like an Orb, A.
Puella Parvula.
Quiet Normal Life, A.
Rabbit Is King of the Ghosts, A.
Re-statement of Romance.
Reader, The.
Reality Is an Activity of the Most August
Imagination.
River of Rivers in Connecticut, The.
Room on a Garden, A.
Sad Strains of a Gay Waltz.
Sea Surface Full of Clouds.
Sense of the Sleight-of-Hand Man, The.
Snow Man, The.
So-and-So Reclining on Her Couch.

Song of Fixed Accord.
Souls of Women at Night, The.
Study of Two Pears.
Sunday Morning.
Table Talk.
Tea at the Palaz of Hoon.
Things of August.
Thinking of a Relation between the Images of Metaphors.
Thirteen Ways of Looking at a Blackbird.
This Solitude of Cataracts.
To an Old Philosopher in Rome.
To the One of Fictive Music.
Two Figures in Dense Violet Night.
Ultimate Poem Is Abstract, The.
Vacancy in the Park.
Valley Candle.
Waving Adieu, Adieu, Adieu.
When was it that the particles became.
World as Meditation, The.
World Without Peculiarity.
Worms at Heaven's Gate, The.

Stevenson, Alec Brock (b. 1895)
Death, my companion, who shall quit me soon.
He Who Loved Beauty.
Hemlock at Sunset, A.
Icarus in November.
Sonnet: "If it be night. . . ."

Stevenson, Anne (b. 1933)
Apology.
By the Boat House, Oxford.
Correspondences, sels.
Daughter's Difficulties as a Wife, A: Mrs. Reuben Chandler to Her Mother in New Orleans.
Demolition.
Epitaph for a Good Mouser.
Fiction-Makers, The.
From an Asylum; Kathy Chattle to Her Mother, Ruth Arbeiter.
Gales.
Giving Rabbit to My Cat Bonnie.
Himalayan Balsam.
In the Orchard.
Larousse Gastronomique.
Making Poetry.
Marriage, The.
North Sea off Carnoustie.
Poem to my Daughter.
Price, The.
Ragwort.
Re-reading Jane.
Respectable House.
Sous-Entendu.
Spirit is too blunt an instrument, The.
Suburb, The.
Suicide.
Temporarily in Oxford.
Utah.
Willow Song.

Stevenson, Matthew (fl. 1654–85)
Elegy upon Old Freeman, An, sels.

Stevenson, Robert Louis (1850–94)
Alcaics; to H. F. B.
Armies in the Fire.
At the Seaside [or Sea-Side].
Auntie's Skirts.
Autumn Fires.
Bed in Summer.
Block City.
Bright is the ring of words.
Browning makes the verses.
Celestial Surgeon, The.
Child's Thought, A.
Christmas at Sea.
Christmas Prayer, A.
Christmas Sermon, A, sels.
Cow, The.
Dumb Soldier, The.
Epitaph: "Angler rose, he took his rod, The."
Escape at Bedtime.
Fair Isle at Sea—thy lovely name.
Far-Farers, The.
Foreign Children.
Foreign Lands.

Fragment, A: "Thou strainest through the mountain fern."
From a Railway Carriage.
Gardener does not love to talk, The.
Golden Keys.
Good and Bad Children.
Good Boy, A.
Good Play, A.
Happy Thought.
Hearts, like doors.
Henry James.
Home no more home to me, whither must I wander?
House Beautiful, The.
I Am a Hunchback.
I saw red evening through the rain.
If This Were Faith.
Ille Terrarum.
In autumn when the woods are red.
In the highlands, in the country places.
In the States.
It's an overcome sooth for age an' youth.
Lamplighter, The.
Land of Counterpane, The.
Land of Nod, The.
Land of Story-Books, The.
Last night we had a thunderstorm in style.
Light-Keeper, The, sels.
Limerick: "There was an old man of the Cape."
Looking Forward.
Marching Song.
Mile an' a bittock, a mile or twa, A.
Moon has a face like the clock in the hall, The.
Morning drum-call on my eager ear, The.
My Bed Is a Boat.
My house, I say. But hark to the sunny doves.
My Shadow.
Not I.
O dull cold northern sky.
Pirate Story.
Rain is raining all around, The.
Requiem: "Under the wide and starry sky."
Rivers and winds among the twisted hills, sels.
Say not of me that weakly I declined.
Sick Child, The.
Sing me a song of a lad that is gone.
So live, so love, so use that fragile hour.
Song of a Traveller, The.
Spaewife, The.
Summer Sun.
Swallows travel to and fro.
Swing, The.
System.
Thought, A.
Ticonderoga: A Legend of the West Highlands.
Time to Rise.
To A Gardener.
To Henry James.
To K. de M.
To Mrs. Will H. Low.
To S.C.
To S. R. Crockett.
To the Muse.
Translations from Martial.
Travel.
Treasure Island, sels.
Tropics vanish, and meseems that I, The.
Unseen Playmate, The.
Vagabond, The.
Verses Written in 1872.
Where Go the Boats?
Whole Duty of Children.
Wind, The.
Windy Nights.
Winter Time [or Winter-Time].
Wishes.
Young Night Thought.

Stevenson, William (1530?–1575) and John Still
Gammer Gurton's Needle, sels.

Stevenson, William Frederick (fl. c.1883)
Life and Impellance.
Planet of Descendance, A.

Steward, Joseph (1752–1822)
God from His Throne with Piercing Eye.
My Soul Would Fain Indulge a Hope.

Steward of Baldynneis [or Stewart of Baldynnis], John (1550–1605?)
To His Darrest Freind.

Stewardess of the Empress Kōka (fl. 12th cent.)
For the sake of a night.

Stewart, Douglas (1913–85)
At the Entrance.
Birdsville Track, The, sels.
Country Song, A.
Garden of Ships, The.
Glencoe, sels.
Leopard Skin.
Silkworms, The.
Terra Australis.
Two Englishmen.

Stewart, Frank
Black Winter.
To a Friend.

Stewart, George Craig (1879–1940)
As I went down to David's town.

Stewart, Harold (b. 1916)
Sage in Unison, The.

Stewart, James McAuley and Harold. See "Malley, Ern"

Stewart, Jane G.
June.

Stewart, Pauline (b. 1962)
Singing down the Breadfruit.

Stewart, Susan (b. 1952)
Gypsy, The.
Memory Cabinet of Mrs. K.   1960.
Mouth of the Wolf.

Stewart, W. (fl. c.1849)
Limerick: "Democracy works (entre nous)."
There was an old chap who said: "Well."

Stewart, William (1481?–1550?)
Thir Lenterne Dayis Ar Luvely Lang.

Stickney, Trumbull (1874–1904)
Age in Youth.
And the last day being come, Man stood alone.
As a sad man, when evenings grayer grow.
At Sainte-Marguerite.
Athenian Garden, An.
Autumn's done; they have the golden corn in, The.
Be still. The Hanging Gardens were a dream.
Departure, The.
Dramatic Fragment.
Dramatic Fragments, sels.
Eride, sels.
He said: "If in his image I was made."
Here in the North I chase an old despair.
In Ampezzo.
In the Past.
Lakeward.
Live blindly and upon the hour. The Lord.
Melancholy year is dead with rain, The.
Mnemosyne.
On Rodin's "L'Illusion, Sœur d'Icare."
On Sandro's Flora.
On Some Shells Found Inland.
On the Concert.
Pity.
Prometheus Pyrphoros, sels.
Quiet after the rain of morning.
Requiescam.
Six o'Clock.
Sonnets from Greece, sels.
You say, Columbus with his argosies.

Stidger, William Leroy (1886–1949)
Day, A.
I Saw God Wash the World.
Lest thou forget in the years between.

Stieler, Kaspar (1632–1707)
Hatred Surely Does Not Kiss.
Night's Delights.

Stigall, John (d. 1942)
Dying.

Stiles, Nina
Thank You, God.

Still, James (b. 1906)
Ballad: "They were a man's words, a ballad of an old time."
On Double Creek.
Spring.
Wolfpen Creek.

Still, John. *See* **Stevenson, William** *and* **John Still**

Stillman, Michael (b. 1940)
In Memoriam John Coltrane.
Lullaby for Suzanne.
Song: "Love is a green girl."
Whiskers Meets Polly.

Stilwell, Joseph W. (1883–1946)
Lyric to Spring.

Stirling, Sir William Alexander, Earl of (1567–1640)
Aurora, *sels.*
Echo, An.

Stirling, Zan
I put my hat upon my head.

Stitch, Wilhelmina
Blessed are they who are pleasant to live with—.
Little roads to happiness, they are not hard to find, The.

Stites, Edgar P. (b. 1837)
I've Reached the Land of Corn and Wine.

Stock, Noel. *See* **Pound, Ezra** *and* Noel Stock

Stockbridge, Patricia
My true love hath my heart and I have his.

Stockenström, Wilma (b. 1933)
L'Agulhas, A Walk.
On the Suicide of Young Writers.
Rank Harvest of Betrayal, The.

Stocking, Jay Thomas (1870–1936)
O Master-Workman of the Race.

Stockton, John H. (1813–77)
Come, Every Soul.

Stockum, Hilda Van
Hut, The.

Stodart, M. A.
One Thing at a Time.

Stoddard, Richard Henry (1825–1903)
Abraham Lincoln.
Little Drummer, The.
Never Again.

Stoddart, Thomas Tod (1810–80)
Death-Wake, The; or, Lunacy, *sels.*
Her, a Statue.

Stoker, Andrew
Limerick: "Student from Pembroke once said, A."

Stokes, Terry (b. 1943)
All Morning.
Crimes of Passion: The Phone Caller.
Crimes of Passion: The Slasher.
Man All Grown Up Is Supposed To, A.
Travis, the Kid Was All Heart.

Stokesbury, Leon (b. 1945)
Adventures in Bronze.
California.
Day Begins at Governor's Square Mall.
Luncheon of the Boating Party, The.
To His Book.
To Laura Phelan: 1880-1906.

Stoloff, Carolyn (b. 1927)
Dinosaurs.

Stone, John A. (b. 1936)
After Love.
Coming around the Horn.
Death.
Early Sunday Morning.
Girl in the Hall, The.

Stone, Phyllis M.
Mr. Pennycomequick.
Topsy-Turvy Land.

Stone, Ruth (b. 1915)
Advice.
Being Human.
Burned Bridge, The.
Cocks and Mares.
Codicil.
Curtains.

Dark Conclusions.
Denouement.
Father's Day.
Green Apples.
Happiness.
How to Catch Aunt Harriette.
Hunger.
I Have Three Daughters.
In an Iridescent Time.
Liberation.
Magnet, The.
My Son.
On the Mountain.
Periphery.
Pokeberries.
Private Pantomime.
Repetition of Words and Weather.
Room.
Secondhand Coat.
Snow.
Song of Absinthe Granny, The.
Talking Fish, The.
That Winter.
Turn Your Eyes Away.
Vernal Equinox.
Watcher, The.
Where I Came From.
Whose Scene?
Wild Asters.
Winter.
Years Later.

Stone, Samuel John (1602–63)
Church's One Foundation, The.

Stone, Walter (1917–59)
Couple.
Nature.
On the Welsh Marches.

Storace, Patricia
Archaeology of Divorce, The.
King Lear Bewildered.
Wedding Song.

Storer, Thomas (1571–1604)
Rivers.

Storey, Violet Alleyn (b. 1899)
Prayer for a Very New Angel.
Prayer for Broken Little Families, A.

Storie-Pahlitzsch, Lori
Dialogue on Finding Someplace to Live.

Storni, Alfonsina (1892–1938)
Ancestral Weight.
I Am Going to Sleep (Suicide Poem).
Lighthouse in the Night.
Men in the City.
My Sister.
Pain.
Sierra.
They've Come.

Story, William Wetmore (1819–95)
Cleopatra.
Contemporary Criticism, A, *sels.*

Stoutenburg, Adrien (1916–82)
Ants and Others.
Avalanche.
Brobdingnag.
Cat at Night.
Cicada.
Traveller's Guide to Antarctica.

Stow, Randolph (b. 1935)
Calenture, The.
Dust.
Enemy, The.
Ghost at Anlaby, The.
Landfall.
My wish for my land is that ladies be beautiful.
Ruins of the City of Hay.
Singing Bones, The.
Thailand Railway, *sels.*

Stowe, Harriet Beecher (1811–96)
Abide in me, O Lord, and I in thee.
Hymn: "When winds are raging."
Still, Still, with Thee.

Strachan, W. J.
Limerick: "Said a parson, addressing his flock."

Strachey, Charles
This prayer, O Lord, of course applies.

Strachey, Lytton (1880–1932)
Cat, The.

Stradling, Sir John (1563–1637)
Abraham's Sacrifice of Isaac.

Stramm, August
Battlefield.
Encounter.
Guard-Duty.
Urdeath.

Strand, Mark (b. 1934)
Always so late in the day.
Babies, The.
Black Maps.
Breath.
Coming of Light, The.
Coming to This.
Courtship.
Dance, The.
Dark Harbor, *sels.*
Dead, The.
Door is before you again and the shrieking, The.
"Dreadful Has Already Happened, The."
Eating Poetry.
Elegy for My Father, *sels.*
End, The.
For Jessica, My Daughter.
Garden, The.
In Celebration.
Keeping Things Whole.
Kite, The.
Last Bus, The.
Late Hour, The.
Letter.
Man in Black, The.
Man in the Mirror, The.
Man in the Tree, The.
Map, The.
Marriage, The.
Moontan.
Morning, A.
My Life.
My Mother on an Evening in Late Summer.
Mysterious Maps, The.
Pot Roast.
Prediction, The.
Remains, The.
Shooting Whales.
Sleeping with One Eye Open.
Story of Our Lives, The.
Tunnel, The.
Violent Storm.
When the Vacation Is Over for Good.
Where Are the Waters of Childhood?
You and It.

Strange, Sharan (b. 1959)
Barbershop Ritual.
Childhood.
Offering.
Still Life.

"Strannik" (Prince Ioann Shakhovskoy, Archbishop of San Francisco) (1902–89)
Solar Loneliness.

Strato [or Straton] (d. 270 B.C.)
Bath-house bench pinched Graphicus' bottom, The.
Epigram: "Boy's cocks, Diodore."
Epigram: "I am provoked."
Epigram: "I delight in the prime of a boy of twelve."
Epigram: "Long hair, endless curls trained by the devoted."
Epigram: "There was this gym-teacher."
Epigram: "Those snooty boys in all their purple drag!"
Give, and take the cash.
Grey already the hair at my temples.
He's a dragon, see.
Heterosexual Poem.
I swore to you, son of Kronos, never.
If my kisses wrong you, then tit for tat.
"Let's start from Zeus."
Meeting a lovely boy face to face.
Numbers in ass, The.
Off with you, boy! Pretended prude!

Once I came across / some beardless doctors.
Pair of brothers love me, A.
Private Poem.
Someone later may hear these playthings, thinking.
To Kyris.
Two Plus Two.
Vive La Différence.
Who knows when love has had its day.
Why must you thrust your loins.

Strauss, Jennifer (b. 1933)
Love Notes.
Tending the Graves.

"Strauss, Yawcob." See **Adams, Charles Follen**

"Streamer, Col. D." See **Graham, Harry**

Strebeck, George (fl. late 18th cent.)
Joyful Sound It Is, A.

Street, Alfred Billings (1811–81)
Settler, The.

Street, T. (b. 1941?)
Tim tryeth truth convicting all that strive.

Streeter, Sebastian (fl. early 19th cent.)
King Shall Reign in Righteousness, A.
Lo, What Enraptured Songs of Praise.

Strelchenko, Vadim Konstantinovich (1912–42)
My Photograph.

Stricker, Meredith
Against Simple Reading.
Bee Mother.
Foreigners.
Island.
Other Side, The.

Strickland, Stephanie
Diringer's The Alphabet: A Key to the History of Mankind.

Strnisa, Gregor
Graves, The.
Priests, The.
Ship, A.

Strobel, Marion (Mrs. James Herbert Mitchell) (b. 1895)
Encounter.
Pastoral: "This is a place of ease."

Strode, William. See **Noel, Henry** and William Strode

Strode, William (1600–1643)
Bracelets.
Chloris in the Snow.
Devonshire Song, A.
Ear-string, An.
Epitaph on the Monument of Sir William Strode.
Girdle, A.
In Commendation of Music.
Justification.
Kisses.
Nightingale, The.
On a Gentlewoman that Sung and Played upon a Lute.
On a Good Leg and Foot.
On Fairford Windows.
On the Death of Mistress Mary Prideaux.
On Westwall Downes [or On Westwell Downs].
Opposite to Melancholy.
Riddle: On a Kiss, A.

Strong, George A. (1832–1912)
Song of Milkanwatha, The, sels.

Strong, Leonard Alfred George (1896–1958)
Appointment, The.
Brewer's Man, The.
Coroner's Jury.
Door, The.
Evening before Rain.
Knowledgeable Child, The.
Lowery Cot.
Mad Woman of Punnet's Town, The.
March Evening.
Memory, A.
Old Dan'l.
Old Man at the Crossing, The.
Old Woman, Outside the Abbey Theater, An.
Rufus Prays.
Two Generations.
Zeke.

Strong, Nathan (1748–1816)
Almighty Sovereign of the skies!
Summer Harvest Spreads the Fields, The.
Swell the Anthem, Raise the Song.

Strong, Phillips Burrows
Tongue, The.

Stroud, William
Rustler.

"Struther, Jan" (Joyce Anstruther Maxtone Graham) (1901–53)
Freedom.
Lament in Spring.

Stryker, Melancthon Woolsey (1851–1929)
Almighty Lord, with one accord.
God of Our Fathers.

Stuart, Alice V. (1899–1981)
Lintie in a Cage.

Stuart, Dabney (b. 1937)
Ballad of the Frozen Field, The.
Exchange.
Mining in Killdeer Alley.
Rescue.
River, The.
Separate Parties.
Soup Jar, The.

Stuart, Francis (b. 1902)
Remembering Yeats.

Stuart, Jesse (1907–84)
Speaks the Whispering Grass.

Stuart, Muriel (1889–1967)
In The Orchard.

Stuart, Ruth McEnery (1856–1917)
Endless Song, The.

Stubbs, Charles William (1845–1912)
Conscience.

Stubbs, William (1825–1901)
Hymn on Froude and Kingsley, A.

Studdert-Kennedy, Geoffrey Anketell ("Woodbine Willie") (1883–1929)
Great Wager, The.
Indifference.
Is it a dream, and nothing more—this faith.
Roses in December.

Stull, Richard
Romance.

Stumbrs, Olafs
Cigars.
Light, Late Song for Solo Voice Without Piano, A.
Married Romantic, A.
Ode to a Country Childhood.

Sturm, Frank Pearce (1879–1942)
Still-Heart.

Su Man-shu (Hsüan-ying) (1884–1918)
Addressed to a Koto-player.
Chanting These Verses on My Way to Yodoe.
Exile in Japan.
Inscribed on Byron's Poetic Works.
Passing by Kamata.
Poems Written during My Sojourn in Japan, sels.
Written during My Stay at White Clouds Monastery on West Lake.

Su Shih (1037–1101)
At the Heng-ts'ui Pavilion of Fa-hui Monastery.
Bathing the Infant.
Drinking at the Lake, First It's Sunny, Then It Rains.
Fisherman, The, sels.
In a boat, Getting Up at Night.
Monk of Auspicious Fortune Monastery Asking Me to Name a Pavilion, A.
On Chao Ch'ang's Flower Paintings in Wang Po-yu's Collection, sels.
Rain at Cold-Food Festival, sels.
Sent to Chief Abbot of Tung-lin Monastery.
Spring Day.
Tune: "As in a Dream; a Song."
Tune: "Immortal at the River."
Tune: "Joy of Eternal Union"—Passing the Seven-league Shallows.
Tune: "Prelude to Water Music."
Tune: "Song of Divination."

Tune: "Water Dragon's Chang" After Chang Chi-fu's Lyric on the Willow Catkin.
Two Poems on Insect Painting by Candidate Yin, sels.

Su Shun-ch'in (1008–48)
Commandeering the Wind.
Summertime.

Su Tung-p'o (1036–1101)
Along the Road to Stone Lake, sels.
At Gold Hill Monastery.
At the Washing of My Son.
Autumn.
Beginning of Autumn: A Poem to Send to Tzu-yu.
Begonias.
Black Muzzle, south sea dog.
Children don't know what worry means!
Days of Rain; the Rivers Have Overflowed.
Days of Rain; the Rivers Have Overflowed: Two Poems, sels.
Eastern Slope, sels.
End of the Year, The.
Epigram.
Following the Rhumes of Chiang Hui-shu.
Harvest Sacrifice.
I travel day and night toward the Yangtze and the sea.
In a Boat, Getting Up at Night.
Lament of the Farm Wife of Wu.
Last Day of the Year, The.
Listening to the River.
Long ago I lived in the country.
Looking from the Pavilion Over the Lake.
Lotus Viewing.
Mid-Autumn Moon.
Moon, Flowers, Man.
New Year's Blizzard, The.
New Year's Eve.
New Year's Eve blizzard kept me from leaving, The.
New Year's Eve—you'd think I could go home early.
On a Painting by Wang the Clerk of Yen Ling.
On the Birth of His Son.
On the Death of His Baby Son.
On the Road to Hsin-ch'eng.
On the Siu Cheng Road.
On the Tower of Gathering Remoteness.
Presented to Liu Ching-wen.
Purple Peach Tree, The.
Rain in the Aspens.
Red Cliff, The.
Remembering Min Ch'e.
Rhyming with Tzu-yu's "Treading the Green."
Roaring waterfall, the.
Seeking Spring Beyond the city.
Shadow of Flowers, The.
Sitting at Night with My Nephew Who Has Just Come from Afar.
Southern Room Over the River, The.
Spring.
Spring night—one hour worth a thousand gold coins.
Spring Scene.
Terrace in the Snow, The.
Thoughts in Exile.
To a Traveler.
Tune: Immortal at the River.
Tune: Partridge Sky.
Tune: Prelude to Water Music.
Tune: Sand of Silk-washing Stream ("Flutter flutter on clothes and cap, jujube flowers fall.")
Tune: Sand of Silk-washing Stream ("Layer on layer of hemp leaves, jute leaves shining.")
Tune: Sand of Silk-washing Stream ("Soft grasses, a plain of sedge fresh with passing rain.")
Tune: Song of River City.
Turning Year, The.
Under the heaven of our holy ruler, all things turn to spring.
Verses: "I am old, sick and lonely."
Weaker the wine, The.

White Crane Hill.
Written on a Painting Entitled "Misty
  Yangtze and Folded Hills."
Su Wu (*fl.* 2d cent.)
Drafted.
To His Wife.
Sub-ok
Spring at Yesan Station.
Subbiah, Shanmuga (b. 1924)
Salutations.
Subramanyam, Kaa Naa (b. 1912)
Situation.
Succorsa, Janice Appleby
My Garden.
Suckling, Sir John (1609–42)
Against Absence.
Against Fruition ("Fie upon hearts that burn
  with mutual fire[!].")
Against Fruition ("Stay here, fond youth, and
  ask no more.")
Aglaura, *sels.*
Ballad[e] [upon a Wedding], A, *sels.*
Barley-Break , A.
Deformed Mistress, The.
Dream, A.
Farewell to Love.
Love and Debt Alike Troublesome.
Love's Clock.
Loves Feast.
Love's Offence.
Love's Siege.
Loving and Beloved.
Metamorphosis, The.
Miracle, The.
My dearest rival, lest [*or* least] our love.
Ode to Lovers.
On King Richard the Third, Who Lies Buried
  under Leicester Bridge.
Pedlar of Small-Wares, A.
Poem with the Answer, A, *sels.*
Session[s] of the Poets, A, *sels.*
Soldier, A.
Song: "I prithee spare me, gentle boy."
Song to a Lute, A.
Sonnet: "Dost see how unregarded now."
Sonnet: "O[h]! for some honest lover's
  ghost."
Sonnet: "Of thee, kind boy, I ask no red and
  white."
Summons to Town, A.
Supplement of an Imperfect Copy of Verses
  of Mr. Will. Shakespeare's, by the Author,
  A.
To a Lady That Forbade to Love before
  Company.
To B.C.
To Master Davenant for Absence.
Upon Christ His Birth.
Upon My Lady Carlisle's [*or* Carlile's]
  Walking in Hampton Court Garden.
Upon My Lord Brohall's Wedding.
Upon Sir John Lawrence's Bringing Water
  over the Hills [to My L. Middlesex His
  House at Witten].
Upon Stephen Stoned.
Woman's Constancy.
Suckling, Sir John (1609– 42) *and* **Owen
Feltham** (c.1602–1668)
Song: "When, dearest, I but think on [*or* of]
  thee."
Sudeley, Baron Seymour of. *See* Seymour, Sir
Thomas
Sueyoshi, Fujiwara No
Crying plovers, The.
Sugita, Hisajo (1890–1946)
Mending his broken *tabi* without becoming a
  Nora.
O flower garment!/ when I take it off.
Suharu, Anryu (b. 1923)
When, with breaking heart.
Suhl, Yuri (1908–86)
And the Earth Rebelled.
Sui Ching-ch'en (*fl* c.1300)
Tune: "Slow Chant"—Kao-tsu's
  Homecoming.

Suibne Geilt (*fl.* 12th cent.)
Bellower with the antlers.
I am in great misery tonight.
I am Suibne the wanderer.
My fixed abode is Glen Bolcain.
Rich tuft of ivy, A.
Starry frost descends, The.
Sweet voice of the Garb.
Though my wanderings are many.
Suilleabhain, Eoghan Rua O. *See* O'Sullivan,
Owen Roe
Suilleabhain, Tadhg Gaelach O. *See* O'Sullivan,
Teig Gaelach
Suknaski, Andrew (b. 1942)
Chinese Camp, Kamloops (circa 1883).
Snake, The.
Sullam, Sarah Copia (1592–1641)
My Inmost Hope.
Sullivan, Charles (b. 1933)
Another Kind of Country.
Houseboat Mouse.
Nights along the River.
Sullivan, Francis (b. 1929)
Prayer: "You may be right, divinity."
Still Life.
Sullivan, Jonny Kyoko
Sagimusume: The White Heron Maiden.
Sullivan, Nancy (b. 1929)
Eclipses.
His Necessary Darkness.
Telling It.
To My Body.
Sullivan, Page
Red Leaf, The.
Sully-Prudhomme, René François Armand
(1839–1907)
Struggle, The.
Sulpicia (*fl.* c.20 B.C.)
At last love has come. I would be more
  ashamed.
Darling, I won't be your hot love.
Do you have a sweet thought, Cerinthus.
Drat my hateful birthday.
Have you heard? The troubles.
I'm grateful, really grateful.
It's nice that though you are casual about
  me.
Let your longing for me, my love.
My hated birthday is here, and I must go.
Sulpicia to Cerinthus.
That you allow yourself this vast neglect of
  me.
Sumangala, *The mother of* (*fl.* 19th cent.)
Free woman, A. At last free!
Sumangalamata (fl. 6th cent. B.C.)
At last free.
Summerfield, Geoffrey
Sci-fi Horrorscopes.
Tall Story for Fred Dibnah.
Washday Battles.
Yesterday the House was Full of Flies.
Summers, Hal (b. 1911)
April Fool.
As I went out this May morning I found.
Cold February.
Leaves in the Yard.
Mild February.
My old cat [is dead].
Summers, Hollis Spurgeon (b. 1916)
Lost Pictures, The.
Report
Summers, Thomas O. (1812–82)
Morning Bright, with Rosy Light, The.
Sun Kuang-hsien (898?–968)
Tune: "Eight-beat Barbarian Tune."
Tune: "Paying Homage at the Golden Gate."
Tune: "Song of a Dandy."
Sun-Ra
Nothing Is.
Plane: Earth, The.
Primary Lesson: The Second Class Citizens.
Sun Yün-feng (1764–1814)
On the Road through Chang-te.
Starting at Dawn.

Trail up Wu Gorge, The.
Suo, Lady (fl. 11th cent.)
That spring night I spent.
Supervielle, Jules (1884–1960)
Early in the morning.
Earth.
Like an ox streaming saliva, yoked to the
  plough.
Missing France.
Rain and the Tyrants.
Return to Paris.
Some day shall I be the one who let.
Sphere.
Traveller, traveller, accept you must go back.
Voyages.
Surkov, Aleksey [*or* Aleksei] **Aleksandrovich**
(1899–1983)
Tenderness.
Surrey, Henry Howard, Earl of (1517?–1547)
Although I had a check.
Another Tribute to Wyatt.
As oft as I behold and see.
Bonum Est Mihi Quod Humiliasti Me.
Complaint by Night of the Lover Not
  Beloved, A.
Complaint of a Lover Rebuked.
Complaint of the Absence of Her Lover
  Being upon the Sea.
Complaint That His Ladie After She Knew of
  His Love Kept Her Face Alway Hidden
  from Him.
Consolation.
Death of Wyatt, The.
Description of Spring, Wherein Each Thing
  Renews Save Only the Lover.
Epitaph on Thomas Clere.
Exhortation to Learn of Others' Trouble.
Frailty and Hurtfulness of Beauty, The.
From Tuscan came my lady's worthy race.
Give place, ye lovers (here before).
Golden gift that nature did thee give, The.
Golden Mean, The.
If care do cause men cry, why do not I
  complain.
If he that erst the form so lively drew.
In Cipres springes [*or* Cyprus springs]
  (wheras [*or* whereas] dame Venus dwelt)..
In Praise of Wyatt's Psalms.
In Windsor Castle.
In winter's just return, when Boreas gan his
  reign.
Lady Again Complains, The.
Laid in my quiet bed, in study as I were.
Love, that doth reign and live within my
  thought.
Love's Rebel.
Of a Lady That Refused to Dance with Him.
Oh loathsome place! where I.
Paraphrase of Part of the Book of
  Ecclesiates, A, *sels.*
Restless Heart, The.
Restless State of a Lover, The.
Sardanapalus.
Satire on London, A.
Since fortune's wrath envieth the wealth.
Such[e] wayward[e] ways [*or* wais] hath
  love, that most[e] part[e] in discord[e].
Though I regarded not.
Too dearly had I bought my green and
  youthful years.
Tribute to Wyatt.
Virgil's Aeneid Book 4, *sels.*
When Windsor Walls.
When youth had led me half the race.
Windsor Castle, *sels.*
Woman's Answer, A.
Wrapt in my careless cloak, as I walk to and
  fro.
Surve, Narayan (b. 1926)
Lifetime.
Süsskind von Trimberg (c.1250–1300)
Power of Thought, The.
Virtuous Wife, The.
Why Should I Wander Sadly.
Sutcliffe, Alice (*fl.* c.1633)
Meditations of Man's Mortalitie; or, A Way
  to True Blessedness, *sels.*

Sutherland, Janet (b. 1957)
  During long walks.
  H ear t h.
  Touching Heartsease.
Sutherland, Robert. *See* **Garioch, Robert**
Sutskever [*or* Sutzkever], Abraham (b. 1913)
  Banks of a River, The.
  Cartload of Shoes, A.
  Here I am, full-grown, flourishing.
  Here I am, sprouted to my full height.
  How will you fill your goblet?
  Like Groping Fingers.
  Mother, *sels.*
  Poems from a Diary, *sels.*
  Poetry.
  Secret Town, The.
  Song for a Dance.
  Toys.
Sutter, Barton (b. 1949)
  Shoe Shop.
Sutton, David (b. 1944)
  Not to Be Born.
Sutu, S. D. R. (d. 1965)
  Night, and on all sides only the folding quiet.
  Thaba Bosio.
Suwo, Lady (*fl.* c.11th cent.)
  Pillowed on your arm / only for the dream of
    a spring night.
**Svetlov, Mikhail Arkadyevich [*or*Arkad'evich]
(1903–64)**
  Friends.
  Grenada.
  Italian, The.
  On Reconnaissance.
  To a Rabfak Student.
  Two.
"Svirepy, Makar." *See* **Oleynikov, Nikolai
  Makarovich**
Swain, Charles (*fl.* c.1870)
  Home Is Where There Is One to Love Us.
  Take the World As It Is, *sels.*
Swain, John D. (d. 1964)
  Would I Be Shrived?
Swain, Leonard (1821–69)
  My Soul, Weigh Not Thy Life.
Swainson, Eric
  Limerick: "I fear, Mr. Lear, you're a clot."
Swan, Jon (b. 1929)
  Father Father Son and Son.
  In Her Song She Is Alone.
  Kingdom, The.
  March Weather.
  Report, The.
  Their Party, Our House.
Swan, Robert
  If you think it crude to be rough and rude.
  Trench Fever.
Swann, Brian (b. 1940)
  Desert in the Sea.
  Paradigms of Fire.
  Quiet.
  Year of the Bird.
Sward, Robert (b. 1933)
  American Heritage.
  Concert.
  Movies, Left to Right.
  Uncle Dog; the Poet at 9.
Swart, Edward Vincent (1911–62)
  Casey Jones has left today.
  Convict.
  This is not a poem but a proem. I want to be
    in the wide.
  Tired of Eating Kisses.
Swarth, Hélène (1859–1941)
  Candles.
  Ecstasy.
Swede, George
  After I step.
  After the search for meaning bills in the
    mail.
  At dawn remembering her bad grammar.
  At my father's.
  At the edge of the precipice I become
    logical.

At the end of myself pencil tip.
August sky, The.
Christmas Eve.
Dawn.
Frozen breaths, The.
In one corner.
In the town dump I find a still-beating heart.
Leaving my loneliness inside her.
Mental hospital my shadow stays outside.
Night begins to gather between her breasts.
On the face.
One button undone.
One by one to the floor all of her shadows.
Panties on the clothesline lingering mist.
Passport check.
Stars crickets.
Summer night.
Swinging on the hanger.
Unhappy wife.
Windless summer day.
Sweeney, Matthew (b. 1952)
  Couple Waiting, A.
  Where Fishermen Can't Swim.
Sweet, Frank Herbert
  Before It Is Too Late.
Swenson, Cole (b. 1955)
  Line.
  Our Town.
Swenson, Karen (b. 1936)
  Woman, Gallup, N. M.
Swenson, May (b. 1919)
  Above the Arno.
  Almanac.
  Analysis of Baseball.
  Bison Crossing Near Mt. Rushmore.
  Bleeding.
  Blindman placed, The.
  Cardinal Ideograms.
  Cat and the Weather.
  Centaur, The.
  Death Invited.
  Dream, A.
  "Feel me to do right," our father said on his
    deathbed.
  Fire Island.
  Fireflies throw.
  First Walk on the Moon.
  Fixture, A.
  Flying Home from Utah.
  Four-Word Lines.
  Frontispiece.
  Garden at St. John's, The.
  Goodbye, Goldeneye.
  Green Red Brown and White.
  He That None Can Capture.
  How Everything Happens.
  How to Be Old.
  In Love Made Visible.
  In the Bodies of Words.
  James Bond Movie, The.
  July 4th.
  Landing on the Moon.
  Lightning waked me, The.It slid under.
  Lion.
  Living Tenderly.
  Morning at Point Dume.
  Motherhood.
  Naked in Borneo.
  News from the Cabin.
  Notes Made in the Piazza San Marco.
  On Its Way.
  Painting the Gate.
  Poet to Tiger, *sels.*
  Poplar's Shadow, The.
  Promontory Moment, The.
  Question.
  Rain at Wildwood.
  Riding the "A."
  Seeing the frog.
  Shape of Death, The.
  Sleeping with Boa.
  Snow by Morning.
  Some Small Shells from the Windward
    Islands.
  Southbound on the Freeway.
  Staying at Ed's Place.
  Stone gullets among.

Strawberrying.
Stripping and Putting on.
Teleology.
Trellis for R, A.
Unconscious came a beauty.
Waking from a Nap on the Beach.
Watch, The.
Waterbird.
Weather.
Willets, The.
Women.
Women / should be / pedestals / moving.
Written While Riding the Long Island Rail
  Road
You are my mirror.
Swift, Joan (b. 1926)
  On the Göta Canal, 1986.
  Oxygen.
Swift, Jonathan (1667–1745)
  As Sonata in Praes o Molli.
  Baucis and Philemon.
  Beautiful Young Nymph Going to Bed, A.
  Behold! a proof of Irish sense!
  Cantata, A.
  Cassinus and Peter.
  Character of Sir Robert Walpole, The.
  Clever Tom Clinch Going to Be Hanged.
  Daphne knows, with equal ease.
  Day of Judgement, The.
  Description of a City Shower, A.
  Description of the Morning, A.
  Dick, a Maggot.
  E I O U, A.
  Epigram on Fasting.
  Epigram on Scolding, An.
  Fool, to put up four crosses at your door.
  Gentle Echo on Woman, A.
  Holyhead. September 25, 1727.
  I Walk before No Man (Composed While
    Asleep).
  In Sickness.
  Ireland.
  Lady's Dressing Room, The.
  Legion Club, The, *sels.*
  Libel on the Reverend Dr. Delany, A, *sels.*
  Life and Character of Dean Swift, The, *sels.*
  Life and Genuine Character of Dr Swift, The,
    sels.
  Mary the Cook-Maid's Letter to Dr.
    Sheridan.
  Mrs. Harris's Petition.
  New Song of Wood's Halfpence, A.
  On a Curate's Complaint of Hard Duty.
  On Dreams.
  On His Own Deafness.
  On Poetry: a Rhapsody, *sels.*
  On Reading Dr. Young's Satires.
  On Stella's Birthday, 1718/1719.
  On the Astrologer and Almanac Maker, John
    Partridge.
  On the Collar of Mrs. Dingley's Lap-Dog.
  On the Irish Club.
  Parson's Case, The, *sels.*
  Phyllis [*or* Phillis] [*or* Progress of Love,
    The].
  Place of the Damned [*or* Damn'd], The.
  Power of Time, The.
  Progress of Beauty, The.
  Progress of Poetry, The.
  Prometheus.
  Riddling Letter, A ("Sir, / Pray discruciate
    what follows: / A long-eared beast, and a
    field-house for cattle.")
  Satire on an Inconstant Lover, A.
  Satirical Elegy on the Death of a Late
    Famous General, A.
  Stella at Wood-Park.
  Stella's Birthday, 1725.
  Stella's Birthday, 1721.
  Stella's Birthday ([March 13,] 1727).
  Three Epigrams.
  To Stella.
  To the Earl of Oxford, Late Lord Treasurer.
  To Their Excellencies the Lords Justices of
    Ireland, the Humble Petition of Frances
    Harris, Who Must Starve, and Die a Maid
    if It Miscarries.

Twelve Articles.
Verses Made for the Women Who Cry Apples, etc, *sels.*
Verses Occasioned by the Sudden Drying Up of St. Patrick's Well, *sels.*
Verses on the Death of Dr. Swift, D.S.P.D, *sels.*
Verses on the Death of Dr. Swift, D.S.P.D., Occasioned by Reading a Maxim in Rochefoucauld.
Virtue conceal'd within our breast.

Swinburne, Algernon Charles (1837–1909)
After Death.
Aholibah.
Anactoria.
Atalanta in Calydon, *sels.*
Ave atque Vale.
Ballad of François Villon, A.
Before Parting.
Before Sunset.
Before the Mirror, *sels.*
By the North Sea, *sels.*
Child's Laughter, A.
Come into the orchard, Anne.
Dialogue, A.
Dolores, *sels.*
Duriesdyke.
Erotion.
Étude Réaliste, *sels.*
Faustine.
Forsaken Garden, A.
Garden of Proserpine, The, *sels.*
Heptalogia, The, *sels.*
Hertha.
Hesperia.
Hope and Fear.
Hymn to Proserpine.
Ilicet.
In Memory of Walter Savage Landor.
In The Orchard.
Interpreters, The.
Itylus.
Kissing her hair, I sat against her feet.
Lake of Gaube, The.
Leave-taking, A.
Leper, The.
Limerick: "There was a young girl of Aberystwyth."
Limerick: "There was a young lady of Norway / Who hung by her toes in a doorway."
Limerick: "There was a young man of Cape Horn."
Love And Sleep.
Love at Sea.
Match, A.
Mill Garden, The.
On Arthur Hugh Clough.
On the Russian Persecution of the Jews.
Oscar Wilde.
Poeta Loquitur.
Return, The.
Sapphics.
Satia Te Sanguine.
Shakespeare.
Sonnets of English Dramatic Poets, *sels.*
Stage Love.
Sundew, The.
Super Flumina Babylonis.
To a Cat.
Triads.
Tristram of Lyonesse, *sels.*
Triumph of Time, The, *sels.*

Swir, Anna
Astonishment.
Youngest Children of an Angel, The.

Swirszczynska, Anna (1909–84)
Conversation Through the Door, A.
First Madrigal, The.
Good Lord Saved Her, The.
Greatest Love, The.
He Is Gone.
He Was Lucky.
I Am Afraid of Fire.
I Starve My Belly for a Sublime Purpose.
I Talk to My Body.
I Wash the Shirt.

Poetry Reading.
Same Inside, The.
Sea and the Man, The.
Second Madrigal, The.
She Does Not Remember.
Terminally Ill.
Thank You, My Fate.
They Lay Dying Side by Side.
Troubles with the Soul at Morning Calisthenics.
Very Sad Conversation at Night, A.
Visit, A.
We Are Going to Shoot at the Heart.
We Survived Them.
When We Wake Up in the Morning.
White Wedding Slippers.

Sỹ, Nguyễn Hoc. *See* **Nam Trân**

Sykes, Arthur A.
Splendid Bankrupt, The.

Sykes, Bobbi (b. 1943)
Cycle.
One Day.

Sylvester, Janet (b. 1950)
Modern Times.

Sylvester, Joshua (1561–1618)
Aestas.
Divine Weeks and Works of Guillaume de Saluste Sieur Du Bartas, The, *sels.*
Fuimus Fumus.
Garden, The.
I hate these phrases: Of power absolute.
Job Triumphant, *sels.*
Job's Epitaph.
Maidens Blush, The, *sels.*
Mundus Qualis.
Of a Husbandman.
Omnia Somnia.
Rome, Conqueror, Conquered.
Saluste du Bartas' Devine Weekes, *sels.*
Sweet mouth, that send'st a musky-rosed breath;.
They say that shadow[e]s of deceased ghosts.
Ubique.
Variable.
When wine runs low, it is not worth the sparing.

Sylvester, Stephen
Limerick: "'How much,' sighed the gentle Narcissus."

Symeon (949–1022)
We awaken in Christ's body.

Symonds, John Addington (1840–93)
Camera Obscura, The.
Lux Est Umbra Dei[1].
On a Picture by Poussin Representing Shepherds in Arcadia.
Rebuke Me Not.
Sonnet (III), The.
To Night, the Mother of Sleep and Death.

Symons, Arthur (1865–1945)
Absinthe-Drinker, The.
Amoris Victima, *sels.*
Amorix Exsul, *sels.*
At Dawn.
At Dieppe, *sels.*
At the Cavour.
Barrel-Organ, The.
Bianca.
Dreams.
During Music.
Emmy ("Emmy's exquisite youth and her virginal air.")
Faint Love.
Grey Wolf, The.
Hallucination.
In Ireland, *sels.*
In Ireland: By the Pool at the Third Rosses.
In Kensington Gardens.
Isolation.
Javanese Dancers.
La Mélinite: Moulin-Rouge.
Laus Virginitatis.
Maquillage.
Morbidezza.
Nerves.
On an Air of Rameau.

Palm Sunday: Naples.
Paris.
Pastel: Masks and Faces.
Prologue: Before the Curtain.
Prologue: In the Stalls.
Scènes de la Vie de Bohème, *sels.*
Stéphane Mallarmé, *sels.*
To a Dancer.
Tune, A.
Venice.
Violet.
Wanderer's Song.
When you were here, ah foolish then!
White Heliotrope.

Symons, Julian (b. 1912)
Central Park.
Hart Crane.
Harvard, Cambridge, Mass.

Synge, John Millington (1871–1909)
Beg-Innish.
Curse, The.
Danny.
Dread.
Epitaph after Reading Ronsard's Lines from Rabelais.
I curse my bearing, childhood, youth.
I read about the Blaskets and Dunquin.
In Glencullen.
In Kerry.
In May.
Is It a Month.
I've Thirty Months.
On a Birthday.
On an Anniversary.
On an Island.
Passing of the Shee, The.
Patch-Shaneen.
Prelude: "Still south I went and west and south again."
Queens.
Question, A.
Rendez-vous Manqué dans la Rue Racine.
They found the path and I found the puddle.
To the Oaks of Glencree.
Winter.
Wish, A.

Syrus, Publilius (1st cent. B.C.)
Sententiae: Maxims.

Sze, Arthur (b. 1950)
Black Java Pepper.
Every Where and Every When.
Leaves of a Dream Are the Leaves of an Onion, The.
Network, The.
Shapes of Leaves, The.

Szumigalski, Anne (b. 1926)
Angels.
In the Heat of the Morning.
Midwife's Story; Two, A.
Visitor's Parking.
Want of ♭ and Want of ♮

Szymborska, Wislawa (b. 1923)
Born of Woman.
Children of the Epoch.
Clothes.
Contribution on Pornography, A.
End and the Beginning, The.
Experiment.
Four in the Morning.
Homecoming.
I Am Too Near.
In Praise of My Sister.
In Praise of Self-Deprecation.
Innocence.
Interview with a Child.
Laughter.
Memory at last has what it sought.
Miracle Mart.
Monologue for Cassandra.
Museum, The.
Once we knew the world well.
Onion.
π deserves our full admiration.
Pietà.
Preparing a Curriculum Vitae.
Reality demands.
Seen From Above.

Starvation Camp near Jaslo.
Still.
Terrorist, He Watches, The.
Theater Impressions.
Under a Certain Little Star.
Unexpected Meeting.
View with a Grain of Sand.
Voices.
Women of Rubens, The.
Words.
Writing a Curriculum Vitae.

T

"T., B. L." *See* **Taylor, Bert Leston**
T., H. H.
Sea and the Sands, The.
"T., J." (*fl.* late 19th cent.)
Sea-Chaplain's Petition to the Lieutenants in the Ward-Room, for the Use of the Quarter-Gallery, A.
Ta' Abbata Sharra (*fl.* 7th cent.)
Ever Watchful.
Ta Hữu Thiện (*fl.* 20th cent.)
Looking For Her.
Tabb, John Banister (1845–1909)
Bicycles! Tricycles!
Bridge, The.
Christ and the Pagan.
Close Quarters.
Echo.
Echoes.
Evolution.
Foot Soldiers.
Mid-Day Moon, The.
Milton.
Rub, A.
Shadow, The.
Sisters, The.
Tenebræ.
Tryst, The.
Whisper.
Winter Twilight, A.
"Tabitha"
Sweet it is to be a child.
Tabito. *See* **Otomo no Tabito**
Tablada, José Juan (1871–1945)
Haiku: "Dragon-fly strives patiently, The."
Red cold / guffaw of summer.
Two Drinking Songs, *sels.*
Tada, Chimako (b. 1930)
Mirror.
Odyssey or "On Absence," The.
Poetry Calendar, A.
Universe of the Rose.
Wind invites wind.
Tadamichi (Fujiwara no Tadamichi) (1097–1164)
As I row over the plain.
Tadic, Novica (b. 1949)
Antipsalm.
At the Hairdresser.
Die.
Dogs Gambol.
Feather Plucked from the Tail of the Fiery Hen, A.
Fool, The.
I Ask.
I Run With a Pair of Compasses Stuck in the Back of My Head.
Jesus.
Laocoon/Serpent.
Little Picture Catalogue.
Man from the Death Institute.
Night Game of the Maker of Faces, The.
Nobody.
Pocket Watch.
Rose, The.
Song to the Lamb.
Text, Silk.
Thief.
Toys, Dream.
Tafari, Levi (b. 1960)
Tongue (De First Instrument), De.

Tagami, Jeff (b. 1954)
Mussel Rock/Lowtide—Santa Cruz, California 1959.
Now It Is Broccoli.
Song of Pajaro.
Tobera.
Tagami Kikusha-Ni (1752–1826)
Wind From Mt. Fuji, The.
Taggard, Genevieve (Mrs. Kenneth Durant) (1894–1948)
American Farm, 1934.
At Last the Women are Moving.
Demeter.
Dilemma of the Elm.
Doomsday Morning.
Enamel Girl, The.
Geraniums, The.
In the Tail of the Scorpion.
Little Girl with Bands on Her Teeth, The.
Millions of Strawberries.
No Abstraction.
Poem to Explain Everything about a Certain Day in Vermont, A.
Solar Myth.
Song for Unbound Hair.
Squirrel near Library.
To the Veterans of the Abraham Lincoln Brigade.
Train: Abstraction.
Try Topic.
With Child.
Taggart, John
Body and Soul: Poem for Two Readers.
Giant Steps.
Monk.
Never Too Late.
Pen Vine and Scroll.
Sainte-Chapelle.
Twenty One Times.
Tagliabue, John (b. 1923)
Bare Arms of Trees, The.
I sought all over the world for a present for you until I found.
Maine Vastly Covered with Much Snow.
Unseen deer through seen shadows leaps through my heart, An.
Tagore, Rabindranath (1861–1941)
Bird, The.
Epigrams, *sels.*
Flute-music.
Gardener, The, *sels.*
Gitanjali, *sels.*
I seem to have loved you in numberless forms, numberless times.
Tahmisic, Husein
Landscapes.
Letter to a Friend.
Limbo.
Red Moon High in the Sky.
Stone and Ashes.
Tahureau, Jacques (1527–55)
Moonlight.
Shadows of His Lady.
Tai Piao-yüan (1244–1310)
As My Way Passed Through T'ung-ch'uan, I Wished to Visit the Policy Critic of the Right, Mei, but Did Not Know Where to Find Him.
Cheng-tao Temple.
Following His Rhymes and Answering the Poems of My Friend Next Door on Recent Events, *sels.*
In the Year Chi-hai (1299), While Returning by Way of Purple Fungus Mountain at Springmouth, I Lamented for Lecture Master Chin.
Painting, *"Mist and Rain on the Spring River,"* by Hsiao Chao, The.
Painting of One Hundred Wild Geese, A.
Returning to Yin-ch'eng Early in the Year *Ting-ch'ou* (1277).
Supervisor, Han Chün-mei, Has Shown Me Five Poems He Has Written Called, The Trees Flourish in Early Summer. I Have Therefore Written Down My Own Ignoble Feelings and Sent Them Via Inspector

Juan. At This Time, Chün-mei Is Lecturing to the Various Scholars on the I-ching, The.
T'ai-shang (*fl.* 10th? cent.)
In Reply to Questions.
Tai Shu-lun (732–89)
Accidental Meeting with an Old Friend While Traveling at Night, An.
Living in the Mountains.
Wang Chao-chün.
Tait, William J. (b. 1918)
Gallow Hill.
Takahashi Shinkichi (b. 1901)
Birth.
Takako Uchino Lento (b. 1941)
Glass.
Takarai [or Enomoto] Kikaku (1661–1707)
Blind child / Guided by his mother, A.
Takiguchi, Masako (b. 1933)
Blue Horse.
Slaughterhouse.
Talbot, Charles Remington. *See* **"Brownjohn, John"**
Talbot, Kirkham
Limerick: "King Henry the Eighth was a Tudor."
Talbot, Norman (b. 1936)
Ballad of Old Women & of How They Are Constrained To Simulate Youth In Order To Avoid Shocking the Young.
Talfourd, Sir Thomas N.
Friend, A.
Taliesin (*fl.* c.550)
Battle of Argoed Llwyfain, The.
Death Song for Owain ab Urien.
Song to the Wind, A.
Tallet, José Zacarías (b. 1983)
Rumba.
"Tallis"
Limerick: "Conclusion I reach at the Tate, The."
TallMountain, Mary
Good Grease.
Hands of Mary Joe, The.
Indian Blood.
Last wolf hurried toward me, The.
Matmiya.
Peeling Pippins.
There Is No Word for Goodbye.
Talpalar, Morris
True Happiness.
Tam'si, Tchicaya U. *See* **U'Tamsi, Felix Tchicaya**
Tản Đà (Nguyễn Khắc Hiếu) (1888–1939)
Barber, The.
Canary in a Cage, The.
Dark Night.
Rail and the Bullfrog, The.
Ship An-Nam, The.
Speaking to My Photo.
State of the World, The.
Still At Play.
Tattered Map, The.
To a Scarecrow.
Troth Between the Hill and the Stream, The.
"Tan Ying" (Liu Pao-chen) (b. 1943)
Drinking the Wind.
T'an Yüan-ch'un (1586–1631)
Heard on a Boat.
Tandori, Dezső (b. 1938)
Utrillo: "La Belle Gabrielle."
Tanfield, Lady Elizabeth (*fl.* 1565–1628)
Epitaph for Sir Lawrence Tanfield.
T'ang Hsien-tsu (1550–1616)
Autumn River.
Cave of Gold Essence—in Ning-tu, The.
Descending the Ridge of Flying Clouds.
Evening View from the Bell Tower at P'ing-ch'ang.
Hsiu-chou.
Inspector Hsü Claims He Has Found the Secret of Youth.
On the Day of Washing the Buddha in the Year Ting-wei (1607), I Dreamed That My

Late Son Shih-ch'ü Was Holding a Book, and Appeared To Be Quite Happy. He Said That He Had Earned His Chin-shih Degree in the Underworld. After We Sighed and Laughed Together for a Long Time, I Woke Up and Wrote This Poem.

Paintings on My Wall Have Been Damaged by the Weather, The.

Spending the Night on the River.

Twenty-two Quatrains on Receiving the Obituary Notice for my Son Shih-Chü, *sels.*

T'ang Wan (*fl.* **12th cent.**)

To the Tune "The Phoenix Hairpin."

T'ang Yen-ch'ien (*fl.* **c.880**)

Walk in the Country, A.

T'ang Yin (**1470–1523**)

Inscribed on a Painting.

Inscribed on a Painting ("At the country inn, thousands of peach trees.")

Inscribed on a Painting of a Cock.

Inscribed on a Painting of a Fisherman.

Inscribed on a Painting of Bamboo.

Inscribed on a Painting ("On the mountain, old trees, still green in autumn.")

Inscribed on a Painting ("Places I go, leaning on my bramble cane, The.")

Inscribed on a Painting ("Thatched hut among the pines, door open near a cliff.")

Miscellaneous Feelings, *sels.*

On a Painting of a Woman Shown Half-Length, *sels.*

On the Butterflies.

Poems Inscribed on Paintings, *sels.*

Rainstorm Has Dragged On for Ten Days Now, and There Is No Fire in the Kitchen. Moistening My Inkstone and Chewing on My Brush, I've Lived in Isolation Like a Monk—and Completed Eight Quatrains to Express My Feelings, A, *sels.*

Scene at Heaven Gate, The.

Song of Peach Blossom Retreat.

Spring—River—Flower—Moon—Night, *sels.*

Tanikawa Shuntaro (**b. 1931**)

August is a dreamless month.

Concerning a Girl.

Everyone possesses something sad.

Family Portrait.

Request.

River.

Sadness.

Stone and Light.

Tannahill, Robert (**1774–1810**)

O! Are Ye Sleepin, Maggie?

Tao-chi (**1642–1707**)

Bend after bend, the long embankment.

Flower-Rain Terrace, The.

Inscribed on a Painting ("Little boat floats by the dock, The.")

Inscribed on a Painting of a Wu-t'ung Tree by Myself.

Inscribed on "Drunk in the Autumn Woods."

Inscribed on My Ink Landscape Painting.

Inscribed on My Large Landscape Hanging Scroll "Listening to a Waterfall."

Inscribed on My Little Painting of Plum Blossom and Bamboo.

Inscribed on the Wall at the Temple of the Auspicious Talisman.

Mood comes on—I want to cross Hsi-ling, The.

Riding a Boat on Wu-ling Stream.

Searching for Herb Brazier and Cinnabar Well, I Also Saw the Waterfall of Singing Strings. Alongside Was the Cliff of the Lord of the Mountain.

Trip to Hua-yang Mountain, A.

Trip to the Village of the River of White Sand, A.

T'ao Ch'ien [*or* **T'ao Yuan-ming**] (**365–427**)

Begging for Food.

Blaming Sons.

Bright blossoms seldom last long.

Bright sun lights out over the western bank.

Drinking Wine, *sels.*

I Return to the Place I Was Born.

Imitating the Old Poems.

In Praise of Poor Scholars.

In the Year with the Cyclical Sign *Mou-shen.*

Long time ago, A.

Man has no roots, A.

Matching a Poem by Secretary Kuo.

Motionless Clouds.

Moving House ("In spring and fall there are many fine days.")

Moving House ("Long time I've wanted to live in the southern village, A.")

Noble ambition spans the four seas, A.

On Being Assigned as Military Adviser to the Garrison Army.

On Returning to My Garden and Field, *sels.*

Once More Fields and Gardens.

Passing Ch'ien-hsi as Military Adviser in the Third Month of the Year Yi-ssu.

Poem in the Form of a Coffin-Puller's Song ("In the old days I had no wine to drink.")

Poem in the Form of a Coffin-Puller's Song ("Plain of wild grasses, broad and tangled, A.")

Poem in the Form of a Coffin-Puller's Song ("What has a life must have a death.")

Poem without a Category ("Brave man has ambitions wide as the four seas, A.")

Poem without a Category ("Sun and moon refuse to slow their pace.")

Reading *The Classic of Hills and Seas.*

Returning to My Home in the Country ("Out here in the fields, few social affairs.")

Returning to My Home in the Country ("So long since I've enjoyed the hills and ponds.")

Seasons Come and Go, The, *sels.*

Shady, Shady.

Stopping Wine.

Substance, Shadow, and Spirit, *sels.*

When I was young and in my prime.

Years ago, when I heard the words of my elders.

T'ao Hung Ching (**T'ao T'ung Ming**) (**452–536**)

Freezing Night.

Tao Tschung Yu, Lyall (*fl.* **18th? cent.**)

Familiar Spirits.

Quarrelling.

Tapahonso, Luci (**b. 1954**)

All I want is the bread to turn out like hers just once.

I Am Singing Now.

Listen.

Tappan, William Bingham (**1794–1849**)

Ransomed Spirit to Her Home, The.

There Is an Hour of Peaceful Rest.

Tarachow, Michael

Walking in the Midst of Others.

Tarkovsky [*or* **Tarkovskii**], **Arseny** [*or* **Arsenii**] **Aleksandrovich** (**1907–89**)

First Meetings.

I dreamed this dream and I still dream of it.

Poet, The.

Sight grows dim—my power.

Tarn, Nathaniel (**b. 1928**)

Journal of the Laguna de San Ignacio, *sels.*

Lyrics for the Bride of God, *sels.*

Tarpley, Natasha (**b. 1971**)

Feel Free.

Tartler, Grete

Sighioara 1982.

Tasso, Torquato (**1544–95**)

Aminta, *sels.*

Godfrey of Bulloigne; or, The Recoverie of Jerusalem, *sels.*

I'd like to be a bee.

Love, the great master of true eloquence.

Now the waves murmur.

To His Mistress in Absence.

What dew or what weeping.

"Woods and the rivers are silent," The.

Tate, Allen (**1899–1979**)

Aeneas at Washington.

Battle of Murfreesboro.

Cross, The.

Death of Little Boys.

Emblems.

Horatian Epode to the Duchess of Malfi.

Idiot greens the meadows with his eyes, The.

Last Days of Alice.

Mediterranean, The.

Mr. Pope.

More Sonnets at Christmas, *sels.*

Mother and Son.

Non Omnis Moriar.

Oath, The.

Ode to the Confederate Dead.

Paradigm, The.

Pauper, A.

Robber Bridegroom, The.

Seasons of the Soul.

Shadow and Shade.

Sonnet: To a Portrait of Hart Crane.

Sonnets at Christmas, *sels.*

Sonnets of the Blood, *sels.*

Subway, The.

Swimmers, The.

To Intellectual Detachment.

To the Lacedemonians.

Traveller, The.

Twelve, The.

Winter Mask.

Wolves, The.

Tate, Garth (**1952–92**)

Last Instructions.

Tate, Greg S. (**b. 1957**)

Tonguing.

Tate, James (**b. 1943**)

Blue Booby lives, The.

Breathing.

Chaste Stranger, The.

Coda.

Conjuring Roethke.

Consolations After an Affair.

Contagion.

Deaf Girl Playing.

Dear Reader.

Dime Found in the Snow, A.

Distance from Loved Ones.

Distant Orgasm, The.

Dreamy cars graze on the dewy boulevard.

For Mother on Father's Day.

Goodtime Jesus.

Guide to the Stone Age, The.

In a Motel on Lake Erie.

In My Own Backyard.

Intimidations of an Autobiography.

Land of Little Sticks, 1945.

Like a Scarf.

Lost Pilot, The.

Love Making.

Manna.

Miss Cho Composes in the Cafeteria.

Missed Opportunity, A.

Motorcyclists, The.

My Great Great Etc. Uncle Patrick Henry.

Neighbors.

Pet Deer, The.

Poem to Some of my Recent Poems.

President Slumming, The.

Rooster.

Rustin Steel is driving the crew to the river. A long.

Soup of Venus, The.

Storm.

Stray Animals.

Teaching the Ape to Write Poems.

Vagabond, The.

Wedding, A.

What the City Was Like.

Wheelchair Butterfly, The.

Tate, Nahum (**1652–1715**)

As Pants the Hart.

Choice, The.

Lord, Have Mercy.

While shepherds watched their flocks by night.

See also **Dryden, John** *and* **Nahum Tate.**

Tate, Nahum (**1652–1715**) *and* **Nicholas Brady**

Lord, Who's the Happy Man.

Tatersal, Robert (*fl.* **c.1734**)

Bricklayer's Labours, The.

Tatham, John (*fl.* **1632–64**)

Ostella forth of Town: To My Heart.

Tati-Loutard, Jean-Baptiste (b. 1939)
Death and Rebirth.
Les Racines Congolaises (1968), *sels.*
Pilgrimage to Loango Strand.
Poèmes de la Mer (1968), *sels.*
Submarine Tombs.
Voices, The.

Taufer, Diana
Mice Are Pets?

Taylor, Andrew (b. 1940)
Beast with Two Backs, The.
Clearing Away.
Developing a Wife.
Fitzroy.
Invention of Fire, The.
Travelling to Gleis-Binario, *sels.*

Taylor, Ann (1782–1866)
Air.
Earth.
Fire.
Maniac's Song, The.
Water.

Taylor, Ann (1783–1824)
Cow, The.
Cow and the Ass, The.
Meadows, The.
Meddlesome Matty.
My Mother.
Notorious Glutton, The.
Pin, The.
Sheep, The.

Taylor, Apirana (b. 1955)
Sad Joke on a Marae.
Taiaha Haka Poem.
Womb, The.

Taylor, Bayard (1825–78)
All or Nothing.
Angelo Orders His Dinner.
Ballad of Hiram Hover, The.
Bedouin Song.
Camerados.
Cimabuella.
Echo Club, The, *sels.*
Gettysburg Ode, *sels.*
Gwendoline.
Nauvoo.
Ode on [*or* to] a Jar of Pickles.
Palabras Grandiosas.
Promissory Note, The.
Sir Eggnogg.

Taylor, Benjamin Franklin (1819–87)
Long Ago, The.

Taylor, Bert Leston ("B. L. T.") (1866–1921)
Aprilly.
Canopus.
Doxology.
Passionate Professor, The.
Those Flapjacks of Brown's.
Upon Julia's Arctics.

Taylor, Caleb J. (1763–1817)
O Jesus, My Savior, I Know Thou Art Mine.

Taylor, Cecil
Garden.

Taylor, Charles S. (b. 1927)
Scandal among the Flowers, A.

Taylor, Edward (1645–1729)
Accusation of the Inward Man, The.
Address to the Soul Occasioned by a Rain, An.
Angels Sung a Carol, The.
Ebb and Flow, The.
Elegy upon the Death of That Holy Man of God Mr. John Allen, An.
Fig for Thee, Oh! Death, A.
God's Determinations [touching his Elect], *sels.*
Huswifery.
Meditation Eight.
Meditation Twelve.
Outward Man Accused, The.
Preparatory Meditations Before My Approach to the Lord's Supper, *sels.*
Thou Art the Tree of Life.
Upon a Spider Catching a Fly.
Upon a Wasp Chilled [*or* Child] with Cold.
Upon Wedlock and Death of Children.

Taylor, Eleanor Ross (b. 1920)
Few Days in the South in February, A.
In the Churchyard.
This Year's Drive to Appomattox.
Welcome Eumenides.

Taylor, Elizabeth (*fl.* c.1680)
Ode: "Ah poor Olinda never boast."
Song: "Strephon has fashion, wit and youth."
Song: "Ye Virgin Pow'rs defend my heart."
To Mertill Who Desired Her to Speak to Clorinda of His Love.

Taylor, Ellen (*fl.* c.1792)
Written by the Barrow Side, Where She Was Sent to Wash Linen.

Taylor, Geoffrey (1900–1957)
Admonition to the Muse.
Cruel, Clever Cat.
English Liberal.
Epitaph: "Nor practising virtue nor committing crime."
Gentlemen.

Taylor, George Lansing (1835–1903)
Dare to Do Right.

Taylor, Hannah
Virtue alone can never die. but lives to.

Taylor, Sir Henry (1800–1886)
Philip van Artevelde, *sels.*

Taylor, Henry (1711–85)
Country Curate, The.

Taylor, Henry (b. 1942)
Artichoke.
As on a Darkling Plain.
At the Swings.
Depressed by the Death of the Horse That He Bought from Robert Bly.
Flying Change, The.
Getting at the Root of the Matter.
In Orbit.
J. V. Cunningham Gets Hung Up on a Dirty, of All Things, Joke.
Not Working.
Riding a One-eyed Horse.
Riding Lesson.
Robert Bly Says Something Too.
Somewhere along the Way.
Speech.
Taking to the Woods.
View from a Cab, The.
Way It Sometimes Is, The.

Taylor, James Bayard (1825–78)
To G. H. B.

Taylor, Jane (1783–1824)
Fairies' Song, The.
Field Daisy, The.
Gleaner, The.
Greedy Richard.
I Like Little Pussy.
Pigs, The.
Recreation.
Squire's Pew, The.
Star, The.
Two Little Kittens.
Violet, The.

Taylor, John (1580–1653)
Comparison betwixt a Whore and a Booke, A, *sels.*
Epigram, A Supposed Construction.
Epigram: "Fair Beatrice tucks her coat up somewhat high."
Epigram: "Look how yon lecher's legs are worn away."
Epigram: "Lusty wench as nimble as an eel, A."
Epigram: "There chanced to meet together in an inn."
Epitaph in the Bermuda Tongue, Which Must Be Pronounced With the Accent of the Grunting of a Hog.
Epitaph in the Utopian Tongue.
Here followeth the unfashionable fashion, or the too too homely Worshipping of God, *sels.*
Libra, September.
London Magazine, 3 526, *sels.*
Odcomb's Complaint, *sels.*
Sculler, The, *sels.*

Sir Gregory Nonsense's News from No Place, *sels.*
Taylor's Arithmetic from One to Twelve, *sels.*
Trumpet of Liberty, The.
Virgo, August.

Taylor, Rachel Annand (1876–1960)
Princess of Scotland, The.

Taylor, Richard
Limerick: "Sexy young student once toyed, A."

"Taylor, Rockie D." *See* Ologboni, Tejumola

Taylor, Rod (b. 1947)
Dakota: October, 1822, Hunkpapa Warrior.

Taylor, William (1765–1836)
Ellenore.
Vision, The.

Tchernichowsky [*or* Tchernichovsky], Saul [*or* Shaul] (1875–1943)
Before the Statue of Apollo.
Bells, The.
Dance of Saul with the Prophets, The.
Death of Tammuz, The.
Grave in Ukraine, A.
I Believe.
Levivot.
They say there is a country.
This Be Our Revenge.
To Ashtaroth and Bel.
To the Sun, *sels.*

Te Aomuhurangi te Maaka (b. 1927)
Go Down, O Sun, Out from the Motu River.
Haka: Hinemutu.

Te Apakura, Irihapeti Rangi
Reply to a Marriage Proposal.

Tê Hanh (b. 1921)
Country Road, The.
Mother.

Te Heuheu Tukino
Lament for Te Heuheu Herea.

Te Kooti Rikirangi (c.1830–1893)
Song of Instruction, A.

Te Puea Herangi (1884–1952)
Remain, Rata.

Te Whetu (*fl.* c.1880)
Sound of My Sneezing Nose, The.

Teasdale, Sara (1884–1933)
Answer, The.
Appraisal.
August Night.
Barter.
Crystal Gazer, The.
Epitaph: "Serene descent, as a red leaf's descending."
Falling Star, The.
February Twilight.
Flight, The.
Full Moon; Santa Barbara.
Gift, The.
Hide and Seek.
I Am Not Yours[, not lost in you].
I might have sung of the world.
I Shall Not Care.
I would live in your love as the sea-grasses live in the sea.
Kiss, The.
Long Hill, The.
Look, The.
Moonlight.
Night.
Night Song at Amalfi.
On the South Downs.
Open Windows.
Over the Roofs.
Philosopher, The.
September Midnight.
Sleepless.
Solitary, The.
Song: "Let it be forgotten, as a flower is forgotten."
Song Making.
Spring Night.
Those who love the most.
Water-Lilies.
Weariness.

"What Do I Care."
Wind, The.
Wisdom.

"Teffi" (Nadezhda Aleksandrovna Lokhvitskaia) (1872–1952)
Before the Map of Russia.

Teft, Elizabeth (*fl.* 1741–47)
On Learning.
On Snuff-Taking.
On Viewing Herself in a Glass.
To a Gentleman Who Disordered a Lady's Handerchief, and Immediately Cut His Thumb.

Tegnér, Esaias (1782–1846)
Frithiof's Saga, *sels.*

Teika (Fujiwara no Teika) (1162–1241)
From the beginning.
I gaze far and long.
I rein in my horse.
Spring night's, The.

Teika, Fujiwara no. *See* **Teika**

Tejada, Roberto (b. 1964)
Honeycomb perfection of this form before me.

"Tekahionwake." *See* **Johnson, Emily Pauline**

Tekeyan, Vahan
Country of Dust, The.
Dream.
Forgetting. Yes, I will forget it all.
Prayer on the Threshold of Tomorrow.
Sacred Wrath.

Tekkan, Yosano
Tanka: "Blood, The."
Tanka: "Except the rare time."
Tanka: "Eyes fixed."
Tanka: "Faintly white."
Tanka: "I'll forget I saw you."
Tanka: "In my mind."
Tanka: "It cries and cries."
Tanka: "Let those grasses."
Tanka: "Noiselessly."
Tanka: "Not unlike a fish."
Tanka: "Plucking feathers."
Tanka: "Poppies in bloom."
Tanka: "Snake."
Tanka: "Their father."
Tanka: "Too emotional."
Tanka: "Unlike their father."
Tanka: "Vast wilderness."
Tanka: "With no flower buds."
Tanka: "With warts and all."
To our baby that died[1].

Telemaque, Harold Milton (b. 1911)
Adina.

Telesilla (*fl.* 5th cent.)
O Artemis and your virgin girls.

Telestes (*fl.* c.401 B.C.)
It was a Phrygian king.
It was a Phrygian, Pelops.

Teller, Judah [or Judd] Leib (1912–72)
Lines to a Tree.
Minor Key.
To the Divine Neighbor.

Templeton, Fiona (b. 1951)
You: The City, *sels.*

Teng Yu-pin (*fl.* late 13th cent.)
Tune: "Wild Geese Have Come Down; Song of Victory"—Idle Leisure.

Tenji, Emperor (626–71)
Because.

Tennant, Robert (1830–79)
Wee Davie Daylicht.

Tennant, William (1784–1848)
Anster Fair, *sels.*

Tennyson, Alfred Tennyson, 1st Baron (1809–92)
Ancient Pistol, peacock Payne.
Arabian Night Garden, An.
Audley Court, *sels.*
Babylon.
Becket, *sels.*
Beggar Maid, The.
Break, break, break.

Brook; An Idyl, The, *sels.*
Buonaparte.
Character, A.
Charge of the Light Brigade, The, *sels.*
Circumstance.
City Child, The.
Crossing the Bar.
Daisy, The.
Dawn, The.
Dedication, A: "Dear, near and true—no truer Time himself."
Dualisms.
Dying Swan, The.
Eagle, The.
Fatima.
Flower in the crannied wall.
Frater Ave Atque Vale.
From Sorrow Sorrow Yet Is Born.
Gardener's Daughter, The, *sels.*
Go By.
Godiva.
Happy, The Leper's Bride.
Hark! the dogs howl! the sleetwinds blow.
Hendecasyllabics.
Hesperides, The.
Higher Pantheism, The.
I ran upon life unknowing, without or science or art.
I Stood on a Tower in the Wet.
Idylls of the King, *sels.*
If I were loved, as I desire to be.
In Memoriam A. H. H, *sels.*
In my youth the growls.
In the Garden at Swainston.
In the Valley of Cauteretz.
June Bracken and Heather.
Kraken, The.
Lady Clare.
Lady of Shalott, The.
Letter, The.
Locksley Hall, *sels.*
Lotus-Eaters, The, *sels.*
Lucretius.
Mariana.
Marriage Morning.
Maud [A Monodrama], *sels.*
May Queen, The, *sels.*
Merlin and the Gleam.
Mermaid, The.
Merman, The.
Miller's Daughter, The.
Milton [Alcaics].
Minnie and Winnie.
Morte d'Arthur, *sels.*
Northern Cobbler, The.
Northern Farmer: New Style.
Northern Farmer: Old Style.
Not only with no sense of shame.
Nothing Will Die.
"O Swallow, Swallow, flying, flying south".
Oak, The.
Ode on the Death of the Duke of Wellington, *sels.*
On the Jubilee of Queen Victoria.
Opening of the Indian and Colonial Exhibition by the Queen.
Owl, The.
Palace of Art, The, *sels.*
Poets and Their Bibliographies.
Poet's Song, The.
Popular, popular, unpopular!
Princess, The, *sels.*
Recollections of The Arabian Nights.
Revenge, The, *sels.*
Rizpah.
Sadness.
Sailor Boy, The.
St. Simeon Stylites.
Sea Dreams, *sels.*
Somebody being a nobody.
Song: "Spirit haunts the year's last hours, A."
Song: "Who can say."
Sonnet: "She took the dappled partridge flecked [or fleckt] with blood."
Spinster's Sweet-Arts, The, *sels.*
St. Agnes' Eve.
Suburban Garden.

Throstle, The.
Tithonus.
To Christopher North.
To E. Fitzgerald.
To the Rev. F. D. Maurice, *sels.*
To Virgil [or Vergil].
To —. With the Following Poem.
Today I saw the dragon-fly.
Ulysses.
Vision of Sin, The, *sels.*
Voice by the Cedar Tree, A.
Voyage, The.
Voyage of Maeldune, The.

Tennyson, Frederick (1807–98)
Glory of Nature, The.
Holy Tide, The.
Old Age.

Teodorescu, Virgil
Arm in Arm.
At Night the Jellyfish Unfold Their Veils.
Ex Voto.
Goodbye.

Terapiano, Yury [or Iurii] Konstantinovich (1892–1980)
Lights shining above the Neva.
Ships that sail forth.

Terence (Publius Terentius Afer) (195?–159 B.C.)
Brothers (Adelphi), The, *sels.*
Girl from Andros (Andria), The, *sels.*
Inscription.

Teresa de Cepeda Y Ahumada (Teresa of Avila) (1515–1582)
(Lines Written on a Bookmark Found in Her Breviary).

Terry, Ellen (1847–1928)
No Funeral Gloom.

Terry, Lucy (1730–1821)
Bar[']s Fight[, August 28, 1746].

Tessimond, Arthur Seymour John (1902–62)
Heaven.
Jamaican Bus Ride.
Not Love Perhaps.
Postscript to a Pettiness.

Teton Sioux Oral Tradition
I Sing for the Animals.
Wolf Song.

Tevakulattar
What She Said ("Bigger than earth, certainly.")

Tewa Oral Tradition
Song of the Sky Loom.

Thacker, Labhshankar (b. 1935)
Poem: "Word is fast asleep, The."

Thackeray, William Makepeace (1811–63)
At the Zoo.
Ballad of Bouillabaisse, The, *sels.*
Damages, Two Hundred Pounds.
Dear Jack, this white mug that with Guinness I fill.
Due of the Dead, The.
Georges, The, *sels.*
King of Brentford's Testament *abr. The.*
Little Billee.
Mr. Molony's Account of the Crystal Palace.
Pocahontas, *sels.*
Sorrows of Werther, The.
Speculators, The.
Tragic Story, A.

Thallus (*fl.* A.D. 1st cent.)
Now the green plane-tree hides the lovers, hides the lovers'/ rites.

Thành, Nguyễn Kim. *See* **Tố Hũ'u**

Thanh Quan, (Lady) (Nguyễn thi Hinh) (*fl.* 19th cent.)
Remembering the Past in the City of the Soaring Dragon.

Tharp, H. M.
Finger Folk.

Thatcher, Charles Robert (1831–82)
Dick Briggs from Australia.
Moggy's Wedding.
Taking the Census.

Thatcher, Thomas (1620–78)
Love Letter to Elizabeth Thatcher, A.

Thaxter, Celia Laighton (1835–94)
August.
Chanticleer.
Cruise of the *Mystery*, The.
Favorite Flower, The.
Jack Frost.
On Easter Day.
Sandpiper, The.
Schumann's Sonata in A Minor.

Thayer, Ernest Lawrence (1863–1940)
Casey at the Bat.

Thayer, Louis E. (1870–1966)
Little Child's Faith, The.

**Thayer, William Roscoe ("Paul Hermes")
(1859–1923)**
Last Hunt, The.

Thể Lữ' (Nguyễn Thú' Lễ) (b. 1907)
Lyre of Myriad Tunes, The.
Opium.

The Yueh-Fu
I want to be your friend.

Theaitetus (fl. 6th cent.)
Already the field, fair with leaves, in her
fruitful bringing to birth.
Krantor.

Thelwall, John (1764–1834)
Anacreontic.
Cell, The.
Lines Written at Bridgewater, 27 July 1797,
sels.
Poems Written Chiefly in Retirement, *sels.*
Poems Written in Close Confinement in the
Tower and Newgate upon a Charge of
Treason, *sels.*
To the Infant Hampden. Written during a
Sleepless Night.

Theocritus (c.310–c.250 B.C.)
Adonis.
Along that footpath, shepherd, past the oaks.
Cyclops, The, *sels.*
Daphnis the fair-skinned, who plays country
songs.
Death of Adonis, The.
Epitaph of Cleonicus.
Epitaph of Hipponax.
Herdsmen, The, *sels.*
Honey Stealer, The.
Hylas and the Water Nymphs.
Idyll 1, *sels.*
Idyll 14, *sels.*
Idylls, *sels.*
Look on this statue, traveller; look well.
19th Idyllium of Theocritus attempted in the
Cumberland Dialect, The.
O NICIAS, there is no other remedy for love.
Ortho's Epitaph.
Rural Journey, The, *sels.*
Take, friend, Orthon of Syracuse' advice.
This bank makes welcome citizen and
foreigner.
This is the grave of Eusthenes the wise.
Those dew-moist roses and that bushy thyme.
Wedding Song: Lullaby for Sleepy Lovers.
What do you gain, poor Thyrsis, by these
tears?
Words are Doric, Doric too the man, The.
You left behind, Eurymedon, an infant child.
You sleep here, Daphnis, on the leafy
ground.

Theodoridas (fl. 3d cent. B.C.)
I am the tomb of a shipwrecked man. Sail
on.
Roused by November seas, wrecked on
Italian rocks.
To the triple goddess of Amarynthus.

Theodulf of Orleans (c.750–821)
Wherefore the Scars of Christ's Passion
Remained in the Body of His Resurrection.

Theognis (fl. c.545 B.C.)
Enjoyment.
Exile.
Fowr Epigrams frae Theognis o Megara, *sels.*
Hope.
Our Course.
Poverty.

Theon (fl. 5th cent.)
For the Cenotaph of a Lost Soldier.

Theophanes (fl. 6th cent.)
I wish I could be.

Theresa [or Teresa], Saint, of Avila (1515–82)
Bookmark.
En las Internas Entrañas.
I Die because I Do Not Die.
I gave myself to Love Divine.
If, Lord, Thy Love for Me Is Strong.
Let Mine Eyes See Thee.
Poem: "Nothing move thee."
Shepherd, Shepherd, Hark.
Soul, thou must seek thyself in Me.
To-Day a Shepherd.

Thesen, Sharon (b. 1946)
Kirk Lonegren's Home Movie Taking Place
Just North of Prince George, with Sound.
Loose Woman Poem.
Mean Drunk Poem.

Thibaudeau, Colleen (b. 1925)
Brown Family, The.
Green Family, The.
Poem: "I do not want only."

Thicknesse, Lily (fl early 20th cent.)
Siena.

Thiele, Colin (b. 1920)
Radiation Victim.
Tom Farley.

Thiên Thê (fl.20th cent.)
Wrecking the Statue of Paul Bert.

Thom, William (1799?–1848)
Blind Boy's Pranks, The.

Thomas à Becket
Columbia, the Gem of the Ocean.

Thomas, Ann (fl. 1784–95)
To Laura, on the French Fleet Parading
before Plymouth.

Thomas Aquinas, Saint (c.1225–1274)
With my heart I worship.
Word went forth, The.

Thomas, Claire Richcreek
Flesh will heal and pain will fade.
Heart Wounds.
Treasures.

Thomas, D. M.
Puberty Tree, The.

Thomas, Delaina (b. 1955)
Turning of the Year, The.

Thomas, Dylan (1914–53)
After the funeral, mule praises, brays.
Among Those Killed in the Dawn Raid Was
a Man Aged a Hundred.
And death shall have no dominion.
Author's Prologue.
Before I knocked and flesh let enter.
Ceremony after a Fire Raid.
Child's Christmas in Wales, A, *sels.*
Conversation of Prayer, The.
Conversation of prayers about to be said,
The.
Countryman's Return, The.
Do not go gentle into that good night.
Ears in the turrets hear.
Especially when the October wind.
Fern Hill.
Force that through the green fuse drives the
flower, The.
Ghost Story.
Hand that signed the paper felled a city, The.
Hunchback in the park, The.
I, in my intricate image, stride on two levels.
I, the first named.
In my craft or sullen art.
In the beginning was the three-pointed star.
Incarnate devil in a talking snake.
It is the sinners' dust-tongued bell claps me
to churches.
January 1939.
Light breaks where no sun shines.
Limerick: "Last time I slept with the Queen,
The."
Marriage of a Virgin, The.
O make me a mask and a wall to shut from
your spies.

On no work of words now for three lean
months in the bloody.
On the Marriage of a Virgin.
Out of a War of Wits.
Over Sir John's Hill.
Parachutist, *sels.*
Poem in October.
Refusal to Mourn the Death, by Fire, of a
Child in London, A.
Sequence of Sonnets, A, *sels.*
Song of the Mischievous Dog, The.
Spire cranes, The. Its statue is an aviary.
There was a saviour.
This bread I break was once the oat.
Tombstone told when she died, The.
Twenty-four years remind the tears of my
eyes.
Under Milk Wood, *sels.*
Vision and Prayer.
Walking in gardens by the sides.
We lying by seasand, watching yellow.
When all my five and country senses see.
When, like a running grave, time tracks you
down.
Winter's Tale, A.

Thomas, Edith Matilda (1854–1925)
Cricket Kept the House, The.
Mrs. Kriss Kringle.
Shooting Star, A.

**Thomas, Edward ("Edward Eastaway") (1878–
1917)**
Adlestrop.
And You, Helen.
As the team's head-brass flashed out on the
turn.
Aspens.
Bob's Lane.
Brook, The.
By the Ford.
Cat, A.
Celandine.
Cherry Trees, The.
Clouds That Are So Light, The.
Cock-Crow.
Combe was ever dark, ancient and dark, The.
Dark Forest, The.
Digging.
February Afternoon.
Fifty Faggots.
Gallows, The.
Glory of the beauty of the morning, The.
Gone, gone again.
Good-Night.
Green Roads, The.
Gypsy, The.
Haymaking.
If I Should Ever by Chance.
In Memoriam (Easter, 1915).
It Rains ("It rains, and nothing stirs within
the fence.")
Liberty.
Lights Out.
Like the Touch of Rain [she was].
Man and Dog.
Mill-Pond, The.
New House, The.
No one cares less than I.
No One So Much as You.
October.
Old Man, or Lad's-Love,—in the name
there's nothing.
Out in the dark over the snow.
Owl, The.
Penny Whistle, The.
Private, A.
Rain, midnight rain, nothing but the wild
rain.
Roads.
Snow.
Some Eyes Condemn.
Sun used to shine while we two walked, The.
Swedes.
Tall Nettles.
Tears.
Thaw.
This is no case of petty right or wrong.
Trumpet, The.

Two Houses.
Two Pewits.
Under the Woods.
Unknown, The.
Unknown Bird, The.
What Shall I Give?
When first I came here I had hope.
When I first came here I had hope.
Will You Come?

Thomas, Elizabeth (1675–1731)
Dream, The; An Epistle to Mr. Dryden.
Epistle to Clemena, Occasioned by an
    Argument She Had Maintained Against the
    Author.
Execration, The.
Forsaken Wife, The.
Jill, A Pindaric Ode, *sels.*
Midnight Thought, A &[;on the Death of
    Mrs. *E. H.* and Her Little Daughter&];.
New Litany, Occasioned by an Invitation to a
    Wedding, A.
On Sir J—— S—— Saying in a Sarcastic
    Manner, My Books Would Make Me Mad;
    an Ode.
Remedia Amoris.
To Almystrea, on her Divine Works.
To Colindra.
Triple League to Mrs Susan Dove, The.
Triumvirate, The.
True Effigies of a Certain Squire: Inscribed
    to Clemena, The.

Thomas, Evan (c.1710–c.1770)
To the Gentlewoman of Llanarth Hall.

Thomas, Gwyn (b. 1936)
Horses.
Little Death.
Microscope.

Thomas, Harry
Limerick: "'Strip,' Leofric said, 'and you'll
    find.'"

Thomas, J. H. (b. 1943)
If the maiden coughs immediately after.

Thomas, Jenny
Space.

Thomas, Joyce Carol (b. 1938)
Bittersweet, *sels.*

Thomas, Lorenzo (b. 1944)
Cameo in Sudden Light.
Clear Channel.
Electricity of Blossoms.
Excitation.
Historiography.
Inauguration.
Instructions for Your New Osiris.
Marvelous Land of Indefinitions, The.
Onion Bucket.
Subway Witnesses, The.
Wonders.

Thomas, Louisa Carroll
What Is Charm?

Thomas, Richard W. (b. 1939)
Amen.
Life after Death.
Martyrdom.
Riots and Rituals.
To the New Annex to the Detroit County
    Jail.
Worker, The.

Thomas, Ronald Stuart (b. 1913)
After Jericho.
Ancients of the World, The.
Ann Griffith.
Aside.
At It.
Blackbird Singing, A.
Centuries.
Coleridge.
Country Clergy, The.
Echoes.
Hand, The.
Here.
Hill Farmer Speaks, The.
In a Country Church.
Ire.
Judgment Day.
Lonely Farmer, The.

Lore.
Madrigal: "Your love is dead, lady, your love
    is dead."
Moor, The.
Nocturne by Ben Shahn.
On the Farm.
One Furrow, The.
Peasant, A.
Person from Porlock, A.
Petition.
Pisces.
Poetry for Supper.
Porch, The.
Postscript.
Rhodri Theophilus Owen.
Selah.
Survivor, The.
They.
View from the Window, The.
Welsh History.
Welsh Landscape.
Welshman to Any Tourist, A.
Woman, The.

Thomas, Rosemary (b. 1901)
Between Two Worlds.

**Thomas, Thomas Jacob ("Sarnicol") (1873–
1945)**
Dic Siôn Dayfydd.

Thomas of Celano (1200?–1255?)
Day of Judgment, The.
Dies Irae.

Thomas of Erceldoune (c.1225–c.1300)
Sir Tristrem, *sels.*

Thompson, Alexander R. (1812–95)
Wayfarers in the Wilderness.

Thompson, Benjamin (1642–1714)
Seaconk Plain Engagement.

Thompson, Cinda
Heirloom.
Tree, The.

Thompson, Clara Ann (b. 1887?)
After-Glow of Pain, The.
Angel's Message, The.
Autumn Day, An.
Autumn Leaves.
Christmas Rush, The.
Church Bells.
Doubt crept into a heart one day, A.
Drift-Wood.
Dying Year, The.
Easter Bonnet, The.
Easter Light, The.
Empty Tomb, The.
His Answer.
Hope.
Hope Deferred.
If Thou Shouldst Return.
I'll Follow Thee.
Johnny's Pet Superstition.
Lullaby: "Hush ye, hush ye! honey, darlin'."
Memorial Day.
Mrs. Johnson Objects.
Not Dead, but Sleeping.
Oh List to My Song!
Old and the New, The.
Opening Service, An.
Out of the Deep.
Parted.
She Sent Him Away.
Skeptic, The.
Storm-Beaten.
Submission.
To My Dead Brother.
Uncle Rube on the Race Problem.
Uncle Rube to the Young People.
Uncle Rube's Defense.
Watcher, The.

Thompson, D'Arcy Wentworth (1860–1948)
That Little Black Cat.
Very Odd Fish, A.

Thompson, Dorothy Brown (b. 1896)
Good Will to Men—Christmas Greetings in
    Six Languages.
Wish.

Thompson, Dunstan (b. 1918)
Ovid on the Dacian Coast.

Thompson, Earle (b. 1950)
Juniper Moon Pulls at My Bones, The.
Love Song: "She is a reed swaying in blue."
Mythology.
No Deposit.
Song: "Woman sits on her porch."

Thompson, Edward (1739?–1786)
Humble Wish; off Porto-Santo, March 29,
    1779, An, *sels.*
Indian maid the demararie october twenty
    seven seventeen eighty one.
To Emma, Extempore; Hyaena, off Gambia,
    June 4, 1779.

Thompson, Eloise Bibb. *See* **Bibb, Eloise**

Thompson, Francis (1859–1907)
Ad Amicam.
Any Saint.
Arab Love-Song, An.
At Lord's.
Contemplation, *sels.*
Counsel of Moderation, A.
Daisy.
End of It, The.
Envoy: "Go, songs, for ended is our brief,
    sweet play."
Ex Ore Infantium.
Fallen Yew, A.
Grace of the Way, *sels.*
Heart, The, *sels.*
Heaven and Hell.
Hound of Heaven, The.
In No Strange Land.
Judgment in Heaven, A, *sels.*
Messages.
Mistress of Vision, The.
Ode to the Setting Sun, *sels.*
Past Thinking of Solomon.
Poppy, The.
Sister Songs, *sels.*
To a Snowflake.
To My Friend.
To Olivia.
To the Dead Cardinal of Westminster.
Too Soon.

Thompson, Irene (b. 1919)
Caravans.
Country Child, The.
Feet.
Holiday Train, The.
Penny Wish, A.
Rainy Nights.
Secret Places.
Swinging.
Town Child, The.
Welcome to Spring.

Thompson, J. W.
Work.

Thompson, James W. (b. 1936)
Constant Labor, A.
Greek Room, The.
Plight, The.
Spawn of Slums, The.
Yellow Bird, The.
You Are Alms.

Thompson, John (1907–68)
Bread Hot from the Oven, The.
Now You Have Burned.
Onion, The.

Thompson, John Randolph (b. 1838)
Lee to the Rear.
Obsequies of Stuart.

Thompson, John Reuben (1823–73)
Burial of Latané, The.
Music in Camp.

Thompson, Larry (b. 1950)
Black Is Best.

Thompson, Maurice (1844–1901)
Address by an Ex-Confederate Soldier to the
    Grand Army of the Republic, An.
Lincoln's Grave, *sels.*
To the South.

Thompson, Priscilla Jane (b. 1882)
Address to Ethiopia.
Adieu, Adieu, Forever.
Adown the heights of Ages.
After the Quarrel.

Afternoon Gossip, An.
Alberta, lovely little dame.
Athelstane.
Autumn ("List to the sad wind, drearily moaning.")
Autumn ("Sun shines bright, but sadly, The.")
Christmas Ghost, A.
Common Occurrence, A.
Consumptive, The.
David and Goliath.
Death and Resurrection.
Domestic Storm, A.
Emancipation.
Evelyn.
Examination, The.
Favorite Slave's Story, The.
Freedom at McNealy's.
Fugitive, The.
Glimpses of Infancy.
Happy Pair, A.
Home Greeting, A.
Husband's Return, The.
Hymn: "Lord, within thy fold I be."
In the Valley.
Inner Realm, The.
Insulted.
Interrupted Reproof, The.
Just How It Happened.
Kindly Deed, A.
King's Favorites, The.
Knight of My Maiden Love.
Lines on a Dead Girl.
Lines to an Old School-House.
Lines to Emma.
Little Wren, A.
Muse's Favor, The.
My Father's Story.
Oh, Whence Comes the Gladness?
Old Freedman, The.
Old Saint's Prayer, The.
Old Year, The.
Prayer, A: "Oh, Lord! I lift my heart."
Precious Pearl, The.
Raphael.
Snail's Lesson, The.
Snow-Flakes, The.
Soft Black Eyes.
Song of the Moon.
Song, The: "Oh, foully slighted Ethiope maid!"
Southern Scene, A.
They Are the Same.
Thwarted.
To a Deceased Friend.
To a Little Colored Boy.
To the New Year.
Tribute to the Bride and Groom, A.
Turncoat, The.
Uncle Ike's Holiday.
Uncle Jimmie's Yarn.
Unromantic Awakening, An.
Valentine, A.
Vineyard of My Beloved, The.
While the Choir Sang.
Winter Night, A.
Thompson, Ralph (b. 1928)
He knows what height is, this hillside dweller.
Thompson, Samuel (1766–1816)
April.
To a Hedgehog.
Thompson, Ted
Limerick: "Having rid Hamelin town of its vermin."
Thompson, Will Henry (1848–1918)
High Tide at Gettysburg, The.
Thompson, William (1712?–1766?)
Happy Life, The.
Sickness, sels.
Thomson, James (1700–1748)
Castle of Indolence, The, sels.
For ever, Fortune, wilt thou prove.
Hymn on Solitude.
Late Spring.
Migrating Birds.
Of a Country Life, sels.

On Beauty [or Beauety], sels.
On the Death of Mr. William Aikman the Painter, sels.
One day the god of fond desire.
Paraphrase of the Latter part of the Sixth Chapter of St. Matthew, A.
Seasons, The, sels.
Signs of Storm.
To the Memory of Sir Isaac Newton, sels.
Thomson, James ("B. V." or "Bysshe Vanolis") (1834–82)
Art, sels.
City of Dreadful Night, The, sels.
In a Christian Churchyard.
In the Room.
Mister MacCall at Cleveland Hall.
Once in a saintly passion.
Shelley, sels.
Sunday at Hampstead, sels.
Sunday up the River, sels.
William Blake.
Thomson, James (1700–1748) and David Mallet
Alfred: A Masque, sels.
Thomson, Mary A. (1834–1923)
O King of Saints, We Give Thee Praise and Glory.
O Sion, Haste, Thy Mission High Fulfilling.
Thoreau, Henry David (1817–62)
Among the worst of men that ever lived.
At Midnight's Hour I Raised My Head.
Between the Traveller and the Setting Sun.
Brother where dost thou dwell?
Dong, sounds the brass in the east.
Each More Melodious Note I Hear.
Fog.
For though the caves were rabbeted.
Forever in My Dream and in My Morning Thought.
Friendship.
Great Friend.
Great God I ask thee for no meaner pelf.
Guido's Aurora.
I am a parcel of vain strivings tied.
I was born upon thy bank, river.
I Was Made Erect and Lone.
I'm Thankful That My Life Doth Not Deceive.
Indeed indeed, I cannot tell.
Inspiration, sels.
Inward Morning, The.
It is no dream of mine.
Men say they know things.
Moon Now Rises to Her Absolute Rule, The.
Music.
My life has been the poem I would have writ.
Nature.
Old Marlborough Road, The.
On fields oer which the reaper's hand has passed.
On Ponkawtasset, since, we took our way.
On the Sun Coming Out in the Afternoon.
Poet's Delay, The.
Pray to What Earth Does This Sweet Cold Belong.
River Swelleth More and More, The.
Rumors from an Aeolian Harp.
Tall Ambrosia.
They Made Me Erect and Lone.
They who prepare my evening meal below.
Though All the Fates Should Prove Unkind.
To a Marsh Hawk in Spring.
To the Maiden in the East.
To the Mountains.
Walden, sels.
Week on the Concord and Merrimack Rivers, A, sels.
What's the Railroad to Me?
When Winter fringes every bough.
Who Sleeps by Day and Walks by Night.
Winter and Spring Scene, A.
Winter Memories.
Thorley, Wilfrid (b. 1878)
Chant for Reapers.
Fan, the Filly.
Happy Sheep, The.
Song for a Ball-Game.

Thornbury, George Walter (1828–76)
Cavalier's Escape, The.
Court Historian, The.
Smith of Maudlin.
Thorne, Cyril Morton (b. 1826)
To My Unborn Son.
Thorne, Tim (b. 1944)
High Country.
Whatever Happened to Conway Twitty?
Thorneley, Thomas
Limerick: "Candid Professor confesses, A."
Limerick: "Cynic says: Now that we know, A."
Limerick: "Fascist, erect and irate, A."
Limerick: "Figure is not anatomical, The."
Limerick: "Life-Force, afflicted with doubt, The."
Limerick: "Man who had lately declared, A."
Limerick: "Millionaire, filled with elation, A."
Limerick: "Mordant and decadent Youth, A."
Limerick: "Novelist, flushed with success, A."
Limerick: "Painter, encumbered with cash, A."
Limerick: "Said a Tripper: 'O joy, to have found.'"
Limerick: "Said the Stoic, tormented by gout."
Limerick: "There was a great German Grammarian."
Thornton, R. K. R.
Limerick: "'Political women,' thought Yeats."
Limerick: "There once was a writer called James."
Thorold Rogers, J. E. (1823–90)
Here X. lies dead, but God's forgiving.
On a Distinguished Politician.
On the Historians Freeman and Stubbs.
Suggestion Made by the Posters of the Globe, A.
Upon the man who's buried here.
Vulgar Error, A.
Thorpe, Adam (b. 1956)
Against the bolts and welder's bloom of rhetoric.
Thorpe, Rose Hartwick (1850–1939)
Curfew Must Not Ring Tonight [or To-Night].
Thorson, Marie
Closed Doors.
Thrale [later Mrs. Piozzi], Hester Lynch Salusbury (1741–1821)
Ode to Society, An.
Winter in Wales, A.
Three Marias, The (Maria Isabella Barreno, Maria Teresa Horta, and Maria Velho da Costa)
Saddle and Cell.
See also Horta, Maria Teresa.
Thribb, E. J. (b. 1960?)
Erratum.
In Memoriam Krishna Menon.
In Memoriam Larry Parnes ("Mr Parnes Shillings and Pence").
In Memoriam Salvador Dali.
In Memoriam the Master—Noel Coward (1900-1973).
Lines on the Award "Pipe Man of the Year" to Magnus Magnusson.
Lines on the Hundredth Anniversary of the Birth of W. Somerset Maugham.
Lines on the Return to Britain of Billy Graham.
Thù'a Phong (Lê Văn Cu') (b. 1914)
Mother's Faith.
Thucydides (b. c.460 B.C.)
Euripides.
Thurman, Judith (b. 1946)
Clockface.
Going Barefoot.
Oil Slick.
Rags.
Zebra.
Thurtle, Ida
Limerick: "Certain young man of Hilgay, A."

Thwaite *(continued)*
Limerick: "Flighty young lady from Loddon, A."
Limerick: "Retired Civil Servant from Gateley, A."
Limerick: "Said a wife to her husband near Scole."
Limerick: "Said the boy driving home towards Clere."
Limerick: "Young man who lived at Holme Hale, A."

Thwaite, Anthony (b. 1930)
Ali Ben Shufti.
At Birth.
At Dunwich.
Dream Time.
Girdle round the Earth, A.
Great Foreign Writer Visits Age-Old Temple, Greeted by Venerable Abbess, 1955.
Marriages.
Mr. Cooper.
On Consulting "Contemporary Poets of the English Language."
Pond, The.
Simple Poem.
Sunday Afternoons.

Thyillos *(fl. between 50 and 450)*
Already swallows build their homes of mud.

Thymocles (Timocles) *(fl. 3d cent. B.C.)*
Remember, do you remember those solemn words.
Remember now? Do you.

Tibble, Anne (b. 1912)
Trials of a Tourist.

Tibullus (Albius Tibullus) (c.59–c.19 B.C.)
Elegies, I.iv: "Yield prompt compliance to the maid's desires."
Odes, *sels.*
Pastoral Elegy, A.
Peace.
Those who the Godhead's soft Behests obey.

Tichborne [or Tichbourne], Chidiock (1558–86)
Tichborne's Elegy.

Tickell, Thomas (1686–1740)
Fragment of a Poem on Hunting, A, *sels.*
On the Prospect of Peace, *sels.*
To the Earl of Warwick, on the Death of Mr. Addison.

Ticknor, Francis Orrery [or Orray] (1822–74)
Little Giffen.

Tico, Tom
After gazing at stars.
Tinkle of chimes, The.
Wisp of spring cloud, A.

Tidjani-Cissé, Ahmed (b. 1947)
Home News.
Of Colours and Shadows.

Tieck, Johann Ludwig (1773–1853)
Autumn Song.

Tiempo, César (Israel Zierlin) (b. 1906)
Harangue on the Death of Hayyim Nahman Bialik.
I Tell of Another Young Death.

Tien Ch'ien (b. 1916)
Freedom is Walking toward Us.

T'ien Hung *(fl. 3d cent. B.C.)*
Dew on the Young Garlic Leaves.

Tietjens, Eunice (1884–1944)
Fullfillment.

Tighe, Mary (1772–1810)
Psyche, *sels.*
Psyche, with Other Poems, 3rd edition, *sels.*
Sonnet Addressed to My Mother.
To Time.

Tikhonov, Nikolai Semionovich (1896–1979)
Ballad of the Blue Envelope, The.
Ballad of the Nails, The.
Fire, the rope, the bullet, and the ax, The.
Gulliver Plays Cards.
We have forgotten how to offer alms.

Tilden, Stephen (1690–1766)
O Heaven Indulge.

Tillam, Thomas *(fl. 17th cent.)*
Upon the First Sight of New England, June 29, 1638.

Tiller, Terence (b. 1916)
Reading a Medal.
Street Performers, 1851.

Tillinghast, Richard (b. 1940)
Dozing on the Porch with an Oriental Lap-Rug.
Envoi: "Go little book, par avion."
Knife, The.
Our Flag Was Still There.
Summer rain, and the voices of children.

Tilton, Theodore (1835–1907)
Even This Shall Pass Away.

Timocles. *See* Thymocles

Timrod, Henry (1828–67)
Carolina.
Charleston.
Christmas.
Cotton Boll, The.
Dreams.
Ethnogenesis.
Faint Falls the Gentle Voice.
I know not why, but all this weary day.
La Belle Juive.
Most men know love but as a part of life.
Ode: "Sleep sweetly in your humble graves."
Retirement.

Tindal, Henrietta (1818–1879)
Birth Wail, The.
Cry of the Oppressed, The.

Tió, Elsa (b. 1950)
I am furious with myself.

"Tipcuca." *See* Wilson, T. P. Cameron

Tipper, Elizabeth *(fl. 1698–1704)*
Pilgrim's Viaticum; or, The Destitute, But Not Forlorn, *sels.*
To a Young Lady that Desired a Verse of My Being Servant One Day, and Mistress Another.

Tippett, James Sterling (1885–1958)
Familiar Friends.
Hang Out the Flag.

Tipping, Richard (b. 1949)
Casino.
Just after Michael's Death, the Game of Pool.
Mangoes are not cigarettes.
Men at Work.
Poet at Work.
When you're feeling kind of bonkers.

Tipputtolar
Red is the battlefield.

Tipton, James
All day.

Tirolien, Guy (b. 1917)
Ghetto.
Little Black Boy's Prayer, A.
Marie Galante.
Soul of the Black Land, The.

Tirumalesh, K. V. (b. 1940)
Face to Face.

Titherage, Dion (1889–1934)
And Her Mother Came Too.

Tjinapirrgarri
Emu Shot.

Tkachenko, Aleksandr Petrovich (b. 1945)
Requiem for Eduard Streltsov.

Tô Giang Tử' (Nguyễn Quang Nha) (b. 1908)
Congratulating a Friend On His New Dentures.

Tô Hũ'u Nguyễn Kim Thành (b. 1920)
Cradlesong, A.
Cuckoo calls its flock—it's when the rice, The.
Elephants.
Orphans.
Prison Thoughts.
Since then, inside me, summer has blazed up.
Song on the River of Perfumes, The.
Three sounds sum up the sense of life.

Todd, Alice
If I take an acorn.
Postman, The.

Todd, Ruthven (b. 1914)
Joan Miró ("After that war, when death had gone away.")
Joan Miró ("Once there were peasant pots and a dry brown hare.")
Mantelpiece of Shells, A.
Of Moulds and Mushrooms.
Paul Klee.
Poem: "I walk at dawn across the hollow hills."
Sea Horse, The.
Trout Flies.
Upon This Rock.

Todhunter, John (1839–1916)
Irish Love Song, An.
Utter Passion Uttered Utterly, An.

Todorovski, Gane
Peaceful Step, A.

Todros ben Judah Abulafia
From Prison.

Toerien, Barend (b. 1921)
Absent Daughter.
Campi Flegrei.
Firmament Displays on High, The.
Quatrain: "My bloodstream chokes on gall and spleen."
Youth.

Tofte, Robert (d. 1620)
Laura, *sels.*

Tolkien, John Ronald Reuel (1892–1973)
Cat on the Mat.
Man in the Moon Stayed up To Late, The.
Oliphaunt.

Toller, Ernst (1893–1939)
Book I Held Grew Cold, The.
Corpses in the Wood.
O Heavy Step of Slow Monotony.
O Master Masons.
O My Swallows!
One Who Struggles, The.
To the Mothers.

Tollerud, Jim
Bird of Power.
Buzz.
Earth.
Elementary.
Eye of God.
Rainier.
Sunrise.
Thirsty Island.
Week-Seek.

Tollet, Elizabeth (1694–1754)
Hypatia, *sels.*
On a Death's Head.
On Loving Once and Loving Often.
On the Prospect from Westminster Bridge.
Rose, The.
To My Brother at St. John's College in Cambridge.
Winter Song.

Tolson, Melvin Beaunearus (1898–1966)
African China.
Black boy / let me get up from the white man's table of fifty sounds.
Dark Symphony.
Ex-Judge at the Bar, An.
Festus Conrad.
Harlem Gallery, *sels.*
Harlem Gallery: Book I, The Curator, The, *sels.*
Legend of Versailles, A.
Lena Lovelace.
Libretto for the Republic of Liberia, *sels.*
Mu.
Note, The.
Old Houses.
Old Pettigrew.
Satchmo.
Toulouse Lautrec.
Victor Garibaldi.
Workaday Morning.

Tomioka, Taeko (b. 1935)
Girlfriend.
Just the Two of Us.
Life Story.
Please Say Something.

Tomkiw, Lydia (b. 1959)
Last Night in Elvisville.

New York Love Song (Part 1—Lower East
    Side), sels.

Tomlinson, Charles (b. 1927)
Ararat.
At Barstow.
At Delft.
Atlantic, The.
Cavern, The.
Chances of rhyme, The.
Charlotte Corday.
Chestnut Avenue: at Alton House, The.
Civilities of Lamplight.
Crane, The.
Death in the Desert, A.
Death of Will, The.
Descartes and the Stove.
Distinctions.
Door, The.
Dream, A.
Farewell to Van Gogh.
Fiascherino.
How still the hawk.
Icos.
In Arden.
In Defence of Metaphysics.
In the Borghese Gardens.
Jam Trap, The.
John Maydew or The Allotment.
Juliet's Garden.
Las Trampas U. S. A.
Macduff.
Mr. Brodsky.
On a Pig's Head.
On the Hall at Stowey.
On Water.
Oxen: Ploughing at Fiesole.
Paring the Apple.
Picture of J. T. in a Prospect of Stone, The.
Poem: "Upended, it crouches on broken
    limbs."
Return to Hinton.
Rhymes.
Shaft seemed like a place of sacrifice, The.
Snow Signs.
Swimming Chenango Lake.
Through Binoculars.
Tramontana at Lerici.
Two Views of Two Ghost Towns.
Ute Mountain.
Winter Encounters.
Word in Edgeways, A.

Tomoana, Paraire Henare (1868–1946)
Full Tide.
Waters of Waiapu, The.

Tompson, Benjamin (1642–1714)
Chelmsfords Fate.
Edmund Davie 1682; Annagram.
Marlburyes Fate.
New-Englands Crisis.
On a Fortification at Boston Begun by
    Women.
Seaconk or Rehoboths Fate.
Supplement, A.
To My Honoured Patron Humphery Davie.
Town Called Providence, Its Fate, The.

**"Tomson, Graham R." See Watson, Rosamund
Marriott**

Tomson, Graham R.
Ballad of the Werewolf, sels.

Tôn Thất Diệm (fl. 20th cent.)
To a Piggy Bank.

Tonkin, S.
Limerick: "Since my overdraft threatens to
    be."

Tonks, Rosemary
Farewell to Kurdistan.
Story of a Hotel Room.

Tooker, Lewis Frank (1855–1925)
Last Fight, The.

Toomer, Jean (1894–1967)
Beehive.
Blue Meridian, The, sels.
Cotton Song.
Delivered at the Knighting of Lord Durgling
    by Great Bruce-Jean.
Evening Song.

Face.
Georgia Dusk.
Harvest Song.
Her Lips Are Copper Wire.
I sit in my room.
It is Everywhere.
Lost Dancer, The.
Merl.
November Cotton Flower.
People.
Portrait in Georgia.
Prayer.
Reapers.
Seventh Street.
Song of the Son.

Toplady, Augustus Montague (1740–78)
Living and Dying Prayer for the Holiest
    Believer in the World, A.

Torlino
Therefore I Must Tell the Truth.

Torregian, Sotère (b. 1941)
Newark Public Library Reading Room, The.
Poem for the Birthday of Huey P. Newton.
Travois of the Nameless.

Torrence, Frederic Ridgely (1875–1950)
Adam's Dying.

Tosh, Peter (1944–1988?)
African.

Toshiko, Takada (b. 1916)
Seacoast at Mera, The.

Toshinari, Fujiwara No
I remember a grass hut.
Twilight.

Toshiyuki (Fujiwara no Toshiyuki)
Although it is not plainly visible to the eye.
    From Kokin Shu
Autumn has come invisibly.
In the Bay of Sumi.

Tóth, Judit (b. 1936)
Dead Embryos.
February. Germination's moment.
Forest.
Masks.
Murmuring.
Outskirts, Afternoon.
To the Newborn.
Two Cities.

"Totius" (1877–1935)
Forgive and Forget.

Toulson, Shirley
Amber.

Toure, Askia M. (b. 1958)
Frontier of rage that exists, The.

Touré, Askia Muhammad (b. 1938)
Floodtide.
JuJu.
O Lord of Light! A Mystic Sage Returns to
    Realms of Eternity!
Tauhid.

Tourneur, Cyril (1575?–1626)
Revenger's Tragedy, The, sels.

Toussaint L'Ouverture, Isaac (1782–1854)
Farewell: "Shores of my native land."

Towanbucket
Limerick: "There once was a doctor who
    said."
Limerick: "There was a French bard who
    said: 'Hell!'"

Towle, Tony (b. 1939)
North.
Painting the Eaves.
Random (Re-arrangeable) Study for Views.

Towne, Anthony (1928–80)
Dead of Winter.

Towne, Charles Hanson (1877–1949)
Around the Corner ("Around the corner I
    have a friend.")
At Nightfall.
Roof-tops, roof-tops, what do you cover?

Townsend, Ann (fl. 20th cent.)
Eighteenth-Century Medical Illustration: The
    Infant in its Little Room.

Townsend, Charles (1789–1870)
On the Lake Poets.

Townsend, Emily
Fish.

Townsend, F. H. (b. 1893)
O Cuckoo! shall I call thee Bird.

Townsend, George Alfred (1841–1914)
Fire Guest, The.

Townsend, Mary Ashley ("Xariffa") (b. 1832)
Creed.

**Townshend [or Townsend], Aurelian (c.1583–
c.1651)**
Dialogue betwixt Time and a Pilgrim[e], A.
Elegie Made by Mr. Aurelian Townshend in
    Remembrance of the Ladie Venetia Digby,
    An.
Let not thy beauty make thee proud.
Paradox, A.
Pure Simple Love.
Though regions far [or farr] divided.
To the Countesse of Salisbury.
To the Lady May.
Upon Kind[e] and True Love.
Youth and Beauty.

Toxaoci
I don't know why you tell me I'm drunk.

Traherne, Thomas (1636–74)
Bible, The.
Christendom.
Christian Ethics, sels.
Dreams.
Eden.
Hosanna.
In Salem dwelt a glorious king.
Innocence.
Insatiableness.
Love.
Meditations on the Six Days of the Creation,
    sels.
My Spirit.
On Christmas-Day.
On Leaping over the Moon.
On the Bible.
Poverty.
Preparative, The.
Rapture, The.
Return, The.
Right Apprehension.
Salutation [or Salutations], The.
Serious and a Curious Night-Meditation, A.
Shadows in the Water.
Thanksgivings for the Beauty of His
    Providence.
Third Century, The, sels.
To the same purpose: he, not long before.
Walking.
Wonder.

Trai, Nguyen (1380–1442)
Cat, The.

Traill, Henry Duff (1842–1900)
After Dilettante Concetti.
Puss and the Boots, The, sels.

Trainin, Avner (b. 1928)
Cat in the Dovecote.
Sunbeams.

Trajan (Marcus Ulpius Traianus) (A.D. 53–117)
Point your nose to the sun.

Trakl, Georg (1887–1914)
De Profundis.
Dejection.
Downfall.
Evening, The.
Grodek.
In the East.
Lament: "Sleep and death, the dusky eagles."
Night.
Rats, The.
Revelation and Decline.
Romance to Night, A.
Summer.
Trumpets.

Trần Cao Vân (1866–1916)
It's mere child's play to die—who'd care to
    try?
On Poulo Condore.

Trần Dạ Tù' (Lê Hà Vĩnh) (b. 1940)
Drinking Song, A.
Gifts as Tokens of Love.

New Lullaby, The.

Trần Đú'c Uyễn (b. 1941)
Letter to My Future Child, A.

Trần Gia Thoai (*fl.* 20th cent.)
Falling Leaf, A.
Night Train, The.

Trân, Hoàng Pham. *See* Nhu'o'ng Tổng

Trần Huiền Ân (Trần Sĩ Huệ) (b. 1937)
My Mother's Son.
Old Vow, The.

Trần Huy Liệu (1901–69)
Down-and-Out Fighter and the Spring
Nymph, A.
Dropping By the Guava Graveyard in So'n-
La.
What's My Crime?

Tran Minh-tong (King)
Bạch-đằng River, The.
Farewell to two envoys from the Yüan court.

Trần Minh Tu'ó'c (b. 1913)
Prison Dreams.

Trần Mộng Tú (*fl.* 20th cent.)
New Year's Wish for a Little Refugee, A.

Trần Tế Xu'o'ng (1870–1907)
Actors.
Best Wishes for the New Year.
Drought.
Lamenting the State of Confucian
Scholarship.
Looking Far Ahead.
Man Has Lost His Way, A.
New-Style Examinations.
No, Thank You!
Poor and Happy.
Tomorrow, should I fail, I'll go away.
What earthly use are these Confucian graphs?

Trần Tuấn Khải (1894–1983)
Our Land, Our Home.

Tranströmer, Tomas (b. 1931)
After a Death.
Allegro.
Below Freezing.
Breathing Space July.
Man Awakened by a Song Above His Roof,
The.
Morning Bird Songs.
Open and Closed Space.
Outskirts.
Scattered Congregation, The.
Sketch in October.
Solitude.
Standing Up, *sels.*
Syros.
Track.

Tranter, John (b. 1943)
Alphabet Murders, The, *sels.*
Backyard.
Crying in Early Infancy, *sels.*
Death Circus, The.
Debbie and Co.
Enzensberger at 'Exiles.'
Glow-boys.
Great Artist Reconsiders the Homeric Simile,
The.
Having Completed My Fortieth Year.
Lufthansa.
Mark finished it himself, choosing midnight.
Moment of Waking, The.
Un-American Women, The.

Trapnell, Anna (c.1622–c.1660)
Cry of a Stone, A, *sels.*

Trapp, Joseph (1679–1747)
Epigram: "King, observing with judicious
eyes, The."

Traubel, Horace Logo (1858–1919)
Chants Communal, *sels.*
How Are You, Dear World, This Morning?

Travis, Nancy (b. 1967)
At My Father's House.
Church Ladies.
Sunbathing.

Traxler, Patricia
Death of a Distant In-law.

Treasone, Grace
Life is like a jagged tooth.

Tree-Leaf Woman
Who speaks the sound of an echo?

Treece, Henry (1912–66)
Conquerors.
Horror.
Magic Wood, The.
That summer, the red may and the white may
made.
Three Pleas.

Trefusis, Elizabeth (*fl* early 19th cent.)
Valentine, A, *sels.*

Tregear, Edward (1846–1931)
Te Whetu Plains.

Tregian, Francis (1548–1608)
Imprisoned Recusant Writes to His Wife, An.

Tregonning, Charley
Cousin Jack Song.

Trejo, Ernesto
Cloud Unfolding, The.

Tremayne, Sydney (b. 1920)
Burial, A.
Legend.
Moses.
Wanting News.

Tremblay, Bill
Home Front.
Mayday.

Tremblay, Gail (b. 1945)
Indian Singing in 20th Century America.
It Is Important.
Medicine Bearer.
Night Gives Old Woman the Word.
Not Sense.
Reflections on a Visit to the Burke Museum,
University of Washington, Seattle.
To Grandmother on Her Going.

Trench, Herbert (1865–1923)
Charge, A.
I Heard a Soldier.
Jean Richepin's Song.
She Comes Not When Noon Is on the Roses.

Trench, M.
Limerick: "Dear Sir, You're quite wrong
about me."

Trench, Richard Chenevix (1807–86)
Power of Prayer, The.

Trevor, Scott
Kite, A.

Trinh Tiên
Woman Writes to Her Daughter Who's
Studying Overseas, A.

Trinh, Tru'o'ng Khuông. *See* Kiên Giang

Trinh, Võ thị Hoài. *See* Minh Đú'c Hoài Trinh

Trinidad, David (b. 1953)
C'est Plus Qu'en Crime, C'est une Faute.
Double Trouble.
Hockney: Blue Pool.
Movin' with Nancy.

Tripathi, Suryakant. *See* "Nirala"

Tripathy, Sunanda (b. 1964)
Tryst.

Trivelpiece, Laurel
Nursery, The.

Tropp, Stephen (b. 1930)
My Wife Is My Shirt.

Trotter, Catherine (1679–1749)
Agnes De Castro, *sels.*
Queen Catharine; or, The Ruines of Love,
sels.
To Mrs. Manley.

Troupe, Quincy (b. 1943)
Boomerang: A Blatantly Political Poem.
Conjuring Against Alien Spirits.
Conversation Overheard.
Day in the Life of a Poet, A.
Dirge: "It is the endless dance of the dead."
For Malcolm Who Walks in the Eyes of Our
Children.
Four and More; for Miles Davis.
Impressions / of Chicago; For Howlin' Wolf.
In Jimmy's Garden.
In Texas Grass.
Leaving Los Angeles.
Poem for Friends.

Poem for "Magic," A.
Poem for My Father.
Reflections on Growing Older.
River Town Packin House Blues.
Sense of Coolness, A.
Snake-Back Solo.
Syntax of the mind grips, The.
View from Skates in Berkeley, The.
You come to me.

Trowbridge, John Townsend (1827–1916)
Circumstance.
Darius Green and His Flying-Machine.
Farmer John.
Filling an Order.
Idyl of Harvest Time, An.
Old Lobsterman, The.
Recollections of "Lalla Rookh."
Vagabonds, The.

Truax, Hawley (1889–1978)
Half of a clasping of the hands.
Morning, Noon, And.

Trubin, Aleksandr (b. 1961)
And we kill blood.

Trubridge, B. A.. *See* "Vrepont, Brian"

Trudell, Dennis
Hotel in Paris.

Trumbull, John (1750–1831)
M'Fingal, *sels.*
Progress of Dulness, The, *sels.*
Prospect of the Future Glory of America.

Tru'o'ng Anh Th&ulodot;y (*fl.* 20th cent.)
First Day of School, The.

Trussell, Donna
Snow,
This Woman.

Truth, Sojourner (1797–1883)
Ain't I a Woman?

**Tryapkin [*or* Triapkin], Nikolai Ivanovich (b.
1918)**
How much there was of everything:
kettledrums and horns and bells!
Verses about the Dog's Inheritance, *sels.*
We banished the tyrant-tsars.

Trypanis, Constantine A.
Cock at Sea.

Tryphon
Terpander.

Ts'ai Yen (162?–239?)
Eighteen Verses Sung to a Tatar Reed
Whistle, *sels.*
Lamentation, The.

Tsakak
I'm gonna die & won't see you all any more.

Tsaloumas, Dimitris (b. 1921)
Autumn Supper.
Consolation.
Falcon Drinking.
Grudge, The.
Note.
Old Friend.
Progressive Man's Indignation, A.
Return of an Ikon.
Rhapsody of Old Men, A, *sels.*

Ts'an, Ts'en. *See* Ts'en Shen

Ts'ao Chih (192–232)
Ballad of the Orioles in the Fields.
Cock-fight, The.
Forsaken Wife, The.
Presented to Piao, the Prince of Pai-ma.
Rhyme-Prose on the Goddess of the Lo.
Roaming Immortal.
Ruins of Lo-yang, The.
Seven Poems of Lament.
Song of Heavenly Ascent.
Song of Lament, A.
Vision, A.
Written on Parting from Mr. Ying.

Ts'ao P'i (187–226)
Deep and boundless, the long autumn night.
In the northwest there is a drifting cloud.
Lotus Lake.
Lotus Pond, The.
Song of Yen.

Ts'ao Sung (*fl.* c.870–c.920)
Protest in the Sixth Year of Ch'ien Fu, A.

Ts'ao Ts'ao (155–220)
Song on Enduring the Cold.
Viewing the Ocean.

Tsatsos, Ioanna (b. 1919)
Chios.
Protest.

Ts'en Shen (Ts'en Ts'an) (715–70)
Autumn Thoughts.
Composed at Sunset at the Dunes of Ho-yen.
Fisherman.
On Climbing the Pagoda of the Temple of
   Gracious Benevolence with Kao Shih and
   Hsüeh Chü.
Replying to "On the Occasion of Morning
   Audience after Snow" Poem by Assistant
   Secretary Wang of the Board of Sacrifices.
Song of the Bay Steed of Governor Wei, A.
Song of the Running Horse River, A:
   Presented on Seeing General Feng Off on
   a Campaign to the West.
Song of the White Snow: Saying Farewell to
   Supervisor Wu Returning to the Capital.

Tseng Jui (fl. c.1300)
Tune: "Sheep on Mountain Slope"—
   Lamenting the Times, sels.

Tso Ssu (fl. 3d cent.)
Day Dreams.
Scholar in the Narrow Street, The.

Tso Yen-nien (fl. 3d cent.)
Call to Arms.

Tsogyel, Yeshe (757?–817?)
Listen.

Ts'ui Hao (704–54)
By the City Gate.
Songs of Ch'ang-kan

Tsui, Kitty
Chinese Banquet, A.
How Can I Show This Poem to Geraldine?
It's in the Name.

Tsung Ch'en (1525–60)
Drinking at the Cave Mouth.
Excursion to the Suburbs, An, sels.
Miscellaneous Words on the Lake, sels.
On Hearing That the Sea-Barbarians Are
   About To Attack Hu-chou—Expressing My
   Feelings to Tzu-yü.
On Things Seen, sels.
Sent to Yü Te-fu upon His Receipt of an
   Official Commission to the Two Che's,
   sels.
Snowstorm: At a Gathering at Chang Chu-
   fu's House, with Tzu-yeh Attending, We
   All Wrote Poems on This Subject—I Got
   the Ryhme-Word, "Hu."
Snowy Mountains.
Song of Chiang-nan, sels.
Song of Meeting.
Song of Selling Flowers.

Tsurayuki (Ki no Tsurayuki) (c.868–c.946)
I went out in the Spring.
Time I went to see my Sister, The. From
   Shui Shu.
When.

Tsvetayeva, Marina Ivanovna (1892–1941)
And, not crying in vain.
André Chénier.
Ars.
Attempt at Jealousy, An.
Bethlehem.
Cycle Akhmatova, The, sels.
Daughter of Jairus, The, sels.
Desk, sels.
Fatal volume, The.
God (3).
Gold that was my hair has turned, The.
Homesickness! that long / Exposed
   weariness!
I bless the daily labor of my hands.
I know the truth—give up all other truths!
I'd like to live with you.
If the soul was born with pinions.
Insomnia, sels.
Magdalene.
March, sels.
Poem of the End, sels.
Praise to the Rich.

Readers of Newspapers.
Two Songs, sels.
We shall not escape Hell, my passionate.
Where does this tenderness come from?
White low sun, low thunderclouds; and back,
   A.
You, walking past me.

**Tsvetkov, Aleksey [or Aleksei] Petrovich (b.
1947)**
I had a dream. I walked in a field of feather
   grass.
Pupil of fever chills and bewilderment, A.
To be mistaken in old age and not to be
   afraid.
What remained of our meetings?
Yes, it's me. I appear thus to myself.

Tsybin, Vladimir Dmitrievich (b. 1932)
Eyes.

Tù' Diễn Dồn
Long Night, The.

Tu Fu (712–76)
Another Spring.
At Horizon's End, Thinking of Li Po.
At the Corner of the World.
Autumn Meditation.
Autumn Thoughts, sels.
Autumn wastes are each day wilder, The.
Banquet at the Tso Family Manor.
Brimming Water.
By the Winding River I.
By the Winding River II.
Chengtu.
Ch'iang Village, sels.
Chüeh-chü.
City of White Emperor, The.
Clear After Rain.
Clear Evening after Rain.
Climbing the Heights.
Coming Home Late at Night.
Country Cottage.
Dawn Over the Mountains.
Deep in Winter.
Dejeuner Sur L'Herbe.
Dreaming of Li Po.
Elegant Women, The.
Emperor, The.
Empty Purse, The.
Excursion, The.
Far Up the River.
Farewell of an Old Man.
Farewell Once More to My Friend Yen at
   Feng Chi Station.
For Li Po.
Frontier Songs, First Series, sels.
Full Moon.
Guest Arrives, A.
Homecoming—Late at Night.
I Pass the Night at General Headquarters.
I Spend the Night in a Room by the River.
Jade Flower Palace.
Journey North.
Loneliness.
Lovely lady, fairest of the time.
Man with No Family to Take Leave of, The.
Meandering River, sels.
Midnight.
Moon Festival.
Moonlight Night.
New Moon.
Night.
Night in the House by the River.
Night in the Villa by the River.
Night Thoughts aboard a Boat.
Night Thoughts While Travelling.
No Word.
On Climbing the Heights on the Ninth Day
   of the Ninth Moon.
On the Border, First Series, sels.
On the River.
On the Spur of the Moment.
Overlooking the Desert.
Passing Chao-ling Again.
Prelude: "This fugitive between the Earth and
   Sky."
Presented to Wei Pa, Gentleman in
   Retirement.

Quatrain: "Before you praise Spring's advent
   note."
Quatrain: "Beyond the gate the cormorant
   had gone and not returned."
Quatrain: "Birds the more white, against
   green stream."
Quatrain: "I lounge on the jetty in the
   fragrance of catalpa."
Quatrain: "Late sun, the stream and the hills;
   the beauty."
Rain, Four Poems, sels.
Random Pleasures.
Recruiting Officer of Shih-hao.
Restless Night.
Restless Night in Camp, A.
Return, The.
Seven Songs Written During the Ch'ien-yüan
   Era, sels.
Seven Songs Written while Living at T'ung-
   ku in 759.
Snow Storm.
Song of P'eng-ya.
Song of the Beautiful Ladies.
Song of the Vermeil Phoenix.
South Wind.
Spring.
Spring Night, A—Rejoicing in Rain.
Spring Prospect.
Spring Rain.
Stars and Moon on the Yangtse.
Strolling along the Riverbank, Looking for
   Flowers, sels.
Summer Night.
Sunset glitters on the beads.
They Say You're Staying in a Mountain
   Temple.
Thinking of My Brothers on a Moonlit Night.
Thoughts on Historical Sites: Wang Chao-
   chün.
Tired Night, A.
To Li Po.
To Li Po at the Sky's End.
To Li Po on a Spring Day.
To My Younger Brother, sels.
To Pi Ssu Yao.
To Wei Pa, a Retired Scholar.
Traveler at Night Writes His Thoughts, A.
Travelling Northward.
Two Poems on Night.
Upon Seeing the Fireflies.
Visiting Tsan, Abbot of Ta-Yun.
Visitors.
Waiting for Audience on a Spring Night.
Willow, The.
Winter Dawn.
Written on the Thirtieth Day, Ninth Month,
   Second Year of the Ta-li Reign [767].
Written on the Wall at Chang's Hermitage.
Yangtse and Han.

Tu Hsün-ho (846–907)
Climbing to a Mountain Monastery.
Traveler's Thoughts.

Tu Mu (803–53)
At Clear Brook in Ch'ih-chou.
Autumn Evening.
Climbing to Lo-yu Plateau, before Leaving
   for Wu-hsing.
Climbing Up to the Lo-yu Plain.
Crane, The.
Early Geese.
Easing My Heart.
Egrets.
Farewell Poem, sels.
Gate Tower of Ch'i-an City, The.
In Ch'i-an, on a Chance Theme, sels.
On the Road.
Pien River Blocked by Ice.
Pond in a Basin.
Pool behind Ch'i-an, The.
Recalling Former Travels, sels.
Red Embankment.
Red Slope, sels.
Retired Official Yüan's High Pavilion, The.
Returning Home.
Sent in Parting.
Shih Ch'ung's 'Golden Valley' Garden.
Sighing over Flowers.

Spring in Chiang-nan.
To Judge Han Ch'o at Yang-chou.
Travelling in the Mountains.
View from the Cliffs.
We Drink Farewell.

Tucker, F. Bland (b. 1895)
All praise to thee, for thou, O king divine.
Our Father, by Whose Name.

Tucker, Mary E. (b. 1838?)
Adieu.
All Alone.
Apple Dumplings.
Arria to Poetus.
Autumn Thoughts.
Beautiful Sea, The.
Beautiful, The! what is not perfect here
   below.
Blight of Love, The.
Burial of a Fairy Queen.
Charley du Bignon.
Child Life.
Christmas Eve, South, 1865.
Christmas, South, 1866.
Crazed.
Crushed Flower, The.
"Did You Call Me, Father?"
Disappointment.
Drink On.
Drunkard's Wife, The.
Evanishings.
Family Portraits.
Father's Love, The.
First Grey Hair, The.
Found—Who Lost?
Gone, with all her sparkling beauty.
Heart's Ease.
Hope.
Hugging the Shore.
Humming-Bird, The.
I Am Fashion's Toy.
I am Weary, Mother.
I Smile, but Oh! My Heart Is Breaking.
"I Was a Stranger and Ye Took Me In."
Kindness.
Kiss? A. Pray tell me, what is in a kiss.
Knitting.
Life.
Life for a Life.
Lift Me Higher.
Light in Darkness.
Lines on the Death of the Rev. S. K.
   Talmage.
Lines to an Old Dress.
Little Bell.
Loew's Bridge: A Broadway Idyl, sels.
Love-letter, A.
Mail Has Come, The.
Mine.
Mistletoe.
Mother's Lament, The.
Mrs. Myrick's Lecture.
My Mother's Voice.
Mysteries of Life.
No Letter.
Old Crib, The.
Only a Blush.
Opium-Eater, The.
Revenge.
Signal Gun, The.
Silvery Fountain.
Soldier Boy's Dream, The.
Speak to Her Tenderly.
Spring.
That Glove.
To Annie.
To Don Juan Baz.
To Fannie.
To Father.
To Mary.
To One Who Sleepeth.
Tryst, The.
Upon Receipt of a Pound of Coffee in 1863.
Wail of the Divorced.
We Met.
Weariness.

Tucker, St. George (1752–1827)
Cynic, The, sels.

Discontented Student, The.
Judge with the Sore Rump, The.

Tuckerman, Frederick Goddard (1821–73)
As sometimes in a grove at morning chime.
Coralie.
Cricket, The.
How Oft in Schoolboy Days.
Infatuation.
Last night I dreamed we parted once again.
November.
Question, The.
Rhotruda.
Sonnet: "And so, as this great sphere (now
   turning slow)."
Sonnets, sels.
Sonnets: First Series.
Sonnets: "Starry flower, the flower-like stars
   that fade, The."
Under the Locust Blossoms.

Tudur Aled (fl. c.1480–c.1525)
Stallion, The.

Tuéni, Nadia (1935–1983)
More distant than the dead sea.
Nothing but a man.
Would you come back if I said the earth.

Tung-shan (807–69)
If you look for the truth outside yourself.

Tu'o'ng Phô (Đỗ thị Đàm) (b. 1900)
Who is that soldier, hero of my heart?

Tuqan, Fadwa (b. 1917)
After Twenty Years.
Behind Bars, Sel.
Face Lost in the Wilderness.
From behind the Bars, sels.
I Won't Sell His Love.
Song of Becoming.

Turberville, George (c.1540–c.1610)
Epitaph of Maister Win Drowned in the Sea,
   An.
Lover to His Lady, The.
Lover Whose Mistress Feared a Mouse, The.
Of Drunkenness.
Of One That Had a Great Nose.
Poor Ploughman to a Gentleman for Whom
   He Had Taken a Little Pains, A.
To an Old Gentlewoman That Painted Her
   Face.
To His Friend.
To His Friend P. of Courting, Traveling,
   Dicing, and Tennis.
To his Love that sent him a Ring wherein
   was gravde, / Let Reason rule.
To Spencer.
Verse in Praise of Lord Henry Howard, Earl
   of Surrey, sels.

Turbyfill, Mark
Benediction.

Turco, Lewis (b. 1934)
Ordinary Evening in Cleveland, An.
Winter Bouquet.

Turk, Marie C.
Thank You, Jesus, for this day.

Turnbull, Gael (b. 1928)
Residues: Thronging the Heart.
They have taken my father.

Turner, Alberta (b. 1921)
Anyone, Lifting.
Drift.
Elm Street.
Fourth Wish.
In Love with Wholes.
Making Old Bones.
Meditation Upon Ought.
On the Nature of Food.
Three Easters.
Water Eased of Its Cliffs by Falling.

Turner, Ann
Clean.
Red-Dress Girl.
Red Flower.

Turner, Brian (b. 1944)
Coming home late through the smoky.
Nichita Stanescu.
Responses to Montale.

Turner, Charles Tennyson (1808–79)
Artist on Penmaenmawr, The.

Brilliant Day, A.
Buoy-Bell, The.
Calvus to a Fly.
Country Dance, A.
Drowned Spaniel, The.
From Harvest to January.
Gout and Wings.
Great Britain Through the Ice: Or, Premature
   Patriotism.
Letty's Globe.
Lion's Skeleton, The.
Old Ruralities: A Regret.
Old Stephen.
On a Vase of Gold-Fish.
On Seeing a Little Child Spin a Coin of
   Alexander the Great.
On Shooting a Swallow in Early Youth.
On the Eclipse of the Moon of October 1865.
Orion.
Seaside: In and Out of the Season, The.
Steam Threshing-Machine, The.
To a "Tenting" Boy.
White Horse of Westbury, The.
Wind on the Corn.

Turner, Darwin T. (b. 1931)
Love.

Turner, Elizabeth (1755–1846)
Canary, The.
How to Write a Letter.
Truth's the Best.
Two Little Miss Lloyds, The.

Turner, Frederick (b. 1943)
April Wind.
On the Pains of Translating Miklós Radnóti.
Spring Evening.

Turner, Godfrey (fl. c.1878)
Journal of Society, The.
Synchoresis.
Tattle.

Turner, Joseph Mallord William (1779–1851)
Foam's Frail Power.

Turner, Judy
Man on the Moon, The.
Rhapsodies.

Turner, Nancy Byrd (b. 1880)
Black and Gold.
Death Is a Door.
First Thanksgiving of All.
God's Plan for Spring.
Let Us Have Peace.
Old Quin Queeribus.
Washington.
When Young Melissa Sweeps.
Whenever I say "America."

Turner, Patty
Looking for Him.

Turner, S. C.
Limerick: "Youth and a maiden from
   Costessey, A."

Turner, Steve (b. 1951)
Christmas Is Really for the Children.

Turner, Walter James (1889–1946)
Dancer, The.
Ecstasy.
Epithalamium: "Can the lover share his soul."
Giraffe and Tree.
Hymn to Her Unknown.
In Time like Glass.
India.
Life and Death.
Lion, The.
Love-song: "Beautiful, delicate bright gazelle,
   The."
Magic.
Marriage.
Men Fade Like Rocks.
Music of a Tree, The.
Navigators, The.
Reflection.
Robber, The.
Romance.
Seven Days of the Sun, The, sels.
Silence.
Soldiers in a Small Camp.
Song: "Lovely hill-torrents are."
Sun has come, I know, The.

Talking with Soldiers.
Tragic Love.
Word Made Flesh, The.

Turner, William Price (b. 1927)
Alien.
Coronary Thrombosis.
University Curriculum.

Turochkin, Nikolai Karpovich. *See* "Otrada, Nikolai Karpovich"

Tusser, Thomas (c.1524–1580)
Five Hundred Points of Good Husbandry, *sels.*

Tuwhare, Hone (b. 1922)
Friend.
Heemi.
Monologue.
No Ordinary Sun.
Ron Mason.
Song in Praise of a Favourite Humming-Top, A.
Talk with My Cousin Alone, A.

Tuwim, Julian [*or* Juljan] (Juljan) (1894–1953)
Prayer, A: "I pray Thee O Lord."
Pursuit.
There Is No Country.

Tvardovsky [*or* Tvardovskii], Aleksandr Trifonovich (1910–71)
From a crumpled wartime diary.
No, I have not been cheated by life.
Vasily Tyorkin, *sels.*

"Twain, Mark" (Samuel Langhorne Clemens) (1835–1910)
Adventures of Huckleberry Finn, The, *sels.*
Aged Pilot Man, The.
Epitaph Placed on His Daughter's Tomb.
He Done His Level Best.
Imitation of Julia A. Moore.
Limerick: "Man hired by John Smith and Co., A."

Tweedy, Henry Hallam (1868–1953)
Eternal God, whose power upholds.
O Gracious Father of Mankind.

Twichell, Chase (b. 1950)
Aisle of Dogs.
Chanel No. 5.
Condom Tree, The.
Shades of Grand Central, The.
Six Belons.

Twiss, Horace (1786 *or* 1787–1849)
Fashion.
Our parodies are ended. These our authors.
Patriot's Progress, The.

Twomey, Catherine (b. c.1960)
Cliona.

Tyler, Parker (1907–74)
Anthology of Nouns.
Nijinsky.

Tyler, Royall (1757–1826)
Anacreontic to Flip.
Contrast, The, *sels.*
Gambling.
Hail to the Joyous Day.
Love Song: "By the fierce flames of love I'm in a sad taking."
Original Epitaph on a Drunkard.
Widower, The.

Tymnes (*fl.* 2d cent. B.C.)
Dear little bird, the Graces' favourite.
Don't let it matter much, Philaenis.
Epigrams, *sels.*
Eumelos had a Maltese dog.

Tynan, Katharine (Katharine Tynan Hinkson) (1861–1931)
Doves, The.
Farewell: "Not soon shall I forget—a sheet."
Holy Family.
Joining the Colours.
Leaves.
Making of Birds, The.
Man of the House, The.
Mater Dei.
Nightingale, The.
Pink Almond.
Sheep and Lambs.
Slow Spring.

Vision, The.
Wild Geese.
Witch, The.

Tysh, Chris
Porné, *sels.*

Tysh, George (b. 1942)
Genitalia.

Tyson, Ian. *See* John, Richard Johnny, Jerome Rothenberg *and* Ian Tyson

Tyutchev, Fyodor [*or* Feodor] Ivanovich (1803–73)
As Ocean's Stream.
At Vshchizh.
Last Love.

Tzara, Tristan (1896–1963)
Approximate Man, The, *sels.*
Chanson Dada.
Dada Manifesto on Feeble and Bitter Love, *sels.*
For Robert Desnos.
Great Lament of my Obscurity Three, The.
Maison Aragon.
Metal Coughdrops.
Poemes Negres, *sels.*
Waking.
Way.
Zurich Chronicle February 1916.
See also **Huelsenbeck, Richard, Marcel Janko** *and* **Tristan Tzara**

Tzu Yeh (*fl.* 3d–4th cent.)
Bare branches tremble, The.
I had not fastened my sash over my gown.
It is night again.

U

U Tam'si Tchicaya (b. 1929)
Bad Blood.
Brush-Fire.
Communion II.
Dance to the Amulets.
Debout, *sels.*
Epitomé (1962), *sels.*
Fragile, *sels.*
Headline to Summarize a Passion.
L'Arc Musical (1970), *sels.*
Le Ventre (1964), *sels.*
Mat to Weave, A.
Promenade, The.
Sea Nocturne.
Viaticum.

Uahupirapi, Dina
Imagination.

Úc, Lâm Thái. *See* **Mộng Tuyết**

Uceda, Julia (b. 1925)
Time Reminded Me.
2976.

Uda, Emperor (*fl.* 9th cent.)
Like a wave crest.

Udall, L. G.
Limerick: "Each Lon was a notable man."
Limerick: "Pulmonary tuberculosis."

Udall [*or* Udal], Nicholas (1305–56)
Ralph Roister Doister, *sels.*

Uflyand [*or* Ufliand], Vladimir (b. 1937)
It has for ages been observed.

Uhland, Ludwig (Johann Ludwig Uhland) (1787–1862)
Castle by the Sea, The.
Durand of Blonden.
Hostess' Daughter, The.
Ichabod! The Glory Has Departed.
In a Lovely Garden Walking.
Leaf falls softly at my feet, A.
Luck of Edenhall, The.
Spirits Everywhere.

Ujejski, Kornel (1823–97)
Polish Eagle, The.

Ukihashi (*fl.* late 17th cent.)
Whether I sit or lie.

Ukon, Lady (*fl.* 10th cent.)
I am forgotten now.

Ulacia, Manuel (b. 1953)
Stone at the Bottom, The.

Ulinover, Miriam (1890–1944)
Havdolah Wine.
In the Courtyard.

Ullman, Leslie (b. 1947)
Dawn Feeding.
Desire.
Dreams by No One's Daughter.
Living Near the Plaza of Thieves.
Mauve.
Peace.
Running.

Uloccanar
What Her Girl Friend Said, Consoling Her when She Was Distressed by the Town's Gossip.
What Her Girl Friend Said, the Lover within Earshot, behind a Fence.

Ulrich, Anton (1633–1714)
Dying Song.

Unaipon, David. *See* **Ngunaitponi**

Unamuno, Miguel de (1864–1936)
Throw Yourself Like Seed.

Under, Marie (1883–1980)
Alone with the Sea.
And a Star Fell.
Morning Joy.

U'ng Bình (1877–1961)
Retired Mandarin's Wife Complains, A.

Ungar, Lynn
Common Prayer.

Ungaretti, Giuseppe (1888–1970)
Agony.
Babel.
Brothers.
Christmas.
I Am a Creature.
Italy.
Morning.
No More Crying Out.
Rivers.
San Martino del Carso.
Soldiers.
Vigil.
You Were Broken.
You Were Shattered.

Unger, Barbara
Pillar of Flame.

Unik, Pierre
Manless Society, The.

Untermeyer, Jean Starr (1886–1970)
Autumn.
Country of No Lack.
Dew on a Dusty Heart.
False Enchantment.
High Tide.
Lake Song.
Passionate Sword, The.
Sinfonia Domestica.

Untermeyer, Louis (1885–1977)
Caliban in the Coal Mines.
Dance of Dust, The.
Dark Chamber, The.
End of the Comedy.
Feuerzauber.
Food and Drink.
Glad Day.
Goliath and David.
Infidelity.
Irony.
Koheleth.
Last Words before Winter.
Long Feud.
Mother Goose Up-to-Date, *sels.*
On Hearing Prokofieff's Grotesque for Two Bassoons, Concertina and Snare-Drums.
Portrait of a Machine.
Prayer for This House.
Prayer: "God, though [*or* although] this life is but a wraith."
Relativities.
Repentance.
Sagging Bough, The.
Scarcely Spring.
Song Tournament: New Style.
To a Vine-clad Telegraph Pole.
Wallflower to a Moonbeam.

Wind Gardens.

Unwin, Richard
Limerick: "My beard's overcrowded. Now that."

Updike, John (b. 1932)
Amish are a surly sect, The.
Bath after Sailing.
Bendix.
Child's Calendar, A, *sels.*
Dea ex Machina.
Dog's Death.
Ex-Basketball Player.
Great Scarf of Birds, The.
I Missed His Book, but I Read His Name.
In Extremis.
Insomnia the Gem of the Ocean.
January.
Love Sonnet.
Meditation on a News Item.
Movie House.
Naked Ape, The.
Newlyweds, The.
On the Inclusion of Miniature Dinosaurs in Breakfast Cereal Boxes.
Player Piano.
Recital.
Report of Health.
Richmond.
Sea Knell.
Seagulls.
September.
Seven Stanzas at Easter.
Snapshots.
Some Frenchmen.
Telephone Poles.
Upon Learning That a Bird Exists Called the Turnstone.
Upon Shaving Off One's Beard.
V. B. Nimble, V. B. Quick.
Vow.
Winter Ocean.

Upham, Thomas Cogswell (1799–1872)
Fear Not, Poor Weary One.

Upton, Charles
Panic Grass, *sels.*

Upton, Lee
Daughter, A.
Debt, The.
Lost Child.

Uraiyur Mutukorran
What the Passersby Said to the Lover Eloping with the Girl.

Urchard, T. (1611–60)
Truly Rich, The.

Urdang, Constance (b. 1922)
All Around Us.
At Frank 'n' Helen's.
Back Far Enough, Down Deep Enough.
Birth of Venus.
Children, The.
Evening of Home Movies, An.
Muse Is Always the Other Woman, The.
My Father's Death.
Old Wives' Tales.
Returning to the Port of Authority: A Picaresque.
This Poem.

Uribe, Armando
I love you and the rosebush.

Urin, Viktor Arkad'evich (b. 1924)
Oh, Maika in a maika, there's the smell of summer.

Urmy, Clarence Thomas (1858–1923)
Old Year, The.

Urrea, Luis Alberto (b. 1955)
Ghost Sickness.

Urriola, Joleen
Mister Snowman.

Uruttiran
Girl Friend Describes the Bull Fight, The.
What She Said to Her Girl Friend, and What Her Girl Friend Said in Reply.

Usborne, Richard (b. 1910)
Epitaph on a Party Girl.

Usha, S. (b. 1954)
To Mother.

Ushakov, Nikolai Nikolaevich (1899–1973)
Craftsmanship.
Lady Macbeth.
Wine.

Usher, Leila (1859–1955)
I Am the Cat.

Ushida, May
Deep in the rippling spring.

U'Tamsi, Felix Tchicaya [or TchiKaya] (Tchicaya U Tam'si) (b. 1929)
Scorner, The.

Uticensis, Cato (95–46 B.C.)
Catoes Morall Distichs: Translated and Paraphras'd, with variations of Expressing, in English verse, *sels.*
Cato's Moral Distichs Englished in Couplets, *sels.*

Utkin, Iosif Pavlovich (1903–44)
Komsomol Song.
Letter.
Tale of Red-Haired Motl, Mister Inspector, Rabbi Isaiah, and Commissar Blokh, The.

Uvavnuk (fl. 19th–20th cent.)
Great sea has set me in motion, The.

Uyematsu, Amy
December 7 always brings christmas early.
Fortune Cookie Blues.
Near Roscoe and Coldwater.
Same Month They Bombed Cambodia, The.

V

"V., B." See Thomson, James

Vacietis, Ojars
Burning Leaves.
Horse Dream.
Of nights / some bear.
Sunday.

Vade, Jean-Joseph (1719–57)
Three Amphigouris.

Vaginov, Konstantin Konstantinovich (1899–1934)
Song of Words.

"Vaidehi" (Janaki Srinivas Murthy) (b. 1945)
Girl in the Kitchen.

Vaiiunaite, Judita
Botticelli. Three candles. Soft lips suggesting a smile.
Four Portraits, *sels.*
Museum Street.
Penelope.

Vakaló, Eléni (b. 1921)
But there was / once / a time.
Genealogy.
My Father's Eye.
Song of the Hanged.

"Vala, Katri" (Karen Alice Heikel) (1901–44)
On the Meadow.
Winter Is Here.

Valek, Miroslav
Apple from the cupboard rolled to the floor, The.
Hearing.
Steel-Rod Benders.

Valentine, Jean (b. 1934)
After Elegies.
Anaesthesia.
April.
Bride's Hours, A.
December 21st.
Dream Barker.
Field, The.
First Love.
Forgiveness Dream.
He Said.
Living Together.
Messenger, The, *sels.*
My Mother's Body, My Professor, My Bower.
Orpheus and Eurydice.
Pilgrims.
Sasha and the Poet ("Sasha: I dreamed you and he.")

Second Dream, The.
Seeing You.
Sex.
Silences; a Dream of Governments.
Snow Landscape, in a Glass Globe.
Tell Me, What Is the Soul.
"X."

Valerius Flaccus, Gaius (d. c.93–5)
Argonautica, The, *sels.*

Valéry, Paul (1871–1945)
Bee, The.
Crusoe had provided all the necessaries and was more or less at leisure in.
Footsteps, The.
Girl with Mind Wandering.
Graveyard by the Sea, The.
Helen.
Helen, the Sad Queen.
Narcissus.

Valle, Isabel
Very Minor Poet Speaks, A.

Vallejo, César (1892–1938)
And don't bother telling me anything.
And what if after so many words.
Anger that Breaks the Man into Chidren, The.
Black Riders, The.
Black Stone on Top of a White Stone.
Distant Footsteps, The.
España, Aparta de me Este Caliz, *sels.*
Have You Anything to Say in Your Defense?
Hungry Man's Wheel, The.
I have a terrible fear of being an animal.
Our Daily Bread.
Poem to Be Read and Sung.
Right Meaning, The.
Rollcall of Bones, The.
Spider, The.
Telluric and Magnetic.
Trilce, *sels.*

Valli, Maria
Crows, The.

Van den Heever, C. M. (1902–57)
Fallen Zulu Commander, The.

Van den Heuvel, Cor
After the shower.
Autumn twilight.
Branch, A.
From behind me.
Geese have gone, The.
Hot night.
In the parking lot.
Late autumn.
My mind takes a leap.
November evening.
Raining at every window.
Shading his eyes.
Shadow in the folded napkin, The.
Starting to rise.
Stick goes over the falls at sunset, A.
Summer breeze.
Sun goes down, The.
Through the small holes.
Tidepool, A.
Twilight.

Van Doesburg, Theo (1883–1991)
Remembrance of the Founts of Night.
Still Life: The Table.

Van Doren, Mark (1894–1973)
Ancient Couple on Lu Mountain, The.
And did the animals in Noah's ark.
Apple Hell.
Burial.
City Songs.
Distant Runners, The.
Dream of Trains, A.
Escape, The.
Family Prime.
Former Barn Lot.
Gardener.
Good Appetite.
History Lesson.
Immortal.
Moments He Remembers, The.
Praise Him Who Makes Us Happy.
Proper Clay.

Pulse, The.
Runaways, The.
Seven Sleepers, The.
Sleep, grandmother, sleep.
Slowly, Slowly Wisdom Gathers.
Whisperer, The.
Why, Lord ("Why Lord, must something in
    us.")
Van Duyn, Mona (b. 1921)
Ballad of Blossom, The.
Falling in Love at Sixty-Five.
Footnotes to "The Autobiography of Bertrand
    Russell," *sels.*
Gardener to His God, The.
Homework.
Into Mexico.
Late Loving.
Leda.
Leda Reconsidered.
Letters from a Father.
Moose in the Morning, Northern Maine.
Open Letter from a Constant Reader.
Sonnet for Minimalists.
Stream, The.
Talker, The.
Twins, The.
View, A.
Vision Test, The.
What the Motorcycle Said.
Wish to Be Believed, The.
Van Dyke, Henry (1852–1933)
America for Me.
America's Welcome Home.
Four Things [a man must learn to do].
Jesus, Thou Divine Companion.
Lost Word of Jesus, A.
Mile with Me, A.
Peace Hymn of the Republic.
These Are the Gifts I Ask.
Toiling of Felix, The, *sels.*
Van Ostaijen, Paul (1896–1928)
Murderers, The.
Van Rooten, Luis d'Antin (1906–73)
Mots d'Heures: Gousses, Rames, *sels.*
Van Sertima, Ivan (b. 1935)
Volcano.
Van Toorn, Peter (b. 1944)
Mountain Study.
Shake'nbake Ballad.
Van Vliet, Eddy (b. 1942)
City is covered with places you, The.
Coastline never alters for the fisherman, The.
Courtyard, The.
Old Champagne Glass.
Party.
Valediction—To My Father.
Van Vriesland, Victor (b. 1891)
Ars Poetica.
Evening.
Van Walleghen, Michael (b. 1938)
Age of Reason, The.
Blue Tango.
Driving into Enid.
Meat.
Van Wyk, Chris (b. 1957)
Ballot and the Bullet, The.
Reason why, The.
Van Zyl, Tania (b. 1908)
Horses of Marini, The.
House with coarse stuccoed, The.
Man with the Hollow Breast, The.
Rope, The.
She Waited.
Two Women.
Vanada, Lillian Schulz
Fuzzy wuzzy, creepy crawly.
Vance, Thomas H.
Frozen Hero, The.
Vando, Gloria
Chimayo.
New York City Mira Mira Blues.
Vanhomrigh, Esther (*fl.* early 18th cent.)
Hail, blushing goddess, beauteous Spring!
"Vanolis, Bysshe." *See* Thomson, James
Vanparanar
Price of Giving Too Much, The.

Woman and Her Dying Warrior, A.
Vanshenkin, Konstantin Iakovlevich (b. 1925)
Urchin, The.
Vardhill, Anna Jane (1781–1852)
To a Skeleton.
Varela, Blanca (b. 1926)
Before the Pacific.
Captain, The.
Nobody will open the door for you.
Things I Say Are True, The.
Varley, Jane
Before Throwing a Chicken into an Iowa
    Valley.
Varma, Archana (b. 1946)
Man.
Vas, István (b. 1910)
Catacombs.
Just This.
Tambour.
What Is Left?
Vashon, George Boyer (1824–78)
Vincent Ogé.
**Vasilyev [*or* Vasil'ev], Pavel Nikolaevich (1910–
37)**
Lines in Honor of Natalya.
Prince Foma.
Salt Riot, The, *sels.*
**Vasilyev [*or* Vasil'ev], Sergey Aleksandrovich
(1911–75)**
Pigeon of My Childhood.
**Vatsyayan, Sachidananda Hirananda. *See*
"Agyeya"**
Vaughan, Henry ("Silurist") (1622?–1695)
Abel's Blood.
Admission.
Anguish.
As time one day by me did pass.
Ascension-Day.
Ascension Hymn ("Dust and clay.")
Begging.
Bird, The.
Book, The.
British [*or* Brittish] Church, The.
Burial.
Charnel-house, The.
Childhood.
Christ's Nativity.
Cock-crowing.
Come, come, what doe I here?
Corruption.
Dawning, The.
Day of Judgement.
Death.
Dedication, The: "My God, thou that didst
    dye for me."
Disorder and Frailty.
Distraction.
Dressing.
Dwelling-Place, The.
Easter-Day.
Easter Hymn.
Eclipse, The.
Epitaph Upon the Lady Elizabeth, Second
    Daughter to his Late Majesty, An.
Evening-Watch, The.
Friends Departed.
H. Scriptures.
Holy Communion, The.
I walked [*or* walkt] the other day to spend
    my hour.
Idle Verse.
Incarnation and Passion, The.
Isaac's Marriage.
Jacob's Pillow, and Pillar.
Joy of My Life! While Left Me Here.
Kingdom of Heaven Compared to a Grain of
    Mustard-Seed, The.
Knot, The.
Lamp[e], The.
Leaves Come Again, The.
Love and Discipline.
Man.
Mans Fall, and Recovery.
Match, The.
Midnight.
Morning-Watch, The.

Mount of Olives.
Mount of Olives ("Sweet, sacred hill! on
    whose fair brow.")
Night, The, *sels.*
Palm-tree, The.
Passion, The.
Peace.
Pilgrimage, The.
Praise.
Pursuit[e], The.
Queer, The.
Quickness.
Rainbow, The.
Regeneration.
Relapse, The.
Religion.
Resolve, The.
Resurrection and Immortality.
Retirement.
Retreat[e], The.
Revival, The.
Rhapsody, A.
Rom. Cap. 8 Ver. 19.
Rules and Lessons.
Sap, The.
Search, The.
Seed Growing Secretly, The.
Shepherds [*or* Shepheards], The.
Shower [*or* Showre], The.
Showre, The.
Silence, and stealth of day[e]s! 'tis now.
Son-Days [dayes].
Starre, The.
Stone, The.
Storm, The.
Sure, there's a tic of bodies! and as they.
Tempest, The.
Timber, The.
To Amoret.
To Amoret Gone from Him.
To Amoret, of the Difference 'twixt Him and
    Other Lovers, and What True Love Is.
To Amoret, Walking in a Starry Evening.
To his retired friend, an Invitation to
    Brecknock, *sels.*
To My Ingenuous Friend, R. W.
To the Best, and Most Accomplished Couple.
To the Most Excellently Accomplished Mrs.
    Katherine Philips.
To the Pious Memory of C. W. Esquire.
Twenty-first Day of the Seventh Month.
Unprofitablenes.
Upon the Priory Grove, His Usual
    Retirement.
Vanity of Spirit.
Waterfall [*or* Water-Fall], The.
World, The (1).
Wreath, The.
Vaughan, Thomas (1622?–1666)
Stone, The.
Vaughan-Thomas, Wynford (b. 1908)
Farewell to New Zealand.
Hiraeth in N.W.3.
To His Not-so-coy Mistress.
Vautor, Thomas (*fl.* c.1590?)
Songs of Divers Airs and Natures, *sels.*
Sweet Suffolk owl, so trimly dight.
**Vaux, Thomas, 2d Baron Vaux of Harrowden
(1510–66)**
Age Looks Back at Youth.
Aged Lover Renounceth Love, The.
Death in Life.
Pleasures of Thinking, The.
Vayilanrevan
What She Said ("In the tiny village.")
**Vaynshteyn [*or* Weinstein], Berysh [*or* Berish]
(Berish Weinstein) (1905–67)**
New York Everywhere, *sels.*
Veale, Peter (b. 1919)
Bold Troubleshooters.
I put my hat upon my head.
Veenendaal, Cornelia
On My Fourteenth Wedding Anniversary I
    Ride on Trains.
Vega (b. 1954)
Brothers Loving Brothers.

Veiga, Marisella
New Refugee, A.

Velacan Maturai
Peace Poem.

Veliyanar Erumai
Horse Did Not Come Back, The.

Venantius Fortunatus (*fl.* 14th cent.)
Stedefast [*or* Steddefast *or* Steadfast]
cross[e], inmong [*or* among] alle [*or* all]
other.
To The Lady Radegund, With Violets.

Venantius Fortunatus, Saint (c.530–c.610)
Standards of the King go forth, The.

Venclova, Tomas
Dialogue in Winter.
In Memory of the Poet. Variant.
Night descended on us with a chill.
Shield of Achilles, The.
Villanelle.

Veneris, Pervigilium
Vigil of Venus, The, *sels.*

Venkorran
What She Said ("Are there others too.")

Venmanipputi
What She Said to Her Girl-Friend.

Venugopalan, T. S. (b. 1929)
Family Pride.

Vere, Mary Ainge De. *See* "Bridges, Madeline"

Vergil. *See* Virgil.

Verhaeren, Emile (1855–1916)
Poor, The.

Verlaine, Paul (1844–96)
Anointed Vessel.
Art Poétique.
Bad Sleeper, A.
Chansons d'Automne.
Clair de Lune.
Clymène, A.
Cortège.
Cythère.
En Bateau.
E's Finch.
Exchange Of Feelings, An.
Fantoches.
Femme et Chatte.
Il Pleut Doucement sur la Ville.
In that café crowded with fools we stood.
la Promenade, A.
L'Allée.
Mandoline.
Nevermore.
Pantomime.
Pensionnaires.
Sagesse, *sels.*
Spleen.
Thousand and Three, A.
You Would Have Understood Me.

Verma, Shrikant (1931–86)
Pleasure Dome, The.

Verstegan [*or* **Verstegen**]**, Richard**
(**Richardowlands**) (1565–1620)
Lullaby: "Upon my lap my sovereign sits."

Vertinsky [*or* **Vertinskii**]**, Aleksandr** [*or* **Viktor**
Fyodorovich] (1889–1957)
In the Moldavian Steppe.

Very, Jones (1831–80)
Autumn Flowers.
Autumn Leaves.
Barberry Bush, The.
Birds of Passage, The.
Clouded Morning, The.
Columbine, The.
Cottage, The.
Created, The.
Cross, The.
Cup, The.
Day of Denial, The.
Dead, The.
Eagles gather on the place of death, The.
Earth, The.
Enoch.
Eye and Ear, The.
Fair Morning, The.

Fear Not: For They That Be With Us.
First Atlantic Telegraph, The.
Forevermore.
Fugitive Slaves, The.
Garden, The.
Grave-Yard, The.
Hand and Foot, The [*or* Hand and the Foot,
The].
Hath the Rain a Father?
I Was Sick and in Prison.
In Him We Live [& Move & Have Our
Being].
Indian's Retort, The.
Jacob Wrestling with the Angel.
John.
Lament of the Flowers, The.
Latter rain, it falls in anxious haste, The.
Lost, The.
Morning Watch, The.
Moses in Infancy.
Mountain, The.
My People Are Destroyed for Lack of
Knowledge.
Nature.
New Birth, The.
New Man, The.
New World, The.
On Finding the Truth.
On the Completion of the Pacific Telegraph.
On Visiting the Graves of Hawthorne and
Thoreau.
One Generation Passeth Away.
Origin of Man, I, The.
Prayer, The.
Prayer of Jabez, too, should be our prayer,
The.
Presence, The.
Promise, The.
Robe, The.
Robin, The.
Serpent, The.
Silent, The.
Slave, The.
Slavery.
Slowness of Belief in a Spiritual World, The.
Son, The.
Song, The: "When I would sing of crooked
streams and fields."
Spheres, The.
Spirit, The.
Spirit Land, The.
Strangers, The.
Sumach Leaves, The.
Take Ye Heed, Watch and Pray.
Thy Brother's Blood.
Today.
Trees of Life, The.
Wild Rose of Plymouth, The.
Winter Rain, The.
Word! it cannot fail; it ever speaks, The.
Yourself.

"Vesey, Paul." *See* Allen, Samuel

"Vestal, Stanley" (Walter Stanley Campbell)
Kit Carson's Last Smoke ("Kit Carson came
to old Fort Lyons.")

Vetus, Gaius Antistius. *See* Antistius Vetus

Vice, Lisa (b. 1951)
Pants.

Vicente, Gil (c.1465–1536)
Song: "If thou art sleeping, maiden."

Victor, Geraldo Bessa (b. 1917)
Note on a Shop in the Muceque.
That old mulemba.

Vidya (**Vijjika**) (*fl.* c.659)
Friends, / you are lucky you can talk.
Hiding in the / cucumber garden.
Please keep an eye on my house for a few
moments.
Substantiations, *sels.*
Sun, The, *sels.*
Wanton, The, *sels.*
You are fortunate, dear friends, that you can
tell.

Vidyakara (*fl.* 11th cent.)
Eleventh-Century Sanskrit, The, *sels.*

Vidyapati (*fl.* 15th cent.)
New Love.

Sad Love.
Twin Hills.

Viên Linh (**Nguyễn Nam**) (b. 1938)
Cold season—birds all head for warmer
climes.
Hundred Tongues, A.

Viereck, Peter (b. 1916)
Blindman's Buff.
Crass Times Redeemed by Dignity of Souls,
sels.
Ennui.
Graves Are Made to Waltz On.
Homecoming.
Kilroy.
Love Song to Eohippus.
1912–1952, Full Cycle.
Poet.
To Helen of Troy (N.Y.).
Vale from Carthage.

Việt Phu'o'ng (b. 1928)
O Life I Love and Cherish Like My Wife!

Vigny, Alfred de (1797–1863)
Helena.
Nature.
Sound of the Horn, The.

Viidikas, Vicki (b. 1948)
Future.

Viiding, Juhan
George Marrow's 1011th Dream.
I am a serf. I work in the sweat of my brow.
I celebrated this day in March.
Speeches in the Interior.

Vijjika. *See* Vidya

Vilakazi, B. W. (1906–47)
Because.
I Heard the Old Song.
In the Gold Mines.
Now I do believe that he has died.
Now I Will Only Believe.
Then I'll Believe.

Vildrac, Charles (b. 1882)
After Midnight.
Relief.

Vilenkin, Nicolai Maksimovich. *See* "Minsky,
Nicolai Maksimovich"

Villa, José Garcia (b. 1914)
To become an archer.

Villakaviralinar
What the Concubine Said When She Heard
the Wife Complain about the Concubine's
Wiles.

Villalongo, José Angel Sr. (*fl.* 20th cent.)
In the Good Old U. S. A.

Villana [*or* **Vallana**] (*fl.* between 10th and 12th
cent.)
After he stripped off my clothes.

Villanueva, Alma (b. 1944)
Crazy Courage.
Even the Eagles Must Gather.
Mother, May I?
Peace #3.
They didn't get me.
To Jesus Villanueva, with Love.
Witches' Blood.

Villanueva, Tino (b. 1941)
Haciendo Apenas la Recolección.

Villiers, George, 2d Duke of Buckingham
(1628–87)
Cabin-Boy, The.
Epitaph upon Thomas, Lord Fairfax, An.

Villon, François (1431–65)
Arbor Amoris.
Ballad against the Enemies of France.
Ballad[e] of Dead Ladies.
Ballad of the Gibbet.
Ballad of the Lords of Old Time.
Ballad of the Women of Paris.
Ballad of Villon and Fat Madge, The.
Ballad Written for a Bridegroom.
Ballade: "Tell me where, in what country,
where."
Ballade to His Mistress.
Ballat o the Hingit.
Ballat o the Leddies o Langsyne.
Complaint of the Fair Armoress [*or*
Armouress], The.

Dispute of the Heart and Body of François Villon, The.
Double Ballad of Good Counsel, A.
Epistle in Form of a Ballad to His Friends.
Epitaph in Form of a Ballad, The.
Fragment on Death, A.
His Mother's Service to Our Lady.
No, I Am Not as Others Are.
Old Lady's Lament for Her Youth, The.
Old Woman's Lamentations, An.
Prayer of the Old Woman.
Rondel: "Good-by, the tears are in my eyes."
To Death, of His Lady.

Vĩnh, Lê Hà. *See* **Trần Dạ Tù'**

Vinkenoog, Simon
(((((Hollanditis)))))).

Vinokurov, Yevgeny [*or* Evgenii] Mikhailovich (b. 1925)
And when my legs had already grown numb.
Every store keeps a book for complaints.
Forget-Me-Nots.
Hamlet.
I ate and drank with you, fellow men.
I feel the reasonableness of existence.
In the Dresden Gallery.
Mother of Judas, The.
My beloved was laundering.
On the hall stand hangs a fur coat.
Poetry Editor.
Prophet, The.
Rhythm.
She sits down to eat, breaks off a piece.
Shows.

Vinz, Mark (b. 1942)
November Song.
Old Doc.
Passages.
Sins of the Fathers.
Variations on a Theme.
Wild West.

Violi, Paul (b. 1944)
Index.
Rifacimento.
Scatter.
When to Slap a Woman.

Viorst, Judith (b. 1931)
Honeymoon is over, The.
Mother Doesn't Want a Dog.
Night Fun.

Virgil [*or* Vergil] (Publius Vergilius Maro) (70–19 B.C.)
Aeneas' firmness.
Aeneas sees his wife.
Aeneas' story.
Aeneid [*or* Eneados, *Aeneis*], The, *sels.*
Aeolus looses the winds.
Camilla goes to war.
Civill Warres of Rome, Discours'd to his Royall Highness, Prince Charles, The, *sels.*
Copa: The Barmaid.
Cupid at work.
Dead Ox, The.
Death of Camilla.
Dido's death.
Dido's last night.
Dido's reproaches, *sels.*
Drances in debate.
Eclogues, *sels.*
End.
Fame, *sels.*
Georgics, *sels.*
Hell's gate.
Honest life, The.
Hostesse, The.
Love and the Creatures.
Love-charm, A.
Loves of Dido and Aeneas, The, *sels.*
Morning after shipwreck.
Orpheus and Eurydice.
Paraphrase on the last speech of Dido in Virgil's Æneas, A, *sels.*
Passion of Dido for Aeneas, The, *sels.*
Promised rain, The.
Release.
Sallad, The.
Scarronides; or, Virgile Travestie, *sels.*
School for calves.

Scythian winters.
Seasons: Winter, The, *sels.*
Second Eclogue, The, *sels.*
Second Pastoral. Or, Alexis, The, *sels.*
Silenus sings.
Snakes.
Three Inscriptions for Statues of Priapus, *sels.*
Turnus kills Pallasy.
Turnus' retreat.
Turnus without sword.
Village, The, *sels.*
Virgils Gnat, *sels.*
Weeds.

Virgil, Anita
Another year!
Awakening.
Behind sunglasses.
Bitterness.
Black spaces, The.
Claiming.
Coal train, The.
Dark, The.
Darkening.
Emerging hot and rosy.
First hot night, The.
Grass path lasts.
Holding you.
Hot afternoon.
Knifing deep.
Laughing softly.
Low tide.
Morning bath.
Mullein.
Not seeing.
Over and over.
Phoebe's cry, A.
Quiet afternoon.
Rainy day, A.
Red flipped out.
She turns the child.
Spring breeze.
Swan's head, The.
Trickling.
Twilight.
Walking the snow-crust.

Virgilio, Nicholas
Adding father's name.
After father's wake.
Alone on the road.
Another autumn.
At the open grave.
Autumn twilight.
Autumn wind, The.
Beyond empty pews.
Cathedral bell, The.
Crow in the snowy pine, A.
Deep in rank grass.
Distant balloon, A.
Empty highway, The.
Flag-covered coffin.
Heat before the storm.
Hinge of the year, The.
In the empty church.
Into the blinding sun.
Junkyard dog, The.
Lily.
Lone red-winged blackbird.
My dead brother.
My gold star mother.
Now the swing is still.
Pressing my forehead.
Sack of kittens, The.
Town barberpole.
Town clock's face, The.
Viet Nam Monument.
Winter evening.

Virruĩnṛu Mūteyiṉaṉaṉār
What He Said after a Quarrel, Remembering His Wedding Night.

Virtue, Vivian (b. 1911)
Hour, The.
Waifs.

Viscusi, Robert
Autobiography.

Visick, Mary
Wordsworth on Lloyd George.

Vita-Finzi, C.
Limerick: "Her husband was *hors de combat.*"
Limerick: "Lecherous young Lilliputian, A."
Limerick: "Some people may think I'm a bit la-di."
Limerick: "Three scribblers whose names end in Bert."
Limerick: "Unperson from West Oceania, An."
Limerick: "When an amorous youth from Atlantis."

Vitiello, Justin
Letter to a Cretan Flute-Maker.

Vītiyār?, Veḷḷi. *See* **Aḷici, Kollaṉ**

Vittorelli, Jacopo (1749–1803)
On a Nun.

Vivian, Mary
Four Scarlet Berries.
Snowdrops.

Vivien, René (1877–1909)
Chanson.
Roses Rising.
Sad Words.
Undine.
Your strange hair, cold light.

Vizenor, Gerald (b. 1934)
Anishinabe Grandmothers.
Family Photograph.
February Park.
Haiku: "August heat."
Indians at the Guthrie.
North to Milwaukee.
Raising the Flag.
Seasons in Santa Fe.
Seven Woodland Crows.
Shaman Breaks.
Surrendered Names.
Thumbing Old Magazines.
Tropisms on John Berryman.
Tyranny of Moths.
Unhappy Diary Days.
White Earth.

Võ Liêm So'n (1888–1949)
Paradise and Hell.

Võ Phiến (Đoan Thế Nho'n) (b. 1925)
Where Have They Gone?

Vogel, David (1891–1943)
How Can I See You, Love.
I saw my father drowning.
There is a last, solitary coach about to leave.

Vogelsang, Arthur (b. 1942)
Nose, the Grand Canyon, and the Sixties, The.
Which Letter?

Voigt, Ellen Bryant (b. 1943)
At the Edge of Winter.
At the Movie: Virginia, 1956.
Blue Ridge.
Claiming Kin.
Dancing with Poets.
Daughter.
Delilah.
Farm Wife.
Farmer, The.
Feast Day, *sels.*
Feast of the Assumption of the Virgin, The.
Field Trip, The.
For My Mother.
Heart is the Target, The.
Jug Brook.
Landscape, Dense with Trees.
Last Class, The.
Lotus Flowers, The.
Song and Story.
Spire, The.
Sweet Everlasting.
Tropics.
Victim, The.
Visit, The.
Why She Says No.
"Wife Takes a Child," The.
Woman Who Weeps.
Year's End.

Volkow, Veronica
Washerwoman, The.

Vollmoeller, Karl Gustav (b. 1878)
Nocturne in G Minor.

Volman, Karen (b. 1967)
Case, The.

Voloshin, Maksimilian Aleksandrovich (Maksimilian Kirilenko-Voloshin) (1877–1932)
Bourgeoisie.
Civil War.
Holy Russia.
In the Bottomless Pit.
Red Guard.
Russia, sels.

Von Freytag-Loringhoven, Else (1874–1927)
Affectionate.
Holy Skirts.

Vopiscus, Flavius (c. 4th cent.)
Epimanes, sels.

Vories, William M. (b. 1880)
Let There Be Light.

Voznesensky [or Voznesenskii], Andrey [orAndrei] Andreievich (b. 1933)
Autumn.
Autumn in Sigulda.
Big Fire at the Architectural College, The.
Call of the Lake, The.
Cashier, The.
Chagall's Cornflowers.
Chorus of Nymphs, A.
Darkmotherscream is a Siberian dance.
Dead Still.
Dogalypse.
Elegy for My Mother.
Epitaph for Vysotsky.
Give Me Peace.
Hunting a hare. Our dogs are raising a racket.
I am Goya.
New York Airport at Night.
Old Song.
Saga.
Someone is beating a woman.
Somewhere a man puts on his shorts.
Two Poems.
War.

"Vrepont, Brian" (B. A. Trubridge) (1882–1955)
Bomber, The.

Vrettakos, Nikiphoros (1912–91)
Liturgy Under the Acropolis, sels.

Vũ Đình Liên (b. 1913)
Old Calligrapher, The.
Our Hearts Are Ancient Citadels.

Vũ Hoàng Chu'o'ng (1916–76)
Beau Ideal, The.
Far Away.
No More Anxiety.
To the Black Nymph.

Vuco, Aleksandar (1897–1985)
Cyril and Methodius, sels.

Vvedensky [orVvedenskii], Aleksandr Ivanovich (1904–41)
I wish I were a wild beast.
Maybe There's a God Around.
Where he was standing leaning against a statue. With a face charged with.

Vysotsky [or Vysotskii], Vladimir Semionovich (1938–80)
And ice below, and above—I toil somewhere in between.
I never believed in mirages.
Unruly Horses.

W

"W., A." (fl. c.1586)
Hopeless Desire Soon Withers and Dies.
In Praise of the Sun.
Upon Visiting His Lady by Moonlight.
Where His Lady Keeps His Heart.

"W., C. A."
To have it out or not? that is the question.

"W——, Miss" (fl. 18th cent.)
Gentleman's Study, in Answer to The Lady's Dressing-Room, The.

Waddell, Helen (1889–1965)
But we, whose sands run low.
December nights are frosts and stars.
Dim grey wastes of the silent hills.
Earth said to Death.
Hitler Speaks.
I shall not go to heaven when I die.
I stood within the empty House of Youth.
New York City.

Waddell, P. Hately (1817–91)
David and Goliath.

Wadding [or Waddinge], Luke (1588–1657)
Christmas day is come; let all prepare for mirth.
For Christmas Day.
For Innocents' Day.
For Saint John's Day.
For Saint Stephen's Day.
For Twelfth Day.
On the Circumcision: New Year's Day.

Waddington, Miriam (b. 1917)
Advice to the Young.
Catalpa Tree.
Icons.
My Lessons in the Jail.
Old Women of Toronto.
Season's Lovers, The.
Ten Years and More.
Women's Jail, The.

Wade, Barrie
Conkers.
Goldfish.
Summer School.
Tadpoles.
Truth.

Wade-Gayles, Gloria (b. 1940)
Inquisition.
Loving Again.

Wade, Thomas (1805–75)
Shelley.
Winter Shore, The.

Wadsworth, William
Snake in the Garden Considers Daphne, The.

Wagenlander, Lydia
Mother's Birthday.

Wagner, Charles L. H.
Let's forget the many troubles.

Wagner, Maryfrances Cusumano
Miss Clement's Second Grade.

Wagoner, David (b. 1926)
Advice to the Orchestra.
Author of American Ornithology Sketches a Bird, Now Extinct, The.
Best Slow Dancer, The.
Breaking Camp.
Calculation, The.
Closing Time.
Death of the Moon, The.
Diary.
Elegy for a Forest Clear-Cut by the Weyerhaeuser Company.
Elegy for Yards, Pounds, and Gallons.
Excursion of the Speech and Hearing Class, The.
Five Dawn Skies in November.
Fruit of the Tree, The.
In the Badlands.
Leaving Something Behind.
Looking for Mountain Beavers.
Loons Mating.
Lost.
Making Camp.
Making Up for a Soul.
Man of the House, The.
Marsh Leaf.
Meeting a Bear.
Muse.
My Father's Garden.
Naval Trainees Learn How to Jump Overboard, The.
On Motel Walls.
Poem about Breath.
Poets Agree to Be Quiet by the Swamp, The.
Shooting of John Dillinger outside the Biograph Theater July 22, 1934, The.
Singing Lesson, The.

Source, The.
Staying Alive.
To a Farmer Who Hung Five Hawks on His Barbed Wire.
Valedictory to Standard Oil of Indiana, A.
Victorian Idyll, A.
Visiting Hour, The.
Walking in a Swamp.
Walking in the Snow.
Walt Whitman Bathing.
Words, The.
Young Girl with a Pitcher Full of Water, A.

Wagstaff, Blanche Shoemaker (b. 1888)
All Paths Lead to You.
Earth Trembles Waiting.
Quiet Waters.

Wah, Fred (b. 1939)
Breathe Dust.

Wain, John (b. 1925)
Anniversary.
Apology for Understatement.
Arrival.
Au Jardin des Plantes.
Brooklyn Heights.
Gentleman Aged Five before the Mirror.
Song about Major Eatherly, A.
This above All Is Precious and Remarkable.
When It Comes.

Wainwright, Jeffrey (b. 1944)
Fierce Dream, The.
Illumination.

Wake, W. Bernard
Limerick: "Student of nuclear fission, A."

Wakefield, Samuel (1799–1895)
Music of His Steps, The.

Wakley, Thirza
Easter Chick, An.
Mouse, The.
Spring Work at the Farm.

Wakolele, Nguno
Southern Africa.

Wakoski, Diane (b. 1937)
Apology, An.
Belly Dancer.
Blue Monday.
Butcher's Apron, The.
Canoer, The.
Father of My Country, The.
For Craig Who Leapt Off a Cliff in to Hummingbird Light.
Girls, The.
Hitchhikers, The.
Hummingbird Light.
Inside Out.
Justice Is Reason Enough.
Light.
Mechanic, The.
Mirror of a Day Chiming Marigold, The.
Moneylight.
My trouble / is that I have the spirit of Gertrude Stein.
Night a Sailor Came to Me in a Dream, The.
Patriotic Poem.
Photos, The.
Placing a $2 Bet for a Man Who Will Never Go to the Horse Races Any More.
Poem for a Little Boy on the Buddha's Birthday.
Poet Recognizing the Echo of the Voice, A.
Realization of difference comes, The.
Ring, The.
Ringless.
Sestina from the Home Gardener.
Singer, The.
Smudging.
Summer.
Thank You for the Valentine.
Thanking My Mother for Piano Lessons.
Valentine for Ben Franklin Who Drives a Truck in California, A.
Walking Past Paul Blackburn's Apt. on 7th St.
Wind Secrets.
You, Letting the Trees Stand as My Betrayer.

Walcott, Derek (b. 1930)
Another Life, sels.
Arkansas Testament, The.

Blues.
Cloud, The.
Codicil.
Country Club Romance, A.
Crusoe's Island.
Elsewhere.
Far Cry from Africa, A.
For Adrian.
Force.
Forest of Europe.
Fortunate Traveller, The.
Frederiksted, Dusk.
Glory Trumpeter, The.
God Rest Ye Merry, Gentlemen.
Gulf, The.
Hotel Normandie Pool, The.
In a Green Night.
In idle August, while the sea soft.
Le loupgarou.
Letter from Brooklyn, A.
Man o' War Bird.
Man Who Loved Islands, The.
Midsummer, *sels.*
Midsummer LIV.
Midsummer, Tobago.
Midsummer: XXXI.
Moon.
Nearing La Guaira.
New World.
Nights in the Gardens of Port of Spain.
Omeros, *sels.*
Port of Spain.
Ruins of a Great House.
Sainte Lucie, *sels.*
Sea Canes.
Sea-Chantey, A, *sels.*
Sea Grapes.
Sea is History, The.
Season of Phantasmal° Peace, The.
Spoiler's Return, The.
Star.
Swamp, The.
Tales of the Islands.
Upstate.
Villa Restaurant, The.
Village Life, A.
Virgins, The.
Voice out of the Sabbaths, A.
Volcano.
Whale, His Bulwark, The.
Winding Up.
Young Wife, The.

Walden, Alfred Islay (1847–84)
Dedicated to a Young Lady Representing the
    Indian Race at Howard University.
Introductory to Second Edition.
Nation's Friend, The.
One to Love.
Transition—S.M, The.
Wish for an Overcoat.

Waldheim, Franklin
Help Wanted.

Waldman, Anne (b. 1945)
Baby's Pantoum.
Because I don't have spit.
Berthe Morisot.
Complaynt.
Evangelle.
Lady Tactics.
Makeup on Empty Space.
Pressure.
Skin / Meat / BONES.
Two Men.

Waldman, Anne *and* Ted Berrigan
Memorial Day: a collaboration, *sels.*

Waldrop, Keith (b. 1932)
Proposition II.
Shipwreck in Haven, A, *sels.*
Wandering Curves.
Will to Will.

Waldrop, Rosemarie (b. 1935)
Inserting the Mirror, *sels.*
Lawn of Excluded Middle.
Relaxed Abalone, The.
Reproduction of Profiles, The, *sels.*
Shorter American Memory of the American
    Character According to Santayana.

Waley, Arthur (1889–1966)
Censorship.

Walker, Alice (b. 1944)
African Images, Glimpses from a Tiger's
    Back.
Black Mail.
Burial.
Chic Freedom's Reflection.
Did This Happen to Your Mother? Did Your
    Sister Throw Up a Lot?
Early Losses: a Requiem.
Enemy, The.
Even as I hold you.
Expect nothing. Live frugally.
Few Sirens, A.
For Two Who Slipped Away Almost
    Entirely.
Forgiveness.
Good Night, Willie Lee, I'll See You in the
    Morning.
In These Dissenting Times, *sels.*
In Uganda an early king chose.
Kiss, The.
Love is not concerned.
Medicine.
My husband says.
On Stripping Bark from Myself.
Once, *sels.*
Outcast.
Poem at Thirty-nine.
Revolutionary Petunias.
S M.
She said: "When I was with him."
Suicide.
Thing Itself, The.
Your soul shines.

Walker, Charlie (b. 1911)
St. George.

Walker, J. (1881–1946)
Love Song of J. Alfred Prufrock, The.

Walker, James (b. 1940)
Safe.

Walker, Jeanne Murray (b. 1944)
For My Daughter's Twenty-First Birthday.
Studying Physics with My Daughter.

Walker, Kath (Oodgeroo Noonuccal) (b. 1920)
Dawn Wail for the Dead.
We Are Going.

Walker, Kevin
My Talk with an Elegant Man.

Walker, Margaret Abigail (b. 1915)
Ballad of the Hoppy-Toad.
Birmingham.
Childhood.
Dark Blood.
For Andy Goodman—Michael Schwerner—
    and James Chaney.
For Gwen, 1969.
For Malcolm X.
For my people [everywhere singing their
    slave songs repeatedly: their].
Girl Held without Bail.
Kissie Lee.
Lineage.
Molly Means.
October Journey.
Poppa Chicken.
Prophets for a New Day.
Since 1619.
Street Demonstration.
We Have Been Believers.
Whores.

Walker, Robert (1958–84)
Solitary Confinement.

Walker, Ted (b. 1934)
Breakwaters.
By the Bridge.
By the Saltings.
Doomed Spaceman, The.
Estuary.
Heron.
Home Is So Sad.
Homing Pigeons.
Lemons.
Mules.
On Scafell Pike.

Owl.
Skimmers.

Walker, William (1623–84)
High o'er the Hills.

Walker, William Sidney (1795–1846)
Too solemn for day, too sweet for night.

Walla, Edna Kingsley
Christmas Eve.

Wallace-Crabbe, Chris (b. 1934)
Abhorring a Vacuum.
And the World was Calm.
Binary.
Bits and Pieces, The, *sels.*
Citizen.
Collective Invention, The.
Dirigible, The.
Double Dactyl.
Life of Ideas, The.
Mental Traveller's Landfall, The.
Nub.
Rebel General, The.
Secular, The.
Shape-Changer, The.
Sonnets to the Left, *sels.*
Sporting the Plaid.
Trace Elements.
Tribunal, The.
Windows, The.

Wallace, Edgar (1875–1932)
Song of the Bounder, THe.
War.

Wallace, Robert (1858–1938)
Aubade: N.Y.C.
Ballad of the Mouse.
Between Equals.
Dog's Song.
Double-Play, The.
Driving By.
Fly in December.
Fresco of Swans and Bears, A.
Girl Writing Her English Paper, The.
In a Spring Still Not Written Of.
In One Place.
Problem in History, A.
Riding in a Stranger's Funeral.
Storm, The.
Under the September Peach.

Wallace, Ronald (b. 1945)
Basketball.
Building an Outhouse.
Condoms.
Facts of Life, The.
Grandmother Grace.
Makings of Happiness, The.
Nightline: An Interview with the General.
1001 Nights.
Real Thing, The.
Sestina for the House.
State Poetry Day.
Thirteen.
Wild Strawberries.

Wallace, William Ross (1819–81)
Hand That Rocks the Cradle Is the Hand
    That Rules the World, The.

Wallach [*or* Wollach], Yona (b. 1946)
Absalom.
All the silly threatening things.
Are These Moods of Mine Memory.
At Sea.
Body, The.
Christina.
Gentle as Moon on Water.
House Is Empty, The.
I Feel Empty.
Jonathan.
Lola.
Love Poem No. 2.
Never Will I Hear the Sweet Voice of God.
Preannual Poem.
Sebastian.
Splitting the Infinite.
This Poem Should Have Etc.
To Live at the Speed of Biography.
To See Long like El Greco.
Two Gardens.
When You're Not a Poet.

Wallāda (*fl.* 11th cent.)
I wonder: is there no way for us to meet again.
If you were just in keeping our pact of love.
To Ibn Zaidun.
Wait till the darkness is deep.

Wallbank, Susan (b. 1943)
Why So Many of Them Die.

Wallenstein, Barry
Blues 1.
Blues 2.

Waller, Edmund (1606–87)
Apologie for Having Loved Before, An.
At Penshurst [Another].
At Penshurst ("While in the park I sing, the listning deer.")
Battle [*or* Battel] of the Summer-Islands, The, *sels.*
Budd, The.
Dancer, The.
Fall, The.
Garden of Bermuda, The.
Of English Verse.
Of Loving at First Sight.
Of My Lady Isabella Playing on the Lute.
Of The Last Verses in the Book, *sels.*
Of the Marriage of the Dwarfs.
On a Girdle.
On St. James's Park, as Lately Improved by His Majesty.
Song: "Go[e], lovely rose[—ous sweet and fair]."
Song: "Stay Phoebus, stay."
Story of Phoebus and Daphne Applied, [etc.], The.
To a Fair Lady Playing with a Snake.
To a Lady in a Garden.
To a Very Young Lady.
To Chloris, upon a Favour Received.
To Mr. Henry Lawes, Who Had Then Newly Set a Song of Mine in the Year 1635.
To One Married to an Old Man.
To Phillis.
To Phyllis.
To the King, on His Navy.
To the Mutable Fair.
Under a Lady's Picture.
Upon Ben Johnson [*or* Jonson].
Upon his Majesties repairing of Pauls.
While I listen to thy voice.

Waller, Sir John
Limerick: "Artist who lived near Montmartre, An."

Waller, Thomas ("Fats"), Andy Razaf *and* **Harry Brooks**
(What Did I Do to Be So) Black and Blue?

Walley, Dean
Limerick: "Inept young person, Miss Muffet, The."

Wallis, George B.
Lovely Rivers and Lakes of Maine, The.

Wallis, Hannah (*fl.* 1787)
Female's Lamentations, The; or, The Village in Mourning.
To a Sick Friend.
To Mrs.———, on the Death of Her Husband.

Wallis, John (1616–1703)
When a twister a-twisting will twist him a twist.

Wallis, Severn Teackle (1816–94)
Prayer for Peace, A.

Walpole, Horace, 4th Earl of Orford (1717–97)
All praise your face, your verses none abuse.
Epitaphs [*or* Epitaph] on Two Piping-Bullfinches of Lady Ossory's, Buried under a Rose-Bush in Her Garden, *sels.*
Estate and an earldom at seventy-four, An!
On the Translation of Anacreon.
To Lady Anne Fitzpatrick, When about Five Years Old, with a Present of Shells, 1772.
To the Gardener at Nuneham.

Walsh, Chad (b. 1914)
Psalm of Christ, The, *sels.*
Quintina of Crosses, A.

Walsh, Christina
Prayer to Isis.
Woman to Her Lover, A.

Walsh, John (1911–1972)
Christmas Tree, The.
I've Got an Apple Ready.
White Rabbit, The.

Walsh, Marnie
Thomas Iron-Eyes.

Walsh, Octavia (1677–1706)
At length my soul the fatal union finds.

Walsh, William (1663–1708)
Despairing Lover, The.
Love and Jealousy.
Lyce.
Phillis's Resolution.
Rivals.

Walsh, William (1663–1708) *and* **Sir George Etherege (1653–91)**
Imperfect Enjoyment, The.
Rivals.
Song: "If she be not as kind as fair."

Walter, Howard Arnold (1883–1918)
I would be true, for there are those [who trust me].

Walter, Nehemiah (1663–1750)
Elegiack Verse on Mr. Elijah Corlet, An.

Walters, Anna (b. 1946)
Hartico.
I Am of the Earth.
I Have Bowed before the Sun.
My Brothers.
Simplicity Aims Circularly.
Teacher Taught Me, A.

Walters, Dorothy (b. 1924)
Flannery O'Connor.

Walters, Elizabeth
Elizabeth Walters is my name.

Walters, Muru (b. 1935)
Haka: The Feathered Albatross.

Walther [*or* Walter] von der Vogelweide (1170?–1230?)
Alas, all my years, where have they disappeared?
Alas, that wisdom, and youth.
Awake! The day is coming now.
Dearly beloved gentle girl.
I sat down on a rock.
"Lady, take this garland."
Now my life has gained some meaning.
There Is a Lady ("There is a lady conquering with glances.")
Translation from Walter von der Vogelweide, A.
Under the Lindens [*or* Lime Tree].
Will anyone tell me what Minne is?
With a Rod No Man Alive.
You excellent women, you valiant men.
You should bid me welcome.

Walton, Alfred Grant
First Impressions.
Recipe for Living.
Sincere Man, The.
World We Make, The.

Walton, Eda Lou (b. 1896)
In Recompense.
Necessary Miracle, A.

Walton, Thelma
God's Gifts to Me.

Walwicz, Ania (b. 1951)
Abattoir, The.
Big Tease.
Daredevil.
Little Red Riding Hood.
Tattoo, The.
Wonderful.

Walworth, Clarence A. (1820–1900)
Holy God, We Praise Thy Name.

Wandor, Michelene (b. 1940)
Eve to Lilith.
Eve's Commentary.
Lilith to Eve.
Ruth's Story, As Told to Lilith.

Wang An-shih (1021–86)
At the Chiang-ning River Mouth.
Autumn sun over the *t'ung* tree.

By a Stream on Mount T'ien-t'ung.
By the River.
Composed on Horseback, Returning from Lakeview Pavilion at Hangchow, Presented to Yü-ju and Lo-tao.
Confiscating Salt.
Fresh Flowers.
Hastily Composed on the Mo-ling Road.
Impromptu; Late Spring at Pan-shan.
In the Mountains.
In the Style of Han Shan and Shih Te, *sels.*
Old Pine, An.
On the Yangtze.
Plum Blossoms on Solitary Hill.
Sketch of Mount Chung, A.
Song of the Radiant Lady.
Tune: "Mountain Hawthorns."
Tune: "Sand of Silk-washing Stream."
Twenty Poems in Imitation of Han-shan and Shih-te, *sels.*
Walking in the Countryside.
Written at Hsiang-kuo Temple on the Occasion of Watching Actors in the Hsing-hsiang Garden of the T'ung-t'ien-chieh Tao-ch'ang.
Written for My Own Amusement.
Written on the Wall of Halfway Mountain Temple.
Written on the Wall of Pan-shan Temple.

Wang Ch'ang-ling (698–757)
Castleside Song.
Following the Army on Campaign, *sels.*
Listening to a Wanderer's "Water Melody."
Sorrow in the Harem, A.

Wang Chi (*fl.* c.700)
In Praise of Carnations.
Sent to Recluse Ch'eng.
'TELL me now, what should a man want.'
Viewing Mr. Yü's Landscape Painting on the Wall.

Wang Chia (*fl.* 9th cent.)
Shrine Festival.

Wang Chien (768?–833?)
Boatman's Song, A.
Hearing That His Friend Was Coming Back from the War.
Palace Poems, *sels.*
Palace Song.
South, The.
Weaving at the Window.
Words of the Newly Wed Wife.

Wang Ch'ing-hui (*fl.* 13th cent.)
Now the lotuses in the imperial lake.

Wang Chiu-ssu (1468–1551)
After Reading the Poems of Master Han Shan, *sels.*
Ballad of Selling a Child.
Ballad of the Fatherless Boy.
Chanting Poems.
For Several Days I Have Not Visited the Garden Pavilion—A Poem Sent to My Pet Crane.
Forced Feelings, *sels.*
Living in the Woods, *sels.*
Miscellaneous Poems on Living in the Woods—In the Manner of Han Shan, *sels.*
Quiet Sitting.
Recording My Happiness.
Rising from Sleep.
Robber of Kuan-shan, The, *sels.*
Song of the Painting of the Long-Life Star.
Thunder in the southern mountains, the third month of the year.

Wang Fan-chih (590–660?)
Grass hovel filled with wind and dust.
Having power is nothing to be concerned about.
I, Fan-chih, wear my socks inside out.
I saw another man die.
No one lives past a hundred.
On the outskirts, dumplings of mud.
That fellow rides a big horse.
Yellow gold's not precious.

Wang I (*fl.* c.120)
Lychee, The.
Lychee-tree, The.

Wang K'ang-chü (*fl.* **4th cent.**)
Refuting the "Invitation to Hiding."
Wang Kuo-wei (1877–1927)
To try to find my heart, it's hard enough.
Tune: "Butterflies Lingering over Flowers."
Tune: "Echoing Heaven's Everlastingness."
Tune: "Immortal at the River."
Tune: "Sand of Silk-washing Stream."
Tune: "Song of Picking Mulberry."
Wang Seng-ta (423–58)
I think of when she sits.
I think of when she sleeps.
Out Early One Morning, I Met an Old
Acquaintance.
To Match the Prince of Lang-yeh's Poem in
the Old Style.
Written for My Neighbor.
Wang Shih-chieng (1634–1711)
After Rain, Visiting the Temple of Heavenly
Peace.
Arriving after Rain at the Temple of
Heavenly Peace.
At Ch'en Ch'u.
Bamboo Branch Song of Han-chia.
Crossing the Yangtze in a Strong Wind.
Dawn at Chiao Mountain, Seeing Off K'un-
lun on His Way Back to Ching-k'ou.
Echoing Old Man Mu's Poem, "Inscribed on
Shen Lang-ch'ien's Little Landscape,
Autumn Willows at Stone Cliff."
Lamenting for My Wife.
Lieh Mountain.
Moonlit Night at Fragrant Mountain Temple.
Mooring at Night at Kao-yu.
Mooring at Night at the River Mouth, I
Heard a Flute—Sent to My Elder Brother
Hsi-ch'iao.
Occasional Poem: Upon Seeing Lotuses
Bloom in a Vase.
On the Way to Huang-ch'ang River.
Quatrain at Chen-chou.
Sailing along the Tai Stream from Stone
Bridge to the Foot of Mo-ho Peak.
Seeing Off Editor Wang Chou-tz'u and
Secretary Lin Shih-lai on Their Mission as
Envoys to the Ryūkyū Islands.
Song of the Ch'in-Dynasty Mirror—Written
for Yüan Sung-li.
Things Seen.
Thinking of the Past on an Autumn Night at
Tz'u-jen Temple.
What Strikes My Eye.
Written beneath Hui Mountain, When Tsou
Liu-yi Comes by for a Visit.
Wang T'ing-hsiang (1474–1544)
Climbing to the Top of the City Walls at
Kan-yü.
Flowering tree does not spare itself, The.
Miscellaneous Poems on Spirit-Valley
Temple, *sels.*
Miscellaneous Poems Written in the Snow.
On New Year's Day of the Year Kuei-ssu
(1533), Releasing Live Creatures.
Song of the Wanderer.
Song of Wu-ch'eng, *sels.*
Songs of Chiang-nan, *sels.*
Traveling by Boat, *sels.*
Written in the Office Precincts.
Wang Ts'an (177–217)
Joining the Army: A Song.
Occasional Verse.
Seven Poems of Lament, *sels.*
Seven Sorrows, *sels.*
Wang Wei (*fl.* **17th cent.**)
After Long Rain.
At My Country Home in Chung-nan.
Autumn.
Autumn Twilight in the Mountains.
Bird and Waterfall Music.
Birdsong Brook.
Cold mountain turns dark green.
Composed on a Spring Day on the Farm.
Deep in the mountain wilderness.
Departure.
Duckweed Pond.
Enjoying Coolness.
Farms at Wei River, The.

In the Hills.
Joys of the Country: Seven Poems, *sels.*
Morning.
On Returning to Sung Mountain.
Red Peonies.
Seeing Someone Off.
Seeking a Mooring.
Song for Wei City, A.
Suffering from Heat.
Thinking of My Brother in Shantung on the
Ninth Day of the Ninth Moon.
To Subprefect Chang.
Twenty Views of Wang-ch'uan, *sels.*
Twilight comes over the monastery Garden.
Verses: "You who come from the old
village."
Visiting the Temple of Accumulated
Fragrance.
Walking at leisure we watch laurel flowers
falling.
Weather Newly Cleared.
Weeping for Ying Yao.
Wang Wei, Lady (b. 699?)
Lady Hsi.
Wang Ya (c.764–835)
Palace Poem.
Song of Autumn Night.
Song of Spring Journeying.
Wang Yen-Shou (*fl.* **2nd cent.**)
Nightmare, The.
Wangsun, The.
Wang-ying, Hsieh. *See* **"Ping Hsin"**
Wang Yü-ch'eng (954–1001)
Journey to a Village.
Journeying to the Village.
Random Thoughts Written in Spring.
Song of the Crow Pecking at My Scarred
Donkey.
**Waniek, Marilyn Nelson (Lynn Nelson) (b.
1946)**
Alderman.
April Rape.
Balance.
Bali Hai Calls Mama.
Ballad of Aunt Geneva, The.
Canticle for Abba Jacob, A.
Chopin.
Chosen.
Daughters, 1900.
Diverne's Waltz.
House on Moscow Street, The.
Letter to a Benedictine Monk.
Levitation with Baby.
Lonely Eagles.
Sacrament of Poverty, The.
Sequence.
Sleepless Nights.
Star-Fix.
Strange beautiful woman, A.
Tuskegee Airfield.
Women's Locker Room.
Warburton, N. J.
Snake on D. H. Lawrence, The.
Warburton, R. E. Egerton (1804–91)
Past and Present.
Ward, Diane (b. 1956)
Absolution.
Approximately.
Crossing.
Glass House.
Immediate Content Recognition.
Limit.
Lovely Stuff.
Re-Verse.
Shakeout.
Tables in Pictures.
Ward, Edward (1667–1731)
Ballad on the Taxes, A.
Extravagant Drunkard's Wish, The.
Journey to Hell, A; or, A Visit Paid to the
Devil, *sels.*
Nuptial Dialogues, *sels.*
South Sea Ballad, A.
Ward, Eunice
Magician, A.

Ward, Jerry W., Jr. (b. 1943)
Comfort-Maker.
Don't Be Fourteen (In Mississippi).
Jazz to Jackson to John.
Ward, Nathaniel (1578–1652)
Mercury shew'd Apollo, Bartas Book.
Mr. Ward of Anagrams Thus.
Poetry's a gift wherein but few excell.
World's a well strung fidle, mans tongue the
quill, The.
Ware, Eugene Fitch ("Ironquill") (1841–1911)
Ballad in "G," A.
He and She.
Manila Bay.
Whist.
Zephyr.
Ware, Henry, Jr. (1794–1843)
Great God, the Followers of Thy Son.
Lift Your Glad Voices in Triumph on High.
Ware, Marianne
Understanding Guyana.
Waring, Anna L. (1823–1950)
My Times Are in Thy Hand.
Waring, Belle
Baby Random.
Back to Catfish.
Breeze in Translation.
Nothing Happened.
Our Lady of the Laundromat.
Refuge at the One Step Down.
Reprieve on the Stoop.
Tip, The.
When a Beautiful Woman Gets on the
Jutiapa Bus.
Waring, II. C.
Quite the Cheese.
**Warner, Anna Bartlett ("Amy Lothrop")
(1827–1915)**
Jesus Loves Me, This I Know.
One More Day's Work for Jesus.
We Would See Jesus.
Warner, Eva
Irony of God.
Warner, Francis
Epithalamium: "This girl all in white is my
crystal of light."
Warner, Rex (b. 1905)
Chough.
Warner, Sylvia Townsend (1893–1978)
Absence, The.
After he had gone the wind rose.
Alarum, The.
Benicasim.
Building in Stone.
Country Thought.
Drawing you, heavy with sleep to lie closer.
El Heroe.
"Elizabeth the Beloved."
Epitaph: "Her grieving parents cradled here."
Epitaph: "I, an unwedded wandering dame."
Epitaph: "I, Richard Kent, beneath these
stones."
Epitaph: "John Bird, a laborer, lies here."
Gloriana Dying.
Green Valley, The.
Journey To Barcelona.
Killing No Murder.
King Duffus.
Modo and Alciphron.
Nelly Trim.
Port Bou.
Rival, The.
Sad Green.
Sailor, The.
Some Make This Answer.
Song for a Street-Song.
Song from the Bride of Smithfield.
Song: "She has left me, my pretty."
Triumph of Sensibility.
Warner, William (1558?–1609)
Albion's England, *sels.*
Warr, Bertram J. (1917–43)
Working Class.
Warr, Michael
Brain on Ice.

Malcolm Is 'Bout More Than Wearing a
Cap.

Warren, Mrs. Mercy (1728–1814)
Limerick: "Maiden at college called Breeze,
A."

Warren, Robert Penn (1905–89)
Amazing Grace in the Back Country.
American Portrait: Old Style.
Apology for Domitian.
Aubade for Hope.
Audubon, *sels.*
Ballad: Between the Boxcars, *sels.*
Ballad of Billie Potts, The.
Bearded Oaks.
Better Than Counting Sheep.
Birth of Love.
Blow, West Wind.
Caribou.
Code Book Lost.
Confederate Veteran Tries to Explain the
Event, A.
Country Burying (1919).
Covered Bridge.
Crime.
Debate: Question, Quarry, Dream.
Dream, Dump-Heap, and Civilization.
English Cocker: Old and Blind.
Evening Hawk.
Evening Hour.
Fairy Story.
Fall Comes in Back-Country Vermont, *sels.*
Flaubert in Egypt.
Garden, The.
Gold Glade.
Heart of Autumn.
Heart of the Backlog.
Heat Lightning.
History during Nocturnal Snowfall.
Infant Boy at Midcentury, *sels.*
Kentucky Mountain Farm, *sels.*
Last Laugh.
Last Meeting.
Letter from a Coward to a Hero.
Letter of a Mother.
Letter to a Friend.
Limited, The.
Little Girl Wakes Early.
Man in the Street.
Masts at Dawn.
Mexico Is a Foreign Country: Four Studies in
Naturalism, *sels.*
Mortmain, *sels.*
Myth on Mediterranean Beach: Aphrodite as
Logos.
Natural History.
Notes on a Life to Be Lived.
Old-Time Childhood in Kentucky.
Original Sin.
Owl, The.
Patriotic Tour and Postulate of Joy.
Penological Study: Southern Exposure, *sels.*
Picnic Remembered.
Pondy Woods.
Pro Sua Vita.
Pursuit.
Rattlesnake Country.
Red Mullet, The.
Revelation.
Riddle in the Garden.
School Lesson Based on Word of Tragic
Death of Entire Gillum Family.
Sila.
Sister Water.
Sky.
Spider has more eyes than I have money,
The.
Tale of Time, *sels.*
Terror.
There's a grandfather's clock in the hall,
watch it closely. The.
Tiberius on Capri, *sels.*
Timeless, Twinned.
To a Face in a Crowd.
To a Little Girl, One Year Old, in a Ruined
Fortress, *sels.*
Two Studies in Idealism: Short Survey of
American and Human History, *sels.*

Vermont Ballad: Change of Season.
Watershed.
Way to Love God, A.
What Voice at Moth-Hour did I hear calling.

Warren, Rosanna (b. 1954)
Daylights.
Funerary Portraits, *sels.*
Garden.
History as Decoration.
In Creve Coeur, Missouri.
Interior at Petworth: From Turner.
Renoir.
To Max Jacob.

Warren, William F. (1833–1929)
I Worship Thee, O Holy Ghost.

Warrior, Emma Lee (b. 1941)
Enemy's Eyes, The.
How I Came to Have a Man's Name.
New Indian Medicine.
Reginald Pugh, The Man Who Came from
the Army.

Warsh, Lewis (b. 1944)
Enmeshment.
Gout.
Precious Mettle.
Static, The.
Suicide Rates, The.

Warton, Joseph (1722–1800)
Dying Indian, The.
Enthusiast: or, The Lover of Nature, The.
Enthusiast, The; or, The Lover of Nature,
sels.
Ode to Evening.
Ode to Fancy, *sels.*
Revenge of America, The.
Verses Written at Montauban in France,
1750.
Wild, The.

Warton, Thomas, the Elder (*fl.* late 17th cent.)
Fashioned After the Manner of Master
Geoffrey Chaucer in His Assembly of
Fowls.
Ode on the Passion.
On the Spirit Adulterated by the Flesh.
Stanzas Imitated From Psalm CXIX.
Stanzas on the Psalms.

Warton, Thomas, the Younger (1728–90)
Come, gentle sleep, death's image though
thou art.
On King Arthur's Round Table, at
Winchester.
On Leander's Swimming over the Hellespont
to Hero.
Pleasures of Melancholy, The, *sels.*
Prologue on the Old Winchester Playhouse
over the Old Butchers' Shambles.
Sonnet: To the River Lodon.
To Mr. Gray.
Verses on Sir Joshua Reynolds's Painted
Window at New College, Oxford.
Written at Stonehenge.
Written in a Blank Leaf of Dugdale's
"Monasticon."

Washbourne, Thomas (1606–87)
Circulation, The.
Upon a Great Shower of Snow That Fell on
May-Day, 1654.

Washburn, Henry Stevenson (1813–1903)
Almighty God, thy constant care.

Washington, Raymond
Freedom Hair.
Moon Bound.
Vision from the Ghetto.

Wasserman, Rosanne (b. 1952)
Putting in a Word.

Wastell, Simon (d. 1632)
Microbiblion, *sels.*

Wat, Aleksander (1900–1967)
Before Breughel the Elder.
Facing Bonnard.
From "Songs of a Wanderer."
Imagerie d'Epinal.
Japanese Archery.
Joke, A.
Notes Written in Obory, *sels.*
Persian Parables, *sels.*

To be a mouse. Preferably a field mouse. Or
a garden mouse—.

Waterbury, Jared Bell (1799–1876)
I Have Fought the Good Fight.
Sinner, Is Thy Heart at Rest?

Waterman, Nixon (1857–89)
Cheer for the Consumer.
Far from the Madding Crowd.
If We Didn't Have to Eat, *sels.*
Johnny's Hist'ry Lesson.
Making a Man.
Rose to the living is more than, A.
To Know All Is to Forgive All.
Whistling Boy.

Watermeyer, G. A. (b. 1917)
Harvest Time.

Waters, Michael (b. 1949)
Keats' Lips.
Miles Weeping.
Mystery of the Caves, The.

**Waters, Muddy McKinley Morganfield (1915–
1983)**
Hoochie Coochie.

Watkins, Edward (b. 1917)
Figures of Authority.

**Watkins, Nayo-Barbara ("Nayo"; Barbara
Malcolm)**
Bedtime Story.
Black Woman Throws a Tantrum.
Easy way out.
First time I was sweet sixteen.
Hard Times A' Coming.
I watched little black boys.
Near Miss.

Watkins, Vernon (1906–67)
Ballad of the Two Tapsters.
Beaver's Story, The.
Collier, The.
Compost Heap, The.
Cwmrhydyceirw Elegiacs.
Dead Words, The.
Demands of the Muse.
Discoveries.
Earth and Fire.
Feather, The.
Fingernail Sunrise.
Fire in the Snow, The.
Foal.
For a Wine Festival.
Furnace of Colors, The.
Healing of the Leper, The.
Heron, The.
Hurdy-Gurdy Man in Winter.
Indolence.
Lady with the Unicorn, The.
Mare lies down in the grass where the nest
of the skylark is hidden, The.
Music of Colours—White Blossom.
Napkin and Stone.
Ode to Swansea.
Old Triton Time.
Peace in the Welsh Hills.
Returning from Harvest.
Returning to Goleufryn.
She That Is Memory's Daughter.
Snow Curlew, The.
Song of the Good Samaritan, The.
Swedenborg's Skull.
Two Decisions.

Watkyns, Rowland (*fl.* 1635–64)
Antipathy.
Bad company is a disease.
Gardener, The.
Periwig, A.
Saul did much care and diligence express.
Strange Monsters.
Upon Christ's Nativity or Christmas.
Worldly Wealth.

Watson, Barbara Bellow
Late Light.

Watson, Clyde (b. 1947)
Dilly Dilly Piccalilli.
Do the Baby Cake-Walk.
Knickerbocker Knockabout.
Phoebe in a Rosebush.
Rock, Rock, Sleep, My Baby.

Watson, Flora Willis
Calendar Rhyme.

Watson, Frank
Limerick: "Said a practical thinker: 'One should.'"

Watson, J. Y.
Soldier, The.

Watson, John Whittaker (1824–90)
Beautiful Snow, The.

Watson, Nancy Dingman
Grasshopper Green.

Watson, Rosamund Marriott ("Graham R. Tomson"; "R. Armytage") (1863–1911)
Ave atque Vale.
Ballad of the Bird-Bride.
Ballad of the Were-Wolf, A.
Cage, The.
Children of the Mist.
Nirvana.
White Bird, The.
White Lady, The.

Watson, Roy W. (b. 1926)
View on Death, A.
Who a Mother Is.

Watson, Thomas (c.1557–1592)
Hecatompathia; or, Passionate Century of Love, *sels.*
My Love is Past.
Tears of Fancy, The, *sels.*

Watson, W. F. N.
Hicche-Hykeres Tale, The.
Limerick: "Couple there was in Blefuscu, A."
Limerick: "Dear Albert, of Saxe-Coburg-Gotha."
Limerick: "Fellow from far Erewhon, A."
Limerick: "Feminine mouth in Utopia, The."
Limerick: "Few things to desire can so prod us."
Limerick: "Lady from Vanity Fair, A."
Limerick: "There was a young lady of Lundy."
Limerick: "Young couple who lived at 'The Laurels', A."

Watson, Wilfred (b. 1911)
Canticle of Darkness.
Emily Carr.
Invocation: "Appear, O Mother, was the perpetual cry."
Lines: I Praise God's Mankind in an Old Woman.
O My Poor Darling.
White Bird, The.

Watson, Sir William (1858–1935)
Epitaph, An.
Epitaph, An: "His friends he loved. His direst earthly foes."
Ode in May.
Song: "April, April, / Laugh thy girlish laughter."
Sonnets to Miranda, *sels.*
To Lord Tennyson.
Wordsworth's Grave.

Watteau, Otto
Limerick: "'Oh, halt!' cried Virginia, 'Enough!'"

Watten, Barrett (b. 1948)
Progress, *sels.*
Radio.
Statistics.

Watterman, Catharine H. (1812–97)
Come unto Me, When Shadows Darkly Gather.

Watts, Alaric Alexander (1797–1864)
Austrian Army, An.

Watts, Isaac (1674–1748)
Adventurous Muse, The.
Broad Is the Road.
Christ hath a garden walled around.
Church the Garden of Christ, The.
Cradle Hymn, A.
Crucifixion to the World by the Cross of Christ.
Day of Judgement [*or* Judgment]; an Ode, The.
Early, my God, without delay.

Edom.
Few Happy Matches.
Flying Fowl, and Creeping Things, Praise Ye the Lord.
For the Lord's Day Evening.
Great God, attend while Zion sings.
Hosanna to Christ.
How doth the little busy bee.
How long, dear Savior, O how long.
Hurry of the Spirits, in a Fever and Nervous Disorders, The.
Innocent Play.
Kind Deeds.
Law Given at Sinai, The.
Look on Him Whom They Pierced, and Mourn.
Man Frail, and God Eternal.
Miracles at the Birth of Christ.
Ninety-fifth.
O God, Our Help in Ages Past.
Our Saviour's Golden Rule.
Passion and Exaltation of Christ, The.
Praise for Mercies Spiritual and Temporal.
Prospect of Heaven Makes Death Easy, A.
Psalm 58.
Shortness and Misery of Life, The.
Sluggard, The.
Spare Us, O Lord, Aloud We Pray.
Submission to Afflictive Providences.
Sweet Muse, Descend.
Through every age, eternal God.
Where-e'er My Flatt'ring Passions Rove.
Where Nothing Dwelt but Beasts of Prey.
Why Do We Mourn Departing Friends?

Watts, May Thielgaard (*fl* 1920s)
Vision.

Watts-Dunton, Theodore (1832–1914)
Coleridge.
Sonnet's Voice, The.

Waugh, Alec (1898–1981)
From Albert to Bapaume.

Waugh, Evelyn (1903–66)
Loved One, The, *sels.*
They told me, Francis Hinsley, they told me you were hung.

Waxman, Natasha
War Rug.

Way, Sophie
Hoping for a Dog.

Wayman, Tom (b. 1945)
Another Poem about the Madness of Women.
Chilean Elegies: 5, The. The Interior.
Despair.
Hating Jews.
Picketing Supermarkets.
Teething.
Wayman in Love.

Wearne, Alan (b. 1948)
Go on, tell me the season is over.
Nightmarkets, The, *sels.*

Weatherly, Tom (b. 1942)
Arroyo.
Autobiography.
Blues for Franks Wooten.
Canto 7: First Thesis.
Cantos, *sels.*
First Monday Scottsboro Alabama.
Imperial Thumbprint.
Mud Water **Shango**.
Times.
Your eyes are mirth.

Weaver, Michael S.
Appaloosa, The.
Beginnings.
Black and White Galaxie, The.
Black Man's Sonata, A.
Blind Solo.
Borders.
Dogs, The.
Imitation of Life.
Improvisation for Piano.
Left Bank Jazz Society, The.
Luxembourg Garden.
Message on Cape Cod, The.
Missing Patriarch, The.
My Father's First Baseball Game.

My Father's Geography.
Picnic, an Homage to Civil Rights, The.
Water Song.
Weekend Equestrian, The.

Webb, Charles Henry ("John Paul") (b. 1834)
At the Ball!
Autumn Leaves.
Shape of History, The.

Webb, Doris
Tragedy, A.

Webb, Francis (1925–73)
Airliner.
Around Costessey, *sels.*
Clouds.
Death at Winson Green, A.
End of the Picnic.
Gunner, The.
Hospital Night.
Laid Off.
Port Phillip Night.
Sea, The.
This Runner.
Tip for Saturday, A.
Towards the Land of the Composer.
Ward Two.
Wild Honey.

Webb, Mary (1881–1927)
Foxgloves.
Green Rain.
Market Day.
Secret Joy, The.
Water-Ousel, The.
Why did you come, with your enkindled eyes.

Webb, Phyllis (b. 1927)
Days of the Unicorns, The.
Imperfect Sestina.
Kropotkin Poems, The, *sels.*
Poetics against the Angel of Death.
Propositions.
Spots of Blood.
Time of Man, The.
To Friends Who Have Also Considered Suicide.

Webb, Thomas Henry Basil (b. 1935)
Ancient Prayer, An.

Webbe, Charles (*fl.* c.1678)
Against Indifference.

Weber, Richard (b. 1932)
Elizabeth in Italy.
Envying the Pelican.
Poet's Day, The.
Primer for Schoolchildren, A.
Visit to Bridge House, A.

Weber, Ron
Concise History of the Vietnam War: 1965–1968, A.

Webster, Augusta Davies ("Cecil Home") (1837–94)
By the Looking-Glass.
Castaway, A, *sels.*
Circe, *sels.*
Enigma No. 6.
Faded.
Love's Mourner.
Medea in Athens, *sels.*
Since first my little one lay on my breast.
Sonnets from Mother and Daughter, *sels.*
That some day Death who has us all for jest.
There's one I miss. A little questioning maid.

Webster, Ed
San Joaquin Valley Poems: 1969.

Webster, H. D. L.
Lorena.

Webster, John (c.1580–1638)
Devil's Law Case, The, *sels.*
Duchess of Malfi, The, *sels.*
White Devil, The, *sels.*

Webster, John (c.1580–1638) *and* William Rowley
Thracian Wonder, The, *sels.*

Webster, Mary Morison
Gallipoli.
Grass hath such a simple faith, The.
I Set Aside.

Illi Morituri.
Ox, The.
Quiet of the Dead, The.
Secret, The.

Webster, W. J.
Prick a maiden nether holly.
To His Coy Mistress.

Weckherlin, Georg Rudolph (1584–1653)
Concerning the King of Sweden.
Love Is Life and Death.
She Is the Greatest Wealth.
To Breisach, Taken by That Supremely
Celebrated Hero, Bernhard, Duke of
Saxony.
To Germany.

Wedde, Ian (b. 1946)
Angel, *sels.*
Beggar at the Gate, The.
Earthly: Sonnets for Carlos, *sels.*
Hardon ("Get One Today").
King Solomon Vistas.
Those Others.

Wedderburn, Robert. *See* **James, John** *and*
Robert Wedderburn

Wedgefarth, W. Dayton
Bum.
Mother in gladness, Mother in sorrow.
Mother's Hands.

Weeden, Craig
Pizza Joint in Cranston, A.

Weekes, Nathaniel (b. c.1730)
Barbados, *sels.*

Weeks, James Eyre (b. 1719?)
On the Great Fog in London, December
1762.

Weeks, Robert Lewis
Appalachian Front.

Weelkes, Thomas (fl. c.1600)
Fara Diddle Dyno.
Madrigal: "Ay me, alas, heigh ho, heigh ho!"
Tan ta ra: cries Mars on bloody rampier.

Weever, John (1576–1632)
De Se.

Wei Chuang (836–910)
Lament of the Lady of Ch'in, The.
Late Rising on Spring Days.
Spoken to Pines and Bamboos.
Tune: "Deva-like Barbarian."
Tune: Deva-like Barbarian ("People all say
the southland's better.")
Tune: Lotus-leaf Cup.
Tune: "Sand of Silk-washing Stream."
Tune: The Taoist Priestess.

Wei Wên-Ti (d. 220)
On the Death of his Father.

Wei Ying-wu (b. 736)
Crossing the Lang-yeh Mountain with a
Friend.
In Imitation of T'ao P'eng-tse.
Longing in My Heart.
On Dewdrop.
On Sound.
Sent to the Taoist Holy Man of Ch'üan-
chiao.
To Send to Li Tan and Yüan Hsi.
Tune: Flirtatious Laughter.
Tune: "Song of Flirtatious Laughter."
West Creek at Ch'u-chou.

Weigl, Bruce (b. 1949)
Ambassador, The.
Amnesia.
Anna Grasa.
Anna's Grace.
Black Hose, The.
Burning Shit at An Khe.
Confusion of Planes We Must Wander in
Sleep, The.
Girl at the Chu Lai Laundry.
Her Life Runs Like a Red Silk Flag.
Him, on the Bicycle.
Last Lie, The.
Meditation at Pearl Street.
Mercy.
Mines.
Monkey.

One, The.
Sailing to Bien Hoa.
Sharing, The.
Shelter.
Song for the Lost Private.
Song of Napalm.
Surrounding Blues on the Way Down.
Temple Near Quang Tri, Not on the Map.
They Name Heaven.
Way of Tet, The.
What Saves Us.

Weil, Simone (1909–43)
Forms of the Implicit Love of God, *sels.*

Weil, Zaro
From My Window.
October wind, An.

Weiman, Andrew (b. 1956)
Andy-Diana DNA Letter.

Wein, Jules Alan
Genesis.

Weiner, Hannah (b. 1928)
Clairvoyant Journal, *sels.*
From *Spoke / Aug 19.*
Little Books / 137 / Silence Mar 22 79.
Little Books / Indians, *sels.*
Remembered Sequel.
Spoke Aug 19, *sels.*

Weiner, Joshua
Who They Were.

Weiners, John (b. 1934)
Act #2.
Acts of Youth, The.
Children of the Working Class.
My Mother.
Poem for museum goers, A.
Poem for Painters, A.
Poem for the Insane, A.
Poem for Trapped Things, A.
Poem for vipers, A.
With Meaning.

Weinfield, Henry
Song for the In-Itself and For-Itself.

Weingarten, Roger (b. 1945)
Blue Bog Children.
Ethan Boldt.
Father Hunger and Son.
Four Seasons of His Discontent.
From the Temple of Longing.
Her Apron through the Trees.
In the Cloud Chamber.
Jungle Gliders.
These Obituaries of Rattlesnakes Being Eaten
by the Hogs.

Weinstein, Berish. *See* **Vaynshteyn, Berysh**

Weise, Christian (1642–1708)
Upon the Birth of a Young and Highly
Desired Son.

Weiser, Conrad (1696–1760)
Jehovah, Lord and Majesty.

Weiss, Neil (b. 1914)
Word, The.

Weiss, Theodore (b. 1916)
Another and Another and.
As You Like It.
Barracks Apt. 14.
Clothes Maketh the Man.
Dab of Color, A.
Egyptian Passage, An.
Every Second Thought, *sels.*
Fire at Alexandria, The.
Last Day and the First, The.
Letter from the Pygmies, A.
Life of. . . , The.
Off to Patagonia.
Pair of Shoes, A.
Preface: "Sonja Henie, the young girl."
Ten Little Rembrandts.
To Forget Me.
Ultimate Antientropy, The.
Web, The.
"Yes, But. . . ."

Weissbort, Daniel (b. 1935)
Mourning.

Weisslitz, E. F.
Baldpate Pond.

Welburn, Ron (b. 1944)
And universals / are not that world.
Avoidances.
Ben Webster: "Did You Call Her Today?"
Black is beautiful.
Bones and Drums.
Cecil County.
Condition Blue/ Dress.
Eulogy for Populations.
Gonsalves.
It is overdue time.
Lyrics shimmy like.
Put u red-eye in.
Tu / cson's of blackmens.
Whichway.
Yellow Wolf Spirit.

Welch, Don
Spade Scharnweber was a white Watusi. His
mother.
We Used to Play.

Welch, James (b. 1940)
Across to the Peloponnese.
Arizona Highways.
Blue like Death.
Christmas Comes to Moccasin Flat.
D-Y Bar.
Day after Chasing Porcupines.
Directions to the Nomad.
Going to Remake This World.
Grandma's Man.
Harlem, Montana.
In My First Hard Springtime.
In My Lifetime.
Lady in a Distant Face.
Magic Fox.
Man from Washington, The.
Never Give a Bum an Even Break.
Only Bar in Dixon, The.
Plea to Those Who Matter.
Please Forward.
Renegade Wants Words, The.
Snow Country Weavers.
Surviving.
Thanksgiving at Snake Butte.
Verifying the Dead.
Visit.
Why I Didn't Go to Delphi.

Welch, Lew (b. 1920)
Chicago Poem.
Empress herself served tea to Su Tung-po,
The.
He Thanks His Woodpile.
Image, as in a Hexagram.
In Answer to a Question From P. W.
Sausalito Trash Prayer.
Song of the Turkey Buzzard.
Taxi Suite, *sels.*
This Book is for Magda.
Whenever I make a new poem.
Wobbly Rock.

Welch, Marie De L. (b. 1905)
Prelude to Commencement.

Welch, Myra Brooks
Touch of the Master's Hand, The.

Weldon, Charles
Poem of the Universe, The.

Welish, Marjorie (b. 1944)
Blood or Color.
Casting Sequences.
Crossing Disappearing behind Them.
If I Blindfold You.
Kiss Tomorrow Goodbye.
Respected, Feared, and Somehow Loved.
Scalpel in Hand.
Skin.
Street Cries.
Veil.
Wild Sleeve.
Within This Book, Called Marguerite.

Weller, Archie (b. 1957)
Ngungalari.
Story of Frankie. . . My Man, The.

Welles, Winifred (1893–1939)
Cruciform.
White Valentine.

**Wellesley, Dorothy, Duchess of Wellington
(1891–1956)**
April 1939.
As Lambs into the Pen.
Asian Desert.
Avebury.
Deserted House, *sels.*
Enemy, The.
Fire.
Fishing.
Horses.
Lenin, *sels.*
Lighthouses.
Lost Lane.
Matrix, *sels.*
Morning After, The.
Mother.
Walled Garden.

Wellman, Mac (b. 1945)
Having Led a Charmed Life, He Had to be
Hanged Twice.
Hollowness, *sels.*
Mad Wolf in Lunar Web, Mad Crow on the
Beach.
Terminal Hip, *sels.*

Wells, Amos Russel (1862–1935)
Ambitious ant would a-travelling go, The.
Considerate Crocodile, The.
Inn That Missed Its Chance, The.
Length of Life, The.

Wells, Anna Maria (1795–1868)
Cow-Boy's Song, The.
Little Maid, The.

Wells, Carolyn (1862–1942)
Alone.
Baker's Dozen of Wild Beasts, A, *sels.*
Diversions of the Re-Echo Club.
How To Tell the Wild Animals.
Limerick: "Canner, Exceedingly Canny, A."
Limerick: "There was a young person called
Tate."
Limerick: "Tutor who tooted a flute, A."
Marvel, A.
Overworked Elocutionist, An.
Oyster-Crabs.
Poster Girl, The.
Puzzled.
Universal Favorite, The.

Wells, H. G.
Limerick: "Mr. Wells of the big cerebellum."
Limerick: "Our novels get longa and longa."

Wells, Marcus Morris (1815–95)
Holy Spirit, Faithful Guide.

Wells, Rollin J. (b. 1848)
Growing Old [or Growing Older].

Welsh, Anne (b. 1922)
Between Seasons.
Many Birds.
Sharpeville Inquiry.
That Way.
Waterfall.

Welshimer, Helen
Dusk.

Welsted, Leonard (1688–1747)
Invitation, The.

Welt, Bernard (b. 1952)
Prose.

Welte, Lou Ann (b. 1923)
Those Last, Late Hours of Christmas Eve.

Welty, Eudora (b. 1909)
Flock of Guinea Hens Seen from a Car, A.

Wen Cheng-ming (1470–1559)
As flowers fall at the river city, memories
come to me.
Chung-i Temple, The, *sels.*
Evening Bell from a Misty Temple.
Hearing a Flute on the River Chi.
Improvised on Horseback to Say Good-bye to
Those Who Are Seeing Me Off, *sels.*
Inscribed on a Painting: Cultivating Leisure,
sels.
Lines Written on New Year's Day—In the
Manner of Liu Hou-ts'un [Liu K'o-chuang
(1187–1269)], *sels.*
Mooring My Boat on the Ssu River and
Watching the Moon.

My Son's One-Year Test: Improvised, *sels.*
New Year's Eve.
On First Returning from Taking the
Examinations: Feelings at Cloud-Stop
Pavilion.
Painting a Picture, The Tranquil Boat—Sent
to Ko Ju-ching.
Recording My Happiness upon Returning
Home.
Staying Overnight at Spirit-Source Temple.
Walking to the Temple of Precious Light.
What It's Like Living in My Studio Late in
Spring, *sels.*
Where among the blue clouds.
While It Was Raining.
Written While Sick.
Year *Chi-wei* (Fifteen Fifty Nine), New
Year's Day, The.
Year Hsin-hai (Fifteen Fifty One), New
Year's Eve: Keeping Watch, The.
Year I-mao (Fifteen Fifty Five), New Year's
Eve, The.

Wen I-to
Last Day, The.

Wen-Ti Chien (6th cent.)
Lo-yang.
Winter Night.

Wen T'ing-yün (812–72)
Crossing South of Li-chou, A.
Early Autumn in the Mountains.
Early Walk on Shang Mountain, An.
Fishing Trapping Song, A.
I remember that year, under the blossoms.
In the Mountains as Autumn Begins.
Last night at midnight.
Passing a Ruined Palace.
People all say the southland's better.
Song Of Chang Ching-Yüan Picking Lotus
Flowers, A.
Song of Distant Waters, A.
Song of Wildfire, A.
Spring Day in the Countryside, A.
Tune: Deva-like Barbarian.
Tune: Deva-like Barbarian ("On the many-
leafed bedscreens, gold flickers and
fades.")
Tune: Dreaming of the South.
Tune: "Lotus-leaf Cup."
Tune: "Pacifying the Western Barbarians."
Tune: "River Messages."
Tune: "Southern Song, A."
Tune: "Telling of Innermost Feelings."

Wen Yi-tuo (1898–1946)
Dead Water.
Miracle.

Wenberi
Wenberi's Song.

Wendel, Ngudia (b. 1940)
We Shall Return, Luanda.

Wendell, Julia (fl. 20th cent.)
In the Pasture of Dead Horses.

Wendt, Ingrid (b. 1944)
After a Class in Seaweed.
Mussels.
Newest Banana Plant Leaf, The.
Teacher I Wanted to Be, The.

Weöres, Sándor (b. 1913)
Chinese Temple.
Ecce Homo.
Elf.
Lost Parasol, The, *sels.*
Monkeyland.
Plain, The.
Rain's pounding away, The.
Saturn Sinking.
To the Spirits of Shakespeare and Velázquez.

Werfel, Franz (1890–1945)
Eternal Road, The, *sels.*
Exaltation.
For I Have Done a Good and Kindly Deed.
Litany of the Rooms of the Dead.
Loneliness.
Song of Life, A.
Strangers Are We All upon the Earth.
Teach Us to Mark This, God.
To a Lark in War-Time.

Wergeland, Henrik Arnold Thaulov (1808–45)
Wall-Flower, The.

Werner, Martina (b. 1929)
Monogram 4.
Monogram 23.
Monogram 29.

Werth, Lloyd E.
I'll be polite in many ways.

Wertheimer, Paul (1874–1948)
Souls.

Wescott, Glenway (b. 1901)
Poet at Night-Fall, The.
Summer Ending, The.

Wesley, Charles (1707–88)
Ah! lovely appearance of death.
Come on, my partners in distress.
During His Courtship.
For His Wife, on Her Birthday.
Free Grace.
Gentle Jesus Meek and Mild.
He Shook off the Beast.
Horrible Decree, The, *sels.*
In Temptation.
Incarnation, The.
Inextinguishable Blaze.
Love Divine, All Loves Excelling.
Morning Hymn.
N T.
None is like Jeshuron's God!
O Thou Eternal Victim Slain.
On Sympathisers with the American
Revolution.
On the Death of His Son.
On Worldly Prelates.
Whole Armour of God, The.
Wrestling Jacob.

Wesley, John (1703–91)
Hymn: "Thou hidden love of God, whose
height."

Wesley, Samuel (1691–1739)
Anacreontic, on Parting with a Little Child.
Epitaph, An: "Here lie I, once a witty fair."
Monument, The.
On the Setting Up of Mr. Butler's Monument
in Westminster Abbey.
Pindaric on the Grunting of a Hog, A.

Wesley-Smith, Peter
Cavendish McKellar.
Walter Spaggot, strange old man.

West, Arthur Graeme
Night Patrol, The.

West, Colin
Jocelyn, my Dragon.
My Gecko and I.
My obnoxious brother Bobby.

West, Gilbert (1703–56)
Stowe, the Gardens of the Rt. Hon. Richard
Lord Viscount Cobham, *sels.*
Triumphs of the Gout, The, *sels.*

West, Jane (1758–1852)
To a Friend on her Marriage, *sels.*
To the Hon. Mrs. C——e.

West, Kathleene
On Track.

West, Marlys
Exciting New Concept of Art Therapy, The.

West, Robert A. (1809–65)
Come, Let Us Tune Our Loftiest Song.

**Westmorland, Mildmay Fane, 2d Earl of (1602–
65)**
Dedication of My First Son, A.
Happy Life, A.
How to Ride Out a Storm.
In Obitum Ben. Jons.
In Praise of Fidelia.
Man Leaves the Batch.
My Carol.
My Close-Committee.
My Country Audit.
My Observation at Sea.
Occasioned by Seeing a Walk of Bay Trees.
Reveille Matin, or Good Morrow to a Friend.
Shamed by the Creature.
To Kiss God's Rod; Occasioned upon a
Child's Sickness.

To Retiredness.
To Sir John Wentworth, Upon His Curiosities and Courteous Entertainment at Summerly in Lovingland.
Upon the Times.

Weston, Mildred (b. 1900)
Departure.
Primitive Place.

Weston, R. P. (1878–1936) *and* **Bert Lee (1880–1945)**
Epitaph: "Beneath this stone lies William Burke."

Westrup, J. M. (1904–75)
Best of All.
Flying.
Furry Home, The.
Growing Rhyme, A.
My Little House.
Poor Snail, The.
Vision Clear, The.

Westwood, Thomas (1814–88)
Night of Spring.
Quest of the Sancgreall, The, *sels.*

Wetzsteon, Rachel (B. 1967)
Dinner at Le Caprice.
Three Songs.

Wever, Robert (*fl.* c.1550)
Lusty Juventus, *sels.*

Wevill, David (b. 1935)
Birth of a Shark, The.
Body of a Rook.
In Love.
Irish Hotel.
Monsoon.
Mystery, The.
Namelessness.
Snow.
Spiders.

Wexionius, Olof (1656–1690?)
On the Death of a Pious Lady.

Whalen, Philip (b. 1923)
Chanson d'Outre Tombe.
Complaint: To the Muse.
Denunciation; or, Unfrock'd Again.
For C.
For Kai Snyder.
Further Notice.
Hymnus Ad Patrem Sinensis.
International Date Line, Monday/Monday 27:XI:67.
Life in the City: In Memoriam Edward Gibbon.
Martyrdom of Two Pagans.
"Never Apologize; Never Explain."
Regalia in Immediate Demand!
Same Old Jazz, The.
Slop Barrel, The.
Sourdough Mountain Lookout.
Take I, 4:11:58.
Technicalities for Jack Spicer.
10:X:57, 45 Years Since the Fall of the Ch'ing Dynasty.
To the Muse.
25:I:68.
2 Variations: All About Love.
Walking beside the Kamogawa, Remembering Nansen and Fudo and Gary's Poem.
Where or When.

Whalley, George (b. 1915)
Affair of Honour.

Wharton, Anne (1659–85)
Elegy on the Earl of Rochester.
Penelope to Ulysses, *sels.*
Song: "How hardly I concealed my tears."
Wit's Abuse.

Wharton, Edith (1862–1937)
Autumn Sunset, An.
Chartres.
Experience.
Last Giustiniani, The.
Life, like a marble block, is given to all.
Mona Lisa.
Mortal Lease, The.
Tomb of Ilaria Giunigi, The.
Two Backgrounds.

Wharton, Thomas Wharton, 1st Marquess of (1648–1715)
Lilli Burleo [*or* Lilliburlero].

Whateley, Mary (1738–1825)
Ode to Truth.
On the Author's Husband Desiring Her to Write Some Verses.
Power of Destiny, The.
Vanity of External Accomplishments, The.

Whately, Richard, Archbishop (1787–1863)
There is a place in distant seas.

Wheatley, John (d. 1830)
Cape of Storms, The.

Wheatley, Phillis (c.1753–1784)
Farewell to America. To Mrs. S. W, A.
Hymn to the Evening, An.
Hymn to the Morning, An.
Liberty and Peace, *sels.*
On Being Brought from Africa to America.
On Imagination.
On the Death of the Rev. Mr. George Whitefield, 1770.
On Virtue.
Thoughts on the Works of Providence.
To a Gentleman and Lady on the Death of the Lady's Brother and Sister, and a Child of the Name Avis, Aged One Year.
To a Lady on the Death of Her Husband.
To His Excellency General Washington.
To Mæcenas.
To S. M., a Young African Painter, on Seeing His Works.
To the King's Most Excellent Majesty.
To the Right Honourable William, Earl of Dartmouth[, His Majesty's Principal Secretary of State for North America].
To the University of Cambridge, in New-England.

Wheeler, Ruth Winant
Prayer for Shut-Ins.

Wheeler, Susan (b. 1955)
Filial Republic, A.
Journal of the Thousand Choices.
Run on a Warehouse.

Wheelock, C. Webster (b. 1939)
Divorcee.

Wheelock, John Hall (1886–1978)
Afternoon: Amagansett Beach.
Amagansett Beach Revisited.
Beethoven.
Black Panther, The.
Dear Men and Women.
Divine Insect, The.
Earth ("Grasshopper, your fairy [*or* tiny] song.")
Earth ("'Planet doesn't explode of itself, A,' said drily.")
Elegy: "Gnu up at the zoo, The."
Gardener, The.
Hippopotamothalamion.
House in the Green Well, The.
Lion-House, The.
Love and Liberation.
Night Thoughts in Age.
Nirvana.
Random Reflections on a Summer Evening.
Silence.
Slow Summer Twilight.
Sunday Evening in the Common.
This Quiet Dust.
Triumph of Love.

Wheelwright, John (1897–1940)
Abel.
And for His Mother.
Bread-Word Giver.
Canal Street.
Father.
Forty Days, *sels.*
Live, Evil Veil.
There Is No Opera like "Lohengrin."
Train Ride.
Two Tongues in a Tower
Why Must You Know?

Whipple, Laura
My dad works late in a coffee shop.

Whisenand, Emma Bridge
Open your eyes that you may see.

Whistler, Laurence (b. 1912)
Form of Epitaph, A.
Portrait in the Guards, A.

Whitbread, Thomas (b. 1931)
CCC, The ("CCC campers near West Cummington.")
Pool, A.
To My Fellow-Mariners, March, '53.

White, Adeline
Autumn Morning.
Christmas Party, The.
Colour.
Over the Fields.

White, Elwyn Brooks (1899–1985)
Chairs in Snow.
Classic Waits for Me, A.
Commuter.
Conch.
Definitions, *sels.*
I Paint What I See.
Listener's Guide to the Birds, A.
Marble-Top.
Red Cow Is Dead, The.
Song of the Queen Bee.
Window Ledge in the Atom Age.

White, Gail
Leopard in Eden, The.

White, Gilbert (1720–93)
Naturalist's Summer-Evening Walk, The.
On the Dark, Still, Dry, Warm Weather Occasionally Happening in the Winter Months.

White, Henry Kirke (1785–1806)
Clifton Grove, *sels.*
To an Early Primrose.

White, J. P. (b. 1940)
In Ecclesiastes I read, "That which is far off and exceeding deep".

White, James L. (1936–81)
Making Love to Myself.

White, Joseph Blanco (1775–1841)
Black Is a Soul.
To Night.

White, Michael
"Claude Monet sur son lit do mort."

White, Shelley
Healing, The.

White, Terence Hanbury (1906–64)
To Myself, after Forty Years.

White, William Allen (1868–1944)
Rhyme of the Dream-Maker Man, A.

White-arm
Child listen / I am singing.

Whitecotton, Moses
Fuller and Warren.

Whitehead, Charles (1804–62)
Lamp, The.

Whitehead, James (b. 1936)
About a Year After He Got Married He Would Sit Alone in an Abandoned Shack in a Cotton Field Enjoying Himself.
Good Linemen Live in a Closed World.
He Remembers How He Didn't Understand What Lieutenant Dawson Meant.
Local Contractor Flees His Winter Trouble and Saves Some Lives in a Knoxville Motel Room, A.
Local Man Goes to the Killing Ground, A.
Local Man Remembers Betty Fuller, A.
Long Tour: The Country Music Star Explains Why He Put off the Bus and Fired a Good Lead Guitar in West Texas.
Narrative Hooper and L.D.O. Sestina with a Long Last Line, The.
Natural Theology, A.

Whitehead, Paul (1710–74)
Apollo and Daphne, *sels.*
Gymnasiad, The, or Boxing Match, *sels.*

Whitehead, William (1715–85)
Charge to the Poets, A, *sels.*
New Night Thoughts on Death; a Parody.
On the Late Improvements at Nuneham, the Seat of the Earl of Harcourt.
Song for Ranelagh.

Sweepers, The.
Venus Attiring the Graces.

Whitman, Roberta Hill (Roberta Hill) (b. 1947)
Beginning the Year at Rosebud, S. D.
Blue Mountain.
Climbing Gannett.
Depot in Rapid City.
Direction.
Dream of Rebirth.
E Uni Que A The Hi A Tho, Father.
Falling Moon.
For Heather, Entering Kindergarten.
From the Sun Itself.
Horses in Snow.
In the Longhouse, Oneida Museum.
In the Madison Zoo.
Leap in the Dark.
Lines for Marking Time.
Midnight on Front Street.
Nation Wrapped in Stone, A.
Night along the Mackinac Bridge.
One More Sign.
Patterns.
Reaching Yellow River.
Seal at Stinson Beach.
Sleeping with Foxes.
Song for Healing.
Star Quilt.
Steps.
Swamp.
Variations for Two Voices.
Waiting for Robinson.
Whispers.
White Land, The.
Winter Burn.
Woman Seed Player.

Whiteside, Mary Brent (d. 1962)
Carpenter, The.
Who Has Known Heights.

Whitfield, James M. (1823–78)
America, it is to thee, *sels.*
From America.
How long, oh gracious God! how long.
Misanthropist, The.
Poem Written for the Celebration of the
     Fourth Anniversary of President Lincoln's
     Emancipation Proclamation, A, *sels.*
Self-Reliance.
To A. H.
To ———: "Approaching night her mantle
     flings."
Yes! strike again that sounding string.

Whiting, William (1825–78)
Eternal Father, Strong to Save.

Whitlow, Carolyn Beard
Book of Routh.
Poem for the Children.
Rockin' A Man, Stone Blind.

Whitman, Albery Allson (1851–1901)
Idyll of the South, An, *sels.*
Lute of Afric's Tribe, The.
Not a Man and Yet a Man, *sels.*
Octoroon, The, *sels.*
Twasinta's Seminoles; Or Rape of Florida,
     sels.

Whitman, Ruth (b. 1922)
Castoff Skin.
Dead Center.
Laughing Gas.
Listening to Grownups Quarreling.

Whitman, S. W.
October.

Whitman, Sarah Helen (1803–78)
Morning-Glory, The.
November Landscape, A.
To ———: "Vainly my heart had with thy
     sorceries striven."

Whitman, Teresa
Super-Brave.

Whitman, Walt (1819–92)
Aboard at a ship's helm.
After the sea-ship, after the whistling winds.
After the supper and talk—after the day is
     done.
Ah poverties, wincings, and sulky retreats.

All the Past We Leave Behind.
America.
Among the Multitude.
Are you the new person drawn toward me?
Army Corps on the March, An.
Artilleryman's Vision, The.
As Adam early in the morning.
As I ebb'd with the ocean of life.
As I lay with my head in your lap camerado.
As I sit writing here, sick and grown old.
As if a phantom caress'd me.
As toilsome I wander'd Virginia's woods.
Base of All Metaphysics, The.
Beat! beat! drums!—blow! bugles! blow!
Beautiful Swimmer, The.
Beauty.
Beginning my studies the first step pleas'd
     me so much.
Behold this swarthy face, these gray eyes.
Bivouac on a Mountain Side.
Boston Ballad [1854], A.
Broadway.
By blue Ontario's shore, *sels.*
By the bivouac's fitful flame.
Cavalry Crossing a Ford.
Centenarian's Story, The.
Chanting the square deific, out of the One
     advancing, out of the sides.
City of orgies, walks and joys.
Clear Midnight, A.
Come, said my soul.
Come up from the fields father, here's a
     letter from our Pete.
Commonplace I sing, The.
Crossing Brooklyn Ferry, *sels.*
Dalliance of the Eagles, The.
Death's Valley.
Dirge for Two Veterans.
Dismantled Ship, The.
Earth, my likeness.
Eidolons.
Evening Lull, An.
Excelsior.
Faces.
Facing west from California's shores.
Fancies at Navesink, *sels.*
Farm Picture, A.
Fast-anchor'd eternal O love! O woman I
     love!
For You O Democracy.
From pent-up aching rivers.
Full of life now, compact, visible.
Give me the splendid silent sun with all his
     beams full-dazzling.
Glimpse through an interstice caught, A.
Good-bye my Fancy!
Good-Bye, My Fancy! ("Good-bye, my
     Fancy! / Farewell dear mate, dear love!")
Halcyon Days.
Hand-Mirror, A.
Hast never come to thee an hour.
Here the frailest leaves of me and yet my
     strongest lasting.
Hours continuing long, sore and heavy-
     hearted.
Hush'd be the camps to-day.
I am the poet of reality.
I dream'd in a dream I saw a city invincible
     to the attacks of the whole of the rest of
     the earth.
I hear America singing, the varied carols I
     hear.
I hear it was charged against me that I
     sought to destroy institutions.
I heard you solemn-sweet pipes of the organ
     as last Sunday morn I pass'd the church.
I saw in Louisiana a live-oak growing.
"I Sing the Body Electric," *sels.*
I sit and look out upon all the sorrows of the
     world, and upon all oppression and shame.
In cabin'd ships at sea.
In paths untrodden.
Italian Music in Dakota.
Joy, shipmate, joy!
Last Invocation, The.
Leaf for hand in hand, A.
Leaves of Grass (1855).

Long I Thought That Knowledge Alone
     Would Suffice.
Mannahatta ("I was asking for something
     specific and perfect for my city.")
March in the ranks hard-prest, and the road
     unknown, A.
Me imperturbe, standing at ease in Nature.
Memories of President Lincoln, *sels.*
Miracles.
My Picture-Gallery.
Native moments—when you come upon
     me—ah you are here now.
Night on the Prairies.
No labor-saving machine.
Noiseless patient spider, A.
Not heat flames up and consumes.
Not heaving from my ribb'd breast only.
Now precedent songs, farewell—by every
     name farewell.
O living always, always dying!
O tan-faced prairie-boy.
O you whom I often and silently come where
     you are that I may be with you.
Of the terrible doubt of appearances.
Old Ireland.
Old War-Dreams.
On the beach at night.
On the beach at night alone.
On the Same Picture.
Once I pass'd through a populous city
     imprinting my brain.
One's-Self I sing, a simple separate person.
Orange Buds by Mail from Florida.
Osceola.
Out of the cradle endlessly rocking.
Ox-Tamer, The.
Passage to India, *sels.*
Patrolling Barnegat.
Pensive on her dead gazing I heard the
     Mother of All.
Pioneers! O Pioneers!
Prairie-grass dividing, its special odor
     breathing, The.
Prayer of Columbus, *sels.*
Promise to California, A.
Proud music of the storm.
Reconciliation.
Recorders ages hence.
Respondez! Respondez! / (The war is
     completed—the price is paid—the title is
     settled beyond recall).
Roots and leaves themselves alone are these.
Rounded Catalogue Divine Complete, The.
Runner, The.
Scented herbage of my breast.
Shut not your doors to me proud libraries.
Sight in camp in the daybreak gray and dim,
     A.
Sleepers, The.
"Sleepers," The, *sels.*
So Long!
Sometimes with one I love I fill myself with
     rage for fear I effuse unreturn'd love.
Song for All Seas, All Ships.
Song of Myself, *sels.*
Song of the Broad-Axe, *sels.*
Song of the Exposition, *sels.*
Song of the Open Road, *sels.*
Song of the Redwood-Tree.
Sparkles from the Wheel.
Spirit whose work is done—spirit of dreadful
     hours!
Spontaneous me, Nature.
Tears! tears! tears! / In the night, in solitude,
     tears.
Thanks in old age—thanks ere I go.
That shadow my likeness that goes to and fro
     seeking a livelihood, chattering, chaffering.
These I singing in spring collect for lovers.
This Compost.
This moment yearning and thoughtful sitting
     alone.
To a Certain Civilian.
To a Common Prostitute.
To a Locomotive in Winter.
To a President.
To a Stranger.

To a Western Boy.
To-day and Thee.
To Him That Was Crucified.
To Old Age.
To the East and to the West.
To the garden the world anew ascending.
To the Man-of-War Bird.
To the Pending Year.
To the States, To Identify the 16th, 17th, or 18th Presidentiad.
To think of time—of all that retrospection.
Torch, The.
Trickle drops! my blue veins leaving!
Untold want by life and land ne'er granted, The.
Vigil strange I kept on the field one night;.
We two boys together clinging.
We two, how long we were fool'd.
What am I after all but a child, pleas'd with the sound of my own name? repeating it over and over.
What think you I take my pen in hand to record?
When I Heard at the Close of Day, *sels.*
When I heard at the close of the day how my name had been receiv'd with plaudits in the capitol, still it was not a happy night for me that follow'd.
When I heard the learn'd astronomer.
When I peruse the conquer'd fame of heroes and the victories of mighty generals, I do not envy the generals.
When I read the book, the biography famous.
Whoever you are holding me now in hand.
Woman waits for me, she contains all, nothing is lacking, A.
Words of the true poems give you more than poems, The.
World below the brine, The.
Wound-Dresser, The.
Years of the modern! years of the unperform'd!
Yonnondio.

Whitmell, Lucy
Christ in Flanders.

Whitney, Anna Temple
Kneeling Camel, The.

Whitney, Isabella (*fl.* **c.1567–c.1573)**
Admonition by the Auctor to all yong Gentilwomen: And to al other Maids being in Love, The, *sels.*
Aucthour Maketh Her Wyll and Testament, The.
I.W. To her unconstant Lover.
Manner of Her Will and What She Left to London and to All Those in It, at Her Departing, The, *sels.*
Sweet Nosegay, A, or Pleasant Posy, *sels.*

Whittaker, Frederick (d. 1963)
Custer's Last Charge.

Whittemore, Elizabeth
My friends are little lamps to me.

Whittemore, Reed (b. 1919)
Clamming.
Day with the Foreign Legion, A.
Departure, The.
On the Suicide of a Friend.
Only the Dead.
Party, The.
Projection, A.
Radio under the Bed, The.
Recall.
Science Fiction.
Still Life.
Storm from the East, A.
Tarantula, The.
Thinking of Tents.
Walk Home, The.

Whittier, John Greenleaf (1807–92)
Abraham Davenport.
All's Well.
Among the Hills, *sels.*
Astræa.
Barbara Frietchie.
Barefoot Boy, The, *sels.*
Bartholdi Statue, The.
Battle Autumn of 1862, The.

Brewing of Soma, The, *sels.*
Brown of Ossawatomie.
Burning Drift-Wood.
Call of the Christian, The.
Cities of the Plain, The.
Clerical Oppressors.
Dead Feast of the Kol-Folk, The.
Dedication: "I would the gift I offer here."
Eternal Goodness, The, *sels.*
Ezekiel.
Farewell, The: "Gone, gone,—sold and gone."
First-Day Thoughts.
For Righteousness' Sake.
Forgiveness.
Furnace Blast, The.
Garden.
Godspeed.
Haschish, The.
Help.
Henchman, The.
Hunters of Men, The.
Hymn: "Thine are all the gifts, O God!"
Ichabod[!].
Immortal Love, Forever Full.
In School-Days.
King Solomon and the Ants.
Laus Deo!
Lost Occasion, The.
Maud Muller on a summer's day, *sels.*
Miriam, *sels.*
My Playmate.
My Triumph.
O Thou! Whose Presence Went Before.
Official Piety.
Over-Heart, The.
Overruled.
Palm-Tree, The.
Proem: "I love the old melodious lays."
Pumpkin, The.
Sisters, The.
Skipper Ireson's Ride.
Snow-Bound [*or* Snow-Bound; a Winter Idyl], *sels.*
Song of Slaves in the Desert.
Telling the Bees.
Tent on the Beach: &[;The Dreamer&];, *sels.*
To My Old Schoolmaster.
What the Birds Said.
Word for the Hour, A.
Worship.

Whittingham, William (1524–79)
Now Israel May Say, and That Truly.

Whyte-Melville, George John
Coyotes are howling, The.

Wickham, Anna (Mrs. Patrick Hepburn) (1884–1947)
Affinity, The.
After Annunciation.
Boor's Wooing, The.
Cherry-Blossom Wand, The.
Creatrix.
Dedication of the Cook.
Dilemma, The.
Divorce.
Envoi: "God, thou great symmetry."
Fired Pot, The.
Friend Cato.
Gift to a Jade.
Happy Mathematician, The.
King Alfred and the Peasant Woman.
Lament of the Red Knight.
Last Round, The.
Letter to a Boy at School.
Meditation at Kew.
Nervous Prostration.
Nursery Song.
Paradox.
Pilgrimage.
Pugilist.
Sehnsucht.
Self-Analysis.
Sick Assailant, The.
Silent Singer, The.
Singer, The.
Slighted Lady, The.

Song: "I was so chill, and overworn, and sad."
Song-Maker, The.
Song of Ophelia the Survivor.
Song of the Lonely Shepherd.
Soul's Liberty.
Sportsman, The.
Tired Woman, The.
To a Crucifix.
To Men.
Vanity.
Weapons.

Widdemer, Margaret (b. 1880)
Invisible Playmate, The.
Oiseaurie.
Rainuv; a Romantic Ballad from the Early Basque.
Rambuncto.

Widerberg, Siv (b. 1931)
At Annika's Place.
Best?
Once I liked pablum.

Wieder, Laurance (b. 1946)
Tower of Babel, The.

Wieners, John (b. 1934)
Acceptance.
Anniversary of Death, An.
Doll.
Glimpse, A.
King Solomon's Magnetic Quiz.
Le Chariot.
Loneliness, The.
Long Nook.
Moon Poems.
My Mother.
Poem for Museum Goers, A.
Poem for Painters, A.
Poem for the Old Man, A.
Poem for Trapped Things, A.
Suck, The.
To H.
Two Years Later.
Waning of the Harvest Moon, The.
What Happened?

Wier, Dara (b. 1949)
Barely There.
Daytrip to Paradox.
Flood, The.
Holidays.
Innate Deception of Unspoiled Beauty, The.
Lucille and Ernie's Master Bedroom.
Lucille's Kumquat Colored Kimono.
Old-fashioned.

Wiesel, Elie (b. 1928)
Ani Maamin, A Song Lost and Found Again, *sels.*
Never shall I forget that night.

Wieseltier, Meir (b. 1941)
Allenby.
Caution Prevents Accidents.
Columns.
Elegies by the Senses, *sels.*
Everyone passes under the moon.
Extended Sonnet on the Death of Isaac Danziger.
God's Fire upon Children ("God's fire upon cities.")
Here in Netanya.
Holy Is the Desire to Proclaim the Existence of God.
Leningrad: Picture Postcard.
Love Poem: "Greyish yellow is the color of the dust."
Note.
On Guard.
Poetry's Buried.
Saul Re-enthroned.
Site.
Song of the last soldier, A.
Take a Look at My Rebels.
Take poems, but don't read them.
Too Short.
Wintry Dawn, *sels.*

Wiggin, Larry
Crickets.
Dreaming.

Fly.
Scouring pans.
Wind.

Wigglesworth, Michael (1631–1705)
Day of Doom, The, *sels.*
For Just Men Light Is Sown.
God's Controversy with New-England.
Prayer unto Christ the Judge of the World,
   A.
Song of Emptiness to Fill up the Empty
   Pages Following, A.
Welcome, Sweet Rest.

Wigmore, Paul
Limerick: "Man called Andronicus (Titus),
   A."

Wigson, John (b. c.1711)
On the Death of Squire Christopher.

Wilberforce, Ernest R.
Just for To-Day.

Wilberforce, Samuel (1805–73)
Impromptu.

Wilbur, Richard (b. 1921)
Advice to a Prophet.
After the last bulletins the windows darken.
All These Birds.
Altitudes.
April 5, 1974.
Aspen and the Stream, The.
Baroque Wall-Fountain in the Villa Sciarra,
   A.
Beasts in their major freedom / Slumber in
   peace tonight.
Beautiful Changes, The.
Bell Speech.
Black November Turkey, A.
Boy at the Window.
Caserta Garden.
Catch, The.
Ceremony.
Christmas Hymn, A.
Cicadas.
Cottage Street, 1953.
Death of a Toad, The.
Digging for China.
Digression, A.
Epistemology.
Event, An.
Exeunt.
Finished Man, A.
Fire-Truck, A.
First Snow in Alsace.
Flippancies, *sels.*
For K. R. on Her Sixtieth Birthday.
For the Student Strikers.
Grasse: The Olive Trees.
Grasshopper, A.
Hamlen Brook.
Hole in the Floor, A.
In a Churchyard.
In Limbo.
In the Elegy Season.
In the Field.
In the Smoking-Car.
John Chapman.
Juggler.
Junk.
Late Aubade, A.
Leaving.
Looking into History.
Love Calls Us to the Things of This World.
Loves of the Puppets.
Lying.
Marginalia.
Matthew VIII, 28 ff.
Merlin Enthralled.
Mill, The.
Miltonic Sonnet for Mr. Johnson on His
   Refusal of Peter Hurd's Official Portrait,
   A.
Mind in its [*or* the] purest play is like some
   bat.
Mind-Reader, The, *sels.*
Museum Piece.
My Father Paints the Summer.
On the Marginal Way.
Pangloss's Song: A Comic-Opera Lyric.
Parable.

Pardon, The.
Part of a Letter.
Piazza di Spagna, Early Morning.
Place Pigalle.
Plain Song for Comadre, A.
Playboy.
Praise in Summer.
Prisoner of Zenda, The.
Proof, The.
Rillons, Rillettes, they taste the same.
Running.
Seed Leaves.
Shame.
She.
Simile for Her Smile, A.
Simplification, A.
Sleepless at Crown Point.
Some Opposites.
Speech for the Repeal of the McCarran Act.
St. Matthew, *sels.*
Still, citizen sparrow, this vulture which you
   call.
Stop.
Summer Morning, A.
Teresa.
Thyme Flowering among Rocks.
To an American Poet Just Dead.
To the Etruscan Poets.
Transit.
Two Voices in a Meadow.
Tywater.
Undead, The.
Voice from under the Table, A.
Walking to Sleep.
Wedding Toast, A.
What is the opposite of *nuts?*.
Winter Deepening, The.
'World Without Objects Is a Sensible
   Emptiness," A."
Writer, The.
Year's End.

Wilcox, Carlos (1794–1827)
Age of Benevolence, The, *sels.*

Wilcox, Ella Wheeler (1850–1919)
Accept My Full Heart's Thanks.
Ad Finem.
Answered Prayers.
Attraction.
Beautiful Land of Nod, The.
Belief.
Dawn.
Days grow shorter, the nights grow longer,
   The.
Engine, The.
Faith.
Fault of the Age, The.
Five Little Brothers.
Friendship.
Friendship After Love.
Holiday, A.
I love your lips when they're wet with wine.
Law, The.
Life.
Life's Journey.
Life's Scars.
Lifting and Leaning.
Love much. Earth has enough of bitter in it.
Mistakes.
Morning Prayer, A.
My Ships.
No classes here! Why, that is idle talk.
Nothing New.
One of Us Two.
Only One Way.
Optimism.
Peace and Love.
Peace at the Goal.
Progress.
Queen's Last Ride, The.
Room beneath the Rafters, The.
Secret Thoughts.
Solitude.
Sonnet, The.
There Comes a Time.
Those We Love the Best.
Two Glasses, The.
Was, Is, and Yet-to-be.

Way of It, The.
What Love Is.
Whatever Is—Is Best.
Will.
Winds of Fate, The.
World, The.
Worthwhile.
You Never Can Tell.

Wilczek, Frank (b. 1951)
Virtual Particles.

Wild, Peter (b. 1940)
Air Raid.
Dog Hospital.
Ice Cream.
Riding Double.
Snakes.
Thomas and Charlie.

Wild, Robert (1609–79)
Alas poore Scholler, whither wilt thou goe,
   sels.
Epitaph for a Godly Man's Tomb, An.
Epitaph on Some Bottles of Sack and Claret
   Laid in Sand.

Wilde, J. (fl. c.1779)
Verses to Miss———.

**Wilde, Lady Jane Francesca ("Speranza")
(1820–96)**
Corinne's Last Love-Song.
Désillusion.
Famine Year, The.
Poet's Destiny, The.
Who Will Show Us Any Good?

**Wilde, Oscar Fingall O'Flahertie Wills (1854–
1900)**
Ave Imperatrix!
Ave Maria, Gratia Plena.
Ballad of Reading Gaol, The, *sels.*
By the Arno.
Disciple, The.
E Tenebris.
Easter Day.
Harlot's House, The.
Hélas!
Impression Du Matin.
Impression du Voyage.
Impressions, *sels.*
Le Jardin des Tuileries.
Les Ballons.
Magdalen Walks.
My Voice.
Picture of Dorian Gray, The, *sels.*
Requiescat.
San Miniato.
Sphinx, The, *sels.*
Symphony in Yellow.
Theocritus.

Wilde, Richard Henry (1789–1847)
Hesperia, *sels.*
Lament of the Captive, The.
To the Mocking-Bird.

Wilkes, H. E.
Q-Boat, The.

Wilkie, William (1721–72)
Grasshopper and the Glowworm, The, *sels.*

Wilkins, Alice
Elephant's Trunk, The.

Wilkinson, Anne (1910–61)
Adam and God.
Daily the Drum.
Falconry.
In June and Gentle Oven.
Leda in Stratford, Ont.
Lens.
Nature Be Damned.
Red and the Green, The.
Variations on a Theme.

Wilkinson, H. E. (b. 1930)
Bread.
Topsy-turvy Land.
What Is It?

Wilkinson, Iris Gulver. *See* "Hyde, Robin"

Wilkinson, John (b. 1953)
Clay when the wire slackens, sheds its velvet
   light.
Every metaphor sounds the same.

He smears.
We'd launch out, but a spiral failure binds so
    close.
Willard, Emma Hart (1787–1870)
    Rocked in the Cradle of the Deep.
Willard, Nancy (b. 1936)
    Angels in Winter.
    Arbor.
    Ballad of Biddy Early, The.
    Blake Leads a Walk on the Milky Way.
    Cat to His Dinner, The.
    Cat's Second Song, The.
    Clearing the Air.
    Feast of St. Tortoise, The.
    How the Hen Sold Her Eggs to the Stingy
        Priest.
    How to Stuff a Pepper.
    Insects, The.
    King of Cats Sends a Postcard to His Wife,
        The.
    Night Light.
    One for the Road.
    Original Strawberry.
    Questions My Son Asked Me, Answers I
        Never Gave Him.
    Saint Pumpkin.
    Sleep of the Painted Ladies, The.
    Speckled Hen's Morning Song to Biddy
        Early, The.
    Why I Never Answered Your Letter.
William of Aquitaine (1071–1127)
    From the Provençal of William of Poitiers.
    I will write a poem about nothing.
    Since now I have a mind to sing.
William of Shoreham (fl. early 14th cent.)
    Marye, maide, milde and fre.
Williams, Anna (1706–83)
    Nunnery, The.
    Verses to Mr. Richardson on his History of
        Sir Charles Grandison.
Williams, Bertye Young (d. 1951)
    Friend Who Just Stands By, The.
Williams, Big Joe (b. 1903)
    President Roosevelt.
Williams, C. K. (b. 1936)
    My Mother's Lips.
Williams, Charles (1886–1945)
    At the "Ye That Do Truly."
    Dream, A.
    From a Walking Song.
    Kings Came Riding.
    Mount Badon.
    Night Song for a Child.
    Taliessin's Song of the Unicorn.
Williams, Sir Charles Hanbury (1709–57)
    Isabella; or, The Morning, sels.
    Song upon Miss Harriet Hanbury, Addressed
        to the Revd Mr Birt.
    Verses: "Poor fellow, what is it to you."
Williams, Charles Kenneth (b. 1936)
    Alzheimer's: The Wife.
    Dream of Mind: The Gap, A.
    Gas Station, The.
    Helen.
    It Is This Way with Men.
    Last Deaths, The.
    Love: Intimacy.
    Love: Shyness.
    Question, The.
    Racists.
    Repression.
    Snow: II.
    Tar.
    World's greatest tricycle rider, The.
Williams, Clarence (1893–1965)
    Gulf Coast Blues.
Williams, Daniel (1927–72)
    We Are the Cenotaphs.
Williams, Dennis
    If a lot of people are laughing.
Williams, Edward (Iolo Morganwg) (1747–1826)
    My Pet Goldfish.
    Poet's Arbour in the Birchwood, The.
Williams, Edward W. (1863–91)
    At Harper's Ferry Just before the Attack.

Williams, Eliseus (1867–1926)
    Heather Flowers.
Williams, Emmett (b. 1925)
    Like Attracts Like.
Williams, Evelyn M. (d. 1959)
    Chestnut Buds.
Williams, Frederick (b. 1947)
    Eighties, De.
Williams, George. See Awoonor, Kofi
Williams, Gwyn (b. 1904)
    Aspects of Now, sels.
Williams, Helen Maria (1762–1827)
    Address to Poetry, An, sels.
    Elegy on a Young Thrush Which Escaped
        from the Writer's Hand.
    On the Death of the Rev. Dr. Kippis.
    Poems, sels.
    Song, A: "No riches from his scanty store."
    Sonnet on Reading the Poem upon the
        Mountain Daisy, by Mr. Burns.
    Sonnet to Hope.
    Sonnet VI. To the Torrid Zone.
    To Dr. Moore, in Anser to a Poetical Epistle
        Written by Him in Wales.
    To Mrs. K————, On Her Sending Me an
        English Christmas Plum-Cake at Paris.
    To the Curlew.
    To the Moon.
Williams, Hugo (b. 1942)
    Broken Dreams.
    Butcher carves veal for two, The.
    Girl.
    Gone Away.
    Love Life.
    Some Kisses from The Kama Sutra.
    Sure.
Williams, John (1664–1729)
    Some Contemplations of the Poor, and
        Desolate State of the Church at Deerfield.
Williams, John (1761–1818)
    Matrimony.
    On Reading Aloud My Early Poems.
Williams, John Lloyd (d. 1945)
    Naming of Private Parts.
Williams, Jonathan (b. 1929)
    Adhesive Autopsy of Walt Whitman, The.
    Anthropophagites See a Sign on NC Highway
        177 That Looks like Heaven, The.
    Bitch-Kitty, The.
    Distances to the Friend, The.
    Fast Ball.
    Hermit Cackleberry Brown, on Human
        Vanity, The.
    Honey Lamb, The.
    Little Tumescence, A.
    Mahler, sels.
    Mrs. Sadie Grindstaff, Weaver and Factotum.
    Ovid, Meet a Metamorphodite.
    Switch Blade; or, John's Other Wife, The.
    Those Troublesome Disguises.
    Three Sayings from Highlands, North
        Carolina.
    Uncle Iv Surveys His Domain from His
        Rocker.
    Vulnerary, A.
Williams, Lucy (b. 1893)
    Origin of the Skagit Indians, The.
Williams, Marilyn
    Images.
Williams, Max
    Empty House, The.
Williams, Miller (b. 1930)
    After the Revolution for Jesus the Associate
        Professor [or a Secular Man] Prepares His
        Final Remarks.
    Aging Actress Sees Herself a Starlet on the
        Late Show, The.
    Caterpillar, The.
    Death of Chet Baker, The.
    Firebreathers at the Café Deux Magots, The.
    Love and How It Becomes Important in Our
        Day to Day Lives.
    On a Photograph of My Mother at Seventeen.
    On the Symbolic Consideration of Hands and
        the Significance of Death.

Poem for Emily, A.
Ruby Tells All.
Why God Permits Evil: For Answers to This
    Question of Interest to Many Write Bible
    Answers Dept. E-7.
Williams, Oscar (b. 1900)
    By Fiat of Adoration.
    Dwarf of Disintegration.
    Golden Fleece, The.
    I Sing an Old Song.
    Last Supper, The.
    Leg in the Subway, The.
    Mirage, The.
    Picture Postcard of a Zoo.
    Praying Mantis Visits a Penthouse, The
        ("Praying mantis with its length of straw,
        The.")
    Shopping for Meat in Winter.
    Variations on a Theme, sels.
Williams, Patrick (b. 1950)
    Baby in the House, A.
    In the Dark.
    Lost Seed.
    Passing Through.
    Rhapsody on Main Street.
    Trails.
Williams, Peter (b. 1937)
    When She Was Here, Li Bo.
Williams, Rhydwen (b. 1916)
    Baboon, The.
Williams, Robert (1830–77)
    On a Woman.
Williams, Roger (c.1603–1683)
    Adulteries, murthers, robberies, thefts.
    Boast not proud English, of thy birth and
        blood.
    Course bread and water's most their fare.
    Courteous Indian, The.
    God gives them sleep on ground, on straw.
    How busie are the sonnes of men?
    I have heard ingenuous Indians say.
    If Birds That neither Sow nor Reap.
    Indians count of men as dogs, The.
    Indians prize not English gold, The.
    Mans restlesse soule hath restlesse eyes and
        ears.
    One step twix't me and death, (twas Davids
        speech).
    Our English gamesters scorne to stake.
    Pagans wild confesse the bonds, The.
    They see Gods wonders that are call'd.
    Truth is a native, naked beauty; but.
    What Habacuck once spake, mine eyes.
    When Sun Doth Rise.
Williams, Sarah (1837–68)
    Is It True?
    Like a drop of water is my heart.
    Old Astronomer to His Pupil, The.
Williams, Sherley Anne (b. 1944)
    Driving Wheel.
    Empress Brand Trim: Ruby Reminisces, The.
    For Ronald King Our Brother.
    House of Desire, The.
    I Sing This Song for Our Mothers: Ruise.
    I Want Aretha to Set This to Music.
    Peacock Poems, The, sels.
    Peacock Poems: 1, The.
    Quartet.
    Say Hello to John.
    She Had Known Brothers.
    Straight Talk from Plain Women.
    This Is a Sad-Ass Poem for a Black Woman
        to Be Writing.
    You Were Never Miss Brown to Me.
Williams, Shirley
    If He Let Us Go Now.
    Killing of the Birds, The.
**Williams, Tennessee (Thomas Lanier Williams)
    (1914–83)**
    Carrousel Tune.
    Crepe de Chine.
    Cried the Fox.
    Gold Tooth Blues.
    Kitchen Door Blues.
    Life Story.
    My Love Was Light.

Sugar in the Cane.
You and I.

Williams, Theodore Chickering (1855–1915)
Hast Thou Heard It, O My Brother.
My Country, to Thy Shore.
When Thy Heart with Joy O'erflowing.

Williams, Thomas Lanier. *See* **Williams, Tennessee**

Williams, Waldo (1904–72)
Daffodil.
In Two Fields.
Summer Cloud, A.

Williams, William ("Pantycelyn") (1717–91)
Guide Me, O Thou Great Jehovah.
I Gaze across the Distant Hills.
View of Christ's Kingdom, A, *sels.*

Williams, William Carlos (1883–1963)
Act, The.
Apology.
Approach to a City.
Après le Bain.
Are the desolate, dark weeks.
Artist, The.
Asphodel, That Greeny Flower, *sels.*
At Kenneth Burke's Place.
At the Ball Game.
Ballad of Faith.
Between Walls.
Bird Song.
Botticellian Trees, The.
Breakfast.
Bull, The.
Burning the Christmas Greens.
Catholic Bells, The.
Children, The.
Classic Scene.
Clouds, The.
Coda.
Complaint.
Complete Destruction.
Daisy.
Dance, The.
Danse Russe.
Dawn.
Dead Baby, The.
Death.
Deceptrices, The.
Descent beckons, the.
Descent of Winter, The, *sels.*
Desert Music, The.
Drink.
Drunkard, The.
El Hombre.
End of the Parade, The.
Exercise No. 2.
First Praise.
Flowers by the Sea.
Folded Skyscraper, A, *sels.*
For Eleanor and Bill Monahan.
4th of July.
Fragment: "As for him who."
Gift, The.
Good Night.
Goodnight, A.
Graceful Bastion, The.
Great Figure, The.
Gulls.
Hard Listener, The.
High Bridge above the Tagus River at Toledo, The.
History of Love, A.
Horse Show, The.
Hounded Lovers, The.
House is yours, The.
Illegitimate Things.
Impromptu: The Suckers.
Intelligent Sheepman and the New Cars, The.
Iris.
It is a small plant.
Italian Garden, The.
Ivy Crown, The.
January.
January Morning.
Jungle, The.
Kora in Hell, *sels.*
Lament: "What face, in the water."

Last Words of My English Grandmother, The.
Late Singer, The.
Le Médecin Malgré Lui.
Lear.
Locust Tree in Flower, The.
Lonely Street, The.
Love Song: First Version, 1915, A.
Love Song: "I lie here thinking of you."
Love Song: "Sweep the house clean."
Marriage.
Mental Hospital Garden, The, *sels.*
Metric Figure.
Mezzo Forte.
Mists Over the River.
Mujer.
Nantucket.
Negro Woman, A.
Ol' Bunk's Band.
On Gay Wallpaper.
Orchestra, The.
Overture to a Dance of Locomotives.
Parable of the Blind, The.
Pastoral: "Little sparrows, The."
Pastoral: "When I was younger."
Paterson.
Paterson: The Falls.
Philomena Andronico.
Pictures from Brueghel, *sels.*
Pink Locust, The.
Poem: "As the cat / climbed over."
Poem: "On getting a card."
Poem: "Rose fades / and is renewed again, The."
Poor, The.
Porous.
Portrait of a Lady.
Predicter of Famine, The.
Prelude to Winter.
Proletarian Portrait.
Puerto Rico Song.
Queen-Anne's-Lace.
Raleigh Was Right.
Raper from Passenack, The.
Red Wheelbarrow, The.
Return to Work, The.
Revelation, The.
Rewaking, The.
Ritualists, The.
River Rhyme.
Rose, The.
Russia.
Sadness of the Sea, The.
Sea-Elephant, The.
Semblables, The.
Short Poem.
Silence.
Slow Movement.
Smell.
Sort of a Song, A.
Sparrow, The.
Sparrows among Dry Leaves.
Spring and All.
St. Matthew; He also told them a parable, *sels.*
These are the desolate, dark weeks.
These Purists.
This Is Just to Say.
This is the time of year.
To.
To a Dog Injured in the Street.
To a Friend Concerning Several Ladies.
To a Poor Old Woman.
To a Solitary Disciple.
To an Elder Poet.
To Be Recited to Flossie on Her Birthday.
To Close.
To Elsie.
To Flossie.
To Ford Madox Ford in Heaven.
To Greet a Letter-Carrier.
To Mark Anthony in Heaven.
To Waken an Old Lady.
Tract.
Tulip Bed, The.
Turtle, The.
Unison, A.

Waiting.
Widow's Lament in Springtime, The.
Willow Poem.
Wind Increases, The.
Woman Walking.
Yachts, The.
Yellow Flower, The.
Yellow Season, The.
Young Housewife, The.
Young Laundryman, The.
Young Sycamore.

Williamson, Greg (b. 1964)
Annual Returns.
Counterfeiter, The.
Walter Parmer.
Waterfall.

Williamson, Jess (b. 1942)
Natural Selection.

Williamson, Roosevelt. *See* **Shahid**

"Willie, Woodbine." *See* **Studdert-Kennedy, Geoffrey Anketell**

Willis, Humphrey (*fl.* 1647)
Time's Whirligig, Or, The Blue-New-Made-Gentleman Mounted.

Willis, Love Maria (1824–1908)
Father, Hear the Prayer We Offer.

Willis, Nathaniel Parker (1806–67)
Ambition.
City Lyrics.
Confessional, The.
Declaration, The.
January 1, 1829.
Lady in the White Dress, Whom I Helped into the Omnibus, The.
Lady Jane, The; a Humorous Novel in Rhyme, *sels.*
Melanie, *sels.*
Psyche, Before the Tribunal of Venus.
To Charles Roux, of Switzerland.
To Helen in a Huff.
To the Lady in the Chemisette with Black Buttons.
Unseen Spirits.

Willis, Paul (b. 1955)
Meeting Like This.

Willmot, Rod
Away from eyes.
Breathing.
Cheeses, pâté.
Her breasts lift with her arms.
Her hand on the doorknob.
Humiliated again.
I find her huddled on the bed.
If I go alone.
Listening.
Mail on the counter.
May rain.
Musty shed.
Novel's end.
Now the spade.
Page of Shelley, A.
Quiet rustle, A.
Shadows in the grass.
Small noise, A.
Weak sun.

Willoby, Henry (1574–1596?)
Willobie His Avisa, *sels.*

Wills, John
Another bend.
Below the dam.
Beyond the porch.
Bittern booms, A.
Bluegill rises, A.
Bluejay sails, A.
Boulders.
Box of nails, A.
Coolness.
Day wears on, The.
Den of the bear.
Dusk from rock to rock a waterthrush.
Evening sun, The.
Forest stands, The.
Goats on the roof.
Hills, The.
I catch.
In an upstairs room.

Larger.
Laurel in bloom.
Looking deeper.
Moon at dawn, The.
Mourning cloak, A.
My hand moves out.
November evening.
Old cow lags, The.
Pebble falls, A.
Rain in gusts.
River, The.
Stagnant pond, A.
Summer drizzle.
Sun lights up a distant ridge another, The.
Water lilies.
Water pools.
White horse.
Winter again.

Willson, Dixie
Mist and All, The.
Tip-Toe Tail.

Willson, Forceythe (1837–67)
Estray, The.
In State, *sels.*
To Hersa.

Wilmot, Frank. *See* **"Maurice, Furnley"**

Wilmot, John. *See* **Rochester, John Wilmot, 2d Earl of.**

Wilner, Eleanor (b. 1931)
Coda, Overture.
Emigration.
Epitaph: "Young then, / we were bored already."
High Noon at Los Alamos.
Reading the Bible Backwards.
Sarah's Choice.

Wilson, Anne (fl. 1778)
Teisa, a Descriptive Poem of the River Tees, Its Towns and Antiquities, *sels.*

Wilson, August (b. 1945)
Theme One: The Variations.

"Wilson, Charlotte." *See* **Baker, Karle Wilson**

Wilson, Edmund (1895–1972)
Disloyal Lines to an Alumnus.
Drafts for a Quatrain.
Easy Exercises in the Use of Difficult Words, *sels.*
Enemies of Promise.
Miniature Dialogue.
Not Here.
Omelet of A MacLeish, The.
On Editing Scott Fitzgerald's Papers.
Something for My Russian Friends.
Voice, The.

Wilson, Edwin H. (b. 1898)
Where Is Our Holy Church?

Wilson, James
Casey's Revenge.

Wilson, James Edward (b. 1907)
When I Am Dead.

Wilson, John (1588–1677)
Armada, 1588, The.

Wilson, John (1591–1667)
Confess We All, before the Lord.
For Lo! My Jonah How He Slumped.
Whoso Would See This Song of Heavenly Choice.

Wilson, John (1627?–1696)
Claudius Gilbert.
Copy of Verses, A.

Wilson, John ("Christopher North") (1785–1854)
Isle of Palms and Other Poems, The, *sels.*
Sonnet VII. Written on Skiddaw, during a Tempest.
Written on the Banks of Wastwater During a Calm.

Wilson, Keith (b. 1927)
Dusk in My Backyard.
Idiot, The.
Lamb, The.
Old Women beside a Church.
Twin Aces.

Wilson, Marjorie
From the Train.
Gates to England, The.

Jungle Trees, The.
Lighthouse, The.
Little Things That Happen, The.
Through the Porthole.

Wilson, Mary
Diary.
Harold Wilson's Selected Poems, *sels.*

Wilson, Ramona (b. 1945)
Bags Packed and We Expected This.
Eveningsong.
Eveningsong 2.
Keeping Hair.
Late in Fall.
Meeting, The.
Overnight Guest.
Reading Indian Poetry.
Spring at Fort Okanogan.
Spring in Virginia.
Summer.

Wilson, Raymond
Davy by Starlight.
Family Holiday.
Never since Eden.
Space Walk.

Wilson, Robert (d. 1600?)
Three Ladies of London, The, *sels.*

Wilson, Robert Noble Denison (1899–1953)
Elegy in a Presbyterian Burying-Ground.

Wilson, Robley, Jr. (b. 1936)
Envoi: "Sun in the mouth of the day."
Mechanical Cow, The.
Military-Industrial Complex, The.
Rejoicing That Attend the Murder of Famous Men, The.
Say Girls in Shoe Ads: "I Go for a Man Who's Tall!"
Sparrow Hills.

Wilson, T. P. Cameron ("Tipcuca") (1889–1918)
Magpies in Picardy, The.
Sportsmen in Paradise.

Wilson, Woodrow (1856–1924)
Limerick: "I went with the Duchess to tea."

Winant, Fran (b. 1943)
Sacred Grove, A.
To Begin.

Winchester, Caleb T. (1847–1920)
Lord Our God Alone Is Strong, The.

Winchester, Elhanan (1751–97)
Behold with Joy.

Winchilsea, Anne Finch, Countess of (1661–1720)
Adam Posed.
Answer, The.
Ballad to Mrs. Catherine Fleming in London from Malshanger Farm in Hampshire, A.
Circuit of Apollo, The.
Enquiry after Peace. A Fragment.
Friendship Between Ephelia and Ardelia.
Hog, the Sheep and Goat, Carrying to a Fair, The.
Introduction, The: "Did I, my lines intend for public[k] view."
Letter to Daphnis, A.
Life's Progress.
Nocturnal Reverie, A.
On Myself.
Pastoral Dialogue between Two Shepherdesses, A.
Petition for an Absolute Retreat, The, *sels.*
Pindaric Poem, A, *sels.*
Reformation.
Sigh, A.
Some Reflections.
Song, A: "Nymph in vain bestows her pains, The."
Song of the Cannibals, A.
Song on the South Sea, A.
Spleen, A.
Spleen, a Pindaric Poem, The, *sels.*
Tale of the Miser and the Poet, A.
To Death.
To Melancholy.
To the Nightingale.
Trail All Your Pikes.
Trail all your pikes, dispirit every drum.

Upon My Lord Winchilsea's Converting the Mount in His Garden to a Terrace.

Wine, Maria (b. 1912)
Love Me.
Woman, you are afraid of the forest.

Wingfield, Sheila (1906–73)
Winter.

Winik, Marion
Foreign Exchange.

Winner, Joseph E. (1837–1918)
Little Brown Jug.

Winner, Robert (b. 1930)
Segregated Railway Diner—1946.

Winner, Septimus ("Alice Hawthorne") (1827–1902)
Coolie Chinee, The.
Lilliputian's Beer Song.
Ten Little Injuns.

Winslow, Pete
I blink and half my life is over.
O god of spring forgive me.

Winstanley, Gerrard (1609?–1676)
Digger's Song, The.

Winstanley, John (1678–1750)
Epigram on Florio.
Epigram on the First of April.
Fanny's Removal in 1714.
Inventory of the Furniture of a Collegian's Chamber, An.
Last Will and Testament, A.
Miss Betty's Singing-Bird.
On a Certain Effeminate Peer.
On a Stingy Beau.
To the Revd. Mr. ——— on His Drinking Sea-Water.

Wintchevsky, Morris (1856–1934)
Child-King, The.
If I Felt Less.

Winter, William (1836–1917)
Heart's Anchor, The.

Winters, Anne (b. 1939)
Mill-Race, The.

Winters, Yvor (1900–1968)
Apollo and Daphne.
At the San Francisco Airport.
Before Disaster.
By the Road to the Air-Base.
Elegy: "Noon is beautiful, The: the perfect wheel."
For the Opening of the William Dinsmore Briggs Room.
Fragment: "I cannot find my way to Nazareth."
Hawk's Eyes.
Inscription for a Graveyard.
John Sutter.
Manzanita, The.
Night of Battle.
Nocturne for October 31st, A.
On Teaching the Young.
Orpheus.
Precision, The.
Rows of Cold Trees, The.
Sir Gawaine and the Green Knight.
Slow Pacific Swell, The.
Song in Passing, A.
Static Autumn.
Summer Commentary, A.
Summer Noon: 1941.
Theseus: A Trilogy.
Time and the Garden.
To a Military Rifle, 1942.
To Emily Dickinson.
To My Infant Daughter.
To the Holy Spirit.

Wintle, Walter D.
Man Who Thinks He Can, The.

Wintu Oral Tradition
Where will you and I sleep?

Wisdome, Robert (d. 1568)
Religious Use of [Taking] Tobacco, A.

Wise, Isaac M. (1819–1900)
In Mercy, Lord, Incline Thine Ear.

Wise, Joseph (b. 1940)
Glory.

Wise, William (b. 1923)
When I grow up.
Wishik, Heather (b. 1950)
Visitation Rights.
Wiswall, Ichabod (1637–1700)
Judicious Observation of That Dreadful
Comet, A.
Witheford, Hubert (b. 1921)
At the Discharge of Cannon Rise the
Drowned.
Barbarossa.
Mid Winter.
What Is Happening Now?
Wither, George (1588–1667)
Britain's Remembrancer Canto 4, *sels.*
Choice, The.
Collection of Emblemes, Ancient and
Moderne, A, *sels.*
Conversion of S. Paul, The.
Epigram: "Women, as some men say,
unconstant be."
Fair Virtue, the Mistress of Philarete, *sels.*
First Song of Moses, The.
For a Poet.
For Scholars and Pupils.
Hallelujah; or, Britain's Second
Remembrancer, *sels.*
I loved a lass, a fair one.
Lord, Many Times Thou Pleased Art.
Ninth Canticle, The.
Prayer of Hezekiah, The.
Prayer of Nehemiah, The.
Shephe[a]rd's Hunting, The, *sels.*
Vox Pacifica, *sels.*
Widow's Hymn, A.
Witherspoon, Naomi Long. *See* **Madgett, Naomi
Long**
Withington, Leonard (1789–1885)
O Saviour of a World Undone.
Witt, Harold (b. 1923)
Dreamscape in Kümmel.
Witt, Sir Robert
Limerick: "Arnolfinis both sat to Van Eyck."
Witting, Amy (b. 1918)
Beauty is the straw I clutch at, but to say
straw.
Blinkered Mind, The.
Curse on Herod, A.
Woddis, Roger (b. 1917)
All Clear.
Believers' Best Buy.
Do not go sober into that dim light.
Doctor, The.
Eat Your Heart Out, Edward Lear!
Ethics for Everyman.
Final Curtain.
I shall vote Centre because.
Limerick: "Said a God-fearing lady called
Whitehouse."
Limerick: "Said Powell: 'Don't call me
insane.'"
Limerick: "There once were two Babes in the
Wood."
Limerick: "There was an Old Man with a
Beard / Who said: 'I demand to be
feared.'"
Moral Tale, A.
Nothing Sacred.
Rewards and Fairies.
Rolling Chinese Wall, The.
Wodehouse, Pelham Grenville (1881–1975)
Gourmet's Love-Song, The.
Outcast, The.
Printer's Error.
To William (Whom We Have Missed).
Wojahn, David (b. 1953)
Armageddon: Private Gabriel Calvin Wojahn
1900–18.
First Six Seals, The.
Homage to Ryszard Kapuściński.
John Berryman Listening to Robert Johnson's
"King of the Delta Blues," January 1972.
Mystery Train: A Sequence, *sels.*
Photo of My Father in a Snowbound Train.
Riding the Empire Builder, 1948.
Satin Doll.

White Lanterns.
Wojtyla, Karol (Pope John Paul II) (b. 1920)
Marble Floor.
Song of the Brightness of Water.
Wolcot, John. *See* **"Pindar, Peter"**
Wolcott, Roger (1679–1767)
Heart Is Deep, The.
Matthew X. 28.
Wolcott, Samuel (1813–86)
Christ for the World! We Sing.
Father! I Own Thy Voice.
Wolf, Leonard (b. 1923)
Peasant, The.
Wolfe, Aaron R. (1821–1902)
Complete in Thee, No Work of Mine.
Parting Hymn We Sing, A.
Wolfe, Charles (1791–1823)
Burial of Sir John Moore &[;after [*or* at]
Corunna&];, The.
Song: "Oh say not that my heart is cold."
To Mary.
Wolfe, Ffrida
Choosing Shoes.
Four and Eight.
Poppies in the Garden, The.
Wolfe, Humbert (1885–1940)
A. E. Housman and a Few Friends.
Blackbird, The.
D. H. Lawrence and James Joyce.
Dead Fiddle, The.
Dean Inge.
G. K. Chesterton.
Gray Squirrel, The.
Green Candles.
Hilaire Belloc.
Iliad.
Journey's End.
Love Is a Keeper of Swans.
Man.
Things Lovelier.
This Is Not Death.
Thrush In the Trenches, A.
Tulip.
Wardour Street.
Waters of Life, The.
You cannot hope.
Wolfe, Thomas Clayton (1900–1938)
For, brother, what are we?
Wolff, David
While We Slept.
Wolfli, Adolf (1864–1930)
From the Cradle to the Graave, or, through
Working and Sweating, Suffering and
Hardship, even through Prayyer into
Damnation, *sels.*
Nostalgic song for my beloved.
Wolfram von Eschenbach (1170?–1220?)
His Own True Wife.
"Its claws have struck through the clouds."
You always sang at break of day.
Wolfskehl, Karl (1869–1948)
And Yet We Are Here!
Shekhinah.
To Be Said at the Seder.
We Go.
Wollach, Yona (b. 1946)
Absalom.
All the silly threatening things.
Are these moods of mine memory.
At Sea.
Body, The.
Christina.
Gentle as moon on water and not like the
cherry tree that said.
House is empty and the trough is broken,
The.
I feel empty, empty as a swimming pool.
Jonathan.
Lola, are you still getting whatever you want.
Love Poem #2.
Poetry (1976), *sels.*
Sebastian.
Splitting the Infinite.
This Poem Should Have Etc.
To Live at the Speed of Biography.

To See Long like El Greco.
Two Gardens.
Two Gardens (1969), *sels.*
When You're Not a Poet.
Wolstenholme-Elmy, Elizabeth (1834–1918)
Woman Free, *sels.*
Woman, Owl. *See* **O'odham, Tohono**
Wong, Janet S. (b. 1962)
Good Luck Gold.
Wong, Nanying Stella
Three Sweatshop Women.
Wong, Nellie (b. 1934)
Can't Tell.
Dreams in Harrison Railroad Park.
Grandmothers' Song.
Heart of Rice Straw, A, *sels.*
How a Girl Got Her Chinese Name.
Ironing.
Mama, come back.
On Plaza Garibaldi.
On Thinking of Photographing My Fantasies.
Picnic.
Red Journeys, *sels.*
Relining Shelves.
Toward a 44th Birthday.
When I Was Growing Up.
Where are you going now?
Where is my country?
Wong, Orlando. *See* **Onuora Oku**
Wonodi, Okogbule (b. 1936)
Planting.
Salute to Icheke.
Woo, David (b. 1959)
Eden.
Expatriates
Grandfather's Rockery.
Great Helmsman, The.
Habit of staring, The.
Wood, Renate
Blood.
Cabbages.
Pilot, The.
Wood, Robert Williams (1868–1955)
Elk, The Whelk, The.
Pecan, The Toucan, The.
Pen-guin. The Sword-fish, The.
Wood, Susan (b. 1946)
Eggs.
Witness.
Wood, Victoria (b. 1953)
Saturday Night.
Wood, William (1606–c.1637)
Kinds of Shel-fish.
Kingly lyon, and the strong arm'd beare,
The.
Princely eagle, and the soaring hawke, The.
Sea's Abundant Progeny, The.
Trees both in hills and plaines, in plenty be.
Woodard, Deborah
Tower.
Woodbridge, Benjamin (1622–84)
Upon the Author. By a Known Friend.
Upon the Tomb of the Most Reverend Mr.
John Cotton.
Woodcock, George (1912–95)
Imagine the South.
Island, The.
Pacifists.
Paper Anarchist Addresses the Shade of
Nancy Ling Perry.
Poem for Garcia Lorca.
Woodhouse, James (1735–1820)
Life and Lucubrations of Crispinus
Scriblerus, The, *sels.*
Woods, John (b. 1926)
Lie closed, my lately loved, in the far bed.
Looking Both Ways Before Crossing.
What Do You Do When It's Spring?
Woods, Margaret Louisa (b. 1856)
Genius Loci.
Tears and Joys.
Woods, Stuart
Limerick: "Couple from old Aberystwyth, A."
Woodsford, David
Limerick: "Hoover, in grim silence, sat, The."

Woodward, Charles (*fl.* c.1731)
Midnight Ramble, The.

Woodward, Kristy
Thanksgiving Prayer, A.

Woodworth, Samuel (1788–1842)
Bucket, The.
Hunters of Kentucky; or, Half Horse and
Half Alligator, The.
Old Oaken Bucket, The.

Woolagoodjah, Sam
Lalai (Dreamtime).

Woolsey, Sarah Chauncey. *See* "Coolidge,
Susan"

Woolson, Constance Fenimore (1840–94)
Detroit River.
Florida Beach, The.
Kentucky Belle.
Love Unexpressed.

"Worcester"
Pastoral; in the Modern Style, A.

Wordsworth, Dorothy (1771–1855)
Address to a Child during a Boisterous
Winter Evening.
After-recollection at Sight of the Same
Cottage.
Cottage in Grasmere Vale, A.
Cottager to Her Infant, (By My Sister), The.
Floating Island at Hawkshead.
Lake was covered all over, The.
Loving and Liking [Irregular Verses
Addressed to A Child].
O thought I!
Sketch, A.
Thoughts on my sick-bed.
When shall I tread your garden path.

Wordsworth, Elizabeth (1840–1932)
Good and Clever.

Wordsworth, William (1770–1850)
Admonition to a Traveller.
Affliction of Margaret—The The.
Alice Fell; or, Poverty.
Among all lovely things my Love had been.
Anecdote for Fathers, Showing how the Art
of Lying may be Taught.
Best portion of a good man's life, The.
By the Sea.
Change in the Year, A.
Change Me, Some God, into that Breathing
Rose.
Character of the Happy Warrior.
Characteristics of a Child Three Years Old.
Childless Father, The.
Complaint, A.
Complaint of a Forsaken Indian Woman, The.
Composed at Neidpath Castle, the Property of
Lord Queensberry,1803.
Composed by the Sea-Side, near Calais,
August, 1802.
Composed in One of the Valleys of
Westmoreland, on Easter Sunday.
Composed Near Calais on the Road Leading
to Ardres, August 7, 1802.
Composed upon an Evening of Extraordinary
Splendour and Beauty.
Composed upon Westminster Bridge[,
September 3, 1802].
Convict, The.
Daffodils.
Dear native brooks, your ways I have
pursued.
Decay of Piety.
Ecclesiastical Sonnets, *sels.*
1801.
Elegiac Stanzas Suggested by a Picture of
Peele Castle, in a Storm [Painted by Sir
George Beaumont].
England, 1802, V.
England, 1802, III.
England, 1802 ("It is not to be thought of.")
Excursion, The, *sels.*
Expostulation and Reply.
Extempore Effusion upon the Death of James
Hogg, *sels.*
Farewell thou little Nook of mountain-
ground.
Farmer of Tilsbury Vale, The.

Female Vagrant, The.
Foster-Mother's Tale.
Fountain, The.
Fragment, A: "Between two sister moorland
rills."
Goody Blake and Harry Gill: A True Story,
sels.
Green Linnet, The.
I watch, and long have watched, with calm
regret.
Idiot Boy, The.
If thou indeed derive thy light from Heaven.
In a Garden in the Grounds of Coleorton,
Leicestershire.
In trellised shed with clustering roses gay.
Inscription for a Monument in Crossthwaite
Curch, in the Vale of Keswick.
Inscription for the Moss-Hut at Dove
Cottage.
Kitten and [the] Falling Leaves, The, *sels.*
Last of the Flock, The.
Lesson, A.
Lines Composed a Few Miles Above Tintern
Abbey on Revisiting the Banks of the Wye
During a Tour, *sels.*
Lines Left upon a Seat in a Yew-Tree which
Stands near the Lake of Esthwaite, on a
Desolate Part of the Shore, yet
Commanding a Beautiful Prospect.
Lines;: "Loud is the Vale! the Voice is up."
Lines Written in Early Spring.
Lines Written near Richmond, upon the
Thames, at Evening.
London 1802.
London, MDCCCII ("O friend! I know not
which way I must look.")
Louisa; After Accompanying Her on a
Mountain Excursion.
Lucy, *sels.*
Lucy Gray; or, Solitude.
Mad Mother, The.
Man is dear to man: the poorest poor.
Memorials of a Tour in Italy, 1837, *sels.*
Michael [A Pastoral Poem].
Most alluring clouds that mount the sky, The.
My heart leaps up when I behold.
Night in June, A.
November, 1806.
Nuns fret not at their convent's narrow
room;.
Nutting.
Ode: Intimations of Immortality [from
Recollections of Early Childhood], *sels.*
Ode to Duty.
Old Man [Travelling], An.
On the Departure of Sir Walter Scott from
Abbotsford, for Naples.
On the Extinction of the Venetian Republic.
Personal Talk.
Pet Lamb, The; A Pastoral.
Pilgrim Fathers, The.
Poems Composed or Suggested During a
Tour, in the Summer of 1833, *sels.*
Poet!—He Hath Put His Heart to School, A.
Prelude; Growth of a Poet's Mind [1850
vers.], The, *sels.*
Recluse; Home at Grasmere, The, *sels.*
Remembrance of Collins, Composed upon the
Thames near Richmond.
Resolution and Independence, *sels.*
Reverie of Poor Susan, The.
River Duddon [A Series of Sonnets], The,
sels.
see also The Wanderer, *Book 1 of* The
Excursion.
Ruth [or, The Influences of Nature].
She was a Phantom of delight.
Simon Lee [the Old Huntsman].
Solitary Reaper, The.
Sonnet: "England! the time is come when
thou shouldst wean."
Sonnet: "Scorn not the sonnet; critic, you
have frowned."
Sonnet: "World is too much with us; late and
soon, The."
Star-Gazers, *sels.*
Steamboats, Viaducts, and Railways.

Stepping Westward.
Strange Fits of Passion Have I Known.
Surprised by Joy—impatient as the Wind.
Tables Turned[: An Evening Scene, on the
Same Subject], The.
These Chairs they have no words to utter.
This prayer I make.
Thorn, The, *sels.*
Thought[s] of a Briton on the Subjugation of
Switzerland.
To a Butterfly, *sels.*
To a Child [Written in Her Album].
To a Distant Friend.
To a Sky-Lark, *sels.*
To H. C.[, Six Years Old].
To Sleep ("Flock of sheep that leisurely pass
by, A.")
To Sleep ("Fond words have oft been spoken
to thee, sleep!")
To Sleep ("O gentle Sleep! do they belong to
thee.")
To the Cuckoo.
To the Daisy ("With little here to do or
see.")
To the Highland Girl of Inversneyde.
To the Men of Kent (October, 1803).
To the Poet, John Dyer.
To the Skylark.
To Toussaint L'Ouverture.
Trosachs, The.
Two April Mornings, The.
Water Fowl.
We Are Seven, *sels.*
Where lies the Land to which yon Ship must
go?
Where lies the truth? has man, In wisdom's
creed.
White Doe of Rylstone, The; or, The Fate of
the Nortons, *sels.*
With Ships the sea was sprinkled far and
nigh.
Written in London, September, 1802.
Written in March [While Resting on the
Bridge at the Foot of Brother's Water].
Yarrow Unvisited [1803].
Yarrow Visited [September, 1814].
Yew-Trees.

Work, Henry Clay (1932–84)
Come Home, Father[!].
Grandfather's Clock.
Kingdom Coming.
Marching through Georgia.
Ship That Never Returned, The.

Worley, Mrs. J. B.
Mighty Hunter, The.

Wormser, Baron (b. 1948)
It's a Party (1959).
Soul Music.

Woroszylski, Wiktor
Early Chaplin, The.
Franz Kafka (I).
Franz Kafka (II).

Worsley-Benison, H.
Song of the Engine, The.

Worth, Kathryn (b. 1898)
(Circus Elephant).
Smells.

Worth, Valerie (b. 1933)
Chairs.
Christmas Lights.
Christmas Ornaments.
Clock.
Crows.
Dinosaurs.
Door.
Duck.
Fireworks.
Goldfish in the Garden Pond.
Magnet.
McDonald's, New Hartford, NY.
Sun, The.
Zinnias, stout and stiff.

Wortman, Denis (1835–1922)
God of the Prophets! Bless the Prophets'
Sons.
Today beneath Benignant Skies.

Wotton, Sir Henry (1568–1639)
Character of a Happy Life, The.
De Morte.
Dialogue betwixt God and the Soul, A.
Hymn to My God in a Night of My Late
   Sickness[e], A.
On a Bank [or Banck] as I Sate [or Sat] a-
   Fishing; a Description of the Spring.
On a Bank [or Banck] asl I Sat [or Sate]
   a-Fishing; a Description of the Spring.
On His Mistress [or Mistris], the Queen of
   Bohemia.
Poem Written by Sir Henry Wotton, in His
   Youth, A.
Tears at the Grave of Sir Albertus Morton.
To John Donne.
Upon the Death of Sir Albert [or us]
   Morton's Wife.
Upon the Sudden Restraint of the Earl[e] of
   Somerset, Then Falling from Favor [or
   Favour].

Woty, William (1731–91)
Lines Written in the Dog-Days.
Mock Invocation to Genius, A, sels.
White Conduit House.

Wratislaw, Theodore (1871–1933)
Eros D'Aute.
Frangipani.
Hothouse Flowers.
Opoponax.
Orchids.
Palm Sunday.
Satiety.
Sonnet Macabre.
White Lilies.

Wray, Ruby Marion (b. 1888)
You'll Never Know.

Wright, Bruce McM. (b. 1918)
African Affair, The.

Wright, C. D. (1932–78)
Complete Birth if the Cool, The.
Further Adventures With You.
Hotels.
Kings' Daughters, Home for Unwed Mothers,
   1948.
Legend of Hell, The.
Lesson, The.
More Blues and the Abstract Truth.
Obedience of the Corpse.
On the Eve of Our Mutually Assured
   Destruction.
One Summer.
Our Dust.
Provinces.
Scratch Music.
Spread Rhythm.
This Couple.
Woman Looking Through a Viewmaster.

Wright, Carolyne (b. 1949)
Return to Seattle: Bastille Day.

Wright, Celeste Turner (b. 1906)
Kineo Mountain.
Noblesse Oblige.
State of Preservation.
Thumbprint.
Yugoslav Cemetery.

Wright, Charles (b. 1935)
April.
Arkansas Traveller.
Bar Giamaica, 1959-60.
Black and Blue.
California Spring.
Chinoiserie.
Clear Night[, thumb-top of a moon, a back-lit
   sky].
Cloud River.
Daughters of Blum, The.
Dead Color.
Delta Traveller.
Dog Creek Mainline.
Dog Day Vespers.
Edvard Munch.
Fever Toy, The.
Hawaii Dantesca.
Homage to Paul Cézanne, sels.
Homecoming.

Laguna Blues.
March Journal.
Morandi.
Negatives.
New Poem, The.
Nightletter.
Northhanger Ridge.
October.
Other Side of the River, The.
Photographs.
Portrait of the Artist with Li Po.
Remembering San Zeno.
Rural Route.
Self-Portrait ("Someday they'll find me out,
   and my lavish hands.")
Sitting at Night on the Front Porch.
Skins, sels.
Smoke.
Snapshot.
Snow.
Spider Crystal Ascension.
Stone Canyon Nocturne.
Tattoos.
Two Stories.
Virgo Descending.
Yellow is for regret, the distal, the second
   hand.

Wright, Charles David
Beautiful Urinals of Paris, The.
Birth of the Cool.
Slag.
Tours.

Wright, David (b. 1920)
Funeral Oration, A.
Kleomedes.
On Himself.
On the Death of an Emperor Penguin in
   Regent's Park, London.
Pastoral: "Afternoon wears on, The."
Peripatetic Letter to Isabella Fey, A, sels.
Rousecastle.
Seven South African Poems, sels.
South African Broadsheets, sels.

**Wright, David McKee (b. 1867 or 1869, d.
1928)**
Moral Story II.
While the Billy Boils.

Wright, Ernest Vincent (1872–1939)
When Father Carves the Duck.

Wright, Frank Lloyd
If you wisely invest in beauty.

Wright, Franz (b. 1953)
After Picasso, sels.
Alcohol.
Blood.
Certain Tall Buildings.
Drinking Back.
Elegy: Breece D'J Pancake.
Entry in an Unknown Hand.
I did not notice.
Joseph Come Back as the Dusk.
Journey, The.
Mosquitoes.
Needle: For a Friend Who Disappeared, The.
Old, The.
Pawtucket Postcards.
Untitled.

Wright, George T. (b. 1925)
Aquarium.

Wright, Hetty. See Wright, Mehetabel

Wright, Ivan Leonard
Want of You, The.

Wright, James (1643–1713)
Out of Horace.

Wright, James (1927–80)
American Twilights, 1957.
Arrangements with Earth for Three Dead
   Friends.
At the Executed Murderer's Grave.
At the Slackening of the Tide.
At Thomas Hardy's Birthplace, 1953.
Autumn Begins in Martins Ferry, Ohio.
Before the [or a] Cashier's Window in a
   Department Store.
Beginning.

Blessing, A.
Breath of Air, A.
Complaint.
Confession to J. Edgar Hoover.
Depressed by a Book of Bad Poetry, I Walk
   toward an Unused Pasture and Invite the
   Insects to Join Me.
Eisenhower's Visit to Franco, 1959.
Evening.
Fit against the Country, A.
For the Marsh's Birthday.
Gesture by a Lady with an Assumed Name,
   A.
Having Lost My Sons, I Confront the
   Wreckage of the Moon: Christmas, 1960.
In Ohio.
In Response to a Rumor that the Oldest
   Whorehouse in Wheeling, West Virginia,
   Has Been Condemned.
In Shame and Humiliation.
Inscription for the Tank.
Jewel, The.
Journey, The.
Late November in a Field.
Life, The.
Lifting Illegal Nets by Flashlight.
Lights in the hallway, The.
Living by the Red River.
Love in a Warm Room in Winter.
Lying in a Hammock at William Duffy's
   Farm in Pine Island, Minnesota.
Mad Fight Song for William S. Carpenter,
   1966, A.
Mantova.
Micromutations.
Milkweed.
Miners.
Minneapolis Poem, The.
Mutterings Over the Crib of a Deaf Child.
My Grandmother's Ghost.
Names in Monterchi: To Rachel.
Northern Pike.
Note Left in Jimmy Leonard's Shack, A.
Ohio Valley Swains.
Ohioan Pastoral.
Old Age Compensation.
Old Dog in the Ruins of the Graves at Arles,
   The.
Old WPA Swimming Pool in Martins Ferry,
   Ohio, The.
On a Phrase from Southern Ohio.
On the Skeleton of a Hound.
Outside Fargo, North Dakota.
Poem about Breasts, A.
Poem by Garnie Braxton, A.
Poem Written under an Archway in a
   Discontinued Railroad Station, Fargo,
   North Dakota, A.
Poems to a Brown Cricket.
Prayer to the Lord Ramakrishna, A.
Private Meeting Place, The.
Quest, The.
Redwings.
Saint Judas.
Sappho.
Saying Dante Aloud.
Secret Gratitude, A.
Simon and the Tarantula.
Small Frogs Killed on the Highway.
Snowfall; a Poem about Spring.
Song for the Middle of the Night, A.
Sparrows in a Hillside Drift.
Speak.
Stages on a Journey Westward.
Three Sentences for a Dead Swan.
To a Beautiful Pear Tree.
To a Salesgirl, Weary of Artificial Holiday
   Trees.
To a Troubled Friend.
To Flood Stage Again.
To the Muse.
To the Poets in New York.
Twilights.
Two Hangovers.
Two Poems about President Harding.
Two Postures beside a Fire.
Vain Advice at the Year's End.

Verona.
Way to Make a Living, A.
What the Earth Asked Me.
Willy Lyons.
Winter Daybreak above Vence, A.
Written in a Copy of Swift's Poems, for
  Wayne Burns.
You and I Saw Hawks Exchanging the Prey.

Wright, Jay (b. 1935)
Benjamin Banneker Sends His *Almanac* to
  Thomas Jefferson.
Cradle Logic of Autumn, The.
Death as History.
End of an Ethnic Dream, The.
Homecoming Singer, The.
Invention of a Garden, The.
Invitation to Madison County, An.
Jalapeña Gypsies.
Journey to the Place of Ghosts.
Lake in Central Park, The.
Meta-A and the A of Absolutes.
Neighborhood House, The.
19.
Sketch for an Aesthetic Project.
Wednesday Night Prayer Meeting.
What is Beautiful.

Wright, John (fl. 1708–27)
Poor Man's Province, The.

Wright, Judith (b. 1915)
And Mr. Ferritt.
At Cooloolah.
Australia 1970.
Beanstalk, Meditated Later, The.
Birds.
Blind Man, The, *sels.*
Bora Ring.
Brother and Sisters.
Bullocky.
Camphor Laurel.
Child, The.
Cup, The.
"Dove-Love."
Drought Year.
Eli, Eli.
Eve to Her Daughters.
Extinct Birds.
Flood Year.
For a Pastoral Family, *sels.*
Gum-trees Stripping.
Habitat, *sels.*
Half-Caste Girl.
Hawthorn Hedge, The.
Ishtar.
Killer, The.
Legend.
Metho Drinker.
Naked Girl and Mirror.
Nigger's Leap, New England.
Night After Bushfire.
Old Prison, The.
Pelicans.
Portrait.
Precipice, The.
Rainforest.
Remittance Man.
Request to a Year.
River Bend.
Rosina Alcona to Julius Brenzaida.
Sanctuary.
Sisters, The.
Skins.
Sonnet for Christmas.
South of My Days.
Storm.
Surfer, The.
Tableau.
To a Child.
To Another Housewife.
Train Journey.
Two Fires, The.
Wings.
Woman to Child.
Woman to Man.

Wright, Kit (b. 1944)
City Rain.
Dad and the Cat and the Tree.
Fortunes of War.

Frozen Man, The.
Greedyguts.
Heads or Tails?
How I See It.
How the Wild South East Was Lost.
Let's Hear it for the Limpet.
Limerick: "Her limp lover Maud couldn't
  pardon."
New World Symphony, A.
Our hamster's life.
Red Boots On.
Sergeant Brown's Parrot.
Underneath the Archers *or* What's All This
  about Walter's Willy?
Unlikely Obbligato of Andersonstown.
Victorian Family Photograph.

Wright, Mehetabel (1697–1750)
Address to Her Husband.
Epitaph on Herself, An.
To an Infant Expiring the Second Day of Its
  Birth.
Wedlock, a Satire.

Wright, Richard (1808–60)
Between the World and Me.
Coming from the woods.
Green cockleburs, The.
Hokku Poems, *sels.*
I Have Seen Black Hands.

Wright, Sarah E. (b. 1927)
To Some Millions Who Survive Joseph E.
  Mander, Sr.
Until They Have Stopped.

Wright, Stephen Caldwell (b. 1946)
Out of the Wailing.

Wrighton, W. T. (1816–80)
Dearest Spot on Earth, The.

Wrigley, Ammon
Owdham Footbo'.

Wrigley, Robert
Parents.
Ravens at Deer Creek.

**Wroth [or Wroath], Mary Sidney, Countess of
Montgomery (1587?–1651?)**
Crown of Sonnets Dedicated to Love, A,
  sels.
He may our prophet, and our tutor prove.
Pamphilia to Amphilanthus, *sels.*
Urania, *sels.*

Wu Chen (1280–1354)
Fantastic Rock, The.
Inscribed on a Painting of Bamboo.
Level forest stretching far and wide, A.
Moonlight Bay.
Ni Tsan Poem Following Rhyme-Words of
  Wu Chen.
Paintings of Fishermen, *sels.*
Poems Inscribed on Paintings of Bamboo,
  sels.
To the Tune "Chiu-ch'üan tzu."

Wu Chia-chi (1618–84)
East of the salt village, low and narrow.
Grain-Barge Wife, The.
My hut, beside the crystal stream.
Old saltman, hair turned white, The.
Returning to the Alluvial Fields, *sels.*
To Ch'eng Fei-t'ao.
Woman Née Wu, The.
Woman Tung.

Wu Chün (469–520)
Song of Spring.

Wu-Men (1183–1260)
Great Way has no gate, The.
Moon and clouds are the same.
One instant is eternity.
Ten thousand flowers in spring, the moon in
  autumn.

**Wu of Han [or Wu Ti or Ou-ty or Liu Ch'e or
Liu Ch'u], Emperor (156–87 B.C.)**
Autumn wind blows white clouds, The.
Autumn wind rises; white clouds fly.
Autumn winds rise.
From the Most Distant Time.
Li Fu-Jên.
People Hide Their Love.
Song of the Autumn Wind.
Summer Song.

Wu of Liang, Emperor (464–519)
Morning sun shines, The.
Water lilies bloom on the Great River.

Wu Tsao (fl. c.1800)
Bitter rain in my courtyard.
For the Courtesan Ch'ing Lin.
In the Home of the Scholar Wu Su-chiang.

Wu Wei-yeh (1609–72)
Ancient Feeling.
At the Mountain of the Mysterious Tomb
  Visiting Master P'ou.
At the River Tower Parting from My
  Younger Brother, Fu-ling.
At Yuen Yang Lake.
Autumn Night—Sleepless.
Ballad of Yüan-yüan.
Broken Lampstand, The.
Climbing P'iao-miao Peak.
Country Scene, *sels.*
Distant roads in the aftermath of war.
Feelings Come As I Pass through Wu-chiang.
Garden Living.
Impromptu.
Lamenting for My Late Daughter.
On the Twenty-fourth of the Third Month, in
  the Year Ting-wei Sailed across Lake T'ai
  from Behind the Mountain.
Passing by Huai-yin I Have Feelings.
Poem of the Western Fields.
Reading the Annals of Emperor Wu of the
  Han Dynasy.
Sailing at Dusk from T'u-sung.
Seeing Off Sun Ling-hsiu on His Journey to
  Chen-ting.
Seeing Off Wang Yüan-chao—Reprise.
Setting out at dawn from T'ung-lu county.
Song to the Tune "Perching Crows."
Tune: "Sand of Silk-washing Stream."
Tune: "Song of River City"—On a Kite.
View of the Countryside.
Visiting the Garden at Monk Wen Ko's
  Home.

Wulff, Michael (b. 1940)
Masculine, Feminine, Neuter. *From* Lore and
  Language of Schoolchildren.

Wurdemann, Audrey (1911–60)
Text.

Wyat, Hester
What makes me write my dearest Freind you
  aske.

Wyatt, Sir Thomas (1503?–1542)
Absence! Absenting causeth me to complain.
Accused though I be without desert.
After great storms the calm returns.
Ah, Robin, / Jolly Robin.
Alas, madam[e], for stealing [or stelying] of
  a kiss [or kysse].
Alas, poor man, what hap have I.
Alas, the grief and deadly wo[e]ful smart[!].
All heavy minds.
And if an eye may save or slay.
Answer that ye made to me, my dear, The
  [or Th'].
As power and wit will me assist.
At last withdraw your cruelty.
At mo[o]st mischief.
Behold, love, thy power how she despiseth!
Blame not my lute, for he must sound [or
  sssnd or Sownde].
Comfort thyself, my wo[e]ful heart.
Courtier's Life, The.
Deem as ye list. Upon good cause.
Deme as Ye List Upon Goode Cause.
Disdain me not without desert.
Divers[e] [or Dyvers] doth[e] use, as I have
  heard and kno[w].
Eche man me telleth I chaunge moost my
  devise.
Enemy [or en'my] of life, decayer of all
  kind, The [or Th'].
Epitaph of Sir Thomas Gravener, [Knight],
  An.
Face that should content me wonders [or
  wondrous] well, A.
Farewell, all my welfare.
Farewell, the reign of cruelty!
Farewell: "What should I say."

For want of [or I] will in woe I plain.
Fortune.
Fortune doth frown.
Fruit of all the service that I serve, The.
Full well it may be seen.
Furious Gun, The.
Give place all ye that doth rejoice.
He is not de[a]d that sometime [or somtyme]
hath a fall.
Heart and service to you proffered, The.
Heart oppressed [or oppress'd] with desperate
thought.
Help[e] me to seek [or seke] for I lost it
there.
How should I / Be so pleasant.
I abide and abide and better abide.
I am as I am and so will I be.
I have sought long with steadfastness.
I love, loved, and so doth she.
I must go walk[e] the woods so wild.
I see that chance hath chosen me.
If chance assigned [or assign'd].
If ever man might him avaunt.
If fancy [or fansy] would favour.
If in the world there be more woe.
If thou wilt mighty be, flee from the rage.
If waker care, if sudden [or sodayne] pale
colo[u]r.
If with complaint the pain might be
expressed.
In aeternum I was once determed.
In Eternum ("In eternum I was once
determed.")
In faith I not [well] what to say.
In mourning wise since daily I increase.
In Spayn.
Is it possible.
It may be good like it who list.
It was my choice, it was no chance.
Joy so short alas, the pain so near, The.
Knot which first my heart did strain, The.
Lament my loss[e], my labo[u]r, and my pain
[or payne].
Like as the bird in the cage enclosed.
Like as the swan towards her death.
Lo, how I seek and sue to have.
Longer to muse.
Love doth again.
Lover Complaineth the Unkindness of His
Love, The.
Lover Having Dreamed Enjoying of His
Love, Complaineth That the Dreame Is Not
either Longer or Truer, The.
Lover Rejoiceth the Enjoying of His Love,
The.
Lover Showeth How He Is Forsaken of Such
as He Sometime Enjoyed, The.
Lover's Appeal, The.
Lux, my fair falcon, and your fellows all.
Lyve thowe gladly, yff so thowe may.
Madam, withouten Many Words.
Me list no more to sing.
Mistrustful minds be moved.
Most wretched heart, most miserable.
My galley charged with forgetfulness.
My hope, alas, hath me abused.
My love took scorn my service to retain.
My pen, take pain a little space.
Mye love toke skorne my servise to retaine.
Now all of change.
Now must I le[a]rn[e] to live [or lyve] at
rest.
O Goodly Hand.
O miserable sorrow withouten cure!
Pass forth, my wonted cries.
Patience, for I have wrong.
Patience for my device.
Patience of all my smart.
Patience though I have not.
Penitential Psalms, sels.
Perdy [or Perdie or Perdye], I said[e] it [or
yt] not.
Pillar [or Piller] perished [or pearisht] is
whe[a]rto I le[a]nt, The.
Process of time worketh such wonder.
Protest, A.
Quondam was I in my lady's grace.

Renouncing of Love, A.
Resound my voice [or voyse], ye woods [or
wodes] that hear [or here] me plain.
Restful place, reviver of my smart, The.
Robyn, A / Joly Robyn.
Satires, sels.
Sighs are my food, drink are my tears.
Since love is such that, as ye wot.
Since Love will needs that I shall love.
Since so ye please to hear me plain.
Since ye delight to know.
Since you will needs that I shall sing.
So unwarely was never no man caught.
Some tyme I fled the fyre that me brent.
Sometime I fled the fire that me brent.
Sometime I sigh, sometime I sing.
Sonnet: 'Each man me telleth.'
Sonnet: 'My galley charged.'
Sonnet: 'The long love.'
Spite hath no power to make me sad.
Stand whoso list upon the slipper top.
Such hap as I am happed in.
Sufficed not, madame, that you did tear.
Supplication, A.
Take heed betime, lest ye be spied.
Tangled [or Tanglid] I was [or was I] in [or
yn] Love's snare.
That time that mirth did steer my ship.
Thenmy of liff decayer of all kynde.
There was never nothing more me pained [or
payned].
Tho' I can not your cruelty constrain.
Thou sleepest fast and I with woeful heart.
Though this the [or thy] port and I thy
servant true.
Throughout the world, if it were sought.
To cause accord or to ag[g]re[e].
To His Heart.
To rail or jest, ye know I use it not.
To seek each where where man doth live.
To wet your eye withouten tear.
To wish and want and not obtain.
V. Innocentia Veritas Viat Fides
Circumdederunt Me Inimici Mei.
What death is worse than this?
What means [or meaneth or menethe] this
when I lie [or lye] alone.
What nedeth these thretning wordes and
wasted wynde?
What no, Perdy [or Perdie or perdie][!] ye
may be sure[!].
What rage is this? What furo[u]r of what
kind [or kynd]?
What should I say.
What vaileth [or 'vaileth] truth [or trouth]?
or by it to take pain [or payn]?
What wourde is that that chaungeth not.
When first mine eyes did view and mark.
Where shall I have at mine own will.
Who hath he[a]rd of such[e] cruelty before.
Who list his wealth and ease retain.
Who so list to hount I knowe where is an
hynde.
Whoso list to hunt, I know where is an hind.
Will ye see what wonders love hath wrought?
With serving still.
Ye know my heart, my lady dear.
Ye old mule, that thin[c]k your self so fair
[or fayre].
You that in love find[e] luck[e] and
[h]abunda[u]nce.
Your looks so often cast.
Wylie, Elinor (1885–1928)
Address to My Soul.
Atavism.
August.
Beauty.
Birthday Sonnet.
Castilian.
Cold-blooded Creatures.
Confession of Faith.
"Desolation Is a Delicate Thing."
Doomsday.
Eagle and the Mole, The.
Epitaph: "For this she starred her eyes with
salt."
Escape.

Full Moon.
Golden Bough.
Hughie at the Inn.
Hymn to Earth.
Innocent Landscape.
Knight Fallen on Evil Days, The.
Lament for Glasgerion.
Let No Charitable Hope.
Little Eclogue.
Little Elegy.
Madman's Song.
Malediction Upon Myself.
Nebuchadnezzar.
Nonsense Rhyme.
O Virtuous Light.
One Person, sels.
Parting Gift.
Pastiche.
Pebble, The.
Pegasus Lost.
Peregrine's Sunday Song.
Peter and John.
Portrait in Black Paint, with a Very Sparing
Use of Whitewash.
Pretty Words.
Prophecy.
Sanctuary.
Sea Lullaby.
Simon Gerty.
Sonnet: "How many faults you might accuse
me of."
This Corruptible.
To a Lady's Countenance.
Velvet Shoes.
Wild Peaches, sels.
Wynne, John Huddlestone (1743–88)
Horse and the Mule, The.
Time's an hand's-breadth; 'tis a tale.

X

"Xariffa." See Townsend, Mary Ashley
Xuân Diệu (1917–85)
Casting Fragrance to the Winds.
Come on, make haste—please, won't you
hurry up?
Distance.
Feelings and Emotions.
Fool In Love, A.
Forever, yes, forever I'll love you.
Foreword to a Book of Poems.
Geologist and Millions of Years, A.
In a Hurry.
It's All in the Heart.
Magic.
New Tiles.
Nothingness.
Orange With the Rind Still Green, An.
Spring Out of Season.
To love is to die a little in the heart.
You Must Say It.
Xuân Quỳnh (1942–88)
Waves.
Xuân Thủy (b. 1912)
You Cannot Lock Up the Mind.
Xuanjing, Zhou (fl. 12th cent.)
Meditating at midnight.
Xue Tao (768–831)
Cicadas.

Y

Y Vân Tử (Nguyễn Trung Ẩn) (b. 1909)
Gaffer in Love, A.
"Ya-Ka-Nes." See Harjo, Patty L.
Yaba, Shita. See Basho and Shita Yaba
Yagi, Mikajo (b. 1924)
Genitals of woods, The.
Marathon runner's legs, A.
Yakamochi (Otomo no Yakamochi) (718–85)
Better never to have met you.
By way of pretext. From Manyo Shu, Part 1
of 4.

Yako

Cry of the stag, The.
Frost lies white, The.
I lie long abed.
I send you a box.
I will come to you.
[These] meetings in dreams.
Mist floats on the Spring meadow.
Now to meet only in dreams.
Over the Spring fields. *From* Manyo Shu, Part 3 of 4.
We were together.
When evening comes. *From* Manyo Shu, Part 4 of 4.
When I see the first.
Wind rustles the bamboos, The.

Yako, St. J. Page
Year's Ending, The.

Yalden, Thomas (1670–1736)
Advice to a Lover.
To Sir Humphry Mackworth, *sels.*

Yamada, Mitsuye (b. 1923)
American Son.
Camp Notes, *sels.*
Cincinnati.
Club, The.
Homecoming.
I Learned To Sew.
Night Before Good-Bye, The.
Obon: Festival of the Dead.

Yamakawa, Tomiko (1879–1909)
I leave all the scarlet flowers.
White roses I tried to braid in my hair, The.

Yamanaka, Lois-Ann
Kala: Saturday Night at the Pahala Theatre.
Yarn Wig.

Yamanoé [*or* Yamanoué] no Okura (Okura) (660?–733?)
Because he is young. *From* Manyo Shu, Part 1 of 4.

Yamato-himé, Empress (*fl.* c.671)
Others may forget you, but not I.

Yambo, Ouologuem (b. 1940)
When Negro Teeth Speak.

Yang Chi (c.1334–c.1383)
Describing My Feelings While Living in Retirement by the Riverside: Seven Poems to the Tune "Ch'ing-p'ing-yüeh."
Describing My Feelings While Living in the Spring Quarters at Chiang-ning: Four Poems to the Tune "Ch'ing-p'ing-yëh," *sels.*
Five-color robe of embroidered silk, A.
From Sand River to Ts'ai Rock, *sels.*
Living in a Riverside Village—mdash;Miscellaneous Impressions, *sels.*
Living in Master Fang's Garden, *sels.*
Living in the Country at Kou-ch'ü in Autumn—mdash;Miscellaneous Impressions, *sels.*
Meeting My Fellow Countryman, Yü Wu-chung.
Miscellaneous Impressions of T'an-chou, *sels.*
Nesting among Clouds.
Noble Scholar Playing the Lute, A.
On Seeing a Firefly in My Room.
Painting of Bamboo by Ni Yün-lin, A.
Paintings of Ladies Engaged in Four Springtime Occupations, *sels.*
Poem Making Fun of Chi-ti for His Eye Illness, A.
Poem on Passing by Hsin-k'ai Lake at Kao-yu in Light Rain, A.
Reviewing the Troops at Kuei lin with Military Inspectors Chiang And Chang. Scenes, *sels.*
Selling My Official Robe.
Spring Days in My Home Town, *sels.*
Spring dreams, more spring dreams.
Studio for Listening to the Snow, The.
Submitting a Memorial Requesting Permission to Return Home and Care for My Parents.
Ten Poems on the Tuan-yang Festival, *sels.*
Thinking of My Friends at Kou-jung Subprefecture, *sels.*
Walking in the Country outside T'ai-yüan on a Spring Day.

Yang Fang (*fl.* 4th cent.)
Joy of Union, The.

Yang Hsiung (52 B.C.–18 A.D.)
Poverty.

Yang of Sui, Emperor (*fl.* 6th–7th cent.)
Spring River Flowers Moon Night.

Yang Shen (1488–1559)
Four Poems from the Sequence "Singing of the Moon," *sels.*
To the Tune "Chao-chün's Sorrow."
To the Tune "Chiang ch'eng tzu."
To the Tune "Child at Play."
To the Tune, "Ch'ing-p'ing Yüeh."
To the Tune "Flowers in the Rain."
To the Tune "Heavenly Immortal."
To the Tune "Heavenly Immortal" ("Waves wash off the peach blossoms.")
To the Tune "Moon Over West River."
To the Tune "New Moon."
To the Tune "Partridge Sky."
To the Tune "Song of the Plum Blossom at the River Town."
To the Tune "Spring in Tien Is Fine."
To the Tune "Stopping My Horse to Listen."
To the Tune "The Southerner."
To the Tune "Yellow Oriole" ("Threads of rain weave lambent light.")
To the Tune "Yellow Oriole" ("Willows weave spring sorrow.")

Yang Shih-ch'i (1365–1444)
Crossing the River.
Dawn: Clear Skies.
Dragon-Tiger Terrace.
Enclosed with a Letter to My Family—For Shu.
Eulogy on My Own Portrait, A.
Evening of My Birthday, The.
Following the Rhymes of Shao-pao Huang's Poem on Being Moved While Visiting the Farmers.
Group of Officials, A, *sels.*
Hsi-li Echoed My Poems, and I Respond to Him, Using the Same Rhymes—Also Sent to Tsung-lien, *sels.*
I Was Received in an Early Audience at Heaven-Gate and Then at Noon I Was Summoned to the Yu-shun Gate. In the Evening I Withdrew, and Improvised This Poem.
Inscribed on a Painting of Bamboo Presented to Lecturer Ch'en Upon His Departure to Resume His Duties at Nanking, *sels.*
Inscribed on the Painting, Stabbing a Tiger, by Chao Tzu-ang, in the Collection of Scholar Yang.
Intendant Yao Shan Has Requested Six Poems on Living in the Mountains, The, *sels.*
Libationer Hu Became Ill from Eating Sunflowers. These Poems Are Playfully Presented to Him and Are Also Intended to Thank Him for the Vegetables He Sent Me, *sels.*
Night Rain: A Wall Collapses—Sent To My Neighbors.
Night Rain beneath the City Walls of P'i-chou.
On the Hall of Precious Virtue.
Painting of Water Buffaloes, A, *sels.*
Recording a Dream.
Red Heart Station.
Rhymed Words Sent to My Eldest Son, *sels.*
Searching for the Ruins of the Pavilion of the Drunken Old Man.
Sent to All My Nephews and Nieces at Tung-ch'eng, *sels.*
Sha-ch'eng, "Sand City" ("In former years I passed this city.")
Sha-ch'eng, "Sand City" ("Overlooking the water, a desolate city.")
Song of the Merchant's Wife.
Ten Miscellaneous Poems Written as a Member of the Imperial Retinue on an Inspection Tour of the Frontier—We Reached Hsüan-fu and Then Returned, *sels.*
Ten Scenes at the Hsiao Family Stone Ridge, *sels.*

Three Poems on Ch'ang-sha, *sels.*

Yang-Ti, Emperor of Sui Dynasty (*fl.* 7th cent.)
Flowers and Moonlight on the Spring River.

Yang Wan-li (1127–1206)
Bubbles on the Water.
Cold Fly.
Cold Lantern, The.
Crossing Ts'en River.
Drying Clothes.
Early Summer Waking from a Nap.
Fallen Blossoms.
Keng-tzu (1180), First Month, Fifth Day, Dawn.
Master Liu Painted a Portrait of Me in My Old Age and Asked Me to Write a Poem About the Picture.
Passing By Waterwheel Bay.
Relaxing in the Evening in My Study.
Replying to a Poem by Li T'ien-lin.
Sitting at Night on the Moon-viewing Terrace.
Sitting at Night on the Moonlit Terrace.
Songs of Depression, *sels.*
Stanza Written in Jest.
Staying Overnight at the Temple of the Holy Vulture.
Trip to Stone Man Peak, A.

Yang Wei-chen (1296–1370)
Bamboo Branch Song of the Seacoast.
Bamboo Branch Song of West Lake.
Horse-Watering Hole, The.
Horseman at the Roadside, The.
Impromptu Inspirations, *sels.*
Painting Her Nails.
Residence of the Emperors of Ch'en, The.
Song of a Dream Journey over the Vast Sea.
Song of the Merchant's Wife.
Song of the Waterfall at Mount Lu.
Songs of Lake Tung-t'ing, *sels.*
Taking the Ferry at Ta-kao at Dawn.
Tu-lu Poem ("Tu-lu, Tu-lu, evil waters running muddy.")

Yang Yi (974–1020)
Blue mist rises from fragrant herbs in the bronze plate.
Lang Mountain Monastery.
Prisons Are Full of Convicts, The.

Yannai (*fl.* 7th cent.)
And It Came to Pass at Midnight.
Celestial Fire, The.

Ya'oz-kest, Itamar (1732–1815)
Smoke Rose.

Yarrow, Ruth
Baby's pee, The.
Low winter moon.
Sunrise path.
Warm rain before dawn.

Yashashchandra, Sitanshu (b. 1941)
Drought.

"Yashin [*or* "Iashin"], Aleksandr Iakovlevich" (Aleksandr Iakovlevich Popov) (1913–68)
Eagle, The.
I am fated to perform a heroic deed.

Yasuda, Kenneth
Crimson dragonfly, A.
On the bench I wait.
Shadow of the trees, The.

Yates, J. Michael (b. 1938)
Great Bear Lake Meditations, The, *sels.*

Yates, John H.
Model Church, The.

Yates, L. E.
Strange Talk.

Yau, John (b. 1950)
Angel Atrapado VIII.
Broken Off by the Music.
Cenotaph.
Chinese Villanelle.
Different Cereal, A.
Edificio Sayonara.
Engines of Gloom and Affection.
New York Map Company (1).
Postcard from Trakl.
Radiant Silhouette I.
Radiant Silhouette II.

Radiant Silhouette III.
Radiant Silhouette IV.
Radiant Silhouette V.
We Are All Vultures.

Ye, Zi
All night I could not sleep.

Yearley, Reg
Limerick: "Naïve young lady of Cork, A."

Yearsley, Ann (1752–1806)
Familiar Poem from Nisa to Fulvia of the Vale.
On Mrs. Montagu.
Poem on the Inhumanity of the Slave Trade, A.
Remonstrance in the Platonic Shade.
Flourishing on an Height, *sels.*
Soliloquy: "What folly to complain."
To Mira, On the Care of her Infant, *sels.*
To Mr. ———, an Unlettered Poet, on Genius Unimproved.

Yeatman, R. J. (1898–1968) *and* **W. C. Sellar**
How I Brought the Good News from Aix to Ghent (or Vice Versa).

Yeats, William Butler (1865–1939)
Acre of Grass, An.
Adam's Curse.
After Long Silence.
All things can tempt me from this craft of verse.
Among School Children.
Apparitions, The.
Are You Content.
At Galway Races.
At The Abbey Theatre.
At the Grey Round of the Hill.
Ballad of Father Gilligan, The.
Before the World Was Made.
Beggar to Beggar Cried.
Black Tower, The.
Brown Penny.
Byzantium.
"Calvary."
Cap and Bells, The.
Cat and the Moon, The.
Choice, The.
Chosen.
Church and State.
Circus Animals' Desertion, The.
Coat, A.
Cold Heaven, The.
Collarbone [*or* Collar-Bone] of a Hare, The.
Coming of Wisdom with Time, The.
Consolation.
Coole Park and Ballylee, 1931.
Coole Park, 1929.
Cradle Song: "Angels are bending, The."
Cradle Song, A: "Angels are stooping, The."
Crazed Girl, A.
Crazy Jane and Jack the Journeyman.
Crazy Jane and the Bishop.
Crazy Jane Grown Old Looks at the Dancers.
Crazy Jane on God.
Crazy Jane on the Day of Judgment.
Crazy Jane on the Mountain.
Crazy Jane Reproved.
Crazy Jane Talks with the Bishop.
Cuchulain Comforted.
Curse of Cromwell, The.
Death.
Deep-sworn Vow, A.
Dialogue of Self and Soul, A.
Dolls, The.
Down by the salley gardens my love and I did meet;.
Dream of Death, A.
Drinking Song, A.
Easter 1916.
Ego Dominus Tuus.
Everlasting Voices, The.
Fallen Majesty.
Fascination of what's difficult, The.
Father and Child.
Fiddler of Dooney, The.
Fisherman, The.
Folly Of Being Comforted, The.
For Anne Gregory.
Four Ages of Man, The.

Fragments: "Locke sank into a swoon."
Friends.
Gratitude to the Unknown Instructors.
Great Day, The.
Gyres! the gyres! Old Rocky Face look forth, The.
Hawk, The.
He Hears the Cry of the Sedge.
He Remembers Forgotten Beauty.
He Thinks of His Past Greatness When a Part of the Constellations of Heaven.
He Thinks of Those Who Have Spoken Evil of His Beloved.
He Wishes for the Cloths of Heaven.
Her Anxiety.
High Talk.
Host of the Air, The.
Hosting of the Sidhe, The.
How but in custom and in ceremony.
I am of Ireland.
In Memory of Eva Gore-Booth and Con Markievicz.
In Memory of Major Robert Gregory.
In the Seven Woods.
Indian to His Love, The.
Indian upon God, The [*or* An].
Irish Airman Foresees His Death, An.
John Kinsella's Lament for Mrs. Mary Moore.
Lady's Third Song, The.
Lake-Isle of Innisfree, The.
Lamentation of the Old Pensioner, The.
Land of Heart's Desire, The, *sels.*
Lapis Lazuli.
Last Confession, A.
Leaders of the Crowd, The.
Leda and the Swan.
Lonely the Sea-Bird Lies at Her Rest.
Long-Legged Fly.
Lover Mourns for the Loss of Love, The.
Lover Tells of the Rose in His Heart, The.
Lullaby: "Beloved, may your sleep be sound."
Mad as the Mist and Snow.
Madness of King Goll, The.
Magi, The.
Man Who Dreamed of Faeryland, The.
Meditations in Time of Civil War, *sels.*
Memory.
Men Improve with the Years.
Meru.
Michael Robartes and the Dancer.
Michael Robartes Bids His Beloved Be at Peace.
Model for the Laureate, A.
Mohini Chatterjee.
Moods, The.
Mother of God, The.
Municipal Gallery Revisited, The.
Never give all the heart, for love.
New Faces, The.
News for the Delphic Oracle.
Nineteen Hundred and Nineteen, *sels.*
Nineteenth Century and After, The.
No Second Troy.
Oil and Blood.
Old Men Admiring Themselves in the Water, The.
Old Stone Cross, The.
On a Political Prisoner.
On Being Asked for a War Poem.
On Hearing That the Students of Our New University Have Joined the Agitation against Immoral Literature.
On Those That Hated "The Playboy of the Western World" 1907.
On Woman.
Pardon, old fathers, if you still remain.
Parnell came down the road, he said to a cheering man.
Parting.
Paudeen.
People, The.
Pilgrim, The.
Pity of Love, The.
Politics.
Prayer for My Daughter, A.

Prayer for My Son, A.
Prayer for Old Age, A.
Purgatory.
Ragged Wood, The.
Red Hanrahan's Song about Ireland.
Renowned Generations, The.
Reprisals.
Resurrection, The, *sels.*
Ribh Considers Christian Love Insufficient.
Rose of the World, The.
Rose Tree, The.
Running to Paradise.
Sailing To Byzantium.
Scholars, The.
Second Coming, The.
Secret Rose, The.
September 1913.
Seven Sages, The.
Sixteen Dead Men.
Solomon and the Witch.
Solomon to Sheba.
Song, A: "I thought no more was needed."
Song of the Happy Shepherd, The.
Song of the Old Mother, The.
Song Of Wandering Aengus, The.
Sorrow of Love, The ("Brawling of a sparrow in the eaves, The.")
Sorrow of Love, The ("Quarrel of the sparrows in the eaves, The.")
Spilt Milk.
Spur, The.
St. Matthew, *sels.*
Statesman's Holiday, The.
Statues, The.
Stick of Incense, A.
Stolen Child, The.
Swift's Epitaph.
Symbols.
That the Night Come.
Those Images.
Thought from Propertius, A.
Three Bushes, The.
Three Hermits, The.
Three Movements.
Three Things.
To a Child Dancing in the Wind.
To a Friend Whose Work Has Come to Nothing.
To a Poet, Who Would Have Me Praise Certain Bad Poets, Imitators of His and Mine.
To a Shade.
To a Squirrel at Kyle-Na-No.
To a Young Beauty.
To a Young Girl.
To an Isle in the Water.
To Be Carved on a Stone at Thoor Ballylee.
To Ireland in the Coming Times.
To the Rose upon the Rood of Time.
Tom O'Roughley.
Tower, The, *sels.*
Travail of Passion, The.
Two Songs of a Fool.
Two Trees, The.
Under Ben Bulben, *sels.*
Upon a Dying Lady.
Upon a House Shaken by the Land Agitation.
Vacillation, *sels.*
Vision, A, *sels.*
Wanderings of Oisin, The, *sels.*
What Then?
Wheel, The.
When Helen Lived.
When you are old and grey and full of sleep.
Whence Had They Come?
Where My Books Go.
White Birds, The.
Who Goes with Fergus?
Wild Old Wicked Man, The.
Wild Swans at Coole, The.
Wisdom.
Youth and Age.

"Yehoash" (Solomon Bloomgarden [*or* Bloomgarten *or* Blumgarden]) (1870–1926)
At the Tomb of Rachel.
Harp of David, The.
Hunting.

Jephthah's Daughter.
Mystery.
Old Song, An.
Prayer, A: "Eternal God, our life is but."
Prophet, The.
Psalm: "Happy is the man whom Thou hast set apart."
Shadows.
Song as Yet Unsung, A.
Song of grass, A, / A song of earth.
Strongest, The.
Terror.
Thanksgiving.
That Is All I Heard.
Tool of Fate, The.
Wanderer, The.
Withered Rose, A.
Yang-Se-Fu.

Yellen, Samuel (b. 1906)
Personal.

Yên Ba
Twenty-Eight Lines for My Wife.

Yen Chi-tao (1030?–1106?)
Drunk with wine, I slap my spring robe.
Tune: "Butterflies Lingering over Flowers."
Tune: "Mountain Hawthorns."

Yen Shu (991–1055)
Tune: "Spring in Jade Pavilion."
Tune: "Treading on Grass."

Yên Thao
My Home.

Yen Yü (fl. c.1200)
My Boat Moored on a River.

Yenser, Stephen (b. 1941)
Blue Guide.
Ember Week, Reseda.

Yeryomenko [or Eremenko], Aleksandr (b. 1950)
Addition to the Opposition.
I look at you from such deep graves.

Yesenin [or Esenin], Sergey [or Sergei] Aleksandrovich (1895–1925)
Bitch, The.
Black Man, The.
Flowers say goodbye to me, The.
From the start, each living thing's.
Goodbye, my friend, goodbye.
I do not regret, complain, or weep.
Letter to My Mother.
My leafless maple tree, your icy coating.
Now piece by piece we slip away.
Only one final trick remains—.
Rowan Tree Fire, The.
To Kachalov's Dog.
Today I asked the money changer.
Years of my youth, years of dissipation.
You feel no love or pity for me.

Yevtushenko, Yevgeny (b. 1933)
Babii Yar.
From a Talk.
I am.

Yevtushenko [or Evtushenko], Yevgeny Aleksandrovich (b. 1933)
Babii Yar.
City of Yes and the City of No, The.
Disbelief in Yourself Is Indispensable.
Half-measures / can kill.
Hand-Rolled Cigarettes.
Heirs of Stalin, The.
I am a purse.
Loss.
Metamorphoses.
Monologue of a Blue Fox.
My love will come.
New York Elegy.
Saints of Jazz are playing, The.
Siberian Wooing.
Sleep, My Beloved.
When your face dawned.

Yi, Hyonggi (b. 1933)
Fallen Petals.
Song of Cricket.

Yi, Kunbae (b. 1940)
Certain Year, A.
Winter Vision, The.

Yi, Sang (1910–38)
Critical Condition, *sels.*
Crow's-Eye View, *sels.*
Flower-tree.
Mirror, The.
Paper Memorial Stone.
Poem No. III.
Poem No. V.
Poem No. VII.
Poem No. X.
Poem No. XV.
Soyŏng Problems.

Yi, Sanghwa (1900–41)
Does Spring Come to These Forfeited Fields?

Yi, Songbu (b. 1942)
Bulldozer, The.
Paddies lean against each other.

Yi, Tongju (1920–79)
Bride, The.
Gang-gang-suwole.

Yi, Yuksa (1904–44)
Grapes, The.
Vertex, The.
Wilderness.

Yin Shih (fl. early 7th cent.)
Parting from the Courtier Sung.

Yo, Shên
Dreaming of a Dead Lady.

Yokobue (fl. 12th cent.)
How can I complain / that you have shaved your hair?

Yoldugu
It would be very pleasant to die with a wolf woman.

Yolen, Jane (b. 1939)
Caterpillar's Lullaby.
Dragon Night.
First Robin.
Graffiti.
Shepherd's Night Count.
Sky scrape, / City scape.
Troll to her Children, The.

Yondo, Elolongue Epanya (b. 1930)
Love.
Lullaby.
My Country.
To You.
Woman!

"Yorick"
Limerick: "Emperor Marcus Aurelius, The."
Limerick: "Old gourmet who's grown somewhat stout, An."

Yorie (1884–1941)
Cat's Eye, The.

York, Sarah E. (1819–51)
I Am Weary of Straying.

Yorke, Philip
Our Gardener here, James Phillips see.

Yoruba Oral Tradition
Invocation of the Creator.

Yosami (fl. 7th–8th cent.)
Day after day I've longed for my husband.
We will never meet again face to face.
You tell me not to long for you.

Yosano, Akiko (1878–1942)
Amidst the notes.
As I am unhappy.
At the beginning.
Bird comes, A / delicately as a little girl.
Come at last to this point.
Hair unbound, in this.
He tempted me to.
I can give myself to her.
I have the delusion / that you are with me.
I remember the days / When the lily.
It is because you always hope, my heart.
Labour Pains.
Last autumn / The three of us tossed acorns.
Left on the beach.
Like tiny golden.
My heart is like the sun / drowned in darkness.
No camellia.
Once, far over the breakers.
Over the old honeymoon cottage.

Purple butterflies / fly at night through my dreams.
She who carries / in her heart a love.
Spring is short.
Sweet and sad / like love overwhelmed.
Swifter than hail.
Tanka: "Agonizing beyond words."
Tanka: "Aster, The."
Tanka: "But for women."
Tanka: "Camellias."
Tanka: "Clear spring, A."
Tanka: "Each shaped."
Tanka: "Earth looks, The."
Tanka: "Evanescent."
Tanka: "Grabbing one of."
Tanka: "Into a pair of stars."
Tanka: "Peony in her hair, The."
Tanka: "Pressing my breasts."
Tanka: "Sea inside my heart, The."
Tanka: "Tell them."
Tanka: "Two chilly."
Tanka: "Warring heaven."
Tanka: "White blossoms bloom."
Tanka: "White tower, A."
Tanka: "Writes poetry."
Tanka: "Young fingers."
That evening when.
This autumn will end.
Uguisu has not come, The.
Wave of coldness, A.
Without a word.
You never touch.

Yoshifusa, Fujiwara No
Years have touched me, The.

Yoshihara, Sachiko (b. 1932)
Blasphemy.
Candle.
I Forget.
Madness.
Resurrection.

Yoshimi, Kondō
Tanka: "Along a street."
Tanka: "Because."
Tanka: "Casting shadows."
Tanka: "Dream, A."
Tanka: "Gloomy rain."
Tanka: "Having crushed."
Tanka: "Having grown up."
Tanka: "How many people came."
Tanka: "Moment, The."
Tanka: "Ocean, The."
Tanka: "Scissors."
Tanka: "Since I work with those."
Tanka: "Soldiers on the ground."
Tanka: "Spoon, A."
Tanka: "Street, The."
Tanka: "Streetcar, A."
Tanka: "White jet clouds."
Tanka: "With headlights on."
Trip to Berlin.
White sky, The.

Yoshiyuki, Rie (b. 1939)
Sacrificial Victim.

Young, Al (b. 1939)
Blues Don't Change, The.
California Peninsula: El Camino Real.
Conjugal Visits.
Curative Powers of Silence, The.
Dance For Ma Rainey, A.
Dance for Militant Dilettantes, A.
Dance of the Infidels.
Dancer, The.
For Poets.
I Arrive In Madrid.
Kiss.
Lester Leaps In.
Little More Traveling Music, A.
Loneliness.
Move Continuing, The.
Myself When I Am Real.
Poem for Players, A.
Ponce de León: A Morning Walk.
Prestidigitator 1, The.
Prestidigitator 2, The.
Studio Up Over In Your Ear.
Topsy: Part 2.
W. H. Auden & Mantan Moreland.

Yes, the Secret Mind Whispers.
Young, Andrew (1885–1971)
Ba Cottage.
Beauty and Love.
Black Rock of Kiltearn.
Christmas Day.
Culbin Sands.
Dead Crab, The.
Dead Mole, A.
Fairy Ring, The.
Field-Glasses.
Heap of Faggots, A.
In Teesdale.
Last Snow.
Man and Cows.
March Hares.
Nest, The.
On the Pilgrims' Road.
Passing the Graveyard.
Prehistoric Camp, A.
Scarecrow, The.
Shepherd's Hut, The.
Song for Autumn.
Stay, Spring.
Stockdoves, The.
Sudden Thaw.
Suilven.
Thistledown.
Wiltshire Downs.
Young, Augustus (b. 1943)
Advice of an Efficiency Expert, The.
After Five Years.
Ballad of Fat Margot.
Elegy for a School-Friend.
Heritage.
Last Refuge, The.
Woman, don't be troublesome.
Young, Barbara (b. 1872)
I Hear It Said.
Young Bear, Ray A. (b. 1950)
Another Face.
Before the Actual Cold.
Black Dog.
Celebration.
Coming Back Home.
Cook, The.
Crow-Children Walk My Circles in the
Snow, The.
Drive to Lone Ranger, A.
Emily Dickinson, Bismarck and the
Roadrunner's Inquiry.
First Dimension of Skunk, The.
From the Spotted Night.
I am walking and I.
In Dream: The Privacy of Sequence.
In Missing.
King Cobra as Political Assassin, The.
Language of Weather, The.
My reflection.
Nothing Could Take Away the Bear-King's
Image.
Our Bird Aegis.
Personification of a Name, The.
Place of O, The.
Place of V, The.
Poem for Diane Wakoski, A.
Race of the Kingfishers.
Remembrance of a Color inside a Forest, A.
Rushing.
Significance of a Water Animal, The.
Song Taught to Joseph, The.
Star Blanket.
These Horses Came.
This House.
This little house swallows.
Through the cracks.
Trains Made of Stone.
Wadasa Nakamoon, Vietnam Memorial.
Waiting to Be Fed.
War Walking Near.
Way the Bird Sat, The.
What We Can.
Young, C. Dale (b. 1969)
Vespers.
Young, David
August at the Lake.

Boxcar Poem, The ("Boxcars drift by /
clanking, The.")
Death of the Novel, The.
In My Own Back Yard.
Mandelstam.
Project for Freight Trains, A.
Thoughts of Chairman Mao.
Young, Dean
Business of Love is Cruelty, The.
Lace.
Other Obit.
Rothko's Yellow.
Storms.
Threshold.
Twilight with Xs.
Upon Hearing of My Friend's Marriage
Breaking Up.
Young, Douglas (1913–73)
Caller rain frae abune.
Deid sall ye ligg, and ne'er a memorie.
For a Wife in Jizzen.
Kirkyaird by the Sea, The, sels.
Last Lauch.
Minnie, I canna caa my wheel.
Sainless.
Shepherd's Dochter, The.
Winter Homily on the Calton Hill.
Young, Edward (1683–1765)
Epistle II: To Mr. Pope, From Oxford, sels.
Epistles to Mr. Pope, sels.
Love of Fame, the Universal Passion, sels.
Night Thoughts, sels.
Satires, sels.
**Young, Edward Hilton, 1st Baron Kennet of
the Dene (1879–1960)**
Mine-Sweeping Trawlers.
Young, Francis Brett (1884–1954)
Bête Humaine.
Gift, The.
Seascape.
Young, Gary (b. 1951)
Four Days: Earthquake.
Young, George W. (1846–1919)
Lips That Touch Liquor.
Young, Kevin (b. 1970)
Casting.
Eddie Priest's Barbershop and Notary.
Escape Artist, The.
Field Trip.
No Offense.
Preserving, The.
Young, Marguerite (b. 1909)
Angels, The.
Noah's Ark.
Whales, The.
Winter Scene.
Young, Michael (b. 1915)
Metronomic Moon, The.
Young, Stanley
Epitaph for a Concord Boy.
Young, Virginia Brady (b. 1911)
At twilight.
Fallen birch leaf.
In a circle of thaw.
On the first day of spring.
Persimmons.
Sight of a lark's, The.
Silence, The.
Violets.
Yozei Emperor (fl. 9th cent.)
Falling from the ridge.
Yü Chi (1272–1348)
After Snow—Impromptu.
Following the Rhymes of Autumn Night
Song by Meng Tzu-chou, Signatory
Official of the Board of Rites.
Following the Rhymes of Bamboo Branch
Songs in Response to Yüan Po-chang.
Getting on Horseback.
Going to the Ministry with Chao Tzu-ch'i.
Hearing Loom and Shuttle.
Inscribed on a Painting.
Inscribed on the Painting, Solitary Crane, in
the Collection of Jao Shih-ying.
Late in the Year K'uei-yu (1333), Staying at
the Temple of the Upper Regions.

Little Landscape by Chao Ch'ien-li, A.
Little Landscape by Yen Wen-kuei, A.
Sent To Be Inscribed on the Temple of P'u-
jun (Universal Fructification) at Lou-fu
Mountain.
Sitting Alone in the Courtyard.
Traveling Early through a Snowy Valley.
What family has built a house beside the
rapids here?
When I Was Young, I Stopped by a Wine
Shop in Chi-men and Wrote This Poem,
Inscribed It and Signed It, "Written by
Lien the Eighteenth." The People of That
District Have Since Taken It To Be a
Poem of [the God] Lü Tung-pin! I Have
Recorded It Here as an Amusement.
Yü Ch'ien (1394–1457)
Poem on Coal, A.
Yu, Ch'ihwan (1908–67)
Flag.
Isle of Ulung, The.
Life.
Rock.
"Yu-ch'uan-tzu."&xbd; See Lu T'ung
Yü, Hsiang. See Hsiang Chi
Yü Hsüan-chi (c.843–868)
Advice to a Neighbour Girl.
Answering Li Ying Who Showed Me His
Poems about Summer Fishing.
At the End of Spring.
Boudoir Lament.
Composed on the Theme "Willows by the
Riverside."
Elegy for the Wife of a Friend.
For Hidden Mist Pavilion.
For Kuo Hsiang.
Letting My Feelings Out.
On a Visit to Ch'ung Chen Taoist Temple.
On the River.
Poem to the Tune "Riverbank Willows."
Regretful Thoughts.
Replying to a Poem by a New Graduate
Lamenting the Loss of His Wife.
Rhyming a Friend's Poem.
Rhyming with a Friend.
Selling Ruined Peonies.
Sent to Wen T'ing-yün on a Winter Night.
Spring Thoughts Sent to Tzu-an.
Staying in the Mountains in Summer.
Telling My Feelings.
To the Minister Liu.
To Tzu-an.
Yü Hu (b. 745)
Thoughts South of the Yangtze.
**Yu Kuang-chung [or Yu Kwang-chung] (b.
1928)**
Mother, I'm hungry.
When I am dead, lay me down between the
Yangtze.
Yü Wu-ling (fl. 9th cent.)
Offered to a Man Who Sells Pines.
Offering Wine.
Yu Xuanji
At Home in the Summer Mountains.
Yüan Chen (779–831)
Airing Painful Memories.
Apricot Garden.
Drunk Too Soon.
Elegy, An: "Last, best-loved daughter of old
Hsieh, you who foolishly ran off."
Elegy, An: "O youngest, best-loved daughter
of Hsieh."
Late Spring.
Mourning My Son.
On Lien-ch'ang Palace.
Pitcher, The.
Recalling When I Was Drunk.
Sent to Lo-t'ien for Thinking of Me after the
Rainfall.
Sobering Up.
Song of the Weaving Woman.
Three Dreams at Chiang-ling.
To the Waters of the Chia-ling.
Yuan Chi (210–163)
Deep night. I cannot sleep.
Regret.

Yüan Chieh (719–72)
Civilization.
Palace of Rocks, THe.
Stone Fish Lake.

Yüan Hao-wen (1190–1257)
Autumn Sentiments.
Crossing the Yellow River: June 12.
On Poetry, *sels.*
Quatrain: "Above the creek dallies a bright moon."
Random Verses on Mountain Life, *sels.*
Song of the Maidens.

Yüan Hung-tao (1568–1610)
Climbing Mount Yang.
On Board a Boat at Chi-ning.
On Receiving My Letter of Termination.
Passing by the Hot Springs at Hua-ch'ing Palace, *sels.*
Pei-mang Cemetery.
Record of My Trip to Mount She, A.
"Slowly, Slowly" Poem, The.
Woman's Room in Autumn, A.

Yüan Mei (1716–98)
Arriving at Hangchou.
Ballad of Peach Blossom Spring.
Busy.
Finding Serenity.
Five Poems on Returning to Hangchou, *sels.*
Flying Bells.
Fog at Liang-hsiang.
Happy about Being Old.
I Know Inside.
In Late Spring of the Year Keng-hsü (1790), I Stayed at the Sun Family's Gemstone Mountain Villa at West Lake. Before Leaving, I Wrote These Poems as Mementos, *sels.*
Ma-wei.
Miscellaneous Feelings in the Sui Garden.
Miscellaneous Poems on Growing Old, *sels.*
Moments of Fullfillment—mdash;Writing Down Miscellaneous, *sels.*
Next Day the Fog Was Even Worse, The.
Night of the Fifteenth, Second Month.
On the Twenty-First Day of the Fifth Month, I Reached Home.
On the Way to Pa-ling.
Rains pass, the mountains' face is washed.
Returning Home.
Rough Ridge.
Summer Day.
Things Seen.
Things Seen on Spring Days.
Winter Night.
Words from the Goblet of Wisdom.
Writing My Feelings.

Yud, Nachum (b. 1888)
Like the Eyes of Wolves.

Yuhara, Prince (*fl.* 8th cent.)
Let us bribe the Moon God.
What am I to do with my sister? *From* Manyo Shu, Part 4 of 4.

Yukitsuna, Sasaki
At the zoo (two poems).
Baker's prayer.
Tanka: "Always loving."
Tanka: "Amid the waves of time."
Tanka: "Beyond doubt."
Tanka: "Bloom finished, The."
Tanka: "Changing."
Tanka: "Child in my arms."
Tanka: "During a trip."
Tanka: "Each morning I awake."
Tanka: "Moonlight, The."
Tanka: "Overtaken by time."
Tanka: "Plaintive, A."
Tanka: "Poetry."
Tanka: "Since puberty."
Tanka: "With a hangover."
Tanka: "With those who."
Tanka: "Writing a series."
Tanka: "Youngster, A."

Yün-k'an Tzu (*fl.* first half of 14th cent.)
Tune: "Greeting the Immortal Guest."

Yün Shou-p'ing (1633–90)
Autumn Plants, Flowers, Bamboo, Rocks.
Chyrsanthemums, *sels.*

Early Summer in the Year Jen-tzu (1672)— Playfully Painted in the Manner of Ts'ao Yün-hsi.
Green Banana Leaves.
Hearing a Flute at Broken Bridge.
In My Boat, Painting a Picture of Going Home by Boat, *sels.*
In the Tenth Month of the Year Jen-tzu (1672) the Imperial Censor Tan Chiang-shang, Mountain Man Wang Shih-ku and I Traveled by Boat to Pi-ling and Moored There. We Lingered Among the Frosty Trees and Red Leaves. Wang Was Entrusted with the Task of Painting a Picture, and We Each Wrote Twelve Poems to Record Our Delightful Experience, *sels.*
Inscribed on a Painting by Shih-ku, *sels.*
Inscribed on a Painting ("Magic mists twirl around the sky.")
Inscribed on a Painting of Sailboats on the River—Seeing Off Yen-chi on His Journey to Ch'ang-an.
Inscribed on a Painting ("Who needs a raft that can invade the stars?")
Inscribed on a Snowscape.
Lament for Myself, A, *sels.*
Lament for the Willows outside the City Walls, A.
Landscape, *sels.*
Mourning for Lü Hui-chiu, *sels.*
On a Landscape by Myself.
On a Painting "Ancient Trees and Flowing Stream."
On a Painting of Mushrooms.
On the Day of the Mid-Autumn Festival of the Year Ping-yin (1686), Together with Chang Han-chan, Ching-fan, and Ching-t'ien, I Saw the Kuei Blossoms at the Northern Garden of Jade Peak, *sels.*
On the Painting "Joys of Village Life," *sels.*
On the Painting, Mist Over Ten Thousand Mountains by Shih-ku, *sels.*
Painting in the Style of Secretary Kao, A.
Painting of Chrysanthemums in the Boneless Style of Hsü Ch'ung-ssu, A.
Painting of Yams, A.
Sadness in the Autumn Chambers.
Seeing Off Mr. Yang on His Journey to Wu-wei Prefecture, *sels.*
Waterside Village.
Written on the Night of the Twenty-ninth of the First Month.

Yun, Tongju (1917–45)
Counting the Stars.
Cross, The.
Prologue, The.

Yungman, Moshe (b. 1922)
Melons.

Yuwaku
I think about you & it's like having spirits come down on me.

Z

"Z., Z."
Here lies a poet—where's the great surprise!

Zabel, Morton Dauwen (b. 1901)
Journal to Stella.

Zabolotsky [*or* Zabolotskii], Nikolai Alekseievich (1903–58)
Circus shines, like a shield, The.
Face of the Horse, The.
Ivanovs, The.
Last Love.
Movement.
Peoples House.
Signs of the Zodiac are fading, The.
Soccer.
Somewhere in a field near Magadan.
Strolling Musicians.
Thistle.
Ugly Girl, The.
Walk, A.
Wedding.

Zach, Natan (b. 1930)
Against Parting.
Against Sadness.
Be attentive to this trembling shade.
Be careful. Open your life.
Death Came for Michael Rockinghorse early one morning.
Give Me What the Tree Has [and what it won't lose].
Greater Courage.
Harvest Month[. A full moon].
How the Days Passed. Who'd have believed they'd.
I Hear Something Falling, said the wind.
In the Course of Time the original.
King Solomon's Camel is a hypocritical creature.
Like Sand.
Max is dead and his sons.
Nameless.
Painter Paints, The.
Poem Too Late, A.
Problem, The.
Prologue to a Poem.
Samson's Hair.
Soft Warm Breeze, A.
War Confession.

Zagajewski, Adam (b. 1945)
At Daybreak.
Auto Mirror.
Betrayal.
Electric Elegy.
Lava.
Moths watched us through.
On the Escalator.
Watching Shoah in a Hotel Room in America.
When Death Came.

Zamora, Daisy (b. 1959)
Celebration of the Body.
Downpour.
Hand Mirror.
Lineage.
Loyal Housewife.
Mother's Day.
Precisely because I do not have.
Report on the Protest in Front of the United States Embassy by the Pino Grande Movement, A.
To Be a Woman.
Vision of Your Body.

Zangwill, Israel (1864–1926)
At the Zoo.
Death's Transfiguration.
Despair and Hope.
Dreams.
Evolution.
In the Morgue.
Inexhaustible.
Israel.
"Might Is Right."
Moses and Jesus.
Oliver Singing.
Seder-Night.
Sundered.
Tabernacle Thought, A.
Theodor Herzl.
To a Pretty Girl.
Vanitas Vanitatum.
Vision.
Why Do We Live?
Yom Kippur.

Zanzotto, Andrea (b. 1921)
Behold the thin green.
Campèa.
Distance.
Epiphany.
How long between the grain and the wind.
If it were not your face that melts.

Zaranka, William
Conceit upon the Feet.
Continuation of *The Cook's Tale*, The.
Cropdusting, The.
Cry of the Child, The.
High-toned Old Fascist Gentleman, A.
In the Ladies' Room at the Bus Terminal.
Lovers' Debouchment.

Memories of Aunt Maria-Martha.
Ode: "Mistah Berrybones, you daid?"
Parachuting Thoor Ballylee.
Peruke of Poets.
Quicksands.
Ragout.
Robert Frost's Left-leaning *Trespassers Will Be Shot* Sign.

Zarin, Cynthia (b. 1959)
Ant Hill, The.
Song.

Zarucchi, Roy
Grape Stakes.

Zarzyski, Paul
Silos.
Trespasses.

Zaturenska, Marya Alexandrovna (Mrs. Horace Gregory) (1902–82)
Bird and the Muse.
Daisy, The.
Descent of the Vulture, The.
Head of Medusa.
Lovers, The.
Tempest, The.
White Dress, The.
Woman at the Piano.

Zavalnyuk [or Zaval'niuk], Leonid Andreievich (b. 1931)
Earlobe.
I love my enemies, those I forgive.

Zavatsky, Bill (b. 1943)
To the Pianist Bill Evans.

Zealand, Karen
Passion at the Chat 'n Chew Diner.
Primitives Knew How Defenseless, The.
Still Life, Untitled, A.

Zeb-un-Nissa, Princess (1638–1702)
Though I am Laila of the Persian romance.

Zeidner, Lisa (b. 1955)
Bach.
Kafka Poem.
Transvestite.

Zeigler, L. L.
Snack, The.

"Zelda" (Zelda Schneurson or Zelda Mishkovsky) (b. 1914)
Wicked Neighbor, The.

Zeldis, Chayyim (b. 1927)
Holy Ones, the Young Ones, The.

Zenmaro, Toki
At the lectern.
At the Van Gogh exibition.
Evidence.
New York.
On Mumonkan[6].
On the birth of my son.
September 1, 1923.
Tanka: "All the young men I know."
Tanka: "Having lived."
Tanka: "How sad it is."
Tanka: "In sullen silence."
Tanka: "It's hazardous."
Tanka: "No news of him."
Tanka: "Nothing."
Tanka: "Old Japan."
Tanka: "Old soldier, An."
Tanka: "On the road."
Tanka: "Tears, tears."
Tanka: "We're poor.'"
Tanka: "Work on the impossible."

Zenodotus (b. c.325 B.C.)
Statue Of Eros, A.

Zepeda, Ofelia
Kitchen Sink.
People on Wayward Journeys.

Zephaniah, Benjamin
According to my Mood.

Zerbe, Evelyn Arcad
In Memory of My Arab Grandmother.

Zesen, Philipp von (1619–89)
Evening Song.
To the Superhuman Adelmund, When She Would Undo the Kiss Already Done.

Zhao, Pan (48–117?)
Needle and Thread.

Zhdanov, Ivan (b. 1948)
Home.
I'm not the branch, only the prebranchness.

Zhenkai, Zhao ("Bei Dao") (b. 1949)
Accomplices.
Answer, The.
August Sleepwalker, The.
Collection, The.
Discovery.
End or a Beginning, An.
Evening Scene, An.
Old Temple, The.
Requiem: "Not the living but the dead."
Résume.
Stretch out your hands too.

Zhigulin, Anatoly [or Anatolii] (b. 1930)
Campfireburners.

Zibu'n-Nisa. See Makhfi

Ziedonis, Imants
How the candle burns.
Inevitability.
That is her memorial.
That was a beautiful summer.

Zierlin, Israel. See Tiempo, César

Zieroth, Dale (b. 1946)
Baptism.
Beautiful woman, you crown the hours.
Hunters of the Deer, The.

Zimmer, Paul (b. 1934)
Apple Blight.
But Bird.
Day Zimmer Lost Religion, The.
Duke Ellington Dream, The.
Eisenhower Years, The.
Failings, The.
Father Animus and Zimmer.
Lord Fluting Dreams of America on the Eve of His Departure from Liverpool.
Phineas Within and Without.
Queen, The.
Sitting with Lester Young.
What Zimmer Would Be.
Zimmer and His Turtle Sink the House.
Zimmer Drunk and Alone, Dreaming of Old Football Games.
Zimmer Imagines Heaven.
Zimmer in Fall.
Zimmer in Grade School.
Zimmer's Head Thudding against the Blackboard.

Zimmerman, Robert. See "Dylan, Bob"

Zimunya, Musaemura Bonus
After the Massacre.
Arrivants.
Kisimiso.
White Poetess.

Zinzendorf, Nikolaus [or Nicolaus] Ludwig, Graf von (1700–1760)
For Us No Night Can Be Happier.
Jesu, to Thee My Heart I Bow.
On Earth There Is a Lamb So Small.
Slain Lamb of God.

Zipper, Arizona
Farmer drives by, A.
Football, The.
I stop to listen.
Right in the middle.
Wedding over, The.

Zivancevic, Nina
Duende.
Florence.
Kindergarten Curse.
Poem with a Tilde in the Title, A.

Znamenskaya [or Znamenskaia], Irina (b. 1952)
Estonia. A private dacha.

Zolotow, Charlotte (b. 1915)
Aren't You Glad.
Autumn.
Bridge, The.
Change.
Riddle, A: "Once when I was very scared."

Zolynas, Al (b. 1945)
Love in the Classroom.
Zen of Housework, The.

Zonas (fl. 90 B.C.)
Make my cup with clay.
Pass me the sweet earthenware jug.
Pomegranate just splitting, a peach just furry, A.

Zorgenfrey [or Zorgenfrei], Wilgelm Aleksandrovich (1882–1938)
Over the Neva.

Zoroaster [orZarathustra] (fl. 7th cent. B.C.)
Sacred Book, The.

"Zozimus." See Moran, Michael

Zu-Bolton, Ahmos, II (b. 1935)
By the 5th Generation Louisiana, After Slavery.
Governor of the Ollie Street, The.
Struggle-Road Dance.

Zuckmayer, Carl (b. 1896)
My Death.

Žukauskas, Albinas
Midwinter Tourists.

Zukofsky, Louis (1904–78)
A, *sels.*
"A-12," *sels.*
1892-1941.
For you I have emptied the meaning.
Green leaf that will outlast the winter.
I walk in the old street.
It's hard to see but think of a sea.
Lines of this new song are nothing, The.
Non Ti Fidar.
Of Dying Beauty.
Poem Beginning "The," *sels.*
Songs of Degrees, *sels.*
29 Poems, *sels.*
29 Songs, *sels.*
Ways, The.

Zulauf, Sander
Separation in Succasunna.

Zuma, Nongejeni (1870–1942)
Praises of Field-marshal J. C. Smuts, The.

Zuni Oral Tradition
History Myth of the Coming of the A' shiwi as Narrated by ᶜKiäklo, *sels.*
Invocation to the U'wannami (Rain-Makers).

Zweig, Martha
Dark Song.

Zweig, Paul (1935–84)
End Circulates in the Wide Space of Summer, The.
Fly on the Water, A.
Poem: "I don't know if I can bear this suddenly."
River, The.

Zweig, Stefan (1881–1942)
Jeremiah, *sels.*

Zwicky, Fay (b. 1933)
Jack Frost.
Reckoning.
Summer Pogrom.
Three Songs of Love and Hate, *sels.*

Zych, Adam
Auschwitz, 1987.

SUBJECT INDEX

*Poems under each subject are listed alphabetically by author. Subjects range from specific (for example, persons) to general (for example, **Faith**).*

*Some subject headings show cross-references to related subjects. Some subjects, such as **Love**, are so broad that they appear here only to refer the user to related subjects and to anthologies. In other cases as well, anthologies are listed that in whole or in part focus on the subject in question. Anthologies that are mainly translations into English are listed under their appropriate countries or languages.*

There may be cross-references to related subjects.

A

AIDS (acquired immune deficiency syndrome)
Ameen. Monologue of a Dying Beast.
Sonnet No. 21.
Campo. Allegory.
Dixon, M. Aunt Ida Pieces a Quilt.
Gunn, T. Lament: "Your dying was a difficult enterprise."
Man With Night Sweats, The.
Missing, The.
Hacker, M. Dusk: July.
Nights of 1964–1966: The Old Reliable.
Head, G. Night Sweats.
Hull, L. Combat Zone/War Stories.
Lassell. How to Watch Your Brother Die.
McHugh, H. What Hell Is.
Moore, H. Memoir.
Sanchez, S. Poem for my Brother, A.
Schreiber, R. Alarming New Development, An.
Valentine, J. "X."
Waniek. Sacrament of Poverty, The.

Aardvarks
Fields, J. Aardvark.

Aaron (Bible)
Herbert, G. Aaron.

Abandonment
Aldiss. Frozen Boy, The.
Alterman. Abandoned, The.
Blake, W. Never Pain to Tell Thy Love.
Bury. False and faithless as thou art.
Cassian. Lady of Miracles.
Clark, T. Like musical instruments / Abandoned in a field.
Daley, V. Mother Doorstep.
Davis, C. Belongings.
Derricotte. Poem for My Father.
Donne. To Mr I. L ("Blessed [or Blest] are your north parts, for all this long time").
Dove, R. Adolescence—III.
Dufault. Letter for Allhallows, A.
Goldsmith, O. Deserted Village, The.
Han-shan. In an Abandoned Garden.
Hayden, R. Incense of the Lucky Virgin.
Sub Specie Aeternitatis.
Hill, G. My little son, when you could command marvels.
Hsü Pen. Deserted Estate at South Garden, The.
Hughes, L. Mama and Daughter.
Hugo, R. Death of the Kapowsin Tavern.
Degrees of Gray in Philipsburg.
Montana Ranch Abandoned.
River Now, The.
Kamienska. On the Cross*.
Keppel, L. Robin Adair.
Kingsley, C. Airly Beacon, Airly Beacon.
Komunyakaa. My Father's Love Letters [or Loveletters].

Kooser. Abandoned Farmhouse.
Landor, W. What News.
Longfellow, H. From Evangeline.
Tale of Acadie, A.
Lorde. Story Books on a Kitchen Table.
Lowell, A. Autumn.
Madhubuti. What Her Man Had Left Her for the Sixth Time That Year / (An Uncommon Occurrence).
Meynell, A. Study, A.
Mickle. Cumnor Hall.
Moore, L. Winter 1967.
Mountain, M. After your visit.
Nash, O. Exit, Pursued by a Bear.
Nowlan. Only when my heart freezes.
Orampokiyar. What Her Girl Friend Said when He Sent a Flattering Minstrel on His Behalf.
Ralegh, W. 'As ye came from the holy land'.
Ransom, J. Lady Lost.
Rich, A. In the Wake of Home.
Rilke. Olive Garden, The.
Scarfe. Merry Window, The.
Sorrentino. Land of Cotton.
Spender, S. Song: "Stranger, you who hide my love."
Spires. Exhumation.
Stickney, T. Departure, The.
Tomlinson, C. Two Views of Two Ghost Towns.
Unknown. Easy rider, see what you done done, Lawd, Lawd.
Weissbort. Mourning.
Wither. I loved a lass, a fair one.
Wright, C. This Couple.
Wyatt, T. Lover Showeth How He Is Forsaken of Such as He Sometime Enjoyed, The.
Lover's Appeal, The.
Yang Wei-chen. Residence of the Emperors of Ch'en, The.
Yeats. John Kinsella's Lament for Mrs. Mary Moore.

Abbey Theatre, Dublin
Strong, L. Old Woman, Outside the Abbey Theater, An.
Yeats. At The Abbey Theatre.

Abbeys. *See* **Monasteries**

Abel. *See* **Cain and Abel**

Abelard and Heloise
Read, S. Sic et Non.

Abishag
Kaufman, S. Abishag.
Spire. Abishag.

Abolitionists
Benét, S. John Brown's Prayer.
Dove, R. David Walker (1785–1830).
Dunbar, P. Douglass.
Forten. To W. L. G. on Reading His "Chosen Queen."
Harper, F. Bible Defence of Slavery.
Bury Me in a Free Land.

Hayden, R. Runagate Runagate.
Rukeyser, M. Soul and Body of John Brown, The.
Whittier. Brown of Ossawatomie.
For Righteousness' Sake.
Williams, E. At Harper's Ferry Just before the Attack.

Aborigines
Campbell, D. Lovers, The.
Davis, J. Desolation.
First-born, The.
One Hundred and Fifty Years.
Warru.
Durack. Lament for the Drowned Country.
Fogarty. No Grudge.
Remember Something Like This.
Marshall-Stoneking. Passage.
Momaday. Carriers of the Dream Wheel.
Mudrooroo. Peaches and Cream.
Song Thirty-Four.
Oodgeroo of the tribe Noonuccal. Last of His Tribe.
No more boomerang.
We are Going.
Walker, K. We Are Going.
Weller. Story of Frankie. . . My Man, The.
Wright, J. Bora Ring.

Abortion
Ai. Abortion.
Country Midwife: A Day, The.
Atkins. Lakefront, Cleveland.
Atkinson. Same Trouble with Beauty You've Always Had, The.
Brooks, G. Mother, The.
Carroll, K. Truth About Karen, The.
Clifton, L. Lost Baby Poem, The.
Gibson, M. Today snow sparks the air like mica—the sun's.
Hewitt, D. This Version of Love.
Hope, A. Massacre of the Innocents.
Jonson, B. To Fine Lady Would-Be.
Moeller. Ten Years Ago.
Peacock, M. Chriseaster.
Piercy. Sabbath of Mutual Respect, The.
Sexton. Abortion, The.
Shiffrin, N. For My Neverborn.
Unknown. Epitaph on a Child Killed by Procured Abortion.
Woddis. Moral Tale, A.

Abraham
Bloch, C. In wings and starched.
Patriarch in black takes, The.
Dickinson, E. Abraham to kill him.
Frost, R. Luke 16:19–26; "There was a rich man."
Lasker-Schüler. Abraham and Isaac.
Muir, E. Abraham.
Nemerov. Nicodemus.
Nichols, R. Harlot's Catch.
Noll. Abraham's Madness.

Owen, W. Parable of the Old Man and the Young, The.
Rilke. Luke 1:39–56: In those days Mary arose.
Schwartz, D. Abraham.
Smart, C. Faith.
Stradling. Abraham's Sacrifice of Isaac.
Wilner, E. Sarah's Choice.

Absalom

Unknown. Dispraise of Absalom, The.
Wallach. Absalom.
Wollach. Absalom.
Zach. Samson's Hair.

Absence

"Akhmatova." To The Beloved.
Allingham. I walk'd in the lonesome evening.
Auden. Song: "Stop all the clocks, cut off the telephone."
Avidan. What I Have to Tell You, Until Next Time.
Baxter, E. In Your Absence.
Bernard. To see the lark, delighted, dare.
Blunden. Late Light.
Browning, E. Face which, duly as the sun, The.
Browning, R. Never the time and the place.
Carew, T. To Her in Absence; a Ship.
Upon Some Alterations in My Mistress, after My Departure into France.
Carver, R. No Need.
Catullus. Carmen 8 ("Break off / fallen Catullus").
Coleridge, S. Day-Dream, The ("If thou wert here, these tears were tears of light!")
If I had but two little wings.
Cooley. Elect, The.
Cowley, A. Spring, The.
Crane, H. Carrier Letter.
Creeley. Signboard, The.
Song: "Those rivers run from that land."
Turn, The.
Crist. She has gone.
Crozier, A. Humiliation in Its Disguises.
Daive. I rise from the depths of my resemblance.
Nomad, A.
De la Mare. Alone.
Dickinson, E. It was not Death, for I stood up.
Parting.
You love me—you are sure.
Donne. To Mr I. L ("Blessed [or Blesst] are your north parts, for all this long time").
Dooley, M. No, Go On.
Draycott. Search.
Drummond, W. Sonnet: "Slide soft, fair forth, and make a crystal plain."
Duncan, R. Passage Over Water.
Gallagher, T. I Stop Writing the Poem.
Kidnap[p]er.
Googe. Out of Sight, Out of Mind.
Graham, W. Letter II.
Greville, F. Absence and Presence.
Grierson. To Miss Laetitia Van Lewen.
Habington. To Castara, Being to Take a Journey.
Upon Castara's Absence.
Upon Castara's Departure.
Hardy, T. Voice, The.
Hashimoto, S. Mirror of Matsuyama, The.
Hass, R. Song: "Afternoon cooking in the fall sun."
Hofmannsthal. Two of Them, The.
Hoskyns. Present in Abscence.
Hotham. Home early.
Hove. Lost Bird.
Hsü Kan. Deepening shadows bring on sorrow, The.
Drifting clouds, distant and vast, The.
Sadly, sadly the season draws to an end.
Hughes, L. So *long* / is in the song.
Inada. Filling the Gap.
Izumi. Lying here alone.
Jago. Absence.
John of the Cross. Spiritual Canticle, The.
Juana Inés de la Cruz. Happy Easter, my Lady.

Knott. Goodbye.
Kopland. Natzweiler.
Ku Hsiung. Tune: "Telling of Innermost Feelings."
Lake, D. Facing Change.
Lawrence, D. Quite Forsaken.
Lewis, A. Song (On Seeing Dead Bodies Floating Off the Cape).
Li Po. In Imitation of Ancient Songs.
Li Shang-yin. "Coming" is an empty word, "going" leaves no trace.
Coming was an empty promise, you have gone, and left no footprint.
Phoenix tail on scented silk, flimsy layer on layer.
Liu Ch'ang-ch'ing. Listening to the Washblock in the Moonlight.
Liu Chün. In Imitation of Hsü Kan ("Since you went away").
Liu Yu Hsi. Willow Branches.
Long, R. Found and Lost.
Lovelace, R. Elinda's [or Ellinda's] Glove.
Lowell, A. Sprig of Rosemary, A.
Lowell, R. Home after Three Months Away.
Mac Low. 27th Dance—Walking—22 March 1964.
"MacDiarmid." Empty Vessel.
Mathews, A. Letter Following.
McClintock, M. Sat down.
Merwin, W. Separation.
Mew. Absence.
Miedzyrzecki. Can You Imagine.
Millay, E. Oh, Oh, you will be sorry for that word!
Monro. Solitude.
Muldoon, P. Why Brownlee left, and where he went.
Nortje. Waiting.
Nye, N. Streets.
Penna. Lady on Streetcar.
Philips, K. To Mrs. M.A. Upon Absence.
Po Chü-i. On a Moonlit Night, Sent to my Brothers and Sisters.
Parrot.
Raine, K. Wilderness, The.
Ransom, J. Winter Remembered.
Ritsos. Distant, The.
Rochester, J. Song: "Absent from thee, I languish still."
Rózewicz. Draft of a Modern Love Poem.
St. John, D. Hush.
Shakespeare, W. Sonnet 97.
Sonnet 113.
What Answer Can I Give?
"Shu Ting." Missing You.
Sidney, P. Sonnet 89: "Now that of absence the most irksome night."
Skelton, J. Knowledge, Acquaintance.
Southwick. Horse on the Wall.
Spenser. Sonnet 89: "Like as the culver on the bared bough."
Stevens, W. Gallant Château.
Stone, R. Curtains.
Su Man-shu. On the bank of Lake Rouge a chestnut steed treads proudly.
Suckling, J. Against Absence.
To Master Davenant for Absence.
Surrey. If care do cause men cry, why do not I complain.
Lady Again Complains, The.
Tatham. Ostella forth of Town: To My Heart.
Tennyson, A. Daisy, The.
Tremayne. Wanting News.
Tu Fu. Parted by death, we swallow remorse.
Rumours that you lodge in a mountain temple.
Tu Mu. Returning Home.
To Judge Han Ch'o at Yang-chou.
Unknown. Banks of Claudy, The.
Girl I Left behind Me, The.
Green is the grass on riverbanks.
I believe in the sun.
I ne have joy, plesauns, nor comfort.
In the courtyard is a marvelous tree.
Lady Prayeth the Return of Her Lover Abiding on the Seas, The.
Lass A-Laundering.
Lover in Winter Plaineth for the Spring, The.

Queen of Hearts, The.
Wandering Gentleman, The.
Vaughan, H. To Amoret Gone from Him.
Villon. Ballade: "Tell me where, in what country, where."
Warner, S. Absence, The.
Weingarten. From the Temple of Longing.
Wen T'ing-yün. Tune: "Pacifying the Western Barbarians."
Wiesel. Behold, God of Abraham, God of mercy.
Wilbur. 'World Without Objects Is a Sensible Emptiness," A."
Wordsworth, W. To a Distant Friend.
Wright, F. Joseph Come Back as the Dusk.

See also **Isolation; Loneliness; Separation**

Abundance

Cowper, W. On Pruning.
Li Tung-yang. Song of the Painting "Catching Fish."
Navajo Oral Tradition. Night Chant, The.
Pankey. Reason, The.
Rogers, P. Abundance and Satisfaction.
Rumi. You're song.
Tryapkin. How much there was of everything: kettledrums and horns and bells!

Acacia

Bialik. Young Acacia, The.
"Field." Leaves.
Wilbur. Part of a Letter.

Academia

Berryman. Professor's Song, A.
Cunningham, J. To a Friend, on Her Examination for the Doctorate in English.
DiPalma. Each moment is surrounded.
Glaser, E. Confluences at San Francisco.
Kleinzahler. Autumnal Sketch, An.
Larkin, P. Posterity.
Matthews, W. Note I Left for Gerald Stern in an Office I Borrowed, and He Would Next, at a Summer Writers' Conference.
Perelman. Marginalization of Poetry, The.
Roethke. Academic.
Whitman, W. When I heard the learn'd astronomer.

Accent

Hare, M. Alfred de Musset.
Lees, J. Jone o' Grinfilt.

Acceptance

Berry, W. September 2.
Blunt, W. As To His Choice of Her.
Bradstreet, A. Here Follows Some Verses upon the Burning of Our House [July 10th, 1966. Copied Out of a Loose Paper].
Cummings, E. Gee i like to think of dead it means nearer because deeper firmer.
It may not always be so; and i say.
Derricotte. Poem for My Father.
Promise, The.
Dickinson, E. It ceased to hurt me, though so slow.
"Why do I love" You, Sir?
Emerson, R. Terminus ("It is time to be old").
"Field." Methinks my love to thee doth grow.
Frost, R. Acceptance.
Harteis. Genetics.
Herbert, Z. Mr. Cogito Meditates on Suffering.
Herrick. To Vulcan.
Hughes, L. Motto.
Joseph, J. Dog body and cat mind, The.
Kipling, R. Refined Man, The.
Levine, P. On My Own.
MacNeice. After long trouble in a taedious way.
Meredith, G. All other joys of life he strove to warm.
Miller, L. Weather of Invention, The.
Mirabai. Heat of Midnight Tears, The.
Olson, C. Kingfishers, The.
Peacock, T. Love and Age.
Po Chü-i. After Eating.
Resignation
Rich, A. Loser, The.
Sadi. Great Physician, The.
Shelley, P. To————: "One word is too often profaned."
Whitman, W. Little one sleeps in its cradle,

The.
Me imperturbe, standing at ease in Nature.
To a Common Prostitute.

Accidents
Antipater of Thessalonica. Am I to blame the drink or the downpour?
When the deep-piled winter snow / melted on her roof.
Atkins. It's Here In The.
Carruth, H. Wreck of the Circus Train, The.
Corso. New York City—1935.
Dickey, J. Falling.
Fox, R. Another Kind of Burning.
Frost, R. Objection to Being Stepped On, The.
"Out, Out—."
Gibson, W. White Dust, The.
Godden, J. Lost.
Jenks, O. Dying Mine Brakeman, The.
Knight, E. Poem of Attrition, A.
Lawrence, D. Collier's Wife, The.
Leonard, T. Its thi lang / wij a thi / guhtr thaht hi.
Livingstone, D. One Time.
Martynov. Idlers.
McDougall, J. Reporting Back.
McElroy, C. Ruth.
Merrill, J. Broken Bowl, The.
Mother Goose. Jack and Gill [or Jill] went up the hill.
Olds, S. First Love.
Oppen. Cars on the highway filled with speech.
Plath. Cut.
Poseidippus. Three-year-old Archianax.
Reznikoff. Amelia was just fourteen and out of the orphan asylum.
Roethke. Elegy for Jane.
Shumaker. Circle of Totems, The.
Stuart, D. Soup Jar, The.
Thomas, R. Worker, The.
Tryphon. Terpander.
Unknown. Henry K. Sawyer.
Jim Crack Corn; or The Blue Tali Fly.
Mischievous Raven, The.
Weber, R. Concise History of the Vietnam War: 1965–1968, A.
See also **Airplane Crashes; Automobile Accidents; Disasters; Nuclear Accidents; Railroad Wrecks; Shipwrecks**

Accordions
Hall, D. Wedding Party.

Accounting and Accountants
Frost, R. Hardship of Accounting, The.

Achilles
Auden. Shield of Achilles, The.
Campion, T. Breake now my heart and dye!
Oh no, she may relent.
Catullus. Carmen 64 ("In old days / driving through soft waters").
Duncan, R. Achilles' Song.
Homer. Achilles kills Lycaon.
Achilles Over the Trench.
Achilles sets out.
Achilles with wild fury in his heart.
Goddess intervenes between Achilles and Agamemnon, The.
Heroes meet again in the underworld, The.
Invocation, The: "Wrath of *Peleus* Son, O Muse, resound, The."
Patroclus's Request to Achilles for his Arms.
Imitated from the Beginning of the Sixteenth Iliad of Homer.
Phœnix pleads with Achilles.
Priam and Achilles.
Shield of Achilles, The.
Thetis and the Nereids.
Vulcan Forges the Shield of Achilles.
Lihn. Goodnight, Achilles.
Santayana. Before a Statue of Achilles.
Venclova. Shield of Achilles, The.
Whittemore, R. Thinking of Tents.

Acorns
Nicholls, J. Journey.
Unknown. Acorn Song, The.

Acquiescence
Brooks, G. Speech to the Young Speech to

the Progress-Toward (Among Them Nora and Henry III).
Herrick. To Fortune.
Hsiang Ssu. Ailing Japanese Monk, The.
Kunitz, S. Knot, The.
MacLeish. What Any Lover Learns.
MacNeice. After long trouble in a taedious way.
Wroth. Sonnet 7: "Love leave to urge, thou know'st thou hast the hand."
Sonnet 48: "How like a fire doth love increase in me[e]."

Acrobatics and Acrobats
Redmond. Dance Bodies #1.
Swenson, M. He That None Can Capture.
See also **Circus; Trapezes and Trapeze Artists**

Actaeon
Bewe. I would I were Actaeon, whom Diana did disguise.
Heppenstall. Actaeon.
Ovid. Acteon.

Acting and Actors
Allston. On Kean's Hamlet.
Cook, E. To Charlotte Cushman.
Coward. Boy Actor, The.
Regarding yours, dear Mrs Worthington.
Garrigue. Movie Actors Scribbling Letters Very Fast in Crucial Scenes.
Ginsberg, A. Blue Angel, The.
Goldsmith, O. David Garrick.
Hassall. Santa Claus.
Henley, W. Ballade of Dead Actors.
Heywood, T. Author to His Book[e], The.
Hristic. Tragedy is over. Blind Oedipus exits, The.
Jonson, B. To Edward Alleyn.
Lloyd, R. Acting, dear Thornton, its perfection draws.
Lucilius. Bad actors love to play great villains.
McKinney, I. Rapt.
Melville, H. Coming Storm, The.
Nguyễn Khuyến. Comedian Gets a Curtain Lecture, The.
O'Hara, F. To the Film Industry in Crisis.
Pasternak, B. Hamlet.
Reid, C. Howl, Howl.
Sandburg, C. They all want to play Hamlet.
Shakespeare, W. Sonnet 23.
Stevens, W. Of Modern Poetry.
Szymborska. Theater Impressions.
Unknown. Epitaph of a Nicene Actor.
Wang An-shih. Written at Hsiang-kuo Temple on the Occasion of Watching Actors in the Hsing-hsiang Garden of the T'ung-t'ien-chieh Tao-ch'ang.
Wilbur. Prisoner of Zenda, The.
Williams, M. Aging Actress Sees Herself a Starlet on the Late Show, The.
See also **Show Business**

Adam and Eve
Allen, P. Eve the fox swung.
Barbu. Timbre.
Beddoes. Carrion Crow, The.
Blake, W. Earth's Answer.
Ghost of Abel, The.
Booth, P. Original Sequence.
Bowers, E. Adam's Song to Heaven.
Chaucer. To His Scribe Adam.
Clive. Mother, The.
Crane, H. Garden Abstract.
Davies, S. Why did my parents send me to the schools.
Donnelly, S. Eve Names the Animals.
Duncan, R. Strains of Sight.
Emerson, R. Dæmonic and the Celestial Love, The.
Enright, D. Days of Adam were 930 years, The.
"Rich soil," remarked the Landlord.
Why didn't we think of clothes before?
Ferry. Adam's Dream.
Graves, R. Quiet Glades of Eden, The.
Hahn, K. Possession: A Zuihitsu.
Hecht, A. Naming the Animals.
Hildegard von Bingen. Antiphon for the Angels.
Hollander, J. Adam's Task.

Hood, T. Reflection, A.
Hope, A. Imperial Adam, naked in the dew.
Hough, G. Age of Innocence.
Housman, A. Occasional Poem.
Hughes, T. Childish Prank, A.
Theology.
Jensen, L. To a Stranger (At the End of a Caboose).
Kipling, R. Glory of the Garden, The.
Lanier. Now Pontius Pilate is to judge the cause.
Lanier, S. Whate'er Has Been.
Lanyer. From Salve Deus Rex Judaeorum.
Our Mother *Eve*, who tasted of the Tree.
Macpherson, J. Fisherman, The.
Manger. Adam and Eve.
Jealous Adam.
Milton. Adam and Eve in the Garden.
Behold alone / The Woman, opportune to all attempts.
Book IX.
Eve tempts Adam.
Satan tempts Eve.
Thus talking hand in hand alone they pass'd.
Uncloistered Virtue.
Muir, E. Adam's Dream.
Navajo Oral Tradition. There Are No People Song.
Randall, J. How shall we walk naked when.
Recipes.
Ridler. Mile from Eden, A.
Roethke. Follies of Adam, The.
Sassoon. Ancient History.
Sisson. Adam and Eve.
Snyder, G. Milton by Firelight.
Sorescu. Adam paced the footpaths of paradise in a.
Sparshott. Naming of the Beasts, The.
Spencer, T. Circle, A.
Stafford, K. Feather Bag, Stick Bag.
Sutcliffe. Of all the Trees that in the Garden grew.
Symons, A. Hallucination.
Thomas, D. Ceremony after a Fire Raid.
Thompson, C. Tree, The.
Tomlinson, C. In Arden.
Unknown. Adam Lay Bound.
Epigram: "While Adam slept, from him his Eve arose."
Very. Serpent, The.
Walcott. Cloud, The.
New World.
White, G. Leopard in Eden, The.
Whitman, W. As Adam early in the morning.
To the garden the world anew ascending.
Williams, W. Marriage in Eden, The.
Winchilsea. Adam Posed.
Wright, J. Eve to Her Daughters.
Yeats. Adam's Curse.
See also **Eve**

Adams, Henry
Auden. Henry Adams / Was mortally afraid of Madams.

Adams, John
MacLow. 1797.
Monks. Twilight's Last Gleaming.

Adams, John Quincy
Benét, R. *et al.* John Quincy Adams.
MacLow. 1825.

Addison, Joseph
Pope, A. Atticus ("Peace to all such! but were there one whose fires").
Tickell. To the Earl of Warwick, on the Death of Mr. Addison.

Adelaide, Empress Consort
Middleton, C. Adelaide's Dream.

Admiration
Aldrich, T. Fannie has the sweetest foot.
Behn, A. To My Lady Morland at Tunbridge.
Bell, M. Mystery of Emily Dickinson, The.
Boyle, K. For Marianne Moore's Birthday.
Burns, R. Of a' the airts the wind can blaw.
Verses Intended to Be Written below a Noble Earl's Picture.
Byron, G. She walks in Beauty like the night.
Carew, T. Comparison, The.
Complement, The.

Song: Good Counsel to a Young Maid.
To A. L.; Persuasions [or Perswasions] to Love.
To My Worthy Friend Master George Sands [or Sandys], on His Translation of the Psalms.
Catullus. De Quintia et Lesbia.
Sappho.
Cavalcanti. Sonnet: He Compares All Things with His Lady, and Finds Them Wanting.
Cavalieri. First, The.
Constable, H. Of his Mistress, upon Occasion of her Walking in a Garden.
Cullen, C. To John Keats, Poet, at Spring Time.
Dante Alighieri. At whiles (yea oftentimes) I muse over.
Elytis. Ode to Santorini.
Ezekiel. Goodbye Party for Miss Pushpa T. S.
Ferlinghetti, L. Pound at Spoleto.
Fisher, R. Paraphrases.
Fort, C. Worker (We Own Two Houses), The.
Gallagher, T. Horse in the drugstore / wants to be admired, The.
Garrigue. Primer of Plato.
Gay, J. Molly Mog [or The Fair Maid of the Inn].
Guiney. Salutation, A.
Guinicelli. Sonnet: He Will Praise His Lady.
Herrick. Upon the Nipples of Julia's Breast.
Hood, T. Parental Ode to My Son, Aged Three Years and Five Months, A.
Johnston, E. Lines: To a Young Gentleman of Surpassing Beauty.
Keats. Addressed to Haydon.
Kinnell. Hen Flower, The.
Koch, K. In Love with You.
To Marina.
Lindsay, V. To a Golden-Haired Girl in a Louisiana Town.
Lowell, R. Alfred Corning Clark.
Marino. Lips and Eyes.
Matthews, J. Paradigm of a Hero.
Melville, H. College Colonel, The.
Sheridan at Cedar Creek.
Meredith, G. When I would image her features.
Nesbit, E. Love's Guerdons.
Owen, M. Urban Cowboy Hat.
Ponsot. La Une, A.
Praed. Talented Man, The.
Raine, K. Old Paintings on Italian Walls.
Ralegh, W. If Cynthia be a queen, a princess, and supreme.
Samio. Tanka: "Call to mind."
Shin, S. From your eyes.
Shirley, J. Would you know what's soft? I dare.
Sidney, P. Eighth Song: "In a grove most rich of shade."
Sonnet 37: "My mouth doth water, and my breast doth swell."
Sonnet 52: "Strife is grown between Virtue and Love, A."
Sonnet 91: "Stella, while now by honour's cruel might."
Sonnet 100: "O tears, no tears, but rain from beauty's skies."
Sonnet 103: "O happy Thames, that didst my Stella bear."
Third Song: "If Orpheus' voice had force to breathe such music's love."
Skoyles. Good Cheer.
Song. Father and Daughter.
Stevenson, R. To K. de M.
Su Tung-p'o. Written on a Painting Entitled "Misty Yangtze and Folded Hills."
Waller, E. Song: "Go[e], lovely rose[—ous sweet and fair]."
Warren, R. Birth of Love.
Whitfield. To A. H.
Wilbur. Piazza di Spagna, Early Morning.
Praise in Summer.
Williams, S. Song upon Miss Harriet Hanbury, Addressed to the Revd Mr Birt.
Wright, K. Unlikely Obbligato of Andersonstown.

Adobes
Carruth, H. Mending the Adobe.

Adolescence
Alexander, E. Zodiac.
Auden. Adolescence.
Booth, P. He was fifteen. And she, Wisconsin.
Brooks, G. Religion.
Clifton, L. There Is a Girl Inside.
Dickey, J. Sheep Child, The.
Dove, R. Adolescence—I.
Adolescence—II.
Dybek. My Neighborhood.
Forché. As Children Together.
Francis, P. Thunder.
Glück, L. From the Suburbs.
Huntington, C. Breaking.
Hyland, G. Fet Walks Melody Home.
Jennings, E. Young Ones, The.
Kirstein. Double Date.
La Loca. Why I Choose Black Men for My Lovers.
Logan, J. Lines to His Son on Reaching Adolescence.
Lorde. Hanging Fire.
Lux. Little Tooth, A.
Matthews, W. Mood Indigo.
McGinley. Portrait of Girl with Comic Book.
McPherson, S. 1943.
Meinke. Helen.
Merrill, J. Matinees.
Olds, S. That Year.
Oles. To a Daughter at Fourteen Forsaking the Violin.
Ondaatje. Burning Hills.
Orr, G. Adolescence.
Nicole at Thirteen.
Pape. Street Music.
Penny, R. I Remember How She Sang.
Rankin, P. Fifteen.
Ransom, J. Vanity of the Bright Young Men, The.
Rukeyser, M. Question, The.
Rutsala. Lovers in Summer.
Sanchez, S. Norma.
Prelude to Nothing.
Seidel. Dimpled Cloud, A.
Sexton. Little Girl, My String Bean, My Lovely Woman.
Shapiro, K. Drug Store.
Waiting in Front of the Columnar High School.
Silverstein, S. Rock 'N' Roll Band.
Smith, P. So Motown taught me all about men. Men worshipped.
Smith, S. Conventionalist, The.
Sorby. Museum Piece.
Souster. Young Girls.
Stanescu. Adolescents on the Sea.
Trinidad. Double Trouble.
Movin' with Nancy.
Turner, W. Romance.
Unknown. Song for a Young Girl's Puberty Ceremony.
Voigt. Field Trip, The.
Wallace, R. Thirteen.
Welch, D. Spade Scharnweber was a white Watusi. His mother.
Wilson, R. Say Girls in Shoe Ads: "I Go for a Man Who's Tall!"

Adonis
Ayres. Death of Adonis, The.
Barnfield. Cherry-lipped Adonis.
Bion. Lament for Adonis.
Doolittle. Adonis.
Shakespeare, W. Even as the sun with purple-colour'd face.
Shelley, P. Elegy on the Death of John Keats, An.
Theocritus. Death of Adonis, The.

Adoption and the Adopted
Brontë, E. Two Children, The.
Erdrich. Shelter.

Adultery and Adulterers
Amis, K. Aberdarcy: The Chaucer Road.
Nothing to Fear.
Berryman. Dream Song 4.
Berssenbrugge. Jealousy.

Bromley, A. My Mother's Face Never Moved.
Brown, T. Conjergal rights! conjergal rights!
Campbell, I. Learned Mistress, A.
Carew, T. Secrecy [or Secresie] Protested.
Dickey, J. Adultery.
Ewart. Old Husband Suspects Adultery, An.
Fumi Saito. Tanka: "Don't resemble me."
Fumiko. Tanka: "Didn't a certain woman."
Hardy, T. In the Restaurant.
Heaney, S. Punishment.
Herrick. Upon Scobble [Epigram].
Hoagland, T. Sweet Rain.
Holst-Warhaft. Matthew 5:27–30; You have heard that it was said.
Hope, A. Gloss to Matthew V 27–28.
Hughes, L. Sister.
Kazantzis. In Memory, 1978.
King, J. Clichés for an Unfaithful Husband.
Lochhead, L. Hickie, The.
Lomax, M. Other Woman, The.
Maguire, S. Spilt Milk.
Maksimovic. For All Mary Magdalenes.
Masters, E. Elsa Wertman.
Meredith, G. It chanced his lips did meet her forehead cool.
Their sense is with their senses all mixed in.
Middleton, T. Women Beware Women.
Morgan, V. Within the Greenhouse Effect.
Ovid. 1.4.
Phillips, A. Summer My Mother Fell in Love and Wanted to Leave My Father, The.
Quarles. On Dinah.
Rufinus Domesticus. How can any man throw out.
Were that woman's postcoital charms.
Who beat you and put you out.
Schwarz, S. Sonnet: "If love is chaste, what bears adultery?"
Sexton. For My Lover, Returning to His Wife.
Shakespeare, W. Sonnet 92.
Shepard, O. It's a Low Down Dirty Shame.
Simmons, J. End of the Affair, The.
Tourneur. Madam, your grace so private?
Tsvetayeva. And, not crying in vain.
Unknown. Josie.
Queen Eleanor's Confession.
Woman's Song, about Men, A.
Volman. Case, The.
Wigglesworth. Adulterers and whoremongers / were there, with all unchaste.

Advent
Hartigan, A. Advent.
Kavanagh, P. Advent.
Rossetti, C. Advent.

Adventure and Adventurers
Brontë, C. Young Man Naughty's Adventure.
Brooks, G. Old Mary.
Brown, S. Odyssey of Big Boy.
Cavafy. Ithaka.
Chapman, G. In meantime flew our ships, and straight we fetch'd.
Deanovich. Connie Deanovich.
Dehn, P. Alternative Endings to an Unwritten Ballad.
Ivanov, G. Tune becomes a flower, The.
James, J. On Leaving the Footpath.
McWatt. Lady Northcote.
Merrill, J. Thousand and Second Night, The.
Nash, O. Adventures of Isabel.
Owen, M. For Emily (Dickinson).
Selman, R. And so I went forth, exhilarated.
I thought the gesture was only about me.
Stevenson, R. Mile an' a bittock, a mile or twa, A.
Tennyson, A. Sailor Boy, The.
Unknown. Now neghes the New Yere and the night passes.
Seafarer, The.
Ship That Sails, The.

Advertising
Adams, F. Double Standard, The.
Benét, S. Hymn in Columbus Circle.
Cummings, E. Poem, or Beauty Hurts Mr. Vinal.
Dawe, B. Copy-writer's Dream, The.
Dickinson, E. I'm Nobody! Who are you?
Fiser. Teaching Myself to Read.

Hughes, L. Neon Signs.
Lord, E. Legend of the Admen, The.
McNair. Before People, The.
Nash, O. Song of the Open Road.
Padilla. Landscapes.
Silverstein, S. Clarence Lee from Tennessee.
Unknown. Advertising Agency Song, The.
Burma-Shave Roadside Signs.
Carnation Milk ("Carnation milk is the best in the land").

See also **Billboards**

Advice
Alcaeus. Philip of Macedon.
Alexander of Pleuron. Epitaph for Cleonicus.
Aristophanes. On the advice of Praxilla.
Bacchylides. Keep to the one path.
This much I know.
Blake, W. Song By an Old Shepherd.
Bland, P. Notes for the Park Keeper.
Burns, R. Epistle to a Young Friend.
Campion, T. Advice to a Girl.
Carew, J. Tiho, the Carib.
"Carroll." Rules and Regulations.
Catullus. Carm. II.
Frae Catullus, VIII.
Chan. How to Organise a Successful Small Business.
Chaucer. Nun's Priest's Tale, The.
Truth.
Creeley. Way, The.
Dante Alighieri. Sonnet: "All my thoughts always speak to me of love."
Davidson, D. Sanctuary.
Dufferin. Charming Woman, The.
Emerson, R. Suum Cuique ("Wilt thou seal up the avenues of Ill?")
To Rhea.
Farjeon, E. Advice to a Child.
Floyd. Lance Corporal Purdue Grace, U. S. M. C.
Greene, R. Maesia's Song.
Grimké, A. At April.
Herbert, G. Perirrhanterium.
Hesiod. Against sloth.
Holm, B. Advice.
Horace. 18th Ode 1st Book, translated or rather Imitated.
Ne'er fash your *thumb* what *gods* decree.
Housman, A. Carpenter's Son, The.
When I was one-and-twenty.
Hughes, L. Mother to Son.
Warning.
Johannes Barbucollas. Don't halt your voyage, sailor, nor drop sail.
Jonson, B. Things that make the happier life, are these, The.
Keyes, S. Advice for a Journey.
Kipling, R. If you can keep your head when all [about you].
Kuan Han-ch'ing. Snow powder, flowery.
Kydios. Beware. There are fawns.
Leonidas of Tarentum. Don't waste yourself, dragging out the life of a vagrant.
Lewis, E. Advice to a Young Lady Lately Married.
Li Ho. High Dike.
Lovelace, R. Advice to My Best Brother, Colonel Francis Lovelace.
MacLeish. Seafarer.
McCord, D. Father and I in the Woods.
Meinke. Advice to My Son.
Meng Chiao. Impromptu.
Millay, E. If in the years to come you should recall.
Niedecker. Grandfather / advised me.
Persius. Unwelcome advice.
Piercy. Seven of Pentacles, The.
Popa. Craftsmen of the Little Box, The.
Ralegh, W. Sir Walter Ra[u]le[i]gh to His Son[ne].
Sidney, P. Echo.
Simmons, J. Lullaby for Rachael.
Smart, C. Praise.
Su Shih. Tune: "As in a Dream; a Song."
Syrus. Sententiae: Maxims.
T'ao Ch'ien. In Praise of Poor Scholars.
Terence. Elder boy is by adoption mine, The.

Theocritus. Take, friend, Orthon of Syracuse' advice.
Tibullus. Elegies 1.iv: "Far from the tender Tribe of Boys remove."
Tu Fu. Single petal swirling diminishes the spring, A.
Unknown. Borrow to your heart's content.
Good Counsel.
Keep away from asps and toads.
Penny.
Uticensis. Interpone tuis, interdum gaudia curis.
What Men in private whisper, never mind.
Vaughan, H. Rules and Lessons.
Virgil. Others may breathing Mettals softer grave.
Whitehead, W. Song for Ranelagh.
Wotton, S. To John Donne.
Zenmaro. On the birth of my son.

Aegean Sea
Flecker. Santorin.
Simpson, L. Aegean.
Spaziani. Aegean, The.

Aeneas
Stanyhurst. Thee whilst thee dawning Aurora fro the Ocean hastned.
Surrey. Then from the seas, the dawning gan arise.
Tate, A. Aeneas at Washington.
Virgil. Aeneas' firmness.
Aeneas' story.
Morning after shipwreck.
Mounting the Pile she unsheaths the Trojan sword.

Aeneid, The (Virgil)
Cowley, A. To Mr. Hobbes [*or* Hobs].
Lowell, R. Falling Asleep over the Aeneid.

Aengus
Yeats. Song Of Wandering Aengus, The.

Aesop
Catullus. To Varus.
Crane, H. Black Tambourine.
Hecht, A. Improvisations on Aesop.

Affection
Adamson. My Tenth Birthday.
"Akhmatova." Ah—you thought I'd be the type.
He whispers: 'I'm not sorry.
I will leave your white house and tranquil garden.
Instead of wisdom—experience, a flat.
Memory of love, you are painful!
To The Beloved.
Amichai. Elegy: "Wind won't come to draw smiles in dream sand, The."
Two Songs of Peace.
We Have Done Our Duty.
Anacreon. Anacreontic on Love, An.
Wish, The.
Ancient Egyptian Oral Tradition. This love is as good.
Andrade, E. Penniless Lovers.
Aristophanes. Son learns how to beat his father, The.
Armantrout. Sense.
Winter.
Armitage, S. Poem.
Auden. Fish in the unruffled lakes.
Bachmann. Songs from an Island.
Barbauld. Rights of Woman, The.
Barnfield. Sighing, and sadly sitting by my Love.
Sometimes I wish that I his pillow were.
Bartusek. Sentence.
Baudelaire. Exotic Scent.
Bawer. On Leaving the Artists' Colony.
Behn, A. Song: Love Armed.
Bennett, G. Sonnet—2: "Some things are very dear to me—."
Bennett, L. Love Letter.
Bernstein, C. Poem: "Here. Forget."
Bernstein, O. This Is a Poem of Love.
Berryman. He Resigns.
Bhartrihari. In former days we'd both agree.
She who is always in my thoughts prefers.
Bible, *N.T.* Be kindly affectioned one to.

Bishop, E. Casabianca.
One Art.
Blaga. I will not crush the world's corolla of wonders.
Blake, W. Clod and [*or* &] the Pebble, The.
Garden of Love, The.
Prince of Love, The.
Bly, R. In the month of May when all leaves open.
Bognini. Earth and sky are infinities / Where our cries cannot venture.
Boland, E. That the Science of Cartography Is Limited.
Bontemps. Idolatry.
Boyd, M. Sonet: "Fra bank [*or* banc] to bank [*or* banc], fra wood [*or* wod] to wood [*or* wod] I rin."
Bradstreet, A. Another.
Before the Birth of One of Her Children.
Letter to Her Husband, Absent upon Public[k] Employment, A.
To Her Father, with Some Verses.
Breton, A. Free Union.
Bridges, R. Going Home.
Brooke, R. Hill, The.
Sonnet: "Oh! Death will find me, long before I tire."
Browning, E. Face which, duly as the sun, The.
L.E.L.'s Last Question.
Sonnet: "And wilt thou have me fashion into speech."
Sonnet: "Belovèd, thou hast brought me many flowers."
Sonnet: "Can it be right to give what I can give?"
Sonnet: "Face of all the world is changed, I think, The."
Sonnet: "I lift my heavy heart up solemnly."
Sonnet: "I never gave a lock of hair away."
Sonnet: "I thought once how Theocritus had sung."
Sonnet: "If I leave all for thee, wilt thou exchange."
Sonnet: "Say over again, and yet once more again."
Browning, R. Lost Mistress, The.
Meeting At Night.
Porphyria's Lover.
Two in the Campagna.
Burns, R. Highland Mary.
O [*or* Oh] wert thou in the cauld blast.
Red, Red Rose, A.
Byron, G. She walks in Beauty like the night.
So we'll go no more a-roving.
Camões. Do This Favour For Me.
Campion, T. Follow thy fair sun unhappy shadow.
My sweetest Lesbia, let us live and love.
When to Her Lute Corinna [*or* Corrina] Sings.
Carew, T. Fly That Flew into My Mistress'[s] Eye, A.
Song, [A]: "Ask me no more where Jove bestows."
To my Friend G.N. from Wrest.
Carver, R. Late Fragment.
No Need.
Catullus. Carm. II.
Carmen 5 ("My sweetest Lesbia, let us live and love").
Carmen 45 ("Phyllis Corydon clutched to him").
Enough, Catullus, of this silly whining.
To A Friend.
Chaucer. Song of Troylus, The.
Cheng Hsieh. Poem for My Wet Nurse, A.
Chevalier. My Old Dutch.
Chōkū. Tanka: "My research."
Clare, J. To Mary: 'It Is the Evening Hour'.
Clark, C. Plainsmen, The.
Cleveland, J. Antiplatonic[k], The.
Clifton, L. Woman who loves, A.
Constable, H. To St Mary Magdalen.
Cope, W. Flowers.
Giving Up Smoking.
Valentine.
Cowley, A. Wish, The.

Crabbe. Marriage Ring, The.
Crashaw. Hymn to Saint Teresa.
Creeley. Act of Love, The.
Cruz Varela. Love Song for Difficult Times.
Cummings, E. If everything happens that can't be done.
If(touched by love's own secret)we,like homing.
Love is more thicker than forget.
O by the by / has anybody seen.
Somewhere i have never travelled, gladly beyond.
Cunningham, J. To My Wife.
Cutts. Only tell her that I love.
Daniel, S. 46.
Behold what hap *Pigmalion* had to frame.
But love whilst that thou mayst be loved again.
Go wailing verse, the infants of my love.
Unto the boundless Ocean of thy beauty.
Davenant. Countess of Anglesey lead Captive by the Rebels, at the Disforresting of Pewsam, The.
Davies, S. Sacred muse that first[e] made love divine [*or* devine].
De la Mare. Ghost, The.
Deloney. Long have I lov'd this bonny Lasse.
Desnos. I've dreamed such dreams of you that you're losing / your reality.
Dickinson, E. If I may have it, when it's dead.
Love a Life can show Below, The.
Love—is that later Thing than Death.
Love—thou art high.
Soul selects her own Society—The The.
Disch. Clouds, The.
Donne. Anniversary [*or* Anniversarie], The.
Canonization, The.
Ecstasy, The.
Funeral[l], The.
Good-Morrow, The.
His Picture.
Nocturnal[l] upon Saint Lucy's [*or* S. Lucies] Day, Being the Shortest Day, A.
Our Love Hath No Decay.
Relic, The.
Song: "Sweetest love, I do not go[e]."
Valediction, A: Forbidding Mourning.
Valediction of the Book, A.
Valediction: Of Weeping, A.
Dove, R. Who can forget the attitude of mothering?
Dowson. Non Sum Qualis Eram Bonae sub Regno Cynara[e].
Drayton. As Love and I, late harboured in one inn.
Since There's No Help.
These verses weare made By Michaell Drayton Esquier Poett Lawreatt the night before hee dyed.
Dryden, J. Song from Troilus and Cressida.
Du Bellay. To Venus.
Duffy, C. Valentine.
Dunbar, P. Negro Love Song, A.
Dunn, D. France.
Dyer, S. Love is Love.
Edson, R. Having to Love Something Else, The.
Elizabeth I. When I was fair and young, then [*or* and] favour graced me;.
Elmslie, K. One Night Stand.
Elytis. Of the Aegean.
"Ephelia." In the Person of a Lady, to Bajazet, Her Unconstant Gallant.
Essex, R. Change thy minde since she doth change.
Ewart. To Margo.
Faiz. Don't Ask Me for That Love Again.
Feirstein. Mark Stern Wakes Up.
Rune-Maker, The.
Fenton, J. In Paris with You.
Nothing.
Forbes, D. Recension Day.
Frost, R. For a Brother.
Fuller, R. Why do we return? Not in the darkened rooms.
Fumiko. Tanka: "Sharing the gentleness."

Gallagher, T. Hug, The.
Gardner, I. Cock-a-Hoop.
In the Museum.
Gascoigne. Farewell, A.
For That He Looked Not upon Her.
Lullaby [*or* Lullabie] of a Lover, The.
Gerstler. Travelogue.
Ginsberg, A. To Aunt Rose.
Giovanni. Winter Poem.
Glück, L. Garden, The.
Gorges. Her [*or* hir] face her [*or* hir] tongue [*or* tong] her [*or* hir] wit.
Graves, R. Friday Night.
In Perspective.
Lost Love.
Pure Death.
She tells her love while half asleep.
Greenwald, T. And, Hinges.
I hear a step. A step.
Greville, F. Absence and Presence.
Cupid, in Myra's faire bewitching eyes.
From Caelica.
Myra.
Sonnet 78: "Little Hearts, where light-wing'd Passion raignes, The."
Sonnet: "Nurse-life wheat within his green husk growing, The."
Gunn, T. High Fidelity.
Tamer and Hawk.
Haavikko. One who writes us is now doing four plays a year, The.
Hall, D. Love-Letter-Burning.
Hall, D. Gold.
Halpern, M. Go Throw Them Out.
Hampton. Yugoslav Story.
Hardy, T. After A Journey.
Going, The.
She Hears The Storm.
Heaney, S. Mossbawn Sunlight.
Hemphill. XXIV.
Herbert, G. Affliction (1).
Bitter-Sweet.
Heredia. Young Dead Woman, A.
Hikmet. Things I Didn't Know I Loved.
Holiday. Fine and Mellow.
Holmes, O. Tartarus.
Hope, A. Return of Persephone, The.
Horace. 3.9: Dialogue between Horace and Lydia, A ("Donec gratus eram").
Horton, G. Lover's Farewell, The.
Housman, A. Because I liked you better.
So Sound You Sleep.
Howe, F. Set golden butter out in a dish.
Hughes, L. Gal's Cry for a Dying Lover.
Gypsy Man.
Night funeral / In Harlem.
Izumi. In the dusk the path.
It is the time of rain and snow.
Janeczko. How to Hug Your Three-Year-Old Daughter.
Johnson, G. I Want to Die While You Love Me.
Johnson, H. Remember not the promises we made.
Jonson, B. Death and Love.
Elegy, An: "Though beauty be the mark of praise."
Her Triumph.
My Picture Left in Scotland.
So White, So Soft, So Sweet.
Song. To Celia ("Come my Celia, let us prove").
Sonnet to the Noble Lady, the Lady Mary Wroth, A.
To Celia.
József. Attila József.
Kanemori. In the mountain village.
Kasa. To love somebody.
Keats. La Belle Dame Sans Merci.
To ———: "Had I a man's fair form, then might my sighs."
Kemble. Sonnet: "If there were any power in human love."
Kenney. Aubade: "Cold snap. Five o'clock."
King, H. Stay For Me There.
Kinzie. Impromptu.
Koch, K. Permanently.

Koethe. Falling Water.
Kovner. Vow.
La Fontaine. Thyrsis And Amaranta.
Landor, W. Torch of Love dispels the gloom, The.
Lanier, S. Song for "The Jacquerie."
Larkin, P. On Wakening.
Leconte de Lisle, C. Palanquin, The.
Leithauser. Ghost of a Ghost, The.
Levertov. Woman Meets an Old Lover, A.
Lewis, A. Goodbye.
Post-Script: for Gweno.
Lewis, C. Impression, An.
Sequence, The.
Li Po. River Merchant's Wife, The; a Letter.
Lodge, T. Phillis 2.
Rosalind's [*or* Rosalynd's] Madrigal[l].
Longfellow, H. Children's Hour, The.
Talk not of wasted affection.
Lovelace, R. Gratiana Dancing [*or* Dauncing] and [*or* &] Singing.
On Sanazar's being honoured with six hundred Duckets by the Clarissimi of Venice, for composing an Elegiack Hexastick of The City. A Satyre.
To Althea, from Prison.
Lowell, A. Seeing you stand once more before my eyes.
Lowell, J. Contrast, A.
Lowell, R. Grandparents.
Lux. Amiel's Leg.
Machi. Tanka: "Letter, The."
MacLeish. Poem in Prose.
Mahone. What Color Is Black?
Mansour, J. Gently stroke a wound.
Tinfoil.
Marichiko. I wish I could be.
Marlowe. Now ore the sea from her old Love comes she.
Martial. Antipathy.
Martinez, D. In a Duplex Near the San Andreas Fault.
Marvell. Definition Of Love, The.
Fair Singer, The.
Gallery, The.
Mower to the Glow-Worms [*or* Glowworms *or* Glo-Worms], The.
Maunick. Seven Sides and Seven Syllables.
May, J. If we could know.
Mayer, B. Sonnet: Kamikaze: "Dawn and night of fighting, lovers like actual wars."
McAuley, J. Because.
Mei Yao Ch'en. Dream at Night, A.
Millay, E. At least, my dear.
I shall go back again to the bleak shore.
Love is not all: it is not meat or drink.
Modern Declaration.
Night is my sister, and how deep in love.
Mitchison. My True Love Hath My Heart.
Miyazawa Kenji. Siwashing it out once in Siuslaw Forest.
Montagu, L. Lover, The; a Ballad.
Montague, J. All Legendary Obstacles lay between.
Montale. Eel, the North Sea siren, The.
Montgomerie, A. Remembers thou in Æsope of a taill.
Moore, T. Did Not.
Echo.
Oft in the stilly night.
Moorsom. Don't be literary, darling, don't be literary.
Muir, E. In Love For Long.
Nathan, L. Toast.
Neruda. In my sky at twilight you are like a cloud.
Tonight I can write the saddest lines.
Nezval. Walker in Prague.
Nikolov, N. Confusion.
Don't Move Away.
Nims, J. Love Poem: "My clumsiest dear, whose hands shipwreck vases."
Notley. Alice Ordered Me to be Made.
Noyes, A. Highwayman, The.
O'Dalaigh, M. My body's self deserts me now.

Olds, S. First Boyfriend.
  Knowing, The.
Ondaatje. For you I have slept.
Ono no Komachi. Following the roads.
Oodgeroo of the tribe Noonuccal. Song: "Life is ours in vain."
Ovid. To his Wife at Rome, when he was sick.
Parker, D. One Perfect Rose.
Parker, M. Thou knowst I lov'd thee well.
Parun. You whose hands are more innocent than mine.
Pasolini. Prayer to My Mother.
Pastan. Because the night you asked me.
Pasternak, B. Cape Mootch.
  Darling, it's frightening! When a poet loves.
  Devotion is a heavy cross.
  In The Wood.
  You're here. We breathe the selfsame air.
Patmore, C. Revelation, The.
  Too soon, too soon comes Death to show.
Paulinus of Nola. To Ausonius.
Paz. Engaged.
Penn. They that love beyond the world, cannot be separated.
Penny, R. Real People Loves One Another, The.
Philips, K. To Mrs. M.A. Upon Absence.
Phillips, S. Apparition, The.
Piatt, S. Lesson in a Picture, A.
  Pique at Parting, A.
  This World.
Po Chü-i. Golden Bells.
Poe. To One in Paradise.
  Valentine, A.
Porter, P. Don't Be Afraid, I Am With You.
Powys. Nunc Dimittis.
Prévert. Barbara remember.
  Dunce, The.
Pushkin. I loved you.
Ralegh, W. As you came from the holy land.
  Concei[p]t begotten by the eyes.
  Excuse, The.
  Love Indestructible.
  Thus now I leave my love in fortunes [handes / bandes].
Raleigh. Walsinghame.
Ravikovitch. Surely You Remember.
  Time Caught in a Net.
Reavey. Dismissing Progress and Its Progenitors.
Reverdy. For the Moment.
Rihaku. River-Merchant's Wife: A Letter, The.
Rilke. Sonnets to Orpheus, The.
Roberts, M. Magnificat.
Rochester, J. Love And Life.
Roethke. For An Amorous Lady.
  I knew a woman, lovely in her bones.
Ronsard. Sonnet For Helen.
Rossetti, C. First Day, The.
  From Monna Innominata.
  I loved you first: but afterwards your love.
  L.E.L.E.L.
  Somewhere or other there must surely be.
Rotella, A. In the garbage bin.
Rowe, E. Chapter II.
Rózewicz. Draft of a Modern Love Poem.
Rucker. Swallow Creek.
Rushing. Sent for You Yesterday.
Ryan, G. Orbit.
St. John, D. Uptown Love Poem.
Salom. Ghazal on signs of Love and Occupation.
Salter. Summer 1983.
Sappho. Some say nothing on earth excels in beauty.
Sassoon. I Shall Find You.
Schnackenberg. Supernatural Love.
Scott, A. Rondel of Luve [or Love], A.
  To luve unluvit it is ane pane.
Shakespeare, W. Clown's Song, The.
  Lover's eyes will gaze an eagle blind, A.
  Sonnet 20.
  Sonnet 29.
  Sonnet 33.
  Sonnet 55.
  Sonnet 98.

Sonnet 124.
Sonnet: "Let me confesse that we two must be twaine."
Sonnet: "What's in the braine that Inck may character."
Sweet-and-Twenty.
Shapiro, K. Twins, The.
Shelley, P. To Jane ("Keen stars were twinkling, The").
To————: "Music, when soft voices die."
Shen Yüeh. I think of when she comes.
Sherwood, G. Love and Life.
Shin, S. From your eyes.
Shwarts. What that street is called—you can read it on the sign.
Sidney, P. Bargain, The.
  Dirge: "Ring out your bells [or belles], let mourning shows [or shewes] be spread."
  Nightingale as soone as Aprill bringeth, The.
  Seventh Song: "Whose senses in so evil consort, their stepdame Nature lays."
  Sonnet 1: "Loving in truth, and fain[e] in verse my love to show."
  Sonnet 2: "Not at [the] first sight, nor with a dribbed shot."
  Sonnet 25: "Wisest scholar of the wight most wise, The."
  Sonnet 31: "With how sad steps, O Moon, thou climb'st the skies!"
  Sonnet 48: "Soul's joy, bend not those morning stars from me."
  Sonnet 49: "I on my horse, and Love on me doth try."
  Sonnet 63: "O Grammer rules, ô now your virtues show."
  Sonnet 72: "Desire, though thou my old companion art."
  Sonnet 81: "O kiss, which dost those ruddy gems impart."
  Sonnet 87: "When I was forced from Stella ever dear."
Sidney, R. Sonnet 25: "Yow that take pleasure in yowr cruelty."
Silverstein, S. Hug o' War.
Simic. Old Couple.
Simpson, L. As birds are fitted to the boughs.
Skelton, J. Mannerly Margery Mylk and Ale.
  To Mistress [or Maystres] Margaret Hussey.
Smith, S. Freddy.
  Human Affection.
Snodgrass, W. Mementos, 1.
Sorescu. Fountains in the Sea.
  Precautions.
  Segment, A.
Southey, R. Love Indestructible.
Sparrow, J. To an Angel in the House.
Spencer, A. Wife-Woman, The.
Spencer, B. Part of Plenty.
Spenser. Eftsoones they heard a most melodious sound.
  Is not thilke the mery moneth of May.
  Penelope for her *Ulisses* sake.
  Sonnet 1: "Happy ye leaves! whenas those lily hands."
  Sonnet 8: "More than most fair [or fayre], full of the living fire [or fyre]."
  Sonnet 10: 'Unrighteous Lord of Love'.
  Sonnet 30: "My love is like to ice, and I to fire."
  Sonnet 54: "Of this world's Theatre in which we stay."
  Sonnet 70: "Fresh Spring the herald of love's mighty king."
  Sonnet 71: "I joy to see how in your drawen work."
  Sonnet 89: "Like as the culver on the bared bough."
Steffen. Falcon to the Falconer, The.
Strand. Coming to This.
Strauss, J. Love Notes.
Stumbrs. Married Romantic, A.
Suckling, J. Constant Lover, A [or The].
Surrey. Love, that doth reign and live within my thought.
Swenson, M. Hair, The.
  Staying at Ed's Place.
Swift, J. Stella's Birthday ([March 13,] 1727).

Swirszczynska. Greatest Love, The.
  Same Inside, The.
Symons, A. When you were here, ah foolish then!
Synge. In May.
Taggart, J. Body and Soul: Poem for Two Readers.
Tagore. I seem to have loved you in numberless forms, numberless times.
Taylor, E. Meditation Twelve.
Teasdale. I Am Not Yours[, not lost in you].
  Sleepless.
Tennyson, A. Duet.
  If Only.
Tessimond. Not Love Perhaps.
Thomas, E. No One So Much as You.
Thomas, L. Cameo in Sudden Light.
  Clear Channel.
Tibullus. Those who the Godhead's soft Behests obey.
Tonks. Story of a Hotel Room.
Traherne. Salutation [or Salutations], The.
Tsaloumas. Return of an Ikon.
Tsurayuki. When.
Tuckerman, F. Coralie.
  Rhotruda.
Tuqan, F. I Won't Sell His Love.
Turberville. To His Friend.
  To his Love that sent him a Ring wherein was gravde, / Let Reason rule.
Turner, D. Love.
Tyutchev. Last Love.
Unknown. Alison.
  Barbara Allan ("It was about the Martinmas time").
  Bear's Song, The.
  Cicada cries out, The.
  Her bracelets tinkle.
  I cannot go to you.
  I don't care.
  I Have a Young Sister.
  Lady Greensleeves.
  Like the tides' flood.
  Lilies are white.
  Love me little, love me long!
  Lullaby: "My little baby sleeps, the little birds sleep."
  Medicine Song of an Indian Lover.
  My Lady's Tears.
  Our love is infinite.
  Over the reeds the.
  Rare Willie Drowned in Yarrow; or, The Water o Gamrie.
  There is a lady sweet and kind.
  To His Love.
  Waly, Waly [Love Be Bonny].
  We are, you and me.
  When I look at her.
  Yoshino River.
Unknown, sometimes at. to Sir Walter Ralegh. Holy Land of Walsingham, The.
Valéry. Footsteps, The.
Van Vliet. City is covered with places you, The.
Venantius Fortunatus. To The Lady Radegund, With Violets.
Verlaine. Nevermore.
Waldrop, R. Lawn of Excluded Middle.
Walker, A. Love is not concerned.
Warsh. Enmeshment.
Whitman, W. Base of All Metaphysics, The.
  I knew a man, a common farmer, the father of five sons.
  Now what my mother told me one day as we sat at dinner / together.
  Sometimes with one I love I fill myself with rage for fear I effuse unreturn'd love.
  Spring.
  When I heard at the close of the day how my name had been receiv'd with plaudits in the capitol, still it was not a happy night for me that follow'd.
  Woman waits for me, she contains all, nothing is lacking, A.
Whitney, I. I.W. To her unconstant Lover.
Wieners. Doll.

Wieseltier. Love Poem: "Greyish yellow is the color of the dust."
Wilcox, E. Friendship After Love.
Williams, C. Snow: II.
Williams, M. Poem for Emily, A.
Williams, W. Love Song: "Sweep the house clean."
Winchilsea. Friendship Between Ephelia and Ardelia.
  Letter to Daphnis, A.
Woods, M. Tears and Joys.
Wordsworth, W. Louisa; After Accompanying Her on a Mountain Excursion.
Wroth. He may our prophet, and our tutor prove.
Wyatt, T. Lover Complaineth the Unkindness of His Love, The.
  Lover Showeth How He Is Forsaken of Such as He Sometime Enjoyed, The.
  Sonnet: 'The long love'.
Wylie. Puritan Sonnet, IV.
Yakamochi. Better never to have met you.
Yeats. Down by the salley gardens my love and I did meet;.
  Drinking Song, A.
  Folly Of Being Comforted, The.
  Lullaby: "Beloved, may your sleep be sound."
  Solomon to Sheba.
  When you are old and grey and full of sleep.
Yevtushenko. Siberian Wooing.
Yosano. Once, far over the breakers.
Zanzotto. Behold the thin green.
  Distance.
Zolynas. Love in the Classroom.

Affliction
Herbert, G. Affliction (1).
Miedzyrzecki. 29-77-02.
Wieseltier. Love Poem: "Greyish yellow is the color of the dust."

Africa
Agard, J. Pan Recipe.
Angelou. Africa.
Aworinde. If a Suite in Praise of the Yoruba Oracle.
Bachri. Cat.
Baker, H. Toward Guinea: For Larry Neal, 1937–1981.
Baraka. Ka 'Ba.
  Kenyatta Listening to Mozart.
Barlow, G. 4½ Months: Halfway Song.
Barlow, J. Columbiad, The.
Bekederemo, J. Epilogue to Casualties.
  For Granny (from Hospital).
  New from Ethiopia and the Sudan, The.
Bennett, G. Heritage.
Berrigan, T. Certain Slant of Sunlight, A.
Bethune, L. Blue Tanganyika.
  Bwagamoyo.
Bolamba. Portrait.
Bond, F. 'After the war,' they used to say, and pictured.
Bontemps. Nocturne at Bethesda.
  Nocturne of the Wharves.
Brathwaite, E. Mmenson.
Brew. Plea for Mercy, A.
Browning, R. Home-Thoughts, from the Sea.
Césaire, A. Ex-Voto for a Shipwreck.
  Macumba Word.
  Miraculous Weapons, The.
  This flat city shortly after dawn.
Crouch, S. Riding Across John Lee's Finger.
Cullen, C. Brown Boy to Brown Girl.
  Heritage.
Cumbo. Ceremony.
Dadié. Ode to Africa.
  Wreath for Africa, A.
Damas. Whitewash.
Dei-Anang. My Africa.
Delius. Distance.
Dempster, R. Africa's Plea.
  Is This Africa.
Diop, B. Kassak.
Diop, D. Africa my Africa.
  Listen, comrades of the flaming centuries.
  Vultures, The.
  Your Presence.
Dipoko. Poem of Villeneuve St Georges, A.

do Espirito Santo. Where Are the Men Seized in this Wind of Madness?
Dumas, H. Root Song.
Dunbar, P. Ode to Ethiopia.
Fawcett, B. Hand, The.
Fuller, R. In Africa.
Gibbon, P. Answer, An.
Giovanni. They Clapped.
Goodison. Guinea Woman.
Guillén, N. Sensemayá.
Hardy, T. Drummer Hodge.
Harper, F. Ethiopia.
Hughes, L. Afro-American Fragment.
  Danse Africaine.
Jacinto, A. Monangamba.
  Poem of Alienation.
Jackson, M. Return from Luluabourg.
Jeffers, L. Flesh of the Young Men Is Burning, The.
Kanié. All That You Have Given Me, Africa.
Kaufman, B. African Dream.
Khaketla, N. White and the Black, The.
Knight, E. Idea of Ancestry, The.
Koch, K. Geography.
Kunene. Echoes, The.
  Elegy.
La Grone. Suncoming.
Laing, K. Africa Sky.
Laleau. Betrayal.
  Legacies.
Lane, P. Girl at the Window.
Lindsay, V. Congo, The.
Long, D. Number Four.
Louw. Oh wide and sad land, alone.
Lumumba. Dawn in the Heart of Africa.
Madhubuti. Change Is Not Always Progress.
  Knocking Donkey Fleas off a Poet from the Southside of Chi.
Mapanje. After Wiriyamu Village Massacre by Protuguese.
  Messages.
Maunick. Seven Sides and Seven Syllables.
McKay, C. Africa.
McNeill, A. Straight Seeking.
Miller, A. Africa Thing, The.
Miller, J. Africa.
Milner-Brown. Who knows? This Africa so richly blest.
Mnthali. Celebration, The.
  My Father.
  Stranglehold of English Lit, The.
Moorer. Africa.
Mpondo. Season of the rains, The.
Naudé. Planting.
Neto. African Poem.
  Farewell at the Moment of Parting.
  Grieved lands of Africa, The.
Nichols, G. Tapestry.
Nicol. Meaning of Africa, The.
Nortje. Waiting.
Parkes, F. Three Phases of Africa.
Phillips, C. Africa Says.
Pressoir. Country Graveyard.
Reed, I. Sermonette.
Rothenberg, J. Praises of the Bantu Kings (1–10).
Roumain. Negro peddler of revolt.
  When the Tom-Tom Beats.
Senghor. "African Image Is Not An Image by Equation. . . , The."
  After this day's hope—see how the Somme, the Seine, and the wild Slav.
  Before night comes I think of you and for you before I fall.
  Elephant of Moissel, hear my pious prayer.
  Joal.
  Kaya-Magan am I! the first person.
  Man and Beast.
  Night of Sine.
  Song of the Initiate.
  Taga for Mbaye Dyôb.
  We shall bathe, my love, in an African presence.
Shange. Bocas: A Daughter's Geography.
Simpson, J. Old Liberia Is Not the Place for Me.
Sontonga. Lord, bless Africa.

Sousa, N. Appeal.
Southerland. Pale Ant.
Soyinka. Ujamaa.
Tati-Loutard. Pilgrimage to Loango Strand.
Tekkan. Tanka: "Vast wilderness."
Tirolien. Soul of the Black Land, The.
U Tam'si Tchicaya. 'Congo is myself' (Lumumba), The.
  I tear at my belly.
  I was naked for the first kiss of my mother.
  Mat to Weave, A.
  What do I want with a thousand stars in broad daylight.
Wakolele. Southern Africa.
Walcott. Far Cry from Africa, A.
Walker, A. African Images, Glimpses from a Tiger's Back.
Walker, M. For my people [everywhere singing their slave songs repeatedly: their].
Weaver, M. My Father's Geography.
Wonodi. Planting.
Wright, B. African Affair, The.
Yondo. My Country.
Yoruba Oral Tradition. Invocation of the Creator.

African Americans
Alexander, E. Boston Year.
  Deadwood Dick.
  Kevin of the N.E. Crew.
  Ladders.
  Ode.
  Today's News.
Allen, H. Upstairs Downstairs.
Allen, S. Moment Please, A.
  View from the Corner.
Angelou. Sepia Fashion Show.
  Still I Rise.
  Thank You, Lord.
Asclepiades. Didyme waved her wand at me.
Aubert, A. Opposite of Green, The.
Baca. There Are Black.
Baraka. Beautiful Black Women.
  Black Art.
  Black Dada Nihilismus.
  Funk Lore.
  I don't love you.
  In the Tradition / (Not a White Shadow but Black People Will Be Victorious).
  Ka 'Ba.
  Leadbelly Gives an Autograph.
  Leroy.
  Nation Is Like Ouselves, The.
  Pause of Joe, The.
  Poem for Black Hearts, A.
  Poem Some People Will Have to Understand, A.
  Rare Birds, The.
  SOS.
  Three Movements and a Coda.
  W. W.
  Wise 1.
  Wise 5.
Barlow, G. Painting Drunken Twilight.
  Place Where He Arose, The.
Barras, J. Peace.
Barrax. For a Black Poet.
Bennett, G. Heritage.
  Song: "I am weaving a song of waters."
  Sonnet—2: "Some things are very dear to me—."
  To a Dark Girl.
  To Usward.
Berryman. I'm scared a lonely. Never see my son.
Bishop, E. Cootchie, Miss Lula's servant, lies in marl.
Black, I. Racist Psychotherapy.
Blake, W. Little Black Boy, The.
Bontemps. God Give to Men.
Brooks, G. Ballad of Rudolph Reed, The.
  Primer for Blacks.
  Third Sermon on the Warpland, The.
  Vacant Lot, The.
  We real cool. We.
  Young Heroes.
Brown, J. *et al.* Say it loud, I'm black and I'm proud.

Brown, M. Survival Motion: Notice.
Brown, S. Odyssey of Big Boy.
Old Woman Remembers, An.
Slim in Atlanta.
Southern Cop.
Sporting Beasley.
Strong Men.
To Sallie, Walking.
Browning, E. Runaway Slave at Pilgrim's Point, The.
Buddy. Callin Buddy / Bolden.
Burroughs, M. Black Pride.
Only in This Way.
To Soulfolk.
Carruth, H. Mountain, The.
Cassells. Soul Make A Path Through Shouting.
Césaire, A. Islands scars of the water.
This flat city shortly after dawn.
Cesaire, A. *et al.* How did you come to develop the concept of Negritude?
Clemmons. Freedom Song for the Black Woman, A.
Cliff. Within the Veil.
Clifton, L. For de Lawd.
Good Times.
In Salem.
In White America.
Listen Children.
Thirty-eighth year, The.
Way It Was, The.
Coicou. Slave's Lament, The.
Coleman, A. Black Baby.
Coleman, H. Black Soldier Remembers, A.
OK Corral East Brothers in the Nam.
Coleman, W. African Sleeping Sickness
American Sonnet (10).
American Sonnet (35).
Coffee.
Emmett Till.
Essay on Language.
Conyus. Confession to Malcolm.
Corbin, L. Ali / Is our prince.
Cornish, S. My brother is homemade.
Corpus. Blkfern-jungal.
Corrie. How Long Has Trane Been Gone.
Corrothers. At the Closed Gate of Justice.
Indignation Dinner, An.
Cortez. How Long Has Trane Been Gone.
Cotter, J. Ned's Psalm of Life for the Negro.
Crane, H. Black Tambourine.
Cullen, C. Black Majesty.
Brown Girl Dead, A.
From the Dark Tower.
Heritage.
Litany of the Dark People, The.
Shroud of Color, The.
Yet Do I Marvel.
Cumbo. Black Sister.
Cuney. No Images.
Dadié. I thank you, Lord, for having made me Black,.
Damas. Blues.
Hiccups.
Just Like the Legend.
Position.
S.O.S.
Sell Out.
So often my feeling of race.
Their Thing.
Danner. At Home in Dakar.
Grandson Is a Hoticeberg, A.
Dent. For Cool Papa Bell.
Derricotte. Blackbottom.
In an Urban School.
St. Peter Claver.
Struggle, The.
Diop, D. For a Black Child.
Listen, comrades of the flaming centuries.
Negro Tramp.
Dove, R. Wingfoot Lake.
DuBois, W. Song of the Smoke, The.
Dumas, H. Zebra Goes Wild Where the Sidewalk Ends, The.
Dunbar, P. Black Samson of Brandywine.
Colored Soldiers, The.
Negro Love Song, A.

Unsung Heroes, The.
We wear the mask that grins and lies.
When Dey 'Listed Colored Soldiers.
Eady. I Just Wanna Testify.
Why Do So Few Blacks Study Creative Writing?
Earley, J. One Thousand Nine-Hundred and Sixty-Eight Winters.
Emanuel, J. Old Black Men Say.
Whitey, Baby.
Encarnacion. Bulosan Listens to a Recording of Robert Johnson.
Evans, M. How Will You Call Me, Brother.
I Am a Black Woman.
Status Symbol.
Vive Noir!
Who Can Be Born Black.
Fauset. Touché.
Ferdinand. Food for Thought.
Figueroa, J. Portrait of a Woman (and a Man).
Finney, N. Uncles.
Fisher, S. Assumption about the Harlem Brown Baby.
Fleming, R. For All Unwed Mothers.
Ford, C. Plaint.
Foster, S. Old Folks at Home[, The].
Garnet. Thus man devotes his brother and destroys.
Garvey. Centenary's Day.
Giovanni. Adulthood.
Beautiful Black Men.
Ego Tripping [(There May Be a Reason Why)].
Genie in the Jar, The.
Nikki-Rosa.
Poem for Flora.
Woman Poem.
Giscombe. (1980).
(1962 At the Edge of Town).
Grandmaster Flash *and* the Furious Five. Message, The.
Grimké, A. Black Finger, The.
Hairston. Alabama Bus.
Hamilton, M. For My Father's Mother Who Has Alzheimer's.
Handy, W. Beale Street Blues.
Harper, F. She's Free!
Harper, M. Grandfather.
High Modes: Vision as Ritual: Confirmation.
History as Apple Tree.
Song: I Want a Witness.
Harris, W. Daddy Poem, A.
Rib Sandwich.
Hayden, R. Aunt Jemima of the Ocean Waves.
Frederick Douglass.
Hemphill. Cordon Negro.
Family Jewels.
To Some Supposed Brothers.
Henderson-Holmes. Failure of an Invention.
Holman, M. Mr. Z.
Howard, V. Monument in Black.
Hughes, L. Be-Bop Boys.
Carol of the Brown King.
Cross.
Dinner Guest: Me.
Dream Boogie.
Dream Variation[s].
Flatted Fifths.
Freedom Train.
Gal's Cry for a Dying Lover.
High to Low.
I too, sing America.
Me and the Mule.
Merry-Go-Round.
Negro Servant.
Negro Speaks of Rivers, The.
Neighbor.
Nightmare Boogie.
Parade.
Porter.
Red Silk Stockings.
Stars.
Sun Song.
Theme for English B.
Trumpet Player.
Uncle Tom.

Weary Blues, The.
When Sue Wears Red.
Hummer, T. Ideal, The.
Ibrahim, A. Africa, Music and Show Business.
Irvine, W. To be Young, Gifted, and Black.
Iverem. Daddy's Friends.
Jackson, A. Make/n My Music.
Jackson, R. After the Dance.
Albert james was black long before me.
Jamal's Lamentation.
Jacobs, H. On Growing Up the Darker Berry.
Jeffers, L. My Blackness Is the Beauty of This Land.
Nina Simone.
When I Know the Power of my Black Hand.
Joans. Black People.
Johnson, F. Tired.
Johnson, H. Bottled [New York].
Sonnet to a Negro in Harlem.
Johnson, J. Brothers.
Fifty Years.
Lift every [or ev'ry] voice and sing.
O Black and unknown bards of long ago.
Jonas, R. Ballade des Belles Milatraisses.
Brother Baptis' on Woman Suffrage.
Jones, G. 3-31-70.
Tripart.
Jordan, J. If You Saw a Negro Lady.
Poem about Intelligence for My Brothers and Sisters, A.
Jordan, N. Be You.
Kaufman, B. I, Too, Know What I Am Not.
Oregon.
Untitled.
Kelly, R. Newark.
Kendrick, D. Solo: The Good Blues.
We are the writing on the wall.
Kgositsile. Song for Ilva Mackay and Mongane.
Knight, E. Another Poem for Me (after Recovering from an O.D.)
For Black Poets Who Think of Suicide.
Hard Rock Returns to Prison from the Hospital for the Criminal Insane.
Idea of Ancestry, The.
My life, the quality of which.
Warden said to me the other day, The.
Komunyakaa. Gift Horse.
Troubling the Water.
"Kush." Message for Langston, A.
Lindsay, V. Congo, The.
Loftin. Weeksville Women.
Long, D. Black Love Black Hope.
Lorde. Between Ourselves.
Coal.
For the Record.
Naturally.
Story Books on a Kitchen Table.
Lowell, R. For the Union Dead.
Mad Negro Soldier Confined at Munich, A.
Madgett. Black Woman.
Images.
Midway.
Madhubuti. America calling.
Awareness
Malcolm Spoke / Who Listened?
My brothers i will not tell you.
Poem to Complement Other Poems, A.
Poet: What Ever Happened to Luther?
Soft: the way her eyes view her children.
WE'RE an Africanpeople.
Marino. Beautiful Slave, The.
McClaurin. I, Woman.
Mask, The.
To a Gone Era.
McElroy, C. Ghost-Who-Walks, The.
Griots Who Know Brer Fox, The.
Illusion.
Tapestries.
This Is the Poem I Never Meant to Write.
Under the Oak Table.
Woman's Song, A.
McKay, C. Harlem Dancer, The.
If we must die—let it not be like hogs.
To the White Fiends.
White House, The.

Melville, H. Formerly a Slave.
Swamp Angel, The.
Moss, T. Lunchcounter Freedom.
Raising a Humid Flag.
Neal, L. Don't say goodbye to the Porkpie
Hat that rolled.
Harlem Gallery: From the Inside.
Nemerov. Negro Cemetery Next to a White
One, A.
Oden. Man White, Brown Girl and All That
Jazz.
Ofeimun. Gong, A.
O'Meally. I was jus.
Patterson, R. Black Power.
From Riot Rimes U.S.A. #78.
What We Know.
Phillips, C. Passing.
Public Enemy. Don't believe the hype.
Party for your Right to Fight.
Queen Latifah. Evil That Men Do, The.
Quigless. Moving.
Randall, D. Abu / 's a stone black
revolutionary.
Blackberry Sweet.
Booker T. and W. E. B.
Different Image, A.
Melting Pot, The.
Roses and Revolutions.
Reed, I. Railroad Bill, a conjure man.
Reynolds, H. Black Maid to the Fair Boy,
The.
Rivers, C. In Defense of Black Poets.
Underground.
Roach. At Guaracara Park.
Roberts, N. Nigger and Some Poofters, A.
Rodgers, C. For Sistuhs Wearin' Straight Hair.
It Is Deep.
Jesus Was Crucified or: It Must Be Deep.
Poem for Some Black Women.
Portrait.
Rosten. Black boy, the night hides you.
Roumain. Dirty Niggers.
Negro peddler of revolt.
When the Tom-Tom Beats.
Rukeyser, M. George Robinson: Blues.
Sadiq. Tuskegee Experiment.
Sanchez, S. Blues.
Homecoming.
Memorial.
Poem at Thirty.
Present.
Song No. 2: "I say. all you young girls
waiting to live."
Song No. 3: "Cain't nobody tell me any
different."
To Anita.
Saunders, R. Generation Gap, The.
Hush Honey.
Lawd, Dese Colored Chillum.
Senghor. To New York.
You held the black face of the warrior
between your hands.
Sepamla. Civilization Aha.
On Judgement Day.
Shange. About Atlanta.
Nappy Edges.
Nappy Edges (A Cross Country Sojourn).
Somebody almost walked off wid alla my
stuff.
Shapiro, K. Nigger.
Sherlock. Jamaican Fisherman.
Sherman, C. Roots.
Simon, L. Nellie Gives into Blanche.
Sinda. To the banquet of the earth.
Smith, P. Blonde White Women.
They say that black people.
What It's Like to Be a Black Girl (For Those
of You Who Aren't).
Soyinka. Telephone Conversation.
Spellman. Did John's Music Kill Him?
When Black People Are.
Stafford, W. Monuments for a Friendly Girl at
a Tenth Grade Party.
Sykes, B. One Day.
Taylor, C. Garden.
Thomas, L. Excitation.
Thompson, C. Mrs. Johnson Objects.

Thompson, L. Black Is Best.
Tirolien. Ghetto.
Little Black Boy's Prayer, A.
Tolson. Birth of John Henry, The.
Dark Symphony.
Ex-Judge at the Bar, An.
Harlem Gallery: Book I, The Curator, The.
Tosh. African.
Toure, A. Frontier of rage that exists, The.
Touré, A. JuJu.
Travis, N. Sunbathing.
Troupe. In Texas Grass.
Poem for My Father.
River Town Packin House Blues.
U Tam'si Tchicaya. Brush-Fire.
Viaticum.
Unknown. Me and My Captain.
Shine and the *Titanic.*
Song: "We raise de wheat."
Vega. Brothers Loving Brothers.
Voigt. At the Movie: Virginia, 1956.
Wade-Gayles. Inquisition.
Walcott. Swamp, The.
Walker, A. It is true--/ I've always loved.
Women.
Walker, M. For my people [everywhere
singing their slave songs repeatedly: their].
Poppa Chicken.
Waller, T. *et al.* (What Did I Do to Be So)
Black and Blue?
Waniek. Balance.
Ballad of Aunt Geneva, The.
Chopin.
Diverne's Waltz.
Tuskegee Airfield.
Ward, J. Don't Be Fourteen (In Mississippi).
Washington. Freedom Hair.
Watkins, N. Bedtime Story.
Hard Times A' Coming.
Weatherly, T. Mud Water Shango.
Weaver, M. Black and White Galaxie, The.
Black Man's Sonata, A.
Imitation of Life.
Left Bank Jazz Society, The.
Luxembourg Garden.
Picnic, an Homage to Civil Rights, The.
Weiss, T. Dab of Color, A.
Welburn. Black is beautiful.
Bones and Drums.
Wheatley, P. On Being Brought from Africa
to America.
Whitlow. Poem for the Children.
Williams, S. I Want Aretha to Set This to
Music.
Peacock Poems: 1, The.
Straight Talk from Plain Women.
You Were Never Miss Brown to Me.
Wormser. It's a Party (1959).
Wright, J. Confession to J. Edgar Hoover.
Wright, J. End of an Ethnic Dream, The.
Wright, R. Between the World and Me.
Green cockleburs, The.
I Have Seen Black Hands.
Young, A. Dance for Militant Dilettantes, A.
Poem for Players, A.

Afterlife
Cameron, N. Visit to the Dead, A.
Castillo, A. Nani Worries about Her Father's
Happiness in the Afterlife.
Ch'on, S. Return to Heaven.
Crane, H. Circumstance, The.
Cummings, E. If there are any heavens my
mother will (all by herself) have.
Dickinson, E. Of nearness to her sundered
Things.
Fenton, J. Kingfisher's Boxing Gloves, The.
Han. Blue Bird.
Hecht, A. Voice at a Seance, A.
Herrick. Plaudite, or End of Life, The.
Hill, G. Not as we are but as we must appear.
Izumi. Will I cease to be.
Kim, Y. Grass Flower.
Lawrence, D. My way is not thy way, and
thine is not mine.
Lazarus, E. New Ezekiel, The.
MacNeice. This Is the Life.

Marvell. Dialogue between Thyrsis and
Dorinda, A.
Merrill, J. Voices from the Other World.
Milosz, O. Strophes.
Shakespeare, W. Ay[e], but to die, and go we
know not where.
Smith, S. Mrs Simpkins never had very much
to do.
Tennyson, A. If Only.
Unknown. Other World, The.
Wallace-Crabbe. Trace Elements.
Wright, J. Willy Lyons.

Afternoon
Bevington, L. Afternoon.
De la Mare. In the Garden.
Dickinson, E. There's a certain Slant of light.
Fichman. Afternoon Light.
Guggenberger. Afternoon.
Howell, C. Reminder to the Current President,
A.
Levertov. Sunday Afternoon.
Longfellow, H. Afternoon in February.
McAuley, J. One Tuesday in Summer.
Merwin, W. Views from the High Camp.
Millay, E. Afternoon on a Hill.
Senghor. Visit.
Stickney, T. Quiet after the rain of morning.
Tóth, J. Outskirts, Afternoon.
Virgil. Quiet afternoon.

Afton River, Scotland
Burns, R. Flow gently, sweet Afton, among
thy green braes.

Afzal Khan
Ghose, Z. Rise of Shivaji, The.

Aggression
Gilbert, S. Thought from Ruddigore, A.
Thought from Ruddigore, A.
Lý Thu'ò'ng Kiệt. Southern emperor rules the
Southern land, The.
Nash, O. Tweedledee and Tweedledoom.
Young, A. Dance for Militant Dilettantes, A.

Agincourt, Battle of (1415)
Drayton. Agincourt.
Shakespeare, W. Before Agincourt.
Unknown. Agincourt Carol, The.

Aging
Alberti. Homecoming of Love Amongst
Illustrious Ruins.
Anacreon. Age.
Ode of Anacreon, An.
Arnold, M. Growing Old.
Auden. Doggerel by a Senior Citizen.
Baillie, J. Song: "What voice is this, thou
evening gale!"
Baker, K. Let Me Grow Lovely.
Barker, J. To My Young Lover.
Bartlett, E. Contre Jour.
Beckett, S. Saint-Lô.
Beer, P. Jane Austen at the Window.
Middle Age.
Berry, W. Ripening.
Betjeman. Senex.
Binyon. Those That Are Gone.
Blake, W. Angel, The.
Bloch, C. Primer.
Blok. On the Islands.
Blood, B. Late.
Bly, R. Dream of Retarded Children, A.
For My Son Noah, Ten Years Old.
Boland, E. Anna Liffey.
Bontemps. To a Young Girl Leaving the Hill
Country.
Booth, P. Was it he said she said or.
Braithwaite. Turn Me to My Yellow Leaves.
Bramfit. Grandparents.
Brasch. Ambulando.
Brodsky, J. Folk Tune.
Brontë, E. Love and Friendship.
Why do I hate that lone green dell?
Brooks, G. Marie Lucille.
Old Mary.
Sunset of the City, A.
Brown, G. Harpoonist.
Browning, R. By the Fire-Side.
Prologue: "Poet's age is sad: for why?, The."
Youth and Art.
Buckley, V. In the faint blue light.

Burns, R. John Anderson my jo, John / When we were first acquent.

Byron, G. So we'll go no more a-roving.
Stanzas for Music ("There's not a joy the world can give like that it takes away").

Campion, T. First Love.

Carew, T. Disdain Returned.

"Carroll." Father William.

Carruth, H. Twilight comes to the little farm.

Causley. Nursery Rhyme of Innocence and Experience.

Celan. Your Hand Full of Hours.

Christopher. Palm Reader, The.

"Chrystos." Portrait of Assimilation.

Chu Shu-chen. Hysteria.

Clampitt. Written in Water.

Clare, J. Decay.

Claudian. Felix, qui patriis. . . and c.:
Imitated from Claudian.
Old Man of Verona, The.

Clifton, L. Climbing.
There Is a Girl Inside.
Thirty-eighth year, The.

Cole, T. Dial, The.

Coleridge, H. Long Time a Child.

Coleridge, S. This Lime-Tree Bower My Prison.

Collins, A. Another Song.

Conn. Summer Afternoon.

Cornford, F. All Souls' Night.
Childhood.

Coward. Fortitude.

Cowley, H. Departed Youth.

Cowper, W. Inscription.
On an Old Woman.
To Mary.
To William Hayley, Esq.: In Reply to His Solicitation to Write with Him in a Literary Work.

Cranch. My Old Palette.

Creeley. Age.
Body.

Cuddihy. Steps.

Cummings, E. Whatever's merely wilful, / and not miraculous.

Cunningham, J. To My Wife.

Daniel, S. 34.
Sonnet 33: 'When men shall find thy flower'.

Davie. Autumn Imagined.
Heigh-ho on a Winter Afternoon.

Davis, O. Thirty Years Rising.

Derricotte. Touching/Not Touching: My Mother.

Dickinson, E. We outgrow love like other things.

Disch. Entropic Villanelle.

Dischell. Chamber, The.

Divakaruni. Visit.

Dobyns. What You Have Come To Expect.

Donne. Autumnal[l], The.
Canonization, The.

Dransfield. Portrait of the Artist as an Old Man.

Eberhart, R. Half-bent Man.
Hardy Perennial.

"Eliot." Two lovers by a moss-grown spring.

Emerson, R. Awed I behold once more.
Terminus ("It is time to be old").

"Ephelia." Maidenhead.

Fazli. Page from the New Diary, A.

Feldman, I. Terminal Laughs.

Fell, A. Pushing Forty.

Field, E. Little Boy Blue.

Flynn, D. Collector, The.

Forché. As Children Together.

Fowler, A. Relative.

Fraser, K. Dresses.

Frost, R. Span of Life, The.
To Earthward.

Galvin, P. Plaisir d'Amour.

Gay, J. Toilette, The.

Ginsberg, A. Charnel Ground, The.
V. Father Death Blues.

Giovanni. Adulthood.
Life I Led, The.

Glück, L. For My Mother.

Goodman, M. Upkeep.

Graves, R. Advice to Colonel Valentine.
Change.

Gray, S. On a Cat, Ageing.

Gregory of Nazianzus, Saint. Where are my wingèd words? Dissolved in air.

Greville, F. Sonnet: "Whenas [or When as] man's life, the light of human lust."

Guthrie, W. Turkey in the Corn.

Hacker, M. Mother II.

Hadas, R. Yes, But.

Hall, D. Mr. Wakeville on Interstate 90.
My son, my executioner.

Halpern, D. Argument.

Hardy, T. Circus-Rider to Ringmaster.
Colonel's Soliloquy, The.
In a Eweleaze near Weatherbury.
In the Night She Came.
When you shall see me in the toils of Time.

Herbert, G. Answer, The.
Mortification.

Herrick. His Age, Dedicated to His Peculiar Friend, Master John Wickes, under the Name of Posthumus.
To a Bed of Tulips.
To a Gentlewoman Objecting to Him His Grey Hairs.
To His Friend, on the Untunable Times.
To His Mistresses.

Hitomaro. Strange old man, A.
Your hair has turned white.

Hoàng Trinh. Forty.

Holmes, J. Metaphor for My Son.

Hong, Y. On Ornament.

Horace. 1.25: Ribald Romeos Less and Less Berattle ("Parcius iunctas quatiunt fenestras").
1.9.
Fourteenth Ode of the Second Book of Horace, The.

Housman, A. Loveliest of trees, the cherry now.

Howe, J. My Last Dance.

Howes, B. 2nd Wind.

Hughes, L. Young Gal's Blues.

Hugo, R. In Your Young Dream.
Places and Ways to Live.

Hummer, T. Apocatastasis Foretold in the Shape of a Canvas of Smoke.

Hunt, L. Rondeau.

Ibn al-Rumi. Compromise, The.

Ignatow, D. Mother, how wrinkled and old must you become.
Two Friends.

Jackson, H. Poppies on the Wheat.

Jamal Isfahani. White hairs.

Jarrell. Aging.
Next Day.
Player Piano, The.

Jeffers, R. Age in Prospect.
But I Am Growing Old and Indolent.

Johnson, J. Girl of fifteen.

Jones, L. et al. Look for You Yesterday, Here You Come Today.

Jong. Aging.

Jonson, B. My Picture Left in Scotland.
To the World [A Farewell for a Gentlewoman, Virtuous and Noble].

Joron, A. Birdsongs are aging, The.

Joseph, J. Warning.

Justice, D. Men at forty / Learn to close softly.

Kalász. Maiden.

Kantaris. Stocking Up.

Kaufman, S. Next Year, in Jerusalem.

Kazantzis. Woman making advances publicly, A.

Keats. In drear-nighted December.

Kennedy, X. In a Prominent Bar in Secaucus [One Day].

Kenyon, J. Finding a Long Gray Hair.

Kim, J. Tavern at Sunset.

Kinsella, T. Oldest Place, The.

Kipling, R. His Apologies.

Kowit. Cosmetics do no good.

Kunitz, S. Touch Me.

Lamb, C. Old Familiar Faces, The.

Landor, W. Love and Age.
When Helen first saw wrinkles in her face.

Larkin, P. Age.
Nothing to Be Said.

Lattimore. Game Resumed.

Levertov. What Wild Dawns There Were.
Woman Alone, A.

Levine, P. Red Dust.

Li Ch'ing-chao. Hopelessness.

Libbey. Juana Bautista Lucero, Circa 1926, to Her Photographer.

Linton. Epicurean.

Lockhart. Lines: "When youthful faith hath fled."

Loftin. Weeksville Women.

Longfellow, H. For age is opportunity no less.
Meeting, The.

Longley, M. Ash Keys.

Louis, A. Practicing Death Songs.

Lu Kuei Meng. To an Old Tune.

Lu Yu. I Get Up at Dawn.

Lum. Riding the North Point Ferry.

Lux. Little Tooth, A.

Machado Ruiz. Ephemeral Past, The.

Maclean, A. Death of an Old Woman.

Marvell. To His Coy Mistress.

Mayakovsky. Mayakovsky's Suicide Note.

McClatchy. My Mammogram.

McClintock, M. Thought i'd / never grow old.

McElroy, C. Queen of the Ebony Isles.

McGinley. Journey toward Evening.

Meehan, M. Gift for my Mother's 90th Birthday.

Mei Yao Ch'en. Friend Advises Me to Stop Drinking, A.

Meredith, W. His Plans for Old Age.

Merrill, J. Black Mesa, The.
Kimono, The.
Mirror.

Merwin, W. Another Year Come.
Grandfather in the Old Men's Home.

Meynell, A. Letter from a Girl to Her Own Old Age, A.

Michelangelo Buonarroti. To Giovanni da Pistoia When the Author Was Painting the Vault of the Sistine Chapel, 1509.

Miles, J. Album.

Millay, E. Grown-up.
Sonnet: "Oh, my belovèd, have you thought of this."
What lips my lips have kissed, and where, and why.

Miller, V. Trimming the Sails.

Milton. Sonnet: "How soon hath Time the suttle [or subtle] theef [or thief] of youth."

Miu Hsi. Poem in the Form of a Coffin-Puller's Song.

Moon, C. Poem at Forty.

Moore, T. I Saw from the Beach.

Morgan, E. Second Life, The.

Moyer. Listen.

Nastasijevic. Gray Moment.

Ndebele. Revolution of the Aged, The.

Nemerov. Boy with Book of Knowledge.
Thirtieth Anniversary Report of the Class of '41.

Newcastle, M. Woman drest by Age, A.

Nguyễn Bỉnh Khiêm. My hair has thinned, my teeth have worn away.

Nguyễn Chí Thiện. All Come to Me.

Nguyễn Công Trú. Wasted Life, A.

Nguyễn Khuyến. Self-Portrayal.

O'Grady, D. In the valleys of the future we shall walk.
Purpose.

Olds, S. Size and Sheer Will.
35/10.

Opitz. Ah Dearest, let us haste us.

Oppen. And if at 80.
Tell the beads of the chromosomes like a rosary.

Ormsby, E. My Mother in Old Age.

Orr, E. In This Motherless Geography.

Ou-yang Hsiu. Old Age.
Song of Liang Chou.
Song of Picking Mulberry ("Ten years ago I was a visitor at the wine jar").
When the Moon is in the River of Heaven.

Ovid. 3.6.

Owen, W. Sonnet, to a Child.
Pagis. Letter, A.
Paley, G. Sad Children's Song, The.
Pao Chao. In Imitation of "The King of Huai-nan."
Park, C. Heavenly Traveler.
Pasolini. Civil Song.
  Lines from the Testament.
Patchen. Street Corner College.
Paulus Silentiarius. Dont' tell me I'm getting gray.
Peacock, T. Love and Age.
Perillo. Skin.
Peters, L. One long jump.
Petrie. Old Pro's Lament, The.
Picirantaiyar. Why My Hair Is Not Gray.
Pilinszky. On the Back of a Photograph.
Plath. Mirror.
Po Chü-i. At the End of Spring.
  Old Age.
Poe. Eldorado.
  Happiest day—the happiest hour, The.
Pollitt. Turning Thirty.
Pope, A. To Mrs. M. B. on Her Birth-Day.
Porter, P. On This Day I Complete My Fortieth Year.
  What I Have Written I Have Written.
Pound, E. Beautiful Toilet, The.
  Tea Shop, The.
Preil, G. Memory of Autumns at Springtime.
Price, R. Twenty-One Years.
Prince, F. Old Age of Michelangelo, The.
Queneau. If You Imagine.
Ralegh, W. Nimphs [or Nymph's] Reply to the Sheepheard [or Shepherd], The.
Randall, J. Rockland.
Rankin, J. Sea-bundle.
Ransom, J. Blue Girls.
  Conrad in Twilight.
Ravikovitch. Dear Mickey.
Reed, H. Chard Whitlow.
Reed, I. Turning Pro.
Reid, C. Howl, Howl.
Rexroth, K. Fifty.
  Only Years.
Rice, J. Sun stuff, star fluff.
Rich, A. Middle-Aged, The.
  Necessities of Life.
  Since we're not young, weeks have to do time.
  Upper Broadway.
Roberson. True we are two grown men.
Robinson, E. Isaac and Archibald were two old men.
  Veteran Sirens.
Rochester, J. Disabled Debauchee, The.
Rossetti, C. Dumb Friend, A.
  Youth gone, and beauty gone if ever there.
Rowse. White Cat of Trenarren, The.
St. John, D. My friend, a man I love as wholly.
Sanchez, S. July.
  Personal Letter No. 3.
Sanders, E. Cutting Prow, The.
Santayana. Minuet on Reaching the Age of Fifty, A.
  Sonnet XXV: "As in the midst of battle there is room."
Sappho. Tonight I've watched.
Sassoon. "When I'm alone"—the words tripped off his tongue.
Saxe, J. Story of Life, The.
Scott, W. Garland for Advancing Years, A
Sexton. Two Sons.
Shakespeare, W. Sonnet 2.
  Sonnet 5: 'Those hours that with gentle work'.
  Sonnet 22.
  Sonnet 60.
  Sonnet 67.
  Sonnet 73.
  Sonnet 104.
Shapcott, T. Blue Paisley Shirt, The.
  Turning Fifty.
Shenstone. Elegy 11: "Ah me, my friend! it will not, will not last!"
Sherwood, G. Disabled Debauchee, The.
Sisson. In Autumn.

Skoyles. Head of Tasso, The.
Smith, C. Thirty-eight: Addressed to Mrs H—y.
Smith, I. Christmas 1971.
Smith, K. Writing in Prison.
Smith, M. City.
Southey, R. Old Man's Comforts and How He Gained Them, The.
Soyinka. To My First White Hairs.
Spender, S. What I expected, was.
Stern, G. Bite, The.
  Peddler's Village.
Stevenson, A. Willow Song.
Stevenson, R. Sing me a song of a lad that is gone.
Su Tung-p'o. Thoughts in Exile.
Supervielle. Early in the morning.
Swenson, M. How to Be Old.
Swift, J. On Stella's Birthday, 1718/1719.
  Stella's Birthday, 1725.
  Stella's Birthday, 1721.
Taggard. No Abstraction.
TallMountain. Hands of Mary Joe, The.
Tản Đà. Still At Play.
T'ao Ch'ien. Poem without a Category ("Sun and moon refuse to slow their pace").
Tarkovsky. Sight grows dim—my power.
Tate, A. Last Days of Alice.
Tennyson, A. June Bracken and Heather.
Teodorescu. Goodbye.
Thomas, E. Gone, gone again.
Tô Giang Tử'. Congratulating a Friend On His New Dentures.
Tomlinson, C. On the Hall at Stowey.
Toomer. Delivered at the Knighting of Lord Durgling by Great Bruce-Jean.
Trần Gia Thoại. Night Train, The.
Troupe. Reflections on Growing Older.
Tsvetayeva. Gold that was my hair has turned, The.
Tu Fu. By the Winding River I.
  Snow Storm.
  To Wei Pa, a Retired Scholar.
  Winter Dawn.
Unknown. Aurora and Tithonus.
  Crossing the river I pluck the lotus flowers;.
  Daughter of the farrier, The.
  Eastern Gate, The.
  Fleeting Time.
  Growing Friendship.
  Will You Love Me When I'm Old?
Vallejo. Distant Footsteps, The.
Van Duyn. Late Loving.
  Stream, The.
Van Vliet. Party.
Vaux. Age Looks Back at Youth.
Verlaine. Exchange Of Feelings, An.
Very. Autumn Flowers.
Võ Phiến. Where Have They Gone?
Vũ Đình Liên. Our Hearts Are Ancient Citadels.
Vũ Hoàng Chu'o'ng. To the Black Nymph.
Wakoski. Moneylight.
Walcott. Codicil.
Waniek. Sleepless Nights.
Warren, R. American Portrait: Old Style.
  Vermont Ballad: Change of Season.
Warton, T. Sonnet: To the River Lodon.
Weigl. Anna's Grace.
Wen T'ing-yün. People all say the southland's better.
Whitman, R. Laughing Gas.
Whittemore, R. Walk Home, The.
Whittier. To My Old Schoolmaster.
Wilbur. For K. R. on Her Sixtieth Birthday.
Wilcox, E. Friendship After Love.
  Life.
Williams, C. Alzheimer's: The Wife.
  World's greatest tricycle rider, The.
Williams, M. On a Photograph of My Mother at Seventeen.
  Ruby Tells All.
Williams, W. Descent beckons, the.
Winslow, P. I blink and half my life is over.
Wollach. Lola, are you still getting whatever you want.
Wright, C. Hawaii Dantesca.

Wright, J. Old Age Compensation.
Wright, J. Brother and Sisters.
  I To my Brothers.
  Sonnet for Christmas.
Wu of Han. Autumn wind blows white clouds, The.
Wyatt, T. Ye old mule, that thin[c]k your self so fair [or fayre].
Xuân Diệu. Come on, make haste—please, won't you hurry up?
  In a Hurry.
  Nothingness.
  Spring Out of Season.
Yeats. Coming of Wisdom with Time, The.
  Crazy Jane Grown Old Looks at the Dancers.
  Crazy Jane Talks with the Bishop.
  Fallen Majesty.
  Folly Of Being Comforted, The.
  Lamentation of the Old Pensioner, The.
  Men Improve with the Years.
  New Faces, The.
  Song, A: "I thought no more was needed."
  Wild Swans at Coole, The.
  Youth and Age.
Yesenin. I do not regret, complain, or weep.
Yevtushenko. Metamorphoses.
Yoshifusa. Years have touched me, The.
Young, A. Move Continuing, The.
Zenmaro. Tanka: "Having lived."
See also Middle Age; Old Age

Agnosticism and Agnostics
  Ginsberg, L. Biography of an Agnostic.
  Hardy, T. Impercipient, The.
See also Doubt

Agoraphobia
  Wayman. Another Poem about the Madness of Women.

Agriculture. See Farming and Farmers
Air
  Ashbery. Melodic Trains.
  Atwood. Variation on the Word Sleep.
  Benedikt. Some Feelings.
  Berrigan, T. Red Shift.
  Clark, T. You (II).
  Dickey, J. Night Bird.
  Duncan, R. Eyesight II.
  Ekelof. If you ask me where I am.
  "Field." Nightfall.
  Frost, F. Snow-Stars.
  Guest, B. Roses.
  Hardy, T. Garden Seat, The.
  Hays, H. January.
  Manhattan.
  Hopkins, G. Blessed Virgin Compared to the Air We Breathe, The.
  Johnson, R. Beam 7.
  Juana Inés de la Cruz. Since Love is shivering.
  Kgositsile. Air, I hear, The.
  Kinzie. In air hard as sand.
  Kleinzahler. Poetics.
  Kuroda. Afternoon 3.
  Landor, W. Gardener, The.
  Levchev. Capriccio 9.
  Levin, P. Citizens and Sky.
  Li Meng-yang. Crossing the Frontier.
  Maiden. Air.
  Millay, E. Above these cares my spirit in calm abiding.
  Nagy, A. Between.
  O'Brien, G. Theory of Climate.
  Peters, L. Parachute Men say.
  Polkowski. World is only air / shining, granular, transparent things, The.
  Raine, K. Air.
  Sanchez, S. Haiku: "Was it yesterday."
  Sartarelli. That Land (4).
  Serge. Asphyxiated Man, The.
  Strand. Marriage, The.
  Swift, J. Oxygen.
  Taylor, A. Air.
  Thompson, R. He knows what height is, this hillside dweller.
  Unknown. Stars stand up in the air, The.
  Virgil. Mullein.
  Wright, J. Breath of Air, A.
  Yün Shou-p'ing. Inscribed on a Painting

("Who needs a raft that can invade the stars?")

Air Conditioning
Greger. Air-Conditioned Air.

Air Plants
Crane, H. Air Plant, The.

Air Travel
Alexopoulos. Night Flight.
Birney. Twenty-third Flight.
Cassity. Flying Friendly Skies.
Davis, J. Day Flight.
Dunn, S. On Hearing the Airlines Will Use a Psychological Profile to Catch Potential Skyjackers.
Grant, J. Planes Landing.
Kooser. Flying at Night.
Larkin, P. Naturally the Foundation Will Bear Your Expenses.
McHugh, H. 20-200 on 747.
  20-200 on 737.
Pasternak, B. Night.
Pudney. On Seeing My Birthplace from a Jet Aircraft.
Rozhdestvensky. Nonflying Weather.
Swenson, M. Flying Home from Utah.
Winters, Y. At the San Francisco Airport.
See also **Airports**

Air Warfare
Akhmadulina. Words Spoken by Pasternak during a Bombing.
Alchin. Song of the Air, A.
Bayliss. Reported Missing.
Bewsher. Dawn Patrol, The.
Bowers, E. Stoic: for Laura von Courten, The.
Brinnin. Ascension: 1925, The.
Ciardi. Journal.
Day, J. Call of the Air, The.
  Dawn.
Day Lewis. Bombers.
Dickey, J. Firebombing, The.
Doolittle, H. Erige Cor Tuum ad Me in Caelum.
Eberhart, R. Dam Neck, Virginia.
  Fury of Aerial Bombardment, The.
Everson, W. Raid, The.
Ewart. When a Beau Goes In.
Field, E. World War II.
Frankau. Eyes in the Air.
Fuller, R. During a Bombardment by V-Weapons.
  Soliloquy in an Air-Raid.
Gilbert, S. Parachutist's Wife, The.
Hall, D. Airstrip in Essex, 1960, An.
Hutcheon. Flight to Flanders, The.
Jarrell. Dead Wingman, The.
  Death of the Ball Turret Gunner, The.
  Eighth Air Force.
  Field Hospital, A.
  Front, A.
  Losses.
  Pilot from the Carrier, A.
  Pilots, Man Your Planes.
  Range in the Desert, The.
  Second Air Force.
Kipling, R. R.A.F. (Aged Eighteen).
Lowell, R. Dead in Europe, The.
MacGreevy. De Civitate Hominum.
MacNeice. Brother Fire.
  Troll's Courtship.
Monk, G. His hands old edging out of time.
Nemerov. Models.
  Night Operations, Coastal Command RAF.
  War in the Air, The.
Popham, H. Usual exquisite boredom of patrols, The.
Redmond. Gods in Vietnam.
Rodgers, W. Raider, The.
Sitwell, D. Still falls the Rain—.
Spender, S. Air Raid Across the Bay at Plymouth.
  Thoughts During an Air Raid.
Tate, J. Lost Pilot, The.
Thomas, D. Ceremony after a Fire Raid.
  Refusal to Mourn the Death, by Fire, of a Child in London, A.
Unknown. Pilot's Psalm, The.
Webb, F. Gunner, The.

Wieseltier. Caution Prevents Accidents.
Wild, P. Air Raid.
Yeats. Irish Airman Foresees His Death, An.
  Reprisals.
Yoshimi. Tanka: "Casting shadows."
  Tanka: "White jet clouds."

Airline Stewardesses
Dickey, J. Falling.

Airplane Crashes
Avidan. Two Memorial Poems.
Erhardt. Amelia Erhardt.
Ewart. When a Beau Goes In.
Jarrell. Front, A.
  Pilot from the Carrier, A.
Rukeyser, M. Ceiling Unlimited.

Airplanes
Akhmadulina. Small Aircraft.
Bawer. View from an Airplane at Night, over California, The.
Berrolino. Landscape, The.
Davis, L. Bob Hosey Is Dead.
Frost, R. Wrights' Biplane, The.
Graham, J. What the End Is For.
Hall, D. Old Pilot, The.
Kirby, J. Aeroplane, The.
McDonald, W. Retired Pilot to Himself, The.
O'Donoghue, B. Apparition, The.
Orlen. Biplane, The.
Pudjipangu. Aeroplane.
Rankine. New Windows.
Roberts, C. Prayer for a Pilot.
Sandburg, C. Bas-Relief.
Starr, J. Flight.
Tranter. Lufthansa.
Unknown. Heavenly Aeroplane, The.
  Pilot's Psalm, The.
Weigl. Sailing to Bien Hoa.
See also **Aviation and Aviators**

Airports
Bozhilov. Wise Ones, The.
Ignatow, D. Night at an Airport.
Roach. Piarco.
Voznesensky. New York Airport at Night.
Winters, Y. At the San Francisco Airport.
See also **Air Travel**

Ajanta, India
Rukeyser, M. Ajanta.

Akhmatova, Anna
Cheney-Coker. Letter to a Tormented Playwright.
Chimombo. Messengers, The.
Gallagher, T. Stepping Outside.
Nortje. Asseverations.
Różewicz. Proofs.
Tsvetayeva. . . . In my melodious city cupolas burn.

Alabama (state)
Brecht, B. Alabama Song.
Fields, J. Alabama.
  Mr. Tut's House A Recollection.
Hairston. Alabama Bus.
Hughes, L. Croon.
  Daybreak in Alabama.
Patterson, R. Birmingham 1963.

Alamo
Miller, J. Defense of the Alamo, The.

Alaska
Cendrars. Aleutian Islands.
Fordham. Alaska.
Haines, J. Train Stops at Healy Fork, The.
Harjo, J. Anchorage.
McElroy, D. Before Breakup on the Chena outside Fairbanks.
Rose. Alaskan Fragments June 1981—Summer Solstice.

Albatrosses
Ewart. Lines: "Other day I was loving a sweet little fruitpie-and-cream, The."
Masefield. Sea Change.

Alcestis
Euripides. Friends, I account the fortune of my wife.

Alchemy and Alchemists
Bogan, L. Alchemist, The.

Chao Meng-fu. Lamenting the Taoist Wei Kung-yüan.
Donne. Love's Alchemy [*or* Alchemie].
Pound, E. Alchemist, The.
Simic. Poem without a Title.

Alcoholism and Alcoholics
Breckenridge. Bottled.
Cavin. Christmas with the Holy Family.
Cunningham, J. Interview with Doctor Drink.
Davis, L. You taught me fear, Momma.
Davitt. Shortening the Road.
Eubulus. Benefits and Abuse of Alcohol, The.
Heaney, S. Casualty.
Hugo, R. Hilltop, The.
  Letter to Logan from Milltown.
Larkin, J. Clifton.
  Genealogy.
  In Western Massachusetts, Sixteen Months Sober.
Logau. Drunkenness.
Louis, A. Something About Being an Indian.
MacDonald, C. Instruction from Bly.
MacIntyre, T. Yellow Bittern, The.
Martial. What'mmmIdoin'? slurs Lyris, feigning shock.
Mei Yao Ch'en. Friend Advises Me to Stop Drinking, A.
Nash, O. Reflections on Ice-breaking.
Notley. Jack Would Speak Through the Imperfect Medium of Alice.
Peacock, M. Our Room.
Peirce. Alcoholic's Son at Ten, The.
  Near Burning.
Roethke. My Papa's Waltz.
Rosenberg, S. Library closing—.
Shen Chou. Taoist Huang Has Died of Alcoholism, The.
Troupe. River Town Packin House Blues.
Wright, J. Metho Drinker.
Yesenin. Black Man, The.
  Years of my youth, years of dissipation.
See also **Drunkards**

Ale
Blake, W. Little Vagabond, The.
Stevenson, W. *et al.* Back and Side Go Bare, Go Bare.
Unknown. Bring us in good ale, and bring us in good ale.
  There was a little man.
  When Jones's Ale Was New.

Aleichem, Sholom
Lieberman, E. Sholom Aleichem.

Alexander the Great, King of Macedon
Carver, R. Wine.
Dryden, J. Alexander's Feast; or, The Power of Music [*or* Musique].
Dugan, A. How We Heard the Name.
Flecker. Santorin.
Jones, E. How Big Was Alexander?
Killigrew, A. Alexandreis.
Kumar, S. Come Back, Alexander.
Rukeyser, M. Speaking Tree, The.
Unknown. Alexander the Great.

Alexander Jannaeus, King of Judah
Cavafy. Alexander Jannai.

Alexander, Sir William
Drummond, W. To Sir W. A.
James I, King of England. Sonnet on Sir William Alexander's Harsh Verses after the English Fashion, A.

Alfonso X, King of Castile and León
Emerson, R. Alphonso of Castile.

Ali, Muhammad
Corbin, L. Ali / Is our prince.

Alice in Wonderland
Ferlinghetti, L. I am waiting for my case to come up.
Tate, A. Last Days of Alice.

Alienation
Allen, P. Kopis'taya.
Anderson, J. Invention of New Jersey, The.
Anderson, L. Dog Show.
Arnold, M. Buried Life, The.
Auden. Walking Tour, The.
Bachmann. Exile.
Baraka. Invention of Comics, The.

Berryman. Traveller, The.
Bly, R. Snowbanks North of the House.
Brooks, G. Bronzeville Man with a Belt in the Back.
Garbageman: the Man with the Orderly Mind.
Bruner. On City Streets.
Burford, W. On the Apparition of Oneself.
Cassian. Please Give This Seat to an Elderly or Disabled Person.
Christopher. Far from Home.
Clare, J. I am: yet what I am none cares or knows.
Written in Northampton County Asylum.
Clarke, G. Baby-Sitting.
Creeley. Moon, The.
Croft, J. D-Zug.
Cruz, V. ALONE/december/night.
Diop, D. Renegade, The.
Duncan, R. Passage Over Water.
Edson, R. Having to Love Something Else, The.
Eliot, T. Burnt Norton.
Gerontion.
Journey of the Magi.
Portrait of a Lady.
Emerson, R. Blight.
Intellect.
Fearing. Dirge: "1-2-3 was the number he played but today the number came 3-2-1."
Frost, R. In Neglect.
Goldberg, L. Dialogue.
Guri. Odysseus.
Hall, D. Exile.
Harry, J. Honesty-Stones.
Hayden, R. Soledad.
Heaney, S. Guttural Muse, The.
Hernton. Poem.
Hongo. Legend, The.
Hopkins, G. To seem the stranger lies my lot, my life.
Howell, C. Liberty and Ten Years of Return.
Jacinto, A. Poem of Alienation.
Justice, D. Missing Person, The.
Komunyakaa. Crack.
Troubling the Water.
Lau, C. On the Fifth Anniversary of My Father's Death.
Lewis, L. Bridget.
Livingston, M. Poor.
Loden. My Night with Philip Larkin.
Lowell, J. Street, The.
Madhubuti. Back Again, Home.
Empty Warriors.
'Marnia. I must be able to protect you.
McDonald, R. Incident in Transylvania.
McKay, C. Outcast.
Meredith, G. Modern Love.
Merwin, W. Fields, The.
Oppen. Anniversary Poem.
Moving over the hills, crossing the irrigation.
Resort.
Paulin. Ulster Unionist Walks the Streets of London, An.
Pinsky. Poem about People.
Pound, E. In A Station of the Metro.
Tea-rose tea-gown, etc.
Ransom, J. Vanity of the Bright Young Men, The.
Reed, I. Poem for Two Daughters.
Rich, A. After Dark.
Stranger, The.
Rilke. Panther, The.
Robinson, E. Mr Flood's Party.
Rodgers, W. Winter's Cold.
Rodriguez, L. We never stopped crossing borders.
Rukeyser, M. Effort at Speech between Two People.
Sandburg, C. Useless Words.
Schnackenberg. Paperweight, The.
Schwartz, D. Young Child and His Pregnant Mother, A.
Seferis. Word for Summer, A.
Senghor. To New York.
Shapiro, K. My grandmother moves to my mind in context of sorrow.
Travelogue for Exiles.

Simon, P. Sound of Silence, The.
Stanton, M. Childhood.
Su Tung-p'o. Tune: Prelude to Water Music.
Tate, J. Contagion.
Tennyson, A. 108.
Tomlinson, C. Mr. Brodsky.
Tranter. Great Artist Reconsiders the Homeric Simile, The.
Twichell. Shades of Grand Central, The.
Unknown. Chinook Songs.
Oxaitoq's Song.
Warren, R. To a Face in a Crowd.
Warsh. Enmeshment.
Wordsworth, W. Sonnet: "World is too much with us; late and soon, The."
Wright, C. Stone Canyon Nocturne.
Wyatt, T. I must go walk[e] the woods so wild.
Yevtushenko. Monologue of a Blue Fox.
Yosano. Wave of coldness, A.
Yoshimi. Tanka: "Since I work with those."

Aliens
Aylen. Undistinguished Visitor, The.
Cunliffe. Alpha-B375-Earth Visitors' Guide. . . Section.
Duggin. Learning My Father's Language.
Finney, E. Supposing.
Gillilan, P. Alien at the Zoo.
Alien goes Shopping.
Kenward. E. T.
What's out there?
Kirkup. Beautiful Strangers, The.
My Thing from Outer Space.
Kitching. I know where I'm going.
Within the space.
Magee, W. Epitaphs for some Space Beasts.
Fungus Fingers, The.
Morgan, E. First Men on Mercury, The.
Morgan, R. Choice, The.
Patten, B. Earth-ling, The.
Pugh. 'Do you think we'll ever get to see Earth, sir?'.
Raine, C. Martian Sends a Postcard Home, A.
Rice, J. On some other planet.
Rowe, A. Destroyers, The.
Rumble. Close Encounter, A.
Unique?
Scriven, R. Marrog, The.
Smith, I. In the late evening.
Strangers.
Unknown. Welcome over the Door of an Old Inn.
Wilson, R. Never since Eden.

All Souls' Day
Atkins. Lisbon.
Lawrence, D. All Soul''s Day.

All Souls' Night
Cornford, F. All Souls' Night.
Glück, L. All Hallows.

Allen, Richard
Heard, J. Rt. Rev. Richard Allen.

Alligators
Agard, J. Don't Call Alligator Long-Mouth Till You Cross River.
Hall, D. Alligator Bride, The.
Nash, O. Purist, The.
Ravenel. Alligator, The.
See also **Crocodiles**

Almanacs
Bishop, E. Sestina: "September rain falls on the house."
Jammes. Child Reads an Almanac, The ("The child reads on; her basket of eggs stands by").
Wright, J. Benjamin Banneker Sends His Almanac to Thomas Jefferson.

Almond Trees and Almonds
Herrick. Upon Sibilla.
Lawrence, D. Bare Almond-Trees.

Alphabet
Dodge, M. Letters at School, The.
Gorey. Utter Zoo Alphabet, The.
Kolatkar. Alphabet, The.
Peacock, M. Spell, The.
Rimbaud, A. Vowels.
Shapiro, K. Alphabet, The.

Unknown. A was an archer, who [or and] shot at a frog.
O, look at the moon.
Alphabet Poems
Calverley. A B C.
Coward. A. Stands for Absolutely Anything.
Disch. Abecedary.
Zewhyexary.
Humphries, B. Edna's Alphabet.
Lear, E. Alphabet, An.
Twenty-Six Nonsense Rhymes.
Logau. A.E.I.O.U.
Mother Goose. Tragical Death of A, Apple Pie, The.
Nemerov. Primer of the Daily Round, A.
Unknown. A was an archer, who [or and] shot at a frog.
ABC, An.
Alphabet, The.
English Alphabet, An.
Lumberman's Alphabet, The.
Sailors' Alphabet, The.
Watts. Austrian Army, An.

Alphonsus Rodriguez, Saint
Hopkins, G. In Honour of St. Alphonsus Rodriguez.

Alps
Beddoes. Alpine Spirit's Song.
Bunting. On the Fly-Leaf of Pound's Cantos.
Coleridge, S. Chamouny; the Hour Before Sunrise. A Hymn.
Dickinson, E. Our lives are Swiss.
Hardy, T. Schreckhorn, The.
MacGreevy. Nocturne of the Self-evident Presence.
Meynell, A. Watershed, The.

Alsace, France
Wilbur. First Snow in Alsace.

Altars
Belloc. Four things in any land must dwell.
Chin. Altar.
Cole, P. Where the Honey Speech's Hedge.
Dowson. Nuns of the Perpetual Adoration.
Herbert, G. Altar, The.
Lampadius. As a symbol.
O'Higgins, B. Mountain Altar, The.
Samio. Tanka: "Reverently."
Sobin, G. On the Nature of the Iconic.
Spenser. Now is this love already forth to come.
Tao-chi. Trip to Hua-yang Mountain, A.
Taylor, E. Bran, a chaff, a very barley [y]awn, A.

Altgeld, John Peter
Lindsay, V. Eagle That Is Forgotten, The.

Alumni
Eberhart, R. I went to see Irving Babbitt.
Gibson, W. Blues for an Old Blue.
Nemerov. Thirtieth Anniversary Report of the Class of '41.
Wilson, E. Disloyal Lines to an Alumnus.

Amaryllis (mythology)
Campion, T. I care not for these ladies.

Amazons
Coleridge, M. White Women, The.
Killigrew, A. Alexandreis.

Ambition
Armuth. Mother, A.
Astell. Ambition.
Attlee. Few thought he was even a starter.
Bast. Empress's Cat, The.
Bottrall. Icarus.
Brydges. To Miss M——, Written by Moonlight, July 18, 1782.
Cary, A. West Country, The.
Ch'ien T'ao. In the quiet of the morning I heard a knock at my door;.
Chu Chen Po. Hedgehog.
Clampitt. Cormorant in His Element, The.
Clifton, L. Climbing.
Cornish, S. Generations 2.
Davies, W. Ambition.
Herrick. Ambition ("In man, ambition is the common'st thing").
Horton, G. George Moses Horton, Myself.
Johnson, M. Ambition.

Juan Chi. Long ago, at fourteen or fifteen.
Li Shang-yin. Poem for My Little Boy.
Longfellow, H. Mezzo Cammin.
Mitchell, K. Monster, The.
Ou-yang Hsiu. Calligraphy Practice.
Ransom, J. Vanity of the Bright Young Men, The.
Ray, H. Ambition.
Romanes. Simple Nature.
Rowe, G. We Are Rising.
Sidney, P. Sonnet 27: "Because I oft, in dark abstracted guise."
Swirszczynska. First Madrigal, The.
T'ao Ch'ien. Imitating the Old Poems.
Poem without a Category ("Brave man has ambitions wide as the four seas, The").
Unknown. I turn the carriage, yoke and set off.
In the house east of here lives an old woman.
Mills of the Gods, The.
We hold a splendid feast today.
Waniek. Sleepless Nights.
Warren, R. Ballad: Between the Boxcars.

Ambulances
Fanthorpe. Resuscitation Team.
Kirchwey. Ambulance.
Larkin, P. Ambulances.

Amen Ra. *See* **Amon Ra**

America
Ahmad. America, America.
Ai. More.
Alarcon, F. Letter To America.
Alexie. Vision (2).
Allen, P. Zen Americana.
Appleman, P. Peace with Honor.
Ashbery. One Thing That Can Save America, The.
Pyrography.
They Dream Only of America.
Awoonor. America.
American Memory of Africa, An.
On Having Been an Experimental Sacred Cow for Four Years, and a Token African on Faculty.
Baca. How We Carry Ourselves.
Balaban. After our war, the dismembered bits.
Dead for Two Years, Erhart Arranges to Meet Me in a Dream.
In Celebration of Spring.
Baraka. Nation Is Like Ouselves, The.
Three Modes of History and Culture.
Barlow, J. Columbiad, The.
From sultry Mobile's gulf-indented shore.
Bates, K. America the Beautiful.
Beecher, H. American Flag, The.
Bellamy, F. Pledge of Allegiance to the Flag.
Benét, S. American Names.
Ballad of William Sycamore, The.
Daniel Boone.
Bentley, N. Third Dungeness Spit Apocalypse.
Berlin. God bless America.
Berrigan, D. My Name.
Bly, R. After the Industrial Revolution, All Things Happen at Once.
Booth, P. Crossing.
Brathwaite, E. Colombe.
Brodsky, J. In the Lake District.
Bromige. Eastward Ho! A Succession.
Brown, M. Survival Motion: Notice.
Bryant, W. Not Yet.
Bursk. Lies.
Campo. Battle Hymn of the Republic, The.
Cardenal. Mosquito Kingdom.
Cary, A. West Country, The.
Chin. How I Got That Name.
We Are Americans Now, We Live in the Tundra.
Clark, T. Going to School in France or America.
Cohan. You're a grand old flag.
Creeley. America, you ode for reality!
Cross, Jr. When Chicken Man Came Home to Roost.
Cruz, V. Areyto.
Cummings, E. I sing of Olaf glad and big.
Next to of course god america i.
O pr / gress verily thou art m.

"Dario." To Roosevelt.
Davidson, L. America.
Davidson, M. Sensation Type and His Friends, The.
Dennis, C. Miracle, The.
Djanikian. When I First Saw Snow.
Dorn, E. Home on the Range, February 1962.
Drake, J. To a Friend.
Dumas, H. America.
Zebra Goes Wild Where the Sidewalk Ends, The.
Ehrhart. Invasion of Grenada, The.
Relative Thing, A.
Emanuel, L. Film Noir: Train Trip Out.
Ferlinghetti, L. I am waiting for my case to come up.
Poet's eye obscenely seeing, The.
Starting from San Francisco.
Floyd. Corporal Kevin Spina, U. S. M. C.
Freneau. On the Emigration to America [and Peopling the Western Country].
Frost, R. America Is Hard to See.
Gift Outright, The.
García Lorca. Ode for Walt Whitman.
Gibbons, R. American Trains.
Gilmore, B. Bow to Allah.
Ginsberg, A. America I've given you all and now I'm nothing.
Bayonne Turnpike to Tuscarora.
Crossing Nation.
Footnote to Howl.
Wichita Vortex Sutra, Part I.
Goll, I. Lackawanna Elegy.
Greenwald, T. Coordinating cities gulls still gull, and, arms binged with wine, as wine.
Grenier. Wrath to Sadness.
Guillén, N. National Police Headquarters.
Gumilyov. Tanka.
Hagedorn, J. Filipino Boogie.
Harmon. I am the Gross National Product.
Invoice No. 13, A Masque of Resignation.
Harms. Tomorrow, We'll Dance in America.
Harper, M. American History.
Hasford. Bedtime Story.
Hayden, R. &[;American Journal&];.
Hemphill. XXIV.
Herbert, G. Religion stands on tip-toe in our land.
Horace. You of course live in the way that is truly right.
Howe, J. Battle Hymn [or Battle-Hymn] of the Republic, The.
Howe, S. Thorow.
Howell, C. Liberty and Ten Years of Return.
Hughes, L. I too, sing America.
Let America Be America Again.
Hugo, R. What Thou Lovest Well Remains American.
Huidobro. Cow Boy.
Inada. From Our Album.
Jarrell. For an Emigrant.
Jeffers, L. My Blackness Is the Beauty of This Land.
Jeffers, R. Shine, Perishing Republic.
Shine, Republic.
Jordan, F. I love America where truth can be shouted from the housetops.
Kaufman, B. Heavy Water Blues.
Key. Star-Spangled Banner, The.
Klepfisz. Bashert.
Kumin, M. Height of the Season, The.
Larkin, P. Faith Healing.
Laughlin, J. Kind-, The.
Lawrence, D. Evening Land, The.
Lazarus, E. 1492.
Levertov. Fragrance of Life, Odor of Death.
In Thai Binh (Peace) Province.
Weeping Woman.
Lincoln, A. Gettysburg Address, The.
Second Inaugural Address.
Lum. Chinese Hot Pot.
MacLeish. Empire Builders.
Invocation to the Social Muse.
Mathews, C. Masses, The.
McCarthy, E. Right of Way.
McClure, M. Reading Frank O'Hara in a Mexican Rainstorm.

McKay, C. America.
Meinke. Supermarket.
Melville, H. America.
Ungar and Rolfe.
Miller, J. Sierras.
Mitchell, A. From Rich Uneasy America to My Friend Christopher Logue.
Moore, M. Love in America.
Nash, O. Columbus.
Nemerov. Boy with Book of Knowledge.
Neruda. America, I do not call your name without hope.
Letter to Miguel Otero Silva, in Caracas.
Stone within stone, and man, where was he?
North, C. Shooting for Line.
O'Grady, D. Great Horse Fair, The.
O'Hara, F. Ave Maria.
You at the Pump.
Ologboni. Changed Mind (or the Day I Woke Up).
Olson, C. Across Space and Time.
Orban, O. Snowfall in Boston.
Ortiz. Travels in the South.
War Poem.
Padgett, R. Early Triangles.
Parkerson. Statistic.
Parra, N. Modern Times.
Patterson, R. From Riot Rimes U.S.A. #78.
Paulding. Neglected Muse! of this our western clime.
Piatt, J. Farther.
To the Statue on the Capitol.
Piercy. Peaceable Kingdom, The.
Preil, G. Memory of Autumns at Springtime.
Prunty. To be Sung on the Fourth of July.
Randall, D. Melting Pot, The.
Revell. Survey.
Roethke. Night Journey.
Romano, R. But My Blood.
Rukeyser, M. Campaign.
Rutsala. American Dream.
Saint. Triple Trouble.
St. John, P. We Are Going to Be Here Now.
Sanchez, S. Right On: White America.
Sandburg, C. Threes.
Schultz, P. For My Father.
Scott-Heron. Winter in America.
Sexton. Firebombers, The.
Sixth Psalm.
Shapiro, D. For the Evening Land.
Shapiro, H. National Cold Storage Company contains, The.
Shapiro, K. Manhole Covers.
Sharma. American Tourist.
Shelley, P. Tribute to America.
Shepherd, R. Skin Trade.
Simpson, L. To the Western World.
Walt Whitman at Bear Mountain.
Smith, I. Dunoon and the Holy Loch.
Smith, S. America.
Snyder, G. I went into the Maverick Bar.
What Happened Here Before.
Spicer, J. Book of Galahad, The.
Steptoe. Such a Boat of Land.
Sternlieb. Right of Way.
Stevenson, R. Ticonderoga: A Legend of the West Highlands.
Supervielle. Some day shall I be the one who let.
Thomas à Becket. Columbia, the Gem of the Ocean.
Thorne, T. Whatever Happened to Conway Twitty?
Tillinghast, R. Our Flag Was Still There.
Tomlinson, C. Word in Edgeways, A.
Toomer. It is Everywhere.
Turner, N. Washington.
Whenever I say "America."
Unknown. State Quiz.
Upton, C. When I was very young.
Very. Slavery.
Walcott. Blues.
Glory Trumpeter, The.
Gulf, The.
Upstate.
Wayman. Despair.
Weaver, M. My Father's Geography.

Weiners. Poem for Painters, A.
Welburn. Bones and Drums.
Whitman, W. America.
  For You O Democracy.
  Full of life now, compact, visible.
  I hear America singing, the varied carols I
    hear.
  Orange Buds by Mail from Florida.
  Prairie-grass dividing, its special odor
    breathing, The.
  Respondez! Respondez! / (The war is
    completed—the price is paid—the title is
    settled beyond recall).
  Song of Myself.
  Spring.
  To-day and Thee.
  To the East and to the West.
  Wound-Dresser, The.
  Years of the modern! years of the
    unperform'd!
  Yonnondio.
Williams, W. To Elsie.
Willis, N. To Charles Roux, of Switzerland.
Woolson. Detroit River.
Wright, J. American Twilights, 1957.
  Stages on a Journey Westward.
Yevtushenko. New York Elegy.
Zimmer. Eisenhower Years, The.
Zukofsky, L. Fifth Movement: Autobiography.
See also **United States**

American Indians. *See* **Americans; Native
Americans**

American Revolution
Bly, R. Poem Against the British.
Calvert, G. Bunker Hill.
Davidson, M. Landing of Rochambeau, The.
Dunbar, P. Black Samson of Brandywine.
Emerson, R. Concord Hymn.
Freneau. To the Memory of the Brave
  Americans.
Hassett. Christmas.
Hopkinson, F. Battle of the Kegs, The.
Kandel. Spring 61.
Kipling, R. American Spirit speaks, The.
Longfellow, H. Paul Revere's Ride (The
  Landlord's Tale).
MacNeice. Jehu.
Seward. Verses Inviting Stella to Tea on the
  Public Fast-Day.
Shuckburg *et al.* Yankee Doodle.
Sigourney. God Save the Plough.
Simms, W. Swamp Fox, The.
Unknown. Boston in Distress.
  Dying Sergeant, The.
  Emily Geiger.
  Farewell to Kingsbridge.
  Little Britain.
Wesley, C. On Sympathisers with the
  American Revolution.
Whitman, W. Centenarian's Story, The.
Young, S. Epitaph for a Concord Boy.

Americans
Allston. America to Great Britain.
Auden. On the Circuit.
Chesterton, G. Ballad of Abbreviations, A.
Chin. Composed Near the Bay Bridge (after a
  wild party).
Deanovich. National Assessment.
Ferlinghetti, L. And Pablo Neruda / that
  Chilean omnivore of poetry.
  Baseball Canto.
Frost, R. Gift Outright, The.
Groch. Friend to Birds.
Hagedorn, J. Natural Death.
Hughes, L. I, Too, Sing America.
  Madam's Calling Cards.
Hugo, R. What Thou Lovest Well Remains
  American.
Jeffers, R. Ave Caesar.
Kipling, R. American Spirit speaks, The.
Knight, E. Idea of Ancestry, The.
Koch, K. You were wearing your Edgar Allan
  Poe printed cotton blouse.
Lawrence, D. English are so nice, The.
Lieberman, E. I Am an American.
Mathews, C. Masses, The.
McGrath, C. What They Drank.

McHugh, H. Oven Loves the TV Set, The.
Mori Ōgai. In Nara (two poems).
Pound, E. Soirée.
Shapiro, K. Boy-Man.
Simic. Crepuscule with Nellie.
Simpson, L. Inner Part, The.
  Runner, The.
Smith, W. American Primitive.
Very. Indian's Retort, The.
Walcott. Certain things here are quietly
  American.
Walker, M. For my people [everywhere
  singing their slave songs repeatedly: their].
Whitman, W. For You O Democracy.
  I hear America singing, the varied carols I
    hear.
  Prairie-grass dividing, its special odor
    breathing, The.
Williams, W. Impromptu: The Suckers.

Amherst, Massachusetts
Wilbur. Altitudes.

Amish, The
Kasdorf. Dying with Amish Uncles.
Owen, J. Visitation, The.
Updike. Amish are a surly sect, The.

Amnesia
Nagy, A. Like one who brought news from
  far.
Plath. Amnesiac.
Weigl. Amnesia.

Amon Ra
Reed, I. I Am a Cowboy in the Boat of Ra.

Amputees
Chernoff. Phantom Pain.
Coleman, H. Black Soldier Remembers, A.
Hood, T. Faithless Nelly Gray.
"MacDiarmid." In the Children's Hospital.
Ormond. Lament for a Leg.
Owen, W. Disabled.
Phạm Hổ. Hand, The.
Sassoon. Does It Matter?[—losing your legs?].
Shapiro, K. Leg, The.

Amsterdam, Netherlands
Garrigue. Amsterdam Letter.

Amusement Parks
Allbery. Carnies.
Brickley. Sheet lightning.
McClintock, M. Merry-go-round, The.
Moore, M. Old Amusement Park.
Pizzarelli. On the merry-go-round.
Rowan. Prometheus at Coney Island.

Anacreon
Antipater of Sidon. This is Anacreon's grave.
  Here lie.

Anarchism and Anarchists
Davis, T. In the Fire Lane.
Woodcock. Paper Anarchist Addresses the
  Shade of Nancy Ling Perry.

Ancestry and Ancestors
Ai Ch'ing. North, The.
Alexandru. Descending.
Ali, A. Snowmen.
Arghezi. Testament.
Aubert, A. Baptism.
Baca. Invasions.
Baker, H. Toward Guinea: For Larry Neal,
  1937–1981.
Bartusek. Royal Progress.
Bennett, G. Heritage.
Blaeser. Certificate of Live Birth.
Blandiana. From a Village.
Blunden. Forefathers.
Boland, E. Oral Tradition, The.
Brathwaite, E. Ancestors.
Brew. Ancestral Faces.
Brooks, G. Sundays of Satin-Legs Smith, The.
Cain, K. Returned American.
Chin. Barbarian Suite.
  Cauldron.
  Floral Apron, The.
Cortez. I See Chano Pozo.
Creeley. And.
Cullen, C. Heritage.
Curnow. Oldest of us burst into tears and
  cried, The.
Dabydeen, D. Coolie Odyssey.

Davidson, D. Descending Chestnut Ridge.
Diop, B. Diptych.
  Spirits.
  Viaticum.
Dobler. 1920 Photo.
Dumas, H. Black Star Line.
Emerson, R. Forerunners.
Feldman, I. Simple outlines, human shapes,
  daily acts, plain poses.
Frost, R. Pride of Ancestry.
Galguera. Alloy.
Geda. Steep eyes of wooden gods.
Gilbert, C. This Bridge Across.
Goldberg, B. Being Pharaoh.
González, A. Before I could call myself Ángel
  González.
Guiterman. Heredity.
Hagedorn, J. Song for My Father.
Hewitt, J. Search, The.
Hovanessian, D. Radio Yerevan.
Howe, S. Thorow.
Jeffers, L. Flesh of the Young Men Is
  Burning, The.
Kennelly. My Dark Fathers.
Kgositsile. In the Mourning.
Kinsella, T. Ancestor.
  His Father's Hands.
Klein, A. Heirloom.
Knight, E. Idea of Ancestry, The.
Komunyakaa. Salt.
Kunene. Elegy.
Levertov. Illustrious Ancestors.
Li K'ai-hsien. Prosperous Villager, The.
Li Tung-yang. To Yung-erh—Imitating a
  Work by Master Jade Stream.
Lowell, A. To Winky.
Lu Yu. Occasional Poem, A.
Lyon, G. Archaeology.
MacBeth. Draft for an Ancestor.
Manyarrows. Lakota Sister/Cherokee Mother.
Mora. Sonrisas.
Muir, E. Absent, The.
  Scotland 1941.
Newman, L. Poem for My Grandmother's
  Grandmother.
Oandasan. Song of Ancient Ways, The.
Olson, C. Chain of memory is resurrection I
  am a vain man, The.
Popa. Other World, The.
Quiller-Couch. Planted Heel, The.
Ramanujan. Elements of Composition.
Randall, D. Ancestors.
Root, J. Small Differences.
Rose. Story Keeper.
Rukeyser, M. Bunk Johnson Blowing.
Sanchez, S. Present.
Seaton, M. Grief.
Senghor. Elephant of Moissel, hear my pious
  prayer.
  In Memoriam.
  Night of Sine.
  Totem, The.
Shapiro, K. Nigger.
Shelton, R. Prophets, The.
Slomkowska. Alphabet by the Pool on a
  Sunday Afternoon, The.
Smart, C. For man is between the pinchers
  while his soul is shaping and purifying.
Smith, M. Stopping to Take Notes.
  Visit to the Village, A.
Sokolov. Everything as in a good old-
  fashioned novel.
Stevenson, R. Say not of me that weakly I
  declined.
Tate, J. My Great Great Etc. Uncle Patrick
  Henry.
Taylor, J. Squire's Pew, The.
Troupe. Sense of Coolness, A.
Unknown. Dynastic Hymn.
  Origin-Legend of the Chou Tribe.
  She Who First Bore Our People.
Valentine, J. Forgiveness Dream.
Walker, M. Lineage.
Wang Shih-chieng. Song of the Ch'in-Dynasty
  Mirror—Written for Yüan Sung-li.
Welburn. Bones and Drums.
Winchilsea. Upon My Lord Winchilsea's

Converting the Mount in His Garden to a Terrace.
Wright, C. Arkansas Traveller.
Yevtushenko. Heirs of Stalin, The.
Young Bear. Wadasa Nakamoon, Vietnam Memorial.
Zamora, D. Lineage.

Anchorage, Alaska
Harjo, J. Anchorage.

Anchors
Blight. Anchor, The.
Cynewulf. Anchor: "Oft I must strive with wind and wave."
Herrick. End of His Work, The.
His Hope or Sheet-Anchor.
Pitter. Portrait of a Gentleman.

Anci
Auvaiyar. Elegy: "If he found a little liquor."
Elegy: "Let day, let night, come no more."
Elegy: "This bright burning pyre."
His Welcome.

Andrea Doria (ship)
Hollander, J. Last Words.

Andrea del Sarto. See Sarto, Andrea del

Andromache
Homer. Andromache's Lamentation.
O my husband... / cut off from life so young! You leave me a widow.
Iremonger. Hector.
Sappho. Andromache's Wedding.

Andromeda
Hopkins, G. Andromeda.
Nicholls, J. Andromeda.

Anemones
Harwood, G. Sea Anemones, The.
Oppen. Words cannot be wholly transparent. And that is the.

Anesthesia
Hull, L. Fiat Lux.

Angels
Abse. Angels.
Alberti. Angels of the Ruins, The.
Apollinaire. I Imagine Angels.
On imagine les anges.
Bialik. And If the Angel Should Ask.
Blake, W. Angel, The.
Bontemps. Nocturne at Bethesda.
Brooks, M. Shade of Columbus, here thy relics rest.
Browning, R. Guardian-Angel, The.
Burns, R. To an Artist.
Carson, C. Slate Street School.
Causley. Angel's Song.
Christopher. 5°.
Cibulka. Mathematics.
Cole, H. 40 Days and 40 Nights.
Cowley, A. Gabriel's Appearance.
Dana, R. Chanting Cherubs, The [A Group by Greenough].
Dante Alighieri. Ladies that have intelligence in love.
Dickinson, E. God's Residence.
Little East of Jordan, A.
Donne. Air[e] and Angels.
Blow Your Trumpets.
Doolittle, H. This is no rune nor riddle.
Doty, M. Harbor Lights.
Doyle, S. Hell To Pay.
"Dylan." Three angels up above the street.
Eberhart, R. Vision.
Field, E. Angel's Visit, The.
Goldensohn, B. Post Mortem as Angels.
Graves, R. Gardener.
Hass, R. Privilege of Being.
Hawker. Are They Not All Ministering Spirits?
Hildegard von Bingen. Antiphon for the Angels.
Hopkins, G. Sonnet: "Shepherd's brow, fronting forked lightning, owns, The."
Howitt, M. Dying Child, The.
Huidobro. Canto I (excerpt).
Hunt, L. Abou Ben Adhem (may his tribe increase!).
Jackson, R. Angels of 1912 and 1972, The.
Jacobsen, R. Guardian Angel.

Johnson, L. Dark Angel, with thine aching lust.
Kamienska. Annunciation.
In the sixth month the angel Gabriel.
Kandel. First they slaughtered the angels.
Kelly, R. In June was a jar had.
Kirchwey. Natural History.
Levertov. Jacob's Ladder, The.
Where is the angel for me to wrestle?
Levi, P. Annunciation.
Levine, P. Angel Butcher.
Lewis, C. Sonnet: "Bible says Sennacherib's campaign was spoiled, The."
Longfellow, H. Legend of Rabbi Ben Levi, The.
Spanish Jew's Tale: Azrael, The.
MacBeth. Poem of Death, A.
Mackey, N. Song of the Andoumboulou.
Song of the Andoumboulou: 6.
Song of the Andoumboulou: 7.
Melville, H. Swamp Angel, The.
Menashe. Annunciation, The.
Merrill, J. Angel.
Mew. Trees Are Down, The.
Milosz, C. On Angels.
Mitchell, S. Annunciation, The.
Nagy, A. Horses and the Angels, The.
Winter Angel.
North, C. Air and Angels.
O'Hara, F. In Favor of One's Time.
Page, P. Images of Angels.
Pagis. Another Testimony.
Footprints.
Pinsky. Dante's Inferno, Canto XXXIV (The Final Canto).
Poe. Israfel.
Porter, A. Another Sarah.
Porter, P. Angel in Blythburgh Church, An.
Radnóti. Angel of Dread, The.
Ramsey, P. Angels take approaches, The.
Some enter by root.
Ray, D. On a Fifteenth-Century Flemish Angel.
Rich, A. Gabriel.
Rilke. Olive Garden, The.
Ross, W. On Angels.
Rossetti, C. Baby lies so fast asleep.
Rózewicz. Fight With An Angel.
Homework Assignment on the Subject of Angels.
Ryuichi. Every Morning After Killing Thousands of Angels.
Sachs, N. In the evening your vision widens.
Schultz, P. My Guardian Angel Stein.
Schuyler, J. Head, A.
Schwartz, D. Sarah.
Sears, E. It came upon the midnight clear.
Seaton, M. Wings.
Seferis. Les Anges Sont Blancs.
Sexton. Consorting with Angels.
Shakespeare, W. Sonnet 144.
Shapiro, K. Exile.
Sickness of Adam, The.
Smith, I. Law and the Grace, The.
Smith, S. Galloping Cat, The.
I rode with my darling in the dark wood at night.
No Categories!
Southwell. New Heaven, New War[re].
Spenser. Guardian Angels.
Stanton, M. Living Apart.
Stevens, W. Angel Surrounded by Paysans.
Szumigalski. Angels.
Tadic. At the Hairdresser.
Taggart, J. Body and Soul: Poem for Two Readers.
Trakl. De Profundis.
Unknown. Fairest Lord Jesus.
My Way's Cloudy.
Wesley, C. Wrestling Jacob.
Wieseltier. God's Fire upon Children ("God's fire upon cities").
Willard, N. Angels in Winter.
Wordsworth, W. She was a Phantom of delight.
Wright, J. Secret Gratitude, A.
Young, M. Angels, The.

Anger
"Akhmatova." Ah—you thought I'd be the type.
Allen, S. Moment Please, A.
Ammuvanar. What Her Girl Friend Said to Him ("Her soft plump shoulders").
Averill. Bad for You.
Awoonor. To the Eminent Scholar and Meddler.
Basheva. Business.
Baugh, E. Carpenter's Complaint, The.
Truth and Consequences.
Bible, O.T. Bible, Proverbs 15:1, The.
Bible, Proverbs 16:32, The.
Blake, W. Poison Tree, A.
Bly, R. Anger Against Children.
Bolamba. Fistful of News, A.
Bromley, A. Slow Men Working in Trees.
Bruner. Angry word is like a boomerang, An.
Chu Shu-chen. Spring Joy.
Clifton, L. Fury.
Darwish, M. Identity Card.
Sirhan Drinks His Coffee in the Cafeteria.
Daryush. Anger Lay by Me All Night Long.
Derricotte. Promise, The.
Saturday Night.
Fogel, A. Necessity, The.
Ford, C. There's No Place to Sleep in This Bed, Tanguy.
Fyleman. Temper.
Glück, L. Labor Day.
Goethe. Ill Humor.
Hacker, M. Fifteen to Eighteen.
Sonnet for Iva.
Hejinian. Mask of Anger, A.
Hernandez, D. Martin and My Father.
Herrick. To the Rose; a Song.
Hodgson, R. Gipsy Girl, The.
Hongo. Yellow Light.
Iverem. Daddy's Friends.
Iverson. Outrage.
James, D. Blind Man Who Sells Brushes, The.
Jemie. Toward a Poetics.
Katrovas. Beating, The.
Kaufman, S. Mothers, Daughters.
Kenyon, J. Portrait of a Figure near Water.
Khodasevich. Ballad: "Oh, quietly mad I'd like to be."
Koroneu. Funeral Eva.
Kunitz, S. Portrait, The.
Kwakiutl Oral Tradition. Warsong of the Kwakiutl.
Laing, K. Many Worlds Are Walked Once.
Lamb, C. et al. Anger in its time and place.
Le Bel. Foot Fire Burn Dance.
Leonard, T. Cold, Isn't It.
Fathers and Sons.
Levine, P. Fox, The.
Horse, The.
Louis, A. Dust World.
Ludvigson. Man Arrested in Hacking Death Tells Police He Mistook Mother-in-Law for Raccoon.
Macy, A. Peppery Man was cross and thin, The.
Mayakovsky. How I Became a Dog.
Mayer, B. Sonnet: "Thousand apples you might put in your theories."
McClure, M. Rant Block.
Meissner. Twisters.
Meng Chiao. Complaint of a Neglected Wife.
Meredith, G. It ended, and the morrow brought the task.
Modern Love.
Myles, E. Maxfield Parrish.
Neruda. Walking [or Walkin'] Around.
O'odham. War Songs.
Overstreet. Count Ten.
Pastorius. Penance, A.
Peacock, M. Anger Sweetened.
Piercy. Just Anger, A.
Rankin, J. Love Affair 36.
Rathenow. No Picture.
Rich, A. Phenomenology of Anger, The.
Rodgers, W. Lovers, The.
Rumi. Light you give off, The.
Sandburg, C. Choose.

Sappho.   Silent on the subject of vengeance.
   When rage invades your burning breast.
Savard.   Descent of Fire, The.
Shershenevich.   Plot with Bitterness.
Shūji.   Tanka: "To do away with anger."
Sidney, P.   Sonnet 74: "Love still a boy, and
   oft a wanton is."
Smith, S.   Anger's Freeing Power.
Soto.   Behind Grandma's House.
Spender, S.   Prisoners, The.
Sulpicia.   That you allow yourself this vast
   neglect of me.
Thomas, D.   Do not go gentle into that good
   night.
Thomas, E.   Execration, The.
Troupe.   Boomerang: A Blatantly Political
   Poem.
Tuqan, F.   Song of Becoming.
Unknown.   Temper.
   Today I lost my temper.
   Warsong of the Kwakiutl.
   Young Girl of Asturias, The.
Waniek.   April Rape.
Warsh.   Enmeshment.
Wickham.   Sick Assailant, The.
Yoshimi.   Trip to Berlin.
Yüan Mei.   Miscellaneous Feelings in the Sui
   Garden.
Zulauf.   Separation in Succasunna.
Zwicky.   Stone Dolphin, The.
See also **Quarrels**

Angkor Wat, Cambodia
Devlin, D.   Ank'hor Vat.

Angola
Andrade, C.   Fourth Poem of a Canto of
   Accusation.
Neto.   We Must Return.

Animal Migration
Bryant, W.   To A Waterfowl.
Field, R.   Something told the wild geese.

Animals
Amherst.   Verses Designed to Be Sent to Mr.
   Adams.
Amirthanayagam.   Elephants Are in the Yard,
   The.
Ammons.   Pet Panther.
Anderson, J.   Blue Animals, The.
Angira.   Look in the Past, A.
"Antler."   Somewhere Along the Line.
Atwood.   Animals in That Country, The.
Auden.   Fish in the unruffled lakes.
   Our hunting fathers told the story.
Avidan.   Minor Mythology.
Barnes, W.   Sam'el Down vrom Lon'on.
Benson, G.   Cat and the Pig, The.
Bishop, E.   Armadillo, The.
Blaser.   Ruler, The.
Blight.   Into the Ark.
Bly, R.   Extra Joyful Chorus for Those Who
   Have Read This Far, An.
Bobrowski.   Latvian Songs.
Brooke, L.   Johnny Crow's Garden.
Brooks, F.   Barnyard Melodies.
Bruchac.   Prayer: "Let my words."
Campbell, J.   Ad Limina.
"Carroll."   Little Man That Had a Little Gun,
   The.
   Lobster Quadrille, A.
Carryl, C.   Camel's Complaint, The.
Causley.   On Being Asked to Write a School
   Hymn.
Ceravolo.   Ho Ho Ho Caribou.
   Spring of Work Storm.
Chang, E.   After the Storm.
Chao Yi.   Rising Early in the Morning.
Chatain.   World of Darkness.
Ch'ien Ch'ien-i.   On the Road to Western Hill.
"Chukovskysr."   Telephone rang, The.
Clairmont.   Answers, The.
Clare, J.   Hares at Play.
Clifton, L.   What spells racoon to me.
Clouts.   Animal Kingdom.
Cooley.   Ararat.
Corso.   Mad Yak, The.
Cunningham, J.   Hymn to Joy.
Daumal.   Clavicles for a Great Poetic Game.
Davies, W.   Dumb World, The.

Dearmer.   Turkish Trench Dog, The.
Dewdney.   Grid Erectile.
Dickey, J.   Heaven of Animals, The.
   Hedge Life.
Dickinson, E.   Little Dog that wags his tail, A.
Donne.   Why are we[e] by all creatures waited
   on?
Dorset.   Peacock "At Home," The.
Duncan, R.   Little Language, A.
Enright, D.   Better Be Kind to Them Now.
Eskimo Oral Tradition.   Magic Words.
Ewing, J.   Burial of the Linnet, The.
Farjeon, E.   Mistress Malone.
Fenton, J.   Wild Ones[, The].
Flint, F.   Eau-Forte.
Follain.   Face the Animal.
Fumiko.   Tanka: "Eyes, The."
   Tanka: "In a posture."
Garrigue.   False Country of the Zoo.
Gates, L.   Killdeer, The.
Godfrey.   Radiant dog on doublecross, and I.
Goodrich.   Higglety, Pigglety, Pop!
Graves, R.   Allie, call the birds in.
Gray, J.   Mishka [is poet among the beasts].
Greig, A.   In the Tool-shed.
Hale, S.   Mary's Lamb [or Mary and Her
   Lamb].
Hall, D.   Sudden Things.
Han Yü.   Mornings the sparrow twitters
   seeking food.
Hayes, A.   Slaughter-House, The.
Holcroft.   Fool's Song.
Hollander, J.   Adam's Task.
Holub.   Experimental Animals.
Howard, R.   Lost Art, A.
Howitt, M.   Cry of the Animals, The.
Hughes, T.   Bull Moses, The.
   I see a bear.
   My Brother Bert.
James, D.   Love of Water Faucets, The.
Jeffers, R.   Hurt Hawks.
Jones, G.   Psalm to the Creatures.
Keithley.   When they leave the world will be
   at peace.
Kennedy, X.   Witnesses, The.
Kinnell.   Another Night in the Ruins.
   Cells Breathe in the Emptiness.
   When one has lived a long time alone.
Kipling, R.   Eddi's Service.
Knott.   Poem: "After your death."
Kumin, M.   Credo.
Lawrence, D.   Glory is of the sun, too, and the
   sun of suns.
   Self-Pity.
Lear, E.   Calico Pie.
   Quangle Wangle's Hat, The.
Levertov.   Come into animal presence.
   Else a great Prince in prison lies.
Levine, P.   Animals Are Passing from Our
   Lives.
Lipska.   That Moment.
Lovelace, R.   Her Muffe.
Lowry, M.   Xochitepec.
Lucretius.   How They Communicate.
MacCaig.   Byre.
   Feeding Ducks.
   Porpoises.
   Summer Farm.
"MacDiarmid."   Parley of Beasts.
MacNeice.   Pet Shop.
Maiden.   Taste.
Masaoka Shiki.   Among the poems I wrote
   with many pictures spread out before me[2].
Mathias, E.   Zoo Manners.
Meredith, W.   On Falling Asleep by Firelight.
Milton.   On the Detraction Which Followed
   upon My Writing Certain Treatises.
   Tenants of Paradise.
Miyazawa Kenji.   Tanka: "With red eyes."
"Monty Python."   All things dull and ugly.
Moore, M.   Monkeys, The.
   Pangolin, The.
   Snakes, Mongooses, Snake-Charmers and the
   Like.
Moss, T.   There will be animals to teach us.
Muir, E.   Animals, The.
Nash, O.   Exit, Pursued by a Bear.

Nemesianus.   When now the third revolving
   Moon appears.
Newcastle, M.   Discourse of Beasts, A.
   Sea Similized to Meadows and Pastures: the
   Mariners, to Shepherds: the Mast, to a May-
   Pole: the Fish, to Beasts, The.
Nichol.   Scraptures: 7th Sequence.
O'Keeffe.   Beasts and Birds.
Okigbo.   Lion-hearted cedar forest, gonads for
   our thunder.
Patchen.   Animal I wanted, The.
   Because It's Good to Keep Things Straight.
Pennant.   Wildebeest of Carmine Street, The.
Plath.   Zoo Keeper's Wife.
Po Chü-i.   Beginning of Summer, The.
Quiller-Couch.   Sage Counsel.
Ransom, J.   Spiel of [the] Three Mountebanks.
Reese, L.   Christmas Folk-Song, A.
Reeves, J.   Animals' Houses.
   Doze, The.
Richards, L.   After a Visit to the Natural
   History Museum.
Rochester, J.   Satire against Reason and
   Mankind, A.
Roethke.   For An Amorous Lady.
   Running Lightly over Spongy Ground.
Roscoe, W.   Butterfly's Ball [and the
   Grasshopper's Feast], The.
Rossetti, C.   Hurt no living thing; / Ladybird,
   nor butterfly.
Rukeyser, M.   All the Little Animals.
Sackville-West.   Young Stock.
Samio.   Tanka: "For a moment."
   Tanka: "On occasion."
Shūji.   Tanka: "Over my."
   Year's end, The.
Sidney, P.   Shepherd Song.
   Such maner time there was (what time I n'ot).
Simic.   Animal Acts.
Squire.   Stockyard, The.
Stein, G.   What Do I See.
Stephens, J.   Cage, The.
   Little things, that run, and quail.
Stern, G.   Behaving Like a Jew.
Stevens, W.   Poetry Is a Destructive Force.
Stevenson, A.   Giving Rabbit to My Cat
   Bonnie.
Stuart, D.   Mining in Killdeer Alley.
Swenson, M.   Hair, The.
   News from the Cabin.
Swirszczynska.   I Talk to My Body.
Szymborska.   In Praise of Self-Deprecation.
   Unexpected Meeting.
Tadic.   Dogs Gambol.
Thackeray.   At the Zoo.
Tippett.   Familiar Friends.
Unknown.   Animal Fair.
   Barnyard, The.
   Birds of a feather flock together.
   Fiddle-I-Fee.
   Friendly Beasts, The.
   Frog went a-courting, away did ride, huh-huh,
   A.
   How They Sleep.
   Incantation Songs of the Klamath Lake People.
   Incantations of Modoc Conjurers.
   Kindness to Animals.
   Kitty Alone.
   Little Lamb, A.
   Martin and His Man.
   Summer Song.
   Tree in the Wood, The.
Vallejo.   I have a terrible fear of being an
   animal.
Van Doren.   And did the animals in Noah's
   ark.
Viiding.   George Marrow's 1011th Dream.
Virgil.   Of Bees.
   Signs of Rain.
Warren, R.   Caribou.
Wells, C.   How To Tell the Wild Animals.
Whitman, W.   Animals.
   Ox-Tamer, The.
   World below the brine, The.
Wilbur.   Beasts in their major freedom /
   Slumber in peace tonight.
Wills, J.   Day wears on, The.

Winchilsea. Hog, the Sheep and Goat, Carrying to a Fair, The.
Wood, W. Kingly lyon, and the strong arm'd beare, The.
Wright, J. In Shame and Humiliation.
Wright, J. Pelicans.
Wright, K. Let's Hear it for the Limpet.
Young Bear. Significance of a Water Animal, The.
Zabolotsky. Face of the Horse, The.
Zarzyski. Silos.
See also **Death of Animals**

Animism
Gardner, I. That "Craning of the Neck."
Rich, A. Trees inside are moving out into the forest, The.

Anne, Queen of England
Unknown. I am Queen Anne, of whom 'tis said.

Anniversaries
Bruner. Wedding Anniversary.
Donne. Anniversary [or Anniversarie], The.
Gray, D. Golden Wedding, The.
Hewett, D. Anniversary.
Lattimore. Anniversary.
Lovelace, R. Anniversary on the Hymeneals of My Noble Kinsman, Thomas Stanley, Esquire, An.
Merwin, W. For the Anniversary of My Death.
Probyn. Anniversaries.
Sluchevsky. Nothing but anniversaries, anniversaries...

Annunciation of the Virgin
Castellanos. Nazareth.
Donne. Annunciation.
Gunn, T. Jesus and His Mother.
Kamienska. Annunciation.
Luke 1:26–38; In the sixth month the angel Gabriel.
Levi, P. Annunciation.
Menashe. Annunciation, The.
Messerli. Annunciation, The.
Mitchell, S. Annunciation, The.
Muir, E. Annunciation, The.
Smith, K. Annunciation.

Antarctica
Stoutenburg. Traveller's Guide to Antarctica.

Anteaters
Moore, M. Pangolin, The.

Antelopes
Senghor. Song of the Initiate.
Yukitsuna. At the zoo (two poems).
See also **Elands**

Anthony, Saint
McGinley. Temptations of Saint Anthony, The.

Anthropology and Anthropologists
Arnett. Powwow.
Daruwalla. Of Mohenjo Daro at Oxford.

Anti-Semitism
Bruck. Pretty soon / when people hear a quiz show expert.
Feinstein, E. Annus Mirabilis 1989.
Lifshin. After the Anti-Semitic Calls on a Local Talk Station.
Rodriguez, J. How Come the Truck-Loads?
Wayman. Hating Jews.
Yevtushenko. Babii Yar*.

Anticipation
Akazome Emon. I should not have waited.
Ashbery. At North Farm.
One Thing That Can Save America, The.
Beresford. Courtship, The.
Berryman. Sonnet 115: "All we were going strong last night this time."
Browning, E. Sonnet: "Belovéd, my Belovéd, when I think."
Browning, R. In Three Days.
Coleridge, S. Blossoming of the Solitary Date-Tree, The.
Das, M. Horses.
Doolittle, H. At Ithaca.
Everwine. From the Meadow.
Ferlinghetti, L. I am waiting for my case to come up.

Fujiwara no Sadaie. You do not come, and I wait.
Hayden, R. Night-Blooming Cereus, The.
Hugo, R. Skykomish River Running.
Ignatow, D. In the Dark.
Kuzmina-Karavayeva. Everything has been checked. My inventory is ready.
Larkin, P. Next, Please.
Lawrence, D. Suspense.
Levy, A. Twilight.
Matthews, M. Realarro.
Meredith, G. Along the garden terrace, under which.
Miles, J. When I was eight, I put in the left-hand drawer.
Mitchell, S. Maps.
Murasaki Shikibu. Someone passes.
Otomo no Sakanoé, L. You say, "I will come."
Palmer, O. Wasting Time.
Shakespeare, W. Sonnet 118.
Shune. All during a night.
Sosei. She said she would come.
Unknown. I waited for my.
Vigny. Helena.
Yevtushenko. I am a purse.

Antietam Campaign (1862)
Unknown. Battle of Antietam Creek, The.

Antigone
Nathan, L. Letter.
Ray, H. Antigone and Oedipus.

Antiques
Cheng Hsieh. Collecting Antiques.
Corke. Chair, Dog, and Clock.
Dickinson, E. We outgrow love like other things.

Antonioni, Michelangelo
Holden, S. In Praise of Antonioni.

Antony (Marc Antony)
Heredia. Antony and Cleopatra.
Lytle, W. Antony and Cleopatra.
Pascal. Tact.
Shakespeare, W. Welcome from Egypt, sir.
Simpson, L. Early in the Morning.
Williams, W. To Mark Anthony in Heaven.

Antrim. *See* **County Antrim, Northern Ireland**

Ants
Benson, A. Ant-Heap, The.
Campbell, D. Anguish of Ants, The.
De la Mare. Immanent.
"Douglas." Ant-Hills.
Frost, R. Departmental.
Jacobsen, R. Rubber.
Johnson, S. *ad. fr.* the Bible, Proverbs, 6, 6.
Joyce, J. Ondt and the Gracehoper, The.
Knott. Ant Dodger.
Lovelace, R. Ant, The.
Makarov. Twenty years / I tamed an ant.
Mori Ōgai. Tanka: "During a break."
Nash, O. Ant has made himself illustrious, The.
Emmet is an ant (archaic), The.
Okudzhava. I need to worship someone.
Rosenblatt. Ant Trap, The.
Sharpless. "Go to the Ant."
Wallace, R. Dog's Song.
Yoshimi. Tanka: "Spoon, A."
Zarin. Ant Hill, The.

Antwerp, Belgium
Ross, A. Antwerp: Musée Des Beaux-Arts.

Anxiety
Atwood. Up.
Auvaiyar. What She Said, Thinking of Him Crossing the Wilderness Alone.
Baillie, J. Song: Woo'd and married and a'.
Berry, W. Peace of Wild Things, The.
Blake, W. Little Boy Lost, The ("Father, father, where are you going?")
Bukowski. I Am Dead But I Know the Dead Are Not Like This.
Cheney, E. Overheard in an Orchard.
Chhotray. Fear.
Chu Shu-chen. Stormy Night in Autumn.
Creeley. Waiting.
Cuddihy. Pendulum, The.
Di Prima. Abyss.

Dickinson, E. You love me—you are sure.
Erwin. For Someone Temporizing.
Frost, R. Armful, The.
Garrigue. Forest.
Gerstler. Ups and Downs.
Gillan. My Daughter at 14: Christmas Dance, 1981.
Hall, D. Shudder [, The].
Hall, H. Walkers at Dusk.
Herbert, G. Conscience.
Hopkins, G. She schools the flighty pupils of her eyes.
Justice, D. Sadness, An Improvisation.
Kapilar. What She Said ("He is from those mountains").
Kumin, M. Excrement Poem, The.
Lagier. Second Class Citizen.
Lifshin. After the Anti-Semitic Calls on a Local Talk Station.
Lowry, M. Death of a Oaxaquenian.
MacNeice. Prognosis.
Magee, W. Are You Ready?
McGough, R. First Day at School.
McGrath, T. Letter for Marian, A.
Moon, C. Poem at Forty.
Mora. Elena.
Immigrants.
Morgan, R. Phobiphilia.
Mullen, H. Jump City.
Oppen. Department of Plants and Structures—obsolete, the old name.
Ovid. 1.2.
Ramanujan. Snakes.
Ronsard. Elegy 19 (A Kiss): "Without a soul, a mind, a breath, or pulse."
Simic. Clouds Gathering.
Stein, G. Teachers taught her, The.
Sweeney, M. Couple Waiting, A.
Trần Té Xuơ'ng. Tomorrow, should I fail, I'll go away.
Trương Anh Thụy. First Day of School, The.
Tù' Diễn Dồn. Long Night, The.
Uloccanar. What Her Girl Friend Said, the Lover within Earshot, behind a Fence.
Vinz. Sins of the Fathers.
Warren, R. Fairy Story.
Weaver, M. Improvisation for Piano.
Weingarten. Four Seasons of His Discontent.
Whitehead, J. About a Year After He Got Married He Would Sit Alone in an Abandoned Shack in a Cotton Field Enjoying Himself.
Wright, C. Laguna Blues.
Young, D. Storms.

Apartheid
Abrahams, P. Me, Colored.
Currey. Landscape of Violence.
Jonker. Child Who Was Shot Dead by Soldiers at Nyanga, The.
Plumpp. Poet.
Rive. Where the Rainbow Ends.
Ross, A. In Bloemfontein.
Sepamla. Measure for Measure.
Unknown. Pass Office Song.
Vilakazi. In the Gold Mines.

Apartments
Ali, A. Previous Occupant, The.
Cooper, J. Rent.
Druk. Communal Krakovyak.
Gunn, T. Apartment Cats.
Hogan, L. New Apartment.
Hughes, L. Madam and the Rent Man.
Rich, A. Living in Sin.

Apathy
Arif. Ghazal.
Atwood. Notes towards a Poem That Can Never Be Written.
Auden. Musée des Beaux Arts.
Clare, J. Written in a Thunder Storm July 15th, 1841.
De la Mare. Pooh!
Enzensberger, H. At Thirty-three.
Holiday, Fear.
Song for Those Who Know.
Hughes, T. View of a Pig.
Ignatow, D. First on TV, A.
Lindsay, V. Leaden-Eyed, The.

Patmore, C. Revelation, The.
Shapiro, K. Hospital.
Stafford, W. Ritual to Read to Each Other, A.
Stevenson, R. Celestial Surgeon, The.
Studdert-Kennedy. Indifference.

Apes
Barker, G. My sister Clarissa spits twice if I kiss her.
Danner. Best Loved of Africa.
Donne. It quickened [*or* quickned] next a toyful[l] ape, and so.
Edson, R. Ape.
Huxley, A. First Philosopher's Song.
Koertge. Thing Is to Not Let Go of the Vine, The.
Robinson, A. Darwinism.
Tate, J. Teaching the Ape to Write Poems.

Aphrodisiacs
McGuckian. Aphrodisiac, The.
Sharpless. In Praise of Cocoa, Cupid's Nightcap.

Aphrodite
Anacreon. Eros, playing among the roses.
Bryher. Blue Sleep.
Euripides. Blessed are they.
"Field." To the Winter Aphrodite.
Homer. Mars and Venus.
Lawrence, D. Man of Tyre went down to the sea, The.
Mimnermus. There Is No Joy Without Aphrodite.
Nossis. Let us go to the temple.
Olson, C. Ring of, The.
Plato. Lais to Aphrodite.
Sappho. On your throne, a marvel of art, immortal.
Song for the Goddess of Love.
Seneca. Medea's Frenzy.
Unknown. Aphrodite reveals herself.
But *Jove* at length with just Resentment fir'd.
When Aphrodite saw the *Aphrodite* of Knidos.
Warren, R. Myth on Mediterranean Beach: Aphrodite as Logos.
See also **Venus (goddess)**

Apocalypse
Bayliss. Apocalypse and Resurrection.
Graves, R. Interruption.
Haines, J. Choosing a Stone.
Dürer's Vision.
Holmes, O. Latter-Day Warnings.
Hummer, T. Apocatastasis Foretold in the Shape of a Canvas of Smoke.
Kovner. Front Page.
Lowell, R. Harriet.
MacLeish. Long Hot Summer.
McAuley, J. One Tuesday in Summer.
McGrath, T. End of the world: it was given to me to see it, The.
Melo Neto. End of the World, The.
Muir, E. Horses.
Reverdy. Inn.
Sherry, J. Hazardous Waste.
Tahmisic. Limbo.
Unknown. Steal Away to Jesus.
Upton, C. When I was very young.
Wilbur. Advice to a Prophet.
Wylie. Doomsday.
See also **End of the World; Judgment Day**

Apollinaire, Guillaume
Ginsberg, A. At Apollinaire's Grave.
Grier. I Am Almost Asleep.
Kaufman, B. Unhistorical Events.
Unknown. Apollinaire said.

Apollo
Bacchylides. Yet of all that Hellas holds.
Byron, G. Canto 4.
Ceravolo. Crocus Turn and Gods, The.
Coolidge, C. In Nora's House with Rilke's Apollo.
Custance. Hyacinthus.
Doolittle, H. Evadne.
Douglas, L. Rejected.
Drayton. Sacrifice to Apollo, The.
Drummond, W. Invocation: "Pheobus, arise! / And paint the sable skies."
"Field." Prologue.

Herrick. Canticle to Apollo, A.
Homer. Apollo Defeats Patroclus.
Irwin, M. Robert Mapplethorpe's Photograph of Apollo (1988).
Melville, H. Ravaged Villa, The.
Meredith, G. Phoebus with Admetus.
Prudentius. Oracles are dumm, The.
Rilke. Archaic Torso of Apollo.
Robinson, A. Search for Apollo, A.
Robinson, E. Many Are Called.
Seneca. Power of love over gods them selves, The.
Shelley, P. Hymn of Apollo.
Stallings. Apollo Takes Charge of His Muses.
Tchernichowsky. Before the Statue of Apollo.
Unknown. And you (O *Delian* Virgins) doe me grace.
O, let not e'er this quarrel be averred!
Veneris. Over sky and land and down under the sea.
Waller, E. Story of Phoebus and Daphne Applied, [etc.], The.
Winchilsea. Circuit of Apollo, The.
Winters, Y. Apollo and Daphne.

Apoplexy. *See* **Strokes**

Apostles
Dickinson, E. Of Paul and Silas it is said.
Herrick. Salutation.
Pound, E. Ballad of the Goodly Fere.
Schwartz, D. Starlight like Intuition Pierced the Twelve.
Smart, C. Let Peter rejoice with the Moon Fish who keeps up the life in the waters by night.
St Philip and St James.
Southwell. Christs Sleeping Friends.
Tate, A. Twelve, The.
Unknown. Matthew, Mark, Luke and John.
Williams, O. Last Supper, The.

Appalachia
Fox, R. Another Kind of Burning.
Weeks, R. Appalachian Front.

Apple Blossoms
Farrar, J. Comparison, A.

Apple Trees and Apples
Barker, G. How many apples grow on the tree?
Bogan, L. Crossed Apple, The.
Booth, P. Original Sequence.
Brown, R. This is no baby skin—.
Causley. Apple-Tree Man, The.
Cummings, E. It's over a(see just).
Dauenhauer. Tlingit Concrete Poem.
De la Mare. Miss T.
Drinkwater. Moonlit Apples.
Dufault. Burden.
"Dylan." Don't ya tell Henry.
Freneau. On Observing a Large Red-Streak Apple.
Frost, R. After Apple-Picking.
Unharvested.
Wood-Pile, The.
Hall, D. Apples.
Handlin. Sunset.
Hazo. Yellow Delicious.
Heitzman. March.
Hotham. Waiting room quiet.
Humphreys, E. Apple Tree and a Pig, An.
Kaufman, S. Apples.
Keats. Sharing Eve's Apple.
Larkin, P. As Bad as a Mile.
Lawrence, D. Medlars and Sorb-Apples.
Mystic.
Leuty. Apple Harvest.
Livesay, D. Eve.
Machi. Tanka: "With a serene look."
Macpherson, J. Garden of the Sexes, The.
Major, C. Apple Core.
Martin, W. Apple Orchard in the Spring, An.
McClintock, M. Twisting inland.
Merriam, E. Counting-out Rhyme.
Meyers, L. Apple-Eater, The.
Mitchison. Midsummer Apple Tree, The.
Murphy, E. Thank you, Mr Rason, for the Apples.
Nagy, A. Horses and the Angels, The.
Nemerov. Primer of the Daily Round, A.

Okamoto. Tanka: "Stark naked."
Parker, H. Apple Blossoms.
Philips, J. Apple-Culture.
Porter, A. Another Sarah.
Roseliep. On the apple.
Ross, D. On Apples.
Rossetti, C. Apple Gathering, An.
Rossetti, D. Orchard-Pit, The.
Salter. Young Girl Peeling Apples.
Sappho. One Girl.
Scannell. Apple-raid, The.
Snodgrass, W. Old Apple Trees.
Stone, R. Green Apples.
Tomlinson, C. Paring the Apple.
Unknown. Girl threw an apple to a cloud, A.
Harry Parry.
I will give my love an apple without e'er a core.
St. Paul's Steeple.
To My Valentine.
Updike. September.
Valek. Apple from the cupboard rolled to the floor, The.
Van Doren. Apple Hell.
Virgil. Not seeing.
Wilbur. John Chapman.
Yeats. Song Of Wandering Aengus, The.

Apprentices
Chaucer. Cook's Tale, The.
Muldoon, P. Sushi.
Unknown. Sheffield 'Prentice, The.

Approval
Hamill, G. Limerick: "'If you're aristocratic,' said Nietzsche."

Apricot Trees and Apricots
Cassian. Vegetable Destiny.
Isanos. Apricot Tree.
Meng Chiao. Don't let freezing hands play with these pearls.
In vain I gather up these stars from the ground.
It must have been a single thread of tears.
T'ang Hsien-tsu. Hsiu-chou.
Yüan Mei. Things Seen.

April
Benét, S. For City Spring.
Bourne, V. Silkworm, The.
Bridges, R. April, 1885.
Browning, R. Home-Thoughts, From Abroad.
Carman, B. *et al.* Earth's Lyric.
Davies, M. Day before April, The.
Dunbar-Nelson. April is on the way!
"Field." Prologue.
Grimké, A. At April.
Grosholz. Remembering the Ardèche.
Gurney, I. April Gale.
Hughes, L. April Rain Song.
Jeffers, R. Gale in April.
Keyes, S. Elegy: "April again, and it is a year again."
Klein, A. Break-up, The.
Levine, P. Sleepless Night, A.
Loveman. (April Rain).
Lowell, A. April.
Masefield. West Wind, The.
Mayer, G. April Poem.
Millay, E. Song of a Second April.
Spring.
Nesbit, E. Dead to the Living, The.
Nyka-Niliunas. Lied.
Oliver, M. Blossom.
Pastan. April.
Ray, H. April.
Sandburg, C. Three Spring Notations on Bipeds.
Snodgrass, W. April Inventory.
Solomos, D. Temptation.
Summers, H. April Fool.
Taylor, B. Aprilly.
Turner, F. April Wind.
Unknown. All Fools' Day.
Watson, S. Song: "April, April, / Laugh thy girlish laughter."
Winstanley, J. Epigram on the First of April.

April Fool's Day
Mayer, G. April Poem.
Unknown. All Fools' Day.

Aquariums
Gunn, T.   Aquarium, The.
Hammial.   Petit Guignol.
Hassall.   Tropical Fish.
Kunio.   Tanka: "After death."
Lowell, R.   For the Union Dead.
Machi.   Tanka: "Somehow this impulse."
Martin, C.   Sharks at the New York Aquarium.
Revell.   Hotel Sander, The.
Wright, G.   Aquarium.
Aquinas, St. Thomas. See Thomas Aquinas, Saint
Arab-Israeli Wars
Pagis.   November '73.
Wieseltier.   Caution Prevents Accidents.
Arabia
Falkner.   Arabia.
Tennyson, A.   Arabian Night Garden, An.
Recollections of The Arabian Nights.
Arabs
Blind.   Fantasy, A.
Darwish, M.   Identity Card.
Hamod, S.   Dying with the Wrong Name.
Kaye/Kantrowitz.   Jerusalem Shadow.
Marshall, J.   Sesame.
Norton, C.   Arab's Farewell to His Horse, The.
Nye, N.   Blood.
My Father and the Figtree.
Small Vases from Hebron, The.
Ravikovitch.   Hovering at a Low Altitude.
Taylor, B.   Bedouin Song.
Thompson, F.   Arab Love-Song, An.
Arachne
Kazantzis.   Arachne.
Aran Islands, Ireland
Unknown.   Arran.
Arawak Indians
Fergus.   Ethnocide.
McFarlane, B.   Arawak Prologue.
Arbor Day
Abbey, H.   What do we plant when we plant the tree?
Morris, G.   Woodman, spare that tree!
Arbus, Diane
Nemerov.   To D———, Dead by Her Own Hand.
Arcadia
Auden.   Vespers.
Symonds.   On a Picture by Poussin Representing Shepherds in Arcadia.
Archaeology and Archaeologists
Betjeman.   Archaeological Picnic, The.
Daruwalla.   Of Mohenjo Daro at Oxford.
Murphy, R.   Archaeology of Love, The.
Rich, A.   Of simple choice they are the villagers; their clothes come.
Sorley.   Barbury Camp.
Storace.   Archaeology of Divorce, The.
Archery
Chuang Tzu.   Need to Win, The.
Gascoigne.   Gascoigne's Woodmanship.
Homer.   Suitors watch Ulysses string the bow, The.
Longfellow, H.   Arrow and the Song, The.
Villa.   To become an archer.
Wat.   Japanese Archery.
Architecture and Architects
"Ern Malley."   Baroque Exterior.
Evans, A.   On Sir John Vanbrugh [Architect].
Fenton, J.   South Parks Road.
Hall, J.   Hous-keping's dead, *Saturio:* wot'st thou where?
Hirsch, E.   When Skyscrapers Were Invented in Chicago.
Jones, A.   Foot, The.
Kipling, R.   Dedication, A: "My new-cut ashlar takes the light."
Melville, H.   Greek Architecture.
Orban, O.   Peace Pillar.
Arctic
Booth, P.   Stefansson Island.
Gunn, T.   From the Highest Camp.
Kibkarjuk.   Song of the Rejected Woman.
Nicholls, J.   Polar Cub.
Spender, S.   Polar Exploration.

Argentina
Mandel, E.   Madwomen of the Plaza de Mayo, The.
Arguments
Publius Terentius Afer.   CHREMES.   Pese anger not thyself so I thee pray.
See also **Quarrels**
Ariadne
Nonnus.   Dionysiaca.
Arion
Ridler.   On a Picture by Michele Da Verona, of Arion as a Boy Riding upon a Dolphin.
Aristocracy
Burns, R.   Verses Intended to Be Written below a Noble Earl's Picture.
Unknown.   Vicar of Bray, The.
Williams, W.   Impromptu: The Suckers.
Aristotle
Cowley, A.   To Mr. Hobbes [*or* Hobs].
Stafford, W.   Humanities Lecture.
Vallejo.   And don't bother telling me anything.
Arithmetic
Adcock, F.   Halfway Street, Sidcup.
Brownjohn.   Common Sense.
"Carroll."   Sum, A.
Arizona (state)
Carruth, H.   Rimrock, Where It Is.
Santos, S.   Near the Desert Test Sites.
Zukofsky, L.   In Arizona / (how many years in the mountains).
Ark, The
"Adunis."   New Noah, The.
Blight.   Into the Ark.
Higgins, F.   Captain Noah.
Kendall, M.   Vision of Noah, The.
Levertov.   Ache of marriage, The.
Mansour, J.   Beyond the breakers.
Nemerov.   Fall Again, The.
Ombres.   Ballad of Noah's Daughter.
Pagis.   Ararat.
Thomas, D.   Author's Prologue.
Tomlinson, C.   Ararat.
Wallace, R.   Problem in History, A.
Warren, R.   Gold Glade.
Wright, J.   Pelicans.
See also **Noah**
Arkansas (state)
Angelou.   My Arkansas.
Ortiz.   Bend in the River.
Unknown.   State of Arkansas, The.
Walcott.   Arkansas Testament, The.
Wright, C.   Arkansas Traveller.
Armada. See Spanish Armada
Armenia and Armenians
Hill, G.   Song from Armenia, A.
Ishkhan.   Armenian Language Is the Home of the Armenian, The.
Siamanto.   Dance, The.
Grief.
Tekeyan.   Country of Dust, The.
Armies
Bible, *O.T.*   There were some shepherds living in the same part of the country.
Braun, V.   New Purpose of Hadrian's Army, The.
Homer.   Night Piece: the Trojans outside Troy.
Joyce, J.   I hear an army charging upon the land.
Melville, H.   Night-March, The.
Pagis.   Siege.
Ts'ao Ts'ao.   Song on Enduring the Cold.
Armistice
Hardy, T.   And There Was a Great Calm.
Hillyer.   Eternal Return, The.
Oxenham.   Where Are You Going, Greatheart?
Sassoon.   Everyone Sang.
Schwartz, D.   Today Is Armistice, a Holiday.
Van Dyke.   America's Welcome Home.
See also **Peace**
Armstrong, Johnie (Scots, *fl.* **1530)**
Unknown.   Johnie Armstrong.
Armstrong, Louis
Allen, S.   I Say, Mr. A.
Fabio.   For Louis Armstrong, A Ju-Ju.

Moerman.   Louis Armstrong.
Tolson.   Satchmo.
Armstrong, William, (*fl.* **1596)**
Unknown.   Kinmont Willie.
Army Life
Brownjohn.   Class Incident from Graves.
Campo.   Battle Hymn of the Republic, The.
Dawe, B.   Weapons Training.
Day, J.   North Sea.
Ewart.   Officers' Mess.
Ferry.   Soldier, The.
Fuller, R.   Spring 1942.
Grenfell, J.   Prayer for Those on the Staff.
Herbert, S.   General inspecting the trenches, The.
Herbert, A.   After the Battle.
Housman, A.   Grenadier.
New Mistress, The.
Jarmain.   Embarkation, 1942.
Jarrell.   Second Air Force.
Kipling, R.   Boots.
Danny Deever.
'Eathen in 'is blindness bows down to wood an' stone, The.
Gentlemen-Rankers.
Gunga Din.
Mandalay.
Kirstein.   Rank.
Lewis, A.   All day it has rained, and we on the edge of the moors.
Infantry.
Mori Ōgai.   Tanka: "Some medals."
Nichols, R.   Noon.
Plumpp.   Clinton.
Rosenberg, I.   Troop ship, The.
Sassoon.   Stand-to: Good Friday Morning.
Service.   Pot of Tea, A.
Shanks.   Going In to Dinner.
Shapiro, K.   Troop Train.
Smith, A.   Political Intelligence.
Stevenson, R.   Armies in the Fire.
Unknown.   I've lost my rifle and bayonet.
Sure, a little bit of shrapnel fell from out the sky one day.
We are Fred Karno's army.
Vogelsang.   Which Letter?
Wang Ts'an.   Joining the Army: A Song.
This frontier post brings me sorrow.
Warner, S.   Some Make This Answer.
West, A.   Night Patrol, The.
Whitman, W.   Bivouac on a Mountain Side.
By the bivouac's fitful flame.
Cavalry Crossing a Ford.
Wieseltier.   On Guard.
Wu Wei-yeh.   Ballad of Yüan-yüan.
Yang Chi.   Reviewing the Troops at Kuei-lin with Military Inspectors Chiang And Chang.
See also **Soldiers**
Arnold, Matthew
Hecht, A.   Dover Bitch, The.
Arranged Marriage. See Marriage, Arranged
Arrows
DuPlessis, R.   Where is the bird?
Longfellow, H.   Arrow and the Song, The.
Mnasalces.   Promachus hangs here.
Radauskas.   Arrow in the Sky.
Yosano.   Tanka: "Warring heaven."
Art and Artists
Alegría.   Ars Poetica.
Allston.   Art.
On Rembrant; Occasioned by His Picture of Jacob's Dream.
On Seeing the Picture of Æolus by Pelegrino Tibalbi, in the Institute at Bologna.
On the Group of the Three Angels Before the Tent of Abraham, by Raffaelle, in the Vatican.
On the Statue of an Angel, by Bienaimé, in the Possession of J.S. Copley Greene, Esq.
To My Venerable Friend, the President of the Royal Academy.
Aretino.   If famous Apelles with his hand of art.
Auden.   Composer, The.
Baraka.   Black Art.
State/meant.

Baudelaire. Gypsies on the Move.
Bawer. On Leaving the Artists' Colony.
Berryman. Life, friends, is boring. We must not say so.
Bishop, E. Monument, The.
  One Art.
Blake, W. On Sir Joshua Reynolds.
  Orator Prigg.
Bogan, L. To an Artist, to Take Heart.
Bridges, R. Art is the true and happy science of the soul.
Brooks, G. Chicago Picasso, The.
Browning, E. Hiram Powers' "Greek Slave."
Browning, R. How It Strikes a Contemporary.
  Youth and Art.
Burns, R. To an Artist.
Campbell, D. Lovers, The.
Carpenter, W. Girl Writing a Letter.
Carruth, H. This Decoration.
Catullus. Carmen 65 ("Grief reached across the world to get me").
Chao Meng-fu. Admonition to Myself, An.
Cheng Hsieh. For Contemporary Artist Pien Wei-Ch'I.
Cherry, K. Bride of Quietness, The.
Clark, T. Suicide with Squirtgun.
Clarke, A. Japanese Print.
Cole, T. Painter, A.
Coleridge, S. Apologia pro Vita Sua.
Connolly, C. On Geoffrey Grigson.
Creeley. Figures, The.
Cummings, E. If i have made, my lady, intricate.
Davie. With the Grain.
Dischell. Chamber, The.
Duchamp. Speculations.
Dugan, A. Against the Text "Art Is Immortal."
Eberhart, R. Cancer Cells, The.
Edson, R. Performance at Hog Theater, A.
Éluard, P. Invention, The.
Emanuel, L. Sleeping, The.
Emerson, R. Art.
Ernst, M. Hundred Headless Woman, The.
Escoffery. Tricks of the Trade.
Fawcett, B. Hand, The.
Ferlinghetti, L. Monet's Lilies Shuddering.
"Field." La Gioconda.
Forbes, J. Four Heads & How to Do Them.
Fox, S. Peaches.
Galbreath. Limerick: "There once was an artist called Pat."
Gergely. Upon a Renaissance Carving.
Goethe. Nature and Art.
Graves, R. Epitaph on an Unfortunate Artist.
Greger. Piranesi in L.A.
Guest, B. Roses.
  Wild gardens overlooked by night lights.
  Parking.
Gumilyov. Sixth Sense, The.
Gunn, T. Confessions of the Life Artist.
  Expression.
Hacker, M. Ballad of Ladies Lost and Found.
Hass, R. Image, The.
Hayes, A. Much Ado About Nothing, Thanksgiving, 1972.
Hecht, A. Death the Painter.
Herbert, Z. What Mr. Cogito Thinks About Hell.
Herlin. Echo of fireplace on the dividing wall, An.
Herrick. Art above Nature, to Julia.
Hewitt, J. From a Museum Man's Album.
Hill, G. Pre-Raphaelite Notebook, A.
Holub. One-Way Conversation About Radio City Music Hall, A.
Hooper, V. Lost in the Galleries.
Hovey. Accident in Art.
Howard, R. Nikolaus Mardruz to his Master Ferdinand, Count of Tyrol, 1565.
  Venetian Interior, 1889.
Hsieh Chin. Song of Cursive Calligraphy.
Hsü Wei. I Tried to Exchange Two Painting for Some Grain But Failed.
Irwin, M. Robert Mapplethorpe's Photograph of Apollo (1988).
Jacobsen, R. Cobalt.

Jeffers, R. Artist, An.
Jennings. Works of Art.
Johnson, J. Before a Painting.
Justice, D. Anonymous Drawing.
Kates. No altarpiece includes the painter.
Kaufman, B. To My Son Parker, Asleep in the Next Room.
Keats. On Seeing the Elgin Marbles.
Khlebnikov, V. Writers of the knife are we!
Kipling, R. Conundrum of the Workshops, The.
  Evarra and His Gods.
  When Earth's last picture is painted and the tubes are twisted / and dried.
Kumin, M. Louise Bourgeois Exhibit.
Kunze, R. End of ARt, The.
Lamb, E. Shimmering beneath the glaze.
Landor, W. On His Seventy-Fifth Birthday.
Lanier, S. Clover.
  To Bayard Taylor.
Le Gallienne. To the Reader.
Lee-Hamilton. Luca Signorelli to His Son.
Levertov. Art.
Li K'ai-hsien. Sent to the Painter, Lu Hsiao-feng.
Li Meng-yang. Song of Lin Liang's Painting "Two Horned Falcons."
Livesay, D. Three Emily's, The.
Lucilius. Eutychus the painter / Fathered twenty sons.
MacLeish. Corporate Entity.
Maiden. New.
Manilius. From whose large mouth for verse all that since live.
Mason, W. Alcander's Flower Garden.
Matsueda. Two Japanese Prints.
Mayakovsky. But Could You?
McClatchy. Found Parable.
Meinke. To a Daughter with Artistic Talent.
Melville, H. Art.
  Attic Landscape, The.
Michelangelo Buonarroti. To Giovanni da Pistoia When the Author Was Painting the Vault of the Sistine Chapel, 1509.
Miedzyrzecki. Golden Age, The.
Miller, J. Countryside.
Miller, L. My Students Catch Me Dancing.
Milosz, C. Sun, The.
Minh Đú'c Hoài Trinh. Selling My Soul.
Moore, M. When I Buy Pictures.
Muldoon, P. Christo's.
Naden. Two Artists, The.
Nguyễn Nhu'o'c Pháp. In a Garret.
Ni Tsan. Inscribed on a Painting by Myself.
Norse. Business of poetry, The.
  Picasso Visits Braque.
Nortje. Newcombe at the Croydon Gallery.
O'Hara, F. Why I Am Not a Painter.
Olsen, W. Unicorn Tapestries, The.
Oppen. Discrete Series 1929–1933.
Ormsby, F. Apples, Normandy, 1944.
O'Shaughnessy, A. Ode: "We are the music-makers."
Pagis. Acrobatics.
Pinkerton, H. On Vermeer's "Young Woman with a Water Jug" (1658) in the Metropolitan Museum.
Plymell. San Fransisco Ward.
Polkowski. Noli Me Tangere.
Porter, P. And No Help Came.
Pound, E. L'Art, 1910.
Proust. My True Love Hath My Heart.
Randall, D. Primitives.
Rankin, P. Two Lovers on Bridge in Winter.
Rannit. Wiiralt Drawing in Chartres.
Ransom, J. Painted Head.
Reed, I. Catechism of d Neoamerican Hoodoo Church.
Revell. Muse.
Rich, A. At a Bach Concert.
  Aunt Jennifer's tigers prance across a screen. They come to you with their descriptions of your soul.
Robinson, A. Art and Life.
Roseliep. Blues are the big thing.
  Sistine Chapel.
Rossetti, C. In An Artist's Studio.

Rossetti, D. For A Venetian Pastoral By Giorgone (In the Louvre).
  For "Our Lady of the Rocks."
Rukeyser, M. Homage to Literature.
  Käthe Kollwitz.
Ryan, K. Outsider Art.
Sadoleto. Poem of Jacobus Sadoletus on the Statue of Laocoon, The.
Salter. Rebirth of Venus, The.
Sanders, E. Cutting Prow, The.
Sapgir. Fearless One.
Scalapino. Picasso and Anarchism.
Schevill. London Pavement Artist.
Seidel. Pol Pot.
Serote. Hell, Well, Heaven.
"Severyanin." Prologue: "Mirra Lokhvitskaia's ashes are now entombed."
Shakespeare, W. Sonnet 68.
Shapiro, K. Poet.
Slessor. Nuremberg.
Smith, S. New Age, The.
  Salon d'Automne.
Smith, V. At an Exhibition of Historical Paintings, Hobart.
Snodgrass, W. Matisse: "The Red Studio."
Sokolov. Artist has to be enslaved, An.
Song. Girl Powdering Her Neck.
Speght. Disswasion hearing her assigne my helpe.
Stevens, W. Anecdote of the Jar.
  So-and-So Reclining on Her Couch.
Stevenson, R. To the Muse.
Stickney, T. On the Concert.
  Requiescam.
Sylvester, J. Cunning Painter, that with curious care, The.
T'ang Hsien-tsu. Paintings on My Wall Have Been Damaged by the Weather, The.
Tate, A. Sonnet: To a Portrait of Hart Crane.
  To Intellectual Detachment.
Tekkan. Tanka: "It cries and cries."
Thế Lũ'. Lyre of Myriad Tunes, The.
Thomas, D. In my craft or sullen art.
Thomson, J. Anear the centre of that northern crest.
Tomlinson, C. Chances of rhyme, The.
  Distinctions.
Tranter. Great Artist Reconsiders the Homeric Simile, The.
  Having Completed My Fortieth Year.
Troupe. View from Skates in Berkeley, The.
Tuckerman, F. His heart was in his garden; but his brain.
Tzara. Chanson Dada.
Unknown. Art.
  Artist, The: disciple, abundant, multiple, restless.
  Limerick: "There was a young artist called Saint."
  Limerick: "Whilst Titian was mixing rose madder."
Vaiiunaite. Botticelli. Three candles. Soft lips suggesting a smile.
Van Duyn. Homework.
Vas. What Is Left?
Vũ Hoàng Chu'o'ng. Beau Ideal, The.
Wagoner, D. Author of American Ornithology Sketches a Bird, Now Extinct, The.
Wakoski. Butcher's Apron, The.
Wang Shih-chieng. Echoing Old Man Mu's Poem, "Inscribed on Shen Lang-ch'ien's Little Landscape, Autumn Willows at Stone Cliff."
Weiners. Poem for Painters, A.
Weiss, T. Dab of Color, A.
Wen Cheng-ming. At the lacquered table—my recent calligraphy.
West, M. Exciting New Concept of Art Therapy, The.
Whitman, W. Eidolons.
Whittemore, R. Departure, The.
Wilbur. Museum Piece.
Williams, H. Blest Poesy! Oh sent to calm.
Williams, W. Artist, The.
  Landscape with the Fall of Icarus.
Wilson, T. Magpies in Picardy, The.

Wordsworth, W. *Poet!*—He Hath Put His Heart to School, A.
Wright, J. Request to a Year.
Xuân Diệu. Foreword to a Book of Poems.
Yeats. Curse of Cromwell, The.
   Lapis Lazuli.
Yevtushenko. Disbelief in Yourself Is Indispensable.
Yün Shou-p'ing. On a Painting "Ancient Trees and Flowing Stream."
See also **Artists' Colonies**

Artemis
Callimachus. Hymn to Artemis.
Euripides. No more, O my spirit.
Ovid. Arethusa Saved.

Arthurian Legend
Frere. I've often wish'd that I could write a book.
Hill, G. Merlin.
Keyes, S. Grail, The.
Layamon. Passing of Arthur, The.
Morris, W. Defense of Guenevere, The.
   Near Avalon.
Spicer, J. Book of Galahad, The.
Squire. Passing of Arthur, The.
Tennyson, A. Lady of Shalott, The.
   Passing of King Arthur, The.
   Pelleas and Ettarre.
Unknown. Marriage of Sir Gawain, The.
   Sir Mordred, traitor false and vile.
Warton, T. On King Arthur's Round Table, at Winchester.
Winters, Y. Sir Gawaine and the Green Knight.

Artichokes
Taylor, H. Artichoke.

Artifacts
Hughes, T. Relic.
Kroetsch. Stone Hammer Poem.

Artificial Insemination
Kay, J. Mummy and Donor and Deirdre.

Artists' Colonies
Robinson, E. Hillcrest.

Ascension Day
Lewis, S. Ascension Thursday.
Smart, C. Ascension of Our Lord Jesus Christ, The.
Vaughan, H. Ascension-Day.
   Friends Departed.
Wheelwright. Second Ascension of Christ, The.

Ashbery, John
Koch, K. Circus, The.

Ashes
Arendt. Lost Bay.
"Field." Your *rose* is *dead,*.
Foster, E. Marriage of True Minds, The.
Gilbo'a. Kingdom of Silence.
Mahapatra, J. Ash.
Mistral, G. Those Who Do Not Dance.
Nobuyuki. Ashtray (two poems).
Popa. Ashes.
Schelling. Isha Upanishad.
Unknown. Ashes to ashes.
Virgilio. Pressing my forehead.

Asia
Merrill, J. Willowware Cup.
Purdy, A. Blue City, The.
Tien Ch'ien. Freedom is Walking toward Us.

Asian-Americans
Chang, D. Foreign Ways.
Chin. Floral Apron, The.
Inada. Projected Scenario of a Performance to Be Given Before the UN.
Lee, L. Cleaving, The.
Lim, S. Lost Name Woman.
   Modern Secrets.
Okita. Notes for a Poem on Being Asian American.
Wong, N. Toward a 44th Birthday.
   When I Was Growing Up.
See also **Chinese, The; Japanese, The**

Aspen Trees
Holan. Reminiscence.
Hopkins, G. Binsey Poplars (Felled 1879).
Ivask, Y. Shall we forget the shiver.
Su Tung-p'o. Rain in the Aspens.
Thomas, E. Aspens.
Wilbur. Aspen and the Stream, The.
See also **Poplars**

Asphodels
Aiken, C. Snowflake on asphodel, clear ice on rose.
Williams, W. Of asphodel, that greeny flower.

Aspirations
Chin. Elegy for Chloe Nguyen.
Hughes, L. Deferred.
Kennedy, X. Keep a hand on your dream.
Rolfe, E. Song: "Keep the dream alive and growing always."

Assassinations and Assassins
Alcaeus. Philip V of Macedon.
Barrax. For Malcolm: After Mecca.
   King: April 4, 1968.
Dickinson, E. Apparently with no surprise.
Emanuel, J. Panther Man.
Faiz. No Sign of Blood.
Felltham. On the Duke of Buckingham, Slain by Felton, the 23rd August, 1628.
Ferlinghetti, L. Assassination Raga.
Giovanni. Adulthood.
Gunn, T. Claus von Stauffenberg.
Justice, D. Assassination, The.
Kazantzis. In Memory, 1978.
Kennedy, X. Down in Dallas, down in Dallas.
Knight, E. It was a funky deal.
Madhubuti. Assassination.
Melville, H. Martyr, The.
Po Chü-i. Everlasting Sorrow, The.
Tomlinson, C. Charlotte Corday.
Unknown. Booth Killed Lincoln.
   Charles Guiteau.
   Zolgotz.

Asses. *See* **Donkeys**

Assistance
Piercy. Gracious Goodness.

Assyrians
Byron, G. Destruction of Sennacherib, The.

Astarte
Tchernichowsky. To Ashtaroth and Bel.

Astraea (mythology)
Wharton, A. Wit's Abuse.

Astrology and Astrologers
Crashaw. Love's Horoscope.
Dickinson, E. Nature assigns the Sun.
Greville, F. *et al.* 56.
Kipling, R. Astrologer's Song, An.
Longfellow, H. Poet's Calendar, The.
McElroy, C. Horoscope.
Sidney, P. Sonnet 26: "Though dusty wits dare scorn astrology."

Astronauts
Connell, C. Space Men.
Dickey, J. So long.
Harmer. Space Explorer's Story, The.
Kirkup. Astronaut, The.
Kitching. If he cried, he cried in private.
   Space Captain.
Moore, J. Astronauts.
Morgan, E. Spacepoem 3: Off Course.
Nicholls, J. Ballad of the Sad Astronaut.
Smith, I. Retired.
Walker, T. Doomed Spaceman, The.
Whittemore, R. Projection, A.

Astronomy and Astronomers
Adcock, F. Blue Glass.
   Ex-Queen Among the Astronomers, The.
Bowers, E. Astronomers of Mont Blanc, The.
Buckley, C. Sun Spots.
Dickinson, E. Nature assigns the Sun.
Donne. Good Friday [*or* Goodfriday], 1613.
   Riding Westward.
Hristic. That night they all gathered on the highest tower.
Keyes, S. Greenwich Observatory.
Louis, A. Indian College Blues.
Nimatullah. Song of Seyd [*or* Seid] Nimetollah of Kuhistan.
Rich, A. Planetarium.
Shore. Astronomer's Journal, An.
Unknown. Stargazer, The.

Very. Slowness of Belief in a Spiritual World, The.
Whitman, W. When I heard the learn'd astronomer.
Williams, S. Old Astronomer to His Pupil, The.

Atheism
Chesterton, G. On Reading "God."
Corso. Hi.
Dunn, S. At the Smithville Methodist Church.
Hardy, T. Impercipient, The.
Lowell, R. For George Santayana.
Okudzhava. I don't believe in God and fate.
Wigglesworth. There also stand a num'rous band.

Athena
Callimachus. On Pallas Bathing, from a Hymn of Callimachus.
Homer. Goddess intervenes between Achilles and Agamemnon, The.
See also **Minerva**

Athens, Greece
Byron, G. Maid of Athens, ere we part.
Elytis. Psalm and Mosaic for a Springtime in Athens.
Muldoon, P. Dancers at the Moy.
Pindar. Athens.
Ritsos. After the Defeat.
Spencer, B. Spring Wind, A.

Athletics and Athletes
Hope, A. Massacre of the Innocents.
Housman, A. To an Athlete Dying Young.
Matthews, W. In Memory of the Utah Stars.
Morris, M. Swimmer.
Tkachenko. Requiem for Eduard Streltsov.
Updike. Ex-Basketball Player.
Whitman, W. Runner, The.
Wickham. Sportsman, The.

Atlanta, Georgia
Fordham. Atlanta Exposition Ode.
Shange. About Atlanta.

Atlantic Ocean
Aiken, C. Hatteras Calling.
Cowper, W. Castaway, The.
Ford, C. Somebody's Gone.
Gheorghe. Moonlit nights on the Atlantic Ocean!
Longfellow, H. Seaweed.
Osundare. Goree.
Sargent, E. Rockall.
Sexton. Crossing the Atlantic.
Tomlinson, C. Atlantic, The.

Atlantis
Crane, H. Atlantis.
Henson, D. Last Atlantean, The.

Atomic Bomb
"Agyeya." Hiroshima.
Ai. Testimony of J. Robert Oppenheimer, The.
Armour. Hiding Place.
Cartier. Poem for a Chorus.
Eberhart, R. On Shooting Particles beyond the World.
Enright, D. Monuments of Hiroshima, The.
Fell, A. August 6, 1945.
Frost, R. U. S. 1946 King's X.
Ginsberg, A. America I've given you all and now I'm nothing.
Haines, J. Dürer's Vision.
Hughes, L. Jim Crow Car.
Levertov. Gathered at the River.
Mura. Hibakusha's Letter (1955), The.
Santos, S. Near the Desert Test Sites.
Seth. Doctor's Journal Entry for August 6, 1945, A.
Sherry, J. Free Radicals.
   Hazardous Waste.
Shomer. Passive Resistance.
Stafford, W. At the Bomb Testing Site.
Wheelock, J. Earth ("'Planet doesn't explode of itself, A,' said drily").
Wilner, E. High Noon at Los Alamos.
See also **Hiroshima, Japan; Nuclear War**

Atoms
Dickinson, E. Of all the Souls that stand create—.

Jonson, B. Hour Glass, The ("Consider this small dust, here in the glass").
Pack, R. Proton Decay.
Raine, K. Scala Coeli.

Atterbury, Francis, Bishop of Rochester
Prior. Epitaph: "Meek Francis lies here, friend, without stop or stay."

Attics
Auden. Up There.
Coulette. Attic, The.
Nemerov. View from an Attic Window, The.
Porter, P. Easiest Room in Hell, The.

Auctions
Byrom. To Henry Wright of Mobberley, Esq. on Buying the Picture of Father Malebranche.
DeLeeuw. Auction Sale—Household Furnishings.
Hardy, T. Bags of Meat.
Levine, P. Buying and Selling.
Olsen, D. Auction; Saturday 2:00.
Reed, H. Auction Sale, The.
Sandburg, C. Auctioneer.
Spark. Going up to Sotheby's.

Auden, Wystan Hugh
Booth, P. Seeing Auden Off.
Brodsky, J. York: In Memoriam W. H. Auden.
Empson. Just a Smack at Auden.
Gergely. Auden in Old Age.
Spender, S. Auden at Milwaukee.
Young, A. W. H. Auden & Mantan Moreland.

Audubon, John James
Alexander, P. At Coueron. My First Gun. Audubon *Enfant*.

Aughrim, Battle of (1691)
Lawless, E. After Aughrim.
Murphy, R. Deep red bogs divided. Green Martyrs. Rapparees. Wolfhound.

August
Atwood. Late August.
Bly, R. August Rain.
Canton. Day-Dreams.
Ch'eng Hsiao. Satire on Paying Calls in August.
Eberhart, R. Loon Call, A.
Garland, H. In August.
Hardy, T. August Midnight, An.
Kenyon, J. August Rain, after Haying.
Lewis, M. August.
Monk, G. Poem for August—or for My Birthday.
Prévert. August Bank Holiday.
Ray, H. August.
Rich, A. August.
Romano, E. August heat.
Rotella, A. Late August.
San Geminiano. August.
Sexton. I Remember.
Snyder, G. Mid-August at Sourdough Mountain Lookout.
Swede. August sky, The.
Tanikawa Shuntaro. August is a dreamless month.
Thaxter. August.
Updike. August.
Wylie. August.
Zhenkai. August Sleepwalker, The.

Augustine, Saint
Grosholz. Back Trouble.
Plunkett. Saint Augustine.

Auks
Hodgson, R. Great Auk's ghost rose on one leg, The.

Aunt Jemima
Hayden, R. Aunt Jemima of the Ocean Waves.

Aunts
Boss. Candy Lady, The.
Browning, E. First Book: Young Aurora's Fostermother.
Campo. Aunt Toni's Heart.
Cather, W. Macon Prairie.
Cooper, J. In the House of the Dying.
Dacey, P. Thumb.

Dybek. Cherry.
Eliot, T. Aunt Helen.
Ginsberg, A. To Aunt Rose.
Graham, H. Waste.
Harrison, T. Study.
Holmes, O. My aunt! my dear unmarried aunt!
Housman, A. Aunts and Nieces or Time and Space.
Jamie. Aunt Janet's Museum.
Michelson, R. Undressing Aunt Frieda.
Miller, V. Remembering Aunt Helen.
Ochester. Canaries in Uncle Arthur's Basement, The.
Orlen. Aga Khan, The.
Reeves, J. My Singing Aunt.
Rich, A. Aunt Jennifer's tigers prance across a screen.
Ríos, A. Language of Great-Aunts, The.
Sexton. Some Foreign Letters.
Stevenson, R. Auntie's Skirts.
Stone, R. How to Catch Aunt Harriette.
Tolson. Old Houses.
Unknown. My Aunt Jane she took me in.
Urdang. Evening of Home Movies, An.
Wojahn. Satin Doll.

Auschwitz, Poland
Amichai. Almost a Love Poem.
Bond, E. If Auschwitz had been in Hampshire.
Borowski. Night over Birkenau. Sun of Auschwitz, The.
Brock, V. Remembering Dresden.
Fainlight, R. Archive Film Material.
Gershon. Experiments with God.
Levi, P. Buna.
MacBeth. Poem of Death, A.
Mandel, E. On the 25th Anniversary of the Liberation of Auschwitz.
McGrath, T. Remembering the Children of Auschwitz.
Porter, P. Annotations of Auschwitz. Your Attention Please.
Quasimodo. Auschwitz.
Rózewicz. Questions about Poetry since Auschwitz.
Rukeyser, M. Breaking Open.
Schiff, H. Discovery.
Sexton. After Auschwitz.
Zych. Auschwitz, 1987.

Australia
Adamson. Elm Tree in Paddington, An.
Brown, F. Last of England! O'er the sea, my dear, The.
Browne, F. Australian Emigrant, The.
Buckmaster. Wilpena Pound.
Campbell, D. Lovers, The.
Catalano. Australia.
Cataldi. 13 November 1983.
Darwin. Visit of Hope to Sydney Cove, near Botany-Bay.
Davidson, R. Gravy Train, The.
Davis, J. Desolation. First-born, The. One Hundred and Fifty Years.
Dransfield. Minstrel. That Which We Call a Rose.
Duggan, L. Five. One. Hearts (1983). One. One.
"Ern Malley." Dürer: Innsbruck, 1495. Sweet William.
Ewart. Short Time.
Freeth. Botany Bay.
Gray, R. Journey: the North Coast.
Harris, R. Sydney.
Hart-Smith. Nullarbor.
Hope, A. Australia.
Humphries, B. Edna's Hymn.
Ingamells. We who are called Australians have no country.
Marshall-Stoneking. Picture Postcard.
McAuley, J. Envoi.
McAuley, J. Terra Australis.
Mead, P. Melbourne or the Bush.
Murphy, E. Thank you, Mr Rason, for the Apples.

Murray, L. People are eating dinner in that country north of Legge's Lake, The.
O'Dowd. Australia.
Oodgeroo of the tribe Noonuccal. No more boomerang. We are Going.
Page, G. Jerry's Plains, 1848.
Porter, P. Australian Garden, An. Last of England, The. Sydney Cove, 1788. Talking to You Afterwards.
Rankin, J. Old Currawong.
Rodriguez, J. Mahogany Ship, The.
Sladen. Summer Christmas in Australia, A.
Slessor. Five Bells. South Country.
Smith, V. Early Arrival: Sydney.
Stewart, D. Terra Australis.
Thorne, T. High Country.
Tranter. Enzensberger at 'Exiles'.
Unknown. Hail South Australia! blessed clime. Hot Day In Sydney, A.
Wallace-Crabbe. Collective Invention, The. Mental Traveller's Landfall, The.
Webb, F. Towards the Land of the Composer.
Wright, J. At Cooloolah. Australia 1970. I To my Brothers.

Authorship and Authors
Belloc. On His Books.
Bradstreet, A. Author to Her Book, The.
Campbell, R. On the Same.
Drummond, W. I know that all beneath the moon decays.
Feldman, I. Terminal Laughs.
Fitzgerald, F. Oblt on Parnassus.
Freneau. To an Author.
Herrick. Argument of His Book, The. Poetry Perpetuates the Poet.
Holmes, O. Cacoëthes Scribendi.
Jago. Hamlet's Soliloquy Imitated.
Joyce, J. Ladies and gents, you are here assembled.
Kennedy, B. On ["Who Wrote Icon Basilike" by Dr.] Christopher Wordsworth, Master of Trinity.
Killigrew, A. Upon the Saying That My Verses Were Made by Another.
Macpherson, J. Boatman, The.
Na-lan Hsing-te. Tune: "Song of Dandy"— Hunting in Autumn.
Nash, O. So That's Who I Remind Me Of.
Ondaatje. Burning Hills.
Paton. I Have Approached.
Piercy. For the Young Who Want To.
Pound, E. Lake Isle, The.
Rich, A. Frame.
Robinson, E. George Crabbe. Verlaine.
Scott, F. Canadian Authors Meet, The.
Traill, H. After Dilettante Concetti.
Updike. I Missed His Book, but I Read His Name.
Wheelwright. There Is No Opera like "Lohengrin."

Autism
Silkin. Death of a Son.

Automation
Moore, M. Four Quartz Crystal Clocks.
Wagoner, D. Valedictory to Standard Oil of Indiana, A.

Automobile Accidents
Fearing. Obituary.
Glück, L. Racer's Widow, The.
Meissner. After Going Off the Road During the Snowstorm.
Shapiro, K. Auto Wreck.
Tate, J. Rustin Steel is driving the crew to the river. A long.
Tranströmer. Solitude.

Automobile Racing
Glück, L. Racer's Widow, The.

Automobiles
Amabile. Twink Drives Back, in a Bad Mood, from a Party in Massachusetts.
Apollinaire. Little Car, The.
Atkins. New Storefront.

Baranczak, S. Three Magi, The.
Barrax. Adagio.
Betjeman. Meditation on the A30.
Bishop, E. Filling Station.
Bishop, J. This Dim and Ptolemaic Man.
Bishop, M. Gas and Hot Air.
Bly, R. Driving toward the Lac Qui Parle River.
Burns, J. Revisionism.
Cain, J. Waiting.
Cendrars. Harvest.
Connor, T. Last of the Poet's Car.
Crist. Dusty pickup, The.
Cummings, E. She being Brand.
Dawe, B. Abandonment of Autos.
Dickey, J. Cherrylog Road.
Dickey, W. Things Kept.
Dufault. Driving Home.
Duggan, L. Three xlvii.
Dyment. As a boy with a richness of needs I wandered.
Eady. Song.
Edson, R. Automobile, The.
Finkel. Gesture.
Flanders, J. Big Cars.
Frost, R. Were I in Trouble.
Gilbert, C. Now.
Guest, B. Way of Being, A.
Haines, J. Flight, The.
Hammial. *Automobiles of the Asylum.*
Hey. True Ballad of the Great Race to Gilmore City, The.
Hope, A. Brides, The.
Hotham. Stalled car.
Huxley, A. Two Realities.
Jarman, M. Black Riviera, The.
Kane, M. Soap Box Derby, The.
Kennedy, X. At a Low Mass for Two Hot-Rodders.
Kharms. Event on the Street, An.
Livingston, M. Car Wash.
McElroy, D. Ode to a Dead Dodge.
McKuen. Thoughts on Capital Punishment.
McMahon, L. Barbie's Ferrari.
Merriam, E. Landscape.
Meyers, B. Suburban Dusk.
Miles, J. Reason.
Mitchell, A. Autobahnmotorwayautoroute.
Mobilio. Step Seven.
Morrison, L. Sidewalk Racer Or, On the Skateboard, The.
Moss, T. Wonder, The.
Murray, L. Portrait of the Autist as a New World Driver.
Nemerov. Fugue.
Oppen. Cars run in a void of utensils, The.
Part of the Forest.
Parker, D. One Perfect Rose.
Pastan. Jump Cabling.
Pierman. Pilgrims.
Pizzarelli. Driving.
Sun brightens.
Wiping the chrome.
Prunty. Elderly Lady Crossing on Green.
Rutsala. American Dream.
Ryan, G. Ode to My Car.
Shapiro, D. To an Idea.
Shapiro, K. Buick.
Silverstein, S. Longmobile.
Stafford, W. Traveling [or Travelling] through the dark I found a deer.
Swenson, M. Bison Crossing Near Mt. Rushmore.
Southbound on the Freeway.
Weaver, M. Black and White Galaxie, The.
Wieseltier. Extended Sonnet on the Death of Isaac Danziger.
Williams, W. Ballad of Faith.
Intelligent Sheepman and the New Cars, The.
Zukofsky, L. Cars once steel and green, now old.

See also **Driving and Drivers**

Autumn
Ackland. What must we do if we cannot do this.
Akhmadulina. Again September, like the swarm of seasons past.
Autumn.
Aldrich, T. October turned my maple's leaves to gold.
Alexander, M. October Journey.
Allingham. Robin Redbreast.
Amichai. Lovers in Fall.
Baba. In the autumn when words sound.
Barker, G. Gardens of Ravished Psyche, The.
Barnes, W. Fall, The.
Basho. On a withered branch.
Bernstein, O. In a Park, in Siena, at Twilight.
Binyon. Now is the time for the burning of the leaves.
Blake, W. To Autumn.
Blandiana. Song.
Bobrowski. Latvian Autumn, The.
Bogan, L. Simple Autumnal.
Bonnefoy. Words of Evening, The.
Bosselaar. Fall.
Braithwaite. Turn Me to My Yellow Leaves.
Brickley. Autumn rain—.
Bridges, R. Garden in September, The.
In autumn moonlight, when the white air wan.
Bronk. Where It Ends.
Brontë, C. Autumn day its course has run—
The Autumn evening falls, The.
Brontë, E. Fall, leaves, fall; die, flowers, away.
O come with me, thus ran the song.
Brooks, G. Sunset of the City, A.
Browning, R. By the Fire-Side.
Bryant, W. Autumn Woods.
Death of the Flowers, The.
November.
October.
To the Fringed Gentian.
Bunya no Asayasu. In a gust of wind the white dew.
Buson. I go.
Campana. Autumn Garden.
Campbell, R. Autumn.
Campbell, W. How One Winter Came in the Lake Region.
Caraion. Enveloping Echo, The.
"Carroll." Humpty Dumpty's Song.
Carruth, H. Emergency Haying.
Cary, A. Autumn.
Ceravolo. Invisible Autumn.
Chesterton, G. Gold Leaves.
Chiang K'uei. Tune: "Pale-golden Willows."
Chin. Autumn Leaves.
Chong, H. Late Autumn.
Chu Shu-chen. Stormy Night in Autumn.
Chu Yün-ming. As I Looked at a Lake, My Thoughts Turned to a Certain Friend.
Chukhonstev. Farewell to Autumn.
Clare, J. Autumn ("I love the fitful gust that shakes").
Autumn ("Thistledown's flying / Though the winds are all still, The").
Decay.
Pleasant Sounds.
'Tis Martinmass, from rig to rig.
Clark, L. August Ends.
Cole, T. Written in Autumn.
Coleridge, S. Written in Early Youth, the Time an Autumnal Evening.
Columella. Autumnal Work.
Corbett, W. Vermont Apollinaire.
Crapsey. November Night.
Cristall. Song: "Through springtime walks, with flowers perfumed."
Cummings, E. Always before your voice my soul.
It's over a(see just).
Wind has blown the rain away and blown, A.
Cushing, J. Autumn Leaves.
Daniel, J. Moment.
Davidson, L. In the dark lobby.
Davies, W. Rich Days.
Day Lewis. Maple and Sumach.
Stand-To, The.
De Vere, A. Autumnal Ode.
Dickinson, E. Morns are meeker than they were, The.
Name—of it—is "Autumn," The.

Dixon, R. Song: "Feathers of the willow, The."
Winter Will Follow.
Djagarov. Autumn.
Dowson. Autumnal.
Drainac. Leaf.
Dunbar, P. Signs of the Times.
Eberhart, R. Loon Call, A.
Spider expects the cold of winter, The.
Eikei. Autumn has come / To the lonely cottage.
Ekelof. Absentia Animi.
Encarnacion. Seattle, Autumn, 1933.
Enright, D. Old field is sad, The.
Fan Ch'eng-ta. Autumn.
Farjeon, E. Down! Down!
Fell, A. Pushing Forty.
Field, R. Something told the wild geese.
Francis, R. Fall.
Freneau. On Observing a Large Red-Streak Apple.
Frost, R. Clear and Colder.
My November Guest.
Fujiwara no Masatsune. From Yoshino / Mountain the autumn.
Galvin, B. Listening to September.
Garland, H. Plowing: A Memory.
Glück, L. All Hallows.
Gould, E. Red in Autumn.
Gray, D. Sonnet: "October's gold is dim—the forests rot."
Gunn, T. Autumn Chapter in a Novel.
Haas, R. Autumn evening.
Han Yü. Sentiments at Autumn.
Hardy, T. Last Chrysanthemum, The.
Haxton. Auspice.
Hayne, P. October.
Heinze. Late Flowers.
Henson, L. Scattered Leaves.
Hitomaro. Colored leaves, The.
Ho Ching-ming. Seeing Off Han Ju-ch'ing as He Returns to the Land Within the Passes.
Hoatson. Autumn.
Hoban. Summer goes, summer goes.
Hong, Y. Maple Leaves.
Hood, T. No sun—no moon!
Ode: Autumn.
Hopkins, G. Hurrahing in Harvest.
Spring and Fall.
Hotham. On the ceiling.
Housman, A. Tell me not here, it needs not saying.
They Say My Verse Is Sad: No Wonder.
Howells, W. November.
Hoyt, C. Hair, in my comb's teeth.
Hsieh Hui-lien. Fulling Cloth for Clothes.
Hsü Chung-hsing. I shake my robe—and mists disperse, leaving clear autumn sky.
Hulme, T. Autumn.
Illyés. Deep Dusk.
Ivask, I. Foliage foliage.
Ivaska. Wild ducks had flown, and early this year.
Jackson, H. September [Days Are Here].
Jakuren. Hanging raindrops, The.
James, J. Cambridge.
Sister Midnight.
Jeffers, R. Autumn Evening.
Jennings, E. Song at the Beginning of Autumn.
Kao Ch'i. Where Does My Sadness Come From?
Keats. To Autumn.
Kenney. Apples on Champlain.
Kim, H. Prayer in Autumn.
Kim, J. Law of Fall, The.
Kim, K. Lyricism of an Autumn Day.
Kinsella, T. Another September.
Kitahara Hakushū. Tanka: "Autumn bellflower."
Kogan. Star.
Kondo. Autumn light.
Kumin, M. Mummies, The.
Kunitz, S. End of Summer.
Lady of the Assembly. Assembly of Ladies, The.
Lawrence, D. Butterfly, the wind blows sea-

ward[, strong beyond the garden wall!].
Ship of Death, The.
Lee, L.　Field of Autumn.
Levertov.　Settling.
Levine, P.　Snails.
　Zaydee.
Lewis, A.　Autumn, 1939.
Li Ch'ing-chao.　Autumn Evening Beside the
　Lake.
　Quail Sky.
　To the Tune, "Plum Blossoms Fall and
　Scatter."
Li Ho.　Autumn Comes.
Li Meng-yang.　Autumn Vista.
　Seeing Off Commander In Chief Li to Yün-
　chung.
Li Po.　Jade Stairs Resentment.
　On the river, every day these heavy rains.
　Tzu-yeh Song.
　Verses: "Clean is the autumn wind."
Li Yi.　Looking in a Mirror the Day before the
　Advent of Autumn.
Linden, M.　Fall Is Here, The.
Liu Tsung-yüan.　Poem to Send to Friends in
　the Capital, A.
Lodge, G.　Fall.
Longfellow, H.　Aftermath.
　Autumn.
　Harvest Moon, The.
Lorde.　What my child learns of the sea.
Lowell, A.　Hoar-Frost.
　Wind and Silver.
Lu Yu.　Autumn Thoughts.
　Autumn Thoughts ("Mornings up before the
　rooster calls").
　Autumn Thoughts ("Sumac showing faint
　traces of red").
　Boating in Autumn.
　Sounds of Autumn.
Lu Yün.　Valley Wind, The.
Ma Chih-yüan.　Autumn Thoughts.
"MacDiarmid."　In the Fall.
MacLeish.　Immortal Autumn.
　Tourist Death.
Maiden.　Green Side, The.
Malroux.　Octet Before Winter.
Manger.　Autumn.
　I Am the Autumn.
Marcinkeviius.　Nemunas.
Masaoka Shiki.　On the eve of death.
Mathews, H.　Sad Birds, The.
Matveyeva.　Eggplants Have Pins and Needles,
　The.
McGough, R.　Just Another Autumn Day.
McGrath, T.　Black Train, The.
Melville, H.　Pontoosuce.
Meng Chiao.　Autumn finds me old and
　poorer.
　Face of the autumn moon freezes, The.
　In autumn moonlight the face turns icy.
　Wind and bamboos strum and speak to each
　other.
Meng Hao Jan.　First of Autumn, The.
Mihalic.　Autumn.
Millay, E.　Autumn.
　God's World.
Milosz, O.　Bridge, The.
Minamoto no Tsunenobu.　In the evening / The
　rice leaves in the garden.
Mo Shih-lung.　Staying Overnight at Blue
　Cloud Temple.
Moore, L.　Farther and farther.
Mori Ōgai.　In Nara (two poems).
Moritz.　Autumn.
Moses, W.　Night Wind in Fall.
Mountain, M.　Faded flowers of the bed sheets
　autumn night.
　Old towel folding it again autumn evening.
Naito Joso.　Autumn cicada, The.
Narbut.　October.
Nashe.　Autumn Hath All the Summer's
　Fruitful Treasure.
Nemerov.　Dying Garden, The.
Ni Tsan.　Inscribed on the Painting, "River in
　Autumn."
Ōe no Chisato.　As I watch the moon.

O'Hara, F.　Poem: "Eager note on my door
　said 'Call me', The."
Ologoudou.　Vespers.
Ou-yang Hsiu.　Thoughts on the First Day of
　Autumn, Sent to Su Tzu-mei.
Parker, D.　Indian Summer.
Parun.　Open Door.
Pasternak, B.　Autumn.
Pawsey.　Thief, The.
Petri.　Morning Coffee.
P'i Jih-hsiu.　Thoughts in Early Autumn:
　Thirty Rhymes Sent to Lu-wang.
Pien Kung.　On the Sixteenth Day I Visit the
　Temple Again.
Pizzarelli.　Moving van zooms, A.
Po Chü-i.　Drunk, Facing Crimson Leaves.
　Lonely Night in Early Autumn.
　Planting Bamboos.
Porumbacu.　Of Autumn.
Posey, A.　Autumn.
Preil, G.　Memory of Autumns at Springtime.
Quigless.　Autumn.
Ransom, J.　Conrad in Twilight.
Rexroth, K.　Buddha took some Autumn
　leaves.
　Half in a dream.
Riley, J.　When the frost is on the punkin and
　the fodder's in the shock.
Rilke.　Autumn Day.
Rimbaud, A.　Farewell: "Autumn already!—But
　why regret an eternal sun if we are embarked
　on."
Robinson, A.　Art and Life.
Robinson, F.　Down rippling, The.
Rossetti, C.　Autumn.
　Bitter for Sweet.
　October Garden, An.
Ryozan.　When I am lonely.
Ryuichi.　October Poem.
Sandburg, C.　Falltime.
Sansom, C.　October.
　Ploughing.
Sarton.　If I could let you go as trees let go.
　Late Autumn.
Sarumaru.　Deep in the mountain.
Savage, D.　Fall of Leaves.
Scannell.　Autumn.
Schuyler, J.　Master of the Golden Glow, The.
Seward.　Behold that tree, in Autumn's dim
　decay.
Shakespeare, W.　Sonnet 73.
Shapiro, K.　Exile.
Shelley, P.　Autumn: A Dirge.
　Ode to the West Wind.
Shelton, R.　On Lake Pend Oreille.
Simic.　Ancient Autumn.
Smith, C.　Sonnet XXXII. (To Melancholy.
　Written on the Banks of the Arun, October
　1785).
　Written in October.
Spiess.　Wispy autumn clouds.
Stevens, W.　Lunar Paraphrase.
Stevenson, R.　Autumn Fires.
　In autumn when the woods are red.
Stickney, T.　Autumn's done; they have the
　golden corn in, The.
　Mnemosyne.
"Struther."　Lament in Spring.
Su Tung-p'o.　Autumn.
　I travel day and night toward the Yangtze and
　the sea.
Summers, H.　Leaves in the Yard.
Tate, A.　Seasons of the Soul.
Teasdale.　September Midnight.
Teika.　I gaze far and long.
Tenji.　Because.
Tennyson, A.　Dedication, A: "Dear, near and
　true—no truer Time himself."
Thomas, D.　Poem in October.
Thomas, E.　Digging.
　October.
Thompson, C.　Autumn Day, An.
　Autumn Leaves.
Thompson, P.　Autumn ("List to the sad wind,
　drearily moaning").
　Autumn ("Sun shines bright, but sadly, The").
Toshinari.　Twilight.

Toshiyuki.　Autumn has come invisibly.
Trakl.　Rats, The.
Ts'ao P'i.　Song of Yen.
Ts'en Shen.　Autumn Thoughts.
Tsung Ch'en.　Drinking at the Cave Mouth.
Tu Fu.　Autumn Meditation.
　Autumn wastes are each day wilder, The.
　Clear After Rain.
　Dejeuner Sur L'Herbe.
　Moon Festival.
　Overlooking the Desert.
Tucker, M.　Autumn Thoughts.
Tuckerman, F.　And change[,] with hurried
　hand, has swept these scenes.
Ungaretti.　Soldiers.
Unknown.　Autumn ("I at my window sit, and
　see").
　Autumn Morning, An.
　Golden Palace, The.
　Robin sang sweetly.
　Turning my chariot I yoke my horses and go.
Untermeyer, J.　Autumn.
Updike.　Great Scarf of Birds, The.
　September.
Van den Heuvel.　Late autumn.
Very.　Autumn Flowers.
　Autumn Leaves.
　Sumach Leaves, The.
Virgilio.　Another autumn.
　Autumn twilight.
　Autumn wind, The.
　Now the swing is still.
　Town barberpole.
Wade, B.　Conkers.
Waller, E.　Fall, The.
Wang An-shih.　Hastily Composed on the Mo-
　ling Road.
Wang T'ing-hsiang.　Climbing to the Top of
　the City Walls at Kan-yü.
Wang Wei.　Autumn.
　In the Hills.
Warren, R.　Heart of Autumn.
Wei Chuang.　Spoken to Pines and Bamboos.
Welburn.　Gonsalves.
Wen T'ing-yün.　Early Autumn in the
　Mountains.
　In the Mountains as Autumn Begins.
White.　Colour.
Whittier.　Battle Autumn of 1862, The.
Wieners.　Waning of the Harvest Moon, The.
Wieseltier.　Allenby.
Williams, W.　Prelude to Winter.
　Yellow Season, The.
Willson, D.　Mist and All, The.
Wilson, R.　Late in Fall.
Wright, J.　Autumn Begins in Martins Ferry,
　Ohio.
Wright, J.　Cradle Logic of Autumn, The.
Wu of Han.　Autumn wind blows white clouds,
　The.
　Autumn wind rises; white clouds fly.
　Autumn winds rise.
　Song of the Autumn Wind.
Wu Wei-yeh.　Autumn Night—Sleepless.
Yang Shen.　To the Tune "Partridge Sky."
Yang Wan-li.　Sitting at Night on the Moonlit
　Terrace.
Yi, H.　Song of Cricket.
Yosano.　Left on the beach.
　Tanka: "Into a pair of stars."
　This autumn will end.
Young, A.　Song for Autumn.
Yü Chi.　Following the Rhymes of Autumn
　Night Song by Meng Tzu chou, Signatory
　Official of the Board of Rites.
　Sent To Be Inscribed on the Temple of P'u-
　jun (Universal Fructification) at Lou-fu
　Mountain.
Yüan Hao-wen.　Autumn Sentiments.
　Quatrain: "Above the creek dallies a bright
　moon."
Yüan Hung-tao.　Woman's Room in Autumn,
　A.
Yün Shou-p'ing.　As we say farewell to
　autumn.
　Autumn Plants, Flowers, Bamboo, Rocks.
　In a hidden spot on the northern mountain.

Painting of Chrysanthemums in the Boneless Style of Hsü Ch'ung-ssu, A.
Sadness in the Autumn Chambers.
Zimmer. Zimmer in Fall.
Zolotow. Autumn.

Aviation and Aviators
Day Lewis. Winged bull trundles to the wired perimeter, The.
Ewart. When a Beau Goes In.
Hall, D. Airstrip in Essex, 1960, An.
Old Pilot, The.
Iremonger. Icarus.
Jarrell. Dead Wingman, The.
Death of the Ball Turret Gunner, The.
Losses.
Kazantzis. Frightened Flier Goes North, The.
Kelly, B. Those Who Wrestle with the Angel for Us.
Snyder, G. Vapor Trails.
Spender, S. Landscape near an Aerodrome, The.
Tate, J. Lost Pilot, The.
Trowbridge, J. Darius Green and His Flying-Machine.
Winters, Y. Nocturne for October 31st, A.
See also **Air Travel; Air Warfare; Airports**

Avignon, France
Robinson, A. Orchard at Avignon, An.

Avoca, Ireland
Moore, T. Meeting of the Waters, The.

Avon River, Canada
Reaney. To the Avon River above Stratford, Canada.

Avon River, England
Southey, R. Ebb Tide, The.

Axes
Adamson. Private, The.
Dimoski. Revenge.
Evans, M. Boss Communication.
Frost, R. Axe-Helve, The.
Morris, G. Woodman, spare that tree!
Nikolov, L. Axes lie next to the river, The.
P'i Jih-hsiu. Woodcutter's Ax, A.
Plath. Words.
Snyder, G. Axe Handles.
Unknown. If all the seas were one sea.
Willmot. Listening.

Ay
Mutamociyar. Ÿ: A Gift of Elephants.
Ÿ: His Hill.

Ayr, Scotland
Burns, R. Flow gently, sweet Afton, among thy green braes.

Azaleas
Izumi. I picked an azalea.
Kim, S. Azaleas, The.
Patmore, C. Azalea, The.
Shin, T. Land of Flowering Azaleas, The.

Aztecs
Cacamatzin. My friends.

B

Baal
Tchernichowsky. To Ashtaroth and Bel.

Baal-Shem-Tov
Klein, A. Baal Shem Tov.

Babel, Tower of
Crouch, N. Tower of Babel, The.
Quarles. On the Babel-Builders.
Sandburg, C. From the four corners of the earth.
Wheelwright. Two Tongues in a Tower.
Wieder. Tower of Babel, The.

Babies
Adisa. Rainbow, The.
Al-Harizi. Lute, The.
Aldis, D. Little.
Armitage, J. To Our Daughter.
Auden. Mundus et Infans.
Avianus. Monkey, The.
Baillie, J. Mother to Her Waking Infant, A.
Barbauld. To a Little Invisible Being Who Is Expected Soon to Become Visible.

Barbu. Dogmatic Egg, The.
Barker, G. Verses for a First Birthday.
Barlow, G. 4½ Months: Halfway Song.
Barnes, J. Clinic Day.
Barnstone, A. To a Friend's Child.
Beers, E. Weighing the Baby.
Bennett, G. Secret.
Blake, W. Cradle Song, A: "Sleep, sleep, beauty bright."
Infant Joy.
Infant Sorrow.
Bloch, C. Eating Babies.
Magnificat.
Bowering, G. In the Forest.
Breton, N. Cradle Song: "Come, little babe."
Brown, R. This is no baby skin—.
Bruce, D. Two Couples.
Byrd. Lulla, My Sweet Little Baby.
Cameron, E. To David—At Six Months.
Campbell, R. Zulu Girl, The.
Causley. Infant Song.
Cave. Written a Few Hours before the Birth of a Child.
Chernoff. How Lies Grow.
Clifton, L. I am accused of tending to the past.
Coleridge, S. O sleep, my babe, hear not the rippling wave.
Cowper, M. On Viewing Her Sleeping Infant.
Davie. Christening, A.
Derricotte. Note on My Son's Face, A.
Diamond, L. Eskimo Baby, An.
Dickey, J. Magus, The.
Dove, R. Pastoral.
Who can forget the attitude of mothering?
Dunbar, P. Little brown baby wif spa'klin' eyes.
Duncan, R. Coming out of the house to die.
Ewart. Haiku: After The Orgies.
Fisher, R. Incredible Henry McHugh, The.
Fitzgerald, R. Errantry.
García Lorca. Baby.
Graves, R. Maternal Despotism; or, The Rights of Infants.
Graves, R. Call it a good marriage—.
Griffin, S. Song My.
Gunn, T. Baby Song.
Guthrie, W. Turkey in the Corn.
Hadas, R. Up and Down.
Halley. Against Dark's Harm.
Hardy, T. New Toy, The.
Hawley, B. Bad Mother, The.
Heaney, S. Peacock's Feather, A.
Herrick. Upon a child.
Ingelow. Little babe, while burns the west.
Jacobsen, J. Primer, The.
Jarrell. Bats.
Johnson, S. Ballad: "Tender infant, meek and mild, The."
Kelly, I. To an Unborn Infant.
Kim Nam-jo. My baby has no name yet.
King, H. Dream Maiden, A.
Kinnell. Under the Maud Moon.
Kinzie. Sound Waves.
Kirchwey. He Considers the Birds of the Air.
Kirkup. Baby's Drinking Song.
Questions and Answers (a ballad).
Koch, K. Girl and Baby Florist Sidewalk Pram Nineteen Seventy Something.
Lamb, C. *et al.* First Tooth, The.
Leigh, H. Natural Child, The.
Lipsitz. Feeding, The.
Locker-Lampson. Terrible Infant, A.
Lorde. Now That I Am Forever with Child.
Luther. Cradle Hymn.
Macdonald, G. Where did You Come From, Baby Dear?
Madan. To Lysander.
Mahon. Unborn Child, An.
Mathis. Seven Months.
McCaig. Poem: "There is a wailing baby under every stone and you walk."
Moffett. Now or Never.
Monkhouse. To a New-Born Child.
Morris, M. Family Pictures.
Mother Goose. Rock-a-bye, baby, thy cradle is green.

Murray, J. Madonna vs. Child.
Nash, O. Come On In, the Senility Is Fine.
Did Someone Say "Babies"?
Reflection on Babies.
Song to Be Sung by the Father of Infant Female Children.
Nesbit, E. Morning Song.
Song: "Oh, baby, baby, baby dear."
Ogilvy. Natal Address to My Child, March 19th 1844, A.
Newly Dead and Newly Born.
Oppen. Sara in Her Father's Arms.
Osgood, F. Ellen Learning to Walk.
Ostriker. Greedy Baby / sucking the sweet tit.
Owen, M. All That Glitters.
Paddock. Original Mind.
Pagis. Pages of an Album.
Philips, A. To Miss Charlotte Pulteney in Her Mother's Arms.
Plath. Candles.
Death and Co.
Event.
Gulliver.
Magi.
Morning Song.
New Year on Dartmoor.
Nick and the Candlestick.
Night Dances, The.
You're.
Probyn. End of the Journey, The.
Raworth. My Face Is My Own, I Thought.
Ray, D. At the Washing of My Son.
Rice, J. Man and Height.
Riley, J. King of Oo-Rinktum-Jing, The.
Rolfe, E. Song: "Keep the dream alive and growing always."
Rosenberg, L. Poem of my Heart, The.
Rossetti, C. Baby lies so fast asleep.
Why did baby die.
Rosten. This is my name / I have my own name.
Rukeyser, M. Night Feeding.
Salter. Summer 1983.
Sampter. Kadia the Young Mother Speaks.
Sanchez, S. To P. J. (2 Yrs Old Who Sed Write a Poem for Me in Portland, Oregon).
Scovell. Days Drawing In.
Seth. How ugly babies are! How heedless.
Sexton. Unknown Girl in the Maternity Ward.
Smith, P. Dylan, Two Days.
Smith, S. But Murderous.
Valuable.
Snyder, G. Changing Diapers.
Kyoto Born in Spring Song.
Stevenson, A. Spirit is too blunt an instrument, The.
Strand. Babies, The.
Swinburne. Baby's feet, like sea-shells pink, A.
Tadic. Toys, Dream.
Thelwall. To the Infant Hampden. Written during a Sleepless Night.
Thomas, E. Triumvirate, The.
Tóth, J. To the Newborn.
Trivelpiece. Nursery, The.
Unknown. Baby, baby.
Baby Dolly.
Bye, bye, baby bunting / Daddy's gone a-hunting.
Catfish and Toad.
Clap Handies.
Cry, baby, cry, / Put your finger in your eye.
Dahn the Plug'ole.
For Baby.
Here's a ball for baby.
How Many Days Has My Baby to Play?
Hush-a-bye, baby, lie still with thy daddy.
Rock-a-bye baby.
Sleep, baby, sleep.
Sleep, baby, sleep, / Our cottage vale is deep.
Song for the Newborn.
Very. Moses in Infancy.
Waldman, A. Baby's Pantoum.
Waring, B. Baby Random.
Wheelwright. And for His Mother.
White, E. Conch.
Whitman, W. From pent-up aching rivers.

Williams, M. Poem for Emily, A.
Wordsworth, D. Cottager to Her Infant, (By My Sister), The.
Wordsworth, W. Mad Mother, The.
Wright, J. Song for the Middle of the Night, A.
Yang Wei-chen. Bamboo Branch Song of the Seacoast.
Yarrow. Baby's pee, The.
Low winter moon.
Sunrise path.
Yearsley. Mira, as they dear Edward's senses grow.
Yeats. Dolls, The.

See also **Infant Death**

Baboons
Belloc. Big Baboon, The.
Campbell, R. Theology of Bongwi, the Baboon, The.
Unknown. Baboon.
Baboon 2.
Old Codger of Broome, The.
Williams, R. Baboon, The.

Baby-Sitting and Baby-Sitters
Avidan. Fire the Babysitter.
Cheng Hsieh. Poem for My Wet Nurse, A.
Clarke, G. Baby-Sitting.
Hashimoto, S. Eleven A.M. on My Day Off, My Sister Phones Desperate for a Babysitter.

Babylon
Bishop, E. Burglar of Babylon, The.
Crsnaru. Lions of Babylon, The.
Mother Goose. To Babylon.
Reznikoff. Babylon: 539 B.C.E.
I.
Sassoon. Babylon that was beautiful is Nothing now.
Soutar. Song: "Whaur yon broken brig hings owre;."
Stickney, T. Be still. The Hanging Gardens were a dream.
Tennyson, A. Babylon.

Bacchus
Emerson, R. Bacchus.
Horace. Being half foxt he praiseth Bacchus.
Nonnus. Dionysiaca.
Redi. Bacchus's Opinion of Wine, and Other Beverages.
Rimbaud, A. Stolen Heart, The.
Shakespeare, W. Drinking Song, A.
Unknown. Bacchus, or the Pirates.
Virgil. Hostesse, The.

Bach, Johann Sebastian
De Vries, P. Theme and Variation.
Fitzgerald, R. Jesu, Joy of Man's Desiring.
Moore, M. Dream.
Okudzhava. In the City Park.
Schnackenberg. Living Room, The.
Zeidner. Bach.

Bachelors
Eberhart, R. New England Bachelor, A.
Flatman. Batchelor's Song, The.
Herrick. Single Life Most Secure.
Upon the Loss[e] of His Mistresses.
Unknown. A, a, a, a,.
I Don't Let the Girls Worry My Mind.
Starving to Death on a Government Claim.
When I was a bachelor, I lived by myself.

Backs
Grosholz. Back Trouble.

Bacon, Sir Francis
Bentley, F. When their lordships asked Bacon.

Badgers
"Carroll." Three Badgers, The.
Clare, J. Badger ("When midnight comes a host of dogs and men")
Clarke, C. Tortoise and Badger.
Ghiselin. Catch, The.
Muldoon, P. Brock.
Phillpotts. Badgers, The.
Thomas, E. Combe was ever dark, ancient and dark, The.

Bagels
Ignatow, D. Bagel, The.

Bagpipes
"MacDiarmid." Bagpipe Music.

MacNeice. Bagpipe Music.
Tomlinson, C. Mr. Brodsky.

Bahamas
Oppen. Bahamas.

Baker, Chet
Ai. Archangel.
Doty, M. Almost Blue.
Hilton, D. Finding a Chet Baker Album in the Dimestore 2-for-$1 Pile.
Hull, L. Lost Fugue for Chet.
Komunyakaa. Speed Ball.
Williams, M. Death of Chet Baker, The.

Baker, Josephine
Cortez. So Many Feathers.

Balaam
Causley. Balaam.
Colman, H. On Balaam, and His Ass.
Keble. Balaam.

Baldness
Chao Meng-fu. Admonition to Myself, An.
Donne. Licentious Person, A.
Herrick. Upon Blanche.
Po Chü-i. On his Baldness.
Unknown. Bald Cavalier, The.

Baldwin, James
Boyle, K. For James Baldwin.
Troupe. In Jimmy's Garden.

Ballet
Bartošová. And That Is Why. . . .
Cornford, F. Grand Ballet.
Dickinson, E. I cannot dance upon my Toes.
Merrill, J. Watching the Dance.
Smith, S. Ballet of the Twelve Dancing Princesses, The.
Wright, S. Out of the Wailing.

Balloons
Bishop, E. Armadillo, The.
Fleming, E. Balloon Seller, The.
Freneau. To Mr. Blanchard, the Celebrated Aeronaut in America.
Fyleman. Balloon Man, The.
Herbert, E. Balloon Man, The.
Knight, E. Green Grass and Yellow Balloons.
Plath. Balloons.
Morning Song.
Pye. Air Balloon, The.
Sandburg, C. Balloon Faces.
Spargur. Tragedy.
Virgilio. Distant balloon, A.
Wilde, O. Les Ballons.

Balls
Aldis, D. Seals all flap, The.
Berryman. Ball Poem, The.
Clark, T. Superballs.
Farjeon, E. Over the garden wall.
Fitzgerald, E. 70.
Pizzarelli. Just before the storm.
Weber, R. Concise History of the Vietnam War: 1965–1968, A.
Wilbur. Juggler.

Ballylee, Ireland
Yeats. Coole Park and Ballylee, 1931.
To Be Carved on a Stone at Thoor Ballylee.

Baltimore, Maryland
Baumel. Doing Time in Baltimore.
Cullen. Incident.
Ginsberg, A. Haunting Poe's Baltimore.
Unknown. Streets of Baltimore.
Weaver, M. Imitation of Life.
Weekend Equestrian, The.

Bamboo
Chang Yü. Retreat of Sun Ching-hsiang, The.
Chao Meng-fu. Pavilion-Where-the-Crane-Came, The.
Chu Yün-ming. Little Landscape, A.
Hsü Chung-hsing. Cane of Ch'iung Bamboo, The.
Hsü Wei. I Once Did a Bamboo Painting for Somebody—Now He Wants Me To Do Another. I Have Written This To Answer Him.
Kao Ch'i. Nodding Off.
Kitahara Hakushū. Tanka: "In the daytime."
Li Ho. New Bamboo in the North Garden at Ch'ang-ku.

Li Tung-yang. Long Handscroll of Bamboo by Wang Meng-tuan, The.
Nam Xuyên. Bamboo hedgerow cut a dark-green swath, The.
Nguyễn Duy Nhuệ. Bamboos of Vietnam.
Pien Kung. Walking Outside the City Walls on the Day of the Cold Food Festival.
Ping. Song of Calling Souls.
Plomer. Bamboo.
Po Chü-i. Bamboo by Li Ch'e Yun's Window, The.
Eating Bamboo-Shoots.
Night Snow.
Painting Bamboo, a Song.
Planting Bamboos.
Rolls. Bamboo.
Shen Chou. Sent in Parting to Yen Kung-su.
Shūji. Tanka: "Stalks growing."
Tai Piao-yüan. Painting, *"Mist and Rain on the Spring River,"* by Hsiao Chao, The.
Tu Fu. Restless Night.
Yakamochi. Wind rustles the bamboos, The.
Yang Chi. Painting of Bamboo by Ni Yün-lin, A.
Yang Wei-chen. Bamboo Branch Song of West Lake.
Yün Shou-p'ing. Autumn Plants, Flowers, Bamboo, Rocks.
Written on the Night of the Twenty-ninth of the First Month.
Zenmaro. On Mumonkan.

Bananas
Edwards, R. When I was three I had a friend.
Unknown. Grasshopper and the Elephant, The.

Bandits. *See* **Highwaymen**

Bands
Palmer, J. Band Played On, The.

Bangkok, Thailand
Clifton, H. Monsoon Girl.
Scott, F. Bangkok.

Banjos
Foster, S. Oh! Susanna.
Kipling, R. Song of the Banjo, The.

Banking and Bankers
Gibbons, S. Continuity.
Kooser. At the Office Early.
Shapiro, K. Girls Working in Banks.
Theocritus. This bank makes welcome citizen and foreigner.
Unknown. War the Source of Riches.

Baptism
Aubert, A. Baptism.
Ciardi. Evil Eye, The.
Coleridge, S. My Baptismal Birthday [*or* Birth-Day].
Crashaw. On the Baptized Ethiopian.
On the Water of Our Lord's Baptism[e].
Heaney, S. Peacock's Feather, A.
Herbert, G. Love ("Thou art too hard for me in Love").
Johnson, A. And Sea.
Unknown. Jesus, Master, O Discover.

See also **Christenings**

Bar Kokba, Simon
Lazarus, E. Bar Kochba.

Bar Mitzvah
Amichai. My son, in whose face there is already a sign.

Barbecues. *See* **Picnics and Barbecues**

Barberries
Very. Barberry-Bush, The.

Barbers
Beardsley. Ballad of a Barber, The.
Fuller, J. Alex at the Barber's.
Gardner, M. Barbershop.
Gray, J. Barber, The.
Kooser. Self-Portrait at Thirty-Nine.
Levine, P. To a Child Trapped in a Barber Shop.
Mother Goose. Barber, barber, shave a pig.
Paquet. Night Dust-off.
Tadic. At the Hairdresser.

Barcelona, Spain
Bellamy, D. Letters of Mina Harker, The.
Cunard. To Eat To-day.

Warner, S. Journey To Barcelona.

Bards
Benson, G. Limerick: "There once was a bard of Hong Kong."
Blake, W. Introduction: "Hear the voice of the Bard!"
Burns, R. Epistle to J. Lapraik, an Old Scotch Bard.
Gray, T. Progress of Poesy, The.
Johnson, J. O Black and unknown bards of long ago.
Keats. How many bards gild the lapses of time!
Korinna. I come tonight to sing you songs.
O'Heffernan. I ask, who will buy a poem?
Owenson. Irish Harp: Fragment I, The.

Barges
Tekkan. Tanka: "In my mind."

Barley
Burns, R. John Barleycorn [a Ballad].

Barmaids
Stephens, J. Glass of Beer, A.

Barns
Blunden. Barn, The.
Heaney, S. Barn, The.
Kenyon, J. Portrait of a Figure near Water.
Lux. Barn Fire.
MacCaig. Byre.
Merton. Elegy for the Monastery Barn.
Morgan, R. Hay Scuttle.
Plumly. Complaint Against the Arsonist.
Pritchard, N. Paysagesque.
Spender, S. Barn, The.
Whitman, W. Big doors of the country barn stand open and ready, The.

Barons' War (1263-1267)
Unknown. Song of Lewes, The.

Baroque
Fenton, J. Lollipops of the Pomeranian Baroque.

Barrel Organs. See **Hurdy-Gurdies**

Barry, Thomas
Fitzgerald, P. Answer to Thomas Barry, An.

Bars and Bartenders
Angel. Tatters.
Auden. September 1, 1939.
Bartsch. Rita's husband gave Rita her walking papers.
Baxter, J. Bar Room Conversation.
Berryman. Henry sats in de bar and was odd.
Brickley. Outside the pub.
Bukowski. Crucifix in a Deathhand.
Coxon, W. Flash Colonial Barman, The.
Croft, J. Greenhalgh's Pub.
Cummings, E. I was sitting in mcsoreley's.   outside it was New York and beauti- / fully snowing.
Elmslie, K. Big Bar.
Espada. Dándole la mano a Mongo.
Shaking Hands with Mongo.
Gallagher, T. Instructions to the Double.
Gunn, T. Fever.
Hecht, A. Third Avenue in Sunlight.
Hughes, L. Bar.
Hugo, R. Hilltop, The.
Letter to Reed from Lolo.
Letter to Welch from Browning.
Milltown Union Bar, The.
Kennedy, X. In a Prominent Bar in Secaucus [One Day].
Kleinzahler. Two Canadian Landscapes.
Kunio. Tanka: "All the way."
Levine, P. Midget, The.
Poem Circling Hamtramck, Michigan, All Night in Search of You, The.
Lim, S. Starlight Haven.
Patchen. State of the Nation, The.
Peacock, M. Buffalo.
Selman, R. We saw everything except that we were gay.
Smith, P. Sweet Daddy.
Snyder, G. I went into the Maverick Bar.
Stephens, J. Glass of Beer, A.
Tolson. Ex-Judge at the Bar, An.
Unknown. Bar, The.
Welch, J. D-Y Bar.

Whitman, W. Glimpse through an interstice caught, A.
Williams, W. Hemmed-in Males.
Young, A. Topsy: Part 2.
See also **Barmaids**

Barters
Blake, M. Barter.
Chin Nung. Three lines of "clerk script" calligraphy.
Moore, M. New York.
Teasdale. Barter.

Barth, Karl
Clemo. On the Death of Karl Barth.

Baseball
Bottoms. Sign for My Father, Who Stressed the Bunt.
Clark, T. Baseball and Classicism.
Corso. Dream of a Baseball Star.
Currie. July the First.
Dent. For Cool Papa Bell.
Djanikian. How I Learned English.
Ferlinghetti, L. Baseball Canto.
Fitzgerald, R. Cobb Would Have Caught It.
Flynn, M. Sandlot Days.
Francis, R. Base Stealer, The.
Catch.
Pitcher.
Gilbert, C. Theory of Curve.
Hoover, P. Baseball.
Humphries, R. Polo Grounds.
Johnson, D. Home Game.
Kizer, C. One to Nothing.
Logan, J. Brothers: Two Saltimbanques, The.
MacDonald, C. Lady Pitcher, The.
Mayer, B. Carlton Fisk is My Ideal.
McDonald, S. Casey—Twenty Years Later.
McDonald, W. Pee Wee Coach, The.
Moore, M. Baseball and Writing.
Hometown Piece for Messrs. Alston and Reese.
Morrison, L. Rural Recreation.
Mosby. To Josh Gibson (Legendary Slugger of the Old Negro Baseball League).
Norworth. Take Me Out to the Ball Game.
Patchen. Origin of Baseball, The.
Petersen. Ballad of Dead Yankees, The.
Rosenberg, L. City Baseball.
Sherman, F. Baseball.
Smith, D. Roundhouse Voices, The.
Soto. Black Hair.
Swenson, M. Analysis of Baseball.
Thayer, E. Casey at the Bat.
Troupe. Poem for My Father.
Wallace, R. Double-Play, The.
Weaver, M. My Father's First Baseball Game.
Williams, W. At the Ball Game.
Wilson, J. Casey's Revenge.

Basketball
Giovanni. Basketball.
Harper, M. Makin' Jump Shots.
Hirsch, E. Fast Break.
Hugo, R. In Your Young Dream.
Komunyakaa. Slam, Dunk, and Hook.
Matthews, W. In Memory of the Utah Stars.
Ridlon. Fernando ("Fernando has a basketball").
Seibles. For Brothers Everywhere.
Troupe. Poem for "Magic", A.
Updike. Ex-Basketball Player.

Bass, Sam
Unknown. Sam Bass.

Bastille Day
Apollinaire. Phantom of Clouds, A.
Lerner, L. 14 July 1956.

Bastogne, Battle of (1944-1945)
Simpson, L. Battle, The.

Baths and Bathing
Adamson. Rimbaud Having a Bath.
Ammons. Foot-Washing, The.
Ammuvanar. What Her Girl Friend Said to Him When He Wanted to Come by Day.
Barlas. My Lady's Bath.
Becker, R. Bath, The.
Beddoes. Bridal Song to Amala.
Blyton, C. Plug-hole Man, The.
Callimachus. On Pallas Bathing, from a Hymn of Callimachus.

Ch'u Yüan. Lord among the Clouds, The.
Clarke, C. What Goes Around Comes Around, or The Proof is in the Pudding.
Davis, T. Susannah.
Ewart. Miss Twye.
Fisher, R. After a Bath.
Fumi Saito. Tanka: "To take a bath."
Gallagher, T. Now That I Am Never Alone.
Gibbs, M. Song of the Bath, The.
Giovanni. Trips.
Godfrey. Bath.
Graves, R. I Wonder What It Feels Like to Be Drowned!
Heaney, S. Girls Bathing, Galway 1965.
Hollo. That Old Sauna High.
Johnson, B. Soap, the Oppressor.
Kipling, R. Naaman's Song.
Lattimore. Bathtubs.
Lawrence, D. Gloire de Dijon.
Gods! The Gods!, The.
Mackey, N. Dream Thief.
Magrelli. Tomorrow morning I will take a shower.
Miller, E. Another Love Affair/Another Poem.
Nash, O. Samson Agonistes.
Okamoto. Tanka: "Stark naked."
Parry, E. Pater's Bathe.
Patchen. Saturday Night in the Parthenon.
Pound, E. Bathtub [or Bath Tub], The.
Rakosi. In a Warm Bath.
Rankin, P. Hot Bath in an Old Hotel.
Samio. Tanka: "Surely by now."
Slutsky. Bathhouse, The.
Snyder, G. Bath, The.
Steele, T. Aubade, An.
Stern, G. Nobody else living knows that song as well as I do.
Swenson, M. Dream, The.
Unknown. Dahn the Plug'ole.
Draw a bucket of water.
First time I saw you, The.
Midwife's Invocation, A.
Wash me in the water.
Vinokurov. My beloved was laundering.
Weingarten. In the Cloud Chamber.
Wesley-Smith. Walter Spaggot, strange old man.
Whitman, W. Twenty-eight young men bathe by the shore.
Yukitsuna. Tanka: "With a hangover."

Bats
Bennett, R. Witch of Willowby Wood, The.
Carrel. Catching.
"Carroll." Mad Hatter's Song, The.
Carter, M. In a small city at dusk.
Dickinson, E. Bat is dun with wrinkled Wings, The.
Jarrell. Bats.
King, E. To the Bat.
Kizer, C. Intruder, The.
Lawrence, D. Bat.
Man and Bat.
McGreevy. Homage to Hieronymus Bosch.
Oliver, M. Bats.
Roethke. Bat, The.
Smith, D. Bats.
Spear, R. Bat, The.
Wilbur. Mind in its [or the] purest play is like some bat.

Battlefields
Aldington. Battlefield.
Soliloquy 2.
Basho. All That Is Left.
Bowes-Lyon. Battlefield.
Bryant, W. Battle-Field, The.
Campbell, T. Hohenlinden.
Collins, W. Ode Written in the Beginning of the Year 1746.
Douglas, K. Vergissmeinnicht.
Emerson, R. Concord Hymn.
Fenton, J. Wind.
Greenberg, U. By the Waters of the Sava.
Heóghusa. Winter Campaign, A.
Herbert, A. Beaucourt Revisited.
Hill, G. Distant Fury of Battle, The.
Holub. Fly, The.
Homer. Achilles kills Lycaon.

Battle.

Clash in Arms of the Achaians and Trojans.

Equity in death.

Hector's flight.

Priam and Achilles.

Johnstone, P. High Wood.

Kao Ch'i. Passing By the Battlefield at Feng-k'ou.

Kennedy, B. Bad luck to this marching.

Li Ho. Arrowhead from the Ancient Battlefield of Ch'ang-p'ing, An.

McCrae, J. In Flanders Fields the poppies blow.

Melville, H. Battle Summers, The.

Inscription: "To them who crossed the flood." Shiloh [A Requiem].

Muir, E. Combat, The.

Murray, P. Redemption.

Peacock, T. War Song of Dinas Vawr, The.

Pope, A. Rape of the Lock, The.

Publius Papinius Statius. Moment of battle, The.

Rimbaud, A. Sleeper in the Valley, The.

Sandburg, C. Grass.

Shūji. Tanka: "Suddenly."

Simonides. For the Spartan Dead at Thermopylai (480 B.C.).

Smith, D. On a Field Trip at Fredericksburg.

Southey. Battle of Blenheim, The.

Stevenson, R. Ticonderoga: A Legend of the West Highlands.

Tipputtolar. Red is the battlefield.

Ts'ao Sung. Protest in the Sixth Year of Ch'ien Fu, A.

Tu Fu. Travelling Northward.

Tyutchev. At Vshchizh.

Unknown. Battle in the balance, The.

Fighting South of the Ramparts.

Hēr Æthoelstān cyning, eorla drihten.

Hymn to the Fallen.

Mice prepare for battle, The.

Warren, R. History among the Rocks.

Whitman, W. Vigil strange I kept on the field one night;.

Wilson, T. Magpies in Picardy, The.

Baucis and Philemon

Ovid. From lofty Roofs the Gods repuls'd before.

Philemon and Baucis.

Swift, J. Baucis and Philemon.

Baudelaire, Charles

Cronin, A. Baudelaire in Brussels.

Duncan, R. After a Passage in Baudelaire.

Schwartz, D. Baudelaire.

Swinburne. Ave atque Vale.

Bavaria

Campbell, T. Lines on Leaving a Scene in Bavaria.

Bay Trees. *See* **Laurels**

Beaches

Ammons. Constant, The.

Arnold, M. Dover Beach.

Beer, P. Jane Austen.

Beevers. Atameros.

Berryman. Traveller, The.

Betjeman. East Anglian Bathe.

Green shutters, shut your shutters! Windyridge.

Bishop, E. Little Exercise.

Bridges, R. Snow Lies Sprinkled on the Beach, The.

Brown, G. Beachcomber.

Brutus. Sand wet and cool, The.

Ceravolo. Wind Is Blowing West, The.

Clampitt. Baroque Sunburst, A.

Beach Glass.

Corben. On The Beach.

Cornford, F. Summer Beach.

Cummings, E. How many moments must(amazing each).

Maggie and milly and molly and may.

Cunningham, J. Miramar Beach.

Davie. Across the Bay.

De Mello Breyner. Beach.

Flute, The.

Dickinson, E. I started Early—Took my Dog.

Doolittle, H. Shrine, The.

Dugan, A. Memorial Service for the Invasion

Beach Where the Vacation in the Flesh Is Over.

Graves, R. Beach, The.

Gregor, A. Sunbather in Late October, A.

Gurney, I. Sea-Marge.

Heaney, S. Strand at Lough Beg, The.

Hillman. *Cleave* and *Cleave.*

Hopkins, G. Sea and the Skylark, The.

Keats. To Ailsa Rock.

Kees. Beach in August, The.

Kellman. Bajan.

Kennedy, X. Emily Dickinson in Southern California.

Koch, C. Shelly Beach.

Kunitz, S. Prophecy on Lethe.

Lamb, E. Broken kite, sprawled.

Lipsitz. Prospect Beach.

Longley, M. Strand, The.

MacCaig. Beach Talk.

Mahon. Chinese Restaurant in Portrush, The.

McGuckian. On Ballycastle Beach.

Meredith, W. Rhode Island.

Merwin, W. Bones, The.

Mitchell, K. Tree Stillness.

Momaday. Winter Holding off the Coast of North America.

Nemerov. Salt Garden, The.

Okigbo. Eyes Watch the Stars.

Parun. Sleeping Youth.

Peruncattan. What She Said ("In his country of cool seas, they say").

Pizzarelli. Tattoo'd man, The.

Under the boardwalk.

Plath. Point Shirley.

Robinson, M. Haunted Beach, The.

Roethke. Her Time.

Rukeyser, M. Children, the Sandbar, That Summer.

Samio. Tanka: "On the sandy beach."

Sandburg, C. Sandhill People.

Satyamurti. Day Trip.

Schick. Last summer.

Schuyler, J. Crystal Lithium, The.

Shakespeare, W. Sonnet 60.

Singer, B. Peterhead in May.

Smith, W. Abruptly all the palm trees rose like parasols.

Spence, M. Lost People, The.

Spenser. Sonnet 75: "One day I wrote her name upon the strand."

Stafford, W. With Kit, Age Seven, at the Beach.

Starbuck, G. Skin Divers, The.

Stevenson, R. At the Seaside [*or* Sea-Side].

Stickney, T. At Sainte-Marguerite.

Sueyoshi. Crying plovers, The.

Swenson, M. Waking from a Nap on the Beach.

Thaxter. Sandpiper, The.

Thomas, D. Author's Prologue.

Thompson, D. Very Odd Fish, A.

Thurman. Going Barefoot.

Tomlinson, C. Fiascherino.

Icos.

Toomer. Merl.

Toshiko. Seacoast at Mera, The.

Unknown. O sea-gulls that are crying.

Warren, R. Myth on Mediterranean Beach: Aphrodite as Logos.

Wheelock, J. Afternoon: Amagansett Beach.

Amagansett Beach Revisited.

Whitman, W. As if a phantom caress'd me.

On the beach at night.

On the beach at night alone.

Wilbur. On the Marginal Way.

Woolson. Florida Beach, The.

Wright, J. At the Slackening of the Tide.

Yeats. To a Child Dancing in the Wind.

Yosano. Left on the beach.

See also **Shores**

Beagles

Coleridge, H. On the Death of Echo, A Favourite Beagle.

Rodgers, W. Beagles.

Bean, Judge Roy

Unknown. Roy Bean.

Beans

Allur Nanmullai. What She Said ("Bare root of the bean is pink, The").

Murray, L. Broad Bean Sermon, The.

Unknown. Hot Boiled Beans.

Beards

Clarke, J. There was an old man with a beard.

Dove, R. This Life.

Lear, E. There was an Old Man with a beard.

Ríos, A. Domingo Limón.

Shen Chou. Drinking at Night with Yen Kung-mou.

Ulinover. Havdolah Wine.

Updike. Upon Shaving Off One's Beard.

Bears

Austin, M. Grizzly Bear.

Bachmann. Invocation of the Great Bear.

Birney. Bear on the Delhi Road, The.

Blue Cloud. Bear: A Totem Dance As Seen by Raven.

Bly, R. Schoolcraft's Diary Written on the Missouri: 1830.

Césaire, A. Three for Bear.

Coxe, L. Squaring the Circle.

Dubie. Elizabeth's War with the Christmas Bear.

Dunbar, P. Cabin Tale, A.

Field, E. Dancing Bear, The.

Frost, R. Bear puts both arms around the tree above her, The.

García Lorca. Ursa Major.

Hogan, L. Bear Fat.

Housman, A. Infant Innocence.

Hughes, T. Bear, The.

I see a bear.

Kelen. Rabbit Shoeshine.

Kinnell. Bear, The.

Lastness.

Kumin, M. Rendezvous, The.

Kuzma. In Love with the Bears.

Kwakiutl Oral Tradition. Prayer to the Black Bear.

Kyger. Destruction.

Levertov. Embroidery (I), An.

To the Reader.

Milton. Tenants of Paradise.

Momaday. Bear, The.

Nash, O. Adventures of Isabel.

Nemerov. Goose Fish, The.

Nicholls, J. Polar Cub.

Reed, J. Lost Silvertip.

Rich, A. Bears.

Roberson. Sonnet.

Roethke. Lady and the Bear, The.

Schwartz, D. Heavy Bear, The.

Smith, W. Polar Bear never makes his bed, The.

Snyder, G. Right in the Trail.

Stafford, W. Woman at Banff, The.

Unknown. Algy met a bear.

Cheerful old bear at the zoo, A.

Song of the Black Bear, The.

Vacietis. Of nights / some bear.

Wagoner, D. Meeting a Bear.

Willard, N. Cat's Second Song, The.

Wills, J. Den of the bear.

Beatings

Aristophanes. Son learns how to beat his father, The.

"Carroll." Duchess's Lullaby, The.

Knight, E. Hard Rock Returns to Prison from the Hospital for the Criminal Insane.

Ross, C. Jack.

Unknown. No more auction block for me.

Beatniks

Baraka. All is One for Monk.

Durem. Problem in Social Geometry—the Inverted Square!

Ginsberg, A. 'Back on Times Square, Dreaming of Times Square'.

Bop Lyrics.

Dream Record: June 8 1955.

Footnote to Howl.

Howl.

Hilton, D. Finding a Chet Baker Album in the Dimestore 2-for-$1 Pile.

Beatrice Portinari
Dante Alighieri.　Sonnet: Of Beatrice de'
Portinari, on All Saints' Day.

Beaufort, South Carolina
Heard, J.　National Cemetery, Beaufort, South
Carolina, The.

Beaumont, Francis
Jonson, B.　To Francis Beaumont.

Beauty
"Æ."　Great Breath, The.
Agathias.　Beautiful Melite, in the throes of
middle age.
"Akhmatova."　I care nothing for battle odes.
Al-Harizi.　Secret Kept, A.
Alcman.　Vendettas end among the gods.
Alexander, C.　All things bright and beauteous.
Allerton.　Beautiful Things.
Alvarez, J.　He: Age doesn't matter when
you're both in love.
Amirthanayagam.　So beautiful that couple.
Anacreon.　Anacreon's Portrait of His Mistress.
Beauty.
Ode 3: "Of late, what time the Bear turned
round."
Picture, The.
Angelou.　Phenomenal Woman.
Antipater of Thessalonica.　Temple of Artemis
at Ephesos, The.
Antonov.　Toward morning, slipping the pistol
under my arm.
Argentarius.　Isias my love, with your scented
breath.
Looking and lusting is not love.
Love is not just a function of the eyes.
Aristophanes.　O glorious Eie, thou miracle of
Sight.
Arnold, M.　Growing Old.
Asclepiades.　Love has found out how to mix.
When soft Irene like a.
Ashbery.　Le Livre Est sur la Table.
Atkinson.　Same Trouble with Beauty You've
Always Had, The.
Bacchylides.　How white.
Baillie, L.　Werena My Heart Licht I Wad
Dee.
Baraka.　Cold Term.
Return of the Native.
Barlas.　Beauty's Anadems.
Barnes, B.　To the Most Beautiful Lady, the
Lady Bridget Manners.
Barnfield.　Affectionate Shepherd, The.
Barras, J.　Peace.
Bates, K.　America the Beautiful.
Baudelaire.　Jewels, The.
She Is Not Satisfied.
Behn, A.　To My Lady Morland at Tunbridge.
Bell, M.　Stars Which See, Stars Which Do
Not See.
Berryman.　Canto Amor.
Binyon.　Beauty.
Blake, W.　Abstinence sows sand all over.
Blind.　Beautiful Beeshareen Boy, The.
Blunden.　One among the Roses.
Blunt, W.　On Her Vanity.
Bogan, L.　Juan's Song.
Question in a Field.
Boker.　My darling's features, painted by the
light.
Braithwaite.　Sic Vita.
Bridges, R.　Art is the true and happy science
of the soul.
I love all beauteous things.
Brock-Broido.　Last Passenger Pigeon in the
Cincinnati Zoo, The.
Browning, E.　Best Thing in the World, The.
Hiram Powers' "Greek Slave."
Sonnet: "Yet, love, mere love, is beautiful
indeed."
Browning, R.　Guardian-Angel, The.
Women and Roses.
Burns, R.　Bonnie Lesley.
Byron, G.　She walks in Beauty like the night.
Stanzas for Music ("There be none of
Beauty's daughters").
Callimachus.　On Pallas Bathing, from a Hymn
of Callimachus.
Campbell, J.　Old Woman, The.

Campion, T.　Are you what your faire lookes
expresse?
Give beauty all her right.
I must complain, yet doe enjoy my Love.
Laura.
There is a Garden in her face.
Thou art not fair for all thy red and white.
Capito.　Lacking grace / beauty.
Cardenal.　Vision from the Blue Window.
Carew, T.　Beautiful Mistress, A.
Comparison, The.
Complement, The.
Disdain Returned.
Divine Mistress, A.
Fancy, A.
Ingrateful[l] Beauty Threatened.
On Sight of a Gentlewoman's Face in the
Water.
On the Marriage of T. K. and C. C.: The
Morning Stormy.
Song, [A]: "Ask me no more where Jove
bestows."
Song: Good Counsel to a Young Maid.
Tinder, The.
To A. L.; Persuasions [or Perswasions] to
Love.
To a Lady That Desired I Would Love Her.
To my Friend G.N. from Wrest.
"Carroll."　Song of the Mock Turtle, The.
Catullus.　De Quintia et Lesbia.
Many think Quintia's beautiful. She's tall.
Quintia is beautiful, many will tell you: to me.
Cavalcanti.　Sonnet: A Rapture Concerning His
Lady.
Sonnet: He Compares All Things with His
Lady, and Finds Them Wanting.
Cawein.　Beauty.
Unimaginative, The.
Chao Luan-luan.　Willow Eyebrows.
Chaucer.　To Rosamounde.
Chiang K'uei.　Tune: "Sparse Shadows"—Plum
Blossoms.
Chivers.　To Isa Sleeping.
Chu Hsi.　Farm by the Lake, The.
Chudleigh.　Song: "Why Damon, why, why,
why so pressing?"
Clampitt.　Written in Water.
Clare, J.　First Love.
Song—Molly Magee.
Clarke, A.　Planter's Daughter, The.
Coatsworth.　Swift things are beautiful.
Conquest.　Rokeby Venus, The.
Constable, H.　Of his Mistress, upon Occasion
of her Walking in a Garden.
Cowley, A.　Beauty, thou wild fantastic ape.
Cowley, H.　Departed Youth.
Cranch.　Evening Primrose, The.
Crashaw.　Bubble, The.
Crinagoras.　Roses used to bloom in spring.
Cruz, V.　Problems With Hurricanes.
Csoori.　Bachelor, The.
Cullen, C.　To John Keats, Poet, at Spring
Time.
Cummings, E.　My love / thy hair is one
kingdom.
Poem, or Beauty Hurts Mr. Vinal.
Pretty a day, A.
Whatever's merely wilful, / and not
miraculous.
White guardians of the universe of sleep.
Who are you,little i.
Cuney.　No Images.
Daniel, S.　46.
Beauty, Time and Love.
Behold what hap *Pigmalion* had to frame.
Half-blown Rose, The.
Lonely Beauty.
Sonnet: "Beauty, sweet love, is like the
morning dew."
Unto the boundless Ocean of thy beauty.
When winter snows upon thy sable hairs.
Dante Alighieri.　For certain he hath seen all
perfectness.
To waning day, to the wide round of shadow.
Darley.　Song, A: "It is not Beauty [or beautie]
I demand[e]."
Davenant.　Lover and Philosopher.

De la Mare.　Epitaph, An: "Here lies a most
beautiful lady."
Three Cherry Trees, The.
Derricotte.　Minks, The.
Dharmakirti.　Proof.
Dickinson, E.　Beauty be not caused—It Is.
I died for Beauty—but was scarce.
Dioscorides.　My downfall: those pink
articulate lips.
Dioscorides.　They are too much for me.
Donne.　Autumnal[l], The.
Undertaking, The.
Doolittle, H.　Song: "You are as gold."
D'Orleans.　Not long ago I hied me apace.
Smiling mouth and laughing eyen° gray, The.
Drayton.　If he, from heaven that filched the
living fire.
Roundelay Between Two Shepherds, A.
To nothing fitter can I Thee compare.
Drummond, W.　Madrigal.
Drummond, W.　Madrigal: "Like the Idalian
Queen[e]."
Stolen Pleasure.
Dunbar-Nelson.　Proletariat Speaks, The.
Duncan, R.　Poetry, a Natural Thing.
Dunn, D.　She sat up on her pillows, receiving
guests.
Edwards, M.　World Is Full of Beauty, The.
Ehrmann.　If You Made Gentler the Churlish
World.
Elizabeth I.　When I was fair and young, then
[or and] favour graced me;.
Éluard, P.　Dawn Dissolves the Monsters.
Lover, secretly behind your smile.
Elytis.　Ode to Santorini.
Emanuel, L.　Blond Bombshell.
Emerson, R.　Each and All.
Harp, The.
Rhodora, The [On Being Asked Whence Is the
Flower].
Empson.　Villanelle.
"Ephelia."　To a Proud Beauty.
Evelyn, M.　Mundus Muliebris.
"Field."　Elsewhere.
Girl, A.
Portrait, A.
So jealous of your beauty.
Fields, J.　Alabama.
Fitzgerald, M.　Rendezvous.
Fletcher, J.　Song: "Oh [or O] fair[e] sweet
face, oh [or O] eyes celestial[l] bright."
Take, oh, take those lips away.
Fumi Saito.　Turbid current.
Garrigue.　Primer of Plato.
Gascoigne.　Sonet Written in Prayse of the
Browne Beautie, A.
Gergely.　Upon a Renaissance Carving.
Giovanni.　Beautiful Black Men.
Poem for Flora.
Glanz-Leyeles.　White Swan.
Godolphin.　Song: "Noe more unto my
thoughts appeare."
Goldsmith, O.　Deserted Village, The.
Song: "When lovely woman stoops to folly."
Gorges.　Her [or hir] face her [or hir] tongue
[or tong] her [or hir] wit.
Gouri.　Silk and Silence.
Graves, R.　Down, wanton, down! Have you
no shame.
Mirror mirror tell me.
Gray, J.　Les Demoiselles de Sauve.
Greene, R.　Samela.
Greville, F.　Absence and Presence.
Cupid, in Myra's faire bewitching eyes.
From Caelica.
Sonnet: "Nurse-life wheat within his green
husk growing, The."
Guinicelli.　Sonnet: He Will Praise His Lady.
Habington.　To Castara, upon Beautie.
Hafiz.　Ode 147: "Beauty alone will not
account for her."
Ode 173: "All the long night we talked of
your long hair."
Han-shan.　Swine gobble dead men's flesh.
Harford, L.　Beauty and Terror.
Harjo, J.　Eagle Poem.
Harris, W.　Daddy Poem, A.

Hemphill. Soft Targets.
Herbert, G. Sonnet: "Sure Lord, there is enough in thee to dry."
Herbert of Cherbury. La Gialletta Gallante, or the Sunburned Exotic Beauty.
Sonnet of Black Beauty.
To One Black, and Not Very Handsome, Who Expected Commendation.
Herrick. Apron of Flowers, The.
Art above Nature, to Julia.
Definition of Beauty, The.
Delight in Disorder.
Epitaph upon a Virgin, An.
Request to the Graces, An.
To Anthea Lying in Bed.
Upon Her Feet.
Upon Julia's Clothes.
Upon Julia's Haire Fill'd with Dew.
Upon the Nipples of Julia's Breast.
Hewett, D. This Version of Love.
Hill, A. Garden Window, The.
Hoagland, E. Anti-Semanticist, The.
Hodgson, R. Gipsy Girl, The.
Holtby, W. Beauty the Lover's Gift?
Homer. Helen and the elders.
Mars and Venus.
Hood, T. Ruth.
Hookes. To Amanda Walking in the Garden.
Hopkins, G. Pied Beauty.
To what serves mortal beauty—dangerous; does set danc.
Horace. 1.5.
Epistle: To Elizabeth, Countess of Rutland.
Hsieh T'iao. Song of the Men of Chin-ling.
Hsin Ch'i-chi. Tune: "Immortal's Auspicious Crane, An"—On Plum Blossoms.
Hughes, L. Harlem Sweeties.
I too, sing America.
My People.
When Sue Wears Red.
Hull, A. Another Rhythm.
Ibn al-Arabi. Oh, her beauty—the tender maid! Its brilliance gives light.
Illyés. Sour-Cherry Trees.
Irwin, M. Robert Mapplethorpe's Photograph of Apollo (1988).
Jaccottet. Daybreak / mingles blood.
Jackson, L. Helen's Burning.
Jacobs, H. On Growing Up the Darker Berry.
Jeffers, L. My Blackness Is the Beauty of This Land.
Jeffers, R. Beauty of Things, The.
Birds and Fishes.
Divinely Superfluous Beauty.
Life from the Lifeless.
Rearmament.
Jennings, E. Ugly Child, The.
Johnson, H. Poem: "Little brown boy."
Johnston, E. Lines: To a Young Gentleman of Surpassing Beauty.
Jones, M. After the Small Pox.
Jonson, B. Elegy [or Elegie], An: "Let me be what I am, as Virgil cold."
Elegy, An: "Though beauty be the mark of praise."
Fair friend, 'tis true, your beauties move.
Her Triumph.
On Lucy Countess[e] of Bedford.
To Mary, Lady Wroth ("Madam[e], had all antiquity [or antiquitie] been lost").
Vision of Beauty, A.
Jordan, N. July 31.
Joyce, J. My dove, my beautiful one.
Juana Inés de la Cruz. Happy Easter, my Lady.
Julianus of Egypt. Lais' Mirror.
Kapilar. What She Said to Her Girl Friend When She Returned from the Hills.
Kapitonos. No charm.
Kaplinski, J. I UNDERSTOOD I UNDERSTOOD.
Karouzos. Triplets for Beautiful Mistra.
Keats. Endymion.
Kenney. Plume.
Kinnell. Saint Francis and the Sow.
Kirsch, S. Legend of Lilja.
Kizer, C. Hera, Hung from the Sky.

Klingsor. Song of the Cat, The.
Knott. Sonnet: "Way the world is not, The."
Koch, K. Energy in Sweden.
Kuan Yün-shih. Tune: "Song of Shou-yang."
Kynaston. To Cynthia.
To Cynthia, on Concealment of Her Beauty.
Lake, P. Introduction to Poetry.
Lamb, C. "Timid grace sits trembling in her eye, A."
Landon. Lady, thy face is very beautiful.
Landor, W. Behold, O Aspasia! I Send You Verses.
Rose Aylmer.
Lawrence, D. Fronleichnam.
Le Gallienne. Beauty Accurst.
Leapor. Strephon to Celia.
Leconte de Lisle, C. Palanquin, The.
Venus de Milo.
Legaré. To a Lily.
Leigh, R. On a Fair Lady, Looking in the Glass.
Li Ho. Temple of the Orchid Fragrance Goddess.
Li Shang-yin. To Tzŭ-chih: among the 'Flowers'.
Willow.
Li Yü. Tune: "Casket of Pearls, A."
Liu E. Teahouse at Hoshioka, A.
Liu Yung. Tune: "Chrysanthemums Fresh."
Lochhead, L. Grim Sisters, The.
Heartbreak Hotel.
Lorde. Naturally.
Lovelace, R. Fair Beggar, The.
Gratiana Dancing [or Dauncing] and [or &] Singing.
To Amarantha, That She Would Dishevel[l] Her Hair[e].
Lowell, A. Artist, The.
Lowell, J. In a Copy of Omar Khayyám.
Lu Chih. Tune: "Intoxication in the East Wind" Autumn Scenery.
Lyly, J. Cards and Kisses.
Lynd. Beauty and the Beast.
Lyttelton. Soliloquy of a Beauty in the Country.
Macedonius. Beauty kissed your mouth, and gave the petals.
MacLeish. Not Marble nor the Gilded Monuments.
MacNeice. Circe.
Madgett. Black Woman.
Marino. Beautiful Slave, The.
Marlatt, D. Trying. a trying child. trying it on for size. the role.
Marston, J. Pigmalion, whose hie love-hating minde.
Martial. You are the most beautiful.
Masefield. On Growing Old.
Mavilis. Olive Tree.
McClintock, M. Sat down.
McHugh, H. Oven Loves the TV Set, The.
McKay, C. To O.E.A E. A.
Meinke. Sonnet on the Death of the Man Who Invented Plastic Roses.
Meleager. Heliodora's Brows.
Petals fall from Heliodora's image, The.
Mendelssohn, F. Every Day.
Meredith, G. She issues radiant from her dressing-room.
When I would image her features.
Michelangelo Buonarroti. I see in your handsome face, my Lord.
Millay, F. And you as well must die, belovèd dust.
Euclid alone has looked on Beauty bare.
Spring.
When I too long have looked upon your face.
Miller, L. My Students Catch Me Dancing.
Milton. Fifth Ode of Horace. Lib. I, The.
Mitford. Song: "Fairest things are those which live, The."
Montagu, L. Between your sheets you soundly sleep.
Saturday: The Small-Pox.
Moore, T. Believe me, if all those endearing young charms.
Morley, H. Parents.

Morton, D. Who Walks with Beauty.
Nabbes. Song, The: "Beauty no more the subject be."
Nam Trân. Beauty and the Poet.
Navajo Oral Tradition. Night Chant, The.
Neruda. Body of a woman, white hills, white thighs.
Nezval. Prague in the Midday Sun.
Nguyễn Công Trú. Ode to All Flowers.
Nguyễn Gia Thiều. Song of Sorrow Inside the Royal Harem, A.
Nossis. Let us go to the temple.
This is Thaumareta's picture, and how well it captures.
Nukada. When spring escapes.
O'Hara, F. Having a Coke with You.
Poem: "O solo mio, hot diggety, nix 'I wather think I can'."
Oliver, M. May, and among the miles of leafing.
Olson, C. Kingfishers, The.
La Chute.
Orerulavanar. What He Said ("Her arms have the beauty").
Ostriker. Warning.
Ou-yang Hsiu. Song of Liang Chou.
Song of the Radiant Lady, Replying to a Poem by Wang Chieh-fu.
Ovid. Elegies 1.5.
P'an Lang. Tune: "Song of the Wine Spring."
Park, S. Opium Poppy, The.
Parnell, T. Elegy, to an Old Beauty, An.
Paulus Silentiarius. And now you comb and braid your hair.
Choicer than all / flush of youth.
Description of Hagia Sophia.
Peele. Bethsabe's Song.
Pettet. Mevlana.
Peyanar. What He Said ("In this time of rain and thunder").
What her girl friend said ("Her eyes").
Phillips, C. Toys.
Philodemus. Oh feet, oh legs, oh thighs / that formed the deathrow.
Sixty sun-decked years Charito has gotten to.
Piatt, S. Lesson in a Picture, A.
Piercy. Barbie Doll.
Pindar. Athens.
Oh! Sovereign of the willing soul.
Plumly. Cedar Waxwing on Scarlet Firethorn.
Po Chü-i. Lotus-gatherer's Song.
Poe. Israfel.
Lake: To———, The.
Sleeper, The.
Stanzas: "How often we forget all time, when lone."
To Helen ("Helen, thy beauty is to me").
Valley of Unrest, The.
Poseidippus. Doricha.
Pound, E. Dance Figure.
Study in Aesthetics, The.
Praed. Beauty and Her Visitors.
Prestwich. How to Choose a Mistress.
Prévert. River, The.
Prince, F. Token, The.
Prior. Nonpareil.
To a Lady: She Refusing to Continue a Dispute with Me, and Leaving Me in the Argument.
Probyn. Frustrated.
Procter, A. Lost Chord, A.
Publius Papinius Statius. Altar of Mercy, The.
Queneau. If You Imagine.
Rakosi. Sandlewood comes to my mind.
Ralegh, W. Nature, that washed her hands in milk.
Ransom, J. Judith of Bethulia.
Reid, A. Lesson for Beautiful Women, A.
Ritsos. Day in May you left me, a day in May I lose you, A.
Roberson. Eclipse.
Robinson, E. Beauty as a Shield.
Roethke. I knew a woman, lovely in her bones.
Rogetsu. Roasting chestnuts.
Romero, L. If Marilyn Monroe.
Rosenberg, I. Beauty.

Rossetti, C. Cousin Kate.
  Luscious and Sorrowful.
  What is pink? A rose is pink.
Rossetti, D. Soul's Beauty.
Rudman, M. Nowhere Water, The.
Rufinus. Her eyes are gold.
  Here Rhodoklea / is a garland.
Rhodope.
  Silvertoed virgin, A.
  You have Hera's eyes Melite.
Rufinus Domesticus. Her foot sparkled like
  silver.
  How could I have known.
  Years have not damaged your beauty, The.
St. John, D. Uptown Love Poem.
St. John, P. Pearle's Poem.
Sanchez, S. Song No. 3: "Cain't nobody tell
  me any different."
Sandburg, C. Flash Crimson.
Sansom, M. To Cleon's Eyes.
Santayana. On a Piece of Tapestry.
  Sonnet XLIII: "Candour of the gods is in thy
  gaze, The."
  Sonnet XLVIII: "Of Helen's brothers, one was
  born to die."
Sappho. Hymn to Venus, An.
  One Girl.
  Sapho's Ode out of Longinus.
  Some say nothing on earth excels in beauty.
  Stars around the luminous moon—how soon
  they.
Schuyler, J. Poem: "This beauty that I see."
Scott, W. Rosabelle.
Sepamla. Odyssey, The.
"Severyanin." Russian Woman.
Seward. Elegy.
Sexton. Snow White and the Seven Dwarfs.
Shakespeare, W. Phoenix and the Turtle, The.
  Sonnet 1.
  Sonnet 5: 'Those hours that with gentle work'.
  Sonnet 14.
  Sonnet 18.
  Sonnet 20.
  Sonnet 53.
  Sonnet 54.
  Sonnet 65.
  Sonnet 94.
  Sonnet 95.
  Sonnet 104.
  Sonnet 106.
  Sonnet 127.
  Sonnet 130.
  Sonnet 132.
Shapiro, K. Cut Flower, A.
Shchipachov. Blue spaces do not see
  themselves, The.
Shelley, P. Hymn to Intellectual Beauty.
  She met me, Stranger, upon life's rough way.
Shen Chou. Inscribed on a Painting.
Shirley, J. Love's Hue and Cry.
  Would you know what's soft? I dare.
Siddal. Lust of the Eyes, The.
Sidney, P. First Song: "Doubt you to whom
  my Muse these notes intendeth [or
  entendeth]."
  Seventh Song: "Whose senses in so evil
  consort, their stepdame Nature lays."
  Sonnet 5: "It is most true that eyes are formed
  to serve."
  Sonnet 11: "In truth, O Love, with what a
  boyish kind."
  Sonnet 25: "Wisest scholar of the wight most
  wise, The."
  Sonnet 52: "Strife is grown between Virtue
  and Love, A."
  Sonnet 9: "Queen Virtue's court, which some
  call Stella's face."
Singer, E. Cant. 5.6 & c.
Skelton, J. To Mistress [or Maystres] Margaret
  Hussey.
Slessor. William Street.
Smart, C. Loveliness.
Smith, D. Near the Docks.
Smith, P. Blonde White Women.
Smith, S. Pretty.
Smith, W. Independence Day.
So Chong-Ju. Winter Sky, The.

Sophocles. Colonus' Praise.
Spenser.
  Sonnet 8: "More than most fair [or fayre], full
  of the living fire [or fyre]."
  Sonnet 10: 'Unrighteous Lord of Love'.
  Sonnet 15: "Ye tradeful merchants that, with
  weary toil."
  Sonnet 64: "Coming [or Comming] to kiss[e]
  her lips [or lyps], (such grace I found)."
  Sonnet 71: "Soverayne beauty which I doo
  admire, The."
  Sonnet 79: "Men call you fair [or fayre], and
  you do[e] credit it."
  Sonnet 81: "Fair [or Fayre] is my love, when
  her fair [or fayre] golden heares."
Stanley, T. Celia Singing.
  Glowworm, The.
Stein, G. Bundles for Them.
  Suppose an Eyes.
Stevens, W. Peter Quince at the Clavier.
Stevenson, A. He Who Loved Beauty.
Stevenson, R. To Henry James.
Strode. On a Good Leg and Foot.
  On Fairford Windows.
Su Shih. Drinking at the Lake, First It's
  Sunny, Then It Rains.
Suckling, J. Sonnet: "Dost see how unregarded
  now."
  Sonnet: "Of thee, kind boy, I ask no red and
  white."
  To B.C.
Suckling, J. et al. Song: "When, dearest, I but
  think on [or of] thee."
Surrey. Frailty and Hurtfulness of Beauty,
  The.
Swift, J. Lady's Dressing Room, The.
  On Stella's Birthday, 1718/1719.
  Progress of Beauty, The.
Swinburne. Aholibah.
  Sapphics.
Symons, A. Faint Love.
Tasso. I'd like to be a bee.
Taylor, E. Meditation Twelve.
Teasdale. Barter.
  Moonlight.
Tekkan. Tanka: "Vast wilderness."
Tennyson, A. To —. With the Following
  Poem.
Theocritus. Hylas and the Water Nymphs.
  I dare not, faith I dare not pipe at Noon.
Thomas, E. Glory of the beauty of the
  morning, The.
Thompson, F. Too Soon.
Traherne. Salutation [or Salutations], The.
Ts'ao Chih. Rhyme-Prose on the Goddess of
  the Lo.
Ts'ao P'i. Lotus Pond, The.
Tu Fu. South Wind.
Tuckerman, F. Question, The.
Turberville. To His Friend.
Unknown. Aphrodite reveals herself.
  Art thou that she than whom none fairer is.
  Beautiful faces are they that wear.
  Brown Is My Love.
  But Jove at length with just Resentment fir'd.
  Changeful Beauty.
  Dark young pine, at the center of the earth
  originating.
  Dear Black Head.
  First of May, The.
  Growing Friendship.
  In beauty may I walk.
  Lovely is the modest girl.
  Madrigal: "My Love in her attire doth show
  her wit."
  Mirror, mirror, tell me.
  Mulberry by the Path.
  My Lady's Tears.
  Not of Itself, But Thee.
  Question, A.
  Some folks in looks take so much pride.
  There are four Graces, two Aphrodites, ten
  Muses.
  There is a lady sweet and kind.
  Time stands still, with gazing on her face!
  Whether I see you now.

Unknown, sometimes at. to Sir Walter
  Ralegh. Holy Land of Walsingham, The.
Vasilyev, P. Lines in Honor of Natalya.
Veneris. Spring, the new, the warb'ling Spring
  appears, The.
Vidyapati. Twin Hills.
Villon. Complaint of the Fair Armoress [or
  Armouress], The.
  Old Lady's Lament for Her Youth, The.
Vinokurov. My beloved was laundering.
Wakoski. Poet Recognizing the Echo of the
  Voice, A.
Wallace, R. In a Spring Still Not Written Of.
Waller, E. Song: "Go[e], lovely rose[—ous
  sweet and fair]."
Wang An-shih. Song of the Radiant Lady.
Waring, B. When a Beautiful Woman Gets on
  the Jutiapa Bus.
Warren, R. Child next door is defective
  because the mother, The.
Wat. From "Songs of a Wanderer."
Webster, A. Faded.
Wen T'ing-yün. Song Of Chang Ching-Yüan
  Picking Lotus Flowers, A.
Whitman, A. Before the world, I hold that
  none of these.
Whitman, W. Beauty.
  Had I the choice to tally greatest bards.
  Leaves of Grass (1855).
  This is the female form.
  Twenty-eight young men bathe by the shore.
  Walt Whitman, a kosmos, of Manhattan the
  son.
Wickham. Song of Ophelia the Survivor.
Wier. Barely There.
Wilbur. Beautiful Changes, The.
  Caserta Garden.
  Piazza di Spagna, Early Morning.
  Still, citizen sparrow, this vulture which you
  call.
  Thyme Flowering among Rocks.
  Transit.
Wilde, L. Poet's Destiny, The.
Williams, S. Song upon Miss Harriet Hanbury,
  Addressed to the Revd Mr Birt.
Williams, S. Straight Talk from Plain Women.
Williams, W. Poem: "Rose fades / and is
  renewed again, The."
Willson, F. Estray, The.
  To Hersa.
Wither. Ninth Canticle, The.
Witting. Beauty is the straw I clutch at, but to
  say straw.
Wordsworth, W. Composed upon an Evening
  of Extraordinary Splendour and Beauty.
  Composed upon Westminster Bridge[,
  September 3, 1802].
  Daffodils.
  To the Highland Girl of Inversneyde.
  To the Skylark.
Wright, F. If you wisely invest in beauty.
Wright, J. What is Beautiful.
Wright, K. Unlikely Obbligato of
  Andersonstown.
Wylie. Beauty.
Yang Wan-li. Stanza Written in Jest.
Yeats. Before the World Was Made.
  Crazed Girl, A.
  Crazy Jane Talks with the Bishop.
  Dream of Death, A.
  Folly Of Being Comforted, The.
  He Remembers Forgotten Beauty.
  Memory.
  Michael Robartes and the Dancer.
  No Second Troy.
  Old Men Admiring Themselves in the Water,
  The.
  Secret Rose, The.
  Symbols.
  Thought from Propertius, A.
  To a Young Beauty.
Yoshifusa. Years have touched me, The.
Young, A. Dance For Ma Rainey, A.
Young, D. Rothko's Yellow.
Zamora, D. Vision of Your Body.
Zenmaro. At the Van Gogh exibition.
Zukofsky, L. In Arizona / (how many years in

the mountains).
Not much more than being.
Of Dying Beauty.

Beavers
Rothenberg, J. Seneca Journal 1: "A Poem of Beavers."
Watkins, V. Beaver's Story, The.
See also **Mountain Beavers**

Bedouins
Gouri. Of the Azazmeh Too.
Guri. Of the Azazmeh Too.
Taylor, B. Bedouin Song.

Bedrooms
Cornford, F. Country Bedroom, The.
Smith, S. Goodnight.
Wier. Lucille and Ernie's Master Bedroom.

Beds
Amen. Cot, The.
Arnold, M. Last Word, The.
Baudelaire. Anywhere Out of the World.
Benét, S. For City Spring.
Cavafy. One Night.
Coleman, W. Bedtime Story.
Davison, P. Bed Time.
"Field." From Baudelaire.
Love rises up some days.
Graham, J. In the Hotel.
Gunn, T. Bed, The.
Herrick. Her Bed.
Hope, A. Bed, The.
Janeczko. Blanket Hog.
Jewsbury. Verses: "I am monarch of troubles a host."
Johnson, S. Translation of Lines by Benserade.
Kao Ch'i. Lying at Leisure during Rain.
Kovner. Dimmed Observation.
Larkin, P. Sad Steps.
Talking in bed ought to be easiest.
Liu Hsün's Wife. Curtain of the Wedding Bed, The.
Lovelace, R. To Lucasta: The Rose.
Lowell, R. Man And Wife.
Madhubuti. Loneliness, A.
Mei Sheng *et al.* Green green, river bank grasses.
Montagu, L. Between your sheets you soundly sleep.
Morley, C. Plumpuppets, The.
Mother Goose. Formed long ago, yet made today.
Ni Dhomhnaill. Labasheedy (The Silken Bed). Leaba Shíoda.
Patrick, L. Sleepin' at the Foot o' the Bed.
Plath. Most Beds are Beds.
Ross, A. Two in Bed.
Shapiro, D. House (Blown Apart).
Shapiro, K. Bed, The.
Sidney, P. Sonnet 98: "Ah bed, the field where joy's peace some do see."
Spires. Beds, The.
Stevenson, R. Bed in Summer.
Land of Counterpane, The.
My Bed Is a Boat.
Stillman, M. Lullaby for Suzanne.
Surrey. Laid in my quiet bed, in study as I were.
Swinburne. Love And Sleep.
Unknown. Get up, get up, you lazy-head.
Go to bed late.
Green, green.
Lord Randal[l].
Updike. Insomnia the Gem of the Ocean.
Willmot. I find her huddled on the bed.

Beech Trees and Beechnuts
Frost, R. Boundless Moment, A.
Wills, J. Looking deeper.

Beef
Unknown. Little More Cider, A.

Beer
Alexie. Reservation Love Song.
Arnold, G. Beer.
Brown, G. Old Women, The.
Bukowski. Crucifix in a Deathhand.
Housman, A. Terence, this is stupid stuff.
Johnson, J. Renewal.

Julian. On Beer.
Leland, C. Hans Breitmann's Party [*or* Barty].
Leonard, T. Jist Ti Let Yi No.
Marquis. Archy Interviews a Pharoah.
Stedman, E. Ballad of Lager Bier, The.
Stephens, J. Glass of Beer, A.
Sterling, A. Under the Anheuser Bush.
Thackeray. Dear Jack, this white mug that with Guinness I fill.
Unknown. Gud Ber.
Webster, A. Enigma No. 6.
Winner, S. Lilliputian's Beer Song.

Bees and Beekeeping
Alkman. Creatures Rest, The.
Apollonides. Beeman Cliton hews / From the flower fed hive.
Basho. Finis.
Baxter, J. Wild Bees.
Bernstein, O. In a Park, in Siena, at Twilight.
Blunden. Forefathers.
Carew, T. Upon a Mole in Celia's Bosom.
Dickinson, E. Bee, The.
Bee his burnished Carriage, A.
Bees are Black, with Gilt Surcingles—.
Come slowly—Eden!
Could I but ride indefinite.
Did the Harebell loose her girdle.
His Feet are shod with Gauze.
Letter to Bee.
Diodorus Zonas. Come tawny bees.
Emerson, R. Humble-Bee, The.
"Field." Penetration.
Frost, R. White-tailed hornet lives in a balloon, The.
Gerstler. BZZZZZZZ.
Graham, H. Opportunity.
Herrick. Captived Bee; or, The Little Filcher, The.
Hine. Wasp, The.
Ho Xuan Huong. Bonze Got Stung By a Bee, The.
Lear, E. Limerick: "There was an Old Man in a tree."
Levin, P. Lost Bee, The.
Planting Roses.
Lewis, R. Humming Bird, The.
Lloyd, D. Wild rose bending.
Lodge, T. Rosalind's [*or* Rosalynd's] Madrigal[1].
Lovelace, R. Black Patch on Lucasta's Face, A.
Martial. Bee's Burial, A.
Mechthild von Magdeburg. Of all that God has shown me.
Mitchison. Old Love and New Love.
Morgan, R. Honey.
Mori Ōgai. Tanka: "Your heart."
Morley, C. Song for a Little House.
Mother Goose. God made the bees.
Mtshali. Inside My Zulu Hut.
Okamoto. All day long having / buried himself.
Orampokiyar. What She Said ("Bees, six tiny legs and wings all lovely").
Patten, B. Bee's Last Journey to the Rose, The.
Philip of Thessalonica. Bronze warship-beaks, old voyage-avid weapons.
Plath. Arrival of the Bee Box, The.
Stings.
Swarm, The.
Wintering.
Robinson, M. Queen Bee, The.
Rummo. Again again again again again.
Sandburg, C. In Tall Grass.
Smith, C. Invitation to the Bee.
Spenser. Sonnet 71: "I joy to see how in your drawen work."
Tasso. I'd like to be a bee.
Toomer. Beehive.
Unknown. Bee-keeper kissed me, The.
Burnie bee, burnie bee.
God made the bees.
If bees stay at home.
No bees, no honey;.
Swarm of bees in May, A.
Valéry. Bee, The.

Virgil. Of Bees.
Watts, I. How doth the little busy bee.

Beethoven, Ludwig van
Clampitt. Beethoven, Opus 111.
Cobbing. Beethoven.
Lanier, S. To Beethoven.
Millay, E. On Hearing a Symphony of Beethoven.
Ray, H. Beethoven.
Rich, A. Ninth Symphony of Beethoven Understood at Last as a Sexual Message, The.
Seaman, E. Double Dactyls.
Spender, S. Beethoven's Death Mask.
Turner, J. Rhapsodies.
Wheelock, J. Beethoven.

Beetles
Dickinson, E. These are the Nights that Beetles love.
Fisher, A. Upside Down.
Kaufman, S. Beetle on the Shasta Daylight.
Kunio. Tanka: "This May Day night."
Miyazawa Kenji. Tanka: "Scattered clouds."
Shūji. Tanka: "As if it came."
Sorrentino. Zoo, The.
Szymborska. Seen from Above.

Beets
Nash, O. Parsnip, children, I repeat, The.

Begging and Beggars
Aikin, L. Beggar Man, The.
Alexander, C. Beggar Boy, The.
Arnold, M. West London.
Ayres. On a Fair Beggar.
Berry, W. Music, A.
Bishop, E. Pink Dog.
Browning, R. Twins, The.
Bruner. Beggar, The.
Casey, P. Merry Jovial Beggar, The.
Coleman, H. Black Soldier Remembers, A.
Coleridge, M. Insincere Wish Addressed to a Beggar, An.
Cummings, E. Right here the other night something.
Davidson, F. Beggars.
Dickinson, E. I never lost as much but twice.
Let me not thirst with this Hock at my Lip.
There comes an hour when begging stops.
Donne. Lame Beggar, A.
Doty, M. Heaven.
Enzensberger, H. Hôtel Fraternité.
Glazkov. Bast shoe idly on the road, A.
Gunn, T. St. Martin and the Beggar.
Herrick. Beggar to Mab, the Fairy [*or* Fairie] Queen, The.
Jackson, H. Grab-Bag.
King, W. Beggar Woman, The.
Kleinzahler. Ebenezer Californicus.
Kuzmina-Karavayeva. And copper and worn my farthing.
I still kept thinking that I was rich.
Lavrin. As I remember, barracks still stand.
Major, C. Blind Old Woman.
Mei Yao Ch'en. Borrowing Rice from Ju-hui.
Moss, T. Beggar, The.
Mother Goose. Hark, hark, the dogs do bark.
Plath. Applicant, The.
Poseidippus. Here in this rough trench lies.
Stephens, J. Glass of Beer, A.
Swirszczynska. Same Inside, The.
T'ao Ch'ien. Begging for Food.
Tennyson, A. Beggar Maid, The.
Thomas, D. Hunchback in the park, The.
Unknown. Dives and Lazarus ("There was a man in olden times").
Gaberlunzie Man, The.
Jovial Beggar, The.
Woes of the Crab, The.
Wroth. Sonnet 2: "Late in the Forest I did Cupid See."
Yeats. Beggar to Beggar Cried.
See also **Homeless, The; Vagabonds**

Belfast, Northern Ireland
Brodsky, J. Belfast Tune.
Carson, C. Belfast Confetti.
Campaign.
Slate Street School.
Craig, M. Ballad to a Traditional Refrain.

Heaney, S. Summer nineteen sixty nine.
MacNeice. Belfast.
Montague, J. Falls Funeral.
Muldoon, P. Aisling.
Paulin. Under the Eyes.

Belgium
Auden. Brussels in Winter.
Craig, M. Ballad to a Traditional Refrain.
Ross, A. Antwerp: Musée Des Beaux-Arts.
Rossetti, D. Antwerp to Ghent.
Sassoon. On Passing the New Menin Gate.

Belief
Bible, *N.T.* He that heareth my word.
Crane, H. To Brooklyn Bridge.
Crane, S. I SAW A MAN PURSUING THE HORIZON.
Dickinson, E. Spirit lasts, but in what mode, The.
Duncan, R. Song of the Borderguard, The.
Empson. Invitation To Juno.
Everson, W. Narrows of Birth, The.
Fifer. What was his creed?
Fullerton. John 14:1–2.
Greene, R. Ideals.
Han Yü. Girl of Mt. Hua, The.
Hanlon, G. Plainsong.
Hewitt, J. Rome Sunday[,] June 1960.
Johnson, S. Do They Return?
Kenyon, J. Suggestion from a Friend.
Killigrew, A. Upon the Saying That My Verses Were Made by Another.
Kiser. My Creed.
Komunyakaa. Nude Study.
Landor, W. You smiled, you spoke, and I believed.
Levertov. Suspended.
Levine, P. Belief.
Lewis, C. Impression, An.
Milosz, C. On Angels.
Morton, J. On Sir Henry Ferrett, M.P.
Nichol. St. Anzas IX.
Ostriker. Everywoman Her Own Theology.
Pack, R. Proton Decay.
Rexroth, K. Sword in a Cloud of Light, A.
Rukeyser, M. This Place in the Ways.
Shūji. Tanka: "Slowly inside me."
Smith, S. God the Eater.
Thayer, L. Little Child's Faith, The.
Unknown. Apostles' Creed, The.
Child's Creed, A.
Firm Belief.
Should Latin, Greek, and Hebrew fail.
Walter, H. I would be true, for there are those [who trust me].

See also **Faith**

Belisarius
Longfellow, H. Belisarius.

Bellbirds
Kendall, H. Bell-Birds.

Belloc, Hilaire
Beerbohm, M. After Hilaire Belloc.
Wolfe, H. Hilaire Belloc.

Bells
Adams, L. Bell Tower.
Bachmann. Psalm: "Be still with me, as all bells are still!"
Becker, C. Door-Bell, The.
Bevington, L. With the Tide: A Cry of Weakness.
Binyon. Belfry, The.
Bungay. Creeds of the Bells.
"Carroll." Fit the Second: The Bellman's Speech.
Chang Chi. Tying Up for the Night at Maple River Bridge.
Chang Yü. Staying Overnight at T'ien-ning Ch'an Temple.
Chin Nung. In the silences between peals of the bell.
Chōkū. Tanka: "New Year's temple bells."
Close, E. Here We Come a-Haying.
Crane, H. Broken Tower, The.
Cummings, E. Anyone lived in a pretty how town.
Dickinson, E. When Bells stop ringing—Church—begins.

Ekelof. Greece.
Farjeon, E. Children's Bells, The.
Field, E. Christmas Song: "Why do the bells for Christmas ring?"
Fordham. Bells of St. Michael.
Guiney. Sunday Chimes in the City.
Heard, J. Sabbath Bells.
Herrick. Bellman, The.
Holub. Brief Reflection on Charlemagne.
Housman, A. Bredon Hill.
When the bells justle in the tower.
Hsü Pen. Mountain Residence of Secretary Cheng Ching-ssu, The.
Ingelow. High Tide on the Coast of Lincolnshire.
Issa. In my life / As in the twilight.
Jackson, L. Ding-Donging.
Jones, R. Bell, The.
Kao Ch'i. In the Mountains, Parting from Master Ning as I Return to West Bank.
Linden, M. Church Bells, The.
Longfellow, H. Bells of San Blas, The.
Christmas Bells.
Matevski. Bells.
McDonald, W. Christmas Bells, Saigon.
Meynell, A. Chimes.
Mo Shih-lung. Staying Overnight at Blue Cloud Temple.
Mori Ōgai. In Nara (two poems).
Tanka: "It will not be heard."
Noin. As I approach / The mountain village.
Spring twilight.
Owen, W. Anthem for Doomed Youth.
Peck, J. Ringers, The.
Poe. Bells, The.
Prescot. Balsham Bells.
Probyn. Changes.
Reverdy. Secret.
Sexton. Ringing the Bells.
Shen Chou. Temple of the Ocean of Awakening.
Sherman, F. Waterfall, The.
Sidney, P. Dirge: "Ring out your bells [or belles], let mourning shows [or shewes] be spread."
Simko. Coming Home.
Slessor. Five Bells.
Smith, M. Chimes.
Swift, J. On His Own Deafness.
Tchernichowsky. Bells, The.
Thompson, C. Church Bells.
Thoreau. Dong, sounds the brass in the east.
Turner, C. Buoy-Bell, The.
Unknown. Bells, The.
Bells of London, The.
Clear full moon.
London Bells.
Sweet little bell.
Upon Arch-bishop Laud, Prisoner in the Tower. 1641.
Virgilio. Beyond empty pews.
Cathedral bell, The.
Warsh. Suicide Rates, The.
Wen Cheng-ming. Evening Bell from a Misty Temple.
Staying Overnight at Spirit-Source Temple.
Whittier. Skipper Ireson's Ride.
Wilbur. Bell Speech.
Williams, W. Catholic Bells, The.
Yüan Mei. Flying Bells.

Belshazzar
Bibb. Belshazzar's Feast.

Ben Bulben, Ireland
Unknown. Deserted Mountain, The.

Benbow, Admiral John
Unknown. Admiral Benbow.

Benches
Spenser. Sonnet 75: "One day I wrote her name upon the strand."

Bennett, Susan Eugenia
Fordham. In Memoriam. Susan Eugenia Bennett.

Beowulf
Amis, K. Beowulf.
Unknown. FROM Beowulf.
Hwæt, wē gār-dena in gēardagum.

Bergman, Ingmar
Duncan, R. Ingmar Bergman's "Seventh Seal."

Berkeley, George
Davie. Fountain, The.

Berkshire Hills, Massachusetts
Ray, H. Among the Berkshire Hills.

Berlin, Germany
Bartsch. Still Life with Cleaning Lady.
Brodsky, J. Berlin Wall Tune, The.
Mahon. Postcard from Berlin, A.
Nobuyuki. In Berlin.
Péret. Staircase with a Hundred Steps, The.
Sisson. Over the Wall: Berlin, May 1975.
Sutskever. Cartload of Shoes, A.
Villanueva, A. Even the Eagles Must Gather.
Yoshimi. Trip to Berlin.

Bermuda
Marvell. Bermudas.
Waller, E. Aid me Bellona, while the dreadful fight.
Garden of Bermuda, The.

Berrigan, Daniel
Rich, A. Burning of Paper instead of Children, The.

Berryman, John
Harper, M. Tongue-tied in Black and White.
Lowell, R. For John Berryman.
Vizenor. Tropisms on John Berryman.
Zaranka. Ode: "Mistah Berrybones, you daid?"

Bertrand de Born
Pound, E. Near Perigord.
Sestina: Altaforte.

Bestiality
Dickey, J. Sheep Child, The.
Djurdjic. Blue Frog Kisses My Sweetheart.

Bethlehem
Brooks, P. O little town of Bethlehem.
Canton. Bethlehem.
Chesterton, F. How Far Is It to Bethlehem?
Parker, K. Long, Long Ago.
Roberts, E. Christmas Morning.
Unknown. Long, Long Ago.
Yeats. Second Coming, The.

Betjeman, Sir John
Causley. Betjeman, 1984.

Betrayal
Archilochus. Stranded ashore from the sea.
Breton, N. Cradle Song: "Come, little babe."
Brown, T. Conjergal rights! conjergal rights!
Burns, R. Hughie Graham.
Cheney-Coker. Poem for a Guerrilla Leader.
Davidson, J. Ballad of Hell, A.
De Tabley. Song of Faith Forsworn, A.
Dickinson, E. That she forgot me was the least.
Drunina. In all ages, always, everywhere, and everywhere.
Goldsmith, O. Song: "When lovely woman stoops to folly."
Graves, R. Lost Jewel, A.
Not at Home.
Wreath, The.
Greenwell, D. Fidelity Rewarded.
Hardy, T. Broken Appointment, A.
Mongrel, The.
Hayes, A. *Much Ado About Nothing*, Thanksgiving, 1972.
Herbert, Z. When Judas, his betrayer, saw.
Speculations on the Subject of Barabbas.
Hill, G. Gasholders, russet among fields.
Mildams, marpools.
Housman, A. Is my team ploughing.
Jonson, B. O God, and his good angels! whither, whither.
Kipling, R. Ulster.
Kossman. When Jesus had thus said, he was troubled.
Judas' Reproach.
Lamb, L. Would I had seen thee dead and cold.
McBride, M. Loneliness.
Meredith, G. It chanced his lips did meet her forehead cool.
It ended, and the morrow brought the task.
Out in the yellow meadows, where the bee.

She issues radiant from her dressing-room.
Yet it was plain she struggled, and that salt.
Milosz, C. Child of Europe.
Muir, E. Castle, The.
Myles, E. Maxfield Parrish.
Nguyễn Đình Chiểu. Elegy for Tru'o'ng
  Định.
Nguyễn Khuyến. Comedian Gets a Curtain
  Lecture, The.
Nguyễn Văn Lạc. Shrimp.
  To a Dead Dog in the River.
Owen, M. Them.
Pasternak, B. Mark 14:26–42; And when they
  had sung.
  Matthew 26:47–56; While he was still
  speaking, Judas came.
Phan chu Trinh. Dogs in the Loft.
Phan Văn Trị. Mosquito, you are blessed with
  all nice things!
  Opera Actors.
Polkowski. I Don't Know That Man.
Ralegh, W. Farewell to False Love, A.
Ransom, J. Winter Remembered.
Shakespeare, W. Sonnet 41.
Sokolov. Recollections of the Cross.
Stevens, W. Good Man Has No Shape, The.
Szymborska. Laughter.
Tản Đà. Canary in a Cage, The.
Tate, J. Rustin Steel is driving the crew to the
  river. A long.
Trần Tế Xu'o'ng. Actors.
Unknown. Betrayal.
  Donal Og.
  Josie.
  Renaud the Woman-killer.
Whittier. Ichabod[!].
Wier. Old-fashioned.
Wyatt, T. And if an eye may save or slay.
  Behold, love, thy power how she despiseth!
  How should I / Be so pleasant.
  Lover Showeth How He Is Forsaken of Such
  as He Sometime Enjoyed, The.
Yevtushenko. Monologue of a Blue Fox.
Zagajewski. Betrayal.

Betrothal
Ammuvanar. What She Said to Her Girl
  Friend.
Causley. My young man's a Cornishman.
Scovell. Betrothal, A.

Biafra. *See* **Civil War, Nigeria**

Bialik, Hayyim Nahman
Tiempo. Harangue on the Death of Hayyim
  Nahman Bialik.

Bible
Abse. Inscription on the Flyleaf of a Bible.
"Akhmatova." Lot's Wife.
Bible, *O.T.* My love is white and ruddy.
Bishop, E. Over 2000 Illustrations and a
  Complete Concordance.
Blanchard, F. Word of God, Across the Ages.
Borges. John 1:14 (1969).
Cowper, W. To Mary Unwin.
Dickinson, E. Bible is an antique Volume,
  The.
Dickinson, P. Moses and the Princess.
Donne. Upon the Translation of the Psalms by
  Sir Philip Sidney, and the Countess of
  Pembroke His Sister.
Giovanni. Poem for Flora.
Halkin, S. To Tarshish.
Hardy, T. Respectable Burgher, The.
Harte, B. Colenso Rhymes for Orthodox
  Children.
Heaney, S. Other Side, The.
Herbert, G. H. Scriptures, The ("Oh Book!
  infinite sweetnesse! let my heart").
  H. Scriptures, The ("Oh that I knew how all
  thy lights combine").
  Thanksgiving, The.
Jabès. Beginning of the Book, The.
  Book, The.
Keats. Fragment: "O grant that like to Peter
  I."
Levi, D. Thou, Zion, old and suffering.
Longfellow, H. Sand of the Desert in an
  Hour-Glass.
Mahon. Ecclesiastes.

McAuley, J. Art of Poetry, An.
Mobilio. Step One.
Moorer. Bible, The.
  Mountain Tops.
Morris, M. Pilate.
Oden. Bible Study.
Piercy. Book of Ruth and Naomi, The.
Plutzik. And in the 51st Year of That Century,
  While My Brother Cried in the Trench,
  While My Enemy Glared from the Cave.
Price, S. Edge, The.
Quarles. On The Gospel.
  On the Holy Scriptures.
Ravikovitch. Human Qualities.
  Like Rachel.
Reznikoff. Isreal I.
Sangster, M. Bit of the Book in the morning,
  A.
Scott, W. Book of Books, The.
Shlonsky. Jezrael.
Simic. Begotten of the Spleen.
  Concerning My Neighbors, the Hittites.
Smart, C. Taste.
Traherne. On the Bible.
Unknown. From a London Bookshop.
  In *Bath* a wanton wife did dwell.
  Old Testament Contents.
  On the Bible.
Vaughan, H. Book, The.
  H. Scriptures.
Wandor. Eve to Lilith.
  Eve's Commentary.
  Lilith to Eve.
  Ruth's Story, As Told to Lilith
Warton, T. Stanzas on the Psalms.
Wesley, C. N T.
Wilbur. Matthew VIII, 28 ff.
  Simplification, A.
Williams, M. Why God Permits Evil: For
  Answers to This Question of Interest to
  Many Write Bible Answers Dept. E-7.
Wilner, E. Reading the Bible Backwards.

Bicycles and Bicycling
Beeching, H. Going Down Hill on a Bicycle.
Jarry. Passion of Jesus Considered as an
  Uphill Race, The.
Laing, K. Race on Gathering Bites.
Malouf. Bicycle.
Piercy. Cyclist, The.
Samio. Tanka: "Monumental."
Shapcott, T. Bicycle Rider, The.
Tzara. Chanson Dada.
Unknown. To a Bicycle.
Weigl. Him, on the Bicycle.
Willard, N. One for the Road.
Williams, C. World's greatest tricycle rider,
  The.

Billboards
Larkin, P. Sunny Prestatyn.
Nash, O. Song of the Open Road.

Bingen, Germany
Norton, C. Bingen on the Rhine.

Biography
Bentley, E. Art of Biography, The.
  George III.
Brooks, G. Jane Addams (September 6, 1860–
  May 21, 1935).
Buchanan, G. Lyle Donaghy, Poet, 1902-1949.
Greacen. Captain Fox sits reading
  metaphysics.
Larkin, P. Posterity.
McFadden, R. Contemplations of Mary.
Stanton, M. Biography.
Violi. Index.
Whitman, W. When I read the book, the
  biography famous.
Wieseltier. Note.
Wollach. To Live at the Speed of Biography.

Birch Trees
Coleridge, M. Lady of Trees, The.
Frost, R. Birches.
  Young Birch, A.
Levy, A. Birch-Tree at Loschwitz, The.
Willmot. Mail on the counter.

Bird Migration. *See* **Animal Migration**

Birds
Agathias. Justice.
  Partridge.
Akahito. Black jewel like, The.
  In Waka Bay when.
Alkman. Creatures Rest, The.
Ammons. City Limits, The.
Argentarius. Blackbird, singing on the highest
  branch / Of the oak.
  Damned bird, why have you ruined my sleep.
Armstrong, M. On a Little Bird.
Arnold, M. Matthias.
Atkins. Probability and Birds in the Yard.
Auden. Decoys, The.
  Epilogue: " 'O where are you going?' said
  reader to rider."
  Their Lonely Betters.
Austin, M. Shoshone Wedding Song.
Awoonor. Weaver bird built in our house,
  The.
Balaban. Along the Mekong.
Bampfylde. To the Redbreast.
Bardeen. Birds' Ball, The.
Bardoloi. Dawn.
Barham. Jackdaw of Rheims, The.
Barnes, W. Lullaby.
Basho *et al.* Call of Two Birds, The.
Bast. Empress's Cat, The.
Bennett, R. Merry Birds.
Bent. Robin, The.
Berry, W. Wild, The.
Bertolino. Landscape, The.
  On a Line by John Ashbery.
Bishop, E. Some Dreams They Forgot.
Blake, W. Birds, The.
  Blossom, The.
  Prince of Love, The.
Blight. Oyster-Eaters, The.
Blind. Entangled.
Blodgett. Fossil.
Bogan, L. Statue and Birds.
Bosley. Bird / sips water / drips music.
Bottomley. Dawn.
Bowen, E. Winged in Gold.
Brautigan. Surprise.
Brennen. Spring.
Breton, A. Postman Cheval.
Brinckman. Fish and Bird.
Brock, V. Sea Birds, The.
Brontë, A. Captive Dove, The.
Brontë, C. House was still—the room was
  still, The.
Browne, J. Rooks are building on the trees,
  The.
Browning, E. Deserted Garden, The.
  First Book: Young Aurora's Fostermother.
Browning, R. In the Doorway.
Bryant, W. Robert of Lincoln.
  To A Waterfowl.
Bunyan. Of the Child with the Bird on the
  Bush.
Campbell, D. Hear, the bird of day.
  Windy Gap.
"Carroll." King-Fisher [*or* King-Fisher's]
  Song, The.
Carter, E. Ode to Wisdom.
Carter, M. In a small city at dusk.
Ceravolo. Sunset.
Ch'en Tzu-ang. Kingfishers nest on South Sea
  islands.
Ch'in Kuan. Returning from Kuang-ling.
Chong, H. Bird.
Cibulka. Sky Full of Swallows.
Clampitt. Syrinx.
Clare, J. Birds' Nests.
  Little trotty wagtail [he went in the rain].
  Yellowhammer, The.
Clark, L. Grumblers.
  Small Birds.
Clark, T. You (IV).
Clarke, A. Japanese Print.
Coatsworth. No Shop Does the Bird Use.
  Swallows, The.
Coleridge, M. L'Oiseau Bleu.
Coleridge, S. Answer to a Child's Question.
  Glycine's Song.

Colonna, V. As a hungry fledgling, who sees and hears.
Constable, H. Diaphenia like the daffadowndilly.
Conyus. Day in the Life of. . . , A.
Cook, E. On Seeing a Bird-Catcher.
Song of the Imprisoned Bird.
Cook, S. Robin in December, The.
Cooper, J. Morning on the St. John's.
Cranch. Bird Language.
Crane, H. Carrier Letter.
Crane, S. Little birds of the night.
Crinagoras. Linguist parrot flicked his flowery wings, The.
Cullinan. M. François le Vaillant Recalls His Travels to the Interior Parts of Africa.
Cummings, E. If everything happens that can't be done.
May my heart always be open to little.
Nine birds(rising / through a gold moment)climb.
Dainty. Birds on the School Windowsill, The.
Davies, W. Truth, The.
De la Mare. Spotted Flycatcher, The.
Thomas Hardy.
Dickey, J. Reincarnation (II).
Dickinson, E. Before you thought of Spring.
Bird came down the Walk[—A], A.
Cat.
"Hope" is the thing with feathers.
Lady feeds Her little Bird, The.
Saddest noise, the sweetest noise, The.
Dipoko. Our Life.
Dissanayake. Freedom.
Dobler. His Depression.
Dodd, W. Outside My Cabin.
Dogen. On Non-dependence of Mind.
Doolittle, H. Birds in Snow.
Dransfield. Strange Bird, A.
Dunbar, P. Sympathy.
Duoduo. Wishful Thinking Is the Master of Reality.
DuPlessis, R. Since the narcissus bud.
Where is the bird?
Eastwick. Cherry Tree.
Eigner. Live / , bird which.
Elmslie, K. Feathered Dances.
Erdrich. I Was Sleeping Where the Black Oaks Move.
Everson, W. Canticle to the Waterbirds, A.
Field, E. Dinkey-Bird, The.
"Field." Goad, The.
Follain. Taxidermist is sitting / before the russet breasts, A.
Francis, R. Waxwings.
Frost, R. Last Word of a Bluebird, The.
Minor Bird, A.
Never Again Would Birds' Song Be The Same.
Oven Bird, The.
Fukui. Now is the time.
Galvin, B. Chickadee.
Listening to September.
Willow, Wishbone, Warblers.
Gibson, W. Michael's Song.
Gilbert, J. Ko-Ko's Song.
Golding, L. O Bird, So Lovely.
Gregor, A. Sunbather in Late October, A.
Groch. Friend to Birds.
Grosholz. Last of the Courtyard, The.
Guest, B. Geese Blood.
Guillén, J. Flight.
Guillén, N. Usurers, The.
Gunn, T. On the Move.
Hackett, J. Fleeing sandpipers, The.
Haines, J. House of the Injured, The.
Hall, H. Listening Macaws, The.
Han. Blue Bird.
Handlin. Cold winter morning.
Hardy, T. Blinded Bird, The.
Selfsame Song, The.
Weathers [or Weather].
Harryman. Allegory.
Hart-Smith. Boomerang.
Hartnett. I have exhausted the delighted range.
Hawkins, R. Birds.
Heaney, S. Saint Francis and the Birds.

Heath-Stubbs. Jays, The.
Henson, D. Last Atlantean, The.
Herlin. Gull inch-perfect over water, the busy crane, The.
Hernandez, D. Pigeons are the spiks of Birdland.
Heywood, J. Egles byrde hath spred his wings, The.
Heywood, T. Matin Song.
Higginson, W. Interstices.
Hirshfield, J. Story, A.
Hitomaro. Plovers cry, The.
Hope, A. Death of the Bird, The.
Hopkins, G. What I Do Is Me.
Windhover, The.
Hove. Lost Bird.
Migratory Bird ("One day he perched on a tree with dew").
Howitt, M. Sea-Gull, The.
Hsü Wei. Abandoning the Plans of Visiting West Lake.
Inscribed on a Painting.
Hughes, T. October robin kept, An.
Rooks love excitement. When I walked in under the rookery.
Hugo, V. Be like the bird, who.
Hull, L. Ornithology.
Issa. Bird in the cage, The.
No mother! No father!
Jaccottet. Distances.
Letter of the 26th June.
Swifts.
Jarrell. Country Life, A.
Mockingbird, The.
Jastrun, T. Seed, The.
Jeffers, R. Birds.
Birds and Fishes.
Johnson, G. Heart of a woman [goes forth with the dawn], The.
Jones, G. Esyllt.
Jones, J. Sometimes I hear God's whisper in.
Joron, A. Birdsongs are aging, The.
Kanemasa. Awaji Island—.
Keats. How many bards gild the lapses of time!
Kelly, B. Of Royal Issue.
Kerouac. Birds singing.
Ki no Tsurayuki. Out in the marsh reeds.
Kim, C. Bird.
Kim, C. Bird, A.
Kinnell. Last Songs.
Kinsella, J. Sick Woman.
Kirchwey. He Considers the Birds of the Air.
Matthew 8:20; And Jesus said to him.
Kirkup. Caged Bird in Springtime, The.
Scarecrows.
Kirschner. Fall of Light, The.
Kitahara Hakushū. Tanka: "Almost invisible."
Tanka: "Spring bird."
Knowles, S. Tails and Heads.
Komunyakaa. Birds on a Powerline.
Kuan Han-ch'ing. Tune: "Song of Great Virtue"—Spring.
Kumin, M. Noted in The New York Times.
Kunze, R. Almost a Spring Poem.
Lake, P. Blue Jay.
Lamb, E. Broken kite, sprawled.
Lear, E. Limerick: "There was an old man of Whitehaven."
Limerick: "There was an Old Man who said, 'Hush!'."
Lehmann, G. What's that bird, Mr Long?
Lennon, J. Fat Budgie, The.
Leopardi. Calm after the Storm, The.
Levertov. Claritas.
Levine, P. Red Dust.
Lewis, J. Footprint on the Air, A.
Lewis, R. Mocking Bird, The.
Li K'ai-hsien. Crossing the ridge, the woodcutter loses his way.
Li Meng-yang. Song of Lin Liang's Painting "Two Horned Falcons."
Spring Vista from the Tower of Illuminated Distance.
Li Po. Birds have vanished into the sky, The.
Linden, M. Bird Song, The.

Livingstone, D. Bateleur.
Lake Morning in Autumn.
Logan, W. Moorhen.
Longenbach. What You Find in the Woods.
Longfellow, H. Birds of Killingworth, The (The Poet's Tale).
Lovelace, R. Falcon, The.
Lyly, J. Trico's Song.
MacCaig. Blue Tit on a String of Peanuts.
Ringed Plover by a Water's Edge.
"MacDiarmid." Ex Vermibus.
On a Raised Beach.
Storm-Cock's Song, The.
Whip-the-World.
Madge. Birds of Tin, The.
Magowan. Days of 1956.
Major, C. Apple Core.
On Trying to Imagine the Kiwi Pregnant.
Manning-Sanders. Come Wary One.
Masaoka Shiki. All the hot night.
Masefield. Sea Change.
McAuley, J. Nocturne.
McCarthy, G. Sound of Guns, The.
Melly. Homage to René Magritte.
Melville, H. Man-of-War Hawk, The.
Meredith, G. We saw the swallows gathering in the sky.
Meyers, B. Daybreak.
Meynell, A. October Redbreast, The.
Roaring Frost, The.
Michelson, M. Bird, The.
Middleton, C. Oystercatchers.
Miller, R. Birds.
Miller, V. Beat Poem by an Academic Poet.
Milosz, C. Earth.
Miyazawa Kenji. Tanka: "Plucked, The."
Monro. Bird at Dawn, The.
Moore, L. Spectacular.
Moore, M. Bird-witted.
To the Peacock of France.
Moore, N. Island and the Cattle, The.
Moorsom. Company of the Birds, The.
Morgan, E. Starlings in George Square, The.
Morgan, R. Passenger Pigeons.
Mother Goose. Aristotle's Story.
Who killed Cock [or poor] Robin? [or Here lies Cock Robin].
Motherwell. I've plucked the berry from the bush, the brown nut from the tree.
Mueller, J. Allegory.
Murakami Kijo. Against far off snow mountains.
Murray, L. Equanimity.
Mutswairo. My Birds.
Nash, O. Grackle's voice is less than mellow.
Up from the Egg; the Confessions of a Nuthatch Avoider.
Nemerov. More Joy in Heaven.
Nesbit, E. Vies Manquées.
Newcastle, M. Excuse for So Much Writ upon My Verses.
Norris, L. Cage Bird and Sky Bird.
Norton, C. Sonnet 7: "Like an enfranchised bird, who wildly springs."
O'Hara, F. Easter.
Okara. Spirit of the Wind.
O'Keeffe. Beasts and Birds.
Oliver, M. In the Pinewoods, Crows and Owl.
Kingfisher rises out of the black wave, The.
Rabbit, The.
Olson, C. Variations Done for Gerald Van De Wiele.
Ou-yang Hsiu. East Wind.
Pack, R. Thrasher in the Willow by the Lake, The.
Page, P. Deaf-Mute in the Pear Tree.
Palgrave. Linnet in November, The.
Park, N. Birds.
Phylip, S. Seagull, The.
P'i Jih-hsiu. Lament for the People of Lung.
Plumly. Cedar Waxwing on Scarlet Firethorn.
Po Chü-i. Red Cockatoo, The.
Rejoicing at the Arrival of Chi'en Hsiung.
Poe. Preface: "Romance, who loves to nod and sing."
Posner. Birds, The.
Prettyman. Still Life: Lady with Birds.

Prévert. First paint a cage.
Quartier Libre.
Probyn. Tête-à-Tête.
Rakosi. Good Morning.
Paraguay.
Ramanujan. In the Zoo.
Rankin, J. Old Currawong.
Ransom, J. Lady Lost.
Somewhere Is Such a Kingdom.
Ratcliffe, S. Space in the light said to be
where one / comes from.
Ravikovitch. Sound of Birds at Noon, The.
Reeves, J. Grasshopper and the Bird, The.
Riley, J. Few of the Bird-Family, A.
Roberts, N. Gull'' Flight, The.
Roethke. Kitty-Cat Bird, he sat on a fence,
The.
Reply, The.
Rose, The.
Rose, M. Little Bird's Song, A.
Rossetti, C. Birthday, A.
Fly away, fly away over the sea.
Green Cornfield, A.
Summer.
Rosten. Aesthetic.
Rózewicz. Questions about Poetry since
Auschwitz.
Rucker. Swallows of Capistrano, The.
Russell, S. Poem: "I keep feeling all space as
my image."
Ryan, M. Not the End of the World.
Saigyo. My heart emptied.
St. John, P. Reading a Story to My Child.
Samio Tanka: "On occasion,"
Sandburg, C. River Roads.
Sandhill People.
Three Spring Notations on Bipeds.
Schwartz, D. Little Morning Music, A.
Small Score, A.
Scott, W. Madge Wildfire Sings.
Seager, M. Birds' Nests.
Segers. In the eggshell after the chick has
hatched.
Shakespeare, W. Phoenix and the Turtle, The.
Song: "Under the greenwood tree."
Shapcott, T. Shadow of War, 1941.
Shen Yüeh. Wild Geese on the Lake.
Simic. Bird calls me, A.
Fork.
Simpson, L. As birds are fitted to the boughs.
Skelton, J. It had a velvet cap.
Smith, S. None of the other birds seem to like
it.
Snodgrass, W. Examination, The.
Magic Flute, The.
Southard. One breaker crashes.
Spenser. Sonnet 89: "Like as the culver on the
bared bough."
Sonnet 73: 'Being my self captived here'.
Spiess. Blue jays in the pines.
Stephens, J. Rivals, The.
Stern, G. Peddler's Village.
Pile of Feathers.
Sternberg. Little birds in a row.
Stevens, W. Of Mere Being.
Stevenson, R. Time to Rise.
Sueyoshi. Crying plovers, The.
Summers, H. Report.
Swan, J. In Her Song She Is Alone.
Swenson, M. Waterbird.
Synge. In Glencullen.
Tagore. Bird, The.
T'ao Ch'ien. Unsettled, a bird lost from the
flock.
Tarn. Section: America (2): Seen as a Bird.
Tate, J. Blue Booby lives, The.
Taylor, E. Meditation 8 (First Series).
Teller. Lines to a Tree.
Tennyson, A. Cradle Song: "What does little
birdie say?"
Throstle, The.
Thomas, D. January 1939.
Over Sir John's Hill.
Thomas, E. Good-Night.
Snow.
Two Pewits.
Unknown Bird, The.

Thomson, J. Migrating Birds.
Todd, R. Joan Miró ("After that war, when
death had gone away").
Toshinari. I remember a grass hut.
Tranströmer. Morning Bird Songs.
Trevor. Kite, A.
Tsaloumas. Falcon Drinking.
Ts'ao Chih. Ballad of the Orioles in the
Fields.
Cock-fight, The.
Tso Ssu. Scholar in the Narrow Street, The.
Tu Fu. Another Spring.
Loneliness.
Tynan. Making of Birds, The.
Unknown. Belfast Lough.
Bird Scarer, The.
Bird Starver's Cry.
Birds, The.
Bird's Nest, The.
Birds' Nests.
Cock-crow Song.
Crow caws in the moonlight, A.
Cutty Wren, The.
Death Song.
Eastern Wall stands high and long;, The.
Examination Question.
Farewell Lament.
Fowls [*or* Foweles *or* Fowles] in the frith.
In the open sea.
Jackdaw of Rheims, The.
Jaybird a-sitting on a hickory limb.
Little Bird, The.
Little cock sparrow sat on a tree, A.
O sea-gulls that are crying.
On May-day, when the lark began to rise.
Once I saw a little bird going hop, hop, hop.
Over the reeds the.
Pinionjay shits pebbles.
Riddle: "Cuckoo and the gowk, the."
Rooks, The.
Since the narcissus bud.
Small bird, forgive me.
Two little dicky birds.
Two Pigeons.
Warning, A.
Whango Tree, The.
When Jenny Wren Was Young.
White Lake, The.
Who Taught Them?
Wind and the Bird, The.
Updike. Great Scarf of Birds, The.
Upon Learning That a Bird Exists Called the
Turnstone.
Van Duyn. Letters from a Father.
Van Vliet. Courtyard, The.
Vaughan, H. Bird, The.
Twenty-first Day of the Seventh Month.
Very. Birds of Passage, The.
Virgil. Claiming.
Grass path lasts.
Phoebe's cry, A.
Virgilio. Empty highway, The.
Wagoner, D. Author of American Ornithology
Sketches a Bird, Now Extinct, The.
Loons Mating.
Walcott. Season of Phantasmal° Peace, The.
Wang Chien. South, The.
Wang Chiu-ssu. For Several Days I Have Not
Visited the Garden Pavilion—A Poem Sent to
My Pet Crane.
Wang T'ing-hsiang. At Arrow Rapids, the
water splashes foam.
Warner, R. Chough.
Warren, R. Heart of Autumn.
Patriotic Tour and Postulate of Joy.
Warsh. Gout.
Warton, T. Fashioned After the Manner of
Master Geoffrey Chaucer in His Assembly of
Fowls.
Watson, R. Ballad of the Bird-Bride.
Cage, The.
White Bird, The.
Webb, M. Green Rain.
Water-Ousel, The.
Whalen. "Never Apologize; Never Explain."
White, E. Listener's Guide to the Birds, A.
Whitman, W. To the Man-of-War Bird.

Wier. Innate Deception of Unspoiled Beauty,
The.
Wilberforce, S. Impromptu.
Wilbur. All These Birds.
Event, An.
Still, citizen sparrow, this vulture which you
call.
Williams, H. To the Curlew.
Williams, O. I Sing an Old Song.
Williams, W. Breakfast.
To Waken an Old Lady.
Williamson, J. Natural Selection.
Wills, J. Bluejay sails, A.
Wood, W. Princely eagle, and the soaring
hawke, The.
Wordsworth, W. Reverie of Poor Susan, The.
Water Fowl.
Wright, J. Invention of a Garden, The.
Wright, J. Birds.
Extinct Birds.
Yakamochi. Over the Spring fields.
Yang Wei-chen. Song of the Waterfall at
Mount Lu.
Yeats. Lonely the Sea-Bird Lies at Her Rest.
White Birds, The.
"Yehoash." That Is All I Heard.
Yosano. Like tiny golden.
Once, far over the breakers.
Young, A. Stockdoves, The.
Young Bear. Song Taught to Joseph, The.
Young, V. Sight of a lark's, The.
Yü Chi. Following the Rhymes of Bamboo
Branch Songs in Response to Yüan Po-chang.
Yün Shou-p'ing. On a Landscape by Myself.
Zhdanov. I'm not the branch, only the
prebranchness.
See also **Waterfowl;** *Names of birds (e.g.,*
Canaries*).*

Birds' Nests
Blind. On a Forsaken Lark's Nest.
Clare, J. Green Woodpecker's Nest, The.
Hen's Nest.
Pewits Nest.
Larcom. Brown Thrush, The.
Unknown. Warning, A.
Young, A. Nest, The.

Birds of Paradise
Coleridge, M. In London Town.
Davies, W. Bird of Paradise, The.
Lovelace, R. Lucasta's Fan[ne], with a
Looking-Glass[e] in It.

Bird-watching
Hudson, D. Some Tips on Watching Birds.
Nash, O. Up from the Egg; the Confessions of
a Nuthatch Avoider.
Van Duyn. Letters from a Father.
Whitman, W. Out of the cradle endlessly
rocking.

Birmingham, Alabama
Giscombe. (1962 At the Edge of Town).
(The Recent Past).
Monkhouse. Limericks.
Patterson, R. Birmingham 1963.
Randall, D. Ballad of Birmingham.
Shoaf. Birmingham, 1962.

Birmingham, England
MacNeice. Birmingham.
Seward. Scene of superfluous grace, and
wasted bloom.

Birth
Acholonu. Nigeria in the Year 1999.
Ai. Country Midwife: A Day, The.
"Alta." One hesitates to bring a child into this
world without fixing.
Antipater of Thessalonica. "They pray for
children? Let them!" cried Polyxo.
Arnold, M. In Utrumque Paratus.
Baudelaire. Anywhere Out of the World.
Bekederemo. Cry of Birth.
Berg, S. May 1970.
Bernstein, C. Dysraphism.
Berryman. Winters close, Springs open, no
child stirs, The.
Blake, W. Infant Sorrow.
Blaser. Ruler, The.
Bloch, C. Rising to Meet It.

Bradstreet, A. Before the Birth of One of Her Children.
Brecht, B. Luke 2:8–20; And in that region there were shepherds.
Mary.
Brooks, G. Birth in a Narrow Room, The.
Bruce, D. Sonnet 2: "Deep in her seventh month, my sister dozes."
Bruck. Birth.
Buckley, V. Origins.
Callimachus. Eileithyia, once more.
Cave. Written a Few Hours before the Birth of a Child.
Chesterton, G. Donkey, The.
Chhotray. Fear.
Cornford, F. Nurse.
Couzyn. Cartography of the Subtle Heart.
Creeley. River wandering down.
Daniels, K. Lying Down.
Di Prima. Song For Baby-O, Unborn.
Domin. Birthdays.
Dove, R. Cameos.
Drummond de Andrade. Seven-Sided Poem.
Duesing. Blossoming.
Durcan. Birth of a Coachman.
Erdrich. Birth.
Evans, M. Who Can Be Born Black.
Fanthorpe. Nativities.
Feinstein, E. Calliope in the Labour Ward.
Fuller, J. *et al.* Born Too Soon.
Gilbert, C. Midwives, The.
Glück, L. Garden, The.
Luke 2:1–7; In those days a decree went out from Caesar Augustus.
Goodison. Birth Stone.
Graves, R. Birth of a Great Man.
Song of Blodeuwedd, The.
Gross, P. Son and Heir.
Hacker, M. Nearly a Valediction.
Hadewijch. Love's Maturity.
Hardy, T. To an Unborn Pauper Child.
Unborn, The.
Harjo, J. For Alva Benson, and for Those Who Have Learned to Speak.
Harper, M. Deathwatch.
Haxton. Auspice.
Hejduk. Sleep of Adam, The.
Hemschemeyer. Giving birth in Greek.
Heraclitus of Halicarnassus. By Heraclides.
Hernández, M. I go on in the dark, lit from within; does day exist?
Herrick. Epitaph upon a Sober Matron, An.
Upon Batt.
Hildegard von Bingen. Alleluia-verse for the Virgin.
Hope, A. Imperial Adam, naked in the dew.
Hughes, T. Yesterday he was nowhere to be found.
Hummer, T. Austerity in Vermont.
Jones, R. First Birth, The.
Joyce, J. Ecce Puer.
Kamienska. Luke 1:26–38; In the sixth month the angel Gabriel.
Kay, J. Baby Lazarus.
That Distance Apart.
What Jenny Knows.
Kennedy, X. On a Child Who Lived One Minute.
Kennelly. Bread.
Kirchwey. Sonogram.
Kunert. Implant.
Lawrence, D. Demiurge.
Le Sueur. Budded with Child.
Leigh, H. Natural Child, The.
Leonidas. Eileithyia, brought safe.
Leonidas of Tarentum. Ambrosia, brought safe.
Atthis hung up the belt with the pompoms.
Levertov. Map of the Western Part of the County of Essex in England, A.
Lochhead, L. Abortion, An.
Lorde. And What About the Children.
Now That I Am Forever with Child.
Ly Ngoc Kieu. Birth, old age.
Lyon, G. Birth.
"MacDiarmid." Repetition Complex.

Macgoye. August the First; Court Martial. The Mother Speaks.
Machi. Tanka: "With a serene look."
Tanka: "Woman, The."
Madhubuti. There was a man who never was.
Men and Birth: The Unexplainable.
Malangatana. To the Anxious Mother.
Mandelstam. Silentium.
Mansour, J. Anti-mnemonic self-vaccination.
Mattera. Giovanni Azania.
Meynell, A. Maternity.
Mihalic. Man Who Decided, The.
Miles, J. Conception.
Miller, E. Jasmine.
Miller, V. On Approaching My Birthday.
Mistral, G. Like those jars that women put out to catch the dew of night.
Sleep Close to Me.
Mitchell, S. Havana Birth.
Murray, J. Madonna vs. Child.
Nemesianus. When now the third revolving Moon appears.
O'Donoghue, B. Weakness, The.
Ogilvy. Newly Dead and Newly Born.
Okamoto. Tanka: "Insect, An."
Olds, S. Language of the Brag, The.
Olson, C. Ring of, The.
Oppen. Eclogue: "Men talking, The."
Ortiz. To Insure Survival.
Paddock. Original Mind.
Parulekar. Birthmarks.
Pastan. Notes from the Delivery Room.
Perses. Lucina, Care.
Plath. Morning Song.
Po Chü-i. Golden Bells.
Ponsot. Multipara: Gravida 5.
Tranquilized, she speaks or does not speak.
Popa. Last News about the Little Box.
Tale About a Tale, The.
Pratt, M. Poem for My Sons.
Prunty. Winter's Tale, A.
Quarles. Born in Winter.
Ridler. Christmas and Common Birth.
Rogers, P. Elinor Frost's Marble-Topped Kneading Table.
Roseliep. Birthcry!
Rossetti, C. Before the paling of the stars.
Sachs, N. Someone.
Samio. Tanka: "Day I was born, The."
Tanka: "No scar."
Sanchez, S. Present.
Sartarelli. Early Spring, An.
That Land (3).
Satchidanandan. Genesis.
Schulman. Present Perfect, The.
Shakely. Definition.
Shange. Oh, I'm 10 Months Pregnant.
Shapiro, K. Recognition of Eve, The.
Shurin. Very Days.
Simmons, J. Join me in celebrating.
Slessor. Sleep.
Smith, B. Mercy.
Smith, S. Sterilization.
Spires. First Day, The.
Robed Heart, The.
Stallworthy, J. Almond Tree, The.
Stevens, W. To the One of Fictive Music.
Stevenson, A. Poem to my Daughter.
Stone, R. Where I Came From.
Stuart, D. Mining in Killdeer Alley.
Suckling, J. Upon Christ His Birth.
Sykes, B. Cycle.
Szymborska. Born of Woman.
Tadic. Dogs Gambol.
Toys, Dream.
Takahashi Shinkichi. Birth.
Taylor, J. Epigram: "Fair Beatrice tucks her coat up somewhat high."
Thomas, D. Vision and Prayer.
Thwaite. At Birth.
Tindal. Birth Wail, The.
Tolson. Birth of John Henry, The.
Townsend, A. Eighteenth-Century Medical Illustration: The Infant in its Little Room.
U Tam'si Tchicaya. I was naked for the first kiss of my mother.

What do I want with a thousand stars in broad daylight.
Unknown. I often pause and wonder.
Midwife's Invocation, A.
Origin-Legend of the Chou Tribe.
She Who First Bore Our People.
Villanueva, A. Witches' Blood.
Wang Chiu-ssu. Recording My Happiness.
Waniek. Chosen.
Whitman, W. Out of the cradle endlessly rocking.
Woman waits for me, she contains all, nothing is lacking, A.
Wilde, O. Ave Maria, Gratia Plena.
Williams, S. Say Hello to John.
Woods, J. What Do You Do When It's Spring?
Wright, C. Kings' Daughters, Home for Unwed Mothers, 1948.
Wright, J. Lake in Central Park, The.
Yeats. Consolation.
Stick of Incense, A.
Yosano. Labour Pains.
Tanka: "But for women."
Young, D. For a Wife in Jizzen.
Yüan Mei. Happy about Being Old.
Writing My Feelings.

Birth Control
Jonson, B. To Fine Lady Would-Be.
Miller, E. She is flat on her back.
Piercy. Homage to Lucille, Dr. Lord-Heinstein.
Twitchell. Condom Tree, The.
Wallace, R. Condoms.

Birth Defects
Gorey. Limerick: "To his club-footed child said Lord Stipple."
Stallworthy, J. Almond Tree, The.

Birthdays
Adamson. My Tenth Birthday.
Amichai. On My Birthday.
Brown, L. Lyric Can Snare, The.
Byron, G. On My Thirty-third Birthday.
On This Day I Complete My Thirty-sixth Year.
De la Mare. Lucy.
Driver. Birthdays.
Geier. On Your Twenty-First Birthday.
Hahn, K. Hula Skirt, 1959, The.
Heard, J. My Husband's Birthday.
Johnson, S. Short Song of Congratulation [*or* To a Young Heir], A.
To Mrs Thrale [on Her Thirty-fifth Birthday].
Jonson, B. Ode. To Sir William Sydney, on His Birthday.
Jordan, J. If You Saw a Negro Lady.
Justice, D. Birthday Candle, A.
Koch, K. Poem for My Twentieth Birthday.
Komunyakaa. Gift Horse.
Kunitz, S. Passing Through.
Kusano Shimpei. Birthday Party.
Kuskin. Rose on My Cake, The.
Li K'ai-hsien. On My Birthday—Sick.
Lorde. Ethiopia for Tifa.
Lowell, J. Sixty-Eighth Birthday.
Madigan. Curtis Fuller.
Meehan, M. Gift for my Mother's 90th Birthday.
Moorer. Birthday Wishes to a Husband.
Birthday Wishes to a Minister of the Gospel.
Birthday Wishes to a Physician.
Mother Goose. Birthdays.
Myles, E. December 9th.
Natambu. Words and Music in America.
Ogilvy. Grannie's Birthday.
Olds, S. Rites of Passage.
Ostriker. Happy birthday, a gray day like the first one—.
Pope, A. To Mrs. M. B. on Her Birth-Day.
Porter, P. On This Day I Complete My Fortieth Year.
Praed. To Helen, with Crabbe's Poems: a Birthday Present.
Robinson, M. Birth-Day, The.
Romero, N. New Suit, The.
Rosen, M. Eddie and the Birthday.
Rossetti, C. Birthday, A.

Rukeyser, M. Rondel: "Now that I am fifty-six."
Salter. Age of Reason, The.
San Garde. Giant's Cake, A.
Sholl. Thinking of You, Hiroshima.
Simmons, J. Birthday Poem, A.
Stafford, W. Twelfth Birthday.
Steele, T. Epitaph: "Here lies Sir Tact, a diplomatic fellow."
Swift, J. On Stella's Birthday, 1718/1719.
  Stella's Birthday, 1721.
  Stella's Birthday, 1725.
  Stella's Birthday ([March 13,] 1727).
Thomas, D. Poem in October.
Thribb. Lines on the Hundredth Anniversary of the Birth of W. Somerset Maugham.
Torregian. Poem for the Birthday of Huey P. Newton.
Tranter. Having Completed My Fortieth Year.
Unknown. Growing Up.
  Monday's child is fair of face.
Wagenlander. Mother's Birthday.
Wesley, C. For His Wife, on Her Birthday.
Wilbur. For K. R. on Her Sixtieth Birthday.
Yang Shih-ch'i. Evening of My Birthday, The.

Birthmarks
Carew, T. Upon a Mole in Celia's Bosom.
Janeway. Rose.
Parulekar. Birthmarks.

Birthplaces
Corso. Birthplace Revisited.
Hardy, T. Domicilium.
Saffarzadeh. Birthplace.

Bishop, Elizabeth
McPherson, S. For Elizabeth Bishop.
Swenson, M. In the Bodies of Words.
Valentine, J. Snow Landscape, in a Glass Globe.

Bismarck, Otto von
Chapman, J. Lines on the Death of Bismarck.

Bison. *See* **Buffaloes**

Bitterness
Amichai. Quick And Bitter.
Auden. His care-free swagger was a fine invention.
Ayton. To an Inconstant One.
  To His Forsaken Mistress.
Berggolts. You took me, hostile, sullen—.
Brown, S. Bitter Fruit of the Tree.
Carew, T. Song: To Her Again[e], She Burning in a Fe[a]ver.
  To Celia, upon Love's Ubiquity.
  To My Inconstant Mistress [or Mistris].
Clarke, L. Soucouyant.
Collins, M. Because the Dawn Breaks.
Crane, S. Heart, The.
Daniel, S. Love.
Daniel, Y. You stand beside me here, each day and every hour.
Di Prima. Paracelsus.
Dunbar, P. Then and Now.
"Elagin." Amnesty.
Eliot, T. Lines for an Old Man.
Ellis, C. Adder's Epigrams.
Ford, C. There's No Place to Sleep in This Bed, Tanguy.
Graves, R. Laureate, The.
Hardy, T. He Abjures Love.
Hartnett. Small Farm, A.
Hughes, T. Her Husband.
Jong. Colder.
Kooser. Widow, A.
Kunitz, S. Thief, The.
Lorde. Conversations in Crisis.
  New York City 1970.
MacNeice. Il Piccolo Rifiuto.
Major, C. Isolate.
Moore, T. When I loved you, I can't but allow.
Owen, M. "Assholes!" her eyes seem grey in this soup this morning.
Park, T. Before Thy Love.
Piercy. Letter to be Disguised as a Gas Bill.
Seward. Sonnet 19.
  Sonnet 32.
Smith, S. In the Night.
  Lightly Bound.

Tennyson, A. My Day.
Wen Cheng-ming. This little courtyard—mdash;the wind is pure.
Yang Shen. To the Tune "The Southerner."

Black (color)
Coleridge, S. Ne Plus Ultra.
Donne. Oh my black[e] soul[e]! now thou art summoned.
Earley, J. One Thousand Nine Hundred and Sixty-Eight Winters.
Freeman, C. Do Not Think.
Herbert of Cherbury. Sonnet of Black Beauty.
Knott. Goodbye.
Lee, D. WE'RE an Africanpeople.
Levertov. Wings, The.
Mahone. What Color Is Black?
Sanchez, S. Haiku: "Was it yesterday."
Sidney, P. Sonnet 7: "When Nature made her chief work, Stella's eyes."
Strand. Man in Black, The.
Thompson, L. Black Is Best.
Turner, N. Black and Gold.
Welburn. Black is beautiful.

Black Hills, South Dakota and Wyoming
Unknown. Dreary Black Hills, The.

Black Holes
Rumble. Black Hole.
Schmitz. Ladder: Roger Vail's Photo of a Rockface in the Carrara (Italy) Marble Quarries, The.

Black Power
Baraka. In the Tradition / (Not a White Shadow but Black People Will Be Victorious).
  Ka 'Ba.
  Last Word, The.
  Sacred Chant for the Return of Black Spirit and Power.
  State/meant.
Cornish, S. Fannie / lou / hamer / never / heard / of.
DuBois, W. Song of the Smoke, The.
Evans, M. Vive Noir!
Ferdinand. 2 B BLK.
Giovanni. My Poem.
Harper, M. High Modes: Vision as Ritual: Confirmation.
  Song: I Want a Witness.
Hoagland, E. Anti-Semanticist, The.
Hughes, L. I too, sing America.
Jackson, R. Big Chill Variations.
Jeffers, L. I do not know the power of my hand.
"Jerry." Mabrak.
Knight, E. Dark Prophecy: I Sing of Shine.
Madhubuti. Poem to Complement Other Poems, A.
Malik de Coteau. Motto Vision 1971.
Miller, E. Men, The.
Ologboni. Black Henry.
Reed, I. Badman of the Guest Professor.
Sanchez, S. Liberation / Poem.
Smith, M. Black and White.
Tolson. Dark Symphony.
See also **African Americans**

Blackberries
Heaney, S. Blackberry-Picking.
Kinnell. Blackberry Eating.
Komunyakaa. Blackberries.
Nicholson, N. Blackberry, The.
Plath. Blackberrying.
Reese, L. Blackberry Blossoms

Blackbirds
Brown, T. Vespers.
Cohen, L. All There Is to Know about Adolph Eichmann.
Craik. Blackbird, The.
DeFoe, M. 13 Ways of Eradicating Blackbirds.
Drayson. Blackbird, The.
Ledwidge. Lament for the Poets: 1916.
Mother Goose. Sing a song of sixpence.
Stevens, W. Thirteen Ways of Looking at a Blackbird.
Stevenson, A. In the Orchard.
Thomas, R. Blackbird Singing, A.

Unknown. Blackbird by Belfast Lough, The.
  Two Little Blackbirds.
Wolfe, H. Blackbird, The.

Blackouts
Dickey, J. Ice Skin, The.

Blacksmiths
Conn. Yard is littered with scrap, with axles, The.
Dibdin, C. Anchorsmiths, The.
Dickinson, E. Dare you see a Soul *at the White Heat?*.
Hopkins, G. Felix Randal the farrier,° O is he dead then? my duty / all ended.
Illyés. Work.
Longfellow, H. Village Blacksmith, The.
Unknown. Blacksmiths, The.
  Smoke-Blackened Smiths.
  Swarte-smeked Smithes.

Blake, William
Auden. Self-educated WILLIAM BLAKE.
Roethke. Supper with Lindsay.
Rossetti, D. William Blake (To Frederick Shields, on His Sketch of Blake's Work-room and Death-room, 3 Fountain Court, Strand).
Rukeyser, M. Homage to Literature.
Thomson, J. William Blake.

Blasphemy
Benét, S. For All Blasphemers.
Bentley, E. After dinner Erasmus.
Chaucer. Envoy to Scogan.
"Field." Trinity.
Wigglesworth. Blasphemers lewd, and swearers shrewd.
Wilbur. Simplication, A.

Blenheim, Battle of (1704)
Addison, J. Poem to His Grace the Duke of Marlborough, A.
Southey, R. Battle of Blenheim, The.

Blessings
Agard, J. By all means / bless the cloth.
Bible, *O.T.* Bible, Psalm 1:1–3, The.
  New Year, The.
Borges. From an Apocryphal Gospel.
Crosby, F. Blind but Happy.
Daniel, Y. To My Friends.
Dawe, B. Beatitudes.
Francis of Assisi. Canticle of Living Creatures.
Frost, R. Answer, An.
Griffiths, A. His left hand, in heat of noonday.
Hadewijch. Madness of love, The.
Herrick. Crutches.
  Good-Night, or Blessing, The.
  Grace for a Child.
  Grace for Children, A.
  To Dianeme ("Show [or Shew] me thy feet; show [or shew] me thy legs, thy thighs").
  Wassaile, The.
Jarrell. Blind Sheep, The.
Kamienska. Those who carry grand pianos / to the tenth floor.
Pavic. Song: "Rejoice eleventh finger reckoner of stars."
  Song: "Rejoice mason of years."
  Song: "Rejoice singer of songs for the deaf."
  Song: "Rejoice you who sleep with a finger in your ear."
Rumi. Don't grieve. Anything you lose comes round.
Shakespeare, W. Epitaph on Himself.
Theocritus. Wedding Song: Lullaby for Sleepy Lovers.
Tremblay, G. It Is Important.
Tsvetayeva. I bless the daily labor of my hands.
Tvardovsky. No, I have not been cheated by life.
Unknown. God Bless You.
  I See the Moon.
  Thanksgiving Hymn.
  Weingarten Travel Blessing, The.
Vaughan, H. To the Best, and Most Accomplished Couple.
Warren, R. Garden, The.
Whittier. Godspeed.

Wu-Men. Moon and clouds are the same.

Blindness

Berry, W. Music, A.
  To Know the Dark.
Bowes-Lyon. Blind Tramp, The.
Campbell, J. Blind Man at the Fair, The.
Cary, P. True Love.
Chesterman. Sir Nicketty Nox.
Chin Nung. Inkstone Inscription for the Blind
  Scholar Ho Yung-kuang, An.
Cibber. Blind Boy, The.
Crashaw. Samson to His De [or a] lilah.
Cristall. Blind Man, The.
Crosby, F. Blind but Happy.
De la Mare. All but blind.
Dickinson, E. Before I got my eye put out.
Doinas, S. Man with Exploded Eyes, The.
Dunn, D. War Blinded.
Echeruo. Melting Pot.
Gibson, W. Sight.
Hardy, T. Blinded Bird, The.
Hemphill. XXII.
Holmes, O. Prelude to a Volume Printed in
  Raised Letters for the Blind.
Illyés. Part of a Novel.
Jarrell. Blind Sheep, The.
Lieberman, L. Unblinding, The.
Mapanje. On His Royal Blindness Paramount
  Chief Kwangala.
Milton. Blind among enemies, O worse than
  chains.
  Blindness of Samson, The.
  On His Blindness.
  On His Deceased Wife.
  To Mr. Cyriack Skinner upon His Blindness.
Nekrasova. Blind Man, The.
Noyes, A. Spring, and the Blind Children.
Pearce, N. Blind.
Pointon. On Her Blindness.
Rabbitt. Power of Faith, The.
Ramke. How Light Is Spent.
Richards, I. Warhead Wakes.
Ritsos. Unanswered.
Roseliep. Blind man's, The.
Rossetti, C. Don't look for the flaws as you
  go.
  Kindness is a language which the.
  Sketch, A.
Sangster, M. Blind Man, The.
Sassoon. Does It Matter?[—losing your legs?].
Saxe, J. Blind Men and the Elephant, The.
Simonov. Blind Man, The.
Smelyakov. Blind Man, The.
Sorescu. With a green scarf I blindfolded.
Swenson, M. Blindman placed, The.
Tabb. Milton.
Tsybin. Eyes.
Williams, W. Luke 6:39.
  Parable of the Blind, The.
Yosano. Come at last to this point.

Blizzards

Akhmadulina. Blizzard.
Pasternak, B. Winter Night.
Rozhdestvensky. Nonflying Weather.
Su Tung-p'o. New Year's Eve blizzard kept
  me from leaving, The.
Yoshimi. Tanka: "With headlights on."

See also **Storms**

Blocks (toys)

Stevenson, R. Block City.

Blood

Ai. Country Midwife: A Day, The.
Alberti. Punishments.
Bachri. Cat.
Benn. Bunch of drifter sons hollered, A.
Berrigan, T. *et al.* Orange Jews.
Blunden. Midnight Skaters, The.
  1916 Seen from 1921.
Bowes-Lyon. Battlefield.
Breytenbach. Dreams Are Also Wounds.
Brontë, C. Lonely Lady, The.
Campbell, T. Hohenlinden.
Caraion. Tomorrow the Past Comes.
Carew, T. Celia Bleeding, to the Surgeon.
Cassian. Blood, The.
Celan. All those sleep shapes, crystalline.
  Tenebrae.

Crashaw. Hymn to Saint Teresa.
Degutyte. Etude in Glass.
Dickinson, E. Name—of it—is "Autumn,"
  The.
Dipoko. Pain.
do Espirito Santo. Where Are the Men Seized
  in this Wind of Madness?
Donne. Flea, The.
Duncan, R. My mother would be a falconress.
Faiz. No Sign of Blood.
"Field." Flaw, A.
Francis, R. Blood stains how to remove from
  cotton.
Garcia. Salmo: Para El.
Gray, J. Crucifix, A.
Gross, H. At the Crossroads.
Gunn, T. Cannibal.
  Faustus Triumphant.
Hall, D. Poet at Twenty, A.
Harper, M. Breaded Meat, Breaded Hands.
Herbert, Z. Hakeldama.
  Speculations on the Subject of Barabbas.
Hernández, M. July 18, 1936–July 18, 1938.
Herrick. Upon a Child That Died [or Dyed].
Hollander, J. Helicon.
Hughes, L. Negro Speaks of Rivers, The.
Iverem. Keeper.
Jackson, R. For Thurman Thomas.
Jarrell. Islands, The.
Joron, A. Baring the Device.
Kastelan. Blood and the Storm.
Kees. Conversation in the Drawingroom, The.
"MacDiarmid." One of the Principal Causes of
  War.
Mayer, G. Drip Drip or Not Bloody Likely
McClintock, M. Drizzling rain, A.
Mitchell, S. Story, A.
Naden. Poet and Botanist.
O'Brien, G. Scroll.
Ochester. Oh, By the Way.
O'Hara, F. Poem: "Eager note on my door
  said 'Call me', The."
Okamoto. Tanka: "Having let flow."
Okigbo. Death lay in ambush.
Orten. Whispered.
Paz. Doomed Garden, A.
Plunkett. I See His Blood upon the Rose.
Prévert. Song in the Blood.
Rathenow. No Picture.
Raworth. Hot Day at the Races.
Rodriguez, L. Heavy blue veins streaked
  across my mother's legs, some of them
  bunched up into dark lumps at her ankles.
Ryuichi. Human House.
Saitō Mokichi. Tanka: "Ever so close."
Sartarelli. That Land (4).
Serge. Hands.
Shafarman. Russia 1914/Bolinas 1988.
Shapiro, D. After.
Sherry, J. Lepidoptery.
Simic. Butcher Shop.
Sorescu. Start.
Stafford, W. Ceremony.
Sternlieb. Right of Way.
Thomas, L. Subway Witnesses, The.
Thomas, R. Welsh Landscape.
Tipputtolar. Red is the battlefield.
Tsung Ch'en. Rebels' cavalry are everywhere,
  The.
Ungaretti. Babel.
Vallejo. Our Daily Bread.
Vaughan, H. Abel's Blood.
Wakoski. Butcher's Apron, The.
Walker, A. Suicide.
Washbourne. Circulation, The.
Whitman, W. Trickle drops! my blue veins
  leaving!
Wieseltier. Leningrad: Picture Postcard.
  "Wintry Dawn."
Wollach. Jonathan.
Wood, R. Blood.
Wright, F. Blood.
Wright, J. Living by the Red River.

Blue (color)

Blumenthal, M. Blue.
Brock-Broido. Hitchcock Blue.

Cardenal. Tahirassawichi in Washington.
  Vision from the Blue Window.
Cherry, K. Reading, Dreaming, Hiding.
Coleridge, M. L'Oiseau Bleu.
Divakaruni. Indigo.
Edwards, R. Blue Room, The.
Francis, R. Blue Winter.
  Exclusive Blue.
Howes, B. Blue Garden, The.
Kelly, R. Coming.
Rein. Calendar of the Air.
Shapcott, T. Blue Paisley Shirt, The.
Tate, J. Blue Booby lives, The.
Unknown. I heard a fly buzz when I died.
Wakoski. Blue Monday.
Wallace, R. Between Equals.

Blue Jays

Barrax. Gift.
Francis, R. Blue Jay [or Bluejay].
Paino. What the Blue Jay Said.

Bluebells

Enoch. Bluebells.
Ewing, J. Bluebells.

Blueberries

Layton. Berry Picking.
Moore, L. Indian Girl.
  Summer noon.

Bluebirds

Coleridge, M. L'Oiseau Bleu.
Frost, R. Last Word of a Bluebird, The.
Higginson, W. Before the descent.
McClintock, M. Bluebird alights, The.
Melville, H. Blue-Bird, The.
Padgett, R. Big Bluejay Composition.

Blues (mood)

Beeks. Parker's Mood.
Davis, T. Rogue and Jar: 4/27/77.
Emanuel, J. Get Up, Blues.
Encarnacion. Bulosan Listens to a Recording
  of Robert Johnson.
Handy, W. Joe Turner Blues.
  St. Louis Blues.
Herndon. Long Blues, The.
Hughes, L. Blues, The.
  Hard Daddy.
  Homesick Blues.
  Miss Blues'es Child.
  Weary Blues, The.
Jefferson, B. Easy Rider Blues.
Jones, P. Song: "I have so little sorrow."
Jordan, N. When A Woman Gets Blue.
Knight, E. Poem for Myself (Or Blues for a
  Mississippi Black Boy), A.
Patterson, R. Surplus Blues.
Patton, C. 34 Blues.
Randall, D. Langston Blues.
Unknown. Railroad Blues, The.
  Southern Blues, The.
Waller, T. *et al.* (What Did I Do to Be So)
  Black and Blue?
Williams, T. Kitchen Door Blues.
Young, A. Blues Don't Change, The.

See also **Melancholy**

Blues (music)

Aubert, A. Bessie Smith's Funeral.
Baker, H. Tobacco Warehouse Blues.
Baraka. Funk Lore.
  In the Tradition / (Not a White Shadow but
  Black People Will Be Victorious).
  Legacy.
Brathwaite, E. Blues.
Brooks, G. Queen of the Blues.
Carr, L. How Long Blues.
Corrie. How Long Has Trane Been Gone.
Cortez. How Long Has Trane Been Gone.
Dent. For Walter Washington.
Dumas, H. Concentration Camp Blues.
Emanuel, J. Get Up, Blues.
Encarnacion. Bulosan Listens to a Recording
  of Robert Johnson.
Ferdinand. Blues (in Two Parts), The.
Handy, W. St. Louis Blues.
Harper, M. For Bud.
  Narrative of the Life and Times of John
  Coltrane: Played by Himself, A.
Hayden, R. Homage to the Empress of the
  Blues.

Boarding Houses

Hernton. D Blues.
Hughes, L. Brass Spittoons.
  Notes on the Broadway Theatre.
  Po' Boy Blues.
  Song for Billie Holiday.
  Weary Blues, The.
Hunter, A. *et al.* Down-Hearted Blues.
Jackson, A. Choosing the Blues.
Jackson, M. Blues Today, The.
Johnson, R. Hellhound on My Trail.
Jones, R. Trouble in mind, I'm blue.
Kaufman, B. Blues Note.
Knight, E. To Dinah Washington.
McClaurin. Mask, The.
Moore, L. Bluesman's Blues, A.
Neal, L. Don't say goodbye to the Porkpie
  Hat that rolled.
Overton, R. Blues in "C."
Patterson, R. Hopping Toad Blues.
  Sundown Blues.
Penny, R. I Remember How She Sang.
Plumpp. Remembered.
Robson, J. Blues for the Lonely*.
Rushing. Good Morning, Blues.
Sadoff. At the Half-Note Café.
Sanchez, S. For Our Lady.
  Liberation / Poem.
Schuyler, J. Let's All Hear It for Mildred
  Bailey!
Senghor. Blues.
Smith, B. Backwater Blues.
  Black Mountain Blues.
  In the House Blues.
Smith, P. So Motown taught me all about
  men. Men worshipped.
Troupe. Snake-Back Solo.
Unknown. Coal Loadin' Blues.
  Depot Blues.
  East St. Louis Blues.
  Four o'Clock Flower Blues ("Four o'clock
  flowers bloom out in the mornin'").
  Gonna Lay My Head Down on Some Railroad
  Line.
  I Rode Southern, I Rode L & N.
  Lowdown Dirty Blues.
  Mississippi Blues.
  Ragged and Dirty.
  Railroad Blues, The.
  Special Rider Blues.
  Train Is Off the Track, The.
  Worried Life Blues.
Walcott. Blues.
Wallenstein. Blues 1.
  Blues 2.
Weatherly, T. Blues for Franks Wooten.
  Times.
Williams, C. Gulf Coast Blues.
Wojahn. John Berryman Listening to Robert
  Johnson's "King of the Delta Blues," January
  1972.
Young, A. Blues Don't Change, The.
Zu-Bolton. Struggle-Road Dance.

Boarding Houses

Acorn. On Saint-Urbain Street.
Kipling, R. Ballad of Fisher's Boardinghouse,
  The.
Larkin, P. Mr Bleaney.

Boasting

Bible, *O.T.* Psalm 52.
Dabydeen, D. Coolie Son.
Hardy, T. Epitaph for George Moore.
Sandburg, C. Primer Lesson.

Boats and Boating

Bishop, E. Arrival at Santos.
  Fish, The.
Blind. Russian Student's Tale, The.
Campbell, R. Fishing Boats in Martigues.
Catullus. Yacht, The.
Chang Yü. Hearing a Song from My Boat.
Chao Meng-fu. Fisherman's Lyric.
  Inscribed on a Landscape by Mi Yüan-hui.
Ch'ien T'ao. Flood.
Chu Hsi. Boats Are Afloat, The.
Chu Yün-ming. Late Spring—Traveling
  through the Mountains.
Chute, M. My Plan.
Clark, T. You (II).

Davison, P. Equinox 1980.
Deutsch. Barges on the Hudson.
Dickey, J. Lifeguard, The.
Dryden, J. By viewing Nature, Natures hand-
  maid, Art.
Duncan, R. New Poem, A.
Eberhart, R. Ship Burning and a Comet All in
  One Day, A.
Emmett. Boatman's Dance ("Ober de
  mountains, slick as an eel").
"Field." As two fair vessels side by side.
Frost, R. Flower-Boat, The.
Gardner, D. Near Hermes.
Gates, L. Rowing.
Hall, D. Long River, The.
Hirshfield, J. In a Net of Blue and Gold.
Hitomaro. My thoughts are with a boat.
Ho Ching-ming. Bamboo Branch Song.
Holmes, O. Old Ironsides.
Holtby, W. Boats in the Bay.
Hsü Chung-hsing. Traveling by Boat at Shun-
  ch'ang.
Hsü Pen. Ballad of the Merchant.
  Hermit Li's Herb Garden Retreat at T'ung-
  ch'uan.
  Tomb of the Singing Girl Ch'iung-i, The.
"Ingoldsby." Lines Left at Mr Theodore
  Hook's House in June, 1834.
Jackson, H. My Lighthouses.
Jeffers, R. Boats in a Fog.
Kao Ch'i. Going Out to the Country on a
  Boat Trip, Sheltering from Rain Beneath a
  Tree.
  Mooring Our Boat at Tan-yang Harbor.
Kikaku. Above the boat.
Kinsella, T. Downstream.
Komunyakaa. Boat People.
Lake, P. In Rough Weather.
Lear, E. Limerick: "There was an Old Man in
  a boat."
Li Meng-yang. Mooring at Hsia-k'ou at Night.
Lin Hung. Sailing at Night on Flowing-sand
  River.
Liu Yung. Tune: "Midnight Music."
Lu Yu. Blue Rapids.
  Rain on the River.
MacCaig. Drifter.
  Half-Built Boat in a Hayfield.
MacLean, S. Black boat, perfect Greek.
Marvell. Bermudas.
Mayer, B. Boats.
McWatt. Boat Builder, The.
  Lady Northcote.
Mei Yao Ch'en. Dappled Horse, The.
Merrill, J. Parrot Fish, The.
Milosz, C. Luke 5:1–11; While the people
  pressed upon him.
Mitchell, S. Matthew 13:1–9; That same day
  Jesus.
Mo Shih-lung. Gathering Lotus with Singing
  Girls.
Moore, J. One Reason I Went to Prison.
Mura. Huy Nguyen: Brothers, Drowning Cries.
Murphy, R. Last Galway Hooker, The.
Ni Tsan. Inscribed on the Painting, "River in
  Autumn."
Okamoto. Tanka: "My mind shattered."
Ou-yang Hsiu. Old fisherman spends his night
  beneath the western cliffs.
Pape. Dinner on the Miami River.
Pien Kung. Inscribed on an Album Leaf
  Painted by Dr. Lin.
  Song of the Transport Workers—Seeing Off
  Fang Wen-yü on His Way to His Post as
  Inspector of Transportation.
Plath. Crossing the Water.
Po Chü-i. Arriving at Hsün-yang.
  Illness.
  Kept Waiting in the Boat at Chiu-K'ou Ten
  Days by an Adverse Wind.
Prismanova. Siren.
Rich, A. We are driven to odd attempts; once
  it would not have occurred to.
Ríos, A. Domingo Limón.
Rossetti, C. Rainbow, The.
Sami Mansei. This world of ours.
Sandburg, C. Lost.

Shanks. Boats at Night.
Shelley, P. Startled by his own thoughts, he
  looked around.
Shen Chou. On the Fifteenth Day of the
  Seventh Month I Came Home Late from the
  City.
Sidney, P. Sonnet 103: "O happy Thames, that
  didst my Stella bear."
Simpson, L. Fine Day for Straw Hats, A.
Spencer, B. Boat Poem.
Stevenson, R. Travel.
  Where Go the Boats?
Stokesbury. California.
Su Shih. In a boat, Getting Up at Night.
Su Tung-p'o. Following the Rhumes of
  Chiang Hui-shu.
  I travel day and night toward the Yangtze and
  the sea.
  In a Boat, Getting Up at Night.
Tadamichi. As I row over the plain.
T'an Yüan-ch'un. Heard on a Boat.
T'ang Yin. Inscribed on a Painting ("On the
  mountain, old trees, still green in autumn").
  On the Butterflies.
Tao-chi. Inscribed on a Painting ("Little boat
  floats by the dock, The").
  Mood comes on—I want to cross Hsi-ling,
  The.
  Riding a Boat on Wu-ling Stream.
  Trip to Hua-yang Mountain, A.
Tsung Ch'en. On Hearing That the Sea-
  Barbarians Are About To Attack Hu-chou—
  Expressing My Feelings to Tzu-yü.
Tu Fu. Dejeuner Sur L'Herbe.
  Excursion, The.
  Night Thoughts aboard a Boat.
Unknown. Boat of Cypress Wood, The.
  Hey, dorolot, dorolot!
  Tru'o'ng Chi, the Lovelorn Boatman.
Wang Chien. Boatman's Song, A.
Wang Shih-chieng. Mooring at Night at Kao-
  yu.
Wang Wei. Seeking a Mooring.
Warren, R. Red Mullet, The.
Wen Cheng-ming. For three years I sadly
  listened.
  Mooring My Boat on the Ssu River and
  Watching the Moon.
  Painting a Picture, The Tranquil Boat—Sent to
  Ko Ju-ching.
Willmot. Musty shed.
Wills, J. Boulders.
Wu Wei-yeh. At the River Tower Parting
  from My Younger Brother, Fu-ling.
  Sailing at Dusk from T'u-sung.
  Song to the Tune "Perching Crows."
Yang Chi. Up at the prow, I wash my mouth,
  dripping water on my robe.
Yang Shen. To the Tune, "Ch'ing-p'ing
  Yüeh."
Yang Shih-ch'i. Night Rain beneath the City
  Walls of P'i-ling.
Yang Wan-li. *Keng-tzu* (1180), First Month,
  Fifth Day, Dawn.
Yang Wei-chen. Taking the Ferry at Ta-kao at
  Dawn.
Yosano. Left on the beach.
Yü Chi. Following the Rhymes of Bamboo
  Branch Songs in Response to Yüan Po-chang.
  Hearing Loom and Shuttle.
  Little Landscape by Yen Wen-kuei, A.
Yüan Hung-tao. On Board a Boat at Chi-ning.
Zukofsky, L. Ways, The.

See also **Ferry Boats; Freighters; Ships and
  Shipbuilding; Yachts**

Bobolinks

Bryant, W. Robert of Lincoln.

Bodies

Ackland. Eyes of body, being blindfold by
  night, The.
Amichai. In My Time, at Your Place.
  Two Songs of Peace.
Anghelaki-Rooke. Body Is the Victory and the
  Defeat of Dreams, The.
Armantrout. Disown.
  Winter.
Auden. Prime.

Bass, E. To Praise.
Benedikt. Thoughts.
Benn. Monologue.
Biaoszewski. *They clanged and clanged.*
Bidart. Ellen West.
Bogan, L. Cartography.
Bowman, C. Mr. X.
Breton, A. Free Union.
Brooks, G. Still Do I Keep My Look, My
  Identity. . . .
Brown, L. Come go with me out to the Field.
Brownstein. Oracle night / the porch is frozen.
Carter, E. Dialogue, A.
Cavafy. Body, remember not only how much
  you were loved.
Cendrars. Great Fetishes, The.
Child, A. Squeeze.
Clarke, C. Rondeau: "They are bodies left
  unburied."
Clifton, L. 11/10 Again.
  Homage to My Hips.
  Lost Baby Poem, The.
Cohen, L. Suzanne takes you down to her
  place near the river.
Comte de Lautréamont. I am filthy. Lice gnaw
  me. Swine, when they look at me, vomit.
  The scabs.
Cooper, J. Waiting.
Couani. Map of the world is felt from the
  inside. Rough around the, The.
Couzyn. Way towards each other is through
  our bodies, The.
Cowley, A. Platonic[k] Love.
Creeley. Body.
Cruz Varela. Love Song for Difficult Times.
Csoori. Bullet, A.
  Tenant Who Lives in Fire, The.
Cuddihy. This Body.
Cummins, J. Sestina.
Daumal. Clavicles for a Great Poetic Game.
Dickinson, E. I am afraid to own a Body.
  Prison gets to be a friend, A.
Donald. Eye for an Eye, An.
  I Expect You Think This Huge Dark Coat.
Donne. Ecstasy, The.
  Holy Ghost, The.
  Love's Progress.
  Resurrection, Imperfect.
D'Orleans. Smiling mouth and laughing eyen°
  gray, The.
Duesing. Reprieve.
Duggan, L. One xxxvii.
Duncan, R. Torso / Passages 18, The.
Eliot, T. Dedication to My Wife, A.
Elizabeth I. Written in Her French Psalter.
Elytis. Autopsy, The.
"Ern Malley." Egyptian Register.
Fatchen. Hullo, Inside.
  Tailpiece.
Felltham. To Phryne.
"Field." Sweet-Briar in Rose.
Follain. Mirror, A.
  Taxidermist is sitting / before the russet
  breasts, A.
Fox, S. Miss Pimberton Of.
Fraser, K. Frammenti Romani.
Fried, E. One Kind of Freedom Speaks.
Fuertes. Human Geography.
Fulton, A. Priming Is a Negligee, The.
Fumiko. Tanka: "As the surgical knife."
  Tanka: "Each year."
  Tanka: "Since that evening."
  Tanka: "With a thunderous crack."
  Tanka: "With sorrow I recall."
Funk, A. After Dark.
Gallagher, T. Each Bird Walking.
Ginsberg, A. After Lalon.
Gizzi. Another Day on the Pilgrimage.
González, A. Before I could call myself Ángel
  González.
Graves, R. Thieves, The.
Greenwald, T. Open mouth open through.
Grimké, A. Black Finger, The.
Gunn, T. Man With Night Sweats, The.
Hacker, M. Mother II.
  Presentation Piece.
Hadas, R. Winged Words.

Hagiwara Sakutaro. Lover of Love.
Harding, S. Noblest bodies are but gilded
  clay.
Hecht, A. Feast of Stephen, The.
Hernández, M. Waltz Poem of Those in Love
  and Inseparable Forever.
Herrick. Body is the Soul's [or Soules]
  poor[e] house, or home, The.
  Life is the body's [or Bodies] light, which
  once declining.
Hilberry. Body and mind, we used to think,
  were two.
Holmes, J. Love of the Flesh, The.
Holst-Warhaft. In the end is the body—what
  we know.
Holub. Vanishing Lung Syndrome.
Howe, M. Without Devotion.
Hsü Pen. Poem on Buddha's Begging Bowl—
  For Hui-ku, His Holiness Ming, A.
Hughes, L. Red Silk Stockings.
Huy Cân. Body, The.
Imre. So, then, the soul craves an earthly
  body.
Ishikawa Takuboku. Tanka: "Has Fate sneaked
  in."
  Tanka: "When I breathe."
Itwaru. Body Rites.
Jackson, L. Head Itself.
  Starved.
Jenyns. Temple of Venus, The.
Jones, A. Foot, The.
Kabir. My friend, this body is His lute. He
  tightens the strings and plays its songs.
Kalász. Maiden.
Kerouac. Arms folded.
Kitahara Hakushū. Tanka: "Strong scent, The."
Komunyakaa. Slam, Dunk, and Hook.
Koneski. Wheat, The.
Kowit. In the morning.
  What chord did she pluck in my soul.
Kruchyonykh. Sahara to America, The.
Kunert. Implant.
Larkin, P. Mr Bleaney.
Laux. China.
Lawrence, D. Body of God, The.
  Demiurge.
  Eloi, Eloi, Lama Sabachthani?
Lee, L. Interrogation, The.
  This Room and Everything in It.
Leyvik. Open up, gate.
Lipska. When our enemies fall asleep.
Loy. Three Moments in Paris.
"MacDiarmid." Scunner.
MacLeish. What the Serpent Said to Adam.
Mahadevi. When the body becomes Your
  mirror.
Maiden. In the Gloaming.
Malroux. Octet Before Winter.
Mansour, J. Tinfoil.
Marlatt, D. Trying. a trying child. trying it on
  for size. the role.
Martinez, V. It Is Not.
Marvell. Dialogue between the Soul and [the]
  Body, A.
McClatchy. Found Parable.
  My Mammogram.
McCombs, D. River and Under the River,
  The.
McOrlan. Weighing-machine, The.
McPherson, S. **His Body.**
Merrill, J. **Body.**
Mirabai. Love has stained my body.
  O friend, understand: the body.
Mitchell, S. Girl Tearing Up Her Face.
Moorsom. Body.
Mora. Mangos y limones.
Morgan, R. As it was in the beginning.
Morley, H. Made Out of Links.
Neruda. Sonnet XVII.
Newcastle, M. Dialogue betwixt the Body and
  the Mind, A.
  Of the Animal Spirits.
  Soul and Body.
  Soul's Garment, The.
Niedecker. News.
Noguere. Soma.
Nowak, T. Psalm To Cheer Up.

O'Brien, G. Scroll.
O'Dalaigh, M. My body's self deserts me
  now.
Olds, S. Language of the Brag, The.
  Pajamas.
Oppenheimer, J. Innocent Breasts, The.
Pagis. Siege.
Palmer, M. Eighth Sky.
  Erolog.
Patmore, C. To the Body.
Paz. Counterparts.
  Touch.
Peacock, M. Have You Ever Faked an
  Orgasm?
Pembroke, M. O Lord, Thou Hast Searched
  and Known Me.
Perelman. Cliff Notes.
Phillips, C. As From a Quiver of Arrows.
  Toys.
Piercy. Friend, The.
Raine, K. Love-Poem: "Yours is the face that
  the earth turns to me."
Ralegh, W. Lie, The.
Ramanujan. Elements of Composition.
Rankin, J. Tale.
Receveur. Night Fear.
Reverdy. Squares.
Rilke. Tombs of the Hetaerae.
Roberts, K. How Late Desire Looks.
Roberts, N. Max Factor Pink.
Robinson, K. Intent to consider.
Rukeyser, M. Endless.
Rutsala. Bodies.
Ryan, G. Cruising.
Samio. Tanka: "No scar."
Sartarelli. Phantasmatikon.
Schelling. Isha Upanishad.
Seale, J. Nape.
Seibles. Who doesn't.
Senghor. Song of the Initiate.
Sexton. Earth, The.
  In Celebration of My Uterus.
  Mr. Mine.
Shūji. Tanka: "My body."
  Tanka: "Over my."
Shwarts. Elegy on an X-ray Photo of My
  Skull.
Sidney, P. What tongue can her perfections
  tell.
Simko. Three Songs.
Smart, C. Author Apologizes to a Lady, for
  His Being a Little Man, The.
Smith, S. Man is a spirit. This the poor flesh
  knows.
  This Englishwoman is so refined.
Snyder, G. Bath, The.
Södergran. Instinct.
Sorescu. Fresco.
  Map.
Soupault. One o'Clock.
Stein, G. Kiss my lips.
Stevenson, A. Spirit is too blunt an
  instrument, The.
Strode. On a Good Leg and Foot.
Sullivan, N. To My Body.
Swenson, M. Question.
Swirszczynska. I Starve My Belly for a
  Sublime Purpose.
  I Talk to My Body.
Tadic. Man from the Death Institute.
Tanikawa Shuntaro. Request.
Teodorescu. At Night the Jellyfish Unfold
  Their Veils.
Tysh, G. Genitalia.
U Tam'si Tchicaya. 'Congo is myself'
  (Lumumba), The.
  I tear at my belly.
Unknown. Have I a body or have I none?
  I have a gentle cock.
  I know moon-rise, I know star-rise.
  Joy and Temperance and Repose.
  When I look at her.
Updike. In Extremis.
Vas. Just This.
Vaughan, H. Resurrection and Immortality.
Virgil. Knowing About Horses.
Virgil. Red flipped out.

Voigt. Heart is the Target, The.
Waldman, A. Skin / Meat / BONES.
Ward, D. Absolution.
Limit.
Wat. Facing Bonnard.
Watkins, N. Near Miss.
Webb, T. Ancient Prayer, An.
Weöres. Ecce Homo.
Whitman, W. Come, said my soul.
I am the poet of the Body and I am the poet of the Soul.
Walt Whitman, a kosmos, of Manhattan the son.
Willmot. Her hand on the doorknob.
Wollach. Body, The.
Never will I hear the sweet voice of God.
Wright, J. Jewel, The.
Wright, J. What is Beautiful.
Yang Shen. To the Tune "Yellow Oriole" ("Threads of rain weave lambent light").
Yeats. Crazy Jane Talks with the Bishop.
Lady's Third Song, The.
Michael Robartes and the Dancer.
Oil and Blood.
Yi, S. Poem No. V.
Yosano. Tanka: "Tell them."
Zach. Against Sadness.
Zamora, D. Celebration of the Body.
Vision of Your Body.
Zhenkai. Requiem: "Not the living but the dead."

See also **Nudity and Nudists**

Boer War
Davidson, J. Battle.
Hardy, T. Christmas Ghost-Story, A.
Colonel's Soliloquy, The.
Departure.
Drummer Hodge.
Embarcation.
Souls of the Slain, The.
Wife in London, A.
Kipling, R. Bridge-Guard in the Karroo.
Chant-Pagan.
Return, The.

Boethius, Anicius Manlius Severinus
Macoubrie. Boethius at Cavalzero.

Bogart, Humphrey
Berg, S. To My Friends.

Bogs
Heaney, S. Bog Queen.
Bogland.
Tollund Man, The.
Smith, S. Our Bog is dood, our Bog is dood.

Bohemian Life
Durem. Problem in Social Geometry—the Inverted Square!
Herbert, S. Lines for a Worthy Person Who Has Drifted by Accident into a Chelsea Revel.

Boleyn, Anne
Bibb. Anne Boleyn.
Petrarch. Whoso list to hunt, I know where is a hind.
Wyatt, T. Who so list to hount I knowe where is an hynde.
Whoso list to hunt, I know where is an hind.

Bolsheviks
Khlebnikov, V. She came and spoke low.
Tsar! Send out a shot!
Unknown. Harry Pollit Was a Bolshie.

Bombs and Bombing
Baggett. Day Before They Bombed Nagasaki, The.
Brecht, B. This Summer's Sky.
Brock, V. Remembering Dresden.
Cartier. Poem for a Chorus.
Cunard. To Eat To-day.
Fiacc. Intimate Letter 1973.
Fisher, R. Entertainment of War, The.
Floyd. Corporal Charles Chungtu, U. S. M. C.
Garioch. Wire, The.
Hitchcock. Scattering Flowers.
Ignatow, D. All Quiet.
Jarrell. Truth, The.
Layne, M. Intersection in the Sky.
Levertov. Fragrance of Life, Odor of Death.

Lipsitz. Feeding, The.
McDonald, W. For Kelly, Missing in Action.
Retired Pilot to Himself, The.
War Games.
Miller, V. Light Reading.
Nagys. Hallesches Tor: Communion.
Randall, D. Ballad of Birmingham.
Receveur. Eagle in the Land of Oz.
Reed, H. Chard Whitlow.
Ridler. At Christmas.
Roberson. Aerialist Narratives, Chapter Three, The.
Salis. Bomb Victim in the Cathedral Speaks to a Child, A.
Seifert. Never Again.
Sexton. Firebombers, The.
Spender, S. Epilogue to a Human Drama.
Rejoice in the Abyss.
Stafford, W. At the Bomb Testing Site.
Szymborska. Terrorist, He Watches, The.
Taggart, J. Twenty One Times.
Todd, R. Joan Miró ("Once there were peasant pots and a dry brown hare").
Weigl. Her Life Runs Like a Red Silk Flag.
Wellesley. Enemy, The.

See also **Air Warfare**

Bonaparte, Josephine
Hollander, J. Appearance and Reality.

Bones
Blumenthal, M. Blue.
Bly, R. Counting Small-Boned Bodies.
Craveirinha. Seed is in Me, The.
Donne. Relic, The.
Fumi Saito. Tanka: "Bones of a fish."
Hollander, J. Lady's-Maid's Song, The.
Hope, A. Meditation on a Bone.
Hughes, T. Relic.
Lorde. Ethiopia for Tifa.
MacLeish. Immortal Helix.
McGinley. Choice of Weapons, A.
Merwin, W. Bones, The.
Milton. On Shakespear[e].
Neruda. Nothing but Death.
Perlman, A. Family Reunion.
Roy, L. Suffering The Sea Change: All My Pretty Ones.
Shakespeare, W. Ariel's Song ("Full fathom [or fadom] five thy father lies").
Epitaph on Himself.
Stevens, W. Postcard from the Volcano, A.
Stow. Singing Bones, The.
Unknown. Epitaph on William Jones.
Thin Flynn.
Wat. By a great, swift water.
Webb, D. Tragedy, A.
Wylie. Full Moon.

See also **Skeletons**

Bonneau, Jennette
Fordham. Death of a Grandparent. Mrs. Jennette Bonneau.

"Bonnie Dundee." *See* **Dundee, John Graham of Claverhouse, 1st Viscount**

Bonsai
Piercy. Work of Artifice, A.

Boobies
Tate, J. Blue Booby lives, The.

Book Clubs
White, E. Classic Waits for Me, A.

Book of Kells. *See* **Kells, Book of**

Books
Adams, F. To a Thesaurus.
Amis, K. Bookshop Idyll, A.
Balaban. Opening Le Ba Khon's Dictionary.
Baugh, E. Old Talk, or West Indian History.
Beer, P. Footbinding.
Belloc. On His Books.
Benedikt. Dossier of the Torturer.
Bogan, L. Man Alone.
Boldman. I read.
Bradstreet, A. Author to Her Book, The.
Brownell, H. Suspiria Noctis.
Browning, R. Sibrandus Schafnaburgensis.
Burke, M. On the twelfth floor.
Burns, J. How these pieces of paper: lined unlined small large crinkled smooth.
Reading.

Burns, R. Book-Worms, The.
Carew, T. Fancy, A.
Catullus. To Varus.
Chang Yü. Lamenting for Kao Ch'ing-ch'iu, Chi-ti.
Reading the Poetry Collection of Lü Fang-ch'ing.
Chu Yün-ming. Painting of the Butterfly Dream by the Master Artist Li Tsai, A.
Coolidge, C. This Garden Being: The Hanging of Books.
Corso. I Held a Shelley Manuscript.
Cummings, E. If everything happens that can't be done.
Dana, R. Pleasure Boat, The [or Pleasure-Boat, The].
Davenant. There, when they thought they saw in well sought Books.
Davidson, M. Dream Dream, The.
Dickinson, E. He ate and drank the precious Words.
Precious—moldering pleasure—'tis, A.
There is no Frigate like a Book.
Disch. Bookmark, A.
Donne. Valediction of the Book, A.
Dove, R. First Book, The.
Drummond, W. Book, The.
Fumi Saito. Tanka: "In my possession."
Giovanni. Ten Years Old.
Glaser, M. Changing Address Books.
Goldbarth. Still Life, Symbolic of Lines, A.
Guiney. In the Reading-Room of the British Museum.
Gumilyov. No flowers will live in my room.
Hadas, R. Moments of Summer.
Harwood, L. "Utopia" The.
Herlin. So many traces, fragile monuments.
Herrick. Argument of His Book, The.
To His Book[e] ("Have I not blessed thee? Then go forth; nor fear").
To My Ill Reader.
Holmes, O. Iris, Her Book.
Hotham. Library book, The.
Ignatow, D. Against the Evidence.
Jabès. To be in the book. To figure in the book of questions, to be part of it.
Jarrell. Author to the Reader, The.
Johnson, L. In Honorem Doriani Creatorisque Eius.
In Honour of Dorian and his Creator.
Keats. Keen, fitful gusts are whispering here and there.
Keyes, S. War Poet.
Kirby, D. To a French Structuralist.
Kleinzahler. San Francisco/New York.
Larkin, P. Fiction and the Reading Public.
Study of Reading Habits, A.
Lawrence, A. Robert Penn Warren's book.
Le Gallienne. Library in a Garden, A.
Leib. In little hands she holds an open book.
Li K'ai-hsien. Not a day goes by without someone borrowing books from me.
Lo Yin. Book-burning Pit, The.
Mallarmé. End / conscience.
Martial. De Libro suo.
Masaoka Shiki. My room.
McCord, D. Books Fall Open.
McOrlan. Modern circus, The.
Mei Yao Ch'en. Offering for the Cat, An.
Milosz, C. And yet the books will be there on the shelves, separate beings.
Milton. On the Detraction Which Followed upon My Writing Certain Treatises.
Mori Ōgai. Tanka: "Frolicking."
Muldoon, P. Making the Move.
Nesbit, E. Among His Books.
Nesbit, W. Who Hath a Book.
Newcastle, M. Common Fate of Books, The.
Excuse for So Much Writ upon My Verses.
Poetresses Petition, A.
O'Meally. It aint no.
Patmore, C. Revelation, The.
P'i Jih-hsiu. Reading.
Po Chü-i. On a Box Containing his Own Works.
Quarles. Booke of *Common Pray'r* excels the rest, The.

Reese, L. Love, Weeping, Laid This Song.
Rich, A. Burning of Paper instead of Children, The.
Rifat. Stars.
Rosenberg, S. Library closing—.
Rowe, G. God Speed.
Shapiro, D. Book of Glass, A.
Shen Chou. Sent in Parting to Yen Kung-su.
Sissman. Upon Finding Dying: An Introduction, by L. E. Sissman, Remaindered at is.
Sosnora. Do you envy, my comrades-in-arms.
Southey, R. Scholar, The.
Stedman, E. Prelude to An American Anthology.
Stevens, R. House was quiet and the world was calm, The.
Poem That Took the Place of a Mountain, The.
Stevenson, R. Armies in the Fire.
Land of Story-Books, The.
Strand. Eating Poetry.
Swirszczynska. He Was Lucky.
Tarkovsky. Poet, The.
Taylor, J. Me thinks I heare some Cavillers object.
Teller. Lines to a Tree.
Thomas, E. On Sir J—— S—— Saying in a Sarcastic Manner, My Books Would Make Me Mad; an Ode.
Thornbury. Court Historian, The.
Tipping. Poet at Work.
Tranter. Enzensberger at 'Exiles'.
Trowbridge, J. Recollections of "Lalla Rookh."
Unknown. Domestic Philosopher, The.
O for a Booke.
Open Sesame.
Vaughan, H. Book, The.
Veenendaal. On My Fourteenth Wedding Anniversary I Ride on Trains.
Wakoski. Light.
Walcott. Volcano.
Walden. Introductory to Second Edition.
Waldman, A. et al. & Now the book is closed.
Weiss, T. Fire at Alexandria, The.
Wen Cheng-ming. Volumes of books, tea and incense.
White, E. Classic Waits for Me, A.
Whitman, W. In cabin'd ships at sea.
Shut not your doors to me proud libraries.
Whoever you are holding me now in hand.
Wordsworth, W. Expostulation and Reply.
Tables Turned[: An Evening Scene, on the Same Subject], The.
Yang Shih-ch'i. Night Rain: A Wall Collapses—Sent To My Neighbors.
Yeats. When you are old and grey and full of sleep.
Yüan Mei. I Know Inside.

Books of Hours
Ramsey, P. Hours, The.

Bookworms
Burns, R. Book-Worms, The.
Cynewulf. Old English Riddle.
Unknown. Moth ate words; a marvellous event, A.

Boone, Daniel
Benét, S. Daniel Boone.

Booth, Edwin
Melville, H. Coming Storm, The.

Booth, John Wilkes
Unknown. Booth Killed Lincoln.

Booth, William
Lindsay, V. General William Booth Enters into Heaven.

Boots
Hall, S. Boot Hill.
Harter. Snowflakes.
Meehan, M. Is There Life after Feminism.
Unknown. Young Lady of Twickenham, The.
Wright, K. Red Boots On.

Borden, Lizzie
Gallagher, T. Instructions to the Double.

Borders (region), Scotland. See **Scottish Borders**

Boredom
Ashbery. Darlene's Hospital.
Atwood. Bored.
Berryman. Life, friends, is boring. We must not say so.
Brownstein. War.
Buzbee. Sunday, Tarzan in His Hammock.
Clampitt. Meridian.
Elliott, A. Stay Behind, The.
Fazli. Page from the New Diary, A.
Hope, A. Observation Car.
Inez. Slumnight.
Justice, D. Variations on Southern Themes.
Keppel, L. Robin Adair.
Larkin, P. Vers de Société.
Lawrence, D. Last Lesson of the Afternoon.
Lee, B. Rain.
Moss, H. Ménage à Trois.
Oppen. Words cannot be wholly transparent. And that is the.
Robinson, E. Help Me Today.
Simic. Book Full of Pictures, A.
Smith, I. How Often I Feel Like You.
Stumbrs. Cigars.
Wen Cheng-ming. Day drags on, as long as a year!, The.
Wickham. Nervous Prostration.
Yang Wan-li. I don't feel like reading another book.

Bores
Betjeman. Reproof Deserved; or After the Lecture.
De la Mare. Pooh!
Edman. La Donna E Perpetuum Mobile.
Horace. As I was walking in the Mall of late.

Borgia, Lucretia
Landor, W. On Seeing a Hair of Lucretia Borgia.

Borneo
Swenson, M. Naked in Borneo.

Bosch, Hieronymus
Antokolsky. Hieronymus Bosch.
MacGreevy. Homage to Hieronymus Bosch.

Boston, Massachusetts
Aiken, C. South End.
Bossidy. Boston.
Boston Toast, A.
Espada. Bully.
Hall, D. Woolworth's.
Houghton, F. Mr. Frost Goes South to Boston.
Lowell, R. At the Indian Killer's Grave.
For the Union Dead.
Public Garden, The.
Where the Rainbow Ends.
McCarthy, T. November in Boston.
Moore, M. In the Public Garden.
Orban, O. Snowfall in Boston.
Plath. Winter's Tale, A.
Revere. Unhappy Boston.
Robinson, E. Boston.
Sexton. Window That Watched the Pru.
Starbuck, G. Communication to the City Fathers of Boston.
Unknown. Boston Burglar, The.
Walcott. Midsummer: XXX.
Whitman, W. Boston Ballad [1854], A.

Boston Tea Party
Orban, O. Snowfall in Boston.
Seward. Verses Inviting Stella to Tea on the Public Fast-Day.

Boswell, James
Moody, E. Dr. Johnson's Ghost.

Bottles
Bishop, M. Song of the Pop-Bottlers.
Kinnell. Milk Bottle, The.
Kunio. Tanka: "In a grove."
Stevens, W. Anecdote of the Jar.

Bourgeoisie
Angelou. Sepia Fashion Show.
Auden. Unknown Citizen, The.
Corso. Marriage.
Cummings, E. Cambridge ladies who live in furnished souls, The.
Enzensberger, H. At Thirty-three.

Middle-Class Blues.
Short History of the Bourgeoisie.
Feirstein. Mark Stern.
Khodasevich. Plainsong.
Larkin, P. Toads.
Lawrence, D. How beastly the bourgeois is.
Worm Either Way.
Levertov. Tenebrae.
Nemerov. Life Cycle of Common Man.
Saarikoski. Potato Thief.
Wickham. Fired Pot, The.

See also **Proletariat**

Bowles, William Lisle
Byron, G. William Lisle Bowles.
Coleridge, S. To the Rev. [or Reverend] W. L. Bowles.

Bowling and Bowlers
Francis, P. Thunder.
Kooser. Genuine Poem, Found on a Blackboard in a Bowling Alley in Story City, Iowa.

Boxing and Boxers
Acorn. Fights, The.
Alexander, E. Today's News.
Cuney. My Lord, What a Morning.
Dugan, A. On Hurricane Jackson.
Dybek. My Father's Fights.
Komunyakaa. Boxing Day.
Lucilius. Cleombrotus the bruiser.
HIS GRATEFUL OPPONENTS SET UP THIS STATUE OF APIS THE BOXER.
Olympicus, the welter-weight.
Reed, I. White Hope.
Smith, D. Championship Fight.
Wickham. Pugilist.

Boyne, Battle of the (1690)
Unknown. Boyne Water, The.

Boyne (river), Ireland
Higgins, F. Father and Son.

Boys
Aldis, D. Hiding.
Beeching, H. Going Down Hill on a Bicycle.
Betjeman. False Security.
Bishop, E. Casabianca.
Blake, W. Little Boy Lost, A ("Nought loves another as itself").
Blind. Beautiful Beeshareen Boy, The.
Bowman, C. Mr. X.
Brecht, B. Three Fragments.
Burroughs, W. My Legs Señor.
"Carroll." Duchess's Lullaby, The.
Catullus. Aurelius, I'm entrusting you with all.
Cheng Hsieh. Song of Surfing on the Bore.
Ciardi. All about Boys and Girls.
Cornish, S. Generations 1.
Davies, M. Fishing Pole, The ("Fishing pole's a curious thing,").
De la Mare. Tired Tim.
Duncan, R. Preface to the Suite: "Childhood, boyhood, young manhood."
Eberhart, R. Horse Chestnut Tree, The.
Field, E. Little Boy Blue.
Flynn, M. Sandlot Days.
Grimberg. For a long time I haven't seen such a young face.
Gunn, T. Allegory of the Wolf Boy, The.
Blackie, The Electric Rembrandt.
Halpern, D. Early Death, An.
Hartwig. Above Us.
Hogg, J. Boy's Song, A.
Holden, J. American Boyhood, An.
Hoover, H. Boy has two jobs, A.
Howes, B. Portrait of the Boy as Artist.
Jewett, S. Country Boy in Winter, A.
Kinnell. First Song.
Kipling, R. If you can keep your head when all [about you].
Kumin, M. Fräulein Reads Instructive Rhymes.
Lamb, M. Two Boys, The.
Lauterbach. Boy Sleeping.
Letts. Boys.
Longfellow, H. My Lost Youth.
Olds, S. One Girl at the Boys Party, The.
Orfalea. War.
Patchen. Street Corner College.

Po Chü-i. Realizing the Futility of Life.
Praed. School and Schoolfellows.
Pratt, M. Waving Hand, A.
Rands. Godfrey Gordon Gustavus
  Gore—
Ray, D. On the Photograph "Yarn Mill," by
  Lewis W. Hine.
Reznikoff. Testimony: The United States
  (1901–1910) Recitative/The South.
Riley, J. Extremes.
  Jack the Giant-Killer.
Rivard. 1966.
Roseliep. Buttoning his fly.
Savage, M. To a School-Boy at Eton, Yes and
  No.
Schuyler, J. Head, A.
Shakespeare, W. Song: "When that I was and
  a little tiny boy."
Snyder, R. Chicago, Summer Past.
Stein, D. Heat.
Tuqan, F. Song of Becoming.
Unknown. Little cock sparrow sat on a tree,
  A.
  Natural History.
  One Little Boy.
  Sad Story of a Little boy That Cried, The.
Wakoski. Poem for a Little Boy on the
  Buddha's Birthday.
Walwicz. Tattoo, The.
Warren, R. Ballad: Between the Boxcars.
Whitman, W. We two boys together clinging.
Whittier. Oh for boyhood's painless play.
Wise, W. When I grow up.
Wright, R. Green cockleburs, The.

See also **Childhood and Children; Youth**

Bradstreet, Anne
Berryman. Winters close, Springs open, no
  child stirs, The.
Norton, J. Funeral Elegy Upon that Pattern
  and Patron of Virtue, A.
Rogers, J. Upon Mrs. Anne Bradstreet, Her
  Poems, Etc.
Woodbridge. Upon the Author. By a Known
  Friend.

Brahma
Emerson, R. Brahma.
Jones, S. Hymn to Na'ra'yena, A.

Brahms, Johannes
Stevens, W. Anglais Mort à Florence.

Brains
Auden. Ode to the Diencephalon.
Dickinson, E. Brain—is wider than the Sky,
  The.
  Brain, within its Groove, The.
Lowell, J. Darkened Mind, The.
Ochester. Oh, By the Way.
Pacheco, A. I hear but my brain doesn't get
  the.
Snodgrass, W. Examination, The.

Brandy
MacNeice. Brandy Glass, The.

Braque, Georges
Norse. Picasso Visits Braque.

Brazil
Oden. Private Letter to Brazil, A.

Bread
Anderson, T. Kneading Bread.
Brontë, C. Like wolf—and black bull or
  goblin hound.
Brooks, G. My Dreams, My Works Must Wait
  Till after Hell.
Burnshaw. Bread.
Crashaw. On the Miracle of Multiplied [or
  Multiplyed] Loaves.
Dickinson, E. Indian Summer.
Dunbar, P. Dinah Kneading Dough.
Fitzgerald, E. 12.
Gheorghe. Cathedral Stones.
Hartnett. Domestic Scene.
Hébert, A. Bread Is Born.
Hecht, A. La Condition Botanique.
Lawrence, D. Matthew 6:7–15; "And in
  praying do not heap up empty."
Levertov. Acolyte, The.
Levy, A. Epitaph: "This is the end of him,
  here he lies."

MacBeth. Poem of Death, A.
Markham, E. Don't Talk to Me about Bread.
  Old Thought for a New Couple, An.
Matthews, W. Realarro.
McGrath, T. Bread of this World; Praises III,
  The.
Merwin, W. Bread.
Moss, T. Wonder, The.
Mother Goose. Willful waste brings woeful
  want.
Neruda. Two happy lovers make one single
  bread.
Padilla. History.
Pankey. Luke: 24:13–32; That very day two
  of them.
Rilke. Last Supper, The.
Roy, L. Bread Man, The.
Schultz, P. Pumpernickel.
Tapahonso. All I want is the bread to turn out
  like hers just once.
Taylor, E. Meditation 8 (First Series).
Thomas, D. This bread I break was once the
  oat.
Tsvetayeva. I bless the daily labor of my
  hands.
Unknown. There were three ghostesses.
Valentine, J. Tell Me, What Is the Soul.
Wilkinson, H. Bread.
Yoshimi. Tanka: "Having crushed."
Yukitsuna. Baker's prayer.

Breakfast
Equi. Breakfast with Jerome.
Gibson, W. Breakfast.
Graham, H. Breakfast.
Griffin, S. Song My.
Harms. Breakfast on the Patio.
Lowry, M. Eye-Opener.
McDonald, D. Breakfast in Bed (Influenza in
  War-time).
Pawsey. Eggs for Breakfast.
Rankine. Man. His Bowl. His Raspberries,
  The.
Rosenblatt. It's in the Egg.
Rossetti, C. Bread and milk for breakfast.
Unknown. Morning.
Vallejo. Our Daily Bread.
Yau. Different Cereal, A.
Yün Shou-p'ing. Inscribed on a Painting
  ("Magic mists twirl around the sky").

Breasts
Adcock, F. Soho Hospital for Women, The.
Bhartrihari. Breasts.
Bible, *N.T.* Blessed be the Paps which Thou
  hast Sucked.
Carew, T. Upon a Mole in Celia's Bosom.
Chernoff. Breasts.
Coleman, W. Breast Examination.
Dunn, S. Routine Things Around the House,
  The.
"Eliza." To a Friend for Her Naked Breasts.
Fumiko. Tanka: "Didn't a certain woman."
  Tanka: "In search of a shore."
  Tanka: "That hill."
Gallagher, T. Breasts.
Hacker, M. Cancer Winter.
Hadas, R. Up and Down.
Herrick. How Roses Came Red.
  Upon Julia's Breasts.
  Upon the Nipples of Julia's Breast.
Jenyns. To a Nosegay in Pancharilla's Breast.
Johnson, A. Conqueror of a Forbidden
  Landscape.
Krustev. Nostalgia for Titian.
Lawrence, D. Song of a Man Who Is Loved.
Martinez, D. In a Duplex Near the San
  Andreas Fault.
Mathis. Seven Months.
McClatchy. My Mammogram.
Miller, E. Rebecca.
Mistral, G. Like those jars that women put out
  to catch the dew of night.
Oppenheimer, J. Innocent Breasts, The.
Ostriker. Greedy Baby / sucking the sweet tit.
Owen, M. Urban Cowboy Hat.
Pratt, M. Poem for My Sons.
Prévert. River, The.
Saitō Mokichi. Tanka: "Often likened."

Sexton. Mr. Mine.
Shakespeare, W. Her lily hand her rosy cheek
  lies under.
Simic. Breasts.
Smith, S. This Englishwoman is so refined.
Spenser. Sonnet 76: "Fair bosom! fraught with
  virtue's richest treasure."
Unknown. Lady Lowbodice.
Vidyapati. Twin Hills.
Virgil. Spring breeze.
Wright, J. Poem about Breasts, A.
Yosano. Tanka: "Pressing my breasts."
  This autumn will end.

Breath
Bateman, C. Conspiracy.
Boldman. Sitting.
Garnett, R. Dealing Scraps.
Herrick. To Julia ("Julia, when thy Herrick
  dies").
Holub. Vanishing Lung Syndrome.
Ishikawa Takuboku. Tanka: "When I breathe."
Kenyon, J. In and Out.
Kinsella, J. Chess Piece Cornered.
Kinzie. But her arm—damp, small.
Mahadevi. So long as this breath fills your
  nostrils.
Nathan, L. Breathing Exercises.
Phillips, C. Mathematics of Breathing, A.
Raworth. Collapsible.
Strand. Breath.
Tate, J. Breathing.
Wagoner, D. Poem about Breath.
Wieseltier. Too Short.

Brecht, Bertolt
Brecht, B. Of Poor B.B.

Brendan, Saint
MacCarthy, D. Voyage, The.
Unknown. Fish at Mass, The.

Breuqhel, Pieter. See Brueghel, Pieter

Bricks and Bricklayers
Ackland. Overnight.
Roche, P. Brick, The.
Tatersal. Bricklayer's Labours, The.

Brides
Akhmadulina. Bride, The.
Daglarca. Cats.
Dyer, L. Epitaph on the Monument of Sir
  William Dyer at Colmworth, 1641.
Hall, D. Alligator Bride, The.
Herrick. Tithe [or Tythe]: To the Bride, The.
Hope, A. Brides, The.
Japanese Oral Tradition. Butterfly Wine.
John of the Cross. Spiritual Canticle, The.
Jonson, B. Now, bride and bridegroom, help
  to sing.
Lovelace, R. Anniversary on the Hymeneals of
  My Noble Kinsman, Thomas Stanley,
  Esquire, An.
Meleager. Upon a Maid That Died [or Dyed]
  the Day She Was Married [or Marryed].
Meredith, G. Flat as to an eagle's eye.
Sappho. Dust of Timas, The.
Scott, W. Lochinvar.
Sikelianos. Village Wedding, The.
Smedley, M. Contrast, A.
Smith, S. I Remember.
Somervile. Inquisitive Bridegroom, The.
Song. Picture Bride.
Unknown. Rosy Apple, Lemon or Pear.
  Slave Marriage Ceremony Supplement.
Valentine, J. Bride's Hours, A.
Veenendaal. On My Fourteenth Wedding
  Anniversary I Ride on Trains.
Yi, T. Bride, The.

See also **Weddings**

Bridges
Alegría. From the Bridge.
Brock, V. Lying on a Bridge.
Crane, H. To Brooklyn Bridge.
Dickinson, E. How brittle are the Piers.
Dromgoole. Building the Bridge.
Fumi Saito. Tanka: "When neither a man."
Guobin. My poem is a bridge, silent, lonely;.
Hardy, T. On Sturminster Foot-Bridge.
Hemphill. XXII.
Holub. Franklin Bridge in Philadelphia, The.

Hoyt, C. Down from the bridge rail.
Jiménez, J. To the bridge of love.
Lecount. Bridge toll-booth—, The.
Levchev. We stopped.
Lindsay, V. Pontoon-Bridge Miracle, The.
McPherson, S. Suspension: Junior Wells on a Small Stage in a Converted Barn.
Mother Goose. London Bridge is broken down.
Nortje. At Lansdowne Bridge.
Plumpp. Poems are not places.
Rossetti, C. Rainbow, The.
Ryuichi. Every Morning After Killing Thousands of Angels.
Shen Chou. South of the Bridge.
Smith, W. Brooklyn Bridge, Brooklyn Bridge.
Stone, R. Burned Bridge, The.
Tabb. Bridge, The.
T'ang Yin. Inscribed on a Painting ("Places I go, leaning on my bramble cane, The").
Tsvetayeva. Poem of the End, The.
Unknown. bridge engineer, Mister Crumpett, A.
Bridge instead of a Wall, A.
Goddess Chiao, The.
Warren, R. Covered Bridge.
Wilbur. Simile for Her Smile, A.
Wollach. Jonathan.
Wordsworth, W. Composed upon Westminster Bridge[, September 3, 1802].
Yang Shih-ch'i. Red Heart Station.
Yü Chi. Going to the Ministry with Chao Tzu-ch'i.
Yün Shou-p'ing. Hearing a Flute at Broken Bridge.
Waterside Village.
Written on the Night of the Twenty-ninth of the First Month.
Zolotow. Bridge, The.

Bridges, Robert
Bagg. Ezra Pound and Robert Bridges.
Hopkins, G. To R. B.

Bridget, Saint
Irvine, J. Invocation to Saint Bride.

British Columbia, Canada
Lowry, M. Christ Walks in This Infernal District Too.
Marlatt, D. Imagine: A Town.
Marty. In the Dome Car of the "Canadian."
Wah. Breathe Dust.

British Empire
Ái Lan. Deathless Autumn, A.
Aytoun, W. et al. Royal Banquet, The.
Cardenal. Mosquito Kingdom.
Chesterton, G. Geography.
Kipling, R. Arithmetic on the Frontier.
Ballad of East and West, The.
Boots.
Ford o' Kabul River.
Gunga Din.
Mandalay.
New Knighthood, The.
Recessional.
Song of the Banjo, The.
Widow at Windsor, The.
Magee, W. British Garden, A.
Martin, E. National Anthem.
Maurice. How cursed that country, how severe its doom.
McDonald, D. Song of Those Who Died, A.
Muldoon, P. Meeting the British.
Murphy, E. Thank you, Mr Rason, for the Apples.
Shepherd, W. Ode on Lord Macartney's Embassy to China.

British Museum, London
Empson. Homage to the British Museum.
Guiney. In the Reading-Room of the Brtish Museum.
MacNeice. British Museum Reading Room, The.

Brittany, France
Browning, R. Hervé Riel.

Broadway, New York City
Hughes, L. Notes on the Broadway Theatre.
Rich, A. Upper Broadway.

Sandburg, C. Broadway.
Whitman, W. Broadway.

Brodsky, Joseph
Walcott. Forest of Europe.

Brontë, Anne
Brontë, C. On the Death of Anne Brontë.

Brontë, Charlotte
"Coolidge." Charlotte Brontë.
Hayne, P. Charlotte Bronté.
Howard, F. Sampler from Haworth.

Brontë, Emily
Brontë, C. On the Death of Emily Jane Brontë.
Day Lewis. Emily Brontë.
Wright, J. Rosina Alcona to Julius Brenzaida.

Bronx, The, New York City
Di Prima. April Fool Birthday Poem for Grandpa.
Drake, J. Bronx.
Esteves. South Bronx Testimonial.
Henderson-Holmes. My First Riot: Bronx, NYC.
Ignatow, D. East Bronx.

Brooklyn Bridge
Crane, H. To Brooklyn Bridge.
Moore, M. Granite and Steel.
Pagis. Photo at the Bridge.
Schulman. For That Day Only.
Shapiro, H. National Cold Storage Company contains, The.
Smith, W. Brooklyn Bridge, Brooklyn Bridge.

Brooklyn, New York City
Berrigan, T. Personal Poem #9.
Blackburn, P. Brooklyn Narcissus.
Di Prima. Backyard.
Eady. Romare Bearden Retrospective at the Brooklyn Museum.
Elovic. Brooklyn Bound.
Espada. Waiting for the Cops.
Gallagher, T. Conversation with a Fireman from Brooklyn.
Jones, P. Day of the Dead.
Montague, J. Cage, The.
Shapiro, H. National Cold Storage Company contains, The.
Wain. Brooklyn Heights.
Whitman, W. Centenarian's Story, The.

Brooks, Van Wyck
Wheelock, J. Dear Men and Women.

Brooks and Streams
Ammons. Serpent Country.
Bastard. Ad Henricum Wottonem.
Blackburn, P. Crossing, The.
Bruchac. There is a stream which rises.
Burns, R. Birks of Aberfeldy, The [Composed on the Spot].
Clough. Highland Glen near Loch Ericht, A.
Frost, R. Brook in the City, A.
West-Running Brook.
Fumi Saito. Tanka: "When I think over."
Hopkins, G. Inversnaid.
Winter with the Gulf Stream.
Kendall, H. Orara.
Lee, L. Interrogation, The.
Lyles. Moon.
McClintock, M. Rowing downstream.
Mezey. Stream Flowing, The.
Mori Ōgai. Tanka: "On a post."
Tanka: "Trying to perch."
Roethke. Lady and the Bear, The.
Ross, W. Creek, shining, The.
Seward. Scene of superfluous grace, and wasted bloom.
Sonnet: "Stranger, when o'er yon slant, warm field no cloud."
Smollett. To Leven Water.
Snyder, G. Source, The.
Spratt. On His Mistress Drown'd.
Tennyson, A. Brook, The.
Thomas, E. Brook, The.
Unknown. Handiwork of God, The.
River, The.
Wagoner, D. Source, The.
Walker, T. By the Bridge.
Wilbur. Hamlen Brook.
"Yehoash." That Is All I Heard.

See also **Rivers**

Brooms
Lear, E. Limericks, I (ii).
Ledwidge. June.
Simic. Brooms.
Unknown. In Praise of the Broom.

Brotherhood
Baraka. Return of the Native.
Bible, O.T. Psalm 133.
Blake, W. Divine Image, The ("To Mercy, Pity, Peace and Love").
Little Black Boy, The.
Burns, R. For A' That and A' That ["Is there, for honest poverty"].
Carew, T. Second Rapture, The.
Clifton, L. Listen Children.
Confucius. Fraternitas.
Corwin, N. Man unto His Fellow Man.
Cronin, J. Motho Ke Motho Ka Batho Babang (A Person Is a Person Because of Other People).
Dadié. World to Come, A.
Dalton, R. Love Poem.
Dame. Seder, The.
Đông Hồ. Poem of Humankind, The.
Encarnacion. Bulosan Listens to a Recording of Robert Johnson.
Frost, R. For a Brother.
Frost, R. Tuft of Flowers, The.
Ginsberg, A. Who Be Kind To.
Grade. To Life I Said Yes.
Hayden, R. In the Morning Time.
Heine. New Jewish Hospital at Hamburg, The.
To Edom.
Hogan, L. New Apartment.
Hughes, L. Projection.
Hunt, L. Abou Ben Adhem (may his tribe increase!).
Johnson, G. Interracial.
Jones, R. Romance of the Poor.
Kim, J. To a Nigerian Friend.
Kipling, R. Ballad of East and West, The.
Lê Thánh-tông. Conduct of Kings, The.
Leib. When I See Another's Pain.
Lum. Chinese Hot Pot.
MacDermot. Cuba.
"MacDiarmid." Farewell to Dostoevski.
MacLeish. Speech to Those Who Say Comrade.
Mason, R. Sonnet of Brotherhood.
Miles, J. Family.
Moore, M. In Distrust of Merits.
Muir, E. Brothers, The.
Nadson. Brother, The.
Nguyễn Trãi. Womb's own flesh and bone—strong brotherhood, A.
Oppen. Wars that are just? A simpler question: In the event.
Park, C. Flute Holes.
Phan Bội Châu. Human Nature.
Phan Trọng Quảng. International Solidarity.
Ransom, J. Armageddon.
Rive. Where the Rainbow Ends.
Rosten. Out of Our Shame.
Rukeyser, M. Hostages, The.
Sandburg, C. Long Shadow of Lincoln: A Litany, The.
Schneour. Like Water down a Slope.
Shelley, P. Over the utmost hill at length I sped.
Slonimski. He Is My Countryman.
London Spring.
Tchernichowsky. Dance of Saul with the Prophets, The.
I Believe.
Thoreau. Friendship.
Trần Tế Xu'o'ng. Best Wishes for the New Year.
Unknown. There is so much of loneliness.
Untermeyer, L. Goliath and David.
Watkins, H. Hard Times A' Coming.
Whitman, W. Full of life now, compact, visible.
I believe in you my soul, the other I am must not abase itself to you.
I dream'd in a dream I saw a city invincible to the attacks of the whole of the rest of the

earth.
I hear it was charged against me that I sought
to destroy institutions.
To Him That Was Crucified.
To the East and to the West.
Wylie. Pebble, The.
Young, A. W. H. Auden & Mantan Moreland.

Brothers
Al-Khansa. Lament for a Brother.
Aldis, D. Little.
Browne, M. Talk to Me, Baby.
"Carroll." Brother and Sister.
Catullus. On the Burial of His Brother.
Chipasula. My Blood Brother.
Convisser. Over the Pass.
Cornish, S. My brother is homemade.
Creeley. World, The.
Currie. Brothers.
Draycott. Search.
"Eliot." I Cannot Choose but Think upon the
Time.
Long years have left their writing on my
brow.
Enzensberger, H. Hôtel Fraternité.
Farrell, J. Bank Thief, The.
Forbes, C. Hand Me Down Blues.
Frost, R. To E.T.
Gunn, T. Cannibal.
Herrick. To His Dying Brother, Master
William Herrick.
Howe, F. Torn Parts: the story.
Hsieh Chin. I still remember Conch-Shell
Slope, west of the River Tzu.
Hughes, T. My Brother Bert.
Keats. To My Brothers.
Kinnell. Two Set Out on Their Journey.
Lake, P. In Rough Weather.
Lamb, C. To John Lamb, Esq.: Of the South-
Sea House.
Lassell. How to Watch Your Brother Die.
Leigh, H. Twins, The.
Leithauser. Old Bachelor Brother.
Levine, P. You Can Have It.
Lopate. Once a long time ago, you remember.
Lovelace, R. Advice to My Best Brother,
Colonel Francis Lovelace.
Mapanje. Making Our Clowns Martyrs.
Melville, H. Timoleon.
Muir, E. Brothers, The.
Notley. One of the Longest Times.
Orfalea. War.
Orr, G. Gathering the Bones Together.
Mother, The.
Po Chü-i. To his Brother Hsing-chien.
To his Brother Hsing-chien, Who was Serving
in Tung-ch'uan.
Robinson, A. Scape-Goat, The.
Robinson, E. Prodigal Son, The.
Ross, A. Two in Bed.
Sanchez, S. To P. J.
To P. J. (2 Yrs Old Who Sed Write a Poem
for Me in Portland, Oregon).
Schulman. For That Day Only.
Serge. Constellation of Dead Brothers.
Shapiro, K. Two-Year-Old Has Had a
Motherless Week, The.
Shklyarevsky. My younger brother is stronger
than me.
Soldati. Surroundings.
Soto. Not Knowing.
Southwick. Brothers.
Stafford, W. Remembering Brother Bob.
Stockum. Hut, The.
Thompson, C. To My Dead Brother.
Thoreau. Brother where dost thou dwell?
Tillinghast, R. Knife, The.
Ts'ao Chih. Presented to Piao, the Prince of
Pai-ma.
Tu Fu. Rumours that you lodge in a mountain
temple.
Turner, F. On the Pains of Translating Miklós
Radnóti.
Unknown. Last Words of the Prophet.
Other Side of the Valley, The.
Twa Brothers, The.
Van Duyn. Twins, The.
Virgilio. My dead brother.

Wallis, H. Female's Lamentations, The; or,
The Village in Mourning.
West, C. My obnoxious brother Bobby.
Wilcox, E. Five Little Brothers.
Young Bear. Our Bird Aegis.

Brown (color)
Grimké, A. At April.

Brown, Andrew
Heard, J. Rev. Andrew Brown, over the Hill
to Rest.

Brown, John
Atkins. Narrative.
Benét, S. John Brown's Prayer.
Hughes, L. October 16[: The Raid].
Lindsay, V. John Brown.
Melville, H. Portent, The.
Rukeyser, M. Soul and Body of John Brown,
The.
Sandburg, C. Osawatomie.
Unknown. John Brown's body lies a-
mould'ring in the grave.
Whittier. Brown of Ossawatomie.

Brown, Mrs. E. Cohrs
Fordham. Mrs. E. Cohrs Brown.

Brown, Sterling A.
Harper, M. Br'er Sterling and the Rocker.

Browning, Elizabeth Barrett
Blagden. To George Sand on her Interview
with Elizabeth Barrett Browning.
Browning, R. Lost Mistress, The.
Dickinson, E. Her—'last Poems'.
Greenwell, D. To Elizabeth Barrett Browning,
in 1851.
To Elizabeth Barrett Browning, in 1861.
Lowell, A. Sisters, The.
Parkes, B. To Elizabeth Barrett Browning.

Browning, Robert
Chesterton, G. From a Spanish Cloister.
Landor, W. To Robert Browning.
Stevenson, R. Browning makes the verses.

Bruce, Robert
Burns, R. Scots, wha hae wi' Wallace bled.
Cook, E. Try Again.
Holland, S. Douglas and the Bruce's Heart.

Brueghel, Pieter
Auden. Musée des Beaux Arts.
Berryman. Winter Landscape.
De la Mare. Brueghel's Winter.
Dubie. February; the Boy Breughel.
Kopland. Breughel's Winter.
Langland, J. Fall of Icarus: Brueghel.
Hunters in the Snow: Brueghel.
Plath. Two Views of a Cadaver Room.
Rutsala. Skaters.
Sandy. Et Quid Amabo Nisi Quod Aenigma
Est.
Williams, W. Dance, The.
Parable of the Blind, The.

Brummell, "Beau" (George Bryan Brummell)
Glassco. Brummell at Calais.

Brussels, Belgium
Auden. Brussels in Winter.

Brutus, Dennis
Awoonor. To Dennis Brutus.

Brutus (Marcus Junius Brutus)
Pinsky. Dante's Inferno, Canto XXXIV (The
Final Canto).
Shakespeare, W. Let me see, let me see; is
not the leaf turned down.

Bryan, William Jennings
Unknown. Free Silver.

Bryant, William Cullen
Lowell, J. Bryant.

Bubbles
Bacon, F. Life.
Breton, A. Spectral Attitudes, The.
Bùi Khải Nguyễn. Soap Bubbles.
Crashaw. Bubble, The.
Drummond, W. Madrigal: "This life, which
seems so fair."
Garrett, G. Bubbles.
Grainger, J. What is fame? An empty bubble.
Herrick. Bubble; a Song, The.
Ushida. Deep in the rippling spring.

Buber, Martin
Harris, M. Martin Buber in the Pub.

Buckingham, George Villiers, 2d Duke of
Dryden, J. Zimri: "In the first rank of These
did Zimri stand."
Felltham. On the Duke of Buckingham, Slain
by Felton, the 23rd August, 1628.
Shirley, J. On the Duke of Buckingham.
Unknown. Epitaph on the Duke of
Buckingham.

Buddha and Buddhism
Adams, H. Buddha and Brahma.
Barry, J. Nun in Ninh Hoa, A.
Cheng Hsieh. Girl from Ch'ang-kan is just
fourteen years old, The.
Cho, C. Nun's Dance, The.
Chōkū. Tanka: "Somewhere around."
Chu. Fireworks.
Đào Duy Từ. Where gather mists and clouds,
a happy world.
Dharmakirti. Proof.
Di Prima. Death Sunyata Chant: A Rite for
Passing Over.
Gates, L. Silent Buddha, The.
Guest, B. Walking Buddha.
Han Yü. Girl of Mt. Hua, The.
Hayashi. Lord Buddha, The.
Ho Xuan Huong. Poking Fun At a Bonze.
Hsü Pen. Poem on Buddha's Begging Bowl—
For Hui-ku, His Holiness Ming, A.
Izumi. In the Autumn, on Retreat at a
Mountain Temple.
Jong. Buddha in the Womb, The.
Kaufman, B. Unanimity Has Been Achieved,
Not a Dot Less for Its Accidentalness.
Kerouac.
179th Chorus.
182nd Chorus.
One Hundred and Eighty-Third Chorus.
229th Chorus.
Lanier, S. Nirvâna.
Masaoka Shiki. Among the poems I wrote
with many pictures spread out before me[2].
McClintock, M. Here's a guy.
Mo Shih-lung. Drinking Wine.
Friend Comes to Visit on a Summer Night, A.
I Went to Gold Mountain to Visit a Ch'an
Master But He Was Not at Home.
To the Monk Wu-hsia on the Occasion of His
Editing the Lotus Sutra.
Nguyễn Bỉnh Khiêm. On Reading the
Buddha's Scriptures.
Nguyễn Khuyến. Scholar-Laureate in
Retirement, A.
Nobuyuki. Stone Buddha (two poems).
Pawar. Buddha, The.
Po Chü-i. Half in the Family, Half Out.
Idle Droning.
Taoism and Buddhism.
Rexroth, K. Further Advantages of Learning.
Rilke. Buddha in Glory.
Shin, S. Gong Dance, The.
Snyder, G. Avocado.
Circumambulating Arunachala.
Tai Piao-yüan. In the Year Chi-hai (1299),
While Returning by Way of Purple Fungus
Mountain at Springmouth, I Lamented for
Lecture Master Chin.
Trai. Cat, The.
Unknown. Stepping Out of the World.
Wang An-shih. Written on the Wall of
Halfway Mountain Temple.
Written on the Wall of Pan-shan Temple.
Whalen. Walking beside the Kamogawa,
Remembering Nansen and Fudo and Gary's
Poem.
Wu Wei-yeh. At the Mountain of the
Mysterious Tomb Visiting Master P'ou.
Broken Lampstand, The.
See also **Zen Buddhism**

"Buffalo Bill" (William Frederick Cody)
Cummings, E. Portrait.

Buffaloes
Andal. O sister of wealth.
Barnes, J. Bone Yard.
Belloc. Bison, The.
Eglington. Buffalo.

Lindsay, V. Flower-fed buffaloes of the spring, The.
Ghosts of the Buffaloes, The.
Mair, C. Song: "Hear me, ye smokeless skies and grass-green earth."
Moore, M. Buffalo, The.
Oliver, M. Ghosts.
Sandburg, C. Buffalo Dusk.
Swenson, M. Bison Crossing Near Mt. Rushmore.
Unknown. Buffalo Skinners, The.
Song of the Promise of the Buffalo.
Song of the Red & Green Buffalo, A.
Two Soldier's Songs.
Yang Shih-ch'i. Herdboy returns, none too early, The.
Yün Shou-p'ing. For a hundred miles the west wind carries the fragrance of millet.

Bugles and Buglers
Tennyson, A. Blow, Bugle, Blow.
Whitman, W. Beat! beat! drums!—blow! bugles! blow!

Buildings and Builders
Ammons. Cracking a Few Hundred Million Years.
Bertrand. Mason Abraham Knupfer is singing, trowel in hand, scaffolded, The.
Braun, V. New Purpose of Hadrian's Army, The.
Brown, G. Press-Gang.
Browning, R. Apparent Failure.
Ch'ien T'ao. Written While Drunk.
Cooper, G. What Robin Told.
Cowper, W. Inscription.
Crane, S. Many workmen / Built a hugh ball of masonry.
Creeley. Invitation, The.
Dugan, A. Love Song: I and Thou.
Fisher, A. Sandpile Town.
Gheorghe. Cathedral Stones.
Graves, R. Fallen Tower of Siloam, The.
Hartnett. Visit to Castletown House, A.
Heaney, S. Scaffolding.
Herlin. Morning space expands the building's.
Keate. Midst the fair range of buildings which, new-reared.
Kelly, R. Bittersweet growing up the red wall.
Komunyakaa. Instructions for Building Straw Huts.
Kunio. Tanka: "From a flour mill."
Lampadius. As a symbol.
Lear, E. There was an Old Man with a beard.
MacLeish. Burying Ground by the Ties.
Mother Goose. House That Jack Built, The.
Murray, L. Flight from Manhattan, The.
Oden. Review from Staten Island.
Ormond. Cathedral Builders.
O'Shaughnessy, A. Ode: "We are the music-makers."
Paz. Along Galeana Street.
Pope, A. Epistle to Lord Burlington.
Reznikoff. About an excavation.
Sandburg, C. Shovel Man, The.
Sidney, P. Sonnet 9: "Queen Virtue's court, which some call Stella's face."
Skeeter. Midwest, Midcentury.
Smith, D. Dome Poem.
Snyder, G. Building.
Staff. Foundations.
Stevenson, R. Block City.
Stockum. Hut, The.
Tomlinson, C. Crane, The.
Tranströmer. Outskirts.
Tu Fu. Jade Flower Palace.
Unknown. King Wen's Park Divine.
Valek. Steel-Rod Benders.
Watts, I. How doth the little busy bee.
Yi, S. Bulldozer, The.
Yoshimi. Tanka: "With headlights on."

Bukowski, Charles
Carver, R. You Don't Know What Love Is.

Bulgaria
Bagryana. Old Fortress, The.

Bull Run, Battles of (1861, 1862)
Lowell, R. March 1, The.
Melville, H. March into Virginia, The.
Unknown. Battle of Bull Run, The.

Bullets
Csoori. Bullet, A.
Dove, R. Teach Us to Number Our Days.
Fumi Saito. Tanka: "In my possession."
Harte, B. What the Bullet Sang.
Melo Neto. Knife All Blade, A.
Pizzarelli. Under the boardwalk.
Rannit. Boris Vilde.
Ritsos. Audible and Inaudible.

Bullfights and Bullfighters
García Lorca. Lament for Ignacio Sánchez Mejías.
Holub. Bullfight.
Jacobsen, J. Matadors, The.
Swenson, M. Death Invited.
Uruttiran. Girl Friend Describes the Bull Fight, The.

Bullfinches
Cowper, W. On the Lamented Death of Mrs. Throckmorton's Bullfinch.

Bulls
Bunting. Brag, sweet tenor bull.
Dinka Oral Tradition. Magnificent Bull, The.
Heaney, S. Outlaw, The.
Hodgson, R. Bull, The.
Holub. Bullfight.
Hughes, T. Bull Moses, The.
Layton. Bull Calf, The.
McClintock, M. Long summer day.
Phelp. Duke Of Buccleuch, The.
Sackville-West. Bull, The.
Unknown. Hoosen Johnny.
Two Bulls, The.
Williams, W. Bull, The.
Wright, R. Coming from the woods.

Bullying and Bullies
Spender, S. Rough.
Walsh, J. I've Got an Apple Ready.
Zu-Bolton. Governor of the Ollie Street, The.

Bunker Hill, Battle of (1775)
Calvert, G. Bunker Hill.
Freeth. Bunker's Hill, or the Soldier's Lamentation.

Bunyan, John
James, J. Of John Bunyan's Life.

Bureaucracy and Bureaucrats
Ashbery. On The Empress's Mind.
Auden. Unknown Citizen, The.
Burke, K. Frigate Jones, the Pussyfooter ("Frigate Jones was very slow and fat").
Davie. Pilate.
Devlin, D. Anteroom: Geneva.
Frost, R. Departmental.
Mayakovsky. In Re Conferences.
Miles, J. Bureau 2.
Slutsky. Clerks.
Unknown. Pass Office Song.

Burglars
Fulton, A. My Diamond Stud.
Hussey, A. Saturday Night.

Burial
Annensky. Black Spring.
Antipater of Thessalonica. When the deep-piled winter snow / melted on her roof.
Beckett, S. Malacoda.
Berryman. Poet's Final Instructions, The.
Carson, J. I am asking you to come back home.
Clarke, C. Rondeau: "They are bodies left unburied."
Cowper, W. Inscription.
Crinagoras. Foul sod covers a bad one here. Though of white marble and dressed straight.
Currey. Burial Flags.
Dickey, J. Sled Burial, Dream Ceremony.
Drummond, W. If of the dead save good nought should he speak.
Eberhart, R. Sea Burial from the Cruiser *Reve.*
Freneau. Indian Burying Ground, The.
Giovanni. Women gather, The.
Gregory of Nazianzus, Saint. Why do you heave apart my stone?
Hardy, T. I found her out there.
Harper, F. Bury Me in a Free Land.
Herrick. To Anthea ("Now is the time, when all the lights wax dim").

Business and Businessmen
Upon a Child That Died [*or* Dyed].
Upon Himselfe Being Buried.
Upon Prue [*or* Prew], His Maid.
Hill, G. Strange church smelled a bit 'high,' of censers, The.
Hsiang Ssu. Ailing Japanese Monk, The.
Hudgins. Burial Detail.
James, T. Mummy of a Lady Named Jemutesonekh XXI Dynasty.
Jeffers, R. Shane O'Neill's Cairn.
Leonidas of Tarentum. Give me one small smothering of earth.
Liu Tsung-yüan. On Covering the Bones of Chang Chin, the Hired Man.
Lu Yün. *Peacock flew, far off to the southeast; A.*
Mackenzie, K. Earth Buried.
Mazzocco. PBS.
McDonald, I. Place They Have to Go, The.
McKinney, I. Visiting My Gravesite: Talbott Churchyard, West Virginia.
Mitchell, K. On the Anniversary Of Your Death.
Nash, O. Tweedledee and Tweedledoom.
Pasternak, B. Magdalene (I).
Philodemus. Here it's rose-time again, chick-peas in season.
Pollard, V. Su Su.
Robinson, A. Etruscan Tombs.
Southerland. Blue Clay.
Stevenson, A. Temporarily in Oxford.
Swenson, C. Our Town.
Tremayne. Burial, A.
Unknown. Hearse Song, The.
Urn for Burial, An.
Vaughan, H. Burial.
Volman. Case, The.
Warren, R. Country Burying (1919).
Webster, J. Dirge, A: "Call for the robin-redbreast and the wren."
Whitman, W. Vigil strange I kept on the field one night;.
Whitney, I. Now London have I (for thy sake).

See also **Cemeteries; Funerals; Graves; Mausoleums; Tombs**

Burke, Edmund
Goldsmith, O. Edmund Burke.

Burlesque. See Striptease

Burma
Kipling, R. Mandalay.

Burne-Jones, Edward
Rossetti, D. For "The Wine of Circe" by Edward Burne-Jones.

Burns, Robert
Burns, R. Rantin, Rovin Robin.
Landor, W. Had We Two Met.
Smith, C. To the Shade of Burns.
Stevenson, R. Fragment, A: "Thou strainest through the mountain fern."
Williams, H. Sonnet on Reading the Poem upon the Mountain Daisy, by Mr. Burns.

Burros. See Donkeys

Bus Terminals
Reznikoff. Highway I was walking on, The.

Buses
Atkins. Late Bus (After a Series of Hold-Ups).
Bishop, E. Moose, The.
Cohen, L. Bus, The.
Cope. Bloody men are like bloody buses.
Espada. Sleeping on the Bus.
Fumiko. Tanka: "Yellow bus, The."
Hongo. Stay with Me.
Knox, E. Last Bus, The.
Levine, P. Ordinary Morning, An.
Lohmann. Lady on a Bus.
McElroy, C. Pike Street Bus.
Okudzhava. Midnight Trolleybus.
Smith, W. Jittery Jim.
Willis, N. Lady in the White Dress, Whom I Helped into the Omnibus, The.
Yukitsuna. Tanka: "Youngster, A."

Business and Businessmen
Baca. So Mexicans Are Taking Jobs from Americans.

Butchering and Butchers

Betjeman. Business Girls.
  Executive.
Brown, G. Trout Fisher.
Ch'en Tzu-ang. Business men boast of their
  skill and cunning.
Codrescu. Poetry Paper.
Dickinson, E. I asked no other thing.
Dugan, A. On Trading Time for Life by
  Work.
Fearing. Dirge: "1-2-3 was the number he
  played but today the number came 3-2-1."
Ginsberg, A. Who Runs America?
Harmon. I am the Gross National Product.
Hughes, L. Madam's Past History.
MacLeish. Corporate Entity.
Mitchell, A. Accountant in His Bath, The.
Mukhopadhyay, V. Monday.
Pitter. Portrait of a Gentleman.
Po Chü-i. Having Climbed to the Topmost
  Peak of the Incense-Burner Mountain.
Pound, E. Semi-private inducement.
Rukeyser, M. Dam, The.
Shapiro, A. Manufacturing.
Smith, S. Villains.
Unknown. Between a Contractor and His
  Wife.
Yau. New York Map Company (1).
See also **Accounting and Accountants;**
  Advertising; Banking and Bankers;
  Capitalism; Commerce

Butchering and Butchers

Brathwaite, E. Ancestors.
Chuang Tzu. Cutting up an Ox.
Duggan, L. Hearts (1983).
Hampton. Crafty Butcher, The.
Hardy, T. Bags of Meat.
Hood, T. Butcher, A.
Lee, L. Cleaving, The.
Levine, P. Angel Butcher.
  Animals Are Passing from Our Lives.
Robinson, E. Reuben Bright.
Simic. Butcher Shop.
Squire. Stockyard, The.
Stern, G. Bull-roarer, The.
Takiguchi. Slaughterhouse.
Tipping. Casino.
Tomlinson, C. On a Pig's Head.
Wakoski. Butcher's Apron, The.
Walwicz. Abattoir, The.
Williams, C. Racists.

Butler, Samuel (1612-1680)

Oldham, J. On Butler who can think without
  rage.
Taylor, G. English Liberal.

Butter

Amis, K. Pendydd.
Calverley. Ballad: "Auld wife sat at her ivied
  door, The."
Lakshminkara. Lay your head on a block of
  butter and chop.
Nash, O. Arthur.
Thorold Rogers. On the Historians Freeman
  and Stubbs.
Unknown. Butter Betty Bought, The.
  Butter Charm.

Buttercups

Howitt, M. Buttercups and Daisies.
Jones, J. Flowers always know what they.
Thaxter. August.
Unknown. Buttercup, A.
  Buttercups golden and gay.

Butterflies

Alexandru. Miserere Nobis.
Arakida Moritaké. Flying Flower, A.
  Haiku: "Falling flower, The."
Breton, A. Spectral Attitudes, The.
Bunyan. Of the Boy and Butterfly.
Chu Yün-ming. Painting of the Butterfly
  Dream by the Master Artist Li Tsai, A.
Collins, M. Trapped.
Davies, W. Example, The.
Dickinson, E. Butterfly upon the Sky, The.
  Fuzzy fellow, without feet, A.
  My Cocoon tightens—Colors tease.
Duncan, R. Roots and Branches.
Friedmann. Butterfly, The.
Frost, R. Tuft of Flowers, The.

Fuller, J. Butterfly, The.
Graves, R. Flying Crooked.
Grimké, A. Butterflies, white butterflies, in the
  sunshine.
Haas, R. Building the dollhouse.
Hagiwara Sakutaro. So Terrifyingly
  Melancholy.
Hawker. Butterfly, The.
Higginson, T. Ode to a Butterfly.
Hopi Oral Tradition. Song of Creation.
Inez. Woman Who Loved Worms, The.
Japanese Oral Tradition. Butterfly Wine.
Kim, K. Sea and the Butterfly, The.
Kolatkar. Butterfly, The.
Lawrence, D. Butterfly, the wind blows sea-
  ward[, strong beyond the garden wall!].
Layton. Butterfly on Rock.
Levertov. Dead Butterfly, The.
Levis. Cocoon, The.
Lindsay, V. King of Yellow Butterflies, The.
Lloyd, D. Over dried grass.
Major, C. On Watching a Caterpillar Become
  a Butterfly.
Merrill, J. To a Butterfly.
Milosz, C. Abundant Catch (Luke 5:4–10).
Moore, M. To a Steam Roller.
Mori Ōgai. Tanka: "Trying to perch."
Morley, C. Song for a Little House.
Muldoon, P. Milkweed and Monarch.
Nabokov. On Discovering a Butterfly.
Noyes, A. Butterfly Garden, The.
Ōshima Ryōta. They look / like newlyweds.
Pilinszky. Stavrogin's Return.
Pizzarelli. Scarecrow.
Redwing. Hoofer, The.
Ríos, A. True Story of the Pins.
Rogers, P. Abundance and Satisfaction.
Rose, M. Butterfly, The.
Roseliep. On the apple.
Rossetti, C. Caterpillar, The.
Rotella, A. At the edge.
  Butterfly lands on Park Place, A.
Sherry, J. Lepidoptery.
Swenson, M. Unconscious came a beauty.
T'ang Yin. On the Butterflies.
Unknown. Butterfly Song.
Vanada. Fuzzy wuzzy, creepy crawly.
Weiners. Poem for Trapped Things, A.
Wieners. Poem for Trapped Things, A.
Wilde, O. Symphony in Yellow.
Willard, N. Sleep of the Painted Ladies, The.
Williams, W. Graceful Bastion, The.
Wills, J. Mourning cloak, A.
Wordsworth, W. To a Butterfly.
Wright, J. Wings.
Yang Chi. Five-color robe of embroidered
  silk, A.
  Up at the prow, I wash my mouth, dripping
  water on my robe.
Yi, S. Poem No. X.
Yosano. Purple butterflies / fly at night
  through my dreams.
  Tanka: "Grabbing one of."

Buzzards

Rossetti, C. Sketch, A.
Warren, R. Pondy Woods.
Welch, L. Song of the Turkey Buzzard.
See also **Vultures**

Byrd, Mary Furman Weston

Fordham. Mrs. Mary Furman Weston Byrd.

Byron, George Gordon Noel Byron, 6th Baron

Arnold, M. When Byron's eyes were shut in
  death.
Auden. You lived and moved among the best
  society.
Browning, E. Stanzas on the Death of Lord
  Byron.
Byron, G. On This Day I Complete My
  Thirty-sixth Year.
Chesterton, G. Sea Replies to Byron, The.
Clare, J. Lord Byron.
Coogler. Byron.
Fortune. Byron's Oak at Newstead Abbey.
Hogg, J. Nor for the crabbed state-creed,
  wayward wight.
Keats. To Lord Byron.
Lamb, L. New Canto, A.

Lang, A. Fashion changes! Maidens do not
  wear, The.
Moore, J. Sketch of Lord Byron's Life.
Nash, O. Very like a Whale.
Parker, D. Lives and Times of John Keats,
  Percy Bysshe Shelley, and George Gordon
  Noel, Lord Byron, The.
Porter, P. On This Day I Complete My
  Fortieth Year.
Praed. Chancery Morals.
Rogers, S. He is now at rest.
Shelley, P. Sonnet to Byron.
Su Man-shu. Inscribed on Byron's Poetic
  Works.

Byzantium

Nordbrandt. Our love is like Byzantium.
Tsatsos. Chios.
Yeats. Byzantium.
  Sailing To Byzantium.

C

Cabbages

"Carroll." "Time has come," the Walrus, The.
Kinnell. Cells Breathe in the Emptiness.
Norman, R. Cabbage.
Ormsby, E. Skunk cabbage with its smug and
  opulent smell, The.
Unknown. Mid-West, The.
Wood, R. Cabbages.

Cadavers. *See* Corpses

Cads

Bowen, C. Rain it raineth all around, The.

Caedmon

Levertov. Caedmon.
Nicholson, N. Caedmon.

Caesar, Julius

Auden. Fall of Rome, The.
Fitzgerald, E. 19.
Heath-Stubbs. July.
Jonson, B. To Clement Edmonds, on His
  Caesar's Commentaries Observed, and
  Translated.
Marlowe. This said, the restles generall
  through the darke.
Martial. If memory serves, we've shared
  together.
  If you and I, Julius, old friend.
Shakespeare, W. Mark Antony Addresses the
  Mob.
Unknown. Julius Caesar.

Cafés

Dobson, R. In a Café.
Gray, S. Apollo Café.
Smith, I. In the Cafe.
  Milk jugs, cups.
Wright, C. Bar Giamaica, 1959-60.

Cain and Abel

Adamo. My Answer.
Blake, W. Ghost of Abel, The.
Byron, G. Oh! thou dead / And everlasting
  witness! whose unsinking.
Capetanakis. Abel.
Gross, H. At the Crossroads.
Hope, A. Imperial Adam, naked in the dew.
Norwalk. Psalm of Love.
Pagis. Autobiography.
  Written in Pencil in the Sealed Railway-Car.
Quasimodo. Man of My Time.
Vaughan, H. Abel's Blood.
Wheelwright. Abel.

Cakes

Cook, E. Mouse and the Cake, The.
Cummings, E. This little bride & groom are.
Harter. Wrinkles.
St. John, D. Wedding Preparations in the
  Country.
Williams, H. To Mrs. K———, On Her
  Sending Me an English Christmas Plum-Cake
  at Paris.

Calcutta, India

Gangopadhyay. Calcutta and I.

Caliban

Browning, R. Caliban upon Setebos; or,
  Natural Theology in the Island.

McDonald, W. Caliban in Blue.
Namjoshi, S. Caliban's Journal.

California (state)
Breit. Sacramento.
Castillo, A. Napa, California.
Cervantes. Como lo Siento.
Freeway 280.
Poema para los Californios Muertos.
Davie. Across the Bay.
In California.
Di Piero. Ice Plant in Bloom.
San Antonio de Padua.
Ferlinghetti, L. After the Cries of the Birds.
Gioia. California Hills in August.
Hass, R. Concerning the Afterlife, the Indians of Central California Had Only the Dimmest Notions.
Late Spring.
Palo Alto.
Spring Rain.
Tahoe in August.
Hillman. Mighty Forms.
Hongo. Mendocino Rose.
Hoyem. Circumambulation of Mt. Tamalpais.
Hughes, L. City.
Jarrell. In Montecito.
Jeffers, R. Carmel Point.
Clouds of Evening.
Koethe. Mission Bay.
Kyger. And with March a Decade in Bolinas.
Levine, P. Waking in March.
Martin, C. Metaphor of Grass in California.
McClure, M. May Morn.
Milosz, C. It Was Winter.
To Robinson Jeffers.
Montague, J. All Legendary Obstacles lay between.
Moyles. Report from California.
Oppen. And Their Winter and Night in Disguise.
Plath. Sleep in the Mojave Desert.
Reed, I. Oakland Blues.
Rich, A. Walking Down the Road.
Ridge, J. Mount Shasta.
Schmitz. California Phrasebook, The.
Sill. California Winter.
Simpson, L. In California.
Snyder, G. Before the Stuff Comes Down.
Burning the small dead.
Hay for the Horses.
Song. Beauty and Sadness.
Spencer, T. Californians, The.
Stokesbury. California.
Troupe. View from Skates in Berkeley, The.
Voigt. Blue Ridge.
Wakoski. Smudging.
Whitman, W. Facing west from California's shores.
Promise to California, A.
Song of the Redwood-Tree.
Winters, Y. John Sutter.
Young, A. California Peninsula: El Camino Real.

Calligraphy
Cheng Hsieh. To Chin Nung.
Chin Nung. Three lines of "clerk script" calligraphy.
Hsieh Chin. Song of Cursive Calligraphy.
Mo Shih-lung. I Waited for Chuang Hsüan-yüan But He Never Came.
Ou-yang Hsiu. Calligraphy Practice.
Wen Cheng-ming. At the lacquered table—my recent calligraphy.
Yün Shou-p'ing. Scorpion's tails, silver hooks.

Calliope (muse)
Graves, R. To Calliope.

Calm
Amichai. To my love, combing her hair.
Bible, O.T. Bible, Proverbs 16:32, The.
Brainard, J. I saw two clouds at morning.
Donne. Calm[e], The.
Garvey. Keep Cool.
Goedicke. One More Time.
Herrick. To Music, to Becalm a Sweet-sick Youth.
Hughes, L. Sea Calm.
Hughes, T. Horses, The.

Kitahara Hakushū. Tanka: "During a fit."
McPherson, S. Phlox Diffusa: A Poem for My Fiftieth Birthday.
Morgan, R. Honey.
Po Chü-i. Temple of Bequeathed Love, The.
Rossetti, C. In Progress.
Warren, R. Masts at Dawn.
Wordsworth, W. By the Sea.
Zeidner. Bach.

Calvary
Awoonor. Easter Dawn.
Robinson, E. Calvary.
See also **Crucifixion, The**

Calves
Gilpin. Two-headed Calf, The.
Hardy, T. Calf, The.
Jones, R. First Birth, The.
Parry, E. I Would Like You for a Comrade.
Tomlinson, C. Macduff.

Calvinism
Clough. Latest Decalogue, The.
Kipling, R. McAndrew's Hymn.
Lowell, R. Mr. Edwards and the Spider.
Millay, E. To a Calvinist in Bali.

Calypso Music
Brode. Calypsomania.

Calypso (mythology)
Morley, C. Forever Ambrosia.

Camaraderie
Djanikian. How I Learned English.
Graves, R. Two Fusiliers.
Jarmain. Embarkation, 1942.
Jonson, B. Epistle Answering to One That Asked to Be Sealed of the Tribe of Ben, An.
Owen, W. Apologia Pro Poemate Meo.
See also **Friendship**

Cambodia and Cambodians
Fenton, J. Cambodia.
Dead Soldiers.
Palmer, M. Sun.
Receveur. Eagle in the Land of Oz.

Cambridge, England
Calverley. Hic Vir, Hic Est.
Cornford, F. Autumn Morning at Cambridge.
In the Backs.
Wordsworth, W. Inside of King's College Chapel, Cambridge.

Cambridge, Massachusetts
Alexander, E. Boston Year.
O'Grady, D. Professor Kelleher and the Charles River.
See also **Harvard University**

Cambridge University
Cornford, F. Autumn Morning at Cambridge.
Davie. On Bertrand Russell's "Portraits from Memory."
Ewart. Semantic Limerick According to Dr. Johnson's Dictionary (Edition of 1765), The.
Semantic Limerick According to the Shorter Oxford English Dictionary (1933), The.
Wordsworth, W. Inside of King's College Chapel, Cambridge.

Cambridgeshire, England
Brooke, R. Old Vicarage, Grantchester, The.

Camden, New Jersey
Cone. Narcissus in Camden.

Camden, William
Jonson, B. To William Camden.

Camellias
Pastan. Camellias.

Camelot
Tennyson, A. Lady of Shalott, The.

Camels
Carryl, C. Camel's Complaint, The.
Chichibabin. Camel.
Kamienska. Matthew 19:16–24; And behold, one came up to him.
Things of This World.
Korn. Thirty-one Camels, The.
Laila Akhyaliyya. Camel.
Lewis, J. How to Tell a Camel.
Tekkan. Tanka: "Eyes fixed."
Vogelsang. Which Letter?
Wagoner, D. Fruit of the Tree, The.

Cameras
Andrews, T. Cinema Vérité: The Death of Alfred, Lord Tennyson.
Ciardi. On a Photo of Sgt. Ciardi a Year Later.
"Ern Malley." Documentary Film.
Kooser. Camera.
Machi. Tanka: "Freezing my smile."
McDonald, W. For Harper, Killed in Action.
Paquet. Group Shot.
Schwartz, L. Pornography.
Yukitsuna. Tanka: "During a trip."
See also **Photography and Photographers**

Camões, Luis de
Andresen. Camoes and the Debt.
Campbell, R. Luis de Camões.

Campaigns, Political. *See* **Voting and Voters**

Campbell, Roy
Currey. In Memoriam: Roy Campbell.

Camping
Kinnell. Night in the Forest.
Kumin, M. Despair.
Plath. Two Campers in Cloud Country.
Reading. Camping Provencial. Notices: (1).
Rexroth, K. Fish Peddler and Cobbler.
Roseliep. Campfire Extinguished.
Snyder, G. August on Sourdough, a Visit from Dick Brewer.
For the Boy Who Was Dodger Point Lookout Fifteen Years Ago.
Late October Camping in the Sawtooths.
Stuart, D. River, The.
Wagoner, D. Breaking Camp.
Making Camp.
Staying Alive.
Wright, C. Other Side of the River, The.

Campuses
Kennedy, X. Golgotha.
See also **Colleges and Universities**

Canaan
Galai. Canaan, oh Canaan!

Canada
Atwood. At the Tourist Centre in Boston.
Bancroft, C. Tadoussac.
Birney. Can. Lit.
Braley, E. Canada-I-O ("Come all ye jolly lumbermen and listen to my song").
Cohen, L. Only Tourist in Havana Turns His Thoughts Homeward, The.
Layton. From Colony to Nation.
Simpson, J. Away to Canada.
Sirr. Understanding Canada.
Unknown. Canada-I-O ("There was a gallant lady all in her tender youth").

Canals
Ch'in Kuan. Along the Grand Canal.
Freneau. On the Great Western Canal of the State of New York.
Kitahara Hakushū. Tanka: "In my heart."
Melville, H. In a Bye-Canal.
"Twain." Aged Pilot Man, The.

Canaries
Amherst. Verses Designed to Be Sent to Mr. Adams.
Heard, J. My Canary.
Jewett, S. Caged Bird, A.
Nash, O. Canary, The.
Ochester. Canaries in Uncle Arthur's Basement, The.
Turner, E. Canary, The.
Unknown. Mary's Canary.

Canberra, Australia
Rowland. Canberra in April.

Cancer (disease)
Adcock, F. Soho Hospital for Women, The.
Auden. Miss Gee.
Avena. Cancer garden, protected by buildings, one unfinished. Still, The.
Benn. Man and Woman Go Through the Cancer Ward.
Blaser. Ruler, The.
Dubie. Funeral, The.
Eberhart, R. Cancer Cells, The.
Espada. Spanish of Our Out–Loud Dreams, The.

Goedicke. In the Waiting Room.
Hacker, M. Cancer Winter.
Haldane, J. Cancer's a Funny Thing.
Hall, J. St. Peregrinus' Cancer.
Hodgins. Death Who.
Kenyon, J. Pharaoh.
Lowell, R. Death from Cancer.
Martinez, D. In a Duplex Near the San
  Andreas Fault.
McClatchy. My Mammogram.
Miller, E. Rebecca.
Olds, S. Glass, The.
  In the Hospital Near the End.
Pinsky. Memorial.
Ryan, M. TV Room at the Children's
  Hospice.
Scovell. Death from Cancer.
Stafford, W. Bess.

Candlemas
Clampitt. Procession at Candlemas, A.
Herrick. Ceremonies for Candlemas[se] Eve.
  Ceremony upon Candlemas Eve.
Madeleva. Candlemas Day.

Candles
Brown, R. Storm high.
Creeley. Warning, The.
Empson. Legal Fiction.
Hwang, K. Candlelight.
Leithauser. Haunted, The.
Lowell, A. Bungler, The.
Millay, E. First Fig.
  Second Fig.
Moffi. Yahrzeit.
Mother Goose. Candle, A.
  To make your candles last for aye.
Phan chu Trinh. Ode to the Candle.
Plath. Candles.
Sachs, N. But look / but look.
Segal, J. Candle.
Seifert. Candlestick, The.
Shūji. Tanka: "Like a long."
Stevens, W. Valley Candle.
Unknown. Riddle: "Little trotty hetty coat."
Virgilio. Hinge of the year, The.
Warsh. Static, The.
Wilbur. For K. R. on Her Sixtieth Birthday.
Willard, N. Cat's Second Song, The.
Wilson, K. Dusk in My Backyard.
Yeryomenko. Addition to the Opposition.
Yoshihara. Candle.
Ziedonis. How the candle burns.

Candy
Bidart. Ellen West.
Ferlinghetti, L. Pennycandystore beyond the
  El, The.
Flynn, M. Decision.
Ford, C. There's No Place to Sleep in This
  Bed, Tanguy.
Hansen, J. Dakota: Five Times Six.
Holden, J. Wisdom Tooth, The.
Nash, O. Reflections on Ice-breaking.
Simpson, L. Chocolates.

Candy Stores
Ferlinghetti, L. Pennycandystore beyond the
  El, The.

Cannibalism and Cannibals
Dali. Art of Picasso, The.
Gilbert, S. Yarn of the *Nancy Bell*, The.
Goodison. Jamaica 1980.
Irwin, W. Constant Cannibal Maiden, The.
Keithley. From Land Logic.
Laleau. Cannibal.
Lummis. Poe-'em of Passion, A.
Reid, C. Perversion, A.
Yambo. When Negro Teeth Speak.
Zeigler. Snack, The.

Canning
Butler, J. Preserves.
Van Duyn. Homework.
Young, K. Preserving, The.

Canoes and Canoeing
Mapanje. Elegy for Mangochi Fishermen, An.
O'Hara, F. Terrestrial Cuckoo, A.
Revard. Birch Canoe.
Unknown. Paddling Song.

Cape Breton Island, Nova Scotia
Bishop, E. Cape Breton.

Cape Cod, Massachusetts
Santayana. Cape Cod.
Shapiro, H. Provincetown, Mass.
Weaver, M. Message on Cape Cod, The.

Cape Horn
Masefield. Rounding the Horn.

Cape of Good Hope
Campbell, R. Rounding the Cape.

Capital Punishment
Alexie. Capital Punishment.
"MacDiarmid." Facing the Chair.
McKuen. Thoughts on Capital Punishment.
Wilde, O. Ballad of Reading Gaol, The.

See also **Executions and Executioners**

Capitalism
Allen, P. Los Angeles, 1980.
Brathwaite, E. Miss Own.
Brecht, B. Late Lamented Fame of the Giant
  City of New York.
Codrescu. Circle Jerk.
Cruickshank, A. God or Mammon.
Dunbar-Nelson. Proletariat Speaks, The.
Ehrlich. Last Merchant, The.
Fulton, A. Risk Management.
Ginsberg, A. II.
Hall, D. One Day, The.
Hikmet. Sad State of Freedom, A.
Jafri. Morsel.
Kandel. First they slaughtered the angels.
Khlebnikov, V. And so the castles of world
  trade.
  Stop Fooling.
Lanier, S. Symphony, The.
Larkin, P. Homage to a Government.
Levine, M. Capitalism.
MacLeish. Empire Builders.
McNeill, A. Saint Ras.
Replansky. Housing Shortage.
Rich, A. In those years, people will say, we
  lost track.
Shapiro, K. Drug Store.
Spender, S. After They Have Tired of the
  Brilliance of Cities.
Wong, N. Toward a 44th Birthday.

See also **Banking and Bankers; Business and
  Businessmen**

Captivity
Bryant, W. African Chief, The.
Davenant. Countess of Anglesey lead Captive
  by the Rebels, at the Disforresting of
  Pewsam.
Dickinson, E. Prison gets to be a friend, A.
Dunbar, P. Sympathy.
Hart, H. Prisoner of Camau, The.
Jewett, S. Caged Bird, A.
Kipling, R. Half-Ballad of Waterval.
Lovelace, R. Lady A. L., My Asylum [in a
  Great Extremity], The.
Lu Yu. Border Mountain Moon.
Po Chü-i. Prisoner, The.
Rilke. Panther, The.
Rowe, E. Expostulation, The.
Rutsala. Bodies.
Sidney, P. Like as the dove which seeled-up
  doth fly.
Sisson. Money.
Steptoe. Wired In.
"Struther." Freedom.
Unknown. Other Side of the Valley, The.
  Song of the Breaking of the Willow.
Very. I Was Sick and in Prison.
Wilde, R. Lament of the Captive, The.
Wroth. Sonnet 14: "Am I thus conquered [or
  conquer'd]? have I lost the powers."
  Sonnet 45.

Caravaggio, Michelangelo Merisi da
Gunn, T. In Santa Maria del Popolo.

Carcassonne, France
Nadaud. Carcassonne.

Card Games
Cataldi. Advice.
"Chorny." Life.
Davis, T. Playing Solitaire.
Frost, R. In Divés' Dive.
Larkin, P. Card-Players, The.
Lyly, J. Cards and Kisses.

Pope, A. Rape of the Lock, The.
Rossetti, C. Queen of Hearts, The.
Saxe, J. Game of Life, The.
Spicer, J. Cardplayers, The.
Tikhonov. Gulliver Plays Cards.
Webster, A. Enigma No. 6.
Wellesley. Enemy, The.

Cardinals (ornithology)
Montgomery, S. Moonrise white cat eating the
  cardinal.

Cargoes
Masefield. Cargoes.

See also **Freighters**

Carib Indians
Carew, J. Cliffs at Manzanilla, The.
Fergus. Ethnocide.

Caribbean Islands. *See* **West Indies**

Caribbean Sea
Barrax. Scuba Diver Recovers the Body of a
  Drowned Child, The.

Caring
Cooper, J. Rent.
Graves, R. Song: How Can I Care?
Piercy. Hand Games.
Stafford, W. Remembering Brother Bob.
Wright, J. Arrangements with Earth for Three
  Dead Friends.
  Mutterings Over the Crib of a Deaf Child.

Carlyle, Thomas
Lowell, J. Emerson.
Parker, D. Thomas Carlyle.

Carmel, California
Jeffers, R. Carmel Point.

Carnivals
Beissel, H. Pans at Carnival.
Bishop, E. Pink Dog.
Brautigan. Boat, A.
Brown, G. Hamnavoe Market.
Itwaru. And in this carnival you offer me.
"Kitchener." Miss Tourist.
St. John, P. Carnival.
Spencer, A. At the Carnival.

Carousels. *See* **Merry-go-rounds**

Carp
Wright, J. Lifting Illegal Nets by Flashlight.

Carpe Diem
Anacreon. Who cares about the filthy rich.
Angelou. Come, And Be My Baby.
Asclepiades. To a Girl.
  What are you saving it for?
Braley, B. Start where you stand and never
  mind the past.
Browning, R. Youth and Art.
Campion, T. My sweetest Lesbia, let us live
  and love.
Carew, T. To A. L.; Persuasions [or
  Perswasions] to Love.
Carson, J. I am asking you to come back
  home.
Catina. Philosophy.
Catullus. Carmen 5 ("My sweetest Lesbia, let
  us live and love").
Clough. Mari Magno II.
Constable, H. Hope, like the hyaena [or
  hyena], coming to be old.
Cowley, A. Age.
Crane, F. Today.
Cummings, E. My father moved through
  dooms of love.
  Ponder,darling,these busted statues.
  What if a much of a which of a wind.
Daniel, S. But love whilst that thou mayst be
  loved again.
  Half-blown Rose, The.
De Vries, P. Bacchanal.
Dowson. Villanelle of the Poet's Road.
Dryden, J. Happy the man, and happy he
  alone.
Fitzgerald, E. 74.
  13.
Fletcher, J. Love's Emblems.
Foley, H. Touch wood, be humble, never dare
  to say.
Gay, J. Youth and Love.
Hafiz. Lesson of the Flowers, The.

Harte, B. California Madrigal.
Herrick. Anacreontic.
  Corinna's Going A-Maying.
  To [the] Virgins, to Make Much of Time.
Horace. Ne'er fash your *thumb* what *gods* decree.
Huang T'ing-chien. Clear Bright.
Jacob, H. Alarm, The.
Jonson, B. Song. To Celia ("Come my Celia, let us prove").
Jordan, T. Careless Gallant, The.
Kaufman, H. This is your hour—creep upon it!
Keats. Fancy.
  Ode on a Grecian Urn.
Khodasevich. Shape ships to seek some shining shore.
Lodge, T. Pluck the Fruit and Taste the Pleasure.
Lovelace, R. To Amarantha, That She Would Dishevel[l] Her Hair[e].
MacLeish. Speech to a Crowd.
Marlowe. Passionate Shepherd [*or* Sheepheard] To His Love, The.
Marvell. To His Coy Mistress.
  Young Love.
Masefield. Laugh and Be Merry.
Meinke. Advice to My Son.
Melville, H. Rosary Beads.
Moore, T. Young May Moon, The.
Morley, T. Sing we and chant it.
Opitz. Ah Dearest, let us haste us.
Palladas. This is all the life there is.
Perry, N. "Next year, next year," we say.
Plato. Apple, The.
Prior. Quid Sit Futurum Cras Fuge Quaerere.
Ralegh, W. Nimphs [*or* Nymph's] Reply to the Sheepheard [*or* Shepherd], The.
Raleigh. Nymph's Reply to the Shepherd, The.
Ransom, J. Blue Girls.
  Old Man Playing with Children.
Rich, A. Floating Poem, Unnumbered, The.
Ronsard. Corinna In Vendome.
Shakespeare, W. Sweet-and-Twenty.
Shaoxuan. Black hair and red cheeks: for how long?
Sidney, P. Fourth Song: "Only joy, now here you are."
Skinner, J. Rolling in Clover.
Southwell. Loss[e] in Delay[e].
Spenser. Song of Bliss.
Stickney, T. Live blindly and upon the hour. The Lord.
Su Tung-p'o. Turning Year, The.
Unknown. Is It Really Worth the While?
  Ladies, you see time flieth.
  Man's years fall short of a hundred.
  Sister, Awake!
Virgil. Copa: The Barmaid.
Waller, E. Song: "Go[e], lovely rose[—ous sweet and fair]."
  To Phillis.
Wang Seng-ta. To Match the Prince of Lang-yeh's Poem in the Old Style.
Wilcox, E. Was, Is, and Yet-to-be.

Carpentry and Carpenters
Baugh, E. Carpenter's Complaint, The.
"Carroll." Walrus and the Carpenter, The.
Carter, J. At the Sign-Painter's.
Carter, M. Bitter Wood.
Davie. With the Grain.
Dickinson, E. Props assist the House, The.
Dove, R. Genie's Prayer Under the Kitchen Sink.
Kurup. Master Carpenter, The.
Shaw, L. Craftsman.
Snyder, G. After weeks of watching the roof leak.
Wilbur. Hole in the Floor, A.

Carpets. *See* **Rugs and Carpets**

Carriages
Moore, M. Carriage from Sweden, A.
Simpson, L. Troika, troika! The snow moon.

"Carroll, Lewis" (Charles Lutwidge Dodgson)
Farjeon, E. Lewis Carroll.

Cars. *See* **Automobiles**
Carson, Kit
  "Vestal." Kit Carson's Last Smoke ("Kit Carson came to old Fort Lyons").
Carving and Carvers
Sidney, P. Graven Thoughts.
Casabianca, Louis
Hemans. Casabianca.
Casement, Roger David
Murphy, R. Casement's Funeral.
Cassandra
Bogan, L. Cassandra.
Jeffers, R. Cassandra.
Robinson, E. Cassandra.
Ronsard. Fragment of a Sonnet.
Caste Systems, Indian
Kambar. Pond Named Ganga, A.
Surve. Lifetime.
Castile. *See* **Spain**
Castlereagh, Robert Stewart, 2d Viscount
Byron, G. Epitaph for Castlereagh, An.
Shelley, P. Similes for Two Political Characters of 1819.
Castles
Bagryana. Old Fortress, The.
Beevers. Atameros.
Carr, M. Castle in the Fire, The.
Corben. Harlech Castle.
Cotton, C. Chatsworth.
De Vere, S. Rock of Cashel, The.
Dunn, S. Happiness.
Hugo, R. Ferniehirst Castle.
Ingram, A. Castle Howard, the Seat of the Rt. Hon. Charles, Earl of Carlisle.
Kellman. Bajan.
Levertov. Psalm Concerning the Castle.
Leyeles. Castles.
Lipska. When our enemies fall asleep.
MacDonagh, D. Warning to Conquerors, A.
Mahony. Blarney castle.
Muir, E. Castle, The.
O'Huiginn, T. Visit to Enniskillen, A.
Po Chü-i. Being on Duty all Night in the Palace and Dreaming of the Hsien-yu Temple.
Poe. Haunted Palace, The.
Reed, H. Château, The.
Rothenberg, J. At the Castle.
Rózewicz. I Build.
Sitwell, D. Trams.
Spires. Robed Heart, The.
Stevenson, R. Song of a Traveller, The.
Tennyson, A. Blow, Bugle, Blow.
Wordsworth, W. Elegiac Stanzas Suggested by a Picture of Peele Castle, in a Storm [Painted by Sir George Beaumont].
Woroszylski. Franz Kafka (II).
Yüan Chen. On Lien-ch'ang Palace.
Castration
Komunyakaa. Nude Study.
MacDonald, C. Objets D'Art.
Castriot, George. *See* **Savonarola, Girolamo**
Castro, Fidel
Agard, J. Waiting for Fidel.
Ferlinghetti, L. One Thousand Fearful Words for Fidel Castro.
Pau-Llosa. Ganaderia.
Updike. Meditation on a News Item.
Catalpa Trees
Waddington, M. Catalpa Tree.
Caterpillars
Alexandru. Miserere Nobis.
Dickinson, E. Caterpillar.
  Fuzzy fellow, without feet, A.
Fisher, A. Caterpillars.
Hackett, J. Time after time.
Houston, L. Dream of the Cabbage Caterpillars, The.
McCord, D. Cocoon.
Rossetti, C. Caterpillar, The.
Serraillier. Tickle Rhyme, The.
Shannon, M. Only My Opinion.
Vanada. Fuzzy wuzzy, creepy crawly.
Williams, M. Caterpillar, The.
Yolen. Caterpillar's Lullaby.

Catfish
Mills, W. Pity.
Unknown. Catfish and Toad.
Cathedrals
Fields, J. Citizen.
Gheorghe. Cathedral Stones.
Hardy, T. In a Cathedral City.
Hecht, A. Meditation.
Johnson, J. Before a Painting.
Karpowicz. Artistic Copy.
Kedrin. Builders.
Longfellow, H. My Cathedral.
Milosz, C. Abundant Catch (Luke 5:4–10).
Ormond. Cathedral Builders.
Wharton, E. Chartres.
Cather, Willa
Stanton, M. Biography.
Catholicism and Catholics
Auden. Macao.
Ayres. Invites Poets and Historians to Write in Cynthia's Praise.
Corbett, R. Proper New Ballad Intituled The Faer Yes Farewell: Or God-A-Mercy Will, A.
Crashaw. To the Noblest and Best of Ladies, the Countess of Denbigh, Perswading Her to Resolution in Religion, and to Render Her Selfe without Further Delay into the Communion of the Catholick Church.
Derricotte. St. Peter Claver.
Devlin, D. Lough Derg.
Disch. Cardinal Detoxes: A Play in One Act, The.
Donne. Show me dear Christ.
Doolittle, H. This is no rune nor riddle.
Eliot, T. Hippopotamus, The.
Gildner. They Have Turned the Church Where I Ate God.
Iwaszkiewicz. Pope in Ancona, The.
Kennedy, X. First Confession.
Lehmann, G. Pope Alexander VI.
Longley, M. Letter to Derek Mahon.
Lowell, R. Beyond the Alps.
  For George Santayana.
Parra, N. Poems of the Pope, The.
Scates. Going to Mass after Fifteen Years.
Sheperd. Who hath not knowne or herd.
Skelton, J. Over this the foresayd lay.
Unknown. Lament for Our Lady's Shrine at Walsingham, A.
Williams, W. Catholic Bells, The.
Cats
Agathias. Justice.
Alegría. Savoir Faire.
Amherst. Verses Designed to Be Sent to Mr. Adams.
Arnold, M. Matthias.
Atkins. Probability and Birds in the Yard.
Auden. Cats and Dog.
Bachri. Cat.
Bancquart. Woman asleep.
Barlas. Cat-Lady, The.
Bast. Body of the Great Cat, The.
  Chang Tuan's Cats.
  Chrysoberyl: The Eye of the Cat.
  Frost Eyebrows was the favorite cat.
  Hywell the Good Weighs the Worth of a Cat.
  Nebamun's Cat.
Bates, C. Gray Thrums.
Baudelaire. Cat, The.
  Cats.
Benson, G. Cat and the Pig, The.
Bishop, E. Lullaby for the Cat.
Bodecker. Cats and Dogs.
Brautigan. Surprise.
Brickley. Spring evening.
Brownjohn. Explorer.
Bruner. Epitaph for a Cat.
Bukowski. Mockingbird had been following the cat, The.
  Startled into Life Like Fire.
Charles, D. Concrete Cat.
Chigetsu. Propriety.
Chōkū. Tanka: "On Christmas Eve."
Coatsworth. Bad Kittens, The.
  On a Night of Snow.
  Open Door, The.
Cox, P. Lazy Pussy, The.

Cranch. Old Cat's Confessions, An.
Crane, H. Chaplinesque.
Cummings, E. (Im)c-a-t(mo).
  Why did you go.
Daglarca. Cats.
De la Mare. Five Eyes.
Delius. Shadow, killer of doves.
Dickinson, E. Cat.
Du Bellay. There are cats (not he).
Eberhart, R. Concord Cats.
Eden. Four-Paws.
Eliot, T. Bustopher Jones: The Cat About
  Town.
  Cat Morgan Introduces Himself.
  Growltiger's Last Stand.
  Gus: The Theatre Cat.
  Macavity: The Mystery Cat.
  Mr Mistoffelees.
  Naming of Cats is a difficult matter.
  Rum Tum Tugger is a Curious Cat.
  Skimbleshanks: The Railway Cat.
  Song of the Jellicles, The.
Enright, D. Egyptian Cat, The.
Ewart. 14-Year-Old Convalescent Cat in the
  Winter, A.
  Jubilate Matteo.
  Lifelines.
  Who Likes the Idea of Guide Cats?
Farjeon, E. Cats sleep / Anywhere.
Field, E. Duel, The.
Fisher, A. Cat in the Snow.
  Listening.
Fisher, R. That Cat!
Flatman. Appeal to Cats in the Business of
  Love, An.
Ford, C. Desire to be in Two Places at Once,
  The.
Francis, A. When cats like him submit to fate.
Fuller, R. Family Cat, The.
Fyleman. Cat, The.
Garrigue. Epitaph for My Cat.
Gasztold. Prayer of the Cat, The.
Georges. Alley Cat.
Gibbons, R. Hoppy.
Graves, R. Cat Goddesses.
Gray, S. On a Cat, Ageing.
Gray, T. Ode on the Death of a Favourite [or
  Favorite] Cat, Drowned in a Tub [or Bowl]
  of Gold Fishes.
Guiterman. Little Lost Pup.
Gunn, T. Apartment Cats.
Hall, D. Alligator Bride, The.
Halpern, D. Dance, The.
Han-shan. Cold Mountain Poem No. 158.
Hardy, T. Last Words To a Dumb Friend.
Hare, M. Alfred de Musset.
Harris, W. Samantha Is My Negro Cat.
Hart, E. Mother Tabbyskins.
Harter. Cat's whiskers, The.
  Only letting in the cat.
  Winter rain.
Heine. Memory, A.
Hemingway. Earnest Liberal's Lament, The.
Hiley. To a Persian Cat.
Hood, T. Choosing Their Names.
Hope, A. House of God, The.
Horn, E. Pussycat sits on a chair.
Hudgins. Two Ember Days in Alabama.
Hughes, T. Esther's Tomcat.
Issa. Cat, The.
Jarrell. Happy Cat, The.
  Lonely Man, The.
Johnston, E. Nelly's Lament for the Pirnhouse
  Cat.
Jortin. Epitaph of Felis, The.
Keats. To a Cat.
Kees. Wet Thursday.
Kinnell. Supper after the Last, The.
Klingsor. Song of the Cat, The.
Kopland. Ulumbo, a Cat.
Kumin, M. Plans.
Kusatao. Cat, The.
La Fontaine. Cat Changed to a Woman, The.
Lear, E. Le Hibou et la Poussiquette.
  Our mother was the pussy-cat, our father was
  the owl.
  (The Owl and the Pussy-Cat).

Leax. Her Seventeenth Winter.
Lee, J. Spring is a Cat, The.
Levertov. Cat as Cat, The.
  Innocent, The.
  Scenes from the Life of the Peppertrees.
Lindsay, V. Mysterious Cat, The.
Lowell, A. To Winky.
Lowell, R. Frederick Kuh, Manx Cat.
Lucas, E. Pekinese / Adore their ease, The.
MacNeice. Death of a Cat, The.
Marquis. Song of Mehitabel, The.
  Tom-Cat, The.
Master. Cat and the Lute, The.
Mathews, H. Offering for the Cat, An.
Matthews, W. Cat, The.
McClintock, M. Dead cat.
McCrea. Pussy-Cat and Puppy-Dog.
McGough, R. My Cat and I.
McKay, L. Night.
Mei Yao Ch'en. Offering for the Cat, An.
Merrill, J. Maisie.
Merwin, W. Burning the Cat.
Miller, M. Cat.
Milne, E. Diamond Cut Diamond.
Milosz, C. To Mrs. Professor in Defense of
  My Cat's Honor and Not Only.
Molony. Cat Washing.
Monro. Cat's Meat.
  Milk for the Cat.
Montague, J. Mother Cat, The.
Moore, M. Peter.
Moore, R. Catalog.
Morley, C. In Honour of Taffy Topaz.
Mother Goose. As I was going to St. Ives.
  Dame Trot and her cat.
  Diddlety, diddlety, dumpty.
  Ding, dong, bell, / Pussy's in the well.
  Pancake Day.
  Pussy-Cat, Pussy-Cat,/ where have you been?
  Sing, sing, / What shall I sing?
  Six little mice sat down to spin;.
Nash, O. Cat, The.
  Kitten, The.
Neruda. Cat's Dream.
  Ode to the Cat.
Nicholls, J. Cat.
Norris, L. Stable Cat, The.
Obeyd-i-Zàkàni. Gorby and the Rats.
Owen, G. This and That.
Pitt. Fable of the Young Man and His Cat,
  The.
Pratt, E. Prize Cat, The.
Rajasekhara. Moonlight.
Rands. Cat of Cats, The.
Reid, A. Curiosity.
Rieu. Lost Cat, The.
Rifat. Stars.
Rilke. Black Cat.
Robinson, E. New England.
Roseliep. Pacing.
Rosenblatt. Cat.
Rossetti, C. Pussy cat, Pussy cat.
  Pussy has a whiskered face.
Rowse. White Cat of Trenarren, The.
Rudnik. Dream.
Sackville-West. Greater cats with golden eyes,
  The.
Scannell. Cat.
Scarfe. Cats.
Sedgwick, H. Leo to His Mistress.
Seferis. Cats of St. Nicholas, The.
Seward. Old Cat's Dying Soliloquy, An.
Sherwood, M. In Memoriam—Leo: A Yellow
  Cat.
Sitwell, D. Cat, The.
Skwirz. Long Distance Calls.
Smart, C. My Cat Jeoffry.
Smith, S. Galloping Cat, The.
  My Cats.
  Singing Cat, The.
Smith, W. Cats are not at all like people.
  Moon.
Spire. Nativité.
Stanfield. Little Cat Angel, The.
Stevenson, A. Epitaph for a Good Mouser.
Stoutenburg. Cat at Night.
Strachey, L. Cat, The.

Summers, H. My old cat [is dead].
Swenson, M. Cat and the Weather.
Swinburne. To a Cat.
Taufer, D. Mice Are Pets?
Taylor, G. Cruel, Clever Cat.
Taylor, J. I Like Little Pussy.
Thomas, E. Cat, A.
Thompson, D. That Little Black Cat.
Tirumalesh. Face to Face.
Tolkien. Cat on the Mat.
Toulson. Amber.
Trai. Cat, The.
Trainin. Cat in the Dovecote.
Turberville. Lover Whose Mistress Feared a
  Mouse, The.
Turner, N. Black and Gold.
Unknown. Cat came fiddling out of a barn, A.
  Catkin.
  Cat's Conscience, A.
  Cats of Kilkenny, The.
  Children's Song.
  Choosing a Kitten.
  Dame Wiggins of Lee.
  Ding dong bell! Pussy's in the well!
  I love little pussy, her coat is so warm.
  Little Robin Redbreast [or Red-breast] sat
  upon a tree.
  Monk and His Pet Cat, The.
  Oh, the Funniest Thing.
  Pangur Bán.
  Pussy.
  Pussy-cat Mew jumped over a coal.
  Pussy cat sits by the fire.
  Saint Jerome and his Lion.
  Scholar and the Cat, The.
  Ten little mice sat in a barn to spin.
  There was a man, and his name was Dob.
  Two gray kits, The.
  Wildcat was walking.
Usher, L. I Am the Cat.
Verlaine. Femme et Chatte.
Virgil. Darkening.
Whalen. Walking beside the Kamogawa,
  Remembering Nansen and Fudo and Gary's
  Poem.
Willard, N. Cat to His Dinner, The.
  King of Cats Sends a Postcard to His Wife,
  The.
Williams, W. Complete Destruction.
  Mujer.
  Poem: "As the cat / climbed over."
Williamson, J. Natural Selection.
Wordsworth, W. Kitten at Play, The.
Wright, K. Dad and the Cat and the Tree.
Yeats. Cat and the Moon, The.
  Two Songs of a Fool.
Yorie. Cat's Eye, The.
Young, V. In a circle of thaw.
Zipper. Right in the middle.
See also **Kittens**

Cattle
Ba. Familiar Oxen.
  Ox-Soldier, The.
Campbell, R. Driving Cattle to Casas Buenas.
Ch'u Kuang-hsi. Cowherd, The; a Song.
Colum, P. Drover, A.
Currey. Jersey Cattle.
García Lorca. Prelude.
Gibson, W. Drove-Road, The.
Hardy, T. Bags of Meat.
Jones, R. First Birth, The.
Mackay-Warna. Cattle Loading.
McNeill, A. Residue.
  Victors, The.
Moore, N. Island and the Cattle, The.
Murray, L. Names of the Humble, The.
Norris, L. Quiet-eyed Cattle, The.
Rabéarivelo. Hide of the black cow is
  stretched, The.
Salis. Song.
Skrzynecki. Cattle.
Stephens, H. Night-herding Song[, A].
Unknown. Herdsman's Song.
See also **Bulls; Cowboys; Cows; Meat**

Catullus
Huxley, A. Second Philosopher's Song.
Landor, W. On Catullus.

MacLeish. You Also, Gaius Valerius Catullus.
Tennyson, A. Frater Ave Atque Vale.
Poets and Their Bibliographies.

Caution
Barberini. Of Caution.
Brodsky, J. Belfast Tune.
Cassian. Orbits.
Creeley. I Know a Man.
Gascoigne. For That He Looked Not upon Her.
Hagedorn, J. Natural Death.
Hewitt, J. Search, The.
Lewis, A. To a Comrade in Arms.
Montagu, L. Lover, The; a Ballad.
Moore, T. Duke is the lad to frighten a lass, The.
Roethke. Monotony Song, The.
Slessor. Up in Mabel's Room.
Sorescu. Precautions.
Tahmisic. Letter to a Friend.
Weigl. Mines.
Whitney, I. Ye virgins that from Cupid's tents.
Wieseltier. Caution Prevents Accidents.
Wroth. Sonnet 39.
Yeats. Never give all the heart, for love.

Cavafy, Constantine P.
Jarman, M. Cavafy in Redondo.

Cavalcanti, Guido
Dante Alighieri. Sonnet: To Guido Cavalcanti.

Cavaliers
Herrick. His Cavalier.

Cavalry
Davidson, D. Sequel of Appomattox.
Housman, A. Lancer.
Newbolt. Gillespie.
Whitman, W. Cavalry Crossing a Ford.

Cavemen
Eshleman, C. Placements I.
Kipling, R. King, The.
Pratt, E. From Stone to Steel ("From stone to bronze, from bronze to steel").
See also **Man, Primitive**

Caves
Cary, A. Sea-Side Cave, The.
Cawein. Caverns.
Chang Yü. Painting ("Jade cave, ten thousand flowering peach trees, A").
Crashaw. Come See the Place Where the Lord Lay.
Eshleman, C. Notes on a Visit to Le Tuc d'Audoubert.
Fairburn. Cave, The.
Holan. Cave of Words, The.
Knott. Sleep.
Lamb, E. Lizard inching, A.
Merrill, J. Power Station, The.
Merwin, W. Bread.
Moraes, D. Kanheri Caves.
Rukeyser, M. Ajanta.
Schwartz, L. Monuments to the Not Yet Lived.
Tomlinson, C. Cavern, The.
Tsung Ch'en. Drinking at the Cave Mouth.
Tu Mu. Red Embankment.
Wang Chiu-ssu. Total failure—mdash;Master Han Shan, A.
Wu Chen. Fantastic Rock, The.

Cecilia, Saint
Auden. Song for St. Cecilia's Day.
Barker, G. Ode against St. Cecilia's Day.
Dryden, J. Alexander's Feast; or, The Power of Music [*or* Musique].

Celan, Paul
"Asya." Celan.

Celandine
Thomas, E. Celandine.
Wordsworth, W. Lesson, A.

Celibacy. *See* **Bachelors; Virginity and Virgins**

Cellars
De la Mare. John Mouldy.
Kumin, M. In the Root Cellar.
Roethke. Root Cellar.

Celts
Smith, S. Celts, The.

Cemeteries
Aldington. Battlefield.
Amichai. Is all this sorrow? I don't know.
Barton, J. Mistress, The.
Belitt. Papermill Graveyard.
Bialik. Graveyard, The.
Bowers, E. Mountain Cemetery, The.
Braithwaite. In a Grave-Yard.
Causley. At the British War Cemetery, Bayeux.
By St. Thomas Water.
Cervantes. Meeting Mescalito at Oak Hill Cemetery.
Clarke, M. In the Graveyard.
Clifton, L. At the Cemetery, Walnut Grove Plantation, South Carolina, 1989.
Coulette. Black Angel, The.
Creeley. Stairway to Heaven.
Dickinson, E. Cemetery, A.
Dorn, E. Air of June Sings, The.
Eberhart, R. Soul Longs to Return Whence It Came, The.
Fairfax, J. Forest of the Dead, The.
Flecker. Town without a Market, The.
Fordham. Magnolia.
Freneau. Indian Burying Ground, The.
Goethe. Anacreon's Grave.
Gu Cheng. Forever Parted: Graveyard.
Haines, J. Flight, The.
Hall, S. Boot Hill.
Hardy, T. Friends Beyond.
Levelled Churchyard, The.
Paying Calls.
Voices from Things Growing in a Churchyard.
Heard, J. National Cemetery, Beaufort, South Carolina, The.
Hill, G. Distant Fury of Battle, The.
Howe, F. Seeking Out His face in a Cup.
Hugo, R. Graves at Elkhorn.
Jentzsch. Terezin, the Graveyard.
Justice, D. Variations on Southern Themes.
Kelly, B. White Pilgrim: Old Christian Cematary, The.
Kunio. Tanka: "Because the folks."
Lawrence, D. Giorno dei Morti.
Levine, P. Cemetery at Academy, California, The.
Lihn. Cemetery in Punta Arenas.
Lilliard. America's Answer.
Longfellow, H. In the Churchyard at Cambridge.
Jewish Cemetery at Newport, The.
Lowell, R. Quaker Graveyard in Nantucket, The.
Marriott. Prairie Graveyard.
Marston, P. Old Churchyard of Bonchurch, The.
Masters, E. Hill, The.
McCarthy, T. Sorrow Garden, The.
McCrae, J. In Flanders Fields the poppies blow.
McDonald, I. Place They Have to Go, The.
Mew. In Nunhead Cemetery.
Miller, J. In Père La Chaise.
Moore, L. Again.
Mori Ōgai. Tanka: "Step by step."
Moritz. April Fool's Day, Mount Pleasant Cemetary.
Nemerov. Negro Cemetery Next to a White One, A.
Neruda. Nothing but Death.
Ochester. Penn Central Station at Beacon, N.Y, The.
Olds, S. Leningrad Cemetery, Winter of 1941.
Park, T. Hymn to the Graveyard.
Ping. Song of Calling Souls.
Ryan, A. Lines: "Gather the sacred dust."
Sandburg, C. Cool Tombs.
Simko. Jewish Cemetery in Prague, The.
Smith, C. Sonnet Written in the Church-Yard at Middleton in Sussex.
Smith, S. Great Unaffected Vampires and the Moon.
Stanton, M. Sunday Graveyard.
Stevenson, R. To S. R. Crockett.
Tate, A. Ode to the Confederate Dead.
Thomson, J. In a Christian Churchyard.

Timrod. Ode: "Sleep sweetly in your humble graves."
Trần Huy Liêu. Dropping By the Guava Graveyard in So'n-La.
Unknown. Graveyard—who makes his home in that yard?, The.
Of Sir Frauncis Walsingham Sir Phillipp Sydney, and Sir Christopher Hatton, Lord Chancelor.
Tomb of Diogenes, The.
Valéry. Graveyard by the Sea, The.
Vallejo. Our Daily Bread.
Warren, R. Evening Hour.
Wilbur. In a Churchyard.
Williams, W. Children, The.
Wilson, R. Elegy in a Presbyterian Burying-Ground.
Winters, Y. To the Holy Spirit.
Wright, C. Yugoslav Cemetery.
Wright, J. Way to Make a Living, A.
Yeats. Under bare Ben Bulben's head.
Yoshimi. Tanka: "Street, The."
Young, A. Passing the Graveyard.
Yüan Hung-tao. Pei-mang Cemetery.
See also **Burial; Graves; Mausoleums; Tombs**

Censorship
Brecht, B. Burning of the Books, The.
Byron, G. Canto the Eleventh.
Clarke, A. Penal Law.
Donne. Raderus.
Duchamp. SURcenSURE.
Hospital. Freedom.
Kunze, R. Low Volume.
Need for Censorship, The.
Lawrence, D. Innocent England
Nash, O. Invocation: "Senator Smoot (Republican, Ut.)"
"Samoylov." Ballad about the German Censor, The.
Vacietis. Burning Leaves.
Waley. Censorship.
Zenmaro. Tanka: "How sad it is."
Tanka: "It's hazardous."

Centaurs
Bowers, E. Centaur Overheard, The.
Swenson, M. Centaur, The.

Centipedes
Kendall, M. Education's Martyr.
Unknown. Centipede was happy quite, A.

Central America. *See* **Latin America and Latin Americans**

Central Park, New York City
Hollander, M. Central Park.
Lowell, R. Central Park.
Symons, J. Central Park.
Wright, J. Lake in Central Park, The.

Ceremonial Songs (genre)
Macuilxochitl. Battle Song.
Unknown. Hunting-Song.
See also **Wedding Songs**

Ceres. *See* **Demeter**

Cereus, Night-blooming
Hayden, R. Night-Blooming Cereus, The.

Certainty
Cullen, C. Brown Boy to Brown Girl.
Jeffers, R. Nova.
Minamoto no Tōru. Like Michinoku.
Van Vliet. Coastline never alters for the fisherman, The.

Ceylon. *See* **Sri Lanka**

Cézanne, Paul
Brutus. Under House Arrest.
Snyder, R. Aging Poet, on a Reading Trip to Dayton, Visits the Air Force Museum and Discovers There a Plane He Once Flew, The.
Strange. Still Life.

Chagall, Marc
Cohen, L. Out of the Land of Heaven.
Ferlinghetti, L. Don't let that horse / eat that violin.
McGinley. On the Farther Wall, Marc Chagall.
Niatum. Homage to Chagall.
Voznesensky. Chagall's Cornflowers.

Chagres River, Panama
Gilbert, J. Beyond the Chagres.

Chainmail
Martinez, D.   Avant-Dernières Pensées.

Chairs
Cambridge, R.   On Seeing a Tapestry Chair-Bottom Beautifully Worked by His Daughter for Mrs Holroyd.
Cook, E.   Old Arm-Chair, The.
Hagiwara Sakutaro.   Chair.
Hardy, T.   Garden Seat, The.
Horn, E.   Pussycat sits on a chair.
Klein, A.   Rocking Chair, The.
Pagis.   Armchairs.
Unknown.   Grandmother's Old Armchair.
White, E.   Chairs in Snow.
Worth, V.   Chairs.

Chameleons
Klappert.   Lord's Chameleons, The.
Moore, M.   To a Chameleon.
Seaton, M.   Theories of Illusion.

Chamois
Hemans.   Chamois Hunter's Love, The.

Chance
Amichai.   Almost a Love Poem.
Archilochus.   There's nothing now.
Bawer.   On Leaving the Artists' Colony.
Bertolino.   Landscape, The.
Bond, E.   If Auschwitz had been in Hampshire.
Cacamatzin.   My friends.
Cataldi.   We Could Have Met.
Creeley.   Song: "Those rivers run from that land."
Dacey, P.   Small Dark Song.
Dimitrova.   Steady.
Eady.   My Mother, If She Had Won Free Dance Lessons.
Ehrhart.   Letter.
Elizabeth I.   Ah silly pugg wert thou so sore afraid.
Gioia.   Summer Storm.
Goedicke.   Coin of the Realm.
Goldstein, L.   Permissive Entry: A Sermon on Fame.
Gouri.   If a flame has fallen among the cedars.
Horace.   Aequam Memento.
Kelly, B.   All Wild Animals Were Once Called Deer.
Kinnell.   Little Sleep's-Head Sprouting Hair in the Moonlight.
Knott.   At the Crossroads.
Madge.   On One Condition.
Melville, H.   Guide and Guard.
Meredith, W.   Accidents of Birth.
Merwin, W.   One of the Lives.
Phillips, D.   Hounds are either the work of wind, The.
Pinsky.   Ginza Samba.
Ralegh, W.   Thus now I leave my love in fortunes [handes / bandes].
Simic.   Elementary Cosmogony.
Szymborska.   Terrorist, He Watches, The.
Tuqan, F.   I Won't Sell His Love.
Wotton, S.   Upon the Sudden Restraint of the Earl[e] of Somerset, Then Falling from Favor [or Favour].
Wyatt, T.   He is not de[a]d that sometime [or somtyme] hath a fall.
   Is it possible.
See also Fate; Fortune; Luck

Chancellorsville, Battle of (1863)
Hudgins.   At Chancellorsville.

Change
Ammons.   Corsons Inlet.
Atwood.   Eventual Proteus.
Auden.   As I walked out one evening.
   So an age ended, and its last deliverer died.
Backus.   Then Laugh.
Berry, W.   Dance, The.
Bible, *O.T.*   Time for Everything, A.
Blamire.   When home we return, after youth has been spending.
Blanco.   Poem Seen in a Motel Fan.
Boss.   My Ringless Fingers on the Steering Wheel Tell the Story.
Brontë, A.   Fragment, A.
Browning, R.   Prologue: "Poet's age is sad: for why?, The."

Bryant, W.   Mutation.
   Rivulet, The.
Carew, T.   Persuasions to Enjoy.
   Upon Some Alterations in My Mistress, after My Departure into France.
Cartwright, W.   On the Great Frost (1634).
Chacko.   Rice.
Chan.   How to Organise a Successful Small Business.
Charles, F.   Letters from Home.
Chipasula.   Friend, Ah You Have Changed!
Ciardi.   On Learning to Adjust to Things.
Clifton, L.   I am running into a new year.
Coleridge, M.   Marriage.
   Moment, A.
Coleridge, S.   Constancy to an Ideal Object.
Coleridge, S.   Garden Year, The.
Congreve.   False Though She Be [to me and love].
Cook, E.   Song of the Modern Time.
Corpi.   Winter Song.
Corso.   Whole Mess. . . Almost, The . . Almost, The.
Cowper, W.   Yardley Oak.
Cranch.   Spirit of the Age, The.
Crane, H.   Van Winkle.
Creeley.   For Love.
Cuddihy.   Pendulum, The.
Cummings, E.   As freedom is a breakfastfood.
Davies, M.   Vow for New Year's, A.
Dawe, G.   Lundys Letter, The.
Day Lewis.   Poem for an Anniversary.
Deanovich.   Connie Deanovich.
   National Assessment.
Dickinson, E.   At Half past Three, a single Bird.
   He touched me, so I live to know.
   New feet within my garden go—.
   Presentiment—is that long Shadow—on the Lawn.
   We outgrow love like other things.
Donne.   Change.
   Devout Fits.
Doty, M.   Difference.
Dove, R. Ö.
   Sunday Greens.
   Wingfoot Lake.
Du Bellay.   Antiquitez de Rome.
"Dylan."   Ballad of a Thin Man.
Edson, R.   Tearing and Merging of Clouds, The.
Eliot, T.   East Coker.
Elizabeth I.   When I was fair and young, then [or and] favour graced me;.
English, T.   Ben Bolt.
Espada.   Bully.
Fincke.   Era of the Vari-Vue, The.
Forbes, J.   Age of Plastic, The.
Franklin, B.   Bits of Wisdom.
Frost, R.   Directive.
   Nothing Gold Can Stay.
Ginsberg, A.   Change: *Kyoto-Tokyo Express*, The.
Giovanni.   Adulthood.
Glück, L.   Cottonmouth Country.
Graham, J.   What the Instant Contains.
Graves, R.   Change.
Haines, J.   Mothball Fleet: Benicia, California.
Hall, D.   Wedding Party.
Hall, J.   Maybe Dats Your Pwoblem Too.
Hardy, T.   According to the Mighty Working.
   Ancient to Ancients, An.
   Going and Staying.
Harjo, J.   Anchorage.
   For Alva Benson, and for Those Who Have Learned to Speak.
Hayden, R.   Full Moon.
Heitzman.   Spaces.
Herbert, C.   Everything changes. We plant.
Hernandez, D.   Martin and My Father.
Herrick.   Fair[e] Days; or, Dawn[e]s Deceitful[l].
   Impossibilities to His Friend.
Hewitt, J.   Postscript, 1984.
Hirschman, J.   Headlands.
Hollander, J.   Old-Fashioned Song, An.
Holmes, O.   Chambered Nautilus, The.

Hooper, V.   Deep Season.
Housman, A.   Oh, when I was in love with you.
Houston, L.   Dream of the Cabbage Caterpillars, The.
Huỳnh Mẫn Đạt.   Old Whore Becomes a Nun, The.
Jarrell.   In Montecito.
Jeffers, R.   Beaks of Eagles, The.
   Summer Holiday.
Jefferys.   We have lived and loved together.
Jonson, B.   Epistle. To Katharine, Lady Aubigny.
Jordan, J.   Roman Poem Number Nine.
Justice, D.   Houses.
Keats.   Bright star[, would I were stedfast as thou art—].
   Seasons four, The.
   Sonnet: "After dark vapours have oppress'd our plains."
Kiser.   Bargain Sale, A.
Komunyakaa.   Way the Cards Fall, The.
Kooser.   Country School.
Landor, W.   What News.
Lauterbach.   Subject to Change.
Lear, E.   Calico Pie.
Lenngren.   Other Fabrics, Other Mores!
Levine, P.   Later Still.
Li Po.   In Yüeh Viewing the Past.
Lovelace, R.   Apostasy of One and But One Lady, The.
   Grasshopper, The.
   Lucasta's World.
Lu Yün.   Valley Wind, The.
Lucy.   Missing Link.
MacNeice.   Figure of Eight.
   Perdita.
   Precursors.
   Snow.
Madhubuti.   Change-up.
   Poem to Complement Other Poems, A.
Majumdar, B.   Time Wins.
Manyarrows.   Today We Will Not Be Invisible Nor Silent.
Mapanje.   At the Metro: Old Irrelevant Images.
Marippittiyar.   Charmer Turned Ascetic, A.
Maxwell, M.   Our Revolutions Must Be Different.
McElroy, C.   Gra'ma was a little bit of a thing.
McGrath, C.   Dialectical Poem #1.
Melville, H.   Afterward.
Melville, P.   Stonebridge Park Estate.
Merwin, W.   Grandmother Watching at Her Window.
Miller, A.   Pruning, The.
Milton.   Consolation.
Montagu, L.   Saturday: The Small-Pox.
Montague, J.   Mount Eagle.
Moody, W.   Departure, The.
Moraga.   Later, she met Joyce.
Murphy, F.   Paper Clip, Historian, Coathanger.
Narihira.   This is not the moon.
Nemerov.   Dependencies, The.
   Western Approaches, The.
Nguyễn Bỉnh Khiêm.   Clouds float through dreams, are nowhere to be seen.
   Rich look grand, the poor seem cheap and mean, The.
Nguyễn Công Trứ.   Officialdom.
"Nirala."   Betrayal, The.
Nye, N.   New Year.
O'Connor, P.   Poems.
Olson, C.   In cold hell, in thicket, how.
   Kingfishers, The.
   Maximus, to Gloucester, Letter 27.
Palazzeschi.   Stranger, The.
Pastan.   After Reading Nelly Sachs.
Patmore, C.   Constancy Rewarded.
Pound, E.   Tea-rose tea-gown, etc.
Publius Papinius Status.   Forest felled, A.
Revell.   New Dark Ages.
Rich, A.   In the Evening.
   Necessities of Life.
   Phenomenology of Anger, The.
   Prospective Immigrants Please Note.
   Walk by the Charles, A.

Riley, J. Old Swimmin'-Hole, The.
Robinson, E. Ballade of Broken Flutes.
Rossetti, C. In Progress.
Passing Away, Saith the World, Passing
Away.
Rossetti, D. Barren Spring.
St. John, P. Carnival.
Sanchez, S. Norma.
Sandburg, C. Languages.
Scott, J. Changing Room.
Servasius. Rivers level granite mountains.
Shakespeare, W. Sonnet 18.
Shapiro, D. Archaic Torsos.
Shelley, P. Lines: "When the lamp is shattered
[or shatter'd]."
Mutability.
Simic. Poem without a Title.
Read Your Fate.
Simonides. Flux.
Smith, S. Grange, The.
Snodgrass, W. Mutability.
Soyinka. Rust and silence fill the thatch.
Spenser. Dame Nature.
Ssu-k'ung Shu. In Heaven.
Stevenson, R. In the States.
Su Tung-p'o. Beginning of Autumn: A Poem
to Send to Tzu-yu.
Sullivan, C. Another Kind of Country.
T'ao Ch'ien. Returning to My Home in the
Country ("So long since I've enjoyed the
hills and ponds").
Tennyson, A. Nothing Will Die.
Thomas, R. View from the Window, The.
Thomson, J. Hymn on the Seasons, A.
Tillinghast, R. Our Flag Was Still There.
Trần Tế Xu'o'ng. Looking Far Ahead.
New-Style Examinations.
No, Thank You!
What earthly use are these Confucian graphs?
Tremblay, G. Indian Singing in 20th Century
America.
Trussell. Snow.
Tuckerman, F. And change[,] with hurried
hand, has swept these scenes.
Unknown. Deor.
Force.
In Taihang born, in Taihang bred.
World is Turned Upside Down, The.
Viidikas. Future.
Vũ Đình Liên. Old Calligrapher, The.
Walker, J. Studying Physics with My
Daughter.
Walker, M. For my people [everywhere
singing their slave songs repeatedly: their].
Wallace-Crabbe. Shape-Changer, The.
Wang Chi. In Praise of Carnations.
Warren, R. Blow, West Wind.
Whitman, W. Old Ireland.
So Long!
Whittier. My Playmate.
Wilbur. Beautiful Changes, The.
Speech for the Repeal of the McCarran Act.
Wordsworth, W. Mutability.
Steamboats, Viaducts and Railways.
Worth, V. Door.
Wright, J. On a Phrase from Southern Ohio.
Yang Shih-ch'i. Dragon-Tiger Terrace.
Yeats. Lamentation of the Old Pensioner, The.
Old Men Admiring Themselves in the Water,
The.
Yi, K. Certain Year, A.
Young, A. California Peninsula: El Camino
Real.
Zolotow. Change.
See also **Transience**

Changelings
Ransom, J. Vanity of the Bright Young Men,
The.
Unknown. Tam Lin.

Channing, William Henry
Emerson, R. Ode, Inscribed to W. H.
Channing.

Chanukah. *See* **Hanukkah**

Chaos
Artaud. Spurt of Blood, The.
Ashbery. Hotel Lautréamont.
Atmanam. Next Page.

Benn. Fragments, / Refuse of the soul.
Bernstein, C. Gradation.
Blind. Chaunts of Life.
Breton, A. Mystery Corset, The.
Breton, A. *et al.* "Factory."
Brownstein. Glass Enclosure, The.
Byron, G. Darkness.
Chu Yün-ming. Drinking.
Daumal. Short Revelation Concerning Death
and Chaos.
Desnos. Language Event Two.
Eich. Old Postcards.
Ekelof. Absentia Animi.
Finkel. In the Clearing.
Ginsberg, A. Friday the Thirteenth.
Glatshteyn. To a Friend Who Wouldn't Bother
to Strain His Noodleboard Because Even So
It Is Hard to Go Hunting When Your Rifle Is
Blunt and Love Is Soft as an Old Blanket.
Görgey. Fragments of Ten Poems.
Heifetz-Tussman. Thunder My Brother.
Hsieh Chin. Playful Poem on a Chicken Egg,
A.
Hughes, T. All the dreary Sunday morning.
John, R. *et al.* Two Songs About a Dead
Person or a Mole—Whichever It Was.
Karpowicz. From Bosch's Hill.
Kelly, R. Looking.
Kharms. Symphony No. 2.
Kowit. Notice.
Kunitz, S. Reflection by a Mailbox.
Lowell, R. For the Union Dead.
Mac Low. Mani-Mani Gatha.
McClatchy. Snake.
Messerli. Essay on Concrete, An.
Millay, E. I will put Chaos into fourteen lines.
O'Brien, G. Theory of Climate.
Phillips, D. Five.
Pilinszky. Fragment from the Golden Age.
Ribemont-Dessaignes. Artichokes.
Riley, J. Silence.
Robinson, K. First Thing.
Severance.
Tribute to Nervous.
Rothenberg, J. That Dada Strain.
Rukeyser, M. Nuns in the Wind.
St. John, P. Carnival.
Shakespeare, W. Richard II.
Sorley. Hundred thousand million mites we
go, A.
Stein, G. Scenes from the Door.
Stevens, W. Connoisseur of Chaos.
Idiom of the Hero.
Szymborska. Seen from Above.
Tadic. Thief.
T'ang Hsien-tsu. Evening View from the Bell
Tower at P'ing-ch'ang.
Van Doesburg. Remembrance of the Founts of
Night.
Still Life: The Table.
Wu Wei-yeh. Autumn Night—Sleepless.
Yeats. Second Coming, The.

Chaplin, Charlie
Crane, H. Chaplinesque.
Kaufman, B. Patriotic Ode on the Fourteenth
Anniversary of the Persecution of Charlie
Chaplin.
Mandelstam. Charlie Chaplin Poem, The.
Orlovsky. Collaboration: Letter to Charlie
Chaplin.
Woroszylski. Early Chaplin, The.

Chapman, George (1559?-1634)
Drayton. Chapman the Translator.
Jonson, B. To My Worthy and Honoured
Friend, Mr George Chapman, on His
Translation of Hesiod's *Works and Days.*
Keats. On First Looking into Chapman's
Homer.

Chapman, John ("Johnny Appleseed")
Lindsay, V. Apple-Barrel of Johnny
Appleseed, The.
Oleson. Ballad of Johnny Appleseed, A.
Wilbur. John Chapman.

Charity
Balfour. Best thing to give, The.
Browning, R. Twins, The.
Chatterton. Excelente Balade of Charitie, An.

Chesterton, G. From a Spanish Cloister.
Crashaw. C[h]aritas Nimia; or, The Dear[e]
Bargain.
Dickinson, E. If I can stop one Heart from
breaking.
Dobson, A. Virtuoso, A.
Euenus. To the Swallow.
Foss, S. Husband and Heathen.
Graves, R. Certain Mercies.
Guiterman. Offer, An.
Herrick. Upon Sibilla.
Hoch. Good and Bad.
Langland, W. Good Works.
Lindsay, V. Net to Snare the Moonlight, A.
Logue, C. London Airport.
Markham, E. How the Great Guest Came.
Moore, M. Charity Overcoming Envy.
Penny, A. Sung by a Choir of Boys Marching
Round the Room.
Pritchard, N. Cloak, The.
Ray, H. Charity.
Triple Benison, The.
Robinson, E. Karma.
Smart, C. Pray Remember the Poor.
Tikhonov. We have forgotten how to offer
alms.
Unknown. I Shall Not Pass This Way Again.
Tell Him So.
Whittier. Hymn: "Thine are all the gifts, O
God!"
See also **Philanthopy and Philanthropists**

Charlemagne
Holub. Brief Reflection on Charlemagne.
Tuckerman, F. Rhotruda.

Charles I, King of England
Cartwright, W. New Year's Gift, A.
Herrick. Bad Season Makes the Poet Sad,
The.
To the King.
To the King, upon His Com[m]ing with His
Army into the West.
To the King, Upon His Welcome to Hampton
Court.
Johnson, L. By the Statue of King Charles [or
I] at Charing Cross.
Jonson, B. Epigram. To the Household. 1630,
An.
New years [or yeares], expect new gifts: sister,
your harp[e].
Lovelace, R. To My Worthy Friend Mr. Peter
Lely [or Lilly].

Charles II, King of England
Dryden, J. In pious times ere [or e'r] priest-
craft did begin.
Lovelace, R. Mock Song, A.
Philips, K. On the Numerous Accesse of the
English to Waite upon the King in Holland.
Rochester, J. Impromptu on Charles II.
Satire on Charles II, A.
Unknown. Me thinks I see our mighty
monarch stand.

Charles VI, King of France
Boland, E. Glass King, The.

Charles, Prince of Wales
Davies, T. Caernarfon, 2 July 1969.

Charles, Ray
Cecil. Richard's Blues.
Dent. Ray Charles at Mississippi State.
Kaufman, B. Blues Note.

Charles River, Massachusetts
O'Grady, D. Professor Kelleher and the
Charles River.
Rich, A. Walk by the Charles, A.

Charleston, South Carolina
Bellamann, H. Charleston Garden, A.
Heard, J. New Organ, The.
Rich, A. Charleston in the Eighteen-Sixties.
Stansbury, M. How He Saved St. Michael's.
Timrod. Charleston.
Ode: "Sleep sweetly in your humble graves."

Charm
Hafiz. Ode 105.
Herrick. Charme, or an Allay for Love, A.
Hutchinson, P. Bright after Dark.
Khlebnikov, V. We chant and enchant.
Martial. In Lesbiam.

Plomer. French Lisette: A Ballad of Maida Vale.
Ransom, J. Vision by Sweetwater.
Sansom, M. NoTL.
Thomas, L. What Is Charm?
Yeats. Memory.

Charms (genre)
Campion, T. Thrice toss[e] these oaken ashes in the air [or ayre].
Herrick. Another Charme for Stables.
Another Charme (variant).
Another ("Let the superstitious wife").
Another to Bring in the Witch.
Charmes.
Spell, The.
Scott, W. Nativity Chant, The.
Shakespeare, W. Thrice the Brinded Cat Hath Mewed.
Unknown. Butter Charm.
Charm, A.
Charm for Love and Lasting Affection, A.
Charm Rhyme, A.

Charon
Belloc. To Dives.
Ficowski. 5.8.1942 / In Memory of Janusz Korczak.
"Field." Prologue.
Landor, W. Dirce.
MacNeice. Charon.
Prior. Epigram: "When Bibo thought fit from the world to retreat."
Simic. Charon's Cosmology.
Virgil. Charon.

Chartres, France
Wharton, E. Chartres.

Chastity
Aristophanes. Repeat after me.
Blake, W. Abstinence sows sand all over.
"Field." Tragic Mary Queen of Scots, The.
Lovelace, R. To Lucasta.
Martial. In Ponticum.
Montagu, L. Lover, The; a Ballad.
Ovid. Arethusa Saved.
Philips, K. Answer to Another Persuading a Lady to Marriage, An.
Shakespeare, W. When I would pray and think, I think and pray.
Theocritus. Idyll.
Thomas, E. Remedia Amoris.
Yeats. Three Bushes, The.

Chattahoochee River, Georgia
Lanier, S. Song of the Chattahoochee.

Chatterton, Thomas
Keats. To Chatterton.

Chaucer, Geoffrey
Akenside. For a Statue of Chaucer at Woodstock.
Drayton. That noble Chaucer, in those former times.
Greene, R. Description of Sir Geoffrey Chaucer, The.
Longfellow, H. Chaucer.
Lydgate. When bright Phoebus passed was the Ram.
Skelton, J. Our natural tongue is rude.
Spenser. Whilom, as antique stories tellen us.
Waller, E. Of English Verse.
Wordsworth, W. Edward VI.

Cheerfulness
Meredith, W. Cheer, The.
Wordsworth, W. Daffodils.

Cheese
Cole, W. What a Friend We Have in Cheeses!
Hall, D. O Cheese.
Roseliep. Blues are the big thing.
Unknown. Sukey [or Suky], you shall be my wife.
Waring, H. Quite the Cheese.

Chekhov, Anton
Levertov. Like Loving Chekhov.
Simpson, L. Chocolates.

Chemical Warfare
Auden. James Honeyman was a silent child.
Cortez. Stockpiling of frozen trees, The.
Kipling, R. Gethsemane [1914–18].
Owen, W. Dulce Et Decorum Est.

Chemistry and Chemists
Lehrer. Elements, The.
Yukitsuna. Tanka: "Writing a series."

Chénier, André Marie de
Tsvetaeva. André Chénier.

Cherry Trees and Cherries
Campion, T. There is a Garden in her face.
Ch'ien Ch'ien-i. Poem Written During a Dream on the Twenty-Third Day of the Intercalary [Month After The] Fourth [Month].
Fraser, K. These Labdanum Hours.
Fumiko. Tanka: "With sorrow I recall."
Gunn, T. Cherry Tree, The.
Herrick. Cherry-ripe.
Upon Mistresse Susanna Southwell, Her Cheeks.
Housman, A. Loveliest of trees, the cherry now.
Illyés. Sour-Cherry Trees.
Issa. In the cherry blossom's shade.
Jito. Sudden Appearance of Cherry Blossoms, The.
Lawrence, D. Cherry Robbers.
Lowry, M. Wild Cherry, The.
Machi. Tanka: "Cherry blossoms."
Mori Ōgai. Tanka: "Close by the host."
Nadir. Adjectives.
Noin. Spring twilight.
Nukada. When spring escapes.
Okamoto. Tanka: "Cherry blossoms."
Tanka: "Cherry petals."
Tanka: "Ten years ago."
Tanka: "They don't appeal to me."
Rossetti, C. Let's Be Merry.
Schneour. Cherries.
Sidney, P. Sonnet 82: "Nymph of the garden where all beauties be."
Takarai Kikaku. Blind child / Guided by his mother, A.
Thomas, E. Cherry Trees, The.
Unknown. Cherry, A.
Secret, The.
Wu of Han. Summer Song.
Yosano. Over the old honeymoon cottage.
Tanka: "Evanescent."

Chesapeake Bay
Galvin, B. Pitch Pines.
Kennedy, G. Chesapeake.

Chess
Fitzgerald, E. 69.
Ibn-Ezra. Song of Chess, The.
Li K'ai-hsien. Poem Expressing My Wife's Response to One I Sent Her, A.
Sent to the Master Physician, "Almond Orchard" Shih.
Wei-ch'i Chess.
Lovelace, R. To Dr. F. B. on His Book of Chess[e].
Middleton, T. Women Beware Women.
Rossetti, D. On the Poet, Arthur O'Shaughnessy—.
Sackville-West. Spinster.
Simic. Prodigy.
Sorescu. Chess.
Yüan Mei. I Know Inside.
Miscellaneous Feelings in the Sui Garden.

Chesterton, Gilbert Keith
Belloc. Lines to a Don.
Wolfe, H. G. K. Chesterton.

Chestnut Trees and Chestnuts
Eberhart, R. Horse Chestnut Tree, The.
Longfellow, H. Village Blacksmith, The.
Saitō Mokichi. Tanka: "Determined to try."
Spear, R. Chestnuts for Verdi.
Tomlinson, C. Chestnut Avenue: at Alton House, The.

Chicago, Illinois
Alexander, M. Chicago.
Anderson, S. Evening Song.
Brooks, F. Foreigners at the Fair.
Coolbrith. Captive of the White City.
Dobyns. Freight Cars.
Equi. Ode to Chicago.
Fordham. Chicago Exposition Ode.
Harte, B. Chicago.

Hirsch, E. For the New World.
When Skyscrapers Were Invented in Chicago.
Piatt, J. Fires in Illinois.
Plumpp. Clinton.
Rexroth, K. Bad Old Days, The.
Ridge, L. Chicago.
Rodgers, C. U Name This One.
Rodriguez, L. Fire.
Sandburg, C. Chicago.
Schmitz. Making Chicago.
Smith, P. What It's Like to Be a Black Girl (For Those of You Who Aren't).
Snyder, R. Chicago, Summer Past.
Squire. Stockyard, The.
Starbuck, G. To His Chi Mistress.
Troupe. Impressions / of Chicago; For Howlin' Wolf.
Unknown. Goin' to Chicago Blues.
Welch, L. Chicago Poem.

Chicanos and Chicanas
Anzaldúa. Horse.
Encarnacion. Bulosan Listens to a Recording of Robert Johnson.
Mora. Depression Days.
La Migra.
Salinas, R. Trip Through the Mind Jail, A.
Soto. Black Hair.
Mexicans Begin Jogging.
Unknown. El Corrido de Gregorio Cortez.
Villanueva, A. To Jesus Villanueva, with Love.

Chickens
Brown, G. Hawk, The.
Burdette. Orphan Born.
Corben. In the eggs.
Gay, J. Song: "Before the barn-door crowing."
Hall, D. Henyard Round, The.
Herbert, Z. Hen is the best example of what living constantly with humans, The.
Kinnell. Supper after the Last, The.
Nash, O. Experiment Degustatory.
Patchen. In the footsteps of the walking air.
Peters, R. Darkling Chicken, The.
Final Soliloquy on a Randy Rooster (in a Key of Yellow).
Pien Kung. Paintings of Various Subjects by Fang Jih-sheng: Baby Chicks Following Their Mother.
Rankine. Eden.
Roberts, E. Hens, The.
Saitō Mokichi. Tanka: "Past the hens."
Shange. Ancestral Messengers/Composition 13.
Shūji. Tanka: "Out of the shade."
Tanka: "Suddenly."
Tekkan. Tanka: "Bliss, The."
Unknown. Chook, chook, chook, chook, chook.
Five Little Chickens.
I went down to my garden patch.
Varley. Before Throwing a Chicken into an Iowa Valley.
Williams, W. Red Wheelbarrow, The.

Child Abuse
Ai. Child Beater.
Avidan. Fire the Babysitter.
Bridges. Lisa's Ritual, Age 10.
Broumas, O. Eye of Heart.
Budbill. What I Heard at the Discount Department Store.
"Carroll." Duchess's Lullaby, The.
Cary, P. Granny's House.
Chock. Belt, The.
Crabbe. Priest attending, found he spoke at times, The.
Emanuel, L. Silence. She Is Six Years Old.
Harjo, J. Legacy.
Hayden, R. Whipping, The.
Kaune. Case Study.
Lorde. Chain.
McCarriston. Billy.
Castle in Lynn, A.
Meinke. This is a poem to my son Peter.
Miller, E. My Father's Garden.
Rabbitt. For Those Who Will Live Forever.
Smith, S. Lord Barrenstock and Epicene.
Papa Love Baby.
Voigt. Victim, The.

Child Labor

Blake, W. Chimney Sweeper, The ("Little black thing among the snow, A").

Chimney Sweeper, The ("When my mother died I was very young").

Cleghorn. Golf Links [lie so near The mill], The.

Cook, E. Our Father.

Cottle. Industrial Evils.

Galvin, B. Photo of Miners, A.

Childhood and Children

Adams, F. Those Two Boys.

Adcock, F. Halfway Street, Sidcup.

"Æ." Frolic.

Germinal.

Ai. Good Shepherd: Atlanta, 1981, The.

Aldis, D. Hiding.

Allbery. Offering.

"Alta." I would be a fool to want more children.

Lorelei.

Alvarez, J. Greg's got custody of Sally and wants.

Ironing Their Clothes.

Amichai. Anniversaries of War.

God Has Mercy [or Pity] on Kindergarten Children.

We Have Done Our Duty.

Angelou. Elegy: "I lay down in my grave."

Antipater of Thessalonica. I was Hermocrateia: twenty-nine / children I bore.

Aristophanes. Peace: A Wedding Song, The.

Armuth. Mother, A.

Arnold, M. Lines Written in Kensington Gardens.

Ashe. Vision of Children, A.

Baillie, J. Child to His Sick Grandfather, A.

Barber, M. Written for My Son, and Spoken by Him at His First Putting on Breeches.

Barlow, G. Painting Drunken Twilight.

Barnes, W. Rustic Childhood.

Barrax. Efficiency Apartment.

Scuba Diver Recovers the Body of a Drowned Child, The.

Strangers Like Us: Pittsburgh, Raleigh, 1945–1985.

Visit.

Bass, E. There are times in life when one does the right thing.

Bastard. De Puero Balbutiente.

Bateman, C. Childhood of a Stranger.

Baumel. Thumbs Up.

Beeching, H. Going Down Hill on a Bicycle.

Bekederemo. Child Asleep, A.

Belloc. Jim Who Ran Away from His Nurse, and Was Eaten by a Lion.

Rebecca, Who Slammed Doors for Fun and Perished Miserably.

Sarah Byng Who Could Not Read and Was Tossed into a Thorny Hedge by a Bull. A Cautionary Tale.

Benn. Lovely Childhood.

Benson, S. Beaten Track, The.

Berg, S. Don't Forget.

Berrigan, T. Kirsten.

Berryman. Ball Poem, The.

Henry sats in de bar and was odd.

Betjeman. False Security.

NW5 and N6.

Beveridge. Catching Webs.

Bevington, L. One more bruised heart laid bare! one victim more!

Bible, O.T. Even a child is known by his doings.

Binyon. Little Dancers, The.

Bishop, E. In the Waiting Room.

Bishop, M. Sales Talk for Annie.

Blake, W. Holy Thursday [II.] ("Is this a holy thing to see").

Holy Thursday [I.] ("'Twas on a Holy Thursday, their innocent faces clean").

Infant Joy.

Infant Sorrow.

Nurse's Song ("When the voices of children are heard on the green / And laughing is heard on the hill").

Nurse's Song ("When the voices of children

are heard on the green / And whisperings [or whisprings] are in the dale").

Bloch, C. Primer.

Blok. Vulture, The.

Bly, R. Anger Against Children.

But if one of those children came near that we have set / on fire.

Bonnefoy. All, the Nothing, The.

Booth, P. Stove.

Boruch. My Son and I Go See Horses.

Bower, R. On Door Jambs.

Boyd, M. Why?

Bradstreet, A. Author to Her Book, The.

In Reference to Her Children, 23 June, 1659 [or 1659].

To My Dear Children.

Braithwaite. City Garden, A.

Brickley. Slipping in the snow.

Brontë, C. Orphan Child, The.

Brontë, E. Mild the mist upon the hill.

Two Children, The.

Upon her soothing breast.

Brooks, G. Bronzeville Woman in a Red Hat.

Children of the Poor, The.

Mother, The.

Parents: People Like Our Marriage Maxie and Andrew, The.

Broughton, T. Lyric.

Brown, A. Friends.

Brown, G. Island School.

Brown, M. Survival Motion: Notice.

Brown, S. Chillen Get Shoes.

Conjured.

Browning, E. Deserted Garden, The.

Part I.

Bruck. Childhood.

Bukowski. Me against the world.

Burns, J. Marble surfaces.

Burns, M. Beginnings.

Burroughs, W. Cold Lost Marbles.

Byron, G. And I have loved thee, Ocean! and my joy.

"Carroll." Duchess's Lullaby, The.

Jabberwocky.

Cary, P. Suppose, my little lady.

Cassian. Part of a Bird.

Catacalos. David Talamántez on the Last Day of Second Grade.

Cave. Poem for Children, A; or, On Cruelty to the Irrational Creation.

Cawthorn. Wit was a strange unlucky child.

Chase, J. One early spring evening when Celia was fourteen.

Chōkū. Tanka: "Town children."

Tanka: "Which child."

Ciardi. Sometimes Even Parents Win.

Clark, T. Daily News.

Superballs.

Clarke, A. Three Poems about Children.

Clarke, G. Baby-Sitting.

Cleghorn. Golf Links [lie so near The mill], The.

Clements, S. Matinee.

Reservation, The.

Susans.

Clewell. Goodbye Note to Debbie Fuller: Pass It On.

Clifton, L. C. C. Rider.

Listen Children.

Coleman, W. Coffee.

Coleridge, H. Long Time a Child.

Coleridge, M. In London Town.

Coleridge, S. Fruit Plucker, The.

Youth and Age.

Cook, E. Our Father.

Song of the Rushlight.

Coolidge, C. Album—A Runthru.

Book of During, IV, The.

Cooper, J. My young mother, her face narrow.

Cornford, F. Childhood.

Ode on the Whole Duty Of Parents.

Cotton, N. To a Child [of] Five Years Old.

Creeley. Company, The.

Sitting Here.

Croft, S. Blue.

Cruickshank, H. Shy Geordie.

Cullen, C. Incident.

Saturday's Child.

Cumming, P. Caesura.

Cummings, E. Hist whist / little ghostthings.

In Just- / spring when the world is mud-.

Little tree / little silent Christmas tree.

Who are you,little i.

Damas. Hiccups.

"Dario." Far Away and Long Ago.

Daryush. Children of wealth in your warm nursery.

Davis, D. My Childhood's Happy Days.

Davis, D. Childhood of a Spy.

De la Mare. Myself.

Reserved.

Dean, D. In the Way Back.

Denning. Night on the Kho Bha Dinh.

Derricotte. Fears of the Eighth Grade.

Dickinson, E. Little Dog that wags his tail, A.

Softened by Time's consummate plush.

Dietz. Gentle Jesus meek and mild.

Dimitrova. Child and Sea.

Divakaruni. Childhood.

Walk, The.

Yuba City School.

Djanikian. How I Learned English.

In the Elementary School Choir.

When I First Saw Snow.

Dobbie. My First Memory, Switzerland, Circa 1947.

Dobyns. Gun, The.

What You Have Come To Expect.

Dodd, W. Of His Life.

Donne. Good-Morrow, The.

Dowson. Villanelle of Sunset.

Doyle, S. This Shade.

Drummond de Andrade. Souvenir of the Ancient World.

Dubie. Diatribe of the Kite, The.

Dugan, A. Thesis, Antithesis and Nostalgia.

Dunbar, P. Little brown baby wif spa'klin' eyes.

Duncan, R. Ark for Lawrence Durrell, An.

Childhood's Retreat.

Durcan. Weeping Headstones of the Isaac Becketts, The.

Eady. Supremes, The.

Eberhart, R. If I could only live at the pitch that is near madness.

Edmond, L. Jardin des Colombières.

Edwards, R. When I was three I had a friend.

Eklund. Boyhood Winter.

Eliot, T. Animula.

Emanuel, L. What Grieving Was Like.

Emerson, R. Awed I behold once more.

Motto to "The Poet."

Erdrich. Windigo.

Farjeon, E. Jenny White and Johnny Black.

Over the garden wall.

Farnsworth. Coloring Book.

Farrar, J. Chanticleer.

Fatchen. Oh Erica, Not Again!

Fell, A. Freeze-Frame.

Ferlinghetti, L. Pennycandystore beyond the El, The.

Field, E. Jest 'fore Christmas.

Little Boy Blue.

Sugar-Plum Tree, The.

Fisher, A. Sandpile Town.

Fitzgerald, R. Figlio Maggiore.

Floyd. Sergeant Brandon Just, U. S. M. C.

Fontanella. For Emma.

Forbes, C. Picture of a Man.

Forché. As Children Together.

Fort, C. Worker (We Own Two Houses), The.

Frame. Yet Another Poem about a Dying Child.

Frost, R. Birches.

Fumiko. Tanka: "My arms."

Fyleman. I Don't Like Beetles.

Galvin, B. Town Pier Parking Lot.

García Lorca. Little Mute Boy, The.

Garrigue. On the Legends of a Dancer.

Gibran. On Children.

Gibson, M. Today snow sparks the air like mica—the sun's.

Gilbert, C. Pushing.

Gildner. Primarily We Miss Ourselves As Children.
Giovanni. Legacies.
Nikki-Rosa.
Glatstein. Lost.
Glück, L. Apple Trees, The.
Descending Figure.
Drowned Children, The.
Gift, The.
Illuminations.
School Children, The.
Goodison. Songs of the Fruits and Sweets of Childhood.
Graham, H. L'Enfant Glacé.
Stern parent, The.
Tender-Heartedness.
Graves, R. I'd Love to Be a Fairy's Child.
Warning to Children.
Wm. Brazier.
Gray, T. Ode on a Distant Prospect of Eton College.
Greacen. Carnival at the River.
Greenaway. Happy Child, A.
When You and I Grow Up.
Gregerson. Salt.
Grimberg. For a long time I haven't seen such a young face.
Grosholz. Eden.
Gunn, T. Courage, a Tale.
Gwynn, R. Drive-In, The.
Hacker, M. Sonnet for Iva.
Hadas, R. Moments of Summer.
Red Hat, The.
Hagiwara Sakutaro. Chair.
Hale, J. Aaron Nicholas, Almost Ten.
Hale, S. Mary's Lamb [or Mary and Her Lamb].
Hall, D. Sleeping Giant, The.
Sudden Things.
Halpern, D. Naming the Unborn.
Hamod, K. Your mother's often gone.
Han Yü. Old men are like little boys.
Pond in a Bowl, The.
Hardy, T. Oxen, The.
Harms. Explaining the Evening News to Corbyn.
Harper, F. Thank God for Little Children.
Harr, L. Sparkler goes out, The.
Harrison, G. Playground, The.
Harte, B. Miss Edith's Modest Request.
Hartwig. Matthew 2:16–18; Then Herod, when he saw.
Harwood, G. Father and Child.
Hashimoto, S. Standing in the Doorway, I Watch the Young Child Sleep.
Hass, R. Late Spring.
Hayden, R. Those Winter Sundays.
Whipping, The.
Hays, H. Sacred Children, The.
Heaney, S. Follower.
Railway Children, The.
Terminus.
Hecht, A. Book of Yolek, The.
"It Out-Herods Herod. Pray You, Avoid It."
Heine. Mein Kind, wir waren Kinder.
Hemans. Child's First Grief, The.
Henderson-Holmes. Friendly Town #1.
Friendly Town #3.
To Hell and Back, with Cake.
Herbert, G. Holy Baptism (2).
Herrick. Grace for a Child.
Hill, G. Princes of Mercia were badger and raven, The.
Hirshfield, J. Justice without Passion.
Hoagland, E. Big Zeb Johnson.
Hogan, L. Lost Girls, The.
Hogg, J. Boy's Song, A.
Holan. At Mother's After Many Years.
Children at Christmas in 1945.
You're thinking of children, of their.
Holt, J. To Mr. Wren, My Valentine Six Year Old.
Hongo. Winnings.
Hood, T. I remember, I remember.
Parental Ode to My Son, Aged Three Years and Five Months, A.
Hopkins, G. At the Wedding March.

Handsome Heart, The.
Spring and Fall.
Horne, F. Mamma!
Housman, A. African Lion, The.
Aunts and Nieces or Time and Space.
Fragment of an English Opera.
Infant Innocence.
Purple William or The Liar's Doom.
Hove. Child's Parliment.
Howes, B. Early Supper.
Howitt, M. Dying Child, The.
Hughes, L. Children's Rhymes.
Genius Child.
Hugo, R. White Center.
Huntington, C. Rhapsody.
Ignatow, D. Ritual Three.
Ingelow. Echo and the Ferry.
Ivaska. For My Godmother.
Jaccottet. Glimpses.
Jackson, M. Red Flag, The.
Jacobsen, J. Only Alice.
Jafri. Morsel.
Jammes. Five Sorrowful Mysteries, The.
Janeczko. How to Hug Your Three-Year-Old Daughter.
Janeway. Rose.
Jarman, M. Children are hiding among the raspberry canes, The.
Jarrell. Cinderella.
Elementary Scene, The.
Lost Children, The.
Sick Child, A.
Thinking of the Lost World.
Truth, The.
Jenner, H. My Savior, hear my prayer.
Jennings, E. Ugly Child, The.
Jensen, L. Age, An.
Ajax Samples, The.
Johnson, H. Poem: "Little brown boy."
Johnson, J. Judeebug's Country.
Jones, J. I can climb our apple tree.
Jones, P. In the Formal Garden.
Jordan, J. Test of Atlanta 1979, The.
Joyce, J. Ecce Puer.
On the Beach at Fontana.
Juarroz. Bottom of things is neither life nor death, The.
Justice, D. Childhood.
Children Walking Home from School through Good Neighborhood.
Poet at Seven, The.
Sonatina in Yellow.
Kahanu. When I was young on an island.
Kaneko. Bailey Gatzert: The First Grade, 1945.
Kasdorf. Leftover Blessings.
Kavanagh, P. Long Garden, The.
Kay, J. Mother Poem (two), The.
Keeshig-Tobias. I grew up on the reserve.
Mother with Child.
Kennedy, X. Help!
Last Child.
Kenny, M. Patty-Poem.
Kerouac. 127th Chorus.
Kerr, K. Touch.
Kicknosway. West Grand Boulevard.
Kinnell. First Song.
Freedom, New Hampshire.
Lackawanna.
Little Sleep's-Head Sprouting Hair in the Moonlight.
Kinzie. Boy.
Kitahara Hakushū. Tanka: "Ailing child, An "
Klein, A. Baal Shem Tov.
Kleinzahler. Lunatic of Lindley Meadow, The.
Kloefkorn. On the Road.
Knight, E. Green Grass and Yellow Balloons.
Poem of Attrition, A.
Knott. Two Vietnam Poems: (1966).
Koch, K. You were wearing your Edgar Allan Poe printed cotton blouse.
Komey. Change, The.
Komunyakaa. Sunday Afternoons.
Venus's-Flytraps.
Krynicki. By entering the grand lottery.
Kudimova. When I still barely rose above the ground.

Kumin, M. Height of the Season, The.
Nuns of Childhood: Two Views, The.
Kunitz, S. Testing-Tree, The.
Kuskin. I woke up this morning.
Question, The.
Rose on My Cake, The.
Lamb, M. Parental Recollections.
Langford. Speak gently; it is better far.
Larkin, P. I Remember, I Remember.
This Be The Verse.
Laughton. Woman with Child, The.
Lauterbach. Boy Sleeping.
Laux. Children's Train, The.
Lawrence, D. Piano, The.
White Horse, The.
Lea, S. Clouded Evening, Late September.
Lee, L. Milkmaid.
Lee, L. Gift, The.
Levertov. Earliest Spring.
Stir the holy grains, set.
Levin, P. Dark Horse.
Levine, P. Belle Isle, 1949.
Milkweed.
Old Testament, The.
On My Own.
To a Child Trapped in a Barber Shop.
Lewis, N. Footprint on the Air, A.
Lihn. Dark Room, The.
Lincoln, A. Memory.
Livesay, D. Waking in the Dark.
Livingston, M. Coming from Kansas.
Lemonade Stand.
Logan, J. Picnic, The.
Longfellow, H. Children's Hour, The.
My Lost Youth.
Lorde. And What About the Children.
Song for a Thin Sister.
Teacher.
What my child learns of the sea.
Woman Thing, The.
Love, M. Initiation.
Lowell, R. Child's Song.
My Last Afternoon with Uncle Devereux Winslow.
Lu Yu. Farm Families.
Night Thoughts.
Lucie-Smith. Wise Child, The.
Lux. Amiel's Leg.
There Were Some Summers.
MacCaig. Intruder in a Set Scene.
Macdonagh, T. Wishes for My Son.
Macgoye. August the First: The Shadow. Patel Speaks.
Machado Ruiz. Portrait.
Machi. Tanka: "Woman, The."
Mackenzie, K. Children go, The.
Mackey, N. Phantom Light of All Our Day, The.
MacLeish. Eleven.
MacNeice. Soap Suds.
Madgett. Offspring.
Mahapatra, J. Main Temple Street, Puri.
Mandelstam. I must read only children's books.
Manhire. Children.
Mapanje. On Being Asked to Write a Poem for 1979.
Martin, D. (On the Merry, Merry-Go-Round).
Marvell. Picture of Little T. C. in a Prospect of Flowers, The.
Mathams. Jesus, friend of little children.
McBain. I wonder why I can't remember.
McCaffrey. Apprehension.
McCarriston. Billy.
McClintock, M. Thought i'd / never grow old.
McDonald, W. Children of Saigon, The.
McFadden, R. Stringer's Field.
McGinley. About Children.
Death at Suppertime.
McGough, R. First Day at School.
McGrath, T. Remembering the Children of Auschwitz.
McPherson, S. Children.
Edge Effect.
For Elizabeth Bishop.
Mead, M. That I not be a restless ghost.
Meek. Walls.

Mehrotra. Roys, The.

Mei Yao Ch'en. Excuse for Not Returning the Visit of a Friend, An.

Meinke. To a Daughter with Artistic Talent.

Meredith, G. Orchard and the Heath, The.

Merrill, J. Broken Home, The.
Days of 1941 and '44.
Scenes of Childhood.
Up and Down.
Vision of the Garden, A.

Mew. Ne Me Tangito.

Meyers, L. Apple-Eater, The.

Meynell, A. Cradle-Song at Twilight.
Parentage.

Miles, J. Doll.
When I was eight, I put in the left-hand drawer.

Millay, E. Childhood Is the Kingdom Where Nobody Dies.
From a Very Little Sphinx.

Miller, V. Adam's Footprint.
Subterfuge.

Milligan, S. Bad Report—Good Manners.

Mitchell, A. Dumb Insolence.

Mitchison. Hartmanswillerkopf.

Mitsui. Photograph of a Child, Japanese-American Evacuation, Bainbridge Island, Washington, March 30, 1942.

Momaday. To a Child Running with Outstretched Arms in Canyon de Chelly.

Moore, H. First Time: 1950.

Moore, T. Oft in the stilly night.

Morgan, R. And this is the fragrance, almost forgotten.

Morley, C. Animal crackers, and cocoa to drink.

Morris, G. Woodman, spare that tree!

Morse, B. Day on the Planet, A.

Moss, T. Party to which Wolves are Invited, The.

Muir, E. Childhood.

Muldoon, P. Right Arm, The.

Muske. Field Trip.

Myers, J. Jake Addresses the World from the Garden.

Nash, O. Come On In, the Senility Is Fine.
Grandpa Is Ashamed.
Parent, The.

Nemerov. Icehouse in Summer, The.
Remorse for Time, The.

Nesbit, E. Dead to the Living, The.
Haunted.

Newcastle, M. Excuse for So Much Writ upon My Verses.

Nguyễn Chí Thiện. Model children of the regime, The.

Nhật Tiến. Two Eyes.

Nicholls, J. Space-Shuttle.

Notley. California Girlhood, A.

Noyes, A. Cure, The.

Nye, N. Yellow Glove.

O'Brien, G. Prophetic Child, The.

Ogilvy. Natal Address to My Child, March 19th 1844, A.

O'Hara, F. Autobiographia Literaria.
Blocks.
Cornkind.
Poem: "There I could never be a boy."

Olds, S. Armor.
I Go Back to May 1937.
Rites of Passage.
Seventh Birthday of the First Child.
Sign of Saturn, The.
Size and Sheer Will.

O'Neill, H. Written on Seeing Her Two Sons at Play.

Oppen. From a Photograph.

Oppenheimer, J. Poem in Defense of Children.

Ostriker. Happy birthday, a gray day like the first one—.

Owen, G. White Stallion / (The Runaway), The.

Owen, W. To a Child.

Pagis. Limits of Physics, The.

Paley, G. Sad Children's Song, The.

Palgrave. Eutopia.

Palmer, M. Or maybe this / is the sacred.

Pankey. As We Forgive Those.

Pāṇṭiyaṉ Aṟivuṭai Nampi. Children.

Paquet. Mourning the Death, by Hemorrhage, of a Child from Honai.

Parry, E. I Would Like You for a Comrade.

Patchen. Mirru.

Patmore, C. Toys, The.

Peacock, M. Buffalo.

Peacock, T. Love and Age.

Peters, L. Isatou died.

Philips, A. Ode: To Miss Margaret Pulteney.

Piatt, S. Answering A Child.
Lesson in a Picture, A.
Palace-Burner, The.

Picasso. Poems: "Hasten on your childhood to the hour when white in."

Pien Kung. Walking Outside the City Walls on the Day of the Cold Food Festival.

Pinsky. Woman, A.

Plath. Child.
Getting There.

Plumpp. Clinton.

Po Chü-i. Children.
Mad Poem Addressed to My Nephews and Nieces, A.
Rising Late, and Playing with A-ts'ui, Aged Two.
Silver Spoon, The.

Poe. "Alone."

Pope, A. Behold the child, by Nature's kindly law.

Porter, A. Perfect Child, The.

Porter, P. Easiest Room in Hell, The.

Pound, E. Girl, A.
River-Merchant's Wife: A Letter, The.

Praed. School and Schoolfellows.

Prior. To a Child of Quality [Five Years Old, the Author Supposed Forty].

Prunty. Winter's Tale, A.

Quigless. Spring.

Rabéarivelo. Rondo for the Poet's Children.

"Rachel." Barren.

Raine, K. Puer Aeternus.

Ramsey, J. Ontogeny.

Ravikovitch. You Can't Kill a Baby Twice.

Ray, H. On the Picture of a Child.

Reaney. Lost Child, The.
School Globe, The.

Reeves, J. Little Brother, The.
Others.

Rich, A. Afterwake, The.
Bears.
Children Playing Checkers at the Edge of the Forest.
In the Wake of Home.
Memory lifts her smoky mirror: 1943.
This.

Riddell, E. Children March, The.

Ridler. For a Child Expected.

Riley, J. Days Gone By, The.
Extremes.
Hired Man's Faith in Children, The.
Life-Lesson, A.
Little Orphant Annie's come to our house to stay.

Rilke. From a Childhood.

Ríos, A. Language of Great-Aunts, The.

Roethke. Child on Top of a Greenhouse.
My Papa's Waltz.
Where Knock Is Open Wide.

Roseliep. Child.

Rosenberg, L. Suburban Childhood, A.

Rossetti, C. Frisky lamb / And a frisky child, A.

Roy, L. Suffering The Sea Change: All My Pretty Ones.

Różewicz. Talent.

Ruiz, J. Gifts.

Rukeyser, M. Boy with His Hair Cut Short.
Children, the Sandbar, That Summer.
Poem Out of Childhood.
That is what they say, who were broken off from love.

Rummo. Here you grew up. On a land which is flat.

Russell, N. Message of the Rain, The.

Rutsala. War of the Worlds, The.

Ryan, M. TV Room at the Children's Hospice.

Sackville-West. Sissinghurst.

St. John, P. Reading a Story to My Child.

Saitō Mokichi. Tanka: "Red pepper pods."

Salis. Bomb Victim in the Cathedral Speaks to a Child, A.

Salter. Age of Reason, The.
Emily Wants to Play.

Sanchez, S. Poem at Thirty.
Song No. 3: "Cain't nobody tell me any different."

Sandburg, C. Three Spring Notations on Bipeds.
Why did the children.

Sanders, E. Leaves of heaven, The.

Sant. Household Fires.

Santos, S. Childhood.

Sappho. Bridal Songs: "Happy bridegroom! / Now your wedding has come true."

Sawyer, A. Sunday Schools.

Scalapino. Or a Play.

Scannell. Hide and Seek.

Schiff, H. When It Happened.

Schulman. For That Day Only.

Schwartz, D. I Am Cherry Alive[; the little girl sang].

Scott, D. Dreadwalk.

Scovell. Poor Mother, The.
Stranger, A.

Scriven, R. Marrog, The.

Senghor. I know not when it was, I still confuse childhood and Eden.

Sergeant. Man Meeting Himself.

Serraillier. Anne and the Field-Mouse.

Sexton. Fortress, The.
Fury of Overshoes.
January 1st.

Shakespeare, W. Song: "When that I was and a little tiny boy."
What Answer Can I Give?

Shapiro, D. Book of Glass, A.

Sholl. Dawn.

Silverstein, S. Listen to the MUSTN'TS, child.
Nobody loves me.
One Inch Tall.
Sick.

Simic. Book Full of Pictures, A.
Prodigy.

Simpson, L. My father in the night commanding No.

Sissoko. Grandmother.

Smith, C. Glow-Worm, The.
I once was happy, when while yet a child.

Smith, D. Roundhouse Voices, The.

Smith, I. Children, The.

Smith, P. Biting Back.

Smith, S. Bog-Face.
One of Many.
Our Bog is dood, our Bog is dood.
Parklands, The.
To carry the child into adult life.

Snyder, G. Dragonfly / Dead on the snow.

Sobiloff. Child's Sight, The.
Snake's Destiny, The.

Södergran. Homecoming.

Sokolov. Beginning, The.

Soloukhin. Lost Songs.

Song. Wind in the Trees, The.

Sorrels. What can I say, but that it's not easy?

Sorrentino. Classic Case, A.

Soto. Behind Grandma's House.
Black Hair.

Soupault. Poems from Saint Pelagia Prison.

Soutar. Hungry Mauchs, The.

Southwick. Child, Invisible Fire.

Spender, S. Elementary School Classroom in a Slum, An.
Empty House.
Rough.

Spires. First Day, The.
Globe.

Stafford, W. First Grade.
Remembering Brother Bob.

Stanton, M. Childhood.

Stefanile. How I Changed My Name, Felice.

Stein, G. Teachers taught her, The.

Stevens, W. In the Carolinas.
Stevenson, R. Auntie's Skirts.
Bed in Summer.
Cow, The.
Escape at Bedtime.
Foreign Children.
Foreign Lands.
Good and Bad Children.
Good Boy, A.
Good Play, A.
Lamplighter, The.
Land of Counterpane, The.
Land of Nod, The.
Land of Story-Books, The.
Looking Forward.
Marching Song.
My Bed Is a Boat.
My Shadow.
Pirate Story.
Sick Child, The.
Swing, The.
System.
Thought, A.
Time to Rise.
Unseen Playmate, The.
Where Go the Boats?
Whole Duty of Children.
Winter Time [or Winter-Time].
Young Night Thought.
Strand. Where Are the Waters of Childhood?
Strange. Childhood.
Stuart, D. Rescue.
Soup Jar, The.
Stumbrs. Ode to a Country Childhood.
Su Tung-p'o. Children don't know what worry
  means!
Surrey. In Windsor Castle.
Sward. Uncle Dog; the Poet at 9.
Swenson, M. Centaur, The.
Swinburne. Child's Laughter, A.
Szymborska. Interview with a Child.
Laughter.
"Tabitha." Sweet it is to be a child.
Taggard. Little Girl with Bands on Her Teeth,
  The.
Tekkan. Tanka: "Unlike their father."
Tennyson, A. City Child, The.
Lullaby: "Sweet and low, sweet and low."
Minnie and Winnie.
Terence. Elder boy is by adoption mine, The.
Thaxter. Favorite Flower, The.
Thayer, L. Little Child's Faith, The.
Thomas, D. Conversation of prayers about to
  be said, The.
Fern Hill.
When I was a boy.
Thompson, C. Mrs. Johnson Objects.
Thompson, F. Ex Ore Infantium.
Tô Hū'u. Cradlesong, A.
Tomlinson, C. Picture of J. T. in a Prospect of
  Stone, The.
Troupe. Boomerang: A Blatantly Political
  Poem.
Tucker, M. Old Crib, The.
Tuckerman, F. How oft in schoolboy-days,
  from the school's sway.
Turner, C. Letty's Globe.
Tvardovsky. From a crumpled wartime diary.
Twomey. Cliona.
Uahupirapi. Imagination.
Unknown. Against Idleness.
Baby, baby.
Bitter Withy, The.
Blue Bell Boy.
Child's Offering, A.
Deeds of Kindess.
Gingerbread Man, The.
Girls and boys come out to play.
Jo Jo, My Child.
Lullaby: "O! hush thee, my darling, sleep
  soundly my son."
Monday's child is fair of face.
Mulberry Bush, The.
Oh My Own Little Daughter, Four Years Old.
On the Death of Mr. Persall's Little Daughter,
  in the Beginning of the Spring, at
  Amsterdam.

Prayer for Love, A.
Sculpture.
There was a little girl.
Three children sliding on the ice.
To My Niece, A.M., with a New Pair of
  Shoes.
Tumbling.
Walk Together Children.
Who Taught Them?
Young Girl in the Choir, The.
Valentine, J. After Elegies.
"X."
Vanshenkin. Urchin, The.
Vasilyev, S. Pigeon of My Childhood.
Vaughan, H. Childhood.
Retreat[e], The.
Villanueva, A. They didn't get me.
Virtue. Waifs.
Voigt. "Wife Takes a Child", The.
Wade, B. Tadpoles.
Wagner, M. Miss Clement's Second Grade.
Wain. Gentleman Aged Five before the
  Mirror.
Walcott. For Adrian.
Walker, A. Enemy, The.
Walker, M. Childhood.
Wallace, R. Facts of Life, The.
1001 Nights.
Walsh, J. I've Got an Apple Ready.
Wang Chiu-ssu. Ballad of Selling a Child.
Waniek. Sacrament of Poverty, The.
Warner, S. Song for a Street-Song.
Warren, R. American Portrait: Old Style.
Little Girl Wakes Early.
Old-Time Childhood in Kentucky.
What Voice at Moth-Hour did I hear calling.
Watson, R. Children of the Mist.
White Lady, The.
Weaver, M. Improvisation for Piano.
Webster, A. Little child she, half defiant
  came, A.
Since first my little one lay on my breast.
There's one I miss. A little questioning maid.
Webster, E. San Joaquin Valley Poems: 1969.
Weigl. Last Lie, The.
Shelter.
Weingarten. From the Temple of Longing.
Wendt. Teacher I Wanted to Be, The.
White, S. Healing, The.
White, T. To Myself, after Forty Years.
Whitman, W. There was a child went forth
  every.
Whittemore, R. Party, The.
Whittier. Hymn: "Thine are all the gifts, O
  God!"
In School-Days.
My Playmate.
Oh for boyhood's painless play.
Widdemer. Invisible Playmate, The.
Wieseltier. God's Fire upon Children ("God's
  fire upon cities").
Wilbur. Boy at the Window.
Digging for China.
Pardon, The.
Wilde, O. Le Jardin des Tuileries.
Willard, N. Arbor.
Williams, C. My Mother's Lips.
Williams, P. Baby in the House, A.
Williams, S. Peacock Poems: 1, The.
Williams, W. To.
Waiting.
Wollach. All the silly threatening things.
Jonathan.
Love Poem #2.
Wong, N. Ma, my heart must be made of rice
  straw.
Woodworth. Old Oaken Bucket, The.
Wordsworth, W. Anecdote for Fathers,
  Showing how the Art of Lying may be
  Taught.
Characteristics of a Child Three Years Old.
My heart leaps up when I behold.
Ruth [or, The Influences of Nature].
To a Child [Written in Her Album].
To H. C.[, Six Years Old].
Work. Come Home, Father[!].
Wright, F. Untitled.

Wright, J. Evening.
Mutterings Over the Crib of a Deaf Child.
Note Left in Jimmy Leonard's Shack, A.
Poem by Garnie Braxton, A.
Sappho.
Song for the Middle of the Night, A.
Twilights.
Wright, J. To a Child.
Wright, K. How the Wild South East Was
  Lost.
Wu Wei-yeh. Lamenting for My Late
  Daughter.
Yamada. Homecoming.
Yamanaka. Kala: Saturday Night at the Pahala
  Theatre.
Yau. Different Cereal, A.
Yearsley. Mira, as they dear Edward's senses
  grow.
Yeats. Among School Children.
Cradle Song, A: "Angels are stooping, The."
Prayer for My Daughter, A.
To a Child Dancing in the Wind.
Young, K. No Offense.
Yukitsuna. Tanka: "Child in my arms."
Tanka: "Youngster, A."
Zarin. Ant Hill, The.
Zimmer. Father Animus and Zimmer.
What Zimmer Would Be.
Zimmer's Head Thudding against the
  Blackboard.
Zulauf. Separation in Succasunna.
See also **Adolescence; Boys; Death in
  Childhood; Girls; Youth**

Chile
Ali, A. I See Chile in My Rearview Mirror
Coleridge, S. Nightingale, The.
de Jesús. Flag of Chile, The.
  Proverbs.
Dobyns. General Matthei Drives Home
  through Santiago.
Jesús. All of a Sudden.
Neruda. They Receive Instructions Against
  Chile.
Parra, N. Modern Times.

Chilembwe, John
Mapanje. Before Chilembwe Tree.

Chillon Castle, Switzerland
Byron, G. Sonnet on Chillon.

Chimney Sweepers
Alcock. Chimney-Sweeper's Complaint, The
  ("Chimney sweeper's boy am I, A").
Blake, W. Chimney Sweeper, The ("Little
  black thing among the snow, A").
Chimney Sweeper, The ("When my mother
  died I was very young").
De la Mare. "Sooeep!"
Graves, R. Wm. Brazier.
Unknown. Eaper Weaper, chimney sweeper.

Chimneys
Bennett, R. Windy Nights.
Graves, R. Under the Pot.
Rózewicz. Massacre of the Boys.
Sachs, N. O the Chimneys.
Summerfield. Tall Story for Fred Dibnah.
Unknown. Chimney-Tops.

China
Auden. Macao.
Spain 1937.
Beer, P. Footbinding.
Benét, W. Merchants from Cathay.
Ch'en Lin. Song: "I watered my horse at the
  Long Wall caves."
Chin. Barbarian Suite.
Exile's Letter: After the Failed Revolution.
Portrait of the Self as Nation, 1990–1991, A.
Prelude.
Ch'iu Chin. To the Tune "The River Is Red."
Chu Yün-ming. Fan from Korea, A.
Clifton, H. Monsoon Girl.
Dao. End or a Beginning, An.
Résumé.
Digby, J. Sooner or Later.
Gu Cheng. Forever Parted: Graveyard.
Han Yü. Officer at the Rapids, The.
Ho Xuan Huong. Shrine of Ts'en Yi-tung,
  The.

Hofmannsthal. Emperor of China Speaks, The.
Hovey. Sea Gypsy, The.
Kuan Yün-shih. Tune: "Butterflies."
Li Ho. Watchman's Drum in the Streets of Officials, The.
Li Hsün. Tune: "Song of the Southern Country."
Lindsay, V. Chinese Nightingale, The.
Liu Ya-tzu. Beyond the stream at Seta stretches an endless view.
Dragons and snakes tangle in my dream; they can hardly recoil.
On the Second Day of the Fifth Month—Written after Drink.
Lo Fu. Song of the Cricket.
Lofting. Mister Beers.
Lu Yu. Border Mountain Moon.
To Show My Sons.
Lý Thu'ò'ng Kiệt. Southern emperor rules the Southern land, The.
Mao Tse-tung. "Spring in Ch'in's Garden" ("Alone I stand in autumn cold").
Tune: "Deva-like Barbarian"—Ta-po-ti.
Tune: "Remembering the Lady of Ch'in"—Loushan Pass.
Tune: "Spring in Ch'in's Garden" ("Northern landscape, / Thousand miles around covered by ice").
Tune: "The Charm of Nien-nu"—Kunlun Mountains.
Merrill, S. Ballade of the Chinese Lover.
Messerli. Angry with China.
Neihardt. Summer turned.
Nguyễn Trãi. Among the great, no smooth and open world.
Womb's own flesh and bone—strong brotherhood, A.
Nordbrandt. China Observed Through Greek Rain in Turkish Coffee.
O'Hara, F. Poem: "At night Chinamen jump."
Po Chü-i. Old Man of Hsin-feng witih the Broken Arm, The.
Pound, E. Enormous tragedy of the dream in the peasant's bent / shoulders, The.
Roberts, N. Mona Lisa Tea Towel, The.
"Shu Ting." Perhaps our cares.
Silko. Prayer to the Pacific.
Song. Lost Sister.
Su Man-shu. Exile in Japan.
Tran Minh-tong (King). Farewell to two envoys from the Yüan court.
Trần Tế Xu'o'ng. New-Style Examinations.
Unknown. China has many people and many heroes.
Wang Chien. South, The.
Wei Chuang. Lament of the Lady of Ch'in, The.
Tune: "Deva-like Barbarian."
Weöres. Chinese Temple.
Whalen. Hymnus Ad Patrem Sinensis.
Wilbur. Digging for China.
Wu Wei-yeh. View of the Countryside.
Yang Wei-chen. Bamboo Branch Song of West Lake.
Yên Thao. My Home.
Yu Kuang-chung. Mother, I'm hungry.
When I am dead, lay me down between the Yangtze.

Chinatowns
Hongo. Four Chinatown Figures.

Chinaware
Gay, J. To a Lady on Her Passion for Old China.
Lister, R. Bone China.
Merrill, J. Willowware Cup.
Moore, M. No Swan So Fine.
Probyn. China Maniacs.

Chinese, The
Cendrars. Frisco-City.
Chin. Composed Near the Bay Bridge (after a wild party).
How I Got That Name.
Chinn. Not Translation, Not Poetry.
Harte, B. Plain Language from Truthful James.
Kerouac. Thrashing Doves, The.
Lau, A. Upside Down Basket, The.

Lei-Lanilau. Kolohe or Communication.
Liu. My Father's Martial Art.
Mar, L. My Mother, Who Came from China, Where She Never Saw Snow.
Ping. Of Flesh and Spirit.
Shiraishi. Chinese Ulysses, A.
Spires. Courtesan with Fan.
Tate, J. Miss Cho Composes in the Cafeteria.
Trần Tế Xu'o'ng. Lamenting the State of Confucian Scholarship.
What earthly use are these Confucian graphs?
Wong, N. How a Girl Got Her Chinese Name.
When I Was Growing Up.

Chipmunks
Gonzales. Chipmunk can't drag it along.
Chipmunk was standing.
Jarrell. Chipmunk's Day, The.
Jones, J. Did you ever have a chipmunk for a friend?
Melville, H. Chipmunk, The.

Chisholm Trail
Unknown. Old Chisholm Trail, The.

Chivalry
Melville, H. Rusty Man, The.

Chocolates
Simpson, L. Chocolates.

Choices
Baraka. Kenyatta Listening to Mozart.
Carruth, H. Lost.
Dante Alighieri. Sonnet: "All my thoughts always speak to me of love."
Di Prima. Abyss.
Dickinson, E. I'm ceded—I've stopped being Theirs.
Dĭmltrova. Steady.
Dugan, A. Not to Choose.
Flynn, M. Decision.
Frost, R. Lovely Shall Be Choosers, The.
Graves, R. Down, wanton, down! Have you no shame.
Sharp Ridge, The.
Whole Love.
Jonson, B. Epode: "Not to know vice at all, and keep[e] true state."
Kenyon, J. Otherwise.
Mahapatra, S. Election, The.
Olson, C. In cold hell, in thicket, how.
Rich, A. Roofwalker, The.
Sandburg, C. Choose.
Wyatt, T. Like as the bird in the cage enclosed.
Yeats. Choice, The.
Zagajewski. Betrayal.

Choking
Char. Man flees suffocation.
Illyés. Sour-Cherry Trees.
Kitahara Hakushū. Tanka: "During a fit."
Ravikovitch. Portrait.
Serge. Asphyxiated Man, The.
Voigt. Daughter.

Cholera
MacKay, C. Mowers: An Anticipation of the Cholera, 1848, The.

Christchurch, New Zealand
Curnow. Skeleton of the Great Moa in the Canterbury Museum, Christchurch, The.

Christenings
McCord, D. Perambulator Poem.
See also **Baptisms**

Christianity and Christians
Awoonor. Easter Dawn.
Bishop, E. Brazil, January 1, 1502.
Blake, W. Vision of Christ that thou dost see, The.
Brecht, B. Peachum's Morning Hymn.
Crashaw. Howres for the Hours of Matines, The.
Dickinson, E. I'm ceded—I've stopped being Theirs.
Donne. Satire 3.
Show me dear Christ.
Dunbar, W. Of Christ's Nativity.
Dunn, S. At the Smithville Methodist Church.
Ferlinghetti, L. Sometime during eternity / some guys show up.

"Field." Lovers, fresh plighting lovers in our age.
Harper, F. Bible Defence of Slavery.
Hayes, A. Pietá.
Herbert, G. British Church, The.
Cross[e], The.
Priesthood, The.
Herrick. Crosses.
Hudgins. Saints and Strangers.
Huxley, A. Christlike is my behaviour.
Jones, D. In the middle silences of this night's course the blackthorn.
Kenyon, J. Back from the City.
Kraujiete. Vagabond's Arising.
Lawrence, D. Retort to Jesus.
Logau. Faith.
MacNeice. Belfast.
McTurk. Query.
Melville, H. Symphonies.
Meredith, G. Garden of Epicurus, The.
Milosz, C. Poor Christian Looks at the Ghetto, A.
Milton. On His Blindness.
Muldoon, P. Our Lady of Ardboe.
Obolduyev. Rod, The.
Paulinus of Nola. Come my true Consort in my Joyes and Care!
Plath. Medusa.
Pressoir. Country Graveyard.
Prudentius. Now, earth, take to thy cold embrace.
O God, the soules pure fi'ry Spring.
Oracles are dumm, The.
Yee night, and darknes, cloudie aire.
Ritsos. End of Dodona II, The.
Rodriguez, L. String Bean.
Roumain. New Negro Sermon.
Ryuichi. My Imperialism.
Saarikoski. Winter solstice.
Sachs, H. Fair Melody: To Be Sung by Good Christians, A.
Savard. Fall, The.
Schneour. Last Words of Don Henriquez, The.
Skelton, J. Now sing we, as we were wont.
Stevens, W. High-Toned Old Christian Woman, A.
Sunday Morning.
Symeon. We awaken in Christ's body.
Thomas, D. Before I knocked and flesh let enter.
Vision and Prayer.
U Tam'si Tchicaya. Communion II.
Unknown. Akathistos Hymn.
Gospel train is moving, The.
Harmony.
Let Us Cheer the Weary Traveler.
Saint Patrick's Breastplate.
Te Deum.
Vaughan, H. British [or Brittish] Church, The.
Retirement.
Very. John.
Wheatley, P. On Being Brought from Africa to America.
Whitman, W. To Him That Was Crucified.
Whittier. Call of the Christian, The.
Wordsworth, W. Decay of Piety.
Inscription for a Monument in Crossthwaite Curch, in the Vale of Keswick.
Work. Kingdom Coming.
Yeats. Ribh Considers Christian Love Insufficient.
Zimmer. Father Animus and Zimmer.

Christmas
Agnew, E. Let me tell to you the story.
Alexander, C. Once in Royal David's City.
Amann. Snow falling.
Appleman, P. Matthew 1:18–25: Now the birth of Jesus Christ took place.
Arrowsmith, P. Christmas Story (1980).
Barrax. Christmas 1959 et Cetera.
Belloc. Noël.
Betjeman. Christmas.
Bottoms. Boy Shepherds' Simile, The.
Bridges, R. Noel; Christmas Eve, 1913.
Brooks, P. Christmas Everywhere.
Canton. Bethlehem.

Causley. Ballad of the Bread Man.
Sailor's Carol.
Chesterton, F. How Far Is It to Bethlehem?
Chesterton, G. House of Christmas, The.
Chute, M. Day before Christmas.
Coatsworth. Barn, The.
Coleridge, M. I saw a stable low and very bare.
Cooper, R. To See the Cross at Christmas.
Corben. After Christmas.
Before Christmas.
Corn. Navidad, St. Nicholas Ave.
Corrothers. Indignation Dinner, An.
Crashaw. Hymne of the Nativity, Sung by the Shepheards, A.
Crowell, G. Eternal Values.
Cullen, C. Christus Natus Est.
Cummings, E. Little tree / little silent Christmas tree.
Dafydd Bach ap Madog Wladaidd. Christmas Revel, A.
Daniels, K. Christmas Party.
De Ledrede. Festival of the Nativity, The.
Dickinson, P. Advent; a Carol.
Djanikian. When I First Saw Snow.
Dunn, G. Journey Back to Christmas.
Falconer, E. Cradle Song at Bethlehem.
Falkner. Christmas Day; the Family Sitting.
Fanthorpe. BC:AD.
What the Donkey Saw.
Farber. Bow down, mountain, to hear the gladness issuing.
Farjeon, E. Advice to a Child.
In the Week When Christmas Comes.
Ferlinghetti, L. Christ Climbed Down / from His bare Tree.
Field, E. Christmas Song: "Why do the bells for Christmas ring?"
Jest 'fore Christmas.
Finch, R. Crib, The.
Fordham. Nativity, The.
Freeman, C. Christmas Morning I.
Frost, F. Christmas in the Wood.
Fuller, R. Peculiar Christmas, A.
Gilmore, B. Bow to Allah.
Glück, L. Nativity Poem.
Godolphin. Hymn: "Lord, when the wise men came from far[r]."
Graves, R. Carol of Patience.
Gregory. Christmas Lullaby for a New-Born Child.
Guiterman. Christmas Exchange, The.
Hardy, T. House of Hospitalities, The.
Oxen, The.
Reminder, The.
Heard, J. Birth of Jesus, The.
Heine. Wise Men Ask the Children the Way, The.
Hendry, H. Silver Bells.
Herbert, G. Christmas.
Hill, G. Picture of a Nativity.
Holan. Children at Christmas in 1945.
Hopkins, G. Moonless darkness stands between.
Hopkins, J. We Three Kings of Orient are.
Horne, F. Kid Stuff.
Hugo, R. December 24 and George McBride Is Dead.
Image. Meditation for Christmas, A.
Jacob, M. Horrible Today, The.
Jennings, E. Afterthought.
Johnson, G. Christmas Rhyme, A.
Johnson, M. Christmas Times.
Krismas Dinnah.
Jones, P. Christmas, Boston Nineteen Eighty Nine.
Jonson, B. Hymn[e] on the Nativity [or Nativitie] of My Saviour, A.
"Kay." Christmas Verse, A.
Kim, J. Christmas.
Kinnell. To Christ Our Lord.
Kipling, R. Eddi's Service.
Kirkup. Shepherd's Tale, The.
Kirsch, S. Stopover.
Kleinzahler. Ebenezer Californicus.
Lattimore. December Fragments.

Levertov. Advent 1966.
Christmas 1944.
Lewis, C. Nativity, The.
Longfellow, H. Christmas Bells.
Three Kings came riding from far away.
Lowell, R. Christmas Eve under Hooker's Statue.
Macdonald, G. Christmas Prayer, A.
MacNeice. Fanfare for the Makers, A.
Maiola. Up on the Moon.
McDonald, W. Christmas Bells, Saigon.
McGinley. City Christmas.
McGrath, T. Bread of this World; Praises III, The.
Middleton, R. Carol of the Poor Children, The.
Millay, E. To Jesus on His Birthday.
Miller, M. How Far to Bethlehem?
Miller, V. Christmas Mourning.
Milosz, C. "Christ has risen." Whoever believes that / Should not behave as we do.
Mitchell, A. Nothingmas Day.
Montgomery, J. Nativity.
Moore, C. Visit from St Nicholas, A.
Moorer. Christmas Eve.
Morgan, E. Computer's First Christmas Card, The.
Morris, W. Outlanders, The.
Nemerov. Eve.
Santa Claus.
Nicholson, N. Shepherds' Carol.
Niedecker. Will You Write Me a Christmas Poem?
Norris, L. Mice in the Hay.
Shepherd's Dog, The.
Opperman. Christmas Carol: "Three outas from the [High] bleak Karoo."
Orban, O. Gypsy Christmas.
Orrery. On Christmas Day.
Osborn, M. Christmas.
Parker, K. Long, Long Ago.
Parry-Williams. Christmas Carol: "Close to a quarter of a century since then."
Pasternak, B. Christmas Star.
Pickthall, M. Child's Song of Christmas, A.
Plath. Winter's Tale, A.
Ray, H. At Christmas-Tide.
Reese, L. Christmas Folk-Song, A.
Ridler. At Christmas.
Roberts, E. Christmas Morning.
Robinson, E. Karma.
Rodgers, W. White Christmas.
Rossetti, C. Before the paling of the stars.
Ruiz, J. Gifts.
Sansom, C. Innkeeper's Wife, The.
It was a night in winter.
Sarton. "Yes," you say, "of course at Christmas".
Sears, E. It came upon the midnight clear.
Selyns. O Christmas Night.
Sexton. Santa.
Shapiro, K. Jew at Christmas Eve, The.
Shaw, L. Groundhog is, at best, a simple soul, The.
Stars in Apple Cores.
Shorter. Skeleton in the Cupboard, The.
Smart, C. Nativity of Our Lord, The.
Smith, I. Christmas 1971.
Snodgrass, C. Poem for Christmas, A.
Southwell. Burning Babe, The.
Child[e] My Choice [or Choyse], A.
New Prince, New Pomp[e].
Stephens, J. Christmas at Freelands.
Stevenson, R. Christmas at Sea.
Christmas Prayer, A.
Stewart, G. As I went down to David's town.
Swede. Christmas Eve.
Tate, N. While shepherds watched their flocks by night.
Tennyson, A. Time draws near the birth of Christ, The.
Thompson, C. Christmas Rush, The.
Thompson, F. Ex Ore Infantium.
Thomson, J. Hymn on the Seasons, A.
Timrod. Christmas.
Traherne. On Christmas-Day.
Tucker, M. Christmas, South, 1866.

Turner, S. Christmas Is Really for the Children.
Unknown. As I Sat on a Sunny Bank.
Carnal and the Crane, The.
Carol, for Candlemas Day.
Christmas Carol: "God bless the master of this house."
Christmas Hymn.
Christmas Song ("Trees are all bare not a leaf to be seen, The").
First Nowell the angel did say, The.
Friendly Beasts, The.
Hay, ay, hay, ay.
Haylle, Comly and Clene.
I syng of a mayden that is makeles.
Jolly Shepherd, The.
Long, Long Ago.
Make we mery bothe more and lasse.
Medieval Poem of the Nativity, A.
Sing, hey! Sing, hey! / For Christmas Day.
Song Bewailing the Time of Christmas, So Much Decayed in England, A.
Songe bewailinge the tyme of Christmas, So much decayed in Englande, A.
This Endris Night.
Twelve Days of Christmas, The.
Upon a Christmas Morning.
Welcome Yule.
Yule Days, The.
Upton, L. Lost Child.
Vaughan, H. Christ's Nativity.
Shepherds [or Shepheards], The.
Wadding. Christmas day is come; let all prepare for mirth.
For Christmas Day.
Waldman, A. Baby's Pantoum.
Watkyns. Upon Christ's Nativity or Christmas.
Watts, I. Cradle Hymn, A.
Miracles at the Birth of Christ.
Wells, A. Inn That Missed Its Chance, The.
Wesley, C. Incarnation, The.
White. Christmas Party, The.
Wilbur. Christmas Hymn, A.
Williams, W. Burning the Christmas Greens.
Wilson, R. Family Holiday.
Wolfe, H. Dean Inge.
Young, A. Christmas Day.
Zinzendorf. For Us No Night Can Be Happier.

Christmas Cards
Morgan, E. Computer's First Christmas Card, The.

Christmas Carols
Alexander, C. Once in Royal David's City.
Brooks, P. O little town of Bethlehem.
Chaundler. Child's Christmas Carol, A.
Craik. God Rest You [or ye] Merry, Gentlemen.
Longfellow, H. Christmas Carols.
Luther. Cradle Hymn.
Rhodes, M. Carol Singers, The.
Sears, E. It came upon the midnight clear.
Tate, N. While shepherds watched their flocks by night.
Unknown. First Nowell the angel did say, The.
I Saw Three Ships Come Sailing In.
Out of Your Sleep Arise and Wake.
Wolfe, H. Dean Inge.

Christmas Eve
Bly, R. Christmas Eve Service at Midnight at St. Michael's.
Chōkū. Tanka: "On Christmas Eve."
Cole, C. Christmas Eve.
Davie. Devil on Ice.
Farjeon, E. Advice to a Child.
Feinstein, S. Christmas Eve.
Hall, D. Christmas Eve in Whitneyville, 1955.
Hardy, T. Oxen, The.
Moore, C. Visit from St Nicholas, A.
Rexroth, K. Sword in a Cloud of Light, A.
Rossetti, C. Christmas Carol, A: "Thank God, thank God, we do believe."
Thompson, P. Christmas Ghost, A.
Tucker, M. Christmas Eve, South, 1865.
Walla. Christmas Eve.

Christmas Roses
Day Lewis. Christmas Rose, The.

Christmas Trees
Bennett, R. Christmas-Tree Song, A.
Ten Little Christmas Trees.
Burford, W. Christmas Tree, A.
Cook, S. Christmas Tree.
Cummings, E. Little tree / little silent
Christmas tree.
De Savitzsky. Christmas Tree, The.
Moorer. Christmas Tree, The.
Rose, M. Little Fir Tree, The.
Smith, L. Christmas Tree.
Tate, J. Miss Cho Composes in the Cafeteria.
Walsh, J. Christmas Tree, The.
Williams, W. Burning the Christmas Greens.
Christmas, the Virgin
Unknown. Cherry-Tree Carol, The.
In the Town.
Sweet Was the Song.
Chrysanthemums
Hardy, T. Last Chrysanthemum, The.
Lee, L. Between Seasons.
MacLeish. Starved Lovers.
McKinney, I. Chrysanthemums.
Mitsune. White chrysanthemum, The.
Ōshima Ryōta. No one spoke.
Pien Kung. On Hearing That San-p'ing's
Newly Brewed Chrysanthemum Wine Is
Ready to Drink—Investigating with a Poem.
On the Sixteenth Day I Visit the Temple
Again.
Po Chü-i. Chrysanthemums in the Eastern
Garden, The.
So Chong-Ju. Beside the Chrysanthemum.
Yün Shou-p'ing. As we say farewell to
autumn.
Chungking, China
Stilwell. Lyric to Spring.
Church of England
Betjeman. Bristol and Clifton.
Corbet. Fairies' Farewell, The.
Herbert, G. British Church, The.
Knox, R. Anglican curate in want, An.
Unknown. Vicar of Bray, The.
Vaughan, H. British [or Brittish] Church, The.
Churches
Arnold, M. Rugby Chapel.
Beer, M. Church in the Heart, The.
Berkeley, S. Mass is over, they have gone in
peace, The.
Bertrand. Mason Abraham Knupfer is singing,
trowel in hand, scaffolded, The.
Betjeman. Diary of a Church Mouse.
Sunday Afternoon Service in St. Enodoc
Church, Cornwall.
Sunday Morning, King's Cambridge.
Blake, W. Little Vagabond, The.
Boldman. In the temple.
Brown, G. Ruined Chapel.
Buckley, V. Good Friday and the Present
Crucifixion.
Burns, R. Kirk's Alarm, The.
Tam o' Shanter. [A Tale].
To a Louse [On Seeing One on a Lady's
Bonnet at Church].
Calas. Columns of the Temple of Olympian
Zeus.
Clemmons. Greater Friendship Baptist Church,
The.
Clifton, L. In White America.
Close, E. Here We Come a-Haying.
Corbet. Upon Fairford Windows.
Crane, H. Broken Tower, The.
Cummings, E. I am a little church(no great
cathedral).
Di Piero. San Antonio de Padua.
Dickinson, E. Some keep the Sabbath going to
Church.
When Bells stop ringing—Church—begins.
Durcan. Divorce Referendum, Ireland, 1986,
The.
Ekelof. Greece.
Emerson, R. We Love the Venerable House.
Farjeon, E. Children's Bells, The.
Fuller, J. St. Sophia.
Giovanni. Knoxville, Tennessee.
Gray, J. Crucifix, A.
Haines, J. Snowbound City, The.

Hamer. Getting Happy.
Hardy, T. Afternoon Service at Mellstock.
Church Romance, A.
Hawker. Poor Man and His Parish Church,
The.
Hayden, R. Those Winter Sundays.
Herbert, G. Perirrhanterium.
Prayer (I).
Herrick. Fairy Temple; or, Oberon's Chapel,
The.
Temple, The.
Hewitt, J. Whit Monday.
Horne, F. On Seeing Two Brown Boys in a
Catholic Church.
Jarman, M. Unholy Sonnets.
Jewett, S. At Home from Church.
Kantaris. Airing the Chapel.
Keats. On Oxford.
Kennedy, X. Hangover Mass.
Larkin, P. Broadcast.
Church Going.
Lawrence, D. Tabernacle.
Leithauser. Old Bachelor Brother.
Levchev. Abandoned Churches.
Lowell, A. Meeting-House Hill.
Mahapatra, J. Taste for Tomorrow.
Marcinkeviius. Landscape With Apparition.
McCarthy, T. Dying Synagogue at South
Terrace, The.
McKay, C. St. Isaac's Church, Petrograd.
McKinney, I. Sunday Morning, 1950.
Melville, H. In a Church of Padua.
Morgan, R. Bellrope.
Mori Ōgai. Tanka: "It will not be heard."
Morrison, M. What the Choir Sang about the
New Bonnet.
Mullen, H. Dance She Does, The.
Norris, K. Mrs. Schneider in Church.
Olds, S. Wedding Vow, The.
Orlovsky. Dream May 18, 1958.
Palazzeschi. Nuns Go Walking.
Paulus Silentiarius. Description of Hagia
Sophia.
Pessoa. &[;Poem 2&];: "Inside, the church
lights up today's rain."
Philipott. To Sir Henry Newton, upon His Re-
edifying the Church of Charleton in Kent.
Po Chü-i. Temple of Bequeathed Love, The.
Porter, P. Angel in Blythburgh Church, An.
Roberts, E. Mr. Wells.
Roseliep. Sistine Chapel.
Seward. Eyam.
Shiffert. Manners.
Simic. Winter Night.
Sisson. Knole.
Spires. Comb and the Mirror, The.
Stevens, W. Gray Stones and Gray Pigeons.
Swift, J. On His Own Deafness.
Synge. Dread.
Taylor, J. Squire's Pew, The.
Taylor, J. Gods *Houses*, almost like *Troyes
Ilion*,.
Thomas, R. In a Country Church.
Thompson, C. Opening Service, An.
Tolson. Lena Lovelace.
Tomlinson, C. Las Trampas U. S. A.
Tranströmer. Scattered Congregation, The.
Travis, N. Church Ladies.
Unknown. Bells of London, The.
It Isn't the Church—It's You.
Ladies' Aid, The.
Last Mass in Hagia Sophia, The.
Little More Cider, A.
Oranges and lemons, say the bells of St.
Clement's.
Preston.
Virgilio. In the empty church.
Waller, E. Upon his Majesties repairing of
Pauls.
Warner, S. Building in Stone.
Country Thought.
Watts, I. Church the Garden of Christ, The.
For the Lord's Day Evening.
Weigl. Temple Near Quang Tri, Not on the
Map.
Whitman, A. Dark rose the walls, a church
and prison joined.

Whitman, W. March in the ranks hard-prest,
and the road unknown, A.
Wilbur. Plain Song for Comadre, A.
Wilson, K. Old Women beside a Church.
Wordsworth, W. Inscription for a Monument
in Crossthwaite Curch, in the Vale of
Keswick.
Inside of King's College Chapel, Cambridge.
Wright, J. Wednesday Night Prayer Meeting.
Zagajewski. Auto Mirror.
Churchill, Winston Leonard Spencer
Stafford, W. Woman at Banff, The.
Churchyards
Collins, W. Ode on the Poetical Character.
"Fane." In an Irish Churchyard.
Gutteridge. Man into a Churchyard.
Mahon. In Carrowdore Churchyard.
McKinney, I. Visiting My Gravesite: Talbott
Churchyard, West Virginia.
Cibber, Colley
Pope, A. Cibber! write all thy verses upon
glasses.
Quoth Cibber to Pope, tho' in verse you
foreclose.
Cicadas
Chao Meng-fu. Song of an Autumn Night.
Chia Tao. Sick cicada, unable now to fly, A.
Eady. Dance, The.
Ho Ching-ming. Night of the Fourteenth.
Li Shang-yin. Cicada.
Masaoka Shiki. On the eve of death.
Naito Joso. Autumn cicada, The.
Ono no Komachi. Cicadas sing, The.
Ou-yang Hsiu. Cicada, The.
Stoutenburg. Cicada.
Tekkan. Tanka: "It cries and cries."
Unknown. Cicada sings, The.
Wilbur. Cicadas.
Xue Tao. Cicadas.
Yü Chi. Following the Rhymes of Autumn
Night Song by Meng Tzu-chou, Signatory
Official of the Board of Rites.
Yukitsuna. Tanka: "Youngster, A."
Cigarettes
Cope, W. Giving Up Smoking.
Ehrhart. One That Died, The.
Mobilio. Step Seven.
Nobuyuki. Ashtray (two poems).
Popa. In the Ashtray.
Rankin, P. To the House Ghost.
Rodgers, C. Group Therapy.
Shaw, A. Crepuscule.
Unknown. Cigarettes will spoil yer life.
Warsh. Precious Mettle.
Yevtushenko. Hand-Rolled Cigarettes.
See also **Smoking and Smokers**
Cigars
Low, S. To a Segar.
Stevens, W. Emperor of Ice-Cream, The.
Stumbrs. Cigars.
Cinderella
Jarrell. Cinderella.
Sexton. Cinderella.
Circe
De Tabley. Circe.
Doolittle, H. Circe.
Gibson, W. Circe.
Gunn, T. Moly.
Homer. Circe.
MacNeice. Circe.
Webster, A. Circe.
Circumcision
Herrick. To His Savior [or Saviour]. The New
Years [or yeers] Gift.
Lowell, R. New Year's Day.
Milton. Upon the Circumcision.
Okigbo. Elegy of the Wind.
Wadding. On the Circumsision: New Year's
Day.
Circus
Amann. Circus tent, The.
Bishop, E. Cirque d'Hiver.
Cable, G. Song of Cayetano's Circus, The.
Caraion. Bits of Silk.
By the Light of the Branches Outside.
Carruth, H. Wreck of the Circus Train, The.

Dickinson, E. I've known a Heaven, like a Tent.
Dove, R. Hill of Beans, A.
Ferlinghetti, L. Constantly risking absurdity.
Jordan, J. What happens when the dog sits on a tiger.
Larkin, P. For Sidney Bechet.
Lawrence, D. When I went to the circus that had pitched on the waste lot.
Lax. Morning Stars, The.
McOrlan. Modern circus, The.
Mezhirov. Ballad about the Circus.
Padgett, R. First Drift.
Pagis. Acrobatics.
Prelutsky. Man on the Flying Trapeze, The.
Pyle. Circus Parade, The.
Shapcott, T. Litanies of Julia Pastrana (1832-1860), The.
Williams, W. Artist, The.
Zabolotsky. Circus shines, like a shield, The.

Cities

Ammons. City Limits, The.
Arnold, M. In Utrumque Paratus.
Ashbery. Rain.
　Rivers and Mountains.
　These Lacustrine Cities.
Auden. Paysage Moralisé.
Bancquart. Town.
Baraka. Poem for Democrats, A.
Bateman, E. Cockney's Garden, The.
Bernstein, C. Matters of Policy.
Bierce. Passing Show, The.
Bishop, E. One Art.
Blackburn, P. Assistance, The.
Borisov. Untitled.
Braithwaite. City Garden, A.
Brooke, R. Song of the Beasts (Sung, on one night, in the cities, in the darkness), The.
Brousek. Walls shriek, The.
Browning, R. Up at a Villa—Down in the City.
Bruner. On City Streets.
　There is a loneliness on city streets.
Brutus. Nightsong: City.
Campana. Genoa.
Cavafy. City, The.
Cavalli. And to see the city again and to see it again.
Cawein. Dead Cities.
Césaire, A. This flat city shortly after dawn.
Chang Yü. Staying Overnight at T'ien-ning Ch'an Temple.
Clarke, C. 14th Street was gutted in 1968.
Clifton, H. Eccles Street, Bloomsday, 1982.
　Euclid Avenue.
Clifton, L. In the Inner City.
Clough. Sic Itur.
Coleridge, M. Day-dream, A.
Cowley, A. Wish, The.
Crane, H. To Brooklyn Bridge.
Crawford, R. Love Song of Tommo Frogley.
Creeley. City, The.
Crow, C. City Park.
Cruz, V. Urban Dream.
Cumbo. Nocturnal Sounds.
Cummings, E. Twentyseven bums give a prostitute the once.
　What a proud dreamhorse pulling(smoothloomingly)through.
Czechowski. Walk Through the City.
Daniels, J. Day of the Two Bodies.
Davies, A. Thirty East Forty-Second Street.
Dewdney. She is liquid darkness occult with desire.
Dharwadker. New Delhi, 1974.
"Dhoomil." City, Evening, and an Old Man: Me, The.
Di Prima. Montezuma.
Disch. Crumbling Infrastructure, The.
Donne. To Sir Henry Wotton ("Sir, more than kisses, letters mingle souls").
Doolittle, H. It is no madness to say.
Douglas, L. Impression de Nuit; London.
Dransfield. Day at a Time.
Drummond de Andrade. Motionless Faces.
Drummond, W. Content and Resolute.
Ehrmann. Away.

Eliot, T. *Boston Evening Transcript*, The.
　Morning at the Window.
　Preludes.
　Rhapsody on a Windy Night.
Euripides. Blessed are they.
Fields, J. Citizen.
Fishback. Complacent Cliff-Dweller, The.
Follain. Buying.
Forché. City Walk-up, Winter 1969.
František. When the great wind blew the streetlights out.
Gangopadhyay. Calcutta and I.
Gilbo'a. Gazelle I send you to the wolves not in the wood they're.
Ginsberg, A. Describe: The Rain on Dasaswamedh Ghat.
　II.
　My Sad Self.
Godfrey. What It Takes.
　What Say.
González, A. City.
Gouri. In the Amorite city spared for my sake from the sword of Joshua.
　Mistake.
　Northern Romance.
Greenwald, T. Coordinating cities gulls still gull, and, arms binged with wine, as wine.
Guest, B. Bleat.
Guha. Winding Sand.
Guilpin. What more variety of pleasures can.
Gunn, T. Map of the City, A.
Harwood, G. Nightfall.
Hearne, B. Commuters.
Hecht, A. Third Avenue in Sunlight.
Heinze. Storm.
Herbert, Z. Naked Town, A.
　Report from the Besieged City.
Herlin. Gull inch-perfect over water, the busy crane, The.
Hollander, J. Lion Named Passion, A.
Holman, F. City Dump, The.
Hsieh T'iao. Song of the Men of Chin-ling.
Hubbell, P. Streetcleaner's Lament, The.
Hughes, L. City.
Huidobro. Express.
Hull, L. Combat Zone/War Stories.
　Love Song During Riot with Many Voices.
Irby. January 1965, Looking on.
Iverem. Earth Screaming.
Jordan, J. Speculations on the Present through the Prism of the Past.
Jussawalla. Sea Breeze, Bombay.
Kaplinski, J. My wife and children were waiting for ice cream.
Kaufman, B. Battle Report.
Kefala. Industrial City.
Kim, K. Dove in Songbukdong, The.
Kitahara Hakushū. Tanka: "Today too."
Kooser. City Limits.
Kovner. Between mountains coils a city.
　Wind.
　Far, Far a City Lies.
Kraujiete. City Girls.
Krohn. Can Tho, *favela* of crowing cocks.
Lane, P. Wind Thoughts.
Lang, A. Tired of Towns.
Lawson, H. Faces in the Street.
Lea, S. Prayer for the Little City.
Lee, L. City in Which I Love You, The.
Lehman. Towards the Vanishing Point.
Lenski, L. Sing a Song of People.
Lerman. Evenings in the Sea.
Levertov. World Outside, The.
Levin, P. Citizens and Sky.
Levy, A. London Plane-Tree, A.
Li K'ai-hsien. Parable, A.
Lihn. Cemetery in Punta Arenas.
Lodge, G. Lower New York.
Logan, J. Trip to Four or Five Towns, A.
Logan, M. Verses on Hearing That an Airy and Pleasant Situation, near a Populous and Commercial Town, Was Surrounded with New Buildings.
Lowell, J. Street, The.
Lowry, M. Christ Walks in This Infernal District Too.

MacNeice. Birmingham.
　Morning Sun.
Mangan, G. Glasgow 1956.
Martial. To Sextus.
Masaoka Shiki. Shitting in the winter turnip field.
Matthews, W. People Like Us.
Maunick. Further off is the measured force the word of the sea.
　I love to encounter you in strange cities.
Mazzocco. Muertes.
McGrath, J. Song.
McKay, C. White City, The.
Meléndez. Oye Mundo/Sometimes.
Merriam, E. Sing a Song of Subways.
Mew. I Have Been Through the Gates.
　Not for that city of the level sun.
Miliauskaite. Temporary City.
Milosz, C. After Paradise.
　Temptation.
Morgan, E. Glasgow Sonnets.
　Starlings in George Square, The.
Mori Ōgai. Tanka: "Insane thought, An."
Morton, W. Dafney's Lamentation.
Moss, H. Roof Garden, The.
Mueller, L. Commuter.
Nagy, A. Four-Light Window, A.
Nash, O. Theatre Hour.
Nekrasova. Street perturbs my mind somehow, The.
Neruda. Ode to the Watermelon.
Noguere. Whirling Round the Sun.
Noyes, A. Barrel-Organ, The.
Nyka-Niliunas. Winter Landscape.
Oldham, J. London.
O'Loughlin. Posthumous.
Olsen, W. Tomorrow.
Oppen. Impossible Poem, The.
　Moving over the hills, crossing the irrigation.
　Power, The Enchanted World.
O'Shaughnessy, A. Ode: "We are the music-makers."
Osherow. Late Night Tête-à-Tête with a Moon in Transit.
Pagis. Logbook.
　Souvenir, The.
Pao Chao. Rhyme-Prose on the Desolate City.
Parra, N. Vices of the Modern World.
Paz. I Speak of the City.
Piercy. Learning Experience.
Plumpp. Another mule kicking.
Po Chü-i. Hermit and Politician.
Poe. City in the Sea, The.
Pope, A. Epistle to Miss [*or* Miss Teresa] Blount, on Her Leaving the Town after the Coronation.
Purdy, A. Blue City, The.
Redmond. Definition of Nature.
Rilke. For, Lord, the Crowded Cities Be.
Roditi. Hand.
Rosenberg, L. City Baseball.
Sandburg, C. Blue Island Intersection.
　Chicago.
　Fog comes / on little cat feet, The.
　Osawatomie.
　People Who Must.
　Prayers of Steel.
　Skyscraper.
Sanders, T. Transit Authority.
Scalapino. Considering How Exaggerated Music Is.
Scott, T. Mankind Toun, The.
Seferis. Word for Summer, A.
Seibles. Trying for Fire.
Sexton. Mr. Mine.
Shapcott, T. City of Home is reached only in dreams, The.
Sheck. Return, The.
Sheikh. Jaisalmer, 1.
Shoaf. Birmingham, 1962.
Shwarts. What that street is called—you can read it on the sign.
Simic. Marvels of the City, The.
Simko. Arrival, The.
Simpson, L. There Is.
Singh, S. On the Slope of this Hill.
Sitwell, D. Trams.

Smith, M.   Asleep in the City.
 Visit to the Village, A.
Snyder, G.   Cartagena.
Sobin, G.   Violet City: Aspects of the
 Transitive.
Steele, F.   Greener Grass.
Stevenson, R.   Block City.
Sulpicia.   Drat my hateful birthday.
Swenson, M.   Garden at St. John's, The.
Swift, J.   Description of a City Shower, A.
 Description of the Morning, A.
T'ang Hsien-tsu.   Evening View from the Bell
 Tower at P'ing-ch'ang.
Tate, J.   What the City Was Like.
Taylor, A.   Fitzroy.
Tennyson, A.   City Child, The.
 Suburban Garden.
Thanh Quan.   Remembering the Past in the
 City of the Soaring Dragon.
Thomas, D.   Countryman's Return, The.
Thomas, R.   Rhodri Theophilus Owen.
Thompson, I.   Rainy Nights.
Thomson, J.   City is of Night, The; perchance
 of Death.
Thurman.   Zebra.
Tóth, J.   Two Cities.
Turner, A.   Clean.
 Red Flower.
Unknown.   Green green the cypress on the
 ridge.
Vaiiunaite.   Museum Street.
Van Vliet.   City is covered with places you,
 The.
Venclova.   In Memory of the Poet. Variant.
Wakoski.   Walking Past Paul Blackburn's Apt.
 on 7th St.
Walker, K.   My Talk with an Elegant Man.
Wang Chien.   South, The.
Wang Shih-chieng.   Bamboo Branch Song of
 Han-chia.
Weiners.   With Meaning.
Weston, M.   Primitive Place.
Wharton, E.   Two Backgrounds.
Whitman, W.   Once I pass'd through a
 populous city imprinting my brain.
 Song of Myself.
 Sparkles from the Wheel.
Whittemore, R.   Departure, The.
Wilbur.   After the last bulletins the windows
 darken.
 Shame.
Williams, W.   Approach to a City.
 Predicter of Famine, The.
Wordsworth, W.   Composed upon Westminster
 Bridge[, September 3, 1802].
Wright, K.   City Rain.
Yang Shih-ch'i.   Sha-ch'eng, "Sand City"
 ("Overlooking the water, a desolate city").
Yang Wei-chen.   Residence of the Emperors of
 Ch'en, The.
Yeats.   Coole Park, 1929.
Yolen.   Sky scrape, / City scape.
Yoshimi.   Tanka: "Streetcar, A."
Zach.   Nameless.
Zagajewski.   At Daybreak.
 On the Escalator.
Zanzotto.   How long between the grain and the
 wind.
Zepeda, O.   People on Wayward Journeys.
Zhenkai.   Discovery.
See also **Towns; Villages**
Citizenship
Ashbery.   One Thing That Can Save America,
 The.
McDonald, D.   Citizen of—the World, A.
Civil Defense
Burke, K.   Civil Defense.
Civil Rights Movement. *See* **Protest, Social**
Civil War, Nigeria
 Unknown.   Song of the Freedman.
Civil War, Spain
Auden.   Spain 1937.
Campbell, R.   Toledo.
Cornford, J.   Full Moon at Tierz; before the
 Storming of Huesca.
 Letter from Aragon, A.
Éluard, P.   November 1936.

García Lorca.   Quarrel, The.
Hernández, M.   July 18, 1936–July 18, 1938.
Hughes, L.   Madrid—1937.
Livesay, D.   Spain.
"MacDiarmid."   Spanish War, The.
MacDonagh, D.   Of what a quality is courage
 made.
Machado Ruiz.   Today's Meditation.
MacNeice.   And I remember Spain.
Orwell.   Italian soldier shook my hand, The.
Simonov.   By the Campfire.
Spender, S.   Port Bou.
 Two Armies.
See also **Spain**
Civil War, United States
Aldrich, T.   By the Potomac.
Bacheller.   Whisperin' Bill.
Ball, C.   Jacket of Gray, The.
Beers, E.   All quiet along the Potomac tonight.
Bell, J.   Though Tennyson,the poet king.
Bierce.   Confederate Flags, The.
 Death of Grant, The.
 Hesitating Veteran, The.
 To E. S. Salomon.
Bishop, E.   From Trollope's Journal.
Breckenridge.   General John Cabell
 Breckinridge.
Bristol.   Crime of the Ages, The.
Bryant, W.   Death of Slavery, The.
 Not Yet.
Carryl, G.   When the Great Gray Ships Come
 In.
Davidson, D.   Lee in the Mountains.
 Sequel of Appomattox.
Dickey, J.   Hunting Civil War Relics at
 Nimblewill Creek.
Dugan, A.   Fabrication of Ancestors.
Dunbar, P.   Colored Soldiers, The.
 Robert Gould Shaw.
 Unsung Heroes, The.
 When Dey 'Listed Colored Soldiers.
Emerson, R.   Boston Hymn.
Emmett.   Dixie [*or* Dixie's Land].
Finch, F.   Blue and the Gray, The.
Foss, S.   House by the Side of the Road, The.
Frost, R.   Black Cottage, The.
Gilmore, P.   When Johnny comes marching
 home again.
Harte, B.   John Burns of Gettysburg.
 Second Review of the Grand Army, A.
Hayden, R.   Dream, The.
Horgan.   Tintype of a Private in the Fifteenth
 Georgia Infantry.
Horton, G.   General Grant—the Hero of the
 War.
Howe, J.   Battle Hymn [*or* Battle-Hymn] of
 the Republic, The.
 Robert E. Lee.
Hudgins.   After the Wilderness.
 Around the campfire we sang hymns.
 Burial Detail.
 Serenades in Virginia.
 Soldier on the Marsh, A.
Irving, M.   Marching Still.
Jarrell.   Description of Some Confederate
 Soldiers, A.
Jordan, J.   Grand Army Plaza.
Kenyon, J.   Gettysburg, July 1, 1863.
Lanier, S.   Dying Words of Stonewall Jackson,
 The.
Larcom.   Volunteer's Thanksgiving, The.
Lazarus, E.   South, The.
Longfellow, H.   Building of the Ship, The.
 Cumberland, The.
 Killed at the Ford.
Lowell, J.   Memoriae Positum R. G. Shaw.
Lowell, R.   For the Union Dead.
Masters, E.   Battle of Gettysburg, The.
 Veterans of the Wars.
Melville, H.   Apparition, The.
 Ball's Bluff.
 Battle Summers, The.
 College Colonel, The.
 Dirge for McPherson, A.
 House-Top, The.
 Malvern Hill.
 March into Virginia, The.

Memorial on the Slain at Chickamauga.
 Portent, The.
 Requiem[:] for Soldiers Lost in Ocean
 Transports, A.
 Sheridan at Cedar Creek.
 Shiloh [A Requiem].
 Stonewall Jackson.
 Swamp Angel, The.
 Uninscribed Monument on One of the
 Battlefields of the Wilderness, An.
 Utilitarian View of the Monitor's Fight, A.
Meredith, W.   Farragut, Farragut / Old Heart
 of Oak.
Milnes.   England and America, 1863.
Olson, C.   Anecdotes of the Late War.
Osgood, K.   Driving Home the Cows.
Palmer, J.   Stonewall Jackson's Way.
Randall, D.   Memorial Wreath.
Randall, J.   My Maryland.
Randolph, I.   Rebel, The.
Ray, H.   Robert G. Shaw.
Read, T.   Sheridan's Ride.
Reed, I.   Chattanooga.
Rhodenbaugh.   Civil War, The.
Rich, A.   Charleston in the Eighteen-Sixties.
Robinson, G.   I Fights Mit Sigel!
Root, G.   Battle Cry [*or* Battle-Cry] of
 Freedom, The.
Ryan, A.   Lines: "Gather the sacred dust."
 Sword of Robert Lee, The.
Sawyer, C.   When This Cruel War Is Over.
Sherwood, K.   Albert Sidney Johnston.
Tate, A.   Battle of Murfreesboro.
 Ode to the Confederate Dead.
Taylor, E.   Few Days in the South in February,
 A.
 This Year's Drive to Appomattox.
Thompson, J.   Lee to the Rear.
 Obsequies of Stuart.
Thompson, J.   Burial of Latané, The.
 Music in Camp.
Thompson, M.   Address by an Ex-Confederate
 Soldier to the Grand Army of the Republic,
 An.
 To the South.
Ticknor.   Little Giffen.
Timrod.   Carolina.
 Charleston.
 Christmas.
 Cotton Boll, The.
 Ethnogenesis.
 Ode: "Sleep sweetly in your humble graves."
Unknown.   Brother Green.
 Confederate Memorial Day.
 Dan Ellis's Boys.
 Enlisted Today.
 Fare You Well, My Darling.
 Goin' 'cross the Mountain.
 Hospital Duties.
 Negro Soldier's Civil War Chant.
 Red, White and Red, The.
Updike.   Richmond.
Wallis, S.   Prayer for Peace, A.
Warren, R.   History among the Rocks.
Whitman, W.   Army Corps on the March, An.
 Artilleryman's Vision, The.
 As I lay with my head in your lap camerado.
 As toilsome I wander'd Virginia's woods.
 Beat! beat! drums!—blow! bugles! blow!
 Bivouac on a Mountain Side.
 By the bivouac's fitful flame.
 Cavalry Crossing a Ford.
 Come up from the fields father, here's a letter
 from our Pete.
 Dirge for Two Veterans.
 Give me the splendid silent sun with all his
 beams full-dazzling.
 March in the ranks hard-prest, and the road
 unknown, A.
 Reconciliation.
 Sight in camp in the daybreak gray and dim,
 A.
 Spirit whose work is done—spirit of dreadful
 hours!
 To a Certain Civilian.
 Vigil strange I kept on the field one night;.
 Wound-Dresser, The.

Whittier. Barbara Frietchie.
Battle Autumn of 1862, The.
Furnace Blast, The.
Laus Deo!
Lost Occasion, The.
What the Birds Said.
Word for the Hour, A.
Williams, E. At Harper's Ferry Just before the Attack.
Woolson. Kentucky Belle.
Work. Marching through Georgia.

Civil Wars, England
Cowley, A. Powers of Darkness.
Daniel, S. It was upon the twilight of that day.
Herrick. Bad Season Makes the Poet Sad, The.
Upon the Troublesome Times.
Milton. On the Lord Gen[eral] Fairfax at the Siege of Colchester.
On the New Forcers of Conscience Under the Long Parliament.
To the Lord General[l] Cromwell[, on the Proposals of Certain Ministers at the Committee for the Propagation of the Gospel or May 1652].
When the Assault Was Intended to the City.
Parker, M. King Enjoys His Own Again, The.
Unknown. Parliament Soldiers, The.

Civilization
Anderson, J. Invention of New Jersey, The.
Belloc. Four things in any land must dwell.
Bible, Apocrypha. Steel Usurps the Forests; Silence Dethrones Dialogue.
Brooks, G. First fight. Then fiddle. Ply the slipping string.
Campbell, D. Anguish of Ants, The.
Cavafy. Waiting for the Barbarians.
Char. Disdained Apparitions.
Dransfield. Day at a Time.
That Which We Call a Rose.
Durcan. Wife Who Smashed Television Gets Jail.
Emerson, R. Water understands / Civilization well, The.
World-Soul, The.
"Ern Malley." Dürer: Innsbruck, 1495.
Ford, C. There's No Place to Sleep in This Bed, Tanguy.
Freneau. On the Civilization of the Western Aboriginal Country.
Hall, D. New Hampshire.
Hall, R. Text for These Distracted Times, A.
Halliday, M. Population.
Harris, W. We Live in a Cage.
Hope, A. Australia.
Under Sedation.
Hughes, L. Letter to the Academy.
Iverem. Earth Screaming.
Jeffers, R. New Mexican Mountain.
Still the mind smiles at its own rebellions.
Johnson, F. Tired.
Johnstone, R. Eden Says No.
Not from our dreams, not from our daft cadres.
Kipling, R. For all we have and are.
White Man's Burden, The.
Mew. Domus Caedet Arborem.
Miller, E. Tomorrow.
Neruda. Walking [or Walkin'] Around.
"Nirala." Betrayal, The.
Oodgeroo of the tribe Noonuccal. No more boomerang.
Radnóti. Seventh Eclogue.
Raine, C. Martian Sends a Postcard Home, A.
Rakosi. Journey Away, A.
Revell. Survey.
Roughton. Building Society Blues.
Sepamla. Civilization Aha.
Shange. Ancestral Messengers/Composition 13.
Shelton, R. Sonora for Sale.
Simpson, L. Riders Held Back, The.
Stafford, W. At Cove on the Crooked River ("At Cove at our camp in the open canyon").
Stephen, J. On a Rhine Steamer.
Stern, G. Morning Harvest.
There Is Wind, There Are Matches.

Stevens, W. Anecdote of the Jar.
Unknown. Money, money, now hay goode day!
Warren, R. Dream, Dump-Heap, and Civilization.
Yeats. Long-Legged Fly.
Meru.

Clairvoyance and Clairvoyants
Weiner, H. How can I describe anything when all these interruptions keep *arriving* and then.

Clams and Clamming
Armour. Covering the Subject.
Ishigaki. Clams.
Tennyson, A. Minnie and Winnie.
Twichell. Six Belons.
Whittemore, R. Clamming.
See also **Oysters; Shells**

Clans
Aytoun, W. Massacre of the Macpherson, The.
MacLean, S. Clan MacLean, The.
See also **Culloden, Battle of**

Clarke, Austin
Weber, R. Visit to Bridge House, A.

Class. *See* **Social Class**

Classicism
Hardy, T. Liddell and Scott.
Jonson, B. Fit of Rhyme [*or* Rime] against Rhyme [*or* Rime], A.
Pinkney, E. Italy.
Poe. To Helen ("Helen, thy beauty is to me").
Sandburg, C. Child of the Romans.
Southern Pacific.
Smith, I. Oban 1955–82.
Tate, A. Aeneas at Washington.
Mediterranean, The.
Wilde, R. Saint Augustine, thy praise was sung by one.

Claustrophobia
O Riordain. Claustrophobia.

Cleanliness
Alvarez, J. How I Learned to Sweep.
Burgess, F. Table Manners.
Table Manners II.
Dove, R. Great Palaces of Versailles, The.
Giles, B. Mrs. Lorris, Who Died of Being Clean.
Henderson-Holmes. Goodhousekeeping #17.
Housman, A. Oh, when I was in love with you.
Hubbell, P. Streetcleaner's Lament, The.
Locke, A. So foul is sin and loathsome in thy sight.
Machi. Tanka: "Trying to wash away."
Monsour. Sweeping.
Reed, H. Naming Of Parts.
Samio. Tanka: "If only."
Silverstein, S. Dirtiest Man in the World, The.
Szymborska. End and the Beginning, The.
Thompson, D. Wish.
Tolson. Old Houses.
Turner, A. Clean.
Unknown. In Praise of the Broom.
Wilbur. Plain Song for Comadre, A.

Clemens, Samuel Langhorne. *See* **"Twain, Mark"**

Cleopatra
Aiken, C. Dead Cleopatra lies in a crystal casket.
Collier, T. Cleopatra Dying.
Heredia. Antony and Cleopatra.
Horace. Nunc est bibendum, Cleopatra's Death.
Hughes, T. Cleopatra to the Asp.
Lytle, W. Antony and Cleopatra.
Pascal. Tact.
Rossetti, C. Study AA Soul), A.
Shakespeare, W. Death of Cleopatra.
Welcome from Egypt, sir.
Simpson, L. Early in the Morning.
Story, W. Cleopatra.

Clergy
Arnold, M. "In harmony with Nature?" Restless fool.
Barham. Jackdaw of Rheims, The.
Boldman. Priest, The.

Bowering, G. Grandfather.
Browning, R. Bishop Orders His Tomb at Saint Praxed's Church, The.
Soliloquy of the Spanish Cloister.
Burns, R. Kirk's Alarm, The.
Burroughs, W. My Legs Señor.
Chaucer. Good Parson, The.
Clarke, A. Irish-American Dignitary.
Cook, E. Idiot-Born, The.
Corbet. On Mr. Rice the Manciple of Christ Church in Oxford.
Crabbe. Vicar, The.
Crashaw. Upon Bishop Andrewes's [*or* Andrewes His] Picture before His Sermons.
Daumal. Jesus before Pilate said nothing.
Doane, W. Preacher's Mistake, The.
Doinas, S. Pythia.
Donne. To Mr. Tilman after He Had Taken Orders.
Dryden, J. Character of a Good Parson, The.
Elliot, E. Poet vs. Parson.
Fletcher, J. Let the bells ring, and let the boys sing.
Gilbert, S. Rival Curates, The.
Graham, H. Breakfast.
Hardy, T. In Church.
Herbert, G. Aaron.
Collar, The.
Priesthood, The.
Windows, The.
Ho Xuan Huong. Buddhist Priest, A.
Hopkins, G. Habit of Perfection, The.
Hughes, L. Madam and the Minister.
Jarman, M. Questions for Ecclesiastes.
Kipling, R. Eddi's Service.
Knox, R. Anglican curate in want, An.
Moorer. Birthday Wishes to a Minister of the Gospel.
Norse. Believing in the Absurd.
Outram. On Hearing a Lady Praise a Certain Rev. Doctor's Eyes.
"Pindar." Susan, the constant slave to mop and broom.
Praed. Vicar, The.
Quarles. On Those That Deserve It.
Roseliep. Brushing my sins.
Sheridan, J. Priestin' of Father John, The.
To the New Ordained.
Stevens, W. Gray Stones and Gray Pigeons.
Strnisa. Priests, The.
Su Tung-p'o. Rhyming with Tzu-yu's "Treading the Green."
Swift, J. Thy curate's place, thy fruitful wife.
"T., J." Sea-Chaplain's Petition to the Lieutenants in the Ward-Room, for the Use of the Quarter-Gallery, A.
Taylor, H. Country Curate, The.
Thomas, R. Country Clergy, The.
Unknown. High Priest, The.
Jackdaw of Rheims, The.
Jolly Jankin.
On a Clergyman's Horse Biting Him.
Preacher's Vacation, The.
Vicar of Bray, The.
Wanted, a Minister's Wife.
Whittier. Clerical Oppressors.
Official Piety.
Yeats. Ballad of Father Gilligan, The.
See also **Rabbis**

Clerks
Buck, B. Song from a Two-Desk Office.
Davidson, J. Thirty Bob a Week.
Hamill, G. Song of the GPO, A.
Robinson, E. Clerks, The.
Roethke. Dolor.
Swan, J. Report, The.
See also **Office Workers**

Cleveland, Ohio
Atkins. Lakefront, Cleveland.
On the Fine Arts Garden, Cleveland.
Turco. Ordinary Evening in Cleveland, An.

Clichés
Grigson. On a Lover of Books.
Guiterman. Everything in Its Place.
Silveira. Different Poem, A.

Cliffs
Bridges, R. Cliff-Top, The.

Chong, C. Summit, The.
Coleridge, S. Blest is the tarn which towering cliffs o'ershade.
Hardy, T. Beeny Cliff.
Hollander, J. Garden, The.
Hooper, V. Seven Doors Away.
Millay, E. Ragged Island.
Shakespeare, W. Dover, the Samphire Cliff.
Tai Piao-yüan. Cheng-tao Temple.
Tao-chi. Inscribed on My Large Landscape Hanging Scroll "Listening to a Waterfall."
Tennyson, A. Blow, Bugle, Blow.
Tsung Ch'en. Drinking at the Cave Mouth.
Wratislaw. Satiety.
Yang Shih-ch'i. Beyond the temple, a hidden cliff.
Yün Shou-p'ing. Brush in rocks, draw a stream.
  Early Summer in the Year Jen-tzu (1672)—Playfully Painted in the Manner of Ts'ao Yün-hsi.

Clive, Robert
Bentley, E. George III.
  Lord Clive.
Warner, S. Alarum, The.

Clocks
Amann. Quietly dozing.
Barnes, W. Wold clock's feäce is still in pleäce, The.
Bishop, E. Two Mornings and Two Evenings.
Dickinson, E. Clock stopped, A.
Fort, C. Town Clock Burning, The.
Ginsberg, L. Clocks.
Graves, R. Counting the Beats.
Hall, D. Alligator Bride, The.
Hawkshawe. Old Kitchen Clock, The.
Herbert, Z. Fathers of a Star, The.
Longfellow, H. Old Clock on the Stairs, The.
Lowell, R. Fall 1961.
Lucas, E. Mr. Coggs.
Mansfield, K. Meeting, The.
McMaster, R. Clockface.
Melo Neto. Knife All Blade, A.
Moore, M. Four Quartz Crystal Clocks.
Morgenstern. Korf's Clock.
Mother Goose. Clock, The.
Peacock, T. Sun-Dial, The.
"Peter." Speed Track, The.
Rich, A. Clock in the Square, A.
Thurman. Clockface.
Tomlinson, C. At Delft.
Virgilio. Town clock's face, The.
Warren, R. There's a grandfather's clock in the hall, watch it closely. The.
Wilbur. Bell Speech.
Work. Grandfather's Clock.
Worth, V. Clock.

See also **Watches**

Clonmacnoise, Ireland
Clarke, A. Pilgrimage.
O'Gillan. Dead at Clonmacnois [or Clonmacnoise], The.
Rolleston. Dead at Clonmacnois, The.
Unknown. End of Clonmacnois, The.

Clothing
Alvarez, J. Naming the Fabrics.
Ball, C. Jacket of Gray, The.
Barber, M. Written for My Son, and Spoken by Him at His First Putting on Breeches.
Boldman. Mist.
Brathwaite, E. Miss Own.
Brown, S. Sporting Beasley.
Burns, R. Wee Willie Gray, an' his leather wallet.
Burrell. Picture of a Fine Gentleman, The.
Butler, W. Nothing to Wear.
Chan Fang-sheng. Folk-Songs.
Cliff. History of Costume, A.
Codrescu. Grammar, A.
Conway, J. Clothes Make the Man.
Davies, S. Sacred muse that first[e] made love divine [or devine].
Dickinson, E. We outgrow love like other things.
Dixon, S. Verses Left on a Lady's Toilet.
Donahue, J. Opiate Phobia.

Dudley, M. Home late.
Eklund. Dressing My Daughter.
Enright, D. Why didn't we think of clothes before?
Feaver. Coat.
Feldman, I. Se Aprovechan.
Fergusson. Braid Claith.
Ferlinghetti, L. Underwear.
Flynn, F. Clothes on the Washing Line.
Ford-Smith. Lala: The Dressmaker.
Fraser, K. Dresses.
Fulton, A. Priming Is a Negligee, The.
Gallagher, T. Black Silk.
Gay, J. Song: "Think of dress in every light."
Goethe. Roman Elegy Ia.
Hacker, M. Part of a True Story.
Hadas, R. House Beside the Sea, The.
Hahn, K. Hula Skirt, 1959, The.
Hall, H. Late Sewing.
Hardy, T. Pink Frock, The.
  Thunderstorm in Town, A.
Harrod, L. Fitting Room.
Hendriks. Will the Real Me Please Stand Up?
Herrick. Art above Nature, to Julia.
  Clothes Do But Cheat and Cozen [or Cousen] Us.
  Delight in Disorder.
  Julia's Petticoat.
  Lily in a Crystal, The.
  Upon Electra.
  Upon Julia's Clothes.
  Upon Julia's Ribband.
Hoberman. Let's dress up in grown-up clothes.
Hoffenstein. You buy yourself a new suit of clothes.
Hsieh Hui-lien. Fulling Cloth for Clothes.
Hudgins. At Chancellorsville.
Hughes, L. When Sue Wears Red.
Ise Tayu. I thought the chrysanthemum bloomed in autumn.
Jackson, L. Only Daughter, The.
Jenyns. Now haste, my Muse, pursue thy destined way.
Johnson, M. Wintah Styles, De.
Jonson, B. Simplex Munditiis.
Kendrick, D. Alone for a Week.
Kowit. Notice.
Kunze, R. Meditation.
Lear, E. New Vestments, The.
Lee, D. Coat, The.
Lochhead, L. Neckties.
Lovelace, R. To a Lady with Child that Asked [or Ask'd] an Old Shirt.
Lovibond. To Miss Kitty Phillips.
Lowell, A. Artist, The.
Machi. Tanka: "As though to let loose."
Mahadevi. (On Her Decision to Stop Wearing Clothes).
Mandel, T. Prospect of Release.
McAuley, J. Cloak, The.
Meredith, G. This I may know: her dressing and undressing.
Mirabai. Love has stained my body.
Moss, H. Persistence of Song, The.
Mother Goose. Daffadowndilly.
Mountain, M. After your visit.
  End of the cold spell.
  Summer night clothes whirling in a dryer.
Nash, O. Requiem: "There was a young belle of old Natchez."
Neruda. Ode to My Socks.
Padgett, R. Tell Us, Josephine.
Patterson, R. Glory, Glory. . . .
Peacock, M. How I Had to Act.
Pinsky. Shirt.
Pizzarelli. Shade springs open, The.
Po Chü-i. Ease.
  Liao-ling[, sheer patterned silk—what is it like?].
Probyn. After.
  Before.
Randall, J. How shall we walk naked when.
Ravikovitch. Dress of Fire, A.
Redmond. Poetic Reflections Enroute To, and During, The Funeral and Burial of Henry Dumas, Poet.
Ristovic. Gingerbread Heart.

Ritsos. Underneath Oblivion.
Robinson, M. Modern Female Fashions.
  Modern Male Fashions.
Romero, N. New Suit, The.
Rossetti, C. Bread and milk for breakfast.
Rotella, A. Undressed.
Roth, H. Her black negligee.
Ryan, G. Cruising.
Sato. In your panties.
Shakespeare, W. Thy gown? Why, ay. Come, tailor, let us see't.
Shen Chou. Bamboo Villa, The.
Smith, W. Cats are not at all like people.
  Said Dorothy Hughes to Helen Hocking.
Snyder, G. No Shoes No Shirt No Service.
Södergran. On Foot I Had to Walk Through the Solar Systems.
Stevenson, R. Auntie's Skirts.
Stillman, M. Whiskers Meets Polly.
Strand. Man in the Tree, The.
Swede. Swinging on the hanger.
Swenson, M. Question.
Tucker, M. Lines to an Old Dress.
Unknown. Brian O'Linn.
  Come the oak before the ash.
  Hems gathered up, sash not yet tied.
  If I should cast off this tattered coat.
  Joshua Lane.
  Madrigal: "My Love in her attire doth show her wit."
Villanueva, A. Crazy Courage.
Walden. Wish for an Overcoat.
Waller, E. On a Girdle.
Weiss, T. Clothes Maketh the Man.
Wen Cheng-ming. Walking to the Temple of Precious Light.
Whitney, I. For Women shall you Taylors have.
Wilbur. Catch, The.
  Love Calls Us to the Things of This World.
Willmot. Humiliated again.
Wu of Han. Li Fu-Jên.
Yang Chi. Selling My Official Robe.
Yosano. Tanka: "Tell them."
Yüan Hung-tao. Woman's Room in Autumn, A.

See also **Jewelry**

Clouds
Aborigine Oral Tradition. Tongues of the lightning Snakes flicker and twist, one to the other, The.
Allard. Passing clouds only a stand of aspens is in light.
Apollinaire. Phantom of Clouds, A.
Aristophanes. Song of the Clouds.
Atkins. Dark Area.
Bogan, L. Train Tune.
Brooke, R. Clouds.
Castellanos. O cloud that wants to be the sky's arrow.
Cavalli. That white cloud in its contrast.
Chang Yü. Mountain Retreat of a Recluse, The.
Chao Meng-fu. Inscribed on the Painting "Spring Dawn at Peach Blossom Spring" by Scholar Shang Te-fu.
Ch'ien T'ao. Flood.
Ch'u Yüan. Lord among the Clouds, The.
Chu Yün-ming. Clouds are swept into the sunset—mdash;a sky beyond the sky.
Coleridge, M. Moment, A.
Cooley. Ararat.
Davies, W. Black Cloud, The.
  Moon and a Cloud, The.
Digby, J. Sooner or Later.
Disch. Clouds, The.
Dyer, J. Prospects.
Frost, R. Lost in Heaven.
Gorham. White Tiger Leaps, The.
Harter. Clouds.
Harwood, L. Final Painting, The.
  "Utopia" The.
  Words, The.
Herrick. Her Bed.
Ho Ching-ming. Ch'ang-an.
  Night of the Fourteenth.
Hsü Pen. Mountain Residence of Secretary

Cheng Ching-ssu, The.
To a Hermit in the Mountains.
Hsü Tsai-ssu. Tune: "Joy All Under
Heaven"—Sunset on the Western Hill.
Jensen, L. Cloud Parade, The.
Kao Ch'i. Going Out to the Country on a
Boat Trip, Sheltering from Rain Beneath a
Tree.
Levertov. Clouds as I see them, rising, The.
Levin, P. Citizens and Sky.
Levine, P. Clouds.
Li Ch'ing-chao. "Fisherman's Honor," The.
Li K'ai-hsien. Drunk, Climbing to the Peak of
Iron Tomb on Wei Mountain.
Li Meng-yang. Crossing the Frontier.
Seeing Off Commander In Chief Li to Yün-
chung.
Littlebird. For the Girls 'cause They Know.
Livingstone, D. On Clouds.
Lowell, A. Night Clouds.
Makidemewabe. Saw the Cloud Lynx.
Masaoka Shiki. Tanka: "Beyond the glass
door."
McClintock, M. Across the sands.
Overtaken.
Miyazawa Kenji. Tanka: "Emerging."
Tanka: "Scattered clouds."
Mo Shih-lung. Flower Shadows.
Morgan, E. King Billy.
Ni Tsan. Inscribed on a Painting.
Pastan. Last Train, The.
Pizzarelli. Driving.
Meteor.
Pope, A. Gulliver in Lilliput.
Radnóti. Clouded Sky.
Ray, H. Cloud Song.
Rossetti, C. Rainbow, The.
Rubadiri. African Thunderstorm, An.
Saitō Mokichi. Tanka: "Aspiration."
Sansom, C. Flotilla.
Sartarelli. That Land (3).
Shelley, P. Cloud, The.
Shen Chou. White clouds like a scarf enfold
the the mountain's waist.
Sitwell, D. Song: "We are the darkness in the
heat of the day."
Stevens, W. Sea Surface Full of Clouds.
Strand. Marriage, The.
Tai Piao-yüan. In the Year Chi-hai (1299),
While Returning by Way of Purple Fungus
Mountain at Springmouth, I Lamented for
Lecture Master Chin.
Tao-chi. Inscribed on "Drunk in the Autumn
Woods."
Riding a Boat on Wu-ling Stream.
Thomas, E. Clouds That Are So Light, The.
Thoreau. Mist.
Tico. Wisp of spring cloud, A.
Ts'ao Chih. Vision, A.
Tsung Ch'en. Song of Meeting.
Unknown. In the north-west there is a high
house.
Spyglass Conversations.
Van den Heuvel. In the parking lot.
Very. Clouded Morning, The.
Virgil. Morning bath.
Virgilio. Lone red-winged blackbird.
Wang Shih-chieng. Mooring at Night at the
River Mouth, I Heard a Flute—Sent to My
Elder Brother Hsi ch'iao.
Wang Yü-ch'eng. Random Thoughts Written
in Spring.
Warren, R. Timeless, Twinned.
Wen Cheng-ming. Floating clouds and worldly
affairs.
Where among the blue clouds.
Williams, W. Clouds, The.
Willmot. Page of Shelley, A.
Wordsworth, W. Daffodils.
Most alluring clouds that mount the sky, The.
Wratislaw. Palm Sunday.
Wright, F. Pawtucket Postcards.
Wu Chen. Ni Tsan Poem Following Rhyme-
Words of Wu Chen.
To the Tune "Chiu-ch'üan tzu."
Wu of Han. Autumn wind rises; white clouds
fly.

Wu Wei-yeh. Seeing Off Wang Yüan-chao—
Reprise.
Yang Chi. Nesting among Clouds.
Pitch-Ball.
Yüan Hung-tao. Eastern mountains/ and
western mountains.
Yüan Mei. Rains pass, the mountains' face is
washed.
Yün Shou-p'ing. Early Summer in the Year
Jen-tzu (1672)—Playfully Painted in the
Manner of Ts'ao Yün-hsi.
Inscribed on a Painting of Sailboats on the
River—Seeing Off Yen-chi on His Journey to
Ch'ang-an.
Painting in the Style of Secretary Kao, A.
Yuwaku. I think about you & it's like having
spirits come down on me.

Clough, Arthur Hugh
Arnold, M. To a Republican Friend, 1848.
Swinburne. On Arthur Hugh Clough.

"Clout, Colin." *See* **Spenser, Edmund**

Clover
Heine. Memory, A.

Clowns
Apollinaire. Phantom of Clouds, A.
Bruner. Clown, The.
Hall, D. Clown, The.
Prelutsky. Bring on the clowns!
Roseliep. Rain.
See also **Circus**

Clumsiness
Lowell, A. Bungler, The.
Nims, J. Love Poem: "My clumsiest dear,
whose hands shipwreck vases."

Coal Mining and Coal Miners
Armstrong, F. Collier Lass, The.
Bryant, W. Meditation on Rhode Island Coal,
A.
Collier, M. North Corridor.
Dalton, J. Agape the sooty collier stands.
Davies, I. High Summer on the Mountains.
Dorn, E. Los Mineros.
Geoghegan, J. Down in a Coal Mine.
Henry, J. Two hundred men and eighteen
killed.
Jenks, O. Dying Mine Brakeman, The.
Lawrence, D. Collier's Wife, The.
Lorde. Coal.
MacBeth. Miner's Helmet, The.
Morgan, A. Union Man.
Nicholson, N. Cleator Moor.
Owen, W. Miners.
Parini. Coal Train.
Pettit. Self-Portrait Approaching Promontory,
Utah.
Unknown. Avondale Mine Disaster, The.
Blue Monday.
Coal Diggin' Blues.
Coal Miner's Goodbye, A.
Miner's Doom, The.
My Sweetie's a Mule in the Mine.
Old Miner's Refrain, The.
That Little Lump of Coal.
Two-Cent Coal.
Untermeyer, L. Caliban in the Coal Mines.
Watkins, V. Collier, The.
Yü Ch'ien. Poem on Coal, A.

Cobblers. *See* **Shoes and Shoemakers**

Coca Cola
Hollander, R. You Too? Me Too—Why Not?
Soda Pop.
O'Hara, F. Having a Coke with You.
Unknown. There was a young lady from Lynn.

Cocaine
Harper, M. Elvin's Blues.
Selman, R. Ill-equipped bride-to-be, I left
home, An.
Unknown. Cocaine Lil [and Morphine Sue].

Cockaigne, Land of
Sissman. Cockaigne: A Dream.
Unknown. Land of Cokaygne, The.

Cockfighting. *See* **Roosters**

Cockroaches
Marquis. Song of Mehitabel, The.
McClintock, M. Hearing.

Padgett, R. *see also* Poema del City 2.
Raven. Roach / came struttin, A.
Rukeyser, M. St. Roach.
Stone, R. Whose Scene?
Wallace, R. Aubade: N.Y.C.

Cocks. *See* **Roosters**

Cocoa
La Fontaine. Saddled Ass, The.
Sharpless. In Praise of Cocoa, Cupid's
Nightcap.

Coconuts
Espada. Coca-Cola and Coco Frio.

Cody, William Frederick. *See* **"Buffalo Bill"**

Coercion
Flanders, M. Have Some Madeira, M'dear?
Kunitz, S. Approach to Thebes, The.

Coffee
Alegría. Documentary.
Coleman, W. Coffee.
Dudley, M. Menstrual cramps.
Hall, D. Je Suis une Table.
Hotham. Coffee.
McClure, M. May Morn.
Nordbrandt. China Observed Through Greek
Rain in Turkish Coffee.
O'Hara, F. Poem: "'Instant coffee with
slightly sour cream'."
Petri. Morning Coffee.
Saffoti. Espresso.
Tucker, M. Upon Receipt of a Pound of
Coffee in 1863.
Unknown. Little More Cider, A.
Walcott. Gulf, The.

Coffins
Ackland. Fanny Brawne's Letter Put
Unopened In Keats's Coffin.
"Adunis." Mirror for the Twentieth Century,
A.
Baugh, E. Carpenter's Complaint, The.
Celan. Night Ray.
Cendrars. Frisco-City.
Hernández, M. War.
Kovner. What's Not in the Heart.
Kunio. Tanka: "Casket on display, A."
Monsour. Emily's Words.
Roseliep. White orchid.
Ryuichi. Standing Coffin.
Terapiano. Lights shining above the Neva.
Virgilio. Flag-covered coffin.

Coins
Goedicke. Coin of the Realm.
Hill, G. Coins handsome as Nero's; of good
substance and.
Hughes, L. Fact.
Tomorrow may be.
Mahadevi. (On Her Decision to Stop Wearing
Clothes).
Nemerov. Money.

Cold
Apache Oral Tradition. Now you will feel no
rain.
Atwood. You Are Happy.
Bertolino. On a Line by John Ashbery.
Brutus. Clammy cement, The.
Bryant, W. November.
Burns, R. O [or Oh] wert thou in the cauld
blast.
Buson. Sound of a Rat, The.
Bynner. Wintry Mind, The.
Carew, T. Song: To Her Again[e], She
Burning in a Fe[a]ver.
To My Mistress [or Mistris], I Burning in
Love.
Ceravolo. Stolen Away.
Ch'en Shih-tao. Cold Night.
Christopher. 5°.
Congreve. See, see, she wakes, Sabina wakes!
Dickey, J. Ice Skin, The.
Dickinson, E. 'Twas warm—at first—like Us.
Ford, R. Twenty Below.
Francis, R. Cold and the colors of cold:
mineral, shell.
Frost, R. There Are Roughly Zones.
Gbadamosi. Death of the Polar Explorers.
Guest, B. Nebraska.
Haines, J. Into the Glacier.

Heath, R.　On the Unusual Cold and Rainy [or Rainie] Weather in the Summer, 1648.
Holtby, W.　Man who hated the spring was cold and narrow, The.
Hughes, T.　November.
Hulme, T.　Embankment (The Fantasia of a Fallen Gentleman on a Cold, Bitter Night), The.
Jones, P.　Christmas, Boston Nineteen Eighty Nine.
Kenney.　Aubade: "Cold snap. Five o'clock."
Li Ho.　Northern Cold, The.
Meng Chiao.　Face of the autumn moon freezes, The.
Moore, L.　Winter 1967.
Mountain, M.　Beneath / leaf mold.
  End of the cold spell.
Nash, O.　Samson Agonistes.
Pizzarelli.　Shade springs open, The.
Po Chü-i.　Bitter Cold, Living in the Village.
Roberts, D.　Cold.
Rossetti, C.　Chill, A.
  There's snow on the fields.
Salis.　Song.
Service.　Cremation of Sam McGee, The.
Simic.　Winter Night.
Snyder.　Late October Camping in the Sawtooths.
Sorescu.　Tear, The.
Spenser.　Sonnet 30: "My love is like to ice, and I to fire."
Thoreau.　Pray to What Earth Does This Sweet Cold Belong.
Tomlinson, C.　Tramontana at Lerici.
Ts'ao Ts'ao.　Song on Enduring the Cold.
Tso Ssu.　Scholar in the Narrow Street, The.
Tsurayuki.　When.
Tu Mu.　Pien River Blocked by Ice.
Unknown.　Cold! Cold! / Wide Lurg Plain is cold tonight.
  Old Fellow from Tyre, The.
  Young Charlottie or, The Frozen Girl.
Warner, S.　After he had gone the wind rose.
Williams, C.　Snow: II.
Yoshimi.　Tanka: "Ocean, The."

Colds (illness)
Adams, C.　To Bary Jade.
Roethke.　Ceiling, The.

Cole, Thomas
Bryant, W.　To Cole, the Painter, Departing for Europe.

Coleridge, Samuel Taylor
Allston.　Coleridge.
Barbauld.　To Mr. S. T. Coleridge.
Coleridge, H.　Dedicatory Sonnet to S. T. Colerige.
  Written on the Anniversary of Our Father's Death.
Coleridge, S.　Father! no amaranths e'er shall wreathe my brow.
De la Mare.　Bards, The.
Ewart.　Lines: "Other day I was loving a sweet little fruitpie-and-cream, The."
Fanthorpe.　Person's Tale, The.
Frost, R.　Most of It, The.
Robinson, M.　Mrs Robinson to the Poet Coleridge.
Shelley, P.　He was a might poet—and.
  You will see Coleridge, he who sits obscure.
Smith, S.　Thoughts about the Person from Porlock.
Thelwall.　Lines written at Bridgwater in Somersetshire, on 27 July 1797, during a Long Excursion in Quest of a Peaceful Retreat.
Thomas, R.　Coleridge.
  Person from Porlock, A.
Watts-Dunton.　Coleridge.

Colette (Sidonie Gabrielle Colette)
Garrigue.　Cortège for Colette.

Colleges and Universities
Bogin, G.　Nineteen.
Frost, R.　Lucretius versus the Lake Poets.
Heaney, S.　Mid-Term Break.
Herrick.　To His Kinsman, Master Thomas Herrick, Who Desired to Be in His Book.
Hill, L.　Tuskegee.

Jarrell.　Soldier Walks under the Trees of the University, The.
Kizer, C.　To a Visiting Poet in a College Dormitory.
Lochhead, L.　Mad Meg on my mantelpiece.
Moore, M.　Student, The.
Moorer.　Claflin's Alumni.
  Dedication Day Poem.
  What We Teach at Claflin.
Olds, S.　I Go Back to May 1937.
Plomer.　Walk in Würzburg, A.
Plumpp.　Clinton.
Shapiro, K.　University.
Spender, S.　One More New Botched Beginning.
Symons, J.　Harvard, Cambridge, Mass.
Travis, N.　At My Father's House.
Turner, W.　University Curriculum.
Unknown.　Miss Buss and Miss Beale.
Voznesensky.　Big Fire at the Architectural College, The.
Waniek.　Letter to a Benedictine Monk.
Wheatley, P.　To the University of Cambridge, in New-England.
Wilbur.　Finished Man, A.
Wilson, E.　Disloyal Lines to an Alumnus.
See also **Students**

Collies
MacCaig.　Praise of a Collie.

Cologne, Germany
Coleridge, S.　Cologne.
  On My Joyful Departure from the Same City.
Slutsky.　Pit of Cologne, The.

Colonialism
Ái Lan.　Deathless Autumn, A.
Bain, A.　Address.
Baxter, J.　New Zealand.
Collymore.　Triptych.
Corcoran.　Apparently in the real past tough men dazzled the illiterate tribes.
Creeley.　America, you ode for reality!
Daniel, S.　Theare be great Prince, such as will tell you howe.
Diop, D.　Vultures, The.
Ferdinand.　Whi / te boys gone.
Gardiner, A.　Natal Hunters, The.
Hải Âu Tử.　Zoo Cages.
Hemans.　England's Dead.
Huỳnh Phú Sổ.　Bread.
Kearns, L.　Environment.
  Foreign Aid.
Kipling, R.　White Man's Burden, The.
Laleau.　Betrayal.
Leonard, T.　Schooner The Mother of Parliaments has anchored in the bay, The.
Livingstone, D.　Sleep of My Lions, The.
Mapanje.　Baobab Fruit Picking; or, Development in Monkey Bay.
Margarido.　You Who Occupy Our Land.
Michael.　Preface: "I stood watching / I the parade of floats."
Mnthali.　Neocolonialism.
Mtshali.　Removal of Our Village, KwaBhanya, The.
Neruda.　United Fruit Co, The.
Nhu'ọ'ng Tổng.　Sense of History, A.
O'Connor, P.　Poems.
Phan Văn Hy.　Ricksha man does quite a simple job, The.
Plomer.　Fall of Rock, A.
Pringle.　Caffer Commando, The.
Reitz, F.　Proclamation, or Paper Bomb, The.
Ruggieri.　Forked Tongue.
Senghor.　Lord Jesus, at the end of this book which I offer you.
Simpson, J.　Old Liberia Is Not the Place for Me.
Tản Đà.　Rail and the Bullfrog, The.
Thiên Thế.　Wrecking the Statue of Paul Bert.
Trần Tế Xu'o'ng.　Drought.
Unknown.　Mbuyazi (Henry Francis Fynn).
Walcott.　Far Cry from Africa, A.
Zimunya.　White Poetess.
See also **British Empire; Imperialism**

Colorado (state)
Berrigan, T.　Certain Slant of Sunlight, A.
Saner.　Fifth Season, The.

Stafford, W.　Holding the Sky.

Colors
Bailey, A.　Green and the Black, The.
Brown, G.　Shroud.
Browne, W.　Happyer those times were, when the Flaxen clew.
Clark, T.　Each colour sits beside.
Crosby, H.　Vision.
de Jesús.　Flag of Chile, The.
Depero.　Colors.
Dickinson, E.　Yellow Man, Purple Man.
Diop, B.　Ball.
Djanikian.　Agami Beach.
Goodman, P.　I planned to have a border of lavender.
Guest, B.　River Road Studio.
Hughes, L.　Little Song.
Ishikawa Takuboku.　Tanka: "Color, The."
Jackson, L.　Grandpa dropped his glasses once.
Jacobsen, R.　Cobalt.
Ma Chih-yüan.　Tune: "Four Pieces of Jade"—Retirement.
Madhubuti.　Poem Looking for a Reader, A.
Mathews, A.　Spectrum.
McPherson, S.　Quilt of Rights.
Milosz, C.　Sun, The.
Mirabai.　Why Mira Can't Go Back to Her Old House.
Mori Ōgai.　Tanka: "Without incident."
Morley, H.　Curve of the Water.
  For Elaine de Kooning.
Needell.　Color, even whiteness, reaches / the body as a name.
Ni Tsan.　On the Fifteenth Day of the Ninth Month of the Year Kuei mao of the Chih-cheng Period (Oct. 22, 1363), I Painted This to Send to the Summoned Scholar, Sheng-po, and Inscribed This Poem on It.
Okamoto.　Tanka: "Flower blooms, A."
  Tanka: "If I were to stand."
Oppenheimer, J.　Love Bit, The.
Peirce.　Divided Touch, Divided Color.
Picasso.　Poems: "Hasten on your childhood to the hour when white in."
Pitter.　Dun-Colour [or Dun-Color].
Rich, A.　Design in Living Colors.
Rossetti, C.　What is pink? A rose is pink.
"Shu Ting."　Longing.
Stevens, W.　Domination of Black ("At night, by the fire").
Tandori.　Utrillo: "La Belle Gabrielle."
Tidjani-Cissé.　Of Colours and Shadows.
Tomlinson, C.　Distinctions.
Toomer.　People.
Unknown.　Green and yellow patchwork across the country lies, A.
Watkins, V.　Furnace of Colors, The.
Worth, K.　Smells.
Yang Chi.　Five-color robe of embroidered silk, A.
Yoshihara.　I Forget.
Young, D.　Project for Freight Trains, A.
Zukofsky, L.　Blue light is the night harbor-slip.

Colosseum, Rome
Browne, M.　Survey of the Amphitheatre, A.
Norse.　Colosseum.
Poe.　Coliseum, The.

Coltrane, John
Baraka.　Am/Trak.
Brathwaite, E.　Naima.
Etter.　Monk's Dream.
Graham, M.　After the War; When Coltrane Only Wanted to Play Dance Tunes.
Greenlee.　Memorial for Trane.
Harjo, J.　Healing Animal.
Harper, M.　Dear John, Dear Coltrane.
  Here Where Coltrane Is.
  Narrative of the Life and Times of John Coltrane: Played by Himself, A.
  Peace on Earth.
Henderson, D.　Coltrane Memorial, A.
  Elvin Jones Gretsch Freak.
Jordan, N.　Silent Prophet, The.
Kelly, R.　Newark.
Kgositsile.　Acknowledgement.

Colts
Mackey, N. John Coltrane Arrived with An Egyptian Lady.
Madhubuti. Don't Cry, Scream.
Mor. Coming of John, The.
Okantah. Afreeka Brass.
Rodgers, C. Written for Love of an Ascension—Coltrane.
Sneeden. Coltrane and My Father.
Spellman. Did John's Music Kill Him?
  John Coltrane: An Impartial Review.
Stillman, M. In Memoriam John Coltrane.
Taggart, J. Giant Steps.
Touré, A. JuJu.

Colts
Frost, R. Runaway, The.
Lindsay, V. Broncho That Would Not Be Broken, The.
See also **Horses**

Columba, Saint. See **Columcille, Saint**

Columbia University
Ferlinghetti, L. And Pablo Neruda / that Chilean omnivore of poetry.
Hughes, L. Theme for English B.

Columbus, Christopher
Brathwaite, E. Colombe.
Cowley, A. To Mr. Hobbes [or Hobs].
Crane, H. Ave Maria.
Durham. Columbus Day.
Freneau. Columbus to Ferdinand.
Frost, R. America Is Hard to See.
Glancy. Christopher.
Gustafson, R. Columbus Reaches Juana, 1492.
MacDermot. Dark foreboding haunts me lest I die, A.
Miller, J. Columbus.
Nash, O. Columbus.
Pierce, A. In Fourteen Hundred and Ninety-.
Robertson, J. Discovery of America, The.
Rukeyser, M. Columbus.
Squire. Sonnet: "There was an Indian, who had known no change."
Stickney, T. You say, Columbus with his argosies.

Columcille, Saint
Dallán Forgaill. Poem in Praise of Colum Cille, A.
Irvine, J. Saint Colm-Cille and the Cairn of Farewell.
Johnson, L. Saint Columba.

Comas
Meredith, G. King Harald's Trance.

Combs
Crane, S. Ah, God, the way your little finger moved.

Comedians
Bernstein, C. Of Time and the Line.

Comets
Eberhart, R. Ship Burning and a Comet All in One Day, A.
Hardy, T. Comet at Yell'ham, The.
Johnson, S. Comets and Princes.
Lalic. Addressing the Comet.
Marvell. Mower to the Glow-Worms [or Glowworms or Glo-Worms], The.
Nicholson, N. Halley's Comet.
Noguere. Soma.

Comfort
Amichai. To my love, combing her hair.
Baraka. Political Poem.
Berry, W. Wild Geese, The.
Cixous. I urgency, I begged. *Give me your dish*, I said, icy.
Clark, T. Touch of human hands—, The.
Crowell, G. Courage to Live.
Dante Alighieri. Gentle thought there is will often start, A.
Emanuel, L. Discovering the Photograph of Lloyd, Earl, and Priscilla.
Enzensberger, H. Short History of the Bourgeoisie.
Fumiko. Tanka: "When the lights go out."
Herrick. Comfort to a Youth That Had Lost His Love.
Hopkins, G. Sonnet: "No worst, there is none. Pitched past pitch of grief."
Jarman, M. Questions for Ecclesiastes.

Keats. Why did I laugh to-night? No voice will tell.
Mayakovsky. You, who live just for orgiastic feasts.
Melville, H. Herba Santa.
Pembroke, M. Psalm 92: Bonum Est Confiteri.
Peseroff. Bluebird.
Pollitt. Small Comfort.
Popa. Owners of the Little Box, The.
Rossetti, C. There's snow on the fields.
Sandburg, C. At a Window.
Tate, J. Consolations After an Affair.
Thayer, L. Little Child's Faith, The.

Comic Strips
Ashbery. Farm Implements and Rutabagas in a Landscape.
Hall, J. Maybe Dats Your Pwoblem Too.
Reaney. Katzenjammer Kids, The.
Sorrentino. Zoo, The.
Wallace-Crabbe. Collective Invention, The.

Commandments. See **Ten Commandments**

Commencement Day
Carrier, C. Commencement.

Commerce
Dyer, J. Urban Progress.
Ginsberg, A. Studying the Signs.
Gwynn, R. Classroom at the Mall, The.
Hacker, M. Elysian Fields.
Koch, K. You were wearing your Edgar Allan Poe printed cotton blouse.
Krynicki. By entering the grand lottery.
Machado Ruiz. Wind, one brilliant day, called, The.
Martin, C. Victoria's Secret.
Mirabai. It's True I Went to the Market.
Penny, A. Sung at Table by the Same Choir.
Quarles. What is the *World?* A great *Exchange* of ware.
Spender, S. Ultima Ratio Regum.
Spenser. Sonnet 15: "Ye tradeful merchants that, with weary toil."
See also **Barter; Business and Businessmen**

Communes
Piatt, S. Palace-Burner, The.
Piercy. Death of the small commune, The.

Communication
Aiken, C. Annihilation.
Ashbery. Train Rising Out of the Sea.
Atwood. Against Still Life.
Behn, A. Lover's Witness.
Booth, P. Supposition with Qualification.
Bowes-Lyon. Feather, The.
Bronk. Mayan Glyphs Unread, The.
"Chorny." Kreutzer Sonata, A.
Clifton, L. 4 Daughters.
Cranch. Gnosis.
Creeley. Act of Love, The.
Cummings, E. May i feel said he.
Davidson. Utterance.
Dooley, M. No, Go On.
Flook. Continental Divide, The.
Gardner, I. That "Craning of the Neck."
Hacker, M. And I shout at Iva, whine at you. Easily.
Harwood, G. In The Park.
Hauge. I stand here, do you understand.
Herrick. His Answer to a Friend.
  Upon Love, by Way of Question and Answer.
Hippolyte. Air between Us (for an Expatriate), The.
Hoffman, D. Signatures.
Jackson, L. Summary for Alastor.
  World and I, The.
Jastrzebska. Bi-lingual.
Joseph, J. Lost Continent, The.
Lum. Going Home.
Mansfield, K. Meeting, The.
Matthews, T. Even the whales now.
McGrath, T. Letter for Marian, A.
Millay, E. Hearing your words, and not a word among them.
Morgan, E. First Men on Mercury, The.
Oppen. And if at 80.
Piercy. Councils.
  Hand Games.
  You Don't Understand Me.

Popa. Other World, The.
Ransom, J. Two in August.
Rich, A. In the Evening.
  That conversation we were always on the edge.
  Valediction Forbidding Mourning, A.
Robinson, E. Tact.
Rukeyser, M. Effort at Speech between Two People.
Sexton. From the Garden.
Stafford, W. Ritual to Read to Each Other, A.
Stevens, W. Continual Conversation with a Silent Man.
Tzara. Way.
Valentine, J. Snow Landscape, in a Glass Globe.
Van Duyn. Wish to Be Believed, The.
Voznesensky. Dogalypse.
Walcott. For Adrian.
Whitman, W. Past and present wilt—I have fill'd them, emptied them, The.
  Spotted hawk swoops by and accuses me, The.
Woolson. Love Unexpressed.

Communion. See **Eucharist**

Communism
Ackland. Communist Poem, 1935.
  Winter.
Bishop, E. Lullaby for the Cat.
Bokov. Commune for Me, The.
Brecht, B. Late Lamented Fame of the Giant City of New York.
Bùi Công Trừng. Fallen Fruit, A.
Cardenal. Unrighteous Mammon (Luke 16:9).
Connolly, C. M is for Marx.
Cornford, J. Full Moon at Tierz before the Storming of Huesca.
Crosby, H. Firebrand.
Cummings, E. Thanksgiving (1956).
Dalton, R. My Neighbor.
Đng Thái Thuyên. Contrasts.
Ehrlich. Louse.
"Elagin." You told me that I was born under a lucky star.
Elliot, E. On Communists.
Ginsberg, A. Kral Majales.
"Golodny." Judge Gorba.
Gondlevsky. May God grant me the memory to recall my life.
Gu Cheng. Forever Parted: Graveyard.
Hikmet. Angina Pectoris.
Hồng Chu'o'ng. It's Me, Your Son.
Khlebnikov, V. Manifesto of the Presidents of the Terrestrial Globe.
Kibirov. Year 1937, The.
Lê Đức Thọ. Fighter's Thoughts of Spring, A.
Lu'u Văn Vong. Paradise.
  Run! Run!
Mandelstam. Poem No. 286 (On Stalin).
Mao Tse-tung. Tune: "Full River Red"—A Reply to Kuo Mo-jo.
Mayakovsky. At the Top of My Voice.
  My most respected / comrades of posterity!
Mitchison. Midsummer Apple Tree, The.
  To Some Young Communists from an Older Socialist.
Mukhopadhyay, S. Task, The.
Nguyễn Chí Thiện. Party holds you down and you lie still, The.
  Party left me in the wilds, The.
Nguyễn Tất Nhiên. Folk Songs For Today.
Niemoller. First they came for the Jews.
Pauker. Garland for a Propagandist.
Petri. By an Unknown Poet from Eastern Europe, 1955.
Phan Trọng Quảng. International Solidarity.
Ponge. Silent World Is Our Only Homeland, The.
Ridge, L. Réveille.
Ryuichi. My Imperialism.
Saarikoski. Winter solstice.
"Sagittarius." Stalin Moy Golubchik.
Serge. Asphyxiated Man, The.
  Dialectic.
Sokolov. Beginning, The.
Tạ Hũ'u Thiện. Looking For Her.
Tế Hanh. Mother.

Tố Hữu. Cradlesong, A.
Since then, inside me, summer has blazed up.
Trần Minh Tu'ó'c. Prison Dreams.
Unknown. Green and yellow patchwork across the country lies, A.
In Taihang born, in Taihang bred.
Magpie screams loudly and up his tail goes, The.
There's no Jade Emperor in the sky.
We lads in the forging-shop have unbounded strength.
Việt Phu'o'ng. O Life I Love and Cherish Like My Wife!
Yoshimi. Tanka: "Since I work with those."
Zorgenfrey. Over the Neva.

Commuting and Commuters
Hearne, B. Commuters.

See also **Suburbs**

Companionship and Companions
Adamson. Action Would Kill It / A Gamble.
"Akhmatova." Along the hard crest of the snowdrift.
Alford, H. You and I.
Ashbery. Love Poem, A.
Atwood. Eventual Proteus.
Is/Not / Not.
You take my hand and.
Auden. Lullaby: "Lay your sleeping head, my love."
Bernstein, O. And Later by Myself.
Berry, W. Except.
Blaser. Ah.
Bly, R. Third Body, A.
Bogan, L. After the Persian.
Broumas, O. Amazon Twins.
Buchanan, G. I suddenly have come to love.
Burns, R. O [*or* Oh] wert thou in the cauld blast.
Red, Red Rose, A.
Carroll, J. Distances, The.
Cataldi. We Could Have Met.
Catullus. Carmen 75 ("Reason blinded by sin, Lesbia").
Carmina, XIII.
Cavalcanti. Sonnet: To His Lady Joan, of Florence.
Cixous. I urgency, I begged. *Give me your dish*, I said, icy.
Cooper, J. Rent.
Creeley. For Love.
Dickinson, E. Wild Nights—Wild Nights!
Donne. Canonization, The.
Duncan, R. And If He Had Been Wrong for Me.
Elliot, A. House-Rules I: Reading.
Emin. Your Hands.
Etherege. To a Lady Asking Him How Long He Would Love Her.
Ford, C. There's No Place to Sleep in This Bed, Tanguy.
Frost, R. Pasture, The.
González, A. Whatever You Want.
Graves, R. Narrow Sea, The.
Gunn, T. Touch.
Gurney, I. Companion—North-East Dug-Out.
Herrick. Not To Love.
To Phyllis to Love and Live with Him.
James, J. After Christopher Wood.
Jennings, K. Just the Two of Us.
Kefala. Sunday Visit.
Kunitz, S. After the Last Dynasty.
Lanier. To Bayard Taylor.
Levertov. Bedtime.
Losing Track.
Li Po. Night with a Friend, A.
Lipska. If there is a God.
Lowell, A. Summer Rain.
Machi. Tanka: "My heart."
MacLeish. Old Gray Couple, The.
MacNeice. Coda.
Mathews, A. Spectrum.
McKay, C. Wild Goat, The.
Meredith, G. He felt the wild beast in him betweenwhiles.
Merwin, W. Travelling Together.
Mihalic. Approaching Storm.
Moore, T. 'Tis the Last Rose of Summer.

Namjoshi, S. *et al.* Because of India, before and after.
Was It Quite Like That?
Nemerov. Blue Suburban.
Nobuyuki. Third-Class Car on a Night Train (three poems).
Oppen. Troubled that you are not, as they say.
Owen, W. Apologia Pro Poemate Meo.
Pao Chao. Presented as a Farewell to Secretary Fu.
Paz. Last Dawn.
Peacock, T. Love and Age.
Perreault, J. Metaphysical Paintings, The.
Petrov, A. Poetry in a Glass Cube.
Rexroth, K. Just us. / In our little house.
Let us sleep together here tonight.
Without me you can only.
Rich, A. After Twenty Years.
Blood-Sister.
Can it be growing colder when I begin.
I wake up in your bed. I know I have been dreaming.
In the Evening.
Old blanket. The crumbs of rubbed wool turning up, The.
Paula Becker to Clara Westhoff.
Rain on the West Side Highway.
Ritchie. Sorting Laundry.
Robinson, E. Companion, The.
Firelight.
Shelley, P. From the Arabic: An Imitation.
Swenson, M. Hair, The.
Swift, J. Stella's Birthday, 1725.
To Stella.
Twelve Articles.
Sykes, B. One Day.
Tandori. Utrillo: "La Belle Gabrielle."
Teodorescu. Arm in Arm.
Tu Mu. Retired Official Yüan's High Pavilion, The.
Unknown. By Heaven!
Ti-ch'ü Song Words.
Vinokurov. I ate and drank with you, fellow men.
Walcott. Village Life, A.
Wright, F. Alcohol.

See also **Friendship**

Compassion
Brecht, B. World's One Hope, The.
Brontë, A. Song.
Bursk. Lies.
Cavafy. Thermopylae.
Crane, H. Chaplinesque.
Creeley. Token, A.
World, The.
Cullen, C. Magnets.
Dante Alighieri. Mine eyes beheld the blessed pity spring.
Davis, T. In the Fire Lane.
Dementyev, A. As long as we feel another's pain.
Dickinson, E. This is my letter to the World.
Donne. What if this present were the world's last night?
Faiz. Fragrant Hands.
Gregg. Shopping-Bag Lady, The.
Hamburger, M. Between the Lines.
Hull, L. Dartmouth Women's Prison, 1992.
Ishikawa Takuboku. Tanka: "What always seemed."
Jeffers, R. Crumbs or the Loaf.
Kirchwey. Ambulance.
Knott. Two Vietnam Poems: (1966).
Levine, P. Coming Home, *Detroit*, 1968.
Maxwell, M. To My Grandmother, Lady-Woman.
North, C. Few Facts about Me, A.
Ponge. Frog, The.
Prigov. People are on the one side understandable.
Rabbitt. Tortoise.
Rutsala. Skaters.
Saitō Mokichi. Tanka: "Snowflakes."
Spender, S. History and Reality.
Unknown. Bird's Nest, The.
Wright, J. Saint Judas.
Wright, K. Frozen Man, The.

Competition
Cheng Hsieh. Contest Snake, The.
Emerson, R. Fable: "Mountain and the squirrel, The."
Fisher, A. Benjamin Jones Goes Swimming.
Jarry. Passion of Jesus Considered as an Uphill Race, The.
O'Hara, F. Hôtel Transylvanie.
Sidney, P. Sonnet 59: "Dear, why make you more of a dog than me?"
Unknown. Foot Race Song.
Winchilsea. Circuit of Apollo, The.

See also **Rivalry**

Complacency
Creeley. Warning, The.
Shapiro, K. Buick.
Yevtushenko. Half-measures / can kill.

Computers
Morgan, E. Computer's First Christmas Card, The.

Comraderie
Hull, L. Dartmouth Women's Prison, 1992.
Tsvetayeva. Desk.
Yi, S. Paddies lean against each other.

Concentration
Patacara. When they plow their fields.
Reznikoff. Jews from Holland, France, and Hungary, and later from.

Concentration Camps
Bienek. Our Ashes.
Vorkuta.
Blumenthal, M. Juliek's Violin.
Ciardi. Gift, The.
Clampitt. Burning Child, The.
Cohen, L. Heirloom.
Ficowski. 5.8.1942 / In Memory of Janusz Korczak.
Fogel, E. Shipment to Maidanek.
Forché. Elegy.
Fried, E. My Girlfriends.
Gergely. Crazed Man in Concentration Camp.
Hecht, A. Book of Yolek, The.
'More Light! More Light!'.
Henderson, D. Alvin Cash/Keep on Dancin'.
Inada. Concentration Constellation.
"J., M." Funeral, The.
Jarrell. Camp in the Prussian Forest, A.
In the Camp There Was One Alive.
Protocols.
Jentzsch. Terezin, the Graveyard.
Kirsch, S. Legend of Lilja.
Koestenbaum, P. Harriet Feigenbaum is a Sculptor.
Kopland. Natzweiler.
Levi, P. Buna.
Mandel, E. On the 25th Anniversary of the Liberation of Auschwitz.
Pagis. Roll Call, The.
Roll-Call In the Concentration Camp.
Pilinszky. On the Wall of a KZ-Lager.
Passion of Ravensbrück.
Popa. Be Seeing You.
Quasimodo. Auschwitz.
Radnóti. Seventh Eclogue.
Simic. Begotten of the Spleen.
Spender, S. Memento.
Szymborska. Starvation Camp near Jaslo.
Unknown. Cradle Song: "Sleep, my child, my little daughter."
From Tomorrow On.

See also **Auschwitz, Poland; Holocaust; Internment**

Conception
Dickinson, E. Solemn thing—it was—I said, A.
Herrick. Tithe [*or* Tythe]: To the Bride, The.
"MacDiarmid." Harry Semen.
Pritam, A. Creative Process, The.

Concerts
Blunden. Concert Party: Busseboom.
North, C. Hospital.
Smith, V. Summer Band Concert.

Concord, Massachusetts
Emerson, R. Concord Hymn.
Musketaquid.
Young, S. Epitaph for a Concord Boy.

Concrete Poetry. *See* **Shaped Poetry**

Confederacy
Ball, C. Jacket of Gray, The.
Bierce. Confederate Flags, The.
Davidson, D. Lee in the Mountains.
Sequel of Appomattox.
Emmett. Dixie [*or* Dixie's Land].
Jonas, S. Lines on the Back of a Confederate Note.
Preston, M. Grave in Hollywood Cemetery, Richmond, A.
Randall, J. My Maryland.
Tate, A. Battle of Murfreesboro.
Ode to the Confederate Dead.
Thompson, M. To the South.
Timrod. Charleston.
Ode: "Sleep sweetly in your humble graves."
Unknown. Confederate Memorial Day.
Walcott. Arkansas Testament, The.
See also **Civil War, America**

Confessions
Blunt, W. To One Who Would Make a Confession.
Clarke, A. Ancient Lights.
Claudian. Punishment in Hell.
Coleridge, S. Spots in the Sun.
Creeley. Hill, The.
Derricotte. Weakness, The.
Dunn, S. On Hearing the Airlines Will Use a Psychological Profile to Catch Potential Skyjackers.
What They Wanted.
Gower, J. Among these othre of Slouthes kinde.
Gunn, T. Confessions of the Life Artist.
Herbert, G. Trinity Sunday.
Hudgins. Praying Drunk.
Hughes, L. Third Degree.
Kennedy, X. First Confession.
Kowit. Lurid Confessions.
Lee-Hamilton. Ipsissimus.
Leonard, T. Jist Ti Let Yi No.
Levchev. Confession and Salute to the Fire.
Melville, H. In a Church of Padua.
Muldoon, P. Cuba.
Pankey. Confession of Cleopas, The.
Pembroke, M. O Lord, Thou Hast Searched and Known Me.
Raab, L. For You.
Whitman, W. As I lay with my head in your lap camerado.
Whitney, I. Aucthour Maketh Her Wyll and Testament, The.
Wright, J. Confession to J. Edgar Hoover.

Confidence
Dimitrova. Introduction to the Beyond.
Levertov. Variation on a Theme by Rilke.
Mandelstam. Enough of snivelling! Shove our papers in the desk.
Meek. Week the Dirigible Came, The.
Piercy. Unlearning to Not Speak.
Stone, R. Advice.
Townshend. Upon Kind[e] and True Love.
Yevtushenko. Disbelief in Yourself Is Indispensable.

Conflict
Bursk. Lies.
Carew, T. To One That Desired to Know My Mistress [*or* Mistris].
Catullus. Carmen 85.
Creeley. Fancy.
Whip, The.
Wife, The.
D'Aguiar. Mama Dot's Treatise.
Đồng Hồ. War.
Dunn, S. At the Smithville Methodist Church.
Levertov. Went with some of my students to work in the People's.
Lorde. Love, Maybe.
MacGowran. Description of an Irish Feast, The.
Mapanje. On Being Asked to Write a Poem for 1979.
Meissner. Twisters.
Melville, H. After the Pleasure Party.
America.
Nobuyuki. Labor Day[1] (four poems).

Ochester. Canaries in Uncle Arthur's Basement, The.
Ovid. Elegies 3.1: "Old wood stands uncut, of long years' space, An."
Smith, S. Via Media Via Dolorosa.
Southwell. Man's Civil[l] War[re].
Turner, G. Synchoresis.
Walcott. Rest, Christ! from tireless war. See, it's midsummer.
Weinfield. Song for the In-Itself and For-Itself.
Wyatt, T. Will ye see what wonders love hath wrought?

Conformity
Auden. Unknown Citizen, The.
Bly, R. Executive's Death, The.
Brooks, G. To Those of My Sisters Who Kept Their Naturals.
Crane, S. "Think as I think," said a man.
Cummings, E. IN) all those who got.
My specialty is living said.
Day Lewis. "Let Us Now Praise Famous Men."
Dickinson, E. Much Madness is divinest Sense.
"Dylan." It's Alright, Ma (I'm Only Bleeding).
Egerton, S. Emulation, The.
Liberty, The.
Foss, S. Calf-Path, The.
Glazkov. Tale of the Cyclopses, The.
Hall, D. Mr. Wakeville on Interstate 90.
Ignatow, D. Dog barks and is for the moment a dog heard, The.
Joseph, J. Warning.
Laing, K. Huge car with the sad voice, The.
Lindsay, V. Congo, The.
McGrath, T. Ode for the American Dead in Asia.
Melville, H. Enthusiast, The.
Ofeimun. Let Them Choose Paths.
Shapiro, K. University.
Stevens, W. Disillusionment of Ten O'Clock.
Unknown. Dry Leaves, Dry Leaves.
Hit betidde somtime in the termes of Judé.
Williams, D. If a lot of people are laughing.

Confusion
Beckett, S. Saint-Lô.
Carew, T. Lover, upon an Accident Necessitating His Departure, Consults with Reason, A.
Creeley. Chasing the Bird.
Fancy.
Dacey, P. How I Escaped from the Labyrinth.
Duesing. Reprieve.
DuPlessis, R. Where is the bird?
Edson, R. Large thing comes in, A.
Lovers.
Gascoyne. Cubical Domes, The.
End Is Near the Beginning, The.
Graves, R. In Broken Images.
Hadas, R. Lair, The.
Karpowicz. From the Skein of the Straight Line.
La Fontaine. Thyrsis And Amaranta.
Larkin, J. Rape.
Leonard, T. Ifyi stull / huuny / wurkt oot.
Levin, P. Lost Bee, The.
Machi. Tanka: "'Until age thirty'."
Mezhirov. We would awaken in a twilight gloom.
Nikolov, N. Confusion.
Piercy. Song of the Fucked Duck.
Plath. Appearance, An.
Smedley, M. Irish Fairy lost her way, An.
Stanton, M. Childhood.
Supervielle. Voyages.
Toomer. I sit in my room.
Violi. Scatter.
Waniek. Bali Hai Calls Mama.
Wen Cheng-ming. These long verandahs seem to be washed clean.
Wetzsteon. Three Songs.
Wilbur. Digression, A.
Winchilsea. Adam Posed.
Wollach. Are these moods of mine memory.

Congo River
Bethune, L. For Singing In Good Mood.
Kgositsile. Gods Wrote, The.
Martinson. On the Congo.
Sanchez, S. Haiku: "Your voice unwrapping."

Congreve, William
Dryden, J. To My Dear Friend Mr Congreve [on His Comedy Called "The Double-Dealer"].

Connaught, Ireland
Mangan, J. Vision of Connaught in the Thirteenth Century, A.

Connecticut (state)
Hall, D. Sleeping Giant, The.
Halleck, F. They burnt their last witch in CONNECTICUT.
McClatchy. Winter without Snow, A.
Stevens, W. River of Rivers in Connecticut, The.

Connecticut River
Stevens, W. River of Rivers in Connecticut, The.

Conquistadors
Baca. Invasions.
Brathwaite, E. Colombe.
Crane, H. Imperator Victus.
De Villagrá. World has no such pleasing joy, The.
Hall, S. Poppies of Wickenburg.
Nahuatl Oral Tradition. Elegy.
Ryan, R. El Dorado.

Conrad, Joseph
Lowry, M. Joseph Conrad.
Walcott. Volcano.

Conscience
Byron, G. Answer to ——'s Professions of Affection.
Franklin, B. Bits of Wisdom.
Graves, R. With Her Lips Only.
Herrick. To His Conscience.
To Oenone ("What conscience, say, is it in thee").
Hopkins, G. Candle Indoors, The.
Rabbitt. For Those Who Will Live Forever.
Shakespeare, W. Sonnet 151.
Shefner. Forest Fire.
Simic. Inner Man, The.
Stevens, W. High-Toned Old Christian Woman, A.
Szymborska. In Praise of Self-Deprecation.
Tanikawa Shuntaro. Everyone possesses something sad.
Unknown. Little Chap Who Follows Me, The.

Conscientious Objectors
Davison, E. Conscientious Objector.
Gardinier. Supremer Sacrifice, The.
Lowell, R. After the Surprising Conversions.
Memories of West Street and Lepke.
Shapiro, K. Conscientious Objector, The.
See also **Pacifism and Pacifists**

Consciousness
Baraka. Minute of Consciousness, The.
Dickinson, E. My Cocoon tightens—Colors tease.
We learned the Whole of Love.
Frost, R. Silken Tent, The.
Glück, L. Wild Iris, The.
Hardy, T. New Year's Eve.
Simic. Inner Man, The.
Sorrentino. Handbook of Versification.
Stafford, W. For Alexis Christa von Hartmann: Proved Not Guilty.
Ritual to Read to Each Other, A.
Walcott. Elsewhere.

Conscription, Military
Forché. Selective Service.
Gibson, W. Conscript, The.
Tso Yen-nien. Call to Arms.

Conservation. *See* **Ecology and Ecologists**

Consolation
Amichai. Is all this sorrow? I don't know.
Atwood. People come from all over to consult me, bringing their limbs.
Brontë, E. When weary with the long day's care.

Cook, E. To My Lyre.
Davis, C. Belongings.
Giovanni. Women gather, The.
Hooks. Woman's Mourning Song, The.
Longfellow, H. Rainy Day, The.
Mahon. Consolations of Philosophy.
Mitchison. Woman Alone.
Rice, H. It's Me Again, God.
Riley, J. Life-Lesson, A.
Strand. For Jessica, My Daughter.
Tsaloumas. Consolation.
Unknown. Beguines who hear these words.
Van Duyn. Open Letter from a Constant
  Reader.
Conspiracy
Bateman, C. Conspiracy.
Blyton, C. Plug-hole Man, The.
Ovid. Mistress keeps her lover on his toes, A.
Constancy. *See* **Fidelity**
Constantinople, Turkey
Montagu, L. Verses Written in the Chiosk [of
  the British Palace], at Pera, Overlooking [the
  City of] Constantinople.
Paulus Silentiarius. Description of Hagia
  Sophia.
Unknown. Last Mass in Hagia Sophia, The.
Constellations
Barnard, M. Pleiades, The.
Berssenbrugge. Constellation Quilt, The.
Bryant, W. Constellations, The.
De la Mare. Ride-by-Nights, The.
Eliot, T. Sweeney Among the Nightingales.
Frost, R. Canis Major.
  On Looking Up by Chance at the
    Constellations.
Graves, R. Star-Talk.
Grennan. Conjunctions.
Greville, F. *et al.* 56.
Hollander, J. Great Bear, The.
  Lion Named Passion, A.
Kinnell. La Bagarède.
Kitching. Space Captain.
Mahon. Globe in North Carolina, The.
Moss, T. Dennis's Sky Leopard.
Nicholls, J. Andromeda.
Rice, J. Sky Seasons.
Rich, A. Orion.
  Planetarium.
Sigourney. Stars, The.
Stevenson, A. Sonnet: "If it be night. . . ."
Storace. Wedding Song.
Tu Fu. Waiting for Audience on a Spring
  Night.
Tuckerman, F. Sonnets: "Starry flower, the
  flower-like stars that fade, The."
Turner, C. Orion.
Unknown. Clear moon brightly shining in the
  night.
  Far far away, the Herdboy Star.
Wilbur. In the Field.
See also **Sky; Stars**
Constitution (ship)
Blackmur. Resurrection.
Holmes, O. Old Ironsides.
Morris, G. Main-Truck; or, A Leap for Life,
  The.
Construction Workers. *See* **Buildings and**
  Builders
Consumerism
"Chrystos." Real Indian Leans Against, The.
Cummings, E. Poem, or Beauty Hurts Mr.
  Vinal.
Lazard. In Answer to Your Query.
Moore, T. Announcement of a New Grand
  Acceleration Company for the Promotion of
  the Speed of Literature.
Nemerov. Life Cycle of Common Man.
Replansky. Housing Shortage.
Unknown. Lydia Pinkham.
Warr, M. Malcolm Is 'Bout More Than
  Wearing a Cap.
Waterman, N. Cheer for the Consumer.
Contempt
Espada. Secret of the Legal Secretary's
  Cigarette Smoke, The.
Herbert, Z. Hen is the best example of what
  living constantly with humans, The.

Levertov. Grace-Note, The.
Millay, E. Oh, Oh, you will be sorry for that
  word!
Petri. Electra.
Rossetti, C. Frog's Fate, A.
Contentment
Baraka. Song Form.
Barnes, B. Content.
Bly, R. In the month of May when all leaves
  open.
  Third Body, A.
Bontemps. God Give to Men.
Brodsky, J. Six Years Later.
Brown, S. Odyssey of Big Boy.
Bunyan. Shepherd Boy Sings [in the Valley of
  Humiliation], The.
Burns, R. Birks of Aberfeldy, The [Composed
  on the Spot].
Byrom. Careless Content.
Calverley. Peace.
Carphyllides. Passer-by, don't blame this
  memorial.
Carruth, H. Twilight comes to the little farm.
Chudleigh. Resolve, The.
Clampitt. Grasmere.
Clare, J. Sabbath Bells.
Claudian. Felix, qui patriis. . . and c.:
  Imitated from Claudian.
Cotton, N. Contentment.
Couzyn. Dawn.
Cowper, W. Contentment.
Creeley. Innocence, The.
  Rain, The.
Davie. Heigh-ho on a Winter Afternoon.
Davies, W. Oh, Sweet Content.
  Truly Great.
De Mello Breyner. I feel the dead in the cold
  of violets.
De Vere, E. Poem: "Were I a king, I could
  command content."
Dekker, T. Art thou poore yet hast thou
  golden Slumbers.
Dekker, T. *et al.* Happy Heart, The.
Dickinson, E. I'm sorry for the Dead—Today.
  Their Height in Heaven comforts not.
Dunn, S. Something Like Happiness.
Duoduo. Looking out from death you will
  always see.
Dyer, S. My mind [*or* minde *or* mynde] to me
  a kingdom [*or* kyngdome] is.
Ehrhart. Time on Target.
Emerson, R. Day's Ration, The.
Garrigue. Song for "Buvez les Vins du
  Postillion"—Advt.
Graves, R. By this exchange of eyes, this
  encirclement.
Greene, R. Maesia's Song.
Greenwell, D. Content, content! within a quiet
  room.
Haines, J. To Turn Back.
Heitzman. March.
Herbert, G. Family [*or* Familie], The.
  JESU is in my heart, his sacred name.
Herrick. His Content in the Country.
  His Grange, or Private Wealth.
Hikmet. Letters from a Man in Solitary.
Holmes, O. Contentment.
Hsieh Ling-yün. Written on the Lake,
  Returning from the Retreat at Stone Cliff.
Ishikawa Takuboku. Tanka: "Sadly."
Kenyon, J. Wood Thrush.
Kyger. And with March a Decade in Bolinas.
Landor, W. Ireland never was contented.
Lanier, S. Nirvâna.
Lawrence, D. Song of a Man Who Is Loved.
Longfellow, H. Day is done, and the darkness,
  The.
Lowell, A. Decade, [A].
Machi. Tanka: "On a day."
Martial. Happy Life, A.
Marvell. Garden, The.
McMullen, A. By the River.
Millay, E. Above these cares my spirit in
  calm abiding.
Ochester. Gift, The.
Parnell, T. Hymn to Contentment, A.
Peacock, T. Love and Age.

Po Chü-i. After Eating.
  Half in the Family, Half Out.
  Lodging with the Old Man of the Stream.
  Writing Again on the Same Theme.
Pomfret, J. Choice, The.
Prince, F. To a Friend on His Marriage.
Robinson, E. Firelight.
Sassoon. I Shall Find You.
Schulman. Present Perfect, The.
Sexton. I Remember.
Shakespeare, W. Sonnet 29.
Sidney, P. Sonnet 39: "Come Sleep, O Sleep."
Sill. California Winter.
Smith, C. To Spring.
  To the Moon.
Swenson, M. Staying at Ed's Place.
T'ao Ch'ien. On Being Assigned as Military
  Adviser to the Garrison Army.
Tennyson, A. If I were loved, as I desire to
  be.
Unknown. Another Little Boy.
  As for me, I delight in the everyday Way.
  Heart's Content.
  I joy not in no earthly bliss.
  If I Might Be an Ox.
  So Han-shan writes you these words.
  Today I sat before the cliff.
Whitman, W. Glimpse through an interstice
  caught, A.
  Who goes there! hankering, gross, mystical,
    nude?
Winchilsea. Give me, O indulgent fate!
Wollach. Lola, are you still getting whatever
  you want.
Wordsworth, D. Cottage in Grasmere Vale, A.
Wordsworth, W. Farmer of Tilsbury Vale,
  The.
  Fragment, A: "Between two sister moorland
    rills."
  Nuns fret not at their convent's narrow room;.
Wotton, S. Character of a Happy Life, The.
Yeats. Are You Content.
  Lake-Isle of Innisfree, The.
See also **Happiness**
Continuity
Amichai. Instructions for a Waitress.
Ammons. Eternal City, The.
Bell, M. Drawn by Stones, by Earth, by
  Things That Have Been in the Fire.
Bethell. Warning of Winter.
Bunting. Weeping oaks grieve, chestnuts raise.
Clampitt. Procession at Candlemas, A.
Creeley. Again.
Eliot, T. Dry Salvages, The.
  Little Gidding.
Hardy, T. Heredity.
Harper, M. High Modes: Vision as Ritual:
  Confirmation.
Hopkins, E. Life in Death.
Kumin, M. Excrement Poem, The.
Levine, P. Milkweed.
Marshall-Stoneking. Passage.
Meek. Vienna in the Rain.
Meynell, A. Song of Derivations, A.
Murray, L. Mitchells, The.
Nemerov. Dependencies, The.
O'Grady, D. Berlin Metro.
Oliver, M. In Blackwater Woods.
Ortiz. Canyon de Chelly.
Rich, A. Readings of History.
Rossetti, D. Sea-Limits, The.
Seferis. Memory II.
Snodgrass, W. Leaving the Motel.
Unknown. I grew from the earth.
Contraception. *See* **Birth Control**
Contrariness
Kaneko Mitsuharu. Opposition.
Melville, H. Parthenon, The.
Shapiro, K. Calling the Child.
Contrition
Unknown. In *Bath* a wanton wife did dwell.
Convalescence
Emerson, R. Give all to love;.
McCarriston. Healing the Mare.
Plath. Among the Narcissi.
Conventionality
Fulton, A. Risk Management.

Hall, D. Mr. Wakeville on Interstate 90.
Thomas, L. Electricity of Blossoms.

Convents
Brownjohn. In a Convent Garden.
Jamie. Black Spiders.
Mew. At the Convent Gate.
Williams, A. Nunnery, The.

See also **Nuns**

Conversation
Ackerman, D. Rumored Conversation with Oneself Continues in Pittsburgh, The.
Adamson. Action Would Kill It / A Gamble.
Ashbery. Life As a Book That Has Been Put Down.
Austin, M. Grizzly Bear.
Bernstein, O. Memories of Her Friend Who Died.
Bond, C. What You Want Means What You Can Afford.
Catullus. Carmen 10 ("Varus, whom I chanced to meet").
Celan. Leaf, Treeless for Bertolt Brecht, A.
Cheng Hsieh. Twenty-eight Characters Sent to Tung-ts'un on the Subject of the Poems He Burned.
Ch'ien T'ao. Moving House.
Coleman, W. Be Quiet, Go Away.
Crane, H. Praise for an Urn.
Cuadra, A. Brief Letter to Donald Walsh (in memoriam).
De la Mare. In the Garden.
Donne. . . . Then, as if he would have sold.
Dorgan, T. Promised Garden, The.
Edman. La Donna E Perpetuum Mobile.
Frost, R. Meeting and Passing.
Gergely. Silences.
Green, M. Sometimes I dress, with women sit.
Gunn, T. Jamesian.
Hodgins. Death Who.
Hsü Wei. Inscribed on a Painting.
Ignatow, D. Lunchtime.
Janowitz, P. Necessary Angel, The.
Jones, J. Sometimes I hear God's whisper in.
Koch, K. Talking to Patrizia.
Larkin, P. Talking in bed ought to be easiest.
Longfellow, H. Fire of Drift-Wood, The.
Lorde. Conversations in Crisis.
Martinez, D. Room itself. The women. The absence of women, The.
Menashe. Annunciation, The.
Meredith, G. At dinner, she is hostess, I am host.
Madam would speak with me. So, now it comes.
My lady unto Madam makes her bow.
Merrill, J. Charles on Fire.
Millay, E. I, being born a woman and distressed.
Mobilio. Third Kind of Interior Word, The.
More, H. Long was Society o'er-run.
Morley, H. For Elaine de Kooning.
Moss, H. Roof Garden, The.
Mother Goose. As Tommy Snooks and Bessy Brooks.
Myers, G. Talking to God.
Niedecker. Fancy Another Day Gone.
Oden. Bible Study.
O'Grady, D. In the valleys of the future we shall walk.
Oppen. Eclogue: "Men talking, The."
Orban, O. Summer on the Lake, A.
Pagis. Conversation.
Po Chü-i. Old Age.
To a Talkative Guest.
Prior. To a Lady: She Refusing to Continue a Dispute with Me, and Leaving Me in the Argument.
Rich, A. Dialogue.
Richardson, J. Retort Perfect, The.
Rilke. Going Blind.
Roethke. Supper with Lindsay.
Rotella, A. Everyone talking at once.
Rumi. What the Flowers Said.
Schuyler, J. Master of the Golden Glow, The.
Scott, D. Dreadwalk.
Segal, J. Rest.
Shurin. Sailed.

Sidney, P. Sonnet 30: "Whether the Turkish new moon minded be."
Simpson, L. Chocolates.
Sitwell, D. Said King Pompey, the emperor's ape.
Stevens, W. Table Talk.
Stevenson, A. Sous-Entendu.
Taylor, J. Recreation.
Thomas, D. Conversation of prayers about to be said, The.
Thomas, E. Sun used to shine while we two walked, The.
Tomlinson, C. Word in Edgeways, A.
Troupe. Conversation Overheard.
Turner, G. Synchoresis.
Unknown. Dead are gone and with them we cannot converse;, The.
Valéry. Girl with Mind Wandering.
Van Duyn. Talker, The.
Van Vliet. Party.
Waldrop, R. Feverish Propositions.
Walker, K. My Talk with an Elegant Man.
Webb, F. Tip for Saturday, A.
Welish. Blood or Color.
Wen Cheng-ming. Fine breeze blows through the temple halls, A.
Young, A. Dancer, The.

Conversion
Crashaw. To the Noblest and Best of Ladies, the Countess of Denbigh, Perswading her to Resolution in Religion, and to render her selfe without further delay into the Communion of the Catholick Church.
Fitzgerald, P. Answer to Thomas Barry, An.
Heywood, J. Wilt thou use turners craft still? ye by my trouth.
Merton. St. Paul.
Ransom, J. Persistent Explorer.
Ritsos. End of Dodona II, The.
Unknown. Christ's Bounty.
I Met the Master.
Mr. Davis's Experience.
Mrs. Saunder's Experience.
Sweetness of Nature, The.
Vicar of Bray, The.
Voznesensky. Old Song.
Wheatley, P. On Being Brought from Africa to America.
Whittier. Call of the Christian, The.
Wither. Conversion of S. Paul, The.

Conviction
Creeley. Way, The.

Cooking and Cooks
Aiken, J. Palace Cook's Tale.
Alexie. Capital Punishment.
Barkar. Canning Season.
Berry, W. Grandmother, The.
Cardona. Old Dream Oven, The.
Chang Yü. Quatrain: "At this remote village, I have no neighbors."
Clifton, L. Cutting Greens.
Divakaruni. Making Samosas.
Ellis, C. On a Gentleman Marrying His Cook.
Forbes, C. Potlicker Blues.
Gardner, I. Widow's Yard, The.
Gilbert, S. Ferdinando and Elvira; or, The Gentle Pieman.
Graves, R. Under the Pot.
Hamod, S. Leaves.
Harper, M. Breaded Meat, Breaded Hands.
Hoffenstein. You hire a cook, but she can't cook yet
Jong. Woman Who Loved to Cook, The.
Katz, B. Recipe.
Kim, H. Fish Cooking.
Kingston, M. Restaurant.
Lorde. From the House of Yemanjá.
Lowell, A. Interlude.
Massinger. Men May Talk of Country-Christmasses.
McGrath, T. Bread of this World; Praises III, The.
Mei Yao Ch'en. Chiang Lin-chi Treats Me to Mudfish.
Meng Hao Jan. Stopping at a Friend's Farm.
Miller, V. Trimming the Sails.

Moody, E. Sappho Burns Her Books and Cultivates the Culinary Arts.
Mother Goose. Pat-a-cake, pat-a-cake, baker's man.
Muldoon, P. Sushi.
Nemerov. Lobsters.
Newcastle, M. Nature's Cook.
Pickard, T. Recipe: Pastime for the Unemployed.
Piercy. What's That Smell in the Kitchen?
Randall, J. Recipes.
Rossetti, C. Mix a pancake, / Stir a pancake.
Saffoti. Espresso.
Shange. Different Love Poem / We Need a Change, A.
Skeeter. Western Trail Cook, 1880.
Strange. Offering.
Tadic. I Ask.
Tapahonso. All I want is the bread to turn out like hers just once.
Unknown. Don't-Care—he didn't care.
Sally, Sally Waters, sprinkle in the pan.
"Vaidehi." Girl in the Kitchen.
Wang Chien. Words of the Newly Wed Wife.
Waniek. Bali Hai Calls Mama.
Willard, N. How to Stuff a Pepper.

Coole, Ireland
Yeats. Coole Park and Ballylee, 1931.
Coole Park, 1929.
In the Seven Woods.
Wild Swans at Coole, The.

Cooper, James Fenimore
Lowell, J. Cooper.

Copernicus, Nicholas
Leapor. Epistle to a Lady, An.

Coral
Lieberman, L. Coral Reef, The.
Percival. Coral Grove, The.

Corinth, Greece
Antipater of Thessalonica. Where is your famous beauty.

Cormac Mac Art
Ferguson, S. Burial of King Cormac, The.

Cormorants
Blight. Cormorants.
Clampitt. Cormorant in His Element, The.
Clifton, L. To the Unborn and Waiting Children.
Isherwood. Common Cormorant [or Shag], The.

Corn
Bakken. How to Eat Corn.
Bly, R. Snowfall in the Afternoon.
Campbell, J. Song of the Corn.
Ch'ien T'ao. New Corn.
Dunbar, P. Corn-Stalk Fiddle, THe.
Gibran. Prophet Speaks of Love, The.
Kitahara Hakushū. Tanka: "Gleaming sliver."
Koianimptiwa. Korosta Katzina Song.
Lanier, S. Waving of the Corn, The.
McAlmon. Frost in the Corn, The.
Po Chü-i. Watching the Reapers.
Sandburg, C. Early Copper.
Unknown. Corn Song.
Guinea Corn.
Lo! ye children of men and the Mother.
Poem to Be Recited Every 8 Years While Eating Unleavened Tamales.
Willard, N. Speckled Hen's Morning Song to Biddy Early, The.

Cornwall, England
Betjeman. Trebetherick.
Gray, J. On the South Coast of Cornwall.
Hawker. Song of the Western Men, The.
Redgrove, P. Minerals of Cornwall, Stones of Cornwall.
Skelton, R. Ballad of a Mine, A.
Strong, L. March Evening.

Corpses
Aldington. Soliloquy 2.
Alegría. From the Bridge.
Baudelaire. Carrion, A.
Bly, R. Counting Small-Boned Bodies.
Breytenbach. Asylum.
Celan. Night Ray.
Das, J. Corpse, The.

Derricotte. On the Turning Up of Unidentified Black Female Corpses.
Dickinson, E. Do People moulder equally.
Djogo. National Hero, The.
Dobson, A. Before Sedan.
Elytis. Sleep of the Brave, The.
Fumi Saito. Tanka: "When I think over."
Geda. Sebastian's Lament, 1943.
Hemans. Image in Lava, The.
High. Lives of thomas—episodes and prayers, The.
Housman, A. Some can gaze and not be sick.
"MacDiarmid." Dead Liebknecht, The.
Meyers, B. Suburban Dusk.
Miyazawa Kenji. River in Hell (two poems).
Neruda. Nothing but Death.
Phillips, C. As From a Quiver of Arrows.
Plath. Two Views of a Cadaver Room.
Radnóti. Picture Postcards.
Rilke. Matthew 27:57–61; When it was evening, there came a rich man.
Ryuichi. Standing Coffin.
Senior. Searching for Grandfather.
Snodgrass, W. Old Apple Trees.
Southerland. Blue Clay.
Stanescu. Marina.
Swinburne. After Death.
Ts'ao Sung. Protest in the Sixth Year of Ch'ien Fu, A.
Unknown. Have I a body or have I none?
Hearse Song, The.
Yeats. Oil and Blood.
Yüan Hao-wen. Song of the Maidens.
Zenmaro. Evidence.

Correggio (Antonio Allegri)
De Vere, A. Correggio's Cupolas at Parma.
Corruption
Baraka. Three Modes of History and Culture.
Blake, W. London ("I wander through [*or* thro'] each chartered [*or* charter'd] street").
To see a World in a Grain of Sand.
Bly, R. Executive's Death, The.
Boethius. Chawcer upon this fyfte meter of the second book.
Byron, G. Answer to ——'s Professions of Affection.
Carter, M. After One Year.
Chaucer. Friar's Tale, The.
Pardoner's Prologue, The.
Donne. Satire 3.
. . . Then, as if he would have sold.
Graves, R. Wigs and Beards.
Hall, D. One Day, The.
Hemphill. Family Jewels.
Holmes, O. Latter-Day Warnings.
Hull, L. Fiat Lux.
Jeffers, R. Stars Go Over the Lonely Ocean, The.
Jonson, B. On English Monsieur.
Krynicki. By entering the grand lottery.
Lindsay, V. What the Moon Saw.
Martial. To the Emperour Titus, upon his Banishing Sycophants.
McClure, M. Senate Hearings.
Milton. Behold alone / The Woman, opportune to all attempts.
Odoyevtseva. Ground Glass.
Ovid. Elegies 3.13.
Sandburg, C. Soiled Dove.
Shakespeare, W. Sonnet 35.
Sonnet 54.
Sonnet 94.
Spenser. Legend of the Knight of the Red Crosse, or of Holinesse, The.
Unknown. Epitaph on the Duke of Buckingham.
Vaughan, H. Town believes thee lost, and didst thou see, The.
Williams, M. Love and How It Becomes Important in Our Day to Day Lives.
Coruña, La, Spain
Wolfe, C. Burial of Sir John Moore [after [*or* at] Corunna], The.
Cosmetics
Berryman. Dream Song 4.
Chao Luan-luan. Willow Eyebrows.
Chu Shu-chen. Morning.

Donne. Phryne.
Herrick. Upon Sibilla.
Hong, Y. On Ornament.
Jonson, B. Simplex Munditiis.
Kowit. Cosmetics do no good.
Lochhead, L. Heartbreak Hotel.
Lucianus. Artificial Beauty.
Naden. Two Artists, The.
Pope, A. Sol through white curtains shot a tim'rous ray.
Potos. Depending on the Light.
Prior. Phillis's Age.
Swift, J. Progress of Beauty, The.
Symons, A. Maquillage.
Tai Piao-yüan. South of the house, north of the house.
T'ang Hsien-tsu. Inspector Hsü Claims He Has Found the Secret of Youth.
Wratislaw. Opoponax.
Yang Wei-chen. Painting Her Nails.
Cosmology
Bendall, M. Conversations on the Plurality of Worlds.
Brown, G. Hierarchy.
Clairmont. Answers, The.
Fox, S. Almagest, Last Letter to Zakarias.
Spark. Litany of Time Past.
Unknown. Rain Song of the Shu'-wi Chai'än (Snake Society), A.
Cosmos
Jones, R. Explanation of the Exhibit, An.
Olson, C. Celestial Evening, October 1967.
Tuckerman, F. Sonnet: "And so, as this great sphere (now turning slow)."
See also **Creation**
Cotswold Hills, England
Gurney, I. High Hills, The.
Thomas, E. Adlestrop.
Cotton
Bontemps. Southern Mansion.
Davis, F. Snapshots of the Cotton South.
Martinson. Cotton.
Timrod. Cotton Boll, The.
Toomer. Cotton Song.
November Cotton Flower.
Unknown. Pick a Bale of Cotton.
Poor Little Johnny.
Roll the Cotton Down.
Whittier. Haschish, The.
Counterfeiting and Counterfeiters
Juana Inés de la Cruz. This coloured counterfeit that thou beholdest.
Williamson, G. Counterfeiter, The.
Counting
Baldwin, A. Ten Little Dicky-Birds.
Bernstein, O. Don't Count.
Cook, S. Launch, The.
Hutchinson, M. Making Tens.
Justice, D. Counting the Mad.
Lehrer. Wernher von Braun.
Livingston, M. Cried a man on the Salisbury Plain.
Mother Goose. One to Ten.
One, two, three, four, / Mary at the cottage door.
Thirty days hath September.
Prévert. Inventory.
Rice, J. Brokendown Countdown.
Rosen, M. One, Two, Three.
Soto. Teaching Numbers.
Unknown. Counting-out Rhyme, A.
One to Ten.
One, two, three, four, five / Once I caught a fish alive.
Thirty days hath September.
Yolen. Shepherd's Night Count.
Country Life
Adams, L. Country Summer.
Ammons. Hardweed Path Going.
Anderson, M. Country Wisdoms.
Ashe. City Clerk, The.
Auden. Thanksgiving for a Habitat.
Baillie, J. Disappointment, A.
Barnes, W. Common a-Took In, The.
Blamire. From where dark clouds of curling smoke arise.

Blunt, W. Old Squire, The.
Boethius. Happy is he, that with fix'd Eyes.
Bogan, L. Old Countryside.
Brereton, C. To Miss A[——]a M[——]a Tra[——]s; an Epistle from Scotland.
Breton, N. Merry Country Lad, The.
Brown, S. Virginia Portrait.
Byron, H. Rural Simplicity.
Centlivre. From the Country, to Mr. Rowe in Town.
Chong, C. Nostalgic Urge.
Clare, J. Cowper, the poet of the fields.
Mole-Catcher, The.
Moors, The.
Muse of the fields, oft have I said farewell.
Noon.
Winter Fields.
Claudian. Old Man of Verona, The.
Clough. Dipsychus.
Coleridge, S. Reflections on Having Left a Place of Retirement.
Colman, G. London Rurality.
Cornford, F. Country Bedroom, The.
Cowley, A. Wish, The.
Cowper, W. My Pet Hare.
Crabbe. Truth in Poetry.
Year revolves, and I explore, The.
Creeley. City, The.
Cunningham, J. Montana Pastoral.
Donne. To Sir Henry Wotton ("Sir, more than kisses, letters mingle souls").
Dunn, D. In the Grounds.
"Dylan." Tiny Montgomery.
Emanuel, L. Film Noir: Train Trip Out.
Fanshawe, S. Ode on His Majesty's Proclamation.
Farewell. Crunking crane heard high amongst the clouds, The.
Francis, R. Silent Poem.
Frost, R. Directive.
Need of Being Versed in Country Things, The.
Gale, N. Country Faith, The.
Garland, H. Goin' Back T'morrer.
Garrigue. After Reading "The Country of the Pointed Firs."
Gashe. Village, The.
Giovanni. Knoxville, Tennessee.
Gogarty. Farrell O'Reilly.
Gonzalez, A. Gasparillo Remembered.
Graves, R. On Dwelling.
Greenaway. Three little girls were sitting on a rail.
Gregg. Adult.
Grierson. To Miss Laetitia Van Lewen.
Hall, D. Names of Horses.
Ox Cart Man.
Hardy, T. In Time of "The Breaking of Nations."
Hart, L. Mountain Greenery.
Henley, S. Verses Addressed to a Friend, Just Leaving a Favourite Retirement.
Herrick. Country Life: To His Brother, M. Tho: Herrick.
Country Life, to the Honored Mr. Endymion Porter[, Groome of the Bed-Chamber to His Maj.], The.
His Content in the Country.
His Grange, or Private Wealth.
To Phyllis to Love and Live with Him.
Hewitt, J. O country people, you of the hill farms.
Hogg, J. Boy's Song, A.
Horace. Praises of a Country Life, The.
Jarrell. Country Life, A.
Jewett, S. Country Boy in Winter, A.
Kavanagh, P. Epic.
Maguire is not afraid of death, the Church will light him a candle.
Spraying the Potatoes.
Keats. Dawlish Fair.
To one who has been long in city pent.
Where be you [*or* ye] going, you [*or* ye] Devon maid?
Kinnell. Farm Picture.
When one has lived a long time alone.
Kumin, M. Saga.
Lanyer. Description of Cooke-ham, The.

Lawrence, D. Love On the Farm.
 Whether or Not.
Lee, J. Lusca.
Lewis, E. You midst gay crowds reside, I, hid
 in shades.
Lloyd, R. Cit's Country Box, The.
Longfellow, H. Fire of Drift-Wood, The.
Longley, M. Gorse Fires.
 West, The.
Lu Yu. Idle Thoughts.
 Idleness.
 My Village Home.
 Sailing on the Lake to the Ching River.
 Snug—the robe sewn from coarse cotton.
Lux. There Were Some Summers.
Mahon. Woods, The.
Martial. Happy Life, A.
Martinson. Dusk in the Country.
Marvell. And now to the abyss I pass.
 Garden, The.
Mason, W. Heroic Epistle to Sir William
 Chambers, An.
Melville, H. Immolated.
Meredith, G. Here Jack and Tom are paired
 with Moll and Meg.
Millay, E. Return, The.
Miller, J. Squirrel Stand.
Murray, L. Noonday Axeman.
Nemerov. At a Country Hotel.
Ovid. Philemon and Baucis.
P'an Yüeh. Rhyme-Prose on the Idle Life.
Plumpp. Clinton.
Pope, A. Epistle to Miss [or Miss Teresa]
 Blount, on Her Leaving the Town after the
 Coronation.
 Happy Life of a Country Parson, The.
Purdy, A. Country North of Belleville, The.
Ramkissoon-Chen. Father.
Randolph, T. Ode to Mr. Anthony Stafford to
 Hasten Him into the Country, An.
Ravenscroft, E. In Derision of a Country Life.
Reaney. Upper Canadian, The.
Reynolds, B. Cranberry Song, The.
Riley, J. Back to Griggsby's Station.
 Country Pathway, A.
 When the frost is on the punkin and the
 fodder's in the shock.
Rogers, S. Wish, A.
Sansom, M. Invitation from a Country
 Cottage, The.
Schuyler, J. Korean Mums.
Senior. Hill Country.
Seymour, F. Life at Richkings.
Shakespeare, W. Song: "Under the greenwood
 tree."
Simic. Ballad: "What's that approaching like
 dust like poverty."
 Old Mountain Road.
Slessor. Country Towns.
Snyder, G. After Work.
Stevenson, R. Translations from Martial.
Stuart, D. Mining in Killdeer Alley.
Su Tung-p'o. Rhyming with Tzu-yu's
 "Treading the Green."
Sylvester, J. Of a Husbandman.
T'ao Ch'ien. Matching a Poem by Secretary
 Kuo.
 Moving House ("In spring and fall there are
 many fine days").
 Moving House ("Long time I've wanted to
 live in the southern village, A").
 Returning to My Home in the Country ("So
 long since I've enjoyed the hills and ponds").
Tate, J. Land of Little Sticks, 1945.
Tennyson, A. City Child, The.
Thomas, E. Haymaking.
Tu Fu. Country Cottage.
Unknown. As long as I was living in the
 village.
 Oak and the Ash, The.
Untermeyer, L. Country of No Lack.
Vaughan, H. Retirement.
Virgil. Honest life, The.
Walcott. Upstate.
Walker, M. Childhood.
Waller, E. At Penshurst [Another].

Wang Wei. Lush, lush, fragrant grasses in
 autumn green.
Warren, R. Renoir.
Waterman, N. Far from the Madding Crowd.
Weöres. Plain, The.
Westmorland. My Country Audit.
 To Retiredness.
Whitman, W. Farm Picture, A.
Williams, M. Love and How It Becomes
 Important in Our Day to Day Lives.
Williams, W. Raleigh Was Right.
 Woman Walking.
Winchilsea. Ballad to Mrs. Catherine Fleming
 in London from Malshanger Farm in
 Hampshire, A.
Wordsworth, W. Inscription for the Moss-Hut
 at Dove Cottage.
Wright, C. Rural Route.
 Two Stories.
Wright, J. Country Dance.
Wright, K. How the Wild South East Was
 Lost.
Wu Wei-yeh. Garden Living.
Yang Chi. Walking in the Country outside
 T'ai-yüan on a Spring Day.
Yeats. Lake-Isle of Innisfree, The.
Yi, T. Gang-gang-suwole.

County Antrim, Northern Ireland
MacNeice. Carrickfergus.
"O'Neill." Grace for Light.

County Cork, Ireland
Mahon. Garage in Co. Cork, A.
 Kinsale.
Millikin. Groves of Blarney [they look so
 charming], The.

County Galway, Ireland
Murphy, R. High Island.
 Sailing to an Island.

County Kerry, Ireland
Synge. In Kerry.

County Mayo, Ireland
Flavell. County of Mayo, The.

County Meath, Ireland
Higgins, F. Father and Son.

County Monaghan, Ireland
Kavanagh, P. Shancoduff.
 Stony Grey Soil.

County Sligo, Ireland
Yeats. Lake-Isle of Innisfree, The.

County Waterford, Ireland
Unknown. God of his goodnes, praysed that he
 be.

Courage
Aeschylus. On the Thessalians Who Fought at
 Marathon.
"Akhmatova." Courage.
"Alta." 29.
Amis, K. Autobiographical Fragment.
Anacreon. Timokritos was bold in war. This is
 his grave.
Anyte. Indeed then, it was your own courage.
Atwood. Notes towards a Poem That Can
 Never Be Written.
Babcock, M. Be Strong!
Brontë, E. No coward soul is mine.
Brooke, R. Hill, The.
Brooks, G. Strong Men, riding horses. In the
 West.
Bunyan. Pilgrim, The.
Cameron, N. Thespians at Thermopylae, The.
Cary, P. Leak in the Dike, The.
Castillo, O. Distances.
Clough. Say not the struggle nought [or
 naught] availeth.
Colesworthy. Be Never Discouraged.
Cook, E. "No!"
Cooke, E. How Did You Die?
Cornaros. Observe how Eros works his magic
 spells.
Coward. Fortitude.
Crowell, G. Courage to Live.
 I think that God is proud of those who bear.
Dickinson, E. I took my Power in my Hand.
Douglas, K. Gallantry.
Emerson, R. In an age of fops and toys.
Euripides. I crossed sand-hills.

Galsworthy. Prayer, The.
Gilbert, J. Abnormal Is Not Courage, The.
Glazkov. Subject for a Story.
Gordon, A. Question not, but live and labor.
Hegemon. Thermopylai.
Herbert, G. Courage.
Housman, A. Loitering with a vacant eye.
Howard, W. Young men!
Jonson, B. On Playwright ("Playwright convict
 of public wrongs to men").
Kennelly. Dream of a Black Fox.
Kushner, A. He who doesn't dance still
 dances.
Legaré. Tallulah.
Lu Yu. Long Sigh.
Ludvigson. Some Notes on Courage.
Lvov, M. To become a man, it's little to be
 born.
McKay, C. Baptism.
 If we must die—let it not be like hogs.
Millay, E. Courage that my mother had, The.
Milton. Consolation.
Mnasalces. Setting their country free.
Moore, J. One Reason I Went to Prison.
Owen, W. Spring Offensive.
Parmenion of Macedon. Thermopylai.
Patterson, R. You Are the Brave.
Ralegh, W. On the Snuff of a Candle.
Rich, A. Trying to Talk with a Man.
Rossetti, C. I do not look for love that is a
 dream.
Rumi. Core of masculinity does not derive
 from being male, The.
 Where is a foot worthy to walk a garden,.
Salter. Frost at Midnight.
Sassoon. Hero, The.
Scannell. Any Complaints?
Schneour. Besieged.
Scott, W. Red Harlaw.
Shakespeare, W. Once more unto the breach,
 dear friends, / once more.
Simonides. Cenotaph at the Isthmos.
 For the Athenian Dead at Plataia.
 On His Friend Megistias, Who Died at
 Thermopylai.
 There is one story.
Slutsky. How They Killed My Grandmother.
Solomon ibn Gabirol. Defiance.
Soupault. Sporting Goods.
Taylor, G. Dare to Do Right.
Thomas, R. Lore.
Thorpe, R. Curfew Must Not Ring Tonight.
Unknown. It Can Be Done.
 (My Daily Creed).
 On the Athenians Who Died at the Hellespont,
 440–39 B.C.
Vallejo. Masses.
Very. Fear Not: For They That Be With Us.
Wagner, C. Let's forget the many troubles.
Walwicz. Daredevil.
Webb, F. Art.
Whittier. Barbara Frietchie.
Wright, J. Mad Fight Song for William S.
 Carpenter, 1966, A.
Wright, J. Legend.
Yevtushenko. From a Talk.
Yosano. Come at last to this point.
Zach. Greater Courage.
Zenmaro. On the birth of my son.

Coureurs de Bois
Le Pan. Coureurs de Bois.

Courtesy
Auden. Dedication: "Private faces in public
 places."
Belševica. That was a very polite fish.
Elwell. Courtesy is a quality of soul /
 refinement impossible to purchase.
Robinson, E. Flammonde.
Unknown. See the Rat—at Least It's Got a
 Hide.

Courtiers
"Anvari." Hors de Combat.
"Carroll." King-Fisher [or King-Fisher's]
 Song, The.
Donne. Satire 4.
 . . . Then, as if he would have sold.
 To Sir Henry Wotton ("Here's no more news,

than virtue, I may as well").
To Sir Henry Wotton ("Sir, more than kisses, letters mingle souls").
Jonson, B. On Court-Worm[e].
Nguyễn Gia Thiều. Song of Sorrow Inside the Royal Harem, A.
Ransom, J. Vaunting Oak.
Steele, T. Epitaph: "Here lies Sir Tact, a diplomatic fellow."
Unknown. Mode of France, The.
Wyatt, T. Myn owne John poyntz sins ye delight to know.

Courtship
Akhmadulina. Fifteen Boys, or Perhaps Even More.
Alexie. Reservation Love Song.
Amaru. Though she's the girl, I am the one who's shy.
Amis, K. Pendydd.
Angira. Request.
Auden. As I walked out one evening.
Awoonor. Lovers' Song.
Ayton. Answer, The.
Rejection, The.
Song: "What means this strangeness now of late."
There is none, no none but I.
To His Coy Mistress.
Upon His Unconstant Mistress.
Baillie, J. Song: Woo'd and married and a'.
Barnes, W. Bit o' Sly Coorten, A.
White an' Blue.
With you first shown to me.
Beckett, S. Song: "Age is when to a man."
Behn, A. Dream, The.
To Lysander.
Bellamy, D. Letters of Mina Harker, The.
Berryman. I wished, all the mild days of middle March.
Betjeman. Subaltern's Love-Song, A.
Blake, W. Never Pain to Tell Thy Love.
Prince of Love, The.
Blamire. Auld Robin Forbes.
Bonin-Rodriguez. Steven Pudenz.
Brooks, G. Lovely Love, A.
Browning, E. Lord Walter's Wife.
Man's Requirements, A.
Sonnet: "First time he kissed me, he but only kissed."
Sonnet: "First time that the sun rose on thine oath, The."
Sonnet: "My letters! all dead paper, mute and white."
Year's Spinning, A.
Browning, R. Light Woman, A.
Burns, R. Ca' the ewes [or yowes] to the knowes.
Comin[g] thro' [or through] the rye, poor body.
Duncan Gray cam here to woo.
Halloween.
Hark, the mavis' evening sang.
I Once was a maid, tho' I cannot tell when.
Mary Morison.
Song: "It was upon a Lammas night."
Whistle, and I'll Come to You, My Lad.
Calverley. In the gloaming to be roaming[, where the crested waves are foaming].
Campbell, T. Freedom and Love.
Campion, T. Advice to a Girl.
Dance, The.
Elegye, An: "Constant to none, but ever false to me."
Follow, follow[e] / Though with mischiefe.
I care not for these ladies.
My sweetest Lesbia, let us live and love.
Now winter nights enlarge.
Shall I come, sweet love, to thee.
So quicke, so hot, so mad is thy fond sute.
Think'st thou to seduce me then with words that have no meaning?
Though your strangenesse frets my hart.
Thus I resolve, and time hath taught me so.
What fair pomp have I spied of glittering ladies.
Carew, T. Boldness[e] in Love.
Song: Good Counsel to a Young Maid.

To A. L.; Persuasions [or Perswasions] to Love.
To a Lady That Desired I Would Love Her.
Carey, H. Roger and Dolly.
Carmichael, R. Young Lass's Soliloquy, A.
"Carroll." King-Fisher [or King-Fisher's] Song, The.
Cassian. Performances.
Causley. My young man's a Cornishman.
Cavalcanti. Sonnet: To His Lady Joan, of Florence.
Chaucer. Franklin's Tale, The.
To Rosamounde.
Cheng Hsieh. Girl from Ch'ang-kan is just fourteen years old, The.
Chudleigh. Song: "Why Damon, why, why, why so pressing?"
Clifton, H. Polly Perkins.
Cook, E. Song of the Ugly Maiden.
Corso. Love Poem for Three for Kaye & Me.
Marriage.
Coward. Irish Song [Rosie O'Grady].
Cowley, A. Change, The.
Cummings, E. As freedom is a breakfastfood.
Daniel, S. Go wailing verse, the infants of my love.
Dante Alighieri. I felt a spirit of love begin to stir.
New love and the gentle heart are the same thing.
Davies, S. Faith (wench) I cannot court thy sprightly eyes.
De la Mare. Some One.
Dickinson, E. Death is the supple Suitor.
God is a distant—stately Lover.
Dodsley. Progress of Love, The.
Donne. Elegie: "Nature's lay ideot, I taught thee to love."
Prohibition, The.
Dove, R. Adolescence—III.
Courtship.
Du Bois. Song: "Scholar first my Love implor'd, A."
Dubois, L. Song: "Scholar first my love implored, A."
Duffy, M. Semi-Skilled Lover.
Dunbar, P. Howdy, Honey, Howdy!
Durcan. Lion Tamer, The.
Eberhart, R. When Doris danced under the oak tree.
"Ephelia." On a Bashful Shepherd.
"Ern Malley." Boult to Marina.
Perspective Lovesong.
Fêng Mêng-lung. Love-Poem.
Fitzgerald, F. Epitaph from *The Great Gatsby.*
Frost, R. Line-Storm Song, A.
Garrigue. Cracked Looking Glass.
To speak of my influences.
Gay, J. To a Young Lady, with Some Lampreys.
Gershwin. Embraceable You.
Gilbert, S. Ferdinando and Elvira; or, The Gentle Pieman.
Godfrey. Our Lady.
Goethe. Roman Elegy Ia.
Grimké, A. Caprichosa.
Hall, J. Call, The.
Hands, E. Favourite Swain, The.
Lob's Courtship.
Perplexity: A Poem.
Widower's Courtship, The.
Hardy, T. Epitaph on a Pessimist.
Hecht, A. Ghost in the Martini, The.
Samuel Sewall.
Herrick. Chop-Cherry.
Conjuration, to Electra, A.
Corinna's Going A-Maying.
To [the] Virgins, to Make Much of Time.
Up Tail[e]s All.
Hood, T. Ballad: Time of Roses.
Hookes. To Amanda Walking in the Garden.
Horace. Dialogue in Imitation of that between Horace and Lydia, A.
8th Ode of Book I. of Horace imitated in the Cumberland Manner and Dialect, The.
Horat. Carm. lib. 4. Ode 13.
To his Friend in Love with a young Girl.
Housman, A. Along the field as we came by.

Oh see how thick the goldcup flowers.
Sloe was lost in flower, The.
Hyland, G. Fet Walks Melody Home.
Ilanakanar, M. When a King Asks for a Chieftain's Daughter.
Johnson, A. Gifts.
Jonson, B. To Celia.
Kapilar. What She Said Her Lover within Earshot.
What She Said ("'O your hair,' he said").
What She Said to Her Girl Friend, Her Foster-Mother within Earshot.
What She Said to Her Girl Friend ("O you, you wear flowers of gold").
Keats. Stanzas: "You say you love; but with a voice."
To ———: "Had I a man's fair form, then might my sighs."
Where be you [or ye] going, you [or ye] Devon maid?
Komunyakaa. Thorn Merchant's Mistress, The.
Lawrence, D. Cherry Robbers.
Drained Cup, The.
Tortoise Gallantry.
Leapor. Strephon to Celia.
Lear, E. Courtship of the Yonghy-Bonghy-Bo, The.
Li Shang-yin. Spring Rain.
Li Yü. Tune: "Deva-like Barbarian" ("Bright flowers and dim moon, enmeshed in thin drifting mist").
Liu Yung. Tune: "Chrysanthemums Fresh."
Livingstone, D. One Time.
Lochhead, L. My Mother's Suitors.
Lowell, A. Hora Stellatrix.
Madhubuti. My brothers i will not tell you.
Marlowe. Passionate Shepherd [or Sheepheard] To His Love, The.
Martial. Martial's Favourites.
Marvell. To His Coy Mistress.
Meredith, G. I think she sleeps: it must be sleep, when low.
Love in the Valley.
Sonnet 29: "Am I failing? For no longer can I cast."
Merrill, S. Ballade of the Chinese Lover.
Miller, E. Another Love Affair/Another Poem.
Monck. On A Romantic Lady.
Montagu, L. Answer to a Love-Letter in Verse, An.
Between your sheets you soundly sleep.
Lady's Resolve, The.
To a Lady Making Love.
Moore, T. Time I've lost in wooing, The.
Mother Goose. Mr. Frog Went a-Courting.
Musaeus. Amaze then tooke him.
Courtship.
Naden. Love Versus Learning.
Natural Selection.
Scientific Wooing.
North, D. Platonic is a pretty name.
Oppian. Loves of the Tortoise, The.
Orampokiyar. What She Said ("In his place, mother, / mud-spattered spotted crabs").
Ovid. Defensive measures.
If in this Town an unflusht Puny be.
Palmer, O. Wasting Time.
Parker, D. One Perfect Rose.
Social Note.
Unfortunate Coincidence.
Parmenion of Macedon. For a little gold, Zeus bought Danae.
Patchen. We go out together into the staring town.
Patmore, C. Love Serviceable.
Paulus Silentiarius. United.
Philips, K. Answer to Another Persuading a Lady to Marriage, An.
Philodemus. —"Hello there.—*Hello there yourself.*
Wax-contoured, in your face a Muse.
Porter, C. Brush Up Your Shakespeare.
Pound, E. River-Merchant's Wife: A Letter, The.
Prior. Les Estreines.
Ode, An: "Merchant, to secure his treasure, The."

Propertius. Me happy, night, night full of brightness.
Rabéarivelo. Imaginary tremolo.
Ralegh, W. Excuse, The.
Nimphs [or Nymph's] Reply to the Sheepheard [or Shepherd], The.
Ocean's Love to Cynthia, The.
Sir Walter Ralegh to the Queen.
Raleigh. Nymph's Reply to the Shepherd, The.
Ranaivo. Choice.
Rankin, J. Man is following me, A.
Ransom, J. Piazza Piece.
Richards, L. Antonio, Antonio.
Ridley. Cushie Butterfield.
Roethke. For An Amorous Lady.
Rossetti, C. Amor Mundi.
Cousin Kate.
No, Thank You, John.
Noble Sisters.
Triad, A.
Rossetti, D. Willowwood ("I sat with Love upon a woodside well").
Rowe, E. To Orestes.
Salter. Young Girl Peeling Apples.
Sedley. Song: Love Still Has Something of the Sea.
Shakespeare, W. Blossom, The.
Juliet: Good-night, good-night! as sweet repose and rest.
Song: "It was a lover and his lass."
Welcome from Egypt, sir.
Shelley, P. Longest Journey, The.
Sidney, P. Bargain, The.
Eighth Song: "In a grove most rich of shade."
Eleventh Song: "Who is it that this darke[o] night."
Fourth Song: "Only joy, now here you are."
Sapphics.
Sonnet 6: "Some lovers speak, when they their Muses entertain."
Sonnet 61: "Oft with true sighs, oft with uncalled tears."
Sonnet 64: "No more, my dear, no more these counsels try."
Sonnet 69: "O joy, too high for my low style to show."
Sonnet 107: "Stella, since thou so right a Princess art."
Sissoko. Like a Flower.
Smith, C. On the Aphorism "L'Amitié est l'Amour sans Ailes."
Stanzas: "Ah! think'st thou, Laura, then, that wealth."
Smith, S. Landrecie.
Soto. Oranges.
Spenser. Sonnet 67: "Like a huntsman after weary chase."
Stevenson, R. Song of a Traveller, The.
Stirling, S. Echo, An.
Strand. Courtship.
Suckling, J. Barley-Break , A.
Love's Siege.
Loving and Beloved.
Ode to Lovers.
Song: "I prithee spare me, gentle boy."
Song: "No, no, fair heretic[k], it needs must be."
Song: "Why so pale and wan, fond lover?"
Sonnet: "Of thee, kind boy, I ask no red and white."
Sullivan, J. Sagimusume: The White Heron Maiden.
Surrey. Love, that doth reign and live within my thought.
Swenson, M. Fireflies throw.
Symons, A. Prologue: Before the Curtain.
Tennyson, A. Marriage Morning.
Song: "Come into the garden, Maud."
Theocritus. Idyll.
Tibullus. Elegies 1.iv: "Far from the tender Tribe of Boys remove."
Elegies, I.iv: "Yield prompt compliance to the maid's desires."
Titherage. And Her Mother Came Too.
Toure, A. Frontier of rage that exists, The.
Unknown. Bailiff's Daughter of Islington, The.
Billy Boy.

Cold Is the North Wind.
Do you carrot all for me?
Dowie Dens of Yarrow, The.
Four on a Sidewalk.
I Go before, my darling.
If You Think Kindly of Me.
Marvelous Encounter at Blue Creek, The.
O excellent sovereigne, most semely to see.
On Top of Old Smoky.
Please, Chung Tzu.
Plum Tree Drops Its Fruit, The.
Polly Perkins.
Quoth John to Joan.
She Says, Cocks Are Crowing!
Songs of Courtship.
Three Knights from Spain.
Visit, The.
Uruttiran. What She Said to Her Girl Friend, and What Her Girl Friend Said in Reply.
Venantius Fortunatus. To The Lady Radegund, With Violets.
Virgil. Queen whom sense of Honor cou'd not move, The.
Wade-Gayles. Inquisition.
Walker, A. Did This Happen to Your Mother? Did Your Sister Throw Up a Lot?
Whalen. Slop Barrel, The.
Whitman, W. Dalliance of the Eagles, The.
Wickham. Boor's Wooing, The.
Williams, W. First Praise.
Willis, N. City Lyrics.
Winik. Foreign Exchange.
Wyatt, T. I have sought long with steadfastness.
If waker care, if sudden [or sodayne] pale colo[u]r.
Madam, withouten Many Words.
Since Love will needs that I shall love.
Sonnet: 'The long love'.
When first mine eyes did view and mark.
Yeats. Cap and Bells, The.

Cousins
Brooks, G. Rites for Cousin Vit, The.
Coleman, W. Cousin Mary.
Eliot, T. Cousin Nancy.
López Velarde. My Cousin Agueda [or Agatha].
McGough, R. Cousin Reggie.
Nerval. Girl Cousin, The.

Coventry, England
Larkin, P. I Remember, I Remember.

Cowardice and Cowards
Boker. Oh! craven, craven! while my brothers fall.
"Carroll." Phantasmagoria.
Eliot, T. Gerontion.
Homer. Hector's flight.
Housman, A. My dreams are of a field afar.
Kipling, R. Coward, The.
Dead Statesman, A.
Heriot's Ford.
Lamb, C. On Mackintosh.
Lawrence, D. Willy Wet-Leg.
Levine, P. Heaven.
Yukitsuna. Tanka: "Moonlight, The."

Cowboys
Adams, J. Cowboy's Life, The.
Alexander, E. Deadwood Dick.
Antrobus. Cowboy, The.
Campbell, D. Song for the Cattle.
Causley. Cowboy Song.
Clark, C. Plainsmen, The.
Dorn, E. Idle Visitation, An.
Vaquero.
Fletcher, C. High-loping Cowboy, The.
Huidobro. Cow Boy.
Kao Ch'i. Old Cowboy, The.
Major, C. I Was Looking for the University.
McElroy, C. With Bill Pickett at the 101 Ranch.
Mercer, J. I'm an Old Cowhand.
Michie. Arizona Nature Myth.
O'Malley, D. Tenderfoot, The.
Reed, I. I Am a Cowboy in the Boat of Ra.
Smith, W. Closing of the Rodeo, The.
Tomlinson, C. At Barstow.
Unknown. Bucking Bronco.

Buffalo Skinners, The.
California Trail.
Cow Boy's Lament.
Cowboy Sayings.
Cowboy's Lament, The.
Cowboy's Life Is a Very Dreary Life, The.
Educated Feller.
I Ride an Old Paint.
I've Got No Use for the Women.
O I'm a jolly old cowboy.
Old Chisholm Trail, The.
Poor Lonesome Cowboy.
Red Whiskey.
Texas Cowboy, The.
When the Work's All Done This Fall.
Whoopee Ti Yi Yo, Git Along Little Dogies.
Zebra Dun, The.
Warren, R. Rattlesnake Country.

Cowper, William
Browning, E. Cowper's Grave.
Clare, J. Cowper, the poet of the fields.

Cows
Avidan. Glimpse of an Open Dream.
Burgess, F. Cinq Ans Après.
Purple Cow.
Clifton, L. My Dream About the Cows.
D'Aguiar. *Cow Perserverance, The.*
Disch. Cow of Our Time, A.
Fatchen. 'Jump over the moon?' the cow declared.
Flook. Discreet.
Frost, R. Cow in Apple Time, The.
Fumiko. Tanka: "Sharing the gentleness."
Hands, E. Written, Originally Extempore, on Seeing a Mad Heifer Run through the Village.
Hardy, T. Calf, The.
Hawkins, R. Cattle.
Herrick. Supreme Fortune Falls Soonest.
Hillyer. Moo!
Howells, W. Robin and the Cows, The.
Kerouac. Arms folded.
Kinnell. Freedom, New Hampshire.
Kocan. Cows graze across the hill.
Lochhead, L. Abortion, An.
MacCaig. Fetching Cows.
McCaffrey. Apprehension.
McNair. Mina Bell's Cows.
Mitcham. Knowledge of Water, A.
Moore, T. Response to Rimbaud's Later Manner.
Mori Ōgai. Tanka: "Under the blue sky."
Mother Goose. Cushy cow bonny, let down thy milk.
Nash, O. Cow is of the bovine ilk, The.
Ni Tsan. Waking from a Nap.
O'Donoghue, B. Weakness, The.
Opperman. Fable of the Speckled Cow.
Pau-Llosa. Ganaderia.
Pierman. Eight Cows.
Reeves, J. Cows.
Roberson. Blue Horses.
Roberts, E. Milking Time.
Roethke. Cow, The.
Sandburg, C. Milk-white moon, put the cows to sleep.
Scully, J. Midsummer.
Shaw, J. Cow.
Stern, G. Cow Worship.
Stevenson, R. Cow, The.
Taylor, A. Cow, The.
Cow and the Ass, The.
Thomson, J. Signs of Storm.
Tomlinson, C. Macduff
Unknown. Farmer's Boy, A.
Four stiff-standers.
Sukey [or Suky], you shall be my wife.
Van Duyn. Ballad of Blossom, The.
Virgil. School for calves.
Wells, A. Cow-Boy's Song, The.
White, E. Red Cow Is Dead, The.
Wills, J. Old cow lags, The.
Young, A. Man and Cows.

Coyote (mythology)
Blue Cloud. Sweat Song.
Ortiz. Telling About Coyote.
Silko. Toe'osh; a Laguna Coyote Story.

Coyotes
Adams, J. Cowboy's Life, The.
Blue Cloud. Sweat Song.
Jewell. Where the coyote called.
Mountain, M. C o y O t e.
Silko. Toe'osh; a Laguna Coyote Story.
Whyte-Melville. Coyotes are howling, The.

Crabbe, George
Robinson, E. George Crabbe.

Crabs and Crabbing
Atwood. Landcrab I.
    Landcrab II.
Dabydeen, D. Catching Crabs.
Fuller, R. Crustaceans.
Heath-Stubbs. July.
Magowan. Paros. A day mild as morning's
    milk.
Oppian. *Hermit-Fish,* unarm'd by Nature left,
    The.
P'i Jih-hsiu. On a Crab.
Plath. Mussel Hunter at Rock Harbor.
Ridler. Crab is in again, his monthly house,
    The.
Rogers, P. Eulogy for a Hermit Crab.
Unknown. Woes of the Crab, The.
Yang Wei-chen. Bamboo Branch Song of the
    Seacoast.
Young, A. Dead Crab, The.

Cracow, Poland. *See* Krakow, Poland

Craftsmanship
Anacreon. Cup, The.
Kipling, R. Dedication, A: "My new-cut ashlar
    takes the light."
Kirkup. Correct Compassion, A.
Lux. Gold on Mule.
Nye, N. Man Who Makes Brooms, The.
Popa. Craftsmen of the Little Box, The.
Sackville-West. Craftsmen.
Snyder, G. Axe Handles.
Ushakov. Craftsmanship.

Crane, Hart
Doty, M. Almost Blue.
Lowell, R. Words for Hart Crane.
Symons, J. Hart Crane.

Cranes (ornithology)
Celan. When you lie in.
Ceravolo. Migratory Noon.
Langland, J. Crane.
Po Chü-i. Cranes, The.
Shih Te. Far, faraway, steep mountain paths.
Tu Mu. Crane, The.
Unknown. Flamingo, what has brought you
    here?
Yüan Mei. Busy.
Yün Shou-p'ing. Through the windy valley.

Cranmer, Thomas
Sisson. Cranmer was person of this parish.
Smith, S. Admire Cranmer!

Crashaw, Richard
Cowley, A. On the Death of Mr. Crashaw.

Crayfish
Apollinaire. Crayfish, The.

Crazy Horse (Oglala Sioux Chief)
Blue Cloud. Crazy Horse Monument.
Clifton, L. Crazy Horse Instructs the Young
    Men But In Their Grief They Forget.
Message of Crazy Horse, The.
Heyen. Steadying, The.
Stafford, W. Report to Crazy Horse.
    Sound from the Earth, A.

Creation
Addison, J. Ode: "Spacious firmament on
    high, The."
Alexander, C. All things bright and beauteous.
Alquit. Light of the World, The.
Anacreon. Mother Nature gave bulls horns.
Aristophanes. CHORUS. Ye Children of Man!
    whose life is a span.
Ballou, S. Almighty God in being was.
Bible, *O.T.* In the beginning God created the
    heaven and the earth.
    Psalm 104.
Blake, W. Tyger, The.
Blind. Chaunts of Life.
Bloch, C. Magnificat.
Blood, B. Late.

Blue Cloud. Spring Equinox.
Boethius. Book III. Metre 6.
Brathwaite, E. Red Rising.
Brewster, M. Stately Structure of This Earth,
    The.
Browning, R. Johannes Agricola in
    Meditation.
Caedmon. Caedmon's Hymn.
Ceravolo. Data.
Chesterton, G. Donkey, The.
De la Mare. Scribe, The.
Dharmakirti. Proof.
Dickinson, E. It's easy to invent a Life.
    Just as He spoke it from his Hands.
Doyle, S. To An Undiscerning Critic.
Dumbrveanu. Genesis.
Emerson, R. Rhodora, The [On Being Asked
    Whence Is the Flower].
Erinna. On the Portrait of a Girl.
Everson, W. South Coast, The.
Ewart. Creation Myth Haiku.
Fordham. Creation.
Fraser, K. Poems for the New.
Fuller, J. Whole New Scene, A.
Gilbo'a. I love this sunlight cold in spaces
    transparent turning blue.
Glück, L. Lamentations.
Grainger, J. Solitude: An Ode.
Gurr. Creation.
Hadewijch II. All things.
Hamburger, M. Treblinka.
Harjo, J. Perhaps the World Ends Here.
Herbert, G. Man.
    Pulley, The.
Herrick. Eye, The.
Hill, G. Genesis.
Hopi Oral Tradition. Song of Creation.
Horton, G. Praise of Creation.
Howe, J. Kosmos.
Hughes, T. Crow's First Lesson.
Jabès. Notebook, Two.
Jackson, L. In the Beginning.
Kayo. War.
Kilmer, J. Trees.
Lawrence, D. Let There Be Light!
Levine, P. Rain Downriver.
MacLeish. Vicissitudes of the Creator.
Macpherson, J. Fisherman, The.
Magrelli. If you melt some lead.
McAuley, J. Seventh Day, The.
Melville, H. Venice.
Miller, A. Mulch.
Monar. Koker.
Moore, M. Book of How, The.
Ndu. Udude.
Nemerov. Creation Myth on a Moebius Band.
Olson, C. Celestial Evening, October 1967.
Ormsby, E. Origins.
Ortiz. Creation.
O'Shaughnessy, A. Ode: "We are the music-
    makers."
Owens, G. Oh, who can make a flower?
Pagis. Testimony.
Pastan. Imperfect Paradise, The.
Patmore, C. To the Body.
Piatt, S. If I had made the world—ah me!
Pritam, A. Creative Process, The.
Quasimodo. To the New Moon.
Rands. World, The.
Rossetti, D. On the Painter Val Prinsep.
Rukeyser, M. He Had a Quality of Growth.
Shapiro, K. Recognition of Eve, The.
    Sickness of Adam, The.
Sorescu. Adam paced the footpaths of paradise
    in a.
Shakespeare created the world in seven days.
Southwell. Vale of Tear[e]s, A.
Stevenson, A. Spirit is too blunt an
    instrument, The.
Swinburne. Aholibah.
Thomas, R. Echoes.
Traherne. Third Day.
Tuckerman, F. Sonnets: "Starry flower, the
    flower-like stars that fade, The."
Unknown. Lo! ye children of men and the
    Mother.
    Songs of Spirits.

That the earth be made safer for men, and
    more stable.
Valéry. Crusoe had provided all the
    necessaries and was more or less at leisure
    in.
Very. Origin of Man, I, The.
Waller, E. Garden of Bermuda, The.
Wilbur. On the Marginal Way.
    Praise in Summer.
    Two Voices in a Meadow.
Williams, L. Origin of the Skagit Indians,
    The.
Wordsworth, W. Excursion, The.
Yeats. Before the World Was Made.
    Rose of the World, The.
Yoruba Oral Tradition. Invocation of the
    Creator.
See also **Cosmology**

Creativity
Allston. Art.
Browne, M. Talk to Me, Baby.
Creeley. Figures, The.
Cummings, E. No man,if men are gods;but if
    gods must.
Hopkinson, A. Origami.
Hovey. Accident in Art.
Jonson, B. Epistle to Elizabeth, Countess of
    Rutland.
Kwiatek. "Nearer God, Nearer Realite."
Levertov. To the Muse.
Liddy. I know nothing but this scene.
Mandel, T. Shade, The.
St. John, P. Reading a Story to My Child.
Seymour, A. Millionaire.
Sluchevsky. Yes, for the multitude of people
    it's hard to avoid.
Snodgrass, W. Matisse: "The Red Studio."

Creatures
Alexander, C. All things bright and beauteous.
Brown, M. Little Black Bug.
Hendriks. Cirrhosis.
Kinnell. Milk Bottle, The.
Morgan, E. First Men on Mercury, The.
Palamas. In the sun-glad nakedness.
Polito. Animal Mimicry.
Shannon, M. Only My Opinion.
Shenstone. To the Virtuosos.
Stephens, J. Little things, that run, and quail.
Tablada. Haiku: "Dragon-fly strives patiently,
    The."
Yeats. High Talk.
See also **Animals**

Cremation
Borowski. Night over Birkenau.
Fogel, E. Shipment to Maidanek.
Jeffers, R. Cremation.
Matthews, W. My Father's Body.
Mobilio. Step One.
Service. Cremation of Sam McGee, The.
Williams, W. Complete Destruction.

Crete
Corso. Paranoia in Crete.
Vitiello. Letter to a Cretan Flute-Maker.

Cricket (game)
Brathwaite, E. Look wha' happen las' week at
    de Oval!
Dance. When the returning sun begins to
    smile.
Lang, A. Brahma.
Moore, E. Victory Calypso, Lord's 1950.
Petty. There's a breathless hush in the Close
    tonight.
Ross, A. Cricket at Oxford.
Sassoon. Blues at Lord's, The.
Scriven, R. Cricketer.
Thompson, F. At Lord's.
Wodehouse, P. Outcast, The.

Crickets
Aristodicus of Rhodes. Cricket, you'll sing no
    more.
Bennett, W. To a Cricket.
Bourne, V. Cricket, The.
Delius. Thinker, The.
Fujiwara no Go-Kyōgoku. Cricket cries, The.
Heath-Stubbs. Winter Cricket.
Hunt, L. To the Grasshopper and the Cricket.

Izumi.   Cricket Heard.
In the Autumn, on Retreat at a Mountain
  Temple.
Keats.   On the Grasshopper and [the] Cricket.
Klein, A.   Rocking Chair, The.
Lear, E.   Incidents in the Life of My Uncle
  Arly.
Lo Fu.   Song of the Cricket.
Lovelace, R.   Ant, The.
McCord, D.   Crickets.
Merwin, W.   Black Jewel, The.
Mnasalces.   No longer, cricket, sitting.
Mountain, M.   Krĭk'ĭt.
Okudzhava.   As a child I came upon a
  grasshopper.
Sandburg, C.   Splinter.
Simonov.   Cricket, The.
Thomas, E.   Cricket Kept the House, The.
Tuckerman, F.   Cricket, The.
Unknown.   BRIGHT moon illumines the night-
  prospect.
Wiggin.   Crickets.
Wright, J.   Poems to a Brown Cricket.
Yi, H.   Song of Cricket.
Zipper.   I stop to listen.

Crime and Criminals
Adamson.   O to be in the news again—now as
  fashion runs.
Alvarez, J.   I check my parents' house while
  they're abroad.
Atkins.   Late Bus (After a Series of Hold-Ups).
Atwood.   Marrying the Hangman.
Bishop, E.   Burglar of Babylon, The.
Boethius.   Chawcer upon this fyfte meter of
  the second book.
Brecht, B.   Ballad of Immoral Earnings.
See the shark with teeth like razors.
Carpenter, W.   Girl Writing a Letter.
Celan.   Leaf, Treeless for Bertolt Brecht, A.
Chōkū.   Tanka: "Kidnapping."
Cooley.   Soul, The.
Cordle.   Lizzie and Joe Catch a Thief.
Davis, T.   In the Fire Lane.
Dickinson, E.   I know some lonely Houses off
  the Road.
Eliot, T.   Macavity: The Mystery Cat.
Enright, D.   Since Then.
Espada.   Waiting for the Cops.
Ewart.   Charles Augustus Milverton.
Fericano.   Poem for William Rummel Serving
  a Life Sentence in a Texas Prison for Not
  Fixing an Air Conditioner.
Gay, J.   Employments of Life, The.
Newgate's Garland.
Gibran.   Crime and Punishment.
Ginsberg, A.   Tonite I walked out of my red
  apartment door on East tenth street's dusk.
Hall, J.   Reign of Terror.
Hardy, T.   In the Servants' Quarters.
Harington.   Of honest Theft. To my good
  friend Master Samuel Daniel.
Hay, G.   Atman.
Henley, W.   Villon's Straight Tip to All Cross
  Coves.
Kingston, M.   Absorption of Rock.
Lewis, L.   Bridget.
McGuire.   Streets of Forbes, The.
Meeks, B.   Las' Rights.
Mei Yao Ch'en.   Meeting the Herdsmen.
Meredith, W.   Effort at Speech.
Miller, P.   Capture of Edwin Alonzo Boyd,
  The.
Mörike.   Prisoner, The.
Mother Goose.   Taffy was a Welshman, Taffy
  was a thief.
Tarts, The.
Tom, Tom the piper's son.
Newbolt.   He Fell among Thieves.
Noyes, A.   He did not come in the dawning.
He did not come at noon.
Highwayman, The.
Polito.   Animal Mimicry.
Ransome-Davies.   Raymond Chandler: The Big
  Sleep.
Raworth.   Collapsible.
Saarikoski.   Potato Thief.
Saitō Mokichi.   Tanka: "Snowflakes."

Service.   Shooting of Dan McGrew, The.
Silvers.   Frankie Silvers.
Sinclair, I.   Hurricane Drummers! Self-Aid in
  Haggerston.
Tadic.   Thief.
Tennyson, A.   Rizpah.
Unknown.   Boston Burglar, The.
Claude Allen.
Crafty Farmer, The.
El Corrido de Gregorio Cortez.
Frank James, the Roving Gambler.
Geordie [An Old Ballad].
Highwayman, The.
Jesse James was a lad who [or that] killed
  many a man.
John Gilbert was a bushranger.
Johnie Armstrong.
Johnson-Jinkson.
Musgrove.
My Handsome Gilderoy.
Peddler and His Wife, The.
Queen of Hearts, The.
Sam Bass.
Sam Hall.
Twenty-one Years.
Wagoner, D.   Shooting of John Dillinger
  outside the Biograph Theater July 22, 1934,
  The.
Warren, R.   Crime.
Zenmaro.   New York.
See also **Prisons and Prisoners**

Crimean War
Forster, W.   Sonnet on the Crimean War.
Simonov.   Lieutenant, The.
Thackeray   Due of the Dead, The.

Cripples
Gerstler.   True Bride, The.
Khodasevich.   Ballad: "Oh, quietly mad I'd
  like to be."
Kipling, R.   Dead Statesman, A.
McGough, R.   Poem With a Limp.
Owen, W.   Disabled.
Sassoon.   Does It Matter?[—losing your legs?].
Simpson, L.   Stumpfoot on 42nd Street.
See also **Handicaps and the Handicapped**

Criticism and Critics
Antiphanes.   Piddle-paddling race of critics,
  rhizome-fanciers.
Belloc.   Lines to a Don.
Brereton, J.   But should some snarling critic
  chance to view.
Browning, R.   Dialogue between Father and
  Daughter.
Bukowski.   Black poets / young, The.
Burrell.   School for Satire, The.
Byron, G.   Behold! in various throngs the
  scribbling crew.
Canto the Eleventh.
Epistle from Mr Murray to Dr Polidori.
Churchill, C.   Character of a Critic.
Ciardi.   To a Reviewer Who Admired My
  Book.
Coleridge, S.   Modern Critics.
Cope, W.   Serious Concerns.
Cullen, C.   To Certain Critics.
Daniel, S.   Poet and Critic.
Davie.   Rejoinder to a Critic.
Doyle, S.   To An Undiscerning Critic.
Drayton.   His Defence Against the Idle Critic.
Dunbar, P.   To a Captious Critic.
Durem.   I Know I'm Not Sufficiently Obscure.
Enright, D.   Evil Days, The.
Ewart.   Black Box, The.
Falconar, M.   Prefatory Epistle, A.
Fields, J.   Owl-Critic, The.
Greenwell, D.   Saturday Review, The.
Han-shan.   There is a poetaster named Wang.
Hemingway.   Valentine.
Herrick.   To Critic[k]s.
To the Detracter.
Upon the Same.
Hewitt, J.   Because I paced my thought by the
  natural world.
Hood, T.   Poet's Fate, The.
Hope, A.   Now Muse assist me, aptly to
  describe.
Jonson, B.   Ode to Himself.

To Censorious Courtling.
To Fool or Knave.
To John Donne ("Who shall doubt, Donne,
  where [or whe'er] I a poet be[e]").
To My Mere English Censurer.
Keats.   All These Are Vile.
Kunitz, S.   Choice of Weapons, A.
Landor, W.   Critic, A.
Lehman.   One Size Fits All: a Critical Essay.
Marston, J.   Fy Satyre fie, shall each
  mechanick slave.
Marvell.   To His Noble Friend, Mr Richard
  Lovelace, upon His Poems.
Nemerov.   On Certain Wits.
Sacrificed Author, A.
To My Least Favorite Reviewer.
O'Hara, F.   Answer to Voznesensky and
  Evtushenko.
Piercy.   Letter to be Disguised as a Gas Bill.
Pope, A.   Essay on Criticism.
On Dennis.
Porter, P.   St Cecilia's Day Epigram.
Randall, D.   Black Poet, White Critic.
Rich, A.   They come to you with their
  descriptions of your soul.
Rochester, J.   Song: "Give me leave to rail at
  you."
Roethke.   Pipling.
Shakespeare, W.   Sonnet 140.
Shelley, P.   Lines to a Reviewer.
Simmons, N.   With Reservations.
Sorescu.   Shakespeare created the world in
  seven days.
Spencer, T.   Critics, The.
Starbuck, G.   On First Looking in on
  Blodgett's Keats's "Chapman's Homer."
Swift, J.   Critics.
Tennyson, A.   Hendecasyllabics.
Popular, popular, unpopular!
To Christopher North.
Whalen.   Chanson d'Outre Tombe.
Wordsworth, W.   Sonnet: "Scorn not the
  sonnet; critic, you have frowned."
Yeats.   On Those That Hated "The Playboy of
  the Western World" 1907.
To a Poet, Who Would Have Me Praise
  Certain Bad Poets, Imitators of His and
  Mine.

Crockett, Davy (David Crockett) (1786-1836)
Unknown.   Davy Crockett.

Crockett, Samuel Rutherford
Stevenson, R.   To S. R. Crockett.

Crocodiles
Barlas.   Memphian Temple, The.
Beddoes.   Crocodile, A.
"Carroll."   Crocodile, The.
Dugan, M.   Herbaceous Plodd.
Nash, O.   Purist, The.
Richards, L.   Monkeys and the Crocodile, The.
Rossetti, C.   My Dream.
Unknown.   If you should meet a crocodile.
See also **Alligators**

Crocuses
Harper, F.   Crocuses, The.
Platt.   Crocuses.
Schuyler, J.   Spring.

Cromwell, Oliver
Brome.   Come a *brimmer* (my bullies) drink
  whole ones or nothing.
On Sir G. B. his defeat.
Lovelace, R.   Mock Song, A.
Marvell.   'Is this, saith one, the Nation that we
  read'
Milton.   To the Lord General[1] Cromwell[, on
  the Proposals of Certain Ministers at the
  Committee for the Propagation of the Gospel
  or May 1652].
Wright, C.   State of Preservation.
Yeats.   Curse of Cromwell, The.

Croquet
MacNeice.   Soap Suds.

Cross, The
Cooper, R.   To See the Cross at Christmas.
Cynewulf.   Dream of the Rood, A.
Everson, W.   Making of the Cross, The.
Herrick.   Crosses.

Kamienska. On the Cross*.
Leslie, S. Holy Cross.
MacCaig. Celtic Cross.
Magee, T. Celtic Cross, The.
Melville, H. Inscription, The: "While yet
  Rolfe's foot in stirrup stood."
O Direain. Trees on a Frosty Night.
Plunkett. I See His Blood upon the Rose.
Sanchez, S. Father and Daughter.
Sexton. With Mercy for the Greedy.
Tate, A. Cross, The.
See also **Crucifixion, The**

Crowds
Baugh, E. Truth and Consequences.
Brontë, C. Obscure and little seen my way.
Davidson, L. Silent crowd, The.
Dryden, J. Vox Populi.
Hoffman, D. Center of Attention, The.
Hughes, L. Subway Rush Hour.
Lowell, J. Street, The.
Mew. Fame.
Pound, E. In A Station of the Metro.
Sandburg, C. I am the people—the mob—the
  crowd—the mass.
Williams, W. At the Ball Game.

Crowns
Coleridge, M. Moment, A.
  Mortal Combat.
Hill, G. On the morning of the crowning we
  chorused our.
Marvell. Coronet, The.
Rossetti, C. Crown of Windflowers, A.

Crows
Alexander, C. Crow, The.
Basho. Autumn evening.
Beddoes. Carrion Crow, The.
Browne, J. Rooks are building on the trees,
  The.
Chang Yü. Painting ("Jade cave, ten thousand
  flowering peach trees, A").
Clarke, P. In Air.
Digby, J. Sooner or Later.
Frost, R. Dust of Snow.
Gates, L. Crow flies off, The.
  Winter dawn;.
Grenier. Crow.
Harr, L. On the old scarecrow.
Henri, A. Crowfield.
Hoban. October Tuesday.
Hughes, T. Crow's Theology.
La Fontaine. Fox and the Crow, The.
Li Meng-yang. Mooring at Hsia-k'ou at Night.
Lindsay, V. Two old crows sat on a fence
  rail.
MacCaig. Solitary crow.
McCord, D. Crows.
Mori Ōgai. Tanka: "On a post."
Mother Goose. Carrion crow sat upon [*or* on]
  an oak, The [*or* A].
  Tweedledum and Tweedledee.
Ortiz. Telling About Coyote.
"Pygge." Crow Resting.
Roethke. Night Crow.
Silko. Preparations.
Sorley. Rooks.
Southard. Old rooster crows, The.
  Perching bolt upright.
Unknown. Caw Caw the Crows Caw Caw.
  He Asked Them What Did They Know &
  They Told Him.
  I sometimes think I'd rather crow.
  Twa Corbies, The.
  Two More about a Crow, in the Manner of
  Zukofsky.
  What the Weather Does.
Worth, V. Crows.
Young, D. Boxcar Poem, The ("Boxcars drift
  by / clanking, The").

Crucifixion, The
"Akhmatova." Crucifixion.
Alabaster. Of the Reed That the Jews Set in
  Our Saviour's Hand.
  Upon the Ensigns of Christ's Crucifying.
Alexander, C. His Are the Thousand Sparkling
  Rills.
  There Is a Green Hill Far Away.
Auden. Luke 23:26–38; And as they led him

away.
Shield of Achilles, The.
Barnes, D. Chuang Tzu and Hui Tzu were
  hundreds of years old.
Beaumont, J. Garden's quit with me: as
  yesterday, The.
Bevington, L. 'Dreamers?' Ah, no! else he
  was a dreamer.
Borges. John 1:14 (1964).
  Luke XXIII.
Brown, C. Good Friday.
Carruth, H. Emergency Haying.
Causley. I Am the Great Sun[, but you do not
  see me].
Colman, H. On the Inscription Over the Head
  of Christ on the Cross.
  On the Strange Apparitions at Christ's Death.
Cowley, A. Christ's Passion.
Crashaw. To Our Blessed Lord upon the
  Choice of His Sepulchre.
Cullen, C. Simon the Cyrenian Speaks.
Daumal. Matthew 27:11–24; Now Jesus stood
  before.
De Brun. Calvary.
Dickinson, E. I should have been too glad, I
  see.
  One Crucifixion is recorded—only.
  "Remember me" implored the Thief!
Donne. Good Friday [*or* Goodfriday], 1613.
  Riding Westward.
  Son, The.
Everson, W. Zone of Death.
Fletcher, P. Ocean of Light.
Fordham. Crucifixion, The.
  Uranne.
Gascoyne. Tenebrae.
Herbert, G. Sacrifice, The.
Herrick. Cross-tree, The.
  His Anthem, to Christ on the Cross.
  His Saviour[']s Words, Going to the Cross[e].
  Observation ("Virgin-Mother stood at distance
  (there), The").
Hill, G. Canticle for Good Friday.
Hine. Here is another poem in a picture.
Hughes, T. God, A.
  Matthew 27:45–56; Now from the sixth hour
  there was darkness.
Jammes. Five Sorrowful Mysteries, The.
Kamienska. On the Cross*.
Kates. No altarpiece includes the painter.
Keble. Fill High the Bowl.
Kennedy, X. Down in Dallas, down in Dallas.
Lanier, S. Ballad of Trees and the Master, A.
Leax. That day the / words.
Lewis, S. To the Good Thief.
Melville, H. Via Crucis.
Morris, M. Joseph of Arimathaea.
  Pilate.
Muir, E. Killing, The.
Nastasijevic. String, The.
O Direain. Trees on a Frosty Night.
Patchen. Pastoral: "Dove walks with sticky
  feet, The."
Prince, F. Soldiers Bathing.
Quarles. Crucified.
  They Gave Him Vinegar and Gall (Matt. 27)
  and Wine Mingled with Myrrh (Mark 15).
Robinson, E. Calvary.
Rodgers, W. It was a lovely night.
Rossetti, C. Good Friday.
Sandburg, C. Early Lynching.
Sexton. In the Deep Museum.
Simovic. Crucifixion.
Sisson. Easter.
Sitwell, D. Still falls the Rain—.
Studdert-Kennedy. Indifference.
Thompson, P. Death and Resurrection.
Unknown. At the time of Matines, Lord, thu
  were itake.
  Crucifixion, The.
  Dream of the Rood, The.
  He Never Said a Mumblin' Word.
  Helpe, crosse, fairest of timbres three.
  Now Goeth Sun under Wood.
  'O, My Heart Is Woe'.
  Seven Virgins, The.
  Swete sone, reu on me.

Thou Who Createdst Everything.
Were you there when they crucified my Lord?
  [(were you there?)].
York Play of the Crucifixion, The.
Very. Cross, The.
Warton, T. Ode on the Passion.
Watts, I. Crucifixion to the World by the
  Cross of Christ.
  Look on Him Whom They Pierced, and
  Mourn.
Wellesley. Avebury.
Yeats. "Calvary."
  I am Judas.
  Two Songs from a Play.
See also **Cross, The; Calvary**

Cruelty
Allen, S. Moment Please, A.
Borawski. Cheers, Cheers for Old Cha Cha
  Ass ("Cheers, cheers for old Patchogue
  High").
Burns, R. Man's Inhumanity to Man.
Carew, T. Cruel Mistress, A.
  Looking-Glass, A.
  To My Mistress [*or* Mistris], I Burning in
  Love.
"Carroll." Lobster, The.
Cheng Hsieh. Mother-in-Law Is Cruel.
Ciardi. Faces.
Claudian. Old Men not staid with Age,
  Virgins with shame.
Crane, S. MAN FEARED THAT HE MIGHT
  FIND AN ASSASSIN, A.
Creeley. Hill, The.
Daniel, S. Beauty, Time and Love.
Dickinson, E. She dealt her pretty words like
  Blades.
Dixon, S. Request of Alexis, The.
Doolittle, H. We have seen how the most
  amiable.
Herrick. Cruelties.
Holden, J. Liberace.
Huntington, C. Rhapsody.
Inez. Absolving You.
Jarrell. Snow-Leopard, The.
Jeffers, L. On Listening to the Spirituals.
  To him who in his absence from himself.
Johnston, E. Address to Nature on its Cruelty,
  An.
Kayamanar. What Her Girl Friend Said,
  Seeing Her Friend Suffer in Silent Dignity
  over Her Husband's Infidelity.
Lane, P. On Being Head of the English
  Department.
Lawrence, D. Cherry Robbers.
Levertov. Innocent, The.
Lovelace, R. La Bourbon, A.
MacCaig. No Interims in History.
Mayakovsky. On Being Kind to Horses.
Milosz, C. To Mrs. Professor in Defense of
  My Cat's Honor and Not Only.
Morris, W. Haystack in the Floods, The.
Piercy. Friend, The.
Shakespeare, W. Sonnet 94.
Shange. It's Not so Good to be Born a Girl/
  Sometimes.
Smith, S. How cruel is the story of Eve.
Spires. Exhumation.
Swinburne. Satia Te Sanguine.
Tsvetayeva. I know the truth—give up all
  other truths!
Vinokurov. On the hall stand hangs a fur coat.
Wetzsteon. Three Songs.
Wyatt, T. At last withdraw your cruelty.
  Heart oppressed [*or* oppress'd] with desperate
  thought.
  If with complaint the pain might be expressed.
  Longer to muse.
  Since ye delight to know.
  Thou sleepest fast and I with woeful heart.
  Who hath he[a]rd of such[e] cruelty before.

Cruelty to Animals
Cave. Poem for Children, A; or, On Cruelty
  to the Irrational Creation.
Clare, J. Badger ("When midnight comes a
  host of dogs and men").
Hardy, T. Blinded Bird, The.
Hodgson, R. Bells of Heaven, The.

Kinnell. Bear, The.
Porcupine, The.
Livingstone, D. Bad Run at King's Rest.
McKuen. Thoughts on Capital Punishment.
Merwin, W. Fly.
Prior. Epigram: "Thy nags (the leanest things alive)."
Stephens, J. Snare, The.
Thomas, E. Gallows, The.

Crum, William
Moorer. Crum Appointment, The.

Crusades
Chesterton, G. Lepanto.
Iwaszkiewicz. Pope in Ancona, The.

Crystals
"MacDiarmid." Crystals like Blood.

Cuba
Baraka. Cuba Libre.
Brooks, M. Composed at the Request of a Lady, and Descriptive of Her Feelings.
Carew, J. Our Home.
Gomez de Avellaneda. On Leaving Cuba, Her Native Land.
Gossett. On the Question of Fans/ The Slave Quarters Are Never Air Conditioned.
Guillén, N. National Police Headquarters.
Jeffers, L. Flesh of the Young Men Is Burning, The.
Lowell, R. Fall 1961.
MacDermot. Cuba.
Padilla. Landscapes.
Pau-Llosa. Frutas.
Roberts, W. On a Monument to Martí.

Cuchulain (Irish legendary hero)
Yeats. Cuchulain Comforted.

Cuckoldry and Cuckolds
Bishop, M. My Friend the Cuckold.
Catullus. Carmen 5 ("My sweetest Lesbia, let us live and love").
Montagu, L. Epitaph: "Here lies John Hughes and Sarah Drew."
Ovid. 1.4.
Shakespeare, W. Spring.
See also **Adultery**

Cuckoos
Alcuin. Lament for the Cuckoo.
Basho. Though I'm in Kyoto.
Basho *et al.* Call of Two Birds, The.
Campbell, D. Pallid Cuckoo.
Cynewulf. Riddle: Cuckoo.
Davies, W. Great Time, A.
Desnos. Cuckoo.
Heywood, J. Of Use.
Hopkins, G. Cuckoo, The.
Kharms. Tricks.
Kipling, R. Cuckoo Song.
Kuan Yun She. Sending Off Spring.
McAuley, J. Late Winter.
Ray, H. Cuckoo Song.
Sanesada. Cuckoo calls. / When I look there is only, A.
Sargant. Cuckoo Wood, The.
Simic. Theory, A.
Song. Cuckoo on Mt. Chiri*, The.
Townsend, F. O Cuckoo! shall I call thee Bird.
Unknown. Cuckoo, The.
Cuckoo calls from the bamboo grove, The.
Cuckoo, cuckoo / What do you do?
Koocoo, The.
Sumer is icumen in.
Though the purity.
Wee jenny wren she lays sixteen, The.
Wordsworth, W. To the Cuckoo.

Cucumbers
Hikmet. Cucumber, The.
Unknown. Cautionary Limerick.

Cuernavaca, Mexico
Belitt. View from the Gorge.
Bernstein, O. Cuernavaca.

Culloden, Battle of (1746)
Burns, R. Lovely lass o' Inverness, The.

Culture
Anzaldúa. Cultures.
Bell, M. Footnote to Enright's "Apocalypse."
Burns, J. Revisionism.

Corn. Contemporary Culture and the Letter "K."
Davie. Meeting of Cultures, A.
Divakaruni. Indian Movie, New Jersey.
"Ern Malley." Culture as Exhibit.
Fenton, J. Lollipops of the Pomeranian Baroque.
This Octopus Exploits Women.
Ginsberg, A. Studying the Signs.
Gnanakoothan. Tamil, it's true, is the breath of my life.
Gonzales, R. Praise the Tortilla, Praise the Menudo, Praise the Chorizo.
Hewitt, J. Once alien here my fathers built their house.
Koch, K. You were wearing your Edgar Allan Poe printed cotton blouse.
Lee, L. Cleaving, The.
Lei-Lanilau. Kolohe or Communication.
MacEwen, G. Breakfast for Barbarians, A.
Machi. Tanka: "As though to let loose."
Meléndez. Oye Mundo/Sometimes.
Nash, O. Exit, Pursued by a Bear.
Okita. Notes for a Poem on Being Asian American.
Olson, C. Kingfishers, The.
Retallack, J. Western CIV, 4 and 5.
Sahay. Our Hindi is a widower's new wife.
Salazar. Taking It Back.
Shapiro, K. Drug Store.
Smith, I. Gaelic Songs.
Oban 1955–82.
Shall Gaelic Die?
Snyder, G. Axe Handles.

Cumberland, England
Nicholson, N. To the River Duddon.

Cumberland, Virginia
Smith, D. Cumberland Station.
Unknown. Cumberland Gap.

Cunningham, James Vincent
Kennedy, X. Terse Elegy for J.V. Cunningham.

Cunningham, Merce
Miller, S. I Was on a Golf Course the Day John Cage Died of a Stroke.
Olson, C. Merce of Egypt.

Cupboards
De la Mare. Cupboard, The.

Cupid
Anacreon. Wounded Cupid. Song, The.
Baillie, J. To Cupid.
Bion. In sleep before me Venus seem'd to stand.
Bridges, R. Eros.
Campion, T. Mistris [*or* Mistress] Since You So Much Desire.
Carew, T. Song: The Willing Prisoner to His Mistress.
Chaucer. Love's Garden.
Drayton. Cupid, I hate thee, which I'd have thee know.
"Eliza." Eliza, The.
Elizabeth I. When I was fair and young, then [*or* and] favour graced me;.
Gay, J. Damon and Cupid.
Greene, R. Night Visitor, A.
Greville, F. Cupid, thou naughty boy, when thou wert loathed.
Farewell to Cupid.
Herrick. Cheat of Cupid; or, The Ungentle Guest, The.
How Lillies Came White.
How Roses Came Red.
Hymne to Love, An.
To Oenone ("Thou saist [*or* sayest] Love[']s dart").
Upon Love ("Love brought me to a silent Grove").
Wounded Cupid, The.
Jonson, B. Why I Write Not of Love.
Knox, E. To the God of Love.
Lodge, T. Rosalind's [*or* Rosalynd's] Madrigal[l].
Lovelace, R. Cupid Far Gone.
Lyly, J. Cards and Kisses.
O Cupid! Monarch over Kings.
Meleager. Burn not too oft who flutters at thy

flame.
By Cypris, Cupid!
Cupid at Venus' breast.
Lost! Cupid!/ One lost Cupid!
Moschus. Idyll 1.
North, D. Platonic is a pretty name.
Ovid. Elegy 9b: "If I heard a voice from heaven say 'Live without'."
Plato. Love Sleeping.
Sedley. To Cloris.
Shakespeare, W. O! And I forsooth in love!
Sidney, P. Long Their Coupled Joys Maintain.
Sonnet 20: "Fly, fly, my friends."
Sonnet 54: "Because I breathe not love to every one."
Sonnet 65: "Love, by sure proof I may call thee unkind."
Stanley, T. Song: "Fool, take up thy shaft again."
Suckling, J. Metamorphosis, The.
To B.C.
Virgil. Cupid at work.
Wroth. Song: "Love a child is ever criing [*or* crying]."
Sonnet 1: "When night's [*or* nights] black mantle could most darknes prove."
Sonnet 2: "Late in the Forest I did Cupid See."

Cups
Anacreon. Cup, The.
Ishikawa Takuboku. Tanka: "Accidentally."
Schuyler, J. Shimmer.

Curfew
Thorpe, R. Curfew Must Not Ring Tonight [*or* To-Night].

Curie, Marie
Dunbar-Nelson. To Madame Curie.
Harris, A. Pioneers.
Hecht, A. La Condition Botanique.
Rich, A. Power.

Curiosity
Dobler. 1920 Photo.
Kinnell. For Robert Frost.
Komunyakaa. "Everybody's Reading Li Po" Silkscreened on a Purple T-Shirt.
Miller, L. My Students Catch Me Dancing.
Olds, S. Connoisseuse of Slugs, The.
Raab, L. Witch's Story, The.
Rankin, P. To the House Ghost.
Reid, A. Curiosity.
Sidney, P. Sonnet 92: "Be your words made (good sir) of Indian ware."
Unknown. Will You Love Me When I'm Old?
Wallace, R. Condoms.
Wither. Author's Resolution, The.

Curses
Alcaeus. Hipponax.
Amis, K. A. E. H.
Ammianus. May the soil cover / your interred corpse.
Browning, E. Curse for a Nation, A.
Burns, R. Here cursing swearing Burton lies.
Graves, R. Travel[l]er's Curse after Misdirection[, The].
Herrick. Another [To His Booke].
Curse. A Song, The.
To the Sour[e] Reader.
Meleager. Mother of gods.
Ovid. Let th'earth deny thee fruit, and stream.
Pavic. Song: "But I'm the one from whom they stole a button from his trouser leg."
Song: "But I'm the one to whom others spit in the hand when he works."
Song: "But I'm the one who carries a garlic clove in the ear."
Quarles. On Judas Iscariot.
Sedley. On a Cock at Rochester.
Simovic. Curses.
Smith, S. Thoughts about the Person from Porlock.
Stephens, J. Glass of Beer, A.
Odell.
Swinburne. After Death.
Synge. Curse, The.
I curse my bearing, childhood, youth.
Thomas, E. Execration, The.
Unknown. Curse, A.

Horse Cursed by the Sun, The.
Sam Hall.
Skin the Goat's Curse on Carey.
Widow's Curse, The.
Wellesley. Mother.
Wright, J. Song for the Middle of the Night, A.
Yeats. Crazy Jane and the Bishop.
Yosano. Tanka: "Grabbing one of."

Custer, George Armstrong
Alexie. Crazy Horse Speaks.
Anderson, J. Rosebud.
Coolbrith. Captive of the White City.
Kelen. Rabbit Shoeshine.
Whittaker. Custer's Last Charge.

Custom
Juvenal. Client, the patron, the age, The.
Osgood, F. Woman.

Cyclamen
"Field." Cyclamens.
Lawrence, D. Sicilian Cyclamens.

Cyclops
Euripides. But, o great offspring of the Ocean King.
Glazkov. Tale of the Cyclopses, The.
Homer. Cave we found, but vacant all within, The.
Cyclops and No-Man.
Ovid. Cyclops.
Theocritus. Cyclops, The ("And so an easier life").
O NICIAS, there is no other remedy for love.
Thus sweetly sad of old, the Cyclops strove.

Cynicism and Cynics
Berggolts. Ordeal, The.
Brooks, G. Speech to the Young Speech to the Progress-Toward (Among Them Nora and Henry III).
Bukowski. Secret, The.
Carter, M. After One Year.
Daniel, S. Love.
Doyle, S. To An Undiscerning Critic.
Frost, R. Demiurge's Laugh, The.
Hardy, T. Christmas: 1924.
He Never Expected Much.
Hughes, J. Knowingness.
Lowell, R. As a Plane Tree by the Water.
Machado Ruiz. Ephemeral Past, The.
McDonald, P. Totalled.
Ojaide. Launching Our Community Developement Fund.
Parker, D. Symptom.
Unfortunate Coincidence.
Raleigh. Lines Suggested by an Edition of Blake's Poems.
Southey, R. Battle of Blenheim, The.
Wilbur. Matthew VIII, 28 ff.

Cypress Trees
Francis, R. Cypresses.
Jeffers, R. Granite and Cypress.
Kelly, R. Life of Intimate Fleeing, A.
Lawrence, D. Cypresses.
Miyazawa Kenji. Tanka: "Emerging."
Tanka: "Snow has fallen."

Cyprus
Durrell. Paphos.
Euripides. Home of Aphrodite, The.

Czechoslovakia
Gouri. And this happened in Prague many years ago?
At the Train Station.
Holan. Children at Christmas in 1945.
Milosz, C. My Faithful Mother Tongue.
Rumens. Geography Lesson.
Seifert. Candlestick, The.
Never Again.
Tsvetayeva. O what tears in eyes now.
Walker, A. Kiss, The.

D

Da Vinci, Leonardo. *See* **Leonardo da Vinci**
Dachshunds
Arnold, M. Geist's Grave.

Daedalus
Alba. Be Daedalus.
Martynov. Daedalus.
Oppen. Daedalus: The Dirge.
Ovid. Daedalus.

Daffodils
Drayton. Daffodil Song, The.
Henri, A. Early Spring.
Herrick. Divination by a Daffadill [*or* Daffodil].
To Daffodils [*or* Daffadills].
Loveman. (April Rain).
Machi. Tanka: "Looking as though."
Majer. Spring / slips / silent / snowdrops.
McGrath, T. Black Train, The.
Mother Goose. Daffadowndilly.
Ropes. Daffodils.
Samio. Tanka: "If only."
Shakespeare, W. Pedlar's Song, The.
Williams, W. Daffodil.
Wordsworth, W. Daffodils.

Dahlias
Saitō Mokichi. Tanka: "Dahlias are black."

Daisies
Burns, R. To a Mountain Daisy [On Turning One Down, with the Plough, in April—1786].
Glück, L. Daisies.
Gray, J. Poem: "Geranium, houseleek, laid in oblong beds."
Herrick. To Daisies, Not to Shut So Soon[e].
Howitt, M. Buttercups and Daisies.
Meynell, A. To a Daisy.
Montgomery, J. Field Flower, A.
Morris, W. Love is enough: though the World be a-waning.
Probyn. Blossom.
Rossetti, C. Where innocent bright-eyed daisies are.
Tennyson, A. Daisy, The.
Williams, H. Sonnet on Reading the Poem upon the Mountain Daisy, by Mr. Burns.
Williams, W. Daisy.
Wordsworth, W. To a Child [Written in Her Album].
To the Daisy ("With little here to do or see").
Zaturenska. Daisy, The.

Dali, Salvador
Gascoyne. Salvador Dali.
Thribb. In Memoriam Salvador Dali.

Damnation and the Damned
Bliss, P. "Almost persuaded," / Now to believe.
Graves, R. Song: Lift-Boy.
Hill, G. Ovid in the Third Reich.
Hunter, W. "Go Bring Me," Said the Dying Fair.
Marie-Madeleine. Crucifixa.
Sappho.
Marlowe. Ah, Doctor Faustus, that I might prevail.
Melvill. Ane Godlie Dreame.
Swift, J. Place of the Damned [*or* Damn'd], The.
Unknown. Ubi Sunt Qui ante Nos Fuerunt?

Damocles
Graves, R. Damocles.

Dams
Hall, D. Town of Hill, The.
Rukeyser, M. Dam, The.
Wills, J. Below the dam.

Dancing and Dancers
Adams, A. Her Dancing Days.
Ai. More.
Alexander, E. Ode.
Alexie. Business of Fancydancing, The.
Altizer. Sonnet 5: "No, I'll not, carrion, comfort you. Comfort."
Amherst. Welford Wedding, The.
Apollinaris Sidonius. Invitation to the Dance.
Auvaiyar. Poet to a Dancer, A.
Ayres. On Lydia Distracted.
Barlas. Beauty's Anadems.
Dancing Girl, The.
Barlow, G. Nook.
Belloc. Tarantella.
Berry, W. Dance, The.

Dancing and Dancers
Berryman. At Henry's bier let some thing fall out well.
King David Dances.
Binyon. Little Dancers, The.
Birney. Bear on the Delhi Road, The.
Bond, S. Tuesday Night Affair.
Boyle, K. Invitation in It, from American Citizen, The.
Brownjohn. Of Dancing.
Buchanan, G. Theatrical Venus.
Burbank, E. I Danced to the Rumble of the Drum.
Bynner. Snake Dance.
Byron, G. Muse of the many-twinkling feet! whose charms.
Camp, J. Female Dancer.
Campbell, J. Mobile-Buck.
Campbell, J. Dancer, The.
Campion, T. Dance, The.
"Carroll." Lobster Quadrille, A.
Chang Heng. Dancers of Huai-nan, The.
Ch'ien Ch'ien-i. Pavilions of dance, terraces of song.
Cho, C. Nun's Dance, The.
Chōkū. Tanka: "Oddly shaped."
Clampitt. Dancers Exercising.
Cogil *et al.* Dem Belly Full.
Cortez. So Many Feathers.
Tapping.
Creeley. Quick-Step.
Crouch, S. Riding Across John Lee's Finger.
Cummings, E. Ladies and gentlemen this little girl.
Custance. Masquerade, The.
Damas. Sleepless Night.
Dandridge, R. Zalka Peetruza.
Davies, S. Sole heir of virtue, and of beauty both.
Davis, T. Boppin' is Safer than Grindin'.
Ded. Soul, like the moon, The.
Di Prima. I Ching.
Dickinson, E. I cannot dance upon my Toes.
Dorfman, A. Last Waltz in Santiago.
Dove, R. Planning the Perfect Evening.
Duncan, R. Presence of the Dance / The Resolution of the Music, The.
Dunn, S. Dancing with God.
Eady. Jazz Dancer.
My Mother, If She Had Won Free Dance Lessons.
Eberhart, R. When Doris danced under the oak tree.
Ferlinghetti, L. Retired Ballerinas, Central Park West.
"Field." Dance of Death, A.
Field, R. Dancing Bear, The.
Garrigue. On the Legends of a Dancer.
Gilbert, C. Directions, The.
Giovanni. Three/Quarters Time.
Gouri. Dance.
Grainger, J. On festal days; or when their work is done.
Gregg. Dark Thing Inside the Day, A.
Grenfell, J. Stately as a Galleon.
Hagedorn, J. Latin Music in New York.
Halpern, D. Dance, The.
Hardy, T. By Her Aunt's Grave.
Wife Waits, A.
Heath, R. Seeing Her Dancing.
Henderson, D. Alvin Cash/Keep on Dancin'.
Holden, J. Dancing School.
Holst-Warhaft. Old Men of Athens, The.
Holtby, W. For the Ghost of Elinor Wylie.
Housman, A. Fancy's Knell.
Hughes, L. Dream Boogie.
Dream Variation[s].
Hutchinson, M. Dancing on the Shore.
Itwaru. And in this carnival you offer me.
Ivask, Y. Ode for the Dancing Khlysty.
Jacobsen, J. Limbo Dancer, The.
Jeffers, R. New Mexican Mountain.
Johnson, H. Bottled [New York].
Joseph, A. Junior High Dance.
Justice, D. Dancer's Life, A.
Kayo. Song of the Initiate.
Kinzie. Impromptu.

Kushner, A. He who doesn't dance still dances.
Lawrence, D. Fronleichnam.
Le Bel. Foot Fire Burn Dance.
Lear, E. Le Hibou et la Poussiquette. (The Owl and the Pussy-Cat).
There was an old person of Skye.
Li Po. For the Dancer of the King of Wu.
Lovelace, R. Gratiana Dancing [or Dauncing] and [or &] Singing.
Loose Saraband, A ("Nay, prethee [or prithee] dear, draw nigher").
MacNeice. Les Sylphides.
Major, C. Large Room with Wood Floor.
McKay, C. Harlem Dancer, The.
McKinney, I. Dance, The.
Mechthild von Magdeburg. I cannot dance, O Lord.
Meireles. Ballad of the Ten Casino Dancers.
Merrill, J. Watching the Dance.
Mezhirov. From the War.
Miller, L. My Students Catch Me Dancing.
Mistral, G. Those Who Do Not Dance.
Morton, J. To Hilda Dancing.
Moss, T. Tornados.
Mother Goose. Cock-a-doodle-doo! / My dame has lost her shoe.
Dance, Thumbkin, dance.
Mullen, H. Dance She Does, The.
Murray, M. I am giving you the dark birds of night.
Naden. Natural Selection.
Neidhart von Reuental. "Sing, my golden cock, I'll give thee grain!"
Nemerov. May Day Dancing, The.
Olson, C. Merce of Egypt.
Oppian. *Dolphins* were Men, (Tradition hands the Tale).
"O'Sullivan." Piper, A [or The].
Page, G. Road Show.
Palmer, J. Band Played On, The.
Po Chü-i. Going to the Mountains with a Little Dancing Girl, Aged Fifteen.
Pound, E. Dance Figure.
Ramkissoon-Chen. When the Hindu Woman Sings Calypso.
Redmond. Dance Bodies #1.
Reed, I. Black Cock, The.
Rimbaud, A. After Bitahatini.
Rodgers, C. We Dance Like Ella Riffs.
Rumi. Daylight, full of small dancing particles.
You that love Lovers.
Sadi. Dancer, The.
St. John, D. Slow Dance.
Sandburg, C. Lines Written for Gene Kelly to Dance To.
Seibles. Who doesn't.
Shange. Dream of Pairing.
Siamanto. Dance, The.
Simpson, L. Riders Held Back, The.
Skinner, J. Tullochgorum.
Smith, M. Last Dance, The.
Smith, P. They say that black people.
Smith, S. Ballet of the Twelve Dancing Princesses, The.
Spellman. Twist, The.
Spencer, B. Castanets.
Egyptian Dancer at Shubra.
Stafford, W. At the Klamath Berry Festival.
Stein, G. Susie Asado.
Stevens, W. Dance of the Macabre Mice.
Stuart, M. In The Orchard.
Sutskever. Song for a Dance.
Symons, A. Javanese Dancers.
La Mélinite: Moulin-Rouge.
To a Dancer.
Synge. On an Island.
Tallet. Rumba.
Tarpley. Feel Free.
Toomer. Lost Dancer, The.
Tu Fu. Coming Home Late at Night.
Tyler, P. Nijinsky.
U Tam'si Tchicaya. Dance to the Amulets.
Unknown. Cock a doodle doo!
Dance of the Rain Gods.
Dance Song.

Harry Parry.
I Am from Ireland.
Mode of France, The.
Old Woman from France, The.
On a Female Rope-Dancer.
Rural Dance about the Maypole, The.
Wooyeo Ball, The.
Urrea. Ghost Sickness.
Van Walleghen. Blue Tango.
Vas. Tambour.
Vinz. Variations on a Theme.
Voigt. Dancing with Poets.
Voznesensky. Darkmotherscream is a Siberian dance.
Wagoner, D. Best Slow Dancer, The.
Wakoski. Belly Dancer.
Wallenstein. Blues 2.
Wang Chiu-ssu. For Several Days I Have Not Visited the Garden Pavilion—A Poem Sent to My Pet Crane.
Wang T'ing-hsiang. Don't ask about the Six Dynasties of the Sui Palace.
Waniek. Diverne's Waltz.
Wickham. Song of the Lonely Shepherd.
Williams, W. Artist, The.
Dance, The.
Danse Russe.
Overture to a Dance of Locomotives.
Philomena Andronico.
Wollach. Christina.
Wordsworth, W. Daffodils.
Wratislaw. Opoponax.
Wright, J. Country Dance.
Wright, S. Out of the Wailing.
Yeats. Among School Children.
Fiddler of Dooney, The.
See also **Ballet; Ghost Dances; Waltzes and Waltzing**

Dandelions
Belitt. Late Dandelions.
Flanders, J. Dandelion Greens.
Kirsch, S. Dandelions for Chains ("Dandelions meet me wherever I am").
Kitahara Hakushū. Tanka: "I sneaked into."
Lowell, J. To the Dandelion.
MacNeice. Nature Notes: Dandelions.
Mayer, G. Dandelions.
McClellan. January Dandelion, A.
Robinson, M. Dandelion Puff, The.
Rosenblatt. Of Dandelions & Tourists.
Stanton, W. Dandelions.
Unknown. Dandelions, The.
O Dandelion.

Daniel
Glück, L. Gretel in Darkness.
Keats. Nebuchadnezzar's Dream.
Rowbotham. Nebuchadnezzar's Kingdom-Come.
Shaw, K. Handwriting on the Wall, The.
Unknown. Didn't my Lord Deliver Daniel.

Dante Alighieri
Bryant, W. Dante.
Emerson, R. Solution.
Keats. Dream, after Reading Dante's Episode of Paolo and Francesca, A.
Longfellow, H. Dante.
Michelangelo Buonarroti. Dante.
Ray, H. Dante.
Wright, J. Saying Dante Aloud.

Danube
Meredith, G. Square along the couch, and stark.

Danziger, Isaac
Wieseltier. Extended Sonnet on the Death of Isaac Danziger.

Daphne
Glück, L. Mythic Fragment.
Undertaking, The.
Kitahara Hakushū. Tanka: "Gasoline."
Ovid. Daphne and Apollo.
Pound, E. Tree, The.
Waller, E. Story of Phoebus and Daphne Applied, [etc.], The.
Winters, Y. Apollo and Daphne.

Dare, Virginia
Benét, R. *et al.* Peregrine White and Virginia Dare.

Darkness
Ackland. Overnight.
Aiken, J. Rhyme for Night.
Al-Khansa. Night, The.
Aldis, D. No One Heard Him Call.
Armstrong, F. Out of the Darkness.
Bartusek. Heliotropism / of branches, now darkened.
Berry, W. To Know the Dark.
Bible, *O.T.* Song: "I am dark, daughters of Jerusalem."
Bly, R. Snowfall in the Afternoon.
Bobrowski. Latvian Songs.
Bowes-Lyon. Blind Tramp, The.
Brodsky, J. I Sit by the Window.
Brontë, E. Spellbound.
Browne, M. Epithalamion/Wedding Dawn.
Byron, G. Darkness.
Carew, T. Beautiful Mistress, A.
Christopher. After Hours.
Clark, T. You (IV).
Cooley. Ararat.
Cornford, F. Single Woman, The.
Creeley. I Know a Man.
Rhythm, The.
Somewhere.
Curzon, D. Instructions to a Seed.
Davidson, L. It is growing dark.
Davis, F. Flowers of Darkness.
Dickinson, E. Lightning is a yellow Fork, The.
We grow accustomed to the Dark.
Dunbar, P. Slow Through the Dark.
Duoduo. At Parting.
Ellis, T. Shooting Back.
Ferguson, J. Auld Daddy Darkness creeps frae his hole.
"Field." They Shall Look on Him.
Foster, E. Morning.
Francis, R. Three darks come down together.
Fraser, K. These Labdanum Hours.
Garrigue. Forest.
Gilbo'a. In Darkness.
Gildner. Primarily We Miss Ourselves As Children.
Graves, R. Jealous Man, A.
Gunn, T. Feel of Hands, The.
Hanzlicek, C. In the Dark Again.
Hemphill. Where Seed Falls.
Herrick. In the Dark None Dainty.
Hewitt, J. Calling on Peadar O'Donnell at Dungloe.
Hill, G. Masque of Blackness, The.
Hippolyte. Reggae Cat (for Boston Jack).
Ho Ching-ming. Night of the Fourteenth.
Hotham. This loneliness.
Hristic. In a dark hour (there are more and more of them now).
Hsü Pen. In Harmony with Kao "The Second" Ch'i's Poem "On Hearing a P'i-p'a Played Next Door."
Hughes, L. Moonlight Night: Carmel.
Izumi. Way I must enter, The.
James, D. Love of Water Faucets, The.
Jarrell. 90 North.
Jewell. Somewhere behind me.
Keller, D. Friends, Outside, Night.
Kirkup. Who's that.
Knott. Funny Poem.
Kojijū. On the Spirit of the Heart as Moon-Disk.
Komunyakaa. Cage Walker, The.
Kooser. Late Lights in Minnesota.
Lane, P. Lake Murry.
Lao Tzu. Tao that can be told, The.
Lawrence, D. Young Wife, A.
Levertov. Closed World, The.
Levis. Magnolia.
Li Ho. In Protest.
Longfellow, H. Children's Hour, The.
Lowell, R. Darkened Mind, The.
Magowan. Zeimbekiko.
Maksimovic. Darkness was born in the forest. I found it there.
McGrath, T. Remembering the Children of Auschwitz.
Meissner. After Going Off the Road During the Snowstorm.

Milton. Samson's Complaint.
Montale. House of the Customs-Men, The.
Moses, W. Dark and Dark.
Neruda. Nothing but Death.
Owl Woman. Songs for the Four Parts of the Night.
Palmer, M. O you in that little bark.
Petrie. Phases of Darkness, The.
Pizzarelli. Spark, A.
Probyn. More than They that Watch for the Morning.
Roethke. In a dark time, the eye begins to see.
Rossetti, C. Remember me when I am gone away.
Rossetti, D. Without Her.
Rotella, A. Opening his.
Saitō Mokichi. Tanka: "Fly, A."
Samio. Tanka: "For a moment."
Selby, S. Spread, The.
Sheck. Return, The.
Shūji. Tanka: "At a corner."
Smith, K. Train.
Snyder, G. How Poetry Comes to Me.
Stafford, W. Traveling [or Travelling] through the dark I found a deer.
Sullivan, N. His Necessary Darkness.
Swinburne. Lake of Gaube, The.
Symons, A. Pastel: Masks and Faces.
Szymborska. Four in the Morning.
T'ang Hsien-tsu. Autumn River.
Tate, J. Contagion.
Teasdale. Hide and Seek.
Thomas, E. Dark Forest, The.
Out in the dark over the snow.
Tomlinson, C. Civilities of Lamplight.
Unknown. Evening darkens until.
Owl Woman's Death Song.
To a Firefly.
Wang Chiu-ssu. Thunder in the southern mountains, the third month of the year.
Welch, L. Empress herself served tea to Su Tung-po, The.
White, J. To Night.
Wieseltier. Holy Is the Desire to Proclaim the Existence of God.
Wright, J. Beginning.
Lights in the hallway, The.
Wroth. Sonnet 19: "Come darkest night, be[e]coming sorrow best."
Sonnet 22: "Like to the Indians, scorched with the sun[ne]."
Sonnet 9.
Yosano. Come at last to this point.
He tempted me to.
Zweig, M. Dark Song.

Darwin, Charles
Edson, R. Darwin Descending.
Melville, H. Epilogue: "If Luther's day expand to Darwin's year."
Naden. Natural Selection.
Solomon Redivivus, 1886.
Niedecker. Darwin.
Robinson, A. Darwinism.
Schnackenberg. Darwin in 1881.

See also **Evolution**

Dating
Ayton. Rejection, The.
Song: "What means this strangeness now of late."
Upon His Unconstant Mistress.
Campbell, T. Freedom and Love.
Collins, M. Story We Know, The.
Cope, W. Exchange of Letters.
Dove, R. Planning the Perfect Evening.
Dunbar, P. Lover's Lane.
Negro Love Song, A.
Francis, P. Thunder.
North, D. Platonic is a pretty name.
Reading. Ballad: "I'll tell you a story / concerning John and Joan."
Correspondence.

Daughters
Andreyev, V. To My Daughter.
Armitage, J. To Our Daughter.
Balamani Amma. To My Daughter.

Baraka. Preface to a Twenty Volume Suicide Note.
Berryman. Song 385.
Besant, L. Telepathy.
Betjeman. Old Land Dog, The.
Boland, E. Pomegranate, The.
Bolger. Dublin Girl, Mountjoy, 1984.
Booth, P. First Lesson.
Brigham. Tell Our Daughters.
Brooks, G. Jessie Mitchell's Mother.
Maxie Allen [always taught her].
Burns, R. Poet's Welcome to His Love-Begotten Daughter [the First Instance that Entitled Him to the Venerable Appellation of Father], A.
Byron, G. Jephtha's Daughter.
Campbell, D. Mothers and Daughters.
Carruth, H. Words for My Daughter from the Asylum.
Carver, R. My Daughter and Apple Pie.
Clarke, A. My mother wept loudly.
Clifton, L. Admonitions.
4 Daughters.
If mama / could see.
Cofer. Unspoken.
Coleman, H. Black Soldier Remembers, A.
Poem for a "Divorced" Daughter.
Coleman, W. Cousin Mary.
Corso. For Miranda.
Creeley. Fire, The.
Sitting Here.
Cumming, P. Spring.
Dobyns. Shaving.
Dove, R. After Reading *Mickey in the Night Kitchen* for the Third Time Before Bed.
Dufferin. Mother's Lament, The.
"Dylan." Tears of Rage.
Eklund. Dressing My Daughter.
Eliot, T. Marina.
Euripides. Agamemnon struggles to avert the sacrifice of his daughter Iphigeneia].
Galvin, B. For a Daughter Gone Away.
Gilbert, C. Circles.
Gillan. My Daughter at 14: Christmas Dance, 1981.
Gillies, V. Young Harper.
Gioia. Counting the Children.
Goodison. I Am Becoming My Mother.
Graves, R. Frosty Night, A.
Griffin, S. Rebecca, sweet-one, little-one.
Hagedorn. Natural Death.
Halliday, C. Ode to My Daugther's Plimsolls and the Mess in Her Room.
Harper, M. Eve (Rachel).
Harrod, L. Fitting Room.
Harwood, G. Mother who gave me life.
Hashimoto, S. Standing in the Doorway, I Watch the Young Child Sleep.
Hogan, L. Daybreak.
Hughes, L. Mama and Daughter.
Hugo, V. Jeanne was on bread and water in a dark room.
Hull, L. Shore Leave.
Jackson, L. Only Daughter, The.
Jamison, B. Ask This of a Mother Whose Daughter Has Been Tortured.
Jarrell. Lost Children, The.
Jonson, B. On My First Daughter.
To Elizabeth, Countess of Rutland.
Joyce, J. Flower Given to My Daughter, A.
Joyce, W. My Daughter's Pundalunda.
Kao Ch'i. Seeing Flowers I Remember My Late Daughter, Shu.
Kaufman, S. Mothers, Daughters.
Notes on My Daughters.
Kees. For My Daughter.
Kgositsile. To My Daughter.
Kinnell. Little Sleep's-Head Sprouting Hair in the Moonlight.
Round– / cheeked girlchild comes awake, A.
Kipling, R. Merrow Down.
Kizer, C. Blessing, The.
Knight, E. Circling the Daughter.
Kumin, M. Envelope, The.
Journey, The.
Making the Jam without You.

Landor, W. Mother, I Cannot Mind My Wheel.
Lepik. Let Me Hold Your Hand.
Li Po. Sent to My Two Little Children in the East of Lu.
Libera. Mother, I may do violence to you.
Livingston, M. Working with Mother.
Longfellow, H. Wreck of the *Hesperus*, The.
Lowell, R. Home after Three Months Away.
Lum. Backup, The.
Lux. Little Tooth, A.
MacCaig. Intruder in a Set Scene.
MacDonald, C. Inheritance.
MacKay, C. Louise on the Door-Step.
Macpherson, J. Beauty of Job's Daughters, The.
Madgett. Offspring.
McDonald, W. Faraway Places.
McElroy, C. In My Mother's Room.
Meinke. To a Daughter with Artistic Talent.
Meynell, A. Girl on the Land, The.
Moraga. For the Color of my Mother.
Msham. Daughter, take this amulet.
Mullen, H. Momma Sayings.
Saturday Afternoon, When Chores Are Done.
Olds, S. Quake Theory.
Quest, The.
35/10.
What If God.
Why My Mother Made Me.
Oppen. Exodus.
Orr, G. Nicole at Thirteen.
Otomo no Sakanoé, L. Sent from the Capital to Her Elder Daughter.
Pastan. Duet for One Voice.
To a Daughter Leaving Home.
Peseroff. Bluebird.
Po Chü-i. Golden Bells.
Ransom, J. Bells for John Whiteside's Daughter.
Reed, I. Poem for Two Daughters.
Rexroth, K. Living Pearl, A.
Rich, A. Woman Mourned by Daughters, A.
Richardson, J. As If Ending.
Rodgers, C. It Is Deep.
Salter. Emily Wants to Play.
Seaton, M. Fear of Shoplifting.
Segal, J. Candle.
Sexton. Little Girl, My String Bean, My Lovely Woman.
Pain for a Daughter.
Shapiro, K. Calling the Child.
Shumaker. Waitress's Kid, The.
Shurin. Material's Daughter.
Siddal. At Last.
Smith, B. Mercy.
Smith, S. Human Affection.
Spender, S. Missing My Daughter.
Stevenson, A. Poem to my Daughter.
Stone, R. I Have Three Daughters.
Tennyson, A. Gardener's Daughter, The.
Thomas, E. If I Should Ever by Chance.
Thwaite. At Birth.
Unknown. Execution of Alice Holt.
Hush, little baby, don't say a word.
Upton, L. Daughter, A.
Vinz. Sins of the Fathers.
Vittorelli. On a Nun.
Walker, A. Forgiveness.
Poem at Thirty-nine.
Walker, J. For My Daughter's Twenty-First Birthday.
Waniek. Daughters, 1900.
Warren, R. Colder Fire.
Whittier. Farewell, The: "Gone, gone,—sold and gone."
Wilbur. Writer, The.
Williams, C. Last Deaths, The.
Williams, M. Poem for Emily, A.
Wilson, K. Dusk in My Backyard.
Winters, Y. To My Infant Daughter.
Wong, N. Where are you going now?
Wright, C. Daughters of Blum, The.
Wright, J. Eve to Her Daughters.
Yeats. Father and Child.
Prayer for My Daughter, A.
Young, D. Shepherd's Dochter, The.

Zealand. Primitives Knew How Defenseless, The.
Zweig, P. River, The.

David (Bible)
Abelard. David's Lament for Jonathan.
Amis, K. After Goliath.
Benét, S. King David.
Berryman. King David Dances.
Bialik. Death of David, The.
Bible, *O.T.* Duty.
Byron, G. Harp the monarch minstrel swept, The.
Cohen, J. Harp of David, The.
Crouch, N. David and Goliath.
Drayton. Our sacred Muse, of Israel's Singer sings.
Graves, R. Goliath and David.
Lamb, C. David in the Cave of Adullam.
Lindsay, V. In Which Roosevelt Is Compared to Saul.
Moore, M. That Harp You Play So Well.
Naylor. Authorship.
Quarles. On Saul and David.
Reznikoff. David.
  I do not believe that David killed Goliath.
Smart, C. David's Song to Saul.
Spire. Abishag.
Steele, T. In the King's Rooms.
Thompson, P. David and Goliath.
Traherne. In Salem dwelt a glorious king.
Untermeyer, L. Goliath and David.
Waddell, P. David and Goliath.
"Yehoash." Harp of David, The.

Davies, Dr. John
Howell, J. Upon Dr. Davies's British Grammar.

Davis, Angela
Cobb, A. Angela Davis.

Davis, Miles
Brathwaite, E. Blues.
Corso. For Miles.
Ford, W. Of Miles Davis.
Harper, M. Alone.
Jauss. Black Orchid.
Kelly, R. Ode to Language.
Komunyakaa. Boxing Day.
Troupe. Four and More; for Miles Davis.
Waters, M. Miles Weeping.
Whitlow. Poem for the Children.

Davis, Thomas Osborne
Ferguson, S. Lament for the Death of Thomas Davis.

Dawn
Antipater of Thessalonica. It is morning, Chrysilla. Some time ago the clarion cock.
Bardoloi. Dawn.
Beckett, S. Alba.
Belloc. Early Morning, The.
Blue Cloud. Spring Equinox.
Campbell, R. Mass at Dawn.
  Sisters, The.
Chiyojo. Cuckoo!/ Cuckoo!
Cooper, J. Morning on the St. John's.
Dana, R. Daybreak.
Daryush. Invalid Dawn.
Davenant. Aubade: "Lark now leaves his watery [*or* wat'ry] nest, The."
Davison, P. Equinox 1980.
De la Mare. Stranger, The.
De Tabley. Nuptial Song.
Dickinson, E. It was a quiet way—.
Dixon, R. Dawning
Drummond, W. Invocation: "Pheobus, arise! / And paint the sable skies."
Dunbar, P. Dawn.
Eifuku. We dressed each other.
Fujiwara no Michinobu. In the dawn, although I know.
Fujiwara no Sadayori. As the mists rise in the dawn.
Gates, L. Winter dawn;.
Gilder, R. Prelude: "Night was dark, though sometimes a faint star, The."
Graves, R. Return of the Goddess [Artemis].
Guiney. When on the marge of evening the last blue light is broken.

Hackett, J. Moon fades into dawn.
  Stillness of dawn, The.
Harmon. Dawn Horse, The.
Harr, L. Pale dawn moon, A.
Hearn, M. At Dawn.
Herlin. Light brush of dawn, A.
Herrick. To Anthea Lying in Bed.
Hitomaro. On the Eastern horizon.
Housman, A. Fairies break their dances, The.
  Reveille.
Hsieh Chin. To Hsiao Shih-ying.
Hudgins. Two Ember Days in Alabama.
Hughes, L. Daybreak in Alabama.
Hughes, T. Roe-Deer.
Irwin, T. With the Dawn.
Izumi. It is the time of rain and snow.
Jaccottet. Dawn.
  Daybreak / mingles blood.
  Swifts.
  Wishes.
Jewell. Last screech owl cry.
Juana Inés de la Cruz. But Venus first.
Kerouac. Birds singing.
Kinsella, T. First Light.
Kitahara Hakushū. Tanka: "Magnolia."
Kumbirai. Dawn.
Lane, P. Spring.
Lawrence, D. Quite Forsaken.
Lee, L. Edge of Day, The.
Levertov. What Wild Dawns There Were.
Lewis, A. Dawn on the East Coast.
Lewis, J. Snail Garden.
Li Ho. Dawn in Stone City.
Li Meng-yang. Oriole at Dawn, An.
Lloyd, D. Quietly shaping.
Lodge, G. Lower New York.
Longfellow, H. Children's Hour, The.
  Daybreak.
Mac Thiên Tích. Morning Bell at Tiêu Monastery, The.
Mahapatra, J. October Morning, An.
Marlowe. Now ore the sea from her old Love comes she.
Meredith, W. Ideogram.
Mibu no Tadami. Since I left her.
Millay, E. Recuerdo.
Milosz, C. Encounter.
Miyazawa Kenji. Tanka: "At dawn."
Montgomerie, A. Night Is Near [*or* Neir] Gone, The.
Morris, W. Summer Dawn.
North, C. Sunrise with Sea Monster.
O'Rahilly. Vision, The.
Ovid. I, 13. Elegy: Ad Auroram, ne properet.
Pagis. Plans.
Parry, R. Miraculous Dawn.
Philips, A. Happy Swain, The.
Po Chü-i. On his Baldness.
  Starting Early from the Ch'u-ch'êng Inn.
Rabéarivelo. Three Dawns.
Ray, H. Dawn's Carol.
Rimbaud. Dawn.
Rossetti, C. "Kookoorookoo! kookoorookoo!" / Crows the cock before the morn.
Sakanoe No Korenori. In the dawn.
Sami Mansei. This world of ours.
Sanesada. Cuckoo calls. / When I look there is only, A.
Sappho. In gold sandals.
Schwartz, D. Little Morning Music, A.
Shakespeare, W. Song: "Hark! hark! the lark at heaven's gate sings."
Shūji. Tanka: "Mr. Nehru."
Sidney, P. Sonnet 99: "When far-spent night persuades each mortal eye."
Sissoko. Dawn in the Valley.
Soyinka. Death in the Dawn.
Stanyhurst. Thee whilst thee dawning Aurora fro the Ocean hastned.
Stevens, W. Brave Man, The.
Swede. At dawn remembering her bad grammar.
  Dawn.
Symons, A. At Dawn.
Teika. From the beginning.
Tennyson, A. Dawn, The.
  Owl, The.

Thomas, D. Light breaks where no sun shines.
Thomas, E. Cock-Crow.
  Trumpet, The.
Thoreau. Guido's Aurora.
Tuckerman, F. Morning comes; not slow, with reddening gold, The.
Under. Morning Joy.
Unknown. Crow caws in the moonlight, A.
  Dawn, The.
  First dawn comes, The.
  First Daylight Song.
  Last Daybreak Song.
  Last Song of the Exploding Stick.
  Salutation of the Dawn, The.
Vaughan, H. Cock-crowing.
Very. Fair Morning, The.
Wagoner, D. Five Dawn Skies in November.
Warren, R. Masts at Dawn.
Wen Cheng-ming. Year Hsin-hai (Fifteen Fifty One), New Year's Eve: Keeping Watch, The.
Westmorland. Reveille Matin, or Good Morrow to a Friend.
Wieselter. "Wintry Dawn."
Wilcox, E. Dawn.
Williams, W. Dawn.
Wu Wei-yeh. Autumn Night—Sleepless.
Yang Chi. Poem on Passing by Hsin-k'ai Lake at Kao-yu in Light Rain, A.
Yosano. Tanka: "Earth looks, The."
Zagajewski. At Daybreak.
See also **Morning; Sunrise**

Dawson, F. W.
Fordham. Tribute to Capt. F. W. Dawson.

Day
Baillie, J. Up! quit thy bower.
Barbauld. Tomorrow.
Belloc. Early Morning, The.
Bible, *O.T.* Psalm 19.
Boldman. Day darkens.
Bourdillon. When Love Is Done.
Bu-er. Cut brambles long enough.
Carlyle, T. Today.
Codrescu. Work.
Coleridge, M. Shadow.
"Coolidge." New Every Morning.
Cummings, E. Impression.
  Out of midsummer's blazing most not night.
De Mello Breyner. Day of sea in the sky, made.
Dickinson, E. First Day's Night had come, The.
Emerson, R. Days.
Herrick. Dream[e]s.
Hesketh. Love's Advocate.
Higginson, W. I look up.
Kalidasa. Salutation to the Dawn.
Lanier, S. Song for "The Jacquerie."
Larkin, P. Days.
Levertov. Variation on a Theme by Rilke.
McCrae, J. In Flanders Fields the poppies blow.
Mother Goose. Thirty days hath September.
Mountain, M. Quiet day, A.
Nicholls, J. Earthrise.
Owen, G. Gathering in the Days.
Park, T. Sun, The.
Roseliep. Morning-Glory, The.
Rossetti, C. Is the moon tired? she looks so pale.
  "Kookoorookoo! kookoorookoo!" / Crows the cock before the morn.
Ryashentsev. April in Town.
Sandburg, C. Skyscraper.
Stevens, W. Brave Man, The.
  Prejudice against the Past, The.
Stevenson, R. Bed in Summer.
  Moon has a face like the clock in the hall, The.
Stidger. Day, A.
Tennant, R. Wee Davie Daylicht.
Thoreau. Guido's Aurora.
Trần Gia Thoại. Falling Leaf, A.
Walcott. Star.
Wilbur. Death of a Toad, The.

Daydreams
Ashbery. Instruction Manual, The.
  Mixed Feelings.

Baudelaire. Exotic Scent.
Breeze. Dreamer.
Brontë, E. Little while, a little while, A.
Ch'ien Ch'ien-i. Fishing cove and long lines of fishermen's huts, A.
Chin Ch'ang-hsü. Spring Grievance.
Coleridge, M. Day-dream, A.
Coleridge, S. Day-Dream, The ("If thou wert here, these tears were tears of light!")
Eshleman, C. Foo to the Infinite.
Eskimo Oral Tradition. Song of Kuk-ook, the Bad Boy, The.
Foster, S. Jeanie with the Light Brown Hair.
Harrison, G. Playground, The.
Hecht, A. Hill, A.
Humphries, R. Heresy for a Class-Room.
"MacDiarmid." Harry Semen.
MacKie, A. Sun's oot. I sit, my pipe alunt and puff, The.
Robinson, E. Miniver Cheevy, child of scorn.
Schimelpfenig. Geography of Lunch, A.
"Shu Ting." Bits of Reminiscence.
Traherne. Dreams.
"Vaidehi." Girl in the Kitchen.
Valéry. Girl with Mind Wandering.
Wade, B. Summer School.
Young, A. Loneliness.
See also **Dreams and Dreaming**
De Hooch, Pieter. *See* **Hooch, Pieter de**
De Soto, Hernando
Harjo, J. New Orleans.
Van Doren. Distant Runners, The.
Deafness
Baranczak, S. N. N. Tries to Remember the Words of a Prayer.
Coleridge, H. To a Deaf and Dumb Little Girl.
Delius. Deaf-and-Dumb School.
Gallagher, T. Deaf Poem.
Glazkov. Deaf-Mutes.
Higgs, B. Deaf is like.
Jones, R. Hearing Aid, The.
Murray, L. Hearing Impairment.
Nastasijevic. Beauty since.
Not one whisper.
Page, P. Deaf-Mute in the Pear Tree.
Ryan, R. Deafness.
Swift, J. On His Own Deafness.
Tate, J. Deaf Girl Playing.
Traxler. Death of a Distant In-law.
Valek. Hearing.
Wright, D. On Himself.
Wright, J. Mutterings Over the Crib of a Deaf Child.
Dean, James
Jones, R. James Dean.
O'Hara, F. For James Dean.
Death and the Dead
Abdullah. Tombs, The.
Abse. Peachstone.
Winter Visit, A.
Abu Dhu'ayb al-Hudhali. Lament for Five Sons Lost in a Plague.
Ackland. Instructions From England 1936.
"Ada." Oh, when this earthly tenement.
Adamovich. Autumn night, in a hotel, the two, An.
Adams, L. Death and the Lady.
Adamson. My House.
Adcock, B. Walking Out.
Adcock, F. Poem Ended by a Death.
"Adeler." Out of the Hurly-Burly.
"Adunis." New Noah, The.
Tree of Fire.
"Æ." Immortality.
Aeschylus. Lament for the Two Brothers Slain by Each Other's Hand.
Agathias. Justice.
"Agyeya." Hiroshima.
Ai. She Didn't Even Wave.
Aichinger. Enumeration.
Aiken, C. Tetélestai.
"Akhmatova." Dedication.
Everything Is Plundered[, betrayed, sold].
When a man dies.
Al-Khansa. Lament for a Brother.
Alberti. Punishments.

Alcaeus. Poet has died, A.
Aldington. Soliloquy 2.
Aldrich, T. Memory.
Alegría. Desire.
From the Bridge.
I Am Root.
We Were Three.
Aleixandre. My Grandfather's Death.
Alexander, M. Her Garden.
Alexandru. Miserere Nobis.
Aliger. Blue Hour, The.
Allen, P. Los Angeles, 1980.
Allen, S. Staircase, The.
Allingham. Dream, A [*or* The].
No funeral gloom, my dears, when I am gone.
Allott. Statue, The.
Alvarez, J. How I Learned to Sweep.
Amann. Names of the dead, The.
Night train passes, A.
Amichai. I have nothing to say about the war.
Is all this sorrow? I don't know.
Little Ruth.
Summer or Its Ending.
Amiel. Death is a matter of mathematics.
Amis, K. A. E. H.
Last War, The.
Ammianus. Dawn after dawn after dawn / then suddenly the Dark One.
Epitaph of Nearchos.
Anacreon. If Profit offered immortality for gold.
Ode of Anacreon, Paraphras'd / The Cup, An.
Anderson, J. In Sepia.
Andrade, C. Fourth Poem of a Canto of Accusation.
Andresen. Small Square, The.
Andrews, M. Elegy on the Death of Mr Sterne.
Angelou. Elegy: "I lay down in my grave."
Angira. Country of the dead, The.
Annensky. Black Spring.
Antipater of Sidon. Already prepared in the golden chamber.
Antipater of Thessalonica. Italian dust covers a Libyan.
Antokolsky. Ballad of the Wondrous Moment.
Applewhite. My Grandfather's Funeral.
Arabov. I'm introducing it as a hunchback.
Arendt. Lost Bay.
Aridjis. Epitaph for a Poet.
Arnold, M. Matthias.
Requiescat.
What though the music of thy rustic flute.
Youth and Calm.
Arp. Kaspar Is Dead.
Asalache. Death of a Chief.
Ashbery. Fear of Death.
How much longer will I be able to inhabit the divine sepulchre.
Saying It to Keep It from Happening.
Ashe. Corpse-bearing.
"Asphodel." Winter Solstice—for Frank.
Aston, A. Everything in the Garden is Lovely.
"Asya." Celan.
Atkins. Narrative.
Atwood. Settlers, The.
This Is a Photograph of Me.
Aubert, A. For Mark James Robert Essex d. 1973.
Auchterlonie. Waiting for the Post.
Auden. Aesthetic Point of View, The.
As I walked out one evening.
Ballad: "O what is that sound [which so thrills the ear]."
Embassy.
From Scars Where Kestrels Hover.
Song: "Stop all the clocks, cut off the telephone."
Augustine. Half Of Me.
My heart was darkened over with grief, and whatever I.
Auslander, J. Elegy: "Fled is the swiftness of all the white-footed ones."
Austin, M. Song of a Man About to Die in a Strange Land.
Auvaiyar. Elegy: "If he found a little liquor."
Elegy: "This bright burning pyre."

Avakkumova. Dead man touched me with his hand, A.
Avidan. Burying Uncle Salomon.
Prehistory.
Awoonor. Song of War.
Songs of Sorrow.
Ayton. On the Prince's Death, to the King.
Bachmann. Early Noon.
"Bagritzky." Watermelon.
Baker, D. Dying in Massachusetts.
Balaban. Graveyard at Bald Eagle Ridge.
News Update.
Bancquart. Baroque.
Counterfable of Orpheus.
Epitaph.
Town.
Vanished, The.
Baraka. Crow Jane.
Incident.
Invention of Comics, The.
Barker, G. And now there is nothing left to celebrate.
In Memory of a Friend.
Barlas. Oblivion! is it not one name of death?
Barlow, G. Mingus Speaks: Found Poems.
Barnes, W. Geate A-Vallen To, The.
Mater Dolorosa.
Sonnet: "In every dream thy lovely features rise."
Wife A-Lost, The.
Barrax. Scuba Diver Recovers the Body of a Drowned Child, The.
Barry, J. Green Hell, Green Death.
Harvest Moon.
Bates, K. Yellow Clover.
Baudelaire. Carrion, A.
Baugh, E. Carpenter's Complaint, The.
Baxter, J. East Coast Journey.
Rata blooms explode, the bow-legged tomcat, The.
Bayly. Mistletoe Bough, The.
Beaumont, F. *et al.* Aspatia's Song.
Beaver. Three images of dying stick in my mind like morbid transfers.
Beckett, S. Alba.
I would like my love to die.
Song: "Age is when to a man."
Beddoes. Death Sweet.
Dirge: "We do lie beneath the grass."
Beer, P. Grave Doubts.
Lemmings die every year. Over the cliff.
Beerbohm, M. On the Imprint of the First English Edition of "The Works of Max Beerbohm."
Behan, B. Repentance.
Behn, A. Epitaph on the Tombstone of a Child, the Last of Seven That Died Before.
On the Death of the Late Earl of Rochester.
Behrens. Trees are rustling outside the open window, The.
Bekederemo. Death of a Lady.
Family Procession, A.
Leader, The.
Order of the Dead, The.
Belloc. Obiter Dicta.
Statue, The.
Benn. Lovely Childhood.
Bennett, G. Sonnet: "He came in silvern armor, trimmed with black."
Benveniste. End To It, An.
Berg, S. Holes, The.
Bernstein, O. Cuernavaca.
Memories of Her Friend Who Died.
Berrigan, T. Dear Margie, hello. It is 5:15 a.m.
Sonnet I: "His piercing pince-nez. Some dim frieze."
Berry, D. Sun goes.
Berry, J. It's Me Man.
Berry, W. Grandmother, The.
Ripening.
Slip, The.
Berryman. 324. An Elegy for W.C.W., The Lovely Man.
At Henry's bier let some thing fall out well.
Grandfather, sleepless in a room upstairs.
Henry sats in de bar and was odd.

Poet's Final Instructions, The.
Thin as a sheet his mother came to him.
This world is gradually becoming a place.
To My Father.
Whether There Is Sorrow in the Demons.
Bertolino. Coons, The.
Beshenkovskaya. In a land whose prosperity
    constantly grows.
Bethune, L. For Singing In Good Mood.
Harlem Freeze Frame.
Betjeman. Death in Leamington.
Five O'Clock Shadow.
House of Rest.
Inevitable.
Remorse.
Bevington, L. Twilight.
Bialik. Death of David, The.
Bible, O.T. Duty.
Psalm 23.
Bidart. Sacrifice, The.
To the Dead.
Bienek. Exodus.
Our Ashes.
Vorkuta.
Bierce. Done with the work of breathing;
    done.
General B. F. Butler.
Binyon. Now is the time for the burning of
    the leaves.
Unreturning Spring, The.
Bion. Lament for Adonis.
Bishop, E. Cootchie, Miss Lula's servant, lies
    in marl.
First Death in Nova Scotia.
Man-Moth, The.
Bishop, J. Hours, The.
Sleep Brought Me Vision.
Blackmur. Elegy for Five, An.
Blagden. To George Sand on her Interview
    with Elizabeth Barrett Browning.
Blaginina. To the Memory of G. N.
    Obolduyev.
Blake, W. Another [Epitaph]: "Here lies John
    Trot, the Friend of all mankind."
Epitaph, An: "I was buried near this dyke [or
    Dike]."
Little Boy Lost, The ("Father, father, where
    are you going?")
Sick Rose, The.
Blamire. Auld Robin Forbes.
Blaser. Ruler, The.
Blight. Death of a Whale.
Blind. Dead abide with us! Though stark and
    cold, The.
Bloch, C. Survivors.
Blok. On Death.
Blossom, L. Disappearing Act.
Blumenthal, M. Juliek's Violin.
Blunden. Death Mask of John Clare, The.
Bly, R. Christmas Eve Service at Midnight at
    St. Michael's.
Looking at New-Fallen Snow from a Train.
Bodenheim. Death.
Bodman. What rich profusion here.
Boland, E. Anna Liffey.
Boleyn, G. O death, rock me asleep.
Bonnefoy. De Natura Rerum.
Booth, P. Hope.
Boss. Candy Lady, The.
Bowers, F. Centaur Overheard, The.
Elegy, An: December, 1970.
Bowles, C. Stanzas.
Brackenbury. Two dead divers hauled up in
    their bell, The.
Bradstreet, A. Before the Birth of One of Her
    Children.
In Memory of My Dear Grandchild Anne
    Bradstreet Who Deceased June 20, 1669,
    Being Three Years and Seven Months Old.
To My Dear and Loving Husband.
To the Memory of My Dear and Ever
    Honored Father Thomas Dudley Esq. Who
    Deceased July 31, 1653, and of His Age 77.
To the Memory of My Dear Daughter in Law,
    Mrs. Mercy Bradstreet.
Braithwaite. House of Falling Leaves, The.
In a Grave-Yard.

Brathwaite, E. Ancestors.
Brecht, B. To Those Born Later.
Breytenbach. Out There.
Bridges, R. I Never Shall Love the Snow
    Again.
When Death to Either Shall Come.
Bringhurst. For the Bones of Josef Mengele,
    Disinterred June 1985.
Brock-Broido. Moving on in the Dark Like
    Loaded Boats at Night, Though There is No
    Course, There is Boundlessness.
Brock, V. Departure.
Brodrick. Epitaph on a Diamond Digger.
On a Government Surveyor.
Brodsky, J. Belfast Tune.
Nature Morte.
Brontë, A. Night.
Reminiscence, A.
Brontë, C. Diving.
Is this my tomb, this humble stone.
On the Death of Anne Brontë.
On the Death of Emily Jane Brontë.
Reason.
Young Man Naughty's Adventure.
Brontë, E. Aye, there it is! It wakes to-night.
Come, walk with me.
Death Scene, A.
Death, that struck when I was most confiding.
Long neglect has worn away.
Night Wind, The.
No coward soul is mine.
Remembrance.
Song: "Linnet in the rocky dells, The."
Stanzas: "I'll not weep that thou art going to
    leave me."
Stanzas to———.
Warning and Reply.
Brooke, R. Great Lover, The.
Hill, The.
Peace.
Soldier, The.
Sonnet: "Oh! Death will find me, long before
    I tire."
Brooks, G. Boy Died in My Alley, The.
In Honor of David Anderson Brooks, My
    Father.
Last Quatrain of the Ballad of Emmett Till,
    The.
Medgar Evers.
Of De Witt Williams on His Way to Lincoln
    Cemetery.
Old Relative.
Rites for Cousin Vit, The.
Southeast Corner.
We real cool. We.
White Troops Had Their Orders but the
    Negroes Looked Like Men.
Broughton, T. Hold, Hold.
Brown, A. Assassination of Charlie Parker,
    The.
Brown, D. Still Later There Are War Stories.
Brown, G. Five Voyages of Arnor, The.
Funeral of Ally Flett, The.
Kirkyard.
Old Fisherman with Guitar.
Brown, M. Created Clay.
Brown, S. Conjured.
Sister Lou.
Browne, W. On the Countess Dowager of
    Pembroke.
Browning, E. Died...
Felicia Hemans.
Grief.
L.E.L.'s Last Question.
Mother and Poet.
Sleep, The.
Sonnet: "How do I love thee? Let me count
    the ways."
Sonnet: "Unlike are we, unlike, O princely
    Heart!"
Stanzas on the Death of Lord Byron.
Browning, R. Bishop Orders His Tomb at
    Saint Praxed's Church, The.
Lines on Swinburne.
Lost Leader, The.
May and Death.
Prospice.

Bruchac. Elegy for Jack Bowman.
Brutus. At a Funeral.
Endurance.
Bryant, W. Death of Lincoln, The.
Death of the Flowers, The.
Thanatopsis.
To the Fringed Gentian.
Buchanan, G. Jill's Death.
Buckley, V. In the faint blue light.
Buckmaster. Seed.
Bukowski. I Am Dead But I Know the Dead
    Are Not Like This.
Bunan. Die while you're alive.
Bunin. Flowers, and tall-stalked grasses, and a
    bee.
Bunting. To Violet [with Prewar Poems].
Burns, R. Death and Doctor Hornbook [A
    True Story].
Epitaph on a Schoolmaster.
Here cursing swearing Burton lies.
Highland Mary.
Lo worms enjoy the seat of bliss.
On a Noisy Polemic.
So vile was poor Wat, such a miscreant slave.
Tam Samson's Elegy.
Ye maggots, feed on Willie's brains.
Burris. Strong's Winter.
Burt, D. On the Death of Lisa Lyman.
Buson. Haiku: "I feel a sudden chill—."
Scattering bloom, The.
Butler, G. In Memoriam, J.A.R., Drowned,
    East London.
Bynner. Death of a Friend.
Pause.
Byron, G. Bright be the place of thy soul!
Destruction of Sennacherib, The.
Stanzas: "And thou art dead, as young and
    fair."
Stanzas: "I heard thy fate without a tear."
Callimachus. Somebody told me you were
    dead.
Someone told me, Heraclitus.
Cameron, N. She and I.
Visit to the Dead, A.
Camões. Do This Favour For Me.
Campbell, D. I Starting from Central Station.
Men in Green.
Campbell, J. Dancer, The.
Campbell, T. Hohenlinden.
Last Man, The.
Campion, T. Lamentation, A.
When thou must home to shades of
    underground [or under ground].
Campo. El Día de los Muertos.
Cao Tân. Our friend would board the
    Thu'o'ng-Tín and go home.
Caraion. Memory.
Carew, T. Another [On the Duke of
    Buckingham].
Another [Epitaph on Lady Mary Villiers]
    ("This little vault, this narrow room").
For a Picture Where a Queen Laments over
    the Tomb of a Slain Knight.
Maria Wentworth.
Carphyllides. Happy Man, A.
Carroll, J. Maybe I'm Amazed.
Carruth, H. Song: So Often, So Long I Have
    Thought.
Carter, E. On the Death of Mrs. Rowe.
Cartier. Poem for a Chorus.
Cassells. Courtesy, A Trenchant Grace, A.
Sung From A Hospice.
Castillo, A. Nani Worries about Her Father's
    Happiness in the Afterlife.
Cather, W. Macon Prairie.
Catullus. Lines from Catullus.
Love and Death.
On the Burial of His Brother.
To A Friend.
Causley. By St. Thomas Water.
Death of a Poet.
Song of the Dying Gunner A.A.1.
Cavafy. Voices.
Cavalli. Ah, yes, to your misfortune.
Celan. Aspen tree, your leaves glance white
    into the dark.

Death Fugue, A.
When you lie in.
Césaire, A. Beat It Night Dog.
In Memory of a Black Union Leader.
Chamberlain, B. Dead Ponies.
Chandler, M. My Own Epitaph.
Chang, E. Bamboo Elegy: Two.
Chang Yü. In a Book-Box I Found the Lost Manuscript of a Poem Sent to Me by the Late Kao [Ch'i].
Lamenting for Kao Ch'ing-ch'iu, Chi-ti.
Chao. Locust Swarm, The.
Chao Meng-fu. Eulogy of the Sagely Virtue of His Imperial Majesty Emperor Shih-tsu, A.
Chapman, G. Death Described by His True Effects.
Homer and the Brazen Head of Rumour.
Chapman, M. African Dirge.
Chappell, F. Second Wind.
Chatterton. Mynstrelle's Songe ("O! synge untoe mie roundelaie").
Chaucer. Experience, though noon auctoritee.
Song of Troylus, The.
Chế Lan Viên. Graves.
Cheney-Coker. Letter to a Tormented Playwright.
Chesterfield. On Lord Ila's Improvements, near Hounslow Heath.
Cheyenne Oral Tradition. Death Song of White Antelope*, The.
Chimombo. Four Ways of Dying.
Chin. Autumn Leaves.
Elegy for Chloe Nguyen.
Chingono. Epitaph, An: "Here lies Stephen Pwanya."
Chivers. Avalon.
Cho, P. Empty as Death.
Never to Meet Again.
Chock. Poem for George Helm: Aloha Week 1980.
Chukhonstev. Elegy: "Cross between a bakehouse and a bell tower, A."
Ciardi. Death's the Classic Look.
Clampitt. What the Light Was Like.
Clare, J. Death.
I am: yet what I am none cares or knows.
Song—Last Day.
Written in Northampton County Asylum.
Claudian. Old Men not staid with Age, Virgins with shame.
Clifton, H. Death of Thomas Merton.
Clifton, L. At Jonestown.
Bodies broken on, The.
Raising of Lazarus, The.
Sam.
Clinton. Tantrum Girl Responds to Death.
Clough. Epi-Strauss-ium.
Codrescu. Grammar, A.
Coleman, E. Liberator, The.
Coleman, H. Remembrance of Things Past.
Coleman, W. Today I Am a Homicide in the North of the City.
Waif of Echo Park, The.
Coleridge, H. On the Death of Echo, A Favourite Beagle.
Think upon Death.
Written on the Anniversary of Our Father's Death.
Coleridge, M. 'But in that Sleep of Death what Dreams may Come?'.
I envy not the dead that rest.
Marriage.
Witch, The.
Coleridge, S. Epitaph: "Stop, Christian passer-by!—Stop, child of God."
Ne Plus Ultra.
W. H. *Eheu!*.
Coleridge, S. Father! no amaranths e'er shall wreathe my brow.
Collins, B. Dead are always looking down on us, they say, The.
Collins, W. Dirge in "Cymbeline."
Ode Written in the Beginning of the Year 1746.
Cook, E. Song of the Rushlight.
Cook-Lynn. My Grandmother's Burial Ground.
Cooke, E. How Did You Die?

Cooke, P. Florence Vane.
Cooley. Elect, The.
Coolidge, C. Book of During, IV, The.
Cooper, D. Drugs.
Cooper, J. Hotel De Dream.
In the House of the Dying.
Long, Disconsolate Lines.
Corbet. Elegy Upon the Death of His Own Father, An.
On the Lady Arabella.
Corman. Deceased.
Cornford, F. Nurse.
Recollection, A.
Watch, The.
Cornish, S. Death of Dr. King.
Corso. Mad Yak, The.
Cothi. Lament for Siôn y Glyn.
Cotton, C. Epitaph on M. H, An.
Cowley, A. It was a dismal and a fearful night.
On the Death of Mr. Crashaw.
Cowper, W. Epitaph on a Hare.
Epitaph on Dr. Johnson.
Inscription.
Cox, M. Sleep Apnea.
Crabbe. Peter Grimes.
Crane, H. Broken Tower, The.
Circumstance, The.
Praise for an Urn.
Crane, S. Man adrift on a slim spar, A.
Many workmen / Built a hugh ball of masonry.
There is a grey thing that lives in the tree-tops.
Crashaw. Death's Lecture.
Epitaph Upon Husband and Wife Who Died and Were Buried Together, An.
Creeley. After Lorca.
And.
Death of Venus, The.
For My Mother: Genevieve Jules Creeley.
Heroes.
Mother's Voice.
Rhythm, The.
World, The.
Cross, Jr. Fifty Gunner, The.
Gliding Baskets.
Rice Will Grow Again.
Csoori. Maybe elegies have ruined me.
Stranger, A.
Thin, Black Band, A.
Cuevish. Before They Made Things Be Alive They Spoke.
Cullen, C. Brown Girl Dead, A.
Only the Polished Skeleton.
Protest.
Cummings, E. Am was. are leaves few this. is these a or.
Gee i like to think of dead it means nearer because deeper firmer.
Great / man / is / gone, A.
If i should sleep with a lady called death.
Nobody loses all the time.
One Fine Day.
One X.
Portrait.
Since feeling is first.
Sonnet IV.
Whatever's merely wilful, / and not miraculous.
When god lets my body be.
Who's most afraid of death?thou.
Cuney. Death Bed, The.
Cunningham, J. Epigram: "Life flows to death as rivers to the sea."
Epitaph for Someone or Other.
Curnow. Oldest of us burst into tears and cried, The.
Cust. Non Nobis.
Custance. Candle-Light.
Peacocks: A Mood.
Cynddelw Brydydd Mawr. Poem on His Death-Bed.
Czechowski. Walk Through the City.
Dacey, P. Small Dark Song.
Damagetus. In the name of the God of strangers, we beg you.

Dana, R. Dying Raven, The.
Husband's and Wife's Grave, The.
Dana, R. At the Vietnam War Memorial, Washington, D. C.
Daniels, K. Ethiopia.
Lying Down.
Dante Alighieri. Beyond the sphere which spreads to widest space.
Death, always cruel, Pity's foe in chief.
Eyes that weep for pity of the heart, The.
That she hath gone to Heaven suddenly.
Thoughts are broken in my memory, The.
Very pitiful lady, very young, A.
Weep, Lovers, with Love's very self doth weep.
Woe's me! by dint of all these sighs that come.
Darley. Pass of Death, The.
Darr. At Sixteen.
Darwish, M. Guests on the sea: Our visit is short.
Victim Number 48.
Daryush. If your loved one prove unworthy, why then.
Daumal. Short Revelation Concerning Death and Chaos.
Davidson, D. Lines for a Tomb.
Redivivus.
Davidson, J. Price, The.
Davie. G. M. B.
Davies, J. Remembrance of My Friend Mr. Thomas Morley, A.
Davies, W. Bird of Paradise, The.
Davis, L. Bob Hosey Is Dead.
Davitt. Mirror, The.
Dawe, B. Family Man, The.
Going.
On the Death of Ronald Ryan.
Day Lewis. Reconciliation.
De Burgos. Poem to My Death.
De Kok. Transfer.
De la Mare. Autumn.
Epitaph, An: "Here lies a most beautiful lady."
Fare Well.
Love Lies Here.
Motley.
Peace.
Revenant, The.
Shubble, The.
Silver Penny, The.
Slim cunning hands at rest, and cozening eyes.
TO E. T.: 1917.
De Mello Breyner. I feel the dead in the cold of violets.
Small Square, The.
De Vere, E. Poem: "Were I a king, I could command content."
Deane, S. Burial, A.
Deanovich. Road Block: Sante Fe, New Mexico.
DeFrees. Letter to an Absent Son.
Delanty. Tie.
Dementyev, A. It's all over...
Denham. Song, A: "Morpheus, the humble god, that dwells."
Denning. Fire Support Burk.
Kim-San.
Movie, The.
Night on the Kho Bha Dinh.
This Time.
Derwood. Elegy: "When in the mirror of a permanent tear."
Desnos. Epitaph: "I lived in those times. For a thousand years."
Di Prima. Death Poems in September.
Death Sunyata Chant: A Rite for Passing Over.
For the Dead Lecturer.
Dibdin, C. Poor Tom.
Dickey, J. Hospital Window, The.
Sled Burial, Dream Ceremony.
Dickinson, E. Admirations—and Contempts—of time, The.
Afraid! Of whom am I afraid?
After a hundred years.
Because I could not stop for Death.
Brain—is wider than the Sky, The.

Brain, within its Groove, The.
Bustle in a House, The.
By a departing light.
Color, Caste, Denomination.
Death is a Dialogue between.
Death is the supple Suitor.
Distance that the dead have gone, The.
Do People moulder equally.
Dropped into the Ether Acre.
He fumbles at your Soul.
Heart asks Pleasure—*first*, The.
How many times these low feet staggered.
I died for Beauty—but was scarce.
I felt a Funeral in my Brain.
I heard a Fly buzz—when I died[—died].
I know that He exists.
I like a look of Agony.
I never lost as much but twice.
I should not dare to leave my friend.
If anybody's friend be dead.
If I may have it, when it's dead.
It was not Death, for I stood up.
I've seen a Dying Eye.
Last Night that She lived, The.
Love—is that later Thing than Death.
More than the Grave is closed to me.
My Life Had Stood—A Loaded Gun.
My Triumph lasted till the Drums.
Of all the Souls that stand create—.
Of nearness to her sundered Things.
Oh give it Motion—deck it sweet.
One dignity delays for all.
Parting.
Safe in their Alabaster Chambers.
Shade upon the mind there passes, A.
So proud she was to die.
Some things that fly there be.
Somehow myself survived the Night.
Sun kept setting—setting—still, The.
That after Horror—that 'twas us.
There comes an hour when begging stops.
There's a certain Slant of light.
There's been a Death, in the Opposite House.
They put Us far apart.
This Consciousness that is aware.
This docile one inter.
Tie the Strings to my Life, My Lord.
'Tis so appalling—it exhilarates.
To die—takes just a little while.
To know just how He suffered—would be
　　dear.
'Twas just this time, last year, I died.
'Twas warm—at first—like Us.
Under the Light, yet under.
Visitor in Marl, A.
What care the Dead, for Chanticleer.
Word is dead, A.
Work of Her that went, The.
World—feels Dusty, The.
Dimitrova. Introduction to the Beyond.
Dimoski. Revenge.
Diop, B. Diptych.
Spirits.
Vanity.
Dixon, M. Aunt Ida Pieces a Quilt.
Dixon, R. Wizard's Funeral, The.
Dlugos. D.O.A.
Dobell, S. Tommy's Dead.
Dobson, R. Being Called For.
Dobyns. Counterparts.
Delicate, Plummeting Bodies, The.
Tomatoes.
Dodd, W. Of His Life.
Dodge, M. Two Mysteries, The.
Doinas, S. Man with Exploded Eyes, The.
Donahue, J. Transfigurations.
Donne. Blossom [*or* Blossome], The.
Computation, The.
Expiration, The.
Funeral[l], The.
Hero and Leander.
Holy Sonnet.
Hymn[e] to God My God, In My Sickness[e].
Hymn to the Saints, and to Marquis
　　Hamilton[, An].
Oh my black[e] soul[e]! now thou art
　　summoned.

Paradox, The.
Pyramus and Thisbe.
Second Anniversary [*or* Anniversarie], The.
Since she whome I lovd, hath payd her last
　　debt.
Song: "Sweetest love, I do not go[e]."
Valediction, A: Forbidding Mourning.
Valediction: Of Weeping, A.
Donnelly, C. Tolerance of Crows, The.
Doolittle, H. Epigram: "Golden one is gone
　　from the banquets, The."
Helen.
Wine Bowl.
D'Orleans. Oft in my thought full busily have
　　I sought.
Doty, M. Bill's Story.
Douglas, K. How to Kill.
Offensive, The.
Simplify Me When I'm Dead.
Dove, R. Event, The.
Oriental Ballerina, The.
Political.
Statistic: The Witness.
Teach Us to Number Our Days.
Thomas at the Wheel.
Zeppelin factory, The.
Dowling, B. Revel, The.
Downar. From The Bramble Hedge.
Dowson. Dregs.
Extreme Unction.
Last Word, A.
Passing of Tennyson, The.
Drennan, W. Wake of William Orr, The.
Drummond de Andrade. Motionless Faces.
Drummond, W. Madrigal: "Daedal of my
　　death, A."
Madrigal: "This world a hunting is."
Redeem Time Past.
To Sir W. A.
Dryden, J. Epilogue to *Tyrannic[k] Love*.
Love's Despair.
Spectre, fiercely staring, thus reply'd, The.
To the Memory of Mr Oldham.
To the Pious Memory of the Accomplished [*or*
　　Accomplisht] Young Lady, Mrs. Anne
　　Killigrew, [Excellent in the Two Sister-Arts
　　of Poesie and Painting].
Du Maurier. Music.
Dubie. Elegy for Integral Domains, The.
Dudek. Dead, The.
Dufault. First Night, A.
Letter for Allhallows, A.
Dugan. Memorial Service for the Invasion
　　Beach Where the Vacation in the Flesh Is
　　Over.
Dunbar, P. Compensation.
Death Song[, A].
Frederick Douglass.
Paradox, The.
When all is done, and my last word is said.
Dunbar, W. Lament for the Makaris.
Translation by Mark Willhardt.
Widow Has Buried Her Second Husband, The.
Dunn, D. Kaleidoscope, The.
She sat up on her pillows, receiving guests.
Supreme Death.
Dunn, S. Routine Things Around the House,
　　The.
Duoduo. Looking out from death you will
　　always see.
Durcan. Ireland 1972.
Tullynoe: Tête-à-Tête in the Parish Priest's
　　Parlour.
Dyer, L. Epitaph on the Monument of Sir
　　William Dyer at Colmworth, 1641.
Eberhart, R. Flux.
Hardy Perennial.
Horse Chestnut Tree, The.
I walked over the grave of Henry James.
Rumination.
Two Loves.
Edson, R. Bringing a Dead Man Back into
　　Life.
Edwards, M. Time to Die, The.
We Are Passing Away.
Egan, T. Drover's Boy, The.
Ehrenstein. Suffering.

Ehrhart. Letter.
One That Died, The.
Eich. Seminar for Backward Pupils.
Eigner. Letter for Duncan.
Eliot, T. Aunt Helen.
Hollow Men, The.
Marina.
Song for Simeon, A.
Wind sprang up at four o'clock, The.
"Eliza." To My Husband.
"Elmo." Our Ernest.
Éluard, P. Dawn Dissolves the Monsters.
Elytis. Sleep of the Brave, The.
Emanuel, L. Dig, The.
What Grieving Was Like.
Emerson, R. Good-bye, proud world! I'm
　　going home.
Teach me I am forgotten by the dead.
Terminus ("It is time to be old").
Visit, The.
Empson. Ignorance of Death.
Missing Dates.
Engman. One Minute of Night Sky.
Enzensberger, H. For the Grave of a Peace-
　　Loving Man.
Erdrich. Shelter.
"Ern Malley." Egyptian Register.
Escoffery. After the Fall.
Farewell to a Jovial Friend.
Mother Jackson Murders the Moon.
Eshleman, C. Lich Gate, The.
Espada. Latin Night at the Pawnshop.
Evans, G. Horse on a Fence.
Evans, H. And Again.
Evans, M. Rebel, The.
Everson, W. Poet Is Dead, The.
Everwine. Counting.
Fairfax, E. Drearie trumpet blew a dreadfull
　　blast, The.
Faiz. So Bring the Order for My Execution.
"Fane." In an Irish Churchyard.
Fanthorpe. At the Ferry.
Fauset. Oblivion.
Fearing. Dirge: "1-2-3 was the number he
　　played but today the number came 3-2-1."
Evening Song.
Fenton, J. Cambodia.
Dead Soldiers.
God, A Poem.
Ferlinghetti, L. Sometime during eternity /
　　some guys show up.
Fernandez, R. Legacy of a Brother.
Ferry. Cythera.
My Parents En Route.
Fiacc. Saint Coleman's Song for Flight/ An
　　Ite Missa Est.
Fiawoo. Soliloquy on Death.
Ficowski. Girl of Six from the Ghetto
　　Begging in Smolna Street in 1942, A.
Field, E. Bachelor Hall.
Little Boy Blue.
Little Peach, The.
"Field." Almoner, An.
Dance of Death, A.
Dying Viper, A.
Lo, my loved is dying, and the call.
My Darling.
Picture, A.
Portrait, A.
Your *rose* is *dead*,.
Figueroa, J. Epitaph: "Old man is gone, The."
Finch, A. Reply From His Coy Mistress, A.
Fisher, R. As he came near death things grew
　　shallower for us.
Fishman, C. Death March.
Fitzgerald, F. Obit on Parnassus.
Flanders, J. Testimony.
Flatman. Thought of Death, A.
Flecker. Prologue: "We Who with Songs
　　Beguile Your Pilgrimage."
Fletcher, J. Fletcher's Lament for his Friend.
Fletcher, J. Last Frontier, The.
Lincoln.
Floyd. Captain James Leson, U. S. M. C.
Corporal Kevin Spina, U. S. M. C.
Sergeant Brandon Just, U. S. M. C.
Flynn, E. After Grave Deliberation.

Forbes, J. Death, an Ode.
Fordham. Dying Girl, The.
Magnolia.
On Parting with a Friend.
To My Mother.
Twilight Musings.
Foscolo. Upon the Death of His Brother Giovanni.
Foster, E. Morning.
Fowler, A. Catacomb Suburb.
Fox, G. It Is Her Cousin's Death.
Francis, R. That Dark Other Mountain.
While I slept, while I slept and the night grew colder.
František. Honeycomb of Bees, The.
When the great wind blew the streetlights out.
Freneau. Indian Burying Ground, The.
Fried, E. One Kind of Freedom Speaks.
Frost, R. Away!
Death of the Hired Man, The.
Departmental.
Fire and Ice.
"Out, Out—."
Stopping by Woods on a Snowy Evening.
To E.T.
Fuller, R. Death.
Memorial Poem.
Fumi Saito. Tanka: "Palm of the hand, The, / is not aware of dying."
Tanka: "Trailing for a while."
Tanka: "Water streams."
Tanka: "White hare, A."
Tanka: "Wood borers."
Fumiko. Tanka: "Since that evening."
Gallagher, T. After the Chinese.
Red Poppy.
Galsworthy. So Might It Be.
García Lorca. Quarrel, The.
Serenata.
Gardinier. Two Girls.
Gardner, I. Cock-a-Hoop.
Telephone rang / in my dream Long Distance from, The.
Garioch. Elegy: "They are lang deid, folk that I used to ken."
Garrett, G. York Harbor Morning.
Garrigue. On the Legends of a Dancer.
Gascoyne. De Profundis.
Tenebrae.
Gay, J. My Own Epitaph.
Gbadamosi. Death of the Polar Explorers.
Sewing-Box, The.
Geda. God's Family.
Repentance: The Devil's Blossom.
George, D. Wreck of the Old 97.
Gibbons, O. Silver swan, who living had no note, The.
Gibson, M. Country Woman Elegy.
Gibson, W. All Being Well.
Gilbert-Lecomte. Son of the Bone Speaks, The.
Gilbo'a. I wanted to write the lips of sleepers.
Kingdom of Silence.
Morning-Selah.
Gilmore, M. Tenancy, The.
Ginsberg, A. After Lalon.
At Apollinaire's Grave.
Death News.
Dream Record: June 8 1955.
Elegy for Neal Cassady.
Hymmnn.
IV.
Memory Gardens.
On Neal's Ashes.
V. Father Death Blues.
Ginsberg, L. Soon at Last My Sighs and Moans.
Giorno. Scum & Slime.
Gioseffi. American Sonnets for My Father.
Giovanni. Women gather, The.
Gladding. Asparagus.
Glaser, E. Coroner.
Glaser, M. Changing Address Books.
Gleim. To Death.
Glissant. O Sun! O age-old labor mutely mixed with ocean.
Glück, L. Apple Trees, The.

Descending Figure.
Drowned Children, The.
Garden, The.
Hyacinth.
Lullaby: "My mother's an expert at one thing."
Phenomenal Survivals of Death in Nantucket.
Racer's Widow, The.
Godfrey. Air.
Reveille.
Goedicke. One More Time.
Without Looking.
Goethe. Anacreon's Grave.
Ecstatic Longing.
Erl-King, The.
Gogarty. Per Iter Tenebricosum.
To Death.
Goldberg, B. Being Pharaoh.
To a Girl Writing Her Father's Death.
Goldsmith, O. Song: "When lovely woman stoops to folly."
This tomb, inscribed to gentle Parnell's name.
Goll, I. Last river leaves for desolation, The.
Your sleep is a closed almond.
"Golodny." Verka the Free.
Gonzáles Martínez. Last Journey.
González, A. Diatribe Against the Dead.
Gonzalez, A. First Friday bell shatters the morning.
Goodman, M. Coming and Going.
Goodman, P. Sonnet 21: "I start awake at night afraid of death."
Googe. Epitaph of the Death of Nicholas Grimald, An.
Gorges. Written upon the death of the most Noble Prince Henrie.
Gouri. Mistake.
Graham, H. Opportunity.
Tender-Heartedness.
Waste.
Graham, J. For My Father Looking for My Uncle.
Graham, W. Baldy Bane.
Grahn. Funeral Plainsong from a Younger Woman to an Older Woman, A.
Hannah.
Graves, R. It Was All Very Tidy.
Narrow Sea, The.
Pure Death.
Sharp Ridge, The.
Gray, C. Funeral Service.
Gray, D. Sonnet: "October's gold is dim—the forests rot."
Gray, T. Descent of Odin, The.
Ode on the Death of a Favourite [or Favorite] Cat, Drowned in a Tub [or Bowl] of Gold Fishes.
Sonnet [on the Death of Mr. Richard West].
Greacen. Summer Day, A.
Greenberg, B. Mother, R.I.P.
Greenberg, U. Penny for you, philosophers of eternity, A.
Greenlee. Memorial for Trane.
Greenwell, D. Christina.
To Christina Rossetti.
Gregerson. Salt.
Gregg. My Father and God.
Gregor, A. Irreconcilables.
Gregory of Nazianzus, Saint. Leave my tomb. Employ your pick.
Where are my wingèd words? Dissolved in air.
Greville, F. 87.
Greville, F. Sonnet: "Whenas [or When as] man's life, the light of human lust."
Griffin, S. Sunday Morning.
Grimald. From A Funeral Song, Upon the Decease of Annes His Mother.
I, in your frutefull woomb conceyved, born was.
Grimké, A. Garden Seat, The.
Grimke, C. Charles Sumner.
Gross, H. At the Crossroads.
Gross, P. Son and Heir.
Grossman, R. Therefore, We Thank Thee, God.
Gruffydd, W. In Memoriam.

Grunthal. All great men were ground to powder.
And thus a monologue keeps flowing.
Guiney. Open, Time, and let him pass.
Gumilyov. Memory.
Worker, The.
Gunn, T. Garden of the Gods, The.
Lament: "Your dying was a difficult enterprise."
My Sad Captains.
Unsettled Motorcyclist's Vision of His Death, The.
Guri. Requiescat.
Gurney, I. Farewell.
First Time In.
Silent One, The.
Gwynn, R. Approaching a Significant Birthday, He Peruses The Norton Anthology of Poetry.
Gwynn, S. On One Dying in a Convent.
Habington. Solum Mihi Superest Sepulchrum.
Hacker, M. Ballad of Ladies Lost and Found.
Dusk: July.
Elevens.
Nights of 1964–1966: The Old Reliable.
Presentation Piece.
Hadas, R. Yes, that.
Hadrian. Adriani Morientis ad Animam Suam.
Adrian's Address to His Soul When Dying.
Animula, vagula, blandula: The Emperor Hadrian to his soul.
My soul, my pleasant soul and witty.
Hahn, K. Possession: A Zuihitsu.
Haines, J. Flight, The.
Hajnal. Jaguar is Getting Ready, The.
Hall, D. Another Elegy.
Christmas Eve in Whitneyville, 1955.
My son, my executioner.
Raisin, The.
Shudder [, The].
Small Fig Tree, A.
White Apples.
Hall, H. Late Sewing.
Hall, J. Kind of Faith, A.
Hall, M. Turn Again to Life.
Hall, S. Boot Hill.
Halleck, F. On the Death of Joseph Rodman Drake.
Halswell. Upon Mr. Hopton's Death.
Hamburger, M. Treblinka.
Hammial. Petit Guignol.
Hamod, S. After the Funeral of Assam Hamady.
Dying with the Wrong Name.
Handlin. Father, You Learn to Die.
Hanzlik. Variation VI.
Who's that driving a black cart.
Hardy, E. Some Time at Eve.
Hardy, T. Afterwards.
At Castle Boterel.
Beeny Cliff.
By Her Aunt's Grave.
Channel Firing.
Choirmaster's Burial, The.
Drummer Hodge.
During Wind and Rain.
Epitaph: "I never cared for Life: Life cared for me."
Fallow Deer at the Lonely House, The.
Friends Beyond.
Going, The.
I found her out there.
If you had known.
Last Words To a Dumb Friend.
Lodging-House Fuchsias, The.
Nettles, The.
Neutral Tones.
Passionate pages of his earlier years, The.
She Hears The Storm.
Subalterns, The.
Thoughts of Phena.
Transformations.
Voice, The.
Where the Picnic Was.
Who's in the next room?—who?
Wife in London, A.
Your Last Drive.

Harington, L. Elegy: "Death be not proud, thy hand gave not this blow."
Harjo, J. Song for the Deer and Myself to Return On.
Harjo, P. Death.
Harper, F. Let the Light Enter!
Night of Death, The.
Harper, M. Mother Speaks: The Algiers Motel Incident, Detroit, A.
Nightmare Begins Responsibility.
Reuben, Reuben.
We Assume: On the Death of Our Son, Reuben Masai Harper.
Harrison, T. Heartless Art, The.
Study.
Harry, J. Honesty-Stones.
Harteis. Mirage.
Harter. Thawing.
Hartnett. All the death-room needs.
Death of an Irishwoman.
Last Vision of Eoghan Rua Ó Súilleabháin, The.
Harwood, G. Death has no features of his own.
Mother who gave me life.
Hassett. Patriot's Day.
Havergal. Just when Thou wilt, O Master, call!
Hawker. Death Song.
Hay, G. Bizerta.
Hayden, R. Broken Dark, The.
Mourning Poem for the Queen of Sunday.
Paul Laurence Dunbar.
Hayiaku. Funeral Song.
Hays, H. For One Who Died Young.
Heaney, S. Casualty.
Funeral Rites.
In Memoriam Francis Ledwidge.
Mid-Term Break.
Ship of Death, A.
When all the others were away at Mass.
Heard, J. Message to a Loved One Dead, A.
Resting.
Heath-Stubbs. Raft drifted, The.
Heavysege. Dead, The.
Hecht, A. Death the Painter.
'More Light! More Light!'.
Transparent Man, The.
Hedin, R. Wreck of the Great Northern, The.
Heine. Memory, A.
Heithaus. What a Little Moonlight Can Do.
Hemans. Effigies, The.
England's Dead.
Grave of a Poetess, The.
Graves of a Household, The.
Hour of Death, The.
Image in Lava, The.
Indian Woman's Death-Song, The.
Magic Glass, The.
Properzia Rossi.
Hemschemeyer. My grandmother had bones as delicate.
My Mother's Death.
Henderson, H. End of a Campaign.
Seven Good Germans.
We Show You That Death as a Dancer.
Hendriks. Hot Summer Sunday.
Henley, W. Margaritæ Sorori [I. M.].
To W. R.
Henry, J. Two hundred men and eighteen killed.
Heraclitus of Halicarnassus. By Heraclides.
Soil is freshly dug, the half-faded wreaths of leaves, The.
Herbert, G. Ah Mater, quo te deplorem fonte?
Dolores.
Death, thou wast once an uncouth hideous thing.
Doomsday.
Life.
Mortification.
Redemption.
Virtue [or Vertue].
Herbert of Cherbury. Elegy over a Tomb.
One Another's Mystery.
Herbert, Z. Elegy of Fortinbras.
Fathers of a Star, The.

Meditations of Mr. Cogito on Redemption.
Our Fear.
Heredia. Young Dead Woman, A.
Hernández, M. I go on in the dark, lit from within; does day exist?
Hernton. Fall Down.
Herrick. Comfort to a Youth That Had Lost His Love.
Dirge of Jephthah's Daughter, The.
Funeral[l] Rites of the Rose, The.
Grace for a Child.
His Answer to a Friend.
His Last Request to Julia.
His Winding-Sheet.
Ode to Master Endymion Porter, upon His Brother's Death, An.
On Himself.
On Himselfe ("I will no longer kiss").
On Himselfe ("I'll [or Il'e] write no more of Love; but now repent").
On Himselfe ("Weepe for the dead, for they have lost this light").
Posting to Printing.
Putrefaction is the end.
To Death.
To His Lovely Mistresses.
To Julia ("Julia, when thy Herrick dies").
To Perilla.
To the Reverend Shade of His Religious Father.
Transfiguration, The.
Upon a child.
Upon Ben Jo[h]nson.
Upon Prue [or Prew], His Maid.
Widow's Tears [or Widdowes Teares]: or, Dirge of Dorcas, The.
Hesketh. Death of a Gardener.
Hewitt, J. Father's Death, A.
Scar, The.
High. Lives of thomas—episodes and prayers, The.
Hildebert. On the Death of Henry the Lion.
Hill, G. Domaine Public.
Down in the orchard.
Guardians, The.
In Memory of Jane Fraser [or Frazer].
Merlin.
Not as we are but as we must appear.
White Ship, The.
Hine. Wasp, The.
Hirsch, E. Fast Break.
Hirshfield, J. Story, A.
Hitomaro. On the shingle.
When she was still alive.
Ho Ching-ming. Song of the Painting "River and Mountains," by Wu Wei.
Hodgins. Death Who.
Hoffmann, H. Story of Augustus Who Would Not Have Any Soup, The.
Hogg, J. Kilmeny.
Holan. From Untitled.
Holden, M. Seaman, 1941.
Höllerer. Held back, like a bow drawn tight.
Holst-Warhaft. In the end is the body—what we know.
Holtby, W. Resurrection.
Holub. Death in the Evening.
Interferon.
On the Origin of the Contrary.
Homer. Achilles Over the Trench.
Briseis mourns Patroclus.
Equity in death.
Execution of the faithless maids.
First to the Corse the weeping Consort flew.
Heroes meet again in the underworld, The.
O my husband... / cut off from life so young! You leave me a widow.
Hongo. Legend, The.
Honig, E. Now, My Usefullness Over.
Hood, T. Bridge of Sighs, The.
Death-Bed, The.
Jack Hall.
Sally Simpkin's Lament, [or John Jones's Kit-Cat-astrophe].
Sea of Death, The.
Sonnet: "It is not death, that sometime in a sigh."

Hooks. Body Inside the Soul, The.
Hope, A. Death of the Bird, The.
Inscription for a War.
Hopkins, E. Life in Death.
Hopkins, G. Felix Randal the farrier,° O is he dead then? my duty / all ended.
Sonnet: "No worst, there is none. Pitched past pitch of grief."
Horace. Aequam Memento.
Nunc est bibendum, Cleopatra's Death.
Horovitz, F. Rain—Birdoswald.
Horton, G. Imploring to Be Resigned at Death.
Housman, A. Along the field as we came by.
Because I liked you better.
Bredon Hill.
For My Funeral.
Here dead lie we because we did not choose.
Is my team ploughing.
Isle of Portland, The.
Night Is Freezing Fast, The.
Rain, it streams on stone and hillock, The.
So Sound You Sleep.
Some can gaze and not be sick.
To an Athlete Dying Young.
When I watch the living meet.
When smoke stood up from Ludlow.
Winter.
With rue my heart is laden.
Houston, L. Scales.
Howard, R. Lost Art, A.
1915: A Pre-Raphaelite Ending, London.
Howe, F. Seeking Out His face in a Cup.
Howe, M. Death, the Last Visit.
Howe, S. In its first dumb form.
Howell, J. Elegy upon His Tomb in Herndon-Hill Church, Erected by His Wife, Who Speaks, An.
Howes, B. Death of a Vermont Farm Woman.
Howitt, M. Dying Child, The.
Hoyt, C. Those camellias.
Hsü Pen. Ballad of the Ferocious Tiger.
Huchel. Ammonite, The.
Meeting.
Melpomene.
Poplars, The.
Psalm.
Roads.
Thrace.
Hudgins. After the Wilderness.
Burial Detail.
Dead Christ.
Elegy for My Father, Who Is Not Dead.
Hereafter, The.
Seventeen.
Huffstickler. Lament for an Old Woman.
Hughes, L. As Befits a Man.
Cross.
Drum.
Gal's Cry for a Dying Lover.
Peace.
Song for a Dark Girl.
Stony Lonesome.
Sylvester's Dying Bed.
Wake.
World War II.
Young Gal's Blues.
Hughes, T. Day He Died, The.
Examination at the Womb-Door.
Heptonstall.
Leaves.
Ravens.
Suddenly his poor body.
Hugo, R. December 24 and George McBride Is Dead.
Elegy: "I expected him to look dead in the casket."
Hull, L. Address.
Letter, The.
Hummer, T. Train Wreck, 1890: My Grandmother Lies Down with the Dead.
What Shines in Winter Burns.
Hummer, T. Heart Attack in the Country, A.
Hunt, L. On the Death of His Son Vincent.
Hunt, S. My Father Today.
Hunter, A. North American Death Song.
Hunter, W. Monologue in a Rand Hospital.

Huy Cận. Dirge, A: "Who died? Why does the music speak such grief?"
Talking With the Pyramid.
Hywel ab Owain Gwynedd. Exultation.
Ibarbourou. Life-Hook.
Ignatow, D. For My Daughter in Reply to a Question.
I see a truck mowing down a parade.
Walt Whitman in the Civil War Hospitals.
Inez. Absolving You.
Ingelow. Cold and Quiet.
High Tide on the Coast of Lincolnshire, 1571, The.
Iwaszkiewicz. Pope in Ancona, The.
"J., M." Funeral, The.
Jabès. Desert, II, The.
Jaccottet. These wood-shadows, timid, patient.
Jackson, H. Last Words.
Jackson, L. Elegy in a Spider's Web.
Jacobsen, J. Limbo Dancer, The.
James, A. Honor (1969).
James, T. Lines on His Companions Who Died in the Northern Seas.
James, T. Mummy of a Lady Named Jemutesonekh XXI Dynasty.
Jammes. Prayer to Go to Paradise with the Donkeys, A.
Jarman, M. Mirror, The.
Jarrell. Black Swan, The.
Death of the Ball Turret Gunner, The.
In the Camp There Was One Alive.
Islands, The.
Knight, Death, and the Devil, The.
Losses.
Seele im Raum.
Sleeping Beauty: Variation of the Prince, The.
Truth, The.
When I was home last Christmas.
Jeffers, R. Antrim.
Coast-Road, The.
Cremation.
Deer Lay Down Their Bones, The.
May-June, 1940.
Original Sin.
Purse-Seine, The.
Vulture.
Jentzsch. Dead Father, The.
Terezin, the Graveyard.
Jewsbury. Summer Eve's Vision, A.
Jito. Even a flaming fire can be snatched.
Johnson, F. My God in Heaven said to me.
Song of the Whirlwind.
Johnson, G. I Want to Die While You Love Me.
When I am dead, withhold, I pray, your blooming legacy.
Johnson, J. Color Sergeant, The.
Glory of the Day Was in Her Face, The.
Go Down Death.
Johnson, L. Collins.
Dark Angel, with thine aching lust.
Destroyer of a Soul, The.
Nihilism.
To a Passionist.
Johnson, L. Death of the Bosun's Mate.
Johnson, S. Empty Heart, An.
On the Death of Dr [or Mr] Robert Levet [a Practiser in Physic].
Johnston, E. Mother's Love, A.
Nelly's Lament for the Pirnhouse Cat.
Johnston, M. In Memoriam.
Johnstone, R. Robot Camera.
Undertakers.
Jones, E. Development of Idiotcy, A.
Jones, M. Stella's Epitaph.
Jonson, B. By this time had they reached the Stygian pool.
Death and Love.
Epitaph on Elizabeth, L. H.
Epitaph on Master Philip Gray, An.
Epitaph on Master Vincent Corbet[t], An.
Hour Glass, The ("Consider this small dust, here in the glass").
Little Shrub Growing By, A.
An Ode To Himself.
On Margaret Ratcliffe.

To the World [A Farewell for a Gentlewoman, Virtuous and Noble].
Jortin. Epitaph of Felis, The.
Juarroz. Any movement kills something.
To die, but far away.
Justice, D. First Death.
Incident in a Rose Garden.
Invitation to a Ghost.
Nostalgia and Complaint of the Grandparents.
On the Death of Friends in Childhood.
Psalm and Lament.
White Notes.
Juvenal. Prepare for Death, if here at Night you roam.
Kang. Grass Leaves.
Kangro. Old Age.
Kao Ch'i. Lament of a Soldier's Wife.
Seeing Flowers I Remember My Late Daughter, Shu.
Karp. Taxi to the Flame, A.
Kasdorf. Dying with Amish Uncles.
Kastelan. Corpse in the House.
Kataiyañ Kaṇṇaṉār. In Praise of a Cremation Ground.
Katrovas. Dog and a Boy, A.
Kavanagh, P. In Memory of My Mother.
Kay, J. He Told Us He Wanted a Black Coffin.
Keating, G. Keen Thyself, Poor Wight.
Keats. Bright star[, would I were stedfast as thou art—].
Song: "I had a dove and the sweet dove died."
Terror of Death, The.
To Chatterton.
Kelen. Gods Ash Their Cigarettes, The.
Kelly, B. All Wild Animals Were Once Called Deer.
Kelly, R. Newark.
Kendrick, D. Inpatient.
26th Person, The.
Kennedy, X. Epitaph for a Postal Clerk.
Kenyon, J. Reading Aloud to My Father.
Travel: After a Death.
Keyes, S. Death and the Plowman.
Elegy: "April again, and it is a year again."
Kgositsile. Acknowledgement.
Air, I hear, The.
Khodasevich. Twilight was turning to darkness outside.
Killigrew, A. On Death.
Kim, C. When That Day Comes.
Kim, C. Death of a Girl in Budapest, The.
Kim, Y. Grass Flower.
Kim, Y. Sea of Lemon, The.
Kim, Y. Message.
Years.
King, H. Stay For Me There.
Kingsley, C. Three Fishers [Went Sailing], The.
Kinnell. Cells Breathe in the Emptiness.
Freedom, New Hampshire.
Last Hiding Places of Snow, The.
Spindrift.
Kinsella, T. Cover Her Face.
Death Bed.
Kipling, R. En-Dor.
Heriot's Ford.
My Boy Jack.
Nativity, A.
Neighbours.
Widower, The.
Kitahara Hakushū. Tanka: "Winter day."
Kizer, C. On a Line from Valéry.
Klappert. Ellie Mae Leaves in a Hurry.
Kleinzahler. East of the Library, Across from the Odd Fellows Building.
Kleist. Song at Graveside.
Knevet. Navigation.
Knight, E. Poem of Attrition, A.
Knopfli. Death Certificate.
Knott. At the Crossroads.
Death.
Funny Poem.
Poem: "After your death."
Two Vietnam Poems: (1966).
Knox, W. Oh! why should the spirit of mortal be proud?

Komey. Oblivion.
Komunyakaa. April Fools' Day.
Landscape for the Disappeared.
We Never Know.
Kooser. Finding, A.
Kopland. Johnson Brothers Ltd.
Natzweiler.
Thanks to the Things.
Ulumbo, a Cat.
Kornilov, B. Under the scraggy fir tree.
Kovner. Lookout on a Rock on the Heights of Mount Hermon.
Krynicki. By entering the grand lottery.
Krysl. Grandmother.
Kudimova. When I still barely rose above the ground.
Kumin, M. How It Is.
Louise Bourgeois Exhibit.
Retrieval System, The.
Kunio. Tanka: "After death."
Tanka: "As night falls."
Tanka: "Because the folks."
Tanka: "On the water."
Tanka: "Stalwartly."
Tanka: "This May Day night."
Kupriyanov. Twilight of Vanity.
Kurup. Master Carpenter, The.
Kuthaiyir. At Her Grave.
Kuznetsov. To Father.
Laing, K. I am the freshly dead husband.
Lake, P. Blue Jay.
Lalic. Voices of the dead. They are not dead.
Who hears.
Lamb, C. Hester.
Old Familiar Faces, The.
Landon. Child Screening a Dove from a Hawk, A.
Marriage Vow, The.
Stanzas on the Death of Mrs Hemans.
Landor, W. Age.
Alas! 'tis very sad to hear.
Death of the Day.
Death Stands above Me[, whispering low].
Maid's Lament, The.
On His Seventy-Fifth Birthday.
Place where soon I think to lie, The.
Rose Aylmer.
Lane, P. Rain Ditch.
Lang, A. On the Death of Lord Tennyson.
Lang, D. Depression, The.
Lanier, S. Nirvâna.
Stirrup-Cup, The.
Lankesh. Mother.
Larkin, P. Ambulances.
Aubade: "I work all day, and get half-drunk at night."
Church Going.
Dublinesque.
Next, Please.
Lassell. How to Watch Your Brother Die.
Lattimore. RMS Lusitania.
Witness to Death.
Lau, C. On the Fifth Anniversary of My Father's Death.
Lawrence, D. All Soul''s Day.
Bride, The.
Build then the ship of death, for you must take.
Cherry Robbers.
Fatality.
Giorno dei Morti.
Hymn to Priapus.
My way is not thy way, and thine is not mine.
New Heaven and Earth.
Service of All the Dead.
Shadows.
Ship of Death, The.
When the ripe fruit falls.
Layne, M. On Hats and Things.
Layton. Cold Green Element, The.
Lazarus, E. Age and Death.
New Ezekiel, The.
Youth and Death.
Le Guin. Child on the Shore, The.
Le Pan. Incident, An.
Lea, S. At the Flyfisher's Shack.

Feud, The.
Wrong Way Will Haunt You, The.
Leaf, E. Her Son.
Leapor. Epistle to a Lady, An.
Mira's Will.
Leconte de Lisle, C. Palanquin, The.
Lee, L. Between Seasons.
Here I Am.
Visions and Interpetations.
Lehmann, J. No Easy Answer.
Leib. In little hands she holds an open book.
Leigh, H. Twins, The.
Leithauser. Haunted, The.
Leonard, T. Its thi lang / wij a thi / guhtr
thaht hi.
Leopardi. To Himself.
Lermontov. Testament, The.
Levertov. Clouds as I see them, rising, The.
Dead Butterfly, The.
Note to Olga (1966), A.
Olga Poems.
What Were They Like?
Levin, P. Shadow Returns, The.
Levine, P. And the Trains Go On.
Angel Butcher.
Baby Villon.
Belief.
Cemetery at Academy, California, The.
Death of Saul, The.
Horse, The.
1933.
Red Dust.
To My God in His Sickness.
Uncle.
Levis. For Zbigniew Herbert, Summer, 1971,
Los Angeles.
Magnolia.
Levitansky. Dream about a Piano, A.
Levy, A. Cross-Road Epitaph, A.
Epitaph: "This is the end of him, here he
lies."
Felo de Se.
In the Mile End Road.
London Poets.
Magdalen.
Old House, The.
On the Threshold.
Reminiscence, A.
Sequel to 'A Reminiscence," The.
Straw in the street where I pass to-day.
Twilight.
Lewis, A. All day it has rained, and we on
the edge of the moors.
Autumn, 1939.
Easter at Christmas.
Song (On Seeing Dead Bodies Floating Off
the Cape).
Unknown Soldier, The.
Lewis, C. Ballade of Dead Gentlemen.
Epitaph, An: "Erected by her sorrowing
brothers."
Evensong.
Joys Once Shared.
Sequence, The.
Lewis, J. Snail Garden.
Lewis, M. Alonzo the Brave and the Fair
Imogine.
Li K'ai-hsien. Earthquake covered Shansi and
Shensi, The.
Lifshin. Yahrtzeit Light, The.
Lightfoot. Wreck of the Edmund Fitzgerald,
The.
Lihn. Cemetery in Punta Arenas.
Goodnight, Achilles.
Of all despondencies, death-despair must be
the worst.
Lilliard. America's Answer.
Lincoln, A. Memory.
Lisboa. Minor Elegy.
Lisnyanskaya. To you, my friends, to you, my
dear ones.
Liu. Mother.
Liu K'o-chuang. Weeping for Hsüeh Tzu-shu.
Liu Tsung-yüan. On Covering the Bones of
Chang Chin, the Hired Man.
Lloyd, H. Unveiling.

Llywelyn Goch ap Meurig Hen. Lament for
Lleucu Llwyd.
Lockhart. Lines: "When youthful faith hath
fled."
Long, R. Refuge.
Longenbach. What You Find in the Woods.
Longfellow, H. Cross of Snow, The.
Dante.
Excelsior.
Hawthorne.
Jewish Cemetery at Newport, The.
Legend of Rabbi Ben Levi, The.
Nature.
Spanish Jew's Tale: Azrael, The.
Longley, M. In Memoriam.
In Memory of Gerard Dillon.
Kindertotenlieder.
Linen Workers, The.
Third Light, The.
Wounds.
Lorde. Father Son and Holy Ghost.
Hanging Fire.
Suffer the Children.
Louis, A. Practicing Death Songs.
Lourie. For All My Brothers and Sisters.
Lovelace, R. Black Patch on Lucasta's Face,
A.
La Bourbon, A.
Lowell, A. Frimaire.
Lowell, R. First Snowfall [or Snow-Fall], The.
Memoriae Positum R. G. Shaw.
Sixty-Eighth Birthday.
Lowell, R. Alfred Corning Clark.
Death and the Bridge.
Falling Asleep over the Aeneid.
For Sale.
Harriet.
History has to live with what was here.
Mr. Edwards and the Spider.
Quaker Graveyard in Nantucket, The.
Sailing Home from Rapallo.
Where the Rainbow Ends.
Lowry, M. Death of a Oaxaquenian.
Epitaph: "Malcolm Lowry."
For Under the Volcano.
Strange Type.
Volcano is dark and suddenly thunder, The.
Lu Yu. Rain Cleared and the Breeze and
Sunshine Are Superb as I Stroll Outside the
Gate, The.
To Show My Sons.
Lu Yün. Peacock flew, far off to the south-
east; A.
Lucan. Pompey's death and apotheosis.
Lucie-Smith. Lesson, The.
Lucilius. Lean Gaius, who was thinner than a
straw.
Lucretius. Lucretius Paraphrased.
Suave Mari Magno.
Threshold Of The New, The.
What has this Bugbear death to frighten Man.
Ludvigson. Man Arrested in Hacking Death
Tells Police He Mistook Mother-in-Law for
Raccoon.
Luzzatto, I. Death, Thou Hast Seized Me.
Lyte. Abide with me[; fast falls the eventide].
Macaulay, T. Horatius at the Bridge.
MacCaig. Two Friends.
"MacDiarmid." At My Father's Grave.
Dead Liebknecht, The.
Empty Vessel.
Farmer's Death.
On a Raised Beach.
Watergaw, The.
MacKay, C. Louise on the Door-Step.
Mackenzie, K. Door swung open, The.
Sick Men Sleeping.
Maclean, A. Death of an Old Woman.
Rain, The.
Waking the Dead.
MacLean, S. Heroes.
MacLeish. Burying Ground by the Ties.
Epistle to Be Left in the Earth.
Immortal Helix.
Mother Goose's Garland.
My Naked Aunt.
Old Gray Couple, The.

Prologue: "And the way goes on in the worn
earth."
MacNeice. Bar-Room Matins.
Charon.
Death of a Cat, The.
Gardener, The.
Sunlight on the garden, The.
This Is the Life.
Maddox. Great Man's Death: An Anecdote,
The.
Madeleva. I Ask My Teachers.
Mahapatra, J. Ash.
Mahon. In Carrowdore Churchyard.
Maiden. Air.
Climbing.
Major, C. Swallow the Lake.
Maksimovic. Bloody Fable.
Malange. This Poem Is Dedicated to Brother
Andries Raditsela.
Malé. My Mother's Homeland.
Mandelstam. I Was Washing Outside in the
Darkness.
Mounds of Human Heads Are Wandering into
the Distance.
Petropolis.
To A. A. A. (Akhmatova).
Tristia.
Mangan, J.
Rest Only in the Grave.
Mansour, J. Gently stroke a wound.
Regulation equipment.
Mapanje. Steve Biko is Dead.
March, A. Let others hail the holidays with
laughter.
Out scouting for sound counsels? How to
prosper?
Marguerite de Navarre. Smell of death is so
powerful, The.
Markham, E. Grandfather's Sermon and
Michael Smith.
Markham, E. In Death Valley.
Marks, L. Code Poem for the French
Resistance.
Marshall, J. Sesame.
Marshall-Stoneking. On the Death of Muriel
Rukeyser.
Marston, P. Inseparable.
Not Thou but I.
Martial. De M. Antonio.
Swan her sweetest Notes sings as she dies,
The.
Martin, C. Easter Sunday, 1985.
Martin, P. Tongues.
Marvell. Damon the Mower.
Dialogue between Thyrsis and Dorinda, A.
Epitaph upon —, An.
To His Coy Mistress.
Masaoka Shiki. Among the poems I wrote
with many pictures spread out before me[2].
On the eve of death.
Masefield. Dead Knight, The.
Sonnet: "There, on the darkened deathbed, dies
the brain."
To-morrow.
Masing. For Polla.
Mason, R. Spark's Farewell to Its Clay, The.
Massinger. Song.
Masters, E. Hill, The.
Mather, C. Go then, my dove, but now no
longer mine.
Mathews, A. At the Wailing Wall.
Mathias, R. Departure in Middle Age.
Mavilis Olive Tree.
Maxton. Elegies.
Maxwell, M. To My Grandmother, Lady-
Woman.
May, J. If we could know.
Mazzocco. Muertes.
PBS.
McAuley, J. Cloak, The.
Pietá.
McAuley, J. Pietá.
McCarthy, T. Sorrow Garden, The.
McCombs, D. River and Under the River,
The.
McCrae, J. In Flanders Fields the poppies
blow.

McCreery. There is no death! The stars go down.
McDonald, I. Place They Have to Go, The.
McDonald, W. For Harper, Killed in Action.
For Kelly, Missing in Action.
McGough, R. Let me die a youngman's death.
Survivor.
McGrath, C. James Wright, Richard Hugo, the Vanishing Forests of the Pacific Northwest.
McGrath, T. Blues for Warren.
Death for the Dark Stranger.
Epitaph: "Again, traveller, you have come a long way led by that star."
Go Ask the Dead.
McHugh, H. Take Care.
Third Person Neuter.
McKay, C. If we must die—let it not be like hogs.
My Mother.
McNair. Minister's Death, The.
My Brother Running: V.
McOrlan. Wood merchant's parlour, The.
McPherson, S. At the Grave of Hazel Hall.
Meehan, M. She has withdrawn from us.
Mei Yao Ch'en. Dream at Night, A.
I Remember the River at Wu Sung.
In Broad Daylight I Dream of My Dead Wife.
Mourning for My Wife.
On the Death of a New Born Child.
On the Death of His Wife.
Sad Remembrance.
Sorrow.
Meilyr Brydydd. Poem on His Death-Bed.
Meleager. Down through the earth as a last gift.
Tread lightly, Stranger!
Upon a Maid That Died [or Dyed] the Day She Was Married [or Marryed].
Whose the hand unloosed Clearista's zone.
Meltzer, D. 17:II:82.
Melville, H. Ball's Bluff.
Dirge: "Stay, Death. Not mine the Christus-wand."
Haglets, The.
Monody.
Time's Betrayal.
Menken. Dying.
Resurgam.
Meredith, G. 30.
Ballad of Past Meridian, A.
Dirge in Woods.
Meredith, W. Dying Away.
To the Thoughtful Reader.
Merrill, J. Annie Hill's Grave.
Broken Home, The.
Country of a Thousand Years of Peace, The.
Friend of the Fourth Decade, The.
Hotel de l'Univers et Portugal.
Merton. Elegy for Ernest Hemingway, An.
Responsory, 1948, A.
Merwin, W. Asians Dying, The.
Ballad of John Cable and Three Gentlemen.
For the Anniversary of My Death.
Strawberries.
Mew. À Quoi Bon Dire.
At the Convent Gate.
Beside the Bed.
In Nunhead Cemetery.
Smile, Death.
Meynell, A. Maternity.
Parentage.
Michelangelo Buonarroti. To Vittoria Colonna.
Miles, J. Conception.
Miljkovic. Ballade: "Wisdom, innocently the sun rises."
Black Horseman.
Millay, E. And you as well must die, belovèd dust.
Buck in the Snow, The.
Childhood Is the Kingdom Where Nobody Dies.
Conscientious Objector.
Elegy before Death.
I dreamed I moved among the Elysian fields.
Moriturus.
Passer Mortuus Est.
Sonnet 17.

Miller, E. Dressed Up.
Miller, J. Closing the House.
Hanging Burley.
Hungry Dead, The.
Miller, M. Closing, A.
Miller, V. Beside a Deathbed.
Mourning, A.
On Approaching My Birthday.
Milosz, C. Dedication: "You whom I could not save / Listen to me."
Encounter.
Mark 5:21–43; And when Jesus had crossed.
On the Book.
With Her*.
Milosz, O. Bridge, The.
Milton. On His Blindness.
On His Deceased Wife.
On Shakespear[e].
On the University Carrier Who Sick'n'd [or Sickened] in the Time of His Vacancy [, Being Forbid to go to London, by Reason of the Plague].
On Time.
Sin and Death.
Sonnet: On the Religious Memorie of Mrs. Catherine Thomason My Christian Freind Deceas'd Decem. 1646.
Mirikitani. Fisherman, The.
Jade.
Shadow in Stone.
Mistral, G. Death Sonnet I.
Martha and Mary.
Mitchell, A. Not a Very Cheerful Song, I'm Afraid.
Mitchell, K. On the Anniversary Of Your Death.
Mitchell, S. Parable of the Sower, The.
Mitchell, S. Dead, The.
Mitchell, S. Immortality.
Mitchison. Hartmanswillerkopf.
Thinking of War.
Mitsuhashi. O bird's singing!
Miu Hsi. Bearer's Song.
Poem in the Form of a Coffin-Puller's Song.
Mnasalces. Aristocrateia, / You've crossed the dark stream.
Mo Shih-lung. Staying Overnight at Blue Cloud Temple.
Mobilio. Step One.
Moffi. Yahrzeit.
Momaday. Colors of Night, The.
Rainy Mountain Cemetery.
Two Figures.
Monar. Judgement Day.
Monck. Verses Written on Her Death-bed at Bath to Her Husband in London.
Monk, M. Verses Written on Her Death-Bed at Bath to Her Husband in London.
Monsour. Emily's Words.
Montagu, L. Epitaph: "Here lie John Hughes and Sarah Drew."
Epitaph: "Here lies John Hughes and Sarah Drew."
On the Death of Mrs. Bowes.
Montague, J. Mother Cat, The.
Montale. Fan, The.
Montgomerie, W. Epitaph: "My brother is skull and skeleton now."
Moon, C. Flock of Birds, A.
Moore, M. Grave, A.
What Are Years?
Moore, M. Fable.
Moore, T. Echo.
Go where glory waits thee.
'Tis the Last Rose of Summer.
Moorer. In Memoriam of E. B. Clark.
Moorsom. Jewels In My Hand.
More, S. Minstrel Boy to the war is gone, The.
Morgan, E. After a Death.
Post-Referendum.
Morgan, R. Death Crown.
Mori. Speaking Through White: For My Mother.
Moritz. April Fool's Day, Mount Pleasant Cemetary.
Moritz. Baltic Summer.

Morris, M. Day my father died, The.
Morris, W. Death Song, A.
Garden By The Sea, A.
Moschus. With thee, sweet Bion, all the grace of Song.
Moses ibn Ezra. End of Man Is Death, The.
Moss, H. Elegy for My Sister.
Game of Chance, A.
Water Island.
Moss, S. For Margaret.
Moss, T. Fisher Street.
Mother Goose. Six little mice sat down to spin;.
Who killed Cock [or poor] Robin? [or Here lies Cock Robin].
Mtshali. Ride upon the Death Chariot.
Muir, E. Child Dying, The.
For Ann Scott-Moncrieff.
Muldoon, P. Big House, The.
Soap-Pig, The.
Munby. Post Mortem.
Mura. Grandfather-in-law.
Murray, L. Lament for the Country Soldiers.
Murray, M. Poem to My Grandmother in Her Death.
Muske. Eulogy, The.
Myles, E. December 9th.
Myrinos. Time topples Statyllios like a doddery oak.
Nagy, A. Ikhnaton's Night.
Lazarus.
To a Poet.
Nagys. Laterna Obscura.
Nairne. Land o' the Leal, The.
Naito Joso. Autumn cicada, The.
Nalungiaq. Heaven and Hell.
Nash, O. Old Men.
Tweedledee and Tweedledoom.
Nashe. Litany in Time of Plague, A.
Nastasijevic. String, The.
Ndlovu. Elegy for the Dead of Soweto.
Nelson, H. My Father Went to Funerals.
Nemerov. Easter.
Elegy for a Nature Poet.
Grace to Be Said at the Supermarket.
Media.
Speculation.
Neruda. Nothing but Death.
Nerval. Grandmother, The.
Nesbit, E. Dead to the Living, The.
Newbolt. Messmates.
Newcastle, M. Common Fate of Books, The.
Nature's Cook.
Soul and Body.
Woman drest by Age, A.
Nezval. Trap Door.
Nguyễn Bính. Girl Next Door, The.
Nguyễn Chí Thiện. All Come to Me.
This land's no joy.
Nguyễn Du. Calling All Souls.
Nguyễn Ngọc Thuận. Prisoner's Funeral, A.
Nguyễn Văn Lạc. To a Dead Dog in the River.
Nhật Tiến. Two Eyes.
Nhu'ọ'ng Tống. Mourning a Hero.
Ní Dhomhnaill. Labasheedy (The Silken Bed).
Ni Tsan. Lamenting Noble Scholar Chu.
Man in Hangchou Spread Word that I Had Died. Chen-chü Heard of This and Was Upset, So I Have Written This To Send Him, A.
Nicarchus of Alexandria. It's true I will die. So what do I care.
Path of glory leads but to the grave, The.
Raven, The.
Nichol. Ferry Me Across.
Nicholls, J. Winter crept.
Nichols, G. Tropical Death.
Nims, J. Trainwrecked Soldiers.
Nordbrandt. Our love is like Byzantium.
Norris, J. Meditation, The.
Norris, L. Elegy for Lyn James.
Nortje. Autopsy.
Norton, C. Obscurity of Woman's Worth.
Notley. Beginning with a stain, as the universe did perhaps.
Poem: "You hear that heroic big land music?"

Nowlan. Suppose This Moment Some Stupendous Question.
Noyes, A. Highwayman, The.
Nyka-Niliunas. Lied.
O Riordain. Death was at hand.
  Ice Cold.
  My Mother's Burying.
Ochester. Relatives, The.
O'Connor, P. Fag-End.
O'Dalaigh, M. On the Death of His Wife.
Odarchenko. And you, Vanya.
  Cap, a sword, flowers, A.
  What a sweet little day, what a day!
Odoyevtseva. Ground Glass.
Ogilvy. Newly Dead and Newly Born.
O'Grady, D. Day concludes burning, The.
  Dying Gaul, The.
  Reading the Unpublished Manuscripts of Louis MacNeice at Kinsale Harbour.
O'Hara, F. Day Lady Died, The.
  Hôtel Transylvanie.
  Ode to Joy.
  Poem: "Eager note on my door said 'Call me', The."
  To My Mother.
O'Hussey. O'Hussey's Ode to the Maguire.
Okamoto. Tanka: "Insect, An."
Okigbo. Death lay in ambush.
Olds, S. Cambridge Elegy.
  Dead Body Itself, The.
  Girl, The.
  Leningrad Cemetery, Winter of 1941.
  Moment of My Father's Death, The.
  Pull, The.
  Race, The.
Oliver, M. Ghosts.
  In the Pinewoods, Crows and Owl.
  Poem for My Father's Ghost.
  Visitor, A.
  Waves, The.
Ologoudou. Liberty.
O'Loughlin. Irish Requiem, An.
  Posthumous.
Olsen, W. Dead Monkey, The.
Olson, C. As the dead prey upon us.
  Cole's Island.
  Death of Europe, The.
  La Chute.
  La Préface.
  Newly Discovered "Homeric" Hymn, A.
  Variations Done for Gerald Van De Wiele.
  What soul / isn't in default?
Olson, E. Plot Improbable, Character Unsympathetic.
Oodgeroo of the tribe Noonuccal. Dawn Wail for the Dead.
O'Rahilly. No help I'll call till I'm put in the narrow coffin.
Orban, O. Requiem: "He tossed a life preserver to the young castaway in '55."
  That strength, which behind the tongue.
Ormond. At His Father's Grave.
Ormsby, F. Day in August, A.
Orr, G. Mother, The.
Orten. Whispered.
Ortleb. On Finding Out that the One You Slept with the Night Before Was Murdered the Next Day.
Ostriker. Anxiety about Dying.
Ovid. 1.15.
  Time was, when we were sow'd, and just began.
  To his Paternall Countrey.
Owen, G. Elegy for His Daughter Ellen.
Owen, W. End, The.
  Futility.
  Miners.
  Next War, The.
  Strange Meeting.
  Unreturning, The.
Padgett, R. Something or Other.
Page, G. Elegist, The.
  Inscription at Villers-Bretonneux.
Pagis. Autobiography.
  Draft of a Reparations Agreement.
Paino. Truth, The.
Painter, C. Elegy for Jack Moffat.

Palladas. Sad and great evil is the expectation of death, A.
P'an Yüeh. Lamenting the Dead.
Paquet. Easter '68.
  In a Plantation.
  It Is Monsoon at Last.
  Morning—A Death.
  Mourning the Death, by Hemorrhage, of a Child from Honai.
  They Do Not Go Gentle.
Park, C. Changtzu 33.
  Distrust.
Park, M. Lowering the Coffin.
Park, T. Hymn to the Graveyard.
Parker, D. Résumé.
Parkerson. Statistic.
Parra, N. Anti-Lazarus, The.
Parry, R. Two Hearts Divided.
Parry-Williams. These Bones.
Pasolini. Day of My Death, The.
  John 12:24–25; Truly, truly, I say to you.
Pastan. Hat Lady, The.
  Turnabout.
Patchen. Body Beside the Ties, The.
  Do the Dead Know What Time It Is?
  From my high love I look at that poor world there.
  In Memory of Kathleen.
  O All Down within the Pretty Meadow.
  O terrible is the highest thing.
Patel, G. Forensic Medicine.
Patmore, C. Azalea, The.
  She Was Mine.
  Too soon, too soon comes Death to show.
Paul the Deacon. Epitaph for His Niece, Sophia.
Paul The Silentiary. Epitaph to Let, An.
Paulinus of Nola. To Ausonius.
Paulus Silentiarius. United.
Payne, B. Lines in Memory of My Father.
Paz. Doomed Garden, A.
  Small Variation.
Peacock, M. Dream Come True.
Peacock, T. Margaret Love Peacock, for Her Tombstone, 1826.
Pearl. Mourning Song.
Pearse, P. Mother, The.
  Prayer to Mother Mary.
Penn. They that love beyond the world, cannot be separated.
"Pereleshin." In the final hour, dear.
Péret. Nungesser und Coli Sind Verreckt.
Perry, N. Too Late.
Perses. Mnasylla, the daughter you lament.
Peters, L. Isatou died.
  One long jump.
Petersen. Ballad of Dead Yankees, The.
Pettet. Rose Garland Sonnet.
Peynetsa. Boy and the Deer, The.
Phan Bội Châu. Mourning Nguyễn Thái Học and Nguyễn Thị Giang.
Philips, K. EPITAPH. On her Son H. P. at St. Syth's Church where her body also lies Interred.
Phillips, A. Photograph & Story in *The Press*: The Mother Whose Children Burned to Death.
Philodemus. Roses are already here.
Piatt, S. Army of Occupation.
  Giving Back the Flower.
  Her Word of Reproach.
Picasso. Bottle of Suze, A.
Pickthall, M. Resurgam.
Pien Kung. At the Lake—Remembering My Dead Son, Yü.
Piercy. Barbie Doll.
  Landed Fish.
Pilinszky. Harbach 1944.
Pindar. Afterlife in Elysium.
Ping. Song of Calling Souls.
Pinkney, E. Widow's Song, The.
Pinsky. Dying.
  Memorial.
Piontek. In the Woods.
Pitcher. Pale Blue Casket, The.
Pitter. 1938.
Plath. All the Dead Dears.

Bee Meeting, The.
Daddy.
Death and Co.
Edge.
Getting There.
Lady Lazarus.
Last Words.
Point Shirley.
Stings.
Plato. Reflections, Written on Visiting the Grave of a Venerated Friend.
Plumly. After Grief.
Po Chü-i. Hat Given to the Poet by Li Chien, The.
  Last Poem.
  Separation.
Poe. Annabel Lee.
  City in the Sea, The.
  Conqueror Worm, The.
  For Annie.
  Lenore.
  Raven, The.
  Sleeper, The.
  To My Mother.
  To One in Paradise.
  Ulalume [*or* Ulalume—a Ballad].
Pollitt. Visitors.
Pomeroy, R. Between Here and Illinois.
Pompeius. Lais, who was a lovely flower.
Popa. Heaven's Ring.
  Other World, The.
  Tale About a Tale, The.
Pope, A. Dying Christian to His Soul, The.
  Epitaph for One Who Would Not Be Buried in Westminster Abbey ("Heroes, and Kings! your distance keep").
  Epitaph on Himself.
Poplavsky. Another Planet.
Porter, D. Lollies Noir.
Porter, P. Don't Be Afraid, I Am With You.
  Exequy, An.
  Talking to You Afterwards.
Pound, E. Coda.
Powys. Nunc Dimittis.
Pozhenyan. Poet and Tsar.
Preston, M. Ready.
Prévert. Familial.
  Last Supper, The.
Prior. Epigram: "When Bibo thought fit from the world to retreat."
  Reasonable Affliction, A.
Prismanova. Siren.
Probyn. Kyrielle.
Rondelet: "Which way he went?"
Procter, A. Envy.
  Philip and Mildred.
  Three Evenings in a Life.
Propertius. Ghosts do exist; death does not finish everything.
Proust. My True Love Hath My Heart.
Prudentius. Now, earth, take to thy cold embrace.
Pudney. Missing.
Purdy, A. Winter Walking.
Qaisi. Outside the Furnace.
Quarles. David's Epitaph on Jonathan.
  I saw him dead; I saw his Body fall.
  On Death.
Quasimodo. To the Fifteen of Piazzale Loreto.
Quiller-Couch. Doom Ferry.
Quinones. February.
Raab, L. Room, The.
Rabbitt. Bernadette Murphy, 1943-1955.
  For Those Who Will Live Forever.
  Over All.
  Tortoise.
Radnóti. Forced March.
  Peace, Horror.
  Picture Postcards.
  Postcard (Found on His body after He Was Killed by the Nazis).
  Seventh Eclogue.
Rakovszky. Difficulties of Falling Asleep.
Ralegh, W. Epitaph on Sir Philip Sidney.
  On the Snuff of a Candle.
  Passionate Man[']s Pilgrimage, The.
  Sir Walter Ra[u]le[i]gh to His Son[ne].

Verses Made the Night before He Died [*or* Dyed].
Verses Made the Night before His Beheading.
Ramanujan. Breaded Fish.
Some People.
Randall, D. Old Witherington.
Randolph, T. On Sir Robert Cotton the Antiquary.
Rankin, J. Forever the Snake.
Rannit. Boris Vilde.
Ransom, J. Here lies a lady of beauty and high degree.
Piazza Piece.
Ravikovitch. Like Rachel.
Man of Mystery.
You Can't Kill a Baby Twice.
Ray, D. Eskimo Girl, The.
Rector. Showing.
Redmond. Poetic Reflections Enroute To, and During, The Funeral and Burial of Henry Dumas, Poet.
Reed, I. Oakland Blues.
Reese, L. Lydia Is Gone This Many a Year.
Regan, J. In Flight.
Reid, A. Curiosity.
Lesson for Beautiful Women, A.
Reisen. Burn Out Burn Quick.
Reverdy. Flower Market.
Rexroth, K. Delia Rexroth.
For Eli Jacobson.
Some day in six inches of.
Reznikoff. I.
Jews from Holland, France, and Hungary, and later from.
Testimony: The United States (1901–1910) Recitative/The South.
Rich, A. Final Notations.
For the Dead.
From a Survivor.
I Dream I'm the Death of Orpheus.
Mourning Picture.
Paula Becker to Clara Westhoff.
Phantasia for Elvira Shatayev.
Readings of History.
Tattered Kaddish.
Woman Mourned by Daughters, A.
Richards, I. End of a Course.
Richards, L. (Bibbily Boo and Wollypotump).
Rickword. Moonrise Over Battlefield.
Riley, J. Out of the Hitherwhere.
Rilke. Be ahead of all parting, as though it already were.
Death.
On the Death of Countess Luise Schwerin.
Swan, The.
Time and again, however well we know the landscape of love.
We are the driving ones.
Rimbaud, A. Sleeper in the Valley, The.
Ríos, A. Mi Abuelo.
Ristovic. About Death and Other Things.
Dead Leaves.
Ritsos. Afternoon is all fallen plaster, black stones, dry thorns, The.
Day in May you left me, a day in May I lose you, A.
Miniature.
Unanswered.
Robinson, A. Dead Friend, The.
Pallor.
Venetian Nocturne.
Robinson, E. Exit.
For a Dead Lady.
Luke 15:20–32; And he arose and came.
Luke Havergal.
Many Are Called.
Old Story, An.
Recalled.
Walt Whitman.
Rochester, J. Song: "Absent from thee, I languish still."
Rodgers, C. Written for Love of an Ascension—Coltrane.
Roditi. Seance.
Roethke. Elegy for Jane.
Flight, The.
Journey to the Interior.

Judge Not.
Slug.
Rogers, S. Boy of Egremond, The.
Rolleston. Dead at Clonmacnois, The.
Root, J. Small Differences.
Rose, B. Unknown Soldier, The.
Rose, P. Terminus.
Rose. Truganinny.
Rossetti, C. After Death.
Amen.
At Home.
Bourne, The.
Buried.
Cardinal Newman.
Chilly Night, A.
Dead before Death.
Dirge, A: "Why were you born when the snow was falling?"
Dream Land.
Easter Monday.
End, An.
Eve.
From the Antique.
Heart Knoweth Its Own Bitterness, The.
Iniquity of the Fathers upon the Children, The.
Passing and Glassing.
Passing Away, Saith the World, Passing Away.
Pause, A.
Poor Ghost, The.
Remember me when I am gone away.
Rest.
Sappho.
Sleeping at last, the trouble and tumult over.
Song: "Oh roses for the flush of youth."
Song: "When I am dead, my dearest."
Sonnet 26: "This Life is full of numbness and of balk."
They lie at rest, our blessed dead.
Triad, A.
Under willows among the graves.
Uphill [*or* Up-Hill].
Verse III.
Wednesday in Holy Week.
Rossetti, D. Lost on Both Sides.
My Sister's Sleep.
Orchard-Pit, The.
Sudden Light.
Rothenberg, J. Water of the Flowery Mill (II), The.
Rowbotham. Bus-Stop on the Somme, The.
Rowe, E. Upon the Death of Her Husband.
Rowswell. Should You Go First.
Różewicz. Busy with Many Jobs.
Forms.
Larva, The.
Posthumous Rehabilitation.
Talent.
Rukeyser, M. Death and the Dancer.
Iris.
Madboy's Song.
Power of Suicide, The.
Then.
Rumi. Don't grieve. Anything you lose comes round.
In the shambles of love, they kill only the best,.
Rutsala. Silence, The.
Ryan, G. Elegy for 6 So Far.
Ryan, R. At the End.
Ryuichi. October Poem.
Standing Coffin.
Sachs, N. Chorus of the Dead.
How long have we forgotten how to listen!
O my mother.
O sister, / where do you pitch your tent?
You / in the night.
Sackville-West. Frost.
September 1939.
Saitō Mokichi. Tanka: "Aspiration."
Tanka: "Nothing to be done?"
Salaam. Our World Is Less Full Now That Mr. Fuller Is Gone.
Salamun. Clumsy Guys.
Salazar. Piñon Nuts.
Samio. Tanka: "Because my room."
Tanka: "Call to mind."

"Samoylov." Ballad about the German Censor, The.
Death of Ivan, The.
Sanchez, S. Blues.
Poem for my Brother, A.
Sandburg, C. Cool Tombs.
Death Snips Proud Men.
Grass.
Losers.
Mist Forms.
Sandhill People.
Southern Pacific.
Santayana. Sonnet XXV: "As in the midst of battle there is room."
Santos, S. Death.
Sapgir. Fearless One.
Sappho. On a Lady Indifferent to Poetry.
Sapphic Fragment.
Someday you will be dead.
These are the ashes of Timas.
This is the dust of Timias.
When Death shall close those Eyes, imperious Dame!
Sarson, H. Shell, The.
Sarton. All Souls.
I am not ready to die.
I did not weep my father.
Letter from Chicago.
Sassoon. At Daybreak.
Counter-Attack.
Death-Bed, The.
General, The.
In Heytesbury Wood.
One Who Watches.
Rear-Guard, The.
To His Dead Body.
Working Party, A.
Schechter. What Were You Patching?
Schelling. Run My Hand Under.
Schmitz. Ladder: Roger Vail's Photo of a Rockface in the Carrara (Italy) Marble Quarries, The.
Schnackenberg. Nightfishing.
Schreiner, O. Cry of South Africa, The.
Schwartz, L. Exiles: Ends.
Schwob. Things Dead.
Scott, D. Prayer for the Little Daughter between Death and Burial.
Scott, D. Forsaken, The.
Scott, W. Caledonia.
Fitz-Eustace's Song.
Madge Wildfire Sings.
Scott, W. Death.
My Mother.
Scott, W. U. S. Sailor with the Japanese Skull, The.
Scovell. Death from Cancer.
Suicide, The.
Scupham. House of Geraniums, A.
Seeger, A. Rendezvous, The.
Seeger, P. Where have all the flowers gone?— long time passing.
Seferis. And if the soul.
Last Day, The.
Our Sun.
Segal, J. Candle.
Rest.
Segalen. Mongol Libation.
Seneca. Deaths of Orphues and Hercules, The.
Learne Lordings, learne to feare and dread th'unweildy.
Seneca's Troas, Act 2. Chorus.
Senior. Searching for Grandfather.
Serge. Constellation of Dead Brothers.
Seth. Doctor's Journal Entry for August 6, 1945, A.
Seward. Sonnet 31.
Sonnet 32.
Sewell, G. Dying Man in His Garden, The.
Sexton. All My Pretty Ones.
Jesus Dies.
Lament: "Someone is dead."
Moss of His Skin, The.
Santa.
Somewhere in Africa.
Starry Night, The.

Truth the Dead Know, The.
Wanting to Die.
Seymour-Smith. He Came to Visit Me.
Shakespeare, W. Ariel's Song ("Full fathom
  [or fadom] five thy father lies").
Ay[e], but to die, and go we know not where.
Clown's Song, The.
Epitaph on Himself.
Ophelia's Song.
Post Mortem.
Song: "Fear no more the heat o' the Sun."
Sonnet 5: 'Those hours that with gentle work'.
Sonnet 64.
Sonnet 66.
Sonnet 71.
Sonnet 72.
Sonnet 73.
Sonnet 74.
Sonnet 81.
Sonnet 86.
Sonnet 107.
Sonnet 110.
Sonnet 146.
When I would pray and think, I think and
  pray.
Shapiro, D. For the Evening Land.
Lateness.
Shapiro, K. Auto Wreck.
Cut Flower, A.
Hospital.
My grandmother moves to my mind in context
  of sorrow.
Necropolis.
Scyros.
Shelley, M. To the air of 'My Phillida, adieu,
  love!'.
Shelley, P. Elegy on the Death of John Keats,
  An.
Music, when soft voices die.
On a Faded Violet.
She met me, Stranger, upon life's rough way.
To Night.
Shelnutt. At the Mass Graveyard.
Memory.
Shen Chou. Taoist Huang Has Died of
  Alcoholism, The.
Shen Yüeh. Lament for Hsieh T'iao.
Shiraishi. Anniversary of Samansa's Death,
  The.
Shirley, J. Death the Leveller.
Shomer. Passive Resistance.
Shurin. Continuous Thunder.
Very Days.
Siamanto. Dance, The.
Grief.
Siddal. At Last.
Dead Love.
Sidney, P. Dirge: "Ring out your bells [or
  belles], let mourning shows [or shewes] be
  spread."
Farewell, A.
Splendidis longum valedico nugis.
Why Fear to Die?
Wronged Lover, The.
Sikelianos. Rehearsing for Death.
Silkin. Space in the Air, A.
Simic. Charon's Cosmology.
Eyes Fastened with Pins.
Toy Factory.
Simko. Thinking of My Father on a Bus to
  Baltimore.
Simmons, J. From the Irish.
Simonides. For the Spartan Dead at
  Thermopylai (480 B.C.).
Simovic. Epitaph: "To the chimney a bull's
  horns."
Epitaphs from Karansko Cemetery.
Simpson, L. Landscape with Barns.
Riders Held Back, The.
Sinda. You shall walk in peace!
Singer, B. Epilogue: "That death might not be
  casual."
Siôn Cent. Vanity of the World, The.
Sirr. Beginnings.
Sissman. Bruisingly cradled in a Harvard
  chair.
Deathplace, A.

Upon Finding Dying: An Introduction, by L.
  E. Sissman, Remaindered at 1s.
Sitwell, D. Prelude.
Skeeter. Western Trail Cook, 1880.
Skelton, J. Phillip Sparow.
Upon a Dead Man's Head.
Skoyles. In Memoriam.
Smedley, M. Cavour.
Face from the Past, A.
Smith, A. Dead stare out of empty sockets,
  The.
Smith, C. Dead Beggar, an Elegy Addressed
  to a Lady, The.
Ode to Death.
Sonnet V. To the South Downs: "Ah, hills
  beloved!—where once, an happy child."
Sonnet Written in the Church-Yard at
  Middleton in Sussex.
To the Shade of Burns.
Smith, D. Roundhouse Voices, The.
Smith, I. Cuillins tower, The.
Oban 1955–82.
Smith, J. Sew a Pocket.
Smith, K. Train.
Smith, P. Poor old lady, she swallowed a fly.
Smith, P. Sweet Daddy.
Smith, S. Angel Boley.
Death Sentence, The.
Exeat.
Le Revenant.
Mrs Simpkins never had very much to do.
Not Waving But Drowning.
Parklands, The.
Private Means is dead.
Quand on n'a pas ce que l'on aime, il faut
  aimer ce que l'on a—.
Reversionary.
Rise from Your Bed of Languor.
Voice from the Tomb (1).
Who Killed Lawless Lean?
Smith, S. El Alamein.
Snodgrass, W. Flat One, A.
Monet: 'Les Nymphéas'.
Snyder, G. Dragonfly / Dead on the snow.
For John Chappell.
Word Basket Woman.
Snyder, R. Blue Sparks in Dark Closets.
Sophocles. Elektra's Keening.
Over come—O bitter sweetness.
Sorescu. Chess.
Sorley. All the Hills and Vales Along.
Stones.
Sorrells. Town I Left.
Sorrentino. Zoo, The.
Soupault. One o'Clock.
Sousa, N. Appeal.
Soutar. Guns, The.
Hungry Mauchs, The.
Song: "Whaur yon broken brig hings owre;."
Southern Bushmen Oral Tradition. Day we
  die, The.
Southey, R. Scholar, The.
Soyinka. Civilian and Soldier.
Death in the Dawn.
Funeral Sermon, Soweto.
Massacre, October '66.
Ujamaa.
Spark. Elegy in a Kensington Churchyard.
Sparrow, J. Epitaph: "This stone, with not
  unpardonable pride."
Speer. Mama Rosanna's Last Bead-Clack.
Spellman. Did John's Music Kill Him?
Spence, L. Stown Bairn, The.
Spender, S. Beethoven's Death Mask.
Funeral, The.
Spenser. What If Some Little Paine the
  Passage Have.
Spires. Exhumation.
First Day, The.
Stafford, W. Bess.
Traveling [or Travelling] through the dark I
  found a deer.
Stanescu. Song.
Winter Ritual.
Stanford, F. Between Love and Death.
Stanley, T. On S. John the Baptist.
Stanton, M. Sunday Graveyard.

Stern, G. Behaving Like a Jew.
Pile of Feathers.
Stevens, W. Death of a Soldier, The.
Flyer's Fall.
Of Heaven Considered as a Tomb.
Owl in the Sarcophagus, The.
Postcard from the Volcano, A.
Sunday Morning.
Table Talk.
Worms at Heaven's Gate, The.
Stevenson, A. Death, my companion, who
  shall quit me soon.
Stevenson, A. Apology.
Epitaph for a Good Mouser.
Stevenson, R. Celestial Surgeon, The.
Epitaph: "Angler rose, he took his rod, The."
It's an owercome sooth for age an' youth.
Pirate Ditty.
Requiem: "Under the wide and starry sky."
So live, so love, so use that fragile hour.
Ticonderoga: A Legend of the West
  Highlands.
To K. de M.
To Mrs. Will H. Low.
Tropics vanish, and meseems that I, The.
Verses Written in 1872.
Stokesbury. To Laura Phelan: 1880-1906.
Stone, J. Death.
End, The.
Prediction, The.
Strand. Dead, The.
Strauss, J. Tending the Graves.
Stricker. Island.
Strode. Epitaph on the Monument of Sir
  William Strode.
Stuart, D. Ballad of the Frozen Field, The.
Su Tung-p'o. On the Death of His Baby Son.
Remembering Min Ch'e.
Tune: Song of River City.
Under the heaven of our holy ruler, all things
  turn to spring.
Suckling, J. Song: "I prithee spare me, gentle
  boy."
Suhl. And the Earth Rebelled.
Summers, H. My old cat [is dead].
Supervielle. Like an ox streaming saliva,
  yoked to the plough.
Surkov. Tenderness.
Surrey. Complaint of a Lover Rebuked.
Epitaph on Thomas Clere.
Tribute to Wyatt.
Sutskever. Friday evening coos up in the attic.
Song for a Dance.
Svetlov. Two.
Swenson, C. Our Town.
Swenson, M. "Feel me to do right," our father
  said on his deathbed.
In the Bodies of Words.
Question.
Shape of Death, The.
Swift, J. In Sickness.
Satirical Elegy on the Death of a Late Famous
  General, A.
Swinburne. After Death.
Forsaken Garden, A.
Garden of Proserpine, The.
Kissing her hair, I sat against her feet.
Return, The.
Swirszczynska. Conversation Through the
  Door, A.
I Wash the Shirt.
They Lay Dying Side by Side.
Sylvester, J. Modern Times.
Symons, A. Wanderer's Song.
Synge. Question, A.
Szymborska. Seen from Above.
Tabb. Echoes.
Tadic. Man from the Death Institute.
Taliesin. Death Song for Owain ab Urien.
TallMountain. Hands of Mary Joe, The.
T'ang Hsien-tsu. My son, you loved telling
  the story of Prince Nata.
On the Day of Washing the Buddha in the
  Year Ting-wei (1607), I Dreamed That My
  Late Son Shih-ch'ü Was Holding a Book,
  and Appeared To Be Quite Happy. He Said
  That He Had Earned His Chin-shih Degree in

the Underworld. After We Sighed and Laughed Together for a Long Time, I Woke Up and Wrote This Poem.

T'ao Ch'ien. Poem in the Form of a Coffin-Puller's Song ("In the old days I had no wine to drink").

Poem in the Form of a Coffin-Puller's Song ("Plain of wild grasses, broad and tangled, A").

Poem in the Form of a Coffin-Puller's Song ("What has a life must have a death").

Tate, A. Cross, The.

Non Omnis Moriar.

Oath, The.

To Intellectual Detachment.

Tate, G. Last Instructions.

Tate, J. Distance from Loved Ones.

Tati-Loutard. Death and Rebirth.

Submarine Tombs.

Voices, The.

Taylor, E. Fig for Thee, Oh! Death, A.

Upon a Spider Catching a Fly.

Taylor, H. As on a Darkling Plain.

Taylor, J. Sonnet on the Death of the Poet J. Keats.

Taylor, W. Ellenore.

Teasdale. Hide and Seek.

Tekeyan. Forgetting. Yes, I will forget it all.

Tennyson, A.

Crossing the Bar.

Dying Swan, The.

Go By.

Hark! the dogs howl! the sleetwinds blow.

If Only.

In Memoriam A.H.H. 35, 50.

In the Garden at Swainston.

In the Valley of Cauteretz.

Lady of Shalott, The.

Old yew, which graspest at the stones.

Passing of King Arthur, The.

Sailor Boy, The.

St. Simeon Stylites.

Song: "Spirit haunts the year's last hours, A."

Sonnet: "She took the dappled partridge flecked [or fleckt] with blood."

Sweet after showers, ambrosial air.

Tithonus.

Thackeray. Dear Jack, this white mug that with Guinness I fill.

Sorrows of Werther, The.

Theognis. Our Course.

Thomas, D. After the funeral, mule praises, brays.

Among Those Killed in the Dawn Raid Was a Man Aged a Hundred.

And death shall have no dominion.

Conversation of prayers about to be said, The.

Death is all metaphors, shape in one history.

Do not go gentle into that good night.

Force that through the green fuse drives the flower, The.

Hand that signed the paper felled a city, The.

When, like a running grave, time tracks you down.

Thomas, E. Cat, A.

Gallows, The.

Lights Out.

Rain, midnight rain, nothing but the wild rain.

Snow.

Thomas, G. Little Death.

Thomas, R. Madrigal: "Your love is dead, lady, your love is dead."

Pisces.

Thompson, C. Not Dead, but Sleeping.

To My Dead Brother.

Thompson, P. Afternoon Gossip, An.

Consumptive, The.

Lines on a Dead Girl.

Song, The: "Oh, foully slighted Ethiope maid!"

To a Deceased Friend.

Thornbury. Smith of Maudlin.

Tichborne. Tichborne's Elegy.

Tiempo. I Tell of Another Young Death.

T'ien Hung. Dew on the Young Garlic Leaves.

Timrod. Ode: "Sleep sweetly in your humble graves."

Tipping. Just after Michael's Death, the Game of Pool.

Todd, R. Joan Miró ("After that war, when death had gone away").

Todorovski. Peaceful Step, A.

Tollet. On a Death's Head.

Tolson. Festus Conrad.

Old Pettigrew.

Tomlinson, C. Death in the Desert, A.

Traherne. Serious and a Curious Night-Meditation, A.

Trakl. De Profundis.

In the East.

Trần Dạ Tù'. New Lullaby, The.

Trần Huy Liệu. Dropping By the Guava Graveyard in So'n-La.

Tranströmer. After a Death.

Track.

Tranter. Death Circus, The.

Traxler. Death of a Distant In-law.

Tremayne. Burial, A.

Troupe. Conjuring Against Alien Spirits.

Day in the Life of a Poet, A.

Ts'ao Chih. Vision, A.

Tsatsos. Protest.

Tsvetayeva. I know the truth—give up all other truths!

Tu Fu. Visiting Tsan, Abbot of Ta-Yun.

Tucker, M. "Did You Call Me, Father?"

Gone, with all her sparkling beauty.

Lift Me Higher.

Tuckerman, F. Coralie.

Turner, N. Death Is a Door.

Turner, P. Looking for Him.

Turner, W. Life and Death.

Tuwhare. Ron Mason.

"Twain." Emmeline Grangerford's "Ode to Stephen Dowling Bots, Dec'd."

Twichell. Aisle of Dogs.

Tzara. For Robert Desnos.

Waking.

Ulacia. Stone at the Bottom, The.

Under. And a Star Fell.

Ungaretti. Agony.

No More Crying Out.

Unknown. Among the dead we come.

Barbara Allan ("It was about the Martinmas time").

Bells of hell go ting-a-ling-a-ling, The.

Beyond.

Blowflies Buzz, The.

Bonny Earl of Murray, The.

Burial Songs.

Cauld Lad of Hilton, The *or* The Wandering Spectre.

Chronicle, A.

Cow Boy's Lament.

Cowboy's Lament, The.

Créide's Lament for Dínertech.

Dead are gone and with them we cannot converse;, The.

Death.

Death of Digenis, The.

Death of Moses, The.

Dew on the leek.

Don't cry / over the happy dead.

Dying Airman, The.

Earl Brand (The Douglas Tragedy).

Egyptian Poem.

Epitaph.

Epitaph for One Killed at Roncesvalles.

Epitaph from a Tomb in Asia Minor.

Epitaph: "Man who in his life trusts in this world, A."

Epitaph of Sardanapalos, The.

Epitaph on a Tomb near Rome.

Feltons Epitaph.

Fighting South of the Ramparts.

Finnegan's Wake.

Funerall Song, A.

Gentle rodent in its cage.

Graves the rain makes wet and sleek, The.

Gravestone at Corinth, A.

Greedy Ned.

Hallelujah, I'm a Bum.

Hearse Song, The.

I am of this world.

I heard a fly buzz when I died.

I know moon-rise, I know star-rise.

I Thank God I'm Free at Las'.

I Wende to Dede.

If I should cast off this tattered coat.

In the wilds there is a dead doe.

Lament for Te Iwi—ika.

Lament, The: "What shall I send you, my dear one, there in the underworld?"

Limerick.

Lonesome Valley.

Lord, Remember Me!

Lyke-Wake Dirge, The [or A].

Man of Words [and not of deeds], A.

No more auction block for me.

Old Codger of Broome, The.

On Bond the Usurer.

On Prince Frederick.

On the Death of Mr. Persall's Little Daughter, in the Beginning of the Spring, at Amsterdam.

On the Funeral of a Rich Miser.

One Morning in May; or, The Young Girl Cut Down in Her Prime.

Other World, The.

Perle, plesaunte to prynces paye.

Poor old lady, she swallowed a fly.

Rare Willie Drowned in Yarrow; or, The Water o Gamrie.

Ruin, The.

Saint, Bird, Angel.

She drank good ale, strong punch and wine.

Ship, The.

Silver swan, who living had no note, The.

Soon I will be done with the troubles of the world.

Springfield Mountain.

St. James Infirmary.

Steal Away to Jesus.

Stormalong!

Swing low, sweet chariot.

Thank God for life!

There were two royal children.

They fought south of the walls.

This is a sailor's grave, while opposite.

This little stone, dear Sabinos.

Thou shalt die.

Three Ravens, The.

Timor Mortis.

Twa Brothers, The.

Twa Corbies, The.

Ubi Sunt Qui ante Nos Fuerunt?

Unquiet Grave, The.

Upon a Maid That Died the Day She Was Married.

We Shall Know.

When I pick up my koto.

When the turuf [or turf] is thy tour [or tower].

Widow's Lament.

Wife of Usher's Well, The.

Untermeyer, L. Irony.

To a Vine-clad Telegraph Pole.

Updike. Bath after Sailing.

Urdang. My Father's Death.

Urrea. Ghost Sickness.

Usborne. Epitaph on a Party Girl.

Valek. Hearing.

Valentine, J. Father, The.

My Mother's Body, My Professor, My Bower.

"X."

Vallejo. Black Riders, The.

Black Stone on Top of a White Stone.

Masses.

Our Daily Bread.

Trilce.

Van Duyn. Stream, The.

Van Vliet. Party.

Vaughan, H. As time one day by me did pass.

Death.

Easter Hymn.

Friends Departed.

Pursuit[e], The.

To the Pious Memory of C. W. Esquire.

Waterfall [or Water-Fall], The.

Venclova. Night descended on us with a chill.

Verlaine. Exchange Of Feelings, An.
Very. Autumn Leaves.
  Cup, The.
  Dead, The.
  Son, The.
  Yourself.
"Vestal." Kit Carson's Last Smoke ("Kit
  Carson came to old Fort Lyons").
Vilakazi. Now I do believe that he has died.
  Now I Will Only Believe.
Villanueva, A. To Jesus Villanueva, with
  Love.
Villiers. Epitaph upon Thomas, Lord Fairfax,
  An.
Villon. Fragment on Death, A.
Vinokurov. And when my legs had already
  grown numb.
  Forget-Me-Nots.
Vinz. Passages.
Virgil. Aeneas' firmness.
  Death of Camilla.
  Dido in the Elysian Fields.
  Dido's death.
  End.
  Orpheus and Eurydice.
  Release.
  Turnus kills Pallasy.
Vittorelli. On a Nun.
Vizenor. Unhappy Diary Days.
Vogel, D. There is a last, solitary coach about
  to leave.
Voigt. For My Mother.
Volman. Case, The.
Voznesensky. Call of the Lake, The.
  Elegy for My Mother.
Vū Hoàng Chu'o'ng. No More Anxiety.
Waddell, H. But we, whose sands run low.
  Earth said to Death.
  I shall not go to heaven when I die.
Wagoner, D. Author of American Ornithology
  Sketches a Bird, Now Extinct, The.
Wain. Gentleman Aged Five before the
  Mirror.
Walcott. Letter from Brooklyn, A.
  Sea Canes.
  Village Life, A.
  Young Wife, The.
Walker, A. Burial.
  Good Night, Willie Lee, I'll See You in the
  Morning.
Wallace, R. Riding in a Stranger's Funeral.
Wallace, R. Grandmother Grace.
Wallis, H. Female's Lamentations, The; or,
  The Village in Mourning.
  To Mrs.———, on the Death of Her Husband.
Walsh, M. Thomas Iron-Eyes.
Walsh, O. At length my soul the fatal union
  finds.
Wang Chiu-ssu. Ballad of the Fatherless Boy.
Wang Shih-chieng. Lamenting for My Wife.
Warner, S. Some Make This Answer.
Warren, R. After Night Flight Son Reaches
  Bedside of Already Unconscious Father,
  Whose Right Hand Lifts in a Spasmodic
  Gesture, as Though Trying to Make Contact:
  1955.
  Better Than Counting Sheep.
  Confederate Veteran Tries to Explain the
  Event, A.
  Country Burying (1919).
  School Lesson Based on Word of Tragic
  Death of Entire Gillum Family.
  There once, on that goat island, I.
  There's a grandfather's clock in the hall,
  watch it closely. The.
  Way to Love God, A.
Warren, R. In Creve Coeur, Missouri.
Warsh. Gout.
Wat. Before Breughel the Elder.
Waters, M. Keats' Lips.
Watson, R. View on Death, A.
Watson, W. O My Poor Darling.
Watts, I. Prospect of Heaven Makes Death
  Easy, A.
Waugh, E. They told me, Francis Hinsley,
  they told me you were hung.
Weatherly, T. Times.

Weaver, M. Water Song.
Webb, F. Death at Winson Green, A.
Webster, A. That some day Death who has us
  all for jest.
Webster, J. Dirge, A: "Call for the robin-
  redbreast and the wren."
  Shrouding of the Duchess of Malfi, The.
Webster, M. Illi Morituri.
Weelkes. Tan ta ra: cries Mars on bloody
  rampier.
Wei Wên-Ti. On the Death of his Father.
Weigl. Temple Near Quang Tri, Not on the
  Map.
Weingarten. Father Hunger and Son.
Welish. Kiss Tomorrow Goodbye.
Welles. White Valentine.
Wellesley. Mother.
Wen Cheng-ming. Written While Sick.
Wendell, J. In the Pasture of Dead Horses.
Werfel. Litany of the Rooms of the Dead.
  Strangers Are We All upon the Earth.
Wesley, C. Ah! lovely appearance of death.
Weston, R. et al. Epitaph: "Beneath this stone
  lies William Burke."
Wevill. Mystery, The.
Whalen. Walking beside the Kamogawa,
  Remembering Nansen and Fudo and Gary's
  Poem.
Wheatley, P. On the Death of the Rev. Mr.
  George Whitefield, 1770.
  Thoughts on the Works of Providence.
  To a Gentleman and Lady on the Death of the
  Lady's Brother and Sister, and a Child of the
  Name Avis, Aged One Year.
Whistler. Form of Epitaph, A.
White, M. "Claude Monet sur son lit du
  mort."
Whitehead, J. He Remembers How He Didn't
  Understand What Lieutenant Dawson Meant.
Whitehead, W. New Night Thoughts on
  Death; a Parody.
Whitlow. Rockin' A Man, Stone Blind.
Whitman, A. But, "if a man die, shall he live
  again?"
  Let scoffers mock, let unbelief deny.
Whitman, W. As if a phantom caress'd me.
  As toilsome I wander'd Virginia's woods.
  Carol of Death, The.
  Come up from the fields father, here's a letter
  from our Pete.
  Death's Valley.
  Hush'd be the camps to-day.
  Joy, shipmate, joy!
  Last Invocation, The.
  Leaves of Grass (1855).
  O Captain! my Captain! our fearful trip is
  done.
  O living always, always dying!
  On the Same Picture.
  Osceola.
  Out of the cradle endlessly rocking.
  Sight in camp in the daybreak gray and dim,
  A.
  Sleepers, The.
  Spring.
  This Compost.
  To think of time—of all that retrospection.
  Vigil strange I kept on the field one night;.
Whitney, I. I whole in body and in minde.
  Rejoice in God that I am gon.
Whittier. Dead Feast of the Kol Folk, The.
  Telling the Bees.
Wickham. Happy Mathematician, The.
Wieseltier. Extended Sonnet on the Death of
  Isaac Danziger.
Wigglesworth. Welcome, Sweet Rest.
Wilbur. Bell Speech.
  Finished Man, A.
  In a Churchyard.
  Merlin Enthralled.
  Mill, The.
  Pardon, The.
  To an American Poet Just Dead.
  Tywater.
  Voice from under the Table, A.
  Year's End.

Wild, R. Epitaph on Some Bottles of Sack
  and Claret Laid in Sand.
Wilde, O. Ballad of Reading Gaol, The.
  Requiescat.
Willard, N. King of Cats Sends a Postcard to
  His Wife, The.
Williams, C. Helen.
Williams, H. On the Death of the Rev. Dr.
  Kippis.
Williams, M. Death of Chet Baker, The.
  On the Symbolic Consideration of Hands and
  the Significance of Death.
Williams, W. Complete Destruction.
  Death.
  Last Words of My English Grandmother, The.
  To a Dog Injured in the Street.
  Widow's Lament in Springtime, The.
Wilson, J. When I Am Dead.
Winchilsea. To Death.
  Trail all your pikes, dispirit every drum.
Winters, Y. Before Disaster.
  Inscription for a Graveyard.
  Song in Passing, A.
  Time and the Garden.
  To the Holy Spirit.
Wojahn. John Berryman Listening to Robert
  Johnson's "King of the Delta Blues," January
  1972.
  Riding the Empire Builder, 1948.
Wolfe, C. To Mary.
Wolfe, H. Journey's End.
Wollach. Body, The.
Wong, N. Mama, come back.
Wood, R. Cabbages.
  Pilot, The.
Wordsworth, W. Lines;: "Loud is the Vale!
  the Voice is up."
  Lucy.
  She was a Phantom of delight.
  Slumber did my spirit seal, A.
  Song: "She dwelt among the untrodden ways."
  Surprised by Joy—impatient as the Wind.
  Two April Mornings, The.
Wright, C. Obedience of the Corpse.
Wright, C. Arkansas Traveller.
  Delta Traveller.
  Hawaii Dantesca.
  Portrait of the Artist with Li Po.
  Sitting at Night on the Front Porch.
Wright, F. Elegy: Breece D'J Pancake.
  Pawtucket Postcards.
Wright, J. Arrangements with Earth for Three
  Dead Friends.
  At the Executed Murderer's Grave.
  At the Slackening of the Tide.
  At Thomas Hardy's Birthplace, 1953.
  Gesture by a Lady with an Assumed Name, A.
  Inscription for the Tank.
  Life, The.
  Minneapolis Poem, The.
  Northern Pike.
  Note Left in Jimmy Leonard's Shack, A.
  Old Age Compensation.
  Old WPA Swimming Pool in Martins Ferry,
  Ohio, The.
  On the Skeleton of a Hound.
  Saint Judas.
  Small Frogs Killed on the Highway.
  Speak.
  Three Sentences for a Dead Swan.
  To the Muse.
  Two Poems about President Harding.
  Way to Make a Living, A.
  Willy Lyons.
Wright, J. Journey to the Place of Ghosts.
Wright, J. Eli, Eli.
  Metho Drinker.
Wright, M. Epitaph on Herself, An.
Wroth. Sonnet 30: "You blessed shades, which
  give mee silent rest."
Wu of Han. Li Fu-Jên.
Wu Wei-yeh. Lamenting for My Late
  Daughter.
  Passing by Huai-yin I Have Feelings.
Wyatt, T. Enemy [or en'my] of life, decayer
  of all kind, The [or Th'].

In mourning wise since daily I increase.
Stand whoso list upon the slipper top.
Wylie. Prophecy.
Sea Lullaby.
Yang Shih-ch'i. I've drawn a salary in the capital for forty years now.
"Yashin." Eagle, The.
Yau. Different Cereal, A.
We Are All Vultures.
Yeats. Byzantium.
Circus Animals' Desertion, The.
Crazy Jane and the Bishop.
Death.
Dream of Death, A.
He Thinks of His Past Greatness When a Part of the Constellations of Heaven.
Irish Airman Foresees His Death, An.
Last Confession, A.
Man Who Dreamed of Faeryland, The.
Sailing To Byzantium.
That the Night Come.
Three Bushes, The.
Three Things.
To a Shade.
Tom O'Roughley.
Two Songs from a Play.
Upon a Dying Lady.
Yesenin. Black Man, The.
Now piece by piece we slip away.
Only one final trick remains—.
Rowan Tree Fire, The.
Yevtushenko. Heirs of Stalin, The.
Yo. Dreaming of a Dead Lady.
Yorke. Our Gardener here, James Phillips see.
Yosano. Tanka: "White tower, A."
Yoshihara. Resurrection.
Yoshimi. Tanka: "Having crushed."
Young, A. W. H. Auden & Mantan Moreland.
Young, A. Passing the Graveyard.
Thistledown.
Young, A. Elegy for a School-Friend.
Young Bear. Our Bird Aegis.
Young, D. Shepherd's Dochter, The.
Young, K. Escape Artist, The.
Young, S. Epitaph for a Concord Boy.
Yü Hsüan-chi. Replying to a Poem by a New Graduate Lamenting the Loss of His Wife.
Yu Kuang-chung. When I am dead, lay me down between the Yangtze.
Yüan Mei. Happy about Being Old.
Writing My Feelings.
Yukitsuna. Tanka: "With those who."
Zach. Death Came for Michael Rockinghorse early one morning.
Max is dead and his sons.
Zagajewski. When Death Came.
Zangwill. Death's Transfiguration.
Zhenkai. Requiem: "Not the living but the dead."
Zuckmayer. My Death.

Death in Childhood
"Adeler." Willie had a purple monkey climbing on a yellow stick.
Ai. Good Shepherd: Atlanta, 1981, The.
Anyte. On this her daughter's tomb.
Atwood. Death of a Young Son by Drowning.
Bagg. Death at Pocono Lake Preserve.
Beaumont, S. Of My Dear Son [or Deare Sonne], Gervase Beaumont.
Behn, A. Epitaph on the Tombstone of a Child, the Last of Seven That Died Before.
Bekederemo. Abiku.
Bishop, E. First Death in Nova Scotia.
Bourdillon. When Love Is Done.
Bradstreet, A. In Memory of My Dear Grandchild Anne Bradstreet Who Deceased June 20, 1669, Being Three Years and Seven Months Old.
In Memory of My Dear Grandchild Elizabeth Bradstreet Who Deceased August, 1665, Being a Year and Half Old.
On My Dear Grandchild Simon Bradstreet, [Who Died on 16TH November, 1669, Being But A Month And One Day Old].
Bridges, R. On a Dead Child.
Carew, T. Another [Epitaph on the Lady Mary Villiers] ("Purest soul that e'er was sent,

The").
Epitaph on the Lady Mary Vill[i]ers.
Carey, M. Wretten by Me at the Death of My 4th Sonne and 5th Child Perigrene Payler.
Wretten by Me att the Same Tyme; on the Death of My 4th, & Only Child, Robert Payler.
Dawe, B. Elegy for Drowned Children.
Dickinson, E. How the Waters closed above Him.
Diodoros of Sardis. Young child of Diodoros's house, A.
Diodorus Zonas. Who in the waters of this reedy lake.
Eichendorff. On My Child's Death.
Field, E. Little Boy Blue.
"Field." Gray mob-cap and a girl's, A.
Fordham. In Memoriam. Alphonse Campbell Fordham.
Queenie.
To an Infant.
Frame. Yet Another Poem about a Dying Child.
Frost, R. "Out, Out—."
Gautier. Her Toys.
Gilman, C. Dead Sister, The.
Glück, L. Mount Ararat.
Goethe. Erl-King, The.
Goodman, P. My Daughter Very Ill.
Gould, H. Dying Child's Request, The.
Halpern, D. Early Death, An.
Harper, M. Nightmare Begins Responsibility.
Reuben, Reuben.
Heaney, S. Limbo.
Mid-Term Break
Heard, J. Solace.
Hecht, A. Book of Yolek, The.
Herrick. Epitaph upon a Child, An.
Upon a Child That Died [or Dyed].
Holmes, O. Iris, Her Book.
Honig, E. 1925.
Hopkinson, A. Chord, The.
Howitt, M. Dying Child, The.
Hunt, L. Epitaph of Erotion, The.
Hwang, K. Prayer.
Jarrell. Come to the Stone.
Lost Children, The.
Protocols.
Jonson, B. Epitaph On Solomon Pavy, [Salomon or Salathiel Pavy], a Child of Q[ueen] El[izabeth's] Chapel.
On My First Daughter.
On My First Son [or Sonne].
Why I Write Not of Love.
Jordan, J. Test of Atlanta 1979, The.
Justice, D. On the Death of Friends in Childhood.
Kao Ch'i. Seeing Flowers I Remember My Late Daughter, Shu.
Kennedy, X. Little Elegy.
Kettle. To My Daughter Betty.
Kinnell. Round– / cheeked girlchild comes awake, A.
Landon. Dying Child, The.
Li K'ai-hsien. Thanking Doctor Jen.
Lucian. Calimachus.
Lucianus. I was Kallimachos, age five.
Mew. To a Child in Death.
Meynell, A. Maternity.
Mezhirov. Ice of Ladoga, The.
Montague, J. Falls Funeral.
Moore, J. Little Libbie.
Moorer. Russia's Resentment.
Morgan, F. February 11, 1977.
Muir, E. Child Dying, The.
Muske. Wish Foundation, The.
O Heigeartaigh. My sorrow, Donncha, my thousand-cherished.
Peters, L. Isatou died.
Philetas. This tombstone heavy with grief announces.
Pien Kung. At the Lake—Remembering My Dead Son, The.
Po Chü-i. Remembering Golden Bells.
Randall, D. Ballad of Birmingham.
Ransom, J. Bells for John Whiteside's

Daughter.
Dead Boy.
Reznikoff. Children.
Rice, S. I sit waiting for one of the two kinds of miracle.
Look! she is dead: no cover can cover her: look.
Rossetti, C. Baby lies so fast asleep.
Why did baby die.
Rózewicz. Massacre of the Boys.
Sachs, N. Already embraced by the arm of heavenly solace.
Dead Child Speaks, A.
O the night of the weeping children!
Schulman. For That Day Only.
Schuyler, J. Head, A.
Scott, W. To L. B. S.
Senior. Children's Hospital.
Epitaph: "Last year the child died."
Shorter. Mother, The.
Sigourney. Request of a Dying Child.
Silkin. Death of a Son.
Simmerman. Child's Grave, Hale County, Alabama.
Soyinka. Abiku.
Strode. On the Death of Mistress Mary Prideaux.
Su Tung-p'o. On the Death of His Baby Son.
Tate, A. Death of Little Boys.
Taylor, E. Upon Wedlock and Death of Children.
Thomas, D. Refusal to Mourn the Death, by Fire, of a Child in London, A.
Thomas, E. Nine times the sun his yearly course had run.
Unknown. After the Inscription on a Greek Stele of a Woman Holding Her Grandchild on Her Knees.
Babes in the Wood, The ("Now ponder well, you parents dear").
Before your hair was ever cut.
Epitaph from Athens.
Kū' siut Song.
Papa's Letter.
Voigt. Year's End.
Watson, S. Epitaph, An: "His friends he loved. His direst earthly foes."
Wesley, C. On the Death of His Son.
Wilde, O. Requiescat.
Wordsworth, W. Childless Father, The.
Education of Nature, The.
Lucy Gray; or, Solitude.
Surprised by Joy—impatient as the Wind.
Wright, J. Flood Year.
Wu Wei-yeh. Lamenting for My Late Daughter.
Yüan Chen. Airing Painful Memories.
Elegy, An: "Last, best-loved daughter of old Hsieh, you who foolishly ran off."

Death in War. *See* War Dead

Death of Animals
Agathias. Justice.
Partridge.
Anyte. Child Myro made this tomb, The.
Cock, A.
Damis set this up, to commemorate.
Argentarius. Here lie a grasshopper and a / Cicada.
Baudelaire. Carrion, A.
Bly, R. Dead Seal [near McClure's Beach], The.
Hollow Tree, A.
Braun, R. Goose.
Lilies, The.
Catullus. Death of Lesbia's Bird, The.
Chamberlain, B. Dead Ponies.
Clark, L. Grumblers.
Cowper, W. Epitaph on a Hare.
Cummings, E. Me up at does.
De Stein. Elegy on the Death of Bingo Our Trench Dog.
Dickey, J. Heaven of Animals, The.
Eberhart, R. For a Lamb.
Frost, R. Draft Horse, The.
Gardner, I. Widow's Yard, The.
Garrigue. Epitaph for My Cat.
Mouse, The.

Gray, T.   Ode on the Death of a Favourite [or Favorite] Cat, Drowned in a Tub [or Bowl] of Gold Fishes.
Hardy, T.   Last Words To a Dumb Friend.
Hayden, R.   Plague of Starlings, A.
Herrick.   Upon His Spaniel[l] Tracie [or Tracy].
Hughes, T.   Old Age Gets Up.
  View of a Pig.
Hummer, T.   Rural Carrier Stops to Kill a Nine-Foot Cottonmouth, The.
Jeffers, R.   Hurt Hawks.
Kinnell.   Hen Flower, The.
Kipling, R.   Power of the Dog, The.
Kitching.   My Gerbil.
Kunitz, S.   Robin Redbreast.
  Wellfleet Whale, The.
Lawrence, A.   Cro-Kill.
Lindsay, V.   Eagle That Is Forgotten, The.
Longfellow, H.   Birds of Killingworth, The (The Poet's Tale).
Lovelace, R.   Fly Caught in a Cobweb, A.
Lowry, M.   Salmon Drowns Eagle.
MacCaig.   Interruption to a Journey.
Mathews, H.   Offering for the Cat, An.
McClure, M.   For the Death of 100 Whales.
Mei Yao Ch'en.   Offering for the Cat, An.
Meireles.   Dead Horse, The.
Meredith, G.   Young Reynard.
Millay, E.   Buck in the Snow, The.
Moran, R.   Cross Country.
Mother Goose.   Who killed Cock [or poor] Robin? [or Here lies Cock Robin].
Musgrave.   Burial of the Dog.
Nguyễn Đình Chiểu.   Loyal Horse, The.
Oliver, M.   Ghosts.
Pound, E.   Lies a dead deer on younder plain.
Randolph, T.   On the Death of a Nightingale.
Ransom, J.   Janet Waking.
Rich, A.   Mare's skeleton in the clearing: another sign of life, The.
Rossetti, C.   Last Rites.
Shapiro, K.   Interlude.
Sharah.   Package for Another World.
Slutsky.   Horses in the Sea.
Snyder, G.   Dead by the Side of the Road, The.
Stafford, W.   Traveling [or Travelling] through the dark I found a deer.
Stern, G.   Dog, The.
Strong, G.   Modern Hiawatha, The.
Theocritus.   What do you gain, poor Thyrsis, by these tears?
Thomas, E.   Gallows, The.
Turner, C.   Drowned Spaniel, The.
Unknown.   Appeal, An.
  Epitaph of a Dog.
  Guinea-Pig Song, A.
  Two gray kits, The.
Updike.   Dog's Death.
Verlaine.   E's Finch.
Watson, S.   Epitaph, An.
Wilbur.   Death of a Toad, The.
  Pardon, The.
Williams, H.   Elegy on a Young Thrush Which Escaped from the Writer's Hand.
Wordsworth, W.   Last of the Flock, The.
Wright, J.   Small Frogs Killed on the Highway.
  Sparrows in a Hillside Drift

Debauchery
Awoonor.   To the Eminent Scholar and Meddler.
Brooks, G.   Rites for Cousin Vit, The.
Chipasula.   Dusk.
Graves, R.   Blue-Fly, The.
Johnson, S.   Short Song of Congratulation [or To a Young Heir], A.
Jonson, B.   On Gut.
Ovid.   Elegies 2.10.
  Elegies 3.1: "Old wood stands uncut, of long years' space, An."
Rochester, J.   Disabled Debauchee, The.
Sherwood, G.   Disabled Debauchee, The.
Thomas, E.   Epistle to Clemena, Occasioned by an Argument She Had Maintained Against the Author.

"W——."   Gentleman's Study, in Answer to The Lady's Dressing-Room, The.
Whitman, W.   Hand-Mirror, A.
Wyatt, T.   Courtier's Life, The.
Debt
Bayly.   Out, John! out, John! what are you about, John?
Cardenal.   He also said to the disciples.
Dickinson, E.   I gave myself to Him——.
Dunbar, P.   Debt, The.
Emerson, R.   Suum Cuique ("Wilt thou seal up the avenues of ill?")
Herrick.   Bell-Man, The.
  Upon Bunce: Epigram.
Horton, G.   Creditor to His Proud Debtor, The.
Hughes, L.   Little Lyric (of Great Importance).
King, B.   If I Should Die Tonight.
Kornilov, V.   Poorer than X.
Mather, J.   File-Hewer's Lamentation, The.
More, H.   Come, neighbour, take a walk with me.
Nguyễn Trãi.   Tired legs won't climb the high road of blue clouds.
Suckling, J.   Love and Debt Alike Troublesome.
Taylor, B.   Promissory Note, The.
Unknown.   I had my good and my.
  Remember it, althought you're far away.
Westmorland.   My Country Audit.
Decadence
Antipater of Sidon.   This is the grave of grey-haired Maronis.
Burns, R.   Lord Galloway.
Cheng Hsieh.   Collecting Antiques.
Cummings, E.   Come,gaze with me upon this dome.
  Space being(don't forget to remember)Curved.
Davis, T.   In the Fire Lane.
Eliot, T.   Burnt Norton.
  Sweeney Among the Nightingales.
  Sweeney Erect.
Ewart.   One for the Anthologies.
Hagedorn, J.   Natural Death.
Kirchwey.   Natural History.
Le Gallienne.   Décadent to His Soul, The.
MacNeice.   Belfast.
  Goodbye to London.
  Individualist Speaks, The.
Meleager.   Foresworn now the love-vows!
Mother Goose.   Curly Locks [!] Curly Locks [!] wilt thou be mine?
Seaman, S.   To a Boy-Poet of the Decadence.
Sitwell, D.   Waltz.
Verma.   Pleasure Dome, The.
Warren, R.   Bearded Oaks.
Wu Chia-chi.   To Ch'eng Fei-t'ao.
Wyatt, T.   Lux, my fair falcon, and your fellows all.
Decalogue. *See* **Ten Commandments**
Decay
Agathias.   Troy.
Auden.   Paysage Moralisé.
Awoonor.   Songs of Sorrow.
Baudelaire.   Carrion, A.
Benn.   Monologue.
Breytenbach.   Asylum.
Brooks.   Throwing Out the Flowers.
Brutus.   This sun on this rubble after rain.
Churchyard.   That humor now, declines for age drawes on.
Clampitt.   Catalpa Tree on West Twelfth Street, A.
Comte de Lautréamont.   I am filthy. Lice gnaw me. Swine, when they look at me, vomit. The scabs.
Crinagoras.   Forehead without scalp, dry shell without yolk of eye.
Davies, H.   Poem: "In the stump of the old tree, where the heart has rotted out."
Dickinson, E.   Crumbling is not an instant's Act.
Disch.   Entropic Villanelle.
Donne.   First Anniversary [or Anniversarie], The.
  From Holy Sonnets.
  Our Love Hath No Decay.
Dransfield.   War of the Roses, The.

Drummond, W.   I know that all beneath the moon decays.
Eberhart, R.   Groundhog, The.
Eglitis.   Winter has already shriveled—spring rushes in with / black burial steeds.
Eliot, T.   Burnt Norton.
  Gerontion.
  Hollow Men, The.
  Portrait of a Lady.
  Preludes.
  Rhapsody on a Windy Night.
  Sweeney Erect.
Frost, R.   Range-finding.
  Wood-Pile, The.
Fumi Saito.   Tanka: "This huge pile."
Ginsberg, A.   Sunflower Sutra.
Glatstein.   If you should be surprised, Nathan.
Graham, J.   Opulence.
Greger.   Notre Dame, Sainte Chapelle, Sacré Coeur by foot—.
  Piranesi in L.A.
Gwynn, R.   Approaching a Significant Birthday, He Peruses The Norton Anthology of Poetry.
Hall, D.   Old Pilot, The.
Heath-Stubbs.   Footnote to Belloc's "Tarantella."
Herbert, G.   Decay.
Herbert, Z.   To Marcus Aurelius.
Herrick.   All Things Decay and Die.
  Putrefaction is the end.
Hughes, T.   Heptonstall Old Church.
Hugo, R.   Death of the Kapowsin Tavern.
  Montana Ranch Abandoned.
Jeffers, R.   Prescription of Painful Ends.
Juan Chi.   Singing of Thoughts.
Kefala.   Freedom fighter, she said, A.
Kelly, R.   Recessional.
Kerouac.   230th Chorus.
Lawrence, A.   Robert Penn Warren's book.
Li Po.   On Climbing the Phoenix Tower at Chinling.
Lowell, R.   As a Plane Tree by the Water.
Matthews, J.   Gravity's the villain in this piece—.
McAuley, J.   Wet Day.
Melo Neto.   Landscape of the Capibaribe River.
Merwin, W.   Losing a Language.
Millay, E.   So she came back into his house again.
Nash, O.   Exit, Pursued by a Bear.
Okamoto.   Tanka: "Cherry petals."
Olson, C.   Kingfishers, The.
Oppen.   Power, The Enchanted World.
Pack, R.   Proton Decay.
Pagis.   Decline of an Empire.
Pao Chao.   Rhyme-Prose on the Desolate City.
Petri.   By an Unknown Poet from Eastern Europe, 1955.
Piercy.   Death of the small commune, The.
Ramanujan.   Elements of Composition.
Rich, A.   Diving into the Wreck.
Robinson, E.   Ballade of Broken Flutes.
  House on the Hill, The.
Rodefer.   Pretext.
Root, J.   Snail Winter.
Saitō Mokichi.   Tanka: "From where."
"Severyanin."   Prologue: "Mirra Lokhvitskaia's ashes are now entombed."
Shelley, P.   Ozymandias [of Egypt].
Shūji.   Tanka: "My body."
Simpson, L.   Inner Part, The.
Slessor.   Choker's Lane.
Southey, R.   Love Indestructible.
Stevens, W.   Worms at Heaven's Gate, The.
Trakl.   Revelation and Decline.
Turner, C.   Lion's Skeleton, The.
Unknown.   Song Bewailing the Time of Christmas, So Much Decayed in England, A.
Vaughan, H.   Friends Departed.
Walker, K.   My Talk with an Elegant Man.
Wilbur.   Junk.
Williams, H.   Sonnet VI. To the Torrid Zone.
Williams, W.   Raleigh Was Right.
Wordsworth, W.   Excursion, The.

I watch, and long have watched, with calm regret.
Wright, J. On the Skeleton of a Hound.
Zenmaro. Tanka: "No news of him."

December
Cane. Tree in December.
Clare, J. December.
Clark, L. Singing in the Streets.
Cranch. December.
Fergusson. Daft Days, The.
Francis, R. December.
Giovanni. December of My Springs, The.
Heard, J. December.
Herford. I heard a bird sing.
Housman, A. Winter.
Keats. Happy Insensibility.
In drear-nighted December.
Kenny, M. December.
Lovelace, R. Grasshopper, The.
Machi. Tanka: "Loneliness."
Ray, H. December.
Sassoon. December Stillness.

Deception
Aeschylus. Chorus sing the doom of Helen, The.
Asclepiades. It is eternally winter.
Barbauld. Tomorrow.
Bayly. Out, John! out, John! what are you about, John?
Bell, M. Stars Which See, Stars Which Do Not See.
Brautigan. Chinese Checker Players, The.
Brecht, B. From a German War Primer.
Brown, D. First Person—1981.
Brownjohn. Negotiation.
Burich. You blow on the hair of your child.
Campion, T. Are you what your faire lookes expresse?
Blame Not My Cheekes.
Elegye, An: "Constant to none, but ever false to me."
I must complain, yet doe enjoy my Love.
Carew, T. Deposition from Love, A.
Looking-Glass, A.
"Carroll." Crocodile, The.
Carryl, G. Sycophantic Fox and the Gullible Raven, The.
Chaucer. Miller's Prologue, The.
Chesterton, G. Aristocrat, The.
Clark, T. Society.
Creeley. If you were going to get a pet.
Son: "What I took in my hand."
Dacey, P. Looking at Models in the Sears Catalogue.
Davis, T. Playing Solitaire.
Dementyev, A. As long as we feel another's pain.
Donne. On His Mistress [or Mistris].
Dunbar, P. Made to Order Smile, The.
We wear the mask that grins and lies.
Dunbar, W. Translation by Mark Willhardt.
Widow Has Buried Her Second Husband, The.
Dunn, S. On Hearing the Airlines Will Use a Psychological Profile to Catch Potential Skyjackers.
What They Wanted.
Duoduo. Untitled.
Elizabeth I. On Monsieur's Departure.
Emerson, R. Maia.
"Ephelia." In the Person of a Lady, to Bajazet, Her Unconstant Gallant.
Floyd. Captain James Leson, U. S. M. C.
Frost, R. Revelation.
Graves, R. Beauty in trouble flees to the good angel.
Friday Night.
Full Moon.
Leda.
Sick Love.
Theseus and Ariadne.
Hall, J. Reel World, The.
Hare, P. Deceit in the Park.
Hayes, A. Much Ado About Nothing, Thanksgiving, 1972.
Heffernan, M. Message, The.
Herrick. Anacreontic.

Chop-Cherry.
Fair[e] Days; or, Dawn[e]s Deceitful[l].
Homer. Cyclops and No-Man.
Horace. 8th Ode of Book I. of Horace imitated in the Cumberland Manner and Dialect, The.
Hughes, T. Childish Prank, A.
Jones, M. Lass of the Hill, The.
King, J. Clichés for an Unfaithful Husband.
Landor, W. You smiled, you spoke, and I believed.
Levchev. Secret Love.
Li K'ai-hsien. Record of a Past Affair, A.
Lingg. Though you can tell me.
Lum. On M. Butterfly.
Mandelstam. For the resounding valor of millennia to come.
Matveyeva. I, he says, am not a warrior.
McBride, M. Loneliness.
McBurney. Croppy Boy, The.
McElroy, C. Horoscope.
Menander. What do you say to this? The thought has just.
Moschus. Into the Mead he comes, nor (seen) doth fright.
Ojaide. When Tomorrow Is Too Long.
Ostriker. Lamenting the Inevitable.
Ovid. 3.13.
To his false Mistress.
Parun. Ballad of the Deceived Flowers.
Peacock, M. Have You Ever Faked an Orgasm?
Plomer. French Lisette: A Ballad of Maida Vale.
Pope, J. Word of Encouragement, A.
Prescod. Vicious Circle.
Prior. Ode, An: "Merchant, to secure his treasure, The."
Phillis's Age.
Scott, W. Oh, what a tangled web we weave.
"Severyanin." Same Old Way, The.
Shakespeare, W. Blind Love.
Set down, set down your honourable load.
Sonnet 95.
Silverstein, S. Sick.
Skoyles. Head of Tasso, The.
Spender, S. Song: "Stranger, you who hide my love."
Stanton, M. Shoplifters.
Stephens, J. Blue Blood.
Su Tung-p'o. Lotus Viewing.
Rhyming with Tzu-yu's "Treading the Green."
Thomas, L. Instructions for Your New Osiris.
Tikhonov. Fire, the rope, the bullet, and the ax, The.
Unknown. Me and My Captain.
On Top of Old Smoky.
Roses are red.
Signifying Monkey, The.
Westphalian Song.
Virgil. Cupid at work.
Queen whom sense of Honor cou'd not move, The.
Warren, R. Mango on the mango tree, The.
Picnic Remembered.
Welch, J. Man from Washington, The.
Wharton, A. Song: "How hardly I concealed my tears."
Whitlow. Book of Routh.
Whitney, I. Ye virgins that from Cupid's tents.
Wroth. Song: "Love a child is ever criing [or crying]."
Sonnet 35: "False [or Faulce] hope which feeds but[t] to destroy, and spill."
Wyatt, T. Mistrustful minds be moved.
To wet your eye withouten tear.
What vaileth [or 'vaileth] truth [or trouth]? or by it to take pain [or payn]?
Ye old mule, that thin[c]k your self so fair [or fayre].
Yeats. Matthew 24:15–31.
Three Bushes, The.

Decisions
Atwood. I made no choice / I decided nothing.
Burrell. Chloe and Myra.

Carew, T. Mediocrity in Love Rejected.
Corbin, A. Love me at last, or if you will not.
Crane, S. Wayfarer / Perceiving the pathway to truth, The.
"Field." Second Thoughts.
Flint, C. Trois, A.
Frost, R. Road Not Taken, The.
Herrick. Neutrality Loathsome.
Khodasevich. Monument, The.
Mihalic. Man Who Decided, The.
Parra, N. I Move the Meeting Be Adjourned.
Patchen. Easy Decision, An.
Roethke. Decision, The.

See also **Free Will**

Decorum
Glück, L. My Neighbor in the Mirror.
Kinnell. To William Carlos Williams.
Meynell, A. Shepherdress, The.
Unknown. See the Rat—at Least It's Got a Hide.

Deer
Argüelles, I. Canto the Tenth.
"Asya." Deer, The.
Benét, S. Daniel Boone.
Benét, W. Fawn in the Snow, The.
Booth, P. Deer Isle.
How to See Deer.
Presence.
Conyus. Upon Leaving the Parole Board Hearing.
Davidson, J. Runnable Stag, A.
Dickinson, E. Wounded Deer—leaps highest, A.
Drinkwater. Deer.
Erdrich. Strange People, The.
Frost, R. Two Look at Two.
Fujiwara No Toshinari. In all the world.
Glück, L. Messengers.
Hardy, T. Fallow Deer at the Lonely House, The.
Harjo, J. Song for the Deer and Myself to Return On.
Hass, R. Image, The.
Hughes, T. Roe-Deer.
Jeffers, R. Deer Lay Down Their Bones, The.
Fawn's Foster-Mother.
Kooser. Finding, A.
Lawrence, D. Doe at Evening, A.
Levien. In the Falling Deer's Mouth.
Lewis, J. Grandmother Remembers, A.
Lovelace, R. La Bella Bona-Roba.
Lyles. Doe's leap, A.
Millay, E. Buck in the Snow, The.
Minamoto no Morotada. In the mountain village.
Miyazawa Kenji. Tanka: "Phosphorescence."
Moore, L. Silent deer the sound of a waterfall.
More, S. Child's Song.
No Ch'ŏn-myŏng. Deer.
Onakatomi Yoshinobu. Deer on pine mountain, The.
Oppen. Psalm: "In the small beauty of the forest."
Papago. There was a mountain, over its black roots [the deer].
Patchen. Deer and the Snake, The.
Petrarch. Whoso list to hunt, I know where is a hind.
Pope, A. To Mr. Gay, Who Wrote Him a Congratulatory Letter on the Finishing His House.
Sarumaru. Deep in the mountain.
Silko. Deer Song.
Sisson. Knole.
Snyder, G. Long Hair.
Two Fawns That Didn't See the Light This Spring.
Spenser. Sonnet 67: "Like a huntsman after weary chase."
Stafford, W. Traveling [or Travelling] through the dark I found a deer.
Tate, J. Pet Deer, The.
Tu Fu. Dawn Over the Mountains.
U Tam'si Tchicaya. Dance to the Amulets.
Unknown. Hunting-Song.
My Hope, My Love.

Wang Chiu-ssu. Song of the Painting of the Long-Life Star.
Warren, R. Sila.
Wyatt, T. Who so list to hount I knowe where is an hynde.
Whoso list to hunt, I know where is an hind.
Yakamochi. Cry of the stag, The.

See also **Hunting and Hunters**

Defeat
Amichai. Elegy: "Wind won't come to draw smiles in dream sand, The."
Arnold, M. Last Word, The.
Avidan. Longterm Hatred.
Bible, *O.T.* David's Lament.
Bynner. What though they conquer us?
Dickinson, E. I took my Power in my Hand.
My Portion is Defeat—today.
Fitzgerald, E. 19.
Foley, M. On the Waterfront.
Glatstein. Ruth.
Herrick. To Virgins.
Hugo, R. Degrees of Gray in Philipsburg.
Hugo, V. Russia 1812.
Jebeleanu. Hannibal.
Komunyakaa. After the Fall of Saigon.
Kovner. On My Words.
Lindsay, V. Broncho That Would Not Be Broken, The.
Padilla. Discourse on Method, The.
Ramanujan. At Forty.
Ransom, J. Prelude to an Evening.
Ritsos. After the Defeat.
Robinson, E. Mighty Runner, A.
Scarborough, G. To the Men Who Lose.
Sedulius Scottus. Heavens, ocean, and all earth, rejoice!
Stevenson, R. O dull cold northern sky.
Thayer, E. Casey at the Bat.
Wright, J. Speak.

Deformities
Elizabeth I. Written in Her French Psalter.
Mother Goose. Tongs.
Warren, R. Child next door is defective because the mother, The.

Degas, Edgar
Wilbur. Museum Piece.

Dehumanization
Craig, C. City Blues.
Mitsui. Destination: Tule Lake Relocation Center, May 20, 1942.
Owen, W. Anthem for Doomed Youth.
Plath. Applicant, The.
Shinder. Prayer.
Simic. Cold, The.

See also **Bureaucracy and Bureaucrats**

Deirdre
Stephens, J. Deirdre.

Deism
Addison, J. Ode: "Spacious firmament on high, The."
Hong, Y. Thunder.
Kerouac. Did I create that sky? Yes, for, if it was.
Masefield. There is no God, as I was taught in youth.

Déjà Vu
Ransom, J. Vision by Sweetwater.

Dejection
"Carroll." Rules and Regulations.
Coleridge, S. Dejection.
Mahon. Dejection.
Shelley, P. Stanzas Written in Dejection, near Naples [*or* —December 1818, near Naples].

See also **Melancholy**

Del Sarto, Andrew. *See* **Sarto, Andrea del**

De la Mare, Walter
Untermeyer, L. Walter de la Mare Tells the Listener about Jack and Jill.

Delaware (state)
Unknown. State Quiz.

Delft, Holland
Mahon. Courtyards in Delft.
Tomlinson, C. At Delft.

Delight
Browning, E. Deserted Garden, The.

Dickinson, E. Delight is as the flight.
Oh Sumptuous moment.
Dunbar, W. Translation by Mark Willhardt.
Widow Has Buried Her Second Husband, The.
Eliot, T. Dedication to My Wife, A.
Fumi Saito. Tanka: "Sweeter than a song."
Marichiko. I hold your head tight.
Shakespeare, W. Sweet-and-Twenty.
Shelley, P. Song: "Rarely, rarely, comest thou."
Stevens, W. Poems of Our Climate, The.
Vidyapati. New Love.
Yang Wan-li. Sitting at Night on the Moonlit Terrace.

Deliverance
Bible, *O.T.* Like unto Them That Dream.
Psalm 59.
Psalm 91.
Psalm 118.
Ciardi. Gift, The.
Jarrell. Jews at Haifa.
Unknown. Didn't my Lord Deliver Daniel.
I to the Lord from My Distress.

Delphi, Oracle of
Lindsay, C. Love or Fame.
Merrill, J. Charioteer of Delphi, The.
Yeats. News for the Delphic Oracle.

Delvaux, Paul
Guthrie, R. Homage to Paul Delvaux.

Demeter
Dove, R. Persephone Underground.
Political.
Greenwell, D. Demeter and Cora.
Unknown. There Ceres, distant from the powers divine.
To Demeter.
Virgil. Hostesse, The.

Democracy
Belloc. On a General Election.
Cummings, E. Thanksgiving (1956).
Euripides. Nothing / Is worse for a city than an absolute ruler.
Freneau. On Mr. Paine's Rights of Man.
Piercy. Councils.
Scott-Heron. Winter in America.
Skovron. Election Eve, with Cat.
Unknown. Equal, An.
Van Wyk. Ballot and the Bullet, The.
Whitman, W. Commonplace I sing, The.
For You O Democracy.
One's-Self I sing, a simple separate person.
Walt Whitman, a kosmos, of Manhattan the son.
Yu Kuang-chung. Mother, I'm hungry.

See also **Voting and Voters**

Demons
Berryman. Whether There Is Sorrow in the Demons.
Burns, R. De'il's [*or* Deil's] Awa wi' th' [*or* the] Exciseman, The.
Chōkū. Tanka: "On Christmas Eve."
Emerson, R. Dæmonic and the Celestial Love, The.
Gippius. Little Demon, The.
Hill, G. Asmodeus.
Milton. Next came one / Who mourn'd in earnest, when the Captive Ark.
Wright, J. Killer, The.

See also **Monsters**

Denial
Browning, E. Denial, A.
"Carroll." My Fairy.
Carver, R. My Daughter and Apple Pie.
Clifton, L. At the Cemetery, Walnut Grove Plantation, South Carolina, 1989.
Dickinson, E. Renunciation—is a piercing Virtue.
Graves, R. Cool Web, The.
She is no liar, yet she will wash away.
Hardy, T. In the Servants' Quarters.
Iverem. Time #2, The.
Lawrence, D. Death Is Not Evil, Evil Is Mechanical.
MacNeice. Mixer, The.
Meynell, A. Renouncement.
Ransom, J. Good Ships.

Rich, A. What Kind of Times Are These.
Wright, F. Pawtucket Postcards.

Denmark
Evald. King Christian.
Oehlenschläger. There Is a Charming Land.

Dentistry and Dentists
Ostriker. Anxiety about Dying.

Dentures
Blyton, C. Night Starvation or The Biter Bit.
Dickey, W. Poet's Farewell to His Teeth, The.
Tô Giang Tử. Congratulating a Friend On His New Dentures.

Denver, Colorado
Ferril. Waltz against the Mountains.

Department Stores
Alexander, E. Ladders.
Derricotte. Weakness, The.
Farber. For a Quick Exit.
Swenson, M. Fixture, A.

Deportation
Unknown. On Queen Caroline.

Depression (economic). *See* **Great Depression**

Depression (psychological). *See* **Melancholy; Mental Illness**

Dereliction
Wordsworth, W. Decay of Piety.

Descartes, René
Dunn, S. Something Like Happiness.
Tomlinson, C. Descartes and the Stove.

Deserts
Ali, A. Desert Landscape.
Austin, M. Song of the Maverick.
Carruth, H. Rimrock, Where It Is.
Coolidge, C. Morning muezzin in orange and a mosquito.
Currey. Burial Flags.
Drummond de Andrade. Travelling in the Family.
Dugan, A. Against the Text "Art Is Immortal."
Forbes, C. Dark Mirror.
Garioch. Property.
Hadewijch. Knowing Love in Herself.
Hall, S. Poppies of Wickenburg.
Holub. Gila Desert in Arizona, The.
Hope, A. Australia.
Illyés. Logbook of a Lost Caravan.
Jabès. Desert, II, The.
Jarrell. Range in the Desert, The.
Karpowicz. Artistic Copy.
Kipling, R. Pelicans in the Wilderness (A Grave near Halfa).
Kirattanar. What Her Girl Friend Said before the elopement.
Korn. Thirty-one Camels, The.
Kunio. Tanka: "I've swept away."
Kunitz, S. Old Cracked Tune, An.
Langworthy. Drifting Sands and a Caravan.
Longfellow, H. Sand of the Desert in an Hour-Glass.
Lowry, M. Death of a Oaxaquenian.
MacLean, S. Going Westwards.
Major, N. Lost in the Desert.
Mandelstam. Bread is poisoned and the air's drunk dry, The.
Markham, E. In Death Valley.
Martinez, V. It Is Not.
McAuley, J. Envoi.
McClintock, M. Glimmering morning.
Eide canyon, A
Mechthild von Magdeburg. Desert Has Many Teachings, The.
Melville, H. In the Desert.
Mora. La Migra.
Morgan, E. Dowser, The.
Patmore, C. Two Deserts, The.
Plath. Sleep in the Mojave Desert.
Rabéarivelo. Cactus.
Robinson, A. Oasis, An.
Rokeah. Negev.
Rossetti, C. I dug and dug amongst the snow.
Sachs, N. Your eyes, O my beloved.
Santos, S. Near the Desert Test Sites.
Shelley, P. Ozymandias [of Egypt].
Shelton, R. Sonora for Sale.
Tomlinson, C. Death in the Desert, A.

Unknown. I walked in a desert.
Whittemore, R. Day with the Foreign Legion, A.
Whittier. Song of Slaves in the Desert.
Woo, D. Eden.
Zukofsky, L. In Arizona / (how many years in the mountains).

Desire
Adamson. Action Would Kill It / A Gamble.
"Æ." Desire.
Alberti. Homecoming of Love Amongst Illustrious Ruins.
Alegría. Savoir Faire.
Alford, H. You and I.
Alvarez, J. He: Age doesn't matter when you're both in love.
Amaru. When his mouth faced my mouth, I turned aside.
Amichai. Quick And Bitter.
3.
Anacreon. Love.
Wounded Cupid. Song, The.
You recount old tales of Thebes.
Andal. We rose before dawn.
Angelou. On Diverse Deviations.
Angus. Invitation.
Antipater of Sidon. Bitto gives to Athena.
Armantrout. Attention.
Arnaut Daniel. Resolute desire that enters, The.
Asclepiades. Didyme waved her wand at me.
To a Girl.
Ashbery. Blessing in Disguise, A.
Lament Upon the Waters, The.
Atwood. Against Still Life.
There Is Only One of Everything.
Variation on the Word *Sleep.*
Woman Who Could Not Live With Her Faulty Heart, The.
Awoonor. Lovers' Song.
Baker, H. Love's an headstrong wild desire.
Rapture, The.
Barker, J. To My Young Lover.
Barlas. Terrible Love.
Barnes, J. Dog Days 1978.
Barnfield. Sighing, and sadly sitting by my Love.
Sometimes I wish that I his pillow were.
Basheva. Business.
Baudelaire. Giantess, The.
Head of Hair, The.
She Is Not Satisfied.
Becker, R. Story I Like to Tell, The.
Beckett, S. Cascando.
Behn, A. In Imitation of Horace.
Song: Love Armed.
Song: "Oh! Love, that stronger art than wine."
Thousand Martyrs I Have Made, A.
To the Fair Clarinda, Who Made Love to Me, Imagin'd More Than Woman.
Bensley. Desires.
Benveniste. Blue Crêpe.
Bergman, D. Blueberry Man.
Bernard. Good time of the year, The.
Berryman. Desires of Men and Women.
Dream Song 4.
Beveridge. Dining Out.
Blake, W. Abstinence sows sand all over.
Question Answered, The [*or* A].
Blandiana. Dance in the Rain.
Blind. Once we played at love together.
Bogan, L. Dream, The.
Masked Woman's Song.
Bogin, G. Nineteen.
Boker. Farewell once more,—and yet again farewell!
If she should give me all I ask of her.
Boland, E. In Her Own Image.
Bold, A. Love-Lowe.
Borson. Lust.
Braley, B. Success ("If you want a thing bad enough").
Breton, N. Assurance, An.
Brooks, G. Ballad of Chocolate Mabbie, The.
Broughton, J. Wondrous the Merge.
Broumas, O. She Loves.
Sleeping Beauty.

Browning, E. Man's Requirements, A.
Sonnet: "Can it be right to give what I can give?"
Sonnet: "Let the world's sharpness, like a clasping knife."
Brownstein. Oracle night / the porch is frozen.
Burns, R. Green sleeves and tartan ties.
Mary Morison.
Tam Glen.
Cady. Starting 1973: What to Do Now that Peace Has Been Announced.
Calbert. Woman Who Loved Things, The.
Callimachus. I despise neo-epic verse sagas.
Campion, T. Be thou then my beauty named.
Beauty, since you so much desire.
Fain would I wed a fair young man that night and day could please me.
First Love.
Follow, follow[e] / Though with mischiefe.
Shall I come, if I swim? wide are the waves, you see.
Sleep, angry beauty, sleep, and fear[e] not me.
So quicke, so hot, so mad is thy fond sute.
Song: "O sweet delight, O more than human[e] bliss[e]."
Campo. For J. W.
Carew, T. Mediocrity in Love Rejected.
To My Worthy Friend Master George Sands [*or* Sandys], on His Translation of the Psalms.
To One That Desired to Know My Mistress [*or* Mistris].
Catti Natanar. What He Said ("As a little white snake").
Catullus. Carmen 5 ("My sweetest Lesbia, let us live and love").
Carmen 45 ("Phyllis Corydon clutched to him").
Catullus to Lesbia.
Many think Quintia's beautiful. She's tall.
Sappho.
Cavafy. Body, remember not only how much you were loved.
One Night.
Return other and take me.
Cavalli. But first one must free oneself.
Far from kingdoms.
Chartier. I turn you out of doors.
Chaucer. Hide, Absolon, thy gilte tresses clere.
Song of Troylus, The.
Cheney-Coker. On Being a Poet in Sierra Leone.
Ch'in Kuan. Tune: "Courtyard Full of Fragrance."
"Chrystos." Getting Down.
Chudleigh. Song: "Why Damon, why, why, why so pressing?"
Ch'ung. Parody of a Lover.
Cisneros, S. You Called Me Corazón.
Clare, J. First Love.
Clark, M. Summer, At Home.
Clark, T. Doors.
Conoley. Heroes, Saints, and Neighbors.
I'd like a little love in the wine-red Afternoon.
Some Gangster Pain.
Cooper, J. My Past.
Corbière. To the Eternal Feminine.
Corn. Older Men.
Cornish, W. You and I and Amyas.
Crane, H. Legend.
Creeley. Ballad of the Despairing Husband.
For W.C.W ("Rhyme is after, The").
Crozier, A. In the time it takes.
Csoori. Bachelor, The.
Cuddihy. Pendulum, The.
Cullen, C. Timid Lover.
Cummings, E. First of all my dreams was of, The.
Goodby Betty,don't remember me.
It is at moments after i have dreamed.
Item.
My sweet old etcetera.
Notice the convulsed orange inch of moon.
Somewhere i have never travelled, gladly beyond.
Thy fingers make early flowers of.
When my sensational moments are no more.

Cummins, J. Sestina.
Cutts. To a Lady, Who Desired Me Not To Be in Love with Her.
Dacre, C. Power of Love, The.
Sappho; or, The Resolve.
Darr. At Sixteen.
Das, J. In Camp.
Davidson, M. Century of Hands.
Davies, M. Love Song: "There is a strong wall about me to protect me."
Davis, T. Desire 1.
Day Lewis. Desire is a witch.
De. Santhal Poems, 1.
De Vere, E. Lively lark stretched forth her wing, The.
Dewdney. She is liquid darkness occult with desire.
Dickinson, E. I cannot live with You.
To see her is a Picture.
Wild Nights—Wild Nights!
Diên Nghi. Her Story.
Dioscorides. My downfall: those pink articulate lips.
Dipoko. Poem of Villeneuve St Georges, A.
Dixon, S. Request of Alexis, The.
Doinas, S. Woman in the Mirror, The.
Donahue, J. Desire's green / and gold corona / in the wavering branch.
Donne. Canonization, The.
Lovers' Infiniteness[e].
Doolittle, H. Helmsman, The.
D'Orleans. Not long ago I hied me apace.
Dove, R. Secret Garden, The.
Sunday Greens.
Dowson. Benedictio Domini
Non Sum Qualis Eram Bonae sub Regno Cynara[e].
Dransfield. Epiderm.
Memoirs of a Velvet Urinal.
Drayton. These verses weare made By Michaell Drayton Esquier Poett Lawreatt the night before hee dyed.
Du Bellay. To Venus.
Duesing. Blossoming.
Duffy, M. I am beset with a dream of fair woman.
Semi-Skilled Lover.
Dumbrveanu. Genesis.
Duncan, R. Eyesight II.
Preface to the Suite: "Childhood, boyhood, young manhood."
Dunn, S. Tenderness.
Truck Stop: Minnesota.
DuPlessis, R. Mirror Poem.
Elenkov. Ten Girls.
"Eliot." How Lisa Loved the King.
Eliot, T. Dedication to My Wife, A.
Elizabeth I. When I was fair and young, then [*or* and] favour graced me;.
Emanuel, L. Desire.
Emerson, R. To Rhea.
"Ephelia." Love's First Approach.
To J.G. on the News of His Marriage.
"Ern Malley." Night Piece.
Euripides. Oh Love! oh Love! whose shafts of fire.
Ewart. Clarissa Harlowe Poem, The.
Office Friendships.
"Field." Caput Tuum Ut Carmelus.
Ebbtide at Sundown.
Fletcher, J. Take, oh, take those lips away.
Fraser, K. Because you aren't here to be what I can't think of I need most.
Frost, R. Fire and Ice.
Frym. Yield, The.
Fujiwara no Sadaie. You do not come, and I wait.
García Lorca. Sleepwalkers' Ballad.
Garrigue. From Venice was that afternoon.
To speak of my influences.
Gascoigne. For That He Looked Not upon Her.
Lullaby [*or* Lullabie] of a Lover, The.
Gerstler. Unforseen, The.
Gibbons, S. Truce, The.
Gill, G. Girl's desire moves among her bangles, The.

Ginsberg, A.   Green Automobile, The.
Kaddish.
Shrouded Stranger, The.
Why Is God Love, Jack?
Giorno.   Life Is a Killer.
Scum & Slime.
Gioseffi.   Toward the Greater Romance, Please Place Roses in my Skull (A Tantric Love Song).
Glück, L.   Elms.
Godfrey.   One or More Together.
Wings.
Goldberg, B.   In the Badlands of Desire.
Goodman, P.   Long Lines: Youth and Age.
Gouri.   Album.
Graves, R.   Quiet Glades of Eden, The.
Symptoms Of Love.
Young Cordwainer, The.
Greene, R.   Palmer's Ode, The.
Greger.   Frog in the Swimming Pool, The.
Greville, F.   Sonnet ("All my senses, like beacon's flame").
Grimké, A.   Brown Girl.
Triolet, A.
Guillén, N.   Don't Know No English.
Gumilyov.   Sixth Sense, The.
Hacker, M.   Another Sunday.
Conclusion: "Did you love well what very soon you left?"
Future Conditional.
Runaways Café I.
Hadas, R.   Mars and Venus.
Three Silences.
Hadewijch II.   If I desire something, I know it not.
Hafiz.   Ode 105.
Hagiwara Sakutaro.   Lover of Love.
Hall, D.   Mangosteens.
Hall, D.   "Reclining Figure."
Hammond, W.   Delay, whose parents Phlegm and Slumber are.
Hardy, T.   To Meet, or Otherwise.
Harms.   Tomorrow, We'll Dance in America.
Harryman.   Matter.
Harwood, L.   As your eyes are blue.
Hawthorne, N.   Oh, Man can seek the downward glance.
Herrick.   Charme, or an Allay for Love, A.
Frozen Zone; or, Julia Disdainful, The.
Hymne to Love, An.
Julia's Petticoat.
Night-Piece, to Julia, The.
To Anthea ("Let's call for Hymen if agreed thou art").
To Electra.
Upon Julia['s] Washing Herself in the River.
Upon Julia's Clothes.
Upon Love, by Way of Question and Answer.
What Kind of Mistress[e] He Would Have.
Hewett, D.   Sunset flames over the city, The.
You Gave Me Hyacinths First a Year Ago.
Hill, G.   And you my spent heart's treasure.
Hirshfield, J.   Of Gravity & Angels.
To Drink.
Ho Xuan Huong.   Girl Caught Napping By Day, A.
On Picking Flowers.
"Hope."   Request.
Horace.   Odes 1.25: Ribald Romeos Less and Less Berattle ("Parcius iunctas quatiunt fenestras").
Odes 1.5.
Hovey.   Song by the Shore, A.
Hsiao-Wei.   For My Wife.
Huang T'ing-chien.   Tune: "Pleasure of Returning to the Fields: A Prelude."
Hughes, L.   Advice.
Hugo, R.   Letter to Welch from Browning.
Ise.   Is it your command.
Izumi.   I picked an azalea.
Jackson, H.   Tides.
Jamie.   Black Spiders.
Jeffers, R.   Divinely Superfluous Beauty.
Maid's Thought, The.
Jennings, E.   First Love.
Thinking of Love.
John of the Cross.   Dark Night, The.

Jonson, B.   Song. To Celia ("Come my Celia, let us prove").
József.   Freight trains are pulling in.
Juana Inés de la Cruz.   Happy Easter, my Lady.
My Divine Lysi.
Kalász.   Maiden.
Kamatari.   Hey! Ho! Hurrah!
Kanemori.   Although I hide it.
Kantaris.   Body Language.
Karandikar.   Knot, The.
Kasa.   I dreamed I held / A sword against my flesh.
I love and fear him.
Kästner.   Moral Taxi Ride, The.
Keats.   Stanzas: "You say you love; but with a voice."
Kenyon, J.   August Rain, after Haying.
Kessler, M.   All their names were Vincent, Ernie, Paul.
Khlebnikov, V.   Once again, once again.
Kim, S.   Song by the Brook.
Kinzie.   Want, predation, sleep.
Kirsch, S.   Air already smells like snow, my lover, The.
Date.
Kirschner.   Fall of Light, The.
Komunyakaa.   Imhotep.
Thorn Merchant's Mistress, The.
Kovner.   Hour's Late, The.
Vow.
Kowit.   What chord did she pluck in my soul.
Kuan Yün-shih.   Tune: "Rapt with Wine, Loudly Singing; Joy in Spring's Coming."
Laird, C.   Sea at Evening, The.
Landor, W.   Thou hast not rais'd, Ianthe, such desire.
Larkin, P.   Wants.
Lasker-Schüler.   To The Barbarian.
Lawrence, D.   Basta!
Desire.
Desire Is Dead.
Grasshopper Is a Burden.
In Trouble and Shame.
Manifesto.
Mess of Love, The.
On the Balcony.
Leapor.   Strephon to Celia.
Leconte de Lisle, C.   Palanquin, The.
Lee, L.   Irises.
Lehman.   Guilt Trip.
Levchev.   Appassionato.
Carmen, or the Made-Up Girl.
Secret Love.
Levertov.   Quest, The.
Sea's Wash in the Hollow of the Heart, The.
Levine, P.   Poem Circling Hamtramck, Michigan, All Night in Search of You, The.
Li Ch'ing-chao.   Tune: "Song of Picking Mulberry."
Li Shang-yin.   Spring Rain.
Lihn.   Dark Room, The.
Lorde.   Conversations in Crisis.
Lovelace, R.   Dialogue.
Love Made in the First Age[: To Chloris].
To a Lady That Desired Me I Would Bear My Part with Her in a Song.
Lowell, A.   Bullion.
Lu Chih.   Tune: "Wu-t'ung Leaves"—Written in Jest at a Banquet.
Lu Yu.   Tune: Phoenix Hairpin.
Lucretius.   Euphemisms of the love-blind.
Lum.   Urban Love Songs.
Lyly, J.   Cards and Kisses.
Mackenzie, K.   Fool, The.
Mager.   Beloved,/ What does it take to put a house in order?
Mahapatra, A.   Spell.
Maitre.   Woman Underneath, The.
Mandel, T.   Say Ja.
Mandelstam.   Tristia.
Manley, D.   Song: "Ah, Dangerous Swain, tell me no more."
Mansfield, K.   Secret Flowers.
March, A.   Know what I'm like? Some captain moors his ship.
Marichiko.   Every morning.

Marlowe.   Men of wealthy Sestos, every year, The.
Martial.   Either get out of the [my] house or conform to my tastes, woman.
Marutanilanakanar.   What Her Girl Friend Said to her.
Marvell.   Ametas and Thestylis Making Hay-Ropes.
Match, The.
Mower's Song, The.
Maunick.   Further off is the measured force the word of the sea.
May, S.   House.
Mayakovsky.   Mayakovsky's Suicide Note.
McAuley, J.   Legendary.
Mechthild von Magdeburg.   God Speaks to the Soul.
How God Answers the Soul.
Melville, H.   After the Pleasure Party.
In a Bye-Canal.
Meredith, G.   He felt the wild beast in him betweenwhiles.
Sonnet 29: "Am I failing? For no longer can I cast."
This golden head has wit in it. I live.
This I may know: her dressing and undressing.
We three are on the cedar-shadowed lawn.
Merrill, J.   Kimono, The.
Octopus, The.
Merry.   Adieu and Recall to Love, The.
Mesens.   Arid Husband, The.
Michelangelo Buonarroti.   Love's Justification.
Millay, E.   Philosopher, The.
Miller, R.   Aspects of Love.
Minamoto no Tōru   Like Michinoku.
Monk, M.   Fire Us with Ice, Burn Us with Snow.
Montagu, L.   Man in Love, A.
Receipt to Cure [or for] the Vapours, A.
To a Lady Making Love.
Moon, T.   Song for Grass Leaf.
Moore, T.   Did Not.
Moraes, D.   Snow on a Mountain.
Morgan, V.   Within the Greenhouse Effect.
Mouré.   She Touched Me.
Muldoon, P.   Something of a Departure.
Mullen, H.   Muse & Drudge.
Muruvalar.   What He Said.
Musgrave.   Exchange of Fire.
Nguyễn Bính.   Girl Next Door, The.
Nguyễn Công Trú'.   Ode to All Flowers.
Nordbrandt.   Our love is like Byzantium.
Norse.   You Must Have Been a Sensational Baby.
North, C.   From the French.
Oates.   Growing Together.
Ofeimun.   Gong, A.
O'Hara, F.   Poem: "I don't know as I get what D.H. Lawrence is driving at."
Poem: "O solo mio, hot diggety, nix 'I wather think I can'."
Ojaide.   What They Said.
Oliver, M.   Blossom.
Olson, C.   Chockablock Once a man was traveling through the woods, and.
Ono no Komachi.   He does not come.
Oppen.   Forms of Love, The.
Orampokiyar.   What She Said ("In his place, mother / field-crabs cut into the pink").
O'Reilly, J.   White Rose, A.
Ovid.   1.5.
'Twas now the mid of Night, when Slumbers close.
Owens, R.   Devils Clowns and Women.
Parra, N.   Pilgrim, The.
Pattanshetti.   Woman / is a problem negative.
Peacock, M.   Desire.
Wheel, The.
Pearse, P.   Renunciation.
Peele.   Bethsabe's Song.
Pennant.   Wildebeest of Carmine Street, The.
Pessoa.   She brings the surprise of being.
Petronius Arbiter.   I had just gone to bed.
Peyanar.   What He Said ("As the deer begin to hide").
Pinsky.   Want Bone, The.
Poe.   To F——.

Pond, L. Ovulation.
Porete. Beloved, what do you want of me?
Porter, D. Lollies Noir.
P. M. T.
Porter, P. Now it's in all the novels, what's pornography to do?
Poseidippus. If Pythias has a customer.
Pound, E. Na Audiart.
Prévert. River, The.
Propertius. Me happy, night, night full of brightness.
Ralegh, W. Concei[p]t begotten by the eyes.
Randolph, T. Milkmaid's Epithalamium, The.
Rankin, J. Love Affair 36.
Ravikovitch. Surely You Remember.
Trying Again.
Rexroth, K. Every morning, I / Wake alone, dreaming my.
I sit at my desk.
You ask me what I thought about.
Rice, H. Prayer for the Young and Lovely, A.
Rich, A. Re-forming the Crystal.
Two Songs.
Ridge, J. Cherokee Love Song, A.
Stolen White Girl, The.
Riley, D. It Really Is the Heart.
Roberts, K. How Late Desire Looks.
Robinson, C. We who have loved, alas! may not be friends.
Robinson, E. John Evereldown.
Tavern, The.
Robinson, K. On the Corner.
Rochester, E. Song: "Nothing ades to Loves fond fire."
Roethke. Her Longing.
I knew a woman, lovely in her bones.
Long Waters, The.
Marrow, The.
Renewal, The.
Rose, The.
Sequel, The.
She.
Swan, The.
Voice, The.
Rokeah. Zealots of Yearning.
Ronsard. Sonnet For Helen.
Rossetti, C. Soeur Louise de la Miséricorde (1674).
What would I give for a heart of flesh to warm me thro'.
Roughton. Soluble Noughts and Crosses; or, California, Here I Come.
Rowe, E. To Orestes.
Rózewicz. Draft for a Contemporary Love Poem.
Rufinus. Rhodope.
Rukeyser, M. Cries From Chiapas.
Eyes of Night-Time.
Looking at Each Other.
Meeting, The.
Samio. Tanka: "Memories open."
Sandburg, C. At a Window.
Evening Waterfall.
Gone.
Joy.
Sansom, M. NoTL.
To My Heavenly Charmer.
Sappho. He is More than a Hero.
High on the upper, outermost bough.
Honestly I'd as soon be dead!
Percussion, salt and honey.
Thank you, my dear.
Sarton. Prothalamion for an Autumn Wedding.
Sassoon. Foot Inspection.
Scalapino. Floating Series 2.
Scannell. Act of Love.
Schuyler, J. Tom.
Schwartz, D. Heavy Bear, The.
Schwitters. Anna Blossom Has Wheels.
Desire.
Seifert. Fingerprints.
Senghor. Song of the Initiate.
Sexton. Farmer's Wife, The.
Shakespeare, W. Song: "It was a lover and his lass."
Sonnet 46.
Sonnet 52.

Sonnet 56.
Sonnet 114.
Sonnet 129.
Sonnet 144.
Sonnet 147.
Sonnet 150.
Shapiro, K. Haircut.
Shelley, M. Stanzas: "Oh, come to me in dreams, my love!"
Shirley, J. Lover that Durst Not Speak to His M[istress], A.
Shūji. Tanka: "Red flowers."
Shurin. Forward or Back.
Sidney, P. Second Song: "Have I caught my heav'nly jewel."
Sonnet 14: "Alas, have I not pain enough, my friend."
Sonnet 39: "Come Sleep, O Sleep."
Sonnet 52: "Strife is grown between Virtue and Love, A."
Sonnet 56: "Fie, school of Patience, fie; your lesson is."
Sonnet 71: "Who will in fairest book of Nature know."
Sonnet 72: "Desire, though thou my old companion art."
Sweeter Saint I Serve, A.
Thou blind man's mark, thou fool's self-chosen snare.
Sitwell, D. Heart and Mind.
King of China's Daughter, The.
Skelton, J. Mannerly Margery Mylk and Ale.
Smith, S. Love me, Love me, I cried to the rocks and the trees.
Snyder, G. For a Far-out Friend.
Four Poems for Robin.
Manichaeans, The.
So Chong-Ju. Flower-Patterned Snake.
Södergran. Instinct.
Spencer, B. Egyptian Dancer at Shubra.
Spenser. Eftsoones they heard a most melodious sound.
For round about, the wals yclothed were.
Legend of the Knight of the Red Crosse, or of Holinesse, The.
Sonnet 30: "My love is like to ice, and I to fire."
Sonnet 73: 'Being my self captived here'.
Steele, T. Aubade, An.
Eros.
Stein, G. Lifting belly. Are you. Lifting.
Stevens, W. Bouquet of Belle Scavoir.
Stramm. Encounter.
Strand. Courtship.
Strauss, J. Love Notes.
Suckling, J. Against Absence.
Miracle, The.
Sonnet: "Dost see how unregarded now."
Sonnet: "Of thee, kind boy, I ask no red and white."
Sulpicia. Sulpicia to Cerinthus.
Surrey. Complaint by Night of the Lover Not Beloved, A.
Since fortune's wrath envieth the wealth.
Too dearly had I bought my green and youthful years.
Swinburne. Love And Sleep.
Sapphics.
Sylvester, J. But, fair Iëmpsar (wife of Potiphar).
Symons, A. To a Dancer.
Taylor, E. Song: "Strephon has fashion, wit and youth."
Tennyson, A. 27.
If I were loved, as I desire to be.
"O Swallow, Swallow, flying, flying south".
Theocritus. O NICIAS, there is no other remedy for love.
Thomas, E. Remedia Amoris.
To Colindra.
Thomson, J. For ever, Fortune, wilt thou prove.
One day the god of fond desire.
Tibullus. Elegies 1.iv: "Far from the tender Tribe of Boys remove."
Timrod. La Belle Juive.
Tollet. On Loving Once and Loving Often.

Tomlinson, C. Death of Will, The.
Traherne. Insatibleness.
Tripathy. Tryst.
Tuckerman, F. Question, The.
Tysh, C. In the morning one often feels.
Uflyand. It has for ages been observed.
Ullman. Desire.
Unknown. Alison.
Aphrodite reveals herself.
Art thou that she than whom none fairer is.
Aurora and Tithonus.
Cock Robin got up early.
Come, come, my companion.
Constant Mouse, The.
Cow Boy's Lament.
CRUEL, you pull away too soon your lips whenas you kiss me.
Do you remember that night?
Down in Yonder Meadow [where the green grass].
Fragrance comes from the scent I wear, The.
Hares on the Mountain.
I love thee for thy fickleness.
Lady, those cherries plenty.
Lavender's Blue.
Love Song: "I will walk into some one's dwelling."
Marvelous Encounter at Blue Creek, The.
My lover will soon be here.
O western wind when wilt thou blow.
Out the southern gate at sundown.
Sing, Muse, the Force, and all-informing Fire.
Song of Songs.
Swampland Mulberries Are Lovely.
There is a lady sweet and kind.
To His Love.
Tune: "Joy in Spring's Coming"—Seven Songs.
Turkish Bakery, The.
Vallejo. Poem to Be Read and Sung.
Vanhomrigh. Hail, blushing goddess, beauteous Spring!
Vaughan, H. To Amoret, of the Difference 'twixt Him and Other Lovers, and What True Love Is.
Villanueva, A. Peace #3.
Virgil. Aeneas' firmness.
But she who Love long since had swallowed down.
Come to my longing Arms, my lovely care.
Love and the Creatures.
Love-charm, A.
Vivien. Roses Rising.
Waldrop, R. Feverish Propositions.
Walton, E. In Recompense.
Walwicz. Tattoo, The.
Warren, R. Birth of Love.
Wearne. Division of O'Dowd, The.
Elise.
Terri.
Weinfield. Song for the In-Itself and For-Itself.
Welish. Veil.
Wetzsteon. Dinner at Le Caprice.
Three Songs.
Whitman, W. As Adam early in the morning.
Fast-anchor'd eternal O love! O woman I love!
From pent-up aching rivers.
I heard you solemn-sweet pipes of the organ as last Sunday morn I pass'd the church.
Not heat flames up and consumes.
O you whom I often and silently come where you are that I may be with you.
To the garden the world anew ascending.
When I heard at the close of the day how my name had been receiv'd with plaudits in the capitol, still it was not a happy night for me that follow'd.
Whittier. Henchman, The.
Wieseltier. Love Poem: "Greyish yellow is the color of the dust."
Wilbur. Playboy.
She.
Voice from under the Table, A.
Wilcox, E. Attraction.
Williams, W. Woman Walking.

Willis, N.   Lady in the White Dress, Whom I
  Helped into the Omnibus, The.
Wordsworth, D.   When shall I tread your
  garden path.
Wright, C.   On the Eve of Our Mutually
  Assured Destruction.
Wright, J.   Lights in the hallway, The.
  Poem about Breasts, A.
  Sappho.
Wright, J.   Cradle Logic of Autumn, The.
Wright, J.   Metho Drinker.
  To a Child.
Wroth.   Song: "Love a child is ever criing [or
  crying]."
Sonnet 35: "False [or Faulce] hope which
  feeds but[t] to destroy, and spill."
Sonnet 39.
Wyatt, T.   For want of [or I] will in woe I
  plain.
  If fancy [or fansy] would favour.
  If thou wilt mighty be, flee from the rage.
  Lover Showeth How He Is Forsaken of Such
    as He Sometime Enjoyed, The.
  So unwarely was never no man caught.
  Sometime I fled the fire that me brent.
  Sonnet: 'The long love'.
Xuân Diệu.   Fool In Love, A.
  Orange With the Rind Still Green, An.
  You Must Say It.
Y Vân Tử'.   Gaffer in Love, A.
Yeats.   Politics.
  What Then?
Yesenin.   Today I asked the money changer.
  You feel no love or pity for me.
Yozei Emperor.   Falling from the ridge.
Yuhara.   Let us bribe the Moon God.
Zabolotsky.   Ivanovs, The.
Zenodotus.   Statue Of Eros, A.
Zivancevic.   Duende.

See also **Erotic Love; Lust**

Desks
Mahon.   Table Talk.
Samio.   Tanka: "With the blue."
Smith, D.   Desks.
Tsvetayeva.   Desk.
Willmot.   Novel's end.

Desolation
Ackerman, D.   Lines Written in a Pittsburgh
  Skyscraper.
Akers.   Night: Volcano, California.
Belloc.   Ha'nacker Mill.
Bobrowski.   Deserted House, The.
Bontemps.   Blight.
Brontë, E.   Remembrance.
Browning, E.   Sonnet: "Thou hast thy calling
  to some palace-floor."
Byron, G.   Darkness.
Campion, T.   Raving warre, begot / In the
  thirstye sands.
Chế Lan Viên.   Silk Threads of Memory.
Cooley.   Ararat.
Creeley.   Marriage, A.
Daryush.   It is pleasant to hang out.
Faiz.   Tyrant, The.
Finch, R.   Last Visit.
Follain.   School and Nature.
Fort, C.   How Old Are the People of the
  World.
Ginsberg, A.   In Back of the Real.
Harteis.   Hermit's Curse, The.
Henri, A.   Adrian Henri's Talking after
  Christmas Blues.
Hill, S.   Looking for Camels.
Hughes, T.   That Moment.
Hugo, R.   Letter to Scanlon from Whitehall.
Jeffers, R.   Place for No Story, The.
Jones, R.   Progress Alley.
Jordan.   When A Woman Gets Blue.
Joseph, L.   Do What You Can.
Knight, E.   Feeling Fucked/Up Up.
Lowry, M.   Delirium in Vera Cruz.
Lux.   Grim Town in a Steep Valley.
McNair.   House in Spring.
Pace, R.   This Is English and I Am Speaking
  It No Matter What.
Ransom, J.   Emily Hardcastle, Spinster.
Ritsos.   Return.

Roberts, G.   Burnt Lands.
Shelley, P.   Tower of Famine, The.
Smith, C.   Unhappy exile, whom his fates
  confine, The.
Southwick.   Ruins, The.
Stanton, M.   Shoplifters.
Thomas, D.   Hand that signed the paper felled
  a city, The.
Tóth, J.   Forest.
Very.   Lament of the Flowers, The.
Wang Shih-chieng.   Mooring at Night at Kao-
  yu.
  Mooring at Night at the River Mouth, I Heard
    a Flute—Sent to My Elder Brother Hsi-
    ch'iao.
Wu Wei-yeh.   Seeing Off Sun Ling-hsiu on
  His Journey to Chen-ting.
Yeats.   Meru.
Zimmer.   Eisenhower Years, The.

Despair
Adamovich.   Autumn night, in a hotel, the two,
  An.
Ai.   Man with the Saxophone, The.
"Akhmatova."   Everything Is Plundered[,
  betrayed, sold].
  Slander.
  Twenty-first. Night. Monday.
  You know, I languish here.
"Aminado."   Honest with Oneself.
Anacreon.   Word has come to me that she.
"Ansky."   Tailor, The.
Arnold, M.   Self-Dependence.
  To Marguerite.
Awoonor.   Agosu if you go tell them.
Baker, D.   Snow Figure.
Baraka.   Poem Some People Will Have to
  Understand, A.
Barber, M.   On Seeing an Officer's Widow
  Distracted.
Barnes, B.   O Powers Celestial, with what
  sophistry.
  Why do I draw this coole releeving ayer.
Beckett, S.   Cascando.
Behn, A.   Song, A.
Berryman.   Sonnet 115: "As usual I'm up
  before the sun."
Beshenkovskaya.   In a land whose prosperity
  constantly grows.
Bialik.   Dance of Despair, The.
Blake, W.   Sick Rose, The.
  Song: "My silks and fine array."
Blamire.   Written on a Gloomy Day, in
  Sickness.
Bly, R.   Snowbanks North of the House.
  When the Dumb Speak.
Brody.   Cry of the Peoples, The.
Bronk.   World, The.
Brontë, E.   F. de Samara to A. G. A.
  I know not how it falls on me.
  It will not shine again.
  Sympathy.
  Wind, I hear it sighing, The.
Browning, E.   Mask, The.
Brutus.   Endurance.
Byron, G.   Lines Written beneath a Picture.
Campion, T.   Breake now my heart and dye!
  Oh no, she may relent.
Cassian.   Morning Exercises.
Castro, R.   Black Mood.
Chin.   We Are Americans Now, We Live in
  the Tundra.
Chitre.   My father travels on the late evening
  train.
Chu Shu-chen.   Morning.
Chudakov.   When they cry: / "Man overboard."
Chukhonstev.   Epistle to Baron Delvig.
Clare, J.   Written in a Thunder Storm July
  15th, 1841.
Clifton, L.   Crazy Horse Instructs the Young
  Men But In Their Grief They Forget.
Coleridge, M.   Other Side of a Mirror, The.
Coleridge, S.   Work Without Hope.
Cowper, W.   Castaway, The.
  Lines Written During a Period of Insanity.
Crashaw.   Against Hope.
Creeley.   Ballad of the Despairing Husband.
  For Love.

Deane, S.   Roots.
Dickinson, E.   Despair's advantage is achieved.
  I cannot live with You.
  It might be lonelier.
  It was not Death, for I stood up.
  Softened by Time's consummate plush.
  There's a certain Slant of light.
Disch.   Zewhyexary.
Dowson.   Last Word, A.
Drummond, W.   Madrigal: "My thoughts hold
  mortal[l] strife."
Dunbar, P.   Ships That Pass in the Night.
  Worn Out.
Éluard, P.   Invention, The.
Faiz.   Rain of Stones Is Finished, The.
Ferlinghetti, L.   In Golden Gate Park that day.
Fletcher, J.   Last Frontier, The.
Fujiwara No Toshinari.   In all the world.
Galai.   To My Generation.
Garrigue.   Upon the Intimation of Love's
  Mortality.
Gascoigne.   Before mine eye to feed my
  greedy will.
  Divorce of a Lover, The ("Divorce me nowe
    good death").
Giorno.   Life Is a Killer.
Godfrey.   Where the Weather Suits My
  Clothes.
Grachova.   Of what use to me are the nights
  full of wine.
Grandmaster Flash *and* the Furious
  Five.   Message, The.
Greville, F.   *Cupid, in Myra's* faire bewitching
  eyes.
Gu Cheng.   Ark.
Hacker, M.   Sonnet for Iva.
Hardy, T.   Darkling Thrush, The.
Hayes, A.   Epistle to the Gentiles.
Hemans.   Indian Woman's Death-Song, The.
Herbert, G.   Affliction (4).
  Collar, The.
  Decay.
  Denial[l].
  Longing.
Hewitt, J.   Postscript, 1984.
Hill, S.   Looking for Camels.
Hillel.   Sun.
Hoffenstein.   You buy some flowers for your
  table.
Homer.   O my husband... / cut off from life so
  young! You leave me a widow.
Hooper, E.   Better a sin which purposed wrong
  to none.
Hope, A.   Return of Persephone, The.
Hopkins, G.   Carrion Comfort.
  I wake and feel the fell of dark, not day.
  Leaden Echo and the Golden Echo, The.
  Sonnet: "No worst, there is none. Pitched past
    pitch of grief."
  Thou art indeed just, Lord, if I contend.
Housman, A.   World goes none the lamer, The.
Hove.   Red Hills of Home.
Hughes, L.   Same in Blues.
Hugo, R.   Brief History.
  Letter to Levertov from Butte.
  My Buddy.
Hull, L.   Combat Zone/War Stories.
Ignatow, D.   Brooding.
Ivanov, G.   Boiling up over the years.
  Fog. The road I usually wander down.
  If you want to live, then live...
  People? What do I care about people?
  They'll not exterminate you now.
Jabès.   Desert, II, The.
Jenkins, L.   In a Tavern.
Kaplan, M.   Knife, The.
Katayev.   For a long time, not a year, not two.
Kayo.   Song of the Initiate.
Keats.   La Belle Dame Sans Merci.
Kerouac.   225th Chorus.
Ki no Tomonori.   In the eternal / Light of the
  spring day.
Kim, K.   Gaslight.
  Lyricism of an Autumn Day.
  Snowy Night.
Kim, T.   When the river breaks loose.
Kintsune.   Flowers whirl away, The.

Kirkpatrick. For a Woman Murdered While Running at Land's End, October 1979.
Knight, E. Report to the Mother.
Kumin, M. Despair.
Kunitz, S. Night Letter.
Kushniroff. Die My Shriek.
Laing, K. Senior Lady Sells Garden Eggs.
Lansdown. Golgotha.
Lear, E. Limericks, II (v).
Levy, A. To Vernon Lee.
Lihn. Of all despondencies, death-despair must be the worst.
Locke, A. Sin and despair have so possess'd my heart.
Lodge, G. Lower New York.
Long, R. Fumetti.
Lorde. Generation.
Lowry, M. Death of a Oaxaquenian.
Macaulay, T. Jacobite's Epitaph, A.
Macdonald, G. Shall the Dead Praise Thee?
MacSweeney. Blackbird: Elegy for William Gordon Calvert.
Mahon. Girls on the Bridge.
Mangan, J. Twenty Golden Years Ago.
March, A. Day's in dread of losing her bright features, The.
Mazur. Fracture Santa Monica.
McAuley, J. Tomb of Heracles, The.
McCarthy, T. Quatrain without Sparrows, Helpful Bells or Hope.
McCord, D. Five Chants.
McGrath, T. End of the Line, The.
Melville, H. Island, The.
Meredith, G. I am to follow her. There is much grace.
Merezhkovsky. She Loves Me, She Loves Me Not.
Mezey. How Much Longer?
Miles, J. Maxim.
Millay, E. Above these cares my spirit in calm abiding.
Mirabai. O friends, I am mad.
Momoi. Quickness of Fear, The.
Montagu, L. Addressed to ———.
Moos. Black Shawl, The.
Morris, W. Apology, An.
Nathan, R. Mountaineer, The.
Nemerov. Redeployment.
Nguyễn Gia Thiều. Song of Sorrow Inside the Royal Harem, A.
Nguyễn Khuyến. On Hearing the Rail Cry.
To a Statue.
Niedecker. I married.
Notley. Poem: "You hear that heroic big land music?"
Odarchenko. There are perfect illustrations.
What a sweet little day, what a day!
O'Hara, F. Meditations in an Emergency.
Olsen, W. Storm Chasers, The.
Oppen. Cars on the highway filled with speech.
Power, The Enchanted World.
Route.
Survival: Infantry.
O'Rahilly. Last Lines.
Panchenko. Ballad of the Shot Heart.
Papaionnou. Nights I stay awake without hope.
Patil. Freak.
"Pereleshin." Path, The.
Pessoa. In the terrible night, natural substance of all nights.
Plath. Event.
Moon and the Yew Tree, The.
Ralegh, W. Fortune hath taken away my love.
If Cynthia be a queen, a princess, and supreme.
Likes to a hermit poor in place obscure.
My Body in the Walls Captived.
Rice, S. Enough is never enough—That voice comes back—Suave.
Ritsos. Not Even Mythology.
Penelope's Despair.
Robinson, M. Stanzas: "In this vain, busy world, where the good and the gay."
Rosenfeld, M. Another While.
Rossetti, C. Better Resurrection, A.

If Only.
L.E.L. E. L.
Old-World Thicket, An.
What would I give for a heart of flesh to warm me thro'.
Rossetti, D. Superscription, A.
Rumi. Outside, the freezing desert night.
Sassoon. Lamentations.
Savard. Descent of Fire, The.
Schwartz, L. Exiles: Ends.
Scovell. Suicide, The.
Sepamla. Silence: 2.
Sexton. Her Kind.
Shelley, P. England in 1819.
Lament, A: "O world! O life! O time!"
Lines Written among the Euganean Hills.
Stanzas Written in Dejection, near Naples [or —December 1818, near Naples].
Shelton, R. Eden After Dark.
Shivarudrappa. This Man.
Sidney, P. Sonnet 19: "On Cupid's bow how are my heart-strings bent."
Sissay. "What Have We Got."
Slingeland. About Writing Poetry.
Slonimski. Remembrance.
Sluchevsky. I told her: the sidewalks are muddy.
Smith, C. Nepenthe.
Ode to Death.
On Passing Over a Dreary Tract of Country, and Near the Ruins of a Deserted Chapel, During a Tempest.
To Spring.
Unhappy exile, whom his fates confine, The.
Smith, D. Cuba Night.
Smith, M. City.
Smith, S. Bereaved Swan, The.
Bog-Face.
I rode with my darling in the dark wood at night.
So Chong-Ju. Nightingale Path, The.
Southwick. Ruins, The.
Speer. Mama Rosanna's Last Bead-Clack.
Spender, S. Memento.
Spenser. Cave of Despair, The.
Spicer, J. Transformations.
Stevenson, R. O dull cold northern sky.
Stickney, T. At Sainte-Marguerite.
Su Tung-p'o. Abandoned earthworks nobody tends.
Lament of the Farm Wife of Wu.
Swift, J. Phyllis [or Phillis] [or Progress of Love, The].
Swinburne. Satia Te Sanguine.
Tản Đà. Rail and the Bullfrog, The.
Tennyson, A. Mariana.
Thomson, J. In the Room.
Thoreau. Poet's Delay, The.
Tố Hữu. Song on the River of Perfumes, The.
Three sounds sum up the sense of life.
Toller. O Heavy Step of Slow Monotony.
Trần Tế Xu'o'ng. Drought.
Tsui. How Can I Show This Poem to Geraldine?
Tsvetayeva. You, walking past me.
Ullman. Peace.
Unknown. Alphabet of Love, The.
Big Chariot, The.
Flood.
Love is a secret feeding fire that gives all creatures.
Miserere, My Maker.
Sometimes I feel like a motherless child.
Untermeyer, L. Koheleth.
Upton, L. Debt, The.
"Vaidehi." Girl in the Kitchen.
Vaughan, H. Anguish.
Very. Forevermore.
Vũ Hoàng Chu'o'ng. Far Away.
Wallace-Crabbe. Sonnet IV.
Walsh, W. Despairing Lover, The.
Weissbort. Mourning.
Weller. Story of Frankie. . . My Man, The.
Whalen. Complaint: To the Muse.
Wieners. Waning of the Harvest Moon, The.
Wieseltier. Holy Is the Desire to Proclaim the Existence of God.

Williams, W. Are the desolate, dark weeks.
Drunkard, The.
Wordsworth, W. Complaint of a Forsaken Indian Woman, The.
Composed Near Calais on the Road Leading to Ardres, August 7, 1802.
Reverie of Poor Susan, The.
Written in London, September, 1802.
Wright, J. Lying in a Hammock at William Duffy's Farm in Pine Island, Minnesota.
Wroth. Song 2: "All night I weep[e], all day I cry, Ay me[e]."
Sonnet 6: "My pain[e], still smothered [or smother'd] in my grievèd bre[a]st."
Sonnet 9: "Be[e] you all pleased [or pleas'd]? your pleasures grieve not[t] me[e]."
Sonnet 30: "You blessed shades, which give mee silent rest."
Sonnet 42: "If ever love had force in huma[i]ne brest?"
Wyatt, T. Absence! Absenting causeth me to complain.
After great storms the calm returns.
Alas, poor man, what hap have I.
All heavy minds.
Comfort thyself, my wo[e]ful heart.
Enemy [or en'my] of life, decayer of all kind, The [or Th'].
Fruit of all the service that I serve, The.
Heart oppressed [or oppress'd] with desperate thought.
I see that chance hath chosen me.
Joy so short alas, the pain so near, The.
Like as the swan towards her death.
Most wretched heart, most miserable.
My galley charged with forgetfulness.
My hope, alas, hath me abused.
Pillar [or Piller] perished [or pearisht] is whe[a]rto I le[a]nt, The.
Restful place, reviver of my smart, The.
Since you will needs that I shall sing.
Sonnet: 'My galley charged'.
There was never nothing more me pained [or payned].
To wish and want and not obtain.
What death is worse than this?
Wylie. Let No Charitable Hope.
Yamada. Cincinnati.
Yesenin. Letter to My Mother.
Zangwill. Moses and Jesus.

Destiny. *See* **Fate**

Destruction

Ai. Testimony of J. Robert Oppenheimer, The.
Aiken, C. Summer.
Atwood. It Is Dangerous to Read Newspapers.
Awoonor. Sea Eats the Land at Home, The.
Bekederemo. Season of Omens.
Bogen, D. House Destroyed by Fire, The.
Brecht, B. Friends, The.
Brooks, G. Boy Breaking Glass.
Brousek. Walls shriek, The.
Brown, S. Schadenfreude.
Chan. Paradise.
Charles, F. Letters from Home.
Ché Lan Viên. On the Way Home.
Clifton, L. Message of Crazy Horse, The.
De Vere, S. Rock of Cashel, The.
Dev Sen. Yellow River, The.
Di Prima. Brief Wyoming Meditation.
Djogo. Black Sheep, The.
Donne. Broken Heart, The.
Duncan, R. Passage Over Water.
Dupin. Waiting with lowered voice.
Duris. Ephesos.
Éluard, P. November 1936.
Emerson, R. Water understands / Civilization well, The.
Fenton, J. Wind.
Frost, R. Fire and Ice.
Gilbo'a. Ends of Things were heard no more, The.
Glancy. Raid on a Cheyenne Village.
Gould, A. Demolisher.
Gouri. Jericho unknowing.
Grahn. Spider Webster's Declaration: He Is Singing the End of the World Again.
Graves, R. Twins.

Gray, T. On Lord Holland's Seat near Margate, Kent.
Hall, H. For a Broken Needle.
Harter. Broken bowl.
Hill, L. Let Him Return.
Hoagland, T. Sweet Rain.
Holub. Brief Thoughts on Cracks.
Homer. Demodocus sings the fall of Troy.
Hoyt, C. Pretty matron, The.
Hughes, T. That Moment.
Ishikawa Takuboku. Tanka: "Accidentally."
Jabès. Desert, The.
Jeffers, R. Summer Holiday.
Jonson, B. Execration upon Vulcan, An.
Kelly, B. White Pilgrim: Old Christian Cemetary, The.
Kinnell. Another Night in the Ruins.
Kirsch, S. Pictures.
Kocbek. Dialectics.
Stick, The.
Komunyakaa. Crack.
Kooser. Shooting a Farmhouse.
Korn. Thirty-one Camels, The.
Kowit. Notice.
Kunitz, S. Approach to Thebes, The.
Last Picnic, The.
Kyger. Destruction.
Lepik. Curse.
Lucan. All great things crush themselves.
Lux. Barn Fire.
Lyttelton. Happiest Pair, The.
Mapanje. Glory Be to Chingwe's Hole.
Mattera. Day They Came for Our House, The.
McGinley. Conquerors, The.
McHugh, H. Earthmoving Malediction.
Melville, H. Iris.
Ravaged Villa, The.
Merrill, J. Urban Convalescence, An.
Momaday. Colors of Night, The.
Morgan, R. Choice, The.
Mother Goose. Three wise men of Gotham.
Nahuatl Oral Tradition. Elegy.
Nichol. Some Nets.
Oppen. Survival: Infantry.
Pagis. Houses.
Lesson in Observation, A.
Parker, P. Love Isn't.
Parun. Ballad of the Deceived Flowers.
Poe. Sonnet—To Science.
Porter, P. May, 1945.
Prior. Dutch Proverb, A.
Pugh. 'Do you think we'll ever get to see Earth, sir?'.
"Ravitch." Verses Written on Sand.
Rich, A. For the Record.
Rowe, A. Destroyers, The.
Rukeyser, M. Sand-Quarry with Moving Figures.
Sandburg, C. Prayers of Steel.
Sapgir. Fearless One.
Sassoon. Post-Mortem, A.
Seferis. Last Stop.
Shelley, P. Tower of Famine, The.
Shelton, R. Sonora for Sale.
Slonimski. Elegy: "No more, no more Jewish townships in Poland."
Smith, D. Near the Docks.
Su Tung-p'o. Lament of the Farm Wife of Wu.
Szymborska. Children of the Epoch.
Tahmisic. Limbo.
Tennyson, A. Babylon.
Trubin. And we kill blood.
Tuqan, F. Song of Becoming.
Unknown. End of Clonmacnois, The.
Kilcash.
Vaughan, H. Charnel-house, The.
Venclova. Villanelle.
Waldrop, K. Wandering Curves.
Watts, I. Day of Judgement [or Judgment]; an Ode, The.
Williamson, G. Walter Parmer.
Winters, Y. Summer Noon: 1941.
Wollach. To Live at the Speed of Biography.
Wordsworth, W. Composed at Neidpath Castle, the Property of Lord

Queensberry, 1803.
Steamboats, Viaducts and Railways.
Wyatt, T. Will ye see what wonders love hath wrought?
Wylie. Doomsday.
Zach. In the Course of Time the original.
Zenmaro. September 1, 1923.
Tanka: "Old Japan."
Detectives
Fearing. Operative No. 174 Resigns.
Hughes, L. Café: 3 A.M.
Orlovsky. Dick Tracy's yellow Hat and Blacksuit.
Ransome-Davies. Raymond Chandler: The Big Sleep.
Determination
Angelou. Still I Rise.
Hughes, T. Crueller than owl or eagle.
Kunitz, S. Knot, The.
Moore, M. I May, I Might, I Must.
Oliver, M. Journey, The.
Piercy. For the Young Who Want To.
Woman in the ordinary pudgy downcast girl, The.
Rich, A. Power.
Sidney, P. Sonnet 64: "No more, my dear, no more these counsels try."
Wyatt, T. Lo, how I seek and sue to have.
What no, Perdy [or Perdie or perdie][!] ye may be sure[!].
Detroit, Michigan
Bly, R. Andrew Jackson's Speech.
Daniels, J. Time, Temperature.
Davis, O. Thirty Years Rising.
Joseph, L. Then.
Levine, P. Belle Isle, 1949.
Coming Home, *Detroit,* 1968.
Ordinary Morning, An.
Snow.
You Can Have It.
Pape. Birds of Detroit.
Developing Countries
Enright, D. Underdeveloped Country, An.
Hove. Country Life.
Ojaide. Ward 6.
Salkey. Remember Haiti, Cuba, Vietnam.
Devil. *See* **Satan**
Devonshire, England
Browne, W. Frolic Mariners of Devon, The.
Herrick. Discontents in Devon.
Dew
Basho. Quick-falling dew.
Bryant, W. To A Waterfowl.
Bunya no Asayasu. In a gust of wind the white dew.
Clare, J. Clock-A-Clay [The Lady Bug].
Halkin, S. Drop of Dew, A.
Herrick. Upon Julia's Haire Fill'd with Dew.
Kao Ch'i. Well of the King of Wu, The.
Kolmar. Toad, The.
Mechthild von Magdeburg. How God Comes to the Soul.
Miles, J. Fields of Learning.
Tasso. What dew or what weeping.
Tenji. Because.
Unknown. Burial Songs.
Dew on the hill.
I syng of a mayden that is makeles.
Wei Ying-wu. On Dewdrop.
Wen I-to. Last Day, The.
Xue Tao. Cicadas.
Dewey, George
Ware, E. Manila Bay.
Diabetes
Hacker, M. Fifteen to Eighteen.
Hoagland, E. Big Zeb Johnson.
Diana
Callimachus. Goddess, how oft you bent the silver bow.
See also **Artemis**
Diana (mythology)
Catullus. Hymn to Diana.
Gallagher, T. Instructions to the Double.
Horace. 3.22: Pine Tree for Diana, The ("Montium custos nemorumque").
Jonson, B. Hymn to Diana.

Killigrew, A. On a Picture Painted by Herself], Representing Two Nimphs of Diana's].
Kleinzahler. Two Canadian Landscapes.
Ralegh, W. Shepherd's Praise of Diana, The.
Simms, W. New Moon, The.
Diaries
Allingham. Writing.
Bishop, E. From Trollope's Journal.
Dibdin, C. Lady's Diary, The.
Dugan, A. On a Seven-Day Diary.
Larkin, P. Forget What Did.
Procter, A. My Journal.
Unknown. Fascinating Poet's Dream, A.
Wilson, M. Diary.
Dickinson, Emily
Bell, M. Mystery of Emily Dickinson, The.
Bly, R. Visiting Emily Dickinson's Grave with Robert Francis.
Carlisle. Emily Dickinson's To-Do List.
Clampitt. Amherst.
Corpi. Emily Dickinson.
Crane, H. To Emily Dickinson.
Dirjan. Poetry Evening.
Finch, A. Dickinson.
Hadas, R. Teaching Emily Dickinson.
Kennedy, X. Emily Dickinson in Southern California.
Longley, M. Emily Dickinson.
Lowell, A. Sisters, The.
Paterson, A. Because I Could Not Dump.
Rich, A. I Am in Danger—Sir—.
Rubin, L. Houses of Emily Dickinson, The.
Wilbur. Altitudes.
Winters, Y. To Emily Dickinson.
Dictionaries
Fields, J. Aardvark.
Hardy, T. Liddell and Scott.
Dido
Ausonius. I am that Dido which thou here do'st see.
Stanyhurst. Thee whilst thee dawning Aurora fro the Ocean hastned.
Surrey. Then from the seas, the dawning gan arise.
Virgil. Dido in the Elysian Fields.
Dido's death.
Dido's last night.
He many waies his labouring thoughts revolves.
Mounting the Pile she unsheaths the Trojan sword.
Release.
Dieting
Burge. Diet, The.
King, S. Breakfast Song in Time of Diet.
Nash, O. I Can't Have a Martini, Dear, but You Take One, or, Are You Going to Sit THere Guzzling All Night?
Unknown. On a Gentleman's Complaining to a Lady That He Could Not Eat Meat.
Digging and Diggers
Gildner. Digging for Indians.
Izumi. As I dig for wild orchids.
Merwin, W. Diggers, The.
Pitter. Digdog.
Stevenson, R. At the Seaside [or Sea-Side].
Su Tung-p'o. White Crane Hill.
Unknown. Digging Sing, A.
Wilbur. Digging for China.
Dikes
Cary, P. Leak in the Dike, The.
Kipling, R. Dykes, The.
Winters, Y. By the Road to the Air-Base.
Dillinger, John
Wagoner, D. Shooting of John Dillinger outside the Biograph Theater July 22, 1934, The.
Dimples
Holland, J. Where Shall the Baby's Dimple Be.
Diners
Atwood. They Eat Out.
Clewell. We Never Close.
St. John, D. Avenues, The.
Waring, B. Tip, The.

Dinosaurs
Armour. Pachycephalosaurus.
Couto. Living in the La Brea Tar Pits.
Equi. Ode to Chicago.
Kovner. Dinosaurs wept angry tears.
Stoloff. Dinosaurs.
Unknown. Ichthyosaurus, The.
Updike. On the Inclusion of Miniature
Dinosaurs in Breakfast Cereal Boxes.
Worth, V. Dinosaurs.

Diocletian
Cowley, A. Garden, The.

Diogenes
Unknown. Tomb of Diogenes, The.

Dionysus
Alcaeus. Evening Song, An.
Apollinaris Sidonius. Invitation to the Dance.
Aristophanes. C'wa nou, what wey suld I chap
o this door?
Euripides. Then listen Thebes, nurse of
Semele.
Graves, R. Ambrosia of Dionysus and Semele,
The.
Randall, D. Hail, Dionysos.

Diplomacy and Diplomats
Barrington, P. I had a duck-billed platypus
when I was up at Trinity.
Donne. To Sir H. W. at His Going
Ambassador to Venice.
Senghor. Elephant of Moissel, hear my pious
prayer.
Weigl. Ambassador, The.

Dirigibles
Meek. Week the Dirigible Came, The.

Disabilities
Owen, W. Disabled.
Pettit. Legless Boy Climbing In and Out of
Chair.

Disappointment
Akazome Emon. I should not have waited.
"Akhmatova." Round my neck a rosary of
fine beads.
Annensky. Small Kulak Landowner.
Baillie, L. Werena My Heart Licht I Wad
Dee.
Behn, A. Disappointment, The.
Clifton, L. Thirty-eighth year, The.
Davis, T. Telepathy.
Derricotte. Saturday Night.
Dickinson, E. I showed her Hights she never
saw.
It would never be Common—more—I said.
Erwin. Land Donation.
Hall, J. Figure a Poem Makes, The.
Hardy, T. Broken Appointment, A.
Herrick. Invitation, The.
Jeffers, R. Self-Criticism in February.
Lazard. Ordinance on Arrival.
Levine, P. Blasting from Heaven.
Machado Ruiz. Ephemeral Past, The.
Meek. Walls.
Meynell, A. Modern Mother, The.
Mototoshi. Your fine promises.
Norton, C. Laura was lightsome, gay, and free
from guile.
Parker, D. One Perfect Rose.
Ralegh, W. Farewell to False Love, A.
Rich, A. Snapshots of a Daughter-in-Law.
Shune. All during a night.
Sosei. She said she would come.
Tate, J. My Great Great Etc. Uncle Patrick
Henry.
Thayer, E. Casey at the Bat.
Wang Seng-ta. Written for My Neighbor.
Wordsworth, W. Yarrow Visited [September,
1814].
Wroth. Sonnet 27: "Fie [*or* Fy] tedious Hope,
why do[e] you still rebel[l]?"
Wyatt, T. Answer that ye made to me, my
dear, The [*or* Th'].
Give place all ye that doth rejoice.
If ever man might him avaunt.

Disarmament
Lehmann, J. This Excellent Machine.
See also **Militarism; Pacifism and Pacifists**

Disasters
Ammons. Eternal City, The.

Graves, R. Fallen Tower of Siloam, The.
Khlebnikov, V. Once again, once again.
Larkin, P. Explosion, The.
McGonagall. Albion Battleship Calamity, The.
Moore, J. Ashtabula Disaster, The.
Peacock, M. Don't think governments end the
world. The blast.
Sherlock. Dinner Party 1940.
Ts'ao Chih. Written on Parting from Mr.
Ying.
Urdang. All Around Us.

Discipline
Herbert, G. Discipline.
Martial. To a Schoolmaster.
Mullen, H. Momma Sayings.
Ross, C. Jack.
Rossetti, C. Seldom "can't."
Stevenson, R. Good and Bad Children.
Unknown. Jemima.
You, North must go.

Discontent
Abrahams, L. Whiteman Blues, The.
Agathias. Restless and discontent.
Akhtar-ul-Iman. Compromise.
Alcaeus. I long for the call to council.
Auden. Roman Wall Blues.
Betjeman. Meditation on the A30.
Brathwaite, E. Naima.
Carter, M. Childhood of a Voice.
Clarke, J. Evidently Chicken Town.
Coleman, W. African Sleeping Sickness.
Cooley. Loom, The.
Creeley. Gift, The.
Dunbar-Nelson. Proletariat Speaks, The.
Enzensberger, H. Middle-Class Blues.
Song for Those Who Know.
Espada. Jorge the Church Janitor Finally
Quits.
Fanthorpe. Not my best side, I'm afraid.
Fields, D. Fine romance! with no kisses!, A.
Gay, J. *et al.* Mary Gulliver to Capt. Lemuel
Gulliver.
Glancy. Kemo Sabe.
Graves, R. Lovers in Winter.
Gunn, T. Autumn Chapter in a Novel.
Hall, J. Maybe Dats Your Pwoblem Too.
Harms. Breakfast on the Patio.
Herbert, G. Affliction (1).
Herrick. Discontents in Devon.
Not To Love.
Ho Xuan Huong. On Being a Concubine.
Jennings, E. Afterthought.
Juan Chi. Years ago, when I was young.
Karandikar. Knot, The.
Kazakova. I am growing calmer.
Keats. Naughty Boy, The.
Kirschner. Fall of Light, The.
Ko. Chongno Street*.
Kunitz, S. Night Letter.
Lear, E. O dear! How disgusting is life!
Leonard, T. Baa baa black sheeep.
Lochhead, L. Mirror's Song.
MacNeice. Nature Morte.
Wolves.
Macy, A. Peppery Man was cross and thin,
The.
Mathew. Poem in Time of Winter.
McCord, D. Five Chants.
McGough, R. Prayer to Saint Grobianus.
Millay, E. Hearing your words, and not a
word among them.
Rendezvous.
Murray, P. Inquietude.
Nguyễn Trãi. For years you wallowed in the
scholar's world.
Nordbrandt. No matter where we go, we
always arrive too late.
O'Brien, S. In Residence: A Worst Case
View.
Ostriker. Exchange, The.
Peseroff. Adolescent.
Phan Bội Châu. My Shadow and I.
Plath. Spinster.
Porter, P. Consumer's Report, A.
Seay. It All Comes Together Outside the
Restroom in Hogansville.
Simpson, L. Suddenly.

Smith, C. Sonnet Written in the Church-Yard
at Middleton in Sussex.
Spicer, J. Song for Bird and Myself.
Tản Đà. State of the World, The.
Toomer. I sit in my room.
Trần Tế Xu'o'ng. Looking Far Ahead.
Unknown. Grumble Family, The.
I would but I can't.
Usha. To Mother.
Vinokurov. Every store keeps a book for
complaints.
Waters, M. Mystery of the Caves, The.
Wickham. Nervous Prostration.
Williams, W. Raleigh Was Right.
Yeats. He Hears the Cry of the Sedge.
Yuan Chi. Deep night. I cannot sleep.

Discothèques
Ginsberg, A. Chances "R."
Merrill, J. Watching the Dance.

Discovery
Carew, T. Ingrateful[l] Beauty Threatened.
Coleridge, S. On a Discovery Made Too Late.
Fulton, A. Wreckage Entrepreneur, The.
Gunn, T. Discovery of the Pacific, The.
Heffernan, M. Message, The.
Hewitt, J. Tryst.
Ignatow, D. Absolutely.
Jarman, M. Children are hiding among the
raspberry canes, The.
Keats. Naughty Boy, The.
Levertov. Overland to the Islands.
Secret, The.
Lewis, L. Urinating Man, The.
MacLeish. Voyage West.
MacNeice. Truisms, The.
McWatt. Stone.
Millay, E. Euclid alone has looked on Beauty
bare.
Padgett, R. Advice to Young Writers.
Shapiro, K. Leg, The.

Disdain
Akhtar-ul-Iman. Compromise.
Ayton. To an Inconstant One.
Boker. Oh! craven, craven! while my brothers
fall.
Campion, T. Follow thy fair sun unhappy
shadow.
Catullus. Carmen 69 ("That no fair woman
will, wonder not why").
Chesterton, G. World State, The.
Creeley. Gift, The.
Memory, The.
Daniel, S. Sonnet 5: 'Whilst Youth and Error'.
Donne. To the Countesse of Bedford ("Honour
is so sublime perfection").
Florian. Send my spinach.
Follain. Face the Animal.
Glück, L. My Neighbor in the Mirror.
Godolphin. Chloris, it is not thy disdain.
Hewitt, J. Glens, The.
Turf-Carrier [*or* Turf Carrier] on Aranmore.
Ho Xuan Huong. Bonze Got Stung By a Bee,
The.
Lorde. Suffer the Children.
Martial. Last night, after five pints of wine.
Nam Trân. Against Tunes in a Minor Key.
Nguyễn Chí Thiện. Party left me in the wilds,
The.
Nguyễn Trãi. Ask to be put in charge of
streams and hills!
Nguyễn Văn Lạc. Shrimp.
To a Dead Dog in the River.
Plath. Daddy.
Ralegh, W. If Cynthia be a queen, a princess,
and supreme.
Sidney, P. Sonnet 104: "Envious wits, what
hath been mine offence."
Tekkan. Tanka: "Bliss, The."
Trần Tế Xu'o'ng. Actors.
Lamenting the State of Confucian Scholarship.
Unknown. Mode of France, The.
Wilbur. Simplification, A.
Wyatt, T. Behold, love, thy power how she
despiseth!
Lover Complaineth the Unkindness of His
Love, The.
Renouncing of Love, A.

Disease

Becker, R. Medical Science.
Beckett, S. Ooftish.
Cavalli. Outside, in fact, there wasn't any change.
Chimombo. Derailment: A Delirium.
Cummings, E. Come,gaze with me upon this dome.
Elliott, A. Angel.
Gumilyov. Plague, The.
Hendriks. Cirrhosis.
Lucretius. Symptoms of plague in Athens.
MacKay, C. Mowers: An Anticipation of the Cholera, 1848, The.
McHugh, H. What Hell Is.
Muldoon, P. Aisling.
Piercy. Crabs.
Scott, D. Apocalypse Dub.
Wilbur. Pangloss's Song: A Comic-Opera Lyric.
Williams, C. Alzheimer's: The Wife.

Disgrace

Sidney, P. Sonnet 21: "Your words my friend (right healthful caustics) blame."

Dishonesty

Cary, P. When lovely woman wants a favour.
Holden, J. Losers.
Nesbit, E. Appeal.
Piercy. Song of the Fucked Duck.
Raab, L. Room, The.

Dishonor

Marie-Madeleine. Vagabonds.
Melville, H. Stonewall Jackson.
Unknown. He that in youthe no vertu will yowes.
Poor But Honest.

Disillusion

Argentarius. Old Story, The.
Bierce. Done with the work of breathing; done.
Browning, R. Patriot, The [An Old Story].
Carew, T. Ingrateful[l] Beauty Threatened.
Catullus. Carmen 72.
Coleridge, S. On a Discovery Made Too Late.
Conoley. I'd like a little love in the wine-red Afternoon.
Dickinson, E. Loss of something ever felt I, A.
Split the Lark—and you'll find the Music.
Ferlinghetti, L. Poet's eye obscenely seeing, The.
Fuller, R. Spring 1942.
Ginsberg, A. America I've given you all and now I'm nothing.
My Alba.
Giovanni. Adulthood.
Hanzlicek, C. C.G. Hanzlicek.
Heitzman. Spaces.
Koch, K. Thanksgiving.
Kuo Mo-jo. Impressions of Shanghai.
Macaulay, T. Jacobite's Epitaph, A.
Meredith, G. 30.
But where began the change; and what's my crime?
Not solely that the Future she destroys.
Sonnet 29: "Am I failing? For no longer can I cast."
Montague, J. Well-beloved, The.
Owen, W. Dulce Et Decorum Est.
Sonnet, to a Child.
Parker, D. Symptom.
Rathbun. Uncool.
Reese, L. Lyric on the Lyric, A.
Robinson, E. Another Dark Lady.
Swift, J. Cassinus and Peter.
Tomlinson, C. Jam Trap, The.
Unknown. Oxaitoq's Song.
Wyatt, T. Myn owne John poyntz sins ye delight to know.
Yeats. Old Stone Cross, The.

Disorder

Bishop, E. Filling Station.
Gunn, T. Wheel of Fortune, The.
Herrick. Delight in Disorder.
Jewell. Disturbing some brush.
Lindsay. Compleynt of the Comoun Weill of Scotland, The.

Merrill, J. Broken Bowl, The.
Mikata Shami. Bound up it always.
Niedecker. Fancy Another Day Gone.
Nobuyuki. Even Invisible Things (two poems).
Peseroff. Adolescent.
Rimbaud, A. Stolen Heart, The.
Spicer, J. Thing Language.
Stevens, W. Connoisseur of Chaos.
Welish. Blood or Color.
Wild Sleeve.
Whitman, W. Beat! beat! drums!—blow! bugles! blow!
Yosano. At the beginning.

Disraeli, Benjamin

Brooks, S. To Disraeli.

Distrust

Amis, K. Last War, The.
Dunn, S. Man Who Closed Shop, The.
Graham, W. Lying Dear, The.
Herrick. Anacreontic.
Distrust ("To safeguard man from wrongs, there nothing must").
Morgan, E. Cinquevalli is falling, falling.
Padilla. Prayer for the End of the Century, A.
Park, P. True Line, The.
Ransom, J. Her Eyes.
Rich, A. Like This Together.
Williams, C. Question, The.

Diversity

Cohen, E. #2, Shoes.
Dunbar, P. Accountability.
Hewitt, J. Frontier, The.
Glens, The.
O country people, you of the hill farms.
Kipling, R. We and They.
Yau. New York Map Company (1).

Dives (Bible)

Unknown. Dives and Lazarus ("There was a man in olden times").

Diving and Divers

Bernstein, O. Imagined Description of Myself, in Another Scene, An.
Brackenbury. Two dead divers hauled up in their bell, The.
Brontë, C. Diving.
Hayden, R. Diver, The.
Knight, E. Poem of Attrition, A.
Livesay, D. Fantasia.
Livingstone, D. One Time.
Meinke. Elegy for a Diver.
Mole, J. Taking the Plunge.
Quennell. Divers, The.
Rich, A. Diving into the Wreck.
Ross, W. Diver, The.
Simpson, R. Diver.

Divining and Diviners

Herrick. Divination by a Daffadill [*or* Daffodil].

Divorce

Alvarez, J. Greg's got custody of Sally and wants.
Amichai. Pity; We Were Such a Good Invention, A.
Bartsch. Rita's husband gave Rita her walking papers.
Boss. My Ringless Fingers on the Steering Wheel Tell the Story.
Byron, G. To Penelope, January 2, 1821.
Coleman, H. Poem for a "Divorced" Daughter.
Dibdin, C. Popular Functionary, A.
Dryden, J. Why Should a Foolish Marriage Vow.
Durcan. Divorce Referendum, Ireland, 1986, The.
Pietà's Over—and, now, my dear, droll, husband, The.
Elliott, A. X-Ray, The.
Enzensberger, H. Divorce, The.
Ferlinghetti, L. People getting divorced.
Fraser, K. History of my feeling for you (or is it the way you change), The.
Green, J. Songs of Divorce.
"H., C. G." Power of Innocence, The.
Hoagland, T. Sweet Rain.
Jarman, M. Gift, The.
Koehn. Divorce.

Kunitz, S. River Road.
Laing, R. If she did not love you, she would not be.
Lowell, R. Katherine's Dream.
Mathis. Getting Out.
McCabe, V. For Starters.
McCarriston. To Judge Faolain, Dead Long Enough: A Summons.
Meredith, G. Dusty Answer, A.
Modern Love.
Merrill, J. Broken Home, The.
Mew. Madeleine in Church.
Nowlan. Beginning.
Olds, S. Victims, The.
Pratt, M. Laughing Place, The.
Rotella, A. Discussing divorce.
Rucker. Swallows of Capistrano, The.
Rudman, M. Nowhere Water, The.
Savard. Daughter's Brooch, The.
Shelnutt. Family.
Snodgrass, W. Mementos, 1.
Sokolov. Garland, The.
Storace. Archaeology of Divorce, The.
Tucker, M. Wail of the Divorced.
Unknown. Divorce Song.
Jamie Douglas.
Weingarten. In the Cloud Chamber.
Wickham. Divorce.
Young, D. Upon Hearing of My Friend's Marriage Breaking Up.

Doctors. See Physicians

Dodgson, Charles Lutwidge. See "Carroll, Lewis"

Dodo Birds

Carlile. Dodo.

Dogs

Abse. Of Itzig and His Dog.
Amherst. Verses Designed to Be Sent to Mr. Adams.
Anderson, J. Ye Bruthers Dogg.
Anderson, L. Dog Show.
Antipater of Thessalonica. Gorgo, a Cretan bitch, on a deer's track.
Arnold, M. Geist's Grave.
Asquith. Hairy Dog, The.
Auden. Cats and Dog.
Bangs, J. My Dog.
Barker, G. Dog, Dog in My Manger.
Beddoes. Sonnet: To Tartar, a Terrier Beauty.
Beerbohm, M. Brave Rover.
Bennett, R. My Dog, Spot.
Berners. Properties of a Good Greyhound, The.
Bishop, E. Pink Dog.
Bodecker. Cats and Dogs.
Brent. I Think I Know No Finer Things than Dogs.
Brereton, E. Three Dogs.
Brickley. Autumn rain—.
Browning, E. Flush or Faunus.
Bruner. Beyond the Grave.
Dog's Vigil, A.
Lonely Dog, The.
Burns, R. On a Dog of Lord Eglinton's.
Catacalos. One Man's Family.
Chute, M. My Dog.
Ciardi. Suburban.
Coleridge, H. On the Death of Echo, A Favourite Beagle.
Cooke, E. Rags.
Cornford, F. Child's Dream, A.
Cowper, W. Beau's Reply.
On a Spaniel Called Beau Killing a Young Bird.
Davidson, L. It is growing dark.
Davies, W. D is for Dog.
Dawe, B. Dogs in the Morning Light.
Drifters.
Day Lewis. Sheepdog Trials in Hyde Park.
Stand-To, The.
De Kok. Transfer.
Dearmer. Turkish Trench Dog, The.
Dickey, J. Madness.
Doane, G. Bishop Doane on His Dog.
Dugan, A. Memorial Service for the Invasion Beach Where the Vacation in the Flesh Is Over.

Dunn, S. Something Like Happiness.
Eisenhuth. Night in the Village.
Fanthorpe. Our Dog Chasing Swifts.
Ferlinghetti, L. Dog trots freely in the street, The.
Field, E. Duel, The.
Fraser, K. Boot, wet sand and more white along the borders defining a trail of lush / chemicals we adhere to.
Frammenti Romani.
Frost, R. Canis Major.
Span of Life, The.
Gasztold. Prayer of the Cat, The.
Gilbert, C. Glimpses.
Girard *et al.* Grave of Marmousette, The.
Giscombe. (1978, Remembering 1962).
Godfrey. Reveille.
Goldsmith, O. Elegy on the Death of a Mad Dog, An.
Greenwell, D. Fidelity Rewarded.
Guiterman. Little Lost Pup.
Gunn, T. Yoko.
Hardy, T. Ah, are you digging on my grave.
Mongrel, The.
Harper, M. Sandra: At the Beaver Trap.
Hodgins. Shooting the Dogs.
Holland, J. To My Dog "Blanco."
Holland, N. Little Dog-Angel, A.
Hope, A. Bounce to Pope.
Hotham. Distant thunder.
Letting.
Hudgins. Seventeen.
Two Ember Days in Alabama.
Hughes, L. Warning.
Hughes, T. Roger the Dog.
Iremonger. Dog, The.
Ishikawa Takuboku. Tanka: "On the roadside."
Tanka: "Young maidens."
Jensen, L. Red Dog, The.
Johnson, S. To Robbers furious, and to Lovers tame.
Johnston, G. Noctambule.
Karpowicz. Dog Which Barked Itself Out, The.
Kinnell. Supper after the Last, The.
Kipling, R. His Apologies.
Power of the Dog, The.
Supplication of the Black Aberdeen.
Klee. Wolf speaks, while chewing, The.
Landor, W. To Our House-Dog Captain.
Lea, B. Wrong Way Will Haunt You, The.
Lee, B. Bad Dog.
Letts. To Scott.
Levertov. Overland to the Islands.
Shlup, shlup, the dog.
Lewis, E. My Dog.
Lewis, J. Stories.
Lucas, S. Curate Thinks You Have No Soul, The.
MacCaig. Praise of a Collie.
MacEwen, P. My Little Dog.
Martin, S. Comic Adventures of Old Mother Hubbard and Her Dog, The.
Masing. For Polla.
Mayakovsky. How I Became a Dog.
McCrea. Pussy-Cat and Puppy-Dog.
McLeod. Lone Dog.
Merrill, J. Victor Dog, The.
Milne, A. Puppy and I.
Mish. Stray Dog.
Momaday. Two Figures.
Monro. Dog.
Montgomerie, A. Remembers thou in Æsope of a taill.
Moore, N. Island and the Cattle, The.
More, S. De Principe Bono et Malo.
Mother Goose. Leg over leg.
Musgrave. Burial of the Dog.
Nash, O. Dog, The.
Nicholls, J. Dog.
Nobuyuki. In Berlin.
Norris, L. Shepherd's Dog, The.
Nurton. My Doggie.
O'Cotter. Malemute Dog, A.
Ondaatje. Biography.
Ortiz. Bony.
Peabody, J. To a Dog.

Peseroff. Dog in the Lifeboat, A.
Pettit. Pavlov's Dog.
Phan Bội Châu. Epitaph for My Dog.
Phillips, D. Hounds are either the work of wind, The.
Pitter. Digdog.
Pope, A. Argus.
Epigram Engraved on the Collar of a Dog Given [*or* Which I Gave] to His Royal Highness.
Procter, A. Homeless.
Retallack, J. Woman Dragged by Welsh Corgis.
Reynolds, E. Little Black Dog, The.
Reznikoff. Highway I was walking on, The.
Rickel. Poem to Begin the Second Decade of AIDS.
Riley, J. Diners in the Kitchen, The.
Rossetti, C. Pussy has a whiskered face.
Salom. Winter.
Schelling. Run My Hand Under.
Schwartz, D. Dogs Are Shakespearean, Children Are Strangers.
Seldon. To My Setter, Scout.
Sidney, P. Sonnet 59: "Dear, why make you more of a dog than me?"
Smith, S. Goodnight.
Squire. To a Bull-Dog.
Starbird. Hound, The.
Stein, G. Dog, A.
Identity A Poem.
Stern, G. Dog, The.
Su Tung-p'o. Black Muzzle, south sea dog.
Sward. Uncle Dog; the Poet at 9.
Swift, J. On the Collar of Mrs. Dingley's Lap-Dog.
Swinburne. To a Cat.
Tekkan. Tanka: "Unlike their father."
Thomas, D. Song of the Mischievous Dog, The.
Thompson, P. Unromantic Awakening, An.
Tickell. Such be the dog, I charge, thou mean'st to train.
Tymnes. Eumelos had a Maltese dog.
Maltese Dog, A.
Unknown. Bingo.
Epitaph of a Dog.
Growing Up.
Little Dog under the Wagon, The.
Maggie.
Old Mother Hubbard.
One leg in front of the other.
One reason a dog is such a lovable.
Pussy cat sits by the fire.
There was a little dog, and he had a little tail.
There was a man, and his name was Dob.
Thin Dog.
Towser Shall Be Tied Tonight.
Unknown, after the Latin of Joachim du Bellay. At thieves I bark; at lovers wag my tail.
Updike. Dog's Death.
Van Duyn. Ballad of Blossom, The.
Viorst. Mother Doesn't Want a Dog.
Virgilio. Junkyard dog, The.
Wallace, R. Dog's Song.
Wang Ya. Palace Poem.
Warren, R. English Cocker: Old and Blind. Sila.
Watson, S. Epitaph, An.
Way. Hoping for a Dog.
Webb, D. Tragedy, A.
Wedgefarth. Bum.
Wilbur. Pardon, The.
Williams, W. To a Dog Injured in the Street.
Wilson, R. Family Holiday.
Wright, J. Old Dog in the Ruins of the Graves at Arles, The.
On the Skeleton of a Hound.
Simon and the Tarantula.
Wright, K. Heads or Tails?
Yesenin. To Kachalov's Dog.
See also **Puppies**; *Names of dogs (e.g.,* **Collies***).*

Dollhouses
Schmitz. Making a Door.

Dolls
Annensky. It happened in Vallen-Koski.

Boland, E. Dolls Museum in Dublin, The.
Boldman. In the doll's.
Burke, M. Rainy winter evening.
Chōkū. Tanka: "Oddly shaped."
Damas. Blues.
Freeman, C. Christmas Morning I.
Gioia. Counting the Children.
Haas, R. Building the dollhouse.
Hemphill. Soft Targets.
Hoyt, C. Leaves moil in the yard.
Jarman, M. Homing Instinct, The.
Levertov. Partial Resemblance.
Livingston, M. Doll.
Miles, J. Doll.
Mole, J. Song of the Hat-Raising Doll.
Palmer, M. Of this cloth doll which.
Peabody, R. Burning the Dolls.
St. John, D. Dolls.
Hush.
Shea, M. Long night, The.
Strnisa. Graves, The.
Yeats. Dolls, The.

Dolphins
Bishop, E. Riverman, The.
Gunn, T. Aquarium, The.
MacCaig. Porpoises.
Zwicky. Stone Dolphin, The.

Dominican Republic
Dove, R. Parsley.

Don Juan
Baudelaire. Don Juan in Hell.
Byron, G. Canto I.
Howard, R. Aubade: Donna Anna to Juan, Still Asleep.
Kirsch, S. Don Juan is coming in the morning.
Lawrence, D. Don Juan.

Don Quixote
Melville, H. Rusty Man, The.
Reavey. Bridge of Heraclitus, The.
Wilbur. Parable.

Donaghy, Lyle (1902-49)
Buchanan, G. Lyle Donaghy, Poet, 1902-1949.

Donkeys
Causley. Balaam.
Chesterton, G. Donkey, The.
Coleridge, S. To a Young Ass.
Colman, H. On Balaam, and His Ass.
Fanthorpe. What the Donkey Saw.
Fyleman. Donkey, The.
Gibson, W. Advice to Travelers.
Hecht, A. Pig.
Hewitt, J. Turf-Carrier [*or* Turf Carrier] on Aranmore.
Howe, F. From a donkey, excuse me, one lesson is given.
Hsü Wei. Returning from the Seventy-Two Mountains.
Jammes. Little Donkey, The.
Prayer to Go to Paradise with the Donkeys, A.
La Fontaine. Donkey and the Lapdog, The.
Li K'ai-hsien. Trip to a Mountain Village, A.
Montgomerie, A. Remembers thou in Æsope of a taill.
Orlen. Big Friend of the Stones.
Palladas. Poor little donkey! It's no joke.
Pasternak, B. Matthew 21:1–11.
Péret. Making Feet and Hands.
Roethke. Donkey, The.
Monotony Song, The.
Sitwell, D. "I Do Like To Be Beside the Seaside."
Taylor, A. Cow and the Ass, The.
Thomas, D. After the funeral, mule praises, brays.
Unknown. Donkey, The.
Donkey, donkey, old and gray.
Donkey Riding.
I had a little mule and his name was Jack.
Lock and Key.
Yungman. Melons.

Donne, John
Coleridge, S. On Donne's Poetry.
Corbet. Epitaph on Dr. Donne, Dean of Paul's, An.
Godolphin. Elegy on D. D.
Passion's excess for thee we need no fear.

Herbert of Cherbury. Having delivered now what praises are.

Jonson, B. To John Donne ("Donne, the delight of Phoebus, and each Muse").

To John Donne ("Who shall doubt, Donne, where [*or* whe'er] I a poet be[e]").

Kenyon, J. Travel: After a Death.

King, H. Upon the Death of My Ever Desired Friend Doctor Donne Dean of Pauls.

Maxton. Elegies.

Rukeyser, M. Homage to Literature.

Simmons, J. John Donne.

Sisson. Letter to John Donne, A.

Wotton, S. To John Donne.

Donnelly, Charles

MacDonagh, D. Of what a quality is courage made.

Dons. *See* **Teaching and Teachers**

Doors

Alexandru. Man.

Andal. O sister of wealth.

O you who guard over.

Auden. Door, The.

Barrington, J. Villanelle VI.

Bayliss. Seven Dreams.

Bennett, R. Windy Nights.

Bible, *O.T.* Song: "I was asleep but my heart stayed awake."

Bower, R. On Door Jambs.

Budenz. Poeta Fui.

Clark, T. Doors.

You (I).

Coleridge, M. Broken Friendship.

Gone.

Witch, The.

Creeley. Door, The.

Csoori. Door Creaked Three Times, The.

Davidson, L. It is growing dark.

Dickinson, E. I laughed a crumbling laugh.

Frost, R. Lockless Door, The.

García Lorca. Casida of Sobbing.

Garrison, T. Closed Door, The.

Greenaway. Which Is the Way to Somewhere Town?

Harter. In the mirror.

Herrick. No Lock against Lechery.

Hooper, V. Drawing Room Drama.

Seven Doors Away.

Hoyt, C. In that empty house.

Imbs. Sleep.

Kafka. Before the Law stands a doorkeeper.

Kerouac. Missing a kick.

Straining at the padlock.

Kunze, R. Return from the Convention.

Kuppner. Passing Through Doorways.

Larkin, P. Mr Bleaney.

Levy, A. Minor Poet, A.

Mackenzie, K. Door swung open, The.

Mackey, N. Dream Thief.

Maiden. In the Gloaming.

Masaoka Shiki. Tanka: "Beyond the glass door."

McKay, C. White House, The.

Merwin, W. Door, A.

To the Hand.

Miller, M. Closing, A.

Monro. Terrible Door, The.

Ponge. Delights of the Door, The.

Rabi'a al-Adawiyya. I am fully qualified to work as a doorkeeper, and for this reason.

O my Lord.

Ralegh, W. My Body in the Walls Captived.

Rands. Godfrey Gordon Gustavus Gore—.

Reed, I. Why I Often Allude to Osiris.

Reznikoff. House-wreckers have left the door and a staircase, The.

Rilke. Isn't the secret intent.

Saarikoski. Revolution.

Shorter. Skeleton in the Cupboard, The.

Smith, W. Jittery Jim.

Stevenson, R. Hearts, like doors.

Thomas, E. Like the Touch of Rain [she was].

Tomlinson, C. Door, The.

Unknown. Prayer is so simple.

Walk down the path.

Waldman, A. *et al.* & Now the book is closed.

Wu Chia-chi. East of the salt village, low and narrow.

Old saltman, hair turned white, The.

Yosano. Tanka: "Pressing my breasts."

Zeidner. Kafka Poem.

Dormice

Cole, C. Dormouse, The.

Herford. Elf and the Dormouse, The.

Dorset, England

Bastard. Ad Henricum Wottonem.

Hardy, T. Domicilium.

Once at Swanage.

Roman road runs straight and bare, The.

Dostoyevsky, Feodor

"MacDiarmid." Farewell to Dostoevski.

Pilinszky. In Memoriam F.M. Dostoevsky.

Doubt

Arnold, M. Dover Beach.

Bontemps. Miracles.

Browning, E. Sonnet: "And wilt thou have me fashion into speech."

Sonnet: "Belovéd, my Belovéd, when I think."

Clark, T. Greeks, The.

Creeley. Token, A.

Dante Alighieri. My lady looks so gentle and so pure.

Dao. Answer, The.

Daryush. You should at times go out.

Davies, W. Inquest, The.

Dickinson, E. Split the Lark—and you'll find the Music.

This World is not Conclusion.

Those—dying then.

Drayton. Sonnet 35: 'Some, misbelieving and profane'.

Fumi Saito. Tanka: "Ever deeper."

Gallagher, T. On Your Own.

Görgey. Thomas.

Herbert, G. Affliction (1).

Hewitt, J. Substance and Shadow.

Hope, A. Luke 24:36–49; As they were saying this, Jesus.

Horikawa. Will he always love me?

Hristic. That night they all gathered on the highest tower.

Hudgins. Elegy for My Father, Who Is Not Dead.

Juarroz. Every word is a doubt.

Lakshminkara. Lay your head on a block of butter and chop.

McWatt. Man in the House, A.

Nesbit, E. Love's Guerdons.

O'Hara, F. Ode: "Idea of justice may be precious, An."

To the Harbormaster.

Pankey. Confession of Cleopas, The.

Petri. By an Unknown Poet from Eastern Europe, 1955.

Piatt, S. Doubt, A.

Procter, A. Woman's Question, A.

Public Enemy. Don't believe the hype.

Ransom, J. Somewhere Is Such a Kingdom.

Rexroth, K. Did you take me because you loved me?

Robinson, A. Sibyl, The.

Rossetti, C. After Communion.

Shapiro, D. House (Blown Apart).

"Shu Ting." Perhaps our cares.

Smart, C. St. Thomas.

Spenser. Sonnet 65: "Doubt which ye misdeeme, fayre love, is vaine, The."

Thompson, C. Doubt crept into a heart one day, A.

Skeptic, The.

Tuckerman, F. As sometimes in a grove at morning chime.

Unknown. Essay on Man.

Twelfth Song of the Thunder.

Williams, C. Question, The.

See also **Agnosticism and Agnostics**

Douglass, Frederick

Bibb. In Memoriam Frederick Douglass.

Cornish, S. Frederick Douglass.

Cotter, J. Frederick Douglass.

Dunbar, P. Douglass.

Frederick Douglass.

Hayden, R. Frederick Douglass.

Heard, J. Welcome to Hon. Frederick Douglass.

Hughes, L. Frederick Douglass: 1817-1895.

Ray, H. In Memoriam Frederick Douglass.

Dover, England

Arnold, M. Dover Beach.

Bond, F. 'After the war,' they used to say, and pictured.

Shakespeare, W. Dover, the Samphire Cliff.

Doves

Ackland. Whether a dove or a seagull lighted there.

Bible, *O.T.* I am the rose of Sharon, and the lily of the valleys.

Brontë, A. Captive Dove, The.

Darley. Dove's Loneliness, The.

Eaton, A. Dove Apologizes to His God for Being Caught by a Cat, The.

Eglitis. In a Naples Bar.

Falconer, E. Doves.

Farber. Dove.

"Field." I sing thee with the stock-dove's throat.

Palimpsest, A.

Trinity.

Keats. Song: "I had a dove and the sweet dove died."

Kerouac. Thrashing Doves, The.

Khlebnikov, V. Feeding the Dove.

Miller, L. What the Women Told Me.

Montagu, L. Verses Written in a Garden.

Mother Goose. Dove and the Wren, The.

Paley, G. In Aix.

Pasternak, B. Into the enormous sky flew.

Probyn. Lai.

Ray, H. My Easter Dove.

Rilke. Dove that ventured outside, flying far from the dovecote.

Robinson, A. Song: "Oh for the wings of a dove."

Shelnutt. Family.

Sidney, P. Like as the dove which seeled-up doth fly.

Stevens, W. Song of Fixed Accord.

Unknown. Turtle-Doves' Nest, The.

Young, A. Stockdoves, The.

See also **Turtle Doves**

Down's Syndrome

Rubin, L. Dinner at the Mongoloid's.

Snyder, R. Mongoloid Child Handling Shells on the Beach, A.

Stallworthy, J. Almond Tree, The.

See also **Mental Retardation**

Dowries

Herrick. Single Life Most Secure.

Ramsay, A. Lass with a Lump of Land.

Dowsing and Dowsers

Morgan, E. Dowser, The.

Dragonflies

Bogan, L. Dragonfly, The.

Harr, L. Until it alights.

Kitahara Hakushū. Tanka: "Each alighted."

McClatchy. Dragonfly, The.

Nemerov. Dragonfly, The.

Rossetti, D. Silent Noon.

Sandy. Hunter's Moon.

Snyder, G. Dragonfly / Dead on the snow

Tennyson, A. Today I saw the dragon-fly.

Wallace, R. Between Equals.

Yasuda. Crimson dragonfly, A.

Young, F. Bête Humaine.

Dragons

Bast. Frost Eyebrows was the favorite cat.

"Carroll." Jabberwocky.

Dove, O. Dragon has come, A.

Fanthorpe. Not my best side, I'm afraid.

Ho Ching-ming. Fish in a Painting.

Hsieh Chin. Inscribed on a Painting of Dragons by Ch'en So-weng.

Hsü Chung-hsing. Cane of Ch'iung Bamboo, The.

Li Tung-yang. Long Handscroll of Bamboo by Wang Meng-tuan, The.

Mo Shih-lung. Saying Good-Bye to Feng the Hermit.
Moore, M. O To Be A Dragon.
Mullineaux. Dragon, The.
Nash, O. Tale of Custard the Dragon, The.
Nicholls, J. Storytime.
Pepler. Concerning Dragons.
Salamun. Clumsy Guys.
Smith, W. Toaster, The.
Stevens, M. Carp, The.
Treece. Magic Wood, The.
Tu Fu. To the south there is a dragon living in a mountain pool.
West, C. Jocelyn, my Dragon.
Wu Wei-yeh. Impromptu.
Yang Shih-ch'i. Dragon-Tiger Terrace.

Drake, Joseph Rodman
Halleck, F. On the Death of Joseph Rodman Drake.

Drake, Sir Francis
Beedome. To the Noble Sir Francis Drake.
Newbolt. Drake's Drum.
Unknown. On Francis Drake.
Upon Sir Francis Drake's Return from His Voyage about the World, and the Queen's Meeting Him.

Drawing
Behn, H. Circles.
Forbes, C. Picture of a Man.
Haines, J. Eye in the Rock, The.
Lipshitz. To a Set of Drawing Pencils.
Merrill, J. Vision of the Garden, A.
Rago. Childhood Painting Lesson.

Dreams and Dreaming
Adams, J. Dream, or the Type of the Rising Sun, A
"Adunis." Passage, The.
Akhmadulina. Small Aircraft.
Alberti. Punishments.
Ali, A. Dream of Glass Bangles, A.
I See Chile in My Rearview Mirror.
Allingham. Dream, A [or The].
Amichai. Look, thoughts and dreams weave over us.
Amis, K. Against Romanticism.
Dream of Fair Women, A.
Anderson, L. Dog Show.
Angira. If.
Antokolsky. From their journeys our dreams return.
Anyidoho. Hero and Thief.
Arnold, M. Longing.
Atwood. Variation on the Word *Sleep*.
Avidan. Glimpse of an Open Dream.
Song of the Self-Made Orphans.
Baca. Voz de la Gente.
Work We Hate and Dreams We Love.
Baillie, J. Reverie, A.
Balaban. Dead for Two Years, Erhart Arranges to Meet Me in a Dream.
Balmont. Vanishing Shadows.
Baraka. New World, The.
Barnes, W. Sonnet: "In every dream thy lovely features rise."
Beddoes. Dream-Pedlary.
Behn, A. Dream, The.
Belloc. Good Advice.
Beneyto. Nocturne in the Women's Prison.
Berg, S. Answer, The.
May 1970.
Berrigan, T. Sonnet: "My dream a drink with Lonnie Johnson we discuss the code."
Bevington, L. 'Dreamers?' Ah, no! else he was a dreamer.
Bishop, E. Summer's Dream, A.
Blake, W. Angel, The.
Dream, A.
Land of Dreams, The.
Little Girl Found, The.
Blockcolski. My Dream.
Blok. Sorcerer sang the spring to sleep, The.
Bloze. Leaves have yellowed like, The.
Bly, R. Dream of Retarded Children, A.
Bogan, L. Dream, The.
Meeting, The.
Bolger. Dublin Girl, Mountjoy, 1984.
Bona. Dream Poem.

Bonnefoy. De Natura Rerum.
Stone, A.
Bowers, E. Le Rêve.
Brecht, B. I, the Survivor.
Breckenridge. General John Cabell Breckinridge.
Breytenbach. Dreams Are Also Wounds.
Brontë, C. Again I find myself alone, and ever.
Dream that stole o'er us in the time.
Pilate's Wife's Dream.
What does she dream of, lingering all alone.
Brontë, E. Day Dream, A.
High waving heather'neath stormy blasts bending.
Stars.
Brooke, R. Sonnet: "Oh! Death will find me, long before I tire."
Brooks, G. Kitchenette Building.
My Dreams, My Works Must Wait Till after Hell.
Brown, D. Illumination.
Browning, E. Sonnet: "I lived with visions for my company."
True Dream, A.
Browning, R. Bad Dreams.
Bad Dreams III.
Women and Roses.
Brydges. On Dreams, October 15, 1782.
Byron, G. All this she told with some confusion and.
Darkness.
Caddel. Wyatt's Dream.
Campbell, T. Soldier's Dream, The.
Campo. Allegory.
Caraion. Winter
Carruth, W. Dreamer of Dreams.
Carter, R. Vietnam Dream.
Cartwright, W. Dream Broke, A.
Cavalieri. Grandmother.
Chao. Locust Swarm, The.
Cherry, K. Reading, Dreaming, Hiding.
Chin Nung. I remember when he took me on a trip to this place.
Chu Yün-ming. Painting of the Butterfly Dream by the Master Artist Li Tsai, A.
Clampitt. Burning Child, The.
Clifton, L. Mary's Dream.
Message of Crazy Horse, The.
Night Vision.
Powell (Officer Charged with the beating of Rodney King).
Clough. I dreamed a dream: I dreamt that I espied.
Codrescu. Work.
Coleridge, M. 'But in that Sleep of Death what Dreams may Come?'.
Coleridge, S. Egypt's might is tumbled down.
If I had but two little wings.
Kubla Khan; or, a Vision in a Dream.
Coleridge, S. Blest is the tarn which towering cliffs o'ershade.
Conkling, G. I will not give thee all my heart.
Conoley. Some Gangster Pain.
Cooper, J. El Sueño de la Razón.
Cornford, F. Child's Dream, A.
"Cornwall." Dream, A.
Corrothers. Snapping of the Bow, The.
Corso. Dream of a Baseball Star.
Creeley. Death of Venus, The.
For No Clear Reason.
Talking.
Three Ladies, The.
Cullen, C. For a Poet.
Cumbo. I'm a Dreamer.
Cummings, E. First of all my dreams was of, The.
It is at moments after i have dreamed.
My sweet old etcetera.
What a proud dreamhorse pulling(smoothloomingly)through.
White guardians of the universe of sleep.
Dabydeen, D. Miranda.
D'Aguiar. Airy Hall's Exits.
Daive. She does not move. Takes the man's.
Daley, V. Vision of Sunday in Heaven, A.
Davis, D. 6 A.M. Thoughts.

Davis, T. C. T. at the Five Spot.
Dawe, B. Copy-writer's Dream, The.
De la Mare. Miss Loo.
Voices.
De' Medici. (To the Virgin).
De Vries, R. On Alabama Ave., Paterson, NJ, 1954.
Desnos. I've dreamed such dreams of you that you're losing / your reality.
Dickey, J. Sled Burial, Dream Ceremony.
Dickinson, E. In Winter in my Room.
We dream—it is good we are dreaming.
Digges. Rough Music.
Donahue, J. Opiate Phobia.
Donne. Dream[e], The.
Doob. My Mother's Blue Vase.
Doolittle, H. At Baia.
Dor. Before sleep Baba arranges extra.
Douglas, L. Dead Poet, The.
Two Loves.
Dove, R. Oriental Ballerina, The.
This Life.
Dransfield. That Which We Call a Rose.
Driscoll, L. Hold Fast Your Dreams.
Dunbar, P. Ere sleep comes down to soothe the weary eyes.
Duncan, R. Often I Am Permitted to Return to a Meadow.
Rites of Participation.
Duoduo. Untitled.
Durston. Hippopotamus, The.
Eady. Success.
Eberhart, R. When Doris danced under the oak tree.
Eliot, T. Wind sprang up at four o'clock, The.
Emerson, R. Memory.
Equi. In a Monotonous Dream.
Erdrich. Strange People, The.
Etter. Monk's Dream.
Everson, W. Narrows of Birth, The.
Faiz. Prison Daybreak, A.
Field, E. Little Boy Blue.
Rock-a-by Lady, The.
Sugar-Plum Tree, The.
Wynken, Blynken and Nod one night.
"Field." Elsewhere.
Foster, E. In Your Words.
Frost, R. After Apple-Picking.
Galvin, B. Old Trip by Dream Train, The.
Gardner, I. Nightmare.
Telephone rang / in my dream Long Distance from, The.
Gascoyne. And the Seventh Dream Is the Dream of Isis.
Geda. I walked out into Lithuania.
George, D. Asenath.
Gilbert, C. Kite-Flying.
Gilbert, S. Dream Kitchen, The.
Gilbert, S. Nightmare, [A or The].
Gilbo'a. Havdala.
Our Dreams.
With the Rain.
Ginsberg, A. So I dream nightly of an embarkation.
Giovanni. Dreams.
Giscombe. All (Facts, Stories, Chance). (1980).
(The Recent Past).
Glancy. Kemo Sabe.
Goethe. To Belinda.
Graham, W. Night City, The.
Graves, R. Hag-Ridden.
In Procession.
Pinch of Salt, A.
Theseus and Ariadne.
Window Sill, The.
Gray, J. Barber, The.
Gunn, T. Wheel of Fortune, The.
Hacker, M. Wagers.
Hadas, R. Journey Out.
Hall, D. Town of Hill, The.
White Apples.
Woolworth's.
Hall, J. Kind of Faith, A.
Hanzlicek, C. C.G. Hanzlicek.
Hardy, T. Self-Unseeing, The.

Harte, B.   Second Review of the Grand Army, A.

Hass, R.   Palo Alto.

Hayden, R.   Bone-Flower Elegy.

Hazard, J.   Whiskey in Whiting, Indiana.

Head, G.   Night Sweats.

Hemans.   Dreaming Child, The.

Land of Dreams, The.

Hemp.   Living Lean.

Hemschemeyer.   My grandmother had bones as delicate.

Henry, J.   Out of the Frying Pan into the Fire.

Herbert, Z.   Trial, The.

Herford.   Snail's Dream, The.

Herrick.   Dream[e]s.

Vine, The.

Vision, The.

Vision to Electra, The.

Hollo.   Le Jazz Hot.

Holmes, O.   Old Man Dreams, The.

Housman, A.   Harlem.

Howes, B.   Chimera.

Hughes, L.   Dream Boogie.

Dream Variation[s].

Harlem.

Morning After.

Same in Blues.

Water-Front Streets.

Hugo, R.   In Your Bad Dream.

In Your Young Dream.

Hunt, L.   Nile, The.

Ignatow, D.   Dream, The.

Imbs.   Sleep.

Issaia.   Dream.

Itwaru.   Body Rites.

Jackson, H.   Dreams.

Jarrell.   Dead Wingman, The.

Girl in a Library, A.

House in the Wood, The.

Jewett, S.   Together.

Jewsbury.   Summer Eve's Vision, A.

Johnson, G.   My Little Dreams.

Johnson, M.   Dream, A.

Johnston, M.   Directions for Dreamfishing.

Jones, E.   Dream, A.

Jonson, B.   Dream[e], The.

Kane, P.   Disciples Asleep at Gethsemane.

Kasa.   I dreamed I held / A sword against my flesh.

Kastelan.   You shine in darkness, you dream under shelter.

Kaufman, B.   African Dream.

Keats.   Dream, A.

Dream, after Reading Dante's Episode of Paolo and Francesca, A.

Garden-Dream, A.

Nebuchadnezzar's Dream.

Kelly, B.   White Pilgrim: Old Christian Cemetary, The.

Kendall, M.   Pure Hypothesis, A.

King, H.   Dream Maiden, A.

Kinsella, T.   Nuchal, a Fragment.

Wormwood.

Kipling, R.   If you can keep your head when all [about you].

Kirkup.   My Thing from Outer Space.

Kitahara Hakushū.   Tanka: "In my heart."

Komey.   Change, The.

Kossman.   Pilate's Wife.

Kovner.   Lord of Dreams.

Kumin, M.   Making the Jam without You.

Kung Tzu-chen.   Tune: "Green Jade Cup."

Kunze, R.   Diary Page 69.

Kuo Mo-jo.   Impressions of Shanghai.

Lane, P.   Girl at the Window.

Larkin, P.   On Wakening.

Lehman.   Heaven.

Lehmann, G.   Roses.

Levertov.   Don't You Hear that Whistle Blowin'.

Runes, The.

Stir the holy grains, set.

Levi, P.   Reveille.

Levine, P.   Soloing.

Waking in March.

Levy, A.   Old House, The.

On the Threshold.

Lewis, J.   Snail Garden.

Li Ch'ing-chao.   Tune: "Telling of Innermost Feelings."

Li Ho.   Dream of Heaven, A.

Li Po.   Song of a Dream Visit to T'ien-mu.

Lim, S.   Modern Secrets.

Litsey.   Dreams Ahead, The.

Longfellow, H.   Golden Mile-Stone, The.

Lowell, R.   Katherine's Dream.

Lowry, M.   Joseph Conrad.

Lu Yu.   In a Dream.

In a Dream I Traveled among Ten Thousand Acres of Lotuses.

Night Thoughts.

Lum.   Chinese Hot Pot.

Ma Chih-yüan.   Tune: "Sailing at Night"—A Song Sequence.

Machado Ruiz.   Last night, as I was sleeping.

Parables, I.

Yesterday, dreamed He was near me.

Mackenzie, K.   Sick Men Sleeping.

MacLeish.   Prologue: "These alternate nights and days, these seasons."

MacNeice.   Bad Dream.

Major, C.   Round Midnight.

Manger.   Autumn.

Matthews, W.   Dream, The.

Matveyeva.   Dream.

McAuley, J.   Dialogue.

McClure, M.   PLEASURE FEARS ME, FOOT ROSE, FOOT BREATH.

McElroy, C.   Dreams of Johnson Grass.

McNair.   Before People, The.

Mei Yao Ch'en.   Dream at Night, A.

In Broad Daylight I Dream of My Dead Wife.

Year Wu-tzu [1048], The, First Month, Night of the Twenty-sixth: A Dream.

Meleager.   Epigram: "At 12 o'clock in the afternoon."

Melvill.   Upon one day as I did mourn full sore.

Melville, H.   Rose Window.

To.

Merrill, J.   Mad Scene, The.

Merton.   Lent in a Year of War.

Merwin, W.   To the Hand.

Mew.   Ne Me Tangito.

Not for that city of the level sun.

Miles, J.   Dear Frank, Here is a poem.

Dream.

Miljkovic.   Sleepers.

Milton.   On His Deceased Wife.

Mitchell, K.   Monster, The.

Miyazawa Kenji.   Daydreaming on the Trail.

Momaday.   Carriers of the Dream Wheel.

Moore, N.   Patient, The.

Morton, W.   Dafney's Lamentation.

Muir, E.   Adam's Dream.

Brothers, The.

Labyrinth, The.

Murray, P.   Rain.

Nabokov.   Execution, The.

Nagys.   Poem.

Nash, O.   Lady from near Rising Sun, A.

Needell.   Color, even whiteness, reaches / the body as a name.

Nguyễn Chí Thiện.   Party holds you down and you lie still, The.

Niedecker.   Subliminal.

Nordbrandt.   Streets.

Norton, C.   Dreams.

Ochester.   Oh, By the Way.

O'Hara, F.   Sleeping on the Wing.

Okara.   Snowflakes Sail Gently Down, The.

Oldham, J.   One night, as I was pondering of late.

Ono no Komachi.   Following the roads.

O'Rahilly.   Vision, The.

O'Reilly, J.   Cry of the Dreamer, The.

Orlen.   Biplane, The.

Orlovsky.   Dream May 18, 1958.

I Dream of St. Francis.

Orpingalik.   Alcheringa Definitions.

O'Shaughnessy, A.   Ode: "We are the music-makers."

Ostriker.   Warning.

Owen, G.   Make Believe.

Owen, G.   White Stallion / (The Runaway), The.

Owen, W.   Strange Meeting.

Pagis.   Honi.

Palmer, M.   Erolog.

Parra, N.   Tablets, The.

Pastan.   September.

Pasternak, B.   In The Wood.

Patmore, C.   Azalea, The.

Pau-Llosa.   Island of Mirrors, The.

Ostiones Y Cangrejos Moros.

Pavic.   Swing over the Calm Source of Our Names, The.

Petrarch.   Visions, The.

Phillips, D.   On Entries Emptiness.

Pierman.   How We Learned about Friction.

"Ping Hsin."   Deliverance.

Plutzik.   Dream about Our Master, William Shakespeare, The.

Po Chü-i.   Being on Duty all Night in the Palace and Dreaming of the Hsien-yu Temple.

Dream of Mountaineering, A.

Dreaming of Yüan Chên.

Dreaming that I went with Li and Yü to Visit Yüan Chên.

Immeasurable pain!

Sleeping on Horseback.

Poe.   Dream-Land [or Dreamland].

Fairyland [or Fairy-Land].

Oh! that my young life were a lasting dream!

To One in Paradise.

Pollak, F.   Dream, The.

Popa.   Dream of the Quartz Pebble, The.

Victims of the Little Box, The.

Pyle.   Waking.

Rakosi.   Journey Away, A.

Rakovszky.   Difficulties of Falling Asleep.

Ransom, J.   Prelude to an Evening.

Rexroth, K.   Fish Peddler and Cobbler.

Rich, A.   I wake up in your bed. I know I have been dreaming.

Jerusalem.

Richardson, F.   Pantry Ghosts, The.

Richardson, J.   On My Late Dear Wife.

Ridge, L.   Dream, The.

Robinson, A.   Pallor.

Robinson, E.   Miniver Cheevy, child of scorn.

Rodgers, W.   Scapegoat.

Rodney.   Anywoman's Lyric.

Roethke.   Dream, The.

Rolfe, E.   Song: "Keep the dream alive and growing always."

Rossetti, C.   Echo.

Mirage.

My Dream.

Old-World Thicket, An.

On the Wing.

Reflection.

Rossetti, D.   Nuptial Sleep.

Orchard-Pit, The.

Severed Selves.

Rózewicz.   Memory of a Dream From the Year 1963.

Return, The.

Ruark.   Sleeping Out with My Father.

Rudnik.   Dream.

Rukeyser, M.   Burning the Dreams.

Sackville-West.   Dream, A.

Sissinghurst.

Salom.   World of dreams, The.

Sanchez, S.   Blues.

Sandburg, C.   Gone.

Prayers of Steel.

Santayana.   Sonnet V: "Dreamt I today [or to-day] the dream of yesternight."

Sarton.   Nursery Rhyme.

Sayres.   Bankrupt.

Schwartz, D.   O Child, Do Not Fear the Dark and Sleep's Dark Possession.

Scovell.   Flowers.

Seifert.   Fingerprints.

"Severyanin."   Minor Elegy, A.

Seward.   Invocation, To the Genius of Slumber Written Oct. 1787.

Sexton.   I'm dreaming the My Lai soldier

again.
Three Green Windows.
Shakespeare, W. "Be cheerful, sir."
Calphurnia here, my wife, stays me at home.
Methought That I Had Broken from the Tower.
Sonnet 27.
Shange. Dream of Pairing.
Shapiro, K. Love for a Hand.
Shelley, M. Stanzas: "Oh, come to me in dreams, my love!"
Sherburne. Dream, The.
Sherman, F. Daisies.
"Shu Ting." Singing Flower, The.
Simic. Empire of Dreams.
Simpson, L. I dreamed that in a city dark as Paris.
Skinner, J. Ballad of the Swimming Angel.
Smelyakov. Monument, The.
Smith, C. To Sleep.
Smith, S. Be Off!
In my dreams I am always saying goodbye and riding away.
My Hat.
Snyder, G. For a Stone Girl at Sanchi.
Spender, S. Daybreak.
Trance, The.
Stafford, W. Vocation.
Stevens, W. Disillusionment of Ten O'Clock.
Stevenson, R. Escape at Bedtime.
Land of Nod, The.
Young Night Thought.
Strange. Offering.
Su Tung-p'o. Southern Room Over the River, The.
Suckling, J. Dream, A.
Suo. That spring night I spent.
Swenson, M. Dream, A.
Swift, J. On Dreams.
Swinburne. Love And Sleep.
Tada. Odyssey or "On Absence," The.
Taggard. Demeter.
Tarkovsky. I dreamed this dream and I still dream of it.
Tati-Loutard. Noonday in Immaturity.
Teika. Spring night's, The.
Tekeyan. Dream.
Thwaite. Dream Time.
Timrod. Dreams.
Tolkien. Cat on the Mat.
Tomlinson, C. Dream, A.
Toomer. Evening Song.
Tree-Leaf Woman. Who speaks the sound of an echo?
Tso Ssu. Day Dreams.
Tu Mu. Easing My Heart.
Turner, W. Romance.
U Tam'si Tchicaya. Bad Blood.
Unknown. All day I hoe weeds.
Ballad of the Western Island in the North Country.
Chinese Sandmen.
Dream.
Dream of the Rood, The.
Dreams.
How They Sleep.
I cannot go to you.
Kalapuya Prophecy, A.
Last night in a dream I returned to my old home.
Limerick: "There was an old man of [or from] Peru / Who dreamt [or dreamed] he was eating his shoe."
Message of King Sakis and the Legend of the Twelve Dreams He Had in One Night, The.
She Lay All Naked in Her Bed.
Vacietis. Horse Dream.
Valentine, J. Dream Barker.
Valéry. Footsteps, The.
Van Doren. Dream of Trains, A.
Voigt. Tropics.
Vũ Đình Liên. Our Hearts Are Ancient Citadels.
Wainwright, J. Fierce Dream, The.
Wakoski. Night a Sailor Came to Me in a Dream, The.
Wang An-shih. Composed on Horseback,

Returning from Lakeview Pavilion at Hangchow, Presented to Yü-ju and Lo-tao.
Warren, R. Dream, Dump-Heap, and Civilization.
Watson, R. Nirvana.
Weaver, M. Blind Solo.
Wen Cheng-ming. For three years I sadly listened.
Wen T'ing-yün. Last night at midnight.
White, W. Rhyme of the Dream-Maker Man, A.
Whitfield. To ———: "Approaching night her mantle flings."
Whitman, W. Old War-Dreams.
Whittier. Tent on the Beach: &[;The Dreamer&];.
Wieners. King Solomon's Magnetic Quiz.
Wilbur. Beasts in their major freedom / Slumber in peace tonight.
In Limbo.
In the Smoking-Car.
Merlin Enthralled.
Walking to Sleep.
Wilde, L. Corinne's Last Love-Song.
Williams, C. Dream of Mind: The Gap, A.
Williams, W. Revelation, The.
Williamson, G. Annual Returns.
Woodard. Tower.
Wordsworth, W. Expostulation and Reply.
Lucy.
Wright, C. Further Adventures With You.
Wright, J. American Twilights, 1957.
Poem about Breasts, A.
Wright, J. End of an Ethnic Dream, The.
Wyatt, T. Lover Showeth How He Is Forsaken of Such as He Sometime Enjoyed, The.
Yakamochi. Better never to have met you.
Now to meet only in dreams.
Yang Chi. Spring dreams, more spring dreams.
Yang Shih-ch'i. Eulogy on My Own Portrait, A.
Recording a Dream.
Yeats. Dream of Death, A.
He Wishes for the Cloths of Heaven.
Host of the Air, The.
Lover Tells of the Rose in His Heart, The.
Rose of the World, The.
To the Rose upon the Rood of Time.
White Birds, The.
Yosano. Once, far over the breakers.
Tanka: "Peony in her hair, The."
Yoshimi. Tanka: "Dream, A."
Young, A. Curative Powers of Silence, The.
Yü Chi. Hearing Loom and Shuttle.
Yüan Chen. Pitcher, The.
Three Dreams at Chiang-ling.
Yüan Mei. Fog at Liang-hsiang.
Yukitsuna. Tanka: "Each morning I awake."

Dress. *See* Clothing

Drinking Water
Bishop, E. Under the Window: Ouro Prêto.
Tate, J. Contagion.

Drinks and Drinking
Ade. R-E-M-O-R-S-E.
Ai. I Can't Get Started.
Alcaeus. And if the wine leaves him witless.
Don't wait for the lamplighter.
Drink on, tho' Night be spent and Sun do shine.
Evening Song, An.
Wet your lungs with wine—the dogstar rises.
Aldrich, H. Catch, A.
Allison, D. When I drink I become / the joy of faggots.
Anacreon. Dark earth drinks the sky, The.
Drink.
Drinking.
Ode of Anacreon, Paraphras'd / The Cup, An.
Paraphras'd from Anacreon.
Upon his drinking a Bowl.
Antimedon. Of Dronkennesse.
Antipater of Thessalonica. Gipsies tell me my life-line's a short one, The.
Yesterday when I'd drunk myself to bed / with water (neat).
Apollonides. Cup clinks out, my friend, The.

Argentarius. Aristomache loved a drink:/ The old chatterbox was fonder.
Come, Gobrys, there are other gods besides the Muses.
Dead, you will lie under a yard of earth.
Drunk I observe the golden dance of stars.
Arnold, G. Beer.
Asclepiades. Get drunk, my boy, don't weep, you're.
On a Ring.
Banus. Eighteen.
Belloc. West Sussex Drinking Song.
Bishop, M. Song of the Pop-Bottlers.
Boyd, M. Beer Drops.
Brecht, B. Three Fragments.
Brome. Come a *brimmer* (my bullies) drink whole ones or nothing.
Brooks, G. We real cool. We.
Bukowski. Crucifix in a Deathhand.
Funny Man.
Burns, R. Auld Lang Syne.
Scotch Drink.
Tam o' Shanter. [A Tale].
Willie Brew'd [or Brewed] a Peck o' Maut.
Cao Bá Quát. Drink and Drown Your Cares.
Celan. I am the first to drink of the blue that still looks for its eye.
Ceravolo. Geological Hymn.
Chang Yüeh. Written When Drunk.
Ch'ien Ch'ien-i. Drinking Wine.
Poem on Drinking Wine with the Degree-Holder Ku.
Ch'in T'ao. Blaming Sons.
Chin Nung. I get so drunk, I could be called the Earl of Dissipation!
Traveler, I've been through a thousand changes, A.
"Chorny." Kreutzer Sonata, A.
Chou Pang-yen. Tune: "Distant Red Window."
Chu Tun-ju. Tune: "Magnolia Blossoms, Abbreviated" ("No one invited me").
Chu Yün-ming. Drinking.
Coolidge, C. Some Glow on the Sill.
Cope, W. Usquebaugh.
Cornish, S. His Fingers Seem to Sing.
Cowley, A. Drinking.
Epicure, The ("Fill the bowl with rosie [or rosy] wine").
Crabbe. Inebriety.
Crane, H. Wine Menagerie, The.
Cunningham, J. Interview with Doctor Drink.
Daniels, K. Christmas Party.
D'Arcy, H. Face upon [or on] the Floor, The.
Davis, J. Desolation.
De Vries, P. Bacchanal.
Ded. I searched for my Self.
Dickinson, E. I taste a liquor never brewed.
Disch. Cardinal Detoxes: A Play in One Act, The.
Dow, P. Drunk Last Night with Friends, I Go to Work Anyway.
Doyle, S. Hell To Pay.
Drummond de Andrade. Seven-Sided Poem.
Dumas, H. Knees of a Natural Man.
Eberhart, R. Ship Burning and a Comet All in One Day, A.
Eubulus. Benefits and Abuse of Alcohol, The.
Ewart. Haiku: After The Orgies.
North American Haiku.
Faiz. Prison Daybreak, A.
Fergusson. Daft Days, The.
Flanders, M. Have Some Madeira, M'dear?
Forbes, C. Potter's Wheel, The.
Garrigue. Song for "Buvez les Vins du Postillion"—Advt.
Glaser, E. Blues for the Nightowl.
Goldsmith, O. Song: "Let school-masters puzzle their brain."
Gorey. Limerick: "From the bathing machine came a din."
Limerick: "Some Harvard men, stalwart and hairy."
Graves, R. Ouzo Unclouded.
Greenwell, D. To Christina Rossetti.
Guest, B. Green Revolutions.
Guillén, N. Wake for Papa Montero.
Gunn, T. Donahue's Sister.

Halleck, F. Song: "There's a barrel of porter at Tammany Hall."
Hardy, T. Great Things.
Harte, B. Willows, The.
Hazard, J. Whiskey in Whiting, Indiana.
Heaney, S. Sloe Gin.
Hecht, A. Ghost in the Martini, The.
Hedylos. Dedication to Aphrodite, A.
Let's drink up: with wine, what original.
Musical Wine-Jar, A.
Herrick. Anacreontic[k] Verse.
Frolic[k], A.
To Live Merrily, and To Trust to Good Verses.
Wassaile, The.
Welcome to Sack, The.
Hoffenstein. Dry.
Holmes, O. Ode for a Social Meeting.
Horace. Being half foxt he praiseth Bacchus.
18th Ode 1st Book, translated or rather Imitated.
Housman, A. Terence, this is stupid stuff.
Hudgins. Praying Drunk.
Hughes, L. Flatted Fifths.
Neighbor.
Hugo, R. Hilltop, The.
Hybrias The Cretan. Song of Hybrias the Cretan.
Illyés. Part of a Novel.
Jacobsen, J. Bush.
Johnston, M. Café of Situations, The.
Drinking Sappho Brand Ouzo.
Sea-Cucumber, The.
Jonson, B. To Celia.
Jonson, E. Water-Drinker, The.
Julian. Beer.
Julianus of Egypt. 'Drink was the end of you, Anacreon'.
I kept singing this, and I will call it out from the grave.
K'ang Hai. Dreaming of Master Chung-lu.
Kendrick, D. 26th Person, The.
Kennedy, X. Hangover Mass.
In a Prominent Bar in Secaucus [One Day].
Kirsch, S. Drinking Vodka.
Komunyakaa. White Port and Lemon Juice.
Kovner. Sun-Watchers.
Landor, W. Had We Two Met.
Larkin, P. Aubade: "I work all day, and get half-drunk at night."
Leonidas of Tarentum. Remember Euboulos [or Eubolus], who lived and died sober?
Li Po. Awakening from Drunkenness on a Spring Day.
Bring the Wine!
Drinking Alone in Moonlight.
Drinking Alone in the Moonlight.
Drinking Alone under Moonlight.
For the Dancer of the King of Wu.
Night with a Friend, A.
Pot of wine among the flowers, A.
Self-abandonment.
To Amuse Myself.
Lin Hung. Drinking Wine.
Liu Tsung-yüan. Drinking at Night in the Western Pavilion of the Fa-hua Temple.
Livingston, M. Lemonade Stand.
Looney. Breaking the Surface.
Louw. Ballad of the Drinker in His Pub.
Lovelace, R. Vintage to the Dungeon, The.
Lowry, M. Eye-Opener.
Lu Chih. Wine in the cup is heavy.
Lu Yu. After Getting Drunk, I Scribble Songs and Poems.
Lucianus. We were all drunk, and Acindynus was determined to keep sober.
Lyly, J. Serving Men's Song, A.
Mac Giolla Ghunna. Yellow Bittern, The.
"MacDiarmid." Jean! Jean! Gin she's no' here it's no' oor bed.
Old Wife in High Spirits.
MacNeice. Alcohol.
Brandy Glass, The.
Madgett. Sally: Twelfth Street.
Mandelstam. I drink to military asters, to all that I'm censured about.
I'll tell you bluntly.

Martial. For every letter drink a glass.
To my Lady Rogers.
Tom never drinks: that I should much commend.
Whenever you drink all night you make.
You drink all night, and promise fairly.
Masefield. Captain Stratton's Fancy.
Mathews, H. Aboard a Boat at Night, Drinking with My Wife.
Back from Green Dragon, Presented to Hsieh Shih-chih.
Merriam, E. Counting-out Rhyme.
Merwin, W. Grandfather in the Old Men's Home.
Messerli. Actually Swallowed.
Mihalic. Drinking Spree Beneath the Open Sky.
Mitcham. Knowledge of Water, A.
Mo Shih-lung. Drinking Wine.
Moorer. Circle, The.
Social Glass, The.
Morice. Alaskan Drinking Song.
Morton, T. Song, The: "Drink and be merry, merry, merry boys."
Mother Goose. Strange Old Woman, A.
Nash, O. Reflections on Ice-breaking.
Nicarchus of Alexandria. Path of glory leads but to the grave, The.
Ome Shushiki. Be careful! Be careful!
Otomo no Tabito. Better get drunk and cry.
To sit silent.
Ou-yang Hsiu. Written for the Pavilion of the Drunken Old Man at Ch'u-chou.
Palladas. Drink to drown my sorrows and restart, A.
Paschen. Confederacy.
Peacock, M. Say You Love Me.
Pettet. Echo.
Phalaicus. This gift, her gold-hemmed saffron gown.
P'i Jih-hsiu. Impromptu on a Hangover.
Pien Kung. On Hearing That San-p'ing's Newly Brewed Chrysanthemum Wine Is Ready to Drink—Investigating with a Poem.
Pima Oral Tradition. Datura Hunting Song.
Po Chü-i. After Getting Drunk, Becoming Sober in the Night.
Better Come Drink Wine with Me.
Drunk, Facing Crimson Leaves.
Fishing in the Wei River.
Question Addressed to Liu Shih-chiu, A.
Prior. Epigram: "When Bibo thought fit from the world to retreat."
Ramsay, A. Up in the Air.
Randall, D. Old Witherington.
Rathbun. Uncool.
Redi. Bacchus's Opinion of Wine, and Other Beverages.
Ristovic. Old Motif.
Robinson, A. Oasis, An.
Robinson, E. Miniver Cheevy, child of scorn.
Mr Flood's Party.
Rochester, J. Upon Drinking in a Bowl.
Roethke. My Papa's Waltz.
Rossetti, C. Better Resurrection, A.
Rumi. Two strong impulses: One.
Sappho. Song for the Goddess of Love.
Scott, J. Plato's Dog.
Shen Chou. Drinking at Night with Yen Kung-mou.
Sheridan, R. Song: "Here's to the maiden [or maid] of bashful fifteen."
Smith, S. Grace of God and the Meth-Drinker, The.
Snyder, G. I went into the Maverick Bar.
Stanizzi. Drink.
Stephen, J. Drinking Song.
Stephens, J. Glass of Beer, A.
What Thomas an Buile Said in a Pub.
Stevenson, W. et al. Back and Side Go Bare, Go Bare.
Su Tung-p'o. Tune: Immortal at the River.
T'ao Ch'ien. Autumn chrysanthemums have beautiful color.
I built my hut in a place where people live.
Old friends know what I like.
Poem in the Form of a Coffin-Puller's Song

("What has a life must have a death").
Prosperity and decline have no fixed dwelling.
Stopping Wine.
Way's been lost for a thousand years, The.
Tekkan. Tanka: "I'll forget I saw you."
Tu Fu. Guest Arrives, A.
Snow Storm.
Turberville. Of Drunkenness.
Tyler, R. Anacreontic to Flip.
Unknown. D . . . dronken.
Drinking Song.
Finnegan's Wake.
Green green the cypress on the ridge.
Here I was and here I drank.
I cannot eat but little meat.
I have no pain, dear mother, now.
Is tell you my mind, Annes Tayliur: Dame.
Judged by the Company One Keeps.
Last Drink, A.
Little More Cider, A.
Love.
Old Woman of Norwich, The.
Omnes Gentes Plaudite!
Riddle: "As I went through yon guttery gap / I met my Uncle Davy."
Rye Whisky.
She drank good ale, strong punch and wine.
Strip Me Naked, or Royal Gin for Ever; a Picture.
Tale of Lord Lovell, The.
Tappster, fille another ale.
There was a young lady from Lynn.
When the Guests First Take Their Seats.
Voznesensky. Darkmotherscream is a Siberian dance.
Walcott. God Rest Ye Merry, Gentlemen.
Wang Ch'ang-ling. Castleside Song.
Wang Chi. 'Tell me now, what should a man want'.
Ward, E. Extravagant Drunkard's Wish, The.
Warsh. Precious Mettle.
Webster, J. Circe.
Wei Chuang. Late Rising on Spring Days.
Wen Cheng-ming. New Year's Eve.
Year I-mao (Fifteen Fifty Five), New Year's Eve, The.
Wilbur. Voice from under the Table, A.
Wilcox, E. Two Glasses, The.
Willard, N. Ballad of Biddy Early, The.
Williams, W. Drink.
Winner, S. Lilliputian's Beer Song.
Wright, J. Journey to the Place of Ghosts.
Yang Shih-ch'i. Crossing the River.
Yeats. Drinking Song, A.
Yen Chi-tao. Tune: "Butterflies Lingering over Flowers."
Yevtushenko. Siberian Wooing.
Young, A. I Arrive In Madrid.
Young, G. Lips That Touch Liquor.
Yü Hsüan-chi. To Tzu-an.
Yüan Chen. Drunk Too Soon.
Recalling When I Was Drunk.
Sobering Up.

See also **Alcoholism and Alcoholics; Drunkards**

Driving and Drivers
Betjeman. Meditation on the A30.
Blackburn, P. El Camino Verde.
Bly, R. Driving toward the Lac Qui Parle River.
Three Kinds of Pleasures.
Creeley. I Know a Man.
Cummings, E. She being Brand.
Dobyns. General Matthei Drives Home through Santiago.
Dove, R. Nigger Song: An Odyssey.
Dufault. Driving Home.
Dunn, S. Looking for a Rest Area.
Ginsberg, A. Bayonne Turnpike to Tuscarora.
Hanzlik. Who's that driving a black cart.
Heaney, S. From the Frontier of Writing.
Peninsula, The.
Hull, L. Fiat Lux.
Ilantiraiyan. Great Wagon, The.
Jarman, M. Homing Instinct, The.
Los Angeles.
Kyger. News bulletin from Keith Lampe.
Lehman. First Offense.

Livingston, M. 4-Way Stop.
Meissner. Twisters.
Miles, J. Reason.
Mitchell, S. Once, Driving West of Billings, Montana.
Parun. Let's Get the Coachman Drunk.
Pettit. Driving Lesson.
Revard. Driving in Oklahoma.
Rukeyser, M. Sand-Quarry with Moving Figures.
Sexton. Road Back, The.
Shapiro, D. Taking a Look.
Van Duyn. Vision Test, The.
Vinokurov. Rhythm.

See also **Automobiles**

Drought
Caraion. Remember.
Lewis, A. Mahratta Ghats, The.
Muske. Little L.A. Villanelle.
Narasimhaswami. Consolation to Empty Pitchers.
Osundare. Who Says That Drought Was Here?
Phạm Quý Thích. Summer Drought.
Su Tung-p'o. Little stream used to cross my land, A.
Trần Tế Xu'o'ng. Drought.
Wright, J. Drought Year.
Yashashchandra. Drought.

Drowning
Adcock, B. Walking Out.
Atwood. Death of a Young Son by Drowning.
This Is a Photograph of Me.
Bagg. Death at Pocono Lake Preserve.
Barrax. Scuba Diver Recovers the Body of a Drowned Child, The.
Benn. Little Aster.
Lovely Childhood.
Bottoms. Drowned, The.
Under the Boathouse.
Brewster, E. Death by Drowning.
Cavafy. Supplication.
Cowper, W. Castaway, The.
Dawe, B. Elegy for Drowned Children.
Derwood. Elegy: "When in the mirror of a permanent tear."
Dickinson, E. Drowning is not so pitiful.
Djanikian. Agami Beach.
Dobson, R. Three Fates, The.
Donne. Burnt Ship, A.
Hero and Leander.
Field, E. Icarus.
Fumi Saito. Tanka: "To take a bath."
Gardner, C. Dead Man Dragged from the Sea, The.
Glaukos. Inscription by the Sea, An.
Glück, L. Drowned Children, The.
Gray, T. Ode on the Death of a Favourite [*or* Favorite] Cat, Drowned in a Tub [*or* Bowl] of Gold Fishes.
Hardy, T. Mongrel, The.
Heaney, S. Limbo.
Hill, G. White Ship, The.
Holden, M. Seaman, 1941.
Hugo, R. Lady in Kicking Horse Reservoir, The.
Jones, D. These Trees Are No Forest of Mourners.
Kingsley, C. Sands of Dee, The.
Lattimore. RMS Lusitania.
Lear, E. Limerick: "There was an Old Man in a boat."
Lowry, M. Salmon Drowns Eagle.
Mechthild von Magdeburg. Fish cannot drown in water, A.
Miles, J. Family.
Moss, H. Water Island.
Mother Goose. Ding, dong, bell, / Pussy's in the well.
Oliver, D. Oracle of the Drowned, The.
Parker, D. Résumé.
Porumbacu. Anesthesia.
Salom. Winter.
Shakespeare, W. Ariel's Song ("Full fathom [*or* fadom] five thy father lies").
Smith, S. Not Waving But Drowning.
Sweeney, M. Where Fishermen Can't Swim.
Thomas, E. Midnight Thought, A &[;on the

Death of Mrs. *E. H.* and Her Little Daughter&];.
"Twain." Emmeline Grangerford's "Ode to Stephen Dowling Bots, Dec'd."
Unknown. Clementine.
Ding dong bell! Pussy's in the well!
Golden Vanity, The.
Jimmy Judge.
Lowlands o' [*or of*] Holland, The.
May Colven [*or* May Colvin].
Samuel Allen.
Sir Patrick Spens [*or* Spence].
Three children sliding on the ice.
Tweed and Till.
Vogel, D. I saw my father drowning.
Whitman, W. Beautiful Swimmer, The.
Wilbur. Marginalia.
Williams, W. Landscape with the Fall of Icarus.
Witheford. At the Discharge of Cannon Rise the Drowned.
Wright, J. In Response to a Rumor that the Oldest Whorehouse in Wheeling, West Virginia, Has Been Condemned.
Note Left in Jimmy Leonard's Shack, A.
To the Muse.
Wright, J. Eli, Eli.

Drug Addiction
Adamson. Passing Through Experiences.
Ai. Archangel.
Baraka. Babylon Revisited.
Barresi. Venice Beach: Brief Song.
Barth, R. Insert, The.
Brooks, G. Coora Flower, The.
Brown, P. I Remember Dexedrine. 1970.
Carroll, J. Paregoric Babies.
Withdrawal Letter.
Chong, H. Note 25.
Clark, T. Going to School in France or America.
Creeley. Chasing the Bird.
Dransfield. Fix.
Fanthorpe. Person's Tale, The.
Forbes, J. Speed, a Pastoral.
Gunn, T. Street Song.
Harrison, W. In Praise of Laudanum.
Hirsch, E. Art Pepper.
Hope, A. Under Sedation.
Hughes, L. Junior Addict.
Hull, L. Hospice.
Jauss. Black Orchid.
Jones, J. Drugs.
Knight, E. Another Poem for Me (after Recovering from an O.D.)
Idea of Ancestry, The.
Welcome Back, Mr. Knight: Love of My Life.
Komunyakaa. Crack.
Speed Ball.
Lerman. Margaret Whiting Tearfully Sings.
Levis. Magnolia.
Mackey, N. Falso Brilhante.
Murray, L. Drugs of War, The.
Orlen. Aga Khan, The.
Sanchez, S. Homecoming.
Summer Words of [*or* for] a Sistuh [*or* Sister] Addict.
Shelton, R. Certain Choices.
Smith, S. Drugs made Pauline vague.
Spicer, J. Song for Bird and Myself.
Thomas, L. Historiography.
Tucker, M. Opium-Eater, The.
Unknown. Cocaine Lil [and Morphine Sue].
Laudanum.
Willie the Weeper.
Waring, B. Refuge at the One Step Down.
Wright, F. Needle: For a Friend Who Disappeared, The.

Drugs
Berrigan, T. Dear Margie, hello. It is 5:15 a.m.
Things To Do in Providence.
Carroll, J. Maybe I'm Amazed.
Cooper, D. Drugs.
Creeley. Chasing the Bird.
Di Prima. Ave.
Ford, C. Bad Habit, The.
Hollo. Discovery of LSD a True Story, The.

Hull, L. Hospice.
Jail, Flames—Jersey, 1971.
Letter, The.
Jackson, R. Tee.
Jarman, M. Black Riviera, The.
Jones, J. Drugs.
Knight, E. Feeling Fucked/Up Up.
Idea of Ancestry, The.
Leonard, T. Paroakial.
McClure, M. Clear—the senses bright—sitting in the black chair—Rocker.
Mirikitani. Jade.
Morgan, E. De Quincey in Glasgow.
Muldoon, P. Gathering Mushrooms.
St. John, D. Meridian.
Selman, R. And so I went forth, exhilarated.
And so I went forth in uniform.
I befriended Mike with the good hash pipe.
Sinclair, I. German Bite.
Smith, S. Marriage I think.
Spicer, J. Song for Bird and Myself.
Unknown. Cocaine Lil [and Morphine Sue].
Weiners. Act #2.
Poem for vipers, A.
Wright, F. Needle: For a Friend Who Disappeared, The.

Drugstores
Whitney, I. Now when thy folke are fed and clad.

Druids
Wordsworth, W. Trepidation of the Druids.

Drums
Andal. We rose before dawn.
Baca. Voz de la Gente.
Barlow, G. 4½ Months: Halfway Song.
Bethune, L. For Singing In Good Mood.
Bolamba. Bonguemba.
Cortez. Tapping.
DiPasquale. Rain.
Etter. Stuffy Turkey.
Hardy, T. Drummer Hodge.
Hernton. Distant Drum, The.
Hughes, L. Danse Africaine.
Kao Ch'i. Ballad of the Neighborhood Shaman.
Komunyakaa. Back Then.
Kyei. Talking Drums, The.
Liu E. House of Red Leaves, The.
MacLeish. End of the World, The.
Momaday. Eagle-Feather Fan, The.
Ni Tsan. To the Retired Scholar Chang.
Okara. Piano and Drums.
Okigbo. Sacrifice.
Olson, C. La Chute.
Quasimodo. Anno Domini MCMXLVII.
Scott of Amwell. Ode: "I hate that drum's discordant sound."
Senghor. French Garden.
Seymour, A. Drums / Then again drums.
Smith, P. They say that black people.
Unknown. King Wen's Park Divine.
Wizard's Chant, The.
Whitman, W. Beat! beat! drums!—blow! bugles! blow!
Wu Wei-yeh. At the Mountain of the Mysterious Tomb Visiting Master P'ou.
Young, K. Escape Artist, The.

Drunkards
Baillie, J. Hooly and Fairly.
Barnes, J. Lying in a Yuma Saloon.
Berryman. Alcoholic.
Burns, R. Johnie Blunt.
Poor Merry-Andrew, in the neuk.
Carver, R. Wine.
Chesterton, G. Rolling English Road, The.
Chin Nung. I get so drunk, I could be called the Earl of Dissipation!
"Chorny." Drunkard's Nocturnes, A.
Chu Yün-ming. Clouds are swept into the sunset—mdash;a sky beyond the sky.
Cummings, E. He as O, A.
Cunningham, J. Interview with Doctor Drink.
D'Arcy, H. Face upon [*or* on] the Floor, The.
Dickinson, E. Drunkard cannot meet a Cork, A.
I taste a liquor never brewed.

Dove, R.   Genie's Prayer Under the Kitchen Sink.
Endrezze-Danielson.   Eclipse.
   Song-Maker.
Evans, G.   Renaissance Drunk, A.
Glazkov.   What Did They Have In Mind?
Graves, R.   Point of No Return.
Herrick.   Vision, The.
Housman, A.   Could man be drunk for ever.
   Terence, this is stupid stuff.
Hsü Chung-hsing.   Who would have thought that a disease of the ordinary world.
Hsü Pen.   Hermit Li's Herb Garden Retreat at T'ung-ch'uan.
Knight, S.   Resentments Composed because of the Clamor of Town Topers Outside My Apartment.
Leland, C.   Wein Geist.
Levine, P.   Sweet Will.
Li K'ai-hsien.   Drunk, Climbing to the Peak of Iron Tomb on Wei Mountain.
Li Po.   Self-abandonment.
Li Tung-yang.   Long Handscroll of Bamboo by Wang Meng-tuan, The.
Lu Yu.   Sailing on the Lake to the Ching River.
   Wild Flower Man, The.
Martial.   Last night, after five pints of wine.
Meinke.   Elegy for a Diver.
Merwin, W.   Drunk in the Furnace, The.
Mo Shih-lung.   On a Cold Day I Climbed Tiger Hill With Professor Ho. At the Time, the Local Prefect Had Prohibited Pleasure Excursions and Feasts, But the Mountain Was Quiet and Tranquil, So We Stayed All Day.
More, H.   Come, neighbour, take a walk with me.
Moriarty, L.   Rondeaux: "Each page a day."
Morice.   Alaskan Drinking Song.
Nash, O.   Say About Seven or Seven-Fifteen.
Notley.   Jack Would Speak Through the Imperfect Medium of Alice.
Ou-yang Hsiu.   Inscribed on the Arbor of the Old Drunkard (Tsui-weng-t'ing) at Ch'u-chou.
Paul, L.   Cynical Portraits.
Po Chü-i.   After Getting Drunk, Becoming Sober in the Night.
Prior.   Epigram: "When Bibo thought fit from the world to retreat."
Randall, D.   Old Witherington.
Robinson, E.   Miniver Cheevy, child of scorn.
   Mr Flood's Party.
Smith, S.   Grace of God and the Meth-Drinker, The.
Södergran.   Question.
Stevenson, R.   Pirate Ditty.
Su Tung-p'o.   Tune: Immortal at the River.
Symons, A.   Absinthe-Drinker, The.
T'ang Yin.   Inscribed on a Painting of a Fisherman.
   Inscribed on a Painting of Bamboo.
Tao-chi.   Inscribed on "Drunk in the Autumn Woods."
Thatcher, C.   Moggy's Wedding.
Tucker, M.   Drunkard's Wife, The.
Turberville.   Of Drunkenness.
Tyler, R.   Original Epitaph on a Drunkard.
Unknown.   Chinook Songs.
   Drunk Man, The.
   Drunkard's Doom, The.
   John Adkins' Farewell.
   Limerick.
   Pig, The.
   Red Whiskey.
   Shickered As He Could Be.
   Tarpauling Jacket.
Ward, E.   Extravagant Drunkard's Wish, The.
Wilbur.   Voice from under the Table, A.
Willard, N.   Ballad of Biddy Early, The.
Williams, W.   Drunkard, The.
Woodward, C.   Midnight Ramble, The.
Work.   Come Home, Father[!].
Wright, J.   Inscription for the Tank.
   Note Left in Jimmy Leonard's Shack, A.
Yang Shih-ch'i.   Not sobered up from my

muddy Kao-yang drunk.
   Searching for the Ruins of the Pavilion of the Drunken Old Man.
Yesenin.   Letter to My Mother.
   My leafless maple tree, your icy coating.
Zimmer.   Zimmer Drunk and Alone, Dreaming of Old Football Games.

See also **Alcoholism and Alcoholics**

Dryads
Doolittle, H.   Acon.

Dryden, John
Behn, A.   On Mr. Dryden, Renegade.
McAuley, J.   Dear John, whoever now takes pen to write.
Piers.   Urania: The Divine Muse. On the Death of John Dryden, Esq.
Thomas, E.   Dream, The; An Epistle to Mr. Dryden.

Du Bois, William Edward Burghardt
Latimer.   For William Edward Burghardt Du Bois on His Eightieth Birthday.
Randall, D.   Booker T. and W. E. B.
Rivers, C.   On the Death of William Edward Burghardt Du Bois by African Moonlight and Forgotten Shores.

Dublin, Ireland
Durcan.   Bewley's Oriental Café, Westmoreland Street.
Ford, R.   Back to Dublin.
Kavanagh, P.   Canal Bank Walk.
   If ever you go to Dublin town.
   Lines Written on a Seat on the Grand Canal, Dublin.
Larkin, P.   Dublinesque.
MacDonagh, D.   Dublin Made Me.
MacNeice.   Dublin.
Montague, J.   Herbert Street Revisited.
O'Connor, P.   Lights of Dublin, The.
Ormsby, F.   At the Jaffé Memorial Fountain, Botanic Gardens.

Duchamp, Marcel
Kennedy, X.   Nude Descending a Staircase.

Ducks
Allingham.   Four Ducks on a Pond.
"Carroll."   Little Man That Had a Little Gun, The.
Donaghy, J.   Duck.
Galvin, B.   Seals in the Inner Harbor.
Grahame, K.   Duck''s Ditty.
Greger.   Garden, The.
Higginson, W.   Ducks land, The.
Ivaska.   Wild ducks had flown, and early this year.
Kao Ch'i.   Song of the Duck Hunters.
Keyser.   In the wake.
King, E.   Duck, The.
Kinnell.   Duck-chasing.
Lear, E.   Duck and the Kangaroo, The.
Lesoro.   Muscovy Drake, The.
Lloyd, D.   Duck feathers.
Masaoka Shiki.   During a trip.
McDonald, W.   Faraway Places.
Mitchell, S.   Feeding the ducks at the Howard Johnson Motel.
Nash, O.   Duck, The.
Noyes, A.   New Duckling, The.
Sandeen.   Nearing Winter.
Swenson, M.   Goodbye, Goldeneye.
Symons, A.   By the Pool at the Third Rosses.
Taylor, A.   Notorious Glutton, The.
Worth, V.   Duck.

Dudevant, Baronne. *See* **"Sand, George"**

Duels
Field, E.   Duel, The.
Unknown.   Dowie Houms o' Yarrow, The.

Dullness
Inez.   Old Lady Across the Hall Has Gone to Live Behind the Door, The.
Mother Goose.   Simple Simon met a pieman.
Pope, A.   Reign of Chaos, The.
Pound, E.   Les Millwin.

Dumbness
Hall, D.   Je Suis une Table.
Lear, E.   Limericks, I (v).

Dumont, Margaret
Hollander, J.   To the Lady Portrayed by Margaret Dumont.

Dumps
Holman, F.   City Dump, The.
Kuzma.   Dump, The.
Nemerov.   Town Dump, The.
Spires.   Woman on the Dump, The.
Stevens, W.   Man on the Dump, The.

Dunbar, Paul Laurence
Corrothers.   Paul Laurence Dunbar.
Cullen, C.   For Paul Laurence Dunbar.
Hayden, R.   Paul Laurence Dunbar.
Linden, M.   Paul Laurence Dunbar.
Ray, H.   In Memoriam Paul Laurence Dunbar.
Spencer, A.   Dunbar.

Dundee, John Graham of Claverhouse, 1st Viscount ("Bonnie Dundee")
Scott, W.   Bonny [*or* Bonnie] Dundee.

Dunes
Ammons.   So I Said I Am Ezra.
Frost, R.   Sand Dunes.

Duns Scotus
Hopkins, G.   Duns Scotus's Oxford.

Dunwich, England
Thwaite.   At Dunwich.

Dürer, Albrecht
"Ern Malley."   Dürer: Innsbruck, 1495.
Haines, J.   Dürer's Vision.
Jarrell.   Knight, Death, and the Devil, The.
"Malley."   Dürer; Innsbruck, 1495.
Moore, M.   Steeple-Jack, The.

Dusk. *See* **Twilight**

Dust
Ackland.   Poem: "You send me a letter from far, from across the sea."
Borges.   John 1:14 (1964).
Cather, W.   Prairie Spring.
Chesterton, G.   Praise of Dust, The.
Chin.   Altar.
Davies, J.   Remembrance of My Friend Mr. Thomas Morley, A.
Dickinson, E.   Death is a Dialogue between.
Douglas, L.   Ode to My Soul.
Faiz.   No Sign of Blood.
"Field."   Mummy Invokes his Soul, The.
Finch, A.   Sapphics for Patience.
Frost, R.   Meeting and Passing.
Gascoyne.   Yves Tanguy.
Gilbo'a.   My Soul Wanders About.
Gunn, T.   Elegy on the Dust.
Johnson, G.   Common Dust.
Kunio.   Tanka: "I've swept away."
Machi.   Tanka: "Trying to wash away."
Ni Tsan.   Following the Rhymes of the Six Poems "Thinking of the Past at Ku-Su and Ch'ien-t'ang."
Po Chü-i.   Five-string[1], The.
Ropes.   Dust.
Rukeyser, M.   George Robinson: Blues.
Saitō Mokichi.   Tanka: "Past the hens."
Spire.   Duster, dust away, my friend.
Tekeyan.   Country of Dust, The.
Tekkan.   Tanka: "Bliss, The."
Unknown.   Ashes to ashes.
Wen Cheng-ming.   On First Returning from Taking the Examinations: Feelings at Cloud-Stop Pavilion.
   These long verandahs seem to be washed clean.
Wheelock, J.   This Quiet Dust.
Wiggin.   Dreaming.
Yang Chi.   Thousands of flowers, thousands of petals.
Yün Shou-p'ing.   Lament for the Willows outside the City Walls, A.

Dutch, The
Canning, G.   Dutch, The.

Dutch Wars
Dryden, J.   Now van to van the foremost squadrons meet.
Sackville, C.   Song Written at Sea in the First Dutch War (1665), the Night before an Engagement.

Duty
Amichai.   We Have Done Our Duty.

Boker. Brave comrade, answer! When you joined the war.
Burich. Citizen's Way, The.
Clough. Duty—that's to say, complying.
Cornford, F. Ode on the Whole Duty Of Parents.
Dimoski. Revenge.
Emerson, R. I Can.
Erdrich. Shelter.
Frost, R. Stopping by Woods on a Snowy Evening.
Han Yü. This morning I can't seem to get out of bed.
Hay, J. Jim Bludso of the Prairie Belle.
Hoagland, T. In the Land of the Lotus Eaters.
Hodgson, W. England to Her Sons.
Hooper, E. Duty.
Hsü Pen. To the Filial Son, Ts'ui.
Huang T'ing-chien. Out in the Snow, Spending the Night at the New Stockade, Extremely Depressed.
Kingsley, C. Three Fishers [Went Sailing], The.
Kipling, R. Eddi's Service.
Li K'ai-hsien. Gazing at Ch'ang-po Mountain.
Li Po. On the river, every day these heavy rains.
Li Shang-yin. Last night's stars, last night's winds.
Lu Yu. Long Sigh.
McCrae, J. In Flanders Fields the poppies blow.
Milton. On His Blindness.
Sonnet: "How soon hath Time the suttle [or subtle] theef [or thief] of youth."
Monk, M. Verses Written on Her Death-Bed at Bath to Her Husband in London.
Moorer. Duty, or Truth at Work.
Nash, O. Kind of an Ode to Duty.
Pasternak, B. Devotion is a heavy cross.
Ralegh, W. Sir Walter Ralegh to the Queen.
Read, S. My men go wearily.
Shakespeare, W. Sonnet 26.
Stafford, W. Traveling [or Travelling] through the dark I found a deer.
Stevenson, A. In the Orchard.
Stevenson, R. Say not of me that weakly I declined.
Unknown. Do It Now!
Village Crier, The.
Watts, I. How doth the little busy bee.
Whittier. Abraham Davenport.
Wordsworth, W. Ode to Duty.
Yang Wei-chen. Tu-lu Poem ("Tu-lu, Tu-lu, evil waters running muddy").

Dwarfs
Ewart. Lines: "Other day I was loving a sweet little fruitpie-and-cream, The."
Merwin, W. Small Woman on Swallow Street.
Smart, C. Author Apologizes to a Lady, for His Being a Little Man, The.
Wallace-Crabbe. Windows, The.

E

Eagles
Altamirano, S. Eagle above Us, The.
Amichai. My son, in whose face there is already a sign.
Duncan, R. Letting the beat go.
Fordham. To the Eagle.
Hale, S. Mole and the Eagle, The.
Harjo, J. Eagle Poem.
Hughes, L. Fact.
Jeffers, R. Beaks of Eagles, The.
Fire on the Hills.
Kavanagh, P. Goldie Sapiens.
Lawrence, D. American Eagle, The.
Towards the sun, towards the south-west.
Lindsay, V. Eagle That Is Forgotten, The.
Lowry, M. Salmon Drowns Eagle.
Momaday. Eagle-Feather Fan, The.
Story of a Well-made Shield, The.
Skelton, R. Eagle.
Tennyson, A. Eagle, The.
Todd, R. Poem: "I walk at dawn across the hollow hills."

Unknown. Ha-Kon-E-Crase, the Eagle Dance.
Villanueva, A. Even the Eagles Must Gather.
Whitman, W. Dalliance of the Eagles, The.
Wylie. Eagle and the Mole, The.
"Yashin." Eagle, The.
Young Bear. Our Bird Aegis.

Ears
Allen, M. What Is It?
Forché. Colonel, The.
Haines, J. Awakening.
Herbert, Z. Rosy Ear.
Lovelace, R. To a Lady That Desired Me I Would Bear My Part with Her in a Song.
Machi. Tanka: "Looking as though."
Masing. For Polla.
Roseliep. Cat, The.
Thoreau. Each More Melodious Note I Hear.
Unknown. Young Man of Devizes, The.
Young Man Who Couldn't See Why, The.
Zimmer. Failings, The.

Earth
Allen, S. Moment Please, A.
Arendt. Ode I.
Atwood. You begin this way.
Auden. Et in Arcadia Ego.
Auvaiyar. Earth's Bounty.
Begay. Mother's Lace.
Bible, O.T. Holy, holy, holy.
Lay not up for yourselves treasures.
Blake, W. And every Space that a Man views around his dwelling-place.
Earth's Answer.
Introduction: "Hear the voice of the Bard!"
To see a World in a Grain of Sand.
Blind. Chaunts of Life.
Bly, R. Extra Joyful Chorus for Those Who Have Read This Far, An.
Bognini. Earth and sky are infinities / Where our cries cannot venture.
Bradstreet, A. Contemplations.
Brathwaite, E. Red Rising.
Bronk. Aspects of the World like Coral Reefs.
Browning, R. Sonnet: "When our two souls stand up erect and strong."
Bryant, W. Thanatopsis.
Césaire, A. Bucolic.
Channing. Hymn of the Earth.
Chao Meng-fu. Lamenting the Taoist Wei Kung-yüan.
Ch'en Tzu-ang. As the crescent moon is born from the Western Sea.
Chia Tao. Evening View as the Snow Clears.
Ch'ien T'ao. Substance, Shadow, and Spirit.
Chu Yi-tsun. West Cliff.
Clairmont. Answers, The.
Clare, J. Loves Lives Beyond the Tomb.
Clifton, L. Message of Crazy Horse, The.
Cowley, A. Drinking.
Cowper, W. Work of Gardening, The.
Crase. Once the Sole Province.
Creeley. Here.
Cummings, E. Bigness of cannon, The.
O sweet spontaneous.
De la Mare. Snow.
Deloney. Weavers Song, The.
Desnos. There once was a leaf with all its lines.
Donne. First Anniversary [or Anniversarie], The.
To Mr. Tilman after He Had Taken Orders.
Valediction: Of Weeping, A.
Dransfield. Strange Bird, A.
Drevniok. Deep snow.
Drinkwater. Town Window, A.
Dumaine. Second Language.
Eberhart, R. Hard Structure of the World, The.
Soul Longs to Return Whence It Came, The.
Under the Hill.
Echeruo. Melting Pot.
Edwards, M. World Is Full of Beauty, The.
Emerson, R. Hamatreya.
Empson. To an Old Lady.
Faber, F. World is wise, for the world is old, The.
Fitzgerald, E. 73.
Fletcher, G. As when the cheerfull Sunne, elamping wide.

Fuertes. Birds Nest in My Arms, The.
Fulton, R. Resolutions.
Gilbert, S. To the Terrestrial Globe.
Grahn. Spider Webster's Declaration: He Is Singing the End of the World Again.
Haines, J. Cloud Factory, The.
Tundra is a living, The.
Halevi. Earth in Spring, The.
Harington. Thus all that day, they spent in divers talke.
Heaney, S. Bog Queen.
Herrick. White Island.
Hewitt, J. Because I paced my thought by the natural world.
Hildegard von Bingen. I am the one whose praise echoes on high.
Hill, G. Genesis.
I was invested in mother-earth, the crypt of roots.
In Piam Memoriam.
Hollo. Shed the Fear.
Hopkins, G. God's Grandeur.
Howe, J. Kosmos.
Hughes, T. Like those flailing flames.
River.
Ingelow. Divided.
Ivask, I. And then I told about the red soil of Oklahoma.
Iverem. Earth Screaming.
Jarrell. Blind Sheep, The.
Jeffers, R. Autumn Evening.
Eye, The.
Life from the Lifeless.
Shine, Perishing Republic.
Jemie. Iroko.
Johnston, G. O Earth, Turn!
Juana Inés de la Cruz. Since Love is shivering.
Kim, M. Bounty, II, The.
Kipling, R. Sestina of the Tramp-Royal.
Kitching. No need to scan the skies.
Koch, K. Geography.
Kusano Shimpei. Skylarks and Fuji.
Lattimore. Report from a Planet.
Lawrence, D. Fidelity and love are two different things, like a flower and a gem.
Lepik. Nobody talks earth's language.
Levertov. O Taste and See.
What It Could Be.
Levine, P. Clouds.
How Much Earth.
Rain Downriver.
Snow.
They Feed They Lion.
To My God in His Sickness.
Li Ho. Ch'ang-ku.
On the Frontier.
Ravine on a Cold Evening.
Up in Heaven.
Li Po. How like a bolt of white silk is this water.
Lovelace, R. To My Noble Kinsman, Thomas Stanley, Esquire, on His Lyric Poems Composed by Master John Gamble.
"MacDiarmid." Bonnie Broukit Bairn, The.
Stick-nest in Ygdrasil, A.
MacLeish. Seafarer.
Speech to a Crowd.
Mahon. Tractatus.
Masaoka Shiki. During an illness.
Masters, E. Fiddler Jones.
Meng Chiao. Edges of the gorges hack up sun and moon, The.
Merriam, E. Landscape.
Merrill, J. Childlessness.
Meyn. At the Planning Commission.
Miles, J. Merchant Marine.
On Inhabiting an Orange.
Millay, E. God's World.
Muir, E. One foot in Eden still, I stand.
Murray, P. Conquest.
Nagy, A. Between.
Neidjie. This earth.
Newcastle, M. Of the Animal Spirits.
Nicholls, J. Earthrise.
Earthset.
Nichols, G. Sugar Cane.

Noguere. Whirling Round the Sun.
Oppian. Prayer, A.
Osundare. Eyeful Glances.
Goree.
  I Sing of Change.
  Our Earth Will Not Die.
  We called the statue.
  Who Says That Drought Was Here?
Ou-yang Hsiu. Tune: "Butterflies Lingering over Flowers" ("Ruffed blue-green garden, red blossoms").
Ovid. To his Paternall Countrey.
Padilla. Fountain, a house of stone, A.
Pagis. Lesson in Observation, A.
Patchen. Temple, A.
Perelman. China.
"Perse." Anabasis.
Peters, L. Parachute Men say.
Petrarch. Now that the sky and earth and wind are still.
Polkowski. World is only air / shining, granular, transparent things, The.
Popa. Burning Shewolf.
Prévert. Song in the Blood.
Puttenham. O mightye Muse.
Quarles. What is the *World?* A great *Exchange* of ware.
"Rachel." Here on Earth.
Raine, K. World, The.
Rands. World, The.
Rexroth, K. Lute Music.
  Lyell's Hypothesis Again.
Rich, A. Dark woman, head bent, listening for something, A.
Roberts, E. People, The.
Robinson, A. Sibyl, The.
  Unum est Necessarium.
Robinson, K. Nursery Rhyme.
Rossetti, C. Advent.
  Buried.
  Horses of the sea, / Rear a foaming crest, The.
  Later Life: A Double Sonnet of Sonnets.
Rukeyser, M. He Had a Quality of Growth.
Rummo. Sky bends over the earth, The.
St. John, P. Lynching and Burning.
Sandburg, C. Be Ready.
  Early Copper.
Santos, S. Nineteen Fifty-five.
Sarton. Prothalamion for an Autumn Wedding.
Schuyler, J. Earth's Holocaust.
Scovell. Flowers.
"Setoun." World's Music, The.
Sexton. Earth, The.
Shūji. Tanka: "To do away with anger."
Sidney, P. Long Their Coupled Joys Maintain.
Sillitoe. Optics.
Simic. Poem: "Every morning I forget how it is."
Smelyakov. Earth.
Smith, I. In the late evening.
Snyder, G. For Nothing.
Southwell. Vale of Tear[e]s, A.
Soyinka. Ujamaa.
Stevens, W. Gubbinal.
  Planet on the Table, The.
  Ultimate Poem Is Abstract, The.
Su Tung-p'o. Abandoned earthworks nobody tends.
Supervielle. Earth.
  Voyages.
Sylvester, J. Ubique.
Sze. Every Where and Every When.
  Network, The.
Taylor, A. Earth.
Taylor, E. Preface, The: "Infinity, when all things it beheld."
Tewa Oral Tradition. Song of the Sky Loom.
Thomas, D. This bread I break was once the oat.
Tomlinson, C. Ararat.
Ts'ao P'i. Lotus Pond, The.
Tsvetaeva. Fatal volume, The.
Tu Mu. Climbing Up to the Lo-yu Plain.
  Shih Ch'ung's 'Golden Valley' Garden.
Tuckerman, F. Sonnet: "And so, as this great sphere (now turning slow)."
Ungaretti. You Were Broken.

Unknown. Hymn to the Earth.
  Hymn to the Orange.
  Small bird, forgive me.
  This Newly Created World.
Vaughan, H. World, The (1).
Virgil. Knifing deep.
Walcott. Elsewhere.
Wen T'ing-yün. Early Walk on Shang Mountain, An.
Weston, M. Departure.
Wheelock, J. Earth ("'Planet doesn't explode of itself, A,' said drily").
White, J. In Ecclesiastes I read, "That which is far off and exceeding deep".
Whitman, S. November Landscape, A.
Whitman, W. Earth, my likeness.
  I am the poet of the Body and I am the poet of the Soul.
  This Compost.
Wilbur. Caserta Garden.
Williams, W. At Kenneth Burke's Place.
Wordsworth, W. Composed upon Westminster Bridge[, September 3, 1802].
Wright, J. Arrangements with Earth for Three Dead Friends.
  At Thomas Hardy's Birthplace, 1953.
  Fit against the Country, A.
  What the Earth Asked Me.
Wylie. Hymn to Earth.
Yeats. Before the World Was Made.
Yosano. Tanka: "Earth looks, The."

Earthquakes
Antiphilus. Earthquaked, my house collapsed.
Cuevish. Before They Made Things Be Alive They Spoke.
Ford, R. Earthquake.
Grainger, J. Then earthquakes, nature's agonizing pangs.
Heard, J. Earthquake of 1886, The.
Hillman. Mighty Forms.
Kirkup. Earth Tremor in Lugano.
Li K'ai-hsien. Earthquake covered Shansi and Shensi, An.
Miller, A. Crack in the Wall Holds Flowers.
Olds, S. Quake Theory.
Seward. On Catania and Syracuse Swallowed Up by an Earthquake, from the Italian of Filicaja.
Tekkan. Tanka: "I'll forget I saw you."
Unknown. Santa Barbara Earthquake, The.
Young, G. Four Days: Earthquake.
Zenmaro. September 1, 1923.

"Eastaway, Edward." *See* **Thomas, Edward**

Easter
Ammons. Easter Morning.
Awoonor. Easter Dawn.
Bennett, R. Easter Praise.
Bertrans de Born. Song of Battle.
Clifton, L. God Send Easter.
Clough. Easter Day. Naples, 1849.
Coleridge, M. When Mary thro' the Garden Went.
Crashaw. Easter Day.
Hardy, T. Drizzling Easter Morning, A.
Heard, J. Easter Morn.
Herbert, G. Easter ("Rise heart; thy Lord is risen. Sing his praise").
  Easter-Wings.
Hope, A. Easter Hymn.
Hopkins, G. That Nature Is a Heraclitean Fire and of the Comfort of the Resurrection.
Hopkins, G. Alleluia! Christ is risen today.
Housman, A. Easter Hymn.
  Loveliest of trees, the cherry now.
John of Damascus. Day of Resurrection, The.
Luther. In the bonds of Death He lay.
Melville, H. Easter.
Meynell, A. Easter Night.
Moorer. Easter; or, Spring-Time.
Nemerov. Easter.
Nicol. African Easter.
Paquet. Easter '68.
Peacock, M. Chriseaster.
Prudentius. Easter Eve.
  For the Kindling of the Light on Easter Eve.
Ray, H. Easter Carol.
Rossetti, C. Easter Monday.

Schaefer, S. Rejoice, Let Alleluias Ring.
Sisson. Easter.
Spenser. Sonnet 68: "Most glorious Lord of Life that on this day."
Thaxter. On Easter Day.
Thompson, C. Easter Light, The.
Truax. Morning, Noon, And.
Turner, A. Three Easters.
Turner, S. Christmas Is Really for the Children.
Updike. Seven Stanzas at Easter.
Vaughan, H. Easter-Day.
  Easter Hymn.
Wakley. Easter Chick, An.
Wilde, O. Easter Day.
Wordsworth, W. Composed in One of the Valleys of Westmoreland, on Easter Sunday.
Yeats. Easter 1916.

Easter Rebellion (1916)
Ledwidge. Lament for the Poets: 1916.
  Lament for Thomas MacDonagh.
MacDonagh, D. Veterans, The.
Yeats. Easter 1916.
  Rose Tree, The.
  Sixteen Dead Men.

Eatherly, Claude R.
Wain. Song about Major Eatherly, A.

Eating
Ackland. When I have said 'I love you' I have said.
Aldis, D. Mouths.
Alexander, E. Nineteen.
Bakken. How to Eat Corn.
Barrax. In the Restaurant.
Belloc. Vulture eats between his meals, The.
Beveridge. Dining Out.
Bloch, C. Eating Babies.
Brooks, G. Bean Eaters, The.
  Sunday Chicken.
Burgess, F. Table Manners.
  Table Manners II.
"Carroll." Phantasmagoria.
  Walrus and the Carpenter, The.
Catullus. *Carmina,* XIII.
Chōkū. Tanka: "Late at night in the kitchen."
Clough. Le Diner.
Cole, W. Two Sad.
Crane, S. Heart, The.
Daryush. It is pleasant to hang out.
De la Mare. Miss T.
Dickey, J. Bread.
Duhamel. Bulimia.
Edson, R. Ape.
Gaspar. Kapital.
Gorman, L. I shut down the lawnmower.
Greiffenberg. On the Fruit-Providing Autumn Season.
Harjo, J. Perhaps the World Ends Here.
Harper, M. Fireplace, The.
Herbert, G. Love bade me welcome[: yet my soul drew back].
Herrick. Custard, The.
  Panegyric to Sir Lewis Pemberton, A.
  Upon Jack and Jill: Epigram.
  Upon Showbread [*or* Shewbread]: Epigram.
Ho Xuan Huong. Snail.
Hoffmann, H. Story of Augustus Who Would Not Have Any Soup, The.
Hull, L. Frugal Repasts.
Ignatow, D. Pleasure, The.
Ishikawa Takuboku. Tanka: "Color, The."
Jacobsen, J. Food.
Jaques, F. There Once Was a Puffin.
Jonson, B. Inviting a Friend to Supper.
  On Gut.
Kalász. Up against That Wall Everywhere.
Kinnell. Supper after the Last, The.
Kinzie. Heat-heavy creatures.
Kossman. Judas' Reproach.
Kovner. Sun-Watchers.
Lee, J. Mango.
Lipsitz. Feeding, The.
Lu Yu. Sitting Outdoors.
MacCaig. Fetching Cows.
MacNeice. Brandy Glass, The.
Madge. Birds of Tin, The.
Martial. Inviting a Friend to Supper.

Merriam, E.   How to Eat a Poem.
Mirikitani.   Soul Food.
Moore, T.   Beautiful Meals.
Morley, C.   Animal crackers, and cocoa to drink.
Mother Goose.   Jack Sprat could eat no fat.
Little Jack Horner/ Sat in a corner.
Pease porridge [or pudding] hot.
Strange Old Woman, A.
Nash, O.   Experiment Degustatory.
Termite, The.
Noyes, A.   Cure, The.
O'Hara, F.   Blocks.
Oliver, M.   Kingfisher rises out of the black wave, The.
Peacock, M.   Anger Sweetened.
Devolution.
Po Chü-i.   Eating Bamboo-Shoots.
Silver Spoon, The.
Rajasekhara.   Moonlight.
Rakosi.   Good Morning.
Ramanujan.   Pleasure.
Richards, L.   Monkeys and the Crocodile, The.
Rodney.   Anywoman's Lyric.
Romero, N.   New Suit, The.
Rosen, M.   Giant Jojo.
Rukeyser, M.   Night Feeding.
Samio.   Tanka: "With the blue."
Smith, P.   Poor old lady, she swallowed a fly.
Smith, W.   Big Gumbo.
Stevenson, R.   Cow, The.
Thought, A.
Strand.   Eating Poetry.
TallMountain.   Good Grease.
Tanikawa Shuntaro.   Family Portrait.
Turner, N.   Old Quin Queeribus.
Unknown.   Betty.
Big rat, big rat.
Greedy Ned.
I cannot eat but little meat.
Limerick: "There was an old man of [or from] Peru / Who dreamt [or dreamed] he was eating his shoe."
Old Woman of Norwich, The.
Piggish young person from Leeds, A.
There was a young lady of Riga.
Webb, T.   Ancient Prayer, An.
Wickham.   Dilemma, The.
Williams, W.   This Is Just to Say.
To a Poor Old Woman.
Wright, E.   When Father Carves the Duck.
See also Food; Gluttony and Gluttons

Eating Disorders
Bidart.   Ellen West.
Hoffmann, H.   Story of Augustus Who Would Not Have Any Soup, The.
Maiden.   Anorexia.
Nash, O.   Curl Up and Diet.
Rankin, P.   For the Obese.

Echo Lake, New Hampshire
Ray, H.   Echo Reverie.

Echo (mythology)
Ray, H.   Echo's Complaint.
Rossetti, C.   Echo.
See also Narcissus (mythology)

Echoes
Barnes, W.   Echo, The.
Bekederemo.   Cry of Birth.
Borkhuis.   Quartet.
Cawein.   Echo.
De la Mare.   Echo.
Hardy, T.   Echo-Elf Answers, The.
Ho Ching-ming.   Rainy Night.
Hollo.   On the occasion of becoming an echo.
Lazarus, E.   Echoes.
Lorde.   Echoes.
Madgett.   Echoes.
Ovid.   Echo.
Pettet.   Echo.
Popa.   Echo.
Sidney, P.   Echo.
Smith, S.   Word, The.
Sobin, G.   Notes on Sound, Speech, Speech-Crystals and the Celestial Echo.
Song.   Cuckoo on Mt. Chiri*, The.
Swift, J.   Gentle Echo on Woman, A.
Tabb.   Echo.

Tennyson, A.   Blow, Bugle, Blow.
Tree-Leaf Woman.   Who speaks the sound of an echo?
Unknown.   If I should cast off this tattered coat.
Yakamochi.   Cry of the stag, The.
Yang Wei-chen.   Horse-Watering Hole, The.

Eclipses
Lockwood.   December Eclipse.
Mathews, H.   Lunar Eclipse.
Mei Yao Ch'en.   Lunar Eclipse.
Pindar.   Pindar on the Eclipse of the Sun.
Roberson.   Eclipse.
Rosen, M.   Total Eclipse.
Unknown.   Moon Eclipse Exorcism.

Ecology and Ecologists
Buckmaster.   End to Myth, An.
Ciardi.   Mystic River.
Cole, T.   Lament of the Forest, The.
Cowper, W.   Poplar Field, The.
Dutton, G.   Stranded Whales, The.
Ellis, C.   Bungaloid Growth.
Hodgson, R.   Hymn to Moloch.
Hopkins, G.   Binsey Poplars (Felled 1879).
Inversnaid.
Hugo, R.   Plans for Altering the River.
Kunitz, S.   War against the Trees, The.
Levertov.   Gathered at the River.
Lindsay, V.   Flower-fed buffaloes of the spring, The.
Milne, E.   Martyred Earth, The.
Morris, G.   Woodman, spare that tree!
Purdy, A.   Dead Seal.
Ransom, W.   Statement on Our Higher Education.
Roethke.   Moss-Gathering.
Snyder, G.   Front Lines.
Mother Earth: Her Whales.
Spender, S.   I think continually of those who were truly great.
Stafford, W.   Baby Ten Months Old Looks at the Public Domain, A.
Stephens, J.   Little things, that run, and quail.
Unknown.   Great Spirit.
Great Spirit, whose dry lands thirst, help us to find.
Song of Cove Creek Dam, The.
We have forgotten who we are.
We join with the earth and with each other.
See also Pollution

Economics and Economists
Bentley, E.   Intrepid Ricardo, The.
Nash, O.   Love Under the Republicans (Or Democrats).
What Do You Want: A Meaningful Dialogue, or a Satisfactory Talk?

Ecstasy
Browning, R.   Now.
Donne.   Ecstasy, The.
Fullerton.   Poetry.
Hull, L.   Holy City, City of Night.
Jackson, L.   Makeshift.
Kwon, I.   Rapture.
Mackey, N.   Slipped Quadrant.
Piercy.   Raisin Pumpernickel.
Scalapino.   Floating Series 1.
Traherne.   On News.

Eden
Alegría.   Ars Poetica.
Auchterlonie.   Tree, The.
Auden.   Vespers.
Beaumont, J.   Garden's quit with me: as yesterday, The.
Bible, O.T.   Genesis.
Chin.   Disorder, The.
Coolbrith.   Longing.
Cotton, N.   On Lord Cobham's Garden.
Crane, H.   Garden Abstract.
Dickinson, E.   Did the Harebell loose her girdle.
Eden is that old-fashioned House.
Wild Nights—Wild Nights!
Donnelly, S.   Eve Names the Animals.
Ferry.   Adam's Dream.
Frost, R.   Winter Eden, A.
Goodison.   Jamaica 1980.
Graves, R.   Conjunction.

Grosholz.   Eden.
Gurney, D.   Lord God Planted a Garden, The.
Hartigan, A.   Brazen Image.
Herbert, G.   Prayer (I).
Hopkins, G.   Spring.
Housman, A.   When Adam walked in Eden young.
Howitt, M.   Cry of the Animals, The.
Hughes, T.   Theology.
Kavanagh, P.   Long Garden, The.
Kendrick, D.   Gethsemane A. D.
Kipling, R.   When Earth's last picture is painted and the tubes are twisted / and dried.
Lanyer.   From Salve Deus Rex Judaeorum.
Larkin, P.   High Windows.
Lawrence, D.   Paradise Re-entered.
Leapor.   Man the Monarch.
MacNeice.   Apple Blossom.
Merton.   Lent in a Year of War.
Milton.   Adam and Eve in the Garden.
Eden.
Eve tempts Adam.
Satan tempts Eve.
Tempter Disarmed, The.
Muir, E.   Adam's Dream.
One foot in Eden still, I stand.
Pagis.   Tropical Greenhouse.
Plath.   Snakecharmer.
Polkowski.   World is only air / shining, granular, transparent things, The.
Probyn.   Ballade of Lovers.
Rabi'a al-Adawiyya.   O my Lord.
Raine, K.   On its way I see.
Ridler.   Mile from Eden, A.
Robinson, A.   Unum est Necessarium.
Rochester, J.   Fall, The.
Rossetti, C.   Blessed that flock safe penned in Paradise.
Later Life: A Double Sonnet of Sonnets.
Shapiro, K.   Exile.
Sickness of Adam, The.
Smith, R.   Apple, The.
Sparshott.   Naming of the Beasts, The.
Sutcliffe.   Of all the Trees that in the Garden grew.
Symons, A.   Hallucination.
Thomas, D.   Incarnate devil in a talking snake.
Tomlinson, C.   In Arden.
John Maydew or The Allotment.
Unknown.   Adam Lay Bound.
Alas, that ever that speche was spoken.
Vaughan, H.   Corruption.
Very.   Garden, The.
Walcott.   Crusoe's Island.
New World.
Wallace-Crabbe.   And the World was Calm.
White, G.   Leopard in Eden, The.
Whitman, W.   To the garden the world anew ascending.
Whittier.   Garden.
See also Adam and Eve

Edinburgh, Scotland
Dunbar, W.   To the Merchantis of Edinburgh.
Fergusson.   Daft Days, The.
Garioch.   Embro to the Ploy.
To Robert Fergusson.

Editors
Betjeman.   Ballad of George R. Sims, The.
Byron, G.   To Mr. Murray.
Cummings, E.   Mr u will not be missed.
Fogel, A.   Printer's Error, The.
Masters, E.   Editor Whedon.
Mo Shih-lung.   To the Monk Wu-hsia on the Occasion of His Editing the Lotus Sutra.

Education
Amichai.   Anniversaries of War.
We Have Done Our Duty.
Awoonor.   On Having Been an Experimental Sacred Cow for Four Years, and a Token African on Faculty.
Barrows, R.   Report Card, The.
Belloc.   Lines to a Don.
Bentley, E.   On Education, December 1789.
Berkeley, G.   On the Prospect of Planting Arts and Learning in America.
Brownjohn.   Common Sense.
Butler, S.   Presbyterian Knight, The.

Chōkū. Imamiya Middle School.
Chung-ch'ang T'ung. Speaking My Mind.
Clark, T. Going to School in France or
    America.
Dickinson, E. Through the Dark Sod—as
    Education.
    Water, is taught by thirst.
Dove, R. Flash Cards.
Eady. Supremes, The.
Enright, D. University Examinations in Egypt.
Finney, E. Our Solar System.
    Supposing.
Forbes, J. Speed, a Pastoral.
Forten. Poem: "In the earnest path of duty."
Ginsberg, A. Sather Gate Illumination.
Guest, B. If So.
Gwynn, R. Classroom at the Mall, The.
Hardy, T. Young Man's Epigram on
    Existence.
Heard, J. Advance of Education, The.
Heath-Stubbs. One thinks of one as a pronoun
    employed principally.
Hecht, A. Mysteries of Caesar, The.
Hoskins, G. Homework, homework.
Kunio. Tanka: "In a grove."
Leonard, T. Poetry.
Lilley. Sewing Lesson, The.
Lorde. Learning to Write.
Louis, A. Indian College Blues.
Lucy. Supervising Examinations.
Martin, C. E. S. L.
McCord, D. History of Education.
Melo Neto. Education by stone: through
    lessons, An.
Milton. To Cyriack Skinner.
Naden. Love Versus Learning.
Nemerov. Sweeper of Ways, The.
    To David, about His Education.
Nguyễn Trãi. For years you wallowed in the
    scholar's world.
Nye, N. Rain.
Pacheco, A. I hear but my brain doesn't get
    the.
Pagis. Final Exam.
Palmer, T. Try, Try Again.
Po Chü-i. Escorting Candidates to the
    Examination Hall.
Praed. Talented Man, The.
Prelutsky. Homework! Oh, homework!
Rodgers, C. Portrait.
Smith, S. Portrait, A.
    Salon d'Automne.
Snodgrass, W. Campus on the Hill, The.
Spender, S. Elementary School Classroom in a
    Slum, An.
Teft. On Learning.
Thomas, E. On Sir J—— S—— Saying in a
    Sarcastic Manner, My Books Would Make
    Me Mad; an Ode.
Tirolien. Little Black Boy's Prayer, A.
Trần Tế Xu'o'ng. Lamenting the State of
    Confucian Scholarship.
    New-Style Examinations.
    No, Thank You!
    What earthly use are these Confucian graphs?
Travis, N. At My Father's House.
Unknown. Arithmetic.
    Diller, a dollar, A.
    Dr. Foster.
    Educated Feller.
    Exhortation to Learning.
Villalongo. In the Good Old U. S. A.
Wang Chiu-ssu. Chanting Poems.
Whitman, W. When I heard the learn'd
    astronomer.
Yang Chi. Poem on Passing by Hsin-k'ai
    Lake at Kao-yu in Light Rain, A.

See also Colleges and Universities; Scholarship
    and Scholars; Students; Teaching and
    Teachers

Edward IV, King of England
Sidney, P. Sonnet 75: "Of all the kings that
    ever here did reign."
Unknown. King Edward the Fourth and a
    Tanner of Tamworth.

Edward VII, King of England
Beerbohm, M. Addition to Kipling's "The
    Dead King (Edward VII), 1910."
Harkness, J. New Song on the Birth of the
    Prince of Wales, A.
Murphy, E. Thank you, Mr Rason, for the
    Apples.
Unknown. Death of King Edward VII, The.

Edwards, Jonathan
Lowell, R. After the Surprising Conversions.
    Mr. Edwards and the Spider.
McGinley. Theology of Jonathan Edwards,
    The.

Eels
Brown, W. Ballad of the Electric Eel.
Diaper. Sex-life of Fish, The.
Guiterman. Song of Hate for Eels.
Montale. Eel, The.
    Eel, the North Sea siren, The.
    Eel, the siren, The.
Muldoon, P. Briefcase, The.
Nash, O. Eel, The.
Oppian. Loves of the Eel, The.
Unknown. Lord Randal[l].

See also Lampreys

Eggs
Barbu. Dogmatic Egg, The.
Blind. On a Forsaken Lark's Nest.
Brooks, G. Egg Boiler, The.
Cook, S. Boiling an Egg.
Day, C. Egg, The.
Gogarty. Leda and the Swan.
Grass. In the Egg.
Herrick. Her Legs.
Hoban. Egg Thoughts.
Hsieh Chin. Playful Poem on a Chicken Egg,
    A.
Hughes, L. Bar.
Iskrenko. To Beat or Not to Beat.
Lamport. Eggomania.
MacLeish. Vicissitudes of the Creator.
Moore, N. Song: "Little onion lay by the
    fireplace, A."
Mother Goose. In marble walls [or halls] as
    white as milk.
Olds, S. Eggs.
Romano, E. August heat.
Rosen, M. Humpty Dumpty went to the moon.
Rosenblatt. It's in the Egg.
Saitō Mokichi. Tanka: "Yolk, The."
Samio. Tanka: "With each quiver."
Soloukhin. Lost Songs.
Ulinover. In the Courtyard.
Unknown. Dirge for Three Trumpets.
    Warning, A.
    Young Girl of Asturias, The.
Willard, N. How the Hen Sold Her Eggs to
    the Stingy Priest.

Egotism and Egotists
Berlin. Couple of Swells, A.
Bierce. Egotist.
Carew, T. Ingrateful[l] Beauty Threatened.
Creeley. Immoral Proposition, The.
Eberhart, R. If I could only live at the pitch
    that is near madness.
Ewart. It's Hard to Dislike Ewart.
Fainlight, R. Future is timid and wayward,
    The.
Ginsberg, A. Salutations to Fernando Pessoa.
Giovanni. Ego Tripping [(There May Be a
    Reason Why)].
González, A. Diatribe Against the Dead.
Holden, J. Falling from Stardom.
Kirsch, S. Stopover.
Landon. Gifts Misused.
Lawrence, D. Death Is Not Evil, Evil Is
    Mechanical.
Meredith, G. Lucifer in Starlight.
Siegel, R. Ego.
Van Duyn. Talker, The.
Waters, M. Hoochie Coochie.

See also Individualism and Individualists

Egrets
Chao Meng-fu. Fisherman's Lyric.
Li Tung-yang. Inscribed on the Painting
    "Meaning of a Poem by Wang Wei."
McNeill, A. Residue.
    Victors, The.
    Wreath for the Suicide Heart, A.
Mo Shih-lung. I Waited for Chuang Hsüan-
    yüan But He Never Came.
Tu Mu. Egrets.
Uda Emperor. Like a wave crest.

Egypt
Bast. Chrysoberyl: The Eye of the Cat.
Blodgett. Snails.
Coleridge, M. Egypt's might is tumbled down.
Coleridge, S. Egypt's might is tumbled down.
Coolidge, C. I came here. I don't know you
    here.
    Morning muezzin in orange and a mosquito.
    New hunt / the morning bent, A.
Douglas, K. On a Return from Egypt.
Dufault. Mud Dauber Wasp, The.
Enright, D. Egyptian Cat, The.
"Ern Malley." Egyptian Register.
Ford, R. Sakhara.
Fyleman. Cat, The.
Giovanni. Ego Tripping [(There May Be a
    Reason Why)].
Hunt, L. Nile, The.
Kipling, R. Naaman's Song.
McKay, C. Africa.
Nagy, A. Ikhnaton's Night.
Pound, E. Papyrus.
Reed, I. I Am a Cowboy in the Boat of Ra.
    Why I Often Allude to Osiris.
Shelley, P. Ozymandias [of Egypt].
Unknown. Go down, Moses.
Warren, R. All is nothing, nothing all.
    Flaubert in Egypt.

Eichmann, Adolf
Levi, P. For Adolf Eichmann.

Einstein, Albert
Bold, A. Special Theory of Relativity, A.
Feinstein, E. Annus Mirabilis 1989.
Jordan, J. Poem about Intelligence for My
    Brothers and Sisters, A.
Kizer, C. Twelve O'Clock.
Moss, H. Einstein's Bathrobe.
    Gift to Be Simple, The.

Eisenhower, Dwight David
Wright, J. Eisenhower's Visit to Franco, 1959.

El Dorado
Poe. Eldorado.

El Greco. See Greco, El

El Salvador
Alegría. Documentary.
Dalton, R. Love Poem.
Forché. Colonel, The.
Mora. Mangos y limones.
Rose. Day They Cleaned Up the Border El
    Salvador, February, 1981, The.

Elands
Jarrell. Seele im Raum.

Eleanor of Aquitaine
Masefield. Rose of the World, The.
Unknown. Queen Eleanor's Confession.

Electricity
Carver, R. Window, The.
Cranch. Spirit of the Age, The.
Dickey, J. Power and Light.
Duchamp. Electricity Breadthwise.
Kunio. Tanka: "From a flour mill."
    Tanka: "Only when."
Lawrence, D. Storm in the Black Forest.
McOrlan. Battery woman.
Merrill, J. Power Station, The.
Smith, W. There Was an Old Lady Named
    Crockett.
Spender, S. Pylons, The.
Thomas, L. Electricity of Blossoms.

Elephants
Aikin, J. Tit for Tat; a Tale.
Amirthanayagam. Elephants Are in the Yard,
    The.
Asquith. Elephant, The.
Belloc. Elephant, The.
Brooks, G. Pete at the Zoo.
Catti Natanar. What He Said ("As a little
    white snake").
Falconer, E. Elephant is like a wall, The.

Field, R. Merry-Go-Round.
Housman, A. Elephant, or the Force of Habit, The.
Jebeleanu. Hannibal.
Kapilar. What She Said to Her Friend ("Colors on the elephant's body, The").
Kipling, R. Municipal.
Kuriyiraiyar. What Her Friend Said Criticizing Him to Give Her Strength.
Lakshminkara. Lay your head on a block of butter and chop.
Lawrence, D. Elephant Is Slow to Mate, The. Two Performing Elephants.
Link, L. Holding Hands.
Livingstone, D. To a Dead Elephant.
Mathias, E. Just Jumbo.
Maturai Ilampalaciriyan Centan Kuttanar. What She Said ("What will happen now?")
Neruda. Gross innocent.
Ochester. Penn Central Station at Beacon, N.Y, The.
Richards, L. Eletelephony.
Sandburg, C. Elephants Are Different to Different People.
Saxe, J. Blind Men and the Elephant, The.
Tolkien. Oliphaunt.
Unknown. Grasshopper and the Elephant, The. Signifying Monkey, The.
Wilkins, A. Elephant's Trunk, The.
Worth, K. (Circus Elephant).
Yüan Hung-tao. Climbing Mount Yang.

Elevators
Bierce. Safety-Clutch.
Cain, J. Empty elevator, An.
Holan. Meeting in a Lift.
Nye, N. Elevator.

Elgin Marbles
Keats. On Seeing the Elgin Marbles.

Elijah (Bible)
Dickinson, E. Elijah's Wagon knew no thill.
Hayes, A. Angel, The.

Eliot, Thomas Stearns
Auden. T. S. Eliot.
Crawford, R. Love Song of Tommo Frogley.
Eliot, T. Lines for Cuscuscaraway and Mirza Murad Ali Beg.
Ferlinghetti, L. Sea and Ourselves at Cape Ann, The.
Francis, R. Mr. Eliot's Day.
Hecht, A. Vice.
Levi, P. New Year's Eve Poem 1965.
Lowell, R. T. S. Eliot.
Rabbitt. For Thomas Stearns Eliot on the Occasion of His One Hundredth Birthday.
Wallace-Crabbe. Double Dactyl.
Weöres. Saturn Sinking.

Elizabeth I, Queen of England
Bradstreet, A. In Honour of That High and Mighty Princess Queen Elizabeth of Happy Memory.
Dubie. Elizabeth's War with the Christmas Bear.
Elizabeth I. Doubt of future foes exiles my present joy, The.
Written with a Diamond On Her Window at Woodstock.
Kipling, R. Looking Glass, The.
Ondaatje. Elizabeth.
Peele. Write write yow Croniclers of Tyme and Fame.
Pembroke, M. To the Thrice-Sacred Queen Elizabeth.
Prayton. Paradice on earth is found, A.
Puttenham. Her Majestie resembled to the crowned piller. Ye must read upward.

Elizabeth II, Queen of England
Kerekere. Greeting to Queen Elizabeth, the Rare White Heron of Single Flight, A.

Elizabeth, Queen Consort of Henry VII
More, S. Rueful Lamentation on the Death of Queen Elizabeth, A.

Elizabeth, Queen of Bohemia
"Eliza." To the Queen of Bohemiah.
Philips, K. On the Death of the Queen of Bohemia.

Wotton, S. On His Mistress [or Mistris], the Queen of Bohemia.

Elk
Ceravolo. Ho Ho Ho Caribou.
Haines, J. Field of the Caribou, The.
Nash, O. Wapiti, The.
Unknown. Song of the Elk.

Ellington, Edward Kennedy (Duke)
Cortez. Rose Solitude.
Dana, R. Elegy for the Duke.
Komunyakaa. Twilight Seduction.

Elm Trees
Clare, J. Fallen Elm, The.
Elliot, E. Drone v. Worker.
"Field." Leaves.
MacLeish. Long Hot Summer.
Melville, H. Malvern Hill.
Plath. Elm.
Taggard. Dilemma of the Elm.
Thomas, E. October.

Elopement
Campbell, T. Lord Ullin's Daughter.
Keats. Eve of St Agnes, The.
Kirattanar. What Her Girl Friend Said before the elopement.
Longfellow, H. Skeleton in Armor [or Armour], The.
Scott, W. Jock of Hazeldean.
Lochinvar.
Unknown. Bleeding Nun, The.
Earl Brand (The Douglas Tragedy).
To His Love.
What Her Mother Said ("If a calving cow").

Elves
Bangs, J. Little Elf, The.
Bateman, D. My Rocking Chair.
Bishop, M. How to Treat Elves.
Chaucer. Wife of Bath's Tale, The.
Cooper, J. Elves and Fairies.
Farjeon, E. For a Mocking Voice.
Herford. Elf and the Dormouse, The.
Keats. La Belle Dame Sans Merci.
Ray, H. Dream of Elfland, A.
Unknown. Tam Lin.
Weöres. Elf.
See also **Fairies**

Emancipation (1863-1865)
Heard, J. General Robert Smalls.
Howe, J. Battle Hymn [or Battle-Hymn] of the Republic, The.
Moorer. Emancipation Day.
Thompson, P. Emancipation.
Freedom at McNealy's.
Hymn: "Lord, within thy fold I be."
Unknown. No more auction block for me.
Slavery chain done broke at last, broke at last, broke at last.
Whittier. Laus Deo!

Embryos
Tóth, J. Dead Embryos.
Traherne. Preparative, The.
Return, The.
Wright, J. Woman to Man.

Emerson, Ralph Waldo
Lee, L. Cleaving, The.
Lowell, J. Emerson.
Ray, H. Emerson.

Emigration
Bennett, L. Colonization in Reverse.
Excitement.
Boyle, K. New Emigration, The.
Browne, F. Australian Emigrant, The.
Bunting. Complaint of the Morpethshire Farmer, The.
Gin the Goodwife Stint.
Cao Tần. Booby had a little sack, The.
Five crackpots got together, talked big things.
Dalton, H. Emigrant Ship, The.
Du Tử' Lê. Dawn of a New Humankind, The.
Hà Huyền Chi. Sea, the World, and the Boat People, The.
Hall, D. Sister on the Tracks, A.
Hemans. Song of Emigration.
Jarrell. For an Emigrant.
McCarthy, T. Emigration Trains, The.
Nhật Tiến. Two Eyes.

Nichols, G. Wherever I Hang.
Trần Mộng Tú. New Year's Wish for a Little Refugee, A.
Viên Linh. Hundred Tongues, A.
Wilner, E. Emigration.

Emmet, Robert
Moore, T. She Is Far from the Land.

Empedocles
Gregory, H. Death and Empedocles 444 B.C.
Mallalieu. Empedocles on Etna.

Empire State Building, New York City
Berrigan, T. Bean Spasms.

Emptiness
Ashbery. As You Came from the Holy Land.
Berg, S. Holes, The.
Berry, W. Wild, The.
Clark, T. Like musical instruments / Abandoned in a field.
Cooper, J. Waiting.
Creeley. Hole, The.
Language, The.
Signboard, The.
Dabydeen, C. Husband, The.
Davies, H. Music in an Empty House.
Ded. Coursing in emptiness.
Dodd, W. Letter.
Eliot, T. Gerontion.
Hollow Men, The.
Fumi Saito. Tanka: "When neither a man."
Graves, R. Not at Home.
Hardy, T. Exeunt Omnes.
Herbert, Z. Drawer.
Howard, R. Among the Missing.
Hsi K'ang. Taoist Song.
Hughes, T. You are a wild look—out of an egg.
Ise Tayu. Only the waning morning moon / visits my garden.
Juarroz. Emptiness of the day, The.
Kees. Heat in the Room, The.
Kerouac. 113th Chorus.
Kim, C. Salt Sea, The.
Kinnell. Another Night in the Ruins.
Kipling, R. Derelict, The.
Knight, E. Cell Song.
Levchev. Abandoned Churches.
Lindsay, V. Leaden-eyed, The.
Lindsay, V. Leaden-Eyed, The.
Mahon. Achill.
Mallarmé. Lace curtain self-destructs, A.
Matthews, J. People in These Houses, The.
Mechthild von Magdeburg. Desert Has Many Teachings, The.
Melo Neto. Emptiness of man is not like, The.
Merwin, W. "Prodigal Son," The.
Mew. I Have Been Through the Gates.
Oppen. Population.
Orr, G. Who'd Want to Be a Man?
Popa. Judges of the Little Box, The.
Quarles. Nahum 2.10.
Rossetti, D. Without Her.
Rumi. Praise to the emptiness that blanks out existence. Existence.
Smith, I. Milk jugs, cups.
Waldman, A. Makeup on Empty Space.
Williams, W. Are the desolate, dark weeks.
Wollach. House is empty and the trough is broken, The.
I feel empty, empty as a swimming pool.
Wright, F. Needle: For a Friend Who Disappeared, The.
Yang Shih-ch'i. Recording a Dream.
Zukofsky, L. Lines of this new song are nothing, The.

Emus
Gellert, L. Emu makes, though prone to fret, The.
Tjinapirrgarri. Emu Shot.

Enchantment
Brontë, E. Spellbound.
Carew, T. Tinder, The.
Clare, J. To Mary: 'I Sleep with Thee, and Wake with Thee'.
Disch. Rapist's Villanelle, The.
Hardy, T. First Sight of Her and After.
Herrick. To Music: A Song.
Keats. La Belle Dame Sans Merci.

End of the World

Khlebnikov, V. We chant and enchant.
Landon. Enchanted Island, The.
Li Po. Poem No. 19 in the Old Manner.
Mathews, H. At Night, Hearing Someone
Singing in the House Next Door.
Spenser. Eftsoones they heard a most
melodious sound.
Wright, F. Depiction of Childhood.
Yeats. Sorrow of Love, The ("Quarrel of the
sparrows in the eaves, The").

End of the World
"Akhmatova." Land not mine, still, A.
Bottomley. End of the World, The.
Browning, R. Childe Roland to the Dark
Tower Came.
Byron, G. Darkness.
Cummings, E. If in beginning twilight of
winter will stand.
Now does our world descend.
What if a much of a which of a wind.
Derricotte. Fears of the Eighth Grade.
Donne. Blow Your Trumpets.
Eady. Dance, The.
Frost, R. Fire and Ice.
Once by the Pacific.
Fulton, A. Everyone Knows the World Is
Ending.
Gascoyne. And the Seventh Dream Is the
Dream of Isis.
End Is Near the Beginning, The.
Graves, R. Warning to Children.
Haines, J. Dürer's Vision.
Jauss. After the End of the World.
Jeffers, R. I Shall Laugh Purely.
MacLeish. End of the World, The.
McGrath, T. End of the world: it was given to
me to see it, The.
Pack, R. Proton Decay.
Patterson, R. When I Awoke.
Puttenham. O mightye Muse.
Shapiro, K. Scyros.
Snyder, G. L M F B R.
Stafford, W. Epitaph Ending in And, The.
Tao-chi. Flower-Rain Terrace, The.
Very. First Atlantic Telegraph, The.
Wade-Gayles. Loving Again.
Wilbur. Advice to a Prophet.
Winters, Y. Summer Noon: 1941.
Wright, C. October.
Wylie. Doomsday.
See also **Apocalypse; Judgment Day**
Endangered Species
Atwood. Elegy for the Giant Tortoises.
Hope, A. Moschus Moschiferus.
Oliver, M. Ghosts.
Endurance
Baca. Cloudy Day.
Bowles, W. Time and Grief.
Brodsky, J. Eclogue IV: Winter.
May 24, 1980.
Brutus. Endurance.
Chichibabin. Camel.
Chōkū. Tanka: "After enduring."
Coleridge, S. Forbearance.
Di Prima. For H.D.
Narrow Path into the Back Country.
Dutton, G. Clach Eanchainn.
Emerson, R. Character.
Gabai. For the Last Time on My Native
Estate...
Hewitt, J. If I had given you that love and
care.
Jeffers, R. Granite and Cypress.
Kim, N. Winter Sea, The.
Kipling, R. Old Men, The.
Kornilov, B. Under the scraggy fir tree.
Kunitz, S. Welcome the Wrath.
Lawrence, D. Race and Battle.
Lovelace, R. Valiant Love.
MacLeish. Snowflake Which Is Now and
Hence Forever, The.
Matveyeva. Wood.
Merrill, J. After Greece.
Mihalic. Maestro, extinguish the candle,
serious times have come.
Muir, E. Difficult Land, The.
Park, T. Before Thy Love.

Shelley, P. But Greece and her foundations
are.
Strange. Still Life.
Voznesensky. Autumn.
Warren, R. To a Face in a Crowd.
Yeats. Travail of Passion, The.
See also **Fortitude**
Endymion
Keats. Endymion.
Millay, E. Oh, sleep forever in the Latmian
cave.
Stirling, S. I Envy Not Endymion.
Enemies
Barrax. In the Restaurant.
Bible, *O.T.* Psalm 83.
Blake, W. Poison Tree, A.
Coleridge, M. Gifts.
De la Mare. Hare, A.
Dickinson, E. Rat is the concisest Tenant,
The.
Elizabeth I. Written on a Wall at Woodstock.
Hardy, T. Man He Killed, The.
Hill, B. Tribute to Robert E. Lee.
Iman. Love Your Enemy.
Kilar, K. Poet's Counsel, A ("Your enemy is
not the kind who wears").
Lovelace, R. Fly Caught in a Cobweb, A.
Matveyeva. I, he says, am not a warrior.
Millay, E. First Fig.
Robinson, E. New Tenants, The.
Unknown. Approaching Dance, The.
Only safe, The.
Other Side of the Valley, The.
Song of the Lenape Warriors Going against
the Enemy, The.
Wellesley. Enemy, The.
Whitman, W. Reconciliation.
Wickham. Pugilist.
Zavalnyuk. I love my enemies, those I
forgive.
Energy
Carruth, H. Being, The.
Ceravolo. Dangers of the Journey to the
Happy Land.
Cowper, W. Inscription.
Gunn, T. My Sad Captains.
Hildegard von Bingen. Antiphon for Divine
Wisdom.
Kendall, M. Ether Insatiable.
Koch, K. Energy in Sweden.
Lawrence, D. We Are Transmitters.
MacCaig. Blue Tit on a String of Peanuts.
Mirabai. All I Was Doing Was Breathing.
Why Mira Can't Go Back to Her Old House.
Sorrentino. Razzmatazz.
Whitman, W. Song of Myself.
Wilbur. Star System, The.
Energy Crisis
Morley, C. Elegy Written in a Country Coal-
Bin.
Engineers
Cope, W. Engineers' Corner.
Donahue, J. Transfigurations.
Kipling, R. McAndrew's Hymn.
Nurses, The.
Unknown. Casey Jones.
England
Ackland. Instructions From England 1936.
Auden. On This Island.
Barker, G. Channel Crossing.
Belloc. Ha'nacker Mill.
Imitation.
South Country, The.
Benson, A. Land of Hope and Glory.
Betjeman. Christmas.
Great Central Railway, Sheffield Victoria to
Banbury.
In Westminster Abbey.
Matlock Bath.
Town Clerk's Views, The.
Binyon. This Is England.
Blake, W. Fields from Islington to Marybone,
The.
Jerusalem.
Prelude: "England! awake! awake! awake!"
When Klopstock England defied.

Bond, E. If Auschwitz had been in
Hampshire.
Bradstreet, A. Old England.
Brome. On Sir G. B. his defeat.
Brooke, R. Old Vicarage, Grantchester, The.
Soldier, The.
Browning, E. Sweetness of England, The.
Browning, R. Home-Thoughts, From Abroad.
Home-Thoughts, from the Sea.
Brownjohn. We are going to see the rabbit.
Burns, R. Such a Parcel of Rogues in a
Nation.
Byron, G. Canto the Eleventh.
Italy versus England.
Causley. Armistice Day.
At the British War Cemetery, Bayeux.
Centlivre. To thee—rude warrior, who, we
once admired.
Chaucer. Canterbury Tales, The.
General Prologue, The.
Chesterton, G. Elegy in a Country
Churchyard.
Rolling English Road, The.
Churchill, C. Ghost, The.
Collins, W. Ode Written in the Beginning of
the Year 1746.
Cowper, W. Boadicea: An Ode.
Darwin. Kew.
Davidson, J. Crystal Palace, The.
Day Lewis. You That Love England.
Deloney. Princely Ditty in Praise of the
English Rose, A.
Drayton. *Satyr* O never ask how I came to
this place.
What spirit can lift you up, to that immortall
praise.
Duffy, C. In Your Mind.
Dunbar, W. Lament for the Makaris.
"Ern Malley." Sweet William.
Gilbert, S. Utopia Anglicized.
Googe. Goyng towards Spayne.
Gorges. Written upon the death of the most
Noble Prince Henrie.
Hardy, T. On an Invitation to the United
States.
Harrison, T. Classics Society.
Durham.
Harry, J. Shot of War, A.
Heath-Stubbs. One thinks of *one* as a pronoun
employed principally.
Hemans. England's Dead.
Homes of England, The.
Henley, W. England, My England.
Herbert, G. British Church, The.
Religion stands on tip-toe in our land.
Hewitt, J. Once alien here my fathers built
their house.
Hill, G. Laurel Axe, The.
Hopkins, G. To seem the stranger lies my lot,
my life.
Housman, A. 1887.
New Mistress, The.
On Wenlock Edge the wood's in trouble.
Hughes, L. Seascape.
Huntington, G. International Hymn.
Hutchinson, P. Fleadh Cheoil.
Jones, D. In the middle silences of this night's
course the blackthorn.
Jonson, B. On the Union.
Keats. Happy is England! I could be content.
Naughty Boy, The.
Kingsley, C. Last Buccaneer, The.
Kinsella, T. Foot of the tower. An angle
where the darkness, The.
Kipling, R. American Spirit speaks, The.
Chant-Pagan.
Dane-Geld.
Land, The.
Puck's Song.
Return, The.
Ulster.
Lanyer. Description of Cooke-ham, The.
Larkin, P. MCMXIV.
Naturally the Foundation Will Bear Your
Expenses.
Lawrence, D. English are so nice, The.
Innocent England.

Lee, L. Home From Abroad.
Lovelace, R. Mock Song, A.
Lowell, R. George III.
Lucas, E. O England, Country of My Heart's Desire.
"MacDiarmid." We must look at the harebell as if.
Mapanje. At the Metro: Old Irrelevant Images.
Marvell. 'Is this, saith one, the Nation that we read'.
Meynell, A. Summer in England, 1914.
Miller, A. I Have Loved England.
Miller, J. At Our Golden Gate.
More, H. Riot; or, Half a Loaf Is Better than No Bread, The.
Mure. O Heavens! O Earth! heer I must pause a space.
Nichols, G. Wherever I Hang.
Nicholson, N. Ravenglass Railway Station, Cumberland.
Norton, C. Voice from the Factories, A.
Noyes, A. Sherwood in the twilight, is Robin Hood awake?
O'Connor, P. Writing in England Now.
"O'Neill." Corrymeela.
Peele. Write write yow Croniclers of Tyme and Fame.
Pembroke, M. To the Thrice-Sacred Queen Elizabeth.
Penny, A. Sung at Table by the Same Choir.
Philips, K. On the 3. of September, 1651.
"Pindar." Hymn to the Guilotine.
Plomer. Murder on the Downs, The.
Porter, P. Last of England, The.
Pound, E. Enormous tragedy of the dream in the peasant's bent / shoulders, The.
Prior. Fable, A: "In Æsop's tales an honest wretch we find."
Raine, K. By the River Eden.
Ralegh, W. As you came from the holy land.
His Petition to Queen Anne of Denmark (1618).
Retallack, J. Secret Life of Gilbert Bond, The.
Sackville, T. Midnight ("Midnight was come, when every vital thing").
Salkey. Song for England, A.
Salter. England.
Shakespeare, W. Henry V at the Siege of Harfleur.
Now is the winter of our discontent.
Once more unto the breach, dear friends, / once more.
Shelley, P. England in 1819.
Song to the Men of England.
Skelton, J. Rose both white and Rede, The.
Smith, C. From Beachy Head.
Spenser. Ruines of Time, The.
Tho when they came to the sea coast, they found.
Swinburne. Forsaken Garden, A.
Thackeray. Mr. Molony's Account of the Crystal Palace.
Thomas, E. Adlestrop.
Thomson, J. et al. Rule, Britannia!
Tomlinson, C. John Maydew or The Allotment.
Return to Hinton.
Unknown. Agincourt Carol, The.
Diggers' Song, The.
England.
England's Sovereigns in Verse.
English Succession, The.
Free Parliament Litany, A.
History.
I don't want to be a soldier.
Lament for Our Lady's Shrine at Walsingham, A.
Of Sir Frauncis Walsingham Sir Phillipp Sydney, and Sir Christopher Hatton, Lord Chancelor.
Song Bewailing the Time of Christmas, So Much Decayed in England, A.
Songe bewailinge the tyme of Christmas, So much decayed in Englande, A.
We four lads from Liverpool are.
Vaughan, H. British [or Brittish] Church, The.
Charnel-house, The.

Walcott. Far Cry from Africa, A.
Wheatley, P. Farewell to America. To Mrs. S. W, A.
Wilde, O. Ave Imperatrix!
Wilson, A. In Praise of Drainage.
Wither. If by mischance the people in the street.
Wordsworth, W. Composed by the Sea-Side, near Calais, August, 1802.
England, 1802, V.
I traveled [or travell'd] among unknown men.
London 1802.
Sonnet: "England! the time is come when thou shouldst wean."
Yeats. On a Political Prisoner.
See also Civil Wars, England
England, Church of. See Church of England
English Channel
Barker, G. Channel Crossing.
Glaze. Outlanders, The.
Smith, C. From Beachy Head.
English, The
Allston. America to Great Britain.
Brooke, R. Soldier, The.
Campbell, T. Ye Mariners of England.
Chapman, G. And, for our tongue, that still is so empayr'd.
Chesterton, G. Secret People, The.
Cleveland, J. How? "Providence", and yet a Scottish crew?
Coward. Mad Dogs and Englishmen.
Cowley, A. London Subverted by the Furies.
Cummings, E. It was a goodly co.
Q:dwo / we know of anything which can.
Defoe, D. Wherever God erects a house of prayer.
Drayton. First Steps Up Parnassus.
O, why should Nature niggardly restraine!
Dryden, J. In pious times ere [or e'r] priest-craft did begin.
Graves, R. For the Rain It Raineth Every Day.
Kay, J. English Cousin Comes to Scotland.
"Kerr." Neutral British Gentleman, The.
Kipling, R. Fuzzy-Wuzzy.
Gentlemen-Rankers.
Ladies, The.
Lawrence, D. English are so nice, The.
How beastly the bourgeois is.
Lees, J. Jone o' Grinfilt.
Leonard, T. This is thi.
Longfellow, H. Rhyme of Sir Christopher, The.
Macaulay, T. Jacobite's Epitaph, A.
MacBeth. Ode to English Food, An.
Miller, A. English Are Frosty, The.
Milligan, S. Teeth.
Milton. To the Lord General[l] Cromwell[, on the Proposals of Certain Ministers at the Committee for the Propagation of the Gospel or May 1652].
Nash, O. England Expects.
O'Rahilly. Last Lines.
Pembroke, M. To the Thrice-Sacred Queen Elizabeth.
Rexroth, K. Observations in a Cornish Teashop.
Shelley, P. Song to the Men of England.
Simpson, L. Runner, The.
Smith, S. Celts, The.
This Englishwoman is so refined.
Stewart, D. Two Englishmen.
Unknown. To Buonaparte.
Wolfe, H. You cannot hope.
Wordsworth, W. Decay of Piety.
Engraving and Engravers
Hsü Chung-hsing. This metal is engraved with Shang-style markings.
Envy
Burrell. School for Satire, The.
Catullus. Carmen 5 ("My sweetest Lesbia, let us live and love").
Chase, J. One early spring evening when Celia was fourteen.
Clare, J. Written in Prison.
Coleridge, M. I envy not the dead that rest.
Cook, E. Lines / Suggested by the Song of a Nightingale.

Dizhur. With tender back glistening.
Donne. Song: "Go and catch a falling star."
"Field." So jealous of your beauty.
Holden, J. Falling from Stardom.
Ishikawa Takuboku. Tanka: "On the roadside."
Kipling, R. My Rival.
Kurup. Master Carpenter, The.
Moore, M. Charity Overcoming Envy.
Perlman, A. Summer Adjustments.
Po Chü-i. Chu Ch'ên Village.
Procter, A. Envy.
Ramanujan. Love Poem for a Wife, 2.
Shakespeare, W. Sonnet 70.
Sidney, P. Sonnet 59: "Dear, why make you more of a dog than me?"
Synge. Dread.
Wilbur. All These Birds.
Williams, W. Drunkard, The.
See also Jealousy
Epic Poetry
Browning, E. From Book 5.
Callimachus. I despise neo-epic verse sagas.
Kavanagh, P. Epic.
Epictetus
Arnold, M. To a Friend.
Epicureanism
Cowley, A. Epicure, The ("Fill the bowl with rosie [or rosy] wine").
Davies, J. Author Loving These Homely Meats, The.
Unknown. I drive my carriage from the Upper East Gate.
Epigrams
Coleridge, S. What is an epigram? a dwarfish whole.
Ellis, C. Adder's Epigrams.
Jonson, B. To My Book.
To My Mere English Censurer.
Landor, W. Epigrams must be curt, nor seem.
Epiphany. See Twelfth Night
Epitaphs
Behn, A. Epitaph on the Tombstone of a Child, the Last of Seven That Died Before.
Brodsky, J. Sir, you are tough, and I am tough.
Cunningham, J. Epitaph for Someone or Other.
Davidson, D. Lines for a Tomb.
Escoffery. After the Fall.
Gay, J. My Own Epitaph.
Hardy, T. Epitaph: "I never cared for Life: Life cared for me."
Hunt, L. Epitaph of Erotion, The.
Jackson, L. Dimensions.
Levy, A. Epitaph: "This is the end of him, here he lies."
Ralegh, W. Epitaph on the Earl of Leicester [or Leceister].
Verses Made the Night before His Beheading.
Shirley, J. Garden, The.
Terence. Inscription.
Unknown. On Leslie Moore.
She drank good ale, strong punch and wine.
Whitman, W. As toilsome I wander'd Virginia's woods.
Equality
Adisa. Women at the Crossroad / (May Elegba Forever Guard the Right Doors).
Barbauld. Rights of Woman, The.
Bruck. Equality, father! Your dream has come true.
Burns, R. For A' That and A' That ["Is there, for honest poverty"].
Carew, T. Rapture, A.
"Carroll." Lobster, The.
Chaucer. Franklin's Tale, The.
Wife of Bath's Tale, The.
Chicago. And then all that has divided us will merge.
Cowper, W. Negro's Complaint, The.
Dickinson, E. Color, Caste, Denomination.
Eady. Why Do So Few Blacks Study Creative Writing?
Euripides. Nothing / Is worse for a city than an absolute ruler.
Jefferson, T. Preamble to the Declaration of Independence.

Eraikkon

Jordan, J. What Would I Do White?
Kipling, R. Equality of Sacrifice.
Lincoln, A. Gettysburg Address, The.
"MacDiarmid." On a Raised Beach.
Pozhenyan. Poet and Tsar.
Public Enemy. Party for your Right to Fight.
Rilke. Someday there will be girls and women whose name will no longer mean.
Shirley, J. Death the Leveller.
Spender, S. Not palaces, an era's crown.
Walsh, C. Woman to Her Lover, A.
Ward, N. Mercury shew'd Apollo, Bartas Book.
Whitman, W. America.
Yeats. Paudeen.

See also **Social Class**

Eraikkon
Ilaveyini. Tiger, The.

Erie Canal
Allen, W. Erie Canal, The.
Unknown. E-ri-e, The.

Erne (river), Ireland
Muldoon, P. Yggdrasill.

Eros. *See* **Cupid**

Erosion
Dugan, A. Against the Text "Art Is Immortal."
Tomlinson, C. Poem: "Upended, it crouches on broken limbs."
Wilbur. On the Marginal Way.

Erotic Love
Abanaki Oral Tradition. Come, my beloved, let us go up the shining mountain, and sit together.
Ackland. When I have said 'I love you' I have said.
Agathias. That old crow-beaked hag.
Ai. Reunion with a Ghost.
Twenty-Year Marriage.
Alcaeus. I despise love. What weighty God.
Altizer. Sonnet 2: "My own heart let me have. More pity on."
Amichai. Quick And Bitter.
To my love, combing her hair.
Anacreon. And why.
Come, all you painters, all you who are the best.
Count, if you can, every leaf on every tree.
Eros cast in wax, molded into a candle, An.
Eros, playing among the roses.
It is lovely to walk fields of tall grass.
Weave garlands of roses for our hair.
Word has come to me that she.
Angira. Request.
Angus. Invitation.
Apollinaire. My darling little Lou how I love you.
Ninth Secret Poem, The.
Argentarius. I can't bear to watch your hips.
Love is not just a function of the eyes.
That's your third sneeze now, my good lamp.
You are a bee, my flower-lovely.
Arnold, M. To Marguerite.
Asclepiades. Dear Lamp, she swore by you.
Didyme waved an olive branch at me.
Didyme waved her wand at me.
Great is a drink of snow.
It is eternally winter.
Think how unspeakably sweet.
When soft Irene like a.
Ashbery. My Erotic Double.
Uncle Henry.
Auden. As I walked out one evening.
Auvaiyar. What She Said, Thinking of Him Crossing the Wilderness Alone.
Averill. Bad for You.
Bangs, C. Touching Each Other's Surfaces.
Barker, G. O Golden Fleece ("O Golden Fleece she is where she lies tonight").
Barlas. My Lady's Bath.
Barnes, B. Soft, lovely, rose-like lips, conjoined with mine.
Would I were Changed.
Barnfield. Affectionate Shepherd, The.
Baudelaire. Jewels, The.
She Is Not Satisfied.

Behn, A. Song, A.
To the Fair Clarinda, Who Made Love to Me, Imagin'd More Than Woman.
Willing Mistriss, The.
Berry, W. Dance, The.
Fear of Love, The.
Berryman. Ah when you drift hover before you kiss.
Bertolino. On a Line by John Ashbery.
Betjeman. Invasion Exercise on the Poultry Farm.
Licorice Fields at Pontefract, The.
Potpourri from a Surrey Garden.
Bhartrihari. Three Poems.
Bible, *O.T.* My love is white and ruddy.
Song of Solomon, The.
Bion. In sleep before me *Venus* seem'd to stand.
Power of Love, The.
Blake, W. Garden of Love, The.
Bly, R. Listening to the Köln Concert.
Bogan, L. Frightened Man, The.
Juan's Song.
Bolamba. Esanzo.
Bold, A. Special Theory of Relativity, A.
Boyse. On Platonic Love.
Breton, A. On the Road to San Romano.
Bridges, R. Eros.
Brooks, G. Ballad of Edie Barrow, The.
Browne, W. Shall I tell you whom I love?
Browning, E. Romance of the Swan's Nest, The.
Sonnet: "Go from me. Yet I feel that I shall stand."
Sonnet: "How do I love thee? Let me count the ways."
Sonnet: "If thou must love me, let it be for nought."
Sonnet: "Thou comest! all is said without a word."
Sonnet: "What can I give thee back, O liberal."
Sonnet: "When our two souls stand up erect and strong."
Sonnet XXIX.
Sonnet: "Yet, love, mere love, is beautiful indeed."
Browning, R. Confessions.
Last Ride Together, The.
Meeting At Night.
Burns, R. Patriarch, The.
Red, Red Rose, A.
Song: "It was upon a Lammas night."
Bury. False and faithless as thou art.
Byron, G. And thus they wandered forth, and hand in hand.
So we'll go no more a-roving.
Stanzas to the Po.
Campbell, I. Learned Mistress, A.
Campion, T. Follow, follow[e] / Though with mischiefe.
I care not for these ladies.
It fell on a summer's [*or* sommers] day.
Secret love or two, I must confess[e], A.
Thou art not fair for all thy red and white.
Carew, T. On the Marriage of T. K. and C. C.: The Morning Stormy.
Rapture, A.
Song, [A]: "Ask me no more where Jove bestows."
Song: Good Counsel to a Young Maid.
Cartwright, W. No Platonic [*or* Platonique] Love.
Song of Dalliance, A.
Cassian. Like Gulliver pulling a hundred ships.
Young Vampire, The.
Catullus. Carmen 5 ("My sweetest Lesbia, let us live and love").
Carmen 58 ("My Lesbia, Caelius, that same Lesbia").
Carmen 61 ("Guardian of Helicon, Urania's son").
Carmina, LV.
Catullus to Lesbia.
Frae Catullus, VIII.
Kisse me, sweet: The warie lover.

Lesbia, live to love and pleasure.
Sappho.
Weep, weep, ye Loves and Cupids all.
Cavafy. Body, remember not only how much you were loved.
One Night.
To Remain.
Cavalcanti. Ballata: Concerning a Shepherd-Maid.
Cephalus. To light young poets' hearts.
Chan Fang-sheng. Folk-Songs.
Chapman, G. Bridal Song: "O come, soft rest of cares, come Night."
Chatterton. Mynstrelle's Songe ("O! synge untoe mie roundelaie").
Cheney-Coker. Poem for a Lost Lover.
"Chrystos." Dream Lesbian Lover.
Getting Down.
Clare, J. First Love.
Silent Love.
To Elia (unsigned).
Clarke, A. Envy of Poor Lovers, The.
Penal Law.
Clarke, C. Rondeau: "They are bodies left unburied."
Cleage. Confession.
Cleveland, J. To the State of Love or The Senses' Festival.
Clifton, H. Monsoon Girl.
Clough. Natura Naturans.
Cook, E. 'Tis well to wake the theme of Love.
Cope, W. You know exactly what to do.
Cornaros. Observe how Eros works his magic spells.
Cortez. Pray for the lovers.
Costello, L. Lines: "If we should ever meet again."
Crashaw. Against Hope.
Bubble, The.
Cullen, C. Brown Boy to Brown Girl.
Wind Bloweth Where It Listeth, The.
Cummings, E. I like my body when it is with your.
I will be / M o ving in the Street of her.
May i feel said he.
My love / thy hair is one kingdom.
My sweet old etcetera.
Cushing, J. Lover Man.
Custance. White Statue, The.
Cynewulf. Three Riddles from *The Exeter Book.*
Dacre, C. Il Trionfo del Amor.
Kiss, The.
To Him Who Says He Loves.
Dafydd ap Gwilym. Rattle Bag, The.
Daniel, S. 46.
Darley. Serenade of a Loyal Martyr.
Song, A: "It is not Beauty [*or* beautie] I demand[e]."
Davie. Rejoinder to a Critic.
Time Passing, Beloved.
Davies, W. Dream, A.
De. Santhal Poems, 1.
De Veaux. Sisters, The.
Dickey, J. Cherrylog Road.
Dickinson, E. Wild Nights—Wild Nights!
You love me—you are sure.
Diop, D. Rama Kam.
Diophanes of Myrina. Thief, and triply so!, A.
Dioscorides. Thracian page-boy / mastered, A.
Dioscorides. They are too much for me.
Dodsley. Stolen Kiss, The.
Dongala. Fantasy under the Moon.
Donne. Bait[e], The.
Canonization, The.
Dream[e], The.
Ecstasy, The.
Elegie: "Nature's lay ideot, I taught thee to love."
Farewell to Love.
Flea, The.
Good-Morrow, The.
Indifferent, The.
Love's Alchemy [*or* Alchemie].
Love's Deity [*or* Deitie].
Love's Growth.

Love's Progress.
Sun[ne] Rising, The.
To His Mistress Going To Bed.
To Mr. C.B.
Dove, R. Persephone Underground.
Dransfield. Memoirs of a Velvet Urinal.
Drayton. Since There's No Help.
These verses weare made By Michaell Drayton Esquier Poett Lawreatt the night before hee dyed.
To the Senses.
Dryden, J. Mercury's Song [to Phaedra].
Song: "SYLVIA the fair, in the bloom of fifteen."
Du Bellay. To Venus.
Duesing. Blossoming.
Send Pictures, You Said...
Wild and Blue.
Dunbar, P. Negro Love Song, A.
Eifuku. We dressed each other.
"Eliot." Two lovers by a moss-grown spring.
Elizabeth I. On Monsieur's Departure.
Éluard, P. Lady Love.
Éluard, P. et al. 32 Positions of Love, The.
Emanuel, L. Sleeping, The.
Emerson, R. Eros.
Give all to love;.
"Ephelia." On a Bashful Shepherd.
"Ern Malley." Perspective Lovesong.
Euripides. Oh Love! oh Love! whose shafts of fire.
Fêng Mêng-lung. Love-Poem.
Fenton, E. Olivia's lewd, but looks devout.
"Field." Ah, Eros doth not always smite.
As two fair vessels side by side.
Constancy.
Lovers, fresh plighting lovers in our age.
Methinks my love to thee doth grow.
Unbosoming.
Fitzgerald, E. 12.
Flaccus, G. Now as Medea walks, dark echoes fill.
Flatman. Appeal to Cats in the Business of Love, An.
Floyd. Private First Class Brooks Morgenstein, U. S. M. C.
Follain. Taxidermist is sitting / before the russet breasts, A.
Francis, R. Swimmer.
Freeman, J. Fifteen.
Fulton, A. My Diamond Stud.
Funk, A. After Dark.
García Lorca. Serenata.
Gibran. Prophet Speaks of Love, The.
Glück, L. Garden, The.
Goldsmith, O. Song: "When lovely woman stoops to folly.
Graham, J. Salmon.
Grahn. Paris and Helen.
Graves, R. Conjunction.
Down, wanton, down! Have you no shame.
Not at Home.
She tells her love while half asleep.
Gray, J. Barber, The.
On A Picture.
Parsifal Imitated from the French of Paul Verlaine.
Greville, F. et al. 56.
Grimké, A. You.
Your Eyes.
Guinicelli. Sonnet: He Will Praise His Lady.
Gunn, T. Bed, The.
Monster, The.
Hacker, M. Aube Provençale.
Ballad of Ladies Lost and Found.
Bloomingdale's.
Eight Days in April.
Noces.
Presentation Piece.
Rondeau after a Transatlantic Telephone Call.
Sources.
Villanelle: "Every day our bodies separate."
Hafiz. Ode 173: "All the long night we talked of your long hair."
Halliday, C. Music.
Hamill, J. Open Window.

Hardy, T. Beeny Cliff.
Neutral Tones.
Hawthorne, N. Oh, Man can seek the downward glance.
Heaney, S. La Toilette.
Heath, R. Seeing Her Dancing.
Hecht, A. Gardens of the Villa D'Este, The.
Old Malediction, An.
Hedylos. Wine and treacherous proposals.
Hemans. Chamois Hunter's Love, The.
Properzia Rossi.
To a Wandering Female Singer.
Herbert, G. Love bade me welcome[: yet my soul drew back].
Herbert, Z. Rosy Ear.
Heredia. Antony and Cleopatra.
Herrick. Fresh Cheese and Cream.
Her Bed.
Her Legs.
No Loathsomnesse in Love.
To Anthea ("Let's call for Hymen if agreed thou art").
To Anthea, Who May Command Him Anything.
To Dianeme ("Show [or Shew] me thy feet; show [or shew] me thy legs, thy thighs").
To Electra ("I'll [or Ile] come to thee in all those shapes").
Upon Julia's Breasts.
Upon Julia's Clothes.
Vine, The.
Vision to Electra, The.
Hesketh. Love's Advocate.
Hill, A. On a Lady, Preached into the Colic, by One of Her Lovers.
Ho Xuan Huong. Swinging.
Hogg, J. When Maggy Gangs Away.
Honestus. I would never marry a young girl or an old woman.
Hong, Y. Spring Fever.
Hope, A. Blason, A.
Horace. Odes 1.9.
Odes 4.7.
Soracte.
Housman, A. When I was one-and-twenty.
Huang O. To the Tune "Red Embroidered Shoes."
Hunt, L. Rondeau: "Nelly kissed me when we met."
Ibycus. In Spring, quince trees.
Ignatow, Y. We were love.
Irenaeus Referendarius. O supercilious delicious Rhodope.
Jacinto, A. Letter from a Contract Worker.
James, J. Sister Midnight.
Jiménez, J. To the bridge of love.
Johnson, G. I Want to Die While You Love Me.
Johnson, L. Decadent's Lyric, A.
Jonson, B. Doing a filthy pleasure is, and short.
Song. To Celia ("Come my Celia, let us prove").
Jordan, J. Grand Army Plaza.
Juana Inés de la Cruz. Happy Easter, my Lady.
My Divine Lysi.
Kantan. What His Friend Said, teasing the man in love.
Kapilar. What She Said ("He is from those mountains").
What She Said to Her Friend ("You ask me to forget him").
Kay, J. Photo in the Locket.
Keats. Bright star[, would I were stedfast as thou art—].
Dawlish Fair.
Eve of St Agnes, The.
Left to herself, the serpent now began.
Song.
Kennelly. Bread.
Kim, Y. Labyrinth.
Kizer, C. Copulating Gods, The.
Koch, K. Sleeping with Women.
Kuan Yun She. Seventh Day Seventh Month.
Kumin, M. After Love.
Laleau. Cannibal.

Lamantia. Winter Day, A.
Lamb, L. My heart's fit to break, yet no tear fills my eye.
Would I had seen thee dead and cold.
Lamb, M. What is Love?
Landon. Girl at Her Devotions, A.
Landor, W. Faesulan Idyll.
Mother, I Cannot Mind My Wheel.
Rose Aylmer.
Laughlin, J. Rhyme.
Lawrence, D. Gloire de Dijon.
New Year's Eve.
True Love at Last.
Young Wife, A.
Le Gallienne. Sunset in the City.
Lee, J. Lusca.
Levertov. Eros at Temple Stream.
Hymn to Eros.
Li Ch'ing-chao. To the Tune, "Plum Blossoms Fall and Scatter."
Tune: Song of Picking Mulberry ("Evening comes with an onslaught of wind and rain").
Liddy. History.
Liu E. I remember when we made our first promises of love.
Livingstone, D. One Time.
Lodge, T. Rosalind's [or Rosalynd's] Madrigal[l].
Lorde. Love Poem.
Meet.
On a Night of the Full Moon.
Lovelace, R. Love Made in the First Age[: To Chloris].
Song: To Lucasta, Going to the War[re]s.
Lowell, A. April.
Frimaire.
Lowell, R. Man And Wife.
Lowry, M. Volcano is dark and suddenly thunder, The.
Lucretius. Address to Venus.
Macedonius. Every year men harvest grapes, not seeing.
I dreamt I held the laughter-loving girl.
You're here! I hadn't dared to hope. Surprise.
MacNeice. Libertine, The.
Shelley and jazz and lieder and love and hymn-tunes.
Madan. Abelard to Eloisa.
Maguire, S. Perfect Timing.
Marino. Out of the Italain.
Marlowe. By this Leander being near the land.
Passionate Shepherd [or Sheepheard] To His Love, The.
Marutanilanakanar. Hunchback and the Dwarf, The.
Marvell. To His Coy Mistress.
Meleager. By Timo's locks.
Counts itself lucky.
Epigram: "At 12 o'clock in the afternoon."
Epigram: "Breath of my life, The—no less."
Inconstant Dawn, thou tak'st thy time.
Lost! Cupid!/ One lost Cupid!
Love cast!
Love like a heavy wave.
More than Apollo's golden lyre.
Something in my soul.
Volatile mosquito.
Meredith, G. 30.
Dusty Answer, A.
Modern Love.
Mew. À Quoi Bon Dire.
Mezey. Confession, A.
Middleton, C. Adelaide's Dream.
Miller, V. Mourning, A.
Milosz, C. After Paradise.
Milton. Eve tempts Adam.
Montagu, L. Between your sheets you soundly sleep.
Moore, E. Nun, The.
Song 3: "As Phyllis the gay, at the break of the day."
Moore, H. Green Place, A.
Moore, T. Love in a Storm.
Moraes, D. Snow on a Mountain.
Mouré. Aspen.
Musaeus. Consummation.
Namjoshi, S. From the Travels of Gulliver.

Namjoshi, S. *et al.* In that particular temple.
Nashe. Choise of valentines, The.
Neruda. Drunk as drunk on turpentine.
  Girl lithe and tawny, the sun that forms.
  Sonnet XVII.
Nesbit, E. Vies Manquées.
Nichols, G. Configurations.
Nossis. Nothing is sweeter than love, all other blessings.
Olds, S. First Boyfriend.
Ovid. Elegies 2.i.
  Elegy 9b: "If I heard a voice from heaven say 'Live without'."
Paranar. What She Said to Her Girl Friend ("On the tall hill").
Parker, D. Unfortunate Coincidence.
Parker, P. Love Isn't.
Parun. You whose hands are more innocent than mine.
Patchen. Character of Love Seen as a Search for the Lost, The.
  In Judgment of the Leaf.
  In Memory of Kathleen.
  'Sea is Awash with Roses, The'.
  While the sun still spends his fabulous money.
Patten, B. Party Piece.
Paulus Silentiarius. Choicer than all / flush of youth.
  Giving her mother's / zealous eye.
  Goodbye: I bite the word back.
  How many stolen glances can we trade.
  I believe the grief of Tantalus in Hell.
  I saw them, caught them in the act.
  Locked in Hippomenes' kisses.
  Man (they say), A.
  Our kisses / Rhodope.
  Our kisses / Rhodope / let us steal.
  Sappho kisses softly.
  Set foot once beyond Nilotic Meroë.
  She lay all night beside me.
  She plucked one thread.
  Slip off that gown.
  Soft are Sappho's kisses.
  These wreaths, Lais.
  United.
Peele. Love.
  Song: "When as [*or* whenas] the rye [*or* rie] reach to the chin."
Petronius Arbiter. Fragment of Petronius, A.
  That night will long delight us, Nealce.
Peyanar. Embracing this woman.
  His heart swells.
Philips, K. Friendship in Emblem, or the Seal, to my Dearest Lucasia.
  L'Amitie: To Mrs. M. Awbrey.
Philodemus. In the middle of the night.
  Oh feet, oh legs, oh thighs / that formed the deathrow.
  Small thing and moreover black is she, A.
  With Demo I fell in love, of Paphian origins.
  Xanthippe, singing at her lyre.
Piercy. Raisin Pumpernickel.
Pilkington, L. Dol and Roger.
  Fair and Softly goes far or, The Wary Physician.
Plato. Aster.
  Sokrates to Agathon.
Po Chü-i. Everlasting Sorrow, The.
Poliziano. Welcome to May.
Porter, P. Affair of the Heart.
Praxilla. Peeking in through.
Prior. Les Estreines.
Probyn. After.
  Barcarolle.
  Before.
  Blossom.
  China Maniacs.
  Lai.
  Love in Mayfair.
Procter, A. Philip and Mildred.
  Woman's Answer, A.
  Woman's Last Word, A.
Propertius. Me happy, night, night full of brightness.
Pushkin. I loved you.
  No, never think, my dear, that in my heart I treasure.

Qaisi. Outside the Furnace.
Raine, K. Love-Poem: "Yours is the face that the earth turns to me."
Ralegh, W. Nimphs [*or* Nymph's] Reply to the Sheepheard [*or* Shepherd], The.
Ranaivo. Old Merina Theme.
  Song of a Common Lover.
Randall, D. Blackberry Sweet.
Rankin, R. Women of Maine, The.
Ransom, J. Equilibrists, The.
Rich, A. Floating Poem, Unnumbered, The.
  I come home from you through the early light of spring.
  I wake up in your bed. I know I have been dreaming.
  My mouth hovers across your breasts.
Rilke. For one human being to love another human being: that is perhaps the.
  Isn't the secret intent.
  Lovers, gratified in each other, I am asking *you.*
  No, we don't accomplish our love in a single year.
  Once the realization is accepted that even between the closest people.
  Time and again, however well we know the landscape of love.
Robinson, A. Posies.
  Tuscan Olives.
Rochester, J. Imperfect Enjoyment, The.
Rodgers, C. Now Ain't That Love?
Rodgers, W. Net, The.
Roethke. I knew a woman, lovely in her bones.
Rogers, P. Hummingbird: a Seduction, The.
Rossetti, C. Bed of Forget-Me-Nots, A.
  Birthday, A.
  Echo from Willow-Wood, An.
  From Monna Innominata.
  If I Were a Queen.
  "Love me, for I love you"—and answer me.
Rossetti, D. Lost on Both Sides.
  Sudden Light.
  Willowwood ("I sat with Love upon a woodside well").
Roumer. Peasant Declares His Love, The.
Rufinus. Amymone.
  Letter from Ephesos.
  Melissias denies she's in love.
Rufinus Domesticus. Her foot sparkled like silver.
Rumi. I, you, he, she, we.
  Minute I heard my first love story, The.
  Turn me like a waterwheel turning a millstone.
Sackville-West. Absence.
  Tess.
  Thus love, bright charlatan, besieged my heart.
St. John, D. My friend, a man I love as wholly.
  Uptown Love Poem.
Sappho. Eros seizes and shakes my very soul.
  He is almost a god, a man beside you.
  Hymn to Venus, An.
  I love / love's delicacy.
  If you had lusted after something noble or decent.
  Must be some girl from the villages.
  Percussion, salt and honey.
  Sapho's Eye out of Longinus.
  Thank you, my dear.
  With his venom.
Schwartz, D. Aria.
Sedley. On the Happy Corydon and Phyllis.
  To Cloris
Seneca. Power of love over gods them selves, The.
Seward. Elegy.
Sexton. That Day.
Shakespeare, W. Beshrew me but I love her heartily;.
  Phoenix and the Turtle, The.
  Sonnet 66.
  Sonnet 116.
  Sonnet 130.
  Sonnet 138.
Shange. Where the Mississippi meets the Amazon.

Sharkey. Hots, The.
Sheridan, R. Geranium, The.
Sidney, P. Bargain, The.
  Second Song: "Have I caught my heav'nly jewel."
  Sonnet 1: "Loving in truth, and fain[e] in verse my love to show."
  Sonnet 31: "With how sad steps, O Moon, thou climb'st the skies!"
  Sonnet 54: "Because I breathe not love to every one."
Sikelianos. Thalero.
Simic. Breasts.
Simmons, J. Goodbye, Sally.
Sinclair, I. Star-breath descends. line.
Skythinos. Epigram: "Great woe, fire & war come on me."
Smith, C. On the Aphorism "L'Amitié est l'Amour sans Ailes."
Smith, W. Pavane for the Nursery, A.
Snyder, G. After Work.
Soutar. Tryst [*or* Trysting Place], The.
Spender, S. Daybreak.
Spenser. In the Bower of Bliss.
  Now is this love already forth to come.
  Sonnet 54: "Of this world's Theatre in which we stay."
  Sonnet 75: "One day I wrote her name upon the strand."
Stein, G. Lifting belly. Are you. Lifting.
Stevenson, R. Swallows travel to and fro.
Strato. Who knows when love has had its day.
Suckling, J. Against Fruition ("Fie upon hearts that burn with mutual fire[!]").
  Constant Lover, A [*or* The].
  Farewell to Love.
  Love's Clock.
  Love's Siege.
  Miracle, The.
  My dearest rival, lest [*or* least] our love.
  Song: "No, no, fair heretic[k], it needs must be."
  Song: "Why so pale and wan, fond lover?"
  Sonnet: "O[h]! for some honest lover's ghost."
  To a Lady That Forbade to Love before Company.
  Upon My Lady Carlisle's [*or* Carlile's] Walking in Hampton Court Garden.
Surrey. Complaint of a Lover Rebuked.
Swenson, M. Riding the A.
Swinburne. In The Orchard.
  Love And Sleep.
Swirszczynska. Second Madrigal, The.
  Thank You, My Fate.
Sylvester, J. Modern Times.
Symons, A. Emmy ("Emmy's exquisite youth and her virginal air").
  Faint Love.
  Morbidezza.
  Nerves.
  White Heliotrope.
Synge. In May.
Tennyson, A. In Memoriam A.H.H. 27, 35.
Tevakulattar. What She Said ("Bigger than earth, certainly").
Thallus. Now the green plane-tree hides the lovers, hides the lovers'/ rites.
Theocritus. O Polyphemus, while your flocks you keep.
Thomas, D. In my craft or sullen art.
Tighe. Psyche; or The Legend of Love.
Tremblay, G. Not Sense.
Tripathy. Tryst.
Troupe. You come to me.
Tsui. How Can I Show This Poem to Geraldine?
Tsvetayeva. Poem of the End, The.
  Where does this tenderness come from?
Turberville. Lover to His Lady, The.
Unknown. All Year Long.
  Alphabet of Love, The.
  At the beginning of winter a cold spirit comes.
  Bakchos the wine-god / dissolver of limbs.
  Cripple Creek.
  Dear Black Head.
  Easy rider, see what you done done, Lawd, Lawd.

Fyllr.
Gift, A.
I fell in love. I kissed her.
I fell in love with her kisses.
I have a gentle cock.
I would be a soft pink rose.
Love-goddess, saviour / Of the sea-wrecked.
Love Me Not [for Comely Grace].
Merry, Merry Is My Lord.
Now is the month of maying.
O restless, caressing eyes.
Oh! the time that is past.
Picking Rushes.
Pitman's Lovesong, A.
Plucking The Rushes.
She Lay All Naked in Her Bed.
Song of the Snow-white Heads.
South of the Great Sea.
There Was a Lady Loved a Swine.
This morning our boat left the.
Unquiet Grave, The.
Will You Love Me When I'm Old?
You, little round-bellied.
Valentine, J. First Love.
Valéry. Footsteps, The.
Van Duyn. Falling in Love at Sixty-Five.
Leda.
Leda Reconsidered.
Verlaine. Anointed Vessel.
Nevermore.
Vidyakara. Four Poems.
Vidyapati. Sad Love.
Villon. Ballad of Villon and Fat Madge, The.
Virgil. Queen whom sense of Honor cou'd not move, The.
Viṟṟūṟu Mūtcyiṉaṉār. What He Said after a Quarrel, Remembering His Wedding Night.
Voznesensky. Dead Still.
Wade-Gayles. Loving Again.
Wadsworth, W. Snake in the Garden Considers Daphne, The.
Wakoski. Inside Out.
Mechanic, The.
Realization of difference comes, The.
Wallace, R. Real Thing, The.
Waller, E. Budd, The.
Waniek. Ballad of Aunt Geneva, The.
Watkins, N. Near Miss.
Webster, A. By the Looking-Glass.
Weigl. What Saves Us.
Weingarten. Jungle Gliders.
Wharton, E. Mortal Lease, The.
Whitman, W. As Adam early in the morning.
From pent-up aching rivers.
Spontaneous me, Nature.
This is the female form.
When I heard at the close of the day how my name had been receiv'd with plaudits in the capitol, still it was not a happy night for me that follow'd.
Whoever you are holding me now in hand.
Wilbur. Late Aubade, A.
Loves of the Puppets.
Pangloss's Song: A Comic-Opera Lyric.
Wilde, L. Corinne's Last Love-Song.
Williams, W. Jungle, The.
Queen-Anne's-Lace.
Rewaking, The.
Wordsworth, W. I traveled [or travell'd] among unknown men.
Wratislaw. Frangipani.
Satiety.
Sonnet Macabre.
Wright, J. Gesture by a Lady with an Assumed Name, A.
Lights in the hallway, The.
Sappho.
Wroth. Sonnet 14: "Am I thus conquered [or conquer'd]? have I lost the powers."
Wu of Han. People Hide Their Love.
Wyatt, T. Is it possible.
Lover Showeth How He Is Forsaken of Such as He Sometime Enjoyed, The.
With serving still.
Xuân Diệu. Distance.
Yalden. Advice to a Lover.
Yang Shen. To the Tune "Heavenly

Immortal."
To the Tune "Moon Over West River."
Yeats. Brown Penny.
Father and Child.
Last Confession, A.
Lullaby: "Beloved, may your sleep be sound."
Ragged Wood, The.
Yondo. Woman!

See also **Sex**

Error
Peacock, M. How I Had to Act.
Popa. Proud Error.
Preston, K. Lapsus Linguae.
Probyn. Masquerading.
Ransom, J. Parting, without a Sequel.
Simic. Errata.
Unknown. Erasers are the nicest things!

Escalators
Zagajewski. On the Escalator.

Escapes
Aeschylus. Chorus recall Helen's flight, The.
Ai. Kid, The.
Alexander, E. Passage.
Bayly. Out, John! out, John! what are you about, John?
Bennett, R. Gingerbread man gave a gingery shout, The.
Brathwaite, R. Vandunk's Four Humours, in Quality and Quantity.
Causley. What has happened to Lulu, mother?
Ciardi. Sometimes Even Parents Win.
Clewell. Disappearing.
Cummings, E. Notice the convulsed orange inch of moon.
Dacey, P. How I Escaped from the Labyrinth.
Dickinson, E. I never hear the word "escape."
Dobyns. Favorite Iraqi Soldier.
Erdrich. Indian Boarding School: The Runaways.
Euripides. Chorus sing of escape, The.
Ewart. Wanting Out.
Farber. For a Quick Exit.
Hanagid. Prison, The.
Harper, F. Eliza Harris.
Slave Mother, The.
Hayden, R. Runagate Runagate.
Kay, J. Dressing Up.
Keats. Naughty Boy, The.
Lazard. Ordinance on Arrival.
Leadbelly. Take this hammer, (huh!) carry it to the captain, (huh!).
Levine, P. And the Trains Go On.
Lucilius. Lean Gaius, who was thinner than a straw.
MacEwen, G. Manzini; Escape Artist.
MacNeice. Woods.
Mandel, E. Houdini.
Mother Goose. Rub a dub dub.
Nichols, R. 1.
Okudzhava. Midnight Trolleybus.
Owen, G. White Stallion / (The Runaway), The.
Po Chü-i. Children.
Old Man with the Broken Arm, The.
Probyn. Anniversaries.
Reznikoff. When the Second World War began.
Robinson, A. To My Muse.
Rodriguez, L. Always Running.
Seward. Eyam.
Shakespeare, W. Methought That I Had Broken from the Tower.
Stafford, W. Runaway Teen.
Stevenson, R. Escape at Bedtime.
Unknown. Hey diddle diddle.
Take this hammer—huh!
Villanueva, A. They didn't get me.
Vũ Hoàng Chu'o'ng. Far Away.
Whitman, A. Runaway, The.
Whitman, W. We two, how long we were fool'd.
Wong, N. Can't Tell.
Wyatt, T. Farewell, the reign of cruelty!
Longer to muse.
Now all of change.
Now must I le[a]rn[e] to live [or lyve] at rest.

Tangled [or Tanglid] I was [or was I] in [or yn] Love's snare.
Wylie. Escape.
Yamada. Club, The.
Yau. Angel Atrapado VIII.
Young, K. Escape Artist, The.
Yu. Isle of Ulung, The.

Eschatology. *See* **End of the World**

Eskimos
Diamond, L. Eskimo Baby, An.
Kayak Song, A.
"Dylan." Quinn the Eskimo.
Koch, K. Geography.
Purdy, A. Lament for the Dorsets.
Ray, D. Eskimo Girl, The.
TallMountain. Indian Blood.
Warren, R. Sila.
Watson, R. Ballad of the Bird-Bride.

Essex, England
Levertov. Map of the Western Part of the County of Essex in England, A.

Essex, Robert Devereux, 2d Earl of
Unknown. Young Earl of Essex's Victory over the Emperor of Germany, The.

Esther, Book of (Bible)
Harper, F. Vashti.
Spencer, A. Before the Feast of Shushan.

Estrangement
Brown, W. Words.
Browning, R. In a Year.
Byron, G. Lines on Hearing That Lady Byron Was Ill.
So we'll go no more a-roving.
Cope, W. At 3 A.M.
Crane, H. Stark Major.
Crozier, L. So this is love, a kind of sad dance.
Di Prima. To My Father—2.
"Dylan." Tears of Rage.
Godfrey. Where the Weather Suits My Clothes.
Harrison, T. Book Ends.
Hogan, L. Heritage.
Jeffers, R. Birth-Dues.
Jong. Colder.
Kantaris. Body Language.
Kapilar. What the Girl Friend Said to the Foster-Mother.
Lowell, R. Man And Wife.
To Speak of Woe That Is in Marriage.
Lu Yu. Tune: Phoenix Hairpin.
Lugovskoy. Woman / that I knew, The.
Major, C. Isolate.
Mansfield, K. Meeting, The.
'Marnia. Accoutrement.
Merrill, J. Renewal, A.
Olson, C. Distances, The.
Ransom, J. Two in August.
Rich, A. After Dark.
In the Evening.
Like This Together.
Mother-in-Law.
Rain on the West Side Highway.
Rumens. Double Bed.
Schoenberger. Taxidermist's Daughter, The.
Scott, L. Ettrick.
Shakespeare, W. Sonnet 89.
Sonnet 120.
Sonnet 148.
Smith, S. Broken Friendship, The.
Stanley-Wrench. Storm, The.
Unknown. Since first I saw your face I resolved to honor and reknown.
Viorst. Honeymoon is over, The.
Whittemore, R. Storm from the East, A.
Wyatt, T. I must go walk[e] the woods so wild.
Young, A. Dance of the Infidels.

Eternity
Amichai. Now, in the storm before the calm.
Ammons. Eternal City, The.
Andreyev, V. Deep scar engraved in the bark's dark silver, A.
Beaumont, S. Description of Love, A.
Betjeman. NW5 and N6.
Bible, *N.T.* He that heareth my word.

Blake, W. Eternity ("He who binds to himself a joy").
To see a World in a Grain of Sand.
Bozhilov. Eternity.
Wise Ones, The.
Bradstreet, A. Contemplations.
There is a path no vulture's eye hath seen.
Brontë, E. I'm happiest when most away.
No coward soul is mine.
Browning, E. Sonnet: "I thought once how Theocritus had sung."
Sonnet: "If thou must love me, let it be for nought."
Browning, R. Last Ride Together, The.
Love.
Bursk. Tearing Up the Tracks.
Byron, G. Incantation, An.
Carlyle, T. Today.
Ch'en Tzu-ang. Song on Climbing the Gate Tower at Yu-chou, A.
Song on Climbing Yu-chou Gate Tower.
Clare, J. Vision, A.
Cornford, F. On August the Thirteenth.
Cowley, A. Muse, The.
Cummings, E. One Fine Day.
Stand with your lover on the ending earth.
Dickinson, E. Because I could not stop for Death.
It was a quiet way—.
Only News I know, The.
Our journey had advanced.
Disch. Argument Resumed; Or, Up Through Tribeca, The.
Donne. Anniversary [or Anniversarie], The.
Douglas, L. Ode to My Soul.
Ehrenburg. I lived obscurely and uncertainly.
Emerson, R. Days.
Spiritual Laws.
Ferlinghetti, L. Cro-Magnons carried stones for books.
River Still To Be Found, A.
Fitzgerald, R. Face of the Waters, The.
Glazkov. Khikhimora.
Glück, L. White Lilies, The.
Hall, D. Shudder [, The].
Heard, J. Eternity.
Herrick. Eternity.
Love What It Is.
White Island.
Hill, G. Not as we are but as we must appear.
Hood, T. Sonnet: "It is not death, that sometime in a sigh."
Horace. 3.30: This Monument Will Outlast (Exegi momumentum aere perennius).
Housman, A. Immortal Part, The.
Hughes, T. Pibroch.
Kaufman, B. Private Sadness.
Keats. Bright star[, would I were stedfast as thou art—].
Larkin, P. Is it for now or for always.
Leopardi. Infinite, The.
Li Ho. On and On for Ever.
Lipkin, S. In the Desert.
Lu Chao-lin. Weary Road, The.
"MacDiarmid." Man and the Infinite.
MacLeish. Pole Star for This Year.
Mandelstam. Body was given to me—what to do with it, A.
Marichiko. I wish I could be.
Mechthild von Magdeburg. How God Answers the Soul.
Meynell, A. To a Daisy.
Moore, T. Response to Rimbaud's Later Manner.
Nemerov. John 3:1–15; Now there was a man.
Ovid. 1.15.
Park, T. Youthful Sea, The.
Pasolini. John 12:24–25; Truly, truly, I say to you.
Paulinus of Nola. To Ausonius.
Penn. They that love beyond the world, cannot be separated.
Poplavsky. Another Planet.
Ralegh, W. Love Indestructible.
Rands. Cat of Cats, The.
Riley, J. Eternity.

Rilke. No, we don't accomplish our love in a single year.
Rimbaud, A. Hunger.
Rist. Eternity, thou thunderous word.
Roberts, G. Night Sky, The.
Rochester, J. Song: "Absent from thee, I languish still."
Roethke. I knew a woman, lovely in her bones.
Rossetti, C. Bed of Forget-Me-Nots, A.
From the Antique.
Life's Parallels, A.
Rest.
Sandburg, C. Sea-wash never ends, The.
Sappho. When Death shall close those Eyes, imperious Dame!
Senghor. Your face, the beauty of a time long past evokes the perfumed robes in faded hues.
Shakespeare, W. Sonnet 109.
Sonnet 116.
Shelley, P. She met me, Stranger, upon life's rough way.
Shūji. During the rainy season.
Smelyakov. Should I ever fall ill.
Smith, W. Pavane for the Nursery, A.
Spencer, T. Day was a year at first, The.
Spenser. Sonnet 75: "One day I wrote her name upon the strand."
Tagore. I seem to have loved you in numberless forms, numberless times.
T'ao Ch'ien. Substance, Shadow, and Spirit.
Tennyson, A. Brook, The.
The Yueh-Fu. I want to be your friend.
Tikhonov. We have forgotten how to offer alms.
Vaughan, H. World, The (1).
Whitman, W. I have heard what the talkers were talking, the talk of the beginning and the end.
Wu-Men. One instant is eternity.
Yeats. Whence Had They Come?
Young, A. Blues Don't Change, The.
See also **Immortality**
Ethiopia
Bekederemo. New from Ethiopia and the Sudan, The.
Christopher. April in New York.
Crashaw. On the Baptized Ethiopian.
Dunbar, P. Ode to Ethiopia.
Lorde. Ethiopia for Tifa.
Plato. We are Eretrians from Euboia.
Etiquette
Alcock. Modern Manners.
Betjeman. How to Get On in Society.
Bishop, E. Manners.
Browning, R. Respectability.
Bruner. On City Streets.
Burgess, F. Leave-Taking.
Table Manners.
Table Manners II.
Chigetsu. Propriety.
Creeley. Way, The.
Elwell. Courtesy is a quality of soul / refinement impossible to purchase.
Important Words.
Politeness is to do and say.
Emerson, R. Manners are the happy way of doing things.
Garcia. Tips for Living.
Gilbert, S. Etiquette.
Guiterman. Of Courtesy.
Herrick. Panegyric to Sir Lewis Pemberton, A Upon Showbread [or Shewbread]: Epigram.
Hoffmann, H. Story of Fidgety Philip, The.
Lydgate. Boy Serving at Table, The.
Martial. I often bow; your hat you never stir. Monsieur Naso, verolè, A.
Sandburg, C. We Must Be Polite.
Smart, C. Elegance.
Mutual Subjection.
Smith, S. Two Friends.
Stevenson, R. Golden Keys.
Good and Bad Children.
Good Boy, A.
Hearts, like doors.
Whole Duty of Children.

Unknown. How pleasant is Saturday night.
If you must yawn, just turn aside.
Jemima.
Manners at Table When Away from Home.
Table Rules for Little Folk[s].
Tom, Jill and Bob.
Waniek. Daughters, 1900.
Warner, S. Some Make This Answer.
Werth. I'll be polite in many ways.
Williams, W. Raper from Passenack, The.
Eton College
Connolly, C. On Himself.
Gray, T. Ode on a Distant Prospect of Eton College.
Etruscan Civilization
Lawrence, D. Cypresses.
Wilbur. To the Etruscan Poets.
Eucharist
Alabaster. Beehould a cluster to itt selfe a vine.
Clarke, A. Martha Blake.
Conder. Bread of Heaven, on Thee We Feed.
Constable, H. To the Blessed Sacrament.
Herbert, G. Agony [or Agonie], The.
Banquet, The.
H[oly] Communion, The.
Love bade me welcome[: yet my soul drew back].
Superliminare.
Hopkins, G. Bugler's First Communion, The.
L'Engle. At Communion.
Lyon, G. Foot-Washing, The.
Meynell, A. General Communion, A.
In Portugal, 1912.
Norris, K. Moon of the First Communion.
Seaver, G. Communion Hymn.
Snider. Communion.
Southwell. Of the Blessed Sacrament of the Altar [or Aulter].
Thomas, D. This bread I break was once the oat.
Unknown. Let Us Break Bread Together.
Lines to the Blessed Sacrament.
Sacrament of the Altar, The.
Vaughan, H. Holy Communion, The.
See also **Last Supper**
Euclid
Lovelace, R. Snail [or Snayl], The.
Millay, E. Euclid alone has looked on Beauty bare.
Europa
Moschus. Into the Mead he comes, nor (seen) doth fright.
Europe
Apollinaire. Little Car, The.
Arabov. Walking the Places I've Never Been.
Barker, G. Channel Crossing.
Bryant, W. To Cole, the Painter, Departing for Europe.
Cussons. 1945.
Douglas, K. On a Return from Egypt.
Goethe. United States, The.
Gustafson, R. In the Yukon.
Ignatow, D. Europe and America.
Jenkins, J., *et al.* In Ferrara.
Lowell, R. Beyond the Alps.
MacLean, S. Cry of Europe, The.
Milosz, C. Child of Europe.
Scarfe. Kitchen Poem.
Sergeant. Inundation, The.
Sirr. Guide to Holland, A.
Whitman, W. Leaves of Grass (1855).
Eurydice
"Alta." Euridice.
Bancquart. Counterfable of Orpheus.
Browning, R. Eurydice to Orpheus.
Conoley. Unchained Melody.
Doolittle, H. At least I have the flowers of myself.
So for your arrogance.
So you have swept me back.
Hill, G. Orpheus and Eurydice.
Lovelace, R. Orpheus to Beasts.
Raine, K. What substance had Euridice.
Valentine, J. Orpheus and Eurydice.

Eutaw Springs, South Carolina, Battle of (1781)
Freneau. To the Memory of the Brave Americans.

Euthanasia
Jeffers, R. Hurt Hawks.
Randall, D. To the Mercy Killers.

Evangelism and Evangelists
Dale, P. Few ever came to help you speak or sell.
Garrett, G. Revival.
Hayden, R. Witch Doctor.
Oden. This Child Is the Mother.
Warren, R. Amazing Grace in the Back Country.

Eve
Berryman. Gislebertus' Eve.
Bull. Eve.
Caedmon. Temptation and Fall of Man, The.
Frost, R. Never Again Would Birds' Song Be The Same.
Gascoyne. Eve.
Harper, M. Eve (Rachel).
Hartigan, A. Brazen Image.
Hejduk. Sleep of Adam, The.
Hodgson, R. Eve, with her basket, was.
Hood, T. Reflection, A.
Hope, A. Imperial Adam, naked in the dew.
Hough, G. Age of Innocence.
Hughes, T. Theology.
Keats. Garden-Dream, A.
Lanier. Eves Apologie.
Manger. Adam and Eve.
Jealous Adam.
Milton. Adam and Eve in the Garden.
As when of old some orator renowed.
Temptation of Eve, The.
Nasrin. Eve Oh Eve.
Pagis. Written in Pencil in the Sealed Railway-Car.
Pastan. Aspects of Eve.
Probyn. Ballade of Lovers.
Ray, H. Vision of Eve, The.
Rossetti, C. Eve.
Sharpless. *Paradise Lost* as a Haiku.
Sinason. In the Beginning.
Sisson. Adam and Eve.
Smith, S. Dream of Comparison, A.
How cruel is the story of Eve.
Spencer, T. Circle, A.
Unknown. Eve am I, great Adam's wife.
Wilbur. She.
Wright, J. Eve to Her Daughters.
Yeats. Adam's Curse.

See also **Adam and Eve**

Evening
Adams, L. Home-coming.
Aldington. Evening.
Allingham. Evening, An.
Arp. Domestic Stones (fragment), The.
Auden. As I walked out one evening.
Embassy.
Avis. Evening star, The.
Baillie, J. Evening.
Barnes, W. Evenen in the Village.
Bernstein, O. And after a Long While.
In a Park, in Siena, at Twilight.
Bialik. At Day's End.
Bierce. Elegy: "Cur foretells the knell of parting day, The."
Blake, W. To the Evening Star.
Bly, R. Surprised by Evening.
Bobrowski. Wanderer, The.
Bowles, W. Sonnet 5: "Evening, as slow thy placid shades descend."
Brickley. Spring evening.
Summer evening.
Bridges, R. Winter Nightfall.
Burke, M. Rainy winter evening.
Campana. Window, The.
Clare, J. Ballad: The Sun Had Grown on Lessening Day.
Evening.
To Mary: 'It Is the Evening Hour'.
Collins, W. Ode to Evening.
Cristall. Evening, Gertrude.
Daive. I rise from the depths of my

resemblance.
Under the wind I saw.
De la Mare. Myself.
Summer Evening.
Thomas Hardy.
Dickinson, E. Lightly stepped a yellow star.
Doolittle, H. Evening.
Eastwick. At Sunset.
Eliot, T. Preludes.
Enright, D. Old field is sad, The.
Fearing. Evening Song.
Fletcher, J. Folding the Flocks.
Foscolo. To Evening.
Frost, R. Stopping by Woods on a Snowy Evening.
Gascoigne. Gascoigne's [*or* Gascoygnes] Good-Night.
Gerhardt. Evensong.
Guest, B. Otranto.
Guiney. When on the marge of evening the last blue light is broken.
Haas, R. Autumn evening.
Han Yü. Evening: for Chang Chi and Chou K'uang.
Hawley, B. Evening.
Hitomaro. Plovers cry, The.
Hodgson, R. Late, Last Rook, The.
Hristic. Evening Quiet.
Hughes, T. Full Moon and Little Frieda.
Issa. In my life / As in the twilight.
Jaccottet. Wishes.
Jeffers, R. Autumn Evening.
Jewell. This evening stillness.
Johnson, L. Beacon of Hope.
Ken. Evening Hymn, An.
Kenyon, J. Let Evening Come.
Kinnell. Another Night in the Ruins.
Kitahara Hakushū. Tanka: "Each alighted."
Tanka: "Spring bird."
Lampman. Winter Evening.
Landor, W. Progress of Evening.
Larkin, P. Coming.
Going.
Lazarus, E. Evening.
Lewis, C. Evensong.
Li Shang-yin. Evening comes. My mind is troubled.
Longfellow, H. Curfew.
Fire of Drift-Wood, The.
Longfellow, S. Again as evening's shadow falls.
Lovelace, R. Another ("As I beheld a winters evening air").
Magrelli. Every evening, bent over the bright.
McBride, M. Going Under of the Evening Land, The.
Merriam, E. Lullaby "Purple."
Merwin, W. Witnesses.
Meynell, A. November Blue.
Miller, T. Evening.
Miller, W. Willie Winkie.
Montgomery, S. Evening lecture.
Mori Ōgai. Tanka: "But for the dew."
Tanka: "During a break."
Moses, W. Dark and Dark.
Moss, H. Persistence of Song, The.
Mountain, M. Old towel folding it again autumn evening.
Patmore, C. Evening Scene, An.
Peyanar. Evening in the yard.
Pizzarelli. Late in the evening.
Porter, F. Island in the Evening, The.
Quigless. Evening.
Radnóti. Seventh Eclogue.
Roethke. In Evening Air.
Sachs, N. In the evening your vision widens.
Saitō Mokichi. Tanka: "From the evening darkness."
Tanka: "What on the other shore."
Sandburg, C. Evening Waterfall.
Scarfe. Ode in Honour.
Senghor. Man and Beast.
Shapiro, D. Tracing of an Evening.
Shin, S. It is Not Time Yet to Light the Candle.
Slonimski. Morning and Evening.
Snyder, G. Work to Do Toward Town.

Stafford, W. For Alexis Christa von Hartmann: Proved Not Guilty.
Stephens, J. Evening.
Stevens, W. Evening without Angels.
Tagore. Bird, The.
Teasdale. February Twilight.
Tekkan. Tanka: "Noiselessly."
Toomer. Georgia Dusk.
Trakl. De Profundis.
Tu Mu. Autumn Evening.
Turner, F. Spring Evening.
Unknown. Aching nostalgia—.
Evening darkens until.
In the evening / The mists trail.
Van den Heuvel. November evening.
Tidepool, A.
Virgilio. Winter evening.
Wang Shih-chieng. Sailing along the Tai Stream from Stone Bridge to the Foot of Mo-ho Peak.
Warren, R. Evening Hawk.
White, G. Naturalist's Summer-Evening Walk, The.
Wordsworth, W. By the Sea.
Composed upon an Evening of Extraordinary Splendour and Beauty.
Wright, C. Complete Birth if the Cool, The.
Yosano. Tanka: "Each shaped."
Tanka: "White tower, A."
Tanka: "Young fingers."
That evening when.
Zesen. Evening Song.

See also **Twilight**

Evening Star
Blake, W. To the Evening Star.
Clare, J. Hesperus! the day is gone.
Jeffers, R. Evening Ebb.
Longfellow, H. Evening Star, The.
Sappho. Oh Hesperus! thou bringest all good things.
Stevens, W. Homunculus et la Belle Étoile.
Martial Cadenza.

See also **Venus (planet)**

Evers, Medgar
Brooks, G. Medgar Evers.
Ignatow, D. For Medgar Evers.

Evictions
Clinton. Eviction.

See also **Inclosure Movement**

Evil
Berryman. Nothing there? nothing up the sky alive.
Bible, *O.T.* Psalm 14.
Psalm 37: "Fret not thyself because of evildoers."
Psalm 50.
Blake, W. Marriage of Heaven and Hell, The.
Boito. Spirit of Evil, The.
Brecht, B. To Those Born Later.
When Evil-Doing Comes Like Falling Rain.
Byrom. On the Origin of Evil.
Byron, G. Sketch from Private Life, A.
Chaucer. Pardoner's Tale, The.
Clare, J. Sonnet: "Ere I had known the world and understood."
Clifton, L. Coming of Kali, The.
Crinagoras. Though of white marble and dressed straight.
Dowriche. So him at first *De Nance* commanded was to kill;.
Drummond, W. Doth then the world go thus, doth all thus move?
Duncan, R. Fire, The.
Elwell. Courtesy is a quality of soul / refinement impossible to purchase.
"Field." Dying Viper, A.
Frost, R. Bearer of evil tidings, The.
Design.
Ginsberg, L. Hymn to Evil.
Goethe. Do you know me now? Skinny, cadaverous bitch.
Graves, R. Succubus, The.
Gray, T. Tophet.
Hecht, A. "It Out-Herods Herod. Pray You, Avoid It."
Herrick. Another Charme (variant).

Neutrality Loathsome.
Spell, The.
Hippolyte. Caribbean Exorcism Poem, A.
Holan. To the Enemies.
Hope, A. Möbius Strip-Tease.
Hughes, L. Bad Man.
Jarrell. Blind Sheep, The.
Johnson, L. To a Passionist.
Kendall, M. Legend of the Crossing-Sweeper.
Kizer, C. Most people from Idaho are crazed rednecks.
Kutilov. Crickety Creek.
Lawrence, D. Root of Our Evil, The.
Lindsay, V. Simon Legree—A Negro Sermon.
Longfellow, H. Rhyme of Sir Christopher, The.
Matveyeva. Laughter of a Faun, The.
McGrath, T. Death for the Dark Stranger.
Merwin, W. Stranger, The.
Mother Goose. For every evil under the sun.
O'Brien, G. Ornamental Syllable.
Osundare. Maddening moon, A.
Pembroke, M. Quid gloriaris? Psalm 52.
Pinsky. Dante's Inferno, Canto XXXIV (The Final Canto).
Poe. Silence.
Polkowski. Noli Me Tangere.
Raine, K. Pythoness, The.
Rózewicz. What Happens.
Sexton. After Auschwitz.
Shakespeare, W. Now is the winter of our discontent.
Shapiro, K. Puritan, The.
Smith, S. Angel Boley.
  Lord Barrenstock and Epicene.
  To the Tune of the Coventry Carol.
Soto. Who Will Know Us?
Stanford, F. Terrorism.
Vaughan, H. Kingdom of Heaven Compared to a Grain of Mustard-Seed, The.
Voloshin. In the Bottomless Pit.
Walcott. God Rest Ye Merry, Gentlemen.
Wesley, C. He Shook off the Beast.
Wheelwright. Live, Evil Veil.
Whitman, W. I sit and look out upon all the sorrows of the world, and upon all oppression and shame.
Williams, M. Why God Permits Evil: For Answers to This Question of Interest to Many Write Bible Answers Dept. E-7.
Young, D. Business of Love is Cruelty, The.

Evolution
Allen, G. Ballade of Evolution, A.
Azevedo. Suicide, The.
Bevington, L. Midnight.
  Morning.
Blight. Evolution.
Ciardi. On Evolution.
Collymore. Monkeys.
Day, C. Yesterday explorers found.
Edson, R. Darwin Descending.
Emerson, R. Nature [1836].
Equi. Ode to Chicago.
Gilman, C. Similar Cases.
Howe, J. Kosmos.
Jones, A. Foot, The.
Karp. Consequences of Waking, The.
Kendall, M. Lay of the Trilobite, The.
  Lower Life, The.
Lawrence, D. Self-Protection.
Lewis, C. Evolutionary Hymn.
Melville, H. Epilogue: "If Luther's day expand to Darwin's year."
Naden. Solomon Redivivus, 1886.
Peskett. Inheritors, The.
  Question of Time, The.
Sandburg, C. Wilderness.
Schnackenberg. Darwin in 1881.
Smith, L. Evolution.
Updike. Naked Ape, The.
Very. Origin of Man, I, The.
Viereck, P. Love Song to Eohippus.
Williamson, J. Natural Selection.

See also **Darwin, Charles; Extinction**

Excavations
Emanuel, L. Dig, The.
Unknown. Clementine.

Weston, M. Primitive Place.

Excrement
Benn. Monologue.
Brecht, B. Three Fragments.
Ciardi. Suburban.
Comte de Lautréamont. I am filthy. Lice gnaw me. Swine, when they look at me, vomit. The scabs.
Herbert, S. General inspecting the trenches, The.
Holan. To the Enemies.
Kumin, M. Excrement Poem, The.
Louis, J. Indian College Blues.
Mansour, J. From an ass to an analyst and back.
Nathan, L. Bladder Song.
Tipton. All day.
Weigl. Burning Shit at An Khe.
Zipper. Farmer drives by, A.

Executions and Executioners
Beckovic. If I knew I'd bear myself proudly.
Breytenbach. We Shall Overcome.
Bruchac. Let the Midnight Special.
Burns, R. Hughie Graham.
Cable, G. Dirge of St. Malo, The.
Chao Meng-fu. Poem of Prefectural Judge Yang T'ien-jui Righting a Wrong.
Chipasula. Hanging, Zomba Central Prison, A.
Dimoski. Revenge.
Fairfax of Cameron. On the Fatal Day January 30, 1648.
  Shortness of Life.
Faiz. So Bring the Order for My Execution.
Frankau. Deserter, The.
Freedman, W. Family, The.
Greene, A. Four roads lead out of the town.
Gunn, T. No Speech from the Scaffold.
Gwynn, R. Among Philistines.
Harington. Tragicall Epigram, A.
Hecht, A. 'More Light! More Light!'.
Herbert, Z. Five Men.
Housman, A. Carpenter's Son, The.
  Eight O'Clock.
  On moonlit heath and lonesome bank.
Khlebnikov, V. She came and spoke low.
Kipling, R. Danny Deever.
Leipoldt. Oom Gert's Story.
Marinoni. At Sunrise.
Melville, H. Billy in the Darbies.
Moritz. In Memory of Titian Tabidze.
Nabokov. Execution, The.
Newbolt. He Fell among Thieves.
Obolduyev. Tongue, The.
Patmore, C. London Fete, A.
Popa. Be Seeing You.
Ralegh, W. Sir Walter Ra[u]le[i]gh to His Son[ne].
Ridge, L. Electrocution.
Ritsos. Underneath Oblivion.
"Ropshin." Guillotine's / Sharp blade?, The.
Simic. Toy Factory.
Smith, S. Death Sentence, The.
  One of Many.
Swift, J. Clever Tom Clinch Going to Be Hanged.
Tekeyan. Sacred Wrath.
Tennyson, A. Rizpah.
Thorpe, R. Curfew Must Not Ring Tonight [*or* To-Night].
Tichborne. Tichborne's Elegy.
Trần Cao Vân. It's mere child's play to die— who'd care to try?
Tsaloumas. They brought him one morning.
Unknown. Croppy Boy, The.
  John Hardy was a desp'rate man.
  Josie.
  Last Words.
  Mary [*or* Marie] Hamilton.
  Night before Larry was stretched, The.
  Queen's Marie, The.
Villon. Epitaph in Form of a Ballad, The.
Wat. Imagerie d'Epinal.
Wyatt, T. In mourning wise since daily I increase.

See also **Capital Punishment; Hanging**

Exercise
Glenn. José Cruz.

Mizejewski. Anaerobics: Elaine Powers, Wheeling, West Virginia.
Pomfret, J. No Barren Leaves.
Swirszczynska. Troubles with the Soul at Morning Calisthenics.

Exhilaration
Browning, R. Now.
Rexroth, K. Frost covers the reeds of the marsh.

Exile
"Adunis." Elegy for the Time at Hand.
Agosin. Disappeared Woman I.
"Akhmatova." I am not one of those who left the land.
Alegría. We Were Three.
"Ansky." Emigrant Song.
Antipater of Thessalonica. Unlucky Nicanor, quenched by the grey and deep.
Auden. Exiles, The.
Bachmann. Exile.
Bancquart. Town.
Bernard. Lark, The.
Berry, J. Old Man in New Country.
Bible, *O.T.* Psalm 137.
Bienek. Exodus.
Bly, R. Dream of Retarded Children, A.
Brecht, B. 1940.
Breeze. Riddym Ravings (The Mad Woman's Poem).
Breytenbach. Dar es-Salaam: Harbour of Peace.
  Eavesdropper.
  Exile, Representative.
Brodsky, J. In the Lake District.
Brontë, E. Loud without the wind was roaring.
  Visionary, The.
Brooke, R. Old Vicarage, Grantchester, The.
Brooks, M. Shade of Columbus, here thy relics rest.
Burns, R. Highland Harry Back Again.
  My heart's in the Highlands, my heart is not here.
Cain, K. Lesson, The.
Caulfield. Photo That Watches, The.
Cheney-Coker. Road to Exile Thinking of Vallejo, The.
Columcille. If I owned all of Alba.
Cuadra, A. In Brief.
Curnow. House and Land.
Dafydd Benfras. From Exile.
Darwish, M. Guests on the sea: Our visit is short.
  Identity Card.
  Sirhan Drinks His Coffee in the Cafeteria.
  We travel like other people, but we return to nowhere. As if travelling.
De Kok. Transfer.
Diop, D. Renegade, The.
Dipoko. Exile.
  Poem of Villeneuve St Georges, A.
Dobbie. Things Grow Up out of the Dark.
Dorfman, A. Vocabulary.
Dowson. Exile.
Driver. Letter to Breyten Breytenbach from Hong Kong.
Duffy, C. Foreign.
Espaillat. You call me by old names: how strange.
Euripides. Ilion, o my city.
  No more, O my spirit.
Fordham. Exile's Reverie, The.
Fortunato. Leaving, The.
Fried, E. Exile.
Han Yü. Written on My Way into Exile.
Hecht, A. Alceste in the Wilderness.
Herbert, G. Religion stands on tip-toe in our land.
Hildebert. Songs you sent me I have read, The.
  To Peter, Bishop of Poitiers, Who Withstood William of Aquitaine and Died in Exile.
Hospital. Mother Tongue, The.
Huỳnh Thúc Kháng. Farewell Song, A.
Inada. From Our Album.
Ivask, I. And then I told about the red soil of Oklahoma.
  We shall return we will stay here.

James, S. Short Wave In Shanghai.
Jastrun, T. Scrap.
Jones, T. Welshman in Exile Speaks, The.
Julius Polyaenus. Although your ears must be plentifully occupied.
Kaye/Kantrowitz. Jerusalem Shadow.
Keegan. Irish Reaper's Harvest Hymn.
Kipling, R. St. Helena Lullaby, A.
Kolmar. Judith.
Kunyayev. It's hard to understand how one can leave.
Lazard. Ordinance on Arrival.
Lazarus, E. Currents.
Leonidas of Tarentum. Far from Italy, far from my native Tarentum.
Levertov. Contraband.
Lovelace, R. Another ("Centaur, siren [or syren], I forgo[e], The").
MacCarthy, D. Paschal Fire, The.
Markham, E. Towards the End of a Century.
McNeill, A. Straight Seeking.
Millay, E. Exiled.
Milosz, C. My Faithful Mother Tongue.
Mphahlele. Exile in Nigeria.
Nabokov. Execution, The.
  To Russia.
Nerber. Castaway.
O'Meallain. Exodus to Connacht.
Ovid. When night falls here, I think of that other night.
Padilla. In Trying Times.
  Nuclear Umbrella.
Pastan. At Home.
Paterson, E. Tribal Homeland.
Patten, B. Earth-ling, The.
Pau-Llosa. Frutas
"Perse." Doors open on the sands, doors open on exile.
Phillips, D. From Arena.
Plato. Leaving behind for ever the thundering Aegean.
Po Chü-i. After Collecting the Autumn Taxes.
  Dreaming that I Went with Li and Yü to Visit Yüan Chēn.
  Rain.
  Song of the Lute.
Raine, K. Written in Exile.
Ralegh, W. Farewell to the Court.
Robinson, E. Aaron Stark.
Rocha. Poem of Return.
Rowe, A. Space Settlement.
Rukeyser, M. Song: "World is full of loss; bring, wind, my love, The."
Schiff, H. German Frontier at Basel: 1942 and 1992, The.
Seneca. O barbarous Corsica, locked in by crags.
Shapiro, K. Exile.
  Travelogue for Exiles.
Simko. Thinking of My Father on a Bus to Baltimore.
Smelyakov. Menshikov.
Smith, I. Exiles have departed, The.
Soprovsky. Notes from the house of the dead.
Soyinka. Massacre, October '66.
Stansbury, J. To Cordelia.
Stewart, F. Black Winter.
Stricker. Against Simple Reading.
Su Man-shu. Exile in Japan.
Thompson, D. Ovid on the Dacian Coast.
Tidjani-Cissé. Home News.
Tô Hū'u. Cuckoo calls its flock—it's when the rice, The.
  Prison Thoughts.
Trân Tuân Khái. Our Land, Our Home.
Unknown. Brunanburg.
  Edward [or Edward, Edward].
  Encountering Sorrow.
  Exile of Erin, The.
  Seafarer.
  Songe bewailinge the tyme of Christmas, So much decayed in Englande, A.
Voznesensky. Autumn in Sigulda.
Walcott. Hotel Normandie Pool, The.
  Midsummer: XXX.
Walker, A. Outcast.
Wat. From "Songs of a Wanderer."

Woodcock. Pacifists.
Wyatt, T. I must go walk[e] the woods so wild.
  Myn owne John poyntz sins ye delight to know.

Existentialism and Existentialists
Crane, S. Man said to the universe, A.
Roethke. Duet.
Tomlinson, C. Juliet's Garden.
Williams, C. Gas Station, The.

Exodus
Bible, O.T. Psalm 78.
  Psalm 114.
Dunbar, P. Ante-Bellum Sermon, An.
Ezechiel of Alexandria. Exodus from Egypt, The.
Moore, T. Sound the Loud timbrel o'er Egypt's dark sea!
Oppen. Exodus.
Reznikoff. Exodus.
Unknown. Go down, Moses.
  Let My People Go.
  Parting of the Red Sea, The.

Experience
Ashbery. As You Came from the Holy Land.
Blake, W. Introduction: "Piping down the valleys wild."
Blunden. Report on Experience.
Brathwaite, E. Clock.
Brontë, E. Old Stoic, The.
  Why do I hate that lone green dell?
Cavafy. Ithaka.
Chaucer. Wife of Bath's Prologue, The.
Cooper, J. Knowledge That Comes through Experience, The.
Crane, S. Little birds of the night.
Csoori. Everyday History.
Cummings, E. All ignorance toboggans into know.
  If everything happens that can't be done.
  May my heart always be open to little.
  Since feeling is first.
  What a proud dreamhorse pulling(smoothloomingly)through.
Dickinson, E. Far from Love the Heavenly Father.
  I stepped from Plank to Plank.
Dunn, S. Tenderness.
Eberhart, R. Rumination.
Emerson, R. Experience.
Fenton, J. Pitt-Rivers Museum, Oxford, The.
Ginsberg, A. Howl.
Giovanni. Alabama Poem.
Golding, L. In The Gallery Where the Fat Men Go.
Hacker, M. Hang-Glider's Daughter, The.
Hope, A. Observation Car.
Hughes, L. Esthete in Harlem.
Kerouac. Poem.
Kipling, R. Nurses, The.
  Sestina of the Tramp-Royal.
Lawrence, D. When the ripe fruit falls.
Levertov. In Mind.
MacLeish. L'An Trentiesme de Mon Eage.
Masters, E. Arlo Will.
Meredith, W. Ritual Mouse, A.
Miles, J. When I was eight, I put in the left-hand drawer.
Prescod. Vicious Circle.
Ransom, J. Blue Girls.
Rich, A. Diving into the Wreck.
Robinson, E. Isaac and Archibald were two old men.
Seferis. Memory II.
Sitwell, E. Green Song.
Smith, P. What It's Like to Be a Black Girl (For Those of You Who Aren't).
Unknown. Song of an Old Gray Wolf.
Van Duyn. Moose in the Morning, Northern Maine.
Wharton, E. Experience.
Whitman, W. Houses and rooms are full of perfumes.
  Trippers and askers surround me.
  When I heard the learn'd astronomer.
Williams, M. After the Revolution for Jesus the Associate Professor [or a Secular Man]

  Prepares His Final Remarks.
  Ruby Tells All.
Winner, R. Segregated Railway Diner—1946.
Wordsworth, W. Sonnet: "World is too much with us; late and soon, The."
Young, A. For Poets.
  Prestidigitator 1, The.
W. H. Auden & Mantan Moreland.

Exploring and Explorers
Atwood. Explorers will come, The.
Barlow, J. On the Discoveries of Captain Lewis.
Bierds. For the Sake of Retrieval.
Bishop, J. O Pioneers!
Booth, P. Stefansson Island.
Donne. Calm[e], The.
Drayton. To the Virginian Voyage.
Dryden, J. By viewing Nature, Natures hand-maid, Art.
Falkner. Arabia.
Fetherling. Explorers as Seen by the Natives.
Frost, R. America Is Hard to See.
Glancy. Christopher.
Hacker, M. Future Conditional.
Hoffman, D. Exploration.
Ingamells. They made impudent inspection of our coast.
Kirkup. Astronaut, The.
MacLeish. Voyage West.
Marvell. Bermudas.
Melville, H. To Ned.
Miller, J. Columbus.
Newlove. Samuel Hearne in Wintertime.
Rumble. Eagle has Landed, The.
Simpson, L. To the Western World.
Smedley, M. North Pole Story, A.
Squire. Sonnet: "There was an Indian, who had known no change."
Unknown. On Francis Drake.
Waniek. Star-Fix.

Explosions
Daniel, J. To Mt. St. Helens.
Field, R. Fourth of July.
Larkin, P. Explosion, The.
Smith, B. American Lunch.
Yukitsuna. Tanka: "Writing a series."

Extinction
Blight. Death of a Whale.
Booth, P. Species.
Brock-Broido. Last Passenger Pigeon in the Cincinnati Zoo, The.
Buckmaster. End to Myth, An.
Carlile. Dodo.
Davis, J. First-born, The.
Dransfield. Endsight.
Enzensberger, H. Vanished Work.
Hope, A. Moschus Moschiferus.
Keithley. When they leave the world will be at peace.
Kumin, M. Noted in The New York Times.
MacBeth. Bedtime Story.
Merwin, W. For a Coming Extinction.
Oliver, M. Ghosts.
Oodgeroo of the tribe Noonuccal. Last of His Tribe.
  We are Going.
Prokosch. Conspirators, The.
Sandburg, C. Buffalo Dusk.

Extrasensory Perception
Graves, R. Foreboding, The.

Extreme Unction
Dowson. Extreme Unction.

Eyeglasses
Clark, T. Eyeglasses.
Fanthorpe. Relief of Myopia, The.
Machi. Tanka: "Trying to wash away."
Rajeevan. Pair of Glasses, A.
Rein. Glimpsed through a Lens.

Eyes
Ackland. Eyes of body, being blindfold by night, The.
  Poem: "You send me a letter from far, from across the sea."
Arnold, M. Absence.
Asquith. Hairy Dog, The.
Barrax. Your Eyes Have Their Silence.

Baudelaire. Cats.
Owls.
Benedikt. Eye, The.
Birney. Slug in Woods.
Bogan, L. Medusa.
Bontemps. "Close Your Eyes!"
Bourdillon. When Love Is Done.
Brodsky, J. Roman Elegies IV.
Brontë, E. O thy bright eyes must answer now.
Celan. Language Mesh.
Coolidge, C. In Nora's House with Rilke's Apollo.
Crashaw. Weeper, The.
Dante Alighieri. My lady carries love within her eyes.
Dickinson, E. I like a look of Agony.
Like Eyes that looked on Wastes.
Donne. Message, The.
Dowson. Extreme Unction.
Duncan, R. Coming out of the house to die.
Eyesight II.
DuPlessis, R. Since the narcissus bud.
Eliot, T. Eyes that last I saw in tears.
Field, E. Wynken, Blynken and Nod one night.
"Field." Already to mine eyelids' shore.
Dying Viper, A.
La Gioconda.
Poet, The.
Field, R. Dancing Bear, The.
Gilbert-Lecomte. Wink.
Graves, R. By this exchange of eyes, this encirclement.
Grenier. Wrath to Sadness.
Grimké, A. Naughty Nan.
Gu Cheng. Generation, A.
Haines, J. Awakening.
Harwood, L. Soft White.
Herrick. Eye, The.
Upon Her Eyes.
Hiley. To a Persian Cat.
Holst-Warhaft. Matthew 5:27–30; You have heard that it was said.
Hopkins, G. She schools the flighty pupils of her eyes.
Hussey, A. Ezra Pound's Eye.
Ishikawa Takuboku. Tanka: "I close my eyes."
Jonson, B. Song, A: "Oh do[e] not wanton with those eyes."
To Celia.
Kandinsky. Sounds.
Kaufman, B. Would You Wear My Eyes?
Kendrick, D. Note to the Ophthalmologist.
Kizer, C. Through a Glass Eye, Lightly.
Knight, E. He sees through stone.
Knott. Goodbye.
Lee, J. Spring is a Cat, The.
Lowell, R. Eye and Tooth.
MacNeice. Grey Ones, The.
Magowan. Susan.
Marino. Beautiful Slave, The.
Marvell. Eyes and Tears.
McClintock, M. First melt, The.
Hamburger Hill.
Peering out.
Merkel, B. Owls.
Merwin, W. Diggers, The.
Glass.
Meynell, A. Cradle-Song at Twilight.
Mirabai. O friends on this Path.
Montgomery, N. Eyewash.
Okamoto. Tanka: "As I gaze upon."
Tanka: "Green leaves."
Okigbo. Eyes Watch the Stars.
Olds, S. Knowing, The.
Pack, R. Thrasher in the Willow by the Lake, The.
Pau-Llosa. Island of Mirrors, The.
Péret. Making Feet and Hands.
Pfeiffer, E. Any Husband to Many a Wife.
Po Chü-i. Separation.
Popa. Eyes of a Wolf.
Porter, P. Non Piangere, Liù.
Porumbacu. Pupil, The.
Rabi'a al-Adawiyya. O my Lord.
Ransom, J. Her Eyes.

Reverdy. Inn.
Rilke. Black Cat.
Roth, H. Her eyes still closed.
Rukeyser, M. Eyes of Night-Time.
Sachs, N. Your eyes, O my beloved.
Sansom, M. To Cleon's Eyes.
Schafer. Battle Lines.
Seay. Options.
Sedley. To Cloris.
Shakespeare, W. Sonnet 130.
Siddal. Lust of the Eyes, The.
Sidney, P. Sonnet 7: "When Nature made her chief work, Stella's eyes."
Sonnet 48: "Soul's joy, bend not those morning stars from me."
Spire. Nativité.
Stein, G. I Am Rose [my eyes are blue].
Suppose an Eyes.
Strachey, L. Cat, The.
Su Shih. On A Toad.
Swenson, M. Seeing the frog.
Symons, A. To a Dancer.
Thompson, P. Soft Black Eyes.
Tsaloumas. Return of an Ikon.
Turberville. Lover to His Lady, The.
Unknown. Alexander's Song.
Since the narcissus bud.
Two little eyes to look to God.
Young Man Who Couldn't See Why, The.
Vakaló. My Father's Eye.
Ward, D. Approximately.
Willmot. Away from eyes.
Wordsworth, D. Lake was covered all over, The.
Wroth. Sonnet 39.
Yang Chi. Poem Making Fun of Chi-ti for His Eye Illness, A.
Yeats. Cat and the Moon, The.
Drinking Song, A.
Zimmer. Failings, The.

Ezra
Ammons. So I Said I Am Ezra.

F

Faces
"Akhmatova." Alone.
Auden. Dedication: "Private faces in public places."
Bogan, L. Song for the Last Act.
Boldman. Face wrapping a champagne glass.
Borges. Luke XXIII.
Brickley. Sheet lightning.
Bridges, R. Eros.
Brontë, A. Fragment, A.
Browning, E. Face which, duly as the sun, The.
Camp, P. Rhyme of Dorothy Rose, The.
Campbell, J. Old Woman, The.
Campion, T. There is a Garden in her face.
Caraion. Archaic Hippocamp.
Carrel. Treacherous Death of Jesse James, The.
Chin. Altar.
Chu Shu-chen. Morning.
Clare, J. First Love.
Secret, The.
Coolidge, C. Crystal Text, The.
Creeley. Just Friends.
Signboard, The.
Dante Alighieri. You that thus wear a modest countenance.
Dash. Me Again.
De la Mare. Widow, The.
Drayton. These verses weare made By Michaell Drayton Esquier Poett Lawreatt the night before hee dyed.
Eigner. In Imitation.
"Field." Elsewhere.
Fyleman. (Mice).
Gallagher, T. Not There.
Gascoyne. Ecce Homo.
Graves, R. Face in the Mirror, The.
Hall, D. Raisin, The.
Harr, L. Sparkler goes out, The.
Hayati. Before there was a trace of this world of men.

Is this darkness the night of Power, or the black falling of your hair?
Herrick. Upon Mistresse Susanna Southwell, Her Cheeks.
Ho Ching-ming. Song of the Painting "River and Mountains," by Wu Wei.
Hughes, L. Chord.
Ishikawa Takuboku. Tanka: "Beastly face."
Tanka: "Mirror in hand."
Jewell. Under ledges.
Keller, D. In the Middle of the Journey.
Khlebnikov, V. Bo-be-o-bee sang the mouth.
It has the unassuming face of a burnt-out candle.
Komunyakaa. Facing It.
Kooser. Self-Portrait at Thirty-Nine.
Lamb, E. Old album, The.
Lewis, A. Unknown Soldier, The.
Li Ch'ing-chao. Hopelessness.
Lindsay, C. To My Own Face.
Lorde. From the House of Yemanjá.
Lovelace, R. Another ("As I beheld a winters evening air").
Black Patch on Lucasta's Face, A.
Scrutiny [or Scrutinie], The.
Marino. Lips and Eyes.
McPherson, S. Ability to Make a Face Like a Spider While Singing Blues: Junior Wells, The.
Michelangelo Buonarroti. I see in your handsome face, my Lord.
Mitchell, S. Face, The.
Girl Tearing Up Her Face.
Moore, M. Face, A.
Nobuyuki. Ashtray (two poems).
Patterson, R. Sundown Blues.
Pinkerton, H. On Dorothea Lange's Photograph "Migrant Mother" (1936).
Pound, E. In A Station of the Metro.
Probyn. Model, The.
Rodgers, C. Poem No. 1.
Sandburg, C. Halsted Street Car.
Sidney, P. Sonnet 9: "Queen Virtue's court, which some call Stella's face."
Simon, L. Nellie Gives into Blanche.
Smedley, M. Face from the Past, A.
Sobin, G. Towards the Blanched Alphabets.
Suckling, J. Constant Lover, A [or The].
Swede. On the face.
Swift, J. Progress of Beauty, The.
Sylvester, J. Sweet mouth, that send'st a musky-rosed breath;.
Symons, A. Maquillage.
Tóth, J. Masks.
Unknown. Beautiful faces are they that wear.
Patience is a virtue.
Tommy.
Valentine, J. After Elegies.
Wang Chiu-ssu. You think I am happy.
Webster, A. By the Looking-Glass.
Faded.
Whitman, W. Faces.
Wyatt, T. Face that should content me wonders [or wondrous] well, A.
Wylie. To a Lady's Countenance.
Yi, S. Soyŏng Problems.
Zanzotto. If it were not your face that melts.

Factories
Ackland. Communist Poem, 1935.
Alexander, M. Chicago.
"Antler." Machines waited for me, The.
Bishop, E. Varick Street.
Blok. Factory, The.
Bryll. In a Fever.
Jago. Iron Industry in Birmingham, The.
Johnston, E. Lines to Ellen, the Factory Girl.
Kelly, R. Bittersweet growing up the red wall.
Lindsay, V. Factory windows are always broken.
Longfellow, H. Ropewalk, The.
Mueller, L. Night Shift at the Fruit Cannery.
Nicholson, N. On the Closing of Millom Ironworks.
Norton, C. Voice from the Factories, A.
Plath. Night Shift.
Reznikoff. Amelia was just fourteen and out of the orphan asylum.

Sandburg, C. Mill-Doors.
Shepherd, R. Skin Trade.
What Cannot Be Kept.
Unik. Manless Society, The.
Unknown. Factory Workers' Song.
Williams, W. Classic Scene.

Faerie Queene, The
Ralegh, W. Vision upon This Concei[p]t of the Faerie [or Faery] Queen[e], A.
Ralegh, W. *et al.* Another of the Same.
Spenser. Amoretti, Sonnet 80.

Failure
Altizer. Sonnet 5: "No, I'll not, carrion, comfort you. Comfort."
Angel. Twice Removed.
Backus. Then Laugh.
Bly, R. August Rain.
Cameron, C. Don't Give Up.
Cary, P. Don't Give Up.
Chin. First Lessons.
Clifton, L. Making of Poems, The.
Coleridge, H. He Lived amidst th' Untrodden Ways.
Cummings, E. Nobody loses all the time.
Dickinson, E. Success is counted sweetest.
Eady. Hank Mobley's.
Edson, R. Floor is something we must fight against. Whilst seemingly, The.
"Elagin." Has my life been a failure? I wonder—.
Ficowski. I did not manage to save.
Finlay, I. Great frog race.
Gilder, R. Failure and Success.
Ginsberg, A. Last Night in Calcutta.
Gioia. Guide to the Other Gallery.
Giovanni. Stars.
Goode. Failure.
Griffin, S. Bad Mother, The.
Guillén, N. Don't Know No English.
Gwynn, R. Anacreontic.
Holden, J. Losers.
Hughes, T. Crow's First Lesson.
Hunt, L. Rondeau: Jenny Kiss'd [or Kissed] Me.
James, C. Book of my enemy has been remaindered, The.
Jonson, B. Ode to Himself.
Kendall, M. Failures.
Knight, E. Report to the Mother.
Kooser. Abandoned Farmhouse.
Kunert. Vain Attempt.
Lake, P. Crime and Punishment.
Lowell, A. Epitaph on a Young Poet Who Died before Having Achieved Success.
Magee, K. Instrumentum Vocale.
Markham, E. Victory in Defeat.
Masefield. Consecration, A.
Meng Chiao. On Failing the Examination.
Miller, J. For Those Who Fail.
Newcastle, M. Poetresses Petition, The.
Piercy. Death of the small commune, The.
Pitter. 1938.
Po Chü-i. Half-recluse, The.
Ray, H. Failure.
Robinson, E. Bewick Finzer.
Clavering.
Rossetti, C. Symbols.
Rukeyser, M. Paper Anniversary.
Sassoon. Counter-Attack.
Shen Chou. To the Tune "Nan-hsiang-tzu."
"Shu Ting." Perhaps these thoughts of ours.
Symons, A. Prologue: In the Stalls.
Trowbridge, J. Farmer John.
Unknown. Never Say Fail.
Optimist / "Somebody Said That It Couldn't Be Done."
Roses are red.
Updike. Player Piano.
Viiding. I celebrated this day in March.
Virgil. Turnus' retreat.
Wilbur. In the Smoking-Car.
Wu Wei-yeh. Seeing Off Sun Ling-hsiu on His Journey to Chen-ting.
Yeats. To a Friend Whose Work Has Come to Nothing.
Zimmer. Zimmer in Grade School.

Fairies
Allingham. Fairies, The.
Bangs, J. Little Elf, The.
Beddoes. Song by Isbrand.
Bishop, M. How to Treat Elves.
Burgess, F. Trapping fairies in West Virginia.
Carman, B. Mr. Moon.
"Carroll." My Fairy.
Cary, A. To Mother Fairie.
Chalmers, P. Puk-Wudjies.
Chaucer. Tale of Sir Thopas, The.
Corbet. Fairies' Farewell, The.
Cox, P. Brownies' Celebration, The.
Doughty. Fairies Feast, The.
Ferguson, S. Fairy Thorn, The.
Fyleman. Fairies.
Fairy Went a-Marketing, A.
Goblin lives in our house, in our house, in our house, A.
Graves, R. I'd Love to Be a Fairy's Child.
Lollocks.
Guiterman. Of Certain Irish Fairies.
Hardy, T. On a Midsummer Eve.
Herford. Elf and the Dormouse, The.
Herrick. Beggar to Mab, the Fairy [or Fairie] Queen, The.
Fairy Temple; or, Oberon's Chapel, The.
Oberon's Feast.
Oberon's Palace.
Temple, The.
Hiott. Tale of Mushrooms.
Housman, A. Fairies break their dances, The.
Keats. Faery Song.
La Belle Dame Sans Merci.
Lowell, J. Hob Gobbling's Song.
Mew. Changeling, The.
Monro. Overheard on a Saltmarsh.
More, H. Inscription in a Beautiful Retreat Called Fairy Bower.
Morley, C. Plumpuppets, The.
Moultrie. Fairy Maimounè, The.
Noyes, A. Sherwood in the twilight, is Robin Hood awake?
Peake. O here it is! And there it is!
Poe. Fairyland [or Fairy-Land].
Pope, A. Belinda still her downy Pillow prest.
Ray, H. On a Nook Called Fairyland.
Riley, J. Little Orphant Annie's come to our house to stay.
Scott, W. Ballad: Alice Brand.
Shakespeare, W. Ariel's Song: "Come unto these yellow sands."
Ariel's Song: "Where the bee sucks, there suck I."
I dreamt a dream tonight.
Smedley, M. Irish Fairy lost her way, An.
Taylor, J. Fairies' Song, The.
Unknown. Thomas the Rhymer [or Rimer].
Wee Wee Man, The.
Wright, J. Evening.
Yeats. Stolen Child, The.

See also **Elves; Goblins**

Fairs
Auden. Fairground.
Clarke, A. Fair at Windgap, The.
Gardinier. Agricultural Show, Flemington, Victoria, The.
Gay, J. Two Monkeys, The.
Hardy, T. Ballad-Singer, The.
Former Beauties.
"MacDiarmid." Cattle Show.
Nguyễn Khuyến. At an Exposition.
Stevens, G. Bartleme Fair.
Thackeray. Mr. Molony's Account of the Crystal Palace.
Unknown. Sledburn Fair.
Tomorrow's the Fair.
Williams, P. Rhapsody on Main Street.
Williams, W. Dance, The.
Winchilsea. Hog, the Sheep and Goat, Carrying to a Fair, The.
Zabolotsky. Peoples House.

Fairy Tales
Ashbery. Märchenbilder.
Baxter, J. Spring-heeled Jack.
Corbet. Proper New Ballad, Intitled The Fairies' Farewell, A.

Corbett, R. Proper New Ballad Intituled The Faer Yes Farewell: Or God-A-Mercy Will, A.
Galvin, J. Independence Day, 1956: A Fairy Tale.
Glück, L. Gretel in Darkness.
Graves, R. To Juan at the Winter Solstice.
Jarrell. House in the Wood, The.
Märchen, The.
Kuznetsov. Atomic Fairy Tale.
Lugovskoy. Bear, The.
Lynd. Beauty and the Beast.
Mueller, L. Reading the Brothers Grimm to Jenny.
Nesbit, E. Goose-Girl, The.
Pack, R. Frog Prince, The.
Smith, S. Fairy Story.
Frog Prince, The.

Fairyland
Alexander, C. Dreams.
Graves, R. Land of Whipperginny, The.
More, H. Inscription in a Beautiful Retreat Called Fairy Bower.

Faith
Aaronson. Homeward Journey, The.
Adamovich. One of them said: "One life is much too little."
There, in some place, some time.
Alabaster. Jesu, thie love within mee is soe maine.
My soule a world is by Contraccion.
Now I have found thee, I will ever more.
Three sortes of teares doe from myne eies distraine.
Upon the Ensignes of Christes Crucifyinge.
Arghezi. Psalm.
Arnold, M. Dover Beach.
Rugby Chapel.
Arthur, K. I Saw Three Ships.
Askew. Ballad Which Anne Askew[e] Made and Sang When She Was in Newgate, The.
Aus of Kuraiza. Apostasy.
"Bagritzky." Origin.
Bangs, J. Blind.
Baxter, R. Now it belongs not to my care.
Bible, Apocrypha. Jeremie .17.
Bible, *N.T.* Though I speak in the tongues of men or of angels: if I have no love, I am.
Bible, *O.T.* I am the resurrection, and the life.
Psalm 23.
Psalm 115.
Blake, W. Divine Image, The ("To Mercy, Pity, Peace and Love").
Lamb, The.
Mock on, Mock on Voltaire, Rousseau.
Night.
Brontë, E. No coward soul is mine.
Visionary, The.
Brooke, R. Heaven.
Browning, R. Bad Dreams.
Bryant, W. To A Waterfowl.
Byrom. My spirit longeth for Thee.
Cane. Tree in December.
Chesterton, G. Convert, The.
Chukhontsev. Farewell to Autumn.
Clark, T. Faith for Tomorrow.
Clough. Dipsychus.
Coleridge, S. Hexameters[; Paraphrase of Psalm XLVI].
Coverdale. Song of the Virgin Mary, The.
Cowper, W. Light Shining out of Darkness.
Crane, H. Recitative.
Crashaw. Against Hope.
Hymn in Adoration of the Blessed Sacrament.
Crowell, G. Courage to Live.
I think that God is proud of those who bear.
Cummings, E. I thank You God for most this amazing.
No time ago / or else a life.
That melancholy / fellow'll play / his handorgan.
Davis, D. I Can Trust.
Dickinson, E. "Faith" is a fine invention.
Faith—is the Pierless Bridge.
How brittle are the Piers.
I know that He exists.
I never lost as much but twice.
I never saw a Moor.

Nearest Dream recedes—unrealized, The.
On a Columnar Self.
Read—Sweet—how others—strove.
This World is not Conclusion.
Those—dying then.
To pile like Thunder to its close.
Donne. "Batter my heart, three-person'd God; for you."
To Mr. Roland Woodward ("Like one who in [or who'in] her third widowhood [or widdowhood] doth profess[e]").
Dowland. Dear, if you change, I'll never choose again.
Drayton. Other Song of the Faithful, for the Mercies of God, An.
Song of the Faithful, A.
Dryden, J. Thus man by his own strength to Heaven would soar.
Dunbar, P. Slow Through the Dark.
Dunn, S. At the Smithville Methodist Church.
Ehrmann. Prayer, A: "Let me do my work each day."
Emerson, R. Character.
Worship.
Fenton, J. God, A Poem.
Fields, J. Ballad of the Tempest.
Floyd. Corporal Kevin Spina, U. S. M. C.
Frost, R. Sitting by a Bush in Broad Daylight.
Gale, N. Country Faith, The.
Gilbert, C. Directions, The.
Glück, L. Celestial Music.
Grossman, R. Therefore, We Thank Thee, God.
Guiney. Wild Ride, The.
Halevi. Hymn for Atonement Day.
Meditation on Communion with God.
Hall, J. Kind of Faith, A.
Hall, J. Praise of Faith, The.
Hardy, T. Impercipient, The.
Harris, R. Isaiah by Kerosene Lantern Light.
Hartnett. There will be a talking of lovely things.
Herbert, G. Affliction: "Kill me not every [or ev'ry] day."
Affliction (1).
Artillery [or Artillerie].
Bag, The.
Banquet, The.
Bitter-Sweet.
Charms and Knots.
Church-Floor[e], The.
Collar, The.
Complaining.
Discipline.
Divinity.
Elixir [or Elixer], The.
Employment (1).
Flower, The.
Forerunners, The.
Glance, The.
Grace.
Holy Baptism (2).
Justice.
Love (1).
Love ("Thou art too hard for me in Love").
Peace.
Pearl. [Matth. 13.45 or Matt. 13:45], The.
Perseverance.
Quidditie [or Quiddity], The.
Search, The.
Sepulchre.
Sin (1).
Sonnet: "My God, where is that ancient heat towards Thee."
Sonnet: "Sure Lord, there is enough in thee to dry."
Superliminare.
Temper (1), The.
Temper (2), The.
Thanksgiving, The.
Windows, The.
Herrick. His Creed.
His Litany to the Holy Spirit.
Hirsch, E. For the Sleepwalkers.
Holmes, O. Our Limitations.
Hooper, V. Lost in the Galleries.

Hopkins, G. Carrion Comfort.
God's Grandeur.
Housman, A. If it chance your eye offend you.
Howe, S. Silence Wager Stories.
Hunt, L. Abou Ben Adhem (may his tribe increase!).
Faith, Hope, and Charity Are the Prospects of Manhood.
Hurston. Faith hasn't got no eyes, but she long-legged.
Jeffers, R. Credo.
John of the Cross. Song of the Soul That Knows God by Faith.
Song of the Soul that Rejoices in Knowing God through Faith.
Stanzas of the Soul that Suffers with Longing to See God.
Johnson, A. And Sea.
Johnson, F. Song of the Whirlwind.
Kalir. To Him Who Is Feared.
Katuvei Ilaveyinanar. Tirumal.
Keats. What the Thrush Said.
Keble. See Lucifer like lightning fall,.
Kemble. Faith.
Kempis, T. Love is a great thing, a great good in every way; it alone lightens what is.
Kipling, R. Recessional.
Kirantaiyar. Hymn to Tirumāl (Viṣṇu).
Knevet. Harp, The.
Knox, R. O God, for as much as without Thee.
Komunyakaa. Instructions for Building Straw Huts.
Kumin, M. Getting the Message.
Kushner, A. What I really wanted.
Kuzmina-Karavayeva. I too have encompassed a lot: a mother thrice—.
Lawrence, D. Hills, The.
Llwyd, M. 1. What? summer now? divisions ring.
Locke, A. Sin and despair have so possess'd my heart.
Longfellow, H. Bells of San Blas, The.
Lowell, J. After the Burial.
In a Copy of Omar Khayyám.
Lowell, R. As a Plane Tree by the Water.
Malone, W. Opportunity.
Markham, E. How the Great Guest Came.
Mayakovsky. No matter how much more waiting I'll have to do.
McAuley, J. In the Twentieth Century.
McKay, C. Pagan Isms, The.
Melville, H. Conflict of Convictions, The.
Epilogue: "If Luther's day expand to Darwin's year."
Swamp Angel, The.
Miguel de Guevara. Raise me up, Lord, who am fallen down.
Milosz, C. Faith.
Milton. On His Blindness.
On Time.
More, H. Patient Joe; or, The Newcastle Collier.
Newman, J. Pillar of the Cloud, The.
Noll. Abraham's Madness.
Okudzhava. I don't believe in God and fate.
O'Meallain. Exodus to Connacht.
O'Rahilly. Time of Change, A.
Palmer, R. My Faith Looks Up to Thee.
Patmore, C. Constancy Rewarded.
Pfeiffer, E. Any Husband to Many a Wife.
Pozzi. To Trust.
Preil, G. Lines on the Rambam.
Quarles. Behold this needle; when the *Arctick* stone.
Ralegh, W. Verses Made the Night before He Died [or Dyed].
Ray, H. Triple Benison, The.
Riley, J. Hired Man's Faith in Children, The.
Robinson, E. Children of the Night, The.
Credo.
Rossetti, C. Comparisons.
Lord Jesus, who would think that I am Thine?
Somewhere or other there must surely be.
Rossetti, D. "Retro Me, Sathana."

Rowbotham. Nebuchadnezzar's Kingdom-Come.
Rowe, E. Hymn: "In vain the dusky night retires."
Rumi. Keep walking, though there's no place to get to.
Turn me like a waterwheel turning a millstone.
Sackville-West. September 1939.
St. John, D. Leap of Faith.
Sangster, M. Prayer for Faith, A.
"Shu Ting." Fairy Tales.
Smart, C. Conclusion of the Matter, The.
Faith.
Fortitude.
Strength.
Smith, P. Annie Pearl Smith Discovers Moonlight.
Smith, S. Dream of Comparison, A.
God the Eater.
Smith, S. Aa my life, my leman said.
Stafford, W. Runaway Teen.
Stevenson, R. If This Were Faith.
Stradling. Abraham's Sacrifice of Isaac.
Swinburne. Higher Pantheism in a Nutshell, The.
Tabb. Sisters, The.
Tenebræ.
Tahmisic. Landscapes.
Tarkovsky. First Meetings.
Taylor, E. Meditation 8 (First Series).
Meditation Eight.
State, a state, oh! dungeon state indeed, A.
Tennyson, A.
In Memoriam A.H.H. 50, 54, 124.
Doubt.
Thomas, L. Electricity of Blossoms.
Thomas, R. In a Country Church.
Thompson, F. Hound of Heaven, The.
Thoreau. If with light head erect I sing.
Thù'a Phong. Mother's Faith.
Traherne. Innocence.
Tranströmer. Scattered Congregation, The.
Tuckerman, F. As sometimes in a grove at morning chime.
Sonnets: First Series.
Unknown. Apostles' Creed, The.
Death.
Faith.
God and Yet a Man, A?
I believe in the sun.
Lonesome Valley.
Roll, Jordan, Roll.
Shema Yisrael.
Sometimes I feel like a motherless child.
Though Mine Eye Sleep Not.
Van Dyke. Four Things [a man must learn to do].
Vaughan, H. Retreat[e], The.
Wreath, The.
Very. Nature.
Slavery.
Slowness of Belief in a Spiritual World, The.
Wallace-Crabbe. Secular, The.
Warren, R. English Cocker: Old and Blind.
Warton, T. On the Spirit Adulterated by the Flesh.
Wesley, C. Come on, my partners in distress.
Wesley, J. Hymn: "Thou hidden love of God, whose height."
Wilcox, E. Faith.
Nothing New.
Optimism.
Wild, R. In a melancholly studdy.
Willard, E. Rocked in the Cradle of the Deep.
Williams, C. Dream of Mind: The Gap, A.
Williams, M. After the Revolution for Jesus the Associate Professor [or a Secular Man] Prepares His Final Remarks.
Winters, Y. Precision, The.
Wolfskehl. To Be Said at the Seder.
Wright, J. Cradle Logic of Autumn, The.
Wroth. Song: "O[h] me[e], the time is [or has] come to part."
Sonnet 6: "My pain[e], still smothered [or smother'd] in my grievèd bre[a]st."
Wyatt, T. After great storms the calm returns.
Farewell: "What should I say."

Give place all ye that doth rejoice.
Supplication, A.
What should I say.
Ye know my heart, my lady dear.
Yoshimi. Tanka: "Having grown up."

Faith Healers
Larkin, P. Faith Healing.

Falcons
Duncan, R. My mother would be a falconress.
Hopkins, G. Windhover, The.
Lovelace, R. Lady with a Falcon on Her Fist, A.
Read, S. Falcon and the Dove, The.
Rossetti, C. Noble Sisters.
Steffen. Falcon to the Falconer, The.
Unknown. I trained me a falcon, for more than a year.
Lover Compareth Himself to the Painful Falconer, The.
Timor Mortis.
Villon. Ballad Written for a Bridegroom.
Wyatt, T. Lux, my fair falcon, and your fellows all.

Falkland, Lucius Cary, Viscount
Conway, H. Falkland at Newbury, 1643.

Fall. *See* **Autumn**

Falling
Azevedo. Suicide, The.
Cherry, K. Pines without peer, The.
Davis, T. Boppin' is Safer than Grindin'.
Ded. This world.
Dickinson, E. It dropped so low—in my Regard.
Fumiko. Tanka: "Knees collapsing."
Grigson. Before a Fall.
Hooks. Body Inside the Soul, The.
Hsü Wei. Returning from the Seventy-Two Mountains.
Ishikawa Takuboku. Tanka: "Somehow."
Jacobsen, J. Primer, The.
Levchev. Capriccio 9.
Makeda (Queen of Sheba). I fell.
Mechthild von Magdeburg. Fish cannot drown in water, A.
Molodovsky. Prayers: I.
Mother Goose. Humpty Dumpty sat on a wall.
Noyes, A. Daddy Fell into the Pond.
Pagis. Footprints.
Palmer, M. Theory of the Flower, The.
Rózewicz. Homework Assignment on the Subject of Angels.
Unknown. Doctor Bell fell down the well.
Optimist fell ten stories, The.
Warren, R. Ballad: Between the Boxcars.
Williams, W. Luke 6:39.

Fame
Ashbery. He cuts down the lakes so they appear straight.
Bible, Apocrypha. Our Fathers.
Bradstreet, A. In Honour of That High and Mighty Princess Queen Elizabeth of Happy Memory.
Brontë, E. Old Stoic, The.
Stanzas to———.
Browning, R. Popularity.
Brownjohn. We are going to see the rabbit.
Butler, S. There is a tall long-sided dame.
Byron, G. Stanzas Written on the Road between Florence and Pisa.
What is the end of fame? 'Tis but to fill.
Calverley. Of Friendship.
Chapman, G. . . . Through the wall, uprore.
Chudleigh. Resolve, The.
Coleridge, S. Epitaph: "Stop, Christian passer-by!—Stop, child of God."
Cowley, A. Motto, The.
Daniel, S. To The Lady Lucie, Countesse of Bedford.
Davies, I. Consider Famous Men, Dai Bach.
Dickinson, E. Be Mine the Doom.
Fame is a bee.
Fame is a fickle food.
I'm Nobody! Who are you?
Of Bronze—and Blaze.
Publication—is the Auction.
"Elagin." Has my life been a failure? I wonder—.

Elenkov. Stone.
Ewart. Haiku: The Season of Celebrity.
Fisher, R. Paraphrases.
Fitzgerald, E. 13.
Flexner, H. Contemporary.
Frost, R. Provide, Provide.
Garioch. Glisk of the Great.
Glazkov. To My Ill-Wishers.
Goldstein, L. Permissive Entry: A Sermon on Fame.
Grainger, J. What is fame? An empty bubble.
Greville, F. Sonnet: "Three things there be in mans opinion dear[e]."
Heard, J. Fame.
Hemans. Woman and Fame.
Herrick. Fame.
Fame Makes Us Forward.
Pillar of Fame, The.
To His Book[e] ("Have I not blessed thee? Then go forth; nor fear").
Horace. Conclusion. After the Manner of Horace, ad librum suum, The.
Hughes, T. Famous Poet.
Jewsbury. Summer Eve's Vision, A.
Jones, M. Epistle to Lady Bowyer, An.
Jonson, B. To Sir Henry Cary.
Keats. Addressed to Haydon.
Terror of Death, The.
Kemble. Wish, A.
Killigrew, A. Upon the Saying That My Verses Were Made by Another.
Lamb, L. New Canto, A.
Lihn. Favorite Little Shrine, A.
Lindsay, C. Love or Fame.
Lowell, J. In an Album.
Sonnet.
Lowry, M. After Publication of Under the Volcano.
Macgillivray. Return, The.
Martial. Post-Obits and the Poets.
McClure, M. Mad Sonnet: Fame.
Merton. Elegy for Ernest Hemingway, An.
Mew. Fame.
Milton. On Shakespear[e].
Nabokov. Fame.
Nathan, L. So you aren't Tolstoy or Saint Francis.
Norton, C. Picture of Sappho, The.
Nye, N. Art of Disappearing, The.
Famous.
Ovid. 1.15.
Parkes. To an Author who Loved Truth More than Fame.
Parra, N. Poems of the Pope, The.
Pasternak, B. To be famous is not in good taste.
Philip of Thessalonica. Sky will extinguish its stars, and the sun, The.
Po Chü-i. Escorting Candidates to the Examination Hall.
In Early Summer Lodging in a Temple to Enjoy the Moonlight.
On Hearing Someone Sing a Poem by Yüan Chên.
Rich, A. Focus.
Robinson, E. Three Quatrains.
Sandburg, C. Soup.
Shakespeare, W. Sonnet 125.
Shelley, P. Ozymandias [of Egypt].
Sidney, P. Sonnet 15: "You that do search for every purling spring."
Sonnet 27: "Because I oft, in dark abstracted guise."
Sonnet 90: "Stella, think not that I by verse seek fame."
Simms, W. Glory and Enduring Fame.
Troupe. Poem for "Magic", A.
Tu Fu. To Pi Ssu Yao.
Unknown. I often pause and wonder.
Turning my chariot I yoke my horses and go.
Updike. Newlyweds, The.
Waller, E. At Penshurst [Another].
Whalen. International Date Line, Monday/ Monday 27:XI:67.
Whitman, W. When I heard at the close of the day how my name had been receiv'd with

plaudits in the capitol, still it was not a happy night for me that follow'd.
Wyatt, T. Stand whoso list upon the slipper top.

See also **Greatness**

Family
Alexander, E. Who I Think You Are.
Ali, A. Cracked Portraits.
Bekederemo. Abiku.
Death of a Lady.
Family Procession, A.
Leader, The.
Order of the Dead, The.
Berryman. Henry's Fate.
When by me in the dusk my child sits down.
Bishop, E. Poem: "About the size of an old-style dollar bill."
Blandiana. From a Village.
Bobrowski. Latvian Songs.
Brooks, G. Parents: People Like Our Marriage Maxie and Andrew, The.
Broumas, O. Landscape with Next of Kin.
Buckley, V. Origins.
Bukowski. Me against the world.
Bursk. Lies.
Chao Meng-fu. Inscribed on Sun An-chih's "Painting of Pines and Catalpas."
Inscribed on the Painting "Spring Dawn at Peach Blossom Spring" by Scholar Shang Te-fu.
Chin. How I Got That Name.
Chock. Chinese Fireworks Banned in Hawaii.
Chu Yün-ming. Fan from Korea, A.
Cisneros, S. His Story.
Coleman, W. Dear Mama (2).
Cooley. Holy Family.
Cooper, J. In the House of the Dying.
Dabydeen, D. Catching Crabs.
Davidson, D. Sanctuary.
De Vries, R. On Alabama Ave., Paterson, NJ, 1954.
Dean, D. In the Way Back.
Deane, S. Fording the River.
Dove, R. Fifth Grade Autobiography.
Drummond de Andrade. Motionless Faces.
Travelling in the Family.
Durcan. Wife Who Smashed Television Gets Jail.
Eberhart, R. Spite Fence.
Emanuel, L. Patient.
Ennis. Drink of Spring, A.
Espada. Niggerlips was the high school name / for me.
Eversley. Just to Be Needed.
Fried, E. My Girlfriends.
Gallagher, T. Woodcutting on Lost Mountain.
Geda. God's Family.
Glück, L. Brown Circle.
From the Suburbs.
Widows.
Goodman, M. Upkeep.
Gorman, L. My family asleep.
Hacker, M. And I shout at Iva, whine at you. Easily.
Elevens.
Hagedorn, J. Smokey's Getting Old.
Hahn, K. Hula Skirt, 1959, The.
Possession: A Zuihitsu.
Hai-Jew, S. Three Gypsies.
Harms. Explaining the Evening News to Corbyn.
Harper, M. Families Album, The.
Heaney, S. Funeral Rites.
Hewitt, J. From a Museum Man's Album.
Hogan, L. Heritage.
Holly. Our family tree is in the sear.
Hongo. Hilo: First Night Back.
Huddle. Cousin.
Hudgins. Telling, The.
Ishikawa Takuboku. Tanka: "Forgetting."
Joans. Black People.
Jordan, J. Female and the Silence of a Man, The.
Kaplinski, J. My wife and children were waiting for ice cream.
Karpowicz. On Opening an Old House.
Kay, J. English Cousin Comes to Scotland.

Kayo. Song of the Initiate.
Kenyon, J. At the Iga: Franklin, New Hampshire.
From Room to Room.
Kinzie. Boy.
Kirsch, S. Pictures.
Kloefkorn. On the Road.
Koch, K. You were wearing your Edgar Allan Poe printed cotton blouse.
Kollar. Late Arrivals.
Ku. War Poems 1.
Kumin, M. For My Great-Grandfather: A Message Long Overdue.
My Father's Neckties.
Retrieval System, The.
Kunitz, S. Father and Son.
Quinnapoxet.
Kushner, D. Grandma in the Shower.
Larkin, P. Ambulances.
Lee, L. Persimmons.
Li K'ai-hsien. In the Second Month of Summer, Taking My Family to the Villages East of the City.
Lilley. Sewing Lesson, The.
Lisella. Song of the Third Generation.
Livingston, M. Coming from Kansas.
Invitation.
Lorde. Time of lamentation and curses is passing, The.
Lu Yu. Idleness.
Lum. Picture of my Mother's Family, A.
Maclean, A. Home Thoughts from Home.
Markham, E. Her story.
Marshall, J. Sesame.
Mathews, A. Letter Following.
McGinley. Giveaway, The.
McGuckian. Lychees.
McNair. My Brother Running: V.
Mei Yao Ch'en. On the Night of the Fifteenth Day of the First Month I Go Out and Return.
Melville, H. Fragments of a Lost Gnostic Poem of the Twelfth [or 12th] Century.
Menander. What do you say to this? The thought has just.
Meng Chiao. In vain I gather up these stars from the ground.
When I tread the earth, I fear to hurt the ground.
Meredith, G. We saw the swallows gathering in the sky.
Miles, J. Belief.
Montague, J. At Last.
Muir, E. Ring, The.
Scotland 1941.
Mullins, B. At the Lakehouse.
Nichols, G. Tapestry.
Niedecker. Fancy Another Day Gone.
Paean to Place.
Norris, K. Poem about Faith, A.
Ochester. Relatives, The.
O'Loughlin. Glasnevin Cemetery.
Ondaatje. Light.
Parker, P. Prologue from "Legacy."
Pasternak, B. Autumn.
Patchen. Easy Decision, An.
Peyanar. His heart swells.
Piercy. My Rich Uncle, Whom I Only Met Three Times.
Po Chü-i. On a Moonlit Night, Sent to my Brothers and Sisters.
Parrot.
Popa. In the Village of My Forefathers.
Prévert. Whale hunt, The.
Raab, L. On the Island.
Ramanujan. In the Zoo.
Ransom, J. First Travels of Max.
Rein. Galya, Mother, and My Daughter Anna.
Rogers, P. Family Is All There Is, The.
Root, J. Small Differences.
Rózewicz. Return, The.
Rutsala. Shack Outside Boise, The.
Sáenz. Resurrections.
Saffoti. Espresso.
Schaeffer. Housewife.
Sexton. All My Pretty Ones.
Shapcott, T. Turning Fifty.
Shapiro, A. Manufacturing.

Slutsky. Burnt.
Smith, S. Tenuous and Precarious.
Sophocles. Think on thy father in the vale of years.
Soto. Braly Street.
Stafford, W. One Home.
Subbiah. Salutations.
Tanikawa Shuntaro. Family Portrait.
Tapahonso. I Am Singing Now.
Tate, A. Not power nor the casual [or storied] hand of God.
Tate, J. Land of Little Sticks, 1945.
My Great Great Etc. Uncle Patrick Henry.
Tennyson, A. Lullaby: "Sweet and low, sweet and low."
Tidjani-Cissé. Home News.
Tremblay, B. Home Front.
Unknown. Girl threw an apple to a cloud, A.
On Prince Frederick.
Please, Chung Tzu.
Walcott. Glory Trumpeter, The.
Walker, A. For Two Who Slipped Away Almost Entirely.
Warren, R. Ballad of Billie Potts, The.
Waters, M. Mystery of the Caves, The.
Wayman. Teething.
Weigl. One, The.
Shelter.
Weiner, J. Who They Were.
Weller. Ngungalari.
Story of Frankie. . . My Man, The.
Wickham. Letter to a Boy at School.
Wong, N. Ma, my heart must be made of rice straw.
Picnic.
Wood, S. Witness.
Wright, C. Return to Seattle: Bastille Day.
Wright, J. Willy Lyons.
Wright, J. I To my Brothers.
Yamada. American Son.
Yang Shih-ch'i. Enclosed with a Letter to My Family—For Shu.
Yang Wei-chen. Tu-lu Poem ("Tu-lu, Tu-lu, evil waters turning muddy").
Yü Chi. What family has built a house beside the rapids here?
Yün Shou-p'ing. Waterside Village.

Family Life
Alvarez, J. Ironing Their Clothes.
Atwood. In this house (in a dying orchard.
Barrax. Domestic Tranquility.
Bell, M. Gemwood.
Berg, S. And the Scream.
Betjeman. Green shutters, shut your shutters! Windyridge.
Bible, O.T. Bible, Psalm 1:1–3, The.
Brissenden. Verandahs.
Bromley, A. Teel St. Trailer Court.
Brooks, G. Religion.
Vacant Lot, The.
Cervantes. Beneath the Shadow of the Freeway.
Clare, J. Country Letter.
Clifton, L. Good Times.
Courtney. Be kind to thy father: for when thou wert young.
Creeley. Gift of Great Value, A.
Derricotte. Poem for My Father.
Di Prima. Poem in Praise of My Husband (Taos).
Divakaruni. Making Samosas.
Doubiago. Signal Hill.
Dove, R. Daystar.
Taking in Wash.
Drummond de Andrade. Family Portrait.
Eady. I Just Wanna Testify.
Eshleman, C. Deeds Done and Suffered by Light.
Flanders, J. Dandelion Greens.
Foley, M. Provincial Adolescence, A.
Gildner. House on Buder Street, The.
Nails.
Giovanni. Nikki-Rosa.
Glück, L. Amazons.
Griffin, S. Love Should Grow Up like a Wild Iris in the Fields.
Hands, E. On an Unsociable Family.

Hartnett. Small Farm, A.
Harwood, G. In The Park.
Hass, R. Concerning the Afterlife, the Indians of Central California Had Only the Dimmest Notions.
Song: "Afternoon cooking in the fall sun."
Hawley, B. Evening.
Hayden, R. Those Winter Sundays.
Hernandez. Sunday morning.
Hogan, L. Heritage.
Holmes, J. Somerset Dam for Supper, The.
Holmes, O. Old Man Dreams, The.
Hughes, L. Piggy-back.
Hughes, P. Handful of Pebbles, Mouthful of Stones.
Jenkins, C. Sunday Morning.
Joseph, L. Sand Nigger.
Kaniyan Punkunran. Every Town a Home Town.
Kaufman, S. Mothers, Daughters.
Kay, J. Dressing Up.
Kenyon, J. At the Iga: Franklin, New Hampshire.
Knight, E. Idea of Ancestry, The.
Kunitz, S. Three Floors.
Lowell, R. My Last Afternoon with Uncle Devereux Winslow.
Lu Yu. Idleness.
McCarriston. Hotel Nights with My Mother.
To Judge Faolain, Dead Long Enough: A Summons.
McElroy, C. Looking for a Country under Its Original Name.
McHugh, H. What Hell Is.
McMichael. I know I'll lose her.
McNair. Minister's Death, The.
Meltzer, D. Eyes, the Blood, The.
Meredith, G. Orchard and the Heath, The.
Merrill, J. Emerald, The.
Millay, E. Lament: "Listen, children: / Your father is dead."
Morley, C. Animal crackers, and cocoa to drink.
Morris, M. Family Pictures.
Moss, H. Long Island Springs.
Muldoon, P. Mixed Marriage, The.
Mura. Nisei Picnic: From an Album, A.
Nash, O. Family Court.
O'Hara, F. Ave Maria.
Orerulavanar. Relations.
Pastan. Passover.
Peacock, M. Those Paperweights with Snow Inside.
Peeradina, S. Sisters.
Peterson, N. Search, The.
Peyanar. Like the red flame.
Pratt, M. Motionless on the Dark Side of the Light.
Place Lost and Gone, the Place Found, The.
Prévert. Familial.
Rich, A. In the Wake of Home.
Woman Mourned by Daughters, A.
Ridge, L. I room at Sodos'—in the little green room.
Riley, J. King of Oo-Rinktum-Jing, The.
Rilke. From a Childhood.
Roethke. My Papa's Waltz.
Rossetti, C. What does the bee do? / Bring home honey.
Salter. Frost at Midnight.
Sandburg, C. Population Drifts.
Senior. Hill Country.
Sexton. Funnel.
Seymour, A. To the Family Home Awaiting Repair.
Shelnutt. Family.
Shinder. Prayer.
Simpson, L. My father in the night commanding No.
Physical Universe.
Smith, S. Emily Writes Such a Good Letter.
So Chong-Ju. Looking at Mt. Mudung.
Stafford, K. Opening the Book.
Stafford, W. Rescued Year, The.
Stanton, M. Childhood.
Storey. Prayer for Broken Little Families, A.
Tekkan. Tanka: "Their father."

Thibaudeau. Brown Family, The.
Green Family, The.
Tsui. Chinese Banquet, A.
Uruttiran. What She Said to Her Girl Friend, and What Her Girl Friend Said in Reply.
Voigt. O mild Christ.
Victim, The.
Weaver, M. Picnic, an Homage to Civil Rights, The.
Whitman, T. Super-Brave.
Wild, P. Ice Cream.
Willard, N. Why I Never Answered Your Letter.
Wright, E. When Father Carves the Duck.
Wright, K. Victorian Family Photograph.
Yamada. Obon: Festival of the Dead.

Famine
Bàng Bá Lâ. They Starved, They Starved.
Bekederemo. New from Ethiopia and the Sudan, The.
Binyon. Hunger.
Jackson, H. In Time of Famine.
Kavanagh, P. Maguire is not afraid of death, the Church will light him a candle.
Ryan, R. Father of Famine.
Walker, A. Few Sirens, A.
Wickham. Nursery Song.
Wilde, L. Famine Year, The.

Fancy. *See* **Imagination**

Fans
Brandling. To a Lady, with a Present of a Fan.
Gossett. On the Question of Fans/ The Slave Quarters Are Never Air Conditioned.
Lovelace, R. Lucasta's Fan[ne], with a Looking-Glass[e] in It.
Mallarmé. Another Fan.
Momaday. Eagle-Feather Fan, The.
Nguyễn Khuyến. To a Discarded Fan.
Pan Chieh-yû. Present from the Emperor's New Concubine, A.
Song of Regret.
Probyn. Tête-à-Tête.
Wickham. Boor's Wooing, The.
Yün Shou-p'ing. Essence of ink, The.

Fantasies
Arnold, M. Longing.
Bernstein, O. Don't Count.
Boyd, M. Sonet: "Fra bank [or banc] to bank [or banc], fra wood [or wod] to wood [or wod] I rin."
Browning, E. Romance of the Swan's Nest, The.
Cannon, E. Unsuspected Fact, An.
"Chrystos." Dream Lesbian Lover.
Clare, J. To Mary: 'I Sleep with Thee, and Wake with Thee'.
Corbière. To the Eternal Feminine.
Cummings, E. My sweet old etcetera.
Than(by yon sunset's wintry glow).
Dabydeen, D. Miranda.
Doolittle, H. At Baia.
Dove, R. Adolescence—III.
"Field." And on My Eyes Dark Sleep by Night.
Gouri. Northern Romance.
Holmes, J. Against the Literal.
Holub. Interferon.
Hughes, L. Flatted Fifths.
Jarrell. Seele im Raum.
Kunene. Thought on June 26.
Lifshin. Penthouse Playboy.
Lowell, R. We imitate, oh horror! tops and bowls.
Mallarmé. Another Fan.
Mitchell, A. Celia Celia.
Naden. Love's Mirror.
Nerval. Fancy, A.
Padgett, R. Symbols of Transformation.
Pound, E. Dance Figure.
Prescod. Women Are Different.
Reed, I. Poetry Makes Rhythm in Philosophy.
Rossetti, C. Echo.
In An Artist's Studio.
Rukeyser, M. Along history, forever.
Sarton. Nursery Rhyme.
Shakespeare, W. "Be cheerful, sir."

Shūji. Tanka: "Flowering poppies."
Year's end, The.
Simic. This Morning.
Soyinka. Bearings III: Amber Wall.
Spivack, K. Love U.S.A.
Stevenson, A. Sous-Entendu.
Suckling, J. Upon My Lady Carlisle's [or Carlile's] Walking in Hampton Court Garden.
Tennyson, A. You must wake and call me early, call me early, mother.
Thế Lữ. Opium.
Ullman. Peace.
Unknown. Pitman's Lovesong, A.
She Lay All Naked in Her Bed.
Walker, A. She said: "When I was with him."
Wilbur. Baroque Wall-Fountain in the Villa Sciarra, A.
Williams, W. Good Night.
Wong, N. On Thinking of Photographing My Fantasies.

Farewell
Alexander, E. Farewell to You.
Beaver. Folk Song: "O I'm off to Hullaboola where the climate's never cooler."
Borowski. Farewell to Maria.
Burgess, F. Leave-Taking.
Catullus. On the Burial of His Brother.
Clare, J. Farewell to the bushy clump close to the river.
Cushing, J. Every Time We Say Goodbye.
Donne. Expiration, The.
Fever, A.
Dryden, J. Love's Despair.
To the Memory of Mr Oldham.
"Dylan." Boots of Spanish Leather.
Elizabeth I. On Monsieur's Departure.
Ennius, Quintus. O father, frendes, my countrey eke, and Priams house farewell.
"Ephelia." First Farewell to J.G G.
Etter. Riding the Rock Island Through Kansas.
Ezekiel. Goodbye Party for Miss Pushpa T. S.
Gay, J. Sweet William's Farewell to Black-Eyed [or Black-Ey'd] Susan.
Hemans. Parting Song, A.
Herrick. His Tears to Thamesis [or Thamasis].
To Dianeme ("Dear[e], though to part it be a hell").
To His Peculiar Friend Master Thomas Shapcott, Lawyer.
Hesketh. Love's Advocate.
Hogg, J. When Maggy Gangs Away.
Holmes, J. Good Night! Good Night!
Housman, A. Now hollow fires burn out to black.
Hsüeh T'ao. Farewell to a Friend.
Jewsbury. Farewell to the Muse, A.
Kemble. Farewell to Italy.
To Mrs. Norton.
Kipling, R. King, The.
Knight, E. Cell Song.
Kochetkov. Ballad About a Smoke-Filled Railway Carriage.
Landon. Farewell!
Song.
Lanyer. Description of Cookham, The.
Li Po. Seeing Meng Hao-jan Off to Kuang-ling.
To Secretary Lu Ch'ien of Jen City.
Li Yü. Tune: "Crows Crying at Nighit."
Tune: "Joy at Meeting."
Lin Hung. Saying Farewell to Magistrate Ch'en Ta-yu.
"Lu Hsün." Sending Off O.E. Who Brought an Orchid Home to Japan.
Na-lan Hsing-te. Tune: "Partridge Sky"—Parting Sorrows.
Naden. Sister of Mercy, The.
Nashe. Litany in Time of Plague, A.
Osgood, F. He bade me "Be Happy," he whisper'd "Forget me;."
Ovid. Dido's farewell.
Paschen. Litany.
Patmore, C. Farewell, A.
Pien Kung. Song of the Transport Workers—Seeing Off Fang Wen-yü on His Way to His Post as Inspector of Transportation.
Po Chü-i. Good-bye to the People of

Hangchow.
Grass on Ancient Plain, a Song of Farewell.
Pope, A. Farewell to London in the Year 1715, A.
Praed. Goodnight to the Season!
Procter, A. Woman's Last Word, A.
Ralegh, W. Farewell to False Love, A.
Farewell to the Court.
Poem Put into My Lady Laiton's Pocket, A.
Rubtsov. Farewell Song.
Shen Yüeh. I Say Goodby to Fan An-ch'eng.
Sidney, P. Splendidis longum valedico nugis.
Sophocles. Listen first, and show what you're made of.
Stevens, W. Farewell to Florida.
Waving Adieu, Adieu, Adieu.
Strand. It is true, as someone has said, that in.
Suckling, J. Farewell to Love.
Swenson, M. Goodbye, Goldeneye.
Tu Fu. Farewell of an Old Man.
Farewell Once More to My Friend Yen at Feng Chi Station.
Tu Mu. Passion too deep seems like none.
Voznesensky. Autumn in Sigulda.
Saga.
Vvedensky. Where he was standing leaning against a statue. With a face charged with.
Walcott. In idle August, while the sea soft.
Walker, A. Good Night, Willie Lee, I'll See You in the Morning.
Wang Wei. Seeing Someone Off.
Wen Cheng-ming. All of you are seeing me off, east of the Emperor's city.
Beneath the Shrine of the Three Loyal Ones.
Floating clouds and worldly affairs.
Wheatley, P. Farewell to America. To Mrs. S. W, A.
Wordsworth, W. Farewell thou little Nook of mountain-ground.
Wyatt, T. Renouncing of Love, A.
Yang Shen. To the Tune "Child at Play."
Yau. Edificio Sayonara.
Yesenin. Goodbye, my friend, goodbye.
Yün Shou-p'ing. War ships, cold tides.

Fargo, North Dakota
Wright, J. Outside Fargo, North Dakota.

Farming and Farmers
Ackland. Lonely Woman, The.
Adams, L. Country Summer.
Agathias. Astrologer, The.
Alexander, M. Iowa Farmer.
Ammons. Hardweed Path Going.
Silver.
Apollonides. Lacking rich acres, thick grape-crops.
Baillie, J. Hay making.
Beaver. Silo Treading.
Benjamin, R. Farmer's Soliloquy, The.
Berry, W. September 2.
Bishop, E. Prodigal, The.
Blind. Reapers.
Sower, The.
Bly, R. Snowfall in the Afternoon.
Bontemps. Black Man Talks of Reaping, A.
Brown, G. Taxman.
Brown, S. After Winter.
Foreclosure.
Bùi Du'o'ng Lịch. To a Watering Scoop.
Bunting. Complaint of the Morpethshire Farmer, The.
Gin the Goodwife Stint.
Calverley. Ballad: "Auld wife sat at her ivied door, The."
Campion, T. Jack and Joan they think no ill.
Carlyle, T. Sower's Song, The.
Carruth, H. Emergency Haying.
Cheng Hsieh. Tune: "Full River Red"—A Four-season Song on the Hardships and Joys of Farming Life.
West wind has come again to the "tower of makeup," The.
Ch'u Kuang-hsi. Farm Routine.
Farmer's Thoughts, A.
Chu Yün-ming. Late Spring—Traveling through the Mountains.
Clampitt. Beethoven, Opus 111.

Farmworkers

Clare, J. Farmyard, The.
Wheat Ripening, The.
Cockrell. Field Work.
Colum, P. Drover, A.
Conn. On Craigie Hill.
Todd.
Creeley. Counterpoint, A.
Cummings, E. Nobody loses all the time.
Di Piero. Ice Plant in Bloom.
Diodorus Zonas. For Demeter winnowing, for the Hours who haunt the furrows.
Dorn, E. On the Debt My Mother Owed to Sears Roebuck.
Dove, R. Small Town.
Eiseley. Deserted Homestead, The.
Elliott, H. For Farmers.
Emerson, R. Musketaquid.
Ennis. Coyne's.
Evans, D. Retired Farmer.
Fallon, P. Meadow, The.
Fan Ch'eng-ta. Consoling the Yü Farmers.
Rejoicing the Spirits.
Finch, A. For Grizzel McNaught (1709–1792).
Frost, R. Code, The.
Death of the Hired Man, The.
Girl's Garden, A.
Impulse, The.
Mowing.
Pasture, The.
Putting in the Seed.
Range-finding.
Strong Are Saying Nothing, The.
Galvin, J. Western Civilization.
Garland, H. Plowing: A Memory.
Gibbon, M. French Peasants.
Gilbert, C. Glimpses.
Glassco. Entailed Farm, The.
Gonzalez, A. Gasparillo Remembered.
Goulbourne. One Acre.
Grossman, A. Great Work Farm Elegy.
Guthrie, W. Turkey in the Corn.
Hall, D. Farm, The.
Henyard Round, The.
Ox Cart Man.
Hardy, T. Calf, The.
Hartnett. Retreat of Ita Cagney, The.
Small Farm, A.
Heaney, S. At a Potato Digging.
Follower.
Harvest Bow, The.
Wife's Tale, The.
Herrick. His Grange, or Private Wealth.
Hiebert. Farmer and the Farmer's Wife, The.
Holmes, O. Ploughman, The.
Howes, B. Death of a Vermont Farm Woman.
Hugo, R. Brief History.
Jackson, H. Poppies on the Wheat.
James, D. Harvest.
Jarrell. Field and Forest.
Jones, E. Song of the Banana Man, The.
Kao Ch'i. Along the River, Seeing the Home of Absconded Farmers.
Kavanagh, P. I May Reap.
Ploughman.
Spraying the Potatoes.
Kinnell. Farm Picture.
Komunyakaa. Banking Potatoes.
Kooser. Abandoned Farmhouse.
Lanier, S. Waving of the Corn, The.
Lawrence, D. Love On the Farm.
Lehmann, G. Saving the Harvest.
Li Shen. Pitying the Farmer.
Liu Tsung-yüan. Beyond the bamboo fence, cooking fire and smoke.
By an ancient road, abundant thistle plants.
Longfellow, H. From Evangeline.
Tale of Acadie, A.
Lu Yu. Snug—the robe sewn from coarse cotton.
MacCaig. Summer Farm.
"MacDiarmid." Farmer's Death.
MacLeish. Eleven.
Marcinkeviius. Father's Winter.
Markham, E. Man with the Hoe, The.
McAlmon. Frost in the Corn, The.
Meredith, G. Phoebus with Admetus.
Messerli. Harrowing.

Mew. Farmer's Bride, The.
Miles, J. When Sanders brings feed to his chickens, some sparrows.
Millay, E. From a Train Window.
Mitsui. Picture of a Japanese Farmer, Woodland, California, May 20, 1942.
Miyazawa Kenji. Tanka: "Silver greeting."
Montoya. Just the other day.
Muir, E. Difficult Land, The.
Muldoon, P. Why Brownlee left, and where he went.
Nguyễn Thiên Túng. Well, The.
Nystrom. Prairie Wind.
Ou-yang Hsiu. Reading the Poems of an Absent Friend.
Peirce. Farmers.
Phạm Quý Thích. Summer Drought.
Phan Văn Trị. Grains of Rice.
Philip of Thessalonica. Sosicles the farmer dedicated these sheaves.
Phổ Đú'c. Buffalo Boy On a Field of Corpses, The.
P'i Jih-hsiu. Song of a Farmer.
Po Chü-i. Watching the Wheat-Reapers.
Ramkissoon-Chen. Father.
Reed, I. White Hope.
Reznikoff. I.
Riley, J. Raggedy Man, The.
Rilke. Sonnets to Orpheus I, 12, The.
Roberts, S. Mowing, The.
Sarton. Prothalamion for an Autumn Wedding.
Senior. Hill Country.
Sexton. Farmer's Wife, The.
Sholl. Farmwife.
Simmons, J. Rogation Day: Portrush.
Skeeter. Midwest, Midcentury.
Snyder, G. Hay for the Horses.
Soto. Field Poem.
Hoeing.
Spender, S. Marginal Field, The.
Stafford, W. Lost in the Centuries.
Steele. Country Greeting.
Su Tung-p'o. Lament of the Farm Wife of Wu.
Sylvester, J. Aestas.
T'ao Ch'ien. Returning to My Home in the Country ("Out here in the fields, few social affairs").
Taylor, H. Somewhere along the Way.
Tennyson, A. Northern Farmer: New Style.
Northern Farmer: Old Style.
Thomas, E. As the team's head-brass flashed out on the turn.
Haymaking.
Thomas, R. Hill Farmer Speaks, The.
Lonely Farmer, The.
Peasant, A.
Tomlinson, C. Oxen: Ploughing at Fiesole.
Toomer. Reapers.
Touré, A. Floodtide.
Trakl. Rats, The.
Trowbridge, J. Idyl of Harvest Time, An.
Trypanis. Cock at Sea.
Turberville. Poor Ploughman to a Gentleman for Whom He Had Taken a Little Pains, A.
Unknown. Boll Weevil Song.
Dear cattle, take old Amyntichus to your heart.
Farmer's Boy, A.
God Speed the Plough!
Ground Thumping Song.
Magpie screams loudly and up his tail goes, The.
Plow, Maro, the plains.
There was a young farmer of Leeds.
This is the way the farmers ride.
We are a people who love to sing.
Voigt. Farmer, The.
Wallace, R. Makings of Happiness, The.
Wang Chiu-ssu. Thunder in the southern mountains, the third month of the year.
Today I am a farmer in the fields.
Warner, S. Rival, The.
Wen T'ing-yün. Song of Wildfire, A.
Whitman, W. Farm Picture, A.
Wither. Planting.
Wordsworth, W. Farmer of Tilsbury Vale,

The.
Solitary Reaper, The.
Wright, J. Milkweed.
Yang Shih-ch'i. Following the Rhymes of Shao-pao Huang's Poem on Being Moved While Visiting the Farmers.
Young, D. Sainless.

Farmworkers
Barnes, J. Dog Days 1978.
Castillo, A. Napa, California.
Dunn, D. Washing the Coins.
Simic. Summer Morning.

Farragut, David Glasgow
Meredith, W. Farragut, Farragut / Old Heart of Oak.

Fascism and Fascists
Hill, G. Christmas Trees.
Penrose, R. Road is Wider Than Long: An Image Diary from the Balkans, July–August 1938, The.
Reed, I. Why I Often Allude to Osiris.

Fashion
Barlow, G. Place Where He Arose, The.
Cawthorn. Englishman at the Table, The.
Clare, J. In poesy's spells some all their raptures find.
Dacey, P. Looking at Models in the Sears Catalogue.
Dickinson, E. Morns are meeker than they were, The.
Hsü Chün-ch'ien. Beginning of Spring—A Stroll with My Wife.
Jonson, B. On English Monsieur.
Kelly, R. Rainmakers, The.
Morrison, M. What the Choir Sang about the New Bonnet.
Nemerov. History of a Literary Movement.
Newcastle, M. Woman drest by Age, A.
Robinson, M. Modern Female Fashions.
Modern Male Fashions.
Rossetti, C. If a pig wore a wig.
Twiss, H. Fashion.
Unknown. As long as I was living in the village.
Whitehead, W. Venus Attiring the Graces.
Williams, S. Monkey, lap-dog, parrot, and her Grace, The.
Yamanaka. Yarn Wig.
See also **Clothing**

Fate
Adams, F. Those Two Boys.
Aeschylus. For me, the tears that welled.
Alver. Iron Nerves.
Arnold, S. Destiny.
Ashbery. Brute Image.
Atwood. It's the story that counts.
Auden. Long time since it seems today, A.
Barker, J. Necessity of Fate, The.
Beadle. Lines to Caste.
Beckett, S. My way is in the sand flowing.
Berberova. I remain with what was not fully said.
Berrigan, T. Red Shift.
Bevington, L. 'Egoisme à Deux'.
Measurements.
Bibb. Destiny.
Blaga. Heraclitus by the Lake.
Blaser. Finder, The.
Boethius. None from thy laws are free.
Bogan, L. Cartography.
Didactic Piece.
Bradstreet, A. Here Follows Some Verses upon the Burning of Our House [July 10th, 1966. Copied Out of a Loose Paper].
Braithwaite. House of Falling Leaves, The.
Brodsky, J. Roman Elegies IV.
Brown, S. Schadenfreude.
Brown, W. Song For a Tourist.
Browning, E. Sonnet: "Let the world's sharpness, like a clasping knife."
Sonnet: "My future will not copy fair my past."
Sonnet: "Unlike are we, unlike, O princely Heart!"
Burns, R. Tam Glen.
To a Mountain Daisy [On Turning One Down, with the Plough, in April—1786].

Burroughs, J. Waiting.
Cacamatzin. My friends.
Caraion. Archaic Hippocamp.
Carew, T. For a Picture Where a Queen Laments over the Tomb of a Slain Knight.
To Celia, upon Love's Ubiquity.
Carruth, H. Lost.
Carter, M. After One Year.
Castellanos. Nazareth.
Cavafy. Nero's Deadline.
Char. Unbending Prayer.
Chaucer. Monk's Tale, The.
Ch'en Tzu-ang. Business men boast of their skill and cunning.
Chia Yi. Rhyme-Prose on the Owl.
Ch'ien T'ao. In the quiet of the morning I heard a knock at my door;.
Cisneros, S. His Story.
Clifton, L. Kali.
Cooke, R. Arachne.
Cowper, W. Boadicea: An Ode.
Crashaw. Against Hope.
Creeley. Kore.
Oh No.
Son: "What I took in my hand."
Window, The.
Daniel, Y. Sentence, The.
Dickinson, E. Belshazzar had a Letter.
Ended, ere it begun.
He fumbles at your Soul.
It dropped so low—in my Regard.
Dryden, J. Happy the man, and happy he alone.
Dunbar, P. Robert Gould Shaw.
Duncan, R. Poem Beginning with a Line by Pindar, A.
Rites of Participation.
Eberhart, R. Flux.
Elizabeth I. Written on a Wall at Woodstock.
Emerson, R. Day's Ration, The.
Fate.
Fate ("Her planted eye to-day controls").
Guy.
Nemesis.
"Ephelia." To One That Asked Me Why I Loved J.G G.
Fainlight, R. Future is timid and wayward, The.
Ferry. Cythera.
Embarkation for Cythera, The.
Fischerova. Who Knows Something About Women?
Fitzgerald, E. I sent my Soul through the Invisible.
Life's Chequer-Board.
74.
73.
Forbes, C. Hand Me Down Blues.
Frost, R. Design.
Draft Horse, The.
Gift Outright, The.
Fulton, A. A.M.: The Hopeful Monster.
Gizzi. Another Day on the Pilgrimage.
Glück, L. Mount Ararat.
Goethe. To Charlotte von Stein.
González, A. Future, The.
Gouri. Thorns.
Graves, R. Mirror mirror tell me.
Gurney, I. Ballad of the Three Spectres.
Generations.
Hardy, T. Hap.
Harmon. Invoice No. 13, A Masque of Resignation.
Harteis. Genetics.
Hecht, A. Jason.
Henley, W. Invictus.
Herbert, G. H. Scriptures, The ("Oh that I knew how all thy lights combine").
Herrick. Man's Dying-Place Uncertain.
Parcæ, The; or, Three Dainty Destinies: The Armilet.
Hood, T. Miss Kilmansegg's Birth.
Poet's Fate, The.
Hope, A. Beyond Phigalia.
Fafnir.
Horace. Hence, ye Profane; I hate ye all.
Housman, A. Along the field as we came by.

Hsieh Chin. To the Fortuneteller Hsüeh T'ieh-yai.
Hughes, L. Bad Luck Card.
Hwang, K. Candlelight.
Ishikawa Takuboku. Tanka: "Has Fate sneaked in."
Ivask, Y. Ode for the Dancing Khlysty.
Jackson, H. Crossed Threads.
Jackson, L. Lullaby, The.
Juana Inés de la Cruz. Green Enravishment of Human Life.
Kastelan. As if it resembled your hair.
Keats. Endymion.
Kenyon, J. Otherwise.
Khlebnikov, V. Once again, once again.
Zangezi: R, K, L, G—.
King, H. Sonnet: "Tell me[e] no more how fair[e] she[e] is."
Kipling, R. Gertrude's Prayer.
Laforgue. Solo by Moonlight.
Landon. Stern Truth.
Lipkin, S. When I was arranging letters into words.
Lovelace, R. Advice to My Best Brother, Colonel Francis Lovelace.
Mahon. Girls on the Bridge.
Mandel, T. Shade, The.
Marvell. Definition Of Love, The.
McAuley, J. Blue Horses, The.
McGirt. Tell me, oh fate, is it decreed.
Melville, H. Camoëns.
Haglets, The.
Immolated.
Mew. Call, The.
Mihalic. Atlantis.
Millay, E. Buck in the Snow, The.
Montale. Fan, The.
Moritz. In that town I was twenty. Snow there lay.
Narihira. I have always known / That at last I would.
Nguyễn Bỉnh Khiêm. Men jostle and men fight with labored breath.
Nobuyuki. And Then.
Pasternak, B. Mary Magdalene (I).
Peacock, M. Wheel, The.
Perreault, J. Boomerang.
Pindar. How *early* has young *Chromius* begun.
Poseidippus. World's a bubble, and the life of man, The.
Procter, A. Woman's Question, A.
Raine, K. Lachesis.
"Rayevsky." You think: won't fate tap.
Robinson, E. Eros Turannos.
Karma.
Roethke. Waking, The.
Sappho. When Death shall close those Eyes, imperious Dame!
Seeger, A. Rendezvous, The.
Seneca. Fate is the master of everything it is vain to fight against fate.
Shakespeare, W. This is the excellent foppery of the world.
Shapiro, K. Auto Wreck.
Shirley, J. Love's Hue and Cry.
"Shu Ting." Assembly Line.
Perhaps these thoughts of ours.
Smith, S. Sigh no more ladies nor gentlemen at all.
Smith, S. Omens.
Sophocles. Chorus sing of the laws of the gods, The.
Chorus: "What man is he that yearneth."
Sparrow, J. Apology and Explanation.
Stefanovich. For all of us destiny is undivided.
Stevens, W. Flyer's Fall.
Stevenson, R. Ticonderoga: A Legend of the West Highlands.
Swirszczynska. Thank You, My Fate.
Tarkovsky. First Meetings.
Theognis. Our Course.
Thrale. Winter in Wales, A.
Todros ben Judah Abulafia. From Prison.
Tomlinson, C. Ararat.
Trowbridge, J. Circumstance.
Tsvetayeva. Single post, a point of rusting, A.
U Tam'si Tchicaya. Viaticum.

Unknown. Alone up here on the mountain.
Burial Songs.
I often pause and wonder.
Mirror, mirror, tell me.
Omens.
Orphan, The.
Vaughan, H. To Amoret, Walking in a Starry Evening.
Virgil. Aeneas' story.
Dido in the Elysian Fields.
Walker, T. Doomed Spaceman, The.
Ward, D. Crossing.
Warren, R. Caribou.
Whateley. Power of Destiny, The.
Wilbur. Marginalia.
Wilcox, E. Way of It, The.
Winds of Fate, The.
Wroth. Sonnet 31: "After long trouble in a taedious way."
Yeats. Leda and the Swan.
Yun. Prologue, The.
Zhdanov. I'm not the branch, only the prebranchness.
Ziedonis. Inevitability.

See also **Fortune; Chance**

Fathers

Alexander, E. Who I Think You Are.
Amichai. I Am a Live Man.
My Father.
Aristophanes. Son learns how to beat his father, The.
Armitage, S. Poem.
Ashbery. Boy, A.
Atwood. Flowers.
Avidan. Two Memorial Poems.
Balaban. Words for My Daughter.
Barrax. Efficiency Apartment.
Visit.
Barry, J. Lessons.
Berg, S. Answer, The.
Berry, J. Girls Can We Educate We Dads?
My Father.
Berryman. Also I love him: me he's done no wrong.
Dream Song 384.
Scholars at the Orchid Pavilion.
To My Father.
Bible, O.T. Honour thy father and thy mother.
Black, S. To Her Father.
Blake, W. Little Boy Lost, The ("Father, father, where are you going?")
Little Boy Lost, A ("Nought loves another as itself").
Bly, R. Busy Man Speaks, A.
My Father's Wedding.
Boldman. Touching the ashes of my father.
Boss. At the Nuclear Rally.
Bottoms. Desk, The.
Boyd, E. On the Death of an Infant of Five Days Old.
Boyd, M. Sunflowers and Saturdays.
Bradstreet, A. To Her Father, with Some Verses.
To the Memory of My Dear and Ever Honored Father Thomas Dudley Esq. Who Deceased July 31, 1653, and of His Age 77.
Brinnin. My Father, My Son.
Brock-Broido. Moving on in the Dark Like Loaded Boats at Night, Though There is No Course, There is Boundlessness.
Bruck. Equality, father! Your dream has come true.
Bukowski. My Old Man.
Burns, M. Beginnings.
Campbell, A. Shabby Old Dad.
Campbell, D. I Starting from Central Station.
Carruth, H. Words for My Daughter from the Asylum.
Chambers, J. Why Are Daddies So Mean?
Chitre. My father travels on the late evening train.
"Chrystos." Portrait of Assimilation.
Clemmons. Love from My Father.
Clifton, L. Sam.
Cokinos. Short-Wave.
Coleman, H. Poem for a "Divorced" Daughter.
Coleman, W. Cousin Mary.

Coleridge, H. Full Well I Know.
Written on the Anniversary of Our Father's
Death.
Coleridge, S. Composed on a Journey
Homeward; the Author Having Received
Intelligence of the Birth of a Son.
Coleridge, S. Father! no amaranths e'er shall
wreathe my brow.
Conn. To My Father.
Cook-Lynn. Grandfather at the Indian Health
Clinic.
Creeley. Fathers.
Croft, S. Blue.
Cummings, E. My father moved through
dooms of love.
Daniels, K. My Father's Desk.
Davis, A. From Him.
Davitt. Mirror, The.
Deane, S. Fording the River.
Derricotte. Poem for My Father.
Dhasal. Stone-masons, My Father, and Me.
Dickens. Joe Gargery's Epitaph on His Father.
Dickey, J. Hospital Window, The.
Dodd, W. Of His Life.
Doubiago. Father.
Dove, R. Anti-Father.
Taking in Wash.
Drummond de Andrade. Travelling in the
Family.
Dugan, A. Elegy: "I know but will not tell."
Dumas, H. Zebra Goes Wild Where the
Sidewalk Ends, The.
Dunbar, P. Little brown baby wif spa'klin'
eyes.
Dybek. My Father's Fights.
Eimers. Another Kimono.
Emanuel, L. Of Your Father's Indiscretions
and the Train to California.
Engman. Atlantis.
Ennis. Road to Patmos, The.
Erdrich. Birth.
Espada. Thirty years ago.
Evans, D. Story of Lava, The.
Fanthorpe. Father in the Railway Buffet.
Fleming, R. For All Unwed Mothers.
Fontanella. Father-Sequence.
Fort, C. Worker (We Own Two Houses), The.
Gardner, I. Telephone rang / in my dream
Long Distance from, The.
Gildner. My Father after Work.
Gillan. Arturo.
Gillilan, S. "Are You There?"
Gioseffi. American Sonnets for My Father.
Glück, L. Departure.
First Memory.
Mythic Fragment.
Goethe. Erl-King, The.
Goldberg, B. To a Girl Writing Her Father's
Death.
Gotera. Dance of the Letters.
Graham, J. For My Father Looking for My
Uncle.
Gregg. Not Saying Much.
Grosholz. Legacies.
Life of a Salesman.
Guest, E. Becoming a Dad.
Hagedorn, J. Song for My Father.
Hall, D. White Apples.
Halpern, D. Naming the Unborn.
Handlin. Father, You Learn to Die.
Harris, W. Daddy Poem, A.
Harwood, G. Father and Child.
Hayden, R. Those Winter Sundays.
Heaney, S. Digging.
Follower.
Hemphill. XXII.
Herbert, Z. Remembering My Father.
Herrick. To the Reverend Shade of His
Religious Father.
Hewitt, J. Father's Death, A.
Higgins, F. Father and Son.
Hirsch, E. My Father's Back.
Hoagland, T. Poem for Men Only.
Sweet Rain.
Hoffenstein. Now, alas, it is too late.
Hollo. Le Jazz Hot.
Holmes, J. Metaphor for My Son.

Hongo. Hilo: First Night Back.
O-Bon: Dance for the Dead.
Howe, M. How Many Times.
Huddle. My Daddy, Whenever He Went Some
Place.
Hudgins. Elegy for My Father, Who Is Not
Dead.
Saints and Strangers.
Hugo, V. Jeanne was on bread and water in a
dark room.
Hull, L. Shore Leave.
Humphreys, E. From Father to Son.
Hunt, S. My Father Scything.
My Father Today.
Ignatow, D. Europe and America.
Jentzsch. Dead Father, The.
Johnson, D. Home Game.
Johnson, L. Reggae fi Dada.
Johnstone, R. He's a high clear forehead.
Jones, R. Certain People.
Jonson, B. On My First Son [or Sonne].
Jordan, J. Clock on Hancock Street.
Daddy at the stove or sink. Large.
Judah ibn Tibbon. Father's Testament, A.
Justice, D. Men at forty / Learn to close
softly.
Kaffka. Father.
Kasdorf. Vesta's Father.
Kavanagh, P. Memory of my Father.
My father played the melodion.
Kenny, M. Molly.
Kessler, M. Secret Love.
Kgositsile. To My Daughter.
Kinnell. When I come back to my father's
house,.
Kinsella, T. His Father's Hands.
Klein, A. Heirloom.
Komunyakaa. Banking Potatoes.
My Father's Love Letters [or Loveletters].
Kopland. Johnson Brothers Ltd.
Kovner. Poem: Alte Zachen.
Kumin, M. My Father's Neckties.
Kunitz, S. Catch, The.
Portrait, The.
Kunze, R. Reply.
Kurup. Master Carpenter, The.
Kuznetsov. To Father.
Kyger. My Father Died This Spring.
Lamkin. Golden Season.
Lau, A. On the Fifth Anniversary of My
Father's Death.
Lee, L. Gift, The.
Here I Am.
Mnemonic.
Story, A.
Weight of Sweetness, The.
Lehman. Difference Between Pepsi and Coke,
The.
Leonard, T. Fathers and Sons.
Lepik. Let Me Hold Your Hand.
Levin, P. Planting Roses.
Levine, P. 1933.
Lim, S. Black and White.
Father from Asia.
Lipkin, J. Father.
Liu. My Father's Martial Art.
Livingston, M. Father.
Logan, J. Letter to a Young Father in Exile.
Lines to His Son on Reaching Adolescence.
Longley, M. In Memoriam.
Wounds.
Lorde. Father Son and Holy Ghost.
Love Poem.
Lowell, R. Commander Lowell.
Home after Three Months Away.
MacBeth. Return, The.
"MacDiarmid." At My Father's Grave.
MacNeice. Truisms, The.
Woods.
Maiden. Air.
Malik de Coteau. Oui Papa.
Manley, F. Dead Letters.
Marcinkeviius. Father's Winter.
Mathews, A. Letter Following.
Maxton. Waking.
Mazur. Family Plot, October.
McAuley, J. Because.

McCarthy, T. Party Shrine.
Sorrow Garden, The.
McCord, D. Father and I in the Woods.
McCuaig. Au Tombeau de Mon Père.
McGrath, T. Offering.
McNair. My Brother Inside the Revolving
Doors.
Meinke. Advice to My Son.
This is a poem to my son Peter.
Melville, P. Homeland.
Merrill, J. Scenes of Childhood.
Merwin, W. Strawberries.
Meynell, A. Father of Women, A [Ad
Sororem E. B.].
Miller, E. Jasmine.
Miller, J. Far Away.
Mitsui. At Bon Odori.
Because of My Father's Job.
Miyazawa Kenji. Tanka: "Red rag."
Montague, J. At Last.
Cage, The.
Last Journey.
Windharp.
Moore, L. Winter 1967.
Moore, M. Silence.
Moss, H. Elegy for My Father.
Moss, T. Lynching, The.
Muldoon, P. Wishbone, The.
Nelson, H. My Father Went to Funerals.
Nemerov. Sacrificed Author, A.
Nesbit, E. Song: "Oh, baby, baby, baby dear."
Ni Dhomhnaill. Labasheedy (The Silken Bed).
Nichols, R. 1.
Nicholson, N. Halley's Comet.
Niedecker. Museum Man! / I wish he'd take
Pa's spitbox!, The.
Nomberg. Russian Cradle Song, A.
Nowlan. Only when my heart freezes.
Noyes, A. Daddy Fell into the Pond.
Nye, N. My Father and the Figtree.
Olds, S. Guild, The.
I Go Back to May 1937.
Last Acts.
Moment of My Father's Death, The.
Race, The.
Saturn.
Victims, The.
Oliver, M. Poem for My Father's Ghost.
Ombres. Morning Hours.
Ondaatje. Letters and Other Worlds.
Ortiz. My Father's Song.
What I Tell Him.
Paley, G. On Mother's Day.
Pankey. As We Forgive Those.
Payne, B. Lines in Memory of My Father.
Peacock, M. Buffalo.
Dream Come True.
Pham Hồ. Hand, The.
Plath. Colossus, The.
Daddy.
Plumly. After Grief.
Out-of-the-Body Travel.
Polito. Animal Mimicry.
Pomeroy, R. Between Here and Illinois.
Prunty. Reading Before We Read, Horoscope
and Weather.
Rabbitt. My Father's Watch.
Ravikovitch. On the Road at Night There
Stands the Man.
Ray, D. In the Third Month.
Ray, H. To My Father.
Reese, L. They say that all little girls adore
their fathers / want to marry.
Rich, A. After Dark.
Rivard. Fall River.
Firestone.
Roberts, E. Father's Story.
Roethke. Elegy for Jane.
My Papa's Waltz.
Rosen, M. This morning my father looks out
of the window, rubs his nose.
Ryan, M. Switchblade.
Ryan, R. Father of Famine.
Sanchez, S. Father and Daughter.
Poem for My Father, A.
Savard. Daughter's Brooch, The.
Schnackenberg. Supernatural Love.

Seidman. Icon.
Seward. Eyam.
Sexton. All My Pretty Ones.
And One for My Dame.
Moss of His Skin, The.
Santa.
Shakespeare, W. Ariel's Song ("Full fathom [or fadom] five thy father lies").
Shange. My father is a retired magician.
Shapiro, G. Tattoo.
Shelton, R. Letter to a Dead Father.
Shomer. Passive Resistance.
Simko. Thinking of My Father on a Bus to Baltimore.
Simmons, J. Reformer to His Father, A.
Simpson, L. My father in the night commanding No.
Working late.
Smith, B. Mercy.
Smith, P. Sweet Daddy.
Smith, S. Correspondence between Mr. Harrison in Newcastle and Mr. Sholto Peach Harrison in Hull.
Smith, W. American Primitive.
Souster. Man Who Finds That His Son Has Become a Thief, The.
Stafford, W. Rescued Year, The.
Stevens, W. Irish Cliffs of Moher, The.
Stewart, P. Singing down the Breadfruit.
Stewart, S. Gypsy, The.
Stone, R. Father's Day.
Storace. King Lear Bewildered.
Strand. "Dreadful Has Already Happened, The."
Stuart, D. Soup Jar, The.
Swirszczynska. I Wash the Shirt.
Tapahonso. Listen.
Tate, J. Lost Pilot, The.
Taylor, E. Few Days in the South in February, A.
Terence. CHREMES. Pese anger not thyself so I thee pray.
Thomas, D. Do not go gentle into that good night.
Tipping. Just after Michael's Death, the Game of Pool.
Travis, N. At My Father's House.
Troupe. Poem for My Father.
Tucker, M. To Father.
Turner, P. Looking for Him.
Ulacia. Stone at the Bottom, The.
Unknown. Edward [or Edward, Edward].
Hush, little baby, don't say a word.
I Sit with My Dolls.
Man's Song, about His Daughter, A.
Our Ship She Lies in Harbour.
Woman's Song, about Men, A.
Urdang. My Father's Death.
Valentine, J. Father, The.
Van Duyn. Letters from a Father.
Van Vliet. Valediction—To My Father.
Vinz. Passages.
Virgilio. After father's wake.
Vittorelli. On a Nun.
Vizenor. Family Photograph.
Vogel, D. I saw my father drowning.
Voigt. Visit, The.
Wakoski. Father of My Country, The.
Placing a $2 Bet for a Man Who Will Never Go to the Horse Races Any More.
Walcott. Letter from Brooklyn, A.
Walker, A. Good Night, Willie Lee, I'll See You in the Morning.
Poem at Thirty-nine.
Wang Chiu-ssu. Ballad of the Fatherless Boy.
Waniek. Daughters, 1900.
Ware, M. Understanding Guyana.
Warren, R. After Night Flight Son Reaches Bedside of Already Unconscious Father, Whose Right Hand Lifts in a Spasmodic Gesture, as Though Trying to Make Contact: 1955.
Watkins, E. Figures of Authority.
Weaver, M. My Father's First Baseball Game.
My Father's Geography.
Webster, E. San Joaquin Valley Poems: 1969.
Wei Wên-Ti. On the Death of his Father.

Weingarten. Father Hunger and Son.
Wheelock, J. Gardener, The.
Whipple, L. My dad works late in a coffee shop.
Whitman, T. Super-Brave.
Whitman, W. Dirge for Two Veterans.
Wishik. Visitation Rights.
Wojahn. Photo of My Father in a Snowbound Train.
Riding the Empire Builder, 1948.
Wong, N. Ironing.
Wordsworth, W. Anecdote for Fathers, Showing how the Art of Lying may be Taught.
Childless Father, The.
Work. Come Home, Father[!].
Wright, E. When Father Carves the Duck.
Wright, J. Evening.
Having Lost My Sons, I Confront the Wreckage of the Moon: Christmas, 1960.
Two Postures beside a Fire.
Yang Shih-ch'i. Enclosed with a Letter to My Family—For Shu.
Yang Wei-chen. Bamboo Branch Song of the Seacoast.
Yeats. Father and Child.
Yi, S. Poem No. II.
Young, K. Field Trip.
Yukitsuna. Tanka: "Since puberty."
Zenmaro. On the birth of my son.

Fatigue. *See* **Weariness**

Faults
Herrick. In the Dark None Dainty.
To the Generous Reader.
Kavanagh, P. Sometimes.
Larkin, P. This Be The Verse.
Shakespeare, W. Sonnet: "Let me confesse that we two must be twaine."
Wakoski. My trouble / is that I have the spirit of Gertrude Stein.

Fauns
Pound, E. Faun, The.

Faust
Ashbery. Faust.
Crane, H. For the Marriage of Faustus and Helen.
Enright, D. Royalties.
Gunn, T. Faustus Triumphant.
Marlowe. Ah, Doctor Faustus, that I might prevail.
Mother Goose. Doctor Faustus was a good man.
Shapiro, K. Progress of Faust, The.

Fawkes, Guy
De la Mare. Please to Remember.
Unknown. Gunpowder Plot, The.

Fear
Ackerman, D. Lines Written in a Pittsburgh Skyscraper.
Al-Khansa. Night, The.
Alabaster. Way feare with thy projectes, noe false fyre, A.
Allur Nanmullai. What He Said ("Heart, knowing, The").
Amis, K. Autobiographical Fragment.
Angelou. Life Doesn't Frighten Me.
Antin. List of the Delusions of the Insane / What They Are Afraid Of, A.
Atkins. Late Bus (After a Series of Hold-Ups).
Auden. Leap Before You Look.
Averill. Bad for You.
Baca. Like an Animal.
Baggett. Day Before They Bombed Nagasaki, The.
Berry, W. Fear of Love, The.
Berryman. Conversation.
I'm scared a lonely. Never see my son.
Blake, W. Little Boy Lost, The ("Father, father, where are you going?")
Bogan, L. Frightened Man, The.
Brett, L. La Pathétique.
Brontë, C. Again I find myself alone, and ever.
Brooks, G. Michael Is Afraid of the Storm.
Brown, D. When I Am 19 I Was a Medic.
Brown, W. Rilke.

Browning, E. Sonnet: "I lift my heavy heart up solemnly."
Browning, R. Prospice.
Burns, R. Cares o' love are sweeter far, The.
To a Mouse[, On Turning Her Up in Her Nest, with the Plough, November, 1785].
Cassian. Other Life, the.
Chao Meng-fu. In the Ancient Manner.
Chappell, F. Cleaning the Well.
Chimombo. Four Ways of Dying.
Clifton, L. Powell (Officer Charged with the beating of Rodney King).
Coleman, H. Night Flare Drop, Tan Son Nhut.
Coleridge, M. Master and Guest.
Collins, W. Ode to Fear.
Cook, E. Surgeon's Knife, The.
Cox, M. Archaic Torso of My Uncle Phil.
Cranch. Ocean, The.
Crapsey. Warning, The.
Cummings, E. Right here the other night something.
Who's most afraid of death?thou.
Daryush. You should at times go out.
Derricotte. Fears of the Eighth Grade.
Dickey, J. Sheep Child, The.
Dickinson, E. I laughed a crumbling laugh.
Narrow Fellow in the Grass, A.
While we were fearing it, it came.
Dimitrova. Introduction to the Beyond.
Djanikian. Agami Beach.
Douglas, K. On a Return from Egypt.
Dove, R. Motherhood.
Nightmare.
Drummond de Andrade. Souvenir of the Ancient World.
Eberhart, R. New England Bachelor, A.
Elizabeth I. Ah silly pugg wert thou so sore afraid.
Doubt of future foes exiles my present joy, The.
Ferlinghetti, L. Frightened / by the sound of my own voice.
Fletcher, J. River[-]God's Song, The.
Foster, E. Hermetic Silence.
Franklin, B. Bits of Wisdom.
Fraser, M. Spring.
Frost, R. Storm Fear.
Fulton, A. A.M.: The Hopeful Monster.
Glück, L. Garden, The.
Gretel in Darkness.
Goedicke. Coin of the Realm.
One More Time.
Goethe. Erl-King, The.
Graves, R. Straw, The.
Gunn, T. Man With Night Sweats, The.
Hacker, M. After the Revolution.
Hajnal. Fear.
Hall, D. Scream, The.
Hardy, T. To an Unborn Pauper Child.
Harjo, J. I Give You Back.
Harms. Tomorrow, We'll Dance in America.
Hayden, R. Soledad.
Hearne, V. Riding a Nervous Horse.
Hecht, A. Hill, A.
Henderson-Holmes. My First Riot: Bronx, NYC.
Herbert, Z. Meditations of Mr. Cogito on Redemption.
Our Fear.
Herrick. On Himselfe ("I fear no earthly powers").
Hewitt, J. Glens, The.
Hristic. In a dark hour (there are more and more of them now).
Hudgins. Hereafter, The.
Hughes, L. Situation.
Sweet Words on Race.
Ishikawa Takuboku. Tanka: "Fearing."
Issaia. Dream.
James, D. Blind Man Who Sells Brushes, The.
Love of Water Faucets, The.
Jarrell. Bird of Night, The.
Johnston, M. Gorey at the Biennale.
Jonson, B. To Fine Lady Would-Be.
Kannan. What Her Girl Friend Said to Him.
Kazantzis. Frightened Flier Goes North, The.
Keats. Terror of Death, The.

Kennelly. Dream of a Black Fox.
Kessler, M. Eli, Eli.
Kharms. Khaldeyev, Naldeyev, and Peppermaldeyev.
Tricks.
Killigrew, A. On Death.
Kitahara Hakushū. Tanka: "Each alighted."
Komunyakaa. After the Fall of Saigon.
Venus's-Flytraps.
Kooser. Child Frightened by a Thunderstorm.
Kovner. On My Words.
To Myself.
Kumin, M. Getting the Message.
Kuzma. Sometimes.
Laing, K. Many Worlds Are Walked Once.
Landor, W. Death Stands above Me[, whispering low].
Larkin, P. Is it for now or for always.
Lawrence, D. Doe at Evening, A.
Song of a Man Who Has Come Through.
Lehman. Fear.
Levertov. Clouds as I see them, rising, The.
Li K'ai-hsien. Colorful frames are erected beside the Yellow River, The.
Lihn. Of all despondencies, death-despair must be the worst.
Lorde. Litany for Survival, A.
Lucilius. Poor Calpurnius, the most Schweikian soldier in the land.
March, A. Day's in dread of losing her bright features, The.
Masaoka Shiki. First of May³, The.
Matevski. Arrive sluggish, arrive weary horses of space.
Mayakovsky. Listen, / if stars are lit.
McGinley. Women of Jericho, The.
McNair. My Brother Inside the Revolving Doors.
Mearns. Antigonish.
Melville, H. To.
Merrill, J. Days of 1941 and '44.
Mew. Farmer's Bride, The.
Milosz, C. Task, A.
Moore, M. Fable.
Myles, E. Sadness of Leaving, The.
Nowlan. Thief, The.
Okamoto. Tanka: "As I gaze upon."
Oliver, M. Lightning.
Ologoudou. Vespers.
Owen, W. Next War, The.
Paddock. Alien.
Patterson, R. From Riot Rimes U.S.A. #79.
Peacock, T. Fear.
Piercy. Rape Poem.
Pilinszky. Celebration of Nadir.
Pinsky. Woman, A.
Po Chü-i. Alarm at First Entering the Yangtze Gorges.
Pollard, V. Su Su.
Ponge. Frog, The.
Popa. Victims of the Little Box, The.
Pope, A. Shut, shut the door, good *John!* fatigu'd, I said.
Pratt, M. Waulking Song: Two.
Radnóti. Angel of Dread, The.
Ralegh, W. On the Snuff of a Candle.
Ramanujan. Snakes.
Ratushinskaya. No, I'm not afraid: after a year.
Receveur. Doper's Dream.
Night Fear.
Reed, H. Château, The.
Reeves, J. Others.
Rilke. First Duino Elegy, The.
Robinson, E. Eros Turannos.
Poem for Max Nordau, A.
Rosenberg, L. Poem of my Heart, The.
Rossetti, C. Pussy cat, Pussy cat.
Rumble. Close Encounter, A.
Rumi. Keep walking, though there's no place to get to.
Sappho. There's a man, I really believe, compares with.
Savard. Carnival Figure of Guatemalan Clay, A.
Seaton, M. Fear of Subways.
Senghor. I walked you to the village where

the granaries are at the threshold of Night.
Visit.
Shakespeare, W. Sonnet 23.
Sonnet 64.
Shange. Where the Heart Is.
Shelley, P. I fear thy kisses, gentle maiden.
Shorter. Mother, The.
Shūji. Tanka: "Stalks growing."
Sidney, P. Why Fear to Die?
Silverstein, S. Whatif.
Simic. Empire of Dreams.
Fear passes from man to man.
Old Couple.
Simmons, J. Fear Test: Integrity of Heroes.
Smith, C. Captive Escaped in the Wilds of America. Addressed to the Hon. Mrs. O'Neill, on.
Smith, T. Two Poems on the Fear of Love.
Sophocles. Think on thy father in the vale of years.
Spicer, J. Cantata.
Stanley, T. Expectation.
Steele, T. Eros.
Stephens, J. In Waste Places.
Stern, G. Peddler's Village.
Stevenson, R. In autumn when the woods are red.
Sick Child, The.
Stone, R. That Winter.
Stumbrs. Light, Late Song for Solo Voice Without Piano, A.
Surrey. Love, that doth reign and live within my thought.
Swenson, M. Hair, The.
Swinburne. Lake of Gaube, The.
Tekkan. Tanka: "Unlike their father."
Tù Diễn Dồn. Long Night, The.
Unknown. Boy in the Barn, The.
Christian's Prayer, The.
Fears and Tears.
Firm Belief.
Timor Mortis.
Walcott. God Rest Ye Merry, Gentlemen.
Wang Fan-chih. I saw another man die.
Waniek. April Rape.
Warr, M. Brain on Ice.
Warren, R. Notes on a Life to Be Lived.
Wat. To be a mouse. Preferably a field mouse. Or a garden mouse—.
Weigl. Mines.
Shelter.
Whitman, R. Listening to Grownups Quarreling.
Whittier. Song of Slaves in the Desert.
Winchilsea. To Death.
Wordsworth, W. Slumber *did* my spirit *seal,* A.
Wright, F. Entry in an Unknown Hand.
Wright, J. Lights in the hallway, The.
Wright, J. Brother and Sisters.
Woman to Man.
Wyatt, T. It may be good like it who list.
Sonnet: 'The long love'.
Ya'oz-kest. Smoke Rose.
Yeats. Who Goes with Fergus?
Yevtushenko. Sleep, My Beloved.
When your face dawned.
Zimmer. Queen, The.

Feasts and Feasting
Aristophanes. Peace: A Wedding Song, The.
Aytoun, W. *et al.* Royal Banquet, The.
Carew, T. Upon a Mole in Celia's Bosom.
Coleridge, M. Unwelcome.
Fisher, A. Thanksgiving Dinner.
Herrick. Invitation, The.
Holtby, W. Trains in France.
Keats. Then by the bed-side, where the faded moon.
MacGowran. Description of an Irish Feast, The.
MacNeice. This Is the Life.
Mo Shih-lung. On a Cold Day I Climbed Tiger Hill With Professor Ho. At the Time, the Local Prefect Had Prohibited Pleasure Excursions and Feasts, But the Mountain Was Quiet and Tranquil, So We Stayed All Day.

Nash, O. Private Dining Room, The.
Novikov. On my right hand I'll seat one of my loves.
Po Chü-i. Light Furs, Fat Horses.
Robinson, A. Celia's Home-Coming.
"Sagittarius." Passionate Profiteer to His Love, The.
Tu Fu. Banquet at the Tso Family Manor.
Song of the Beautiful Ladies.
Winter Dawn.
Unknown. Of this day's glorious feast and revel.
Wilbur. Wedding Toast, A.

February
Akhmadulina. Blizzard.
Bodecker. When Skies are Low and Days are Dark.
Given. Song for February, A.
Gregg. To Be Here.
Heath-Stubbs. February.
Kenyon, J. February: Thinking of Flowers.
Kinsella, T. Mirror in February.
Longfellow, H. Afternoon in February.
Pasternak, B. February. Get your ink and weep.
Ray, H. February.
Ríos, A. What a Boy Can Do.
Schuyler, J. February.
Shapiro, D. Taking a Look.
Summers, H. Mild February.
Teasdale. February Twilight.
Tóth, J. February. Germination's moment.
Unknown. In the month of February.

Federal Bureau of Investigation
Di Prima. Fragmented Address to the FBI.
Durem. Award.

Feebleness
Herrick. Crutches.

Feet
Herrick. To Dianeme ("Show [*or* Shew] me thy feet; show [*or* shew] me thy legs, thy thighs").
Upon Her Feet.
Hughes, L. Feet O' Jesus.
Jacobsen, J. Limbo Dancer, The.
Jones, A. Foot, The.
Kassiane. Troparion.
Lyon, G. Foot-Washing, The.
Major, C. Large Room with Wood Floor.
McKay, L. Night.
Neruda. Ode to My Socks.
To the Foot from Its Child.
Walking [*or* Walkin'] Around.
Patmore, C. To the Body.
Pettet. Mevlana.
Plumly. My Mother's Feet.
Probyn. After.
Before.
Rilke. Pietà.
Sandburg, C. Fog comes / on little cat feet, The.
Sutskever. Cartload of Shoes, A.
Swinburne. Baby's feet, like sea-shells pink, A.
Symons, A. Javanese Dancers.
Thompson, I. Feet.
Tsvetayeva. Magdalene.
Wickham. Song of the Lonely Shepherd.
Williams, W. Overture to a Dance of Locomotives.
Poem: "As the cat / climbed over."
Yevtushenko. Siberian Wooing.
See also **Toes**

Fellowship. See Brotherhood

Feminism and Feminists
"Alta." Yesterday i had a wild thot. hearing james brown on the radio singing *say it.*
Aristophanes. Home front, The.
Repeat after me.
Armstrong, F. Women of My Land.
"Astra." Daughters.
Barbauld. Rights of Woman, The.
Chaucer. Wife of Bath's Prologue, The.
Wife of Bath's Tale, The.
Ch'iu Chin. To the Tune "The River Is Red."
Chudleigh. To the Ladies.

Daiches. To Kate, Skating Better than Her Date.
Egerton, S. Emulation, The.
Fell, A. Significant Fevers.
Gallagher, T. Conversation with a Fireman from Brooklyn.
Hacker, M. Ballad of Ladies Lost and Found.
Hamilton, C. March of the Women, The.
Hugo, R. To Women.
Jong. Seventeen Warnings in Search of a Feminist Poem.
Kizer, C. One.
Three.
Two.
Lawrence, D. It's no good, the women are in eruption.
Levertov. Hypocrite women, how seldom we speak.
Lewis, L. Bridget.
Macaulay, F. Women's Marseillaise, The.
Markman. They lived out in a women's house.
Meehan, M. Is There Life after Feminism.
Millay, E. To Inez Milholland.
Mirikitani. Breaking Tradition.
Morgan-Browne. Purple, White and Green, The.
Morgan, R. Damn you, lady, get out of my blood for good.
Oliver, M. Strawberry Moon.
"O'Neill." Her Sister.
Osgood, F. Woman.
Ostriker. Propaganda Poem: Maybe for Some Young Mamas.
Parker, P. For Willyce.
My lady ain't no lady.
There Is a Woman in This Town.
Polwhele. Thou, who with all the poet's genuine rage.
Reeve, C. Sacred Heliconian spring, The.
Rich, A. Final Notations.
Ninth Symphony of Beethoven Understood at Last as a Sexual Message, The.
Snapshots of a Daughter-in-Law.
Translations.
Riley, D. Affections Must Not.
Rodgers, C. Feminism.
Rukeyser, M. Myth.
Sanchez, S. Poem for my Most Intelligent 10:30 AM Class/Fall 1985, A.
Scott, M. Women of the Future.
Selman, R. They called the next panel, "New Lesbians."
Thousands of cheers filled the chalky air.
We lay in an attic under beamed eaves.
Stone, R. Liberation.
Tompson. On a Fortification at Boston Begun by Women.
Truth. Ain't I a Woman?
Tsui. It's in the Name.
Unknown. Cloe to Artimesa.
Villanueva, A. Witches' Blood.
Ward, N. Mercury shew'd Apollo, Bartas Book.
Ware, E. He and She.

Fences
Blue Cloud. Old Man's Lazy, The.
Dickey, J. Fence Wire.
Dudley, M. At the backyard fence.
Eberhart, R. Spite Fence.
Frost, R. Mending Wall.
McCord, D. Pickety fence, The.
McKay, D. Barbed Wire Fence Meditates upon the Goldfinch, A.
Stow. Singing Bones, The.

See also **Walls**

Fencing and Fencers
Manifold. Fencing School.
Yuan Chi. Regret.

Ferns
Hughes, T. Fern.

Ferry Boats
Dibdin, C. Jolly Young Waterman, The.
Doty, M. Night Ferry.
Grosholz. On the Ferry, Toward Patras.
Ho Ching-ming. Ch'en-hsi County.
Housman, A. Crossing alone the nighted ferry.
Liu E. Waiting for the Ferry at Inchŏn.

Millay, E. Recuerdo.
Rossetti, C. Ferry Me across the Water.
Ferry me across the water, / Do, boatman, do.
Sexton. Letter Written on a Ferry While Crossing Long Island Sound.
Teika. I rein in my horse.

Fertilizer
Grainger, J. Compost.

Festivals
Apollinaire. Phantom of Clouds, A.
Chu. Fireworks.
Faiz. Tyrant, The.
Garioch. Embro to the Ploy.
Li K'ai-hsien. Colorful frames are erected beside the Yellow River, The.
Night of the First Full Moon, The.
On the Cold Food Festival, Entertaining at the Southern Estate—the Guests Were Li Chiu-ho, Ma Nan-yeh, Wei Tung-kao, Li Hu-ch'uan, Huang K'ung-ts'un, Li Lung-t'ang, and Hu Hu-shan.
Maiden. Taste.
Meredith, G. Here Jack and Tom are paired with Moll and Meg.
Nguyễn Khuyến. French National Holiday, The.
Ofeimun. Naming Day, A.
Pien Kung. Walking Outside the City Walls on the Day of the Cold Food Festival.
Po Chü-i. To Li Chien.
Unknown. Golden Palace, The.
Po, po, po, po.
Wang Chia. Shrine Festival.

Feuds
Aytoun, W. Massacre of the Macpherson, The.
Day, J. Rowan County Crew, The.
Lea, S. Feud, The.
Unknown. Lads of Wamphray, The.
Lord Maxwell's Last Goodnight.

Fever
Akhmadulina. Fever.
Bryll. In a Fever.
Dobson, R. Fever, The.
Gunn, T. Fever.
Pilkington, L. Fair and Softly goes far or, The Wary Physician.
Plath. Fever 103°.
Shakespeare, W. Sonnet 147.

Fiacre, Saint
Irvine, J. Saint Fiacre.

Fiddles and Fiddlers
Burns, R. Green sleeves and tartan ties.
Evans, E. Seven Fiddlers, The.
Hardy, T. Country Wedding, The.
Kinnell. First Song.
Masters, E. Earth keeps some vibration going, The.
Fiddler Jones.
Neilson, J. Take Down the Fiddle, Karl!
Yeats. Fiddler of Dooney, The.

See also **Violins**

Fidelity
Auden. Lullaby: "Lay your sleeping head, my love."
Bàng Bá Lân. If in a Future Life We Meet Again.
Barrett, E. Woman.
Beer, P. Faithful Wife, The.
Berry, W. Dance, The.
Blamire. Siller Croun, The.
Boker. As stands a statue on its pedestal.
Brontë, E. Visionary, The.
Browning, E. Man's Requirements, A.
Sonnet: "How do I love thee? Let me count the ways."
Sonnet: "I never gave a lock of hair away."
Sonnet: "If thou must love me, let it be for nought."
Browning, R. Bad Dreams.
Burns, R. Come, let me take thee to my breast.
Open the Door to Me, Oh!
Red, Red Rose, A.
Campion, T. Shall I then hope when faith is fled?
Cary, P. Samuel Brown.

Chang Chi. Faithful Wife, A.
Chaucer. Complaint unto Pity, The.
Crane, S. Should the wide world roll away.
Daniel, S. Sonnet 33: 'When men shall find thy flower'.
Donne. Anniversary [or Anniversarie], The.
Indifferent, The.
Legacy [or Legacie], The.
Lovers' Infiniteness[e].
On His Mistress [or Mistris].
Our Love Hath No Decay.
Relic, The.
Dowson. Non Sum Qualis Eram Bonae sub Regno Cynara[e].
"Ern Malley." Perspective Lovesong.
"Field." Constancy.
Ford, T. There is a Lady sweet and kind.
Greenwell, D. Fidelity Rewarded.
Gunn, T. Monster, The.
Hardy, T. Postponement.
Hartmann von Aue. I said I would always live for her.
Harwood, G. Wine is drunk, the woman known, The.
Heinrich von Veldeke. Tristan had no choice.
Herrick. Bracelet.
Love Me Little, Love Me Long.
To Anthea, Who May Command Him Anything.
Housman, A. Shades of night were falling fast, The.
Jonson, B. Epistle. To Katharine, Lady Aubigny.
Kim, T. My mind is a lake.
Lawrence, D. Fidelity and love are two different things, like a flower and a gem.
Lewis, A. Post-Script: for Gweno.
Lodge, T. Phillis 2.
McAuley, J. In a Late Hour.
Meredith, G. But where began the change; and what's my crime?
Their sense is with their senses all mixed in.
You like not that French novel? Tell me why.
Millay, E. Modern Declaration.
Montagu, L. Verses Written in a Garden.
Moore, T. Irish Peasant to His Mistress, The.
Mullen, H. Roadmap.
Nesbit, E. Wife of All Ages, The.
O'Neal. Shades of Pharoah Sanders Blues for My Baby.
Paulinus of Nola. To Ausonius.
Philips, K. To Mrs. M.A. Upon Absence.
Poe. Annabel Lee.
Ponsot. La Une, A.
Matins and Lauds.
Prassinos. Hair Tonic.
Procter, A. Woman's Answer, A.
Ralegh, W. Fortune hath taken away my love.
Rist. She Boasts of Her Constancy.
Robinson, E. Luke Havergal.
Rochester, J. Love And Life.
Rossetti, C. From Monna Innominata.
Meeting.
Sackville-West. Greater cats with golden eyes, The.
Shakespeare, W. Sonnet 31.
Sonnet 116.
Sherwood, G. Love and Life.
Sidney, P. Bargain, The.
Sonnet 91: "Stella, while now by honour's cruel might."
Stanley, T. Changed, Yet Constant.
Suckling, J. Constant Lover, A [or The].
Surrey. Love, that doth reign and live within my thought.
Taylor, B. Bedouin Song.
Trefusis. Valentine, A.
Tuqan, F. I Won't Sell His Love.
Unknown. By Heaven!
First month of winter: cold air comes.
Frail frail, lone-growing bamboo.
Kudzu Spreads Till It Darkens the Brier, The.
Lament of the Border Widow, The.
Love me little, love me long!
Love Me Not [for Comely Grace].
Song of the Snow-white Heads.
Southeast the Peacock Flies.

There is a lady sweet and kind.
Unquiet Grave, The.
When ice on the pond is three feet thick.
Young Beichan.
Vaiiunaite. Penelope.
Vaughan, H. To Amoret, of the Difference 'twixt Him and Other Lovers, and What True Love Is.
Volkow. Washerwoman, The.
Wickham. Paradox.
Slighted Lady, The.
Winchilsea. Letter to Daphnis, A.
Wyatt, T. Deem as ye list. Upon good cause.
Quondam was I in my lady's grace.
Sometime I sigh, sometime I sing.
Sonnet: 'The long love'.
Supplication, A.
Ye know my heart, my lady dear.
Yakamochi. We were together.
Yeats. Folly Of Being Comforted, The.
Yi, T. Bride, The.
Young, A. Woman, don't be troublesome.

Field-Glasses
Young, A. Field-Glasses.

Fields and Pastures
Alexandru. Descending.
Ashbery. Grand Abacus.
Betjeman. Licorice Fields at Pontefract, The.
Bible, *O.T.* Song: "Come, my beloved."
Bowes-Lyon. Pastoral: "This field has buried men; is browed."
Brand, M. Lost.
Brown, L. Come go with me out to the Field.
Browning, R. Meeting At Night.
Two in the Campagna.
Ch'ien T'ao. New Corn.
Clare, J. Hares at Play.
Conyus. Day in the Life of. . . , A.
Cowper, W. Poplar Field, The.
De la Mare. Crazed.
Voices.
Duncan, R. Often I Am Permitted to Return to a Meadow.
Enright, D. Old field is sad, The.
Flynn, M. Down in the field.
Frost, R. Cow in Apple Time, The.
Pasture, The.
Glatstein. Ruth.
Glück, L. Field Flowers.
Goldberg, L. When You Will Walk in the Field.
Goodison. Gleanings.
Griffiths, A. His left hand, in heat of noonday.
Gunn, T. For Signs.
Heaney, S. Field Work.
Herrick. To Meadows [*or* Meddowes].
High. Lives of thomas—episodes and prayers, The.
Hitomaro. On the Eastern horizon.
Hugo, R. Open Country.
Ingelow. Dappled sky, a world of meadows, A.
Izen. As the late night passes.
Izumi. As I dig for wild orchids.
Jarrell. Field and Forest.
Jewell. This evening stillness.
Lovelace, R. Ant, The.
Marlowe. Passionate Shepherd [*or* Sheepheard] To His Love, The.
Marvell. And now to the abyss I pass.
Mower's Song, The.
Masaoka Shiki. Shitting in the winter turnip field.
Merwin, W. Low Fields and Light.
Miles, J. Fields of Learning.
Millay, E. I dreamed I moved among the Elysian fields.
Mitchison. Unfertile Heart, The.
Miu Hsi. Bearer's Song.
Mori Ōgai. Tanka: "Under the blue sky."
Naito Joso. Fields and mountains.
Newcastle, M. Sea Similized to Meadows and Pastures: the Mariners, to Shepherds: the Mast, to a May-Pole: the Fish, to Beasts, The.
Nowak, T. Psalm of the Field.
Pasternak, B. In The Wood.

Petrarch. Alone and pensive, the most deserted fields.
Pierman. Eight Cows.
Pritchard, N. Paysagesque.
Ray, H. Pastoral: "Annette came through the meadows."
Roberts, S. Pea-Fields, The.
Roethke. Far Field, The.
Meadow Mouse, The.
Rossetti, C. Green Cornfield, A.
Rossetti, D. Silent Noon.
Rumi. Out beyond ideas of wrongdoing and rightdoing.
Sartarelli. Phantasmatikon.
Stafford, K. Proposal.
Stephens, J. White Fields.
Tarpley. Feel Free.
Tate, J. Love Making.
Taylor, A. Meadows, The.
Thomas, D. I, in my intricate image, stride on two levels.
Thoreau. On fields oer which the reaper's hand has passed.
Tsogyel. Listen.
Unknown. Down in Yonder Meadow [where the green grass].
Vacietis. Of nights / some bear.
Van Doren. Immortal.
Weöres. Plain, The.
Wilbur. Exeunt.
Grasshopper, A.
Two Voices in a Meadow.
Wilcox, E. Attraction.
Wordsworth, W. Solitary Reaper, The.
Wratislaw. Hothouse Flowers.
Wright, J. Late November in a Field.
Young, A. Field-Glasses.

Fig Trees and Figs
Causley. Figgie Hobbin.
Dove, R. This Life.
Hall, D. Small Fig Tree, A.
Lawrence, D. Bare Fig-trees.
Figs.
Nye, N. My Father and the Figtree.

Fights
Blake, W. Jerusalem.
Browning, R. Woman's Last Word, A.
"Carroll." Brother and Sister.
Cockrell. Fist Fight.
Coleridge, M. Mortal Combat.
Gunn, T. Apartment Cats.
Hazard, J. Whiskey in Whiting, Indiana.
Hiley. To a Persian Cat.
Lawrence, D. What Would You Fight For?
McKay, C. If we must die—let it not be like hogs.
Millay, E. Hearing your words, and not a word among them.
Orfalea. War.
Ransom, J. Captain Carpenter rose up in his prime.
Trakl. Rats, The.
Ts'ao Chih. Cock-fight, The.
Unknown. Ojibwa War Songs.
Whitman, R. Listening to Grownups Quarreling.

Figureheads (ship)
Adams, L. Figurehead, The.

Filipinos. *See* **Philippines**

Financiers. *See* **Banking and Bankers**

Finches
Knight, H. Bullfinch in Town, The.
Ochester. 110 Year Old House.
Singer, B. Birdsong.
Wordsworth, W. Green Linnet, The.

Fingers
Buzzi. Finger-nails.
Dacey, P. Thumb.
Davies, H. Poem: "It doesn't look like a finger it looks like a feather of broken glass."
Eglitis. I see how the grasping fingers of lovers do not let go, till.
Fitzgerald, E. 71.
Hartnett. I think sometimes / of the fingernail slotted.
Kitahara Hakushū. Tanka: "Almost invisible."

Kuroda. Afternoon 3.
Malroux. Fingers probe.
Montgomery, S. Evening lecture.
Nezval. City With Towers.
O'Neill, M. My fingers are antennae.
Randolph, T. Upon the Loss[e] of His Little Finger.
Simic. Bestiary for the Fingers of My Right Hand.
Tagami. Now It Is Broccoli.
Unknown. Finger Play.
Yang Wei-chen. Painting Her Nails.
Yosano. Tanka: "Young fingers."

Finland
Brecht, B. 1940.
Hacker, M. Rune of the Finland Woman.
Jacobsen, J. Reindeer and Engine.
Lönnrot. It is my desire, it is my wish.

Finnsburg, Battle of
Unknown. Battle of Finnsburg, The.

Fionn (legendary king of Fenians)
Unknown. Praise of Fionn, The.

Fir Trees
Murphy, R. Epitaph on a Fir-Tree.

Fire Engines
Baxter, J. Firemen, The.
Wilbur. Fire-Truck, A.
Williams, W. Great Figure, The.

Fire Island
Cole, H. Ascension on Fire Island.
Herbert, Z. Two Drops.
O'Hara, F. True Account of Talking to the Sun at Fire Island, A.

Fire and Fires
Ackland. Overnight.
"Adunis." Passage, The.
Tree of Fire.
Anderson, P. Houses Burning; Quebec.
Atwood. Morning in the Burned House.
Averill. Renewal.
Balaban. Thoughts Before Dawn.
Baxter, J. Firemen, The.
Wild Bees.
Bekederemo. Season of Omens.
Binyon. Now is the time for the burning of the leaves.
Bishop, E. Armadillo, The.
Casabianca.
Bly, R. But if one of those children came near that we have set / on fire.
Bobrowski. Latvian Autumn, The.
Place of Fire.
Bogen, D. House Destroyed by Fire, The.
Bradley, G. Fire Fetched Down, The.
Bradstreet, A. Here Follows Some Verses upon the Burning of Our House [July 10th, 1966. Copied Out of a Loose Paper].
Brew. Search, The.
Bromige. Log.
Point is not the point—, The.
Brown, S. Schadenfreude.
Brydges. To Miss M———, Written by Moonlight, July 18, 1782.
Buckley, V. Man, a woman, straighten up from where, A.
Byron, G. Darkness.
Campbell, D. Man in the Honeysuckle, The.
Carberry. It takes a mighty fire.
Cardiff. Where Fire Burns.
Carew, T. Song: To Her Again[c], She Burning in a Fe[a]ver.
To My Mistress [*or* Mistris], I Burning in Love.
Carr, M. Castle in the Fire, The.
Cecco Angiolieri, da Siena. Sonnet: Of All He Would Do.
Celan. Alchemical.
Night Ray.
Chao Meng-fu. To a Pyrotechnist.
Clifton, L. Move.
Coleman, H. Remembrance of Things Past.
Coleridge, M. Fire, the lamp, and I, were alone together, The.
Csoori. Tenant Who Lives in Fire, The.
Daryush. Children of wealth in your warm nursery.

Davis, C.   Years, The.
Dickinson, E.   Dare you see a Soul *at the White Heat?*.
Donne.   I am a little world made cunningly.
Doolittle, H.   In no wise is the pillar-of-fire.
Sea Violet.
Drayton.   If he, from heaven that filched the living fire.
Dugan, A.   Winter for an Untenable Situation.
Duncan, R.   Fire, The.
Tribal Memories.
Eberhart, R.   Ship Burning and a Comet All in One Day, A.
Espada.   Mrs. Baez Serves Coffee on the Third Floor.
"Field."   From Baudelaire.
Fleming, E.   Fires.
Frost, R.   Fire and Ice.
Garland, H.   Fighting Fire.
Prairie Fires.
Gilbo'a.   Ends of Things were heard no more, The.
Glazkov.   Subject for a Story.
Graham, H.   Tender-Heartedness.
Grahn.   Hannah.
Graves, R.   Under the Pot.
Groch.   Friend to Birds.
Gunn, T.   Faustus Triumphant.
Hall, D.   Love-Letter-Burning.
Halpern, D.   Street Fire.
Hamburger, M.   Treblinka.
Harper, M.   Fireplace, The.
Harte, B.   Chicago.
Harter.   Mattress Fire.
Hassett.   Mother's Day.
Hemphill.   Soft Targets.
Henderson-Holmes.   My First Riot: Bronx, NYC.
Herlin.   Echo of fireplace on the dividing wall, An.
Herrick.   Scar[e]-Fire, The.
Herschberger.   Lumberyard, The.
Hirsch, E.   Man on a Fire Escape.
Hitchcock.   Scattering Flowers.
Holan.   At Mother's After Many Years.
Homer.   Clash in Arms of the Achaians and Trojans.
Huchel.   Thrace.
Jaccottet.   Right at the end of night.
Jacobsen, J.   Limbo Dancer, The.
Jeffers, R.   Fire on the Hills.
Jonson, B.   Execration upon Vulcan, An.
Hour Glass, The ("Consider this small dust, here in the glass").
Karp.   Taxi to the Flame, A.
Kees.   Heat in the Room, The.
Kennedy, X.   Lighting a Fire.
Khlebnikov, V.   It has the unassuming face of a burnt-out candle.
King, H.   Sonnet: "Tell me[e] no more how fair[e] she[e] is."
Kinnell.   Under the Maud Moon.
Kukai.   Singing Image of Fire.
Landor, W.   Torch of Love dispels the gloom, The.
Lehman.   Spontaneous Combustion.
Levchev.   Confession and Salute to the Fire.
Levine, P.   Coming Home, *Detroit*, 1968.
Longfellow, H.   Golden Mile-Stone, The.
Lorde.   Summer Oracle.
Lovelace, R.   Fly about a Glass[e] of Burnt Claret, A.
Loving.   Black Horse Rider, The.
Lowell, J.   Darkened Mind, The.
Lux.   Barn Fire.
MacNeice.   Brother Fire.
Martinez, D.   Fuego.
Matuzeviius.   Writing in the Fire, The.
McDonald, W.   Once You've Been to War.
McGrath, T.   Coal Fire in Winter, A.
Mechthild von Magdeburg.   Fish cannot drown in water, A.
Merrill, J.   Charles on Fire.
Merton.   Elegy for the Monastery Barn.
Merwin, W.   Burnt Child, The.
Monk, M.   Fire Us with Ice, Burn Us with Snow.

Moore, M.   To a Chameleon.
Morgan, R.   Phobiphilia.
Mori Ōgai.   Tanka: "Insane thought, An."
Moss, T.   Lynching, The.
Musgrave.   Exchange of Fire.
Nemerov.   Marriage of Heaven and Earth, The.
Neruda.   Poetry.
Neto.   African Poem.
North, C.   Leap Year.
O'Connor, M.   Fire.
Patchen.   Naked Land, The.
Pau-Llosa.   Ostiones Y Cangrejos Moros.
Peabody, R.   Burning the Dolls.
Peele.   Bethsabe's Song.
Love.
Piatt, J.   Fires in Illinois.
Piatt, S.   Palace-Burner, The.
Piercy.   Noon of the Sunbather.
Plumly.   Complaint Against the Arsonist.
Porter, P.   Non Piangere, Liù.
Raab, L.   Witch's Story, The.
Ralegh, W.   Love Indestructible.
Ravikovitch.   Dress of Fire, A.
Reavey.   How many fires.
Redmond.   Distance.
My tongue paints a path of fire.
Ristovic.   Despair.
Rivard.   Firestone.
Roberts, G.   Burnt Lands.
Robinson, F.   Brief day ending.
Rodriguez, L.   Fire.
Roseliep.   Campfire Extinguished.
Rossetti, C.   Flint.
Roy, L.   Ride, The.
Rudnik.   Dream.
Ruffin.   Hotel Fire: New Orleans.
Rukeyser, M.   Burning the Dreams.
Sachs, N.   Rushing at Times Like Flames.
Scannell.   Incendiary.
Scott, A.   Rondel of Luve [or Love], A.
Shapiro, K.   Exile.
Sissoko.   Brush Fire.
Slutsky.   Burnt.
Smith, D.   Near the Docks.
Smith, S.   Persian, The.
Snyder, G.   Burning the small dead.
Sorrentino.   Land of Cotton.
Southwell.   Burning Babe, The.
Spenser.   Sonnet 30: "My love is like to ice, and I to fire."
Stafford, W.   Looking West.
Stevenson, R.   Armies in the Fire.
Autumn Fires.
Swirszczynska.   I Am Afraid of Fire.
Taggart, J.   Twenty One Times.
Tate, A.   Fire I praise was once perduring flame, The.
Near to me as my flesh, my flesh and blood.
Tati-Loutard.   Noonday in Immaturity.
Taylor, A.   Fire.
Taylor, J.   As Gold is better that's in fire tride.
Ts'ao Chih.   Written on Parting from Mr. Ying.
U Tam'si Tchicaya.   Brush-Fire.
Unknown.   Brooklyn Theater Fire, The.
First Song of the Exploding Stick.
Milwaukee Fire, The.
Miramichi Fire, The.
Old Fellow from Tyre, The.
Vacietis.   Burning Leaves.
Virgil.   Until Jove let it be, no colonist.
Voznesensky.   Big Fire at the Architectural College, The.
Warren, R.   In Creve Coeur, Missouri.
Watson, R.   Ballad of the Were-Wolf, A.
Weigl.   Burning Shit at An Khe.
Weiss, T.   Fire at Alexandria, The.
Welch, L.   He Thanks His Woodpile.
Whitman, W.   By the bivouac's fitful flame.
Whittier.   Burning Drift-Wood.
Wieseltier.   God's Fire upon Children ("God's fire upon cities").
Williamson, G.   Walter Parmer.
Wright, C.   State of Preservation.
Wright, J.   Night After Bushfire.
To a Child.
Two Fires, The.

Wright, R.   Between the World and Me.
Yannai.   Celestial Fire, The.
Yosano.   Tanka: "Peony in her hair, The."
Tanka: "Warring heaven."
Yün Shou-p'ing.   Lament for the Willows outside the City Walls, A.
Zenmaro.   September 1, 1923.
Zenodotus.   Statue Of Eros, A.
Zhigulin.   Campfireburners.
Zu-Bolton.   Struggle-Road Dance.

Firearms. *See* **Guns**

Firecats
Stevens, W.   Earthy Anecdote.

Fire-eaters
Williams, M.   Firebreathers at the Café Deux Magots, The.

Firefighters
Aiken, C.   Habeas Corpus Blues, The.
Baxter, J.   Firemen, The.
Gallagher, T.   Conversation with a Fireman from Brooklyn.
Hampton.   Fire station's delight, The.
Harris, R.   Ambition, The.

Fireflies
Charles, F.   Fireflies.
Chine-Jo.   Fireflies' light, The.
Fleischman.   Fireflies.
Frost, R.   Fireflies in the Garden.
Gorman, L.   My family asleep.
Kinzie.   Canicula.
Kitahara Hakushū.   Tanka: "In the daytime."
Marvell.   Mower to the Glow-Worms [or Glowworms or Glo-Worms], The.
Mercer, J.   Glow-Worm, The.
Roberts, E.   Firefly.
Saitō Mokichi.   Tanka: "Nothing to be done?"
Tanka: "What on the other shore."
Smith, C.   Glow-Worm, The.
Strange.   Childhood.
Swenson, M.   Fireflies throw.
T'ang Hsien-tsu.   Spending the Night on the River.
Tu Fu.   Upon Seeing the Fireflies.
Unknown.   Chant to the Fire-Fly.
To a Firefly.
Valle, I.   Very Minor Poet Speaks, A.
Willmot.   Now the spade.

See also **Glowworms**

Fireworks
Chock.   Chinese Fireworks Banned in Hawaii.
Chu.   Fireworks.
Deutsch.   Fireworks.
Fumi Saito.   Tanka: "Crooked fireworks."
Fumiko.   Tanka: "With a thunderous crack."
Hotham.   Quietly.
Peck, R.   Four of July.
Swenson, M.   July 4th.
Worth, V.   Fireworks.

First Church of The Millennium. *See* **Shakers (First Church of The Millennium)**

First World War. *See* **World War I**

Fish
Aaronson.   Pesci Misti.
Adamson.   Gutting the Salmon.
Alexander, P.   Fish Fact.
Allard.   Alone tonight one fish ripples the lake.
Barker, G.   How many apples grow on the tree?
Sonnet of Fishes.
Belloc.   Good Advice.
Belševica.   That was a very polite fish.
Bierds.   Seizure.
Bishop, E.   Fish, The.
Blight.   Evolution.
Garfish.
Blunden.   Pike, The.
Brinckman.   Fish and Bird.
Brooke, R.   Fish, The.
Heaven.
Carrel.   Catching.
"Carroll."   Crocodile, The.
Humpty Dumpty's Song.
Carruth, H.   When howitzers began.
Castellanos.   Great fish's eyes never shut, The.
Catherine of Siena (A. K. A. Saint Catherine).   We were enclosed.

Cendrars. Fish Cove.
Chuang Tzu. Man Is Born in Tao.
Cobbing. Alphabet of Fishes.
Cope, J. Flying Fish, The.
Cynewulf. Fish in River: "My house is not quiet, I am not loud."
Davies, M. Fishing Pole, The ("Fishing pole's a curious thing, A").
De la Mare. Alas, Alack!
Dickey, J. Movement of Fish, The.
Donne. Bait[e], The.
Dove, R. Fish in the Stone, The.
Dumas, H. Knees of a Natural Man.
Eigner. Letter for Duncan.
Enright, D. Egyptian Cat, The.
Farber. How They Brought the Good News by Sea.
Fumi Saito. Tanka: "Bones of a fish."
Fumiko. Tanka: "Wiggling out."
Gander. Table Laid with Horrors, A.
Gray, T. Ode on the Death of a Favourite [or Favorite] Cat, Drowned in a Tub [or Bowl] of Gold Fishes.
Guest, B. Twilight Polka Dots.
Hackett, J. Deep within the stream.
Half of the minnows.
Harwood, G. Mid-Channel.
Hassall. Tropical Fish.
Heyen. Snapper, The.
Hitchcock. One Whose Reproach I Cannot Evade, The.
Ho Ching-ming. Fish in a Painting.
Horace. Conservation.
Howes, B. Sea School.
Hsü Wei. Two Fish by a Willow Embankment.
Hughes, T. Pike, three inches long, perfect.
Hummer, T. Worldly Beauty.
Hunt, L. To a Fish.
Ignatow, D. Fisherwoman, The.
Jaques, F. There Once Was a Puffin.
Jeffers, R. Birds and Fishes.
Purse-Seine, The.
Karp. Consequences of Waking, The.
Keats. Swarms of minnows show their little heads.
Kelly, B. Leaving, The.
Kim, H. Fish Cooking.
Kinnell. Avenue Bearing the Initial of Christ into the New World, The.
Kwakiutl Oral Tradition. Prayer to the Sockeye Salmon.
Lawrence, D. Little Fish.
Lowell, R. Fishnet.
MacCaig. Kingfisher.
Mackey, N. Memphite Recension.
MacLeish. Vicissitudes of the Creator.
Major, C. Beaulieu.
Malangatana. Woman.
McAuley, J. Legendary.
McCaffery. Little Hans.
Mei Yao Ch'en. Chiang Lin-chi Treats Me to Mudfish.
Fish Peddler.
Melville, H. Maldive Shark, The.
Song from Mardi.
We fish, we fish, we merrily swim.
Mills, W. Pity.
Milosz, C. Abundant Catch (Luke 5:4–10).
Montague, J. Trout, The.
Moore, M. Fish, The.
Nagys. Poem.
Nemerov. Goose Fish, The.
Noguere. Soma.
Okamoto. Tanka: "Having let flow."
Pagis. Ararat.
Péret. Making Feet and Hands.
Perlman, A. Family Reunion.
Pizzarelli. Tiny fish.
Pollitt. Two Fish.
Rao, B. Fish.
Rosenblatt. Fish.
Ichthycide.
Ross, W. Fish dripping, A.
Rossetti, C. When fishes set umbrellas up.
Sandburg, C. Fish Crier.
Shen Chou. South of the Bridge.

Sitwell, S. Mrs. Busk.
Smedley, M. Sorrowful Sea-Gull, The.
Stevens, M. Carp, The.
Tate, J. Blue Booby lives, The.
Tekkan. Tanka: "Not unlike a fish."
Thomas, R. Pisces.
Thompson, D. Wish.
Tsung Ch'en. Drinking at the Cave Mouth.
Unknown. Fish weeps in the, The.
Fisherman's Rhyme.
Fowls [or Foweles or Fowles] in the frith.
Goddess Chiao, The.
One, two, three, four, five / Once I caught a fish alive.
Wang Shih-chieng. Quatrain at Chen-chou.
Wang T'ing-hsiang. On New Year's Day of the Year Kuei-ssu (1533), Releasing Live Creatures.
Waring, B. Back to Catfish.
Warren, R. Red Mullet, The.
Wills, J. Bluegill rises, A.
Wood, W. Sea's Abundant Progeny, The.
Wright, G. Aquarium.
Wright, J. Northern Pike.
Wu Wei-yeh. Climbing P'iao-miao Peak.
Yang Shen. To the Tune "Chiang ch'eng tzu."
Yeats. Three Movements.
Yoshimi. Tanka: "Because."

See also names of fish (e.g., **Trout**).

Fishing and Fishermen
Ammuvanar. What She Said ("Fishermen who go, The").
Ausonius. No fish has ever told another of danger.
Bacon, L. Flyfisherman in Wartime.
Balaban. Dragonfish, The.
Barrax. Visit.
Basse. Angler's Song, The.
Bianor. In the clear water by the beach.
Bishop, E. At the Fishhouses.
Fish, The.
Brown, A. Fisherman goes out at dawn, The.
Brown, G. Haddock Fishermen.
Old Fisherman with Guitar.
Trout Fisher.
Browne, M. Talk to Me, Baby.
Bunting. Fishermen.
Chang Chi. Coming at Night to a Fisherman's Hut.
Chang Chih-ho. Before dusk on the lake, the moon just full.
Near the rim of Hsi-sai Mountain, white egrets fly.
Oh, about the joy of owning a crab hut at Sung-chiang!
Chao Meng-fu. Fisherman's Lyric.
Chiyojo. Grazing.
Chock. Bait, The.
Chu Yün-ming. Clouds are swept into the sunset—mdash;a sky beyond the sky.
Crabbe. Priest attending, found he spoke at times, The.
Curnow. Canst Thou Draw Out Leviathan with an Hook.
Davies, M. Fishing Pole, The ("Fishing pole's a curious thing, A").
Dickey, J. Shark's Parlor, The.
Donne. Bait[e], The.
Dunbar, P. Boy's Summer, A.
D'Urfey. Fisherman's Song, The.
Eigner. Letter for Duncan.
Farjeon, E. Blackfriars.
Field, E. Wynken, Blynken and Nod one night.
Fujiwara no Sadayori. As the mists rise in the dawn.
Gascoigne. Farewell, A.
Grosholz. Old Fisherman, The.
Guest, E. Out Fishin'.
Hall, D. Another Elegy.
Hall, J. Reel World, The.
Hamilton, G. Don's Holiday.
Hanzlicek, C. Room for Doubt.
Harwood, G. Mid-Channel.
Hay, G. To a Loch Fyne Fisherman.
Heaney, S. Hazel Stick for Catherine Ann, A.
Howes, B. Out Fishing.

Hsieh Chin. Wait until I too hang up my carriage.
Huang T'ing-chien. Song of the Clear River.
Hughes, L. Catch.
Hughes, T. Stealing Trout.
Hugo, R. Letter to Wagoner from Port Townsend.
Ignatow, D. Fisherwoman, The.
Jeffers, R. Purse-Seine, The.
Kahanu. When I was young on an island.
Kao Ch'i. Spring Day—Remembering Living on the River, A.
Kingsley, C. Three Fishers [Went Sailing], The.
Kunitz, S. Catch, The.
Quinnapoxet.
Lang, A. Last Chance, The.
Lea, S. At the Flyfisher's Shack.
Leonidas. Theris, the old man who lived by his fish traps.
Leslie, K. Halibut Cove Harvest.
Li K'ai-hsien. Parable, A.
Staying Overnight on the Banks of Embroidered River.
Li Tung-yang. Song of the Painting "Catching Fish."
Li Yü. One scull in the spring wind, one leaf of a boat.
Tune: The Fisherman.
Liu E. Waiting for the Ferry at Inchŏn.
Lorde. Fishing the White Water.
Lowell, R. Drunken Fisherman, The.
Lu Kuei Meng. Fisherman on a Southern Stream.
Lu Yu. Tune: "Immortal at the Magpie Bridge."
MacCaig. Crofter's Kitchen, Evening.
Drifter.
Maccius. Your pleasure, Priapus, is the island coast.
"MacDiarmid." With the Herring Fishers.
Mapanje. Elegy for Mangochi Fishermen, An.
Martinson. Cable Ship, The.
Merrill, J. Parrot Fish, The.
Pier: Under Pisces, The.
Merwin, W. Finding a Teacher.
Mills, W. Pity.
Rituals along the Arkansas.
Milosz, C. Luke 5:1–11; While the people pressed upon him.
Mirikitani. Fisherman, The.
Mitchison. Dick and Colin at the Salmon Nets.
Montague, J. Trout, The.
Moody, E. To a Gentleman Who Invited Me to Go A-Fishing.
Morgan, R. Hollow, The.
Mueller, L. Mermaid, The.
Nairne. Caller Herrin'.
Nemerov. Casting.
Newbolt. Master and Man.
Nguyễn Đình Chiểu. Fisherman Speaks His Mind, A.
Ni Tsan. Painting "Solitary Fisherman by a Spring River" The.
O'Hara, F. Captains Courageous.
Ou-yang Hsiu. Fisherman.
Old fisherman spends his night beneath the western cliffs.
Phan Thanh Giản. Fishermen and Cormorants.
Philip of Thessalonica. His anchor, seaweed-probing, boat-securing.
Plutzik. Jim Desterland.
Pu Chü-i. Fishing in the Wei River.
Rao, B. Fish.
Ray, H. Fisherman's Story, The.
Richards, L. Some Fishy Nonsense.
Roethke. Lady and the Bear, The.
Ropes. Disappointed Shrimper, The.
St. John, P. Song.
Schnackenberg. Nightfishing.
Scovell. Boy Fishing, The.
Shen Yüeh. Fishing Rod, The.
Shumaker. Circle of Totems, The.
Smith, D. Fisherman's Whore, The.
Smithyman. Hint for the Incomplete Angler.
Stafford, W. In the Deep Channel.

Stevens, W. Thinking of a Relation between the Images of Metaphors.

Stevenson, R. Epitaph: "Angler rose, he took his rod, The."

Su Shih. Fisherman drinks, The.

Su Tung-p'o. Epigram.

T'ang Hsien-tsu. Autumn River.
Spending the Night on the River.

T'ang Yin. Inscribed on a Painting of a Fisherman.

Todd, R. Trout Flies.

Trowbridge, J. Old Lobsterman, The.

Ts'en Shen. Fisherman.

Unknown. Fishermen's Song.
Lines are cast and the nets are set and waiting, The.
To Astarte.

Voznesensky. Call of the Lake, The.

Wang Shih-chieng. Quatrain at Chen-chou.

Wen T'ing-yün. Fishing Trapping Song, A.

Whitman, W. Torch, The.

Whittier. Skipper Ireson's Ride.

Williams, W. Ritualists, The.

Wood, S. Witness.

Wright, J. Lifting Illegal Nets by Flashlight.

Wu Chen. Level forest stretching far and wide, A.

Wu Chia-chi. Grain-Barge Wife, The.

Yang Shih-ch'i. Eulogy on My Own Portrait, A.

Yeats. Fisherman, The.

Yevtushenko. Hand-Rolled Cigarettes.

Young, K. Casting.

Yü Chi. What family has built a house beside the rapids here?

Yün Shou-p'ing. Waterside Village.

See also **Clams and Clamming; Crabs and Crabbing;** *Names of fish (e.g.,* **Trout***).*

Fitts, Dudley
Gregory, H. Elegy and Flame.

Fitzgerald, Edward
Browning, R. To Edward FitzGerald.
Tennyson, A. To E. Fitzgerald.

Fitzgerald, F. Scott
Preston, K. Effervescence and Evanescence.
Wilson, E. On Editing Scott Fitzgerald's Papers.

Fixation
Mew. My heart is lame with running after yours so fast.

Flags
Beecher, H. American Flag, The.
Bellamy, F. Pledge of Allegiance to the Flag.
Bierce. Confederate Flags, The.
Cohan. You're a grand old flag.
de Jesús. Flag of Chile, The.
Dickinson, E. Success is counted sweetest.
Hardy, T. Middle-Age Enthusiasms.
Key. Star-Spangled Banner, The.
Kirby, J. Union Jack, The.
Morgan, E. Itinerary.
Shapiro, D. For the Evening Land.
Smelyakov. Portrait.
Smith, K. Train.
Thomas, L. Subway Witnesses, The.
Yu. Flag.

Flags, United States
Bennett, H. Flag Goes By, The.
Cohan. You're a grand old flag.
Daly, J. Toast to the Flag, A.
Drake, J. American Flag, The.
Fordham. Stars and Stripes.
Key. Star-Spangled Banner, The.
Tippett. Hang Out the Flag.
Unknown. Our Flag.
Whittier. Barbara Frietchie.

Flamingos
Rilke. Flamingos, The.
Unknown. Flamingo, what has brought you here?

Flanders, Belgium
Armstrong, J. Another Reply to "In Flanders Fields."
Ford, F. Old Houses of Flanders, The.
Grenfell, J. Into Battle.
McCrae, J. In Flanders Fields the poppies blow.

Mitchell, J. Reply to "In Flanders Fields."

Flapjacks. *See* **Pancakes**

Flattery
Carryl, G. Sycophantic Fox and the Gullible Raven, The.
Ewart. It's Hard to Dislike Ewart.
Herrick. To His Kinswoman, Mrs. Penelope Wheeler.
Howitt, M. Spider and the Fly, The.
La Fontaine. Fox and the Crow, The.
Shakespeare, W. Sonnet 85.
Sonnet 138.
Unknown. "How Quick You Are!"

Fleas
Coleridge, S. On Donne's First Poem.
De Morgan. Great Fleas [have little fleas upon their backs to / bite 'em].
Donne. Flea, The.
Greig, D. To a Flea in a Glass of Water.
Issahakian. For you fleas too.
Lindsay, V. Little Turtle, The.
Nichols, R. Harlot's Catch.
Roseliep. Flea . .
Sandburg, C. Englishman in the old days, An.
Unknown. Flea and a fly in a flue, A.
Poem to Answer the Question: How Old Are Fleas?

Flies
Aubert, A. Silence.
Blake, W. Fly, The.
Carew, T. Fly That Flew into My Mistress'[s] Eye, A.
Carey. Nulla Fides.
Clare, J. Clock-A-Clay [The Lady Bug].
De la Mare. Fly, The.
Dickinson, E. I heard a Fly buzz—when I died[—died].
Ewart. Haiku: The Season of Celebrity.
Googe. Fly, The.
Gorman, L. Billboard girl.
Gouri. Mistake.
Graves, R. Blue-Fly, The.
Herrick. Amber Bead, The.
Holub. Fly, The.
On the Origin of the Contrary.
Howitt, M. Spider and the Fly, The.
Issahakian. Don't kill that fly!
Kerouac. In my medicine cabinet.
Lear, E. There was an old person of Skye.
Little, G. Fallen horse.
Lovelace, R. Fly about a Glass[e] of Burnt Claret, A.
Lowell, R. Harriet.
Morris, M. Pre-Carnival Party.
Mountain, M. One fly everywhere the heat.
Nash, O. Fly, The.
Nemerov. Truth.
Ní Chuilleanáin. Dead Fly.
Noyes, A. Cure, The.
Oldys. On a Fly Drinking out of [*or* from] His Cup.
Page, P. Evening Dance of the Grey Flies.
Patmore, C. Flesh-Fly and the Bee, The.
Perreault, J. Readymade.
"Pindar." To a Fly, Taken out of a Bowl of Punch.
Pizzarelli. BuzzZ.
Po Chü-i. After Collecting the Autumn Taxes.
Rilke. Black Cat.
Saitō Mokichi. Tanka: "Fly, A."
Smith, P. Poor old lady, she swallowed a fly.
Summerfield. Yesterday the House was Full of Flies.
Taylor, E. Upon a Spider Catching a Fly.
Tomlinson, C. Jam Trap, The.
Turner, C. Calvus to a Fly.
Unknown. Flea and a fly in a flue, A.
I heard a fly buzz when I died.
Jim Crack Corn; or The Blue Tali Fly.
Wallace, R. Fly in December.
Wiggin. Fly.
Yang Wan-li. Cold Fly.
Yeats. Long-Legged Fly.

Flight
Allingham. Swing Song, A.
Arakida Moritaké. Flying Flower, A.
Arendt. Ode I.

Bishop, E. Invitation to Miss Marianne Moore.
Brownstein. Stepping Out.
Brutus. Prayer: "O let me soar on steadfast wing."
"Carroll." Mad Hatter's Song, The.
Coatsworth. And Stands There Sighing.
Davis, L. Bob Hosey Is Dead.
De la Mare. Ride-by-Nights, The.
Dickey, J. Night Bird.
Dickinson, E. Bees are Black, with Gilt Surcingles—.
Donahue, J. Opiate Phobia.
Dransfield. Flying.
Duncan, R. Letting the beat go.
Guillén, J. Flight.
Gunn, T. Tamer and Hawk.
Hall, D. Old Pilot, The.
Hughes, T. My idleness curdles.
Hugo, V. Be like the bird, who.
Imbs. Wind Was There, The.
Kumin, M. Noted in The New York Times.
Li Po. Ancient Airs.
Lovelace, R. Falcon, The.
MacCaig. Solitary crow.
Magee, J. High Flight.
Mataka. Ornithology.
McClatchy. Dragonfly.
Melville, H. Man-of-War Hawk, The.
Merwin, W. Fly.
Meyers, B. Pigeons.
Mother Goose. Old Mother Goose.
Old Woman, Old Woman.
Noguere. Barney Bigard.
Probyn. As the Flower of the Grass.
Regan, J. In Flight.
Roberts, N. Gull'' Flight, The.
Rossetti, C. Fly away, fly away over the sea.
Sexton. To a Friend Whose Work Has Come to Triumph.
Sherman, F. Kite, A.
Smith, S. No Categories!
Spender, S. Icarus.
Stanton, M. Living Apart.
Stevenson, R. Swing, The.
T'ang Yin. On the Butterflies.
Tennyson, A. Cradle Song: "What does little birdie say?"
Thompson, R. He knows what height is, this hillside dweller.
Tranter. Lufthansa.
Trevor. Kite, A.
Ts'ao Chih. Vision, A.
Unknown. Baby Seeds.
Grey goose and gander.
Lady and the Magpie, The.
Once I saw a little bird going hop, hop, hop.
There was an old woman tossed up in a basket.
Van Walleghen. Age of Reason, The.
Very. Birds of Passage, The.
Wallace, R. Between Equals.
Warren, R. Evening Hawk.
Wilbur. All These Birds.
Wright, J. Poem by Garnie Braxton, A.
Yü Chi. Following the Rhymes of Bamboo Branch Songs in Response to Yüan Po-chang.
When I Was Young, I Stopped by a Wine Shop in Chi-men and Wrote This Poem, Inscribed It and Signed It, "Written by Lien the Eighteenth." The People of That District Have Since Taken It To Be a Poem of [the God] Lü Tung-pin! I Have Recorded It Here as an Amusement.
Yüan Mei. Flying Bells.
Yüan Mei. Things Seen.

Flirtation
Asclepiades. Although she's a girl, Dorkion.
Ayton. Song, A: On His Mistress.
Blok. In the Restaurant.
Burge. Disillusion.
Campbell, D. Small-town Gladys.
Clare, J. Oh sweet is the sound o' the dove's clapping wings.
Cockburn, C. Caution, The.
Congreve. Doris.
Cullen, C. Timid Lover.
Davies, W. Flirt, The.

Gascoigne.　For That He Looked Not upon Her.
Gay, J.　O Polly, you might have toy'd and kist.
Godfrey.　Our Lady.
　Wings.
Grimké, A.　Caprichosa.
Gunn, T.　Fever.
Herrick.　Lips Tongueless[e].
　Sho[o]e Tying, The.
　Silken Snake, The.
Lawrence, D.　Passing Visit to Helen.
Lennox, C.　Art of Coquetry, The.
Montagu, L.　To a Lady Making Love.
Nerval.　Girl Cousin, The.
Prior.　Ode, An: "Merchant, to secure his treasure, The."
Stanley, T.　Divorce, The.
Stevenson, A.　Sous-Entendu.
Stuart, M.　In The Orchard.
Surrey.　Love, that doth reign and live within my thought.
Theocritus.　Damoetas and Daphnis.
Unknown.　Hems gathered up, sash not yet tied.
Verlaine.　L'Allée.
Walwicz.　Big Tease.
Waring, B.　Breeze in Translation.
Wyatt, T.　Lover Showeth How He Is Forsaken of Such as He Sometime Enjoyed, The.
　Sonnet: 'The long love'.

Flodden Field, Battle of (1513)
Aytoun, W.　Then the Provost he uprose.
Elliot, J.　Flowers of the Forest, The.
Scott, W.　Battle, The ("By this, though deep the evening fell").
Unknown.　Battle of Flodden, The.

Flood, The
Bible, *O.T.*　And God saw that the wickedness of man was great.
Gasztold.　Noah's Prayer.
Halsall.　Return to Ararat.
Kendall, M.　Vision of Noah, The.
Lewis, C.　Late Passenger, The.
Merwin, W.　Noah's Raven.

Floods
Bloom, V.　Wat A Rain.
Bly, R.　Schoolcraft's Diary Written on the Missouri: 1830.
Brown, S.　Foreclosure.
Ch'ien T'ao.　Flood.
Clare, J.　Flood, The.
Davis, T.　C.T.'s variation.
Duris.　Ephesos.
Erdrich.　I Was Sleeping Where the Black Oaks Move.
Foulcher.　After the Flood.
Goedicke.　Lucky.
Holub.　Brief Thoughts on Floods.
Keithley.　Fourth Day of the Flood, The.
Knight, E.　Poem to Galway Kinnell, A.
Liu Ya-tzu.　Filled with Emotions on the Moon-ferrying Bridge at Arashiyama.
Marvell.　Eyes and Tears.
McAuley, J.　Song of Shem.
Mu Hua.　Rhyme-Prose on the Sea.
Ovid.　Floods, by nature enemies to land, The.
Phạm Quý Thích.　Summer Drought.
Plisetsky.　Pipe, The.
Quarles.　On the Two Great Floods.
Su Tung-p'o.　Days of Rain; the Rivers Have Overflowed.
Wier.　Flood, The.
Wright, J.　To Flood Stage Again.
Wright, J.　Beanstalk, Meditated Later, The.
　Flood Year.
Wu Chia-chi.　In the morning they build embankments against floods.

Florence, Italy
Hoffman, D.　È, the Feasting Florentines.
Lawrence, D.　Bat.
Levy, A.　Reminiscence, A.
Raine, K.　Daisies of Florence.
Swenson, M.　Above the Arno.
Zivancevic.　Florence.

Florida
Becker, R.　In Pompano Beach, Florida.

Bishop, E.　Florida.
Hughes, L.　Florida Road Workers.
Rakosi.　Florida.
Sholl.　Distinct Call of the Alligator, The.
Stevens, W.　Farewell to Florida.
　Nomad Exquisite.
Unknown.　Removal, The.
Woolson.　Florida Beach, The.

Florists
Koch, K.　Girl and Baby Florist Sidewalk Pram Nineteen Seventy Something.
Roethke.　Old Florist.

Flowers
Allard.　Snow by the window paper flowers gathering dust.
Amichai.　Look, thoughts and dreams weave over us.
Arakida Moritaké.　Flying Flower, A.
Ashbery.　Picture of Little J. A. in a Prospect of Flowers, The.
Atwood.　Flowers.
Basho.　Finis.
　Worshipping at the Great Shrine At Ise.
Benn.　Little Aster.
Betjeman.　Licorice Fields at Pontefract, The.
Binyon.　Harebell and Pansy.
Blake, W.　Blossom, The.
　Garden of Love, The.
Blunden.　Vlamertinghe.
Bodecker.　Garden Calendar.
Bromley, A.　Teel St. Trailer Court.
Brooke, R.　Old Vicarage, Grantchester, The.
Brooks, G.　Coora Flower, The.
Browning, E.　Deserted Garden, The.
　Sonnet: "Belovèd, thou hast brought me many flowers."
Browning, R.　Flower's Name, The.
Bryant, W.　Death of the Flowers, The.
　Painted Cup, The.
Carruth, H.　This Decoration.
Cavalcanti.　Sonnet: To His Lady Joan, of Florence.
Celan.　Psalm: "No one kneads us again out of earth and clay."
Ceravolo.　Dangers of the Journey to the Happy Land.
Chang Yü.　In a Boat on the Cha River.
Chao Meng-fu.　Inscribed on a Wall Painting of Assembled Immortals.
Chatterton.　There Lackethe Somethynge Stylle.
Ch'ien Ch'ien-i.　No Flowers.
　Poem on Drinking Wine with the Degree-Holder Ku.
Ch'in Kuan.　Spring Rain.
Chiyojo.　From the mind.
Chōkū.　Tanka: "Arrowroot flowers."
Chu Shu-chen.　Plaint.
Clare, J.　First Love.
Cole, C.　Pimpernel.
Coleridge, M.　Poison flower that in my garden grew, The.
Compiuta Donzella.　In the season when the world leafs and flowers.
Constable, H.　Of his Mistress, upon Occasion of her Walking in a Garden.
Cook, S.　Flowers in Town, The.
　Spring Flower, The.
Cooper, J.　Morning on the St. John's.
Cope, W.　Flowers.
Crane, H.　To Emily Dickinson.
Creeley.　Flower, The.
Crist.　She has gone.
Crouch, S.　Chops Are Flyin.
Cummings, E.　If everything happens that can't be done.
　In time of daffodils(who know.
Custance.　Candle-Light.
Davies, W.　Hill-Side Park, The.
Day Lewis.　Christmas Rose, The.
　Two Songs.
Dayre.　Morning Compliments.
De la Mare.　Lucy.
　Me.
　Two gardens see!—this, of enchanted flowers.
De Tabley.　Study of a Spider, The.
Dickinson, E.　Apparently with no surprise.
　Bloom—is Result—to meet a Flower.

Clover's simple Flame, The.
　Come slowly—Eden!
　Did the Harebell loose her girdle.
　My nosegays are for Captives.
Dobell, S.　Chanted Calendar, A.
Doolittle, H.　At Baia.
　Evening.
　Garden.
　Sea Rose.
　Sea Violet.
　White World.
Dorn, E.　Song, A.
Duncan, R.　Glimpse, A.
DuPlessis, R.　Since the narcissus bud.
Emerson, R.　Humble-Bee, The.
　Rhodora, The [On Being Asked Whence Is the Flower].
Enright, D.　Flowers.
Fainlight, R.　Archive Film Material.
Faiz.　Fragrant Hands.
Farjeon, E.　First Gathering.
　Flower-Seller, The ("Flower-seller's fat, The").
"Field."　Penetration.
　Sullenness.
　Unbosoming.
Foster, J.　Moving.
Francis, R.　Bouquets.
　Exclusive Blue.
Fraser, K.　Flowers.
　Frammenti Romani.
Freneau.　Wild Honey Suckle, The.
Frost, R.　Leaves Compared with Flowers.
　Subverted Flower, The.
　Tuft of Flowers, The.
Fumi Saito.　Tanka: "Even the black gloves."
　Tanka: "Sweeter than a song."
Fumiko.　Tanka: "Although blooming."
　Tanka: "Each year."
　Tanka: "That hill."
Gascoigne.　World as Garden, The.
Gates, L.　On the jewelweed.
Ginsberg, A.　In Back of the Real.
Glück, L.　Field Flowers.
　Mock Orange.
Goethe.　Found.
Gonzalez, A.　Little Rosebud Girl.
Goodison.　Kenscoff.
Graham, J.　Opulence.
Graves, R.　Gardener.
　Troll's Nosegay, The.
Gray, J.　Poem: "Geranium, houseleek, laid in oblong beds."
Guest, B.　Heavy violets there is no way.
Gunn, T.　Messenger, The.
　Moly.
Hafiz.　Lesson of the Flowers, The.
Hamburger, M.　Weeding.
Hardy, T.　Lodging-House Fuchsias, The.
Harr, L.　Late snowfall;.
　Until it alights.
Harter.　White flowers.
Harwood, G.　Sea Anemones, The.
Hatsui Shizue.　Scattered petals gather on the road.
Hayden, R.　Night-Blooming Cereus, The.
Heath, R.　On Clarastella walking in Her Garden.
Heinze.　Late Flowers.
Hemans.　Night-Blooming Flowers.
Herbert, G.　Flower, The.
　Life.
Herrick.　Meditation for His Mistress[e], A.
　To Blossoms.
　To Daffodils [or Daffadills].
　To Marygolds.
　To Violets.
　Why Flowers Change Color.
Hitchcock.　Scattering Flowers.
Hitomaro.　When I gathered flowers.
Ho Ching-ming.　Alone I stand, facing the flowers' shade.
Ho Xuan Huong.　On Picking Flowers.
Hoffenstein.　You buy some flowers for your table.
Holland, R.　Foolish Flowers.
Hope, A.　Flower Poem.
Hoshino.　O brightness / of peony's buds.

Housman, A. I hoed and trenched and weeded.
When green buds hang in the elm like dust.
Howitt, M. Buttercups and Daisies.
Hoyt, C. Those camellias.
Hsüeh T'ao. Willow Catkins.
Hunt, L. Story of Rimini, The.
Izumi. Come quickly—as soon as.
I cannot say.
Jackson, R. Lady's Way.
Jennings, E. Her Garden.
Jenyns. To a Nosegay in Pancharilla's Breast.
Jones, J. Flowers always know what they.
Jones, P. In the Formal Garden.
In the Park.
Kao Ch'i. Seeking out Hermit Hu.
Kaplinski, J. White clover will not ask anything.
Keats. Sweet Peas.
Kenyon, J. Peonies at Dusk.
Ki no Tsurayuki. No, the human heart.
Kim, S. Flowers in the Mountains.
King, H. Contemplation upon Flowers, A.
Kinnell. Flower Herding on Mount Monadnock.
Kintsune. Flowers whirl away, The.
Kitahara Hakushū. Tanka: "After letting my wife."
Tanka: "Autumn bellflower."
Tanka: "My uncle."
Tanka: "Strong scent, The."
Komunyakaa. Venus's-Flytraps.
Kovner. Of All My Loves.
Kung Tzu-chen. Miscellanies of the Year Chi-hai.
Lamb, E. Leaving all the morning glories closed.
Pausing.
Landor, W. Faesulan Idyll.
Lawrence, D. Andraitx—Pomegranate Flowers.
Bavarian Gentians.
Flowers and Men ("Flowers achieve their own floweriness and its's a miracle").
Le Gallienne. Ballad of London, A.
Library in a Garden, A.
Lee, L. Irises.
Levertov. Earliest Spring.
Li Ch'ing-chao. Tune: "Magnolia Blossoms, Abbreviated" ("From the pole of the flower vendor").
Li Shang-yin. Fallen Flowers.
For Lotus Flower.
Hibiscus Flowers.
In a Day.
Peonies.
Liu K'o-chuang. Leaving the City.
Liu Yu Hsi. Bamboo Branch Song.
Lloyd, D. Quietly shaping.
Lovelace, R. To Lucasta: The Rose.
Lowell, A. Autumn.
Garden by Moonlight, The.
Left Behind.
Petals.
Weather-Cock Points South, The.
Lu Yu. How I Sailed on the Lake till I Came to the Eastern Stream.
Wild Flower Man, The.
Macdonald, G. Things We Can Depend On.
Machi. Tanka: "This day in March."
Mackenzie, K. Ginger-flowers.
Madgett. Woman with Flower.
Mahadevi. So long as this breath fills your nostrils.
Mansfield, K. Secret Flowers.
Marvell. Picture of Little T. C. in a Prospect of Flowers, The.
Masaoka Shiki. During a trip.
First of May, The.
Tanka: "Day I had in mind, The."
Tanka: "Hawkers."
Tanka: "Illuminated."
Tanka: "In the house."
Tanka: "Makes me writhe."
Upon receiving potted peonies for a gift.
McGuckian. Collusion.
Orchid House, The.

McPherson, S. Phlox Diffusa: A Poem for My Fiftieth Birthday.
Mechthild von Magdeburg. How God Comes to the Soul.
Meenakshi. If Hot Flowers Come to the Street.
Meleager. Heliodora's Brows.
White violets flower.
Moore, J. Springburst.
Mori Ōgai. Tanka: "Trying to perch."
Tanka: "Your heart."
Mountain, M. Empty mailbox.
Faded flowers of the bed sheets autumn night.
Myles, E. Maxfield Parrish.
Naden. Poet and Botanist.
Neilson, J. Flowers in the Ward.
Nezahualcoyotl. Flower Songs.
Nezval. Lilac by the Museum on St. Wenceslas Square, The.
Nguyễn Trãi. Hibiscus, The.
Notley. Alice Ordered Me to be Made.
White Peacock, The.
Okamoto. Tanka: "Flower blooms, A."
Tanka: "Green leaves."
Tanka: "If I were to stand."
Tanka: "Where."
Okigbo. Passion Flower.
Oliver, M. Old Whorehouse, An.
Olson, C. Perfume / of flowers! A haw, The.
Ombres. Twelve.
Ono no Komachi. As certain as color.
Imperceptible / It withers in the world.
Ou-yang Hsiu. Spring Walk to the Pavilion of Good Crops and Peace.
Owens, G. Oh, who can make a flower?
Pagis. Siege.
Parun. Ballad of the Deceived Flowers.
Pizzarelli. Late in the evening.
Plath. Among the Narcissi.
I Am Vertical.
Po Chü-i. Buying Flowers.
Flower, A.
Flower Market, The.
Planting Flowers on the Eastern Embankment.
Pope, A. Garden, The.
Pound, E. Ts'ai Chi'h.
Prince, F. Babiaantje, The.
Raine, K. Daisies of Florence.
Rakosi. Menage, The.
Reese, L. Blackberry Blossoms.
Revell. Other the Wings, The.
Robinson, A. Posies.
Unum est Necessarium.
Rodriguez, J. Nasturtium Scanned.
Roethke. Carnations.
Geranium, The.
Shape of the Fire, The.
Transplanting.
Roseliep. Buttoning his fly.
Morning-Glory, The.
Unable.
Rossetti, C. Comparisons.
Crown of Windflowers, A.
Hope and Joy.
I dug and dug amongst the snow.
October Garden, An.
Passing and Glassing.
Why did baby die.
Rossetti, D. Woodspurge, The.
Rotella, A. Vase of peonies.
Rufinus. Here Rhodoklea / is a garland.
Russell, S. Poem: "I keep feeling all space as my image."
Samio. Tanka: "Because my room."
Tanka: "In the evening wind."
Sandburg, C. There Are Different Gardens.
Schuyler, J. Korean Mums.
Roof Garden.
Scott, W. Flowers and Trees.
Scovell. Flowers.
Seifert. Garland on the Wrist, A.
Seward. To the Poppy.
Sexton. Fury of Flowers and Worms, The.
Shakespeare, W. Flowers of Perdita, The.
Sonnet 99.
With fairest flowers,/ Whilst summer lasts.
Shapiro, D. After.

Shapiro, K. Cut Flower, A.
Shea, M. Held it.
Shelley, P. On a Faded Violet.
Shen Chou. Lady Picking Flowers, A.
Shepherd, R. White Days.
Shimoni. Flower Pot, The.
Shindo Chie. Space.
Shūji. Tanka: "After rainfall."
Tanka: "Red flowers."
Sitwell, D. Swans, The.
Sitwell, S. Kingcups.
Skelton, J. To Mistress Margery Wentworth.
Smart, C. For the doubling of flowers is the improvement of the gard'ner's talent.
Smith, C. Invitation to the Bee.
Sonnet Written at the Close of Spring [or Elegiac Sonnet].
Smith, W. Bachelor's-Buttons.
So Chong-Ju. Beside a Chrysanthemum.
Peony Afternoon.
Spiess. Marsh marigold.
Stein, G. From Stanzas in Meditation.
Stevenson, A. Himalayan Balsam.
Stevenson, R. To A Gardener.
Su Shih. Hibiscus.
Su Tung-p'o. Begonias.
Moon, Flowers, Man.
Swede. At my father's.
Swinburne. Before the Mirror.
Sundew, The.
Sylvester, J. Garden, The.
T'ang Yin. Inscribed on a Painting ("Places I go, leaning on my bramble cane, The").
Tao-chi. Bend after bend, the long embankment.
Flower-Rain Terrace, The.
Inscribed on My Little Painting of Plum Blossom and Bamboo.
Taylor, J. Violet, The.
Tekkan. Tanka: "With no flower buds."
Tennyson, A. City Child, The.
Flower in the crannied wall.
Song: "Come into the garden, Maud."
Thomson, J. Late Spring.
Tsung Ch'en. Song of Selling Flowers.
Tu Fu. Another Spring.
Sunset glitters on the beads.
Tu Mu. Sighing over Flowers.
Tuckerman, F. Coralie.
Turner, A. *Meditation Upon Ought.*
Unknown. Chalcan Female Song.
Crossing the river I pluck the lotus flowers;.
First time I saw you, The.
Flowers, flowers, high-no!
Forget-Me-Not, The.
Love Song: "Beautiful is she, this woman."
Lyric by Nine.
March winds and April showers.
Since the narcissus bud.
To Demeter.
When I look at her.
Urriola. Mister Snowman.
Vaughan, H. I walked [or walkt] the other day to spend my hour.
Venantius Fortunatus. To The Lady Radegund, With Violets.
Very. Autumn Flowers.
Columbine, The.
Lament of the Flowers, The.
Walker, A. Enemy, The.
Wang An-shih. Fresh Flowers.
Wang Chien. Palace Song.
Wat. Joke, A.
Wellesley. Walled Garden.
Wen Cheng-ming. As flowers fall at the river city, memories come to me.
Whitman, S. Morning-Glory, The.
Whitman, W. Orange Buds by Mail from Florida.
These I singing in spring collect for lovers.
Wilbur. In a Churchyard.
In the Field.
Williams, W. Flowers by the Sea.
Iris.
It is a small plant.
Ivy Crown, The.
Locust Tree in Flower, The.

Pink Locust, The.
Yellow Flower, The.
Willmot. Her breasts lift with her arms.
  If I go alone.
Wolfe, F. Four and Eight.
Wratislaw. Hothouse Flowers.
  White Lilies.
Wu of Han. People Hide Their Love.
  Summer Song.
Wu Wei-yeh. Ancient Feeling.
Xuân Diệu. Casting Fragrance to the Winds.
Yamakawa. I leave all the scarlet flowers.
  White roses I tried to braid in my hair, The.
Yang Chi. Thousands of flowers, thousands of
  petals.
Yang Shen. To the Tune "Stopping My Horse
  to Listen."
Yang-Ti, Emperor of Sui Dynasty. Flowers
  and Moonlight on the Spring River.
Yang Wan-li. Fallen Blossoms.
Yi, S. Precipice.
Yosano. I remember the days / When the lily.
  No camellia.
  Tanka: "Aster, The."
  Tanka: "Camellias."
  Tanka: "White blossoms bloom."
Yüan Mei. Busy.
Yukitsuna. Tanka: "Bloom finished, The."
Yün Shou-p'ing. Painting of Chrysanthemums
  in the Boneless Style of Hsü Ch'ung-ssu, A.
Zenmaro. Tanka: "No news of him."
Ziedonis. That was a beautiful summer.

Flutes
Austin, M. Shoshone Wedding Song.
Browning, E. Musical Instrument, A.
De Mello Breyner. Flute, The.
Fyleman. Fairy Flute, The.
Han. Oaten Pipe.
Hongo. Something Whispered in the
  Shakuhachi.
Kabir. Flute of interior time is played whether
  we hear it or not, The.
Krohn. My Flute.
Li Po. Spring Night in Lo-Yang—Hearing a
  Flute.
Lowell, A. Music.
Mirabai. Song of the flute, O sister, is
  madness, The.
Muldoon, P. Lass of Aughrim, The.
Okigbo. Lament of the Flutes.
Shen Chou. White clouds like a scarf enfold
  the the mountain's waist.
T'ang Yin. Inscribed on a Painting ("On the
  mountain, old trees, still green in autumn").
Tao-chi. Inscribed on My Ink Landscape
  Painting.
Unknown. Amateur Flute, The.
  Old [*or* Ould] Orange Flute, The.
  Tutor who tooted the flute, A.
Yün Shou-p'ing. Hearing a Flute at Broken
  Bridge.

Foals
Hughes, T. Yesterday he was nowhere to be
  found.
Juhász, F. Birth of the Foal.
Watkins, V. Foal.
See also **Horses**

Fog
Clare, J. November.
Clark, L. Fog in November, trees have no
  heads.
Dickinson, E. Sun and Fog contested, The.
Dodd, W. Like Deer Our Bodies.
Eberhart, R. Flux.
Greenwald, T. And, Hinges.
Guiney. Fog.
Hotham. Fog.
  Morning fog.
Jacobsen, J. Sea Fog, The.
Jarrell. Front, A.
Jeffers, R. Boats in a Fog.
Kiyowara Fukuyabu. River-Fog.
Lu Yu. Rain on the River.
McClintock, M. Twisting inland.
Merriam, E. Windshield Wiper.
Moore, L. In the Fog.
Oppen. Forms of Love, The.

Piercy. Quiet Fog, The.
Pratt, C. Fog has settled, The.
Raworth. Hot Day at the Races.
Samio. Tanka: "Day I was born, The."
Sandburg, C. Fog comes / on little cat feet,
  The.
  Lost.
T'ang Yin. Fog of night envelops the
  flowering trees, The.
Thoreau. Fog.
Unknown. Northern har, A.
Weeks, J. On the Great Fog in London,
  December 1762.
Yüan Mei. Next Day the Fog Was Even
  Worse, The.

Folly
"Akhmatova." Instead of wisdom—experience,
  a flat.
Deloney. Long have I lov'd this bonny Lasse.
Drayton. As Love and I, late harboured in one
  inn.
Euripides. But, o great offspring of the Ocean
  King.
Goldsmith, O. Song: "When lovely woman
  stoops to folly."
Mapanje. On His Royal Blindness Paramount
  Chief Kwangala.
More, H. Riot; or, Half a Loaf Is Better than
  No Bread, The.
Pope, A. Essay on Criticism, An.
Prior. Fable, A: "In Æsop's tales an honest
  wretch we find."
Sandburg, C. They have yarns / Of a
  skyscraper so tall they had to put hinges.
Suckling, J. Barley-Break, A.
Traherne. To the same purpose: he, not long
  before.
Unknown. Rakes of Mallow, The.
Yeats. Down by the salley gardens my love
  and I did meet;.

Food
Aaronson. Pesci Misti.
Alexander, E. Who I Think You Are.
Ancient Egyptian Oral Tradition. This love is
  as good.
Automedon. Having dined yesterday on a
  goat's foot.
Barkan. Two Grandmas.
Barker, G. How many apples grow on the
  tree?
Belloc. On Jam.
Bond, S. Tuesday Night Affair.
Brown, S. After Winter.
Brownstein. Jet Set Melodrama.
Burns, R. To a Haggis.
Chong, H. Note 25.
Cisneros, S. Good Hot Dogs.
Cornish, S. Your Mother.
Coward. Any Part of Piggy.
Crinagoras. Here are grapes ready to turn to
  wine.
Davidson, M. Framing.
Davies, J. Author Loving These Homely
  Meats, The.
De la Mare. Miss T.
Dunbar, P. When de Co'n Pone's Hot.
Emanuel, L. What Ely Was.
Erdrich. Windigo.
Evans, M. When in Rome.
Flanders, J. Dandelion Greens.
Gibson, W. Essay on Lunch.
Gloria. Milkfish.
Gonzales, R. Praise the Tortilla, Praise the
  Menudo, Praise the Chorizo.
Greenwald, T. Coordinating cities gulls still
  gull, and, arms binged with wine, as wine.
Guest, E. Lemon Pie.
  Sausage.
Herrick. Custard, The.
  Grace for Children, The.
  To His Book[e] ("Make haste away, and let
  one be").
  Upon Jack and Jill: Epigram.
Hongo. Who Among You Knows the Essence
  of Garlic?
Hood, T. Epicurean Reminiscences of a
  Sentimentalist.

Ishikawa Takuboku. Tanka: "Words from."
Jonson, B. Cocklorrel woulds needs have the
  devil his guest.
  Hymn to Comus.
  Inviting a Friend to Supper.
Kākkai Pātiṇiyār Naccellaiyār. What Her Girl
  Friend Said to her lover on his return.
Kasdorf. When our women go crazy, they're
  scared there won't be.
Kenyon, J. Potato.
King, B. Pessimist, The.
Kinzie. Heat-heavy creatures.
Kollar. Sunday Matinee.
Kuriyiraiyar. What Her Friend Said Criticizing
  Him to Give Her Strength.
Lawrence, D. Food of the north tastes too
  much of the fat of the pig, The.
Lee, L. Eating Alone.
Levertov. Stir the holy grains, set.
Levine, P. Simple Truth, The.
Li Ch'ing-chao. Day of Cold Food, The.
Long, D. Number Four.
Lyly, J. Serving Men's Song, A.
MacBeth. Ode to English Food, An.
Major, C. Beaulieu.
Margolis, G. For the Woman at the Fast-Food
  Fish Place Who Called Me Pig.
Martial. Inviting a Friend to Supper.
McDonald, W. Children of Saigon, The.
McKay, C. Tropics in New York, The.
McOrlan. Horse butcher, The.
"Meredith." We may live without poetry,
  music and art.
Mitchell, A. Giving Potatoes.
Moody, F. Sappho Burns Her Books and
  Cultivates the Culinary Arts.
Moore, M. To a Chameleon.
Moore, T. Oh Dick! You may talk of your
  writing and reading.
Morley, C. Animal crackers, and cocoa to
  drink.
Mother Goose. King Arthur.
  To sleep easy at night.
Mus. Conserves.
Nash, O. I Can't Have a Martini, Dear, but
  You Take One, or, Are You Going to Sit
  THere Guzzling All Night?
  Parsnip, children, I repeat, The.
  Private Dining Room, The.
Nemerov. Grace to Be Said at the
  Supermarket.
  Lobsters.
Newcastle, M. Dissert, A.
  Nature's Cook.
Nichols, G. Like a Beacon.
Norris, K. Stomach.
Padgett, R. Lucky Strikes.
Parra, N. Inflation.
Peacock, M. Devolution.
Phillips, C. Sunday.
Piercy. Attack of the Squash People.
Pilinszky. Paraphrase.
Pizzarelli. Brim-shadow, The.
Po Chü-i. Eating Bamboo-Shoots.
Prelutsky. Spaghetti Nut, The.
Ransom, J. Survey of Literature.
Rexroth, K. Observations in a Cornish
  Teashop.
Richardson, F. Pantry Ghosts, The.
Rieu. Lost Cat, The.
Rios, A. Chinese Food in the Fifties.
Rosen, M. Christmas Dinner.
Rossetti, C. Three plum buns / To eat here at
  the stile.
Rotella, A. Breakfast alone.
Roumer. Peasant Declares His Love, The.
"Sagittarius." Passionate Profiteer to His Love,
  The.
Salimon. Food-Factory Kitchen.
Scott, W. Fire, with well-dried logs supplied,
  The.
Shen Chou. Bamboo Villa, The.
Smith, B. American Lunch.
Smith, S. Salad, A.
Snyder, G. Song of the Taste.
Soto. Soup, The.
Spencer, B. Part of Plenty.

Steele, T. Joseph.
Stevenson, A. Larousse Gastronomique.
Strand. Pot Roast.
Swenson, M. Salt, The.
Swift, J. Epigram on Fasting.
Swirszczynska. White Wedding Slippers.
Tadic. I Ask.
TallMountain. Good Grease.
Taylor, B. Those Flapjacks of Brown's.
Taylor, E. Meditation 150 (Second Series).
Tu Fu. For Li Po.
Turk. Thank You, Jesus, for this day.
Turner, A. On the Nature of Food.
Tyler, R. Love Song: "By the fierce flames of love I'm in a sad taking."
Unknown. Dish for a Poet, A.
 Dried Apple Pies.
 Gingerbread Man, The.
 I Had But Fifty Cents.
 If ("If all the land were apple-pie").
 Little King Boggen, he built a fine hall.
 Little Man and Maid, The.
 Miss Foggerty's Cake.
 Mr. Finney's Turnip.
 On a Gentleman's Complaining to a Lady That He Could Not Eat Meat.
 On Tomato Ketchup.
 Scones.
 Suet Dumpling, The.
 There was an old man of Tobago.
 Visit from Mr. Fox, A.
Untermeyer, L. Food and Drink.
Updike. On the Inclusion of Miniature Dinosaurs in Breakfast Cereal Boxes.
Virgil. Hostesse, The.
Weigl. Last Lie, The.
Wells, C. Universal Favorite, The.
Wendt. After a Class in Seaweed.
Whitney, I. And now let mee dispose such things.
Wilbur. *Rillons, Rillettes,* they taste the same.
Willmot. Cheeses, pâté.
Wodehouse, P. Gourmet's Love-Song, The.
Yang Shih-ch'i. Following the Rhymes of Shao-pao Huang's Poem on Being Moved While Visiting the Farmers.
Zach. War Confession.
See also **Cooking and Cooks; Eating; Gluttony and Gluttons**
Food Poisoning
Unknown. Dog Shark.
Fools
Barnes, W. Sam'el Down vrom Lon'on.
Bernard. To see the lark, delighted, dare.
Browne, W. Love who will, for I'll love none.
Burns, R. Holy Fair, The.
 So vile was poor Wat, such a miscreant slave.
Cameron, N. Compassionate Fool, The.
Clare, J. Lout, The: "For Sunday's play he never makes excuse."
Creeley. Counterpoint, A.
Cummings, E. May my heart always be open to little.
Donne. Triple Fool[e], The.
Egerton, S. Liberty, The.
"Ephelia." To a Proud Beauty.
Farquhar. Song, A.
Franklin, B. Bits of Wisdom.
Hewitt, J. Ireland.
Hoskyns. Upon a Fool.
Jonson, B. On Don Surly.
 To Fool or Knave.
Juvenal. Fortune a Goddess is to Fools alone.
Landor, W. Plays.
Leonovich. I have to write a page.
Logau. Fools and Wise Men.
Lovelace, R. Fool much bit by fleas put out the light, A.
Mackenzie, K. Fool, The.
Martial. To a Friend an Epigram: Of him.
Pope, A. Another [Epigram].
 Epigram from the French: "Sir, I admit your general [or gen'ral] Rule."
Prior. Epigram: "Yes, every poet is a fool."
Ralegh, W. Sir Walter Ra[u]le[i]gh to His Son[ne].
Ristovic. Time of fools is coming.

Shakespeare, W. Motley's the Only Wear.
Shen Chou. Returning Home at Dusk from Town, on the Fifteenth of the Seventh Month.
Tadic. Fool, The.
Unknown. He Who Knows ("He who knows not and knows not [that he knows not]").
 Silly boy, wert you but wise.
 When people see the man of Cold Mountain.
 Wise men, you have cast me aside.
 You can lead a horse to water.
Yeats. Symbols.
See also **Jesters**
Football
Brooke, R. New Boy's View of Rugger.
Dyson, E. Friendly Game of Football, A.
Gildner. First Practice.
Hirsch, E. After the Last Practice.
Holden, J. Losers.
Jackson, R. For Thurman Thomas.
Jenkins, L. Football.
Komunyakaa. White Port and Lemon Juice.
Mason, W. Football.
Rice, G. Alumnus Football.
Saunders, A. Funky Football.
Updike. September.
Wright, J. Autumn Begins in Martins Ferry, Ohio.
Wrigley, A. Owdham Footbo'.
See also **Soccer**
Forbidden Fruit
Carew, T. Secrecy [or Secresie] Protested.
Hewitt, J. Tryst.
Milton. As when of old some orator renowed.
Shakespeare, W. At the Moated Grange.
Sharpless. *Paradise Lost* as a Haiku.
Ford, Ford Madox
Lowell, R. Ford Madox Ford ("Lobbed ball plops, then dribbles to the cup, The").
 Ford Madox Ford ("Taking Ford's dictation on Samuel Butler").
Williams, W. To Ford Madox Ford in Heaven.
Fordham, Alphonse Campbell
Fordham. In Memoriam. Alphonse Campbell Fordham.
Fordham, Edward
Fordham. Mr. Edward Fordham.
Forest Fires
Melville, H. Uninscribed Monument on One of the Battlefields of the Wilderness, An.
Reed, J. Lost Silvertip.
Snyder, G. Text, The.
Foresters
Unknown. I Have Been a Foster.
Forests
Ausonius. Oft in her Glass the musing Shepherd spies.
Bernstein, O. At Woods' Edge.
Bialik. Pool, The.
Birney. Slug in Woods.
Blake, W. Laughing Song.
 Tyger, The.
 Blind. Entangled.
Bly, R. Solitude Late at Night in the Woods.
Brautigan. Boat, A.
Bryant, W. Inscription for the Entrance to a Wood.
Buson. That axe that I hear.
Casement. Forest Thoughts.
Chu Yi-tsun. Deepening-Green Pavilion.
Chu Yün-ming. Landscape Painted on a Fan—Echoing a Poem by Wen Cheng-ming, A.
Clare, J. Gipsies seek wide sheltering woods again, The.
Cole, T. Lament of the Forest, The.
Coleridge, M. Witches' Wood, The.
Cowley, M. Piney Woods.
Dafydd ap Gwilym. Woodland Mass, The.
D'Annunzio. Rain in the Pine Wood.
Davenant. Countess of Anglesey lead Captive by the Rebels, at the Disforresting of Pewsam, The.
Dickey, J. By Canoe through the Fir Forest.
Doolittle, H. Pursuit.
Dransfield. In the forest, in unexplored.
Eliot, T. Usk.

Emerson, R. Waldeinsamkeit.
Finkelstein, N. Track.
Frost, F. Christmas in the Wood.
Frost, R. Come In.
 In winter in the woods alone.
 Stopping by Woods on a Snowy Evening.
Galvin, B. Pitch Pines.
Garrigue. Forest.
Gascoyne. Cage, The.
Graves, R. Gift of Sight.
Hagiwara Sakutaro. So Terrifyingly Melancholy.
Hall, D. Poet at Twenty, A.
Harasymowicz. Woods.
Hardy, T. In a Wood.
Henderson, D. Song of Devotion to the Forest.
Herbert of Cherbury. Sonnet Made upon the Groves near Merlou [or Merlow] Castle.
Holub. Forest, The.
Hoover, P. Heart's Ease.
Hughes, T. Modest Proposal, A.
Jarrell. House in the Wood, The.
Kenyon, J. Depression in Winter.
Kipling, R. Way Through The Woods, The.
Lampman. In November.
Lanier, S. Ballad of Trees and the Master, A.
Larkin, P. Is it for now or for always.
Lee-Hamilton. Among the Firs.
Lin Pu. Trail among the Pines, A.
Longenbach. What You Find in the Woods.
MacLean, S. Hallaig.
MacNeice. Woods.
Mandelstam. Shy speechless sound, The.
 Whoever Finds a Horseshoe.
McGrath, C. James Wright, Richard Hugo, the Vanishing Forests of the Pacific Northwest.
McGrath, T. Remembering the Children of Auschwitz.
Merrill, J. Pyroxenes, The.
Merwin, W. Asians Dying, The.
Murray, L. Noonday Axeman.
Nicholls, J. Timeless.
Okamoto. Tanka: "Twenty days."
Okigbo. Banks of reed.
 For he was a shrub among the poplars.
 Image insists, An.
 Lion-hearted cedar forest, gonads for our thunder.
 Suddenly becoming talkative.
Oliver, M. Sleeping in the Forest.
Pritchard, N. Cassandra and Friend.
 Landscape with Nymphs and Satyrs.
 Narrow Path, The.
Publius Papinius Statius. Forest felled, A.
Randall, J. Valediction, A.
Ransom, J. First Travels of Max.
Ray, H. Wood Carols.
Reeves, W. Passing of the Forest, The.
Roberts, G. Burnt Lands.
Rolls. Rain Forest.
Rukeyser, M. Then I Saw What the Calling Was.
Sacchetti. Catch: On a Wet Day.
Saitō Mokichi. Tanka: "All that past life."
Siddal. Silent Wood, A.
Simic. Ballad: "What's that approaching like dust like poverty."
Smith, S. I rode with my darling in the dark wood at night.
 Little Boy Lost.
Södergran. Forest Lake.
Sousa, N. Appeal.
Tasso. "Woods and the rivers are silent," The.
Thomas, E. Combe was ever dark, ancient and dark, The.
 Dark Forest, The.
 Green Roads, The.
Tomlinson, C. In Arden.
Tóth, J. Forest.
Treece. Horror.
 Magic Wood, The.
Tuckerman, F. Dark fens of cedar; hemlock-branches gray.
Unknown. Glyn Cynon Wood.
 My Hope, My Love.
Very. Indian's Retort, The.

Wagoner, D. Lost.
  Staying Alive.
Wang Chiu-ssu. I love the serenity of living
  in the woods.
Warren, R. Caribou.
Whittemore, R. Departure, The.
Wills, J. Forest stands, The.
Wordsworth, W. Nutting.
Wright, J. Fit against the Country, A.
  On the Skeleton of a Hound.
Wright, J. Rainforest.
Wright, R. Coming from the woods.
Wrigley, R. Ravens at Deer Creek.
Yagi. Genitals of woods, The.
Yeats. Ragged Wood, The.

Forges
Heaney, S. Casualty.
  Forge, The.

Forgetfulness
"Akhmatova." Instead of wisdom—experience,
  a flat.
Amichai. If I forget thee, Jerusalem.
Ammuvanar. What She Said ("Friend, listen").
Avidan. Recurring Opportunity.
Bennett, L. Home Sickness.
Bensley. One's Correspondence.
Benson, S. Now I Have Nothing[. Even the
  joy of loss].
Bromige. Log.
Browning, R. Memorabilia.
Carpenter, W. Keeper, The.
Davidson, M. Sensation Type and His Friends,
  The.
Forbes, D. Recension Day.
Garrigue. Song for "Buvez les Vins du
  Postillion"—Advt.
Hall, D. Exile.
Hardy, T. Tess's Lament.
Ishikawa Takuboku. Tanka: "Forgetting."
Jackson, H. Two Truths.
Katayev. When I lie down to die.
Kennedy, X. To Someone Who Insisted I
  Look up Someone.
Levertov. Woman Meets an Old Lover, A.
Merwin, W. Losing a Language.
Millay, E. What lips my lips have kissed, and
  where, and why.
Mura. Natives, The.
Nagy, A. Like one who brought news from
  far.
O'Neill, R. I made a house of houselessness.
Osgood, F. Forgive and Forget.
Ou-yang Hsiu. Old Age.
Pagis. I Was Before I Was, who now.
Parra, N. Poems of the Pope, The.
Rossetti, C. First Day, The.
Smith, C. Nepenthe.
Sorescu. Segment, A.
Stickney, T. Pity.
Strand. Always so late in the day.
Swinburne. Anactoria.
Swirszczynska. She Does Not Remember.
Szymborska. End and the Beginning, The.
Teasdale. Water-Lilies.
Unknown. Walking the Wide Road.
Wevill. Namelessness.
Williams, C. Alzheimer's: The Wife.
Wyatt, T. Supplication, A.

Forgiveness
Aengus the Culdee. Prayer for Forgiveness, A.
Balfour. Best thing to give, The.
Benét, W. Brazen Tongue.
Berryman. Also I love him: me he's done no
  wrong.
Bible, *O.T.* Bless the Lord, O my soul.
  Psalm 130.
Bidart. Confessional.
Chesterton, G. Ballade D'une Grande Dame.
Coleridge, S. Epitaph: "Stop, Christian passer-
  by!—Stop, child of God."
Columcille. Prayer for the Virgin.
Craveirinha. Seed is in Me, The.
Dickinson, E. Of God we ask one favor.
  "Remember me" implored the Thief!
Dombrovsky. I'm at the bottom again. The
  baron's there.
Donne. Hymn to God the Father, A.

If poisonous [*or* poysonous] mineral[l]s, and if
  that tree.
Frost, R. Forgive, O Lord, my little jokes on
  Thee.
Glatstein. How much Christian, so to speak,
  can I get?
  "You have heard that it was said, 'An eye'."
Goldberg, L. Prodigal Son, The.
Gouri. Piyyut for the New Year.
Graves, R. Hedges Freaked With Snow.
  In Her Only Way.
Hardy, T. Burghers, The.
  Peace-Offering, The.
Herbert, G. Love bade me welcome[: yet my
  soul drew back].
Herrick. His Prayer for Absolution.
Hope, A. Easter Hymn.
Inez. Absolving You.
Jackson, H. Two Truths.
Katayev. When I lie down to die.
Keech. True to the Best.
Kipling, R. Supplication of the Black
  Aberdeen.
Maksimovic. For Maria Magdalenes.
Markham, E. Outwitted.
Meynell, A. Beyond Knowledge.
Olds, S. After 37 Years My Mother
  Apologizes for My Childhood.
Orampokiyar. What Her Girl Friend Said,
  When the Woman Was About to Take Back
  Her Unfaithful Husband.
Osgood, F. Forgive and Forget.
Pankey. As We Forgive Those.
Pratt, J. Words and Thoughts.
Reznikoff. Day of Atonement.
Robinson, E. Unforgiven, The.
Rossetti, C. Ash Wednesday.
Rózewicz. Posthumous Rehabilitation.
Sangster, M. Forgiven.
Seward. Sonnet 32.
Shalom. Guard me, Oh God, from hating man
  my neighbor.
Shurin. Temptation.
Smith, S. I forgive you, Maria.
Springer, T. Giving and Forgiving.
Szymborska. Under a Certain Little Star.
Tate, N. Lord, Have Mercy.
Tennyson, A. We Kiss'd Again with Tears.
Trần Hiền Ân. My Mother's Son.
Unknown. Short Sermon.
  Whirlpool, The.
Waddington, M. Ten Years and More.
Warren, R. Revelation.
Whittier. Forgiveness.
Willard, N. Clearing the Air.
Williams, W. This Is Just to Say.

Forks
Simic. Fork.
Unknown. Lyric by Nine.

Fort McHenry, Maryland
Key. Star-Spangled Banner, The.

Fort Sumter, South Carolina
Timrod. Charleston.

Fortitude
Allen, E. Endurance.
Kipling, R. If you can keep your head when
  all [about you].
  Winners, The.
Moore, M. Nevertheless.
Smart, C. Fortitude.
Unknown. Don't Quit.
Wilcox, E. Solitude.
  Worthwhile.

See also **Endurance**

Fortune
Aeschylus. There is the sea.
Barnfield. Philomel.
Blamire. I've gotten a rock, I've gotten a reel.
Chudleigh. Wish, The.
Cockburn, A. Flowers of the Forest, The.
Crashaw. Against Hope.
Cummings, E. That melancholy / fellow'll
  play / his handorgan.
Cunningham, J. Epigram: "Good Fortune,
  when I hailed her recently."
Dekker, T. *et al.* Fortune and Virtue.

Drummond, W. Doth then the world go thus,
  doth all thus move?
Emerson, R. Guy.
Fynn, H. Adieu, to Fortune.
Gray, T. Now the golden morn aloft.
Greville, F. Sonnet: "Three things there be in
  mans opinion dear[e]."
Gunn, T. Wheel of Fortune, The.
Halevi. Fortune's Treachery.
Hardy, T. Hap.
Harington. Author, of His Own Fortune, The.
Herrick. Supreme Fortune Falls Soonest.
  To Fortune.
Horace. Remember, when blinde Fortune knits
  her brow.
Housman, A. Lads in their hundreds to
  Ludlow come in for the fair, The.
Juvenal. Fortune a Goddess is to Fools alone.
Koch, K. Locks.
MacNeice. After long trouble in a taedious
  way.
Narihira. I have always known / That at last I
  would.
Pindar. Greatness of *Mind* and *Fortune* too.
Rózewicz. What luck I can pick.
Shakespeare, W. Sonnet 29.
Sinda. You shall walk in peace!
Spalding, S. Fate.
Unknown. A! Mercy, Fortune; have pitee on
  me.
  Birds and their chatter overwhelm me with
  feeling, The.
  I think of all the places I've been.
  Sneezing.
  Wele, thu art a waried thing.
Virgil. MelibŒus. O fortunate old man!
Wyatt, T. Fortune.
  Fortune doth frown.
  In faith I not [well] what to say.
  Lover Rejoiceth the Enjoying of His Love,
  The.
Wylie. Hughie at the Inn.

See also **Fate; Luck; Chance**

Fortunetelling and Fortunetellers
Agathias. Astrologer, The.
Christopher. Palm Reader, The.
Churchill, C. Ghost, The.
Dante Alighieri. Earnest I look'd.
Diogenes Laertius. Tauromancy at Memphis.
Gauradas. Dear Echo, do me a favour; it's
  somewhat . . . *Some what?*.
Gildner. Meeting the Reincarnation Analyst.
Hardy, T. Echo-Elf Answers, The.
Homer. Here open'd Hell, all Hell I here
  implor'd.
Hsieh Chin. To the Fortuneteller Hsüeh T'ieh-
  yai.
Ríos, A. Madre Sofía.
Shakespeare, W. Jesu preserve your royal
  Majesty!
Stevenson, R. Spaewife, The.
Williams, T. Crepe de Chine.

Fossils
Blodgett. Fossil.
Dove, R. Fish in the Stone, The.
Ferlinghetti, L. Cro-Magnons carried stones
  for books.
Ferril. Time of Mountains.
Kendall, M. Fossil, A.
Lewis, J. Fossil, 1975.
McWatt. Stone.
Merrill, B. Fossil, The.

Fountains
Bogan, L. Roman Fountain.
Davidson, L. Silent crowd, The.
Davie. Fountain, The.
Duncan, R. Drinking Fountain, The.
Eberhart, R. Garden God, The.
Herrick. To the Water Nymphs, Drinking at
  the Fountain.
Jennings, E. Fountain.
Levertov. Fountain, The.
Longfellow, H. Talk not of wasted affection.
Lowell, J. Fountain, The.
Pettet. Echo.
Pound, E. Ts'ai Chi'h.
Rapin. Of Gardens.

Rilke. Roman Fountain.
Samio. Tanka: "When the gardener."
Sitwell, S. Fountains ("Proud fountains, wave your plumes").
Spaziani. Rome has a thousand fountains, and in May they sing.
Spenser. In the Bower of Bliss.
Wilbur. Baroque Wall-Fountain in the Villa Sciarra, A.
Wordsworth, W. Fountain, The.

Fourth of July
Cox, P. Brownies' Celebration, The.
Field, M. Fourth of July.
Fisher, A. Benjamin Jones Goes Swimming.
Hollander, J. Late Fourth, A.
Lowell, R. Fourth of July in Maine.
McGrath, T. End of the Line, The.
Peck, R. Four of July.
Pierpont, J. Fourth of July, The.
Swenson, M. July 4th.
Unknown. Independence Bell—July 4, 1776.
Williams, W. 4th of July.

Fox, Charles James
Scott, W. Nelson, Pitt, Fox.
Wordsworth, W. Lines;: "Loud is the Vale! the Voice is up."

Foxes
Angell, B. Fox's Song.
Carryl, G. Sycophantic Fox and the Gullible Raven, The.
Clare, J. Vixen, The.
Davies, E. Wily Fox, The.
Dickey, J. Dog Sleeping on My Feet, A.
Dyer, J. Tenants of an Abandoned Castle.
Dyment. Fox.
Fuller, J. Can-Can.
Grennan. Conjunctions.
Hughes, T. Thought-Fox, The.
Kennelly. Dream of a Black Fox.
Kirchwey. Matthew 8:20; And Jesus said to him.
Knowles, S. Fox Dancing.
La Fontaine. Fox and the Crow, The.
Levine, P. Fox, The.
Llwyd, H. Fox's Counsel, The.
Masefield. Fellow Mortal, A.
Fox knew well, that before they tore him, The.
Meredith, G. Young Reynard.
Milne, A. Three Foxes, The.
Montale. Eel, the North Sea siren, The.
Mozeen. Kilruddery Hunt, The.
Parry, R. Fox, The.
Rich, A. Abnegation.
Sackville-West. To Any M.F.H F. H.
Unknown. Owl and the Fox, The.
"Pax vobis," quod the fox.
Put your finger in Foxy's hole.
Visit from Mr. Fox, A.
Williams, T. Cried the Fox.
Wylie. Escape.

Foxgloves
Holland, R. Foolish Flowers.
Webb, M. Foxgloves.
Wolfe, F. Four and Eight.

France
Apollinaire. Stanzas Against Forgetting.
Ba. Nobility.
Barbauld. On the Expected General Rising of the French Nation.
Beckett, S. Dieppe.
Cannan. Rouen.
Caraion. Song from the Occupation Time.
Cendrars. Back then I was still young.
Clark, T. Going to School in France or America.
Claudian. For France.
Clifton, L. Women You Are Accustomed To, The.
Dehn, P. St. Aubin d'Aubigne.
Desnos. Night Watchman of Pont-au-Change, The.
Dove, R. Great Palaces of Versailles, The.
"Eliza." Epistle to John Walker, Esq., An.
Flecker. Riouperoux.
Grosholz. Remembering the Ardèche.
Hacker, M. Days of 1992.
Hopkins, G. Duns Scotus's Oxford.

Jonson, B. On English Monsieur.
Lincoln, M. Kings of France.
McOrlan. Hairdresser's, The.
Moore, M. To the Peacock of France.
O'Loughlin. Bunkers, The.
Paley, G. In Aix.
Péret. Hymn of the Patriotic War Veterans. Nungesser und Coli Sind Verreckt.
"Perse." Doors open on the sands, doors open on exile.
Ponge. Silent World Is Our Only Homeland, The.
Pound, E. Provincia Deserta.
Prévert. Barbara.
Rivers, C. Four Sheets to the Wind and a One-Way Ticket to France.
Selman, R. Avec Amour.
Shepherd, R. Lucky One, The.
Supervielle. Some day shall I be the one who let.
U Tam'si Tchicaya. Promenade, The.
Unknown. Humble Petition of the British Jacobins to their Brethren of France, The.
Mode of France, The.
Updike. Some Frenchmen.
Warton, J. Verses Written at Montauban in France, 1750.
Weaver, M. Luxembourg Garden.
My Father's Geography.
Whittier. Bartholdi Statue, The.
Wordsworth, W. England, 1802, III.
Wright, J. Winter Daybreak above Vence, A.

Francis of Assisi, Saint
Heaney, S. Saint Francis and the Birds.
Hecht, A. At the Frick.
Kinnell. Saint Francis and the Sow.
Miller, V. Trimming the Sails.
Orlovsky. I Dream of St. Francis.

Franco, Francisco
Wright, J. Eisenhower's Visit to Franco, 1959.

Franco-Prussian War
Rimbaud, A. Poster of Our Dazzling Victory at Saarbrucken, A.

Franconia Mountains
Ray, H. Lines Written on a Farewell View of the Franconia Mountains at Twilight.

Frankenstein
Barlow, G. Painting Drunken Twilight.
Field, E. Bride of Frankenstein, The.
Lochhead, L. Dreaming Frankenstein.
Young, D. Business of Love is Cruelty, The.

Franklin, Aretha
Giovanni. Poem for Aretha.

Franklin, Benjamin
Harris, A. Pioneers.

Fraternity. *See* Brotherhood

Fratricide
Very. Thy Brother's Blood.

Free Will
Atwood. Torture.
Auden. Long time since it seems today, A.
Frost, R. Road Not Taken, The.
Jonson, B. Epode: "Not to know vice at all, and keep[e] true state."
Rumi. Friend remarks to the Prophet, "Why is it," A.
Whittier. Overruled.
Wroth. Sonnet 48: "How like a fire doth love increase in me[e]."

Freedom
"Ada." Lines.
Adams, J. Cowboy's Life, The.
Ai. Twenty-Year Marriage.
Alegría. From the Bridge.
Angelou. Caged Bird.
"Antler." Ungag our souls!! Unstrangle our souls!! Unsmother our souls!!
Auden. Free One, A.
They wondered why the fruit had been forbidden.
Baranczak, S. February 8, 1980: And No One Has Warned Me.
Barbauld. Eighteen Hundred and Eleven.
On the Expected General Rising of the French Nation.
Barbour, J. Freedom [or Fredome].

Barry, M. Hymn of Freedom.
Bell, J. Bondsman's gloomy night has passed, The.
Bennett, L. Jamaica oman cunny sah!
Berggolts. Friends repeat: "All means are good."
Blake, W. Prince of Love, The.
Borowski. Two Countries.
Brathwaite, E. Citadel.
Brontë, E. When weary with the long day's care.
Browning, E. Hiram Powers' "Greek Slave."
Runaway Slave at Pilgrim's Point, The.
Browning, R. Why I Am a Liberal.
Brutus. Prayer: "O let me soar on steadfast wing."
Bryant, W. Conjunction of Jupiter and Venus, The.
Damsel of Peru, The.
Burns, R. De'il's [or Deil's] Awa wi' th' [or the] Exciseman, The.
For A' That and A' That ["Is there, for honest poverty"].
Scots, wha hae wi' Wallace bled.
Tree of Liberty, The.
Byron, G. Canto the Eleventh.
Sonnet on Chillon.
Stanzas: "When a man hath no freedom to fight for at home."
Carew, T. Song: The Willing Prisoner to His Mistress.
Causley. One day at a Perranporth pet-shop.
Cavalli. But first one must free oneself.
Now that the time seems all mine.
Char. Argument.
Disdained Apparitions.
Ch'ien T'ao. Returning to the Fields.
Chin. Composed Near the Bay Bridge (after a wild party).
Chukhonstev. Chaadayev on Basmannaya.
Chung-ch'ang T'ung. Speaking My Mind.
Clifton, L. To Bobby Seale.
Cohan. You're a grand old flag.
Coleman, E. Liberator, The.
Collins, W. Ode Written in the Beginning of the Year 1746.
Comfort, A. Notes for My Son.
Cornish, S. Cross Over the River.
Cowper, W. Negro's Complaint, The.
Craik. Friendship.
Crane, H. To Brooklyn Bridge.
Creeley. Ballad of the Despairing Husband.
Crouch, S. Like a Blessing.
Cruz, V. Puerta Rica.
Cullen, C. Wind Bloweth Where It Listeth, The.
Cummings, E. Am was. are leaves few this. is these a or.
As freedom is a breakfastfood.
If(touched by love's own secret)we,like homing.
Dao. Accomplices.
Darwish, M. Guests on the sea: Our visit is short.
Daryush. If your loved one prove unworthy, why then.
Dickinson, E. Could I but ride indefinite.
No Rack can torture me.
They shut me up in Prose.
Diop, D. Africa my Africa.
Listen, comrades of the flaming centuries.
do Espirito Santo. Where Are the Men Seized in this Wind of Madness?
Donne. "Batter my heart, three-person'd God; for you."
Canonization, The.
Doolittle, H. Helmsman, The.
Dove, R. Geometry.
Lady Freedom Among Us.
Dumas, H. Root Song.
Dunbar, P. Ante-Bellum Sermon, An.
Sympathy.
Duoduo. Untitled.
Du'o'ng Bá Trạc. Prison Life.
Egerton, S. Liberty, The.
Eliot, T. Burnt Norton.
Éluard, P. To Her of Whom They Dream.

Emerson, R. Freedom.
Give all to love;.
Merlin II.
Feaver. Coat.
Ferlinghetti, L. Dog trots freely in the street, The.
Francis, E. Rotogravure.
Fried, E. One Kind of Freedom Speaks.
Fuller, M. Freedom and Truth.
Gildner. Cabbage in Polish is kapusta—kapoosta.
Glück, L. Undertaking, The.
Gunn, T. Aquarium, The.
Tamer and Hawk.
Hacker, M. Open Windows.
Harper, F. Slave Mother, The.
Hayden, R. Frederick Douglass.
Runagate Runagate.
Hemans. Corinne at the Capitol.
Herbert, G. Religion stands on tip-toe in our land.
Herrera. Mission Street Manifesto.
Hirshfield, J. For the Women of Poland: December 1981.
Holly. Wreath of Holly, A.
Howe, J. Battle Hymn [or Battle-Hymn] of the Republic, The.
In the beauty of the lilies Christ.
Hughes, L. Dream Boogie.
Dream Variation[s].
Freedom Train.
Freedom will not come.
Let America Be America Again.
Words Like Freedom.
Hughes, T. Bull Moses, The.
Jaguar, The.
Huy Cận. Two Wooden Men, The.
Jarrell. Emancipators, The.
Woman at the Washington Zoo, The.
Jeffers, L. How High the Moon.
When I Know the Power of my Black Hand.
Jeffers, R. Coast-Road, The.
Shine, Republic.
Jefferson, T. Preamble to the Declaration of Independence.
Johnson, J. Fifty Years.
Lift every [or ev'ry] voice and sing.
Jordan, F. I love America where truth can be shouted from the housetops.
Jordan, J. I Must Become a Menace to My Enemies.
Joseph, J. Warning.
Kalvos. Altar of the Fatherland, The.
Keats. Song: "I had a dove and the sweet dove died."
Kefala. Freedom fighter, she said, A.
Kendrick, D. Sidney, Looking for her Mother.
Key. Star-Spangled Banner, The.
Kgositsile. Song for Ilva Mackay and Mongane.
Khlebnikov, V. Lone Performer, The.
Kim, C. Aerin I.
Bird.
Kim, Y. Sea of Lemon, The.
Kipling, R. Ode to Liberty.
Kirillov. We uncountable dread legions of Labor.
Kupriyanov. Epidemic / of freedom, An.
Lazarus, E. In Exile.
Levy, A. Magdalen.
Lewis, J. Time and Music.
Lincoln, A. Gettysburg Address, The.
Logau. Freedom.
Lovelace, R. To Althea, from Prison.
To Lucasta[, from Prison].
Vintage to the Dungeon, The.
Lowell, J. Letter Six—The Pious Editors' Creed.
Lucretius. Euphemisms of the love-blind.
MacLeish. Brave New World.
MacNeice. Fanfare for the Makers, A.
Sunlight on the garden, The.
Madgett. Midway.
Mandelstam. &[;Last Poems&];.
Mazzocco. Muertes.
McBride, M. Red Letters.
Meinke. Supermarket.

Milosz, C. Incantation.
Milton. On the Detraction Which Followed upon My Writing Certain Treatises.
Mnthali. Celebration, The.
Moore, T. Harp That Once through Tara's Halls, The.
Sound the Loud timbrel o'er Egypt's dark sea!
More, S. Minstrel Boy to the war is gone, The.
Moss, T. Lunchcounter Freedom.
Nagy, A. Sincerity.
To Freedom.
Nasrin. Border.
Character.
Neruda. Poet's Obligation.
Newcastle, M. Claspe, The.
Nguyễn Văn Năng. I Shall Not Die.
Norris, L. Pit Ponies, The.
Nortje. At Rest from the Grim Place.
Norton, C. Sonnet 7: "Like an enfranchised bird, who wildly springs."
Voice from the Factories, A.
Notley. Désamère.
O Riordain. Freedom.
Ofeimun. Handle for the Flutist, A.
Ologoudou. Liberty.
Oppenheimer, J. Poem in Defense of Children.
Paine, T. These are the times that try men's.
Park, N. Birds.
Parra, N. Inflation.
Patterson, R. Black Power.
Paulding. Neglected Muse! of this our western clime.
Perreault, J. Shoe.
Phan Trọng Quảng. Independence Day.
Pheraios. War Hymn.
Philips, K. Answer to Another Persuading a Lady to Marriage, An.
Piercy. Noon of the Sunbather.
Sabbath of Mutual Respect, The.
Pierpont, J. Fourth of July, The.
Pilkington, L. Song, A.
Po Chü-i. On Being Sixty.
Releasing a Migrant 'Yen' (Wild Goose).
Too Brilliant.
Polkowski. Noli Me Tangere.
Poole, E. Last Prayer.
Pound, E. Enormous tragedy of the dream in the peasant's bent / shoulders, The.
Raine, K. Eudaimon.
Ransom, J. Dog.
Ray, H. To My Father.
Reason. O Freedom! Freedom! O! how oft.
Spirit Voice, The; or Liberty Call to the Disfranchised (State of New York).
Reed, I. Railroad Bill, a conjure man.
Rilke. Someday there will be girls and women whose name will no longer mean.
Roethke. I knew a woman, lovely in her bones.
Rossetti, C. Promises like Pie-Crust.
Sandburg, C. Harbor, The.
Limited.
Seng-ts'an. Mind of Absolute Trust, The.
Sidney, P. Sonnet 47: "What, have I thus betrayed my liberty?"
Simpson, J. First of August in Jamaica, The. "No, Master, Never!"
Twilight Hour, The.
Skeeter. California, 1852.
Midwest, Midcentury.
Smith, S. Anger's Freeing Power.
Stafford, W. For Alexis Christa von Hartmann: Proved Not Guilty.
Steffen. Falcon to the Falconer, The.
Stewart, D. Silkworms, The.
"Struther." Freedom.
Sumangalamata. At last free.
Swenson, M. Weather.
Sykes, B. Cycle.
T'ao Ch'ien. Green pine grows in eastern garden, A.
Taylor, J. Trumpet of Liberty, The.
Tế Hanh. Mother.
Thomas à Becket. Columbia, the Gem of the Ocean.
Thompson, P. Emancipation.

Fugitive, The.
Prayer, A: "Oh, Lord! I lift my heart."
Tien Ch'ien. Freedom is Walking toward Us.
Tirolien. Ghetto.
Tolson. Festus Conrad.
Unknown. Christian's Prayer, The.
Freedom a Come Oh!
Freedom in the Air.
Go down, Moses.
I Thank God I'm Free at Las'.
Keep Your Eyes on the Prize.
Let My People Go.
No more auction block for me.
No More Beneath the Oppressive Hand.
O Freedom! / O Freedom!
Preamble to the Constitution of the United States.
Promises of Freedom.
Slavery chain done broke at last, broke at last, broke at last.
Swing low, sweet chariot.
We'll soon be free.
Uvavnuk. Great sea has set me in motion, The.
Vashon. Vincent Ogé.
Viiding. Speeches in the Interior.
Villanueva, A. Even the Eagles Must Gather.
Walker, M. For my people [everywhere singing their slave songs repeatedly: their].
Washington. Freedom Hair.
Watson, R. White Bird, The.
Weller. Ngungalari.
Wendel. We Shall Return, Luanda.
Wheatley, P. To the Right Honourable William, Earl of Dartmouth[, His Majesty's Principal Secretary of State for North America].
Whitman, A. Is manhood less because man's face is black?
Whitman, W. Commonplace I sing, The.
We two, how long we were fool'd.
Years of the modern! years of the unperform'd!
Whittier. Bartholdi Statue, The.
Laus Deo!
Lost Occasion, The.
Proem: "I love the old melodious lays."
Wilbur. Still, citizen sparrow, this vulture which you call.
Willis, N. To Charles Roux, of Switzerland.
Wordsworth, W. England, 1802 ("It is not to be thought of").
Foster-Mother's Tale.
Thought[s] of a Briton on the Subjugation of Switzerland.
To the Skylark.
Wright, J. Wednesday Night Prayer Meeting.
Wroth. Sonnet 14: "Am I thus conquered [or conquer'd]? have I lost the powers."
Sonnet 45.
Wyatt, T. If chance assigned [or assign'd].
Now must I le[a]rn[e] to live [or lyve] at rest.
Renouncing of Love, A.
Tangled [or Tanglid] I was [or was I] in [or yn] Love's snare.
Zangwill. At the Zoo.
Zu-Bolton. Struggle-Road Dance.

Freedom Train
Hughes, L. Freedom Train.

Freemasonry
Morris, R. Level and the Square, The.

Freezers
Armour. Hiding Place.

Freighters
Greenberg, A. Freight Train, Freight Train.
Levertov. Don't You Hear that Whistle Blowin'.
See also **Cargoes**

French Revolution
Barbauld. On the Expected General Rising of the French Nation.
Coleridge, S. France.
"Pindar." Hymn to the Guillotine.
Serge. Dialectic.
Tomlinson, C. Charlotte Corday.
Williams, H. To Dr. Moore, in Anser to a Poetical Epistle Written by Him in Wales.

French, The
Ái Lan. Deathless Autumn, A.
Hải Âu Tử'. Zoo Cages.
Hood, T. To Henrietta, on Her Departure for Calais.
Huỳnh Thúc Kháng. Comedy of the World, The.
Nguyễn Đình Chiểu. Blind Poet Looks at the World Outside, A.
Fleeing From Bandits.
Waiting for the East Wind.
Nguyễn Khuyến. At an Exposition.
Comedian Gets a Curtain Lecture, The.
On Hearing the Rail Cry.
To a Discarded Fan.
To a Statue.
O'Hara, F. Ode: Salute to the French Negro Poets.
Phan Bội Châu. Alarm Clock, The.
My Shadow and I.
To a Cuckoo.
Phan chu Trinh. Game of Chess, A.
Opera Actors.
Phan Trọng Quảng. Ricksha Man's Impromptu, A.
Phan Văn Hy. Ricksha man does quite a simple job, The.
Phan Văn Trị. Mosquito, you are blessed with all nice things!
Opera Actors.
T. P. Verses for the End of an Era.
Thiên Thê. Wrecking the Statue of Paul Bert.
Trần Cao Vân. It's mere child's play to die—who'd care to try?
Trần Tế Xu'o'ng. Lamenting the State of Confucian Scholarship.
New-Style Examinations.
No, Thank You!
What earthly use are these Confucian graphs?
Unknown. Epigram: "Says a Reverend Priest to a less Rev'rend friend."
Fourteenth of July, The.

Freud, Sigmund
Auden. In Memory of Sigmund Freud.
Heseltine, P. Limerick: "Young things who frequent picture-palaces, The."
Nemerov. Sigmund Freud.
Unknown. Limerick: "Young men who frequent picture palaces."
Wayman. Wayman in Love.

Friars
Chaucer. Friar's Prologue, The.
Ransom, J. Necrological.

Friends, Society of
Green, M. On Barclay's Apology for the Quakers.
Harriman, C. William Penn owned millions of.
Mollineux. Epistle, An: "Is Friends fled, or Love grown cold?"
Whittier. First-Day Thoughts.

Friendship
Ackerly. Prayer of an Unemployed Man.
Alcaeus. You who were once my friend.
Aldrich, T. Catch, A.
Amirthanayagam. There Are Many Things I Want to Tell You.
Annand. I Winna Let On.
Argentarius. Old Story, The.
Ashbery. Friends.
Train Rising Out of the Sea.
Auden. For Friends Only.
Augustine. Half Of Me.
Awoonor. First Circle, The.
Ayton. Upon Platonic Love: To Mistress Cicely Crofts, Maid of Honour.
Bekederemo. Abiku.
Belloc. They Say That in the Unchanging Place.
Berryman. Dream Song 45.
Winter-Piece to a Friend Away, A.
Bishop, E. Letter to N.Y.
Manuelzinho.
Shampoo, The.
Blackmur. Elegy for Five, An.
Blake, W. On Hayley.
Poison Tree, A.
To H[ayley].

Bly, R. After Drinking All Night with a Friend, We Go Out in a Boat at Dawn to See Who Can Write the Best Poem.
Late at Night During a Visit of Friends.
Bowles, W. To a Friend.
Braley, B. Loyalty.
Brett, L. My Mother's Friend.
Brontë, E. Love and Friendship.
Brown, A. Friends.
Brown, D. Still Later There Are War Stories.
Browning, E. L.E.L.'s Last Question.
Sleep, The.
Browning, R. Light Woman, A.
Waring.
Brutus. They hanged him, I said dismissively.
Burns, R. Auld Lang Syne.
To James Smith.
Callimachus. Someone told me, Heracleitus.
Calverley. Of Friendship.
Campbell, A. There is always a place for you at my table.
To My Friend.
Campion, T. Were My Heart as Some Men's Are.
Cheney-Coker. Letter to a Tormented Playwright.
Chin. Song of the Sad Guitar.
Chin Nung. Wearing a Worn-Out Coat.
Chipasula. Friend, Ah You Have Changed!
"Chrystos." For Sharol Graves.
Ciardi. What Johnny Told Me.
Clark, T. Friends.
Coleridge, H. To a Friend.
Coleridge, M. Contents of an Ink-bottle, The.
Friends—With a Difference.
Gifts.
Gone.
Mortal Combat.
Coleridge, S. Scars Remaining, The.
To William Wordsworth.
Colesworthy. Little word in kindness spoken, A.
Cook, E. To the Late William Jerdan.
Cooper, J. Long, Disconsolate Lines.
Corrothers. Me 'n' Dunbar.
Corso. I Met This Guy Who Died.
Cowley, A. It was a dismal and a fearful night.
On the Death of Mr William Hervey.
Cowper, W. Animals Enjoying Life.
Contemporaries all surpassed, see one.
Friendship.
My Pet Hare.
Craik. Friendship.
Creeley. Damon & Pythias.
For friendship / make a chain that holds.
Cuadra, A. Brief Letter to Donald Walsh (in memoriam).
Cullen, C. Tableau.
Dabydeen, D. Catching Crabs.
Dante Alighieri. Sonnet: "Guido, I wish that you and Lapo and I."
Sonnet: To Guido Cavalcanti.
Davies, J. Remembrance of My Friend Mr. Thomas Morley, A.
Davis, J. Warru.
Dawson, G. To a Friend.
Day Lewis. At Lemmons.
Derricotte. Friendship, The.
Dickinson, E. Are Friends Delight or Pain?
I should not dare to leave my friend.
I showed her Hights she never saw.
If anybody's friend be dead.
My friend must be a Bird.
Donne. To Mr I. L ("Blessed [or Blesst] are your north parts, for all this long time").
To Mr I. L ("Of that short Roll of friends writ in my heart").
To Mr. C.B.
Duncan, R. Among my friends love is a great sorrow.
Dunn, S. Men Talk.
Durem. Friends.
Edwards, R. When I was three I had a friend.
Eimers. No Friends of the Heart.
English, T. Ben Bolt.
Farjeon, E. Jenny White and Johnny Black.

"Field." Ah, Eros doth not always smite.
Field, R. Some People.
Fischer, H. There is a mystic borderland that lies.
Foss, S. House by the Side of the Road, The.
Frost, R. Telephone, The.
Time to Talk, A.
Fulton, A. What I Like.
Gallagher, T. Hug, The.
Gershwin. Babbitt and the Bromide, The.
Ginsberg, A. Green Automobile, The.
Googe. Of Money.
Grahn. Funeral Plainsong from a Younger Woman to an Older Woman, A.
Graves, R. At First Sight.
Green, M Sometimes I dress, with women sit.
Greville, F. Sonnet: "Three things there be in mans opinion dear[e]."
Gudzenko. Ballad about Friendship, A.
Guest, E. Friend's Greeting, A.
Gurney, I. Companion—North-East Dug-Out.
Hacker, M. Against Silence.
Eight Days in April.
Elevens.
Nights of 1964–1966: The Old Reliable.
Halevi. On Parting with Moses ibn Ezra.
Han Yü. Evening: for Chang Chi and Chou K'uang.
Hartnett. Person as Dreamer: We Talk about the Future, The.
Harwood, G. In The Park.
Haynes, C. Any Wife or Husband.
Herbert, G. Church-Porch, The.
Unkindness.
Herrick. His Age, Dedicated to His Peculiar Friend, Master John Wickes, under the Name of Posthumus.
To His Friend to Avoid Contention of Words.
To His Honoured and Most Ingenious Friend Mr. Charles Cotton.
Hill, G. Gasholders, russet among fields.
Mildams, marpools.
Horace. Horatian Canons of Friendship, The.
Housman, A. Shake hands, we shall never be friends, all's over.
Hsieh Chin. Wait until I too hang up my carriage.
Hsieh Ling-yün. Replying to a Poem from My Cousin Hui-lien.
Hsieh T'iao. In a Provincial Capital Sick in Bed.
Huang Tsun-hsien. Spending the Night in an Inn at Swatow and Writing about My Feelings, Sent to Liang Shih-wu.
Hughes, L. Poem: "I loved my friend."
Hughes, T. Six Young Men.
Ignatow, D. Two Friends.
Ivaska. K. H.
Jennings, E. Friendship.
Relationships.
Jones, J. Did you ever have a chipmunk for a friend?
Jordan, J. Grand Army Plaza.
Juan Chi. This summer's burning heat.
Kalidasa. This life on earth's a poison tree.
Keats. Bright star[, would I were stedfast as thou art—].
Keller, D. Friends, Outside, Night.
Kemble. To Mrs. Norton.
Kim, J. To a Nigerian Friend.
Kim, T. Banana Plant, The.
King, H. Change, The.
Klee. Friend, A.
Koch, K. Circus, The.
Lamb, C. Old Familiar Faces, The.
Langhorne. Studley Park.
Lawrence, D. Lies About Love.
Lazarus, E. Youth and Death.
Leapor. To Artemisia.—'Tis to her we sing.
Lear, E. Daddy Long-legs and the Fly, The.
Levchev. Last night I was coming back home alone.
Levi, P. To my Friends.
Levin, P. Meeting of Friends, A.
Levy, A. To Vernon Lee.
Lewis, N. Footprint on the Air, A.

Lewis, R. If you had a friend strong, simple, true.

Li K'ai-hsien. Earthquake covered Shansi and Shensi, The.

Li Ling. Parting from Su Wu.

Li Po. Facing Wine with Memories of Lord Ho.

To Tan-Ch'iu.

Li Yü. Tune: "Crows Crying at Night."

Longfellow, H. Arrow and the Song, The.

Lovelace, R. Grasshopper, The.

Lowell, A. To a Friend.

Lowell, R. To Delmore Schwartz.

Lu Yu. Harp Song.

Lucilius. Lean Gaius, who was thinner than a straw.

MacCaig. Two Friends.

MacGill. Matey.

Macgoye. Omera.

Maclean, A. Waking the Dead.

Malouf. Judas Touch, The.

Marinoni. Who Are My People?

Martial. If memory serves, we've shared together.

Masefield. Being her friend, I do not care, not I.

Word, The.

Mathams. Jesus, friend of little children.

Mayer, B. Birthday Sonnet for Grace.

McHugh, H. Third Person Neuter.

Meng Hao Jan. Stopping at a Friend's Farm.

Merrill, J. Black Mesa, The.

Friend of the Fourth Decade, The.

Manos Karastefanís.

Miles, S. Hares, The.

Montagu, L. Lover, The; a Ballad.

Moore, T. Meeting of the Waters, The.

Moorsom. Jewels In My Hand.

Moraga. Later, she met Joyce.

Morley, H. For Elaine de Kooning.

Moses ibn Ezra. Without My Friends the Day Is Dark.

Moss, T. Anointing, An.

Muldoon, P. Soap-Pig, The.

Nash, O. Friend in Need Will Be Around in Five Minutes, A.

Nelson, F. Human Heart, The.

Nemerov. Blue Suburban.

Nesbit, E. Among His Books.

Nguyễn Bỉnh Khiêm. Time and again you've seen them win or lose.

Ni Tsan. On the Fifteenth Day of the Ninth Month of the Year Kuei-mao of the Chih-cheng Period (Oct. 22, 1363), I Painted This to Send to the Summoned Scholar, Sheng-po, and Inscribed This Poem on It.

O'Connor, P. My prayer is that I have friends.

Okikaze. Who shall I have for friends.

Olson, C. Death of Europe, The.

Om Ui-Gil. Sitting at Night.

Pao Chao. Imitating the Old Poems.

Parra, N. Who are my friends / the sick / the weak / the poor in spirit.

Parry, J. New Friends and Old Friends.

Pasternak, B. Meeting.

Patchen. State of the Nation, The.

Paz. Friendship.

Pereira. Burden, The.

Philips, K. Friendship.

Friendship in Emblem, or the Seal, to my Dearest Lucasia.

Friendship in Embleme, or the Seal. To my dearest Lucasia.

Friendship's Mystery, To My Dearest Lucasia.

L'Amitie: To Mrs. M. Awbrey.

On Rosania's Apostasy, and Lucasia's Friendship.

To Mrs M. A. at Parting.

To My Excellent Lucasia, On Our Friendship.

To the Excellent Mrs A. O. upon her receiving the name of Lucasia.

To the Queen of Inconstancy, Regina Collier, in Antwerp.

Piercy. Friend, The.

Planché. Self-Evident.

Po Chü-i. At the End of Spring.

Being Visited by a Friend During Illness.

Dreaming that I Went with Li and Yü to Visit Yüan Chēn.

Pouring Out My Feelings after Parting from Yüan Chen.

Thinking of the Past.

To Li Chien.

To Liu Yü-hsi.

Pomfret, J. Choice, The.

Porta. I'm walking out on Rome.

Porter, C. Friendship.

Pushkin. October.

Quarles. Best-Beloved, The.

Ramsay, A. Friendship in Perfection.

Robinson, C. We who have loved, alas! may not be friends.

Robinson, E. How Annandale Went Out.

Old Story, An.

Rochester, J. Platonic Lady, The.

Roethke. Chums, The.

Rossetti, C. After Communion.

Dumb Friends.

From Sunset to Star Rise.

Promises like Pie-Crust.

Sackville-West. Nostalgia.

St. John, D. My friend, a man I love as wholly.

Wavelength.

Sanchez, S. Song No. 3: "Cain't nobody tell me any different."

Sangster, M. In Gratitude for Friends.

Sappho. My lovely friends.

Schafer. Battle Lines.

Seay. Ballet of Happiness, The.

Seth. Protocols.

Seward. Invocation, To the Genius of Slumber Written Oct. 1787.

Lady Eleanor Butler.

To Miss Ponsonby.

Sexton. Big heart.

Seymour, A. My Aim.

Shakespeare, W. Sonnet 30.

Sonnet 42.

Sonnet 104.

Sonnet 133.

Sonnet 134.

Shelton, R. Certain Choices.

Sheridan, J. Joe's No Saint.

Shin, S. If you call / I will come to you.

Shwarts. Remembrance of Strange Hospitality.

Silverstein, S. Friendship.

Hug o' War.

Nobody loves me.

Smith, C. Captive Escaped in the Wilds of America. Addressed to the Hon. Mrs. O'Neill, The.

On the Aphorism "L'Amitié est l'Amour sans Ailes."

Smith, S. Broken Friendship, The.

Freddy.

Pleasures of friendship are exquisite, The.

Two Friends.

Smith, W. Interlude.

Spencer, A. Creed.

Stanley, T. La Belle Confidente.

Stephens, J. Seumas Beg.

Stevenson, R. It's an owercome sooth for age an' youth.

Mile an' a bittock, a mile or twa, A.

My Shadow.

Verses Written in 1872.

Su Tung-p'o. End of the Year, The.

To a Traveler.

Swift, J. In Sickness.

Twelve Articles.

Swinburne. To a Cat.

Talfourd. Friend, A.

T'ao Ch'ien. Old friends know what I like.

Tao Tschung Yu. Quarrelling.

Tarachow. Walking in the Midst of Others.

Tennyson, A. In the Garden at Swainston.

To E. Fitzgerald.

The Yueh-Fu. I want to be your friend.

Theocritus. We had not got half way, nor yet discerned.

Thompson, F. To My Friend.

Thoreau. Friendship.

Tiempo. I Tell of Another Young Death.

Towne, C. Around the Corner ("Around the corner I have a friend").

Troupe. View from Skates in Berkeley, The.

Tsaloumas. Old Friend.

Tsui. How Can I Show This Poem to Geraldine?

Tsvetayeva. Desk.

Tu Fu. Drifting clouds pass by all day long.

Farewell Once More to My Friend Yen at Feng Chi Station.

Flocks of chicken clucking from every corner.

Presented to Wei Pa, Gentleman in Retirement.

Visitors.

Unknown. And Yet the Earth Remains Unchanged.

Auld Lang Syne.

By Heaven!

Confide In a Friend.

Epitaph: "My friend, judge not me."

Fellowship.

Friend, A.

Friend is a person, A.

(Friends).

Friendship.

Friendship needs no studied phrases.

Green, green.

Growing Friendship.

I would but I can't.

It's a funny thing, but true.

Make Me Worthy of My Friends.

Money and a Friend.

No one is too small to be able to help.

Oath of Friendship.

Oaths of Friendship.

Old Codger of Droome, The.

Only safe, The.

Only way to have a friend, The.

Plucking The Rushes.

Seeds of Kindness.

There's happiness in little things.

Three Friends.

To me nothing seems as splendid nor as praiseworthy.

Van Dyke. Mile with Me, A.

Vaughan, H. To My Ingenuous Friend, R. W.

Walcott. Sea Canes.

Village Life, A.

Wang Chien. Hearing That His Friend Was Coming Back from the War.

Weaver, M. Left Bank Jazz Society, The.

Wen Cheng-ming. As flowers fall at the river city, memories come to me.

Beneath the Shrine of the Three Loyal Ones.

Floating clouds and worldly affairs.

In the past when I saw friends off.

Whitman, W. As toilsome I wander'd Virginia's woods.

I dream'd in a dream I saw a city invincible to the attacks of the whole of the rest of the earth.

I saw in Louisiana a live-oak growing.

In paths untrodden.

Not heat flames up and consumes.

Recorders ages hence.

Whittemore, E. My friends are little lamps to me.

Whittemore, R. On the Suicide of a Friend.

Wier. Old-fashioned.

Wilcox, E. Accept My Full Heart's Thanks.

Friendship.

Friendship After Love.

Williams, B. Friend Who Just Stands By, The.

Winchilsea. Friendship Between Ephelia and Ardelia.

Wordsworth, W. Tables Turned[: An Evening Scene, on the Same Subject], The.

To a Child [Written in Her Album].

Wyatt, T. Lux, my fair falcon, and your fellows all.

Yang Chi. Meeting My Fellow Countryman, Yü Wu-chung.

Yang Shih-ch'i. Even ordinarily, parting is difficult.

Yeats. Friends.

Young, B. I Hear It Said.

Yukitsuna. Tanka: "With those who."

Yün Shou-p'ing. As we say farewell to

autumn.
Painting of Yams, A.
Zavalnyuk. I love my enemies, those I forgive.

Frietchie, Barbara
Whittier. Barbara Frietchie.

Frisbees
Pizzarelli. Flinging the frisbee.

Frog Prince, The
Bloch, C. I and Thou.
Smith, S. Frog Prince, The.

Frogs
Basho. Ancient pool. Sound.
Old pond, / frog jumps in.
Old pond— / The sound, An.
Belloc. Frog, The.
Bertolino. Frog Voices.
Bose, B. Frogs.
Bruchac. Birdfoot's Grampa.
Dickinson, E. His Mansion in the Pool.
Evans, D. Bullfrogs.
Ewing, J. Friend in the Garden, A.
Finlay, I. Great frog race.
Fyleman. Frog, The.
Greger. Frog in the Swimming Pool, The.
Heaney, S. Death of a Naturalist.
Hoban. Tin Frog, The.
Homer. Ascend my shoulders, firmly keep thy seat.
Hughes, T. Bullfrog.
Kinnell. First Song.
Vapor Trail Reflected in the Frog Pond.
La Fontaine. Aesop's Fable of the Frogs.
McGough, R. Cousin Nell.
Mother Goose. Mr. Frog Went a-Courting.
Mountain, M. Frog.
Pack, R. Frog Prince, The.
Phaedrus. Proud Frog, The.
Pizzarelli. Waterbug running by the frogulp.
Ponge. Frog, The.
Richards, L. Some Fishy Nonsense.
Robinson, M. Brown Frog, The.
Rossetti, C. Frog's Fate, A.
Hopping frog, hop here and be seen.
Rothenberg, J. Song of Quavering, A.
Saitō Mokichi. Tanka: "Frog."
Schevill. Green Frog at Roadstead, Wisconsin.
Smith, S. Frog Prince, The.
Swenson, M. Seeing the frog.
Unknown. Battle in the balance, The.
Cause of War, The.
Centipede was happy quite, A.
"Croak!" said the Toad, "I'm hungry, I think."
Frog, The.
Wallace-Crabbe. Nub.
Wright, J. Small Frogs Killed on the Highway.
Young Bear. Wadasa Nakamoon, Vietnam Memorial.

Frontiers
Chin. Barbarians Are Coming, The.
Heaney, S. From the Frontier of Writing.
Li Meng-yang. Crossing the Frontier.

Frost
Basho. It would melt.
Begay. Mother's Lace.
Davis, C. Years, The.
Dickinson, E. Apparently with no surprise.
Doolittle, H. Blue-geese, white-geese, you may say.
Gould, H. Frost looked forth, one still, clear night, The.
Herrick. Farewell Frost; or, Welcome the Spring.
Lovelace, R. Grasshopper, The.
O'Brien, G. Ornamental Syllable.
O'Hussy. O'Hussey's Ode to the Maguire.
Pike, C. Jack Frost.
Sackville-West. Frost.
Sandburg, C. Splinter.
"Setoun." Jack Frost.
Shipman. Streams are fettered, and with us as rare, The.
Smeeton. Jack Frost in the Garden.
T'ang Yin. Inscribed on a Painting of a Fisherman.
Thaxter. Jack Frost.

Yakamochi. Frost lies white, The.
Zwicky. Jack Frost.

Frost, Robert
Brooks, G. Of Robert Frost.
Hillyer. Letter to Robert Frost, A.
Houghton, F. Mr. Frost Goes South to Boston.
Kinnell. For Robert Frost.
Lowell, R. Robert Frost.
Matveyeva. Robert Frost.
Salter. Frost at Midnight.

Fruit Trees and Fruit
Adisa. Discover Me.
Agard, J. English Girl Eats Her First Mango.
Alarcon, F. Ode to Tomatoes.
Bible, *O.T.* Psalm 1.
Das, M. Learner
Diodorus Zonas. Pomegranate just splitting, a peach just furry, A.
Dooley, M. At Les Deux Magots.
Elmslie, K. Fruit.
"Field." She is singing to Thee, *Domine!.*
Forché. On Returning to Detroit.
Garrigue. Catch What You Can.
Goodison. Songs of the Fruits and Sweets of Childhood.
Gorham. Empress Receives the Head of a Taiping Rebel, The.
Greiffenberg. On the Fruit-Providing Autumn Season.
Hadewijch. Love's Maturity.
Hall, D. Mangosteens.
Harpur, C. Basket Of Summer Fruit, A.
Harrison, T. Kumquat for John Keats, A.
Huelsenbeck, R. We hardly had gotten the man's pants down.
Jaccottet. Fruit.
Keats. To Autumn.
Kelly, B. Leaving, The.
Kyger. Caption for a Miniature.
Lee, J. Mango.
Levertov. O Taste and See.
MacLeish. Ars Poetica.
Maguire, S. Fall, The.
Mahadevi. Vein of sapphires, A.
Mayer, G. Bilberries.
McClintock, M. Letting my tongue.
McKay, C. Flame-Heart.
Tropics in New York, The.
Millay, E. Never May the Fruit Be Plucked.
Milosz, C. Earth.
Moore, M. Nevertheless.
Nine Nectarines and Other Porcelain.
Newcastle, M. Of the Theme of Love.
Park, S. Fruit Tree.
Pau-Llosa. Frutas.
Philip of Thessalonica. Yellow-coated pomegranate, figs like lizards' necks, A.
Piercy. September Afternoon at Four O'Clock.
Pizzarelli. Bright awning is cranked, A.
Fat lady, The.
Rankine. Man. His Bowl. His Raspberries, The.
Rilke. Where in what ever-blissfully watered gardens, upon what trees.
Rossetti, C. Summer.
What is pink? A rose is pink.
Worrying Fruit.
Scovell. Betrothal, A.
Strange. Still Life.
Tipping. Mangoes are not cigarettes.
Williams, W. This Is Just to Say.
Zonas. Pomegranate just splitting, a peach just furry, A.

Fry, Elizabeth
Hood, T. Friendly Address, A.

Fuchsia
Colum, P. Fuchsia Hedges in Connacht.
Hardy, T. Lodging-House Fuchsias, The.

Fujiyama
Kusano Shimpei. Skylarks and Fuji.

Fulfillment
Blake, W. Question Answered, The [*or* A].
Bly, R. Third Body, A.
Bontemps. God Give to Men.
Browning, R. Now.
Chuang Tzu. Man Is Born in Tao.

Creeley. Song: "What's in the body you've forgotten."
Cullen, C. From the Dark Tower.
Donne. Good-Morrow, The.
Equi. Words Read by Lightning.
Espada. Tony Went to the Bodega but He Didn't Buy Anything.
Keats. Portrait, A.
Kushner, A. And if you sleep, and if the sheets are clean.
McGough, R. Away from you.
Olson, C. Chockablock Once a man was traveling through the woods, and.
Peyanar. What her girl friend said ("Her eyes").
Robinson, E. Three Quatrains.

Fuller, Margaret
Hacker, M. Ballad of Ladies Lost and Found.
Masters, E. Margaret Fuller Slack.

Fun
"Æ." Frolic.
Croft, S. Blue.
Fisher, R. Funny Folk.
Herrick. Anacreontic.
Frolic[k], A.
Hsü Chün-ch'ien. Sitting Up with My Wife on New Year's Eve.
Hughes, L. Advice.
Keech. Discovery.
Mason, W. Football.
Viorst. Night Fun.
See also **Play; Pleasure; Libraries and Librarians**

Funerals
Aiken, C. Lovers, The.
Amann. Winter burial.
Amis, K. Fforestfawr.
Applewhite. My Grandfather's Funeral.
Arnold, M. But when the Gods and Heroes heard, they brought.
Asalache. Death of a Chief.
Ashe. Corpse-bearing.
Auden. Song: "Stop all the clocks, cut off the telephone."
Bancquart. Epitaph.
Barlow, G. Salt.
Beaumont, S. Upon a Funeral.
Bensko. Watching TV, the Elk Bones Up on Metaphysics.
Bowering, G. Está Muy Caliente.
Bromley, A. My Mother's Face Never Moved.
Brown, G. Funeral of Ally Flett, The.
Carleton, W. Country Doctor, The.
Crabbe. Pauper's Funeral, The.
Cullen, C. Brown Girl Dead, A.
Dawe, B. At Shagger's funeral there wasn't much to say.
Going.
De Roche. Aunt Laura Moves toward the Open Grave of Her Father.
Dickinson, E. I felt a Funeral in my Brain.
Dobyns. Counterparts.
Donne. Funeral[l], The.
Dubie. Funeral, The.
Ganges, The.
Dunn, D. She sat up on her pillows, receiving guests.
Eady. I Just Wanna Testify.
Evans, M. Rebel, The.
Gonzalez, A. First Friday bell shatters the morning.
Graves, R. 1805.
Greacen. St Andrew's Day, blind November fumbling.
Summer Day, A.
Hall, D. Funeral, The.
Hardy, T. Choirmaster's Burial, The.
Heaney, S. Funeral Rites.
Henderson, D. Do Nothing Till You Hear from Me.
Herbert, Z. Elegy of Fortinbras.
Herrick. Funeral[l] Rites of the Rose, The.
Housman, A. Bredon Hill.
Hughes, L. As Befits a Man.
Ballad of the Man Who's Gone.
Dead in There.
Night funeral / In Harlem.

Justice, D. First Death.
Kay, J. He Told Us He Wanted a Black Coffin.
Kennedy, X. At a Low Mass for Two Hot-Rodders.
Komunyakaa. April Fools' Day.
Kovner. Far, Far a City Lies.
Lewis, J. Country Burial.
Longfellow, H. Hawthorne.
Longley, M. Detour.
Lowell, R. Death of the Sheriff, The.
Maclean, A. Waking the Dead.
McKinney, I. Chrysanthemums.
Meleager. Upon a Maid That Died [or Dyed] the Day She Was Married [or Marryed].
Melville, H. Dirge for McPherson, A.
Merrill, J. Annie Hill's Grave.
Millay, E. Dirge Without Music.
Miller, E. Dressed Up.
Mitchell, K. On the Anniversary Of Your Death.
Montague, J. Falls Funeral.
Mother Goose. Who killed Cock [or poor] Robin? [or Here lies Cock Robin].
Muske. Eulogy, The.
Nastasijevic. Burial.
Pagis. Souvenir, The.
Plath. Bee Meeting, The.
Poe. Lenore.
Prévert. Song of the snails on their way to a funeral.
Probyn. Changes.
Ransom, J. Bells for John Whiteside's Daughter.
    Emily Hardcastle, Spinster.
Ravikovitch. King over Israel.
    Requiem after Seventeen Years.
    War's End.
Redmond. Poetic Reflections Enroute To, and During, The Funeral and Burial of Henry Dumas, Poet.
Salaam. Our World Is Less Full Now That Mr. Fuller Is Gone.
Schulman. Burial of a Fisherman in Hydra.
Sexton. Truth the Dead Know, The.
Snodgrass, W. Old Apple Trees.
Soyinka. Funeral Sermon, Soweto.
Spender, S. Funeral, The.
Stanford, F. Island Funeral.
Stanley, T. Exequies, The.
Synge. Question, A.
Tati-Loutard. Submarine Tombs.
Thomas, D. After the funeral, mule praises, brays.
Towne, A. Dead of Winter.
Traxler. Death of a Distant In-law.
Unknown. Beowulf's Funeral.
    Cowboy's Lament, The.
    Finnegan's Wake.
    Funeral of Scyld Shefing, The.
    Funeral Pyre, The.
Walker, A. Burial.
Wallace, R. Riding in a Stranger's Funeral.
Wilcox, E. Queen's Last Ride, The.
Williams, M. On the Symbolic Consideration of Hands and the Significance of Death.
Williams, W. Tract.
Wolfe, C. Burial of Sir John Moore &[;after [or at] Corunna&];, The.
Yoshimi. Tanka: "How many people came."

Furnaces
MacBeth. Poem of Death, A.
Merwin, W. Drunk in the Furnace, The.
Roseliep. After Beethoven.

Furniture
Ashbery. Melodic Trains.
Davidson, M. Feeling Type and His Friends, The.
DiPalma. Table, The.
Ferril. Empire Sofa, The.
Maiden. In the Gloaming.
McGuckian. Presence, The.
McHugh, H. What Could Hold Us.
Nemerov. Singular Metamorphosis, A.
Tsaloumas. Autumn Supper.
Wheeler, S. Run on a Warehouse.

Winstanley, J. Inventory of the Furniture of a Collegian's Chamber, An.

Fuseli, Henry
Blake, W. To Hunt.

Future
Adams, F. Those Two Boys.
Ashbery. Brute Image.
Atwood. Up.
Auden. Door, The.
Avidan. Some Futureplans.
"Bagritzky." Till Eulenspiegel.
Benson, S. Blue Book 18 Pages 1–4.
Berberova. I remain with what was not fully said.
Braley, B. Start where you stand and never mind the past.
Brecht, B. To Those Born Later.
Breeze. Dreamer.
Browning, E. Sonnet: "My future will not copy fair my past."
Chōkū. Tanka: "From the water's depth."
Clark, T. Daily News.
Coleridge, M. Unwelcome.
Cummings, E. If(touched by love's own secret)we,like homing.
Dante Alighieri. Earnest I look'd.
Dao. Answer, The.
Davidson, D. Randall, my son, before you came just now.
de Carvalho. I Come from a South.
Desnos. Trance Event.
Dipoko. Our Life.
Dodd, W. Outside My Cabin.
Dupin. Waiting with lowered voice.
Ehrhart. To Those Who Have Gone Home Tired.
Everwine. From the Meadow.
Fainlight, R. Future is timid and wayward, The.
Fuller, J. *et al.* Born Too Soon.
Fumiko. Tanka: "Knees collapsing."
Glazkov. Races will disappear.
González, A. Future, The.
Gray, R. Flames and Dangling Wire.
Greville, F. Sonnet: "Man, dream[e] no more of curious mysteries."
Hardy, T. If you had known.
    Strange House, The.
Harms. My Androgynous Years.
Hartnett. There will be a talking of lovely things.
Hawthorne, N. Oh could I raise the darken'd veil.
Haxton. Auspice.
Heath-Stubbs. To a Poet a Thousand Years Hence.
Herbert, C. Everything changes. We plant.
Hill, G. Processes of generation; deeds of settlement.
Hirsch, E. For the New World.
Housman, A. Lads in their hundreds to Ludlow come in for the fair, The.
Hsü Chung-hsing. This metal is engraved with Shang-style markings.
Irtenev. When I burn up without a trace.
Jaccottet. Reason.
Jarrell. On the Railway Platform.
Jastrun, T. Scrap.
Jeffers, R. Granite and Cypress.
    Watch the Lights Fade.
Kalász. Hymn: "Where should I seat you, where."
Kao Ch'i. Silkworm Song of Torchlit Fields.
Kelly, R. Recessional.
Kenyon, J. Otherwise.
Khlebnikov, V. Manifesto of the Presidents of the Terrestrial Globe.
Kipling, R. Storm Cone, The.
Kuzmina-Karavayeva. Everything has been checked. My inventory is ready.
Larkin, P. Arundel Tomb, An.
    Next, Please.
MacNeice. Prospect.
Madhubuti. Union of Two, The.
Marinetti. Correction of proofs + desires in speed.
    Futurism Wants to Transform the Variety

Theater into a Theater of Amazement, Record-setting, and Body-madness.
    We had stayed up all night, my friends and I, under hanging mosque lamps.
Mayakovsky. My most respected / comrades of posterity!
Meyers, B. Suburban Dusk.
Milosz, C. Incantation.
Morgan, R. We will grow old, and older.
Mueller, M. Evolution: A Science Fiction.
Ofeimun. Let Them Choose Paths.
O'Hara, F. Poem: "'Instant coffee with slightly sour cream'."
Osundare. I Sing of Change.
Padilla. History.
Pagis. Pages of an Album.
Pasolini. Day of My Death, The.
Rich, A. Prospective Immigrants Please Note.
Ríos, A. Mi Abuelo.
Rossetti, C. Cobwebs.
Sachs, N. But Perhaps [God needs the longing, wherever else should it dwell].
Sandburg, C. Broken-Face Gargoyles.
Shchirovsky. I really don't want to die now.
Stanescu. Song.
Stevens, W. Postcard from the Volcano, A.
Strand. Prediction, The.
Tate, J. Dime Found in the Snow, A.
Tati-Loutard. Noonday in Immaturity.
Toomer. It is Everywhere.
Trần Đức Uyển. Letter to My Future Child, A.
Tu Fu. To Pi Ssu Yao.
Wallace-Crabbe. Nub.
Wen Cheng-ming. Smiling, we set the testing tray before the hall.
White, E. Conch.
Whitman, W. Full of life now, compact, visible.
    Recorders ages hence.
    To the Pending Year.
    Years of the modern! years of the unperform'd!
Wieseltier. Here in Netanya.
Wilcox, E. Was, Is, and Yet-to-be.
Yü Chi. Sitting Alone in the Courtyard.

G

Gabriel
Dickinson, E. Robin is a Gabriel, The.
Rich, A. Gabriel.
Richards, G. Almighty spake, and Gabriel sped, Th'.

Galatea
Ovid. *Pygmalion* off'ring, first, approach'd the Shrine.

Galilee, Israel
Barnes, D. Chuang Tzu and Hui Tzu were hundreds of years old.

Galileo
Jarrell. Emancipators, The.

Gallantry
Scott, W. Lochinvar.

Galley Slaves
Kipling, R. Song of the Galley-Slaves.

Gallipoli Campaign (1915)
Stallworthy, J. War Story.

Gallows. See Hanging

Galoshes
Bacmeister. Galoshes.
Taylor, B. Upon Julia's Arctics.

Galuppi, Baldassaro
Browning, R. Toccata of Galuppi's, A.

Galveston, Texas
Howes, B. On Galveston Beach.

Galway. See County Galway, Ireland

Gambling and Gamblers
Baker, M. Porkskin Panorama.
Cavafy. Days of 1908.
    Days of 1908.
Clairmont. Hero in the Land of Dough, A.
Dickinson, E. We lose—because we win.
Frost, R. In Divés' Dive.

Gotera. Gambling.
Hacker, M. Wagers.
Hawthorn. Deathbed, A.
Hongo. Winnings.
Hughes, L. Situation.
Krynicki. By entering the grand lottery.
Long, D. One Time Henry Dreamed the Number.
Lyly, J. Cards and Kisses.
Ortiz. Telling About Coyote.
Piercy. Kid on Her Way, A.
Sandburg, C. Crapshooters.
Studdert-Kennedy. Great Wager, The.
Tyler, R. Gambling.
Unknown. John Hardy.
  Root Hog or Die.
Wakoski. Placing a $2 Bet for a Man Who Will Never Go to the Horse Races Any More.
Young, A. Studio Up Over In Your Ear.

Games
Anderson, L. Red Hot.
Armour. Good sportsmanship we hail, we sing.
Atwood. Game after Supper.
Blind. Once we played at love together.
Bond, J. Rotation.
Brautigan. Chinese Checker Players, The.
Burns, R. Johnie Blunt.
Clare, J. Shepherd Boy, The.
Cleghorn. Golf Links [lie so near The mill], The.
Cummings, E. May i feel said he.
Custance. Hyacinthus.
Dehn, P. Game of Consequences, A.
Dent. For Cool Papa Bell.
Fatchen. It's a Bit Rich.
Fitzgerald, E. 70.
  69.
Gilbert, C. This Bridge Across.
Graves, R. Hide and Seek.
Harper, M. Makin' Jump Shots.
Huntington, C. Hackeysack Players, The.
Jackson, R. For Thurman Thomas.
Johnson, A. Grandma.
Laughlin, J. Step on His Head.
Mason, W. Football.
McDonald, W. War Games.
Mosby. To Josh Gibson (Legendary Slugger of the Old Negro Baseball League).
Mother Goose. Intery, mintery, cutery corn.
Patchen. Mirru.
Perreault, J. Boomerang.
Popa. He.
  Hide-and-Seek.
  Nail, The.
  Rose Thieves, The.
Roy, L. Triple Overtime.
Sachs, N. Someone.
Stevenson, R. Good Play, A.
  Marching Song.
  Pirate Story.
  Unseen Playmate, The.
Swenson, M. Analysis of Baseball.
Tadic. Die.
Tate, G. Tonguing.
Teasdale. Hide and Seek.
Todd, R. Paul Klee.
Troupe. Poem for "Magic", A.
Unknown. Children's Ball-Bouncing Song.
  Foot Race Song.
  Getting Berries.
  Getting Firewood.
  Inter, mitzy, titzy, tool.
  Lying Down.
  Pieces of Snot.
Vidyakara. Four Poems.
Wen Cheng-ming. Day drags on, as long as a year!, The.

See also **Card Games; Sports**

Gandhi, Mohandas Karamchand
O'Higgins, M. Vaticide.
Shapiro, K. In India.

Ganges River, India
Dubie. Ganges, The.
Péret. Staircase with a Hundred Steps, The.

Shange. Where the Mississippi meets the Amazon.

Gangs and Gangsters
Cohen, E. Drive-By Shooting.
Fenton, J. Wild Ones[, The].
Gunn, T. Black Jackets.
Muldoon, P. Sightseers, The.
  Weepies, The.
Muske. Field Trip.
Soto. Morning They Shot Tony Lopez, Barber and Pusher Who Went Too Far, 1958, The.

Gannets. *See* **Boobies**

Ganymede
Heywood, T. Jupiter and Ganimede.

Garages
Bethell. Detail.
Mahon. Garage in Co. Cork, A.

Garbage and Garbage Men
Allard. Thawing ice the garbage blooming out of it.
Berry, W. Wild, The.
Fulton, A. Wreckage Entrepreneur, The.
Fumi Saito. Tanka: "Bones of a fish."
Grennan. Wing Road.
Howell, C. Memories of Mess Duty and the War.
Levchev. Secret Love.
Nemerov. Town Dump, The.
North, C. Little Cape Cod Landscape.
Sansom, C. Dustman, The.
Shūji. During the rainy season.
Silverstein, S. Sarah Cynthia Sylvia Stout Would Not Take the Garbage Out.
Tranter. Glow-boys.
Unknown. Dustman, The.
Wilbur. After the last bulletins the windows darken.
  Junk.

García Lorca, Federico
Dudek. García Lorca.
Duncan, R. Drinking Fountain, The.
Manifold. Garcia Lorca Murdered in Granada.
Woodcock. Poem for Garcia Lorca.

Garda, Lake, Italy
Tennyson, A. Frater Ave Atque Vale.

Gardens and Gardening
Akenside. Inscription for a Grotto.
"Akhmatova." Lord is not merciful to reapers and gardeners, The.
  Summer Garden.
Alexander, M. Her Garden.
Allen, A. My Mother's Garden.
Anzaldúa. Cultures.
Argüelles, I. Canto the Tenth.
Arkell. What is a Garden?
Armstrong, J. Art of Preserving Health, The.
Arnold, M. Lines Written in Kensington Gardens.
Aston, A. Everything in the Garden is Lovely.
Auden. Their Lonely Betters.
Avena. Cancer garden, protected by buildings, one unfinished. Still, The.
Barker, G. Gardens of Ravished Psyche, The.
Barnfield. Affectionate Shepherd, The.
Bateman, E. Cockney's Garden, The.
Beaver. Déjeuner Sur l'Herbe.
Becker, R. Gardener, The.
Bellamann, H. Charleston Garden, A.
Bernstein, O. And after a Long While.
Bethell. Erica.
  Time.
  Warning of Winter.
Bialik. I have a garden and I have a well.
Bible, *O.T.* Genesis.
  Song of Solomon, The.
Bishop, E. Manuelzinho.
Blake, W. Garden of Love, The.
Bodecker. Garden Calendar.
Boileau-Despéaux. Epistle to My Gardener.
  Garden of Writing, The.
Bridges, R. Garden in September, The.
Brooke, L. Johnny Crow's Garden.
Brown, T. My Garden.
Browne, W. Vision V.
Browning, E. Deserted Garden, The.
Browning, R. Flower's Name, The.

Sibrandus Schafnaburgensis.
Sordello.
Brownjohn. In a Convent Garden.
Bullock, M. Garden.
Burns, R. Gardener wi' His Paidle; or, The Gardener's March, The.
Campana. Autumn Garden.
Campion, T. There is a Garden in her face.
Chang, E. After the Storm.
Chang Yü. Retreat of Sun Ching-hsiang, The.
Chao Meng-fu. Pavilion-Where-the-Crane-Came, The.
Chaucer. Love's Garden.
  Parliament of Fowls, The.
Chesterfield. On Lord Ila's Improvements, near Hounslow Heath.
Chu Yün-ming. For Several Years I Have Wanted To Grow a Garden, But Have Never Finished One. This Year It Is Already Halfway Through Summer, and This Has Made Me Despondent.
Ciardi. Suburban.
Clare, J. To a Bower.
  Wish, The.
Coleridge, M. Poison flower that in my garden grew, The.
Coleridge, S. Garden Year, The.
Collins, A. Another Song.
Columella. Autumnal Work.
Combs. Just after Noon with Fierce Shears.
Cornford, F. On August the Thirteenth.
Cornwall. Sowing Seeds.
Cotton, N. On Lord Cobham's Garden.
Cowley, A. Garden, The.
  Wish, The.
Cowper, W. On Pruning.
  Shrubbery, The.
  Task, The.
  Work of Gardening, The.
Crane, H. Garden Abstract.
Creeley. Door, The.
Cummings, E. Sonnet IV.
Curry. Gardens.
Darwin. Kew.
  Poppy, The.
Das, M. Growing Tip, The.
Davie. Gardens No Emblems.
Davies, W. No Man's Wood.
Dawe, B. Homo Suburbiensis.
Day Lewis. Snowfall on a College Garden.
De la Mare. In the Garden.
  Myself.
  Two gardens see!—this, of enchanted flowers.
de Lille. Gardens, The.
De Tabley. Philoctetes.
Denby. Villa D'Este.
Dobson, A. Garden Song, A.
Doddridge, P. Meditations on the Sepulchre in the Garden.
Donne. Twicknam [*or* Twickenham] Garden.
Doolittle, H. Garden.
  Heat.
  Sheltered Garden.
Dorgan, T. Promised Garden, The.
Douglas, L. Apologia.
  Two Loves.
Downie. Her Garden.
Driscoll, L. My garden is a pleasant place.
Druce. Apropos of Garden Statuary: A Disquisition upon a Minor Genre.
Drummond de Andrade. Souvenir of the Ancient World.
Dunn, D. Gardeners.
  In the Grounds.
Durrell. In the Garden: Villa Cleobolus.
Dyer, J. Prospects.
Edmond, L. Jardin des Colombières.
Emerson, R. Days.
  Gardener.
  In my garden three ways meet.
Enright, D. Kyoto Garden, A.
Ewart. Wanting Out.
Ewing, J. Garden Lore.
Farjeon, E. Over the garden wall.
Finney, N. Uncles.
Flanders, J. Planting Onions.

Frost, R. Girl's Garden, A.
Winter Eden, A.
Gardner, J. Feat of Gardening, The.
Garrigue. Cortège for Colette.
Gascoigne. World as Garden, The.
Gilbert, S. Florist's Vade-Mecum, The.
Giles, J. Leasowes: Or, A Poetical Description
of the Late Mr. Shenstone's Rural
Retirement, The.
Ginsberg, A. Strange New Cottage in
Berkeley, A.
Glück, L. Garden, The.
White Lilies, The.
Witchgrass.
Graves, R. Gardener.
Greger. Garden, The.
Gregory, H. Chinese Garden, The.
Greig, A. In the Tool-shed.
Grigson. Landscape Gardeners, The.
Grimald. Garden, The.
Guest, B. Wild gardens overlooked by night
lights. Parking.
Guillaume de Lorris et al. Garden of Amour,
The.
Gunn, T. Breaking Ground.
Garden of the Gods, The.
Last Days at Teddington.
Martial.
Pope's Carnations Knew Him.
Gurney, D. Lord God Planted a Garden, The.
Haas, R. Rain mixed with sleet.
Habergham. Seeds of Love, The.
Hafiz. Lesson of the Flowers, The.
Hajnal. That's All?
Hamburger, M. Garden, Wilderness.
Weeding.
Han-shan. In an Abandoned Garden.
Han Yü. Flowering Plums.
My ceramic lake in dawn, water settled clear.
Hardy, T. Garden Seat, The.
Hecht, A. Gardens of the Villa D'Este, The.
La Condition Botanique.
Herbert, G. Paradise.
Herlin. Warmth of the wind-break wall, The.
Herrick. To a Bed of Tulips.
Hesketh. Death of a Gardener.
Hill, A. Garden Window, The.
Hines, P. My Garden.
Hitchcock. One Whose Reproach I Cannot
Evade, The.
Hofmannsthal. Emperor of China Speaks, The.
Hollander, J. Garden, The.
Hollander, M. Central Park.
Holub. Garden of Old People, The.
Homer. Gardens of Alcinous, The.
Horace. Conservation.
Howells, W. November.
Hsü Chung-hsing. I shake my robe—and mists
disperse, leaving clear autumn sky.
Huchel. Garden of Theophrastus, The.
Hugo, R. Way a Ghost Dissolves, The.
Hunt, L. Story of Rimini, The.
Ingraham. She Would Have Roses.
Ingram, A. Castle Howard, the Seat of the Rt.
Hon. Charles, Earl of Carlisle.
Irvine, J. Saint Fiacre.
Jago. Instructions on landscaping.
James I, King of Scotland. King is Quair,
The.
Jarrell. In a Hospital Garden.
Jennings, E. Her Garden.
In a Garden.
Johnson, R. Beam 30, The Garden.
Jones, L. Who Loves a Garden.
Kalász. Up against That Wall Everywhere.
Kavanagh, P. Long Garden, The.
Kendrick, D. Gethsemane A. D.
Kinzie. Sun and Moon.
Kipling, R. Glory of the Garden, The.
Kirkup. Scarecrows.
Kitahara Hakushū. Tanka: "I sneaked into."
Knight, R. Landscape, The.
Kumin, M. Mummies, The.
Kunitz, S. Round, The.
Snakes of September, The.
Lady of the Arbour. Flower and the Leaf,
The.

Lady of the Assembly. Assembly of Ladies,
The.
Landor, W. Gardener, The.
Lawrence, D. Trees in the Garden.
Layton. Cold Green Element, The.
Layzer. Lawn Roller, The.
Le Gallienne. Library in a Garden, A.
Leithauser. In a Japanese Moss Garden.
Levin, P. Planting Roses.
Lindon. My Garden.
Lowell, A. Garden by Moonlight, The.
Lowell, R. Public Garden, The.
Lu Yu. Vegetable Garden.
Lucas, T. Town Garden, A.
Lydgate. Complaint of the Black Knight, The.
MacNeice. Gardener, The.
Sunlight on the garden, The.
Macpherson, J. Garden of the Sexes, The.
Garden shut, a fountain sealed, A.
Magee, W. British Garden, A.
Martial. De Hortis Julii Martialis.
Marvell. Garden, The.
Mower Against Gardens, The.
To My Lord Fairfax.
Masaoka Shiki. Tanka: "Nobody with me."
Mason, W. Against Formal Gardens.
To a Gravel Walk.
Maurice. Chiswick.
Mayer, B. Garden, The.
McClatchy. Snake.
Weeds.
McCord, D. Mr. Bidery's Spidery Garden.
McMaster, R. Back Steps Lookout.
Melville, H. Ravaged Villa, The.
Meredith, G. Garden of Epicurus, The.
Merrick, A. Hartwell Gardens.
Merwin, W. What is a Garden.
Millay, E. Hardy Garden, The.
So she came back into his house again.
Spring in the Garden.
Miller, A. Mulch.
Pruning, The.
Miller, E. My Father's Garden.
Millikin. Groves of Blarney [they look so
charming], The.
Milton. Eden.
Minhinnick. Grandfather in the Garden.
Mirabai. O friend, understand: the body.
Mole, J. Trick, The.
Moraes, D. Gardener.
More, T. Child's Song.
Morris, W. Garden By The Sea, A.
Thunder in the Garden.
Moss, H. Roof Garden, The.
Mother Goose. Mary, Mary, quite contrary.
Nemerov. Salt Garden, The.
Nesbit, E. At Parting.
Newcastle, M. 'Poet I am neither born, nor
bred," A.
Noyes, A. Butterfly Garden, The.
O'Brien, G. Ornamental Syllable.
Prophetic Child, The.
Orr, G. Weeds, The.
Ōshima Ryōta. And Then.
Ovid. Golden Age, The.
Pagis. Siege.
Pasternak, B. Weeping Garden, The.
Paz. Doomed Garden, A.
Stanzas for an Imaginary Garden.
Peacocke. Railway Allotments.
Philip of Thessalonica. Yellow-coated
pomegranate, figs like lizards' necks, A.
Piercy. Seven of Pentacles, The.
Vegetable Love.
Pitter. Diehards, The.
Other People's Glasshouses.
Pizzarelli. Piece of buttered popcorn, A.
Plath. Manor Garden, The.
Po Chü-i. Chrysanthemums in the Eastern
Garden, The.
Planting Flowers on the Eastern Embankment.
Written when Governor of Soochow.
Poliziano. She Finds Herself in a Garden.
Pomfret, J. No Barren Leaves.
Pope, A. Garden, The.
Gardens of Alcinous, The.
To Mr. Gay, Who Wrote Him a

Congratulatory Letter on the Finishing His
House.
Porter, C. Old-Fashioned Garden, An.
Porter, P. Australian Garden, An.
Pound, E. Garden, The.
Pratt, S. Cottage Pictures.
Prayton. Paradice on earth is found, A.
Prunty. Vegetable Garden, The.
Raine, C. Gardener, The.
Randolph, T. On a Maid of Honour Seen by a
Scholar in Somerset Garden.
On Grafting.
Rapin. Of Roses and Hyacinths.
"Ravitch." Verses Written on Sand.
Redgrove, P. Negotium Perambulans.
Reed, H. Naming Of Parts.
Reid, C. Gardeners, The.
Revell. Sirius.
Rich, A. Design in Living Colors.
Rilke. Gently gripped by the.
Robinson, E. Garden, The.
Roethke. Cuttings ("Sticks-in-a-drowse droop
over sugary loam").
Cuttings ("This urge, wrestle, resurrection of
dry sticks").
Transplanting.
Weed Puller.
Rosenberg, I. Garden of Joy, The.
Rossetti, C. October Garden, An.
On Keats, 18 January, 1948 (Eve of St
Agnes).
Shut Out.
Rossetti, D. Silent Noon.
Saba. King's Garden World, A.
Sackville-West. Frost.
Garden, The.
Pruning in March.
Rose, The.
Saigyo. In Winter.
Samio. Tanka: "When the gardener."
Sassoon. I Shall Find You.
In Heytesbury Wood.
Schuyler, J. Roof Garden.
Senghor. French Garden.
Sewell, G. Dying Man in His Garden, The.
Shakespeare, W. Richard II.
Shirley, J. Garden, The.
Shūji. Tanka: "Its bloom finished."
Shwarts. Beast Flower.
Simmons, J. October in the Country: [1983].
Playing with Fire.
Sims. Garden Song, A.
Sitwell, D. Gardener Janus Catches a Naiad.
Sitwell, S. In the Potting Shed.
In the Winter.
Snow, A. Gardener.
Southerland. Night in Nigeria.
Spark. Kensington Gardens.
Spenser. Bower of Bliss, The.
Garden of Adonis, The.
In the Bower of Bliss.
Stanley-Wrench. Hinterland.
Steele, T. Wartburg, 1521–22, The.
Stein, G. In This Way.
Stevens, W. Banal Sojourn.
Room on a Garden, A.
Stevenson, R. Autumn Fires.
Gardener does not love to talk, The.
To A Gardener.
Translations from Martial.
Stickney, T. Athenian Garden, An.
Eride, V.
Strand. Garden, The.
Suckling, J. Upon My Lady Carlisle's [or
Carlile's] Walking in Hampton Court Garden.
Swenson, M. Garden at St. John's, The.
Swinburne. Forsaken Garden, A.
Garden of Proserpine, The.
Mill Garden, The.
Sylvester, J. Garden, The.
T'ao Ch'ien. I plant beans at the foot of the
southern hill.
Returning to My Home in the Country.
When I was young, I did not fit into the
common mold.
Tennyson, A. Arabian Night Garden, An.
Gardener's Daughter, The.

In Memoriam.
Princess, The.
Recollections of The Arabian Nights.
Somersby, Lincolnshire; after Leaving the
  Refectory.
Song: "Come into the garden, Maud."
Song: "Spirit haunts the year's last hours, A."
Suburban Garden.
Thomas, D. Walking in gardens by the sides.
Thomas, E. Digging.
Thomson, J. Late Spring.
Tomlinson, C. In the Borghese Gardens.
Juliet's Garden.
Ts'ao Chih. Forsaken Wife, The.
Ts'ao P'i. Lotus Lake.
Turner, N. Old Quin Queeribus.
Unknown. Falling Snow.
I have a newe gardin.
In My Garden.
International Chainpoem.
Man of Words [and not of deeds], A.
Mary, Mary, quite contrary.
Richmond Gardens: A Poem.
Rise and Progress of the Present Taste in
  Planning Parks, Pleasure Grounds, Gardens,
  etc, The.
Seeds of Love, The.
Van Doren. Gardener.
Van Duyn. Gardener to His God, The.
Verlaine. L'Allée.
Voigt. At the Edge of Winter.
Wadsworth, W. Snake in the Garden
  Considers Daphne, The.
Wakoski. Sestina from the Home Gardener.
Waller, E. At Penshurst [Another].
Garden of Bermuda, The.
On St. James's Park, as Lately Improved by
  His Majesty.
Wang An-shih. Impromptu; Late Spring at
  Pan-shan.
Warren, R. Garden, The.
Warren, R. Garden.
Warton, J. Wild, The.
Wellesley. Walled Garden.
West, G. Stowe, the Gardens of the Rt. Hon.
  Richard Lord Viscount Cobham.
White, M. "Claude Monet sur son lit do
  mort."
Whitehead, W. On the Late Improvements at
  Nuneham, the Seat of the Earl of Harcourt.
Whittier. Garden.
Wilbur. Caserta Garden.
Wilde, O. Le Jardin des Tuileries.
Willard, N. Arbor.
Williams, P. Lost Seed.
Williams, W. Italian Garden, The.
Tulip Bed, The.
Widow's Lament in Springtime, The.
Winchilsea. Upon My Lord Winchilsea's
  Converting the Mount in His Garden to a
  Terrace.
Winters, Y. Time and the Garden.
Wollach. Two Gardens.
Wordsworth, W. Excursion, The.
In a Garden in the Grounds of Coleorton,
  Leicestershire.
Wright, J. Invention of a Garden, The.
Wu Chia-chi. My hut, beside the crystal
  stream.
Yeats. Ancestral Houses.
Down by the salley gardens my love and I did
  meet;.
Yorke. Our Gardener here, James Phillips see.
Yüan Mei. Busy.

Garfield, James Abram
Unknown. Charles Guiteau.

Gargoyles
Rabbitt. Gargoyle.
Sandburg, C. Broken-Face Gargoyles.
Gargoyle.
Shaw, R. Gargoyle.

Garlic
Foster, J. Garlic.
Horace. Counterblast against Garlic, A.

Garrison, William Lloyd
Ray, H. William Lloyd Garrison.

Garters
Davies, S. On a Pair of Garters.

Gasoline Stations
Bishop, E. Filling Station.
Espada. Rednecks.
Grass. Gasco.

Gates
Andal. O you who guard over.
Awoonor. At the Gates.
Booth, P. Crossing.
Daryush. It is pleasant to hang out.
Dickinson, E. Soul selects her own Society—
  The The.
Gorham. Princess Parade.
Homer. Gardens of Alcinous, The.
Macaulay, T. Horatius at the Bridge.
Mew. At the Convent Gate.
Mo Shih-lung. Saying Good-bye to a Singing
  Girl Who Has Decided to Become a Nun.
Mountain, M. He leans on the gate going
  staying.
Ni Tsan. To the Retired Scholar Chang.
Probyn. Blossom.
Shapiro, D. After.
Tai Piao-yüan. Cheng-tao Temple.
T'ang Yin. Scene at Heaven Gate, The.
Unknown. East Gate Willows.
Eastern Gate, The.
Wang Shih-chieng. After Rain, Visiting the
  Temple of Heavenly Peace.
Wen Cheng-ming. In the sixth month, outside
  the gate.
Yang Shih-ch'i. I Was Received in an Early
  Audience at Heaven-Gate and Then at Noon
  I Was Summoned to the Yu-shun Gate. In
  the Evening I Withdrew, and Improvised This
  Poem.
Yang Wei-chen. Bamboo Branch Song of
  West Lake.
Yasuda. On the bench I wait.

Gauguin, Paul
Hearne, V. Gauguin's White Horse.
Saitō Mokichi. Tanka: "Self-portrait, A."
Walcott. Gauguin.

Gawaine, Sir
Unknown. This kyng lay at Camylot upon
  Krystmasse.
Winters, Y. Sir Gawaine and the Green
  Knight.

Gazelles
Lawrence, D. Gazelle calf, O my children,
  The.
Moore, T. Gazelles, The.
Rilke. Gazelle, The.

Geese
Aesop. Swan and the Goose, The.
Berry, W. Wild Geese, The.
Braun, R. Goose.
Lilies, The.
Carroll, J. Withdrawal Letter.
Cheng Hsieh. For Contemporary Artist Pien
  Wei-Ch'I.
Coatsworth. And Stands There Sighing.
Field, R. Something told the wild geese.
Glück, L. Messengers.
Ho Ching-ming. Ch'ang-an.
Imbs. Wind Was There, The.
Ise. As the first spring mists appear.
Issa. Wild Goose, Wild Goose.
Kikaku. Above the boat.
Li Meng-yang. Spring Vista from the Tower
  of Illuminated Distance.
Li Shang-yin. About Geese.
Lu Kuei Meng. Lone Wild Goose, A.
Mao Tse-tung. Loushan Pass.
Masaoka Shiki. Wild geese cry, The.
McCosker. Full Moon that Strikes the Earth
  Cold.
Mei Yao Ch'en. Boat-pullers, The.
Mother Goose. Goosey, goosey, gander[,
  where *or* whither shall I wander? shall I
  wander?].
Mountain, M. Gosling following its neck to
  the bug.
Nesbit, E. Goose-Girl, The.
Oliver, M. Wild Geese.

Piercy. Last Scene in the First Act.
Postcard from the Garden.
Po Chü-i. Releasing a Migrant 'Yen' (Wild
  Goose).
Sandburg, C. Bas-Relief.
Southey, R. To a Goose [*or* Gosse].
Spiess. Long wedge of geese, A.
Stafford, W. Late at Night.
Stallworthy, J. Poem about Poems about
  Vietnam, A.
Tai Piao-yüan. Painting of One Hundred Wild
  Geese, A.
Tao-chi. Inscribed on My Large Landscape
  Hanging Scroll "Listening to a Waterfall."
Tu Mu. Early Geese.
Tynan. Wild Geese.
Unknown. Cackle, cackle, Mother Goose.
Grey goose and gander.
"Pax vobis," quod the fox.
Three grey geese in a green field grazing.
When the Rain Raineth.
Wire, briar, limber-lock.
Van den Heuvel. Geese have gone, The.
Waniek. Bali Hai Calls Mama.
Warren, R. Heart of Autumn.
Tell Me a Story.
Whitman, W. Wild gander leads his flock
  through the cool night, The.
Yü Chi. After Snow—Impromptu.
Yüan Hung-tao. Woman's Room in Autumn,
  A.
Yün Shou-p'ing. Sadness in the Autumn
  Chambers.

Gems
Dickinson, E. 'Tis little I— could care for
  Pearls.
Douglas, L. Impression de Nuit; London.
Ellis, P. "Scientists find universe awash in
  tiny diamonds."
Herrick. Amber Bead, The.
To Julia ("How rich and pleasing thou, my
  Julia, art").
To the Right Honourable Mildmay, Earl of
  Westmorland.
Kao Ch'i. Ballad of the Deserted Mansion.
Lowther. Stone Diary, A.
McGuckian. Laurentia.
Rossetti, C. Flint.
Slater, F. Stars in Sand.
Spenser. Sonnet 15: "Ye tradeful merchants
  that, with weary toil."
Summers, H. As I went out this May morning
  I found.
Taylor, J. Star, The.

Generals
Betjeman. Old Land Dog, The.
Bierce. General B. F. Butler.
Dobyns. General Matthei Drives Home
  through Santiago.
Garman. Bury the Great Horse.
Graves, R. General Elliott, The.
Sassoon. General, The.
Sherwood, K. Albert Sidney Johnston.
Wallace, R. Nightline: An Interview with the
  General.

Generosity
Browning, E. Sonnet: "What can I give thee
  back, O liberal."
Hughes, L. Preference.
Ilam Peruvaluti. This World Lives Because.
Kapilar. Kāri Sober.
Martial. In Lupum.
McGinley. Giveaway, The.
Muruvalar. He has held.
Perevin Muruvalar. Elegy: "He has held."
Peruvatuti. This World Lives Because.
Rossetti, C. Don't look for the flaws as you
  go.
Spencer, A. Creed.
Trainin. Sunbeams.
Unknown. (My Daily Creed).
Walter, H. I would be true, for there are those
  [who trust me].
Werth. I'll be polite in many ways.

Genetics and Geneticists. *See* **Evolution**

Geneva, Switzerland
Reid, A. Geneva.

Genius
Browning, E.   To George Sand: A Recognition.
Cotter, J.   On Hearing James W. Riley Read.
Glazkov.   To My Friends.
Graeme.   Mortified Genius, The.
Hughes, L.   Genius Child.
Kizer, C.   Twelve O'Clock.
Menken.   Genius is power.
Merry.   Genius, or Muse, whate'er thou art! whose thrill.
Robinson, E.   Ben Jonson Entertains a Man from Stratford.
Smith, S.   Sterilization.

Gentians
Bryant, W.   To the Fringed Gentian.
Lawrence, D.   Bavarian Gentians.

Geodes
Merrill, J.   Geode, the troll's melon.

Geography and Geographers
Chesterton, G.   Geography.
Donne.   Hymn[e] to God My God, In My Sickness[e].
Koch, K.   Geography.

Geology and Geologists
Ciardi.   Goodnight.
Day, C.   Yesterday explorers found.
Pratt, E.   Precambrian [or Pre-Cambrian] Shield, The.
Redgrove, P.   Minerals of Cornwall, Stones of Cornwall.
Rexroth, K.   Lyell's Hypothesis Again.
Snyder, G.   What Happened Here Before.
Solheim.   Cambrian Night.
Xuân Diệu.   Geologist and Millions of Years, A.

Geometry
Dove, R.   Geometry.
Kenward.   Technicians.
See also **Euclid**

George I, King of England
Browne, S.   Epigram: "King to Oxford sent a troop of horse, The."
Trapp.   Epigram: "King, observing with judicious eyes, The."

George II, King of England
Carey, H.   Lilliputian Ode on Their Majesties' Accession, A.
Unknown.   What mean these loud aerial cracks I hear?

George III, King of England
Byron, G.   Vision of Judgment, The.
Carey, H.   Lilliputian Ode on Their Majesties' Accession, A.
Koch, K.   You were wearing your Edgar Allan Poe printed cotton blouse.
Lowell, R.   George III.
"Pindar."   George III Visits Whitbread's Brewery.

George V, King of England
Betjeman.   "New King Arrives in His Capital by Air. . . "—Daily Newspaper.
Hayward, C.   King George V.

George VI, King of England
Ngani.   Praises of King George VI.

Georgia (state)
Bottoms.   In a U-Haul North of Damascus.
Broonzy.   Southern Blues, The.
Brown, S.   Slim in Atlanta.
Davis, F.   Robert Whitmore.
Dickey, J.   In the Marble Quarry.
Dove, R.   Planning the Perfect Evening.
Evans, M.   Daufuskie.
Hughes, L.   Sun Song.
Jones, R.   Contempt.
Lanier, S.   Song of the Chattahoochee.
McElroy, C.   This Is the Poem I Never Meant to Write.
Toomer.   Georgia Dusk.
Portrait in Georgia.
Work.   Marching through Georgia.

Geraniums
Clark, M.   Red Geraniums.
Cornford, F.   On August the Thirteenth.
Dorn, E.   Geranium.
Gibson, W.   Geraniums.

Jacobsen, J.   Motion, The.
Lawrence, D.   Red Geranium and Godly Mignonette.
Oppen.   Discrete Series 1929–1933.
Roethke.   Geranium, The.

German (language)
Buckley, V.   Teaching German Literature.
Graham, V.   Ein Complaint.
Morgenstern.   Ghost.

Germans, The
Caraion.   Song from the Occupation Time.
Heyen.   Riddle: "From Belsen a crate of gold teeth."
Jacob, M.   In Search of the Traitor.
Leland, C.   Breitmann in Paris.
There's a liddle fact of hishdory vitch few hafe oonderdstand.
Wein Geist.
Smith, S.   On the Death of a German Philosopher.
Tsvetayeva.   O what tears in eyes now.
They took quickly, they took hugely.

Germany
Bachmann.   Early Noon.
Bartsch.   Rita's husband gave Rita her walking papers.
Bowers, E.   Prince, The.
Brecht, B.   From a German War Primer.
War Has Been Given a Bad Name.
Brock, V.   Remembering Dresden.
Celan.   Death Fugue, A.
Eich.   Seminar for Backward Pupils.
Éluard, P.   Nazi Song.
Enright, D.   No Offence.
Fenton, J.   German Requiem, A.
Gershon.   Race.
Huelsenbeck, R.   We hardly had gotten the man's pants down.
Logau.   Booty from the German War.
German Language, The.
Longfellow, H.   Nuremberg.
Lowell, R.   Exile's Return, The.
"Martin."   Dreams in German.
Maxton.   Deutschland.
Nagys.   Hallesches Tor: Communion.
Norton, C.   Bingen on the Rhine.
Plomer.   Walk in Würzburg, A.
Porter, P.   May, 1945.
Schiff, H.   German Frontier at Basel: 1942 and 1992, The.
Shanks.   High Germany.
Sisson.   Over the Wall: Berlin, May 1975.
Sorley.   To Germany.
Tranter.   Enzensberger at 'Exiles'.
Lufthansa.
Weckherlin.   To Germany.
Yevtushenko.   Babii Yar.
Žukauskas.   Midwinter Tourists.

Germs
Atwell.   Some Little Bug.
Nash, O.   Germ, The.

Gethsemane
Hemans.   Agony in the Garden, The.
Kane, P.   Disciples Asleep at Gethsemane.
Kipling, R.   Gethsemane [1914–18].
Pasternak, B.   Garden of Gethsemane, The.
Hamlet.
Mark 14:26–42; And when they had sung.
Pratt, E.   From Stone to Steel ("From stone to bronze, from bronze to steel").
Southwell.   Christs Sleeping Friends.
Sinnes Heavie Loade.
Unknown.   Sory beverech [or beverech] it is, and sore it is abought [or abouth], A.

Gettysburg, Battle of (1863)
Harte, B.   John Burns of Gettysburg.
Kenyon, J.   Gettysburg, July 1, 1863.
Masters, E.   Battle of Gettysburg, The.
Gettysburg.
Thompson, W.   High Tide at Gettysburg, The.

Ghana
Ama Ata Aidoo.   Cornfields in Accra.
Laing, K.   Same Corpse, The.

Ghettos
Ackerman, D.   Lines Written in a Pittsburgh Skyscraper.

Dumas, H.   Concentration Camp Blues.
Friedmann.   Butterfly, The.
Glatstein.   Back to the Ghetto.
Goulbourne.   This Is the Place Where.
Klein, A.   Autobiographical.
Lorde.   New York City 1970.
Meléndez.   Oye Mundo/Sometimes.
Milosz, C.   Poor Christian Looks at the Ghetto, A.
Rodgers, C.   U Name This One.
Slonimski.   Elegy: "No more, no more Jewish townships in Poland."
Steptoe.   Wired In.
Voznesensky.   Call of the Lake, The.

Ghost Dances and Ghost Dancers
Arapaho Oral Tradition.   Ghost Dance Songs.

Ghosts
Addison, J.   In this grave age, when comedies are few.
Alcott, L.   Our Little Ghost.
Alegría.   Nocturnal Visits.
Alexander, C.   They shorten'd the corp, and they pack'd.
Anthony, G.   Autumn Evening.
Avakkumova.   Dead man touched me with his hand, A.
Baillie, J.   Ghost of Edward.
Ghost of Fadon, The.
Baker, H.   Toward Guinea: For Larry Neal, 1937–1981.
Balaban.   After our war, the dismembered bits.
Baraka.   Masked Angel Costume / The Sayings of Mantan Moreland.
Beddoes.   Carrion Crow, The.
Phantom-Wooer, The.
Song by Isbrand.
Bernstein, O.   Memories of Her Friend Who Died.
Binyon.   Those That Are Gone.
Blair, R.   Oft in the lone church-yard at night I've seen.
Whilst some affect the sun, and some the shade.
Bonnefoy.   De Natura Rerum.
Bontemps.   Southern Mansion.
Bridges, R.   Going Home.
Brown, S.   After the Vietnam War.
Byron, G.   Grim reader, did you ever see a ghost?
Saul.
Cassian.   Ghost.
Causley.   By St. Thomas Water.
Colonel Fazackerley [Butterworth-Toast].
Cavafy.   Voices.
Chōkū.   Tanka: "Phantom appears, A."
Churchill, C.   Ghost, The.
Clare, J.   To Mary: 'It Is the Evening Hour'.
Coleman, W.   American Sonnet (35).
Coleridge, S.   I woke, and we were sailing on.
Loud wind never reached the ship, The.
Colvin, I.   Flying Dutchman, The.
Cornford, F.   All Souls' Night.
Crabbe.   Priest attending, found he spoke at times, The.
De la Mare.   Ghost, The.
Listeners, The.
Revenant, The.
Solitude.
Dickinson, E.   Distance that the dead have gone, The.
Digges.   Rough Music.
Donne.   Apparition, The.
Dryden, J.   Epilogue to *Tyrannic[k] Love.*
Spectre, fiercely staring, thus reply'd, The.
Edwards, R.   Recollections of an Old Spook.
Emanuel, L.   Dig, The.
"Ern Malley."   Coda.
Fanthorpe.   Father in the Railway Buffet.
Fuller, R.   Why do we return? Not in the darkened rooms.
Gilbert, C.   This Bridge Across.
Graves, R.   Welsh Incident.
Gregg.   Adult.
Hall, D.   Mount Kearsarge.
Hardy, T.   Garden Seat, The.
Haunter, The.
My spirit will not haunt the mound.

Phantom Horsewoman, The.
Souls of the Slain, The.
Strange House, The.
Harjo, J.　For Anna Mae Aquash Whose Spirit Is Present Here and in the Dappled Stars.
Harper, M.　Ghost of Soul-making, The.
Heath-Stubbs.　Simcox was one of several rather uninteresting.
Hecht, A.　Ghost in the Martini, The.
Still Life.
Hill, G.　And it seemed, while we waited, he began to walk towards us.
Hiott.　Tale of Mushrooms.
Holtby, W.　For the Ghost of Elinor Wylie.
Hood, T.　Sally Simpkin's Lament, [or John Jones's Kit-Cat-astrophe].
Hooper, V.　Drawing Room Drama.
Housman, A.　In midnights of November.
When I watch the living meet.
Howard, R.　Among the Missing.
Hugo, R.　Way a Ghost Dissolves, The.
Jentzsch.　Terezin, the Graveyard.
Johnson, S.　Do They Return?
Justice, D.　Beyond the Hunting Woods.
Keesing.　Queer Thing, A.
Kipling, R.　Looking Glass, The.
Komunyakaa.　Dead at Quang Tri, The.
Lawrence, D.　Nostalgia.
Leithauser.　Ghost of a Ghost, The.
Levi, P.　Survivor, The.
Levy, A.　Old House, The.
Lindsay, L.　Auld Robin Gray.
Livesay, D.　Uninvited, The.
Longfellow, H.　Cross of Snow, The.
Haunted Houses.
Lowell, R.　Ghost is someone: death has left a hole, A.
MacLean, S.　Hallaig.
Maiden.　Air.
Foundations, The.
Mallet.　William and Margaret.
Mearns.　Antigonish.
Merrill, J.　Correct but cautious, that first night, we asked.
Moody, A.　Dr. Johnson's Ghost.
Morgenstern.　Ghost.
Nagy, A.　Ghost, The.
Nesbit, E.　Gray Folk, The.
Haunted.
Villeggiature.
Nguyễn Du.　Calling All Souls.
Noyes, A.　Highwayman, The.
Olson, C.　As the dead prey upon us.
Owen, W.　Shadwell Stair.
Park, M.　Lowering the Coffin.
Peacock, T.　Ghosts, The.
Phillips, D.　Hounds are either the work of wind, The.
Phillips, S.　Apparition, The.
Piatt, S.　Army of Occupation.
Poe.　Conqueror Worm, The.
Haunted Palace, The.
Pollitt.　Visitors.
Pope, A.　Dull, Sullen Prisoners.
Propertius.　Ghosts do exist; death does not finish everything.
Ramanujan.　Some People.
Rankin, P.　To the House Ghost.
Ransom, J.　Spectral Lovers.
Ravikovitch.　War's End.
Reid, A.　Ghosts.
Rilke.　Black Cat.
Robinson, A.　Dead Friend, The.
Robinson, E.　Why He Was There.
Robinson, M.　Haunted Beach, The.
Rossetti, C.　Chilly Night, A.
Poor Ghost, The.
Rückert.　Barbarossa.
Sassoon.　At Daybreak.
Scott, A.　Coronach.
Scupham.　House of Geraniums, A.
Senghor.　Visit.
Shakespeare, W.　Angels and ministers of grace defend us!
Hamlet.
Let me see, let me see; is not the leaf turned down.

Where wilt thou lead me? Speak; I'll go no further.
Sitwell, D.　Extract from Romance.
Smith, I.　Ghost, The.
Smith, S.　Le Revenant.
Parklands, The.
Wanderer, The.
Soyinka.　Abiku.
Civilian and Soldier.
Stafford, W.　Both Ways.
Stevens, W.　Rabbit Is King of the Ghosts, A.
Tao Tschung Yu.　Familiar Spirits.
Tekkan.　Tanka: "Plucking feathers."
Tennyson, A.　I shall not see thee. Dare I say.
Thomas, D.　Ghost Story.
I, the first named.
Trench, H.　She Comes Not When Noon Is on the Roses.
Tu Fu.　Snow Storm.
Unknown.　Cauld Lad of Hilton, The *or* The Wandering Spectre.
Dark House, The.
Ghost & Shaman.
Should Latin, Greek, and Hebrew fail.
Suffolk Miracle, The.
There were three ghostesses.
There were two ghostesses.
Three Ghostesses.
Wife of Usher's Well, The.
Virgil.　Dido in the Elysian Fields.
Wallace-Crabbe.　Trace Elements.
Waniek.　House on Moscow Street, The.
Weaver, M.　Appaloosa, The.
Whitman, W.　As if a phantom caress'd me.
Whittier.　Sisters, The.
Wordsworth, W.　Lucy Gray; or, Solitude.
She was a Phantom of delight.
Wright, J.　My Grandmother's Ghost.
Yeats.　All Souls' Night.
Apparitions, The.
Crazy Jane and Jack the Journeyman.
To a Shade.
Young, A.　Shepherd's Hut, The.

Giants
Alver.　Children of the Wind.
Baudelaire.　Giantess, The.
Brooks, G.　Jane Addams (September 6, 1860– May 21, 1935).
Hall, D.　Sleeping Giant, The.
Major, C.　Giant Red Woman.
Mayer, G.　Count Carrots.
Millay, E.　Bean-Stalk, The.
Namjoshi, S.　From the Travels of Gulliver.
Reader.　When Paul Bunyan was ill we sent.
Riley, J.　Jack the Giant-Killer.
Rosen, M.　Giant Jojo.
Smith, W.　Big Gumbo.

Gibbon, Edward
Hardy, T.　Lausanne: In Gibbon's Old Garden: 11–12 p.m.
Landor, W.　Distribution of Honours for Literature.

Gibraltar
Blunt, W.　Gibraltar.

Gifts and Giving
Alford, J.　Thanks Be to God.
Antiphilus.　Gifts to a Lady.
Anyte.　Big enough for an ox, the cauldron.
To shock-haired Pan and the nymphs who protect the cow-byres.
Balfour.　Best thing to give, The.
Betjeman.　Christmas.
Bible, *O.T.*　Song: "Come, my beloved."
Browning, E.　Sonnet: "Belovèd, thou hast brought me many flowers."
Bruner.　Beggar, The.
Greater Gift, The.
Causley.　My young man's a Cornishman.
Nursery Rhyme of Innocence and Experience.
Clark, T.　Greeks, The.
Coleridge, M.　Broken Friendship.
Corben.　Before Christmas.
Creeley.　Gift, The.
Crinagoras.　This silver thing I send you for your birthday.
This wingtip feather from a hook-beaked eagle.

Davenant.　For the Lady Olivia Porter; a Present upon a New Year's Day.
Davies, M.　Let Me Be a Giver.
Dickinson, E.　'Tis customary as we part.
Doolittle, H.　Acon.
Gift, The.
Wine Bowl.
Eliot, T.　Now when Jesus was born.
Emerson, R.　Give all to love;.
Erucius of Cyzicus.　I, the priest of Rhea, long-haired.
Ewing, J.　Gifts.
Farjeon, E.　Advice to a Child.
Fisher, A.　Fair Exchange.
Fiskin.　Magi, The.
Freeman, C.　Christmas Morning I.
Frost, R.　Gift Outright, The.
Fulton, A.　Self-Storage.
Gay, J.　To a Young Lady, with Some Lampreys.
Gruber, A.　My Neighbor's Roses.
Guiterman.　Christmas Exchange, The.
Of Giving.
Hafiz.　Oft have I said, I say it once more.
Herrick.　New-Year's [or New-Yeares] Gift Sent to Sir Simeon Steward, A.
Primrose, The.
Ring Presented to Julia, A.
Ternarie of Littles, upon a Pipkin of Jellie [or Jelly] Sent to a Lady, A.
To His Saviour, a Child; a Present, by a Child.
Holtby, W.　Beauty the Lover's Gift?
Hsieh Chin.　Government wine of Peking is sweeter than honey, The.
Huddle.　My Daddy, Whenever He Went Some Place.
Ignatow, D.　Mystique.
Irvine, W.　To be Young, Gifted, and Black.
Irving, M.　Wedding Gift, The.
Kim, S.　Gift of Love.
Komunyakaa.　Gift Horse.
Lamantia.　Time Traveler's Potlatch.
Landon.　Gifts Misused.
Leonidas.　Theris, whose hands were cunning.
Leonidas of Alexandria.　You send me reams of snowy paper.
Leonidas of Tarentum.　Sheep-folds, holy spring of the Nymphs.
Silver Eros the ankle bracelet, The.
Li Po.　In Reply When Lesser Officials of Chung-tu Brought a Pot of Wine and Two Fish to My Inn as Gifts.
Lowell, A.　Autumn.
Lugovskoy.　Bear, The.
Martial.　Roman Presents.
Roman Thank-You Letter, A.
Milton.　On His Blindness.
Momaday.　Gift, The.
Moorer.　Accompanying a Gift ("From thy patient, who while here").
Accompanying a Gift ("One whose love will never end").
Murillo.　Conversation in Front of a Helicopter.
Park, H.　Song for Empty Cup.
Po Chü-i.　Feelings Wakened by a Mirror.
Hat Given to the Poet by Li Chien, The.
Red Cockatoo, The.
Sentimental Poem.
Silver Spoon, The.
Too Brilliant.
Prince, F.　Token, The.
Procter, A.　Love Token, A.
Rabéarivelo.　Rondo for the Poet's Children.
Raine, K.　Heirloom.
Reader.　When Paul Bunyan was ill we sent.
Roethke.　Her Reticence.
Rossetti, C.　My Gift.
O sailor, come ashore, / What have you brought for me?
Ruiz, J.　Gifts.
Sandall.　Song: "Love that is hoarded, moulds at last."
Sandburg, C.　Englishman in the old days, An.
Santayana.　With you a part of me hath passed away.
Schuyler, J.　Stone Knife, A.

Seiler. Lake, The.
Shange. You are sucha fool / i haveta love you.
Shelley, P. To————: "One word is too often profaned."
"Shu Ting." Gifts.
Skoyles. Head of Tasso, The.
Snow, K. Gifts.
Sorrentino. Oranges Returned, The.
Springer, T. Giving and Forgiving.
Sun Kuang-hsien. Tune: "Paying Homage at the Golden Gate."
Teasdale. Gift, The.
Tomlinson, C. Picture of J. T. in a Prospect of Stone, The.
Tsvetayeva. Bethlehem.
Unknown. Beyond the Profit of Today.
Child's Offering, A.
For Baby.
Giving.
Her saffron gown.
I went downtown.
In the garden a strange tree grows.
My Neighbor's Reply.
Riddle Song, The.
Short Sermon.
South of the Great Sea.
Theris, whose hands were cunning.
Twelve Days of Christmas, The.
Understanding.
Walton, T. God's Gifts to Me.
Wilcox, E. Morning Prayer, A.
Williams, W. Gift, The.
Wright, J. Request to a Year.
Wyatt, T. To seek each where where man doth live.
Yakamochi. I send you a box.
Yeats. Never give all the heart, for love.
Yü Wu-ling. Offering Wine.

Ginkgo Trees
Bell, M. These Green-going-to-Yellow.
Nemerov. Ginkgoes in Fall.
Yosano. Like tiny golden.
Tanka: "Each shaped."

Ginsberg, Allen
Berrigan, T. Red Shift.
Derricotte. Allen Ginsberg.
Ferlinghetti, L. He is one of the prophets come back.
Ginsberg, A. After Lalon.
My Alba.
Salutations to Fernando Pessoa.
So I dream nightly of an embarkation.
This Form of Life Needs Sex.
Why Is God Love, Jack?
Hollander, J. Helicon.
Peters, R. Blessing a Bride and Groom; a Wedding Night Poem.

Giraffes
Beveridge. Domesticity of Giraffes, The.
Hood, T. On the Death of the Giraffe.
Moore, M. To a Giraffe.
Plumly. Giraffe.
Unknown. Giraffe.
Yukitsuna. Tanka: "Each morning I awake."

Girdles
Waller, E. On a Girdle.

Girls
Ashbery. Thoughts of a Young Girl.
Barlas. Dancing Girl, The.
Bell, M. Mystery of Emily Dickinson, The.
Blaga. Soul of the Village, The.
Blake, W. Little Girl Found, The.
Little Girl Lost, A.
Boccaccio. I am a young maiden, and I willingly.
Brooks, G. Narcissa.
Brownstein. Jet Set Melodrama.
Campbell, D. Small-town Gladys.
Campion, T. Advice to a Girl.
There is a Garden in her face.
Cassells. Soul Make A Path Through Shouting.
Chiricahua Apache Oral Tradition. Song for Girls' Puberty Rites.
Ciardi. All about Boys and Girls.
Desnos. St Merri district, The.

Dickinson, E. I'm "wife"—I've finished that.
Duhamel. Feminism.
Elenkov. Ten Girls.
Eliot, T. La Figlia Che Piange.
Elytis. Axion Esti, The.
Embiricos. Caryatids, The.
Ewart. Lifelines.
"Field." Girl, A.
Gill, G. Girl's desire moves among her bangles, The.
Glanz-Leyeles. White Swan.
Gorman, L. Beyond the laughing billboard girl.
Billboard girl.
Down the billboard girl's bare belly.
One AM.
Greenaway. Three little girls were sitting on a rail.
Heaney, S. New Song, A.
Hemans. Evening Prayer, at a Girls' School.
Hitomaro. When I gathered flowers.
Hogg, J. When Maggy Gangs Away.
Höllerer. Held back, like a bow drawn tight.
Holmes, R. Little girl's heart must be wide and, A.
Hugo, V. She had no shoes on, she had freed her hair.
Hull, A. Another Rhythm.
Ishikawa Takuboku. Tanka: "Young maidens."
Johnson, J. Girl of fifteen.
Koneski. Wheat, The.
Kraujiete. City Girls.
Li Ho. Girl Combs Her Hair, A.
Li Po. Girl of Yueh, The.
Girls of Yueh, The.
Li Shang-yin. At eight stealing a mirror glance.
Lorde. Story Books on a Kitchen Table.
MacLean, S. Cry of Europe, The.
MacLeish. Where the Hayfields Were.
Maiden. New.
Mansour, J. Regulation equipment.
McClintock, M. Small girl, A.
McGinley. Portrait of Girl with Comic Book.
McGough, R. My Cat and I.
Miles, J. Travelers.
Morus. In Praise of a Girl.
Moss, T. Anointing, An.
Nash, O. Adventures of Isabel.
Ochester. In the Library.
Olds, S. One Girl at the Boys Party, The.
Pajamas.
Padgett, R. Strawberries in Mexico.
Page, P. Young Girls.
Paz. Girl.
Peacock, M. Good Girl.
Phylip, S. Seagull, The.
"Pindar." Ode to a Country Hoyden.
Pizzarelli. Girl / loosens her bra, The.
Poliziano. She Finds Herself in a Garden.
Pound, E. Girl, A.
Radauskas. Salesgirl.
Randall, D. Blackberry Sweet.
Ravikovitch. Time Caught in a Net.
Riley, J. Extremes.
Rilke. Gazelle, The.
Roughton. Soluble Noughts and Crosses; or, California, Here I Come.
Rózewicz. Moment.
Sanchez, S. Song No. 2: "I say. all you young girls waiting to live."
Sandburg, C. Little girl saw her first troop parade and asked, "What are those?", The.
Sappho. One Girl.
Shurin. Blue Shade.
Simic. Ballad: "What's that approaching like dust like poverty."
Stevens, W. Plot Against the Giant, The.
Symons, A. Morbidezza.
Tanikawa Shuntaro. Concerning a Girl.
Tuckerman, F. Coralie.
Ulinover. Havdolah Wine.
Unknown. Girl.
Jemima.
Natural History.
Near the East Gate.
Wakoski. Girls, The.

Walwicz. Little Red Riding Hood.
Weatherly, T. Mud Water Shango.
Wen-Ti Chien. Lo-yang.
Williams, W. Lonely Street, The.
Wordsworth, W. Solitary Reaper, The.
Wright, F. Depiction of Childhood.
Yeats. Politics.
See also **Adolescence; Childhood and Children; Youth**

Giving. *See* **Gifts and Giving**

Glaciers
"Eliza." Epistle to John Walker, Esq., An.
Haines, J. Into the Glacier.
McClure, M. Moiré.

Glasgow, Scotland
Mangan, G. Glasgow 1956.
Heraclitus at Glasgow Cross.
Morgan, E. Glasgow Sonnets.
King Billy.

Glass and Glassblowers
Brownstein. Glass Enclosure, The.
Davies, H. Poem: "It doesn't look like a finger it looks like a feather of broken glass."
Degutyte. Etude in Glass.
Gorham. White Tiger Leaps, The.
Hoffmann, R. Deceptively Like a Solid.
Merrill, J. Octopus, The.
Morton, J. Epitaph: "Glassblower lies here at rest, A."
Rabéarivelo. Black glassmaker, The.
Scully, J. Glass Blower, The.
Shapiro, D. Book of Glass, A.
Supervielle. Earth.
Ward, D. Glass House.
Yoshimi. Tanka: "Along a street."

Glasses. *See* **Eyeglasses**

Glencoe, Scotland
Stewart, D. Sigh, wind in the pine.

Globes
Donne. Valediction: Of Weeping, A.
Reaney. School Globe, The.
Turner, C. Letty's Globe.

Glory
Bacchylides. Yet of all that Hellas holds.
Bible, *O.T.* Holy, holy, holy.
Psalm 24.
Psalm 29.
Borges. John 1:14; And the Word became flesh and dwelt among us.
Disch. Argument Resumed; Or, Up Through Tribeca, The.
Donne. Anniversary [*or* Anniversarie], The.
"Field." Beloved, my glory in thee is not ceased.
Fellowship.
Francis of Assisi. Canticle of Living Creatures.
Garrick. Heart of Oak.
Garrigue. Mouse, The.
Hankey. I Love to Tell the Story.
Hawthorne, N. I Left My Low amd Humble Home.
Herrick. Posting to Printing.
Homer. Sarpedon's Speech.
Wen Cheng-ming. This man of leisure for twenty years.

Glossolalia
Morgan, R. Gift of Tongues, The.

Gloucester, Massachusetts
Dorn, E. From Gloucester Out.
Olson, C. Librarian, The.
Maximus, to Gloucester, Letter 27.

Gloves
Bond, H. Glove, The.
Cleage. Confession.
Cornford, F. To a Fat Lady Seen from the Train.
Fumi Saito. Tanka: "Even the black gloves."
Jonson, B. Glove, The.
Lovelace, R. Elinda's [*or* Ellinda's] Glove.
Nye, N. Yellow Glove.
Roseliep. He removes his glove.
Tucker, M. That Glove.

See also **Mittens**

Glowworms

Cowper, W. Nightingale and the Glowworm, The.

Marvell. Mower to the Glow-Worms [*or* Glowworms *or* Glo-Worms], The.

McCord, D. Glowworm.

Ropes. Glow-Worms.

Stanley, T. Glowworm, The.

Wordsworth, W. Among all lovely things my Love had been.

See also **Fireflies**

Gluttony and Gluttons

Alcman. Alkman's Supper.

Belloc. Vulture eats between his meals, The.

Cook, E. Mouse and the Cake, The.

Jonson, B. Hymn to Comus.

On Gut.

Kizer, C. Food of Love.

Langland, W. Glutton [*or* Glutton in the Tavern], The.

Moore, T. Oh Dick! You may talk of your writing and reading.

Oakman. Glutton, The.

Shakespeare, W. Sonnet 75.

Taylor, A. Notorious Glutton, The.

Unknown. Greedy Jane.

Wright, K. Greedyguts.

Glyn, Elinor

Unknown. Elinor Glyn.

Gnats

Beaumont, J. Gnat, The.

Graves, R. One Hard Look.

Yoshimi. Tanka: "Having crushed."

Gnomes

Druce. Apropos of Garden Statuary: A Disquisition upon a Minor Genre.

Goats

Anyte. Children have put purple, The.

Children have tied you, billy-goat, with bright, The.

Look at the horned goat of Dionysus.

Dennis, N. Maltese Goat.

Erucius of Cyzicus. Kleson's goat snorted all night through the dark.

Herford. Smile of the Goat has a meaning that few, The.

Kelly, B. Song: "Listen: there was a goat's head hanging by ropes in a tree."

Magowan. Zeimbekiko ("Old man gets up turns, An").

Shange. Ancestral Messengers/Composition 13.

Simic. Old Mountain Road.

Stephens, J. Goat Paths, The.

Unknown. Billy Goat.

Goat, The.

Old Hogan's goat was feeling fine.

Wills, J. Goats on the roof.

Zarzyski. Trespasses.

Goblins

Fyleman. Goblin lives in our house, in our house, in our house, A.

Herrick. Ceremony upon Candlemas Eve.

Monro. Overheard on a Saltmarsh.

Prelutsky. Mother Goblin's Lullaby.

Riley, J. Little Orphant Annie's come to our house to stay.

Nine Little Goblins, The.

Shakespeare, W. Either I mistake your shape and making quite.

See also **Elves; Fairies; Ghosts**

God

Abse. Of Itzig and His Dog.

"Ada." Lines.

"Adunis." New Noah, The.

Ai. Good Shepherd: Atlanta, 1981, The.

"Akhmatova." Lord is not merciful to reapers and gardeners, The.

Alabaster. O starry Temple of unvalted space.

Alcuin. Night Prayer, A.

Alexander, C. All things bright and beauteous.

Alexander, M. Psychotropic Squalls, The.

Alford, H. Come, ye thankful people, come.

Ali, A. In the Mountains.

Allen, P. Taku Skanskan.

Allen, S. To Satch.

Ambrose. Eternal, Thou.

Amergin. Mystery, The.

Amichai. God Has Mercy [*or* Pity] on Kindergarten Children.

Ammons. Hymn: "I know if I find you I will have to leave the earth."

"Angelus Silesius." God is a pure no-thing.

God, whose love and joy.

It Depends on You.

Apollinaire. Zone.

Appleman, P. Waiting for the Fire.

Arghezi. Gulf.

Psalm.

Arvey, V. All that I am.

Ashbery. Lament Upon the Waters, The.

Askew. Ballad Which Anne Askew[e] Made and Sang When She Was in Newgate, The.

Atwood. Resurrection.

Auden. Petition.

Augustine. My heart was darkened over with grief, and whatever I.

Aworinde. If a Suite in Praise of the Yoruba Oracle.

Baba Kuhi of Shiraz. In the market, in the cloister—only God I saw.

Babcock, M. Be Strong!

This Is My Father's World.

Ballou, S. Almighty God in being was.

Bancquart. Sea.

Bangs, J. Blind.

Baranczak, S. N. N. Tries to Remember the Words of a Prayer.

Barbauld. Summer Evening's Meditation, A.

To the Poor.

Barker, G. Dog, Dog in My Manger.

Reverend Arbuthnot-Armitage-Brown, The.

Baudelaire. Fuses I and II.

Baxter, J. Colin, you can tell my words are crippled now.

Small grey cloudy louse that nests in my beard, The.

Benton, P. Psalm 23: "Lord is my shepherd; I shall not want, The."

Berryman. Certainty Before Lunch.

Lauds.

Nothing there? nothing up the sky alive.

Betjeman. In Westminster Abbey.

Bialik. Pool, The.

Bible, *N.T.* End To Tears, An.

Bible, *O.T.* Bible, Isaiah 40:31, The.

Bible, Psalm 1:1–3, The.

Bless the Lord, O my soul.

Genesis.

Holy, holy, holy.

It is a good thing to give thanks.

My son, forget not my law; but let thine heart keep my commandments.

New Year, The.

Psalm 19.

Psalm 23.

Psalm 023: "Lord is my shepherd; I shall not, The."

Psalm 100.

Psalm 147: "Praise ye the Lord."

Psalm 148.

They that go down to the sea in.

Bishop, J. Hunchback, The.

Blake, W. Book of Urizen [*or* First Book of Urizen], The.

Divine Image, The ("To Mercy, Pity, Peace and Love").

Jerusalem.

Little Boy Found, The.

Little Vagabond, The.

To Nobodaddy.

To see a World in a Grain of Sand.

Tyger, The.

Blaser. Even on Sunday.

Bly, R. NOTL.

Waking from Sleep.

Boethius. All human kind on earth.

Boetius. Libr. 3. Metr. 6.

Book III. Metre 6.

None from thy laws are free.

Bonhoeffer. Who am I? They often tell me.

Bontemps. Golgotha is a mountain, a purple mound.

Miracles.

Nocturne at Bethesda.

Booth, P. Original Sequence.

Borges. Everness.

Bowring. God Is Love.

Bradstreet, A. Here Follows Some Verses upon the Burning of Our House [July 10th, 1966. Copied Out of a Loose Paper].

To My Dear Children.

Braithwaite. Rye Bread.

Breytenbach. Breyten Prays for Himself.

Brontë, C. Orphan Child, The.

Brontë, E. No coward soul is mine.

Brooks, G. Maxie Allen [always taught her].

Preacher: Ruminates Behind the Sermon, The.

Brown, S. Sister Lou.

Browne, W. Vision V.

Browning, E. Sleep, The.

Browning, R. Epilogue: "On the first of the Feast of Feasts."

Johannes Agricola in Meditation.

Porphyria's Lover.

Prospice.

Bruner. God's ways are strange; He chastens those.

Bryant, W. To A Waterfowl.

Bunin. At the gates of Zion, over Kedron.

Burns, R. *First Six Verses* of the Ninetieth Psalm, The.

Holy Willie's Prayer.

Byron, G. Ah! didst *thou* tempt my mother?

Campbell, R. Counsel.

St John of the Cross: Song of the Soul That Is Glad to Know God by Faith.

St John of the Cross: Songs of the Soul in Rapture.

Campion, T. Author of light, revive my dying spright.

Heart's Music.

O Come Quickly!

Seek the Lord, and in His ways persever.

To music bent is my retired mind.

Carruth, W. Each in His Own Tongue.

Catherine of Siena (A. K. A. Saint Catherine). We were enclosed.

Causley. Bible Story.

Cawein. Three Elements, The.

Celan. Alchemical.

Jugs, The.

Psalm: "No one kneads us again out of earth and clay."

Tenebrae.

Zürich, the Stork Inn.

Ceravolo. Data.

Fill and Illumined.

Chaucer. Truth.

Chon, P. Mischief.

Ch'u Yüan. Great Arbiter of Fate, The.

Clampitt. Sun Underfoot Among the Sundews, The.

Clare, J. First Love.

Hymn to the Creator.

Clarkson. Behold, the King of glory now is come.

Clifton, L. Kali.

Prayer.

Clough. Dipsychus.

What we, when face to face we see.

Cohen, J. Eternal Jew, The.

Cole, H. 40 Days and 40 Nights.

Coleridge, S. He prayeth best, who loveth best.

To Nature.

Collins, A. Song: "My straying thoughts, reduced stay."

Collymore. Ballad of an Old Woman.

Colman, H. On Balaam, and His Ass.

Colonna, V. I see in my mind, surrounding God.

Constable, H. To St Mary Magdalen.

Cook, E. Song for the Workers, A.

Coolbrith. Longing.

Corso. Hi.

Cowley, A. Garden, The.

Cowper, W. Light Shining out of Darkness.

Lines Written During a Period of Insanity.

Cranch. Correspondences.

Crane, H. Broken Tower, The.
Crane, S. Ah, God, the way your little finger moved.
God lay dead in Heaven.
Little ink more or less!, A.
Crashaw. Ecstacy, An.
Hymn to Saint Teresa.
Creeley. Awakening, The.
Cruz Varela. Invocation.
Cullen, C. For a Mouthy Woman.
For Amy Lowell.
Shroud of Color, The.
Yet Do I Marvel.
Cummings, E. I am a little church(no great cathedral).
I thank You God for most this amazing.
When any mortal(even the most odd).
Cust. Non Nobis.
Dante Alighieri. Ladies that have intelligence in love.
That lady of all gentle memories.
Davenant. Praise and Prayer.
Davies, S. To him with trumpets and with flutes.
Day Lewis. Offertorium.
De la Mare. Last Chapter, The.
DeBary. Under a Wiltshire Apple Tree.
Ded. At the end of a crazy-moon night.
I drag a boat over the ocean.
I was passionate.
This world.
Dickinson, E. Alter! When the Hills do—.
Brain—is wider than the Sky, The.
Drowning is not so pitiful.
God is a distant—stately Lover.
God is indeed a jealous God.
He fumbles at your Soul.
"Heavenly Father"—take to thee.
I am afraid to own a Body.
I gave myself to Him—.
I got so I could take his name.
I never saw a Moor.
Infinite a sudden Guest, The.
It was a quiet way—.
It would have starved a Gnat.
Love—is that later Thing than Death.
My Life Had Stood—A Loaded Gun.
Of God we ask one favor.
One who could repeat the Summer day, The.
Only News I know, The.
Publication—is the Auction.
Spring is the Period.
Struck, was I, not yet by Lightning.
There comes an hour when begging stops.
This was a Poet—It is That.
To know just how He suffered—would be dear.
Trees like Tassels—hit—and swung, The.
Truth—is as old as God.
Wild Nights—Wild Nights!
Dodson, O. Black Mother Praying.
Donne. "Batter my heart, three-person'd God; for you."
Father of heaven, and him, by whom.
Good Friday [or Goodfriday], 1613. Riding Westward.
Hymn[e] to God My God, In My Sickness[e].
Satire 3.
Doolittle, H. Helen.
Dorsey, T. Take My Hand, Precious Lord.
Douglas, L. Apologia.
Drayton. Song of the Faithful, A.
Driscoll, L. Thanksgiving.
Drummond de Andrade. Seven-Sided Poem.
Drummond, W. Book, The.
Du Bellay. It was the time, when rest, soft sliding downe.
Dunbar, P. Compensation.
Not they who soar, but they who plod.
Spiritual, A.
Duncan, R. This Place Rumord to Have Been Sodom.
Torso / Passages 18, The.
Dunn, D. Gardeners.
Dunn, S. Dancing with God.
Eady. My Mother is a God Fearing Woman.
Eberhart, R. Fury of Aerial Bombardment,

The.
On a Squirrel Crossing the Road in Autumn, in New England.
Echeruo. Man and God Distinguished.
Elizabeth, Queen of Bohemia. Verses by the Princess Elizabeth, Given to Lord Harington, of Exton, Her Preceptor.
Elliot, E. Plaint.
Emerson, R. Dæmonic and the Celestial Love, The.
Dear brother, would you know the life.
I Can.
Everson, W. Canticle to the Waterbirds, A.
South Coast, The.
Ewer. How odd / Of God.
Fairfax of Cameron. On the Fatal Day January 30, 1648.
Felsted. Thanks for Hearing.
Fenton, J. God, A Poem.
"Field." Beloved, now I love God first.
Fields, J. Jolly fat widows, The.
Fitzgerald, E. I sent my Soul through the Invisible.
73.
Fletcher, G. As when the cheerfull Sunne, elamping wide.
Francis of Assisi. Canticle of Living Creatures.
Prayer of St. Francis of Assisi for Peace.
Francis Xavier. Hymn.
Frost, R. Bereft.
Forgive, O Lord, my little jokes on Thee.
Sitting by a Bush in Broad Daylight.
Fuller, J. Whole New Scene, A.
Fuller, M. Sistrum.
Fullerton. John 14:1–2.
Poetry.
Gaba. Great Hymm.
Great Hymn.
Garnet. Hear ye not how, from all high points of Time.
Gascoigne. Gascoigne's Good-Morrow.
Gascoigne's Woodmanship.
Gascoyne. Rex Mundi.
Geda. God's Family.
Gershon. Experiments with God.
Gilbert-Lecomte. Preface or The Drama of Absence in an Eternal Heart.
Gilbo'a. Havdala.
Gillilan, S. "Are You There?"
Gilmore, J. He Leadeth Me.
Ginsberg, A. Why Is God Love, Jack?
Gioia. Prayer.
Giovanni. Poem for Flora.
Glück, L. Gift, The.
Lamentations.
Grahn. They Say She Is Veiled.
Gray, J. Parsifal Imitated from the French of Paul Verlaine.
Greenwell, D. Christina.
Gregg. Gnostics on Trial.
My Father and God.
Greiffenberg. I look.
On the Fruit-Providing Autumn Season.
Zealous Admonition to Praise.
Griffiths, A. His left hand, in heat of noonday.
Grimke, C. Parting Hymn, A.
Grosholz. Holy Week.
Gunn, T. Pope's Carnations Knew Him.
Halevi. God, Whom Shall I Compare to Thee?
Heal Me, My God.
Halkin, S. Before your wonders I stand, my world.
Hall, D. Small Fig Tree, A.
Hall, J. Praise of Godly Love Out of 1 John. 4, The.
Proverb, XXX.
Han. I Do Not Know.
Hardy, T. New Year's Eve.
Harper, F. Ethiopia.
Heard, J. Hope Thou in God.
I Will Look Up.
Herbert, G. Affliction (1).
Altar, The.
Artillery [or Artillerie].
Bitter-Sweet.
Church-Floor[e], The.

Church-Lock and Key.
Clasping of Hands.
Collar, The.
Decay.
Denial[l].
Discipline.
Easter-Wings.
Elixir [or Elixer], The.
Employment (1).
Evensong [or Even-Song].
Family [or Familie], The.
Forerunners, The.
Frailty.
Grace.
Hope.
Invitation, The.
Jordan.
Jordan (2)(II): "When first my lines [or verse] of heavenly [or heav'nly] joy[e]s made mention."
Judgement.
Justice.
L'Envoy.
Man.
Misery [or Miserie].
Obedience.
Odour. 2. Cor. 2, The.
Paradise.
Pearl. [Matth. 13.45 or Matt. 13:45], The.
Perseverance.
Posy [or Posie], The.
Praise (2).
Prayer (I).
Pulley, The.
Redemption.
Search, The.
Sepulchre.
Sion.
Sonnet: "Sure Lord, there is enough in thee to dry."
Thanksgiving, The.
True Hymn, A.
Unkindness.
Vanity [or Vanitie] (1).
Whitsunday.
Windows, The.
World, The.
Herrick. Calling, and Correcting.
God to Be First Served.
God's Mercy.
Neutrality Loathsome.
No Coming to God without Christ.
Right Hand, The.
To Find[e] God.
To God ("Come to me God; but do not come").
To Marygolds.
Upon Time.
What God Is.
Hildebert. For Whitsuntide.
Prayer to God the Father.
Hildegard von Bingen. Antiphon for the Holy Spirit.
I am the one whose praise.
I am the one whose praise echoes on high.
Soul is kissed by God, The.
Hirsch, E. Unearthly Voices.
Hodgson, R. Mystery, The.
Holan. Resurrection.
To the Enemies.
Hölderlin. In the Days of Socrates.
Holmes, O. Living Temple, The.
Our Limitations.
Tartarus.
Holst-Warhaft. John 1:1 and 14.
Holt, C. Dear heavenly Father.
Hooper, E. Better a sin which purposed wrong to none.
Hope, A. House of God, The.
Hopkins, G. At the Wedding March.
Carrion Comfort.
God's Grandeur.
In the Valley of the Elwy.
Pied Beauty.
Spring and Fall.
Thou art indeed just, Lord, if I contend.
What I Do Is Me.

Housman, A.   Mark 16:19–20; So then the Lord Jesus, after.
Howe, S.   Silence Wager Stories.
Hudgins.   Southern Crescent Was on time, The.
Hughes, L.   High to Low.
Pennsylvania Station in New York, The.
Personal.
Huidobro.   Ars Poetica.
Hume, A.   Of Gods Omnipotencie.
Hunt, L.   Abou Ben Adhem (may his tribe increase!).
To Percy Shelley.
To the Same.
Ibn Abithur.   Sanctification.
Ibn-Ezra.   God Everywhere.
Living God, The.
Ignatow, D.   He Puts Me to Rest.
Ingelow.   Divided.
Isaac ben Abun.   All the Hosts of Heaven speak the mighty word.
Jabès.   To be in the book. To figure in the book of questions, to be part of it.
Jackson, L.   In the Beginning.
Jacob, M.   1914.
Jammes.   Prayer to Go to Paradise with the Donkeys, A.
Jana Bai.   Cast off all shame.
Jeffers, R.   Birds and Fishes.
Birth-Dues.
Noon.
Shine, Perishing Republic.
Jemie.   Toward a Poetics.
Jenner, H.   My Savior, hear my prayer.
Jennings, E.   I wish, God, for some end I do not will.
John of the Cross.   Dark Night, The.
Stanzas of the Soul that Suffers with Longing to See God.
Johnson, A.   Grandma.
Johnson, F.   My God in Heaven said to me.
Singing Hallelujia.
Song of the Whirlwind.
Johnson, J.   Go Down Death.
Lift every [or ev'ry] voice and sing.
Johnson, R.   Beam 30, The Garden.
Jones, E.   Genesis.
Jones, J.   Our Wonderful World.
Sometimes I hear God's whisper in.
We have tulips in our flower bed.
Jones, P.   Christmas, Boston Nineteen Eighty Nine.
Prayer.
Jones, S.   Hymn to Na'ra'yena, A.
Jonson, B.   Hymn[e] to God the Father, A.
To Heaven.
Juana Inés de la Cruz.   Because my Lord was born to suffer.
Julian of Norwich.   God wants to be thought of.
Kamienska.   Prayer That Will Be Answered, A.
Kaplinski, J.   White clover will not ask anything.
Kavanagh, P.   Canal Bank Walk.
Kayo.   War.
Kelly, B.   Courting the Famous Figures at the Grotto of Improbable Thought.
Kelly, R.   Rainmakers, The.
Kempis, T.   Love is a great thing, a great good in every way; it alone lightens what is.
Kenyon, A.   Bat, The.
Briefly It Enters, and Briefly Speaks.
Kerouac.   Flies.
Kessler, M.   Eli, Eli.
Kharms.   Un-Now.
Kipling, R.   Dedication, A: "My new-cut ashlar takes the light."
Evarra and His Gods.
Glory of the Garden, The.
Rabbi's Song, The.
Recessional.
Klein, A.   For the Sisters of the Hôtel Dieu.
Kolmar.   Sacrifice, The.
Kowit.   Cosmetics do no good.
Krandievskaya.   Those who would not accept went past.

Kumin, M.   Getting the Message.
Kunze, R.   Refuge Even Beyond Refuge.
Lamdan.   Israel.
Langton, S.   O Holy Ghost.
Lanier, S.   To Beethoven.
Lasker-Schüler.   Zebaoth.
Lawrence, D.   Body of God, The.
"And in praying do not heap up empty."
Eloi, Eloi, Lama Sabachthani?
Hands of God, The.
Lord's Prayer.
Man of Tyre went down to the sea, The.
Pax.
When wilt thou teach the people.
Lax.   Morning Stars, The.
Ledwidge.   God's Remembrance.
Leib.   Psalmodist.
Leslie, S.   Forest Song.
Levertov.   God then.
Suspended.
Task, The.
Levi, P.   Shemà.
Levin, P.   Night Coach.
Levine, P.   To My God in His Sickness.
Levy, A.   Ballad of Religion and Marriage, A.
Lewis, R.   If you had a friend strong, simple, true.
Libbey.   Spring And.
Lima, J.   Enormous Hand, The.
Linden, M.   God's Electric Power.
Lipkin, S.   He who appointed weight to the wind.
Lipska.   If there is a God.
Locke, A.   So foul is sin and loathsome in thy sight.
Lorde.   When the Saints Come Marching In.
Lowell, R.   Death and the Bridge.
Mr. Edwards and the Spider.
Watchmaker God.
Lowry, M.   Death of a Oaxaquenian.
Luther.   In the very midst of life.
Mighty Fortress Is Our God, A.
Lyon, G.   Inventing Sin.
Salvation.
"MacDiarmid."   With the Herring Fishers.
Macdonald, G.   Here lie I, Martin Elginbrodde.
Where did You Come From, Baby Dear?
Machado Ruiz.   Lord, you have ripped away from me what I loved most.
Mackey, N.   John Coltrane Arrived with An Egyptian Lady.
Magee, J.   High Flight.
Mahon.   Ecclesiastes.
Maksimovic.   For the Barren Woman.
Then the Pharisees went and.
Mandelstam.   Thy image, wavering, agonizing.
Marbod of Rennes.   Prayer to God the Father.
Marvell.   Bermudas.
Masing.   Only the Mists are Real.
To Every Believer.
Mathias, R.   God Is.
Maura.   Creation of Light, The.
Mayakovsky.   Listen.
McGinley.   Day after Sunday, The.
McHugh, H.   Third Person Neuter.
Mechthild von Magdeburg.   Effortlessly, / Love flows from God into man.
Fish cannot drown in water, A.
God Speaks to the Soul.
God's Absence.
How the Soul Speaks to God.
Of all that God has shown me.
True love in every moment praises God.
Meinke.   Poet, Trying to Surprise God, The.
Melville, H.   Camoëns.
Conflict of Convictions, The.
In the Desert.
Whale, The.
Merton.   Reader, The.
Merwin, W.   Leviathan.
Meynell, A.   To a Daisy.
Michelangelo Buonarroti.   I see in your handsome face, my Lord.
To the Supreme Being.
Miguel de Guevara.   Raise me up, Lord, who am fallen down.
Miller, T.   Evening.

Milosz, C.   To Robinson Jeffers.
Milton.   On His Blindness.
Praise the Lord.
Sonnet: "How soon hath Time the suttle [or subtle] theef [or thief] of youth."
To Cyriack Skinner.
Mirabai.   Heat of Midnight Tears, The.
Song of the flute, O sister, is madness, The.
Mistral, G.   Like those jars that women put out to catch the dew of night.
Mitchell, A.   Quite Apart from the Holy Ghost.
Molodovsky.   God of Mercy.
"Monty Python."   All things dull and ugly.
Moon, T.   Signpost.
Moore, M.   Book of How, The.
Moore, T.   Sound the Loud timbrel o'er Egypt's dark sea!
Morgan, A.   God the Artist.
Morris, M.   Give T'anks.
Moss, S.   God Poem.
Muir, E.   Incarnate One, The.
Myers, F.   Dear God.
Talking to God.
Nahman of Bratzlav.   From "The Torah of the Void."
Nemerov.   Primer of the Daily Round, A.
Nerval.   Mute Phenomena, The.
Newman, J.   Chorus of Angels.
Sensitiveness.
Nichol.   Ferry Me Across.
Nichols, G.   Caribbean Woman Prayer.
Norris, K.   Sky Is Full of Blue and Full of the Mind of God, The.
Olds, S.   What If God.
Ormond.   Cathedral Builders.
To a Nun.
Orten.   Last Poem, The.
Owens, G.   Oh, who can make a flower?
Padgett, R.   Lucky Strikes.
Pagis.   Another Testimony.
Final Exam.
Testimony.
Palladas.   God's philosophical and so can wait.
Parra, N.   Lord's Prayer.
Pastan.   Imperfect Paradise, The.
Patchen.   Deer and the Snake, The.
Lions of fire, The.
Origin of Baseball, The.
Temple, A.
Patrick, S.   St Patrick's Breastplate.
Saint Patrick's Breastplate; or, The Deer's Cry.
Peacock, M.   Good Girl.
Pembroke, M.   Gods boundles bownties gods promise ever abyding.
O Lord, Thou Hast Searched and Known Me.
Psalm 57: Miserere Mei, Deus.
Psalm 58: Si Vere Utique.
Psalm 84: "How lovely is thy dwelling."
Psalm 92: Bonum Est Confiteri.
Psalm 100: "O all you lands, the treasures of your joy."
Quid gloriaris? Psalm 52.
Voce mea ad Dominum Psalm 142.
Penstone.   Praise to God for things we see.
Pereira.   Paradox, The.
"Pereleshin."   Path, The.
Persand.   Rain Storm.
Phillips, C.   Sunday.
Piatt, S.   Answering A Child.
If I had made the world—ah me!
No Help.
Pique at Parting, A.
Sad Spring-Song.
Plath.   Metamorphosis.
Plutzik.   And in the 51st Year of That Century, While My Brother Cried in the Trench, While My Enemy Glared from the Cave.
Pope, A.   All are but parts of one stupendous whole.
Messiah: A Sacred Eclogue in Imitation of Virgil's Pollio.
Universal Prayer [Deo Opt. Max.], The.
What if the foot, ordain'd the dust to tread.
Porete.   Beloved, what do you want of me?
Pound, E.   Ballad for Gloom.
Prabhu.   For the Lord of Caves.
Pratt, E.   Truant, The.

Prévert. Pater Noster.

Prince, F. Question, The.

Probyn. More than They that Watch for the Morning.

Procter, A. Three Evenings in a Life.

Purdy, A. Wilderness Gothic.

Pushkin. Prophet, The.

Quarles. Behold this needle; when the *Arctick* stone.

My Beloved Is Mine, and I Am His; He Feedeth among the Lillies.

On God's Favour.

On God's Law.

On the Life of Man.

Rab. Kingdom of God, The.

Raine, K. Written in Exile.

Ralegh, W. Verses Made the Night before His Beheading.

Ravikovitch. Man of Mystery.

Ray, H. God's Ways, Not Our Ways.

Reese, L. Christmas Folk-Song, A.

Rein. Black Music.

Rice, H. God, Are You There?

He Was One of Us.

It's Me Again, God.

Legend of the raindrop, The.

Prayer for the Young and Lovely, A.

Richards, G. Almighty spake, and Gabriel sped, Th'.

Rilke. Sonnets to Orpheus I, 12, The.

Rimbaud, A. Farewell: "Autumn already!—But why regret an eternal sun if we are embarked on."

Rinckhart. Now thank we all our God

Robbins, H. And have the bright immensities.

Roberts, C. Prayer for a Pilot.

Robinson, A. Idea, The.

Valley, The.

Rodgers, C. It Is Deep.

Testimony.

Rodgers, W. Lent.

Scapegoat.

Roethke. Decision, The.

In a dark time, the eye begins to see.

Marrow, The.

Rogers, P. Elinor Frost's Marble-Topped Kneading Table.

Rossetti, C. After Communion.

Before the mountains were brought forth, before.

Blessed that flock safe penned in Paradise.

Christmas Carol, A: "Thank God, thank God, we do believe."

God Is Everywhere.

Heart Knoweth Its Own Bitterness, The.

Long Barren.

Lowest Place, The.

My Gift.

They lie at rest, our blessed dead.

Twice.

Two Pursuits.

Rossetti, D. Blessed damozel leaned out, The.

On the Painter Val Prinsep.

Rothenberg, J. Realtheater Piece Two.

Rowe, E. Chapter II.

Expostulation, The.

Rukeyser, M. Nuns in the Wind.

Place at Albert Bay, The.

Rumi. Say Yes Quickly.

Totally conscious, and appropos of nothing, he comes to see me.

When it's cold and raining.

Sachs, N. But Perhaps [God needs the longing, wherever else should it dwell].

Chorus of the Stars.

Sandburg, C. They Ask: Is God, Too, Lonely?

Sangster, M. In Gratitude for Friends.

Sangster, M. Oh, face to face with trouble.

Sargent, E. Planet Jupiter, The.

Schiff, H. Discovery.

Scott, W. Mistress Severin.

Sexton. Earth, The.

No So. Not So.

Welcome Morning.

Shalom. At evening when flicker.

Drink wonder, my heart, drink in the wonder.

Shange. I Sat Up One Night.

Shelley, P. Made One With Nature.

Shwarts. Elegy on an X-ray Photo of My Skull.

Sidney, P. Lord, the Lord my shepherd is, The.

Simmons, J. Eden.

Singer, E. Cant. 5.6 & c.

Slutsky. God.

Small, A. Second Coming.

Smart, C. Conclusion of the Matter, The.

Gratitude.

Long-Suffering of God.

My Cat Jeoffry.

Psalm 58.

Smith, G. Penitential Cries of Jupiter Hammond, The.

Smith, S. America.

Smith, S. Away, melancholy, / Away with it, let it go.

Distractions and the Human Crowd.

God the Eater.

Mother, among the dustbins and the manure.

No Categories!

Snider. Communion.

Snow, E. Song of the Desert.

Södergran. Question.

There is no one in this world who has time.

Sölle. I don't as they put it believe in god.

Solomon ibn Gabirol. Almighty! what is man?

Song of the Wind and the Rain.

Sorescu. Shakespeare created the world in seven days.

Southerland. Pale Ant.

Southey, R. Old Man's Comforts and How He Gained Them, The.

Southwell. At Home in Heaven.

Spellman. Twist, The.

Spencer, A. Creed.

Spenser. Is not thilke the mery moneth of May.

Spicer, J. God must have a big eye to see everything.

God's other eye is good and gold. So bright.

Yes, be like God. I wonder what I thought.

Squire. Dilemma, The.

Stafford, W. With My Crowbar Key.

Stephens, J. What the Devil Said.

What Thomas an Buile Said in a Pub.

Stevenson, R. Epitaph: "Angler rose, he took his rod, The."

House Beautiful, The.

If This Were Faith.

Last night we had a thunderstorm in style.

Stickney, T. He said: "If in his image I was made."

Stowe. Abide in me, O Lord, and I in thee.

Still, Still, with Thee.

Strange. Offering.

Strnisa. Priests, The.

Strong, N. Almighty Sovereign of the skies!

Stryker. Almighty Lord, with one accord.

Sullivan, N. His Necessary Darkness.

Swinburne. Leper, The.

Sylvester, J. Cunning Painter, that with curious care, The.

Symonds. Lux Est Umbra Dei[1].

Tadic. Antipsalm.

At the Hairdresser.

Tarkovsky. Firsy Meetings.

Tate, G. Last Instructions.

Tate, J. Teaching the Ape to Write Poems.

Taylor, E. God's Selecting Love in the Decree.

Meditation 8 (First Series).

Meditation Twelve.

Preface, The: "Infinity, when all things it beheld."

Reflexion, The.

Upon a Spider Catching a Fly.

Taylor, J. Gods *Houses,* almost like *Troyes Ilion,*.

Teller. To the Divine Neighbor.

Tennyson, A.

In Memoriam A.H.H. 54, 124.

Flower in the crannied wall.

Higher Pantheism, The.

Wish, that of the living whole, The.

Teresa de Cepeda Y Ahumada. (Lines Written on a Bookmark Found in Her Breviary).

Theresa. I Die because I Do Not Die.

Thomas Aquinas. With my heart I worship.

Thomas, D. In the beginning was the three-pointed star,.

Thomas, R. Ann Griffith.

Echoes.

Pisces.

Thompson, F. Hound of Heaven, The.

Thompson, P. In the Valley.

Thomson, J. Hymn on the Seasons, A.

Traherne. Bible, The.

Salutation [*or* Salutations], The.

To the same purpose: he, not long before.

Wonder.

Tranter. Backyard.

Trapnell, A. O he is a rest that requires.

Trench, R. Power of Prayer, The.

Tsvetayeva. God (3).

Tucker, F. All praise to thee, for thou, O king divine.

Tucker, M. Mysteries of Life.

Tuckerman, F. As sometimes in a grove at morning chime.

Sonnets: First Series.

Sonnets: "Starry flower, the flower-like stars that fade, The."

Turner, N. God's Plan for Spring.

U Tam'si Tchicaya. Scorner, The.

Unknown. Abraham Lincoln's Creed.

All-knowing God, 'tis thine to know.

All Through the Night.

Apostles' Creed, The.

Been in the Storm So Long

Beguines who hear these words.

Beulah Railway, The.

Bible, Matthew 5:3–12, The.

Bless Him ("Bless Him, O constant companions").

Blessed Be the Holy Will of God.

Chants to the Deity.

Child's Creed, A.

Child's Offering, A.

Christian's Prayer, The.

Christmas Carol: "God bless the master of this house."

Didn't my Lord Deliver Daniel.

Freedom in the Air.

Friendly Beasts, The.

Give Thanks.

God Be with You.

God made the bees.

God of Might, God of Right.

God's A-Gonna Trouble the Water.

Good Lord in That Heaven.

Handiwork of God, The.

Highest Divinity.

Hospital Duties.

Hymn of Unity.

I believe in the sun.

I saw some lovely things today.

I See the Moon.

I syng of a mayden that is makeles.

I Vision God [standing].

I walked in a desert.

I'm a-rollin', I'm a-rollin', I'm a-rollin', through an unfriendly world.

I'm glad the sky is painted blue.

Little Black Train Is A-Comin'.

Lord Is King, The.

Lord of the World.

Lord's Prayer, The.

Make Me Worthy of My Friends.

My Choice.

My heart was split, and a flower.

Nobody Knows the Trouble I've Had.

Now I lay me down to sleep.

Peace Be Still.

Prayer for Every Day.

Prayer is so simple.

Psalm 137.

Psalm 58.

Questions of Ethne Alba, The.

Sent from the Power.

Sing, my soul, his wondrous love.

Slave Marriage Ceremony Supplement.

Soon I will be done with the troubles of the world.
Stand by Me.
Steal Away to Jesus.
Take My Hand, Precious Lord.
Te Deum.
Thanks.
Thanksgiving Hymn.
Thanksgivings, The.
This Little Light of Mine.
Thou Great God.
Though Mine Eye Sleep Not.
Timor Mortis.
Two little eyes to look to God.
We'll soon be free.
Who'll Be a Witness for My Lord?
Whose Hand.
U'Tamsi. Scorner, The.
Valéry. Crusoe had provided all the necessaries and was more or less at leisure in.
Vallejo. Have You Anything to Say in Your Defense?
Van Duyn. Gardener to His God, The.
Van Dyke. Four Things [a man must learn to do].
Vaughan, H. Anguish.
Book, The.
Cock-crowing.
Knot, The.
Love and Discipline.
Midnight.
Regeneration.
Retirement.
Vanity of Spirit.
Very Created, The.
Cup, The.
Earth, The.
Eye and Ear, The.
First Atlantic Telegraph, The.
Forevermore.
Hand and Foot, The [or Hand and the Foot, The].
In Him We Live [& Move & Have Our Being].
Lost, The.
Mountain, The.
Prayer, The.
Presence, The.
Promise, The.
Silent, The.
Slavery.
Spheres, The.
Spirit, The.
Winter Rain, The.
Word! it cannot fail; it ever speaks, The.
Yourself.
Villon. Epitaph in Form of a Ballad, The.
Vrettakos. Poet, The.
Vysotsky. And ice below, and above—I toil somewhere in between.
Walton, T. God's Gifts to Me.
Walworth. Holy God, We Praise Thy Name.
Waniek. Canticle for Abba Jacob, A.
Warren, R. Way to Love God, A.
Warton, T. Stanzas on the Psalms.
Washburn, H. Almighty God, thy constant care.
Watts, I. Day of Judgement [or Judgment]; an Ode, The.
Man Frail, and God Eternal.
O God, Our Help in Ages Past.
Psalm 58.
Webb, F. Art.
Wesley, C. Come on, my partners in distress.
None is like Jeshurun's God!
Westmorland. Man Leavens the Batch.
To Kiss God's Rod; Occasioned upon a Child's Sickness.
Wheatley, P. On Being Brought from Africa to America.
Thoughts on the Works of Providence.
Whitfield. Self-Reliance.
Whitman, W. Chanting the square deific, out of the One advancing, out of the sides.
I believe in you my soul, the other I am must not abase itself to you.

I have said that the soul is not more than the body.
Whitney, I. I whole in body and in minde.
Whittier. All's Well.
Garden.
Over-Heart, The.
Overruled.
Palm-Tree, The.
Wickham. To Men.
Wiesel. Behold, God of Abraham, God of mercy.
Never shall I forget that night.
Wieseltier. God's Fire upon Children ("God's fire upon cities").
Wilbur. Proof, The.
Tywater.
Williams, M. Why God Permits Evil: For Answers to This Question of Interest to Many Write Bible Answers Dept. E-7.
Williams, P. In the Dark.
Williams, W. Guide Me, O Thou Great Jehovah.
Wilson, E. Disloyal Lines to an Alumnus.
Winters, Y. Precision, The.
Wither. Prayer of Hezekiah, The.
Wolfli. And now: And now: here begins Our Voyage, hunters and naturalists of indefatigable enthusiasm.
Nostalgic song for my beloved.
Wollach. Love Poem #2.
Wordsworth, W. By the Sea.
Wright, C. Clear Night[, thumb-top of a moon, a back-lit sky].
Wright, J. Speak.
Wright, J. Meta-A and the A of Absolutes.
Wyatt, T. After great storms the calm returns.
Ya'oz-kest. Smoke Rose.
Yeats. Crazy Jane on God.
Indian upon God, The [or An].
Paudeen.
Rose of the World, The.
Yoruba Oral Tradition. Invocation of the Creator.
Young, A. I Arrive In Madrid.
Myself When I Am Real.
Young, M. Noah's Ark.
Zach. Like Sand.
Zukofsky, L. For you I have emptied the meaning.
Zweig, P. Fly on the Water, A.

God's Protection
Clough. That there are powers above us I admit.
Colman, H. On the Three Children in the Fiery Furnace.
Elliot, E. God Save the People.
Emerson, R. Worship.
Herbert, G. Affliction (4).
Evensong [or Even-Song].
Invitation, The.
L'Envoy.
Kunitz, S. Benediction.
Lorde. Seboulisa, mother of power.
MacNeice. Prayer Before Birth.
Prudentius. Yee night, and darknes, cloudie aire.
Rous. I to the Hills Will Lift Mine Eyes.
Smart, C. Gratitude.
Unknown. All other love is like the mone.
All other love is like the moon.
Got a Home in That Rock.
Whittier. Furnace Blast, The.

Gods and Goddesses
Alcman. Vendettas end among the gods.
Ancient Sumerian Oral Tradition. Inanna sang.
Andal. I was sent forth from the power.
Archilochus. There's nothing now.
Aristophanes. CHORUS. Ye Children of Man! whose life is a span.
Arnold, M. Forth from the east, up the ascent of Heaven.
Awoonor. At the Gates.
Easter Dawn.
Barnes, B. Would I were Changed.
Bast. Body of the Great Cat, The.
Nebamun's Cat.
Baudelaire. Cat, The.

Bekederemo. Olokun.
Blunt, W. St. Valentine's Day.
Bly, R. Busy Man Speaks, A.
Brontë, C. Dream that stole o'er us in the time.
Carew, T. Cruel Mistress, A.
To the King, at His Entrance into Saxham: By Master John Crofts.
Catullus. Roman Epithalamion.
Césaire, A. In Order to Speak.
Chimombo. Obituary.
Clifton, L. Coming of Kali, The.
Kali.
Coleridge, S. Visit of the Gods, The.
Columella. Autumnal Work.
Crashaw. In the Glorious Epiphanie of Our [or Ovr] Lord God[, A Hymn. Svng as by the Three Kings].
Craveirinha. Three Dimensions.
Cummings, E. No man,if men are gods;but if gods must.
Davies, S. Cosmus hath more discoursing in his head.
Der von Kürenberg. "Late at night I stood on a battlement."
Di Prima. If he did not come apart in her hands, he fell.
Disch. Ballade of the New God.
Dlugos. Healing the World from Battery Park.
Dobson, R. Three Fates, The.
Doinas, S. Man with Exploded Eyes, The.
Doolittle, H. Evadne.
We have seen how the most amiable.
Dove, R. Demeter's Prayer to Hades.
Duncan, R. Chords Passages 14.
Structure of Rime XVIII.
Eliot, T. Dry Salvages, The.
Elytis. Axion Esti, The.
Enheduanna. From The Hymn to Inanna.
Erucius of Cyzicus. I, the priest of Rhea, long-haired.
Euripides. Maenads on Cithaeron, The.
There Are No Gods.
Fairfax, E. Drearie trumpet blew a dreadfull blast, The.
Fanthorpe. Nativities.
Foscolo. Upon the Death of His Brother Giovanni.
Fumi Saito. Tanka: "Ever deeper."
Geda. Steep eyes of wooden gods.
Graves, R. Cat-Goddesses.
Friday Night.
In Her Praise.
Problems Of Gender.
Return of the Goddess [Artemis].
Weather of Olympus, The.
White Goddess, The.
Greene, R. Samela.
Gunn, T. Garden of the Gods, The.
Herbert, Z. From Mythology.
Hesiod. Bronze Age, The.
When first Both Gods and Men had one Times Birth.
Hollo. On the occasion of becoming an echo.
Holub. Garden of Old People, The.
Homer. Goddess intervenes between Achilles and Agamemnon, The.
Juno seduces Jove.
Thetis Asks Jove to Revenge Her Son Achilles.
Vulcan Forges the Shield of Achilles.
Hope, A. Fafnir.
Hsieh Chin. Song of Cursive Calligraphy.
Huchel. Ammonite, The.
Jones, S. Hymn to Indra, A.
Jonson, B. Hymn to Diana.
Kipling, R. Gods of the Copybook Headings, The.
Sacrifice of Er-Heb, The.
Kizer, C. Muse of Water, A.
Klee. Wolf speaks, while chewing, The.
Koroneu. Funeral Eva.
Kuo P'o. Poem on the Wandering Immortal.
Kwakiutl Oral Tradition. Healing Prayer to the Salmon-Berry Vines.
Laing, K. Godhorse.
Lawrence, D. Gods! The Gods!, The.

Man of Tyre went down to the sea, The.
Maximus.
Levertov.　To the Reader.
Li Ho.　Magic Strings.
　Piece for Magic Strings, A.
Li Po.　Song of a Dream Visit to T'ien-mu.
Lorde.　Seboulisa, mother of power.
Louw.　Gods Are Mighty, The.
Lucretius.　*Gods*, by right of Nature, must possess, The.
Madhubuti.　Gods, The.
Marvell.　Mower Against Gardens, The.
McPherson, S.　Edge Effect.
Merrill, J.　After Greece.
Milton.　Next came one / Who mourn'd in earnest, when the Captive Ark.
Moschus.　Into the Mead he comes, nor (seen) doth fright.
Munivar.　On the marriage platform made of gold.
Nahuatl Oral Tradition.　Song for the Festival of Tlaloc, the Rain God.
Namjoshi, S.　Caliban's Journal.
Namjoshi, S. *et al.*　In that particular temple.
Nemerov.　Companions, The.
Nguyễn Khuyến.　Scholar-Laureate in Retirement, A.
Nossis.　Let us go into the temple.
　Most honoured Hera, who descends from heaven.
Nowak, T.　Psalm To Cheer Up.
Okara.　Spirit of the Wind.
Okigbo.　Overture.
　Water Maid.
Olson, C.　Distances, The.
　In cold hell, in thicket, how.
Philodemus.　This stone incorporates three gods:/ the head is unmistakably goat-horned Pan's.
Pindar.　Fourteenth Olympick Ode, The.
Po Chü-i.　To Li Chien.
Poseidippus.　On sea and land alike.
Rakosi.　Origins.
Ralegh, W.　Shepherd's Praise of Diana, The.
Reed, I.　I Am a Cowboy in the Boat of Ra.
Rilke.　Lovers, gratified in each other, I am asking *you*.
Ritsos.　End of Dodona II, The.
　Marpessa's Choice.
　Requiem on Poros.
Saarikoski.　No, Quetzalcoatl, don't come back.
Santayana.　Sonnet XLIII: "Candour of the gods is in thy gaze, The."
Schelling.　Isha Upanishad.
Shapiro, D.　Lateness.
Shelton, R.　Sonora for Sale.
Shurin.　Agora.
　Temptation.
Slessor.　Fixed Ideas.
Smith, S.　River God, The.
Sophocles.　Chorus sing of the laws of the gods, The.
　What is God singing in his profound.
Soyinka.　Huge with Time, a wombfruit lanced.
Spenser.　Dame Nature.
　Mutability.
Stanescu.　Second Elegy, Getic.
Stevens, W.　Less and Less Human, O Savage Spirit.
Swinburne.　Garden of Proserpine, The.
　Hertha.
T'ang Hsien-tsu.　Evening View from the Bell Tower at P'ing-ch'ang.
Theocritus.　Along that footpath, shepherd, past the oaks.
　Wedding Song: Lullaby for Sleepy Lovers.
Tibullus.　Those who the Godhead's soft Behests obey.
Unknown.　And you (O *Delian* Virgins) doe me grace.
　First Merseburg Spell.
　I was sent forth from the power.
　Lord among the Clouds, The.
　Lord of the River.
　Mountain Spirit, The.
　On Proclus's Great Nose.

Second Merseburg Spell.
　To the Sun.
　Twelfth Song of the Thunder.
Villon.　Ballad[e] of Dead Ladies.
Virgil.　Release.
Wade-Gayles.　Loving Again.
Wadsworth, W.　Snake in the Garden Considers Daphne, The.
Wang Shih-chieng.　Seeing Off Editor Wang Chou-tz'u and Secretary Lin Shih-lai on Their Mission as Envoys to the Ryūkyū Islands.
Welish.　Respected, Feared, and Somehow Loved.
Wu Wei-yeh.　Impromptu.
Yang Chi.　Meeting My Fellow Countryman, Yü Wu-chung.
Yang Shen.　To the Tune "Child at Play."
Yoshimi.　Tanka: "Dream, A."
Yüan Mei.　On the Way to Pa-ling.

Goebbels, Joseph
Snodgrass, W.　Magda Goebbels ("This is the needle that we give").

Goethe, Johann Wolfgang von
Emerson, R.　Solution.
Richter, M.　Light?
Thackeray.　Sorrows of Werther, The.

Gogh, Vincent van.　See Van Gogh, Vincent

Gold
Bast.　Chang Tuan's Cats.
Blake, W.　I saw a chapel all of gold.
Bowes-Lyon.　Pastoral: "This field has buried men; is browed."
Crabbe.　Marriage Ring, The.
Crane, H.　Key West.
Doolittle, H.　Song: "You are as gold."
Elliott, H.　For Farmers.
Frost, R.　Nothing Gold Can Stay.
Gray, T.　Ode on the Death of a Favourite [*or* Favorite] Cat, Drowned in a Tub [*or* Bowl] of Gold Fishes.
Greenwell, D.　Broken Chain, The.
Greiffenberg.　I look.
Hall, D.　Gold.
Hall, S.　Poppies of Wickenburg.
Hopkins, G.　My own heart let me more have pity on; let.
Keller, D.　Mussels.
Kipling, R.　Runes on Weland's Sword, The.
Lansing.　Gold in the Mud, The.
Lee-Hamilton.　Sunken Gold.
Oppen.　Gold on Oak Leaves.
Pettet.　Annul.
Po Chü-i.　Lodging with the Old Man of the Stream.
T'ang Hsien-tsu.　Cave of Gold Essence—in Ning-tu, The.
Unknown.　Make Me Worthy of My Friends.
Wong, J.　Good Luck Gold.

Gold Mining and Gold Miners
Brodrick.　Joe's Luck.
Garland, H.　Gold-Seekers, The.
Harris, J.　When mama came here as a gold panner.
Harte, B.　Dow's Flat.
Lux.　Gold on Mule.
Montross, P.　Oh, My Darling Clementine.
Service.　Cremation of Sam McGee, The.
　Spell of the Yukon, The.
Skeeter.　California, 1852.
Unknown.　Californian, The.
　Days of 'Forty-Nine [*or* '49], The.
　Dreary Black Hills, The.
　Joe Bowers.
　Lousy Miner.
　Miner's Lament, The.
　National Miner, The.
　San Francisco Company, The.
　Sweet Jane.
　When I Went Off to Prospect.
Winters, Y.　John Sutter.

Golden Age
Browne, W.　Golden Age, The.
Metastasio.　Age of Gold.
Ovid.　Golden Age, The.
Tasso.　Pastoral[l], A: "Oh [*or* O] happy golden age."

Whittier.　My Triumph.

Golden Rule, The
Edwards, M.　Do As You Would Be Done By.

Goldfinches
Ammons.　Mechanism.

Goldfish
Brandreth.　Ode to a Goldfish.
Fisher, R.　O Goldfish!
Turner, C.　On a Vase of Gold-Fish.
Williams, E.　My Pet Goldfish.
Worth, V.　Goldfish in the Garden Pond.

Goldilocks
Kuzma.　In Love with the Bears.

Golem
Colombo.　How They Made the Golem.

Golf
Boynton, H.　Golfer's Rubaiyat, The.
Cleghorn.　Golf Links [lie so near The mill], The.
Lowell, R.　Ford Madox Ford ("Lobbed ball plops, then dribbles to the cup, The").
Mathison.　Victory on the Last Green.

Goliath
Crouch, N.　David and Goliath.
Graves, R.　Goliath and David.
Thompson, P.　David and Goliath.
Untermeyer, L.　Goliath and David.

Good
Blake, W.　Marriage of Heaven and Hell, The.
Hardy, T.　Unkept Good Fridays.
O'Reilly, J.　What Is Good?
Polkowski.　Noli Me Tangere.
Stevens, W.　Good Man Has No Shape, The.
Unknown.　Comparatives.

Good Friday
Auden.　Terce.
Brown, C.　Good Friday.
Clarke, A.　Tenebrae.
Donne.　Good Friday [*or* Goodfriday], 1613. Riding Westward.
Hardy, T.　Unkept Good Fridays.
Herbert, G.　Good Friday.
Herrick.　Good Friday: Rex Tragicus, or, Christ Going to His Cross[e].
Hill, G.　Canticle for Good Friday.
Longley, M.　Letter to Derek Mahon.
Rossetti, C.　Good Friday.
Thomas, R.　Pisces.

Good Hope, Cape of.　See Cape of Good Hope

Good Samaritan
Cummings, E.　Man who had fallen among thieves, A.

Gore-Booth, Eva
Yeats.　In Memory of Eva Gore-Booth and Con Markievicz.

Gorillas
"Antler."　Somewhere Along the Line.
Danner.　Best Loved of Africa.
Wain.　Au Jardin des Plantes.

Gospel Music
Duesing.　Wild and Blue.
Evans, M.　And the Old Women Gathered.

Gossip and Gossips
Auden.　Love Feast, The.
Bruner.　Monk and the Peasant, The.
Chu Ch'ing-yü.　Palace Poem.
Day, B.　Three Gates.
Fraser, G.　Lean Street.
Hitomaro.　Gossip grows like weeds.
Hoch.　Good and Bad.
Johnson, A.　Gifts.
Leapor.　Headache, The.
Linden, M.　Gossip.
Mibu no Tadami.　Yes, I am in love.
O'Hara, F.　Personal Poem.
Parker, M.　Whither away good neighbour.
Sappho.　People do gossip.
Shakespeare, W.　Sonnet 121.
Sidney, P.　Sonnet 92: "Be your words made (good sir) of Indian ware."
Suo.　That spring night I spent.
Suwo.　Pillowed on your arm / only for the dream of a spring night.
Taylor, J.　Recreation.
Turner, G.　Journal of Society, The.
Tattle.

Uloccanar. What Her Girl Friend Said, the Lover within Earshot, behind a Fence.
Unknown. Sir, so suspicious.
Wordsworth, W. Personal Talk.
Wright, K. Underneath the Archers *or* What's All This about Walter's Willy?

See also **Rumor; Reputation**

Govan, Saint
Prys-Jones. Saint Govan.

Government
Beecher, H. American Flag, The.
Bly, R. Johnson's Cabinet Watched by Ants.
Butler, S. Presbyterian Knight, The.
"Chrystos." I Have Not Signed a Treaty with the United States Government.
Clarke, L. Soucouyant.
Daumal. Jesus before Pilate said nothing.
Emerson, R. Ode, Inscribed to W. H. Channing.
Ennis. Coyne's.
Freneau. On Mr. Paine's Rights of Man.
Haines, J. Poem Like a Grenade, A.
Herbert, Z. Elegy of Fortinbras.
Herrick. Ill Government.
Power in the People, The.
Hsieh Chin. Government wine of Peking is sweeter than honey, The.
Hsieh T'iao. In a Provincial Capital Sick in Bed.
Hsü Pen. Ballad of the Merchant.
Kao Ch'i. Along the River, Seeing the Home of Absconded Farmers.
Kipling, R. Death-Bed, A.
Li K'ai-hsien. Prosperous Villager, The.
Record of a Past Affair, A.
Lorde. Revolution Is One Form of Social Change.
Lowell, J. Letter Six—The Pious Editors' Creed.
McTair. Politics Kaiso.
More, S. Quis Optimus Reipublicae Status.
Parra, N. Discourse of the Good Thief, The.
Po Chü-i. After Collecting the Autumn Taxes.
Light Furs, Fat Horses.
Watching the Reapers.
Written when Governor of Soochow.
Sandburg, C. Death Snips Proud Men.
Shelley, P. England in 1819.
Steptoe. Election Time.
Wordsworth, W. 1801.
Yeats. Church and State.
Old Stone Cross, The.

Goya y Lucientes, Francisco José de
Duncan, R. Poem Beginning with a Line by Pindar, A.
Ferlinghetti, L. In Goya's greatest scenes we seem to see.
Petrie. Church of San Antonio de la Florida, The.
Voznesensky. I am Goya.

Grace
Ammons. Grace Abounding.
Armour. Good sportsmanship we hail, we sing.
Askew. Ballad Which Anne Askew[e] Made and Sang When She Was in Newgate, The.
Bontemps. God Give to Men.
Borges. John 1:14; And the Word became flesh and dwelt among us.
Brown, S. To Sallie, Walking.
Campion, T. Author of light, revive my dying spright.
Creeley. Fire, The.
Dickinson, E. Love a Life can show Below, The.
Sweetest Heresy received, The.
Donne. From Holy Sonnets.
Oh my black[e] soul[e]! now thou art summoned.
Emerson, R. Grace.
Glück, L. Gift, The.
Herbert, G. Conscience.
Grace.
Love bade me welcome[: yet my soul drew back].
Temper (2), The.
Hewitt, J. Rome Sunday[,] June 1960.

Hopkins, G. Handsome Heart, The.
To what serves mortal beauty—dangerous; does set danc.
Windhover, The.
Jewsbury. Verses: "I am monarch of troubles a host."
Kendrick, D. Gethsemane A. D.
Landor, W. Rose Aylmer.
Lanier. To the Lady Arabella.
Levertov. Grace-Note, The.
Ralegh, W. Passionate Man[']s Pilgrimage, The.
Shakespeare, W. Sonnet 53.
Sitwell, D. Princess, The.
Stevenson, R. Thought, A.
Taylor, E. Meditation 8 (First Series).
Thy grace, dear Lord's my golden wrack I find.
Thompson, F. Hound of Heaven, The.
Unknown. Graces of the Holy Ghost, The.
Love Me Not [for Comely Grace].
On a Female Rope-Dancer.
Very. Promise, The.
Warren, R. Amazing Grace in the Back Country.

Grackles
Nash, O. Grackle's voice is less than mellow.

Graffiti
Alexander, E. Kevin of the N.E. Crew.
Dugan, A. Thesis, Antithesis and Nostalgia.
Larkin, P. Sunny Prestatyn.
Martin, C. Speech Against Stone.
Meinke. Helen.
Philips, K. Upon the graving of her Name upon a Tree in Barnelmes Walks.
Snodgrass, W. Men's Room in the College Chapel, The.
Viereck, P. Kilroy.
Yolen. Graffiti.

Graham, Billy (William Franklin Graham)
Thribb. Lines on the Return to Britain of Billy Graham.

Grammar
Carryl, G. How a Girl Was Too Reckless of Grammar [by Far].
Cope, W. Uncertainty of the Poet, The.
Dunn, S. Let's See If I Have It Right.
Koch, K. Permanently.
Sidney, P. Sonnet 63: "O Grammer rules, ô now your virtues show."

Grand Canyon
Vogelsang. Nose, the Grand Canyon, and the Sixties, The.

Grand Pré, Nova Scotia
Carman, B. Low Tide on Grand Pré.

Grand Rapids, Michigan
Moore, J. Grand Rapids.

Grandchildren
Bradstreet, A. On My Dear Grandchild Simon Bradstreet, [Who Died on 16TH November, 1669, Being But A Month And One Day Old].
Brickley. Summer evening.
Giovanni. Legacies.
Po Chü-i. On a Box Containing his Own Works.
Sanchez, S. Father and Daughter.
Sissoko. Grandmother.
Wang Chiu-ssu. Recording My Happiness.
Yang Shih-ch'i. Evening of My Birthday, The.

Granddaughters
Bradstreet, A. In Memory of My Dear Grandchild Elizabeth Bradstreet Who Deceased August, 1665, Being a Year and Half Old.

Grandfathers
Alexander, E. Who I Think You Are.
Allbery. Offering.
Baillie, J. Child to His Sick Grandfather, A.
Berryman. Grandfather, sleepless in a room upstairs.
Berssenbrugge. Chronicle.
Bishop, E. Manners.
Bowering, G. Grandfather.
Bruchac. Birdfoot's Grampa.
Chappell, F. Cleaning the Well.

Child, L. Thanksgiving Day.
Clarke, G. Taid's Grave.
Clements, A. Elegy.
Di Prima. April Fool Birthday Poem for Grandpa.
Dove, R. Roast Possum.
Downie. Great-Grandfather.
Fox, S. Grandmother.
Gloria. Whisper, The.
Gotlieb. Late Gothic.
Graham, H. Grandpapa.
Harper, M. Grandfather.
Harris, W. Grandfather Poem, A.
Hendriks. Hot Summer Sunday.
Henson, L. Grandfather.
Inada. Father of My Father.
Jackson, L. Grandpa dropped his glasses once.
Kooser. In January, 1962.
Kumin, M. For My Great-Grandfather: A Message Long Overdue.
Levine, P. Zaydee.
Mahon. Grandfather.
Merwin, W. Grandfather in the Old Men's Home.
Minhinnick. Grandfather in the Garden.
Mosby. To Josh Gibson (Legendary Slugger of the Old Negro Baseball League).
Mura. Grandfather-in-law.
Niedecker. Grandfather / advised me.
Ríos, A. Mi Abuelo.
Scott, D. Grampa.
Senior. Searching for Grandfather.
Sexton. Funnel.
Shapiro, D. Dead Will Not Praise You, The.
Song. Easter: Wahiawa, 1959.
Woo, D. Grandfather's Rockery.
Work. Grandfather's Clock.
Zach. War Confession.

Grandmothers
Adams, P. My Grandmother.
Alexander, M. Her Garden.
Allbery. Offering.
Allen, P. Grandmother.
Bahe. Grandmother Sleeps.
Barkan. Two Grandmas.
Barnes, W. Grammer's Shoes.
Bekederemo. For Granny (from Hospital).
Bernstein, C. When My Grandmother Said "Pussy."
Berry, W. Grandmother, The.
Berssenbrugge. Chronicle.
Bishop, E. Sestina: "September rain falls on the house."
Bona. Dream Poem.
Boruch. Krakow and the Girl of Twelve.
Butler, G. Great-great-grandmother.
Cavalieri. Grandmother.
Cervantes. Beneath the Shadow of the Freeway.
Refugee Ship.
Chappell, F. My Grandmother Washes Her Feet.
Cornish, S. When / my / grandmother / died.
Crane, H. My Grandmother's Love Letters.
Cullen, C. For My Grandmother.
Davis, T. It's All the Same.
De la Mare. Cupboard, The.
Derricotte. Feeding, The.
Weakness, The.
Downie. Her Garden.
Field, E. Both My Grandmothers ("Both my grandmas came from far away").
Forché. Morning Baking, The.
Fox, S. Grandmother.
Galguera. Second Childhood.
Gidlow. I know myself linked by chains of fire.
Giovanni. Legacies.
Goodison. Guinea Woman.
Gotlieb. Late Gothic.
Hartnett. For My Grandmother, Bridget Halpin.
Hemschemeyer. My grandmother had bones as delicate.
Hummer, T. Sorrow.
Train Wreck, 1890: My Grandmother Lies Down with the Dead.

Irving, M. Wedding Gift, The.
Iverem. Murmur.
Jackson, D. Grandmother Jackson.
Jarman, M. Mirror, The.
Jennings, E. My Grandmother.
Johnson, A. Grandma.
Jordan, J. Sunflower Sonnet Number One.
Justice, D. First Death.
Kageyama, C. Mama.
Kaufman, S. Nechama.
Krysl. Grandmother.
Kushner, D. Grandma in the Shower.
Lau, A. Upside Down Basket, The.
Livesay, D. Green Rain.
Lockwood. Victorian Grandmother.
Long, D. Number Four.
Malangatana. To the Anxious Mother.
Maxwell, M. To My Grandmother, Lady-
  Woman.
McElroy, C. Gra'ma was a little bit of a
  thing.
  This Is the Poem I Never Meant to Write.
Milligan, S. Granny.
Murray, M. Poem to My Grandmother in Her
  Death.
Ogilvy. Grannie's Birthday.
Oliver, M. Grandmothers, The.
O'Loughlin. Glasnevin Cemetery.
Patterson, R. Glory, Glory. . . .
Plath. Point Shirley.
Popa. Other World, The.
Redmond. Love Necessitates.
St. John, D. Iris.
Sapia. Grandmother, a Caribbean Indian,
  Described by My Father.
Satchidanandan. Genesis.
Schultz, P. Ode.
Shafarman. Russia 1914/Bolinas 1988.
Shange. Different Love Poem / We Need a
  Change, A.
Shapiro, K. My grandmother moves to my
  mind in context of sorrow.
Sholl. Dogwood blossoms, lovely and full—.
  Whitecaps.
Silko. In Cold Storm Light.
  It Was a Long Time Before.
  Long Time Ago.
Sissoko. Grandmother.
Slingeland. Babouchka.
Slutsky. How They Killed My Grandmother.
Smith, J. Mandolin.
Snyder, G. Old dutch woman would spend
  half a day, The.
Soto. Behind Grandma's House.
Southerland. Pale Ant.
TallMountain. Matmiya.
Thaxter. Favorite Flower, The.
Ulinover. Havdolah Wine.
Villanueva, A. To Jesus Villanueva, with
  Love.
Vizenor. Anishinabe Grandmothers.
Walker, A. Medicine.
Walker, M. Lineage.
Wallace, R. Grandmother Grace.
Weigl. Anna Grasa.
Williams, W. Last Words of My English
  Grandmother, The.
Wilson, R. Keeping Hair.
Wong, N. Grandmothers' Song.
Wright, C. More Blues and the Abstract
  Truth.
Wright, J. My Grandmother's Ghost.
Wright, J. Request to a Year.
Zamora, D. Hand Mirror.
Zerbe. In Memory of My Arab Grandmother.

Grandparents
"Carroll." Poeta Fit, Non Nascitur.
Forché. Morning Baking, The.
Gildner. Primarily We Miss Ourselves As
  Children.
Gioseffi. Bicentennial Anti-Poem for Italian-
  American Women.
Hsü Pen. To the Filial Son, Ts'ui.
Justice, D. Nostalgia and Complaint of the
  Grandparents.
Lowell, R. Grandparents.
Lux. Night above the Town.

Moss, H. Long Island Springs.
Nash, O. Come On In, the Senility Is Fine.
Orlen. Ukranian Pastorals.
Salazar. Piñon Nuts.
Zarucchi. Grape Stakes.

Granicus, Battle of (334 B.C.)
Dugan, A. How We Heard the Name.

Grant, Ulysses Simpson
Bierce. Death of Grant, The.
Horton, G. General Grant—the Hero of the
  War.
Sandburg, C. Cool Tombs.

Grapes
Adams, L. Grapes Making.
Anacreon. Cup, The.
Cervantes. Raisins are my currency.
Chao Meng-fu. Song of an Autumn Night.
Saitō Mokichi. Tanka: "Often likened."
Unknown. Father and His Children, The.
Yi, Y. Grapes, The.

Grass
Ashbery. They Dream Only of America.
Beveridge. In the Park.
Bly, R. Poem Against the British.
  Snowfall in the Afternoon.
Bold, A. Grass basks greedily in the sun.
Bowering, G. Grass, The.
Dickinson, E. Narrow Fellow in the Grass, A.
  Presentiment—is that long Shadow—on the
  Lawn.
Fumi Saito. Tanka: "Seeds of the grass."
Goldberg, L. Blade of Grass Sings to the
  River, The.
Gorman, L. I shut down the lawnmower.
Gosse. Lying in the Grass.
Haines, J. To Turn Back.
Hall, D. Granite and Grass.
Harr, L. Hot summer wind, A.
Holtby, W. Man who hated the spring was
  cold and narrow, The.
Jacobsen, R. Green Light.
Kim, S. Grass lies flattened.
Kim, Y. Grass Flower.
Kremer. Epiphany.
Kunze, R. Kind of Hope, A.
Larkin, P. Cut grass lies frail.
Lauterbach. For Example (5): Song of the
  Already Sung.
Lloyd, D. Over dried grass.
Lovelace, R. Grasshopper, The.
Lynd. Solitary, The.
MacCaig. Fetching Cows.
Madhubuti. Loneliness, A.
Magowan. Zeimbekiko.
Martin, C. Metaphor of Grass in California.
Mayer, B. It moves across and over / across
  the ground.
Mei Sheng *et al.* Green green, river bank
  grasses.
Neruda. Two happy lovers make one single
  bread.
Ni Dhomhnaill. Labasheedy (The Silken Bed).
  Leaba Shíoda.
Sandburg, C. Grass.
  In Tall Grass.
So Chong-Ju. Fresh Green, The.
Stuart, J. Speaks the Whispering Grass.
Swenson, M. Cardinal Ideograms.
Tekkan. Tanka: "Let those grasses."
Tu Fu. Traveler at Night Writes His Thoughts,
  A.
Unknown. Green, green.
  On a Clergyman's Horse Biting Him.
  Piggish young person from Leeds, A.
  Seeds of Love, The.
  There was a young farmer of Leeds.
Untermeyer, L. Long Feud.
Van Doren. Former Barn Lot.
Virgil. Grass path lasts.
Virgilio. Deep in rank grass.
Warner, S. Sad Green.
Webster, M. Grass hath such a simple faith,
  The.
Whitman, W. Grass.
Willmot. Shadows in the grass.
Winters, Y. By the Road to the Air-Base.

Yün Shou-p'ing. For a hundred miles the west
  wind carries the fragrance of millet.

Grasshoppers
Aristodicus of Rhodes. On a Pet Grasshopper.
Clare, J. Grasshoppers.
Cowley, A. Grasshopper, The.
Cummings, E. R-p-o-p-h-e-s-s-a-g-r.
Hunt, L. To the Grasshopper and the Cricket.
Joyce, J. Ondt and the Gracehoper, The.
Keats. On the Grasshopper and [the] Cricket.
Lovelace, R. Grasshopper, The.
McClatchy. Grasshopper.
McClintock, M. Grasshopper, A.
Morin, C. High June.
Okudzhava. As a child I came upon a
  grasshopper.
Reeves, J. Grasshopper and the Bird, The.
Stanley, T. Grasshopper thrice-happy! who.
Unknown. Grasshopper and the Elephant, The.
  Grasshopper Wings.
Watson, N. Grasshopper Green.
Wilbur. Grasshopper, A.

Gratitude
Agard, J. By all means / bless the cloth.
Balaban. For Miss Tin in Hue.
Brodsky, J. May 24, 1980.
Brontë, E. My Comforter.
Browning, E. Sonnet: "What can I give thee
  back, O liberal."
Congreve. False Though She Be [to me and
  love].
Dunn, S. Routine Things Around the House,
  The.
Everson, W. Canticle to the Waterbirds, A.
Felsted. Thanks for Hearing.
Glück, L. Gratitude.
Gray, C. Misses Norman lived on Marine
  Square, The.
Herrick. To the Most Virtuous Mistress Pot,
  Who Many Times Entertained Him.
Hsü Kan. Steep, steep the lofty mountain
  peak.
Koch, K. Thank You.
Lawrence, D. Wild Common, The.
Liu Chih. Tune: "Decorous and Pretty"—
  Respectfully Offered to Circuit Inspector
  Kao.
Maltseva. To the Muse.
Meek. Walls.
Meng Chiao. Wanderer's Song.
Merwin, W. Stranger, The.
Prunty. Note of Thanks, A.
Rossetti, C. Christmas Carol, A: "Thank God,
  thank God, we do believe."
Snyder, G. Prayer for the Great Family.
T'ao Ch'ien. Begging for Food.
Thomas, E. No One So Much as You.
Tvardovsky. No, I have not been cheated by
  life.
Voznesensky. Elegy for My Mother.
Woodward, K. Thanksgiving Prayer, A.
Zavalnyuk. I love my enemies, those I
  forgive.
See also **Thankfulness**

Graves
Beddoes. Dirge: "We do lie beneath the
  grass."
Beer, P. Grave Doubts.
Behn, A. Epitaph on the Tombstone of a
  Child, the Last of Seven That Died Before.
Belloc. Statue, The.
Berryman. Dream Song 384.
Betjeman. Lord Cozens Hardy.
Blair, R. New Dawn, A.
Blodgett. Snails.
Brontë, A. Night.
Browning, R. Bishop Orders His Tomb at
  Saint Praxed's Church, The.
  Childe Roland to the Dark Tower Came.
Campbell, R. Buffel's Kop.
Carver, R. Walk, A.
Catullus. On the Burial of His Brother.
Chesterton, G. Elegy in a Country
  Churchyard.
  English Graves, The.
Clampitt. Amherst.
Clarke, G. Taid's Grave.

Coleridge, S. Knight's Tomb, The.
Crashaw. Epitaph Upon Husband and Wife Who Died and Were Buried Together, An.
Creeley. Fathers.
Dao. Accomplices.
Davidson, D. Lines for a Tomb.
Dickinson, E. Ample make this Bed.
Color of the Grave is Green, The.
Mine—by the Right of the White Election!
Not any higher stands the Grave.
We do not play on Graves.
Doddridge, P. Meditations on the Sepulchre in the Garden.
Donne. Relic, The.
Durcan. Weeping Headstones of the Isaac Becketts, The.
Eberhart, R. Concord Cats.
I walked over the grave of Henry James.
"Field." After Soufrière.
Sometimes I do despatch my heart.
Fowler, A. Catacomb Suburb.
František. Honeycomb of Bees, The.
Girard et al. Grave of Marmousette, The.
Glück, L. Mount Ararat.
González, A. Diatribe Against the Dead.
Gutteridge. Man into a Churchyard.
Hall, D. Sister on the Tracks, A.
Hardy, T. Ah, are you digging on my grave.
Nettles, The.
Poet, A.
Rain on a Grave.
Harper, F. Bury Me in a Free Land.
Harper, M. Alice.
Hayden, R. Paul Laurence Dunbar.
Heredia. Young Dead Woman, A.
Hernández, M. I go on in the dark, lit from within; does day exist?
Herrick. To Anthea ("Now is the time, when all the lights wax dim").
To Laurels.
Upon Ben Jo[h]nson.
Upon His Departure Hence.
Housman, A. Because I liked you better.
Rain, it streams on stone and hillock, The.
With rue my heart is laden.
Hudgins. Burial Detail.
Jarrell. Come to the Stone.
Johnson, H. Invocation: "Let me be buried in the rain."
Kipling, R. Grave, The.
Kramer, L. Red Cross telegram, The.
Ku. War Poems 7.
Kunze, R. Kind of Hope, A.
Kupriyanov. Twilight of Vanity.
Landon. Song.
Lawrence, D. Giorno dei Morti.
Leithauser. Buried Graves, The.
Levertov. Despair.
Levy, A. Sequel to 'A Reminiscence," The.
Longfellow, H. Jewish Cemetery at Newport, The.
Lorde. Father Son and Holy Ghost.
Lowell, R. At the Indian Killer's Grave.
Sailing Home from Rapallo.
Macdonald, G. Here lie I, Martin Elginbrodde.
MacNeice. Introduction, The.
Mangan, J. Rest Only in the Grave.
Marcinkeviius. Landscape With Apparition.
Mazur. Family Plot, October.
McKinney, I. Visiting My Gravesite: Talbott Churchyard, West Virginia.
Millay, E. In the Grave No Flower.
Milnes. Sir Walter Scott at the Tomb of the Stuarts in St. Peter's.
Moore, M. Grave, A.
Morgan, E. De Quincey in Glasgow.
King Billy.
Muldoon, P. Milkweed and Monarch.
Ndu. Udude.
Orlovsky. Snail Poem.
Ormond. Lament for a Leg.
Orten. Whispered.
Pagis. End of the Questionnaire.
Siege.
Paquet. Graves Registration.
Parra, N. Discourse of the Good Thief, The.

Philips, K. On the Death of My First and Dearest Childe, Hector Philipps.
Pitter. Coffin-Worm, The.
Po Chü-i. On an Ancient Tomb East of the Village.
Preston, M. Grave in Hollywood Cemetery, Richmond, A.
Receveur. August 17, 1970.
Reznikoff. Jews from Holland, France, and Hungary, and later from.
Roethke. Flight, The.
Roseliep. Ordering my tombstone.
Rossetti, C. Song: "When I am dead, my dearest."
Under willows among the graves.
Sandburg, C. Cool Tombs.
Sassoon. Prehistoric Burials.
Shakespeare, W. With fairest flowers,/ Whilst summer lasts.
Shin, K. Visiting a Rural Town.
Shin, T. Land of Flowering Azaleas, The.
Simmerman. Child's Grave, Hale County, Alabama.
Slessor. Beach Burial.
Spark. Elegy in a Kensington Churchyard.
Stanton, M. Sunday Graveyard.
Stevenson, A. Temporarily in Oxford.
Stevenson, R. Requiem: "Under the wide and starry sky."
Strnisa. Graves, The.
Tchernichowsky. Grave in Ukraine, A.
Tomlinson, C. Death in the Desert, A.
Trakl. Downfall.
Turner, A. Anyone, Lifting.
Unknown. Epitaph on the Duke of Buckingham.
Unquiet Grave, The.
Virgilio. Adding father's name.
At the open grave.
Warner, S. "Elizabeth the Beloved."
Whistler. Form of Epitaph, A.
Whitman, W. As toilsome I wander'd Virginia's woods.
Dirge for Two Veterans.
Wieseltier. Note.
Poetry's Buried.
Wilde, O. Requiescat.
Wright, C. Yugoslav Cemetery.
Wright, J. Way to Make a Living, A.
See also **Burial; Cemeteries; Mausoleums; Tombs**

Graves, Robert
Ewart. Robert Graves.
Graves, R. Face in the Mirror, The.
My Name and I.

Gravevards. See Cemeteries

Gravity
Gustafson, R. In the Yukon.
Wilbur. Juggler.

Gray, Thomas
Smith, C. Sonnet V. To the South Downs: "Ah, hills beloved!—where once, an happy child."
Warton, T. To Mr. Gray.
Wilbur. In a Churchyard.

Great Britain. See England; Northern Ireland; Scotland; Wales

Great Depression
Dove, R. Hill of Beans, A.
Hughes, L. Madam's Past History.
Lang, D. Depression, The.
Moore, M. Americans in 1933–4–5–6–7–8–, Etc.
Unknown. Arizona.
Wright, J. Old WPA Swimming Pool in Martins Ferry, Ohio, The.

Great Lakes
Merton. Aubade: Lake Erie.
Sandburg, C. Lost.
Sangster, C. Thousand Islands, The.

Great Wall, China
Blunden. At the Great Wall of China.
Ch'en Lin. Song: "I watered my horse at the Long Wall caves."
Chu Ch'ing-yü. Great Wall, The.
Na-lan Hsing-te. Tune: "Big String of Words A"—The Great Wall.

Wang Shih-chieng. Song of the Ch'in-Dynasty Mirror—Written for Yüan Sung-li.
Yang Wei-chen. Horse-Watering Hole, The.

Greatness
Andreyev, D. For the Unveiling of a Memorial.
Bible, Apocrypha. Our Fathers.
Bible, O.T. Psalm 8.
Byron, G. Thou glorious mirror, where the Almighty's form.
Cummings, E. All ignorance toboggans into know.
Glazkov. To My Friends.
Guest, E. Equipment.
Guiterman. On the Vanity of Earthly Greatness.
Howard, R. Nadar.
Martial. Thence to the gates cast round thine eye, and see.
Piercy. Woman in the ordinary pudgy downcast girl, The.
"Samoylov." Old Derzhavin.
Shao Yung. Thoughts on T'ien-chin Bridge.
Spender, S. I think continually of those who were truly great.
Unknown. Beyond the Profit of Today.
Voznesensky. Epitaph for Vysotsky.
Wordsworth, W. England, 1802, III.
See also **Fame**

Greco, El
Birney. El Greco: Espolio.
Starbuck, G. High Renaissance.
Wollach. To See Long like El Greco.

Greece
Bacchylides. Peace.
Boyle, K. Poem for February First 1975, A.
Bryant, W. Conjunction of Jupiter and Venus, The.
Byron, G. Isles of Greece, the isles of Greece!, The.
On This Day I Complete My Thirty-sixth Year.
Written After Swimming from Sestos to Abydos.
Capetanakis. Isles of Greece, The.
Cavafy. Ithaka.
Chamberlain, K. Yerokastrinos.
Chapman, G. . . . Through the wall, uprore.
Davidson, D. On a Replica of the Parthenon.
Doolittle, H. Islands, The.
Lais.
Dryden, J. What Greece, when learning flourished, only knew.
Duncan, R. Chords Passages 14.
Durrell. Delos.
Nemea.
Ekelof. Greece.
Elenkov. Amphora / as an emotion.
Elytis. Aegean Melancholy.
Axion Esti, The.
In the beginning the light And the first hour.
Intelligible sun of Justice and you, gloryfying myrtle.
Ode to Santorini.
Euripides. Delphic Dawn.
Nothing / Is worse for a city than an absolute ruler.
Golding, A. . . . This Damsell was not famous for the place.
Gouri. Piraeus.
You're no king.
Graves, R. Ouzo Unclouded.
Grosholz. On the Ferry, Toward Patras.
Hölderlin. Patmos.
Horace. Ode.
Kalvos. Altar of the Fatherland, The.
Karouzos. Triplets for Beautiful Mistra.
Kazantzakis. O sun, great Oriental, my proud mind's golden cap.
Lawrence, D. Argonauts, The.
Melville, H. Attic Landscape, The.
Merrill, J. After Greece.
Charioteer of Delphi, The.
Correct but cautious, that first night, we asked.
Samos.
Niedecker. So he said / on radio.

O'Grady, D. Here, because of the shock, the sudden.
Petri. Electra.
Rakosi. Origins.
Ritsos. Our Land.
Sarton. At Lindos.
Seferis. Last Stop.
Our country is closed in [enclosed], all mountains.
Shelley, P. But Greece and her foundations are.
Chorus: "World's great age begins anew, The."
Sikelianos. Return, The.
Thalero.
Spenser. *Penelope* for her *Ulisses* sake.
Spicer, J. Transformations.
Tada. Odyssey or "On Absence," The.
Taggart, J. Never Too Late.
Tranströmer. Syros.
Tsatsos. Chios.
Protest.
Venclova. Shield of Achilles, The.
Wilde, O. Impression du Voyage.
Yenser, S. Blue Guide.

Greed
Adams, J. Wants of Man, The.
Anacreon. If Profit offered immortality for gold.
Berryman. Desires of Men and Women.
Bierce. Statesmen, The.
Burns, R. Such a Parcel of Rogues in a Nation.
Charles, F. Letters from Home.
Chaucer. Pardoner's Prologue, The.
Pardoner's Tale, The.
Coleman, W. Aunt Jessie.
Cowley, A. Against Fruition.
Cummings, E. Greedy the people, The.
Ehrlich. Last Merchant, The.
Emerson, R. Hamatreya.
Wealth.
Frym. Yield, The.
Guest, E. What's In It for Me?
Herbert, G. Size, The.
Holmes, O. Contentment.
Horace. 2.18.
Idley. Covetousness.
Khlebnikov, V. And so the castles of world trade.
Stop Fooling.
Lucilius. Asclepiades the Miser was horrified.
Of a covetous Niggard, and a needie Mouse.
Treasure.
May, E. To a Covetous Churl.
McBride, M. Loneliness.
Melville, H. Time's Betrayal.
Quarles. Philippians 1.23.
Robinson, E. Aaron Stark.
Sexton. With Mercy for the Greedy.
Smith, S. Villains.
Stickney, T. You say, Columbus with his argosies.
Taylor, J. Greedy Richard.
Tennyson, A. Northern Farmer: New Style.
Traherne. Insatiableness.
Unknown. Greedy man is he who sits, The.
Greedy Ned.
Money, money, now hay goode day!
War the Source of Riches.
Whittier. Haschish, The.
Wilbur. Matthew VIII, 28 ff.
Wordsworth, W. Written in London, September, 1802.

Green (color)
Barry, J. Green Hell, Green Death.
García Lorca. Sleepwalkers' Ballad.
Graves, R. Variables of Green.
Jiménez, J. Green was the maiden, green, green!
Lawrence, D. Green.
Lee, B. In the Green Shade.
Machi. Tanka: "Only the green."
Merrill, J. Green Eye, The.
Mother Goose. Walnut, A.
Schuyler, J. I Think.
Stevens, W. Candle a Saint, The.

Greene, Graham
McGinley. Muted Screen of Graham Greene, The.
Greene, Nathanael
Freneau. To the Memory of the Brave Americans.
Greenhouses
Cowper, W. Task, The.
Hardy, T. Frozen Greenhouse, The.
Morgan, E. My Greenhouse.
Pitter. Other People's Glasshouses.
Roethke. Big Wind.
Child on Top of a Greenhouse.
Greenland
Diamond, L. Greenland Winter, A.
Gregory, Lady Augusta
Yeats. Municipal Gallery Revisited, The.
Gregory, Robert
Yeats. In Memory of Major Robert Gregory.
Grenada
Fergus. Lament for Maurice Bishop.
Greyhounds
Berners. Properties of a Good Greyhound, The.
Grief
Abelard. David's Lament for Jonathan.
"Adunis." Elegy for the Time at Hand.
Agathias. Restless and discontent / I lie awake all night long.
"Akhmatova." Ah—you thought I'd be the type.
Dedication.
He whispers: 'I'm not sorry.
Angel. Twice Removed.
Antipater of Sidon. Never again, Orpheus.
Anyte. Throwing her arms around her father.
Auden. Stop All the Clocks, Cut Off the Telephone.
Augustine. My heart was darkened over with grief, and whatever I.
Bacchylides. Keep to the one path.
Barnes, W. Wind at the Door, The.
Bates, K. Yellow Clover.
Berry, W. Grief.
Bertolino. Coons, The.
Bible, *O.T.* Duty.
Blake, W. On Another's Sorrow.
Bogan, L. Juan's Song.
Bowles, W. Time and Grief.
Bridges, R. Elegy on a Lady, Whom Grief for the Death of Her Betrothed Killed.
Brody. Lamentations.
Brontë, E. Day Dream, A.
If grief for grief can touch thee.
Stanzas: "Often rebuked, yet always back returning."
Browning, E. Bereavement.
Face which, duly as the sun, The.
Felicia Hemans.
Grief.
Sonnet: "If I leave all for thee, wilt thou exchange."
Bryant, W. Death of the Flowers, The.
Burns, R. Red, Red Rose, A.
Buson. No poem you need.
Byron, G. Stanzas: "I heard thy fate without a tear."
Camões. Do This Favour For Me.
Campbell, R. Counsel.
Catullus. Carmen 65 ("Grief reached across the world to get me").
Death of Lesbia's Bird, The.
Love and Death.
On the Burial of His Brother.
Celan. All those sleep shapes, crystalline.
Chang Yü. In a Book-Box I Found the Lost Manuscript of a Poem Sent to Me by the Late Kao [Ch'i].
Chao Meng-fu. Song of an Autumn Night.
Ch'ien Ch'ien-i. No Flowers.
Chivers. Avalon.
Chōkū. Tanka: "Imagining."
Christine de Pisan. Fountain of tears, river of grief.
Clifton, L. For de Lawd.
Coleman, W. Waif of Echo Park, The.

Coleridge, M. "My True Love Hath My Heart and I Have His."
Crinagoras. On the Death of Cleopatra-Selene.
Csoori. Postponed Nightmare.
Daniel, S. If this be love, to draw[e] a weary [or wearie] breath.
Sonnet: "Care-charmer Sleep[e], son[ne] of the sable night."
Dante Alighieri. All ye that pass along Love's trodden way.
Beyond the sphere which spreads to widest space.
Canst thou indeed be he that still would sing.
Death, always cruel, Pity's foe in chief.
Gentle thought there is will often start, A.
Love hath so long possessed me for his own.
Love's pallor and the semblance of deep ruth.
Mine eyes beheld the blessed pity spring.
Stay now with me, and listen to my sighs.
Very bitter weeping that ye made, The.
Woe's me! by dint of all these sighs that come.
You that thus wear a modest countenance.
De la Mare. Widow, The.
De Vere, A. Sorrow.
Di Prima. To My Father—2.
Dickinson, E. After great pain a formal feeling comes—.
Bustle in a House, The.
Butterfly upon the Sky, The.
I can wade Grief.
I measure every Grief I meet.
Đinh An. Visiting an Old Friend.
Djagarov. Night.
Dombrovsky. I'm at the bottom again. The baron's there.
Donne. Triple Fool[e], The.
Valediction, A: Forbidding Mourning.
Dorfman, A. I Just Missed the Bus and I'll Be Late for Work.
D'Orleans. Oft in my thought full busily have I sought.
Dove, R. Blown apart by loss, she let herself go.
Draycott. Search.
Dryden, J. To the Memory of Mr Oldham.
Duesing. Wild and Blue.
Duncan, R. Structure of Rime XXIII.
Dunn, D. Kaleidoscope, The.
"Dylan." Tears of Rage.
Ehrenstein. Home-Coming.
Homer.
Elizabeth I. On Monsieur's Departure.
Emanuel, L. What Grieving Was Like.
Erinna. Epitaph on a Betrothed Girl.
Evans, M. Where Have You Gone?
"Field." After Soufrière.
Beloved, my glory in thee is not ceased.
My lady has a lovely rite.
Ford, C. Somebody's Gone.
Gallagher, T. Spacious Encounter.
García Lorca. Ballad of Black Grief.
Casida of Sobbing.
Gascoigne. For That He Looked Not upon Her.
Gibbons, R. We say a heart breaks—like.
Gibson, M. Country Woman Elegy.
Gilbert, S. Ko-Ko's Song.
Ginsberg, A. To Aunt Rose.
Gorbanevskaya. Sukhanovo.
Gray, T. Death of Hoel, The.
Sonnet [on the Death of Mr. Richard West].
Gregg. Night Music.
Grimald. From A Funeral Song, Upon the Decease of Annes His Mother.
I, in your frutefull woomb conceyved, born was.
Gumilyov. Tram That Lost Its Way, The.
Gunn, T. Monster, The.
Hailsham. If Grief Could Burn Out.
Hardy, T. Bereft.
Harteis. Mirage.
Hayes, A. Pietá.
Heaney, S. Wedding Day.
Heard, J. Bereft.
Heine. I, a Most Wretched Atlas.
Hemphill. Homocide.

Herbert, G. Affliction (1).
Affliction (3).
Ah Mater, quo te deplorem fonte? Dolores.
Confession.
Heredia. Young Dead Woman, A.
Herrick. Anacreontic.
Observation ("Virgin-Mother stood at distance (there), The").
Hill, A. Alone in an Inn at Southampton, April the 25th, 1737.
Hitomaro. In the sea of ivy clothed Iwami.
Plovers cry, The.
When she was still alive.
Honestus. Very day one son was drowned, The.
Hopkins, G. Felix Randal the farrier,° O is he dead then? my duty / all ended.
Sonnet: "No worst, there is none. Pitched past pitch of grief."
Spring and Fall.
Housman, A. Bredon Hill.
Howard, A. Good Shepherd's Sorrow for the Death of His Beloved Son, The.
Hsiao-Wei. For My Wife.
Hsin Ch'i-chi. Tune: Ugly Rogue.
Huang E. Pearl-teardrops roll and gather.
Hummer, T. Sorrow.
Isakovsky. Enemy had burned his cottage home, The.
Ishikawa Takuboku. Tanka: "Just for fun."
Tanka: "Young maidens."
Johnson, J. Glory of the Day Was in Her Face, The.
Johnson, S. Empty Heart, An.
Jonson, B. On My First Son [or Sonne].
Song: "Slow, slow fresh fount, keep time with my salt tears."
Julianus of Egypt. Anastasia, the Graces blossom and you were their flower.
On a Young Wife.
Though you rule the dead, under the earth, who never smile.
Kavanagh, P. In Memory of My Mother.
King, J. Grief Plucked Me Out of Sleep.
Kipling, R. Son, A.
Knight, E. As You Leave Me.
Kochetkov. Ballad About a Smoke-Filled Railway Carriage.
Kopland. Johnson Brothers Ltd.
Kornilov, B. My Nightingale.
Kovner. Dinosaurs wept angry tears.
While at Prayer.
Lake, D. Facing Change.
Larkin, P. If grief could burn out.
Lawrence, D. Brooding Grief.
Hymn to Priapus.
Sorrow.
Lehmann, J. No Easy Answer.
Leib. In little hands she holds an open book.
When I See Another's Pain.
Leiser, J. Kol Nidra.
Leopardi. Calm after the Storm, The.
Lewis, C. Grief's Circle.
Joys Once Shared.
Sequence, The.
Li K'ai-hsien. Poem about Fan the Fourth, A.
Li Po. Moon over the Mountain Pass, The.
Li Yü. Tune: Pure Serene Music ("Since we parted, spring half over").
Licymnios. Ten thousand rivers of tears.
Lindsay, C. To My Own Face.
Littledale. When My Dog Died.
Liu E. On the Road to Pyongyang—An Improvisation.
Longfellow, H. Cross of Snow, The.
Lopate. Once a long time ago, you remember.
Lorde. Suffer the Children.
Lovelace, R. In Allusion to the French Song.
Vintage to the Dungeon, The.
Lowell, J. After the Burial.
Lucie-Smith. Lesson, The.
Lynd. Solitary, The.
Lysohorsky. 22.6.1941.
"MacDiarmid." At My Father's Grave.
Marcinkeviius. Landscape With Apparition.
Markham, E. Victory in Defeat.
Marston, P. Not Thou but I.

Marvell. Mourning.
Mathews, H. Out and Back on the Fifteenth Night of the First Month.
Mayakovsky. Mayakovsky's Suicide Note.
Melville, H. Martyr, The.
Monody.
Michitsuna. Have you any idea.
Mihalic. Large Grieving Women.
Millay, E. Lament: "Listen, children: / Your father is dead."
Song of a Second April.
Time does not bring relief; you all have lied.
Miller, V. On Approaching My Birthday.
Milton. On His Deceased Wife.
Mnasalces. Aristocrateia, / You've crossed the dark stream.
Moffat. Passing of Sorrow, The.
Monro. Solitude.
Montagu, L. Receipt to Cure [or for] the Vapours, A.
Moore, J. One Reason I Went to Prison.
Moritz. Some Lines on My Mother's Illness.
Morley, H. Lizard's heart throbs, The.
Morpurgo. Sonnet: "My soul surcharged with grief now loud complains."
Moses ibn Ezra. On My Sorrowful Life.
Nathan, R. Sonnet: "Because my grief seems quiet and apart."
Neto. Grieved lands of Africa, The.
Nguyễn Chí Thiện. Travel with grief— goodbye to joy!
Ni Tsan. Lamenting Noble Scholar Chu.
Nobuyuki. Humans Bought and Sold (two poems).
Oakes. Away loose-reined careers of poetry!
O'Dalaigh, M. Invocation: "Last night my soul departed."
Oden. Carousel, The.
Okamoto. Tanka: "Innately reserved."
Olds, S. First Love.
Orr, G. Gathering the Bones Together.
Mother, The.
Who'd Want to Be a Man?
Owen, W. Hospital Barge at Cérisy.
Pastan. Five Stages of Grief, The.
Pasternak, B. Marburg.
Patchen. O now the drenched land wakes.
Patmore, C. Farewell, A.
She Was Mine.
Pembroke, M. If Ever Hapless Woman Had a Cause.
Peretz. In the Silent Night.
Three Seamstresses, The.
Perses. Death came before Marriage, Philaenion.
Mnasylla, the daughter you lament.
Petröczi. Swift Floods.
Philips, K. EPITAPH. On her Son H. P. at St. Syth's Church where her body also lies Interred.
On the Death of My First and Dearest Childe, Hector Philipps.
Piatt, S. Her Word of Reproach.
No Help.
Pilkington, L. Sorrow.
Po Chü-i. On the Way to Hangchow: Anchored on the River at Night.
Remembering Golden Bells.
To the Distant One.
Poe. Annabel Lee.
For Annie.
Porter, P. Exequy, An.
What I Have Written I Have Written.
Prudentius. Hymn Before Sleep.
Raine, K. Spell Against Sorrow.
Ralegh, W. Farewell to the Court.
Reese, L. In Time of Grief.
Richardson, J. On My Late Dear Wife.
Richardson, M. Sonnet: "I still shall smile and go my careless way."
Robinson, E. Reuben Bright.
Rodriguez, J. In-flight Note.
Roethke. Sequel, The.
Rosenberg, I. Spiritual Isolation.
Rossetti, C. Remember me when I am gone away.
Song: "When I am dead, my dearest."

Rossetti, D. Woodspurge, The.
Sáenz. Resurrections.
Sandeen. Plaint of Flowers, A.
Sarton. I did not weep my father.
Schneour. Forsaken.
Seward. Sonnet 13.
Shakespeare, W. Clown's Song, The.
Sonnet 40.
Sonnet 50.
Sonnet 90.
What Answer Can I Give?
Shelley, P. Dirge, A: "Rough wind, that moanest loud."
Lament, A: "O world! O life! O time!"
Sherburne. Weeping and Kissing.
Sidney, P. Nightingale as soone as Aprill bringeth, The.
Then do I thinke in deed, that better it is to be private.
Skoyles. In Memoriam.
Smith, C. Verses Intended to Have Been Prefixed to the Novel of Emmeline, but Then Suppressed.
Solomon ibn Gabirol. Stanzas: "With tears thy grief thou dost bemoan."
Wine and Grief.
Spenser. Sonnet 89: "Like as the culver on the bared bough."
"Stephany." Who collects the pain.
Surrey. Complaint by Night of the Lover Not Beloved, A.
Te Heuheu Tukino. Lament for Te Heuheu Herea.
Tekeyan. Forgetting. Yes, I will forget it all.
Tennyson, A. Break, break, break.
Dark house, through which once more I stand.
I held it truth, with him who sings.
If Only.
Lincolnshire Wolds and Lincolnshire Sea.
Sweet after showers, ambrosial air.
Thomas, D. In my craft or sullen art.
Tighe. To Time.
Tsvetaeva. Yesterday he could still look in my eyes, yet.
Tu Fu. Lovely lady, fairest of the time.
Man with No Family to Take Leave of, The.
Snow Storm.
Turner, A. Anyone, Lifting.
Tuwim. There Is No Country.
Unknown. At sixty I, Dionysios of Tarsos, lie here.
Blackbird calls in grief, The.
Chilling breath of midwinter arrives, The.
Green green the cypress on the ridge.
Grief.
I am of this world.
Kilcash.
Lament for Our Lady's Shrine at Walsingham, A.
Moon Is Rising, The.
My Buried Friends.
My grief on the ocean.
Stars stand up in the air, The.
Two Laments.
Unquiet Grave, The.
Wife's Lament, The.
Voznesensky. I am Goya.
Wallis, H. Female's Lamentations, The; or, The Village in Mourning.
Wang Wei. Weeping for Ying Yao.
Webster, A. That some day Death who has us all for jest.
Wen T'ing-yün. Tune: "Southern Song, A."
Wharton, A. Elegy on the Earl of Rochester.
Whitman, W. Come up from the fields father, here's a letter from our Pete.
O Captain! my Captain! our fearful trip is done.
Whitney, I. I.W. To her unconstant Lover.
Whittier. Telling the Bees.
Wieseltier. Extended Sonnet on the Death of Isaac Danziger.
Wilde, O. Requiescat.
Williams, W. Widow's Lament in Springtime, The.
Wratislaw. Sonnet Macabre.
Wright, J. Complaint.

Poem Written under an Archway in a Discontinued Railroad Station, Fargo, North Dakota, A.

Wroth. Sonnet 28: "Griefe, killing griefe: have nott my torments binn."

Sonnet 9.

Wyatt, T. Alas, the grief and deadly wo[e]ful smart[!].

All heavy minds.

At mo[o]st mischief.

Blame not my lute, for he must sound [or sssnd or Sownde].

If in the world there be more woe.

Lover's Appeal, The.

Sighs are my food, drink are my tears.

Yearsley. Soliloquy: "What folly to complain."

Yeats. Down by the salley gardens my love and I did meet;.

Yesenin. Bitch, The.

Yosano. Tanka: "White blossoms bloom."

Young, M. Metronomic Moon, The.

Zenmaro. Tanka: "How sad it is."

See also **Sorrow; Mourning and Mourners**

Grieve, Christopher Murray. *See* **"MacDiarmid, Hugh"**

Grocers

Chesterton, G. Song against Grocers, The.

Espada. Tony Went to the Bodega but He Didn't Buy Anything.

Joseph, L. There I Am Again.

Simic. Grocery.

Stanton, M. Grocery Store, The.

Shoplifters.

Voznesensky. Cashier, The.

Williams, C. Racists.

Groundhogs

Eberhart, R. Groundhog, The.

Frost, R. Drumlin Woodchuck, A.

Kumin, M. Woodchucks.

Shaw, L. Groundhog is, at best, a simple soul, The.

Grouse

Baillie, J. Blackcock, The [*or* The Black Cock].

Growth

Ashbery. Boy, A.

Spring Day.

Bangs, J. Little Elf, The.

Bloch, C. Magnificat.

Brooke, R. Sonnet: In Time of Revolt.

Brooks, G. Big Bessie Throws Her Son into the Street.

Celan. I am the first to drink of the blue that still looks for its eye.

Cummings, E. Am was. are leaves few this. is these a or.

If everything happens that can't be done.

Curzon, D. Instructions to a Seed.

Dickinson, E. We outgrow love like other things.

Duncan, R. Preface to the Suite: "Childhood, boyhood, young manhood."

Eberhart, R. Rumination.

Evans, M. Mushrooms grew / Overnight.

Field, R. General Store.

Fraser, K. Poems for the New.

Gatty. Three Little Pigs, The.

Gilbo'a. Watchful Wakeful.

Glenn. José Cruz.

Gonzalez, A. Little Rosebud Girl.

Graham, J. What the Instant Contains.

Hadas, R. Red Hat, The.

Hardy, T. Second Attempt, A.

Herbert, G. Paradise.

Holmes, O. Chambered Nautilus, The.

Holt, C. Dear heavenly Father.

Hoover, H. Boy has two jobs, A.

Housman, A. Loitering with a vacant eye.

Hsieh Chin. Poem on a Little Pine, A.

Hudgins. Seventeen.

Ignatow, D. Absolutely.

Kipling, R. 'Eathen in 'is blindness bows down to wood an' stone, The.

Major, C. Giant Red Woman.

Merwin, W. Last One, The.

Namjoshi, S. From the Travels of Gulliver.

Nash, O. Kitten, The.

O'Hara, F. Poem: "There I could never be a boy."

Palma. Coming of Age.

Plath. Mushrooms.

Popa. Little box grows [gets] her first teeth, The.

Raine, K. Rose.

Roethke. Cuttings ("Sticks-in-a-drowse droop over sugary loam").

Cuttings ("This urge, wrestle, resurrection of dry sticks").

Rowe, G. His Manhood.

Rumi. You're song.

Serote. Growing, The.

Seymour, A. My Aim.

Smith, W. Big Gumbo.

Song. Mehinaku Girl in Seclusion, A.

Sorby. Museum Piece.

Southwell. Times [*or* Tymes] Go[e] By Turn[e]s.

Stevenson, R. Looking Forward.

My Shadow.

Trivelpiece. Nursery, The.

Turner, N. Old Quin Queeribus.

Unknown. Deeds of Kindess.

Go to bed late.

Growing Up.

Planting Initiation Song.

Two Laments.

Wang T'ing-hsiang. Flowering tree does not spare itself, The.

Whitman, W. There was a child went forth every.

Wilbur. Seed Leaves.

Wise, W. When I grow up.

Wordsworth, W. My heart leaps up when I behold.

Guadalajara, Mexico

Ashbery. Instruction Manual, The.

Guadeloupe

Tirolien. Marie Galante.

Guatemala

Castillo, O. Distances.

Espada. Mi Vida: Wings of Fright.

Jordan, J. Poem for Guatemala.

Stevens, W. Arrival at the Waldorf.

Guerrillas

Heaney, S. Requiem for the Croppies.

Kipling, R. Arithmetic on the Frontier.

Guest, Edgar A

Nash, O. Lines to a World-famous Poet Who Failed to Complete a World-famous Poem; or, Come Clean, Mr. Guest!

Untermeyer, L. Edgar A. Guest Considers "The Old Woman Who Lived in a Shoe" and the Good Old Verities at the Same Time.

Guests

Auden. For Friends Only.

Barbauld. Washing-Day.

Bishop, E. House Guest.

Bruce, D. Two Couples.

Ch'êng Hsiao. Satire on Paying Calls in August.

Cheng Hsieh. Small Garden, The.

Ch'ien T'ao. In the quiet of the morning I heard a knock at my door;.

Moving House.

Child, L. Thanksgiving Day.

Coleridge, M. Master and Guest.

De la Mare. Feckless Dinner-Party, The.

Dickinson, E. Infinite a sudden Guest, The.

Hall, D. Wedding Party.

Haynes, C. Any Wife or Husband.

Hitchcock. One Whose Reproach I Cannot Evade, The.

Hoyt, C. While the guests order.

Hurley, J. Tea Party.

Jonson, B. Inviting a Friend to Supper.

Kao Ch'i. In the Mountains, Parting from Master Ning as I Return to West Bank.

Kastelan. Corpse in the House.

Li K'ai-hsien. Night of the First Full Moon, The.

Liu E. On the Road to Pyongyang—An Improvisation.

Liu Ya-tzu. For Guests after Their Visit.

Martial. Inviting a Friend to Supper.

Mayer, B. Midwinter Day.

Mo Shih-lung. Friend Comes to Visit on a Summer Night, A.

Mori Ōgai. Tanka: "Close by the host."

O'Hara, F. Poem: "Eager note on my door said 'Call me', The."

Pastan. At Home.

Patchen. Easy Decision, An.

Po Chü-i. Being Visited by a Friend During Illness.

Dreaming that I went with Li and Yü to Visit Yüan Chên.

Invitation to Hsiao Ch'u-shih.

Lodging with the Old Man of the Stream.

Stopping the Night at Jung-yang.

To a Talkative Guest.

Rilke. Guest, The.

Robinson, E. And again Jesus spoke to them.

Shen Chou. Paying a Sick-call to Yao Ts'un-tao in the Rain.

Tai Piao-yüan. As My Way Passed Through T'ung-ch'uan, I Wished to Visit the Policy Critic of the Right, Mei, but Did Not Know Where to Find Him.

T'ang Yin. Inscribed on a Painting ("Thatched hut among the pines, door open near a cliff").

Unknown. Golden Palace, The.

Preparations.

Welcome over the Door of an Old Inn.

Vaiiunaite. Nausicaa.

Watson, R. White Bird, The.

Wu Wei-yeh. Poem of the Western Fields.

Yeats. Secret Rose, The.

Yi, Y. Grapes, The.

See also **Hospitality; Visiting and Visitors**

Guggenheim, John Simon

Hollander, J. No Foundation.

Guilt

Aeschylus. She-kin, show our force. Join hands!

Alterman. Abandoned, The.

Balaban. After our war, the dismembered bits.

Berrigan, D. My Name.

Bidart. Sacrifice, The.

Blake, W. Sick Rose, The.

Brecht, B. To Those Born Later.

Brontë, C. Again I find myself alone, and ever.

Bruner. Atonement.

Cary, A. Sea-Side Cave, The.

Clampitt. Cormorant in His Element, The.

Cross, Jr. When Chicken Man Came Home to Roost.

Cruz Varela. Kaleidoscope.

Dunbar, P. Debt, The.

Eich. Geometrical Place.

Elizabeth I. Written on a Wall at Woodstock.

"Field." Flaw, A.

Gibson, W. Back.

Goldsmith, O. Song: "When lovely woman stoops to folly."

Gunn, T. High Fidelity.

Gurney, I. Target, The.

Hall, D. By the Exeter River.

Herbert, G. Conscience.

Hughes, L. Dinner Guest: Me.

Jarrell. Eighth Air Force.

Jennings, E. My Grandmother.

Landor, W. Maid's Lament, The.

Lehman. Guilt Trip.

Levi, P. Survivor, The.

Lipska. That Moment.

Merrill, J. Renewal, A.

Miles, J. Belief.

Morgan, E. Pilate at Fortingall.

Morgan, V. Within the Greenhouse Effect.

Morris, M. Joseph of Arimathaea.

Muir, E. Oedipus.

Pennant. Wildebeest of Carmine Street, The.

Rabbitt. For Those Who Will Live Forever.

Racine. My time's too short, your highness. It was I.

Replansky. Housing Shortage.

Rózewicz. Lament: "I turn to you high priests."

Posthumous Rehabilitation.

Saitō Mokichi. Tanka: "By the road."
Sarton. Tortured, The.
Shelnutt. O Hero.
Sobiloff. Snake's Destiny, The.
Spender, S. Double Shame, The.
Szymborska. Under a Certain Little Star.
Very. Slavery.
  Thy Brother's Blood.
Wain. Song about Major Eatherly, A.
Warren, R. Amazing Grace in the Back
  Country.
  Crime.
  Pursuit.
  Red Mullet, The.
  Revelation.
Weigl. Her Life Runs Like a Red Silk Flag.
Wright, C. California Spring.
Young, D. Upon Hearing of My Friend's
  Marriage Breaking Up.

Guinea Hens
Welty. Flock of Guinea Hens Seen from a
  Car, A.

Guitars
Cornford, F. Guitarist Tunes Up, The.
García Lorca. Guitar.
  Six Strings, The.
Kunio. Tanka: "Only when."
Leipoldt. On My Old Ramkiekie.
Penrose, R. Road is Wider Than Long: An
  Image Diary from the Balkans, July–August
  1938, The.

Guiteau, Charles J.
Unknown. Charles Guiteau.

Gulls
Ackland. Whether a dove or a seagull lighted
  there.
Allen, E. Sea-Birds.
Dafydd ap Gwilym. Seagull, The.
De la Mare. Storm, The.
Howitt, M. Sea-Gull, The.
Kanemasa. Guardian of the gate.
Nakasuk. Magic Words to Feel Better.
Nash, O. Sea-Gull, The.
Phylip, S. Seagull, The.
Roberts, N. Gull'' Flight, The.
Sandburg, C. Harbor, The.
Schwartz, D. Ballet of the Fifth Year, The.
Smedley, M. Sorrowful Sea-Gull, The.
Unknown. O sea-gulls that are crying.
Updike. Seagulls.
Warren, R. Gull's Cry.
Williams, W. Gulls.
Wright, J. Poem by Garnie Braxton, A.

Gunpowder Plot. *See* **Fawkes, Guy**

Guns
Ai. Kid, The.
Alexander, P. At Coueron. My First Gun.
Blunden. Vlamertinghe.
Bowes-Lyon. Battlefield.
Brown, G. Hawk, The.
Carson, C. Bloody Hand.
Cassity. Technique on the Firing Line.
Charles, D. Bang! the starter's gun—.
Chon, P. Mischief.
Coleridge, M. In London Town.
Cummings, E. Bigness of cannon, The.
Dickinson, E. My Life Had Stood—A Loaded
  Gun.
Dobler. His Depression.
Dobyns. Gun, The.
Escoffery. No Man's Land.
Galvin, J. Independence Day, 1956: A Fairy
  Tale.
Gurney, I. First Time In.
Haines, J. Flight, The.
Hardy, T. Channel Firing.
Heaney, S. From the Frontier of Writing.
Howell, C. Reminder to the Current President,
  A.
Joans. .38, The.
Karpowicz. Rifle, The.
Kirsanov. ...Back then I cut off a lock.
Kunio. Tanka: "Hands picking a rose."
  Tanka: "Woman."
Laing, A. Original Sin.
Manifold. Defensive Position.
Melville, H. Swamp Angel, The.

Mother Goose. Sam, The Sportsman.
Mountain, M. Pick-up truck.
Owen, W. Anthem for Doomed Youth.
  Arms and the Boy.
  On Seeing a Piece of Our Artillery Brought
    into Action.
Quasimodo. Anno Domini MCMXLVII.
Ransom, W. Grandpa's .45.
Reed, H. Naming Of Parts.
Robinson, E. Richard Cory.
Sackville-West. Out with a Gun.
Sandburg, C. A. E. F.
Sassoon. General, The.
Sorescu. Start.
Spender, S. Ultima Ratio Regum.
Unknown. Epigram: "Says a Reverend Priest
  to a less Rev'rend friend."
  Gunpowder Plot Day.
  Riddle: "Long slick black feller."
  Riddle: "Wooden belly iron back."
Whitman, W. Artilleryman's Vision, The.
Wilson, R. Military-Industrial Complex, The.
Wright, F. Pawtucket Postcards.
Yeats. To a Squirrel at Kyle-Na-No.
Yeryomenko. Addition to the Opposition.
Young, K. Casting.

**Gustavus II (Gustavus Adolphus), King of
Sweden**
Carew, T. In Answer of an Elegiacal[l] Letter,
  Upon the Death of the King of Sweden [from
  Aurelian Townsend, Inviting Me to Write on
  That Subject].

Guy Fawkes Day. *See* **Fawkes, Guy**

Guyana
Matthews, M. Guyana not Ghana.
Seymour, A. First of August.
  Slaves / Humming in the twilight by the
    shanty door.

Gymnastics and Gymnasts. *See* **Acrobatics and
Acrobats**

Gypsies
Bashford, S. Where do the gipsies come from?
Baudelaire. Gypsies on the Move.
Blunden. Idlers, The.
Clare, J. Gipsies seek wide sheltering woods
  again, The.
  Gipsies: "Snow falls deep; the forest lies
    alone, The."
Cofer. What the Gypsy Said to Her Children.
Field, R. Gypsies.
García Lorca. Preciosa and the Wind.
Hodgson, R. Gipsy Girl, The.
Hovey. Sea Gypsy, The.
Hughes, R. Gipsy-Night.
Keats. Meg Merrilies [*or* Merrilees].
King, D. Gipsy Man.
Kipling, R. Gipsy Trail, The.
Langhorne. Gypsies.
Levertov. Gypsy's Window, The.
Mandelstam. Last night I tell you, I do not
  lie.
Monsour. Emily's Words.
Service. Men That Don't Fit In, The.
Thomas, E. Gypsy, The.
Unknown. Gypsy Laddie, The.
  Johnny Faa, the Lord of Little Egypt.
  Wraggle Taggle Gipsies, The.
Wright, J. Jalapeña Gypsies.

H

Habits
Ai. I Can't Get Started.
Akhtar-ul-Iman. Compromise.
Atwood. You take my hand and.
Meek. Week the Dirigible Came, The.
O'Reilly, J. Builder's Lesson, A.
Plath. Love Letter.
Smith, I. Sitting here by the foreshore day
  after day.

Hades
Aristophanes. C'wa nou, what wey suld I chap
  o this door?
Claudian. Ye mighty Demons, whose
  tremendous sway.

Hope, A. Return of Persephone, The.
Pound, E. Canto 1.
Rukeyser, M. In the Underworld.
Swinburne. Garden of Proserpine, The.
Unknown. By Heraclides.
  To Demeter.
Virgil. Hell's gate.
  Orpheus and Eurydice.

Hael, Ifor
Evans, E. Hall of Ifor Hael, The.

Hagar
Bibb. Expulsion of Hagar, The.

Haggard, Sir Henry Rider
Stephen, J. To R. K.

Haggis
Burns, R. To a Haggis.

Haiku (form)
Roseliep. Campfire Extinguished.
Snyder, G. They Didn't Hire Him.
Wilbur. Sleepless at Crown Point.

Hail
Hopkins, G. Hailstorm in May.

Hair
Asquith. Hairy Dog, The.
Avidan. General Truths.
Baudelaire. Head of Hair, The.
Beardsley. Ballad of a Barber, The.
Berni. Hair of fine silver, shaggy and twisted.
Betjeman. Licorice Fields at Pontefract, The.
Bhartrihari. If the forest of her hair.
Bishop, E. Shampoo, The.
Bogan, L. Medusa.
Cardiff. Combing.
Causley. Tom Bone.
Cheng Hsieh. To Chin Nung.
Ch'ien Ch'ien-i. Miscellaneous Poems Written
  While in Jail.
Clarke, C. Hair: A Narrative.
Cornish, S. Sam's World ("Sam's mother
  has").
Cowper, W. On an Old Woman.
Crawford, R. Herr-Knit Bunnet, The.
Dafydd ab Edmwnd. Girl's Hair, A.
Damas. Just Like the Legend.
Dickinson, E. 'Tis customary as we part.
Dove, R. Blown apart by loss, she let herself
  go.
  Nightmare.
Erdrich. Butcher's Wife, The.
Euphorion. When first Eudoxos cut his lovely
  hair.
"Field." Embalmment.
Gray, S. Girl with Long Dark Hair.
Hafiz. Ode 105.
Hayati. Before there was a trace of this world
  of men.
Hecht, A. Giant Tortoise.
Herrick. Art above Nature, to Julia.
  Upon Julia's Haire Fill'd with Dew.
Hitomaro. This morning I will not.
  Your hair has turned white.
Housman, A. Oh who is that young sinner
  with the handcuffs on his wrists?
Hoyt, C. Hair, in my comb's teeth.
Jackson, A. Choosing the Blues.
Kastelan. As if it resembled your hair.
Keeshig-Tobias. Mother with Child.
Knott. Hair Poem.
Landor, W. On Seeing a Hair of Lucretia
  Borgia.
Lee, L. Early in the Morning.
Liu E. Boiling Falls.
Love, M. Initiation.
Lovelace, R. To Amarantha, That She Would
  Dishevel[l] Her Hair[e].
Lucilius. On an Old Woman.
  Some say you dye your hair, Nikylla.
Marichiko. I cannot forget.
Martial. I send you a lock of hair.
McOrlan. Hairdresser's, The.
Mikata Shami. Bound up it always.
Miliauskaite. In the damp places.
Mori Ōgai. Tanka: "Should I stroke it."
Moss, T. Raising a Humid Flag.
  Tornados.
Mullen, H. Saturday Afternoon, When Chores
  Are Done.

Hairdressers

Parnell, T. How flame the glories of Belinda's hair.
Patmore, C. To the Body.
Piercy. Hello Up There.
Po Chü-i. On his Baldness.
Pope, A. Rape of the Lock, The.
Pound, E. River-Merchant's Wife: A Letter, The.
Probyn. As the Flower of the Grass.
Randall, D. On Getting a Natural.
Ravikovitch. Hovering at a Low Altitude.
Rich, A. Suppose you want to write.
Rotella, A. Clutching a fist of hair.
  His footsteps in the room.
Rózewicz. Pigtail.
Rudnik. Lady in the Barbershop, The.
Rukeyser, M. Boy with His Hair Cut Short.
Shaoxuan. Black hair and red cheeks: for how long?
Sherman, C. Roots.
Spenser. Sonnet 37: "What guile [or guyle] is this, that those her golden tresses."
Swinburne. Kissing her hair, I sat against her feet.
Thackeray. Tragic Story, A.
Theodoridas. To the triple goddess of Amarynthus.
Toomer. Face.
  Portrait in Georgia.
Tsvetayeva. Gold that was my hair has turned, The.
Tucker, M. First Grey Hair, The.
Unknown. Betty.
  Dear Black Head.
  Dirge for Three Trumpets.
  Inky gloss of your mane, The.
  Song of the Snow-white Heads.
Virgil. She turns the child.
Washington. Freedom Hair.
Watkyns. Periwig, A.
Welles. White Valentine.
Wen Cheng-ming. Walking to the Temple of Precious Light.
Wilson, R. Keeping Hair.
Wollach. Absalom.
Wright, R. Green cockleburs, The.
Wu Chia-chi. Old saltman, hair turned white, The.
Yang Wan-li. Master Liu Painted a Portrait of Me in My Old Age and Asked Me to Write a Poem About the Picture.
Yeats. For Anne Gregory.
Yosano. At the beginning.
  Hair unbound, in this.
  Tanka: "Writes poetry."
Young, K. Eddie Priest's Barbershop and Notary.
Zach. Samson's Hair.

Hairdressers

Jackson, A. Choosing the Blues.
Love, M. Initiation.
Strange. Barbershop Ritual.
Young, K. Eddie Priest's Barbershop and Notary.

Haiti

Cullen, C. Black Majesty.
Iverem. Time #2, The.
Pressoir. Black Island.
  Country Graveyard.

Hales, John

King, A. Under Mr. Hales Picture.

Halevi, Judah

Heine. If, Jerusalem, I Ever Should Forget Thee.

Halloween

Aldis, D. Hallowe'en Pumpkin, A.
Barry, J. Harvest Moon.
Burns, R. Halloween.
Cummings, E. Hist whist / little ghostthings.
Glück, L. All Hallows.
Karp. Taxi to the Flame, A.
Livingston, M. Lazy Witch.
Moorer. Hallowe'en.
Prelutsky. It's Halloween.
  Skeleton Parade.
Turner, N. Black and Gold.

Ham

Hood, T. Sonnet to Vauxhall.
McGinley. Notes for a Southern Road Map.
Smith, D. Smithfield Ham.
Unknown. Riddle: "Riddlum riddlum ranty pole."

Hamer, Fannie Lou

Davis, T. Remembering Fannie Lou Hamer.

Hamlet

Allston. On Kean's Hamlet.
Herbert, Z. Elegy of Fortinbras.
Manley, F. Dead Letters.
Pasternak, B. Hamlet.
Sandburg, C. They all want to play Hamlet.
Sharpless. Hamlet.
Vinokurov. Hamlet.

Hammers and Hammering

Bogan, L. Roman Fountain.
Boldman. I hammer a nail.
Brown, S. Southern Road.
Gustafson, R. Of Green Steps and Laundry.
Herbert, Z. Passion of Our Lord painted by an anonymous hand from the Circle of Rhenish Masters, The.
Hooks. Body Inside the Soul, The.
Leadbelly. Take this hammer, (huh!) carry it to the captain, (huh!).
Unknown. Smoke-Blackened Smiths.
  Take this hammer—huh!
  We lads in the forging-shop have unbounded strength.

Hammocks

Monsour. Dream of Dying, A.

Hamsters

Wright, K. Our hamster's life.

Handball

Dunn, S. Day and Night Handball.
Lattimore. Game Resumed.

Handicaps and the Handicapped

Cook, E. Idiot-Born, The.
Donne. Lame Beggar, A.
Hugo, R. Freaks at Spurgin Road Field, The.
Mazur. Fracture Santa Monica.
Mungoshi. Dotito is our brother.
Owen, W. Disabled.
Sassoon. Does It Matter?[—losing your legs?].
Shapcott, T. Near the School for Handicapped Children.
Simic. Great Infirmities.
Thomas, D. Hunchback in the park, The.
Wordsworth, W. Idiot Boy, The.
See also **Amputees; Birth Defects; Blindness; Cripples; Deafness; Mental Retardation**

Hands

Atwood. You begin this way.
Bancquart. Curriculum vitae.
Behn, A. Oh, how the hand the lover ought to prize.
Bly, R. Taking the hands of someone you love.
Brooks, G. Medgar Evers.
Brown, S. Conjured.
Cassian. Sand.
Celan. Matière de Bretagne.
Clark, T. Touch of human hands—, The.
Couzyn. My father's hands.
Creeley. Figures, The.
  For friendship / make a chain that holds.
  People, The.
Cross, Jr. Accident, An.
Dacey, P. Thumb.
Dadié. Hands
Dickinson, E. Caterpillar.
Dorsey, T. Take My Hand, Precious Lord.
Drummond de Andrade. Dirty Hand, The.
Emin. Your Hands.
Feinstein, S. Sonnets for Stan Gage (1945–1992).
Finch, A. Sapphics for Patience.
Finkel. Hands.
Fumi Saito. Tanka: "Palm of the hand, The, / is not aware of dying."
Gergely. Encelado and the Facts.
Grimké, A. Your Hands.
Gunn, T. Feel of Hands, The.
  Man With Night Sweats, The.

Hall, D. Second Stanza for Dr. Johnson, A.
Harrison, T. Hands, The.
Herrick. Right Hand, The.
Housman, A. As through the wild green hills of Wyre.
Hoyt, C. While the guests order.
Ignatow, D. Mystique.
Ishikawa Takuboku. Tanka: "I work."
Jackson, L. Take hands. / There is no love now.
Jeffers, L. I do not know the power of my hand.
Johnson, L. Nihilism.
Johnson, S. Ballad: "I put my hat upon my head."
Keats. To Fanny Brawne.
Keens-Douglas. Wukhand.
Knott. Death.
Kunio. Tanka: "Hands picking a rose."
Latta. Hand reaches up, A.
Lecount. Bridge toll-booth—, The.
Lovelace, R. Her Muffe.
Lowell, A. Sprig of Rosemary, A.
Magowan. Susan.
Minty. Look to the Back of the Hand.
Moss, H. Hand, The.
Park, N. Hands.
Phillips, C. As From a Quiver of Arrows.
Piercy. Friend, The.
Randolph, T. Upon the Loss[e] of His Little Finger.
Rossetti, C. Twice.
St. John, P. Ocean of the Streams of Story.
Saitō Mokichi. Tanka: "Nothing to be done?"
Serge. Hands.
Shapiro, K. Love for a Hand.
Shea, M. Walk's end.
Snyder, G. After Work.
Stein, G. Leave, A.
TallMountain. Hands of Mary Joe, The.
Tate, J. Love Making.
Thomas, D. Hand that signed the paper felled a city, The.
Thomas, R. Hand, The.
Tsaloumas. Return of an Ikon.
Ungaretti. Vigil.
Unknown. Midwife's Invocation, A.
  My Mother's Hands.
  Warm hands, warm.
Valentine, J. Seeing You.
Vallejo. Poem to Be Read and Sung.
Ward, D. Glass House.
Wills, J. My hand moves out.
Wright, R. I Have Seen Black Hands.
Yosano. Tanka: "Writes poetry."

Handwriting

Barbauld. On a Lady's Writing.
Nemerov. Writing.
Reid, A. Lesson in Handwriting, A.

Hanging

Atwood. Marrying the Hangman.
Auden. Terce.
Bartusek. Strangled, The.
Borges. Luke 23:39–43; One of the criminals.
Brutus. They hanged him, I said dismissively.
Cecco Angiolieri, da Siena. Sonnet: Of Why He Is Unchanged.
Chipasula. Hanging, Zomba Central Prison, A.
Fumiko. Tanka: "One day I saw."
Housman, A. Carpenter's Son, The.
  Eight O'Clock.
  On moonlit heath and lonesome bank.
Kipling, R. Danny Deever.
Lowell, J. Boss, The.
Melville, H. Portent, The.
Parker, D. Résumé.
Patmore, C. London Fete, A.
Plath. Hanging Man, The.
Scott, D. Epitaph: "They hanged him on a clement morning, swung."
Swift, J. Clever Tom Clinch Going to Be Hanged.
Unknown. Geordie [An Old Ballad].
  Hang Me, O Hang Me, and I'll Be Dead and Gone.
  Hanging of Sam Archer, The.
  Murder of Maria Marten by W. Corder, The.

Night before Larry was stretched, The.
Receipt to Cure a Love Fit, A.
Sam Hall.
Vinokurov. Mother of Judas, The.
Waugh, E. They told me, Francis Hinsley, they told me you were hung.
Yukitsuna. Tanka: "With those who."
See also **Executions and Executioners; Lynchings**

Hangovers
P'i Jih-hsiu. Impromptu on a Hangover.
Yukitsuna. Tanka: "With a hangover."

Hanks, Nancy
Lindsay, V. Nancy Hanks, Mother of Abraham Lincoln.

Hansel and Gretel
Glück, L. Gretel in Darkness.
McGrath, T. Remembering the Children of Auschwitz.
Morgan, R. Two Gretels were exploring the forest, The.
Sexton. Hansel and Gretel.

Hanukkah
Chaikin. Light Another Candle.
Lazarus, E. Kindle the Taper.

Happiness
Atwood. You Are Happy.
Avidan. What I Have to Tell You, Until Next Time.
Baumel. Doing Time in Baltimore.
Blake, W. Echoing [or Ecchoing] Green, The.
Laughing Song.
Bozhilov. Troubles.
Brecht, S. Thanksgiving (1974).
Brennen. Spring.
Brontë, E. How still, how happy! These [or Those] are words.
Brown, S. Schadenfreude.
Browne, W. Happyer those times were, when the Flaxen clew.
Carew, T. To My Cousin (C.R.) Marrying My Lady (A.)
Carney. (Little Things).
Carphyllides. Happy Man, A.
Cassian. Part of a Bird.
Ch'ien T'ao. Matching a Poem by Secretary Kuo.
Chōkū. Tanka: "Late at night in the kitchen."
Clifton, L. Good Times.
Cowley, A. Wish, The.
Crane, F. Today.
Creeley. Air: "The Love of a Woman."
Crosby, F. Blind but Happy.
Cummings, E. I am so glad and very.
You shall above all things be glad and young.
Curzon, D. Proverbs 6:6.
Davies, W. Example, The.
Disch. Argument Resumed; Or, Up Through Tribeca, The.
In Praise of New York.
Doolittle, H. White World.
Dove, R. Bistro Styx, The.
Demeter Mourning.
Dryden, J. Happy the man, and happy he alone.
Song from Troilus and Cressida.
Dunn, S. Happiness.
Euripides. What is wisdom: What gift of the gods.
Farley, R. Thinking Happiness.
Ferlinghetti, L. Heaven was only.
Fernández. If You Happy Would Be.
Frost, R. Happiness Makes Up in Height for What It Lacks in Length.
Glazkov. Simple Man, A.
Graves, R. By this exchange of eyes, this encirclement.
Harjo, P. Wishes.
Heard, J. Happy Heart, A.
Herrick. Anacreontic.
Four[e] Things Make Us Happy Here.
Horace. To Maecenas.
Hughes, L. Dream Boogie.
World War II.
Hughes, T. Bull Moses, The.
Jarrell. Happy Cat, The.

Jefferson, T. Preamble to the Declaration of Independence.
Justice, D. But That Is Another Story.
Kamatari. Hey! Ho! Hurrah!
Keats. Pleasure Thermometer, The.
Kinnell. Crying only a little bit.
Kizer, C. Afternoon Happiness.
Klee. Happy one, who is almost / an idiot, The.
Landon. Mask of Gaiety, The.
Larkin, P. High Windows.
Lawrence, D. Bat.
Layton. Birth of Tragedy, The.
Leonard, P. Happiness is like a crystal.
Lovelace, R. Grasshopper, The.
Lu Chih. Tune: "Song of the Lunar Palace."
Lux. Amiel's Leg.
Lyttelton. Happiest Pair, The.
Machi. Tanka: "Woman, The."
Marlowe. Passionate Shepherd [or Sheepheard] To His Love, The.
Martial. Happy Life, The.
Martin, D. (On the Merry, Merry-Go-Round).
McAuley, J. Seventh Day, The.
Meredith, G. Here Jack and Tom are paired with Moll and Meg.
Meredith, W. Preponderance, The.
Milne, A. Happiness.
Montague, J. Hearth Song.
More, H. Epilogue: "Child! we must quit these visionary scenes."
Nagy, A. Sincerity.
Nash, O. Anatomy of Happiness, The.
Oliver, M. Poppies send up their, The.
Sunrise.
Olson, C. What soul / isn't in default?
Padgett, R. Poema del City 2.
Palmer, M. Notes for Echo Lake 2.
Paman. On Christmas Day to My Heart.
Parker, D. Comment.
Pomfret, J. Choice, The.
Pope, A. Ode on Solitude.
Porter, P. 'In the New World Happiness is Allowed'.
Pound, E. Salutation.
Powys. Nunc Dimittis.
Prévert. Dunce, The.
Ravenscroft, T. Sing we now merily.
Rich, A. Miracle Ice Cream.
Robinson, E. Cliff Klingenhagen had me in to dine.
Rodriguez, J. Eskimo Occasion.
Roethke. Waking, The.
Rogers, S. Wish, A.
Romanes. Simple Nature.
Rumi. Out beyond ideas of wrongdoing and rightdoing.
Ryokan. First days of spring—the sky.
Sandburg, C. Happiness.
Seay. Ballet of Happiness, The.
Shao Yung. Song of Delight.
Shelley, P. Song: "Rarely, rarely, comest thou."
Shurin. Saturated.
Silveira. Different Poem, A.
Smith, C. Sonnet Written at the Close of Spring [or Elegiac Sonnet].
Smith, S. Conviction IV.
Stafford, W. Gift, The.
Stevens, W. Crude Foyer.
Stevenson, R. Happy Thought.
Unseen Playmate, The.
Stickney, T. Athenian Garden, An.
Stitch. Little roads to happiness, they are not hard to find, The.
Stone, R. Happiness.
Subbiah. Salutations.
Talpalar. True Happiness.
T'ao Ch'ien. Bank to bank, the stream is wide.
Teasdale. On the South Downs.
Thomas, E. Glory of the beauty of the morning, The.
Thorley. Happy Sheep, The.
Trần Tế Xu'o'ng. Poor and Happy.
Tu Fu. Dejeuner Sur L'Herbe.
Returning from court day after day, I pawn

my spring clothes.
Visitors.
Unknown. Aubade: "O, Lady, awake! The azure moon."
Bible, Matthew 5:3–12, The.
Centipede was happy quite, A.
Minutes of Gold.
There's happiness in little things.
Today I sat before the cliff.
Tune: "Sheep on Mountain Slope"—Boudoir Thoughts.
Uguisu on the flowering plum, The.
Utitia' q's Song.
Upton, L. Daughter, A.
Utkin. Tale of Red-Haired Motl, Mister Inspector, Rabbi Isaiah, and Commissar Blokh, The.
Virgil. Fiery Sun was mounted now on hight, The.
Wallace-Crabbe. Sonnet IV.
Wang Chiu-ssu. You think I am happy.
West, K. On Track.
Westmorland. Happy Life, A.
Whitman, W. Day when I rose at dawn from the bed of perfect health, refresh'd, The.
Halcyon Days.
There is that in me.. . . I do not know what it is.. . . but I know it is in me.
When I heard at the close of the day how my name had been receiv'd with plaudits in the capitol, still it was not a happy night for me that follow'd.
Wickham. Happy Mathematician, The.
Wilbur. Wedding Toast, A.
What's Good for the Soul is Good for Sales.
Winchilsea. Give me, O Indulgent fate!
Wollach. Lola, are you still getting whatever you want.
Woolson. Florida Beach, The.
Wordsworth, W. These Chairs they have no words to utter.
Wotton, S. Character of a Happy Life, The.
To John Donne.
Wright, J. Out of Horace.
Wright, J. Blessing, A.
Northern Pike.
Way to Make a Living, A.
Yang Chi. After my illness, so hard to be a traveler.
Yoshifusa. Years have touched me, The.
Yüan Hung-tao. "Slowly, Slowly" Poem, The.
See also **Contentment**

Harbors and Ports
Bethell. Long Harbour, The.
Channing. Harbor, The.
Crane, H. Harbor Dawn, The.
Galvin, B. Seals in the Inner Harbor.
Hardy, T. Harbour Bridge, The.
O'Hara, F. Blocks.
Plath. Green Rock, Winthrop Bay.
Quiller-Couch. Harbour of Fowey, The.
Radauskas. Harbor.
Sandburg, C. Harbor, The.
Tranströmer. Syros.

Harding, Warren Gamaliel
Wright, J. Two Poems about President Harding.

Hardy, Thomas
Beerbohm, M. Luncheon, A.
Day Lewis. Birthday Poem for Thomas Hardy.
De la Mare. Scholars.
Thomas Hardy.
Dubie. Thomas Hardy.
Wright, J. At Thomas Hardy's Birthplace, 1953.

Hares
Clare, J. Hares at Play.
Cowper, W. Epitaph on a Hare.
Davies, G. Dance, The.
De la Mare. Hare, A.
Fumi Saito. Tanka: "White hare, A."
Lear, E. Limericks, II (v).
MacCaig. Interruption to a Journey.
Miles, S. Hares, The.
Nicholson, N. Cowper's Tame Hare.
Smart, C. To the Rev. Mr. Powell.
Unknown. Names of the Hare, The.

Riddle: "Hopper o'ditches, A."
Two Laments.
Yeats. Two Songs of a Fool.
Young, A. March Hares.
See also **Rabbits**

Harlem, New York City
Baraka. Return of the Native.
Bethune, L. Harlem Freeze Frame.
Cortez. Under the Edge of February.
Dana, R. Elegy for the Duke.
Davis, T. Zoom (The Commodores).
Espada. Dándole la mano a Mongo.
Shaking Hands with Mongo.
Henderson, D. Do Nothing Till You Hear
from Me.
Keep on Pushing.
Walk with de Mayor of Harlem.
Hernton. Jitterbugging in the Streets.
Housman, A. Harlem.
Hughes, L. Comment on Curb.
Esthete in Harlem.
Good morning, daddy!
Harlem.
Harlem Sweeties.
Island.
Jazzonia.
Juke Box Love Song.
Neighbor.
Night funeral / In Harlem.
Passing.
Prime.
Projection.
Theme for English B.
Weary Blues, The.
Johnson, H. Sonnet to a Negro in Harlem.
McKay, C. Harlem Dancer, The.
Harlem Shadows.
Neal, L. Harlem Gallery: From the Inside.
Patterson, R. Harlem Suite.
Rivers, C. Still Voice of Harlem, The.
Train Runs Late to Harlem, The.
Rukeyser, M. Ballad of Orange and Grape.
Senghor. To New York.
Tolson. African China.
Harlem Gallery: Book I, The Curator, The.
Mu.

Harper's Ferry, West Virginia
Atkins. Narrative.
Williams, E. At Harper's Ferry Just before the
Attack.

Harps and Harpists
Coleridge, S. Eolian Harp, The.
Cook, E. 'Tis well to wake the theme of
Love.
Emerson, R. Merlin I.
"Fane." Siren, The.
Gillies, V. Young Harper.
Mac Siomoin. Silence, The.
Mechthild von Magdeburg. Effortlessly, / Love
flows from God into man.
Melville, H. Aeolian Harp, The.
Millay, E. Ballad of the Harp-Weaver, The.
Moore, T. Dear Harp of My Country.
Harp That Once through Tara's Halls, The.
Minstrel Boy, The.
Owenson. Irish Harp: Fragment I, The.
Pitter. Military Harpist, The.
Po Chü-i. Harp, The.

Harpur, Charles
Wright, J. Extinct Birds.

Harrison, Benjamin
Hollander, J. Historical Reflections.

Harvard University
Cummings, E. Little joe gould has lost his
teeth and doesn't know where.
Eberhart, R. I went to see Irving Babbitt.
Sissman. In and Out.
Symons, J. Harvard, Cambridge, Mass.
Wheatley, P. To the University of Cambridge,
in New-England.

Harvest
Alford, H. Come, ye thankful people, come.
Anh Tho'. Harvesting at Sunset.
Anyidoho. Hero and Thief.
Atwood. November.
Auden. As I walked out one evening.

Beaver. Silo Treading.
Blind. Reapers.
Bold, A. And Now.
Carlyle, T. Sower's Song, The.
Carruth, H. Emergency Haying.
Cendrars. Harvest.
De la Mare. Scarecrow, The.
Duck. Soon as the harvest hath laid bare the
plains.
Fallon, E. August.
Fallon, P. Meadow, The.
Fitzgerald, E. 73.
Gibran. Prophet Speaks of Love, The.
Glück, L. All Hallows.
Goodison. Gleanings.
Herrick. Hock-Cart, or Harvest Home, The.
Hesiod. Summer.
Hood, T. Ruth.
Hope, A. Hay Fever.
Hopkins, G. Hurrahing in Harvest.
Hutchinson, M. Harvest.
James, D. Harvest.
Kao Ch'i. Picking Tea: A Ballad.
Khlebnikov, V. It has the unassuming face of
a burnt-out candle.
Lawrence, D. Youth Mowing, A.
Li K'ai-hsien. Compassion for the Farmers.
Longfellow, H. Aftermath.
Lu Yu. It Has Snowed Repeatedly and We
Can Count On a Good Crop of Wheat and
Barley.
Mechthild von Magdeburg. I cannot dance, O
Lord.
Melville, H. Afterward.
Meynell, A. Threshing Machine, The.
P'i Jih-hsiu. Lament of a Woman Acorn-
gatherer.
Prunty. Vegetable Garden, The.
"Rachel." Aftergrowth.
Roberts, S. Potato Harvest, The.
Rossetti, C. Amen.
Sarton. Prothalamion for an Autumn Wedding.
Shimoni. Gleaning.
Soyinka. Harvest of Hate.
Season.
Su Tung-p'o. Harvest Sacrifice.
New Year's Eve blizzard kept me from
leaving, The.
Tanikawa Shuntaro. Concerning a Girl.
Toomer. Harvest Song.
Reapers.
Trowbridge, J. Idyl of Harvest Time, An.
Unknown. Grain for Emperor Huan.
Harvest Song.
Watermeyer. Harvest Time.
Watkins, N. Returning from Harvest.
Wordsworth, W. Solitary Reaper, The.
Wu Chen. To the Tune "Chiu-ch'üan tzu."
Zach. Harvest Month[. A full moon].

Harvey, Gabriel (1545?–1630)
Spenser. To the Right Worshipfull, My
Singular Good Frend, Master Gabriell
Harvey, Doctor of the Lawes.

Hashish
Whittier. Haschish, The.

Hate
"Akhmatova." Ah—you thought I'd be the
type.
Amichai. Quick And Bitter.
Ammianus. Epitaph of Nearchos.
Avidan. Longterm Hatred.
What I Have to Tell You, Until Next Time.
Baraka. Agony. An. As Now.
Poem Some People Will Have to Understand,
A.
Bennett, G. Hatred.
Bodker. Fury's Field.
Browning, R. Soliloquy of the Spanish
Cloister.
Bruner. Retaliation.
Chesterton, G. World State, The.
Creeley. Self-Portrait.
Damas. Whitewash.
Dickinson, E. I had no time to hate, because.
Duncan, R. Up Rising.
Ehrmann. Hate and the Love of the World,
The.

"Ephelia." To One That Asked Me Why I
Loved J.G G.
Feldman, I. Terminal Laughs.
"Field." As two fair vessels side by side.
Foss, S. Despise not any man that lives.
Frances, J. Song of Hate.
Frost, R. For a Brother.
Frost, R. Beyond Words.
Fire and Ice.
Fumiko. Tanka: "Yellow bus, The."
Harjo, J. Transformations.
Herbert of Cherbury. Ditty: "Why dost thou
hate return instead of love."
Hope, A. Fafnir.
Johnson, L. Destroyer of a Soul, The.
Jonson, B. Little Shrub Growing By, A.
Kaufman, S. Mothers, Daughters.
Lawrence, D. Eloi, Eloi, Lama Sabachthani?
History.
Lowry, M. Wild Cherry, The.
Machi. Tanka: "Although."
MacNeice. Belfast.
McElroy, C. Illusion.
McKay, C. Enslaved.
White House, The.
Moore, T. When I loved you, I can't but
allow.
Neruda. Dictators, The.
O'Hara, F. Poem: "Hate is only one of many
responses."
Ostriker. Lamenting the Inevitable.
Pasolini. Southern Dawn.
Pembroke, M. O Lord, Thou Hast Searched
and Known Me.
Petri. Night Song of the Personal Shadow.
Piatt, S. Pique at Parting, A.
Piercy. Letter to be Disguised as a Gas Bill.
Rape Poem.
Plath. Daddy.
Prelutsky. Homework! Oh, homework!
Ryan, G. If I Had a Gun.
Schafer. Battle Lines.
Sepamla. Odyssey, The.
Shakespeare, W. Sonnet 145.
Shelley, P. Hate-Song, A.
Shore. High Holy Days.
Soyinka. Harvest of Hate.
Stephens, J. Hate.
Suckling, J. Barley-Break , A.
Unknown. Edward [*or* Edward, Edward].
'Tis a little journey.
Warren, R. Child next door is defective
because the mother, The.
Watkins, N. Easy way out.
Wickham. Paradox.
Wyatt, T. Is it possible.
Wylie. Full Moon.
Yosano. Tanka: "Agonizing beyond words."
Zu-Bolton. By the 5th Generation Louisiana,
After Slavery.

Hats
Adams, C. My Infundibuliform Hat.
Bezymensky. About a Hat.
Bishop, E. Manuelzinho.
Burns, R. To a Louse [On Seeing One on a
Lady's Bonnet at Church].
Cleage. Confession.
Cook, E. My Old Straw Hat.
Duncan. Hat Factory, The.
Hall, D. Second Stanza for Dr. Johnson, A.
Harper, M. Bandstand.
Hill, E. When Polly Buys a Hat.
Jastrun, T. Hat.
Johnson, S. Ballad: "I put my hat upon my
head."
Kyger. Philip Whalen's Hat.
Layne, M. On Hats and Things.
Lear, E. Limerick: "There was an Old Man
who supposed."
Quangle Wangle's Hat, The.
Little, L. My Yellow Straw Hat.
Mole, J. Song of the Hat-Raising Doll.
Neal, L. Don't say goodbye to the Porkpie
Hat that rolled.
Pastan. Hat Lady, The.
"Peter." Saint Wears a Halo, The.
Pizzarelli. Stranger passing, A.

Po Chü-i. Hat Given to the Poet by Li Chien, The.
Probyn. Frustrated.
Shange. My father is a retired magician.
Smith, S. Magna Est Veritas.
  My Hat.
Stafford, W. One of the Years.
Thompson, C. Easter Bonnet, The.
Travis, N. Church Ladies.
Unknown. In Praise of the Hat.
  Stackalee.
  Staffs and Hats.

Haunted Houses
Bontemps. Southern Mansion.
"Carroll." Phantasmagoria.
Causley. Colonel Fazackerley [Butterworth-
  Toast].
De la Mare. Feckless Dinner-Party, The.
Donne. Apparition, The.
Edwards, R. Recollections of an Old Spook.
Hardy, T. Strange House, The.
Hill, G. Asmodeus.
Longfellow, H. Haunted Houses.
Nesbit, E. Haunted.
Robinson, E. Haunted House.

Havana, Cuba
Komunyakaa. Boxing Day.

Hawaii
Birney. Twenty-third Flight.
Blanding. Aloha Oe.
Chock. Chinese Fireworks Banned in Hawaii.
Dean, D. In the Way Back.
Hahn, K. Hula Skirt, 1959, The.
Lei-Lanilau. Kolohe or Communication.
Mazzocco. Honolulu.

Hawks
Blackburn, P. Net of Place, The.
Blue Cloud. Hawk Nailed to a Barn Door.
Brodsky, J. Hawk's Cry in Autumn, The.
Brown, G. Hawk, The.
"Ern Malley." Sonnets for the Novachord.
Flanner. Hawk Is a Woman.
Gorman, L. Down the billboard girl's bare
  belly.
Gunn, T. Tamer and Hawk.
Hackett, J. Searching on the wind.
Hopkins, G. Windhover, The.
Hotham. Every night.
Hughes, T. Hawk Roosting.
Jeffers, R. Hurt Hawks.
  Rock and Hawk.
Jonson, B. To Sir Henry Goodyere.
Melville, H. Man-of-War Hawk, The.
Palmer, H. Wounded Hawk, The.
Thomas, D. Over Sir John's Hill.
Thoreau. To a Marsh Hawk in Spring.
Tomlinson, C. How still the hawk.
Unknown. Hawk Chant of the Saginaws.
  Sparrow-Hawk, A.
Warren, R. Evening Hawk.
Yeats. Hawk, The.
Yukitsuna. Tanka: "Beyond doubt."

Hawthorn (botany)
Brown, T. I Bended unto Me.
Heaney, S. Haw Lantern, The.
Unknown. Hawthorn, The.
Wright, J. Hawthorn Hedge, The.

Hawthorne, Nathaniel
Alcott, A. Sonnet 19: "Romancer, far more
  coy than that coy sex!"
Fogle. Hawthorne Garland, A.
Longfellow, H. Hawthorne.
Lowell, J. Hawthorne.
Lowell, J. Hawthorne.
Melville, H. Monody.
Noguere. Secret, The.
Very. On Visiting the Graves of Hawthorne
  and Thoreau.

Hay and Haymaking
Barnes, W. Sam and Bob.
Clampitt. Stacking the Straw.
Dickinson, E. I'm sorry for the Dead—Today.
Hay, G. Atman.
Hodgins. Making Hay.
MacLeish. Where the Hayfields Were.
Moon, T. Signpost.

Steele, T. Timothy.
Whitman, W. Big doors of the country barn
  stand open and ready, The.

Haydn, Franz Joseph
Holcroft. To Haydn.
Transt, römer. Allegro.

Haydon, Benjamin Robert
Browning, E. On a Portrait of Wordsworth by
  B. R. Haydon.
Keats. Addressed to Haydon.

Haymaking. *See* **Hay and Haymaking**

Haze. *See* **Fog**

Hazlitt, William
Coleridge, S. W. H. *Eheu!*.
Guiney. W. H.

Heads
Bradstreet, A. Letter to Her Husband, Absent
  upon Public[k] Employment, A.
Carnevali. Queer Things.
Carter, E. Dialogue, A.
Conquest. Agents, The.
Davidson, M. Troth.
Di Cicco. Head Is a Paltry Matter, The.
Forbes, J. Four Heads & How to Do Them.
Gorey. Limerick.
Hall, D. Second Stanza for Dr. Johnson, A.
Hollo. Mescalito.
Hoyt, C. Hallowe'en mask, A.
Jackson, L. Ding-Donging.
Johnson, S. Ballad: "I put my hat upon my
  head."
Lear, E. There was a Young Person of Ayr.
Major, C. Balance and Beauty.
Mandelstam. Mounds of Human Heads Are
  Wandering into the Distance.
Meredith, W. Thoughts on One's Head.
Nokan. My head is immense.
Okamoto. Tanka: "I measure."
Pettet. Mevlana.
Pope, A. Another [Epigram].
Samio. Tanka: "Reverently."
Schuyler, J. Head, A.
Skelton, J. Upon a Dead Man's Head.
Sparrow, J. To an Angel in the House.
Unknown. Baby, baby.
  Tommy.
Wieners. Glimpse, A.

Health Clubs
Merrill, J. Family Week at Oracle Ranch.

Hearne, Samuel
Newlove. Samuel Hearne in Wintertime.

Hearst, William Randolph
Taylor, B. Doxology.

Hearts
Altizer. Sonnet 2: "My own heart let me have.
  More pity on."
Alvarez, J. Woman's Work.
Atwood. Woman Who Could Not Live With
  Her Faulty Heart, The.
Behn, A. Song: Love Armed.
Bernstein, O. Games.
Berryman. There sat down, once, a thing on
  Henry's heart.
Binyon. Harebell and Pansy.
Bogan, L. Song for the Last Act.
Boldman. In the temple.
Bourdillon. When Love Is Done.
Breton, A. Poem-Object.
Browning, E. My Heart and I.
  To George Sand: A Recognition.
Browning, R. Meeting at Night.
Bu-er. Late Indian summer's.
Burns, R. My heart's in the Highlands, my
  heart is not here.
Bynner. Wintry Mind, The.
Campo. Aunt Toni's Heart.
Carew, T. Celia Bleeding, to the Surgeon.
Chamberlain, K. Yerokastrinos.
Clare, J. First Love.
Clark, T. Superballs.
Clough. Put forth thy leaf, thou lofty plane.
Coleridge, M. Broken Friendship.
  "He Knoweth Not That the Dead Are Thine."
  Only a little shall we speak of thee.
Cope, W. Valentine.
Cowper, W. Animals Enjoying Life.

Crane, S. Heart, The.
Crashaw. Hymn to Saint Teresa.
  On the Name of Jesus.
  To the Noblest and Best of Ladies, the
  Countess of Denbigh, Perswading her to
  Resolution in Religion, and to render her
  selfe without further delay into the
  Communion of the Catholick Church.
Cummings, E. I carry your heart with me(i
  carry it in).
Cunningham, J. To My Wife.
Dante Alighieri. Day agone, as I rode sullenly,
  A.
  Gentle thought there is will often start, A.
  Love hath so long possessed me for his own.
  My lady looks so gentle and so pure.
  Sonnet: "Love and the gentle heart are one
  same thing."
  Stay now with me, and listen to my sighs.
  To every heart which the sweet pain doth
  move.
Davis, T. Playing Solitaire.
Dickinson, E. Heart asks Pleasure—*first*, The.
  This dirty—little—Heart.
Dietz. Gentle Jesus meek and mild.
Digby, J. One Night Away from Day.
Donne. Blossom [*or* Blossome], The.
  Broken Heart, The.
  Legacy [*or* Legacie], The.
  Message, The.
Dorgan, T. Promised Garden, The.
Drayton. Cryer, The.
  Heart, The.
Dryden, J. One Happy Moment.
Duggan, L. Hearts (1983).
Eimers. No Friends of the Heart.
"Field." Love rises up some days.
  Sometimes I do despatch my heart.
  Unbosoming.
Foscolo. To Evening.
Frost, R. Dust of Snow.
Hardy, T. In a Cathedral City.
Hemans. Stranger's heart! Oh! wound it not!,
  The.
Herbert, G. Altar, The.
Herrick. To Oenone ("What conscience, say,
  is it in thee").
Hikmet. Angina Pectoris.
Holmes, R. Little girl's heart must be wide
  and, A.
Hopkins, G. My own heart let me more have
  pity on; let.
Ishikawa Takuboku. Tanka: "Fearing."
  Tanka: "Sadly."
Jewsbury. My heart's in the kitchen, my heart
  is not here.
  To My Own Heart.
Johnson, G. Heart of a woman [goes forth
  with the dawn], The.
Kambala. KYE HO! Wonderful!
King, H. Sonnet: "Tell me[e] no more how
  fair[e] she[e] is."
Kirsanov. New Heart, The.
Kitahara Hakushū. Tanka: "In my heart."
Kojijū. On the Spirit of the Heart as Moon-
  Disk.
Kunitz, S. Touch Me.
Larkin, P. If grief could burn out.
Lawrence, D. Go deeper than love, for the
  soul has greater depths.
Levchev. Abandoned Churches.
Liu E. On the Night of the Sixteenth of the
  Eighth Month: Watching the Moon from the
  Deck of the Ship, Aimo-maru in the Black
  Water Sea.
Lovelace, R. To Lucasta ("Like to the sentinel
  stars, I watch all night").
Lowell, R. Colloquy in Black Rock.
Machado Ruiz. Lord, you have ripped away
  from me what I loved most.
Machi. Tanka: "Freezing my smile."
  Tanka: "My heart."
  Tanka: "This day in March."
Marson. Repose.
Masefield. Her heart is always doing lovely
  things.

Mechthild von Magdeburg. How God Answers the Soul.
Mew. I Have Been Through the Gates.
Mirabai. O friends on this Path.
Mistral, G. Rose, The.
Mitchison. To Some Young Communists from an Older Socialist.
Unfertile Heart, The.
Miyazawa Kenji. Tanka: "Lightning."
Mori Ōgai. Tanka: "Your heart."
Nguyễn Bính. Two Hearts.
Ni Tsan. Woodpecker, The.
Norton, C. Sonnet 7: "Like an enfranchised bird, who wildly springs."
Paschen. Confederacy.
Philips, K. Friendship in Embleme, or the Seal. To my dearest Lucasia.
Friendship's Mystery, To My Dearest Lucasia.
Prior. Les Estreines.
Rabi'a al-Adawiyya. I am fully qualified to work as a doorkeeper, and for this reason.
Receveur. Eagle in the Land of Oz.
Rexroth, K. Heart of Herakles, The.
Rilke. Panther, The.
Sonnets to Orpheus, The.
Root, J. Naming the Shells.
Rossetti, C. Birthday, A.
My Gift.
Twice.
Rózewicz. What luck I can pick.
Sackville-West. Thus love, bright charlatan, besieged my heart.
Saigyo. My heart emptied.
Saitō Mokichi. Tanka: "What on the other shore."
Sarton. Prothalamion for an Autumn Wedding.
Scovell. Betrothal, A.
Shakespeare, W. Sonnet 151.
Shapiro, D. Sentences.
Shelley, P. From the Arabic: An Imitation.
Lines: "When the lamp is shattered [or shatter'd]."
Shūji. Tanka: "Slanted."
Sidney, P. Bargain, The.
Song: "O fair! O sweet! when I do look on thee."
Sitwell, D. Extract from Romance.
Heart and Mind.
Spenser. Sonnet 37: "What guile [or guyle] is this, that those her golden tresses."
Spires. Robed Heart, The.
Stevenson, R. Hearts, like doors.
Supervielle. Sphere.
Swede. In the town dump I find a still-beating heart.
Sylvester, J. Ubique.
Tasso. Now the waves murmur.
Teasdale. Song Making.
Thomas, D. When all my five and country senses see.
Thomas, R. Lonely Farmer, The.
Unknown. Boat of Cypress Wood, The.
Clear full moon.
Moon is full, The.
Prayer for Love, A.
See! Here, My Heart.
Thy heart is like some icy lake.
Warren, R. Debate: Question, Quarry, Dream.
Watson, R. Cage, The.
Williams, S. Like a drop of water is my heart.
Wright, J. At Thomas Hardy's Birthplace, 1953.
Jewel, The.
Yang Shen. To the Tune "Moon Over West River."
Yeats. Never give all the heart, for love.
Song, A: "I thought no more was needed."
Yosano. Tanka: "Sea inside my heart, The."
Tanka: "White blossoms bloom."

Heat
Baumel. Thumbs Up.
Boldman. In the heat.
Bryant, W. Midsummer.
Ch'u Ch'uang I. Tea.
Doolittle, H. Heat.
Eigner. It Sounded.
Giovanni. Knoxville, Tennessee.

Graves, R. Cool Web, The.
Hampton. In Andrea's Garden.
Hass, R. Late Spring.
Hotham. Up late.
Jacobsen, J. Shade-Seller, The.
Kusano Shimpei. 4 Or 5 Tadpoles.
Lampman. Heat.
Loftin. Weeksville Women.
Mackenzie, K. Heat.
McDonald, W. Last Still Days in a Bunker, The.
Mountain, M. At dusk hot water from the hose.
Oden. Riven Quarry, The.
Ovid. Elegies 1.5.
Powell, J. It was fever that made the world.
Radauskas. Hot Day.
Shurin. Saturated.
Spenser. Sonnet 30: "My love is like to ice, and I to fire."
Tomlinson, C. Las Trampas U. S. A.
Unknown. Hot Day In Sydney, A.
Old Fellow from Tyre, The.
Warm hands, warm.
Virgil. Hot afternoon.
Walcott. Midsummer, Tobago.
Wang Wei. Suffering from Heat.
Warren, R. Rattlesnake Country.

Heather
Bethell. Erica.
Williams, E. Heather Flowers.

Heaven
Abelard. Hymn for the Close of the Week.
Alabaster. O starry Temple of unvalted space.
Atwood. Resurrection.
Bailey, P. What Is Heaven?
Baraka. Dope.
Baranczak, S. N. N. Tries to Remember the Words of a Prayer.
Barlow, J. Eager he look'd. Another train of years.
Bernstein, O. More Questions.
Bible, O.T. From the Sermon on the Mount.
Lay not up for yourselves treasures.
Psalm 19.
They that go down to the sea in.
Binney. Eternal Light!
Bishop, E. Seascape.
Blake, W. Marriage of Heaven and Hell, The.
To see a World in a Grain of Sand.
Boethius. Boetius. Libr. 3. Metr. 6.
Bowers, E. Adam's Song to Heaven.
Bradstreet, A. As weary pilgrim, now at rest.
Contemplations.
Brontë, E. No coward soul is mine.
Stanzas: "Often rebuked, yet always back returning."
Brooke, R. Heaven.
Brooks, G. Hunchback Girl: She Thinks of Heaven.
Brown, S. Sister Lou.
Byron, G. Vision of Judgment, The.
Campion, T. O Come Quickly!
Carney. (Little Things).
Cary, P. Nearer Home.
Chao Meng-fu. Eulogy of the Sagely Virtue of His Imperial Majesty Emperor Shih-tsu, A.
Chapman, G. Peace of Death, The.
Ch'ien T'ao. Substance, Shadow, and Spirit.
Ch'on, S. Return to Heaven.
Clare, J. Vision, A.
Coleridge, M. Friends—With a Difference.
Impromptu.
Coleridge, S. Kubla Khan; or, A Vision in a Dream.
Collins, A. Another Song.
Cranch. Spirit of the Age, The.
Crashaw. I Am the Doore.
On the Assumption.
To the Infant Martyrs.
Upon the Infant Martyrs.
Cullen, C. For a Lady I Know.
Cummings, E. If there are any heavens my mother will (all by herself) have.
Dante Alighieri. Eyes that weep for pity of the heart, The.
Ladies that have intelligence in love.

Middle of life's journey; I, The.
That she hath gone to Heaven suddenly.
Davenant. Praise and Prayer.
Dickey, J. Heaven of Animals, The.
Dickinson, E. "Arcturus" is his other name.
God's Residence.
"Heaven"—is what I cannot reach!
I dwell in Possibility.
I never saw a Moor.
I reason, Earth is short.
Immortal is an ample word.
I've known a Heaven, like a Tent.
My nosegays are for Captives.
Parting.
Pit—but Heaven over it, A.
There is a Zone whose even Years.
'Tis so much joy! 'Tis so much joy!
What is—"Paradise."
What mystery pervades a well!
Disch. Garage Sale as a Spiritual Exercise, The.
Doddridge, P. Hymn: "Ye golden lamps of heaven, farewell."
Meditations on the Sepulchre in the Garden.
Dolben. He Would Have His Lady Sing.
Donne. Hymn to the Saints, and to Marquis Hamilton[, An].
To Mr. Tilman after He Had Taken Orders.
Dunbar, W. Amendis to the Telyouris and Sowtaris for the Turnament Maid on Thame, The.
Egerton, S. Blasphemous wretch! How canst thou think on.
Emerson, R. Spiritual Laws.
Ficowski. Assumption of Miriam from the Street in the Winter of 1942, The.
"Field." Girl, A.
Loved, on a sudden thou didst come to me.
Fumi Saito. Tanka: "Crooked fireworks."
Glancy. Then.
Graves, R. Conjunction.
Greger. Garden, The.
Hall, D. Sister on the Tracks, A.
Hartnett. Wounded otter, A.
Hays, H. January.
Hendriks. Recollections of the Sun.
Herbert, G. Church Lock-and-Key.
Heaven.
Obedience.
Paradise.
Pilgrimage, The.
Star[re], The.
Herrick. Comfort to a Youth That Had Lost His Love.
His Creed.
To Heaven.
White Island.
Hooper, E. Heart, heart, lie still.
Hopkins, G. Handsome Heart, The.
Heaven-Haven.
Housman, A. Easter Hymn.
So then the Lord Jesus, after.
Howard, R. Giovanni da Fiesole on the Sublime.
Hsü Chung-hsing. This metal is engraved with Shang-style markings.
Hudgins. Elegy for My Father, Who Is Not Dead.
Hughes, L. Heaven, Heaven, Heaven Is the Place.
Hughes, T. River.
Ingelow. Divided.
Izen. As the late night passes.
Jammes. Prayer to Go to Paradise with the Donkeys, A.
Jewsbury. To My Own Heart.
Johnson, F. My God in Heaven said to me.
Singing Hallelujia.
Johnson, R. Ark 34, Spire on the Death of L.Z.
Jonson, B. To Heaven.
Kaufman, B. Untitled.
Kavanagh, P. Sanctity.
Keats. Ode: "Bards of passion and of mirth."
Kendall, M. Legend of the Crossing-Sweeper.
Kennedy, X. Nothing in Heaven Functions as It Ought.

Kipling, R. When Earth's last picture is painted and the tubes are twisted / and dried.
Knott. Hair Poem.
Krichevsky. Exhausted from depression.
Kunio. Tanka: "On the snow."
Lang, A. Tired of Towns.
Lasker-Schüler. Chronica.
Lehman. Heaven.
Levertov. Contraband.
Levine, P. Heaven.
Li Ho. Don't Go Out of the Door.
Li Po. Ancient Airs.
Lindsay, V. General William Booth Enters into Heaven.
Liu E. Pleasures of Shinbashi.
Lodge, T. Minde through thee divines on endlesse things, The.
Lovelace, R. Falcon, The.
To My Noble Kinsman, Thomas Stanley, Esquire, on His Lyric Poems Composed by Master John Gamble.
Lowell, J. What [or And what] Is So Rare as a Day in June?
Lowry, R. Beautiful River.
March, A. Let others hail the holidays with laughter.
Masefield. Port of Many Ships.
McFarlane, B. Arawak Prologue.
Melville, H. Spirit appeared to me, and said, A.
Moore, T. Thy Heaven.
Morris, W. Apology, An.
Nairne. Land o' the Leal, The.
Nalungiaq. Heaven and Hell.
Nemerov. Backward Look, The.
Newcastle, W. Love's Sun.
Newton, J. Glorious Things of Thee Are Spoken.
Palmer, M. Or maybe this / is the sacred.
Parra, N. Lord's Prayer.
Patchen. Naked Land, The.
Patmore, C. 'Twas when the spousal time of May.
Phillips, C. Sunday.
Pindar. Afterlife in Elysium.
Plath. Sheep in Fog.
Popa. Heaven's Ring.
Tale About a Tale, The.
Pope, A. Universal Prayer [Deo Opt. Max.], The.
Pound, E. Heaven conserve thy course in quietness.
Prayton. Paradice on earth is found, A.
Procter, A. Lost Chord, A.
Philip and Mildred.
Quarles. My Beloved Is Mine, and I Am His; He Feedeth among the Lillies.
On a Feast.
Ralegh, W. Passionate Man[']s Pilgrimage, The.
Randolph, T. On Grafting.
Ransetsu. Deep in the night.
Rice, H. Legend of the raindrop, The.
Riley, J. Out of the Hitherwhere.
Roberts, G. Night Sky, The.
Robinson, E. Credo.
Matthew 22:1–14; And again Jesus spoke to them.
Supremacy.
Rogers, P. Good Heavens.
Rossetti, C. Buried.
Lord Jesus, who would think that I am Thine?
Marvel of marvels, if I myself shall behold.
Pause, A.
They lie at rest, our blessed dead.
Uphill [or Up-Hill].
Rossetti, D. Blessed damozel leaned out, The.
Sanders, E. Leaves of heaven, The.
Serote. Hell, Well, Heaven.
Sexton. Earth, The.
Shakespeare, W. Sonnet 94.
Shelley, P. To————: "One word is too often profaned."
Shirley, J. Garden, The.
Sigourney. Stars, The.
Smith, P. Annie Pearl Smith Discovers Moonlight.

Smith, S. Heavenly City, The.
Smith, W. Pavane for the Nursery, A.
Snodgrass, W. Monet: 'Les Nymphéas'.
Southey, R. Love Indestructible.
Southwell. At Home in Heaven.
New Heaven, New War[re].
Seek[e] Flowers of Heaven.
Spenser. Bower of Bliss, The.
Sonnet 71: "Soverayne beauty which I doo admire, The."
Stevens, W. Of Heaven Considered as a Tomb.
Waving Adieu, Adieu, Adieu.
Stricker. Island.
Sylvester, J. Ubique.
T'ang Hsien-tsu. Cave of Gold Essence—in Ning-tu, The.
Tappan. There Is an Hour of Peaceful Rest.
Tate, N. As Pants the Hart.
Taylor, E. Meditation 8 (First Series).
Oh that I was the Bird of Paradise!
Tekeyan. Dream.
Tekkan. Tanka: "With no flower buds."
Tomlinson, C. John Maydew or The Allotment.
Traherne. Bible, The.
Innocence.
Unknown. Beulah Railway, The.
City Called Heaven.
Fair is Our Lord's Own City.
Good Lord in That Heaven.
Heaven.
I got a home in dat Rock.
In Bath a wanton wife did dwell.
Jerusalem, my happy home.
Lord's Prayer, The.
Roll Jordan, roll.
Sometimes I feel like a motherless child.
Soul's Desire, The.
Swing low, sweet chariot.
Ubi Sunt Qui ante Nos Fuerunt? [or Contempt of the World].
Walk Together Children.
Van Dyke. Four Things [a man must learn to do].
Vaughan, H. Friends Departed.
Peace.
Pilgrimage, The.
Resolve, The.
Sap, The.
Very. Birds of Passage, The.
Forevermore.
Nature.
Wang Chi. 'Tell me now, what should a man want'.
Washburn, H. Almighty God, thy constant care.
Watts, I. Prospect of Heaven Makes Death Easy, A.
Psalm 58.
Wellesley. April 1939.
Wickham. Pilgrimage.
Wolfli. And now: And now: here begins Our Voyage, hunters and naturalists of indefatigable enthusiasm.
Wordsworth, W. If thou indeed derive thy light from Heaven.
Wright, J. Quest, The.
Wu Wei-yeh. Passing by Huai-yin I Have Feelings.
Yeats. Cold Heaven, The.
He Thinks of His Past Greatness When a Part of the Constellations of Heaven.
He Wishes for the Cloths of Heaven.
Running to Paradise.
Yosano. Tanka: "Warring heaven."
Yü Chi. Following the Rhymes of Autumn Night Song by Meng Tzu-chou, Signatory Official of the Board of Rites.
Zimmer. Zimmer Imagines Heaven.

Hebrew
Reznikoff. Hebrew of your poets, Zion, The.

Hebrides
Longley, M. Hebrides, The.

Hector
Homer. Achilles with wild fury in his heart.
Hector Arms.

Hector's flight.
Night Piece: the Trojans outside Troy.
O my husband... / cut off from life so young!
You leave me a widow.
Iremonger. Hector.
Muir, E. Ballad of Hector in Hades.

Hedgehogs
Chu Chen Po. Hedgehog.
Kenward. Composition, The.
King, E. Hedgehog is a little beast, The.
Muldoon, P. Hedgehog.
Thompson, S. To a Hedgehog.
Unknown. There were three jovial Welshmen.

Hedonism
Cummings, E. Since feeling is first.
Housman, A. Think no more, lad; laugh, be jolly.
Melville, H. After the Pleasure Party.

Heine, Heinrich
Lazarus, E. Venus of the Louvre.
Lewisohn, L. Heinrich Heine.
Pound, E. Translator to Translated.

Helen of Troy
Aeschylus. Chorus recall Helen's flight, The.
Chorus sing the doom of Helen, The.
Alcaeus. Her heart so stricken, Helen.
Doolittle, H. Helen.
So we were together.
Euripides. And Pergamos, / City of the Phrygians.
Ilion, o my city.
Grahn. Paris and Helen.
Homer. Helen and the elders.
Jackson, L. Helen's Burning.
Landor, W. Passed Ruin'd Ilion.
Lloyd, E. Helen like the Rose.
Marlowe. Ah, Doctor Faustus, that I might prevail.
End of Doctor Faustus, The.
Helen.
Poe. To Helen ("Helen, thy beauty is to me").
Read, S. White Isle of Leuce, The.
Ronsard. Sonnet For Helen.
Sappho. Some prefer a glory of horsemen; warships.
Valéry. Helen.
Waller, E. Under a Lady's Picture.
Wilbur. Voice from under the Table, A.
Yeats. Leda and the Swan.
When Helen Lived.

Helicopters
Mishler. Ceremony.

Heliogabalus
Hollander, J. Heliogabalus.

Hell
Alabaster. Way feare with thy projectes, noe false fyre, A.
Baraka. I don't love you.
Barry, J. Green Hell, Green Death.
Bayliss. Apocalypse and Resurrection.
Belloc. To Dives.
Blake, W. Marriage of Heaven and Hell, The.
Boland, E. Pomegranate, The.
Brontë, E. Stanzas: "Often rebuked, yet always back returning."
Burns, R. Kellyburnbraes.
Callimachus. Does Charidas lie beneath you? If you mean.
Since you are dead, Timon, tell me which.
Coleridge, M. Wilderspin.
Cowley, H. Invocation. To Horror.
Crashaw. But Men loved Darkness[e] Rather Than [or Then] Light.
Dickinson, E. Parting.
Pit—but Heaven over it, A.
Dove, R. Political.
Doyle, S. Hell To Pay.
Elizabeth, Queen of Bohemia. Verses by the Princess Elizabeth, Given to Lord Harington, of Exton, Her Preceptor.
Ford, F. That Exploit of Yours.
Graves, R. Sharp Ridge, The.
Gray, T. Descent of Odin, The.
Greenwell, D. Demeter and Cora.
Greer, J. Rodin's "Gates of Hell."
Greville, F. 99.

Herbert, Z. Pan Cogito's Thoughts on Hell.
  What Mr. Cogito Thinks About Hell.
Herrick. Barley-Break; or, Last in Hell.
Hill, G. Ovid in the Third Reich.
Homer. Here open'd Hell, all Hell I here
  implor'd.
Housman, A. Hell Gate.
  Mill-stream, now that noises cease, The.
Howard, R. Giovanni da Fiesole on the
  Sublime.
Huch. Arrival in Hell.
Keats. Dream, after Reading Dante's Episode
  of Paolo and Francesca, A.
Kelen. First Circle, The.
Kelly, R. Loom, The.
Kennedy, X. Nothing in Heaven Functions as
  It Ought.
Krichevsky. Exhausted from depression.
Lindsay, V. Simon Legree—A Negro Sermon.
Lister, R. Lament of an Idle Demon.
Lucilius. Eutychides, who wrote the songs.
Mandel, T. Jews in Hell.
Marlowe. First will I question with thee about
  hell.
Marquis. Tom-Cat, The.
McHugh, H. What Hell Is.
Melvill. Ane Godlie Dreame.
Milosz, C. Proof.
Milton. Occupations of Hell.
Miyazawa Kenji. River in Hell (two poems).
Muir, E. Good Man in Hell, The.
Naden. Pessimist's Vision, The.
Nalungiaq. Heaven and Hell.
Nesbit, E. Great Industrial Centre, A.
Olson, C. In cold hell, in thicket, how.
Owen, W. Strange Meeting.
Porter, P. Easiest Room in Hell, The.
Rabi'a al-Adawiyya. O my Lord.
Rich, A. Lucifer in the Train.
Robinson, E. Supremacy.
Rochester, J. Rochester to the Post Boy.
Seneca. Seneca's Troas, Act 2. Chorus.
Serote. Hell, Well, Heaven.
Shakespeare, W. Sonnet 129.
Shapiro, K. Poets of Hell, The.
Shelley, P. Hell is a city much like London.
Simic. Fork.
Södergran. Hell.
Sorescu. Fresco.
Stanton, M. Living Apart.
Symons, A. Emmy ("Emmy's exquisite youth
  and her virginal air").
Tate, J. Cross, The.
Thompson, F. To the Dead Cardinal of
  Westminster.
Tsvetayeva. We shall not escape Hell, my
  passionate.
Unknown. Dere's no hidin' place down dere.
  Stackolee.
  Whale, The.
Winters, Y. Summer Noon: 1941.

Hell's Angels
Gunn, T. Black Jackets.

Heloise. *See* Abelard and Heloise

Help
Bible, *O.T.* Psalm 3.
  Psalm 46.
  Psalm 121.
Dickinson, E. These Strangers, in a foreign
  World.
Dorsey, T. Take My Hand, Precious Lord.
Ezekiel. Family.
Fitzgerald, E. 72.
Graves, R. Grotesques.
Grosholz. Eden.
Hale, E. Lend a Hand.
Unknown. Courtesy Tips.
  No one is too small to be able to help.

Hemingway, Ernest
Merton. Elegy for Ernest Hemingway, An.
Updike. Meditation on a News Item.
Walcott. Swamp, The.

Hemlocks
Ammons. Bonus.
Dickinson, E. I think the Hemlock likes to
  stand.
Stevenson, A. Hemlock at Sunset, A.

Hengist
Borges. Hengest Cyning.

Henley, Margaret
Henley, W. Margaritæ Sorori [I. M.].

Henry I, King of England
Lee-Hamilton. Henry I to the Sea.
Rossetti, D. White Ship, The.

Henry II, King of England
Unknown. Queen Eleanor's Confession.

Henry V, King of England
Unknown. King Henry Fifth's Conquest of
  France.

Henry VIII, King of England
Harington. Groome of the Chambers religion
  in King Henry the eights time, A.
Harington, J. Groom of the Chamber's
  Religion in King Henry the Eighth's Time,
  A.
Skelton, J. Rose both white and Rede, The.
Unknown. Thenne wax I wounder wroth, as I
  well might.

Henry the Navigator
Clouts. Prince Henry the Navigator.

Hens
Clare, J. Hen's Nest.
Kinnell. Hen Flower, The.
Magowan. Zeimbekiko.
  Zeimbekiko ("Old man gets up turns, An").
McGonagall. Hen It Is a Noble Beast, The.
Morgenstern. Hen, The.
Mother Goose. Black Hen, The.
  Hickety, pickety, my black hen.
Pawsey. Browny Hen, The.
Pitter Hen under Bay-Tree.
Ransom, J. Janet Waking.
Roberts, E. Hens, The.
Roseliep. Black hen, The.
Tadic. Feather Plucked from the Tail of the
  Fiery Hen, A.
Unknown. Clever Hen, The.
  Clucking Hen, The.
  What the Farmyard Fowl are Saying.
Welty. Flock of Guinea Hens Seen from a
  Car, A.
Wilbur. Black November Turkey, A.
Willard, N. Speckled Hen's Morning Song to
  Biddy Early, The.
See also **Chickens**

Heraclitus
Cory, W. Heraclitus.
Dugan, A. From Heraclitus.
Fore. They told me, Heraclitus, they told me
  you were dead.
Hanlon, G. They told me, Heraclitus, they told
  me you were dead.
Hopkins, G. That Nature Is a Heraclitean Fire
  and of the Comfort of the Resurrection.
MacNeice. Variation on Heraclitus.
Vallejo. And don't bother telling me anything.

Herbs
Duncan, R. Glimpse, A.
Emerson, R. Blight.
Goodison. From the Garden of the Women
  Once Fallen.
Miliauskaite. In the damp places.
Ruark. Basil.
Thomas, E. Old Man, or Lad's-Love,—in the
  name there's nothing.

Hercules
Martynov. It seems to me I'm resurrected.
Rogers, S. To the Fragment of a Statue of
  Hercules, Commonly Called the Torso.
Seneca. Deaths of Orpheus and Hercules, The.
  Learne Lordings, learne to feare and dread
  th'unweildy.
Sophocles. Listen first, and show what you're
  made of.

Herding
Joyce, J. Tilly.
Stephens, H. Night-herding Song[, A].
Su Tung-p'o. Long ago I lived in the country.
See also **Shepherds and Shepherdesses**

Heresy and Heretics
Kendall, M. Fossil, A.
Lysohorsky. Ballad of Jan Palach, Student and
  Heretic.

Wigglesworth. Apostates and run-aways.
Wordsworth, W. Foster-Mother's Tale.

Hermits
Bibb. Hermit, The.
Birney. Bushed.
Chang Yü. Mountain Retreat of a Recluse,
  The.
Chao Meng-fu. Living in Retirement at Te-
  ch'ing.
Chia Tao. Looking for a Recluse but Failing
  to Find Him.
Chin Nung. Who bought a mountain and
  became a hermit there?
Ch'iu Wei. Visiting a Recluse on West
  Mountain and Not Finding Him In.
Chu Yün-ming. Little Landscape, A.
Coleridge, S. This Hermit good lives in that
  wood.
Davies, W. Hermit, The.
Drayton. With solitude what sorts, that here's
  not wondrous rife?
Dufault. Black Jess.
Gunn, T. Last Man, The.
Han Yü. To the Wooden Hermit.
Harteis. Hermit's Curse, The.
Hsü Pen. Hermit Feng's Residence on the
  Lake.
  Hermit Li's Herb Garden Retreat at T'ung-
  ch'uan.
  To a Hermit in the Mountains.
Kao Ch'i. Seeking out Hermit Hu.
Kinnell. When one has lived a long time
  alone.
Liu Ch'ang-ch'ing. Encountering a Snowstorm,
  I Stay with the Recluse of Mount Hibiscus.
  Sent to the Taoist of Dragon Mountain, Hsü
  Fa-leng.
Logan, J. He told the crowd "The devils."
Lowell, R. Skunk Hour.
Marippittiyar. Charmer Turned Ascetic, A.
Matthews, T. Private But Sulphurous.
Melville, H. Recluse, The.
Mo Shih-lung. Saying Good-Bye to Feng the
  Hermit.
Oliver, M. Strawberry Moon.
P'an Yüeh. Rhyme-Prose on the Idle Life.
Pien Kung. First Day of Spring, The.
Po Chü-i. Half-recluse, The.
  Hermit and Politician.
  Invitation to Hsiao Ch'u-shih.
  Mad Poem Addressed to My Nephews and
  Nieces, A.
Ray, H. Hermit and the Soul, The.
Ssu-k'ung Shu. In the Mountains.
Stevenson, A. He Who Loved Beauty.
Tai Piao-yüan. As My Way Passed Through
  T'ung-ch'uan, I Wished to Visit the Policy
  Critic of the Right, Mei, but Did Not Know
  Where to Find Him.
Supervisor, Han Chün-mei, Has Shown Me
  Five Poems He Has Written Called, The
  Trees Flourish in Early Summer. I Have
  Therefore Written Down My Own Ignoble
  Feelings and Sent Them Via Inspector Juan.
  At This Time, Chün-mei Is Lecturing to the
  Various Scholars on the I-ching, The.
T'ang Yin. Inscribed on a Painting ("At the
  country inn, thousands of peach trees").
Unknown. Hermit Marbán, The.
  Hermit's Song, The.
  I came once to sit on Cold Mountain.
  Marban, a Hermit Speaks.
  Place where I spend my days, The.
  When people see the man of Cold Mountain.
Walcott. Winding Up.
Wang Chiu-ssu. Total failure—mdash;Master
  Han Shan, A.
Wang K'ang-chü. Refuting the "Invitation to
  Hiding."
Wang T'ing-hsiang. Miscellaneous Poems
  Written in the Snow.
Welch, L. Image, as in a Hexagram.
Whalen. Further Notice.
Wu Wei-yeh. Poem of the Western Fields.
Yang Shih-ch'i. Beyond the temple, a hidden
  cliff.
Yeats. Three Hermits, The.

Yüan Hung-tao. On Receiving My Letter of Termination.
Yün Shou-p'ing. As old age approaches.

Hero and Leander
Byron, G. Written After Swimming from Sestos to Abydos.
Campion, T. Shall I come, if I swim? wide are the waves, you see.
Chapman, G. New light gives new directions, Fortunes new.
Donne. Hero and Leander.
Hubbard, P. Subjectivity at Sestos.
Marlowe. By this Leander being near the land. Men of wealthy Sestos, every year, The.
Musaeus. Amaze then tooke him. Courtship.
Warton, T. On Leander's Swimming over the Hellespont to Hero.

Herod the Great
Causley. Innocent's Song.
Hanzlik. Clap Your Hands for Herod.
Unknown. Give Thanks.
Witting. Curse on Herod, A.

Heroes and Heroines
Auden. Ballad: "O what is that sound [which so thrills the ear]."
From Scars Where Kestrels Hover.
Bishop, M. Who'd Be a Hero (Fictional)?
Brooks, G. "Negro" Hero.
Browning, E. From Book 5.
Browning, R. Hervé Riel.
Byron, G. Canto I.
Campbell, T. Hohenlinden.
"Carroll." Jabberwocky.
Collins, W. Ode Written in the Beginning of the Year 1746.
Comfort, A. Song for the Heroes.
Creeley. Heroes.
Cummings, E. My father moved through dooms of love.
De la Mare. Peace.
Djogo. National Hero, The.
Dolmatovsky. Hero.
"Dylan." Quinn the Eskimo.
Emerson, R. Forerunners.
Encarnacion. Threading the Miles.
Foss, S. Man from the Crowd, The.
Ginger. Name, A.
"Golodny." Stallion, The.
Gunn, T. Byrnies, The.
Hemans. Casabianca.
Heóghusa. Winter Campaign, A.
Herbert, Z. Elegy of Fortinbras.
Hodgson, W. Back to Rest.
Homer. Achilles kills Lycaon.
Equity in death.
Heroes meet again in the underworld, The.
Invocation, The: "Wrath of *Peleus* Son, O Muse, resound, The."
Horace. Translation from Horace.
Joseph, A. My Father's Heroes.
Kefala. Party, The.
Kiên Giang. Hero of Our Times, The.
Lauterbach. For Example (5): Song of the Already Sung.
Layne, M. Beautiful Ladies.
Longfellow, H. Skeleton in Armor [or Armour], The.
Lowell, R. For the Union Dead.
Lysohorsky. Ballad of Jan Palach, Student and Heretic.
MacLean, S. Heroes.
Marvell. To My Lord Fairfax.
Matthews, J. Paradigm of a Hero.
Melville, H. Commemorative of a Naval Victory.
Montague, J. Old Mythologies.
Moore, M. Hero, The.
Nguyễn Công Trú. Hero's Will, A.
Nichols, G. Wha Me Mudder Do.
O'Hussey. O'Hussey's Ode to the Maguire.
Olds, S. Language of the Brag, The.
Pindar. Greatness of *Mind* and *Fortune* too.
Prigov. Whenever I live, like simple.
Ravikovitch. Private View, A.
Rilke. "We Must Die Because We Have Known Them."

Rowe, G. His Prime.
Sassoon. Glory of Women.
Seferis. Last Stop.
Silius Italicus. Again she Arms prepares: One Captain may.
Simpson, L. Heroes, The.
Smith, S. El Alamein. Slugabed.
Spender, S. I think continually of those who were truly great. Seascape.
Stoddard, R. Abraham Lincoln.
Szymborska. Pietà.
Taylor, C. Garden.
Thayer, E. Casey at the Bat.
Tu'o'ng Phổ. Who is that soldier, hero of my heart?
Unknown. China has many people and many heroes.
Emily Geiger.
Hēr Æthoelstān cyning, eorla drihten.
Homage to the Tru'ng queens.
Hwæt, wē gār-dena in gēardagum.
Wallace-Crabbe. Collective Invention, The.
Warner, S. El Heroe.
Whitman, A. Upon the shells by Carribea's wave.

Heroin. *See* **Drug Addiction**

Herons
Annand. Heron.
Basho. Lightning-gleam, A.
Booth, P. Heron.
Galvin, B. Great Blue.
Gardner, I. That "Craning of the Neck."
Kizer, C. Great Blue Heron, The.
Ledwidge. Ardan Mór.
Li Ch'ing-chao. As in a Dream.
Lowell, A. Hoar-Frost.
Roberts, T. Blue Heron, The.
Walker, T. Heron.
Watkins, V. Heron, The.
Wright, J. Old Age Compensation.

Herrick, Robert
Herrick. On Himselfe ("I fear no earthly powers").
On Himselfe ("I will no longer kiss").
On Himselfe ("I'll [*or* Il'e] write no more of Love; but now repent").
On Himselfe ("Let me not live, if I not love").
On Himselfe ("Weepe for the dead, for they have lost this light").
To his book's end this last line he'd have placed.
Upon Himself ("Mop-eyed I am, as some have said").
Upon the Loss[e] of His Mistresses.

Herring
"Carroll." Three Badgers, The.
"MacDiarmid." With the Herring Fishers.
Nairne. Caller Herrin'.

Herzl, Theodor
Zangwill. Theodor Herzl.

Hess, Dame Myra
Fitzgerald, R. Jesu, Joy of Man's Desiring.

Hiawatha
"Carroll." Hiawatha's Photographing.

Hicks, Edward
Helwig. For Edward Hicks.

Highlands of Scotland. *See* **Scottish Highlands**

Highwaymen
Mutukorran. What the Passersby Said to the lover eloping with the girl.
Noyes, A. He did not come in the dawning. He did not come at noon. Highwayman, The.
Unknown. Brennan on the Moor. Mulberry Mountain.

Highways. *See* **Roads**

Hiking and Hikers
Betjeman. Hike on the Downs, A.
Bowden, M. Miller Canyon Trail No. 106.
Carruth, H. Lost.
Convisser. Over the Pass.
Francis, R. Identity.
Kenyon, J. Depression in Winter.
McPherson, S. Wings and Seeds.

Revard. October, Isle of Skye.
Rossetti, D. Hill Summit, The.

Hills and Mountains
Ammons. Close-up. Mountain Talk.
Beddoes. Alpine Spirit's Song.
Berlin. God bless America.
Bible, *O.T.* "All night the cicada chirps."
Bogan, L. Last Hill in a Vista.
Bontemps. Golgotha is a mountain, a purple mound.
To a Young Girl Leaving the Hill Country.
Borges. Matthew 5:1–12; Seeing the crowds, he went up on the mountain.
Brontë, E. Stanzas: "Often rebuked, yet always back returning."
Chang Yü. In a Boat on the Cha River. Mountain Retreat of a Recluse, The. Staying Overnight at T'ien-ning Ch'an Temple.
Chao Meng-fu. Inscribed on a Landscape by Mi Yüan-hui.
Inscribed on the Painting "Spring Dawn at Peach Blossom Spring" by Scholar Shang Te-fu.
Ch'ien T'ao. New Corn. Reading the Book of Hills and Seas.
Chin Nung. Evening Scene at Twin Forests.
Ch'u Yüan. Spirit of the Mountain, The.
Chu Yün-ming. Landscape Painted on a Fan— Echoing a Poem by Wen Cheng-ming, A.
Late Spring—Traveling through the Mountains.
Making Fun of the Well at the Inn below the Mountain.
Coleridge, M. Lady of Trees, The.
Coleridge, S. Blest is the tarn which towering cliffs o'ershade.
Crane, S. On the horizon, the peaks assembled.
There Was Set Before Me a Mighty Hill.
Creeley. Hill, The.
Crowe, W. Up to thy summit, Lewesdon, to the brow.
De la Mare. Crazed.
Di Prima. I Ching.
Dickinson, E. Alter! When the Hills do—. Mountains grow—unnoticed, The.
Douglas, L. Two Loves.
Ellis, S. Weathered Ides Grant Young Flesh.
Emerson, R. Fable: "Mountain and the squirrel, The."
Ferril. Time of Mountains.
"Field." Eros.
Francis, R. That Dark Other Mountain.
Frost, R. Meeting and Passing.
Fumiko. Tanka: "That hill."
Garner. Summer Solstice.
Hall, D. Sleeping Giant, The.
Han-shan. Cold Mountain Poems.
Han Yü. Fine weather since yesterday. Gazing as I climbed a high peak. North of the great lake of K'un-ming,. Southern Mountains.
Hardy, T. Schreckhorn, The.
Harwood, L. "Utopia" The.
Hecht, A. Hill, A.
Ho Ching-ming. Bamboo Branch Song.
Ho Xuan Huong. Man-and-Wife Mountain, The.
Hoyem. Circumambulation of Mt. Tamalpais.
Hsieh Chin. Sandal Mountain.
Hsieh Ling-yün. Journeying by Stream: Following Chin-chu Torrent I Cross the Mountains.
HSü Ling. Teleg Song.
Hsü Pen. Hermit Feng's Residence on the Lake.
Mountain Residence of Secretary Cheng Ching-ssu, The.
Hs'üan-Chi. On a Visit to Ch'ung Chen Taoist Temple.
Hughes, L. Porter.
Hughes, T. Bear, The.
Huntington, W. Lowlands.
Jackson, H. Cheyenne Mountain.
Kao Ch'i. Cold Spring. Well of the King of Wu, The.

Kapilar. What Her Friend Said to the foster-mother (who is guarding her carefully).
Kavanagh, P. Shancoduff.
Kellman. King, The.
Kipling, R. Sea and the Hills, The.
Komunyakaa. Boat People.
Kooser. City Limits.
Kuan Yün-shih. Tune: "Butterflies."
Lanier, S. From the Flats.
Leopardi. Infinite, The.
Li Ho. Southern hills, how mournful!, The.
Li K'ai-hsien. Drunk, Climbing to the Peak of Iron Tomb on Wei Mountain.
Li Po. In the Mountains on a Summer Day.
On the Mountain: Question and Answer.
T'ien-mu Mountain Ascended in a Dream: A Farewell Song.
Liu Tsung-yüan. Viewing Mountains with His Reverence Hao Ch'u: To My Friends and Relatives in the Capital.
Lu Chao-lin. Mount Wu Is High.
MacGreevy. Nocturne of the Self-evident Presence.
MacLeish. Pony Rock.
Mayer, B. It moves across and over / across the ground.
McClintock, M. Poppy, A.
Meng Chiao. Excursion to the Dragon Pool Temple on Chung-nan, An.
Wandering on Mount Chung-nan.
Meynell, A. Watershed, The.
Milton. On the Late Massacre [or Massacher] in Piedmont [or Piemont].
Mirabai. All I Was Doing Was Breathing.
Love has stained my body.
Mo Shih-lung. Staying Overnight at Blue Cloud Temple.
Muir, E. Childhood.
Na-lan Hsing-te. Tune: "Remembering the Lady of Ch'in—At the Mouth of Dragon Pool."
Ni Tsan. Man in Hangchou Spread Word that I Had Died. Chen-chü Heard of This and Was Upset, So I Have Written This To Send Him, A.
On the Twentieth Day.
Painting "Solitary Fisherman by a Spring River" The.
Okigbo. Lustra.
Petrarch. Alone and pensive, the most deserted fields.
Pettit. Self-Portrait Approaching Promontory, Utah.
Pien Kung. Song of the Woodcutter of the Sea.
Po Chü-i. Alarm at First Entering the Yangtze Gorges.
Dream of Mountaineering, A.
Going to the Mountains with a Little Dancing Girl, Aged Fifteen.
Having Climbed to the Topmost Peak of the Incense-Burner Mountain.
Madly Singing in the Mountains.
Passing T'ien-mên Street in Ch'ang-an and Seeing a Distant View of Chung-nan Mountains.
Pruning Trees.
Temple, The.
Raine, K. To My Mountain.
Ravikovitch. Hovering at a Low Altitude.
Robinson, E. Dark hills at evening in the west.
Rossetti, C. Uphill [or Up-Hill].
Rukeyser, M. Alloy.
Shen Chou. Inscribed on a Painting.
Temple of the Ocean of Awakening.
White clouds like a scarf enfold the the mountain's waist.
Silko. Alaskan Mountain Poem #1.
Sissman. Big Rock-Candy Mountain, The.
Smith, C. Sonnet V. To the South Downs: "Ah, hills beloved!—where once, an happy child."
Snyder, G. Mid-August at Sourdough Mountain Lookout.
Stafford, W. Holding the Sky.
Survey, A.

Stern, G. Nice Mountain.
Stevens, W. Thirteen Ways of Looking at a Blackbird.
Stuart, D. Mining in Killdeer Alley.
Su Tung-p'o. On the Road to Hsin-ch'eng.
Tai Piao-yüan. In the Year Chi-hai (1299), While Returning by Way of Purple Fungus Mountain at Springmouth, I Lamented for Lecture Master Chin.
Tao-chi. Inscribed on the Wall at the Temple of the Auspicious Talisman.
Trip to Hua-yang Mountain, A.
Tennyson, A. Somersby, Lincolnshire; after Leaving the Refectory.
Thomas, R. Lonely Farmer, The.
Tomlinson, C. Ute Mountain.
Ts'ao Chih. Ruins of Lo-yang, The.
Tsung Ch'en. Snowy Mountains.
When you enter Chin-hua Mountain.
Tu Hsün-ho. Climbing to a Mountain Monastery.
Tu Mu. Travelling in the Mountains.
Unknown. Monastery on Mount Hill-and-Stream, The.
On Top of Old Smoky.
Pilgrimage Song.
There's no Jade Emperor in the sky.
Vaughan, H. Mount of Olives ("Sweet, sacred hill! on whose fair brow").
Twenty-first Day of the Seventh Month.
Wang Shih-chieng. Bamboo Branch Song of Han-china.
Wang T'ing-hsiang. Miscellaneous Poems Written in the Snow.
Wang Wei. On Returning to Sung Mountain.
Williams, T. Cried the Fox.
Wills, J. Hills, The.
Winters, Y. By the Road to the Air-Base.
Wordsworth, W. Trosachs, The.
Wu Chen. Inscribed on a Painting of Bamboo.
Wu Wei-yeh. Climbing P'iao-miao Peak.
Yang Chi. Describing My Feelings While Living in Retirement by the Riverside: Seven Poems to the Tune "Ch'ing-p'ing-yüeh."
Yang Shih-ch'i. Dawn: Clear Skies.
Forty *li* through Chü-yang Pass.
I Was Received in an Early Audience at Heaven-Gate and Then at Noon I Was Summoned to the Yu-shun Gate. In the Evening I Withdrew, and Improvised This Poem.
Searching for the Ruins of the Pavilion of the Drunken Old Man.
Yang Wan-li. Trip to Stone Man Peak, A.
Yeats. Now the eleven disciples went to Galilee.
Yi, S. Bulldozer, The.
Yü Chi. Inscribed on a Painting.
Late in the Year K'uei-yu (1333), Staying at the Temple of the Upper Regions.
Sitting Alone in the Courtyard.
Yüan Chieh. Civilization.
Yüan Hao-wen. Clustered trees filled with the sounds of autumn.
Winding creek and scattered maple groves, A.
Yüan Hung-tao. Climbing Mount Yang.
Eastern mountains/ and western mountains.
Record of My Trip to Mount She, A.
"Slowly, Slowly" Poem, The.
Yüan Mei. Ballad of Peach Blossom Spring.
Rains pass, the mountains' face is washed.
Rough Ridge.
Yün Shou-p'ing. In a hidden spot on the northern mountain.
Painting in the Style of Secretary Kao, A.
See also **Mountain Climbing**

Hilo, Hawaii
Hongo. Hongo Store 29 Miles Volcano Hilo, Hawaii, The.

Hinduism and Hindus
Katuvan Ilaveyinanar. Tirumal.
Kirantaiyar. Hymn to Tirumāl (Viṣṇu).
Nakkiranar. Murukaṉ: His Places.
Murukaṉ, the Red One.
Parthasarathy. Speaking of Places.
Snyder, G. No Shoes No Shirt No Service.
Yeats. Indian upon God, The [or An].

Hippies
Dickey, J. False Youth: Autumn: Clothes of the Age.

Hippopotamuses
Barrington, P. I had a hippopotamus; I kept him in a shed.
Belloc. Hippopotamus, The.
Clouts. Dawn Hippo.
Cole, J. Hippopotamus.
Durston. Hippopotamus, The.
Eliot, T. Hippopotamus, The.
Guiterman. Habits of the Hippopotamus.
Jackson, L. Fun.
Leithauser. Trauma.
Roethke. Hippo, The.
Wheelock, J. Hippopotamothalamion.
Young, V. At twilight.

Hips
Clifton, L. Homage to My Hips.
Magowan. Days of 1956.

Hiroshige, Ando
Perlberg. Hiroshige.

Hiroshima, Japan
"Agyeya." Hiroshima.
Baggett. Day Before They Bombed Nagasaki, The.
Cartier. Poem for a Chorus.
Eich. Geometrical Place.
Enright, D. Monuments of Hiroshima, The.
Levertov. Gathered at the River.
Levine, P. Horse, The.
Mirikitani. Shadow in Stone.
Salter. Welcome to Hiroshima.
Seth. Doctor's Journal Entry for August 6, 1945, A.
Sitwell, D. Shadow of Cain, The.

Hispanics. *See* **Chicanos and Chicanas**

History and Historians
"Akhmatova." And people will think this like.
Ali, A. Dacca Gauzes, The.
Anzaldúa. Cultures.
Atwood. Marrying the Hangman.
Auden. Fall of Rome, The.
Baca. 43.
Mu Tío Baca el Poeta de Socorro.
Baraka. Three Modes of History and Culture.
Barclay, E. Human Greatness.
Barry, J. In the Footsteps of Genghis Khan.
Baugh, E. Old Talk, or West Indian History.
Bentley, N. Third Dungeness Spit Apocalypse.
Berryman. Boston Common.
Bly, R. After the Industrial Revolution, All Things Happen at Once.
Boland, E. That the Science of Cartography Is Limited.
Bold, A. June 1967 at Buchenwald.
Bond, E. If Auschwitz had been in Hampshire.
Bontemps. Golgotha is a mountain, a purple mound.
Brathwaite, E. Citadel.
Mmenson.
Xango.
Bynner. What though they conquer us?
Campbell, J. Antiquary, The.
Cardenal. Mosquito Kingdom.
Carew, J. Dreamtime Lives Again, The.
Cherry, K. History.
Chin. Floral Apron, The.
Prelude.
Chinn. Not Translation, Not Poetry.
Christopher. Terminus.
Clark, T. Mountain Men.
Cleveland, J. Epitaph on the Earl of Strafford.
Cliff. History of Costume, A.
Clifton, L. I am accused of tending to the past.
Colman, G. On Sir Nathaniel Wraxall the Historian.
Conyus. I rode with Geronimo.
Cronin, A. Responsibilities.
Cummings, E. All nearness pauses, while a star can grow.
Davidson, D. On a Replica of the Parthenon.
Davidson, M. Landing of Rochambeau, The.
Thinking the Alps.
Davis, J. One Hundred and Fifty Years.

Deane, S. History Lessons.
Deloney. Weavers Song, The.
Digges. Rock, Scissors, Paper.
Drainac. Classic Verses.
Drayton. First Steps Up Parnassus.
  What spirit can lift you up, to that immortall
  praise.
Duggan, L. Town on the Ten Dollar Note,
  The.
Durham. Columbus Day.
Durrell. Sarajevo.
Dutton, G. Street.
Eliot, T. Little Gidding.
Emerson, R. Solution.
Evans, M. Status Symbol.
Ferlinghetti, L. Cro-Magnons carried stones
  for books.
Fortune. Upon the future life we build.
Frost, R. Peaceful Shepherd, The.
Fulton, R. Museums and Journeys.
Gibson, M. Wars.
Gillies, V. Ericstane Brooch, The.
Ginsberg, A. Café in Warsaw.
Giovanni. Ego Tripping [(There May Be a
  Reason Why)].
Glancy. Christopher.
Glazkov. Declaration.
  To My Ill-Wishers.
Gould, J. We Exist.
Graves, R. End of Play.
Gregg. Strong Pomegranate Flowers and Seeds
  of the Mind.
Gregor, A. History.
Grenier. Has Faded in Part But Magnificent
  Also Late for RC / Mirrors.
Gu Cheng. Forever Parted: Graveyard.
Guiterman. Ancient History.
Gunn, T. Claus von Stauffenberg.
Gustafson, R. In the Yukon.
Halleck, F. They burnt their last witch in
  CONNECTICUT.
Hardy, T. One We Knew.
  Rome: Building a New Street in the Ancient
  Quarter.
  Zermatt: To the Matterhorn.
Harper, M. American History.
  Goin' to the Territory.
  History as Apple Tree.
  Zocalo.
Harry, J. Poem Films Itself, The.
Hass, R. Palo Alto.
Hopkinson, A. Chord, The.
Howard, R. Again for Hephaistos, the Last
  Time.
Hristic. To Phaedrus.
Hughes, J. Dog Day Lesson.
Hugo, R. Ferniehirst Castle.
Jarman, M. Shrine and the Burning Wheel,
  The.
Jeffers, R. I Shall Laugh Purely.
Jonson, B. Mind of the Frontispiece to a
  Book, The.
Kaplinski, J. I UNDERSTOOD I
  UNDERSTOOD.
Kaufman, B. Geneology.
Kennelly. Running Battle, A.
Khodasevich. Amidst a smoking desolation.
Kipling, R. Land, The.
Knox, C. Rune, A.
Koch, C. Shelly Beach.
Kooser. Gilbert Stuart Portrait of Washington,
  The.
Kusano Shimpei. Skylarks and Fuji.
Kushner, A. We don't get to choose our
  century.
Landon. History of the Lyre, A.
Larkin, P. Arundel Tomb, An.
Lear, E. Limericks, II (i).
Li Ho. Arrowhead from the Ancient
  Battlefield of Ch'ang-p'ing, An.
Li Po. In Yüeh Viewing the Past.
Lowell, R. History has to live with what was
  here.
Lux. History Books.
Machado Ruiz. On the Banks of the Duero.
MacLeish. Poet Speaks from the Visitors'
  Gallery, A.

Mayakovsky. It's already past one. You'll
  have gone to bed.
Mazur. Lilacs on Brattle Street.
McCarthy, T. Dying Synagogue at South
  Terrace, The.
McGrath, C. What They Drank.
McGrath, T. . . . All that winter, in the black
  cold, the buzz-saw screamed and whistled.
Melville, P. Homeland.
Morgan, E. Coin, The.
Muir, E. Ring, The.
Nemerov. Historical Judas, The.
  Ultima Ratio Reagan.
O'Grady, D. Berlin Metro.
O'Hara, F. In Memory of My Feelings.
Olson, C. Kingfishers, The.
  Praises, The.
Osaki. Amnesiac.
Padilla. History.
  Prayer for the End of the Century, A.
Park, S. Opium Poppy, The.
Paz. I Speak of the City.
Perelman. Cliff Notes.
Pinsky. Ginza Samba.
Plumpp. Living Truth, The.
  Turf Song.
  When the Spirit Spray-Paints the Sky.
Popa. Tale About a Tale, The.
Porter, P. And No Help Came.
Prior. Written in the Beginning of Mezeray's
  History of France.
Rabéarivelo. You delude yourself.
Randall, J. Recipes.
Reed, I. Dualism.
Rich, A. Culture and Anarchy.
  In those years, people will say, we lost track.
  Living Memory.
  Readings of History.
  Whatever it was: the grains of the glacier
  caked in the boot-cleats.
Rodefer. Pretext.
Rodriguez, J. Mahogany Ship, The.
Różewicz. What Happens.
Sackville, T. Midnight ("Midnight was come,
  when every vital thing").
Salamun. Homage to a Hat and Uncle Guido
  and Eliot.
Sandburg, C. I am the people—the mob—the
  crowd—the mass.
  Old Timers.
Seidel. Pol Pot.
Shurin. Continuous Thunder.
Sidney, P. Sonnet 30: "Whether the Turkish
  new moon minded be."
Simpson, L. Story About Chicken Soup, A.
Slessor. Five Bells.
Smith, C. From Beachy Head.
Smith, M. Dis-ya dutty, a we create it.
Smith, S. How cruel is the story of Eve.
Snyder, G. Building.
  What Happened Here Before.
Sorescu. Historiotherapy.
Sze. Every Where and Every When.
Szymborska. Once we knew the world well.
Tate, A. Mediterranean, The.
Taylor, E. This Year's Drive to Appomattox.
Thomas, R. Centuries.
Thornbury. Court Historian, The.
Thorold Rogers. On the Historians Freeman
  and Stubbs.
Tranter. Alphabet Murders, The.
Unknown. History.
Upton, C. When I was very young.
Vaughan, H. Charnel-house, The.
Violi. Scatter.
Walcott. Sea is History, The.
Waterman, N. Johnny's Hist'ry Lesson.
Webb, C. Shape of History, The.
Whitman, W. On the Same Picture.
  To-day and Thee.
Whittemore, R. Walk Home, The.
Wilbur. Looking into History.
  Speech for the Repeal of the McCarran Act.
Wojahn. Homage to Ryszard Kapuściński.
Wright, C. Our Dust.
Wright, J. At Cooloolah.

Xuân Diệu. Geologist and Millions of Years,
  A.
Yeats. Lapis Lazuli.
Yevtushenko. Hand-Rolled Cigarettes.
Hitchhiking and Hitchhikers
Ciardi. Faces.
Corso. Poets Hitchhiking on the Highway.
Wakoski. Hitchhikers, The.
Hitler, Adolf
Auden. Refugee Blues.
Enzensberger, H. Portrait of a House
  Detective.
Gunn, T. Claus von Stauffenberg.
Waddell, H. Hitler Speaks.
Ho Chi Minh
Ho Chi Minh. Song of a Cotton Yarn, The.
Weber, R. Concise History of the Vietnam
  War: 1965–1968, A.
Hobbes, Thomas
Cowley, A. To Mr. Hobbes [or Hobs].
Hass, R. Concerning the Afterlife, the Indians
  of Central California Had Only the Dimmest
  Notions.
Hoboes. *See* **Vagabonds**
Hogarth, William
Johnson, S. Epitaph on William Hogarth, An.
Hogue, La, Battle of (1692)
Cummings, E. No time ago / or else a life.
Holbein, Hans
MacKellar, D. Fancy Dress.
"Holiday, Billie" (Eleanora Fagan McKay)
Dove, R. Canary.
Heithaus. What a Little Moonlight Can Do.
Hughes, L. Song for Billie Holiday.
Jackson, A. Billie in Silk.
May, K. Valentine's Day.
Neal, L. Lady's Days.
O'Hara, F. Day Lady Died, The.
Holidays
Buchanan, G. May Morning.
Chesterton, G. Certain Evening, A.
Clare, J. 'Tis Martinmass, from rig to rig.
Dame. Seder, The.
Davidson, J. Holiday at Hampton Court.
Durham. Columbus Day.
Glaser, M. Preparations for Seder.
Herrick. Ceremonies for Candlemas[se] Eve.
Longfellow, H. Holiest of all holidays are
  those, The.
Nguyễn Khuyến. French National Holiday,
  The.
Petri. Gratitude.
Smith, S. Holiday, The.
Zabolotsky. Peoples House.
See also **Listings for specific Holidays**
Holland. *See* **Netherlands**
Holly
De la Mare. Holly, The.
Farjeon, E. Holly and Mistletoe.
Unknown. Green Groweth the Holly.
  Holver and Hivy made a gret party.
  Riddle: "Highty, tighty, paradighty, clothed
  [all] in green."
Hollyhocks
Van Doren. Gardener.
Hollywood, California
Jarrell. Thinking of the Lost World.
Shapiro, K. Hollywood.
Holmes, Oliver Wendell
Lowell, J. Holmes.
Holocaust
Amichai. Little Ruth.
Bobrowski. Kaunas 1941.
Bold, A. June 1967 at Buchenwald.
Bond, E. How We See.
Borowski. Farewell to Maria.
  Night over Birkenau.
Brett, L. I keep forgetting.
  La Pathétique.
  Leaving You.
  My Mother's Friend.
Breytenbach. Lullaby.
Brock, V. Remembering Dresden.
Bruck. Childhood.
  Equality, father! Your dream has come true.

Pretty soon / when people hear a quiz show expert.
Celan. Aspen tree, your leaves glance white into the dark.
  Death Fugue, A.
  In Prague.
  Tenebrae.
Clampitt. Burning Child, The.
Fainlight, R. Archive Film Material.
Ficowski. Girl of Six from the Ghetto Begging in Smolna Street in 1942, A.
  Assumption of Miriam from the Street in the Winter of 1942, The.
  Both Your Mothers.
  Execution of Memory, The.
  5.8.1942 / In Memory of Janusz Korczak.
  I did not manage to save.
Fogel, E. Shipment to Maidanek.
Fried, E. My Girlfriends.
Friedmann. Butterfly, The.
Gardinier. Two Girls.
Gershon. I Was Not There.
  Race.
Glaser, M. English-Speaking Persons Will Find Translations.
Glatstein. Lost.
Gouri. Heritage.
  Pictures of Jews.
Greenberg, U. We were not likened to dogs among the Gentiles—They pity a dog.
Hacker, M. Days of 1992.
Hamburger, M. Treblinka.
Harris, R. Riding Over Belmore Park.
Hecht, A. Book of Yolek, The.
  "It Out-Herods Herod. Pray You, Avoid It."
  'More Light! More Light!'.
Herbert, Z. Biology Teacher.
Heyen. Passover: the Injections.
  Riddle: "From Belsen a crate of gold teeth."
Hill, G. Ovid in the Third Reich.
  September Song.
Holan. To the Enemies.
Holub. Interferon.
Huchel. Roads.
Jarrell. Camp in the Prussian Forest, A.
  In the Camp There Was One Alive.
  Protocols.
Jentzsch. Terezin, the Graveyard.
Kirsch, S. Legend of Lilja.
Klepfisz. Bashert.
  Perspectives on the Second World War.
Kolmar. Judith.
Kovner. Far, Far a City Lies.
  My Sister.
  Of All My Loves.
  To the Things That Are Immortal.
Kramer, L. Red Cross telegram, The.
Levi, P. Buna.
  Reveille.
  Shemà.
  Survivor, The.
Levine, P. Survivor, The.
Lifshin. I Remember Haifa Being Lovely But.
MacBeth. Poem of Death, A.
MacLean, S. Death Valley.
Mahon. Disused Shed in Co. Wexford, A.
"Martin." Dreams in German.
McGrath, T. Remembering the Children of Auschwitz.
Meltzer, D. What do I know of journey.
Michelson, R. Undressing Aunt Frieda.
Mihalic. Under the Microscope.
Milosz, C. Campo dei Fiori.
  Poor Christian Looks at the Ghetto, A.
Molodovsky. God of Mercy.
Moraes, D. Altermann, sipping wine, reads with a look.
Murray, L. Dog Fox Field.
Olds, S. That Year.
Olson, C. La Préface.
Pagis. Autobiography.
  Draft of a Reparations Agreement.
  Europe, Late.
  Needless Return.
  Roll Call, The.
  Roll-Call In the Concentration Camp.
  Scrawled in Pencil in a Sealed Car.

Souvenir, The.
  Testimony.
  Written in Pencil in the Sealed Railway-Car.
Pilinszky. Frankfurt.
  French Prisoner, The.
  Harbach 1944.
  On the Wall of a KZ-Lager.
  Passion of Ravensbrück.
Pillen. Ascensions, The.
Plath. Daddy.
  Mary's Song.
Porter, P. Annotations of Auschwitz.
Quasimodo. Auschwitz.
Radnóti. Postcard (Found on His body after He Was Killed by the Nazis).
Ranasinghe. Holocaust 1944.
Reznikoff. Children.
  Jews from Holland, France, and Hungary, and later from.
  When the Second World War began.
Rich, A. Memory lifts her smoky mirror: 1943.
Rothenberg, J. Dos Geshray (The Scream).
Rózewicz. In the Midst of Life.
  Massacre of the Boys.
  Pigtail.
  She Looked At the Sun.
  Survivor, The.
  Warning.
Sachs, N. Already embraced by the arm of heavenly solace.
  Chorus of the Dead.
  Chorus of the Stars.
  Dead Child Speaks, A.
  How long have we forgotten how to listen!
  O sister, / where do you pitch your tent?
  O the Chimneys.
  O the night of the weeping children!
Sandy. Threads.
Schiff, H. German Frontier at Basel: 1942 and 1992, The.
  When It Happened.
Schuyler, J. Let's All Hear It for Mildred Bailey!
Sexton. After Auschwitz.
Shapiro, G. Tattoo.
Sillitoe. Synagogue in Prague.
Simpson, L. Story About Chicken Soup, A.
Sklarew. Holocaust.
  Teaching the Children.
Slonimski. Elegy: "No more, no more Jewish townships in Poland."
Slutsky. Burnt.
  How They Killed My Grandmother.
Spender, S. History and Reality.
  Memento.
Stallworthy, J. Letter from Berlin, A.
Sutskever. Cartload of Shoes, A.
  How will you fill your goblet?
  1980.
  Toys.
Szymborska. Still.
Vogel, D. How Can I See You, Love.
Voznesensky. Call of the Lake, The.
Wiesel. Behold, God of Abraham, God of mercy.
  Never shall I forget that night.
Yevtushenko. Babii Yar.
Zach. Against Parting.
  Nameless.
Zagajewski. Watching Shoah in a Hotel Room in America.

Holy Baptism. See Baptism
Holy Communion. See Eucharist
Holy Family
Farren. Stable Straw.
Rukeyser, M. Holy Family.
Tynan. Holy Family.
Unknown. Cherry-Tree Carol, The.
Whitman, W. Swiftly Arose.
Holy Ghost
Herbert, G. Whitsunday.
Herrick. His Litany to the Holy Spirit.
Ridler. Now as Then.
Sassoon. Christ and the Soldier.
Holy Innocents
Wadding. For Innocents' Day.

Holy Spirit
Constable, H. To God the Holy Ghost.
Donne. Holy Ghost, The.
  Show me dear Christ.
"Field." Sweet-Briar in Rose.
Hildegard von Bingen. Antiphon for the Holy Spirit.
  Holy Spirit, / giving life to all life.
Langton, S. Hymn to the Holy Spirit.
Mangan, J. Hymn for Pentecost.
Mechthild von Magdeburg. Effortlessly, / Love flows from God into man.
Unknown. Graces of the Holy Ghost, The.
Very. Lost, The.
  Silent, The.
Yeats. Matthew 28:16–20; Now the eleven disciples went to Galilee.
Holy Thursday
Blake, W. Holy Thursday [II.] ("Is this a holy thing to see").
  Holy Thursday [I.] ("'Twas on a Holy Thursday, their innocent faces clean").
Home
Adamson. Home, The Spare Room, The.
Aldis, D. No One Heard Him Call.
Alexander, E. Who I Think You Are.
Arnot. Woman at Home.
Ashbery. Rain Moving In.
Awoonor. Sea Eats the Land at Home, The.
Bancquart. Vanished, The.
Bartusek. Home.
Berlin. God bless America.
Berssenbrugge. Tan Tien.
Blamire. When home we return, after youth has been spending.
Bone, F. Prayer for a Little Home, A.
Brontë, A. Home.
Brooks, C. Our Island Home.
Brooks, G. Ballad of Rudolph Reed, The.
Brown, D. Coming Home.
Bunner, H. Home Sweet Home with Variations.
Burns, R. My heart's in the Highlands, my heart is not here.
Cariaga. Plantings.
Chang Yü. Hearing a Song from My Boat.
Channing. Harbor, The.
Ch'ien Ch'ien-i. Miscellaneous Poems Written While in Jail.
Ch'ien T'ao. LONG time ago, A.
Cibulka. Kremenez.
Clare, J. After Reading in a Letter Proposals for Building a Cottage.
  My Early Home.
Claudian. Old Man of Verona, The.
Clifton, H. Distaff Side, The.
Clifton, L. In the Inner City.
Clinton. Eviction.
Clough. Come home, come home! and where an home hath he.
Coffey. Nightfall, Midwinter, Missouri.
Colum, P. Old Woman of the Roads, The.
Cowley, M. Long Voyage, The.
Cunningham, A. Hame, Hame, Hame.
Das, K. Hot Noon in Malabar.
Davies, A. Thirty East Forty-Second Street.
Davies, W. Sweet Stay-at-Home.
Ded. I was passionate.
"Dhoomil." City, Evening, and an Old Man: Me, The.
Di Prima. Backyard.
  Notes on the Art of Memory.
Dickey, J. Coming Back to America.
Dobson, A. Wanderer, The.
Donahue, J. Desire's green / and gold corona / in the wavering branch.
Donne. Jealosie.
  To Sir Henry Wotton ("Sir, more than kisses, letters mingle souls").
Dove, R. Dusting.
Doyle, S. This Shade.
Dudley, M. Home late.
Edey *et al.* Trot Along, Pony.
Edwards, M.
Edwards, R. Recollections of an Old Spook.
Emanuel, L. Desire.
Finkel. In the Clearing.

Forbes, C. Home.
Foster, S. My Old Kentucky Home[, Good Night!].
Old Folks at Home[, The].
Frase. Homegoing.
Fraser, G. Home Town Elegy.
Frost, R. Death of the Hired Man, The.
Galvin, B. Old Trip by Dream Train, The.
Gerstler. Travelogue.
Gioia. In Cheever Country.
Gnanakoothan. Tamil, it's true, is the breath of my life.
Gregg. Night Music.
Guest, E. Home.
Hamilton, E. My Ain Fireside.
Harjo, J. Song for the Deer and Myself to Return On.
Harris, J. Home to me is laughter.
Harris, W. Rib Sandwich.
Hayes, N. Shiny Little House, The.
Heard, J. Welcome Home.
Helwig. Considerations.
Herrick. Thanksgiving to God for His House, A.
Hewitt, J. Substance and Shadow.
Hicky. When a man turns homeward through the moonfall.
Hines, N. Home!
Holan. Resurrection.
Hooper, V. Argument for Resurrection.
Hotham. Coffee.
Home early.
Housman, A. Recruit, The.
Hughes, L. Croon.
Po' Boy Blues.
Hunter, S. Traveling Back.
Ishkhan. Armenian Language Is the Home of the Armenian, The.
Ivask, I. And then I told about the red soil of Oklahoma.
Jackson, R. Sunday Brunch.
Johnson, L. Mystic and Cavalier.
Kahn, G. Pilgrim from the East, The.
Kalász. Impromptu.
Kaplinski, J. We started home, my son and I.
Kasdorf. Where We Are.
Keeshig-Tobias. I grew up on the reserve.
Kilmer, J. House with Nobody in It, The.
Roofs.
Kim, K. Homesickness.
Kim, K. Home.
Mother's Letter from the North.
King, S. Hearth and Home.
Kipling, R. Recall, The.
Kirsch, S. Stopover.
Kuppner. Passing Through Doorways.
Lanyer. Description of Cooke-ham, The.
Lapidus. Exmatriate.
Larkin, P. Home is so sad. It stays as it was left.
Lawrence, D. End of Another Home Holiday.
Lee, L. Home From Abroad.
Li K'ai-hsien. Crossing the ridge, the woodcutter loses his way.
Jade trees from the rear courtyard of the empire of Ch'en.
Llawdden. No Place Like Home.
Longfellow, H. Golden Mile-Stone, The.
Longley, M. Remembering Carrigskeewaun.
West, The.
Lovelace, R. Another ("Centaur, siren [or syren], I forgo[e], The").
Lu Yu. Herd-Boy, The.
Lydston. Family, The.
Lyons, J. Island Muse.
MacCaig. Kingfisher.
Macdonald, G. Baby-Sermon, A.
Shortest and Sweetest of Songs, The.
MacKie, A. Sun's oot. I sit, my pipe alunt and puff, The.
Maclean, A. Home Thoughts from Home.
Mahon. Ford Manor.
Malé. My Mother's Homeland.
Marinoni. For a New Home.
Masefield. West Wind, The.
Mathews, A. Two Months Married.
May, S. House.

McCrae, H. Song of the Rain.
Meek. Walk Around the Lake, A.
Merwin, W. Odysseus.
Millay, E. On the wide heath at evening overtaken.
Moldaw. 64 Panoramic Way.
Mphahlele. Homeward Bound.
Ni Tsan. You ask when I will go back home.
Nichols, G. Like a Beacon.
Norton, C. My Childhood's Home.
Okamoto. Tanka: "Selfish woman."
Okigbo. From flesh into phantom.
Ozog. Song of the Field.
Pagis. Souvenir, The.
Paschen. Confederacy.
Patterson, R. I've Got a Home in That Rock.
Pavese. Words from Confinement.
Payne, J. Home, Sweet Home!
Peters, L. We have come home.
Phạm Hổ. Sea, The.
Philip of Thessalonica. Sky will extinguish its stars, and the sun, The.
Piercy. Spring Offensive of the Snail, The.
Pinsky. Street, The.
Po Chü-i. New thatched hall, five spans by three, A.
Writing Again on the Same Theme.
Radnóti. Seventh Eclogue.
Raine, K. Message from Home.
Ravikovitch. Portrait.
Rexroth, K. Here is Klito's little shack.
Robinson, E. House on the Hill, The.
Rodgers, C. For Sistuhs Wearin' Straight Hair.
Rummo. Here you grew up. On a land which is flat.
Samio. Tanka: "Surely by now."
Sappho. Oh Hesperus! thou bringest all good things.
Schaeffer. Housewife.
Shapcott, T. City of Home is reached only in dreams, The.
Simko. Coming Home.
Simmons, J. Westport House, Portrush.
Snodgrass, W. Mutability.
Södergran. Homecoming.
Sophocles. Many marvels walk through the world.
Spence, L. Carse, The.
Great Tay of the Waves.
Stafford, W. One Home.
Starr, J. Flight.
Stein, D. Searching for Schüpfen.
Stevenson, R. Ille Terrarum.
To S. R. Crockett.
Stickney, T. Quiet after the rain of morning.
Storie-Pahlitzsch. Dialogue on Finding Someplace to Live.
Stricker. Foreigners.
Swain, C. Home Is Where There Is One to Love Us.
Swenson, M. Staying at Ed's Place.
T'ao Ch'ien. Returning to My Home in the Country.
Returning to My Home in the Country ("Out here in the fields, far social affairs").
Thorne, T. High Country.
Tremblay, B. Home Front.
Troupe. Conjuring Against Alien Spirits.
Ts'ui Hao. Songs of Ch'ang-kan.
Turk. Thank You, Jesus, for this day.
Unknown. At Fifteen I Went Off to the Army;.
Deep river, my home is over Jordan.
Flamingo, what has brought you here?
For Sale or Rent.
Good Lord in That Heaven.
Heart's Content.
I Wonder How My Home Is.
Steal Away to Jesus.
That Mountain Far Away.
Wa-Sissica, the War Song.
"What makes a home?"
Zion me wan go home.
Untermeyer, J. Autumn.
Untermeyer, L. Prayer for This House.
Utkin. Tale of Red-Haired Motl, Mister

Inspector, Rabbi Isaiah, and Commissar Blokh, The.
Van Doren. Family Prime.
Vando. New York City Mira Mira Blues.
Voznesensky. Old Song.
Wang T'ing-hsiang. Song of the Wanderer.
Waniek. House on Moscow Street, The.
Wayman. Teething.
Welshimer. Dusk.
Wen Cheng-ming. In the sixth month, outside the gate.
Whittemore, R. Still Life.
Wickham. Dilemma, The.
Wilson, K. Dusk in My Backyard.
Wordsworth, D. Cottage in Grasmere Vale, A.
Wordsworth, W. Farewell thou little Nook of mountain-ground.
see also The Wanderer, *Book 1 of* The Excursion.
Wright, C. Homecoming.
Virgo Descending.
Wrighton. Dearest Spot on Earth, The.
Wroth. Sonnet 35: "False [or Faulce] hope which feeds but[t] to destroy, and spill."
Wu Chen. Inscribed on a Painting of Bamboo.
Level forest stretching far and wide, A.
Yamada. I Learned To Sew.
Yang Chi. Nesting among Clouds.
Thousands of flowers, thousands of petals.
Yang Shen. To the Tune "Yellow Oriole" ("Threads of rain weave lambent light").
Yü Chi. Sent To Be Inscribed on the Temple of P'u-jun (Universal Fructification) at Lou-fu Mountain.
Yu Xuanji. At Home in the Summer Mountains.
Zhdanov. Home.
Znamenskaya. Estonia. A private dacha.
Zolynas. Zen of Housework, The.

Homecoming
Adcock, B. Southbound.
Blake, W. Dream, A.
Cain, K. Returned American.
Carew, T. Upon Master Walter Montagu's Return from Travel.
Carrier, C. Journey.
Chacko. Rice.
Chan Fang-sheng. Sailing Homeward.
Chong, C. Native Village.
Dickey, J. Coming Back to America.
Dobyns. Freight Cars.
Gay, J. *et al.* Mary Gulliver to Capt. Lemuel Gulliver.
Gibson, W. Back.
Goldberg, L. Prodigal Son, The.
Gudzenko. Not from old age our death will come.
Ho Ch'e Ch'ang. Homecoming.
Homer. Penelope hesitates.
Howell, C. Liberty and Ten Years of Return.
Hsieh Chin. Wait until I too hang up my carriage.
Huang T'ing-chien. Upon Passing the Homestead.
Kao Ch'i. On a Painting by Hsia Kuei Entitled "Returning in Wind and Snow to a Village Home."
Returning to Lotus Village.
Kavanagh, P. In Memory of My Mother.
Keppel, L. Robin Adair.
Kipling, R. Return, The.
Knight, E. Poem for Myself (Or Blues for a Mississippi Black Boy), A.
Welcome Back, Mr. Knight: Love of My Life.
Levine, P. Survivor, The.
Li P'in. Crossing Han River.
Mahon. I am going home by sea.
Mapanje. Making Our Clowns Martyrs.
Markham, E. Late Return.
Mazur. May, Home after a Year Away.
Melville, H. Return of the Sire de Nesle A.D. 16, The.
Muir, E. Return of the Greeks, The.
Nguyễn Ý Thuần. Homecoming.
O'Grady, D. Homecoming.
Owen, W. Send-Off, The.
Po Chü-i. Stopping the Night at Jung-yang.

Ransom, J. Prelude to an Evening.
Riley, J. When she comes home again! A thousand ways.
Robinson, A. Celia's Home-Coming.
Robinson, E. Prodigal Son, The.
Rossetti, C. Italia, Io Ti Saluto!
Salkey. Dry River Bed.
Schuyler, J. Elizabethans Called It Dying, The.
Scott, D. Homecoming.
Shen Chou. On the Fifteenth Day of the Seventh Month I Came Home Late from the City.
Smith, P. Dylan, Two Days.
Su Tung-p'o. Following the Rhumes of Chiang Hui-shu.
Sui Ching-ch'en. Tune: "Slow Chant"—Kao-tsu's Homecoming.
T'ao Ch'ien. I Return to the Place I Was Born.
Returning to My Home in the Country.
Tsvetayeva. And, not crying in vain.
Unknown. At Fifteen I Went Off to the Army;.
Dead are gone and with them we cannot converse;, The.
Home.
Return from Battle.
Show Me The Way.
Walcott. He yawned and watched the lilac horns of his island.
Wang Chien. Hearing That His Friend Was Coming Back from the War.
Wilner, E. Coda, Overture.
Wilson, T. Sportsmen in Paradise.
Wordsworth, W. Composed at Rydal on May Morning, 1838.
Wright, C. Return to Seattle: Bastille Day.
Yamada. Homecoming.
Yang Shih-ch'i. I've drawn a salary in the capital for forty years now.
Yüan Mei. On the Twenty-First Day of the Fifth Month, I Reached Home.
Returning Home.
Zimunya. Arrivants.
Kisimiso.

Homeless, The
Ashbery. Street Musicians.
Baraka. Legacy.
Berryman. Boston Common.
Ch'en Tzu-lung. Ballad of the Little Cart, A.
Clifton, L. Miss Rosie.
Colum, P. Old Woman of the Roads, The.
Dickey, J. Bums, on waking.
Doty, M. Broadway.
Ford-Smith. Aux Leon...Women.
Fulton, A. Wreckage Entrepreneur, The.
Gregg. Lies and Longing.
Shopping-Bag Lady, The.
Hirschman, J. X L E B.
Hughes, L. Vagabonds.
Hughes, T. November.
Imlah. Goldilocks.
Jones, R. Romance of the Poor.
Kirchwey. Rogue Hydrant, August.
Kleinzahler. East of the Library, Across from the Odd Fellows Building.
Komunyakaa. "Everybody's Reading Li Po" Silkscreened on a Purple T-Shirt.
Procter, A. Homeless.
Randall, D. Bag Woman.
Spires. Woman on the Dump, The.
Stevenson, R. Ille Terrarum.
Thomas, D. Hunchback in the park, The.
Tố Hữu. Orphans.
Unknown. Soup Kitchen Song.
Virtue. Waifs.
Williams, W. To a Poor Old Woman.

Homer
Alpheios. Andromache's lament is still in our ears.
Antipater of Sidon. Reporter of the courage of heroes.
Antipater of Thessalonica. Homer said everything beautifully, but to call.
Carver, R. Wine.
Coffey. Homer where born where buried of whom the son.

Cowper, W. Inscription.
Eberhart, R. Garden God, The.
Ehrenstein. Homer.
Emerson, R. Solution.
Kavanagh, P. Epic.
On Looking into E. V. Rieu's Homer.
Keats. On First Looking into Chapman's Homer.
To Homer.
Lang, A. Odyssey, The.
MacKie, A. Sun's oot. I sit, my pipe alunt and puff, The.
Philip of Thessalonica. Sky will extinguish its stars, and the sun, The.
Pound, E. Canto 1.
Reese, L. Love, Weeping, Laid This Song.
Unknown, after the Latin of George Buchanan. Cure for Poetry, A.

Homesickness
Alexander, E. Letter: Blues.
Ashe. City Clerk, The.
Bennett, L. Home Sickness.
Berry, J. Lucy's Letter.
Blind. Fantasy, A.
Blunden. At the Great Wall of China.
Borges. John 1:14 (1969).
Brooke, R. Old Vicarage, Grantchester, The.
Browning, R. Home-Thoughts, From Abroad.
Byron, G. Lachin y Gair.
Cao Tân. Our friend would board the *Thu'o'ng-Tín* and go home.
Clare, J. Flitting, The.
Coleridge, S. Lines Written in the Album at Elbingerode, in the Hartz Forest.
Cunningham, A. Hame, Hame, Hame.
Drainac. Then, the drops were freezing on black branches of ancient ash trees.
Ferry. Soldier, The.
Gerstler. Travelogue.
Heissenbüttel. Homesick.
Ho Ching-ming. Ch'en-hsi County.
Rainy Night.
Homer. Landfall.
Hughes, L. Homesick Blues.
Kao Ch'i. Walk to the Eastern River Bank, A.
Kefala. Sunday Visit.
Kim, T. Banana Plant, The.
Lewis, A. In Hospital: Poona (1).
Li Po. Spring Night in Lo-Yang—Hearing a Flute.
Still Night Thoughts.
Liu Tsung-yüan. Poem to Send to Friends in the Capital, A.
MacLeish. American Letter.
MacNeice. Nostalgia.
Masefield. West Wind, The.
McKay, C. Outcast.
Tropics in New York, The.
Pilinszky. One Fine Day.
Porter, P. 'In the New World Happiness is Allowed'.
Ransom, J. Amphibious Crocodile.
Rowe, A. Space Settlement.
Ryan, R. Winter in Minneapolis.
Senghor. Long, long between your hands you held the warrior's black face.
Theognis. I've been a gangrel bodie, I've been to Sicilie.
Tsvetayeva. Homesickness! that long / Exposed weariness!
Tu Fu. Chengtu.
Unknown. Away from Home.
Don't Walk beside the Big Carriage.
Guinea Corn.
Lament of Hsi-Chün.
My Heart Is in Merioneth.
Oak and the Ash, The.
Sad Song.
Song of Sorrow.
We Pick Ferns, We Pick Ferns.
Wang Shih-chieng. Thinking of the Past on an Autumn Night at Tz'u-jen Temple.
Wang Wei. Thinking of My Brother in Shantung on the Ninth Day of the Ninth Moon.
Wen Cheng-ming. In the past when I saw friends off.

Wright, J. Outside Fargo, North Dakota.
Yang Shih-ch'i. I've drawn a salary in the capital for forty years now.

Homesteaders
Unknown. Little Old Sod Shanty.

Homophobia
Anzaldúa. Interface.
Avicolli. Rape Poem, The.
Bergman, D. Blueberry Man.
Borawski. Cheers, Cheers for Old Cha Cha Ass ("Cheers, cheers for old Patchogue High").
Invisible History.
Crew, L. Gay Psalm from Fort Valley, A.
De la Tierra. De Ambiente.
Everhard. Curing Homosexuality.
Gates, B. Deadly Weapon.
Hughes, L. Café: 3 A.M.
Morse, C. Fairy Straighttalk.
Norse. We Bumped Off Your Friend the Poet.
Parker, P. My Brother.
Prologue from "Legacy."
Where Will You Be?

Homosexuality and Homosexuals
Adamson. Action Would Kill It / A Gamble.
Allison, D. When I drink I become / the joy of faggots.
Argentarius. Epigram: "Hetero-sex is best for the man of a serious turn of mind."
Barnfield. Sighing, and sadly sitting by my Love.
Sometimes I wish that I his pillow were.
Barrington, J. Dirty Panes.
Bass, E. For Barbara, who said She Couldn't Visualize Two Women Together.
Baudelaire. Femmes Damnées.
Behn, A. Song, A.
To the Fair Clarinda, Who Made Love to Me, Imagin'd More Than Woman.
Blaser. Even on Sunday.
Broumas, O. Amazon Twins.
Rapunzel.
Sleeping Beauty.
Snow White.
Campo. Aunt Toni's Heart.
Battle Hymn of the Republic, The.
El Día de los Muertos.
Cataldi. 13 November 1983.
We Could Have Met.
Catullus. Aurelius, I'm entrusting you with all.
Cavafy. And I Lounged and Lay on Their Beds.
In Despair.
Clarke, C. Of Althea and Flaxie.
Clinton. Tantrum Girl Responds to Death.
Cooper, D. No God.
Creeley. All That Is Lovely in Men.
De Veaux. Sisters, The.
Dickinson, E. You love me—you are sure.
Duffy, C. Oppenheim's Cup and Saucer.
DuPlessis, R. Mirror Poem.
Fraser, K. Song: "I love you, Mrs. Acorn. Would your husband mind."
García Lorca. Ode for Walt Whitman.
Gilbert, T. Against Homosexuality.
Ginsberg, A. Chances "R."
This Form of Life Needs Sex.
Hacker, M. Ballad of Ladies Lost and Found.
Dusk: July.
Eight Days in April.
Gramercy Park.
Harms. Explaining the Evening News to Corbyn.
My Androgynous Years.
Head, G. Night Sweats.
Hecht, A. Feast of Stephen, The.
Hemphill. Homocide.
Where Seed Falls.
XXIV.
Hoagland, T. One Season.
Hughes, L. Café: 3 A.M.
Kay, J. Mummy and Donor and Deirdre.
Kirstein. Double Date.
Klepfisz. Dinosaurs and Larger Issues.
Knight, E. For Freckle-Faced Gerald.
Koestenbaum, W. 1975.
Komunyakaa. Troubling the Water.

Lorde. Meet.
Lowell, R. Words for Hart Crane.
Marie-Madeleine. Words of Old Age*.
Martial. Martial's Favourites.
McHugh, H. Note Delivered by a Female
  Impersonator.
Meredith, W. Wholesome.
Mew. On the Road to the Sea.
Moraga. Loving in the War Years.
Morgan, R. Damn you, lady, get out of my
  blood for good.
Mouré. She Touched Me.
Mueller, I. Invisibility Poem: Lesbian.
Namjoshi, S. et al. Was It Quite Like That?
Norse. I Would Not Recommend Love.
O'Hara, F. Homosexuality.
O'Neill, R. Dream of Sappho, A.
  Sister, The.
Owens, R. Devils Clowns and Women.
Parker, P. For Willyce.
Pasolini. Civil Song.
  Southern Dawn.
Peacock, M. Have You Ever Faked an
  Orgasm?
Philips, K. L'Amitie: To Mrs. M. Awbrey.
Plymell. San Fransisco Ward.
Pratt, M. All the Women Caught in Flaring
  Light.
Prince, F. Old Age of Michelangelo, The.
Rainey. Prove It on Me Blues.
Rickel. Night Sweats 2.
  Poem to Begin the Second Decade of AIDS.
Roberts, M. Magnificat.
Roberts, N. Nigger and Some Poofters, A.
Rochester, J. Song: "Love a woman? You're
  [or Y'are] an ass."
Sassoon. Foot Inspection.
Scannell. Protest Poem.
Schuyler, J. Tom.
Seaton, M. Christmas in the Midwest.
  Harlem.
Selman, R. Avec Amour.
  Old man waves to me through iron bars, The.
  One of us had to be the first to lead.
  They called the next panel, "New Lesbians."
Seward. Elegy.
Shakespeare, W. Sonnet 20.
Shurin. City of Men.
  His Promise.
Simon, L. Bernice Got Next to Isis.
Smith, S. Lord Barrenstock and Epicene.
Strato. Epigram: "I delight in the prime of a
  boy of twelve."
  Epigram: "There was this gym-teacher."
  Heterosexual Poem.
  Vive La Différence.
Tsui. Chinese Banquet, A.
  How Can I Show This Poem to Geraldine?
Unknown. Limerick: "There was a young
  Fellow of King's."
  Surprise, Surprise.
  Woman-love can't touch my heart.
Verlaine. Bad Sleeper, A.
  In that café crowded with fools we stood.
  Thousand and Three, A.
Weiners. Act #2.
Whitman, W. In paths untrodden.
  Not heat flames up and consumes.
  Recorders ages hence.
  When I heard at the close of the day how my
    name had been receiv'd with plaudits in the
    capitol, still it was not a happy night for me
    that follow'd.
  Whoever you are holding me now in hand.
Wieners. Acceptance.
  Doll.
  King Solomon's Magnetic Quiz.
  Loneliness, The.
  To H.
Williams, S. She Had Known Brothers.
Wright, J. Sappho.

Honesty
Campion, T. Heart's Music.
  Were My Heart as Some Men's Are.
Cheng Hsieh. Contest Snake, The.
Cleage. Confession.
Cowper, W. Friendship.

Creeley. Somebody Died.
Donne. Song: "Go and catch a falling star."
Herbert, G. Courage.
Larkin, P. Talking in bed ought to be easiest.
McBride, M. Red Letters.
Meredith, G. Their sense is with their senses
  all mixed in.
Milosz, C. Task, A.
Nesbit, E. Appeal.
Rukeyser, M. Poem as Mask, The.
Unknown. Keep this in mind, and all will go.
Walton, A. Sincere Man, The.
Wyatt, T. Throughout the world, if it were
  sought.
Wylie. Let No Charitable Hope.

Honey
Ancient Egyptian Oral Tradition. This love is
  as good.
Ashbery. They Dream Only of America.
Brooks, G. My Dreams, My Works Must Wait
  Till after Hell.
Doolittle, H. Fragment 113: "Not honey, / not
  the plunder of the bee."
  Socratic.
Kelly, R. In June was a jar had.
Lima, J. Distribution of Poetry.
Makeda (Queen of Sheba). Wisdom is.
Morgan, R. Honey.
Mother Goose. God made the bees.
Rauter. Peach.
Rumi. This marriage be wine with halvah,
  honey dissolving in milk.
Sandburg, C. In Tall Grass.
Toomer. Beehive.
Unknown. God made the bees.
  I eat my peas with honey.
Virgil. Of Bees.
Watts, I. How doth the little busy bee.

Honeymoons
Corso. Marriage.
Durcan. Honeymoon Postcard.
Herrick. Epithalamy to Sir Thomas Southwell
  and His Lady, An.
Updike. Newlyweds, The.
Yosano. Over the old honeymoon cottage.

Honeysuckle
Freneau. Wild Honey Suckle, The.

Hong Kong
Ravikovitch. How Hong Kong Was Destroyed.

Honor
Berryman. Scholars at the Orchid Pavilion.
Bible, N.T. Though I speak in the tongues of
  men or of angels: if I have no love, I am.
Bible, O.T. Honour thy father and thy mother.
Browne, W. Shall I tell you whom I love?
Cameron, N. Thespians at Thermopylae, The.
Cavafy. Thermopylae.
Chaucer. Lack of Steadfastness.
  Lak of Stedfastnesse.
Collins, W. Ode Written in the Beginning of
  the Year 1746.
Crane, S. Youth, A.
Daniel, S. Ulysses and the Siren [or Syren].
Del Giudice. Rules to Live By.
Dickinson, E. Sown in dishonor!
Donne. To the Countesse of Bedford ("Honour
  is so sublime perfection").
Dunbar, W. In Prais of Wemen.
  In Praise of Women.
Fu Hsüan. Gentle Wind [fans the calm night],
  A.
Garcia. Tips for Living.
Gay, J. Honour plays a bubble's part.
Goldsmith, O. Song: "When lovely woman
  stoops to folly."
Greenlee. Memorial for Trane.
Guinicelli. Sonnet: He Will Praise His Lady.
Herrick. God to Be First Served.
Jonson, B. O God, and his good angels!
  whither, whither.
  Ode. To Sir William Sydney, on His Birthday.
  To Celia.
  To Sir Henry Cary.
Keith, J. Definitions.
Kiser. My Creed.
Legaré. Tallulah.

Lovelace, R. Mock Charon, A.
  Song: To Lucasta, Going to the War[re]s.
MacNeice. Elegy for Minor Poets.
Mandeville. On Honour.
Martial. Motto to Richard Lovelace, Lucasta.
  Posthume Poems.
McKay, C. If we must die—let it not be like
  hogs.
Melville, H. College Colonel, The.
  Stonewall Jackson.
Middleton, T. Changeling, The.
Murray, L. Lament for the Country Soldiers.
Philips, K. On the Welsh Language.
Pindar. Fourteenth Olympick Ode, The.
Po Chü-i. Fifteenth Volume, The.
Scarfe. Ode in Honour.
Shakespeare, W. Before Agincourt.
  Sonnet 25.
Stanley, T. Pythagoric letter, two ways spread,
  The.
Suckling, J. Loving and Beloved.
Tasso. Pastoral[l], A: "Oh [or O] happy
  golden age."
Unknown. Down to the Mire.
  Poor But Honest.
Vega. Brothers Loving Brothers.
Villiers. Epitaph upon Thomas, Lord Fairfax,
  An.
Wilde, L. Désillusion.
Yang Chi. Selling My Official Robe.
Zukofsky, L. "A"-11 River That Must Turn
  Full After I Stop Dying.

Hooch, Pieter de
Mahon. Courtyards in Delft.
Tomlinson, C. Paring the Apple.

Hoopoes
Darley. Hoopoe.

Hope
Adamovich. When we return to Russia...
"Akhmatova." Dedication.
Alegría. Ars Poetica.
Ali, A. Desert Landscape.
Allnutt. Comfortable Words.
Arnold, M. Self-Dependence.
Atwood. In this house (in a dying orchard.
Avidan. Moment Ago, A.
Baca. Oppression.
Barannikov. May there always be sun!
Bible, O.T. Psalm 42.
Bly, R. Poem in Three Parts.
Booth, P. Hope.
Brecht, B. World's One Hope, The.
Brontë, E. Anticipation.
  Hope was but a timid friend.
  Prisoner, The.
Byron, G. Stanzas for Music.
Carrier, C. Pro Patria.
Carstairs. Addressed to a Beech Tree.
Channing. Poet's Hope, A.
Chimombo. Death Song, A.
Clark, T. Faith for Tomorrow.
Cohen, M. Sometimes in Winter.
Coleridge, S. On a Discovery Made Too Late.
  Work Without Hope.
Collins, A. Song.
Cornford, F. Single Woman, The.
Crane, H. Ave Maria.
Crashaw. Against Hope.
Cruz, V. Today Is a Day of Great Joy.
Cullen, C. Brown Boy to Brown Girl.
  From the Dark Tower.
Dame. Seder, The.
Di Prima. Revolutionary Letter #1.
Dickinson, E. "Hope" is the thing with
  feathers.
  I dwell in Possibility.
Diop, D. Vultures, The.
Dipoko. From My Parisian Diary.
Divakaruni. Restroom.
Driscoll, L. Hold Fast Your Dreams.
Eedes. No Love, to Love of Man and Wife.
Faiz. Prison Evening, A.
Fanning, R. Shoelace.
Galvin, B. Willow, Wishbone, Warblers.
Gillilan, S. Be hopeful, friend, when clouds
  are dark and days are.

Ginsberg, A.　In Back of the Real.
　Sunflower Sutra.
Giovanni.　Poem For My Nephew.
Glazkov.　Path Is Long, The.
Graves, R.　Love without hope, as when the
　young bird-catcher.
　Lovers in Winter.
Halpern, D.　Naming the Unborn.
Hardy, T.　Darkling Thrush, The.
　To an Unborn Pauper Child.
Heard, J.　Hope! Thou vain, delusive maiden.
Herbert, G.　Hope.
　Size, The.
Herrick.　His Hope or Sheet-Anchor.
　Impossibilities to His Friend.
Hillel.　Sun.
Hopkins, G.　Leaden Echo and the Golden
　Echo, The.
Horton, G.　On Liberty and Slavery.
　Slave's Complaint, The.
Hudgins.　Hereafter, The.
Hughes, L.　Hope.
Jarrell.　Hope.
　Jews at Haifa.
Jeffers, L.　I do not know the power of my
　hand.
Julius Polyaenus.　Hope is what skims time
　always from our lives.
Kenyon, J.　Let Evening Come.
　Once There Was Light.
Kinzie.　Impromptu.
　Xenophilia.
Kiser.　Unsubdued.
Knight, E.　Green Grass and Yellow Balloons.
Korn.　Thirty-one Camels, The.
Landon.　Farewell!
Levertov.　Beginners.
Lodge, G.　Fall.
Lum.　Backup, The.
MacLeish.　Pole Star for This Year.
MacNeice.　Prospect.
Mahon.　Everything Is Going to Be All Right.
Martynov.　Seashore, The.
McNair.　Before People, The.
Melville, H.　Immolated.
　Shelley's Vision.
Menken.　Aspiration.
Momaday.　Gift, The.
Moorer.　Door of Hope, The.
Mora.　Immigrants.
Morris, W.　Message of the March Wind, The.
Mouré.　La Gueule.
Muir, E.　Good Man in Hell, The.
　Horses, The ("Barely a twelvemonth after").
Neruda.　America, I do not call your name
　without hope.
Nguyễn Đình Chiểu.　Waiting for the East
　Wind.
Olson, C.　Distances, The.
Piercy.　Sun, The.
Pratt, M.　Poem for My Sons.
Prince, F.　To a Friend on His Marriage.
Pugh.　Sometimes things don't go, after all.
Ratushinskaya.　Try to cover your shivering
　shoulders in rags of the oldest.
Ray, H.　Aspiration.
　Triple Benison, The.
Rossetti, C.　Aloof.
　Comparisons.
　Hope and Joy.
　If Only.
　Song: "She sat and sang alway."
Rukeyser, M.　Who in one lifetime sees all
　causes lost.
Ryan, R.　Lake of the Woods, The.
Sanchez, S.　Anthem, An.
Sassoon.　Everyone Sang.
Shelley, P.　England in 1819.
　Lines Written among the Euganean Hills.
Shkapskaya.　My body had no entrance, and
　the black.
"Shu Ting."　Fairy Tales.
Sidney, P.　Get Hence Foule Griefe.
Simmons, J.　For Thomas Moore.
Smart, C.　Hope.
Stanley, T.　Expectation.
Strand.　For Jessica, My Daughter.

Su Tung-p'o.　At the Washing of My Son.
Swinburne.　Hope and Fear.
Tekeyan.　Country of Dust, The.
Thomas, E.　When I first came here I had
　hope.
Thomas, E.　To Colindra.
Thomas, L.　Wonders.
Thompson, C.　Hope.
　Hope Deferred.
Trần Đú'c Uyển.　Letter to My Future Child,
　A.
Trần Mộng Tú.　New Year's Wish for a Little
　Refugee, A.
Trần Tế Xu'o'ng.　Man Has Lost His Way, A.
Tucker, M.　Hope.
Turner, N.　Whenever I say "America."
Unknown.　High Resolve.
　My Hope, My Love.
Very.　Forevermore.
Wagner, C.　Let's forget the many troubles.
Walker, M.　For my people [everywhere
　singing their slave songs repeatedly: their].
Warren, R.　Aubade for Hope.
　When the century dragged, like a great wheel
　stuck at dead center.
Way.　Hoping for a Dog.
Wen Cheng-ming.　Smiling, we set the testing
　tray before the hall.
Williams, H.　Sonnet to Hope.
Wordsworth, W.　Composed Near Calais on
　the Road Leading to Ardres, August 7, 1802.
Wright, C.　Hawaii Dantesca.
Wright, J.　Arrangements with Earth for Three
　Dead Friends.
Wright, K.　How I See It,
Wroth.　Song: "I, that ame of all most crost."
　Sonnet 27: "Fie [or Fy] tedious Hope, why
　do[e] you still rebel[l]?"
Wyatt, T.　I abide and abide and better abide.
Wylie.　Let No Charitable Hope.
Yosano.　It is because you always hope, my
　heart.
Zu-Bolton.　By the 5th Generation Louisiana,
　After Slavery.
Zukofsky, L.　Green leaf that will outlast the
　winter.
See also **Optimism**

Hopi, The
Rose.　Naayawva Taawi.
　Story Keeper.
Tomlinson, C.　Death in the Desert, A.

Hopkins, Gerard Manley
Gibbon, M.　Poetry of Gerard Manley Hopkins,
　The.
McMahon, L.　Hopkins and Whitman.

Hopper, Edward
Ray, D.　Midnight Diner by Edward Hopper,
　A.

Horace
Auden.　Horatians, The.
Durrell.　On First Looking into Loeb's Horace.
Godley, A.　After Horace.
Montagu, L.　Verses Addressed to the Imitator
　of the First Satire of the Second Book of
　Horace: An Attack on Pope.
Tennyson, A.　Poets and Their Bibliographies.

Horatius
Macaulay, T.　Horatius.
　Horatius at the Bridge.

Horn, Cape. *See* **Cape Horn**

Horse Racing
Foster, S.　Gwine to Run All Night; or, De
　Camptown Races.
Gordon, A.　How We Beat the Favourite.
Hart, K.　Flemington Racecourse.
Larkin, P.　At Grass.
Moore, M.　Tom Fool at Jamaica.
Parone.　Morning Track, The.
Paterson, A.　Father Riley's Horse.
Unknown.　Galway Races.
Wakoski.　Placing a $2 Bet for a Man Who
　Will Never Go to the Horse Races Any
　More.
Yeats.　At Galway Races.

Horse Shows
Sidney, P.　Sonnet 41: "Having this day my
　horse, my hand, my lance."

Horseback Riding
Baillie, J.　Horse and His Rider, The.
Betjeman.　Hunter Trials.
Browning, R.　Last Ride Together, The.
Campbell, R.　Sisters, The.
Chu Yün-ming.　Shrine of General Pien, The.
Cummings, E.　All in green went my love
　riding.
Francis, R.　Boy Riding Forward Backward.
Guiney.　Wild Ride, The.
Hardy, T.　Circus-Rider to Ringmaster.
Hsü Wei.　On the Road Through the Wu-i
　Mountains—Making Fun of Chia-tse for
　Falling Off His Horse.
King, H.　Moonlight Ride, A.
Li K'ai-hsien.　Gazing at Ch'ang-po Mountain.
Li Tung-yang.　Following the Rhymes of Yang
　T'ing-ho's Poem, "On the Road Back,
　Accompanying the Imperial Retinue on a
　Visit to the Tombs of Former Emperors."
Longfellow, H.　Paul Revere's Ride (The
　Landlord's Tale).
Morris, W.　Haystack in the Floods, The.
Mother Goose.　Ride a cock-horse [*or* a-cock
　horse] to Banbury Cross, / To see a fine lady
　upon a white horse.
　This is the way the ladies ride.
Po Chü-i.　Escorting Candidates to the
　Examination Hall.
　Visiting the Hsi-lin Temple.
Roethke.　Elegy for Jane.
Sidney, P.　Sonnet 41: "Having this day my
　horse, my hand, my lance."
　Sonnet 49: "I on my horse, and Love on me
　doth try."
Stevenson, R.　Windy Nights.
T'ang Yin.　Galloping around, north and south.
Taylor, H.　Riding Lesson.
Unknown.　Here goes my lord.
　This is the way the farmers ride.
　This is the way the gentlemen ride.
Virgil.　Knowing About Horses.
Weaver, M.　Weekend Equestrian, The.
Wen Cheng-ming.　Beneath the Shrine of the
　Three Loyal Ones.
Westwood.　Night of Spring.
Wu Wei-yeh.　Setting out at dawn from T'ung-
　lu county.
Yang Shih-ch'i.　Crossing the River.
Yang Wei-chen.　Horse-Watering Hole, The.
　Horseman at the Roadside, The.
Yü Chi.　Getting on Horseback.

Horses
Ai.　Before You Leave.
Ammons.　Silver.
Apollinaire.　Horse Calligram.
Ayres.　Cynthia on Horseback.
Baca.　Mantanza to Welcome Spring.
Baillie, J.　Horse and His Rider, The.
Barnes, J.　Paiute Ponies.
Barnes, K.　Mare, A.
Bensko.　Wild Horses of Assateague Island,
　The.
Berryman.　Whether There Is Sorrow in the
　Demons.
Bible, *O.T.*　Hast thou given the horse
　strength?
Blaser.　Suddenly.
Blind.　Fantasy, A.
Bloomfield.　Ploughman's Horse, The.
Blunt, W.　St. Valentine's Day.
Boland, E.　War Horse, The.
Boruch.　My Son and I Go See Horses.
Bowering, G.　Dobbin.
Burns, R.　Tam o' Shanter. [A Tale].
Buson.　Tethered horse, A.
Campbell, R.　Horses on the Camargue.
　Sisters, The.
Cattanar.　What He Said to his charioteer, on
　his way back.
Chamberlain, B.　Dead Ponies.
Chin.　Cauldron.
Clifton, L.　C. C. Rider.
Coatsworth.　Circus-Postered Barn, The.
　Daniel Webster's Horses.
　Old Mare, The.
Comfort, A.　Lovers, The.

Conn. Todd.
Corrington. For a Woodscolt Miscarried.
Corso. New York City—1935.
Creeley. Gift of Great Value, A.
Rescue.
Cummings, E. All in green went my love riding.
What a proud dreamhorse pulling(smoothloomingly)through.
Das, M. Horses.
Dickey, J. Dusk of Horses, The.
Dickinson, E. I like to see it lap the Miles.
Dove, R. Horse and Tree.
Drummond, W. Trojan Horse, The.
Edey et al. Trot Along, Pony.
Éluard, P. To Ride.
Espaillat. Metrics.
Fawkes. Elegy on the Death of Dobbin, the Butterwoman's Horse, An.
Field, E. Fly-Away Horse, The.
Johnny's Team.
Field, R. Merry-Go-Round.
Ford, C. January wraps up the wound of his arm.
Forrest-Thomson. Strike.
Frankau. Gun Teams.
Frost, R. Draft Horse, The.
Runaway, The.
Gallagher, T. Horse in the drugstore / wants to be admired, The.
Garland, H. Horses Chawin' Hay.
Glück, L. Horse.
Goodge. How We Drove the Trotter.
Guiney. Wild Ride, The.
Hall, D. Names of Horses.
Harjo, J. She Had Some Horses.
Harmon. Dawn Horse, The.
Heaney, S. Terminus.
Hearne, V. Gauguin's White Horse.
Riding a Nervous Horse.
Hewitt, J. King's Horses, The.
Hogan, L. Celebration: Birth of a Colt.
Holmes, W. Old Brown Horse, The.
Hopkins, G. Felix Randal the farrier,° O is he dead then? my duty / all ended.
Hsü Wei. From Chekiang I Went to Hsin-an and Climbed Even-with-the-Clouds Mountain. On the Way Back There Were Many Beautiful Sights at the Inns Where I Stayed and Yet I Could Not Write One Word of Poetry. When I Got Back to the Main Road I Wrote These Four Lines to Make Fun of Myself.
Hughes, T. Horses, The.
Yesterday he was nowhere to be found.
Juhász, F. Birth of the Foal.
Kapilar. What She Said ("And all those horses").
Kennelly. Horse's Head, The.
Larkin, P. At Grass.
Wedding-Wind.
Lawrence, D. White Horse, The.
Lea, S. Museum.
Levin, P. Dark Horse.
Levine, P. Horse, The.
Lindsay, V. Broncho That Would Not Be Broken, The.
Little, G. Fallen horse.
Loving. Black Horse Rider, The.
Macedonius. You neigh and whinny, seeming to invite.
Matevski. Arrive sluggish, arrive weary horses of space.
Mathews, H. Dappled Horse, The.
Mayakovsky. On Being Kind to Horses.
McAuley, J. Blue Horses, The.
McCarriston. Healing the Mare.
McGrath, T. End of the Line, The.
Mei Yao Ch'en. Dappled Horse, The.
Merrill, J. Charioteer of Delphi, The.
Mistral, F. Mares of the Camargue, The.
Miu Hsi. Bearer's Song.
Moody, M. Say This of Horses.
Moore, L. Eternal Landscape, The.
Moore, M. Tom Fool at Jamaica.
Muir, E. Horses.
Horses, The ("Barely a twelvemonth after").

Muldoon, P. Dancers at the Moy.
Nagy, A. Horses and the Angels, The.
Sincerity.
Nguyễn Đình Chiểu. Loyal Horse, The.
Norris, L. Pit Ponies, The.
Norton, C. Arab's Farewell to His Horse, The.
O'Grady, D. Great Horse Fair, The.
O'Malley, D. Tenderfoot, The.
Owen, G. White Stallion / (The Runaway), The.
Palladas. I was promised a horse but what I got instead.
Perlman, A. At Fifty in the Crystal-Dead Eye of the Center.
Po Chü-i. Sleeping on Horseback.
Purdy, A. Cariboo Horses, The.
Reeves, J. Four Horses, The.
Mr Kartoffel's a whimsical man.
Renton. Foal, The.
Shadow of Himself, The.
Rexroth, K. Horse.
Roberson. Blue Horses.
Rossetti, C. Horses of the sea, The.
Horses of the sea, / Rear a foaming crest, The.
Rothenberg, J. 12th Horse-Song of Frank Mitchell (Blue), The.
Roy, L. Ride, The.
Sabina. 13th Horse Song of Frank Mitchell, The.
Sexton. Pain for a Daughter.
Shalamov. Pegasus.
Slutsky. Horses in the Sea.
Snyder, G. All through the Rains.
Spicer, J. 6.
Stephens, J. To the Four Courts, Please.
Stevens, W. Room on a Garden, A.
Swenson, M. Centaur, The.
Weather.
Taylor, H. Flying Change, The.
Riding a One-eyed Horse.
Teika. I rein in my horse.
Thomas, D. January 1939.
Thomas, E. Horses.
Tudur Aled. Stallion, The.
Turner, C. White Horse of Westbury, The.
Ullman. Dawn Feeding.
Unknown. Educated Feller.
Evening darkens until.
Horse Cursed by the Sun, The.
Old Gray Mare.
On a Clergyman's Horse Biting Him.
On Buying a Horse.
Poor Old Horse.
Shoe the little horse.
Song of the Horse.
Turning my chariot I yoke my horses and go.
War God's Horse Song, The.
Widdecombe [or Widdicombe] Fair.
You can lead a horse to water.
Zebra Dun, The.
Vacietis. Horse Dream.
Van Doren. Distant Runners, The.
Van Zyl. Horses of Marini, The.
Viereck, P. Love Song to Eohippus.
Virgil. Knowing About Horses.
Vysotsky. Unruly Horses.
Watkins, V. Foal.
Mare lies down in the grass where the nest of the skylark is hidden, The.
Weaver, M. Appaloosa, The.
Wei Ying-wu. Tune: "Song of Flirtatious Laughter."
Weigl. Sharing, The.
Wellesley. Horses.
Wen Cheng-ming. I sit on horseback at Twin Bridges.
Wine of parting flowed and flowed, The.
Wendell, J. In the Pasture of Dead Horses.
Whitman, W. Gigantic beauty of a stallion, fresh and responsive to my caresses, A.
Wills, J. White horse.
Woolson. Kentucky Belle.
Wordsworth, W. Lucy.
Wright, J. Blessing, A.
Outside Fargo, North Dakota.
Poems to a Brown Cricket.

Yang Chi. Reviewing the Troops at Kuei-lin with Military Inspectors Chiang And Chang.
Yang Shih-ch'i. Crossing the River.
Red Heart Station.
Yang Wei-chen. Horse-Watering Hole, The.
Yeats. Michael Robartes Bids His Beloved Be at Peace.
Zabolotsky. Face of the Horse, The.
See also **Colts; Foals; Horse Racing; Horse Shows; Horseback Riding**

Horseshoes
Hopkins, G. Felix Randal the farrier,° O is he dead then? my duty / all ended.
Howard, R. Tremendous Trifles.
Mother Goose. For want of a nail[, the shoe was lost].
Unknown. Shoe the little horse.
Worth, V. Magnet.

Hospitality
Al-Lajjam al-Harrani. His banquets cure most ills.
Archilochus. Stranded ashore from the sea.
Belloc. On a Dead Hostess.
Dickinson, E. Soul that hath a Guest, The.
Gurney, I. La Gorgue.
Hardy, T. At an Inn.
Herrick. To the Most Virtuous Mistress Pot, Who Many Times Entertained Him.
Upon Showbread [or Shewbread]: Epigram.
Hugo, R. Places and Ways to Live.
Jonson, B. Inviting a Friend to Supper.
Kipling, R. Ballad of East and West, The.
Lowell, J. Yussouf.
Martial. Inviting a Friend to Supper.
Robinson, E. Cliff Klingenhagen had me in to dine.
Unknown. Hospitality in Ancient Ireland.
See also **Guests**

Hospitals
Adcock, F. Soho Hospital for Women, The.
Atwood. Flowers.
Betjeman. Five O'Clock Shadow.
Buckley, V. In the faint blue light.
Cervantes. From the Bus to E. L. at Atascadero State Hospital.
Cooper, J. Infusion Room, The.
Cox, M. Sleep Apnea.
Daniels, K. Not Singing.
Dickey, J. Hospital Window, The.
Dransfield. Visiting Hour (Repatriation Hospital).
Engman. Staff.
Flecker. In Hospital.
Funk, W. Tubes.
Garrett, G. In the Hospital.
Gibson, W. Conscript, The.
Godley, E. Ninety-Nine.
Goedicke. In the Waiting Room.
Graves, R. Surgical Ward: Men.
Hall, D. Tubes.
Harwood, G. Hospital Evening.
Hayden, R. Broken Dark, The.
Hogan, L. Friday Night.
Holan. In the Yard of the Policlinic.
Howard, R. Far Cry after a Close Call, A.
Ignatow, D. Sunday at the State Hospital.
Jarrell. Field Hospital, A.
In a Hospital Garden.
Kavanagh, P. Hospital, The.
Kenyon, J. Coats.
Kinsella, T. Lady of Quality, A.
Kitahara Hakushū. At a hospital in Tokyo during the summer of 1911.
Levertov. Malice of Innocence, The.
Lewis, A. In Hospital: Poona (1).
"MacDiarmid." In the Children's Hospital.
Mackenzie, K. Hospital—Retrospections, The.
McManus, J. Spike Logic.
Melville, H. Camoëns.
Merwin, W. St. Vincent's.
Moore, M. Transfusion.
Muldoon, P. Field Hospital, The.
Muske. Pediatrics.
Nash, O. Notes for the Chart in 306.
North, C. Hospital.
Owen, W. Conscious.
Disabled.

Hospital Barge at Cérisy.
Mental Cases.
Peacock, M. Chriseaster.
Petrosky. V.A. Hospital.
Plath. Stones, The.
Tulips are too excitable, it is winter here, The.
Plymell. San Fransisco Ward.
Porter, P. Happening at Sordid Creek.
Preygel. Hospital, The.
Randall, D. George.
Sassoon. Death-Bed, The.
Schuyler, J. Sleep.
Senior. Children's Hospital.
Serge. Asphyxiated Man, The.
Sexton. Unknown Girl in the Maternity Ward.
You, Doctor Martin, walk.
Sholl. Hospital State, The.
Sissman. Deathplace, A.
Slutsky. Hospital.
Snodgrass, W. Flat One, A.
Operation, The.
Steele, T. Wait.
Swede. Mental hospital my shadow stays outside.
Tate, J. Like a Scarf.
Ulacia. Stone at the Bottom, The.
Viiding. George Marrow's 1011th Dream.
Waring, B. Baby Random.
Warner, S. Benicasim.
Webb, F. Hospital Night.
Ward Two.
Whitman, W. Sight in camp in the daybreak gray and dim, A.
Williams, W. Between Walls.
Spring and All.
Yi, S. Paper Memorial Stone.
Zagajewski. When Death Came.

Hotels
Betjeman. Arrest of Oscar Wilde at the Cadogan Hotel, The.
Campbell, D. Hotel Marine.
Christopher. Far from Home.
Davidson, L. In the dark lobby.
Doty, M. Harbor Lights.
Emanuel, J. Black Man, 13th Floor.
Graham, J. In the Hotel.
Klein, A. For the Sisters of the Hôtel Dieu.
Kumin, M. At the End of the Affair.
Liddy. Strand Hotel, Rosslare, The.
Lindsay, V. Jazz of This Hotel, The.
Lowry, M. Delirium in Vera Cruz.
McGinley. Lament for Lost Lodgings.
Merrill, J. Hotel de l'Univers et Portugal.
Moss, H. At the Algonquin.
O'Grady, D. Finn's Wishes.
Price, R. Twenty-One Years.
Rossetti, C. Uphill [or Up-Hill].
Ryan, G. In the Purple Bar.
Shenstone. Written at [or in] an Inn at Henley.
Tonks. Story of a Hotel Room.
Unknown. Stirling's Hotel.
Wevill. Irish Hotel.
Wright, C. Hotels.

See also **Motels**

Hottentots
Breytenbach. First Prayer for the Hottentotsgod.

Houdini, Harry
Mandel, E. Houdini.

Hourglasses
Herrick Hour-Glass, The.
Jonson, B. Hour-Glass [or Houre-Glasse], The.

House Painting
Hemschemeyer. Painters, The.

Housekeeping
Alvarez, A. How I Learned to Sweep.
Brown, R. I have a neighbor.
Campbell, R. On the Same.
Di Prima. Quarrel, The.
Dove, R. Dusting.
Gallagher, T. I Stop Writing the Poem.
Halley. Housewife's Letter: To Mary.
Henderson-Holmes. Goodhousekeeping #17.
Hoskins, G. Homework, homework.
Kenyon, J. Finding a Long Gray Hair.

Mayhall. Tracing Back.
Schuyler, J. Song: "I'm about to go shopping."
Taylor, E. Huswifery.
Turner, N. When Young Melissa Sweeps.
Waldman, A. Baby's Pantoum.
Walker, A. Women.
Wong, N. Ironing.

See also **Housewives**

Houses
Abbey, H. What do we plant when we plant the tree?
Adamson. My House.
Ashbery. Old Complex, The.
Atwood. Morning in the Burned House.
Auden. Thanksgiving for a Habitat.
Ayres. Invites His Nymph to His Cottage.
Blanding. Vagabond House.
Blumenthal, M. Marriage, A.
Bobrowski. Deserted House, The.
Sanctuary.
Bowering, G. House, The.
Bradstreet, A. Here Follows Some Verses upon the Burning of Our House [July 10th, 1966. Copied Out of a Loose Paper].
Bronk. Strong Room of the House, The.
Brooks, G. Vacant Lot, The.
Browning, R. House.
Love in a Life.
Cain, J. Empty room.
Caraion. Winter.
Carew, T. To Saxham.
Carpenter, W. Fire.
Carruth, H. Mending the Adobe.
Carter, E. Dialogue, A.
Carver, R. Cobweb, The.
Chang Chi. Coming at Night to a Fisherman's Hut.
Ch'ien T'ao. Moving House.
Written While Drunk.
Clare, J. After Reading in a Letter Proposals for Building a Cottage.
Clark, T. Eyeglasses.
Coleridge, M. Deserted House, The.
Coleridge, S. Eolian Harp, The.
Colum, P. Old Woman of the Roads, The.
Coward. Stately Homes of England, The.
Cowley, A. Wish, The.
Creeley. House, The.
Daniel, Y. House, A.
Davie. Priory of St Saviour, Glendalough, The.
Davies, H. Music in an Empty House.
Davies, W. No Man's Wood.
Dawson, W. House of Pride, The.
Day Lewis. At Lemmons.
De la Mare. Old Summerhouse, The.
Sleeper, The.
Dickinson, E. Eden is that old-fashioned House.
God's Residence.
I know some lonely Houses off the Road.
Props assist the House, The.
D'Lettuso. Old Houses.
Dodd, W. Of Rain and Air.
Dransfield. Portrait of the Artist as an Old Man.
Dugan, A. Love Song: I and Thou.
Duncan, R. Coming out of the house to die.
Fisher, A. Houses are faces.
Forbes, C. My Father's House.
Ford, F. Old Houses of Flanders, The.
Frost, R. Black Cottage, The.
Directive.
Fyleman. (Mice).
Garrigue. Country Villa.
Ginsberg, A. Strange New Cottage in Berkeley, A.
Glassco. Quebec Farmhouse.
Goedicke. Lucky.
Gorman, L. For the smell.
Gould, A. Demolisher.
Graham, J. San Sepolcro.
Grass. Saturn.
Graves, R. Not at Home.
Gray, T. On Lord Holland's Seat near Margate, Kent.

Grennan. Woman at Lit Window.
Grosholz. Legacies.
Guest, B. Defensive Rapture.
Prairie Houses.
Gunn, T. Last Days at Teddington.
Haas, R. Building the dollhouse.
Hadas, R. House Beside the Sea, The.
Hagiwara Sakutaro. Chair.
Hall, D. Alligator Bride, The.
Hall, J. Hous-keeping's dead, *Saturio:* wot'st thou where?
Hanzlik. Cottage Behind the Railway, The.
Hardy, T. Domicilium.
Fallow Deer at the Lonely House, The.
Hartnett. Visit to Castletown House, A.
Hass, R. House.
Heaney, S. Summer Home.
Herbert, G. Redemption.
World, The.
Herrick. Thanksgiving to God for His House, A.
Hopkins, G. In the Valley of the Elwy.
Howells, W. Empty House, The.
Howes, B. 2nd Wind.
Hoyt, C. In that empty house.
Huchel. Spindle, The.
Huddle. Gregory's House.
Iverem. Murmur.
Jamie. Aunt Janet's Museum.
Jarrell. Happy Cat, The.
Jones, D. On a Picture of Your House.
Jones, J. Our Wonderful World.
Justice, D. Beyond the Hunting Woods.
Men at forty / Learn to close softly.
Kao Ch'i. Ballad of the Deserted Mansion.
Karpowicz. On Opening an Old House.
Keller, H. Friends, Outside, Night.
Kenyon, J. From Room to Room.
Kilmer, J. House with Nobody in It, The.
Koch, K. Variations on a Theme by William Carlos Williams.
Kooser. Shooting a Farmhouse.
Kunitz, S. Three Floors.
Larkin, P. Home is so sad. It stays as it was left.
Leithauser. In Minako Wada's House.
Levertov. Invocation: "Silent, about-to-be-parted-from house."
Levy, A. Old House, The.
Linderman. Cabins.
Lowell, R. For Sale.
Lu Yu. My Village Home.
MacNeice. House on a Cliff.
Maiden. Foundations, The.
Malouf. For Two Children.
Masaoka Shiki. Tanka: "In the house."
Matthews, J. People in These Houses, The.
Mayer, B. House Cap.
McNair. House in Spring.
Mead, P. There.
Melville, P. Homeland.
Merwin, W. Door, A.
Millay, E. Second Fig.
Miller, M. Closing, A.
Mobilio. Step Seven.
Montale. House of the Customs-Men, The.
Morley, C. Song for a Little House.
Moss, H. Water Island.
Mother Goose. House That Jack Built, The.
Old Mother Goose.
Mountain, M. Wood pile.
Mtshali. Inside My Zulu Hut.
Nash, O. Turtle lives 'twixt plated decks, The.
Navajo Oral Tradition. Night Chant, The.
Nesbit, E. Gray Folk, The.
Nye, N. House Made of Rain, The.
Orban, O. Peace Pillar.
Padilla. Fountain, a house of stone, A.
Paley, G. Sad Children's Song, The.
Parmenter-Newell. Dream House.
Pembroke, M. Psalm 84: "How lovely is thy dwelling."
Plath. Point Shirley.
Plumly. For Esther.
Po Chü-i. Climbing the Terrace of Kuan-yin and Looking at the City of Ch'ang-an.

Grand Houses at Lo-yang, The.
Winter Night.
Rakosi. Founding of New Hampshire, The.
Randall, J. Rockland.
Ransom, J. Old Mansion.
Reynolds, L. To the New Owner.
Reznikoff. House-wreckers have left the door and a staircase, The.
Roberson. Poor Houses, The.
Robinson, E. House on the Hill, The.
Romano, J. Old Houses.
Ryuichi. Human House.
Samio. Tanka: "Why does a room."
Seifert. Never Again.
Seymour, A. To the Family Home Awaiting Repair.
Shange. Where the Heart Is.
Smith, S. Grange, The.
Smith, W. Floor and the Ceiling, The.
Spender, S. Empty House.
Stanley-Wrench. Hinterland.
Stanton, M. Childhood.
Stevens, W. Gallant Château.
House was quiet and the world was calm, The.
Stevenson, R. House Beautiful, The.
My house, I say. But hark to the sunny doves.
Swenson, M. Question.
Taylor, A. Fitzroy.
Tenji. Because.
Thomas, E. New House, The.
Thoreau. For though the eaves were rabbeted.
Tomlinson, C. On the Hall at Stowey.
Tu Fu. Visitors.
Turner, A. Elm Street.
Unknown. Eastern Wall stands high and long;, The.
I will give my love an apple without e'er a core.
In the north-west there is a high house.
Planting Initiation Song.
Shall we stay in the.
Song of Lo-fu, The.
Wide Walls.
Untermeyer, L. Prayer for This House.
Van Zyl. House with coarse stuccoed, The.
Vaughan, H. Friends Departed.
Walcott. Ruins of a Great House.
Waldman, A. *et al.* & Now the book is closed.
Walker, T. Home Is So Sad.
Wallace, R. Sestina for the House.
Weaver, M. Beginnings.
Water Song.
Westrup. My Little House.
Whitlow. Book of Routh.
Wilbur. Altitudes.
Wilde, O. Harlot's House, The.
Williams, M. Empty House, The.
Williams, W. House is yours, The.
Wills, J. Beyond the porch.
Wollach. House is empty and the trough is broken, The.
Wordsworth, W. Excursion, The.
Inscription for the Moss-Hut at Dove Cottage.
see also The Wanderer, *Book 1 of* The Excursion.
Wright, C. Virgo Descending.
Wylie. Prophecy.
Yeats. Ancestral Houses.
Yü Chi. What family has built a house beside the rapids here?
Zenmaro. Tanka: "Old soldier, An."

See also **Home**

Housewives
Antipater of Sidon. Lysidice, I'm anxious to find out the meaning.
Bodecker. Hurry, hurry, Mary dear.
Boland, E. Woman in Kitchen.
Dove, R. Daystar.
Gilligan. Household Dilemma.
Hallack. Divine Office of the Kitchen, The.
Halley. Housewife's Letter: To Mary.
Hutchinson, R. Suburban Wife's Song.
Jarrell. Next Day.
Mew. Farmer's Bride, The.
Pande, M. Two Women Knitting.
Pastan. Marks.

Riley, D. Affections Must Not.
Scarfe. Kitchen Poem.
Sexton. Housewife.
Risk, The.
Shuttle. Gone Is the Sleepgiver.
Unknown. Epitaph.
My Love.
Williams, W. Young Housewife, The.
Young, A. California Peninsula: El Camino Real.
Zamora, D. Loyal Housewife.

See also **Housekeeping**

Housman, Alfred Edward
Auden. A. E. Housman.
Pound, E. Mr. Housman's Message.

Hudson River, New York
Goodman, P. Lordly Hudson, The.
Lowell, R. Mouth of the Hudson, The.
Weiss, T. Egyptian Passage, An.

Hughes, Langston
Blockcolski. Langston Hughes.
Brooks, G. Langston Hughes.
Danner. Rhetoric of Langston Hughes, The.
Forbes, C. Reading Walt Whitman.
Henderson, D. Do Nothing Till You Hear from Me.
Knight, E. For Langston Hughes.
Madgett. Simple.
Randall, D. Langston Blues.

Hughes, Ted
Cope, W. Policeman's Lot, A.
Larkin, P. Limerick: "There was an old fellow of Kaber."

Huguenots
Bridges, R. Psalm: "While Northward the hot sun was sinking o'er the trees."

Human Folly
Bensley. Bloomsbury Snapshot.
Blake, W. Human Abstract, The.
Bradstreet, A. Contemplations.
Burns, R. Poor Merry-Andrew, in the neuk.
Chaucer. Lack of Steadfastness.
Coleridge, S. Ode to Tranquillity.
De Vries, P. Sacred and Profane Love, or, There's Nothing New under the Moon Either.
Ezekiel. There's only this.
Ferlinghetti, L. World is a beautiful place, The.
Hall, D. Grace, A.
Hart, L. I Wish I Were in Love Again.
Herbert, G. Justice.
Hesiod. Iron Age, The.
Horace. I often wish'd, that I had clear.
Jeffers, R. Eagle Valor, Chicken Mind.
Original Sin.
Juan Chi. In North Ward they do many strange dances.
Juvenal. Let Observation with extensive View.
Little do folks the heav'nly Powers mind.
Kerouac. Poem.
Kim, C. Aerin I.
McGough, R. Prayer to Saint Grobianus.
Muktibodh. Void inside us, The.
Munib-ur-Rahman. Tall Buildings.
Murray, L. Quality of Sprawl, The.
No Ch'ŏn-myŏng. Watching the Stars.
Ovid. Narcissus on the grassy Verdure lies.
Owen, W. Arms and the Boy.
On Seeing a Piece of Our Artillery Brought into Action.
Palladas. Think of your conception, you'll soon forget.
Parra, N. Vices of the Modern World.
Patchen. Origin of Baseball, The.
While the sun still spends his fabulous money.
Phan Bội Châu. Character.
Epitaph for My Dog.
Pindar. How *early* has young *Chromius* begun.
Prévert. Pater Noster.
Rumi. Strange Business.
Scott, W. Lucy Ashton's Song.
Shapiro, K. Fly, The.
Sophocles. Chorus sing of the doom of Thebes' royal family, The.
Chorus: "What man is he that yearneth."
Speech of Ajax.
Tản Đà. To a Scarecrow.

Verma. Pleasure Dome, The.
Warren, R. Man in the Street.

Human Race. *See* **Mankind**

Humility
Astell. Ambition.
In Emulation of Mr Cowleys Poem Call'd The Motto.
A'Zmi, K. Humiliation.
Bensley. Charity.
Bible, *O.T.* Psalm 131.
Blake, W. Clod and [*or* &] the Pebble, The.
Buddha. Unlimited Friendliness.
Bunyan. Shepherd Boy Sings [in the Valley of Humiliation], The.
Carew, T. On the Marriage of T. K. and C. C.: The Morning Stormy.
Chaucer. Franklin's Prologue, The.
Ch'iao Chi. Tune: "Sheep on Mountain Slope."
Chudleigh. Resolve, The.
Coleridge, S. Forbearance.
Curzon, D. Proverbs 6:6.
Dante Alighieri. So gentle and so virtuous she appears.
Di Piero. Near Damascus.
Emerson, R. Experience.
Fogel, A. Necessity, The.
Foss, S. House by the Side of the Road, The.
Frost, R. Demiurge's Laugh, The.
Herbert, G. Church-Lock and Key.
Humility.
Misery [*or* Miserie].
Posy [*or* Posie], The.
Sighs and Groans [*or* Grones].
Hsin Ch'i-chi. Tune: "Partridge Sky"—Written at the Po-shan Monastery.
Hubert. Joseph in Carcere.
Kipling, R. If you can keep your head when all [about you].
Recessional.
Knevet. Contrition.
Kublanovsky. He who gave weight to the wind.
Kuzmina-Karavayeva. Even in repentance there is pleasure.
Ma Chih-yüan. Tune: "Slow Chant."
Mechthild von Magdeburg. God's Absence.
Mei Yao Ch'en. Eating Shepherd's-purse.
Mitchell, A. Icarus Schmicarus.
Norris, A. Humble Heart, A.
Pasternak, B. To be famous is not in good taste.
Porter, A. Oaks and Squirrels.
Ransom, J. Amphibious Crocodile.
Robinson, E. Cliff Klingenhagen had me in to dine.
Rochester, J. Rochester Extempore.
Rossetti, C. Lowest Place, The.
Rubisova. Humility is the eye of the needle.
Stanley, T. Paraphrase Upon Part of the CXXXIX Psalm, A.
Surrey. When that repentant tears hath cleansed clear from ill.
Taylor, E. Bran, a chaff, a very barley [y]awn, A.
State, a state, oh! dungeon state indeed, A.
Taylor, J. Violet, The.
Ts'en Shen. Composed at Sunset at the Dunes of Ho-yen.
Tseng Jui. Cock's crow means profit, The.
Unknown. I love thee for thy fickleness.
To Show How Humble.
Wang Fan-chih. Grass hovel filled with wind and dust.
That fellow rides a big horse.
Wang Kuo-wei. Tune: "Sand of Silk-washing Stream."
Wilbur. Finished Man, A.
Wright, J. Out of Horace.

Hummingbirds
Corbett, W. Vermont Apollinaire.
Corman. Container, The.
Dickinson, E. Hummingbird, A.
Within my Garden, rides a Bird.
Dubie. Hummingbirds.
Eberhart, R. Vision.
Howitt, M. Hummingbird, The.

Kennedy, X. Hummingbird.
Lawrence, D. Humming-Bird.
Lewis, R. Humming Bird, The.
Littlebird. Hummingbird.
Paz. Exclamation.
Rogers, P. Hummingbird: a Seduction, The.
Tucker, M. Humming-Bird, The.

Hunchbacks

Brooks, G. Hunchback Girl: She Thinks of
Heaven.
Ibn al-Rumi. To a Hunchback.
Nicarchus of Alexandria. Diodorus the
hunchback / Went to Socles the quack.
Soyinka. Hunchback of Dugbe, The.
Thomas, D. Hunchback in the park, The.

Hundred Years War

Holub. Fly, The.
Unknown. King Henry Fifth's Conquest of
France.

Hungary

Csoori. My Masters.
We were good, good and obedient.
Cummings, E. Thanksgiving (1956).
Feinstein, E. Annus Mirabilis 1989.
Petri. Christmas 1956.
Electra.
Reed, I. Dualism.

Hunger

Angira. Manna.
Atwood. More and more frequently the edges.
Auden. Healthy Spot, A.
Binyon. Hunger.
Bishop, J. Hunger and Thirst.
Carter, M. University of Hunger.
Ceravolo. Ho Ho Ho Caribou.
Ch'en Tzu-lung. Little cart jolting and banging
through the yellow haze of dusk, The.
Ch'ien T'ao. LONG time ago, A.
Chin. Disorder, The.
Clampitt. Beethoven, Opus 111.
Coicou. Lord's Prayer, The.
Dadié. In Memoriam.
Dickinson, E. I had been hungry, all the
Years.
It would have starved a Gnat.
Drainac. My hunger is infinite and my hands
always empty.
Edwards, A. Give Me Three Grains of Corn,
Mother.
"Field." Eros.
Fyleman. Punch and Judy.
Gerstler. Ups and Downs.
Grass. Saturn.
Hadewijch. Love's Constancy.
Hernández, M. Lullaby of the Onion.
Ho Ching-ming. Ballad of the Government
Granary Clerk.
Hsü Wei. I Tried to Exchange Two Painting
for Some Grain But Failed.
Ignatow, D. Mystique.
Pleasure, The.
Ireland, W. To starve, or not to starve? that is
the question.
Keithley. From Land Logic.
Komunyakaa. Banking Potatoes.
Levertov. O Taste and See.
Levine, P. They Feed They Lion.
Li K'ai-hsien. Trip to a Mountain Village, A.
Liu E. New Year's Eve.
Livingston, M. Poor.
Lorde. Litany for Survival, A.
Woman Thing, The.
Mahadevi. When I am hungry.
McClintock, M. Hungry / without money—.
Mei Yao Ch'en. Dappled Horse, The.
Merwin, W. Bread.
Miller, A. Hungry Black Child, The.
Orban, O. Peace Pillar.
Peruncittiranar. Bard's Family, A.
Pilinszky. Frankfurt.
French Prisoner, The.
Paraphrase.
Reed, H. Château, The.
Rice, H. He Was One of Us.
Richards, L. Poor unfortunate Hottentot, A.
Rimbaud, A. Hunger.
Rothenberg, J. Hunger.

Samik. Hunger.
Schwartz, D. Heavy Bear, The.
Shen Chou. Painting of Peach Blossom
Spring, A.
Stone, R. Hunger.
Stumbrs. Married Romantic, A.
Swenson, M. Salt, The.
Swirszczynska. I Starve My Belly for a
Sublime Purpose.
Szymborska. Starvation Camp near Jaslo.
T'ang Yin. Ten days of wind and rain,
depressing darkness!
Thomas, E. Owl, The.
Todd, R. Sea Horse, The.
Toomer. Harvest Song.
Tsaloumas. Autumn Supper.
Tsung Ch'en. Song of Selling Flowers.
Vallejo. Hungry Man's Wheel, The.
Walker, A. Few Sirens, A.
Wickham. Pugilist.
Yang Shih-ch'i. Following the Rhymes of
Shao-pao Huang's Poem on Being Moved
While Visiting the Farmers.
Yu Kuang-chung. Mother, I'm hungry.

Hunt, Leigh

Dehn, P. Jenny kiss'd me when we met.
Keats. To Leigh Hunt, Esq.
Written on the Day That Mr. Leigh Hunt Left
Prison.

Hunting and Hunters

Amirthanayagam. Elephants Are in the Yard,
The.
Atwood. Dream 2: Brian the Still-Hunter.
Auden. Decoys, The.
Barnes, J. Tracking Rabbits: Night.
Beer, P. Lion Hunts.
Berryman. Winter Landscape.
Blunden. Winter: East Anglia.
Blunt, W. Old Squire, The.
St. Valentine's Day.
Brontë, A. Song.
Brontë, C. Young Man Naughty's Adventure.
"Carroll." Little Man That Had a Little Gun,
The.
Causley. I saw a jolly hunter.
Chiyojo. My hunter of dragonflies.
Clare, J. Badger ("When midnight comes a
host of dogs and men").
Mole-Catcher, The.
Clarke, C. Tortoise and Badger.
Coleridge, S. Hunting Song.
Cope, J. Rock Painting.
Cox, M. Geese.
Cummings, E. All in green went my love
riding.
Daniel, G. After a Storm, Going a Hawking.
Davidson, J. Runnable Stag, A.
Davies, S. Scene after Hunting at
Swallowfield in Berkshire, A.
Davis, J. Warru.
De la Mare. Hi! handsome hunting man.
Dickey, J. After the Night Hunt.
Springer Mountain.
Dickinson, E. Cat.
My Life Had Stood—A Loaded Gun.
Donaghy, J. Duck.
Dow, P. Duck Pond at Mini's Pasture, a
Dozen Years Later, The.
Driver. Ballad of Hunters, A.
Drummond, W. Madrigal: "This world a
hunting is."
Dunbar. A-Hunting.
Ehrhart. Hunting.
Erdrich. Jacklight.
Strange People, The.
Faiz. Once Again the Mind.
Fielding. Hunting Song.
Finkel. Hunting Song.
Follain. Black Meat.
Ford, R. Revenge of the Hunted.
Francis, R. December.
Fuller, J. Can-Can.
Garnet. Proud Nimrod first the bloody chase
began.
Gascoigne. Gascoigne's Woodmanship.
Gascoyne. Rex Mundi.
Graham, H. It was a winter's morning.

Graves, J. John Peel.
Harjo, J. Song for the Deer and Myself to
Return On.
Harper, M. Drive In, The.
Harris, R. Literary Excellence.
Hartnett. Possibility That Has Been
Overlooked Is the Future, The.
Hemans. Chamois Hunter's Love, The.
Herbert, G. Affliction (4).
Howe, J. Soul-Hunter, The.
Hughes, T. Modest Proposal, A.
Hummer, T. What Shines in Winter Burns.
Isidorus. On a Fowler.
Jarrell. Bird of Night, The.
Jonson, B. To Sir Henry Goodyere.
Kao Ch'i. Song of the Duck Hunters.
Kapilar. What She Said to Her Girl Friend.
Karpowicz. Hunting.
Kibkarjuk. Song of the Rejected Woman.
Killigrew, A. On a Picture Painted by
Herself[, Representing Two Nimphs of
Diana's].
Kinnell. Bear, The.
To Christ Our Lord.
Kumin, M. Woodchucks.
Kunitz, S. Robin Redbreast.
Kwakiutl Oral Tradition. Prayer to the Black
Bear.
Prayer to the Sockeye Salmon.
Lanier, S. Revenge of Hamish, The.
Lawrence, D. Mountain Lion.
Leonidas of Tarentum. Good hunting, rabbit-
catcher and bird-catcher.
Theromachos of Crete came to hang up.
Li K'ai-hsien. Meeting Trappers on the Road
in Heavy Snow.
Lorde. Woman Thing, The.
Lovelace, R. La Bella Bona-Roba.
Love Enthroned.
Lowbury. Huntsman, The.
Lowry, M. Salmon Drowns Eagle.
Lu Lun. Select fine arrows and call for
falcons.
Mahon. St. Eustace.
Masefield. Fox knew well, that before they
tore him, The.
Meredith, G. Young Reynard.
Miller, J. Squirrel Stand.
Mother Goose. Sam, The Sportsman.
Mozeen. Kilruddery Hunt, The.
Newcastle, M. Hunting of the Hare, The.
O'Hara, F. Hunter, The.
Orr, G. Gathering the Bones Together.
Page, P. Stories of Snow.
Petrarch. Whoso list to hunt, I know where is
a hind.
Peynetsa. Boy and the Deer, The.
Pima Oral Tradition. Datura Hunting Song.
Popa. Hunter.
Pope, A. Hunting and Fishing.
Pound, E. Return, The.
Robinson, W. Horse & Rider.
Rodgers, W. Beagles.
San Geminiano. Sonnets of the Months:
September.
Scott, W. Hunting Song.
Senghor. Midnight Elegy.
Song of the Initiate.
Senior. Birdshooting season the men.
Simms, C. Three Years in Glen Garry.
Skrzynecki. Hunting Rabbits.
Souster. Hunter, The.
Soutar. Guns, The.
Spenser. Sonnet 67: "Like a huntsman after
weary chase."
Starbird. Hound, The.
Stein, G. Valentine to Sherwood Anderson, A.
White hunter is nearly crazy, A.
Surrey. Then from the seas, the dawning gan
arise.
Tai Piao-yüan. Painting of One Hundred Wild
Geese, A.
TallMountain. Good Grease.
Thayer, W. Last Hunt, The.
Thesen. Kirk Lonegren's Home Movie Taking
Place Just North of Prince George, with
Sound.

Tu Mu. Egrets.
Unknown. Buffalo Skinners, The.
Bye, bye, baby bunting / Daddy's gone a-hunting.
Carmen Possum.
Cheerful Horn, The.
Fowls [*or* Foweles *or* Fowles] in the frith.
Hunt is up, the hunt is up, The.
Hunter's Song.
Hunting-Song.
Magic Words for Hunting Caribou.
Magic Words for Hunting Seal.
Round and round the cornfield.
Scholar and the Cat, The.
Song of the Fallen Deer.
Sun rises red amid radiant clouds, The.
There were three jovial Welshmen.
Visit from Mr. Fox, A.
Voznesensky. Hunting a hare. Our dogs are raising a racket.
Whitehead, P. Hunting Song.
Whitman, A. Saville in Trouble.
Wordsworth, W. Simon Lee [the Old Huntsman].
Worley, M. Mighty Hunter, The.
Wyatt, T. Who so list to hount I knowe where is an hynde.
Whoso list to hunt, I know where is an hind.
Zieroth. Hunters of the Deer, The.
Hurdy-Gurdies
Calverley. Lines on Hearing the Organ.
Epstein, D. Barrel Organ, The.
Fleming, E. Hurdy-Gurdy Man, The.
Noyes, A. Barrel-Organ, The.
Symons, A. Barrel-Organ, The.
Watkins, V. Hurdy-Gurdy Man in Winter.
Huron, Lake
Herschberger. Huron, The.
Hurricanes
Carew, J. Dreamtime Lives Again, The.
Crane, H. Hurricane, The.
Cruz, V. Problems With Hurricanes.
Freneau. Hurricane, The.
Unknown. Wasn't That a Mighty Storm?
See also **Storms**
Husbands
Boyle, K. Invitation in It, from American Citizen, The.
Bradstreet, A. Letter to Her Husband, Absent upon Public[k] Employment, A.
To My Dear and Loving Husband.
Browning, R. Any Wife to Any Husband.
Carey, H. Maid's Husband, The.
Chudleigh. Unhappy they, who by their duty led.
DeFrees. Letter to an Absent Son.
Donne. Jealosie.
Egerton, S. Emulation, The.
"Eliza." To My Husband.
Fumiko. Tanka: "Boxes of sleeping pills."
Tanka: "Eyes, The."
Tanka: "Yellow bus, The."
Gay, J. *et al.* Mary Gulliver to Capt. Lemuel Gulliver.
Graves, R. Slice of Wedding Cake, A.
Haynes, C. Any Wife or Husband.
Heard, J. My Husband's Birthday.
Herrick. Upon Blanche.
Hiranandani. Husband.
Homer. Ulysses Reunited with Penelope.
King, H. Dream Maiden, A.
Lee, L. Gift, The.
Lewis, C. Ballade of Dead Gentlemen.
Lowell, R. To Speak of Woe That Is in Marriage.
Madan. To Lysander.
McGinley. 5:32, The.
Mesens. Arid Husband, The.
Millay, E. Sonnet 17.
Nash, O. Perfect Husband, The.
Word to Husbands, A.
Nesbit, E. Husband of To-Day, The.
Ouloguem. Minotaur Next Door, The.
Pape. Minotaur Next Door, The.
Peyanar. Embracing the young mother from behind.
Philips, K. To My Antenor, March 16, 1661/2.

Rabéarivelo. Wife is like a blade of grass, A.
Rowe, E. Upon the Death of Her Husband.
Rubin, L. Brother-in-Law, The.
Sawyer, A. Lines, / Written on Seeing My Husband's Picture, painted when he was young: "Those are the features, those the smiles."
Sexton. And One for My Dame.
Shaw, A. Crepuscule.
Stevenson, R. So live, so love, so use that fragile hour.
Thomas, E. New Litany, Occasioned by an Invitation to a Wedding, A.
Thompson, P. Husband's Return, The.
Unknown. Henpecked Husband, A.
Villon. Ballad Written for a Bridegroom.
Wallis, H. To Mrs.———, on the Death of Her Husband.
West, J. Married, poor soul! your empire's over.
Winchilsea. Letter to Daphnis, A.
Wright, M. Address to Her Husband.
Hutchinson, Anne
Stanford, A. Brother Symmes conversed with her on the ship.
Hyacinths
Eliot, T. Song for Simeon, A.
Glück, L. Hyacinth.
Prince, F. Babiaantje, The.
Sadi. Hyacinths to Feed Thy Soul.
Sappho. One Girl.
Hyde, Douglas
Clarke, A. Burial of An Irish President.
Hyenas
Kipling, R. Hyænas [*or* Hyenas], The.
Tahmisic. Red Moon High in the Sky.
Unknown. Hyena.
Hyena Addressing Her Young Ones, The.
Hymns
Crashaw. Apologie for the Precedent Hymnes on Tereas, An.
In the Glorious Epiphanie of Our [*or* Ovr] Lord God[, A Hymn. Svng as by the Three Kings].
Davies, S. To him with trumpets and with flutes.
Lucie-Smith. Hymn Tunes, The.
Scott, W. Rebecca's Hymn.
Thomson, J. Hymn on the Seasons, A.
Unknown. And you (O *Delian* Virgins) doe me grace.
Hymn to the Earth.
Limerick.
There Ceres, distant from the powers divine.
Hypnosis and Hypnotists
Joron, A. Shade of a Grammarian.
Hypocrisy and Hypocrites
Blake, W. On Hayley.
On Sir Joshua Reynolds.
Bly, R. Johnson's Cabinet Watched by Ants.
Brecht, B. Peachum's Morning Hymn.
Browning, E. Man's Requirements, A.
Browning, R. Soliloquy of the Spanish Cloister.
Burns, R. Address to the Unco Guid, or the Rigidly Righteous.
Holy Willie's Prayer.
Butler, S. For his religion it was fit.
Hypocrisy will serve as well.
Byron, G. Byron on Southey.
"Carroll." Lobster, The.
Clough. Latest Decalogue, The.
Coleridge, S. Spots in the Sun.
Congreve. Hue and Cry after Fair Amoret, A.
Connolly, C. To Osbert Sitwell.
Creeley. Wait for Me.
Cummings, E. Come,gaze with me upon this dome.
Next to of course god america i.
Season 'tis,my lovely lambs, The.
DeBary. Tomorrow I will haul down the flag of hypocrisy.
Dennis, C. Miracle, The.
Dickinson, E. Mine—by the Right of the White Election!
Euripides. Of all things which are living and can form a judgment.

Graves, R. Sick Love.
Harington. Groome of the Chambers religion in King Henry the eights time, A.
Harper, F. Double Standard, A.
Hemingway. Chapter Heading.
Hughes, L. American Heartbreak.
Hutchinson, P. Look, No Hands.
Jonson, B. On Don Surly.
On the Town's Honest Man.
Kipling, R. Tommy.
Knight, E. On Watching Politicians Perform at Martin Luther King's Funeral.
Lawrence, D. Commandments.
Retort to Jesus.
Levertov. Hypocrite women, how seldom we speak.
Lindsay, V. At Mass.
Why I Voted the Socialist Ticket.
Lucianus. Beard-wagging stick-waving beggarman Cynic, A.
MacLeish. Hypocrite Auteur.
Mahsati. Better to live as a rogue and a bum.
Mapanje. Cheerful Girls at Smiller's Bar, The.
Meredith, G. At dinner, she is hostess, I am host.
It is no vulgar nature I have wived.
Milosz, C. Child of Europe.
Montagu, L. Epistle from Mrs. Yonge to Her Husband.
Mudrooroo. Peaches and Cream.
Pau-Llosa. Ganaderia.
Piercy. Peaceable Kingdom, The.
Pope, A. Epigram in a Maid of Honour's Prayer-Book.
Sporus.
Praed. Chancery Morals.
Robinson, M. Stanzas: "In this vain, busy world, where the good and the gay."
Shapiro, K. Drug Store.
Sidney, P. Sonnet 31: "With how sad steps, O Moon, thus climb'st the skies!"
Swinburne. Higher Pantheism in a Nutshell, The.
Tennyson, A. Character, A.
Unknown. Hyena.
"May Grace be with you all" said the bishop.
Whittier. Clerical Oppressors.
Woddis. Ethics for Everyman.
Yeats. On Hearing That the Students of Our New University Have Joined the Agitation against Immoral Literature.
Zavalnyuk. Earlobe.

I

Ibn Ezra, Moses
Halevi. On Parting with Moses ibn Ezra.
Ibsen, Henrik
Bentley, E. "Susaddah!" exclaimed Ibsen.
Dubie. Fox Who Watched for the Midnight Sun, The.
Ibycus
Lazarus, E. Cranes of Ibycus, The.
Icarus
Abse. Brueghel in Naples.
Auden. Musée des Beaux Arts.
Benét, S. Winged Man.
Bottrall. Icarus.
Field, E. Icarus.
Iremonger. Icarus.
Langland, J. Fall of Icarus: Brueghel.
Mitchell, A. Icarus Schmicarus.
Nowlan. I, Icarus.
Ovid. Daedalus.
Rukeyser, M. Waiting for Icarus.
Sexton. To a Friend Whose Work Has Come to Triumph.
Simpson, L. Goodnight, The.
Spender, S. Icarus.
Stevenson, A. Icarus in November.
Stickney, T. On Rodin's "L'Illusion, Sœur d'Icare."
Williams, W. Landscape with the Fall of Icarus.
Ice
De la Mare. Ice.
Dickey, W. Arrival of the Titanic, The.

"Field." Dance of Death, A.
To the Winter Aphrodite.
Fletcher, J. Skaters, The.
Fontanella. Image of the frozen lake, The.
Frost, R. Fire and Ice.
Harper, M. Drive In, The.
Klein, A. Break-up, The.
Livesay, D. Uninvited, The.
Longley, M. Freeze-up annexes the sea even, The.
MacCaig. Sleet.
Monk, M. Fire Us with Ice, Burn Us with Snow.
Nemerov. Icehouse in Summer, The.
Ridler. Mile from Eden, A.
Roditi. Aurora Borealis.
Spenser. Sonnet 30: "My love is like to ice, and I to fire."
Thoreau. When Winter fringes every bough.
Wilbur. Stop.

Ice Cream
Kaplinski, J. My wife and children were waiting for ice cream.
Laing, A. Grace for Ice-Cream, A.
Stevens, W. Emperor of Ice-Cream, The.

Ice Skating and Ice Skaters. *See* **Skating and Skaters**

Icebergs
Bishop, E. Imaginary Iceberg, The.
Cowper, W. On the Ice Islands Seen Floating in the German Ocean.
Hardy, T. Convergence of the Twain, The.
Melville, H. Berg, The.

Iceland
Auden. Journey to Iceland.
Hajnal. After all, what have I become?

Icicles
Frost, R. Beyond Words.
Roberson. Poor Houses, The.

Idaho (state)
Kizer, C. Most people from Idaho are crazed rednecks.
Unknown. Way Out in Idaho.

Idealism and Idealists
Collins, M. If life were never bitter.
"Elagin." I know that a gangster will not murder me.
Herrick. No Loathsomnesse in Love.
Hughes, L. As I Grew Older.
Lawrence, D. Mess of Love, The.
Ransom, J. Address to the Scholars of New England.
Unknown. I will give my love an apple without e'er a core.
Wyatt, T. *In aeternum* I was once determed.

Identity Crisis
Arnold, M. Self-Dependence.
Baraka. Agony, An. As Now.
Bona. Amazone.
Bronk. I Thought It Was Harry.
Dame. On the road to Damascus, Maryland.
Derricotte. Struggle, The.
Dickinson, E. I'm Nobody! Who are you?
Francis, R. Identity.
Galguera. Alloy.
Hagedorn, J. Filipino Boogie.
Hall, J. Maybe Dats Your Pwoblem Too.
Hayden, R. Names.
Hogan, L. Truth Is, The.
Honig, E. Being Somebody.
Hughes, L. Theme for English B.
Hughes, T. Wodwo.
Jarrell. Woman at the Washington Zoo, The.
Jiménez, J. I am not I.
Kaufman, B. I, Too, Know What I Am Not.
Kumin, M. After Love.
Libbey. Juana Bautista Lucero, Circa 1926, to Her Photographer.
MacDonald, C. Inheritance.
Madgett. Exits and Entrances.
McElroy, C. Queen of the Ebony Isles.
Mirikitani. Doreen had a round face.
Myers, J. Not Thinking of Himself.
Nguyễn Hữu Chu. Neither Fish Nor Fowl.
Ojibway Oral Tradition. Calling-One's-Own.
Olson, C. In cold hell, in thicket, how.

Peacock, M. Spell, The.
Rilke. Lovers, gratified in each other, I am asking *you.*
Rivard. Change My Evil Ways.
Rodgers, C. Group Therapy.
St. John, P. We Are Going to Be Here Now.
Selman, R. Minds I admired, the strong-bodied, The.
Spires. Interrogations of the Sparrow.
Stafford, W. First Grade.
Stephens, J. Twins, The.
Stone, R. My Son.
Trussell. This Woman.
Waldman, A. Complaynt.
Wong, N. When I Was Growing Up.
Where is my country?

Idleness
Emerson, R. Apology, The.
Keats. Ode on Indolence.
McDonald, D. Breakfast in Bed (Influenza in War-time).
Po Chü-i. After Collecting the Autumn Taxes.
Sidney, P. Sonnet 18: "With what sharp checks I in myself am shent."
Silverstein, S. Jimmy Jet and His TV Set.
Simic. Against Whatever It Is That's Encroaching.
Spender, S. Unemployed.
Tu Fu. On the Spur of the Moment.
Unknown. As for me, I delight in the everyday Way.
Watts, I. Sluggard, The.
Welch, L. This Book is for Magda.
Whalen. Chanson d'Outre Tombe.

See also **Sloth**

Idolatry
Bible, *O.T.* Psalm 115.
Bunin. Stone Idol, The.
Greville, F. Manicheans did no idols make, The.
Sonnet: "Three things there be in mans opinion dear[e]."
Hollo. Italics.
Kipling, R. Evarra and His Gods.
Lindsay, V. To a Golden-Haired Girl in a Louisiana Town.
MacNeice. Leaving Barra.
Milton. With these came they who, from the bord'ring flood.
Symons, A. Javanese Dancers.
Unknown. Worship of Cromm Cruaich, The.
Wigglesworth. Thus everyone before the throne.

Ignorance
Aiken, C. Annihilation.
Beckett, S. Gnome.
Brooks, G. "Pygmies Are Pygmies Still, Though Percht on Alps."
Bunting. To Violet [with Prewar Poems].
Chinn. Skin Color from the Sun.
Cornford, F. To a Fat Lady Seen from the Train.
Cowper, W. Lines Written upon a Window-Shutter at Weston.
Cummings, E. All ignorance toboggans into know.
Old age sticks / up Keep.
Derricotte. Blackbottom.
Donne. Soules Ignorance in This Life and Knowledge in the Next, The.
Goedicke. Without Looking.
Heffernan, M. Message, The.
Hewitt, J. From the Tibetan.
Hitchcock. Song of Expectancy.
Hoffenstein. You hire a cook, but she can't cook yet.
Holmes, J. Against the Literal.
Hughes, T. Childish Prank, A.
Joseph, J. Back to Base.
Komunyakaa. Salt.
Machi. Tanka: "On a day."
Madgett. Images.
Ransom, J. Man without Sense of Direction.
Rossetti, C. Sketch, A.
Sackville-West. Extract from Solitude.
Stafford, W. Both Ways.

Stevens, W. Sense of the Sleight-of-Hand Man, The.
Weöres. To the Spirits of Shakespeare and Velázquez.

Illegitimacy
Allingham. Girl's Lamentation, The.
Breton, N. Cradle Song: "Come, little babe."
Burns, R. Poet's Welcome to His Love-Begotten Daughter [the First Instance that Entitled Him to the Venerable Appellation of Father], A.
Rantin Laddie, The.
Hughes, L. Mulatto.
Leigh, H. Natural Child, The.
Marson. Brown Baby Blues.
Masters, E. Elsa Wertman.
Sexton. Unknown Girl in the Maternity Ward.
Smith, S. Valuable.
Unknown. Limerick.

Illinois (state)
Bly, R. Three Kinds of Pleasures.
Brooks, G. Lovers of the Poor, The.
Kinnell. First Song.
Schmitz. Making Chicago.
Unknown. El-a-noy.

Illiteracy
Belloc. Sarah Byng Who Could Not Read and Was Tossed into a Thorny Hedge by a Bull. A Cautionary Tale.
Jacinto, A. Letter from a Contract Worker.
Meredith, W. Illiterate, The.
Mora. Señora X No More.
Murphy, R. Reading Lesson, The.

Illness
Akhmadulina. Fever.
Baillie, J. Child to His Sick Grandfather, A.
Bartlett, E. 999 Call.
Belloc. Henry King, Who Chewed Bits of String, and Was Early Cut Off in Dreadful Agonies.
Blackmur. Elegy for Five, An.
Blake, W. Sick Rose, The.
Bradstreet, A. Deliverance from a Fit of Fainting.
For Deliverance from a Fever.
Breytenbach. Menace of the Sick.
Broumas, O. Touched.
Browning, R. Confessions.
Burns, R. Duncan Gray cam here to woo.
Byron, G. Lines on Hearing That Lady Byron Was Ill.
Carroll, J. Paregoric Babies.
Cassells. Sung From A Hospice.
Cave. Ah! why from me art thou for ever flown.
Chimombo. Derailment: A Delirium.
Ch'in Chia. Ch'in Chia's Wife's Reply.
Chinnov. Sometimes, you give way to sickness.
Coleman, W. Aunt Jessie.
Cooper, J. Infusion Room, The.
Cornford, F. Watch, The.
Cowper, M. World Not Our Rest, The.
Cowper, W. To Mary.
Daniel, S. Love.
Daryush. Invalid Dawn.
Off Duty.
Disch. Convalescing in London.
Donne. Canonization, The.
Hymn[e] to God My God, In My Sickness[e].
Oh my black[e] soul[e]! now thou art summoned.
Dunn, D. France.
Ezekiel. Family.
Fatchen. Oh Erica, Not Again!
"Field." Almoner, An.
Picture, A.
Fitzgerald, R. Entreaty.
Garrett, G. In the Hospital.
Gilbert, S. Nightmare, [A *or* The].
Glück, L. Descending Figure.
Godley, E. Ninety-Nine.
Goedicke. In the Waiting Room.
Graves, R. Symptoms Of Love.
Gray, J. Night Nurse Goes Her Round, The.
Green, M. From The Spleen.

Gunn, T. Man With Night Sweats, The.
 Missing, The.
Gurney, I. Farewell.
Harata Tangikuku. Invalid's Song.
Harteis. Star Trek III.
Hayden, R. Broken Dark, The.
Hayley. To Mr. William Long, On His
 Recovery from a Dangerous Illness, 1785.
Head, G. Night Sweats.
Hemans. Thoughts During Sickness: II.
 Sickness Like Night.
Herford. There was a young lady of
 Twickenham.
Herrick. To Music, to Becalm a Sweet-sick
 Youth.
Hewitt, J. Scar, The.
Hikmet. Angina Pectoris.
Holtby, M. Answer to a Kind Enquiry.
Holtby, W. For the Ghost of Elinor Wylie.
Hopkins, G. Felix Randal the farrier,° O is he
 dead then? my duty / all ended.
Hove. Other Syllabus, The.
Howard, R. Far Cry after a Close Call, A.
 1915: A Pre-Raphaelite Ending, London.
Hsiang Ssu. Ailing Japanese Monk, The.
Hsü Chung-hsing. Who would have thought
 that a disease of the ordinary world.
Hsü Wei. On the Road Through the Wu-i
 Mountains—Making Fun of Chia-tse for
 Falling Off His Horse.
Hughes, L. Madam and the Wrong Visitor.
Hunt, L. Rondeau.
Ishikawa Takuboku. Tanka: "Forgetting."
 Tanka: "Sadly."
Jarrell. Sick Child, A.
Jewsbury. Verses: "I am monarch of troubles
 a host."
Jonson, B. To Sickness.
Jortin. Epitaph of Felis, The.
Kao Ch'i. Ballad of the Neighborhood
 Shaman.
Kavanagh, P. Hospital, The.
Kendrick, D. Inpatient.
Kinsella, J. Sick Woman.
Kinsella, T. Tear.
Kinzie. Orchard dying, The.
Kitahara Hakushū. Tanka: "Ailing child, An."
 Tanka: "During a fit."
La Fontaine. Thyrsis And Amaranta.
Lawrence, D. Healing.
Li K'ai-hsien. On My Birthday—Sick.
Lowell, R. My Last Afternoon with Uncle
 Devereux Winslow.
Ly Ngoc Kieu. Birth, old age.
"MacDiarmid." Two Parents, The.
Machado Ruiz. Look, our Spaniard's yawning.
Mackenzie, K. Sick Men Sleeping.
Mai Thảo. Coaxing My Illness.
Marvell. Dialogue between the Soul and [the]
 Body, A.
Masaoka Shiki. Tanka: "Makes me writhe."
 Tanka: "On a young pine."
 Upon receiving potted peonies for a gift.
Maura. Each Day.
McAuley, J. Convalescence.
McCarriston. Healing the Mare.
McClure, M. Rant Block.
McManus, J. Spike Logic.
McOrlan. Horse butcher, The.
McPherson, S. Sisters.
Merrill, J. Country of a Thousand Years of
 Peace, The.
Metcalfe. Visit the Sick.
Miller, V. Bout with Burning.
Moritz. Some Lines on My Mother's Illness.
Nash, O. Notes for the Chart in 306.
 Oh to Be Odd!
Nashe. Litany in Time of Plague, A.
Ngân Giang. Getting Well.
Ni Tsan. Inscribed on a Painting by Myself.
Olds, S. Dead Body Itself, The.
 Pull, The.
Olson, C. Librarian, The.
Orampokiyar. What Her Girl Friend Said to
 the foster-mother ("If you think, mother").
Ormsby, F. Day in August, A.

Orpingalik. In a Time of Sickness.
Ovid. To his Wife at Rome, when he was
 sick.
Paulin. Anastasia McLaughlin.
Pien Kung. First Day of Spring, The.
 New Year's Day—Following the Rhymes of
 Inspector Luan-chiang.
Plath. Among the Narcissi.
 Fever 103°.
 Stones, The.
Po Chü-i. Being Visited by a Friend During
 Illness.
 Illness.
 Illness and idleness give me much leisure.
 Last Poem.
 On Being Sixty.
 Sick Leave.
 Since I lay ill, how long has passed?
 To a Portrait Painter who Desired Him to Sit.
Praed. To Helen.
Purdy, A. Poem: "You are ill and so I lead
 you away."
Ransom, J. Conrad in Twilight.
Reader. When Paul Bunyan was ill we sent.
Rich, A. Final Notations.
Rickel. Night Sweats 2.
Rimbaud, A. Girls Looking for Lice.
Robinson, E. Mortar.
Roethke. Infirmity.
Rogers, S. Written in a Sick Chamber.
Rukeyser, M. George Robinson: Blues.
Scott, D. Apocalypse Dub.
Scovell. Poor Mother, The.
Shapcott, T. Post Operative.
Shen Chou. Paying a Sick-call to Yao Ts'un-
 tao in the Rain.
Sissman. Bruisingly cradled in a Harvard
 chair.
Snodgrass, W. Flat One, A.
Solomon ibn Gabirol. His Illness.
Sophocles. What is God singing in his
 profound.
Speer. Mama Rosanna's Last Bead-Clack.
Spivack, K. Judgment, The.
Stevenson, R. Land of Counterpane, The.
Stow. Calenture, The.
Swift, J. In Sickness.
 To Stella.
Swirszczynska. Terminally Ill.
 Visit, A.
Symons, A. Nerves.
T'ang Yin. Galloping around, north and south.
Tate, A. Mother and Son.
Teasdale. Open Windows.
Tennyson, A. Song: "Spirit haunts the year's
 last hours, A."
Thomas, E. Nine times the sun his yearly
 course had run.
Tu Fu. Visitors.
Unknown. Doctor Bell fell down the well.
 Young Lady of Twickenham, The.
Vallejo. Have You Anything to Say in Your
 Defense?
Van Duyn. Letters from a Father.
Villanueva, A. To Jesus Villanueva, with
 Love.
Voigt. Year's End.
Walker, A. Medicine.
Wallis, H. To a Sick Friend.
Wang Shih-chieng. Lamenting for My Wife.
Wen Cheng-ming. I remove my court gown
 and part from the Emperor's precincts.
 Written While Sick.
Whitman, W. Evening Lull, An.
Whitney, I. Now when thy folke are fed and
 clad.
Williams, C. Helen.
Williams, W. Raper from Passenack, The.
Winchilsea. Spleen, The.
Wojahn. White Lanterns.
Wordsworth, D. Thoughts on my sick-bed.
 When shall I tread your garden path.
Wordsworth, W. Idiot Boy, The.
Wotton, S. Hymn to My God in a Night of
 My Late Sickness[e], A.
Wright, J. Tableau.
Wu Chia-chi. Woman Née Wu, The.

Yang Chi. After my illness, so hard to be a
 traveler.
 Poem Making Fun of Chi-ti for His Eye
 Illness, A.
Yang Shih-ch'i. After the rain, the vegetables
 from your garden.
Yüan Hung-tao. On Receiving My Letter of
 Termination.
Yün Shou-p'ing. Facing you, on the wall,
 across from your bed.

Illusion

Ashbery. Forties Flick.
 Illustration.
Boker. My darling's features, painted by the
 light.
Carew, T. To T. H., a Lady Resembling My
 Mistress.
Crane, S. I SAW A MAN PURSUING THE
 HORIZON;.
Cullen, C. Only the Polished Skeleton.
Dickinson, E. I many times thought Peace had
 come.
 I met a King this afternoon!
Dunbar, P. We wear the mask that grins and
 lies.
Dunn, S. Happiness.
Emerson, R. Maia.
Guest, B. Emphasis Falls on Reality, An.
Hall, J. Reel World, The.
Jarman, M. Black Riviera, The.
Johnson, G. Lost Illusions.
Keats. Modern Love.
Koch, K. One Train May Hide Another.
Kunitz, S. Illumination, The.
Laughlin, J. Inn at Kirchstetten, The.
Lehman. Moment of Truth, The.
Leland, C. Ballad: "Der noble Ritter Hugo."
Levine, P. Old Testament, The.
Mandelstam. I'll tell you bluntly.
Martynov. Seashore, The.
Okudzhava. Everything here is curtained in
 darkness.
Rich, A. Newsreel.
Slessor. Choker's Lane.
Stafford, W. Bi-Focal.
Whitman, W. Are you the new person drawn
 toward me?
 Eidolons.
 Of the terrible doubt of appearances.
Wyatt, T. Ye old mule, that thin[c]k your self
 so fair [*or* fayre].
Zeidner. Transvestite.
Zukofsky, L. Lines of this new song are
 nothing, The.

Imagination

Ai. Man with the Saxophone, The.
Akenside. Creative Process, The.
Ammons. Corsons Inlet.
 He Held Radical Light.
 Laser.
 Triphammer Bridge.
Baudelaire. Exotic Scent.
Baxter, J. Spring-heeled Jack.
Bishop, E. Little Exercise.
 Sleeping on the Ceiling.
Blackmore, S. In the wide womb of
 possibility.
Brontë, E. Aye, there it is! It wakes to-night.
 Little while, a little while, A.
 O thy bright eyes must answer now.
 When weary with the long day's care.
Brooks, G. Anniad, The.
Browning, R. By the Fire-Side.
Brownstein. Paris Visitation.
 War.
Burns, R. Mary Morison.
Calverley. In the gloaming to be roaming[,
 where the crested waves are foaming].
Carr, M. Castle in the Fire, The.
"Carroll." Mad Gardener's Song, The.
Ceravolo. Spring in This World of Poor
 Mutts.
Char. Poet, conserver of the infinite faces of
 the living, The.
Coulette. Attic, The.
Creeley. Again.

Wicker Basket, A.
Wife, The.
Crsnaru. Lions of Babylon, The.
Cummings, E. No man,if men are gods;but if gods must.
Dacre, C. Power of Love, The.
Davidson, J. Imagination.
Davies, W. Mind's Liberty, The.
Day, J. Moving Object.
Dickinson, E. I cannot dance upon my Toes.
I never saw a Moor.
Donne. Sapho To Philaenis.
Song: "Go and catch a falling star."
Dorfman, A. Vocabulary.
Dove, R. Banneker.
Geometry.
Driscoll, L. Hold Fast Your Dreams.
Duncan, R. Often I Am Permitted to Return to a Meadow.
Durcan. Backside to the Wind.
Elenkov. Ten Girls.
Eliot, T. La Figlia Che Piange.
Finney, E. Our Solar System.
Freneau. Power of Fancy, The.
Galindo. Short Story, A.
Giovanni. Poem For My Nephew.
Gogarty. To a Friend.
Graves, R. Death Room, The.
Warning to Children.
Greig, A. In the Tool-shed.
Guest, B. Wild gardens overlooked by night lights. Parking.
Hacker, M. Days of 1992.
Hass, R. Heroic Simile.
Hernández, M. Tomb of the Imagination.
Herrick. Upon Julia's Clothes.
Hewitt, J. Substance and Shadow.
Hill, G. Imaginative Life, The.
Holub. Boy's Head, A.
Fairy Tale.
Vanishing Lung Syndrome.
Howe, S. In its first dumb form.
Hutchinson, P. Amhrán na mBréag.
James, D. Love of Water Faucets, The.
Jarrell. Cinderella.
Girl in a Library, A.
Sick Child, A.
Johnstone, R. Robot Camera.
Keats. Ode on a Grecian Urn.
Kinnell. When one has lived a long time alone.
Komunyakaa. Smokehouse, The.
Lasker-Schüler. George Grosz.
Lazarus, E. City Visions.
Lee, D. Billy Batter.
Levchev. Carmen, or the Made-Up Girl.
Levertov. In Mind.
Lindsay, V. When the Mississippi Flowed in Indiana.
Lodge, T. Minde through thee divines on endlesse things, The.
Longfellow, H. Children's Hour, The.
Lorde. Summer Oracle.
Lowell, R. Epilogue: "Those blessèd structures, plot and rhyme."
Lux. Solo Native.
MacCaig. Things in Each Other.
"MacDiarmid." Harry Semen.
Manger. Rachel Goes to the Well for Water ("Rachel stands by the mirror and plaits").
Maran. "Tropicals."
Markham, E. After Reading Shakspere.
McDonald, P. Christmas.
Pleasures of the Imagination.
Mearns. Antigonish.
Mehrotra. Roys, The.
Millay, E. From a Very Little Sphinx.
Mitsui. Photograph of a Child, Japanese-American Evacuation, Bainbridge Island, Washington, March 30, 1942.
Morse, B. Day on the Planet, A.
Moss, H. Underwood.
Muir, E. Childhood.
Muske. Painter's Daughter, The.
Newcastle, M. Discourse of Melancholy, A.
Imagination.
Nicholls, J. Space-Shuttle.

Nims, B. On a Cold Autumn Day.
Oldham, J. One night, as I was pondering of late.
Oppen. From Virgil.
Orlovsky. Dick Tracy's yellow Hat and Blacksuit.
Otalantaiyar. What He Said in the Desert.
Owen, G. Make Believe.
Shed in Space.
Paz. Stanzas for an Imaginary Garden.
Perelman. Let's Say.
Plath. Most Beds are Beds.
Porter, P. Annotations of Auschwitz.
Rabéarivelo. Reading.
You built yourself a tower in the wind.
Rakosi. Unswerving Marine.
Rankin, T. Fifteen.
Two Lovers on Bridge in Winter.
Ravikovitch. Time Caught in a Net.
Ray, H. Fancy and Imagination.
Richards, L. After a Visit to the Natural History Museum.
Rilke. As once the winged energy of delight.
Robinson, E. Miniver Cheevy, child of scorn.
Rokeah. Beyond Imagination.
Rossetti, C. Somewhere or other there must surely be.
Rózewicz. Transformations.
Rutsala. Late at Night.
Samio. Tanka: "For a moment."
Schultz, P. My Guardian Angel Stein.
Schuyler, J. Greetings from the Chateau.
Scriven, R. Marrog, The.
Shakespeare, W. Song: "Tell me where is fancy [or Fancie] bred."
Silverstein, S. One Inch Tall.
Rock 'N' Roll Band.
Simpson, L. My father in the night commanding No.
Smith, S. Fairy Story.
My Hat.
Our Bog is dood, our Bog is dood.
So Chong-Ju. Untitled.
Sokolov. Everything as in a good old-fashioned novel.
Sorrentino. Classic Case, A.
Sosnora. Do you envy, my comrades-in-arms.
Stafford, W. Allegiances.
Stanton, M. Biography.
Childhood.
Stevens, W. Final Soliloquy of the Interior Paramour.
Mrs. Alfred Uruguay.
Plain Sense of Things, The.
Puella Parvula.
Snow Man, The.
To the One of Fictive Music.
Stevenson, R. Armies in the Fire.
Block City.
Dumb Soldier, The.
Good Play, A.
Land of Counterpane, The.
Land of Nod, The.
Land of Story-Books, The.
My Bed Is a Boat.
Pirate Story.
Unseen Playmate, The.
Stone, R. Secondhand Coat.
Suckling, J. Upon My Lady Carlisle's [or Carlile's] Walking in Hampton Court Garden.
Swenson, M. Centaur, The.
Szymborska. View with a Grain of Sand.
T'ang Yin. Inscribed on a Painting of Bamboo.
Thomas, D. Turning of the Year, The.
Thoreau. On fields oer which the reaper's hand has passed.
They who prepare my evening meal below.
Timrod. I know not why, but all this weary day.
Tu Mu. Caught in a storm outside Cloud Gate Abbey.
Milky in the spring grotto stone fattens, sprouts goose-quills.
Tuckerman, F. His heart was in his garden; but his brain.
Turner, A. *Meditation Upon* Ought.

Turner, W. Romance.
Talking with Soldiers.
Unknown. If all the world were [or was] paper.
Mr Nobody.
Vogelsang. Nose, the Grand Canyon, and the Sixties, The.
Wang Shih-chieng. What Strikes My Eye.
Warton, J. O warm, enthusiastic maid.
Wheatley, P. On Imagination.
Whitman, W. Glimpse through an interstice caught, A.
Grass.
Whittemore, R. Party, The.
Wieners. Glimpse, A.
Wilbur. In the Elegy Season.
Walking to Sleep.
Williams, W. There is neither beginning nor end to the imagination.
Wise, W. When I grow up.
Wollach. Sebastian.
Wordsworth, W. Lucy.
Yarrow Visited [September, 1814].
Woroszylski. Franz Kafka (I).
Yau. Radiant Silhouette IV.
Yeats. Those Images.
Yukitsuna. Tanka: "Beyond doubt."
Tanka: "Writing a series."
Zukofsky, L. Lines of this new song are nothing, The.

Imayavarampan Netunceralatan
Kumattur Kannanar. Where the Lilies Were in Flower.

Immigration and Immigrants
Adcock, F. Immigrant
Atwood. Disembarking at Quebec.
Baca. Immigrants in Our Own Land.
Capone. In Answer to Their Questions.
Chin. First Lessons.
Portrait of the Self as Nation, 1990–1991, A.
Clements, A. Elegy.
Dabydeen, C. Dubious Foreigner.
Patriot.
Dabydeen, D. Catching Crabs.
D'Aguiar. Letter from Mama Dot.
Divakaruni. Yuba City School.
Djanikian. How I Learned English.
Dobler. 1920 Photo.
Espada. Thirty years ago.
Fenyves. Exile.
Ferlinghetti, L. Poet's eye obscenely seeing, The.
Ferrarelli. Emigrant/Immigrant ("From the people").
Emigrant/Immigrant ("Slight accent, A").
Field, E. Both My Grandmothers ("Both my grandmas came from far away").
Freneau. On the Emigration to America [and Peopling the Western Country].
Galguera. Second Childhood.
Geddes, G. Inheritors, The.
Gilbert, S. Mafioso.
Ginsberg, A. IV.
Gioseffi. Bicentennial Anti-Poem for Italian-American Women.
Gotera. Madarika.
Hamod, S. Dying with the Wrong Name.
Hernandez, D. Welcome.
Hewitt, J. Once alien here my fathers built their house.
Ignatow, D. Europe and America.
Jarrell. For an Emigrant.
Kageyama, C. Mama.
Karp. Still-Life in the Coat Factory Office.
Kaufman, S. Nechama.
Keane, E. Soufrière.
Larkin, M. Immigrant Daughter's Song.
Lazarus, E. Currents.
In Exile.
New Colossus, The.
Lee, L. Cleaving, The.
Furious Versions.
MacLeish. Burying Ground by the Ties.
Mar, L. My Mother, Who Came from China, Where She Never Saw Snow.
McCarthy, E. Right of Way.
McCarthy, T. November in Boston.

Melville, P.　Stonebridge Park Estate.
Merwin, W.　Fields, The.
Mitsui.　Katori Maru, October 1920.
Mora.　Immigrants.
　La Migra.
Nichols, G.　Wherever I Hang.
Ochester.　Relatives, The.
Oresick.　Passion and Woe in Marriage: A
　Ukrainian Love Story, The.
Papaleo.　American Dream: First Report.
Pavic.　Great Serbian Migration 1690.
Porter, P.　Last of England, The.
Prunty.　To be Sung on the Fourth of July.
Rich, A.　Prospective Immigrants Please Note.
Rose, P.　Wind Debates Asian Immigration,
　The.
Schultz, P.　For My Father.
　My Guardian Angel Stein.
Seiler.　Digging in the Streets of Gold.
Shapiro, K.　My grandmother moves to my
　mind in context of sorrow.
Soto.　Mexicans Begin Jogging.
Suknaski.　Chinese Camp, Kamloops (circa
　1883).
Tru'o'ng Anh Thuy.　First Day of School, The.
Unknown.　Mid-West, The.
　Welcome over the Door of an Old Inn.
Uyematsu.　Near Roscoe and Coldwater.
　Same Month They Bombed Cambodia, The.
Vando.　New York City Mira Mira Blues.
Veiga.　New Refugee, A.
Villanueva, A.　To Jesus Villanueva, with
　Love.
Wilbur.　Speech for the Repeal of the
　McCarran Act.
Yamanaka.　Yarn Wig.

Immortality
"Ada."　Oh, when this earthly tenement.
"Æ."　Immortality.
Amichai.　We Will Live Forever.
Arnold, M.　Shakespeare.
Ashbery.　How much longer will I be able to
　inhabit the divine sepulcher.
Atwood.　They Eat Out.
Bible, *N.T.*　Christ's Promise.
　End To Tears, An.
　Last Day, The.
Bly, R.　Poem in Three Parts.
Bozhilov.　Eternity.
Bridges, R.　Emily Brontë: Du hast
　Diamanten.
Catullus.　Carmen 40.
Chao Meng-fu.　Inscribed on a Wall Painting
　of Assembled Immortals.
Clare, J.　Invite to Eternity, An.
Cowley, A.　Muse, The.
Cummings, E.　So shy shy shy(and with a).
Custance.　Statues.
Daniel, S.　34.
　46.
Dickinson, E.　Because I could not stop for
　Death.
　It is an honorable Thought.
　Only News I know, The.
　Parting.
　Soul's Superior instants, The.
　We thirst at first—'tis Nature's Act.
Dobyns.　Delicate, Plummeting Bodies, The.
Donne.　Good-Morrow, The.
　Holy Sonnet.
Drayton.　Sonnet 6: 'How many paltry, foolish,
　painted things'.
Dugan, A.　Against the Text "Art Is
　Immortal."
Duggan, L.　Ten ii.
Elder.　Carried Away.
Eliot, T.　Whispers of Immortality.
Emerson, R.　Eros.
Enright, D.　Days of Adam were 930 years,
　The.
Gallagher, T.　Instructions to the Double.
Ginsberg, A.　Poem Rocket.
Glück, L.　Field Flowers.
Graves, R.　To Bring the Dead to Life.
Hall, D.　My son, my executioner.
Hardy, T.　His Immortality.
　Shelley's Skylark.

Hemans.　Woman and Fame.
Herbert, G.　Death, thou wast once an uncouth
　hideous thing.
　Virtue [*or* Vertue].
Herrick.　His Creed.
　To His Peculiar Friend Master Thomas
　Shapcott, Lawyer.
Ho Ching-ming.　Seeing Off Han Ju-ch'ing as
　He Returns to the Land Within the Passes.
Hopkins, E.　Life in Death.
Hsü Chung-hsing.　Who would have thought
　that a disease of the ordinary world.
Hsü Wei.　Mushroom Gatherer Deep in the
　Mountains Among the White Clouds, A.
Jackson, L.　Poet's Corner, The.
Jeffers, R.　Post Mortem.
Jefferson, J.　Immortality.
Johnson, L.　Nihilism.
Keats.　Ode: "Bards of passion and of mirth."
Kublanovsky.　He who gave weight to the
　wind.
Landor, W.　Passed Ruin'd Ilion.
Lanyer.　Description of Cookham, The.
Lipkin, S.　He who appointed weight to the
　wind.
McCreery.　There is no death! The stars go
　down.
Meynell, A.　Song of Derivations, A.
Milton.　On Shakespear[e].
"Minsky."　Immortality.
Mitchell, S.　Immortality.
Moorer.　Immortality.
Naden.　Pantheist's Song of Immortality, The.
Ovid.　1.15.
Paulinus of Nola.　To Ausonius.
Pembroke, W.　Song: "Soules joy, now I am
　gone."
Pien Kung.　Inscribed on an Album Leaf
　Painted by Dr. Lin.
Pinkney, E.　Voyager's Song, The.
Poseidippus.　Doricha.
Reese, L.　Love, Weeping, Laid This Song.
Ritsos.　Marpessa's Choice.
Robinson, E.　Man against the Sky, The.
　Walt Whitman.
Rodriguez, J.　Lifetime Devoted to Literature,
　A.
Rogers, P.　Objects of Immortality, The.
Shakespeare, W.　Sonnet 55.
　Sonnet 81.
　Sonnet 107.
Shen Chou.　To the Tune "Nan-hsiang-tzu."
Southey, R.　Love Indestructible.
Spenser.　Sonnet 75: "One day I wrote her
　name upon the strand."
Swenson, M.　In the Bodies of Words.
Swinburne.　From too much love of living.
Tennyson, A.　Nothing Will Die.
　Tithonus.
Tsung Ch'en.　When you enter Chin-hua
　Mountain.
Unknown.　George Washington.
　There Is No Death.
　years of a lifetime do not reach a hundred,
　The.
Vaughan, H.　Easter Hymn.
　Resurrection and Immortality.
　Waterfall [*or* Water-Fall], The.
Very.　Cross, The.
　New Birth, The.
Waller, E.　Of English Verse.
Wheatley, P.　To a Gentleman and Lady on the
　Death of the Lady's Brother and Sister, and a
　Child of the Name Avis, Aged One Year.
Whitman, W.　Joy, shipmate, joy!
　On the beach at night.
　Woman waits for me, she contains all, nothing
　is lacking, A.
Wolfe, H.　Iliad.
Wu Wei-yeh.　Passing by Huai-yin I Have
　Feelings.
　Reading the Annals of Emperor Wu of the
　Han Dynasy.
Yeats.　Sailing To Byzantium.
Yüan Mei.　Finding Serenity.
　Next Day the Fog Was Even Worse, The.

Yün Shou-p'ing.　Inscribed on a Painting
　("Magic mists twirl around the sky").

Imperfections
Creeley.　Immoral Proposition, The.
Fumi Saito.　Tanka: "Ever deeper."
Herrick.　No Loathsomnesse in Love.
　To the Generous Reader.
Martinez, D.　Fuego.
Stevens, W.　Poems of Our Climate, The.
Su Tung-p'o.　Tune: Prelude to Water Music.
Zimmer.　Failings, The.

Imperialism
Appleman, P.　Peace with Honor.
Blok.　Scythians, The.
Brathwaite, E.　Citadel.
Cardenal.　Mosquito Kingdom.
Chin.　Portrait of the Self as Nation, 1990–
　1991, A.
Conyus.　Day in the Life of. . . , A.
Daley, V.　When London Calls.
Di Prima.　Goodbye Nkrumah.
Fawcett, B.　Hand, The.
French, W.　Queen's After-Dinner Speech, The.
Hamilton, M.　For My Father's Mother Who
　Has Alzheimer's.
Kipling, R.　Recessional.
　White Man's Burden, The.
Lim-Wilson.　Inventing the Filipino.
Lucie-Smith.　Imperialists in Retirement.
McGrath, T.　Fresco: Departure for an
　Imperialist War.
McOrlan.　Produce from the colonies.
Mitchell, A.　Remember Suez?
Montague, J.　Wild Sports of the West.
Muir, E.　Combat, The.
Mutabaruka.　Free Up de Lan, White Man.
Pagis.　Decline of an Empire.
Ryuichi.　My Imperialism.
Thomas, D.　Incarnate devil in a talking snake.
Unknown.　Hope.
Wilde, O.　Ave Imperatrix!
Xuân Thǔy.　You Cannot Lock Up the Mind.

Impermanence. *See* **Transience**

Impotence
Adcock, F.　Happy Ending.
Automedon.　Impotent Lover, The.
Behn, A.　Disappointment, The.
Djogo.　Wooden Handle, The.
Everson, W.　Kingfisher Flat.
Harington.　Against an Old Lecher.
Herrick.　To His Mistresses.
Huang O.　To the Tune "Red Embroidered
　Shoes."
Levy, A.　On the Threshold.
Ovid.　Elegies 3.6.
Rochester, J.　Against Constancy.
　Disabled Debauchee, The.
　Imperfect Enjoyment, The.
　Song of a Young Lady to Her Ancient Lover,
　A.
Sherwood, G.　Disabled Debauchee, The.
Strato.　Grey already the hair at my temples.
Unknown.　One Writing against His Prick.

Impressionism and Impressionists
Mueller, L.　Monet Refuses the Operation.
Waldman, A.　Berthe Morisot.

Incantations
Shakespeare, W.　Thrice the Brinded Cat Hath
　Mewed.

Incense
Doolittle, H.　*Amen.*
Ginsberg, A.　After Yeats.
Li K'ai-hsien.　Night of the First Full Moon,
　The.
Po Chü-i.　Having Climbed to the Topmost
　Peak of the Incense-Burner Mountain.
Thoreau.　Smoke.
Wen Cheng-ming.　Quiet courtyard fills with
　greenery.
　Tea bowls, incense burning—a good feeling
　here!
Wratislaw.　Palm Sunday.
Yang Shen.　To the Tune "Flowers in the
　Rain."
　To the Tune "New Moon."

Incest
Borawski. English Was Only a Second Language.
Bridges. Lisa's Ritual, Age 10.
Bruck. Equality, father! Your dream has come true.
Cavin. Christmas with the Holy Family.
Couzyn. World War II.
Emanuel, L. Silence. She Is Six Years Old.
Fallon, P. Airs and Graces.
Howe, M. How Many Times.
Kumin, M. Saga.
Lorde. Chain.
Mitchell, S. Sons and Fathers.
Moraga. La Dulce Culpa.
Olds, S. What If God.
Smukler. Shower, The.
Verlaine. Pensionnaires.
Wakoski. Justice Is Reason Enough.

Inclosure Movement
Freeth. Cottager's Complaint, on the Intended Bill for Enclosing Sutton-Coldfield, The.

Incomprehensibility
Catullus. Death of Lesbia's Bird, The.
Crane, S. Why?
"Dylan." Ballad of a Thin Man.
Ford, C. Bad Habit, The.
Hewitt, J. O country people, you of the hill farms.

Inconstancy
Behn, A. To Alexis in Answer to His Poem Against Fruition.
Brown, T. Oaths.
Burns, R. Banks O' Doon, The.
  Bonie Doon.
  Ye flowery banks o' bonie Doon.
Edson, R. Large thing comes in, A.
Hood, T. Faithless Nelly Gray.
Jonson, B. Another. In Defense of Their Inconstancy [or Inconstancie]. A Song.
Karpowicz. From the Skein of the Straight Line.
Maguire, S. Fall, The.
Montagu, L. Answer to a Love-Letter in Verse, An.
Pilkington, L. Song, A: "Strephon, your breach of faith and trust."
Ralegh, W. Advice, The.
Stevenson, R. To Henry James.
Tabb. Shadow, The.
Thomas, E. Forsaken Wife, The.
Tollet. On Loving Once and Loving Often.

Indecision. *See* **Decisions**

Independence
Arnold, M. Self-Dependence.
Bennett, L. Independance wid a vengeance.
  Independence Twenty-One.
Eberhart, R. Concord Cats.
Eliot, T. Cousin Nancy.
Frost, R. Silken Tent, The.
Galvin, J. Independence Day, 1956: A Fairy Tale.
Henley, W. Invictus.
Ho Chi Minh. Song of a Cotton Yarn, The.
Huy Cận. Two Wooden Men, The.
Lê Đức Thọ. Fighter's Thoughts of Spring, A.
Lưu Văn Vong. Run! Run!
Miles, J. In the town where every man is king.
Mora. Cortez's Horse.
Ogilvy. Grannie's Birthday.
Phan Trọng Quảng. Independence Day.
T. P. Verses for the End of an Era.
Tế Hanh. Mother.
Twomey. Cliona.
Unknown. Against Idleness.
  Ground-Thumping Song.
  You can lead a horse to water.
Virtue. Hour, The.
Xuân Diệu. New Tiles.
Young, A. Dance For Ma Rainey, A.

India
Ali, A. Dacca Gauzes, The.
Berryman. Henry sats in de bar and was odd.
Birney. Bear on the Delhi Road, The.

Brooks, C. Lines: Composed at the Old Temples of Maralipoor.
Chacko. Rice.
Das, K. Hot Noon in Malabar.
  Introduction: "I don't know politics but I know the names."
Dharmaraj. Full of rain, the word.
Dharwadker. New Delhi, 1974.
Divakaruni. Indian Movie, New Jersey.
Ginsberg, A. Describe: The Rain on Dasaswamedh Ghat.
Gnanakoothan. Tamil, it's true, is the breath of my life.
Joshi. Passing through Rajasthan.
Jussawalla. Sea Breeze, Bombay.
Kipling, R. Gunga Din.
  Mandalay.
Lewis, A. Mahratta Ghats, The.
Li Tung. For the Monk San-tsang on His Return to the Western Regions.
Mahapatra, J. Main Temple Street, Puri.
  Monsoon Day Fable, A.
  Sanskrit.
  Summer Poem, A.
  Taste for Tomorrow.
Meenakshi. If Hot Flowers Come to the Street.
Meredith, W. Jain Bird Hospital in Delhi, The.
Moraes, D. Babur.
Namjoshi, S. *et al.* Because of India, before and after.
  Was It Quite Like That?
Narain. Towards Delhi.
"Nirala." Betrayal, The.
Orlovsky. Lepers Cry.
Padgaonkar. Salaam, / to everyone, salaam.
Pant. Almora Spring.
Parthasarathy. Speaking of Places.
Pichamurti. National Bird.
Ramanujan. At Forty.
  Elements of Composition.
  Pleasure.
Rukeyser, M. Ajanta.
Sahay. Our Hindi is a widower's new wife.
Shapiro, K. In India.
Sheikh. Jaisalmer, 1.
Singh, S. On the Slope of this Hill.
Tagore. Flute-music.
Verma. Pleasure Dome, The.

Indian Summer
Campbell, W. Indian Summer.
Dickinson, E. Indian Summer.
Garland, H. Indian Summer.

Indiana (state)
Fitzgerald, R. July in Indiana.
Wagoner, D. Valedictory to Standard Oil of Indiana, A.

Indians, American. *See* **Native Americans**

Indifference
Baraka. Preface to a Twenty Volume Suicide Note.
Bobyshev. Indifference— / A house.
Byrom. Careless Content.
Castillo, O. Apolitical Intellectuals.
Catullus. Carmen 39.
Chudakov. When they cry: / "Man overboard."
Cohen, E. Drive-By Shooting.
Cruz Varela. Invocation.
Csoori. We were good, good and obedient.
Cummings, E. Anyone lived in a pretty how town.
Dacey, P. Small Dark Song.
Dowson. Flos Lunae.
Hands, E. On an Unsociable Family.
Kornilov, V. Snow.
Levine, P. Coming Home, *Detroit*, 1968.
Melo Neto. End of the World, The.
Melville, H. Pebbles.
Montagu, L. Lover, The; a Ballad.
"Rayevsky." O, he who flashed above the moon afar.
Steele, T. In the King's Rooms.
Thackeray. Sorrows of Werther, The.
Wakoski. Realization of difference comes, The.
Wollach. Christina.

Individualism and Individualists
Arnold, M. Self-Dependence.
Berry, J. One.
Brownjohn. Of Dancing.
Chan. How to Organise a Successful Small Business.
Clark, L. There was a man whose nose was long.
Clough. In the Great Metropolis.
Coleridge, S. Phantom.
Crane, S. "Think as I think," said a man.
Dugan, M. Herbaceous Plodd.
"Dylan." It's Alright, Ma (I'm Only Bleeding).
Emerson, R. Ode, Inscribed to W. H. Channing.
Frost, R. Road Not Taken, The.
Glazkov. Four Paths.
Graves, R. Portrait, The.
Harper, F. Mission of the Flowers, The.
Huxley, A. Fifth Philosopher's Song.
Jordan, N. Be You.
Kao Ch'i. Song of the Man of Green Hill, The.
Keane, S. Once the wind.
Lawrence, D. Don'ts.
Lear, E. Jumblies, The.
MacNeice. Individualist Speaks, The.
Madgett. Offspring.
O'Hara, F. My Heart.
Parsons, C. Different.
Po Chü-i. To Liu Yü-hsi.
Reeves, J. Mr Kartoffel's a whimsical man.
Rilke. Once the realization is accepted that even between the closest people.
Saxe, J. Game of Life, The.
Smith, I. Law and the Grace, The.
Soloukhin. Wolves.
"Strannik." Solar Loneliness.
Walker, A. On Stripping Bark from Myself.
  Outcast.
Wesley-Smith. Walter Spaggot, strange old man.
Whitman, W. One's-Self I sing, a simple separate person.
  Torch, The.
Wyatt, T. I am as I am and so will I be.
Yeats. Coat, A.

See also **Egotism and Egotists**

Indonesia and Indonesians
Brissenden. Walking down Jalan Thamrin.
Fenton, J. Dead Soldiers.

See also **Borneo**

Indulgences
Sheridan, R. On Lady Anne Hamilton.

Industrial Revolution
Bishop, E. Varick Street.
Bisset. Next day they rambled round the town, and swore.
Seward. Scene of superfluous grace, and wasted bloom.
  While neighbouring cities waste the fleeting hours.
Unknown. Factory Girl's Come-All-Ye, The.

Industrialization
Ama Ata Aidoo. Cornfields in Accra.
Cranch. Spirit of the Age, The.
Dransfield. Endsight.
Eberhart, R. Hard Structure of the World, The.
Goldsmith, O. Deserted Village, The.
Hall, D. Foundations of American Industry, The.
Hopkins, G. God's Grandeur.
Kerouac. 146th Chorus.
Kim, K. Dove in Songbukdong, The.
Kinnell. Tragedy of Bricks, The.
Ko. Chongno Street*.
  Sky, The.
Kumin, M. Chain, The.
Larkin, P. Going, Going.
Lawrence, D. Evening Land, The.
Levine, M. Capitalism.
Levine, P. They Feed They Lion.
Mardhekar. Forest of yellow bamboo trees, The.
Munib-ur-Rahman. Tall Buildings.
Nesbit, E. Great Industrial Centre, A.

Sexton. Mr. Mine.
Spender, S. Landscape near an Aerodrome, The.
Trần Tế Xu'o'ng. Looking Far Ahead.
Wagoner, D. Valedictory to Standard Oil of Indiana, A.
Welch, L. Chicago Poem.

Ineptitude
Burns, R. On Elphinston's Translation of Martial.
Curbelo. Listening to a White Man Play the Blues.

Infant Death
Balk, C. Yellow Hills in Back, The.
Bawer. Grand Central Station, 20 December 1987.
Boyd, E. On the Death of an Infant of Five Days Old.
Carey, M. Upon ye Sight of My Abortive Birth.
Crashaw. To the Infant Martyrs.
  Upon the Infant Martyrs.
Davies, W. Inquest, The.
Geier. On Your Twenty-First Birthday.
Grogan. Elizabeth, Listening.
Harper, M. We Assume: On the Death of Our Son, Reuben Masai Harper.
Hartnett. Lament for Tadhg Cronin's Children.
Hewett, D. Anniversary.
Huddle. Two Facts.
Jonson, B. On My First Daughter.
Kennedy, X. On a Child Who Lived One Minute.
Lamb, C. On an Infant Dying as Soon as Born.
Marvell. Picture of Little T. C. in a Prospect of Flowers, The.
McAuley, J. Pietá.
McAuley, J. Pietà.
Melville, H. Chipmunk, The.
Muir, E. Child Dying, The.
Muske. Intensive Care.
Philips, K. EPITAPH. On her Son H. P. at St. Syth's Church where her body also lies Interred.
  On the Death of My First and Dearest Childe, Hector Philipps.
Piatt, S. No Help.
Tekkan. To our baby that died[1].
Unknown. Cruel Mother, The.
Williams, W. Dead Baby, The.
Wright, M. To an Infant Expiring the Second Day of Its Birth.
See also **Death in Children**

Infanticide
Boake. At Devlin's Siding.
Browning, E. Runaway Slave at Pilgrim's Point, The.
Davies, W. Inquest, The.
Hall, D. By the Exeter River.
Smith, S. But Murderous.
Unknown. Mary [*or* Marie] Hamilton.
  Queen's Marie, The.

Infants. *See* **Babies**

Infatuation
Arnold, M. Calais Sands.
Behn, A. To the Fair Clarinda, Who Made Love to Me, Imagin'd More Than Woman.
Clare, J. To Mary: 'I Sleep with Thee, and Wake with Thee'.
Cope, W. Two Cures for Love.
Dante Alighieri. Love hath so long possessed me for his own.
  Love's pallor and the semblance of deep ruth.
Duesing. Reprieve.
Herrick. Epitaph upon a Virgin, An.
  To Oenone ("Thou saist [*or* sayest] Love[']s dart").
  Upon a Black Twist, Rounding the Arm of the Countess of Carlisle.
  Upon Love ("Love brought me to a silent Grove").
Housman, A. Oh, when I was in love with you.
Koch, K. In Love with You.
  To Marina.
  To You.

Locker-Lampson. Mr. Placid's Flirtation.
Mayer, B. Carlton Fisk is My Ideal.
Meredith, G. We three are on the cedar-shadowed lawn.
Ralegh, W. Concei[p]t begotten by the eyes.
Ridley. Cushie Butterfield.
Shirley, J. Love's Hue and Cry.
Sidney, P. Eleventh Song: "Who is it that this dark[e] night."
Sonnet 16: "In nature apt to like when I did see."
Sonnet 21: "Your words my friend (right healthful caustics) blame."
Sonnet 47: "What, have I thus betrayed my liberty?"
Sonnet 49: "I on my horse, and Love on me doth try."
Sonnet 53: "In martial sports I had my cunning tried."
Sonnet 54: "Because I breathe not love to every one."
Sonnet 61: "Oft with true sighs, oft with uncalled tears."
Sonnet 64: "No more, my dear, no more these counsels try."
Sonnet 69: "O joy, too high for my low style to show."
Sonnet 74: "Love still a boy, and oft a wanton is."
Sonnet 92: "Be your words made (good sir) of Indian ware."
Sonnet 107: "Stella, since thou so right a Princess art."
Suckling, J. Upon My Lady Carlisle's [*or* Carlile's] Walking in Hampton Court Garden.
Surrey. Since fortune's wrath envieth the wealth.
Tuckerman, F. Infatuation.
Unknown. Gracius and gay.
  So well is me begone.
Wyatt, T. It was my choice, it was no chance.

Infidelity
Abse. In My Fashion.
Alexander, E. Nineteen.
Allur Nanmullai. What She Said ("As the lovely new flowers").
Angelou. Pickin Em Up and Layin Em Down.
Auden. Lullaby: "Lay your sleeping head, my love."
Behn, A. To Alexis in Answer to his Poem against Fruition.
Bernard. Men, a word of wisdom. Give.
Berssenbrugge. Jealousy.
Bhavani. Avatars.
Bible, *O.T.* And it came to pass, after the year was expired.
Bromley, A. My Mother's Face Never Moved.
Brooks, G. Vacant Lot, The.
Browning, E. Bianca Among the Nightingales.
Browning, R. Any Wife to Any Husband.
Byron, G. When we two parted.
Callimachus. Kallignotos swore to Ionis—no one.
Campbell, T. Jilted Nymph, The.
Campion, T. Secret love or two, I must confess[e], A.
Carew, T. Deposition from Love, A.
Carey. To the Tune—"But I Fancy Lovely Nancy."
Catullus. Carmen 70 ("Lesbia says she'ld rather marry me").
Chattopadhyay. Forgive Me.
Chaucer. Cook's Tale, The.
  Miller's Prologue, The.
  Miller's [*or* Milleres] Tale, The.
Cleveland, J. Antiplatonic[k], The.
Cummings, E. It may not always be so; and i say.
Dabydeen, C. Husband, The.
Dancer. Variety, The.
Deloney. Long have I lov'd this bonny Lasse.
Dickey, J. Adultery.
Donne. Change.
  Elegie: "Nature's lay ideot, I taught thee to love."
  Message, The.

Song: "Go and catch a falling star."
  Woman's Constancy.
Dowson. Non Sum Qualis Eram Bonae sub Regno Cynara[e].
Dugan, A. Adultery.
Egerton, S. To One Who Said I Must Not Love.
Elizabeth I. Doubt of future foes exiles my present joy, The.
"Ephelia." In the Person of a Lady, to Bajazet, Her Unconstant Gallant.
Essex, R. Change thy minde since she doth change.
Feirstein. Mark Stern Wakes Up.
  Rune-Maker, The.
García Lorca. Unfaithful Wife, The.
Godolphin. Song: "'Tis affection but dissembled."
Graves, R. Lament for Pasiphaë.
  Never Such Love.
  Straw, The.
  With Her Lips Only.
Grosholz. Legacies.
Handy, W. St. Louis Blues.
  Yellow Dog Blues.
Hardy, T. Burghers, The.
  Contretemps, The.
  Newcomer's Wife, The.
  Wife Waits, A.
Harington. Of an Heroical Answer of a Great Roman Lady to Her Husband.
Harrington, J. Inconstancy.
Hecht, A. Dover Bitch, The.
Heffernan, M. Message, The.
Herrick. Chop-Cherry.
  Upon Scobble [Epigram].
Ho Xuan Huong. On Being a Concubine.
Housman, A. Along the field as we came by.
Howard, S. *et al.* To the Unconstant Cynthia: a Song.
Hughes, L. Gypsy Man.
Hughes, T. Kreutzer Sonata.
Hunter, A. *et al.* Down-Hearted Blues.
Jong. Parable of the Four-Poster.
Juvenal. But say you, if each private Family.
  Woman stops at nothing, when she wears, A.
Kayamanar. What Her Girl Friend Said, Seeing Her Friend Suffer in Silent Dignity over Her Husband's Infidelity.
Kenrei Mon-in Ukyo no Daibu. My heart, like my clothing / is saturated with your fragrance.
Klappert. Ellie Mae Leaves in a Hurry.
Koch, K. To Marina.
Kollar. Late Arrivals.
Lindsay, V. At Mass.
Lomax, M. Other Woman, The.
Lovelace, R. Scrutiny [*or* Scrutinie], The.
  Song: To Lucasta, Going to the War[re]s.
Lowell, R. At the Altar.
Maccius. I swore, love, by your / dominion, to rest.
Mataka. Next Door.
McElroy, C. Caledonia.
  Horoscope.
McFadden, R. Bigamy.
Meleager. Love's night and a lamp.
  Pour this wine.
Meredith, G. I play for Seasons; not Eternities!
Millay, E. Thursday.
Montagu, L. Epistle from Mrs. Yonge to Her Husband.
Nesbit, E. Husband of To-Day, The.
Netumpalliyattan. What She Said about Her Unfaithful, Estranged Husband.
Nguyễn Tất Nhiên. Folk Songs For Today.
Nguyễn Ý Thuần. Homecoming.
Orampokiyar. What Her Girl Friend Said to the Foster-Mother ("In his fields, mother").
  What Her Girl Friend Said, When the Woman Was About to Take Back Her Unfaithful Husband.
  What She Said ("Green creepers planted inside the house").
  What She Said ("Hovering like the heron").
Ovid. 2.8.

Palladas. Cuckolded husbands have no certain sign.
Parker, M. Thou knowst I lov'd thee well.
Paulus Silentiarius. Epigram: "Kissing Hippomenes, I crave."
Philodemus. With the night half over.
Pilkington, L. Song, A.
Plumly. Infidelity.
Pope, A. Two or Three; a Recipe [or Receipt] to Make a Cuckold.
Pound, E. Temperaments, The.
Pratt, M. Laughing Place, The.
Rainey. See See Rider, see what you done done!
Ralegh, W. Farewell to False Love, A.
Raleigh. Walsinghame.
Ravenscroft, T. Hey ho, what shall I say?
Rochester, J. Against Constancy.
Ramble in St. James's Park, A.
Sadi. Dancer, The.
Savard. Daughter's Brooch, The.
Sedley. Song: "Phillis is my only joy."
Shakespeare, W. Ha' not you seen, Camillo?
I had been happy, if the general camp.
Song: "Sigh no more, ladies, sigh no more."
Sonnet 110.
Sonnet 138.
Spring.
Sidney, P. Sonnet 91: "Stella, while now by honour's cruel might."
Stevenson, A. Love Letter, A: Ruth Arbeiter to Major Paul Maxwell.
Strato. Off with you, boy! Pretended prude!
Private Poem.
Suckling, J. Constant Lover, A [or The].
Song: "Why so pale and wan, fond lover?"
Swift, J. Satire on an Inconstant Lover, A.
Taylor, A. Beast with Two Backs, The.
Thomas, R. Madrigal: "Your love is dead, lady, your love is dead."
Unknown. Clever Skipper, The.
Crowned with flowers, I saw fair Amarillis.
Demon Lover, The.
First Lawcase, The.
Frankie Blues.
Frankie was a good waoman.
Graces, if the beautiful Dionysios.
I am constantly wounded.
Josie.
Little Musgrave and Lady Barnard.
Little Sparrow.
May no man slepe in youre halle.
My cares comen ever anew.
Oh! What is the matter?
Only Jealousy of Emer, The.
Queen Eleanor's Confession.
Shickered As He Could Be.
Trail to Mexico, The.
Walker, A. My husband says.
Waring, B. Our Lady of the Laundromat.
Wedde. By day and also by night and you are.
"If thy wife is small bend down to her and."
Wickham. Slighted Lady, The.
Williams, C. Question, The.
Williams, C. Gulf Coast Blues.
Wither. I loved a lass, a fair one.
Wyatt, T. Accused though I be without desert.
Ah, Robin, / Jolly Robin.
Farewell: "What should I say."
Lover Having Dreamed Enjoying of His Love, Complaineth That the Dreame Is Not either Longer or Truer, The.
Lover Showeth How He Is Forsaken of Such as He Sometime Enjoyed, The.
Spite hath no power to make me sad.
Whoso list to hunt, I know where is an hind.
Yeats. Host of the Air, The.

See also **Adultery and Adulterers**

Infinity
Dickinson, E. Infinite a sudden Guest, The.
Dowden, E. Two Infinities.
Dugan, A. Note: The Sea Grinds Things Up.
Hadewijch II. All things.
Hirsch, E. Watcher, The.
Jiménez, J. I unpetalled you, like a rose.

Neruda. Loving is a journey with water and with stars.
Shakespeare, W. *Juliet:* Good-night, good-night! as sweet repose and rest.

Inflation
Gilbert, S. There lived a King, as I've been told.
Parra, N. Inflation.

Ingratitude
Hayden, R. Those Winter Sundays.
Herbert, G. Unkindness.
Seward. Sonnet: Ingratitude.
Smith, C. To a Querulous Acquaintance.

Inheritance
Atwood. How little I know / about you finally.
Dennis, C. Loss.
Donne. Disinherited.
Dryden, J. Crown Prince of Dullness, The.
Espada. Niggerlips was the high school name / for me.
Gerrard. Remonstrance, A.
Herrick. Lyric[k] for Legacies.
Hewitt, J. From a Museum Man's Album.
Hogan, L. Truth Is, The.
Jacob, H. To Geron.
Johnson, S. Short Song of Congratulation [or To a Young Heir], A.
Olds, S. Guild, The.
Wolfe, T. For, brother, what are we?
Wordsworth, W. Michael [A Pastoral Poem].

Injuries
Alegría. Nocturnal Visits.
Amichai. Ibn Gabirol.
Ammons. Silver.
Berry, D. Sun goes.
Breytenbach. Dreams Are Also Wounds.
Creeley. Man, The.
Cross, Jr. Accident, An.
Denning. Kim-San.
Erwin. Land Donation.
Faiz. You Tell Us What to Do.
Floyd. Private Ian Godwin, U. S. M. C.
Frost, R. Not to Keep.
Fumi Saito. Tanka: "Crooked fireworks."
Grosholz. Back Trouble.
Jaccottet. Wound seen from afar.
Kooser. Very old are forever, The.
Mackenzie, K. Hospital—Retrospections, The.
Mansour, J. Gently stroke a wound.
McDonald, W. Veteran.
Nowak, T. Psalm To Cheer Up.
Olds, S. Latest Injury, The.
Orr, G. Parable, A.
Paquet. Basket Case.
Easter '68.
Night Dust-off.
They Do Not Go Gentle.
Petrosky. V.A. Hospital.
Po Chü-i. Old Man with the Broken Arm, The.
Ritsos. Audible and Inaudible.
Rossetti, C. Hurt no living thing; / Ladybird, nor butterfly.
Utkin. Letter.
White, S. Healing, The.
Yoshimi. Tanka: "Scissors."

Injustice
Aubert, A. For Mark James Robert Essex d. 1973.
Berry, J. Fantasy of an African Boy.
Bierce. Hesitating Veteran, The.
Bontemps. Black Man Thinks of Reaping, A.
Brecht, B. World's One Hope, The.
Browning, R. Heretic's Tragedy, The.
"Carroll." Long Tale, A.
"Chrystos." I Walk in the History of My People.
Conyus. I rode with Geronimo.
Cullen, C. Scottsboro, Too, Is Worth Its Song.
Dennis, C. Loss.
Diop, D. Challenge.
For a Black Child.
Listen, comrades of the flaming centuries.
Dunbar, P. Haunted Oak, The.
Graham, J. From the New World.

Grahn. Ella, in a Square Apron, Along Highway 80.
Hall, D. Small Fig Tree, A.
Harper, F. Slave Auction, The.
Lindsay, V. Abraham Lincoln Walks at Midnight.
Lorde. Revolution Is One Form of Social Change.
Millay, E. Justice Denied in Massachusetts.
Moorer. Injustice of the Courts.
Owen, W. Parable of the Old Man and the Young, The.
Po Chü-i. Light Furs, Fat Horses.
Robinson, M. January, 1795.
Stanzas: "In this vain, busy world, where the good and the gay."
Rodriguez, L. Speaking with Hands.
Shakespeare, W. Sonnet 66.
Sophocles. Numberless wonders / terrible wonders walk the world but none the match for man—.
Stanley, T. Ode XV.
Stevens, W. Idiom of the Hero.
Sui Ching-ch'en. Tune: "Slow Chant"—Kao-tsu's Homecoming.
Tkachenko. Requiem for Eduard Streltsov.
U Tam'si Tchicaya. I am no longer master of my tears.
Unknown. Song: "We raise de wheat."
Wang An-shih. Confiscating Salt.
Whittier. For Righteousness' Sake.
Furnace Blast, The.
Hunters of Men, The.
Williams, W. Impromptu: The Suckers.

See also **Protest, Social**

Inkwells
Coleridge, M. Contents of an Ink-bottle, The.
Morley, C. To a Post-Office Inkwell.

Innisfree, Ireland
Yeats. Lake-Isle of Innisfree, The.

Innocence
Aldrich, T. Fannie has the sweetest foot.
Atkins. New Storefront.
Ayton. On the Prince's Death, to the King.
Blake, W. Book of Thel, The.
Introduction: "Piping down the valleys wild."
Lily, The.
To see a World in a Grain of Sand.
Brontë, E. Tell me, tell me, smiling child.
Bryant, W. Oh fairest of the rural maids!
Campbell, D. Small-town Gladys.
Cassian. Part of a Bird.
Clark, T. In those first days.
Coleridge, H. Long Time a Child.
Cruz Varela. Kaleidoscope.
Curbelo. Listening to a White Man Play the Blues.
Dobyns. Gun, The.
Donne. Good-Morrow, The.
Drayton. Since There's No Help.
Egerton, S. Blasphemous wretch! How canst thou think or say.
Eliot, T. Hippopotamus, The.
Elizabeth I. Written on a Wall at Woodstock.
Gunn, T. Innocence.
Herbert, G. Holy Baptism (2).
Holmes, O. Iris, Her Book.
Hummer, T. Mississippi 1955 Confessional.
Jackson, L. Only Daughter, The.
Summary for Alastor.
Jarman, M. Supremes, The.
Jiménez, J. Green was the maiden, green, green!
Jones, R. Explanation of the Exhibit, An.
Jordan, J. All the world moved next to me strange.
Kavanagh, P. Innocence.
Knight, E. Circling the Daughter.
Lamb, C. "Timid grace sits trembling in her eye, A."
Lanyer. From Salve Deus Rex Judaeorum.
Our Mother *Eve,* who tasted of the Tree.
Lea, S. Clouded Evening, Late September.
Levertov. In Mind.
Innocent, The.
Overland to the Islands.
Lewis, A. Sentry, The.

MacNeice. Apple Blossom.
Autobiography.
Mahon. Girls on the Bridge.
Miller, L. Substitute, The.
Moore, T. In the morning of life, when its cares are unknown.
Nemerov. Remorse for Time, The.
Ni Dhomhnaill. Poem for Melissa.
Ofeimun. Naming Day, A.
Olds, S. I Go Back to May 1937.
Oliver, M. Old Whorehouse, An.
Oppen. Quotations.
Palgrave. Eutopia.
Philips, K. To My Excellent Lucasia, On Our Friendship.
Ransom, J. Janet Waking.
Necrological.
Vaunting Oak.
Rich, A. Children Playing Checkers at the Edge of the Forest.
Robinson, E. Souvenir.
Schorr. Amusement.
Segal, J. Candle.
Smith, C. Glow-Worm, The.
Sorrentino. Razzmatazz.
Stanley, T. Love's Innocence.
Thelwall. To the Infant Hampden. Written during a Sleepless Night.
Thomas, D. Fern Hill.
Refusal to Mourn the Death, by Fire, of a Child in London, A.
Thoreau. Rumors from an Aeolian Harp.
Traherne. Innocence.
On News.
Unknown. Now for that slawnders sake.
Wallace-Crabbe. Windows, The.
Waller, E. To a Fair Lady Playing with a Snake.
Warren, R. Picnic Remembered.
Sirocco.
Whittier. In School-Days.
Williams, C. Gas Station, The.
Last Deaths, The.
Wordsworth, W. To the Highland Girl of Inversneyde.
Xuân Diệu. Fool In Love, A.
Yeats. To a Child Dancing in the Wind.

Inns
Chang Yü. To the Innkeeper at Five Rivers, Sun Pen.
Fairfax of Cameron. Upon the New Building at Appleton.
Gwerfyl Mechain. Hostess of the Ferry Inn, The.
Hardy, T. At an Inn.
Heath-Stubbs. Footnote to Belloc's "Tarantella."
Laughlin, J. Inn at Kirchstetten, The.
Longfellow, H. Prelude: The Wayside Inn.
Rossetti, C. Uphill [or Up-Hill].
Smith, I. Sitting here by the foreshore day after day.
Warren, R. Ballad of Billie Potts, The.
See also **Hotels; Motels**

Insanity. *See* **Madness**

Insects
Avison. Nameless One, A.
Barnes, D. Transfiguration.
Brooks, G. Birth in a Narrow Room, The.
Brown, M. Little Black Bug.
Browning, R. In a Gondola.
Clare, J. Clock-A-Clay [The Lady Bug].
D'Aguiar. Mama Dot's Treatise.
Dickinson, E. Further in Summer than the Birds.
Dufault. Mud Dauber Wasp, The.
Fumi Saito. Tanka: "Wood borers."
Han Yü. Don't shoo the morning flies away.
Hardy, T. August Midnight, An.
Huang T'ing-chien. On a Painting of Ants and Butterflies.
Short on brains, long on stupidity, the mantis seizes the cicada.
Hughes, T. To Paint a Water Lily.
Issa. From the bough / floating down river.
Issahakian. Even with insects—.
Johnson, L. Beacon of Hope.

Kitahara Hakushū. At a hospital in Tokyo during the summer of 1911.
Laing, K. Race on Gathering Bites.
Lamb, E. Still. . . some echo.
Le Gallienne. Ballad of London, A.
Li Shang-yin. Boudoir Feelings.
Longfellow, H. Birds of Killingworth, The (The Poet's Tale).
Mathews, A. Woodniche.
McCord, D. Plane Geometer.
Mei Yao Ch'en. Swarming Mosquitoes.
Mitchell, S. Tent Caterpillars.
Miyazawa Kenji. Tanka: "Plucked, The."
Mountain, M. Gosling following its neck to the bug.
Okamoto. Tanka: "Insect, An."
Tanka: "Where."
Oleynikov. Beetle, The.
Parmenion of Macedon. Gutsy bugs grabbed grub from me till disgusted, The.
Perreault, J. Readymade.
Pizzarelli. Waterbug running by the frogulp.
Plath. Frog Autumn.
Pratt, M. Not a breath of air.
Roethke. Minimal, The.
Shapiro, K. Fly, The.
Interlude.
Shurin. Temptation.
Spenser. Sonnet 71: "I joy to see how in your drawen work."
Taylor, E. Upon a Spider Catching a Fly.
Unknown. Cicada cries out, The.
Fly's Wedding, The.
West, C. My obnoxious brother Bobby.
Wheelock, J. Divine Insect, The.
Willard, N. Insects, The.
Wright, J. Depressed by a Book of Bad Poetry, I Walk toward an Unused Pasture and Invite the Insects to Join Me.
Wright, J. Invention of a Garden, The.
Yang Wan-li. Cold Fly.

Insomnia and Insomniacs
Berryman. Sonnet 115: "As usual I'm up before the sun."
Bukowski. I Am Dead But I Know the Dead Are Not Like This.
Burns, R. Simmer's a pleasant time.
Chu Shu-chen. Stormy Night in Autumn.
Davis, D. 6 A.M. Thoughts.
Devi. This Night.
Eimers. History of Navigation, A.
Geiger. Insomnia.
Hardy, T. Lying Awake.
Hayden, R. Broken Dark, The.
Kipling, R. City of Sleep, The.
Knight, H. Written to a Near Neighbour in a Tempestuous Night.
Lalic. Insomnia.
Lea, S. Insomnia: The Distances.
Li Ch'ing-chao. Tune: Telling of Innermost Feelings ("Night comes and, drowsy with drink, I'm slow to shed my /ornaments ornaments").
Lindsay, V. Abraham Lincoln Walks at Midnight.
Lu Yu. Night Thoughts.
Masini. Nightscape.
Montagu, L. Between your sheets you soundly sleep.
Nemerov. Insomnia I.
Pavlovic. Questionnaire of Sleeplessness.
Po Chü-i. Pine Sounds.
Song of the Rear Palace.
Prunty. Insomnia.
Rich, A. Afterwake, The.
Insomniacs, The.
Shakespeare, W. Sonnet 61.
Sidney, P. Sonnet 40: "As good to write as for to lie and groan."
Sonnet 98: "Ah bed, the field where joy's peace some do see."
Tu Fu. Restless Night.
Unknown. That Cypress Boat Is Drifting.
Updike. Insomnia the Gem of the Ocean.
Wilbur. Walking to Sleep.
Wright, C. Hotels.

Inspiration
Alegría. Summing Up.
Berrigan, T. Sonnet LV: "Grace to be born and live as variously as possible."
Berryman. Henry's Fate.
Blake, W. Introduction: "Piping down the valleys wild."
Brecht, B. Bad Time for Poetry.
Brodsky, J. Seven Strophes.
Bryant, W. I cannot forget with what fervid devotion.
"Cornwall." Poet's Thought, A.
Crane, S. Scaped.
Creeley. Door, The.
Drayton. Ode Written in the Peak[e], An.
Dufault. Mud Dauber Wasp, The.
Emerson, R. Art.
Merlin I.
Fanthorpe. Person's Tale, The.
Herrick. Not Every Day Fit for Verse.
Holmes, O. Sympathies.
Horace. Epistle: To Elizabeth, Countess of Rutland.
Jonson, B. And must I sing? What subject shall I choose?
Keats. How many bards gild the lapses of time!
On Sitting Down to Read "King Lear" Once Again.
Lanier, S. Clover.
Lazarus, E. Echoes.
Melville, H. Art.
Monroe, A. To W. S. M.
Ovid. Elegies 3.1: "Old wood stands uncut, of long years' space, An."
Park, S. Fruit Tree.
Persius. Prologue of Persius, The.
Pound, E. Virginal, A.
Robinson, E. Sonnet: "Oh for a poet—for a beacon bright."
Rogers, P. Doomsayers, The.
Santos, S. Inspiration.
Service. Inspiration.
"Severyanin." Russian Woman.
Shakespeare, W. Sonnet 78: 'So oft have I invok'd thee'.
Sidney, P. Sonnet 1: "Loving in truth, and fain[e] in verse my love to show."
Sonnet 15: "You that do search for every purling spring."
Sonnet 28: "You that with allegory's curious frame."
Sonnet 41: "Having this day my horse, my hand, my lance."
Sonnet 74: "I never drank of Aganippe well."
Sonnet 90: "Stella, think not that I by verse seek fame."
Stevenson, R. Happy Thought.
Su Tung-p'o. Following the Rhumes of Chiang Hui-shu.
Thoreau. If with light head erect I sing.
Tomlinson, C. Death of Will, The.
Watts-Dunton. Coleridge.
Wheatley, P. To S. M., a Young African Painter, on Seeing His Works.
Wilbur. Love Calls Us to the Things of This World.
Young, A. Prestidigitator 2, The.

Instinct
Chuang Tzu. Cutting up an Ox.
Cowper, W. Beau's Reply.
Stevens, W. Poetry Is a Destructive Force.
Thomas, D. Before I knocked and flesh let enter.

Institutionalization
Bogan, L. Evening in the Sanitarium.
Carruth, H. Words for My Daughter from the Asylum.
Dowson. To One in Bedlam.
Gardinier. Supremer Sacrifice, The.
Hecht, A. Transparent Man, The.
Kocan. Sleepers, The.
Lowell, R. In the Ward.
Waking in the Blue.
Morgan, R. Heirloom.
Sexton. Flee on Your Donkey.

Music Swims Back to Me.
Ringing the Bells.
Szumigalski. Visitor's Parking.

Insults
Belloc. Frog, The.
Bunting. What the Chairman Told Tom.
Burns, R. Extempore—On Being Shown a
  Beautiful Country Seat Belonging to Maxwell
  of Cardoness.
Catullus. Carmen 92 ("Lesbia loads me night
  & day with her curses").
Clifton, L. What spells racoon to me.
Holub. Man Cursing the Sea.
Tekkan. Tanka: "Snake."
Wasserman, R. Putting in a Word.

Integrity
Ashbery. Le Livre Est sur la Table.
Creeley. Like They Say.
Ho Xuan Huong. Cake-That-Drifts-in-Water,
  The.
Jeffers, R. Answer, The.
Klepfisz. About My Father.
Rich, A. Integrity.
Shakespeare, W. Sonnet 125.

Intellect and Intellectuals
Ammons. Pet Panther.
Carter, E. Dialogue, A.
Castillo, O. Apolitical Intellectuals.
Chin. Elegy for Chloe Nguyen.
Coleridge, M. Clever Woman, A.
Cummings, E. Since feeling is first.
Dickinson, E. Brain—is wider than the Sky,
  The.
Drummond, W. Content and Resolute.
Dyer, S. My mind [or minde or mynde] to me
  a kingdom [or kyngdome] is.
Eberhart, R. In a hard intellectual light / I will
  kill all delight.
Emerson, R. Intellect.
Thought.
Frost, R. At Woodward's Gardens.
Garrison, W. Freedom for the Mind.
Gilbert, S. Bunthorne's Song.
Graham, J. Mind.
Gurney, I. Townshend? I knew him well,
  queer ways he had.
Herrick. His Desire.
Hood, T. Lament of Toby the Learned Pig,
  The.
Jones, D. Perishing Bird, The.
Jordan, J. Poem about Intelligence for My
  Brothers and Sisters, A.
Kendall, M. Woman's Future.
Lear, E. Limerick: "There was an old person
  of Basing."
Maran. Silence.
Moore, M. Mind, Intractable Thing, The.
Mind Is an Enchanting Thing, The.
More, H. From The Slave Trade.
Nemerov. Blue Swallows, The.
Brainstorm.
Pitchford. Lobotomy.
Pope, A. What if the foot, ordain'd the dust to
  tread.
Ransom, J. Vanity of the Bright Young Men,
  The.
Shapiro, K. Intellectual, The.
Shelley, P. Hymn to Intellectual Beauty.
Simic. Harsh Climate.
Sparshott. Reply to the Committed Intellectual.
Stern, G. I Remember Galileo.
Su Tung-p'o. On the Birth of His Son.
Tate, A. To Intellectual Detachment.
Traherne. Preparative, The.
Wheelock, J. Earth ("'Planet doesn't explode
  of itself, A,' said drily").
Wilbur. Mind in its [or the] purest play is like
  some bat.
Wordsworth, W. Sweet is the lore which
  Nature brings;.
Wright, J. End of an Ethnic Dream, The.
See also **Mind; Rationalism and Rationalists;**
  Reason; Libraries and Librarians

Interment. *See* &bd;Burial

International Brigade. *See* **Civil War, Spain**

Internment
Hongo. Redness: Thinking it Through.

Mura. Argument: on 1942, An.
Letters from Poston Relocation Camp (1942–
  45).
Okita. In Response to Executive Order 9066:
  All Americans of Japanese Descent Must
  Report to Relocation Centers.
Nice Thing About Counting Stars, The.
Uyematsu. December 7 always brings
  christmas early.
Wong, N. Can't Tell.

Interracial Love and Marriage
"Alta." Yr eyes dark and aware.
Bennett, L. Back To Africa, Miss Mattie?
Durand, O. Black Man's Son, The.
Eady. Sherbet.
Hacker, M. Against Silence.
Hughes, L. Cross.
Marson. Brown Baby Blues.
Maunick. Seven Sides and Seven Syllables.
Middleton, C. Adelaide's Dream.
Moreton. Ballad: "Altho' a slave me is born
  and bred."
Rhys, J. Obeah Night.
Ridge, J. Stolen White Girl, The.
Roumer. Ten Lines.
Sholl. Midnight Vapor Light Breakdown.
Tolson. African China.

Intolerance
Ginsberg, A. Uptown.
Halliday, M. Vegetable Wisdom.

Introspection
Bromley, A. Slow Men Working in Trees.
Brontë, E. All hushed and still within the
  house.
Had there been falsehood in my breast
I know not how it falls on me.
My Comforter.
Self-Interrogation.
Clifton, L. Turning into my own.
Crane, S. Heart, The.
Creeley. Rain, The.
Dunbar, P. Ere sleep comes down to soothe
  the weary eyes.
Kerouac. Buddha.
Kirsch, S. Date.
Lodge, G. Pastoral: "Slopes of the sun and
  vine, and thou dark stream."
Meissner. After Going Off the Road During
  the Snowstorm.
Melville, H. Afterward.
Of Mortmain.
Moody, W. Harmonics.
Nemerov. Salt Garden, The.
Olson, C. Celestial Evening, October 1967.
Maximus, to Himself.
Rexroth, K. Signature of All Things, The.
Rich, A. Necessities of Life.
Storm Warnings.
Smith, S. After-Thought, The.
Southwick. Sun Speaks, The.
Stickney, T. Here in the North I chase an old
  despair.
Unknown. Self-Examination, The.
Very. Lost, The.
Walcott. Hotel Normandie Pool, The.
Wilbur. Aspen and the Stream, The.
Hole in the Floor, A.
Wordsworth, W. Inner Vision, The.

Inventions and Inventors
Blumenthal, M. Inventors.
Corbett, E. Inventor's Wife, The.
Fuller, J. *et al.* Born Too Soon.
Gildner. Cabbage in Polish is kapusta—
  ka*poo*sta.
Holub. Inventions.
Hughes, T. My Uncle Dan's an inventor, you
  may think.
Meinke. Sonnet on the Death of the Man Who
  Invented Plastic Roses.
Nemerov. Extract from Memoirs.
Spender, S. Icarus.

Invocation
Herrick. His Prayer to Ben[.] Jo[h]nson.
MacNeice. Invocation: "Dolphin plunge,
  fountain play."

Iowa (state)
Alexander, M. Iowa Farmer.

Browne, M. Iowa.
Hollo. Amazing Grace.
Kooser. Genuine Poem, Found on a
  Blackboard in a Bowling Alley in Story City,
  Iowa.
Schmitz. Mile Hill.
Wallace, R. Grandmother Grace.

Iphigenia
Aeschylus. And then the old leader of the
  Achaian fleet.

Iran and Iranians
Aldrich, T. When the Sultan Goes to Ispahan.
Farrokhzad. O Realm Bejewelled.
See also **Persians**

Ireland
Alcock. Written in Ireland.
Allingham. Eviction, The.
Lord Crashton: The Absentee Landlord.
Banim. Soggarth Aroon.
Berryman. 324. An Elegy for W.C.W., The
  Lovely Man.
Betjeman. Ireland with Emily.
Bigg. Irish Picture, An.
Boland, E. Famine Road, The.
That the Science of Cartography Is Limited.
Clifton, H. Distaff Side, The.
Cochrane, S. Irish Sweaters.
Colum, P. Poor Scholar of the 'Forties, A.
Davis, T. Nation Once Again, A.
Davitt. Shortening the Road.
Dawe, G. Names.
Deane, A. Cult of the Celtic, The.
Deane, S. Return.
Donatus. Land Called Scotia, The.
Dunn, D. Washing the Coins.
Durcan. Backside to the Wind.
Birth of a Coachman.
Going Home to Mayo, Winter, 1949.
Irish Hierarchy Bans Colour Photography.
Ennis. Alice of Daphne, 1799.
Coyne's.
"Fane." In an Irish Churchyard.
Ford, R. Back to Dublin.
Fordham. Song to Erin.
French, W. Queen's After-Dinner Speech, The.
Graves, R. Broken Girth, The.
Heaney, S. Bogland.
In Memoriam Francis Ledwidge.
Requiem for the Croppies.
Singing School.
Traditions.
Heffernan, W. Kathaleen Ny-Houlahan [*or*
  Kathleen-Ni-Houlahan].
Heóghusa. On Maguire's Winter Campaign.
Hewitt, J. Glens, The.
Irishman in Coventry, An.
Postscript, 1984.
Ulster Names.
Howard-Jones. Hibernia.
Hughes, L. Seascape.
Hutchinson, P. Fleadh Cheoil.
Frost is All Over, The.
Gaeltacht.
True Story Ending in False Hope, A.
Joyce, J. Right Heart in the Wrong Place,
  The.
Kavanagh, P. Clay is the word and clay is the
  flesh.
If ever you go to Dublin town.
Long Garden, The.
Maguire is not afraid of death, the Church will
  light him a candle.
Kennelly. Limerick Train, The.
Kinsella, T. Foot of the tower. An angle
  where the darkness, The.
His Father's Hands.
Kipling, R. Ulster.
Lancaster, O. Eireann.
Landor, W. Ireland never was contented.
Leonard, T. Ulstir fur fucks sake.
Letts. Irish Skies.
Longley, M. Wounds.
Lucy. Missing Link.
MacDonagh, D. Dublin Made Me.
MacNeice. Belfast.
Dublin.
Nightmare leaves fatigue.

MacWard *et al.* Dark Rosaleen.
Magee, T. Celts, The.
Maxton. Ode.
  Urgent Letter, An.
McCarthy, T. Toast.
McFadden, R. First Letter to an Irish Novelist.
McGuckian. To a Cuckoo at Coolanlough.
McNeill, L. Hill Daughter.
Montague, J. Like dolmens round my
  childhood, the old people.
Moore, M. Spenser's Ireland.
Moore, T. Dear Harp of My Country.
  Harp That Once through Tara's Halls, The.
  Minstrel Boy, The.
  Oh! blame not the bard, if he fly to the
  bowers.
  Oh! where's the slave so lowly.
  Pastoral Ballad by John Bull, A.
  Petition of the Orangemen of Ireland, The.
  Sweet Innisfallen.
Muldoon, P. Christo's.
  Ireland.
  Ma.
  Sightseers, The.
Murphy, R. Gate Lodge.
  Luttrell, Master of Luttrellstown.
O'Gnive. Downfall of the Gael, The.
O'Grady, D. Here, because of the shock, the
  sudden.
O'Loughlin. Glasnevin Cemetery.
  Irish Requiem, An.
O'Rahilly. Last Lines.
  Time of Change, A.
  Vision, The.
Ormsby, F. Home.
Owenson. Irish Harp: Fragment I, The.
Paulin. Impossible Pictures, The.
Pearse, P. I am Ireland.
Skinner, K. Cold Irish Earth, The.
Smedley, M. Irish Fairy lost her way, An.
Spenser. Tho when they came to the sea
  coast, they found.
Squire. Numerous Celts.
Stevens, W. Irish Cliffs of Moher, The.
Swift, J. Ireland.
  On the Irish Club.
Symons, A. By the Pool at the Third Rosses.
  In Ireland: By the Pool at the Third Rosses.
Synge. Prelude: "Still south I went and west
  and south again."
Thomas, D. Fern Hill.
Unknown. Alfrid's Itinerary through Ireland.
  Arran.
  Croppy Boy, The.
  Fair Hills of Ireland, The.
  General wonder in our land.
  Go to Old Ireland.
  Hospitality in Ancient Ireland.
  I Am from Ireland.
  Kevin Barry.
  Little Black Rose.
  Orange Lily, The.
  Shan Van Vocht, The.
  Wearin' o' the Green, The.
  Wearing of [*or* Wearin' o'] the Green, The.
Whitman, W. Old Ireland.
Wilde, L. Who Will Show Us Any Good?
Wright, J. Remittance Man.
Yeats. Easter 1916.
  Hosting of the Sidhe, The.
  I am of Ireland.
  Lake-Isle of Innisfree, The.
  Many ingenious lovely things are gone.
  Municipal Gallery Revisited, The.
  On a Political Prisoner.
  Pardon, old fathers, if you still remain.
  Parnell came down the road, he said to a
  cheering man.
  Prayer for My Daughter, A.
  Red Hanrahan's Song about Ireland.
  Rose Tree, The.
  September 1913.
  To Ireland in the Coming Times.

See also **Northern Ireland;** *individual counties*
  (*e.g.,* **County Donegal, Ireland**).
Ireland, Northern. See **Northern Ireland**
Iris (flower)
Barrington, P. White Iris, A.
Donnelly, D. Blue Flag.
Foster, J. Irises, The.
Glück, L. Wild Iris, The.
Griffin, S. Love Should Grow Up like a Wild
  Iris in the Fields.
Rukeyser, M. Iris.
St. John, D. Iris.
Sobin, G. Irises.
Williams, W. Iris.
Irish, The
"Æ." On Behalf of Some Irishmen Not
  Followers of Tradition.
Carson, C. Insular Celts, The.
Clarke, J. Fighting Race, The.
Deane, A. Cult of the Celtic, The.
"Doyle." Ulsterman, An.
Hartnett. Death of an Irishwoman.
  Pity the man who English lacks.
Heaney, S. Docker.
Hewitt, J. Ireland.
  Irishman in Coventry, An.
  Once alien here my fathers built their house.
  Scar, The.
Hovey. Barney McGee.
Howard-Jones. Hibernia.
Hutchinson, P. Gaeltacht.
Leonard, T. Summer's Day, A.
McBurney. Croppy Boy, The.
McCarthy, T. Emigration Trains, The.
Moore, T. Irish Antiquities.
Muldoon, P. Anseo.
  Cuba.
  Quoof.
O Direain. That Face.
O'Connor, P. Exiles.
O'Meallain. Exodus to Connacht.
Unknown. Finnegan's Wake.
  Poor Paddy Works on the Railway.
Iron
Lawrence, D. Things made by iron and
  handled by steel are born.
Snyder, G. Some Good Things to Be Said for
  the Iron Age.
Unknown. Red Iron Ore.
Iron Lungs
Plumly. Iron Lung, The.
Irony
Alcaeus. Philip of Macedon.
Argentarius. Welcome, old friend, long-necked
  bottle.
Baca. 43.
Carter, M. Mouth Is Always Muzzled, A.
Creeley. Gift of Great Value, A.
Dacey, P. How I Escaped from the Labyrinth.
Dobler. 1920 Photo.
Eady. Supremes, The.
Flaccus. X finds gold and leaves his noose for
  Y.
Hardy, T. Country Wedding, The.
Harms. Breakfast on the Patio.
Ibn al-Rumi. Weighing-In, The.
Irenaeus Referendarius. Why is the floor,
  Chrysilla.
Matthews, T. Robert Sat.
McDonald, I. Life/Death.
Mew. My heart is lame with running after
  yours so fast.
Rhianus. Archinos, this retsina bottle contains.
Sidney, P. Sonnet 63: "O Grammer rules, ô
  now your virtues show."
  What length of verse can serve brave
  Mopsa's good to show?
Smith, S. I forgive you, Maria.
Stevenson, R. System.
Wilbur. Parable.
Wright, C. Lesson, The.
Isaac
Bloch, C. In wings and starched.
  Patriarch in black takes, The.
Clough. Genesis XXIV.
Cole, P. Isaac: a Poise.
  Where the Honey Speech's Hedge.

Gilbo'a. Isaac.
Gouri. Heritage.
Owen, W. Parable of the Old Man and the
  Young, The.
Stradling. Abraham's Sacrifice of Isaac.
Vaughan, H. Isaac's Marriage.
Wilner, E. Sarah's Choice.
Ishmael
Palmer, H. Ishmael.
Ishtar
Levertov. Song for Ishtar.
Isis
Doolittle, H. We have seen how the most
  amiable.
Gascoyne. And the Seventh Dream Is the
  Dream of Isis.
Simon, L. Bernice Got Next to Isis.
Walsh, C. Prayer to Isis.
Islam. *See* **Muslims and Islam**
Islands
Allfrey. Love for an Island.
Arnold, M. To Marguerite.
Auden. On This Island.
Berrigan, T. Sonnet III: "Stronger than
  alcohol, more great than song."
Bishop, E. Crusoe in England.
Bogan, L. Night.
Brathwaite, E. Citadel.
Brinnin. Letter from an Island.
Brooks, C. Our Island Home.
Brown, G. Fish and Corn.
  Kirkyard.
  Saint.
Campbell, R. Tristan da Cunha.
Cendrars. Aleutian Islands.
Césaire, A. Islands scars of the water.
  Lagoonal Calendar.
  On the Islands of All Winds.
Chan. Paradise.
Dumas, H. Island within Island.
Elmslie, K. Island Celebration.
Foscolo. To Zante.
Fulton, R. Remembering an Island.
Hölderlin. Patmos.
Kanemasa. Awaji Island—.
Kennelly. In the Sea.
Landon. Enchanted Island, The.
McFarlane, B. Arawak Prologue.
McNeill, A. Saint Ras.
Melville, H. Archipelago, The.
  Enviable Isles, The.
  Island, The.
  Rolfe and the Palm.
Millay, E. Ragged Island.
Nanton. I.
Pagis. Epilogue to Robinson Crusoe.
  Logbook.
Phillips, C. You Are Here.
Raab. N. On the Island.
Rankin, J. Sea-bundle.
Reid, A. Isle of Arran.
Roach. Love Overgrows a Rock.
Rose. Alaskan Fragments June 1981—Summer
  Solstice.
Russell, T. Sonnet: Suppos'd to Be Written at
  Lemnos.
Sargent, E. Rockall.
Smith, I. Lewis 1928–45.
Stevenson, R. Fair Isle at Sea—thy lovely
  name.
  To S.C.
Tennyson, A. Duet.
Unknown. Arran.
Walcott. Crusoe's Island.
Wordsworth, D. Floating Island at Hawkshead.
Yeats. Lake-Isle of Innisfree, The.
  Sorrow of Love, The ("Quarrel of the
  sparrows in the eaves, The").
Yenser, S. Blue Guide.
Yu. Isle of Ulung, The.
Isolation
"Bagritzky." Origin.
Kaufman, B. Heavy Water Blues.
Mandelstam. For the resounding valor of
  milennia to come.
Shchirovsky. I don't enclose the universe in
  my grasp.

See also **Absence; Loneliness; Separation**
Isolde. *See* **Tristram and Isolde**
Israel
　Amichai.　Almost a Love Poem.
　　Jews in the Land of Israel.
　　Patriotic Reflections.
　Avidan.　Three Self-Plagiarisms.
　Bible, *O.T.*　David's Lament.
　　Psalm 136.
　Byron, G.　Oh! weep for those that wept by
　　Babel's stream.
　Curzon, D.　Tour of Ein Kerem, A.
　Gilbo'a.　Song of Blue and Red, A.
　Ginsberg, A.　Galilee Shore.
　Greenberg, U.　At Your Feet, Jerusalem.
　Guri.　But We Shall Bloom.
　Hame'iri.　Passover in Jerusalem.
　Housman, A.　When Israel out of Egypt came.
　Jarrell.　Jews at Haifa.
　Jordan, J.　Intifada.
　Kaufman, S.　Déjà Vu.
　Kovner.　Lookout on a Rock on the Heights of
　　Mount Hermon.
　Lazarus, E.　Banner of the Jew, The.
　　New Ezekiel, The.
　Nye, N.　Small Vases from Hebron, The.
　Pagis.　Picture Postcard from Our Youth.
　Pasolini.　Southern Dawn.
　Ravikovitch.　King over Israel.
　　You Can't Kill a Baby Twice.
　Scott, W.　Rebecca's Hymn.
　Shalom.　They That Sow at Night.
　Shlonsky.　Jezra:l.
　Sillitoe.　Synagogue in Prague.
　Spark.　Canaan.
　Spire.　Hear, O Israel! / Will you never tire of
　　repeating in your prayers.
　Tchernichowsky.　They say there is a country.
　Zach.　Soft Warm Breeze, A.
Italians, The
　Barolini.　Having the Wrong Name for Mr.
　　Wright.
　Bona.　Amazone.
　Browning, R.　Italian in England, The.
　Capone.　In Answer to Their Questions.
　Clements, A.　Why I Don't Speak Italian.
　Gillan.　Arturo.
　　Growing Up Italian.
　　Public School No. 18: Paterson, New Jersey.
　Gioseffi.　Bicentennial Anti-Poem for Italian-
　　American Women.
　Leto.　For Talking.
　　Mary Morelle Show, The.
　Palma.　Coming of Age.
　Repetto.　6th grade—our lady of pompeii.
　Romano, R.　Bucket, The.
　　But My Blood.
　　So I Lost My Temper.
　Rossetti, C.　Enrica, 1865.
　Saffoti.　Espresso.
　Stefanile.　How I Changed My Name, Felice.
　Viscusi.　Autobiography.
　Wagner, M.　Miss Clement's Second Grade.
Italy
　Aretino.　If famous Apelles with his hand of
　　art.
　Auden.　Good-Bye to the Mezzogiorno.
　Bona.　Dream Poem.
　Brinnin.　Hotel Paradiso e Commerciale.
　Browning, E.　Casa Guidi Windows.
　　Part I.
　　Part II.
　Browning, R.　Love among the Ruins.
　　Sordello.
　　Up at a Villa—Down in the City.
　Byron, G.　Italy versus England.
　Campana.　Genoa.
　Christopher.　April in New York.
　Clements, A.　Why I Don't Speak Italian.
　Cranch.　In the Palais Royal Garden I stood
　　listening to-day.
　Denby.　Villa D'Este.
　Dickinson, E.　Our lives are Swiss.
　Divakaruni.　Outside Pisa.
　Filicaia.　Italia.
　Fitzgerald, R.　Figlio Maggiore.
　Garrigue.　Country Villa.

Gilbert, S.　Mafioso.
Gregor, A.　Poem: "So many pigeons at
　Columbus."
Guest, B.　Otranto.
Hecht, A.　Hill, A.
Hugo, R.　Map of Montana in Italy, A.
　View from Cortona, A.
Jacobsen, R.　Catacombs in San Callisto, The.
Kemble.　Farewell to Italy.
Lawrence, D.　Cypresses.
Marinetti.　Correction of proofs + desires in
　speed.
Milton.　On the Late Massacre [*or* Massacher]
　in Piedmont [*or* Piemont].
O'Hara, F.　Rogers in Italy.
Pasolini.　Day of My Death, The.
Pinkney, E.　Italy.
Porta.　I'm walking out on Rome.
Pound, E.　Enormous tragedy of the dream in
　the peasant's bent / shoulders, The.
Quasimodo.　19 January 1944.
Robinson, E.　To My Muse.
Rossetti, C.　Italia, Io Ti Saluto!
St. John, D.　Terraces of Rain.
Shelley, P.　Lines Written among the Euganean
　Hills.
Simpson, L.　On the lawn at the villa.
Stickney, T.　Autumn's done; they have the
　golden corn in, The.
　In Ampezzo.
Svetlov.　Italian, The.
Swinburne.　Super Flumina Babylonis.
Tennyson, A.　Daisy, The.
　Frater Ave Atque Vale.
Weiss, T.　Life of. . . , The.
Wright, J.　Journey, The.
Zanzotto.　Campèa.
Itching
Nash, O.　Requiem: "There was a young belle
　of old Natchez."
　Taboo to Boot.
Paniker, K.　Itch, The.
Ivy
Brontë, A.　Home.
Unknown.　Holver and Hivy made a gret party.
　Ivy, chefe of trees it is.

J

Jack and Jill
Kipling, R.　Flight of the Bucket, The.
Loomis.　Jack and Jill.
Jack the Ripper
Miller, V.　Light Reading.
Jackson, Andrew
Bly, R.　Andrew Jackson's Speech.
　Three Presidents.
Davidson, D.　Twilight on Union Street.
Lindsay, V.　Statue of Old Andrew Jackson,
　The.
MacLow.　1829.
Jackson, "Hurricane"
Dugan, A.　On Hurricane Jackson.
Jackson, Mahalia
Prettyman.　When Mahalia Sings.
Jackson, Thomas Jonathan ("Stonewall")
Lanier, S.　Dying Words of Stonewall Jackson,
　The.
Melville, H.　Stonewall Jackson.
Palmer, J.　Stonewall Jackson's Way.
Stevens, W.　American Sublime, The.
Jacob (Bible)
Burns, R.　Patriarch, The.
Dickinson, E.　Little East of Jordan, A.
Lasker-Schüler.　Jacob ("Jacob: a bull among
　his herd").
Levertov.　Jacob's Ladder, The.
Quarles.　On Jacob's Purchase.
Schwartz, D.　Jacob.
Vaughan, H.　Jacob's Pillow, and Pillar.
Very.　Jacob Wrestling with the Angel.
Wesley, C.　Wrestling Jacob.
Jacob, Max
Warren, R.　To Max Jacob.

Jaguars
Hajnal.　Jaguar is Getting Ready, The.
Hughes, T.　Jaguar, The.
　Second Glance at a Jaguar.
Jails. *See* **Prisons and Prisoners**
Jam- and Jelly-making
Belloc.　On Jam.
Kumin, M.　Making the Jam without You.
Jamaica, West Indies
Bennett, L.　Independance wid a vengeance.
　Independence Twenty-One.
　Jamaica oman cunny sah!
Escoffery.　No Man's Land.
Goodison.　Jamaica 1980.
Hendriks.　Jamaican Small Gal.
Maxwell-Hall.　Jamaica Market.
Roberts, W.　Maroon Girl, The.
　Valediction: "Before the seas again divide."
Salkey.　Away.
Simpson, L.　Jamaica.
Unknown.　Our tropic fruits, nurs'd 'neath a
　torrid sky.
Virtue.　Hour, The.
**James IV, King of Scotland VIII, King of
England**
Aytoun, W.　Then the Provost he uprose.
James VIII, King of Scotland. *See* **James IV,
King**
James, Henry
Gunn, T.　Jamesian.
Kees.　Henry James at Newport.
Ransom, J.　Old Mansion.
Stevenson, R.　Henry James.
James, Jesse
Benét, W.　Jesse James was a two-gun man.
Carrel.　Treacherous Death of Jesse James,
　The.
Unknown.　Jesse James was a lad who [*or*
　that] killed many a man.
Jamestown, Virginia
Moore, M.　Enough.
Tati-Loutard.　Pilgrimage to Loango Strand.
January
Bishop, E.　Brazil, January 1, 1502.
Clare, J.　January.
Ford, C.　January wraps up the wound of his
　arm.
Gibson, D.　January.
Hays, H.　January.
Heath-Stubbs.　January.
Rakosi.　January of a Gnat, The.
Ray, H.　January.
Robinson, M.　January, 1795.
Updike.　January.
Williams, W.　January.
Janus
Carew, T.　To the New Year [For the Countess
　of Carlisle].
Japan
Ai Lan.　Deathless Autumn, A.
DiPalma.　Annotations Tropes and Lacunae of
　the Itoku Master.
Eimers.　Another Kimono.
Fenollosa.　I remember an ancient Chinese
　picture kept over there in Daitokuji.
　Separated East, The.
Ginsberg, A.　Change: *Kyoto-Tokyo Express,*
　The.
Hecht, A.　Japan.
Hsü Pen.　Saying Goodbye to a Monk from
　Japan.
Inada.　Father of My Father.
Kunio.　Tanka: "Late summer day."
Leithauser.　In a Japanese Moss Garden.
　In Minako Wada's House.
Mahon.　Snow Party, The.
Miyazawa Kenji.　Pictures of the Floating
　World.
　Snow on Saddle Mountain, The.
Mura.　Listening.
Nobuyuki.　Returning from Abroad.
Retallack, J.　Japanese Presentation I and II.
Ryuichi.　My Imperialism.
Shūji.　Tanka: "Spoken in response."
Song.　Girl Powdering Her Neck.

Su Man-shu. Exile in Japan.
Shouldn't I pilfer wantonly this famed
  fragrance of a foreign land?
Thwaite. Great Foreign Writer Visits Age-Old
  Temple, Greeted by Venerable Abbess, 1955.
Zenmaro. Tanka: "It's hazardous."
Tanka: "Old Japan."
Tanka: "Work on the impossible."

Japanese, The
Cummings, E. YgUDuh / ydoan / yunnuhstan.
Dickey, J. Performance, The.
Elmslie, K. Japanese City.
Inada. From Our Album.
Inez. Woman Who Loved Worms, The.
Kageyama, C. Mama.
Kaneko. Bailey Gatzert: The First Grade,
  1945.
Logue, M. Sweet Oranges.
Matsueda. Two Japanese Prints.
Mirikitani. Breaking Tradition.
Mura. Argument: on 1942, An.
Okita. In Response to Executive Order 9066:
  All Americans of Japanese Descent Must
  Report to Relocation Centers.
Uyematsu. Fortune Cookie Blues.
Yamada. American Son.
Cincinnati.
Yi, S. Does Spring Come to These Forfeited
  Fields?

Jasmine
Lorde. Night-Blooming Jasmine, The.
McKay, C. Jasmine.

Jason
Apollonius Rhodius. Stealing the Golden
  Fleece.
Dickinson, E. Finding is the first Act.
Flaccus, G. Now as Medea walks, dark echoes
  fill.
Glover, D. Old Jason, the Argonaut, The.
Williams, O. Golden Fleece, The.

Jays
"Field." Flaw, A.
Rogers, P. Next Story, The.
Unknown. Jaybird a-sitting on a hickory limb.
See also **Blue Jays**

Jazz
Ai. Archangel.
Allen, S. I Say, Mr. A.
Ashanti. Just Another Gig.
Aubert, A. Bessie.
Bessie Smith's Funeral.
Baker, H. Of Walter White's Father in the
  Rain.
Tobacco Warehouse Blues.
Baraka. All is One for Monk.
Am/Trak.
In the Tradition / (Not a White Shadow but
  Black People Will Be Victorious).
Barlow, G. Mingus Speaks: Found Poems.
Barresi. Venice Beach: Brief Song.
Berrigan, T. String of Pearls.
Blackburn, P. Listening to Sonny Rollins at
  the Five-Spot.
Brathwaite, E. Clock.
Brodey. Lennie Tristano, No Wind.
Little Light.
Brooks, G. Third Sermon on the Warpland,
  The.
We real cool. We.
Brown, A. Assassination of Charlie Parker,
  The.
Brown, S. Cabaret.
Ma Rainey.
Buckley, C. Nostalgia.
Playing for Time.
Buddy. Callin Buddy / Bolden.
Carruth, H. Freedom and Discipline.
Castro, M. Blew It.
Cecil. Richard's Blues.
Chase, K. What You Can't See.
Coolidge, C. Of What The Music to Me.
Rhymes with Monk.
Cooper, J. Wanda's Blues.
Corrie. How Long Has Trane Been Gone.
Corso. For Miles.
Cortez. How Long Has Trane Been Gone.
Rose Solitude.

Solo Finger Solo.
Tapping.
Crane, H. For the Marriage of Faustus and
  Helen.
Crouch, S. Revelation, The.
Up on the Spoon.
Cummings, E. God pity me whom (god
  distinctly has).
Cushing, J. Autumn Leaves.
Every Time We Say Goodbye.
Lover Man.
Dana, R. Elegy for the Duke.
Davis, F. Jazz Band.
Davis, T. C. T. at the Five Spot.
C.T.'s variation.
Expandable Language.
Rogue and Jar: 4/27/77.
Diop, B. Ball.
Doty, M. Almost Blue.
Dove, R. Canary.
Listen to the sound of my horn. . . .
Eady. Hank Mobley's.
Jazz Dancer.
William Carlos Williams.
Espada. Majeski Plays the Saxophone.
Etter. Monk's Dream.
Stuffy Turkey.
Evans, M. Boss Communication.
Fabio. For Louis Armstrong, A Ju-Ju.
Feinstein, S. Christmas Eve.
Sonnets for Stan Gage (1945–1992).
Ford, W. Of Miles Davis.
Giovanni. Genie in the Jar, The.
Graham, M. After the War; When Coltrane
  Only Wanted to Play Dance Tunes.
Harjo, J. Healing Animal.
Harper, M. Alone.
Bandstand.
Dear John, Dear Coltrane.
Driving the Big Chrysler across the Country of
  My Birth.
For Bud.
Narrative of the Life and Times of John
  Coltrane: Played by Himself, A.
Reuben, Reuben.
Harvey, S. Mighty Tropicale Orchestra, The.
Hayden, R. Soledad.
Henderson, D. Coltrane Memorial, A.
Elvin Jones Gretsch Freak.
Lee Morgan.
Sonny rollins seeking.
Thelonious Sphere Monk.
Heyward, D. Jasbo Brown.
Hirsch, E. Art Pepper.
Hollo. Le Jazz Hot.
Hughes, L. Be-Bop Boys.
Jazz Band in a Parisian Cabaret.
Jazzonia.
Song for Billie Holiday.
Hull, L. Lost Fugue for Chet.
Ornithology.
Hummer, T. Poem in the Shape of a
  Saxophone.
Inada. Blues for Dan Morin.
Jackson, A. Make/n My Music.
Ohnedaruth.
Jackson, R. Shadows.
Jauss. After the End of the World.
Black Orchid.
Jeffers, L. How High the Moon.
Joseph, A. My Father's Heroes.
Kaufman, B. Battle Report.
Mingus.
Walking Parker Home.
War Memoir: Jazz, Don't Listen to It at Your
  Own Risk.
Keane, E. Week Seven.
Kelly, R. Newark.
Ode to Language.
Kerouac. 221st Chorus.
Kgositsile. Acknowledgement.
For Art Blakey and the Jazz Messengers.
Kleinzahler. Like cities, like storms.
Love Poem.
Komunyakaa. Elegy for Thelonious.
February in Sydney.

Speed Ball.
Twilight Seduction.
Kostakis. Circle with a Hole in the Middle,
  The.
Fire Parcel.
Lagrone. I Heard the Byrd.
Lang, D. Depression, The.
Lange, A. Fine Line, A.
Larkin, P. For Sidney Bechet.
Lewis, J. To The Great Hard-Bop Pianists.
Lindsay, V. Jazz of This Hotel, The.
Long, D. Black Love Black Hope.
Longley, M. Words for Jazz Perhaps.
Lux. Night above the Town.
Lyle. Tampa Red's Contemporary Blues.
Mackey, N. Capricorn Rising.
John Coltrane Arrived with an Egyptian Lady.
Madgett. Echoes.
Plea for My Heart's Sake.
Madhubuti. Don't Cry, Scream.
Knocking Donkey Fleas off a Poet from the
  Southside of Chi.
Madigan. Curtis Fuller.
Stereo Time with Booker Little.
Matthews, W. Buddy Bolden Cylinder, The.
Mingus at the Showplace.
May, K. Valentine's Day.
McClure, M. For Monk.
Jazz at the Intergalactic Nightclub.
McGrath, T. Guiffre's Nightmusic.
McPherson, S. Some Metaphysics of Junior
  Wells.
Suspension: Junior Wells on a Small Stage in
  a Converted Barn.
Miller, V. Dirge in Jazz Time.
Mitchell, A. From Rich Uneasy America to
  My Friend Christopher Logue.
Moerman. Louis Armstrong.
Mor. Coming of John, The.
Natambu. Words and Music in America.
Neal, L. Don't say goodbye to the Porkpie
  Hat that rolled.
O'Hara, F. Day Lady Died, The.
Okantah. Afreeka Brass.
Southern Road.
Redmond. Distance.
Reed, I. Lake Bud.
Rivard. Baby Vallejo.
Rivers, C. Underground.
Rodgers, C. We Dance Like Ella Riffs.
Written for Love of an Ascension—Coltrane.
Rukeyser, M. Bunk Johnson Blowing.
Homage to Literature.
Sadiq. Tuskegee Experiment.
Sandburg, C. Jazz Fantasia.
Schuyler, J. Let's All Hear It for Mildred
  Bailey!
Shange. Okra to greens.
Rite-ing.
Simic. Crepuscule with Nellie.
Simmons, J. Didn't He Ramble.
Sneeden. Coltrane and My Father.
Spellman. Did John's Music Kill Him?
John Coltrane: An Impartial Review.
Spicer, J. Song for Bird and Myself.
Taggart, J. Giant Steps.
Thomas, L. Historiography.
Tolson. Mu.
Satchmo.
Troupe. Four and More; for Miles Davis.
Poem for My Father.
Snake-Back Solo.
Unknown. It Don't Mean a Thing (If It Ain't
  Got That Swing).
Ward, J. Jazz to Jackson to John.
Weaver, M. Left Bank Jazz Society, The.
Welburn. Ben Webster: "Did You Call Her
  Today?"
Williams, M. Death of Chet Baker, The.
Wojahn. Satin Doll.
Yevtushenko. Saints of Jazz are playing, The.
Young, A. Lester Leaps In.
Zavatsky. To the Pianist Bill Evans.
Zimmer. But Bird.
Duke Ellington Dream, The.
Sitting with Lester Young.

Jealousy
"Akhmatova." Ah—you thought I'd be the type.
He whispers: 'I'm not sorry.
Ammuvanar. Six Said by the Concubines to Him.
Baillie, L. Werena My Heart Licht I Wad Dee.
Berssenbrugge. Jealousy.
Brown, S. Chillen Get Shoes.
Browning, R. My Last Duchess [Ferrara].
Bukowski. Funny Man.
Callimachus. I despise neo-epic verse sagas.
Campion, T. Though your strangenesse frets my hart.
Carew, T. To One That Desired to Know My Mistress [or Mistris].
Carmichael, R. Young Lass's Soliloquy, A.
Catullus. Sappho.
Coleridge, S. Jealousy.
Other Side of a Mirror, The.
Creeley. Memory, The.
D'Arcy, H. Face upon [or on] the Floor, The.
Davies, W. No Man's Wood.
When I in praise of babies speak.
Dickinson, E. God is indeed a jealous God.
Doolittle, H. At Ithaca.
"Ephelia." To J.G. on the News of His Marriage.
To My Rival.
Fox, G. She Lay Wrapped.
Friedrich von Hausen. When I parted from my Good.
Glück, L. Horse.
Graves, R. Cat-Goddesses.
Jealous Man, A.
Greene, R. Love and Jealousy.
Gumilyov. Tanka.
Gunn, T. Road Map, The.
Hall, D. Jealous Lovers, The.
Hardy, T. To Carrey Clavel.
Heaney, S. Dream of Jealousy, A.
Herrick. How Marigolds Came Yellow.
Johnson, E. Jealousy.
Jonson, B. Against Jealousy [or Jealousie].
Kemble. Petition, A.
Khodasevich. Ballad: "Oh, quietly mad I'd like to be."
Kipling, R. Bill 'Awkins.
Koch, K. Down at the docks.
Lamb, C. et al. First Tooth, The.
l'Hermite. Jealousy.
Lovelace, R. Cupid Far Gone.
Lucilius. Diophon, seeing / another man.
Manley, D. Song: "Ah, Dangerous Swain, tell me no more."
Mayer, B. Sonnet: "Beauty of songs your absence I should not show."
Meleager. Mother of gods.
Night and Night's longing.
Meredith, G. Their sense is with their senses all mixed in.
Nugent, R. To Clarissa.
O'Hara, F. Hôtel Transylvanie.
Ono no Komachi. In the daytime.
Ovid. 1.4.
Mistress keeps her lover on his toes, A.
Poe. Annabel Lee.
Ralegh, W. Excuse, The.
Ranaivo. Song of a Young Girl.
Ransom, J. Vaunting Oak.
Rossetti, D. Lost on Both Sides.
Sappho. He is more than a hero.
Scève. Délie.
Scott, A. To luve unluvit it is ane pane.
Service. Shooting of Dan McGrew, The.
Shakespeare, W. Now is the winter of our discontent.
Sonnet 29.
Sonnet 41.
Sonnet 61.
Sidney, P. Love and Jealousy.
Strato. Off with you, boy! Pretended prude!
Theocritus. Tom, Will, and Dick, and I, a jovial Crew.
Tsaloumas. Grudge, The.
Tsvetaeva. Attempt at Jealousy, An.

Unknown. But Jove at length with just Resentment fir'd.
Fair Margaret and Sweet William.
Josie.
Lily of the West, The.
Sheffield 'Prentice, The.
Two Sisters, The.
Widow's Old Broom, The.
You that are jealous and have a wife.
Waniek. Women's Locker Room.
Whitman, W. Sometimes with one I love I fill myself with rage for fear I effuse unreturn'd love.

See also **Envy**

Jeffers, Robinson
Everson, W. Man-Fate, The.
Poet Is Dead, The.
Milosz, C. To Robinson Jeffers.

Jefferson, Thomas
MacLeish. Brave New World.
MacLow. 1801.
Monks. Twilight's Last Gleaming.

Jehovah's Witnesses
Jones, G. 3-31-70.

Jellyfish
Doty, M. Difference.
Fumiko. Tanka: "In search of a shore."
Kahanu. When I was young on an island.
Kendall, M. Philanthropist and the Jelly-fish, The.
Moore, M. Jelly-Fish, A.
Teodorescu. At Night the Jellyfish Unfold Their Veils.

Jeremiah (Bible)
Kalir. Prophet Jeremiah and the Personification of Israel, The.

Jericho
Gouri. Jericho unknowing.
Guri. Jericho.
McGinley. Women of Jericho, The.

Jerome, Saint
Moore, M. Leonardo Da Vinci's.

Jerusalem
Amichai. I have nothing to say about the war.
If I forget thee, Jerusalem.
Letter.
Mayor.
This year I traveled far.
Bible, O.T. I Return unto Zion.
Song: "I am dark, daughters of Jerusalem."
Song: "I was asleep but my heart stayed awake."
Blake, W. But turning toward Ololon in terrible majesty Milton.
Jerusalem.
Prelude: "England! awake! awake! awake!"
Deloney. Our Savior Christ tracing the bordering hills,.
Fichman. In the Old City.
Halevi. Jerusalem.
Longing for Jerusalem.
Heine. By the Waters of Babylon.
If, Jerusalem, I Ever Should Forget Thee.
Kaufman, S. Next Year, in Jerusalem.
Kaye/Kantrowitz. Jerusalem Shadow.
Kovner. I Don't Know if Mount Zion would recognize itself.
Litvinoff. If I Forget Thee.
Mathews, A. At the Wailing Wall.
Melville, H. Hostel, The.
Via Crucis.
Pasternak, B. Evil Days, The.
Matthew 21:1–11.
Ravikovitch. Who Art Thou, O Great Mountain.
Rich, A. Jerusalem.
Rokeah. Jerusalem.
Tuqan, F. Face Lost in the Wilderness.
Tuwhare. Friend.
Unknown. Hierusalem, my happy [or happie] home.
Jerusalem, my happy home.
Prayer for Redemption.

See also **Zion**

Jesters
Storace. King Lear Bewildered.

Yeats. Cap and Bells, The.

See also **Fools**

Jesuits
Scott, F. Brébeuf and His Brethren.

Jesus Christ
Adams, F. To the Christians.
"Akhmatova." Crucifixion.
Alabaster. Divine Sonnet, A.
Jesu, thie love within mee is soe maine.
Night, the starles[e] night of passion, The.
Of the Reed That the Jews Set in Our Saviour's Hand.
To Christ.
Upon the Ensigns of Christ's Crucifying.
What meaneth this, that Christ an hymne did singe.
When without tears I looke on Christ, I see.
Alcuin. In the Refectory.
Inscription in Monastic Refectory.
On the Cross ("Adore the lifted standard of the Cross").
Prayer at Night ("He lay with quiet heart in the stern asleep").
Alexander, C. His Are the Thousand Sparkling Rills.
Once in Royal David's City.
There Is a Green Hill Far Away.
Amis, K. New Approach Needed.
Andrade, E. Fable.
Appleman, P. Mary.
Matthew 1:18–25: Now the birth of Jesus Christ took place.
Arif. To a Despondent Evening.
Arnold, M. Progress.
Askew. Ballad Which Anne Askew[e] Made and Sang When She Was in Newgate, The.
Auden. From "The Prolific and the Devourer."
Terce.
Avison. Dumbfounding, The.
Bacon, L. Wake the Song of Jubilee.
Baldwin, W. Christ, My Beloved.
Baraka. When We'll Worship Jesus.
Barnes, D. Chuang Tzu and Hui Tzu were hundreds of years old.
Barrett, E. Woman.
Bates, K. Despised and Rejected.
Berkeley, S. Mass is over, they have gone in peace, The.
Berrigan, D. Prayer: "I left Cornell / with half a wit; six mismated socks."
Berryman. Carpenter's Son, The.
Bevington, L. 'Dreamers?' Ah, no! else he was a dreamer.
Bible, N.T. Blessed be the Paps which Thou hast Sucked.
Christ's Promise.
Luke 7; She Began To Wash His Feet with Teares and Wipe Them with the Haires of Her Head.
Bible, O.T. There were some shepherds living in the same part of the country.
Birney. El Greco: Espolio.
Blake, W. Introduction: "Piping down the valleys wild."
Jerusalem.
Lamb, The.
Night.
Prince of Love, The.
To Tirzah.
Was Jesus Humble? or did he.
Bolton, S. His Monument.
Borges. John 1:14 (1969).
One of the criminals.
Luke XXIII.
Seeing the crowds, he went up on the mountain.
Bowes-Lyon. Blind Tramp, The.
Brecht, B. And in that region there were shepherds.
Mary.
Breytenbach. There Is Life.
Brodsky, J. Nature Morte.
Brontë, C. Pilate's Wife's Dream.
Brooks, P. Christmas Everywhere.
O little town of Bethlehem.
Brooks, W. Pilate Remembers.

Brown, C. Good Friday.
Browning, R. Epistle Containing the Strange Medical Experience of Karshish, the Arab Physician, An.
Byrd. Lulla, My Sweet Little Baby.
Campbell, J. When Rooks Fly Homeward.
Cardenal. Unrighteous Mammon (Luke 16:9).
   I Am the Great Sun[, but you do not see me].
Causley. Ballad of the Bread Man.
Chesterton, G. Donkey, The.
Clarkson. Behold, the King of glory now is come.
Clemo. Christ in the Clay-Pit.
Clifton, L. God Send Easter.
   How Is He Coming Then.
   Spring Song.
Clough. Across the sea, along the shore,.
Cohen, L. Suzanne takes you down to her place near the river.
Coleridge, M. I saw a stable low and very bare.
Coleridge, S. My Baptismal Birthday [or Birth-Day].
Columbanus. Boyhood of Christ, The.
Corrington. On the Flesh of Christ.
Crashaw. Come See the Place Where the Lord Lay.
   Hymne of the Nativity, Sung by the Shepheards, A.
   In the Glorious Epiphanie of Our [or Ovr] Lord God[, A Hymn. Svng as by the Three Kings].
   Neither Durst Any Man From That Day Ask Him Any More Questions.
   On the Name of Jesus.
   On the Water of Our Lord's Baptism[e].
   On the Wounds of Our Crucified Lord.
   To Our Blessed Lord upon the Choice of His Sepulchre.
   To the Noblest and Best of Ladies, the Countess of Denbigh, Perswading her to Resolution in Religion, and to render her selfe without further delay into the Communion of the Catholick Church.
   Upon the Asse That Bore Our Saviour.
Crossman. My Song Is Love Unknown.
Cullen, C. Christus Natus Est.
Cummings, E. No time ago / or else a life.
Cusack. Cross Talk.
   Summer Reflection.
Da Todi. Stabat Mater, The.
Daumal. Jesus before Pilate said nothing.
   Now Jesus stood before.
Davie. Pilate.
Day Lewis. Christmas Rose, The.
De Brun. Calvary.
Dickey, J. Magus, The.
Dickinson, E. At least—to pray—is left—is left.
   God is a distant—stately Lover.
   I shall know why—when Time is over.
   One crown that no one seeks.
   Word made Flesh is seldom, A.
Dietz. Gentle Jesus meek and mild.
Donne. Hymne to Christ, at the Author's Last Going into Germany, A.
   Oh my black[e] soul[e]! now thou art summoned.
   Resurrection, Imperfect.
   Son, The.
   Spit in my face ye [or you] Jew[e]s, and pierce my side.
   What if this present were the world's last night?
   Why are we[e] by all creatures waited on?
   Wilt thou love God, as he thee? [or thee!] then digest.
Drunina. In all ages, always, everywhere, and everywhere.
Dunbar, W. In Praise of Women.
   Of Christ's Nativity.
Eliot, T. And at the end of eight days, when he was circumcised.
   Now when Jesus was born.
Fairfax, E. Drearie trumpet blew a dreadfull blast, The.

Fanthorpe. Nativities.
Farren. Immolation.
   Stable Straw.
Ferlinghetti, L. Christ Climbed Down / from His bare Tree.
   Sometime during eternity / some guys show up.
"Field." Constancy.
   They Shall Look on Him.
Flecknoe. On the Death of Our Lord.
Fletcher, P. Hymn, An: "Wake, O my soul; awake, and raise."
   Ocean of Light.
Fordham. Christ Child, The.
   Nativity, The.
Frear. Young Workman, The.
Fuller, R. Peculiar Christmas, A.
Gascoigne. Gloze Upon This Text, *Dominus iis opus habet*, A.
Gascoyne. Ecce Homo.
Gergely. Magdalene.
Glatstein. Matthew 5:38–48; "You have heard that it was said, 'An eye'."
Glück, L. Luke 2:1–7; In those days a decree went out from Caesar Augustus.
   Nativity Poem.
Graves, R. In the Wilderness.
Gregg. Esta.
Greville, F. 99.
Greville, F. Sonnet: "Down[e] in the depth of mine iniquity."
   Sonnet: "Man, dream[e] no more of curious mysteries."
Griffin, S. Miracle.
Griffiths, A. Lo, between the Myrtles Standing.
Gumilyov. I, who could have been the best of poems.
Gunn, T. Jesus and His Mother.
Hall, D. Matthew 21:18–22; In the morning.
   Small Fig Tree, A.
Hammon. Evening Thought, An [: Salvation by Christ with Penetential Cries].
Hankey. I Love to Tell the Story.
Hardy, T. Unkept Good Fridays.
Harper, F. He "Had Not Where to Lay His Head."
   Let the Light Enter!
   Sir, We Would See Jesus.
Harris, R. Call, The.
Hartwig. Who Says.
Havergal. Just when Thou wilt, O Master, call!
Hayden, R. Full Moon.
Hayes, A. Pietá.
Heard, J. Birth of Jesus, The.
Hecht, A. Pig.
Herbert, G. Aaron.
   Affliction: "Kill me not every [or ev'ry] day."
   Affliction (3).
   Agony [or Agonie], The.
   Bag, The.
   Bunch of Grapes, The.
   Dawning, The.
   Dialogue, A.
   Dulness[e].
   Easter-Wings.
   Good Friday.
   Grieve Not the Holy Spirit, etc.
   Holy Baptism (1).
   JESU is in my heart, his sacred name.
   Longing.
   Love bade me welcome[: yet my soul drew back].
   Love-Joy.
   Love ("Thou art too hard for me in Love").
   Mary [or Marie] Magdalene.
   Our Life Is Hid with Christ in God.
   Redemption.
   Reprisal[l], The.
   Sacrifice, The.
   Son[ne], The.
   Sunday.
   Thanksgiving, The.
Herbert, Z. When Judas, his betrayer, saw.
   Meditations of Mr. Cogito on Redemption.
   Passion of Our Lord painted by an anonymous

hand from the Circle of Rhenish Masters, The.
   Speculations on the Subject of Barabbas.
Herebert. Crist, buyere of alle icoren.
   Jesu our raunsoun.
   Thou king of wele and blisse.
Herrick. Christ's Sadness.
   Good Friday: Rex Tragicus, or, Christ Going to His Cross[e].
   His Offering, with the Rest, at the Sepulcher.
   His Saviour[']s Words, Going to the Cross[e].
   No Coming to God without Christ.
   To Christ.
Hibernicus Exul. O Christ, receive these souls in thy Mother's house.
Hildebert. In Honour of the Holy Spirit.
   Nor God, nor man, the image thou dost see.
   Shepherd cheerfully, The.
Hill, G. Lachrimae Amantis.
   Lachrimae Verae.
Holst-Warhaft. In the end is the body—what we know.
Hope, A. Easter Hymn.
   Gloss to Matthew V 27–28.
   As they were saying this, Jesus.
Hopkins, G. Lantern Out of Doors, The.
   Moonless darkness stands between.
   Spring.
   Starlight Night, The.
   What I Do Is Me.
   Windhover, The.
Hopkins, J. Alleluia! Christ is risen today.
Hopper, E. Jesus Saviour, Pilot Me.
Housman, A. Easter Hymn.
   So then the Lord Jesus, after.
Hristic. That night they all gathered on the highest tower.
Hudgins. Dead Christ.
Hughes, L. Feet O' Jesus.
Hughes, T. God, A.
   Now from the sixth hour there was darkness.
Hurston. Faith hasn't got no eyes, but she long-legged.
Ita. Jesukin.
Jarry. Passion of Jesus Considered as an Uphill Race, The.
Johnson, J. Go Down Death.
Johnson, L. Church of a Dream, The.
Jones, D. In the middle silences of this night's course the blackthorn.
Jonson, B. Hymn[e] on the Nativity [or Nativitie] of My Saviour, A.
Jordan, J. All the world moved next to me strange.
Joyce, J. Ballad of Joking Jesus, The.
Kamienska. Now as they went on their way.
Kane, P. Disciples Asleep at Gethsemane.
Kenyon, J. Back from the City.
Kinsella, T. Carol: "Garden and gardener He made."
Kipling, R. Nativity, A.
   Sons of Martha, The.
Kirchwey. And Jesus said to him.
Kossman. When Jesus had thus said, he was troubled.
   Pilate's Wife.
Kunitz, S. He runs before the wise men: He.
Lanier. Now Pontius Pilate is to judge the cause.
Lanier, S. Ballad of Trees and the Master, A.
Lawrence, D. Commandments.
   Demiurge.
   My name is Jesus, I am Mary's son.
   Quetzalcoatl Looks Down on Mexico.
   Retort to Jesus.
Leax. Incarnation Poem.
Leslie, S. Holy Cross.
Lindsay, V. I heard Immanuel singing.
Llwyd, M. 1. What? summer now? divisions ring.
Lowell, R. Drunken Fisherman, The.
Luther. Cradle Hymn.
   From heaven above to earth I come.
   From Heaven High I Come to You.
   In the bonds of Death He lay.
Lvov, V. That yellowed body of the Lord.

"MacDiarmid." Harry Semen.
Innumerable Christ, The.
Maksimovic. Then the Pharisees went and.
Martin, C. Easter Sunday, 1985.
Marvell. Clorinda and Damon.
Coronet, The.
Mason, R. Ecce Homunculus.
On the Swag.
McAuley, J. In the Twentieth Century.
Jesus.
McClellan. Feet of Judas, The.
Melville, H. Arch, The.
Merton. Cana.
Mew. Madeleine in Church.
Meynell, A. Christ in the Universe.
Fugitive, The.
Michael of Kildare. Swet Jesus.
Middleton, E. Unhappy merchant, Thus
  t'expose thy Lord.
Milosz, C. "Christ has risen." Whoever
  believes that / Should not behave as we do.
Luke 5:1–11; While the people pressed upon
  him.
Mark 5:21–43; And when Jesus had crossed.
Matthew 28:1–6; Now after the sabbath.
Matthew 4:1–11; Then Jesus was led up by
  the spirit.
Temptation.
With Her.
Milton. Hymn on the Morning of Christ's
  Nativity [or On the Morning of Christ's
  Nativity].
Mitchell, C. Soul of Jesus Is Restless, The.
Mitchell, S. And behold, a lawyer.
Matthew 13:1–9; That same day Jesus.
Mitchell, S. Descent of the Child, The.
Moorer. Benefits of Sorrow.
Sympathy.
Morris, M. Joseph of Arimathaea.
Pilate.
Mtshali. Ride upon the Death Chariot.
Muir, E. Incarnate One, The.
Killing, The.
Nemerov. Carol: "Now is the world
  withdrawn all."
John 3:1–15; Now there was a man.
Nicodemus.
Sacrificed Author, A.
Santa Claus.
Nowak, T. Psalm Ajar.
O Direain. Trees on a Frosty Night.
O'Dalaigh, G. Under Sorrow's Sign.
O'Flynn. God?
O'Higgins, M. Young Poet.
Okigbo. Passion Flower.
Olson, E. Ballad of the Scarecrow Christ.
O'Shaughnessy, A. Line of Beauty, The.
O'Sullivan, T. Poem to the Heart of Jesus, A.
Owen, W. At a Calvary near the Ancre.
Pankey. Luke: 24:13–32; That very day two
  of them.
Parra, N. Who are my friends / the sick / the
  weak / the poor in spirit.
Pasternak, B. Christmas Star.
Evil Days, The.
Garden of Gethsemane, The.
Hamlet.
Magdalene (I).
Mark 14:26–42; And when they had sung.
Matthew 21:1–11.
Matthew 26:47–56; While he was still
  speaking, Judas came.
Miracle, The.
Patrick, S. St Patrick's Breastplate.
Saint Patrick's Breastplate; or, The Deer's Cry.
Patterson, R. Harlem Suite.
Peacock, M. Devolution.
Perronet. All hail the Power of Jesus' name!
Pickthall, M. Bridegroom of Cana, The.
Pilinszky. Paraphrase.
Plumpp. I Told Jesus.
Plunkett. I Saw the Sun at Midnight, Rising
  Red.
I See His Blood upon the Rose.
Stars Sang in God's Garden, The.
Pound, E. Ballad of the Goodly Fere.
Powell, C. Nativity.

Prudentius. Hymn for Morning.
Quarles. I saw him dead; I saw his Body fall.
I wish a greater knowledge, then t'attaine.
On Our Saviour's Passion.
Upon the Day of Our Saviour's Nativity.
Ralegh, W. On the Card[e]s, and Dice.
Ransom, J. Armageddon.
Our Two Worthies.
Ray, H. Prayer: "O Christ, who in
  Gethsemane."
Rilke. John 11:30–44; Now Jesus had not yet
  come to the village.
But Mary stood weeping outside the tomb.
On the third day there was a marriage.
Last Supper, The.
Mary at Peace with the Risen Lord.
Matthew 26:17–29.
When it was evening, there came a rich man.
Olive Garden, The.
On the Marriage at Cana.
Pietà.
Robinson, E. Calvary.
Rock. He Is the Lonely Greateness.
Rodgers, W. It was a lovely night.
Rossetti, C. Before the paling of the stars.
Better Resurrection, A.
Bruised Reed Shall He Not Break, A.
Easter Monday.
If Only.
Long Barren.
Lord Jesus, who would think that I am Thine?
Lowest Place, The.
Three Enemies, The.
Wednesday in Holy Week.
Rothenberg, J. Visions of Jesus.
Roumain. New Negro Sermon.
Rukeyser, M. Holy Family.
Sandburg, C. Early Lynching.
Sassoon. Christ and the Soldier.
Schneour. Last Words of Don Henriquez, The.
Sexton. For God While Sleeping.
Jesus Dies.
Shelton, M. When Jesus walked upon the
  earth.
Sheperd. Who hath not knowne or herd.
Sisson. Adam and Eve.
Easter.
Skelton, J. O benign Jesu, my sovereign Lord
  and King.
Smart, C. Ascension of Our Lord Jesus Christ,
  The.
Crucifixion of Our Blessed Lord.
Epiphany.
Smith, S. Airy Christ, The.
Was he married, did he try.
Southwell. Burning Babe, The.
Child[e] My Choice [or Choyse], A.
Christ[e]'s Childhood[e].
Christs Sleeping Friends.
New Heaven, New War[re].
New Prince, New Pomp[e].
Sinnes Heavie Loade.
Spenser. Sonnet 68: "Most glorious Lord of
  Life that on this day."
Staff. Portrait.
Steele, P. Cana.
Stewart, G. As I went down to David's town.
Stocking. O Master-Workman of the Race.
Stone, S. Church's One Foundation, The.
Suckling, J. Upon Christ His Birth.
Tabb. Christ and the Pagan.
Tadic. Jesus.
Tate, J. Goodtime Jesus.
Tate, N. While shepherds watched their flocks
  by night.
Taylor, E. Christ's Reply.
Reflexion, The.
View, all ye eyes above, this sight which
  flings.
Tennyson, A. Sweet after showers, ambrosial
  air.
Thaxter. On Easter Day.
Theodulf of Orleans. Wherefore the Scars of
  Christ's Passion Remained in the Body of
  His Resurrection.
Thomas Aquinas. With my heart I worship.
Word went forth, The.

Thomas, D. This bread I break was once the
  oat.
Thompson, C. Empty Tomb, The.
Thompson, F. Ex Ore Infantium.
Hound of Heaven, The.
Thompson, P. Death and Resurrection.
Traherne. Wonder.
Trapnell, A. O he is a rest that requires.
Tsvetayeva. Bethlehem.
Magdalene.
Turk. Thank You, Jesus, for this day.
Tynan. Sheep and Lambs.
U Tam'si Tchicaya. Scorner, The.
Unknown. Bitter Withy, The.
Child's Creed, A.
CHRIST was the Word that spake it.
Christ's Bounty.
Coventry Carol.
Crucifixion, The.
Deep Spring.
Down in the Valley.
Down to the Mire.
Easter Song, An.
Fairest Lord Jesus.
Give Me Jesus.
Here I ame and fourthe I mouste.
His Son's / A Jew.
I Met the Master.
I saw a Peacock with a fiery tail.
I syng of a mayden that is makeles.
I Wonder as I Wander.
Jesu Crist, heovene king.
Jesu that is most of might.
Jesus Borned in Bethlea.
Jesus on the Sabbath.
Joys of Mary, The.
Keening of Mary, The.
Kindely is now my coming.
Little Cradle Rocks Tonight in Glory, The.
Lo, how a rose is growing.
Lord Jesus Christ, in whose hand is the breath.
Men rent me on rode.
My folk, now answere me.
My folk, what habbe I do thee.
Now Goeth Sun under Wood.
Preparations.
Ride in, kind Saviour!
See! Here, My Heart.
Senful man, bethink and see.
Somer is comen and winter gon.
Song of Childbirth, The.
Song of the Woman, The.
Steal Away to Jesus.
"Stond well, moder, under Rode."
Swete Jesu, king of blisse.
Swete Jhesu, king of blisse.
This Endris Night.
Water and nblod for thee I swete.
Were you there when they crucified my Lord?
  [(were you there?)].
When I See on Rood.
When the Lord climbed.
Ye that passen [or pasen] by the weye [or
  weiye].
U'Tamsi. Scorner, The.
Van Dyke. Lost Word of Jesus, A.
Vaughan, H. British [or Brittish] Church, The.
Burial.
Christ's Nativity.
H. Scriptures.
Incarnation and Passion, The.
Lamp[e], The.
Match, The.
Midnight.
Mount of Olives.
Passion, The.
Peace.
Rainbow, The.
Search, The.
Shepherds [or Shepheards], The.
Wreath, The.
Very. Cross, The.
Garden, The.
Morning Watch, The.
New Birth, The.
Serpent, The.
Son, The.

Wadding. On the Circumsision: New Year's Day.
Walcott. God Rest Ye Merry, Gentlemen.
Walsh, C. Quintina of Crosses, A.
Walther von der Vogelweide. Now my life has gained some meaning.
Warner, E. Irony of God.
Watkyns. Gardener, The.
Upon Christ's Nativity or Christmas.
Watts, I. Passion and Exaltation of Christ, The.
Wellesley. April 1939.
Wesley, C. Gentle Jesus Meek and Mild.
In Temptation.
Whiteside. Carpenter, The.
Whitman, W. To Him That Was Crucified.
Whitmell. Christ in Flanders.
Whittier. Dedication. "I would the gift I offer here."
Over-Heart, The.
Wickham. To a Crucifix.
Wilbur. And when he came to the other side. Matthew VIII, 28 ff.
Wilde, O. Ave Maria, Gratia Plena.
E Tenebris.
Williams, W. Gift, The.
Wojahn. First Six Seals, The.
Wolfe, H. Dean Inge.
Wright, J. Saint Judas.
Wright, J. Eli, Eli.
Yeats. "Calvary."
I am Judas.
Now the eleven disciples went to Galilee.
Stick of Incense, A.
Two Songs from a Play.
Zangwill. Moses and Jesus.

Jewelry
Gillies, V. Ericstane Brooch, The.
Fellow Passenger.
Graves, R. With a Gift of Rings.
Herrick. Seest thou those diamonds which she wears.
To Julia ("How rich and pleasing thou, my Julia, art").
Kirchwey. Natural History.
Pope, A. Sol through white curtains shot a tim'rous ray.
Stanley, T. Bracelet, The.
Wakoski. Ring, The.

See also **Rings**

Jews
Abse. Footnote Extended, A.
Amichai. Jews in the Land of Israel.
Patriotic Reflections.
Antin. Real Estate.
Auden. And as they led him away.
Refugee Blues.
Bibb. Wandering Jew, The.
Bobrowski. Elderblossom.
Boss. At the Nuclear Rally.
Bruck. Equality, father! Your dream has come true.
Celan. Death Fugue, A.
Zürich, the Stork Inn.
Cohen, L. Genius, The.
Daumal. Now Jesus stood before.
Davie. Pilate.
Durcan. Jewish Bride, The.
Ewer. How odd / Of God.
Feldman, I. Scene of a Summer Morning.
Ficowski. Girl of Six from the Ghetto Begging in Smolna Street in 1942, A.
Assumption of Miriam from the Street in the Winter of 1942, The.
Both Your Mothers.
Execution of Memory, The.
Florsheim. Jewish Singles Event, The.
Gershon. Experiments with God.
Race.
Glaser, M. Preparations for Seder.
Glatstein. How much Christian, so to speak, can I get?
Goldensohn, B. Marrano, The.
Gouri. Heritage.
In the Amorite city spared for my sake from the sword of Joshua.

Pictures of Jews.
Window-Dreaming with SAS.
Guri. Pictures of the Jews.
Hamburger, M. Treblinka.
Harris, R. Riding Over Belmore Park.
Hecht, A. 'More Light! More Light!'.
Jarrell. Jews at Haifa.
Kaye/Kantrowitz. Jerusalem Shadow.
Klein, A. Autobiographical.
Heirloom.
Klepfisz. About My Father.
Bashert.
Few Words in the Mother Tongue, A.
Kolmar. Judith.
Kovner. Dinosaurs wept angry tears.
Sun-Watchers.
Kramer, L. Shoemaker's Wife, The.
Kumin, M. Chain, The.
Living Alone with Jesus—.
Lazarus, E. In Exile.
New Ezekiel, The.
Levine, P. Old Testament, The.
Lifshin. Being Jewish in a Small Town.
Yahrtzeit Light, The.
Longfellow, H. Jewish Cemetery at Newport, The.
Legend of Rabbi Ben Levi, The.
Mayne, S. Before Passover.
Melville, H. Concerning Hebrews.
Merrill, J. Correct but cautious, that first night, we asked.
Miller, J. Far Away.
Moore, T. Weep, Children of Israel.
Moraes, D. Altermann, sipping wine, reads with a look.
Narovchatov. Wolf Cub.
Niemoller. First they came for the Jews.
Ostriker. Eighth and the Thirteenth, The.
Meditation in Seven Days, A.
Parnell, T. From the black beach and broad expanse of sea.
Plath. Daddy.
Preil, G. Lines on the Rambam.
Quarles. Meditatio Septima.
Rakosi. Israel.
Sandlewood comes to my mind.
Services.
Ranasinghe. Holocaust 1944.
Ravikovitch. Human Qualities.
Reznikoff. Hebrew of your poets, Zion, The.
Highway I was walking on, The.
Jews from Holland, France, and Hungary, and later from.
Joshua at Schechem.
When the Second World War began.
Rich, A. Yom Kippur 1984.
Rosenberg, I. Jew, The.
Rosenberg, L. Edith B——and her mother on a Sunday afternoon.
Rothenberg, J. At the Castle.
Dos Geshray (The Scream).
Poland / 1931 "The Wedding."
Portrait of a Jew Old Country Style.
Structural Study of Myth, The.
Rukeyser, M. Despisals.
To be a Jew in the twentieth century.
Sachs, N. Chorus of the Dead.
O the Chimneys.
Sadoff. Nazis.
Seiler. Digging in the Streets of Gold.
Shapiro, K. Alphabet, The.
Shore. High Holy Days.
Simko. Jewish Cemetery in Prague, The.
Simpson, L. Story About Chicken Soup, A.
Sklarew. What Is a Jewish Poem?
Slonimski. Elegy: "No more, no more Jewish townships in Poland."
Spender, S. History and Reality.
Stern, G. Behaving Like a Jew.
Dancing, The.
Sutskever. Friday evening coos up in the attic.
Swinburne. On the Russian Persecution of the Jews.
Szymborska. Still.
Tsvetayeva. Dense as a horse mane is.
Unknown. His Son's / A Jew.
Hugh of Lincoln.

Weiner, J. Who They Were.
Wiesel. Behold, God of Abraham, God of mercy.
Wieseltier. Take a Look at My Rebels.
Yevtushenko. Babii Yar.
Zach. Nameless.
Zukofsky, L. Fifth Movement: Autobiography.

Jezebel
Higgins, F. Song for the Clatter-Bones.

Joan of Arc
Clifton, L. To Joan.
Lowell, M. Rouen, Place de la Pucelle.
Ludvigson. Jeanne d'Arc.
Péret. Joan of Arc.
Roberts, M. Rite de Passage.
Svetlov. To a Rabfak Student.

Job (Bible)
Ashbery. Cæsura.
Lax. Morning Stars, The.
Macpherson, J. Beauty of Job's Daughters, The.
Plumly. Will Work for Food.
Rosenberg, D. Job Speaks.
Sandys, G. Again when all the radiant sons of light.
"O Father, I acknowledge," Job replied.
Sewell, E. Job.
Shelton, R. Job the Father.
Sholl. Yes, I said it.
Sylvester, J. Job's Epitaph.
Leviathan.

Jockeys
Higgins, F. Old Jockey, The.

See also **Horse Racing**

Jogging and Joggers. *See* **Running and Runners**

John XXIII, Pope
Hewitt, J. Rome Sunday[,] June 1960.

"John Henry" (folk hero)
Unknown. John Henry.

John Paul II, Pope
Jordan, J. Lolek.

John, Saint
Wheelwright. Bread-Word Giver.
Wilbur. Wedding Toast, A.
Wylie. Peter and John.

John of Austria
Chesterton, G. Lepanto.

John the Baptist, Saint
Constable, H. To St John Baptist.
Drummond, W. For the Baptiste.
Smart, C. Nativity of St. John the Baptist, The.

"Johnny Appleseed." *See* **Chapman, John**

Johnson, Lionel
Yeats. In Memory of Major Robert Gregory.

Johnson, Lyndon Baines
Duncan, R. Up Rising.
Weber, R. Concise History of the Vietnam War: 1965–1968, A.
Wilbur. Miltonic Sonnet for Mr. Johnson on His Refusal of Peter Hurd's Official Portrait, A.

Johnson, Samuel
Cowper, W. Epitaph on Dr. Johnson.
Dunbar, P. Then and Now.
Jenyns. Doctor Johnson.
Epitaph on Dr Samuel Johnson.
Moody, E. Dr. Johnson's Ghost.
"Pindar." Town Eclogue, A.
Synge. To the Oaks of Glencree.

Johnston, James Hugo
Johnson, M. James Hugo Johnston.

Jonah (Bible)
Bancquart. Portrait of Jonah with woman.
Drayton. Song of Jonah in the Whale's Belly, The.
Jarrell. Jonah.
Marquis. Noah an' Jonah an' Cap'n John Smith.
Melville, H. Whale, The.
Merwin, W. Leviathan.
Owen, G. Jonah and the Whale.
Salamun. Jonah.
Shapiro, D. In a Blind Garden.

Unknown. I to the Lord from My Distress.
Jonathan (Bible)
  Bible, *O.T.* David's Lament.
Jones, Ebenezer
  Betjeman. Incident in the Early Life of Ebenezer Jones, Poet, 1828, An.
Jones, John Paul
  Unknown. Paul Jones's Victory.
  Yankee Man-of-War, The.
Jonson, Ben
  Beaumont, F. Letter to Ben Jonson, A.
  Carew, T. To Ben Jonson.
  Cartwright, W. Where shall we find a Muse like thine, that can.
  Cleveland, J. Elegy on Ben Jonson, An.
  Godolphin. On Ben Jonson.
  Herrick. His Prayer to Ben[.] Jo[h]nson.
    My Ben!
    Ode for Ben Jonson, An.
    Upon Ben Jo[h]nson.
    Upon M. Ben Jo[h]nson: Epigram.
  Howell, J. Upon the Poet of His Time, Ben Jonson: His Honoured Friend and Father.
  Johnson, S. Then Jonson came, instructed from the school.
  King, H. To My Dead Friend Ben: Johnson.
  Oldham, J. Plain Humour, shown with her whole various face.
  Randolph, T. Answer to Mr. Ben Jonson's Ode, to Persuade Him Not to Leave the Stage, An.
    Gratulatory to Mr. Ben Johnson for His Adopting of Him to Be His Son, A.
  Suckling, J. First that broke silence was good old Ben, The.
  Swinburne. Ben Jonson.
  Waller, E. Upon Ben Johnson [*or* Jonson].
  Westmorland. In Obitum Ben. Jons.
  Wilson, E. Nursery Vignette.
Joseph (Bible, O.T.)
  Avidan. Glimpse of an Open Dream.
  George, D. Asenath.
  Herbert, G. Joseph's Coat.
  Hubert. Joseph in Carcere.
  Nemerov. September, the First Day of School.
  Reznikoff. Israel II.
  Sylvester, J. But, fair Iëmpsar (wife of Potiphar).
Joseph, Saint
  Chesterton, G. Joseph.
  "MacDiarmid." Harry Semen.
  Rilke. Joseph's Suspicion.
  Tynan. Man of the House, The.
Joshua (Bible)
  Gouri. In the Amorite city spared for my sake from the sword of Joshua.
  Kennedy, X. Joshua.
  Ostriker. Story of Joshua.
  Unknown. Joshua fit de battle of Jericho [*or* ob Jerico].
Journalism and Journalists
  Forché. Memory of Elena, The.
  Mathews, C. Journalist, The.
  McFadden, R. For the Record.
  Moorer. Southern Press, The.
  Ofeimun. Beyond Fear.
  Sandburg, C. Buttons.
  Wolfe, H. You cannot hope.
  See also **Magazines; Newspapers**
Jowett, Benjamin
  Beeching, H. First come I. My name is Jowett.
Joy
  Anacreon. Love.
  Bachmann. Kind of Loss, A.
  Bangs, J. Today, whatever may annoy.
  Barannikov. May there always be sun!
  Beam. Time is.
  Bible, *N.T.* End To Tears, An.
  Bible, *O.T.* Like unto Them That Dream.
  Blake, W. Eternity ("He who binds to himself a joy").
    Infant Joy.
  Bonnefoy. All, the Nothing, The.
  Bose, B. Frogs.
  Braithwaite. Sic Vita.

Brome. Epithalamy.
Brontë, E. Fair sinks the summer evening now.
Brown, G. Old Women, The.
Browning, E. Deserted Garden, The.
  Sonnet: "I lived with visions for my company."
Browning, R. Now.
Buddha. Unlimited Friendliness.
Bunin. Flowers, and tall-stalked grasses, and a bee.
Carter, E. Ode to Wisdom.
Cavafy. One Night.
Chalkhill. Coridon's Song.
Chang Yü. Merchant's Joy, The.
Chōkū. Tanka: "Bulky oil lamp, A."
Ch'u Kuang-hsi. Cowherd, The; a Song.
Chu. Sound of Rain, The.
Coleridge, M. Solo.
Cowper, W. Animals Enjoying Life.
Crashaw. Against Hope.
Cullen, C. From Life to Love.
Cummings, E. Darling!because my blood can sing.
  If everything happens that can't be done.
  You shall above all things be glad and young.
Dacre, C. Kiss, The.
Dante Alighieri. To every heart which the sweet pain doth move.
Dawe, B. Going.
Dawe, G. Solstice.
DeBary. Tomorrow I will haul down the flag of hypocrisy.
Dickey, J. In the Marble Quarry.
Dickinson, E. Did Our Best Moment last.
  I can wade Grief.
Dioscorides. Thracian page-boy / mastered, A.
Donne. Ecstasy, The.
Dryden, J. Song from The Indian Emperor.
Dunbar, P. Little brown baby wif spa'klin' eyes.
  Old Cabin, The.
Eedes. No Love, to Love of Man and Wife.
Emerson, R. Water understands / Civilization well, The.
Etter. Great Northern.
Evans, M. Who Can Be Born Black.
"Field." To Christina Rossetti.
Gay, J. Cotillion.
Glück, L. Nativity Poem.
Goedicke. After the Second Operation.
Hamer. Getting Happy.
Hardy, T. First or Last.
Hong, Y. Maple Leaves.
Hopkins, G. Hurrahing in Harvest.
Howe, F. First Chance Twice.
Hsü Chün-ch'ien. Beginning of Spring—A Stroll with My Wife.
Hulme, T. Embankment (The Fantasia of a Fallen Gentleman on a Cold, Bitter Night), The.
Ishikawa Takuboku. Tanka: "Accidentally."
Jeffers, R. Joy.
Jonson, B. To Sir Henry Cary.
K'ang Hai. Sitting by Myself.
Kazantzakis. O sun, great Oriental, my proud mind's golden cap.
Keats. Fancy.
Kharms. Khaldeyev, Naldeyev, and Peppermaldeyev.
Killigrew, A. Farewel to Worldly Joyes, A ("Farewel to unsubstantial joyes").
Levertov. Ache of marriage, The.
  Matins.
  Triple Feature.
Liu E. Pleasures of Shinbashi.
Lovelace, R. Dialogue.
Lu Yu. Boating in Autumn.
Mao Tse-tung. Long March, The.
Martial. De M. Antonio.
Mathews, H. Aboard a Boat at Night, Drinking with My Wife.
McCord, D. Blesséd Lord, What It Is to Be Young.
Meng Chiao. After Passing the Examination.
Miles, S. Plumbers.
Milton. To the Lord General[l] Cromwell[, on

the Proposals of Certain Ministers at the Committee for the Propagation of the Gospel *or* May 1652].
Mitchell, S. Girl Tearing Up Her Face.
Moore, T. Go where glory waits thee.
Nabbes. Song: "What a dainty life the milkmaid leads!"
Nashe. Spring.
Nasrin. Eve Oh Eve.
Nguyễn Chí Thiện. Travel with grief—goodbye to joy!
Nicaenetus. Not in the city, Philoterus.
Oliver, M. Blossom.
"O'Sullivan." Piper, A [*or* The].
Owenson. Joy a fix'd state—a tenure, not a start!
Peele. Write write yow Croniclers of Tyme and Fame.
Phillips, C. Reach, The.
Pilinszky. Fragment from the Golden Age.
Po Chü-i. Chrysanthemums in the Eastern Garden, The.
  Going Alone to Spend a Night at the Hsien-Yu Temple.
  To his Brother Hsing-chien.
Ray, H. Shadow and Sunrise.
Reverdy. For the Moment.
Riley, J. When she comes home again! A thousand ways.
Rilke. Isn't the secret intent.
Roethke. Moment, The.
Rosenberg, I. Garden of Joy, The.
Rossetti, C. Birthday, A.
  Hope and Joy.
Rukeyser, M. Reading Time : 1 Minute 26 Seconds.
Rumi. Say Yes Quickly.
  Someone Digging in the Ground.
  Tonight with wine being poured.
Ryashentsev. April in Town.
Sandburg, C. Joy.
Sarton. Small Joys.
"Severyanin." Spring Day.
Sexton. Welcome Morning.
Sherburne. Weeping and Kissing.
Sidney, P. Sonnet 69: "O joy, too high for my low style to show."
Sikelianos. Return, The.
So Chong-Ju. Fresh Green, The.
Sri Sri. Man walks on the bridge and gives away the change in his, A.
Steele, T. Eros.
Strode. Opposite to Melancholy.
Swift, J. Satirical Elegy on the Death of a Late Famous General, A.
Swirszczynska. Thank You, My Fate.
T'ang Yin. Fog of night envelops the flowering trees, The.
Tao-chi. Inscribed on a Painting ("Little boat floats by the dock, The").
Teasdale. Answer, The.
Thoreau. Winter Memories.
Tolson. Victor Garibaldi.
Tzara. Waking.
Unknown. Fairest Lord Jesus.
  I loathe the twin seas.
  May Day.
  My Choice.
  My Lord Summons Me.
  Of this day's glorious feast and revel.
  Only rule is enjoy yourself, The.
  There's happiness in little things.
Watts, M. Vision.
Whitman, W. I saw in Louisiana a live-oak growing.
  We two, how long we were fool'd.
Wilbur. Hamlen Brook.
Wilde, L. Corinne's Last Love-Song.
Woods, M. Tears and Joys.
Wordsworth, W. Daffodils.
Wright, J. Blessing, A.
Wu Wei-yeh. Garden Living.
Yang Shen. To the Tune "Heavenly Immortal."
Yü Chi. Sent To Be Inscribed on the Temple of P'u-jun (Universal Fructification) at Lou-fu Mountain.

Yüan Chieh. Stone Fish Lake.
Yüan Mei. Miscellaneous Feelings in the Sui Garden.
Zolotow. Aren't You Glad.

Joyce, James
Daiches. Ulysses' Library.
"MacDiarmid." In the Fall.
It was Landor who first said.
We must look at the harebell as if.
McDonald, W. For Kelly, Missing in Action.
Shapiro, K. Poets of Hell, The.
Walcott. Volcano.
Wolfe, H. D. H. Lawrence and James Joyce.

Judas Iscariot
Cullen, C. Judas Iscariot.
De la Mare. Ballad of Christmas, A.
Drunina. In all ages, always, everywhere, and everywhere.
Herbert, Z. Hakeldama.
Matthew 27:3–10; When Judas, his betrayer, saw.
Kossman. John 13:21–30; When Jesus had thus said, he was troubled.
Judas' Reproach.
Malouf. Judas Touch, The.
Mason, R. Judas Iscariot / sat in the upper.
McClellan. Feet of Judas, The.
Middleton, E. Unhappy merchant, Thus t'expose thy Lord.
Miller, V. Judas.
Nemerov. Historical Judas, The.
Nowak, T. Psalm Ajar.
Pasternak, B. Garden of Gethsemane, The.
Matthew 26:47–56; While he was still speaking, Judas came.
Pinsky. Dante's Inferno, Canto XXXIV (The Final Canto).
Spender, S. Judas Iscariot.
Unknown. It wes upon a Shere [*or* Scere] Thorsday that ure [*or* oure] Louerd [*or* Lord] aros.
Judas.
Vinokurov. Mother of Judas, The.
Wellesley. April 1939.
Wright, J. Saint Judas.
Yeats. I am Judas.

Judges
"Carroll." Long Tale, A.
Chao Meng-fu. Poem of Prefectural Judge Yang T'ien-jui Righting a Wrong.
Davie. Pilate.
Hölderlin. In the Days of Socrates.
Kipling, R. Gallio's Song.
Gehazi.
Kyger. News bulletin from Keith Lampe.
McCarriston. To Judge Faolain, Dead Long Enough: A Summons.
Ristovic. Law, The.
Roethke. "Judge not, that you be not."
Smart, C. Psalm 58.
Unknown. On Rÿneveld, an Unpopular Dutch Judge.
Roy Bean.
Watts, I. Psalm 58.

Judgment
Adams, J. Wants of Man, The.
Aeschylus. Chorus sing the doom of Helen, The.
Bible, *O.T.* Psalm 037: "Fret not thyself because of evildoers."
Psalm 72.
Psalm 98.
Carew, T. To the Reader of Master William Davenant's Play [*The Wits*].
Cassells. Sung From A Hospice.
Cowper, W. Lines Written During a Period of Insanity.
Di Prima. Death Sunyata Chant: A Rite for Passing Over.
Dickinson, E. This is my letter to the World.
Emerson, R. Prudence.
Jarrell. Variations.
Miller, L. Substitute, The.
Rankin, P. For the Obese.
Ransom, J. Armageddon.
Simic. Cold, The.

Tate, J. My Great Great Etc. Uncle Patrick Henry.
Unknown. Little Black Train Is A-Comin'.
Mere, The.
Wright, J. At the Executed Murderer's Grave.

Judgment Day
Bible, *N.T.* Last Day, The.
Claudian. Punishment in Hell.
Clough. What we, when face to face we see.
Cowley, A. Resurrection, The.
Cruz Varela. Kaleidoscope.
Evans, S. Fifteen Days of Judgment, The.
Faiz. So Bring the Order for My Execution.
Farewell. Quaerè.
Fletcher, P. Against a Rich Man Despising Poverty.
Hart, K. Last Day, The.
Herbert, G. Death, thou wast once an uncouth hideous thing.
Doomsday.
Judgement.
Herrick. Upon Himselfe Being Buried.
Hill, G. Requiem for the Plantagenet Kings.
Johnson, J. Judgment Day, The.
Kipling, R. Last Chantey, The.
Kunitz, S. For the Word Is Flesh.
Lattimore. Rise and Shine.
Macaulay, T. Dies Iræ.
"MacDiarmid." Crowdieknowe.
Monar. Judgement Day.
Nicholson, N. Carol for the Last Christmas Eve.
Stickney, T. And the last day being come, Man stood alone.
Swift, J. Day of Judgement, The.
Thomas of Celano. Day of Judgment, The.
Dies Irae.
Unknown. Heavenly Aeroplane, The.
I know moon-rise, I know star-rise.
Muspilli.
My Lord, what a mornin' [*or* morning when de stars begin to fall].
Vaughan, H. Day of Judgement.
Very. New World, The.
Watts, I. How doth the little busy bee.
How long, dear Savior, O how long.
Whittier. Abraham Davenport.
Yeats. Crazy Jane on the Day of Judgment.
Second Coming, The.

See also **Apocalypse; End of the World**

Judith (Apocrypha)
Bibb. Judith.
Menken. Judith.
Ransom, J. Judith of Bethulia.
Stanton, M. Judith Recalls Holofernes.

Juggling and Jugglers
Morgan, E. Cinquevalli is falling, falling.
Unknown. Draw me nere [*or* near], draw me nere [*or* near].
Wilbur. Juggler.

Julius Caesar. *See* **Caesar, Julius**

July
Clare, J. July.
Cole, W. Back Yard, July Night.
Fitzgerald, R. July in Indiana.
Heath-Stubbs. July.
MacCaig. July Evening.
Pierpont, J. Fourth of July, The.
Posey, A. July.
Ray, H. July.
Sanchez, S. July.
Wilbur. My Father Paints the Summer.

Jumping
Mother Goose. Jack be nimble.
Leg over leg.
Peters, L. Parachute Men say.

June
Aridjis. Rain is Falling, The.
Burns, R. Red, Red Rose, A.
Ch'ien T'ao. Reading the Book of Hills and Seas.
Clare, J. June.
Davies, W. All in June.
Dickinson, E. I'm sorry for the Dead—Today.
Feinstein, E. June.
Fordham. June.

Jacobsen, R. Rubber.
Kelly, R. In June was a jar had.
Larkin, P. Cut grass lies frail.
Lawrence, D. Andraitx—Pomegranate Flowers.
Ledwidge. June.
Lowell, J. Prelude to Part the First.
What [*or* And what] Is So Rare as a Day in June?
MacNeice. June Thunder.
Mew. June, 1915.
Pawsey. June.
Ray, H. June.
Roberts, S. Mowing, The.
Sackville-West. Rose, The.
Schuyler, J. I Think.
Tennyson, A. June Bracken and Heather.
Unknown. Full carly in the morning.
Wilkinson, A. In June and Gentle Oven.

Jungles
Banker, I. Lion Thoughts.
Barry, J. Green Hell, Green Death.
Brown, D. Eating the Forest.
First Person—1981.
Returning Fire.
When I Am 19 I Was a Medic.
Buzbee. Sunday, Tarzan in His Hammock.
Haring. Jungle.
Koertge. Thing Is to Not Let Go of the Vine, The.
Lane, P. At the Edge of the Jungle.
Lewis, A. Jungle, The.
McDonald, W. Once You've Been to War.
Murray, L. Louvres.
Nguyễn Chí Thiện. Jungle night—it rains and rains, roofs leak, A.
Questel. Bush, The.
Saxena. Black panther is sleeping on the crags, The.
Smith, S. Jungle Husband, The.
Weigl. Amnesia.
Sharing, The.
Surrounding Blues on the Way Down.
Williams, W. Jungle, The.
Worth, K. (Circus Elephant).
Wright, J. Rainforest.

Juniper Trees
Behn, A. On *a* Juniper-Tree, Cut Down to Make Busks.
Francis, R. Juniper.

Junk and Junkyards
Dickey, J. Cherrylog Road.
Disch. Garage Sale as a Spiritual Exercise, The.
Kunitz, S. Chariot.
Merwin, W. Drunk in the Furnace, The.
Pierman. Pilgrims.
Unknown. Ol' Clothes.
Wilbur. Junk.

Jupiter (god)
Fields, J. Jupiter and Ten.
Heywood, T. Jupiter and Ganimede.

Jupiter (planet)
Sargent, E. Planet Jupiter, The.

Justice
Austin, A. Jameson's Ride.
Ba. Justice is Done.
Nobility.
Bible, *O.T.* Heathen Are Come into Thine Inheritance, The.
Psalm 14.
Psalm 17.
Psalm 62.
Psalm 73.
Psalm 107.
Bowen, C. Rain it raineth all around, The.
Brown, J. *et al.* Say it loud, I'm black and I'm proud.
Browning, R. Instans Tyrannus.
Burns, R. Holy Willie's Prayer.
Callimachus. Goddess, how oft you bent the silver bow.
Cardenal. Unrighteous Mammon (Luke 16:9).
Carew, T. Upon My Lord Chief Justice's Election of My Lady Anne Wentworth [*or* A.W.] for His Mistress.
Carson, C. Judgement.
Castillo, O. Before the Scales, Tomorrow.

Chapman, G. Justice.
Coleridge, S. Good Great Man, The.
Cutler, B. Doing Justice.
Dante Alighieri. Middle of life's journey; I, The.
Davies, W. Inquest, The.
De la Mare. In the Dock.
do Espirito Santo. Where Are the Men Seized in this Wind of Madness?
Eich. Seminar for Backward Pupils.
Elizabeth I. Written on a Wall at Woodstock.
Elytis. Intelligible sun of Justice and you, gloryfying myrtle.
Emerson, R. Astræa.
Fericano. Poem for William Rummel Serving a Life Sentence in a Texas Prison for Not Fixing an Air Conditioner.
"Golodny." Judge Gorba.
Hall, D. Small Fig Tree, A.
Hawkins, W. Death of Justice, The.
Holub. Brief Reflection on Charlemagne.
"Hope." Youth.
Hughes, L. Freedom Train.
  Justice.
  Who But the Lord?
Jonson, B. On Lieutenant Shift.
Julianus of Egypt. Julianus Sees a Magistrate's Axe.
Kinsella, T. Another September.
Kinzie. Sun and Moon.
Kipling, R. Gallio's Song.
  Gehazi.
Lawrence, D. When wilt thou teach the people.
Leonard, T. And their judges spoke with one dialect.
Levi, P. Shemà.
Linden, M. All We Ask Is Justice.
Masters, E. Carl Hamblin.
Nicarchus of Alexandria. Law should have ear-plugs, not bandaged eyes, The.
Ofeimun. Judgement Day.
Ogundipe-Leslie. On Reading an Archeological Article.
O'Hara, F. Ode: "Idea of justice may be precious, An."
Pembroke, M. Psalm 58: Si Vere Utique.
  Psalm 92: Bonum Est Confiteri.
Quarles. Luke 6.25.
Reznikoff. Day of Atonement.
Rice, H. He Was One of Us.
Roethke. "Judge not, that you be not."
"Samoylov." Ivan and the Serf.
Sepamla. If you still have bacon and eggs for breakfast.
Shefner. Forest Fire.
Smart, C. Psalm 58.
Unknown. Fortune's Legacy.
  "Guilty or Not Guilty?"
  Preamble to the Constitution of the United States.
  Psalm 58.
  Whatsoever things are true.
Wallace-Crabbe. Tribunal, The.
Wang Fan-chih. Having power is nothing to be concerned about.
Watts, I. Psalm 58.
Whittier. Cities of the Plain, The.
Williams, W. Impromptu: The Suckers.
See also **Injustice**

Justification
Emerson, R. Compensation ("Why should I keep holiday").
Page, G. Jerry's Plains, 1848.
Rich, A. Women.

Juvenile Delinquency
Brooks, G. We real cool. We.
Cutler, B. Doing Justice.

K

Kabul, Afghanistan
Kipling, R. Ford o' Kabul River.
Kafka, Franz (1883-1924)
Holub. Jewish Cemetery at Olsany, Kafka's Grave, April, Sunny Weather, The.

Muir, E. To Franz Kafka.
Stanton, M. Letter to Kafka.
Woroszylski. Franz Kafka (I).
  Franz Kafka (II).
Kahlo, Frida
Alexander, E. Painting / (Frida Kahlo).
Dove, R. Sonnet in Primary Colors.
Kalamazoo, Michigan
Sandburg, C. Sins of Kalamazoo are neither scarlet nor crimson, The.
Kalankaykkanni Narmuticceral
Kappiyarrukkappiyanar. Harvest of War.
Kangaroos
Field, B. Kangaroo, Kangaroo!
Gray, R. Dusk, The.
Lawrence, D. Kangaroo.
Lear, E. Duck and the Kangaroo, The.
Kansas (state)
Bynner. Haskell.
Etter. Riding the Rock Island Through Kansas.
Justice, D. Crossing Kansas by Train.
Stafford, W. Ceremony.
  Rescued Year, The.
Unknown. Kansas Boys.
Kansas City, Kansas and Missouri
Beeks. Parker's Mood.
Dahlberg. Kansas City West Bottoms.
Karate
Kicknosway. West Grand Boulevard.
Katharine of Aragón, Queen of England
Bibb. Catharine of Arragon.
Causley. Ballad for Katharine of Aragon, A.
Katmandu, Nepal
Justice, D. Here in Katmandu.
Katsushika Hokumei
Enright, D. Laughing Hyena, after [or by] Hokusai, The.
Katydids
Freneau. To a Caty-did.
Katzenjammer Kids
Reaney. Katzenjammer Kids, The.
Kavanagh, Patrick
Kavanagh, P. If ever you go to Dublin town.
Kayaks
Diamond, L. Kayak Song, A.
Villanueva, A. Peace #3.
Keats, John
Ackland. Fanny Brawne's Letter Put Unopened In Keats's Coffin.
Brown, L. Green arbor that I once knew, A.
Browning, E. By Keats's soul, the man who never stepped.
Byron, G. John Keats.
Clare, J. To the Memory of John Keats.
Cullen, C. To John Keats, Poet, at Spring Time.
"Ern Malley." Colloquy with John Keats.
Harrison, T. Kumquat for John Keats, A.
Hood, T. False Poets and True.
  Sonnet Written in Keats's *Endymion*.
Hunt, L. To John Keats.
Keats. Naughty Boy, The.
Landor, W. Keats.
Lanier, S. Clover.
Longfellow, H. Keats.
Lowell, A. To John Keats.
Lowell, J. To the Spirit of Keats.
Masters, E. Keats to Fanny Brawne.
Parker, D. Lives and Times of John Keats, Percy Bysshe Shelley, and George Gordon Noel, Lord Byron, The.
Reynolds, J. To Keats: On Reading His Sonnet Written in Chaucer.
Rossetti, C. On Keats, 18 January, 1948 (Eve of St Agnes).
Rossetti, D. John Keats.
Rukeyser, M. Homage to Literature.
Shelley, P. Elegy on the Death of John Keats, An.
Skirrow. Ode on a Grecian Urn Summarized.
Taylor, J. Sonnet on the Death of the Poet J. Keats.
Waters, M. Keats' Lips.
Kells, Book of
Colum, P. Book of Kells, The.

Kennedy, John Fitzgerald
Berry, W. November Twenty-sixth Nineteen Hundred and Sixty-three.
Bly, R. Three Presidents.
Ferlinghetti, L. Assassination Raga.
Kennedy, X. Down in Dallas, down in Dallas.
Plisetsky. Papers have been sold. In them it's all made clear, The.
Kennedy, Robert Francis
Ferlinghetti, L. Assassination Raga.
Justice, D. Assassination, The.
Kensington Gardens, London
Arnold, M. Lines Written in Kensington Gardens.
Spark. Kensington Gardens.
Symons, A. In Kensington Gardens.
Unknown. Poor Adam and Eve were from Eden turned out.
Kent, England
"Asphodel." On the Pilgrim's Way in Kent, as It Leads to the Coldrum Stones.
Bozhilov. Kentish Sestinas.
Davidson, J. In Romney Marsh.
Gray, T. On Lord Holland's Seat near Margate, Kent.
Rochester, J. Tunbridge Wells.
Waller, E. At Penshurst ("While in the park I sing, the listning deer").
Wright, K. How the Wild South East Was Lost.
Kentucky
Cotter, J. Answer to Dunbar's "After a Visit."
Foster, S. My Old Kentucky Home[, Good Night!].
Tate, A. Swimmers, The.
Warren, R. American Portrait: Old Style.
Williams, W. To Elsie.
Kerouac, Jack
Corso. I Met This Guy Who Died.
Ginsberg, A. Malest Cornifici Tuo Catullo.
  Memory Gardens.
  Sunflower Sutra.
  Sweet Levinsky in the night.
Kerouac. Hymn.
Kerry. *See* **County Kerry, Ireland**
Kesey, Ken
Ginsberg, A. First Party at Ken Kesey's with Hell's Angels.
Kew Gardens, London
Noyes, A. Barrel-Organ, The.
Key West, Florida
Crane, H. Key West.
Stevens, W. Idea of Order at Key West, The.
  Two Figures in Dense Violet Night.
Keys
Bishop, E. One Art.
Coleman, E. Liberator, The.
Forbes, C. Home.
Hernton. Fall Down.
Hussey, A. Saturday Night.
Merwin, W. To the Hand.
Stafford, W. With My Crowbar Key.
Stevenson, R. Golden Keys.
Kidd, William
Unknown. Captain Kidd ("You captains brave and bold, hear our cries, hear our cries").
Kidnapping and Kidnappers
Heywood, T. Jupiter and Ganimede.
Reed, I. Beware: Do Not Read This Poem.
Unknown. Bear's Song, The.
Kilcash, Ireland
Unknown. Kilcash.
Killi Parananuru
Alattur Killar. Guide to Patrons, A.
Kilār, Ā. Guide to Patrons, A.
Killing and Killers
Aubert, A. How It's Done.
Baraka. Incident.
Bickerstaffe. What a charming thing's a battle!
Brown, S. Sam Smiley.
Causley. On Being Asked to Write a School Hymn.
Coleman, W. Emmett Till.
Cowper, W. On a Spaniel Called Beau Killing a Young Bird.

Daniels, J. Day of the Two Bodies.
Darwish, M. Sirhan Drinks His Coffee in the Cafeteria.
Steps in the Night.
Escoffery. No Man's Land.
Fried, E. Measures Taken, The.
Gibson, W. Back.
Guest, B. Geese Blood.
Gurney, I. Target, The.
Hammial. Sadie.
Hodgins. Shooting the Dogs.
Holub. Experimental Animals.
Huchel. Winter Billet.
Hughes, T. Esther's Tomcat.
Hawk Roosting.
Kreutzer Sonata.
Joseph, L. There I Am Again.
Kandel. First they slaughtered the angels.
Kelly, B. Song: "Listen: there was a goat's head hanging by ropes in a tree."
Komunyakaa. Tiger Lady.
Kooser. Shooting a Farmhouse.
Kunitz, S. Foreign Affairs.
MacNeice. Grey Ones, The.
Troll's Courtship.
Owen, W. Strange Meeting.
Ryuichi. Every Morning After Killing Thousands of Angels.
Saitō Mokichi. Tanka: "Self-portrait, A."
Sidney, P. Sonnet 48: "Soul's joy, bend not those morning stars from me."
Unknown. Edward.
Poor Lazarus.
Varley. Before Throwing a Chicken into an Iowa Valley.
Vopiscus. Thousand, a thousand, a thousand, A.
Voznesensky. Old Song.
Weigl. Surrounding Blues on the Way Down.
Whalen. Regalia in Immediate Demand!
Yoshimi. Tanka: "Spoon, A."
Zarzyski. Trespasses.

Kimonos
Eimers. Another Kimono.
Merrill, J. Kimono, The.

Kindness
Alford, J. Thanks Be to God.
Bangs, J. On File.
Belloc. Frog, The.
Bible, N.T. Be kindly affectioned one to.
Blunden. Watchers, The.
Buchanan, G. Lewis Mumford.
Buddha. Unlimited Friendliness.
Carey, H. Maid's Husband, The.
Carney. (Little Things).
Chang Yü. Presented to a Lady within the Palace.
Chaucer. Gentilesse.
Chicago. And then all that has divided us will merge.
Colesworthy. Little word in kindness spoken, A.
Courtney. Be kind to thy father: for when thou were young.
Dietz. Help us to do the things we should.
Elwell. Politeness is to do and say.
Foley, J. Drop a Pebble in the Water.
Foresman. How to Forget.
Ginsberg, A. Who Be Kind To.
Glück, L. Gratitude.
Gordon, A. Question not, but live and labor.
Hale, S. Mary's Lamb [or Mary and Her Lamb].
Hemans. Stranger's heart! Oh! wound it not!, The.
Hongo. Stay with Me.
Keech. Love Is Kind.
True to the Best.
King, H. If we give love and sympathy.
Kramer, L. Shoemaker's Wife, The.
Langford. Speak gently; it is better far.
Laughlin, J. Kind-, The.
Lawrence, D. English are so nice, The.
Mandelstam. Still far from patriarch or sage.
Martial. Kindest thing of all is to comply, The.
Martynov. Be kind / Be iron—.

Metcalf, R. These Are Not Lost.
Nelson, F. Human Heart, The.
Nichols, C. Boomerang, The.
O'Reilly, J. What Is Good?
Piercy. Homage to Lucille, Dr. Lord-Heinstein.
Plath. Kindness glides about my house.
Reed, M. One Year to Live.
Rossetti, C. Kindness is a language which the.
Sandall. Song: "Love that is hoarded, moulds at last."
Sangster, M. Our Own.
Seymour, A. My Aim.
Shimon. I Know Something Good about You.
Springer, T. Giving and Forgiving.
Stevenson, R. Golden Keys.
Thompson, P. Kindly Deed, A.
Tucker, M. Kindness.
Unknown. Be ye kind one to another.
Deeds of Kindess.
Gentle Word, A.
John Wesley's Rule.
(My Daily Creed).
Somebody's Mother.
Watts, I. Our Saviour's Golden Rule.
Werth. I'll be polite in many ways.
Wilcox, E. Morning Prayer, A.
Williams, W. Raper from Passenack, The.
Wordsworth, W. Best portion of a good man's life, The.
Man is dear to man: the poorest poor.
Wright, J. Sappho.

King Lear
Keats. On Sitting Down to Read "King Lear" Once Again.
Salter. Refrain.
Storace. King Lear Bewildered.
Williams, W. Lear.

King, Martin Luther, Jr
Barrax. King: April 4, 1968.
Brooks, G. Martin Luther King, Jr.
Cornish, S. Death of Dr. King.
Fort, C. For Martin Luther King.
Giovanni. Funeral of Martin Luther King, Jr, The.
Hairston. Alabama Bus.
Harper, M. Martin's Blues.
Hernandez, D. Martin and My Father.
Jordan, J. In Memoriam: Martin Luther King, Jr.
Madhubuti. Assassination.
Sarton. Easter, 1968.
Troupe. Day in the Life of a Poet, A.

King, William Lyon Mackenzie
Scott, F. W. L. M. K.

Kingfishers
Davies, W. Kingfisher, The.
Fenton, J. Kingfisher's Boxing Gloves, The.
Heath-Stubbs. Kingfisher, The.
Hopkins, G. What I Do Is Me.
Hussey, D. Kingfisher, The.
Olson, C. Kingfishers, The.

Kings
Allingham. Swing Song, A.
Bartusek. Royal Progress.
Belloc. Henry King, Who Chewed Bits of String, and Was Early Cut Off in Dreadful Agonies.
Bishop, E. Twelfth Morning; or What You Will.
Boethius. Book 3, metrum 4.
Browne, W. O! should all Potentates whose higher birth.
Browning, R. Solomon and Balkis.
Byron, G. Harp the monarch minstrel swept, The.
To Belshazzar.
"Carroll." "Time has come," the Walrus, The.
Causley. Figgie Hobbin.
Césaire, A. Ex-Voto for a Shipwreck.
Cullen, C. Black Majesty.
De Vere, E. Poem: "Were I a king, I could command content."
Dickinson, E. Belshazzar had a Letter.
I met a King this afternoon!
Donne. Anniversary [or Anniversarie], The.
Dowriche. So him at first De Nance commanded was to kill;.

DuBois, W. Song of the Smoke, The.
Engle, P. Portrait of a King's Mistress, Nude.
Fairfax of Cameron. On the Fatal Day January 30, 1648.
"Field." Fifty Quatrains.
Fiskin. Magi, The.
Gergely. Encelado and the Facts.
Gnosis.
Gheorghe. Unicorn, The.
Gilbert, S. There lived a King, as I've been told.
Goethe. King in Thule, The.
Gouri. You're no king.
Greene, R. Shepherd's Wife's Song, The.
Greville, F. Sonnet 78: "Little Hearts, where light-wing'd Passion raignes, The."
Hall, H. Upon the King's Return from Flanders, 1695.
Herbert, Z. Return of the Proconsul, The.
Herrick. Ill Government.
King and No King, A.
Power in the People, The.
Hill, G. Requiem for the Plantagenet Kings.
Homer. Gardens of Alcinous, The.
Priam and Achilles.
Lalic. King and the Singer, The.
Landor, W. Georges, The.
Lê Thánh-tông. Conduct of Kings, The.
King's Portrait, A.
Leapor. Man the Monarch.
Li Ho. King of Ch'in Drinks Wine, The.
Lincoln, M. Kings of France.
Lovelace, R. To Lucasta[, from Prison].
MacNeice. Jehu.
Mansour, J. From an ass to an analyst and back.
Milne, A. King's Breakfast, The.
Mocikiranar. Not Rice, Not Water.
Montague, J. Deer Park.
More, S. De Principe Bono et Malo.
Quis Optimus Reipublicae Status.
Mother Goose. King of France, the king of France / with forty thousand men, The.
Old King Cole was a merry old soul.
Nguyễn Trãi. Ask to be put in charge of streams and hills!
Philips, K. On the 3. of September, 1651.
Pindar. Each element to water yields.
Pope, A. Epigram Engraved on the Collar of a Dog Given [or Which I Gave] to His Royal Highness.
Quarles. On Saul and David.
Richards, L. (Bibbily Boo and Wollypotump).
Rochester, J. Satire on Charles II, A.
Rossetti, C. After Communion.
Saba. King's Garden World, A.
Seneca. 'Tis not wealth that makes a king.
Shelley, P. England in 1819.
Ozymandias [of Egypt].
Sidney, P. Sonnet 75: "Of all the kings that ever here did reign."
Such maner time there was (what time I n'ot).
Stafford, W. Story That Could Be True, A.
Stevens, W. Emperor of Ice-Cream, The.
Stevenson, R. Happy Thought.
Suckling, J. On King Richard the Third, Who Lies Buried under Leicester Bridge.
Tu Fu. Passing Chao-ling Again.
Unknown. Cause of War, The.
England's Sovereigns in Verse.
English Succession, The.
Great Summons, The.
King and Subjects.
King Arthur.
King John and the Abbot of Canterbury.
King of Connacht, The.
King Wen's Park Divine.
Lavender's Blue.
Preparations.
Sir Patrick Spens [or Spence].
There's no Jade Emperor in the sky.
To Archbishop Lang.
Verlaine. L'Allée.
Virgil. Drances in debate.
Walker, A. In Uganda an early king chose.
Wickham. King Alfred and the Peasant Woman.

Wieseltier. Saul Re-enthroned.
Wither. If by mischance the people in the street.
Wordsworth, W. Edward VI.
Yeats. Model for the Laureate, A.
See also Individual names of kings (e.g., **Edward VII, King of England.***)*

Kingston, Jamaica
Berry, J. Back to Hometown Kingston.

Kipling, Rudyard
Carryl, G. Ballad: "As I was walkin' the jungle round, a-killin' of tigers an' time."
O'Hara, F. Captains Courageous.
Stephen, J. To R. K.

Kirk, Henry
Unknown. To the Poets.

Kisses
Ackland. What must we do if we cannot do this.
Alexander, E. Zodiac.
Amaru. When his mouth faced my mouth, I turned aside.
Angus. Mary's Song.
Barker, G. My sister Clarissa spits twice if I kiss her.
Barrington, J. Dirty Panes.
Behn, A. Willing Mistriss, The.
Bell, M. What They Do to You in Distant Places.
Berryman. Ah when you drift hover before you kiss.
Beveridge. Dining Out.
Bevington, L. With the Tide: A Cry of Weakness.
Browning, E. Romance of the Swan's Nest, The.
Sonnet: "First time he kissed me, he but only kissed."
To George Sand / A Desire.
Browning, R. In a Gondola.
Budenz. Poeta Fui.
Bunting. Came to me— / Who?
Burkard. Raincoat, A.
Burns, R. Song: "Ae fond kiss, and then we sever."
Byron, G. And thus they wandered forth, and hand in hand.
Campion, T. Thou art not fair for all thy red and white.
Catullus. Carmen 5 ("My sweetest Lesbia, let us live and love").
Kisse me, sweet: The warie lover.
Cavalli. To simulate the burning of the heart, the humiliation.
Ceravolo. Spring in This World of Poor Mutts.
"Chrystos." Your Tongue Sparkles.
Cleveland, J. To the State of Love or The Senses' Festival.
Cummings, E. Thy fingers make early flowers of.
Up into the silence the green.
Dacre, C. Kiss, The.
Donne. Expiration, The.
D'Orleans. Your mouth hit saith me "Bas me, bas me, sweet."
Dove, R. Adolescence—I.
Drayton. Since There's No Help.
Drummond, W. Kisses Desired.
Duhamel. Bulimia.
Dunbar, P. Her Thought and His.
Negro Love Song, A.
Espada. Rednecks.
"Field." Already to mine eyelids' shore.
Fleming, P. How He Should Like to Be Kissed.
Fletcher, J. Take, oh, take those lips away.
Foster, E. In Your Words.
Gallagher, T. One kiss.
García Lorca. Variations.
Gay, J. Sweet William's Farewell to Black-Eyed [*or* Black-Ey'd] Susan.
Gibbons, S. Truce, The.
Gray, J. On A Picture.
Grier. Kissing Natalia.
Hardy, T. Thunderstorm in Town, A.
Two Lips.

Harteis. Genetics.
Herrick. Barley-Break; or, Last in Hell.
Chop-Cherry.
Kiss[e], A.
Kisses Loath[e]some.
Kissing and bussing differ both in this.
Love Palpable.
Tithe [*or* Tythe]: To the Bride, The.
To Dianeme ("Give me one kiss").
To Electra.
Upon a Virgin Kissing a Rose.
Upon Jack and Jill: Epigram.
Hughes, L. Suicide's Note.
Hunt, J. You Kissed Me.
Hunt, L. Rondeau.
Rondeau: Jenny Kiss'd [*or* Kissed] Me.
Inez. Instructions for the Erection of a Statue to Myself in Central Park.
Jackson, L. Take hands. / There is no love now.
Jonson, B. Doing a filthy pleasure is, and short.
To the Same [Celia].
Lawrence, D. Kisses in the Train.
Lightning.
Le Gallienne. Beauty Accurst.
Lenier. Finale.
Leontius Scholasticus. My little cup, go now and taste.
Levchev. We stopped.
Lyly, J. Cards and Kisses.
Macdonald, G. Sweet Peril.
Machi. Tanka: "Gazing upwards."
Makarov. Life lasts the course of a kiss.
Millay, E. What lips my lips have kissed, and where, and why.
Mitchison. Old Love and New Love.
Moore, T. Did Not.
Kiss, The.
Mother Goose. Georgie Porgie, pudding and pie.
Nathan, L. Bladder Song.
Neruda. Loving is a journey with water and with stars.
Nesbit, E. Kiss, The.
Ovid. 1.5.
Patmore, C. Kiss, The.
Paulus Silentiarius. Come, give me kisses, Rhodope.
I believe the grief of Tantalus in Hell.
Paz. Engaged.
Petronius Arbiter. Fragment of Petronius, A.
Plato. Kiss, The.
Porter, C. Old-Fashioned Garden, An.
Ríos, A. Teodoro Luna's Two Kisses.
Ronsard. Elegy 19 (A Kiss): "Without a soul, a mind, a breath, or pulse."
Rossetti, C. Baby lies so fast asleep.
Rossetti, D. Kiss, The.
Nuptial Sleep.
Willowwood ("I sat with Love upon a woodside well").
Rudaki. Came to me— / Who?
Rufinus Domesticus. Europa kisses sweetly.
Kiss from her! Her mouth, coming even close to your own, how, A.
Schwartz, D. Aria.
"Severyanin." Minor Elegy, A.
Shakespeare, W. At the Moated Grange.
Even as the sun with purple-colour'd face.
If I profane with my unworthiest hand.
Shange. Its Happenin / But You Dont Know Abt It.
Shelley. Love's Philosophy.
Shuttle. Passion.
Sidney, P. Sonnet 74: "I never drank of Aganippe well."
Sonnet 81: "O kiss, which dost those ruddy gems impart."
Sonnet 82: "Nymph of the garden where all beauties be."
Stella's Kiss.
Spenser. Sonnet 64: "Coming [*or* Comming] to kiss[e] her lips [*or* lyps], (such grace I found)."
Stanley, T. Speaking and Kissing.
Stein, G. Kiss my lips.

Stirling, S. I Envy Not Endymion.
Strode. Kisses.
Riddle: On a Kiss, A.
Swenson, M. Trellis for R, A.
Swinburne. Anactoria.
Kissing her hair, I sat against her feet.
Swir. Astonishment.
Youngest Children of an Angel, The.
Tate, J. Love Making.
Teasdale. Kiss, The.
Look, The.
Tekkan. Tanka: "Poppies in bloom."
Tennyson, A. We Kiss'd Again with Tears.
Thomas, L. Excitation.
Toomer. Her Lips Are Copper Wire.
Tucker, M. Kiss? A. Pray tell me, what is in a kiss.
Ulinover. In the Courtyard.
Unknown. Bee-keeper kissed me, The.
Betrayal.
Did you eever, iver, over.
I Kissed You.
"I pray you, cum kiss me."
Keep your kiss to yourself.
Kiss'd yestreen, and kiss'd yestreen.
Vaiiunaite. Nausicaa.
Walker, A. Kiss, The.
Waniek. Canticle for Abba Jacob, A.
Warner, S. After he had gone the wind rose.
Watts, M. Vision.
Wendt. Teacher I Wanted to Be, The.
Wharton, E. Mortal Lease, The.
Whitman, W. Behold this swarthy face, these gray eyes.
Winik. Foreign Exchange.
Wyatt, T. Alas, madam[e], for stealing [*or* stelying] of a kiss [*or* kysse].
Lover Showeth How He Is Forsaken of Such as He Sometime Enjoyed, The.
Young, A. Curative Powers of Silence, The.
Kiss.

Kitchens
Brooks, G. Mrs. Small went to the kitchen for her pocketbook.
Causley. Old Mrs Thing-um-e-bob.
Crist. She has gone.
Davis, T. Boppin' is Safer than Grindin'.
Dove, R. Sunday Greens.
Gilbert, S. Dream Kitchen, The.
Harjo, J. Perhaps the World Ends Here.
Hartnett. Domestic Scene.
Jewsbury. My heart's in the kitchen, my heart is not here.
Kamienska. Saint Martha.
Mistral, G. Martha and Mary.
Morley, C. Animal crackers, and cocoa to drink.
Nelson, E. Kitchens.
Okamoto. Tanka: "Having let flow."
Rutsala. Silence, The.
Salimon. Food-Factory Kitchen.
Scarfe. Kitchen Poem.
Stevens, W. Emperor of Ice-Cream, The.
Wong, N. Relining Shelves.
Wright, C. State of Preservation.
Zepeda, O. Kitchen Sink.

Kites (toys)
Bowden, S. Kite, completed thus, is borne along, The.
Chōkū. Tanka: "Which child."
Cohen, L. Kite Is a Victim, A.
Gilbert, C. Kite-Flying.
Hesketh. Boy with Kite.
MacEwen, P. Kite, The.
O'Keeffe. Kite, The.
Ríos, A. What a Boy Can Do.
Roseliep. Sky.
Snodgrass, W. Lovers Go Fly a Kite, The.
Strand. Kite, The.
Swenson, M. Goodbye, Goldeneye.
Trevor. Kite, A.
Valentine, J. Seeing You.
Wu Wei-yeh. Tune: "Song of River City"— On a Kite.

Kittens
Bast. Empress's Cat, The.
Hywell the Good Weighs the Worth of a Cat.

Eden. Four-Paws.
Follen, E. Three little kittens [they] lost their mittens.
Hood, T. Choosing Their Names.
MacCaig. Byre.
Mother Goose. As I was going to St. Ives.
Mountain, M. On this cold.
Nash, O. Kitten, The.
Prentiss. Kitty.
Taylor, J. Two Little Kittens.
Thomas, E. Cat, A.
Twichell. Aisle of Dogs.
Unknown. Two Little Kittens[, one stormy night].
Virgilio. Sack of kittens, The.
Willard, N. King of Cats Sends a Postcard to His Wife, The.
Williams, W. Mujer.

Klee, Paul
Todd, R. Paul Klee.

Knees
Cornford, F. Peasant Woman, A.
Morgenstern. Knee, The.

Knife-Grinding and Knife-Grinders
Canning, G. *et al.* Friend of Humanity and the Knife Grinder, The.
Nightingale. Scissor-Man, The.
Whitman, W. Sparkles from the Wheel.

Knight, Etheridge
Sanchez, S. Hospital/Poem.

Knighthood and Knights
Askew. Ballad Which Anne Askew[e] Made and Sang When She Was in Newgate, The.
Browning, R. Childe Roland to the Dark Tower Came.
Heretic's Tragedy, The.
Butler, S. Presbyterian Knight, The.
Chatterton. Bristowe Tragedie: or, The Dethe of Syr Charles Bawdin.
Chaucer. Tale of Sir Thopas, The.
Wife of Bath's Tale, The.
Chesterman. Sir Nicketty Nox.
De Tabley. Knight in the Wood, The.
Guiney. Knight Errant, The.
Wild Ride, The.
Hawes, S. True Knight [*or* True Knighthood], The.
Herbert, Z. Passion of Our Lord painted by an anonymous hand from the Circle of Rhenish Masters, The.
Herebert. What is he, this lordling, that cometh from the fight?
Ingelow. Winding-up Time.
Keats. La Belle Dame Sans Merci.
Masefield. Dead Knight, The.
Mayer, G. Ballad: "Knight went down to the river's rim, A."
Melville, H. Medallion, The.
Merry. Sir Roland; a Fragment.
Morris, W. Haystack in the Floods, The.
Poe. Eldorado.
Procter, A. Legend of Provence, A.
Rowlands. Sir Eglamour.
Sandburg, C. Horses and Men in the Rain.
Scott, W. Lochinvar.
Spenser. In the Bower of Bliss.
Tai Piao-yüan. South of the house, north of the house.
Taylor, J. Squire's Pew, The.
Tennyson, A. Arabian Night Garden, An.
Unknown. Sir Mordred, traitor false and vile.
Sun rises red amid radiant clouds, The.
Three Ravens, The.
Wickham. Lament of the Red Knight.
Winters, Y. Sir Gawaine and the Green Knight.
Yang Wei-chen. Horseman at the Roadside, The.

Knights of Pythias
Kipling, R. New Knighthood, The.
Linden, M. For the Good of the Pythian Order.

Knitting and Knitters
Bowes-Lyon. Woman Knitting, A.
Gardinier. On a Grey-haired Old Lady Knitting at an Orchestral Concert.
Holub. Crocheting.
Kuskin. Knitted Things.
Tucker, M. Knitting.

Knives
Acklais. Give me your silver knife, right here.
Adamson. Gutting the Salmon.
Borges. Dagger, The ("A dagger rests in a drawer").
Cook, E. Surgeon's Knife, The.
Fumiko. Tanka: "As the surgical knife."
García Lorca. Quarrel, The.
Goldbarth. Life is Happy.
Hampton. Women who Speak with Steak Knives.
Kirsch, S. Seven Skins.
Melo Neto. Knife All Blade, A.
Mirabai. I was going to the river for water.
O'Dalaigh, M. On the Gift of a Knife.
Po Chü-i. Pruning Trees.
Radnóti. Angel of Dread, The.
Sackville-West. Pruning in March.
Tess.
Schuyler, J. Stone Knife, A.
Stanford, F. Inventory.
Symons, A. Nerves.
Thomas, D. January 1939.
Tillinghast, R. Knife, The.
Unknown. Dirge for Three Trumpets.
Walwicz. Big Tease.
Little Red Riding Hood.
Tattoo, The.
Wratislaw. Hothouse Flowers.

Knowledge
Adamson. Dreaming Up Mother.
"Asya." Deer, The.
Atwood. Procedures for Underground.
Baraka. New World, The.
Bartsch. Deposition.
Basho. Worshipping at the Great Shrine At Ise.
Berry, W. To Know the Dark.
Bhatt. What Is Worth Knowing?
Bible, *O.T.* Psalm 139.
Bishop, E. At the Fishhouses.
Boethius. Book 3, Metrum 11.
Bogan, L. Knowledge.
Booth, P. Species.
Bowers, E. Adam's Song to Heaven.
Brett, L. Leaving You.
Byron, G. Ah! didst *thou* tempt my mother?
Caraion. Ultimate Argument.
Carrier, C. Prospect Before Us, The.
Chapman, G. Learning ("So Learned Men in Controversies Spend").
Chaudhari, B. Meaning of Things, The.
Cooper, J. Knowledge That Comes through Experience, The.
Cope, W. Two Cures for Love.
Couani. Obvious, The.
Cowley, A. Tree of Knowledge, The.
Cranch. Gnosis.
Creeley. Somebody Died.
Crompton. Epigram LXVII: Time, the Interpreter.
Cummings, E. You shall above all things be glad and young.
Daive. Lost in contemplation of its end.
Davies, S. I know my soul hath power to know all things.
Ded. I searched for my Self.
Dickinson, E. To know just how He suffered—would be dear.
Donne. Soules Ignorance in This Life and Knowledge in the Next, The.
Dove, R. Demeter's Prayer to Hades.
Emerson, R. Limits.
Enzensberger, H. Song for Those Who Know.
Erhardt. Amelia Erhardt.
Fennelly. Poem Not to Be Read at Your Wedding.
Frost, R. For Once, Then, Something.
From Plane to Plane.
Revelation.
Garrigue. Catch What You Can.
Ginsberg, A. PsalmIII: "To God: to illuminate all men. Beginning with Skid Road."
Gonzáles Martínez. Last Journey.
Greville, F. Mind of man is this world's true dimension, The.
Guiney. In the Reading-Room of the Brtish Museum.
Habington. "Nox Nocti Indicat Scientiam."
Hadewijch II. You who want.
Hardy, T. If you had known.
Herbert, G. Pearl. [Matth. 13.45 *or* Matt. 13:45], The.
Howe, S. Sabbath and sweet spices.
Hughes, T. Man Seeking Experience Enquires His Way of a Drop of Water, The.
Jabès. Desert, The.
Jackson, L. Nothing so far but moonlight.
Jeffers, R. Science.
Kavanagh, P. To Hell with Commonsense.
Kennedy, X. Hummingbird.
Kirsanov. New Heart, The.
Koch, K. Taking a Walk with You.
Levertov. Contraband.
Runes, The.
Levine, P. Cemetery at Academy, California, The.
On My Own.
Lin Hung. Drinking Wine.
March, A. Much as a man who takes delight in dreaming.
May, J. If we could know.
McClatchy. Found Parable.
McHugh, H. Place Where Things Got.
Michaux. He who knows how to shave the razor, will know how to erase the.
Moore, M. To a Snail.
Murray, J. Madonna vs. Child.
Nathan, L. Hole.
Nemerov. Boy with Book of Knowledge.
To David, about His Education.
Oppen. Not to reduce the thing to nothing.
Tell the life of the mind, the mind creates the finite.
Orr, E. In This Motherless Geography.
Parsons, C. Different.
P'i Jih-hsiu. Reading.
Pinsky. Serpent Knowledge.
Po Chü-i. Lao Tzŭ.
Philosophers: Lao-Tzu, The.
Pope, A. Know Thyself.
Pound, E. Tree, The.
Quarles. I wish a greater knowledge, then t'attaine.
Raine, K. Message from Home.
Rajeevan. Pair of Glasses, A.
Rege, S. Old Leaves from the Chinese Earth.
Rich, A. To the Days.
Robinson, E. Mortar.
Roethke. Marrow, The.
Sackville-West. Extract from Solitude.
St. John, D. I know the moon is troubling.
Sandburg, C. Why repeat? I heard you the first time.
Shelley, P. Sonnet: "Lift not the painted veil which those who live."
Shih Te. Since apes are still able to learn.
Sluchevsky. I told her: the sidewalks are muddy.
Snyder, G. My home was at Cold Mountain from the start.
Sorescu. Carbon Paper.
Perseverance.
Stein, G. On Her Way.
Swinburne. Triads.
Symons, A. When you were here, ah foolish then!
Szymborska. Once we knew the world well.
Taylor, B. Night the Second: All or Nothing.
Tennyson, A. To —. With the Following Poem.
Thomas, E. On Sir J—— S—— Saying in a Sarcastic Manner, My Books Would Make Me Mad; an Ode.
Unknown. I was born almost ten thousand years ago.
Very. Eye and Ear, The.
Wang Fan-chih. Yellow gold's not precious.
Ward, D. Approximately.
Waterman, N. To Know All Is to Forgive All.

Zach. How the Days Passed. Who'd have believed they'd.
Zavalnyuk. Earlobe.

Knox, George L.
Bibb. Lines to the Hon. George L. Knox.
Muir, E. Scotland 1941.

Knoxville, Tennessee
Giovanni. Knoxville, Tennessee.

Kollwitz, Käthe
Rukeyser, M. Käthe Kollwitz.

Koran
Jami. Even from earthly love thy face avert not.

Korean War
Chakravarty, A. Fire.
Cho, C. At Toriwon.
McGrath, T. Ode for the American Dead in Asia.
Olds, S. Solitary.
Park, P. True Line, The.

Koreans
Kim, T. Boatsong of the Sungari, The.
Park, P. True Line, The.

Krafft-Ebing, Richard Von
Gogarty. On First Looking into Krafft-Ebing's *Psychopathosexualis* [*or* Psychopathia Sexualis].

Krakow [*or* Cracow], **Poland**
Gebirtig. Waiting for Death.

Ku Klux Klan
Baraka. Wise 5.
Hayden, R. Night, Death, Mississippi.
Hughes, L. Ku Klux.
Special Bulletin.
St. John, P. Lynching and Burning.
Spellman. When Black People Are.

Kubla Khan
Chao Meng-fu. Eulogy of the Sagely Virtue of His Imperial Majesty Emperor Shih-tsu, A. Lamenting the Taoist Wei Kung-yüan.
Coleridge, S. Kubla Khan; or, A Vision in a Dream.
Smith, S. Thoughts about the Person from Porlock.

Kumanan
Peruncittiranar. Bard's Family, A.

Kutakko Ilanceral Irumporai
Kiḻr. Parade, A.
Perunkunrur Kilar. Parade, A.

Kyoto, Japan
Enright, D. Kyoto Garden, A.
Yosano. Tanka: "Two chilly."

L

L'Ouverture, Toussaint. *See* **Toussaint L'Ouverture, François**

La Coruna, Spain. *See* **Coruna, La, Spain**

La Hogue, Battle of. *See* **Hogue, La, Battle of (1692)**

La Plata, Missouri
Barnes, J. Last Look at La Plata, Missouri.

Labor Day
Glück, L. Labor Day.
Nobuyuki. Labor Day[1] (four poems).

Labor Unions
Hayes, A. Joe Hill.
Hill, J. Preacher and the Slave, The.
Morgan, A. Union Man.
Sandburg, C. Ice Handler.
Unknown. My Sweetie's a Mule in the Mine.
Old Chisholm Trail, The.
See also **Strikes and Strikers**

Labor and Laborers
Abdullah. Tombs, The.
Adiga. Do something, brother.
Aiken, C. Road, The.
Alegría. Documentary.
Allbery. Assembler.
Alvarez, J. Woman's Work.
Angira. Manna.
Annensky. Small Kulak Landowner.
Babcock, M. Be Strong!

Baca. So Mexicans Are Taking Jobs from Americans.
Work We Hate and Dreams We Love.
Baillie, J. Hay making.
Baraka. Poem Some People Will Have to Understand, A.
Barrows, R. Report Card, The.
Belloc. Good Advice.
Bersohn. Dignity of Labor, The.
Bevington, L. Morning.
Bible, *O.T.* Even a child is known by his doings.
Go to the ant, thou sluggard;.
Boileau-Despéaux. Epistle to My Gardener.
Garden of Writing, The.
Braley, B. Thinker, The.
Braun, V. New Purpose of Hadrian's Army, The.
Brown, G. Taxman.
Brown, S. Call Boy.
Southern Road.
Bunting. What the Chairman Told Tom.
Burke, M. On the twelfth floor.
Campbell, R. Serf, The.
Carter, J. At the Sign-Painter's.
Cary, A. To Solitude.
Cary, P. Don't Give Up.
Casey, T. Drill, Ye Tarriers, Drill.
Césaire, A. In Memory of a Black Union Leader.
Chang Yü. Retreat of Liu Kuo-pao, The.
Ch'en Lin. Song: "I watered my horse at the Long Wall caves."
Chin. Autumn Leaves.
Chipasula. Those Rainy Mornings.
Chock. Working Construction.
Ciardi. All about Boys and Girls.
Codrescu. Work.
Coleridge, S. Work Without Hope.
Collier, M. Womans Labour, an epistle, The.
Conyus. Six Ten Sixty-Nine.
Cook, E. Song for the Workers, A.
Crane, S. Many workmen / Built a hugh ball of masonry.
Crowell, G. Common tasks are beautiful if we.
Cullen, C. For a Lady I Know.
Davie. With the Grain.
Dickinson, E. Robin is a Gabriel, The.
Dietz. Help us to do the things we should.
Dove, R. Great Palaces of Versailles, The.
Satisfaction Coal Company, The.
Zeppelin factory, The.
DuBois, W. Song of the Smoke, The.
Dunbar, P. Not they who soar, but they who plod.
Elliot, E. Child, is thy father dead?
Engle, P. Twilight.
Enzensberger, H. Vanished Work.
Espada. Secret of the Legal Secretary's Cigarette Smoke, The.
Fanthorpe. You Will Be Hearing from Us Shortly.
Field, E. What Grandma Knew.
Flecknoe. Ant, The.
Fort, C. Worker (We Own Two Houses), The.
Frear. Young Workman, The.
Frost, R. Mowing.
"Out, Out—."
Tuft of Flowers, The.
Wood-Pile, The.
Fulton, A. Risk Management.
García. I Ain't Going to Hurry No More.
Gibran. On Work.
Gibson, M. Invisible Work.
Gilman, C. To Labor.
Ginsberg, A. Strange New Cottage in Berkeley, A.
Glück, L. School Children, The.
Goethe. Nature and Art.
Goodison. Birth Stone.
Gordon, A. Question not, but live and labor.
Gotlieb. Three-handed Fugue.
Gould, A. Demolisher.
Grahn. Hannah.
Gumilyov. Worker, The.

Hall, D. Foundations of American Industry, The.
Han Yü. Leaves fall turning turning to the ground.
Hayden, R. Those Winter Sundays.
Hayes, A. Joe Hill.
Heaney, S. Mossbawn Sunlight.
When all the others were away at Mass.
Herrick. End of His Work, The.
Hesiod. Summer.
Hill, G. Ovid in the Third Reich.
Hill, J. Preacher and the Slave, The.
Hood, T. Song of the Shirt, The.
Hooper, E. Duty.
Hopkins, G. God's Grandeur.
Housman, A. When smoke stood up from Ludlow.
Hove. Country Life.
You Will Forget.
Hughes, L. Florida Road Workers.
Necessity.
Hutchinson, L. Verses Written by Mrs. Hutchinson.
Ingelow. Little babe, while burns the west.
Iolo Goch. Labourer, The.
Irtenev. Ditchdigger, The.
Ishikawa Takuboku. Tanka: "I work."
Jacinto, A. Letter from a Contract Worker.
Monangamba.
Johnson, M. What's de Use ob Wukin in de Summer Time at All.
Johnson, S. *ad. fr.* the Bible, Proverbs, 6, 6.
Johnston, E. Lines to Ellen, the Factory Girl.
Working Man, The.
Jones, E. Song of the Low, The.
Jones, R. Mechanic, The.
Jordan, J. If You Saw a Negro Lady.
Kalász. Legacy.
Kazarnovsky. Chinese Laundry.
Keens-Douglas. Wukhand.
Kelly, B. Leaving, The.
Kendall, M. Underground.
Kennelly. Thatcher, The.
King, B. Pessimist, The.
Kipling, R. Sons of Martha, The.
Koch, K. Thank You.
Kornilov, V. Johnny.
"Korzhavin." I was never an ascetic.
Krasnikov. Come on, Mama, we'll slake the lime.
Larkin, P. Aubade: "I work all day, and get half-drunk at night."
Dedicated, The.
Toads.
Toads Revisited.
Lawrence, D. Morning Work.
Work.
Le Gallienne. I meant to do my work today.
Lê Thánh–tông. King's Portrait, A.
Leapor. Sacrifice: An Epistle to Celia, The.
Leonard, T. Scream, A.
Simple Simon.
Levine, P. Sweet Will.
You Can Have It.
Littlefield, M. O Son of Man, Thou Madest Known.
Liu Cheng. Poem without a Category.
Longfellow, H. Village Blacksmith, The.
Lu Yu. Autumn Thoughts ("Mornings up before the rooster calls").
Farm Families.
Sitting Outdoors.
"MacDiarmid." Ah, Lenin, you were richt. But I'm a poet.
MacLean, S. Highland Woman, A.
MacLeish. Burying Ground by the Ties.
Madhubuti. America calling.
Mandelstam. To A. A. A. (Akhmatova).
Mar, L. My Mother, Who Came from China, Where She Never Saw Snow.
Markham, E. Forgotten Man, The.
Man with the Hoe, The.
Martin, E. Trade.
Masefield. Consecration, A.
Massey. Worker, The.
Mayakovsky. On Being Kind to Horses.

McCarthy, T. Feeding Ground.
Word "Silk", The.
McKay, C. Fetchin Water.
Tired Worker, The.
Mechthild von Magdeburg. True love in every moment praises God.
Merriam, E. Lazy Thought, A.
Merwin, W. What is a Garden.
Meynell, A. Girl on the Land, The.
Milnes. England and America, 1863.
Mizejewski. Anaerobics: Elaine Powers, Wheeling, West Virginia.
Mnthali. My Father.
Monro. Man Carrying Bale.
Montoya. Just the other day.
Moore, L. From the Field.
Moraga. Half-Breed.
More, H. Hackney Coachman, The; Or, The Way to Get a Good Fare.
Morgan, A. Work; a Song of Triumph ("Work / Thank God for the might of it").
Morris, M. For Consciousness.
Mother Goose. Curly Locks [!] Curly Locks [!] wilt thou be mine?
Mphande. Why the Old Woman Limps.
Nash, O. Introspective Reflection.
Nemerov. Sunday at the End of Summer.
Niedecker. In the great snowfall before the bomb.
Niemoller. First they came for the Jews.
Olson, C. Praises, The.
Ou-yang Hsiu. Reading the Poems of an Absent Friend.
Pastan. Notes from the Delivery Room.
Pfeiffer, E. Peace to the odalisque, the facile slave.
Piercy. To Be of Use.
Pinsky. Shirt.
Po Chü-i. Lazy Man's Song.
Rabi'a al-Adawiyya. I am fully qualified to work as a doorkeeper, and for this reason.
Randall, D. George.
Replansky. Two Women.
Reznikoff. Amelia was just fourteen and out of the orphan asylum.
Ridge, L. Réveille.
Riley, J. Raggedy Man, The.
Rilke. For one human being to love another human being: that is perhaps the.
Rivard. Torque.
Rivers, C. Train Runs Late to Harlem, The.
Rodgers, C. It Is Deep.
Rukeyser, M. Alloy.
George Robinson: Blues.
Rumi. Someone Digging in the Ground.
Sandburg, C. Blue Island Intersection.
Chicago.
Child of the Romans.
Horses and Men in the Rain.
Ice Handler.
Jack was a swarthy, swaggering son-of-a-gun.
Mill-Doors.
Psalm of Those Who Go Forth before Daylight.
What the people learn out of lifting and hauling and waiting and losing.
Work Gangs.
Sandy. Threads.
Scott, W. Hour with thee! When earliest day, An.
Scovell. City Worker, The.
Shange. Tango.
Shapiro, D. House (Blown Apart).
Shelley, P. Song to the Men of England.
Shlonsky. Toil.
Shūji. Tanka: "On the way home."
Shurin. Material's Daughter.
Sigourney. To a Shred of Linen.
Skipsey. "Get up!" the caller calls, "Get up!"
Smith, S. Childe Rolandine.
Smith, W. Cats are not at all like people.
Snyder, G. Hay for the Horses.
Sokolov. Artist has to be enslaved, An.
Soyinka. Ujamaa.
Spender, S. Unemployed.
Spenser. *Penelope* for her *Ulisses* sake.
Steele, T. Timothy.

Steptoe. O' yes.
Stevenson, R. To A Gardener.
Stickney, T. Requiescam.
Six o'Clock.
Su Tung-p'o. New Year's Eve—you'd think I could go home early.
Swift, J. Description of the Morning, A.
On a Curate's Complaint of Hard Duty.
Swirszczynska. When We Wake Up in the Morning.
Synge. On an Island.
Tagami. Now It Is Broccoli.
Song of Pajaro.
Thomas, R. Worker, The.
Thoreau. If with light head erect I sing.
Tindal. Cry of the Oppressed, The.
Toomer. Reapers.
Tranströmer. Open and Closed Space.
Outskirts.
Troupe. River Town Packin House Blues.
Tsvetayeva. I bless the daily labor of my hands.
Tu Fu. By the Winding River II.
Unamuno. Throw Yourself Like Seed.
Unknown. All day I hoe weeds.
Always Finish.
Another Little Boy.
Big rat, big rat.
Can't You Line It?
Day-Dreamer.
Factory Girl's Come-All-Ye, The.
Freighting from Wilcox to Globe.
Go Down, Old Hannah.
God Speed the Plough!
Green and yellow patchwork across the country lies, A.
Ground-Thumping Song.
However they talk, whatever they.
In everything you do.
In Praise of the Broom.
Jerry, Go an' Ile That Car.
John Henry.
John Henry was a lil [*or* little] baby.
Lavender's Blue.
Lining Track.
No bees, no honey;.
One, two, whatever you do.
Pick a Bale of Cotton.
Plucking The Rushes.
Poor Paddy Works on the Railway.
Shovelling Iron Ore.
Take this hammer—huh!
Tamping Ties ("Tamp 'em up solid").
This Sun Is Hot.
Track-lining Song.
Unloading Rails.
Way Out in Idaho.
We lads in the forging-shop have unbounded strength.
When John Henry was a little babe.
Winner never quits, A.
Women Transport Corps.
Working on the Railway.
Ushakov. Craftsmanship.
Vinokurov. Prophet, The.
Virgil. Dead Ox, The.
Until Jove let it be, no colonist.
Voznesensky. Autumn.
Wang Chien. Words of the Newly Wed Wife.
Waniek. Balance.
Warner, S. Epitaph: "John Bird, a laborer, lies here."
Warr, B. Working Class.
Wat. Before Breughel the Elder.
Watts, I. How doth the little busy bee.
Whipple, L. My dad works late in a coffee shop.
Whitehead, W. Sweepers, The.
Whiteside. Carpenter, The.
Whitman, W. I hear America singing, the varied carols I hear.
Whittier. Dedication: "I would the gift I offer here."
Wilbur. Plain Song for Comadre, A.
Summer Morning, A.
Winters, A. Mill-Race, The.
Wise, W. When I grow up.

Wither. Husbandman, The.
Spade and the Wreath, The.
Wong, N. Three Sweatshop Women.
Yang Shih-ch'i. On the Hall of Precious Virtue.
Yeats. Adam's Curse.
Yorke. Our Gardener here, James Phillips see.
Yoshimi. Tanka: "Ocean, The."
Zenmaro. Tanka: "How sad it is."
Tanka: "In sullen silence."
Tanka: "'We're poor'."
Ziedonis. Inevitability.
Zolynas. Zen of Housework, The.

Labrador, Canada
Crane, H. North Labrador.
Sandburg, C. Love in Labrador.

Labyrinthitis
Hummer, T. Inner Ear.

Labyrinths
Gioia. Maze Without a Minotaur.
Gregg. Strong Pomegranate Flowers and Seeds of the Mind.
Muir, E. Labyrinth, The.

Lade, Sir John
Johnson, S. Short Song of Congratulation [*or* To a Young Heir], A.

Ladybirds
Clare, J. Clock-A-Clay [The Lady Bug].
Farber. Ladybug's Christmas.
Mother Goose. Ladybird, Ladybird fly away home.
Rossetti, C. I caught a little ladybird / That flies far away.
Unknown. Ladybird.

Lafayette, Marie Joseph, Marquis de
Madison. Lafayette.

Lake District, England
Wordsworth, W. Composed at Rydal on May Morning, 1838.

Lakes and Ponds
Allard. Alone tonight one fish ripples the lake.
Amalrik. Lake Baskunchak.
Ashbery. On Autumn Lake.
Basho. Old pond:/ frog-jump-in.
Old pond— / The sound, An.
Bayliss. Seven Dreams.
Beddoes. Lake / Is a river curled and asleep like a snake, The.
Belitt. Winter Pond.
Blaga. Heraclitus by the Lake.
Blunden. Midnight Skaters, The.
Bly, R. Sunset at a Lake.
Byron, G. Sonnet to Lake Leman.
Campbell, W. Winter Lakes, The.
Chiang K'uei. Tune: "Charm of Nien-nu."
Chu Hsi. Farm by the Lake, The.
Thoughts While Reading.
Chu Yün-ming. As I Looked at a Lake, My Thoughts Turned to a Certain Friend.
Clark, T. You (III).
Coleridge, M. Lady of Trees, The.
Coxe, L. Lake, The.
Creeley. Way, The.
Ded. At the end of a crazy-moon night.
Durrell. Vega.
Eberhart, R. Loon Call, A.
Eimers. Night Without Stars, A.
Frost, R. Spring Pools.
Fumi Saito. Tanka: "Snow seeping."
Tanka: "To take a bath."
Tanka: "Water streams."
Garrigue. Shore.
Gioia. Country Wife, The.
Glück, L. Pond, The.
Greger. Frog in the Swimming Pool, The.
Guest, B. Twilight Polka Dots.
Han Yü. My ceramic lake in dawn, water settled clear.
Pond in a Bowl, The.
Harteis. Mirage.
Hughes, T. Lake, The.
Kapilar. Then and Now.
Kelly, B. Leaving, The.
Kunitz, S. Goose Pond's imaginary snows.
Lane, P. Lake Murry.
Levertov. Quest, The.

Li Ch'ing-chao. Autumn Evening Beside the Lake.
Lin Pu. Autumn Day, An—Leisurely Boating on West Lake.
Lloyd, D. Duck feathers.
Lochhead, L. What The Pool Said, On Midsummer's Day.
Major, C. Swallow the Lake.
Malouf. For Two Children.
Marriott. Beaver Pond.
Masaoka Shiki. During a trip.
McLaughlin, K. Suicide Pond.
McQueen. To Ben, at the Lake.
Millay, E. Armenonville.
Mullins, B. At the Lakehouse.
Noyes, A. Daddy Fell into the Pond.
Oliver, M. At Blackwater Pond the tossed waters have settled.
Ou-yang Hsiu. Tune: "Song of Picking Mulberry"—Recollections of West Lake.
P'an Lang. Written on Lake View Tower.
Percival. To Senaca Lake.
Pizzarelli. Piece of buttered popcorn, A.
Plath. Crossing the Water.
Poe. Lake: To———, The.
Pound, E. Canto 49.
Pritchard, N. Paysagesque.
Reed, I. Lake Bud.
Scott, F. Lakeshore.
Scott, F. Unnamed Lake, The.
Seiler. Lake, The.
Seward. Lake, The; Or, Modern Improvement in Landscape.
Shapiro, D. To an Idea.
Simpson, R. Lake.
Smith, T. Two Poems on the Fear of Love.
Southard. Across the still lake.
Stickney, T. In the Past.
Lakeward.
Su Tung-p'o. Little stream used to cross my land, A.
Looking from the Pavilion Over the Lake.
Supervielle. Missing France.
Tu Mu. Pond in a Basin.
Voznesensky. Call of the Lake, The.
Wilbur. Marginalia.
Wills, J. Stagnant pond, A.
Wilson, J. Written on the Banks of Wastwater During a Calm.
Wordsworth, D. Lake was covered all over, The.
Wu Chen. Ni Tsan Poem Following Rhyme-Words of Wu Chen.
Yüan Chieh. Civilization.
Stone Fish Lake.

Lalemant, Gabriel
Scott, F. Brébeuf and His Brethren.

Lamb, Charles
Coleridge, S. This Lime-Tree Bower My Prison.

Lamb, Mary
Landor, W. To the Sister of Charles Lamb.

Lambs
Blake, W. Lamb, The.
Tyger, The.
Brock-Broido. Carrowmore.
Campbell, D. Pallid Cuckoo.
Davies, W. Child's Pet, A.
Eastwick. Wolf and the Lambs, The.
Eberhart, R. For a Lamb.
Fogel, A. Necessity, The.
Hale, S. Mary's Lamb [or Mary and Her Lamb].
Howitt, M. Sale of the Pet Lamb, The.
Hughes, T. Ravens.
Larkin, P. First Sight.
MacCaig. Gone Are the Days.
Mew. Fame.
Roberson. Blue Horses.
Rossetti, C. Frisky lamb / And a frisky child, A.
Lambs at Play.
Tadic. Song to the Lamb.
Tekeyan. Sacred Wrath.
Unknown. Little Lamb, A.
Mary had a little lamb.
Wordsworth, W. Pet Lamb, The; A Pastoral.
Bobrowski. Pruzzian Elegy.

Lament (form)
Daniel, S. Sonnet 5: 'Whilst Youth and Error'.
De la Mare. Sunk Lyonesse.
Drayton. To His Coy Love, A Canzonet.
Fumi Saito. Tanka: "When I think over."
Morton, W. Dafney's Lamentation.
Oodgeroo of the tribe Noonuccal. Dawn Wail for the Dead.
Rowe, E. Expostulation, The.
Sidney, P. Sonnet 33: "I might, unhappy word, O me, I might."
Spenser. Sonnet 10: 'Unrighteous Lord of Love'.
Surrey. Epitaph on Thomas Clere.
Unknown. Lament, The: "What shall I send you, my dear one, then in the underworld?"
Sweet, sweet, sweet, let me go.
Wyatt, T. Resound my voice [or voyse], ye woods [or wodes] that hear [or here] me plain.
See also **Lament** in Title, First Line, and Last Line Index

Lamplighting and Lamplighters
Farjeon, E. Light the Lamps Up, Lamplighter!
"O'Sullivan." Lamplighter, The.
Stevenson, R. Lamplighter, The.
Tomlinson, C. Civilities of Lamplight.

Lampreys
Diaper. Lamprey, glowing with uncommon fires, The.
Gay, J. To a Young Lady, with Some Lampreys.
See also **Eels**

Lancashire, England
Carew, T. To Saxham.
Connor, T. Lancashire Winter.

Landlords and Landladies
Atwood. Landlady, The.
Bunner, H. Behold the Deeds!
Dickinson, E. Rat is the conciest Tenant, The.
Farewell. Adieu to My Landlady, An.
Herbert, G. Redemption.
Hughes, L. Ballad of the Landlord.
Madam and the Rent Man.
Joans. Scenery.
Montague, J. Wild Sports of the West.
Soyinka. Telephone Conversation.
Wells, A. Inn That Missed Its Chance, The.

Landor, Walter Savage
Landor, W. For an Epitaph at Fiesole.
Moore, M. W. S. Landor.
Parker, D. Walter Savage Landor.
Swinburne. In Memory of Walter Savage Landor.

Landscape
Bawer. View from an Airplane at Night, over California, The.
Bozhilov. Kentish Sestinas.
Cardenal. Vision from the Blue Window.
Cendrars. Aleutian Islands.
Clare, J. Ploughman Singing.
Cuddihy. Steps.
Di Prima. Tassajara, 1969.
Divakaruni. Indigo.
Drake, J. Bronx.
Eliot, T. New Hampshire.
Rannoch, by Glencoe.
Usk.
Virginia.
Elytis. Origin of Landscape or the End of Mercy, The.
Garioch. Wire, The.
Ginsberg, A. Wales Visitation.
Hardy, T. In Front of the Landscape.
Hewitt, J. Glens, The.
Ram's Horn, The.
Holub. Franklin Bridge in Philadelphia, The.
Jonson, B. To Sir Robert Wroth.
Karpowicz. On Opening an Old House.
Kinnell. Supper after the Last, The.
Kinzie. Xenophilia.
Knight, R. Landscape, The.
Lanier, S. From the Flats.
Mead, P. Cinema Point.
Melo Neto. Landscape of the Capibaribe River.

Melville, H. Attic Landscape, The.
Enviable Isles, The.
Inscription, The: "While yet Rolfe's foot in stirrup stood."
Padilla. Fountain, a house of stone, A.
Landscapes.
Paz. Landscape.
Plumly. Toward Umbria.
Ritsos. Our Land.
Rukeyser, M. Homage to Literature.
Sandburg, C. Nocturne in a Deserted Brickyard.
Seward. Lake, The; Or, Modern Improvement in Landscape.
Sikelianos. Thalero.
Spender, S. Mask.
Stow. Singing Bones, The.
Su Tung-p'o. Written on a Painting Entitled "Misty Yangtze and Folded Hills."
Tahmisic. Landscapes.
Van Duyn. View, A.
Wright, J. In Ohio.
Quest, The.

Landscapes
Anh Tho'. Harvesting at Sunset.
Auden. In Praise of Limestone.
Brown, G. Island School.
Carrier, C. Prospect Before Us, The.
Cary, A. Katrina on the Porch.
Cherry, K. Going Down on America.
Chong, C. Summit, The.
Darwish, M. We walk towards a land not of our flesh.
Dunbar, R. Summit gain'd how glorious the reward, The.
Graves, R. Lost Acres.
Gunn, T. Iron Landscapes (and the Statue of Liberty).
Hilberry. Body and mind, we used to think, were two.
Kim, Y. May.
Kim, Y. Landscape I.
Kleinzahler. Two Canadian Landscapes.
Madge. Landscape I.
Melville, H. Enviable Isles, The.
Pontoosuce.
Ostriker. Minor Van Gogh (He Speaks), A.
Park, C. Landscape, A.
Patchen. Saturday Night in the Parthenon.
Ridler. Backgrounds to Italian Paintings: Fifteenth Century.
Smith, C. Sonnet V. To the South Downs: "Ah, hills beloved!—where once, an happy child."
Stickney, T. Requiescam.
Su Tung-p'o. Red Cliff, The.
Thomas, R. Welsh Landscape.
Tran Minh-tong (King). Bạch-đằng River, The.
Tu Fu. Clear Evening after Rain.
Wright, C. Northhanger Ridge.
Wright, J. Night After Bushfire.
Yi, K. Winter Vision, The.

Landslides
Ammons. Clarity.

Language
Adams, F. To a Thesaurus.
Agard, J. Listen Mr Oxford Don.
Albiach. "Theatre."
Allen, P. Zen Americana.
Andrews, B. Appetizers'.
DDD.
Gestalt me out! Slang to the point of meat-eating, imperative ornament, dislike.
Impatient Heart, The.
Methodology.
West West.
While.
Antin. Real Estate.
Armantrout. Language of Love.
Ashbery. Life As a Book That Has Been Put Down.
Paradoxes and Oxymorons.
Aubert, A. Opposite of Green, The.
When the Wine Was Gone.
Auden. Their Lonely Betters.
Ball, H. Complete Sound-Poems of Hugo Ball,

The.
Flight out of Time.
Baraka. Wise 3.
Barker, G. Reverend Arbuthnot-Armitage-
Brown, The.
Bell, M. These Green-going-to-Yellow.
Benson, S. Beethoven's Sixth Symphony.
Berkson, B. Rebecca Cutlet.
Bernstein, C. Wait.
Bible, *O.T.* And the whole earth was of one
language, and of one speech.
Bienek. Resistance.
Bishop, M. Naughty Preposition, The.
Boland, E. Anna Liffey.
Boldman. Leaves blowing into a sentence.
Borkhuis. Inside Language.
Bozhilov. Kentish Sestinas.
Breytenbach. Struggle for the Taal, The.
Brown, L. Lyric Can Snare, The.
Burn. For the Common Market.
Cage. Lecture on Nothing.
Campion, T. Think'st thou to seduce me then
with words that have no meaning?
Carryl, G. How a Girl Was Too Reckless of
Grammar [by Far].
Cassian. Vowel.
Castro, M. Blew It.
Causley. Old Mrs Thing-um-e-bob.
Celan. Language Mesh.
Chapman, G. And, for our tongue, that still is
so empayr'd.
Cibulka. Kremenez.
Clare, J. Fragment: "Language has not the
power to speak what love indites."
Clifton, L. I am accused of tending to the
past.
Codrescu. Poetry Paper.
Coleman, W. Essay on Language.
ISM, The.
Collobert. III.
Coolidge, C. On Induction of the Hand.
Cope, W. Uncertainty of the Poet, The.
Corn. Contemporary Culture and the Letter
"K."
Cortez. Phraseology.
Creeley. Language, The.
Crouch, S. Blackie Thinks of His Brothers.
Cuadra, A. Brief Letter to Donald Walsh (in
memoriam).
Cunliffe. Alpha-B375-Earth Visitors'
Guide. . . Section.
Darragh. Footnote at "Figure of Speech."
Lattice at "Split."
Lattice at/of (Com)pare (Dis)pair.
"Legion" to "Lent" for "R."
"Luteous" to "Lymph" for "F."
Sis Boom Ba.
Throwing Out at / of (Com)pare (Dis)pair, A.
Volcanic tuff.
Davidson, M. Century of Hands.
Et in Leucadia Ego.
Davie. Hearing Russian Spoken.
With the Grain.
Davies, A. New Sentience, The.
Thirty East Forty-Second Street.
Day, J. From momentary work, a wrench, to
just fall forward.
Moving Object.
De la Mare. Antiques.
Desnos. Hour farther witch art in Heaven.
Like.
When children slap their father's face.
Dickinson, E. Could mortal lip divine.
DiPalma. Annotations Tropes and Lacunae of
the Itoku Master.
Bed, The.
Motion of the Cypher.
We Forego Mimicry.
Djanikian. How I Learned English.
Drayton. First Steps Up Parnassus.
O, why should Nature niggardly restraine!
Duncan, R. Little Language, A.
Dunn, S. Let's See If I Have It Right.
Eady. Sherbet.
Eberhart, R. I went to see Irving Babbitt.
Eigner. Temporary language, A.
Elmslie, K. Stage Duo.

Equi. In a Monotonous Dream.
Eskimo Oral Tradition. Magic Words.
Finch, R. Words.
Finlay, I. Garden Poem.
Fordham. Saxon Legend of Language, The.
Foster, E. Morning.
Francis, R. Hogwash.
Gibson, M. Learning a New Language.
Gildner. Cabbage in Polish is kapusta—
ka*poos*ta.
Gillan. Public School No. 18: Paterson, New
Jersey.
Giovanni. Poem (for Langston Hughes), A.
Glancy. First Reader Santee Training School,
1873, The.
Glatshteyn. To a Friend Who Wouldn't Bother
to Strain His Noodleboard Because Even So
It Is Hard to Go Hunting When Your Rifle Is
Blunt and Love Is Soft as an Old Blanket.
Glück, L. Illuminations.
Gnanakoothan. Tamil, it's true, is the breath
of my life.
Goldsworthy. After Babel.
Görgey. Fragments of Ten Poems.
Graves, R. Cool Web, The.
In Broken Images.
Tilth.
Guest, B. Words.
Guillén, N. Don't Know No English.
Sensemayá.
Gumilyov. Words.
Hacker, M. After the Revolution.
Hadas, R. Forgetting Greek.
Pass it on, II.
Three Silences.
Hale, J. Desmet, Idaho, March 1969.
Hall, D. Je Suis une Table.
Peaches.
Hardy, T. Liddell and Scott.
Harrison, T. Classics Society.
On Not Being Milton.
Them and [uz].
Harryman. Allegory.
That Can Not Be Taken Away From It.
Hartnett. Pity the man who English lacks.
Harwood, L. Words, The.
Hass, R. Meditation at Lagunitas.
Heaney, S. Alphabets.
Traditions.
Hemensley. Sulking in the Seventies.
Herbert, G. Son[ne], The.
Higgins, B. Genesis.
Holbrook, W. Varitalk.
Holmes, O. Aestivation [an Unpublished
Poem, by My Late Latin Tutor].
Hoover, P. Desire.
Howe, S. In its first dumb form.
Say that a ballad.
Hsü Wei. Inscribed on a Painting.
Huelsenbeck, R. *et al.* L'amiral cherche une
maison à louer.
Hutchinson, P. Frost is All Over, The.
Inada. Kicking the Habit.
Inman, P. Centered.
Colloam.
Field dodd.
Subtracted Words.
XX.
Ishkhan. Armenian Language Is the Home of
the Armenian, The.
Jabès. Desert, The.
Notebook, Two.
Jackson, L. All things that wake enjoy the
sun.
World and I, The.
Jastrzebska. Bi-lingual.
Jonson, B. Fit of Rhyme [*or* Rime] against
Rhyme [*or* Rime], A.
Joyce, J. *Bronze by gold heard the hoofirons,
steelyringing.
Kalász. Time's No Grammar.
Kaneko. Bailey Gatzert: The First Grade,
1945.
Kelly, R. Ode to Language.
Khlebnikov, V. Zangezi: R, K, L, G—.
Koch, K. Permanently.
Kruchyonykh. Declaration of the Word as

Such.
Pomade.
Laleau. Betrayal.
Landor, W. Death Stands above Me[,
whispering low].
Lange, A. Perugia.
Lee, L. Persimmons.
Lehrer. Wernher von Braun.
Leonard, T. Ifyi stull / huuny / wurkt oot.
Its thi lang / wij a thi / guhtr thaht hi.
Poetry.
Right inuff / ma language is disgraceful.
This is thi.
Lepik. Nobody talks earth's language.
Levertov. Caedmon.
O Taste and See.
Lipkin, S. Conjunction.
Longfellow, H. Picture-Writing.
Looney. Breaking the Surface.
Lorde. Coal.
Lucretius. How They Communicate.
Lum. Going Home.
Lux. Solo Native.
Mac Low. Almost Casanova Electricity.
Lack of Balance but not Fatal, A.
7th Light Poem: For John Cage—17 June
1962.
"MacDiarmid." Weapon, The.
Mackey, N. Alphabet of Ahtt.
Magee, K. Tedium Drum, Part IV.
Mahapatra, J. Sanskrit.
Maiden. Language.
Mandel, T. Realism.
Marichiko. Who is there? Me.
Martin, C. E. S. L.
Speech Against Stone.
Maunick. Letter to Ellen Conroy Kennedy.
McCaffery. Can there be a collision between
picture and application?
Little Hans.
McHugh, H. Inflation.
McOrlan. Horse butcher, The.
Meredith, W. Rhode Island.
Merrill, J. Lost in Translation.
Merwin, W. Home for Thanksgiving.
Last One, The.
Losing a Language.
Michaux. Tomorrow.
Milosz, C. My Faithful Mother Tongue.
Montague, J. Grafted Tongue, A.
Mora. Elena.
Mountain, M. K k k k k.
Nash, O. Very like a Whale.
Needell. Color, even whiteness, reaches / the
body as a name.
Nemerov. Makers, The.
Translation.
Nichol. Scraptures: 7th Sequence.
St. Anzas IX.
St. Anzas VI.
Noguere. Scribes, The.
O'Bruadair. Change, The.
New Style, The.
Olson, C. Moon Is the Number 18, The.
These Days.
Oppen. Words cannot be wholly transparent.
And that is the.
Ortiz de Montellano. Space Between, The.
Palmer, M. Eighth Sky.
Project of Linear Inquiry, The.
Recursus.
Sun.
Parker, D. One Perfect Rose.
Pastan. Grammar Lesson.
Patchen. Moon, Sun, Sleep, Birds, Live.
Paz. Brotherhood.
Pembroke, M. To the Thrice-Sacred Queen
Elizabeth.
Perelman. Broken Mirror, The.
Chronic Meanings.
Let's Say.
Seduced by Analogy.
Things.
Philips, K. On the Welsh Language.
Phillips, D. From Arena.
I Held the Vein, But Death.
On Entries Emptiness.

Plath. Magi.
Plumpp. Turf Song.
Prévert. Dunce, The.
Questel. Judge Dreadword.
Ramke. Buchenwald.
Retallack, J. Here's Looking at You Francis Bacon.
Not a Cage.
Western CIV, 4 and 5.
Reznikoff. Highway I was walking on, The.
Rimbaud, A. Vowels.
Ríos, A. Language of Great-Aunts, The.
Nani.
Rothenberg, J. Aleph Poem.
Russell, N. Message of the Rain, The.
Sabina. 13th Horse Song of Frank Mitchell, The.
Sahay. Our Hindi is a widower's new wife.
Salazar. Piñon Nuts.
Salter. Summer 1983.
Sanchez, S. Nigger.
Sandburg, C. Languages.
Little girl, be careful what you say.
Precious Moments.
Primer Lesson.
Useless Words.
Schwitters. Third movement.
Shapiro, K. Dirty word hops in the cage of the mind like the Pondicherry vulture, The.
Sherry, J. Lepidoptery.
What should be the title of a king. Too, how also to include. What happened when.
Silliman. Lucky my ears 'pop' at the hilltop.
Not this. / What then?
Simic. Errata.
Singer, B. Sort of Language, A.
Sisson. Usk, The.
Smith, I. Shall Gaelic Die?
Sobin, G. Premises.
Towards the Blanched Alphabets.
Spender, S. Word bites like a fish, The.
Spicer, J. 6.
Duet for a Chair and a Table.
Thing Language.
Starbuck, G. Spell against Spelling, The.
Stein, G. Which I wish to say is this.
Stevens, W. Of the Manner of Addressing Clouds.
Sze. Black Java Pepper.
Tafari. Tongue (De First Instrument), De.
Taggart, J. Body and Soul: Poem for Two Readers.
Monk.
Thomas, D. Before I knocked and flesh let enter.
Thomas, L. Electricity of Blossoms.
Trần Tế Xu'o'ng. Lamenting the State of Confucian Scholarship.
New-Style Examinations.
No, Thank You!
Tyler, P. Anthology of Nouns.
Tzara. Dada Manifesto on Feeble and Bitter Love.
Great Lament of my Obscurity Three, The.
Maison Aragon.
[Part One].
Ullman. Living Near the Plaza of Thieves.
Unknown. Aborigine Sound Poem.
Americana IX.
Bald Mountain Zaum-Poems.
Magic Words.
Why English Is So Hard!
Vaginov. Song of Words.
Vallejo. And what if after so many words.
Trilce.
Very. Promise, The.
Voznesensky. Dogalypse.
Walcott. Codicil.
Waldrop, R. To explore the nature of rain I opened the door because inside the workings of language clear vision is impossible.
Wallace-Crabbe. Life of Ideas, The.
Waters, M. Keats' Lips.
Watten. Statistics.
Weaver, M. Luxembourg Garden.
Welish. Scalpel in Hand.

Wellman, M. Of Power, Money, Cheese, Real Estate, Conboberation, Hoohah.
Williamson, G. Waterfall.
Wilson, E. Miniature Dialogue.
Wolfli. Nostalgic song for my beloved.
Wordsworth, D. Loving and Liking [Irregular Verses Addressed to A Child].
Wylie. Pretty Words.
Yang Chi. Submitting a Memorial Requesting Permission to Return Home and Care for My Parents.
Yoshimi. Tanka: "Since I work with those."
Yukitsuna. Tanka: "Always loving."
Zenmaro. Tanka: "It's hazardous."

Lanterns
Brown, S. Long Track Blues.
Chao Meng-fu. To a Pyrotechnist.
Chōkū. Tanka: "Bulky oil lamp, A."
Coleridge, M. Street Lanterns.
Frost, R. Draft Horse, The.

Lanyon, Peter
Graham, W. Thermal Stair, The.

Laos and Laotians
McDonald, W. For Harper, Killed in Action.

Lapwings
Blake, W. O lapwing, thou fliest around the heath.
Yakamochi. I will come to you.

Larches
Eastwick. Larch Wood Secrets.

Larkin, James
Clarke, A. Inscription for a Headstone.

Larkin, Philip
Karr. Post-Larkin Triste.
Loden. My Night with Philip Larkin.
Ruark. Larkin.

Larks
Blake, W. Lark's Song, The.
Blind. On a Forsaken Lark's Nest.
Bunyan. Upon the Lark and the Fowler.
Eastwick. Morning.
Graves, R. Love without hope, as when the young bird-catcher.
Hardy, T. Shelley's Skylark.
Henley, W. Margaritæ Sorori [I. M.].
Hopkins, G. Caged Skylark, The.
Sea and the Skylark, The.
Woodlark, The.
Hughes, T. All the dreary Sunday morning.
I suppose you just gape and let your gaspings.
Lark begins to go up, The.
Like those flailing flames.
My idleness curdles.
Kavanagh, P. Praying.
Leighton, R. Bunch of Larks, The.
Rosenberg, I. Returning, We Hear the Larks.
Shakespeare, W. Song: "Hark! hark! the lark at heaven's gate sings."
Shelley, P. To a Skylark.
Smart, C. For Saturday.
Unknown. Lark, The.
Werfel. To a Lark in War-Time.
Wordsworth, W. To the Skylark.

Las Vegas, Nevada
Hays, H. Case, The.

Last Judgment
Atwood. Resurrection.
Borges. Matthew XXV:30.
Howard, R. Giovanni da Fiesole on the Sublime.
Shelley, P. England in 1819.

Last Rites. *See* **Extreme Unction**

Last Supper
Prévert. Last Supper, The.
Rilke. Last Supper, The.
Matthew 26:17–29.
Southwell. Of the Blessed Sacrament of the Altar [*or* Aulter].
Williams, O. Last Supper, The.

Latin
Cummings, E. Noster was a ship of swank, The.
Hecht, A. Mysteries of Caesar, The.
Unknown. Latin is a dead tongue.

Latin America and Latin Americans
Alexander, E. Ode.

Cofer. What the Gypsy Said to Her Children.
Espada. Jorge the Church Janitor Finally Quits.
Hagedorn, J. Latin Music in New York.
Hernandez, D. Armitage Street.
Rodriguez, L. Fire.
Rose. Day They Cleaned Up the Border El Salvador, February, 1981, The.

Latter-Day Saints, Church of Jesus Christ of.
See **Mormons**

Lauder, William
Edwards, T. To the Editor of Mr. Pope's Works.

Laughter
Al-Harizi. Lightning, The.
Avena. Cancer garden, protected by buildings, one unfinished. Still, The.
Bartsch. Deposition.
Baxter, J. Small grey cloudy louse that nests in my beard, The.
Blake, W. Laughing Song.
Browning, R. Memorabilia.
Catullus. Carmen 31 ("Apple of islands, Sirmio, & bright peninsulas, set").
Ch'in Kuan. Along the Grand Canal.
Corso. Zizi's Lament.
Creeley. Wicker Basket, A.
Davies, W. Her Merriment.
Day Lewis. Two Songs.
Dipoko. From My Parisian Diary.
Dunbar, P. We wear the mask that grins and lies.
Enoch. Laughter.
Foix. When I Sleep, Then I See Clearly.
Gilbert-Lecomte. Son of the Bone Speaks, The.
Graham, J. Soul Says.
Greenaway. School is over.
Hadewijch. Love's Maturity.
Hall, D. Clown, The.
Howes, B. Early Supper.
Hughes, L. Homesick Blues.
Johnson, G. I Want to Die While You Love Me.
Jonker. When You Laugh.
Keats. Why did I laugh to-night? No voice will tell.
Kinnell. Crying only a little bit.
Lovelace, R. Lucasta Laughing.
Matveyeva. Laughter of a Faun, The.
McGrath, J. Song.
Page, P. Young Girls.
Prunty. Reading Before We Read, Horoscope and Weather.
Ríos, A. Teodoro Luna's Two Kisses.
Rotella, A. Only I laugh.
Sanchez, S. Haiku.
Sandburg, C. Bundles.
Schwartz, D. Sarah.
Seferis. Wreck "Thrush", The.
Shannon, M. Only My Opinion.
Smith, S. Conventionalist, The.
Persian, The.
Swinburne. Child's Laughter, A.
Swirszczynska. Sea and the Man, The.
Unknown. Me and My Captain.
Sunshine and Music.
Wagoner, D. Loons Mating.
Woroszylski. Early Chaplin, The.
Zenmaro. At the lectern.
See also **Mirth**

Laughton, Charles
Brecht, B. Letter to the Actor Charles Laughton concerning the Work on the Play "The Life of Galileo."

Laundry and Laundering
Alvarez, J. Ironing Their Clothes.
Barbauld. Washing-Day.
Barrax. Domestic Tranquility.
Burnand. Tubby or not tubby—there's the rub.
Collier, M. Washerwoman, The.
Dobson, R. Folding the Sheets.
Elmslie, K. Duo-Tang.
Ewing, J. Dolls' Wash, The.
Ferlinghetti, L. Away above a harborful.
Fordham. Washerwoman, The.
Gallagher, T. I Stop Writing the Poem.

Gustafson, R. Of Green Steps and Laundry.
Hochman. Goldfish Wife, The.
Kazarnovsky. Chinese Laundry.
Kendrick, D. Alone for a Week.
McCrea. Wash-Day.
Merrill, J. Mad Scene, The.
Moss, T. Fisher Street.
Nagy, A. Storm.
North, C. Hospital.
Pizzarelli. Bearded lady, The.
Rankine. Eden.
Ritchie. Sorting Laundry.
Rosenberg, S. In the laundermat.
Seifert. It was afternoon or later.
Smith, B. Laundry.
Steele, T. Sheets, The.
Stone, R. In an Iridescent Time.
Summerfield. Washday Rattles.
Swirszczynska. I Wash the Shirt.
Updike. Bendix.
Weigl. Girl at the Chu Lai Laundry.
Wesley-Smith. Walter Spaggot, strange old
man.
Wilbur. Love Calls Us to the Things of This
World.
Williams, W. Young Laundryman, The.
Yang Wan-li. Drying Clothes.
Young, A. Shepherd's Hut, The.
Young, C. Vespers.

Laurels
Bogan, L. Several Voices Out of a Cloud.
Herrick. Mount of the Muses, The.
To Laurels.
To Mistress Katherine Bradshaw, the Lovely,
That Crowned Him with Laurel.
Westmorland. Occasioned by Seeing a Walk
of Bay Trees.
Wills, J. Laurel in bloom.
Winchilsea. Circuit of Apollo, The.

Laurentian Mountains, Canada
Scott, F. Laurentian Shield.

Lautrec, Henri de Toulouse-. *See* **Toulouse-
Lautrec, Henri de**

Lavender
Fleming, E. Lavender Bush, The.
Goodman, P. I planned to have a border of
lavender.
McClatchy. Weeds.
Unknown. Lavender's Blue.

Law and Lawyers
Auden. Law like Love.
Bartusek. Sentence.
Blamire. Wey, Ned, man! thou luiks sae
down-hearted.
"Carroll." Long Tale, A.
Clarke, A. Penal Law.
Cordle. Lizzie and Joe in Court.
Cutler, B. Doing Justice.
De la Mare. In the Dock.
Donne. Epithalamion for Lawyers, An.
Poet Turned Lawyer, The.
Satire 5.
Empson. Legal Fiction.
Gay, J. Air: "Fox may steal your hens, sir,
A."
Greville, F. Chorus Primus of Bashaws or
Cadis.
Herbert, Z. Trial, The.
Housman, A. Laws of God, the Laws of Man,
The.
Kelly, R. Life of Intimate Fleeing, A.
Landor, W. Case at Sessions, A.
Levchev. We stopped.
Moorer. Injustice of the Courts.
Legal Mouse, A.
Quarles. On God's Law.
Sandburg, C. Lawyers Know Too Much, The.
Sepamla. Law that says, The.
Small, A. What abou' de Law?
Su Tung-p'o. New Year's Eve—you'd think I
could go home early.
Thackeray. Damages, Two Hundred Pounds.
Tolson. Ex-Judge at the Bar, An.
Unknown. Beneath this smooth stone by the
bone of his bone.
Case to the Civilians, A.
Lawyers themselves uphold the commonweal.

Waldheim. Help Wanted.
Lawes, Henry
Milton. To Mr. H. Lawes On His Airs.
Philips, K. To Mr. Henry Lawes.
Waller, E. To Mr. Henry Lawes, Who Had
Then Newly Set a Song of Mine in the Year
1635.
Lawns
Empson. Rolling the Lawn.
Lawrence, David Herbert
O'Hara, F. Poem: "I don't know as I get what
D.H. Lawrence is driving at."
Warburton, N. Snake on D. H. Lawrence, The.
Wolfe, H. D. H. Lawrence and James Joyce.
Lawrence, Edward
Milton. To Mr. Lawrence.
Lazarus (Bible)
Browning, R. Epistle Containing the Strange
Medical Experience of Karshish, the Arab
Physician, An.
Chesterton, G. Convert, The.
Clifton, L. Raising of Lazarus, The.
Colman, H. On Lazarus Raised From Death.
Crashaw. Upon Lazarus His Teares.
Frost, R. Luke 16:19–26; "There was a rich
man."
Nagy, A. Lazarus.
Parra, N. Anti-Lazarus, The.
Procter, A. Homeless.
Rilke. John 11:30–44; Now Jesus had not yet
come to the village.
Tennyson, A. When Lazarus left his charnel-
cave.
Unknown. Dives and Lazarus ("There was a
man in olden times").
Yeats. "Calvary."
Laziness
Bible, *O.T.* Go to the ant, thou sluggard;.
Chaucer. Cook's Tale, The.
Chukhonstev. Epistle to Baron Delvig.
Dunbar, P. In the Morning.
Herrick. Ass[e], The.
Long and Lazy [or Lazie].
Hesiod. Against sloth.
Hoskyns. Epitaph, An: On a Man for Doing
Nothing.
Hughes, T. Moon-transport.
Martynov. Idlers.
Mayer, G. Old Mrs. Lazibones.
McGirt. Nothing to Do.
When de Sun Shines Hot.
Murray, R. Wasted Day, The.
Nash, O. Introspective Reflection.
Persius. Argument.
Po Chü-i. Lazy Man's Song.
Prior. Epitaph, An: "Interred [or Interr'd]
beneath this marble stone."
Roethke. Sloth, The.
Shao Yung. Song on Being Too Lazy to Get
Up.
Sidgwick, H. Strenuous Life, The.
Unknown. diller, a dollar, A.
Get up, get up, you lazy-head.
Nancy Dawson was so fine.
Watts, I. Sluggard, The.
Wilde, O. Hélas!
Yang Chi. Wu Shan-yang.
Leadership
Antokolsky. Paul the First.
Csoori. My Masters.
Dryden, J. Crown Prince of Dullness, The.
Holland, J. God, Give Us Men!
Jonson, B. To Sir Horace Vere.
To William, Earl[e] of Pembroke.
Kipling, R. Servant When He Reigneth, A.
Leonard, T. Feed Ma Lamz.
Lindsay, V. Abraham Lincoln Walks at
Midnight.
Robinson, E. Master, The.
Taylor, B. Night the Second: All or Nothing.
Unknown. Ode to the Toad.
Warren, R. There once, on that goat island, I.
Zu-Bolton. Governor of the Ollie Street, The.
Leander. *See* **Hero and Leander**
Leap Year
Johnson, M. Leap Yeah Party, De.

Lear, Edward
Auden. Edward Lear.
Lear, E. Self-Portrait of the Laureate of
Nonsense.
Lear, King. *See* **King Lear**
Learning
Atwood. You begin this way.
Beckett, S. Gnome.
Berkeley, G. On the Prospect of Planting Arts
and Learning in America.
Chōkū. Tanka: "Bulky oil lamp, A."
Chung-ch'ang T'ung. Speaking My Mind.
Cowley, A. Against Fruition.
Das, M. Learner.
Ded. To learn the scriptures is easy.
Divakaruni. Yuba City School.
Gibson, M. Learning a New Language.
Glück, L. Illuminations.
Graves, R. Plea to Boys and Girls, A.
Judah ibn Tibbon. Father's Testament, A.
Lisella. Song of the Third Generation.
Lorde. Black Mother Woman.
McElroy, C. You will learn to speak.
Meredith, W. Ritual Mouse, A.
Mora. Señora X No More.
Pacheco, A. I hear but my brain doesn't get
the.
Pinsky. Serpent Knowledge.
Sandburg, C. We Must Be Polite.
What the people learn out of lifting and
hauling and waiting and losing.
Scott, D. Marrysong.
Shelley, P. To a Skylark.
Simic. Lesson, The.
Snyder, G. Axe Handles.
Sorrentino. Razzmatazz.
Subramanyam. Situation.
Leaves
Amann. Names of the dead, The.
Barnes, W. Sonnet: Leaves.
Bennett, R. Fluttering Leaves.
Binyon. Now is the time for the burning of
the leaves.
Unreturning Spring, The.
Boldman. Just past sunset.
Leaves blowing into a sentence.
Brontë, A. Lines Composed in a Wood on a
Windy Day.
Cardiff. Leaves like Fish.
Chin. Autumn Leaves.
Chōkū. Tanka: "Nowhere on the leaves."
Compiuta Donzella. In the season when the
world leafs and flowers.
Cook, S. Gathering Leaves.
Cooper, G. October's Party.
Wind and the Leaves, The.
Crapsey. November Night.
Cullen, C. Leaves.
Cummings, E. L(a.
Davies, W. Leaves.
Desnos. There once was a leaf with all its
lines.
"Field." Leaves.
Lo, my loved is dying, and the call.
Frost, R. Gathering Leaves.
In Hardwood Groves.
Leaf-Treader, A.
Leaves Compared with Flowers.
Fumi Saito. Tanka: "This huge pile."
Garnett, R. Fading-Leaf and Fallen-Leaf.
Graves, R. By this exchange of eyes, this
encirclement.
Hackett, J. Stillness of dawn, The.
Wind gives way to calm.
Harumichi no Tsuraki. Wind has stopped, The.
Housman, A. When green buds hang in the
elm like dust.
Hughes, T. Leaves.
Ignatow, D. Simultaneously, five thousand
miles apart.
Johnson, L. Church of a Dream, The.
Keble. November.
Lâm thị Mỹ Dạ. Like Leaves.
Larkin, P. Trees are coming into leaf, The.
Levchev. Last night I was coming back home
alone.

Liu E. Boiling Falls.
Poem on Falling Leaves.
Masaoka Shiki. Frozen in the ice.
McClintock, M. Rowing downstream.
McDonald, W. Winter Before the War, The.
Moon, T. Ode to Fallen Leaves.
Mordecai. Starapple Tree.
Mori Ōgai. Tanka: "It will not be heard."
Mountain, M. Beneath / leaf mold.
In / the / woods.
Noin. After the storm / On Mount Mimuro.
Nukada. When spring escapes.
O'Hara, F. Les Étiquettes Jaunes.
Okamoto. Tanka: "Green leaves."
Pace, R. This Is English and I Am Speaking
It No Matter What.
Po Chü-i. Cranes, The.
Pomfret, J. No Barren Leaves.
Prévert. Song of the snails on their way to a
funeral.
Pritchard, N. Landscape with Nymphs and
Satyrs.
Rexroth, K. Buddha took some Autumn
leaves.
Robinson, E. Pity of the Leaves, The.
Robinson, E. New Language, The.
Rossetti, C. Caterpillar, The.
Who has seen the wind? / Neither I nor you.
Saitō Mokichi. Tanka: "All that past life."
Seferis. Poplar Leaf, The.
Sergeant. Man Meeting Himself.
Seward. Behold that tree, in Autumn's dim
decay.
Shannon, M. Only My Opinion.
Shea, M. Red-flashing lights.
Shelley, P. Ode to the West Wind.
"Shu Ting." Maple Leaf.
Sone Yoshitada. Lower leaves of the trees,
The.
Southard. Now the leaves are still.
On a leaf, a leaf.
Still sunlit, one tree.
Spenser. Sonnet 1: "Happy ye leaves! whenas
those lily hands."
Spire. Nativité.
Steele, F. Markings.
Stephens, J. Wind stood up, and gave a shout.
Stokesbury. California.
Sullivan, P. Red Leaf, The.
Summers, H. Leaves in the Yard.
Sze. Shapes of Leaves, The.
Thompson, C. Autumn Leaves.
Tynan. Leaves.
Unknown. Anglo-American Chainpoem.
Leaves had a wonderful frolic, The.
On Asuka River.
Very. Autumn Leaves.
Sumach Leaves, The.
Wang Wei. Seeking a Mooring.
Webb, C. Autumn Leaves.
Willmot. Quiet rustle, A.
Wills, J. I catch.
Young, V. Fallen birch leaf.
Yü Chi. Getting on Horseback.
Yüan Hung-tao. Record of My Trip to Mount
She, A.
Yün Shou-p'ing. Early Summer in the Year
Jen-tzu (1672)—Playfully Painted in the
Manner of Ts'ao Yün-hsi.
Painting of Chrysanthemums in the Boneless
Style of Hsü Ch'ung-ssu, A.
Zukofsky, L. Green leaf that will outlast the
winter.

See also **Autumn**

Lebanon and Lebanese
Joseph, L. Sand Nigger.
Melville, H. Guide and Guard.
Scollard. As I came down from Lebanon.

Leda
Bowes-Lyon. Leda.
Doolittle, H. Leda.
Gogarty. Leda and the Swan.
Graves, R. Leda.
Jordan, J. Female and the Silence of a Man,
The.
Meinke. Helen.

Millay, E. I dreamed I moved among the
Elysian fields.
Sappho. People do gossip.
Spenser. Therein was writ, how often
thundering Jove.
Van Duyn. Leda.
Leda Reconsidered.
Yeats. Leda and the Swan.

Ledwidge, Francis
Heaney, S. In Memoriam Francis Ledwidge.

Lee, Robert Edward
Davidson, D. Lee in the Mountains.
Hill, B. Tribute to Robert E. Lee.
Howe, J. Robert E. Lee.
Ryan, A. Sword of Robert Lee, The.
Thompson, J. Lee to the Rear.

Leeds, England
Harrison, T. On Not Being Milton.
Unknown. Poem for Jacqueline Hill.

Legree, Simon
Lindsay, V. Simon Legree—A Negro Sermon.

Legs
Brown, L. Lyric Can Snare, The.
Burroughs, W. My Legs Señor.
Carnevali. Queer Things.
Durem. Vet's Rehabilitation.
Fraser, K. Poem in Which My Legs Are
Accepted.
Gorman, L. Her long paper legs.
Graves, R. Legs, The.
Herrick. Her Legs.
To Dianeme ("Show [*or* Shew] me thy feet;
show [*or* shew] me thy legs, thy thighs").
Mother Goose. Riddle: "Two legs sat upon
three legs."
Nash, O. Octopus, The.
Ormond. Lament for a Leg.
Receveur. Eagle in the Land of Oz.
Scarfe. Merry Window, The.
Seibles. Who doesn't.
Taylor, J. Epigram: "Fair Beatrice tucks her
coat up somewhat high."
Unknown. Young Girl of Asturias, The.
Whitman, W. Runner, The.
Williams, W. Portrait of a Lady.

Leicester, Robert Dudley, Earl of
Ralegh, W. Epitaph on the Earl of Leicester
[*or* Leceister].

Leisure
Adcock, F. Three-toed sloth is the slowest
creature we know, The.
Benlowes. Pleasures of Retirement, The.
Davidson, J. Crystal Palace, The.
Davies, W. Leisure.
Hsü Pen. Following the Rhymes of Kao Chi-
ti's Poem: "We Had Planned to Travel to
Cloud Cliff But Couldn't Because of Rain."
Mountain of green trees and orioles
everywhere!
Jewett, S. At Home from Church.
Kuan Han-ch'ing. Tune: "Four Pieces of
Jade"—Idle Leisure.
Lu Chih. Be a loafer / Wash off the dust of
fame and gain in the vast waves.
Lu Yu. Idle Thoughts.
Martial. Happy Life, A.
McGinley. Evening Musicale.
Village Spa.
Nabbes. Song: "What a dainty life the
milkmaid leads!"
Ou-yang Hsiu. Reading the Poems of an
Absent Friend.
Po Chü-i. Illness and idleness give me much
leisure.
Quiet House in Ch'ang-lo Ward, A.
Quiller-Couch. Harbour of Fowey, The.
Revett. Ode: Hastening His Friend into the
Country.
Rossetti, C. Reflection.
Snyder, G. Walk, A.
Ssu-k'ung Shu. In the Country.
Stevens, W. Ordinary Women, The.
Stickney, T. In Ampezzo.
Su Tung-p'o. Lotus Viewing.
T'ao Ch'ien. Reading *The Classic of Hills and
Seas.*

Thompson, W. Happy Life, The.
Unknown. Hob upon a Holiday ("Hob yawned
three times and rubbed his eyes").
Proposal, A.
Tune: "Wild Geese Have Come Down; Song
of Victory."
Wang Chiu-ssu. Quiet Sitting.
Wang T'ing-hsiang. Written in the Office
Precincts.
Wang Wei. Enjoying Coolness.
Wen Cheng-ming. This man of leisure for
twenty years.
Wishing to try retirement, I requested release
from duty.
Westmorland. To Retiredness.
Wright, J. Lying in a Hammock at William
Duffy's Farm in Pine Island, Minnesota.
Yang Wan-li. Early Summer Waking from a
Nap.

Lemmings
Beer, P. Lemmings die every year. Over the
cliff.
Masefield. Lemmings, The.

Lemonade
Unknown. There was a young lady from Lynn.

Lemons
Cowley, A. Written in Juice of Lem[m]on.
Hadas, R. Lair, The.
Harter. Bitter tea.

Lenin, Vladimir Ilyich
Klyuyev. Lenin has the spirit of an Old
Believer.
"MacDiarmid." First Hymn to Lenin.
Skeleton of the Future, The.
Orlovsky. Dream May 18, 1958.
Paulin. Impossible Pictures, The.
Wellesley. So I came down the steps to Lenin.

Leningrad, Russia. *See* **St. Petersburg, Russia**

Lennon, John
Unknown. We four lads from Liverpool are.

Lent
Herrick. To Keep a True Lent.

Lent Magdalene
Rodgers, W. Lent.

Leonardo da Vinci
Bly, R. Leonardo's Secret.
Dowden, E. Leonardo's "Mona Lisa."
Eberhart, R. Cancer Cells, The.
"Field." La Gioconda.
Moore, M. Leonardo Da Vinci's.
Rossetti, D. For "Our Lady of the Rocks."
Shelley, P. On the Medusa of Leonardo da
Vinci in the Florentine Gallery.

Leopards
Jarrell. Snow-Leopard, The.
Kariara. Leopard lives in a Muu tree, A.
Lowell, A. To Winky.
White, G. Leopard in Eden, The.
Yukitsuna. At the zoo (two poems).

Leopold III, King of the Belgians
Berryman. Moon and the Night and the Men,
The.

Lepanto, Battle of (1571)
Chesterton, G. Lepanto.

Leprosy and Lepers
Bunin. At the gates of Zion, over Kedron.
Kipling, R. Gehazi.
Rabéarivelo. Cactus.
Swinburne. Leper, The.

Lesblans. *See* **Homosexuality and Homosexuals**

Lethargy
Justice, D. Lethargy.

Letter Carriers. *See* **Mail and Mailmen**

Letters
Ackland. Poem: "You send me a letter from
far, from across the sea."
Aiken, J. Do It Yourself.
Amichai. Letter.
Apollinaire. Post Card.
Ashbery. Rain.
Thoughts of a Young Girl.
Atwood. Postcard.
Auden. Letter, The.
Barber, M. Conclusion of a Letter to the Rev.
Mr. C——, The.

Barker, G. I sent a letter to my love.
Beaver. (Frank O'Hara).
Beer, P. Letter, The.
Bellamy, D. Letters of Mina Harker, The.
Bennett, L. Love Letter.
Bensley. One's Correspondence.
Berry, J. Lucy's Letter.
Berryman. Winter-Piece to a Friend Away, A.
Bethell. Response.
Bishop, E. Letter to N.Y.
Blight. Letter, The.
Bradstreet, A. Another.
Browning, E. Sonnet: "My letters! all dead paper, mute and white."
Clare, J. Country Letter.
Clark, T. You (III).
Comfort, A. Letter to an American Visitor.
Corman. Deceased.
Cowley, A. Written in Juice of Lem[m]on.
Crane, H. My Grandmother's Love Letters.
Creeley. Invoice, The.
Dabydeen, D. Coolie Son.
Daryush. Still-Life.
Desnos. Letter to Youki.
Deutsch. Destruction of Letters.
Dickinson, E. Way I read a Letter's—this, The.
Dixon, S. Lines Occasioned by the Burning of Some Letters.
Dransfield. Self-analysis.
Emerson, R. Letters.
Fainlight, R. Handbag.
Gallagher, T. Unanswered Letter.
Under Stars.
Graham, H. Waste.
Graves, R. Not at Home.
Gregory, H. Postman's Bell Is Answered Everywhere, The.
Hadas, R. Lair, The.
Hall, D. Love-Letter-Burning.
Hands, E. Lob's Courtship.
Hardy, T. Wife in London, A.
Harper, M. Lecturing on the Theme of Motherhood.
Heard, J. Love Letters.
Hughes, L. Little Old Letter.
Personal.
Jacinto, A. Letter from a Contract Worker.
Jarrell. Burning the Letters.
Kinnell. Correspondence School Instructor Says Goodbye to His Poetry Students, The.
Kinsella, T. Artists' Letters.
Koch, K. To Marina.
Kunert. News from Behind the Seven Hills.
Kunitz, S. Night Letter.
Kushner, A. Envelope looks so peculiar, The.
Landon. Lines Written Under a Picture of a Girl Burning a Love-Letter.
Leapor. Epistle of Deborah Dough, The.
Lear, E. To Ann Lear.
To Lady Wyatt.
Leong, R. Aerogrammes.
Livesay, D. Children's Letters, The.
Lorde. Learning to Write.
Lowell, A. Letter, The.
Lu Yu. Harp Song.
Phoenix Hairpins.
Machi. Tanka: "From the moment."
Tanka: "Letter, The."
Madhubuti. Poem Looking for a Reader, A.
Maiden. New.
Marshall-Stoneking. Picture Postcard.
Mathews, A. Letter Following.
McClure, M. From the Window of the Beverly Wilshire Hotel.
Meinke. Dear Reader.
Meredith, G. I think she sleeps: it must be sleep, when low.
Meredith, W. Illiterate, The.
Merrill, J. Body.
Friend of the Fourth Decade, The.
Meynell, A. Letter from a Girl to Her Own Old Age, A.
Moss, H. Burning Love Letters.
Mura. Letters from Poston Relocation Camp (1942–45).
Myers, G. Dear God.

Nagys. Poem.
Neruda. Letter to Miguel Otero Silva, in Caracas.
Piercy. Letter to be Disguised as a Gas Bill.
Po Chü-i. Letter, The.
Praed. Talented Man, The.
Radnóti. Letter to My Wife.
Picture Postcards.
Rankin, R. Women of Maine, The.
Ransom, J. Parting, without a Sequel.
Raworth. Empty Pain-Killer Bottles, The.
Rexroth, K. Two flowers in a letter.
Riddell, E. Letter, The.
Rossetti, C. Postman, The.
Rottman. APO 96225.
Schuyler, J. Stone Knife, A.
Scott, J. Typing the Letters.
Sexton. Letter Written on a Ferry While Crossing Long Island Sound.
Some Foreign Letters.
Shapiro, A. Letter said you had to speak to me, The.
Smith, S. Emily Writes Such a Good Letter.
Jungle Husband, The.
Soldati. Surroundings.
Sorrentino. Oranges Returned, The.
Stewart, F. To a Friend.
Tennyson, A. Letter, The.
Tidjani-Cissé. Home News.
Tsaloumas. Note.
Tucker, M. Love-letter, A.
Tuqan, F. Face Lost in the Wilderness.
Turner, E. How to Write a Letter.
Unknown. I sent a letter to my love.
I've lost my rifle and bayonet.
Meaning of a Letter, The.
Van Duyn. Letters from a Father.
Vitiello. Letter to a Cretan Flute-Maker.
Vogelsang. Which Letter?
Walcott. Letter from Brooklyn, A.
Waldman, A. Two Men.
Walker, A. Suicide.
Whitman, W. Come up from the fields father, here's a letter from our Pete.
Wickham. Letter to a Boy at School.
Wilbur. Part of a Letter.
See also **Mail and Mailmen**
Leukemia
Hecht, A. Transparent Man, The.
Levet, Robert
Johnson, S. On the Death of Dr [*or* Mr] Robert Levet [a Practiser in Physic].
Leviathan
Levertov. Ache of marriage, The.
Merwin, W. Leviathan.
Sylvester, J. Leviathan.
Levita, Elijah
Unknown. Epitaph: "Stone cries from the wall, The."
Lewis, Meriwether
Barlow, J. On the Discoveries of Captain Lewis.
Li Po
Grier. On the Subject of Waves.
Komunyakaa. "Everybody's Reading Li Po" Silkscreened on a Purple T-Shirt.
Tu Fu. Dreaming of Li Po.
No Word.
To Li Po.
To Li Po on a Spring Day.
Wright, C. Portrait of the Artist with Li Po.
Liars. *See* **Lies and Lying**
Liberace
Holden, J. Liberace.
Liberalism and Liberals
Browning, R. Lost Leader, The.
Why I Am a Liberal.
Hummer, T. Ideal, The.
Jackson, R. Lonely Affair, A.
Liberia
Tolson. On the Founding of Liberia.
Liberty. *See* **Freedom**
Liberty Bell
Bible, *O.T.* Inscription on the Liberty Bell.
Unknown. Independence Bell—July 4, 1776.

Liberty, Statue of
Bierce. To the Bartholdi Statue.
Dove, R. Lady Freedom Among Us.
Gunn, T. Iron Landscapes (and the Statue of Liberty).
Lazarus, E. New Colossus, The.
Whittier. Bartholdi Statue, The.
Libraries and Librarians
Brown, S. Chapter One.
Deane, S. Scholar II.
Ellis, T. View of the Library of Congress from Paul Laurence Dunbar High School.
Giovanni. Ten Years Old.
Hristic. In the big library scholars sit and read books.
Jarrell. Girl in a Library, A.
Jonson, B. Execration upon Vulcan, An.
Le Gallienne. Library in a Garden, A.
MacNeice. British Museum Reading Room, The.
O'Meally. It aint no.
Rosenberg, S. Library closing—.
Steele, T. Library, The.
Unknown. Domestic Philosopher, The.
Weiss, T. Fire at Alexandria, The.
Lice
Burns, R. To a Louse [On Seeing One on a Lady's Bonnet at Church].
Mathews, H. Shih-hou Pointed Out to Me that from Ancient Times There Had Never Been a Poem on the Subject of Lice.
Mei Yao Ch'en. Shih-hou Pointed Out to Me That from Ancient Times There Had Never Been a Poem on the Subject of Li.
Rimbaud, A. Girls Looking for Lice.
Rosenberg, I. Immortals, The.
Louse Hunting.
Villa. To become an archer.
Lies and Lying
Amichai. Song of Lies on Sabbath Eve, A.
Auden. Their Lonely Betters.
Ausonius. I am that Dido which thou here do'st see.
Belloc. Matilda told such Dreadful Lies.
Bernstein, O. More Questions.
Bible, *O.T.* Psalm 52.
Bolton, F. Insult before Gift-Giving.
Brown, S. Schadenfreude.
Campion, T. Elegye, An: "Constant to none, but ever false to me."
Catullus. Carmen 70 ("Lesbia says she'ld rather marry me").
Chaucer. Canon Assistant's Tale, The.
Chernoff. How Lies Grow.
Clarke, C. What Goes Around Comes Around, or The Proof is in the Pudding.
Coleridge, M. Insincere Wish Addressed to a Beggar, An.
True to myself am I, and false to all.
Dabydeen, D. Coolie Son.
Donne. Lame Beggar, A.
Dunbar, P. We wear the mask that grins and lies.
"Ephelia." To J. G.
Garrigue. Upon the Intimation of Love's Mortality.
Gregg. Lies and Longing.
Hardy, T. Her Dilemma.
Housman, A. Purple William or The Liar's Doom.
Inez. Warrior Daughters.
Jones, R. Caught.
Kay, J. Stincher, The.
Keller, D. In the Middle of the Journey.
Kipling, R. Dead Statesman, A.
Lie, The.
Laing, K. I am the freshly dead husband.
Lawrence, D. I Am in a Novel.
Lies About Love.
Lear, E. Limerick: "There was an old person of Gretna."
Maxwell. Rumplestiltskin.
Nash, O. Golly, How Truth Will Out.
Nesbit, E. Appeal.
Ofeimun. Beyond Fear.
Poet Lied, The.
Okamoto. Tanka: "They don't appeal to me."

Parker, D. Comment.
Social Note.
Unfortunate Coincidence.
Parra, N. Sentences.
Pilkington, L. Song, A: "Lying is an occupation."
Plautus Titus Maccius. From Amphitryon.
Pope, J. Word of Encouragement, A.
Rabbitt. Tortoise.
Ralegh, W. Lie, The.
Robinson, E. How Annandale Went Out.
Uncle Ananias.
Shakespeare, W. Sonnet 138.
Silverstein, S. Sick.
Taylor, J. Epigram: "There chanced to meet together in an inn."
Unknown. Lady and the Magpie, The.
Song of Lies, The.
Weigl. Song of Napalm.
Wilbur. Lying.
Yukitsuna. Tanka: "Moonlight, The."

Life

Adcock, B. Walking Out.
Aiken, C. Things, The.
Aklais. Dedication.
Alegría. Documentary.
Savoir Faire.
Summing Up.
Ali, A. History of Paisley, A.
Allestry. What art thou, love? Whence are those charms.
"Alta." 29.
Amichai. I Am a Live Man.
Ammons. Cut the Grass.
Easter Morning.
Angel. River Has No Hair to Hold Onto, The.
Angelou. Life Doesn't Frighten Me.
Arnold, M. To Marguerite.
Ashbery. Darlene's Hospital.
Young Prince and the Young Princess, The.
Auden. Precious Five.
Ausonius. To His Wife.
Austin, A. Is Life Worth Living?
Awoonor. Something has happened to me.
Bachmann. Kind of Loss, A.
Bacon, F. Life.
Bailey, P. We live in deeds, not years; in thoughts, not breaths.
Bancquart. Curriculum vitae.
Epitaph.
Banks. What I Live For.
Baraka. Minute of Consciousness, The.
Barbauld. Life! I know not what thou art.
Bartusek. Sentence.
Strangled, The.
Baxter, J. Small grey cloudy louse that nests in my beard, The.
Beaumont, J. Cheat, The.
Beaver. Angels' Weather.
Beckett, S. My way is in the sand flowing.
What would I do without this world faceless incurious.
Beedome. Question and Answer, The.
Belloc. World's a stage. The trifling entrance fee, The.
Berkson, B. Melting Milk.
Berrigan, T. Red Shift.
Berryman. Life, friends, is boring. We must not say so
Sympathy, A Welcome, A.
Bevington, L. Afternoon.
Bible, *N.T.* He that heareth my word.
Bible, *O.T.* Time for Everything, A.
Blackburn, P. Park Poem.
Blake, W. Sick Rose, The.
Blind. Sower, The.
Blunden. Report on Experience.
Bognini. Suddenly an old man on the threshold of the age.
We are men of the new world a tree prompts us to harmony.
Bonnefoy. Words of Evening, The.
Borson. Rain.
Bowden, M. Miller Canyon Trail No. 106.
Braithwaite. Sic Vita.
Turn Me to My Yellow Leaves.

Breytenbach. Exile, Representative.
There Is Life.
Brodsky, J. Six Years Later.
Bromige. He thought it humanity's lot for ever to be persuading a huge rock up a mountainside.
Bronk. Life Supports.
Metonymy as an Approach to a Real World.
Brooks, G. Sadie and Maud.
Vacant Lot, The.
Brown, G. Funeral of Ally Flett, The.
Brown, S. Odyssey of Big Boy.
Browning, E. Felicia Hemans.
Sonnet: "When our two souls stand up erect and strong."
Browning, R. Master Hugues of Saxe-Gotha.
Pisgah-Sights. I.
Pisgah-Sights. II.
Buchanan, G. Jill's Death.
Bùi Khải Nguyễn. Soap Bubbles.
Bukowski. Crucifix in a Deathhand.
Burich. You blow on the hair of your child.
Burke, M. On the twelfth floor.
Burns, R. Epistle to a Young Friend.
Campbell, D. Here, under pear-trees, on the broad verandahs.
Campbell, J. Mors et Vita.
Campbell, T. River of Life, The.
Cao Bá Quát. Drink and Drown Your Cares.
Good luck, bad luck are both the Maker's works.
Caraion. Bits of Silk.
Carroll, J. Distances, The.
Heroin.
Carruth, H. Wreck of the Circus Train, The.
Carter, M. Being, always to arrange.
Mouth Is Always Muzzled, A.
Carver, R. Late Fragment.
Cassian. Then.
Cavafy. As Much As You Can.
City, The.
Ceravolo. New Realism.
Chakrabarti. Amalkanti is a friend of mine.
Chế Lan Viên. Graves.
Cheng Hsieh. Song of Surfing on the Bore.
Ch'ien T'ao. Chill and harsh the year draws to its close;.
Chimombo. Death Song, A.
Chiyojo. From the mind.
Cho, P. Empty as Death.
Never to Meet Again.
Ch'on, S. Namelessness.
Return to Heaven.
Chong, H. Parting.
Chong, H. Going by far.
Note 25.
Cibulka. Sky Full of Swallows.
Clark, T. As I walked out early.
What the day weaves.
Clark, T. Take time to live.
Clifton, L. Cutting Greens.
December.
Cohan. Life's a Funny Proposition after All.
Coleridge, M. I envy not the dead that rest.
Coleridge, S. Epitaph: "Stop, Christian passer-by!—Stop, child of God."
Psyche.
Collobert. III.
Cooper, J. Praise.
Corpus. Blkfern-jungal.
Couani. Never-Dead, The.
Cranch. Ocean, The.
Creeley. Song: "What's in the body you've forgotten."
Cronin, A. Elegy for the Nightbound.
Trembling with engines, gulping oil, the river.
Csoori. Everyday History.
Maybe elegies have ruined me.
Cullen, C. From Life to Love.
Protest.
Cummings, E. Anyone lived in a pretty how town.
As freedom is a breakfastfood.
If everything happens that can't be done.
May my heart always be open to little.
My father moved through dooms of love.
Out of midsummer's blazing most not night.

Cunningham, J. Epigram: "Life flows to death as rivers to the sea."
Cunningham, J. Miller, The.
On a Certain Alderman.
Custance. Masquerade, The.
Daive. Woman measures, A.
D'Ambrosio, C. Morning.
Dante Alighieri. Middle of life's journey; I, The.
Davies, W. Leisure.
De la Mare. Last Chapter, The.
Ded. This world.
Del Giudice. Rules to Live By.
"Dhoomil." City, Evening, and an Old Man: Me, The.
Di Prima. Short Note on the Sparseness of the Language.
Dickinson, E. Between the form of Life and Life.
I am alive—I guess.
My Life Had Stood—A Loaded Gun.
That it will never come again.
This is my letter to the World.
Water, is taught by thirst.
Word is dead, A.
DiPalma. When Torrid Rhymes with Forehead.
Doane, G. Life Sculpture.
Doinas, S. Ascent, The.
Dolben. We hurry on, nor passing note.
Doolittle, H. White World.
Dove, R. Fish in the Stone, The.
Lost Brilliance.
This Life.
Downar. From The Bramble Hedge.
Dowson. Vitae Summa Brevis Spem Nos Vetat Incohare Longam.
Drainac. Dreams worn out like small coins taken out of circulation.
Drummond de Andrade. Dead in Frock Coats, THe.
Motionless Faces.
Residue.
Drummond, W. Madrigal: "This life, which seems so fair."
Dryden, J. Song from Troilus and Cressida.
Dugan, A. Last Statement for a Last Oracle.
Dunbar, P. Common Things.
Dunn, S. Something Like Happiness.
Eberhart, R. Hard Structure of the World, The.
Hardy Perennial.
Human Being Is a Lonely Creature, The.
New Hampshire, February.
Rumination.
Ehrenburg. Potter of Jaen, The.
Ehrmann. I ponder on life.
Eigner. Live / , bird which.
Temporary language, A.
Eisner. Autumn nears. The branches yellow.
Ekelof. If you ask me where I am.
Eliot, T. Dry Salvages, The.
Emerson, R. Blight.
Day's Ration, The.
Nominalist and Realist.
"Ern Malley." Palinode.
Petit Testament.
Sybilline.
Young Prince of Tyre.
Faiz. You Tell Us What to Do.
Ferlinghetti, L. River Still To Be Found, A.
Field, E. Lower East Side: The George Bernstein Story.
"Field." Life Plastic.
Palimpsest, A.
Prologue.
Follain. Buying.
Forché. Burning the Tomato Worms.
Island, The.
Fortune. O, Life of Dreams! O, Dreams of Life!
Francis, R. Hound, The.
Fraser, K. Flowers.
Frost, R. Master Speed, The.
On the Heart's Beginning to Cloud the Mind.
Road Not Taken, The.
Stopping by Woods on a Snowy Evening.
Fuller, M. Freedom and Truth.

Fulton, A.   A.M.: The Hopeful Monster.
Powers of Congress.
Gambold.   Mystery of Life, The.
Gangnus.   Firing back at my heavy heart.
Gay, J.   My Own Epitaph.
Gensei.   Poem without a Category.
George, G.   Quasi Quasi . . . as If Repeated.
Gheorghe.   Moonlit nights on the Atlantic
Ocean!
Gilbert, S.   To the Terrestrial Globe.
Gillan.   Ebba Dawson: Mardel Rest Home,
Haskell, New Jersey.
Gioia.   Maze Without a Minotaur.
Giorno.   Life Is a Killer.
Giovanni.   Life I Led, The.
Godfrey.   In Front of a Large Number of
People.
Goethe.   Ecstatic Longing.
Goldbarth.   How the World Works: An Essay.
Life is Happy.
Nile, The.
Goldstein, L.   Permissive Entry: A Sermon on
Fame.
Graham, J.   Way Things Work, The.
Greville, F.   Sonnet: "Nurse-life wheat within
his green husk growing, The."
Gu Cheng.   Epigraph: "In the sea of life."
Guiterman.   Of Giving.
Gumilyov.   No flowers will live in my room.
Gunn, T.   Confessions of the Life Artist.
Habington.   Cogitabo Pro Peccato Meo.
Hadas, R.   Sentimental Education.
Hadewijch II.   Tighten.
Hagedorn, J.   Smokey's Getting Old.
Something about You.
Hall, D.   Mr. Wakeville on Interstate 90.
Raisin, The.
Hammond, W.   On the Same [Death of My
Dear Brother, Mr. H.S., Drowned]: The Boat.
Han-shan.   From my father and mother I
inherited land enough.
Man lives his life in a dust bowl.
Han.   Ferryboat and the Traveler, The.
Silence of Love, The.
Hanzlicek, C.   C.G. Hanzlicek.
Hardy, T.   Epitaph: "I never cared for Life:
Life cared for me."
Necessitarian's Epitaph, A.
Placid Man's Epitaph, A.
Harford, L.   Experience.
Harjo, J.   Remember the sky that you were
born under.
Harper, F.   Let the Light Enter!
Harry, J.   Poem Films Itself, The.
Harryman.   My Story.
Harteis.   Genetics.
Havergal.   Just when Thou wilt, O Master,
call!
Hayden, R.   Whipping, The.
Heaney, S.   Casting and Gathering.
Heine.   Looking Back.
Hejinian.   Moment yellow, just as four years
later when, A.
Hendryson.   Prayer for a Tenspeed Heart.
Henley, W.   To Robert Louis Stevenson.
To W. R.
Henry, P.   Is life so dear, or peace so sweet.
Herbert, G.   H. Scriptures, The ("Oh that I
knew how all thy lights combine").
Life.
Pilgrimage, The.
Herbert, Z.   Elegy of Fortinbras.
Heredia.   Young Dead Woman, A.
Herrick.   Four[e] Things Make Us Happy Here.
Life is the body's [or Bodies] light, which
once declining.
Hikmet.   Since I was thrown inside.
Hillyer.   As One Who Bears beneath His
Neighbor's Roof.
Hirshfield, J.   Story, A.
Hoccleve.   After that hervest inned had his
sheves.
Hoffman, D.   Special Train, A.
Holub.   Suffering.
Hongo.   Pier, The.
Hooper, E.   Better a sin which purposed wrong
to none.

Duty.
Heart, heart, lie still.
Hopkins, G.   Thou art indeed just, Lord, if I
contend.
Hoskyns.   Epitaph, An: On a Man for Doing
Nothing.
Housman, A.   Be still, my soul, be still; the
arms you bear are brittle.
From far, from eve and morning.
Immortal Part, The.
Is my team ploughing.
Terence, this is stupid stuff.
Howard, R.   Among the Missing.
Hsieh Ling-yün.   Climbing a Solitary Islet in
the River.
Passing White Banks Pavilion.
Hughes, L.   Advice.
Esthete in Harlem.
Life Is Fine.
Mother to Son.
Motto.
Still Here.
Hughes, T.   Crueller than owl or eagle.
Moon-Hops.
Hutchinson, L.   Verses Written by Mrs.
Hutchinson.
Hutchinson, P.   Be born a saint; or keep.
Hwang, K.   Candlelight.
Icaza.   Responding Voice.
Ignatow, D.   Brooding.
Rescue the Dead.
Ilantiraiyan.   Great Wagon, The.
Ingelow.   Little babe, while burns the west.
Story, A.
Jaccottet.   Letter of the 26th June.
Jacinto, A.   Poem of Alienation.
Jacob, M.   I thought he was bankrupt.
Jamie.   Way We Live, The.
Jarrell.   Country Life, A.
Well Water.
Jeffers, R.   Ante Mortem.
Purse-Seine, The.
Jewell.   Some unknown sound.
Jonson, B.   To William Roe ("When Nature
bids us leave to live, 'tis late").
József.   Seventh, The.
To Sit, to Stand, to Kill, to Die.
Juarroz.   Bottom of things is neither life nor
death, The.
Kabir.   Between the conscious and the
unconscious, the mind has put up a swing.
Kalidasa.   This life on earth's a poison tree.
Kang.   Rotation (1).
Kao Ch'i.   Returning to Lotus Village.
Kaufman, B.   Grandfather Was Queer, Too.
Heavy Water Blues.
Kavanagh, P.   To Hell with Commonsense.
Keats.   Human Seasons, The.
Kees.   Beach in August, The.
Kennelly.   Island, The.
Kerouac.   113th Chorus.
211th Chorus.
Two Hundred and Twenty-Eighth Chorus.
Khodasevich.   Monkey.
Killigrew, A.   On Death.
Kim, C.   Death of a Girl in Budapest, The.
Kim, H.   Absolute Solitude, The.
Kim, N.   Music.
Kim, Y.   Elegy: "Because of you I have
lived."
King, B.   Sum of Life, The.
King, H.   Sic Vita.
Kinnell.   Milk Bottle, The.
Kinsella, T.   All is Emptiness, and I Must
Spin.
Downstream.
Oldest Place, The.
Route of the Táin, The.
Kipling, R.   Envoi: "There's a whisper down
the field where the year has shot her yield."
Neighbours.
Kizer, C.   Most people from Idaho are crazed
rednecks.
Knight, E.   My life, the quality of which.
Koch, K.   One Train May Hide Another.
Koethe.   Falling Water.
Kornilov, V.   Johnny.

Kovner.   Sun-Watchers.
Laing, K.   Godhorse.
Huge car with the sad voice, The.
Lake, P.   Crime and Punishment.
Lamantia.   Romantic Movement, The.
Landon.   Lines of Life.
Secrets.
Small Miseries.
Stern Truth.
Lanier, S.   Nirvâna.
Larbaud.   Alma Perdida.
Images.
Larkin, P.   Days.
Nothing to Be Said.
Lavrin.   As I remember, barracks still stand.
Lawrence, D.   We Are Transmitters.
Layman P'ang.   My daily affairs are quite
ordinary.
Lea, S.   Insomnia: The Distances.
Lear, E.   O dear! How disgusting is life!
Levertov.   Living.
O Taste and See.
Levine, P.   Blasting from Heaven.
Clouds.
Genius.
How Much Earth.
Rain Downriver.
Salami.
Sweet Will.
Levy, A.   Epitaph: "This is the end of him,
here he lies."
Lewis, H.   Life's Morning.
Li Ho.   Don't Go Out of the Door.
Sing Loud.
Li Shang-yin.   Where is it, the sad lyre which
follows the quick flute?
Li Yü.   Tune: "Ripples Sifting Sand: A Song."
Tune: "Song of Tzu-yeh."
Livada.   Horoscope.
Lo Yin.   Thinking of the Way Home, a Song.
Long, R.   Have a Nice Day.
Longfellow, H.   Nature.
Rainy Day, The.
Village Blacksmith, The.
Lovelace, R.   La Bourbon, A.
Lowell, A.   Petals.
Lowell, R.   Book of Wisdom, The.
We imitate, oh horror! tops and bowls.
Lowry, M.   Wild Cherry, The.
Lum.   Riding the North Point Ferry.
Mac Low.   1st Dance—Making Things New—
6 February 1964.
"MacDiarmid."   Harry Semen.
On a Raised Beach.
Machado Ruiz.   Parables, I.
MacLeish.   Seafarer.
MacLow.   1st Dance—Making Things New—6
February 1964.
MacNeice.   Prayer Before Birth.
Mahapatra, A.   Spell.
Malroux.   Octet Before Winter.
Mandelstam.   Body was given to me—what to
do with it, A.
Mansour, J.   Anti-mnemonic self-vaccination.
Tinfoil.
Marais.   Here We have No Firm Dwelling-
Place.
March, A.   Much as a man who takes delight
in dreaming.
Out scouting for sound counsels? How to
prosper?
Marks, L.   Code Poem for the French
Resistance.
Martial.   If you and I, Julius, old friend.
Martin, A.   Malcolm MacKerral.
Mase.   It's Simply Great.
Masefield.   Word, The.
Masters, E.   Jennie McGrew.
Lucinda Matlock.
Mathews, A.   Caedmon.
Matveyeva.   Dream.
Mayakovsky.   What About You?
McAuley, J.   Gnostic Prelude.
Released on Parole.
McClellan.   Hydromel and Rue.
McClure, M.   Mad Sonnet: Grace.
McDonald, I.   Life/Death.

McHugh, H. Take Care.
McPherson, S. Wings and Seeds.
Meek. Walk Around the Lake, A.
Melville, H. To.
Menken. Infelix.
Meredith, G. 30.
   Ballad of Past Meridian, A.
   Hymn to Colour.
Meredith, W. Accidents of Birth.
   Preponderance, The.
Merrill, J. Last Words.
Messerli. NARRATOR: Suddenly someone wakes
   me. Still half-asleep, I see standing in front.
Mihalic. Maestro, extinguish the candle,
   serious times have come.
Momaday. Delight Song of Tsoai-Talee, The.
Montagu, L. Addressed to ———.
Moon, C. Flock of Birds, A.
Moore, T. I Saw from the Beach.
Moorsom. Don't be literary, darling, don't be
   literary.
Mordecai. Easy Life.
Mori Ōgai. Tanka: "Never have I."
Mother Goose. Solomon Grundy.
Muir, E. Voyage, The.
Mulford. Valentine.
Murasaki Shikibu. This life of ours would not
   cause you sorrow.
Murray, L. People are eating dinner in that
   country north of Legge's Lake, The.
Nagy, A. Lazarus.
Nathan, L. Bladder Song.
Nemerov. Life, A.
   Life Cycle of Common Man.
Neruda. Past.
   Sexual Water.
   Walking [or Walkin'] Around.
Neto. Grieved lands of Africa, The.
Ngân Giang. Getting Well.
Nguyễn Bỉnh Khiêm. Before the world of
   power you'll fold your arms.
Nguyễn Công Trú'. Looking Forward to
   Retirement.
   Officialdom.
Nguyễn Khuyến. Scholar-Laureate in
   Retirement, A.
   Self-Portrayal.
Ni Dhomhnaill. Aubade: "It's all the same to
   morning what it dawns on."
Nichol. St. Anzas VI.
Niedecker. So he said / on radio.
No Ch'ŏn-myŏng. Behind Prison Bars.
North, C. Elizabethan & Nova Scotian Music.
   Few Facts about Me, A.
   Leap Year.
   Shooting for Line.
Nortje. Newcombe at the Croydon Gallery.
Ochester. New Day.
O'Dalaigh, G. Under Sorrow's Sign.
Ofeimun. Poet Lied, The.
O'Grady, D. Purpose.
O'Hara, F. In Favor of One's Time.
   In Memory of My Feelings.
   Poem: "'Instant coffee with slightly sour
   cream'."
   Steps.
Okamoto. Tanka: "If I were to stand."
Okigbo. Hurrah for Thunder.
Oldham, P. Noon.
Oliver, M. In Blackwater Woods.
O'Loughlin. Posthumous.
Olson, C. Chain of memory is resurrection I
   am a vain man, The.
   Distances, The.
Ondaatje. Light.
Oodgeroo of the tribe Noonuccal. Song: "Life
   is ours in vain."
Oppen. But So As by Fire.
   Occurrences, The.
Ormsby, F. Landscape with Figures.
Osgood, K. Driving Home the Cows.
"Otrada." Football.
Ovid. 1.15.
Padgett, R. Sandwich Man, The.
Padilla. Man on the Edge.
Pagis. Limits of Physics, The.
   Pages of an Album.

Palmer, M. Painted Cup, The.
Pao Chao. Have you not seen the grasses on
   the riverbank?
   Water spilled on level ground.
Park, C. Flute Holes.
Park, C. Changtzu 33.
   Distrust.
   Heavenly Traveler.
Park, T. Sun, The.
Parker, D. Résumé.
Parra, N. Anti-Lazarus, The.
Parulekar. Birthmarks.
Pasternak, B. Hamlet.
   May It Be.
   Snow is falling, snow is falling.
Patel, G. Forensic Medicine.
Paz. Pause.
Penfold, N. Woman with the Wild-Grown
   Hair Relaxes after Another Long Day, The.
Perreault, J. Boomerang.
Peters, L. One long jump.
Phạm Hổ. Tall Trees.
Piatt, S. In Her Prison.
Piercy. Seven of Pentacles, The.
"Ping Hsin." Deliverance.
Pitcher. Pale Blue Casket, The.
Plath. Appearance, An.
   Life, A.
   Mystic.
Plumly. Birthday.
Po Chü-i. Climbing the Ling-ying Terrace and
   Looking North.
   Golden Bells.
   Realizing the Futility of Life.
Pomfret, J. Choice, The.
Pope, A. Behold the child, by Nature's kindly
   law.
Porter, P. Consumer's Report, A.
Pound, E. And the days are not full enough.
Prévert. Pater Noster.
Price, S. Edge, The.
Prior. Human Life.
Procter, A. Three Evenings in a Life.
Quarles. On the Life of Man.
Radnóti. Clouded Sky.
Ralegh, W. On the Life of Man.
Ramke. How Light Is Spent.
Ransom, J. Here lies a lady of beauty and
   high degree.
Ray, H. Life.
   Life's Boundary.
Reese, L. Little Song of Life, A.
   Tears.
Rexroth, K. Long lifetime, A.
   Racoon.
Rice, G. Alumnus Football.
Rich, A. Can it be growing colder when I
   begin.
   Dark woman, head bent, listening for
   something, A.
   Living Memory.
   Tattered Kaddish.
Rilke. Call me to the one among your
   moments.
   Time and again, however well we know the
   landscape of love.
Robinson, A. Art and Life.
Robinson, E. Man against the Sky, The.
Rocha. Poem of Return.
Rodney. Anywoman's Lyric.
Rodriguez, J. About this Woman.
Roethke. Decision, The.
   Judge Not.
Rossetti, C. Birthday, A.
   Cobwebs.
   Don't look for the flaws as you go.
   From the Antique.
   Life's Parallels, A.
Sappho.
   Sonnet 26: "This Life is full of numbness and
   of balk."
   Uphill [or Up-Hill].
   Wednesday in Holy Week.
   World, The.
Rossetti, D. Choice, The.
   Sea-Limits, The.
Rowe, E. Expostulation, The.

Rukeyser, M. All the Little Animals.
Rumi. Morning: a polished knifeblade.
   You are the notes, and we are the flute.
Sackville-West. Extract from Solitude.
St. John, P. Carnival.
Saitō Mokichi. Tanka: "All that past life."
   Tanka: "Confinement."
Salinas, P. Wake up. Day calls you.
Sandburg, C. Aprons of Silence.
   Blue Island Intersection.
   Broken-Face Gargoyles.
   Caboose Thoughts.
   Chicago.
   Early Copper.
   Gone.
   Happiness.
   Jack was a swarthy, swaggering son-of-a-gun.
   Mag.
   Mill-Doors.
   People Who Must.
   People, Yes, The.
   Poetry is any page from a sketchbook of
   outlines of a.
   Shovel Man, The.
   Sins of Kalamazoo are neither scarlet nor
   crimson, The.
   Soup.
   Southern Pacific.
   What the people learn out of lifting and
   hauling and waiting and losing.
Sangster, C. Our life is like a forest, where
   the sun.
Sassoon. Picture-Show.
Saxe, J. Story of Life, The.
Sayres. Bankrupt.
Scalapino. Flush / a Play.
Schnackenberg. Darwin in 1881.
Schultz, P. I'm Not Complaining.
Schwartz, D. Passionate Shepherd to His
   Love, The.
"Severyanin." Russian Woman.
Sexton. Rowing.
"Shahryar." Still Life.
Shakespeare, W. Seven Ages of Man, The.
   Song: "When that I was and a little tiny boy."
   Tomorrow, and Tomorrow, and Tomorrow.
Shange. I live in music.
Shapiro, D. Archaic Torsos.
Shapiro, H. Montauk Highway.
Sheck. Return, The.
Shelley, P. Sonnet: "Lift not the painted veil
   which those who live."
Shelnutt. At the Mass Graveyard.
Sherwood, G. Love and Life.
Shin, K. Reed had been weeping, The.
Shin, S. Gong Dance, The.
"Shu Ting." Assembly Line.
Shwarts. Elegies on the Cardinal Points.
Simic. Great Infirmities.
   Lesson, The.
   Poem: "Every morning I forget how it is."
Sirr. Collector's Marginalia, The.
Skovron. Election Eve, with Cat.
Slessor. Fixed Ideas.
   Last Trams.
Smith, C. Sonnet Written in the Church-Yard
   at Middleton in Sussex.
Smith, I. This is the land God gave to Andy
   Stewart.
Smith, M Stopping to Take Notes.
Smith, S. Dream of Comparison, A.
Snodgrass, W. After experience taught me that
   all the ordinary.
   April Inventory.
Snow, C. Mask Series.
Song. Poem: "Water wears away a rock."
Sorescu. Chess.
Soyinka. Bearings III: Amber Wall.
Spender, S. Sonnet: "You were born; must
   die; were loved; must love."
Stafford, W. Ask Me.
   Gift, The.
Stanley, T. Pythagoric letter, two ways spread,
   The.
   Quickness.
Stevens, W. Men Made Out of Words.

Sunday Morning.
Table Talk.
Stevenson, R. Morning drum-call on my eager ear, The.
Strand. Mysterious Maps, The.
Story of Our Lives, The.
Suckling, J. Song: "I prithee spare me, gentle boy."
Supervielle. Return to Paris.
Swinburne. Chorus: "Before the beginning of years."
Garden of Proserpine, The.
Match, A.
Swirszczynska. Poetry Reading.
Symons, A. Prologue: In the Stalls.
Sze. Network, The.
Szymborska. Preparing a Curriculum Vitae.
Reality demands.
Taggard. Demeter.
T'ao Ch'ien. Bright blossoms seldom last long.
Man has no roots, A.
When I was young and in my prime.
Years ago, when I heard the words of my elders.
Tasso. I'd like to be a bee.
What dew or what weeping.
Taylor, A. Fitzroy.
Taylor, H. Flying Change, The.
Thomas, D. Force that through the green fuse drives the flower, The.
This bread I break was once the oat.
Twenty-four years remind the tears of my eyes.
Thomas, R. Lore.
Thoreau. I am a parcel of vain strivings tied.
My life has been the poem I would have writ.
Tố Hũ'u. Three sounds sum up the sense of life.
Toomer. It is Everywhere.
Trần Gia Thoại. Night Train, The.
Tranter. Enzensberger at 'Exiles'.
Treasone. Life is like a jagged tooth.
Trivelpiece. Nursery, The.
Troupe. Conversation Overheard.
Tsaloumas. Falcon Drinking.
Ts'ao Chih. Roaming Immortal.
Tu Fu. By the Winding River I.
Night in the House by the River.
Tucker, M. Life.
Mysteries of Life.
Tuckerman, F. Sonnets: First Series.
U Tam'si Tchicaya. I was naked for the first kiss of my mother.
What do I want with a thousand stars in broad daylight.
Ungaretti. Vigil.
Unknown. Be Merry.
Great Summons, The.
Green, green.
I been rebuked and I been scorned.
I cross the river to pluck hibiscus.
I turn the carriage, yoke and set off.
I'm a-rollin', I'm a-rollin', I'm a-rollin', through an unfriendly world.
It's in Your Face.
Life owes me nothing. Let the years.
Life's a Game.
Little Things.
Little work, a little play, A.
Nobody Knows the Trouble I've Had.
On and on, always on and on.
Playing the Game.
Prayer of a Woman in Charge of Berry Picking in Knights Inlet.
Rabbit goes soft-foot, pheasant's caught.
Speeding carriage climbs through eastern gate, A.
Thank God for life!
'Tis a little journey.
Ubi Sunt Qui ante Nos Fuerunt? [or Contempt of the World].
Until life goes out.
What care I though the world reprove.
Wide Walls.
Will You Love Me When I'm Old?

years of a lifetime do not reach a hundred, The.
Vallejo. Our Daily Bread.
Van Doren. Good Appetite.
Van Duyn. Sonnet for Minimalists.
Vaughan, H. Pursuit[e], The.
Quickness.
Vice. Pants.
Viidikas. Future.
Violi. Scatter.
Võ Liêm So'n. Paradise and Hell.
Walden. Transition—S.M, The.
Wallace-Crabbe. And the World was Calm.
Sonnet IV.
Walton, A. Recipe for Living.
World We Make, The.
Wang Chi. Sent to Recluse Ch'eng.
Wang Fan-chih. No one lives past a hundred.
Ware, E. Whist.
Warren, R. When the century dragged, like a great wheel stuck at dead center.
Waterman, N. Making a Man.
Wearne. Division of O'Dowd, The.
Elise.
Terri.
Webb, F. Clouds.
Webster, A. That some day Death who has us all for jest.
Wellman, M. Having Led a Charmed Life, He Had to be Hanged Twice.
Of Power, Money, Cheese, Real Estate, Conboberation, Hoohah.
Wells, A. Length of Life, The.
Werfel. Song of Life, A.
Wharton, E. Life, like a marble block, is given to all.
Wheeler, S. Journal of the Thousand Choices.
Whistler. Form of Epitaph, A.
Whitman, A. Mind knows no death. Life is the "first and last."
Whitman, W. Beat! beat! drums!—blow! bugles! blow!
Leaves of Grass (1855).
Miracles.
O living always, always dying!
When I read the book, the biography famous.
Wieseltier. Here in Netanya.
Too Short.
Wilbur. Digression, A.
Leaving.
Star System, The.
'World Without Objects Is a Sensible Emptiness," A."
Wilcox, E. Life.
Life's Journey.
Williams, W. Horse Show, The.
Love Song: "Sweep the house clean."
Pastoral: "Little sparrows, The."
Winchilsea. Life's Progress.
Wordsworth, D. Thoughts on my sick-bed.
Wordsworth, W. Best portion of a good man's life, The.
Sonnet: "World is too much with us; late and soon, The."
These Chairs they have no words to utter.
Wotton, S. De Morte.
Wright, C. Scratch Music.
Wright, C. Laguna Blues.
Wright, D. Funeral Oration, A.
Wright, F. If you wisely invest in beauty.
Wright, F. Entry in an Unknown Hand.
Wright, J. American Twilights, 1957.
Inscription for the Tank.
Life, The.
Mutterings Over the Crib of a Deaf Child.
Northern Pike.
Secret Gratitude, A.
What the Earth Asked Me.
Wylie. Hughie at the Inn.
Yang Hsiung. Poverty.
Yau. Angel Atrapado VIII.
Yeats. Four Ages of Man, The.
Gyres! the gyres! Old Rocky Face look forth, The.
Meru.
New Faces, The.

Scholars, The.
Wild Old Wicked Man, The.
Yesenin. Now piece by piece we slip away.
Yevtushenko. Metamorphoses.
Yosano. Tanka: "Evanescent."
Young, A. Little More Traveling Music, A.
Myself When I Am Real.
Yu. Life.
Yü Hsüan-chi. Replying to a Poem by a New Graduate Lamenting the Loss of His Wife.
Yüan Mei. Writing My Feelings.
Yun. Prologue, The.
Zach. Be careful. Open your life.
Zangwill. Dreams.
Zhenkai. Accomplices.
Zolotow. Aren't You Glad.
Zweig, P. Poem: "I don't know if I can bear this suddenly."

Lifeguards

Dickey, J. Lifeguard, The.
Stuart, D. River, The.

Light

Adams, L. Light at Equinox.
Allard. Passing clouds only a stand of aspens is in light.
Alquit. Light of the World, The.
Ammons. City Limits, The.
Aristophanes. O glorious Eie, thou miracle of Sight.
Armantrout. Getting Warm.
Bachmann. Paris.
Bangs, J. Philosophy.
Barbu. Dioptric.
Bawer. View from an Airplane at Night, over California, The.
Berssenbrugge. Experience.
Blake, W. To Morning.
Bourdillon. When Love Is Done.
Bronk. Where It Ends.
Brown, D. Illumination.
Brown, R. I want to understand light years.
Browning, E. Best Thing in the World, The.
Bruce, D. Sonnet 4: "Wet streets, black trees, a gold leaf smacked."
Bu-er. Cut brambles long enough.
Byron, G. Darkness.
Cain, J. Waiting.
Campion, T. My sweetest Lesbia, let us live and love.
Carew, T. Beautiful Mistress, A.
Ceravolo. New Realism.
Coleridge, M. In Dispraise of the Moon.
Colonna, V. I see in my mind, surrounding God.
Congreve. See, see, she wakes, Sabina wakes!
Cook, E. Song of the Rushlight.
Cooley. Loom, The.
Cooper, J. Morning on the St. John's.
Cowley, A. Hymn: To Light.
Creeley. World, The.
Crouch, S. Like a Blessing.
Di Prima. Paracelsus.
Dickey, J. Power and Light.
Dickinson, E. Light exists in Spring, A.
Poets light but Lamps, The.
There's a certain Slant of light.
Dlugos. Healing the World from Battery Park.
Donne. Nocturnal[l] upon Saint Lucy's [or S. Lucies] Day, Being the Shortest Day, A.
Equi. Breakfast with Jerome.
Farjeon, E. Light the Lamps Up, Lamplighter!
"Field." They Shall Look on Him.
Fletcher, P. Ocean of Light.
Ford, C. Overturned Lake, The.
Gilbo'a. I love this sunlight cold in spaces transparent turning blue.
Goodison. Always homing now soul toward light.
Graham, J. San Sepolcro.
Graves, R. Lament for Pasiphaë.
Greiffenberg. On the Ineffable Inspiration of the Holy Spirit.
Gu Cheng. Generation, A.
Guest, B. Wild gardens overlooked by night lights. Parking.
Gunn, T. Map of the City, A.
Hall, H. White Day's Death.

Hays, H. Manhattan.
Heaney, S. Mossbawn Sunlight.
Herrick. Life is the body's [or Bodies] light,
  which once declining.
Hildegard von Bingen. Alleluia-verse for the
  Virgin.
  Antiphon for the Angels.
  Song to the Creator.
Izumi. Way I must enter, The.
Jabès. Beginning of the Book, The.
Jaccottet. Distances.
  I rise with an effort and look out.
  Serenity.
Johnson, L. Beacon of Hope.
Johnson, R. Beam 30, The Garden.
Juarroz. Lamp lit, A.
Knott. (Poem) (Chicago) (The Were-Age).
Kooser. Late Lights in Minnesota.
Krynicki. I Can't Help You.
Kunitz, S. When the light falls, it falls on her.
Landor, W. Torch of Love dispels the gloom,
  The.
Lawrence, D. Let There Be Light!
Lea, S. Telescope.
Levine, P. Belief.
Lyles. Summer stillness.
MacLow. 59th Light Poem: for La Monte
  Young and Marian Zazeela—6 November
  1982.
MacNeice. Star-Gazer.
Marvell. Mower to the Glow-Worms [or
  Glowworms or Glo-Worms], The.
Masaoka Shiki. Shitting in the winter turnip
  field.
  Tanka: "Illuminated."
Maura. Creation of Light, The.
Melville, H. In the Desert.
Millay, E. First Fig.
Milton. Blind among enemies, O worse than
  chains.
  On His Blindness.
Miyazawa Kenji. Tanka: "In the blue rays."
Moore, L. Homeplace, The.
Mouré. La Gueule.
Nichol. St. Anzas VI.
"O'Neill." Grace for Light.
Patacara. When they plow their fields.
Prabhu. For the Lord of Caves.
Probyn. More than They that Watch for the
  Morning.
Raine, K. Images.
Ratcliffe, S. Beginning in the light as heard,
  wheel on stone.
Rich, A. Focus.
  Insusceptibles, The.
  Integrity.
Richter, M. Light?
Roberts, D. Dazzle.
Roethke. Light Listened.
Roseliep. Morning-Glory, The.
Sartarelli. That Land (4).
Schuyler, J. Shimmer.
Senghor. Pearls.
Shea, M. Bolted space.
Sitwell, D. Aubade: "Jane, Jane, / Tall as a
  crane."
Snyder, G. How Poetry Comes to Me.
Stanley, T. Glowworm, The.
Stevens, W. Homunculus et la Belle Étoile.
Symonds. Lux Est Umbra Dei[1].
Symons, A. Pastel: Masks and Faces.
Tabb. Tenebræ.
Tanikawa Shuntaro. Stone and Light.
Tennyson, A. Marriage Morning.
Thomas, D. Light breaks where no sun shines.
Thomas, L. Electricity of Blossoms.
Thoreau. Haze.
Touré, A. O Lord of Light! A Mystic Sage
  Returns to Realms of Eternity!
Towle. Painting the Eaves.
Tysh, G. Genitalia.
Unknown. Beautiful faces are they that wear.
  This Little Light of Mine.
Walcott. Star.
Wallace, R. Driving By.
Wat. Facing Bonnard.
Waters, M. Mystery of the Caves, The.

Webb, F. Port Phillip Night.
Wen-Ti Chien. Lo-yang.
White, J. To Night.
Wieseltier. "Elegies By the Senses."
Wilbur. Star System, The.
Wollach. This Poem Should Have Etc.
Wright, J. Beginning.
Wroth. Sonnet 22: "Like to the Indians,
  scorched with the sun[ne]."
Wylie. O Virtuous Light.
Yosano. Tanka: "Each shaped."
Yukitsuna. Tanka: "Moonlight, The."
Zepeda, O. Kitchen Sink.

Lighthouses
Bishop, E. Seascape.
Clampitt. Baroque Sunburst, A.
Gibson, W. Flannan Isle.
Jackson, H. My Lighthouses.
Lowry, M. Lighthouse invites the storm and
  lights it, The.
Matveyeva. Lighthouse.
Stevenson, R. Brilliant kernel of the night,
  The.
Storni. Lighthouse in the Night.
Wellesley. Lighthouses.
Wilson, M. Lighthouse, The.

Lightning
Aborigine Oral Tradition. Tongues of the
  lightning Snakes flicker and twist, one to the
  other, The.
Ai. She Didn't Even Wave.
Al-Harizi. Lightning, The.
Alexander, W. Lightning.
Brickley. Sheet lightning.
Chernoff. Man Struck Twenty Times by
  Lightning, The.
Ded. On the way to God the difficulties.
Dickinson, E. Lightning is a yellow Fork, The.
Greiffenberg. On the Ineffable Inspiration of
  the Holy Spirit.
Hester. Lightning Rod Salesman, The.
Hoyt, C. In that lightning flash.
Kinnell. Another Night in the Ruins.
Lawrence, D. Lightning.
  Storm in the Black Forest.
Macdonald, G. Baby-Sermon, A.
McClintock, M. Tonight. . . wishing.
Mitchell, S. Once, Driving West of Billings,
  Montana.
Miyazawa Kenji. Tanka: "Lightning."
Montagu. Epitaph: "Here lie John Hughes
  and Sarah Drew."
Oliver, M. Lightning.
Pagis. Final Exam.
Stevenson, R. Last night we had a
  thunderstorm in style.
Swenson, M. Lightning waked me, The.It slid
  under.
Unknown. At Great Torrington, Devon.
  Dance-Song of the Lightning.
  Song of the Rain Chant.
  Songs of Spirits.
Warren, R. Heat Lightning.
Wollach. When You're Not a Poet.

Lightning Bugs. See **Fireflies**
Lilacs
Harjo, J. Santa Fe.
Lowell, A. Lilacs.
Miliauskaite. These are lilacs.
Roseliep. Piano practice.
Whitman, W. Spring.
Wright, R. Coming from the woods.

Lilies
Allard. Deep in my notebook a lily pad floats
  away.
Beddoes. Crocodile, A.
Bible, O.T. I am the rose of Sharon, and the
  lily of the valleys.
Bozhilov. Lilies.
Constable, H. Diaphenia like the
  daffadowndilly.
"Eliot." Two lovers by a moss-grown spring.
Glück, L. White Lilies, The.
Gregory, H. Chinese Garden, The.
Guest, B. Red Lilies.
Guinicelli. Sonnet: He Will Praise His Lady.
Hackett, J. Moon fades into dawn.

Herrick. How Lillies Came White.
Howe, J. In the beauty of the lilies Christ.
Keats. La Belle Dame Sans Merci.
Legaré. To a Lily.
Machi. Tanka: "My heart."
Miyazawa Kenji. Tanka: "In the blue rays."
  Tanka: "Lightning."
  Tanka: "Scattered clouds."
Pizzarelli. Bending back.
Robinson, A. Pallor.
Rotella, A. Left to the wind.
  Waterlilies.
Rumi. What the Flowers Said.
Scalapino. Floating Series 1.
Sexton. From the Garden.
Shefner. Lily, The.
Smart, C. On a Bed of Guernsey Lilies.
Symons, A. Morbidezza.
Tennyson, A. Song: "Come into the garden,
  Maud."
Thaxter. On Easter Day.
Unknown. Lily Events.
  Maudle-in Ballad, A.
Virgilio. Lily.
Wills, J. Water lilies.
Wratislaw. White Lilies.

Lilies of the Valley
Silkin. Lilies of the Valley.
Lilith
Gregg. Lilith.
Norris, K. Lilith and the Doctor.
Limbo
Coleridge, S. Limbo.
Jacobsen, J. Limbo Dancer, The.
Levy, A. Ballad of Religion and Marriage, A.
Limestone
Auden. In Praise of Limestone.
Lincoln, Abraham
Benét, S. John Brown's Prayer.
Bryant, W. Death of Lincoln, The.
Cooke, E. Born without a Chance.
Fletcher, J. Lincoln.
Hughes, L. Lincoln Monument: Washington.
Lindsay, V. Abraham Lincoln Walks at
  Midnight.
Masters, E. Anne Rutledge.
McClellan. Daybreak.
McGirt. Memory of Lincoln and the Yankees.
Meigs, M. Abraham Lincoln.
Melville, H. Martyr, The.
Ray, H. Lincoln.
Robinson, E. Master, The.
Sandburg, C. Cool Tombs.
  Long Shadow of Lincoln: A Litany, The.
Shulman, M. Honest Abe Lincoln.
Stoddard, R. Abraham Lincoln.
Unknown. Abraham Lincoln's Creed.
  Booth Killed Lincoln.
Whitman, W. O Captain! my Captain! our
  fearful trip is done.
  Spring.
Lincolnshire, England
Ingelow. High Tide on the Coast of
  Lincolnshire, 1571, The.
Lindbergh, Charles Augustus
Unknown. Lindbergh.
Lindsay, Vachel
Ginsberg, A. To Lindsay.
Linen
Longley, M. Linen Industry, The.
Linnets
Bridges, R. I Heard a Linnet Courting.
Brontë, E. Song: "Linnet in the rocky dells,
  The."
Webster, A. Since first my little one lay on
  my breast.
Wordsworth, W. Green Linnet, The.
Lions
Banker, I. Lion Thoughts.
Beer, P. Lion Hunts.
Belloc. Jim Who Ran Away from His Nurse,
  and Was Eaten by a Lion.
  Lion, the Lion, he dwells in the waste, The.
Blake, W. Little Girl Found, The.
Carruth, H. Wreck of the Circus Train, The.
Duncan, R. Song of the Borderguard, The.

Edgar, M. Lion and Albert, The.
Ginsberg, A. Lion for Real, The.
Glazkov. I strolled around the zoo.
Herrick. Upon Umber: Epigram.
Heywood, J. Egles byrde hath spred his wings, The.
Housman, A. African Lion, The.
Jacobsen, J. Bush.
Kikaku. bantam rooster, A.
MacLeish. End of the World, The.
Mother Goose. Lion and the unicorn, The.
Nash, O. Lion, The.
Patchen. Lions of fire, The.
Richards, L. Poor unfortunate Hottentot, A.
Sackville-West. Greater cats with golden eyes, The.
Smith, S. Reversionary.
　Sunt Leones.
Swenson, M. Lion.
Turner, C. Lion's Skeleton, The.
Unknown. Lion.
　Saint Jerome and his Lion.
　Signifying Monkey, The.
　Song of the Lioness for Her Cub.
Watson, W. O My Poor Darling.
Wheelock, J. Lion-House, The.

Lips
Benedikt. Divine Love.
Berni. Hair of fine silver, shaggy and twisted.
Chapman, G. Bridal Song: "O come, soft rest of cares, come Night."
Conquest. Agents, The.
Dowson. Non Sum Qualis Eram Bonae sub Regno Cynara[e].
DuPlessis, R. Back arched like a bow.
Giscombe. All (Facts, Stories, Chance).
Herrick. Captived Bee; or, The Little Filcher, The.
Knott. (Poem) (Chicago) (The Were-Age).
Marino. Lips and Eyes.
Mitchison. Old Love and New Love.
Miyazawa Kenji. Tanka: "Bloodshot."
Shakespeare, W. At the Moated Grange.
　Sonnet 128.
　Sonnet 130.
Simon, L. Bernice Got Next to Isis.
Toomer. Evening Song.
　Her Lips Are Copper Wire.

Lisbon, Portugal
Atkins. Lisbon.

Listening and Listeners
Ammons. Little Thing Like That, A.
Halliday, M. Vegetable Wisdom.
Herrick. Canticle to Apollo, A.
Sachs, N. How long have we forgotten how to listen!
Stewart, F. To a Friend.
Tapahonso. Listen.
Tomlinson, C. Word in Edgeways, A.
Zukofsky, L. In Arizona / (how many years in the mountains).

Literature
Berryman. Professor's Song, A.
Birney. Can. Lit.
Brown, W. England, Autumn.
Connolly, C. It was late last night when my lord came home.
Donne. To Mr. R. W ("Kindly I envy thy song's [or songs] perfection").
Donnell. Canadian Prairies View of Literature, The.
Kenzheyev. Poets have often noticed.
Kunio. Tanka: "I've swept away."
"MacDiarmid." Ah, Lenin, you were richt. But I'm a poet.
　Water Music.
Mazur. Lilacs on Brattle Street.
Merwin, W. Night Singing.
Mnthali. Stranglehold of English Lit, The.
Nemerov. History of a Literary Movement.
Ransom, J. Survey of Literature.
Reed, I. Badman of the Guest Professor.
Rukeyser, M. Homage to Literature.
Smith, S. Souvenir de Monsieur Poop.
Stevens, W. Poem That Took the Place of a Mountain, The.
Tennyson, A. Poets and Their Bibliographies.

Waller, E. Of English Verse.
See also **Authorship and Authors; Criticism and Critics**

Lithuania
Bagryana. River Run.
Bobrowski. Lithuanian Well, The.
Geda. I walked out into Lithuania.
Milosz, C. With Her*.
Nagys. Laterna Obscura.
Preil, G. Memory of Autumns at Springtime.
Zwicky. Summer Pogrom.

Little, Malcolm. *See* **Malcolm X**

Little Red Riding Hood
Sholl. Riding Hood.

Livingstone, David
Monette. Into the Dark.

Lizards
Alexander, W. Psychotropic Squalls, The.
Bethune, L. Today Tutu Is Beating the Same Burru As Me.
Casalinuovo. Lizard's Tango, The.
García Lorca. Mister Lizard is Crying.
Grennan. Lizards in Sardinia.
Jones, R. Contempt.
Lamb, E. Lizard inching, A.
Lawrence, D. Lizard ran out on a rock and looked up, listening, A.
Magowan. Zeimbekiko ("Old man gets up turns, An").
Morley, H. Lizard's heart throbs, The.
Murray, R. Lizard, The.
Pender. Lizard, The.
Pinto, J. I had a pet lizard called Albert.
Robinson, R. Jarrangulli.
Roethke. Lizard, The.
　Wish for a Young Wife.
Rossetti, C. When fishes set umbrellas up.
Rotella, A. From green to grey.
Stafford, W. At the Bomb Testing Site.
West, C. My Gecko and I.
Wu Chen. Fantastic Rock, The.

Llamas
Belloc. Llama, The.
Nash, O. Lama, The.

Lobsters
"Carroll." Lobster, The.
　Lobster Quadrille, A.
Grennan. Incident.
Jackson, L. Fun.
Lowell, R. Water.
Nemerov. Lobsters.
Sexton. Lobster.
Snodgrass, W. Lobsters in the Window.
Sorrentino. September in Kittery.

Locker Rooms
Mitchell, N. Locker Room, The.

Locomotives
Cranch. Locomotive, The.
MacLeish. Grazing Locomotives.
Wilcox, E. Engine, The.
See also **Trains; Railroads**

Locusts
Chao. Locust Swarm, The.
Kinzie. Canicula.
Pound, E. Locusts a-wing, multiply.
Unknown. Coyote and the Locust, The.
　Locust, The.

London, England
Adcock, F. Immigrant.
Arnold, M. West London.
Bancks. Description of London, A.
Bateman, E. Cockney's Garden, The.
Blake, W. Fields from Islington to Marybone, The.
　London ("I wander through [or thro'] each chartered [or charter'd] street").
Bridges, R. London Snow.
Bromwich. Wandsworth Common.
Chesterton, G. Old Song, The.
Colman, G. London Rurality.
Cronin, A. Responsibilities.
Davidson, J. London.
Defoe, D. London.
Disch. Convalescing in London.
Douglas, L. Impression de Nuit; London.

Dower. New River Head, a Fragment, The.
Dowson. Benedictio Domini.
Dryden, J. New London, The.
　Yet London, empress of the northern clime.
Dunbar, W. To the City of London [or In Honour of the City of London].
Ewart. Dell, The.
Flecker. Ballad of the Londoner.
Ford, S. Hail, glorious day; mayst thou be writ in gold.
Forster, W. Poor of London, The.
French, W. Mountains of Mourne, The.
Ginsberg, A. Studying the Signs.
Guilpin. What more variety of pleasures can.
Guiney. Lights of London, The.
　Sunday Chimes in the City.
W. H.
Herrick. His Return to London.
Housman, A. Eight O'Clock.
Howell, C. Liberty and Ten Years of Return.
Johnson, S. London: A Poem.
Keats. Lines on the Mermaid Tavern.
Le Gallienne. Ballad of London, A.
Lee, L. Sunken Evening [in Trafalgar Square].
Levy, A. London Plane-Tree, A.
　London Poets.
　Straw in the street where I pass to-day.
Lloyd, C. London Rain.
MacNeice. Goodbye to London.
　London Rain.
　September has come and I wake.
　Streets of Laredo, The.
　Whit Monday.
Mason, R. Latter-day Geography Lesson.
McOrlan. Produce from the colonies.
Meynell, A. November Blue.
Morris, C. Country and Town.
Morton, J. Spring in London.
Mother Goose. London Bridge is broken down.
Motteux. Song, A: "Slaves to London, I'll deceive you."
Nortje. Cosmos in London.
Noyes, A. Barrel-Organ, The.
Oldham, J. London.
Owen, W. Shadwell Stair.
Pope, A. Farewell to London in the Year 1715, A.
Pound, E. Portrait d'une Femme.
Robinson, M. London's Summer Morning.
Rowland. London.
Shelley, P. Hell is a city much like London.
　You are now / In London, that great sea.
Spender, S. Rejoice in the Abyss.
Spires. Sunday Afternoon at Fulham Palace.
Summers, H. Report.
Surrey. Satire on London, A.
Swift, J. Description of a City Shower, A.
Thomas, D. Countryman's Return, The.
　Refusal to Mourn the Death, by Fire, of a Child in London, A.
Thomson, J. William Blake.
Tollet. On the Prospect from Westminster Bridge.
Tonks. Farewell to Kurdistan.
Unknown. Annette Myers.
　Bells of London, The.
　Cries of London, The.
　Let dirty streets be paved with flow'ry green.
　London Bells.
　London Lickpenny.
　Oranges and lemons, say the bells of St. Clement's.
　St. Paul's Steeple.
　Which is the way to London Town.
Vaughan, H. Town believes thee lost, and didst thou see, The.
Waller, E. On St. James's Park, as Lately Improved by His Majesty.
Ward, E. South Sea Ballad, A.
Whitney, I. And now let mee dispose such things.
　And (though I am perswade) that I.
　Aucthour Maketh Her Wyll and Testament, The.
　Now London have I (for thy sake).
　Rejoice in God that I am gon.

Wilde, O. Impression Du Matin.
Symphony in Yellow.
Wordsworth, W. Composed upon Westminster Bridge[, September 3, 1802].
London 1802.

Londonderry, Northern Ireland
Mahon. Derry Morning.

Loneliness
Abrahams, P. Lonely Road.
Ackerly. Prayer of an Unemployed Man.
Ackland. Lonely Woman, The.
Aiken, J. John's Song.
Akers. Night: Volcano, California.
Allingham. I walk'd in the lonesome evening.
Alma-Tadema, L. If no one ever marries me—
.
Ammuvanar. What She Said ("My body").
"Amorous Lady." Letter to My Love—All Alone, Past 12, in the Dumps, A.
Arnold, M. To Marguerite.
Arrowsmith, P. Political Activist Living Alone.
Ashby. Stranger in This Land, A.
Ayton. Valediction.
Barnes, W. Wife A-Lost, The.
Baumel. Doing Time in Baltimore.
Berryman. He Resigns.
I'm scared a lonely. Never see my son.
Sometimes the night echoes to prideless wailing.
Betjeman. House of Rest.
Blaga. Psalm.
Bly, R. Snowbanks North of the House.
Brodsky, J. To Urania.
Brontë, A. Captive Dove, The.
Brontë, C. Again I find myself alone, and ever.
Lonely Lady, The.
Brontë, E. If grief for grief can touch thee.
Sun has set, and the long grass now, The.
Brooks, G. Preacher: Ruminates Behind the Sermon, The.
Sunset of the City, A.
Browne, M. Epithalamion/Wedding Dawn.
Bruner. There is a loneliness on city streets.
Bunin. Loneliness.
Catullus. Carmen 69 ("That no fair woman will, wonder not why").
Velluti, the lorn heart, the sexless voice.
Chang Chiu-ling. Since you left, my lover.
Chin. Composed Near the Bay Bridge (after a wild party).
Chōkū. Tanka: "From the water's depth."
"Chrystos." Night Visits.
Chu Shu-chen. Alone.
Morning.
Sorrow.
Spring Joy.
Clare, J. Shepherd Boy, The.
Song: "I peeled bits of straw and I got switches too."
Coleridge, H. She was a queen of noble Nature's crowning.
Coleridge, S. Blossoming of the Solitary Date-Tree, The.
Cope, W. Lonely Hearts.
Cortez. Lonely Woman.
Crane, S. I explain the silvered passing of a ship at night.
Creeley. Door, The.
Moon, The.
Whip, The.
Csoori. Thin, Black Band, A.
Cummings, E. L(a.
Wind has blown the rain away and blown, A.
Darley. Dove's Loneliness, The.
Das, J. Corpse, The.
De la Mare. Alone.
Old Men, The.
Derricotte. Saturday Night.
Deutsch. Solitude.
Dickinson, E. Shade upon the mind there passes, A.
There is another Loneliness.
Dischell. Chamber, The.
Dobyns. What You Have Come To Expect.
Doty, M. Harbor Lights.

Eberhart, R. Human Being Is a Lonely Creature, The.
Edson, R. Large thing comes in, A.
Eimers. No Friends of the Heart.
Emerson, R. Good-bye, proud world! I'm going home.
Thine eyes still shined for me, though far.
Enright, D. Old field is sad, The.
Ferry. Soldier, The.
Field, E. Unwanted.
"Field." Life Plastic.
Field, R. Skyscrapers.
Forché. City Walk-up, Winter 1969.
Frost, R. Acquainted with the Night.
Bereft.
Desert Places.
Impulse, The.
Loneliness.
Most of It, The.
Fujiwara no Go-Kyōgoku. Cricket cries, The.
Garland, H. Plowing: A Memory.
Gatsos. How very much I loved you only I know.
Gibbons, R. We say a heart breaks—like.
Goldberg, B. Possibilities, The.
Gould, J. We Exist.
Greenwell, D. Scherzo, A.
Hacker, M. Elevens.
Runaways Café I.
Hardy, T. Bereft.
Fallow Deer at the Lonely House, The.
Harmer. Space Explorer's Story, The.
Harrison, G. Alone in the Grange.
Hartnett. Death of an Irishwoman.
Hitomaro. In the empty mountains.
Ho Hsun. Traveler with his heavy heart, The.
Ho Xuan Huong. Woman Lies Alone, A.
Hogan, L. Thought, A.
Holub. Fairy Tale.
Horovitz, F. Women.
Hotham. This loneliness.
Hovey. At Sea.
Hsi K'ang. Sent to the Hsiu-ts'ai on His Entry into the Army.
Hughes, L.
Hope.
Miss Blues'es Child.
Poem: "I loved my friend."
Stony Lonesome.
Hunter, A. Pastoral Song, A.
Ignatow, D. Mother, how wrinkled and old must you become.
Inez. Old Lady Across the Hall Has Gone to Live Behind the Door, The.
Ion of Chios. Don't leave me.
Ishikawa Takuboku. Tanka: "I close my eyes."
Tanka: "When I breathe."
Issahakian. For you fleas too.
Izumi. Lying here alone.
Jackson, L. Take hands. / There is no love now.
Jacobsen, R. Express train 1256 races alongside hidden, remote villages. House.
Jarrell. Game at Salzburg, A.
Lonely Man, The.
Jastrzebska. Bi-lingual.
Jennings, K. Couples.
Jewett, S. Widows' House, The.
Jones, R. Birds, The.
Jordan, N. When A Woman Gets Blue.
Kalász. Hymn: "Where should I seat you, where."
Kamienska Annunciation.
Kantan. What She Said ("Only the dim-witted say it's evening").
Kantaris. Not-loving.
Karandikar. Knot, The.
Kayamanar. What Her Girl Friend Said, Seeing Her Friend Suffer in Silent Dignity over Her Husband's Infidelity.
Kennedy, X. B Negative.
Kerouac. Mexican Loneliness.
Khodasevich. In Front of the Mirror.
Ki No Washika. No.
Kim, C. Aerin 4.
Kim, N. Heart's Flag.
Kinnell. Burn, The.

Kitahara Hakushū. At a hospital in Tokyo during the summer of 1911.
Tanka: "After lunch."
Knight, E. Poem to Galway Kinnell, A.
Kovner. Tashlich.
Krasnikov. Come on, Mama, we'll slake the lime.
Kuznetsov. Should I see a cloud high up in the sky.
Landor, W. What News.
Levine, P. At the Fillmore.
Poem Circling Hamtramck, Michigan, All Night in Search of You, The.
Li Ch'ing-chao. Alone in the Night.
Li Po. Verses: "Clean is the autumn wind."
Li Shang-yin. I Wake Up Alone.
Lihn. Six Poems of Loneliness.
Linden, M. Lonely World.
Louis, A. Practicing Death Songs.
Lowell, A. Letter, The.
Madonna of the Evening Flowers.
Lowry, M. Delirium in Vera Cruz.
Lu Chao-lin. Lotuses on the Crooked Pond.
Lu Chi. She Thinks of Her Beloved.
Machi. Tanka: "Loneliness."
MacNeice. Autobiography.
For X.
Nostalgia.
Madgett. Plea for My Heart's Sake.
Mahon. Achill.
Masters, E. Lost Orchard, The.
Matthews, W. Note I Left for Gerald Stern in an Office I Borrowed, and He Would Next, at a Summer Writers' Conference.
McBride, M. Loneliness.
McElroy, C. In My Mother's Room.
Queen of the Ebony Isles.
Mei Sheng et al. Green green, river bank grasses.
Merwin, W. Departure's Girl-friend.
Metcalfe. Visit the Sick.
Meynell, A. Shattered Lute, A.
Mezhirov. Loneliness chases me.
Michitsuna. Have you any idea.
Milaipperun Kantan. What She Said ("Only the dim-witted say it's evening").
Millay, E. On the wide heath at evening overtaken.
Mo Shih-lung. I Waited for Chuang Hsüan-yüan But He Never Came.
Modisane. Lonely.
Monro. Solitude.
Mountain, M. Smoke from a neighbor's chimney loneliness.
Muneyuki. I can feel the loneliness.
Na-lan Hsing-te. Tune: "Remembering the Prince."
Okamoto. Tanka: "Twenty days."
Ono no Komachi. So lonely am I.
Oxenham. Art thou lonely, O my brother?
Papaionnou. Nights I stay awake without hope.
Park, M. April.
Love.
Partridge, F. My Days Go On.
Petri. By an Unknown Poet from Eastern Europe, 1955.
Petronius Arbiter. Man in the middle of the street.
Phan Bội Châu. My Shadow and I.
Pilinszky. Fable. "Once upon a time / there was a lonely wolf."
Po Chü-i. Invitation to Hsiao Ch'u-shih.
On being Removed from Hsün-yang and Sent to Chung-chou.
Porter, C. Nobody's Chasing Me.
Pushkin. October.
Raine, K. Lachesis.
Randall, D. Old Witherington.
Rankin, P. Fifteen.
Revell. Sirius.
Rexroth, K. Every morning, I / Wake alone, dreaming my.
Half in a dream.
Night without end. Loneliness.
Once I shone afar like a.
Rice, H. God, Are You There?

Rich, A. Rain on the West Side Highway.
Song: "You're wondering if I'm lonely."
Rivard. Change My Evil Ways.
Robinson, E. Mr Flood's Party.
Robson, J. Blues for the Lonely*.
Rodgers, C. One.
Poem for Some Black Women.
What Color Is Lonely.
Rossetti, C. At Home.
Chilly Night, A.
Hoping Against Hope.
Sappho.
Rutsala. Late at Night.
Ryan, G. Elegy for 6 So Far.
Sanchez, S. Summary.
Sandburg, C. They Ask: Is God, Too, Lonely?
Sappho. Moon has veil'd her Silver Light, The.
Pleiades disappear, The.
Sarton. Fruit of Loneliness.
"Yes," you say, "of course at Christmas".
Sassoon. "When I'm alone"—the words tripped off his tongue.
Seth. All you who sleep tonight.
Sexton. Window That Watched the Pru.
Shakespeare, W. Sonnet 29.
Shūji. Tanka: "Suddenly."
Sitwell, D. Cat, The.
Smith, I. Chinese Poem.
Spire. Lonely.
Stickney, T. Mnemosyne.
Su Tung-p'o. Verses: "I am old, sick and lonely."
Surrey. Complaint by Night of the Lover Not Beloved, A.
Swede. Leaving my loneliness inside her.
Swirszczynska. Very Sad Conversation at Night, A.
Teasdale. Spring Night.
Tennyson, A. Mariana.
Tessimond. Not Love Perhaps.
Thomson, J. William Blake.
Tóth, J. Forest.
Ts'ao Chih. Seven Poems of Lament.
Tu Fu. Loneliness.
Lovely lady, fairest of the time.
Man with No Family to Take Leave of, The.
Tynan. Wild Geese.
Unknown. Alone, I live alone.
Company in Loneliness.
Donal Og.
Green green, river bank grasses.
How terrible it is to trust no one.
I think of all the places I've been.
Months go by like water in a waterfall, The.
Night without end. I cannot sleep.
Seafarer.
There is a mystery in human hearts.
There is so much of loneliness.
Well, the war is done.
Widow's Lament.
Van Duyn. Open Letter from a Constant Reader.
Venkorran. What She Said ("Are there others too").
Walker, T. Home Is So Sad.
Webster, A. Circe.
Wei Ying-wu. Longing in My Heart.
Wells, C. Alone.
Wen-Ti Chien. Winter Night.
Werfel. Loneliness.
Whalen. Complaint: To the Muse.
Wheelock, C. Divorcee.
Whitman, W. As if a phantom caress'd me.
I saw in Louisiana a live-oak growing.
This moment yearning and thoughtful sitting alone.
When I peruse the conquer'd fame of heroes and the victories of mighty generals, I do not envy the generals.
Wither. Sonnet: "I that erstwhile the world's sweet air did draw."
Sonnet: "I wandered out a while agone."
Wordsworth, W. Daffodils.
Wright, F. Journey, The.
Wright, J. For the Marsh's Birthday.
Having Lost My Sons, I Confront the

Wreckage of the Moon: Christmas, 1960.
Inscription for the Tank.
Northern Pike.
Poem about Breasts, A.
Poems to a Brown Cricket.
Speak.
Wright, J. Half-Caste Girl.
Wyatt, T. What means [*or* meaneth *or* menethe] this when I lie [*or* lye] alone.
Wylie. Let No Charitable Hope.
Little Eclogue.
Yakamochi. Better never to have met you.
[These] meetings in dreams.
Mist floats on the Spring meadow.
Yang Hsiung. Poverty.
Yang Shen. To the Tune "Heavenly Immortal" ("Waves wash off the peach blossoms").
Yang Shih-ch'i. Night Rain beneath the City Walls of P'i-chou.
Yeats. Crazy Jane and Jack the Journeyman.
Wind Blows out of the Gates of the Day, The.
Yên Ba. Twenty-Eight Lines for My Wife.
Yondo. Love.
To You.
Young, A. Loneliness.
Topsy: Part 2.
See also **Isolation; Absence; Separation**

Long Island, New York
Lazarus, E. Long Island Sound.
Moss, H. Long Island Springs.
Sissman. On the Island.
Swenson, M. Fire Island.
Written While Riding the Long Island Rail Road.
Wheelock, J. Afternoon: Amagansett Beach.
Amagansett Beach Revisited.
Whitman, W. As I ebb'd with the ocean of life.
Centenarian's Story, The.

Longfellow, Henry Wadsworth
Betjeman. Longfellow's Visit to Venice.
"Carroll." Hiawatha's Photographing.
Lowell, J. Poe and Longfellow.
Ray, H. Longfellow.

Longing
Akahito. I wish I were close.
Alford, H. You and I.
Allingham. I walk'd in the lonesome evening.
Allur Nanmullai. What He Said ("Heart, knowing, The").
Ammuvanar. What She Said ("My body").
Anacreon. Wish, The.
Argentarius. I can't bear to watch your hips.
Arnold, M. Longing.
Asclepiades. In a fit, Philaenion bit me.
Austin, M. Song of the Maverick.
Auvaiyar. What She Said, Thinking of Him Crossing the Wilderness Alone.
Averill. Renewal.
Barnes, W. Wind at the Door, The.
Bates, K. If You Could Come.
Baudelaire. Giantess, The.
Bennett, L. Home Sickness.
Love Letter.
Berkeley, S. Parting, The.
Bernard. Joy! a heart so overflowing.
When—presto—turf and trees are green.
Berryman. Your shining—where?—rays my wide room with gold.
Bible, *O.T.* Psalm 42.
Boker. Ah, lute, how well I know each tone of thee.
Boland, E. In Her Own Image.
Brathwaite, E. Naima.
Brontë, E. F. de Samara to A. G. A.
Shall Earth no more inspire thee.
Brooks, G. To be in love.
Browning, E. Sonnet: "Belovéd, my Belovéd, when I think."
Sonnet: "If I leave all for thee, wilt thou exchange."
Browning, R. In Three Days.
Lovers' Quarrel, A.
Never the time and the place.
Burns, R. Highland Harry Back Again.
Mary Morison.
My heart's in the Highlands, my heart is not

here.
Simmer's a pleasant time.
Carew, T. Divine Mistress, A.
To Her in Absence; a Ship.
To My Mistress[e] in My Absence.
Catullus. Carmen 8 ("Break off / fallen Catullus").
Carmen 55.
There on th'extreamest Beach, and farthest Sand.
Chivers. Lily Adair.
Chou Pang-yen. Tune: Palace of Night Revels.
"Chrystos." Getting Down.
Clare, J. I am—yet what I am none cares or knows.
Secret Love.
Written in Prison.
Clark, M. Summer, At Home.
Clifton, L. Climbing.
Coleridge, S. Day-Dream, The ("If thou wert here, these tears were tears of light!")
If I had but two little wings.
Love.
Cometas. Phyllis, loving Demophoon.
Conoley. Heroes, Saints, and Neighbors.
Coolbrith. Longing.
Craik. Douglas, Douglas, Tender and True.
Cranch. Ocean, The.
Crane, H. Carrier Letter.
Creeley. Song: "Those rivers run from that land."
Csoori. Bachelor, The.
Cummings, E. Always before your voice my soul.
Das, J. In Camp.
Dickinson, E. I many times thought Peace had come.
Lady feeds Her little Bird, The.
Diên Nghi. Her Story.
Dietmar von Aist. Yonder on the linden tree there sang a merry little bird.
Dodd, W. Letter.
Donne. Fever, A.
Doubiago. Signal Hill.
Du Bellay. To Venus.
"Dylan." Boots of Spanish Leather.
"Eliza." Dart, The.
Elizabeth I. On Monsieur's Departure.
Emanuel, L. Patient.
Emerson, R. To Rhea.
Euripides. I crossed sand-hills.
"Field." Unbosoming.
Forché. Morning Baking, The.
Ford, C. Somebody's Gone.
Foscolo. To Zante.
Foster, S. Jeanie with the Light Brown Hair.
Friedrich von Hausen. Help! How Minne has deserted me.
Fujiwara no Go-Kanesuke. River Izumi, The.
Gallagher, T. Under Stars.
García Lorca. Sleepwalkers' Ballad.
Garrigue. Catch What You Can.
Stranger, The.
Gershon. Uphold Me.
Ginsberg, A. Lion for Real, The.
Goethe. Diary, The.
Hunter's Song at Nightfall, The.
Sonnet: "To work away in art's traditional measure."
Graham, W. Letter II.
Gregg. Lies and Longing.
Grimké, A. Garden Seat, The.
When the green lies over the earth, my dear.
Gunn, T. Autobiography.
Hacker, M. Aube Provençale.
Hafiz. Ode 173: "All the long night we talked of your long hair."
Hardy, T. Curtains now are drawn, The.
Last Leaf, The.
Voice, The.
Hawthorne, N. Oh, Man can seek the downward glance.
Hayden, R. Ballad of Sue Ellen Westerfield, The.
Herbert, G. Longing.
Hewett, D. In Moncur Street.
Hewitt, J. Ireland.

Hill, G. Splendidly-shining darkness.
Hirshfield, J. Of Gravity & Angels.
Hitomaro. Bay of Tsunu, The.
In the sea of ivy clothed Iwami.
Hồ Dzềnh. Shilly-Shally.
Ho Xuan Huong. Confession.
Elegy for the Prefect of Vĩnh-tu'ờ'ng.
Homer. Landfall.
Housman, A. Far in a western brookland.
When the lad for longing sighs.
Howells, W. Forlorn.
Hsiao-Wei. For My Wife.
Hsieh T'iao. Jade Steps Plaint.
Hsü Kan. Wife's Thoughts, The.
Hughes, L. Afro-American Fragment.
Ion of Chios. Don't leave me.
Jeffers, R. Maid's Thought, The.
Jewett, S. Together.
John of the Cross. Spiritual Canticle, The.
Jong. Parable of the Four-Poster.
Juana Inés de la Cruz. Happy Easter, my
Lady.
Kapilar. What Her Friend Said to the Foster-
Mother.
What Her Friend Said to the foster-mother
(who is guarding her carefully).
What She Said to Her Girl Friend.
Kaufman, S. Notes to my Daughters.
Keats. Endymion.
To Fanny.
What can I do to drive away.
Keens-Douglas. Trinidad If Ah Let You.
Keppel, L. Robin Adair.
Kim, C. Aerin I.
Bird.
Kim, T. When the river breaks loose.
Kipling, R. Rebirth.
Recall, The.
Kirschner. Fall of Light, The.
Komunyakaa. Imhotep.
Ku Hsiung. Tune: "Telling of Innermost
Feelings."
Tune: Telling of Innermost Feelings ("Long
nights when he neglects me—where's he
gone?")
Kynaston. To Cynthia.
Laforgue. Solo by Moonlight.
Landor, W. Rose Aylmer.
Lawrence, D. Search for Love.
Lee, J. Lusca.
Lee, L. Here I Am.
Lehman. Arrival at Kennedy.
Lewis, A. Dawn on the East Coast.
In Hospital: Poona (1).
Song (On Seeing Dead Bodies Floating Off
the Cape).
Li Ch'ing-chao. Alone in the Night.
To the Tune, "Plum Blossoms Fall and
Scatter."
Li Po. Calling on a Taoist Priest in Tai-t'ien
Mountain but Failing to See Him.
River Merchant's Wife, The; a Letter.
Written in Behalf of My Wife.
Li Shang-yin. Bite back passion. Spring now
sets.
Night Rains: to my Wife up North.
Lilley. You Have to Strike Back.
Liu Yung. Tune: "Jade Butterflies."
Lodge, T. Shepherd's Sorrow, Being
Disdained in Love, The.
Louis, A. Practicing Death Songs.
Lovelace, R. In Allusion to the French Song.
Lowell, A. Garden by Moonlight, The.
Luân Hoán. Washing My Wife's Clothes.
"MacDiarmid." Wheesht, wheesht, my foolish
hert.
Mackenzie, K. Shall then another do what I
have done.
MacLeish. Voyage to the Moon.
Madan. Abelard to Eloisa.
Mahon. Achill.
Majumdar, B. Time Wins.
Mallarmé. Breeze from the Sea.
Marutanilanakanar. What Her Girl Friend Said
to her.
Matthews, W. Mood Indigo.

McGrath, T. Epitaph: "Again, traveller, you
have come a long way led by that star."
Meleager. Epigram: "At 12 o'clock in the
afternoon."
Sounds of love are needles in my ears, The.
Melville, H. Since as in night's deck-watch ye
show.
Meredith, G. He found her by the ocean's
moaning verge.
Love in the Valley.
Message from her set his brain aflame, A.
Their sense is with their senses all mixed in.
This was the woman; what now of the man?
Merrill, J. Vision of the Garden, A.
Mew. Farmer's Bride, The.
Mirabai. All I Was Doing Was Breathing.
Mitchell, S. Of Earthly Love.
Moon, T. Song for Grass Leaf.
Moraes, D. Snow on a Mountain.
Morgan, V. Within the Greenhouse Effect.
Mörike. Beauty Rohtraut.
Mother Goose. Bobby Shaftoe's [or Shafto's]
gone to sea.
Motoyoshi Prince. I am unhappy. / I do not
care what happens.
Murillo. Angel in the Deluge.
Muruvalar. What She Said.
Nannakaiyar. What She Said ("When he
said").
Neruda. Girl lithe and tawny, the sun that
forms.
Nguyễn Bính. Two Hearts.
Nguyễn Đình Thi. Yearning.
Ni Dhomhnaill. Marvellous Grass.
Nukada. Longing for you.
Olds, S. Monarchs.
Olson, C. As the dead prey upon us.
O'Rahilly. Brightness of brightness lonely met
me where I wandered.
Ou-yang Hsiu. Song of "Night After Night,"
A.
Ovid. 1.3.
Pace, R. This Is English and I Am Speaking
It No Matter What.
P'an Yüeh. Thinking of My Wife.
Paranar. What She Said to Her Girl Friend
("On the tall hill").
Partridge, F. My Days Go On.
Patil. Freak.
Paulin. Lyric Afterwards, A.
Paulus Silentiarius. And now you comb and
braid your hair.
Pearse, P. Renunciation.
Petrarch. She used to let her golden hair fly
free.
Peyanar. What He Said ("As wild oxen
bellowed").
What He Said ("Red earth, The").
Piatt, S. In Her Prison.
Piercy. Raisin Pumpernickel.
Po Chü-i. How can the tide of the river be
compared to your love?
Poe. To One in Paradise.
Pommy-Vega. Ah certainty of love in the
hand.
Here before the sunrise blue and in this
solitude.
Porter, C. Night and Day.
Pound, E. O Atthis.
River-Merchant's Wife: A Letter, The.
Propertius. Me happy, night, night full of
brightness.
Quasimodo. Antico Inverno.
Ralegh, W. Like to a hermit[e] poor[e][,] in
place obscure.
Ravikovitch. Tirzah and the Wide World.
Rexroth, K. Every morning, I / Wake alone,
dreaming my.
I pass the day tense, day-.
I sit at my desk.
I wish I could be.
Rich, A. Loser, The.
Paula Becker to Clara Westhoff.
Since we're not young, weeks have to do
time.
Riddell, E. Letter, The.
Rihaku. River-Merchant's Wife: A Letter, The.

Rilke. Not wooing, no longer shall wooing,
voice that has outgrown it,.
Robinson, E. Luke Havergal.
Rollings. Light Years and the Love Lost in
the Oleanders.
Rossetti, C. Echo from Willow-Wood, An.
Hoping Against Hope.
Twilight Night.
Rotella, A. Barefoot through clover.
Rucker. Swallows of Capistrano, The.
Rudaki. Quatrain: "With you away—despair!"
Rukeyser, M. Believing in those inexorable
laws.
Song: "World is full of loss; bring, wind, my
love, The."
Rumi. Human shape is a ghost, The.
Strange Business.
Sa Nguyễn. Dress of Hà-Đông silk, The.
Sachs, N. But Perhaps [God needs the
longing, wherever else should it dwell].
Sappho. Hymn to Venus, An.
I longed to.
Moon has veil'd her Silver Light, The.
Some say nothing on earth excels in beauty.
Scève. Délie.
Schuyler, J. Sunday.
Scott, A. To luve unluvit it is ane pane.
Scott, W. Hour with thee! When earliest day,
An.
Seay. It All Comes Together Outside the
Restroom in Hogansville.
Selman, R. I befriended Mike with the good
hash pipe.
Shakespeare, W. Sonnet 20.
Sonnet 57.
Shapiro, K. Sickness of Adam, The.
Shin, T. Shoe, A.
Shizuka. How I long for the man who
climbed Mt. Yoshino.
"Shu Ting." Longing.
Sidney, P. Sonnet 89: "Now that of absence
the most irksome night."
Skelton, J. Knowledge, Acquaintance.
Smith, C. Stanzas: "Ah! think'st thou, Laura,
then, that wealth."
Smith, I. In the Cafe.
Smith, M. Last Dance, The.
Smith, S. In the Night.
Snyder, G. Four Poems for Robin.
So Chong-Ju. Nightingale Path, The.
Stevenson, R. To Mrs. Will H. Low.
Stewardess of the Empress Kōka. For the sake
of a night.
Stickney, T. As a sad man, when evenings
grayer grow.
Surrey. If care do cause men cry, why do not
I complain.
Swift, J. To Stella.
T'ao Ch'ien. Motionless Clouds.
Teasdale. Flight, The.
Sleepless.
Theocritus. O NICIAS, there is no other remedy
for love.
Thicknesse. Siena.
Thomas, L. Cameo in Sudden Light.
Ts'ao Chih. Forsaken Wife, The.
Ts'ao P'i. Deep and boundless, the long
autumn night.
Tsvetayeva. Poem of the End, The.
Tu Mu. Gate Tower of Ch'i-an City, The.
Tuckerman, F. Dark fens of cedar; hemlock-
branches gray.
Last night I dreamed we parted once again.
Turner, D. Love.
Unknown. Alone, I live alone.
Distant and faint the Herd-Boy Star.
Go hert, hurt with adversité.
Hiraeth.
If I were but a bird.
Jinny.
Lass A-Laundering.
Loon upon the Lake, The.
Love me little, love me long!
Lover in Winter Plaineth for the Spring, The.
Mountain Spirit, The.
Sad Song.
Swift Is That Falcon.

Tru'o'ng Chi, the Lovelorn Boatman.
When ice on the pond is three feet thick.
Wife's Complaint, The.
Wolde God that it were so.
Unknown, at. to John Donne. Aubade.
Updike. Report of Health.
Valéry. Footsteps, The.
Vidyapati. Sad Love.
Võ Phiến. Where Have They Gone?
Walton, E. In Recompense.
Wang Kuo-wei. Tune: "Butterflies Lingering over Flowers."
Wang Ts'an. Land of the Ching tribes is not my home, The.
Wang Wei. Farms at Wei River, The.
Webster, A. There's one I miss. A little questioning maid.
Wei Ying-wu. To Send to Li Tan and Yüan Hsi.
Wen T'ing-yün. Tune: Dreaming of the South.
Whitman, W. I heard you solemn-sweet pipes of the organ as last Sunday morn I pass'd the church.
O you whom I often and silently come where you are that I may be with you.
Wickham. Divorce.
Williams, C. Gas Station, The.
Willis, N. Confessional, The.
Winslow, P. O god of spring forgive me.
Wordsworth, W. With Ships the sea was sprinkled far and nigh.
Wright, C. October.
Wright, F. Journey, The.
Wright, J. Complaint.
For the Marsh's Birthday.
Poems to a Brown Cricket.
To the Muse.
Wroth. From Pamphilia to Amphilanthus.
Sonnet 26: "Deare cherish this, and with it[t] my soules will."
Wyatt, T. Absence! Absenting causeth me to complain.
As power and wit will me assist.
Comfort thyself, my wo[e]ful heart.
For want of [*or* I] will in woe I plain.
Heart oppressed [*or* oppress'd] with desperate thought.
If fancy [*or* fansy] would favour.
It may be good like it who list.
Knot which first my heart did strain, The.
Lover Rejoiceth the Enjoying of His Love, The.
Such hap as I am happed in.
Sufficed not, madame, that you did tear.
There was never nothing more me pained [*or* payned].
Though this the [*or* thy] port and I thy servant true.
What death is worse than this?
Xuân Diệu. To love is to die a little in the heart.
Xuân Quỳnh. Waves.
Zeidner. Bach.

Longshoremen
Heaney, S. Docker.

Lookout Mountain, Battle of (1863)
Hayden, R. On Lookout Mountain.

Loons
Carruth, H. Loon on Forrester's Pond, The.
Eberhart, R. Loon Call, A.
Unknown. Loon upon the Lake, The.

Lorelei
Heine. Lorelei.

Los Angeles, California
Allen, P. Los Angeles, 1980.
Greger. Piranesi in L.A.
Hongo. Yellow Light.
Jarman, M. Los Angeles.
Jarrell. Thinking of the Lost World.
Muske. Little L.A. Villanelle.
Rivers, C. Watts.
Rodriguez, L. Always Running.
We never stopped crossing borders.
Trinidad. C'est Plus Qu'en Crime, C'est une Faute.
Hockney: Blue Pool.
Troupe. Leaving Los Angeles.

Waugh, E. They told me, Francis Hinsley, they told me you were hung.
See also **Hollywood, California**

Loss
Adamovich. There was...what?—Pale sunsets, wide expanses.
"Akhmatova." Your white house and tranquil garden, I shall leave.
Allen, D. Lost Love.
Alterman. Red Ridinghood.
Antin. Definitions for Mendy.
Antipater of Sidon. Already prepared in the golden chamber.
Never again, Orpheus.
Ruins of Corinth, The.
Archilochus. Shield, The.
Aridjis. Epitaph for a Poet.
Atwood. At first I was given centuries.
Ayton. Sonnet: on Loss.
Bachmann. Kind of Loss, A.
Barr, B. Tremendous Mood Swings.
Bartošová. And That Is Why. . . .
Bell, M. Gemwood.
Benson, S. Now I Have Nothing[. Even the joy of loss].
Berg, S. To My Friends.
Berrigan, T. Red Shift.
Berryman. Ball Poem, The.
Sonnet 115: "As usual I'm up before the sun."
Bishop, E. One Art.
Blok. At first she turned the whole thing to a joke.
Girl was singing in the choir with fervor, A.
On the Railway.
Blokh. Random talk has blown in.
Boe, M. Sunday Afternoon at the State Hospital.
Bogan, L. After the Persian.
Brontë, A. Reminiscence, A.
Brooks, G. Appendix to the Anniad.
Browne, M. Talk to Me, Baby.
Browning, E. Sonnet: "My letters! all dead paper, mute and white."
Year's Spinning, A.
Browning, R. Any Wife to Any Husband.
In a Year.
Lost Leader, The.
Lost Mistress, The.
Waring.
Youth and Art.
Burns, R. Lovely lass o' Inverness, The.
Song: "Ae fond kiss, and then we sever."
Byron, G. Childe Harold's Pilgrimage Canto III.
So we'll go no more a-roving.
Caicedo. Nochebuena.
Canning, J. Indian Gone!, The.
Carew, T. Deposition from Love, A.
Catullus. Carmen 58 ("My Lesbia, Caelius, that same Lesbia").
Carmen 65 ("Grief reached across the world to get me").
Death of Lesbia's Bird, The.
Love and Death.
On the Burial of His Brother.
Cavafy. In Despair.
Chế Lan Viên. Waning Night, The.
Chernoff. Lost and Found.
"Chrystos." Night Visits.
Ciardi. On Learning to Adjust to Things.
Clare, J. To Elia (unsigned).
Cofer. Fever.
Coleridge, H. She was a queen of noble Nature's crowning.
Coleridge, S. Glycine's Song.
Cooper, J. Long, Disconsolate Lines.
Crane, H. Above the fresh ruffles of the surf.
Sad Indian, The.
Stark Major.
Creeley. To and / back and forth.
Cronin, J. Group Photo from Pretoria Local on the Occasion of a Fourth Anniversary (Never Taken).
Csoori. Everyday History.
My Masters.
Postponed Nightmare.

Cullen, C. Wind Bloweth Where It Listeth, The.
Cummings, E. In heavenly realms of hellas dwelt.
Noster was a ship of swank, The.
When my sensational moments are no more.
When what hugs stopping earth than silent is.
Why did you go.
Damagetus. Epitaph of a Sailor.
Dame. Lilith.
Daniel, Y. To My Friends.
Dante Alighieri. All ye that pass along Love's trodden way.
Beyond the sphere which spreads to widest space.
Darley. Serenade of a Loyal Martyr.
To Helene.
De la Mare. Fare Well.
Reserved.
Deane, S. Fording the River.
Delanty. Gift, The.
Dickey, J. Leap, The.
Dickey, W. Shortest Day, The.
Dickinson, E. Except the Heaven had come so near.
Her sweet Weight on my Heart a Night.
Loss of something ever felt I, A.
Now I knew I lost her.
We miss a Kinsman more.
You love me—you are sure.
Dioscorides. Zephyr, kindliest of winds.
Donne. Broken Heart, The.
Computation, The.
To Mr I. L ("Blessed [*or* Blesst] are your north parts, for all this long time").
Dove, R. Blown apart by loss, she let herself go.
Drummond, W. To His Lute.
Dufferin. Countess of Dufferin, The.
Dunn, S. Vanishings, The.
"Dylan." Boots of Spanish Leather.
Eliot, T. Eyes that last I saw in tears.
Hollow Men, The.
Journey of the Magi.
Emerson, R. Give all to love;.
"Ephelia." First Farewell to J.G G.
Euripides. Agamemnon struggles to avert the sacrifice of his daughter Iphigeneia].
Ilion, o my city.
Fenton, J. Wind.
"Field." My lady has a lovely rite.
Fletcher, J. Fletcher's Lament for his Friend.
Fuller, R. Translation.
Garrigue. After Reading "The Country of the Pointed Firs."
Gautier. Her Toys.
Gergely. Crazed Man in Concentration Camp.
Gibson, W. Question, The.
Ginsberg, A. Café in Warsaw.
Elegy for Neal Cassady.
Gioseffi. Some Slippery Afternoon.
Glatstein. Lost.
Godfrey. Where the Weather Suits My Clothes.
Goldberg, B. Possibilities, The.
Gouri. Holiday's End.
Graham, J. What the End Is For.
Graves, R. Lost Love.
Guiterman. Little Lost Pup.
Gumilyov. Memory.
Gunn, T. Autobiography.
Butcher's Son, The.
Hacker, M. Against Silence.
Handy, W. Joe Turner Blues.
Hardy, T. I said to Love.
Hass, R. Meditation at Lagunitas.
Hayden, R. Road in Kentucky, A.
Hecht, A. Old Malediction, An.
Hemans. Lost Pleiad, The.
Herrick. Upon the Loss[e] of His Mistresses.
Vine, The.
Hewitt, J. King's Horses, The.
Ho, H. Snowfall on the Seas.
Ho Xuan Huong. Elegy for the Prefect of Vĩnh-tu'ờ'ng.
Hogan, L. Lost Girls, The.
Hongo. Hilo: First Night Back.

Housman, A. Land of Lost Content, The.
Howard, R. Tremendous Trifles.
Howe, J. My Last Dance.
Hsiang Chi. Song of Kai-hsia.
Hsin Ch'i-chi. Tune: "Full River Red."
Hsü Tsai-ssu. Tune: "Clear River, a
    Prelude"—Lovesickness.
Hughes, L. Homecoming.
    Lament over Love.
    Young Gal's Blues.
Hugo, V. At dawn tomorrow, time of
    whitening fields.
Hwang, T. Small Love Song, A.
Ingelow. Dappled sky, a world of meadows,
    A.
Jackson, L. Summary for Alastor.
Jarrell. Second Air Force.
    Truth, The.
Jonson, B. Execration upon Vulcan, An.
    To the World [A Farewell for a Gentlewoman,
    Virtuous and Noble].
    Why I Write Not of Love.
Justice, D. In Bertram's Garden.
Keats. In drear-nighted December.
Keller, D. Friends, Outside, Night.
Kim, N. Winter Sea, The.
Kim, S. Gift of Love.
Kim, T. When the river breaks loose.
Kim, Y. Elegy: "Because of you I have
    lived."
King, H. Summer Lost.
King, H. Change, The.
    Forfeiture, The.
Kipling, R. Bridegroom, The.
    For to Admire.
    Gertrude's Prayer.
    Lovers' Litany, The.
    Mesopotamia.
    Widower, The.
Kirsanov. ...Back then I cut off a lock.
Knight, E. Feeling Fucked/Up Up.
Koch, K. To Marina.
"Korzhavin." How difficult to live without
    you!
Kovner. Poem: Alte Zachen.
    Scientists Are Mistaken, The.
Kumin, M. How It Is.
Kushner, A. Remembering Love.
Lamb, C. Hester.
    Old Familiar Faces, The.
Landor, W. Alas! 'tis very sad to hear.
    Rose Aylmer.
Larkin, P. No Road.
    So through that unripe day you bore your
    head.
Lasker-Schüler. To Senna Hoy.
Lawrence, D. Last Words to Miriam.
    On the Balcony.
Lear, E. Calico Pie.
Lee, L. Eating Alone.
Lehman. Arrival at Kennedy.
    Moment of Truth, The.
Levine, P. Buying and Selling.
Levy, A. On the Threshold.
Lewis, A. Song (On Seeing Dead Bodies
    Floating Off the Cape).
Li Po. Climbing Phoenix Terrace at Chin-ling.
    Moon over Mountain Pass.
Li Shang-yin. Lamp glows deep in the mica
    screen.
    Ma-wei.
Liu Yu Hsi. Coming Again to Heng-yang, I
    Mourn for Liu Tsung-yüan.
Long, R. What Happens.
Longfellow, H. Cross of Snow, The.
    Hawthorne.
Lowell, A. Patterns.
"Lu Hsün." Lamenting Yang Ch'uan.
Lum. Urban Love Songs.
Lysohorsky. 22.6.1941.
Macaulay, T. Jacobite's Epitaph, A.
Makarov. Life lasts the course of a kiss.
Mataka. Next Door.
McCarthy, T. Dying Synagogue at South
    Terrace, The.
McGrath, T. End of the Line, The.
Meleager. Goat-foot Pan has quit his flocks.

Lost! Cupid!/ One lost Cupid!
    Love's night and a lamp.
    Pour this wine.
Meng Chiao. Nipping chill, the frost killed
    spring.
Meredith, G. I am to follow her. There is
    much grace.
    It chanced his lips did meet her forehead cool.
    Love Dies.
    Love's Grave.
    Message from her set his brain aflame, A.
    This was the woman; what now of the man?
    'Tis Christmas weather, and a country house.
Meynell, A. Maternity.
Mihalic. Autumn.
    Elegy: "From the old settlements only the
    writings."
Millay, E. If I should learn, in some quite
    casual way.
    What lips my lips have kissed, and where, and
    why.
Miller, V. Remembering Aunt Helen.
Milton. Mulciber.
Moffat. In This New Year.
Moffi. Putting an End to the War Stories.
Moore, T. Journey Onwards, The.
    Oft in the stilly night.
Morgan, R. Damn you, lady, get out of my
    blood for good.
Mother Goose. Lucy Locket lost her pocket.
Moulton. Shall I complain because the feast is
    o'er.
Mura. To H.N.
Neruda. Past.
    Poem.
Nesbit, E. Among His Books.
Ng Shao. New Wife, The.
Olds, S. Cambridge Elegy.
Oliver, M. In Blackwater Woods.
Pacheco, J. Boundaries.
Paddock. Silos, The.
Park, M. Lowering the Coffin.
Philips, K. To the Queen of Inconstancy,
    Regina Collier, in Antwerp.
Phillips, A. Photograph & Story in The Press:
    The Mother Whose Children Burned to
    Death.
Po Chü-i. Losing a Slave-Girl.
Poe. Happiest day—the happiest hour, The.
    Sleeper, The.
    To One in Paradise.
    Valley of Unrest, The.
Popa. Be Seeing You.
Prokofiev. Betrothed, The.
Publius Papinius Statius. And so Death took
    him. Yet be comforted.
Pushkin. I loved you.
Rabbitt. Tortoise.
Ralegh, W. Poem Entreating of Sorrow, A.
Ransom, J. Dead Boy.
Raworth. Nothing.
Reese, L. Singer, The.
Rexroth, K. Half in a dream.
    Once I shone afar like a.
    This flesh you have loved.
Rich, A. Loser, The.
    Of simple choice they are the villagers; their
    clothes come.
    Old blanket. The crumbs of rubbed wool
    turning up, The.
Roethke. Visitant, The.
Rogers, D. Desert.
Rossetti, C. Cousin Kate.
    Echo.
    Grown and Flown.
    Youth gone, and beauty gone if ever there.
Rucker. Swallow Creek.
Rukeyser, M. Song: "World is full of loss;
    bring, wind, my love, The."
    Waiting for Icarus.
Ryan, G. Too Bad.
Salaam. Our World Is Less Full Now That
    Mr. Fuller Is Gone.
Sanchez, S. Father and Daughter.
Sappho. Bridal Songs: "Happy bridegroom! /
    Now your wedding has come true."
Sassoon. Lamentations.

Seay. Options.
"Severyanin." Same Old Way, The.
Seward. Invocation, To the Genius of Slumber
    Written Oct. 1787.
Sexton. Wedding Night, The.
Shakespeare, W. I had been happy, if the
    general camp.
    Sonnet 42.
    Sonnet 49.
    Sonnet 86.
    Sonnet 87.
    Sonnet 90.
    Sonnet 134.
Shange. I Sat Up One Night.
Shapiro, K. Haircut.
    Leg, The.
Shelley, M. To the air of 'My Phillida, adieu,
    love!'.
Shelley, P. On a Faded Violet.
Shen Yüeh. Song of Woe.
Sheridan, R. Lines by a Lady on the Loss of
    her Trunk.
Shin, T. Shoe, A.
Sidney, P. Double Sestine [or Sestina].
    Sonnet 18: "With what sharp checks I in
    myself am shent."
Simmons, J. Long Way After Ronsard, A.
Simms, W. Lost Pleiad, The.
Smith, I. Clearances, The.
So Chong-Ju. Nightingale Path, The.
Soldati. Surroundings.
Soloukhin. To Make Birds Sing.
Sorrentino. Good Night!
Southwick. Horse on the Wall.
Soyinka. He escape the lynch days. He
    survives.
Spender, S. Double Shame, The.
Staff. Kingdom.
Stafford, W. Farm on the Great Plains, The.
Stanley, T. Love Deposed.
Stern, G. Expulsion, The.
    Kissing Stieglitz Goodbye.
Storey. Prayer for Broken Little Families, A.
Stricker. Other Side, The.
Swirszczynska. He Is Gone.
Tennyson, A. 27.
    Hark! the dogs howl! the sleetwinds blow.
    If Only.
Terapiano. Ships that sail forth.
Thomas, E. Triple League to Mrs Susan Dove,
    The.
Thomas, L. Instructions for Your New Osiris.
Thoreau. Brother where dost thou dwell?
Tikhonov. Gulliver Plays Cards.
Ts'ui Hao. By the City Gate.
Tu Fu. Recruiting Officer of Shih-hao.
Tu Mu. At Clear Brook in Ch'ih-chou.
Tymnes. Maltese Dog, A.
Unknown. Adieu, the years are a broken song.
    Alphabet of Love, The.
    Chant from the Iroquois Book of Rites.
    Dubbement dere of down and dales, The.
    I can no longer untangle my hair.
    Last Mass in Hagia Sophia, The.
    Lost, yesterday, somewhere.
    My Little Maid.
    On Prince Frederick.
    TEHKARIHHOKEN! / Continue to listen!
Urin. Oh, Maika in a maika, there's the smell
    of summer.
Verlaine. Nevermore.
Whitman, W. O Captain! my Captain! our
    fearful trip is done.
    Spring.
    Yonnondio.
Whittier. Farewell, The: "Gone, gone,—sold
    and gone."
Wilcox, E. Friendship After Love.
    One of Us Two.
Wilde, O. Requiescat.
Williams, P. Passing Through.
Williams, W. Are the desolate, dark weeks.
    Hemmed-in Males.
Wordsworth, W. Complaint, A.
    Last of the Flock, The.
    Song: "She dwelt among the untrodden ways."

Surprised by Joy—impatient as the Wind.
Written in London, September, 1802.
Wright, C. Scratch Music.
Wright, F. Alcohol.
Joseph Come Back as the Dusk.
Wright, J. Having Lost My Sons, I Confront the Wreckage of the Moon: Christmas, 1960.
Wroth. Song: "I, that ame of all most crost."
Sonnet 29: "Fly hence O! joy noe longer heere abide."
Wu of Han. Li Fu-Jên.
Wyatt, T. Help[e] me to seek [or seke] for I lost it there.
My love took scorn my service to retain.
Where shall I have at mine own will.
Yeats. Crazy Jane Reproved.
Lover Mourns for the Loss of Love, The.
Never give all the heart, for love.
Yesenin. Bitch, The.
Flowers say goodbye to me, The.
I do not regret, complain, or weep.
Years of my youth, years of dissipation.
You feel no love or pity for me.
Yevtushenko. Loss.
New York Elegy.
Yüan Chen. Mourning My Son.
Zabolotsky. Last Love.
Somewhere in a field near Magadan.
Zealand. Passion at the Chat 'n Chew Diner.
Zenmaro. Tanka: "No news of him."

Lot (Bible)
"Akhmatova." Lot's Wife.
Goldbarth. Lot's Wife.
Helwig. Lot.
Hope, A. Lot and His Daughters I.
Lot and His Daughters II.
Housman, A. Half-way, for one commandment broken.
Kaufman, S. His Wife.
Nemerov. Lot Later.
Ransom, C. Lot's Wife.

Lotus
Bu-er. Cut brambles long enough.
Chu Ch'ing-yü. Gathering Lotus.
Ded. Coursing in emptiness.
Hsü Wei. Fifth day of the fifth month.
Lotus.
Ishikawa Takuboku. Tanka: "Like a white lotus."
Kambala. KYE HO! Wonderful!
Kunio. Tanka: "On the cloudy water."
Mo Shih-lung. Gathering Lotus with Singing Girls.
Tao-chi. Inscribed on My Ink Landscape Painting.
Ts'ao P'i. Lotus Lake.
Wang Shih-chieng. Occasional Poem: Upon Seeing Lotuses Bloom in a Vase.
Yang Wei-chen. Song of a Dream Journey over the Vast Sea.
Yosano. Tanka: "Earth looks, The."

Louisiana
Dent. Return to English Turn.
Komunyakaa. Landscape for the Disappeared.
Kyei. African in Louisiana.
Whitman, W. I saw in Louisiana a live-oak growing.

Love. See **Affection; Companionship and Companions; Courtship; Dating; Desire; Erotic Love; Lust; Sex; Sexuality**

Lovebirds
Hippolyte. Revo Lyric.
Hood, T. Ballad: Time of Roses.
Rankin, P. Two Lovers on Bridge in Winter.
Tomlinson, C. In the Borghese Gardens.
Unknown. Cock Robin got up early.
Unknown, at. to John Donne. Aubade.
Wright, J. For the Marsh's Birthday.

Lovelace, Richard
Marvell. To His Noble Friend, Mr Richard Lovelace, upon His Poems.

Lowell, Amy
Cullen, C. For Amy Lowell.
Cummings, E. Slightly before the middle of Congressman Pudd.
Ridge, L. Amy Lowell.

Lowell, James Russell
Lowell, J. Lowell.

Lowell, Robert
Bishop, E. North Haven.

Lowry, Malcolm
Lowry, M. Epitaph: "Malcolm Lowry."

Loyalty
Browning, E. Sonnet: "I never gave a lock of hair away."
Sonnet: "My poet, thou canst touch on all the notes."
Browning, R. Light Woman, A.
Burns, R. O [or Oh] wert thou in the cauld blast.
Red, Red Rose, A.
Creeley. She Went to Stay.
Hardy, T. Broken Appointment, A.
Hewitt, J. If I had given you that love and care.
Housman, A. As through the wild green hills of Wyre.
Kim, S. Azaleas, The.
Kim, T. Banana Plant, The.
My mind is a lake.
Kipling, R. Gunga Din.
Ulster.
Kuzmin. If they say: "you must suffer both torture and burning"—.
Lovelace, R. To Lucasta[, from Prison].
Melville, H. Enthusiast, The.
Nguyễn Bỉnh Khiêm. Time and again you've seen them win or lose.
Nguyễn Đình Chiểu. Loyal Horse, The.
Nguyễn Khuyến. Widow's Reply to a Matchmaker, The.
Peele. Farewell to Arms, A.
Ralegh, W. Advice, The.
Shin, S. If you call / I will come to you.
Sidney, P. Sonnet 54: "Because I breathe not love to every one."
Smith, C. Stanzas: "Ah! think'st thou, Laura, then, that wealth."
Su Tung-p'o. Black Muzzle, south sea dog.
Unknown. Constant Mouse, The.
Wroth. Sonnet 26: "Deare cherish this, and with it[t] my soules will."

Luanda, Angola
Wendel. We Shall Return, Luanda.

Luck
Angelou. On Aging.
Cao Bá Quát. Good luck, bad luck are both the Maker's works.
Ewing, J. Little Kings and Queens of the May.
Fitzgerald, R. Favour.
Gibson, W. Wishing-Well, The.
Glazkov. I strolled around the zoo.
Googe. Of Money.
Hay, J. Good Luck and Bad ("Good luck is the gayest of all gay girls").
Heath-Stubbs. Unpredicted, The.
Herrick. Coming of Good Luck, The.
Hewitt, J. Local Poet, A.
Howes, B. Rune for C, A.
Hughes, L. Bad Luck Card.
Luck.
Jackson, L. Lullaby, The.
Rossetti, C. Queen of Hearts, The.
Södergran. Pain.
Virgil. MelibŒus. O fortunate old man!
Wong, J. Good Luck Gold.
Wyatt, T. He is not de[a]d that sometime [or somtyme] hath a fall.

See also **Chance; Fate; Fortune; Chance**

Lucretius
Tennyson, A. Lucretius.

Luddites
Harrison, T. On Not Being Milton.

Lullabies
Auden. Lullaby: "Lay your sleeping head, my love."
Bennett, G. Secret.
Bishop, E. Lullaby for the Cat.
Blake, W. Cradle Song, A: "Sweet dreams form a shade."
Breytenbach. Lullaby.

Bumstead. Summer Lullaby, A.
Causley. Mary's Song.
Charles I, King of England. On a Quiet Conscience.
Coleridge, S. O sleep, my babe, hear not the rippling wave.
Colum, P. Cradle Song,A: "O men from the fields!"
Cox, P. Mouse's Lullaby, The.
Davis, D. Aunt Chloe's Lullaby.
Dekker, T. et al. Cradle Song, A: "Golden slumbers kiss your eyes."
Field, E. Norse Lullaby.
Wynken, Blynken and Nod one night.
Fumi Saito. Turbid current.
Gascoigne. Lullaby [or Lullabie] of a Lover, The.
Herrick. Upon a child.
Jacobsen, J. Primer, The.
Marais. Radio Cradle-song.
Mother Goose. Bye, baby bunting.
Hush-a-bye, baby[, on the tree-top].
Rock-a-bye, baby, thy cradle is green.
Prelutsky. Mother Goblin's Lullaby.
Rivner. Lullaby: "Nocturnal, my panther, has eyes that spark, The."
Sidney, P. Sleep, baby mine, Desire; nurse Beauty singeth.
Stephens, H. Night-herding Song[, A].
Tennyson, A. Lullaby: "Sweet and low, sweet and low."
Minnie and Winnie.
Unknown. All the Pretty Little Horses.
Coventry Carol.
Evening.
Give Thanks.
Lullaby: "My little baby sleeps, the little birds sleep."
Lullaby: "Puva, puva, puva."
Lullaby: "Sleep, baby, sleep."
Lullaby: "Someone would like to have you for her child."
Sleep, baby, sleep, / Our cottage vale is deep.
Wordsworth, D. Cottager to Her Infant, (By My Sister), The.
Yondo. Lullaby.

See also **Cradle Song in Title and First Line Index**

Lumbering and Lumbermen
Abbey, H. What do we plant when we plant the tree?
Calhoun, J. Peter Amberley.
Drummond, W. Log Jam, The.
Frost, R. In winter in the woods alone.
Gorbovsky. Woodcutting.
Kinnell. Man Splitting Wood in the Daybreak, The.
Morris, G. Woodman, spare that tree!
Nelson, C. How We Make Lumber Out of Trees.
Rosen, M. This morning my father looks out of the window, rubs his nose.
Scott, D. At the Cedars.
Snyder, G. Getting in the Wood.
Unknown. Canada-I-O ("There was a gallant lady all in her tender youth").
Farmer and the Shanty Boy, The.
Johnny Carroll's Camp.
Little Brown Bulls, The.
Lumberman's Alphabet, The.
Michigan-I-O.
Once More a-Lumbering Go.
Roving Shanty Boy, The.
Shanty Boys and the Pine, The.
Turner's Camp on the Chippewa.
Wild Mustard River, The.
Wagoner, D. Elegy for a Forest Clear-Cut by the Weyerhaeuser Company.
To a Farmer Who Hung Five Hawks on His Barbed Wire.

Lunch
Hughes, L. Jim Crow Car.
Ignatow, D. Lunchtime.
Kitahara Hakushū. Tanka: "After lunch."
O'Hara, F. Step Away from Them, A.
Po Chü-i. After Eating.
Schimelpfenig. Geography of Lunch, A.

Lungs
Berry, D. Sun goes.

Lungworms
Fuller, R. Autobiography of a Lungworm.

Lust
Adaios of Macedon. If you see someone beautiful / hammer it out right then.
Agathias. It is not wine that makes me reel / Not juice of grape I crave.
Manifesto.
Antipater of Sidon. This is Anacreon's grave. Here lie.
Antiphilus. Even then I said.
Argentarius. Here's to Lysidice: pour in ten ladles, boy.
Asclepiades. Leave the rags, you tiny lusts.
Night long and wintry / the Pleiades half set.
Nikarete's face, sweetly moistened.
To you, Kypris, Lysidike.
Auden. Love Feast, The.
Automedon. That Asiatic striptease girl / who goes in for those.
Baraka. New World, The.
Baudelaire. Giantess, The.
Behn, A. To Alexis in Answer to his Poem against Fruition.
Berryman. Dream Song 4.
Betjeman. Late-Flowering Lust.
Senex.
Blackburn, P. Once-over, The.
Slogan, The.
Brutus. Simple lust is all my woe, A.
Burns, R. Charlie He's My Darling.
Calbert. Woman Who Loved Things, The.
Catullus. Less pub than brothel, and you, the regulars.
Clare, J. Song—Molly Magee.
Clarke, C. Kittatinny Tunnel in that holy place you let me hit.
Clifton, L. There Is a Girl Inside.
Crane, H. National Winter Garden.
Crinagoras. Turn on your left side, back to your right again.
Cummings, E. God pity me whom (god distinctly has).
Twentyseven bums give a prostitute the once.
Da Ponte. Little lady, you are not going to like this.
Dickinson, E. Wild Nights—Wild Nights!
Dobyns. Desire.
Drayton. To His Coy Love, A Canzonet.
Drummond, W. For a Lady's Summons of Non-Entry.
Dryden, J. Song: "SYLVIA the fair, in the bloom of fifteen."
Emanuel, L. Of Your Father's Indiscretions and the Train to California.
Erucius of Cyzicus. How massively, with what a fine stiff rise.
Euripides. Chorus sing of escape, The.
Flaccus. Flaccus gave me, the silver lamp.
Fraser, K. Your sky against my starfish I know how big.
Frym. Yield, The.
García Lorca. Unfaithful Wife, The.
Garnett, R. Dealing Scraps.
Giacosa et al. And first, a sip of wine. It comes from Spain.
Goethe. Diary, The.
Graham, W. Letter VI.
Graves, R. Blue-Fly, The.
Down, wanton, down! Have you no shame.
Succubus, The.
Griffin, P. To His Importunate Mistress.
Gunn, T. Modes of Pleasure.
Habington. Against Them Who Lay Unchastity to the Sex of Women.
Hacker, M. Bloomingdale's.
Future Conditional.
Hatton, R. Epithalamium: "Hymen hath together tied."
Herrick. Julia's Petticoat.
Poet Loves a Mistress, but Not to Marry, The.
Vine, The.
Vision, The.
Hill, S. Ram, The.
Holan. Meeting in a Lift.

Horace. 2.8.
Irenaeus Referendarius. Eyes filled with speaking fire.
Jackson, R. Circumstances.
Jennings, E. Thinking of Love.
Johnson, L. Dark Angel, with thine aching lust.
Jonson, B. Doing a filthy pleasure is, and short.
On Groin.
Jordan, J. Sunflower Sonnet Number One.
Kicknosway. Mr. Muscle-On.
Kim, Y. Labyrinth.
Kunitz, S. She wept, she railed, she spurned the meat.
Kwon, I. Apocalypse, The.
Lawrence, D. Passing Visit to Helen.
Leconte de Lisle, C. Palanquin, The.
Lifshin. Penthouse Playboy.
Marie-Madeleine. Vagabonds.
Marlowe. Elegies.
Martial. Ad Flaccum.
Either get out of the [my] house or conform to my tastes, woman.
May, E. To Barba.
Mayer, B. Work in Progress.
Meleager. All that he is . . . does . . . is attractive.
Epigram: "And now I, Meleager, am among them."
Epigram: "At 12 o'clock in the afternoon."
Epigram: "I was thirsty."
Eyes / flatterers of Soul.
'Tis Timarion.
Melville, H. After the Pleasure Party.
Miles, S. Hares, The.
Millay, E. I too beneath your moon, almighty Sex.
Miller, V. Dirge in Jazz Time.
Musset. To Julie.
Norse. I Would Not Recommend Love.
O'Hara, F. Poem: "I don't know as I get what D.H. Lawrence is driving at."
Olds, S. Greed and Aggression.
Sex without Love.
Ovid. Elegies 1.5.
Pace, R. Tingel-Tangel.
Paulus Silentiarius. Giving her mother's / zealous eye.
On a Bath-House in which Both Men and Women Bathe.
Petronius Arbiter. Fragment of Petronius, A.
Philodemus. Naked warmth of you is still, The.
Strumming and patter / the meaningful glances, The.
White violets again and lyre orchestras.
Pitter. But for Lust.
Plato. Alexis.
Plautus Titus Maccius. From Mostellaria.
Po Chü-i. On Being Sixty.
Porter, P. Now it's in all the novels, what's pornography to do?
Racine. My time's too short, your highness. It was I.
Read, S. Sic et Non.
Rich, A. Two Songs.
Ríos, A. Inquietude of a Particular Matter, The.
Robinson, E. John Evereldown.
Rochester, J. Ramble in St. James's Park, A.
Ronsard. Sonnet For Helen.
Rufinus. Leaving the Boys Behind.
Rhodope, Melite and Rhodoklea / contested.
Sanchez, S. Poem for My Father, A.
Shakespeare, W. Sonnet 129.
Sidney, P. Fourth Song: "Only joy, now here you are."
Skythinos. Epigram: "Great woe, fire & war come on me."
Southerne. Song: "Pursuing beauty, men descry."
Stevenson, A. Sous-Entendu.
Strato. Bath-house bench pinched Graphicus' bottom, The.
Epigram: "I am provoked."
Epigram: "I delight in the prime of a boy of twelve."
Epigram: "Long hair, endless curls trained by the devoted."
Give, and take the cash.
Meeting a lovely boy face to face.
To Kyris.
Suckling, J. Upon My Lady Carlisle's [or Carlile's] Walking in Hampton Court Garden.
Swinburne. Aholibah.
Taylor, J. Epigram: "Lusty wench as nimble as an eel, A."
Unknown. Constant Mouse, The.
Could I but become a crimson rose.
Hares on the Mountain.
I wish I were the wind, and you.
Standing beside you, fiddler.
Sthenelais.
Till the good morning star.
Tumult in the street!, A.
Villiers. Cabin-Boy, The.
Vivien. Chanson.
Walker, A. She said: "When I was with him."
Walsh, W. et al. Imperfect Enjoyment, The.
Song: "If she be not as kind as fair."
Waniek. Balance.
Whitman, W. Native moments—when you come upon me—ah you are here now.
Spontaneous me, Nature.
Wilbur. Loves of the Puppets.
Wither. Epigram: "Women, as some men say, unconstant be."
Wyatt, T. For want of [or I] will in woe I plain.
If thou wilt mighty be, flee from the rage.
So unwarely was never no man caught.
Such hap as I am happed in.
Y Vân Tủ'. Gaffer in Love, A.
See also **Erotic Love; Sex**

Lutes
Al-Harizi. Lute, The.
Campion, T. When to Her Lute Corinna [or Corinna] Sings.
Drummond, W. To His Lute.
Landon. Sappho's Song.
Mallarmé. Lace curtain self-destructs, A.
Master. Cat and the Lute, The.
Po Chü-i. Five-string[1], The.
Old Lute, The.
Song of the Lute.
"Shu Ting." Longing.
Suckling, J. Song to a Lute, A.
Waller, E. Of My Lady Isabella Playing on the Lute.
Wilde, O. Hélas!
Wyatt, T. At mo[o]st mischief.
Blame not my lute, for he must sound [or sssnd or Sownde].
Lover Complaineth the Unkindness of His Love, The.

Luther, Martin
Lee-Hamilton. Luther to a Bluebottle Fly.
Melville, H. Epilogue: "If Luther's day expand to Darwin's year."
Steele, T. Wartburg, 1521–22, The.

Lying. See Lies and Lying

Lynching
Brown, S. Sam Smiley.
Derricotte. Note on my Son's Face, A.
Dunbar-Nelson. April is on the way!
Dunbar, P. Haunted Oak, The.
Durem. I Know I'm Not Sufficiently Obscure.
Emanuel, J. Emmett Till.
Evans, M. I Am a Black Woman.
Ford, C. Plaint.
Freeman, C. I Saw Them Lynch.
Gilmore, M. Fourteen Men.
Harjo, J. Strange Fruit.
Hayden, R. Night, Death, Mississippi.
Hill, L. So Quietly.
Hughes, L. Song for a Dark Girl.
Jeffers, L. Tuskegee, Tuskegee!
Lorde. Afterimages.
McKay, C. Lynching, The.
Moorer. Eutawville Lynching, The.
Lynching.
Retribution.
Moss, T. Lynching, The.

Patchen. Nice Day for a Lynching.
Rosten. Black boy, the night hides you.
St. John, P. Lynching and Burning.
Scott, D. Epitaph: "They hanged him on a clement morning, swung."
Skeeter. Western Trail Cook, 1880.
Tate, A. Swimmers, The.
Toomer. Portrait in Georgia.
Toure. Frontier of rage that exists, The.
Whitehead, J. Local Man Goes to the Killing Ground, A.
Wright, R. Between the World and Me.

Lynx
Eaton, C. Lynx, The.
Unknown. Magic Song.

Lyonnesse, Cornwall
De la Mare. Sunk Lyonesse.
Hardy, T. When I set out for Lyonnesse.

Lysergic Acid (LSD)
Ginsberg, A. Wales Visitation.
Hollo. Discovery of LSD a True Story, The.
Tada. Universe of the Rose.
Waldman, A. Evangelie.

M

"MacDiarmid, Hugh" (Christopher Murray Grieve)
Morgan, E. To Hugh MacDiarmid.

McKay, Eleanora Fagan. *See* **"Holiday, Billie"**

McKinley, William
Unknown. Zolgotz.

MacLeish, Archibald
Sandburg, C. On a Flimmering Floom You Shall Ride.

Mac Liammóir, Micheál
Durcan. Micheál Mac Liammóir.

MacNeice, Louis
Auden. Cave of Making, The.
MacNeice. Autobiography.
Mahon. In Carrowdore Churchyard.

McPherson, James Birdseye
Melville, H. Dirge for McPherson, A.

Macbeth
Ushakov. Lady Macbeth.

Machines
Ammons. Needs.
"Antler." Machines waited for me, The.
Bacon, L. Horatian Variation.
Benét, S. Nightmare Number Three.
Blaga. Twentieth Century.
Frost, R. Egg and the Machine, The.
Glück, L. Daisies.
Kenney. Sawmill.
Kipling, R. McAndrew's Hymn.
Komunyakaa. Temples of Smoke.
Kunert. Realization.
Kunio. Tanka: "Hidden."
Kyger. It's been a long time.
Leib. Psalmodist.
Levertov. Those Who Want Out.
McOrlan. Weighing-machine, The.
Miyazawa Kenji. Tanka: "Left alone."
Moore, M. To a Steam Roller.
Mueller, I. Night Shift at the Fruit Cannery.
Mueller, M. Evolution: A Science Fiction.
Nash, O. Up from the Wheelbarrow.
Reed, H. Naming Of Parts.
Schultz, P. Answering Machine, The.
Snyder, G. Removing the Plate of the Pump on the Hydraulic System of the Backhoe.
Tomlinson, C. Crane, The.
Tóth, J. Murmuring.
Turner, C. Steam Threshing-Machine, The.
Unknown. John Henry was a lil [*or* little] baby.
When John Henry was a little babe.
Untermeyer, L. Portrait of a Machine.
Wilcox, E. Engine, The.
Wordsworth, W. Steamboats, Viaducts, and Railways.
Yoshimi. Tanka: "With headlights on."

Mad Song (genre)
"Carroll." Mad Gardener's Song, The.
Herrick. Mad Maid's Song, The.

Holcroft. Fool's Song.
Unknown. Tom o'Bedlam.

Madness
Allison, D. To the Bone.
Antin. List of the Delusions of the Insane / What They Are Afraid Of, A.
Ariosto. Orlando's Madness.
Armstrong, J. Madness.
Arnot. Woman at Home.
Baraka. Preface to a Twenty Volume Suicide Note.
Bayliss. Apocalypse and Resurrection.
Berrigan, T. Sonnet LXXVII: "It is 3:17 a.m. in New York city, yes, it is."
Berryman. I can't get him out of my mind, out of my mind.
I've found out why, that day, that suicide.
Bishop, E. Visits to St. Elizabeths.
Blake, W. Mad Song.
To Flaxman.
Boland, E. Glass King, The.
Breeze. Riddym Ravings (The Mad Woman's Poem).
Buddy. Callin Buddy / Bolden.
Carkesse. His Rule of Behaviour: If You Are Civil, I Am Sober.
On the Doctors' Telling Him that till He Left off Making Verses He Was Not Fit to be Discharged.
"Carroll." Mad Gardener's Song, The.
Carson, C. Asylum.
Chin. Cauldron.
Chukhonstev. Chaadayev on Basmannaya.
Clare, J. I am: yet what I am none cares or knows.
Crosby, H. Vision.
Cummings, E. Love is more thicker than forget.
De la Mare. Motley.
Dickinson, E. First Day's Night had come, The.
I think I was enchanted.
Much Madness is divinest Sense.
DiPalma. Pink maniac, A.
Doolittle, H. Gift, The.
Dowson. To One in Bedlam.
Drayton. As other men, so I myself do muse.
Eady. My Mother, If She Had Won Free Dance Lessons.
Fitzgerald, E. 74.
Floyd. Private Ian Godwin, U. S. M. C.
Galvin, P. Madwoman of Cork, The.
Garrett, G. Buzzard.
Ginsberg, A. Howl.
Gubanov. Palette of Grief.
Guest, B. Sassafras.
Hadewijch. Madness of love, The.
Hagedorn, J. Solea.
Herrick. Mad Maid's Song, The.
Hill, G. Mad are predators. Too often lately they harbour, The.
Howard, R. Nikolaus Mardruz to his Master Ferdinand, Count of Tyrol, 1565.
Hugo, R. What Thou Lovest Well Remains American.
Irving, M. Marching Still.
Jarrell. Seele im Raum.
Jeffers, R. Cassandra.
Jones, P. Song: "I have so little sorrow."
Justice, D. Counting the Mad.
On a Painting by Patient B of the Independence State Hospital for the Insane.
Kaufman, B. Would You Wear My Eyes?
Kenyon, J. Travel: After a Death.
Komunyakaa. Cage Walker, The.
Levertov. Mad Song.
Levine, P. On the Edge.
Levis. For Zbigniew Herbert, Summer, 1971, Los Angeles.
Lillard. Bushed.
Livingston, M. Why?
Lovelace, R. Cupid Far Gone.
McClure, M. May Morn.
McDonald, N. Hatters, The.
Melville, H. Berg, The.
Merry. Madness.

Mew. Farmer's Bride, The.
Ken.
Mirabai. O friends, I am mad.
Song of the flute, O sister, is madness, The.
Morgan, R. Heirloom.
Invisible woman in the asylum corridor, The.
Mozeen. Bedlamite, The.
Ni Tsan. Inscribed on a Painting by Myself.
Nichol. Monotones.
Okara. To Adhiambo.
Opie. To a Maniac.
Oppen. Route.
Owen, W. Mental Cases.
Padgett, R. First Drift.
Parra, N. Pilgrim, The.
Plath. Life, A.
Po Chü-i. To Liu Yü-hsi.
Poe. Conqueror Worm, The.
Pretorius. Madman, The.
Ratti. Division.
Rimbaud, A. Hunger.
Roberts, M. Madwoman at Rodmell.
Roethke. Heard in a Violent Ward.
In a dark time, the eye begins to see.
Rukeyser, M. Rational Man.
St. John, D. Dolls.
Iris.
Samio. Tanka: "Why does a room."
Satchidanandan. Genesis.
Seneca. Medea's Frenzy.
Senior. To the Madwoman in My Yard.
Sexton. Flee on Your Donkey.
Noon Walk on the Asylum Lawn.
Ringing the Bells.
Shakespeare, W. Sonnet 147.
Shange. Elegance in the extreme.
Sitwell, O. Madwoman in the Park, The.
Smith, C. On Being Cautioned against Walking on an Headland Overlooking the Sea, because It Was Frequented by a Lunatic.
Smith, S. Deserter, The.
Sophocles. Chorus.
Stein, G. White hunter is nearly crazy, A.
Stevenson, A. From an Asylum; Kathy Chattle to Her Mother, Ruth Arbeiter.
Stickney, T. Age in Youth.
Pity.
Strong, L. Mad Woman of Punnet's Town, The.
Symons, A. Nerves.
Szumigalski. Visitor's Parking.
Tate, J. Like a Scarf.
Taylor, A. Maniac's Song, The.
Tennyson, A. Lucretius.
Tucker, M. Crazed.
Unknown. Loving Mad Tom.
There was a Mad Man.
There Was a Man and He Was Mad.
Tom o'Bedlam.
Viiding. George Marrow's 1011th Dream.
Watts, I. Hurry of the Spirits, in a Fever and Nervous Disorders, The.
Wayman. Another Poem about the Madness of Women.
Weaver, M. Appaloosa, The.
Weiner, H. Little Books / 137 / Silence Mar 22 79.
Weiners. Poem for the Insane, A.
Whitehead, J. Local Man Remembers Betty Fuller, A.
Wilbur. What is the opposite of *nuts?*.
Williams, W. To Elsie.
Wojahn. First Six Seals, The.
Wollach. Splitting the Infinite.
Wordsworth, W. Mad Mother, The.
Wylie. Nebuchadnezzar.
Yeats. Crazed Girl, A.
Crazy Jane Talks with the Bishop.
Yoshihara. Madness.

See also **Mental Illness**

Madonnas
Doolittle, H. We have seen her.
We have seen her/ the world over.
Krustev. Nostalgia for Titian.
Muldoon, P. Bearded Woman, by Ribera, The.
Rossetti, D. For "Our Lady of the Rocks."

Madrid, Spain
Hughes, L. Madrid—1937.
O'Hara, F. Madrid.
Young, A. I Arrive In Madrid.
Magazines
Aiken, J. Do It Yourself.
Codrescu. Paper on Humor.
Gioia. My Confessional Sestina.
Wilbur. Playboy.
See also **Journalism and Journalists;**
Newspapers
Magdalene, Mary. *See* **Mary Magdalene**
Maggots
Soutar. Hungry Mauchs, The.
Magi
Baranczak, S. Three Magi, The.
Cooke, E. Perfect Gift, The.
"Dario." Three Kings, The.
Dickey, J. Magus, The.
Eliot, T. Journey of the Magi.
    Matthew 2:1–12; Now when Jesus was born.
Erskine, J. Kings and Stars.
Fiskin. Magi, The.
Garrett, G. Magi, The.
Glück, L. Magi, The.
Godolphin. Hymn: "Lord, when the wise men
    came from far[r]."
Guthrie, R. Magi, The.
Hawker. Mystic Magi, The.
Heine. Three Holy Kings from Morgenland.
    Wise Men Ask the Children the Way, The.
Hopkins, J. We Three Kings of Orient are.
Hughes, L. Carol of the Brown King.
Kunitz, S. He runs before the wise men: He.
Longfellow, H. Three Kings came riding from
    far away.
Merwin, W. Carol of the Three Kings.
Norris, L. Camels, the Kings' Camel, The.
Pilling. Adoration of the Magi, The.
Plath. Magi.
Ralegh, W. On the Card[e]s, and Dice.
Tsvetayeva. Bethlehem.
Williams, C. Kings Came Riding.
Williams, W. Gift, The.
Yeats. Magi, The.
Magic
Antiphanes. When Cytherea slipped her wily
    sash off.
Baraka. Ka 'Ba.
Blossom, L. Disappearing Act.
Byron, G. Incantation, An.
Campbell, J. Cunjah Man, De.
Césaire, A. First Problem.
    Magic.
Cummings, E. Now air is air and thing is
    thing:no bliss.
    That melancholy / fellow'll play / his
    handorgan.
Dickinson, E. Ah, Necromancy Sweet!
    I think I was enchanted.
Eliot, T. Usk.
Eskimo Oral Tradition. Magic Words.
Henderson-Holmes. Goodhousekeeping #17.
Holub. Zito the Magician.
Hutchinson, P. Bright after Dark.
Jacobs, H. It is not just.
Jenkins, L. Walking through a Wall.
Keats. La Belle Dame Sans Merci.
Kumin, M. Credo.
Kunitz, S. Testing-Tree, The.
Kuskin. Knitted Things.
La Fontaine. Cat Changed to a Woman, The.
Lazarus, E. Elixir, The.
Lorde. Summer Oracle.
Lu Yu. Pedlar of Spells, The.
MacEwen, G. Manzini; Escape Artist.
Mandel, E. Houdini.
McDonald, I. Poison-maker, The.
McElroy, C. This Is the Poem I Never Meant
    to Write.
Miliauskaite. In the damp places.
Millay, E. Ballad of the Harp-Weaver, The.
Muir, E. Merlin.
Oppen. Occurrences, The.
Patchen. Magical Mouse, The.
Popa. Tenants of the Little Box, The.
Raab, L. Magic Problems.

Reed, I. Black Cock, The.
    Sermonette.
Reeves, J. My Singing Aunt.
Shange. My father is a retired magician.
Smiler Narautjarri. Witch Doctor's Magic
    Flight, The.
Unknown. Another Man Done Gone.
    First Nowell the angel did say, The.
    For the nightemare.
    Good medicin for sor eyen.
    Imploration for Clear Weather.
    Incantation Songs of the Klamath Lake People.
    Incantations of Modoc Conjurers.
    Juce of lekes with gotes galle.
    Magic Formula.
    Magic Song.
    Magic Words.
    Medicine Songs.
    Sixth Song of the Holy Young Men.
    Two Magicians, The.
    Wizard's Chant, The.
    You May Go But This Will Bring You Back.
Virgil. Love-charm, A.
Ward, E. Magician, A.
Magnolias
Kitahara Hakushū. Tanka: "Magnolia."
Sexton. Wedding Night, The.
Yosano. Tanka: "Young fingers."
Magpies
Glover, D. Magpies, The.
Unknown. Lady and the Magpie, The.
    Magpie screams loudly and up his tail goes,
    The.
    Tune: Magpie on the Branch.
Wilson, T. Magpies in Picardy, The.
Magritte, René
Melly. Homage to René Magritte.
Maguire, Hugh, Lord of Fermanagh
O'Hussey. O'Hussey's Ode to the Maguire.
Maguire, Molly
Collins, W. Captain Molly.
Mahon, Derek
Longley, M. Letter to Derek Mahon.
Mail and Mailmen
Auden. Night Mail, The.
Bennett, R. Postman's Knock.
Cholmondeley-Pennell. Night Mail North, The.
Gibson, W. Advice to Travelers.
Hamill, G. Song of the GPO, A.
Jarrell. Hope.
Jenkins, L. Appointed Rounds.
Kennedy, X. Epitaph for a Postal Clerk.
Kinnell. Getting the Mail.
Kostakis. Fire Parcel.
Kunitz, S. Reflection by a Mailbox.
Machi. Tanka: "Arriving."
Manley, F. Dead Letters.
Mountain, M. Empty mailbox.
    Seed catalog in the mailbox cold drizzle.
Pizzarelli. Opening the mailbox.
Robinson, F. Today too.
Rossetti, C. Postman, The.
Sansom, C. Postman, The.
Swede. After the search for meaning bills in
    the mail.
Tucker, M. Mail Has Come, The.
Unknown. Meaning of a Letter, The.
    Omagh Post Office Rhyme.
Van den Heuvel. Through the small holes.
Whitman, W. Orange Buds by Mail from
    Florida.
Williams, W. To Greet a Letter-Carrier.
See also **Letters**
Maine (state)
Booth, P. Jake's Wharf.
    Stove.
Clampitt. Baroque Sunburst, A.
Eberhart, R. Spite Fence.
Garrett, J. York Harbor Morning.
Levertov. Brass Tacks.
Lowell, R. Fourth of July in Maine.
    Skunk Hour.
    Soft Wood.
    Water.
McNair. House in Spring.
Millay, E. Exiled.

Morris, H. Maine Lake at Night.
Nowlan. For Jean Vincent d'Abbadie, Baron
    St.-Castin.
Rankin, R. Women of Maine, The.
Toomer. Merl.
Van Duyn. Moose in the Morning, Northern
    Maine.
Wallis, G. Lovely Rivers and Lakes of Maine,
    The.
Wright, C. Kineo Mountain.
Malachy, Saint
Merton. St. Malachy.
Malaga, Spain
Hutchinson, P. Malaga.
Malaiyaman Tirumutikkari
Kapilar. Kāri Sober.
    True Protocol of Poets, The.
Malawi
Chipasula. Love Poem for My Country, A.
Mapanje. On His Royal Blindness Paramount
    Chief Kwangala.
Malcolm X (Malcolm Little)
Alba. For Malcolm X.
Baraka. Poem for Black Hearts, A.
Barrax. For Malcolm: After Mecca.
Brooks, G. Malcolm X.
Clifton, L. Malcolm.
Conyus. Confession to Malcolm.
Fields, J. Aardvark.
Hayden, R. El-Hajj Malik El-Shabazz.
Henderson, D. They Are Killing All the
    Young Men.
Jackson, M. I Remember ("I remember /
    January, / 1968").
Knight, E. It was a funky deal.
    Portrait of Malcolm X.
    Sun came, Miss Brooks—, The.
Madhubuti. Malcolm Spoke / Who Listened?
Neal, L. Malcolm X—an Autobiography.
Patterson, R. At That Moment.
Troupe. For Malcolm Who Walks in the Eyes
    of Our Children.
Walker, M. For Malcolm X.
Warr, M. Malcolm Is 'Bout More Than
    Wearing a Cap.
Whitlow. Poem for the Children.
Maldon, Battle of (991)
Unknown. Battle of Maldon, The.
Malls. *See* **Shopping Malls**
Malta
Forbes, J. Malta.
Man, Primitive
Avidan. Prehistory.
Day, C. Yesterday explorers found.
Heaney, S. Tollund Man, The.
See also **Cavemen**
Man in the Moon
Hewett, D. Moon-Man.
Unknown. Man in the moon, The.
Manchuria
Ravikovitch. Private View, A.
Mandalay, Burma
Kipling, R. Mandalay.
Mandela, Nelson
Lorde. Evening News, The.
Soyinka. "No!" He Said.
Mandelstam, Osip
Young, D. Mandelstam.
Mangan, James Clarence
Kinsella, T. Clarence Mangan.
Mangoes
Adisa. Cultural Trip, A.
Bethune, L. Today Tutu Is Beating the Same
    Burru As Me.
Crane, H. Mango Tree, The.
Cruz, V. Problems With Hurricanes.
Mora. Mangos y limones.
Waniek. Canticle for Abba Jacob, A.
Manhattan. *See* **New York City**
Manila Bay, Battle of (1898)
Ware, E. Manila Bay.
Manitoba, Canada
Purdy, A. Wilderness Gothic.

Mankind

Ai. Testimony of J. Robert Oppenheimer, The.
Aiken, C. Tetélestai.
Allston. Word: Man, A.
Amichai. Man in his life has no time to have, A.
Onus of Mercy, The.
Testimonies.
"Antler." Somewhere Along the Line.
Arnold, M. "In harmony with Nature?"
Restless fool.
Arp. People.
Ashbery. Hotel Lautréamont.
Avidan. Longterm Hatred.
Baraka. Balboa, the Entertainer.
Beaver. Day 20.
Bede. Sparrow's Flight, A.
Benn. Fragments, / Refuse of the soul.
Berry, W. Slip, The.
Berryman. Gislebertus' Eve.
Traveller, The.
Bishop, E. In the Waiting Room.
Blake, W. And every Space that a Man views around his dwelling-place.
Divine Image, A ("Cruelty has a Human heart").
Divine Image, The ("To Mercy, Pity, Peace and Love").
Human Abstract, The.
To see a World in a Grain of Sand.
Bognini. Suddenly an old man on the threshold of the age.
We are men of the new world a tree prompts us to harmony.
Bonhoeffer. Who am I? They often tell me.
Bowman, C. Demographics.
Bradley, G. Fire Fetched Down, The.
Browning, R. Parting at Morning.
Bryant, W. Crowded Street, The.
Burns, R. Epistle to a Young Friend.
For A' That and A' That ["Is there, for honest poverty"].
Campbell, T. Last Man, The.
Char. Man flees suffocation.
Collymore. Monkeys.
Conquest. Horror Comic.
Couani. Obvious, The.
Cowley, A. Garden, The.
Crane, S. "It Was Wrong to Do This" Said the Angel.
Cruickshank, A. Let Us Be Frank.
Cummings, E. No man,if men are gods;but if gods must.
Now does our world descend.
Pity this busy monster,manunkind.
When serpents bargain for the right to squirm.
Davie. Christening, A.
Davies, S. I know my soul hath power to know all things.
De la Mare. All That's Past.
Depestre. Ballad of a Little Lamp.
Dickey, W. Suburban.
Donne. To the Countess of Salisbury.
Drummond de Andrade. Dirty Hand, The.
Drummond, W. Madrigal: "This world a hunting is."
Dryden, J. Song from The Indian Emperor.
Dunbar, P. Slow Through the Dark.
Duoduo. Wishful Thinking Is the Master of Reality.
Ehrhart. Making the Children Behave.
Éluard, P. Dawn Dissolves the Monsters.
Enzensberger, H. Portrait of a House Detective.
Eskimo Oral Tradition. Magic Words.
Finch, R. Collective Portrait, The.
Flecknoe. Ant, The.
Frase. Fish Story: How Language Carries Us into the Unknown.
Frost, R. Vantage Point, The.
Gay, J. Employments of Life, The.
Gilbo'a. I'll grab hold of a butt of dream.
Glatstein. If you should be surprised, Nathan.
Gray, T. Ode on a Distant Prospect of Eton College.
Greville, F. Chorus Sacerdotum.
Guilpin. What more variety of pleasures can.

Guiterman. Brief Essay on Man.
Gunn, T. Last Man, The.
Hardy, T. Heredity.
I said to Love.
Hass, R. Human Wishes.
Hejinian. Polar Circle, The.
Herbert, G. Justice.
Man.
Pulley, The.
Hesiod. Iron Age, The.
Hewitt, J. Ram's Horn, The.
Holan. In the Yard of the Policlinic.
Holmes, O. Sympathies.
Holub. Crocheting.
Wings.
Hopkins, G. Lantern Out of Doors, The.
Sea and the Skylark, The.
Sonnet: "Shepherd's brow, fronting forked lightning, owns, The."
To His Watch.
Horace. Hence, ye Profane; I hate ye all.
Howe, F. What We Learned.
Huchel. Psalm.
Ignatow, D. Ritual Three.
Jarrell. Islands, The.
Jeffers, L. To him who in his absence from himself.
Jeffers, R. Inquisitors, The.
Science.
Jemie. Iroko.
Johnson, G. Common Dust.
Jones, E. Genesis.
Jonson, B. To William, Earl[e] of Pembroke.
Kaufman, B. Geneology.
To My Son Parker, Asleep in the Next Room.
Kayo. War.
Keats. Human Seasons, The.
Kerouac. Two Hundred and Twenty-Eighth Chorus.
Khlebnikov, V. Suppose I make a timepiece of humanity.
Khodasevich. To a Guest.
King, H. Sic Vita.
Kipling, R. If you can keep your head when all [about you].
Kirillov. We uncountable dread legions of Labor.
Knevet. Habitation, The.
Krohn. Farmer's Song at Can Tho.
Landor, W. On Man.
Lao Tzu. All things pass.
Lawrence, D. Elemental.
Gods! The Gods!, The.
My way is not thy way, and thine is not mine.
When wilt thou teach the people.
Levertov. Beginners.
God then.
Levi, P. Shemà.
Levine, P. Animals Are Passing from Our Lives.
How Much Earth.
Lipska. That Moment.
What Happened to Professor White on Leaving the Hat Store.
Lowry, M. Volcano is dark and suddenly thunder, The.
MacCaig. Basking Shark.
"MacDiarmid." Black leaf owre a white leaf twirls, A.
Man and the Infinite.
On a Raised Beach.
Problem Child, The.
With the Herring Fishers.
Mahapatra, J. October Morning, An.
Markham, E. Man with the Hoe, The.
Melo Neto. Emptiness of man is not like, The.
Meredith, G. 30.
Meredith, W. Major Work, A.
Merwin, W. For a Coming Extinction.
Millay, E. Apostrophe to Man.
Miller, J. In Men Whom Men Condemn as Ill.
Milton. On the Detraction Which Followed upon My Writing Certain Treatises.
Montoya. Just the other day.
Muir, E. Animals, The.
Muktibodh. Void inside us, The.
Neruda. Stone within stone, and man, where

was he?
Walking [*or* Walkin'] Around.
We Are Many.
Newcastle, M. Dialogue betwixt Man, and Nature, A.
Okamoto. Tanka: "Cherry petals."
Oliver, M. Wild Geese.
Olson, C. Chain of memory is resurrection I am a vain man, The.
In cold hell, in thicket, how.
Pacosz. Seed Is the Light of the Earth, The.
Padgett, R. Lucky Strikes.
Pagis. Biped is quite a strange creature, The.
Tropical Greenhouse.
Parra, N. I Move the Meeting Be Adjourned.
Man's mother is very sick, A.
Pembroke, M. Psalm 58: Si Vere Utique.
Po Chü-i. Climbing the Ling-Ying Terrace and Looking North.
Lodging with the Old Man of the Stream.
Pope, A. Bliss of man, The (could pride that blessing find).
Essay on Criticism, An.
Placed on this isthmus of a middle state.
What would this Man? Now upward will he soar.
Pound, E. Meditatio.
Return, The.
Pozdnyayev. Remembrance of Five Loaves.
Pratt, E. From Stone to Steel ("From stone to bronze, from bronze to steel").
Truant, The.
Quarles. Can he be fair that withers at a blast.
Quasimodo. Man of My Time.
Raine, K. Human Form Divine, The.
Raleigh. Wishes of an Elderly Man[, Wished at a Garden Party, June 1914].
Ravikovitch. Human Qualities.
Poem of Explanations.
Rexroth, K. Long lifetime, A.
Rich, A. For the Record.
Rivard. Later History.
Robinson, K. Pontoon.
Rochester, J. Satire against Reason and Mankind, A.
Rossetti, C. One Certainty, The.
Wednesday in Holy Week.
Rózewicz. In the Midst of Life.
What luck I can pick.
Rukeyser, M. Myth.
Sachs, N. But look / but look.
Sandburg, C. Jack was a swarthy, swaggering son-of-a-gun.
People, Yes, The.
They Ask: Is God, Too, Lonely?
Wilderness.
Scalapino. Considering How Exaggerated Music Is.
Or a Play.
Schultz, P. Quality, The.
Scott, T. Mankind Toun, The.
Senghor. Man and Beast.
Sexton. After Auschwitz.
Shakespeare, W. Seven Ages of Man, The.
Sherwood, G. Satire against Reason and Mankind, A.
Shirley, J. Death the Leveller.
Sisson. Nature of Man, The.
Smith, B. Black Mountain Blues.
Smith, S. Away, melancholy, / Away with it, let it go.
Distractions and the Human Crowd.
Man is a spirit. This the poor flesh knows.
New Age, The.
Sophocles. Numberless wonders / terrible wonders walk the world but none the match for man—.
Southwell. Look[e] Home.
Sri Sri. Man walks on the bridge and gives away the change in his, A.
Stefanovich. For all of us destiny is undivided.
Supervielle. Earth.
Swift, J. Day of Judgement, The.
Swirszczynska. Same Inside, The.
Sea and the Man, The.
Tate, J. Guide to the Stone Age, The.
Tennyson, A. 108.

Tidjani-Cissé. Of Colours and Shadows.
Tirolien. Ghetto.
Vallejo. I have a terrible fear of being an
  animal.
Rollcall of Bones, The.
Varma. Man.
Vaughan, H. Corruption.
Man.
Tempest, The.
World, The (1).
Very. Created, The.
Origin of Man, I, The.
Wat. To be a mouse. Preferably a field
  mouse. Or a garden mouse—.
Whitman, W. Animals.
I hear America singing, the varied carols I
  hear.
On the Same Picture.
One's-Self I sing, a simple separate person.
Song of Myself.
Wickham. To Men.
Wilbur. Ceremony.
Williams, D. We Are the Cenotaphs.
Williams, W. Clouds, The.
Winchilsea. Spleen, The.
Wolfe, H. Man.
Wordsworth, W. Lines Written in Early
  Spring.
Man is dear to man: the poorest poor.
Wright, J. In Shame and Humiliation.
Secret Gratitude, A.
Yeats. Four Ages of Man, The.
Sorrow of Love, The ("Brawling of a sparrow
  in the eaves, The").
Zach. Like Sand.
Prologue to a Poem.
Mannequins
Corbière. To the Eternal Feminine.
Sheck. Mannequins.
Manners. *See* **Etiquette**
Man-of-War Birds
Whitman, W. To the Man-of-War Bird.
Mantis. *See* **Praying Mantis**
Maori
Habib. Moment of Truth.
Kemp, J. "When the Wild Goose Finds Food
  He Calls His Comrades"—*I Ching.*
Te Kooti Rikirangi. Song of Instruction, A.
Unknown. Land Is Gone, The.
Walters, M. Haka: The Feathered Albatross.
Maple Trees
Hong, Y. Maple Leaves.
Koch, K. Down at the docks.
Pratt, C. Fog has settled, The.
Weil, Z. October wind, An.
Wright, J. To a Troubled Friend.
Maps
Alexander, E. Ode.
Ashbery. Rivers and Mountains.
Bishop, E. Map, The.
Bitar. Kinshasa.
Blaser. Suddenly.
Bogan, L. Cartography.
Caddy, C. Three-Inch Reflector.
"Carroll." Fit the Second: The Bellman's
  Speech.
Couani. Map of the world is felt from the
  inside. Rough around the, The.
Gunn, T. Map of the City, A.
Hammial. Jane.
Hogan, L. Map.
Holmes, J. Map of My Country, A.
Le Pan. Incident, An.
Mullen, H. Roadmap.
Nemerov. Low-Level Cross-Country.
Mapmaker on His Art, The.
Oden. Private Letter to Brazil, A.
Sorescu. Historiotherapy.
Map.
Strand. Map, The.
Mysterious Maps, The.
Tranter. Alphabet Murders, The.
Marathon, Battle of (490 B.C.)
Graves, R. Persian Version, The.
Gurney, I. Towards Lillers.
Marathon (race)
Mann, C. Comrades Marathon, The.

Wilbur. Running.
Marble
Dickey, J. In the Marble Quarry.
March
Bronk. March, Upstate.
Caraion. Always, In March.
Coatsworth. March.
Davies, M. Day before April, The.
Dickinson, E. Dear March, Come in.
We like March—his shoes are Purple.
Housman, A. March.
Ledwidge. Twilight in Middle March, A.
Levine, P. Mad Day in March.
Machi. Tanka: "This day in March."
McGough, R. MARCH ingorders.
McKay, D. March Snow.
Merwin, W. Thorn Leaves in March.
Nyka-Niliunas. March.
Ray, H. March.
Sackville-West. Pruning in March.
Smith, I. Cuillins tower, The.
Poem in March.
This is the land God gave to Andy Stewart.
Stevens, W. Not Ideas about the Thing but the
  Thing Itself.
Vacancy in the Park.
Swan, J. March Weather.
Wordsworth, W. Change in the Year, A.
Written in March [While Resting on the
  Bridge at the Foot of Brother's Water].
Marching and Marches
Bennett, H. Flag Goes By, The.
Emerson, R. Days.
Gurney, I. Towards Lillers.
Hopkins, G. At the Wedding March.
Mao Tse-tung. Long March, The.
Melville, H. Night-March, The.
Owen, W. Dulce Et Decorum Est.
Radnóti. Forced March.
Saunders, M. Remembering Day.
Stevenson, R. Marching Song.
Ts'ao Ts'ao. Song on Enduring the Cold.
Wilson, T. Magpies in Picardy, The.
See also **Parades**
Margaret, Saint
Constable, H. To Saint Margaret.
Marigolds
Driscoll, L. Marigolds.
Herrick. How Marigolds Came Yellow.
To Marygolds.
Williams, W. Negro Woman, A.
Wither. Marigold, The.
Marijuana
Degutyte. In Jazz Rhythms.
Hughes, E. Gauge.
Knight, E. As You Leave Me.
Owen, M. "Assholes!" her eyes seem grey in
  this soup the hangars.
Padgett, R. Strawberries in Mexico.
Marin County, California
Jeffers, R. Clouds of Evening.
Marin, John
Booth, P. Marin.
Mariners. *See* **Sailing and Sailors**
Marion, Francis
Simms, W. Swamp Fox, The.
Markets
Balaban. Along the Mekong.
Bloom, V. Longsight Market.
Brabazon. Victoria Market.
Brown, G. Hamnavoe Market.
Dumas, H. Knees of a Natural Man.
Falconer, E. Marketing.
Forbes, J. Potlicker Blues.
Goodison. Kenscoff.
Hall, D. Ox Cart Man.
Johnson, A. Granny in de Market Place.
Kinnell. Avenue Bearing the Initial of Christ
  into the New World, The.
Labriola. Orgy (That Is, Vegetable Market, at
  Sarno).
Mangan, D. Heraclitus at Glasgow Cross.
"Maurice." Victoria Markets Recollected in
  Tranquility, The.
Mirabai. It's True I Went to the Market.
Po Chü-i. Flower Market, The.

Reese, L. Lavender Woman, The.
St. John, P. Pearle's Poem.
Simon, L. Hattie Went to Market.
T'ang Yin. Scene at Heaven Gate, The.
Unknown. As I was going to sell my eggs.
Cries of London, The.
Linstead Market.
Van Vliet. Old Champagne Glass.
Markiewicz, Constance Georgine, Countess
Day Lewis. Remembering Con Markiewicz.
Yeats. In Memory of Eva Gore-Booth and
  Con Markievicz.
Marlborough, John Churchill, 1st Duke of
Addison, J. Poem to His Grace the Duke of
  Marlborough, A.
Southey, R. Battle of Blenheim, The.
Swift, J. Satirical Elegy on the Death of a
  Late Famous General, A.
Marlowe, Christopher
Swinburne. Christopher Marlowe.
Marpessa
Ritsos. Marpessa's Choice.
Marriage
Abid ibn al-Abras. Arab Chieftain to His
  Young Wife, An.
Adcock, F. Wife to Husband.
Ai. She Didn't Even Wave.
Twenty-Year Marriage.
Aig-Imoukhuede. One Wife for One Man.
Akhmadulina. Bride, The.
Alma-Tadema, L. If no one ever marries
  me—.
Amherst. Song for the Single Table on New
  Year's Day, A.
Amichai. Pity; We Were Such a Good
  Invention, A.
Ammuvanar. What Her Girl Friend Said on
  Her Wedding Day.
Ancient Sumerian Oral Tradition. Inanna sang.
Apache Oral Tradition. Now you will feel no
  rain.
Applewhite. Marriage Portrait.
Ashbery. Decoy.
Atwood. Habitation.
Auden. Carry her over the water.
Ausonius. To His Wife.
Ayton. Posy, A: "Dear love, I am resolved
  with thee to live."
Baillie, L. Werena My Heart Licht I Wad
  Dee.
Bàng Bá Lân. If in a Future Life We Meet
  Again.
Barber, M. Conclusion of a Letter to the Rev.
  Mr. C——, The.
Barlas. Terrible Love.
Barnes, W. Bachelor, The.
Bateman, E. It's a Great Big Shame.
Beddoes. Bridal Song to Amala.
Beer, P. Faithful Wife, The.
Behrens. Wedding in the Port.
Bergman, A. Letter.
Berrigan, T. Red Shift.
Berrigan, T. *et al.* Orange Jews.
Berry, W. Grandmother, The.
Berryman. Canto Amor.
Bevington, L. Wrestling.
Bishop, E. Washing hangs upon the line, A.
Blackburn, T. Lucky Marriage, The.
Blake, W. London ("I wander through [*or*
  thro'] each chartered [*or* charter'd] street").
Blamire. O Donald! ye are just the man.
Blumenthal, M. Marriage, A.
Blunden. Forefathers.
Bly, R. Third Body, A.
Bogan, L. Betrothed.
Bradstreet, A. To My Dear and Loving
  Husband.
Brautigan. Chinese Checker Players, The.
Breckenridge. Unlocking the Doors.
Brodrick. Joe's Luck.
Brodsky, J. Six Years Later.
Brontë, E. Day Dream, A.
Brooke, R. Sonnet Reversed.
Brooks, G. Ballad of Late Annie, The.
Bronzeville Mother Loiters in Mississippi. /
  Meanwhile, a Mississippi Mother Burns
  Bacon.

Kitchenette Building.
Old-Marrieds, The.
To be in love.
Broome. Widow and Virgin Sisters, The.
Brown, T. Conjergal rights! conjergal rights!
Browning, E. Year's Spinning, A.
Browning, R. Any Wife to Any Husband.
Life in a Love.
Love in a Life.
My Last Duchess [Ferrara].
Bruce, D. Sonnet 4: "Wet streets, black trees, a gold leaf smacked."
Buchanan, G. Song for Straphangers.
Bukowski. Funny Man.
Burns, R. John Anderson my jo, John / When we were first acquent.
Kellyburnbraes.
Tam Glen.
Whistle o'er the Lave o't.
Burr, A. Lynmouth Widow, A.
Butler, M. Listen.
Bynner. Episode of Decay.
Campbell, A. Before and After Marriage.
Carew, T. Hymeneal[l] Dialogue, An.
Hymeneal Song on the Nuptials of the Lady Anne Wentworth and the Lord Lovelace, An.
On the Marriage of T. K. and C. C.: The Morning Stormy.
Carey, H. Sally in Our Alley.
"Carroll." "You are old," said the youth, "and your jaws are too weak."
Caruthers. Prayer of Any Husband.
Cary, P. Dorothy's Dower.
Psalm of Marriage.
Cassells. These Are Not Brushstrokes.
Catullus. Carmen 61 ("Guardian of Helicon, Urania's son").
Roman Epithalamion.
Cave. Elegy on a Maiden Name, An.
Chapman, G. Bridal Song: "O come, soft rest of cares, come Night."
Chappell, F. My Mother Shoots the Breeze.
Chatterton. There Lackethe Somethynge Stylle.
Chaucer. Experience, though noon auctoritee.
Franklin's Tale, The.
Wife of Bath's Prologue, The.
Cherry, K. Bride of Quietness, The.
Chin. Song of the Sad Guitar.
Christine de Pisan. In Praise of Marriage.
Marriage is a lovely thing.
Chu Yün-ming. Remembering My Late Wife.
Chudleigh. To the Ladies.
Ciardi. To Judith Asleep.
Cillactor. Married life for a poor man.
Clare, J. Married to a Soldier.
Clarke, A. Marriage.
Clifton, H. Id.
Coleridge, M. Marriage.
Compiuta Donzella. In the season when the world leafs and flowers.
Corso. Marriage.
Song: "Oh, dear! Oh, me! Oh, my!"
Cotton, N. Early Thoughts of Marriage.
Crabbe. Marriage Ring, The.
Crashaw. Epitaph Upon Husband and Wife Who Died and Were Buried Together, An.
On Marriage.
Creeley. Ballad of the Despairing Husband.
Marriage, A.
Naughty Boy.
Wait for Me.
Way, The.
Wife, The.
Criswell. Newlyweds, The.
Crozier, L. So this is love, a kind of sad dance.
Cullen, C. Wind Bloweth Where It Listeth, The.
Cummings, E. If there are any heavens my mother will (all by herself) have.
Cunningham, J. Holiday Gown.
Dabydeen, C. Husband, The.
Daryush. If your loved one prove unworthy, why then.
Dasgupta, P. Man: 1961.
Davie. Autumn Imagined.

Davies, S. Contention betwixt a Wife, a Widow, and a Maid, A.
Day, C. To My Wife.
Who Drags the Fiery Artist Down?
De Tabley. Nuptial Song.
Derricotte. Promise, The.
Di Prima. Poem in Praise of My Husband (Taos).
Dickinson, E. Her sweet Weight on my Heart a Night.
I'm "wife"—I've finished that.
Ourselves were wed one summer—dear.
Rearrange a "Wife's" affection!
She rose to His Requirement—dropt.
Title divine—is mine!
Wife—at Daybreak I shall be, A.
Divakaruni. Brides Come to Yuba City, The.
Donahue, J. Transfigurations.
Donne. Antiquary.
Epithalamion for Lawyers, An.
Epithalamion Made at Lincoln's Inn [or Lincolnes Inne].
Flea, The.
Dove, R. Beauty and the Beast.
Drayton. By night within my bed, I roamed here and there.
Dryden, J. Why Should a Foolish Marriage Vow.
Dufferin. Charming Woman, The.
Mother's Lament, The.
Dugan, A. Love Song: I and Thou.
Duke, R. To Caelia.
Durcan. Divorce Referendum, Ireland, 1986, The.
Edson, R. Ape.
Having to Love Something Else, The.
Eedes. No Love, to Love of Man and Wife.
Egerton, S. Emulation, The.
On My Wedding Day.
To One Who Said I Must Not Love.
Eimers. History of Navigation, A.
"Eliot." Armgart, to many minds the first success.
Eliot, T. Dedication to My Wife, A.
Then no doubt it's all for the best.
Yes a very important discovery.
Engle, P. Twilight.
"Ephelia." To J.G. on the News of His Marriage.
Eratosthenes. Meditation, Followed by Excellent Advice.
Erdrich. Shelter.
Euripides. Of all things which are living and can form a judgment.
Ezekiel. When the female railway clerk.
Ferlinghetti, L. In Golden Gate Park that day.
Field, E. April Fool, The.
"Field." Come, Gorgo, put the rug in place.
I love you with my life—'tis so I love you.
So jealous of your beauty.
Finch, A. O, love, in your sweet name enough.
Flatman. Batchelor's Song, The.
On Marriage.
Fletcher, J. River[-]God's Song, The.
Flook. Continental Divide, The.
Florsheim. Jewish Singles Event, The.
Fordham. Marriage.
Foster, E. Marriage of True Minds, The.
Frost, R. Love and a Question.
Fu Hsüan. Woman.
Fulton, A. Powers of Congress.
Gerstler. Marriage.
Gilbert, J. Meaning Well.
Gilbert, S. Parachutist's Wife, The.
Gioia. Summer Storm.
Glück, L. From the Suburbs.
Horse.
Goldensohn, B. Honeymoon.
Goldsmith, O. Double Transformation, The.
Goodman, M. Man and Wife.
Gould, G. You were young--but that was scarcely to your credit.
Graves, R. Call it a good marriage—.
Henry and Mary.
Slice of Wedding Cake, A.
Hacker, M. Eight Days in April.

Halevi. Marriage Song.
Hardy, T. Bride-Night Fire, The.
In the Night She Came.
Harington, J. Author to His Wife, of a Woman's Eloquence, The.
Harington, J. Husband to Wife.
Wife to Husband.
Harms. Tomorrow, We'll Dance in America.
Harper, M. Elvin's Blues.
Hatton, R. Epithalamium: "Hymen hath together tied."
Hawaiian Oral Tradition. Here all seeking is over.
Haynes, C. Any Wife or Husband.
Heaney, S. Cana Revisited.
Mother of the Groom.
Hearson. Nomenclaturik.
Herder. Esthonian Bridal Song.
Herrick. Entertainment, or Porch-Verse, at the Marriage of Mr. Henry Northleigh [or Hen. Northly] and the Most Witty Mrs. Lettice Yard, The.
Epitaph upon a Sober Matron, An.
Epithalamy to Sir Thomas Southwell and His Lady, An.
Nuptiall Song, or Epithalamie, on Sir Clipseby Crew and His Lady, A.
Poet Loves a Mistress, but Not to Marry, The.
Single Life Most Secure.
Hershenson. Husbands and Wives.
Hesiod. As Drones, oppressive Habitants of Hives.
Hewett, D. This Version of Love.
Hill, S. Looking for Camels.
Hiranandani. Husband.
Ho Xuan Huong. On Being a Concubine.
Hodgson, R. Silver Wedding.
Holbrook, D. Maternity Gown.
Hollo. Wasp Sex Myth (One).
Wasp Sex Myth (Two).
Homer. Ulysses Reunited with Penelope.
Hope, A. Advice to Young Ladies.
Howard, R. 1915: A Pre-Raphaelite Ending, London.
Hughes, T. Her Husband.
Ignatow, D. Suite for Marriage, A.
Ingelow. Long White Seam, The.
Seven Times Three—Love.
Irving, M. Wedding Gift, The.
Jackson, R. Jamal's Lamentation.
Jarrell. Man Meets a Woman in the Street, A.
Jemmat. Rural Lass, The.
Jennings, E. One Flesh.
John of the Cross. Christmas Ballad.
Jonson, B. Epithalamion: or, a Song.
On Giles and Joan.
Justice, D. But That Is Another Story.
Kahn, G. Makin' Whoopee.
Kayamanar. What Her Girl Friend Said, Seeing Her Friend Suffer in Silent Dignity over Her Husband's Infidelity.
Kelly, B. Young Wife's Lament.
Kessler, M. All their names were Vincent, Ernie, Paul.
Kiên Giang. Beauties in White.
Kim, K. Conflict.
Kipling, R. Bridegroom, The.
Sergeant's Weddin', The.
Koethe. Falling Water.
Kovner. Sun-Watchers.
Kuan Tao Shêng. Married Love.
Kunio. Tanka: "Hidden."
Kunitz, S. Touch Me.
Landon. Enchanted Island, The.
Marriage Vow, The.
Larkin, P. Maiden Name.
Self's the Man.
Wedding-Wind.
Whitsun Weddings, The.
Lawrence, D. Wedding Morn.
Young Wife, A.
Lear, E. The Owl and the Pussy-Cat.
Lei-Lanilau. Kolohe or Communication.
Leithauser. Old Bachelor Brother.
Lesser. Degli Sposi.
Levertov. About Marriage.

Ache of marriage, The.
Embroidery (I), An.
Levis. Story.
Levy, A. Ballad of Religion and Marriage, A.
Lewis, E. Advice to a Young Lady Lately Married.
Lewis, M. Alonzo the Brave and the Fair Imogine.
Lewisohn, L. Together.
Li Po. River Merchant's Wife, The; a Letter.
Li Shang-yin. Ma-wei.
Linden, M. Marriage Vow.
Lindsay, L. Auld Robin Gray.
Lindsay, M. Love's Anniversaries.
Liu Hsün's Wife. Curtain of the Wedding Bed, The.
Loden. My Night with Philip Larkin.
Logghe. Marriage.
Lovelace, R. Anniversary on the Hymeneals of My Noble Kinsman, Thomas Stanley, Esquire, An.
Lowell, A. Decade, [A].
Lowell, R. Frederick Kuh, Manx Cat.
Man And Wife.
To Speak of Woe That Is in Marriage.
Lu Yün. Peacock flew, far off to the southeast, The.
Lucan. Cato at his wedding.
Lucilius. Cleombrotus the bruiser.
Ludlow. Socrates Snooks.
M–rt–n. Humble Wish, The.
"MacDiarmid." O wha's the bride that carries the bunch.
MacDonagh, D. Prothalamium.
MacLeish. Old Gray Couple, The.
Poem in Prose.
Unfinished History.
MacNeice. For X.
Les Sylphides.
Madhubuti. Union of Two, The.
Magrelli. Side by side after the meal.
Marson. To Wed or Not to Wed.
Martial. Epigram: "Wife, there are some points on which we differ from each other."
Since your marriage you have lost the look.
Masters, E. Margaret Fuller Slack.
Mathews, A. Spectrum.
Two Months Married.
Mathews, H. Marrying Again.
Mayhall. Tracing Back.
McCarthy, T. Toast.
McElroy, C. Caledonia.
McGinley. Midcentury Love Letter.
McGough, R. Cousin Nell.
40— Love.
McKinney, I. Visiting My Gravesite: Talbott Churchyard, West Virginia.
McPherson, S. 1943.
Mei Yao Ch'en. Marrying Again.
On the Death of His Wife.
Second Marriage.
Meredith, G. At dinner, she is hostess, I am host.
Dusty Answer, A.
He found her by the ocean's moaning verge.
Hymn to Colour.
It is no vulgar nature I have wived.
Love Dies.
Modern Love.
Their sense is with their senses all mixed in.
'Tis Christmas weather, and a country house.
Yet it was plain she struggled, and that salt.
Merrill, J. Emerald, The.
Mew. Farmer's Bride, The.
Middleton, T. Song: "In a maiden-time professed."
You'll say the gentleman is somewhat simple.
Miller, E. Rebecca.
Milton. Unfallen Love.
Mirikitani. Soul Food.
Momaday. Four Notions of Love and Marriage.
Montagu, L. Epistle from Mrs. Yonge to Her Husband.
On the Death of Mrs. Bowes.
Moore, E. Why, Celia, is your spreading waist.

Moore, M. Marriage.
Morgan, V. Still Life.
Morley, C. Washing the Dishes.
Moses ibn Ezra. Dying Wife to Her Husband, A.
Moss, H. Ménage à Trois.
Moss, T. Dennis's Sky Leopard.
Mothibi. Speech.
Muir, E. Combat, The.
Song: "Why should your face so please me."
Munivar. On the marriage platform made of gold.
Mura. Grandfather and Grandmother in Love.
Musgrave. Exchange of Fire.
Naden. Love Versus Learning.
Pessimist's Vision, The.
Nash, O. Love Under the Republicans (Or Democrats).
Reprise.
Song to Be Sung by the Father of Infant Female Children.
Strange Case of Mr. Ormantude's Bride, The.
Word to Husbands, A.
Nesbit, E. Goose-Girl, The.
Newcastle, M. Poet I am neither born, nor bred, A.
Niedecker. I married.
Norton, C. Laura was lightsome, gay, and free from guile.
Oden. Man White, Brown Girl and All That Jazz.
O'Hehir. Questions and Answers.
Olds, S. I Go Back to May 1937.
Wedding Vow, The.
Orampokiyar. What Her Girl Friend Said, When the Woman Was About to Take Back Her Unfaithful Husband.
Oresick. Passion and Woe in Marriage: A Ukrainian Love Story, The.
Ostriker. Exchange, The.
In the Twenty-Fifth Year of Marriage, It Goes On.
Ouloguem. Dear Husband.
Ozog. Village for a Wedding.
Paley, G. Quarrel.
Palladas. Cuckolded husbands have no certain sign.
When he comes up to the bedroom.
Pastan. Because the night you asked me.
Camellias.
Patmore, C. Constancy Rewarded.
'Twas when the spousal time of May.
Peacock, M. Wheel, The.
Peele. Song: "When as [or whenas] the rye [or rie] reach to the chin."
Peretz. Three Seamstresses, The.
Peseroff. Hardness Scale, The.
Pfeiffer, E. So the river—yes, the river; I have come to that at last.
Philips, A. Happy Swain, The.
Philips, K. Answer to Another Persuading a Lady to Marriage, An.
Piercy. Battle of Wills Disguised, A.
Pilkington, L. Fair and Softly goes far or, The Wary Physician.
Wish, By a Young Lady, The.
"Pindar." Ode: "That I have often been in love, deep love."
Plath. Applicant, The.
Wreath for a Bridal.
Zoo Keeper's Wife.
Pollitt. Turning Thirty.
Porter, P. Talking to You Afterwards.
Pound, E. River-Merchant's Wife: A Letter, The.
Prince, F. To a Friend on His Marriage.
Prior. Reasonable Affliction, A.
Probyn. Kyrielle.
Procter, A. Woman's Question, A.
Ranaivo. Love Song: "Do not love me, my friend."
Ransom, J. Emily Hardcastle, Spinster.
Rege, P. Pact, The.
Rich, A. Snapshots of a Daughter-in-Law.
Rihaku. River-Merchant's Wife: A Letter, The.
Rilke. John 2:1–12; On the third day there

was a marriage.
On the Marriage at Cana.
Robinson, E. Eros Turannos.
Rochester, J. To My More Than Meritorious Wife.
Rolls. Bamboo.
Rosenberg, L. In the End We Are All Light.
Rossetti, C. Bride Song.
Cousin Kate.
Maude Clare.
Rossetti, D. Nuptial Sleep.
Rotella, A. In his wedding band watching the clouds pass.
Rowe, E. Chapter II.
Rufinus Domesticus. We who find no joy in celebrity.
Rumens. Double Bed.
Rumi. This marriage be wine with halvah, honey dissolving in milk.
St. John, P. Ocean of the Streams of Story.
Sandburg, C. Mag.
Soiled Dove.
Sangster, M. Our Own.
Santos, S. Married Love.
Savage, M. Letter to Miss E. B. on Marriage.
Schulman. Present Perfect, The.
Schwartz, D. Passionate Shepherd to His Love, The.
Scott, D. Marrysong.
Scott, W. Lochinvar.
Madge Wildfire Sings.
Seaman, S. Plea for Trigamy, A.
Sedley. Marriage and Money.
See! Hymen comes; how his torch blazes!
Serote. Poem, A: "Gasp sounded, The."
Shakespeare, W. I do not know / One of my sex; no woman's face remember.
Sonnet 67.
Sonnet 116.
Sherry, J. Pay Cash Only.
Sidney, P. Long Their Coupled Joys Maintain.
Simmons, J. After Eden.
Honeymoon, The.
Simpson, L. Man Who Married Magdalene, The.
Sims. Garden Song, A.
Smith, S. Autumn.
I Remember.
Lady "Rogue" Singleton.
Major Macroo.
Marriage I think.
Octopus, The.
Smith, S. Aa my life, my leman said.
So Chong-Ju. Looking at Mt. Mudung.
Sorby. Museum Piece.
Soto. Fair Trade.
Southwick. Rain's Marriage, The.
Sparshott. Three Seasons.
Spender, S. Polar Exploration.
Trance, The.
Stanescu. Engagement.
Stephen, J. She's not a faultless woman; no!
Stephens, J. Red-haired Man's Wife, The.
Stevenson, A. Daughter's Difficulties as a Wife, A: Mrs. Reuben Chandler to Her Mother in New Orleans.
Marriage, The.
Stevenson, R. So live, so love, so use that fragile hour.
Storace. Archaeology of Divorce, The.
Wedding Song.
Strand. Courtship.
Marriage, The.
Strong, L. Brewer's Man, The.
Stumbrs. Married Romantic, A.
Su Tung-p'o. Children don't know what worry means!
Su Wu. Drafted.
To His Wife.
Suckling, J. Upon My Lord Brohall's Wedding.
Sugita. Mending his broken tabi without becoming a Nora.
Swift, J. Phyllis [or Phillis] [or Progress of Love, The].
Three Epigrams.
Synge. On an Island.

Tạ Hũ'u Thiện. Looking For Her.
Taylor, A. Developing a Wife.
Taylor, E. Upon Wedlock and Death of Children.
Tennyson, A. Lady Clare.
  Marriage Morning.
  Northern Farmer: New Style.
Tessimond. Heaven.
Thomas, D. On the Marriage of a Virgin.
Thomas, E. Epistle to Clemena, Occasioned by an Argument She Had Maintained Against the Author.
  New Litany, Occasioned by an Invitation to a Wedding, A.
Thwaite. Marriages.
Tollet. What cruel laws depress the female kind.
Twichell. Chanel No. 5.
Ullman. Peace.
Unknown. Bridegroom, beloved of my heart.
  Bridge instead of a Wall, A.
  Chirp Chirp the Katydids.
  Daughter of the farrier, The.
  Epithalamium: "Lo! Hymen passes through th' admiring crowds."
  Folk Song.
  Frail frail, lone-growing bamboo.
  Get Up and Bar the Door.
  Gwan! Gwan! Cry the Fish Hawks.
  Henpecked Husband, A.
  How! hey! it is non les.
  Husband's Message, The ("Now shall I unseal myself to yourself alone").
  Jack Jingle.
  Knight and Shepherd's Daughter, The.
  Know er thou knitte; prove er thou preise it.
  Lament of Hsi-Chün.
  Little Man and Maid, The.
  Lovely the young peach tree.
  Man, bewar of thine wowing.
  Man once married who hunts wife once more, A.
  Marriage.
  Married and Single Life.
  May Colven [or May Colvin].
  Merry, Merry Is My Lord.
  My Pretty [Little] Pink.
  Old Man's Song, about His Wife, The.
  Our Goodman.
  Our Ship She Lies in Harbour.
  Paper of Pins.
  Proposal, A.
  Railroad Man for Me, A.
  Rare Willie Drowned in Yarrow; or, The Water o Gamrie.
  Rejoice, O Bridegroom!
  Riddling Knight, The.
  Rosy Apple, Lemon or Pear.
  Shady grove, my true love.
  Show Me The Way.
  Slave Marriage Ceremony Supplement.
  Song Ballet (I Was Sixteen Years of Age).
  Southeast the Peacock Flies.
  Sukey [or Suky], you shall be my wife.
  "There's not a husband whom storms don't benight."
  To Mr. Punchinello.
  To wed, or not to wed? That is the question.
  Upon a Maid That Died the Day She Was Married.
  Whan'll we be marry'd.
  What Her Girl Friend Asked and What She Replied Regarding His Return.
  Wife Wrapt [or Wrapped] in Wether's Skin, The.
  Yong wyf and an harvest-gos, A.
Updike. Newlyweds, The.
Valentine, J. Bride's Hours, A.
Van Duyn. Late Loving.
Vaughan, H. Isaac's Marriage.
Villon. Ballad Written for a Bridegroom.
Viorst. Honeymoon is over, The.
Virgil. How hard a fate enthrals the wretched maid.
Virrừru Mũteyinaṇānār. What He Said after a Quarrel, Remembering His Wedding Night.
Võ Phiến. Where Have They Gone?

Wakoski. Moneylight.
Wallace, R. Wild Strawberries.
Walsh, C. Woman to Her Lover, A.
Waniek. Bali Hai Calls Mama.
Ward, E. Dialogue between a Squeamish Cotting Mechanic and His Sluttish Wife, in the Kitchen.
Weever. De Se.
Wendt. Mussels.
West, J. Married, poor soul! your empire's over.
Wharton, E. Last Giustiniani, The.
Whateley. On the Author's Husband Desiring Her to Write Some Verses.
Whitehead, J. About a Year After He Got Married He Would Sit Alone in an Abandoned Shack in a Cotton Field Enjoying Himself.
Whittemore, R. Storm from the East, A.
Wickham. Meditation at Kew.
  Nervous Prostration.
  Slighted Lady, The.
Wier. Lucille's Kumquat Colored Kimono.
Wilcox, E. Holiday, A.
  Way of It, The.
Williams, J. Matrimony.
Williams, W. Marriage.
Winchilsea. Letter to Daphnis, A.
  Reformation.
Wolstenholme-Elmy. Marriage, which might have been a mateship sweet.
Wong, N. Ironing.
  Where are you going now?
Wright, M. Address to Her Husband.
  Wedlock, a Satire.
Yang Fang. Joy of Union, The.
Yau. Edificio Sayonara.
Yeats. Collarbone [or Collar-Bone] of a Hare, The.
Yevtushenko. Siberian Wooing.
Yi, T. Bride, The.
Yosano. As I am unhappy.
Yüan Chen. Airing Painful Memories.
Zamora, D. Loyal Housewife.

See also **Monogamy and Monogamists; Polyandry; Wedding Songs; Weddings**

Marriage, Arranged
Sappho. Bridal Songs: "Happy bridegroom! / Now your wedding has come true."

Mars (god)
Brecht, B. God of War, The.
Ehrenstein. Ares.
Hadas, R. Mars and Venus.
Leonidas of Alexandria. Upon Venus Putting on Mars His Armes.
Longley, M. Sulpicia.
Ovid. Elegy 9b: "If I heard a voice from heaven say 'Live without'."

Mars (planet)
Berrigan, T. Bean Spasms.
Bold, A. Last Men on Mars.
Lowell, R. March 1, The.
Maiola. Up on the Moon.
Rabbitt. For Thomas Stearns Eliot on the Occasion of His One Hundredth Birthday.
Urdang. Evening of Home Movies, An.
Whittemore, R. Science Fiction.

Marshes
Bromige. Choice.
Everwine. Marsh, New Year's Day, The.
Johnson, E. Marshlands.
Kusano Shimpei. Birthday Party.
Lanier, S. Marshes of Glynn, The.
Lawrence, D. Doe at Evening, A.
Niedecker. Paean to Place.
  Will You Write Me a Christmas Poem?
Wills, J. Bittern booms, A.

Marsyas
Roberts, G. Marsyas.

Martí, José
Roberts, W. On a Monument to Martí.

Martial Arts
Liu. My Father's Martial Art.

Martin, Saint
Gunn, T. St. Martin and the Beggar.

Martyrs
Alabaster. What meaneth this, that Christ an hymne did singe.
Behn, A. Thousand Martyrs I Have Made, A.
Bialik. City of Slaughter, The.
Blumenthal, W. Da Silva Gives the Cue.
Borges. John 1:14 (1964).
Buckmaster. Vanzetti.
Campbell, A. Shabby Old Dad.
Chaucer. General Prologue, The.
Crashaw. Hymn to Saint Teresa.
  To the Infant Martyrs.
  Upon the Infant Martyrs.
Dickinson, E. Martyr Poets—did not tell, The.
  Through the strait pass of suffering.
Drennan, W. Wake of William Orr, The.
Eleazar. Thy Faithful Sons.
Gomez. Elegy: "I die for Your holy word without regret."
Görgey. Thomas.
Hecht, A. 'More Light! More Light!'.
Herrick. Dirge of Jephthah's Daughter, The.
  To Groves.
Johnson, L. Te Martyrum Candidatus.
Kim, Y. Sea of Lemon, The.
Lamb, C. Salome.
"Learsi." Martyrdom.
Lowell, R. Colloquy in Black Rock.
MacNeice. Springboard, The.
Milosz, C. Campo dei Fiori.
Milton. On the Late Massacre [or Massacher] in Piedmont [or Piemont].
Moritz. In Memory of Titian Tabidze.
Oleynikov. Beetle, The.
Oliver, M. Sunrise.
Phan Văn Trị. Rice Mill, The.
Pickthall, M. Père Lalement.
  Two Souls.
Pratt, E. Martyrdom of Brébeuf and Lalemant, 16 March 1649, The.
Quarles. Of St Stephen.
Read, S. My men go wearily.
Schneour. Last Words of Don Henriquez, The.
Sepamla. I Remember Sharpeville.
Shengeli. 27 July 1830.
Smith, S. Sunt Leones.
Stanley, T. On S. John the Baptist.
Suckling, J. Upon Stephen Stoned.
Svetlov. To a Rabfak Student.
Tagami. Tobera.
Unknown. John Brown's body lies a-mould'ring in the grave.
Vaughan, H. Incarnation and Passion, The.
Voznesensky. Call of the Lake, The.
Vuco. Cyril and Methodius.
Weiners. With Meaning.
Wilde, L. Who Will Show Us Any Good?
Yun. Cross, The.

Marvell, Andrew
MacLeish. You, Andrew Marvell.

Marx, Karl
Connolly, C. M is for Marx.
Enzensberger, H. Karl Heinrich Marx.
Vallejo. And don't bother telling me anything.
Wayman. Wayman in Love.

Mary II, Queen of England
Unknown. Maria to Henric.

Mary Magdalene
"Akhmatova." Crucifixion.
Barrett, E. Woman.
Channing. Murillo's Magdalen.
Clarke, C. Palm Leaf of Mary Magdalene.
Constable, H. To Saint Mary Magdalen.
  To St Mary Magdalen.
Crashaw. On Mary Magdalene.
  Saint Mary Magdalene or the Weeper.
  Weeper, The.
Hecht, A. Man Who Married Magdalene, The.
Herbert, G. Mary [or Marie] Magdalen.
Hughes, T. Matthew 27:45–56; Now from the sixth hour there was darkness.
Kingsley, H. At Glastonbury.
Levy, A. Magdalen.
Lewis, S. Mary Magdalene.
Maksimovic. For All Mary Magdalenes.
Marbod of Rennes. Hymn of the Magdalen.

Mew. "Find rest in Him!" One knows the parsons' tags.
Milosz, C. Matthew 28:1–6; Now after the sabbath.
Pasternak, B. Magdalene (I).
Rilke. John 20:11–18; But Mary stood weeping outside the tomb.
Mary at Peace with the Risen Lord.
Matthew 27:57–61; When it was evening, there came a rich man.
Southwell. Marie [or Mary] Magdalens Complaint at Christs Death.
Tsvetayeva. Magdalene.
Unknown. Akathistos Hymn.

Mary Queen of Scots
Bell, H. Mary, Queen of Scots.
Elizabeth I. Doubt of future foes exiles my present joy, The.
"Field." Tragic Mary Queen of Scots, The.
Harington. Tragicall Epigram, A.
Southwell. At Fotheringay.

Mary, the Virgin
Alabaster. To the Blessed Virgin.
Appleman, P. Mary.
Matthew 1:18–25; Now the birth of Jesus Christ took place.
Brecht, B. Luke 2:8–20; And in that region there were shepherds.
Mary.
Brooke, R. Mary and Gabriel.
Brooks, G. Penitent Considers Another Coming of Mary, A.
Campbell, J. O Glorious Childbearer.
Castellanos. Nazareth.
Clifton, L. Anna Speaks of the Childhood of Mary Her Daughter.
Astrologer Predicts at Mary's Birth, The.
Island Mary.
Mary.
Mary's Dream.
Coleridge, M. Our Lady.
When Mary thro' the Garden Went.
Columcille. Prayer to the Virgin.
Constable, H. To Our Blessed Lady.
Coverdale. Song of the Virgin Mary, The.
Crashaw. On the Blessed Virgins Bashfulnesse.
Tear[e], The.
Cullen, C. Mary, Mother of Christ.
Curzon, D. Tour of Ein Kerem, A.
da Todi. Stabat Mater, The.
Dickey, J. Magus, The.
Donne. Annunciation.
Doolittle, H. We have seen her.
We have seen her/ the world over.
Fallon, P. Assumption.
Mater Dei.
Gardner, A. Mary, The Mother of Jesus.
Glazkov. Conversation of a Private and the Virgin.
Glück, L. Luke 2:1–7; In those days a decree went out from Caesar Augustus.
Gore-Booth. Heretic's Pilgrimage, A.
Griffin, G. To a Seagull.
To the Blessed Virgin Mary.
Gunn, T. Jesus and His Mother.
Hawker. Aishah Schechinah.
Herbert, G. Ana(Mary-Army)gram.
Herebert. Holy moder, that bere Crist.
Thou wommon boute fere.
Herrick. Observation ("Virgin-Mother stood at distance (there), The").
Hopkins, G. Blessed Virgin Compared to the Air We Breathe, The.
May Magnificat, The.
Jackson, L. Virgin, The.
Jammes. Five Sorrowful Mysteries, The.
Jennings, E. Visitation, The.
Kamienska. Luke 10:38–42; Now as they went on their way.
Keegan. Irish Reaper's Harvest Hymn.
Kipling, R. Sons of Martha, The.
Lee, A. Motherhood.
L'Engle. O Simplicitas.
Levi, P. Annunciation.
Lope de Vega Carpio. At Dawn the Virgin Is Born.

Lowell, R. Beyond the Alps.
Mac Con Brettan. I call you with honest words.
"MacDiarmid." Harry Semen.
Problem Child, The.
Marbod of Rennes. Hymn of the Magdalen.
Mistral, G. Martha and Mary.
Mitchell, S. Vermeer.
Muir, E. Annunciation, The.
O Direain. Invitation to Mary.
O'Donoghue, B. Apparition, The.
O'Riordan. Hymn to the Virgin Mary.
Pasternak, B. Christmas Star.
Patchen. I have lighted the candles, Mary.
Rilke. John 11:30–44; Now Jesus had not yet come to the village.
Luke 1:39–56: In those days Mary arose.
Mary's Visitation.
Robinson, E. Gift of God, The.
Schnackenberg. Living Room, The.
Smith, S. Dream of Comparison, A.
Tynan. Mater Dei.
Unknown. Hail, Queen of Heaven.
Hymn to the Virgin.
I syng of a mayden that is makeles.
Keening of Mary, The.
Litany to Our Lady.
Mary Weeps for Her Child.
Mary's Dream.
Now Fade the Rose and Lily-Flower.
Now Goeth Sun under Wood.
Our Lady's Song.
Seven Virgins, The.
Song of the Woman, The.
"Stond well, moder, under Rode."
Virgin Mary, The.
Vaughan, H. Knot, The.
Voigt. Feast of the Assumption of the Virgin, The.
Wilde, O. San Miniato.
Williams, W. For Eleanor and Bill Monahan.
Yeats. Mother of God, The.

Maryland (state)
Clifton, L. Slave Cabin, Sotterly Plantation, Maryland, 1989.
Dame. On the road to Damascus, Maryland.
Randall, J. My Maryland.
Smith, D. Cumberland Station.

Masefield, Caroline Louisa
Masefield. C. L. M.

Masefield, John
Untermeyer, L. John Masefield Relates the Story of Tom, Tom, the Piper's Son.

Masks
Allen, P. Night Vision.
Brecht, B. Mask of Evil, The.
Browning, E. Mask, The.
Custance. Masquerade, The.
Doubiago. Self.
Dunbar, P. We wear the mask that grins and lies.
Gregory, H. On a Celtic Mask by Henry Moore.
Hoyt, C. Hallowe'en mask, A.
Komunyakaa. Untitled Blues.
Landon. Mask of Gaiety, The.
Levertov. People at Night.
Lim, S. Lost Name Woman.
Probyn. Masquerading.
Rexroth, K. Racoon.
Rukeyser, M. Poem as Mask, The.
Senghor. Negro Mask.
Prayer to the Masks.
Sorescu. Carnival.
Thomas, D. O make me a mask and a wall to shut from your spies.
Tóth, J. Masks.
Zimmer. Zimmer in Grade School.

Masochism
Davies, S. In Francum.
Hernton. Long Blues, The.
Koch, K. To win the love of women one should first discover.

Massachusetts (state)
Baker, D. Dying in Massachusetts.
Bishop, E. In the Waiting Room.
Brinnin. Cape Ann; a View.

Eberhart, R. On a Squirrel Crossing the Road in Autumn, in New England.
Eliot, T. Cape Ann.
Emerson, R. Concord Hymn.
Longfellow, H. Rhyme of Sir Christopher, The.
Lowell, R. For the Union Dead.
Orban, O. Snowfall in Boston.
Plath. Point Shirley.
Shapiro, H. Provincetown, Mass.
Terry, L. Bar['s Fight[, August 28, 1746].
Tompson. On a Fortification at Boston Begun by Women.
Unknown. Boston Burglar, The.
Wilbur. Running.

Massacre of the Innocents
Hanzlik. Clap Your Hands for Herod.
Hartwig. Matthew 2:16–18; Then Herod, when he saw.
Who Says.
Hope, A. Massacre of the Innocents.
Lowell, R. Holy Innocents, The.
Rózewicz. Massacre of the Boys.
Shaw, L. To a Christmas Two-Year-Old.
Unknown. Give Thanks.

Massacres
Baruch of Worms. Elegy: "Those reckless hosts rush to the wells."
Bialik. City of Slaughter, The.
Breytenbach. Lullaby.
Chin. Exile's Letter: After the Failed Revolution.
Darwish, M. Psalm 2.
Getsi. Oradour-sur-Glane. Silence.
Jeffers, R. Antrim.
Lowell, R. At the Indian Killer's Grave.
Mapanje. After Wiriyamu Village Massacre by Protuguese.
Milton. On the Late Massacre [or Massacher] in Piedmont [or Piemont].
Sexton. I'm dreaming the My Lai soldier again.
Small, J. Pig-Sticking Season, The.
Suhl. And the Earth Rebelled.
Wu Chia-chi. Woman Tung.
Zimunya. After the Massacre.
Zwicky. Summer Pogrom.

Masts
Campbell, R. Choosing a Mast.

Maternity
Hemschemeyer. Giving birth in Greek.
Jeffers, R. Haunted Country.
Kiên Giang. Beauties in White.
Mistral, G. Song.

Mathematics and Mathematicians
Baumel. Thirty-Six Poets.
Cibulka. Mathematics.
Cowley, A. Number, Weight, and Measure.
Dove, R. Flash Cards.
Holub. Zito the Magician.
Karpowicz. From the Skein of the Straight Line.
Kendall, M. Pure Hypothesis, A.
Kovner. To Myself.
Kunio. Tanka: "In a grove."
Machi. Tanka: "Loneliness."
Millay, E. Euclid alone has looked on Beauty bare.
Phillips, C. Mathematics of Breathing, A.
Tekkan. Tanka: "Unlike their father."
Unknown. Arithmetic.
Learn to Count.
Lover's Arithmetic, The.
Welish. Wild Sleeve.
Wickham. Happy Mathematician, The.
See also **Arithmetic**

Matisse, Henri
Sanders, E. Cutting Prow, The.
Snodgrass, W. Matisse: "The Red Studio."

Matterhorn
Hardy, T. Zermatt: To the Matterhorn.

Maturity
Cummings, E. Pretty a day, A.
DeClue. Ijajee's Story.
Gallagher, T. Breasts.
Hill, G. Guardians, The.

Holmes, J. Against the Literal.
Jonson, B. Ode. To Sir William Sydney, on His Birthday.
Kipling, R. If you can keep your head when all [about you].
Lipska. What Happened to Professor White on Leaving the Hat Store.
Liu. Mother.
Lovelace, R. Love Enthroned.
Moore, T. In the morning of life, when its cares are unknown.
Orlen. Biplane, The.
Paquet. Basket Case.
Pasolini. Part of a Letter to the Codignola Boy.
Ransom, J. First Travels of Max.
Rukeyser, M. Boys of These Men Full Speed.
Shakespeare, W. Sonnet 102.
Shepherd, R. White Days.
Smith, S. To carry the child into adult life.
Stephens, M. After Asia.
Unknown. Girl's Song, A.
Waller, E. Budd, The.
Wordsworth, W. My heart leaps up when I behold.

Mausoleums
"MacDiarmid." Skeleton of the Future, The.
Schmitz. Queen of Heaven Mausoleum.

See also **Cemeteries; Graves; Monuments; Tombs**

May
Auden. May with its light behaving.
Bly, R. In the month of May when all leaves open.
Browning, R. Home-Thoughts, From Abroad. May and Death.
Buchanan, G. May Morning.
Dafydd ap Gwilym. Duw gwyddiad mai da y gweddai.
De la Mare. There blooms no bud in May.
Dekker, T. et al. May.
Dixon, R. Judgment of the May, The.
Dunbar, W. Poet's Dream, The.
Hardy, T. Afterwards.
Hass, R. Late Spring.
Herrick. Corinna's Going A-Maying.
Maypole is up, The.
Hopkins, G. May Magnificat, The.
Hovell-Thurlow. May! queen of blossoms.
Kim, Y. May.
Kumin, M. May 10th.
Lanier, S. Song for "The Jacquerie."
Larkin, P. Trees are coming into leaf, The.
Linden, M. May.
Lowell, J. May is a pious fraud of the almanac.
Masaoka Shiki. First of May[3], The.
McGough, R. May.
Milton. Song: on [or of] May Morning.
Neilson, J. May.
Nemerov. May Day Dancing, The.
Oliver, M. May, and among the miles of leafing.
Patmore, C. 'Twas when the spousal time of May.
Poliziano. She Finds Herself in a Garden. Welcome to May.
Pritchard, N. Springtime.
Ray, H. May.
May's Invocation after a Tardy Spring.
Rosenfeld, M. Jewish May, The.
Rossetti, C. May.
May-Time.
Singer, B. Peterhead in May.
Spenser. Is not thilke the mery moneth of May.
Teasdale. Over the Roofs.
Tolson. Victor Garibaldi.
Tranströmer. Man Awakened by a Song Above His Roof, The.
Unknown. Fisherman's Rhyme.
Here we come a-piping.
May Day.
May in the Green-Wood.
May-Time.
Now is the month of maying.

Old May Song.
On May-day, when the lark began to rise.
Updike. May.
Watson, S. Ode in May.
Wickham. Lament of the Red Knight.
Williams, W. Bird Song.
Locust Tree in Flower, The.
Tulip Bed, The.
Wordsworth, W. Composed at Rydal on May Morning, 1838.
Wyatt, T. You that in love find[e] luck[e] and [h]abunda[u]nce.

May Day
Herrick. May-pole is up, The.
Kunio. Tanka: "This May Day night."
Unknown. On Mayday we dance.

Maya
Bernstein, O. Cuernavaca.
Jones, S. Hymn to Na'ra'yena, A.

Mayflower (ship)
Ellsworth. Mayflower, The.

Mayo. See **County Mayo, Ireland**

Mead
Cynewulf. Honey-Mead: "I am valued by men, fetched from afar."

Meadows. See **Fields and Pastures**

Meadowsweet
Allingham. Meadowsweet.

Meat
Chu Yün-ming. Making Fun of the Well at the Inn below the Mountain.
Coward. Any Part of Piggy.
Edson, R. Ape.
Elenkov. Sauna.
Elytis. Autopsy, The.
Follain. Black Meat.
Hardy, T. Bags of Meat.
Harper, M. Breaded Meat, Breaded Hands.
Herrick. Grace for a Child.
Upon Showbread [or Shewbread]: Epigram.
Jewsbury. My heart's in the kitchen, my heart is not here.
Joseph, L. There I Am Again.
Levine, P. Salami.
McClure, M. Moiré.
Melville, H. Maldive Shark, The.
Mountain, M. One fly everywhere the heat.
Unknown. On a Gentleman's Complaining to a Lady That He Could Not Eat Meat.
Van Walleghen. Meat.
Waldman, A. Skin / Meat / BONES.
Watson, C. Knickerbocker Knockabout.
Wilbur. Rillons, Rillettes, they taste the same.
Wu Chia-chi. To Ch'eng Fei-t'ao.
Yün Shou-p'ing. Scorpion's tails, silver hooks.

Meath. See **County Meath, Ireland**

Mechanics
McMullen, R. It happens working.
Wakoski. Mechanic, The.

Medals
Mori Ōgai. Tanka: "Some medals."

Medea
Apollonius Rhodius. Now rising shades a solemn scene
Ovid. Medea rejuvenates Aeson.
Medea's invocation. display.
Seneca. Medea's Frenzy.
Webster, A. Oh smooth adder/ who with fanged kisses changedst my natural blood.

Medicine
Belloc. On Hygiene.
Browning, R. Epistle Containing the Strange Medical Experience of Karshish, the Arab Physician, An.
Burns, R. Death and Doctor Hornbook [A True Story].
Giscombe. (1962 At the Edge of Town).
Huang E. Pearl-teardrops roll and gather.
Kenyon, J. Bottles.
Kwakiutl Oral Tradition. Healing Prayer to the Salmon-Berry Vines.
Li K'ai-hsien. On My Birthday—Sick.
Longfellow, H. Day is done, and the darkness, The.
Meredith, G. Melampus.

Rich, A. 5:30 A.M.
Smelyakov. Should I ever fall ill.
Unknown. Magic Formula.
Walwicz. Daredevil.

See also **Hospitals; Illness; Nurses; Physicians**

Meditation
Baudelaire. Owls.
Brutus. Under House Arrest.
De Vere, E. SITTING alone upon my thought, in melancholy mood.
Emerson, R. Apology, The.
Hamburger, M. Garden, Wilderness.
Hecht, A. Meditation.
Heyen. Tie, The.
Hopkinson, A. Origami.
Kerouac. Buddha.
How to Meditate.
Kung Tzu-chen. Tune: "Decorous and Pretty."
Kunze, R. Meditation.
Kyger. News bulletin from Keith Lampe.
Liu Tsung-yüan. Meditation Hall.
Mahadevi. So long as this breath fills your nostrils.
Mo Shih-lung. Meditation Rock, The.
Oppen. Discrete Series 1929–1933.
Padilla. Discourse on Method, The.
Ponsot. Analogue.
Steele, T. Wartburg, 1521–22, The.
Sumangalamata. At last free.
Thompson, F. From stones and poets you may know.
Tillinghast, R. Dozing on the Porch with an Oriental Lap-Rug.
Unknown. Sent from the Power.
Whatsoever things are true.
Very. Columbine, The.
Wang Chiu-ssu. Quiet Sitting.
Wang Kuo-wei. To try to find my heart, it's hard enough.
Wild, R. In a melancholly studdy.
Wordsworth, W. Inner Vision, The.
Wyatt, T. Prologue: "Love, to give law unto his subject hearts."
Xuanjing. Meditating at midnight.
Yang Wan-li. Sitting at Night on the Moon-viewing Terrace.
Yosano. Tanka: "Aster, The."

Mediterranean Sea
Lawrence, D. Middle of the World.
Santayana. Ode V: "Of thee the Northman by his beachèd galley."
Tate, A. Mediterranean, The.

Medusa
Alousi. Medusa Cement.
Bogan, L. Medusa.
Clampitt. Medusa.
Drummond, W. Statue of Medusa, The.
Hayden, R. Perseus.
Marino. Head of Medusa on a Rotella of Michelangelo da Caravaggio, in the Gallery of the Grand Duke of Tuscany, The.
Sarton. Muse as Medusa, The.
Shelley, P. On the Medusa of Leonardo da Vinci in the Florentine Gallery.

Melampus
Meredith, G. Melampus.

Melancholy
Bensko. Elk on Mutability, The.
Blamire. Written on a Gloomy Day, in Sickness.
Blumenthal, M. Blue.
Bridges, R. Melancholia.
Brontë, E. Wind, I hear it sighing, The.
Brooks, G. Crazy Woman, The.
Burton, R. Authors [or Author's] Abstract of Melancholy, The.
Byrom. My spirit longeth for Thee.
Byron, G. Childe Harold's Pilgrimage Canto III.
Ch'u Kuang-hsi. Farmer's Thoughts, A.
Clare, J. O could I be as I have been.
Silent Love.
To Elia (unsigned).
Coleridge, S. Dejection.
Nightingale, The.
This Lime-Tree Bower My Prison.
Cope, W. Depression.

Cornford, F.   She Warns Him.
Costello, L.   Lines: "If we should ever meet again."
Cranch.   Pines and the Sea, The.
Davis, W.   January.
Deane, J.   On a dark night.
Dyer, G.   In deep distress, I cried to God.
Emerson, R.   Teach me I am forgotten by the dead.
"Field."   She is singing to Thee, *Domine!*.
Fletcher, J.   Melancholy.
Ginsberg, A.   My Sad Self.
Headly.   Child of the potent spell and nimble eye.
Hemans.   Indian Woman's Death-Song, The.
   Second Sight.
Herrick.   His Litany to the Holy Spirit.
Huang Tsun-hsien.   To Send Away Melancholy.
Hughes, L.   Neighbor.
Hugo, R.   Letter to Bell from Missoula.
Jackson, L.   Sad Boy, The.
Kavanagh, P.   Wet Evening in April.
Keats.   Ode on Melancholy.
Kenyon, J.   From the Nursery.
Kung Tzu-chen.   Lute Song, The.
Lake, P.   Crime and Punishment.
Landon.   Poet's Love, The.
Lewis, C.   Naked Seed, The.
Li Shang-yin.   In a Day.
Marquis.   Reverie.
Matthews, J.   People in These Houses, The.
McGough, R.   Survivor.
Middleton, T.   Melancholy.
Montagu, L.   Receipt to Cure [*or* for] the Vapours, A.
Neruda.   Melancholy inside Families.
Newcastle, M.   Discourse of Melancholy, A.
Norris, K.   Lilith and the Doctor.
Pao Chao.   Imitating the Old Poems.
Patterson, R.   Surplus Blues.
Plath.   Poppies in July.
Radcliffe, A.   Rondeau: "Soft as yon silver ray that sleeps."
Revell.   Other the Wings, The.
Robinson, E.   Charles Carville's Eyes.
Rossetti, C.   At Home.
   If Only.
Shelley, M.   On Reading Wordsworth's Lines on Peele Castle.
Shelley, P.   Stanzas Written in Dejection, near Naples [*or* —December 1818, near Naples].
Sidney, P.   Sonnet 99: "When far-spent night persuades each mortal eye."
Smith, C.   Sonnet XXXII. (To Melancholy. Written on the Banks of the Arun, October 1785).
   Sonnet V. To the South Downs: "Ah, hills beloved!—where once, an happy child."
   Written in October.
Smith, S.   Away, melancholy, / Away with it, let it go.
Stern, G.   Nobody else living knows that song as well as I do.
Stevens, W.   Anglais Mort à Florence.
Swinburne.   Itylus.
Szymborska.   Four in the Morning.
T'ang Hsien-tsu.   Descending the Ridge of Flying Clouds.
Thompson, N.   Next, in a low-browed cave, a little hell.
Thomson, J.   Anear the centre of that northern crest.
Tuckerman, F.   Sometimes I walk where the deep water dips.
Unknown.   On Melancholy.
   Water Is Wide, The.
   What care I though the world reprove.
Wakoski.   Blue Monday.
Wen T'ing-yün.   Tune: "Lotus-leaf Cup."
Wordsworth, W.   Daffodils.
   Sonnet: "World is too much with us; late and soon, The."
Wyatt, T.   What rage is this? What furo[u]r of what kind [*or* kynd]?
Yearsley.   Soliloquy: "What folly to complain."
Zenmaro.   Tanka: "Having lived."

Zimmer.   Queen, The.
See also **Blues (mood); Dejection**

Meleager
Ovid.   Meleager.

Melons
Juan Chi.   Tung-ling melons—men say that long ago.
Mei Yao Ch'en.   Melon Girl.
Wollach.   Love Poem #2.
Yungman.   Melons.

Melville, Herman
Aiken, C.   Herman Melville.
Auden.   Herman Melville.
Crane, H.   At Melville's Tomb.
Elmslie, K.   Japanese City.
Koch.   You were wearing your Edgar Allan Poe printed cotton blouse.
Martin, C.   Satyr, Cunnilinguent: To Herman Melville.
Muir, E.   Scotland 1941.

Memorial Day
Anania.   Memorial Day.
Collins, W.   Ode Written in the Beginning of the Year 1746.
Finch, F.   Blue and the Gray, The.
Heard, J.   Decoration Day.
McCrae, J.   In Flanders Fields the poppies blow.
O'Hara, T.   Bivouac of the Dead, The.
Peterson, H.   O gallant brothers of the generous South.
Saunders, M.   Remembering Day.
Thompson, C.   Memorial Day.

Memories
Nesbit, E.   Gray Folk, The.

Memory
Adamovich.   There was...what?—Pale sunsets, wide expanses.
Akahito.   Mists rise over, The.
Akhmadulina.   I Swear.
"Akhmatova."   And people will think this like. Instead of a Preface.
   Memory of love, you are painful!
   Your white house and tranquil garden, I shall leave.
Aldrich, T.   Memory.
Alegría.   From the Bridge.
Alexander, M.   Memory.
Ali, A.   Cracked Portraits.
Allingham.   At Ballyshannon, Co. Donegal.
   Four Ducks on a Pond.
Amichai.   Anniversaries of War.
   Little Ruth.
   My Father.
Antin.   Real Estate.
Apollinaire.   Shadow.
Aragon.   Lilacs and the Roses, The.
Arnold, M.   Absence.
Aseyev.   How shall I tell you.
Ashbery.   Houseboat Days.
   Other Tradition, The.
   Rain.
Āttiraiyaṉār.   Poet's Memory Is Counsel, A.
Atwood.   Bored.
Aubert, A.   Feeling Through.
Auden.   On This Island.
   Question, The ("To ask the hard question is simple").
   Since.
   Taller to-day, we remember similar evenings.
Bagryana.   River Run.
Balaban.   News Update.
Ball, S.   Nocturnal.
Baraka.   In Memory of Radio.
Barr, T.   Antique Shop.
Bates, K.   To One Who Waits.
   Yellow Clover.
Baudelaire.   Head of Hair, The.
Baxter, E.   In Your Absence.
Belloc.   Tarantella.
Berg, S.   And the Scream.
Berggolts.   Ordeal, The.
Bernstein, O.   Memories of Her Friend Who Died.
Berrigan, T.   Certain Slant of Sunlight, A.
Berry, W.   Wild, The.

Bethell.   Response.
Bezymensky.   About a Hat.
Binyon.   Those That Are Gone.
Bishop, J.   Hours, The.
Blake, W.   Song: "Memory, hither come."
Blok.   Before the Court.
Blood, B.   Late.
Blunden.   1916 Seen from 1921.
Bly, R.   Remembering in Oslo the Old Picture of the Magna Carta.
Boethius.   Book 3, Metrum 11.
Boland, E.   Black Lace Fan My Mother Gave Me, The.
   I remember the way the big windows washed.
Bontemps.   Idolatry.
Borowski.   Sun of Auschwitz, The.
Brathwaite, E.   Ancestors.
Breeze.   Lovin wasn easy all de time.
Brett, L.   I keep forgetting.
Brew.   Search, The.
Brodsky, J.   Café Trieste: San Francisco.
Bromige.   Logical Positivist, The.
Bromley, A.   My Mother's Face Never Moved.
Brontë, A.   Memory.
Brontë, E.   All hushed and still within the house.
   Aye, there it is! It wakes to-night.
   Mild the mist upon the hill.
   O Dream, where art thou now?
   Remembrance.
   Stanzas to———.
   Warning and Reply.
   What winter floods, what showers of spring.
   Wind, I hear it sighing, The.
Brooke, R.   New Boy's View of Rugger.
Brooks, G.   Anniad, The.
   Bean Eaters, The.
Brooks, W.   Pilate Remembers.
Brown, D.   First Person—1981.
   Still Later There Are War Stories.
Browning, E.   L.E.L.'s Last Question.
Browning, R.   Appearances.
   By the Fire-Side.
   Confessions.
   Memorabilia.
Bruner.   Remembrance.
Brush.   Waiting for the End of the War.
Bryant, F.   Cathexis.
Buckley, V.   Man, a woman, straighten up from where, A.
Byron, G.   Lines Written beneath a Picture.
   Stanzas: "And thou art dead, as young and fair."
   Stanzas for Music.
   Stanzas for Music ("There's not a joy the world can give like that it takes away").
Callimachus.   Someone spoke of your death, Herakleitos. It brought me.
   Flight.
Campana.   Autumn Garden.
Canning, G. *et al.*   Rogero's Song.
Caraion.   Memory.
Carew, T.   To T. H., a Lady Resembling My Mistress.
Carlile.   Train Whistles in the Wind and Rain.
Carter, M.   Childhood of a Voice.
Cassian.   Blood, The.
   Part of a Bird.
Cataldi.   Advice.
Causley.   Armistice Day.
   Eden Rock.
Cavafy.   Body, remember not only how much you were loved.
   One Night.
   Return often and take me.
Césaire, A.   In Memory of a Black Union Leader.
   Mississippi.
Chế Lan Viên.   Human Skull, The.
   On the Way Home.
   War Elephant, The.
Ch'en Yü-yi.   Tune: "Immortal at the River"—Ascending a Little Tower at Night.
Cheney-Coker.   Philosopher, The.
   Poem for a Lost Lover.
Chesterton, G.   Donkey, The.

Chipasula. Tramp.
"Chrystos." Your Tongue Sparkles.
Ch'ung. Parody of a Lover.
Ciardi. On a Photo of Sgt. Ciardi a Year Later.
Cisneros, S. Good Hot Dogs.
Clampitt. Burning Child, The.
Clare, J. Love's memories haunt my footsteps still.
Stanzas: "Black absence hides upon the past."
Clark, L. Singing in the Streets.
Clements, S. Susans.
Cohen, L. Heirloom.
Coleman, W. Cousin Mary.
Mastectomy.
Coleridge, M. Only a little shall we speak of thee.
Coleridge, S. Written in Early Youth, the Time an Autumnal Evening.
Cook, E. To the Late William Jerdan.
Coolidge, C. Album—A Runthru.
Corman. Tortoise, The.
Corso. Birthplace Revisited.
Cory, W. Heraclitus.
Cowley, A. On the Death of Mr William Hervey.
Cox, M. In This His Suit.
Crane, H. Emblems of Conduct.
Passage.
Repose of Rivers.
Creeley. Company, The.
Edge, The.
Fire, The.
For My Mother: Genevieve Jules Creeley.
Hole, The.
House, The.
Just Friends.
Memory Gardens.
People, The.
Cronin, J. Naval Base (Part III), The.
Cuddihy. Steps.
Cullen, C. Youth Sings a Song of Rosebuds.
Cummings, E. In time of daffodils(who know.
Love is more thicker than forget.
Dabydeen, C. Dubious Foreigner.
Dacre, C. Power of Love, The.
Daini no Sanmi. From Mt. Arima / over the bamboo plains of Ina.
Dana, R. At the Vietnam War Memorial, Washington, D. C.
Daniels, K. My Father's Desk.
Dante Alighieri. That lady of all gentle memories.
Thoughts are broken in my memory, The.
Darr. At Sixteen.
Daruwalla. Of Mohenjo Daro at Oxford.
Darwish, M. Guests on the sea: Our visit is short.
Davie. Barnsley and District.
Devil on Ice.
Time Passing, Beloved.
Davis, O. Thirty Years Rising.
De la Mare. Fare Well.
Lucy.
Miss Loo.
Old Men, The.
Widow, The.
Winter.
Deane, S. Brethren, The.
Deutsch. Memory.
Di Prima. Backyard.
Notes on the Art of Memory.
Dickey, W. Things Kept.
Dickinson, E. Heart! We [or Heart, we] will forget him!
No Passenger was known to flee.
Pain—has an Element of Blank.
To flee from memory.
DiPalma. Memory's wedge / makes a valley.
Wrong Side of the Door, The.
Ditlevsen. Self Portrait 4.
Djanikian. Agami Beach.
When I First Saw Snow.
Djurdjic. Unfulfilled Love.
Dobbie. My First Memory, Switzerland, Circa 1947.
Dodd, W. Like Deer Our Bodies.

Dooley, M. At Les Deux Magots.
Doolittle, H. Helen.
Lethe.
So you have swept me back.
Dove, R. Dusting.
Fifth Grade Autobiography.
Wingfoot Lake.
Dowson. Non Sum Qualis Eram Bonae sub Regno Cynara[e].
Spleen.
Drainac. Classic Verses.
Drayton. Satyr O never ask how I came to this place.
Drummond de Andrade. In the middle of the road there was a stone.
Duffy, C. In Your Mind.
Dugan, A. Memories of Verdun.
Winter for an Untenable Situation.
Duncan, R. Tribal Memories.
Turning into a restful roomfull.
Dunn, D. Kaleidoscope, The.
Dunn, S. Vanishings, The.
"Dylan." Boots of Spanish Leather.
Edwards, M. To a Loved One of Other Days.
Ehrenburg. I lived obscurely and uncertainly.
Ehrenstein. Home-Coming.
Ehrhart. Confirmation, A.
To Those Who Have Gone Home Tired.
"Elagin." I like these foreign shores and I have never.
"Eliot." Long years have left their writing on my brow.
Two lovers by a moss-grown spring.
Eliot, T. Burnt Norton.
La Figlia Che Piange.
Rhapsody on a Windy Night.
Emanuel, L. On Waking after Dreaming of Raoul.
What Grieving Was Like.
Emerson, R. Memory.
Past, The.
Thine eyes still shined for me, though far.
English, T. Ben Bolt.
Equi. Date With Robbe-Grillet, A.
Evans, G. Eye Blade.
Revelation in the Mother Lode.
Fainlight, R. Handbag.
Faiz. Rain of Stones Is Finished, The.
Fanshawe, C. When last we parted, thou wert young and fair.
Fearing. Resurrection.
Feldman, I. Terminal Laughs.
Fell, A. Freeze-Frame.
Ferlinghetti, L. 26.
Ficowski. Execution of Memory, The.
Field, E. Bachelor Hall.
"Field." I sing thee with the stock-dove's throat.
Fitzgerald, R. Rain in my ears: impatiently there raps.
Flynn, D. Collector, The.
Forché. Elegy.
Foscolo. To Zante.
Fowler, A. Relative.
Frase. Put a Woman into the Memory Box.
Frost, R. Directive.
Fujiwara no Kiyosuke. I may live on until.
Fulton, R. Museums and Journeys.
Remembering Walls.
Fumiko. Tanka: "Eyes, The."
Galguera. Second Childhood.
Gallagher, T. Woodcutting on Lost Mountain.
Galvin, B. Green Evening, A.
Galvin, P. My Father Spoke with Swans.
Gardner, D. Near Hermes.
Garland, H. Plowing: A Memory.
Geda. Sebastian's Lament, 1943.
Gerstler. Unforseen, The.
Gibson, M. Wars.
Gilbert, C. Pushing.
Gildner. Primarily We Miss Ourselves As Children.
Gillan. In memory we are walking.
Ginsberg, A. Hymmnn.
IV.
Memory Gardens.
To Aunt Rose.

Giovanni. Nikki-Rosa.
Glatstein. I still remember the half-lit meaning.
Glazkov. Poetograd.
Glück, L. First Memory.
Pond, The.
Godfrey. Our Lady.
Goldbarth. Nile, The.
Gondlevsky. May God grant me the memory to recall my life.
Gouri. Pictures of Jews.
Graves, R. Plea to Boys and Girls, A.
Recalling War.
Greacen. Carnival at the River.
Father and Son.
Grenier. Has Faded in Part But Magnificent Also Late for RC / Mirrors.
Griffin, G. Song: "Place in thy memory, dearest, A."
Grimké, A. Butterflies, white butterflies, in the sunshine.
Garden Seat, The.
Grosholz. Last of the Courtyard, The.
On the Ferry, Toward Patras.
Remembering the Ardèche.
Grunthal. And thus a monologue keeps flowing.
Gumilyov. Turkey, The.
Gunn, T. Autobiography.
Gurney, I. To His Love.
Habington. Recogitabo Tibi Omnes Annos Meos.
Hacker, M. Hang-Glider's Daughter, The.
Haines, J. Mothball Fleet: Benicia, California.
Hall, D. Airstrip in Essex, 1960, An.
By the Exeter River.
Farm, The.
Foundations of American Industry, The.
Old Pilot, The.
Hamilton, M. For My Father's Mother Who Has Alzheimer's.
Hamod, S. After the Funeral of Assam Hamady.
Hardy, T. After A Journey.
Afterwards.
Ah, are you digging on my grave.
Ancient to Ancients, An.
Beyond the Last Lamp.
Mound, The.
One We Knew.
Shut Out That Moon.
Superseded, The.
To Lizbie Browne.
Voice, The.
Where the Picnic Was.
Harjo, J. Remember the sky that you were born under.
Skeleton of Winter.
Harms. Explaining the Evening News to Corbyn.
My Androgynous Years.
Harryman. My Story.
Harteis. Mirage.
Hass, R. Meditation at Lagunitas.
Hathaway, W. War Hope.
Hayden, R. Ballad of Sue Ellen Westerfield, The.
Those Winter Sundays.
Whipping, The.
Heaney, S. Anahorish.
Terminus.
When all the others were away at Mass.
Hecht, A. Hill, A.
Heine. Looking Back.
Heitzman. March.
Hejinian. Moment yellow, just as four years later when, A.
Helwig. Considerations.
Hemans. Parting Song, A.
Hemschemeyer. I Remember the Room Was Filled with Light.
Herrick. Upon His Sister-in-Law, Mistress Elizabeth Herrick.
Hesketh. Love's Advocate.
Hikmet. Things I Didn't Know I Loved.
Hill, G. Domaine Public.
Hillman. Cleave and Cleave.

Hine. Côte de Liesse.
Letting Go.
Hirsch, E. After the Last Practice.
My Father's Back.
Hitomaro. Plovers cry, The.
Hoagland, T. In the Land of the Lotus Eaters.
One Season.
Hoàng Trinh. Forty.
Hogan, L. Lost Girls, The.
New Apartment.
Holan. Memory II.
Reminiscence.
Hollo. Godlike.
Holub. Gila Desert in Arizona, The.
Hongo. Hilo: First Night Back.
O-Bon: Dance for the Dead.
Hood, T. I remember, I remember.
Hoover, P. Theory.
"Hope." Kashmiri Song.
Howard, R. 1915: A Pre-Raphaelite Ending,
London.
Howe, S. Bride's Day.
Howes, B. Letter from the Caribbean, A.
Hoyt, H. Memory.
Hsiao-Wei. For My Wife.
Hudgins. Around the campfire we sang
hymns.
Hughes, L. Negro Speaks of Rivers, The.
Hugo, R. Freaks at Spurgin Road Field, The.
White Center.
Hull, L. Holy City, City of Night.
Hunt, L. Rondeau: Jenny Kiss'd [or Kissed]
Me.
Hunter, S. Traveling Back.
Ignatow, D. Journey, The.
Irby. Heredom.
Irwin, W. Reminiscence.
Ivaska. For My Godmother.
That which has remained unlived.
To the Memory of a Poet.
Izumi. Will I cease to be.
Jackson, H. Poppies on the Wheat.
Jackson, L. Forgiven Past, The.
Jarman, M. Cavafy in Redondo.
Mirror, The.
Jarrell. Burning the Letters.
Dead Wingman, The.
Elementary Scene, The.
Player Piano, The.
When I was home last Christmas.
Jentzsch. Terezin, the Graveyard.
Johnston, M. Sea-Cucumber, The.
Jonson, B. Mind of the Frontispiece to a
Book, The.
Jordan, J. Daddy at the stove or sink. Large.
Joseph, A. Junior High Dance.
Joseph, L. Mama Remembers.
Justice, D. Invitation to a Ghost.
Men at forty / Learn to close softly.
On the Death of Friends in Childhood.
Sonatina in Yellow.
Kalász. Up against That Wall Everywhere.
Kapilar. What She Said to Her Friend ("You
ask me to forget him").
Kavanagh, P. Memory of my Father.
October.
Kay, J. Photo in the Locket.
Stincher, The.
Keesing. Reverie of a Mum.
Kefala. Freedom fighter, she said, A.
Kemble. Farewell to Italy.
Petition, A.
To Mrs. Norton.
Kenny, M. Molly.
Kessler, M. All their names were Vincent,
Ernie, Paul.
Keyes, S. Elegy: "April again, and it is a year
again."
Kgositsile. Air, I hear, The.
For Art Blakey and the Jazz Messengers.
Ki no Tsurayuki. Out in the marsh reeds.
Kinnell. For Robert Frost.
River That Is East, The.
To William Carlos Williams.
When I come back to my father's house,.
Kirsch, S. Pictures.
Knight, E. Poem of Attrition, A.

Koch, K. Circus, The.
Energy in Sweden.
To Marina.
With Janice.
Koethe. Falling Water.
Komey. Change, The.
Oblivion.
Komunyakaa. Break from the Bush, A.
Report from the Skull's Diorama.
Korkiya. Stanzas: "With youthful loss of
memory, in my voiceless land."
Kovner. Poem: Alte Zachen.
To the Things That Are Immortal.
While at Prayer.
Krynicki. By entering the grand lottery.
Kumin, M. Envelope, The.
How It Is.
Nuns of Childhood: Two Views, The.
Kunitz, S. Passing Through.
Touch Me.
Kuppner. Passing Through Doorways.
Kushner, A. Remembering Love.
Kuzmina-Karavayeva. I too have encompassed
a lot: a mother thrice—.
Lalic. Inscribed in the Silver of the Sea.
Lamb, C. Old Familiar Faces, The.
Landon. Lines Written Under a Picture of a
Girl Burning a Love-Letter.
Song.
Landor, W. Memory.
Rose Aylmer.
What News.
Lang, A. Twilight on Tweed.
Lankesh. Mother.
Lanyer. Description of Cookham, The.
Larkin, P. I Remember, I Remember.
So through that unripe day you bore your
head.
Laughlin, E. Unknown, The.
Lauterbach. Here and There.
Laux. China.
Lawrence, D. Argonauts, The.
Hymn to Priapus.
Piano.
Lea, S. At the Flyfisher's Shack.
Telescope.
Lee, J. My Father's Country.
Lee, L. I Ask My Mother to Sing.
Mnemonic.
Lehmann, G. What's that bird, Mr Long?
Leonidas of Tarentum. Night and mist, what
bones you have eaten.
Lerman. Evenings in the Sea.
Levertov. Intrusion.
Note to Olga (1966), A.
Woman Meets an Old Lover, A.
Levi, P. Shemà.
Levine, P. Genius.
I Remember Clifford.
Levy, A. Old House, The.
Lewis, A. Post-Script: for Gweno.
Lewis, J. Stories.
Lewis, J. Grandmother Remembers, A.
Li Ch'ing-chao. Tune: "Southern Song, A."
Li Ho. Sing Loud.
Li Po. Exile's Letter.
Li Shang-yin. Crooked River.
Lim, S. Father from Asia.
Lincoln, A. Memory.
Lindsay, V. Eagle That Is Forgotten, The.
Liu E. I remember when we made our first
promises of love.
Livesay, D. Green Rain.
Lochhead, L. Grim Sisters, The.
Lodge, G. On an Æolian Harp.
Long, R. What Happens.
Longfellow, H. Fire of Drift-Wood, The.
Golden Mile-Stone, The.
Meeting, The.
My Lost Youth.
Longley, M. Ash Keys.
Remembering Carrigskeewaun.
Lorde. Movement Song.
Lowell, A. Seeing you stand once more before
my eyes.
Lowell, J. Remembered Music.
"Lu Hsün." In Remembrance of the Forgotten.

Lu Yu. Night Thoughts.
Lukonin. To Kolya Otrada.
MacCaig. Aspects.
"MacDiarmid." Crystals like Blood.
Eemis-Stane, The.
MacDonagh, D. Veterans, The.
Macedonius. Praise memory and forgetfulness!
Macgoye. August the First: The Shadow. Patel
Speaks.
Mackintosh, E. In Memoriam[, Private D.
Sutherland].
Maclean, A. Rain, The.
MacNeice. Soap Suds.
Madgett. Souvenir.
Mandelstam. I'll chase through the gypsy
camp of dark streets.
Mansour, J. Anti-mnemonic self-vaccination.
Mapanje. We Wondered about the Mellow
Peaches.
Marston, P. Vain Wish, A.
Marvell. Gallery, The.
Mason, R. Old Memories of Earth.
Matevski. Bells.
Matthews, J. Paradigm of a Hero.
Mayer, B. Birthday Sonnet for Grace.
Carlton Fisk is My Ideal.
Mazur. Phonic.
McAuley, J. Because.
McCarriston. Billy.
Castle in Lynn, A.
McCarthy, G. Arrival.
Finding the Way Back.
Sound of Guns, The.
McClellan. To Theodore.
McDonald, W. Hauling Over Wolf Creek Pass
in Winter.
Once You've Been to War.
Veteran.
McFadden, R. Contemplations of Mary.
Stringer's Field.
McGinley. 5:32, The.
McKay, C. Flame-Heart.
Jasmine.
Tropics in New York, The.
McKean. After Listening to Jack
Teagarden. . . .
McPherson, S. Helen Todd: My Birthname.
Mei Yao Ch'en. Dream at Night, A.
I Remember the River at Wu Sung.
On the Death of His Wife.
Melville, H. Stonewall Jackson.
Menken. Memory, A.
Merrill, J. Broken Home, The.
Days of 1941 and '44.
Days of 1964.
Last Words.
Manos Karastefanís.
Scenes of Childhood.
Up and Down.
Urban Convalescence, An.
Vision of the Garden, A.
Meynell, A. Renouncement.
Mibu no Tadami. Since I left her.
Millay, E. Cameo, The.
Only until this cigarette is ended.
Time does not bring relief; you all have lied.
What lips my lips have kissed, and where, and
why.
Miller, V. Remembering Aunt Helen.
Milosz, C. And yet the books will be there on
the shelves, separate beings.
Screens will be set there.
Mitchell, S. Dead, The.
Miyazawa Kenji. Siwashing it out once in
Siuslaw Forest.
Moffi. Putting an End to the War Stories.
Moldaw. 64 Panoramic Way.
Montague, J. Lament for the O'Neills.
Like dolmens round my childhood, the old
people.
Moore, T. Echo.
Go where glory waits thee.
Journey Onwards, The.
Long, Long Be My Heart with Such Memories
Filled.
Oft in the stilly night.
Moorsom. Jewels In My Hand.

Mora. Depression Days.
Gentle Communion.
Morgan, V. Within the Greenhouse Effect.
Morris, G. Woodman, spare that tree!
Morton, D. Old Ships.
Moss, H. Elegy for My Sister.
Moultrie. Forget Thee?
Muir, E. Animals, The.
Muldoon, P. Soap-Pig, The.
Mura. Colors of Desire, The.
To H.N.
Nagys. Poem.
Nam Xuyên. Bamboo hedgerow cut a dark-green swath, The.
Nelson, C. How We Make Lumber Out of Trees.
Nemerov. Blue Suburban.
Models.
Nesbit, E. Among His Books.
Newbolt. Felix Antonius.
Nezval. Walker in Prague.
Nguyễn Khuyến. Old Age.
Nichol. Some Nets.
Nortje. Cosmos in London.
Notley. Beginning with a stain, as the universe did perhaps.
California Girlhood, A.
Oandasan. Grandmothers Land.
Oden. Carousel, The.
O'Hara, F. In Favor of One's Time.
In Memory of My Feelings.
Oldham, P. Noon.
Olofsson. Autobiography.
O'Loughlin. Posthumous.
Olsen, C. Storm Chasers, The.
Olson. Chain of memory is resurrection I am a vain man, The.
Ondaatje. Burning Hills.
Oppen. Cars run in a void of utensils, The.
Forms of Love, The.
Part of the Forest.
Orban, O. Requiem: "He tossed a life preserver to the young castaway in '55."
Orlen. Ukranian Pastorals.
Osaki. Amnesiac.
Ostriker. Leaf Pile, The.
Owen, W. Roads also have their wistful rest, The.
Unreturning, The.
Pack, R. Thrasher in the Willow by the Lake, The.
Page, G. Late Night Radio.
Pagis. Final Exam.
Letter, A.
Picture Postcard from Our Youth.
Story, The.
Paley, G. Love.
People in My Family.
Paquet. Group Shot.
Pasternak, B. Fresco Come to Life.
Mary Magdalene (I).
On Early Trains.
Paulin. In the Lost Province.
Payne, B. Lines in Memory of My Father.
Peacock, T. Love and Age.
Peters, L. Home Coming.
Petri. Christmas 1956.
Gratitude.
Phanias. Here Lysis set an empty tomb.
Phillips, C. Africa Says.
Picasso. Poems: "Hasten on your childhood to the hour when white in."
Pierman. How We Learned about Friction.
Pilinszky. Afterword.
Passion of Ravensbrück.
Pilkington, L. Memory, a Poem.
Pinsky. Long Branch Song, A.
Planché. Self-Evident.
Plath. Green Rock, Winthrop Bay.
Plumpp. When the Spirit Spray-Paints the Sky.
Po Chü-i. Dreaming that I Went with Li and Yü to Visit Yüan Chên.
Poe. To F——.
Polwhele. Visit to the Author's Paternal Seat, A.
Porter, C. Old-Fashioned Garden, An.

Porter, P. Easiest Room in Hell, The.
Pound, E. Doria.
Prévert. Barbara remember.
Prince, F. Babiaantje, The.
Probyn. Song Out of Season, A.
Proust. My True Love Hath My Heart.
Raine, C. Onion, Memory, The.
Raine, K. Images.
Ramanujan. Breaded Fish.
Randall, D. Souvenirs.
Ransom, J. Antique Harvesters.
Equilibrists, The.
Ravikovitch. Surely You Remember.
Reaney. School Globe, The.
Reese, L. Lavender Woman, The.
Rein. Glimpsed through a Lens.
Rexroth, K. How long, long ago.
In the park a crow awakes.
Signature of All Things, The.
Rich, A. From the Prison House.
Living Memory.
Newsreel.
Riley, J. Old Swimmin'-Hole, The.
Rilke. On the Death of Countess Luise Schwerin.
Roberts, N. Max Factor Pink.
Robinson, A. Dead Friend, The.
Stornelli and Strambotti.
Valley, The.
Robinson, E. Souvenir.
Rodriguez, L. Heavy blue veins streaked across my mother's legs, some of them bunched up into dark lumps at her ankles.
Roethke. Dream, The.
Romano, R. Bucket, The.
Rossetti, C. Echo.
First Day, The.
From Sunset to Star Rise.
Memory.
Remember me when I am gone away.
Song: "She sat and sang alway."
Rossetti, D. Memory.
Sudden Light.
Woodspurge, The.
Różewicz. Return, The.
Ruark. Vacant Lot, A.
Rubtsov. Good Filya.
Rukeyser, M. Woman as Market.
Rutsala. Silence, The.
World, The.
Sa Nguyên. Dress of Hà-Đông silk, The.
Sackville-West. Beechwoods at Knole.
Valediction.
St. John, D. Quote Me Wrong Again and I'll Slit the Throat of Your Pet Iguana.
Salinas, R. Trip Through the Mind Jail, A.
Salkey. Away.
Samio. Tanka: "Call to mind."
Tanka: "Memories open."
Sanchez, S. Poem at Thirty.
Poem for my Brother, A.
Sanjō Emperor. Involuntary, / I may live on.
Santayana. With you a part of me hath passed away.
Santos, S. Childhood.
Sassoon. Aftermath.
Two Old Ladies.
Scalapino. Flush / a Play.
Scannell. Apple-raid, The.
Schmitz. Ladder: Roger Vail's Photo of a Rockface in the Carrara (Italy) Marble Quarries, The.
Schnackenberg. Darwin in 1881.
Scott, A. Coronach.
Scott, J. Plato's Dog.
Seferis. Cats of St. Nicholas, The.
Last Stop.
Segal, J. Candle.
Seibles. Trying for Fire.
Seifert. Fingerprints.
Selman, R. Avec Amour.
Old man waves to me through iron bars, The.
Selvinsky. I Saw It.
Senghor. Luxembourg 1939.
Serote. Ofay-Watcher Looks Back.
Seward. In scenes paternal, not beheld through years.

Sexton. I Remember.
January 1st.
What's That.
Seymour, A. Millionaire.
Shakespeare, W. Sonnet 30.
Sonnet 55.
Sonnet 77.
Shange. Where the Heart Is.
Shapiro, K. Nigger.
Shchirovsky. Dance of the Soul.
Shelley, P. To————: "Music, when soft voices die."
Shelnutt. Memory.
Shen Yüeh. Four Recollections.
I think of when she comes.
"Shu Ting." Bits of Reminiscence.
Maple Leaf.
Silko. Where Mountain Lion Lay [or Laid] Down with Deer.
Sillitoe. Synagogue in Prague.
Simic. Empire of Dreams.
Lesson, The.
Wall, A.
Simko. Thinking of My Father on a Bus to Baltimore.
Simmons, J. Archæologist, The.
Simovic. One Evening.
Sissman. Bruisingly cradled in a Harvard chair.
Slonimski. Remembrance.
Smith, C. I once was happy, when while yet a child.
Smith, I. Christmas 1971.
Clearances, The.
Snodgrass, W. Mementos, 1.
Ten Days Leave.
Snyder, G. Autumn Morning in Shokoku-ji, An.
For the Boy Who Was Dodger Point Lookout Fifteen Years Ago.
Four Poems for Robin.
Looking at Pictures to Be Put Away.
Sobin, G. On the Nature of the Iconic.
Soloukhin. Lost Songs.
Song. Out of Our Hands.
Wind in the Trees, The.
Sorrentino. Good Night!
September in Kittery.
Soto. Braly Street.
Not Knowing.
Who Will Know Us?
Soupault. Route.
Spencer, T. Return.
Spender, S. Ice.
Spires. Globe.
Stanescu. Song.
Stern, G. Dancing, The.
Expulsion, The.
Faces I Love, The.
Kissing Stieglitz Goodbye.
Stevens, W. Debris of Life and Mind.
Stevenson, A. Suburb, The.
Stevenson, R. To S. R. Crockett.
Stickney, T. In the Past.
Mnemosyne.
Pity.
Stidger. Lest thou forget in the years between.
Strand. Pot Roast.
Where Are the Waters of Childhood?
Strelchenko. My Photograph.
Stuart, D. Soup Jar, The.
Surrey. In Windsor Castle.
Svetlov. Friends.
Swenson, M. Seeing the frog.
Swinburne. Anactoria.
Before the Mirror.
Sundew, The.
Symons, A. Tune, A.
White Heliotrope.
Szymborska. Laughter.
Memory at last has what it sought.
Tabb. Echoes.
Mid-Day Moon, The.
T'ao Ch'ien. Bright blossoms seldom last long.
Peering into the depths of the stream.
Tapahonso. I Am Singing Now.

Tate, J. What the City Was Like.
Tati-Loutard. News of My Mother.
Taylor, A. Clearing Away.
Taylor, H. As on a Darkling Plain.
Way It Sometimes Is, The.
Teasdale. Water-Lilies.
Tekeyan. Forgetting. Yes, I will forget it all.
Tennyson, A. If any vision should reveal.
If Only.
In the Valley of Cauteretz.
Somersby, Lincolnshire; after Leaving the
Refectory.
Thanh Quan. Remembering the Past in the
City of the Soaring Dragon.
Thomas, D. When I was a boy.
Thomas, E. Celandine.
In Memoriam (Easter, 1915).
Thomas, L. Wonders.
Thoreau. Music.
They who prepare my evening meal below.
Tillinghast, R. Knife, The.
Toshinari. I remember a grass hut.
Trinidad. Double Trouble.
Trowbridge, J. Recollections of "Lalla
Rookh."
Tsvetaeva. Homesickness! that long /
Exposed weariness!
Tsvetkov. Yes, it's me. I appear thus to
myself.
Tu Fu. Winter Dawn.
Tuckerman, F. How well do I recall that walk
in state.
Under the mountain, as when first I knew.
"Upper chamber in a darkened house, An."
Tuqan, F. Face Lost in the Wilderness.
Uceda. Time Reminded Me.
Ulacia. Stone at the Bottom, The.
Unknown. Do you remember that night?
I Wonder How My Home Is.
Last year in the spring when the birds were
calling.
Memory System, A.
Psalm 137.
Simple rustic you seemed, A.
That Mountain Far Away.
Today I lost my temper.
Until life goes out.
Wanderer, The ("Who liveth alone longeth for
mercy").
Urrea. Ghost Sickness.
Utkin. Tale of Red-Haired Motl, Mister
Inspector, Rabbi Isaiah, and Commissar
Blokh, The.
Van Doren. Moments He Remembers, The.
Van Duyn. Stream, The.
Van Vliet. City is covered with places you,
The.
Party.
Vasilyev, S. Pigeon of My Childhood.
Vaughan, H. Friends Departed.
Verlaine. Exchange Of Feelings, An.
Nevermore.
Villanueva, A. To Jesus Villanueva, with
Love.
Villon. Ballade: "Tell me where, in what
country, where."
Vinokurov. Shows.
Võ Phiến. Where Have They Gone?
Voigt. Claiming Kin.
Voznesensky. I am Goya.
Vũ Hoàng Chu'o'ng. To the Black Nymph.
Walcott. Glory Trumpeter, The.
Letter from Brooklyn, A.
Village Life, A.
Walker, J. Studying Physics with My
Daughter.
Wallace, R. Grandmother Grace.
Wang An-shih. At the Chiang-ning River
Mouth.
Waniek. House on Moscow Street, The.
Waring, B. Reprieve on the Stoop.
Warner, S. Green Valley, The.
Warren, R. Blow, West Wind.
Debate: Question, Quarry, Dream.
Warsh. Suicide Rates, The.
Weigl. Her Life Runs Like a Red Silk Flag.
One, The.

Sailing to Bien Hoa.
Shelter.
Weiner, H. Remembered Sequel.
Weingarten. In the Cloud Chamber.
Wen Cheng-ming. As flowers fall at the river
city, memories come to me.
Wendell, J. In the Pasture of Dead Horses.
Whalen. Slop Barrel, The.
Wheeler, S. Run on a Warehouse.
Wheelock, J. Dear Men and Women.
White, E. Chairs in Snow.
Whitman, W. As toilsome I wander'd
Virginia's woods.
By that long scan of waves, myself call'd
back, resumed upon myself.
Glimpse through an interstice caught, A.
My Picture-Gallery.
Old War-Dreams.
Once I pass'd through a populous city
imprinting my brain.
Out of the cradle endlessly rocking.
Whittier. Burning Drift-Wood.
Telling the Bees.
To My Old Schoolmaster.
Wieners. Two Years Later.
Wiesel. Never shall I forget that night.
Wilbur. Finished Man, A.
Mill, The.
Pardon, The.
Piazza di Spagna, Early Morning.
Williams, C. Repression.
Williams, W. To a Dog Injured in the Street.
Willis, N. Confessional, The.
Wingfield. Winter.
Wojahn. Satin Doll.
Wollach. Are these moods of mine memory.
Wong, N. Mama, come back.
Woodworth. Old Oaken Bucket, The.
Wordsworth, D. Thoughts on my sick-bed.
Wordsworth, W. Complaint, A.
Daffodils.
Remembrance of Collins, Composed upon the
Thames near Richmond.
Surprised by Joy—impatient as the Wind.
To a Butterfly.
Worth, K. (Circus Elephant).
Wright, C. Kings' Daughters, Home for
Unwed Mothers, 1948.
This Couple.
Wright, C. Black and Blue.
Other Side of the River, The.
Wright, J. On a Phrase from Southern Ohio.
Redwings.
Wright, J. End of an Ethnic Dream, The.
Wroth. Sonnet 101.
Wyatt, T. Lover Showeth How He Is Forsaken
of Such as He Sometime Enjoyed, The.
Supplication, A.
Xuân Diệu. Orange With the Rind Still Green,
An.
Yakamochi. When I see the first.
Yamato-himé. Others may forget you, but not
I.
Yang Chi. Submitting a Memorial Requesting
Permission to Return Home and Care for My
Parents.
Yau. Cenotaph.
Postcard from Trakl.
Radiant Silhouette III.
Yeats. Circus Animals' Desertion, The.
He Thinks of His Past Greatness When a Part
of the Constellations of Heaven.
People, The.
To a Young Girl.
When you are old and grey and full of sleep.
Yesenin. Black Man, The.
Flowers say goodbye to me, The.
Yi, H. Song of Cricket.
Yosami, the wife of Hitomaro. We will never
meet again face to face.
Yosano. Tanka: "Into a pair of stars."
Young, K. Preserving, The.
Yüan Chen. Airing Painful Memories.
Yukitsuna. Tanka: "Plaintive, A."
Zach. Against Sadness.
Max is dead and his sons.
Zamora, D. Downpour.

Zhenkai. Old Temple, The.
Zych. Auschwitz, 1987.

Memphis, Tennessee
Brown, S. Memphis Blues.
Handy, W. Beale Street Blues.
Tarpley. Feel Free.
Tomkiw. Last Night in Elvisville.

Men
Ai. Before You Leave.
Alexandru. Man.
Allur Nanmullai. What She Said ("Bare root
of the bean is pink, The").
Arp. Man. The Woman, The.
Atwood. Eventual Proteus.
Men with the heads of eagles.
This story was told to me by another traveller.
Barlow, G. Place Where He Arose, The.
Behn, A. To Alexis in Answer to his Poem
against Fruition.
Bernstein, O. Imagined Description of Myself,
in Another Scene, An.
Betham-Edwards. Power of Women, THe.
Blamire. I've gotten a rock, I've gotten a reel.
Bogan, L. Masked Woman's Song.
Men loved wholly beyond wisdom.
Brooks, G. Strong Men, riding horses. In the
West.
Burns, R. Green grow the rashes, O.
Green grow the rashes, O; / Green grow the
rashes, O; / The lasses they hae wimble
bores.
On a Dog of Lord Eglinton's.
Campo. For J. W.
Catullus. Aurelius, I'm entrusting you with all.
Césaire, A. On the Islands of All Winds.
Chudleigh. 'Tis hard we should be by the men
despised.
Clark, T. Sons of Promise.
Clifton, L. Wishes for Sons.
Cope, W. Bloody men are like bloody buses.
Crouch, S. Chops Are Flyin.
Dacre, C. Similie.
De la Mare. Hare, A.
Di Cicco. Male Rage Poem.
Dickey, W. January White Sale.
Duncan, R. Torso / Passages 18, The.
Dunn, S. Man Who Closed Shop, The.
Eberhart, R. Marrakech.
Edson, R. Feeding the Dog.
"Ephelia." In the Person of a Lady, to
Bajazet, Her Unconstant Gallant.
Euripides. Of all things which are living and
can form a judgment.
Foley, M. Brothers and Sisters.
Gallagher, T. Black Silk.
Garrick. Jupiter and Mercury.
Gilbert, C. Beginning by Value.
Gilmore, M. Eve-Song.
Glück, L. Labor Day.
Palais des Arts.
Greville, F. Mind of man is this world's true
dimension, The.
Gross, P. Son and Heir.
Gunn, T. Innocence.
Hands, E. Favourite Swain, The.
Handy, W. St. Louis Blues.
Harryman. Male, The.
Hawthorne, N. Oh, Man can seek the
downward glance.
Hecht, A. Feast of Stephen, The.
Hill, S. Rain, The.
Ho Xuan Huong. Man-and-Wife Mountain,
The.
Ode to the Fan.
Scolding Some Dunces.
Swinging.
Hoagland, T. Poem for Men Only.
Holiday. Fine and Mellow.
Hoover, H. Boy has two jobs, A.
Houston, J. Judging Lear.
Hughes, L. Bad Man.
Gypsy Man.
Isler. Little Things, The.
Iverem. Daddy's Friends.
Janowitz, P. Reach.
Jiles. Tallness.
Johnston, E. Lines: To a Young Gentleman of

Surpassing Beauty.
Working Man, The.
Justice, D. Men at forty / Learn to close softly.
Kapilar. What Her Friend Said to Her, before the Rains.
Keller, D. Friends, Outside, Night.
In the Middle of the Journey.
Kipling, R. Female of the Species, The.
If you can keep your head when all [about you].
Kizer, C. Hera, Hung from the Sky.
Lawrence, D. How beastly the bourgeois is.
Lear, E. Limerick: "There was an Old Man in a tree."
There was an Old Man with a beard.
Levertov. Abel's Bride.
Mutes, The.
Lowry, M. Eye-Opener.
Lvov, M. To become a man, it's little to be born.
"MacDiarmid." One of the Principal Causes of War.
Madgett. Black Woman.
Martinez, D. Room itself. The women. The absence of women, The.
Mataka. Next Door.
McCarriston. Hotel Nights with My Mother.
McKay, C. St. Isaac's Church, Petrograd.
McWatt. Man in the House, A.
Montagu, L. Answer to a Love-Letter in Verse, An.
Ill fates pursue me, may I never find.
Mountain, M. He leans on the gate going staying.
Muldoon, P. Why Brownlee left, and where he went.
Naden. Love's Mirror.
Nasrin. At the Back of Progress. . . .
Nathan, L. Body Count.
Nelson, C. How We Make Lumber Out of Trees.
Neruda. Walking [or Walkin'] Around.
Nguyễn Công Trứ. Ode to All Flowers.
Norse. I'm Not a Man.
Nowlan. Rites of Manhood, The.
Orr, G. Who'd Want to Be a Man?
Ortleb. Militerotics.
Pace, R. Tingel-Tangel.
Padilla. Man on the Edge.
Parker, D. Social Note.
Song of One of the Girls.
Parker, M. Whither away good neighbour.
Parun. Sleeping Youth.
Pilkington, L. Song, A.
Pitchford. Surgery.
Plath. Gulliver.
Prescod. Women Are Different.
Probyn. Tête-à-Tête.
Queen Latifah. Evil That Men Do, The.
Questel. Bush, The.
Rainey. See See Rider, see what you done done!
Rich, A. From a Survivor.
Phenomenology of Anger, The.
Re-forming the Crystal.
Trying to Talk with a Man.
Waking in the Dark.
Roberson. Eclipse.
True we are two grown men.
Roberts, E. Mr. Wells.
Robinson, M. Modern Male Fashions.
Rotella, A. Holding his gaze.
Leading him in.
Ryan, G. If I Had a Gun.
Samio. Tanka: "On the sandy beach."
Sanchez, S. Prelude to Nothing.
Scalapino. How can I help myself, as one woman said to me about wanting.
Schuyler, J. Royals.
Senior. Birdshooting season the men.
Shakespeare, W. Song: "Sigh no more, ladies, sigh no more."
Shelnutt. Triumph of Children, The.
Shurin. Exorcism of the Straight/Man/Demon.
Simmons, J. Experience.
Influence of Natural Objects, The.

Smith, P. So Motown taught me all about men. Men worshipped.
Smith, S. Landrecie.
Sölle. He needs you.
Sri Sri. Man walks on the bridge and gives away the change in his, A.
Stanley-Wrench. Man in the Moon, The.
Stevenson, R. Looking Forward.
Suckling, J. Constant Lover, A [or The].
Szymborska. Born of Woman.
Taylor, E. Song: "Strephon has fashion, wit and youth."
Thomas, D. I, in my intricate image, stride on two levels.
Thomas, E. Forsaken Wife, The.
Tomlinson, C. Word in Edgeways, A.
Troupe. Reflections on Growing Older.
Unknown. Marvelous Encounter at Blue Creek, The.
Railroad Bill, Railroad Bill.
Sally, Sally Waters, sprinkle in the pan.
Stackolee.
Tired as I Can Be.
Vaynshteyn. Mangin Street.
Vega. Brothers Loving Brothers.
Villanueva, A. Crazy Courage.
"W——." Gentleman's Study, in Answer to The Lady's Dressing-Room, The.
Waldman, A. Two Men.
Walker, A. Did This Happen to Your Mother? Did Your Sister Throw Up a Lot?
Ward, N. Mercury shew'd Apollo, Bartas Book.
Waters, M. Hoochie Coochie.
West, K. On Track.
Whitman, W. I knew a man, a common farmer, the father of five sons.
Williams, C. It Is This Way with Men.
Williams, S. She Had Known Brothers.
Williams, W. Hemmed-in Males.
Marriage.
Wilson, K. Twin Aces.
Yeats. Men Improve with the Years.
Zach. Poem Too Late, A.
Zenmaro. Tanka: "All the young men I know."
Zukofsky, L. For you I have emptied the meaning.

Menageries. See Zoos

Menopause
"Astra." Bloody Pause.
Koestenbaum, P. Harriet Feigenbaum is a Sculptor.
Piercy. Something to Look Forward To.

Menstruation
"Alta." Euch, are you having your period?
Bass, E. Tampons.
Clifton, L. Wishes for Sons.
Dove, R. After Reading *Mickey in the Night Kitchen* for the Third Time Before Bed.
Millay, E. Menses.
Moos. Spendthrifts.
Olds, S. Eggs.
Moment, The.
Peacock, M. Smell.
Piercy. Something to Look Forward To.
Ridler. Crab is in again, his monthly house, The.

Mental Illness
Betjeman. Huxley Hall.
Bishop, E. Faustina, or Rock Roses.
Bishop, M. Dementia Praecox.
Bogan, L. Evening in the Sanitarium.
Cowper, W. Shrubbery, The.
Davis, C. Out of Work, Out of Touch, Out of Sorts.
Dobler. His Depression.
Dobyns. Black Dog, Red Dog.
Doty, M. Bill's Story.
Espada. Music of Astronomy, The.
Fallon, P. Himself.
"Field." Sullenness.
Frost, R. Servant to Servants, A.
Ginsberg, A. IV.
Kaddish.
Hecht, A. Third Avenue in Sunlight.
Hughes, L. Neighbor.

Jastrzebska. My Illness and Other Animals.
Justice, D. Counting the Mad.
Keats. Ode on Melancholy.
Kenyon, J. Depression in Winter.
Knight, E. Hard Rock Returns to Prison from the Hospital for the Criminal Insane.
Kocan. Bill.
Sleepers, The.
Krichevsky. Exhausted from depression.
Levy, A. Cross-Road Epitaph, A.
Lowell, R. Waking in the Blue.
Maiden. Anorexia.
Mew. Ken.
On the Asylum Road.
Morgan, E. De Quincey in Glasgow.
Post-Referendum.
Mori Ōgai. Tanka: "Insane thought, An."
North, C. Note to Tony Towle (After WS), A.
Okamoto. Tanka: "Cockscomb, A."
Tanka: "Ten years ago."
Opie. To a Maniac.
Owen, W. Chances, The.
Mental Cases.
Page, P. Schizophrenic.
Peterson, N. Search, The.
Plath. Tulips are too excitable, it is winter here, The.
Saitō Mokichi. Tanka: "Dahlias are black."
Tanka: "Ever so close."
Sexton. Flee on Your Donkey.
Music Swims Back to Me.
Ringing the Bells.
You, Doctor Martin, walk.
Smith, S. Away, melancholy, / Away with it, let it go.
Deserter, The.
Tipping. When you're feeling kind of bonkers.
Unknown. Limerick.
Zenmaro. At the Van Gogh exibition.
See also **Madness; Psychiatry and Psychiatrists**

Mental Retardation
Blackburn, T. Hospital for Defectives.
Gunn, T. As Expected.
Hugo, R. Letter to Wagoner from Port Townsend.
Marty. In the Dome Car of the "Canadian."
Murray, L. Dog Fox Field.
Wilson, K. Idiot, The.
See also **Down's Syndrome**

Mephistopheles. See Satan

Mercenaries
Housman, A. Epitaph on an Army of Mercenaries.
"MacDiarmid." Another Epitaph on an Army of Mercenaries.

Merchants
Brathwaite, E. Miss Own.
Chang Yü. Merchant's Joy, The.
Dickinson, E. I asked no other thing.
Herrick. Upon Rook: Epigram.
Hsü Pen. Ballad of the Merchant.
Johnson, A. Granny in de Market Place.
Lê Thánh-tông. Merchants.
Lu Yu. Merchant's Joy, The.
Mei Yao Ch'en. Fish Peddler.
Whitney, I. Yf they that keepe what I you leave.
Yang Shih-ch'i. Song of the Merchant's Wife.
See also **Business and Businessmen; Clerks**

Mercury (god)
Dryden, J. Mercury's Song [to Phaedra].
Komunyakaa. Slam, Dunk, and Hook.
Lawrence, D. Maximus.
Svetlov. On Reconnaissance.

Mercury (planet)
Morgan, E. First Men on Mercury, The.

Mercy
"Ada." Lines.
Amichai. God Has Mercy [or Pity] on Kindergarten Children.
Onus of Mercy, The.
Bible, *O.T.* My son, forget not my law; but let thine heart keep my commandments.
Psalm 6.
Psalm 23: "Lord is my shepherd; I shall not, The."

Psalm 72.
Psalm 100.
Psalm 102.
Psalm 103.
Psalm 118.
Psalm 136.
Bishop, E.   Fish, The.
Cooper, J.   Infusion Room, The.
Donne.   If poisonous [*or* poysonous] mineral[l]s, and if that tree.
Elytis.   Origin of Landscape or the End of Mercy, The.
Hardy, T.   Burghers, The.
Often when warring for he wist not what.
Herbert, G.   Discipline.
Herrick.   Calling, and Correcting.
God's Mercy.
To Heaven.
Hughes, L.   Feet O' Jesus.
Johnson, F.   Singing Hallelujia.
Levine, P.   Angel Butcher.
Mitchell, S.   Luke 10:25–37; And behold, a lawyer.
Mitchell, S.   Tent Caterpillars.
Molodovsky.   God of Mercy.
Nahman of Bratzlav.   From "The Torah of the Void."
Pembroke, M.   Gods boundles bownties gods promise ever abyding.
Psalm 57: Miserere Mei, Deus.
Prudentius.   Hymn Before Sleep.
Ralegh, W.   Passionate Man[']s Pilgrimage, The.
Reznikoff.   Day of Atonement.
Shakespeare, W.   Mercy.
Sonnet 145.
Sidney, P.   Sonnet 40: "As good to write as for to lie and groan."
Södergran.   Question.
Tuckerman, F.   Rhotruda.
Unknown.   Epitaph: "My friend, judge not me."
Prayer of a Woman in Charge of Berry Picking in Knights Inlet.
Sweet, sweet, sweet, let me go.
Villon.   Epitaph in Form of a Ballad, The.
Weigl.   Mercy.
Wheatley, P.   On Being Brought from Africa to America.
Whittier.   King Solomon and the Ants.
Wright, J.   Two Poems about President Harding.

Merlin
Drayton.   Poly-Olbion.
Hill, G.   Merlin.
Norris, L.   Merlin and the Snake's Egg.
Tennyson, A.   Merlin and the Gleam.
Wilbur.   Merlin Enthralled.

Mermaid Tavern, London
Keats.   Lines on the Mermaid Tavern.

Mermaids and Mermen
Calverley.   In the gloaming to be roaming[, where the crested waves are foaming].
Darley.   Mermaidens' Vesper-Hymn, The.
De la Mare.   Sam.
Goethe.   Fisherman, The.
Hennell.   Mermaiden, A.
Hughes, L.   Catch.
King, B.   Mermaid, The.
"Macleod."   Moon-Child, The.
Mueller, L.   Mermaid, The.
Nash, O.   Mermaid, The.
Richards, L.   Mermaidens, The.
Spires.   Comb and the Mirror, The.
Tennyson, A.   Mermaid, The.
Merman, The.
Unknown.   Clerk Colvill.
Mermaid, The.

Merrimac (ship)
Longfellow, H.   Cumberland, The.
See also **Monitor (ship)**

Merriment
McGinley.   City Christmas.
Unknown.   Green green the cypress on the ridge.

Merry-Go-Rounds
Field, R.   Merry-Go-Round.

Hughes, L.   Merry-Go-Round.
Martin, D.   (On the Merry, Merry-Go-Round).
McAuley, J.   Merry-go-round.
Oden.   Carousel, The.
Rilke.   Merry-go-round, The.

Messengers
Doolittle, H.   Hermes of the Ways.
Frost, R.   Bearer of evil tidings, The.
Glück, L.   Messengers.
Gunn, T.   Messenger, The.
Kunene.   "Advice" to a Young Poet.
Lawrence, D.   Maximus.
Meleager.   Dorcas, be off! & tell her this.
Mitchell, S.   Annunciation, The.
Nagy, A.   Like one who brought news from far.
Richards, G.   Almighty spake, and Gabriel sped, Th'.
Tennyson, A.   "O Swallow, Swallow, flying, flying south".
Warren, R.   Patriotic Tour and Postulate of Joy.

Messiah
Gascoyne.   Rex Mundi.
Gilbo'a.   My Soul Wanders About.
Halkin, S.   Here is much burning anger, mighty hate.
Karni.   Put me into the breach with every rolling stone.
Leib.   Hush, hush, do not speak.
Yeats.   Matthew 24:15–31.
Second Coming, The.

Metaphor
Collins, B.   Death of Allegory, The.
Davie.   With the Grain.
Dove, R.   History.
Elenkov.   Amphora / as an emotion.
Levertov.   Cat as Cat, The.
Lowell, A.   Meeting-House Hill.
Lux.   Solo Native.
MacLeish.   Hypocrite Auteur.
Marvell.   Definition Of Love, The.
Nash, O.   Very like a Whale.
Plath.   Metaphors.
Sidney, P.   Sonnet 9: "Queen Virtue's court, which some call Stella's face."
Sklarew.   How Metaphor Can Save Your Life.
What Is a Jewish Poem?
Stevens, W.   Motive for Metaphor, The.
To Henry Church.
Tranter.   Great Artist Reconsiders the Homeric Simile, The.
Williams, W.   Sort of a Song, A.

See also **Symbols**

Metaphysics
Barbauld.   To Mr. S. T. Coleridge.
MacNeice.   London Rain.
McPherson, S.   Some Metaphysics of Junior Wells.
Perreault, J.   Metaphysical Paintings, The.
Stevens, W.   Glass of Water, The.
Tomlinson, C.   In Defence of Metaphysics.

Meteors and Meteorites
Huntington, W.   Cold Meteorite, The.
Pizzarelli.   Meteor.
Thomas, E.   Shooting Star, A.
Vaughan, H.   To Amoret, of the Difference 'twixt Him and Other Lovers, and What True Love Is.

Methodism
Anstey.   Hearken, Lady Betty, hearken.
Lloyd, E.   Religion and the Lower Classes.

Metric System
Wagoner, D.   Elegy for Yards, Pounds, and Gallons.

Mexican War
Baca.   Mu Tío Baca el Poeta de Socorro.
Hoffman, C.   Monterey.
Unknown.   Maid of Monterey, The.

Mexico
Ashbery.   Instruction Manual, The.
Baca.   So Mexicans Are Taking Jobs from Americans.
Belitt.   View from the Gorge.
Bernstein, O.   Cuernavaca.
Birney.   Sinalóa.

Campo.   El Día de los Muertos.
Grier.   Mountain Town—Mexico.
Kerouac.   Mexican Loneliness.
Lawrence, D.   Quetzalcoatl Looks Down on Mexico.
Lowry, M.   For *Under the Volcano*.
McClure, M.   Reading Frank O'Hara in a Mexican Rainstorm.
McGrath, C.   Sunrise and Moonfall, Rosarito Beach.
Miles, J.   Seasons Greetings, Love and Revolution.
Paz.   Hymn Among the Ruins.
Ríos, A.   At Kino Viejo, Mexico.
Salkey.   Postcard from Mexico, 16.X.1973.
Soto.   Mexicans Begin Jogging.
Urrea.   Ghost Sickness.
Van Duyn.   Into Mexico.
Welch, L.   In Answer to a Question From P. W.
Whitman, A.   Hail! home of exiles and of Seminoles!
We leave thee with thy guests, thou sunny maid!
Williams, W.   Desert Music, The.
Wong, N.   On Plaza Garibaldi.
Wright, J.   Minneapolis Poem, The.

Mexico City
Twichell.   Aisle of Dogs.
Young, A.   Ponce de León: A Morning Walk.

Mice
Alexander, C.   Fieldmouse, The.
Ariston.   If you mice are looking for *food.*
Barbauld.   Mouse's Petition, The.
Bennett, R.   Witch of Willowby Wood, The.
Betjeman.   Diary of a Church Mouse.
Blight.   Death of a Whale.
Bodecker.   Cats and Dogs.
Broughton, T.   Hold, Hold.
Brown, M.   Little Black Bug.
Burns, R.   To a Mouse[, On Turning Her Up in Her Nest, with the Plough, November, 1785].
Callimachus.   Mousetrap, The.
"Carroll."   Long Tale, A.
Charles, D.   Concrete Cat.
Ciardi.   I Wouldn't.
Clare, J.   Clock-A-Clay [The Lady Bug].
Mouse's Nest.
Coatsworth.   Mouse, The.
Cole, C.   Three Mice.
Cook, E.   Mouse and the Cake, The.
Cox, P.   Mouse's Lullaby, The.
Cummings, E.   Four III.
Me up at does.
Mouse)Won / derfully is.
Dickinson, E.   Papa above!
Dixon, M.   Place, Places.
Dugan, A.   Funeral Oration for a Mouse.
Edson, R.   Mouse Dinners.
Fisher, A.   Mouse Dinner.
Fyleman.   (Mice).
Garrigue.   Mouse, The.
Gasztold.   Prayer of the Cat, The.
Graves, R.   One Hard Look.
Gray, S.   On a Cat, Ageing.
Gunn, T.   Last Days at Teddington.
Harter.   Thawing.
Henryson.   Tale of the Upland Mouse and the Burgess Mouse, The.
Herford.   Elf and the Dormouse, The.
Homer.   Ascend my shoulders, firmly keep thy seat.
Hughes, T.   Cat and Mouse.
Kinsella, J.   Chess Piece Cornered.
Klingsor.   Song of the Cat, The.
Kunitz, S.   Waltzer in the House, The.
Levertov.   Innocent, The.
Lucilius.   Asclepiades the Miser was horrified.
Marsh, D.   Mice.
Meredith, W.   Ritual Mouse, A.
Mitchell, L.   House of the mouse, The.
Moorer.   Legal Mouse, A.
Morgenstern.   Midnightmouse, The.
Mori Ōgai.   Tanka: "Frolicking."
Mother Goose.   Hickory, dickory, dock.

Six little mice sat down to spin;.
Three blind mice, see how they run!
Norris, L. Mice in the Hay.
Patchen. Magical Mouse, The.
Richards, L. Mouse, The.
Roethke. Meadow Mouse, The.
Rossetti, C. City Mouse and the Garden Mouse, The.
Pussy cat, Pussy cat.
Serraillier. Anne and the Field-Mouse.
Mouse in the Wainscot, The.
Sharp, W. Field Mouse, The.
Sharpe, R. *et al.* Country Mouse and the City Mouse, The.
Starbuck, G. New Strain.
Stevens, W. Dance of the Macabre Mice.
Stroud, W. Rustler.
Sullivan, C. Houseboat Mouse.
Taufer, D. Mice Are Pets?
Tolkien. Cat on the Mat.
Trai. Cat, The.
Tsaloumas. Old Friend.
Tu Fu. Travelling Northward.
Unknown. Battle in the balance, The.
Cat came fiddling out of a barn, A.
Cause of War, The.
Mice prepare for battle, The.
Mouse in her room woke Miss Dowd, A.
Ten little mice sat in a barn to spin.
Worldes blisse, have good day!
Wakley. Mouse, The.
Wallace, R. Ballad of the Mouse.
Wat. To be a mouse. Preferably a field mouse. Or a garden mouse—.
Westrup. Furry Home, The.
Willard, N. Cat to His Dinner, The.
Williams, W. Mujer.

Michael, Saint
Alcuin. Sequence for Saint Michael, A.
Ransom, J. First Travels of Max.

Michaelmas
Nicholson, N. Michaelmas.

Michelangelo Buonarroti
Allston. On a Falling Group in the Last Judgement of Michael Angelo, in the Cappella Sistina.
On Michael Angelo.
Browning, R. "Moses" of Michael Angelo, The.
Michelangelo Buonarroti. To Giovanni da Pistoia When the Author Was Painting the Vault of the Sistine Chapel, 1509.
Morley, H. Rondanini Pieta, The.
Prince, F. Old Age of Michelangelo, The.

Michigan (state)
Joseph, L. Do What You Can.
Levine, P. Poem Circling Hamtramck, Michigan, All Night in Search of You, The.
Rain Downriver.

Microbes
Ade. Microbe's Serenade, The.

Microcosm
Ammons. Corsons Inlet.
Bradstreet, A. Contemplations.
Dowden, E. Two Infinities.
Frost, R. Design.
Whitman, W. I believe a leaf of grass is no less than the journey-work of the stars.

Microscopes
Dickinson, E. "Faith" is a fine invention.
Thomas, G. Microscope.

Midas
Bowes-Lyon. Pastoral: "This field has buried men; is browed."
Moss, H. King Midas.
Ovid. King Midas.
"Pindar." Epigram: "Midas, they say, possessed the art of old."

Middle Age
"Astra." Bloody Pause.
Now or Never.
Beer, P. Middle Age.
Brasch. Ambulando.
Clifton, L. Thirty-eighth year, The.
Donne. Autumnal[1], The.
Hall, D. To a Waterfowl.

Hansen, J. Loved One, The.
Hardy, T. Middle-Age Enthusiasms.
Heath-Stubbs. Lady's Complaint, The.
Jarrell. Next Day.
Justice, D. Men at forty / Learn to close softly.
Kunitz, S. End of Summer.
Lattimore. Game Resumed.
Longfellow, H. Mezzo Cammin.
McGough, R. 40—   Love.
Patten, B. Ode on Celestial Music.
Porter, P. Sex and the Over Forties.
Prior. Phillis's Age.
Rankin, P. Middle Age.
Rich, A. Middle-Aged, The.
Rukeyser, M. Rondel: "Now that I am fifty-six."
Santayana. Minuet on Reaching the Age of Fifty, A.
Schuyler, J. Growing Dark.
Shapiro, H. Montauk Highway.
Simpson, L. Middleaged Man, The.
Smith, C. Thirty-eight: Addressed to Mrs H—y.
Sorrells. From a Correct Address in a Suburb of a Major City.
Swift, J. On Stella's Birthday, 1718/1719.
Tucker, M. First Grey Hair, The.
Wang Wei. At My Country Home in Chung-nan.

Middle Ages
Auden. Ode to the Medieval Poets.
Browning, R. Grammarian's Funeral, A.
Hill, G. Requiem for the Plantagenet Kings.
Schneour. Middle Ages draw near. Do you hear, sensitive man, do you feel, The.

Middlesex, England
Betjeman. Middlesex.
Slough.

Midgets
Levine, P. Midget, The.

Midnight
Bevington, L. Midnight.
Brown, G. Haddock Fishermen.
Bunin. It was near midnight when I entered.
Cornford, F. Single Woman, The.
Donne. Nocturnal[1] upon Saint Lucy's [or S. Lucies] Day, Being the Shortest Day, A.
Fichman. Midnight.
Hughes, L. Jam Session.
Izumi. Watching the moon.
Komunyakaa. Boat People.
Lakides. Armed Forces.
Lane, P. Midnight Song.
Leadbelly. Midnight Special, The.
Mistral, G. Midnight.
Patchen. Midnight Special.
Unknown. Cool breezes—I sleep by the open window.
Whitman, W. Clear Midnight, A.
Xuanjing. Meditating at midnight.

Midsummer
"Carroll." Little Man That Had a Little Gun, The.
Hardy, T. On a Midsummer Eve.

Mignonettes
Lawrence, D. Red Geranium and Godly Mignonette.

Migraine
Dunbar, W. Magryme, The.

Migrant Workers. See Farmworkers

Migration
Bryant, W. To A Waterfowl.
Freneau. On the Emigration to America [and Peopling the Western Country].
Hope, A. Death of the Bird, The.
Hughes, L. Good morning, daddy!
Ise. As the first spring mists appear.
Lane, P. Migration.
Meredith, W. We saw the swallows gathering in the sky.
Thomson, J. Migrating Birds.
Warren, R. Heart of Autumn.
Wilbur. Event, An.

Milan, Italy
Levine, P. And the Trains Go On.

Militarism
Carryl, G. When the Great Gray Ships Come In.
Cortez. Stockpiling of frozen trees, The.
Ginsberg, A. Pentagon Exorcism.
Hardy, T. Channel Firing.
"M." On the Frequent Review of the Troops.

Military Justice
Kipling, R. Danny Deever.

Military Life. *See* **Army Life**

Milk and Milking
Corso. Mad Yak, The.
Dallas, R. Milking before Dawn.
Frost, R. Cow in Apple Time, The.
Herrick. Upon Sibilla.
Kinnell. Milk Bottle, The.
Lee, L. Milkmaid.
Maguire, S. Spilt Milk.
Monro. Milk for the Cat.
Montague, J. Drink of Milk, A.
Mother Goose. Cushy cow bonny, let down thy milk.
Nash, O. Cow is of the bovine ilk, The.
Roberts, E. Milking Time.
Shwarts. Remembrance of Strange Hospitality.
Taylor, E. Meditation 150 (Second Series).
Yeats. Spilt Milk.

Milkmaids
Clare, J. Ballad: The Sun Had Grown on Lessening Day.
Mother Goose. Milk Maid, The.
Randolph, T. Milkmaid's Epithalamium, The.

Milkmen
Lux. Milkman and His Son, The.
Sansom, C. Milkman, The.

Milkweed
Frost, R. Pod of the Milkweed.
Levine, P. Milkweed.
Wilbur. Two Voices in a Meadow.
Wright, J. Milkweed.

Milky Way, The
Basho. Wild sea—/ In the distance, A.
Hsieh Chin. Playful Poem on a Chicken Egg, A.
Li Po. Viewing the Waterfall at Mount Lu.
Liu E. Boiling Falls.
Wei Ying-wu. Tune: Flirtatious Laughter.
Yang Wei-chen. Song of the Waterfall at Mount Lu.
Yüan Mei. Ma-wei.
Yün Shou-p'ing. Inscribed on a Snowscape.

Mill, John Stuart
Bentley, E. J. S. Mill.

Millay, Edna St. Vincent
Untermeyer, L. Edna St. Vincent Millay Exhorts Little Boy Blue.

Millennium
Brock-Broido. Domestic Mysticism.
Stafford, W. Epitaph Ending in And, The.
Vaughan, H. Dawning, The.
Whittier. Astræa.
Yeats. Second Coming, The.

Miller, Glenn
Kerouac. 179th Chorus.

Millet, Jean François
Markham, E. Man with the Hoe, The.

Mills and Millers
Allingham. Mill, A.
Barnes, W. Leeburn Mill.
Chaucer. Miller's [or Milleres] Tale, The.
Coppard. Unfortunate Miller, The.
Cunningham, J. Miller, The.
Doudney. Water Mill, The.
Eastwick. Miller, Miller.
Johnson, G. Old Rustic Mill, The.
Lucas, E. Windmill, The.
Robinson, E. Miller's wife had waited long, The.
Swinburne. Mill Garden, The.
Tomlinson, C. John Maydew or The Allotment.
Unknown. Dishonest Miller, The.
Jolly Miller, The.
Wilbur. Mill, The.

Milton, John
Addison, J.   But Milton next, with high and haughty stalks.
Blake, W.   Jerusalem.
Bridges, R.   Johannes Milton, Senex.
Collins, W.   High on some cliff, to heaven up-piled.
Deane, S.   Reading *Paradise Lost* in Protestant Ulster 1984.
Dryden, J.   Lines Printed under the Engraved Portrait of Milton [In Tonson's Folio of the "Paradise Lost"].
Longfellow, H.   Milton.
Marvell.   On Mr Milton's "Paradise Lost."
Myles, E.   December 9th.
Pope, A.   Milton's strong pinion now not heaven can bound.
Ray, H.   Milton.
Snyder, G.   Milton by Firelight.
Tabb.   Milton.
Tennyson, A.   Milton [Alcaics].
Watts, I.   Adventurous Muse, The.
Wordsworth, W.   London 1802.

Mind
Lodge, T.   Minde through thee divines on endlesse things, The.

See also **Intellect and Intellectuals**

Minerals
Dupin.   Mineral Kingdom.
Levertov.   What It Could Be.
"MacDiarmid."   Crystals like Blood.
Redgrove, P.   Minerals of Cornwall, Stones of Cornwall.
Thomas, D.   I, in my intricate image, stride on two levels.

See also **Mining and Miners**

Minerva
Hood, T.   To Minerva.

See also **Athena**

Mining and Miners
Ammons.   Prospecting.
Clemo.   Christ in the Clay-Pit.
Dorn, E.   Mourning Letter, March 29 1963.
Galvin, B.   Photo of Miners, A.
Geoghegan, J.   Down in a Coal Mine.
Gibson, W.   White Dust, The.
Heaney, S.   Singer's House, The.
Huddle.   Almost Going.
   Holes Commence Falling.
Larkin, P.   Explosion, The.
MacColl, D.   Miners' Response, The.
McKinney, I.   Deep Mining.
   Twilight in West Virginia: Six O'Clock Mine Report.
Menai.   Where shall the eyes a darkness find.
Merwin, W.   Burning Mountain.
Miljkovic.   Miners.
More, H.   Patient Joe; or, The Newcastle Collier.
Owen, W.   Miners.
Page, P.   Photos of a Salt Mine.
Sizemore.   Drill Man Blues.
Skelton, R.   Ballad of a Mine, A.
Skipsey.   Mother Wept.
Snyder, G.   Fire in the Hole.
   Milton by Firelight.
Tomlinson, C.   Shaft seemed like a place of sacrifice, The.
"Twain."   He Done His Level Best.
Unknown.   Avondale Mine Disaster, The.
   Clementine.
   Dreary Black Hills, The.
   Dynamite Song.
   Hard-working Miner, The.
   I'm Only a Broken-down Miner.
   Lament while Descending a Shaft.
   Miner Boy, The.
   Oh, Give Me the Hills.
   Only a Miner.
   Tramp Miner's Song.
Untermeyer, L.   Caliban in the Coal Mines.
Watkins, V.   Collier, The.
Wright, J.   Miners.
Yalden.   Miner thus through perils digs his way, The.

See also **Coal Mining and Coal Miners; Gold Mining and Gold Miners**

Ministers. *See* Clergy

Mink
Derricotte.   Minks, The.

Minnesota (state)
Ai.   Ice.
Bly, R.   Driving toward the Lac Qui Parle River.
Etter.   Great Northern.
Kooser.   Late Lights in Minnesota.
Ryan, R.   Winter in Minneapolis.
Wright, J.   Blessing, A.
   Lying in a Hammock at William Duffy's Farm in Pine Island, Minnesota.
   Minneapolis Poem, The.

Minotaur
Gioia.   Maze Without a Minotaur.
Wright, F.   Depiction of Childhood.

Minstrels
Chatterton.   Mynstrelle's Songe ("O! synge untoe mie roundelaie").
Dransfield.   Minstrel.
Goethe.   Minstrel, The.
Moore, T.   Minstrel Boy, The.
More, S.   Minstrel Boy to the war is gone, The.
Scott, W.   Caledonia.
   Minstrel, The.
Unknown.   Deor's Lament.
   Widsith, the Minstrel.

Miracles
Aiken, C.   Miracles.
Angira.   Manna.
Appleman, P.   Mary.
Awoonor.   This Earth, My Brother.
Bontemps.   Miracles.
Caraion.   Deornamentation.
Crashaw.   On the Miracle of Loaves.
   On the Miracle of Multiplied [*or* Multiplyed] Loaves.
   To Our Lord, upon the Water Made Wine.
Creeley.   Kore.
Diop, B.   Animism.
Donne.   Relic, The.
   Song: "Go and catch a falling star."
Drayton.   Sonnet 35: 'Some, misbelieving and profane'.
Ghalib, A.   For the raindrop, joy is in entering the river.
Ginsberg, A.   Galilee Shore.
Griffin, S.   Miracle.
Herbert, G.   Whitsunday.
Herrick.   Widow's Tears [*or* Widdowes Teares]: or, Dirge of Dorcas, The.
Jackson, L.   Wind Suffers of Blowing, The.
Masters, E.   Business Reverses.
McGough, R.   Poem With a Limp.
Merton.   Cana.
Milosz, C.   And when Jesus had crossed.
Pasternak, B.   Evil Days, The.
   Miracle, The.
Pickard, T.   Gypsy Music in Krakow.
Plath.   Black Rook in Rainy Weather.
Seferis.   Les Anges Sont Blancs.
Shaw, E.   Looking Inside the Miracle.
Smart, C.   Crucifixion of Our Blessed Lord.
Smith, G.   Penitential Cries of Jupiter Hammond, The.
Sobin, G.   What the music.
Tate, J.   Manna.
Vaughan, H.   Religion.
Wang Yen-Shou.   Wangsun, The.
Wen Yi-tuo.   Miracle.
Whitman, W.   Miracles.
Wilbur.   Matthew 8:28–34; And when he came to the other side.

Mirages
Aaron, J.   Sighting, The.

Mirrors
Abse.   Footnote Extended, A.
Aiken, C.   Dear Uncle Stranger.
"Akhmatova."   In the Looking Glass.
Ammons.   Reflective.
Andresen.   Mirrors, The.
Apollinaire.   I Imagine Angels.
   On imagine les anges.

Atwood.   Tricks With Mirrors.
Barnfield.   Sighing, and sadly sitting by my Love.
Bartusek.   Love Song.
Bogan, L.   Man Alone.
Browning, R.   Love in a Life.
Burns, R.   How daur ye ca' me "Howlet-face."
Caddy, C.   Three-Inch Reflector.
Carew, T.   Looking-Glass, A.
   On His Mistress Looking in a Glass.
"Carroll."   Welcome Queen Alice.
Chu Shu-chen.   Morning.
Coleridge, M.   Other Side of a Mirror, The.
Corn.   Infinity Effect at the Hôtel Soubise.
Cronin, J.   Motho Ke Motho Ka Batho Babang (A Person Is a Person Because of Other People).
Doinas, S.   Woman in the Mirror, The.
Drayton.   These verses weare made By Michaell Drayton Esquier Poett Lawreatt the night before hee dyed.
Finkelstein, N.   Track.
Follain.   Mirror, A.
Foster, E.   Marriage of True Minds, The.
Garrigue.   Cracked Looking Glass.
   Primer of Plato.
Gascoyne.   Salvador Dali.
Graves, R.   Face in the Mirror, The.
   Foreboding, The.
   Pier-Glass, The.
Hadewijch II.   You who want.
Hardy, T.   Moments of Vision.
Harter.   Grandmother's mirror.
   In the mirror.
Hemans.   Mirror in the Deserted Hall, The.
Hemphill.   Family Jewels.
Herbert of Cherbury.   In a Glass-Window for Inconstancy.
Hitomaro.   Strange old man, A.
Hsieh Chin.   To the Fortuneteller Hsüeh T'ieh-yai.
Ishikawa Takuboku.   Tanka: "Mirror in hand."
Jarman, M.   Mirror, The.
Joron, A.   Baring the Device.
Kastelan.   Blood and the Storm.
Kgositsile.   Mirrors, Without Song.
Kipling, R.   Looking Glass, The.
Kowit.   Cosmetics do no good.
   In the morning.
La Fontaine.   Man and His Image, The.
Lalic.   Roll Call of Mirrors.
Levertov.   Seeing for a Moment.
Li Ch'ing-chao.   Hopelessness.
Lochhead, L.   Hickie, The.
   Mirror's Song.
Lovelace, R.   Lucasta's Fan[ne], with a Looking-Glass[e] in It.
Lowell, R.   Fat Man in the Mirror, The.
Lowry, M.   Delirium in Vera Cruz.
   Sestina in a Cantina.
Mahadevi.   When the body becomes Your mirror.
Mayer, B.   Midwinter Day.
Merwin, W.   Glass.
Montgomery, S.   Crying.
Noguere.   Whirling Round the Sun.
Plath.   Mirror.
Po Chü-i.   Feelings Wakened by a Mirror.
Pope, A.   Sol through white curtains shot a tim'rous ray.
Prior.   Lady Who Offers Her Looking-Glass to Venus, The.
Probyn.   Model, The.
Rakosi.   Lord, What is Man?
Reed, I.   Beware: Do Not Read This Poem.
Rossetti, C.   Passing and Glassing.
Rossetti, D.   Without Her.
Rosten.   This is my name / I have my own name.
Satyamurti.   Reflections.
Shakespeare, W.   Sonnet 3.
Shirley, J.   To a Lady Upon a Looking-Glass Sent.
Simic.   Charon's Cosmology.
Swenson, M.   You are my mirror.
Swinburne.   Before the Mirror.
Symons, A.   La Mélinite: Moulin-Rouge.

Tada. Mirror.
Traherne. Shadows in the Water.
Tree-Leaf Woman. Who speaks the sound of an echo?
Troupe. Sense of Coolness, A.
Wain. Gentleman Aged Five before the Mirror.
Wang Shih-chieng. Song of the Ch'in-Dynasty Mirror—Written for Yüan Sung-li.
Waniek. Strange beautiful woman, A.
Webster, A. By the Looking-Glass.
Wen Cheng-ming. Year I-mao (Fifteen Fifty Five), New Year's Eve, The.
Whitman, W. Eidolons.
Hand-Mirror.
Williams, M. Images.
Williams, W. Mists Over the River.
Yi, S. Mirror, The.
Poem No. XV.
Yüan Mei. Arriving at Hangchou.
Yukitsuna. Tanka: "Poetry."
Zagajewski. Auto Mirror.
Zamora, D. Hand Mirror.

Mirth
Herrick. Hock-Cart, or Harvest Home, The.
Lyric to Mirth, A.
To Live Merrily, and To Trust to Good Verses.
Hunt, L. To the Grasshopper and the Cricket.
Lowry, M. Strange Type.
Milton. Mirth and Poetry.
To Cyriack Skinner.
Rodriguez, J. Eskimo Occasion.
Smart, C. Mirth.
Unknown. Aphrodite reveals herself.
See also **Laughter; Merriment**

Misanthropy
Ivanov, G. People? What do I care about people?
Whitfield. Misanthropist, The.
Wylie. Eagle and the Mole, The.

Miscarriages
Ai. But What I'm Trying to Say Mother Is.
"Alta." 104.
Balk, C. Yellow Hills in Back, The.
Bierds. Stillness, the Dancing, The.
Corrington. For a Woodscolt Miscarried.
Fraser, K. Flowers.
Gibson, M. Country Woman Elegy.
Hecht, A. Vow, The.
Plath. Barren Woman.
Tóth, J. Dead Embryos.

Mischief
Herrick. Upon Pagget.
Horace. Part of the Seventh Epistle of the First Book of Horace Imitated: And Address'd to a Noble Peer.
Kicknosway. West Grand Boulevard.
Nichols, G. I am the rain.
Unknown. Mr Nobody.
O, let not e'er this quarrel be averred!

Misfortune
Agathias. Restless and discontent / I lie awake all night long.
Antiphanes. Lost Bride, The.
Anyte. On this her daughter's tomb.
Asclepiades. Drink, Asklepiades.
Beckett, S. Ooftish.
Bozhilov. Troubles.
Burns, R. To a Mouse[, On Turning Her Up in Her Nest, with the Plough, November, 1785].
Callimachus. Kallignotos swore to Ionis—no one.
Our guest's wound went unnoticed.
Cowper, W. Shrubbery, The.
Dickinson, E. One need not be a Chamber—to be Haunted.
Dobell, S. Tommy's Dead.
Elizabeth I. Ah silly pugg wert thou so sore afraid.
Erinna. Epitaph on a Betrothed Girl.
Fumiko. Tanka: "Boxes of sleeping pills."
Gaetulicus. Here, by the seashore, there lies / Archilochus.
Gray, T. Hymn to Adversity.
Halpern, M. That's Our Lot.

Harris, R. Call, The.
Harte, B. Mrs. Judge Jenkins[; Being the Only Genuine Sequel to "Maud Muller"].
Hegesippus. Hang that day with black, that night, sinister, moonless.
Julianus of Egypt. Anastasia, the Graces blossom and you were their flower.
On a Young Wife.
Lanier, S. Revenge of Hamish, The.
Lindsay, L. Auld Robin Gray.
More, H. Riot; or, Half a Loaf Is Better than No Bread, The.
Mother Goose. Trip upon trenchers, and dance upon dishes.
Perses. Death came before Marriage, Philaenion.
Petrarch. Ever mine [*or* myn] hap[pe] is slack and slo[w] in coming [*or* commyng].
Piatt, S. Giving Back the Flower.
Ralegh, W. Fortune hath taken away my love.
Shakespeare, W. Sonnet 29.
Shepherd, R. Brotherhood.
Stickney, T. Six o'Clock.
Tuckerman, F. "Upper chamber in a darkened house, An."
Unknown. Stackalee.
Three Sons, The.
Wotton, S. Upon the Sudden Restraint of the Earl[e] of Somerset, Then Falling from Favor [*or* Favour].
Wyatt, T. Lover Showeth How He Is Forsaken of Such as He Sometime Enjoyed, The.
Since love is such that, as ye wot.
Where shall I have at mine own will.

Mishima, Yukio
Cole, W. Mysterious East.

Misogyny
Ai. Mother's Tale, The.
Clare, J. Song: "I peeled bits of straw and I got switches too."
Patmore, C. Warning, A.
Pollitt. Onion.
Rich, A. From an Old House in America.
Rochester, J. Song: "Love a woman? You're [*or* Y'are] an ass."
Swift, J. Gentle Echo on Woman, A.

Missionaries
Burke, J. Missionary Hymm.
Campbell, J. I'm far from what I call my home.
Gates, E. Your Mission.
Heber. From Greenland's Icy Mountains.
Johnson, H. Magalu.
Linden, M. Missionary, The.
Moorer. Africa.
Pickthall, M. Père Lalement.
Two Souls.
Pratt, E. Martyrdom of Brébeuf and Lalemant, 16 March 1649, The.
Sinclair, K. Memorial to a Missionary.
Unknown. First Stone of the New Castle, The.
He is coming, Adzed-Head.

Mississippi (state)
Brooks, G. Bronzeville Mother Loiters in Mississippi. / Meanwhile, a Mississippi Mother Burns Bacon.
Crouch, S. No New Music.
Emanuel, J. Church Burning: Mississippi.
Hayden, R. Night, Death, Mississippi.
Knight, E. Poem for Myself (Or Blues for a Mississippi Black Boy), A.
Miller, E. Mississippi.
Plumpp. Clinton.

Mississippi River
Crane, H. River, The.
Davis, T. C.T.'s variation.
Funk, A. After Dark.
Garland, H. On the Mississippi.
Hayden, R. Night, Death, Mississippi.
Ransom, J. Antique Harvesters.
Shange. Where the Mississippi meets the Amazon.

Missouri (state)
Barnes, J. Last Look at La Plata, Missouri.
Sunday Dreamer's Guide to Yarrow, Missouri, A.
Justice, D. Childhood.

Knight, E. Poem to Galway Kinnell, A.
Sterling, A. Meet Me in St. Louis, Louis.

Missouri River
Brown, S. Foreclosure.
Unknown. Shenandoah.

Mist
Bishop, E. Cape Breton.
Boldman. Mist.
Bridges, R. Garden in September, The.
Brontë, E. Mild the mist upon the hill.
Clare, J. November.
Gates, L. Rowing.
Jaccottet. Daybreak / mingles blood.
Kangro. Trees Walk Farther Away, The.
Keats. To Autumn.
Lamb, E. Far shore, The.
Marcinkevicius. Nemunas.
Masing. Only the Mists are Real.
Paz. Here.
Sandburg, C. Mist Forms.
Southard. Mist.
Spiess. Asparagus bed.
Swede. Panties on the clothesline lingering mist.
Tao-chi. Inscribed on "Drunk in the Autumn Woods."
Unknown. Mist, The.
Wang Shih-chieng. Echoing Old Man Mu's Poem, "Inscribed on Shen Lang-ch'ien's Little Landscape, Autumn Willows at Stone Cliff."
Things Seen.
Watson, R. Children of the Mist.
Willson, D. Mist and All, The.
Yün Shou-p'ing. Inscribed on a Painting ("Magic mists twirl around the sky").
See also **Fog**

Mistletoe
Bayly. Mistletoe Bough, The.
Cullen, C. Under the Mistletoe.
Tucker, M. Mistletoe.

Mistresses
Ausonius. Mistresse, A.
Cakalacanar. What She Said to Him, after Meeting His Concubine.
Catullus. Less pub than brothel, and you, the regulars.
Donne. On His Mistress [*or* Mistris].
Self[e] Accuser, A.
Engle, P. Portrait of a King's Mistress, Nude.
Herrick. To His Mistresses.
Upon the Loss[e] of His Mistresses.
What Kind of Mistress[e] He Would Have.
Li K'ai-hsien. Poem about Fan the Fourth, A.
Marvell. To His Coy Mistress.
Pan Chieh-yü. Song of Regret.
Pao Chao. In Imitation of "The King of Huai-nan."
Pratt, J. Words and Thoughts.
Ranaivo. Song of a Young Girl.
Rilke. Flamingos, The.
Shakespeare, W. Sonnet 130.
Sweet-and-Twenty.
Shirley, J. To His Mistress.
Smith, S. Infelice.
Suckling, J. Sonnet: "O[h]! for some honest lover's ghost."
Tu Fu. Song of the Beautiful Ladies.
Unknown. All Seasons in One.
Marrying maiden / Undertakings bring misfortune, The.
My mistress loves no woodcocks.
Waniek. Ballad of Aunt Geneva, The.
Wright, J. Gesture by a Lady with an Assumed Name, A.

Misunderstanding
Baird, M. Do not make things too easy.
Creeley. Gift, The.
Donne. Pyramus and Thisbe.
Hewitt, J. Turf-Carrier [*or* Turf Carrier] on Aranmore.
Koch, K. Taking a Walk with You.
Mezhirov. We are huddled in a crowd before Kolpino.
Murray, L. Hearing Impairment.
Rich, A. Like This Together.
They come to you with their descriptions of

your soul.
Trying to Talk with a Man.
Unknown. Since first I saw your face I
resolved to honor and reknown.

Mites
Frost, R. Considerable Speck, A.
Merrill, B. Mite, The.
Shapiro, K. Interlude.

Mithridates the Great
Emerson, R. Mithridates.

Mittens
Allen, M. Mitten Song, The.
Follen, E. Three little kittens [they] lost their
mittens.
Hughes, L. This Little House Is Sugar.

See also **Gloves**

Moas
Curnow. Skeleton of the Great Moa in the
Canterbury Museum, Christchurch, The.

Mobile Bay, Battle of (1864)
Meredith, W. Farragut, Farragut / Old Heart
of Oak.

Mobility
Jordan, J. Roman Poem Number Nine.
Kunitz, S. Summing-up, The.

Mockingbirds
Bukowski. Mockingbird had been following
the cat, The.
Drake, J. Mocking-Bird, The.
Fordham. To the Mock-Bird.
Hayden, R. Mourning Poem for the Queen of
Sunday.
Heard, J. My Mocking Bird.
Hovey. Mocking-Bird, The.
Jarrell. Mockingbird, The.
Lanier, S. Mocking Bird, The.
Moore, M. Bird-witted.
Unknown. Mocking-Bird's Song, The.
Wilde, R. To the Mocking-Bird.

Models
Dickey, W. January White Sale.
Emanuel, L. When Father Decided He Did
Not Love Her Anymore.
Foerster. Life Drawing.
Gerstler. Ups and Downs.
Hill, S. Ram, The.
Nabokov. Ode to a Model.
Probyn. Model, The.
Rossetti, C. In An Artist's Studio.
Wearne. Division of O'Dowd, The.
Terri.

Moderation
Cullen, C. Song in Spite of Myself.
Herrick. Moderation.
Plumptre, A. To thee, whose cautious step and
specious air.
Thompson, F. Counsel of Moderation, A.
Wylie. Nonsense Rhyme.

Modern Man
Ackerman, D. Rumored Conversation with
Oneself Continues in Pittsburgh, The.
"Adunis." Mirror for the Twentieth Century,
A.
Allen, P. Kopis'taya.
Ashbery. Caesura.
Auden. Unknown Citizen, The.
Avidan. Three Self-Plagiarisms.
Baraka. Political Poem.
Bishop, E. Varick Street.
Bissett. Christ I Wudint Know Normal if I
Saw It When.
Blaga. Twentieth Century.
Bond, E. How We See.
Bronk. At Tikal.
Burliuk *et al.* Slap in the Face of Public
Taste, A.
Christopher. After Hours.
Ciardi. Back through the Looking Glass to
This Side.
Cummings, E. Plato told / him:he couldn't.
Season 'tis,my lovely lambs, The.
Davidson, J. Crystal Palace, The.
De la Mare. Reserved.
Di Cicco. Flying Deeper into the Century.
"Dylan." It's Alright, Ma (I'm Only

Bleeding).
Quinn the Eskimo.
"Ern Malley." Documentary Film.
Fearing. Dirge: "1-2-3 was the number he
played but today the number came 3-2-1."
Ferlinghetti, L. In Goya's greatest scenes we
seem to see.
Lost Parents.
Sea and Ourselves at Cape Ann, The.
Fletcher, J. Song of the Moderns.
Fuertes. We're OK.
Gardner, I. Loud Song, Mother, A.
Ginsberg, A. II.
Greger. Air-Conditioned Air.
Gwynn, R. Among Philistines.
Hardy, T. I said to Love.
Hollo. Wasp Sex Myth (One).
Wasp Sex Myth (Two).
Iwaszkiewicz. How Does the Negative
Look. . . .
Jacobsen, R. Green Light.
Jeffers, R. Unnatural Powers.
Jones, R. James Dean.
Joseph, L. Do What You Can.
Kipling, R. New Knighthood, The.
Kleinzahler. Case in Point, A.
Ko. Chongno Street*.
Sky, The.
Kovner. Front Page.
Lamantia. Voice of Earth Mediums.
Le Pan. Net and the Sword, The.
Levchev. Capriccio 9.
Lowell, R. For the Union Dead.
MacCaig. Gone Are the Days.
Mahon. Glengormley.
Mardhekar. Forest of yellow bamboo trees,
The.
McDonald, P. Cash Positive.
Merrill, J. Urban Convalescence, An.
Monro. Every Thing.
Mukhopadhyay, V. Monday.
Munib-ur-Rahman. Tall Buildings.
Nathan, L. At the Well.
Nemerov. Life Cycle of Common Man.
Olson, C. In cold hell, in thicket, how.
Poem 143.
Oppen. And Their Winter and Night in
Disguise.
Anniversary Poem.
Book of Job and a Draft of a Poem to Praise
the Paths of the Living, The.
Impossible Poem, The.
Parra, N. Vices of the Modern World.
Patchen. While the sun still spends his
fabulous money.
Pound, E. Tea-rose tea-gown, etc.
Rich, A. Dark woman, head bent, listening for
something, A.
Richter, M. Light?
Rodefer. My mind to me mangles iron. An
error is mirror to the truth.
Pretext.
Shapiro, K. Hospital.
Shteiger. No one waits down below, as when
we were young.
Simon, P. Sound of Silence, The.
Smith, A. Common Man, The.
Snyder, G. This Tokyo.
Spires. Good Friday. Driving Weekend.
Steele, T. Wartburg, 1521–22, The.
Stern, A. Europa.
Stevens, W. Of Modern Poetry.
Tranter. Un-American Women, The.
Updike. Dea ex Machina.
On the Inclusion of Miniature Dinosaurs in
Breakfast Cereal Boxes.
Verma. Pleasure Dome, The.
Warren, R. To a Face in a Crowd.
Whitman, W. One's-Self I sing, a simple
separate person.
Years of the modern! years of the
unperform'd!
Williams, C. Last Deaths, The.
Wright, C. Stone Canyon Nocturne.
Yeats. Second Coming, The.

Modesty
Horace. Country Parson turn'd in Years, The.

Lowell, J. Sonnet.
Martial. I often bow; your hat you never stir.
Out of an Epigram of Martial.
To His Book[e].
Po Chü-i. Mad Poem Addressed to My
Nephews and Nieces, A.
Smart, C. Mutual Subjection.
Waller, E. Song: "Go[e], lovely rose[—ous
sweet and fair]."
Wylie. Let No Charitable Hope.

Moles
De la Mare. All but blind.
Fisher, A. Moles.
Gonzales. Mole makes his pole redhot.
Hale, S. Mole and the Eagle, The.
Joseph, J. Back to Base.
Milosz, C. Poor Christian Looks at the Ghetto,
A.
Rossetti, C. Handy Mole who plied no shovel,
A.
Stafford, W. Moles.
Wylie. Eagle and the Mole, The.
Young, A. Dead Mole, A.

Moloch
Garnet. Down let the shrine of Moloch sink.
Ginsberg, A. Howl.
II.

Mona Lisa
Dowden, E. Leonardo's "Mona Lisa."
"Field." La Gioconda.
Jacobsen, J. Only Alice.
Pater. Mona Lisa.
Roberts, N. Mona Lisa Tea Towel, The.
Wharton, E. Mona Lisa.

Monaghan. *See* **County Monaghan, Ireland**

Monasteries
Chia Tao. Spending the Night at a Mountain
Temple.
Chu Yi-tsun. Majestic Valley.
Hirsch, E. Unearthly Voices.
Huang T'ing-chien. Passing Hung-fu
Monastery with Yüan-ming: Inscribed in Jest.
Kim, K. Lord's Day, The.
Li Shang-yin. Written on a Monastery Wall.
Lu Yu. Leaving the Monastery Early in the
Morning.
Mei Yao Ch'en. Solitary Falcon above the
Buddha Hall of the Monastery of universal
Purity, A.
Merton. Elegy for Ernest Hemingway, An.
Reader, The.
Mo Shih-lung. I Went to Gold Mountain to
Visit a Ch'an Master But He Was Not at
Home.
Pagis. Siege.
Seferis. Cats of St. Nicholas, The.
Simovic. Notation in Gold.
Snyder, G. December.
Ssu-k'ung Shu. Oxhead Temple.
Su Man-shu. Written during My Stay at White
Clouds Monastery on West Lake.
Su Tung-p'o. At Gold Hill Monastery.
Unknown. All alone in my little cell.
Lament for Our Lady's Shrine at Walsingham,
A.
Lament over the Ruins of the Abbey of Teach
Molaga.
Monastery on Mount Hill-and-Stream, The.
Warton, T. Written in a Blank Leaf of
Dugdale's "Monasticon."
Williams, W. Semblables, The.
Wu Wei-yeh. Visiting the Garden at Monk
Wen Ko's Home.
Yang Yi. Lang Mountain Monastery.

See also **Monks**

Monday
Hughes, L. Blue Monday.
Mukhopadhyay, V. Monday.
Wakoski. Blue Monday.

Monet, Claude
Ferlinghetti, L. Monet's Lilies Shuddering.
Haxton. Traveling Company.
Hayden, R. Monet's "Waterlilies."
Hollander, J. Effet de Neige.
Huntington, C. Hackeysack Players, The.
Mueller, L. Monet Refuses the Operation.

Snodgrass, W. Monet: 'Les Nymphéas'.
White, M. "Claude Monet sur son lit do mort."

Money

Alexie. Business of Fancydancing, The.
Armour. Money.
Belloc. Fatigue.
Berg, S. Cold Cash.
Berrigan, T. Red Shift.
Berry, J. Fantasy of an African Boy.
Bishop, E. Washing hangs upon the line, A.
Brooks, G. Maxie Allen [always taught her].
Brownstein. Jet Set Melodrama.
Burns, R. Twa bonny [or bony] lads were Sandy and Jockie.
Cardenal. Luke 16:1–9; He also said to the disciples.
Unrighteous Mammon (Luke 16:9).
"Carroll." White Knight's Song, The.
Cary, P. Dorothy's Dower.
Chaucer. Complaint of Chaucer to His [Empty] Purse, The.
Clairmont. Hero in the Land of Dough, A.
Connor, T. She Was One of the Early Birds.
Crane, S. Impact of a dollar upon the heart, The.
Cronin, A. Elegy for the Nightbound.
Davies, W. Money.
Davison, P. Money Cry, The.
Dumas, H. America.
Feirstein. Mark Stern.
Flynn, M. Decision.
Forbes. Love Poem.
Garioch. In Princes Street Gairdens.
Ginsberg, A. American Change.
Googe. Of Money.
Gorman, L. My family asleep.
Guest, E. What's In It for Me?
Hall, J. Figure a Poem Makes, The.
Hammerstein. Money Isn't Everything!
Hardy, T. By Her Aunt's Grave.
Hatton, D. Christmas Bills.
Hays, H. Case, The.
Herrick. Lyric[k] for Legacies.
Money Gets the Mastery [or Masterie].
Money Makes the Mirth.
Upon Bunce: Epigram.
Horace. 2: Moderation.
Ode.
Howard, V. Monument in Black.
Hoyt, C. While the guests order.
Hughes, L. 50–50.
Little Lyric (of Great Importance).
Request.
What?
Jarrell. In Nature There Is Neither Right nor Left nor Wrong.
Jonas, S. Lines on the Back of a Confederate Note.
Jones, M. Soliloquy on an Empty Purse.
Jonson, B. On Lieutenant Shift.
Kharms. There I was sitting on one leg.
Kolatkar. Old woman grabs, An.
Lecount. Bridge toll-booth—, The.
Lincoln, A. Ten Rules of Conduct for Individuals and Nations.
Liu K'o-chuang. From "Ten Poems Recording Things that Happened at the Year's End."
Lowell, R. Skunk Hour.
Lu Yu. Pedlar of Spells, The.
McClintock, M. Hungry / without money—.
Morgan, A. Union Man.
Mother Goose. I love sixpence, jolly [or pretty] little sixpence.
Murphy, R. Elixir.
Nemerov. Dialogue.
Money.
Ultima Ratio Reagan.
North, C. Elizabethan & Nova Scotian Music.
Outram. Annuity, The.
Paulus Silentiarius. Gold cut the knot of otherwise.
Perelman. Money.
Petrov, A. Poetry in a Glass Cube.
Pizzarelli. With no money.
Pound, E. Canto XLV.
Raine, K. Worry about Money.

Roethke. Reckoning, The.
Sandburg, C. Soiled Dove.
Sedley. Marriage and Money.
Sisson. Money.
Smith, W. American Primitive.
Soto. Fair Trade.
Spender, S. Ultima Ratio Regum.
Swift, J. Mrs. Harris's Petition.
To Their Excellencies the Lords Justices of Ireland, the Humble Petition of Frances Harris, Who Must Starve, and Die a Maid if It Miscarries.
Tennyson, A. Northern Farmer: New Style.
Thomas, L. Clear Channel.
Tu Fu. By the Winding River I.
Unknown. Borrow to your heart's content.
Chairs to Mend.
Hush, little baby, don't say a word.
In the house east of here lives an old woman.
Man upon mold, whatsoever thou be.
Mode of France, The.
Money and a Friend.
Money and the Mare.
Money, money, now hay goode day!
My Purse.
No bees, no honey;.
Old woman was sweeping her house, and she found, An.
Other Side of the Valley, The.
Penny.
Pop Goes the Weasel.
Winner never quits, A.
Voznesensky. Cashier, The.
Whitney, I. Yf they that keepe what I you leave.
Wilbur. Finished Man, A.
Williamson, G. Annual Returns.
Yang Chi. Selling My Official Robe.
Yeats. Brown Penny.

Mongolia

Ai Ch'ing. North, The.
Bunting. Vestiges.

Mongolism. See Down's Syndrome

Monitor (ship)

Melville, H. Utilitarian View of the Monitor's Fight, A.

Monkeys

"Adeler." Willie had a purple monkey climbing on a yellow stick.
Avianus. Monkey, The.
Colum, P. Monkeys.
Fleming, M. Sonnet, A: "O lovely O most charming pug."
Frost, R. At Woodward's Gardens.
Gay, J. Two Monkeys, The.
Khodasevich. Monkey.
Kirschner. Two Blue Swans.
Li Po. Autumn Cove.
Mole, J. Musical monkey is dressed like a flunkey, The.
Moore, M. Monkeys, The.
Olsen, W. Dead Monkey, The.
Richards, L. Monkeys and the Crocodile, The.
Shiffert. Monkeys on Mt. Hiei.
Stein, G. Dog, A.
Swenson, M. Motherhood.
Unknown. Pop Goes the Weasel.
Signifying Monkey, The.
Wang Chiu-ssu. Song of the Painting of the Long-Life Star.
Weigl. Monkey.
Weöres. Monkeyland.
Williams, W. Jungle, The.
Yün Shou-p'ing. On a Landscape by Myself.

Monks

Browning, R. Grammarian's Funeral, A.
Soliloquy of the Spanish Cloister.
Clarke, A. Pilgrimage.
Dowson. Carthusians.
Evans, S. How the Abbey of Saint Werewulf Juxta Slingsby Came by Brother Fabian's Manuscript.
Everson, W. Narrows of Birth, The.
Hemingway. Earnest Liberal's Lament, The.
Ho Xuan Huong. Bonze Got Stung By a Bee, The.
Poking Fun At a Bonze.

Hsü Chung-hsing. Trees are ancient, thick with patterns of moss, The.
Hsü Pen. Saying Goodbye to a Monk from Japan.
Hsü Wei. Buddhist Monk Cut and Burned His Own Flesh to Make The Rains Stop—A Man From His Native Place Asked Me to Write a Poem to Send to Him, A.
Kao Ch'i. In the Mountains, Parting from Master Ning as I Return to West Bank.
Nodding Off.
Well of the King of Wu, The.
Liu Ch'ang-ch'ing. Saying Goodby to the Monk Ling-ch'e.
Meng Hao Jan. Paying a Visit to Monk Yung's Cloister.
Merton. Elegy for the Monastery Barn.
Mo Shih-lung. Meditation Rock, The.
Pien Kung. On the Sixteenth Day I Visit the Temple Again.
Rakosi. Menage, The.
Ransetsu. Fields and mountains turn.
Shen Chou. South of the Bridge.
Temple of the Ocean of Awakening.
Simovic. Notation in Gold.
Smith, S. Weak Monk, The.
Unknown. Monk and His Pet Cat, The.
Pangur Bán.
Waniek. Letter to a Benedictine Monk.
Wen Cheng-ming. Fine breeze blows through the temple halls, A.
Floating threads of spider webs hang.
These long verandahs seem to be washed clean.
Walking to the Temple of Precious Light.
Wu Wei-yeh. At the Mountain of the Mysterious Tomb Visiting Master P'ou.
Yang Shih-ch'i. Beyond the temple, a hidden cliff.
Yang Wei-chen. Residence of the Emperors of Ch'en, The.
See also Clergy; Monasteries

Monmouth, James Scott, Duke of

Behn, A. Silvio's Complaint: A Song, To a Fine Scotch Tune.
Dryden, J. In pious times ere [or e'r] priest-craft did begin.

Monogamy and Monogamists

Aig-Imoukhuede. One Wife for One Man.
James, W. Hogamous, higamous.
Nash, O. Third Jungle Book, The.
Shelley, P. Longest Journey, The.

Monotony

Barnes, J. Dog Days 1978.
Bell, M. Senilio Passes, Singing.
Disch. Bookmark, A.
Icaza. Responding Voice.
MacNeice. Nature Morte.
Mori Ōgai. Tanka: "Some medals."
Muske. Little L.A. Villanelle.
Roethke. Monotony Song, The.
Smith, S. Childe Rolandine.

Monsters

Auden. Chimaeras, The.
"Carroll." Jabberwocky.
Celan. Death Fugue, A.
Clifton, L. Shapeshifter Poems.
Cranch. Locomotive, The.
Dickey, J. Sheep Child, The.
Ehrhart. Making the Children Behave.
Éluard, P. Dawn Dissolves the Monsters.
Meetings.
Erdrich. Windigo.
Fletcher, P. Say Muses, say; who now in those rich fields.
Gardner, C. If you ever come to our house.
Graves, R. Hide and Seek.
Gunn, T. From the Highest Camp.
Heath-Stubbs. Vision of Beasts, A.
Homer. Ulysses Insults over the Cyclops.
Housman, A. Aunts and Nieces or Time and Space.
Hughes, L. Genius Child.
Kirkup. My Thing from Outer Space.
Kunert. Every Day.
Implant.
Lee, D. I Eat Kids Yum Yum!

Legaré. Tallulah.
Levi, P. Annunciation.
Mitchell, K. Monster, The.
Nguyễn Chí Thiện. Model children of the regime, The.
O'Neill, R. Master-Mistress, The.
Pepler. Concerning Dragons.
Raab, L. Attack of the Crab Monsters.
Sudden Appearance of a Monster at a Window.
Robinson, K. Pontoon.
Sartarelli. Phantasmatikon.
Silverstein, S. Slithergadee has crawled out of the sea, The.
Tadic. Dogs Gambol.
Tennyson, A. Kraken, The.
Unknown. FROM Beowulf.
Hwæt, wē gār-dena in gēardagum.
Wang Yen-Shou. Nightmare, The.

See also **Demons**

Mont Blanc
Coleridge, S. Chamouny; the Hour Before Sunrise. A Hymn.
Shelley, P. Mont Blanc.

Montana (state)
Anderson, J. Rosebud.
Cunningham, J. Montana Pastoral.
Haste. Wind, The.
Hugo, R. Degrees of Gray in Philipsburg.
Lady in Kicking Horse Reservoir, The.
Letter to Bell from Missoula.
Letter to Levertov from Butte.
Letter to Scanlon from Whitehall.
Map of Montana in Italy, A.
Stafford, W. Montana Eclogue.
Welch, J. Christmas Comes to Moccasin Flat.
Harlem, Montana.
Zarzyski. Silos.

Monterrey, Mexico
Hoffman, C. Monterey.

Months
Andrade, E. Friend is sometimes desert, A.
Barker, G. January jumps about.
Bodecker. One Year.
Coleridge, S. Garden Year, The.
Herrick. Four Sweet Months, The.
Longfellow, H. Poet's Calendar, The.
Mother Goose. Thirty days hath September.
Shurin. Agora.
Spenser. Pageant of the Seasons and the Months, The.
Unknown. By this [*or* thys] fire [*or* fyre] I warm[e] my handes [*or* handys].
Months, The.
Thirty days hath September.

Montreal, Quebec
Hoffmann, R. Deceptively Like a Solid.
Klein, A. Montreal.

Monuments
Bishop, E. Monument, The.
Carrier, C. Pro Patria.
Daniel, S. 46.
Emerson, R. Concord Hymn.
Hemans. Effigies, The.
Horace. 3.30: This Monument Will Outlast (Exegi momumentum aere perennius).
Howard, V. Monument in Black.
Johnstone, P. High Wood.
Kavanagh, P. Lines Written on a Seat on the Grand Canal, Dublin.
King, A. Inscription on Monument of Dorothy, Lady Hubert.
Komunyakaa. Facing It.
Lovelace, R. Black Patch on Lucasta's Face, A.
Lowell, R. For the Union Dead.
Melville, H. Inscription: "To them who crossed the flood."
Mew. Cenotaph, The.
Page, G. Smalltown Memorials.
Philipott. To Sir Henry Newton, upon His Re-edifying the Church of Charleton in Kent.
Rossetti, D. Sonnet, A [*or* The: "Sonnet is a moment's monument"].
Sandburg, C. Washington Monument by Night.

Shakespeare, W. Sonnet 55.
Smelyakov. Monument, The.
Stevens, W. Dance of the Macabre Mice.
Ziedonis. That is her memorial.

Moods
Ashbery. Crazy Weather.
Ayton. Answer, The.
Upon His Unconstant Mistress.
Donne. Devout Fits.
Frost, R. Mood Apart, A.
Kiser. Bargain Sale, A.
Manilius. What Constellations rise with the Lion. The great Dog.
Unknown. It's a funny thing, but true.
Sluggy and slowe, in spetinge muiche.
Yang Wan-li. Relaxing in the Evening in My Study.
Yeats. Moods, The.

Moon
Abanaki Oral Tradition. Come, my beloved, let us go up the shining mountain, and sit together.
Aldington. Evening.
Allard. Icicle the moon drifting through it, An.
Allen, P. Meditations on the Moon.
Alterman. Moon.
"Asphodel." Full Moon in Malta.
Auden. Moon Landing.
This lunar beauty.
Barker, G. Section VI.
Bast. Chrysoberyl: The Eye of the Cat.
Baxter, J. Spring-heeled Jack.
Bayliss. Seven Dreams.
Behn, H. Circles.
Berryman. Moon and the Night and the Men, The.
Berssenbrugge. Experience.
Best, C. Sonnet of the Moon, A.
Bishop, E. Man-Moth, The.
Bold, A. Moon.
Bowering, G. Moon Shadow.
Boyce. Ballad of Morgan the Moon, The.
Braithwaite. Golden Moonrise.
Brecht, B. Alabama Song.
Brickley. Deserted wharf.
Byron, G. So we'll go no more a-roving.
Carman, B. Mr. Moon.
Chang Chiu-ling. Watching the Moon with Thoughts of Far Away.
Ch'ien Ch'ien-i. Crescent moon hangs on the tip of the willows, A.
Chikako. On this summer night.
Chin Nung. Who bought a mountain and became a hermit there?
Chiyojo. Grazing.
Clare, J. To Mary: 'It Is the Evening Hour'.
Coleridge, M. In Dispraise of the Moon.
Witches' Wood, The.
Creeley. Moon, The.
Daive. Space instead of furniture.
Davies, W. Moon, The.
Moon and a Cloud, The.
Nailsworth Hill.
De la Mare. Moonlight.
Silver.
Dickey, J. So long.
Dickinson, E. I watched the Moon around the House.
Moon, The.
Moon upon her fluent Route, The.
Dongala. Fantasy under the Moon.
Doolittle, H. Moonrise.
Downie. Starlight.
Drennan, J. On the Telescopic Moon.
Dufault. On Aesthetics, More or Less.
Duncan, R. Chords Passages 14.
Moon, The.
Eliot, T. Rhapsody on a Windy Night.
Empson. To an Old Lady.
Escoffery. Mother Jackson Murders the Moon.
Ewart. Creation Myth Haiku.
Fainlight, R. Another Full Moon.
Faiz. Vista.
Fatchen. 'Jump over the moon?' the cow declared.
"Field." Penetration.
Follen, E. Oh! Look at the Moon.

García Lorca. Memory.
Moon Rises, The.
Gifford, F. Moon Folly.
Glück, L. Mock Orange.
Goethe. To the Moon.
Graves, R. Full Moon.
Problems Of Gender.
Guillén, N. Moon.
Proposition.
Gunn, T. For Signs.
Haas, R. Moon at the window.
Hackett, J. Moon fades into dawn.
Handlin. Full autumn moon, A.
Hardy, T. Shut Out That Moon.
Harr, L. Pale dawn moon, A.
Harries, N. Dog-watch.
Hayden, R. Full Moon.
Hendryson. What Is Repeated, What Abides.
Henson, D. Last Atlantean, The.
Hewett, D. Moon-Man.
Higginson, W. Evening star.
Summer moon.
Hood, T. No sun—no moon!
Hopkins, G. Moonrise.
Horovitz, F.
Hotham. Sun and moon.
Housman, A. White in the moon the long road lies.
Hsieh Ling-yün. Exchange of Poems by Tung-yang Stream, An.
Hsü Pen. Deserted Estate at South Garden, The.
Hsüeh T'ao. Moon, The.
Hubbell, P. Travelers, The.
Hughes, L. Moonlight Night: Carmel.
Winter Moon.
Hughes, T. Full Moon and Little Frieda.
Harvest Moon, The.
Moon-Hops.
Moon-transport.
Moon-wind.
Hulme, T. Above the Dock.
Inez. Slumnight.
Izumi. Although the wind.
I cannot say.
Watching the moon.
Way I must enter, The.
Jacob, M. Moon Poem.
James, D. Harvest.
Jennings, E. Her Garden.
Jewell. That breeze brought it.
Where the coyote called.
Jonson, B. Hymn to Diana.
Keats. Bright star[, would I were stedfast as thou art—].
Kenward. Moon.
Kerouac. Straining at the padlock.
Keyes, S. Moon is a poor woman, The.
King, H. Moonlight Ride, A.
Kinnell. Little Sleep's-Head Sprouting Hair in the Moonlight.
Kitahara Hakushū. Tanka: "Gleaming sliver."
Kleinzahler. San Francisco/New York.
Knight, S. Thoughts on the Sight of the Moon.
Knott. Sleep.
Kojijū. On the Spirit of the Heart as Moon-Disk.
Kunio. Tanka: "Because the folks."
Kusatao. Cat, The.
Lauterbach. For Example (5): Song of the Already Sung.
Lawrence, D. Aware.
Moonrise.
White Blossom, A.
Leopardi. To the Moon.
Levertov. Song for Ishtar.
Li K'ai-hsien. Night of the Seventeenth, The.
Staying Overnight on the Banks of Embroidered River.
Li Po. Jade Stairs Resentment.
Still Night Thoughts.
Li Shang-yin. First calls of the migrant geese, no more cicadas.
Li Tung-yang. Following the Rhymes of Yang T'ing-ho's Poem, "On the Road Back,

Accompanying the Imperial Retinue on a Visit to the Tombs of Former Emperors."
Lindsay, V. Moon's the North Wind's cooky, The.
Little, G. Now ice-covered.
Lloyd, D. Moonlit sleet.
Longfellow, H. Harvest Moon, The.
Little Moon, The.
Lowell, A. Garden by Moonlight, The.
Interlude.
Wind and Silver.
Loy. Lunar Baedeker.
Lu T'ung. Eclipse of the Moon, The.
Lu Yu. Evening in the Village.
I Walk Out into the Country at Night.
Lyles. Moon.
Macdonald, G. Things We Can Depend On.
Wind and the Moon, The.
Mackey, N. Memphite Recension.
MacLeish. Voyage to the Moon.
Maiola. Up on the Moon.
Masaoka Shiki. Fresh from the Void.
Tanka: "Beyond the glass door."
Masing. To Every Believer.
Mayer, G. April Poem.
McClintock, M. Hamburger Hill.
McGrath, T. Guiffre's Nightmusic.
Mei Yao Ch'en. Crescent moon shines, The.
Meyers, B. Daybreak.
Michie. Arizona Nature Myth.
Miliauskaite. On winter nights, when my grandmother.
Millay, E. Oh, sleep forever in the Latmian cave.
Miller, M. Universe, The.
Milnes. Lady Moon, Lady Moon, where are you roving?
Miyazawa Kenji. Tanka: "Bloodshot."
Tanka: "Dark seaweeds."
Tanka: "Phosphorescence."
Montagu, L. Hymn to the Moon.
Montgomery, S. Moonrise white cat eating the cardinal.
Moore, T. Young May Moon, The.
Morley, H. Parents.
Murasaki Shikibu. Someone passes.
Naden. Moonlight and Gas.
Nemerov. Backward Look, The.
Goose Fish, The.
Newbolt. Moonset.
Nezval. Moon over Prague.
Nichol. Monotones.
Nicholls, J. Moonscape.
Nukada. At Nigitazu we wait for the moon.
Ochester. New Day.
Ōe no Chisato. As I watch the moon.
Okigbo. Lustra.
Olson, C. Moon Is the Number 18, The.
Oppen. Troubled that you are not, as they say.
Osundare. Frantic as a prentice poet.
Maddening moon, A.
Moon is an exile, The.
Ou-yang Hsiu. When the Moon is in the River of Heaven.
Park, M. Traveler, The.
Patmore, C. Two Deserts, The.
Pavese. August Moon.
Philodemus. Double-horned, nocturnal Moon.
"Ping Hsin." Deliverance.
Pizzarelli. Fat lady, The.
Plath. Moon and the Yew Tree, The.
Rival, The.
Plomer. To the Moon and Back.
Po Chü-i. In Early Summer Lodging in a Temple to Enjoy the Moonlight.
Starting Early from the Ch'u-ch'êng Inn.
Traveler's Moon, The.
Porter, D. P. M. T.
Poulsson. Judging by Appearances.
Quasimodo. To the New Moon.
Raab, L. For You.
Rabéarivelo. What invisible rat.
Radnóti. Clouded Sky.
Rajasekhara. Moonlight.
Ransetsu. Fields and mountains turn.
Ravikovitch. Sinking Rising.
Ray, H. Vision of Moonlight, A.

"Rayevsky." O, he who flashed above the moon afar.
Reese, L. One Night.
Renton. Crescent Moon.
Rich, A. Amends.
Rogers, P. Abundance and Satisfaction.
Roseliep. Child.
Rossetti, C. Is the moon tired? she looks so pale.
O Lady Moon, your horns point toward the east.
Rossetti, D. Match with the Moon, A.
Rotella, A. After the full moon.
Rumble. Eagle has Landed, The.
Rushing. Sent for You Yesterday.
Sandburg, C. Auctioneer.
Balloon Faces.
Milk-white moon, put the cows to sleep.
Moist Moon People.
Nocturne in a Deserted Brickyard.
Sanjō Emperor. Involuntary, / I may live on.
Sappho. Evening Star who gathers everything.
Glow and beauty of the stars, The.
Stars around the luminous moon—how soon they.
Saunders, R. You Made It Rain.
Seiler. Lake, The.
Sergeant. Inundation, The.
Shakespeare, W. In Such a Night.
Moonlight.
Shea, M. Terminal.
Shelley, P. One stood on my path who seemed.
To the Moon.
Waning Moon, The.
Shen Chou. Moon in a Winecup, The.
Wine Cup and Bright Moon.
Shen Yüeh. Response to Wang Ssu-yüan's Poem on the Moon, A.
Shih Te. You can see the moon's brightness.
Shūji. Tanka: "After rainfall."
Sidney, P. Sonnet 31: "With how sad steps, O Moon, thou climb'st the skies!"
Simms, W. New Moon, The.
Simpson, L. Working late.
Smith, C. To the Moon.
Smith, W. Moon.
Solomos, D. Temptation.
Sorrentino. Magic Composer.
Southard. Down to dark leaf-mold.
In the garden pool.
Spiess. Dirt road, A.
Stanley-Wrench. Man in the Moon, The.
Steele, T. Joseph.
Stevens, W. God is Good. It Is a Beautiful Night.
Lunar Paraphrase.
Motive for Metaphor, The.
Two Figures in Dense Violet Night.
Stevenson, R. Mile an' a bittock, a mile or twa, A.
Moon has a face like the clock in the hall, The.
Stewart, F. To a Friend.
Stoutenburg. Cat at Night.
Strand. Moontan.
Prediction, The.
Su Tung-p'o. Begonias.
Moon, Flowers, Man.
Tune: Prelude to Water Music.
Supervielle. Missing France.
Swede. After I step.
Swenson, M. First Walk on the Moon.
Landing on the Moon.
Tahmisic. Red Moon High in the Sky.
T'ang Yin. Inscribed on a Painting ("Thatched hut among the pines, door open near a cliff").
Teasdale. Full Moon; Santa Barbara.
Tolkien. Man in the Moon Stayed up To Late, The.
Toomer. Beehive.
Traherne. On Leaping over the Moon.
Tu Fu. Full Moon.
I Pass the Night at General Headquarters.
Moon Festival.
New Moon.

Night Thoughts While Travelling.
Stars and Moon on the Yangtse.
Tuqan, F. After Twenty Years.
Turner, J. Man on the Moon, The.
Under. And a Star Fell.
Unknown. All other love is like the moon.
Aubade: "O, Lady, awake! The azure moon."
Bedtime.
BRIGHT moon illumines the night-prospect.
bright moon, oh how white it shines, The.
Clear full moon.
Holy is the moon and our own Selene.
I See the Moon.
Man in the Moon ("Man in the moon came tumbling down").
Man in the Moon ("Man in the moon was caught in a trap, The").
Man in the Moon ("Mon in the mone stond and strit").
Moon Eclipse Exorcism.
Moon is full, The.
Moon penny bright as silver.
Moon Sings, The.
Net of Moon, The.
O, look at the moon.
Prayer to the Young Moon.
Purity of the moonlight, The.
Re-birth.
Thanks.
They Went to the Moon Mother.
Though the purity.
Vaughan, H. Twenty-first Day of the Seventh Month.
Verlaine. Clair de Lune.
Virgilio. Now the swing is still.
Wagoner, D. Death of the Moon, The.
Wallace, R. Fresco of Swans and Bears, A.
Washington. Moon Bound.
Weigl. They Name Heaven.
Westrup. Flying.
Wieseltier. Site.
Willard, N. Night Light.
Williams, H. To the Moon.
Williams, W. To a Solitary Disciple.
Wills, J. In an upstairs room.
Moon at dawn, The.
Wollach. Gentle as moon on water and not like the cherry tree that said.
Wright, J. Beginning.
Having Lost My Sons, I Confront the Wreckage of the Moon: Christmas, 1960.
Secret Gratitude, A.
Wright, J. Train Journey.
Wu Chen. Moonlight Bay.
Wu Wei-yeh. Feelings Come As I Pass through Wu-chiang.
Yakamochi. When I see the first.
Yang Chi. Noble Scholar Playing the Lute, A.
Yang Shen. To the Tune "New Moon."
To the Tune "The Southerner."
Yang-Ti, Emperor of Sui Dynasty. Flowers and Moonlight on the Spring River.
Ye. All night I could not sleep.
Yeats. Cat and the Moon, The.
Sorrow of Love, The ("Quarrel of the sparrows in the eaves, The").
Yosano. Sweet and sad / like love overwhelmed.
Tanka: "Tell them."
Young, M. Metronomic Moon, The.
Young, V. Silence, The.
Yü Chi. Inscribed on the Painting, Solitary Crane, in the Collection of Jao Shih-ying.
Yüan Hung-tao. "Slowly, Slowly" Poem, The.
Yuhara. Let us bribe the Moon God.
Yün Shou-p'ing. Inscribed on a Painting ("Who needs a raft that can invade the stars?")
Zach. Harvest Month[. A full moon].
Zimmer. Failings, The.

Moonshiners
De la Mare. Moonshine.

Moore, Henry
Gregory, H. On a Celtic Mask by Henry Moore.
Hall, D. "Reclining Figure."

Moore, Marianne
Bishop, E. Invitation to Miss Marianne Moore.
Boyle, K. For Marianne Moore's Birthday.

Moore, Sir John
Wolfe, C. Burial of Sir John Moore [after [or at] Corunna], The.

Moore, Thomas
Trowbridge, J. Recollections of "Lalla Rookh."

Moors (geography)
Channing. Barren Moors, The.
Coleridge, M. Master and Guest.
Dickinson, E. I never saw a Moor.
Eliot, T. Rannoch, by Glencoe.
Garioch. Wire, The.
Kunio. Tanka: "From a flour mill."

Moors (people)
Flecker. War Song of the Saracens.

Moose
Bishop, E. Moose, The.
Duncan, R. Poetry, a Natural Thing.
Stafford, W. Woman at Banff, The.
Van Duyn. Moose in the Morning, Northern Maine.

More, Sir Thomas (Saint Thomas More)
Cunningham, J. Friend, on This Scaffold Thomas More Lies Dead.

Morgan, John Hunt
Woolson. Kentucky Belle.

Morisot, Berthe
Waldman, A. Berthe Morisot.

Mormons
Taylor, B. Nauvoo.
Unknown. Marching to Utah.

Morning
Ambrose. Hymn: "Framer of the earth and sky."
Ammons. Easter Morning.
Arp. Domestic Stones (fragment), The.
Atwood. Morning in the Burned House.
Auden. Lauds.
Baillie, J. Morning.
Baraka. Ballad of the Morning Streets.
Song Form.
Belloc. Early Morning, The.
Bernstein, O. What She Wanted to Be.
Blake, W. Morning.
To Morning.
Bly, R. Poem in Three Parts.
Waking from Sleep.
Boyle, K. Poem on Getting Up Early in the Morning (or Even Late in the Morning), When One is Old, A.
Brontë, E. Stars.
Browning, R. Pippa's Song.
Burns, R. Up in the Morning Early.
Cain, J. Someone's newspaper.
Campbell, W. Morning on the Shore.
Carlyle, T. Morning.
Cassian. Morning Exercises.
Chao Yi. Rising Early in the Morning.
Charles, F. Omens of the Morning.
Ch'ien Wen-Ti. Getting Up in Winter.
Chin. Aubade: "Waking is this easy."
Chu Shu-chen. Morning.
Clare, J. Ploughman Singing.
Cleveland, J. Upon Phillis Walking in a Morning before Sun-Rising.
Congreve. See, see, she wakes, Sabina wakes!
Cotton, C. Morning Quatrains, The.
Couzyn. Dawn.
Coward. Convalescence.
Cristall. Morning, Rosamonde.
Cummings, E. Raise the shade.
Dalmon. Early Morning Meadow Song.
Davenant. City Morning, The.
Davies, W. Early Morn.
Dawe, B. Morning Becomes Electric.
Dawson, M. Late for Breakfast.
Dickinson, E. Safe in their Alabaster Chambers.
Will there really be a "morning"?
Donne. Break[e] of Day.
Sun[ne] Rising, The.
Drainac. Landscape.

Drummond, W. Invocation: "Pheobus, arise! / And paint the sable skies."
Dunbar, P. In the Morning.
Dunbar, W. Poet's Dream, The.
Eliot, T. Morning at the Window.
Field, R. Summer Morning, A.
Finch, R. Turning.
Fletcher, J. Satyr's Song.
Fulton, A. A.M.: The Hopeful Monster.
Gascoigne. Gascoigne's Good-Morrow.
Ginsberg, A. We Rise on Sun Beams and Fall in the Night.
Grenier. Sunday Morning.
Guiney. When on the marge of evening the last blue light is broken.
Hacker, M. Aube Provençale.
Hackett, J. Bitter morning, A.
Handlin. Cold winter morning.
Harjo, J. Early morning woman.
Hartnett. Last Vision of Eoghan Rua Ó Súilleabháin, The.
Heard, J. Matin Hymn.
Morn.
Heine. Morning After, The.
Herbert, G. Mattens.
Herlin. Morning space expands the building's.
Herrick. Matins [or Mattens], or Morning Prayer.
Heywood, T. Matin Song.
Hitchcock. May All Earth Be Clothed in Light.
Hollander, J. Morning in the Islands.
Hopkinson, F. Arise and see the glorious sun.
Hotham. Morning fog.
Morning quiet.
Housman, A. In the morning, in the morning.
Reveille.
Huang Ching-jen. Traveling at Break of Day.
Huang Tsun-hsien. Recuperating in Chang Villa.
Hughes, L. Blues at Dawn.
Hughes, T. Horses, The.
Stealing Trout.
Jacobsen, R. Rubber.
Jarrell. Nestus Gurley.
Kantaris. Awakening to Snow.
Kaufman, B. Cocoa Morning.
Keats. To Hope.
Kenney. Aubade: "Cold snap. Five o'clock."
Kunitz, S. Round.
Kuskin. I woke up this morning.
Lawrence, D. Morning Work.
Lee, L. Early in the Morning.
Levertov. Matins.
Levine, P. Ordinary Morning, An.
To My God in His Sickness.
Livingstone, D. Lake Morning in Autumn.
Longfellow, H. Daybreak.
Lowell, R. Waking Early Sunday Morning.
Lowry, M. Eye-Opener.
Lu Yu. Impressions.
MacNeice. Morning Sun.
Slow Movement.
Sunday Morning.
Mahon. Everything Is Going to Be All Right.
Maiden. Dew.
Malroux. Every morning the curtain rises.
McCarthy, G. Finding the Way Back.
McClintock, M. Glimmering morning.
Meredith, W. Poem about Morning.
Merton. Aubade: Lake Erie.
Merwin, W. Rain Travel.
Mihalic. Morning Roar of the City, The.
Mother Goose. One misty, moisty morning.
Muir, E. Wayside Station, The.
Muldoon, P. Avenue, The.
Nash, O. Morning Prayer.
Nesbit, E. Morning Song.
Ni Dhomhnaill. Aubade: "It's all the same to morning what it dawns on."
Olson, C. Variations Done for Gerald Van De Wiele.
Ovid. I, 13. Elegy: Ad Auroram, ne properet.
Padgett, R. With Lee Remick at Midnight.
Padilla. Daily Habits.
Patmore, C. Across the sky the daylight crept.
Pavese. Grappa in September.

Pavlovic. Morning Inscription.
Petri. Morning Coffee.
Plath. Sheep in Fog.
Rakosi. Good Morning.
Raworth. My Face Is My Own, I Thought.
Revard. On the Bright Side.
Roethke. Carnations.
Ronsard. Time to be up, Marie, young sleepyhead!
Samio. Tanka: "When the gardener."
Sanchez, S. Haiku.
Sandburg, C. Halsted Street Car.
Saxe, J. Early Rising.
Schwartz, D. In the Naked Bed, in Plato's Cave.
Sexton. Welcome Morning.
Shakespeare, W. Song: "Hark! hark! the lark at heaven's gate sings."
Sonnet 33.
Shlonsky. Morning in My City.
Simic. Summer Morning.
Simpson, L. Early in the Morning.
Morning Light, The.
Sissoko. Dawn in the Valley.
Slonimski. Morning and Evening.
Southerland. Recitation.
Spender, S. Awaking.
Stern, G. Morning Harvest.
There Is Wind, There Are Matches.
Stevens, W. Nomad Exquisite.
Stevenson, R. Winter Time [or Winter-Time].
Supervielle. Early in the morning.
Swift, J. Description of the Morning, A.
Tennyson, A. Marriage Morning.
Thaxter. Chanticleer.
Thomas, E. Glory of the beauty of the morning, The.
Thoreau. Guido's Aurora.
Thurman. Zebra.
Tranströmer. Man Awakened by a Song Above His Roof, The.
Ullman. Dawn Feeding.
Ungaretti. Morning.
Unknown. Cloudy morning.
Cock-crow Song.
My Lord, what a mornin' [or morning when de stars begin to fall].
Sister, Awake!
Vallejo. Our Daily Bread.
Vaughan, H. Morning-Watch, The.
Very. Clouded Morning, The.
Fair Morning, The.
Wang Wei. Morning.
Warren, R. Garden.
Wilbur. Late Aubade, A.
Love Calls Us to the Things of This World.
Summer Morning, A.
Wilde, O. Impression Du Matin.
Williams, W. January Morning.
Wordsworth, W. Composed upon Westminster Bridge[, September 3, 1802].
Wright, C. California Spring.
Yakamochi. I lie long abed.
Yau. Broken Off by the Music.
Yukitsuna. Tanka: "Each morning I awake."

Morning Glories
Chiyojo. Morning glory!, The.
Pitkin. Blue Morning Glory.
Whitman, S. Morning-Glory, The.

Morocco
Cavalli. Moroccans with the carpets, The.
Currey. Marrakech.
Eberhart, R. Marrakech.

Morris, William
Unknown. Rondel: "Behold the works of William Morris."

Mortality
Adams, L. April Mortality.
Aiken, C. Tetélestai.
Ainsworth, H. Fire in my meditation burned.
Alvarez, J. Sonnet 1: "Everything that happens to me these days."
Amichai. Man in his life has no time to have, A.
Atwood. Last Poem.
Auchterlonie. Meditation of a Mariner.

Auden. Lullaby: "Lay your sleeping head, my love."
Avidan. Longterm Hatred.
Barbauld. Life! I know not what thou art.
Barbu. Dogmatic Egg, The.
Beam. Time is.
Bernstein, O. Of All the Splendor.
Season when Nothing's in Place, A.
Time to Leave.
Bible, *O.T.* Lord, Make Me to Know Mine End.
Psalm 90.
Blake, W. Caverns of the Grave Ive seen, The.
To Tirzah.
Bly, R. August Rain.
Hollow Tree, A.
Kneeling Down to Look [or Peer] into a Culvert.
Night.
When the Dumb Speak.
Boker. Blood, blood! The lines of every printed sheet.
Leaden eyelids of wan twilight close, The.
Bonnefoy. Well, The.
Bradstreet, A. Before the Birth of One of Her Children.
Brontë, E. Self-Interrogation.
Burkard. Raincoat, A.
Burns, R. To a Mountain Daisy [On Turning One Down, with the Plough, in April—1786].
Campion, T. Come, Cheerful Day!
Lamentation, A.
What if a day, or a month, or a year[e].
When thou must home to shades of underground [or under ground].
Where are all thy beauties now, all hearts enchaining? [or harts enchayning?].
Carew, T. Song, [A]: "Ask me no more where Jove bestows."
Celan. When you lie in.
Colman, H. On Mortality.
Cory, W. Mimnermus in Church.
Cowper, W. On a Similar Occasion for the Year 1790.
On a Similar Occasion for the Year 1792.
Stanzas Subjoined to the Yearly Bill of Mortality of the Parish of All Saints, Northampton; for the Year 1787.
Crane, S. If I should cast off this tattered coat.
Cullen, C. For Amy Lowell.
Leaves.
Daniel, S. When winter snows upon thy sable hairs.
Desnos. Midway.
Dickinson, E. Because I could not stop for Death.
Exultation is the going.
"Heavenly Father"—take to thee.
My Life Had Stood—A Loaded Gun.
Somehow myself survived the Night.
'Tis not that Dying hurts us so.
Visitor in Marl, A.
Wounded Deer—leaps highest, A.
Disch. Convalescing in London.
Donne. Anniversary [or Anniversarie], The.
Farewell to Love.
First Anniversary [or Anniversarie], The.
Song: "Sweetest love, I do not go[e]."
Dowson. Vitae Summa Brevis Spem Nos Vetat Incohare Longam.
Drummond, W. Word a Hunt, A.
Dunbar, P. All Erdly Joy Returns in Pane.
Ehrhart. ". . . the light that cannot fade. . . ."
Emerson, R. Good-bye, proud world! I'm going home.
Hamatreya.
Ewart. 14-Year-Old Convalescent Cat in the Winter, A.
Fitzgerald, E. Some We Loved.
Fletcher, J. Last Frontier, The.
Forbes, J. Death, an Ode.
Glück, L. Garden, The.
Graves, R. In Her Praise.
Greville, F. 87.

Gwynn, R. Anacreontic.
Release.
Habington. Solum Mihi Superest Sepulchrum.
Hajnal. Jaguar is Getting Ready, The.
Hall, D. Ruminant pillows! Gregarious soft boulders!
Tubes.
Hall, J. Job. I.
Hawes, S. Epitaph of Graunde [or La Graunde] Amoure, The.
Herbert, G. Church Monuments.
Employment: "He that is weary, let him sit."
Frailty.
Mortification.
Time.
Virtue [or Vertue].
Herbert, Z. Remembering My Father.
Herrick. Anacreontic.
His Own Epitaph.
Man's Dying-Place Uncertain.
To the Reverend Shade of His Religious Father.
Upon a Young Mother of Many Children.
Upon His Departure Hence.
Upon the Troublesome Times.
Hopkins, G. Spring and Fall.
Housman, A. Be still, my soul, be still; the arms you bear are brittle.
I hoed and trenched and weeded.
Rain, it streams on stone and hillock, The.
With rue my heart is laden.
Jaccottet. Don't worry, you'll get there! You're close.
Right at the end of night.
Jackson, L. Starved.
Jarrell. Author to the Reader, The.
Jeffers, R. Age in Prospect.
Justice, D. Men at forty / Learn to close softly.
Kabir. Hopeful Spiritual Athlete, The.
Keats. Ode on a Grecian Urn.
Terror of Death, The.
Why did I laugh to-night? No voice will tell.
Kennedy, X. On a Child Who Lived One Minute.
King, H. Sic Vita.
Stay For Me There.
King, J. Moments.
Kinnell. Little Sleep's-Head Sprouting Hair in the Moonlight.
Knox, W. Oh! why should the spirit of mortal be proud?
Lansdown. Behind the Veil.
Larkin, P. Aubade: "I work all day, and get half-drunk at night."
Lawrence, D. Death Is Not Evil, Evil Is Mechanical.
Lee, L. Final Thing, A.
Lewis, A. Sentry, The.
To a Comrade in Arms.
Lodge, G. Strong saturation of sea! O widely flown.
Longfellow, H. Mezzo Cammin.
Lu Kuei Meng. To an Old Tune.
Lucretius. Dissolution of the world proovd from the mortality of every part, The.
MacLeish. Signature for Tempo.
MacNeice. Sunlight on the garden, The.
Malroux. In October.
Markham, E. Leaf from the Devil's Jest-Book, A.
Marvell. Picture of Little T. C. in a Prospect of Flowers, The.
McAuley, J. Gnostic Prelude.
In a Late Hour.
Melville, H. Epilogue: "If Luther's day expand to Darwin's year."
Pontoosuce.
Tom Deadlight.
Meredith, G. Dirge in Woods.
Hymn to Colour.
Thrush in February, The.
Merwin, W. For the Anniversary of My Death.
Small Woman on Swallow Street.
Millay, E. At least, my dear.
First Fig.

Lament: "Listen, children: / Your father is dead."
Poet and His Book, The.
Milosz, C. Encounter.
Milosz, O. Bridge, The.
Mitchell, S. Of Earthly Love.
Miu Hsi. Poem in the Form of a Coffin-Puller's Song.
Moore, M. Fable.
More, S. Rueful Lamentation on the Death of Queen Elizabeth, A.
Morris, M. Pre-Carnival Party.
Swimmer.
Newcastle, M. Dissert, A.
Ní Chuilleanáin. Dead Fly.
Oldys. On a Fly Drinking out of [or from] His Cup.
Oliver, M. In Blackwater Woods.
Oppen. Population.
Owen, W. Anthem for Doomed Youth.
Exposure.
Send-Off, The.
Terre, A.
Palladas. Think of your conception, you'll soon forget.
Pao Chao. In Imitation of "The King of Huai-nan."
Parun. Let's Get the Coachman Drunk.
Pasternak, B. Mary Magdalene (I).
Poe. Eldorado.
Popa. In the Ashtray.
Porter, A. Oaks and Squirrels.
Poseidippus. World's a bubble, and the life of man, The.
Prince, F. Question, The.
Proctor, T. Respice Finem.
Ptolemy. From the Greek.
Ransom, J. Piazza Piece.
Ratushinskaya. Try to cover your shivering shoulders in rags of the oldest.
Ritsos. Marpessa's Choice.
Robinson, E. Pity of the Leaves, The.
Roseliep. Ordering my tombstone.
Rosenberg, L. Poem of my Heart, The.
Rudaki. Young or old we die.
Sackville-West. Greater cats with golden eyes, The.
Santayana. Echo.
Scott, W. To L. B. S.
Shakespeare, W. Song: "Fear no more the heat o' the Sun."
Sonnet 19.
Sonnet 65.
Shapiro, D. Lord I sleep and I sleep.
Shapiro, K. Cut Flower, A.
Shaw, R. Shut In.
"Shu Ting." Perhaps these thoughts of ours.
Simonides. Flux.
Simpson, L. Early in the Morning.
Skelton, J. Upon a Dead Man's Head.
Smith, S. Rise from Your Bed of Languor.
Sophocles. Many marvels walk through the world.
Spender, S. One More New Botched Beginning.
Spenser. Mutability.
Stanescu. Homo Plangens.
Marina.
Stanley, T. Quickness.
Stern, G. Bite, The.
Stickney, T. Athenian Garden, An.
Be still. The Hanging Gardens were a dream.
Sylvester, J. Omnia Somnia.
T'ao Ch'ien. Substance, Shadow, and Spirit.
Tate, A. Non Omnis Moriar.
Ode to the Confederate Dead.
Taylor, E. This Year's Drive to Appomattox.
Tennyson, A. Tithonus.
Tóth, J. Murmuring.
Tryapkin. How much there was of everything: kettledrums and horns and bells!
Tuckerman, F. As when, down some broad River dropping, we.
Unknown. Captive's Song.
Ch'i-yü-ko.
Dew on the leek.
Flowers will do us no good on our

tombstones.
I Shall Not Pass This Way Again.
I turn the carriage, yoke and set off.
Kindely is now my coming.
Lonesome Valley.
Man's years fall short of a hundred.
Steal Away to Jesus.
Thus Passeth.
What Yo' Gwine to [or t'] Do When Yo' [or de] Lamp Burn Down?
Wrecche mon, why artou proud.
Updike. Bath after Sailing.
Sea Knell.
Vaughan, H. Death.
Joy of My Life! While Left Me Here.
Quickness.
Vogel, D. There is a last, solitary coach about to leave.
Warren, R. Sky.
Watts, I. Shortness and Misery of Life, The.
Submission to Afflictive Providences.
Webster, J. Vanitas Vanitatum.
Wharton, E. Autumn Sunset, An.
Experience.
Life, like a marble block, is given to all.
Whitman, W. And as to you Death, and you bitter hug of mortality, it is idle to try to alarm.
This Compost.
Whitney, I. Aucthour Maketh Her Wyll and Testament, The.
Whittemore, R. Walk Home, The.
Wieseltier. Columns.
"Elegies By the Senses."
"Wintry Dawn."
Winchilsea. Spleen, The.
Wolfli. And now: And now: here begins Our Voyage, hunters and naturalists of indefatigable enthusiasm.
Wordsworth, W. Most alluring clouds that mount the sky, The.
Trosachs, The.
Yeats. Get all the gold and silver that you can.
Yosano. This autumn will end.
Zenmaro. Evidence.

Morticians. See Undertakers

Moscow, Russia
Fleming, P. To the Great City of Moscow, as He Was Leaving June 25, 1636.
"Korzhavin." I could be in Paris or Vienna.
Shwarts. Elegies on the Cardinal Points.

Moses
Alexander, C. Burial of Moses, The.
Allen, S. Harriet Tubman aka Moses.
Anacreon. Spare me the man.
Bell, J. Modern Moses, or "My Policy" Man.
Bringhurst. Deuteronomy.
Dickinson, E. It always felt to me—a wrong.
Dickinson, P. Moses and the Princess.
"Eliot." Death of Moses, The.
Gilbo'a. Moses.
Hope, A. Luke 24:36–49; As they were saying this, Jesus.
Hopkins, G. Soliloquy of One of the Spies Left in the Wilderness, A.
Moran, M. Pharao's Daughter.
Naden. Moonlight and Gas.
Nemerov. John 3:1–15; Now there was a man.
Schwartz, L. Monuments to the Not Yet Lived.
Unknown. Angels Came a-Mustering, The.
Death of Moses, The.
Go down, Moses.
Moses supposes his toeses are roses.
Railroad Section Leader's Song.
Very. Moses in Infancy.
Whalen. Complaint: To the Muse.
Wither. First Song of Moses, The.
Zangwill. Moses and Jesus.

Mosquitoes
Bryant, W. To a Mosquito.
Coolidge, C. Morning muezzin in orange and a mosquito.
"Ern Malley." Culture as Exhibit.
Issa. Mosquito at my ear.
Issahakian. Mosquito at my ear—.

Jones, R. Mosquito, The.
Kinzie. Among mosquitoes.
Lawrence, D. Mosquito Knows, The.
Lindsay, V. Little Turtle, The.
Mei Yao Ch'en. Swarming Mosquitoes.
P'i Jih-hsiu. Mosquitoes.
Roseliep. After Tosca.
Wright, F. Mosquitoes.

Moss
Blind. Entangled.
Chu Yün-ming. Landscape Painted on a Fan—Echoing a Poem by Wen Cheng-ming, A.
Hsü Chung-hsing. Trees are ancient, thick with patterns of moss, The.
Irby. January 1965, Looking on.
Kao Ch'i. Moss below the Stairs.
Mayer, B. It moves across and over / across the ground.
Ni Tsan. On the Twentieth Day.
Roethke. Moss-Gathering.
Yang Shih-ch'i. White Stone Slope.

Motels
Grosholz. Outer Banks, The.
Jacob, M. In Search of the Traitor.
Snodgrass, W. Leaving the Motel.
Wagoner, D. On Motel Walls.

See also **Hotels**

Mothers
Abu Dulama. Behold my mother!
Acosta. My Mother Pieced Quilts.
Adamson. Dreaming Up Mother.
My House.
Ai. But What I'm Trying to Say Mother Is.
She Didn't Even Wave.
Allen, A. My Mother's Garden.
Allen, E. Rock Me to Sleep[, Mother].
"Alta." Lorelei.
Alvarez, J. Naming the Fabrics.
Amichai. My Mother Once Told Me.
Armantrout. Incidence.
Armuth. Mother, A.
Auvaiyar. Mothers.
Baba. Since I don't know my mother.
Baillie, J. Mother to Her Waking Infant, A.
Baker, J. My Trundle Bed.
Bàng Bá Lâ. Mother, I Am Still Here With You.
Barber, M. Written for My Son, and Spoken by Him at His First Putting on Breeches.
Barker, G. To My Mother.
Benét, S. Nonsense Song, A.
Bennett, G. Secret.
Berrigan, T. Certain Slant of Sunlight, A.
Besant, L. Telepathy.
Bible, *O.T.* Honour thy father and thy mother.
Virtuous Woman, The.
Birney. Gray Woods Exploding, The.
Blok. Vulture.
Bly, R. Busy Man Speaks, A.
Boe, M. Sunday Afternoon at the State Hospital.
Boyd, E. On the Death of an Infant of Five Days Old.
Bradstreet, A. Before the Birth of One of Her Children.
In Reference to Her Children, 23 June, 1659 [or 1659].
Breeze. Natural High.
Brett, L. Leaving You.
Brine. Somebody's Mother.
Brooks, G. Big Bessie Throws Her Son into the Street.
Jessie Mitchell's Mother.
Maxie Allen [always taught her].
Mrs. Small went to the kitchen for her pocketbook.
Broumas, O. Snow White.
Brown, W. Mother, Home, Heaven.
Browning, E. Mother and Poet.
Bruner. Remembrance.
Budbill. What I Heard at the Discount Department Store.
Burkard. Raincoat, A.
Campbell, D. Mothers and Daughters.
Campbell, R. Zulu Girl, The.
Campion, T. Fain would I wed a fair young man that night and day could please me.

Carruth, H. Death, The.
Song: So Often, So Long I Have Thought.
Causley. What has happened to Lulu, mother?
Cavafy. Supplication.
Celan. Aspen tree, your leaves glance white into the dark.
Cisneros, S. Muddy Kid Comes Home.
Clements, S. Reservation, The.
Clemmons. Revelation.
Clifton, L. Admonitions.
Fury.
If mama / could see.
My Mama moved among the days.
Thirty-eighth year, The.
Twenty-one years of my life you have been.
Clinton. Eviction.
Clive. Mother, The.
Cofer. Unspoken.
Coleman, W. American Sonnet (10).
Dear Mama (2).
Collymore. Ballad of an Old Woman.
Colum, P. Interior.
Conn. Summer Afternoon.
Cook, E. Old Arm-Chair, The.
Cooley. Macular Degeneration.
Cooper, G. Only One Mother.
Cooper, J. My young mother, her face narrow.
Corbet. Certain True Woords Spoken Concerning One Benet Corbett after Her Death.
Cornish, S. Sam's World ("Sam's mother has").
Your Mother.
Corso. Sea Chanty.
Cowper, W. On the Receipt of My Mother's Picture out of Norfolk, the Gift of My Cousin Ann Bodham.
Creeley. Cracks, The.
For My Mother: Genevieve Jules Creeley.
Memory Gardens.
Mother's Voice.
She Went to Stay.
Croft, S. Blue.
Crowell, G. Definition.
Dabydeen, D. Coolie Mother.
Davey, F. She'd Say.
Davis, L. I look at my hands, Momma.
You taught me fear, Momma.
DeFrees. Letter to an Absent Son.
Derricotte. Christmas Eve: My Mother Dressing.
Note on my Son's Face, A.
Touching/Not Touching: My Mother.
Dickey, J. Birth, A.
Buckdancer's Choice.
Dickinson, E. Work of Her that went, The.
Diop, D. For My Mother.
Dobell, S. "How's My Boy?"
Dobyns. Tomatoes.
Dodson, O. Black Mother Praying.
Doob. My Mother's Blue Vase.
Dorcey. First Love.
Dorn, E. On the Debt My Mother Owed to Sears Roebuck.
Doty, M. Harbor Lights.
Doubiago. My mother is a poem I'll never be able to write.
Dove, R. After Reading *Mickey in the Night Kitchen* for the Third Time Before Bed.
Bird Frau, The.
Motherhood.
Pastoral.
Who can forget the attitude of mothering?
Doyle, S. This Shade.
Dromgoole. Old Ladies.
Drown. To Mother.
Dufferin. Mother's Lament, The.
Duggin. For My Mother, Who Lives.
Duncan, R. My mother would be a falconress.
Dunn, S. Routine Things Around the House, The.
Eady. My Mother, If She Had Won Free Dance Lessons.
My Mother is a God Fearing Woman.
Eberhart, R. Soul Longs to Return Whence It Came, The.

Edson, R. Having to Love Something Else, The.
Ehrmann. Mother.
Erdrich. Birth.
Fainlight, R. Handbag.
Feldman, I. Dream, The.
Ficowski. Both Your Mothers.
Fisher, A. On Mother's Day.
Flanders, J. Nightingales in America.
Fordham. Mother's Recall.
To My Mother.
Foscolo. Upon the Death of His Brother Giovanni.
Fowler, A. Relative.
Fuller, R. Metamorphoses.
Gallagher, T. Each Bird Walking.
Gay, J. Mother, the Nurse, and the Fairy, The.
Gbadamosi. Flying Home.
Sewing-Box, The.
Getsi. Oradour-sur-Glane. Silence.
Gidlow. I know myself linked by chains of fire.
Gilbert, C. Circles.
Gilbo'a. Circle of Weeping, The.
Gildner. Poems.
Gillilan, S. Reading Mother, The.
Ginsberg, A. Hymmnn.
IV.
Kaddish.
Giovanni. Mothers.
Mother's Habits.
Gloria. Whisper, The.
Glück, L. For My Mother.
Lullaby: "My mother's an expert at one thing."
Pomegranate.
School Children, The.
Godfrey. My Mother, Life.
Goedicke. In the Ocean.
Goodison. Birth Stone.
I Am Becoming My Mother.
Grafflin. To My Son.
Graves, R. Frosty Night, A.
Greenberg, B. Mother, R.I.P.
Griffin, S. Awful Mother, The.
Bad Mother, The.
Stories and Poems.
Teeth.
Grimald. From A Funeral Song, Upon the Decease of Annes His Mother.
I, in your frutefull woomb conceyved, born was.
Grimke, C. Angel's Visit, The.
Grosholz. Eden.
Guri. His Mother.
"H., H. E." Riddle, The.
Hacker, M. Fifteen to Eighteen.
Mother II.
Nearly a Valediction.
Sonnet for Iva.
Hadas, R. Three Silences.
Up and Down.
Hagedorn, H. Mother.
Hai-Jew, S. Kinged.
Hall, J. St. Peregrinus' Cancer.
Halley. Against Dark's Harm.
Halpern, D. Early Death, An.
Ham, J. Exiles.
Hardy, T. Lacking Sense, The.
Harper, F. Slave Mother, The.
Harper, M. Lecturing on the Theme of Motherhood.
Mama's Report.
Harris, J. When mama came here as a gold panner.
Harrod, L. Fitting Room.
Harryman. Mothering.
Harwood, G. Mother who gave me life.
Hashimoto, S. Mirror of Matsuyama, The.
Hawley, B. Bad Mother, The.
Hayden, R. Whipping, The.
Heaney, S. Mother of the Groom.
When all the others were away at Mass.
Heard, J. Mother.
Heine. Sonnet to My Mother, A.
Hemschemeyer. First Love.
My Mother's Death.

Herbert, G. Ah Mater, quo te deplorem fonte? Dolores.
Herbert, Z. Mother.
Herder. Esthonian Bridal Song.
Herrick. Upon a Young Mother of Many Children.
Herzberg. Reunion.
Holan. At Mother's After Many Years.
Mother.
Holmes, R. Little girl's heart must be wide and, A.
Hove. Country Life.
Hoye. You are like an everlasting friendship.
Hughes, L. Letter.
Mama and Daughter.
Mother to Son.
Ignatow, D. Mother, how wrinkled and old must you become.
Ilanakanar, M. Mothers.
Ingraham. She Would Have Roses.
Woman Back in the Kitchen, The.
Ishikawa Takuboku. Tanka: "Just for fun."
Tanka: "Words from."
Iverem. Murmur.
Jackson, L. In the Beginning.
Jackson, R. 1973.
Jamison, B. Ask This of a Mother Whose Daughter Has Been Tortured.
Jarrell. Bats.
Death of the Ball Turret Gunner, The.
Lost Children, The.
Johnson, F. Lonely Mother, The.
Johnston, E. Mother's Love, A.
Jones, R. Caught.
Joron, A. Zirkus.
Joseph, L. Mama Remembers.
Justice, D. Variations on Southern Themes.
Kākkai Pāṭiṇiyār Naccellaiyār. Mothers.
Kalász. Legacy.
Kaufman, S. Apples.
I Hear You.
Mothers, Daughters.
Notes to my Daughters.
Kavanagh, P. In Memory of My Mother.
Kavarpentu. Mothers.
Kay, J. That Distance Apart.
Keeshig-Tobias. Mother with Child.
Keesing. Reverie of a Mum.
Kelly, I. To an Unborn Infant.
Kendrick, D. Sidney, Looking for her Mother.
Kennedy, X. Mother's Nerves.
Kerouac. One Hundred and Forty-Ninth Chorus.
Kgositsile. To Mother.
Kim, J. Mother-thought.
Kim, K. Mother's Letter from the North.
Kim, M. Bounty, II, The.
Kinnell. Last Hiding Places of Snow, The.
Kipling, R. Unknown Female Corpse.
Kirschner. Blueness of Stars, The.
Kizer, C. Blessing, The.
Intruder, The.
Knight, E. Report to the Mother.
Komunyakaa. My Father's Love Letters [or Loveletters].
Kumin, M. Envelope, The.
Voice From the Roses, A.
Kuzmina-Karavayeva. Who am I, Lord? Just an impostor.
Lake, P. Blue Jay.
Landon. Dying Child, The.
Landor, W. Mother, I Cannot Mind My Wheel.
Lanjewar. I Never Saw You.
Lankesh. Mother.
Lapidus. Exmatriate.
Laughton. Woman with Child, The.
Layton. Keine Lazarovitch, 1870-1959.
Le Guin. Child on the Shore, The.
Leaf, E. Dear Mother.
Ledwidge. My Mother.
Lee, L. Final Thing, A.
I Ask My Mother to Sing.
Lesser. Woman from Chianciano.
Levertov. Dragonfly-Mother, The.
Olga Poems.
Levine, P. Soloing.

Libera. Mother, I may do violence to you.
Lifshin. I Remember Haifa Being Lovely But.
Lim, S. Starlight Haven.
Lindsay, V. Nancy Hanks, Mother of Abraham Lincoln.
Liu. Mother.
Livingston, M. Working with Mother.
Lloyd, H. Unveiling.
Lochhead, L. Abortion, An.
Lorde. Black Mother Woman.
From the House of Yemanjá.
Hanging Fire.
Now That I Am Forever with Child.
Story Books on a Kitchen Table.
Lowell, R. Sailing Home from Rapallo.
Soft Wood.
"MacDiarmid." Two Parents, The.
MacDonald, C. Inheritance.
Late Mother, The.
Macgoye. August the First; Court Martial. The Mother Speaks.
Machi. Tanka: "Woman, The."
Maclean, A. Rain, The.
Madgett. Offspring.
Makeda (Queen of Sheba). Wisdom is.
Malangatana. To the Anxious Mother.
Malé. My Mother's Homeland.
Markman. And / mother why did you tell me.
Marsh, D. Mice.
Marshall, J. Sesame.
Martin, S. Comic Adventures of Old Mother Hubbard and Her Dog, The.
Masefield. C. L. M.
Mason, R. Footnote to John II: 4.
Masters, M. At My Mother's Bedside.
Mathis. Seven Months.
Matthews, M. Realarro.
Maxwell, R. Mother's Joy, A.
Mazur. Phonic.
McAuley, J. Because.
McBain. I wonder why I can't remember.
McElroy, C. In My Mother's Room.
Ruth.
McGinley. Adversary, The.
McKay, C. My Mother.
Meehan, M. She has withdrawn from us.
Meyers, L. Apple-Eater, The.
Meynell, A. Cradle-Song at Twilight.
Girl on the Land, The.
Maternity.
Modern Mother, The.
Parentage.
Miles, J. Belief.
Conception.
Millay, E. Ballad of the Harp-Weaver, The.
Courage that my mother had, The.
Milne, A. Disobedience.
Moffett. Now or Never.
Monsour. Sweeping.
Montague, J. Locket, The.
Mother Cat, The.
Moraga. For the Color of My Mother.
Half-Breed.
La Dulce Culpa.
Morgan, R. As it was in the beginning.
Little heart, little heart.
Mori. Speaking Through White: For My Mother.
Moritz. Baltic Summer.
Some Lines on My Mother's Illness.
Morley, H. Rondanini Pieta, The.
Morrison, M. Nobody Knows but Mother.
Moss, S. For Margaret.
Mother Goose. There was an old woman who lived in a shoe.
Moyer. Listen.
Muir, E. Childhood.
Muldoon, P. Ma.
Mullen, H. Momma Sayings.
Murray, M. My mother talked of breakfast or laundry.
Muske. August, Los Angeles, Lullaby.
Wyndmere, Windemere.
Nagase. Mother.
Naiman. My mother has died, but I visit her weekly.
Nesbit, E. Song: "Oh, baby, baby, baby dear."

Nichols, G. Wha Me Mudder Do.
Nowlan. Mother and Son.
Ofeimun. Naming Day, A.
Ogilvy. Natal Address to My Child, March 19th 1844, A.
O'Hara, F. Ave Maria.
Poem: "There I could never be a boy."
To My Mother.
O'Kane. My Mother's Prayer.
Olds, S. For My Daughter.
Latest Injury, The.
Mother, The.
New Mother.
Power of My Mother, The.
Quake Theory.
What If God.
Why My Mother Made Me.
Ormsby, F. Winter Offerings.
Orr, G. Mother, The.
Weeds, The.
Ostriker. Leaf Pile, The.
Propaganda Poem: Maybe for Some Young Mamas.
Parra, N. Tablets, The.
Pasolini. Prayer to My Mother.
Pastan. Duet for One Voice.
Letter to a Son at Exam Time.
Pearse, P. Mother, The.
Perillo. Sweaters, The.
Peseroff. Bluebird.
Peyanar. Embracing the young mother from behind.
Like the red flame.
Philips, A. To Miss Charlotte Pulteney in Her Mother's Arms.
Piatt, S. This World.
Pitter. Maternal Love Triumphant or Song of the Virtuous Female Spider.
Plath. Disquieting Muses, The.
Morning Song.
Parliament Hill Fields.
Plumly. My Mother's Feet.
Poe. To My Mother.
Ponmutiyar. Mother's List of Duties, A.
Ponsot. Tranquilized, she speaks or does not speak.
Power, K. Sestina for Jaime.
Pratt, M. All the Women Caught in Flaring Light.
Child Taken from the Mother, The.
Poem for my Sons.
Punkanuttiraiyar. Mothers.
Raine, K. Heirloom.
Ramsey, H. Home and Mother.
Mother.
Ranasinghe. Holocaust 1944.
Randell. Watching Women with Children.
Ray, H. To My Mother.
Rebelo. Poem for a Militant.
Rexroth, K. Delia Rexroth.
Rich, A. This.
Riley, D. Affections Must Not.
Ríos, A. Nani.
Rodgers, C. It Is Deep.
Portrait.
Rodriguez, L. Speaking with Hands.
Rogers, D. Desert.
Rosenberg, L. Poem of my Heart, The.
Ross, C. Old Mothers.
Rossetti, C. Chilly Night, A.
Lambs at Play.
Rudman, M. Nowhere Water, The.
Rukeyser, M. Night Feeding.
Question, The.
Sachs, N. Already embraced by the arm of heavenly solace.
Dead Child Speaks, A.
O my mother.
O the night of the weeping children!
We mothers.
St. John, P. Pearle's Poem.
Salter. Emily Wants to Play.
What Do Women Want?
Samio. Tanka: "Day I was born, The."
Tanka: "No scar."
Sanders, E. Leaves of heaven, The.
Sant. Household Fires.

Santos, S. Childhood.
Sappho. Evening Star who gathers everything.
Sarton. I did not weep my father.
Sassoon. Reconciliation.
Schechter. What Were You Patching?
Schultz, P. For My Mother.
Schwartz, D. Baudelaire.
Young Child and His Pregnant Mother, A.
Scott, W. My Mother.
Selvinsky. Portrait of My Mother.
Senesh. To My Mother.
Sexton. Child Bearers, The.
Two Sons.
Shelton, T. Patches.
Sholl. This old woman.
Shorter. Mother, The.
Shumaker. Waitress's Kid, The.
Siddal. At Last.
Simic. Spoons with Realistic Dead Flies on Them.
Smith, B. American Lunch.
Smith, M. Revolutionary.
Smith, P. Biting Back.
Smith, S. Human Affection.
Landrecie.
Mother, among the dustbins and the manure.
Mother love is a mighty benefaction.
Sornberger. Thinking of My Mother Who Fifteen Years Later, Has Gone East to See the Leaves.
Standing. Room to go to, A.
Stanford, F. Terrorism.
Stein, R. Lines to Mother.
Stevens, W. In the Carolinas.
World Without Peculiarity.
Stevenson, A. Apology.
From an Asylum; Kathy Chattle to Her Mother, Ruth Arbeiter.
Poem to my Daughter.
Stevenson, R. Sick Child, The.
Strand. My Mother on an Evening in Late Summer.
Pot Roast.
Swenson, M. Motherhood.
Swirszczynska. Conversation Through the Door, A.
Szymborska. Born of Woman.
Tagami. Now It Is Broccoli.
Tanikawa Shuntaro. River.
Tate, A. Mother and Son.
Tate, J. Distance from Loved Ones.
For Mother on Father's Day.
Tennyson, A. Cradle Song: "What does little birdie say?"
Thompson, C. Tree, The.
Thù'a Phong. Mother's Faith.
Tighe. Sonnet Addressed to My Mother.
Titherage. And Her Mother Came Too.
Toller. One Who Struggles, The.
To the Mothers.
Townsend, A. Eighteenth-Century Medical Illustration: The Infant in its Little Room.
Trinh Tiên. Woman Writes to Her Daughter Who's Studying Overseas, A.
Tucker, M. My Mother's Voice.
Tuqan, F. Behind Bars, Sel.
Twomey. Cliona.
Unknown. Carpenter's Wife, The ("O whare hae ye been, my dearest dear").
Cradle Song: "Sleep, my child, my little daughter."
Cruel Mother, The.
Execution of Alice Holt.
I syng of a mayden that is makeles.
Mother.
Mother's Song, The.
My Mother's Hands.
Old Mother, The.
One, two, buckle my shoe.
Somebody's Mother.
When Mother reads aloud, the past.
Wife of Usher's Well, The.
Untermeyer, J. Autumn.
Upton, L. Debt, The.
Usha. To Mother.
Valentine, J. My Mother's Body, My

Professor, My Bower.
Seeing You.
Vallejo. Right Meaning, The.
Van Duyn. Stream, The.
Villanueva, A. To Jesus Villanueva, with Love.
Vinokurov. Mother of Judas, The.
Virgilio. My gold star mother.
Voigt. Claiming Kin.
For My Mother.
Voznesensky. Elegy for My Mother.
Wagenlander. Mother's Birthday.
Wakoski. Poem for a Little Boy on the Buddha's Birthday.
Waldman, A. Complaynt.
Wallace, W. Hand That Rocks the Cradle Is the Hand That Rules the World, The.
Waniek. Bali Hai Calls Mama.
Levitation with Baby.
Warren, R. Revelation.
There's a grandfather's clock in the hall, watch it closely. The.
Watson, R. Who a Mother Is.
Webster, A. Little child she, half defiant came, A.
Love's Mourner.
Since first my little one lay on my breast.
Wedgefarth. Mother in gladness, Mother in sorrow.
Mother's Hands.
Weiners. My Mother.
Wellesley. Mother.
Wesley-Smith. Cavendish McKellar.
Wheelwright. And for His Mother.
Whitman, W. Now what my mother told me one day as we sat at dinner / together.
Sleepers, The.
Wieners. My Mother.
Williams, C. My Mother's Lips.
Williams, W. Horse Show, The.
Wojahn. White Lanterns.
Wong, N. Dreams in Harrison Railroad Park.
I dream red dreams, an oasis of fire and light.
Ma, my heart must be made of rice straw.
Mama, come back.
Where are you going now?
Wordsworth, W. Affliction of Margaret—The The.
Complaint of a Forsaken Indian Woman, The.
Mad Mother, The.
Wright, C. Kineo Mountain.
Yamada. Homecoming.
I Learned To Sew.
Night Before Good-Bye, The.
Yang Shih-ch'i. Herdboy returns, none too early, The.
Yeats. Song of the Old Mother, The.
Yesenin. Letter to My Mother.
Young, C. Vespers.
Yun. Counting the Stars.
Zamora, D. Mother's Day.
Ziedonis. That is her memorial.

Mother's Day
Becker, E. Mother's Day.
Ross, C. Old Mothers.
Wallace, W. Hand That Rocks the Cradle Is the Hand That Rules the World, The.

Mothers-in-Law
Adams, A. Unrecorded Speech.
Cheng Hsieh. Mother-in-Law Is Cruel
Ciardi. Censorship.
Ludvigson. Man Arrested in Hacking Death Tells Police He Mistook Mother-in-Law for Raccoon.
Rich, A. Mother-in-Law.
Smith, S. Octopus, The.
Sornberger. Place to begin is not your death, The.
Unknown. Prince Robert.
Unexpected Pleasure, An.
Wang Chien. Words of the Newly Wed Wife.

Moths
Baildon. Moth, A.
Bostok. Pregnant again.
Crapsey. Warning, The.
Cynewulf. Book Moth: "Moth ate a word. To me it seemed, A."

Davies, H.   Music in an Empty House.
De Casseres.   Moth-Terror.
Gittings.   Great Moth, The.
Hackett, J.   Moon fades into dawn.
Jackson, M.   Moths, The.
Keyser.   Rainy summer night.
Krynicki.   I Can't Help You.
Kunze, R.   Meditation.
Leithauser.   Haunted, The.
Ni Dhomhnaill.   Labasheedy (The Silken Bed).
  Leaba Shíoda.
O Riordain.   Moths, The.
Revell.   Other Wings, The.
Robinson, F.   Down rippling, The.
Roseliep.   Banker, The.
  Seance.
Saitō Mokichi.   Tanka: "From the evening
  darkness."
Samio.   Tanka: "With each quiver."
Snodgrass, W.   Lying Awake.
Stevens, W.   Hibiscus on the Sleeping Shores.
Vizenor.   Tyranny of Moths.
Williams, W.   Prelude to Winter.
Zagajewski.   Moths watched us through.

Motion
Bartošová.   And That Is Why. . . .
Creeley.   To and / back and forth.
Greenwald, T.   I hear a step. A step.
Gunn, T.   On the Move.
Hughes, T.   Thought-Fox, The.
Juarroz.   Any movement kills something.
Levertov.   Wavering.
Lovelace, R.   Gratiana Dancing [or Dauncing]
  and [or &] Singing.
Mitchell, S.   Rapture.
Mori Ōgai.   Tanka: "White swan."
Prunty.   Ferris Wheel, The.
Stevens, W.   Curtains in the House of the
  Metaphysician, The.
  Pleasures of Merely Circulating, The.

Motion Pictures
Ashbery.   Forties Flick.
Baca.   Main Character.
Bentley, N.   Cecil B. De Mille.
Berryman.   Dispossessed, The.
Collier, M.   Cave, The.
Creeley.   Bresson's Movies.
Cummings, E.   O pr / gress verily thou art m.
Day Lewis.   Newsreel.
Deanovich.   Connie Deanovich.
Dlugos.   D.O.A.
Dobyns.   What You Have Come To Expect.
Duncan.   In Ingmar Bergman's "Seventh Seal."
Field, E.   Curse of the Cat Woman.
Garrigue.   Movie Actors Scribbling Letters
  Very Fast in Crucial Scenes.
Gorbanevskaya.   This world / is amazingly flat.
Gwynn, R.   Drive-In, The.
Hayden, R.   Double Feature.
Heseltine, P.   Limerick: "Young things who
  frequent picture-palaces, The."
Hollander, J.   Movie-Going.
Jackson, R.   Violation, A.
Jones, P.   Why I Like Movies.
Kunio.   Tanka: "Even while."
Lehman.   Moment of Truth, The.
Levertov.   Triple Feature.
Magrelli.   I sit, in treatment, at the movies,
  devoted.
McGough, R.   If Life's a Lousy Picture, Why
  Not Leave before the End.
Milosz, C.   Screens will be set there.
Moss, H.   Movies for the Home.
Muldoon, P.   Weepies, The.
O'Hara, F.   Ave Maria.
  Image of Leda, An.
  To the Film Industry in Crisis.
Rich, A.   Newsreel.
Schmitz.   Star & Garter Theater.
Updike.   Movie House.
Ward, D.   Re-Verse.
Whittemore, R.   Day with the Foreign Legion,
  A.
Wilbur.   Prisoner of Zenda, The.
Yamanaka.   Kala: Saturday Night at the Pahala
  Theatre.
Yoshimi.   Tanka: "Soldiers on the ground."

Zagajewski.   Watching Shoah in a Hotel Room
  in America.
See also **Show Business**
Motorcycles and Motorcycling
Ferlinghetti, L.   Ladakh Buddhess Biker.
Gunn, T.   On the Move.
  Unsettled Motorcyclist's Vision of His Death,
  The.
Hughes, T.   Motorbike, A.
Jordan, J.   Speculations on the Present through
  the Prism of the Past.
Mtshali.   Farewell to My Scooter.
Van Duyn.   What the Motorcycle Said.
Walker, A.   Kiss, The.
Mount Saint Helens, Washington
Daniel, J.   To Mt. St. Helens.
Rose.   Loo-wit.
Mount Tamalpais
Hoyem.   Circumambulation of Mt. Tamalpais.
Oppen.   Impossible Poem, The.
Mountain Beavers
Wagoner, D.   Looking for Mountain Beavers.
Mountain Climbing
Auden.   Climbers, The.
Birney.   David and I that summer cut trails on
  the Survey.
Carmichael, A.   Last Defile, The.
Chong, C.   Summit, The.
Greig, A.   Winter Climbing, The.
Haines, J.   On the Mountain.
Hardy, T.   Zermatt: To the Matterhorn.
Huntington.   From Green Mountain.
Justice, D.   Here in Katmandu.
Kinnell.   Flower Herding on Mount
  Monadnock.
Mangan, K.   Above the Tree Line.
Mo Shih-lung.   On a Cold Day I Climbed
  Tiger Hill With Professor Ho. At the Time,
  the Local Prefect Had Prohibited Pleasure
  Excursions and Feasts, But the Mountain
  Was Quiet and Tranquil, So We Stayed All
  Day.
Rich, A.   Phantasia for Elvira Shatayev.
Snyder, G.   John Muir on Mt. Ritter.
Stafford, W.   Story, A.
Walker, T.   On Scafell Pike.
Mountain Lions
Lawrence, D.   Mountain Lion.
Mountain Men
Clark, T.   Mountain Men.
Mountains
Abanaki Oral Tradition.   Come, my beloved,
  let us go up the shining mountain, and sit
  together.
"Adunis."   Song of a Man in the Dark.
Ammons.   Little Thing Like That, A.
Auden.   Mountains.
Barker, G.   Section VI.
Blackburn, P.   Net of Place, The.
Blaga.   In the Mountains.
Bontemps.   Golgotha is a mountain, a purple
  mound.
Bowers, E.   Mountain Cemetery, The.
Brecht, B.   Three Fragments.
Burns, R.   My heart's in the Highlands, my
  heart is not here.
Chōkū.   Tanka: "Arrowroot flowers."
Chong, C.   Summit, The.
Clarke, C.   Kittatinny Tunnel in that holy place
  you let me hit.
Conforti.   On the mountain slope.
Dickinson, E.   Sweet Mountains—Ye tell Me
  no lie.
Doinas, S.   Ascent, The.
Duggan, L.   Five. One.
  One. One.
Ford, C.   Overturned Lake, The.
Frost, R.   Fountain, a Bottle, a Donkey's Ears
  and Some Books, A.
Fumi Saito.   Tanka: "White hare, A."
  Tanka: "Wood borers."
Gates, L.   Crow flies off, The.
Gregg.   Night Music.
Gu Cheng.   Discovery.
Gunn, T.   From the Highest Camp.
Haines, J.   Cloud Factory, The.
  On the Mountain.

Hall, D.   Mount Kearsarge.
Hernández, M.   Tomb of the Imagination.
Holmes, O.   Nearing the Snow-Line.
Hotham.   Fog.
Jennings, H.   Prose Poem.
Karouzos.   Triplets for Beautiful Mistra.
Kovner.   I Don't Know if Mount Zion would
  recognize itself.
Lookout on a Rock on the Heights of Mount
  Hermon.
Kunio.   Tanka: "Stalwartly."
Lawrence, D.   Men in New Mexico.
Levertov.   Open Secret.
  Presence.
  Witness.
Li K'ai-hsien.   Gazing at Ch'ang-po Mountain.
Li Po.   Birds have vanished into the sky, The.
  Conversations in the Mountains.
  In the Mountains on a Summer Day.
  Poem No. 19 in the Old Manner.
  Summit Temple, The.
  To Tan Ch'iu.
Lloyd, D.   At the bottom.
Magowan.   Paros. A day mild as morning's
  milk.
McClellan.   Lines to Mount Glen.
Melville, H.   Guide and Guard.
Miyazawa Kenji.   Snow on Saddle Mountain,
  The.
  Tanka: "At dawn."
  Tanka: "Silver greeting."
  Tanka: "Unsettled."
Mountain, M.   In her old voice the mountains.
Mphahlele.   Homeward Bound.
Murakami Kijo.   Against far off snow
  mountains.
Naito Joso.   Fields and mountains.
Olson, C.   Song of Ullikummi, The.
Ortiz.   Canyon de Chelly.
Ou-yang Hsiu.   Distant Mountains.
Palmer, M.   Dearest Reader.
Papago.   There was a mountain, over its black
  roots [the deer].
Po Chü-i.   Dream of Mountaineering, A.
Ransetsu.   Fields and mountains turn.
Ridge, J.   Mount Shasta.
Robinson, E.   Vickery's Mountain.
Roditi.   Hand.
Sarumaru.   Deep in the mountain.
Smith, B.   Black Mountain Blues.
Snyder, G.   Meeting the Mountains.
  Path to Han-shan's place is laughable, The.
Song.   Cuckoo on Mt. Chiri*, The.
Spicer, J.   Phonemics.
Stein, G.   It is not a range of a mountain.
Strand.   I recall that I stood before the
  breaking waves.
Su Tung-p'o.   On the Siu Cheng Road.
Tai Piao-yüan.   As My Way Passed Through
  T'ung-ch'uan, I Wished to Visit the Policy
  Critic of the Right, Mei, but Did Not Know
  Where to Find Him.
T'ai-shang.   In Reply to Questions.
Ts'ao Ts'ao.   Viewing the Ocean.
Tu Fu.   Written on the Wall at Chang's
  Hermitage.
Unknown.   Cold Mountain is full of weird
  sights.
  I loathe the twin seas.
  Invocation To Dsilyi N'Eyani.
  On Komochi Mountain.
  One of the Awl Songs.
  Song to the Mountains.
  Wonderful, this road to Cold Mountain.
Wagoner, D.   Breaking Camp.
Wang Wei.   Cold mountain turns dark green.
Whalen.   Sourdough Mountain Lookout.
Wilcox, E.   Attraction.
Wordsworth, W.   Farewell thou little Nook of
  mountain-ground.
Yi, K.   Winter Vision, The.
Young, A.   Prehistoric Camp, A.
See also **Hills and Mountains**
Mourning and Mourners
Auden.   Song: "Stop all the clocks, cut off the
  telephone."
Beckett, S.   I would like my love to die.

Behn, A. On the Death of the Late Earl of Rochester.
Bible, *O.T.* From the Sermon on the Mount.
Bion. Lament for Adonis.
Bly, R. Mourning Pablo Neruda.
Bradstreet, A. In Memory of My Dear Grandchild Anne Bradstreet Who Deceased June 20, 1669, Being Three Years and Seven Months Old.
In Memory of My Dear Grandchild Elizabeth Bradstreet Who Deceased August, 1665, Being a Year and Half Old.
On My Dear Grandchild Simon Bradstreet, [Who Died on 16TH November, 1669, Being But A Month And One Day Old].
To the Memory of My Dear and Ever Honored Father Thomas Dudley Esq. Who Deceased July 31, 1653, and of His Age 77.
To the Memory of My Dear Daughter in Law, Mrs. Mercy Bradstreet.
Brontë, C. On the Death of Anne Brontë.
On the Death of Emily Jane Brontë.
Browning, E. Died...
Felicia Hemans.
Grief.
Stanzas on the Death of Lord Byron.
Bruner. Dog's Vigil, A.
Selfishness.
Time's Hand Is Kind.
Byron, G. Bright be the place of thy soul!
Stanzas: "And thou art dead, as young and fair."
Callimachus. Someone told me, Heraclitus.
Carew, T. Another [Epitaph on the Lady Mary Villiers] ("Purest soul that e'er was sent, The").
Catullus. On the Burial of His Brother.
Chang Yü. Lamenting for Kao Ch'ing-ch'iu, Chi-ti.
Chatterton. Mynstrelle's Songe ("O! synge untoe mie roundelaie").
Chên. Elegy, An.
Chin Nung. Written at the End of Master Ho-ching's Collected Works.
Chivers. Avalon.
Chu Yün-ming. Remembering My Late Wife.
Collins, W. Dirge in "Cymbeline."
Cornish, S. Death of Dr. King.
Dante Alighieri. Whatever while the thought comes over me.
Ye pilgrim-folk, advancing pensively.
Dickinson, E. Bustle in a House, The.
Last Night that She lived, The.
Of nearness to her sundered Things.
Dobson, A. Before Sedan.
Donne. Valediction, A: Forbidding Mourning.
Douglas, L. Dead Poet, The.
Dove, R. Demeter Mourning.
Dowson. You would have understood me, had you waited.
Drennan, W. Wake of William Orr, The.
Drummond, W. Sextain: "Sith gone is my delight and only pleasure."
Dufferin. Countess of Dufferin, The.
"Eliza." To My Husband.
Euripides. Friends, I account the fortune of my wife.
"Field." Beloved, my glory in thee is not ceased.
Finch, F. Blue and the Gray, The.
Gardinier. Two Girls.
Garioch. At Robert Fergusson's Grave[, October 1962].
Gill, G. Girl's desire moves among her bangles, The.
Ginsberg, A. Kaddish.
Gray, C. Funeral Service.
Gray, T. Sonnet [on the Death of Mr. Richard West].
Grenfell, J. First To Go, The.
Gurney, I. To His Love.
Hardy, T. If you had known.
Last Words To a Dumb Friend.
Hartnett. Lament for Tadhg Cronin's Children.
Hayden, R. Mourning Poem for the Queen of Sunday.
Herrick. Mad Maid's Song, The.

To His Dying Brother, Master William Herrick.
To His Lovely Mistresses.
Upon a Maid[e].
Upon a Maid ("Gone she is a long, long way").
Upon His Sister-in-Law, Mistress Elizabeth Herrick.
Hewitt, J. Local Poet, A.
Hidalgo. No.
Hitomaro. I sit at home.
When I left my girl.
When she was still alive.
Ho Xuan Huong. On Hearing a Woman Mourn Her Husband.
Homer. Briseis mourns Patroclus.
First to the Corse the weeping Consort flew.
Hongo. Pier, The.
Hooks. Woman's Mourning Song, The.
Howard, A. Good Shepherd's Sorrow for the Death of His Beloved Son, The.
Hsieh Chin. I still remember Conch-Shell Slope, west of the River Tzu.
Hughes, L. Wake.
Hughes, T. Day He Died, The.
Hugo, R. Elegy: "I expected him to look dead in the casket."
Hugo, V. At dawn tomorrow, time of whitening fields.
Jeffers, R. May-June, 1940.
Jito. On the Death of the Emperor Temmu.
Johnson, J. Go Down Death.
Johnston, E. Nelly's Lament for the Pirnhouse Cat.
Jones, E. Development of Idiotcy, A.
Jones, R. Leaving Town after the Funeral.
Jonson, B. On My First Son [*or* Sonne].
Keating, G. Mourn for Yourself.
Kumin, M. How It Is.
Landon. Stanzas on the Death of Mrs Hemans.
Landor, W. Rose Aylmer.
Lawrence, D. Sorrow.
Li K'ai-hsien. Thanking Doctor Jen.
Li Po. Facing Wine with Memories of Lord Ho.
Liu K'o-chuang. Weeping for Hsüeh Tzu-shu.
MacNeice. Tam Cari Capitis.
Marvell. Mourning.
Mason, H. I asked unanswerable questions a child asks.
Mathews, H. Sad Remembrance.
Mei Yao Ch'en. Mourning for My Wife.
On the Death of His Wife.
Sorrow.
Miller, J. Far Away.
Moschus. With thee, sweet *Bion,* all the grace of Song.
Moss, H. Elegy for My Father.
Nastasijevic. To My Dead Sister.
Nguyễn Bính. Girl Next Door, The.
Ni Tsan. Lamenting Noble Scholar Chu.
Norton, J. Funeral Elegy Upon that Pattern and Patron of Virtue, A.
Olson, C. Death of Europe, The.
P'an Yüeh. In Mourning for His Dead Wife.
Lamenting the Dead.
Paul the Deacon. Epitaph for His Niece, Sophia.
Pien Kung. At the Lake—Remembering My Dead Son, Yü.
Propertius. Ghosts do exist; death does not finish everything.
Ralegh, W. Ocean's Love to Cynthia, The.
Ransom, J. Agitato Ma Non Troppo ("I have a grief").
Reese, L. Death's Guerdon.
Rice, S. Enough is never enough—That voice comes back—Suave.
I sit waiting for one of the two kinds of miracle.
Rich, A. Mourning Picture.
Valediction Forbidding Mourning, A.
Robinson, A. Stornelli and Strambotti.
Robinson, E. Reuben Bright.
Roethke. Elegy for Jane.
Rossetti, C. After Death.
Remember me when I am gone away.

Song: "When I am dead, my dearest."
Why did baby die.
Sappho. Dust of Timas, The.
Here lies the dust of Timas.
Schnackenberg. Angels Grieving over the Dead Christ.
Scott, W. Jock of Hazeldean.
Scott, W. My Mother.
Sexton. Truth the Dead Know, The.
Shakespeare, W. Sonnet 71.
Shelley, P. Elegy on the Death of John Keats, An.
Shen Chou. Consoling Wu Te-cheng on the Death of His Son.
Sitwell, D. Prelude.
Sophocles. Do not you mark how *passionate, how wild.*
Elektra's Keening.
Over come—O bitter sweetness.
Sutton, D. Not to Be Born.
T'ang Hsien-tsu. On the Day of Washing the Buddha in the Year Ting-wei (1607), I Dreamed That My Late Son Shih-ch'ü Was Holding a Book, and Appeared To Be Quite Happy. He Said That He Had Earned His Chin-shih Degree in the Underworld. After We Sighed and Laughed Together for a Long Time, I Woke Up and Wrote This Poem.
Tennyson, A. Dark house, by which once more I stand.
Rizpah.
Troupe. Day in the Life of a Poet, A.
Unknown. Chant from the Iroquois Book of Rites.
I waited for my.
Songs from the Great Feast to the Dead.
TEHKARIHHOKEN! / Continue to listen!
Tru'o'ng Chi, the Lovelorn Boatman.
Unquiet Grave, The.
Wife of Usher's Well, The.
Van Duyn. Stream, The.
Vaughan, H. Joy of My Life! While Left Me Here.
Wallace, R. Riding in a Stranger's Funeral.
Whitman, W. Hush'd be the camps to-day.
Spring.
Vigil strange I kept on the field one night;.
Wilbur. To an American Poet Just Dead.
Wordsworth, W. Surprised by Joy—impatient as the Wind.
Wright, J. At the Slackening of the Tide.
Gesture by a Lady with an Assumed Name, A.
Wu Chia-chi. Woman Tung.
Wu Wei-yeh. Lamenting for My Late Daughter.
Yamato-himé. Others may forget you, but not I.
Yeats. Crazy Jane Reproved.
John Kinsella's Lament for Mrs. Mary Moore.
Yosami, the wife of Hitomaro. Day after day I've longed for my husband.
Yüan Chen. Elegy, An: "O youngest, best-loved daughter of Hsieh."
See also **Funerals; Grief**

Mouths
Aldis, D. Mouths.
Carnevali. Queer Things.
Creeley. Language, The.
Hadewijch II. If I desire something, I know it not.
Swenson, M. Cardinal Ideograms.
Sylvester, J. Sweet mouth, that send'st a musky-rosed breath;.
Tate, G. Tonguing.

Movies. See Motion Pictures

Moving and Movers
Bottoms. In a U-Haul North of Damascus.
Brown, F. Last of England! O'er the sea, my dear, The.
Campbell, D. Duchesses.
Divakaruni. Restroom.
Dunn, D. Removal from Terry Street, A.
Engle, P. Moving In.
Forrest-Thomson. Strike.
Foster, J. Moving.
Gunn, T. Last Days at Teddington.
Haines, J. Flight, The.

Hamod, S. So we move now.
Hemp. Living Lean.
Jacobsen, J. Motion, The.
Kamienska. Those who carry grand pianos / to the tenth floor.
Kim, T. Boatsong of the Sungari, The.
Matthews, T. Private But Sulphurous.
McGuckian. Little House, Big House.
Park, Y. Departing Boat, The.
Shapiro, K. October 1.
Smith, D. Cumberland Station.

Mowing and Mowers
Ammons. Needs.
Brand, M. Lost.
Frost, R. Mowing.
Tuft of Flowers, The.
Gosse. Lying in the Grass.
Lawrence, D. Youth Mowing, A.
Marvell. Damon the Mower.
Mower Against Gardens, The.
Mower to the Glow-Worms [or Glowworms or Glo-Worms], The.
Mower's Song, The.
Meredith, W. Old Field Mowed, An.
Relph. Hay-Time; or, The Constant Lovers. A Pastoral.
Roberts, S. Mowing, The.
Thomas, E. Haymaking.
Toomer. Reapers.

Mozart, Wolfgang Amadeus
Broughton, T. Serenade for Winds.
Graves, R. Corner Knot, The.
Hemans. Mozart's Requiem.
Meynell, A. To Silence.
Unknown. Limerick: "As Mozart composed a sonata."

Mud
Berrigan, T. *et al.* Orange Jews.
Cisneros, S. Muddy Kid Comes Home.
Cummings, E. In Just- / spring when the world is mud-.
Durston. Hippopotamus, The.
Heaney, S. Mud Vision, The.
Higginson, W. Holding the water.
Hsü Wei. On the Road Through the Wu-i Mountains—Making Fun of Chia-tse for Falling Off His Horse.
Kambala. KYE HO! Wonderful!
Kao Ch'i. Moss below the Stairs.
Knight, E. Poem for Myself (Or Blues for a Mississippi Black Boy), A.
Lansing. Gold in the Mud, The.
Li K'ai-hsien. Recording a Weird Happening.
Weatherly, T. Mud Water Shango.
Yosano. Tanka: "Clear spring, A."

Muffs
Lovelace, R. Her Muffe.
See also **Gloves; Mittens**

Muhammad
Rumi. Friend remarks to the Prophet, "Why is it," A.

Mulberry Trees
Ch'ien Ch'ien-i. Poem Written During a Dream on the Twenty-Third Day of the Intercalary [Month After The] Fourth [Month].
Chōkū. Tanka: "Nowhere on the leaves."
Unknown. Swampland Mulberries Are Lovely.

Mules
Ammons. Silver.
Chappell, F. My Father Washes His Hands.
Hughes, L. Me and the Mule.
Jones, R. Mule.
Merrill, B. Mule, The.
Plumpp. Another mule kicking.
Unknown. Kicking Mule, The.
My Sweetie's a Mule in the Mine.
Walker, T. Mules.

Mummies
"Field." Mummy Invokes his Soul, The.
Gardner, I. In the Museum.
Heaney, S. Punishment.
Tollund Man, The.
James, T. Mummy of a Lady Named Jemutesonekh XXI Dynasty.
Marquis. Archy Interviews a Pharoah.

McPherson, S. Wanting a Mummy.
Po Chü-i. Temple, The.

Munch, Edvard
Hall, D. Scream, The.
Mahon. Girls on the Bridge.
Weiners. Poem for museum goers, A.
Wieners. Poem for Museum Goers, A.
Wright, C. Edvard Munch.

Murasaki Shikibu
Guest, B. Wild gardens overlooked by night lights. Parking.

Murder and Murderers
Adams, E. Ashland Tragedy, The.
Aeschylus. Clytemnestra triumphant over the bodies of Agamemnon and Cassandra. She-kin, show our force. Join hands!
Ai. Good Shepherd: Atlanta, 1981, The.
Kid, The.
Alexander, C. They shorten'd the corp, and they pack'd.
Antonov. Toward morning, slipping the pistol under my arm.
Atwood. Robber Bridegroom, The.
Avidan. Song of the Self-Made Orphans.
Barlas. Beauty's Anadems.
Terrible Love.
Beardsley. Ballad of a Barber, The.
Bible, *O.T.* And the Lord discomfited Sisera, and all his chariots, and all his host.
First Murderer, The.
Brecht, B. See the shark with teeth like razors.
Brooks, G. Bronzeville Mother Loiters in Mississippi. / Meanwhile, a Mississippi Mother Burns Bacon.
Brown, S. Southern Cop.
Browning, R. Assassins.
Do you see this square old yellow Book, I toss.
Laboratory, The [Ancien Régime].
Porphyria's Lover.
Byron, G. Byron on Southey.
Carew, T. Another [On the Duke of Buckingham].
Cary, A. Sea-Side Cave, The.
Chaucer. Canon Assistant's Tale, The.
Christopher. April in New York.
Cohen, E. Drive-By Shooting.
Coleridge, M. Fire, the lamp, and I, were alone together, The.
Cronin, J. Lullaby: "But who killed Johannes, mama . . . ?"
Custance. Hyacinthus.
Davies, W. Inquest, The.
Davis, T. Lament for the Death of Eoghan Ruadh O'Neill.
Derricotte. Minks, The.
On the Turning Up of Unidentified Black Female Corpses.
Drennan, W. Wake of William Orr, The.
"Elagin." Amnesty.
Emanuel, J. Panther Man.
Espada. Majeski Plays the Saxophone.
Ewart. Charles Augustus Milverton.
Felltham. On the Duke of Buckingham, Slain by Felton, the 23rd August, 1628.
Fitzgerald, E. 19.
Forché. Memory of Elena, The.
Fuller, R. Love and Murder.
Gregg. Shopping-Bag Lady, The.
Harjo, J. Legacy.
Harper, M. Fireplace, The.
Hartwig. Matthew 2:16–18; Then Herod, when he saw.
Hayman, J. Murdered Girl Is Found on a Bridge, The.
Herbert, Z. Return of the Proconsul, The.
Hongo. Legend, The.
Housman, A. Farewell to barn and stack and tree.
True Lover, The.
Jarrell. Eighth Air Force.
Joans. Scenery.
.38, The.
Jordan, J. Test of Atlanta 1979, The.
Kennedy, X. Loose Woman.
Khodasevich. Twilight.

Kipling, R. Ballad of Fisher's Boardinghouse, The.
Kirkpatrick. For a Woman Murdered While Running at Land's End, October 1979.
Knott. Two Vietnam Poems: (1966).
Ludvigson. Man Arrested in Hacking Death Tells Police He Mistook Mother-in-Law for Raccoon.
Madhubuti. Assassination.
Merwin, W. Last One, The.
Meynell, A. Parentage.
Middleton, T. Changeling, The.
Morris, W. Haystack in the Floods, The.
Shameful Death.
Morrison, B. Ower t'ills o Bingley.
Nemerov. Murder of William Remington, The.
Newbolt. He Fell among Thieves.
Olds, S. Girl, The.
That Year.
Page, G. Premeditations.
Palladas. Murderer & Sarapis, The.
Patchen. From my high love I look at that poor world there.
Petrie. Murderer, The.
Plath. Daddy.
Plomer. Murder on the Downs, The.
Quasimodo. Man of My Time.
Rainey. See See Rider, see what you done done!
Ruff. Delia Holmes ("Delia, Delia, why didn't you run?")
Schwartz, D. For the One Who Would Take Man's Life in His Hands.
Service. Shooting of Dan McGrew, The.
Shakespeare, W. If we should fail?
Othello and Desdemona.
Set down, set down your honourable load.
Vaulting Ambition.
Sidgwick, F. Cheerful Chilterns, The.
Sidney, P. Sonnet 20: "Fly, fly, my friends."
Simmons, J. Claudy.
Smith, S. Bag-Snatching in Dublin.
But Murderous.
Murderer, The.
One of Many.
Who Killed Lawless Lean?
Snodgrass, W. Magda Goebbels ("This is the needle that we give").
Stephens, J. Wind stood up, and gave a shout.
Unknown. Annette Myers.
Babylon; or, The Bonnie Banks o' Fordie.
Bad Man Ballad.
Ballad of William Bloat, The.
Bonny Earl of Murray, The.
Cruel Mother, The.
Death of Samuel Adams, The.
Edwin in the Lowlands Low.
Ella Speed.
Ellen Flannery.
Execution of Alice Holt.
Feltons Epitaph.
Florella; or, The Jealous Lover.
Frankie Blues.
Frankie was a good waoman.
Gosport Tragedy, The.
Hugh of Lincoln.
John Adkins' Farewell.
John Hardy.
Johnson-Jinkson.
Josie.
Little Musgrave and Lady Barnard.
Lord Randal.
Lula Vires.
Murder of Goins, The.
Murder of Maria Marten by W. Corder, The.
Now for that slawnders sake.
Pearl Bryan.
Peddler and His Wife, The.
Poem for Jacqueline Hill.
Poor Ellen Smith.
Poor Naomi.
Pretty Polly.
Prince Robert.
Robin Hood's Death.
Rose Connoley.
Sam Hall.
Silvery Tide, The.

Stackalee.
Three Butchers, The.
Two Sisters, The.
Wexford Girl, The.
Young Hunting.
Ushakov. Lady Macbeth.
Van Ostaijen. Murderers, The.
Vaughan, H. Abel's Blood.
Walker, A. Revolutionary Petunias.
Walker, M. For Andy Goodman—Michael
Schwerner—and James Chaney.
Warren, R. Ballad of Billie Potts, The.
Crime.
Webster, J. I am Duchess of Malfy still.
Wilde, O. Ballad of Reading Gaol, The.
Willard, N. Clearing the Air.
Wordsworth, W. Sweet is the lore which
Nature brings;.
Wright, J. At the Executed Murderer's Grave.
Life, The.
Secret Gratitude, A.
Wright, R. Between the World and Me.

Murfreesboro, Battle of (1862–1863)
Tate, A. Battle of Murfreesboro.

Muses
"Akhmatova." Muse, The.
Archilochus. Sergeant to Enyalios.
Arnold, M. Austerity of Poetry [or Jacopone
da Todi].
Artemidorus. Pastoral Muses once were
scattered, The.
Baillie, J. Ye are the spirits who preside.
Barbauld. To Mr. S. T. Coleridge.
Washing-Day.
Blake, W. To the Muse.
Bradstreet, A. Prologue, The: "To sing of
wars, of captain[e]s, and of kings."
Brodsky, J. Roman Elegies IV.
Collins, W. Passions; an Ode for [or to]
Music, The.
Cowley, A. Muse, The.
Creeley. Door, The.
Crinagoras. How long in these empty thermals
near the cold.
De Mello Breyner. Muse teach me the song.
Drayton. March strongly forth, my Muse,
whilst yet the temperate air.
Ode Written in the Peak[e], An.
Éluard, P. Lady Love.
Emerson, R. Solution.
Test, The.
Equi. Bouquet of Objects, A.
Euenus. B kw rm.
Ewart. Lifelines.
Glück, L. Poem: "In the early evening, as
now, a man is bending."
Goodman, P. Saint Harmony my patroness.
Gray, T. Progress of Poesy, The.
Grimald. Garden, The.
Hacker, M. Muses, The.
Halley. I'd Rather See than be One, but.
Herrick. His Winding-Sheet.
Mount of the Muses, The.
Hood, T. First Attempt in Rhyme, A.
Horace. Our rural Ancestors, with little blest.
Power of song, The.
Jacobsen, J. When the Five Prominent Poets.
Jewsbury. Farewell to the Muse, A.
Jonson, B. And must I sing? What subject
shall I choose?
Elegy [or Elegic], An: "Let me be what I am,
as Virgil cold."
To Lucy, Countess[e] of Bedford, with Mr.
Donnes Satire's [or Satyres].
Killigrew, A. Upon the Saying That My
Verses Were Made by Another.
Leapor. On Winter.
Sacrifice: An Epistle to Celia, The.
Leonidas of Tarentum. Far from Italy, far
from my native Tarentum.
Sun whirls an axle on fire, The.
Levertov. Illustration [—a Footnote], The.
She and the Muse.
To the Muse.
Lucilius. Here I am launching my Second
Book of Epigrams—.
Lyon, G. Visit, A.

Maltseva. To the Muse.
Miller, V. Prayer to my Muse.
Norris, K. Three Small Songs for the Muse.
Ovid. Elegies 3.1: "Old wood stands uncut, of
long years' space, An."
Persius. *Friend:* Your Satyrs, let me tell you,
are too fierce.
Prologue of Persius, The.
Pitter. Portrait of a Gentleman.
Plato. Sappho.
Puttenham. O mightye Muse.
Ray, H. Invocation to the Muse.
Revell. Muse.
Robinson, A. To My Muse.
Rowe, E. Forgo the charming Muses! No, in
spite.
Rowlands. Prologue: "Under the shadow of
the gloomy night."
Sappho. Muse of the Golden Throne.
Shakespeare, W. Sonnet 78: 'So oft have I
invok'd thee'.
Shepherd, R. Skin Trade.
Sidney, P. Sonnet 1: "Loving in truth, and
fain[e] in verse my love to show."
Sonnet 3: "Let dainty wits cry on the sisters
nine."
Sonnet 6: "Some lovers speak, when they their
Muses entertain."
Smith, C. Partial Muse, has from my earliest
hours, The.
Smith, S. My Muse sits forlorn.
Who Is This Who Howls and Mutters?
Spenser. Shepherd's Calendar, 'June', The.
Sonnet 1: "Happy ye leaves! whenas those lily
hands."
Stallings. Apollo Takes Charge of His Muses.
Stevenson, R. To the Muse.
Taylor, G. Admonition to the Muse.
Unknown. Hymn to Castor and Pollux.
Nine Lyric Poets, The.
Sing, Muse, the Force, and all-informing Fire.
Urdang. Muse Is Always the Other Woman,
The.
Wagoner, D. Muse.
Walcott. Upstate.
Waniek. Levitation with Baby.
Wheatley, P. To Mæcenas.
Whitman, W. Muse in the New World, The.
Wither. *Sun* hath run his course through all
the Signes, The.
Woodbridge. Upon the Author. By a Known
Friend.
Woty. I now solicit not the Muses nine.
Wright, J. To the Muse.
Yeats. Those Images.

Museums
Allston. On the Luxembourg Gallery.
Atwood. Night in the Royal Ontario Museum,
A.
Auden. Our Bias.
Beer, P. In a Country Museum.
Boland, E. Dolls Museum in Dublin, The.
Cliff. History of Costume, A.
De la Mare. In the Local Museum.
Di Prima. American Indian Art: Form and
Tradition.
Dickey, W. Tutankhamen.
Duggan, L. Town on the Ten Dollar Note,
The.
Empson. Homage to the British Museum.
Fenton, J. Pitt-Rivers Museum, Oxford, The.
Fields, J. Mr. Tut's House A Recollection.
Fox, S. Miss Pimberton Of.
Fuller, R. Coptic Socks.
Fulton, R. Museums and Journeys.
Gardner, I. In the Museum.
Gates, L. Lights are going out, The.
Gioia. Guide to the Other Gallery.
Gunn, T. Expression.
Hewitt, J. From a Museum Man's Album.
Hollander, J. No Foundation.
Hooper, V. Lost in the Galleries.
Lamb, E. Still. . . some echo.
Lewis, J. In the Egyptian Museum.
MacNeice. Museums offer us, running from
among the buses.

McPherson, S. Museum of the Second
Creation, The.
Mueller, L. Historical Museum, Manitoulin
Island.
Pastan. At the Train Museum.
Plath. Morning Song.
Rich, A. Love in the Museum.
Ross, A. Antwerp: Musée Des Beaux-Arts.
Szymborska. Museum, The.
Pietà.
Vaiiunaite. Museum Street.
Weiners. Poem for museum goers, A.
Wieners. Poem for Museum Goers, A.
Wilbur. Museum Piece.
Yeats. Municipal Gallery Revisited, The.

Mushrooms
Evans, M. Mushrooms grew / Overnight.
Fleming, E. Toadstools.
Harasymowicz. Woods.
Hiott. Tale of Mushrooms.
Hsü Wei. Mushroom Gatherer Deep in the
Mountains Among the White Clouds, A.
Jacob, M. Moon Poem.
Mackenzie, K. Autumn Mushrooms.
Magee, W. Fungus Fingers, The.
McGough, R. Phew.
Muldoon, P. Gathering Mushrooms.
Plath. Mushrooms.
Samio. Tanka: "Surely by now."
Smith, W. Morels.
Todd, R. Of Moulds and Mushrooms.
Young, A. Fairy Ring, The.
Yün Shou-p'ing. On a Painting of Mushrooms.

Music Festivals
Hutchinson, P. Fleadh Cheoil.
Whitman, A. Lute of Afric's Tribe, The.

Music Halls
Davidson, J. In a Music-Hall.
Levine, P. At the Fillmore.
Rukeyser, M. Paper Anniversary.

Music Lessons
Oles. To a Daughter at Fourteen Forsaking the
Violin.

Music and Musicians
Ai. Archangel.
Man with the Saxophone, The.
Aiken, C. Calyx of the Oboe Breaks, The.
"Akhmatova." In the Evening.
Al-Harizi. Lute, The.
Alexander, E. Farewell to You.
Allen, S. I Say, Mr. A.
To Satch.
Alterman. Beyond Melody.
Andrade, E. Music.
Angell, B. Street Music.
Annand. Mavis, mavis.
Armantrout. Getting Warm.
Ashanti. Just Another Gig.
Ashbery. Syringa.
Atkins. Dark Area.
Aubert, A. Bessie.
Auden. Composer, The.
Babcock, M. This Is My Father's World.
Baker, H. Of Walter White's Father in the
Rain.
Tobacco Warehouse Blues.
Bantock. Bard.
Baraka. All is One for Monk.
Am/Trak.
In the Tradition / (Not a White Shadow but
Black People Will Be Victorious).
Rare Birds, The.
Barbu. Timbre.
Barnfield. To His Friend Master R.L., In
Praise of Music and Poetry.
Barresi. Venice Beach: Brief Song.
Baugh, E. Country Dance.
Beardsley. Three Musicians, The.
Behn, R. French Horn.
Bernstein, O. What She Didn't Say.
Berrigan, T. Sonnet I: "His piercing pince-nez.
Some dim frieze."
String of Pearls.
Berry, W. Music, A.
Berryman. At Henry's bier let some thing fall
out well.

Blackburn, P. Listening to Sonny Rollins at the Five-Spot.

Blake, W. Introduction: "Piping down the valleys wild."

Blumenthal, M. Juliek's Violin.

Bly, R. Listening to the Köln Concert.

Bogan, L. M., Singing.

Musician.

Boker. Ah, lute, how well I know each tone of thee.

Bolamba. Esanzo.

Braithwaite. To ———: "Half in the dim light from the hall."

Brathwaite, E. Clock.

Naima.

Brett, L. La Pathétique.

Brinnin. At the Band Concert.

Brodey. Lennie Tristano, No Wind.

Little Light.

Brooks, G. First fight. Then fiddle. Ply the slipping string.

Third Sermon on the Warpland, The.

Broughton, T. Serenade for Winds.

Brown, G. Old Fisherman with Guitar.

Brown, S. Ma Rainey.

Browning, E. Musical Instrument, A.

Browning, R. Abt Vogler.

Master Hugues of Saxe-Gotha.

Toccata of Galuppi's, A.

Buckley, C. Nostalgia.

Playing for Time.

Bunimovich. Moscow: Summer '86.

Burns, R. Red, Red Rose, A.

Butts, A. Massenet / Never wrote a Mass in A.

Byron, G. Stanzas for Music ("There be none of Beauty's daughters").

Cage. 25 Mesostics Re and Not Re Mark Tobey.

Campbell, J. 'Sciplinin' Sister Brown.

Campion, T. Follow your saint, follow with accents sweet.

Laura.

To music bent is my retired mind.

When to Her Lute Corinna [or Corrina] Sings.

Carruth, H. At his last gig in horrid Amsterdam.

Freedom and Discipline.

Castro, M. Blew It.

Cather, W. Spanish Johnny.

Cawein. Music.

Cecil. Richard's Blues.

Ceravolo. Celebration.

Crocus Turn and Gods, The.

Chang Heng. Dancers of Huai-nan, The.

Chase, K. What You Can't See.

Chaucer. Miller's [or Milleres] Tale, The.

Cherry, K. Raiment We Put On, The.

Chin. Song of the Sad Guitar.

Chon, P. Piano, The.

Clampitt. Syrinx.

Clark, T. Like musical instruments.

Codrescu. Imagination of Necessity, The.

Cole, T. Lines Suggested by Hearing Music on the Boston Common at Night.

Coleman, W. But, ruby my dear.

Coleridge, M. Day-dream, A.

Impromptu.

Collins, W. Passions; an Ode for [or to] Music, The.

Congreve. Music has charms to soothe a savage breast.

Cook, E. To My Lyre.

Coolidge, C. Of What The Music to Me.

Rhymes with Monk.

Cooper, J. Wanda's Blues.

Cornford, F. Guitarist Tunes Up, The.

Cornish, S. His Fingers Seem to Sing.

Corso. For Miles.

Cortez. I See Chano Pozo.

Solo Finger Solo.

Cranch. Music.

Crane, H. Black Tambourine.

Broken Tower, The.

For the Marriage of Faustus and Helen.

Crashaw. Epithalamion.

Music[k]'s Duel[l].

Creeley. Chasing the Bird.

They.

Crouch, S. No New Music.

Revelation, The.

Up on the Spoon.

Cullen, C. Night Rain.

Cummings, E. God pity me whom (god distinctly has).

Cushing, J. Autumn Leaves.

Every Time We Say Goodbye.

Lover Man.

Damas. Hiccups.

Davenant. Aubade: "Lark now leaves his watery [or wat'ry] nest, The."

Davidson, J. In a Music-Hall.

Davies, S. To him with trumpets and with flutes.

Davis, D. Miss Liza's Banjer.

Davis, F. Jazz Band.

Davis, T. C. T. at the Five Spot.

Expandable Language.

Rogue and Jar: 4/27/77.

Zoom (The Commodores).

De la Mare. Faint Music.

Dent. For Lil Louis.

Ray Charles at Mississippi State.

Derricotte. Blackbottom.

Di Prima. I Ching.

On Sitting Down to Write, I Decide Instead to Go to Fred Herko's Côncert.

Dickinson, E. Better—than Music! For I—who heard it.

He fumbles at your Soul.

I would not paint—a picture.

Trees like Tassels—hit—and swung, The.

Digges. Rough Music.

Dove, R. Canary.

Event, The.

Listen to the sound of my horn. . . .

Drummond, W. To His Lute.

Dryden, J. Alexander's Feast; or, The Power of Music [or Musique].

Duffy, C. Prayer.

Dunbar-Nelson. Music! Lilting, soft and languorous.

Dunbar, P. Corn-Stalk Fiddle, THe.

When Malindy Sings.

Duncan, R. Bending the Bow.

Passages 37.

Presence of the Dance / The Resolution of the Music, The.

Eady. Hank Mobley's.

Romare Bearden Retrospective at the Brooklyn Museum.

Ekelof. Like ankle-rings, this music.

Emanuel, J. Get Up, Blues.

Emerson, R. Merlin I.

Music.

Saadi.

Enright, D. Apocalypse.

Eshleman, C. Foo to the Infinite.

Espada. Dándole la mano a Mongo.

Latin Night at the Pawnshop.

Majeski Plays the Saxophone.

Shaking Hands with Mongo.

Espaillat. Metrics.

Evans, M. Boss Communication.

I Am a Black Woman.

Fabio. For Louis Armstrong, A Ju-Ju.

Feinstein, S. Christmas Eve.

Sonnets for Stan Gage (1945–1992).

Ferdinand. Blues (in Two Parts), The.

Finkelstein, N. Track.

Fletcher, J., et al. Music.

Ford, W. Of Miles Davis.

Frost, L. Rock 'n' Roll.

Frost, R. Never Again Would Birds' Song Be The Same.

Fuller, M. Sistrum.

Gardner, D. Near Hermes.

Garioch. I Was Fair Beat.

Gilbo'a. I've Come to the Simplest Words.

Rain Falls and Floods.

Gillies, V. Young Harper.

Gioia. Lives of the Great Composers.

Giovanni. Genie in the Jar, The.

Graham, D. Soul.

Graham, W. Johann Joachim Quantz's Five Lessons.

Greig, A. Maid and I, The.

Grosholz. Last of the Courtyard, The.

Guillén, N. Wake for Papa Montero.

Guiney. At a Symphony.

Hagedorn, J. Latin Music in New York.

Han. Oaten Pipe.

Hardy, T. Selfsame Song, The.

Harjo, J. Bird.

Healing Animal.

Sonata for the Invisible.

Harper, F. Songs for the People.

Harper, M. Alone.

Bandstand.

Dear John, Dear Coltrane.

Driving the Big Chrysler across the Country of My Birth.

Elvin's Blues.

For Bud.

Here Where Coltrane Is.

Narrative of the Life and Times of John Coltrane: Played by Himself, A.

Peace on Earth.

Harvey, S. Mighty Tropicale Orchestra, The.

Harwood, G. New Music.

Nightfall.

Heard, J. Music.

Heithaus. What a Little Moonlight Can Do.

Hemans. Corinne at the Capitol.

Mozart's Requiem.

Henderson, D. Coltrane Memorial, A.

Elvin Jones Gretsch Freak.

Lee Morgan.

Sonny rollins seeking.

Thelonious Sphere Monk.

Herbert, G. Church-Music[k].

Herbert, Z. Drawer.

Herrick. Canticle to Apollo, A.

Music, thou soul of heaven, care-charming spell.

To M. Henry Lawes, the Excellent Composer[,] of his Lyrics.

To Music.

To Music: A Song.

To Music, to Becalm a Sweet-sick Youth.

Heyward, D. Jasbo Brown.

Hicky. No Friend Like Music.

Hirsch, E. Art Pepper.

Hirshfield, J. Justice without Passion.

Hodgson, R. Song of Honor [or Honour], The.

Hollander, J. Old Guitar, The.

Horace. Power of song, The.

Hudgins. Around the campfire we sang hymns.

Hughes, L. Be-Bop Boys.

Boogie: 1 A.M.

Daybreak in Alabama.

Dream Boogie: Variation.

Easy Boogie.

Juke Box Love Song.

Notes on the Broadway Theatre.

Trumpet Player.

Weary Blues, The.

When Sue Wears Red.

Hughes, T. Cadenza.

Hugo, R. My Buddy.

Hull, L. Lost Fugue for Chet.

Hummer, T. Poem in the Shape of a Saxophone.

Hutchinson, P. True Story Ending in False Hope, A.

Huy Cận. Dirge, A: "Who died? Why does the music speak such grief?"

Ibrahim, A. Africa, Music and Show Business.

Illyés. Part of a Novel.

While the Record Plays.

Inada. Blue Gene.

Blues for Dan Morin.

Great Bassist, The.

Wintersong.

Jackson, A. Billie in Silk.

Make/n My Music.

Ohnedaruth.

Jackson, R. Lady's Way.

Jackson, R. Shadows.

Jarman, M. Homing Instinct, The.
Supremes, The.
Jauss. After the End of the World.
Jeffers, L. How High the Moon.
Jewett, S. At Home from Church.
Jewsbury. Farewell to the Muse, A.
Johnson, L. Decadent's Lyric, A.
Johnson, S. Epitaph upon the Celebrated
Claudy Phillips, Musician, Who Died Very
Poor, An.
Jordan, J. October 23, 1983.
Joseph, A. My Father's Heroes.
Justice, D. Mrs. Snow.
Variations for Two Pianos.
Kabir. Flute of interior time is played whether
we hear it or not, The.
Kanavi. On Bismillah Khan's Shehnai.
Kaufman, B. Battle Report.
Blues Note.
Unanimity Has Been Achieved, Not a Dot
Less for Its Accidentalness.
Kavanagh, P. My father played the melodion.
Kazin. Accordionist, The.
Keats. How many bards gild the lapses of
time!
Kees. Guide to the Symphony.
Kelly, R. Loom, The.
Newark.
Kerouac. 221st Chorus.
Kgositsile. For Art Blakey and the Jazz
Messengers.
Spirits Unchained.
Kim, N. Music.
Kipling, R. Song of the Banjo, The.
Kirkup. Old Gramophone Records.
Kitahara Hakushū. Tanka: "Ailing child, An."
Kizer, C. Muse of Water, A.
Kleinzahler. Like cities, like storms.
Love Poem.
Knight, E. As You Leave Me.
III. Healing Song.
Komunyakaa. Elegy for Thelonious.
Kostakis. Circle with a Hole in the Middle,
The.
Fire Parcel.
Krohn. My Flute.
Kyger. It's been a long time.
Lagrone. I Heard the Byrd.
Laleau. Legacies.
Lamb, C. Free Thoughts on Several Eminent
Composers.
Lang, D. Depression, The.
Lange, A. Fine Line, A.
Mbizo.
White Line, A.
Langland, W. Entertainment Industry, The.
Lanier, S. To Beethoven.
Lawrence, D. Piano.
Levine, P. I Remember Clifford.
Soloing.
Levitansky. Dream about a Piano, A.
Lewis, J. Time and Music.
Lewis, J. To The Great Hard-Bop Pianists.
Lewis, R. Mocking Bird, The.
Li Po. Listening to a Monk from Shu Playing
the Lute.
Li Shang-yin. Richly painted zither, for no
reason, has fifty strings, The.
Lin Hung. Inscribed on the Painting
"Pleasures of the Lute by the River."
Lindsay, V. Jazz of This Hotel, The.
Lloyd, D. Moonlit sleet.
Long, D. Black Love Black Hope.
Longfellow, H. Spirit of Poetry, The.
Longley, M. Words for Jazz Perhaps.
Lovelace, R. To a Lady That Desired Me I
Would Bear My Part with Her in a Song.
To Lucasta.
Lowell, A. Music.
Lux. Night above the Town.
Lyle. Tampa Red's Contemporary Blues.
Mac Low. Pieces O'six—XXIV.
"MacDiarmid." Bagpipe Music.
Mackey, N. Capricorn Rising.
John Coltrane Arrived with an Egyptian Lady.
MacNeice. Bagpipe Music.
Madgett. Plea for My Heart's Sake.

Madhubuti. Knocking Donkey Fleas off a Poet
from the Southside of Chi.
Madigan. Curtis Fuller.
Stereo Time with Booker Little.
Mapanje. On African Writing.
Marley. Trenchtown Rock.
Marston, P. Love's Music.
Masaoka Shiki. Spring night.
Master. Cat and the Lute, The.
Masters, E. In Memory of Bryan Lathrop.
Matthews, W. Buddy Bolden Cylinder, The.
Mingus at the Showplace.
May, S. Double Bass.
Mayakovsky. For a Violin, Somewhat
Nervously.
McClatchy. Dragonfly.
McClure, M. For Monk.
Jazz at the Intergalactic Nightclub.
McGinley. Evening Musicale.
McGrath, T. Guiffre's Nightmusic.
McKean. After Listening to Jack
Teagarden. . . .
McNeill, A. Don.
McPherson, S. Some Metaphysics of Junior
Wells.
Suspension: Junior Wells on a Small Stage in
a Converted Barn.
Meek. Vienna in the Rain.
Meltzer, D. 18:VI:82.
17:II:82.
Meredith, G. Phoebus with Admetus.
Merrill, J. Victor Dog, The.
Mew. Forest road, The.
Meynell, A. Singers to Come.
"Mighty Chalkdust." Brain Drain.
Millay, E. On Hearing a Symphony of
Beethoven.
Miller, S. I Was on a Golf Course the Day
John Cage Died of a Stroke.
Milton. To Mr. H. Lawes On His Airs.
Mirabai. Song of the flute, O sister, is
madness, The.
Mitchell, A. From Rich Uneasy America to
My Friend Christopher Logue.
Moerman. Louis Armstrong.
Montague, J. Lament for the O'Neills.
Moore, L. Bluesman's Blues, A.
Moore, M. Mind Is an Enchanting Thing, The.
Moore, T. Harp That Once through Tara's
Halls, The.
Mor. Coming of John, The.
Moses ibn Ezra. Garden of Song, The.
Moss, H. Piano Practice.
Nam Trân. Against Tunes in a Minor Key.
Natambu. Funky Butt Legacy Song (An Epic
in Progress), The.
Neal, L. Don't say goodbye to the Porkpie
Hat that rolled.
Harlem Gallery: From the Inside.
Lady's Days.
Nerval. Fancy, A.
Noguere. Barney Bigard.
Noyes, A. Barrel-Organ, The.
Nye, N. Hugging the Jukebox.
O'Hara, F. Day Lady Died, The.
Radio.
Okantah. Afreeka Brass.
Southern Road.
Okara. Piano and Drums.
Okudzhava. In the City Park.
Opie. Stanzas Written under Aeoluo' Harp.
Oppen. Moving over the hills, crossing the
irrigation
O'Shaughnessy, A. Ode: "We are the music-
makers."
Ostriker. Eighth and the Thirteenth, The.
"O'Sullivan." Piper, A [or The].
Ou-yang Hsiu. Cicada, The.
Overton, R. Blues in "C."
Pagis. Europe, Late.
Paman. On Christmas Day to My Heart.
Pasternak, B. Piano, trembling, makes the lips
grow dry, The.
Patterson, R. Hopping Toad Blues.
Philips, K. To Mr. Henry Lawes.
Pinsky. Ginza Samba.
Pitter. Military Harpist, The.

Plath. Snakecharmer.
Po Chü-i. Old Lute, The.
Song of the Lute.
Poe. Israfel.
Pordage. To Lucia Playing on Her Lute,
Another.
Prior. Ode, An: "Merchant, to secure his
treasure, The."
Procter, A. Lost Chord, A.
Radauskas. Star, Sun, Moon.
Randall, D. Langston Blues.
Randolph, T. Song, A: "Music, thou queen of
souls, get up and string."
Ratcliffe, S. Space in the light said to be
where one / comes from.
Ravikovitch. Sound of Birds at Noon, The.
Ray, H. Perfect Orchestra, The.
Two Musicians, The.
Redmond. Dance Bodies #1.
Distance.
Reed, I. Lake Bud.
Rein. Black Music.
Ribemont-Dessaignes. Sliding Trombone.
Rich, A. At a Bach Concert.
Ninth Symphony of Beethoven Understood at
Last as a Sexual Message, The.
Rilke. Everything that touches us, me and
you.
Rivard. Baby Vallejo.
Rivers, C. Underground.
Roberts, E. Orpheus.
Robinson, A. Search for Apollo, A.
Robinson, E. L'Envoi.
Octaves.
Robson, J. Blues for the Lonely*.
Rodgers, C. We Dance Like Ella Riffs.
Rodriguez, W. Accordian Player, The.
Roethke. Partner, The.
Roseliep. After Beethoven.
Piano practice.
Rukeyser, M. Bunk Johnson Blowing.
Rumi. All day and night, music.
You that love Lovers.
Sanchez, S. To Anita.
Sandburg, C. Jazz Fantasia.
Schuyler, J. Grand Duo.
Greetings from the Chateau.
Let's All Hear It for Mildred Bailey!
Man in Blue, A.
Sexton. Music Swims Back to Me.
Shakespeare, W. Sonnet 8.
Sonnet 128.
Shange. I live in music.
Okra to greens.
Shelley, P. Hymn of Pan.
Ode to the West Wind.
To————: "Music, when soft voices die."
Shepherd, R. Lucky One, The.
Shin, S. Flute.
Shwarts. Elegy on an X-ray Photo of My
Skull.
Silverstein, S. Rock 'N' Roll Band.
Simic. Crepuscule with Nellie.
Simmons, J. Didn't He Ramble.
Simonov. Blind Man, The.
Skelton, J. Than, if this noble kyng.
Smart, C. David's Song to Saul.
For the spiritual musick is as follows.
Smith, I. Gaelic Songs.
Smith, J. Mandolin.
Sneeden. Coltrane and My Father.
Sobin, G. What the music.
Spellman. Did John's Music Kill Him?
John Coltrane: An Impartial Review.
Spender, S. Beethoven's Death Mask.
Spicer, J. Orfeo.
Song for Bird and Myself.
Ssu-k'ung Shu. In Illness, Dismissing My
Singing Girl.
Stern, G. Coleman Valley Road.
Romance.
Stevens, W. Anglais Mort à Florence.
Arrival at the Waldorf.
Peter Quince at the Clavier.
Sad Strains of a Gay Waltz.
To the One of Fictive Music.

Stevenson, R. Land of Nod, The.
Song of a Traveller, The.
Strode. In Commendation of Music.
On a Gentlewoman that Sung and Played upon a Lute.
Swirszczynska. First Madrigal, The.
Sylvester, J. Variable.
Symons, A. Prologue: In the Stalls.
Tune, A.
Taggart, J. Giant Steps.
Taylor, C. Garden.
Thaxter. Schumann's Sonata in A Minor.
Theocritus. We had not got half way, nor yet discerned.
Thomas, L. Excitation.
Historiography.
Onion Bucket.
Wonders.
Thompson, J. Music in Camp.
Thoreau. Dong, sounds the brass in the east.
Each More Melodious Note I Hear.
Music.
Thorne, T. Whatever Happened to Conway Twitty?
Tolson. Mu.
Touré, A. O Lord of Light! A Mystic Sage Returns to Realms of Eternity!
Troupe. Four and More; for Miles Davis.
Impressions / of Chicago; For Howlin' Wolf.
Leaving Los Angeles.
Snake-Back Solo.
Tu Fu. Banquet at the Tso Family Manor.
Turner, J. Rhapsodies.
Unknown. Blind Musicians, the blind musicians, The.
He measured out his spirit tower.
It Don't Mean a Thing (If It Ain't Got That Swing).
My Lord Summons Me.
Northwest the tall tower stands.
O magnificent and many.
When I pick up my koto.
Updike. Player Piano.
Recital.
Vow.
Vacietis. Sunday.
Vas. Tambour.
Vũ Hoàng Chu'o'ng. Beau Ideal, The.
Wakoski. Thanking My Mother for Piano Lessons.
Valentine for Ben Franklin Who Drives a Truck in California, A.
Wallenstein. Blues 1.
Blues 2.
Wang Ch'ang-ling. Listening to a Wanderer's "Water Melody."
Weatherly, T. Times.
Welburn. Ben Webster: "Did You Call Her Today?"
Gonsalves.
Whitfield. Yes! strike again that sounding string.
Whitman, W. Italian Music in Dakota.
Proud music of the storm.
Williams, W. Dance, The.
Ol' Bunk's Band.
Orchestra, The.
Wojahn. Assassination of John Lennon as Depicted by the Madame Tussaud Wax Museum, Niagara Falls, Ontario, 1987, The.
At Graceland with a Six Year Old, 1985.
Buddy Holly Watching Rebel Without a Cause, Lubbock, Texas, 1956.
Colorizing: Turner Broadcasting Enterprises, Computer Graphics Division, Burbank, California, 1987.
Custom Job: Hank Williams, Jr., and the Death Car, 1958.
Fab Four Tour Deutschland: Hamburg, 1961.
Homage: Light from the Hall.
John Berryman Listening to Robert Johnson's "King of the Delta Blues," January 1972.
Matins: James Brown and His Famous Flames Tour the South, 1958.
"Mystery Train" Janis Joplin Leaves Port Arthur for Points West, 1964.
Tattoo, Corazon: Ritchie Valens, 1959.

Trashmen Shaking Hands with Hubert Humphrey at the Opening of Apache Plaza Shopping Center, Suburban Minneapolis, August 1963, The.
Woody Guthrie Visited by Bob Dylan: Brooklyn State Hospital, New York, 1961.
Wolfli. Nostalgic song for my beloved.
Wong, N. On Plaza Garibaldi.
Wordsworth, W. Mutability.
Wormser. It's a Party (1959).
Soul Music.
Wright, J. End of an Ethnic Dream, The.
19.
What is Beautiful.
Xuân Diệu. Magic.
Yang Chi. Noble Scholar Playing the Lute, A.
Yeats. Crazed Girl, A.
Fiddler of Dooney, The.
Yosano. Amidst the notes.
Young, A. Dance of the Infidels.
Lester Leaps In.
Little More Traveling Music, A.
Studio Up Over In Your Ear.
Young, K. Eddie Priest's Barbershop and Notary.
Zabolotsky. Strolling Musicians.
Zagajewski. Electric Elegy.
Zavatsky. To the Pianist Bill Evans.
Zeidner. Bach.
Zimmer. But Bird.
Duke Ellington Dream, The.
Sitting with Lester Young.
Zolynas. Love in the Classroom.
Zukofsky, L. Non Ti Fidar.
See also **Blues (music); Gospel Music**

Musk Oxen
Hall, D. Long River, The.
Moore, M. Arctic Ox, The.

Muslims and Islam
Ali, A. In the Mountains.
Diop, B. Desert.
Hamod, S. After the Funeral of Assam Hamady.
Hunt, L. Abou Ben Adhem (may his tribe increase!).
Jordan, J. Intifada.
Melville, H. By the Jordan.
Saunders, R. Hush Honey.
Tahmisic. Landscapes.
Whittier. Palm-Tree, The.

Mussels
Farewell. There's Life in a Mussel; a Meditation.
Keller, D. Mussels.
Plath. Mussel Hunter at Rock Harbor.

Mustaches
Coogler. Mustacheless Bard, A.
Edson, R. Way Things Are, The.

Mutability
Cummins, J. Sestina.
Donne. His Picture.
Field, R. Some People.
Forbes, D. Recension Day.
Hewett, D. Sunset flames over the city, The.
Huchel. Eastern River.
Levy, A. London Poets.
Mackenzie, K. Children go, The.
Ralegh, W. Thus now I leave my love in fortunes [handes / bandes].
Shakespeare, W. Sonnet 64.
Sonnet 116.
Sweet-and-Twenty.
Spenser. Mutability.
Stumbrs. Ode to a Country Childhood.
Szymborska. Interview with a Child.
Taylor, J. Squire's Pew, The.
Wyatt, T. Sonnet: 'Each man me telleth'.

Mutiny
Kocan. Mutineer's Ballad, The.

Mystery
Angelou. Phenomenal Woman.
Barlas. Memphian Temple, The.
Blake, W. Revival of the Eternal Man.
Chang Yü. Pavilion for Listening to Fragrance, The.
Cole, T. I saw a Cave of sable depth profound.

Cullen, C. Yet Do I Marvel.
Dickinson, E. Some things that fly there be.
Diop, B. Diptych.
Eberhart, R. Loon Call, A.
Engonopoulos. On Boetian Roads.
Ewart. Owl Writes a Detective Story, The.
Fanshawe, C. Enigma.
"Field." Embalmment.
Gorey. Limerick.
Koch, K. To You.
Lampadius. As a symbol.
Landon. Power of Words, The.
Lion-Face. KYE HO! Wonderful!
Melville, H. Prelusive.
Mo Shih-lung. To the Monk Wu-hsia on the Occasion of His Editing the Lotus Sutra.
Muldoon, P. Why Brownlee left, and where he went.
Olson, C. Cole's Island.
Popa. Victims of the Little Box, The.
Prévert. Pater Noster.
Rich, A. Diving into the Wreck.
Mare's skeleton in the clearing: another sign of life, The.
Of simple choice they are the villagers; their clothes come.
Shelley, P. Sonnet: "Lift not the painted veil which those who live."
Shelnutt. Triumph of Children, The.
Stevenson, R. Spaewife, The.
Strachey, L. Cat, The.
Thackeray. Tragic Story, A.
Unknown. Love is a secret feeding fire that gives all creatures.
Whitman, W. There is that in me.. . . I do not know what it is.. . . but I know it is in me.
Yeats. He Remembers Forgotten Beauty.
Magi, The.
Yesenin. Today I asked the money changer.

Mysticism
Brock-Broido. Domestic Mysticism.
Fenton, J. Pitt-Rivers Museum, Oxford, The.
Galvin, B. Great Blue.
Komunyakaa. Imhotep.
Lawrence, D. Mystic.
Li Ho. Magic Strings.
Piece for Magic Strings, A.
Machado Ruiz. Come sing with me in chorus: it's nothing, all we know.
Po Chü-i. Tune: "Flower unlike Flower."
Robinson, R. Jarrangulli.
Rumi. Daylight, full of small dancing particles.
Do you think I know what I'm doing?
I, you, he, she, we.
Touré, A. O Lord of Light! A Mystic Sage Returns to Realms of Eternity!
Whitman, W. When I heard the learn'd astronomer.

Mythology
Aborigine Oral Tradition. Mapooram.
Platypus, The.
Star-Tribes, The.
Two Sisters, The.
Alcaeus. Come tip a few with me.
Leaving the Peloponnese.
Anacreon. Artemon once traveled in shadows.
Eros, playing among the roses.
Muses kidnapped Eros, they bound him, The.
Weaving a garland long ago.
Antipater of Thessalonica. You can explore your every desire.
Antiphilus. Here is the river Eurotas.
Aristophanes. Song of the Clouds.
Armantrout. Necromance.
Auden. Atlantis.
Baudelaire. She Is Not Satisfied.
Blake, W. Book of Urizen [or First Book of Urizen], The.
Revival of the Eternal Man.
Boland, E. Pomegranate, The.
Carew, T. Second Rapture, The.
Song, [A]: "Ask me no more where Jove bestows."
Catullus. Attis.

Carmen 64 ("In old days / driving through soft waters").
Cavafy. Ithaka.
Chapman, G. In meantime flew our ships, and straight we fetch'd.
Claudian. Ye mighty Demons, whose tremendous sway.
"Cornwall." Dream, A.
Crane, H. Atlantis.
Darley. Rebellion of the Waters, The.
Davidson, M. Troth.
Doolittle, H. Holy Satyr.
Lais.
Dunbar, P. Black Samson of Brandywine.
Duncan, R. Fire, The.
Eliot, T. Sweeney Among the Nightingales.
Ewart. Haiku: After The Orgies.
Gheorghe. Unicorn, The.
Gifford, H. In the Praise of Music.
Glück, L. Hyacinth.
Mythic Fragment.
Golding, A. . . . This Damsell was not famous for the place.
Grahn. Paris and Helen.
Graves, R. Conjunction.
In Procession.
Harjo, J. Book of Myths, The.
Hecht, A. Goliardic Song.
Hesiod. Anatomy of Winter, The.
Heywood, T. Jupiter and Ganimede.
Hill, G. Orpheus and Eurydice.
Horace. Ode.
Housman, A. Crossing alone the nighted ferry.
Jones, S. Hymn to Su'rya, A.
Keats. Left to herself, the serpent now began.
Pleasure Thermometer, The.
Kizer, C. Hera, Hung from the Sky.
Lanier, S. To Richard Wagner.
Lawrence, D. Argonauts, The.
Licymnios. Hypnos, seeing how.
MacCaig. Midnight, Lochinver.
Marlowe. By this Leander being near the land.
Montague, J. Old Mythologies.
Moore, M. Charity Overcoming Envy.
Morton, T. Poem, The: "Rise Oedipus, and if thou canst unfold."
Ngunaitponi. Song of Hungarrda, The.
Ortiz. Creation.
Ovid. Arethusa Saved.
Echo.
Elegies 2.i.
Rape of Lucrece, The.
'Twas now the mid of Night, when Slumbers close.
Palladas. By what right do they call Zeus a lover?
Parmenion of Macedon. For a little gold, Zeus bought Danae.
Petri. Electra.
Plato. Lais to Aphrodite.
Plumpp. Poet.
Prudentius. Oracles are dumm, The.
Roberts, M. Demeter Grieving.
Rodgers, W. Home Thoughts from Abroad.
Rossetti, D. For Spring By Sandro Botticelli.
Rothenberg, J. Structural Study of Myth, The.
Rukeyser, M. In the Underworld.
Santayana. On an Unfinished Statue.
Sonnet XLVIII: "Of Helen's brothers, one was born to die."
Sarton. At Lindos.
Spenser. For round about, the wals yclothed were.
Penelope for her *Ulisses* sake.
Stampa. All the planets in heaven, all the stars.
Tada. Odyssey or "On Absence," The.
Telestes. It was a Phrygian king.
Tennyson, A. Tithonus.
Tighe. Psyche; or The Legend of Love.
Unknown. Death of Digenis, The.
Lake of the Returned Sword, The.
Song of the Rising Sun Dance.
Songs of Spirits.
This altar for the Gods.
To Demeter.

Veneris. Over sky and land and down under the sea.
Villon. Ballad[e] of Dead Ladies.
Wilbur. Lying.
Woolagoodjah. Lalai (Dreamtime).
Yeats. Leda and the Swan.

N

Nabokov, Vladimir
Kenyon, J. Reading Aloud to My Father.
Nagasaki, Japan
Hall, R. Wedding Day at Nagasaki.
Nakedness
Al-Harizi. Secret Kept, A.
Browning, R. Rhyme for a Child Viewing a Naked Venus in a Painting [of "The Judgement of Paris"].
Cassian. Puberty.
Creeley. Pool, The.
Donne. Epithalamion for Lawyers, An.
To His Mistress Going To Bed.
DuPlessis, R. She will lie naked.
Hacker, M. Saturday Morning.
Herrick. Lily in a Crystal, The.
Upon Electra.
Levchev. Appassionato.
MacLeish. My Naked Aunt.
Mew. Monsieur Qui Passe.
Okamoto. Tanka: "Stark naked."
Oppen. Morality Play: Preface, A.
Pembroke, M. O Lord, Thou Hast Searched and Known Me.
Scott, W. Mistress Severin.
Tekkan. Tanka: "I'll forget I saw you."
Warren, R. Birth of Love.
Wollach. Two Gardens.
Wright, J. Prayer to the Lord Ramakrishna, A.
Zamora, D. Vision of Your Body.
Nalli
Vanparanar. Price of Giving Too Much, The.
Names
Aichinger. In Which Names.
Alakoye. Eshu.
Alexander, P. Audubon *Enfant.*
Alvarez, J. Bilingual Sestina.
Ashbery. Myrtle.
Bagryana. Only One, The.
Barolini. Having the Wrong Name for Mr. Wright.
Bast. Chang Tuan's Cats.
Belloc. Frog, The.
Benét, S. American Names.
Bentley, E. Wynkyn de Worde.
Berrigan, D. My Name.
Betham-Edwards. In a Letter to A.R.C. on Her Wishing to Be Called Anna.
Blake, W. Infant Joy.
Boland, E. Inscriptions: "About holiday rooms there can be."
Brooks, G. Primer for Blacks.
Brown, D. Patrols.
Browning, E. To George Sand: A Recognition.
Cave. Elegy on a Maiden Name, An.
Chaudhari, B. Naming of Things, The.
Cherry, K. History.
Raiment We Put On, The.
Chin. How I Got That Name.
Cisneros, S. Muddy Kid Comes Home.
You Called Me Corazón.
Clarke, P. My name is Sluggery-wuggery.
Clements, S. Susans.
Clifton, L. Crazy Horse Names His Daughter.
Cole, W. Mutual Problem.
Cox, M. Poem for the Name Mary.
Crashaw. On the Name of Jesus.
Crouch, S. Riding Across John Lee's Finger.
Czechowski. Walk Through the City.
Davies, A. Personality syndrome, The.
Dickinson, E. I'm ceded—I've stopped being Theirs.
Diop, D. Your Presence.
Donnelly, S. Eve Names the Animals.
Elliot, E. John. In the sound of that rebellious word.

Espada. Niggerlips was the high school name / for me.
Thirty years ago.
Foix. I Arrived in that Town, Everyone Greeted Me and I Recognized no One. When I Was Going to Read My Verses, the Devil, Hidden Behind a Tree, Called Out to Me Sarcastically and Filled My Hands with Newspaper Clippings.
Gillan. Arturo.
Graves, R. My Name and I.
Gunn, T. Pope's Carnations Knew Him.
Gunnars. Changeling VIII.
Hamod, S. Dying with the Wrong Name.
Hayden, R. 'Mystery Boy' Looks for Kin in Nashville.
Names.
Hewitt, J. Ulster Names.
Hill, G. Pet-name, a common name. Best-selling brand, curt, A.
Hollander, J. Adam's Task.
Hood, T. Choosing Their Names.
Hs'üan-Chi. On a Visit to Ch'ung Chen Taoist Temple.
Hughes, L. Madam and the Census Man.
Jackson, R. Jamal's Lamentation.
Kim Nam-jo. My baby has no name yet.
Lamb, C. Family Name, The.
Lamb, C. *et al.* Choosing a Name.
Larkin, P. Maiden Name.
Leto. Mary Morelle Show, The.
Levertov. I Learned That Her Name Was Proverb.
Locker-Lampson. My Life Is a———.
Mackey, N. Ghede Poem.
Madgett. Nomen.
Majaj. Recognized Futures.
Maxwell. Rumplestiltskin.
McDonald, R. Hollow Thesaurus, The.
Miller, E. Mississippi.
Mirikitani. Jade.
Mora. Señora X No More.
Moss, H. Geography: a Song.
Mullen, H. Momma Sayings.
Nash, O. Ill Met by Zenith.
Nemerov. Makers, The.
Neruda. Too Many Names.
Newman, L. Poem for My Grandmother's Grandmother.
O'Loughlin. Cuchulainn.
Palmer, M. O you in that little bark.
Patchen. Empty Dwelling Places.
Patten, B. How the New Teacher Got Her Nickname.
Pavic. Swing over the Calm Source of Our Names, The.
Preston, K. Lapsus Linguae.
Quasimodo. To the Fifteen of Piazzale Loreto.
Reed, H. Naming Of Parts.
Repetto. 6th grade—our lady of pompeii.
Ridler. Choosing a Name.
Root, J. Naming the Shells.
Rose. Naming Power.
Rosen, M. *et al.* Humpty Dumpty.
Rosten. This is my name / I have my own name.
Salazar. Taking It Back.
Senghor. I will pronounce your name, Naëtt, I will declaim you, Naëtt!
Seymour, A. Name Poem.
Sigourney. Indian Names.
Simon, L. Nellie Gives into Blanche.
Spenser. Sonnet 75: "One day I wrote her name upon the strand."
Stafford, W. Preservation.
Story That Could Be True, A.
Steele, T. Timothy.
Stefanile. How I Changed My Name, Felice.
Stevenson, R. Ticonderoga: A Legend of the West Highlands.
Strange. Barbershop Ritual.
Szymborska. Still.
View with a Grain of Sand.
Taylor, J. Epigram, A Supposed Construction.
Tekkan. To our baby that died[1].
Tsui. It's in the Name.
Unknown. All Fools' Day.

Angel of Death, The.
Ichthyosaurus, The.
Updike. I Missed His Book, but I Read His Name.
Wagner, M. Miss Clement's Second Grade.
Wallace-Crabbe. Life of Ideas, The.
Wallis, G. Lovely Rivers and Lakes of Maine, The.
Warner, S. El Heroe.
Wasserman, R. Putting in a Word.
Whitman, W. What am I after all but a child, pleas'd with the sound of my own name? repeating it over and over.
Wilbur. *Rillons, Rillettes*, they taste the same.
Williams, S. You Were Never Miss Brown to Me.
Winchilsea. Adam Posed.
Wollach. Christina.
Wong, N. How a Girl Got Her Chinese Name.
Wright, J. Minneapolis Poem, The.
See also **Place Names**

Nampi Netunceliyan
Muruvalar. He has held.
Perevin Muruvalar. Elegy: "He has held."

Namur, Belgium
Prior. English Ballad, on the Taking of Namur by the King of Great Britain, 1695, An.

Nantucket, Massachusetts
Glück, L. Phenomenal Survivals of Death in Nantucket.
Lowell, R. Quaker Graveyard in Nantucket, The.
Teasdale. Wisdom.
Williams, W. Nantucket.

Naples, Italy
Freeman, A. Naples Again.
Hugo, R. Napoli Again.

Napoleon I
Barlow, J. Advice to a Raven in Russia [December, 1812].
Browning, R. Incident of the French Camp.
De la Mare. Napoleon.
Dubie. Apocrypha of Jacques Derrida, The.
Holub. Napoleon.
Kipling, R. St. Helena Lullaby, A.
Madge. Poem: "Walls of the maelstrom are painted with trees, The."
Plath. Swarm, The.
Shelley, P. Feelings of a Republican on the Fall of Bonaparte.
Tennyson, A. Buonaparte.
Unknown. Boney.
To Buonaparte.

Napoleon III
Rimbaud, A. Poster of Our Dazzling Victory at Saarbrucken, A.

Napoleonic Wars
Barlow, J. Advice to a Raven in Russia [December, 1812].
Browning, R. Incident of the French Camp.
Byron, G. Eve of Waterloo, The.
Davie. Year 1812, The.
Hardy, T. Men Who March Away.
Hugo, V. Russia 1812.
Tennyson, A. Buonaparte.
Wordsworth, W. November, 1806.
To the Men of Kent (October, 1803).

Nara Japan
Mori Ogai. In Nara (two poems).

Narcissism and Narcissists
Eberhart, R. If I could only live at the pitch that is near madness.
Housman, A. Look not in my eyes, for fear.
Mayer, G. Narcissus.
Reid, A. Lesson for Beautiful Women, A.
Symons, A. Laus Virginitatis.
Zamora, D. Hand Mirror.

Narcissus (botany)
Plath. Among the Narcissi.
White, E. Window Ledge in the Atom Age.

Narcissus (mythology)
Horan. Farewell to Narcissus.
Mayer, G. Echo and Narcissus.
Narcissus.

Narcotics. *See* **Drug Addiction**

Naseby, Battle of (1645)
Macaulay, T. Battle of Naseby, The.

Nash, Richard ("Beau")
Brereton, J. On Mr. Nash's Picture at Full Length.

Nasturtiums
Hale, R. Big Nasturtiums, The.

Nationalism
Deanovich. National Assessment.
McFarlane, J. On National Vanity.
Padilla. Landscapes.
Sandburg, C. Old Timers.
Threes.
Smith, M. Black and White.

Native Americans
Alexie. Business of Fancydancing, The.
Crazy Horse Speaks.
Evolution.
Translated from the American.
Vision (2).
Allen, P. Taku Skanskan.
Baca. Invasions.
Main Character.
Baker, M. Porkskin Panorama.
Bazil. Uncertain Admission.
Belford. Carrier Indians.
Bird, D. Can I Say.
Blue Cloud. Crazy Horse Monument.
Bly, R. Schoolcraft's Diary Written on the Missouri: 1830.
Brathwaite, E. Xango.
Breton, A. Go For Broke.
Bruchac. Birdfoot's Grampa.
Bryant, W. Indian at the Burial-Place [*or* Burying-Place] of His Fathers, An.
Bynner. Haskell.
Canning, J. Indian Gone!, The.
Cardenal. Tahirassawichi in Washington.
Carew, J. Dreamtime Lives Again, The.
Carruth, H. Mending the Adobe.
Rimrock, Where It Is.
Cawein. Dead Cities.
"Chrystos." For Sharol Graves.
Real Indian Leans Against, The.
Today Was a Bad Day Like TB.
Clements, S. Deer Cloud.
Matinee.
Reservation, The.
Cook, E. Indian Hunter, The.
Cook-Lynn. Grandfather at the Indian Health Clinic.
Coolbrith. Captive of the White City.
Corso. Spontaneous Requiem For the American Indian.
Crane, H. Sad Indian, The.
De Villagrá. World has no such pleasing joy, The.
Di Prima. American Indian Art: Form and Tradition.
Brief Wyoming Meditation.
Dumas, H. Concentration Camp Blues.
Erdrich. Dear John Wayne.
Ewart. North American Haiku.
Fandel. Indians.
Fordham. Cherokee, The.
Freneau. Indian Burying Ground, The.
Indian Convert, The.
Indian Student; or, Force of Nature, The.
On the Civilization of the Western Aboriginal Country.
Glancy. Christopher.
First Reader Santee Training School, 1873, The.
Goll, I. Lackawanna Elegy.
Gould, J. We Exist.
Groch. Friend to Birds.
Gustafson, R. Columbus Reaches Juana, 1492.
Haines, J. Eye in the Rock, The.
Train Stops at Healy Fork, The.
Halleck, F. Red Jacket.
Harjo, J. Autobiography.
For Anna Mae Aquash Whose Spirit Is Present Here and in the Dappled Stars.
Grace.
Sonata for the Invisible.

Woman Hanging from the Thirteenth Floor Window, The.
Harper, M. History as Apple Tree.
Harte, B. Truthful James to the Editor.
Hemans. Indian Woman's Death-Song, The.
Henson, L. We Are a People.
Hogan, L. New Apartment.
Truth Is, The.
Hugo, R. Letter to Welch from Browning.
Map of Montana in Italy, A.
Hunter, A. North American Death Song.
Jeffers, R. Inquisitors, The.
New Mexican Mountain.
Johnson, E. Cattle Thief, The.
Ojistoh.
Jordan, J. Poem for Guatemala.
Poem for Nana.
Keeshig-Tobias. I grew up on the reserve.
Kenny, M. Winkte.
Klein, A. Indian Reservation: Caughnawaga.
Koch, K. Thanksgiving.
Lawrence, D. Men in New Mexico.
Lindsay, V. Ghosts of the Buffaloes, The.
Longfellow, H. To the Driving Cloud.
Louis, A. Couch Fantasy.
First of the Month, The.
Indian College Blues.
Practicing Death Songs.
Rhetoric Leads to Cliché.
Something About Being an Indian.
That Great Wingless Bird.
Lowell, R. At the Indian Killer's Grave.
Mair, C. I love you better than I love my race.
Major, C. Lost in the Desert.
Manyarrows. Lakota Sister/Cherokee Mother.
McFadden, D. Lennox Island.
McGrath, T. . . . All that winter, in the black cold, the buzz-saw screamed and whistled.
Merwin, W. Native, The.
Moore, L. Indian Girl.
Nanton. I.
Neihardt. III. THE COUNCIL ON THE POWDER.
Summer turned.
Newlove. Pride, The.
Niedecker. War.
O'Grady, D. Great Horse Fair, The.
Oleson. Ballad of Johnny Appleseed, A.
Ortiz. Creation.
Travels in the South.
Upstate.
Pape. Indian Ruins Along Rio de Flag.
Plato. Natives of America, The.
Purdy, A. Remains of an Indian Village.
Ridge, J. Stolen White Girl, The.
Romero, L. If Marilyn Monroe.
Rose. I Expected My Skin and My Blood to Ripen.
Naayawva Taawi.
Sáenz. Resurrections.
Sandburg, C. Alice Corbin is gone.
Early Copper.
Scott, D. At Gull Lake; August, 1810.
Forsaken, The.
On the Way to the Mission.
Seymour, A. Name Poem.
Sigourney. Indian Names.
Silko. In Cold Storm Light.
It Was a Long Time Before.
Long Time Ago.
Simons. Return to Mankiller Flats, Oklahoma.
Sirr. Understanding Canada.
Smith, R. Making the Snowshoes.
Snodgrass, W. Powwow.
Squire. Sonnet: "There was an Indian, who had known no change."
Stafford, W. At the Klamath Berry Festival.
Returned to Say.
TallMountain. Indian Blood.
Taylor, R. Dakota: October, 1822, Hunkpapa Warrior.
Terry, L. Bar[']s Fight[, August 28, 1746].
Thompson, E. Indian maid the demararie october twenty seven seventeen eighty one.
Tomlinson, C. Ute Mountain.
Unknown. American Indian, The.
Fare Thee Well.

Little Mohea, The.
Shenandoah.
Song of Bekotsidi, The.
Song of Greatness, A.
Tewa Song of War.
Very. Indian's Retort, The.
Walden. Dedicated to a Young Lady Representing the Indian Race at Howard University.
Walsh, M. Thomas Iron-Eyes.
Warton, J. Dying Indian, The.
Welch, J. Christmas Comes to Moccasin Flat.
Harlem, Montana.
Man from Washington, The.
Whitman, A. Old Sac Village, The.
Thus, San Augustine's church and prison joined.
Whitman, W. Now what my mother told me one day as we sat at dinner / together.
Osceola.
Yonnondio.
Williams, R. Adulteries, murthers, robberies, thefts.
Boast not proud English, of thy birth and blood.
Wordsworth, W. Complaint of a Forsaken Indian Woman, The.
Young Bear. Drive to Lone Ranger, A.
From the Spotted Night.
Song Taught to Joseph, The.
Zuni Oral Tradition. Following their road of exit, they stooped over and came out.

Nativity, The. *See* **Christmas**

Naturalists
Bentley, E. "Dinner-time?" said Gilbert White.
Heaney, S. Death of a Naturalist.
White, G. Naturalist's Summer-Evening Walk, The.

Nature
Ackerman, D. Beija-Flor.
Addison, J. Ode: "Spacious firmament on high, The."
"Akhmatova." Alone.
Alcman. Fragment: "Mountain summits sleep, glens, cliffs, and caves, The."
Alexander, C. All things bright and beauteous.
Alexandru. Prayer.
Amergin. Amergin's Charm.
Amichai. We did it in front of the mirror.
Ammons. Arc Inside and Out, The.
Corsons Inlet.
Cut the Grass.
Gravelly Run.
Hymn: "I know if I find you I will have to leave the earth."
Terrain.
Anacreon. Dark earth drinks the sky, The.
Grasshopper, The.
Andrews, B. West West.
"Antler." Somewhere Along the Line.
Armstrong, J. Art of Preserving Health, The.
Arnold, M. "In harmony with Nature?"
Restless fool.
Lake, The.
Quiet Work.
Ashbery. Rivers and Mountains.
These Lacustrine Cities.
Atwood. Landcrab II.
Auden. Fall of Rome, The.
Babcock, M. This Is My Father's World.
Balaban. Graveyard at Bald Eagle Ridge.
Bangs, J. Blind.
Bartusek. Love Song.
Baudelaire. Correspondences.
Giantess, The.
Bazil. Uncertain Admission.
Beattie, J. Youth of a Poet, The.
Belševica. Willow-catkins threw off their narrow shoes.
Bennett, G. Sonnet—2: "Some things are very dear to me—."
Berberova. Eagles and butterflies (and some other things).
Berry, J. Pods Pop and Grin.
Berry, W. Peace of Wild Things, The.
Bethell. Pause.
Bevington, H. Nature Study, After Dufy.

Bevington, L. Morning.
Bialik. Pool, The.
Bible, Apocrypha. Steel Usurps the Forests; Silence Dethrones Dialogue.
Bible, *O.T.* Psalm 147: "Praise ye the Lord."
Bishop, E. Brazil, January 1, 1502.
Cold spring, A.
North Haven.
Blaga. In the Mountains.
Twentieth Century.
Blandiana. Song.
Bloomfield. Spring.
Summer.
Bly, R. After Drinking All Night with a Friend, We Go Out in a Boat at Dawn to See Who Can Write the Best Poem.
In the month of May when all leaves open.
Bobrowski. Deserted House, The.
Latvian Autumn, The.
Lithuanian Well, The.
Place of Fire.
Sanctuary.
Shadowland.
Wanderer, The.
Boccaccio. I am a young maiden, and I willingly.
Two Dreams, The.
Bogan, L. Night.
Bolamba. Fistful of News, A.
Portrait.
Bold, A. Grass basks greedily in the sun.
Bonnefoy. Tree, the Lamp, The.
Booth, P. How to See Deer.
Borowski. Sun of Auschwitz, The.
Bowers, E. Mountain Cemetery, The.
Bowles, C. There is a tongue in every leaf.
Bowman, C. Demographics.
Boyse. Triumphs of Nature, The.
Braithwaite. City Garden, A.
Brathwaite, E. Red Rising.
Breytenbach. There Is Life.
Bridges. How She Operates.
Bridges, R. Sky's unresting cloudland, that with varying play, The.
Brontë, E. Shall Earth no more inspire thee.
Stanzas: "Often rebuked, yet always back returning."
Tell me, tell me, smiling child.
Why do I hate that lone green dell?
Brooke, R. Hill, The.
Broughton, T. Lyric.
Brown, A. Friends.
Brown, P. Leaving.
Browne, W. Happyer those times were, when the Flaxen clew.
Browning, E. Sonnet: "Yet, love, mere love, is beautiful indeed."
Browning, R. Pippa's Song.
Brownstein. Oracle night / the porch is frozen.
Bruchac. Birdfoot's Grampa.
Prayer: "Let my words."
Bryant, W. Fountain, that springest on this grassy slope.
Oh fairest of the rural maids!
Thanatopsis.
Brydges. To Miss M——, Written by Moonlight, July 18, 1782.
Buckmaster. Wilpena Pound.
Bunin. Endless downpour; misty wood.
Burns, R. My heart's in the Highlands, my heart is not here.
To a Mouse[, On Turning Her Up in Her Nest, with the Plough, November, 1785].
Byron, G. There be who say, in these enlightened days.
Campbell, D. Man in the Honeysuckle, The.
Campion, T. I care not for these ladies.
Carew, J. Dreamtime Lives Again, The.
Carew, T. Love's Force.
Spring, The.
To my Friend G.N. from Wrest.
To My Worthy Friend Master George Sands [*or* Sandys], on His Translation of the Psalms.
Carman, B. *et al.* Earth's Lyric.
Carroll, J. Withdrawal Letter.
Carter, M. Childhood of a Voice.

Carver, R. Window, The.
Causley. I am the song that sings the bird.
Ch'en Liang. Tune: "Water Dragon's Chant"—Loathsome Spring.
Ch'en Yü-yi. Sitting on a Rock by Mountain Stream.
Chesterton, G. Oneness of the Philosopher with Nature, The.
Chiang K'uei. Tune: "Dim Fragrance"—Plum Blossoms.
Ch'ien T'ao. Returning to the Fields.
Chong, H. Bird.
Chong, H. Going by far.
Chu Yi-tsun. Listening-to-the-Rain Studio. Tune: "Song of the Southern Country"— Spring Thoughts at Pearl River.
West Cliff.
Chuang Tzu. Man Is Born in Tao.
Clampitt. Sun Underfoot Among the Sundews, The.
Clare, J. Eternity of Nature, The.
Evening.
February.
Oh sweet is the sound o' the dove's clapping wings.
Poets Love Nature.
Secret Love.
We Passed by Green Closes.
Clark, L. August Ends.
Clark, T. Each colour sits beside.
High piled cumulus.
Our boat touches the bank.
Stag comes home at last, The.
Clerk. Country Seat, The.
Coatsworth. Swift things are beautiful.
Cole, T. Painter, A.
Coleridge, S. Nightingale, The.
Picture; or, The Lover's Resolution, The.
Reflections on Having Left a Place of Retirement.
This Lime-Tree Bower My Prison.
To Nature.
Work Without Hope.
Written in Early Youth, the Time an Autumnal Evening.
Coleridge, S. Garden Year, The.
Conoley. Unchained Melody.
Coolbrith. Longing.
Cotton, C. Chatsworth.
Cowley, A. Garden, The.
Cowper, W. My Pet Hare.
Task, The.
Cranch. Correspondences.
Crane, S. Each small gleam was a voice.
Creeley. Innocence, The.
Song: "Those rivers run from that land."
Cronin, A. Trembling with engines, gulping oil, the river.
Crsnaru. Lions of Babylon, The.
Cruickshank, H. Ponnage Pool, The.
Cummings, E. I thank You God for most this amazing.
O sweet spontaneous.
When serpents bargain for the right to squirm.
Wherelings whenlings / (daughters of if but offspring of hopefear).
D'Annunzio. Rain in the Pine Wood.
Darley. My bower is in a green dell.
Darwin. Kew.
Das, M. Leaf in His Ear, The.
Davidson, L. America.
Davies, S. Praise of Dancing, The.
De la Mare. All That's Past.
Miracle, The.
Reserved.
Dev Sen. Yellow River, The.
Dewdney. August a haze amniotic our dream aether and lens of distance. Tree sentinels in.
She is liquid darkness occult with desire.
Dickinson, E. Banish Air from Air.
Bring me the sunset in a cup.
Earth has many keys, The.
Further in Summer than the Birds.
I had been hungry, all the Years.
I taste a liquor never brewed.
Narrow Fellow in the Grass, A.
Nature—sometimes sears a Sapling.

Nature—the Gentlest Mother is.
Sky is low—the Clouds are mean, The.
This is my letter to the World.
Trees like Tassels—hit—and swung, The.
Digges. To a Milkweed.
Dimoski. Rest.
Doolittle, H. Moon in Your Hands, The.
White World.
Dove, R. Fish in the Stone, The.
Dowden, E. Two Infinities.
Downar. From The Bramble Hedge.
Drake, J. Bronx.
Drayton. These verses weare made By
Michaell Drayton Esquier Poett Lawreatt the
night before hee dyed.
Drummond, W. Book, The.
Duck. On Richmond Park.
Dufault. Burden.
Duffy, C. Plainsong.
Duggan, L. Five. One.
One. One.
Dumbrveanu. Seeds of Flight.
Dunn, D. Gardeners.
Dupin. From a thread in space, endless and
unbroken. Without unravelling.
Dyer, S. Love is Love.
Eberhart, R. Concord Cats.
Hard Structure of the World, The.
On a Squirrel Crossing the Road in Autumn,
in New England.
Sea-Hawk.
Spider expects the cold of winter, The.
Ehrhart. Confirmation, A.
Eigner. Environs.
Elenkov. Poet.
Ellis, S. Your Poems at Daybreak, the
Destruction of Knossos by Afternoon.
Elytis. In the beginning the light And the first
hour.
Origin of Landscape or the End of Mercy,
The.
Embiricos. Caryatids, The.
Emerson, R. Awed I behold once more.
Blight.
Circles.
Dear brother, would you know the life.
Each and All.
Experience.
In my garden three ways meet.
Musketaquid.
Nature [1836].
Song of Nature.
Waldeinsamkeit.
Xenophanes.
Esolen. Northwestern Mathematics.
Everson, W. South Coast, The.
Fallon, P. Spring Song.
Fell, A. Desire.
Felsted. Thanks for Hearing.
Fenton, J. For the context of the basidiocarp
Singer states.
Kingfisher's Boxing Gloves, The.
Lollipops of the Pomeranian Baroque.
South Parks Road.
Ferlinghetti, L. Wounded wilderness of Morris
Graves, The.
Finch, A. Nocturnal Reverie, A.
Finkel. In the Clearing.
Fitzgerald, M. Rendezvous.
Fletcher, J. Green Symphony.
Frase. On Returning.
Freneau. On the Religion of Nature.
On the Uniformity and Perfection of Nature.
Frost, R. Design.
Directive.
Fountain, a Bottle, a Donkey's Ears and Some
Books, A.
Lucretius versus the Lake Poets.
Vantage Point, The.
Fuller, M. Sistrum.
Garioch. Merulius Lacrymans.
Giles, J. Leasowes: Or, A Poetical Description
of the Late Mr. Shenstone's Rural
Retirement, The.
Ginsberg, A. Easter Sunday.
Goethe. May Song.

Meeting, the Departure, The.
Nature and Art.
Goldbarth. Life is Happy.
Goldsmith, O. Deserted Village, The.
Goodman, P. My Daughter Very Ill.
Graves, R. Interruption.
Love Story, A.
Nature's Lineaments.
Return of the Goddess [Artemis].
She tells her love while half asleep.
Song of Blodeuwedd, The.
To Juan at the Winter Solstice.
Greenwell, D. Scherzo, A.
Gregg. Dark Thing Inside the Day, A.
Grennan. Facts of Life, Ballymoney.
Sunday Morning Through Binoculars.
Greville, F. Chorus Sacerdotum.
Grigson. Landscape Gardeners, The.
Guest, B. Nebraska.
Sassafras.
Gunn, T. Faustus Triumphant.
Last Man, The.
Gurney, I. Sea-Marge.
Hacker, M. Languedocienne.
Hall, D. Granite and Grass.
New Hampshire.
Hamilton, M. For My Father's Mother Who
Has Alzheimer's.
Han-shan. Clambering up the Cold Mountain
path.
Han. I Do Not Know.
Hardy, T. Five Students, The.
In a Wood.
Middle-Age Enthusiasms.
Nature's Questioning.
Harris, R. Literary Excellence.
Harry, J. Walking, when the Lake of the Air
is Blue with Spring.
Hart-Smith. Nullarbor.
Hartnett. For My Grandmother, Bridget
Halpin.
Hartwig. Above Us.
Harwood, G. Clair de Lune.
Haxton. Traveling Company.
Heaney, S. Anahorish.
Song: "Rowan like a lip-sticked girl, A."
Hejinian. Polar Circle, The.
Hemans. Indian Woman's Death-Song, The.
Nature's Farewell.
Herrick. Art above Nature, to Julia.
Country Life: To His Brother, M. Tho:
Herrick.
Putrefaction is the end.
To Find[e] God.
Upon Time.
Hesketh. Death of a Gardener.
Hewitt, J. Because I paced my thought by the
natural world.
Ram's Horn, The.
Substance and Shadow.
Hikmet. Letters from a Man in Solitary.
Things I Didn't Know I Loved.
Hildegard von Bingen. I am the one whose
praise echoes on high.
Hill, G. Two Chorale-Preludes: On Melodies
by Paul Celan.
Hogan, L. Bear Fat.
Map.
Hogg, J. Kilmeny.
Holan. Memory II.
Hollander, J. Old-Fashioned Song, An.
Variations on a Fragment by Trumbull
Stickney.
Holmes, O. Living Temple, The.
Holub. Crocheting.
Hood, T. I remember, I remember.
Hoole. Cumberland Rocks.
Hopkins, G. God's Grandeur.
Pied Beauty.
That Nature Is a Heraclitean Fire and of the
Comfort of the Resurrection.
Horace. Odes 1.9.
Soracte.
Hsieh Ling-yün. Passing through My Shih-
ning Estate.
Spending the Night on Stone Gate Mountain.

Hsü Wei. Abandoning the Plans of Visiting
West Lake.
Huang T'ing-chien. Living in Exile at Ch'ien-
nan.
Huchel. Melpomene.
Hudgins. Persistence of Nature in Our Lives,
The.
Hughes, T. Fern.
Heptonstall Old Church.
October robin kept, An.
Pibroch.
Roe-Deer.
Stealing Trout.
Thrushes.
Hunt, L. To Hampstead.
Huss. Green Refrain, The.
Hwang, T. Smaller Love Song, A.
Ignatow, D. Rescue the Dead.
Inada. Kicking the Habit.
Jacobsen, J. Hourglass.
Jacobsen, R. Green Light.
Rubber.
James, J. Side Window.
Jarrell. Field and Forest.
Jeffers, R. Boats in a Fog.
Noon.
Place for No Story, The.
Unnatural Powers.
Jewett, S. At Home from Church.
Johnson, R. Ark 34, Spire on the Death of
L.Z.
Johnston, E. Address to Nature on its Cruelty,
An.
Jones, J. Our Wonderful World.
Kavanagh, P. Canal Bank Walk.
Keats. Happy Insensibility.
Kelly, B. All Wild Animals Were Once Called
Deer.
Kemble. Sonnet: "If there were any power in
human love."
Kennelly. Island, The.
Khlebnikov, V. Four Poems.
Persons, people, and the years.
Kim, H. Prayer in Autumn.
Tears.
Kim, J. Law of Fall, The.
Kim, S. Flowers in the Mountains.
Kim, S. Grass lies flattened.
Kim, Y. May.
Kingsley, C. River's Song, The.
Kinnell. Lastness.
Supper after the Last, The.
When one has lived a long time alone.
Kinsella, T. Another September.
Oldest Place, The.
Route of the Táin, The.
Kinzie. Want, predation, sleep.
Xenophilia.
Kizer, C. On a Line from Valéry.
Knight, R. Landscape, The.
Kopland. Thanks to the Things.
Kraujiete. In Chalk Rooms.
Kruchyonykh. Sahara to America, The.
Ku T'ai-ch'ing. Tune: "Ripples Sifting
Sand"—Accompanying My Husband on a
Spring Outing to Stone Pavilion.
Kuan Yün-shih. Tune: "Butterflies."
Kunene. Echoes, The.
Kunze, R. Diary Page 69.
Return from the Convention.
Kuo P'o. Poem on the Wandering Immortal.
Lady of the Assembly. Assembly of Ladies,
The.
Lamantia. Voice of Earth Mediums.
Landor, W. On His Seventy-Fifth Birthday.
Lange, A. Sonnet for the Season.
Lanier, S. Clover.
To Bayard Taylor.
Lanyer. Description of Cookham, The.
Lao Tzu. All things pass.
Every being in the universe.
Lawrence, D. Elemental.
Glory is of the sun, too, and the sun of suns.
Proper Pride.
Self-Protection.
Wild Common, The.
Lazarus, E. South, The.

Le Gallienne. I meant to do my work today.
Leapor. On Winter.
Lee, B. In the Green Shade.
Leib. Psalmodist.
Leithauser. In a Japanese Moss Garden.
Leonard, T. Miracle of the Burd and the Fishes, The.
Levertov. Gathered at the River.
Living.
Those Who Want Out.
Li Ching. Tune: "Sand of Silk-washing Stream."
Li Ho. Ch'ang-ku.
Grave of Little Su, The.
Ravine on a Cold Evening.
Li Po. Poem by the Bridge at Ten-shin.
To Tan-Ch'iu.
You ask why I make my home in the mountain forest.
Li Shan-fu. My Detacted Villa.
Li Shang-yin. Day after day spring's glory vies with the glorious sun.
Lodge, G. Pastoral: "Slopes of the sun and vine, and thou dark stream."
Longfellow, H. Aftermath.
My Cathedral.
Nature.
Snow-Flakes.
Spirit of Poetry, The.
Longley, M. Ash Keys.
Frozen Rain.
Lönnrot. It is my desire, it is my wish.
Louis, A. Wakinyan.
Lu Chih. Tune: "Intoxication in the East Wind" Autumn Scenery.
Lucretius. Address to Venus.
Dissolution of the world proovd from the mortality of every part, The.
Epicurus praised.
First principles of Epicurean physics.
Thus like a Sayler by the Tempest hurl'd.
Lydgate. Complaint of the Black Knight, The.
Ma Chih-yüan. Tune: "Four Pieces of Jade"—Retirement.
MacCaig. Basking Shark.
Explicit Snow.
Feeding Ducks.
July Evening.
Loch Sionascaig.
Looking Down on Glen Canisp.
Shore Road, The.
Things in Each Other.
"MacDiarmid." Water Music.
Mackey, N. Kiche Manitou.
Macklin. Nearsighted, The.
MacNeice. House on a Cliff.
Nature Notes: Dandelions.
Madge. Solar Creation.
Mahon. Woods, The.
Markham, E. Prayer, A: "Teach me, Father, how to go."
Marlowe. Passionate Shepherd [or Sheepheard] To His Love, The.
Martynov. Lord of Nature.
Marvell. Mower Against Gardens, The.
Mason, W. Against Formal Gardens.
Alcander's Flower Garden.
Some Early gardenists.
Matthews, W. People Like Us.
McDonald, W. Hauling Over Wolf Creek Pass in Winter.
McGrath, J. Song.
McPherson, S. Wings and Seeds.
Mead, P. Melbourne or the Bush.
Melville, H. Attic Landscape, The.
Haglets, The.
Little Good Fellows, The.
Malvern Hill.
Pontoosuce.
Meng Chiao. Stopping on a Journey at the East Water Pavilion at Lo-ch'eng.
Meng Hao Jan. Stopping at a Friend's Farm.
Meredith, G. 30.
Dirge in Woods.
Love in the Valley.
Melampus.
Merrick, A. Hartwell Gardens.

Merrill, J. Syrinx.
Messerli. Scared Cows.
This That and Then.
Mew. Afternoon Tea.
In the Fields.
Meynell, A. Rainy Summer, The.
Miljkovic. Shepherd's Flute.
Millay, E. God's World.
Milosz, C. Sun, The.
To Mrs. Professor in Defense of My Cat's Honor and Not Only.
Mitchell, A. Nature Poem.
Mnthali. Celebration, The.
Mole, J. Musical monkey is dressed like a flunkey, The.
Momaday. Delight Song of Tsoai-Talee, The.
Headwaters.
Monar. Koker.
Montale. Eel, The.
Eel, the North Sea siren, The.
"Monty Python." All things dull and ugly.
Morley, H. Curve of the Water.
Morris, W. Love is enough: though the World be a-waning.
Mphande. Wood-Cutter, The.
Mueller, I. Another Time Track.
Murray, P. Returning Spring.
Na-lan Hsing-te. Tune: "Butterflies Lingering over Flowers"—Leaving the Border.
Nashe. Spring.
Nemerov. Companions, The.
Dependencies, The.
Elegy for a Nature Poet.
Holding the Mirror Up to Nature.
Salt Garden, The.
Singular Metamorphosis, A.
Nesbit, E. Great Industrial Centre, A.
Newcastle, M. Dialogue betwixt Man, and Nature, A.
Dissert, A.
Landscape, A.
Nature's Cook.
Nezval. Trap Door.
Nguyễn Trãi. Ask to be put in charge of streams and hills!
Nicholls, J. Timeless.
Niedecker. Element Mother, The.
Paean to Place.
War.
North, C. Note to Tony Towle (After WS), A.
Norwalk. Psalm of Love.
Oden. Review from Staten Island.
O'Hara, F. Easter.
Oliver, M. Climbing the Chagrin River.
Ghosts.
In Blackwater Woods.
Landscape.
Some Questions You Might Ask.
Wild Geese.
Olson. Praises, The.
Oppian. Great Chain of Being, The.
Prayer, A.
Ormsby, F. Soldier Bathing.
Orrick. Little Things.
Osundare. Excursion.
Goree.
Our Earth Will Not Die.
We called the statue.
Who Says That Drought Was Here?
Ou-yang Hsiu. Old fisherman spends his night beneath the western cliffs.
Tune: "Butterflies Lingering over Flowers" ("Ruffed blue-green garden, red blossoms").
Tune: "Treading on Grass."
Ovid. Flood recedes, The.
Golden Age, The.
Owen, W. From My Diary, July 1914.
Pacheco, J. On the Fragile Labyrinth.
Park, C. Flute Holes.
Landscape, A.
Parun. Open Door.
Patchen. Deer and the Snake, The.
Like a Mourningless Child.
Pastoral: "Dove walks with sticky feet, The."
Patel, R. Whirlwind.
Patmore, C. Evening Scene, An.
Paz. Pause.

Peele. Song: "When as [or whenas] the rye [or rie] reach to the chin."
Penstone. Praise to God for things we see.
Philips, A. Happy Swain, The.
Philips, K. To Mr. Henry Lawes.
Piatt, S. In A Queen's Domain.
Piercy. Development, The.
Postcard from the Garden.
Plath. Wreath for a Bridal.
Plomer. Namaqualand after Rain.
Plumly. Hedgerows.
Po Chü-i. Being on Duty all Night in the Palace and Dreaming of the Hsien-yu Temple.
Going to the Mountains with a Little Dancing Girl, Aged Fifteen.
Planting Bamboos.
Planting Flowers on the Eastern Embankment.
Spring River, The.
Poe. Stanzas: "How often we forget all time, when lone."
Valley of Unrest, The.
Pollard, V. Belize Suite.
Ponge. Prairie, The.
Popa. Burning Shewolf.
Pope, A. Epistle to Lord Burlington.
Essay on Criticism, An.
Intended for Sir Isaac Newton.
What if the foot, ordain'd the dust to tread.
Porter, P. Australian Garden, An.
Pound, E. Papyrus.
Pozhenyan. Clear fall afternoon beckons, A.
Pratt, M. Place Lost and Gone, the Place Found, The.
Preil, G. How to Read the First Line.
Pyon. Spring Rain.
Raine, K. Heirloom.
Message from Home.
Natura Naturans.
Wilderness, The.
Randall, J. Valediction, A.
Rands. World, The.
Rankin, J. Old Circles.
Ray, H. At Nature's Shrine.
Instability.
Nature's Minor Chords.
Nature's Uplifting.
Redmond. Definition of Nature.
Reed, H. Naming Of Parts.
Reid, A. Isle of Arran.
James Bottle's Year.
Revard. October, Isle of Skye.
Rilke. First Duino Elegy, The.
Ristovic. Out in the Open.
Rivard. Naive Invocation.
Roberson. Blue Horses.
Roberts, M. Demeter Grieving.
Robinson, E. Poem for Max Nordau, A.
Torrent, The.
Roethke. Bring the Day!
Far Field, The.
Field of Light, A.
Genesis.
Give Way, Ye Gates.
Her Time.
Long Waters, The.
Minimal, The.
Rose, The.
Sequel, The.
Shape of the Fire, The.
Thing, The.
Visitant, The.
Words for the Wind.
Rossetti, C. Cobwebs.
Frisky lamb / And a frisky child, A.
Green Cornfield, A.
Song: "Two doves upon the selfsame branch."
Summer.
What is pink? A rose is pink.
Who has seen the wind? / Neither I nor you.
Rossetti, D. Even So.
Silent Noon.
Rubtsov. Good Filya.
Ryan, R. Lake of the Woods, The.
Sackville-West. Beechwoods at Knole.
Land, The.
St. John, P. Carnival.

Saxena. Black panther is sleeping on the crags, The.

Schuyler, J. Father or Son.

Schwartz, D. Small Score, A.

Scott, W. Madge Wildfire Sings.

Seferis. Wreck "Thrush", The.

Seward. Elegy.

Eyam.

Sonnet VII: "By Derwent's rapid stream as oft I strayed."

Shakespeare, W. Sonnet 15.

Sonnet 68.

Sonnet 98.

Shapiro, D. Commentary Text Commentary Text Commentary Text.

Shapiro, K. Travelogue for Exiles.

Shchipachov. Blue spaces do not see themselves, The.

Little Birch Tree, The.

Shelley, P. Love's Philosophy.

Made One With Nature.

Mont Blanc.

To a Skylark.

Shelton, R. Because the Moon Comes.

Shen Yüeh. Spending the Night in the Eastern Park.

"Shu Ting." Gifts.

Simic. Summer Morning.

Sirr. Collector's Marginalia, The.

Slessor. South Country.

Smart, C. On a Bed of Guernsey Lilies.

St. Philip and St. James.

Smelyakov. Should I ever fall ill.

Smith, C. I once was happy, when while yet a child.

Sonnet V. To the South Downs: "Ah, hills beloved!—where once, an happy child."

Smith, I. Lewis 1928–45.

Smith, S. Away, melancholy, / Away with it, let it go.

Lady "Rogue" Singleton.

Pretty.

Smollett. To Leven Water.

Snyder, G. Burning Island.

By Frazier Creek Falls.

Milton by Firelight.

Old Woman Nature.

Path to Han-shan's place is laughable, The.

Piute Creek.

Ripples on the surface of the water.

Södergran. Homecoming.

There is no one in this world who has time.

Song. Poem: "Water wears away a rock."

Southwell. Vale of Tear[e]s, A.

Spencer, A. 1975.

Spenser. Dame Nature.

Stafford, W. Montana Eclogue.

Oregon Message, An.

Preservation.

Well rising without sound, The.

Stevens, M. Carp, The.

Stevens, W. Banal Sojourn.

Dry Loaf.

Nomad Exquisite.

Sense of the Sleight-of-Hand Man, The.

Stevenson, R. House Beautiful, The.

Stickney, T. Athenian Garden, An.

In Ampezzo.

Lakeward.

Stone, W. Nature.

Stricker. Foreigners.

Su Shih. Tune: "Joy of Eternal Union"—Passing the Seven-league Shallows.

Su Tung-p'o. On a Painting by Wang the Clerk of Yen Ling.

On the Road to Hsin-ch'eng.

Presented to Liu Ching-wen.

Roaring waterfall, the.

Tune: Partridge Sky.

Written on a Painting Entitled "Misty Yangtze and Folded Hills."

Swenson, M. Stripping and Putting on.

Swinburne. Triads.

Sylvester, J. Cunning Painter, that with curious care, The.

Symons, A. Violet.

Synge. Prelude: "Still south I went and west and south again."

Szymborska. View with a Grain of Sand.

Tablada. Haiku: "Dragon-fly strives patiently, The."

T'ao Ch'ien. Autumn chrysanthemums have beautiful color.

When I was young, I did not fit into the common mold.

Taylor, A. Earth.

Tennyson, A. 124.

Flower in the crannied wall.

In Memoriam.

Nothing Will Die.

Wish, that of the living whole, The.

Tennyson, F. Glory of Nature, The.

Teodorescu. Ex Voto.

Thomas, D. This bread I break was once the oat.

Thompson, D. Very Odd Fish, A.

Thompson, F. Nature one hour appears a thing unsexed.

Thoreau. Haze.

Inward Morning, The.

It is no dream of mine.

Mist.

Nature.

Poet's Delay, The.

Pray to What Earth Does This Sweet Cold Belong.

Winter and Spring Scene, A.

Thorne, T. High Country.

Todd, R. Of Moulds and Mushrooms.

Tomlinson, C. John Maydew or The Allotment.

Traherne. Walking.

Trakl. Summer.

Tremayne. Legend.

Tu Fu. Autumn Meditation.

Autumn wastes are each day wilder, The.

Clear After Rain.

Clear Evening after Rain.

Country Cottage.

Homecoming—Late at Night.

Quatrain: "Late sun, the stream and the hills; the beauty."

South Wind.

Sunset glitters on the beads.

Written on the Thirtieth Day, Ninth Month, Second Year of the Ta-li Reign [767].

Tu Mu. Retired Official Yüan's High Pavilion, The.

Tuckerman, F. And change[,] with hurried hand, has swept these scenes.

How oft in schoolboy-days, from the school's sway.

Sonnets: First Series.

Thin little leaves of wood fern, ribbed and toothed.

Yet, even 'mid merry boyhood's tricks and scapes.

Turner, N. God's Plan for Spring.

Ungaretti. You Were Broken.

You Were Shattered.

Unknown. Fourth month: summer already, The.

Great Spirit, whose dry lands thirst, help us to find.

Handiwork of God, The.

I saw some lovely things today.

Incantations of Modoc Conjurers.

Marban, a Hermit Speaks.

Richmond Gardens: A Poem.

Rise and Progress of the Present Taste in Planning Parks, Pleasure Grounds, Gardens, etc, The.

Sea, The.

Smallest basil leaf was heard to whimper, The.

Song to the Trees and Streams.

Songs and Chants.

Southern Paiute Poetry.

Spring breeze stirs a springtime heart.

Sumer is icumen in.

Sweetness of Nature, The.

When, lo, by break of morning.

Wild Man Comes to the Monastery, The.

Untermeyer, L. Song Tournament: New Style.

Uvavnuk. Great sea has set me in motion, The.

Van Duyn. Ballad of Blossom, The.

View, A.

Varma. Man.

Vaughan, H. Love and Discipline.

Regeneration.

Very. Nature.

Silent, The.

Song, The: "When I would sing of crooked streams and fields."

Virgil. Love and the Creatures.

Waddell, H. Earth said to Death.

Wagoner, D. Five Dawn Skies in November.

Making Camp.

Source, The.

Walcott. Midsummer LIV.

Wallace, R. In a Spring Still Not Written Of.

Waller, E. On St. James's Park, as Lately Improved by His Majesty.

Walton, T. God's Gifts to Me.

Wang An-shih. By a Stream on Mount T'ien-t'ung.

Sketch of Mount Chung, A.

Wang I. Lychee-tree, The.

Wang Shih-chieng. Lieh Mountain.

On the Way to Huang-ch'ang River.

Wang Wei. Birdsong Brook.

Warren, R. Gold Glade.

Sky.

Warton, J. Wild, The.

Wat. From "Songs of a Wanderer."

Watts, I. Flying Fowl, and Creeping Things, Praise Ye the Lord.

Wellman, M. Mad Wolf in Lunar Web, Mad Crow on the Beach.

Two hollow eyes follow a cat's crie.

Wen T'ing-yün. Early Walk on Shang Mountain, An.

Wen Yi-tuo. Dead Water.

Westmorland. To Sir John Wentworth, Upon His Curiosities and Courteous Entertainment at Summerly in Lovingland.

Whisenand. Open your eyes that you may see.

White, S. Healing, The.

Whitehead, W. On the Late Improvements at Nuneham, the Seat of the Earl of Harcourt.

Whitman, W. Day when I rose at dawn from the bed of perfect health, refresh'd, The.

Give me the splendid silent sun with all his beams full-dazzling.

Italian Music in Dakota.

Me imperturbe, standing at ease in Nature.

Proud music of the storm.

Spontaneous me, Nature.

To a President.

We two, how long we were fool'd.

When I heard at the close of the day how my name had been receiv'd with plaudits in the capitol, still it was not a happy night for me that follow'd.

World below the brine, The.

Whittemore, R. Departure, The.

Whittier. Over-Heart, The.

Prelude: "Along the roadside, like the flowers of gold."

Wieseltier. Song of the last soldier, A.

Wilbur. Ceremony.

Hamlen Brook.

Part of a Letter.

Wilcox, C. Sultry noon, not in the summer's prime, A.

Wilcox, E. Attraction.

Wilkinson, A. Nature Be Damned.

Williams, H. Blest Poesy! Oh sent to calm.

Sonnet to Twilight.

Williams, W. Raleigh Was Right.

Wilson, J. Sonnet III. Written at Midnight, on Helm Crag.

Sonnet VII. Written on Skiddaw, during a Tempest.

Written on the Banks of Wastwater During a Calm.

Wilson, R. Sparrow Hills.

Winchilsea. Nocturnal Reverie, A.

Wolfe, C. Song: "Oh say not that my heart is cold."

Wordsworth, D. Cottage in Grasmere Vale, A.
Floating Island at Hawkshead.
Loving and Liking [Irregular Verses Addressed to A Child].
Thoughts on my sick-bed.
Wordsworth, W. Composed at Neidpath Castle, the Property of Lord Queensberry,1803.
Composed upon an Evening of Extraordinary Splendour and Beauty.
Education of Nature, The.
Excursion, The.
Expostulation and Reply.
Farewell thou little Nook of mountain-ground.
Lines Written in Early Spring.
Sonnet: "World is too much with us; late and soon, The."
Sweet is the lore which Nature brings;.
Tables Turned[: An Evening Scene, on the Same Subject], The.
This prayer I make.
To a Butterfly.
Trosachs, The.
Written in London, September, 1802.
Written in March [While Resting on the Bridge at the Foot of Brother's Water].
Wotton, S. On a Bank [or Banck] asl I Sat [or Sate] a-Fishing; a Description of the Spring.
Wright, C. California Spring.
Dead Color.
Self-Portrait ("Someday they'll find me out, and my lavish hands").
Stone Canyon Nocturne.
Wright, J. Depressed by a Book of Bad Poetry, I Walk toward an Unused Pasture and Invite the Insects to Join Me.
Fit against the Country, A.
Wright, J. At Cooloolah.
Rainforest.
Wu-Men. Moon and clouds are the same.
Ten thousand flowers in spring, the moon in autumn.
Wyatt, T. Resound my voice [or voyse], ye woods [or wodes] that hear [or here] me plain.
Xuân Diệu. Magic.
Yang Chi. Wu Shan-yang.
Yeats. Coole Park, 1929.
Her Anxiety.
Indian to His Love, The.
Lake-Isle of Innisfree, The.
Sorrow of Love, The ("Brawling of a sparrow in the eaves, The").
Yen Shu. Tune: "Treading on Grass."
Yi, S. Poem No. VII.
Young, A. For Poets.
Young, A. Sudden Thaw.
Young, D. Sainless.
Young, M. Metronomic Moon, The.
Zabolotsky. Walk, A.
Zanzotto. If it were not your face that melts.
Zealand. Still Life, Untitled, A.
Zhenkai. Accomplices.

Nautilus (mollusk)
Holmes, O. Chambered Nautilus, The.

Nauvoo, Illinois
Taylor, B. Nauvoo.

Navaho, The
Pape. Storm Pattern.
Unknown. War God's Horse Song, The.

Naval Battles
Campbell, T. Battle of the Baltic.
Day, J. North Sea.
Defoe, D. Word's gone out, and now they spread the main, The.
Donne. Burnt Ship, A.
Dryden, J. Now van to van the foremost squadrons meet.
Hemans. Casabianca.
Melville, H. Commemorative of a Naval Victory.
Temeraire, The.
Utilitarian View of the Monitor's Fight, A.
Sackville, C. Song Written at Sea in the First Dutch War (1665), the Night before an Engagement.

Smith, C. Sea View, The.
Whitman, W. Battle of the *Bonhomme Richard* and the *Serapis.*

Navels
Shakely. Definition.

Navy, France
Browning, R. Hervé Riel.
Cory, W. Ballad for a Boy, A.
Thomas. To Laura, on the French Fleet Parading before Plymouth.

Navy, Great Britain
Campbell, T. Ye Mariners of England.
Causley. Chief Petty Officer.
Cleveland, R. Destroyers Off Jutland.
Corbett, N. Sailing of the Fleet, The.
Cory, W. Ballad for a Boy, A.
Garrick. Heart of Oak.
Head, S. Destroyers.
Hopwood. Mystery Ships, The.
Kipling, R. White Horses.
"Klaxon." Destroyers.
Newbolt. Admirals All.
Noyes, A. Search-Lights, The.
Owen, W. It was a navy boy, so prim, so trim.
Waller, E. To the King, on His Navy.
Young, E. Mine-Sweeping Trawlers.

Navy Life
Burns, R. Silver Tassie, The.
Ross, A. Destroyers in the Arctic.

Navy, United States
Carryl, G. When the Great Gray Ships Come In.
Haines, J. Mothball Fleet: Benicia, California.
Holmes, O. Old Ironsides.
Meredith, W. Farragut, Farragut / Old Heart of Oak.
Rooney. Men behind the Guns, The.

Nazis
Abse. Footnote Extended, A.
Bobrowski. Kaunas 1941.
Borawski. Invisible History.
Brecht, B. 1940.
War Has Been Given a Bad Name.
Bringhurst. For the Bones of Josef Mengele, Disinterred June 1985.
Char. Leaves of Hypnos No. 128.
Éluard, P. Nazi Song.
Ficowski. Pawiak 1943.
Getsi. Oradour-sur-Glane. Silence.
Hamburger, M. Between the Lines.
Hecht, A. 'More Light! More Light!'.
Heyen. Riddle: "From Belsen a crate of gold teeth."
Hill, G. Christmas Trees.
Ovid in the Third Reich.
Klepfisz. Death Camp.
Lerner, L. Years Later.
MacLean, S. Death Valley.
Niemoller. First they came for the Jews.
Plath. Daddy.
Lady Lazarus.
Pratt, E. From Stone to Steel ("From stone to bronze, from bronze to steel").
Sadoff. Nazis.
Snodgrass, W. Albert Speer.

Nebraska (state)
Guest, B. Nebraska.
Sandburg, C. Limited.
Sunset from Omaha Hotel Window.
Stanton, M. Biography.
Unknown. Kinkaiders, The.

Nebuchadnezzar
Keats. Nebuchadnezzar's Dream.
Wylie. Nebuchadnezzar.

Necrophilia. *See* **Corpses**

Need
Ammons. Needs.
Berry, W. Wild Geese, The.
Burns, R. Grace at Kirkudbright.
Cataldi. It's Easy.
Ceravolo. Spring in This World of Poor Mutts.
Cooper, J. Rent.
Creeley. For W.C.W ("Rhyme is after, The").

Dickinson, E. Undue Significance a starving man attaches.
Drayton. These verses weare made By Michaell Drayton Esquier Poett Lawreatt the night before hee dyed.
Galvin, B. Town Pier Parking Lot.
Koertge. Ubiquity of the Need for Love, The.
Kuzmina-Karavayeva. And copper and worn my farthing.
Mayakovsky. Listen, / if stars are lit.
Now listen! / If the stars shine.
McNair. My Brother Inside the Revolving Doors.
Meynell, A. Modern Mother, The.
Nobuyuki. And Then.
Nye, N. Famous.
Shakespeare, W. Sonnet 75.
Tsvetayeva. You, walking past me.
Walker, A. Did This Happen to Your Mother? Did Your Sister Throw Up a Lot?
Whitman, W. Not heaving from my ribb'd breast only.
Young, A. Dance of the Infidels.
See also **Poverty**

Needles
Bowes-Lyon. Woman Knitting, A.
Cole, H. 40 Days and 40 Nights.
Hall, H. For a Broken Needle.
Kamienska. Matthew 19:16–24; And behold, one came up to him.
Things of This World.
Lear, E. Limericks, I (ii).
Monkhouse. Limericks.
Mother Goose. Old Mother Twitchett had [or has] but one eye.
Rossetti, C. Pin has a head, but has no hair, A.
Unknown. Ode to the Sewing Needle.
Pop Goes the Weasel.
Thread the needle   thread the needle.
Zhao. Needle and Thread.

Nefertiti
Unknown. Queen Nefertiti.

Neglect
Hewitt, J. If I had given you that love and care.
Mahon. Disused Shed in Co. Wexford, A.
Mother Goose. Little Boy Blue, come blow [up] your horn[!].
Silverstein, S. Sarah Cynthia Sylvia Stout Would Not Take the Garbage Out.
Wilbur. Shame.

Negro Spirituals. *See* **Spirituals**

Negroes. *See* **African Americans**

Neighbors
"Alta." Loving your neighbor is all very fine when you have nice.
Biggar. Your Neighbor.
Bower, R. Clothespin, The.
Bronk. Body, The.
Brown, R. I have a neighbor.
Storm high.
Chang Yü. Quatrain: "At this remote village, I have no neighbors."
Dennis, C. Window in Spring, The.
Eady. My Mother, If She Had Won Free Dance Lessons.
Evans, D. Neighbors.
Frost, R. Mending Wall.
Guest, E. Kindly Neighbor, The.
Heaney, S. Other Side, The.
Heywood, J. Quiet Neighbour, A.
Hogan, L. Our Houses.
Hughes, T. My Brother Bert.
Hugo, R. What Thou Lovest Well Remains American.
Jamie. Way We Live, The.
Lawrence, D. Commandments.
Love Thy Neighbour.
Lochhead, L. Grim Sisters, The.
Mathews, H. My Neighbor to the South, the Office Clerk Hsiao, Came in the Evening to Say Good-bye.
Millay, E. Portrait by a Neighbour.
Pape. Minotaur Next Door, The.
Pinsky. Street, The.

Rodgers, C. Slave Ritual.
Smith, A. Roslyn Malamud the Coup.
Tate, J. Neighbors.
Unknown. (My Daily Creed).
Wang Chiu-ssu. Rising from Sleep.
Williams, W. Exercise No. 2.
Yang Chi. Eastern neighbor, western neighbor.
Yang Shih-ch'i. Recording a Dream.
Young, A. Studio Up Over In Your Ear.

Nelson, Horatio Nelson, Viscount
Campbell, T. Battle of the Baltic.
Durrell. Ballad of the Good Lord Nelson, A.
Graves, R. 1805.
Melville, H. *Temeraire,* The.
Newbolt. Admirals All.
Palgrave. Trafalgar.
Seaman, S. England Expects?
Unknown. Death of Nelson, The.

Nepal
Justice, D. Here in Katmandu.
Kipling, R. Sacrifice of Er-Heb, The.

Neptune (god)
Campion, T. Hymn in Praise of Neptune, A.
Homer. Neptune Goes to the Greeks.
Spires. Comb and the Mirror, The.

Nero
Boethius. Book 3, metrum 4.
Cavafy. Nero's Deadline.
Herrick. Cruelties.

Neruda, Pablo
Bly, R. Mourning Pablo Neruda.
Lowther. Last Letter to Pablo.

Nests. *See* Birds' Nests

Netanya, Israel
Wieseltier. Here in Netanya.

Netherlands
Canning, G. Dutch, The.
Cary, P. Leak in the Dike, The.
Unknown. Lowlands o' [*or* of] Holland, The.

Nettles
Bowen, E. Nettles in May.
Thomas, E. Tall Nettles.

Nevada (state)
Emanuel, L. What Ely Was.
Hass, R. Tahoe in August.
Stafford, W. Vacation.

New Brunswick, Canada
Unknown. Banks of the Gaspereaux, The.

New Deal
Whitbread. CCC, The ("CCC campers near West Cummington").

New England
Betjeman. Longfellow's Visit to Venice.
Bradstreet, A. New England.
Braithwaite. House of Falling Leaves, The.
Eliot, T. Cousin Nancy.
Harper, M. History as Apple Tree.
Hooper, E. Better a sin which purposed wrong to none.
Lowell, A. Lilacs.
Lowell, R. Fourth of July in Maine.
Myles, E. New England Wind.
Rakosi. Origins.
Robinson, E. New England.
Thoreau. On Ponkawtasset, since, we took our way.
Tillam. Upon the First Sight of New England, June 29, 1638.
Walcott. Midsummer: XXXI.
Wheatley, P. Farewell to America. To Mrs. S. W, A.
Wild, P. Air Raid.

New Guinea
McAuley, J. New Guinea.

New Hampshire (state)
Brown, R. I want to understand light years.
Eliot, T. New Hampshire.
Hall, D. Granite and Grass.
New Hampshire.
Ruminant pillows! Gregarious soft boulders!
Kinnell. Flower Herding on Mount Monadnock.
Freedom, New Hampshire.
McKay, C. Spring in New Hampshire.
McNair. My Brother Running: V.

Rakosi. Founding of New Hampshire, The.

New Jersey (state)
Ammons. Corsons Inlet.
Anderson, J. Invention of New Jersey, The.
Baraka. Contract. (For The Destruction and Rebuilding of Paterson), A.
De Vries, R. On Alabama Ave., Paterson, NJ, 1954.
Galler. Jersey Marsh, The.
Kennedy, X. In a Prominent Bar in Secaucus [One Day].
Pinsky. Long Branch Song, A.
Whitman, W. Patrolling Barnegat.
Williams, W. Paterson.
Preface: "Rigor of beauty is the quest. But how will you find beauty when it is locked."
Semblables, The.

New Mexico (state)
De Villagrá. World has no such pleasing joy, The.
Deanovich. Road Block: Sante Fe, New Mexico.
Dorn, E. When the Fairies.
Jeffers, R. New Mexican Mountain.
Lawrence, D. Men in New Mexico.
Pettit. Sparrow of Espanola.
Snyder, G. I went into the Maverick Bar.
Wilson, K. Old Women beside a Church.

New Orleans, Louisiana
Cassity. U-24 Anchors off New Orleans.
Dent. For Lil Louis.
Harjo, J. New Orleans.
Jonas, R. Ballade des Belles Milatraisses.
Komunyakaa. Untitled Blues.
Larkin, P. For Sidney Bechet.
Natambu. Funky Butt Legacy Song (An Epic in Progress), The.
Shoaf. Solo, New Orleans.

New Year
Amherst. Song for the Single Table on New Year's Day, A.
Avison. New Year's Poem.
Baranczak, S. Three Magi, The.
Berryman. New Year's Eve.
Bible, *O.T.* New Year, The.
Brathwaite, E. New Year Letter.
Burns, R. Auld Lang Syne.
Carew, T. New Year's Sacrifice: To Lucinda, A.
To the New Year [For the Countess of Carlisle].
Chōkū. Tanka: "Phantom appears, A."
Clare, J. Old Year's gone away, The.
Clifton, L. I am running into a new year.
Davenant. For the Lady Olivia Porter; a Present upon a New Year's Day.
Droste-Hülshoff. Last Day of the Year (New Year's Eve), The.
Fischer, H. New Leaf, A [*or* The].
Fordham. Passing of the Old Year.
Gerondi. Hymn for the Eve of the New Year.
Guest, E. Lord, Make a Regular Man out of Me.
Hardy, T. New Year's Eve.
Herrick. New-Year's [*or* New-Yeares] Gift Sent to Sir Simeon Steward, A.
Hsü Chün-ch'ien. Sitting Up with My Wife on New Year's Eve.
Huang Ching-jen. Sentiments on New Year's Eve in the Year Kuei-ssu.
Jonson, B. New years [*or* yeares], expect new gifts: sister, your harp[e].
Kao Ch'i. Silkworm Song of Torchlit Fields.
Linden, M. Last Day of the Year; or, New Year's Eve, The.
New Year's Morning; or, the First Day of the Year.
Liu E. New Year's Eve.
Lowell, R. New Year's Day.
Mother Goose. I saw three ships come sailing by.
Patchen. At the New Year.
Pien Kung. New Year's Day—Following the Rhymes of Inspector Luan-chiang.
Powers, H. New Year, The.
Sarton. Small Joys.
Shore. High Holy Days.

Su Tung-p'o. End of the Year, The.
Last Day of the Year, The.
New Year's Eve—you'd think I could go home early.
Thompson, P. Old Year, The.
To the New Year.
Tolson. Festus Conrad.
Unknown. Christmas Carol: "God bless the master of this house."
New Year, The.
New Year Carol, A.
Wang T'ing-hsiang. On New Year's Day of the Year Kuei-ssu (1533), Releasing Live Creatures.
Wen Cheng-ming. New Year's Eve.
There was no reason to expect sadness.
Written While Sick.
Year *Chi-wei* (Fifteen Fifty Nine), New Year's Day, The.
Year Hsin-hai (Fifteen Fifty One), New Year's Eve: Keeping Watch, The.
Year I-mao (Fifteen Fifty Five), New Year's Eve, The.
Wilbur. Year's End.

New York City
Applewhite. Prayer for My Son.
Baumel. Thumbs Up.
Bell, M. These Green-going-to-Yellow.
Benét, S. Metropolitan Nightmare.
Berrigan, T. Bean Spasms.
Red Shift.
Bishop, E. Invitation to Miss Marianne Moore.
Letter to N.Y.
Blackburn, P. Slogan, The.
Stone found me in bright sunlight, The.
Blake, J. Sidewalks of New York, The.
Blumenthal, M. Washington Heights, 1959.
Brecht, B. Late Lamented Fame of the Giant City of New York.
Brutus. Off to Philadelphia in the morning.
Christopher. April in New York.
Clampitt. Catalpa Tree on West Twelfth Street, A.
Clifton, H. Euclid Avenue.
Corn. Navidad, St. Nicholas Ave.
Corso. New York City—1935.
Cortez. I Am New York City.
Crane, H. Tunnel, The.
Cummings, E. I was sitting in mcsoreley's. outside it was New York and beauti- / fully snowing.
Dickey, J. Coming Back to America.
Disch. Argument Resumed; Or, Up Through Tribeca, The.
In Praise of New York.
Doty, M. Broadway.
Eiseley. And as for Man.
Equi. Words Read by Lightning.
Esteves. South Bronx Testimonial.
Farber. Manhattan Lullaby.
Feirstein. Mark Stern.
Mark Stern Wakes Up.
Ferlinghetti, L. And Pablo Neruda / that Chilean omnivore of poetry.
Retired Ballerinas, Central Park West.
Reading Yeats.
Field, E. Tulips and Addresses.
Field, R. Manhattan Lullaby.
Fitzgerald, R. Imprisoned, The.
García Lorca. Ode for Walt Whitman.
Ginsberg, A. 'Back on Times Square, Dreaming of Times Square'.
Charnel Ground, The.
My Sad Self.
Glanz-Leyeles. Madison Square.
Gunn, T. Iron Landscapes (and the Statue of Liberty).
Hacker, M. Elysian Fields.
Halliday, M. Seventh Avenue.
Hart, L. Manhattan.
Hays, H. Manhattan.
Holub. One-Way Conversation About Radio City Music Hall, A.
Hopkins, L. Flash.
Hughes, L. Pennsylvania Station in New York, The.
Projection.

Johnson, H.　Bottled [New York].
Johnson, J.　My City.
Kees.　Aspects of Robinson.
Kennedy, X.　B Negative.
Kerouac.　Hymn.
Kleinzahler.　San Francisco/New York.
Koch, K.　Thanksgiving.
Lehman.　Arrival at Kennedy.
Lerman.　Margaret Whiting Tearfully Sings.
Lodge, G.　Lower New York.
Logan, W.　New York.
Lorde.　New York City 1970.
Lowell, R.　Opposite House, The.
Masini.　Nightscape.
Merrill, J.　Urban Convalescence, An.
Miller, S.　I Was on a Golf Course the Day
　John Cage Died of a Stroke.
Moore, M.　New York.
Nash, O.　Theatre Hour.
Newton, B.　Owed to New York.
Oden.　Private Letter to Brazil, A.
　Review from Staten Island.
O'Hara, F.　How to Get There.
　Rhapsody.
　Step Away from Them, A.
　Steps.
　You Are Gorgeous and I'm Coming.
Olds, S.　Summer Solstice, New York City.
Orlovsky.　Poems from Subway to Work.
Padgett, R.　After the Broken Arm.
　Strawberries in Mexico.
Paley, G.　On Mother's Day.
Pietri.　Old Buildings, The.
Polito.　Animal Mimicry.
Pomeroy, R.　High Wind at the Battery.
Ponsot.　Rockefeller the Center.
Reznikoff.　Winter Sketches.
Rich, A.　Upper Broadway.
　Wherever in this city, screens flicker.
Rodriguez, J.　New York Sonnet.
Rukeyser, M.　This is the cripples' hour on
　Seventh Avenue.
Sapia.　Grandmother, a Caribbean Indian,
　Described by My Father.
Schuyler, J.　Let's All Hear It for Mildred
　Bailey!
Senghor.　To New York.
Simpson, L.　Stumpfoot on 42nd Street.
Sissman.　Day in the City, A.
Sobin, G.　Violet City: Aspects of the
　Transitive.
Tate, J.　Contagion.
Towne, C.　Roof-tops, roof-tops, what do you
　cover?
Urdang.　Returning to the Port of Authority: A
　Picaresque.
Vaynshteyn.　Mangin Street.
Waddell, H.　New York City.
Walcott.　Blues.
　God Rest Ye Merry, Gentlemen.
　Village Life, A.
Ware, M.　Understanding Guyana.
Whitman, W.　City of orgies, walks and joys.
　Give me the splendid silent sun with all his
　beams full-dazzling.
　Mannahatta ("I was asking for something
　specific and perfect for my city").
Willis, N.　City Lyrics.
Wright, J.　To the Poets in New York.
Yau.　New York Map Company (1).
Young, A.　Dance of the Infidels.
Zenmaro.　New York.

See also **Broadway, New York City; Bronx,
The, New York City; Brooklyn, New York
City; Harlem, New York City; Rockefeller
Center, New York City**

New York (state)
Allen, W.　Erie Canal, The.
Harper, M.　Grandfather.
Hecht, A.　Sestina d'Inverno.
Hollander, J.　State of Nature, A.
Moss, H.　Long Island Springs.
Unknown.　E-ri-e, The.
Walcott.　Upstate.
Wilbur.　Sleepless at Crown Point.

New Yorker (magazine)
Balaban.　Along the Mekong.

New Zealand
Baxter, J.　East Coast Journey.
　New Zealand.
Curnow.　Landfall in Unknown Seas.
Frame.　Foxes, The.
Vaughan-Thomas.　Farewell to New Zealand.
Newark, New Jersey
Rodgers, C.　Newark, for Now (68).
Newfoundland, Canada
Crane, H.　North Labrador.
Hayman, R.　Pleasant Life in Newfoundland,
　The.
Newgate Prison, London
Hood, T.　Friendly Address, A.
Newman, John Henry, Cardinal
Rossetti, C.　Cardinal Newman.
News
Bishop, E.　12 O'Clock News.
Leapor.　Epistle of Deborah Dough, The.
Leonard, T.　This is thi.
Nye, N.　Blood.
Rosen, M.　Here is the News.
　Here is the News from space.
Salter.　Chernobyl.
Newspapers
Atwood.　It Is Dangerous to Read Newspapers.
Burich.　What do I expect from tomorrow's
　day?
Cain, J.　Someone's newspaper.
Crane, S.　Newspaper is a collection of half
　injustices, A.
Dobson, R.　Country Press.
Eliot, T.　*Boston Evening Transcript*, The.
Jarrell.　Nestus Gurley.
Lehman.　Towards the Vanishing Point.
Masters, E.　Carl Hamblin.
　Daisy Fraser.
　Editor Whedon.
Moorer.　Southern Press, The.
Nemerov.　Picture, A.
Nye, N.　Nobody's newspaper tells what the
　Costa Ricans did.
Owen, W.　Smile, Smile, Smile.
Paulin.　Personal Column.
Plomer.　Headline History.
Prunty.　Reading Before We Read, Horoscope
　and Weather.
St. John, D.　Quote Me Wrong Again and I'll
　Slit the Throat of Your Pet Iguana.
Stanton, M.　Grocery Store, The.
Tsvetayeva.　Readers of Newspapers.
Whittier.　Tent on the Beach: [The Dreamer].
Wilbur.　After the last bulletins the windows
　darken.
Wolfe, H.　You cannot hope.
See also **Journalism and Journalists; Magazines**
Newton, Sir Isaac
Blake, W.　Mock on, Mock on Voltaire,
　Rousseau.
Jarrell.　Emancipators, The.
Pope, A.　Intended for Sir Isaac Newton.
Thomson, J.　All–intellectual eye, our solar
　round.
Unknown.　Sir Isaac Newton.
Newts
Hinsley.　My Newts.
Yang Wei-chen.　Painting Her Nails.
Niagara Falls
Bishop, M.　Public Aid for Niagara Falls.
Drake, J.　Niagara.
Neal, J.　There's a fierce gray Bird, with a
　bending beak.
Nicaragua
Cardenal.　Mosquito Kingdom.
　Tahirassawichi in Washington.
"Dario."　Far Away and Long Ago.
Rodriguez, M.　June 10.
Zamora, D.　Report on the Protest in Front of
　the United States Embassy by the Pino
　Grande Movement, A.
Nigeria
Acholonu.　Nigeria in the Year 1999.
Bekederemo.　Epilogue to Casualties.
Maunick.　Where does this poem come from?
Ojaide.　Launching Our Community
　Developement Fund.

Southerland.　Blue Clay.
　Night in Nigeria.
See also **Civil War, Nigeria**
Night
Akahito.　Black jewel like, The.
Akers.　Night: Volcano, California.
"Akhmatova."　In the Evening.
Al-Harizi.　Secret Kept, A.
Alcaeus.　Evening Song, An.
Alcman.　Fragment: "Mountain summits sleep,
　glens, cliffs, and caves, The."
Amann.　Night train passes, A.
Ashbery.　Morning Jitters.
　Young Prince and the Young Princess, The.
Ausonius.　Evening on the Moselle.
Bachmann.　Invocation of the Great Bear.
　Paris.
　Psalm: "Be still with me, as all bells are still!"
Baillie, J.　Ghost of Edward.
Ball, S.　Nocturnal.
Baraka.　Three Movements and a Coda.
Barbauld.　Summer Evening's Meditation, A.
Barnes, W.　Winter Night, A.
Basho.　Cool it is, and still.
　Fall of night.
Beddoes.　To Night.
Bekederemo.　Night Rain.
Benét, W.　Night.
Bernstein, O.　What She Didn't Say.
Berryman.　Conversation.
Bethell.　Midnight.
Bialik.　Midnight Prayer.
Bible, *O.T.*　Song: "At night on my bed I
　longed for."
Bishop, E.　Man-Moth, The.
Blaga.　Anno Domini.
　In the Mountains.
Blair, R.　New Dawn, A.
Blake, W.　Night.
Bly, R.　Extra Joyful Chorus for Those Who
　Have Read This Far, An.
　Night.
　Solitude Late at Night in the Woods.
Bogan, L.　Night.
Boland, E.　Nocturne.
Borowski.　Night over Birkenau.
Bourdillon.　When Love Is Done.
Bradbury, R.　Switch on the Night.
Brecht, B.　First Psalm (Posthumous).
Bristol.　Night.
Bromley, A.　Slow Men Working in Trees.
Brontë, A.　Night.
Brontë, C.　What does she dream of, lingering
　all alone.
Brooke, R.　Day That I Have Loved.
　Song of the Beasts (Sung, on one night, in the
　cities, in the darkness), The.
Brown, J.　Rhapsody, Written at the Lakes in
　Westmorland, A.
Brownell, H.　Night-Quarters.
Browning, R.　Meeting At Night.
Brutus.　At night.
　Nightsong: City.
Byron, G.　She walks in Beauty like the night.
　So we'll go no more a-roving.
Campion, T.　Now winter nights enlarge.
Cane.　Hymn to Night.
Carlyle, T.　Today.
Carter, E.　Ode to Wisdom.
Carver, R.　Window, The.
Causley.　Coming from Evening Church.
Cawein.　Orgie.
Celan.　Little night: when you.
Cervantes.　Colorado Blvd.
Césaire, A.　Different Horizon.
Chang Chi.　Tying Up for the Night at Maple
　River Bridge.
Chikako.　On this summer night.
Chipasula.　Dusk.
Chōku.　Tanka: "Late at night in the kitchen."
　Tanka: "Train speeds on, The."
Chu Yi-tsun.　Tune: "Song of the Southern
　Country."
Clough.　Darkness.
Codrescu.　Work.
Congreve.　See, see, she wakes, Sabina wakes!
Cope, W.　At 3 A.M.

Crane, H.   In Shadow.
Crane, S.   I explain the silvered passing of a ship at night.
   Little birds of the night.
Crawford, I.   Battle, A.
   Dark Stag, The.
Creeley.   Chasing the Bird.
   Somewhere.
   Son: "What I took in my hand."
Cristofor.   Night Traveller.
Cronin, A.   Elegy for the Nightbound.
Cullen, C.   Night Rain.
Cumbo.   Nocturnal Sounds.
Cummings, E.   Impression.
Darwish, M.   Steps in the Night.
Davies, W.   Nightfall.
Davies, W.   Hour of Magic, The.
Davis, F.   Flowers of Darkness.
   Four Glimpses of Night.
de Jesús.   Curfew.
De la Mare.   Peace.
   Silver.
De Tabley.   Nuptial Song.
Deane, S.   Power Cut.
Ded.   On the way to God the difficulties.
Desnos.   St Merri district, The.
Devi.   This Night.
Dickinson, E.   First Day's Night had come, The.
   Good Morning—Midnight.
   Of Bronze—and Blaze.
   Wild Nights—Wild Nights!
Diop, B.   Diptych.
Djagarov.   Night.
Dodd, W.   Of Rain and Air.
Dogen.   On the Treasury of the True Dharma Eye.
Doolittle, H.   Evening.
Dove, R.   Nigger Song: An Odyssey.
Dransfield.   Endsight.
Drayton.   Night and Day.
Drinkwater.   Moonlit Apples.
Drummond, W.   Madrigal: "Unhappie [or Unhappy] Light."
Eberhart, R.   Concord Cats.
Edwards, M.   I Love the Night.
Ehrhart.   Night Patrol.
Eigner.   For Sleep.
Eisenhuth.   Night in the Village.
Ekelof.   For night comes.
   If you ask me where I am.
Eliot, T.   Rhapsody on a Windy Night.
"Ern Malley."   Night Piece.
Evans, M.   Mushrooms grew / Overnight.
Farber.   Manhattan Lullaby.
   Taking Turns.
Farjeon, E.   Good Night.
   Light the Lamps Up, Lamplighter!
   Night Will Never Stay, The.
Fatchen.   Night Walk.
Ferguson, J.   Auld Daddy Darkness creeps frae his hole.
"Field."   Nightfall.
Field, R.   Manhattan Lullaby.
Finch, A.   Nocturnal Reverie, A.
Fontanella.   In the nighttime someone in my place.
Fox, S.   In the evening.
Fraire.   If night takes the form of a whale and.
Francis, R.   Dog-Day Night.
   Night Train.
Frost, R.   Acquainted with the Night.
   Two Tramps in Mud Time.
   Were I in Trouble.
Fumiko.   Tanka: "When the lights go out."
García Lorca.   Sketches.
   Sleepwalkers' Ballad.
Garstin.   Nocturne: "Red flame flowers bloom and die, The."
Gheorghe.   Moonlit nights on the Atlantic Ocean!
Gilbo'a.   Our Dreams.
Ginsberg, A.   Last Night in Calcutta.
Gioia.   Country Wife, The.
Glaser, E.   Undead White European Male.
Glück, L.   Night Piece.
   Pond, The.

Godfrey.   What It Takes.
Goedicke.   On the Night in Question.
Goethe.   Meeting, the Departure, The.
Goldbarth.   Hey Sweetie.
Goodison.   Always homing now soul toward light.
Gould, A.   Observed Observer, The.
Gouri.   Piraeus.
Graves, R.   Frosty Night, A.
Greger.   Air-Conditioned Air.
Grimké, A.   For the Candle Light.
Grunthal.   And thus a monologue keeps flowing.
Gu Cheng.   Generation, A.
Guha.   Winding Sand.
Hagiwara Sakutaro.   Spring Night.
Haines, J.   Foreboding.
   If the Owl Calls Again.
Hall, H.   Walkers at Dusk.
Hanson, P.   So Beautiful Is the Tree of Night.
Hardy, T.   Shut Out That Moon.
Hare, A.   Walking at Night.
Harrison, J.   Lullaby for a Daughter.
Hayden, R.   O Daedalus, Fly Away Home.
Heard, J.   Night.
Hemans.   Night-Blooming Flowers.
Herrick.   Dream[e]s.
   Night-Piece, to Julia, The.
   No Difference in the Dark [or i'th'dark].
   To Daisies, Not to Shut So Soon[e].
Hitchcock.   Song of Expectancy.
Hitomaro.   On the Eastern horizon.
Hongo.   Yellow Light.
Hood, T.   Nocturnal Sketch, A.
Hopkins, G.   How looks the night? There does not miss a star.
   Tom's Garland: Upon the Unemployed.
Horovitz, F.   Night-Piece.
Hotham.   Every night.
   Night comes.
Housman, A.   Crossing alone the nighted ferry.
Hoyt, C.   In that lightning flash.
Hughes, L.   Chord.
   My People.
Hughes, T.   Thought-Fox, The.
Hugo, V.   Good night! Good night! / Far flies the light.
Hwang Chin-i.   I cut in two / A long November night.
Ishikawa Takuboku.   Tanka: "Has Fate sneaked in."
   Tanka: "Sorrow."
Issahakian.   For you fleas too.
Izen.   As the late night passes.
Jaccottet.   Letter of the 26th June.
   Right at the end of night.
Jarrell.   Bird of Night, The.
Jeffers, R.   Night.
   Watch the Lights Fade.
Jennings, E.   At Night.
   In the Night.
Jewell.   Finding this cavern.
John of the Cross.   Dark Night, The.
Johnson, J.   Mother Night.
Jones, L. et al.   World Is Full of Remarkable Things, The.
József.   Freight trains are pulling in.
Juan Chi.   Deep in the night and unable to sleep.
Juvenal.   Prepare for Death, if here at Night you roam.
Kanemasa.   Awaji Island—.
Kannan.   What Her Girl Friend Said to Him.
Kaplinski, J.   Like a black hedgehog.
Keats.   In drear-nighted December.
Kelly, B.   Leaving, The.
Kenney.   Apples on Champlain.
Kerouac.   146th Chorus.
Keyser.   Rainy summer night.
Kingsley, C.   "Watchman, what of the night?"
Kinsella, T.   Endymion.
Kitahara Hakushū.   Tanka: "Ailing child, An."
   Tanka: "Gasoline."
Kolmar.   Judith.
Komunyakaa.   Starlight Scope Myopia.
Kooser.   Late Lights in Minnesota.
Kovner.   Dimmed Observation.

Kumin, M.   Sound of Night, The.
Kunio.   Tanka: "As night falls."
Kunitz, S.   Image-Maker, The.
   Science of the Night, The.
Lalic.   Love in July.
Lane, P.   Nocturne: "Listening for the sound."
Lanier, S.   Song for "The Jacquerie."
Larkin, P.   Night-Music.
   Sad Steps.
Le Gallienne.   Ballad of London, A.
Lehman.   Spontaneous Combustion.
Lehmann, G.   Song for Past Midnight.
Leuty.   Night, The.
Levchev.   Last night I was coming back home alone.
Levertov.   Eye Mask.
Levin, P.   Night Coach.
Levine, P.   Simple Truth, The.
Lewis, A.   Sentry, The.
Li Ho.   For the Examination at Ho-nan-fu:
   Songs of the Twelve Months.
Li Po.   Verses: "Clean is the autumn wind."
Li Shang-yin.   Night Chill.
Lin Hung.   Sailing at Night on Flowing-sand River.
Linden, M.   Silent Night, The.
Livingston, M.   Night / creeps in, The.
Lloyd, D.   Longest night, The.
Longfellow, H.   Day is done, and the darkness, The.
   Hymn to the Night.
   Night.
Lovelace, R.   Night! loathed [or loathèd] jailor of the locked-up [or lock'd up] sun.
Lowell, A.   Garden by Moonlight, The.
   Interlude.
   Night Clouds.
Lowell, R.   Night Sweat.
Loy.   Three Moments in Paris.
Lu T'ung.   Eclipse of the Moon, The.
Lu Yu.   I Walk Out into the Country at Night.
   Sitting Up at Night.
   Tune: "Immortal at the Magpie Bridge"—On Hearing the Cuckoo at Night.
Lyles.   Summer night.
MacCaig.   Spate in Winter Midnight.
"MacDiarmid."   Eemis-Stane, The.
Machado Ruiz.   Summer Night.
Mackey, N.   Memphite Recension.
MacLeish.   You, Andrew Marvell.
Mahon.   Globe in North Carolina, The.
Mandelstam.   I Was Washing Outside in the Darkness.
Mangan, G.   Nights in Black Valley.
Marichiko.   I cannot forget.
Marlowe.   Now ore the sea from her old Love comes she.
Martin, J.   God's Dark.
Marvell.   Mower to the Glow-Worms [or Glowworms or Glo-Worms], The.
Masaoka Shiki.   All the hot night.
   Spring night.
   Tanka: "Illuminated."
   Tanka: "On a young pine."
   Tanka: "Peacefully."
   Wild geese cry, The.
Masini.   Nightscape.
Mayakovsky.   It's already past one. You'll have gone to bed.
McAuley, J.   Nocturne.
McClellan.   September Night, A.
McClintock, M.   Hearing.
   Tonight. . . wishing.
McCord, D.   This Is My Rock.
McGough, R.   Bully night / I do not like.
McGrath, T.   Guiffre's Nightmusic.
   Nocturne Militaire.
McKay, L.   Night.
McMaster, R.   Back Steps Lookout.
   Clockface.
McOrlan.   Battery woman.
Mead, P.   There.
Mei Yao Ch'en.   Swarming Mosquitoes.
Melville, H.   Night-March, The.
Meng Hao Jan.   Night on the Great River.
   Passing the Night on a River in Chien-te.

Spending the Night at the Hillside Lodge of Master Yeh and Waiting for My Friend Ting.
Meredith, W. Recollection of Bellagio.
Merriam, E. Lullaby "Purple."
Merwin, W. Voyage to Labrador.
Meynell, A. At Night.
Mezey. Confession, A.
Michelson, M. Hymn to Night, A.
Mihalic. Drinking Spree Beneath the Open Sky.
Miliauskaite. On winter nights, when my grandmother.
Millay, E. Night is my sister, and how deep in love.
Miller, V. Aubade: "I press against the emptiness."
Miyazawa Kenji. Tanka: "Bloodshot."
Montague, J. Walking Late.
Montale. Day and Night.
 Little Testament.
Montgomerie, A. Night Is Near [or Neir] Gone, The.
Moore, T. Echo.
 Oft in the stilly night.
Mori Ōgai. Tanka: "Close by the host."
 Tanka: "Step by step."
Mother Goose. To sleep easy at night.
Mountain, M. On this cold.
 Summer night clothes whirling in a dryer.
Nagy, A. Ikhnaton's Night.
Nguyên Chí Thiện. Jungle night—it rains and rains, roofs leak, A.
Nicholls, J. Earthset.
Nicholson, J. On a Calm Summer's Night.
Nobuyuki. Third-Class Car on a Night Train (three poems).
Nortje. Up Late.
Nyka-Niliunas. Before Dawn.
Olsen, W. Tomorrow.
Ono no Komachi. He does not come.
Oppen. Animula.
Orten. Last Poem, The.
Osundare. Frantic as a prentice poet.
Otsuji. Winter midnight.
Owl Woman. Songs for the Four Parts of the Night.
Padgett, R. Poema del City 2.
 With Lee Remick at Midnight.
Paquet. Night Dust-off.
Pasternak, B. Night.
Patchen. In the footsteps of the walking air.
Patterson, R. Night-Piece.
Plumly. Complaint Against the Arsonist.
Po Chü-i. Rain.
 Sitting at Night.
 Village Night.
 Winter Night.
Popa. Ashes.
 Eyes of a Wolf.
Pope, A. Reign of Chaos, The.
Porumbacu. From what once was, from the crazy nights.
Posey, A. Nightfall.
Rabéarivelo. Black glassmaker, The.
 Hide of the black cow is stretched, The.
Radcliffe, A. Night.
Ransetsu. Deep in the night.
Reese, L. One Night.
Reeves, J. Time to go home!
Reznikoff House-wreckers have left the door and a staircase, The.
Rice, J. I am. . . Star Counting.
Rilke. First Duino Elegy, The.
Robinson, E. John Evereldown.
Rodgers, W. Stormy Night.
Roethke. In a dark time, the eye begins to see.
Rossetti, C. From Sunset to Star Rise.
 Is the moon tired? she looks so pale.
Rotella, A. Starrynightenteryourmirror.
Rukeyser, M. Eyes of Night-Time.
 Night-Music.
 Time Exposures.
Rumi. Totally conscious, and appropos of nothing, he comes to see me.
Sachs, N. But look / but look.
 You / in the night.

St. John, D. Avenues, The.
Salom. Walking at Night.
Samio. Tanka: "On a starry night."
Sanchez, S. Poem at Thirty.
Sandburg, C. Nocturne in a Deserted Brickyard.
 Skyscraper.
 Window.
Sappho. Moon has veil'd her Silver Light, The.
Sassoon. Falling Asleep.
Scott, W. Melrose Abbey.
Senghor. After this day's hope—see how the Somme, the Seine, and the wild Slav.
 Before night comes I think of you and for you before I fall.
 I am alone in the plains.
 I walked you to the village where the granaries are at the threshold of Night.
 Visit.
Sexton. Starry Night, The.
Sharp, W. Field Mouse, The.
Shelley, P. Stanzas—April, 1814.
 To Jane ("Keen stars were twinkling, The").
 To Night.
Shen Yüeh. Spending the Night in the Eastern Park.
Shirley, J. Good-night.
Shūji. Tanka: "As if it came."
 Tanka: "Over my."
 Tanka: "Red flowers."
Sidney, P. Night.
 Sonnet 99: "When far-spent night persuades each mortal eye."
Sidney, R. Songe 17: "Sun is set, and masked night, The."
Simpson, L. After Midnight.
Sitwell, D. Madwoman in the Park, The.
Slessor. Choker's Lane.
 Night-Ride, The.
Smith, C. To the Moon.
Smith, S. Goodnight.
Snyder, G. Pine Tree Tops.
Solomon ibn Gabirol. Night, and the heavens beam serene with peace.
Sorrentino. Classic Case, A.
Soto. Soup, The.
Soupault. Condemned.
Soyinka. Night.
Spires. Good Friday. Driving Weekend.
Stevens, W. Candle a Saint, The.
 Girl in a Nightgown.
 God is Good. It Is a Beautiful Night.
 Re-statement of Romance.
 Reader, The.
Stevenson, A. Sonnet: "If it be night. . . ."
Stevenson, R. Bed in Summer.
 Escape at Bedtime.
 Moon has a face like the clock in the hall, The.
 Sick Child, The.
 Windy Nights.
 Young Night Thought.
Stumbrs. Light, Late Song for Solo Voice Without Piano, A.
Su Shih. In a boat, Getting Up at Night.
 Tune: "Prelude to Water Music."
Su Tung-p'o. In a Boat, Getting Up at Night.
 Spring night—one hour worth a thousand gold coins.
Sueyoshi. Crying plovers, The.
Sullivan, C Nights along the River.
Sutu. Night, and on all sides only the folding quiet.
Swede. Night begins to gather between her breasts.
 Summer night.
Swinburne. Garden of Proserpine, The.
Symonds. To Night, the Mother of Sleep and Death.
Szymborska. Four in the Morning.
Tahmisic. Letter to a Friend.
 Stone and Stars.
T'an Yüan-ch'un. Heard on a Boat.
Taylor, J. Fairies' Song, The.
Star, The.

Teasdale. August Night.
 Night.
Teika. Spring night's, The.
Teller. Minor Key.
Thomas, E. Out in the dark over the snow.
Thompson, P. Winter Night, A.
Todd, R. Paul Klee.
Toshinari. I remember a grass hut.
Trakl. Downfall.
 Evening, The.
 Grodek.
 Rats, The.
 Revelation and Decline.
 Romance to Night, A.
Tranströmer. Track.
Trench, H. She Comes Not When Noon Is on the Roses.
Trudell. Hotel in Paris.
Ts'ao P'i. Deep and boundless, the long autumn night.
Tsurayuki. When.
Tsvetayeva. Black as[—] the centre of an eye, the centre, a blackness.
Tu Fu. Coming Home Late at Night.
 Homecoming—Late at Night.
 Midnight.
 New Moon.
 Night.
 Night in the House by the River.
 Night Thoughts While Travelling.
 Restless Night.
 Restless Night in Camp, A.
 Summer Night.
 Tired Night, A.
 Traveler at Night Writes His Thoughts, A.
 Travelling Northward.
 Two Poems on Night.
 Waiting for Audience on a Spring Night.
Unknown. Bright moon white and silver, The.
 Clear full moon.
 Crow caws in the moonlight, A.
 How Is the Night?
 In the Night.
 Moon is full, The.
 Night was growing cold, The.
 Our love is infinite.
 Shall we stay in the.
 Though the purity.
Van den Heuvel. Hot night.
Venclova. Night descended on us with a chill.
Very. Morning Watch, The.
Vogel, D. How Can I See You, Love.
Walcott. God Rest Ye Merry, Gentlemen.
 Nights in the Gardens of Port of Spain.
Wallāda. Wait till the darkness is deep.
Wang Shih-chieng. Moonlit Night at Fragrant Mountain Temple.
Warren, R. Birth of Love.
Webb, F. Hospital Night.
 Port Phillip Night.
Weiners. Acts of Youth, The.
Welch, L. Empress herself served tea to Su Tung-po, The.
Westwood. Night of Spring.
Wheatley, P. Hymn to the Evening, An.
White, J. To Night.
Whitman, W. Night on the Prairies.
 On the beach at night.
Whittemore, R. Still Life.
Wilbur. After the last bulletins the windows darken.
Williams, H. To the Moon.
Williams, W Good Night.
 Goodnight, A.
Wilson, K. Dusk in My Backyard.
Winchilsea. Nocturnal Reverie, A.
Wordsworth, W. I watch, and long have watched, with calm regret.
Wright, C. Clear Night[, thumb-top of a moon, a back-lit sky].
Wright, J. Camphor Laurel.
Wroth. From Pamphilia to Amphilanthus.
 Sonnet 1: "When night's [or nights] black mantle could most darknes prove."
 Sonnet 19: "Come darkest night, be[e]coming sorrow best."
Yakamochi. Frost lies white, The.

Yang Wan-li. Cold Lantern, The.
  Sitting at Night on the Moon-viewing Terrace.
Ye. All night I could not sleep.
Yolen. Dragon Night.
  Shepherd's Night Count.
Yosano. At the beginning.
  Hair unbound, in this.
Yoshimi. Tanka: "Spoon, A."
Yuhara. Let us bribe the Moon God.
Yukitsuna. Tanka: "Amid the waves of time."
Zabolotsky. Signs of the Zodiac are fading, The.

See also **Evening**

Nightclubs
Davis, F. Jazz Band.
Elmslie, K. Amazon Club.
Hughes, L. Jam Session.
  Jazz Band in a Parisian Cabaret.
  Jazzonia.
  Neon Signs.
MacNeice. Night Club.
McClure, M. Jazz at the Intergalactic Nightclub.
Scott, F. Night Club.
Tolson. Mu.
Weaver, M. Left Bank Jazz Society, The.

Nighthawks
Berry, W. September 2.

Nightingales
Arnold, M. Philomela.
Barnfield. Philomel.
Blake, W. Lark's Song, The.
Blind. Russian Student's Tale, The.
Bridges, R. Nightingales.
Browning, E. Bianca Among the Nightingales.
Carstairs. Nightingale.
Clare, J. Nightingale, The.
Coleridge, S. Nightingale, The.
Cook, E. Lines / Suggested by the Song of a Nightingale.
Cowper, W. Nightingale and the Glowworm, The.
Fulbert of Chartres. To the Nightingale.
Kornilov, B. My Nightingale.
Lindsay, V. Chinese Nightingale, The.
Marvell. Mower to the Glow-Worms [*or* Glowworms *or* Glo-Worms], The.
Milton. O Nightingale, that on yon bloomy Spray.
Monro. Nightingale near the House, The.
Randolph, T. On the Death of a Nightingale.
Ransom, J. Philomela.
Sidney, P. Nightingale as soone as Aprill bringeth, The.
Sitwell, D. Prelude.
Smith, C. On the Departure of the Nightingale.
Tynan. Nightingale, The.
Unknown. Happy Nightingale, The.
  Sparrow-Hawk, A.
Winchilsea. To the Nightingale.
Yakamochi. Mist floats on the Spring meadow.

Nightmares
Browning, R. Bad Dreams.
Cisneros, S. Poet Reflects On Her Solitary Fate, The.
Douglas, L. To Sleep.
Dove, R. Nightmare.
Fatchen. I often meet a monster.
Fumiko. Tanka: "For this."
Gardner, I. Nightmare.
Glück, L. Night Piece.
Graves, R. Lost Jewel, A.
Harper, M. Nightmare Begins Responsibility.
Holtby, W. Trains in France.
Hugo, R. In Your Bad Dream.
Jeffers, R. Apology for Bad Dreams.
MacNeice. Bad Dream.
Sarton. Tortured, The.
Summerfield. Sci-fi Horrorscopes.
Trypanis. Cock at Sea.
Tsvetkov. I had a dream. I walked in a field of feather grass.
Wang Yen-Shou. Nightmare, The.
Warren, R. Original Sin.

See also **Dreams and Dreaming**

Nihilism
Crane, S. Man said to the universe, A.
Creeley. Rhythm, The.
Hull, L. Holy City, City of Night.
Lowell, R. Nihilist as Hero, The.
Rochester, J. Upon Nothing.
Seneca. Seneca's Troas, Act 2. Chorus.

Nijinsky, Vaslav
Tyler, P. Nijinsky.

Nile, Battle of the (1798)
Moore, M. New York.

Nile (river)
Blind. Beautiful Beeshareen Boy, The.
"Carroll." Crocodile, The.
Hunt, L. Nile, The.
Unknown. Nile the Hermit.

1960s
Allen, D. Short History of the Vietnam War Years, A.
"Dylan." Ballad of a Thin Man.
  It's Alright, Ma (I'm Only Bleeding).
García. Barrio Beateo.
Ginsberg, A. Crossing Nation.
  Wichita Vortex Sutra, Part I.
Hacker, M. Nights of 1964–1966: The Old Reliable.
Hilton, D. Finding a Chet Baker Album in the Dimestore 2-for-$1 Pile.
La Loca. Why I Choose Black Men for My Lovers.
Piercy. Learning Experience.
Smith, P. What It's Like to Be a Black Girl (For Those of You Who Aren't).
Tillinghast, R. Our Flag Was Still There.
Van Duyn. What the Motorcycle Said.

Niobe
Ray, H. Niobe.
Tsatsos. Chios.

Nixon, Richard Milhous
Di Prima. Brief Wyoming Meditation.
Hayes, A. *Much Ado About Nothing,* Thanksgiving, 1972.
Whalen. Regalia in Immediate Demand!
Woddis. Final Curtain.

Nkrumah, Kwame
Di Prima. Goodbye Nkrumah.

Noah
"Adunis." New Noah, The.
Brown, W. Noah.
Caedmon. Noah's Flood.
Chesterton, G. Wine and Water.
Drayton. Hundred years the Ark in the building was, A.
Duncan, R. Ballad of Mrs. Noah, The.
Heath-Stubbs. History of the Flood, The.
  Kingfisher, The.
Higgins, F. Captain Noah.
Kendall, M. Vision of Noah, The.
Lewis, C. Late Passenger, The.
"MacDiarmid." Parley of Beasts.
Marquis. Noah an' Jonah an' Cap'n John Smith.
Mayer, G. Noah.
McGough, R. Noah's Ark.
Muir, E. Ballad of the Flood.
Ombres. Ballad of Noah's Daughter.
Reeves, J. Noah was an Admiral.
Unknown. Hammer, Ring.
Van Doren. And did the animals in Noah's ark.
Wilbur. Still, citizen sparrow, this vulture which you call.
Young, M. Noah's Ark.

Nobility
Brough, R. My Lord Tomnoddy's the son of an Earl,.
Campion, T. What fair pomp have I spied of glittering ladies.
Gray, T. On Lord Holland's Seat near Margate, Kent.
Lanyer. Description of Cooke-ham, The.
Unknown. Encountering Sorrow.
  Knight and Shepherd's Daughter, The.

Noises
Ball, H. Flight out of Time.

Bateman, D. My Rocking Chair.
Dickinson, E. Saddest noise, the sweetest noise, The.
Dunbar, P. When Malindy Sings.
Eigner. It Sounded.
Francis, R. Sound I Listened For, The.
Hewitt, J. King's Horses, The.
Kinnell. After Making Love We Hear Footsteps.
Lovelace, R. To a Lady That Desired Me I Would Bear My Part with Her in a Song.
Marinetti. Landscape Heard, A.
Marsh, D. Mice.
McAuley, J. Dialogue.
McElroy, C. Illusion.
McHugh, H. Spilled.
Morgan, E. Loch Ness Monster's Song, The.
Plath. Night Shift.
Unknown. Bald Mountain Zaum-Poems.
  Smoke-Blackened Smiths.

Noon
Arp. Domestic Stones (fragment), The.
Bachmann. Early Noon.
Clampitt. Meridian.
Clare, J. Noon.
Corbett, W. Cold Lunch.
Dickinson, E. It's like the Light.
Jeffers, R. Noon.
Meynell, A. Study, A.
Montale. To rest at noon, pale and absorbed.
Moore, L. Summer noon.
Mori Ōgai. Tanka: "On a post."
Nichols, R. Noon.
Radauskas. Harbor.
Xuanjing. Meditating at midnight.

Normandy, Invasion of (1944)
Simpson, L. Carentan O Carentan.

North Carolina (state)
Glück, L. Cottonmouth Country.
Mahon. Globe in North Carolina, The.

"North, Christopher" (John Wilson)
Tennyson, A. To Christopher North.

North Dakota (state)
MacDonald, C. Instruction from Bly.
Wright, J. Outside Fargo, North Dakota.
  Poem Written under an Archway in a Discontinued Railroad Station, Fargo, North Dakota, A.
  To Flood Stage Again.

North Pole
Hejinian. Polar Circle, The.
Jarrell. 90 North.
Roughton. Soluble Noughts and Crosses; or, California, Here I Come.
Worth, V. Magnet.

North, The, United States
Alexander, E. Letter: Blues.
Crouch, S. Blackie Thinks of His Brothers.
Momaday. Winter Holding off the Coast of North America.

North Wind
Lindsay, V. Moon's the North Wind's cooky, The.
Mphahlele. Exile in Nigeria.
Unknown. Blow, Northern Wind.
  Cold Is the North Wind.

Northern Ireland
Bentley, N. Londonderry Air, The.
Deane, S. Derry.
  Northern Ireland: Two Comments.
Heaney, S. Casualty.
  Strand at Lough Beg, The.
  Ulster Twilight, An.
  Whatever You Say Say Nothing.
Kipling, R. Ulster.
MacNeice. Carrickfergus.
Paulin. Of Difference Does It Make.
  Settlers.
Unknown. Omagh Post Office Rhyme.

See also **Listings for specific Counties**

Northumberland, England
Halleck, F. Alnwick Castle.

Northwest Territories, Canada
Yates, J. I persist in a little fabric between me and the world.

Noses
Allen, M. What Is It?
Bierce. Nose.
Clark, L. There was a man whose nose was long.
Dufferin. Mother's Lament, The.
Forrester. To My Nose.
Herrick. Upon Lulls.
Lear, E. Dong with a Luminous Nose, The.
Milligan, S. Granny.
Pope, A. Gulliver in Lilliput.
Smith, I. Nose went away by itself, The.
Starbird. Hound, The.
Turberville. Of One That Had a Great Nose.
Unknown. Choosing a Kitten.
Of Tyndarus, That Frumped a Gentlewoman.
On Proclus's Great Nose.
Williams, W. Smell.

Nostalgia
Adcock, B. Southbound.
Bernstein, C. When My Grandmother Said "Pussy."
Berrigan, T. Red Shift.
Boss. At the Nuclear Rally.
Buckley, C. Nostalgia.
Carlile. Train Whistles in the Wind and Rain.
Carnevale. Walking by the Cliffside Dyeworks.
Cassity. Epigoni Go French Line.
Cavalieri. First, The.
Chappell, F. My Grandmother Washes Her Feet.
Chong, C. Nostalgic Urge.
Clare, J. O could I be as I have been.
Coleridge, M. Where a Roman Villa Stood, above Freiburg.
Coleridge, S. Lines Written in the Album at Elbingerode, in the Hartz Forest.
Conn. On Craigie Hill.
Yard is littered with scrap, with axles, The.
Cook, E. Song of the Modern Time.
Daniel, Y. House, A.
Daniels, K. My Father's Desk.
Davie. Remembering the 'Thirties.
Dawe, G. Likelihood of Snow, The/ The Danger of Fire.
Delone. Ballad of Fate.
Dickey, J. Shark's Parlor, The.
Doolittle, H. Blue-geese, white-geese, you may say.
Drainac. Then, the drops were freezing on black branches of ancient ash trees.
Durcan. Around the corner from Francis Bacon.
Eliot, T. Marina.
Emanuel, L. Self-Portrait at Eighteen.
Fiacc. First Movement.
Frost, R. Range-finding.
García. Barrio Beateo.
Gilmore, M. Saturday Tub, The.
Ginsberg, A. After Yeats.
Glaser, M. Changing Address Books.
English-Speaking Persons Will Find Translations.
Googe. Goyng towardes Spayne.
Hamod, S. Leaves.
Hardy, T. After A Journey.
Lines to a Movement in Mozart's E-Flat Symphony.
Old Furniture.
Heissenbüttel. Homesick.
Heitzman. March.
Hemans. Nature's Farewell.
Hernandez, D. Armitage Street.
Holden, J. Against Paradise.
Howells, W. November.
Hughes, L. Po' Boy Blues.
Hugo, R. Places and Ways to Live.
Hunt, L. To Hampstead.
Hwang, S. Small Love Song, A.
Ivanov, G. I imagine everything wrapped in a beatific mist.
Jarrell. Player Piano, The.
Jones, R. Progress Alley.
Sweep.
Justice, D. Thinking about the Past.

Kipling, R. King, The.
Lovers' Litany, The.
Kleinzahler. Hamburger.
Kumin, M. For My Great-Grandfather: A Message Long Overdue.
Height of the Season, The.
Lamb, C. Old Familiar Faces, The.
Lawrence, D. Nostalgia.
Piano.
Lehman. Arrival at Kennedy.
Levis. Widening Spell of the Leaves, The.
Lewis, A. All day it has rained, and we on the edge of the moors.
Li Po. Thinking of East Mountain.
Lim, S. Black and White.
Longley, M. Leaving Inishmore.
Lysaght, S. Deserted Home, A.
MacBeth. Renewal, The.
MacNeice. Nostalgia.
Mahon. Achill.
McDonald, P. Pleasures of the Imagination.
Sunday in Great Tew.
McElroy, C. From Homegrown: An Asian-American Anthology of Writers.
McFadden, R. First Letter to an Irish Novelist.
My Mother's Young Sister.
McGuckian. Little House, Big House.
McMahon, L. Little Elegy for the Age.
Melville, H. Aeolian Harp, The.
Archipelago, The.
Temeraire, The.
Meng Hao Jan. Night on the Great River.
Meredith, G. It is the season of the sweet wild rose.
Mezey. Stream Flowing, The.
Mitsui. Because of My Father's Job.
Monette. Brother of the Mount of Olives.
Montague, J. Hearth Song.
Mura. To H.N.
Myers, J. Have a Nice Day.
Neale. Oh, Give Us Back the Days of Old!
Norton, C. My Childhood's Home.
O Direain. Axle Song.
O'Grady, D. Homecoming.
Okita Nice Thing About Counting Stars, The.
Patchen. Street Corner College.
Peacock, T. In the days of old.
Pound, E. E. P. Ode Pour l'Election de Son Sepulchre.
Ramke. Nostalgia.
Reed, I. Reactionary Poet, The.
Rich, A. Living Memory.
Riley, J. Days Gone By, The.
Robinson, E. Miniver Cheevy, child of scorn.
Ruark. For a Suicide, a Little Early Morning Music.
Ryan, J. Pawntickets.
Ryan, M. Switchblade.
Sackville-West. Nostalgia.
Schwartz, L. 78's.
Shengeli. Derzhavin.
Simmons, J. One of the Boys.
Stephano Remembers.
Smith, I. Lewis 1928–45.
Smith, J. Mandolin.
Snodgrass, W. Mementos, 1.
Song. Father and Daughter.
Spender, S. I think continually of those who were truly great.
Stafford, W. Farm on the Great Plains, The.
Stevenson, R. Bright is the ring of words.
Home no more home to me, whither must I wander?
I saw red evening through the rain.
Stickney, T. Quiet after the rain of morning.
Su Tung-p'o. Beginning of Autumn: A Poem to Send to Tzu-yu.
Taylor, H. Flying Change, The.
Tennyson, A. Break, break, break.
Thorson. Closed Doors.
Trinidad. Movin' with Nancy.
Tu Fu. Passing Chao-ling Again.
Tynan. Farewell: "Not soon shall I forget—a sheet."
Unknown. Aching nostalgia—.
Auld Lang Syne.
Vaughan, H. Retreat[e], The.

Victor, G. That old mulemba.
Villanueva, T. Haciendo Apenas la Recolección.
Voigt. Landscape, Dense with Trees.
Wang Yü-ch'eng. Journey to a Village.
Warton, T. Sonnet: To the River Lodon.
Weaver, M. Blind Solo.
Weigl. Meditation at Pearl Street.
Williams, W. Raleigh Was Right.
Wong, N. Dreams in Harrison Railroad Park.
Woodworth. Bucket, The.
Wright, C. Arkansas Traveller.
Other Side of the River, The.
Wright, J. Sisters, The.
Wu of Han. Song of the Autumn Wind.
Yeats. He Remembers Forgotten Beauty.
Young, D. Other Obit.

Nothingness
Amichai. Like our bodies' imprint.
Beck, T. Sonnet to Nothing.
Benn. Fragments, / Refuse of the soul.
Bevington, L. Midnight.
Cage. Lecture on Nothing.
Coolidge, C. Saturday Night.
Creeley. Fancy.
Cummings, E. Now does our world descend.
DiPalma. Bed, The.
Donne. Negative Love.
Ekelof. Like ankle-rings, this music.
Fletcher, P. To Thomalin.
Gilbert-Lecomte. Preface or The Drama of Absence in an Eternal Heart.
Hadewijch II. Tighten.
Hood, T. No sun—no moon!
Jabès. Notebook, Two.
Jackson, L. Nothing so far but moonlight.
Juana Inés de la Cruz. This coloured counterfeit that thou beholdest.
Juarroz. Bell is full of wind, The.
Every word is a doubt.
Keats. Terror of Death, The.
Kroll, J. Sestina: "Is this the object."
MacLeish. End of the World, The.
Mandelstam. &[;Last Poems&];.
O how much I would like—.
Matthews, J. People in These Houses, The.
Mihalic. Metamorphosis.
Murray, L. Quality of Sprawl, The.
Padgett, R. Nothing in that drawer.
Pagis. Outside the Line.
Piatt, S. If I had made the world—ah me!
Piercy. Death of the small commune, The.
Raine, K. World, The.
Reverdy. Inn.
Robinson, E. Man against the Sky, The.
Rodgers, W. Neither Here nor There.
Roethke. Duet.
Slonimski. Elegy: "No more, no more Jewish townships in Poland."
Smith, S. Dream of Comparison, A.
Stanescu. Marina.
Stramm. Urdeath.
Tahmisic. Stone and Ashes.
Venclova. Villanelle.
Wright, C. October.
Wright, F. Needle: For a Friend Who Disappeared, The.
Zych. Auschwitz, 1987.
See also **Nihilism**

Notre Dame Cathedral
Mandelstam. Notre Dame.
Péret. Staircase with a Hundred Steps, The.

Nottingham, England
Unknown. Nottamun Town.

Nova Scotia, Canada
Bishop, E. First Death in Nova Scotia.
Poem: "About the size of an old-style dollar bill."
Carman, B. Low Tide on Grand Pré.
Lochhead, D. Winter Lanscape—Halifax.
Stansbury, J. To Cordelia.

Novels
Bishop, M. Who'd Be a Hero (Fictional)?
Campbell, R. On Some South African Novelists.
Cope, W. Exchange of Letters.
Joyce, J. Blurb for *Anna Livia Plurabelle,* A.

MacLeish. Critical Observations.
Nemerov. Style.

Novelty
Browning, E. Poet hath the child's sight in his breast, The.
Herrick. Nothing New.
Olson, C. Celestial Evening, October 1967.
Wollach. Preannual Poem.

November
Atwood. November.
Berrigan, D. Beautiful Ruined Orchard, The.
Bridges, R. November.
Bryant, W. November.
Cary, A. November.
Clare, J. November.
Clark, L. Fog in November, trees have no heads.
Coleridge, H. November.
Crapsey. November Night.
Frost, R. My November Guest.
Harvey, F. November.
Hollander, M. Central Park.
Honig, E. November through a Giant Copper Beech.
Hood, T. No sun—no moon!
Howells, W. November.
Hughes, T. November.
Jeffers, R. November Surf.
Lampman. In November.
Ray, H. November.
Sandeen. Nearing Winter.
Santos, S. Late November.
Toomer. November Cotton Flower.
Vinz. November Song.
Voigt. At the Edge of Winter.
Whitman, S. November Landscape, A.
Wills, J. November evening.
Willson, D. Mist and All, The.
Wright, J. Late November in a Field.

Nuclear Accidents
May, S. Mildmay Grove.
Meinke. Atomic Pantoum.
Paley, G. In Aix.
Salter. Chernobyl.
Swift, J. On the Göta Canal, 1986.
Tranter. Glow-boys.
See also **Radiation and Radiation Sickness**

Nuclear Energy
Ginsberg, A. What new element before us unborn in nature? Is there a.
Kuznetsov. Atomic Fairy Tale.
Williams, C. Tar.

Nuclear War
Bold, A. Last Men on Mars.
Goedicke. Coin of the Realm.
Hall, R. Wedding Day at Nagasaki.
Hine. Survivors, The.
Hoffman, D. Seals in Penobscot Bay, The.
Hogan, L. Daybreak.
Kizer, C. Twelve O'Clock.
Lowell, R. Fall 1961.
Mazur. Lilacs on Brattle Street.
McGinley. Conquerors, The.
Mitchell, A. Fifteen Million Plastic Bags.
Porter, P. Your Attention Please.
Richards, I. Warhead Wakes.
Salter. Welcome to Hiroshima.
Sassoon. Post-Mortem, A.
Strand. When the Vacation Is Over for Good.
Wain. Song about Major Eatherly, A.
When It Comes.
See also **Atomic Bomb; Radiation and Radiation**

Nudity and Nudists
Baudelaire. Jewels, The.
Campbell, R. Sisters, The.
Cavafy. Days of 1908.
Days of 1908.
Crane, H. National Winter Garden.
Cunningham, J. Epitaph for Someone or Other.
Dacey, P. Porno Love.
Ded. Soul, like the moon, The.
Donne. To His Mistress Going To Bed.
Duesing. Send Pictures, You Said...
Elenkov. Sauna.

Feldman, I. Se Aprovechan.
Foerster. Life Drawing.
Graves, R. Naked and the Nude, The.
Herrick. Upon Julia's Clothes.
Kennedy, X. Nude Descending a Staircase.
Kinnell. Last Gods.
Kirby, D. To a French Structuralist.
Lawrence, D. "Gross, Coarse, Hideous" (Police Description of My Pictures).
Innocent England.
Mahadevi. (On Her Decision to Stop Wearing Clothes).
McMahon, L. Devolution of the Nude.
Mitchell, N. Locker Room, The.
Nikolov, N. Window, The.
Perreault, J. Metaphysical Paintings, The.
Pritchard, N. Springtime.
Shakespeare, W. Her lily hand her rosy cheek lies under.
Smith, S. Salon d'Automne.
Spire. Nudities.
Swenson, M. Naked in Borneo.
Unknown. First time I saw you, The.
Wagoner, D. Walt Whitman Bathing.
Wilbur. Playboy.

Number Poems (genre)
Swenson, M. Cardinal Ideograms.

Numbers
Amichai. Onus of Mercy, The.
Brown, D. Patrols.
Carter, H. 'Tis a favorite project of mine.
Donne. Primrose[, Being at Montgomery Castle, upon the Hill, on Which It Is Situate], The.
Esolen. Northwestern Mathematics.
Gioia. Counting the Children.
József. Seventh, The.
Khlebnikov, V. Zangezi: R, K, L, G—.
Mitchell, A. Accountant in His Bath, The.
Mother Goose. One, two, / Buckle my shoe.
Overstreet. Count Ten.
Péret. My Final Agonies.
Popa. Forgetful Number.
Rothenberg, J. Numerology.
Soto. Teaching Numbers.
Stein, G. Kneeling.
Swenson, M. Cardinal Ideograms.
Unknown. One, two, buckle my shoe.
One, two, three, four, five / Once I caught a fish alive.

Nuns
Betjeman. Felixstowe, or, The Last of Her Order.
Brinnin. Nuns at Eve.
Brownjohn. Nuns in a Convent Garden.
Clarke, A. Intercessors.
Davidson, J. Ballad of a Nun, A.
Di Prima. To the Unnamed Buddhist Nun Who Burned Herself to Death on the Night of June 3, 1966.
Divakaruni. Walk, The.
Dowson. Nuns of the Perpetual Adoration.
Durcan. Sister Agnes Writes to Her Beloved Mother.
Eglitis. In a Naples Bar.
Hopkins, G. Heaven-Haven.
Huỳnh Mẫn Đạt. Old Whore Becomes a Nun, The.
Jamie. Black Spiders.
Jones, B. Portrait of a Nun.
Klein, A. For the Sisters of the Hôtel Dieu.
Kumin, M. Nuns of Childhood: Two Views, The.
Lluellyn. Epithalamium: To Mistress M. A.
Miles, J. Beach Party Given by T. Shaughnessy for the Sisters.
Milton. Lady That in the Prime.
Mo Shih-lung. Saying Good-bye to a Singing Girl Who Has Decided to Become a Nun.
Murray, R. Carmelite.
Ormond. To a Nun.
Palazzeschi. Nuns Go Walking.
Pope, A. Life of a Nun.
Procter, A. Legend of Provence, A.
Ristovic. Monastic Outhouse.
Rukeyser, M. Nuns in the Wind.
Swenson, M. Fixture, A.

Tekkan. Tanka: "Noiselessly."
Unknown. Bleeding Nun, The.
I am a young girl, gay.
Motet: "I am a young girl."
Williams, A. Nunnery, The.

Nuremberg, Germany
Cunard. To Eat To-day.
Longfellow, H. Nuremberg.
Slessor. Nuremberg.

Nursery Rhymes
"Carroll." Little Man That Had a Little Gun, The.
Fatchen. 'Jump over the moon?' the cow declared.
Kennedy, X. Help!
Owen, G. Owl and the astronaut sailed through space, The.
Rosen, M. Here is the News from space.
Unknown. As I was going to sell my eggs.
As I was walking down the lake.
Cock a doodle doo!
Four-and-twenty tailors went to kill a snail.
"How many miles is it to Babylon?"
Lavender's Blue.
Lion and the unicorn, The.
Little Robin Red-breast.
Man in the wilderness asked of me, The.
Mulberry Bush, The.
Old Woman of Norwich, The.
Ride a cock-horse to Banbury Cross.
Ring-a-ring o'roses.
Rock-a-bye baby.
Rub-a-dub-dub.
Sam, Sam, the butcher man.
See-saw, Margery Daw.
Sukey [*or* Suky], you shall be my wife.
There was an old woman tossed up in a basket.
What a to-do to die today.
You, North must go.

Nurses
Betjeman. Death in Leamington.
Blake, W. Nurse's Song ("When the voices of children are heard on the green / And laughing is heard on the hill").
Brontë, C. Nurse believed the sick man slept, The.
Cornford, F. Nurse.
Daryush. Off Duty.
Eigner. How it comes about.
Fagg, M. Mrs Nightingale.
Fuller, J., *et al.* Red Light District Nurse, The.
Gray, J. Night Nurse Goes Her Round, The.
Kendrick, D. Inpatient.
Kipling, R. Nurses, The.
Lawrence, A. To be a nurse is.
Levertov. Malice of Innocence, The.
Locker-Lampson. Terrible Infant, A.
Mitchell, S. Nurse, The.
Mộng Tuyết. Red Cross, The.
Moorer. Negro Heroines.
Po Chü-i. Remembering Golden Bells.
Symons, A. I. Hérodiade.
Unknown. Hospital Duties.
"Valueless, A Duffer!" says the Sister's face.
Waring, B. Baby Random.
Whitman, W. Wound-Dresser, The.

Nursing Homes
Naiman. My mother has died, but I visit her weekly.

Nymphs
Carew, T. Pastoral[l] Dialogue, A.
Song: Good Counsel to a Young Maid.
Doolittle, H. Oread.
Hermocreon. Nymphs of the surface, whom Hermokreon gave.
Herrick. To the Water Nymphs, Drinking at the Fountain.
Homer. Thetis and the Nereids.
Hood, T. Water Lady, The.
Leonidas of Tarentum. Nymphs of water, daughters of Doros.
Milton. Oracles are dumm, The.
Moiro. Hail, forest nymphs, daughters of the river.
Monro. Overheard on a Saltmarsh.

More, H. Inscription in a Beautiful Retreat Called Fairy Bower.
Pastorius. Penance, A.
Piccolo. Veneris Venefica Agrestis.
Pritchard, N. Landscape with Nymphs and Satyrs.
Radcliffe, A. Song of a Spirit.
Seward. Speech of the Nymph.
Sidney, P. Sonnet 82: "Nymph of the garden where all beauties be."
Sitwell, D. Waltz.
Snodgrass, W. Monet: 'Les Nymphéas'.
Theocritus. Hylas and the Water Nymphs.
Unknown. Inscription for a Statue of Pan.
Wilbur. Ceremony.
Winchilsea. Adam Posed.

O

O'Connor, Flannery
Walters, D. Flannery O'Connor.
O'Connor, Rory
Clarke, A. They are the spit of virtue now.
O'Hara, Frank
Beaver. (Frank O'Hara).
Berrigan, T. Red Shift.
Koch, K. Circus, The.
O'Hara, F. Day Lady Died, The.
O'Neill, Owen Roe
Davis, T. Lament for the Death of Eoghan Ruadh O'Neill.
O'Neill, Shane
Jeffers, R. Shane O'Neill's Cairn.
Oafs
Francis, R. Yes, What?
Oak Trees
Chorley, H. Brave Old Oak, The.
Cowper, W. Yardley Oak.
Diodorus Zonas. Spare the mother of acorns, man. Cut down some paliurus.
Drayton. Then Frome (a nobler flood) the Muses doth implore.
Herrick. All Things Decay and Die.
La Grone. Lines to the Black Oak.
Locker-Lampson. Old Oak Tree at Hatfield Broadoak, The.
Ransom, J. Parting, without a Sequel.
Roberson. Sonnet.
Scott, W. To an Oak Tree.
Synge. To the Oaks of Glencree.
Tennyson, A. Oak, The.
Warren, R. Bearded Oaks.
Whitman, W. I saw in Louisiana a live-oak growing.
Oases
Anyte. Ease your weary limbs, stranger, under this elm—.
I, Hermes, have been set up.
Sit down in the shade of this fine spreading laurel.
Cameron, N. Green, Green Is El Aghir.
Unknown. Needles of the lofty pine, The.
On a Statue of Pan.
See also **Deserts**
Obesity
Bloch, C. Eating Babies.
Chaucer. Syn I fro Love escaped am so fat.
Dabydeen, C. Fat Men, The.
Eliot, T. Bustopher Jones: The Cat About Town.
Unknown. Whistle, Daughter, Whistle.
Obituaries
Holman, M. Mr. Z.
Lowell, R. Alfred Corning Clark.
Oblivion
Amichai. Like our bodies' imprint.
Apollinaire. Stanzas Against Forgetting.
Barlas. Oblivion! is it not one name of death?
Bobrowski. Elderblossom.
Borges. Everness.
Brooks, G. When You Have Forgotten Sunday: The Love Story.
Catullus. Carmen 5 ("My sweetest Lesbia, let us live and love").

Davenant. Lover and Philosopher.
Dowson. Dregs.
Eberhart, R. On a Squirrel Crossing the Road in Autumn, in New England.
Hughes, L. Blues at Dawn.
Ivask, Y. Shall we forget the shiver.
Jackson, L. All things that wake enjoy the sun.
Lawrence, D. Build then the ship of death, for you must take.
Shadows.
Tabernacle.
"MacDiarmid." Eemis-Stane, The.
Oliver, M. Little Owl Who Lives in the Orchard.
Pilinszky. Passion of Ravensbrück.
Ritsos. Underneath Oblivion.
Samio. Tanka: "On the sandy beach."
Shelnutt. At the Mass Graveyard.
Soupault. Condemned.
Wigglesworth. Wallowing in all kind of sin.
Obscenity
Gogarty. On First Looking into Krafft-Ebing's *Psychopathosexualis* [*or* Psychopathia Sexualis].
Lawrence, D. Innocent England.
Shapiro, A. Manufacturing.
Vas. Just This.
"W——." Gentleman's Study, in Answer to The Lady's Dressing-Room, The.
See also **Pornography**
Obscurity
Baugh, E. Getting There.
De Vere, E. Poem: "Were I a king, I could command content."
Durem. I Know I'm Not Sufficiently Obscure.
Gioia. Guide to the Other Gallery.
Rich, A. Focus.
Rossetti, C. Frog's Fate, A.
Williamson, G. Counterfeiter, The.
Observatories
Keyes, S. Greenwich Observatory.
See also **Astonomy and Astronomers**
Obsessions
Akhmadulina. Small Aircraft.
Belloc. Juliet.
Bernard. When—presto—turf and trees are green.
Berryman. Canto Amor.
Coleridge, S. Recollections of Love.
Damas. Obsession.
Dryden, J. One Happy Moment.
Eberhart, R. Two Loves.
Ellis, S. Weathered Ides Grant Young Flesh.
Gay, J. Molly Mog [or The Fair Maid of the Inn].
Katrovas. Black English.
Kizer, C. Food of Love.
Lamb, M. Helen.
Lawrence, D. Release.
Moore, T. Thee, Thee, Only Thee.
Nash, O. Curl Up and Diet.
Tate, J. Deaf Girl Playing.
Williams, W. Love Song: First Version, 1915, A.
Wroth. Sonnet 23: "When every one to pleasing pastime hies."
Wyatt, T. Process of time worketh such wonder.
Occult, The
Cassian. Vowel.
King, F. Séance.
Moffett. Diehard.
Reid, A. Spell for Sleeping, A.
Occupations
Chakrabarti. Amalkanti is a friend of mine.
Eady. Supremes, The.
Ocean. *See* **Sea**
October
Aldrich, T. October turned my maple's leaves to gold.
Alexander, M. October Journey.
Amann. Circus tent, The.
Bonnefoy. Words of Evening, The.
Brodsky, J. October Tune.
Bronk. Where It Ends.

Cooper, G. October's Party.
Fordham. October.
Gibson, M. October Elegy.
Hayne, P. October.
Henri, A. Crowfield.
Herlin. Sky has recovered its haze-blue tints, The.
Jackson, H. October.
October's Bright Blue Weather.
Kavanagh, P. Clay is the word and clay is the flesh.
October.
Levertov. October.
Linden, M. October Is Here.
Malroux. In October.
Narbut. October.
Nathan, R. Now Blue October.
O'Hara, F. How to Get There.
Piersanti. When Slow October Changes Color.
Pushkin. October.
Ray, H. October.
Rossetti, C. October.
October Garden, An.
Sansom, C. October.
Snyder, G. Late October Camping in the Sawtooths.
Thomas, D. Especially when the October wind.
Poem in October.
Thomas, E. October.
Tranströmer. Sketch in October.
Walker, M. October Journey.
Octopuses
Hilton, A. Octopus.
Merrill, J. Octopus, The.
Nash, O. Octopus, The.
Smith, S. Octopus, The.
Odysseus. *See* **Ulysses**
Oedipus
Aeschylus. Lament for the Two Brothers Slain by Each Other's Hand.
Blackburn, T. Oedipus.
Dryden, J. When Athens all the Graecian state did guide.
Engonopoulos. On Boetian Roads.
Euripides. Daughter, I must commend thy noble heart.
Muir, E. Oedipus.
Publius Papinius Statius. Now wretched *Oedipus,* depriv'd of Sight.
Ray, H. Antigone and Oedipus.
Rukeyser, M. Myth.
Seneca. Fate is the master of everything it is vain to fight against fate.
Sophocles. Chorus: "What man is he that yearneth."
Colonus' Praise.
Offa, King of Mercia
Hill, G. Coins handsome as Nero's; of good substance and.
He adored the desk, its brown-oak inlaid with ebony.
King of the perennial holly-groves, the riven sandstone.
Mad ware predators. Too often lately they harbour, The.
Not strangeness, but strange likeness. Obstinate.
Pet-name, a common name. Best-selling brand, curt, A.
Princes of Mercia were badger and raven, The.
So much for the elves' wergild, the true governance.
Office Workers
Buck, B. Song from a Two-Desk Office.
Dawe, B. Beatitudes.
Ewart. Office Friendships.
Field, E. What Grandma Knew.
Madhubuti. Back Again, Home.
Page, P. Stenographers, The.
Roethke. Dolor.
Swan, J. Report, The.
Williams, W. Return to Work, The.
Wong, N. Toward a 44th Birthday.

See also **Clerks; Secretaries**

Officers, Military
Amherst. From a Young Woman to an Old Officer Who Courted Her.
Grenfell, J. Prayer for Those on the Staff.
Herbert, A. After the Battle.
Mackintosh, E. In Memoriam[, Private D. Sutherland].
Prévert. Quartier Libre.
Sassoon. Base Details.
To Any Dead Officer.

Ogres
Auden. August 1968.
Graves, R. Ogres and Pygmies.
See also **Monsters**

Ohio (state)
Allbery. Produce.
Anania. Second-Hand Elegy, A.
Harper, F. To the Union Savers of Cleveland.
Wright, J. At the Executed Murderer's Grave.
Autumn Begins in Martins Ferry, Ohio.
In Ohio.
In Response to a Rumor that the Oldest Whorehouse in Wheeling, West Virginia, Has Been Condemned.
Ohioan Pastoral.
Old WPA Swimming Pool in Martins Ferry, Ohio, The.
Yamada. Cincinnati.

Ohio River
Emmett. Boatman's Dance ("Ober de mountains, slick as an eel").
Harper, F. Slave Mother, The.
Ransom, J. Antique Harvesters.
Sandburg, C. When I asked for fish in the restaurant facing the Ohio River.
Wright, J. Three Sentences for a Dead Swan.

Oil
Ginsberg, A. Who Runs America?
North, C. Year of the Olive Oil, The.
Thurman. Oil Slick.
Unknown. Ashes to ashes.

Oil Industry
Ginsberg, A. Who Runs America?

Oisin
Liddy. History.
Unknown. Praise of Fionn, The.

Okinawa, Japan
Schmitz. Picture of Okinawa, A.

Oklahoma (state)
Barnes, J. Captive Stone, The.
Harjo, J. Autobiography.
Stevens, W. Life Is Motion.
Van Walleghen. Driving into Enid.

Old Age
Ambapali. Black and glossy as a bee and curled was my hair.
Anacreon. Only now that my hair is gray.
When you see my gray hair and chin.
Angelou. On Aging.
Apollonides. Cup clinks out, my friend, The.
Appleman, P. So What.
Arnold, M. Growing Old.
Ashbery. Fear of Death.
Atwood. Daguerreotype Taken in Old Age.
Baker, K. Let Me Grow Lovely.
Barber, M. To Mrs. Francis-Arabella Kelly.
Barnes, W. When We That Now Ha' Childern Wer Childern.
Basho. Some of them with staves.
Beckett, S. Song: "Age is when to a man."
Bergman, A. Letter.
Betjeman. Late-Flowering Lust.
Senex.
Youth and Age on Beaulieu River, Hants.
Birney. My Love Is Young.
Blackburn, P. Phone Call to Rutherford.
Blake, W. In a Myrtle [*or* Mirtle] Shade.
Infant Sorrow.
Blunden. Almswomen.
Bogan, L. Crows, The.
Bosman. Old I Am.
Boyle, K. Poem on Getting Up Early in the Morning (or Even Late in the Morning), When One is Old, A.
Breytenbach. Struggle for the Taal, The.

Brontë, E. Love and Friendship.
Brooks, G. Bean Eaters, The.
Brown, G. Old Women, The.
Browning, R. Grow old along with me!
Bruner. "Whom the Gods Love die young" I used to quote.
Bunting. When the sword of sixty comes nigh his head.
Campbell, J. Old Woman, The.
Cardiff. Grey Woman.
Carleton, W. Over the Hill to the Poor-House.
"Carroll." Father William.
White Knight's Song, The.
"You are old," said the youth, "and your jaws are too weak."
Carter, M. Bent.
Cassian. Please Give This Seat to an Elderly or Disabled Person.
Castellanos. Hecuba's Testament.
Chandler, M. My Own Epitaph.
Chasin. City Pigeons.
Chesterton, G. Gold Leaves.
Ch'ien T'ao. Blaming Sons.
Chin Nung. I get so drunk, I could be called the Earl of Dissipation!
Chōkū. Tanka: "Among the hundreds."
Chu Shu-chen. Spring has come. I try to forget.
Clarke, C. Older American, The.
Clausen. After Touch.
Clive. Old Age.
Coleridge, H. Long Time a Child.
Coleridge, S. Youth and Age.
Corbett, E. Three wise old women were they, were they.
Cornford, F. Childhood.
Cummings, E. Old age sticks / up Keep.
De la Mare. All That's Past.
Last Chapter, The.
Nod.
Old Men, The.
Old Susan.
DeBary. Tomorrow I will haul down the flag of hypocrisy.
Dementyev, A. It's all over...
"Der Nistor." At the Doors.
Ditlevsen. Old Folk, The.
Dixon, R. Both Less and More.
Donne. Canonization, The.
Doolittle, H. In Time of Gold.
Dransfield. Pioneer Lane.
Dromgoole. Old Ladies.
Drown. To Mother.
Eberhart, R. Youth and Age.
Eliot, T. Gerontion.
Lines for an Old Man.
Emerson, R. Terminus ("It is time to be old").
Empson. To an Old Lady.
Feldman, I. Old Men, The.
Felltham. To Phryne.
Fitzgerald, R. Song for September.
Foley, M. *Sois sage, ô ma douleur. . .* I don't.
Fowler, L. Gather Ye Rosebuds.
Francis, R. Reading of the Psalm, The.
Fritsch, H. How Old Are You?
Frost, R. Old Man's Winter Night, An.
Provide, Provide.
Gallagher, T. Each Bird Walking.
Gentry. Aunt Lucy.
Gergely. Auden in Old Age.
Gibson, W. Ice, The.
Gilligan. Mortgage.
Googe. To Doctor Bale.
Graves, R. Broken Girth, The.
Grotesques.
Green, F. Old Couple, The.
Grenfell, J. Stately as a Galleon.
Grosholz. Old Fisherman, The.
Gruffydd, O. Old, old/ To live on, wretched to behold.
Guiney. Open, Time, and let him pass.
Gunn, T. Breaking Ground.
"H., H. E." Riddle, The.
Hacker, M. Imaginary Translation.
Hall, D. By the Exeter River.
Hammond, M. Golden Age.
Han Yü. Old men are like little boys.

Harasymowicz. Old Age.
Hardy, T. Ancient to Ancients, An.
He Never Expected Much.
I look into my glass.
Near Lanivet, 1872.
Superseded, The.
Harrison, G. Alone in the Grange.
Hartnett. Person as Dreamer: We Talk about the Future, The.
Sonnet: "I saw magic on a green country road."
Hecht, A. Meditation.
Henry, J. Old Man.
Very Old Man.
Herbert, G. Forerunners, The.
Herrick. His Age, Dedicated to His Peculiar Friend, Master John Wickes, under the Name of Posthumus.
On Himselfe ("I will no longer kiss").
To a Gentlewoman Objecting to Him His Grey Hairs.
To Perilla.
Hewitt, J. Local Poet, A.
Higgins, F. Old Jockey, The.
Ho Ch'e Ch'ang. Homecoming.
Holloway, J. Ulysses.
Holmes, O. Last Leaf, The.
Old Man Dreams, The.
Holtby, W. Beauty the Lover's Gift?
Hopkins, G. Leaden Echo and the Golden Echo, The.
Hoskins, K. Baucis and Philemon.
Howe, F. First Chance Twice.
Irving, M. Marching Still.
Isidorus. Now Endymion dedicates / his cold bed's failure to the moon.
Jeffers, R. Age in Prospect.
Deer Lay Down Their Bones, The.
Fawn's Foster-Mother.
Promise of Peace.
Jennings, E. One Flesh.
Johnson, G. I Am Growing Old.
Johnson, G. Old Black Men.
Johnson, L. Seventies, The.
Jonas, G. Temporal.
Jones, D. Old Woman, An.
Jones, R. Age.
Joseph, J. Warning.
Julianus of Egypt. Lais' Mirror.
Justice, D. Nostalgia and Complaint of the Grandparents.
Winter Ode to the Old Men of Lummus Park, Miami, Florida, A.
Juvenal. *Jove* grant large space of life, and length of days.
K'ang Hai. When I have chanted my new poems.
Kangro. Old Age.
Keary. Old Age.
Kerouac. In my medicine cabinet.
Kingsley, C. Young and Old.
Kinsella, T. Tear.
Kipling, R. Old Men, The.
Kleinzahler. Hamburger.
Kolatkar. Old woman grabs, An.
Kooser. Very old are forever, The.
Kung Tzu-chen. Miscellanies of the Year Chi-hai.
Kurup. Master Carpenter, The.
Laing, K. Senior Lady Sells Garden Eggs.
Lamb, C. Old Familiar Faces, The.
Landor, W. Age.
Alas! 'tis very sad to hear.
No charm can stay, no medicine can assuage.
On His Seventy-Fifth Birthday.
Layton. Grand Finale.
Lea, S. Wrong Way Will Haunt You, The.
Lear, E. There was an Old Man who forgot.
Levertov. Old Adam, The.
Li Ch'ing-chao. Tune: "Pure Serene Music."
Li Po. My white hair of thirty thousand feet.
Linden, M. Life's Golden Sunset.
Prospect of the Future, The.
Linton. Epicurean.
Lipkin, J. Father.
Liu Tsung-yüan. Feeling Old Age.

Written in Jest on Elder Stonegate's Eastern Balcony.
Liu Ya-tzu. Strange Tears.
Loftin. Weeksville Women.
Longfellow, H. Nature.
Too Late?
Lowell, J. Auspex.
Sixty-Eighth Birthday.
Lowell, R. Grandparents.
Lowery. Smell of Old Newspapers Is Always Stronger after Sleeping in the Sun, The.
Lu Yu. Stone on the Hilltop, The.
Written in a Carefree Mood.
Ludlow. Too Late.
Ly Ngoc Kieu. Birth, old age.
"MacDiarmid." Old Wife in High Spirits.
Wheesht, wheesht, my foolish hert.
Macdonald, G. Turn from Self.
Macedonius. She who shook and swayed among the chorus.
Madgett. New Day.
Mahon. Refusal to Mourn, A.
Mangan, J. Twenty Golden Years Ago.
Mapanje. These Too Are Our Elders.
Marshall-Stoneking. Passage.
Masefield. On Growing Old.
Mason, C. When I Am Old.
Mason, R. Body of John.
Massinger. Song.
Mathews, H. Back from Green Dragon, Presented to Hsieh Shih-chih.
Matthews, T. Cowboy Film.
McHugh, H. Take Care.
McNair. Hunt Walking.
Mei Yao Ch'en. On the Thirteenth Day of the Eleventh Month I Went to the Granary for the First Time since My Illness.
Melville, H. Old Age in His Ailing.
Meng Chiao. Autumn finds me old and poorer.
Bones of the lonely-wretched spend no quiet nights.
Old and sick, many strange broodings.
Song of the Old Man of the Hills.
Mew. À Quoi Bon Dire.
Meynell, A. Letter from a Girl to Her Own Old Age, A.
Mezey. If I Should Die Before I Wake.
Milosz, C. Felicitous Life, A.
Mimnermus. There Is No Joy Without Aphrodite.
Montague, J. Like dolmens round my childhood, the old people.
Morris-Jones. "Old age never comes alone"—it brings sighs.
Mother Goose. There was an old woman lived under a hill.
Mountain, M. In her old voice the mountains.
Mphande. Why the Old Woman Limps.
Murray, L. Widower in the Country, The.
Nash, O. Come On In, the Senility Is Fine.
Old Men.
Peekaboo, I Almost See You.
Portrait of the Artist as a Prematurely Old Man.
Nemerov. Brief Journey West, The.
Nesbit, E. Things That Matter, The.
Newbolt. Felix Antonius.
Nguyễn Bỉnh Khiêm. Self-Reflection.
Nguyễn Khuyến. Old Age.
Niatum. Apology.
Old Woman Awaiting the Greyhound Bus.
Nicholson, N. Halley's Comet.
O Brolchain. I give Thee thanks, my King.
My sins in their completeness.
O'Hara, F. In Hospital.
Okikaze. Who shall I have for friends.
Oppen. Resort.
Outram. Annuity, The.
Owen, G. Shed in Space.
Owen, W. Parable of the Old Man and the Young, The.
Paley, G. People in My Family.
Parker, D. Little Old Lady in Lavender Silk, The.
Parker, P. I Followed a Path.

Pasternak, B. O had I known that it ends like this.
Paulus Silentiarius. Sober man, I'll take the wine, A.
Peacock, T. In Respect of the Elderly.
Peele. Farewell to Arms, A.
Peters, R. Reflecting on the Aging-Process.
Philodemus. I, who used to score five, even nine times.
Seven plus thirty years are gone.
Po Chü-i. Children.
Looking in the Lake.
Old Age.
Old Man of Hsin-feng witih the Broken Arm, The.
Poems in Depression, at Wei Village.
Realizing the Futility of Life.
To a Portrait Painter who Desired Him to Sit.
Pope, W. Old Man's Wish, The.
Prior. Pass we the ills, which each man feels or dreads.
Rakosi. Unswerving Marine.
Ralegh, W. 'As ye came from the holy land'.
Raleigh. Wishes of an Elderly Man[, Wished at a Garden Party, June 1914].
Randall, D. George.
Rands. Cat of Cats, The.
Ransom, J. Captain Carpenter rose up in his prime.
Miss Euphemia.
Old Man Playing with Children.
Piazza Piece.
Reed, H. Chard Whitlow.
Reisen. Healing.
Ríos, A. Man Who Became Old, The.
Roberts, E. Mr. Wells.
Robinson, E. Mr Flood's Party.
Rochester, J. Song of a Young Lady to Her Ancient Lover, A.
Roethke. First Meditation.
I'm Here.
Infirmity.
Rogers, S. Man's Going Hence.
Roseliep. Sky.
Rosenberg, L. In the End We Are All Light.
Ross, C. Old Mothers.
Rufinus. Did I not say we grow old.
Russell, N. Message of the Rain, The.
Saitō Mokichi. Tanka: "Determined to try."
Santayana. Minuet on Reaching the Age of Fifty, A.
Satyamurti. Day Trip.
Schwartz, D. Poem: "Old man in the crystal morning after snow."
Scott, W. Garland for Advancing Years, A.
Seifert. Fingerprints.
Garland on the Wrist, A.
Selvinsky. Portrait of My Mother.
Sexton. Two Sons.
Shakespeare, W. Madrigal, A: "Crabbed age and youth cannot live together."
Sonnet 73.
Shao Yung. Arriving in Lo-yang Again.
Sharpless. Costa Geriatrica.
Shengeli. Derzhavin.
Sherwood, G. Song of a Young Lady to Her Ancient Lover, A.
Shih Te. I laugh at my failing strength in old age.
Sidney, P. Old Age.
Simic. Old Couple.
Sitwell, D. Poet Laments the Coming of Old Age, The.
Smith, I. Old Woman.
Smith, M. Fall.
Smith, S. Autumn.
Snodgrass, W. April Inventory.
Southey, R. Old Man's Comforts and How He Gained Them, The.
Stafford, W. Strokes.
Steele, T. In the King's Rooms.
Stephens, J. Danny Murphy.
Stickney, T. Requiescam.
Strong, L. Old Dan'l.
Zeke.
Su Tung-p'o. Beginning of Autumn: A Poem to Send to Tzu-yu.

Tune: Immortal at the River.
Verses: "I am old, sick and lonely."
Surrey. Laid in my quiet bed, in study as I were.
Swenson, M. How to Be Old.
Swift, J. Satirical Elegy on the Death of a Late Famous General, A.
Swirszczynska. Greatest Love, The.
Second Madrigal, The.
She Does Not Remember.
Talbot, N. Ballad of Old Women & of How They Are Constrained To Simulate Youth In Order To Avoid Shocking the Young.
T'ang Hsien-tsu. Inspector Hsü Claims He Has Found the Secret of Youth.
Tao-chi. Inscribed on My Little Painting of Plum Blossom and Bamboo.
Teasdale. Long Hill, The.
Moonlight.
Tennyson, A. Tithonus.
Ulysses.
Tennyson, F. Old Age.
Thomas, D. Do not go gentle into that good night.
Thomas, R. Lore.
Survivor, The.
Thompson, P. Old Freedman, The.
Tsvetkov. To be mistaken in old age and not to be afraid.
Tu Fu. Farewell of an Old Man.
Masses of flowers and plants envelop the riverbanks.
Presented to Wei Pa, Gentleman in Retirement.
'Tis not I pity the flowers are about to die.
Turberville. To an Old Gentlewoman That Painted Her Face.
Turner, A. Making Old Bones.
Tyutchev. Last Love.
Unknown. At Fifteen I Went Off to the Army;.
Before my back was bent I was eloquent.
Emancipation.
I am olde whan age doth apele.
Lais' Mirror.
My Mother's Hands.
Old Man's Song, about His Wife, The.
Old Mother, The.
Old-Saxon Fragment.
On a Gentleman's Complaining to a Lady That He Could Not Eat Meat.
Somebody's Mother.
Song of a Woman Abandoned by the Tribe.
Song of an Old Gray Wolf.
Song of the Old Woman.
Tune: "Tartar Tune of Eighteen Beats."
Will You Love Me When I'm Old?
Van Duyn. Falling in Love at Sixty-Five.
Letters from a Father.
Stream, The.
Vaux. Aged Lover Renounceth Love, The.
Villon. Old Lady's Lament for Her Youth, The.
Waddington, M. Old Women of Toronto.
Walcott. Glory Trumpeter, The.
Letter from Brooklyn, A.
Oak inns creak in their joints as light declines, The.
Walker, A. Medicine.
Waller, E. Old Age.
Wang An-shih. Fresh Flowers.
Wang Chien. At home I loved to wear old clothes.
Wang Chiu-ssu. Quiet Sitting.
Warren, R. English Cocker: Old and Blind.
Wei Chuang. Spoken to Pines and Bamboos.
Wen Cheng-ming. I remove my court gown and part from the Emperor's precincts.
New Year's Eve.
Weöres. Saturn Sinking.
Wheelock, J. Dear Men and Women.
Night Thoughts in Age.
Whitman, W. Centenarian's Story, The.
Hours continuing long, sore and heavy-hearted.
Thanks in old age—thanks ere I go.
To Old Age.
Willard, N. Arbor.
Williams, M. On a Photograph of My Mother

at Seventeen.
Ruby Tells All.
Williams, W. Last Words of My English Grandmother, The.
To a Poor Old Woman.
To Waken an Old Lady.
Wordsworth, W. Fountain, The.
Old Man [Travelling], An.
Simon Lee [the Old Huntsman].
Wright, F. Old, The.
Wright, J. Poem Written under an Archway in a Discontinued Railroad Station, Fargo, North Dakota, A.
Y Vân Tử'. Gaffer in Love, A.
Yang Shen. To the Tune "Song of the Plum Blossom at the River Town."
Yang Shih-ch'i. Eulogy on My Own Portrait, A.
Even ordinarily, parting is difficult.
Sha-ch'eng, "Sand City" ("In former years I passed this city").
Yates, J. Model Church, The.
Yeats. Acre of Grass, An.
Apparitions, The.
Are You Content.
Coming of Wisdom with Time, The.
Lamentation of the Old Pensioner, The.
Old Man Stirs the Fire to a Blaze, An.
Old Men Admiring Themselves in the Water, The.
Prayer for Old Age, A.
Sailing To Byzantium.
Scholars, The.
Spur, The.
When you are old and grey and full of sleep.
Wild Old Wicked Man, The.
Yesenin. Only one final trick remains—.
Yevtushenko. Saints of Jazz are playing, The.
Yü Chi. Late in the Year K'uei-yu (1333), Staying at the Temple of the Upper Regions.
Yüan Mei. Arriving at Hangchou.
Finding Serenity.
Happy about Being Old.
I Know Inside.
Night of the Fifteenth, Second Month.
Yün Shou-p'ing. As old age approaches.
Zabolotsky. Last Love.
Somewhere in a field near Magadan.
Zagajewski. Electric Elegy.
See also **Pensions and Pensioners; Retirement and Retirees**

"Old Ironsides." *See* Constitution (ship)

Oldham, John
Dryden, J. To the Memory of Mr Oldham.

Olive Trees and Olives
Housman, A. Olive in its orchard, The.
Mavilis. Olive Tree.
North, C. Year of the Olive Oil, The.
Robinson, A. Tuscan Olives.
Spencer, B. Olive Trees.
Wilbur. Grasse: The Olive Trees.

Oliver Twist
Philip, M. Oliver Twist.

Olympics
Fagg, M. Golden Road to Barcelona: 1992, The.

Omar Khayyám
Lowell, J. In a Copy of Omar Khayyám.

Omens
Angira. If.
Aworinde. If a Suite in Praise of the Yoruba Oracle.
Bekederemo. Season of Omens.
Bernstein, O. At Woods' Edge.
Mene Mene.
Breytenbach. Firewing.
Brownstein. Oracle night / the porch is frozen.
Burns, R. Tam Glen.
Burr, A. Lynmouth Widow, A.
Chia Yi. Rhyme-Prose on the Owl.
"Ern Malley." Sybilline.
Graves, R. On Portents.
Spoils.
Holub. Interferon.
Jacob, M. War.
Johnson, S. Comets and Princes.

Melville, H. Portent, The.
Mpondo. Season of the rains, The.
Poe. Raven, The.
Samio. Tanka: "Fish skeleton, A."
Smith, S. Omens.
Stevenson, R. Ticonderoga: A Legend of the West Highlands.
Unknown. Marrying maiden / Undertakings bring misfortune, The.
Prophetic Powers.
Warren, R. Apology for Domitian.
Zach. Soft Warm Breeze, A.

Omnipotence
Bible, *O.T.* Psalm 8.
Psalm 104.
Psalm 107.
Psalm 114.
Psalm 139.
Psalm 147.
Psalm 90.
Eberhart, R. Two Loves.
Williams, M. Why God Permits Evil: For Answers to This Question of Interest to Many Write Bible Answers Dept. E-7.

Onions
Cynewulf. Riddle: "I'm a strange creature, for I satisfy women."
Duffy, C. Valentine.
Flanders, J. Planting Onions.
Gibson, M. Onion, The.
Goodison. I Am Becoming My Mother.
Hernández, M. Lullaby of the Onion.
Ishikawa Takuboku. Tanka: "As if in water."
Kirsch, S. Seven Skins.
Kooser. Onion Woman, The.
Moore, N. Song: "Little onion lay by the fireplace, A."
Nye, N. Traveling Onion, The.
Raine, C. Onion, Memory, The.
Swift, J. Onyons.

Ontario, Canada
Everson, R. Stranded in My Ontario.
Klein, A. Winter Night: Mount Royal.
Ondaatje. Burning Hills.
Purdy, A. Country North of Belleville, The.
Wilderness Gothic.

Ontario, Lake
Ray, H. Thought of Lake Ontario, A.

Opera
Ade. Il Janitoro.
Ashbery. Faust.
Levchev. Carmen, or the Made-Up Girl.
Levy, N. Rigoletto.
Tannhauser.
"Meredith." Aux Italiens.
Merrill, J. Matinees.
Nash, O. Ill Met by Zenith.
Roseliep. After Tosca.

Ophelia
Manger. Autumn.
Wickham. Song of Ophelia the Survivor.

Opium
Coleridge, S. Kubla Khan; or, A Vision in a Dream.
Darwin. Poppy, The.
Lowell, M. Opium Fantasy, An.
O'Neill, H. Ode to the Poppy.
Seward. To the Poppy.
Thế Lữ'. Opium.
Tucker, M. Evanishings.
Opium-Eater, The.
Unknown. Willie the Weeper.

Opossums
Unknown. Carmen Possum.

Oppenheimer, Joseph Suss
Ai. Testimony of J. Robert Oppenheimer, The.

Opportunity
Browning, R. Youth and Art.
Carlyle, T. Today.
Graham, H. Opportunity.
Hardy, T. Midnight on the Great Western.
Howard, R. Waste not, want not, is a maxim I.
Ingalls, J. Opportunity.
Machiavelli. Opportunity.
Malone, W. Opportunity.

Shakespeare, W. Opportunity.
Sill. Opportunity.

Opposites
Browning, E. Sonnet: "Unlike are we, unlike, O princely Heart!"
Emerson, R. Brahma.
Graves, R. In Broken Images.
Melville, H. Art.
Unknown. Essay on Man.
Talk not of strength, till your heart has known.
Wilbur. What is the opposite of *nuts?*.

Oppression
Agard, J. Pan Recipe.
Alexie. Vision (2).
Anzaldúa. Horse.
Awoonor. First Circle, The.
Ba. Nobility.
Baca. I Am Here.
Oppression.
Bly, R. Romans Angry about the Inner World.
Brecht, B. World's One Hope, The.
Breytenbach. Firewing.
Struggle for the Taal, The.
Bunimovich. Moscow: Summer '86.
Campbell, A. Cry "Infidel!"
Carter, M. After One Year.
Cervantes. Poem for the Young White Man Who Asked Me How I, An Intelligent, Well-Read Person Could Believe in the War Between Races.
Chamberlayne, W. Bad Landlord, The.
Chudleigh. To the Ladies.
Unhappy they, who by their duty led.
Clarke, J. Determination.
Corrothers. Snapping of the Bow, The.
Crane, H. Black Tambourine.
Cummings, E. Thanksgiving (1956).
Dent. Return to English Turn.
Diop, D. Listen, comrades of the flaming centuries.
Time of Martyrdom, The.
Dombrovsky. They wanted me dead, the bastards.
Dove, R. Elevator Man, 1949.
Parsley.
Du'o'ng Bá Trạc. Prison Life.
"Elagin." You told me that I was born under a lucky star.
Garnet. Thus man devotes his brother and destroys.
Harper, F. Ethiopia.
Herbert, Z. What I Saw.
Heywood, J. Wilt thou use turners craft still? ye by my trouth.
Hikmet. Sad State of Freedom, A.
Hogan, L. Friday Night.
Hubert. Joseph in Carcere.
Hughes, L. Dream Boogie.
Harlem.
I too, sing America.
Huỳnh Phú Sổ. Bread.
Ignatow, D. For Medgar Evers.
Inada. Projected Scenario of a Performance to Be Given Before the UN.
Jastrun, T. Polish Knot, The.
Jayaprabha. Burn this Sari.
Johnson, L. Great Insohreckshan, Di.
Jolobe. Making of a Servant, The.
Jordan, J. Intifada.
Korvin-Piotrovsky. Farewell, Captain. In bygone days.
"Korzhavin." Poem about Youth and Romanticism, A.
Laing, K. Tatale Swine.
Lorde. Sisters in Arms.
Lysohorsky. Ballad of Jan Palach, Student and Heretic.
Macgoye. August the First: The Watchman Speaks.
Mandel, T. Say Ja.
Mandelstam. I Was Washing Outside in the Darkness.
Markham, E. Man with the Hoe, The.
Mayakovsky. At the Top of My Voice.
Can't Stand It.
How I Became a Dog.
Last Statement.

Menard. Negro's Lament, The.
Milne, A. Bad Sir Brian Botany.
Mnthali. Stranglehold of English Lit, The.
Moraga. For the Color of My Mother.
Moss, T. Lessons from a Mirror.
Mutabaruka. You Ask Me.
Niemoller. First they came for the Jews.
Obolduyev. Tongue, The.
Ofeimun. Handle for the Flutist, A.
Olson, C. Kingfishers, The.
Osgood, F. Woman.
Pasternak, B. Hamlet in Russia, A Soliloquy.
  Highest Sickness, The.
  To a Friend.
Phan Bội Châu. Alarm Clock, The.
  Human Nature.
  My Shadow and I.
  You Eat the Figs, So Sit Beneath the Tree.
Phan chu Trinh. Dogs in the Loft.
  Game of Chess, A.
  Impromptu.
Piercy. Unlearning to Not Speak.
Pietri. Old Buildings, The.
Plumly. Will Work for Food.
Po Chü-i. Red Cockatoo, The.
Pound, E. Commission.
Raine, K. Eudaimon.
Rebelo. Poem.
Reed, I. Catechism of d Neoamerican Hoodoo
  Church.
Rich, A. Burning of Paper instead of Children,
  The.
  Culture and Anarchy.
  From an Old House in America.
  Hunger.
Ritsos. Missing, The.
"Samoylov." Ivan and the Serf.
Sanchez, S. On Watching a World Series
  Game.
Sepamla. I Remember Sharpeville.
Shapiro, K. University.
Shershenevich. Plot with Bitterness.
Sigourney. To the First Slave Ship.
Soyinka. Apologia (Nkomati).
Stricker. Other Side, The.
Tản Đà. Ship An-Nam, The.
Tindal. Cry of the Oppressed, The.
Tolson. Dark Symphony.
Trần Cao Vân. On Poulo Condore.
Troupe. Boomerang: A Blatantly Political
  Poem.
Tù' Diễn Dồn. Long Night, The.
Unknown. Flood.
  Fourteenth of July, The.
  Go Down, Old Hannah.
Viiding. I am a serf. I work in the sweat of
  my brow.
Walker, A. Women.
Walker, M. For my people [everywhere
  singing their slave songs repeatedly: their].
Waniek. Chopin.
Washington. Moon Bound.
Watkins, N. Bedtime Story.
Whitfield. How long, oh gracious God! how
  long.
Woo, D. Great Helmsman, The.
Yeats. Fascination of what's difficult, The.
Yevtushenko. Half-measures / can kill.
Yi, Y. Vertex, The.
  Wilderness.
Young, A. Poem for Players, A.
Zhenkai. Answer.
Zorgenfrey. Over the Neva.
See also **Apartheid; Dehumanization; Sexism;**
Slavery; Tyranny

Optimism
Alexander, C. All things bright and beauteous.
Balamani Amma. To My Daughter.
Bangs, J. I never knew a night so black.
Browning, R. Pippa's Song.
Cibber. Blind Boy, The.
Clough. Say not the struggle nought [*or*
  naught] availeth.
Creeley. Invitation, The.
Galvin, B. Great Blue.
Hardy, T. When the clouds' swoln bosoms
  echo back the shouts of the many and strong.

Holub. Boy's Head, A.
Howard, R. Difference, The.
Jackson, L. Toward the Corner.
Morgan, E. Second Life, The.
Parker, D. Comment.
Radford, D. Novice, A.
Reid, A. Scotland.
Rukeyser, M. Yes.
Russell, G. It Might Have Been Worse.
Smith, S. Away, melancholy, / Away with it,
  let it go.
Teasdale. Philosopher, The.
Unknown. Brian O'Linn.
  High Resolve.
  Optimist / "Somebody Said That It Couldn't
  Be Done."
Wagner, C. Let's forget the many troubles.
Wilcox, E. Optimism.
Yevtushenko. City of Yes and the City of No,
  The.
Zukofsky, L. In Arizona / (how many years in
  the mountains).

Oracles
Euripides. Delphic Dawn.
Hooper, V. Reading, A.
Housman, A. Oracles, The.
Milton. Oracles are dumm, The.

Orange Trees and Oranges
Baker, T. For Geraldine.
Ferland. Orange.
Sitwell, S. Red-Gold Rain, The.
Sorrentino. Zukofsky.
Soto. Oranges.
Unknown. Hymn to the Orange.
Wakoski. Smudging.
Walcott. In a Green Night.
Wen Cheng-ming. This little courtyard—
  mdash;the wind is pure.
Xuân Diệu. Orange With the Rind Still Green,
  An.

Orange (color)
MacBeth. Orange Poem, The.
O'Hara, F. Why I Am Not a Painter.

Oratory
Antin. David ross called up from syracuse and
  wanted to know if.
Emerson, R. Orator.
Garioch. Did Ye See Me?
Unknown. Thorn Vine on the Wall.
Wells, C. Overworked Elocutionist, An.

Orchards
Ancient Sumerian Oral Tradition. Inanna sang.
Barnes, W. My Orcha'd in Linden Lea.
Doolittle, H. Orchard.
Dufault. In an Old Orchard.
Eliot, T. New Hampshire.
Emin. In the orchard at twilight.
Frost, R. Good-by and Keep Cold.
Jaccottet. Fruit.
Johnson, R. William Stukeley made his own
  Stonehenge.
Kenney. Plume.
Kinzie. Orchard dying, The.
Machej. Orchards in July.
Masters, E. Lost Orchard, The.
Oliver, M. Through Ruddy Orchards.
Robinson, A. Orchard at Avignon, An.
Sandburg, C. Wind Song.
Snodgrass, W. Old Apple Trees.
Stevenson, A. In the Orchard.
Stuart, M. In The Orchard.

Orchids
Ch'en Tzu-ang. Orchids grow through spring
  and summer.
Ch'u Yüan. Lord among the Clouds, The.
  Yüan, Ch'ü.
Doolittle, H. At Baia.
Gentry. Aunt Lucy.
Izumi. As I dig for wild orchids.
Roethke. Orchids.
Roseliep. White orchid.
Symons, A. Violet.
Wratislaw. Orchids.

Order
Ammons. Corsons Inlet.
Bible, *O.T.* Time for Everything, A.

Creeley. Window, The.
Eberhart, R. Hard Structure of the World, The.
Francis of Assisi. Cantica: Our Lord Christ:
  Of Order.
Herbert, G. Family [*or* Familie], The.
McClure, M. White Boot.
Meredith, G. Lucifer in Starlight.
Stevens, W. Connoisseur of Chaos.
  Idea of Order at Key West, The.
  Sad Strains of a Gay Waltz.
  To Henry Church.

Oregon (state)
Kaufman, B. Oregon.
Miller, J. Pilgrims of the Plains.
Nabokov. Lines Written in Oregon.

Organs and Organists
Brown, T. Wesley in Heaven.
Heard, J. New Organ, The.
Lewis, D. Lost Chord, The.
Stevens, G. Organist, The.

Orient
Ginsberg, A. After Yeats.
Ni Dhomhnaill. Venio ex Oriente.

Original Sin
Byron, G. Ah! didst *thou* tempt my mother?
Chaucer. Nun's Priest's Tale, The.
Donne. If poisonous [*or* poysonous]
  mineral[l]s, and if that tree.
Gumilyov. Progeny of Cain, The.
Nash, O. Ha! Original Sin!
Thomas, D. Incarnate devil in a talking snake.
Unknown. Adam Lay Bound.
  Alas, that ever that speche was spoken.
Vaughan, H. Corruption.
Very. Garden, The.
Warren, R. Original Sin.

Orioles
Chin Ch'ang-hsü. Spring Grievance.
Dickinson, E. One of the ones that Midas
  touched.
  To hear an Oriole sing.
Dunbar, P. Summer in the South.
Kees. Conversation in the Drawingroom, The.
Li Meng-yang. Oriole at Dawn, An.
Lowell, R. Fall 1961.
Po Chü-i. Hearing the Early Oriole.
Yang Chi. Describing My Feelings While
  Living in Retirement by the Riverside: Seven
  Poems to the Tune "Ch'ing-p'ing-yüeh."
Yang Shen. To the Tune "Chao-chün's
  Sorrow."
Yün Shou-p'ing. Inscribed on a Painting of
  Sailboats on the River—Seeing Off Yen-chi
  on His Journey to Ch'ang-an.

Orion (constellation)
Rich, A. Orion.
Turner, C. Orion.

Orkney Islands
Fowler, W. In Orknay.

Ormonde, Elizabeth Preston Butler, Countess
of
Shirley, J. To the Excellent Pattern of Beauty
  and Virtue, Lady Elizabeth, Countess of
  Ormonde.

Oronsay, Scotland
Irvine, J. Saint Colm-Cille and the Cairn of
  Farewell.

Orphans
Avidan. Song of the Self-Made Orphans.
Barnes, W. Readen ov a Head-Stwone.
Brontë, C. Orphan Child, The.
Cervantes. Refugee Ship.
Dobell, S. Orphan's Song, The.
Ficowski. Both Your Mothers.
Laughlin, J. Kind-, The.
Levine, P. On My Own.
Linden, M. Orphan Girl, An.
Lysohorsky. 22.6.1941.
Menander. What do you say to this? The
  thought has just.
Riley, J. Little Orphant Annie's come to our
  house to stay.
Rossetti, C. Iniquity of the Fathers upon the
  Children, The.
Rukeyser, M. That is what they say, who
  were broken off from love.

Stein, D. Searching for Schüpfen.
Tố Hữu. Orphans.
Unknown. Babes in the Wood, The ("Now ponder well, you parents dear").
Orphan, The.

Orpheus
"Alta." Euridice.
Antipater of Sidon. Never again, Orpheus.
Bancquart. Counterfable of Orpheus.
Browning, R. Eurydice to Orpheus.
Gascoyne. Orpheus in the Underworld.
Graham, J. Orpheus and Eurydice.
What the End Is For.
Herrick. Orpheus he went (as poets tell).
Hill, G. Orpheus and Eurydice.
Horace. Power of song, The.
Kinsella, J. Orpheus.
Lisle. Power of Music, The.
Lovelace, R. Orpheus to Beasts.
Orpheus to Woods.
Rich, A. I Dream I'm the Death of Orpheus.
Rilke. Be ahead of all parting, as though it already were.
Rukeyser, M. Poem as Mask, The.
Seneca. Deaths of Orphues and Hercules, The.
Unknown. Thus Sung Orpheus to His Strings.
Valentine, J. Orpheus and Eurydice.
Virgil. Orpheus and Eurydice.
Winchilsea. Answer, The.
Winters, Y. Orpheus.

Ostriches
Freeman, M. Ostrich is a Silly Bird, The.
Lovelace, R. Lucasta's Fan[ne], with a Looking-Glass[e] in It.
Moore, M. He "Digesteth Harde Yron."
Wilkins, M. Ostrich *is a silly bird*, The.

Ottawa, Ontario
Kleinzahler. Spleen.

Otterburn, Battle of (1388)
Unknown. Battle of Otterburn [*or* Oterborne], The.
Chevy Chase.

Otters
Hartnett. Possibility That Has Been Overlooked Is the Future, The.
Wounded otter, A.
Heaney, S. Otter, The.
Hughes, T. Otter, An.
Mac Low. Giant Otters.
Giant Philosophical Otters.
Swenson, M. Waterbird.

Ouija Boards
Merrill, J. Life like the periodical not yet.
Voices from the Other World.

Outlaws. *See* **Crime and Criminals**

Ovenbirds
Frost, R. Oven Bird, The.

Ovibos. *See* **Musk Oxen**

Ovid (Publius Ovidius Naso)
Ficowski. Ovid Twice Exiled.
Hill, G. Ovid in the Third Reich.
Jones, D. Summer Is a Poem by Ovid.
Ovid. Elegies 2.i.
Prior. Written in an Ovid.
Ransom, J. Philomela.
Thompson, D. Ovid on the Dacian Coast.
Walcott. Hotel Normandie Pool, The.

Owain Gwynedd, Prince of North Wales
Gray, T. Triumphs of Owen, The.

Owen, Anne
Philips, K. To the Excellent Mrs A. O. upon her receiving the name of Lucasia.

Owen, Wilfred
Hughes, T. Wilfred Owen's Photographs.

Owls
Baudelaire. Owls.
Browne, J. Great Brown Owl, The.
"Carroll." Lobster, The.
Chia Yi. Rhyme-Prose on the Owl.
Crum, L. "Good Night," Says the Owl.
De la Mare. Owl, The.
Doolittle, H. You look at me, a hut or cage contains.
Dufault. Owl.
Ewart. Owl Writes a Detective Story, The.

Fields, J. Owl-Critic, The.
Haines, J. If the Owl Calls Again.
Harwood, G. Father and Child.
Hubbell, P. Owl of the Greenwood.
Huchel. Meeting.
Jarrell. Bird of Night, The.
Jewell. Last screech owl cry.
Lardner. Hail to Thee, Blithe Owl.
Lear, E. Le Hibou et la Poussiquette.
Our mother was the pussy-cat, our father was the owl.
(The Owl and the Pussy-Cat).
There was an Old Man with a beard.
Merkel, B. Owls.
Moss, T. Owl In Daytime, The.
Mountain, M. Hoot.
Munkittrick. Song of the Owl, The.
Oliver, M. In the Pinewoods, Crows and Owl.
Little Owl Who Lives in the Orchard.
O'odham. Healing Songs.
Owen, G. Owl and the astronaut sailed through space, The.
Owl Woman. Songs for the Four Parts of the Night.
Richards, E. Wise old owl lived in an oak, A.
Schuyler, J. Korean Mums.
Shelley, P. Aziola, The.
Smith, D. Sea Owl.
Snodgrass, W. Owls.
Stevens, W. On the Adequacy of Landscape.
Tennyson, A. Owl, The.
Thomas, E. Owl, The.
Thomas, R. Ancients of the World, The.
Thomson, J. Signs of Storm.
Tu Fu. Travelling Northward.
Unknown. Boy in the Barn, The.
Limerick.
Owl and the Fox, The.
Owl / whose home was in the hemlock, The.
Song of the Owl.
Van Duyn. Ballad of Blossom, The.
Winchilsea. Nocturnal Reverie, A.

Oxen
"Dario." Far Away and Long Ago.
Dyer, J. My Ox Duke.
Edson, R. Ox, The.
Hamilton, G. Old Ox, The.
Hardy, T. Oxen, The.
Lu Yu. Herd-Boy, The.
Ranaivo. Humped Ox, The.
Simpson, L. White Oxen.
Tomlinson, C. Oxen: Ploughing at Fiesole.
Unknown. If I Might Be an Ox.
Twelve Oxen, The.
Virgil. Dead Ox, The.
Webster, M. Ox, The.
Whitman, W. Ox-Tamer, The.

Oxford, England
Auden. Oxford.
Fenton, J. Pitt-Rivers Museum, Oxford, The.
Grigson. Above the High.
Hall, D. Christ Church Meadows, [Oxford].
Hopkins, G. Duns Scotus's Oxford.
Johnson, L. Oxford.
Keats. On Oxford.
Letts. Spires of Oxford, The.
Ransom, J. Philomela.
Russell, T. To Oxford.

Oysters
"Carroll." Walrus and the Carpenter, The.
Heaney, S. Oysters.
Howard, R. Oystering.
Wildflowers.
Kaṇṇaṉār. What Her Girl Friend Said to him ("Near the salt pans").
Ponge. Oyster, the size of an average pebble, is of more rugged appearance, The.
See also **Clams and Clamming; Shells**

P

Pacific Ocean
Frost, R. Once by the Pacific.
Gunn, T. Discovery of the Pacific, The.
Jeffers, R. Coast-Road, The.
Eye, The.
Gray Weather.

Silko. Prayer to the Pacific.
Whitman, W. Facing west from California's shores.
Winters, Y. On Teaching the Young.
Slow Pacific Swell, The.

Pacifism and Pacifists
Beissel, H. In the one-two domestic goose one-two one-two step.
Belloc. Pacifist, The.
Cummings, E. I sing of Olaf glad and big.
Ezekiel. Patriot, The.
Homer. Goddess intervenes between Achilles and Agamemnon, The.
Kasdorf. Mennonites.
Lowell, R. After the Surprising Conversions.
Christmas Eve under Hooker's Statue.
Memories of West Street and Lepke.
Michie. Dooley Is a Traitor.
Shapiro, K. Conscientious Objector, The.
Tremblay, B. Home Front.
Unknown. Hymn: "O God of Hosts, thine Ear incline."
Whittier. Brown of Ossawatomie.
See also **Conscientious Objectors**

Paganism and Pagans
Eberhart, R. Soul Longs to Return Whence It Came, The.
"Field." Fellowship.
Milton. With these came they who, from the bord'ring flood.
Sappho. As the full moon slowly rose.
At last, on delicate feet.
Sidney, P. Double Sestine [*or* Sestina].
Tabb. Christ and the Pagan.
Unknown. Plain of Adoration, The.
Wordsworth, W. Sonnet: "World is too much with us; late and soon, The."

Pain
Adamson. Passing Through Experiences.
"Æ." Pain.
"Akhmatova." Memory of love, you are painful!
Amichai. Ibn Gabirol.
Anacreon. Eros, playing among the roses.
Armantrout. Winter.
Baraka. Agony, An. As Now.
Barnes, J. Dog Days 1978.
Benedikt. Dossier of the Torturer.
Nipplewhip, The.
Bloch, C. Rising to Meet It.
Bozhilov. Lilies.
Breytenbach. Breyten Prays for Himself.
Brontë, E. If grief for grief can touch thee.
O thy bright eyes must answer now.
Brook, D. School of Pain, The.
Bruner. Gift, The.
Bryant, W. Mutation.
Carew, T. To My Inconstant Mistress [*or* Mistris].
Carson, C. Knee, The.
Cassian. Blood, The.
Ghost.
Catullus. Carmen 85.
Cave. Ah! why from me art thou for ever flown.
Ceravolo. Conception.
Chế Lan Viên. Silk Threads of Memory.
Waning Night, The.
War Elephant, The.
Chernoff. Phantom Pain.
Chipasula. Talking of Sharp Things.
Chu Shu-chen. Old Anguish, The.
Stormy Night in Autumn.
Clare, J. Love's Pains.
Coleridge, S. Dejection.
Cooper, J. Infusion Room, The.
Creeley. Flower, The.
Csoori. Postponed Nightmare.
Cullen, C. Protest.
Saturday's Child.
Song in Spite of Myself.
Damas. There are nights with no name.
Daniel, S. If this be love, to draw[e] a weary [*or* wearie] breath.
Sonnet: "Care-charmer Sleep[e], son[ne] of the sable night."
Daryush. Off Duty.

Di Prima. For H.D.
Dickinson, E. After great pain a formal feeling comes—.
I can wade Grief.
I heard a Fly buzz—when I died[—died].
I'm "wife"—I've finished that.
Much Madness is divinest Sense.
Pain—expands the Time.
Pain—has an Element of Blank.
There is a Languor of the Life.
There is a pain—so utter.
'Tis not that Dying hurts us so.
'Twas like a Maelstrom, with a notch.
Wounded Deer—leaps highest, A.
Đỗ Tấn Xuân. Words of Comfort.
Dryden, J. Ah, how sweet it is to love! Love's Despair.
Dunn, S. Vanishings, The.
Empson. Villanelle.
"Ephelia." To J. G.
Fainlight, R. Stubborn.
Garrett, G. In the Hospital.
Gascoyne. Ecce Homo.
Glück, L. First Memory.
Goldbarth. Still Life, Symbolic of Lines, A.
Grahn. Ella, in a Square Apron, Along Highway 80.
Funeral Plainsong from a Younger Woman to an Older Woman, A.
Gray, J. Femmes Damnées.
Greenwell, D. Broken Chain, The.
Grosholz. Back Trouble.
Gunn, T. Innocence.
Man With Night Sweats, The.
Hagedorn, J. Solea.
Hans. Hurt.
Hartnett. I have exhausted the delighted range.
I think sometimes / of the fingernail slotted.
Hayden, R. Road in Kentucky, A.
Whipping, The.
Henry, J. "Pain, who made thee?" thus I said once.
Hongo. O-Bon: Dance for the Dead.
Horton, G. Troubled with the Itch and Rubbing with Sulphur.
Howe, F. First Chance Twice.
Hsü Wei. Buddhist Monk Cut and Burned His Own Flesh to Make The Rains Stop—A Man From His Native Place Asked Me to Write a Poem to Send to Him, A.
Hughes, L. Dream Boogie: Variation.
Jaccottet. Wound seen from afar.
Jarrell. Field Hospital, A.
90 North.
Kipling, R. Power of the Dog, The.
Larkin, J. Rape.
Levertov. Ache of marriage, The.
Li Shang-yin. Bite back passion. Spring now sets.
Lovelace, R. To Lucasta ("Like to the sentinel stars, I watch all night").
Lu Yu. Phoenix Hairpins.
Macgoye. August the First; Court Martial. The Mother Speaks.
Mackenzie, K. Hospital—Retrospections, The.
Mathis. Seven Months.
McGough, R. Poem With a Limp.
Merry. Adieu and Recall to Love, The.
Mew. In Nunhead Cemetery.
Meynell, V. Sympathy.
Mirabai. O friends, I am mad.
Moraga. For the Color of my Mother.
Moss, H. Wars, The.
Oppian. Loves of the Tortoise, The.
Ostriker. Leaf Pile, The.
Owen, W. Greater Love.
Hospital Barge at Cérisy.
Partridge, F. My Days Go On.
Piercy. When a friend dies.
Po Chü-i. Immeasurable pain!
Ponsot. "Love is not Love."
Procter, A. Lost Chord, A.
Ralegh, W. Sweet Unsure.
Ramanujan. Pleasure.
Ravikovitch. Private View, A.
Rexroth, K. Half in a dream.

Rich, A. That conversation we were always on the edge.
Ridler. Crab is in again, his monthly house, The.
Rimbaud, A. Stolen Heart, The.
Robinson, E. Pain.
Rossetti, C. Chilly Night, A.
From Monna Innominata.
Introspective.
Roy, L. Triple Overtime.
Sackville-West. Out with a Gun.
Salkey. Inside.
Sandburg, C. At a Window.
Sarton. Tortured, The.
Schultz, P. For My Mother.
Scovell. Stranger, A.
Seibert. Casey Jones.
Sexton. Pain for a Daughter.
Shapiro, A. Letter said you had to speak to me, The.
Shapiro, K. Hospital.
Shelley, P. Lament, A: "O world! O life! O time!"
Sidney, P. Sonnet 1: "Loving in truth, and fain[e] in verse my love to show."
Sonnet 14: "Alas, have I not pain enough, my friend."
Sonnet 16: "In nature apt to like when I did see."
Smith, S. Lads of the village, we read in the lay, The.
Snodgrass, W. Flat One, A.
Södergran. Pain.
Soyinka. Fado Singer.
Stern, G. Coleman Valley Road.
Stevenson, R. I saw red evening through the rain.
Suckling, J. Love's Offence.
Song: "I prithee spare me, gentle boy."
Tanikawa Shuntaro. Everyone possesses something sad.
Thomas, C. Flesh will heal and pain will fade.
Heart Wounds.
Thompson, C. After-Glow of Pain, The.
Unknown. Is it not sure a deadly pain.
It's raining, it's pouring.
Thus I complain my grevous hevynesse.
Young Lady of Twickenham, The.
Valéry. Bee, The.
Wetzsteon. Three Songs.
Whitman, W. I sit and look out upon all the sorrows of the world, and upon all oppression and wrong.
Wieseltier. Holy Is the Desire to Proclaim the Existence of God.
Wilcox, E. Life.
Solitude.
Those We Love the Best.
Williams, C. Alzheimer's: The Wife.
Wordsworth, W. Complaint, A.
Wright, J. Prayer to the Lord Ramakrishna, A.
Wroth. Sonnet 6: "My pain[e], still smothered [or smother'd] in my grievèd bre[a]st."
Sonnet 101.
Wyatt, T. Alas, the grief and deadly wo[e]ful smart[!].
All heavy minds.
I love, loved, and so doth she.
If with complaint the pain might be expressed.
Sighs are my food, drink are my tears.
Thou sleepest fast and I with woeful heart.
Yosano. Tanka: "Agonizing beyond words."
Tanka: "But for women."
Zarzyski. Trespasses.

Paine, Thomas
Freneau. On Mr. Paine's Rights of Man.
Mather, J. God save great Thomas Paine.

Painting and Painters
Alexander, E. Painting / (Frida Kahlo).
Anacreon. Come, all you painters, all you who are the best.
Picture, The.
Ashbery. Painter, The.
Auden. Musée des Beaux Arts.
Ausonius. To One that Painted Eccho.
Baraka. Politics of Rich Painters, The.
Berryman. Winter Landscape.

Bishop, E. Large Bad Picture.
Poem: "About the size of an old-style dollar bill."
Bishop, J. Recollection, A.
Blake, W. Sir Joshua Reynolds.
Bly, R. Remembering in Oslo the Old Picture of the Magna Carta.
Boland, E. From the Painting "Back from Market" by Chardin.
I remember the way the big windows washed.
Brooks, S. Poem by a Perfectly Furious Academician.
Browning, R. Andrea del Sarto.
Face, A.
Guardian-Angel, The.
Pictor Ignotus.
Bryant, W. To Cole, the Painter, Departing for Europe.
Cage. 25 Mesostics Re and Not Re Mark Tobey.
Cary, A. Katrina on the Porch.
Order for a Picture, An.
Cassells. These Are Not Brushstrokes.
Channing. Murillo's Magdalen.
Cheng Hsieh. For Contemporary Artist Pien Wei-Ch'I.
Conquest. Rokeby Venus, The.
Coolidge, C. Jerome in His Study.
Corso. Rembrandt—Self Portrait.
Cranch. My Old Palette.
Cronin, A. Lines for a Painter.
D'Arcy, H. Face upon [or on] the Floor, The.
De la Mare. Brueghel's Winter.
Deutsch. Poem, The: "Painter of Dante's awful ferry-ride, The."
Dickinson, E. I would not paint—a picture.
Drake, J. National Painting, The.
Engle, P. Portrait of a King's Mistress, Nude.
Enright, D. Laughing Hyena, after [or by] Hokusai, The.
Escoffery. Tricks of the Trade.
Ferlinghetti, L. Don't let that horse / eat that violin.
Sarolla's women in their picture hats.
Ferry. Cythera.
"Field." La Gioconda.
Portrait, A.
Foster, E. Poetry and Joy.
Fulton, A. Priming Is a Negligee, The.
Fumi Saito. Tanka: "Don't resemble me."
Gilder, R. Hour in a Studio, An.
Giscombe. Bro Duncanson.
Glassco. Cardinal's Dog, The.
Graham, J. At Luca Signorelli's Resurrection of the Body.
Gray, J. Crucifix, A.
Guest, B. Wild gardens overlooked by night lights. Parking.
Gunn, T. In Santa Maria del Popolo.
Hall, D. Scream, The.
Halleck, F. et al. National Painting [or Paintings], The.
Harper, M. Zocalo.
Harris, C. Framed.
Hearne, V. Gauguin's White Horse.
Hecht, A. At the Frick.
Death the Painter.
Herbert, Z. Painter.
Herrick. Upon Umber: Epigram.
Hine. Here is another poem in a picture.
Ho Ching-ming. Fish in a Painting.
Song of the Painting "River and Mountains," by Wu Wei.
Holub. How to Paint a Perfect Christmas.
Howard, R. Giovanni da Fiesole on the Sublime.
Hsieh Chin. Inscribed on a Painting of Dragons by Ch'en So-weng.
Hsü Wei. I Once Did a Bamboo Painting for Somebody—Now He Wants Me To Do Another. I Have Written This To Answer Him.
Inscribed on a Painting of Windy Bamboo, to Be Presented to Tzu-kan.
Huang T'ing-chien. To Go with Shih K'o's Painting of an Old Man Tasting Vinegar.
Hughes, T. To Paint a Water Lily.

Hugo, R.　Milltown Union Bar, The.
Johnson, J.　Before a Painting.
Johnston, M.　Sea-Cucumber, The.
Jonson, B.　Picture of the Body, The.
Justice, D.　Anonymous Drawing.
　On a Painting by Patient B of the
　　Independence State Hospital for the Insane.
Kates.　No altarpiece includes the painter.
Komunyakaa.　Nude Study.
Kopland.　Breughel's Winter.
Langland, J.　Fall of Icarus: Brueghel.
Lawrence, D.　Innocent England.
Li K'ai-hsien.　Poem about Fan the Fourth, A.
Li Meng-yang.　Song of Lin Liang's Painting
　"Two Horned Falcons."
Li Shang-yin.　Wang Chao-chün.
Lin Ya-tzu.　By Flower-and-Moon Pavilion, I
　stay my carriage.
Lochhead, L.　Mad Meg on my mantelpiece.
Longley, M.　Man Lying on a Wall.
Lovelace, R.　Painture [or Peinture].
　To My Worthy Friend Mr. Peter Lely [or
　　Lilly].
Lowell, R.　Epilogue: "Those blessèd
　structures, plot and rhyme."
Markham, E.　Man with the Hoe, The.
Marvell.　After two sittings, now our Lady
　State.
McClatchy.　Capriccio of Roman Ruins and
　Sculpture with Figures, A.
McGuckian.　Sitting, The.
Mei Yao Ch'en.　On Seeing a Painting of
　Plants and Insects by Chü-ning.
Melville, H.　Bench of Boors, The.
　Fruit and Flower Painter.
Michelangelo Buonarroti.　To Giovanni da
　Pistoia When the Author Was Painting the
　Vault of the Sistine Chapel, 1509.
Mitchell, S.　Vermeer.
Mueller, L.　Monet Refuses the Operation.
Muldoon, P.　Bearded Woman, by Ribera, The.
Muske.　Painter's Daughter, The.
Nemerov.　Old Picture, An.
O'Hara, F.　Having a Coke with You.
　Why I Am Not a Painter.
Ostriker.　Minor Van Gogh (He Speaks), A.
Palmer, M.　Dearest Reader.
　O you in that little bark.
Picasso.　9.1.59: II.
　9.1.59: VI.
Pinkerton, H.　On Vermeer's "Young Woman
　with a Water Jug" (1658) in the Metropolitan
　Museum.
Plumly.　After Whistler.
Po Chü-i.　Painting Bamboo, a Song.
　To a Portrait Painter who Desired Him to Sit.
Prévert.　First paint a cage.
Raine, K.　Old Paintings on Italian Walls.
Ray, D.　Midnight Diner by Edward Hopper,
　A.
　On a Fifteenth-Century Flemish Angel.
Ridler.　Backgrounds to Italian Paintings:
　Fifteenth Century.
　On a Picture by Michele Da Verona, of Arion
　as a Boy Riding upon a Dolphin.
Rilke.　Flamingos, The.
Rodriguez, J.　Nu-plastik Fanfare Red.
Roseliep.　Under.
Rossetti, C.　In An Artist's Studio.
Rossetti, D.　For A Venetian Pastoral By
　Giorgone (In the Louvre).
　For Spring By Sandro Botticelli.
　On the Painter Val Prinsep.
Rowlands.　Epigram 29: "Gentlewoman of the
　dealing trade, A."
Rukeyser, M.　Birth of Venus, The.
Salter.　Young Girl Peeling Apples.
Sandburg, C.　People Who Must.
Sanders, E.　Cutting Prow, The.
Schwartz, L.　Self-Portrait.
Scott, J.　Helen Paints a Room (1984).
Service.　My Madonna.
Shapiro, K.　Dome of Sunday, The [or A].
Shen Chou.　Painting of Peach Blossom
　Spring, A.
　To the Tune "Nan-hsiang-tzu."

Smith, V.　At an Exhibition of Historical
　Paintings, Hobart.
Snodgrass, W.　Matisse: "The Red Studio."
Song.　Beauty and Sadness.
Stanton, M.　Portrait by Bronzino, A.
Stickney, T.　In Ampezzo.
　On Sandro's Flora.
Su Tung-p'o.　On a Painting by Wang the
　Clerk of Yen Ling.
　Written on a Painting Entitled "Misty Yangtze
　　and Folded Hills."
Swenson, M.　Painting the Gate.
Szymborska.　Women of Rubens, The.
Tai Piao-yüan.　Painting of One Hundred Wild
　Geese, A.
T'ang Yin.　Inscribed on a Painting.
　Scene at Heaven Gate, The.
Tao-chi.　Inscribed on My Ink Landscape
　Painting.
　Mood comes on—I want to cross Hsi-ling,
　　The.
　Riding a Boat on Wu-ling Stream.
Thomas, R.　View from the Window, The.
Tomlinson, C.　Farewell to Van Gogh.
　Paring the Apple.
Unknown.　Here let the Muse perform the
　painter's art.
　I'm glad the sky is painted blue.
Very.　Sumach Leaves, The.
Violi.　Index.
Walcott.　Gauguin.
Wang Chi.　Viewing Mr. Yü's Landscape
　Painting on the Wall.
Wat.　Facing Bonnard.
Weiners.　Poem for Painters, A.
Weiss, T.　Ten Little Rembrandts.
Wen Cheng-ming.　Volumes of books, tea and
　incense.
Wharton, E.　Two Backgrounds.
Wheatley, P.　To S. M., a Young African
　Painter, on Seeing His Works.
White, E.　I Paint What I See.
White, M.　"Claude Monet sur son lit do
　mort."
Whitman, W.　Death's Valley.
Wilbur.　Museum Piece.
　My Father Paints the Summer.
Williams, W.　Dance, The.
　Hunters in the Snow, The.
　Parable of the Blind, The.
Wollach.　To See Long like El Greco.
Wordsworth, W.　Elegiac Stanzas Suggested by
　a Picture of Peele Castle, in a Storm [Painted
　by Sir George Beaumont].
Wu Chen.　Ni Tsan Poem Following Rhyme-
　Words of Wu Chen.
Wyatt, T.　In Spayn.
Wylie.　Castilian.
Yang Chi.　Painting of Bamboo by Ni Yün-lin,
　A.
Yü Chi.　Little Landscape by Chao Ch'ien-li,
　A.
Yün Shou-p'ing.　Essence of ink, The.
　Facing you, on the wall, across from your bed.
　Inscribed on a Painting of Sailboats on the
　　River—Seeing Off Yen-chi on His Journey to
　　Ch'ang-an.
　On a Painting "Ancient Trees and Flowing
　　Stream."
Zivancevic.　Poem with a Tilde in the Title, A.

Paleontology and Paleontologists
Harte, B.　Society Upon the Stanislaus, The.
"Twain."　Imitation of Julia A. Moore.
See also **Dinosaurs; Evolution; Extinction;**
　Fossils

Palestine
Byron, G.　On Jordan's Bank.
Darwish, M.　Psalm 2.
　Sirhan Drinks His Coffee in the Cafeteria.
　Victim Number 48.
Lindsay, V.　John Brown.
Pagis.　Decline of an Empire.
Ravikovitch.　You Can't Kill a Baby Twice.
See also **Israel**

Palm Sunday
Block, A.　Willow-Boughs, The.
Chesterton, G.　Donkey, The.

Symons, A.　Palm Sunday: Naples.
Wratislaw.　Palm Sunday.

Palm Trees
Abd-ar-Rahman I.　Palm Tree, The.
Campion, T.　Thus I resolve, and time hath
　taught me so.
Crane, H.　Royal Palm.
Cuney.　No Images.
Melville, H.　Rolfe and the Palm.
Stevens, W.　Of Mere Being.
Unknown.　Ode to the Betel Palm.
Whittier.　Palm-Tree, The.

Pan (god)
Anyte.　Why, country Pan, sitting still.
Arnold, M.　Lines Written in Kensington
　Gardens.
Browning, E.　Flush or Faunus.
　Musical Instrument, A.
"Cornwall."　Sonnet; A Still Place.
Diodorus Zonas.　Pan Asks about Daphnis.
Eliot, T.　Mr. Apollinax.
Emerson, R.　Patient Pan, The.
Fletcher, J.　God of Sheep, The.
Frost, R.　Pan with Us.
Glaukos.　Pan and the Nymphs.
Keats.　Hymn to Pan.
Kyger.　Pan as the Son of Penelope.
Leonidas.　For that goatfucker, goatfooted.
Leonidas of Tarentum.　For that goatfucker,
　goatfooted.
Lyly, J.　Pan's Song.
Marvell.　Clorinda and Damon.
Meleager.　Goat-foot Pan has quit his flocks.
Nicarchus of Alexandria.　Take note who
　stoop.
Plato.　Pan Piping.
Robinson, A.　Valley, The.
Shelley, P.　Hymn of Pan.
Theocritus.　Daphnis the fair-skinned, who
　plays country songs.
Unknown.　Inscription for a Statue of Pan.

Panama
Gilbert, J.　Beyond the Chagres.
Unknown.　Golden Island; or, the Darian Song,
　The.

Pancakes
Prelutsky.　Pancake Collector, The.
Rossetti, C.　Mix a pancake, / Stir a pancake.
Taylor, J.　Those Flapjacks of Brown's.
Tchernichowsky.　Levivot.

Pandas
Seaton, M.　Theories of Illusion.

Pansies
Binyon.　Harebell and Pansy.

Pantheism and Pantheists
Bryant, W.　Thanatopsis.
Coleridge, S.　Religious Musings.
Kavanagh, P.　One, The.
Naden.　Pantheist's Song of Immortality, The.
Ortiz.　Creation.
Swinburne.　Higher Pantheism in a Nutshell,
　The.
Tennyson, A.　Higher Pantheism, The.
Wordsworth, W.　By the Sea.

Panthers
"Carroll."　Lobster, The.
Nash, O.　Panther is like a leopard, The.
Rilke.　Panther, The.
Saxena.　Black panther is sleeping on the
　crags, The.
Wheelock, J.　Black Panther, The.

Papacy
Housman, A.　Pope, The.
See also **Catholicism; Listings for Individual**
　Popes

Paperweights
Schnackenberg.　Paperweight, The.

Parachuting and Parachutists. *See* **Sky Diving**
and Sky Divers

Parades
Field, R.　Parade.
Harte, B.　Second Review of the Grand Army,
　A.
Hughes, L.　Parade.
Ignatow, D.　I see a truck mowing down a
　parade.

Miles, J. Maxim.
Sassoon. Suicide in [the] Trenches.
Stevenson, R. Young Night Thought.
Whitman, W. Boston Ballad [1854], A.
See also **Marching and Marchers**

Paradise. *See* **Heaven**

Paradise Lost
Marvell. On Mr Milton's "Paradise Lost."
See also **Milton, John**

Paradoxes
Ashbery. Paradoxes and Oxymorons.
Carruth, H. At his last gig in horrid Amsterdam.
Catullus. *Carmina*, LXXXV.
Creeley. Time.
Dunn, S. Happiness.
Eberhart, R. Hardy Perennial.
Gallagher, T. Not There.
Hart, L. I Wish I Were in Love Again.
Hewison. Limerick: "Said an erudite sinologue: 'How'."
Matthews, J. Gravity's the villain in this piece—.
Pastan. Because the night you asked me.
Rankin, P. Bedtime Story.
Sidney, P. Sonnet 6: "Some lovers speak, when they their Muses entertain."
Stafford, W. Report from an Unappointed Committee.
Stern, G. Nobody else living knows that song as well as I do.
Wier. Daytrip to Paradox.

Parakeets
Causley. One day at a Perranporth pet-shop.
Steinbergh. Letting the Parakeet Fly.

Paralysis
Ponsot. Residual Paralysis.

Paranoia
Khodasevich. Through the Window.
Ludvigson. Widow, The.
Sexton. Noon Walk on the Asylum Lawn.
Shakespeare, W. Sonnet 118.
Spicer, J. Conspiracy.
Strand. Tunnel, The.
Wright, F. Entry in an Unknown Hand.

Pardons and Pardoners
Chaucer. Pardoner's Prologue, The.
Vallejo. Our Daily Bread.

Parenthood
"Aleichem." Sleep, My Child.
Beers, E. Which Shall It Be?
Bible, *O.T.* Psalm 127.
Bowering, G. I am slowly dying, water evaporating.
Buckley, V. Parents.
Bukowski. Three Oranges.
Burns, R. Poet's Welcome to His Love-Begotten Daughter [the First Instance that Entitled Him to the Venerable Appellation of Father], A.
Dove, R. Daystar.
Gilmore, M. Nationality.
Guest, E. Becoming a Dad.
Harwood, G. In The Park.
Hoffman, D. Special Train, A.
Hood, T. Parental Ode to My Son, Aged Three Years and Five Months, A.
Housman, A. Fragment of an English Opera.
Jarman, M. Gift, The.
Jonson, B. On My First Daughter.
Kay, J. Mummy and Donor and Deirdre.
Kinnell. After Making Love We Hear Footsteps.
Kooser. At the End of the Weekend.
Leib. Door and Window Bolted Fast.
Lorde. What my child learns of the sea.
Macdonagh, T. Wishes for My Son.
MacNamee. Childless.
Madgett. Offspring.
McGinley. Velvet Hand, The.
Meredith, W. Parents.
Meynell, A. Parentage.
Miedzyrzecki. Penguins.
Olds, S. That Moment.
Oppenheimer, J. Father Poem.
Osgood, F. Ellen Learning to Walk.

Plath. Morning Song.
Rich, A. Afterwake, The.
Ridler. For a Child Expected.
Shakespeare, W. Sonnet 2.
Simpson, L. Goodnight, The.
Smith, D. August, on the Rented Farm.
Stafford, W. With Kit, Age Seven, at the Beach.
Stuart, D. Separate Parties.
Su Tung-p'o. On the Birth of His Son.
Taylor, E. Upon Wedlock and Death of Children.
Traherne. Rapture, The.
Unknown. Little Chap Who Follows Me, The.
Walker, J. Studying Physics with My Daughter.
Weaver, M. Improvisation for Piano.
Wesley, S. Anacreontic, on Parting with a Little Child.
Whittemore, R. Party, The.
Wilson, E. Lakeside.
Yeats. Prayer for My Daughter, A.

Parents
Ali, A. Dream of Glass Bangles, A.
Houses.
Avidan. Song of the Self-Made Orphans.
Ball, S. Nocturnal.
Berryman. Sympathy, A Welcome, A.
Blake, W. Infant Sorrow.
Bly, R. Driving My Parents Home at Christmas.
For My Son Noah, Ten Years Old.
Brigham. Will's Love, The.
"Carroll." Three Badgers, The.
Causley. Eden Rock.
Ciardi. Censorship.
Sometimes Even Parents Win.
Coolidge, C. Album—A Runthru.
Cornford, F. Ode on the Whole Duty Of Parents.
Cullen, C. Fruit of the Flower.
Cummings, E. If there are any heavens my mother will (all by herself) have.
Ellis, T. Kiss in the Dark, A.
Emanuel, J. Sleeping, The.
Ferlinghetti, L. Lost Parents.
Ferry. My Parents En Route.
Galvin, P. My Father Spoke with Swans.
Gbadamosi. Reading, The.
Gershon. I Was Not There.
Gillan. My Daughter at 14: Christmas Dance, 1981.
Gladding. Asparagus.
Glück, L. Paradise.
Goldbarth. Still Life, Symbolic of Lines, A.
Goldberg, B. Being Pharaoh.
Graves, R. Parent to Children.
Grosholz. Eden.
Gwynn, R. Drive-In, The.
Hall, D. My son, my executioner.
Hamod, S. Leaves.
Hemschemeyer. I Remember the Room Was Filled with Light.
Herrick. God to Be First Served.
Hongo. Hongo Store 29 Miles Volcano Hilo, Hawaii, The.
Hsü Pen. To the Filial Son, Ts'ui.
Huddle. Two Facts.
Jarrell. Player Piano, The.
Kinnell. Lackawanna.
Kirschner. Two Blue Swans.
Komunyakaa. My Father's Love Letters [or Loveletters].
Kunitz, S. Quinnapoxet.
Larkin, P. This Be The Verse.
Laughlin, J. Step on His Head.
Lee, D. Billy Batter.
There was a man who never was.
Lum. Backup, The.
"MacDiarmid." Two Parents, The.
Magee, K. Instrumentum Vocale.
McAuley, J. Because.
Merrill, J. Broken Home, The.
Childlessness.
Merwin, W. Lament for the Makers.
Mirikitani. Suicide Note.
Mizejewski. Parents Sleeping.

Morley, H. Parents.
Moss, T. Party to which Wolves are Invited, The.
Muldoon, P. Mixed Marriage, The.
Nash, O. Parent, The.
Olds, S. I Go Back to May 1937.
Oppen. Sara in Her Father's Arms.
Parker, P. Prologue from "Legacy."
Phillips, A. Summer Mother Fell in Love and Wanted to Leave My Father, The.
Rosen, M. Night Before His Parents' First Trip to Europe His Mother Writes a Letter "To Our Children", The.
Rossetti, C. Why did baby die.
Rottman. APO 96225.
Seiler. Digging in the Streets of Gold.
Senior. Ancestral Poem.
Silverstein, S. Clarence Lee from Tennessee.
Simic. Book Full of Pictures, A.
Simpson, L. My father in the night commanding No.
Skoyles. Good Cheer.
Sorrentino. Zukofsky.
Spires. Globe.
Stafford, W. Both Ways.
Story That Could Be True, A.
Vocation.
With Kit, Age Seven, at the Beach.
Unknown. Limerick.
Upton, L. Lost Child.
Vinz. Sins of the Fathers.
Wallace, R. Facts of Life, The.
Wevill. Mystery, The.
Whalen. "Never Apologize; Never Explain."
Wrigley, R. Parents.
Yau. Edificio Sayonara.

Pari
Kapilar. Farewell to Pāri's Hill.
His Hill.
Memory of the Hill, A.
Pāri! Pāri! they cry.
Pāri's Green Land, Remembered.
Pāri's Hill Is Partial to Dancers.
Then and Now.
Waterfalls and Liquor ("Waterfalls sounded").
Pari. That Month.
Pāri's daughters. That month.

Paris, France
Apollinaire. Phantom of Clouds, A.
Bancquart. Town.
Vanished, The.
Bishop, E. Two Mornings and Two Evenings.
Cranch. In the Palais Royal Garden I stood listening to-day.
Cummings, E. Two X.
Desnos. Night Watchman of Pont-au-Change, The.
St Merri district, The.
Dipoko. From My Parisian Diary.
Poem of Villeneuve St Georges, A.
Dove, R. Bistro Styx, The.
Island Women of Paris, The.
Fenton, J. In Paris with You.
Greger. Notre Dame, Sainte Chapelle, Sacré Coeur by foot—.
Leland, C. Breitmann in Paris.
Malroux. Octet Before Winter.
McOrlan. Accessories shop, The.
Produce from the colonies.
Millay, E. Armenonville.
Miller, J. In Père La Chaise.
Milosz, C. Bypassing rue Descartes.
Piatt, S. Palace-Burner, The.
Pitchford. 104 Boulevard Saint-Germain.
Pound, E. In A Station of the Metro.
Prévert. August Bank Holiday.
Ransom, J. Amphibious Crocodile.
Rapin. Of Gardens.
Rivers, C. Four Sheets to the Wind and a One-Way Ticket to France.
Mourning Letter from Paris, A.
Senghor. In Memoriam.
Luxembourg 1939.
Supervielle. Return to Paris.
Symons, A. Paris.
Tzara. For Robert Desnos.
Wilbur. Place Pigalle.

Young, A. Dance of the Infidels.

Parker, Charlie
Ashanti. Just Another Gig.
Barlow, G. Mingus Speaks: Found Poems.
Brathwaite, E. Blues.
Brown, A. Assassination of Charlie Parker, The.
Corso. Requiem for "Bird" Parker, Musician.
Creeley. Chasing the Bird.
Crouch, S. Up on the Spoon.
Dodson, O. Yardbird's Skull.
Harjo, J. Bird.
Harper, M. "Bird Lives": Charles Parker [in St. Louis].
Hull, L. Ornithology.
Jackson, R. Shadows.
Kaufman, B. Walking Parker Home.
Kerouac. 239th Chorus: "Charley Parker Looked like Buddha."
Lagrone. I Heard the Byrd.
May, K. Valentine's Day.
Mitchell, A. Goodbye.
Neal, L. Don't say goodbye to the Porkpie Hat that rolled.
Reed, I. Poetry Makes Rhythm in Philosophy.
Spicer, J. Song for Bird and Myself.
Thomas, L. Historiography.
Zimmer. But Bird.

Parks
Aiken, C. South End.
Argüelles, I. Canto the Tenth.
Arnold, M. Lines Written in Kensington Gardens.
Atkins. On the Fine Arts Garden, Cleveland.
Baruch. Popcorn-Popper, The.
Bland, P. Notes for the Park Keeper.
Brickley. Sheet lightning.
Caraion. Enveloping Echo, The.
Crow, C. City Park.
Davies, W. Hill-Side Park, The.
Duck. On Richmond Park.
Fisher, A. Snowy Benches.
Hare, P. Deceit in the Park.
Ignatow, D. Park.
Ingram, A. Castle Howard, the Seat of the Rt. Hon. Charles, Earl of Carlisle.
Jones, P. In the Park.
Kirby, D. To a French Structuralist.
Langhorne. Studley Park.
Livingston, M. Envoi: Washington Square Park.
Lowell, R. Public Garden, The.
Machi. Tanka: "Cherry blossoms."
Millay, E. Armenonville.
Moss, H. Crossing the Park.
Nagy, A. Four-Light Window, A.
Nemerov. Statues in the Public Gardens, The.
Oden. Carousel, The.
Pasternak, B. Hamlet.
Pizzarelli. Drop of ocean.
Redmond. Definition of Nature.
Samio. Tanka: "When the gardener."
Smith, I. In the Park.
Stevens, W. Vacancy in the Park.
Thomas, D. Hunchback in the park, The.
Ts'ao P'i. Lotus Lake.
Turner, W. Magic.
Unknown. King Wen's Park Divine.
Rise and Progress of the Present Taste in Planning Parks, Pleasure Grounds, Gardens, etc, The.
Vaughan, H. Upon the Priory Grove, His Usual Retirement.
Waller, E. On St. James's Park, as Lately Improved by His Majesty.
Westmorland. To Sir John Wentworth, Upon His Curiosities and Courteous Entertainment at Summerly in Lovingland.

Parliament, Great Britain
Carey. Fig for the Lower House, A.
Hughes, T. Wilfred Owen's Photographs.
Milton. On the New Forcers of Conscience Under the Long Parliament.
O'Connor, P. Fag-End.
Oliver, D. We followed the river to Fortune's Wheel.
Unknown. Free Parliament Litany, A.

Vaughan, H. Charnel-house, The.

Parma, Italy
De Vere, A. Correggio's Cupolas at Parma.
Lear, E. Limericks, I (v).

Parmigianino
Ashbery. Self-Portrait in a Convex Mirror.

Parnell, Charles Stewart
Yeats. Parnell came down the road, he said to a cheering man.

Parodies
Borges. From an Apocryphal Gospel.
"Carroll." Crocodile, The.
Father William.
Hiawatha's Photographing.
White Knight's Song, The.
Chaucer. Tale of Sir Thopas, The.
Koch, K. Variations on a Theme by William Carlos Williams.
Unknown. Patience is a virtue.
Pilot's Psalm, The.

Parrots
Bridges, R. Poor Poll.
Chukhonstev. Parrot, The.
Dove, R. Parsley.
Flecker. Parrot, The.
Frere. Boy and the Parrot, The.
Gibson, W. Parrots, The.
Han-shan. Parrots dwell in the west country.
Magee, W. Gran's Green Parrot.
Marchant. Little Miss and Her Parrot.
Po Chü-i. Crow Cries at Night, The.
Too Brilliant.
Sitwell, S. "Psittachus Eois Imitatrix Ales ab Indis."
Skelton, J. Parrot's Soliloquy.
Smith, S. Who Killed Lawless Lean?
Unknown. Old Woman of Gloucester, The.
Parrot, The.
Wright, J. For the Marsh's Birthday.
Wright, K. Sergeant Brown's Parrot.

Parsifal. *See* **Arthurian Legend**

Parthenon
Davidson, D. On a Replica of the Parthenon.
Keats. On Seeing the Elgin Marbles.
Melville, H. Parthenon, The.
Patchen. Saturday Night in the Parthenon.

Parties
Alexander, E. Ode.
Auden. At the Party.
Love Feast, The.
Avison. Party, The.
Belloc. Juliet.
Bensley. One's Correspondence.
Betjeman. False Security.
Brown, P. I Remember Dexedrine. 1970.
Bukowski. Funny Man.
Carson, C. Céilí.
Ceravolo. Celebration.
Chin. Composed Near the Bay Bridge (after a wild party).
Couto. Tea Party.
De la Mare. Feckless Dinner-Party, The.
Drayton. Since There's No Help.
Eady. Song.
Elmslie, K. Amazon Club.
Ezekiel. Goodbye Party for Miss Pushpa T. S.
Fisher, R. Funny Folk.
Ginsberg, A. First Party at Ken Kesey's with Hell's Angels.
Hacker, M. Gramercy Park.
Hernton. Poem.
Hsin Ch'i-chi. Tune: "Green Jade Cup"— Lantern Festival.
Hurley, M. Tea Party.
Jenyns. Nor can I for my soul delight.
Kefala. Party, The.
Kendrick, D. 26th Person, The.
Kuskin. Rose on My Cake, The.
Leland, C. Hans Breitmann's Party [or Barty].
Masaoka Shiki. Tanka: "Day I had in mind, The."
McCullers. Slumber Party.
McGinley. Office Party.
Miles, J. Beach Party Given by T. Shaughnessy for the Sisters.
Nash, O. Say About Seven or Seven-Fifteen.

Nye, N. Art of Disappearing, The.
Olds, S. One Girl at the Boys Party, The.
Rites of Passage.
Patten, B. Party Piece.
Po Chü-i. After Getting Drunk, Becoming Sober in the Night.
Read, S. Garden Party.
Reeves, J. Waiting, waiting, waiting.
Rosen, M. Eddie and the Birthday.
Tranströmer. Below Freezing.
Tranter. Un-American Women, The.
Unknown. He measured out his spirit tower.
We hold a splendid feast today.
When the Guests First Take Their Seats.
Waniek. Sleepless Nights.
Wilbur. Leaving.
Wood, V. Saturday Night.
Zimunya. Kisimiso.

Parting
"Akhmatova." Ah—you thought I'd be the type.
Amichai. Letter.
Quick And Bitter.
Ammuvanar. What She Said ("Friend, his seas swell and roar").
Arnold, M. Parting.
To My Friends, Who Ridiculed a Tender Leave-Taking.
Austin, A. Last Night, The.
Bachmann. Songs from an Island.
Barnes, W. Sonnet: "In every dream thy lovely features rise."
Barr, T. Antique Shop.
Berkeley, S. Parting, The.
Bernstein, O. Mene Mene.
Of All the Splendor.
Time to Leave.
Berryman. Parting as Descent.
Blok. Gray Morning.
Boker. Farewell once more,—and yet again farewell!
Bowes-Lyon. Feather, The.
Bradstreet, A. Before the Birth of One of Her Children.
Bridges, R. I Will Not Let Thee Go.
Brontë, E. F. de Samara to A. G. A.
Brooke, R. Chilterns, The.
Brown, P. Leaving.
Browning, R. Parting at Morning.
Bruner. Good-by can be a happy word.
Brydges. Lines Written Immediately after Parting from a Lady.
Burkard. Raincoat, A.
Burns, R. Farewell, A [or The]: "It was a' for our rightfu' king."
Red, Red Rose, A.
Silver Tassie, The.
Song: "Ae fond kiss, and then we sever."
Byron, G. Fare thee well! and if for ever.
Lines to Mr Hodgson.
Maid of Athens, ere we part.
When we two parted.
Carew, T. Pastoral[l] Dialogue, A.
To My Mistress[e] in My Absence.
Carver, R. No Need.
Catullus. Enough, Catullus, of this silly whining.
On the Burial of His Brother.
Cavalli. Before when you left you would always forget.
Ch'in Chia. To His Wife.
Chong, H. Parting.
Coleridge, M. We Never Said Farewell[, nor even looked].
Coleridge, S. On My Joyful Departure from the Same City.
Cornford, F. Parting in Wartime.
Crawford, L. Kathleen Mavourneen.
Creeley. Just Friends.
Cummings, E. Goodby Betty, don't remember me.
De la Mare. Good-bye.
Di Prima. Narrow Path into the Back Country.
Dickinson, E. Auctioneer of Parting, The.
Frigid and sweet Her parting Face.
Parting.
'Tis customary as we part.

Dimitrova. If.
Djagarov. Autumn.
Doinas, S. Moment of Parting.
Dongala. Fantasy under the Moon.
Donne. His Parting from Her.
  Song: "Sweetest love, I do not go[e]."
  Valediction, A: Forbidding Mourning.
Dove, R. Thomas at the Wheel.
Dowson. O Mors! Quam Amara Est Memoria Tua Homini Pacem Habenti In Substantiis Suis.
Drayton. As Love and I, late harboured in one inn.
  Since There's No Help.
Duoduo. At Parting.
"Dylan." Boots of Spanish Leather.
Eifuku. We dressed each other.
Elizabeth I. On Monsieur's Departure.
Evans, M. Where Have You Gone?
Ewing, J. Gifts.
Ezekiel. Goodbye Party for Miss Pushpa T. S.
Fanshawe, C. When last we parted, thou wert young and fair.
Feaver. Coat.
"Field." Second Thoughts.
Fuller, R. Good-bye for a Long Time.
Glück, L. Departure.
Gomez de Avellaneda. On Leaving Cuba, Her Native Land.
González, A. City.
  Whatever You Want.
Googe. Goyng towards Spayne.
Gorbanevskaya. Sukhanovo.
Haavikko. Days become years. Years.
Hacker, M. Conclusion: "Did you love well what very soon you left?"
Hardy, T. Going, The.
  In the vaulted way, where the passage turned.
Harper, F. Slave Auction, The.
Hass, R. Bashō, A Departure.
Hayden, R. Ballad of Sue Ellen Westerfield, The.
  Road in Kentucky, A.
Heard, J. Parting, The.
  Parting Kiss, The.
Hemans. Parting Song, A.
Henry VIII, King of England. To His Lady.
Herrick. Lovers How They Come and Part.
  To His Dying Brother, Master William Herrick.
  To Larr [or Lar].
Hine. Letting Go.
Ho, H. Snowfall on the Seas.
Hood, T. To a False Friend.
Horton, G. Lover's Farewell, The.
Housman, A. White in the moon the long road lies.
Hovey. At Sea.
Hsieh Chin. To Hsiao Shih-ying.
Hughes, L. Request.
Huidobro. Express.
Hwang, T. Small Love Song, A.
Irby. Sequence.
Ise Tayu. Today is the anniversary of our parting.
Ivaska. K. H.
Jones, G. Esyllt.
Jonson, B. To William Roe ("Roe (and my joy to name) th'art now, to go").
Kang. Grass Leaves.
Kastelan. Parting.
Kipling, R. Lovers' Litany, The.
Knight, E. As You Leave Me.
Lawrence, D. Butterfly, the wind blows seaward[, strong beyond the garden wall!].
  Winter's Tale, A.
Lewis, A. Christmas Holiday.
  Goodbye.
  Post-Script: for Gweno.
Leyvik. Open up, gate.
Li Ling. Parting from Su Wu.
Li Po. Presented to Wang Lun.
  River Merchant's Wife, The; a Letter.
  Seeing a Friend Off.
  Taking Leave of a Friend.
Litchfield. Good-By.
Lorde. Movement Song.

Lovelace, R. Dialogue.
  Song: "If to be absent were to be."
  Song: To Lucasta, Going to the War[re]s.
Lowell, A. Taxi, The.
Lu Yu. Sending Tzu-lung Off to a Post in Chi-chou.
'Marnia. Accoutrement.
Mathews, H. My Neighbor to the South, the Office Clerk Hsiao, Came in the Evening to Say Good-bye.
McGrath, T. Fresco: Departure for an Imperialist War.
Menard. Good-bye! Off for Kansas.
Merrill, J. Renewal, A.
Merwin, W. Departure's Girl-friend.
Mew. À Quoi Bon Dire.
  Sea Love.
Meynell, A. Parted.
Mitsui. Destination: Tule Lake Relocation Center, May 20, 1942.
Mountain, M. After your visit.
Muldoon, P. Avenue, The.
  Something of a Departure.
Myles, E. Sadness of Leaving, The.
Nashe. Litany in Time of Plague, A.
Nathan, L. Day the Perfect Speakers Left, The.
Nesbit, E. At Parting.
Nikolayeva. Seven Beginnings.
Oliver, M. Journey, The.
O'Neill, R. I made a house of houselessness.
Oppen. Anniversary Poem.
Paranar. What Her Friend Said to Her, within the Lover's Hearing.
Patmore, C. Farewell, A.
  Parting.
Philips, K. Lucasia, Rosania and Orinda Parting at a Fountain, July 1663.
  Parting with Lucasia; a Song.
  To Mrs M. A. at Parting.
Phillips, C. Africa Says.
Piatt, J. Taking the Night-Train.
Pinkney, E. On Parting.
Po Chü-i. Letter, The.
  Parting from the Winter Stove.
  Pouring Out My Feelings after Parting from Yüan Chen.
  To Li Chien.
Pound, E. Virginal, A.
Pratt, M. Waving Hand, A.
Probyn. Rondelet: "Which way he went?"
Procter, A. Woman's Last Word, A.
Prokofiev. Betrothed, The.
Ralegh, W. Fortune hath taken away my love.
Randall, D. Souvenirs.
Rexroth, K. As the wheel follows the hoof.
Rich, A. Valediction Forbidding Mourning, A.
Rilke. Time and again, however well we know the landscape of love.
Robinson, E. John Gorham.
  Unforgiven, The.
Rochester, J. Upon [His] Leaving His Mistress.
Rodriguez, J. In-flight Note.
Rossetti, C. Echo from Willow-Wood, An.
  Twilight Night.
Rotella, A. After he leaves.
Sackville-West. Nostalgia.
Saigyo. Woman Forsaken in Love, A.
Scott, A. Bequest of His Heart, A.
Scott, W. Farewell Thou Minstrel Harp.
  Fitz-Eustace's Song.
  Rover's Adieu [or Farewell], The.
Shakespeare, W. Sonnet 87.
Sharah. Parting Roundel.
Shelley, P. On Fanny Godwin.
Shen Chou. Lady Picking Flowers, A.
Shirome. If I were only sure.
Sidney, P. Eleventh Song: "Who is it that this dark[e] night."
  Farewell, A.
Smith, S. In my dreams I am always saying goodbye and riding away.
Stein, G. Let us describe how they went. It was a very windy night and the road.
Stickney, T. Autumn's done; they have the

golden corn in, The.
  Departure, The.
Strobel. Encounter.
Su Tung-p'o. End of the Year, The.
Su Wu. To His Wife.
Swenson, M. "Feel me to do right," our father said on his deathbed.
Swinburne. Before Parting.
  In The Orchard.
  Leave-taking, A.
Swirszczynska. Very Sad Conversation at Night, A.
Symons, A. When you were here, ah foolish then!
Tai Piao-yüan. Returning to Yin-ch'eng Early in the Year Ting-ch'ou (1277).
TallMountain. There Is No Word for Goodbye.
Teasdale. Gift, The.
Teika. From the beginning.
Terapiano. Ships that sail forth.
The Yueh-Fu. *I* want to be your friend.
Thomas, E. Like the Touch of Rain [she was].
Thompson, P. Adown the heights of Ages.
Tregian. Imprisoned Recusant Writes to His Wife, An.
Trussell. Snow.
Ts'ao Chih. Presented to Piao, the Prince of Pai-ma.
Tsung Ch'en. On the spring river, you depart.
  Song of Meeting.
Tu Mu. Sent in Parting.
  We Drink Farewell.
Tucker, M. Adieu.
Tuckerman, F. Last night I dreamed we parted once again.
Unknown. A! Mercy, Fortune; have pitee on me.
  Alas, departing is ground of wo!
  Another Man Done Gone.
  Corydon's Farewell, on Sailing in the Late Expedition Fleet.
  Crow caws in the moonlight, A.
  Fare Thee Well.
  Farewell, Unkind! Farewell! to me, no more a father!
  First dawn comes, The.
  Love Song: "Like pain of fire runs down my body my love to you, my dear!"
  Old *Chüeh-chü.*
  On and on, always on and on.
  On His Mistress Going from Home [Song].
  Red River Valley.
  Stone Castle Music.
  They're Leaving Memphis in Droves.
  When I went with you.
  You May Go But This Will Bring You Back.
Valek. Apple from the cupboard rolled to the floor, The.
Van Vliet. City is covered with places you, The.
  Coastline never alters for the fisherman, The.
  Valediction—To My Father.
Walker, A. Even as I hold you.
Wang An-shih. By the River.
Wang Chiu-ssu. For Several Days I Have Not Visited the Garden Pavilion—A Poem Sent to My Pet Crane.
Warner, S. After he had gone the wind rose.
Weller. Ngungalari.
Wen Cheng-ming. Wine of parting flowed and flowed, The.
Whitman, A. Thus ends my lay: Reluctantly I leave.
Whitman, W. After the supper and talk—after the day is done.
  Good-bye my Fancy!
  Good-Bye, My Fancy! ("Good-bye, my Fancy! / Farewell dear mate, dear love!")
  Once I pass'd through a populous city imprinting my brain.
  So Long!
  What think you I take my pen in hand to record?
Whittier. Godspeed.
Wilbur. Leaving.
Williams, H. Gone Away.

Williams, S. If He Let Us Go Now.
Wingfield. Winter.
Winters, Y. At the San Francisco Airport.
Wolfe, C. To Mary.
Wollach. Never will I hear the sweet voice of God.
Wu of Han. Summer Song.
Wu Wei-yeh. Broken Lampstand, The.
Wyatt, T. Lover's Appeal, The.
Yang Shen. To the Tune "Child at Play."
To the Tune "The Southerner."
Yang Shih-ch'i. Even ordinarily, parting is difficult.
Yeats. Parting.
Yesenin. Goodbye, my friend, goodbye.
Yi, H. Fallen Petals.
Yin Shih. Parting from the Courtier Sung.
Yosano. He tempted me to.
That evening when.
Without a word.
Yü Wu-ling. Offering Wine.
Zach. Against Parting.
Poem Too Late, A.

Partridges

Li Tung-yang. Trip to Yüeh-lu Temple, A.
Pinar. Another Song of the Same Woman, to Some Partridges, Sent to Her Alive.

Passion

Arnaut Daniel. Resolute desire that enters, The.
Arnold, M. Growing Old.
Atwood. Torture.
Auden. That night when joy began.
Ayton. Exercise of Affection, The.
Barnes, B. Why do I draw this coole releeving ayer.
Baudelaire. Cats.
Beaumont, S. Description of Love, A.
Beaumont, J. Love's Mystery.
Behn, A. Disappointment, The.
Song: "How strongly does my passion flow."
Song: "Oh! Love, that stronger art than wine."
Berggolts. Friends repeat: "All means are good."
You took me, hostile, sullen—.
Blok. Before the Court.
I want to live, live to distraction.
On the Islands.
Bly, R. In the month of May when all leaves open.
Bogan, L. Knowledge.
Brodsky, J. Six Years Later.
Brontë, E. D.G.C. to J.A.
Last Words.
Shall Earth no more inspire thee.
Brooks, G. To be in love.
Brown, R. Dancing the Shout to the True Gospel; or, The Song Movement Sisters Don't Want Me to Sing.
Brown, S. Schadenfreude.
Browning, E. Sonnet: "How do I love thee? Let me count the ways."
Burns, R. Cares o' love are sweeter far, The.
Campbell, J. Pariah, The.
Campion, T. Beauty, since you so much desire.
I care not for these ladies.
Mistris [or Mistress] Since You So Much Desire.
When thou must home to shades of underground [or under ground].
Carew, T. Mediocrity in Love Rejected.
Prayer to the Wind, A.
Rapture, A.
Catullus. Carmen 75 ("Reason blinded by sin, Lesbia").
Carmen 92 ("Lesbia loads me night & day with her curses").
Carmen 72.
Carmen 85.
Sappho.
Cortez. So Long.
Cowley, A. Michal her modest flames sought to conceal.
Crabbe. Marriage Ring, The.
Crane, H. River, The.

Creeley. Marriage, A.
Way, The.
Cullen, C. Song in Spite of Myself.
Cummings, E. Now air is air and thing is thing:no bliss.
Custance. Candle-Light.
Statues.
White Statue, The.
Davies, W. Fleeting Passion, A.
Donne. Canonization, The.
Doolittle, H. Fragment 113: "Not honey, / not the plunder of the bee."
Drayton. To the Reader of These Sonnets.
Duncan, R. Among my friends love is a great sorrow.
"Eliot." Felix Holt, the Radical.
"Ephelia." To One That Asked Me Why I Loved J.G G.
Flatman. Appeal to Cats in the Business of Love, An.
Fleming, P. Concerning Himself.
Foley, H. Touch wood, be humble, never dare to say.
Garrigue. Movie Actors Scribbling Letters Very Fast in Crucial Scenes.
Upon the Intimation of Love's Mortality.
Gatsos. How very much I loved you only I know.
Gergely. Magdalene.
Gioseffi. Toward the Greater Romance, Please Place Roses in my Skull (A Tantric Love Song).
Glazkov. Khikhimora.
Goethe. Meeting, the Departure, The.
To Charlotte von Stein.
Graves, R. In Perspective.
Metaphor, The.
Never Such Love.
Succubus, The.
Gregg. Adult.
Strong Pomegranate Flowers and Seeds of the Mind.
Hacker, M. Another Sunday.
Noces.
Sources.
Hajnal. That's All?
Heard, J. Slumbering Passion.
Heinrich von Morungen. Alas, shall I not see again.
Herbert of Cherbury. Ditty: "If you refuse me once, and think again."
Hewitt, J. Tryst.
Hirshfield, J. Justice without Passion.
Horace. First Ode of the Fourth Book of Horace, The.
Ibycus. In the Spring the quince and the.
Jewsbury. To My Own Heart.
Jiménez, J. To the bridge of love.
Johnson, A. Identikit, The.
Johnson, L. To a Passionist.
Jonson, B. Fair friend, 'tis true, your beauties move.
Nymph's Passion, A.
Kabir. To Be a Slave of Intensity.
Kemal Khojandi. One Final Fling.
Khodasevich. To a Guest.
Twilight.
Kim, S. Song by the Brook.
"Korzhavin." For certain, I did not live thus in this world.
Kowit. When he pressed his lips to my mouth.
Kwon, I. Rapture.
Lamb, M. What is Love?
Lawrence, D. Go deeper than love, for the soul has greater depths.
History.
Kisses in the Train.
Last Words to Miriam.
Lightning.
Passing Visit to Helen.
Release.
Lazarus, E. Elixir, The.
Lenier. Finale.
Levine, P. At the Fillmore.
Li Yü. Tune: "Deva-like Barbarian" ("Bright flowers and dim moon, enmeshed in thin drifting mist").

Liddy. History.
Lovelace, R. Lucasta's World.
Mackey, M. Kama Sutra of Kindness: Position No. 2, The.
Mallarmé. Between the reeds I saw their bodies gleam.
Marlowe. Elegies.
Passionate Shepherd [or Sheepheard] To His Love, The.
Marston, P. Love's Music.
Martial. Don't pay any attention.
Matthews, J. Cheerleaders, The.
Mayakovsky. Mayakovsky's Suicide Note.
McClellan. Love is a flame that burns with sacred fire.
Melville, H. Fruit and Flower Painter.
Merrill, J. Days of 1964.
Mirabai. O friends, I am mad.
Naden. Sister of Mercy, The.
Nekrasova. Rublyov XVth Century.
O'Hara, F. Blocks.
Hôtel Transylvanie.
Ovid. Elegies 1.2.
Elegies 1.3.
Elegies 1.4.
Elegies 1.5.
Elegies 2.1.
Come then sick youth unto my sacred skill.
Owen, M. For Emily (Dickinson).
Paino. What the Blue Jay Said.
Parnell, T. Here all the passions, for their greater sway.
Pasternak, B. Feasts, The.
I too have been in love, and my sleepless.
Philodemus. Death has torn ten years from us.
Pickard, T. Detente.
Valentine.
Pilinszky. Passion of Ravensbrück.
Poe. Preface: "Romance, who loves to nod and sing."
Ransom, J. Address to the Scholars of New England.
Good Ships.
Spiel of [the] Three Mountebanks.
Rexroth, K. Fires / Burn in my heart.
Now the fireflies of our youth.
Rich, A. Paula Becker to Clara Westhoff.
Since we're not young, weeks have to do time.
Sleeping, turning in turn like planets.
Robinson, M. Canzonet.
Roethke. Her Words.
Ronsard. Elegy 19 (A Kiss): "Without a soul, a mind, a breath, or pulse."
Rossetti, C. Bed of Forget-Me-Nots, A.
Sackville-West. Valediction.
Sandburg, C. Population Drifts.
Sansom, M. To My Heavenly Charmer.
Shakespeare, W. Sonnet 116.
Shelley, P. Lines: "When the lamp is shattered [or shatter'd]."
Love's Philosophy.
Shirley, J. Lover that Durst Not Speak to His M[istress], A.
"Shu Ting." Singing Flower, The.
Sikelianos. Rehearsing for Death.
Smelyakov. Lovely Leda.
Spender, S. Ice.
Stirling, S. Echo, An.
Story, W. Cleopatra.
Swinburne. Anactoria.
Symons, A. Bianca.
Teasdale. I Am Not Yours[, not lost in you].
Tennyson, A. "O Swallow, Swallow, flying, flying south".
Theocritus. O Polyphemus, while your flocks you keep.
Thomson, J. Once in a saintly passion.
Tsvetayeva. Where does this tenderness come from?
U Tam'si Tchicaya. Headline to Summarize a Passion.
Unknown. Here's a jolly couple! Oh the jolly jolly cuple!
I have two sicknesses, Love.
I will give my love an apple without e'er a core.

Prayer yo Hymen.
Tune: "Joy in Spring's Coming"—Seven Songs.
When I am dead and thou wouldst try.
With your beautiful hair and seemly.
Would you be a man in fashion?
Voznesensky. Epitaph for Vysotsky.
Wharton, A. Song: "How hardly I concealed my tears."
Wheelock, J. Black Panther, The.
Whitman, S. To ———: "Vainly my heart had with thy sorceries striven."
Whitman, W. Native moments—when you come upon me—ah you are here now.
Once I pass'd through a populous city imprinting my brain.
Wilde, O. Hélas!
Wordsworth, W. Lucy.
Wright, J. Quest, The.
To the Muse.
Wroth. Sonnet 1: "When night's [or nights] black mantle could most darknes prove."
Sonnet 101.
Sonnet 24.
Sonnet 48: "How like a fire doth love increase in me[e]."
Wyatt, T. Lover Showeth How He Is Forsaken of Such as He Sometime Enjoyed, The.
Perdy [or Perdie or Perdye], I said[e] it [or yt] not.
Since love is such that, as ye wot.
Take heed betime, lest ye be spied.
Your looks so often cast.
Xuân Diệu. Forever, yes, forever I'll love you.
Orange With the Rind Still Green, An.
You Must Say It.
Yakamochi. We were together.
Yang Fang. Joy of Union, The.
Yang Shen. To the Tune "Moon Over West River."
Yeats. Indian to His Love, The.
Yosano. Come at last to this point.
Zeb-un-Nissa. Though I am Laila of the Persian romance.
Zeidner. Bach.

Passivity
Fort, C. Town Clock Burning, The.
Nash, O. I Never Even Suggested It.
Warren, R. Spider has more eyes than I have money, The.
Wilbur. Shame.

Passover
Hame'iri. Passover in Jerusalem.
Hayes, A. Angel, The.
Heyen. Passover: the Injections.
Kollar. Late Arrivals.
Pastan. Passover.
Rilke. Matthew 26:17–29.

Past
"Adunis." Elegy for the Time at Hand.
Ai. Twenty-Year Marriage.
Ali, A. Previous Occupant, The.
Angelou. Still I Rise.
Antokolsky. From their journeys our dreams return.
Bagryana. Only One, The.
Baraka. In Memory of Radio.
Bernstein, O. Her Words from the Corner.
Blamire. When home we return, after youth has been spending.
Blunt, W. To One Who Would Make a Confession.
Bly, R. Remembering in Oslo the Old Picture of the Magna Carta.
Boethius. Chawcer upon this fyfte meter of the second book.
Bogen, D. Last Installment, The.
Boland, E. Black Lace Fan My Mother Gave Me, The.
Bold, A. Stars.
Bontemps. Return, The.
Southern Mansion.
Braley, B. Start where you stand and never mind the past.
Browning, R. Apparent Failure.
Love among the Ruins.
Brush. Again.

Bunting. Vestiges.
Byron, G. Where'er we tread 'tis haunted, holy ground.
Calas. Columns of the Temple of Olympian Zeus.
Caraion. Tomorrow the Past Comes.
Carew, T. Love's Force.
Carlile. Train Whistles in the Wind and Rain.
Chế Lan Viên. Waning Night, The.
Ch'ien T'ao. Matching a Poem by Secretary Kuo.
Chōkū. Tanka: "My research."
Clare, J. To a Bower.
Clark, T. Superballs.
Clifton, L. I am accused of tending to the past.
Crane, H. Enrich my resignation as I usurp those far.
My Grandmother's Love Letters.
Reliquary.
Creeley. Here.
Cullen, C. Litany of the Dark People, The.
Davidson, D. Sanctuary.
Dickey, J. Buckdancer's Choice.
Dickinson, E. After a hundred years.
Glass was the Street—in tinsel Peril.
Dobson, A. Wanderer, The.
Doinas, S. Woman in the Mirror, The.
Words, The.
Doolittle, H. Helen.
Dove, R. Fifth Grade Autobiography.
Dugan, A. Winter for an Untenable Situation.
Duncan, R. Sleep is a Deep and Many Voiced Flood.
Durrell. Delos.
Eady. Supremes, The.
"Eliot." Two lovers by a moss-grown spring.
Eliot, T. Dry Salvages, The.
Elytis. In the beginning the light And the first hour.
Emanuel, L. Discovering the Photograph of Lloyd, Earl, and Priscilla.
Emerson, R. Past, The.
English, T. Ben Bolt.
Enzensberger, H. Short History of the Bourgeoisie.
Everwine. From the Meadow.
Faiz. Don't Ask Me for That Love Again.
Ferlinghetti, L. Retired Ballerinas, Central Park West.
Fisher, R. On the open side, look out.
Frost, R. Directive.
Fumiko. Tanka: "As the surgical knife."
Fyleman. Cat, The.
Galvin, B. Green Evening, A.
González, A. Yesterday was Wednesday all morning.
Gould, A. Observed Observer, The.
Greville, F. Sonnet: "Man, dream[e] no more of curious mysteries."
Guiterman. Ancient History.
Gumilyov. Tram That Lost Its Way, The.
Haines, J. Mothball Fleet: Benicia, California.
Hampton. Yugoslav Story.
Hanzlicek, C. Last Trains, The.
Harper, M. Families Album, The.
Hartnett. Visit to Castletown House, A.
Hayden, R. Locus.
'Mystery Boy' Looks for Kin in Nashville.
Herbert, Z. Drawer.
Herrick. His Age, Dedicated to His Peculiar Friend, Master John Wickes, under the Name of Posthumus.
Hill, G. Idylls of the King.
Processes of generation; deeds of settlement.
Hoagland, E. Gorée ten miles offshore beckons.
Hollander, J. There was an end to hearts and rhymes.
Why have I locked myself inside.
Housman, A. Land of Lost Content, The.
Howe, J. My Last Dance.
Howe, S. Thorow.
Jackson, L. Ding-Donging.
Jarrell. Augsburg Adoration, The.
When I was home last Christmas.
Jeffers, R. Haunted Country.

Jones, R. Progress Alley.
Justice, D. Houses.
Kendall, M. Fossil, A.
Khodasevich. In Front of the Mirror.
Kipling, R. Merrow Down.
Way Through The Woods, The.
Kizer, C. Bitch.
Kooser. Country School.
Year's End.
Kumin, M. Chain, The.
Lauterbach. Clamor.
Lawrence, D. History.
Humming-Bird.
Nostalgia.
Lerman. Margaret Whiting Tearfully Sings.
Linderman. Cabins.
Lindsay, V. Chinese Nightingale, The.
Lu Yu. I Had Occasion to Tell a Visitor about an Old Trip I Took.
MacCaig. Gone Are the Days.
Machi. Tanka: "Letter, The."
Mandelstam. Finder of a Horseshoe, The.
I'll chase through the gypsy camp of dark streets.
Masters, E. Gettysburg.
Matthews, W. Note I Left for Gerald Stern in an Office I Borrowed, and He Would Next, at a Summer Writers' Conference.
McElroy, C. Dreams of Johnson Grass.
Ghost-Who-Walks, The.
Under the Oak Table.
Melville, H. Battle Summers, The.
Mezhirov. We would awaken in a twilight gloom.
Milosz, C. Encounter.
Morgan, V. Still Life.
Mura. Argument: On 1942, An.
Nemerov. Blue Suburban.
Neruda. Past.
Ni Tsan. Following the Rhymes of the Six Poems "Thinking of the Past at Ku-Su and Ch'ien-t'ang."
Nims, J. Freight.
Nukada. Does that bird.
O Direain. That Face.
Olson, C. Chockablock Once a man was traveling through the woods, and.
Maximus, to Gloucester, Letter 27.
Peters, L. Home Coming.
Plumpp. Clinton.
Po Chü-i. Resignation.
Thinking of the Past.
Porumbacu. From what once was, from the crazy nights.
Pound, E. E. P. Ode Pour l'Election de Son Sepulchre.
Pozdnyayev. Remembrance of Five Loaves.
Procter, A. My Journal.
Rankine. Eden.
Ray, D. On the Photograph "Yarn Mill," by Lewis W. Hine.
Reed, I. Reactionary Poet, The.
Rexroth, K. How long, long ago.
In the park a crow awakes.
Rich, A. Sleeping, turning in turn like planets.
We are driven to odd attempts; once it would not have occurred to.
Robinson, E. Miniver Cheevy, child of scorn.
Octaves.
Roethke. Slug.
Rossetti, C. Passing and Glassing.
Summer Is Ended.
Ryan, J. Pawntickets.
Saigyo. In Winter.
Salinas, R. Trip Through the Mind Jail, A.
Schuyler, J. Salute.
Scott, L. Ettrick.
Seferis. Our country is closed in [enclosed], all mountains.
Serote. Ofay-Watcher Looks Back.
Sexton. Funnel.
Some Foreign Letters.
What's That.
Shakespeare, W. Sonnet 30.
Shao Yung. Arriving in Lo-yang Again.
Smedley, M. Face from the Past, A.
Smelyakov. Locomotives' graveyard, The.

Spender, S. One More New Botched Beginning.
Stevens, W. Cuisine Bourgeoise.
Stevenson, R. Sing me a song of a lad that is gone.
Stickney, T. On Some Shells Found Inland.
Su Tung-p'o. Long ago I lived in the country.
Summerfield. Washday Battles.
Svetlov. Friends.
Thomas, D. January 1939.
  Twenty-four years remind the tears of my eyes.
Thomas, R. Centuries.
Tsvetkov. What remained of our meetings?
Unknown. When Mother reads aloud, the past.
Upton, L. Daughter, A.
Urmy. Old Year, The.
Verlaine. Exchange Of Feelings, An.
Vogel, D. I saw my father drowning.
Vũ Đình Liên. Old Calligrapher, The.
Wang Chiu-ssu. Today I am a farmer in the fields.
Warren, R. Letter from a Coward to a Hero.
Wen Cheng-ming. This man of leisure for twenty years.
  Where among the blue clouds.
Whitman, W. Now precedent songs, farewell—by every name farewell.
  Proud music of the storm.
  To-day and Thee.
Whittemore, R. Clamming.
Wilbur. Pardon, The.
Wilcox, E. Was, Is, and Yet-to-be.
Wojahn. Homage to Ryszard Kapuściński.
Wong, N. Grandmothers' Song.
Wright, C. Bar Giamaica, 1959-60.
  Black and Blue.
  Two Stories.
Xuân Diệu. Distance.
Yau. We Are All Vultures.
Yeats. Circus Animals' Desertion, The.
  Ego Dominus Tuus.
Young, K. Field Trip.
Yüan Mei. Words from the Goblet of Wisdom.
Zhdanov. Home.

Pasternak, Boris
"Akhmatova." Boris Pasternak.
McGinley. Last Year's Discussion: The Nobel Russian.
Yoshimi. Tanka: "How many people came."

Pastoral Verse
Barnfield. Affectionate Shepherd, The.
Clare, J. Pastoral Poesy.
Clerk. Country Seat, The.
Drayton. Daffodil Song, The.
Roundelay: "*Motto* Tell me, thou skilful shepherd's swain."
Marlowe. Passionate Shepherd [*or* Sheepheard] To His Love, The.
"Ophelia." Snaith Marsh; a Yorkshire Pastoral.
Pratt, S. Cottage Pictures.
Ralegh, W. Nimphs [*or* Nymph's] Reply to the Sheepheard [*or* Shepherd], The.
Raleigh. Nymph's Reply to the Shepherd, The.
Sidney, P. Double Sestine [*or* Sestina].
  My sheep are thoughts, which I both guide and serve.
Spenser. Shepherd's Calendar, 'June', The.
Winchilsea. Pastoral Dialogue between Two Shepherdesses, A.

Pastures. See **Fields and Pastures**

Paterson, New Jersey
Williams, W. Episode 17.
  Paterson.
  Preface: "Rigor of beauty is the quest. But how will you find beauty when it is locked."

Paths
Bradstreet, A. There is a path no vulture's eye hath seen.
Bromige. Choice.
Del Renzio. Can You Change a Shilling?
Han-shan. Cold Mountain Poems.
Kinnell. Under the Maud Moon.
Mirabai. O friends on this Path.
Mitchell, S. Maps.
Moore, L. Homeplace, The.

Ngatho. Footpath.
Ofeimun. Let Them Choose Paths.
Patten, B. Terrible Path, The.
Pritchard, N. Narrow Path, The.
Riley, J. Country Pathway, A.
Rossetti, C. Amor Mundi.
Snyder, G. Path to Han-shan's place is laughable, The.
  Riprap.

Patience
Barbauld. To the Poor.
Bible, *O.T.* Psalm 13.
Burroughs, J. Waiting.
Carey, H. Sally in Our Alley.
Creeley. For No Clear Reason.
Davison, E. Owl, The.
Emerson, R. Forbearance.
"Field." Maids, not to you my mind doth change.
Fields, J. Jolly fat widows, The.
Graves, R. Carol of Patience.
  Not at Home.
Hardy, T. Waiting Both.
Herbert, G. Size, The.
Herrick. To Fortune.
Hewitt, J. How have I served you? I have let you waste.
Hollo. Mescalito.
Hopkins, G. My own heart let me more have pity on; let.
  Sonnet: "Patience, hard thing! the hard thing but to pray."
Horne, F. Patience. . . patience.
Jennings, E. Delay.
Kavanagh, P. Sometimes.
Kim, H. Winter Tree.
"Klingle." Be Patient.
Markham, E. Third Wonder, The.
Olds, S. New Mother.
Quarles. Epigram: "My soul, sit thou a patient looker-on."
Rossetti, C. Study AA Soul), A.
Sangster, M. Patience with the Living.
Sidney, P. Psalm 13.
  Sonnet 56: "Fie, school of Patience, fie; your lesson is."
Tekeyan. Sacred Wrath.
Thompson, C. His Answer.
Unknown. Hit betidde somtime in the termes of Judé.
  Learn to wait—life's hardest lesson.
  Morning Prayer.
  Patience is a virtue.
  Temper.
Uticensis. What Men in private whisper, never mind.
Viiding. I am a serf. I work in the sweat of my brow.
Wickham. Sick Assailant, The.
Wyatt, T. Patience, for I have wrong.
  Patience for my device.
  Patience of all my smart.
  Patience though I have not.
Yeats. Down by the salley gardens my love and I did meet;.

Patients. See **Institutionalism; Hospitals; Illness; Mental Illness**

Patriarchy
Grahn. History of Lesbianism, A.
Jordan, J. Some people despise me be- / cause I have a Venus mound.
Myles, E. Woman like Me, A.
Piercy. Barbie Doll.
Plath. Lady Lazarus.
Rich, A. From a Survivor.
  Hunger.
  I come home from you through the early light of spring.
  Paula Becker to Clara Westhoff.
  Your small hands, precisely equal to my own.
Stein, G. Patriarchal poetry their origin their history their origin.

Patrick, Saint
Donnchadh Mor O'Dala. At Saint Patrick's Purgatory.
Leslie, S. Saint Patrick.
McFadden, R. March.

Patrick, S. St Patrick's Breastplate.
  Saint Patrick's Breastplate; or, The Deer's Cry.
Unknown. Praise of Fionn, The.
  White Lake, The.

Patriotic Songs, America
Bates, K. America the Beautiful.
Cohan. Over There.
Dwight. As down a lone valley with cedars o'erspread.
Hopkinson, J. Hail, Columbia.
Hosking. Land of the Free.
Howe, J. Battle Hymn [*or* Battle-Hymn] of the Republic, The.
Key. Star-Spangled Banner, The.
Root, G. Battle Cry [*or* Battle-Cry] of Freedom, The.
Shuckburg *et al.* Yankee Doodle.
Smith, S. America.
Van Dyke. America for Me.

Patriotic Songs, Confederacy
Randall, J. My Maryland.
See also **Patriotic Songs, America**

Patriotic Songs, England
Garrick. Heart of Oak.
Thomson, J. *et al.* Rule, Britannia!

Patriotism and Patriots
Ai Ch'ing. North, The.
"Akhmatova." I heard a voice, within me, call.
Barry, J. Lessons.
Bennett, H. Flag Goes By, The.
Betjeman. In Westminster Abbey.
Brooke, R. Soldier, The.
Browning, R. Patriot, The [An Old Story].
Carberry. It takes a mighty fire.
Cheney-Coker. On Being a Poet in Sierra Leone.
Chipasula. Going Back Patiently.
  Manifesto on Ars Poetica.
  My Friendly People.
  Talking of Sharp Things.
Cohen, L. Killers that run, The.
Cummings, E. Come,gaze with me upon this dome.
  I sing of Olaf glad and big.
  Next to of course god america i.
Cunningham, A. Hame, Hame, Hame.
Đặng Phu'o'ng. Day of Mourning at Yên-Báy, The.
Dawe, G. Names.
Duggan, E. Invasion.
Emerson, R. In an age of fops and toys.
Filicaia. Italy.
Hemans. Homes of England, The.
Henley, W. England, My England.
Herschell. Kid Has Gone to the Colors, The.
Hewitt, J. Ireland.
  Scar, The.
Holly. This Is a Fatherland to Me.
Housman, A. New Mistress, The.
Howe, J. Battle Hymn [*or* Battle-Hymn] of the Republic, The.
Huỳnh Mẫn Đạt. Old Hound, The.
Keats. Happy is England! I could be content.
Kipling, R. Recessional.
"Korzhavin." Or did I really fall out of love with my country?—.
Kunyayev. It's hard to understand how one can leave.
Lanier, S. To Richard Wagner.
Larkin, P. MCMXIV.
Lazarus, E. New Colossus, The.
Letts. Harbour, The.
Lieberman, E. I Am an American.
Lu Yu. To Show My Sons.
Manning, F. Grotesque.
Miller, A. I Have Loved England.
Moore, T. Dear Harp of My Country.
  Harp That Once through Tara's Halls, The.
  Pro Patria Mori.
Moorer. Loyalty to the Flag.
Nguyễn Đình Chiểu. Fisherman Speaks His Mind, A.
Nguyễn Duy Nhuệ. Bamboos of Vietnam.
Nguyễn Hũ'u Huân. Carrying a Cangue Around the Neck.
Ofeimun. Prologue: "I have come down."

Ogundipe-Leslie. Song at the African Middle Class.

Orwell. As One Non-Combatant to Another.

Owen, W. Dulce Et Decorum Est.

Peck, R. Four of July.

Phan Bội Châu. In a Canton Jail.

Phan Văn Hy. Ricksha man does quite a simple job, The.

Phan Văn Trị. Grains of Rice.

Rice Mill, The.

Pound, E. These fought in any case.

Pyon. Non-gae.

Sassoon. Fight to a Finish.

Scott of Amwell. Ode: "I hate that drum's discordant sound."

Scott, W. Caledonia.

Pibroch of Donuil Dhu.

Spring-Rice. I vow to thee, my country, all earthly things above.

Squire. Dilemma, The.

Stewart, F. Black Winter.

Stow. My wish for my land is that ladies be beautiful.

Tản Đà. Barber, The.

Troth Between the Hill and the Stream, The.

Thomas, E. This is no case of petty right or wrong.

Tố Hữu. Prison Thoughts.

Trần Cao Vân. It's mere child's play to die—who'd care to try?

Trần Huy Liệu. What's My Crime?

Tran Minh-tong (King). Bạch-đằng River, The.

Trần Tuấn Khải. Our Land, Our Home.

Turner, C. Great Britain Through the Ice: Or, Premature Patriotism.

Unknown. Columbia.

God Save the King.

Homage to the Trưng queens.

Our Flag.

We mean to thrash these Prussian Pups.

Van Dyke. America for Me.

Việt Phương. O Life I Love and Cherish Like My Wife!

Whitman, W. Beat! beat! drums!—blow! bugles! blow!

I hear America singing, the varied carols I hear.

Whittier. Barbara Frietchie.

Wordsworth, W. Composed by the Sea-Side, near Calais, August, 1802.

I traveled [*or* travell'd] among unknown men.

Yu. Flag.

Patrons

Jonson, B. Epigram. To the Household. 1630, An.

To Lucy, Countess[e] of Bedford, with Mr. Donnes Satire's [*or* Satyres].

Lanyer. Description of Cookham, The.

Paul, Saint

Constable, H. To St. Peter and St. Paul.

Corbet. Distracted Puritan, The.

Dobson, R. Eutychus.

Kipling, R. At His Execution.

Gallio's Song.

Merton. St. Paul.

Ransom, J. Our Two Worthies.

Wesley, C. He Shook off the Beast.

Wither. Conversion of S. Paul, The.

Pawnbrokers and Pawnshops

Alexie. Evolution

Espada. Latin Night at the Pawnshop.

Ryan, J. Pawntickets.

Payne, D. A.

Fordham. Dedicated to the Right Rev'd D. A. Payne.

Peace

Ackland. What must we do if we cannot do this.

Akhmadulina. Remembrance of Yalta.

"Akhmatova." Railings of iron.

Aldington. Field Manoeuvres.

Aliger. Summer days are noticeably shortening, The.

Amichai. Two Songs of Peace.

Ashbery. Poem: "While we were walking under the top."

Bacchylides. Pæan of Bacchylides, On Peace, The.

Peace.

Balaban. April 30, 1975.

In Celebration of Spring.

Berberova. Eagles and butterflies (and some other things).

Berry, W. Peace of Wild Things, The.

Bible, *O.T.* Psalm 133.

Bly, R. After Long Busyness.

Asian Peace Offers Rejected without Publication.

Brainard, J. I saw two clouds at morning.

Brooke, R. Peace.

Bryant, W. After a Tempest.

Autumn Woods.

Buchanan, G. War-and-Peace.

Byron, G. She walks in Beauty like the night.

Cady. Starting 1973: What to Do Now that Peace Has Been Announced.

Campbell, T. Soldier's Dream, The.

Ch'ang Chien. Visit to the Broken Hill Temple, A.

Chang Yü. Retreat of Liu Kuo-pao, The.

Chapman, G. Learning ("So Learned Men in Controversies Spend").

Peace of Death, The.

Chōkū. Tanka: "Town children."

Clifton, L. Let There Be New Flowering.

Codrescu. Grammar, A.

Collins, W. Ode to Evening.

Cooke, R. Arachne.

Corwin, N. Man unto His Fellow Man.

Cowper, W. Nightingale and the Glowworm, The.

Crane, H. Enrich my resignation as I usurp those far.

Creeley. For No Clear Reason.

Cummings, E. All nearness pauses,while a star can grow.

De la Mare. Ghost, The.

Peace.

Dehn, P. Armistice.

Dixon, R. To Peace.

Đông Hồ. String of Pearls, The.

Doolittle, H. Or is it a great tide that covers the rock-pool.

Drummond de Andrade. Motionless Faces.

Dunbar, P. Ere sleep comes down to soothe the weary eyes.

Edman. Peace.

Eliot, T. Song for Simeon, A.

Enzensberger, H. For the Grave of a Peace-Loving Man.

Fanshawe, S. Ode on His Majesty's Proclamation.

Fordham. Ode to Peace.

Fosdick, H. Prince of Peace His Banner Spreads, The.

Francis of Assisi. Prayer of St. Francis of Assisi for Peace.

Goldberg, L. Will there yet come days of forgiveness and grace.

Halkin, S. Reward.

Hardy, T. According to the Mighty Working.

And There Was a Great Calm.

Christmas Ghost-Story, A.

Harper, F. Songs for the People.

Henry, P. Is life so dear, or peace so sweet.

Herbert, G. L'Envoy.

Peace.

Herbert, Z. To Marcus Aurelius.

Herrick. Farewell Frost; or, Welcome the Spring.

Power and Peace.

Holmes, O. Prologue.

Hopkins, G. Peace.

Howe, J. Mother's Day Proclamation of 1870.

Hsieh Ling-yün. Written on the Lake, Returning from the Retreat at Stone Cliff.

Hsü Pen. Hermit Feng's Residence on the Lake.

Mountain of green trees and orioles everywhere!

Hughes, L. Projection.

Joseph, J. Rose in the Afternoon.

Kaufman, B. Private Sadness.

Kazakova. I am growing calmer.

King, J. Moments.

Kipling, R. American Spirit speaks, The.

Knevet. Vote, The.

Krohn. Farmer's Song at Can Tho.

Kunio. Tanka: "Casket on display, A."

Landor, W. Foreign Ruler, A.

On His Seventy-Fifth Birthday.

Larkin, P. Coming.

Lawrence, D. Pax.

What Would You Fight For?

Layman P'ang. When the mind is at peace.

Lee, J. Firebell for Peace.

Lincoln, A. Second Inaugural Address.

Longley, M. Peace.

MacNeice. Apple Blossom.

Meredith, W. On Falling Asleep by Firelight.

Moore, M. In Distrust of Merits.

Muldoon, P. Truce.

Nemerov. Easter.

Nguyễn Trãi. Both favor and disgrace you have full known.

Ollivierre. Talk War.

Patchen. Pastoral: "Dove walks with sticky feet, The."

"Pereleshin." In the final hour, dear.

Po Chü-i. Ease.

Pozhenyan. Clear fall afternoon beckons, A.

Radnóti. Peace, Horror.

Ransom, J. Spiel of [the] Three Mountebanks.

Rossetti, C. From the Antique.

Rubtsov. Good Filya.

Rukeyser, M. Even during war, moments of delicate peace.

Ryokan. To lazy to be ambitious.

Sandburg, C. A. E. F.

For You.

Seng-ts'an. Mind of Absolute Trust, The.

Shao Yung. Song of Delight.

Shūji. Tanka: "Slowly inside me."

Simic. Summer Morning.

Sophocles. Colonus' Praise.

Southerland. Two Fishing Villages.

Stafford, W. At the Un-National Monument along the Canadian Border.

Stevens, W. House was quiet and the world was calm, The.

Studdert-Kennedy. Is it a dream, and nothing more—this faith.

Sutherland, J. H ear t h.

Szymborska. Reality demands.

T'ao Ch'ien. In the Year with the Cyclical Sign *Mou-shen.*

Tennyson, A. For I Dipped [*or* Dipt] into the Future.

Thomas, R. Country Clergy, The.

Tibullus. Peace.

Timrod. Christmas.

Retirement.

Tolson. Legend of Versailles, A.

Tran Minh-tong (King). Farewell to two envoys from the Yüan court.

Tranströmer. Allegro.

Open and Closed Space.

Tường Phố. Who is that soldier, hero of my heart?

Turner, N. Let Us Have Peace.

Unknown. Deep river, my home is over Jordan.

Hierusalem, my happy [*or* happie] home.

Hymn: "O God of Hosts, thine Ear incline."

Lark, The.

Shalom Aleichem.

Soon I will be done with the troubles of the world.

Translation of "Pax Bello Potior."

When this blasted war is over.

Vaughan, H. Peace.

Velacan Maturai. Peace Poem.

Villanueva, A. Peace #3.

Vinkenoog. (((((((Hollanditis))))))).

Voznesensky. Give Me Peace.

Walcott. Season of Phantasmal° Peace, The.

Wallis, S. Prayer for Peace, A.

Wang An-shih. Tune: "Sand of Silk-washing Stream."

Wang Wei. To Subprefect Chang.

Whitman, A.   End of the Whole Matter, The.
Whitman, W.   Base of All Metaphysics, The.
 Halcyon Days.
 Reconciliation.
Whittier.   Battle Autumn of 1862, The.
 Lost Occasion, The.
Wilbur.   Grasshopper, A.
Wilde, O.   E Tenebris.
Wilson, T.   Sportsmen in Paradise.
Winchilsea.   Enquiry after Peace. A Fragment.
Winters, Y.   Before Disaster.
Wither.   Sun hath run his course through all
 the Signes, The.
Wordsworth, W.   Fragment, A: "Between two
 sister moorland rills."
 These Chairs they have no words to utter.
Yang Shih-ch'i.   Sha-ch'eng, "Sand City" ("In
 former years I passed this city").
Yeats.   Michael Robartes Bids His Beloved Be
 at Peace.
Yukitsuna.   Tanka: "Child in my arms."

Peace, Isabel
Fordham.   Lines to Mrs. Isabel Peace.

Peach Trees and Peaches
Abse.   Peachstone.
Atwood.   Late August.
Blake, W.   Angel, The.
Chang Yü.   Painting ("Jade cave, ten thousand
 flowering peach trees, A").
Ch'ien Ch'ien-i.   Willow catkins beyond the
 garden wait for evening tides.
Cole, W.   Two Sad.
Fox, S.   Peaches.
Fraser, K.   These Labdanum Hours.
Graves, R.   Blue-Fly, The.
Hall, D.   Peaches.
Lee, L.   From blossoms comes.
 Weight of Sweetness, The.
Li Shang-yin.   Little Peach Blossoms in the
 Garden.
Nye, N.   Going for Peaches, Fredericksburg,
 Texas.
Rauter.   Peach.
Ríos, A.   La Sequia.
Shelnutt.   O Hero.
Su Tung-p'o.   Purple Peach Tree, The.
T'ang Yin.   Inscribed on a Painting ("At the
 country inn, thousands of peach trees").
 Song of Peach Blossom Retreat.
Tao-chi.   Riding a Boat on Wu-ling Stream.
Tsung Ch'en.   On Hearing That the Sea-
 Barbarians Are About To Attack Hu-chou—
 Expressing My Feelings to Tzu-yü.
Unknown.   Lovely the young peach tree.
 Peach Tree Young and Fresh.
Wang Chien.   Palace Song.
Warren, R.   Riddle in the Garden.
Yang Shen.   To the Tune "Heavenly Immortal"
 ("Waves wash off the peach blossoms").
Yüan Mei.   Ballad of Peach Blossom Spring.
 Things Seen on Spring Days.

Peacock, Margaret Love
Peacock, T.   Margaret Love Peacock, for Her
 Tombstone, 1826.

Peacocks
Custance.   Peacocks: A Mood.
Dickey, W.   Things Kept.
Hall, D.   Apples.
Lawrence, D.   Peacock.
Moore, M.   To the Peacock of France.
Peyanar.   What He Said ("Because peacocks
 moved like you").
Pichamurti.   National Bird.
Roberts, W.   Peacocks.
Sedgwick, M.   I'll Buy a Peacock Bird.
Stevens, W.   Domination of Black ("At night,
 by the fire").

Pear Trees and Pears
Doolittle, H.   Orchard.
 Pear Tree.
Millay, E.   Pear Tree, The.
Page, P.   Deaf-Mute in the Pear Tree.
Po Chü-i.   At the End of Spring.
Stevens, W.   Study of Two Pears.
Unknown.   Harry Parry.
 Return from Battle.
 That Broad and Spreading Sweet Pear.

Pearls
Allen, P.   Night Vision.
Chao Meng-fu.   Inscribed on a Wall Painting
 of Assembled Immortals.
Dickinson, E.   Her breast is fit for pearls.
 'Tis little I— could care for Pearls.
Duffy, C.   Warming Her Pearls.
"Field."   Girl, A.
Holmes, O.   Chambered Nautilus, The.
Huang E.   Pearl-teardrops roll and gather.
Roth, H.   Argument ended.
Senghor.   Pearls.
Shakespeare, W.   Ariel's Song ("Full fathom
 [or fadom] five thy father lies").
Thompson, P.   Precious Pearl, The.
Unknown.   Perle, plesaunte to prynces paye.
Wang Chien.   South, The.
Wang T'ing-hsiang.   On New Year's Day of
 the Year Kuei-ssu (1533), Releasing Live
 Creatures.
Wilde, L.   Poet's Destiny, The.
Yakamochi.   I send you a box.

Peas
Jones, H.   On a Fine Crop of Peas Being
 Spoiled by a Storm.
Unknown.   I eat my peas with honey.

Peasants
"Æ."   Exiles.
"Akhmatova."   You know, I languish here.
Auden.   Epilogue: " 'O where are you going?'
 said reader to rider."
"Bagritzky."   Black bread and a faithful wife.
Bokov.   Salt.
Campbell, J.   I Am the Mountainy Singer.
Clare, J.   Peasant Poet, The.
Cornford, F.   Peasant Woman, A.
E'tesami.   To His Father on Praising the
 Honest Life of the Peasant.
Ewart.   Wanting Out.
Gheorghe.   Cathedral Stones.
Gibbon, M.   French Peasants.
Hsü Chung-hsing.   How brave the peasant who
 lives beside the lake.
Lewis, A.   Peasants, The.
Merwin, W.   Peasant.
Ozog.   Village for a Wedding.
Po Chü-i.   Lodging with the Old Man of the
 Stream.
Unknown.   Cutty Wren, The.
Wickham.   King Alfred and the Peasant
 Woman.

Pedantry and Pedants
Edwards, T.   To the Editor of Mr. Pope's
 Works.
 Tongue-Doughty Pedant.
Nash, O.   Purist, The.
Whitman, W.   When I heard the learn'd
 astronomer.
See also **Scholarship and Scholars**

Peddling and Peddlers
Dowland.   Fine knacks for ladies, cheape
 choise brave and new.
Hoare, F.   Pedlar Jim.
Mew.   Pedlar, The.
Morin, C.   Lace Pedlar, The.
Rands.   Pedlar's Caravan, The.
Richards, L.   Old Joe Jones and his old dog
 Bones.
Ridley.   Cushie Butterfield.
Suckling, J.   Pedlar of Small-Wares, A.
Unknown.   Chapmen.
 Cries of London, The.
 Fine knacks for ladies, cheap, choice, brave
 and new!

Peeping Toms. *See* **Voyeurism and Voyeurs**
Peewees [*or* **Peewits**]. *See* **Pewees** [*or* **Pewits**]
Pelicans
Jeffers, R.   Pelicans.
Lear, E.   Pelican Chorus, The.
Wright, J.   Pelicans.

Penelope (mythology)
Doolittle, H.   At Ithaca.
Harrison, J.   Penelope.
Hartigan, A.   No Easy Harbour.
Homer.   Penelope hesitates.
 Thus, many tales Ulysses told his wife.
 Ulysses Reunited with Penelope.

Kyger.   Pan as the Son of Penelope.
Millay, E.   Ancient Gesture, An.
Muir, E.   Return of the Greeks, The.
Ritsos.   Penelope's Despair.
Spenser.   *Penelope* for her *Ulisses* sake.
Stevens, W.   World as Meditation, The.

Penguins
Miller, R.   Penguin on the Beach.
Wright, D.   On the Death of an Emperor
 Penguin in Regent's Park, London.

Peninsular War (1808–14)
Wolfe, C.   Burial of Sir John Moore [after
 [*or* at] Corunna], The.

Pennsylvania (state)
Daly, T.   Pennsylvania Places.
Djanikian.   How I Learned English.
Lanier, S.   Clover.
Littlebird.   Pennsylvania Winter Indian 1974.
Stern, G.   Dancing, The.

Penshurst, England
Waller, E.   At Penshurst [Another].
 At Penshurst ("While in the park I sing, the
 listning deer").

Pensions and Pensioners
Barber, M.   On Seeing an Officer's Widow
 Distracted.
Collier, J.   Pluralist and Old Soldier, The.
See also **Old Age; Retirement and Retirees**

Pentagon (building)
Bates, G.   Pentagonia.

Pentecost
De Vere, A.   Dominica Pentecostes.
Mangan, J.   Hymn for Pentecost.

Peonies
Hsü Wei.   To Hsü Shih-t'ing.
Kenyon, J.   Peonies at Dusk.
Kim, Y.   Till The Peonies Bloom.
Van Duyn.   Sonnet for Minimalists.
Yosano.   Tanka: "Peony in her hair, The."

Peppers
Matveyeva.   Hymn to the Pepper.
Mother Goose.   Peter Piper picked a peck of
 pickled pepper[s].
Saitō Mokichi.   Tanka: "Red pepper pods."

Peppertrees
Levertov.   Scenes from the Life of the
 Peppertrees.

Perception
Allen, P.   Night Vision.
Averill.   Bad for You.
Barth, R.   Postscript.
Baudelaire.   Which One Is Genuine?
Bernstein, O.   Only from Afar.
Bly, R.   Remembering in Oslo the Old Picture
 of the Magna Carta.
Bogan, L.   Late.
Brooks, G.   To be in love.
Cassity.   Junker-Lied.
Catullus.   To Varus.
Ciardi.   On a Photo of Sgt. Ciardi a Year
 Later.
Coleridge, S.   Apologia pro Vita Sua.
Creeley.   For Love.
 Man, The.
Cummings, E.   For prodigal read generous.
 If up's the word;and a world grows greener.
 So shy shy shy(and with a).
 Somewhere i have never travelled, gladly
 beyond.
 This little bride & groom are.
D'Ambrosio, C.   Morning.
De la Mare.   All but blind.
Dickinson, E.   Perception of an object costs.
 Tint I cannot take—is best, The.
Doolittle, H.   Moon in Your Hands, The.
Edson, R.   Way Things Are, The.
Emerson, R.   Astræa.
 Illusions.
 Memory.
Equi.   Words Read by Lightning.
Fenton, J.   This Octopus Exploits Women.
 Wild Ones[, The].
Fox, S.   Almagest, Last Letter to Zakarias.
Gascoyne.   Yves Tanguy.
Graves, R.   In Perspective.
Hadas, R.   Kaleidoscope.

Harte, B.　What the Bullet Sang.
Hillman.　Thoreau's Fossil Lilies.
Hoban.　Windows.
Hollander, J.　Morning in the Islands.
Jackson, L.　Prisms.
Jarrell.　Orient Express, The.
　Seele im Raum.
Kabir.　How Much Is Not True.
　Knowing nothing shuts the iron gates; the new
　　love opens them.
Keller, D.　In the Middle of the Journey.
Kipling, R.　Conundrum of the Workshops,
　The.
　Looking Glass, The.
　We and They.
Knott.　Feeding the Sun.
Levertov.　Seeing for a Moment.
　Witness.
Lewis, M.　August.
"MacDiarmid."　We must look at the harebell
　as if.
Martin, C.　Size Is Relative.
Martinez, D.　Necessary Story.
Milan, J.　Woman, 2.
Murray, L.　Equanimity.
Nemerov.　Companions, The.
Newcastle, M.　Dialogue betwixt the Body and
　the Mind, A.
Oppen.　Not to reduce the thing to nothing.
Pasman.　Black Hairs, The.
Ransom, J.　Painted Head.
Reed, H.　Judging Distances.
Rich, A.　Can it be growing colder when I
　begin.
Schuyler, J.　Freely Espousing.
Shakespeare, W.　Sonnet 130.
Sillitoe.　Optics.
Smith, S.　Not Waving But Drowning.
Snow, C.　Mask Series.
Snyder, G.　Through the Smoke Hole.
Stevens, W.　Idea of Order at Key West, The.
　Snow Man, The.
　Study of Two Pears.
　Thinking of a Relation between the Images of
　　Metaphors.
　Thirteen Ways of Looking at a Blackbird.
　To Henry Church.
Stevenson, R.　Foreign Children.
Strand.　Keeping Things Whole.
Summers, H.　As I went out this May morning
　I found.
Swenson, M.　In Love Made Visible.
Thurman.　Going Barefoot.
Warr, M.　Brain on Ice.
Wheeler, S.　Journal of the Thousand Choices.
Whitman, W.　Of the terrible doubt of
　appearances.
Williams, W.　Short Poem.
Wollach.　To See Long like El Greco.
Wordsworth, W.　Yarrow Visited [September,
　1814].
Wright, C.　Dead Color.
Percy, Sir Henry
Unknown.　Battle of Otterburn [or Oterborne],
　The.
　Chevy Chase.
Perfection
Chase, J.　One early spring evening when Celia
　was fourteen.
Dacey, P.　Looking at Models in the Sears
　Catalogue.
Dante Alighieri.　For certain he hath seen all
　perfectness.
Donne.　Negative Love.
Eberhart, R.　In a hard intellectual light / I will
　kill all delight.
Glatstein.　Matthew 5:38–48; "You have heard
　that it was said, 'An eye'."
Herrick.　His Request to Julia.
Jordan, J.　Sunflower Sonnet Number Two.
McWatt.　Boat Builder, The.
Olson, C.　As the dead prey upon us.
Plutzik.　Premonition, The.
Raine, K.　Statues.
Stevens, W.　Asides on the Oboe.
　Poems of Our Climate, The.
Tomlinson, C.　Rhymes.

Viiding.　I celebrated this day in March.
Wright, J.　Birds.
Yeats.　Before the World Was Made.
Perfumes
Donne.　Perfume, The.
Herrick.　To His Mistresses.
Mackenzie, K.　Ginger-flowers.
Pound, E.　Portrait d'une Femme.
Symons, A.　White Heliotrope.
Unknown.　Fragrance comes from the scent I
　wear, The.
　Out the southern gate at sundown.
Wratislaw.　Frangipani.
　Opoponax.
　Satiety.
Perplexity
Creeley.　For No Clear Reason.
Eady.　Sherbet.
Persecution
Auden.　Refugee Blues.
Bienek.　Exodus.
Bobrowski.　Elderblossom.
Breytenbach.　Out There.
Brutus.　Robben Island Sequence.
"Carroll."　Long Tale, A.
Cheney-Coker.　Outsider, The.
Glatstein.　How much Christian, so to speak,
　can I get?
Longfellow, H.　Jewish Cemetery at Newport,
　The.
Macgoye.　August the First: The Watchman
　Speaks.
MacNeice.　Turf-Stacks.
Nasrin.　At the Back of Progress. . . .
Niemoller.　First they came for the Jews.
Winner, R.　Segregated Railway Diner—1946.
Persephone
Boland, E.　Pomegranate, The.
Cassity.　Gardens of Proserpine, The.
Creeley.　Kore.
Daumal.　Persephone That Is to Say Double
　Issue.
Dove, R.　Persephone Abducted.
　Persephone, Falling.
　Persephone Underground.
Glück, L.　Pomegranate.
Hope, A.　Return of Persephone, The.
Lawrence, D.　Bavarian Gentians.
Muske.　Wish Foundation, The.
Swinburne.　Garden of Proserpine, The.
　Hymn to Proserpine.
Unknown.　There Ceres, distant from the
　powers divine.
　To Demeter.
Perseus
Hayden, R.　Perseus.
Levy, A.　Reminiscence, A.
MacNeice.　Perseus.
Perseverance
Baca.　Oppression.
Berry, J.　It's Me Man.
Braley, B.　Success ("If you want a thing bad
　enough").
Cameron, C.　Don't Give Up.
　Success.
Carew, T.　Eternity of Love Protested.
Castillo, O.　Distances.
Chan.　Paradise.
Clark, T.　Like musical instruments /
　Abandoned in a field.
Clough.　Say not the struggle nought [or
　naught] availeth.
Cooke, E.　Plug.
Creeley.　Marriage, A.
　Oh No.
Dao.　End or a Beginning, An.
Disch.　Entropic Villanelle.
Eliot, T.　East Coker.
　Little Gidding.
Espada.　Mrs. Baez Serves Coffee on the Third
　Floor.
Herbert, G.　Employment: "He that is weary,
　let him sit."
Holden, J.　Liberace.
Hopkins, G.　Carrion Comfort.
Jackson, H.　My Lighthouses.
Jarrell.　Knight, Death, and the Devil, The.

Jefferys.　We have lived and loved together.
Kipling, R.　Last Lap, The.
　Old Men, The.
Kiser.　Unsubdued.
Longfellow, H.　Excelsior.
Lovelace, R.　Apostasy of One and Bùt One
　Lady, The.
Mihalic.　Maestro, extinguish the candle,
　serious times have come.
Moore, M.　Nevertheless.
Newbolt.　Vitaï Lampada.
Nobuyuki.　Stone Buddha (two poems).
Palmer, T.　Try, Try Again.
Piercy.　To Be of Use.
Rich, A.　Can it be growing colder when I
　begin.
Rogers, P.　Eulogy for a Hermit Crab.
Sandburg, C.　Upstream.
Sargent, E.　Rockall.
Smith, M.　Dis-ya dutty, a we create it.
Song.　Out of Our Hands.
Sorescu.　Perseverance.
Stanton, F.　Keep a-Goin'.
Tennyson, A.　Ulysses.
Unknown.　Pluck Wins.
　Young Man Who Couldn't See Why, The.
Warren, R.　To a Face in a Crowd.
Whitfield.　Self-Reliance.
Whitman, W.　Noiseless patient spider, A.
Williams, W.　Pink Locust, The.
Young, A.　Dance For Ma Rainey, A.
Persia. See Iran
Persian Wars (500 B.C.–449 B.C.)
Graves, R.　Persian Version, The.
Hope, A.　Inscription for a War.
Simonides.　For the Spartan Dead at
　Thermopylai (480 B.C.).
Persians
Graves, R.　Persian Version, The.
Persimmon Trees
Young, V.　Persimmons.
Peru
Bryant, W.　Damsel of Peru, The.
Coolidge, C.　Peru Eye, the Heart of the Lamp.
Garrigue.　Of History More Like Myth.
Vallejo.　Telluric and Magnetic.
Peruncattan
Kirattanar.　Young will not wear it, The.
Kutavayir Kirattanar.　Elegy: "Young will not
　wear it, The."
Peruvaluti, King
Nettimaiyar.　Your bards are wearing lotuses.
Pessimism
Auden.　Epilogue: " 'O where are you going?'
　said reader to rider."
Belloc.　Is there any reward?
Carruth, H.　On Being Asked to Write a Poem
　Against the War in Vietnam.
Coward.　There Are Bad Times Just around the
　Corner.
Creeley.　Turn, The.
Durcan.　Honeymoon Postcard.
Hardy, T.　Epitaph on a Pessimist.
Hoffenstein.　You buy yourself a new suit of
　clothes.
Howard, R.　Difference, The.
Irwin, W.　Worried Skipper, The.
King, B.　Pessimist, The.
　Sum of Life, The.
Knox, R.　To a Pessimist.
Lowell, R.　Waking Early Sunday Morning.
Meredith, G.　Not solely that the Future she
　destroys.
Naden.　Pessimist's Vision, The.
Nims, J.　Philosopher.
Parker, D.　Prophetic Soul.
　Symptom.
Reid, A.　Scotland.
Strand.　Violent Storm.
Unknown.　Pessimist's a cheerless man, The.
Yevtushenko.　City of Yes and the City of No,
　The.
Peter Rabbit
McPherson, S.　Peter Rabbit.
Peter, Saint
Browning, E.　Look, The.
　Meaning of the Look, The.

Constable, H. To St. Peter and St. Paul.
Hardy, T. In the Servants' Quarters.
Herrick. Peter-penny, The.
Rossetti, C. St. Peter once: "Lord, dost Thou wash my feet?"
Unknown. When in my pilgrimage I reach.
Wylie. Peter and John.

Peter the Great
Smelyakov. Peter and Aleksey.

Peterloo Massacre (1819)
Bamford. Touch him, aye! touch him, if you dare.
Shelley, P. Song to the Men of England.

Petra, Jordan
Burgon. Pedra.

Petrarch (Francesco Petrarca)
Carducci. Petrarch.
Russell, T. Sonnet to Valclusa.
Sidney, P. Sonnet 15: "You that do search for every purling spring."

Petrels
Whitman, W. To the Man-of-War Bird.

Pets
Arnold, M. Geist's Grave.
Asquith. Hairy Dog, The.
Auden. Cats and Dog.
Barrington, P. I had a hippopotamus; I kept him in a shed.
Brandreth. Ode to a Goldfish.
Calverley. Disaster.
Clark, L. Grumblers.
Cornford, F. Child's Dream, A.
Cowper, W. Epitaph on a Hare.
On the Lamented Death of Mrs. Throckmorton's Bullfinch.
Creeley. If you were going to get a pet.
Davies, W. Child's Pet, A.
Du Bellay. There are cats (not he).
Fisher, R. O Goldfish!
That Cat!
Who are my pets.
Gardner, C. If you ever come to our house.
Gross, P. Verbal Gerbil.
Hale, S. Mary's Lamb [or Mary and Her Lamb].
Hardy, T. Last Words To a Dumb Friend.
Hassall. Tropical Fish.
Herrick. Upon His Spaniel[l] Tracie [or Tracy].
Hughes, T. My Brother Bert.
Roger the Dog.
Issa. Bird in the cage, The.
Jennings, E. My animals are made of wool and glass.
Katrovas. Dog and a Boy, A.
Kitching. My Gerbil.
Kumin, M. Retrieval System, The.
Larkin, P. Take One Home for the Kiddies.
Lee, B. Bad Dog.
Lowell, R. Frederick Kuh, Manx Cat.
MacCaig. Praise of a Collie.
MacNeice. Pet Shop.
Magee, W. Gran's Green Parrot.
Nicholls, J. Cat.
Dog.
Nurton. My Doggie.
Patten, B. Mum won't let me keep a rabbit.
Pinto, J. I had a pet lizard called Albert.
Ransom, J. Janet Waking.
Roethke. Meadow Mouse, The.
Rowse. White Cat of Trenarren, The.
Scannell. Cat.
Schelling. Run My Hand Under.
Sedgwick, M. I'll Buy a Peacock Bird.
Sidney, P. Sonnet 83: "Good brother *Philip,* I have borne you long."
Smart, C. My Cat Jeoffry.
Smith, S. My Tortoise.
Snyder, G. Nansen.
Taufer, D. Mice Are Pets?
Toulson. Amber.
Turner, E. Canary, The.
Unknown. Gentle rodent in its cage.
Maggie.
Monk and His Pet Cat, The.
My Pet Koala.
Thin Dog.

Verlaine. E's Finch.
Walsh, J. White Rabbit, The.
Weaver, M. Dogs, The.
West, C. My Gecko and I.
My obnoxious brother Bobby.
Williams, E. My Pet Goldfish.
Wright, K. Our hamster's life.
Yeats. Two Songs of a Fool.

Pewees [or Pewits]
Thomas, E. Two Pewits.

Peyote
Blockcolski. Peyote Vision.

Phantoms
Graves, R. Sea Horse, The.

Pheasants
Hart-Smith. Golden Pheasant. Mating Pair.
Hitomaro. Pheasant of the mountain, The.
Kitahara Hakushū. Tanka: "Winter day."
Plath. Pheasant.
Pope, A. Hunting and Fishing.
Samio. Tanka: "With the blue."
Unknown. Rabbit goes soft-foot, pheasant's caught.
Song of the Pheasant.

Philadelphia, Pennsylvania
Baraka. Pause of Joe, The.
Brutus. Off to Philadelphia in the morning.
Holub. Franklin Bridge in Philadelphia, The.
Kemble. To the Wissahiccon.
Unknown. Philadelphia ("Philadelphia is a handsome town").
Weaver, M. Black Man's Sonata, A.

Philanthropy and Philanthropists
Anderson, M. Closed Mill.
Dobson, A. Virtuoso, A.
Guiterman. Offer, An.
Hollander, J. No Foundation.
Kendall, M. Philanthropist and the Jelly-fish, The.
Unknown. Old Woman of Leeds, The.
See also **Charity**

Philately and Philatelists
Spingarn, L. Philatelic Lessons: The German Collection.

Philiphaugh, Battle of (1645)
Unknown. Battle of Philiphaugh, The.

Philippines
Kipling, R. White Man's Burden, The.
Lim-Wilson. Inventing the Filipino.

Philips, James
Philips, K. To My Antenor, March 16, 1661/2.

Philistines
Pound, E. Les Millwin.

Phillips, Wendell
Ray, J. Wendell Phillips.

Philomela
Arnold, M. Philomela.
Ransom, J. Philomela.
Sidney, P. Nightingale as soone as April bringeth, The.

Philosophy and Philosophers
Auden. Voltaire at Ferney.
Baraka. Balboa, the Entertainer.
Bendall, M. Conversations on the Plurality of Worlds.
Blaga. Heraclitus by the Lake.
Blake, W. Mock on, Mock on Voltaire, Rousseau.
Bromige. Logical Positivist, The.
Carson, C. Irish for No, The.
Ch'en Tzu-ang. Business men boast of their skill and cunning.
Collins, M. Positivists, The.
Cowley, A. Philosophy, the great and only heir.
Cunningham, J. Metaphysical Amorist, The.
Dacre, C. Female Philosopher, The.
Deutsch. Homage to the Philosopher.
Douglas, L. Apologia.
Dove, R. Persephone Abducted.
Dunn, S. Something Like Happiness.
Emerson, R. Humble-Bee, The.
Empson. Dissatisfaction with Metaphysics.
Foss, S. Philosopher, A.
Francis, R. Waxwings.

Gascoigne. Gascoigne's Woodmanship.
Glycon. Everything's laughter / everything dust.
Herford. Metaphysics.
Holub. Immanuel Kant.
Larkin, P. Days.
Lo Yin. Sent to the Ch'an Master Wu-hsiang.
Manifold. Makhno's Philosophers.
Mason, W. Some Early gardenists.
Melville, H. Fragments of a Lost Gnostic Poem of the Twelfth [or 12th] Century.
Meredith, G. Garden of Epicurus, The.
Murphy, R. Philosopher and the Birds, The.
O'Brien, G. Interior Prisoner, The.
Ostriker. I Brood about Some Concepts, for Example.
Po Chü-i. Philosophers: Lao-Tzu, The.
Preil, G. Lines on the Rambam.
Rumi. Little by little, wean yourself.
Smith, S. Distractions and the Human Crowd.
On the Death of a German Philosopher.
Stevens, W. To an Old Philosopher in Rome.
To Henry Church.
Tomlinson, C. In Defence of Metaphysics.
Unknown. How was I born? Where from? Why did I come.
Whitman, W. Base of All Metaphysics, The.
Wollach. Love Poem #2.
Zagajewski. Lava.

Phoebus Apollo. *See* **Apollo**

Phoenix
Adams, J. On the Phoenix.
Carew, T. Song, [A]: "Ask me no more where Jove bestows."
Darley. O Blest Unfabled Incense Tree.
Doolittle, H. *Amen.*
Du Bellay. I saw the bird that can the sun endure.
Greiffenberg. I look.
Homer. Phœnix pleads with Achilles.
Lewis, R. Humming Bird, The.
Merrill, J. About the Phoenix.
Nemerov. Phoenix comes of flame and dust, The.
Po Chü-i. Chuang Tzu, The Monist.
Read, S. Phoenix, bird of terrible pride.
Shakespeare, W. Phoenix and the Turtle, The.
Smith, A. News of the Phoenix.
Tao-chi. Inscribed on a Painting of a Wu-t'ung Tree by Myself.
Tu Fu. Song of the Vermeil Phoenix.
Wilbur. Cottage Street, 1953.
Yün Shou-p'ing. Inscribed on a Snowscape.

Photography and Photographers
Alegría. Documentary.
Amis, K. Mightier than the Pen.
Ashbery. City Afternoon.
Atwood. Daguerreotype Taken in Old Age.
This Is a Photograph of Me.
"Carroll." Hiawatha's Photographing.
Cassells. Courtesy, A Trenchant Grace, A.
Chernoff. Lost and Found.
Ciardi. On a Photo of Sgt. Ciardi a Year Later.
Coles, D. Photograph in a Stockholm Newspaper for March 13, 1910.
Couzyn. You Have Shown Me a Strange Image, and We Are Strange Prisoners.
Cranch. Photograph, The.
Cronin, J. Group Photo from Pretoria Local on the Occasion of a Fourth Anniversary (Never Taken).
Dickey, W. Arrival of the Titanic, The.
Dobler. 1920 Photo.
Drummond de Andrade. Dead in Frock Coats, THe.
Durcan. Irish Hierarchy Bans Colour Photography.
Ellis, T. Shooting Back.
Emanuel, L. Discovering the Photograph of Lloyd, Earl, and Priscilla.
Self-Portrait at Eighteen.
Etter. Well You Needn't.
Ferry. Photographs from a Book: Six Poems.
Fuller, R. Middle of a War, The.
Galvin, B. Photo of Miners, A.

Golding, L. In The Gallery Where the Fat Men Go.
Hai-Jew, S. Three Gypsies.
Harper, M. Three O'Clock Love Song.
Heyen. Tie, The.
Holden, M. Photograph of Haymaker, 1890.
Hughes, M. Six Young Men.
Kinzie. Sound Waves.
Kirsch, S. Pictures.
Komunyakaa. Untitled Blues.
Kooser. Camera.
Kumin, M. Family Man, A.
Larkin, P. Lines on a Young Lady's Photograph Album.
Levis. Widening Spell of the Leaves, The.
Lim, S. Black and White.
Lowell, R. Epilogue: "Those blessèd structures, plot and rhyme."
Lum. Picture of my Mother's Family, A.
Machi. Tanka: "Freezing my smile."
McElroy, C. From Homegrown: An Asian-American Anthology of Writers.
Mordecai. Shooting the Horses.
Nemerov. Picture, A.
Oppen. From a Photograph.
Orlen. Ukranian Pastorals.
Ormsby, F. War Photographers, The.
Osbey. Portrait.
Peseroff. Hardness Scale, The.
Pinkerton, H. On Dorothea Lange's Photograph "Migrant Mother" (1936).
Prettyman. Photograph.
Raworth. Empty Pain-Killer Bottles, The.
Ray, D. Eskimo Girl, The.
On the Photograph "Yarn Mill," by Lewis W. Hine.
Rivard. Summons.
Shepherd, R. What Cannot Be Kept.
Simko. Arrival, The.
Strelchenko. My Photograph.
Stuart, D. Rescue.
Suknaski. Chinese Camp, Kamloops (circa 1883).
Tadic. Little Picture Catalogue.
Taylor, A. Developing a Wife.
Tucker, M. Family Portraits.
Updike. Snapshots.
Wakoski. Photos, The.
Wallace, R. Makings of Happiness, The.
Warren, R. In Creve Coeur, Missouri.
Warsh. Suicide Rates, The.
Wilbur. Looking into History.
Wood, R. Cabbages.
Wright, C. Negatives.
Snapshot.
Wright, K. Victorian Family Photograph.
Yau. Cenotaph.
Yoshimi. Tanka: "Because."
Zarucchi. Grape Stakes.

See also **Cameras**

Physicians
Aiken, C. Doctors' Row.
Belloc. Henry King, Who Chewed Bits of String, and Was Early Cut Off in Dreadful Agonies.
On Hygiene.
Betjeman. Five O'Clock Shadow.
Browning, R. Epistle Containing the Strange Medical Experience of Karshish, the Arab Physician, An.
Burns, R. Death and Doctor Hornbook [A True Story].
Campbell, J. Ol' Doc' Hyar.
Carleton, W. Country Doctor, The.
Doctor's Story, The.
Davis, F. Arthur Ridgewood, M.D.
Fitzgerald, R. Wind at Your Door, The.
Gibson, W. Conscript, The.
Hoffman, O. Five best doctors anywhere, The.
Inez. Warrior Daughters.
Johnson, S. On the Death of Dr [*or* Mr] Robert Levet [a Practiser in Physic].
Jonson, B. To Doctor Empiric[k].
Kirkup. Correct Compassion, A.
Li K'ai-hsien. Sent to the Master Physician, "Almond Orchard" Shih.
Thanking Doctor Jen.

Logau. Physicians' Fortune, The.
Miles, J. Doctor Who Sits at the Bedside of a Rat, The.
Moorer. Birthday Wishes to a Physician.
Morgan, R. Invisible woman in the asylum corridor, The.
Piercy. Homage to Lucille, Dr. Lord-Heinstein.
Plumly. Reading with the Poets.
Po Chü-i. Since I lay ill, how long has passed?
Prior. Remedy Worse than the Disease, The.
Robinson, E. How Annandale Went Out.
Sadiq. Tuskegee Experiment.
Seth. Doctor's Journal Entry for August 6, 1945, A.
Stallworthy, J. Letter from Berlin, A.
Unknown. Archaic Song of Dr. Tom the Shaman.
Doctor Bell fell down the well.
Vinz. Old Doc.
Williams, W. Complaint.
Le Médecin Malgré Lui.
To Close.

See also **Hospitals; Medicine; Nurses**

Physics and Physicists
Auden. After Reading a Child's Guide to Modern Physics.
Bold, A. Special Theory of Relativity, A.
Brown, R. I want to understand light years.
Dali. Art of Picasso, The.
Harris, M. Physics One.
Jordan, J. Poem about Intelligence for My Brothers and Sisters, A.
Kendall, M. Ether Insatiable.
Lucretius. First principles of Epicurean physics.

Pianos
Chon, P. Piano, The.
Frost, R. Investment, The.
Gillies, V. Piano-Tuner, The.
Jordan, J. October 23, 1983.
Joyce, J. Twilight turns from amethyst, The.
Justice, D. Variations for Two Pianos.
Kamienska. Those who carry grand pianos / to the tenth floor.
Lawrence, D. Piano, The.
Madgett. Echoes.
Oppen. O withering seas.
Ruark. Visitor, The.
Tranströmer. Allegro.
Updike. Player Piano.
Weissbort. Mourning.

Picasso, Pablo
Cassells. These Are Not Brushstrokes.
Dali. Art of Picasso, The.
Ford, C. There's No Place to Sleep in This Bed, Tanguy.
Norse. Picasso Visits Braque.
Scalapino. Picasso and Anarchism.

Pickles
Dillard, R. Meditation for a Pickle Suite.
Gyorgy. Xenia.
Taylor, B. Ode on [*or* to] a Jar of Pickles.

Picnics and Barbecues
Adamson. My Tenth Birthday.
Betjeman. Archaeological Picnic, The.
Bhartrihari. Three Poems.
Causley. Eden Rock.
Elmslie, K. Picnic.
Hardy, T. Where the Picnic Was.
Holman, M. Picnic: the Liberated.
Lofting. Picnic.
Logan, J. Picnic, The.
Muldoon, P. Truce.
Roethke. Thing, The.
Su Tung-p'o. Rhyming with Tzu-yu's "Treading the Green."
Tagami. Mussel Rock/Lowtide—Santa Cruz, California 1959.
Toomer. Georgia Dusk.
Unknown. Picnics.
Warren, R. Renoir.
Weaver, M. Picnic, an Homage to Civil Rights, The.
Wong, N. Picnic.

Pies
Guest, E. Lemon Pie.

Le Gallienne. Melton Mowbray Pork Pie, A.
Merriam, E. Counting-out Rhyme.

Piety
Aristophanes. CHORUS. Ye Children of Man! whose life is a span.
Bible, *N.T.* Luke 7; She Began To Wash His Feet with Teares and Wipe Them with the Haires of Her Head.
Bible, *O.T.* Psalm 1.
Psalm 119.37.
Chaucer. Friar's Tale, The.
Donne. Devout Fits.
Euripides. There Are No Gods.
Herrick. Chewing [of] the Cud, The.
His Offering, with the Rest, at the Sepulcher.
To Keep a True Lent.
Juvenal. Little do folks the heav'nly Powers mind.
Ovid. From lofty Roofs the Gods repuls'd before.
Virgil. Fiery Sun was mounted now on hight, The.

Pigeons
Bennett, R. Pigeons, The.
Bishop, E. Two Mornings and Two Evenings.
Brock-Broido. Last Passenger Pigeon in the Cincinnati Zoo, The.
Farjeon, E. Mistress Peck-Pigeon.
Katrovas. My Friends the Pigeons.
Kavanagh, P. Leave Them Alone.
Knight, E. Crazy pigeon strutting outside my cell.
McGinley. Trinity Place.
Merwin, W. Fly.
Meyers, B. Pigeons.
Moore, M. Pigeons.
Pinsky. First Early Mornings Together.
Reid, A. Pigeons.
Rossetti, C. On the Wing.
Walker, T. Homing Pigeons.
Wang Wei. Composed on a Spring Day on the Farm.

Pigs
Artaud. All Writing Is Garbage.
Baker, M. Porkskin Panorama.
Benson, G. Cat and the Pig, The.
Blake, W. I saw a chapel all of gold.
Blunden. Poor Man's Pig, The.
Corso. Song: "Oh, dear! Oh, me! Oh, my!"
Cullen, C. Unknown Color, The.
Cussons. Barn-yard, The.
Edson, R. Performance at Hog Theater, A.
Éluard, P. Pig.
Farber. Hog at the Manger.
Fergusson. Sow of Feeling, The.
Forrest. St. Anthony and His Pig; a Cantata.
Gatty. Three Little Pigs, The.
Gay, J. Wild Boar and the Ram, The.
Geddes, G. Transubstantiation.
Gunn, T. Moly.
Hecht, A. Pig.
Hood, T. Lament of Toby the Learned Pig, The.
Little Piggies, The.
Hsü Pen. Ballad of the Ferocious Tiger.
Hughes, T. View of a Pig.
Humphreys, E. Apple Tree and a Pig, An.
Kinnell. Saint Francis and the Sow.
Lawrence, D. Food of the north tastes too much of the fat of the pig, The.
Lehmann, G. Pigs, The.
Levine, P. Animals Are Passing from Our Lives.
McBride, M. Loneliness.
McKay, C. If we must die—let it not be like hogs.
Milosz, C. Readings.
Monkhouse. Limericks.
Mother Goose. Barber, barber, shave a pig.
This little pig went to market.
Tom, Tom the piper's son.
Mountain, M. Pig and i spring rain.
Nash, O. Pig, if I am not mistaken, The.
Padgett, R. Detach, Invading.
Pawsey. Greedy Little Pig, The.
Ristovic. Flirting with a Pig.

Rochester, J. Song: "Fair Chloris in a pigsty lay."
Rossetti, C. If a pig wore a wig.
Siegel, R. Ego.
Smith, D. Pulling a Pig's Tail.
Southey, R. Ode to a Pig while His Nose Was Being Bored.
Taylor, J. Pigs, The.
Unknown. As I Went to Bonner.
Judged by the Company One Keeps.
Pig, The.
Riddle: "As I went down that yella bank."
Roasted Sucking Pig.
Seven Little Pigs.
There Was a Lady Loved a Swine.
To market, to market, to buy a fat pig.
Watson, C. Knickerbocker Knockabout.
Wesley, S. Pindaric on the Grunting of a Hog, A.
Wilbur. Matthew 8:28–34; And when he came to the other side.
Matthew VIII, 28 ff.

Pike (fish)
Hughes, T. Pike, three inches long, perfect.

Pilgrim Fathers
Bacon, L. Pilgrim Fathers, The.
Ellsworth. Mayflower, The.
Emerson, R. Boston Hymn.
Hemans. Landing of the Pilgrim Fathers [in New England], The.
Lowell, R. Children of Light.
Tillam. Upon the First Sight of New England, June 29, 1638.
Very. Wild Rose of Plymouth, The.

Pilgrimages and Pilgrims
Bradstreet, A. As weary pilgrim, now at rest.
Bridges, R. O weary pilgrims, chanting of your woe.
Bunyan. Pilgrim, The.
Chaucer. Canterbury Tales, The.
General Prologue, The.
Miller's [*or* Milleres] Tale, The.
Clarke, A. Pilgrimage.
Clive. Old Age.
Dante Alighieri. Ye pilgrim-folk, advancing pensively.
Donnchadh Mor O'Dala. At Saint Patrick's Purgatory.
Donne. Song: "Go and catch a falling star."
Graves, R. Travel[l]er's Curse after Misdirection[, The].
Hall, D. Woolworth's.
Hardy, T. Hap.
Hemans. Landing of the Pilgrim Fathers [in New England], The.
Herbert, G. Pilgrimage, The.
Kendall, H. Christmas Creek.
Lear, E. Self-Portrait of the Laureate of Nonsense.
Lewis, C. Pilgrim's Problem.
Melville, H. Hostel, The.
Medallion, The.
Mo Shih-lung. Saying Good-Bye to Feng the Hermit.
Nadaud. Carcassonne.
Rossetti, C. Uphill [*or* Up-Hill].
Senghor. Song of the Initiate.
Shakespeare, W. If I profane with my unworthiest hand.
Spender, S. Marston, dropping it in the grate, broke his pipe.
Sutskever. 1980.
Unknown. City Called Heaven.
Vaughan, H. Pilgrimage, The.
Search, The.
Wright, J. Bullocky.
Yeats. Pilgrim, The.
Young, A. On the Pilgrims' Road.
Young, C. Vespers.

Pilots
"H., M. C. D." Hymn for Airmen.
Jarrell. Pilot from the Carrier, A.
Kipling, R. R.A.F. (Aged Eighteen).
Roberts, C. Prayer for a Pilot.
Waniek. Star-Fix.
Tuskegee Airfield.
Wood, R. Pilot, The.

See also **Air Warfare**
Pindar
Antipater of Sidon. Pindar.
Duncan, R. Poem Beginning with a Line by Pindar, A.
Horace. 4.2: Praise of Pindar, The ("Pindarum quisquis studet aemulari").

Pine Island, Minnesota
Wright, J. Lying in a Hammock at William Duffy's Farm in Pine Island, Minnesota.

Pine Trees
Ariwara no Yukihira. I must leave you, but.
Bachmann. Invocation of the Great Bear.
Boldman. Sitting.
Cherry, K. Pines without peer, The.
Chu Yün-ming. Little Landscape, A.
Conforti. On the mountain slope.
De Mello Breyner. Beach.
Doolittle, H. Oread.
Flanders, J. Testimony.
Foster, J. Lynn.
Galvin, B. Pitch Pines.
Hakutsu. O pine-tree standing.
Time it takes, The.
Harr, L. After the snowfall.
Harter. Pine needles.
Hsieh Chin. Poem on a Little Pine, A.
Hsü Wei. Painting of People Strolling through a Pine Forest, A.
Jakuren. Hanging raindrops, The.
Li Po. In the Mountains on a Summer Day.
Li Tung-yang. Inscribed on the Painting "Meaning of a Poem by Wang Wei."
Trip to Yüeh-lu Temple, A.
Masaoka Shiki. Tanka: "On a young pine."
Monroe, B. In the Pines.
Monroe, H. Pine at Timber-Line, The.
Muldoon, P. Yggdrasill.
Nagy, A. Pinetree.
Pagis. Conversation.
Po Chü-i. Pine Sounds.
Pine-trees in the Courtyard, The.
Song of the pines.
Pratt, M. Not a breath of air.
Sidney, P. Graven Thoughts.
Southard. Hushed, the lake-shore's pines.
T'ang Yin. Inscribed on a Painting ("Thatched hut among the pines, door open near a cliff").
Unknown. Aching nostalgia—.
Wang An-shih. Old Pine, An.
Wen Cheng-ming. Around the temple, pines and cedars.
In the sixth month, outside the gate.
Whitman, W. Spring.
Yang Shih-ch'i. White Stone Slope.
Yü Chi. Inscribed on a Painting.
Inscribed on the Painting, Solitary Crane, in the Collection of Jao Shih-ying.
Yüan Hung-tao. Pei-mang Cemetery.
Yün Shou-p'ing. Inscribed on a Snowscape.
Zanzotto. Epiphany.

Pinkham, Lydia
Unknown. Lydia Pinkham.

Pioneers
Benét, S. Ballad of William Sycamore, The.
Bowering, G. Grandfather.
Brewster, E. Great-Aunt Rebecca.
Clark, C. Pioneers.
Clark, T. Mountain Men.
Crawford, V. Pioneer Woman.
Cronwright. Song of the Wagon-whip, A.
Davidson, D. Descending Chestnut Ridge.
Dorn, E. Home on the Range, February 1962.
Emerson, R. Forerunners.
Fisher, A. *et al.* Pioneers.
Freneau. On the Civilization of the Western Aboriginal Country.
Goldsmith, O. Lonely Settler, The.
Haines, J. There Are No Such Trees in Alpine, California.
Harris, A. Pioneers.
Mair, C. I love you better than I love my race.
McLachlan. Arrival, The.
Miller, J. Westward Ho!
Moore, M. New York.

Nowlan. For Jean Vincent d'Abbadie, Baron St.-Castin.
Parkes, B. Lilian's Second Letter.
Pfeiffer, E. Lost Light, The.
Piatt, J. Farther.
Rich, A. Face to Face.
From an Old House in America.
Ridge, J. And shall we view these miracles and more.
Sanchez, S. Right On: White America.
Smith, W. Tempest, The.
Stafford, W. Prairie Town.
Street, A. Settler, The.
Unknown. Boys of Sanpete County, The.
Handcart Song, The.
State of Arkansas, The.
Tittery-Irie-Aye.
Walker, C. St. George.
Whitman, W. Pioneers! O Pioneers!

Pipers
Blake, W. Introduction: "Piping down the valleys wild."
"O'Sullivan." Piper, A [*or* The].

Piracy and Pirates
Allison, Y. Derelict.
Cowley, A. Cheer up, my mates, the wind does fairly blow.
Kingsley, C. Last Buccaneer, The.
Komunyakaa. Boat People.
Masefield. Captain Stratton's Fancy.
Meigs, M. Pirate Don Durk of Dowdee, The.
Pessoa. Ah, pirates, pirates, pirates!
Stevenson, R. Pirate Ditty.
Pirate Story.
Unknown. Bacchus, or the Pirates.
Captain Kidd ("You captains brave and bold, hear our cries, hear our cries").
Captain Ward and the *Rainbow.*
Flying Cloud, The.
Sir Andrew Barton.

Pitt, William
Burns, R. On Mr. Pitt's [*or* Pit's] Hair-Powder Tax.

Pittsburgh, Pennsylvania
Ackerman, D. Lines Written in a Pittsburgh Skyscraper.
Rumored Conversation with Oneself Continues in Pittsburgh, The.
Anderson, M. Closed Mill.
Invention of Pittsburgh, The.
Emanuel, L. Desire.
Stern, G. Dancing, The.

Pity
Altizer. Sonnet 2: "My own heart let me have. More pity on."
Bond, F. Pity Wasted.
Cameron, N. Compassionate Fool, The.
Chaucer. Complaint unto Pity, The.
Introduction to the Pardoner's Prologue and Tale.
Coleridge, S. Dungeon, The.
Love.
To a Young Ass.
Dante Alighieri. At whiles (yea oftentimes) I muse over.
Stay now with me, and listen to my sighs.
Eberhart, R. When Doris danced under the oak tree.
Fisher, A. Moles.
Garrigue. False Country of the Zoo.
Gray, W. She Is More to Be Pitied than Censured.
Hardy, T. Her Dilemma.
Hayes, A. Pietá.
Hewitt, J. How have I served you? I have let you waste.
Holub. Napoleon.
Hopkins, G. My own heart let me more have pity on; let.
Howe, F. From a donkey, excuse me, one lesson is given.
Howitt, M. Cry of the Animals, The.
Hughes, L. Lover's Return.
Jaccottet. I rise with an effort and look out.
Keats. To Fanny.
Li Ho. At Ch'ang-ku, Reading: To Show to My Man Pa.

Lovelace, R.   La Bourbon, A.
Lukonin.   To Kolya Otrada.
Mathews, H.   Dappled Horse, The.
Mayer, B.   Generic Elbows.
Millay, E.   Pity me not because the light of day.
Morris, M.   Swimmer.
Ravikovitch.   Hovering at a Low Altitude.
Rossetti, C.   After Death.
Saigyo.   My heart emptied.
Schuyler, J.   Self-Pity Is a Kind of Lying, Too.
Shakespeare, W.   Sonnet 111.
Sidney, P.   Sonnet 45: "Stella oft sees the very face of woe."
Su Tung-p'o.   Lament of the Farm Wife of Wu.
   New Year's Eve—you'd think I could go home early.
Ukon.   I am forgotten now.
Unknown.   Summer Song.
Wain.   When It Comes.
Wilbur.   Undead, The.
Wollach.   Absalom.
Wright, J.   American Twilights, 1957.
   At the Executed Murderer's Grave.
   Inscription for the Tank.
   What the Earth Asked Me.
Yeats.   Pity of Love, The.

Pixies. *See* **Fairies**

Pizarro, Francisco
Warton, J.   Revenge of America, The.

Place Names
Barnes, W.   Woak Hill.
Benét, S.   American Names.
Daly, T.   Pennsylvania Places.
Gbadamosi.   Padraic's Point.
James, S.   Inner Mongolia—The Grasslands.
"Kerr."   American Traveller, The.
Sigourney.   Indian Names.
Simms, C.   St Kilda-Wren, 1957.
Unknown.   Paris 1912.
Vando.   Chimayo.

Plague
Hecht, A.   Tarantula or the Dance of Death.
Kees.   Coming of the Plague, The.
Melville, H.   In the Desert.
Nashe.   Litany in Time of Plague, A.
Toomer.   November Cotton Flower.

Plains. *See* **Prairies**

Planets
Bold, A.   Tenth Planet, The.
Cole, N.   Saturn.
Finney, E.   Our Solar System.
Kendall, M.   Ether Insatiable.
Kenward.   Planets.
Kitching.   Planets turn in stately dance, The.
   Swirling world stands still, The.
MacCaig.   Stars and Planets.
"MacDiarmid."   Bonnie Broukit Bairn, The.
McClintock, M.   Look it's clear.
Notley.   Désamère.
Rice, J.   On some other planet.
Rogers, D.   Late, Watching Television.

Plants
Alegría.   I Am Root.
Austin, M.   Shoshone Wedding Song.
Barry, J.   Floating Petals.
Beaver.   Day 20.
Belševica.   To be roots. In that deepest earth where no ray.
Breton, A.   Postman Cheval.
Butler, M.   Listen.
Farber.   Jubilate Herbis.
Field, E.   Plant Poem.
Gu Cheng.   Discovery.
Howes, B.   Blue Garden, The.
Keats.   Ode on Melancholy.
Kendall, M.   Education's Martyr.
Levine, P.   Later Still.
Madgett.   Woman with Flower.
Masaoka Shiki.   My room.
Mayer, B.   Aeschyleans, The.
Mazur.   Spring Planting.
McFadden, D.   House Plants.
McKay, C.   Flame-Heart.
McPherson, S.   Waiting for Lesser Duckweed: On a Proposal of Issa's.

Miljkovic.   In Praise of Plants.
Millay, E.   So she came back into his house again.
Moore, M.   Nevertheless.
Napier, F.   Houseplant.
Nichols, G.   Sugar Cane.
Pagis.   Armchairs.
Perreault, J.   Readymade.
Phillips, C.   Reach, The.
Rabéarivelo.   Cactus.
Roethke.   Cuttings ("Sticks-in-a-drowse droop over sugary loam").
   Cuttings ("This urge, wrestle, resurrection of dry sticks").
   Moss-Gathering.
   Root Cellar.
   Transplanting.
Rossetti, C.   Summer.
Rossetti, D.   Woodspurge, The.
Sackville-West.   Dream, A.
Saitō Mokichi.   Tanka: "By the road."
Sappho.   Song for the Goddess of Love.
Stevenson, R.   To A Gardener.
Swinburne.   Sundew, The.
Tate, J.   Consolations After an Affair.
Taylor, A.   Clearing Away.
Thoreau.   I am a parcel of vain strivings tied.
Unknown.   Planting Initiation Song.
   Plucking The Rushes.
   Two Soldier's Songs.
   Wind blows, one can smell the wild rosemary.
Wilbur.   Seed Leaves.
Williams, W.   It is a small plant.
Wills, J.   Pebble falls, A.
Wormser.   It's a Party (1959).
Yün Shou-p'ing.   Lament for the Willows outside the City Walls, A.
See also **Flowers; Trees;** *names of plants (e.g.,* **Cactus***).*

Plath, Sylvia
Berryman.   Your face broods from my table, Suicide.
Herzberg.   On the Death of Sylvia Plath.
Sexton.   Sylvia's Death.
Wilbur.   Cottage Street, 1953.

Plato
Boethius.   Book 3, Metrum 11.
Callimachus.   "Goodbye Sun!" said the Ambracian.
Leontius Scholasticus.   Orpheus, dying, not all Music died.
Mahon.   Death and the Sun.
Sidney, P.   Sonnet 21: "Your words my friend (right healthful caustics) blame."
Unknown.   Eagle of the tomb, whose tomb is this? Why.
   On Plato's Grave.
   Spirit of Plato.
Yeats.   What Then?

Platonic Love
Cartwright, W.   No Platonic [*or* Platonique] Love.
Cowley, A.   Platonic[k] Love.
Donne.   Air[e] and Angels.
   Ecstasy, The.
Habington.   Reward of Innocent Love, The.
Herbert of Cherbury.   Platonic Love.
Koertge.   Ubiquity of the Need for Love, The.
North, D.   Platonic is a pretty name.
Philips, K.   To My Excellent Lucasia, On Our Friendship.
St. John, D.   My friend, a man I love as wholly.
Vaughan, H.   To Amoret, of the Difference 'twixt Him and Other Lovers, and What True Love Is.

Platypuses
Aborigine Oral Tradition.   Platypus, The.
Barrington, P.   I had a duck-billed platypus when I was up at Trinity.
Herford.   Platypus, The.

Play
"Æ."   Frolic.
Aldis, D.   Kick a Little Stone.
Ammons.   Pet Panther.
Ashbery.   Paradoxes and Oxymorons.
Benson, G.   Play No Ball.

Benson, S.   Beaten Track, The.
Blake, W.   Nurse's Song ("When the voices of children are heard on the green / And laughing is heard on the hill").
Bold, A.   And Now.
Bonar.   Length of Days.
Carew, T.   To the Reader of Master William Davenant's Play [*The Wits*].
Charles, D.   Getting Dirty.
Chōkū.   Tanka: "Town children."
Chon, P.   Mischief.
Ciardi.   All about Boys and Girls.
   What Johnny Told Me.
Cook, S.   Gathering Leaves.
Davie.   Fountain, The.
Davies, W.   To W.S.—On his Wonderful Toys.
Dickinson, E.   God is indeed a jealous God.
Dimitrova.   Child and Sea.
Equi.   Sometimes I Get Distracted.
Ginsberg, A.   Bop Lyrics.
Greenaway.   School is over.
Gunn, T.   Aquarium, The.
Harrison, G.   Playground, The.
Harryman.   Magic (or Rousseau).
Hartwig.   Above Us.
Hoberman.   Let's dress up in grown-up clothes.
Hughes, L.   Little Song.
   Piggy-back.
Hugo, V.   She had no shoes on, she had freed her hair.
Ishikawa Takuboku.   Tanka: "Words from."
Keech.   Discovery.
Kennedy, X.   Little Elegy.
Lee, D.   Dickery Dean.
Li Po.   Ch'iu-p-u teems with white gibbons.
Lihn.   Dark Room, The.
Livingston, M.   Lemonade Stand.
Millay, E.   From a Very Little Sphinx.
Moore, L.   Sometimes.
Mother Goose.   Dance to your [*or* thee] daddy.
   Ring-a-ring o' roses.
Piatt, S.   Palace-Burner, The.
Po Chü-i.   Rising Late, and Playing with A-ts'ui, Aged Two.
Ransom, J.   Old Man Playing with Children.
Rossetti, C.   Frisky lamb / And a frisky child, A.
   I caught a little ladybird / That flies far away.
Rózewicz.   Transformations.
Scannell.   Hide and Seek.
Schwartz, D.   I Am Cherry Alive[; the little girl sang].
Smith, I.   Children, The.
Smith, W.   Around My Room.
Snyder, G.   Hop, Skip, and Jump.
Soto.   Behind Grandma's House.
Stafford, W.   At the Playground.
Stanescu.   Evocation.
Stein, G.   Identity A Poem.
Stevenson, R.   At the Seaside [*or* Sea-Side].
   Block City.
   Dumb Soldier, The.
   Gardener does not love to talk, The.
   Good Play, A.
   Land of Counterpane, The.
   Land of Story-Books, The.
   Pirate Story.
   Swing, The.
Summers, H.   Leaves in the Yard.
Tân Đà.   Still At Play.
Tranter.   Debbie and Co.
Turner, A.   Red-Dress Girl.
Unknown.   Billy, Billy, come and play.
   Draw a pail of water.
   Girls and boys come out to play.
   Here we come gathering nuts an' [*or* in] May.
   Mena, deena, deina, duss.
   One I love, two I love.
   Pussy.
   Ring-a-ring o'roses.
   See-saw, Margery Daw.
   Tae titly.
   Tumbling.
Verlaine.   Femme et Chatte.
Wang Chiu-ssu.   Rising from Sleep.
Watson, R.   White Lady, The.
Watts, I.   Innocent Play.

Wordsworth, W. Kitten at Play, The.
Wright, J. Camphor Laurel.

Playhouses. *See* **Theater and Theaters**

Playmates
Jaques, F. There Once Was a Puffin.
Mearns. Antigonish.
Rossetti, C. Lambs at Play.
Stafford, W. First Grade.
Stevenson, R. Gardener does not love to talk,
  The.
  Marching Song.
  My Shadow.
  Unseen Playmate, The.
Taylor, J. I Like Little Pussy.
Widdemer. Invisible Playmate, The.
Yeats. To a Squirrel at Kyle-Na-No.

Pleasure
Benedikt. Dossier of the Torturer.
  Nipplewhip, The.
Bold, A. And Now.
Broumas, O. Tryst.
Browning, E. Best Thing in the World, The.
Burns, R. Come, let me take thee to my
  breast.
  Twa bonny [*or* bony] lads were Sandy and
  Jockie.
Catullus. Carmen 31 ("Apple of islands,
  Sirmio, & bright peninsulas, set").
Coleridge, S. Kubla Khan; or, A Vision in a
  Dream.
Collins, W. Ode to Evening.
Cowley, A. Epicure, The.
Crozier, L. Poem for Sigmund.
Daniel, S. Shadows.
Davidson, D. Redivivus.
Dickinson, E. Heart asks Pleasure—*first*, The.
  I taste a liquor never brewed.
Dryden, J. Ah, how sweet it is to love!
Duhamel. Bulimia.
Ekelof. Hangman / what will you do with my
  arms?
Godfrey. So Let's Look at It Another Way.
Gruber, A. My Neighbor's Roses.
Gunn, T. Modes of Pleasure.
Hacker, M. Canzone: "Consider the three
  functions of the tongue."
  Noces.
Hardy, T. Great Things.
Herrick. On Himselfe ("I fear no earthly
  powers").
  On Himselfe ("Let me not live, if I not love").
Johnson, S. Short Song of Congratulation [*or*
  To a Young Heir], A.
MacLeish. Starved Lovers.
Marvell. Dialogue Between The Resolved Soul
  and Created Pleasure, A.
Okamoto. Tanka: "Green leaves."
Paniker, K. Itch, The.
Payne, D. Long hast thou slumber'd, O my
  sounding Lyre!
Petronius Arbiter. Fragment of Petronius,
  Paraphras'd, A.
  Out of Petronius.
Prunty. Note of Thanks, A.
Ralegh, W. Sweet Unsure.
Ramanujan. Pleasure.
Ronsard. Elegy 19 (A Kiss): "Without a soul,
  a mind, a breath, or pulse."
Rossetti, C. Worrying Fruit.
Shuttle. Old Man, The.
Sidney, P. Get Hence Foule Griefe.
Southwell. Man's Civil[l] War[re].
Stein, G. Why do you feel differently about a
  very little snail and a big one.
Strode. Justification.
T'ao Ch'ien. Noble ambition spans the four
  seas, A.
Thelwall. Anacreontic.
Tysh, C. In the morning one often feels.
Unknown. My Neighbor's Reply.
Wilbur. Simile for Her Smile, A.
Wilde, O. Hélas!
Wright, C. Legend of Hell, The.

Pleiades
Hemans. Lost Pleiad, The.
Stevenson, A. Sonnet: "If it be night. . . ."
Whitman, W. On the beach at night.

Plowing and Plowmen
Bosman. Seed.
Clare, J. Frightened Ploughman, The.
  Ploughboy, The.
Colum, P. Plower, The.
Heaney, S. Follower.
Hopkins, G. Harry Ploughman.
Housman, A. When smoke stood up from
  Ludlow.
Jones, S. Ploughman, in Imitation of Milton,
  The.
Muir, E. Horses.
Quarles. On the Ploughman [*or* Plough-Man].
Sansom, C. Ploughing.
Stevens, W. Ploughing on Sunday.
T'ang Yin. Song of Peach Blossom Retreat.
Thomas, E. As the team's head-brass flashed
  out on the turn.
Unknown. To a Schoolboy.
Wang Shih-chieng. Things Seen.

Plum Trees and Plums
Atwood. Late August.
Chasin. Word *Plum*, The.
Chiang K'uei. Tune: "Sparse Shadows"—Plum
  Blossoms.
Corbett, W. Wickson Plums.
Davidson, L. On my return.
Dooley, M. At Les Deux Magots.
Gogarty. Plum Tree by the House, The.
Han Yü. Flowering Plums.
Hitomaro. When I gathered flowers.
Huang T'ing-chien. Inscribed on a Scroll
  "Plum Blossoms by the Water."
Ise. Shall I come to see.
Li Ch'ing-chao. To the Tune "A Hilly
  Garden."
  Tune: "Pure Serene Music."
Ma Chih-yüan. Voice are still / The moon's
  bright.
Mao Tse-tung. Tune: "Song of Divination"—
  On the Plum Tree, after a Poem by Lu Yu.
Mirabai. Wild woman of the forests, The.
Mother Goose. Little Jack Horner/ Sat in a
  corner.
Po Chü-i. Rejoicing at the Arrival of Chi'en
  Hsiung.
Ransetsu. One plum blossom blooms.
Su Shih. Plum Blossoms.
Sutskever. Poetry.
Toomer. Song of the Son.
Unknown. Ballad of the Western Island in the
  North Country.
Wang An-shih. Plum Blossoms on Solitary
  Hill.
Wen Cheng-ming. Fine breeze blows through
  the temple halls, A.
  Hearing a Flute on the River Chi.
Williams, W. This Is Just to Say.
  To a Poor Old Woman.
Wu Chia-chi. My hut, beside the crystal
  stream.
Yang Chi. Studio for Listening to the Snow,
  The.
Yang Shen. To the Tune, "Ch'ing-p'ing
  Yüeh."
Yün Shou-p'ing. Written on the Night of the
  Twenty-ninth of the First Month.

Plumbing and Plumbers
Dove, R. Genie's Prayer Under the Kitchen
  Sink.
King, S. Difference, The.
Kunio. Tanka: "All the way."
Lu Yu. Tune: "Song of Divination"—On the
  Plum Tree.
Miles, J. Plumbers.
Niedecker. Nursery Rhyme.

Plymouth, England
Spender, S. Air Raid Across the Bay at
  Plymouth.

Poaching and Poachers
Unknown. Lincolnshire Poacher, The.
Wright, J. Lifting Illegal Nets by Flashlight.

Pocahontas
Bibb. Capt. Smith and Pocahontas.
Sandburg, C. Cool Tombs.
Thackeray. Wearied arm, and broken sword.

Poe, Edgar Allan
Ford, C. Bad Habit, The.
Fortune. Edgar Allan Poe.
Ginsberg, A. Haunting Poe's Baltimore.
Koch, K. You were wearing your Edgar Allan
  Poe printed cotton blouse.
Levine, P. On the Edge.
Longfellow, H. Couplet: February 24, 1847.
Lowell, J. Poe and Longfellow.
Smith, S. After-Thought, The.
Spicer, J. Improvisations on a Sentence by
  Poe.
Very. Forevermore.

Poetic Meter
Longfellow, H. Couplet: February 24, 1847.
  Peradventure of old, some bard in Ionian
  Islands.
Tennyson, A. Hendecasyllabics.

Poetics
Abu Dulama. Traders in Beauty and Delight.
Adamson. O to be in the news again—now as
  fashion runs.
"Akhmatova." I will leave your white house
  and tranquil garden.
Alexander, A. For Raftery.
Amichai. Ibn Gabirol.
Ansen. Fit of Something against Something,
  A.
Antin. Real Estate.
Antipater of Sidon. Erinna's *Distaff*.
Arghezi. Testament.
Ashbery. Paradoxes and Oxymorons.
  What Is Poetry.
Avidan. Practical Poems.
Baraka. Balboa, the Entertainer.
Baranczak, S. December 14, 1979: A Poetry
  Reading.
  February 8, 1980: And No One Has Warned
  Me.
Beaver. (Frank O'Hara).
Beckovic. No one will write poetry anymore.
Bernstein, C. Dysraphism.
  Klupzy Girl, The.
  Of Time and the Line.
Bernstein, O. This Is a Poem of Love.
Birney. Poet-Tree.
Bly, R. Possibility of New Poetry, The.
Bozhilov. Eternity.
  Troubles.
Bradstreet, A. In Honour of That High and
  Mighty Princess Queen Elizabeth of Happy
  Memory.
  Prologue, The: "To sing of wars, of
  captain[e]s, and of kings."
Breton, A. On the Road to San Romano.
Bromige. Eastward Ho! A Succession.
Browning, E. Fifth Book.
Browning, R. How It Strikes a Contemporary.
  Prologue: "Poet's age is sad: for why?, The."
Brownstein. Stepping Out.
Bryant, W. Poet, The.
Buckley, V. Teaching German Literature.
Burlingame. Small poems, The.
Burris. Strong's Winter.
Campo. For J. W.
"Carroll." Poeta Fit, Non Nascitur.
Char. Argument.
Ch'en Yü-yi. Spring Morning.
Clerk. Country Seat, The.
Clifton, L. My Dream About the Poet.
Clouts. After the poem the coastline took.
Coleridge, S. Homeric Hexameter, The.
  Metrical Feet.
Cooley. History of Poetry, The.
Coolidge, C. Crystal Text, The.
Cope, W. Uncertainty of the Poet, The.
Corcoran. Nobody Thinks Hard Enough for
  Poetry.
Cowley, A. Muse, The.
Cruz Varela. Love Song for Difficult Times.
Csoori. Bachelor, The.
Cullen, C. Yet Do I Marvel.
Cummings, E. Four III.
  If i have made, my lady, intricate.
  Little joe gould has lost his teeth and doesn't
  know where.

No man, if men are gods; but if gods must.
Since feeling is first.
Daniel, S. Go wailing verse, the infants of my love.
Poet and Critic.
Das, M. Growing Tip, The.
Desnos. Ars Poetica.
Like.
Dickinson, E. I dwell in Possibility.
I reckon—when I count at all.
They shut me up in Prose.
To learn the Transport by the Pain.
DiPalma. Prerogative of Lieder, The.
Dirjan. Poetry Evening.
Dissanayake. Freedom.
Drayton. To the Reader of These Sonnets.
What spirit can lift you up, to that immortall praise.
Drummond, W. Sextain: "With elegies, sad songs, and mourning lays."
Duncan, R. New Poem, A.
Poetry, a Natural Thing.
Structure of Rime XVIII.
Structure of Rime XXIII.
Eigner. In Imitation.
Emerson, R. Motto to "The Poet."
Poet ("To clothe the fiery thought").
Test, The.
"Ern Malley." Sonnets for the Novachord.
Ferlinghetti, L. And Pablo Neruda / that Chilean omnivore of poetry.
"Field." Prologue.
Forbes, J. Monkey's Pride.
Foster, E. Poetry and Joy.
Fullerton. Poetry.
Fumi Saito. Tanka: "Trailing for a while."
Gallagher, T. Deaf Poem.
I Stop Writing the Poem.
Instructions to the Double.
Gergely. Auden in Old Age.
Gilbo'a. Ancient Song.
Watchful Wakeful.
Gildner. Cabbage in Polish is kapusta—kapoosta.
Ginsberg, A. Last Night in Calcutta.
Gioia. Next Poem, The.
Giovanni. Poem (for Langston Hughes), A.
Goethe. Sonnet: "To work away in art's traditional measure."
Gray, T. Behold, where Dryden's less presumptuous car.
Guiterman. Whole Duty of a Poem, The.
Gwala. In Defence of Poetry.
Gwynn, R. Approaching a Significant Birthday, He Peruses The Norton Anthology of Poetry.
Hacker, M. Feeling and Form.
Halley. I'd Rather See than be One, but.
Harris, W. Grandfather Poem, A.
Harrison, T. Heartless Art, The.
Harry, J. Poem Films Itself, The.
Hartnett. Enamoured of the miniscule / of the careful and compact.
Hathaway, W. Poem in Response to Doom, A.
Hecht, A. Lot of Night Music, A.
Hejinian. No form at all—it's impossible to imagine its being.
Hemensley. Look! she said you can see.
My poem's in the oven where it.
Place was famed for, The.
Poem by John Thorpe, A.
Herbert, G. Jordan.
Jordan (2)(II): "When first my lines [or verse] of heavenly [or heav'nly] joy[e]s made mention."
Quidditie [or Quiddity], The.
Sonnet: "My God, where is that ancient heat towards Thee."
Sonnet: "Sure Lord, there is enough in thee to dry."
Herbert, Z. Biology Teacher.
Five Men.
Herrick. His Prayer for Absolution.
Holan. Cave of Words, The.
Holmes, O. At the "Atlantic" Dinner, December 15, 1874.
Huchel. Garden of Theophrastus, The.

Huidobro. Ars Poetica.
Hulme, T. Embankment (The Fantasia of a Fallen Gentleman on a Cold, Bitter Night), The.
Hummer, T. Poem in the Shape of a Saxophone.
Inez. Woman Who Loved Worms, The.
Jaccottet. Don't worry, you'll get there!
You're close.
Jacinto, A. Poem of Alienation.
Jacobsen, J. When the Five Prominent Poets.
Jemie. Toward a Poetics.
Jennings, K. Couples.
Johnston, M. In Memoriam.
Jonson, B. Elegy [or Elegie], An: "Let me be what I am, as Virgil cold."
Fit of Rhyme [or Rime] against Rhyme [or Rime], A.
Sonnet to the Noble Lady, the Lady Mary Wroth, A.
To John Donne ("Who shall doubt, Donne, where [or whe'er] I a poet be[e]").
Justice, D. Variations on a Text by Vallejo.
Kamienska. Prayer That Will Be Answered, A.
Kao Ch'i. Song of the Man of Green Hill, The.
Kapilar. True Protocol of Poets, The.
Klee. Poem.
Knight, E. Haiku: "Eastern guard tower."
To Make a Poem in Prison.
Koch, K. Stones of Time, The.
Kovner. How Many Poems Were Lost.
Kruchyonykh. Pomade.
Kunene. When My Poems were Lost.
Lake, P. Introduction to Poetry.
Lalic. Tree in the wind remembered like a letter.
Landor, W. Does it become a girl so wise.
Passed Ruin'd Ilion.
Laughlin, J. Then and Now.
Lauterbach. Mimetic.
Layton. Birth of Tragedy, The.
Leapor. Mira's Will.
Leib. Psalmodist.
Leonard, T. Good Style.
Poetry.
Levchev. Confession and Salute to the Fire.
Levine, P. Genius.
Li Po. Ancient Airs.
Lima, J. Distribution of Poetry.
Liu E. Teahouse at Hoshioka, A.
Liu Ya-tzu. To a Friend, Using the Same Rhymes of a Peom He Sent Me.
Lloyd, R. Old England has not lost her prayer.
Longfellow, H. Milton.
Lovelace, R. On Sanazar's being honoured with six hundred Duckets by the Clarissimi of Venice, for composing an Elegiack Hexastick of The City. A Satyre.
To My Noble Kinsman, Thomas Stanley, Esquire, on His Lyric Poems Composed by Master John Gamble.
Lowell, J. Science and Poetry.
Lowell, R. Epilogue: "Those blessèd structures, plot and rhyme."
Lu Yu. Shown to My Son Yü.
MacDonald, C. Instruction from Bly.
MacLeish. Ars Poetica.
Mann, C. Poet's Progress, The.
Mapanje. On Being Asked to Write a Poem for 1979.
Marinetti. Correction of proofs + desires in speed.
We had stayed up all night, my friends and I, under hanging mosque lamps.
Marvell. On Mr Milton's "Paradise Lost."
Masters, E. Petit, the Poet.
Mayakovsky. My most respected / comrades of posterity!
Screaming My Head Off.
Mayer, B. Generic Elbows.
McCarriston. Revision.
McElroy, C. Pike Street Bus.
McGough, R. Poem for a Dead Poet.
McPherson, S. At the Grave of Hazel Hall.
Messerli. From Hear to Air.

Miljkovic. Everyone Will Write Poetry.
Millay, E. I will put Chaos into fourteen lines.
Milosz, C. Dedication: "You whom I could not save / Listen to me."
Milton. To Mr. H. Lawes On His Airs.
Minuchihri. I send you my verses.
Recantation.
Moore, M. Poetry.
Mori Ōgai. Tanka: "Let a poem be."
Nash, O. Very like a Whale.
Natambu. Words and Music in America.
Neruda. Poetry.
Tonight I can write the saddest lines.
Newcastle, M. Of the Theme of Love.
Nichol. Some Nets.
Niedecker. In the great snowfall before the bomb.
Nortje. Asseverations.
Oppen. And Their Winter and Night in Disguise.
Cars on the highway filled with speech.
Gold on Oak Leaves.
It is difficult now to speak of poetry.
Little Pin: Fragment, The.
Not the symbol but the scene this pavement leads.
O withering seas.
Tell the beads of the chromosomes like a rosary.
Translucent Mechanics, The.
Orten. Last Poem, The.
Ou-yang Hsiu. Reading the Poems of an Absent Friend.
Ovid. Elegies 2.1.
Elegies 2.i.
Padgett, R. First Drift.
Pagis. Outside the Line.
Parra, N. Letters from the Poet Who Sleeps in a Chair.
Pastan. After Reading Nelly Sachs.
Elegy.
Letter to a Son at Exam Time.
Patchen. Moon, Sun, Sleep, Birds, Live.
Perelman. Marginalization of Poetry, The.
Pessoa. "Startling Reality of Things," The.
Petronius Arbiter. Why do you frown on me, you puritans.
Petrov, A. Poetry in a Glass Cube.
Poetry in an empty dress.
Poetry in the Underground Passage.
Poetry Visits an Old Lady.
Philips, K. On the Death of My First and Dearest Childe, Hector Philipps.
Phillips, C. Passing.
Piombino. Pyramids, The.
Po Chü-i. On Hearing Someone Sing a Poem by Yüan Chên.
Poe. Enigma, An.
Stanzas.
Pound, E. Coda.
Ité.
Pratt, S. Cottage Pictures.
Preil, G. How to Read the First Line.
Rashidi Samarqandi. Complaint to a Court Poet.
Rathenow. After David Samuilow.
Ravikovitch. Surely You Remember.
"Ravitch." Verses Written on Sand.
Reeves, J. W.
Rich, A. In a Classroom.
Ridge, L. Amy Lowell.
Rosen, M., et al. Humpty Dumpty.
Rózewicz. Draft for a Contemporary Love Poem.
Draft of a Modern Love Poem.
Forms.
Questions about Poetry since Auschwitz.
Rummo. Again again again again again.
Ryuichi. My Imperialism.
Salamun. Homage to a Hat and Uncle Guido and Eliot.
"Samoylov." Poem not flowery but bare, A.
Sanchez, S. To P. J.
To P. J. (2 Yrs Old Who Sed Write a Poem for Me in Portland, Oregon).
Sandburg, C. Poetry is any page from a

sketchbook of outlines of a.
Ten Definitions of Poetry.
Scarfe. Kitchen Poem.
Schwartz, D. Sonnet on Famous and Familiar
    Sonnets and Experiences.
Scott, J. Helen Paints a Room (1984).
Scott of Amwell. Ode: Written After Reading
    Some Modern Love-Verses.
Service. Inspiration.
Sexton. Obsessive Combination of Ontological
    Inscape, Trickery and Love, An.
Shakespeare, W. Sonnet 54.
    Sonnet 55.
Shange. Advice.
Sidney, P. Sonnet 1: "Loving in truth, and
    fain[e] in verse my love to show."
    Sonnet 15: "You that do search for every
    purling spring."
    Sonnet 74: "I never drank of Aganippe well."
    What length of verse can serve brave
    Mopsa's good to show?
Silveira. Different Poem, A.
Simpson, R. All Friends Together.
Skelton, J. Than, if this noble kyng.
Smart, C. For the spiritual musick is as
    follows.
Smith, D. Spring Poem, The.
Snyder, G. As for Poets.
    Axe Handles.
    How Poetry Comes to Me.
    What You Should Know to Be a Poet.
Šopov. Poem.
Southey, R. Cataract of Lodore, The.
Spencer, A. 1975.
Spicer, J. Thing Language.
Stafford, W. Near.
Stern, G. Bite, The.
Stevens, W. Planet on the Table, The.
Su Tung-p'o. On a Painting by Wang the
    Clerk of Yen Ling.
    Roaring waterfall, the.
    Thoughts in Exile.
Sutskever. Poetry.
Swirszczynska. Poetry Reading.
Szymborska. In Praise of My Sister.
Tate, J. Miss Cho Composes in the Cafeteria.
Teasdale. I might have sung of the world.
Tekkan. Tanka: "With warts and all."
Thomas, D. In my craft or sullen art.
Thoreau. My life has been the poem I would
    have writ.
Tranter. Alphabet Murders, The.
Tu Fu. Banquet at the Tso Family Manor.
    To Pi Ssu Yao.
Unknown. Limerick: "Well, it's partly the
    shape of the thing."
Valek. Steel-Rod Benders.
Wallace, R. Double-Play, The.
    In a Spring Still Not Written Of.
Warsh. Suicide Rates, The.
Watts-Dunton. Sonnet's Voice, The.
Weiners. With Meaning.
Welch, L. Whenever I make a new poem.
Wheatley, P. To Mæcenas.
Whitman, W. I am the poet of the Body and I
    am the poet of the Soul.
    Song of Myself.
Wieners. To H.
Wieseltier. Poetry's Buried.
Wilbur. Event, An.
Williams, J. On Reading Aloud My Early
    Poems.
Wither. Sun hath run his course through all
    the Signes, The.
Wollach. When You're Not a Poet.
Wordsworth, W. Sonnet: "Scorn not the
    sonnet; critic, you have frowned."
    To the Poet, John Dyer.
Yang Wan-li. Replying to a Poem by Li
    T'ien-lin.
Yeats. Adam's Curse.
    When you are old and grey and full of sleep.
Yukitsuna. Tanka: "Poetry."
Zach. Max is dead and his sons.
    Painter Paints, The.
    Problem, The.
    Prologue to a Poem.

Zephaniah. According to my Mood.
Zukofsky, L. Lines of this new song are
    nothing, The.

Pogroms. See **Massacres**
Poison
Balaban. Along the Mekong.
Enzensberger, H. Poison, The.
Harasymowicz. Woods.
Herbert, Z. Return of the Proconsul, The.
Kizer, C. On a Line from Valéry.
McDonald, I. Poison-maker, The.
Miyazawa Kenji. Tanka: "At last."
Unknown. Lord Randal[l].
Poker
Masson. My Poker Girl.
Unknown. Root Hog or Die.
Wilson, K. Twin Aces.
Pokuttelini
Auvaiyar. Young Chieftain, A.
Poland
Baranczak, S. December 14, 1979: A Poetry
    Reading.
Borowski. Project: Flag.
    Two Countries.
Bryll. In a Fever.
Herbert, Z. Report from the Besieged City.
Hirshfield, J. For the Women of Poland:
    December 1981.
Jastrun, T. Polish Knot, The.
Klepfisz. Bashert.
Milosz, C. Dedication: "You whom I could
    not save / Listen to me."
    My Faithful Mother Tongue.
Reznikoff. When the Second World War
    began.
Rothenberg, J. Poland / 1931 "The Wedding."
Slonimski. Elegy: "No more, no more Jewish
    townships in Poland."
Swirszczynska. Conversation Through the
    Door, A.
Wat. Imagerie d'Epinal.
Police States
"Akhmatova." Requiem: "No foreign sky
    protected me."
Baranczak, S. December 14, 1979: A Poetry
    Reading.
    February 8, 1980: And No One Has Warned
    Me.
Brutus. Sounds Begin Again, The.
Chipasula. Love Poem for My Country, A.
de Jesús. Curfew.
Hecht, A. 'More Light! More Light!'
Jesús. All of a Sudden.
Ofeimun. Handle for the Flutist, A.
Ratushinskaya. But only not to think about the
    journey.
Serge. Dialectic.
Police Stations and Police
Adams, E. Action Rhyme.
Baranczak, S. Three Magi, The.
Beerbohm, M. Police Station Ditties.
Betjeman. Arrest of Oscar Wilde at the
    Cadogan Hotel, The.
Brooks, G. "Negro" Hero.
Brown, S. Southern Cop.
Chesterton, G. Christmas Carol, A: "God rest
    you merry gentlemen."
Clifton, L. Powell (Officer Charged with the
    beating of Rodney King).
Cortez. Give me the Red on the Black of the
    Bullet (for Claude Reece Jr.)
    Rape.
Cummings, E. Two X.
Daniels, J. Day of the Two Bodies.
Deanovich. Road Block: Sante Fe, New
    Mexico.
Digby, J. One Night Away from Day.
Durem. Award.
Eady. False Arrest.
Espada. Waiting for the Cops.
Fogarty. Remember Something Like This.
Garioch. Fair Cop, A.
Gilbert, S. Policeman's Lot, A [or The].
Hamilton, B. Poem to a Nigger Cop.
Hughes, L. Third Degree.
    Who But the Lord?

Inez. Slumnight.
Jacob, M. Horrible Today, The.
Jones, J. Drugs.
Kharms. Event on the Street, An.
Komunyakaa. Cage Walker, The.
Laing, K. Tatale Swine.
Lehman. First Offense.
Levertov. Grace-Note, The.
Lowell, R. Opposite House, The.
Mayer, G. Song: "Does the policeman sleep
    with his boots on."
McGough, R. P.C. Plod versus the Dale St.
    Dog Strangler.
Mora. La Migra.
Muske. Field Trip.
Nobuyuki. Labor Day[1] (four poems).
Randall, D. Idiot, The.
Rich, A. Frame.
Ritsos. Search.
Sadoff. Civil Rights.
Sanchez, S. Definition for Blk/Children.
Simpson, L. Precinct Station, The.
    26th Precinct Station.
Tremblay, B. Mayday.
Unknown. Railroad Bill, Railroad Bill.
Weiners. Poem for vipers, A.
Wright, K. Sergeant Brown's Parrot.

Politics and Politicians
Allen, S. View from the Corner.
Atwood. Torture.
Auden. Statesmen.
Avidan. Election Speech for the Presidency of
    the United States of Chinamerica.
Baxter, J. Harry Fat and Uncle Sam.
Behn, A. Cabal at Nickey Nackey's, The.
Bekederemo. Casualties are not only
Belloc. Epitaph on the Politician Himself.
    On a General Election.
    This, the last ornament among the peers.
Bierce. Safety-Clutch.
    Statesmen, The.
Boyle, K. Poem for February First 1975, A.
Bramston. Time's Changes.
Brutus. Their Behaviour.
Burnett, W. My Shadow.
Catullus. Carmen 10 ("Varus, whom I chanced
    to meet").
Cervantes. Poem for the Young White Man
    Who Asked Me How I, An Intelligent, Well-
    Read Person Could Believe in the War
    Between Races.
Chesterton, G. Elegy in a Country
    Churchyard.
Chipasula. Going Back Patiently. those who
    are dead.
Cohen, L. Killers that run, The.
Cummings, E. Next to of course god america
    i.
    Politician is an arse upon, A.
    Salesman is an it that stinks excuse, A.
    Way to hump a cow is not, The.
Daley, V. Tall Hat.
Davie. Barnsley and District.
Dennis, C. Miracle, The.
Dodge, M. Mayor of Scuttleton burned his
    nose, The.
Duffy, C. Politico.
Durcan. Divorce Referendum, Ireland, 1986,
    The.
    Irish Hierarchy Bans Colour Photography.
Earley, T. Rebel's Progress.
Ferlinghetti, L. Sandinista Avioncitos.
Freneau. To a Noisy Politician.
Ginsberg, A. America I've given you all and
    now I'm nothing.
Giovanni. Seduction.
Gossett. On the Question of Fans/ The Slave
    Quarters Are Never Air Conditioned.
Gowar. Rat Trap.
Halley. I'd Rather See than be One, but.
Harper, F. Aunt Chloe's Politics.
Hartnett. Gaelic is the conscience of our
    leaders.
Hathaway, J. Congressman Visits the Grade
    School, The.
Hayes, A. Much Ado About Nothing,
    Thanksgiving, 1972.

Hippolyte. Revo Lyric.
Hollo. Dream of Instant Total Representation, The.
Hone. This is THE MAN—all shaven and shorn.
Hove. Child's Parliment.
Jarrell. State, The.
Jeffers, R. Stars Go Over the Lonely Ocean, The.
Jones, M. Election Reflection.
Jonson, B. To the Same [Robert, Earl of Salisbury] [Upon the Accension of the Treasurership to Him].
Jordan, J. Poem About My Rights.
Kipling, R. Dead Statesman, A.
Klein, A. Political Meeting.
Kleinzahler. Spleen.
Knight, E. On Watching Politicians Perform at Martin Luther King's Funeral.
Laing, K. Same Corpse, The.
Langland, W. Civil Service, The.
Lawrence, D. Hibiscus and Salvia Flowers.
Leland, C. There's a liddle fact of hishdory vitch few hafe oondershtand.
Lindsay, V. What the Moon Saw.
　Why I Voted the Socialist Ticket.
Logue, C. I shall vote Labour because.
Lorde. Sisters in Arms.
Lowell, J. Boss, The.
　Misconception, A.
Lucy. Senior Members.
Macartney. Kyrielle: Party Politics.
Maxton. Urgent Letter, An.
McClure, M. Senate Hearings.
"Mighty Sparrow." Get to Hell Outa Here.
Miles, J. Campaign, The.
Moore, T. Tory Pledges.
Namjoshi, S. et al. We Can Compose Ourselves.
Nemerov. To the Rulers.
Nguyễn Trãi. Both favor and disgrace you have full known.
Ojaide. Launching Our Community Developement Fund.
Okigbo. Elegy for Alto.
Parker, P. My lady ain't no lady.
Parra, N. Discourse of the Good Thief, The.
Pau-Llosa. Ganaderia.
Petty. Great Poll-Tax Victory of '88, The.
"Pindar." Epigram: "Midas, they say, possessed the art of old."
Po Chü-i. Hermit and Politician.
Pope, A. Wharton ("Wharton! the scorn and wonder of our days").
Praed. Chancery Morals.
Prior. Fable, A: "In Æsop's tales an honest wretch we find."
Rich, A. Dark woman, head bent, listening for something, A.
Scott, F. W. L. M. K.
Selman, R. And so I went forth in uniform.
　One of us had to be the first to lead.
　Thousands of cheers filled the chalky air.
Shakespeare, W. Richard II.
Shelley, P. Similes for Two Political Characters of 1819.
Shūji. Tanka: "Mr. Nehru."
Sidney, P. Sonnet 30: "Whether the Turkish new moon minded be."
Small, J. Pig-Sticking Season, The.
Smith, A. Political Intelligence.
Swift, J. As I strole the city, oft I.
Szymborska. Children of the Epoch.
Taylor, B. Canopus.
Tolson. Legend of Versailles, A.
Unknown. Age of War, The.
　Dodger, The.
　Old-Saxon Fragment.
Waniek. Alderman.
Ware, M. Understanding Guyana.
Warren, R. Terror.
Whitman, W. To a President.
Whittier. King Solomon and the Ants.
Wilbur. Miltonic Sonnet for Mr. Johnson on His Refusal of Peter Hurd's Official Portrait, A.

Woddis. Doctor, The.
　I shall vote Centre because.
Wright, J. Eisenhower's Visit to Franco, 1959.
Yeats. Politics.
Zagajewski. Electric Elegy.
Zenmaro. Tanka: "Work on the impossible."

Pollock, Jackson
Dunn, S. He/She.
McClure, M. Ode to Jackson Pollock.
McGinley. Squeeze Play.

Pollution
Armstrong, J. Urban Pollution.
Bennett, R. Smoke Animals.
Cronin, A. Trembling with engines, gulping oil, the river.
Fincke. Era of the Vari-Vue, The.
Ginsberg, A. Homework.
Hall, J. White Trash.
Kendall, M. Underground.
Kizer, C. On a Line from Valéry.
Meredith, W. Country Stars.
Merriam, E. Landscape.
　Windshield Wiper.
Meyn. At the Planning Commission.
Seward. Scene of superfluous grace, and wasted bloom.
Welch, L. Sausalito Trash Prayer.
See also **Ecology and Ecologists**

Polyandry
Aig-Imoukhuede. One Wife for One Man.
See also **Marriage; Monogamy and Monogamists**

Pomegranates
Boland, E. Pomegranate, The.
Glück, L. Pomegranate.
Lawrence, D. Andraitx—Pomegranate Flowers.

Pompeii, Italy
Akhmadulina. Volcanoes.
Goldberg, B. In the Middle of Things, Begin.
Hemans. Image in Lava, The.
Mahon. Disused Shed in Co. Wexford, A.
Ray, H. Listening Nydia.
Stevens, W. Postcard from the Volcano, A.

Ponds. *See* **Lakes and Ponds**

Ponies
Mother Goose. Dapple-gray.
Unknown. I had a little pony.
Wright, J. Blessing, A.

Pool (game)
Bond, J. Rotation.
Brooks, G. We real cool. We.
Pizzarelli. Fwap!

Poorhouses
Carleton, W. Over the Hill to the Poor-House.

Popcorn
Baruch. Popcorn-Popper, The.
Pizzarelli. Piece of buttered popcorn, A.

Pope, Alexander
Cowper, W. Then Pope, as harmony itself exact.
Crabbe. Our Pope, they say, once entertained the whim.
Edwards, T. To the Editor of Mr. Pope's Works.
Gay, J. Mr. Pope's Welcome from Greece.
Ingram, A. Female mind like a rude fallow lies, A.
Montagu, L. Epitaph: "Here lies John Hughes and Sarah Drew."
Verses Addressed to the Imitator of the First Satire of the Second Book of Horace: An Attack on Pope.
When God created thee, one would believe.
Tate, A. Mr. Pope.
Unknown. On the Death of Mr. Pope.
　Spoken Extempore on the Death of Mr. Pope.
Winchilsea. Answer, The.

Poplar Trees
Cowper, W. Poplar Field, The.
Hopkins, G. Binsey Poplars (Felled 1879).
Huchel. Poplars, The.
Leuty. Poplars.
Swenson, M. Poplar's Shadow, The.
See also **Aspen Trees**

Poppies
Alexander, W. Explosive Decibel Journeys.

Corke. November Poppies.
Darwin. Poppy, The.
Doolittle, H. Sea Poppies.
Glück, L. Red Poppy, The.
Hall, S. Poppies of Wickenburg.
Jackson, H. Poppies on the Wheat.
Loving. Black Horse Rider, The.
Magowan. Paros. A day mild as morning's milk.
McClintock, M. Poppy, A.
Mitchison. Thinking of War.
Oliver, M. Poppies send up their, The.
O'Neill, H. Ode to the Poppy.
Park, S. Opium Poppy, The.
Plath. Poppies in July.
　Poppies in October.
Ropes. Poppies.
Schneour. Poppies.
Seward. To the Poppy.
Shūji. Tanka: "Flowering poppies."
Stephens, J. In the Poppy Field.
Tekkan. Tanka: "Poppies in bloom."
Warner, S. Drawing you, heavy with sleep to lie closer.
Wolfe, F. Poppies in the Garden, The.
Yosano. Tanka: "Warring heaven."

Porcupines
Kinnell. Porcupine, The.

Pornography
"Alta." Bitter Herbs.
Anderson, J. Ode to Pornography.
Cooper, D. Being Aware.
　No God.
Fincke. Era of the Vari-Vue, The.
Lifshin. Penthouse Playboy.
Logan, J. Saturday Afternoon at the Movies.
McClatchy. Found Parable.
Pitt-Kethley. God made the sex-shop keeper.
Pizzarelli. Girl / loosens her bra, The.
Porter, P. Now it's in all the novels, what's pornography to do?
Schwartz, L. Pornography.
Spires. Mutoscope.
Wallace, R. Thirteen.
Yamanaka. Kala: Saturday Night at the Pahala Theatre.
See also **Obscenity**

Porter, Cole
Bentley, N. On Lady A———.
Lardner. Parodies of Cole Porter's "Night and Day."

Portland, Maine
Longfellow, H. My Lost Youth.

Portraits
Ashbery. Self-Portrait in a Convex Mirror.
Blood, B. Stop!—Gaze thro' this hushed gallery! The air.
Brant, B. Her name is Helen.
Browning, E. On a Portrait of Wordsworth by B. R. Haydon.
Browning, R. My Last Duchess [Ferrara].
Chesterfield. On Mr. Nash's Present of His Own Picture at Full Length.
Cowper, W. On the Receipt of My Mother's Picture out of Norfolk, the Gift of My Cousin Ann Bodham.
De la Mare. Portrait, A.
Donne. His Picture.
　Phryne.
Drummond de Andrade. Family Portrait.
Edwards, T. Sonnet on a Family Picture.
Eliot, T. Lines for Cuscuscaraway and Mirza Murad Ali Beg.
Ferlinghetti, L. Ladakh Buddhess Biker.
Field, E. Unwanted.
Graves, R. Face in the Mirror, The.
Halleck, F. Red Jacket.
Hardy, T. On the Portrait of a Woman About to Be Hanged.
Holden, M. Photograph of Haymaker, 1890.
Holmes, O. Dorothy Q.
Howard, R. Nadar.
Howells, W. Royal Portraits, The.
Huddle. Cousin.
Jonson, B. Picture of the Body, The.
King, A. Under Mr. Hales Picture.

Kooser. Gilbert Stuart Portrait of Washington, The.
Leapor. On Winter.
Lovelace, R. Upon the Curtain[e] of Lucasta's Picture [It Was Thus Wrought].
Melville, H. Formerly a Slave.
Praed. Portrait of a Lady in the Exhibition of the Royal Academy.
Rossetti, C. In An Artist's Studio.
Rowlands. Epigram 29: "Gentlewoman of the dealing trade, A."
Sandburg, C. Sins of Kalamazoo are neither scarlet nor crimson, The.
Sawyer, A. Lines, / Written on Seeing My Husband's Picture, painted when he was young: "Those are the features, those the smiles."
Schwartz, L. Self-Portrait.
Stein, G. How do you like what you have.
Tate, A. Sonnet: To a Portrait of Hart Crane.
Thibaudeau. Poem: "I do not want only."
Wetzsteon. Dinner at Le Caprice.
Wilbur. Miltonic Sonnet for Mr. Johnson on His Refusal of Peter Hurd's Official Portrait, A.
Wylie. Castilian.
See also **Painting and Painters; Photography and Photographers**

Ports. See **Harbors and Ports**

Portugal
Andresen. Camoes and the Debt.
Ginsberg, A. Salutations to Fernando Pessoa.
Lear, E. Limericks, II (iv).
Mapanje. After Wiriyamu Village Massacre by Protuguese.
Martinez, D. Avant-Dernières Pensées.
Wyatt, T. In Spayn.

Porvaikkopperunar Kiḷḷi
Cattantaiyar. King Kiḷḷi in Combat.
Nakkannaiyar. Woman in Love with a Captive King, A.

Possums. See **Opossums**

Posterity
Emerson, R. Limits.
Enright, D. Posterity was always a great reader.
Heath-Stubbs. To a Poet a Thousand Years Hence.
Herrick. Upon His Verses.
Jonson, B. Epistle to Elizabeth, Countess of Rutland.
MacLeish. Epistle to Be Left in the Earth.
Shapiro, K. Manhole Covers.
Spence, L. Carse, The.
Whitman, W. Full of life now, compact, visible.
No labor-saving machine.

Postmen. See **Mail and Mailmen**

Potatoes
Donnell. Potatoes.
Drevniok. Deep snow.
Heaney, S. Digging.
Hugo, R. Way a Ghost Dissolves, The.
Kavanagh, P. Clay is the word and clay is the flesh.
Spraying the Potatoes.
Kenyon, J. Potato.
Komunyakaa. Banking Potatoes.
McGough, R. Potato clock, a potato clock, A.
Mitchell, C. Giving Potatoes.
Plath. Poems, Potatoes.
Roseliep. Sailor, The.
Saarikoski. Potato Thief.
Unknown. Potato Peel.
Riddle a riddle as I suppose, A.

Potomac River
Aldrich, T. By the Potomac.
Beers, E. All quiet along the Potomac tonight.
Hovey. Evening on the Potomac.

Pottery and Potters
Bell, M. Drawn by Stones, by Earth, by Things That Have Been in the Fire.
Diop, B. Viaticum.
Dumbrveanu. Genesis.
"Field." Life Plastic.
Forbes, C. Potter's Wheel, The.

Hollander, J. Mad Potter, The.
Komunyakaa. Back Then.
Miller, E. What the Women Told Me.
Miyazawa Kenji. Tanka: "Like cracks."
Todd, R. Joan Miró ("Once there were peasant pots and a dry brown hare").

Pound, Ezra
Bagg. Ezra Pound and Robert Bridges.
Berryman. Cage, The.
Bunting. On the Fly-Leaf of Pound's Cantos.
Ferlinghetti, L. Pound at Spoleto.
Hussey, A. Ezra Pound's Eye.
Lowell, R. Ezra Pound.
MacLeish. Epistle to the Rapalloan.
Ezry.
Morton, J. Another Canto.
Nichols, R. Talking of Ezra Pound and long-dead pantos.
Scott, J. Typing the Letters.
Snyder, G. Axe Handles.
Widdemer. Rainuv; a Romantic Ballad from the Early Basque.

Poverty
Al-Ifriqi al-Mutayyam. My wife complains I pray no more.
Alcaeus. Poverty's the worst savage crime.
Alterman. Introduction: "Joy of the poor knocked on the door, The."
Andrade, E. Penniless Lovers.
Antokolsky. Ballad of the Wondrous Moment.
Arnold, M. West London.
Ashbery. Street Musicians.
Awoonor. Agosu if you go tell them.
Barbauld. To the Poor.
Bible, *O.T.* From the Sermon on the Mount.
Bishop, E. Pink Dog.
Blake, W. Holy Thursday [II.] ("Is this a holy thing to see").
Holy Thursday [I.] ("'Twas on a Holy Thursday, their innocent faces clean").
London ("I wander through [or thro'] each chartered [or charter'd] street").
Bly, R. Sunday in Glastonbury.
Bokov. Salt.
Borges. Matthew 25:14–30; "For it will be as when a man."
Brecht, B. From a German War Primer.
Breeze. Lovin wasn easy all de time.
Brooks, G. Bean Eaters, The.
Lovers of the Poor, The.
Bruner. If Lincoln Should Return.
Bunting. Gin the Goodwife Stint.
Burns, R. For A' That and A' That ["Is there, for honest poverty"].
Carleton, W. Over the Hill to the Poor-House.
Carter, M. University of Hunger.
Cassells. Courtesy, A Trenchant Grace, A.
Causley. Timothy Winters.
Cecco Angiolieri, da Siena. Sonnet: Of Why He Would Be a Scullion.
Chao Yi. Writing Poetry in the Back Garden.
Chaucer. Complaint of Chaucer to His [Empty] Purse, The.
Ch'en Tzu-lung. Ballad of the Little Cart, A.
Cheng Hsieh. Poem for My Wet Nurse, A.
Chin Nung. Wearing a Worn-Out Coat.
Christopher. After Hours.
Clare, J. My Mary.
Clifton, L. Good Times.
Coleman, W. Aunt Jessie.
Dear Mama (2).
Coleridge, M. Insincere Wish Addressed to a Beggar, An.
Conoley. Heroes, Saints, and Neighbors.
Cope, W. *Variation on Belloc's "Fatigue".*
Cornish, S. Your Mother.
Cortez. I'm A Worker.
Crabbe. Letter I.
Peter Grimes.
Poor-House, The.
Priest attending, found he spoke at times, The.
Slum Dwelling, A.
Village life, and every care that reigns.
Crouch, S. No New Music.
Cullen, C. Saturday's Child.
Davidson, J. Thirty Bob a Week.
Davidson, M. Framing.

Davies, I. Mrs. Evans Fach, You Want Butter Again.
Davies, W. Heap of Rags, The.
Dekker, T. *et al.* Happy Heart, The.
Dharmaraj. Full of rain, the word.
Dickinson, E. None can experience stint.
Dipoko. From My Parisian Diary.
Drainac. My hunger is infinite and my hands always empty.
Dugan, A. To a Red-headed Do-good Waitress.
Dunbar-Nelson. Proletariat Speaks, The.
Dunbar, P. Common Things.
Companion's Progress, A.
Dyer, J. Happy Workhouse and the Good Effects of Industry, The.
Elliot, E. Child, is thy father dead?
Emerson, R. Chartist's Complaint, The.
Espada. Mi Vida: Wings of Fright.
Ferry. Guest Ellen at the Supper for Street People, The.
Fletcher, P. Against a Rich Man Despising Poverty.
Forrest-Thomson. Strike.
Forster, W. Poor of London, The.
Fraser, G. Lean Street.
García Lorca. At the Poorhouse.
Garrett, G. Luck's Shining Child.
Gaspar. Kapital.
Giovanni. Nikki-Rosa.
Goulbourne. One Acre.
This Is the Place Where.
Guxnawu. Song for the Richest Woman in Wrangell.
Hacker, M. Elysian Fields.
Hadewijch. Love has subjugated me.
Han-shan. Cold Mountain Poem No. 158.
Hardy, T. Reminder, The.
Hendriks. Jamaican Small Gal.
Hewitt, J. Irishman in Coventry, An.
Turf-Carrier [or Turf Carrier] on Aranmore.
Hoagland, E. Big Zeb Johnson.
Holcroft. Gaffer Gray.
Hood, T. Song of the Shirt, The.
Hove. Other Syllabus, The.
You Will Forget.
Howitt, M. Sale of the Pet Lamb, The.
Hsü Wei. I Tried to Exchange Two Painting for Some Grain But Failed.
Hughes, L. Ballad of the Man Who's Gone.
Cross.
Down and Out.
Ennui.
Madam and the Rent Man.
Necessity.
Hugo, R. What Thou Lovest Well Remains American.
Hunt, L. Rondeau.
Ignatow, D. Pleasure, The.
Ishikawa Takuboku. Tanka: "I work."
Ivanov, G. I imagine everything wrapped in a beatific mist.
James, N. May poverty, without offence, approach.
Johnson, S. Poverty in London.
Jones, E. Song of the Low, The.
Jones, M. Soliloquy on an Empty Purse.
Jones, P. Prayer.
Jones, R. Progress Alley.
Romance of the Poor.
Jones, S. Poverty, in Imitation of Milton.
Jordan, N. I have seen them trying.
Kalász. Legacy.
Kao Ch'i. Returning to Lotus Village.
Kenyon, J. Back from the City.
Kitahara Hakushū. Tanka: "After letting my wife."
Knight, E. Report to the Mother.
Kornilov, V. Poorer than X.
Kumin, M. Saga.
Kuzminsky. I'm cold. I'm destitute and absurd.
Lamb, M. Two Boys, The.
Landon. Dying Child, The.
Poor, The.
Langhorne. Poor, The.

Latter. With tearful eye, how frequent have I seen.

Li K'ai-hsien. Commiserating with the Poor. Jade trees from the rear courtyard of the empire of Ch'en.

Sent to the Painter, Lu Hsiao-feng.

Li Tung-yang. Song of the Painting "Catching Fish."

Lihn. Torture Chamber.

Lincoln, A. Ten Rules of Conduct for Individuals and Nations.

Lindsay. Compleynt of the Comoun Weill of Scotland, The.

Liu E. New Year's Eve.

Livingston, M. Poor.

Long, D. One Time Henry Dreamed the Number.

Longley, M. Ghetto.

Lovelace, R. Grasshopper, The.

Lowell, J. His Throne Is with the Outcast.

Lucilius. Of a covetous Niggard, and a needie Mouse.

MacLean, S. Calvary.

Madgett. Simple.

Markham, E. Forgotten Man, The.

Third Wonder, The.

Matthews, W. People Like Us.

Mayakovsky. But Could You?

McCarthy, T. Claud Cockburn.

McGrath, T. Long Way Outside Yellowstone, A.

McLachlan. We Live in a Rickety House.

Mei Yao Ch'en. Little Village, A.

On the Night of the Fifteenth Day of the First Month I Go Out and Return.

Poverty on the Bank.

Meredith, W. Korean Woman Seated by a Wall, A.

Meynell, A. Lady Poverty was fair, The.

Millay, E. Ballad of the Harp-Weaver, The.

Milligan, S. Christmas 1970.

Mitchison. Tennessee Snow.

Mordecai. Last Lines.

Murray, L. Tin Wash Dish, The.

Neto. Farewell at the Moment of Parting.

O'Hare. Shoofly, The.

Oppen. Power, The Enchanted World.

Peacock, T. Rich and Poor; or, Saint and Sinner.

Peruncittiranar. Bard's Family, A.

Peters, L. I am asking about the way ahead.

Plumly. Will Work for Food.

Po Chü-i. Bitter Cold, Living in the Village.

Old charcoal seller, An.

Porter, P. And No Help Came.

Prévert. August Bank Holiday.

Raine, K. Worry about Money.

Ravenscroft, T. Sing we now merily.

Rexroth, K. Bad Old Days, The.

Richards, L. Poor unfortunate Hottentot, A.

Ridge, L. I room at Sodos'—in the little green room.

Rimbaud, A. Farewell: "Autumn already!—But why regret an eternal sun if we are embarked on."

Roberson. Poor Houses, The.

Robinson, A. Scape-Goat, The.

Roland-Holst. Small Paths.

Salkey. Dry River Bed.

Scovell. Poor Mother, The.

Seaton, M. Fear of Shoplifting.

Shakespeare, W. Sonnet 125.

Shange. About Atlanta.

Simic. Strictly for Posterity.

Simpson, L. There Is.

Smith, C. Dead Beggar, an Elegy Addressed to a Lady, The.

Smith, I. In the Park.

Smith, K. Possessions.

Smith, M. I an I Alone; or Goliath.

Revolutionary.

So Chong-Ju. Looking at Mt. Mudung.

Soutar. Hungry Mauchs, The.

Spender, S. Elementary School Classroom in a Slum, An.

In railway halls, on pavements near the traffic.

Stephens, J. To the Four Courts, Please.

Sterling, A. What You Goin' to Do When the Rent Comes 'Round?

Stevens, W. Dry Loaf.

Good Man Has No Shape, The.

Stevenson, R. System.

Stone, R. Pokeberries.

Su Tung-p'o. Lament of the Farm Wife of Wu.

Swift, J. Phyllis [or Phillis] [or Progress of Love, The].

Synge. Winter.

Tai Piao-yüan. Supervisor, Han Chün-mei, Has Shown Me Five Poems He Has Written Called, The Trees Flourish in Early Summer. I Have Therefore Written Down My Own Ignoble Feelings and Sent Them Via Inspector Juan. At This Time, Chün-mei Is Lecturing to the Various Scholars on the I-ching, The.

T'ang Yin. Ten days of wind and rain, depressing darkness!

Taylor, J. Gleaner, The.

Taylor, R. Princess of Scotland, The.

Traherne. Poverty.

Trần Tế Xu'o'ng. Poor and Happy.

Tsaloumas. Consolation.

Tsvetayeva. If the soul was born with pinions.

Tu Fu. Empty Purse, The.

Guest Arrives, A.

Long hoe, long hoe, handle of white wood.

To Pi Ssu Yao.

Tucker, M. Christmas Eve, South, 1865.

Unknown. Between a Contractor and His Wife.

Brian O'Linn.

Eastern Gate, The.

"Guilty or Not Guilty?"

Hallelujah, I'm a Bum.

Heavily flapping are the bustards' plumes.

I know I am poor.

Orphan Girl, The.

Poor But Honest.

Poor Girl's Meditation, The.

Poverty Knock.

Song, A: "While a thousand fine projects are planned ev'ry day."

Starving to Death on a Government Claim.

Wang An-shih. Walking in the Countryside.

Wang Chiu-ssu. Ballad of Selling a Child.

Wang Fan-chih. On the outskirts, dumplings of mud.

Waniek. Sacrament of Poverty, The.

Watkins, N. Hard Times A' Coming.

Watts, I. Praise for Mercies Spiritual and Temporal.

Weiners. Children of the Working Class.

Whitlow. Rockin' A Man, Stone Blind.

Whitney, I. I whole in body and in minde.

Now for the people in thee left.

Wickham. Pilgrimage.

Williams, P. Trails.

Williams, W. Pastoral: "When I was younger."

Poor, The.

Proletarian Portrait.

To a Poor Old Woman.

Wordsworth, W. Alice Fell; or, Poverty.

Female Vagrant, The.

Wright, A. Poor Man's Province, The.

Wu Chia-chi. Grain-Barge Wife, The.

Yang Chi. Eastern neighbor, western neighbor.

Yang Hsiung. Poverty.

Yang Shih-ch'i. On the Hall of Precious Virtue.

Yang Wan-li. Stanza Written in Jest.

Yüan Chen. Airing Painful Memories.

Zenmaro. Tanka: "All the young men I know."

Tanka: "'We're poor'."

See also **Need**

Power

Adisa. Women at the Crossroad / (May Elegba Forever Guard the Right Doors).

Atwood. Procedures for Underground.

Torture.

Auden. Epitaph on a Tyrant.

Baraka. Wise 5.

Blake, W. Tyger, The.

Bloch, C. Rising to Meet It.

Brutus. Their Behaviour.

Cataldi. Advice.

Chuang Tzu. Need to Win, The.

Chudleigh. To the Ladies.

Clampitt. Amaranth and Moly.

Cortez. Pray for the lovers.

Dickey, J. Power and Light.

Dickinson, E. I can wade Grief.

One crown that no one seeks.

Eberhart, R. Sea-Hawk.

Emerson, R. Self-Reliance.

Enheduanna. From The Hymn to Inanna.

Ewart. To the Virgins, to Make the Most of Time.

Ferlinghetti, L. Frightened / by the sound of my own voice.

Greiffenberg. On the Ineffable Inspiration of the Holy Spirit.

Hacker, M. Rune of the Finland Woman.

Hanlon, G. Plainsong.

Harper, M. Song: I Want a Witness.

Hayden, R. Wheel, The.

Herrick. On Himselfe ("I fear no earthly powers").

Power and Peace.

Hildegard von Bingen. Song to the Creator.

Hollo. Italics.

Horace. Country Parson turn'd in Years, The.

Jeffers, L. When I Know the Power of my Black Hand.

Jeffers, R. Unnatural Powers.

Juvenal. Favourite's fall, The.

Kellman. King, The.

Kemble. Sonnet: "If there were any power in human love."

Kizer, C. Hera, Hung from the Sky.

Knox, E. Director, The.

Kwakiutl Oral Tradition. Warsong of the Kwakiutl.

Landon. Power of Words, The.

Lawrence, D. Lord's Prayer.

Levertov. God then.

Lucan. All great things crush themselves.

Shame, no Statist.

Sit: sit all.

Lugovskoy. Woman / that I knew, The.

Mayakovsky. I know the force of words, I know their clarion call.

Milosz, C. Incantation.

Nemerov. Sparrow in the Zoo, The.

Oppen. Power, The Enchanted World.

Oppian. *Hermit-Fish,* unarm'd by Nature left, The.

Pace, R. Tingel-Tangel.

Pembroke, M. Gods boundles bownties gods promise ever abyding.

Pound, E. Canto 49.

Prunty. Elderly Lady Crossing on Green.

Public Enemy. Party for your Right to Fight.

Ransom, J. Judith of Bethulia.

Robinson, E. Richard Cory.

Romanes. Simple Nature.

Rossetti, C. God Is Everywhere.

Sackville, T. Midnight ("Midnight was come, when every vital thing").

Sanchez, S. Song No. 2: "I say. all you young girls waiting to live."

Simon, P. Richard Cory.

Snodgrass, W. Examination, The.

Spenser. Who lists to see, what ever nature, arte.

Stevens, W. Emperor of Ice-Cream, The.

Thomas, D. Hand that signed the paper felled a city, The.

Thomas, L. Cameo in Sudden Light.

Tolson. Dark Symphony.

Unknown. Hoatchunk' Narwoanar, or Winnebago War Song.

Ode to the Toad.

Sent from the Power.

Warsong of the Kwakiutl.

Vinokurov. She sits down to eat, breaks off a piece.

Voigt. Delilah.

Waldrop, K. Wandering Curves.

Walker, M. For my people [everywhere singing their slave songs repeatedly: their].
Wang Yen-Shou. Wangsun, The.
Warren, R. All is nothing, nothing all.
Waters, M. Keats' Lips.
Whitman, W. Animals.
Wickham. Sportsman, The.
Wilbur. She.
Wroth. Sonnet 7: "Love leave to urge, thou know'st thou hast the hand."

Prague, Czechoslovakia
Celan. In Prague.
Gouri. And this happened in Prague many years ago?
At the Train Station.
Lysohorsky. Ballad of Jan Palach, Student and Heretic.
Nezval. City With Towers.
Lilac by the Museum on St. Wenceslas Square, The.
Moon over Prague.
Prague in the Midday Sun.
Walker in Prague.
Rathenow. Prague.
Sillitoe. Synagogue in Prague.
Simko. Jewish Cemetery in Prague, The.
Woroszylski. Franz Kafka (I).

Prairies
Bates, K. America the Beautiful.
Bryant, W. Prairies, The.
Cather, W. Macon Prairie.
Prairie Spring.
Clampitt. Woodlot, The.
Clark, C. Plainsmen, The.
Dickinson, E. To make a prairie it takes a clover and one bee.
Donnell. Canadian Prairies View of Literature, The.
Ferril. Empire Sofa, The.
Guest, B. Prairie Houses.
Marriott. Prairie Graveyard.
Peterson, R. Midwest Town.
Ponge. Prairie, The.
Reiter, T. Rights of Way.
Sandburg, C. Prairie Waters by Night.
Stafford, W. Prairie Town.
Whitman, W. Night on the Prairies.
Prairie-grass dividing, its special odor breathing, The.

Praxiteles
Unknown. Spoken by Venus on Seeing Her Statue Done by Praxiteles.

Prayer
Abse. Of Itzig and His Dog.
"Æ." Prayer: "Let us leave our island woods grown dim and blue."
Aengus the Culdee. Prayer for Forgiveness, A.
Alakoye. Eshu.
Ambrose. O Strength and Stay upholding all creation.
Angelou. Thank You, Lord.
Angilbert. Angilbert's Prayer.
Anthony, G. Autumn Evening.
Applewhite. Prayer for My Son.
Arghezi. Psalm.
Aristophanes. Good morrow to the morn next to my gold.
Ashbery. Painter, The.
Awoonor. This Earth, My Brother.
Babcock, M. School Days.
Barrax. In the Restaurant.
Barry, M. Hymn of Freedom.
Basho. Worshipping at the Great Shrine At Ise.
Beedome. Petition, The.
Begay. Mother's Lace.
Berrigan, D. Prayer: "I left Cornell / with half a wit; six mismated socks."
Betjeman. In Westminster Abbey.
Bible, *O.T.* It is a good thing to give thanks. Psalm 6.
Psalm 77.
Bienek. Resistance.
Bobrowsky. Free Fire Zone.
Bradstreet, A. Deliverance from a Fit of Fainting.
Here Follows Some Verses upon the Burning

of Our House [July 10th, 1966. Copied Out of a Loose Paper].
Upon My Dear and Loving Husband His Going into England.
Brew. Plea for Mercy, A.
Breytenbach. Breyten Prays for Himself.
First Prayer for the Hottentotsgod.
Bridges, R. Ethick.
Brontë, E. Old Stoic, The.
Brooks, G. Religion.
Browning, R. Guardian-Angel, The.
Brutus. Prayer: "O let me soar on steadfast wing."
Burns, R. Holy Willie's Prayer.
Callimachus. Goddess, how oft you bent the silver bow.
Campbell, J. When Ol' Sis' Judy Pray.
Caprani. Prizefighter's Prayer, The.
Carruth, H. Words for My Daughter from the Asylum.
Cavafy. Supplication.
Celan. Tenebrae.
Char. Unbending Prayer.
Chesterton, G. Prayer in Darkness, A.
Clare, J. Lord, hear my prayer when trouble glooms.
Clifton, L. Prayer.
Clough. Qui Laborat, Orat.
Coleridge, H. Jesus Praying.
Prayer.
Coleridge, S. He prayeth best, who loveth best.
He prayeth well, who loveth well.
Columcille. Prayer to the Virgin.
Conder. Day by Day the Manna Fell.
Congreve. Song: "Pious Selinda goes to prayers."
Cook, E. Our Father.
Cooke, E. Are You You?
Cortez. Pray for the lovers.
Crashaw. C[h]aritas Nimia; or, The Dear[e] Bargain.
Ecstacy, An.
Howres for the Hours of Matines, The.
Ode, which Was Prefixed to a Little Prayer-Book Givin to a Young Gentlewoman, An.
On Mr. G. Herberts Booke, The Temple.
On the Name of Jesus.
Two Went Up into the Temple To Pray.
Crouch, S. Revelation, The.
Cummings, E. Noster was a ship of swank, The.
Cuney. Death Bed, The.
Davenant. Praise and Prayer.
Day, J. Prayer: "Grant that no Hobgoblins fright me."
De la Mare. Motley.
De Vere, S. Right Use of Prayer, The.
Deane, J. Offertory.
Desnos. Hour farther witch art in Heaven.
Dickinson, E. At least—to pray—is left—is left.
"Heavenly Father"—take to thee.
My period had come for Prayer.
Of Course—I prayed.
Prayer is the little implement.
Dietz. Help us to do the things we should.
Dodson, O. Black Mother Praying.
Donne. Hymn to God the Father, A.
Dove, R. Demeter's Prayer to Hades.
Duffy, C. Prayer.
Dyer, G. In deep distress, I cried to God.
Ehrmann. Prayer, A: "Let me do my work each day."
Eliot, T. Song for Simeon, A.
Faiz. Tyrant, The.
Farren. While now I lay me down to sleep.
"Field." My lady has a lovely rite.
Francis of Assisi. Canticle of the Sun.
Prayer of St. Francis of Assisi for Peace.
Galsworthy. Prayer, The.
Garnet. Down let the shrine of Moloch sink.
Gascoigne. Gascoigne's [or Gascoygnes] Good-Night.
Ghalib, A. Even at prayer, our eyes look inward.
Gillies, A. Two Prayers.

Gioia. Prayer.
Gladden. O Master, Let Me Walk with Thee.
Gogan. Mountain Drive.
Prayer of a Pagan Woman.
Goodison. Keith Jarrett—Rainmaker.
Guest, E. Lord, Make a Regular Man out of Me.
Hall, D. Grace, A.
Matthew 21:18–22; In the morning.
Hallack. Divine Office of the Kitchen, The.
Harjo, J. Eagle Poem.
Hayati. Is this darkness the night of Power, or the black falling of your hair?
Hayden, R. Incense of the Lucky Virgin.
Heaney, S. Poor Women in a City Church.
Heard, J. Unuttered Prayer.
Heginbothom. Great God, let all my tuneful pow'rs.
Hemans. Evening Prayer, at a Girls' School.
Herbert, G. Antiphon: "Let all the world in ev'ry corner sing / My God and King."
Bag, The.
Denial[l].
Jordan.
Mattens.
Obedience.
Praise (2).
Prayer (I).
Temper (1), The.
Wreathèd garland of deservèd praise, A.
Herrick. Grace for a Child.
His Litany to the Holy Spirit.
His Prayer for Absolution.
Matins [or Mattens], or Morning Prayer.
Thanksgiving to God for His House, A.
To God: an Anthem, Sung in the Chapel at White-Hall, Before the King.
To God ("Come to me God; but do not come").
Hewitt, J. Whit Monday.
Hildebert. Prayer to God the Father.
Holt, C. Dear heavenly Father.
Hopi Oral Tradition. Song of Creation.
Hudgins. Praying Drunk.
Hughes, L. Gal's Cry for a Dying Lover.
Hull, L. Style of Prayer, A.
Hunter, A. *et al.* Down-Hearted Blues.
Hwang, K. Prayer.
Jarman, M. Unholy Sonnets.
Jennings, E. Teresa of Avila.
Jonson, B. To Heaven.
Kamienska. Prayer That Will Be Answered, A.
Karni. Woman's Prayer, A.
Kasa. To love somebody.
Keats. Fragment of an Ode to Maia Written on May Day, 1818.
Keble. Hezekiah's Display.
Samuel's Prayer.
Ken. Evening Hymn, An.
Glory to Thee, My God, This Night.
Killigrew, A. Upon the Saying That My Verses Were Made by Another.
Kipling, R. Rabbi's Song, The.
Recessional.
Kremer. Epiphany.
Kunene. Elegy.
Kung Tzu-chen. Miscellanies of the Year Chi-hai.
Kwakiutl Oral Tradition. Healing Prayer to the Salmon-Berry Vines.
Prayer to the Black Bear.
Prayer to the Sockeye Salmon.
Landon. Girl at Her Devotions, A.
Larkin, P. Faith Healing.
Lawrence, D. Hands of God, The.
Lord's Prayer.
Matthew 6:7–15; "And in praying do not heap up empty."
Lewis, C. Prayer: "Master, they say that when I seem."
Sonnet: "Bible says Sennacherib's campaign was spoiled, The."
Lohmann. Nothing So Wise.
Lucretius. Address to Venus.
Lyte. Abide with me[; fast falls the eventide].
Mac an Bhaird, G. Morning Prayer.

Macdonald, G. Shall the Dead Praise Thee?
Machado Ruiz. Rainbow at Night.
Mackey, N. Falso Brilhante.
MacNeice. Prayer Before Birth.
Markham, E. Prayer, A: "Teach me, Father, how to go."
Masters, E. Supplication.
McGirt. Century Prayer, The.
McGough, R. Prayer to Saint Grobianus.
McKay, C. St. Isaac's Church, Petrograd.
McNeill, A. Hello Ungod.
Melvill. Ane Godlie Dreame.
Merton. Evening Prayer.
  Reader, The.
Mew. Old Shepherd's Prayer.
Meyers, B. Pigeons.
Miller, V. Without Ceremony.
Milne, A. Vespers.
Moore, M. Cumae.
Mordecai. Easy Life.
Morris, M. Give T'anks.
Nahuatl Oral Tradition. Song for the Festival of Tlaloc, the Rain God.
Newcastle, M. Common Fate of Books, The.
Newman, J. Pillar of the Cloud, The.
Nicholson, N. For Hokey and Henrietta.
Nowak, T. Psalm of the Field.
Nye, N. Small Vases from Hebron, The.
Okara. One Night at Victoria Beach.
  Spirit of the Wind.
Okigbo. Overture.
O'odham. War Songs.
Orten. Last Poem, The.
Ortiz. Bend in the River.
Pasolini. Prayer to My Mother.
Peele. Bethsabe's Song.
Pembroke, M. O Lord, Thou Hast Searched and Known Me.
  Voce mea ad Dominum Psalm 142.
Ponsot. "Love is not Love."
Poole, E. Last Prayer.
Pope, A. Universal Prayer [Deo Opt. Max.], The.
Quarles. Booke of Common Pray'r excels the rest, The.
  Wherefore Hidest Thou Thy Face, and Holdest Me for Thine Enemy [or Enemie]?
Ralegh, W. Verses Made the Night before His Beheading.
Ray, H. Evening Prayer.
  Prayer: "O Christ, who in Gethsemane."
Rice, H. God, Are You There?
  It's Me Again, God.
  Prayer for the Young and Lovely, A.
Ridler. Prayer in a Pestilent Time.
Rimbaud, A. After Bitahatini.
Roberts, C. Prayer for a Pilot.
Rossetti, C. Christmas Carol, A: "Thank God, thank God, we do believe."
Sachs, N. Rushing at Times Like Flames.
St. John, P. Sunday.
Sandburg, C. Prayer after World War.
Schuyler, J. Our Father.
Serge. Hands.
Simmons, J. Rogation Day: Portrush.
Sisson. Temple, The.
Smart, C. Hope.
Smith, K. Heaven which art in Heaven Our Father in Heaven.
Snow, E. Song of the Desert.
Sophocles. What is God singing in his profound.
Spender, S. Rejoice in the Abyss.
Stevenson, R. Epitaph: "Angler rose, he took his rod, The."
  Good Boy, A.
  House Beautiful, The.
  Last night we had a thunderstorm in style.
  System.
  Thought, A.
Stoddard, R. Never Again.
Sutskever. Friday evening coos up in the attic.
Tadic. Antipsalm.
Tate, J. Manna.
Taylor, E. Dull. Dull indeed! What shall it e'er be thus?
  Huswifery.

Tekeyan. Prayer on the Threshold of Tomorrow.
Thomas, D. Conversation of Prayer, The.
  Conversation of prayers about to be said, The.
  Vision and Prayer.
Thomas of Celano. Dies Irae.
Thompson, C. Out of the Deep.
Thompson, P. Old Saint's Prayer, The.
Thoreau. Smoke.
Trench, R. Power of Prayer, The.
Tsvetayeva. White low sun, low thunderclouds; and back, A.
Tu Fu. Visiting Tsan, Abbot of Ta-Yun.
Tuckerman, F. Sonnets: "Starry flower, the flower-like stars that fade, The."
Ungar. Common Prayer.
Unknown. Been in the Storm So Long.
  Beguines who hear these words.
  Christ's Bounty.
  Each prayer is answered.
  Evening Prayer, An.
  Fragrant the Prayer.
  Great Spirit.
  Great Spirit, whose dry lands thirst, help us to find.
  Hermit's Song, The.
  I been rebuked and I been scorned.
  I lie down with God, and may God lie down with me.
  I saw some lovely things today.
  I'm a-rollin', I'm a-rollin', I'm a-rollin', through an unfriendly world.
  Invocation to the U' wannami.
  Lark, The.
  Limerick.
  Lord, Remember Me!
  Lord's Prayer, The.
  Matthew, Mark, Luke and John, / Hold the horse till I leap on.
  Night Prayer.
  Now I lay me down to sleep.
  Poet's Prayer, The.
  Prayer: "Be thou my vision, O Lord of my heart."
  Prayer for Love, A.
  Prayer is so simple.
  Prayer of a Woman in Charge of Berry Picking in Knights Inlet.
  Prayer to the Sockeye Salmon.
  Psalm 137.
  Rain Song of the Shu'-wi Chai' än (Snake Society), A.
  Te Deum.
Untermeyer, L. Prayer for This House.
Van Duyn. Gardener to His God, The.
Van Dyke. Peace Hymn of the Republic.
Vaughan, H. Begging.
  Match, The.
  Mount of Olives.
  Praise.
Very. Prayer, The.
  Prayer of Jabez, too, should be our prayer, The.
  Take Ye Heed, Watch and Pray.
Waring, A. My Times Are in Thy Hand.
Watts, I. Man Frail, and God Eternal.
Wesley, C. During His Courtship.
  None is like Jeshurun's God!
Wheeler, R. Prayer for Shut-Ins.
Whittier. Dedication: "I would the gift I offer here."
Wilcox, E. Answered Prayers.
Wilde, O. E Tenebris.
Willard, E. Rocked in the Cradle of the Deep.
Winchilsea. To Death.
Wither. Prayer of Hezekiah, The.
  Prayer of Nehemiah, The.
Woodward, K. Thanksgiving Prayer, A.
Wright, J. Confession to J. Edgar Hoover.
  Prayer to the Lord Ramakrishna, A.
Wu Chen. To the Tune "Chiu-ch'üan tzu."
Wyatt, T. Prologue: "Love, to give law unto his subject hearts."
Yeats. Mohini Chatterjee.
  Prayer for My Daughter, A.
  Prayer for My Son, A.
Yukitsuna. Baker's prayer.

Zuni Oral Tradition. Invocation to the U'wannami (Rain-Makers).

Praying Mantis
McCord, D. Mantis.
Miller, R. Mantis.
Zach. King Solomon's Camel is a hypocritical creature.

Preaching and Preachers
Arnold, M. Progress.
Barker, G. Reverend Arbuthnot-Armitage-Brown, The.
Berryman. Carpenter's Son, The.
Clough. Across the sea, along the shore,.
Conn. To My Father.
Dickinson, E. He fumbles at your Soul.
Doane, W. Preacher's Mistake, The.
Dobson, R. Eutychus.
Herrick. Upon Parson Beanes.
Hill, J. Preacher and the Slave, The.
Hudgins. Saints and Strangers.
Kipling, R. At His Execution.
Knight, E. II. Song of the Reverend Gatemouth Moore.
MacKay, C. Three Preachers, The.
McGinley. Theology of Jonathan Edwards, The.
Melville, H. Rose Window.
Moorer. Southern Pulpit, The.
Outram. On Hearing a Lady Praise a Certain Rev. Doctor's Eyes.
Questel. Near Mourning Ground.
Roethke. Judge Not.
Thomson, J. Paraphrase of the Latter part of the Sixth Chapter of St. Matthew, A.
Tolson. Old Pettigrew.
Unknown. Let Us Cheer the Weary Traveler.
  Vicar of Bray, The.
Wakefield. Music of His Steps, The.
Warren, R. Amazing Grace in the Back Country.
Zu-Bolton. Governor of the Ollie Street, The.
See also Clergy

Predators
Hendriks. Cirrhosis.
Hughes, T. That Moment.
Lindsay, V. Spider and the Ghost of the Fly, The.
Lovelace, R. Lady with a Falcon on Her Fist, A.
Melville, H. Maldive Shark, The.
Owen, W. Arms and the Boy.
Rossetti, C. Handy Mole who plied no shovel, A.
Taylor, E. Upon a Spider Catching a Fly.
Tomlinson, C. How still the hawk.
Wilson, E. Lakeside.

Predestination
Ainger, A. God Is Working His Purpose Out.
Antipater of Thessalonica. In my stars there's three times ten.
Carter, M. Being, always to arrange.
Hardy, T. Subalterns, The.
Hughes, T. Whether you say it, think it, know it.
Moore, M. Book of How, The.
Nemerov. Western Approaches, The.
Palladas. Ignorant of all logic and all law.

Pregnancy
Allen, L. Belly Woman's Lament.
"Alta." First Pregnancy.
Baraka. For Hettie.
Barbauld. To a Little Invisible Being Who Is Expected Soon to Become Visible.
Bostok. Foetus kicks.
  Pregnant again.
Brereton, J. Unborn.
Bruce, D. Sonnet 2: "Deep in her seventh month, my sister dozes."
  Two Couples.
Carroll, K. Truth About Karen, The.
Clive. Mother, The.
Crane, H. Stark Major.
Curzon, D. Tour of Ein Kerem, A.
Daniels, K. Women's Room in Pennsylvania Station, The.
Denning. Kim-San.
Di Prima. Song For Baby-O, Unborn.

Dimitrova. Woman Pregnant, A.
Dove, R. Cameos.
  History.
  Weathering Out.
Durcan. Sister Agnes Writes to Her Beloved Mother.
Ellis, J. Sarah Hazard's Love Letter.
Ennis. Alice of Daphne, 1799.
Erdrich. Birth.
Fish. What Is Beyond Us.
Fleming, R. For All Unwed Mothers.
Fraser, K. Poems for the New.
Goto. I listen to the pulse of a life / different from mine.
Grennan. Conjunctions.
Gunn, T. Baby Song.
Hacker, M. 1973.
Harjo, J. Early morning woman.
Head, G. Night Sweats.
Hikmet. Evening Walk, The.
Ho Xuan Huong. Unwed Mother, An.
Holbrook, D. Maternity Gown.
Hoyt, C. Pretty matron, The.
Johnson, A. Gifts.
Jones, B. Portrait of a Pregnant Woman.
Jong. Buddha in the Womb, The.
Jonker. Pregnant Woman.
Kinzie. Sound Waves.
Klappert. Ellie Mae Leaves in a Hurry.
Lawrence, D. Youth Mowing, A.
Le Sueur. Budded with Child.
Lorde. Now That I Am Forever with Child.
Mahon. Ford Manor.
  Unborn Child, An.
Major, C. On Trying to Imagine the Kiwi Pregnant.
Makeda (Queen of Sheba). I fell.
Maksimovic. For the Barren Woman.
Mayer, B. We've solved the problem, the problem is solved.
McPherson, S. Pregnancy.
Norris, K. Advent.
Olds, S. May 1968.
Ostriker. Propaganda Poem: Maybe for Some Young Mamas.
Pastan. Notes from the Delivery Room.
Plath. Metaphors.
Pritam, A. Annunciation, The.
Rilke. Mary's Visitation.
Rukeyser, M. All the Little Animals.
Schwartz, D. Young Child and His Pregnant Mother, A.
Shange. Oh, I'm 10 Months Pregnant.
Shuttle. Early Pregnancy.
  Expectant Mother.
  Maritimes.
Sorrells. To a Child Born in Time of Small War.
Stevenson, A. Suburb, The.
Swenson, M. Motherhood.
Taggard. With Child.
Takahashi Shinkichi. Birth.
Unknown. Child Waters.
  I have a newe gardin.
  I loved / secretly.
  Not long ago I met a clerk.
Waly, Waly [Love Be Bonny].
Voigt. "Wife Takes a Child", The.
Wickham. After Annunciation.
  King Alfred and the Peasant Woman.
Williams, W. Raper from Passenack, The.
Wright, J. Woman to Child.
  Woman to Man.

Prehistoric Man. *See* **Cavemen; Man, Primitive**

Prejudice
Atkins. Late Bus (After a Series of Hold-Ups).
Baca. So Mexicans Are Taking Jobs from Americans.
Baraka. Agony, An. As Now.
Cassells. Soul Make A Path Through Shouting.
Chinn. Skin Color from the Sun.
Coicou. Slave's Lament, The.
Derricotte. Weakness, The.
Divakaruni. Yuba City School.
Durand, O. Black Man's Son, The.
Durcan. Jewish Bride, The.

Eady. Sherbet.
Fanthorpe. You Will Be Hearing from Us Shortly.
Gbadamosi. Scene 6 The Boat Passage.
Gillan. In memory we are walking.
  Public School No. 18: Paterson, New Jersey.
Henderson-Holmes. Battle, Over and Over Again, The.
Hewitt, J. From the Tibetan.
Kipling, R. Tommy.
Kramer, L. Shoemaker's Wife, The.
Levine, P. Old Testament, The.
McElroy, C. Foul Line—1987.
Moore, M. Labors of Hercules, The.
Moorer. Prejudice.
Mura. Argument: on 1942, An.
  Grandfather-in-law.
Neto. Farewell at the Moment of Parting.
Ostriker. Lamenting the Inevitable.
Reed, I. Jacket Notes.
Roberts, N. Nigger and Some Poofters, A.
Rodriguez, L. We never stopped crossing borders.
Saunders, R. Lawd, Dese Colored Chillum.
Scannell. Popular Mythologies.
Smart, C. Moderation.
Steptoe. Such a Boat of Land.
Viscusi. Autobiography.
Walton, A. First Impressions.
See also **Racial Prejudice; Racism and Racists; Sexism**

Presbyterianism and Presbyterians
Dryden, J. Presbyterians, The.
Milton. On the New Forcers of Conscience Under the Long Parliament.
Paulin. Presbyterian Study.
Wilson, R. Elegy in a Presbyterian Burying-Ground.

Presence
Creeley. Fire, The.
  Like They Say.
Knott. Goodbye.
Levertov. Thread, The.
  Wings, The.
Olson, C. Cole's Island.
Young, A. Blues Don't Change, The.
  Yes, the Secret Mind Whispers.

Presents. *See* **Gifts and Giving**

Presidency, The, United States
Hollander, J. Historical Reflections.
Jeffers, R. Woodrow Wilson.
Kendrick, D. Solo: The Good Blues.
Moorer. Presidents, The.
Steptoe. Election Time.
Taylor, H. Speech.
Unknown. Our Presidents.
Whitman, W. To the States, To Identify the 16th, 17th, or 18th Presidentiad.
Williams, B. President Roosevelt.

Presley, Elvis
Eady. Young Elvis.
Tomkiw. Last Night in Elvisville.

Presumption
Belševica. Don't be oversure of your cherry-tree.
Cummings, E. Space being(don't forget to remember)Curved.
Wright, C. March Journal.

Pretension
Burns, R. No more of your titled acquaintances boast.
Campion, T. Heart's Music.
Donne. Satire 4.
Eliot, T. Portrait of a Lady.
Gilbert, S. Bunthorne's Song.
Herbert, G. Jordan (2)(II): "When first my lines [*or* verse] of heavenly [*or* heav'nly] joy[e]s made mention."
Jonson, B. On English Monsieur.
"Pindar." Town Eclogue, A.
Shapiro, K. University.
Tranter. Having Completed My Fortieth Year.

Pride
Aeschylus. Beseech you, think not I am silent thus.
  Clytemnestra triumphant over the bodies of Agamemnon and Cassandra.

"Alta." Yesterday i had a wild thot. hearing james brown on the radio singing *say it.*
Angelou. Phenomenal Woman.
Archilochus. That good shield I threw away.
Aristophanes. Since first to exhibit his Plays he began.
Bennett, G. To a Dark Girl.
Bottrall. Icarus.
Breeze. Natural High.
Brooks, G. Primer for Blacks.
  To Those of My Sisters Who Kept Their Naturals.
Brown, J. *et al.* Say it loud, I'm black and I'm proud.
Brown, S. Sporting Beasley.
  To Sallie, Walking.
Burns, R. No more of your titled acquaintances boast.
Clifton, L. Listen Children.
Collins, M. Callaloo.
Craig, C. City Blues.
Disch. In Praise of New York.
Dove, R. Sunday Greens.
Emanuel, J. Old Black Men Say.
Emerson, R. Good-bye, proud world! I'm going home.
Enright, D. Flowers.
  Lucifer Broods.
Euripides. But, o great offspring of the Ocean King.
Gillan. Growing Up Italian.
Gonzales, R. Praise the Tortilla, Praise the Menudo, Praise the Chorizo.
Grigson. Before a Fall.
Herbert, G. Church Monuments.
  Flower, The.
  Vanity [*or* Vanitie] (1).
Herrick. To Dianeme ("Sweet, be not proud of those two eyes").
Hewitt, J. Ulster Names.
Hopkins, G. Of virtues I most warmly bless.
Hughes, L. Ballad of the Girl Whose Name Is Mud.
  Madam and the Census Man.
Jeffers, R. Rock and Hawk.
Knott. Two Vietnam Poems: (1966).
Landon. Mask of Gaiety, The.
Landor, W. Called Proud.
  Proud word you never spoke, but you will speak.
Lawrence, D. Proper Pride.
Leigh, R. Greatness in Little.
Levine, P. Animals Are Passing from Our Lives.
Longfellow, H. Rhyme of Sir Christopher, The.
Lorde. Naturally.
Lowell, J. Contrast, A.
Lucie-Smith. Lesson, The.
McKay, C. If we must die—let it not be like hogs.
McOrlan. Hairdresser's, The.
Mechthild von Magdeburg. God's Absence.
Meredith, G. Lucifer in Starlight.
Otomo no Tabito. Better get drunk and cry.
Owen, W. Parable of the Old Man and the Young, The.
Parmenion of Macedon. Protection of a cheap coat suffices, The.
Popa. Enemies of the Little Box, The.
Pope, A. Essay on Criticism, An.
Sandburg, C. Primer Lesson.
Scott, W. Boat Song.
  Madge Wildfire Sings.
Sewell, G. Dying Man in His Garden, The.
Shelley, P. Ozymandias [of Egypt].
Sherwood, G. Satire against Reason and Mankind, A.
Sidney, P. Sonnet 27: "Because I oft, in dark abstracted guise."
  Sonnet 31: "With how sad steps, O Moon, thou climb'st the skies!"
  Sonnet 53: "In martial sports I had my cunning tried."
Smith, S. My Cats.
Stevenson, R. Foreign Children.
Sylvester, J. Leviathan.

Thomas, E. Forsaken Wife, The.
Thomson, J. One day the god of fond desire.
Turner, N. Whenever I say "America."
Unknown. One, two, whatever you do.
Tamping Ties ("Tamp 'em up solid").
Wa-Sissica, the War Song.
Villalongo. In the Good Old U. S. A.
Whitman, W. Woman waits for me, she contains all, nothing is lacking, A.
Whittier. Cities of the Plain, The.
Forgiveness.
Wordsworth, W. Lines Left upon a Seat in a Yew-Tree which Stands near the Lake of Esthwaite, on a Desolate Part of the Shore, yet Commanding a Beautiful Prospect.
Wright, J. In Shame and Humiliation.

Priests. *See* **Clergy**

Prillerman, Byrd
Johnson, M. Sister Johnson's Speech.
To Professor Byrd Prillerman.

Primitive Man. *See* **Man, Primitive**

Primroses
Cranch. Evening Primrose, The.
Donne. Primrose[, Being at Montgomery Castle, upon the Hill, on Which It Is Situate], The.
Herrick. Primrose, The.
Shaw, A. Crepuscule.
White, H. To an Early Primrose.

Prince Edward Island, Canada
McFadden, D. Lennox Island.

Princes and Princesses
Aiken, J. Palace Cook's Tale.
Ayton. On the Prince's Death, to the King.
Beardsley. Ballad of a Barber, The.
Corbin, L. Ali / Is our prince.
Daniel, S. Theare be great Prince, such as will tell you howe.
Gorges. Written upon the death of the most Noble Prince Henrie.
Holland, H. Epitaph on Prince Henry.
Li K'ai-hsien. Not a day goes by without someone borrowing books from me.
Lynd. Beauty and the Beast.
McGough, R. Cousin Nell.
Moore, T. Duke is the lad to frighten a lass, The.
Mörike. Beauty Rohtraut.
Oxenham. Everymaid.
Rossetti, C. Royal Princess, A.
Sitwell, D. King of China's Daughter, The.
Smith, S. Ballet of the Twelve Dancing Princesses, The.
Tate, J. Pet Deer, The.
Yü Chi. Little Landscape by Chao Ch'ien-li, A.

Princeton University
Eberhart, R. Half-bent Man.

Printing and Printers
Adams, F. Composed in the Composing Room.
Bartlett, E. Charlotte, Her Book.
Cranch. Printing-Press, The.
Dobson, R. Country Press.
Fogel, A. Printer's Error, The.
Glover, D. Printers.
Hughes, L. Madam's Calling Cards.
Joyce, J. Ladies and gents, you are here assembled.
McGough, R. Italic.
Phipson. Press, The.
Unknown. Pan in Battle.
Wodehouse, P. Printer's Error.

Prisoners of War
Dickey, J. Performance, The.
Freneau. Hospital Prison Ship, The.
Gardiner, A. Natal Hunters, The.
Lee, J. German Prisoners.
Levertov. Pilots, The.
Rukeyser, M. Breaking Open.
Trần Huy Liệu. Down-and-Out Fighter and the Spring Nymph, A.
Tu Fu. Spring Prospect.
Unknown. Last Words.

Prisons and Prisoners
Adamo. Great Escape, The.

Adamson. O to be in the news again—now as fashion runs.
Passing Through Experiences.
"Akhmatova." Dedication.
Alexie. Capital Punishment.
Awoonor. They Shall Know.
Baca. Cloudy Day.
How We Carry Ourselves.
I Applied for the Board.
Immigrants in Our Own Land.
It Started.
Like an Animal.
There Are Black.
Barth, R. P.O.W.s.
Beckwith. Two Worlds.
Berrigan, D. Rehabilitative Report: We Can Still Laugh.
Berry, J. Poem for the Wife of an Imprisoned Leader *especially for Winnie Mandela.*
Berryman. Dream Song 45.
Biaoszewski. *They clanged and clanged.*
Blake, W. Crystal Cabinet, The.
Prince of Love, The.
Boleyn, G. O death, rock me asleep.
Borowski. Project: Flag.
Brontë, E. Prisoner, The.
Brown, S. Southern Road.
Brutus. At night.
Clammy cement, The.
Endurance.
Letters to Martha.
On the Island.
Poems About Prison.
Sounds Begin Again, The.
Under House Arrest.
Bryusov. Stonemason, stonemason, in your white apron.
Bùi Công Trù'ng. Fallen Fruit, A.
Byron, G. Sonnet on Chillon.
Canning, G. *et al.* Rogero's Song.
Carkesse. On the Doctors' Telling Him that till He Left off Making Verses He Was Not Fit to be Discharged.
Ceraman Kanaikkal Irumporai. King's Last Words, A.
Ch'ien Ch'ien-i. Fishing cove and long lines of fishermen's huts, A.
Miscellaneous Poems Written While in Jail.
Nightly the watchman's rattle startles my sleep.
Spluttering burnt-out lamp blazes in the dusk.
Ch'ien T'ao. Returning to the Fields.
Chipasula. Hanging, Zomba Central Prison, A.
Clifton, L. To Bobby Seale.
Cobbett. Elegy in Newgate.
Coleridge, S. Dungeon, The.
Conyus. Great Santa Barbara Oil Disaster OR, The.
Upon Leaving the Parole Board Hearing.
Cook, E. Song of the Imprisoned Bird.
Coolbrith. Captive of the White City.
Cruickshank, A. Convict Song, The.
Dalton, R. My Neighbor.
Daniel, Y. To My Friends.
Đào Duy Kỳ. At Condore Port.
Darwish, M. Earth Poem.
Prison.
Sirhan Drinks His Coffee in the Cafeteria.
Dawe, B. On the Death of Ronald Ryan.
De Hearn. Shut-In, The.
De la Mare. In the Dock.
Desnos. Letter to Youki.
Dickinson, E. I never hear the word "escape."
Mine—by the Right of the White Election!
Of Paul and Silas it is said.
Prison gets to be a friend, A.
Dombrovsky. They wanted me dead, the bastards.
When they brought us a pear jacket.
Donne. Oh my black[e] soul[e]! now thou art summoned.
Donnelly, C. Flowering Bars, The.
Dunbar, P. Sympathy.
Du'o'ng Bá Trạc. Prison Life.
Eich. Inventory.
Elizabeth I. Written on a Wall at Woodstock.

Written with a Diamond On Her Window at Woodstock.
Éluard, P. To Her of Whom They Dream.
Faiz. Fragrant Hands.
Prison Daybreak, A.
Prison Evening, A.
Fitzgerald, R. Wind at Your Door, The.
Freneau. Hospital Prison Ship, The.
Frost, R. Line-Gang, The.
Fuentes. In This Place.
Gouri. Pictures of Jews.
Graves, R. Certain Mercies.
Love without hope, as when the young bird-catcher.
Gunn, T. In the Tank.
Tamer and Hawk.
Hamburger, M. Between the Lines.
Hanagid. Prison, The.
Harris, W. We Live in a Cage.
Helwig. Words from Hell.
Henderson, D. Alvin Cash/Keep on Dancin'.
Hernández, M. Tomb of the Imagination.
Hernton. Fall Down.
Hikmet. Evening Walk, The.
Letters from a Man in Solitary.
Letters from Chankiri Prison.
Since I was thrown inside.
Hogan, M. Spring.
Housman, A. Oh who is that young sinner with the handcuffs on his wrists?
Howard, L. Humours of the King's Bench Prison, a Ballad, The.
Howe, F. Scattered Light.
Hull, L. Jail, Flames—Jersey, 1971.
Huỳnh Thúc Kháng. Farewell Song, A.
Irumporai. King's Last Words, A.
Jacob, M. In Search of the Traitor.
Jarrell. Prisoners.
Jastrun, T. Hat.
Johnson, G. Heart of a woman [goes forth with the dawn], The.
Jordan, J. Poem Against the State (Of Things): 1975.
Joseph, J. Dog body and cat mind, The.
Kaufman, B. Jail Poems.
Keats. Written on the Day That Mr. Leigh Hunt Left Prison.
Kelly, R. Newark.
Kim, N. Spring Comes to the Hills and Fields.
This autumn, in blue prisoner's garb, hands tied behind my back.
Kinzie. Ringing Words.
Kipling, R. Half-Ballad of Waterval.
Knight, E. Cell Song.
Crazy pigeon strutting outside my cell.
For Freckle-Faced Gerald.
Haiku: "Eastern guard tower."
Hard Rock Returns to Prison from the Hospital for the Criminal Insane.
He sees through stone.
Idea of Ancestry, The.
To Make a Poem in Prison.
Warden said to me the other day, The.
WASP Woman Visits a Black Junkie in Prison, A.
Kocbek. Longing for Jail, A.
Koestenbaum, P. Sonnet 37: "I'd decided I initiate most."
Kunze, R. Hymn To a Woman Under Interrogation.
L'Estrange. Mr L'Estrange's Verses in the Prison at Lynn.
Levine, P. Heaven.
Lovelace, R. To Althea, from Prison.
To Lucasta[, from Prison].
Vintage to the Dungeon, The.
Lowell, R. After the Surprising Conversions.
In the Cage.
Memories of West Street and Lepke.
Lowry, M. Sestina in a Cantina.
Lysohorsky. At a Sunlit Window.
Machi. Tanka: "As though to let loose."
MacNamara, F. Convict's Tour to Hell, A.
Madan. Abelard to Eloisa.
Mandelstam. You took away all the oceans and all the room.
Mariah. Christmas 1962.

Mazzocco. PBS.
McAuley, J. Released on Parole.
Melvill. Sonnet sent to Blackness to Mr. John Welsch, by the Lady Culross, A.
Melville, H. In the Prison Pen.
Meredith, W. Partial Accounts.
Merrill, J. To a Butterfly.
Messerli. Closure.
Mishler. Ceremony.
More, H. Come, neighbour, take a walk with me.
Morris, W. In Prison.
Mutabaruka. You Ask Me.
Nagys. Hallesches Tor: Communion.
Nakkannaiyar. Woman in Love with a Captive King, A.
Neruda. Poet's Obligation.
Nguyễn Chí Thiện. Jungle night—it rains and rains, roofs leak, A.
Model children of the regime, The.
Party holds you down and you lie still, The.
This land's no joy.
Nguyễn Đình Kiên. Back In Prison.
Prison Impromptu.
Nguyễn Ngọc Thuận. Prisoner's Funeral, A.
Nguyễn Văn Năng. Prison Cell, A.
No Ch'ŏn-myŏng. Behind Prison Bars.
Nortje. Letter from Pretoria Central Prison.
O'Dalaigh, G. Child in Prison, A.
O'Donovan Rossa. Returned Picture, The.
Olds, S. Solitary.
Padilla. Man on the Edge.
Self-Portrait of the Other.
Paton. Prison House, The.
Paulin. Surveillances.
Pavese. Words from Confinement.
Petri. To Be Said Over and Over Again.
Phan Bội Châu. In a Canton Jail.
Phan chu Trinh. Breaking Rocks on Poulo Condore.
Piatt, S. In Her Prison.
Pilinszky. Passion of Ravensbrück.
Plomer. Prisoner, The.
Po Chü-i. Prisoner, The.
Red Cockatoo, The.
Rabémanganjara. In hermetic enclosure.
Lament: "Blue, so blue that eye of sky."
Radnóti. Seventh Eclogue.
Ralegh, W. My Body in the Walls Captived.
Ratushinskaya. No, I'm not afraid: after a year.
Reese, D. Ol' Hannah.
Revard. Coming of Age in the County Jail.
Rich, A. From the Prison House.
Rilke. Panther, The.
Rogers, S. Captivity.
Rossetti, C. Verse II.
Rukeyser, M. Columbus.
Saitō Mokichi. Tanka: "Confinement."
Selvinsky. Sebastopol.
Smith, K. Night Whispers, The.
Smith, M. In Prison.
Smith, S. Commuted Sentence, The.
Soyinka. Prisoner.
Spender, S. Prisoners, The.
Spenser. Sonnet 73: 'Being my self captived here'.
Spicer, J. Song of a Prisoner.
Su Tung-p'o. Under the heaven of our holy ruler, all things turn to spring.
Surrey. In Windsor Castle.
Prisoned in Windsor, He Recounteth His Pleasure There Passed.
Swart. Convict.
Tennyson, A. 27.
Thelwall. Cell, The.
Tố Hữu. Cuckoo calls its flock—it's when the rice, The.
Prison Thoughts.
Trần Cao Vân. On Poulo Condore.
Trần Huy Liệu. Dropping By the Guava Graveyard in So'n-La.
What's My Crime?
Trần Minh Tu'ó'c. Prison Dreams.
Tregian. Imprisoned Recusant Writes to His Wife, An.
Tsvetayeva. Blatant as factory buildings.

Tu Fu. Moonlight Night.
Spring Prospect.
Tucker, M. Soldier Boy's Dream, The.
Tuqan, F. Behind Bars, Sel.
Unknown. Been in the Pen So Long.
Bird in a Cage, The.
Boston Burglar, The.
Clonmel Jail.
Convicts' Rum Song.
Down in the valley, valley so low.
Female Transport, The.
Glance, A.
Other Side of the Valley, The.
Poor Lazarus.
Portland County Jail.
Song of the Breaking of the Willow.
Young Beichan.
Valentine, J. Tell Me, What Is the Soul.
Waddington, M. Women's Jail, The.
Walcott. Forest of Europe.
Walker, M. Girl Held without Bail.
Walker, R. Solitary Confinement.
Watts-Dunton. Coleridge.
Wayman. Despair.
Wheelock, J. Black Panther, The.
Lion-House, The.
Whitney, I. Now for the people in thee left.
Wilde, O. Ballad of Reading Gaol, The.
Condemned Man, The.
Wither. If by mischance the people in the street.
Wordsworth, W. Convict, The.
Nuns fret not at their convent's narrow room;.
Wright, J. American Twilights, 1957.
Wright, J. Old Prison, The.
Yang Yi. Prisons Are Full of Convicts, The.
Young, A. Conjugal Visits.

Privacy
Auden. Dedication: "Private faces in public places."
Dickinson, E. I'm Nobody! Who are you?
Ellis, T. Kiss in the Dark, A.
González, A. Inventory of Places Propitious for Love.
Halpern, M. Go Throw Them Out.
Harris, W. We Live in a Cage.
Lane, P. Sexual Privacy of Women on Welfare.
McGinley. Triolet Against Sisters.
Miller, L. My Students Catch Me Dancing.
Sidney, P. Sonnet 54: "Because I breathe not love to every one."
Then do I thinke in deed, that better it is to be private.
Tate, J. In My Own Backyard.

See also **Solitude**
Privateers
McCarthy, T. Shopkeepers at the Party Meeting.

Prizefighting and Prizefighters
Caprani. Prizefighter's Prayer, The.
Procne
Quennell. Procne.
Procrastination
Ceravolo. Wind Is Blowing West, The.
Crabbe. Delay Has Danger.
Procrastination.
Le Gallienne. I meant to do my work today.
Martial. Procrastination.
Masson. When I Get Time.
Perry, N. "Next year, next year," we say.
Taylor, H. Not Working.
Prodigal Son
Bishop, E. Prodigal, The.
Bunin. Flowers, and tall-stalked grasses, and a bee.
Goldberg, L. Prodigal Son, The.
Kipling, R. Prodigal Son, The.
Merwin, W. "Prodigal Son," The.
Rilke. Departure of the Prodigal Son*, The.
Luke 15:11–19; And he said, "There was a man."
Robinson, E. Luke 15:20–32; And he arose and came.
Prodigal Son, The.
Tsvetayeva. And, not crying in vain.

Prodigality
Moore, M. Americans in 1933–4–5–6–7–8–, Etc.
Progress
Atwood. Is/Not / Not.
Auden. Moon Landing.
Cummings, E. O pr / gress verily thou art m.
Pity this busy monster,manunkind.
Davidson, L. America.
Eberhart, R. On Shooting Particles beyond the World.
Fenton, J. Kingfisher's Boxing Gloves, The.
South Parks Road.
Gilman, C. Similar Cases.
Gunn, T. Considering the Snail.
Halliday, M. Population.
Hardy, T. Christmas: 1924.
Hoffenstein. Progress.
Holub. Helping Hand, A.
Horace. New Buildings.
Hugo, R. Plans for Altering the River.
Linden, M. To the Wheel of Progress.
Mahon. Consolations of Philosophy.
McPherson, S. Waiting for Lesser Duckweed: On a Proposal of Issa's.
Nash, O. Up from the Wheelbarrow.
Nobuyuki. Fiery Declarations (two poems).
Phillips, D. If It's Only Rhythm.
Praed. Chaunts of the Brazen Head, The.
Sandburg, C. Four Preludes on Playthings of the Wind.
Snyder, G. L M F B R.
Spender, S. Not palaces, an era's crown.
Tomlinson, C. Return to Hinton.
Tsaloumas. Progressive Man's Indignation, A.
Wilcox, E. Progress.
Williams, M. Love and How It Becomes Important in Our Day to Day Lives.
Wordsworth, W. Steamboats, Viaducts and Railways.
Proletariat
Khlebnikov, V. We don't live in castles.
See also **Bourgeoisie**
Prometheus
Aeschylus. Beseech you, think not I am silent thus.
Bradley, G. Fire Fetched Down, The.
Byron, G. Prometheus.
Dyer, S. PROMETHEUS, when first from heaven high.
Mastoraki. Prometheus.
Rowan. Prometheus at Coney Island.
Swift, J. Prometheus.
Promises
Bible, *O.T.* Psalm 2.
Browning, E. Sonnet: "First time that the sun rose on thine oath, The."
Donne. On His Mistress [*or* Mistris].
Herrick. Rainbow; or Curious Covenant, The.
To His Conscience.
Howell, T. Acre of performance is worth a, An.
Johnson, H. Remember not the promises we made.
Larkin, P. Is it for now or for always.
Liu E. I remember when we made our first promises of love.
Mototoshi. Your fine promises.
Olds, S. Wedding Vow, The.
Robinson, E. Vickery's Mountain.
Rossetti, C. Promises like Pie-Crust.
Shakespeare, W. *Juliet*: Good-night, good-night! as sweet repose and rest.
Shirley, J. Two Gentlemen That Broke Their Promise of a Meeting.
Smart, C. To the Rev. Mr. Powell.
Spenser. Sonnet 65.": "Doubt which ye misdeeme, fayre love, is vaine, The."
Swift, J. Twelve Articles.
Unknown. Frail frail, lone-growing bamboo.
Oaths of Friendship.
Wyatt, T. Farewell: "What should I say."
What should I say.
Yeats. Deep-sworn Vow, A.
Zach. Like Sand.
Propaganda
Chōkū. Tanka: "Imagining."

Day Lewis. Where Are the War Poets?

Propertius, Sextus
Adcock, F. Note on Propertius I.5.
Lowell, R. Ghost is someone: death has left a hole, A.

Property
Burns, R. Extempore—On Being Shown a Beautiful Country Seat Belonging to Maxwell of Cardoness.
Carpenter, W. Fire.
Davis, C. Belongings.
Dickinson, E. I am afraid to own a Body.
Eich. Inventory.
Garioch. Property.
Imlah. Goldilocks.
Kamienska. Things of This World.
Lawrence, D. Lord Tennyson and Lord Melchett.
Norris, J. My Estate.
Padilla. Fountain, a house of stone, A.
Park, N. Hands.
Pound, E. Portrait d'une Femme.
Sandburg, C. Who shall speak for the people?
Smith, K. Possessions.
Tate, J. In My Own Backyard.
Whitman, W. Animals.
Wickham. Soul's Liberty.

Prophecy and Prophets
Alexander, W. Psychotropic Squalls, The.
Andreyev, V. Rebecca.
Barnes, D. Transfiguration.
Benét, S. John Brown's Prayer.
Bialik. Prophet, Go, Flee!
Byron, G. All this she told with some confusion and.
Saul.
Chagy. Haggai.
Conquest. Agents, The.
Cowley, A. 34. Chapter of the Prophet Isaiah, The.
Drayton. Poly-Olbion.
Eliot, T. Luke 2:21–40; And at the end of eight days, when he was circumcised.
Ginsberg, A. Prophecy, A.
Glazkov. Raven, The.
Hemans. Second Sight.
Hill, G. They slew by night.
Hindley, C. Mother Shipton's Prophecies.
Jackson, L. Helen's Burning.
Johnson, L. Mystic and Cavalier.
Markov. Stendhal.
McGrath, T. End of the world: it was given to me to see it, The.
Notley. Désamère.
O'Brien, G. Prophetic Child, The.
Osundare. Sand Seer, The.
Parker, M. King Enjoys His Own Again, The.
Patchen. In the footsteps of the walking air.
Poe. Stanzas.
Pushkin. Prophet, The.
Sachs, N. Your eyes, O my beloved.
Shakespeare, W. Sonnet 14.
Sonnet 106.
Sherlock. Beauty Too of Twisted Trees, A.
Skelton, J. Than, if this noble kyng.
Strand. Mysterious Maps, The.
Tennyson, A. Babylon.
Tindal. Birth Wail, The.
Unknown. Ezekiel Saw the Wheel.
Kalapuya Prophecy, A.
Prophetic Powers.
Vallejo. Black Stone on Top of a White Stone.
Vinokurov. Prophet, The.
Virgil. Signs of Rain.
Walker, M. Prophets for a New Day.
Wilbur. Advice to a Prophet.
Wojahn. First Six Seals, The.
Yeats. Matthew 24:15–31.
See also **Oracles**

Proserpina [*or* Proserpine]. *See* **Persephone**

Prostitution and Prostitutes
Alcaeus. So lovely . . . / so tender.
Argentarius. Melissa means honeybee; yes, you're true.
Psyllus lies here. Procuring was his trade.
Barry, J. Nights in Nha Trang.

Bassus. I am not going to turn into gold.
Benn. Cycle.
Blind. Russian Student's Tale, The.
Boldman. JANUARY FIRST.
Brecht, B. Ballad of Immoral Earnings.
Breton, A. Man and Woman Absolutely White, A.
Brooks, G. Coora Flower, The.
Browne, I. Letter from a Captain in Country Quarters to his Corinna in Town, A.
Cavafy. And I Lounged and Lay on Their Beds.
Chaucer. Cook's Tale, The.
Clifton, H. Id.
Monsoon Girl.
Coleman, H. OK Corral East Brothers in the Nam.
Cooper, D. Being Aware.
Couzyn. World War II.
Crawford, R. Love Song of Tommo Frogley.
Cullen, C. For Daughters of Magdalen.
Cummings, E. Twentyseven bums give a prostitute the once.
Donne. Klockius so deeply hath sworn[e], ne'er more to come.
Self[e] Accuser, A.
Dowson. Non Sum Qualis Eram Bonae sub Regno Cynara[e].
Eldridge, P. To a Courtesan a Thousand Years Dead.
Eliot, T. Sweeney Erect.
Gray, W. She Is More to Be Pitied than Censured.
Hardy, T. Ruined Maid, The.
Henley, W. To W. R.
Hillman. At a Motel.
Huddle. Words.
Hughes, L. Red Silk Stockings.
Huỳnh Mẫn Đạt. Old Whore Becomes a Nun, The.
Irtenev. Camelia.
Jana Bai. Cast off all shame.
Johnson, F. Scarlet Woman, The.
Kendrick, D. Solo: The Good Blues.
Knight, E. As You Leave Me.
Violent Space, The.
Komunyakaa. Saigon Bar Girls, 1975.
Lassell. Dino.
Going Rate, The.
Leonidas of Tarentum. Antiginides' two daughters, Melo.
Li Ho. Ravine on a Cold Evening.
Lovelace, R. La Bella Bona-Roba.
Mapanje. Cheerful Girls at Smiller's Bar, The.
Messages.
Masters, E. Daisy Fraser.
Matveyeva. Procurers.
McOrlan. Wood merchant's parlour, The.
Mirikitani. Jade.
Nashe. Choise of valentines, The.
Nicarchus of Alexandria. Sweet Nicarete, who served Athene's shuttle.
Osbey. In These Houses of Swift Easy Women.
Pace, R. Tingel-Tangel.
Pasolini. Civil Song.
Southern Dawn.
Peters, L. Song: "Clawed green-eyed."
Philip of Thessalonica. I, a ship, built on the profits / from my master's amorous trade.
Philodemus. Hello. Hello. Hello. What's your name? —"Hello there.—*Hello there yourself.* This *quidam* gives that *quidam* for *one* round.
Piper, L. Sweet Ethel.
Plomer. French Lisette: A Ballad of Maida Vale.
Poseidippus. You who visit in turn.
Pyon. Non-gae.
Rexroth, K. For a Masseuse and Prostitute.
Rodgers, W. Net, The.
Rufinus. I do not enjoy.
Waterfront Girls, The.
Rufinus Domesticus. Ah, Melissa, where's your famous golden beauty.
Shaw, A. Courtesan.
Simmons, J. Cavalier Lyric.

Simpson, L. Man Who Married Magdalene, The.
Smith, D. Fisherman's Whore, The.
Sulpicia. That you allow yourself this vast neglect of me.
Swift, J. Beautiful Young Nymph Going to Bed, A.
Taylor, J. Epigram: "Look how yon lecher's legs are worn away."
Me thinks I have some Cavillers object.
Unknown. Nico's bedroom talents entice men.
Peter hath lost his purse, but will conceal it.
Poor But Honest.
Sthenelais.
Villon. Ballad of Villon and Fat Madge, The.
Old Lady's Lament for Her Youth, The.
Walker, M. Whores.
Weigl. Song for the Lost Private.
Way of Tet, The.
Whitman, W. To a Common Prostitute.
Wilbur. Place Pigalle.
Wilde, O. Harlot's House, The.
Impression Du Matin.
Williams, C. Gas Station, The.
Wright, J. Gesture by a Lady with an Assumed Name, A.
In Response to a Rumor that the Oldest Whorehouse in Wheeling, West Virginia, Has Been Condemned.

Protest, Social
Alexie. On the Amtrak from Boston to New York City.
Aristophanes. Home front, The.
Atwood. Notes towards a Poem That Can Never Be Written.
Baca. Immigrants in Our Own Land.
Bly, R. After the Industrial Revolution, All Things Happen at Once.
At a March against the Vietnam War.
Breton, A. War.
Brooks, G. First fight. Then fiddle. Ply the slipping string.
Lovers of the Poor, The.
Bursk. Lies.
Cambridge, A. Fashion.
Castillo, O. Distances.
Chesterton, G. Secret People, The.
Clampitt. Amaranth and Moly.
Clough. Latest Decalogue, The.
Cole, G. And you'll say a nation totters.
Collins, M. Because the Dawn Breaks.
Conquest. Bagpipes at the Biltmore.
Cornish, S. Brother of the Streets.
Montgomery.
Cullen, C. Scottsboro, Too, Is Worth Its Song.
Cummings, E. Season 'tis, my lovely lambs, The.
Two X.
Davidson, J. Labourer's Wife, A.
Thirty Bob a Week.
Davie. Barnsley and District.
Thanks to industrial Essex.
Dickinson, E. Much Madness is divinest Sense.
Dorn, E. Home on the Range, February 1962.
Mourning Letter, March 29 1963.
Dugan, A. Adultery.
Du'o'ng Bá Trạc. Prison Life.
"Dylan." Blowin' in the Wind.
Emerson, R. Ode, Inscribed to W. H. Channing.
Enright, D. Unlawful Assembly.
Fishman, C. Death March.
Floyd. Private Jack Smith, U. S. M. C.
Fort, C. For Martin Luther King.
Garrigue. Written in London after a Protest Parade.
Gilbert, C. Theory of Curve.
Ginsberg, A. America I've given you all and now I'm nothing.
Death to Van Gogh's Ear!
Goodman, P. April 1962.
Gurney, I. Strange Hells.
Hairston. Alabama Bus.
Hale, J. Cinque.
Custer Lives in Humbolt County.
Hayes, A. Joe Hill.

Hood, T. Song of the Shirt, The.
Hughes, L. Harlem.
Un-American Investigators.
Huỳnh Thúc Kháng. Comedy of the World, The.
Farewell Song, A.
Ignatow, D. All Quiet.
Kearns, L. Environment.
Lawrence, D. How beastly the bourgeois is.
Stand up, but not for Jesus!
Levertov. Went with some of my students to work in the People's.
Lochhead, L. Mirror's Song.
Lorde. Revolution Is One Form of Social Change.
Lowell, R. After the Surprising Conversions.
March 1, The.
Memories of West Street and Lepke.
"Lu Hsün." Call to Arms.
Madgett. Alabama Centennial.
Mapanje. On Being Asked to Write a Poem for 1979.
May, S. Mildmay Grove.
McElroy, C. Foul Line—1987.
McKay, C. If we must die—let it not be like hogs.
Millay, E. Apostrophe to Man.
Moorer. Jim Crow Cars.
Mudrooroo. Peaches and Cream.
Mutabaruka. Revolutionary Poets.
Nguyễn Đình Kiên. Back In Prison.
Prison Impromptu.
Nye, N. Nobody's newspaper tells what the Costa Ricans did.
Rebellion against the North Side.
Onuora Oku. Reflection in Red.
Peacock, T. Rich and Poor; or, Saint and Sinner.
Phan Bội Châu. Alarm Clock, The.
Human Nature.
In a Canton Jail.
Rights.
To a Cuckoo.
Phan chu Trinh. Breaking Rocks on Poulo Condore.
Opera Actors.
Phan Văn Hy. Ricksha man does quite a simple job, The.
Picasso. Bottle of Suze, A.
Piercy. Low Road, The.
Posner. On a Recent Protest against Social Conditions.
Randall, D. Ballad of Birmingham.
Raymond, V. People, No, The.
Rexroth, K. Bad Old Days, The.
Rich, A. Burning of Paper instead of Children, The.
From the Prison House.
Rukeyser, M. For Kay Boyle.
Rational Man.
Sadoff. Civil Rights.
Seeger, P. Where have all the flowers gone?—long time passing.
Sepamla. Measure for Measure.
Shelley, P. Song to the Men of England.
Sóng Hồng. To be a poet—if it means to hum with winds.
Stafford, W. Peace Walk.
Starbuck, G. Of Late.
Tản Đà. Tattered Map, The.
Tôn Thất Diệm. To a Piggy Bank.
Trần Cao Vân. On Poulo Condore.
Tremblay, B. Mayday.
Troupe. Boomerang: A Blatantly Political Poem.
Tsatsos. Protest.
Unknown. Ain't Gonna Let Nobody Turn Me Round.
Diggers' Song, The.
Free Silver.
Get on Board, Little Children.
Grain for Emperor Huan.
I don't want to be a soldier.
Poor But Honest.
Song of the Freedman.
Soup Kitchen Song.
We shall overcome.

Walker, A. Chic Freedom's Reflection.
Walker, M. For my people [everywhere singing their slave songs repeatedly: their].
Girl Held without Bail.
Street Demonstration.
Wayman. Despair.
Picketing Supermarkets.
Teething.
Weaver, M. Picnic, an Homage to Civil Rights, The.
Whittier. Astræa.
Wilbur. For the Student Strikers.
Williams, F. Eighties, De.
Wormser. Soul Music.
Wright, S. Until They Have Stopped.
Zamora, D. Report on the Protest in Front of the United States Embassy by the Pino Grande Movement, A.

Protestantism and Protestants
Donne. Show me dear Christ.
Herbert, G. British Church, The.
Hill, G. Christmas Trees.
Maxton. At the Protestant Museum.
Ormsby, F. Spot the Ball.
Survivors.

Proust, Marcel
Disch. Bookmark, A.
Ewart. Hymn to Proust.
Jarrell. Man Meets a Woman in the Street, A.

Provence, France
Procter, A. Legend of Provence, A.
Wilbur. Grasse: The Olive Trees.
Williams, W. To Ford Madox Ford in Heaven.

Providence
Hewitt, J. Whit Monday.
Wheatley, P. Thoughts on the Works of Providence.

Providence, Rhode Island
Berrigan, T. Things To Do in Providence.

Prudes
Nash, O. First Limick.

Psyche (mythology)
Duncan, R. Poem Beginning with a Line by Pindar, A.
Keats. Ode to Psyche.
Tighe. From Psyche.
Illumined bright now shines the splendid dome.
'Mid the thick covert of that woodland shade.
Willis, N. Psyche, Before the Tribunal of Venus.

Psychiatry and Psychiatrists
Clements, S. Deer Cloud.
Ezekiel. Family.
Lister, R. Mind Reborn in Streatham Common, A.
Pinsky. Invocation: "It's crazy to think one could describe them."
Some Terms.
Their Speech, Compared with Wisdom and Poetry.
See also **Mental Illness**

Psychoanalysis and Psychoanalysts
Anderson, B. Deuce: 12:23 a.m.
Durrell. Ballad of the Oedipus Complex.
Endrezze-Danielson. Notes from an Analyst's Couch.
Everhard. Curing Homosexuality.
Ewart. Psychoanalysis.
Jennings, E. Interrogator, The.
Randall, D. Analysands.

Psychological Testing
West, M. Exciting New Concept of Art Therapy, The.
Wieners. Two Years Later.

Puberty
Cassian. Puberty.
Chase, J. One early spring evening when Celia was fourteen.
Chiricahua Apache Oral Tradition. Song for Girls' Puberty Rites.
Hampton. In Andrea's Garden.
Hirsch, E. Skokie Theatre, The.
Marlatt, D. Trying. a trying child. trying it on for size. the role.
Thomas, D. Puberty Tree, The.

Unknown. Song for a Young Girl's Puberty Ceremony.
Yukitsuna. Tanka: "Since puberty."

Publishing and Publishers
Byron, G. To Mr. Murray.
"Carroll." Poeta Fit, Non Nascitur.
Hall, J. Figure a Poem Makes, The.
Hecht, A. From the Grove Press.
Herrick. To the Right Honourable Mildmay, Earl of Westmorland.
Koch, K. Supposing that one walks out into the air.
Thank You.
Larkin, P. Limerick: "There was an old fellow of Kaber."
McGinley. Publisher's Party.
Morton, J. Someone asked the publisher.
Vinokurov. Poetry Editor.

Pudding
Cole, C. Pudding Charms.
Mother Goose. King Arthur.
Roberts, M. Little Pudding.

Puddles
Frost, R. Spring Pools.
Mitchell, A. Watch Your Step—I'm Drenched.
Mother Goose. Doctor Foster went to Gloucester [*or* Glo'ster].

Puerto Ricans
Espada. Spanish of Our Out–Loud Dreams, The.
Tony Went to the Bodega but He Didn't Buy Anything.
Luciano. You're Nothing but a Spanish Colored Kid.

Puerto Rico
Clarke, C. San Juan: 1979.
Cruz, V. Puerta Rica.
Espada. Coca-Cola and Coco Frio.
Niggerlips was the high school name / for me.

Pumpkins
Aldis, D. Hallowe'en Pumpkin, A.
Barry, J. Harvest Moon.
Goodison. From the Garden of the Women Once Fallen.
Mother Goose. Pumpkin-Eater, The.
Nye, N. What Brings Us Out.
Poulsson. Judging by Appearances.
Willard, N. Saint Pumpkin.

Punctuation
Bishop, M. What Hath Man Wrought Exclamation Point.
Erwin. Playing for Keeps.

Punishment
Agathias. Justice.
Bible, *O.T.* Psalm 37: "Fret not thyself because of evildoers."
Burns, R. Holy Willie's Prayer.
Claudian. Punishment in Hell.
Emerson, R. Nemesis.
Erdrich. Indian Boarding School: The Runaways.
Erucius of Cyzicus. Even though he lies underground.
Gibran. Crime and Punishment.
Graham, H. L'Enfant Glacé.
Stern parent, A.
Graves, R. Wreath, The.
Hayden, R. Whipping, The.
Heaney, S. Punishment.
Kerr, K. Touch.
Leto. For Talking.
Lucian. I am Priapus. I was put here according to custom.
Merwin, W. Lament for the Makers.
Mitchell, A. Dumb Insolence.
Moore, T. Argument, An.
Mother Goose. Little Polly Flinders.
Olds, S. Unjustly Punished Child.
Palladas. Murderer & Sarapis, The.
Patchen. Lions of fire, The.
Patmore, C. Toys, The.
Pembroke, M. Psalm 58: Si Vere Utique.
Ransom, J. Man without Sense of Direction.
Reznikoff. Testimony: The United States (1901–1910) Recitative/The South.
Ross, C. Jack.

Shakespeare, W. When I would pray and think, I think and pray.
Sharpless. Low Church.
Unknown. Bitter Withy, The.
Don't-Care—he didn't care.
Queen of Hearts, The.
There was a little girl.
Warren, R. Wet Hair: If Now His Mother Should Come.
Webster, A. Little child she, half defiant came, A.
Wright, J. Song for the Middle of the Night, A.

Puns
"Ingoldsby." Lines Left at Mr Theodore Hook's House in June, 1834.

Puppets and Puppeteers
Brickley. Puppet, The.
Kondo. Autumn light.
Ku T'ai-ch'ing. Tune: "Partridge Sky"— Puppet Theater.
Marchant. Young Master's Account of a Puppet Show.
Ravikovitch. Marionette.
Symons, A. Prologue: Before the Curtain.
T'ang Yin. Galloping around, north and south.
Tiller. Street Performers, 1851.
Wilde, O. Harlot's House, The.
Yang Shen. To the Tune "Partridge Sky."

Puppies
Kipling, R. His Apologies.
Milne, A. Puppy and I.

Puritanism and Puritans
Butler, S. Presbyterian Knight, The.
Corbet. Distracted Puritan, The.
Equi. Puritans.
Longfellow, H. Rhyme of Sir Christopher, The.
Lowell, R. After the Surprising Conversions.
Quarles. On Those That Deserve It.
Shapiro, K. Puritan, The.
Unknown. Zealous Puritan, The.
Wylie. Puritan Sonnet, IV.

Purity
Blunt, W. As To His Choice of Her.
Ciardi. Evil Eye, The.
Drayton. Sonnet 35: 'Some, misbelieving and profane'.
Gilbert, S. Bunthorne's Song.
Herbert, G. Superliminare.
Koianimptiwa. Korosta Katzina Song.
Kunitz, S. Vita Nuova.
Lamb, C. "Timid grace sits trembling in her eye, A."
Levine, P. Genius.
Lindsay, V. General William Booth Enters into Heaven.
Lovelace, R. Her Muffe.
MacNeice. Individualist Speaks, The.
Mei Yao Ch'en. On the Death of a New Born Child.
Millay, E. Love is not all: it is not meat nor drink.
Robinson, M. Temple of Chastity, The.
Sidney, P. Sonnet 72: "Desire, though thou my old companion art."
Smith, I. Glass of Water, The.
Vaiiunaite. Penelope.
Yang Shih-ch'i. White Stone Slope.

Pursuit
Crane, S. I SAW A MAN PURSUING THE HORIZON.
There was set before me a mighty hill.
Doolittle, H. Pursuit.
Eady. January.
Ignatow, D. Bagel, The.
Mallarmé. Between the reeds I saw their bodies gleam.
Rankin, J. Man is following me, A.
Silverstein, S. Slithergadee has crawled out of the sea, The.
Tahmisic. Red Moon High in the Sky.
Unknown. Run, Nigger, Run!

Pushers
Gunn, T. Street Song.

See also **Drug Addiction**
Pushkin, Aleksandr Sergeyevich
Akhmadulina. Again September, like the swarm of seasons past.
I Swear.
"Akhmatova." Pushkin.
Coles, D. Natalya Nikolayevna Goncharov.
"Samoylov." Pestel, the Poet, and Anna.
Terapiano. Lights shining above the Neva.

Pussy Willows
Unknown. Catkin.

Pygmalion
Marston, J. O gracious gods, take compassion.
Pigmalion, whose hie love-hating minde.
Ovid. *Pygmalion* off'ring, first, approach'd the Shrine.
Pygmalion seeing these to spend their times.
Pygmalion's Statue Comes to Life.

Pygmies
Graves, R. Ogres and Pygmies.

Pym, John
Drummond, W. On Pym.

Pyramids
Giovanni. Ego Tripping [(There May Be a Reason Why)].
Huy Cận. Talking With the Pyramid.
Mattawa. Pyramid of Khufu, The.

Pyramus and Thisbe
Cowley, A. Epitaph of Pyramus and Thisbe.
Donne. Pyramus and Thisbe.

Pythons
Belloc. Python I should not advise, A.

Q

Quail
Smith, W. Quail in Autumn.
Trowbridge, J. Idyl of Harvest Time, An.

Quakers. *See* **Friends, Society of**
Quarrels
Behn, A. Defiance, The.
Bekederemo. For Granny (from Hospital).
Besant, G. Telepathy.
Blaser. Suddenly.
"Carroll." "You are old," said the youth, "and your jaws are too weak."
Di Prima. Quarrel, The.
Dunn, S. He/She.
Frost, R. From Plane to Plane.
Goodman, M. Man and Wife.
Harte, B. Society Upon the Stanislaus, The.
Heard, J. Quarrel, The.
Hughes, L. Early Evening Quarrel.
"J., W." City Eclogue.
Jordan, J. Daddy at the stove or sink. Large.
Justice, D. But That Is Another Story.
Keech. Little Words.
Kharms. Beginning of a Beautiful Day (A Symphony), The.
Mayakovsky. Past one o'clock. You must have gone to bed.
Meredith, G. Modern Love.
Miyazawa Kenji. Tanka: "Red rag."
Mother Goose. Tweedledum and Tweedledee.
Muldoon, P. Sushi.
Nash, O. I Never Even Suggested It.
Okai. 999 Smiles.
Padilla. Song of the Juggler.
Paley, G. Quarrel.
Philips, K. On the 3. of September, 1651.
Phillips, S. Apparition, The.
Piatt, S. Her Word of Reproach.
Prince, F. Token, The.
Prior. To a Lady: She Refusing to Continue a Dispute with Me, and Leaving Me in the Argument.
Salom. Walking at Night.
Seth. Protocols.
Shakespeare, W. Sonnet 40.
Sonnet 120.
Stanley, T. Repulse, The.
To Celia Pleading Want of Merit.
Tao Tschung Yu. Quarrelling.
Thompson, P. After the Quarrel.
Domestic Storm, A.

Unknown. Catfish and Toad.
Cats of Kilkenny, The.
Coffee and Tea.
Jolly Pinder of Wakefield, The.
Two Little Kittens[, one stormy night].
Wallace, R. Wild Strawberries.
Warsh. Static, The.
Yi, S. Poem No. III.
Yukitsuna. Tanka: "Since puberty."

See also **Anger**
Quarries
Nicholson, N. Rockferns.
Rukeyser, M. Sand-Quarry with Moving Figures.

Quebec (city), Canada
Anderson, P. Houses Burning; Quebec.
Atwood. Disembarking at Quebec.
Ray, H. Quebec.

Quebec (province), Canada
Ashbery. On Autumn Lake.
Glassco. Quebec Farmhouse.
Gustafson, R. Wednesday at North Hatley.
Klein, A. Indian Reservation: Caughnawaga.
Rocking Chair, The.

Queen Anne's Lace
Williams, W. Queen-Anne's-Lace.

Queens
Angus. Alas! Poor Queen.
Beddoes. Bridal Song to Amala.
Campbell, D. Australian Dream, The.
"Carroll." Welcome Queen Alice.
Crosby, H. Telephone Directory.
Graves, R. Queen Mother to New Queen.
Housman, A. 1887.
Lawson, H. English Queen, The.
Levin, P. Lost Bee, The.
Newcastle, M. Courting the Faerie Queen.
Pfeiffer, E. Lost Light, The.
Ralegh, W. His Petition to Queen Anne of Denmark (1618).
If Cynthia be a queen, a princess, and supreme.
Sir Walter Ralegh to the Queen.
Robinson, M. Queen Bee, The.
Synge. Queens.
Unknown. I am Queen Anne, of whom 'tis said.
Lavender's Blue.
On Queen Caroline.
Queen Nefertiti.
Queen, Queen Caroline.
Wickham. Lament of the Red Knight.
Wotton, S. On His Mistress [*or* Mistris], the Queen of Bohemia.

See also Names of specific queens (e.g., **Elizabeth I, Queen of England**).

Questions
Auden. Question, The ("To ask the hard question is simple").
Beckett, S. What would I do without this world faceless incurious.
Browning, E. Sonnet: "My poet, thou canst touch on all the notes."
De la Mare. Last Chapter, The.
DiPalma. Prerogative of Lieder, The.
Dunbar, P. Mystery, The.
Duncan, R. Among my friends love is a great sorrow.
"Dylan." Blowin' in the Wind.
Ehrhart. To Those Who Have Gone Home Tired.
Eigner. In Imitation.
Emerson, R. Sphinx is drowsy, The.
Etherege. To a Lady Asking Him How Long He Would Love Her.
Hanzlik. Variation VI.
Herrick. Upon Love, by Way of Question and Answer.
Hoagland, T. Question, The.
Hoffenstein. Progress.
Howe, F. Set golden butter out in a dish.
Ignatow, D. For My Daughter in Reply to a Question.
Iwaszkiewicz. How Does the Negative Look. . . .
Johnson, A. Granny in de Market Place.

Mapanje. Another Fools' Day Touches Down: Shush.
Melville, H. Spirit appeared to me, and said, A.
Merriam, L. At the Door.
Morgenstern. Police Inquiry, The.
Newcastle, M. Discourse of Beasts, A.
Oppen. Gesture, The.
Patchen. Naked Land, The.
Piatt, S. Answering A Child.
Prince, F. Question, The.
Procter, A. Woman's Question, A.
Rumi. I have lived on the lip.
Salamun. Jonah.
Samio. Tanka: "Why does a room."
Sandburg, C. Who shall speak for the people?
Santayana. Cape Cod.
Shapiro, D. Dead Will Not Praise You, The.
Sholl. Catechism.
Sidney, P. Sonnet 31: "With how sad steps, O Moon, thou climb'st the skies!"
Sorrentino. Oranges Returned, The.
Zukofsky.
Unknown. Examination Question.
South Mount soaring high.
Will You Love Me When I'm Old?
Wallace-Crabbe. Binary.
Welburn. Whichway.
Williams, C. Question, The.
Wright, J. What the Earth Asked Me.

Quests
"Æ." Desire.
Browning, R. Childe Roland to the Dark Tower Came.
Camões. Rev'rend Father stood inculcating, The.
Graves, R. White Goddess, The.
Guiney. Wild Ride, The.
Guri. Odysseus.
Halkin, S. To Tarshish.
Hoffman, D. Exploration.
Hollo. Journey, 1966.
Lope de Vega Carpio. To-Morrow.
McWatt. Boat Builder, The.
Melville, H. Of Mortmain.
O'Grady, D. Tipperary.
O'Hara, F. Ode to Tanaquil Leclercq: "Smiling through my own memories of painful excitement your wide eyes."
"Platonov." Wanderer, The.
Poe. Eldorado.
Pound, E. Return, The.
Roethke. Journey to the Interior.
Rossetti, C. I do not look for love that is a dream.
Unknown. Loving Mad Tom.
Wonderful, this road to Cold Mountain.
Warren, R. Pursuit.
Whitman, W. Song of Myself.
Walt Whitman.
Wright, J. Quest, The.
Zuni Oral Tradition. Following their road of exit, they stooped over and came out.

Quilts and Quilting
Acosta. My Mother Pieced Quilts.
Beer, P. In a Country Museum.
Bruce, D. Sonnet 4: "Wet streets, black trees, a gold leaf smacked."
Dixon, M. Aunt Ida Pieces a Quilt.
Fleming, E. Patchwork Quilt, The.
McPherson, S. Quilt of Rights.
Peirce. Quilts.
Rich, A. Aunt Jennifer's tigers prance across a screen.
Smith, D. Quilt in the Bennington College Library, A.
Ward, J. Comfort-Maker.

Quince Trees and Quinces
Antiphilus. Quince Preserved through the Winter, Given to a Lady, A.
Ni Dhomhnaill. As for the Quince.

Quotidian
Blamire. Epistle to Her Friends at Gartmore.
Child, A. Wishes.
Crowell, G. I have found such joy in simple things.
Unknown. Little Things.

R

Rabbis
Bloch, C. White Petticoats.
Glatstein. Bratzlav Rabbi to His Scribe, The.
Klein, A. Baal Shem Tov.
Rabbi Yom-Tob of Mayence Petitions His God.

Rabbits
Allen, M. What Is It?
Bradley, C. Skippets, the Bad One.
Brownjohn. We are going to see the rabbit.
Cassian. rabbit, The.
Clare, J. Hares at Play.
Coatsworth. Song of the Rabbits outside the Tavern, The.
Cowper, W. My Pet Hare.
Gould, E. My New Rabbit.
King, E. Rabbit, The.
Kirby, J. Timid Bunnies.
Larkin, P. Myxomatosis.
Levertov. Springtime, The.
Li K'ai-hsien. Meeting Trappers on the Road in Heavy Snow.
Night of the Seventeenth, The.
McKuen. Thoughts on Capital Punishment.
Milosz, C. Encounter.
Moore, L. Again.
Richards, I. Warhead Wakes.
Roberts, E. Rabbit, The.
Skrzynecki. Hunting Rabbits.
Stephens, J. Snare, The.
Stevens, W. Rabbit Is King of the Ghosts, A.
Stevenson, A. Giving Rabbit to My Cat Bonnie.
Stone, P. Topsy-Turvy Land.
Unknown. Big Rabbit goes to see his baby.
Bunny Rabbit.
Rabbit goes soft-foot, pheasant's caught.
Railroad Section Leader's Song.
Voigt. At the Edge of Winter.
Walsh, J. White Rabbit, The.

See also **Hares**

Raccoons
Bertolino. Coons, The.
Rexroth, K. Racoon.
Whittemore, R. Science Fiction.

Rachel (Bible)
Burns, R. Patriarch, The.
Ravikovitch. Like Rachel.
"Yehoash." At the Tomb of Rachel.

Rachmaninov, Sergei
Carruth, H. Freedom and Discipline.
O'Hara, F. On Rachmaninoff's Birthday.

Racial Prejudice
Agard, J. Half-caste.
Allen, H. Upstairs Downstairs.
Allen, L. I Fight Back.
Allen, S. Moment Please, A.
Anzaldúa. We Call Them Greasers.
Awoonor. American Memory of Africa, An.
Baldwin, J. Lover's Question, A.
Blake, W. Little Black Boy, The.
Boyle, K. Communication to Nancy Cunard, A.
Brooks, G. Ballad of Rudolph Reed, The.
Bronzeville Woman in a Red Hat.
Riot.
Rites for Cousin Vit, The.
Brown, S. Crispus Attucks McCoy.
Old Lem.
Sam Smiley.
Slim Greer.
Southern Cop.
Browning, E. Runaway Slave at Pilgrim's Point, The.
Burroughs, M. Everybody but Me.
Cataldi. Advice.
Cervantes. Poem for the Young White Man Who Asked Me How I, An Intelligent, Well-Read Person Could Believe in the War Between Races.
Clifton, L. Bodies broken on, The.
Cobb, A. Searching, The.
Cofer. What the Gypsy Said to Her Children.
Coleman, W. Emmett Till.

Cornish, S. Montgomery.
Corrothers. At the Closed Gate of Justice.
Cullen, C. For a Lady I Know.
Incident.
Tableau.
Uncle Jim.
Dale, L. Prejudice against Colour.
Damas. S.O.S.
Sleepless Night.
So often my feeling of race.
Whitewash.
Diop, D. Time of Martyrdom, The.
Durham. Justiniano Lamé Has Been Killed.
Emanuel, J. Old Black Men Say.
Greenfield, F. Oh God Forbid.
Hacker, M. 1973.
Harper, M. American History.
Goin' to the Territory.
Grandfather.
Harris, W. Daddy Poem, A.
Hemphill. Cordon Negro.
Family Jewels.
Horne, F. On Seeing Two Brown Boys in a Catholic Church.
Hughes, L. Backlash Blues, The.
Children's Rhymes.
Cross.
Dream Boogie.
Island.
Merry-Go-Round.
Ultimatum: Kid to Kid.
Where? When? Which?
Inada. Projected Scenario of a Performance to Be Given Before the UN.
Jacinto, A. Monangamba.
Johnson, G. Prejudice.
Jones, G. Tripart.
Jordan, J. Poem About My Rights.
What Would I Do White?
Kelen. Rabbit Shoeshine.
Khaketla, N. White and the Black, The.
Klein, A. *In re* Solomon Warshawer.
Leonard, T. On Knowing the Difference Between Prejudice, Discrimination, and Oppression.
Lorde. Power.
Revolution Is One Form of Social Change.
"MacDiarmid." With the Herring Fishers.
Major, C. Vietnam #4.
Mapanje. At the Metro: Old Irrelevant Images.
Marson. Kinky Hair Blues.
Politeness.
McElroy, C. Foul Line—1987.
McKay, C. Tiger.
White House, The.
Mnthan. My Father.
Moss, T. Interpretation of a Poem by Frost.
Neto. Farewell at the Moment of Parting.
Ortiz. Creation.
Patchen. Nice Day for a Lynching.
Quigless. Moving.
Randall, D. Black Poet, White Critic.
Melting Pot, The.
Ross, A. In Bloemfontein.
Small, A. There's Somethin'.
Smith, A. Roslyn Malamud the Coup.
Soyinka. Telephone Conversation.
Trejo. Cloud Unfolding, The.
U Tam'si Tchicaya. I am no longer master of my tears.
Mat to Weave, A.
Unknown. Learn to Count.
Scottsboro.
Walcott. Blues.
Gulf, The.
Walker, A. It is true--/ I've always loved.
Waller, T. *et al.* (What Did I Do to Be So) Black and Blue?
Ward, J. Don't Be Fourteen (In Mississippi).
Welch, J. Harlem, Montana.
Williams, C. Racists.
Wong, N. When I Was Growing Up.
Young, A. Dance for Militant Dilettantes, A.
Poem for Players, A.

See also **Apartheid; Racism and Racists**

Racing and Racers. *See* **Horse Racing; Track Athletics**

Racism and Racists
Alexander, E. Boston Year.
  Ladders.
Alexie. On the Amtrak from Boston to New York City.
Allen, S. Moment Please, A.
"Alta." Yr eyes dark and aware.
Aubert, A. Opposite of Green, The.
Baraka. Nation Is Like Ouselves, The.
  Wise 5.
Black, I. Racist Psychotherapy.
Blake, W. Little Black Boy, The.
Booth, P. Stations.
Brooks, G. Ballad of Rudolph Reed, The.
  Bronzeville Mother Loiters in Mississippi. / Meanwhile, a Mississippi Mother Burns Bacon.
  Bronzeville Woman in a Red Hat.
  Chicago *Defender* Sends a Man to Little Rock, The.
  "Negro" Hero.
  White Troops Had Their Orders but the Negroes Looked Like Men.
Brown, S. Bitter Fruit of the Tree.
  Slim in Atlanta.
  Strong Men.
Brutus. Off to Philadelphia in the morning.
Bryant, F. Cathexis.
Campbell, J. Pariah, The.
Cervantes. Poem for the Young White Man Who Asked Me How I, An Intelligent, Well-Read Person Could Believe in the War Between Races.
  Poema para los Californios Muertos.
Chin. Portrait of the Self as Nation, 1990–1991, A.
Chinn. Not Translation, Not Poetry.
  Skin Color from the Sun.
Clarke, C. Hair: A Narrative.
  San Juan: 1979.
Coffin, F. Ajax' Conclusion.
Coleman, W. Dear Mama (2).
  Women of my Color.
Cornish, S. His Fingers Seem to Sing.
Cortez. Give me the Red on the Black of the Bullet (for Claude Reece Jr.)
  Rape.
Cullen, C. Incident.
  Uncle Jim.
Cummings, E. YgUDuh / ydoan / yunnuhstan.
Daniels, J. Time, Temperature.
Daniels, K. Bus Ride.
Davidson, D. Sequel of Appomattox.
Davis, D. Nigger's Got to Go, De.
Derricotte. Note on my Son's Face, A.
  On the Turning Up of Unidentified Black Female Corpses.
Dove, R. Arrow.
  Elevator Man, 1949.
  Great Palaces of Versailles, The.
Dunbar, P. Harriet Beecher Stowe.
Eady. False Arrest.
  Sherbet.
  Song.
  Thrift.
  William Carlos Williams.
Espada. Niggerlips was the high school name / for me.
  Rednecks.
  Sleeping on the Bus.
Forbes, C. Poet's Shuffle, The.
Ford, C. Plaint.
Fortune. Bartow Black.
Garcia. Salmo: Para El.
Gibbons, R. White Beach.
Giscombe. (1962 at the edge of town).
Glancy. First Reader Santee Training School, 1873, The.
Goldensohn, B. American Innocents, Oberlin, Ohio, 1954.
Griffin, S. I like to think of Harriet Tubman.
Hairston. Alabama Bus.
Harjo, J. Strange Fruit.

Harper, M. American History.
  Nightmare Begins Responsibility.
Harris, C. Policeman Cleared in Jaywalking Case.
Harris, W. Daddy Poem, A.
Harte, B. Plain Language from Truthful James.
  Truthful James to the Editor.
Hayden, R. &[;American Journal&];.
  Frederick Douglass.
  Monet's "Waterlilies."
  'Mystery Boy' Looks for Kin in Nashville.
Heard, J. Black Sampson, The.
Hemphill. Family Jewels.
Henderson-Holmes. To Hell and Back, with Cake.
Hill, L. Tuskegee.
Holman, M. Mr. Z.
Housman, A. Harlem.
Hughes, L. As I Grew Older.
  Ballad of the Landlord.
  Children's Rhymes.
  Comment on Curb.
  Cross.
  Dinner Guest: Me.
  Dream Boogie: Variation.
  Freedom Train.
  Good morning, daddy!
  Harlem.
  I too, sing America.
  Island.
  Jim Crow Car.
  Lincoln Monument: Washington.
  Mulatto.
  Notes on the Broadway Theatre.
  Parade.
  Porter.
  Same in Blues.
  Song for a Dark Girl.
  Tell Me.
  Theme for English B.
  Ultimatum: Kid to Kid.
Ignatow, D. Harold.
Iman. Love Your Enemy.
Iverem. Keeper.
Jackson, R. Lonely Affair, A.
Johnson, J. Color Sergeant, The.
Jordan, J. 1977: Poem for Mrs. Fannie Lou Hamer.
  Poem Against the State (Of Things): 1975.
Joseph, L. Sand Nigger.
Kay, J. Photo in the Locket.
Kizer, C. Race Relations.
Klepfisz. About My Father.
Knight, E. Hard Rock Returns to Prison from the Hospital for the Criminal Insane.
Knott. (Poem) (Chicago) (The Were-Age).
Komunyakaa. Untitled Blues.
Leonard, T. And their judges spoke with one dialect.
Levertov. Long Way Round, The.
Lorde. Afterimages.
  For the Record.
  Suffer the Children.
Madgett. Race Question, The.
Madhubuti. Don't Cry, Scream.
  My brothers i will not tell you.
Maunick. Letter to Ellen Conroy Kennedy.
McElroy, C. Ghost-Who-Walks, The.
McKay, C. Lynching, The.
  White House, The.
Morris, M. To an Expatriate Friend.
Moss, T. Lunchcounter Freedom.
Mura. Argument: on 1942, An.
Ologboni. Changed Mind (or the Day I Woke Up).
Parker, P. My lady ain't no lady.
Parkerson. Statistic.
Paterson, E. Dispossessed.
  Tribal Homeland.
Randall, D. Idiot, The.
  Melting Pot, The.
Randall, J. When Something Happens.
Rankine. New Windows.
Redmond. Love Necessitates.
Reed, I. Jacket Notes.
  Railroad Bill, a conjure man.

Rich, A. Frame.
Ridge, L. I room at Sodos'—in the little green room.
Rose, P. Wind Debates Asian Immigration, The.
Sanchez, S. Right On: White America.
Shoaf. Birmingham, 1962.
Skeeter. Midwest, Midcentury.
Small, A. What abou' de Law?
Smith, P. Blonde White Women.
Soto. Fair Trade.
Spellman. When Black People Are.
Stafford, W. Serving with Gideon.
Stein, J. Grand Tradition of Western Culture, The.
Thompson, C. Uncle Rube on the Race Problem.
  Uncle Rube to the Young People.
Toomer. People.
Travis, N. Sunbathing.
Unger, B. Pillar of Flame.
Unknown. Concert's what the English like, A.
Uyematsu. December 7 always brings christmas early.
Villalongo. In the Good Old U. S. A.
Wade-Gayles. Inquisition.
Walcott. Blues.
  Glory Trumpeter, The.
Walker, A. Thing Itself, The.
Walker, M. For my people [everywhere singing their slave songs repeatedly: their].
  Since 1619.
Waniek, M. Alderman.
  Ballad of Aunt Geneva, The.
  Diverne's Waltz.
Washington. Moon Bound.
Wayman. Hating Jews.
Weaver, M. Borders.
  Picnic, an Homage to Civil Rights, The.
Welch, J. Harlem, Montana.
Whitman, A. Is manhood less because man's face is black?
Williams, W. Impromptu: The Suckers.
Winner, R. Segregated Railway Diner—1946.
Wright, J. On a Phrase from Southern Ohio.
Wright, R. Between the World and Me.
Yamanaka. Yarn Wig.
Young, K. Field Trip.
  No Offense.

See also **Racial Prejudice**

Radcliffe, James, 3d Earl of Derwentwater
Unknown. Lord Derwentwater.

Radiation and Radiation Sickness
Thiele, C. Radiation Victim.

See also **Nuclear Accidents; Nuclear War**

Radio
Baraka. In Memory of Radio.
  Major Bowes' Diary.
  SOS.
Bennett, R. Wireless.
Cokinos. Short-Wave.
Fogarty. No Grudge.
Hoffenstein. Mr. Vachel Lindsay Discovers Radio.
Marais. Radio Cradle-song.
O'Hara, F. Radio.
Page, G. Late Night Radio.
Rutsala. War of the Worlds, The.
Sherlock. Dinner Party 1940.
Taylor, H. Speech.
Thorne, T. Whatever Happened to Conway Twitty?
Whittemore, R. Radio under the Bed, The.
Wojahn. Homage: Light from the Hall.
Zagajewski. Electric Elegy.

Radishes
Bodecker. Radish is / the only dish, The.
Issa. Man pulling radishes, The.
Piercy. Vegetable Love.

Raftery, Anthony
Alexander, A. For Raftery.

Ragworts
Stevenson, A. Ragwort.

Railroad Wrecks
Carruth, H. Wreck of the Circus Train, The.
George, D. Wreck of the Old 97.

Hedin, R. Wreck of the Great Northern, The.
Hummer, T. Train Wreck, 1890: My Grandmother Lies Down with the Dead.
Moore, J. Ashtabula Disaster, The.
Nims, J. Trainwrecked Soldiers.
Unknown. Casey Jones.
 Wreck of the Royal Palm, The.
Wright, C. Dog Creek Mainline.

Railroads
Ashbery. Melodic Trains.
Betjeman. Great Central Railway, Sheffield Victoria to Banbury.
 Metropolitan Railway, The.
Booth, P. Crossing.
 Stations.
Broonzy. Southern Blues, The.
Brown, S. Call Boy.
 Long Track Blues.
 Southern Road.
Buckley, C. Train in the Desert—1916.
Carr, L. How Long Blues.
Casey, T. Drill, Ye Tarriers, Drill.
Collier, M. North Corridor.
Conyus. Six Ten Sixty-Nine.
Cooper, J. Wanda's Blues.
Cornford, F. Parting in Wartime.
Cranch. Locomotive, The.
Crane, H. River, The.
Craveirinha. Three Dimensions.
Delmore Brothers. Wabash Cannonball, The.
Dickey, J. Folk Singer of the Thirties, A.
Dickinson, E. I like to see it lap the Miles.
Eiseley. And as for Man.
Ezekiel. When the female railway clerk.
Francis, R. Night Train.
Frost, R. On the Heart's Beginning to Cloud the Mind.
Galvin, B. For a Daughter Gone Away.
Gibbons, R. American Trains.
Gioia. In Cheever Country.
Glück, L. Departure.
Greenberg, A. Freight Train, Freight Train.
Hall, D. Sister on the Tracks, A.
Hanzlicek, C. Last Trains, The.
Heaney, S. Railway Children, The.
Hope, A. Observation Car.
Hudgins. Southern Crescent Was on time, The.
Hughes, L. Homesick Blues.
Jackson, M. Red Flag, The.
James, E. Sunnyland.
Jefferson, B. Easy Rider Blues.
Jones, R. Trouble in mind, I'm blue.
Justice, D. Train.
Khlebnikov, O. From three sources, / vital sources flowing in dull shades of red.
Lattimore. Note on the L and N.
Leadbelly. Midnight Special, The.
Lindsay, V. Flower-fed buffaloes of the spring, The.
MacLeish. Burying Ground by the Ties.
 Grazing Locomotives.
Merwin, W. Wheels of the Trains, The.
Monroe, B. In the Pines.
Nash, O. Riding on a Railroad Train.
Nemerov. Low-Level Cross-Country.
Nims, J. Freight.
Parini. Coal Train.
Pasternak, B. On Early Trains.
Peacocke. Railway Allotments.
Plumly. For Esther.
Reed, I. Railroad Bill, a conjure man.
Roethke. Night Journey.
Rukeyser, M. Campaign.
Sandburg, C. Caboose Thoughts.
 Child of the Romans.
 Jack was a swarthy, swaggering son-of-a-gun.
 Southern Pacific.
 Work Gangs.
Seibert. Casey Jones.
Shapiro, K. Terminal.
Sissman. Big Rock-Candy Mountain, The.
Slessor. Last Trams.
Soto. Who Will Know Us?
Stafford, W. Observation Car and Cigar.
Swenson, M. Written While Riding the Long Island Rail Road.

Thoreau. What's the Railroad to Me?
Troupe. In Texas Grass.
Unknown. Beulah Railway, The.
 Calling Trains.
 Can't You Line It?
 Casey Jones.
 Echo Canyon.
 Hallelujah, I'm a Bum.
 Henry K. Sawyer.
 Jay Gould's Daughter.
 Jerry, Go an' Ile That Car.
 John Henry was a lil [or little] baby.
 Old Section Boss, The.
 Poor Paddy Works on the Railway.
 Railroad Bill, Railroad Bill.
 Railroad Blues, The.
 Railroad Cars Are Coming, The.
 Railroad Man for Me, A.
 Railroad Section Leader's Song.
 Rock Island Line, The.
 Tamping Ties ("Tamp 'em up solid").
 Utah Iron Horse, The.
 Way Out in Idaho.
 When John Henry was a little babe.
 Working on the Railway.
 Wreck of the Royal Palm, The.
Van Doren. Dream of Trains, A.
Warren, R. Ballad: Between the Boxcars.
Whitman, W. To a Locomotive in Winter.
Wilbur. In the Smoking-Car.
 Stop.
Wojahn. "Mystery Train" Janis Joplin Leaves Port Arthur for Points West, 1964.
Wordsworth, W. Steamboats, Viaducts and Railways.
Wright, C. Dog Creek Mainline.
Wright, J. Outside Fargo, North Dakota.
 Poem Written under an Archway in a Discontinued Railroad Station, Fargo, North Dakota, A.
Young, D. Boxcar Poem, The ("Boxcars drift by / clanking, The").

See also **Trains; Locomotives**

Railway Stations
Eberhart, R. Analogue of Unity in Multeity.
Fontanella. Victoria Station.
Hughes, L. Pennsylvania Station in New York, The.
Loseff. Reading Milosz.
Nicholson, N. Ravenglass Railway Station, Cumberland.
Smith, D. Cumberland Station.
 Looking for the Melungeon.
Thomas, E. Adlestrop.
Wilbur. Stop.
Wright, J. Poem Written under an Archway in a Discontinued Railroad Station, Fargo, North Dakota, A.

Railway Travel
Ashbery. Leaving the Atocha Station.
Barnes, W. An' while I went 'ithin a train.
De la Mare. Railway Junction, The.
Handy, W. Yellow Dog Blues.
Hardy, T. Faintheart in a Railway Train.
Jarrell. Orient Express, The.
Joshi. Passing through Rajasthan.
Nash, O. Riding on a Railroad Train.
Piatt, J. Taking the Night-Train.
Slessor. Night-Ride, The.
Stevenson, R. From a Railway Carriage.
Wilbur. In the Smoking-Car.

Rain
Acton, H. Beads of spring rain.
Akhmadulina. Fairy Tale about Rain, A.
"Akhmatova." Lord is not merciful to reapers and gardeners, The.
Alexandru. Prayer.
Amann. Billboards.
Apache Oral Tradition. Now you will feel no rain.
Apollinaire. It's Raining.
Aridjis. Rain is Falling, The.
Banus. Eighteen.
Bates, C. Who Likes the Rain?
Bekederemo. Night Rain.
Benét, S. Rain after a Vaudeville Show.

Bishop, E. Sestina: "September rain falls on the house."
Blandiana. Dance in the Rain.
Bly, R. August Rain.
Bodecker. Small Rains.
Boldman. I hammer a nail.
Bontemps. Return, The.
Borson. Rain.
Bowen, C. Rain it raineth all around, The.
Boyle, K. Thunderstorm in South Dakota.
Brecht, B. When Evil-Doing Comes Like Falling Rain.
Brickley. Autumn rain—.
 Puppet, The.
Brock-Broido. Carrowmore.
Brock, V. Man in the Rain, The.
Browne, J. Little Raindrops.
Bunin. Endless downpour; misty wood.
Burke, M. Rainy winter evening.
Cattanar. What He Said to his charioteer, on his way back.
Cavalli. Rain brings me back, The.
Chang Yü. Quatrain: "At this remote village, I have no neighbors."
Charles, D. Bang! the starter's gun—.
Ch'ien Ch'ien-i. Poem Written During a Dream on the Twenty-Third Day of the Intercalary [Month After The] Fourth [Month].
Chu. Sound of Rain, The.
Clare, J. Sudden Shower.
Clark, T. You (I).
Clifton, H. Monsoon Girl.
Coatsworth. What Could Be Lovelier than to Hear.
Collins, M. To F. C.
Cooper, J. Morning on the St. John's.
Crawford, R. Rain.
Creeley. Rain, The.
Cullen, C. Night Rain.
Cummings, E. Now comes the good rain farmers pray for(and).
D'Annunzio. Rain in the Pine Wood.
Davies, H. Poem: "In the stump of the old tree, where the heart has rotted out."
Davies, W. Rain, The.
Dharmaraj. Full of rain, the word.
Dickinson, E. Like Rain it sounded till it curved.
DiPasquale. Rain.
Dipoko. Exile.
Dobbie. Things Grow Up out of the Dark.
Dodd, W. Of Rain and Air.
Dransfield. Rainpoem.
Dudley, M. Lulling me to sleep.
Duggan, L. South Coast Haiku.
Edwards, R. Rain, The.
Eigner. If you weep, I think that.
Evans, M. Rain.
"Field." Lo, my loved is dying, and the call.
Foix. When I Sleep, Then I See Clearly.
Fu Hsien. Ruinous Rains.
Gallagher, T. Sudden Journey.
Gates, L. On the jewelweed.
Gilbo'a. Rain Falls and Floods.
 Watchful Wakeful.
 With the Rain.
Goldberg, B. Monsoon.
Gonzales, R. South Texas Summer Rain.
Goodison. Keith Jarrett—Rainmaker.
Gorman, L. I hear her sew.
Graves, R. For the Rain It Raineth Every Day.
Haas, R. Rain mixed with sleet.
Haines, J. Cloud Factory, The.
Hall, D. Pluvia.
Hardy, T. Rain on a Grave.
 Thunderstorm in Town, A.
 Weathers [or Weather].
Harter. Winter rain.
Harwood, L. Soft White.
Hass, R. Spring Rain.
Hassett. Thanksgiving.
Henson, L. Rain.
Heyen. Passover: the Injections.
Higginson, W. This spring rain.
Ho Ching-ming. Alone I stand, facing the

flowers' shade.
Rainy Night.
Hooper, V. Argument for Resurrection.
Hotham. This loneliness.
Hoyt, C. In that lightning flash.
Hsü Wei. Buddhist Monk Cut and Burned His Own Flesh to Make The Rains Stop—A Man From His Native Place Asked Me to Write a Poem to Send to Him, A.
Hughes, L. April Rain Song.
In time of silver rain.
Strange Hurt.
Hughes, T. Heptonstall.
Jacobs, H. It is not just.
Jenner, E. Signs of Rain.
Jewell. Fall wind in pinyons.
Johnson, H. Invocation: "Let me be buried in the rain."
Jones, R. Front Window, The.
K'ang Hai. Dreaming of Master Chung-lu.
Listening to the Rain.
Kao Ch'i. Lying at Leisure during Rain.
Kapilar. What Her Friend Said to Her, before the Rains.
Kees. Wet Thursday.
Kenyon, J. August Rain, after Haying.
Kerouac. Birds singing.
Keyser. Rainy summer night.
Kgositsile. Gods Wrote, The.
Kinnell. Under the Maud Moon.
Komunyakaa. After the Fall of Saigon.
Kooser. At the Office Early.
Kung Tzu-chen. Miscellanies of the Year Chi-hai.
Tune: "Butterflies Lingering over Flowers."
Kunze, R. Refuge Even Beyond Refuge.
Kuzmin. What rain! / Our sail is drenched.
Lane, P. Rain Ditch.
Larkin, P. Card-Players, The.
Whitsun Weddings, The.
Laughlin, J. Then and Now.
Lecount. Bridge toll-booth—, The.
Lee, B. Rain.
Levertov. Way Through, The.
Levine, P. Rain Downriver.
Lewis, A. All day it has rained, and we on the edge of the moors.
Li Ch'ing-chao. Day of Cold Food, The.
Li Tung-yang. Inscribed on the Painting "Meaning of a Poem by Wang Wei."
Trip to Yüeh-lu Temple, A.
Libbey. Spring And.
Livesay, D. Green Rain.
Livingston, M. Cried a man on the Salisbury Plain.
Longfellow, H. Rain in Summer.
Loveman. (April Rain).
Low, P. Wet Weather.
Lowell, A. Shower, A.
Summer Rain.
Lyles. Summer night.
Macdonald, G. Sweet Peril.
Machi. Tanka: "Gazing upwards."
Maclean, A. Rain, The.
MacNeice. Glass Falling.
June Thunder.
London Rain.
Mahadevi. It was like a stream.
Mahon. Kinsale.
Marais. Dance of the Rain, The.
Masaoka Shiki. Tanka: "Illuminated."
View of my garden, A.
McAuley, J. Wet Day.
McCarthy, G. Hooded Legion, The.
McClintock, M. Dead cat.
Drizzling rain, A.
While we wait.
McCord, D. Summer Shower.
To Walk in Warm Rain.
McCrae, H. Song of the Rain.
McCrea. Rain.
Merriam, E. Weather.
Merrill, J. Childlessness.
Merwin, W. Rain Travel.
What is a Garden.
Meynell, A. Rainy Summer, The.
Milosz, C. After Paradise.

Mitchell, K. Night Rain.
Mori Ōgai. Tanka: "But for the dew."
Tanka: "During a break."
Morris, W. Haystack in the Floods, The.
Thunder in the Garden.
Mother Goose. Rain, rain, go to Spain.
Mountain, M. Pig and i spring rain.
Rain.
Seed catalog in the mailbox cold drizzle.
Mpondo. Season of the rains, The.
Mullins, B. At the Lakehouse.
Muske. Little L.A. Villanelle.
Myles, E. New England Wind.
Na-lan Hsing-te. Tune: "Autumn Waters"— Listening to Rain.
Nahuatl Oral Tradition. Song for the Festival of Tlaloc, the Rain God.
Nichols, G. I am the rain.
Nims, J. Philosopher.
Nordbrandt. China Observed Through Greek Rain in Turkish Coffee.
Nyka-Niliunas. Theology of Rain.
Oliver, M. Rain in Ohio.
Page, P. Stories of Snow.
Pasternak, B. Hops.
Weeping Garden, The.
Patchen. Biography of Southern Rain.
Persand. Rain Storm.
Pessoa. [Poem 2]: "Inside, the church lights up today's rain."
Petri. Night Song of the Personal Shadow.
Peyanar. What He Said ("As wild oxen bellowed").
What He Said ("Because peacocks moved like you").
What He Said ("In this time of rain and thunder").
Plomer. Seven Rainy Months.
Po Chü-i. Pine-trees in the Courtyard, The.
Rain.
Prévert. Barbara.
Barbara remember.
Pyon. Spring Rain.
Rankin, J. Old Circles.
Raworth. Hot Day at the Races.
Ray, H. Voices of the Rain.
Rice, H. Legend of the raindrop, The.
Robinson, A. Song: "Oh for the wings of a dove."
Robinson, R. Jarrangulli.
Roseliep. Blind man's, The.
Rain.
Rotella, A. From her neon window.
Surrendering to a rain-washed stone.
Russell, N. Message of the Rain, The.
Saitō Mokichi. Tanka: "Yolk, The."
Sappho. Cool Retreat, A.
Schwartz, D. Dark and Falling Summer, The.
Seifert. It was afternoon or later.
Shakespeare, W. Song: "When that I was and a little tiny boy."
Shapiro, D. Sentences.
Shea, M. Warehouse-theatre's.
Shelley, P. Cloud, The.
Shen Chou. Paying a Sick-call to Yao Ts'un-tao in the Rain.
Shepherd, R. Where When Was.
Shibafune. In the spring evening.
Shūji. During the rainy season.
Tanka: "After rainfall."
Sitwell, D. Mauve summer rain, The.
Song: "We are the darkness in the heat of the day."
Skinner, K. Cold Irish Earth, The.
Smelyakov. Dancing, phosphorescent drops.
Southard. Patter of rain, A.
Southwick. Rain's Marriage, The.
Soyinka. I think it rains.
Spiess. Lean-to of tin.
Spires. Good Friday. Driving Weekend.
Stanley-Wrench. Storm, The.
Stevens, W. Room on a Garden, A.
Stevenson, R. Rain is raining all around, The.
Stickney, T. Melancholy year is dead with rain, The.
Stidger. I Saw God Wash the World.
Su Tung-p'o. Days of Rain; the Rivers Have

Overflowed.
In a Boat, Getting Up at Night.
Looking from the Pavilion Over the Lake.
Rain in the Aspens.
Tune: Partridge Sky.
Tune: Sand of Silk-washing Stream ("Layer on layer of hemp leaves, jute leaves shining").
Tune: Sand of Silk-washing Stream ("Soft grasses, a plain of sedge fresh with passing rain").
Swenson, C. Line.
Swenson, M. Rain at Wildwood.
Swift, J. Description of a City Shower, A.
T'ang Hsien-tsu. Hsiu-chou.
Tao-chi. Flower-Rain Terrace, The.
T'ao Ch'ien. Motionless Clouds.
Taylor, E. Address to the Soul Occasioned by a Rain, An.
Thomas, E. It Rains ("It rains, and nothing stirs within the fence").
Like the Touch of Rain [she was].
Rain, midnight rain, nothing but the wild rain.
Thompson, I. Rainy Nights.
Tico. Tinkle of chimes, The.
Tillinghast, R. Summer rain, and the voices of children.
Tranströmer. Man Awakened by a Song Above His Roof, The.
Tu Fu. Clear After Rain.
Light rain doesn't slick the road.
Spring Night, A—Rejoicing in Rain.
This southern rain nourishes the mossy stones.
Unknown. Daisies and Grasses.
Dance of the Rain Gods.
Doctor Foster went to Gloucester.
Inky, dinky spider.
It's raining, it's pouring.
Little waist, blow on the hilltop.
March winds and April showers.
Mocking-Bird's Song, The.
Rain on the green grass.
Rain, rain, go away.
Riddle: "Round the house and round the house / and there lies a black glove in the window."
Song for the Sun That Disappeared behind the Rainclouds.
Song of the Rain Chant.
St. Swithin's Day, if thou dost rain.
Van den Heuvel. Raining at every window.
Shading his eyes.
Vaughan, H. Showre, The.
Very. Hath the Rain a Father?
Latter rain, it falls in anxious haste, The.
Winter Rain, The.
Virgil. Promised rain, The.
Virgil. Rainy day, A.
Wang Shih-chieng. After Rain, Visiting the Temple of Heavenly Peace.
Mooring at Night at Kao-yu.
Wang Wei. After Long Rain.
Warren, R. Vermont Ballad: Change of Season.
Warsh. Suicide Rates, The.
Watson, R. Ballad of the Were-Wolf, A.
Webb, M. Green Rain.
Weil, Z. From My Window.
Welish. Crossing Disappearing behind Them.
Wen Cheng-ming. On First Returning from Taking the Examinations: Feelings at Cloud-Stop Pavilion.
Weöres. Rain's pounding away, The.
Wesley-Smith. Cavendish McKellar.
Wevill. Monsoon.
Wilbur. My Father Paints the Summer.
Williams, W. Red Wheelbarrow, The.
Willmot. May rain.
Wills, J. Rain in gusts.
Wordsworth, W. Written in March [While Resting on the Bridge at the Foot of Brother's Water].
Wright, C. This Couple.
Wright, J. Living by the Red River.
Wright, K. City Rain.
Yang Chi. On Seeing a Firefly in My Room.
Studio for Listening to the Snow, The.
Yang Shen. To the Tune "Song of the Plum

Blossom at the River Town."
To the Tune "Yellow Oriole" ("Threads of rain weave lambent light").
Yang Shih-ch'i. Dawn: Clear Skies.
Night Rain: A Wall Collapses—Sent To My Neighbors.
Yarrow. Warm rain before dawn.
Yoshimi. Tanka: "Along a street."
Tanka: "Gloomy rain."
Yü Chi. Sitting Alone in the Courtyard.
Yüan Mei. Rains pass, the mountains' face is washed.
Things Seen on Spring Days.
Yukitsuna. Tanka: "Plaintive, A."
Yün Shou-p'ing. Green Banana Leaves.
Zuni Oral Tradition. Invocation to the U'wannami (Rain-Makers).

Rainbows
Baugh, E. Colour-Scheme.
Birney. Bushed.
Dacey, P. Prisms.
Davies, W. Great Time, A.
De la Mare. Rainbow, The.
Dickinson, E. Delight is as the flight.
Dunbar, P. Place Where the Rainbow Ends, The.
Herrick. Rainbow; or Curious Covenant, The.
Hopkins, G. Rainbow, The.
Lawrence, D. Rainbow, The.
Littlebird. In a Double Rainbow.
"MacDiarmid." Watergaw, The.
Patmore, C. Rainbow, The.
Rossetti, C. Rainbow, The.
Rotella, A. Rainbow, A.
Southard. This morning's rainbow.
Strong, L. Door, The.
Turner, C. Drowned Spaniel, The.
Unknown. If there be a rainbow in the eve.
Rainbow i'th'morning.
Rainbow, rainbow.
Song for the Sun That Disappeared behind the Rainclouds.
Vaughan, H. Rainbow, The.
Wordsworth, W. My heart leaps up when I behold.
Wright, J. Legend.
Yang Chi. Poem on Passing by Hsin-k'ai Lake at Kao-yu in Light Rain, A.

Rainey, Gertrude ("Ma")
Brown, S. Ma Rainey.
Okantah. Southern Road.
Young, A. Dance For Ma Rainey, A.

Ralegh, Sir Walter
Elizabeth I. Ah silly pugg wert thou so sore afraid.
King, H. Elegy upon S[ir] W[alter] R[aleigh], An.
Lowell, R. Lady Ralegh's Lament.
Unknown. On Sir Walter Rawleigh at His Execution.

Rameau, Jean Philippe
Symons, A. On an Air of Rameau.

Rameses II, King of Egypt
Shelley, P. Ozymandias [of Egypt].
Unknown. In the days of old Rameses, are you on, are you on?

Rams. *See* **Sheep**

Ranches
Galvin, J. Western Civilization.
Haste. Wind, The.
Hugo, R. Montana Ranch Abandoned.

Rape
Acholonu. Other Forms of Slaughter.
Adamson. Rimbaud Having a Bath.
Alexander, E. Kevin of the N.E. Crew.
Avicolli. Rape Poem, The.
Barker, G. O Golden Fleece ("O Golden Fleece she is where she lies tonight").
Bowes-Lyon. Leda.
Bridges. Lisa's Ritual, Age 10.
Chao Meng-fu. Poem of Prefectural Judge Yang T'ien-jui Righting a Wrong.
Chin. Portrait of the Self as Nation, 1990–1991, A.
Christopher. Terminus.
Cortez. Rape.

Derricotte. On the Turning Up of Unidentified Black Female Corpses.
Desnos. Ars Poetica.
Disch. Rapist's Villanelle, The.
Donne. Apparition, The.
"Batter my heart, three-person'd God; for you."
Endrezze-Danielson. Exodus.
Field, E. Bride of Frankenstein, The.
Graham, J. From the New World.
Hagedorn, J. Solea.
Irby. Sequence.
Jackson, R. Violation, A.
Jordan, J. Case in Point.
Female and the Silence of a Man, The.
Poem About My Rights.
Larkin, J. Rape.
Larkin, P. Deceptions.
Lovelace, R. Mock Charon, A.
McCarriston. Castle in Lynn, A.
Nasrin. At the Back of Progress. . . .
Nelson, M. April Rape.
Olds, S. Girl, The.
Ovid. Rape of Lucrece, The.
Pamphilus. To the Swallow.
Pickard, T. Rape.
Piercy. Rape Poem.
Pope, A. Rape of the Lock, The.
Pratt, M. Waulking Song: Two.
Ravikovitch. Hovering at a Low Altitude.
Rochester, J. Song: "Fair Chloris in a pigsty lay."
Sexton. I'm dreaming the My Lai soldier again.
Shakespeare, W. Her lily hand her rosy cheek lies under.
Shange. It's Not so Good to be Born a Girl/ Sometimes.
Shkapskaya. My body had no entrance, and the black.
Spenser. Therein was writ, how often thundering Jove.
Unknown. Three Butchers, The.
Walker, A. Thing Itself, The.
Walsh, W. *et al.* Imperfect Enjoyment, The.
Waniek.
April Rape.
Chosen.
Williams, W. Raper from Passenack, The.
Wong, N. Relining Shelves.
Yeats. Leda and the Swan.

Raphael Santi
Allston. On the Group of the Three Angels Before the Tent of Abraham, by Raffaelle, in the Vatican.
Hardy, T. Cardinal Bembo's Epitaph on Raphael.
Ray, H. Raphael.

Rastafarianism
Cogil *et al.* Dem Belly Full.
Das, M. Leaf in His Ear, The.
Hippolyte. Reggae Cat (for Boston Jack).
"Jerry." Mabrak.
McNeill, A. Saint Ras.
Michael. Preface: "I stood watching / I the parade of floats."
Scott, D. Dreadwalk.

Rathel, James M.
Heard, J. In Memory of James M. Rathel.

Rationalism and Rationalists
Blake, W. Mock on, Mock on Voltaire, Rousseau.
Poe. Sonnet—To Science.
See also **Intellect and Intellectuals; Reason**

Rats
Atkins. Probability and Birds in the Yard.
Atwood. Rat Song.
Buson. Sound of a Rat, The.
Davies, W. Rat, The.
De la Mare. Five Eyes.
Dickinson, E. Rat is the concisest Tenant, The.
Du Bellay. There are cats (not he).
Edson, R. Rat's Legs, The.
Garston. To the Rats.
Gowar. Rat Trap.
Han-shan. Cold Mountain Poem No. 158.

Hughes, T. Song of a Rat.
Lear, E. Limerick: "There was an Old Man who supposed."
Mathews, H. Sharing Lodging with Hsieh Shih-hou.
Mei Yao Ch'en. Offering for the Cat, An.
Mew. Trees Are Down, The.
Moore, N. Song: "Little onion lay by the fireplace, A."
Neruda. Cat's Dream.
Nye, N. Hello.
Obeyd-i-Zàkànì. Gorby and the Rats.
Olson, E. Plot Improbable, Character Unsympathetic.
Pitter. Digdog.
Rabéarivelo. What invisible rat.
Raven. Assailant.
Smith, S. Pretty.
Toomer. Reapers.
Trakl. Rats, The.
Unknown. Big rat, big rat.
Children's Song.
Little Tim Sprat.
What Became of Them?
Wu Wei-yeh. Broken Lampstand, The.

Rattlesnakes
Warren, R. Rattlesnake Country.

Ravens
Barlow, J. Advice to a Raven in Russia [December, 1812].
Carryl, G. Sycophantic Fox and the Gullible Raven, The.
Coleridge, S. Raven, The.
Dana, R. Dying Raven, The.
Dyer, J. Tenants of an Abandoned Castle.
Euwer. True Facts of the Case, The.
Hughes, T. Ravens.
Lalic. Raven's Monologue.
Nicarchus of Alexandria. Raven, The.
Poe. Raven, The.
Unknown. Three Ravens, The.
Twa Corbies, The.
Wrigley, R. Ravens at Deer Creek.

Reading and Readers
Antin. Private Occasion in a Public Place, A.
Ashbery. But What Is the Reader to Make of This?
Berrigan, T. Things To Do in Providence.
Berry, D. On Reading Poems to a Senior Class at South High.
Boland, E. Oral Tradition, The.
Brode. Breakfast with Gerard Manley Hopkins.
Brown, R. I have a neighbor.
Brownell, H. Suspiria Noctis.
"Carroll." Poeta Fit, Non Nascitur.
Carruth, H. Ray.
Cherry, K. Reading, Dreaming, Hiding.
Chin Nung. Inscribed on the Wall of a Rice Cake Shop.
Chu Hsi. Thoughts While Reading.
Cotter, J. Book's Creed, The.
Cummings, E. For prodigal read generous.
De la Mare. Old Susan.
Dickinson, E. There is no Frigate like a Book.
Dove, R. First Book, The.
Fiser. Teaching Myself to Read.
Forbes, C. Poet's Shuffle, The.
Reading Walt Whitman.
Glancy. First Reader Santee Training School, 1873, The.
Gotera. Dance of the Letters.
Harper, F. Learning to Read.
Herrick. Another [To His Booke].
To My Ill Reader.
To the Sour[e] Reader.
To Vulcan.
Jonson, B. To the Reader ("Pray thee, take care, that tak'st my book[e] in hand").
Keats. On First Looking into Chapman's Homer.
On Sitting Down to Read "King Lear" Once Again.
Kemble. Lines.
Kenyon, J. Reading Aloud to My Father.
Knott. Goodbye.
Kooser. Selecting a Reader.

Kung Tzu-chen. Miscellanies of the Year Chi-hai.
Larkin, P. Fiction and the Reading Public. Study of Reading Habits, A.
Laughlin, J. Inn at Kirchstetten, The.
Leonard, T. Fathers and Sons.
Levertov. To the Reader.
Lisella. Song of the Third Generation.
Longfellow, H. Day is done, and the darkness, The.
Loseff. Reading Milosz.
Madhubuti. Poem Looking for a Reader, A.
Mahon. Death and the Sun.
Martial. To His Book[e].
Meinke. Dear Reader.
Meredith, G. You like not that French novel? Tell me why.
Milosz, C. Readings.
Moore, M. Poetry.
Murphy, R. Reading Lesson, The.
Nelson, M. Chopin.
Palmer, M. Theory of the Flower, The.
Parkes, B. To Elizabeth Barrett Browning.
Patmore, C. Revelation, The.
Po Chü-i. Aboard a Boat, Reading Yüan Chen's Poems.
Mad Poem Addressed to My Nephews and Nieces, A.
My servant wakes me: 'Master, it is broad day'.
On Board Ship: Reading Yüan Chên's Poems.
Poem on the Wall, The.
Procter, A. My Journal.
Rich, A. Diving into the Wreck.
Sangster, M. Bit of the Book in the morning, A.
Selvinsky. Reader of Poetry, The.
Shapiro, D. Book of Glass, A.
Sentences.
Singh, K. On Reading a Love Poem.
Stevens, W. House was quiet and the world was calm, The.
Large Red Man Reading.
Reader, The.
To Henry Church.
Tate, J. Dear Reader.
Tomlinson, C. Dream, A.
Unknown. Do you have the poems of Han-shan in your house?
When Mother reads aloud, the past.
Walcott. Volcano.
Waniek.
Chopin.
Wen Cheng-ming. Quiet courtyard fills with greenery, The.
Staying Overnight at Spirit-Source Temple.
Tea bowls, incense burning—a good feeling here!
Whitman, W. Whoever you are holding me now in hand.
Williams, J. On Reading Aloud My Early Poems.
Yang Wan-li. Passing By Waterwheel Bay.
Relaxing in the Evening in My Study.
Yeats. When you are old and grey and full of sleep.

Reagan, Ronald W.
Smith, K. Living with the Boss.

Reality
Albiach. "Theatre."
Andrews, B. Rich little circle south.
Armantrout. Garden, The.
Baraka. Poem for Deep Thinkers, A.
Bely. By-street was bathed in sun, The.
Benson, S. As sincerely as possible.
Blue Book 18 Pages 1–4.
Berkson, B. Melting Milk.
Bernstein, C. Whose Language.
Bronk. Corals and Shells.
Brooks, G. Kitchenette Building.
Brutus. Sand wet and cool, The.
Burliuk et al. Slap in the Face of Public Taste, A.
Carpenter, W. Girl Writing a Letter.
Cherry, K. Going Down on America.
Child, A. Motive for Mayhem, A.
Surplus.

Ciardi. On a Photo of Sgt. Ciardi a Year Later.
Clark, T. Society.
Clary. Unlikely one will guide me; I won't know I'm being helped, An.
Collins, M. Because the Dawn Breaks.
Collobert. III.
Couani. What a man, what a moon, what a fish, what a chip, what a block.
Creeley. City, The.
Token, A.
Cummings, E. As freedom is a breakfastfood.
Love is a place.
My sweet old etcetera.
Now air is air and thing is thing:no bliss.
This little bride & groom are.
When serpents bargain for the right to squirm.
Daniel, S. Shadows.
DiPalma. Each moment is surrounded.
Empire Smoke, Forgeries, Salient and The Ritz.
Poem: "In danger of which."
Sheaf Mark.
Dove, R. Anti-Father.
Drummond de Andrade. Residue.
Duchamp. 1914 Box, The.
World in Yellow, A.
Duncan, R. Close.
Edson, R. Way Things Are, The.
Equi. Date With Robbe-Grillet, A.
Erhardt. Amelia Erhardt.
Ferlinghetti, L. Frightened / by the sound of my own voice.
Sarolla's women in their picture hats.
Gergely. Encelado and the Facts.
Glück, L. Celestial Music.
Guest, B. Emphasis Falls on Reality, An.
If So.
Words.
Halliday, M. Reality U.S.A.
Harryman. Realism.
Huxley, A. Two Realities.
Jarrell. Märchen, The.
Jeffers, R. Boats in a Fog.
Jones, R. Front Window, The.
Keats. Modern Love.
Kerouac. 113th Chorus.
225th Chorus.
Kim, Y. Hotel North.
Kruchyonykh. Sahara to America, The.
Lauterbach. For Example (1): Stepping Out.
Lawrence, D. Demiurge.
Red Geranium and Godly Mignonette.
Levertov. Seeing for a Moment.
Lifshin. Penthouse Playboy.
Mackey, N. Slipped Quadrant.
Song of the Andoumboulou: 12.
Song of the Andoumboulou: 7.
Mandel, T. Realism.
Mansour, J. From an ass to an analyst and back.
Marinetti. They are Coming.
We had stayed up all night, my friends and I, under hanging mosque lamps.
Markham, E. After Reading Shakspere.
Mayakovsky. Screaming My Head Off.
Mayer, B. Earthworker's God is Healed, The.
McCaffery. Homines qouque si taceant, vocem invenient libri.
McClatchy. Found Parable.
McClure, M. Hymn to Saint Geryon.
McDonald, R. Hollow Thesaurus, The.
McHugh, H. 20-200 on 747.
Millay, E. Love is not all: it is not meat nor drink.
Naden. Love's Mirror.
Neruda. Too Many Names.
Olson, C. Moon Is the Number 18, The.
Orpingalik. Alcheringa Definitions.
Palmer, M. Eighth Sky.
Paz. Here.
Perelman. Things.
Péret. On All Fours.
Pessoa. "Startling Reality of Things," The.
Petrov, A. Poetry in an empty dress.
Picabia. Eunuch Unique.
Piombino. My Lady Carries Stones.

Prassinos. Conversation, A.
Rabbitt. For Those Who Will Live Forever.
Rankin, P. Fifteen.
Ransom, J. Somewhere Is Such a Kingdom.
Ray, D. Midnight Diner by Edward Hopper, A.
Rexroth, K. Prolegomena To A Theodicy.
Robinson, E. Octaves.
Schuyler, J. Letter to a Friend: Who Is Nancy Daum?
Schwartz, L. Monuments to the Not Yet Lived.
Schwitters. Murder Machine 43.
Sexton. Self in 1958.
Shakespeare, W. Sonnet 130.
Shchirovsky. I really don't want to die now.
Sherry, J. Radiant.
Snyder, G. Milton by Firelight.
Truth / like the belly of a woman turning, The.
Soupault. Comrade.
Stafford, W. Twelfth Birthday.
Stanton, M. Biography.
Stevens, W. Angel Surrounded by Paysans.
Holiday in Reality.
Not Ideas about the Thing but the Thing Itself.
So-and-So Reclining on Her Couch.
Strand. Keeping Things Whole.
Templeton, F. Act II - Crossing At the Tracks.
Tzara. Dance of the Greased Women, The.
Metal Coughdrops.
Unknown. I will give my love an apple without e'er a core.
Pawnee War-Song.
Von Freytag-Loringhoven. Affectionate.
Waldrop, R. Feverish Propositions.
Ward, D. Tables in Pictures.
Welish. Casting Sequences.
If I Blindfold You.
Scalpel in Hand.
Wheeler, S. Journal of the Thousand Choices.
Whitman, W. I am the poet of reality.
That shadow my likeness that goes to and fro seeking a livelihood, chattering, chaffering.
Wilbur. Hole in the Floor, A.
Thyme Flowering among Rocks.
Williams, W. Paterson.
Wordsworth, W. Yarrow Visited [September, 1814].
Woroszylski. Franz Kafka (I).
Yeats. Meru.

Reaping and Reapers
Bontemps. Black Man Talks of Reaping, A.
Dowson. Last Word, A.
Hood, T. Ruth.
Po Chü-i. Watching the Reapers.
Toomer. Harvest Song.
Reapers.
Wordsworth, W. Solitary Reaper, The.

Reason
Avidan. Practical Poems.
Ayton. Exercise of Affection, The.
Bevington, L. Afternoon.
Blake, W. Mock on, Mock on Voltaire, Rousseau.
Brontë, C. Reason.
Brontë, E. O thy bright eyes must answer now.
Carew, T. Lover, upon an Accident Necessitating His Departure, Consults with Reason, A.
Love's Force.
Chaucer. Lak of Stedfastnesse.
Dickinson, E. I reason, Earth is short.
Donne. If poisonous [or poysonous] mineral[l]s, and if that tree.
Dove, R. Geometry.
Fraser, K. Because you aren't here to be what I can't think of I need most.
Googe. Fly, The.
Jaccottet. Reason.
Kavanagh, P. To Hell with Commonsense.
Kendall, M. Lower Life, The.
Levertov. Contraband.
Quest, The.

Matthews, W. Psychopathology of Everyday
  Life, The.
Miles, J. Reason.
Milosz, C. Incantation.
Newcastle, M. Discourse of Beasts, A.
Olson, C. Poem 143.
Plath. Death of Myth-making, The.
Pope, A. On a Certain Lady at Court.
Robinson, M. Canzonet.
Rochester, J. Satire against Reason and
  Mankind, A.
Rukeyser, M. Rational Man.
Sherwood, G. Satire against Reason and
  Mankind, A.
Sidney, P. Love and Reason.
Sonnet 5: "It is most true that eyes are formed
  to serve."
Sonnet 10: "Reason, in faith thou art well
  served, that still."
Sonnet 18: "With what sharp checks I in
  myself am shent."
Sonnet 71: "Who will in fairest book of
  Nature know."
Sitwell, D. Heart and Mind.
Smith, C. Written near a Port on a Dark
  Evening.
Suckling, J. Barley-Break , A.
Tate, A. To Intellectual Detachment.
Tollet. On Loving Once and Loving Often.
Turberville. To his Love that sent him a Ring
  wherein was gravde, / Let Reason rule.
Vinokurov. I feel the reasonableness of
  existence.
Whitman, W. When I heard the learn'd
  astronomer.
Wollach. Love Poem #2.
Zenmaro. Tanka: "Nothing."

See also **Intellect and Intellectuals; Rationalism
and Rationalists**

Rebellions and Rebels
Bat-Miriam. Like this before you, just as I
  am.
Brathwaite, E. New World A-Comin'.
Brome. On Sir G. B. his defeat.
Brooke, R. Sonnet: In Time of Revolt.
Browning, R. Italian in England, The.
Collins, M. Because the Dawn Breaks.
Colman, H. On Balaam, and His Ass.
Darwish, M. On Wishes.
Drummond, W. Against the king, sir, now
  why would ye fight?
If of the dead save good nought should be
  said.
Duncan, R. My mother would be a falconress.
Emerson, R. Uriel.
Fenton, J. Wild Ones[, The].
Heaney, S. Requiem for the Croppies.
Holloway, S. Old Sam.
Johnson, L. Great Insohreckshan, Di.
Joseph, J. Dog body and cat mind, The.
Kaneko Mitsuharu. Opposition.
Kipling, R. Ulster.
Lawrence, D. Don'ts.
Lindsay, V. Factory windows are always
  broken.
McBurney. Croppy Boy, The.
Mihalic. Under the Microscope.
Mure. O Heavens! O Earth! heer I must pause
  a space.
Owen, M. "Assholes!" her eyes seem grey in
  this soup the hangars.
"Pindar." Hymn to the Guilotine.
Pope, A. Shut, shut the door, good *John*!
  fatigu'd, I said.
Rich, A. Phenomenology of Anger, The.
Rukeyser, M. For Kay Boyle.
Small, J. Eating the Elephant Whole.
Smith, M. Go Blow Fire, A.
Tu Fu. Lovely lady, fairest of the time.
Unknown. Croppy Boy, The.
Humble Petition of the British Jacobins to
  their Brethren of France, The.
Popular Negro Song, A.
Rising in the North, The.
Song of the King of the Eboes.
Upon Arch-bishop Laud, Prisoner in the
  Tower. 1641.

Walker, A. Outcast.
Waniek. Ballad of Aunt Geneva, The.
Whitman, W. We two boys together clinging.
Wieseltier. Take a Look at My Rebels.
Wordsworth, W. Foster-Mother's Tale.
Yeats. Upon a House Shaken by the Land
  Agitation.
Yên Thao. My Home.

See also **Revolution and Revolutionaries**

Rebirth
Ai. More.
Alegría. Desire.
Alexandru. Miserere Nobis.
Amichai. Four Resurrections in the Valley of
  the Ghosts.
Anacreon. Ode 46: "See—the young, the rosy
  Spring."
Awoonor. This Earth, My Brother.
Bachmann. Settlement.
Songs from an Island.
Balaban. For Mrs. Cam, Whose Name Means
  "Printed Silk."
Beaver. More than 9 Lives.
Bernstein, O. And after a Long While.
Bevington, L. Midnight.
Bible, *N.T.* Christ's Promise.
Last Day, The.
Bontemps. My Heart has Known its Winter.
Brodsky, J. Elegy.
Césaire, A. In Order to Speak.
Cheney-Coker. Philosopher, The.
Clifton, L. Crazy Horse Instructs the Young
  Men But In Their Grief They Forget.
There Is a Girl Inside.
Collins, A. Song.
Confucius. Great Digest, The.
Cook, S. Flowers in Town, The.
"Coolidge." New Every Morning.
Cross, Jr. Rice Will Grow Again.
Cullen, C. For My Grandmother.
Cummings, E. I thank You God for most this
  amazing.
Now does our world descend.
When god lets my body be.
Daumal. Persephone That Is to Say Double
  Issue.
Doolittle, H. It is no madness to say.
Drayton. Since There's No Help.
Enzensberger, H. Portrait of a House
  Detective.
Ferlinghetti, L. I am waiting for my case to
  come up.
Frost, R. Onset, The.
Gheorghe. Unicorn, The.
Gilbo'a. Morning-Selah.
Glück, L. Cottonmouth Country.
Gouri. Holiday's End.
Graves, R. Survivor, The.
Grimké, A. At April.
Hardy, T. For Life I had never cared greatly.
Herbert, Z. Remembering My Father.
Hirsch, E. Unearthly Voices.
Holan. Resurrection.
Houston, L. Dream of the Cabbage
  Caterpillars, The.
Hughes, L. In time of silver rain.
József. Seventh, The.
Kinnell. Saint Francis and the Sow.
Kovner. On My Words.
Kunitz, S. Vita Nuova.
Kunze, R. Kind of Hope, A.
Larkin, J. In Western Massachusetts, Sixteen
  Months Sober.
Lawrence, D. Fatality.
Levine, P. Belief.
Mahapatra, J. Sanskrit.
Mandelstam. Mounds of Human Heads Are
  Wandering into the Distance.
Martin, C. Easter Sunday, 1985.
Masaoka Shiki. Tanka: "Dipped."
McGrath, J. Song.
McKay, C. Baptism.
McMahon, L. Convalescence.
Mitchell, S. Havana Birth.
Nichols, G. Epilogue: "I have crossed an
  ocean."
Osundare. I Sing of Change.

Plumly. After Grief.
Popa. Burning Shewolf.
Ravikovitch. Sinking Rising.
Rossetti, C. Caterpillar, The.
Shut Out.
Rowe, A. Destroyers, The.
Sandburg, C. Falltime.
Sandy. Threads.
Shelley, P. But Greece and her foundations
  are.
Szymborska. Reality demands.
Theater Impressions.
Tabb. Evolution.
Tagore. I seem to have loved you in
  numberless forms, numberless times.
Tati-Loutard. Death and Rebirth.
Taylor, J. As Gold is better that's in fire tride.
Tekeyan. Dream.
Prayer on the Threshold of Tomorrow.
Vallejo. Masses.
Vaughan, H. Ascension Hymn ("Dust and
  clay").
I walked [*or* walkt] the other day to spend my
  hour.
Venclova. In Memory of the Poet. Variant.
Wilbur. April 5, 1974.
Williams, W. Spring and All.
Wright, J. On the Skeleton of a Hound.
Young, A. Thistledown.
Zagajewski. When Death Came.

See also **Renewal; Regeneration**

Rebuilding
Ammons. Eternal City, The.
Popa. Benefactors of the Little Box, The.
Xuân Diệu. New Tiles.

Recipes
Katz, B. Recipe.

Recognition
Browning, R. Popularity.
Cornford, F. Avenue, The.
Dickinson, E. Like Eyes that looked on
  Wastes.
Levertov. People at Night.
MacNeice. Elegy for Minor Poets.
Mura. Recognitions.
Narain. Towards Delhi.
Raab, L. Magic Problems.

Reconciliation
Aiken, C. Quarrel, The.
Chaucer. Pardoner's Tale, The.
Heard, J. Sunshine after Cloud.
Herrick. To the Rose; a Song.
Lovelace, R. To Elinda.
Melville, H. America.
Meredith, G. He found her by the ocean's
  moaning verge.
Oliver, M. Visitor, A.
Petrarch. How oft have I, my dear [*or* dere]
  and cruel[l] foe.
Ransom, J. Armageddon.
Robinson, E. Story of the Ashes and the
  Flame, The.
Shakespeare, W. Sonnet 119.

Record Players
Schwartz, L. 78's.

Red (color)
Donne. Oh my black[e] soul[e]! now thou art
  summoned.
Field, E. Red.
Hughes, L. When Sue Wears Red.
Mathias, E. All in Red.
Okamoto. Tanka: "Cockscomb, A."
Rodriguez, J. Nu-plastik Fanfare Red.
Ryan, K. Outsider Art.
Tablada. Red cold / guffaw of summer.

Red Jacket (Seneca Chief)
Halleck, F. Red Jacket.

Red Sea
Unknown. Parting of the Red Sea, The.

Redemption
Auden. Ballad of Barnaby, The.
Beaumont, J. Garden's quit with me: as
  yesterday, The.
Campion, T. Author of light, revive my dying
  spright.
Seek the Lord, and in His ways persever.

Christopher. After Hours.
Donne. "Batter my heart, three-person'd God; for you."
Good Friday [or Goodfriday], 1613. Riding Westward.
Oh my black[e] soul[e]! now thou art summoned.
Dunbar, W. On the Resurrection of Christ.
Graves, R. Point of No Return.
Harjo, J. Legacy.
Herbert, G. Holy Baptism (1).
Love (2).
Parody [or Parodie], A.
Pulley, The.
Redemption.
Sion.
World, The.
Herrick. To Julia, the Flaminica Dialis, or Queen-Priest.
Hopkins, G. God's Grandeur.
Lynch, T. Lift Up Your Heads, Rejoice!
Merton. Cana.
Meynell, A. "I Am the Way."
Moore, M. To a Giraffe.
Murray, P. Redemption.
Nemerov. Carol: "Now is the world withdrawn all."
Ralegh, W. Passionate Man[']s Pilgrimage, The.
Robinson, E. Children of the Night, The.
Rossetti, C. Heart Knoweth Its Own Bitterness, The.
Smart, C. Epiphany.
Spenser. Sonnet 68: "Most glorious Lord of Life that on this day."
Thomas, D. There was a saviour.
Thompson, F. Hound of Heaven, The.
Unknown. Blow Your Trumpet, Gabriel.
He who would acclaim Cleanness in becoming style.
Nobody Knows the Trouble I've Had.
Out of Your Sleep Arise and Wake.
What Yo' Gwine to [or t'] Do When Yo' [or de] Lamp Burn Down?
Vaughan, H. Regeneration.
Very. I Was Sick and in Prison.
Wesley, C. Free Grace.
Wilbur. Proof, The.
Wilde, O. E Tenebris.

Redwings
Wright, J. Redwings.

Redwood Trees. *See* **Sequoia Trees**

Reeds
Shin, K. Reed had been weeping, The.

Refinement
Lovelace, R. Song: "Strive not, vain Lover, to be fine."
Stone, R. How to Catch Aunt Harriette.

Reflections
Apollinaire. I Imagine Angels.
On imagine les anges.
Atwood. Tricks With Mirrors.
Behn, A. Angellica's Lament.
Burns, R. Of a' the airts the wind can blaw.
Carew, T. To T. H., a Lady Resembling My Mistress.
Chōkū. Tanka: "From the water's depth."
Creeley. Awakening, The.
Kind of Act Of, The.
D'Ambrosio, C. Morning.
Elytis. Anniversary.
Ferlinghetti, L. Heaven was only.
Frost, R. For Once, Then, Something.
Graves, R. Foreboding, The.
Hitomaro. Strange old man, A.
Jarrell. Game at Salzburg, A.
Kinnell. Spindrift.
Knight, E. Belly Song.
Knott. Shorts / Excerpts ("I keep a TV monitor on my chest").
Lochhead, L. Hickie, The.
Lovelace, R. Song: "Strive not, vain Lover, to be fine."
MacCaig. Things in Each Other.
MacNeice. Perdita.
Mechthild von Magdeburg. How the Soul Speaks to God.

Moss, T. Lessons from a Mirror.
Pack, R. Thrasher in the Willow by the Lake, The.
Rexroth, K. Delia Rexroth.
Fish Peddler and Cobbler.
Signature of All Things, The.
Stafford, W. Ask Me.
Tennyson, A. Marriage Morning.
Tu Fu. Stars and Moon on the Yangtse.
Wilbur. Aspen and the Stream, The.
Yi, S. Mirror, The.
Young, A. Move Continuing, The.

Refugees
Auden. Refugee Blues.
Balaban. For Miss Tin in Hue.
Bowes-Lyon. Refugee, A.
Boyle, K. New Emigration, The.
Breytenbach. Exile, Representative.
Browning, R. Italian in England, The.
Cao Tần. Our friend would board the *Thu'o'ng-Tín* and go home.
Davidson, D. Refugees.
Dickinson, E. These Strangers, in a foreign World.
Dunne, S. Refugees at Cobh.
Espada. Mi Vida: Wings of Fright.
Fogarty. Remember Something Like This.
Grade. At night and in the wind and the rain.
Hậu Điền. Biding Our Time.
Jarrell. For an Emigrant.
Refugees, The.
Jussawalla. Sea Breeze, Bombay.
Komunyakaa. Boat People.
Krichevsky. Refugees.
Lazarus, E. New Colossus, The.
Li K'ai-hsien. Sent to the Painter, Lu Hsiao-feng.
Luân Hoán. Washing My Wife's Clothes.
McCarthy, G. Fall of Da Nang, The.
Mura. Huy Nguyen: Brothers, Drowning Cries.
Nortje. Up Late.
Paterson, E. Tribal Homeland.
Schiff, W. When It Happened.
Seferis. Last Stop.
Shapcott, T. Shadow of War, 1941.
Shurin. Very Days.
Spender, S. History and Reality.
Trần Mộng Tú. New Year's Wish for a Little Refugee, A.
Tu Fu. I have brothers, younger brothers in a place far away.
Song of P'eng-ya.
Yang Shih-ch'i. Sha-ch'eng, "Sand City" ("Overlooking the water, a desolate city").

Regeneration
Berry, W. Slip, The.
Clifton, L. To my Friend, Jerina.
Hopkins, G. God's Grandeur.
Oliver, M. Rabbit, The.
Shapiro, K. Leg, The.
Vaughan, H. Regeneration.
Whitman, W. And as to you Death, and you bitter hug of mortality, it is idle to try to alarm.
Grass.
See also **Rebirth**; **Renewal**

Reggae
Onuora Oku. Reflection in Red.

Regret
Ade. R-E-M-O-R-S-E.
Batterham. Once.
Berggolts. Ordeal, The.
Brooks, G. Mother, The.
Brown, R. Fry says a word.
Burns, R. To a Mouse[, On Turning Her Up in Her Nest, with the Plough, November, 1785].
Cambridge, A. Virgin Martyr, The.
Carver, R. Wine.
Ch'in Chia. To His Wife.
Congreve. False Though She Be [to me and love].
Dame. Lilith.
Doob. My Mother's Blue Vase.
Doolittle, H. So you have swept me back.
Dransfield. Portrait of the Artist as an Old Man.

Drayton. *Satyr* O never ask how I came to this place.
Dunbar, P. Debt, The.
Ehrenburg. I lived obscurely and uncertainly.
Elizabeth I. When I was fair and young, then [or and] favour graced me;.
Enzensberger, H. Short History of the Bourgeoisie.
Ficowski. I did not manage to save.
"Field." Ebbtide at Sundown.
Foley, M. On the Waterfront.
Foster, E. Hermetic Silence.
Glazkov. Path Is Long, The.
Hacker, M. Sonnet for Iva.
Hall, D. Tubes.
Harte, B. Mrs. Judge Jenkins[; Being the Only Genuine Sequel to "Maud Muller"].
Hayden, R. Ballad of Sue Ellen Westerfield, The.
Heine. Looking Back.
Hewitt, J. Search, The.
Hippolyte. Caribbean Exorcism Poem, A.
Hollo. Godlike.
Housman, A. When the bells justle in the tower.
Hull, L. Letter, The.
Johnstone, R. Fruit of Knowledge, The.
Various instants I'm not with you.
Koch, K. To Marina.
"Korzhavin." For certain, I did not live thus in this world.
Kunitz, S. Illumination, The.
Landon. Gifts Misused.
Laux. Ghosts.
Levine, P. Uncle.
Li Yü. Tune: Crows Crying at Night.
Tune: Song of Tzu-yeh.
Mahon. Bruce Ismay's Soliloquy.
Masters, E. Fiddler Jones.
Meredith, G. Not solely that the Future she destroys.
Meredith, W. Botanical Trope, A.
Merrill, J. Renewal, A.
Millay, E. At least, my dear.
Moeller. Ten Years Ago.
Nabokov. To Russia.
Olds, S. After 37 Years My Mother Apologizes for My Childhood.
Owen, W. Strange Meeting.
Terre, A.
Wild with All Regrets.
Patmore, C. Toys, The.
Pessoa. In the terrible night, natural substance of all nights.
Po Chü-i. Resignation.
Pound, E. Villanelle: The Psychological Hour.
Ransom, J. Parting, without a Sequel.
Ravikovitch. Dear Mickey.
Rein. Galya, Mother, and My Daughter Anna.
Roberts, K. How Late Desire Looks.
Robinson, E. Miniver Cheevy, child of scorn.
Rossetti, C. Soeur Louise de la Miséricorde (1674).
Rossetti, D. One Hope, The.
Superscription, The.
Schuyler, J. Salute.
Seifert. Fingerprints.
Garland on the Wrist, A.
Sexton. Lament: "Someone is dead."
Sidney, P. Sonnet 33: "I might, unhappy word, O me, I might."
Skelton, J. Mannerly Margery Mylk and Ale.
Spires. Apology.
Su Tung-p'o. Long ago I lived in the country.
T'ao Ch'ien. Poem in the Form of a Coffin-Puller's Song ("What has a life must have a death").
Timrod. Cotton Boll, The.
Tu Fu. By the Winding River II.
U'ng Binh. Retired Mandarin's Wife Complains, A.
Unknown. I had a little pony.
Yes, there are stingy people.
Updike. Report of Health.
Vaughan, H. Retreat[e], The.
Wakoski. Apology, An.
Wurdemann. Text.

Yeats. Down by the salley gardens my love
and I did meet;.
Men Improve with the Years.
People, The.
Yesenin. To Kachalov's Dog.
Yuan Chi. Regret.

Reincarnation
Bishop, M. We Have Been Here Before.
Han. Blue Bird.
Hardy, T. Transformations.
Hopkins, E. Life in Death.
Kerouac. Poem.
Levine, P. Fox, The.
Mahon. Lives.
Meynell, A. Song of Derivations, A.
Mirabai. It's True I Went to the Market.
Mo Shih-lung. Drinking Wine.
Rossetti, D. Sudden Light.
Rumi. Don't grieve. Anything you lose comes
round.
Stevens, W. Good Man Has No Shape, The.
Watson, R. Nirvana.

Reindeer
Jacobsen, J. Reindeer and Engine.
Moore, C. Visit from St Nicholas, A.

Rejection
"Akhmatova." Ah—you thought I'd be the
type.
Angus. Mary's Song.
"Anvari." Hors de Combat.
Argentarius. You loved Menophila when you
were rich.
Ayton. Answer, The.
Rejection, The.
Upon His Unconstant Mistress.
Barrington, P. Take me in your arms, Miss
Moneypenny-Wilson.
Beckett, S. Cascando.
Behn, A. Song: Love Armed.
Bickerstaffe. Expostulation, An.
Borowski. Farewell to Maria.
Browning, E. Denial, A.
Sonnet: "I lift my heavy heart up solemnly."
Burns, R. Open the Door to Me, Oh!
Callimachus. Sleep cold at someone's.
Campion, T. Shall I come, sweet love, to thee.
Shall I then hope when faith is fled?
So quicke, so hot, so mad is thy fond sute.
Carew, T. Spring, The.
To My Inconstant Mistress [or Mistris].
Cavalli. To simulate the burning of the heart,
the humiliation.
Chaucer. To Rosamounde.
Clare, J. When I was young I fell in love and
got but little good on't.
Coleridge, M. Clever Woman, A.
Creeley. Invoice, The.
Daniel, S. Half-blown Rose, The.
Dante Alighieri. Even as the others mock,
thou mockest me.
Darley. To Helene.
Dixon, S. Request of Alexis, The.
Donne. Damp[e], The.
Love's Deity [or Deitie].
Douglas, L. Rejected.
Dove, R. Aircraft.
Drayton. Night and Day.
Dryden, J. Disdain Punished.
Love's Despair.
Durcan. Lion Tamer, The.
"Eliot." How Lisa Loved the King.
"Ephelia." To J.G. on the News of His
Marriage.
To My Rival.
Fell, A. And Again.
Field, E. Unwanted.
"Field." Sweeter Far than the Harp, More
Gold than Gold.
Gilbert, S. Ko-Ko's Song.
Glück, L. Hesitate to Call.
Graves, R. Song: How Can I Care?
Gunn, T. Carnal Knowledge.
Monster, The.
Hafiz. Ode 487: "With last night's wine still
singing in my head."
Hai-Jew, S. Kinged.
Hemans. Properzia Rossi.

Herbert, G. Denial[l].
Herrick. Cruell Maid, The.
Hope, A. Meditation on a Bone.
Horace. Dialogue in Imitation of that between
Horace and Lydia, A.
First Ode of the Fourth Book of Horace, The.
Tibullus, pull yourself together!
Howell, C. Liberty and Ten Years of Return.
Huddle. Vermont.
Ise. Is it your command.
Ivanov, G. If you want to live, then live...
James, C. Book of my enemy has been
remaindered, The.
Jamíl. Salsabíl.
Jonson, B. To Celia.
Joyce, J. Post Ulixem Scriptum.
Keats. Stanzas: "You say you love, but with a
voice."
Ki No Washika. No.
Kizer, C. Bitch.
Lamb, C. "Timid grace sits trembling in her
eye, A."
Landon. Girl at Her Devotions, A.
Landor, W. Maid's Lament, The.
Layne, M. Collect Call.
Levchev. Secret Love.
Liu Hsün's Wife. Curtain of the Wedding
Bed, The.
Lovelace, R. To Lucasta ("Like to the sentinel
stars, I watch all night").
Lowell, A. Carrefour.
'Marnia. I want to love you very much.
Meredith, G. Madam would speak with me.
So, now it comes.
Merrill, S. Ballade of the Outcasts.
Meynell, A. Renouncement.
Millay, E. Love me no more, now let the god
depart.
Muzahim al-Ugaili. Earth outside, The.
O'Hara, F. Meditations in an Emergency.
Ovid. O! Love! how cold, and slow to take
my part!
Pan Chieh-yû. Song of Regret.
Pasternak, B. Marburg.
Perillo. Sweaters, The.
Perunkaṭunkō. What She Said ("Though he
lives in the same town").
Prince, F. Wind in the Tree, The.
Racine. My time's too short, your highness. It
was I.
Ralegh, W. Nimphs [or Nymph's] Reply to
the Sheepheard [or Shepherd], The.
Ocean's Love to Cynthia, The.
Poem Put into My Lady Laiton's Pocket, A.
Raleigh. Nymph's Reply to the Shepherd, The.
Richards, L. Antonio, Antonio.
Richardson, M. Sonnet: "I still shall smile and
go my careless way."
Rochester, E. Song: "Nothing ades to Loves
fond fire."
Rossetti, C. No, Thank You, John.
Scovell. Vain Girl Jilted, The.
Seward. Sonnet 12.
Sonnet 19.
Shelley, P. To————: "One word is too
often profaned."
Sidney, P. Eighth Song: "In a grove most rich
of shade."
Ninth Song: "Go, my flock, go get you
hence."
Sonnet 31: "With how sad steps, O Moon,
thou climb'st the skies!"
Smith, S. Lady "Rogue" Singleton.
Stanley, T. Divorce, The.
Stirling, S. Echo, An.
Sulpicia. Sulpicia to Cerinthus.
Surrey. Complaint of a Lover Rebuked.
Swinburne. Leave-taking, A.
Satia Te Sanguine.
Tate, J. Deaf Girl Playing.
Theocritus. Neteheard.
O NICIAS, there is no other remedy for love.
Tom, Will, and Dick, and I, a jovial Crew.
Tsvetayeva. I didn't want this, not.
Unknown. Art thou that she than whom none
fairer is.

There's Someone I Think Of.
Welcome be ye when ye go.
Whitman, W. Sometimes with one I love I fill
myself with rage for fear I effuse unreturn'd
love.
Wroth. Duke's Song, The.
Wyatt, T. Disdain me not without desert.
Like as the swan towards her death.
Pass forth, my wonted cries.
Renouncing of Love, A.
That time that mirth did steer my ship.
When first mine eyes did view and mark.

Relatives
Brathwaite, E. Ancestors.
Herrick. To His Kinsman, Master Thomas
Herrick, Who Desired to Be in His Book.
Kumin, M. For My Great-Grandfather: A
Message Long Overdue.
Lorde. And What About the Children.

Relativity
Auden. Law like Love.
Bateman, C. Distances.
Bold, A. Special Theory of Relativity, A.
Carew, T. To the Reader of Master William
Davenant's Play [The Wits].
Cummings, E. Space being(don't forget to
remember)Curved.
Horovitz, F. Irthing Valley.
Snodgrass, W. These trees stand very tall
under the heavens.

Relief
Hoffenstein. I'm fond of doctors and drivers
of hacks.
Thompson, J. Work.
Unknown. Ode on a Storm.

Religion
Abse. Of Itzig and His Dog.
Alabaster. My soule a world is by
Contraccion.
Now I have found thee, I will ever more.
Three sortes of teares doe from myne eies
distraine.
Upon the Ensignes of Christes Crucifyinge.
Apollinaire. Zone.
Atkins. Lisbon.
Awoonor. Easter Dawn.
Weaver bird built in our house, The.
Azmi, K. I and I.
Bangs, J. Blind.
Barham. Jackdaw of Rheims, The.
Barker, J. Fidelia Arguing with Her Self on
the Difficulty of Finding the True Religion.
Barlas. Memphian Temple, The.
Baudelaire. Fuses I and II.
Belloc. Four things in any land must dwell.
Bentley, E. "No, sir," said General Sherman.
Betjeman. Matlock Bath.
Blake, W. Garden of Love, The.
Mock on, Mock on Voltaire, Rousseau.
Blaser. Even on Sunday.
Borges. From an Apocryphal Gospel.
Braithwaite. Rye Bread.
Burns, R. Epistle to a Young Friend.
Holy Fair, The.
Kirk's Alarm, The.
Butler, S. For his religion it was fit.
Byron, G. Spirit pass'd before me: I beheld,
A.
Calbert. Woman Who Loved Things, The.
Campbell, A. Divine Mission, The.
Chatterton. Methodist, The.
Sunday: A Fragment Transcribed from a Ms.
in Chatterton's Handwriting.
Chesterton, G. Antichrist, or the Reunion of
Christendom; an Ode.
Clifton, L. At Jonestown.
Coicou. Lord's Prayer, The.
Corbett, R. Proper New Ballad Intituled The
Faer Yes Farewell: Or God-A-Mercy Will, A.
Creeley. After Lorca.
Davies, I. Lay Preacher Ponders, The.
Di Prima. I Fail as a Dharma Teacher.
Dickinson, E. I'm ceded—I've stopped being
Theirs.
Some keep the Sabbath going to Church.
'Tis little I— could care for Pearls.

Disch. Ballade of the New God.
Cardinal Detoxes: A Play in One Act, The.
Doane, W. Preacher's Mistake, The.
Donne. Canonization, The.
Satire 3.
To the Countess of Bedford ("Madam, /
Reason is our soul's left hand, Faith her
right").
To the Countesse of Bedford ("Honour is so
sublime perfection").
Douglas, L. Rejected.
Dove, R. Receiving the Stigmata.
Dryden, J. Confessio Fidei.
Reason and Religion.
Thus man by his own strength to Heaven
would soar.
Dunbar, P. Spiritual, A.
Dunn, S. Something Like Happiness.
Durand, O. Francie-the-Possessed.
Eliot, T. Hippopotamus, The.
Song for Simeon, A.
Fallon, P. Herd, The.
Flanders, J. Nightingales in America.
Freneau. Indian Convert, The.
"G., E. O." My Church ("My church has but
one temple").
Glazkov. Boyarina Morozova, The.
Greacen. Ten New Commandments.
Green, M. Seeker, The.
Gregg. Gnostics on Trial.
Han Yü. Girl of Mt. Hua, The.
Hardy, T. Christmas: 1924.
Dream Question, A.
Respectable Burgher, The.
Harington. Groome of the Chambers religion
in King Henry the eights time, A.
Harmon. Ceremon(y)(ies) of Mutability, The.
Hayden, R. Those Winter Sundays.
Heath-Stubbs. Year of Our Lord two thousand
one hundred and seven, The.
Herbert, G. Religion stands on tip-toe in our
land.
Hewitt, J. Rome Sunday[,] June 1960.
Tryst.
Hill, J. Preacher and the Slave, The.
Hope, A. Advice to Young Ladies.
House of God, The.
Hudgins. Southern Crescent Was on time,
The.
Hughes, L. Song for a Dark Girl.
Hummer, T. Spring Comes to Mid-Ohio in a
Holy Shower of Stars.
Huxley, A. Burning Wheel, The.
Johnson, L. Church of a Dream, The.
Jones, D. In the middle silences of this night's
course the blackthorn.
Kaufman, B. Oregon.
Kelly, B. Courting the Famous Figures at the
Grotto of Improbable Thought.
Klepfisz. My Mother's Sabbath Days.
Knott. Funny Poem.
Knox, R. O God, for as much as without
Thee.
Kumin, M. Living Alone with Jesus—.
Larkin, P. Church Going.
High Windows.
Water.
Laux. Children's Train, The.
Lawrence, D. Quetzalcoatl Looks Down on
Mexico.
Lorde. When the Saints Come Marching In.
Winds of Orisha, The.
Lovelace, R. Apostasy of One and But One
Lady, The.
Lyon, G. Foot-Washing, The.
MacCaig. Celtic Cross.
Mackey, N. Slipped Quadrant.
MacLean, S. Highland Woman, A.
Mapanje. From Florrie Abraham Witness,
December 1972.
Mathews, A. Caedmon.
McGinley. Day after Sunday, The.
How to Start a War.
McHugh, H. Third Person Neuter.
McLachlan. We Live in a Rickety House.
Melville, H. Fragments of a Lost Gnostic

Poem of the Twelfth [or 12th] Century.
Ungar and Rolfe.
Mew. Ken.
Millay, E. Make bright the arrows.
Milton. On the Late Massacre [or Massacher]
in Piedmont [or Piemont].
Mitchell, C. Soul of Jesus Is Restless, The.
Moore, T. Argument, An.
Moorer. Southern Pulpit, The.
Muldoon, P. Our Lady of Ardboe.
Mullen, H. Dance She Does, The.
Nash, O. Seven Spiritual Ages of Mrs.
Marmaduke Moore, The.
Nemerov. Boom!
Newman, J. Sensitiveness.
Nimatullah. Song of Seyd [or Seid]
Nimetollah of Kuhistan.
Nye, N. Man Who Makes Brooms, The.
Obeyd-i-Zākānì. Gorby and the Rats.
Olsen, W. Unicorn Tapestries, The.
Ostriker. Everywoman Her Own Theology.
Paddock. Epiphany.
Parnell. On Bishop Burnet's Being Set on
Fire in His Closet.
Pastan. Passover.
Plato. Advice to Young Ladies.
Po Chü-i. Going Alone to Spend a Night at
the Hsien-Yu Temple.
Temple, The.
Visiting the Hsi-lin Temple.
Prettyman. When Mahalia Sings.
Questel. Near Mourning Ground.
Raine, K. Written in Exile.
Ralegh, W. As you came from the holy land.
Randall, J. To William Wordsworth from
Virginia.
Reed, I. I Am a Cowboy in the Boat of Ra.
Rexroth, K. Wednesday of Holy Week, 1940.
Robbins, H. And have the bright immensities.
Robinson, A. Sibyl, The.
Rodriguez, L. String Bean.
St. John, D. Wavelength.
St. John, P. Sunday.
Salter. Age of Reason, The.
Sassoon. "They."
Scott, F. Bangkok.
Brébeuf and His Brethren.
Scott, W. Mistress Severin.
Senghor. Totem, The.
Sexton. With Mercy for the Greedy.
Sharpless. Moment of Eschatological Doubt,
A.
Sheperd. Who hath not knowne or herd.
Sidney, P. Splendidis longum valedico nugis.
Skelton, J. Over this the foresayd lay.
Spender, S. Landscape near an Aerodrome,
The.
Spenser. Sonnet 71: "Soverayne beauty which
I doo admire, The."
Stafford, W. Religion Back Home.
Stevens, W. Sunday Morning.
Stevenson, R. Epitaph: "Angler rose, he took
his rod, The."
Stone, S. Church's One Foundation, The.
Su Shih. Sent to Chief Abbot of Tung-lin
Monastery.
Swinburne. Higher Pantheism in a Nutshell,
The.
Tabb. Sisters, The.
Tadic. I Run With a Pair of Compasses Stuck
in the Back of My Head.
Text, Silk.
Taylor, E. View, all ye eyes above, this sight
which flings.
Thompson, F. Hound of Heaven, The.
Thribb. In Memoriam Krishna Menon.
Lines on the Return to Britain of Billy
Graham.
Touré, A. JuJu.
Travis, N. Church Ladies.
Unknown. Abraham Lincoln's Creed.
Christian has trousers on.
Each prayer is answered.
George Washington.
Lament for Our Lady's Shrine at Walsingham,
A.
My army cross over.

Old [or Ould] Orange Flute, The.
Old-Time Religion.
Seven Songs and Song Pictures.
To Caelia.
Upon Arch-bishop Laud, Prisoner in the
Tower. 1641.
Vicar of Bray, The.
Wizard's Chant, The.
Vaughan, H. Religion.
Retirement.
Voigt. Woman Who Weeps.
Waller, E. Upon his Majesties repairing of
Pauls.
Ware, M. Understanding Guyana.
Warton, T. Stanzas Imitated From Psalm
CXIX.
Weaver, M. Water Song.
Whittier. Worship.
Wilbur. Matthew VIII, 28 ff.
Wild, R. In a melancholly studdy.
Williams, W. Semblables, The.
Wolfe, H. Gray Squirrel, The.
Wright, J. Sketch for an Aesthetic Project.
Wednesday Night Prayer Meeting.
Yeats. Church and State.
Wisdom.
Zangwill. Moses and Jesus.

See also **Faith**

Religious Life
Arnold, M. Dover Beach.
Beer, M. Church in the Heart, The.
Betjeman. Huxley Hall.
Bunyan. Pilgrim, The.
Campbell, R. Mass at Dawn.
Crane, H. Emblems of Conduct.
Crashaw. On Mr. G. Herberts Booke, The
Temple.
Davie. Priory of St Saviour, Glendalough,
The.
Dickinson, E. Ourselves we do inter with
sweet derision.
Elizabeth, Queen of Bohemia. Verses by the
Princess Elizabeth, Given to Lord Harington,
of Exton, Her Preceptor.
Fenton, J. Kingfisher's Boxing Gloves, The.
Gascoigne. From depth of dole wherein my
soul doth dwell.
Gerstler. Unforseen, The.
Habington. Cupio Dissolvi.
Hall, J. Song of Esechia, The.
Han Yü. Girl from Flower Mountain, The.
Harvey, C. Church Festivals.
Herbert, G. Affliction (1).
Dulness[e].
H[oly] Communion, The.
Invitation, The.
Perirrhanterium.
Herrick. Thanksgiving to God for His House,
A.
Hopkins, G. I wake and feel the fell of dark,
not day.
To seem the stranger lies my lot, my life.
Jonson, B. To Heaven.
Kasdorf. Mennonites.
Kim, K. Lord's Day, The.
Langland, W. Wolleward and wete-shoed went
I forth after.
Leax. Fire Burns Low, The.
Lee, J. Vocation.
Mathews, A. Caedmon.
Melvill. Sonnet sent to Blackness to Mr. John
Welsch, by the Lady Culross, A.
Melville, H. Pillow, The.
Nemerov. Boom!
Owen, M. African Sunday.
Quarles. Galatians 6.14.
Matthew 9.12.
Roethke. Right Thing, The.
Rowe, E. Hymn: "In vain the dusky night
retires."
Sawyer, A. Sunday Schools.
Snyder, G. December.
Taylor, E. Bran, a chaff, a very barley [y]awn,
A.
Dull. Dull indeed! What shall it e'er be thus?
Huswifery.

Toplady. Living and Dying Prayer for the Holiest Believer in the World, A.
Traherne. Contentment is a sleepy thing.
Unknown. Corpus Christi Carol, The.
Hit betidde somtime in the termes of Judé.
I Would Be Clad in Christ's Skin.
Vaughan, H. Disorder and Frailty.
Dressing.
Holy Communion, The.
Jacob's Pillow, and Pillar.
Mans Fall, and Recovery.
Stone, The.
Very. Created, The.
Fear Not: For They That Be With Us.
Presence, The.
Wesley, C. Whole Armour of God, The.
Whittier. Ezekiel.
Winchilsea. Some Reflections.
Wordsworth, W. Decay of Piety.
See also **Clergy; Convents; Monasteries; Monks; Nuns; Rabbis**

Rembrandt, Harmenszoon van Rijn
Allston. On Rembrant; Occasioned by His Picture of Jacob's Dream.
Corso. Rembrandt—Self Portrait.
Weiss, T. Ten Little Rembrandts.

Remorse
Benét, W. Brazen Tongue.
Blake, W. Night II (Enion's Lament).
Brontë, E. Come, walk with me.
If grief for grief can touch thee.
O Dream, where art thou now?
Coleridge, S. Invocation, An: "Hear, sweet spirit, hear the spell."
Dickinson, E. Remorse—is Memory—awake.
Donne. Hymn to God the Father, A.
Housman, A. Rain, it streams on stone and hillock, The.
Johnstone, R. Fruit of Knowledge, The.
Kinzie. Sun and Moon.
Lawrence, D. Piano.
Mahon. Bruce Ismay's Soliloquy.
Nemerov. Remorse for Time, The.
Nishi. Remorse Came Slowly.
O'Sullivan, M. Busk, Pierce.
Sangster, M. Sin of Omission, The.
Tichborne. Tichborne's Elegy.
Waugh, E. They told me, Francis Hinsley, they told me you were hung.

Renaissance
Hill, G. Pre-Raphaelite Notebook, A.
Simpson, L. Riders Held Back, The.

Renewal
"Antler." Ungag our souls!! Unstrangle our souls!! Unsmother our souls!!
Arapaho Oral Tradition. Ghost Dance Songs.
Atwood. In this house (in a dying orchard).
Averill. Renewal.
Burns, R. John Barleycorn [a Ballad].
Campbell, T. Freedom and Love.
Cornford, A. And it came to pass just as they had foretold.
Cummings, E. Spring is like a perhaps hand.
Dafydd ap Gwilym. Duw gwyddiad mai da y gweddai.
Donne. Father of heaven, and him, by whom.
To Mr. R. W ("Kindly I envy thy song's [or songs] perfection").
Gunn, T. Butcher's Son, The.
Haxton. Auspice.
Hill, G. Veni Coronaberis.
Jeffers, R. Shiva.
Johnson, J. Renewal.
Kenyon, J. Pardon.
Lawrence, D. New Heaven and Earth.
MacBeth. Renewal, The.
Martynov. It seems to me I'm resurrected.
Merrill, J. Renewal, A.
Morgan, R. Ghosts in the Carpet.
Olson, C. Chain of memory is resurrection I am a vain man, The.
Pasternak, B. From Superstition.
Roethke. Renewal, The.
Rossetti, C. First Spring Day, The.
Shakespeare, W. Sonnet 56.
Sonnet: "What's in the braine that Inck may character."

Smith, S. New Age, The.
Southwell. Times [*or* Tymes] Go[e] By Turn[e]s.
Thoreau. Music.
Unknown. Songs of the Arapaho.
Songs of the Kiowa.
Songs of the Paiute.
Songs of the Sioux.
Williams, W. Paterson: The Falls.
Rewaking, The.
Wordsworth, W. I watch, and long have watched, with calm regret.
Zukofsky, L. I walk in the old street.
See also **Rebirth; Regeneration**

Renoir, Pierre Auguste
Warren, R. Renoir.

Repentance
"Æ." Reconciliation.
Alabaster. Night, the starless[e] night of passion, The.
Now that the midd day heate doth scorch my shame.
Ashby. Latter Day Psalms.
Behan, B. Repentance.
Berkeley, S. Mass is over, they have gone in peace, The.
Campion, T. Awake, awake, thou heavy sprite [*or* spright].
Delanty. Thrust & Parry.
Dickinson, E. Renunciation—is a piercing Virtue.
Donnchadh Mor O'Dala. At Saint Patrick's Purgatory.
Donne. Blow Your Trumpets.
Fitzgerald, P. Answer to Thomas Barry, An.
Gogarty. Airman's Breastplate, The.
Herbert, G. Cross[e], The.
Discipline.
Mary [*or* Marie] Magdalene.
Parody [*or* Parodie], A.
Reprisal[l], The.
Rose, The.
Sighs and Groans [*or* Grones].
Sin's Round.
Storm, The.
Trinity Sunday.
Herrick. Calling, and Correcting.
Jonson, B. Hymn[e] to God the Father, A.
Kavanagh, P. Advent.
Keating, G. Keen Thyself, Poor Wight.
Kennelly. Pilgrim, The.
Kipling, R. Supplication of the Black Aberdeen.
Kuzmina-Karavayeva. Even in repentance there is pleasure.
MacDonagh, D. Ballade which Villon Made.
Macdonagh, T. Lifting of the Cloud, The.
Melvill. Ane Godlie Dreame.
Milton. On His Blindness.
Montgomerie, A. Away Vane World.
Murray, R. Wasted Day, The.
O'Sullivan, T. Poem to the Heart of Jesus, A.
Pope, A. Epigram in a Maid of Honour's Prayer-Book.
Rossetti, C. Ash Wednesday.
Stampa. Deeply repentant of my sinful ways.
Tate, N. As Pants the Hart.
Thomas of Celano. Day of Judgment, The.
Thompson, F. To the Dead Cardinal of Westminster.
Toplady. Living and Dying Prayer for the Holiest Believer in the World, A.
Unknown. Joyce's Repentance, The.
Vaughan, H. Admission.
Mans Fall, and Recovery.
Match, The.
Relapse, The.

Repression
Bangs, J. On File.
Bly, R. Executive's Death, The.
Bruner. Prayer for Strength.
Cullen, C. Timid Lover.
Cully. Repressed Theme.
Kleiser. Most Vital Thing in Life, The.
Mandelstam. By denying me the seas, the right to run and fly.
Milton. On His Blindness.

Osgood, F. Ah! woman still.
Ping. Of Flesh and Spirit.
Shapiro, K. Buick.
Williams, C. Repression.
Williams, W. Slow Movement.

Reproach
Bible, *O.T.* Psalm 74.
Bly, R. Executive's Death, The.
"Carroll." Duchess's Lullaby, The.
Chaucer. Envoy to Scogan.
To His Scribe Adam.
Li Po. Jewel Stairs' Grievance, The.
MacLeish. You Also, Gaius Valerius Catullus.
Yosano. Tanka: "Camellias."

Reptiles
Po Chü-i. Chuang Tzu, The Monist.

Reputation
Bible, *O.T.* Bible, Proverbs 22:1, The.
Bruner. Sinner, The.
Graves, R. 1805.
Herrick. Poetry Perpetuates the Poet.
Robinson, E. Flammonde.
Shakespeare, W. Sonnet 111.
Yeats. Father and Child.

Rescues
Fanthorpe. Not my best side, I'm afraid.
Ficowski. I did not manage to save.
Ransom, J. Lady Lost.
Sutskever. 1980.

Reservations, Native American
Klein, A. Indian Reservation: Caughnawaga.
Warrior. Reginald Pugh, The Man Who Came from the Army.

Resistance
Carew, T. Boldness[e] in Love.
"Dario." To Roosevelt.
Desnos. Night Watchman of Pont-au-Change, The.
Gubanov. Palette of Grief.
Herrick. To Virgins.
Jordan, J. 1977: Poem for Mrs. Fannie Lou Hamer.
Klepfisz. About My Father.
Kuznetsov. Mushrooms.
Libbey. Come Into the Night Grove.
Meynell, A. Renouncement.
Nobuyuki. Fiery Declarations (two poems).
Rukeyser, M. Don Baty, the Draft Resister.
Unknown. Thy heart is like some icy lake.
Wyatt, T. What no, Perdy [*or* Perdie *or* perdie][!] ye may be sure[!].

Respectability
Eberhart, R. New England Bachelor, A.
Frere. And certainly they say, for fine behaving.
Frost, R. Considerable Speck, A.
Holmes, O. At the "Atlantic" Dinner, December 15, 1874.
Stafford, W. Well rising without sound, The.
Taylor, J. Gods *Houses,* almost like *Troyes Ilion,*.

Responsibility
Brooks, G. Kitchenette Building.
Browning, E. Curse for a Nation, A.
Giovanni. December of My Springs, The.
Heyen. Riddle: "From Belsen a crate of gold teeth."
Hoagland, T. In the Land of the Lotus Eaters.
Joseph, J. Warning.
Kipling, R. Refined Man, The.
Knight, E. I. Slim's Song.
Mordecai. Last Lines.
Peacock, M. Good Girl.
Rich, A. For the Record.
Rukeyser, M. Despisals.
Stafford, W. With Kit, Age Seven, at the Beach.
Su Tung-p'o. Under the heaven of our holy ruler, all things turn to spring.
Turner, A. *Meditation Upon* Ought.
Wang K'ang-chü. Refuting the "Invitation to Hiding."
Wright, C. Self-Portrait ("Someday they'll find me out, and my lavish hands").

Rest
Aldington. Field Manoeuvres.

Amichai. Lovers in Fall.
Bernstein, O. And Later by Myself.
Byron, G. So we'll go no more a-roving.
Cowper, W. Inscription.
Daniel, S. Sonnet: "Care-charmer Sleep[e], son[ne] of the sable night."
Dimoski. Rest.
Dowson. Villanelle of Sunset.
Frost, R. Acceptance.
Gascoigne. Lullaby [or Lullabie] of a Lover, The.
Hardy, T. Drizzling Easter Morning, A.
Herbert, G. Pulley, The.
Herrick. End of His Work, The.
Hsieh Ling-yün. Written on the Lake, Returning from the Retreat at Stone Cliff.
Keats. To one who has been long in city pent.
Levine, P. Sleepless Night, A.
Liu Cheng. Poem without a Category.
Lovelace, R. Ant, The.
Mackenzie, K. Door swung open, The.
Mangan, J. Rest Only in the Grave.
Melville, H. Return of the Sire de Nesle A.D. 16, The.
Mother Goose. Forehead, Eyes, Cheeks, Nose, Mouth, and Chin.
Nesbit, E. Song: "Oh, baby, baby, baby dear."
Pagis. Plans.
Po Chü-i. After Eating.
  Early Levée, An.
  Ease.
  Sick Leave.
Poe. For Annie.
Rossetti, C. Cardinal Newman.
  Rest.
  Sleeping at last, the trouble and tumult over.
  Uphill [or Up-Hill].
Segal, J. Rest.
Sidney, P. Sonnet 39: "Come Sleep, O Sleep."
Smith, C. Sonnet Written in the Church-Yard at Middleton in Sussex.
Su Tung-p'o. Tune: Immortal at the River.
Timrod. Retirement.
Tranströmer. Open and Closed Space.
Trapnell, A. O he is a rest that requires.
Unknown. Egyptian Poem.
  I climb the road to Cold Mountain.
  Rest.
Vaughan, H. Evening-Watch, The.
Wen T'ing-yün. People all say the southland's better.
Whitman, W. Evening Lull, An.
Wordsworth, W. Water Fowl.
Wu Chen. Moonlight Bay.
Yang Chi. Nesting among Clouds.
Yeats. Michael Robartes Bids His Beloved Be at Peace.
Yüan Mei. Rough Ridge.

Restaurants
Betjeman. Huxley Hall.
Cummings, E. Item.
Hall, J. Eat and Walk.
Keats. Lines on the Mermaid Tavern.
Mahon. Chinese Restaurant in Portrush, The.
Margolis, G. For the Woman at the Fast-Food Fish Place Who Called Me Pig.
McElroy, C. Foul Line—1987.
Pettit. Sparrow of Espanola.
Rios, A. Chinese Food in the Fifties.
Trinidad. C'est Plus Qu'en Crime, C'est une Faute.
Unknown. I Had But Fifty Cents.
Urdang. At Frank 'n' Helen's.
Wetzsteon. Dinner at Le Caprice.
Worth, V. McDonald's, New Hartford, NY.

Restlessness
Alexander, M. Memory.
  People of Unrest.
Cawthorn. Wit was a strange unlucky child.
Chu Shu-chen. Plaint.
Edson, R. Lovers.
Elovic. Brooklyn Bound.
K'ang Hai. Listening to the Rain.
Lane, P. Spring.
Levy, A. March Day in London, A.
Longfellow, H. Seaweed.
Lowell, R. At the Altar.

Lowry, M. Joseph Conrad.
Prince, F. Babiaantje, The.
Robinson, A. Darwinism.
Tu Fu. Restless Night.
Wen Cheng-ming. Hearing a Flute on the River Chi.
Wordsworth, D. Cottager to Her Infant, (By My Sister), The.
Young, A. I Arrive In Madrid.

Restraint
Bible, *O.T.* Lord, Make Me to Know Mine End.
Collins, M. Trapped.
Drayton. O, why should Nature niggardly restraine!
Drummond de Andrade. Looking for Poetry.
Glück, L. Palais des Arts.
Hill, G. Masque of Blackness, The.
Kizer, C. Bitch.
Lawrence, D. Passing Visit to Helen.
Newcastle, M. Claspe, The.
Philips, K. Answer to Another Persuading a Lady to Marriage, An.
Piercy. Work of Artifice, A.
Rilke. No, we don't accomplish our love in a single year.
Unknown. Bird's Nest, The.
  Pussy.
Wallace, R. Condoms.
Zimmer. Queen, The.

Resurrection, The
Bible, *O.T.* I am the resurrection, and the life.
Coverdale. Of the Resurrection.
Crashaw. Easter Day.
Dickinson, E. Safe in their Alabaster Chambers.
Doddridge, P. Christ's Resurrection and Ascension.
Donne. Resurrection.
  Resurrection, Imperfect.
Goethe. Christ Is Arisen.
Herbert, G. Dawning, The.
  Easter ("Rise heart; thy Lord is risen. Sing his praise").
Hooper, V. Argument for Resurrection.
Hopkins, G. That Nature Is a Heraclitean Fire and of the Comfort of the Resurrection.
Milosz, C. "Christ has risen." Whoever believes that / Should not behave as we do. Now after the sabbath.
Murray, L. Easter 1984.
Neale. Hymn for Easter Morn.
Pankey. That very day two of them.
Rilke. But Mary stood weeping outside the tomb.
Rossetti, C. Better Resurrection, A.
Shaw, L. For They Shall See God.
Spenser. Sonnet 68: "Most glorious Lord of Life that on this day."
Thompson, C. Empty Tomb, The.
Unknown. I Have Labored Sore.
  Steal Away to Jesus.
Updike. Seven Stanzas at Easter.
Vaughan, H. Easter-Day.
Wordsworth, W. Composed in One of the Valleys of Westmoreland, on Easter Sunday.

Retirement and Retirees
Adaios of Macedon. John spared his patient labouring ox.
Ammons. Creepy little creepers are insinuatingly.
Collins, J. Tomorrow.
Dove, R. Satisfaction Coal Company, The.
Jacobsen, J. Hourglass.
Kessler, M. Secret Love.
Lu Yu. Sitting Up at Night.
Marvell. Garden, The.
Ní Chuilleanáin. Swineherd.
Po Chü-i. Golden Bells.
  Written when Governor of Soochow.
Reed, I. White Hope.
Smith, I. Retired.
Thelwall. Day of my double birth, if such the year.
  Lines written at Bridgwater in Somersetshire, on 27 July 1797, during a Long Excursion in Quest of a Peaceful Retreat.

Wang An-shih. Impromptu; Late Spring at Pan-shan.
Wen Cheng-ming. Wishing to try retirement, I requested release from duty.
Yeats. Lamentation of the Old Pensioner, The.
See also **Old Age; Pensions and Pensioners**

Retribution
Eberhart, R. Fury of Aerial Bombardment, The.
Sassoon. Blighters.
Warren, R. Red Mullet, The.

Reunions
Arnold, M. Lake, The.
Barr, T. Antique Shop.
Beckett, S. Alba.
Blake, W. Little Boy Found, The.
Browning, E. Sonnet: "Thou comest! all is said without a word."
Burns, R. Auld Lang Syne.
Carew, T. Upon Master Walter Montagu's Return from Travel.
Devlin, D. Renewal by Her Element.
Dickinson, E. Return, The.
Donne. Valediction, A: Forbidding Mourning.
Hughes, L. Lover's Return.
Ingelow. Long White Seam, The.
Kipling, R. Widower, The.
Kizer, C. Semele Recycled.
Kunitz, S. Father and Son.
Livingston, M. Coming from Kansas.
Meredith, G. He found her by the ocean's moaning verge.
Mickle. There's Nae Luck about the House.
Montague, J. All Legendary Obstacles lay between.
Owen, W. Unreturning, The.
Peyanar. What her Girl Friend Said ("Saying to himself").
  What her Girl Friend Said ("Your arms are beautiful again").
Rich, A. Face to Face.
Rossetti, C. Birthday, A.
Rukeyser, M. More of a Corpse Than a Woman.
Smith, I. Oban 1955–82.
Tu Fu. Presented to Wei Pa, Gentleman in Retirement.
  Return, The.
  To Wei Pa, a Retired Scholar.
Unknown. Dis Long Time, Gal.
  Husband's Message, The ("Now shall I unseal myself to yourself alone").
Yevtushenko. My love will come.

Revelation (Bible)
Blake, W. Mental Traveller, The.
Herrick. To God ("Do with me, God! as Thou didst deal with John").
Lowry, R. Beautiful River.
Spenser. Sonnet 12: "I saw an ugly beast come from the sea."
  Sonnet 13: "I saw a woman sitting on a beast."
  Sonnet 14: "Then might I see upon a white horse set."
  Sonnet 15: "I saw new Earth, new Heaven, said Saint John."
Trapnell, A. Therefore John read how that thou wouldst.

Revelry
Ch'u Kuang-hsi. Streets of Ch'ang-an, The.

Revenge
Aeschylus. Clytemnestra triumphant over the bodies of Agamemnon and Cassandra.
Alcman. Vendettas end among the gods.
Archilochus. Stranded ashore from the sea.
Brontë, A. Song.
Campo. Allegory.
Carew, T. To My Inconstant Mistress [or Mistris].
Congreve. False Though She Be [to me and love].
Davenant. 'Tis, in good truth, a most wonderful thing.
Dickinson, E. Mine Enemy is growing old.
Donne. Apparition, The.
Ehrenburg. Retribution.
Elizabeth I. Written on a Wall at Woodstock.

Gay, J. Wild Boar and the Ram, The.
Gbadamosi. Sango's son came down to the river.
Graves, R. Wreath, The.
Herbert, G. Reprisal[1], The.
Herrick. Bubble; a Song, The.
Holden, J. Liberace.
Homer. Achilles with wild fury in his heart.
Hughes, T. Kreutzer Sonata.
Kasischke. Woman Kills Sweetheart with Bowling Ball.
Kipling, R. Heriot's Ford.
Kunene. Thought on June 26.
Landon. Revenge.
Lanier, S. Revenge of Hamish, The.
Lea, S. Feud, The.
Lepik. Curse.
Lovelace, R. Cupid Far Gone.
McKay, C. Enslaved.
Melville, H. Martyr, The.
Meredith, G. King Harald's Trance.
Merson. Spaniard That Blighted My Life, The.
Merwin, W. Last One, The.
Millay, E. Oh, Oh, you will be sorry for that word!
Milton. Deliverer, The.
Immortal Hate.
On the Late Massacre [or Massacher] in Piedmont [or Piemont].
Pagis. Autobiography.
Petri. Electra.
Plath. Lady Lazarus.
Sansom, M. Song: "Foolish eyes, thy streams give over."
Shakespeare, W. That Cassio loves her, I do well believe it.
Shaw, C. Search, The.
Smith, S. Revenge, Timotheus cries, and in that shout.
Teasdale. I Shall Not Care.
Tourneur. Madam, your grace so private?
Tucker, M. Revenge.
Unknown. Fair and scornful, do thy worst.
Homage to the Tru'ng queens.
Laily Worm and the Machrel of the Sea, The.
There's Someone I Think Of.
Virgil. Dido's death.
Walker, M. Kissie Lee.

Revere, Paul
Longfellow, H. Paul Revere's Ride (The Landlord's Tale).

Revivalism and Revivalists
Garrett, G. Revival.
Marson. Gettin de Spirit.
Warren, R. Amazing Grace in the Back Country.
See also **Evangelism and Evangelists; Religion**

Revolution and Revolutionaries
Ackland. Communist Poem, 1935.
Alcock. Instructions, Supposed to Be Written in Paris, for the Mob in England.
"Aminado." Honest with Oneself.
"Antler." Ungag our souls!! Unstrangle our souls!! Unsmother our souls!!
Auden. Epilogue: " 'O where are you going?' said reader to rider."
Baraka. Cuba Libre.
When We'll Worship Jesus.
Bienek. Resistance.
Brown, S. Old Woman Remembers, An.
Browning, E. Part II.
Buchanan, G. Revolutionary Revolution.
Speaker in the Square, A.
Bùi Công Trừng. Fallen Fruit, A.
Burns, R. Scots, wha hae wi' Wallace bled.
Carson, C. Hamlet.
Cervantes. Para un Revolucionario.
Cheney-Coker. Poem for a Guerrilla Leader.
Chin. Exile's Letter: After the Failed Revolution.
Collins, M. Callaloo.
Crosby, H. Firebrand.
Đặng Phu'o'ng. Day of Mourning at Yên-Báy, The.
Đào Duy Kỳ. At Condore Port.
Dhasal. Stone-masons, My Father, and Me.
Di Prima. April Fool Birthday Poem for

Grandpa.
Revolutionary Letter #1.
Duffy, C. Politico.
Duoduo. When the People Stand Up out of the Hard Cheese.
Faiz. Don't Ask Me for That Love Again.
Ferlinghetti, L. Sandinista Avioncitos.
Fiacc. British Connection, The.
Frost, R. Semi-Revolution, A.
Galanskov. Night is dark, The.
Ginsberg, A. Vow, A.
Giovanni. For Saundra.
My Poem.
"Gorky." Song of the Stormy Petrel.
Gossett. On the Question of Fans/ The Slave Quarters Are Never Air Conditioned.
Gwala. New Dawn, The.
Haines, J. Poem Like a Grenade, A.
Harper, M. Song: I Want a Witness.
Hippolyte. Revo Lyric.
Hitchcock. United States Prepare for the Permanent Revolution, The.
Hồ Văn Hảo. Revolutionary Youth.
Hồng Chu'o'ng. It's Me, Your Son.
Hughes, L. Letter to the Academy.
Militant.
Warning.
Jackson, R. Lonely Affair, A.
Jeffers, L. Flesh of the Young Men Is Burning, The.
Jordan, J. Poem Against the State (Of Things): 1975.
Poem for Guatemala.
Knight, E. On the Yard.
"Korzhavin." Imitation of Monsieur Beranger.
Lamantia. Voice of Earth Mediums.
Lanjewar. I Never Saw You.
Lawrence, D. O! start a revolution, somebody!
Lê Đù'c Thọ. Fighter's Thoughts of Spring, A.
Lorde. Sisters in Arms.
Macaulay, T. Radical War Song, A.
Machado Ruiz. Meditation for this Day.
Mao Tse-tung. Long March, The.
Loushan Pass.
"Spring in Ch'in's Garden" ("Alone I stand in autumn cold").
Mataka. Ornithology.
Maxwell, M. Our Revolutions Must Be Different.
McFadden, R. First Letter to an Irish Novelist.
Meeks, B. Coup-clock Clicks, The.
Michael. Preface: "I stood watching / I the parade of floats."
Milosz, C. Bypassing rue Descartes.
Moraes, D. Babur.
Mtshali. Day We Buried Our Bully, The.
Mutabaruka. Revolutionary Poets.
Nguyễn Đình Chiểu. Blind Poet Looks at the World Outside, A.
Elegy for Tru'o'ng Định.
Storm, The.
Nguyễn Hữ'u Huân. Carrying a Cangue Around the Neck.
Như'o'ng Tống. Mourning a Hero.
Okigbo. Elegy for Slit-Drum.
Padilla. Discourse on Method, The.
Parkes, F. Lilian's Second Letter.
Petri. Christmas 1956.
Phan Bội Châu. Alarm Clock, The.
Mourning Nguyễn Thái Học and Nguyễn Thị Giang.
Phan Trọng Quảng. Independence Day.
Ricksha Man's Impromptu, A.
Pope, A. Shut, shut the door, good *John*! fatigu'd, I said.
Pound, E. Canto 32.
Randall, D. Abu / 's a stone black revolutionary.
Roses and Revolutions.
Rebelo. Poem.
Reed, I. Reactionary Poet, The.
Rodgers, C. U Name This One.
Rodriguez, M. June 10.
Rossetti, C. Royal Princess, A.
Saarikoski. Revolution.
Scott, D. For the Last Time, Fire.

Scott-Heron. Revolution Will Not Be Televised!, The.
Senghor. In Memoriam.
Serge. Dialectic.
Shengeli. 27 July 1830.
Smith, M. Revolutionary.
Sykes, B. Cycle.
Tản Đà. Tattered Map, The.
Troth Between the Hill and the Stream, The.
Teller. Minor Key.
Trần Minh Tu'ó'c. Prison Dreams.
Tryapkin. We banished the tyrant-tsars.
Unknown. Cutty Wren, The.
Diggers' Song, The.
In Taihang born, in Taihang bred.
Revolutionaries, The.
We are a people who love to sing.
Upton, C. When I was very young.
Voloshin. Bourgeoisie.
Walker, M. For my people [everywhere singing their slave songs repeatedly: their].
Watkins, N. Bedtime Story.
Xuân Thủy. You Cannot Lock Up the Mind.
Yeats. Great Day, The.
Zimunya. After the Massacre.
See also **Rebellion and Rebels**

Revolutionary War, American. *See* **American Revolution**

Rewards
Bible, *O.T.* Psalm 17.
Coleridge, S. Good Great Man, The.

Reynolds, Sir Joshua
Blake, W. Sir Joshua Reynolds.
Goldsmith, O. Sir Joshua Reynolds.

Rhine (river), Germany
Coleridge, S. Cologne.

Rhinoceroses
Nash, O. Rhinoceros, The.

Rhode Island (state)
Bryant, W. Meditation on Rhode Island Coal, A.
Meredith, W. Rhode Island.

Rhythm
Creeley. Rhythm, The.
Jeffers, R. Rearmament.
Johnson, L. Bass Culture.
Reed, I. Poetry Makes Rhythm in Philosophy.
Springer, T. Harmony.
Vinokurov. Rhythm.

Ribbons
Carew, T. Upon a Ribbon [or Ribband].
Herrick. Bracelet.
Upon a Black Twist, Rounding the Arm of the Countess of Carlisle.
Upon Julia's Ribband.
Waller, E. On a Girdle.

Rice
Bobrowsky. Journey, The.
Chin Nung. Three lines of "clerk script" calligraphy.
Cross, Jr. Rice Will Grow Again.
Kākkai Pāṭiṇiyār Naccellaiyār. What Her Girl Friend Said to her lover on his return.
Krohn. Farmer's Song at Can Tho.
Liu E. New Year's Eve.
Mocikiranar. Not Rice, Not Water.
Phan Văn Trị. Grains of Rice.
Po Chü-i. Climbing the Ling-ying Terrace and Looking North.
Strange. Offering.
Su Tung-p'o. I planted rice before Spring Festival.
Unknown. Children's Song.
On and on, always on and on.

Richard I (Richard Coeur de Lion), King of England
Chaucer. Lak of Stedfastnesse.

Richard III, King of England
Shakespeare, W. Set down, set down your honourable load.
Suckling, J. On King Richard the Third, Who Lies Buried under Leicester Bridge.

Richard, Earl of Cornwall
Unknown. Song of Lewes, The.

Richardson, Samuel
Edwards, T. To the Author of Clarissa.

Williams, A. Verses to Mr. Richardson on his History of Sir Charles Grandison.

Riches. *See* **Wealth**

Riddles

Clare, J. Secret Love.
Crane, S. Unwind my riddle.
Cynewulf. Anchor: "Oft I must strive with wind and wave."
Book Moth: "Moth ate a word. To me it seemed, A."
Fish in River: "My house is not quiet, I am not loud."
Honey-Mead: "I am valued by men, fetched from afar."
Horn: "Time was when I was weapon and warrior."
Riddle: Cuckoo.
Swan, The.
Weathercock, The: "I puff my breast out, my neck swells."
Dickinson, E. Narrow Fellow in the Grass, A.
Riddle we can guess, The.
Fanshawe, C. Riddle, A: "'Twas in heaven pronounced, and 'twas muttered in hell."
Hayden, R. Sphinx.
Lindsay, V. Two old crows sat on a fence rail.
Lochhead, L. Riddle-Me-Ree.
MacLeish. What Riddle Asked the Sphinx.
Mother Goose. Candle, A.
I have a little sister, they call her Peep-Peep.
In marble walls [*or* halls] as white as milk.
Man in the wilderness asked [of] me [*or* said to me], The [*or* A].
Old Mother Twitchett had [*or* has] but one eye.
Parnell, T. Riddle, A: "Upon a bed of humble clay."
Poe. Valentine, A.
Reeves, J. Spells.
Robinson, E. How Annandale Went Out.
Rossetti, C. Pin has a head, but has no hair, A.
Riddle, A: "There is one that has a head without an eye."
Sidney, P. Sonnet 37: "My mouth doth water, and my breast doth swell."
Swift, J. Riddling Letter, A ("Sir, / Pray discruciate what follows: / A long-eared beast, and a field-house for cattle").
Unknown. Bishop of Canterbury, The.
Captain Wedderburn's Courtship.
Devil's Nine Questions, The.
Four stiff-standers.
From house to house he goes.
I Have a Young Sister.
I'm called by the name of a man.
In Spring I look gay.
Moth ate words; a marvellous event, A.
My dress is silent when I tread the ground.
Present to a Lady, A.
Riddle: "Highty, tighty, paradighty, clothed [all] in green."
Riddle: "Land was white, The."
Riddle Song, The.
Riddle: "White bird featherless / Flew from Paradise."
Riddle: "White sheep, white sheep, on a blue hill."
Riddles.
Riddles Wisely Expounded.
Riddling Knight, The.

Rifles

Kunio. Tanka: "On the snow."
Sandburg, C. A. E. F.

Righteousness

Bible, *O.T.* Psalm 1.
Psalm 11.
Psalm 19.
Psalm 37: "Fret not thyself because of evildoers."
Psalm 50.
Psalm 58.
Daniel, Y. New Year March: A Declaration, The.
Kutilov. Crickety Creek.

Lindsay, V. Statue of Old Andrew Jackson, The.
MacNeice. Under the surface of flux and of fear there is an underground movement.
Ralegh, W. Lie, The.
Shakespeare, W. Sonnet 94.

Rilke, Rainer Maria

Coolidge, C. In Nora's House with Rilke's Apollo.
Goodison. On Becoming a Tiger.
Rich, A. Paula Becker to Clara Westhoff.
Waldman, A. Evangelie.

Rimbaud, Arthur

Aiken, C. Prelude LVI: "Rimbaud and Verlaine, precious pair of poets."
Berrigan, T. Sonnet LXX: "Sweeter than sour apples flesh to boys."
MacLeish. Aeterna Poetae Memoria.
Moore, T. Response to Rimbaud's Later Manner.

Rings

Crabbe. Marriage Ring, The.
Darley. To Helene.
Donne. Jet Ring Sent, A.
"Field." I love you with my life—'tis so I love you.
Graves. With a Gift of Rings.
Herrick. Ring Presented to Julia, A.
Lovelace, R. Sonnet: "Depose your finger of that Ring."
Merrill, J. Emerald, The.
Rankin, P. Fifteen.
Smith, I. In the Cafe.
Sitting here by the foreshore day after day.
Turberville. To his Love that sent him a Ring wherein was gravde, / Let Reason rule.
Wakoski. Ring, The.
Ringless.

Riots and Rioters

Bly, R. Andrew Jackson's Speech.
Brooks, G. Riot.
Rites for Cousin Vit, The.
Brown, S. Old Woman Remembers, An.
Bryll. In a Fever.
Cruz, V. Urban Dream.
Joseph, L. Then.
Levertov. Gulf, The.
Linden, M. Riot, A.
Melville, H. House-Top, The.
More, H. Riot; or, Half a Loaf Is Better than No Bread, The.
Murray, P. Harlem Riot, 1943.
Mr. Roosevelt Regrets.
Olds, S. May 1968.
Parsons, W. To a Friend in Love during the Riots.
Smith, A. Roslyn Malamud the Coup.

Risorgimento

Landor, W. Regeneration.

Rituals

Barrax. Domestic Tranquility.
Carew, T. New Year's Sacrifice: To Lucinda, A.
To the King, at His Entrance into Saxham: By Master John Crofts.
"Chrystos." For Sharol Graves.
Fields, J. Citizen.
Fuller, M. Sistrum.
Herrick. Perfume, The.
Spell, The.
Steam in Sacrifice.
To Julia, the Flaminica Dialis, or Queen-Priest.
To the Reverend Shade of His Religious Father.
Higo. Ritual Murder.
Jones, P. Day of the Dead.
Kaufman, B. African Dream.
Knight, E. He sees through stone.
Kolmar. Sacrifice, The.
Lyon, G. Foot-Washing, The.
Mattawa. Watermelon Tales.
McGrath, T. Reading the Names of the Vietnam War Dead.
Momaday. Carriers of the Dream Wheel.
Moore, L. Eternal Landscape, The.
Moore, M. Cumae.
Okigbo. Elegy of the Wind.

Plumpp. Remembered.
Ransom, J. First Travels of Max.
Rimbaud, A. After Bitahatini.
Rodgers, C. Slave Ritual.
Rothenberg, J. Crazy Dog Events.
Shange. Rite-ing.
Strange. Barbershop Ritual.
Unknown. Incantation Songs of the Klamath Lake People.
Invocation to the U' wannami.
Prayer upon Cutting down the Sacred Tree.
Whittier. Dead Feast of the Kol-Folk, The.
Yamada. Obon: Festival of the Dead.
Yeats. Collarbone [*or* Collar-Bone] of a Hare, The.
Zuni Oral Tradition. Invocation to the U'wannami (Rain-Makers).

Rivalry

Behn, A. To My Lady Morland at Tunbridge.
Carew, T. Fly That Flew into My Mistress'[s] Eye, A.
Corrothers. Me 'n' Dunbar.
"Ephelia." To My Rival.
Suckling, J. My dearest rival, lest [*or* least] our love.

See also **Competition**

Rivera, Diego

White, E. I Paint What I See.

Rivers

Adams, L. River in the Meadows, The.
"Adunis." Tree of Fire.
Agard, J. Don't Call Alligator Long-Mouth Till You Cross River.
Aldrich, T. By the Potomac.
Ammons. Serpent Country.
Ashbery. Myrtle.
Ausonius. Evening on the Moselle.
Ayton. Sonnet: On the River Tweed.
Bagryana. River Run.
Balaban. Along the Mekong.
Bansode. Woman.
Belloc. Evenlode, The.
Bennett, R. Growing River, The.
Berry, W. Slip, The.
Bevington, L. With the Tide: A Cry of Weakness.
Bible, *O.T.* Psalm 1.
Bishop, E. One Art.
Bly, R. Schoolcraft's Diary Written on the Missouri: 1830.
Bobrowski. Shadowland.
Bolamba. In a Storm.
Boldman. Walking with the river.
Boncho. Long, long river, The.
Bowles, W. To the River Itchin, near Winton.
Tweed Visited, The.
Bryant, W. Green River.
Night Journey of a River, The.
Burns, R. Flow gently, sweet Afton, among thy green braes.
Byron, G. Stanzas to the Po.
Cardenal. Tahirassawichi in Washington.
Carew, T. To My Mistress Sitting by a River's Side; an Eddy.
Carman, B. Low Tide on Grand Pré.
Ceravolo. Spring of Work Storm.
Chan Fang-sheng. Folk-Songs.
Chang Yü. To the Innkeeper at Five Rivers, Sun Pen.
Chao Meng-fu. Inscribed on a Landscape by Mi Yüan-hui.
Chaucer. Love's Garden.
Cheng Hsieh. Inscribed on a Painting.
Chiang Ch'un-lin. Tune: "Magnolia Blossoms, Slow"—Traveling on the Yangtze.
Chin Nung. Evening Scene at Twin Forests.
Mooring in the Rain at Sung-ling.
Ch'u Yüan. Lord of the River Hsiang.
Clare, J. Love's memories haunt my footsteps still.
Cohen, L. Suzanne takes you down to her place near the river.
Coleridge, S. Sonnet to the River Otter.
Cooper, J. Morning on the St. John's.
Cowper, W. Comparison, A.
Crabbe. Sailing upon the River.

Crane, H. Repose of Rivers.
River, The.
Creeley. Memory, The.
River wandering down.
Cronin, J. River That FLows through Our
Land, The.
Cruickshank, H. Ponnage Pool, The.
Davie. Ox-Bow.
De la Mare. Voices.
Deane, S. Fording the River.
Dickinson, E. I like to see it lap the Miles.
Đông Hồ. River, The.
Doolittle, H. Pursuit.
Dove, R. Event, The.
Dowson. Spleen.
Dyer, J. Prospects.
Eliot, T. Dry Salvages, The.
Virginia.
Emerson, R. Musketaquid.
Two Rivers.
Erdrich. I Was Sleeping Where the Black
Oaks Move.
Faiz. You Tell Us What to Do.
Farjeon, E. Tide in the river, The.
Ferlinghetti, L. River Still To Be Found, A.
Ferril. Time of Mountains.
Fletcher, J. River[-]God's Song, The.
Fordham. Maiden and River.
Foster, S. Old Folks at Home[, The].
Francis, R. Like Ghosts of Eagles.
Gardner, D. Fire Music.
Gates, L. At the river-bend.
Glazkov. My Wife.
Goldberg, L. Blade of Grass Sings to the
River, The.
Goll, I. Last river leaves for desolation, The.
Goodison. Wedding in Hanover.
Gorman, L. Her long paper legs.
Hackett, J. Deep within the stream.
Wind gives way to calm.
Hall, D. Long River, The.
Hardy, T. On Sturminster Foot-Bridge.
Harumichi no Tsuraki. Wind has stopped, The.
Hay, J. Jim Bludso of the Prairie Belle.
Heaney, S. Broagh.
New Song, A.
Hemans. Indian Woman's Death-Song, The.
Herrick. To Dean-bourn, a Rude River in
Devon, by Which Sometimes He Lived.
Upon Julia Weeping.
Ho Ching-ming. Ballad of Yi River.
Hollander, J. Variations on a Fragment by
Trumbull Stickney.
Holmes, O. Two Streams, The.
Hsieh Chin. Sandal Mountain.
Hsieh Ling-yün. Exchange of Poems by Tung-
yang Stream, An.
HSü Ling. Teleg Song.
Huang T'ing-chien. Song of the Clear River.
Huchel. Eastern River.
Hughes, L. Life Is Fine.
Negro Speaks of Rivers, The.
Suicide's Note.
Hughes, T. River.
Hugo, R. Plans for Altering the River.
River Now, The.
Skykomish River Running.
Hunt, L. Nile, The.
Issa. From the bough / floating down river.
Jewell. Mountain shadow.
Kemble. To the Wissahiccon.
Kingsley, C. River's Song, The.
Kinnell. River That Is East, The.
Kinsella, T. Nuchal, a Fragment.
Kipling, R. Ford o' Kabul River.
Ku K'uang. On the River.
Lanier, S. Song of the Chattahoochee.
Lattimore. Max Schmitt in a Single Scull.
Lauterbach. Subject to Change.
Lawrence, D. River Roses.
Li Ch'ing-chao. As in a Dream.
Li K'ai-hsien. Recording a Weird Happening.
Li Meng-yang. Autumn Vista.
Wild Wind.
Liu E. On the Road to Pyongyang—An
Improvisation.
Lowry, R. Beautiful River.

Lu Yu. Blue Rapids.
Rain on the River.
MacCaig. Old Edinburgh.
"MacDiarmid." Water Music.
MacLeish. What Any Lover Learns.
Marais. Deep River.
Martinson. On the Congo.
McCombs, D. River and Under the River,
The.
McMullen, A. By the River.
Mei Yao Ch'en. I Remember the Blue River.
I Remember the River at Wu Sung.
Melo Neto. Landscape of the Capibaribe
River.
Meredith, W. Ideogram.
Merrill, J. Current, The.
Meynell, A. Watershed, The.
Miljkovic. Agon.
Miyazawa Kenji. River in Hell (two poems).
Tanka: "Unsettled."
Murray, P. Conquest.
Narihira. Even in the age.
Nasrin. Border.
Nemerov. "Good-bye," said the river, "I'm
going downstream."
Ni Tsan. On the Fifteenth Day of the Ninth
Month of the Year Kuei-mao of the Chih-
cheng Period (Oct. 22, 1363), I Painted This
to Send to the Summoned Scholar, Sheng-po,
and Inscribed This Poem on It.
Noin. After the storm / On Mount Mimuro.
Okamoto. Tanka: "My mind shattered."
Okara. Call of the River Nun, The.
Oliver, M. Climbing the Chagrin River.
Ondaatje. Walking to Bellrock.
Opoku. River Afram.
Orampokiyar. What She Said ("In the full
river").
Orr, G. Elegy: "Not only doesn't the Ohio."
Ortiz. Bend in the River.
Ou-yang Hsiu. In the Evening I Walk by the
River.
Pape. Indian Ruins Along Rio de Flag.
Pfeiffer, E. So the river—yes, the river; I have
come to that at last.
Pien Kung. Inscribed on an Album Leaf
Painted by Dr. Lin.
Pizzarelli. Tiny fish.
Plisetsky. Pipe, The.
Plomer. Tugela River.
Po Chü-i. Evening View at River Pavilion,
Inviting Guest.
Spring River, The.
Posey, A. Song of the Oktahutchee.
Power, K. Sestina for Jaime.
Raine, K. By the River Eden.
Ridler. River God's Song.
Rilke. Tombs of the Hetaerae.
Robinson, M. Canzonet.
Roditi. Hand.
Roethke. Meditation at Oyster River.
Rukeyser, M. Dam, The.
Saitō Mokichi. Tanka: "What on the other
shore."
Sandburg, C. River Roads.
Sarton. After a Train Journey.
Servasius. Rivers level granite mountains.
Simms, C. Otter, Redewetter.
Simms, W. By the Swannanoa.
Sitwell, S. River God, The.
Smith, A. Steamer left he black and oozy
wharves, The.
Smith, S. River God, The.
Souster. On the Rouge.
Southerland. Night in Nigeria.
Spence, L. Carse, The.
Great Tay of the Waves.
Spiess. Light river wind, A.
Shooting the rapids!
Stafford, W. Ask Me.
At Cove on the Crooked River ("At Cove at
our camp in the open canyon").
Ceremony.
In the Deep Channel.
Prairie Town.
Stevens, W. Metaphor as Degeneration.

River of Rivers in Connecticut, The.
This Solitude of Cataracts.
Stevenson, R. Where Go the Boats?
Stickney, T. I heard a river thro' the valley
wander.
Storer. Rivers.
Su Tung-p'o. At Gold Hill Monastery.
Following the Rhumes of Chiang Hui-shu.
Sutskever. Banks of a River, The.
T'ang Hsien-tsu. Spending the Night on the
River.
Tanikawa Shuntaro. River.
Tartler. Sighioara 1982.
Tasso. "Woods and the rivers are silent," The.
Tekkan. Tanka: "Except the rare time."
Tillinghast, R. Knife, The.
Tsung Ch'en. On the spring river, you depart.
Tu Fu. Brimming Water.
Dejeuner Sur L'Herbe.
Far Up the River.
Stars and Moon on the Yangtse.
Tu Mu. Pien River Blocked by Ice.
Ungaretti. Rivers, The.
Unknown. bridge engineer, Mister Crumpett,
A.
Bạch-đằng River, The.
Crossing the river I pluck the lotus flowers;.
Goddess Chiao, The.
On Asuka River.
Tweed and Till.
Yoshino River.
Very. Moses in Infancy.
Wakoski. Canoer, The.
Wang An-shih. By the River.
Wang Shih-chieng. Quatrain at Chen-chou.
Warner, S. Drawing you, heavy with sleep to
lie closer.
Warton, T. Sonnet: To the River Lodon.
Wat. By a great, swift water.
Joke, A.
Watson, R. Children of the Mist.
Weatherly, T. Mud Water Shango.
Wei Ying-wu. West Creek at Ch'u-chou.
Wen Cheng-ming. Painting a Picture, The
Tranquil Boat—Sent to Ko Ju-ching.
Wen T'ing-yün. Crossing South of Li-chou, A.
Tune: "River Messages."
Wilbur. Aspen and the Stream, The.
Williams, W. January Morning.
Mists Over the River.
River Rhyme.
Willis, P. Meeting Like This.
Wills, J. River, The.
Wilson, A. In Praise of Drainage.
Woolson. Detroit River.
Wordsworth, W. Composed upon Westminster
Bridge[, September 3, 1802].
Dear native brooks, your ways I have pursued.
Lines Written near Richmond, upon the
Thames, at Evening.
Wright, J. Living by the Red River.
To the Poets in New York.
Wright, J. Eli, Eli.
River Bend.
Wu Wei-yeh. At the River Tower Parting
from My Younger Brother, Fu-ling.
Yang Chi. Noble Scholar Playing the Lute, A.
Yang Shih-ch'i. Crossing the River.
Yang-Ti, Emperor of Sui Dynasty. Flowers
and Moonlight on the Spring River.
Yang Wan-li. Crossing Ts'en River.
Keng-tzu (1180), First Month, Fifth Day,
Dawn.
Yü Chi. After Snow—Impromptu.
Yüan Hao-wen. Crossing the Yellow River:
June 12.
Yüan Hung-tao. On Board a Boat at Chi-ning.
Yukitsuna. Tanka: "Always loving."
Zieroth. Baptism.
Zukofsky, L. Not much more than being.
Zweig, P. River, The.
See also **Brooks and Streams; Listings for
specific Rivers**
Roaches. *See* **Cockroaches**
Roads
Aiken, C. Road, The.
Alterman. Memento of Roads.

Ashbery. Poem: "While we were walking under the top."
Avidan. Recurring Opportunity.
Blackburn, P. El Camino Verde.
Bly, R. Three Kinds of Pleasures.
Buckley, V. Origins.
Cervantes. Como lo Siento.
Freeway 280.
Chesterton, G. Rolling English Road, The.
Dransfield. Minstrel.
Drummond de Andrade. In the middle of the road there was a stone.
Fenton, J. South Parks Road.
Frost, R. Middleness of the Road, The.
Road Not Taken, The.
García Lorca. Little Infinite Poem.
Goodison. Road of the Dread, The.
Gouri. Album.
Piyyut for the New Year.
Gray, R. Flames and Dangling Wire.
Hardy, T. Roman road runs straight and bare, The.
Heaney, S. On the Road.
Hsü Ling. Waters of Lung-t'ou, The.
Huchel. Roads.
Hughes, L. Florida Road Workers.
Ishikawa Takuboku. Tanka: "On the roadside."
Janevski. Song of the Eternal Sailor, The.
Johnson, H. Road, The.
King, H. Moonlight Ride, A.
Kipling, R. Way Through The Woods, The.
Larkin, P. No Road.
Levertov. Merritt Parkway.
Masefield. Roadways.
Merwin, W. Diggers, The.
Highway, The.
Mew. On the Asylum Road.
Morgan, E. Itinerary.
Mori Ōgai. Tanka: "Step by step."
Muir, E. Road, The.
Nash, O. Song of the Open Road.
Ní Chuilleanáin. Old Roads.
Ozog. Song of the Field.
Pagis. Honi.
Perreault, J. Shoe.
Pizzarelli. Moving van zooms, A.
Renton. Fork of the Road, The.
Sáenz. Resurrections.
Sidney, P. Sonnet 84: "Highway, since you my chief Parnassus be."
Slessor. Last Trams.
Song. Beauty and Sadness.
Swenson, M. Bison Crossing Near Mt. Rushmore.
Tế Hanh. Country Road, The.
Tekeyan. Forgetting. Yes, I will forget it all.
Unknown. Meeting in the Road.
Welburn. Yellow Wolf Spirit.
Wright, J. Brother and Sisters.
Wu Wei-yeh. Distant roads in the aftermath of war.
Yüan Mei. Fog at Liang-hsiang.
Zenmaro. Tanka: "On the road."
See also **Streets**

"Rob Roy" (Robert MacGregor, Scottish freebooter)
Unknown. Rob Roy.

Robbe-Grillet, Alain
Equi. Date with Robbe-Grillet, A.

Robbers. *See* **Crime and Criminals**

Robeson, Paul
Brooks, G. Paul Robeson.

Robespierre, Maximilien Marie Isidore
Lowell, R. Robespierre and Mozart as Stage.

Robin Hood
Keats. Robin Hood.
Noyes, A. Sherwood in the twilight, is Robin Hood awake?
Peacock, T. Robin Hood and the Grey Friars.
Unknown. Birth of Robin Hood, The.
Bold Pedlar and Robin Hood, The.
Death of Robin Hood, The.
Jolly Pinder of Wakefield, The.
Little John a Begging.
Robin Hood and Allen [*or* Allin] -a-Dale.
Robin Hood and Guy of Gisborne.

Robin Hood and Little John.
Robin Hood and Maid Marian.
Robin Hood and Queen Katherine.
Robin Hood and the Bishop.
Robin Hood and the Bishop of Hereford.
Robin Hood and the Curtal Friar.
Robin Hood and the Monk.
Robin Hood and the Potter.
Robin Hood and the Tanner.
Robin Hood and the Three Squires.
Robin Hood and the Tinker.
Robin Hood Newly Revived.
Robin Hood Rescuing Three Squires.
Robin Hood Rescuing Will Stutly.
Robin Hood's Chase.
Robin Hood's Death.
Robin Hood's Golden Prize.
Robin Hood's Progress to Nottingham.

Robins
Allen, M. Angleworms.
Allingham. Robin Redbreast.
Alma-Tadema, L. Bed-Time.
Robin, The.
Bridges, R. Gay Robin Is Seen No More.
Cheney, E. Overheard in an Orchard.
Cooper, G. What Robin Told.
De la Mare. Robin, A.
Dickinson, E. Come show thy Durham Breast.
Robin is a Gabriel, The.
Fallis. Wise Johnny.
Herrick. To Robin Redbreast.
Upon Mistress Elizabeth Wheeler under the Name of Amarillis.
Higginson, W. Robin listens, A.
Howells, W. Robin and the Cows, The.
Kunitz, S. Robin Redbreast.
Lee, D. You Too Lie down.
Melville, H. Little Good Fellows, The.
Mother Goose. Catch.
North wind doth blow, The.
Who killed Cock [*or* poor] Robin? [*or* Here lies Cock Robin].
Rogers, S. Epitaph on a Robin Redbreast, An.
Rossetti, C. Bread and milk for breakfast.
Rye. Redbreast smoulders in the waste of snow, The.
Scott, W. Madge Wildfire Sings.
Unknown. Little Robin Red-breast.
Little Robin Redbreast [*or* Red-breast] sat upon a tree.
Robin and a robin's son, A.
Robin Redbreast's Testament.
Secret, The.
Warning, A.
Welcome, little Robin.
When the Snow is on the Ground.
Very. Robin, The.
Webster, J. Dirge, A: "Call for the robin-redbreast and the wren."
Yolen. First Robin.

Robinson Crusoe
Bishop, E. Crusoe in England.
Jammes. Amsterdam.
Pagis. Epilogue to Robinson Crusoe.
Walcott. Crusoe's Island.

Robinson, Edwin Arlington
Hall, D. T. R.

Robinson, Jackie
Knight, E. Belly Song.

Robots
Owen, G. Message Understood.
Wallace-Crabbe. Amen.

Rochester, John Wilmot, 2d Earl of
Behn, A. On the Death of the Late Earl of Rochester.
Wharton, A. Elegy on the Earl of Rochester.

Rockefeller Center, New York City
Cardenal. Room 5600.
White, E. I Paint What I See.

Rockefeller, John Davison
Cardenal. Room 5600.

Rockets
Boyce. Ballad of Morgan the Moon, The.
Brathwaite, E. New Year Letter.
Cook, S. Launch, The.
Kitching. If he cried, he cried in private.

Magee, W. Giant Rocket.
Masson. Enough.
McDonald, W. Rocket Attack.
Owen, G. Space Shot.
Probyn. As the Flower of the Grass.
Rice, J. Brokendown Countdown.
Man and Height.
Rockets and quasars.
Smith, W. There Was an Old Lady Named Crockett.
Zarzyski. Silos.
See also **Space and Space Travel**

Rocking Chairs
Bateman, D. My Rocking Chair.
Klein, A. Rocking Chair, The.
Wayman. Teething.

Rocks. *See* **Stones and Rocks**

Rocky Mountains
Birney. David and I that summer cut trails on the Survey.
Frémont. On Recrossing the Rocky Mountains after Many Years.

Rodeos
Smith, W. Closing of the Rodeo, The.

Rodin, Auguste
Greer, J. Rodin's "Gates of Hell."
Stickney, T. On Rodin's "L'Illusion, Sœur d'Icare."

Roethke, Theodore
Berry, D. Theodore Roethke Foots It.
Brinnin. Roethke Plain.
Murphy, R. Poet on the Island, The.
Niatum. Lines for Roethke Twenty Years after His Death.

Roland
MacLeish. Too-Late Born, The.
Unknown. In wrath and grief away the Paynims fly.

Roller Skating and Roller Skaters
Adcock, B. Roller Rink.
Livingston, M. 74th Street.
See also **Skating and Skaters**

Roller-Coasters
Schorr. Amusement.
Souster. Flight of the Roller Coaster.

Roman Catholicism. *See* **Catholicism and Catholics**

Romanticism and Romantics
Cope, W. Triolet.
Gifford, W. Lo, Della Crusca! In his closet pent.
"Korzhavin." Poem about Youth and Romanticism, A.
Kulchitsky. 194.
Lowell, A. Hora Stellatrix.
Mew. My heart is lame with running after yours so fast.
Muir, E. Scotland 1941.
Robinson, E. Miniver Cheevy, child of scorn.
Stevens, W. Re-statement of Romance.
Stevenson, R. Song of a Traveller, The.

Rome, Italy
Appleman, P. Peace with Honor.
Auden. Roman Wall Blues.
Beddoes. Humble Beginnings.
Boethius. Lib. 2. Metrum 5.
Bradstreet, A. Apology, An.
Braun, V. New Purpose of Hadrian's Army, The.
Brodsky, J. Roman Elegies.
Browning, R. Two in the Campagna.
Catullus. Carmen 10 ("Varus, whom I chanced to meet").
Cavafy. Waiting for the Barbarians.
Cawein. Rome.
Chaucer. Monk's Tale, The.
Cowper, W. Boadicea: An Ode.
Cunningham, J. Rome.
DiPalma. Hadrian's Lane.
Du Bellay. Antiquitez de Rome.
Gibson, W. Wishing-Well, The.
Hardy, T. Rome: Building a New Street in the Ancient Quarter.
Hemans. Corinne at the Capitol.
Herbert, Z. Return of the Proconsul, The.
To Marcus Aurelius.

Hildebert. Rome.
Hirsch, E. Watcher, The.
Holland, J. Laocöon! thou great embodiment.
Horace. 3.5: Carthaginian Peace, The.
Kunitz, S. Thief, The.
Kushner, A. No better fate is given than to die in Rome.
Martial. De Hortis Julii Martialis.
McClatchy. Capriccio of Roman Ruins and Sculpture with Figures, A.
Melville, H. Arch, The.
Meredith, G. Square along the couch, and stark.
Milosz, C. Campo dei Fiori.
Namatianus. Roma.
Pagis. Decline of an Empire.
Pasolini. Roman Evening.
Philips, K. On the Welsh Language.
Rutilius. Roma.
Sisson. Carmen Saeculare.
Spenser. Ruines of Time, The.
Who lists to see, what ever nature, arte.
Sylvester, J. Rome, Conqueror, Conquered.
Tomlinson, C. In the Borghese Gardens.
Vas. Catacombs.
Wieseltier. Take a Look at My Rebels.
Wilbur. Baroque Wall-Fountain in the Villa Sciarra, A.
Piazza di Spagna, Early Morning.

Romeo and Juliet
Belloc. Juliet.
Miles, J. Maxim.
Unknown. Silver Dagger, The.

Romney Marsh, England
Davidson, J. In Romney Marsh.

Roofing and Roofers
Grennan. Men Roofing.
Kennelly. Thatcher, The.
Moss, H. Roof Garden, The.
Rich, A. Roofwalker, The.
Roethke. Ceiling, The.
Samio. Tanka: "On a starry night."
Snyder, G. After weeks of watching the roof leak.
Williams, C. Tar.

Rooks
"Field." Nests in Elms.
Plath. Black Rook in Rainy Weather.

Rooming Houses. *See* **Boarding Houses**

Roosevelt, Franklin Delano
Hollander, J. Danish Wit.
Williams, B. President Roosevelt.

Roosevelt, Theodore
Bly, R. Three Presidents.
"Dario." To Roosevelt.
Espada. Bully.
Hall, D. T. R.
Lindsay, V. In Which Roosevelt Is Compared to Saul.

Roosters
Bishop, E. Roosters.
Chang Yü. In the Evening, Walking in the Western Fields.
Chaucer. Nun's Priest's Tale, The.
Currey. Cock-Crow.
Dickey, J. Gamecock.
Farrar, J. Chanticleer.
Gardner, I. Cock-a-Hoop.
Gay, J. Song: "Before the barn-door crowing."
Hall, D. Henyard Round, The.
Kikaku. bantam rooster, A.
Lingg. Though you can tell me.
MacLeish. Genius, The.
Mei Yao Ch'en. Elegy for a White Cock.
Meleager. What have you got to crow about.
Mountain, M. My neighbor's rooster hops the stick i throw.
Odarchenko. And you, Vanya.
Okamoto. Tanka: "Cockscomb, A."
Polkowski. I Don't Know That Man.
Roseliep. In white tulips.
Rossetti, C. "Kookoorookoo! kookoorookoo!" / Crows the cock before the morn.
Sedley. On a Cock at Rochester.
Stevens, W. Bantams in Pine-Woods.
Swede. Dawn.

T'ang Yin. Inscribed on a Painting of a Cock.
Unknown. Cock-A-Doodle-Do.
Cock-Crow.
I have a gentle cock.
I sometimes think I'd rather crow.
Wang Chiu-ssu. Rising from Sleep.
Wen Cheng-ming. Year Hsin-hai (Fifteen Fifty One), New Year's Eve: Keeping Watch, The.
Yang Shih-ch'i. On the Hall of Precious Virtue.
See also **Chickens**

Rope
Clifton, L. Climbing.
Fumiko. Tanka: "One day I saw."
Kennedy, X. Little Elegy.
Longfellow, H. Ropewalk, The.
Unknown. High Skip, The.

Rosary
Rogers, R. Rosary, The.

Roses
Ackland. Blossom into a rose as you are bidden.
Ashbery. White Roses.
Bachmann. In the Storm of Roses.
Bethell. Elect.
Bible, O.T. I am the rose of Sharon, and the lily of the valleys.
Bishop, E. Faustina, or Rock Roses.
Blake, W. My Pretty Rose-Tree.
Sick Rose, The.
Blunden. One among the Roses.
Brontë, E. Love and Friendship.
Broome. Rose-Bud, The.
Brown, L. Come go with me out to the Field.
Browne, W. Vision V.
Browning, R. Flower's Name, The.
Women and Roses.
Burns, R. Banks O' Doon, The.
Bonie Doon.
Red, Red Rose, A.
Ye flowery banks o' bonie Doon.
Clare, J. Love's Emblem.
Coleridge, M. Gifts.
Desbordes-Valmore. Roses of Saadi, The.
Desnos. If, like winds semaphored by a rose.
Dickinson, E. Essential oils—are wrung.
Go not too near a House of Rose.
Doolittle, H. Garden.
Sea Rose.
Dowson. Nuns of the Perpetual Adoration.
Dunbar, P. Summer in the South.
"Eliot." Roses.
Eliot, T. Dedication to My Wife, A.
Little Gidding.
"Field." Goad, The.
Sweet-Briar in Rose.
Your *rose is dead,*.
Frost, R. Rose Family, The.
Gibbons, S. Continuity.
Godfrey. Show Me a Rose.
Goethe. Rosebud in the Heather.
Guest, B. Roses.
Guinicelli. Sonnet: He Will Praise His Lady.
Habington. To Roses in the Bosom[e] of Castara.
Hardy, T. If you had known.
Herbert, G. Rose, The.
Herrick. Funeral[l] Rites of the Rose, The.
How Roses Came Red.
Meditation for His Mistress[e], A.
Upon a Virgin Kissing a Rose.
Upon Roses.
Hodgson, R. Mystery, The.
Hood, T. Ballad: Time of Roses.
Jacobsen, J. Only Alice.
Jiménez, J. I unpetalled you, like a rose.
Joseph, J. Rose in the Afternoon.
Kunio. Tanka: "Hands picking a rose."
Landor, W. Gardener, The.
Lawrence, D. Gloire de Dijon.
I Am like a Rose.
River Roses.
Lehmann, G. Roses.
Levertov. Gypsy's Window, The.
Lloyd, D. Wild rose bending.
Magowan. Susan.
Masaoka Shiki. View of my garden, A.

Meinke. Sonnet on the Death of the Man Who Invented Plastic Roses.
Melville, H. Rosary Beads.
Rose Farmer, The.
Meredith, G. It is the season of the sweet wild rose.
Miles, G. Said the Rose.
Millay, E. Hardy Garden, The.
Mistral, G. Rose, the.
Moore, T. 'Tis the Last Rose of Summer.
Naden. Pantheist's Song of Immortality, The.
North, C. Little Cape Cod Landscape.
Noyes, A. Song: "What is there hid in the heart of a rose."
Okamoto. Tanka: "As I gaze upon."
O'Reilly, J. White Rose, A.
Parker, D. One Perfect Rose.
Pilinszky. Stavrogin's Farewell.
Stavrogin's Return.
Plunkett. I See His Blood upon the Rose.
Probyn. Kyrielle.
Raine, K. Rose.
Randall, D. Roses and Revolutions.
Rapin. Of Roses and Hyacinths.
Rilke. Rose, Oh Pure Contradiction.
Rose, oh pure contradiction, joy.
Robinson, E. Garden, The.
Roethke. Rose, The.
Ronsard. Corinna In Vendome.
Rossetti, C. Comparisons.
October Garden, An.
Summer Is Ended.
Summer Wish, A.
Rotella, A. During our argument.
Sackville-West. Rose, The.
Seferis. Mathios Paskalis among the Roses.
Sitwell, D. Extract from Romance.
Skelton, J. Rose both white and Rede, The.
Skoyles. Head of Tasso, The.
Stein, G. I Am Rose [my eyes are blue].
Swinburne. Match, A.
Tada. Universe of the Rose.
Tadic. Rose, The.
Tollet. Rose, The.
Unknown. Rose, The.
Moses supposes his toeses are roses.
Of a Rose, a Lovely Rose.
Roses are red.
To My Valentine.
Very. Wild Rose of Plymouth, The.
Villanueva, A. Crazy Courage.
Waller, E. Budd, The.
Song: "Go[e], lovely rose[—ous sweet and fair]."
Waterman, N. Rose to the living is more than, A.
Wilbur. Beautiful Changes, The.
Williams, S. Like a drop of water is my heart.
Williams, W. Act, The.
Rewaking, The.
To Flossie.
Yeats. Lover Tells of the Rose in His Heart, The.
Secret Rose, The.
To the Rose upon the Rood of Time.

Rosh Hashanah
Kovner. Tashlich.
Shapiro, H. Feast of the Ram's Horn.

Rothko, Mark
Emanuel, L. Sleeping, The.

Rouen, France
Cannan. Rouen.

Roundheads (English political party)
Unknown. Character of a Roundhead, The.

Rousseau, Jean Jacques
Blake, W. Mock on, Mock on Voltaire, Rousseau.
Davie. Rousseau in His Day.
Harryman. Magic (or Rousseau).

Rowing and Rowers
Bly, R. After Drinking All Night with a Friend, We Go Out in a Boat at Dawn to See Who Can Write the Best Poem.
Eberhart, R. Loon Call, A.
Kipling, R. Galley-Slave, The.
Lattimore. Max Schmitt in a Single Scull.
Sexton. Rowing.

Strand. Morning, A.

Royal Society
Cowley, A. Philosophy, the great and only heir.
Unknown. King and Subjects.

Royalty
Belloc. Imitation.
Brown, B. Jonathan Bing.
Burns, R. O'er the Water to Charlie.
Carew, T. For a Picture Where a Queen Laments over the Tomb of a Slain Knight.
Ch'u Yüan. Yüan, Ch'ü.
Coleridge, H. To a Lofty Beauty, from Her Poor Kinsman.
Daniel, G. Landscape, The.
De' Medici. (To the Virgin).
Dickinson, E. Mine—by the Right of the White Election!
One dignity delays for all.
Dryden, J. Crown Prince of Dullness, The.
Garioch. Heard in the Cougate.
Graves, R. Henry and Mary.
Herbert, Z. End of a Dynasty, The.
Howells, W. Royal Portraits, The.
Kao Ch'i. On a Painting of the Radiant Emperor's Night Revels by Candlelight.
Landor, W. Georges, The.
Rose Aylmer.
Marquis. Archy Interviews a Pharoah.
Martynov. Lord of Nature.
Milne, A. Buckingham Palace.
Rossetti, C. If I Were a Queen.
Royal Princess, A.
Seneca. 'Tis not wealth that makes a king.
Smith, S. Lord Barrenstock and Epicene.
Thornbury. Court Historian, The.
Unknown. Dance Song.
History.
Lament of Hsi-Chün.
On Prince Frederick.
Sir Orfeo.
Vasilyev, P. Prince Foma.
Villon. Ballad of the Lords of Old Time.
Wang An-shih. Song of the Radiant Lady.
Wilner, E. Epitaph: "Young then, / we were bored already."
Yeats. Fallen Majesty.
Zivancevic. Poem with a Tilde in the Title, A.
See also **Kings; Princes and Princesses; Queens**

Rubens, Peter Paul
Allston. Rubens.
Blake, W. To English Connoisseurs.
Szymborska. Women of Rubens, The.

Rugs and Carpets
Cavalli. Moroccans with the carpets, The.
Durcan. Turkish Carpet, The.
Longley, M. Amish Rug, An.
Morgan, R. Ghosts in the Carpet.

Ruins
Alberti. Angels of the Ruins, The.
Homecoming of Love Amongst Illustrious Ruins.
Antipater of Sidon. Ruins of Corinth, The.
Antipater of Thessalonica. Watered by the Strymon and great Hellespont.
Aragon. Poem to Shout in the Ruins.
Bagrayana. Old Fortress, The.
Bernstein, O. Cuernavaca.
Berryman. Dream Song 45.
Bianor. Sardis, the old city of Gyges and Alyattes.
Binyon. House That Was, The.
Bowles, W. Netley Abbey.
Brodsky, J. Elegy.
Bromige. Edible World, The.
Brooks, C. Lines: Composed at the Old Temples of Maralipoor.
Browning, R. Love among the Ruins.
Carruth, H. Rimrock, Where It Is.
Cavafy. City, The.
Coleridge, S. House That Jack Built, The.
Cummings, E. Ponder,darling,these busted statues.
Dafydd ap Gwilym. Ruin, The.
Davies, S. Crooked bank still winds to something new, The.
DiPalma. Hadrian's Lane.

Doolittle, H. From The Walls Do Not Fall.
Dove, R. Sightseeing.
Drummond, W. Content and Resolute.
Éluard, P. November 1936.
Emanuel, L. Dig, The.
Gardner, E. Sonnet Written in Tintern Abbey, Monmouthshire.
Goldsmith, O. Deserted Village, The.
Gouri. And of all that was theirs only the letters were left.
Herlin. Echo of fireplace on the dividing wall, An.
Hirsch, E. Watcher, The.
Hood, T. Silence.
Howells, W. Empty House, The.
Hsü Pen. Deserted Estate at South Garden, The.
Hugo, R. Death of the Kapowsin Tavern.
Izumi. Although the wind.
Jewell. Cliff dweller ruins.
Kao Ch'i. Ballad of the Deserted Mansion.
Levertov. Fragrance of Life, Odor of Death.
Li Po. At Su Terrace Viewing the Past.
In Yüeh Viewing the Past.
McCarthy, T. Dying Synagogue at South Terrace, The.
McClatchy. Capriccio of Roman Ruins and Sculpture with Figures, A.
Melville, H. Ravaged Villa, The.
Merrill, J. Power Station, The.
Pao Chao. Rhyme-Prose on the Desolate City.
Pape. Indian Ruins Along Rio de Flag.
Paz. Hymn Among the Ruins.
Peacock, T. Newark Abbey.
Purdy, A. Remains of an Indian Village.
Quasimodo. Anno Domini MCMXLVII.
Robinson, E. Garden, The.
House on the Hill, The.
Salis. Bomb Victim in the Cathedral Speaks to a Child, A.
Scott, W. Melrose Abbey.
Shelley, P. Ozymandias [of Egypt].
Smith, C. On Passing Over a Dreary Tract of Country, and Near the Ruins of a Deserted Chapel, During a Tempest.
Sorley. Barbury Camp.
Sotheby. Netley Abbey; Midnight.
Spenser. Who lists to see, what ever nature, arte.
Tennyson, A. Princess, The.
Tu Fu. Jade Flower Palace.
Unknown. Lament for Our Lady's Shrine at Walsingham, A.
Ruin, The.
Vaughan, H. Friends Departed.
Walcott. Ruins of a Great House.
Wen T'ing-yün. Passing a Ruined Palace.
Weston, M. Primitive Place.
Wordsworth, W. Yarrow Visited [September, 1814].
Yang Shih-ch'i. Dragon-Tiger Terrace.
Yüan Hung-tao. Climbing Mount Yang.
Zhenkai. Old Temple, The.

Rukeyser, Muriel
Cooper, J. Hotel De Dream.
Marshall-Stoneking. On the Death of Muriel Rukeyser.
Olds, S. Solitary.

Rum
Masefield. Captain Stratton's Fancy.
Unknown. Convicts' Rum Song.

Rumor
Bruner. Monk and the Peasant, The.
Herrick. Lips Tongueless[e].
Meinloh von Sevelingen. Woe then to the gossips! They show their evil will.
Rutter, O. Rumour.
Unknown. Buzz Buzz, the Blue Flies.
See also **Fame; Gossip and Gossips; Reputation**

Running and Runners
Charles, D. Bang! the starter's gun—.
Freeman, M. Ostrich is a Silly Bird, The.
Gildner. Runner, The.
Housman, A. To an Athlete Dying Young.
Kelly, R. Life of Intimate Fleeing, A.
Lucilius. Marcus in the armed hoplites' race.
Recent earthquake, A.

MacCaig. Ringed Plover by a Water's Edge.
Roach. At Guaracara Park.
Robinson, E. Mighty Runner, A.
Sorescu. Start.
Sorley. Song of the Ungirt Runners, The.
Spenser. Amoretti, Sonnet 80.
Webb, F. This Runner.
Welch, J. Harlem, Montana.
Whitman, W. Runner, The.
Wilbur. Running.
Williams, T. Cried the Fox.
Yagi. Marathon runner's legs, A.

Russell, Lucy, Countess of Bedford
Jonson, B. On Lucy Countess[e] of Bedford.
To Lucy, Countess[e] of Bedford, with Mr. Donnes Satire's [*or* Satyres].

Russia
Adamovich. When we return to Russia...
"Akhmatova." Courage.
I am not one of those who left the land.
I heard a voice, within me, call.
Introduction.
Requiem.
Voronezh.
"Aminado." Honest with Oneself.
Andreyev, D. Night winds! Dark mountainous skies.
Antokolsky. Paul the First.
Aseyev. Dark Blue Hussars.
How shall I tell you.
Avakkumova. Russia can't be grasped by the mind.
Barlow, J. Advice to a Raven in Russia [December, 1812].
Bely. Despair.
Berggolts. Conversation with a Neighbor.
My Country.
Berryman. Soviet Union, The.
Blok. Russia.
Bokov. Commune for Me, The.
Brodsky, J. In the Lake District.
To Urania.
Browning, R. Assassins.
Bunin. To My Country.
Cendrars. Back then I was still young.
Creeley. She Went to Stay.
Delone. Ballad of Fate.
Drofenko. Sketches from History.
"Elagin." I like these foreign shores and I have never.
Fraser, G. Rostov.
Glazkov. Conversation of a Private and the Virgin.
Prayer: "Lord, stand up for the Soviets."
Gondlevsky. May God grant me the memory to recall my life.
Grachova. Of what use to me are the nights full of wine.
Hejinian. No form at all—it's impossible to imagine its being.
Herbert, S. Less Nonsense.
Kenzheyev. Poets have often noticed.
Kharms. Symphony No. 2.
Khlebnikov, O. From three sources, / vital sources flowing in dull shades of red.
Khlebnikov, V. And so the castles of world trade.
Khodasevich. Monument, The.
Klyuyev. Lenin has the spirit of an Old Believer.
Kornilov, V. Sky, The.
"Korzhavin." Or did I really fall out of love with my country?—.
Krandievskaya. Those who would not accept went past.
Kublanovsky. My Russia, mine!
Kulchitsky. I love Russia.
Kunyayev. It's hard to understand how one can leave.
Larbaud. Images.
Mandelstam. I must read only children's books.
I Was Washing Outside in the Darkness.
Leningrad.
Stalin Epigram, The.
Mayakovsky. Can't Stand It.

In Re Conferences.
Last Statement.
Moore, L. Silent deer the sound of a waterfall.
Nabokov. Execution, The.
To Russia.
What is the evil deed I have committed?
Nekipelov. Alabushevo.
Ostriker. Eighth and the Thirteenth, The.
Pasternak, B. Fresco Come to Life.
Hamlet in Russia, A Soliloquy.
Highest Sickness, The.
To a Friend.
Plisetsky. Pipe, The.
Ratushinskaya. Why is the snow pale blue?
Salter. Chernobyl.
Seaton, M. Wings.
Simonov. Remember, Alyosha, the roads of Smolensk.
Simpson, L. Why Do You Write about Russia?
Sluchevsky. I told her: the sidewalks are muddy.
Nothing but anniversaries, anniversaries...
Smelyakov. Menshikov.
Smith, I. How Often I Feel Like You.
Smolensky. No matter how I shout—there's no reply.
Sokolov. Beginning, The.
Solovyov. Panmongolism! The word's barbaric.
Soprovsky. Notes from the house of the dead.
Svetlov. Italian, The.
"Teffi." Before the Map of Russia.
Tryapkin. We banished the tyrant-tsars.
Tsvetayeva. . . . In my melodious city cupolas burn.
Turberville. To Spencer.
Unknown. Harry Pollit Was a Bolshie.
Vinokurov. I ate and drank with you, fellow men.
Voloshin. Bourgeoisie.
Holy Russia.
In the Bottomless Pit.
Red Guard.
Voznesensky. Chagall's Cornflowers.
Chorus of Nymphs, A.
Saga.
Vysotsky. I never believed in mirages.
Williams, W. Russia.
Yevtushenko. Babii Yar.
Yevtushenko. Heirs of Stalin, The.
Loss.
Zukofsky, L. Fifth Movement: Autobiography.

Russian Revolution
Đng Thái Thuyên. Contrasts.
Ehrenburg. Sons of Our Sons, The.
Ehrlich. Louse.
"Golodny." Verka the Free.
Ivanov, G. Covered with a glory that had lost its luster.
They'll not exterminate you now.
Kharms. Symphony No. 2.
Khlebnikov, V. She came and spoke low.
Tsar! Send out a shot!
Kulchitsky. Mayakovsky.
Kuzmina-Karavayeva. I too have encompassed a lot: a mother thrice—.
Manifold. Makhno's Philosophers.
Mayakovsky. My most respected / comrades of posterity!
Ode on the Revolution.
On Trash.
Selvinsky. I Saw It.
Mighty Ocean, The.
Serge. Dialectic.
Smelyakov. Portrait.
Tomlinson, C. Dream, A.
Vasilyev, P. Prince Foma.
Võ Liêm So'n. Paradise and Hell.

Russians, The
Davie. Hearing Russian Spoken.
Ivanov, G. Even the graves are not tended in Russia.
Ivanov, V. Russian Mind, The.
Kerouac. Two Hundred and Nineteenth Chorus.
Narovchatov. Wolf Cub.

Turner, J. Man on the Moon, The.
Yevtushenko. Babii Yar*.

Rustum
Arnold, M. Then Sohrab with his sword smote Rustum's helm.

Ruth (Bible)
Hood, T. Ruth.
Lewis, D. Ruth.

Rutledge, Anne
Masters, E. Anne Rutledge.

Rydal Water, England
Drinkwater. Sunrise on Rydal Water.

S

Sabbath
Bialik. Queen Sabbath.
Clare, J. Sabbath Bells.
Dickinson, E. Some keep the Sabbath going to Church.
Halevi. Sabbath, My Love.
Heine. Princess Sabbath.
Herbert, G. Sunday.
Luria, I. Sabbath of Rest, A.
MacNeice. Sunday Morning.
Molodovsky. Song of the Sabbath.
Rivner. Wicked clamor, my ear grows deaf, The.
Sampter. Summer Sabbath.
Schneour. Welcome, Queen Sabbath.
Unknown. Keep Ye Holy Sabbath Rest.
Light and Rejoicing to Israel.
Outgoing Sabbath.
Thou Beautiful Sabbath.
Vaughan, H. Son-Days [dayes].
See also **Sunday**

Sacco-Vanzetti Case
Buckmaster. Vanzetti.
Millay, E. Justice Denied in Massachusetts.
Williams, W. Impromptu: The Suckers.

Sacraments. *See* Baptism; Eucharist; Extreme Unction; Marriage

Sacrifices
Aeschylus. And then the old leader of the Achaian fleet.
Angelou. Many and More.
Bloch, C. In wings and starched.
Bloze. Leaves have yellowed like, The.
Browning, E. Sonnet: "If I leave all for thee, wilt thou exchange."
Byron, G. Jephtha's Daughter.
Carew, T. Cruel Mistress, A.
Chin. Turtle Soup.
Chipasula. Those Rainy Mornings.
Coleridge, S. To Nature.
Colman, H. On the Inscription Over the Head of Christ on the Cross.
Da Todi. Stabat Mater, The.
Davenport, R. Sacrifice, A.
Durand, O. Francie-the-Possessed.
Emerson, R. Give all to love;.
To Rhea.
Erucius of Cyzicus. Glaukon and Korydon, mountain herdsmen.
Euripides. Agamemnon struggles to avert the sacrifice of his daughter Iphigeneia].
Fumiko. Tanka: "In a posture."
Ginger. Name, A.
Heaney, S. Tollund Man, The.
Herbert, G. Obedience.
Herrick. Ass[e], The.
Good Friday: Rex Tragicus, or, Christ Going to His Cross[e].
Hymne to Love, An.
Perfume, The.
Scar[e]-Fire, The.
Steam in Sacrifice.
Homer. Ulysses Invokes the Dead.
Horovitz, F. Messenger, The.
Housman, A. If it chance your eye offend you.
Hughes, T. God, A.
James, S. Inner Mongolia—The Grasslands.
Jeffers, R. But I Am Growing Old and Indolent.

Kipling, R. Sacrifice of Er-Heb, The.
Knott. Feeding the Sun.
Kolmar. Sacrifice, The.
Laleau. Sacrifice.
Leonidas. His poor mother gives Mikythos'.
Philokles offers his bouncing.
Theris, whose hands were cunning.
Li Shang-yin. Written on a Monastery Wall.
Marks, L. Code Poem for the French Resistance.
Mathews, A. Caedmon.
McGrath, T. Offering.
Mphande. Why the Old Woman Limps.
Nakkiranar. Murukan: His Places.
Noll. Abraham's Madness.
Okigbo. Sacrifice.
Parra, N. Who are my friends / the sick / the weak / the poor in spirit.
Parun. You whose hands are more innocent than mine.
Po Chü-i. To Li Chien.
Rodgers, W. Scapegoat.
Smart, C. Faith.
Sobin, G. On the Nature of the Iconic.
Theocritus. Those dew-moist roses and that bushy thyme.
Tu Fu. Sharpen the sword in the Sobbing Waters.
Unknown. Dark young pine, at the center of the earth originating.
Dynastic Hymn.
Origin-Legend of the Chou Tribe.
Twelfth Song of the Holy Young Men.
Wilner, E. Sarah's Choice.
Zamora, D. To Be a Woman.

Sacrilege
Whittier. Official Piety.

Sadism and Sadists
Arp. Great Unrestrained Sadist, The.
Derricotte. Boy at the Paterson Falls.
Koch, K. To win the love of women one should first discover.

Sadness
Allingham. I walk'd in the lonesome evening.
Arnold, M. To Marguerite.
Baraka. Invention of Comics, The.
Bernstein, O. Only from Afar.
Berryman. There sat down, once, a thing on Henry's heart.
Bogan, L. Didactic Piece.
Breeze. Lovin wasn easy all de time.
Brontë, E. Had there been falsehood in my breast.
Campana. Window, The.
Castro, R. Black Mood.
I was born at birth of blossoms.
Cheng Hsieh. West wind has come again to the "tower of makeup," The.
Ch'in Chia. Ch'in Chia's Wife's Reply.
Chipasula. Because the Wind Remembers.
Chōkū. Tanka: "Somewhere around."
Chu Shu-chen. Old Anguish, The.
Cortez. Lonely Woman.
Creeley. Air: "The Love of a Woman."
Crozier, A. Humiliation in Its Disguises.
Delanty. Gift, The.
Djagarov. Autumn.
Đỗ Tấn Xuân. Words of Comfort.
Dobyns. Black Dog, Red Dog.
What You Have Come To Expect.
Donne. Song: "Sweetest love, I do not go[e]."
Dowson. Exile.
Elytis. Aegean Melancholy.
Fletcher, J. Fletcher's Lament for his Friend.
Hagiwara Sakutaro. So Terrifyingly Melancholy.
Hauer. Vision.
Herbert, G. Storm, The.
Herrick. Christ's Sadness.
Hove. Lost Bird.
Red Hills of Home.
Howells, W. November.
Hughes, L. Miss Blues'es Child.
Jackson, A. Sad Boy, The.
James, E. Sunnyland.
James, J. Sister Midnight.
Jones, R. Weepers, The.

Justice, D. Sadness, An Improvisation.
Kao Ch'i. Where Does My Sadness Come From?
Kasa. To love somebody.
Kaufman, B. Private Sadness.
Kenyon, J. Pharaoh.
Kirschner. Blueness of Stars, The.
Knott. Two Vietnam Poems: (1966).
Korn. Put Your Word to My Lips.
Larkin, P. Home is so sad. It stays as it was left.
Lee, B. Rain.
Levine, P. Buying and Selling.
   Midget, The.
Li K'ai-hsien. Recording a Weird Happening.
Longfellow, H. Day is done, and the darkness, The.
Lu Yu. I Walk Out into the Country at Night.
MacNeice. And love hung still as crystal over the bed.
Mahon. Dejection.
Mandelstam. I must read only children's books.
March, A. As someone on his back for months of illness.
Matthews, W. Note I Left for Gerald Stern in an Office I Borrowed, and He Would Next, at a Summer Writers' Conference.
McNair. Before People, The.
Millay, E. Ashes of Life.
Moore, T. Oft in the stilly night.
Mori Ōgai. In Nara (two poems).
Nasrin. Another Life.
Nemerov. View from an Attic Window, The.
Neruda. Tonight I can write the saddest lines.
Nokan. My head is immense.
Pan Chieh-yü. Poem in Rhyme-Prose Form.
Park, M. Love.
Paulin. Ulster Unionist Walks the Streets of London, An.
Paulus Silentiarius. And now you comb and braid your hair.
Phillips, A. Photograph & Story in *The Press*: The Mother Whose Children Burned to Death.
Piatt, S. Sad Spring-Song.
Po Chü-i. Feelings Wakened by a Mirror.
   Going to the Mountains with a Little Dancing Girl, Aged Fifteen.
   Light Furs, Fat Horses.
   Traveler's Moon, The.
Pound, E. Green robe, green robe, lined with yellow.
Ray, H. Broken Heart.
   Shadow and Sunrise.
Rexroth, K. I am sad this morning.
   In the park a crow awakes.
Rich, A. Mirror in Which Two Are Seen as One, The.
Roethke. Dolor.
Rossetti, C. At Home.
   Why did baby die.
Rubtsov. Farewell Song.
Rucker. Swallows of Capistrano, The.
Rutsala. Shack Outside Boise, The.
Saba, U. Winter Noon.
Sappho. Honestly I'd as soon be dead!
Schaeffer. Housewife.
Shakespeare, W. Sonnet 20.
Shapiro, H. After the love-making.
Shelley, P. On a Faded Violet.
   Stanzas—April, 1814.
Shorter. Mountain Maid, The.
Siddal. Worn Out.
Soyinka. Prisoner.
Stanescu. Evocation.
Su Tung-p'o. Mid-Autumn Moon.
   Tune: Song of River City.
Supervielle. Some day shall I be the one who let.
Tanikawa Shuntaro. Sadness.
Trakl. De Profundis.
Tu Fu. Climbing the Heights.
Unknown. At Fifteen I Went Off to the Army;.
   Sad Song.

Song of Sorrow.
Why am I always so depressed?
Walker, A. S M.
Waters, M. Miles Weeping.
Wen Cheng-ming. There was no reason to expect sadness.
Year *Chi-wei* (Fifteen Fifty Nine), New Year's Day, The.
Wild, R. In a melancholly studdy.
Williams, H. To the Moon.
Williams, W. Sadness of the Sea, The.
Wright, J. Breath of Air, A.
Wu Wei-yeh. Setting out at dawn from T'ung-lu county.
Yakamochi. Over the Spring fields.
Yang Shih-ch'i. Sha-ch'eng, "Sand City" ("In former years I passed this city").
Yeats. To the Rose upon the Rood of Time.
Zach. Against Sadness.
Zivancevic. Kindergarten Curse.
   Poem with a Tilde in the Title, A.

Sailing and Sailors
Adamson. Sibyl.
Aiken, J. How to Make a Sailor's Pie.
Allingham. Homeward Bound.
Antipater of Sidon. Priapos of the Harbor.
Antiphilus. Give me a mattress on the ship's poop some day.
Beddoes. Sailors' Song.
Bentley, N. Third Dungeness Spit Apocalypse.
Berryman. Conversation.
Bishop, E. Imaginary Iceberg, The.
   Unbeliever, The.
Bogan, L. Putting to Sea.
Bontemps. Nocturne of the Wharves.
Boyle, K. To a Seaman Dead on Land.
Brickley. Outside the pub.
Brownell, H. Burial of the Dane, The.
Browning, R. Hervé Riel.
Burr, G. Sailing, Sailing.
Byron, G. Lines to Mr Hodgson.
Campbell, R. Choosing a Mast.
Campbell, T. Ye Mariners of England.
"Carroll." Fit the Second: The Bellman's Speech.
Carson, R. Old Sailor Looking at a Container Ship.
Catullus. Attis.
   Yacht, The.
Causley. Chief Petty Officer.
Cavafy. Supplication.
Chan Fang-sheng. Sailing Homeward.
Clough. Come home, come home! and where an home hath he.
   Mari Magno II.
   Qua Cursum Ventus.
Corbett, E. Three wise old women were they, were they.
Crane, H. Phantom Bark, The.
Crane, S. I explain the silvered passing of a ship at night.
Cunningham, A. Sea-Song, A.
Curnow. Landfall in Unknown Seas.
Davenant. Winter Storms, The.
Davies, W. Child and the Mariner, The.
   Sheep.
Dawe, G. Seamen's Mission.
Day Lewis. Conflict, The.
De la Mare. Silver Penny, The.
Dibdin, C. Poor Tom.
Dickinson, E. Exultation is the going.
   Wild Nights—Wild Nights!
Dobell, S. "How's My Boy?"
Donne. Calm[e], The.
Doolittle, H. Shrine, The.
Drayton. To the Virginian Voyage.
Drummond, W. Sonnet: "Slide soft, fair forth, and make a crystal plain."
Eberhart, R. Sea Burial from the Cruiser *Reve*.
Fêng Mêng-lung. Love-Poem.
Fields, J. Alarmed Skipper, The.
   Ballad of the Tempest.
Garrick. Heart of Oak.
Gascoyne. Truth is Blind, The.
Gay, J. Sweet William's Farewell to Black-Eyed [*or* Black-Ey'd] Susan.

Gilbert, S. Captain Reece.
   Yarn of the *Nancy Bell*, The.
Greenaway. When You and I Grow Up.
Gu Cheng. Epigraph: "In the sea of life."
Gumilyov. On polar and on southern seas.
Hammial. Sadie.
Harvey, S. Mighty Tropicale Orchestra, The.
Heaney, S. North.
Henson, D. Last Atlantean, The.
Hill, G. Guardians, The.
Hillyer. Over Bright Summer Seas.
Holden, M. Seaman, 1941.
Holmes, O. Sea Dialogue, A.
Homer. Landfall.
Hovey. Sea Gypsy, The.
Howell, C. Liberty and Ten Years of Return.
Hsü Pen. Following the Rhymes of Kao Chi-ti's Poem: "We Had Planned to Travel to Cloud Cliff But Couldn't Because of Rain."
Hughes, L. Sailor.
   Seascape.
Janevski. Song of the Eternal Sailor, The.
Kelly, R. Loom, The.
Kipling, R. Ballad of Fisher's Boardinghouse, The.
   Last Chantey, The.
   McAndrew's Hymn.
   Nurses, The.
Kornilov, B. High Seas on the Caspian.
Lear, E. Jumblies, The.
   Limericks, II (iv).
   (The Owl and the Pussy-Cat).
Leonidas of Tarentum. Spring on the Coast.
Levertov. Leaving Forever.
Lewis, A. Song (On Seeing Dead Bodies Floating Off the Cape).
Li Ch'ing-chao. "Fisherman's Honor," The.
Lightfoot. Wreck of the Edmund Fitzgerald, The.
Longfellow, H. Tide rises, the tide falls, The.
   Wreck of the *Hesperus*, The.
Lowell, R. Salem.
   We imitate, oh horror! tops and bowls.
Lowry, M. Joseph Conrad.
Lu Yu. How I Sailed on the Lake till I Came to the Eastern Stream.
Lucy. Longshore Intellectual.
MacCaig. Basking Shark.
MacLeish. Prologue: "These alternate nights and days, these seasons."
   Seafarer.
Manifold. Fife Tune.
Martinson. On the Congo.
Marvell. Bermudas.
Masefield. All through the windless night the clipper rolled.
   Cargoes.
   Crowd, The.
   Rounding the Horn.
   Sea-Fever.
Mathew. Wynyard Sailor.
Mayer, B. Port, The.
Melville, H. Billy in the Darbies.
   Commemorative of a Naval Victory.
   Haglets, The.
   Island, The.
   Since as in night's deck-watch ye show.
   To Ned.
   Tom Deadlight.
Merwin, W. Odysseus.
Mew. Rambling Sailor, The.
Miles, J. Merchant Marine.
Miller, J. Columbus.
Miller, V. How far is it to you by foot?
Mitchell, W. Tacking Ship Off Shore.
Monkhouse. To a New-Born Child.
Mori Ōgai. Tanka: "Far and near."
Morris, T. Sapphics: At the Mohawk-Castle, Canada.
Moschus. Ocean, The.
Moss, H. Tourists.
Mother Goose. Bobby Shaftoe's [*or* Shafto's] gone to sea.
   I saw three ships come sailing by.
Murphy, R. Pat Cloherty's Version of *The Maisie*.
   Sailing to an Island.

Nash, O. Columbus.
Newbolt. Messmates.
O'Hara, F. To the Harbormaster.
Oppian. *Dolphins* were Men, (Tradition hands the Tale).
Petrarch. Galley, The.
  My Galley.
Philips, K. Sea-Voyage from Tenby to Bristol, A.
Pierce, A. In Fourteen Hundred and Ninety-.
Po Chü-i. On Board Ship: Reading Yüan Chên's Poems.
Poe. To Helen ("Helen, thy beauty is to me").
Pound, E. Canto 1.
  Canto 2.
  Seafarer, The.
Preston, J. Sunfish Races.
Probyn. Barcarolle.
Prys. Poem to Show the Trouble That Befell Him When He Was at Sea, A.
Rakosi. Fluteplayers from Finmarken.
  Unswerving Marine.
Ravikovitch. Dear Mickey.
Ray, H. Boat Song.
Riley, J. Sea-Song from the Shore, A.
Robinson, E. Lost Anchors.
Rooney. Men behind the Guns, The.
Roseliep. Sailor, The.
Ross, A. Destroyers in the Arctic.
Rossetti, C. O sailor, come ashore, / What have you brought for me?
Sackville-West. Absence.
Sargent, E. Life on the Ocean Wave, A.
Scott, W. Gallant Ship, The.
Seferis. And if the soul.
Shakespeare, W. Sea Song, A: "Master, the swabber, the boatswain and I, The."
Shelley, M. To the air of 'My Phillida, adieu, love!'.
Simpson, L. To the Western World.
Smith, C. From Beachy Head.
Snyder, G. Things to Do around a Ship at Sea.
Spence, L. Prows O' Reekie, The.
Stephens, J. Seumas Beg.
Stevenson, R. Christmas at Sea.
  Far-Farers, The.
  Good Play, A.
  My Bed Is a Boat.
  Sing me a song of a lad that is gone.
Strnisa. Ship, A.
Tate, A. Mediterranean, The.
Tennyson, A. Crossing the Bar.
  Lullaby: "Sweet and low, sweet and low."
Thompson, E. I've served my country nine and twenty years.
Thyillos. Already swallows build their homes of mud.
Tikhonov. Ballad of the Nails, The.
Trypanis. Cock at Sea.
Tucker, M. Hugging the Shore.
Turner, C. Buoy-Bell, The.
Unknown. Battle of Brunanburh.
  Bay of Biscay, The.
  Canada-I-O ("There was a gallant lady all in her tender youth").
  Captain Bunker.
  Dance the Boatman.
  Fifteen Ships on Georges Banks.
  Girls around Cape Horn, The.
  Haul Away, My Rosy.
  Heaving the Lead Line.
  In the open sea.
  Jolly Soldier.
  Lightning Flash, The.
  Lowlands o' [*or of*] Holland, The.
  Mæg ic be me sylfum so???ogied wrecan.
  Paddy, Get Back.
  Red Iron Ore.
  Reuben Ranzo.
  Sailor Boy's Song.
  Sailors' Alphabet, The.
  Sea, The.
  Seafarer, The.
  Sir Patrick Spens [*or* Spence].
  Stiff winds blow.
  Tarpauling Jacket.

Tempest, The.
Whale, The.
Wind Sou'west, The.
Young Allan.
Updike. Bath after Sailing.
Walcott. He yawned and watched the lilac horns of his island.
Warren, R. Masts at Dawn.
Westmorland. In Praise of Fidelia.
Whitman, W. In cabin'd ships at sea.
  Song for All Seas, All Ships.
Williams, W. Yachts, The.
Wyatt, T. My galley charged with forgetfulness.
  Sonnet: 'My galley charged'.

St. Agnes' Eve
Keats. Eve of St Agnes, The.
Tennyson, A. St. Agnes' Eve.

St. Crispin's Day
Shakespeare, W. Before Agincourt.

St. David's Day
Unknown. In Honour of St. David's Day.

St. John's Day
Wadding. For Saint John's Day.

Saint Lawrence (river), Canada
Ray, H. On the rapids of the St. Lawrence.

St. Louis, Missouri
Sterling, A. Meet Me in St. Louis, Louis.

Saint Lucia (island nation)
Ford-Smith. Aux Leon...Women.

St. Mark's Eve
Keats. Eve of St. Mark, The.

St. Patrick's Day
MacCarthy, D. Paschal Fire, The.

Saint Peter's Church, Rome
Milnes. Sir Walter Scott at the Tomb of the Stuarts in St. Peter's.
Wojtyla. Marble Floor.

Saint Petersburg [*formerly* Leningrad], Russia
"Akhmatova." Introduction.
  Requiem: "No foreign sky protected me."
Annensky. Petersburg.
Hejinian. No them at all—it's impossible to imagine its being.
"Korzhavin." Leningrad.
Mandelstam. Leningrad.
  Petersburg Strophes.
Olds, S. Leningrad Cemetery, Winter of 1941.
Osherow. Late Night Tête-à-Tête with a Moon in Transit.
Wieseltier. Leningrad: Picture Postcard.

St. Stephen's Day
Hewitt, J. Saint Stephen's Day.
Wadding. For Saint Stephen's Day.

St. Valentine's Day. *See* **Valentine's Day**

Saints
Chao Meng-fu. Lamenting the Taoist Wei Kung-yüan.
Constable, H. To St Mary Magdalen.
Coolidge, C. Jerome in His Study.
Cowper, W. Light Shining out of Darkness.
Crashaw. Hymn to Saint Teresa.
Derricotte. Weakness, The.
Dickinson, E. I taste a liquor never brewed.
Donne. Canonization, The.
  Relic, The.
Farjeon, E. Mistress Malone.
Fitzgerald, E. 27.
Hall, J. St. Peregrinus' Cancer.
Herrick. To Groves.
Hill, G. In Piam Memoriam.
Johnson, L. Church of a Dream, The.
Kamienska. Saint Martha.
Kavanagh, P. Sanctity.
Keats. Then by the bed-side, where the faded moon.
Kendall, M. Legend of the Crossing-Sweeper.
Kerouac. Two Hundred and Nineteenth Chorus.
MacLeish. What Riddle Asked the Sphinx.
McGinley. Giveaway, The.
Mew. Madeleine in Church.
Miyazawa Kenji. Tanka: "Snow has fallen."
Mor. Coming of John, The.
O'Brien, G. Scroll.

O'Flynn. Sainthood.
Ormond. To a Nun.
Park, H. Ode to Merciful Bodhisattva.
Shakespeare, W. If I profane with my unworthiest hand.
Smart, C. Elegance.
Tennyson, A. St. Simeon Stylites.
Thomson, J. Once in a saintly passion.
Unknown. Epigram: "Says a Reverend Priest to a less Rev'rend friend."
  I Am from Ireland.
Yevtushenko. Saints of Jazz are playing, The.
Yüan Chieh. Civilization.

Salads
Ishikawa Takuboku. Tanka: "Color, The."
Smith, S. Salad, A.
Virgil. Sallad, The.
Wells, C. Universal Favorite, The.

Salem, Massachusetts
Lowell, R. Salem.

Sales Clerks. *See* **Clerks**

Salesmen
Cavalli. Moroccans with the carpets, The.
Cummings, E. Salesman is an it that stinks excuse, A.
Elder. One Foot in the Door.
Gillies, V. Fellow Passenger.
Grosholz. Life of a Salesman.
Kunio. Tanka: "As night falls."
Levine, P. Buying and Selling.
Sandburg, C. Fish Crier.
Unknown. Tune: "Eternal Longing."

Salisbury, England
Hardy, T. In a Cathedral City.

Salmon
Adamson. Gutting the Salmon.
Fallon, P. Weir Bridge.
Lowry, M. Salmon Drowns Eagle.
Mitchison. Dick and Colin at the Salmon Nets.
Philip, M. Salmon Courage.
Unknown. Prayer to the Sockeye Salmon.

Salt
Ammuvanar. What She Said ("Fishermen who go, The").
Barlow, G. Salt.
Bokov. Salt.
Brousek. Walls shriek, The.
Di Prima. For H.D.
Dove, R. Nightmare.
Gander. Table Laid with Horrors, A.
Goldbarth. Lot's Wife.
Holst-Warhaft. Matthew 5:13; You are the salt of the earth.
  Old Men of Athens, The.
McClintock, M. I eat alone.
Merrill, J. Upward Look, An.
Page, P. Photos of a Salt Mine.
Phillips, C. Reach, The.
Wang An-shih. Confiscating Salt.
Winters, A. Mill-Race, The.
Wu Chia-chi. East of the salt village, low and narrow.
  Old saltman, hair turned white, The.

Saltus, Thaddeus
Fordham. To Rev. Thaddeus Saltus.

Salvation
Awoonor. Weaver bird built in our house, The.
Bible, *N.T.* Matthew Ten Twenty-Five– Ten Twenty-Six.
Bible, *O.T.* Psalm 037: "Fret not thyself because of evildoers."
Bliss, P. "Almost persuaded," / Now to believe.
Bradstreet, A. As weary pilgrim, now at rest.
Clarkson. Behold, the King of glory now is come.
Crane, H. Recitative.
Cullen, C. Shroud of Color, The.
Dana, R. Husband's and Wife's Grave, The.
Donne. "Batter my heart, three-person'd God; for you."
  Blow Your Trumpets.
  Oh my black[e] soul[e]! now thou art summoned.

This is my play's [or playes] last scene, here
  heavens appoint.
Wilt thou love God, as he thee? [or thee!]
  then digest.
Doolittle, H. From The Walls Do Not Fall.
Eliot, T. Hippopotamus, The.
  Song for Simeon, A.
Farewell. Privy-Love for My Landlady.
Graves, R. Song: Lift-Boy.
Greville, F. Sonnet: "Down[e] in the depth of
  mine iniquity."
Hammon. Evening Thought, An [: Salvation
  by Christ with Penetential Cries].
Heaney, S. On the Road.
Hecht, A. Prospects.
Herbert, G. Bunch of Grapes, The.
  Clasping of Hands.
  Conscience.
  Dialogue, A.
  Divinity.
  Easter-Wings.
  Grieve Not the Holy Spirit, etc.
  Holy Baptism (1).
  Peace.
  Perseverance.
  Redemption.
Herrick. To Christ.
Hewitt, J. Calling on Peadar O'Donnell at
  Dungloe.
Holtby, W. Resurrection.
Hudgins. When I Was Saved.
Hunter, W. "Go Bring Me," Said the Dying
  Fair.
Hyde, A. And canst thou, sinner slight.
Jonson, B. Hymn[e] on the Nativity [or
  Nativitie] of My Saviour, A.
Lansdown. Behind the Veil.
Lindsay, V. General William Booth Enters
  into Heaven.
Lyon, G. Salvation.
Marlowe. Ah, Doctor Faustus, that I might
  prevail.
Mitchell, S. Good Samaritan et Al, The.
Oliver, M. In Blackwater Woods.
Ralegh, W. Verses Made the Night before His
  Beheading.
Tate, A. Cross, The.
Unknown. Nobody Knows the Trouble I've
  Had.
  Ubi Sunt Qui ante Nos Fuerunt?
  Worldes bliss ne last no throwe.
  Zion's Sons and Daughters.
Very. Autumn Leaves.
  Garden, The.
Wesley, C. Come on, my partners in distress.
  None is like Jeshuron's God!
Whittier. Over-Heart, The.

Salvation Army
Robinson, E. Karma.
Unknown. Roll the Chariot.

Samarkand
Spaziani. Journey in the Orient.

Samos, Greece
Merrill, J. Samos.

Samson
Avidan. General Truths.
Clemmons. Love Letter.
Crashaw. Samson to His De [or a] lilah.
Gouri. My Samsons.
Graves, R. Angry Samson.
Gwynn, R. Among Philistines.
Longfellow, H. Warning, The.
Milton. Blindness of Samson, The.
  But what is strength without a double share.
  Consolation.
  Deliverer, The.
Roditi. Aurora Borealis.
Zach. Samson's Hair.

San Francisco, California
Corso. Ode to Coit Tower.
Di Prima. Letter to Jeanne (at Tassajara).
Ferlinghetti, L. Starting from San Francisco.
Ginsberg, A. Sunflower Sutra.
Harper, M. Three O'Clock Love Song.
Hughes, L. City.
Logan, J. San Francisco Poem.
Moldaw. 64 Panoramic Way.

Rukeyser, M. Bunk Johnson Blowing.
Villanueva, A. They didn't get me.
Welch, L. Sausalito Trash Prayer.

Sanctuaries
Ammons. Triphammer Bridge.
"Field." Poet, The.
Levertov. Those Who Want Out.
Sackville-West. To Any M.F.H F. H.

Sand
Baker, D. Castles in the Sand.
Barnes, D. Transfiguration.
Blake, W. To see a World in a Grain of Sand.
Bursk. Tearing Up the Tracks.
Chang Yü. In a Boat on the Cha River.
Chin Nung. In the silences between peals of
  the bell.
Creeley. All That Is Lovely in Men.
Fisher, A. Sandpile Town.
Fraser, K. Boot, wet sand and more white
  along the borders defining a trail of lush /
  chemicals we adhere to.
Frost, R. Neither Out Far Nor In Deep.
Gascoyne. Yves Tanguy.
Gray, J. Femmes Damnées.
Harper, F. Grain of Sand, A.
Hays, H. For One Who Died Young.
Kellman. Bajan.
Kinzie. In air hard as sand.
Kuroda. Afternoon 3.
Longfellow, H. Sand of the Desert in an
  Hour-Glass.
  Tide rises, the tide falls, The.
McClintock, M. Across the sands.
McPherson, S. Edge Effect.
Millay, E. Second Fig.
Mitchell, A. Speck Speaks, A.
Rossetti, C. I dug and dug amongst the snow.
Rossetti, D. Even So.
Spenser. Sonnet 75: "One day I wrote her
  name upon the strand."
Staff. Foundations.
Stevenson, R. At the Seaside [or Sea-Side].
Swenson, M. Sand, The.
Szymborska. View with a Grain of Sand.
Tao-chi. Inscribed on My Little Painting of
  Plum Blossom and Bamboo.
  Trip to the Village of the River of White
  Sand, A.
Thomas, D. We lying by seasand, watching
  yellow.
Unknown. Footprints made on the sands of.
Wen Cheng-ming. I sit on horseback at Twin
  Bridges.
Yang Shih-ch'i. Sha-ch'eng, "Sand City"
  ("Overlooking the water, a desolate city").
Young, A. Culbin Sands.
Yü Chi. Getting on Horseback.
Zach. Like Sand.

"Sand, George" (Amandine Aurore Lucie
Dupin, Baronne Dudevant)
Browning, E. To George Sand / A Desire.
  To George Sand: A Recognition.
Parker, D. George Sand.

Sandpipers
Bishop, E. Sandpiper.
Carruth, H. Summer's Early End at Hudson's
  Bay.
Thaxter. Sandpiper, The.

Sanitary Engineering and Sanitary Engineers.
  See Sewers; Garbage and Garbage Men

Santa Barbara, California
Conyus. Great Santa Barbara Oil Disaster OR,
  The.

Santa Claus
De la Mare. Santa Claus.
Moore, C. Visit from St Nicholas, A.
Moore, M. Saint Nicholas.
Nemerov. Santa Claus.
Sexton. Santa Claus.
Thomas, E. Mrs. Kriss Kringle.
Unknown. Santa Claus.

Santayana, George
Lowell, R. For George Santayana.
Stevens, W. To an Old Philosopher in Rome.

Sappho
Brown, R. Sappho's Reply.

Cope, J. Sappho.
Dacre, C. Sappho; or, The Resolve.
Hemans. Last Song of Sappho, The.
Herrick. Apron of Flowers, The.
Johnson, H. Summer Matures.
Landon. Sappho's Song.
Lowell, A. Sisters, The.
Norton, C. Picture of Sappho, The.
Paulus Silentiarius. Soft are Sappho's kisses.
Pinytos. Epitaph: Sappho.
Plato. Sappho.
Poseidippus. Doricha.
  Doricha, your soft bones are.
Rossetti, C. Sappho.
Smith, E. Ode to Sappho.
Swinburne. Sapphics.
Wright, J. Sappho.

Sarah (Bible)
Nemerov. Nicodemus.
Schwartz, D. Sarah.
Wilner, E. Sarah's Choice.

Sarajevo
Durrell. Sarajevo.
Hugo, R. Yards of Sarajevo, The.

Saratoga, New York
Halleck, F. Field of the Grounded Arms, The.

Sarto, Andrea del
Browning, R. Andrea del Sarto.

Saskatchewan, Canada
Mandel, E. From the North Saskatchewan.
Newlove. Double-headed Snake, The.
Wah. Breathe Dust.

Satan
Auden. Et in Arcadia Ego.
  From "The Prolific and the Devourer."
Baudelaire. Litany to Satan.
Belloc. On Lady Poltagrue, A Public Peril.
Berryman. Whether There Is Sorrow in the
  Demons.
Blake, W. Book of Urizen [or First Book of
  Urizen], The.
Bloom, V. Sun-a-shine, Rain-a-fall.
Brooks, M. Shade of Columbus, here thy
  relics rest.
Burns, R. Address to the Deil.
  To an Artist.
Byron, G. Ah! didst *thou* tempt my mother?
Causley. Infant Song.
Chesterton, G. Aristocrat, The.
  Donkey, The.
Coleridge, M. Devil's Funeral, The.
Coleridge, S. Devil's Thoughts, The.
Crane, S. Sage lectured brilliantly, The.
Cullen, C. For a Mouthy Woman.
Cummings, E. In Just- / spring when the
  world is mud-.
Dekker, T. *et al.* And why on me? why
  should the envious world.
Dickinson, E. Narrow Fellow in the Grass, A.
Djurdjic. Lucifer has bad habits.
Enright, D. Lucifer Broods.
Goethe. Do you know me now? Skinny,
  cadaverous bitch.
  Spirit of Evil, The.
Gowar. Rat Trap.
Grunthal. Constant starburst showers us, A.
Hann. After Reading the Life of Mrs.
  Catherine Stubbs in Isaac Ambrose's "War
  with the Devils."
Herbert, Z. Devil, A.
Herrick. Another Charme (variant).
Hope, A. Möbius Strip-Tease.
Iskander. Devil and the Shepherd, The.
Johnson, L. Dark Angel, with thine aching
  lust.
Jonson, B. Cocklorrel woulds needs have the
  devil his guest.
Kipling, R. Conundrum of the Workshops,
  The.
Lawrence, D. Root of Our Evil, The.
Lindsay, V. Simon Legree—A Negro Sermon.
Lister, R. Lament of an Idle Demon.
Lowell, R. At the Altar.
Marlowe. But may I raise up spirits when I
  please?
Meredith, G. Lucifer in Starlight.
Milton. As when of old some orator renowed.

Book IX.
Immortal Hate.
Satan tempts Eve.
Satan's Journey.
Sin and Death.
Montague, J. Wild Sports of the West.
Montale. Precautions.
Moore, T. Copy of an Intercepted Despatch from His Excellency Don Strepitoso Diabolo.
Olds, S. Satan Says.
Pagis. Another Testimony.
Parra, N. Lord's Prayer.
Rankin, P. Bedtime Story.
Rich, A. Lucifer in the Train.
Rossetti, C. Three Enemies, The.
Savard. Carnival Figure of Guatemalan Clay, A.
Shelley, P. Devil, I safely can aver, The.
Snyder, G. Milton by Firelight.
Sologub. Devil's Swing, The.
Southey, R. Devil, The.
Strnisa. Priests, The.
Thomas, D. Incarnate devil in a talking snake.
Tolson. Old Pettigrew.
Unknown. Demon Lover, The.
Devil in Texas, The.
Did you eever, iver, over.
Hell in Texas.
Whale, The.
Wesley, C. Sinners, abhor the Fiend.
Wylie. Knight Fallen on Evil Days, The.

Satie, Erik
Curtis, S. Satie, at the End of Term.
Merrill, J. Angel.

Satire and Satirists
Donne. Satire 3.
Horace. As I was walking in the *Mall* of late.
Horatian Canons of Friendship, The.
I often wish'd, that I had clear.
Pope: Each Mortal has his Pleasure: None deny.
Phocylides. On the Problem of Choosing a Wife.

Satiric Verse
"Carroll." Duchess's Lullaby, The.
Father William.
Mad Hatter's Song, The.
Melodies.
Dunbar, W. Amendis to the Telyouris and Sowtaris for the Turnament Maid on Thame, The.
Foote, S. Great Panjandrum [Himself], The.
Harte, W. Above all flattery, all thirst of gain.
In Albion then, with equal lustre bright.
Mitchell, J. Nothingmas Day.
Pope, A. Alas, young man! your days can ne'er be long;.
Swift, J. On Reading Dr. Young's Satires.
Unknown. I saw a Peacock with a fiery tail.
See also **Satire and Satirists**

Saturday
Mullen, H. Saturday Afternoon, When Chores Are Done.
Smart, C. For Saturday.
Unknown. How pleasant is Saturday night.
See also **Sabbath**

Saudi Arabia
Kazantzis. In Memory, 1978.

Saul (Bible)
Alterman. Saul.
Bible, *O.T.* David's Lament.
Byron, G. Saul.
Song of Saul before His Last Battle.
Levine, P. Death of Saul, The.
Lindsay, V. In Which Roosevelt Is Compared to Saul.
Merton. St. Paul.
Quarles. On Saul and David.
Smart, C. David's Song to Saul.
Tchernichowsky. Dance of Saul with the Prophets, The.
Wieseltier. Saul Re-enthroned.
Wither. Conversion of S. Paul, The.

Saunas. *See* **Baths and Bathing**

Sausages
Guest, E. Sausage.

Savonarola, Girolamo
Beerbohm, M. Savonarola ("Savonarola looks more grim today").

Scarecrows
Braine. Mr. Scarecrow.
Brownjohn. In a Convent Garden.
De la Mare. Scarecrow, The.
Franklin, M. Scarecrow stood in a field one day, A.
Harr, L. Indian summer.
On the old scarecrow.
Kirkup. Scarecrows.
McClintock, M. Peering out.
Pizzarelli. Scarecrow.
Tản Đà. To a Scarecrow.
Thompson, I. Rainy Nights.
Young, A. Scarecrow, The.

Scheherazade
Hudgins. Telling, The.
St. John, P. Ocean of the Streams of Story.

Schoenberg, Arnold
Revell. Other the Wings, The.

Scholarship and Scholars
Bast. Chang Tuan's Cats.
Baudelaire. Cats.
Belloc. Lines to a Don.
Bentley, E. "Dinner-time?" said Gilbert White.
Bialik. Talmud Student, The.
Browning, R. Grammarian's Funeral, A.
Chin Nung. Inkstone Inscription for the Blind Scholar Ho Yung-kuang, An.
Inscribed on the Wall of a Rice Cake Shop.
Clarke, A. Scholar, The.
Colum, P. Poor Scholar of the 'Forties, A.
Cornford, F. Scholar, The.
Crabbe. Schools.
Cunningham, J. To a Friend, on Her Examination for the Doctorate in English.
Đng Trần Côn *et al.* Song of a Soldier's Wife, The.
Davis, F. Giles Johnson, Ph.D.
Deane, S. Scholar I.
Scholar II.
Ehrenburg. Sons of Our Sons, The.
Foley, M. Lucky Eugene.
Frost, R. Lesson for Today, The.
Hacker, M. Imaginary Translation.
Hall, D. Professor Gratt.
Heine. If, Jerusalem, I Ever Should Forget Thee.
Hristic. In the big library scholars sit and read books.
Ibn-Chasdai. Poor Scholar, The.
Juan Chi. Long ago, at fourteen or fifteen.
Li Shang-yin. Poem for My Little Boy.
Lu Yu. Merchant's Joy, The.
Matthews, T. Happy Arabia.
McClatchy. Grasshopper.
McCord, D. Baccalaureate.
Mother Goose. Ten O'Clock Scholar, [The].
Nguyễn Công Trú'. Scholars and soldiers marshaled in two files!
Nguyễn Khuyến. Scholar-Laureate in Retirement, A.
To a Discarded Fan.
To Some Students Caught Nodding in Class.
Nguyễn Trãi. Among the great, no smooth and open world.
Round shape water takes inside the gourd, A.
Nguyễn Văn Lạc. Shrimp.
Phillpotts. Miniature.
Phùng Khắc Khoan. Advice to Students.
Pien Kung. Paintings of Various Subjects by Fang Jih-sheng: Baby Chicks Following Their Mother.
Po Chü-i. Quiet House in Ch'ang-lo Ward, A.
Ponsot. "Love is not Love."
Reid, C. Perversion, A.
Salzman, E. Double Dactyls.
Shapiro, K. Going to School.
Stevens, W. Of the Manner of Addressing Clouds.
Tao Tschung Yu. Familiar Spirits.
Trần Tế Xu'o'ng. Tomorrow, should I fail, I'll go away.
Unknown. Certain scholar named Mr. Wang, A.

Epigram: "Gold priests, wooden chalices."
Exhortation to Learning.
Fleeting Time.
Scholar and the Cat, The.
Scholar's Life, The.
Wither. For Scholars and Pupils.
Wu Wei-yeh. Poem of the Western Fields.
Yeats. Gratitude to the Unknown Instructors.
Scholars, The.
See also **Pedantry and Pedants; Students; Teaching and Teachers**

School and Schools
Barrows, R. Report Card, The.
Baumel. Thumbs Up.
Baxter, J. In the Lecture Room.
Berry, D. On Reading Poems to a Senior Class at South High.
Blake, W. School-Boy, The.
Bottoms. Desk, The.
Brook, D. School of Pain, The.
Brooks, G. We real cool. We.
Brown, G. Books.
Island School.
Burns, M. Beginnings.
Bynner. Haskell.
Canning, G. *et al.* Rogero's Song.
Carson, C. Slate Street School.
Cassells. Soul Make A Path Through Shouting.
Catacalos. David Talamántez on the Last Day of Second Grade.
Clare, J. Schoolboys in Winter.
Clewell. Goodbye Note to Debbie Fuller: Pass It On.
Crabbe. Schools.
De la Mare. Scholars.
Deane, S. Brethren, The.
Derricotte. In an Urban School.
Divakaruni. Walk, The.
Yuba City School.
Dixon, H. Description of a Good Boy, The.
Djanikian. In the Elementary School Choir.
Dove, R. Flash Cards.
Dumas, E. Our School Now Closes Out.
Durham. Columbus Day.
Elder. School Cadets.
Elmusa. Little Piece of Sky, A.
Flynn, M. Down in the field.
Follain. School and Nature.
Gildner. First Practice.
Glancy. First Reader Santee Training School, 1873, The.
Glück, L. School Children, The.
Greenaway. School is over.
Hale, S. Mary's Lamb [*or* Mary and Her Lamb].
Harrison, G. Playground, The.
Hathaway, J. Congressman Visits the Grade School, The.
Hemans. Evening Prayer, at a Girls' School.
Henderson-Holmes. Battle, Over and Over Again, The.
Herzing. Small Boy, Dreaming, A.
Hoban. Summer goes, summer goes.
Holden, J. Dancing School.
Hood, T. Ode on a Distant Prospect of Clapham Academy.
Hughes, J. Dog Day Lesson.
Humphries, R. Heresy for a Class-Room.
Huws. Goodbye to Regal.
Kaneko. Bailey Gatzert: The First Grade, 1945.
Kinsella, T. Model School, Inchicore.
Koch, K. Schoolyard in April.
Komunyakaa. White Port and Lemon Juice.
Kooser. Country School.
Lane, P. On Being Head of the English Department.
Lawrence, D. Last Lesson of the Afternoon.
Leonard, T. Paroakial.
Leto. For Talking.
Levine, P. On My Own.
Lifshin. Being Jewish in a Small Town.
Lorde. Hanging Fire.
Lu Yu. Farm Families.
Madgett. Images.
Magee, W. Are You Ready?

Major, C. I Was Looking for the University.
Maran. "Tropicals."
McGough, R. First Day at School.
He Who Owns the Whistle Rules the World.
McPherson, S. Helen Todd: My Birthname.
Milligan, S. Bad Report—Good Manners.
Moore, A. Girls' School.
Moore, M. Student, The.
Moore, R. Though the New Teacher Is a Trifle Odd.
Moorer. Negro Schools, The.
Tree of Knowledge, The.
Mora. Señora X No More.
Morse, B. Day on the Planet, A.
Muldoon, P. Anseo.
O'Grady, D. This introspective exile here today.
O'Meally. I was jus.
Piercy. Learning Experience.
Pierman. How We Learned about Friction.
Randall, J. To William Wordsworth from Virginia.
Rich, A. In a Classroom.
Memory lifts her smoky mirror: 1943.
Ríos, A. Domingo Limón.
St. John, P. Reading a Story to My Child.
Sanchez, S. Norma.
Shaw, D. Retrospection.
Silverstein, S. Sick.
Smith, S. To School!
Spender, S. Elementary School Classroom in a Slum, An.
Stafford, W. School Days.
Swift, J. Description of the Morning, A.
Thompson, P. Examination, The.
Lines to an Old School-House.
Tirolien. Little Black Boy's Prayer, A.
Tru'o'ng Anh Thuy. First Day of School, The.
Unknown. Unhappy Schoolboy, The.
Wenest thou, usher, with thyn cointise.
Voigt. Field Trip, The.
Wade, B. Summer School.
Wagner, M. Miss Clement's Second Grade.
Warren, R. School Lesson Based on Word of Tragic Death of Entire Gillum Family.
Waterman, N. Johnny's Hist'ry Lesson.
Wells, C. Overworked Elocutionist, An.
Whittier. In School-Days.
To My Old Schoolmaster.
Williamson, G. Walter Parmer.
Wong, N. How a Girl Got Her Chinese Name.
Yamanaka. Yarn Wig.
Yeats. Among School Children.
Zimmer. Father Animus and Zimmer.
Zimmer in Grade School.
Zimmer's Head Thudding against the Blackboard.
See also **Colleges and Universities**
Schoolmasters. *See* **Teaching and Teachers**
Schubert, Franz
Schuyler, J. Grand Duo.
Schwartz, Delmore
Berryman. I can't get him out of my mind, out of my mind.
This world is gradually becoming a place.
Lowell, R. To Delmore Schwartz.
Science Fiction
Amis, K. Science Fiction.
Revard. Discovery of the New World.
Science and Scientists
Abse. Letter to Alex Comfort.
Auden. Ode to Terminus.
Barbauld. To Mr. S. T. Coleridge.
Brontë, C. Reason.
Cokinos. Short-Wave.
Cowley, A. Philosophy, the great and only heir.
Cummings, E. Pity this busy monster,manunkind.
Space being(don't forget to remember)Curved.
Dunbar-Nelson. To Madame Curie.
Edson, R. Counting Sheep.
Fenton, J. For the context of the basidiocarp Singer states.
Kingfisher's Boxing Gloves, The.
South Parks Road.
Fox, S. Almagest, Last Letter to Zakarias.

Harte, B. Society Upon the Stanislaus, The.
Holub. Brief Reflection on Cats Growing in Trees.
Experimental Animals.
Suffering.
Hope, A. On an Engraving by Casserius.
Jarrell. Emancipators, The.
Jeffers, R. Science.
Kovner. Scientists Are Mistaken, The.
Lawrence, D. Self-Protection.
Lehrer. Wernher von Braun.
Lindsay, V. Horrid Voice of Science, The.
Lipska. What Happened to Professor White on Leaving the Hat Store.
Lowell, J. Science and Poetry.
Magrelli. If you melt some lead.
Merrill, J. Laboratory Poem.
Naden. Scientific Wooing.
Nash, O. Purist, The.
Patmore, C. Science, the agile ape, may well.
Peskett. Bottles in the Zoological Museum.
Poe. Sonnet—To Science.
Pope, A. Intended for Sir Isaac Newton.
Seaton, M. Theories of Illusion.
Tate, J. Teaching the Ape to Write Poems.
Updike. V. B. Nimble, V. B. Quick.
Scopes Trial
Unknown. Bryan's Last Battle.
See also **Evolution**
Scorn
Carew, T. Looking-Glass, A.
To My Mistress Sitting by a River's Side; an Eddy.
Daniel, S. Sonnet 33: 'When men shall find thy flower'.
Sonnet 5: 'Whilst Youth and Error'.
Donne. Apparition, The.
Glück, L. Horse.
Korran. What She Said to Her Girl Friend ("No, we will not make vows to the ever-winning goddess").
Kumin, M. Voice From the Roses, A.
Moore, T. When I loved you, I can't but allow.
Philips, K. To the Queen of Inconstancy, Regina Collier, in Antwerp.
Robinson, E. Miniver Cheevy, child of scorn.
Sidney, P. Sonnet 31: "With how sad steps, O Moon, thou climb'st the skies!"
Theocritus. Neteheard.
Unknown. Fair and scornful, do thy worst.
I been rebuked and I been scorned.
Wilde, L. Désillusion.
Scorpions
Plomer. Scorpion, The.
Yün Shou-p'ing. Scorpion's tails, silver hooks.
Scotland
Auden. Night Mail, The.
Aytoun, W. Massacre of the Macpherson, The.
Brereton, C. To Miss A[——]a M[——]a Tra[——]s; an Epistle from Scotland.
Burns, R. Birks of Aberfeldy, The [Composed on the Spot].
Ca' the ewes [or yowes] to the knowes.
Farewell, A [or The]: "It was a' for our rightfu' king."
Halloween.
John Barleycorn [a Ballad].
Kirk's Alarm, The.
My heart's in the Highlands, my heart is not here.
Scotch Drink.
Scots, wha hae wi' Wallace bled.
Such a Parcel of Rogues in a Nation.
Tam o' Shanter. [A Tale].
To a Haggis.
To William Simpson, Ochiltree.
Campbell, T. Lord Ullin's Daughter.
Carstairs. On Loch Leven.
Crawford, R. Herr-Knit Bunnet, The.
Rain.
Scotland in the 1890s.
Dunbar, W. Lament for the Makaris.
Fordham. Highland Mary.
Fraser, G. Home Town Elegy.
Fulton, R. Remembering an Island.
Garioch. To Robert Fergusson.

Graham, H. Cockney of the North, The.
Gray, S. Scotland.
Johnston, E. Working Man, The.
Jonson, B. On the Union.
Keats. Naughty Boy, The.
Lang, A. Twilight on Tweed.
Leonard, T. Right inuff / ma language is disgraceful.
Lindsay. Compleynt of the Comoun Weill of Scotland, The.
MacCaig. Old Edinburgh.
"MacDiarmid." Scotland small? Out multiform, our infinite Scotland *small*?
Sic Transit Gloria Scotia.
We must look at the harebell as if.
Macgillivray. Return, The.
MacLean, S. Calvary.
Clan MacLean, The.
MacNeice. Bagpipe Music.
Mangan, G. Glasgow 1956.
Heraclitus at Glasgow Cross.
Morgan, E. De Quincey in Glasgow.
Pilate at Fortingall.
Muir, E. Scotland 1941.
Scotland's Winter.
Mure. O Heavens! O Earth! heer I must pause a space.
Powell, A. Caledonia.
Reid, A. Scotland.
Retallack, J. Biographia Literaria.
Scott, W. Boat Song.
Caledonia.
Farewell Thou Minstrel Harp.
Lochinvar.
Melrose Abbey.
Pibroch of Donuil Dhu.
Smith, I. Gaelic Stories.
Highlanders.
Lewis 1928–45.
Listen, I have flown through darkness towards joy.
Oban 1955–82.
Poem in March.
Shall Gaelic Die?
Smith, W. Glenaradale.
Southey, R. Inchcape Rock, The.
Spence, L. Carse, The.
Stown Bairn, The.
Stevenson, A. North Sea off Carnoustie.
Taylor, R. Princess of Scotland, The.
Tomlinson, C. Mr. Brodsky.
Unknown. Geordie [An Old Ballad].
Mary [or Marie] Hamilton.
Sir Patrick Spens [or Spence].
Tam Lin.
Watson, J. Soldier, The.
Scots, The
Burns, R. Scotch Drink.
Scots, wha hae wi' Wallace bled.
Such a Parcel of Rogues in a Nation.
To a Haggis.
Verses Intended to Be Written below a Noble Earl's Picture.
Cleveland, J. Nature herself doth Scotchmen beasts confess.
Crawford, R. Scotland in the 1890s.
Duffy, C. In Your Mind.
Garioch. At Robert Fergusson's Grave[, October 1962].
Embro to the Ploy.
To Robert Fergusson.
Imlah. Goldilocks.
Kay, J. English Cousin Comes to Scotland.
Kipling, R. McAndrew's Hymn.
Leonard, T. Right inuff / ma language is disgraceful.
This is thi.
"MacDiarmid." Thistle's Characteristics, The.
Weapon, The.
Martin, A. Forest.
Malcolm MacKerral.
Muir, E. Scotland 1941.
Nash, O. Genealogical Reflection.
Pratt, E. Gathering, The.
Scott, A. Scotch God / Kent His / Faither.
Scott, W. Blue Bonnets over the Border.
Smith, I. Highlanders.

Lewis 1928–45.
Listen, I have flown through darkness towards joy.
Oban 1955–82.
Stevenson, R. Ticonderoga: A Legend of the West Highlands.
Unknown. Sir Patrick Spens [*or* Spence].

Scott, Sir Walter
Dunn, D. Green Breeks.
Milnes. Sir Walter Scott at the Tomb of the Stuarts in St. Peter's.
Wordsworth, W. On the Departure of Sir Walter Scott from Abbotsford, for Naples.

Scottish Borders
Elliot, J. Flowers of the Forest, The.
Scott, W. Dreary Change, The.
Lochinvar.

Scottish Highlands
Burns, R. My heart's in the Highlands, my heart is not here.
Stevenson, R. In the highlands, in the country places.

Scottsboro Case
Boyle, K. Communication to Nancy Cunard, A.
Cullen, C. Scottsboro, Too, Is Worth Its Song.
Unknown. Scottsboro.

Screams
Carrel. Catching.
Creeley. Turn, The.
Ezekiel. Song to be Shouted Out.
Fisher, R. Incredible Henry McHugh, The.
Gilbo'a. Our Dreams.
Hall, D. Scream, The.
Mihalic. Screams in the Dark.
Sachs, N. Landscape of Screams.
Yukitsuna. Tanka: "Overtaken by time."

Scribes
Bast. Nebamun's Cat.
Chaucer. To His Scribe Adam.
Unknown. Scribe, The.
See also Secretaries; Stenographers

Sculpture and Sculptors
Browning, E. Hiram Powers' "Greek Slave."
Byron, G. Canto 4.
Cawein. Mnemosyne.
Cherry, K. Bride of Quietness, The.
Danner. Convert, The.
"Dario." Victory of Samothrace, The.
De Tabley. Knight in the Wood, The.
Fuller, M. Flaxman.
Goldman, M. Crack, The.
Hall, D. "Reclining Figure."
Keats. On Seeing the Elgin Marbles.
Leconte de Lisle, C. Venus de Milo.
Logan, R. On a Prize Crucifix by a Student Sculptor.
Mathews, C. Sculptor, The.
Meinke. Helen.
Moore, M. No Swan So Fine.
Ray, H. Sculptor's Vision, The.
Tireles Sculptor, The.
Rogers, S. To the Fragment of a Statue of Hercules, Commonly Called the Torso.
Sadoleto. Poem of Jacobus Sadoletus on the Statue of Laocoon, The.
Santayana. Before a Statue of Achilles.
Scollard. Bit of Marble, A.
Stickney, T. On Rodin's "L'Illusion, Sœur d'Icare."
Walker, T. Owl.
Wolfe, H. Tulip.
Yeats. Statues, The.
Zukofsky, L. 1892-1941.

Sea
Aeschylus. There is the sea.
Akahito. In Waka Bay when.
"Akhmatova." Land not mine, still, A.
Alexander, W. Explosive Decibel Journeys.
Alkman. Creatures Rest, The.
Ammons. So I Said I Am Ezra.
Ammuvanar. What Her Girl Friend Said to Him ("Your sands are furrowed").
What She Said ("Friend, his seas swell and roar").
Antipater of Sidon. My house is simple, lying beside the sea.

Antipater of Thessalonica. All sea is sea. How mad it is to blame.
Apollinaire. Listen to the sea.
Arendt. Lost Bay.
Arnold, M. Dover Beach.
To Marguerite.
Ashbery. Painter, The.
Atkins. Lakefront, Cleveland.
Auden. On This Island.
Awoonor. Sea Eats the Land at Home, The.
Baker, H. Ode to the Sea.
Bancquart. Portrait of Jonah with woman.
Sea.
Woman asleep.
Bansode. Woman.
Barrax. There was a song.
Baxter, J. East Coast Journey.
Beaver. Angels' Weather.
Beckett, S. Dieppe.
Beddoes. Sailors' Song.
Beer, P. Jane Austen.
Beevers. Atameros.
Bekederemo. Olokun.
Bentley, N. Third Dungeness Spit Apocalypse.
Betjeman. East Anglian Bathe.
Bierds. For the Sake of Retrieval.
Bishop, E. At the Fishhouses.
Cootchie, Miss Lula's servant, lies in marl.
Large Bad Picture.
Map, The.
Riverman, The.
Seascape.
Twelfth Morning; or What You Will.
Blight. Down from the Country.
Landfall, The.
Booth, P. Marin.
Borkhuis. Quartet.
Braithwaite. House of Falling Leaves, The.
Watchers, The.
Bridges, R. Who has not walked upon the shore.
Brock, V. Sea Birds, The.
Brontë, A. Lines Composed in a Wood on a Windy Day.
Brooke, R. Song of the Beasts (Sung, on one night, in the cities, in the darkness), The.
Brooks, C. Lines: Composed at the Old Temples of Maralipoor.
Brown, G. Beachcomber.
Browning, R. Meeting At Night.
Parting at Morning.
Brownstein. War.
Brutus. At night.
Byron, G. And I have loved thee, Ocean! and my joy.
Camões. Rev'rend Father stood inculcating, The.
Carew, J. Tiho, the Carib.
Carlile. Listening to Beethoven on the Oregon Coast.
"Carroll." Lobster Quadrille, A.
Carver, R. Cobweb, The.
Cary, A. Katrina on the Porch.
Catherine of Siena (A. K. A. Saint Catherine). We were enclosed.
Causley. Tell me, tell me, Sarah Jane.
Cendrars. Fish Cove.
Césaire, A. Bucolic.
On the Islands of All Winds.
Chang Yü. Song of the Old Oak.
Chapman, G. In meantime flew our ships, and straight we fetch'd.
Ch'ien T'ao. Reading the Book of Hills and Seas.
Chin. Repulse Bay.
Chivers. Wind, The.
Chōkū. Tanka: "Phantom appears, A."
Chon, P. Piano, The.
Clampitt. Beach Glass.
Clifton, L. Lost Baby Poem, The.
Corn. Naskeag.
Corso. Sea Chanty.
Cowper, W. Light Shining out of Darkness.
To Mr. Newton [on His Return from Ramsgate].
Crabbe. Letter I.
Winter Views Serene.

Cranch. Ocean, The.
Crane, H. Above the fresh ruffles of the surf.
At Melville's Tomb.
Ave Maria.
Crane, S. Man adrift on a slim spar, A.
Cronin, J. Naval Base (Part III), The.
Cummings, E. How many moments must(amazing each).
Maggie and milly and molly and may.
Curnow. You Will Know When You Get There.
Daive. Lost in contemplation of its end.
Daniel, S. Unto the boundless Ocean of thy beauty.
Darley. Rebellion of the Waters, The.
Darwish, M. Guests on the sea: Our visit is short.
Davison, P. Equinox 1980.
De Mello Breyner. Day of sea in the sky, made.
Ded. I drag a boat over the ocean.
Demetrio. Training.
Dickinson, E. Exultation is the going.
I started Early—Took my Dog.
Wild Nights—Wild Nights!
Dimitrova. Child and Sea.
Dixon, R. By the Sea.
do Espirito Santo. Where Are the Men Seized in this Wind of Madness?
Dolben. Sea Song, A.
Doolittle, H. Blue-geese, white-geese, you may say.
Hermes of the Ways.
Or is it a great tide that covers the rock-pool.
Oread.
Dove, R. Fish in the Stone, The.
Du Maurier. Music.
Dudek. Coming Suddenly to the Sea.
Dugan, A. Note: The Sea Grinds Things Up.
Plague of Dead Sharks.
Duncan, R. Achilles' Song.
DuPlessis, R. She will lie naked.
Eberhart, R. Ship Burning and a Comet All in One Day, A.
Eliot, T. River is within us, the sea is all about us, The.
Elytis. Anniversary.
Ode to Santorini.
Of the Aegean.
Emerson, R. Sea-Shore.
Waves.
Falconer, W. "All hands unmoor!" proclaims a boisterous cry.
Fatchen. Oh Erica, Not Again!
Fenton, J. This Octopus Exploits Women.
Ferlinghetti, L. Sea and Ourselves at Cape Ann, The.
Forbes, C. Dark Mirror.
Home.
Fraser, K. Boot, wet sand and more white along the borders defining a trail of lush / chemicals we adhere to.
Frost, R. Neither Out Far Nor In Deep.
Once by the Pacific.
West-Running Brook.
Garrett, G. York Harbor Morning.
Gates, L. Killdeer, The.
Gilder, R. On the Bay.
Glissant. O Sun! O age-old labor mutely mixed with ocean.
Glück, L. Phenomenal Survivals of Death in Nantucket.
Googe. Coming Homeward out of Spain.
Gouri. You're no king.
Graves, R. Beach, The.
Song of Blodeuwedd, The.
Gray, J. Le Voyage À Cythère.
Grosholz. Old Fisherman, The.
Guiterman. Sea-Chill.
H. H. T. Sea and the Sands, The.
Hackett, J. Fleeing sandpipers, The.
Hadas, R. House Beside the Sea, The.
Haida. Song for Smooth Waters.
Hall, D. Blue Wing, The.
Hardison. Marina.
Hardy, T. Beeny Cliff.
Once at Swanage.

Harwood, G. Clair de Lune.
Harwood, L. Final Painting, The.
Soft White.
Hawthorne, N. Ocean has its silent caves, The.
Hays, H. Case, The.
Hemans. Last Song of Sappho, The.
Song of Emigration.
Hill, G. Wreaths.
Hirschman, J. Headlands.
Hirshfield, J. In a Net of Blue and Gold.
Hoban. Old Man Ocean, how do you pound.
Hollander, J. Hall of Ocean Life.
Morning in the Islands.
Holtby, W. Boats in the Bay.
Holub. Man Cursing the Sea.
Hooper, V. Reading, A.
Hsieh Chin. Inscribed on a Painting of
Dragons by Ch'en So-weng.
Hsü Wei. Colossal:/ Like towers and pavilions
from the flat plain.
Hughes, L. Feet O' Jesus.
Sea Calm.
Hughes, T. Relic.
Still-Life.
Hugo, R. Salt Water Story.
Irwin, T. Iphione.
Ivask, I. We shall return we will stay here.
Jacob, V. Baltic, The.
Jacobsen, J. Limbo Dancer, The.
Jarman, M. Cavafy in Redondo.
Jeffers, R. Evening Ebb.
Eye, The.
November Surf.
Place for No Story, The.
Watch the Lights Fade.
Johnstone, R. Robot Camera.
Joseph, J. Lost Continent, The.
Joyce, J. On the Beach at Fontana.
Kangro. Late Flowers, Wind, Sea, Sand and
Fish.
Kannaṉār. What Her Girl Friend Said to him
("Near the salt pans").
Keane, S. Once the wind.
Keats. On the Sea.
Kennelly. Island, The.
Kim, C. Salt Sea, The.
Kim, K. Sea and the Butterfly, The.
Kingsley, C. Sands of Dee, The.
Kinnell. Spindrift.
Kipling, R. Dykes, The.
Last Chantey, The.
Sea and the Hills, The.
Kircher. Looking at the Sea.
Komunyakaa. Break from the Bush, A.
Laing, D. Lines on the Sea.
Laing, K. One Hundred Lines for the Coast.
Laird, C. Sea at Evening, The.
Landon. Sappho's Song.
Larkin, P. To the Sea.
Lawrence, D. Butterfly, the wind blows sea-
ward[, strong beyond the garden wall!].
Spray.
Whales Weep Not!
Le Guin. Child on the Shore, The.
Lear, E. Jumblies, The.
Leonidas of Tarentum. Spring on the Coast.
Leopardi. Infinite, The.
Lepik, A. Sea, The.
Li Po. Ancient Air.
Liu E. Waiting for the Ferry at Inchŏn.
Lodge, G. Strong saturation of sea! O widely
flown.
Tuckanuck, I.
Longfellow, H. Seaweed.
Sound of the Sea, The.
Tide rises, the tide falls, The.
Longley, M. Freeze-up annexes the sea even,
The.
Lorde. What my child learns of the sea.
Lowell, R. Near the Ocean.
Water.
Lowry, M. Sestina in a Cantina.
Wild Cherry, The.
MacCaig. Midnight, Lochinver.
"MacDiarmid." On the Ocean Floor.
MacEwen, G. Sea Things.

Machado Ruiz. Lord, you have ripped away
from me what I loved most.
Machi. Tanka: "All the more."
Tanka: "Looking as though."
Mackey, N. Dream Thief.
Phantom Light of All Our Day, The.
MacNeice. Leaving Barra.
Thalassa.
Mallarmé. Breeze from the Sea.
Mandelstam. Silentium.
Mansour, J. Beyond the breakers.
Marvell. Bermudas.
Masaoka Shiki. Fresh from the Void.
Wild geese cry, The.
Masefield. Cardigan Bay.
Sea-Fever.
Wanderer's Song, A.
Matthews, W. Come Come.
Matveyeva. Lighthouse.
Maunick. Further off is the measured force the
word of the sea.
Mayer, B. Boats.
McClintock, M. Twisting inland.
McDonald, E. Itherness.
McGough, R. Cousin Reggie.
Melo Neto. Daily Space.
Melville, H. Far Off-Shore.
Maldive Shark, The.
Pebbles.
Song from Mardi.
Meredith, W. Open Sea, The.
Merrill, J. Remora.
Merwin, W. Voyage to Labrador.
Messerli. Going to Sea.
Mew. Sea Love.
Meynell, V. Frozen Ocean, The.
Miles, J. Beach Party Given by T.
Shaughnessy for the Sisters.
Miljkovic. Sea Before I Start Dreaming, The.
Sea Without Poets.
Millay, E. Above these cares my spirit in
calm abiding.
Exiled.
Hearing your words, and not a word among
them.
Ragged Island.
Miller, J. At Our Golden Gate.
Milton. But now my oat proceeds.
Fifth Ode of Horace. Lib. I, The.
Mirabai. O friend, understand: the body.
Montale. Eel, the siren, The.
Moore, L. Until I Saw the Sea.
Moore, M. Fish, The.
Grave, A.
Jelly-Fish, A.
Morris, W. Garden By The Sea, A.
Morrison, L. Surf.
Moschus. Ocean, The.
Mother Goose. Three wise men of Gotham.
Mu Hua. Rhyme-Prose on the Sea.
Muldoon, P. Briefcase, The.
Muratori. Sensible Qualities.
Murford. Storm and Calm: Sent from Embden
to M. Edw. Ma. and M. Tho. Ly, The.
Nemerov. Salt Garden, The.
Neruda. Poet's Obligation.
Newcastle, M. Sea Similized to Meadows and
Pastures: the Mariners, to Shepherds: the
Mast, to a May-Pole: the Fish, to Beasts,
The.
Noguere. Barney Bigard.
Okamoto. Tanka: "To the sea, to the sea."
Okara. One Night at Victoria Beach.
Okigbo. Water Maid.
Oliver, M. Waves, The.
Oppen. Animula.
Bahamas.
Book of Job and a Draft of a Poem to Praise
the Paths of the Living, The.
Gold on Oak Leaves.
Silver as / The needle's eye.
Taste, The.
Translucent Mechanics, The.
Pacheco, J. Song to Be Written on a Wave.
Padilla. Sometimes I plunge into the ocean,
for a long time.
Palmer, H. Aunt Zillah Speaks.

Park, T. Youthful Sea, The.
Pau-Llosa. Ostiones Y Cangrejos Moros.
Paz. Key of Water, The.
Percival. Coral Grove, The.
Pessoa. Portuguese Sea, The.
Petrarch. Galley, The.
Phạm Hồ. Sea, The.
Phylip, S. Seagull, The.
Pien Kung. Song of the Woodcutter of the
Sea.
Pizzarelli. Drop of ocean.
Plath. Blackberrying.
Point Shirley.
Plomer. Azure, or green, or purple when the
sun.
Po Chü-i. Taoism and Buddhism.
Poe. Annabel Lee.
City in the Sea, The.
To Helen ("Helen, thy beauty is to me").
To One in Paradise.
Pollard, V. Belize Suite.
Pound, E. Canto 1.
Portrait d'une Femme.
Pratt, E. Silences.
Pritchard, N. Burnt Sienna.
Probyn. Barcarolle.
Raab, L. On the Island.
Rabéarivelo. Here is.
Rankin, J. Sea and Other Stories, The.
Sea-bundle.
Ravikovitch. Tirzah and the Wide World.
Reeves, J. Sea is a hungry dog, The.
Ribemont-Dessaignes. Sliding Trombone.
Rich, A. Insusceptibles, The.
Roethke. Rose, The.
Rossetti, C. By the Sea.
Horses of the sea, / Rear a foaming crest, The.
What are heavy? Sea-sand and sorrow.
Wind has such a rainy sound, The.
Rossetti, D. Even So.
Sea-Limits, The.
Rukeyser, M. Believing in those inexorable
laws.
St. John, P. Song.
Sunday.
Saitō Mokichi. Tanka: "Aspiration."
Sandburg, C. Be Ready.
Sea-wash never ends, The.
Sargent, E. Life on the Ocean Wave, A.
Schick. Last summer.
Schuyler, J. Crystal Lithium, The.
Seferis. Wreck "Thrush", The.
Shakespeare, W. Sea Song, A: "Master, the
swabber, the boatswain and I, The."
Shelley, P. Time.
Shin, S. Catapulting a Stone.
Shuttle. Maritimes.
Sikelianos. Return, The.
Silko. Prayer to the Pacific.
Silverstein, S. Slithergadee has crawled out of
the sea, The.
Simpson, L. Fine Day for Straw Hats, A.
Singer, B. SOS Lifescene.
Smith, C. Sea View, The.
Sonnet Written in the Church-Yard at
Middleton in Sussex.
Smith, D. March Storm, Poquoson, Virginia,
1963.
Smith, I. Dunoon and the Holy Loch.
Oban 1955–82.
Southard. In the sea, sunset.
Spender, S. Seascape.
Spenser. In the Bower of Bliss.
Spicer, J. Phonemics.
Stanescu. Adolescents on the Sea.
Stephens, J. Main-Deep, The.
Shell, The.
Stevens, W. Idea of Order at Key West, The.
Sea Surface Full of Clouds.
Stevenson, A. North Sea off Carnoustie.
Stevenson, R. At the Seaside [or Sea-Side].
Fair Isle at Sea—thy lovely name.
Stickney, T. At Sainte-Marguerite.
Strand. I recall that I stood before the
breaking waves.
Supervielle. Like an ox streaming saliva,
yoked to the plough.

Swenson, M. Stone gullets among.
Waking from a Nap on the Beach.
Swinburne. I Will Go Back to the Great
Sweet Mother.
Return, The.
Swirszczynska. Sea and the Man, The.
Tadamichi. As I row over the plain.
Tanikawa Shuntaro. August is a dreamless
month.
Tati-Loutard. Pilgrimage to Loango Strand.
Submarine Tombs.
Voices, The.
Tennyson, A. Break, break, break.
Crossing the Bar.
Duet.
Eagle, The.
Kraken, The.
Lincolnshire Wolds and Lincolnshire Sea.
Lullaby: "Sweet and low, sweet and low."
Todd, R. Sea Horse, The.
Ts'ao Ts'ao. Viewing the Ocean.
Tucker, M. Beautiful Sea, The.
U Tam'si Tchicaya. Sea Nocturne.
Under. Alone with the Sea.
Unknown. Battle of Brunanburh.
Golden Vanity, The.
I loathe the twin seas.
If all the seas were one sea.
In the open sea.
Like the tides' flood.
Mæg ic be me sylfum so???ogied wrecan.
Sea, The.
Seafarer, The.
Shell Secrets.
Sir Patrick Spens [*or* Spence].
Song: "In the middle of the sea."
South of the Great Sea.
Stiff winds blow.
Untermeyer, J. High Tide.
Updike. Sea Knell.
Winter Ocean.
Uvavnuk. Great sea has set me in motion,
The.
Valentine, J. First Love.
Van den Heuvel. Summer breeze.
Venclova. Shield of Achilles, The.
Walcott. Sea is History, The.
Wallace, R. Real Thing, The.
Wang T'ing-hsiang. Climbing to the Top of
the City Walls at Kan-yü.
Warner. Port Bou.
Watts-Dunton. Sonnet's Voice, The.
Webb, F. End of the Picnic.
Sea, The.
Webster, A. Enigma No. 6.
Westmorland. My Observation at Sea.
Whitman, A. Upon the shells by Carribea's
wave.
Whitman, W. After the sea-ship, after the
whistling winds.
As I ebb'd with the ocean of life.
By that long scan of waves, myself call'd
back, resumed upon myself.
Facing west from California's shores.
Had I the choice to tally greatest bards.
In cabin'd ships at sea.
Out of the cradle endlessly rocking.
Patrolling Barnegat.
Song for All Seas, All Ships.
To the Man-of-War Bird.
World below the brine, The.
You sea! I resign myself to you also—I guess
what you mean.
Wilde, O. Impression du Voyage.
Williams, W. Flowers by the Sea.
Sadness of the Sea, The.
Yachts, The.
Winters, A. Mill-Race, The.
Wollach. At Sea.
Wordsworth, W. By the Sea.
Wright, J. Miners.
Old Age Compensation.
Way to Make a Living, A.
Wyatt, T. My galley charged with
forgetfulness.
Sonnet: 'My galley charged'.
Wylie. Sea Lullaby.

Yang Wei-chen. Song of a Dream Journey
over the Vast Sea.
Yeats. White Birds, The.
Yorie. Cat's Eye, The.
Yosano. Tanka: "Sea inside my heart, The."
Yoshimi. Tanka: "Ocean, The."
Young, F. Seascape.
Yü Chi. Inscribed on the Painting, Solitary
Crane, in the Collection of Jao Shih-ying.
Yukitsuna. Tanka: "Amid the waves of time."
Zhenkai. August Sleepwalker, The.
See also **Sailing and Sailors**
Sea Battles. *See* **Naval Battles**
Sea Creatures
De la Mare. Sunk Lyonesse.
Fenton, J. This Octopus Exploits Women.
Graves, R. Sea Horse, The.
Ishigaki. Shellfish.
Kinnell. Spindrift.
Moore, M. Fish, The.
Sea Unicorns and Land Unicorns.
Tennyson, A. Kraken, The.
Todd, R. Sea Horse, The.
Williams, W. Sea-Elephant, The.
Sea Gulls. *See* **Gulls**
Sea Hawks
Eberhart, R. Sea-Hawk.
Sea Monsters and Sea Serpents
Kingsley, C. Whelming the dwellings of men,
and the toils of the slow-/ footed oxen.
Morgan, E. Loch Ness Monster's Song, The.
Tennyson, A. Kraken, The.
Westwood. Motionless sat the shadow at the
helm.
Sea Shells. *See* **Shells**
Sea Voyages. *See* **Voyages**
Seacoasts. *See* **Beaches; Shores**
Seafaring and Seafarers. *See* **Sailing and Sailors**
Seals
Aldis, D. Seals all flap, The.
Bly, R. Dead Seal [near McClure's Beach],
The.
Eberhart, R. Seals, Terns, Time.
Field, R. Performing Seal, The.
Hoffman, D. Seals in Penobscot Bay, The.
Lowell, R. Soft Wood.
Murphy, R. Seals at High Island.
Purdy, A. Dead Seal.
Scalapino. How can I help myself, as one
woman said to me about wanting.
Unknown. Magic Words for Hunting Seal.
Spring Fiord.
Seamstresses
Bishop, E. House Guest.
Clifton, H. Seamstress, The.
Peretz. Three Seamstresses, The.
Seashores. *See* **Shores; Beaches**
Seasickness
Unknown. Mistress Towl.
Seasons
Antipater of Thessalonica. To Epicles.
Barker, G. January jumps about.
Blake, W. Earth's Answer.
Boccaccio. Two Dreams, The.
Bogan, L. Zone.
Borkhuis. Quartet.
Bradstreet, A. Four Seasons of the Year, The.
Bridges, R. While yet we wait for spring, and
from the dry.
Brock-Broido. Domestic Mysticism.
Brodsky, J. Hawk's Cry in Autumn, The.
Brontë, E. Song.
Browning, R. Love.
Lovers' Quarrel, A.
Bryant, W. Winter Piece, A.
Cary, A. November.
Chang Yü. Pavilion for Listening to
Fragrance, A.
Ch'on, S. Namelessness.
Clare, J. Decay.
February.
Clough. Put forth thy leaf, thou lofty plane.
Coleridge, S. Garden Year, The.
Collins, W. Ode to Evening.
Compiuta Donzella. In the season when the
world leafs and flowers.

Cristall. Song: "Through springtime walks,
with flowers perfumed."
Cullen, C. Leaves.
Cummings, E. All ignorance toboggans into
know.
In time of daffodils(who know.
Cutler, J. Through the Year.
Delany. Solace.
Dickinson, E. As imperceptibly as Grief.
It was a quiet way—.
Donne. Love's Growth.
Nocturnal[l] upon Saint Lucy's [*or* S. Lucies]
Day, Being the Shortest Day, A.
Eberhart, R. Spider expects the cold of winter,
The.
Emerson, R. In my garden three ways meet.
Figueroa, J. This tree my time keeper.
Frost, R. Oven Bird, The.
"Gander." (The Twelve Months).
Greiffenberg. On the Fruit-Providing Autumn
Season.
Hadewijch. Love's Constancy.
Han-shan. From my father and mother I
inherited land enough.
Han Yü. When white dew descends on the
hundred grasses.
Hesketh. Death of a Gardener.
Holcroft. Seasons, The.
Horace. 1.9.
Housman, A. Winter.
Hove. Lost Bird.
Migratory Bird ("One day he perched on a
tree with dew").
Humphries, R. Seasons, The.
Juan Chi. This summer's burning heat.
K'ang Hai. Sitting by Myself.
Keats. Human Seasons, The.
Seasons four, The.
To Autumn.
Kim, H. Winter Tree.
Kim, K. Spring.
Kovatattan. What Her Girl Friend Said to Her
("These fat cassia trees").
Levine, P. Later Still.
Lorde. What my child learns of the sea.
Lovelace, R. Grasshopper, The.
Lu Yu. Stone on the Hilltop, The.
MacNeice. August.
Spring Voices.
Magee, W. British Garden, A.
Mandel, T. Prospect of Release.
McAuley, J. Keep the season: let the hive.
Melville, H. Little Good Fellows, The.
Pontoosuce.
Meriluoto. Still.
Mezey. Against Seasons.
Millay, E. Hardy Garden, The.
Morris, W. Summer Dawn.
Mother Goose. Spring is showery, flowery,
bowery;.
Nannakaiyar. What She Said ("Bird and
beast").
Nicholls, J. Season Song.
Nicholson, N. For Hokey and Henrietta.
Patmore, C. Round the Year.
Plath. Couriers, The.
Po Chü-i. Beginning of Summer, The.
Illness.
Pine-trees in the Courtyard, The.
Pope, A. Garden, The.
Praed. Goodnight to the Season!
Pratt, E. Come Not the Seasons Here.
Randall, J. To William Wordsworth from
Virginia.
Ransom, J. Vaunting Oak.
Reeves, J. Sea is a hungry dog, The.
Robinson, E. New Language, The.
Rossetti, C. First Day, The.
Fly away, fly away over the sea.
Grown and Flown.
If Only.
Under willows among the graves.
Rossetti, D. Barren Spring.
Salkey. Song for England, A.
Sartarelli. Early Spring, An.
Sexton. Window That Watched the Pru.
Shakespeare, W. Sonnet 97.

Sonnet 98.
Spring.
Shelley, P. Ode to the West Wind.
Sitwell, D. Green Song.
Spenser. Pageant of the Seasons and the Months, The.
Stevens, W. Metamorphosis.
Motive for Metaphor, The.
Stevenson, R. Autumn Fires.
House Beautiful, The.
In autumn when the woods are red.
Su Tung-p'o. Autumn.
Presented to Liu Ching-wen.
T'ao Ch'ien. By and by, the seasons come and go.
Tate, A. Seasons of the Soul.
Thomson, J. Hymn on the Seasons, A.
Unknown. All Seasons in One.
Clear moon brightly shining in the night.
In the seventh month the Fire-star declines.
Januar: by this fire [*or* thys fyre] I warme my handes.
Season Song.
There Ceres, distant from the powers divine.
Vaughan, H. Love and Discipline.
Waddell, H. December nights are frosts and stars.
Earth said to Death.
Walcott. In a Green Night.
Ward, J. Comfort-Maker.
Warren, R. Vermont Ballad: Change of Season.
Wilbur. April 5, 1974.
In the Elegy Season.
Wright, J. Fit against the Country, A.
To a Troubled Friend.
Xuân Diêu. Spring Out of Season.
Yeats. Wheel, The.
Young, D. In My Own Back Yard.
Zolotow. Change.

Seattle, Washington
Wright, C. Return to Seattle: Bastille Day.

Seaweed
Dauenhauer. Kelp.
Lawrence, D. Sea-weed sways and sways and swirls.
Longfellow, H. Seaweed.
McPherson, S. Seaweeds.
Melville, H. Tuft of Kelp, The.
Miyazawa Kenji. Tanka: "Dark seaweeds."
Teasdale. I would live in your love as the sea-grasses live in the sea.

Seclusion
Donne. London Street, A.
Hayden, R. Soledad.
Levertov. Closed World, The.
Mahon. Woods, The.
Ralegh, W. Like to a hermit[e] poor[e][,] in place obscure.
Shapiro, K. Intellectual, The.
Stafford, W. Oregon Message, An.

Second Coming
Browning, R. Earth Breaks Up.
Ferlinghetti, L. Christ Climbed Down / from His bare Tree.
Yeats. Second Coming, The.

See also **Millennium**

Second World War. *See* **World War II**

Secrecy and Secrets
Akazome Emon. In my heart's depth.
"Akhmatova." Land not mine, still, A.
Ammuvanar. What She Said to Her Girl Friend.
Blaeser. Certificate of Live Birth.
Blake, W. Never Pain to Tell Thy Love.
Brontë, A. Fragment, A.
Brontë, E. My Comforter.
Browning, E. Deserted Garden, The.
Browning, R. Meeting At Night.
Brutus. Postscripts 2.
Burns, R. Whistle, and I'll Come to You, My Lad.
Byron, G. When we two parted.
Campbell, R. Counsel.
Carew, T. Secrecy [*or* Secresie] Protested.
Carroll, K. Truth About Karen, The.

Catullus. Carmen 5 ("My sweetest Lesbia, let us live and love").
Causley. Tom Bone.
Clare, J. Secret, The.
Secret Love.
Clifton, L. Listen Children.
Coleman, J. Poem for a "Divorced" Daughter.
Creeley. Innocence, The.
Cruz, V. Going Uptown to Visit Miriam.
Daniels, K. Women's Room in Pennsylvania Station, The.
Davis, T. Desire 1.
De la Mare. Portrait, A.
Donne. Perfume, The.
Undertaking, The.
Doolittle, H. In no wise is the pillar-of-fire.
Dove, R. Adolescence—I.
Dunbar, P. We wear the mask that grins and lies.
Emerson, R. Sphinx is drowsy, The.
"Field." Palimpsest, A.
Frost, R. Secret Sits, The.
Gershon. At a Reception.
Gray, J. Femmes Damnées.
Hacker, M. After the Revolution.
Bloomingdale's.
Hall, D. Mr. Wakeville on Interstate 90.
Hill, G. Turtle Dove, The.
Holden, J. Losers.
Hughes, L. Personal.
Jonson, B. Nymph's Passion, A.
Kanemori. Although I hide it.
Kizer, C. Antique Father.
Knight, E. He sees through stone.
Landon. Secrets.
Levertov. Secret, The.
Li Shang-yin. Ma-wei.
Lifshin. Midwest is Full of Vibrators, The.
Liu Ling-hsien. Inscribed on a Plantain Leaf To Show to a Certain Person.
MacEwen, G. Open Secrets.
Mobilio. Third Kind of Interior Word, The.
Muldoon, P. Hedgehog.
Nesbit, E. Things That Matter, The.
Noguere. Secret, The.
Otomo no Sakanoé, L. Do not smile to yourself.
Rexroth, K. Oh the anguish of these secret meetings.
Rich, A. They come to you with their descriptions of your soul.
Whatever it was: the grains of the glacier caked in the boot-cleats.
Rilke. Mary at Peace with the Risen Lord.
Rodgers, C. Poem No. 1.
Romano, R. Bucket, The.
Rossetti, C. Winter: My Secret.
Sachdev. Well, The.
Sackville-West. Thus love, bright charlatan, besieged my heart.
Shorter. Watcher in the Wood, The.
Swenson, M. Fireflies throw.
Tanikawa Shuntaro. Everyone possesses something sad.
Teasdale. Those who love the most.
Tindal. Birth Wail, The.
Toshiyuki. In the Bay of Sumi.
Tsvetayeva. Gold that was my hair has turned, The.
Unknown. Can you keep a secret?
Secret, The.
Wang Seng-ta. Out Early One Morning, I Met an Old Acquaintance.
Wharton, A. Song: "How hardly I concealed my tears."
Whitney, I. I.W. To her unconstant Lover.
Wollach. When You're Not a Poet.
Wu of Han. People Hide Their Love.
Wyatt, T. Lover Showeth How He Is Forsaken of Such as He Sometime Enjoyed, The.
Xuân Diêu. Distance.
Yeats. Secret Rose, The.

Secretaries
Espada. Secret of the Legal Secretary's Cigarette Smoke, The.
Page, P. Stenographers, The.
Piercy. Secretary Chant, The.

Redgrove, P. Secretary, The.
See also **Scribes; Stenographers**

Sectarianism
Lord, P. Your Church and Mine.

Security
Alvarez, J. I check my parents' house while they're abroad.
Brooke, R. Safety.
Browning, E. Sonnet: "Thou comest! all is said without a word."
Brutus. Postscripts 2.
Colum, P. Old Woman of the Roads, The.
Cowper, W. My Pet Hare.
Cullen, C. For a Poet.
Davis, T. In the Fire Lane.
Diop, B. Viaticum.
Dobyns. Shaving.
Eady. Romare Bearden Retrospective at the Brooklyn Museum.
Frost, R. Provide, Provide.
Grosholz. Eden.
Herrick. Bellman, The.
Jackson, L. Makeshift.
Koch, K. Locks.
Kunze, R. Refuge Even Beyond Refuge.
Kwiatek. "Nearer God, Nearer Realite."
Lawrence, D. Song of a Man Who Is Loved.
Levertov. Christmas 1944.
Levi, P. Shemà.
Lyte. Abide with me[; fast falls the eventide].
McGinley. Velvet Hand, The.
Milosz, C. To Robinson Jeffers.
Rathenow. After David Samuilow.
Roethke. Reckoning, The.
Rous. I to the Hills Will Lift Mine Eyes.
Simpson, L. Goodnight, The.
Tonks. Story of a Hotel Room.
Unknown. In Praise of the Hat.
Staffs and Hats.
Valentine, J. Seeing You.
Voznesensky. Dead Still.

Seduction
Agard, J. English Girl Eats Her First Mango.
Antipater of Thessalonica. You can explore your every desire.
Antiphilus. Here is the river Eurotas.
Ayres. Invites His Nymph to His Cottage.
Bancks. Fragment, A: "In Cloe's chamber, she and I."
Bassus. I'll never have a river of gold.
Baxter, J. Bar Room Conversation.
Behn, A. Disappointment, The.
Willing Mistriss, The.
Burbidge. She Bewitched Me.
Campion, T. Blame Not My Cheekes.
Follow your saint, follow with accents sweet.
It fell on a summer's [*or* sommers] day.
Think'st thou to seduce me then with words that have no meaning?
Thrice toss[e] these oaken ashes in the air [*or* ayre].
Cleveland, J. To the State of Love or The Senses' Festival.
Cockburn, C. Vain Advice, The.
Coleridge, M. Moment, A.
Da Ponte. Little lady, you are not going to like this.
Dabydeen, D. Miranda.
Donne. Flea, The.
DuPlessis, R. Back arched like a bow.
Egerton, S. Repulse to Alcander, The.
Ewart. Clarissa Harlowe Poem, The.
Fraser, K. Song: "I love you, Mrs. Acorn. Would your husband mind."
Frym. Manifesto.
Gay, J. 'Tis woman that seduces all mankind!
Gershon. At a Reception.
Gilmore, M. Eve-Song.
Giovanni. Seduction.
Grimké, A. Naughty Nan.
Hafiz. Ode 44: "Last night, as half asleep I dreaming lay."
Hall-Evans. Seduction.
Hardy, T. Dark-Eyed Gentleman, The.
Hedylos. Wine, the toasts that could not be refused, The.
Herrick. Art above Nature, to Julia.

Delight in Disorder.
Upon Julia's Clothes.
Homer.   Juno seduces Jove.
Jarman, M.   Cavafy in Redondo.
Jones, M.   Lass of the Hill, The.
Jonson, B.   O God, and his good angels!
whither, whither.
Song. To Celia ("Come my Celia, let us
prove").
Kalász.   Hymn: "Where should I seat you,
where."
King, J.   Hymn: "For you I would put on
embroidered robes."
Landor, W.   Thou hast not rais'd, Ianthe, such
desire.
Lifshin.   With So Many Voices.
Longley, M.   Sulpicia.
Lorde.   On a Night of the Full Moon.
Lowell, A.   Carrefour.
Lugovskoy.   Woman / that I knew, The.
Lum.   On M. Butterfly.
Macedonius.   They had the nerve to name you
Constance.
Marlowe.   By this Leander being near the land.
Marvell.   Fair Singer, The.
Mayer, B.   Work in Progress.
Meleager.   You're in love with love.
Mew.   Monsieur Qui Passe.
Michaux.   Simplicity.
Middleton, T.   Women Beware Women.
Nesbit, E.   Villeggiature.
Orampokiyar.   What She Said ("Hovering like
the heron").
O'Sullivan, O.   Volatile Kerryman, The.
Palladas.   Zeus isn't such a raving Casanova.
Perillo.   Skin.
Ransom, J.   Judith of Bethulia.
Rochester, J.   Rochester to the Post Boy.
Twelve months must pass ere you can yet
arrive.
Shakespeare, W.   Even as the sun with purple-
colour'd face.
Set down, set down your honourable load.
Smith, J.   Solitary Canto to Chloris the
Disdainful, A.
Spenser.   Amoretti, Sonnet 18.
In the Bower of Bliss.
Stevens, W.   Plot Against the Giant, The.
Symons, A.   Bianca.
Unknown.   In the Meadow There's a Dead
Deer.
Jolly Jankin.
Late last night, a girl came.
Not long ago I met a clerk.
Poor But Honest.
Sun rises red amid radiant clouds, The.
Waly, Waly [Love Be Bonny].
Webb, M.   Why did you come, with your
enkindled eyes.
Wyatt, T.   Lover Showeth How He Is Forsaken
of Such as He Sometime Enjoyed, The.

Seeds
Buckmaster.   Seed.
Craveirinha.   Seed is in Me, The.
Curzon, D.   Instructions to a Seed.
Finch, A.   Sapphics for Patience.
Graham, J.   Of Forced Sightes and Trusty
Ferefulness.
Housman, A.   I hoed and trenched and
weeded.
Lofting.   Mister Beers.
Marshall, J.   Sesame.
Mitchell, S.   Matthew 13:1–9; That same day
Jesus.
Parable of the Sower, The.
Mitchison.   Unfertile Heart, The.
Molodovsky.   Prayers: I.
Nemerov.   Cabinet of Seeds Displayed, A.
Oleson.   Ballad of Johnny Appleseed, A.
Pasolini.   Day of My Death, The.
Patacara.   When they plow their fields.
Reiter, T.   Rights of Way.
Thomas, D.   After the funeral, mule praises,
brays.
Unknown.   Baby Seeds.
Piggish young person from Leeds, A.

Seeds of Love, The.
There was a young farmer of Leeds.
Vaughan, H.   Seed Growing Secretly, The.
Wade, B.   Conkers.
Webb, D.   Tragedy, A.
Wilbur.   Seed Leaves.
Young, A.   Thistledown.

Seine (river), France
Bell, M.   Stars Which See, Stars Which Do
Not See.

Self
Adamson.   Home, The Spare Room, The.
"Akhmatova."   In the Looking Glass.
Alegría.   From the Bridge.
I Am Root.
Alexander, E.   Painting / (Frida Kahlo).
Alvarez, J.   Sonnet 42: "Sometimes the words
are so close I am."
Ammons.   Chasm.
So I Said I Am Ezra.
Angel.   Man in a Window.
Api.   Another Me.
Apollinaire.   I Imagine Angels.
On imagine les anges.
Arbuthnot.   Know Yourself.
Ashbery.   Paradoxes and Oxymorons.
These Lacustrine Cities.
Atwood.   More and more frequently the edges.
Auden.   Lullaby: "Din of work is subdued,
The."
Prime.
Baca.   Like an Animal.
Baraka.   Agony, An. As Now.
Funk Lore.
Poem Some People Will Have to Understand,
A.
Barbauld.   Life! I know not what thou art.
Baudelaire.   Fuses I and II.
Benedikt.   Thoughts.
Berg, S.   To My Friends.
Berssenbrugge.   Experience.
Bhartrihari.   In former days we'd both agree.
Bitar.   Looking You in the Back of the Head.
Blackburn, P.   At the Well.
Blake, W.   Fly, The.
Blandiana.   Links.
Blaser.   Universe is Part of Ourselves, The.
Blight.   Down from the Country.
Bogan, L.   Man Alone.
Bonar.   Be True [or Be True Thyself].
Bonitaz Nuño.   Smoke.
Brodsky, J.   I Sit by the Window.
Bronk.   Plainest Narrative, The.
Brontë, E.   Stanzas: "Often rebuked, yet
always back returning."
Brooks, G.   My Dreams, My Works Must Wait
Till after Hell.
Sundays of Satin-Legs Smith, The.
Browning, R.   House.
Catacalos.   David Talamántez on the Last Day
of Second Grade.
Cataldi.   13 November 1983.
Catullus.   To Varus.
Cervantes.   Freeway 280.
Césaire, A.   Lagoonal Calendar.
Ch'iao Chin.   Tune: "Overtures"—On Myself.
Chu Tun-ju.   Tune: "Charm of Nien-nu, The."
Ch'u Yüan.   Yüan, Ch'ü.
Chung Ssu-ch'eng.   Tune: "Sprig of Flowers,
A"—Written for My "Ugly Studio."
Clare, J.   Written in Northampton County
Asylum.
Clark, T.   Poem: "Tiny new emotions, The."
Clifton, L.   If mama / could see.
Coleridge, M.   L'Oiseau Bleu.
Other Side of a Mirror, The.
Shadow.
Coleridge, S.   Phantom.
Coolidge, C.   Glance in White Space.
Cooper, J.   Knowledge That Comes through
Experience, A.
Crane, S.   Heart, The.
Creeley.   Edge, The.
Pool, The.
Self-Portrait.
Wife, The.
Cronin, J.   Motho Ke Motho Ka Batho Babang

(A Person Is a Person Because of Other
People).
Cuadra, A.   In Brief.
Cummings, E.   I am a little church(no great
cathedral).
Maggie and milly and molly and may.
Daive.   I rise from the depths of my
resemblance.
Darwish, M.   Identity Card.
Words.
Davidson, M.   Dream Dream, The.
Davies, A.   Personality syndrome, The.
Davis, T.   Desire 1.
Day, J.   Moving Object.
De la Mare.   Me.
Ded.   Coursing in emptiness.
I searched for my Self.
Dennis, C.   Nuts and Raisins.
Dickinson, E.   I am alive—I guess.
Me from Myself—to banish.
Of Bronze—and Blaze.
One need not be a Chamber to be Haunted.
Dimitrova.   If.
Donne.   I am a little world made cunningly.
Doolittle, H.   At least I have the flowers of
myself.
Doty, M.   Broadway.
Doubiago.   Self.
Dransfield.   Self-analysis.
Druk.   Drukascripts.
Drummond de Andrade.   Seven-Sided Poem.
Duncan, R.   Close.
Roots and Branches.
Songs of an Other.
Eliot, T.   Little Gidding.
Elizabeth I.   On Monsieur's Departure.
Elmslie, K.   Squatter in the Foreground.
Emanuel, L.   Self-Portrait at Eighteen.
Flynn, M.   Down in the field.
František.   When the great wind blew the
streetlights out.
Fumi Saito.   Tanka: "Cluster, A."
Tanka: "Don't resemble me."
Fumiko.   Tanka: "Didn't a certain woman."
Tanka: "Wiggling out."
Fyodorov.   Servile Blood.
Gallagher, T.   Black Silk.
Sudden Journey.
Galvin, B.   Town Pier Parking Lot.
García Lorca.   Great Sadness, The.
Gibson, W.   Advice to Travelers.
Ginsberg, A.   End, The.
González, A.   Before I could call myself Ángel
González.
Gorbanevskaya.   And where am I from? From
an anecdote.
Graves, R.   From the Embassy.
Green, M.   From The Spleen.
Greenwell, D.   Scherzo, A.
Habington.   Cogitabo Pro Peccato Meo.
Hadewijch II.   All things.
If I desire something, I know it not.
You who want.
Hajnal.   After all, what have I become?
Hall, J.   Proverb, XXX.
Hanzlicek, C.   C.G. Hanzlicek.
In the Dark Again.
Harryman.   Magic (or Rousseau).
My Story.
Hayden, R.   Names.
Hejinian.   Moment yellow, just as four years
later when, A.
Solitude flared out, The.
Herbert, G.   Jordan (2)(II): "When first my
lines [or verse] of heavenly [or heav'nly]
joy[e]s made mention."
Herbert of Cherbury.   One Another's Mystery.
Hoban.   Small, Smaller.
Hoccleve.   After that hervest inned had his
sheves.
Holub.   Immanuel Kant.
Hoover, P.   Theory.
Hopkins, G.   Candle Indoors, The.
I wake and feel the fell of dark, not day.
My own heart let me more have pity on; let.
Housman, A.   Oh, when I was in love with
you.

Hsin Ch'i-chi. Tune: "Partridge Sky"—Written at the Po-shan Monastery.

Huang Ching-jen. Mixed Emotions.

Hughes, L. Cross.
Final Curve.

Huidobro. Canto I (excerpt).

Izumi. Watching the moon.

Jackson, L. Dimensions.

Jarrell. Woman at the Washington Zoo, The.

Jiménez, J. I am not I.

Jones, E. Study in Blue.

Jones, J. Flowers always know what they.
I am glad I'm who I am.

József. Attila József.

Juan Chi. Autumn's onset means cooling breezes.

Juarroz. Prompting of my shadow, The.

Justice, D. Missing Person, The.
Suicides, The.

Kaufman, B. Grandfather Was Queer, Too.

Keats. Ode on Indolence.

Khodasevich. In Front of the Mirror.

Kinzie. Heat-heavy creatures.

Klee. Poem.

Knight, E. Belly Song.
Report to the Mother.
Welcome Back, Mr. Knight: Love of My Life.

Knott. Death.
Sonnet: "Way the world is not, The."

Koch, K. Alive for an Instant.
Girl and Baby Florist Sidewalk Pram Nineteen Seventy Something.

Kuan Han-ch'ing. Tune: "Sprig of Flowers, A"—Not Bowing to Old Age.

Kunert. Implant.
Realization.

Kung Tzu-chen. My neighbor's child cries in the middle of the night.

Kunio. Tanka: "Casket on display, A."

Kwiatek. "Nearer God, Nearer Realite."

Larkin, P. Self's the Man.

Lawrence, D. Eloi, Eloi, Lama Sabachthani?
I Am in a Novel.
Wild Common, The.

Le Bel. Boxing the Female.

Leapor. Epistle of Deborah Dough, The.
Mira's Will.

Lee-Hamilton. Ipsissimus.

Levertov. In Mind.

Levine, P. Baby Villon.

Li Ho. High Dike.

Libbey. Juana Bautista Lucero, Circa 1926, to Her Photographer.

"Limonov." I would hold another person in my thoughts.

Lovelace, R. Song: "In mine one [or own] monument I lie [or lye]."

Lowell, R. Fat Man in the Mirror, The.

"Lu Hsün." Self-mockery.

Machado Ruiz. Portrait.

MacLow. 6th Dance—Doing Things With Pencils—17-18 February 1964.

Macpherson, J. Lost Soul, A.

Malroux. Every morning the curtain rises.

Marichiko. Who is there? Me.

McClintock, M. Broken window, A.

McClure, M. Hymn to Saint Geryon.

McHugh, H. In Light of Time.

Mechthild von Magdeburg. Desert Has Many Teachings, The.
How the Soul Speaks to God.

Menken. Infelix.
Myself.

Merrill, J. Remora.
Syrinx.

Merwin, W. For the Anniversary of My Death.
One of the Lives.

Mihalic. Man Who Decided, The.

Mo Shih-lung. I Went to Gold Mountain to Visit a Ch'an Master But He Was Not at Home.
Saying Good-bye to a Singing Girl Who Has Decided to Become a Nun.

Momaday. Delight Song of Tsoai-Talee, The.

Morgenstern. Police Inquiry, The.

Mountain, M. Pig and i spring rain.

Nabokov. Fame.

Nathan, L. Hole.
Just Looking, Thank You.

Nemerov. Angel and Stone.
Companions, The.
Salt Garden, The.

Neruda. Ode to the Cat.
Poetry.
We Are Many.

Nguyễn Văn Năng. I Shall Not Die.

Notley. One of the Longest Times.

O'Dalaigh, M. My body's self deserts me now.

O'Hara, F. To the Harbormaster.

Okamoto. Tanka: "Ten years ago."

Oliver, M. Journey, The.

Olson, C. As the dead prey upon us.

Owen, W. Wild with All Regrets.

Pagis. I Was Before I Was, who now.

Pao Chao. Have you not seen the grasses on the riverbank?

Paquet. In a Plantation.

Pasolini. Part of a Letter to the Codignola Boy.

Pasternak, B. To be famous is not in good taste.

Paz. Small Variation.

Peacock, M. Spell, The.

Pessoa. If, after I die they should want to write my biography.

Piatt, S. Doubt, A.

Piercy. Unlearning to Not Speak.

Plath. I Am Vertical.
Nick and the Candlestick.

Plumpp. When the Spirit Spray-Paints the Sky.

Popa. Dream of the Quartz Pebble, The.

Prévert. I'm the way I am.

Quarles. I wish a greater knowledge, then t'attaine.

Rakosi. Lord, What is Man?

Ramanujan. Self-Portrait.

Ray, H. Self-Mastery.

Rich, A. Delta.
Integrity.
Rain on the West Side Highway.
They come to you with their descriptions of your soul.
Trying to Talk with a Man.
Upper Broadway.

Rivard. Change My Evil Ways.

Robinson, K. Intent to consider.

Rochester, J. Rochester to the Post Boy.

Rodgers, C. Group Therapy.

Roethke. Journey to the Interior.
Renewal, The.

Rossetti, C. Verse II.
Verse III.

Rossetti, D. Severed Selves.

Roy, L. Ride, The.

Rukeyser, M. Then I Saw What the Calling Was.

St. John, P. Carnival.

Samio. Tanka: "Loud voice, A."

Schultz, P. I'm Not Complaining.

Schwartz, D. Heavy Bear, The.
Young Child and His Pregnant Mother, A.

Seng-ts'an. Mind of Absolute Trust, The.

Senghor. Kaya-Magan am I! the first person.

Sexton. Self in 1958.

Shakespeare, W. Sonnet 80.
Sonnet 88.
Sonnet 89.

Shange. I Sat Up One Night.

Shelley, P. Made One With Nature.

Shih Te. I laugh at my failing strength in old age.

Shin, T. Vertigo.

Simic. My Shoes.

Simko. Coming Home.

Sinha. Diamond of Character, The.

Slessor. To Myself.

Sorescu. Carbon Paper.

Sorrentino. Zukofsky.

Soupault. Life-Saving Medal.

Southwick. Ruins, The.

Stein, G. I Am Rose [my eyes are blue].

Stevens, W. Idiom of the Hero.

Man on the Dump, The.
On the Adequacy of Landscape.
Re-statement of Romance.

Stone, R. Advice.

Strelchenko. My Photograph.

Su Shih. Tune: "Immortal at the River."

Supervielle. Traveller, traveller, accept you must go back.

Sutskever. Banks of a River, The.

Swede. At the end of myself pencil tip.
In one corner.

Swirszczynska. I Talk to My Body.

Szymborska. Children of the Epoch.

Tada. Poetry Calendar, A.

T'ao Ch'ien. Bright sun lights out over the western bank.
Green pine grows in eastern garden, A.

Taylor, E. Bran, a chaff, a very barley [y]awn, A.

Teasdale. I Am Not Yours[, not lost in you].

Templeton, F. Act II - Crossing At the Tracks.

Thomas, D. I, in my intricate image, stride on two levels.

Thomas, E. Lights Out.

Thoreau. I am a parcel of vain strivings tied.
Music.

Ts'ao Chih. Song of Lament, A.

Ts'ao P'i. Lotus Pond, The.

Tsvetkov. Yes, it's me. I appear thus to myself.

Tuckerman, F. Sonnets: First Series.

Unknown. (Invocation for Storing Corn).
Sir Orfeo.

Van den Heuvel. After the shower.

Viiding. Speeches in the Interior.

Wakoski. My trouble / is that I have the spirit of Gertrude Stein.

Walcott. Hotel Normandie Pool, The.

Wallace-Crabbe. Abhorring a Vacuum.

Wang An-shih. Had I been an ox or horse.

Wang Fan-chih. I, Fan-chih, wear my socks inside out.

Waniek. Strange beautiful woman, A.

Waters, M. Keats' Lips.

Watten. Isolate and.

Weinfield. Song for the In-Itself and For-Itself.

Weöres. Ecce Homo.

Wheelwright. And for His Mother.

Whitman, W. Ah poverties, wincings, and sulky retreats.
Are you the new person drawn toward me?
As I lay with my head in your lap camerado.
Did you read in the seabooks of the oldfashioned frigate-fight?
Grass.
Hand-Mirror, A.
Houses and rooms are full of perfumes.
I believe a leaf of grass is no less than the journey-work of the stars.
I believe in you my soul, the other I am must not abase itself to you.
I have heard what the talkers were talking, the talk of the beginning and the end.
I saw in Louisiana a live-oak growing.
One's-Self I sing, a simple separate person.
Past and present wilt—I have fill'd them, emptied them, The.
Song of Myself.
Swift wind! Space! My Soul! Now I know it is true what I guessed at;.
That shadow my likeness that goes to and fro seeking a livelihood, chattering, chaffering.
There is that in me.. . . I do not know what it is.. . . but I know it is in me.
There was a child went forth every.
Trippers and askers surround me.
Walt Whitman.
Walt Whitman, an American, one of the roughs, a kosmos.
Who goes there! hankering, gross, mystical, nude?
Woman waits for me, she contains all, nothing is lacking, A.

Whittemore, R. Clamming.

Wilbur. Leaving.
Williams, W. Danse Russe.
Winchilsea. On Myself.
Wollach. I feel empty, empty as a swimming pool.
To Live at the Speed of Biography.
Woods, J. Looking Both Ways Before Crossing.
Wright, D. On Himself.
Wyatt, T. Lover Rejoiceth the Enjoying of His Love, The.
Yang Wan-li. I finish chanting my new poems.
Yeats. Dialogue of Self and Soul, A.
Yosano. Amidst the notes.
Zhenkai. Answer.

Self-Deceit
Bruchac. Prayer: "Let my words."
Coleridge, S. On a Discovery Made Too Late.
Crane, S. I SAW A MAN PURSUING THE HORIZON;.
Holden, J. Losers.
Jeffers, R. Self-Criticism in February.
MacNeice. Alcohol.
Mixer, The.
Rich, A. Power.
Selman, R. Next came Bob, but before him I had Phil.
Smith, S. Infelice.
Snodgrass, W. Locked House, A.
Southwick. Horse on the Wall.
Whittier. Haschish, The.

Self-Doubt
Aiken, C. Dear Uncle Stranger.
Bly, R. Anger Against Children.
Brown, W. Rilke.
Doolittle, H. Centaur Song.
Herbert, G. Love bade me welcome[: yet my soul drew back].
Hill, G. Lachrimae Amantis.
Jeffers, R. Love the Wild Swan.
Olson, C. Maximus, to Himself.
Porta. Age of unhappiness has arrived, or is it, The.
Rich, A. Dialogue.
Roofwalker, The.
Shakespeare, W. Sonnet 46.
Sonnet 76.
Stern, G. I Hate My Moaning.
Szymborska. In Praise of Self-Deprecation.
TallMountain. Indian Blood.
Walcott. Codicil.
Wright, C. Laguna Blues.
Wylie. Malediction Upon Myself.

Self-Knowledge
Aiken, C. Dear Uncle Stranger.
Ammons. Chasm.
Reflective.
So I Said I Am Ezra.
Api. Another Me.
Arnold, M. Self-Dependence.
Behn, A. Angellica's Lament.
Berg, S. Don't Forget.
Berry, J. One.
Booth, P. Supposition with Qualification.
Brooks, G. To Those of My Sisters Who Kept Their Naturals.
Carrier, C. Perspective.
Carruth, H. Lost.
Clifton, L. Turning into my own.
Conn. Under the Ice.
Creeley. Awakening, The.
Cummings, E. Maggie and milly and molly and may.
Derricotte. Blackbottom.
Ginsberg, A. Sather Gate Illumination.
Gregg. Copperhead, The.
Harjo, J. Autobiography.
I Give You Back.
Hogan, L. Truth Is, The.
Hollander, J. Angler's Story, The.
Jeffers, R. Self-Criticism in February.
Jordan, J. Poem About My Rights.
Kenyon, J. Here.
Kinnell. Room, The.
Knott. At the Crossroads.
Larkin, P. Reasons for Attendance.

Lawrence, D. Death Is Not Evil, Evil Is Mechanical.
Go deeper than love, for the soul has greater depths.
Levertov. Long Way Round, The.
MacCaig. Summer Farm.
Maclean, A. Home Thoughts from Home.
Macpherson, J. Lost Soul, A.
Manyarrows. Today We Will Not Be Invisible Nor Silent.
Meehan, M. Is There Life after Feminism.
Mirabai. All I Was Doing Was Breathing.
Olson, C. In cold hell, in thicket, how.
Newly Discovered "Homeric" Hymn, A.
Oppen. Discrete Series 1929–1933.
Myself I Sing.
Owen, W. Show, The.
Paz. Brotherhood.
Qaisi. Outside the Furnace.
Ramanujan. Self-Portrait.
Ransom, J. Amphibious Crocodile.
Raut. Snake.
Repetto. 6th grade—our lady of pompeii.
Rich, A. August.
Can it be growing colder when I begin.
Every peak is a crater. This is the law of volcanoes.
Stranger, The.
Rodgers, C. Some Me of Beauty.
Roethke. Open House.
Rumi. Human shape is a ghost, The.
We take long trips.
Satyamurti. Reflections.
Shakespeare, W. Sonnet 121.
Shin, T. Vertigo.
Sinha. Diamond of Character, The.
Smith, C. Partial Muse, has from my earliest hours, The.
Stafford, W. Story That Could Be True, A.
Stanton, M. Sunday Graveyard.
Stevens, W. Of Modern Poetry.
Subramanyam. Situation.
Swenson, M. You are my mirror.
Tản Đà. Speaking to My Photo.
Timrod. Dreams.
Toomer. Prayer.
Unknown. Toltecs were wise, The.
Very. Lost, The.
Villalongo. In the Good Old U. S. A.
Williams, M. Images.
Williams, W. Slow Movement.
Wright, C. Self-Portrait ("Someday they'll find me out, and my lavish hands").
Wylie. Let No Charitable Hope.
Malediction Upon Myself.
Yeats. Two Trees, The.
Yi, S. Mirror, The.
Zamora, D. Lineage.
Mother's Day.
Zukofsky, L. Cars once steel and green, now old.

Self-Pity
Hodgins. Self-Pity.
Lawrence, D. Self-Pity.
Lu Yu. Feeling Sorry for Myself.
Tune: "Bean Leaves Yellow."
Nguyễn Trãi. He tends the tree who wants to eat the fruit.
Schuyler, J. Self-Pity Is a Kind of Lying, Too.
Sidney, P. Complaint of Love.
Su Tung-p'o. Abandoned earthworks nobody tends.
Tichborne. Tichborne's Elegy.
Unknown. Sometimes I go about pitying myself.
Song of the Thunders.
Westmorland. Shamed by the Creature.
Wroth. Sonnet 42: "If ever love had force in huma[i]ne brest?"
Wylie. Malediction Upon Myself.

Self-Reliance
Arnold, M. Self-Dependence.
Brontë, E. Stanzas: "Often rebuked, yet always back returning."
Ceravolo. Data.
Clifton, L. She Lived.
Cofer. What the Gypsy Said to Her Children.

Conkling, G. I will not give thee all my heart.
Cunningham, N. Giving.
Đào Duy Kỳ. At Condore Port.
Dove, R. Canary.
Emerson, R. Self-Reliance.
Henley, W. Invictus.
Ho, H. For the Poor.
Jordan, N. Be You.
'Marnia. I must be able to protect you.
Melville, H. In a Garret.
Miles, J. In the town where every man is king.
Mora. La Migra.
Nguyễn Bỉnh Khiêm. Self-Reflection.
Po Chü-i. New thatched hall, five spans by three, A.
Rich, A. Dark lintels, the blue and foreign stones, The.
Song: "You're wondering if I'm lonely."
Rilke. For one human being to love another human being: that is perhaps the.
Rose. Naayawva Taawi.
Shange. Advice.
Smith, M. Go Blow Fire, A.
Smith, S. Rise from Your Bed of Languor.
Whalen. Further Notice.
Xuân Diệu. It's All in the Heart.
Zealand. Passion at the Chat 'n Chew Diner.

Self-Restraint
Catullus. Carmen 8 ("Break off / fallen Catullus").

Self-Righteousness
Burns, R. Holy Willie's Prayer.
Fainlight, R. Stubborn.
Hiranandani. Husband.
MacNeice. Over the roofs and cranes, blistered cupola and hungry smokestack.
Wylie. Malediction Upon Myself.

Selfishness
Ammons. Coming Right Up.
Bierce. Egotist.
Blake, W. Clod and [or &] the Pebble, The.
Bruner. Selfishness.
Cary, P. Legend of the Northland, A.
Cook, E. Mouse and the Cake, The.
Dancer. Variety, The.
Dickinson, E. Mine—by the Right of the White Election!
Foster, J. Irises, The.
Graham, H. Englishman's Home, The.
Hildegard von Bingen. Now in the people.
Lawrence, D. Intimates.
True Love at Last.
McBride, M. Loneliness.
McHugh, H. Oven Loves the TV Set, The.
North, C. Few Facts about Me, A.
Okamoto. Tanka: "Selfish woman."
Sadi. Dancer, The.
Shakespeare, W. Sonnet 62.
Shapiro, K. Intellectual, The.
Shteiger. No one waits down below, as when we were young.
Swift, J. To Stella.
Tennyson, A. Character, A.
Unknown. Other Side of the Valley, The.
Wang K'ang-chü. Refuting the "Invitation to Hiding."
Wesley, C. On Worldly Prelates.

Semele
Graves, R. Ambrosia of Dionysus and Semele, The.
Kizer, C. Semele Recycled.

Senegal
Damas. Et Cetera.
Davis, T. Double Take at Relais de L'Espadon.
Senghor. Elephant of Moissel, hear my pious prayer.
Night of Sine.

Senility
Hall, D. By the Exeter River.
Kudimova. When I still barely rose above the ground.
Levertov. Old Adam, The.
Paulin. Anastasia McLaughlin.
Prévert. Quartier Libre.

Sennacherib, King of Assyria
Byron, G. Destruction of Sennacherib, The.
Senses
Bogan, L. Spirit's Song.
Cassian. Temptation.
Catullus. *Carmina*, XIII.
Cavalli. This time I won't permit the blue, glimpsed.
Coolidge, C. Disturbing the Sallies Forth.
Davidson, D. Redivivus.
Davidson, M. Feeling Type and His Friends, The.
Dickinson, E. I heard a Fly buzz—when I died[—died].
  Light exists in Spring, A.
Drayton. To the Senses.
Inez. Instructions for the Erection of a Statue to Myself in Central Park.
Kendall, M. Philanthropist and the Jelly-fish, The.
Lazarus, E. Evening.
Meynell, A. To the Body.
Nekrasova. Blind Man, The.
O'Connor, P. Raspberry in the Pudding, The.
O'Neill, M. My fingers are antennae.
Roethke. Prayer: "If I must of my Senses lose."
Schuyler, J. Freely Espousing.
Shakespeare, W. Lover's eyes will gaze an eagle blind, A.
  Sonnet 151.
Sidney, P. Seventh Song: "Whose senses in so evil consort, their stepdame Nature lays."
Swenson, M. Blindman placed, The.
Swinburne. Triads.
Tarkovsky. Sight grows dim—my power.
Thomas, D. When all my five and country senses see.
Tsogyel. Listen.
Valéry. Bee, The.
Warren, R. Code Book Lost.
Sensitivity
Kim, Y. Hotel North.
  Landscape I.
Levertov. O Taste and See.
More, H. Sensibility: A Poetical Epistle to the Hon. Mrs Boscawen.
Nemerov. View from an Attic Window, The.
Owen, W. Insensibility.
Sensuality
Apollinaris Sidonius. Invitation to the Dance.
Baudelaire. Exotic Scent.
Behn, A. Dream, The.
Bhartrihari. If the forest of her hair.
Catullus. Carmen 45 ("Phyllis Corydon clutched to him").
Cavafy. Return often and take me.
Chase, J. One early spring evening when Celia was fourteen.
Conoley. Some Gangster Pain.
Cummings, E. My love / thy hair is one kingdom.
  Since feeling is first.
Éluard, P. Lover, secretly behind your smile.
Ferlinghetti, L. Away above a harborful.
Hacker, M. Canzone: "Consider the three functions of the tongue."
Hirsch, E. Skokie Theatre, The.
Julian of Norwich. I understood that.
Levertov. Eros at Temple Stream.
Lifshin. With So Many Voices.
Maitre. Woman Underneath, The.
Merwin, W. West Wall.
Mirabai. All I Was Doing Was Breathing.
  Why Mira Can't Go Back to Her Old House.
Orampokiyar. What Her Girl friend Said to the Foster-Mother ("In his fields, mother").
Paz. Touch.
Phillips, J. Sweethearts.
Pound, E. Alba ("As cool as the pale wet leaves").
Rich, A. Floating Poem, Unnumbered, The.
Stein, G. Lifting belly. Are you. Lifting.
Unknown. I drive my carriage from the Upper East Gate.
  Song of Songs.
Villakaviralinar. What the Concubine Said

When She Heard the Wife Complain about the Concubine's Wiles.
Virgil. Sallad, The.
Voigt. Heart is the Target, The.
Wakoski. Belly Dancer.
Whitman, W. From pent-up aching rivers.
  To the garden the world anew ascending.
  Twenty-eight young men bathe by the shore.
  Walt Whitman, a kosmos, of Manhattan the son.
Wright, C. This Couple.
Yeats. Chosen.
Zeb-un-Nissa. Though I am Laila of the Persian romance.

Separation
Akahito. I wish I were close.
Allingham. I walk'd in the lonesome evening.
Amichai. Quick And Bitter.
Ariwara no Yukihira. I must leave you, but.
Arnett. Song of the Breed.
Arnold, M. Farewell, A: "My horse's feet beside the lake."
  To Marguerite.
Ashbery. Rivers and Mountains.
Atwood. Postcard.
Awoonor. Lovers' Song.
Ayton. Valediction.
A'Zmi, K. Humiliation.
Baraka. Agony, An. As Now.
Beckett, S. Cascando.
Beer, P. Faithful Wife, The.
Berry, W. Except.
Berryman. He Resigns.
Bhartrihari. In former days we'd both agree.
Black, S. To Her Father.
Blue Cloud. Old Man's Lazy, The.
Boyle, K. Thunderstorm in South Dakota.
Bradstreet, A. Another.
Brontë, E. Last Words.
Brown, W. Words.
Browning, E. Sonnet: "Go from me. Yet I feel that I shall stand."
Browning, R. In Three Days.
  Last Ride Together, The.
  Lovers' Quarrel, A.
  Waring.
Brownstein. Last spell cast came late one afternoon in a brown study. I was studying my-, The.
Burns, R. Highland Harry Back Again.
  Highland Mary.
  Red, Red Rose, A.
  Silver Tassie, The.
Burnshaw. Strange to be torn away from your embrace.
Buson. I go.
Byron, G. Epistle to Augusta.
  Fare thee well! and if for ever.
  When we two parted.
Carew, T. Excuse of Absence, An.
  To Her in Absence; a Ship.
Cartwright, W. Valediction: "Bid me not go where neither suns nor showers [show'rs]."
Cary, P. Jacob.
Cassian. Sand.
Catullus. Carmen 8 ("Break off / fallen Catullus").
Chang, D. Foreign Ways.
Chattopadhyay. Forgive Me.
Ch'in Chia. Ch'in Chia's Wife's Reply.
Chong, C. Native Village.
Chu Shu-chen. Spring Joy.
Chu Yün-ming. Drinking.
Cofer. What the Gypsy Said to Her Children.
Cole, T. Lago Maggiore.
Coleridge, M. We Never Said Farewell[, nor even looked].
Coleridge, S. If I had but two little wings.
Cornford, F. Parting in Wartime.
Cory, D. Miss You.
Cory, W. Separation, A.
Creedon. Litany.
Creeley. America, you ode for reality!
  Ballad of the Despairing Husband.
Crozier, A. Then in the smoke.
Cummings, E. Up into the silence the green.
  When my sensational moments are no more.

Dacey, F. Farewell: "I search / for the straight path."
Dasgupta, P. Man: 1961.
Dixon, M. Place, Places.
Donne. Computation, The.
  His Picture.
  Legacy [or Legacie], The.
  Valediction, A: Forbidding Mourning.
Doubiago. Signal Hill.
Dowson. Exile.
Drayton. Since There's No Help.
Duncan, R. Passage Over Water.
Eliot, T. Portrait of a Lady.
Elliot, J. Flowers of the Forest, The.
Elytis. Aegean Melancholy.
  Of the Aegean.
Fearing. Love, 20 Cents the First Quarter Mile.
Ferlinghetti, L. In Golden Gate Park that day.
  Third World Calling.
"Field." After Soufrière.
Forché. As Children Together.
Fortunato. Leaving, The.
Gallagher, T. Kidnap[p]er.
García. I Ain't Going to Hurry No More.
Garnett, R. Dealing Scraps.
Ginsberg, A. Message.
Glück, L. Hesitate to Call.
  Horse.
Googe. Out of Sight, Out of Mind.
Graves, R. Full Moon.
Greville, F. Myra.
Grigson. Above the High.
Guest, B. Santa Fe Trail.
Hacker, M. If we talk, we're too tired to make love; if we.
  Rondeau after a Transatlantic Telephone Call.
  Villanelle: "Every day our bodies separate."
Hadas, R. Red Hat, The.
Halevi. On Parting with Moses ibn Ezra.
  Parting.
Han. Silence of Love, The.
Hardy, T. After the Visit.
  At Castle Boterel.
  I say, "I'll seek her side."
  In a Cathedral City.
  In Death Divided.
  On the Departure Platform.
  Walk, The.
Henry VIII, King of England. To His Lady.
Herrick. His Sailing from Julia.
Hewett, D. You Gave Me Hyacinths First a Year Ago.
Hitomaro. Bay of Tsunu, The.
  Colored leaves, The.
  In the empty mountains.
  In the sea of ivy clothed Iwami.
  My girl is waiting for me.
"Hope." Kashmiri Song.
Horton, G. Division of an Estate.
Housman, A. As through the wild green hills of Wyre.
  He would not stay for me; and who can wonder?
  Now hollow fires burn out to black.
  White in the moon the long road lies.
Hsi K'ang. Sent to the Hsiu-ts'ai on His Entry into the Army.
Hsü Kan. Wife's Thoughts, The.
Hughes, L. Afro-American Fragment.
  So *long* / is in the song.
Ignatow, D. Brooding.
Ingelow. Dappled sky, a world of meadows, A.
Ismail. Wall, The.
Jacinto, A. Letter from a Contract Worker.
James, E. Sunnyland.
Janowitz, P. Reach.
Jarman, M. Supremes, The.
Jewsbury. Partings.
Johnson, J. Sence You Went Away.
Joyce, J. Crazy Quilt.
Judah ibn Tibbon. Father's Testament, A.
Kapilar. What She Said to Her Friend ("You ask me to forget him").
  What the Girl Friend Said to the Foster-Mother.

Katrovas.   Black English.
Sky.
Kaufman, S.   Notes to my Daughters.
Keats.   Endymion.
Kendrick, D.   Alone for a Week.
Kinnell.   Vow, The.
Kipling, R.   Widower, The.
Kizer, C.   Race Relations.
Semele Recycled.
Knight, E.   Upon Your Leaving.
Komunyakaa.   My Father's Love Letters [or
Loveletters].
Tu Do Street.
Kumin, M.   Woodchucks.
Kunitz, S.   After the Last Dynasty.
Father and Son.
Laforgue.   Solo by Moonlight.
Lakides.   Armed Forces.
Larkin, P.   Within the dream you said.
Levertov.   Divorcing.
In California During the Gulf War.
Like Loving Chekhov.
Li Ch'ing-chao.   I let the incense grow cold.
To the Tune, "Plum Blossoms Fall and
Scatter."
Year after year I have watched.
Li Po.   River Merchant's Wife, The; a Letter.
Sent to My Two Little Children in the East of
Lu.
Separation on the River Kiang.
Tzu-yeh Song.
Li Shang-yin.   Thoughts in the Cold.
When will I be home? I don't Know.
Li Yü.   Tune: "Pure Serene Music."
Tune: Pure Serene Music ("Since we parted,
spring half over").
Lilley.   You Have to Strike Back.
Llewellyn, K.   Finished.
Long, R.   Goodbye.
Lovelace, R.   Song: "If to be absent were to
be."
Song: To Lucasta, Going to the War[re]s.
Lowell, R.   Frederick Kuh, Manx Cat.
Lu Yu.   Harp Song.
Lu Yün.   For Ku Yen-hsien, A Poem for Him
to Give to His Wife.
MacNeice.   And love hung still as crystal over
the bed.
For X.
Mao Wen-hsi.   Tune: Drunk among the
Flowers.
Marvell.   Definition Of Love, The.
Mastin.   From the Telephone.
McGinley.   Midcentury Love Letter.
McMichael.   I know I'll lose her.
Merwin, W.   Rain Travel.
Separation.
Travelling Together.
When you go away the wind clicks around to
the north.
Mew.   In Nunhead Cemetery.
Meynell, A.   After a Parting.
Miedzyrzecki.   29-77-02.
Milosz, C.   Screens will be set there.
Mishra.   Robinson Crusoe.
Monro.   Terrible Door, The.
Montale.   Personae Separatae.
Moore, T.   Journey Onwards, The.
Moraga.   Later, she met Joyce.
Morgan, R.   Damn you, lady, get out of my
blood for good.
Mudrooroo.   Hide and Seek.
Mura.   Letters from Poston Relocation Camp
(1942–45).
Nannakaiyar.   What She Said ("When he
said").
Netumpalliyattan.   What She Said about Her
Unfaithful, Estranged Husband.
Okita.   Notes for a Poem on Being Asian
American.
Olds, S.   On The Subway.
Olson, C.   Newly Discovered "Homeric"
Hymn, A.
Ozog.   Song of the Field.
P'an Yüeh.   Thinking of My Wife.
Pasternak, B.   Meeting.
Philips, K.   Lucasia, Rosania and Orinda

Parting at a Fountain, July 1663.
Orinda to Lucasia.
Plath.   Parliament Hill Fields.
Rival, The.
Po Chü-i.   Feelings Wakened by a Mirror.
Sentimental Poem.
Separation.
To his Brother Hsing-chien, Who was Serving
in Tung-ch'uan.
Pope, A.   Epistle to Miss [or Miss Teresa]
Blount, on Her Leaving the Town after the
Coronation.
Pound, E.   River-Merchant's Wife: A Letter,
The.
Radnóti.   Letter to My Wife.
Ranaivo.   Carry me.
Song of a Young Girl.
Ransom, J.   Spectral Lovers.
Two in August.
Reed, H.   Judging Distances.
Rexroth, K.   If I thought I could get away.
Rich, A.   Rain on the West Side Highway.
Richardson, J.   As If Ending.
Ridler.   At Parting.
Rihaku.   River-Merchant's Wife: A Letter, The.
Riley, J.   When she comes home again! A
thousand ways.
Rodriguez, L.   Always Running.
Romero, L.   If Marilyn Monroe.
Root, W.   Estrangements.
Rossetti, C.   Aloof.
Echo from Willow-Wood, An.
From Monna Innominata.
Hoping Against Hope.
Meeting.
Remember me when I am gone away.
Rossetti, D.   Blessed damozel leaned out, The.
Rotella, A.   Phone call.
Rucker.   Swallow Creek.
Rukeyser, M.   Meeting, The.
Sangster, M.   Forgiven.
Sappho.   Thank you, my dear.
Schneour.   Forsaken.
Senghor.   You held the black face of the
warrior between your hands.
Seward.   Sonnet 19.
Shakespeare, W.   Sonnet 36.
Sonnet 44.
Sonnet 57.
Sonnet 97.
Sonnet 98.
Sonnet 99.
Sonnet: "Let me confesse that we two must be
twaine."
Sweet-and-Twenty.
Shapiro, K.   Haircut.
V-Letter.
Shin, T.   Shoe, A.
Sholl.   Dawn.
Outside the Depot.
Sidney, P.   Sonnet 87: "When I was forced
from Stella ever dear."
Sonnet 89: "Now that of absence the most
irksome night."
Smith, S.   Time be brief.
Snodgrass, W.   Locked House, A.
Spender, S.   Double Shame, The.
Song: "Stranger, you who hide my love."
Ssu-k'ung Shu.   Rebellion Over, I See Off a
Friend Who Is Returning North, The.
Stampa.   I am now so weary with waiting.
Stanescu.   Engagement.
Stern, G.   Waving Good-by.
Stevenson, R.   Swallows travel to and fro.
Strand.   Marriage, The.
Strong, L.   Brewer's Man, The.
Su Tung-p'o.   Mid-Autumn Moon.
Tune: Prelude to Water Music.
Su Wu.   Drafted.
Tarachow.   Walking in the Midst of Others.
Tennyson, A.   Fatima.
Thicknesse.   Siena.
Thomas, E.   Like the Touch of Rain [she was].
Thompson, P.   Adown the heights of Ages.
Ts'ao Chih.   Forsaken Wife, The.
Tu Fu.   Dreaming of Li Po.
I have a sister, little sister, living in Chung-li.

Moonlight Night.
Spring Prospect.
They Say You're Staying in a Mountain
Temple.
Tuckerman, F.   Last night I dreamed we parted
once again.
Unknown.   Blue Blue Your Collar.
bright moon, oh how white it shines, The.
Farewell Folk Song.
First month of winter: cold air comes.
Going on always on and on.
Green green, river bank grasses.
He's Gone Away.
In the garden a strange tree grows.
Last night in a dream I returned to my old
home.
Lover in Winter Plaineth for the Spring, The.
Show Me The Way.
Southern Blues, The.
Swift Is That Falcon.
Wife's Complaint, The.
Wife's Lament, The.
Updike.   Report of Health.
Van Doren.   Ancient Couple on Lu Mountain,
The.
Vaughan, H.   Retreat[e], The.
Voigt.   At the Movie: Virginia, 1956.
Wang Wei.   Composed on a Spring Day on
the Farm.
Waniek.   Star-Fix.
Webster, A.   There's one I miss. A little
questioning maid.
Wei Ying-wu.   Sent to the Taoist Holy Man of
Ch'üan-chiao.
To Send to Li Tan and Yüan Hsi.
Tune: Flirtatious Laughter.
Wen Cheng-ming.   While It Was Raining.
Wen T'ing-yün.   I remember that year, under
the blossoms.
Tune: Deva-like Barbarian.
Tune: Dreaming of the South.
Wevill.   Namelessness.
Whitman, R.   Laughing Gas.
Whitman, W.   Good-Bye, My Fancy! ("Good-
bye, my Fancy! / Farewell dear mate, dear
love!")
Hours continuing long, sore and heavy-hearted.
Williams, H.   Song, A: "No riches from his
scanty store."
Willis, N.   Confessional, The.
Winchilsea.   Letter to Daphnis, A.
Winner, R.   Segregated Railway Diner—1946.
Winters, Y.   At the San Francisco Airport.
Woods, J.   Lie closed, my lately loved, in the
far bed.
Wordsworth, W.   Complaint, A.
Wright, C.   Dead Color.
March Journal.
Wroth.   Sonnet 24.
Wu Chün.   Song of Spring.
Wyatt, T.   Farewell: "What should I say."
Yen Shu.   Tune: "Spring in Jade Pavilion."
Yi, H.   Fallen Petals.
Yo.   Dreaming of a Dead Lady.
Yü Hu.   Thoughts South of the Yangtze.
Yun.   Counting the Stars.
Zangwill.   Sundered.
Zanzotto.   How long between the grain and the
wind.
Ziedonis.   That was a beautiful summer.
Zolynas.   Love in the Classroom.

See also **Absence; Isolation; Loneliness**

September
Bridges, R.   Garden in September, The.
Galvin, B.   Green Evening, A.
Greenaway.   Three little girls were sitting on a
rail.
Gutteridge.   In September 1939.
Housman, A.   Tell me not here, it needs not
saying.
Howitt, M.   September.
Jackson, H.   September [Days Are Here].
Kinnell.   Blackberry Eating.
Kinsella, T.   Another September.
Lawrence, D.   Bavarian Gentians.
MacNeice.   September has come and I wake.
Magee, W.   Are You Ready?

Pastan. September.
Perry, T. For Nicholas, Born in September.
Ray, H. September.
Roethke. Carnations.
Taylor, J. Libra, September.
Turner, C. Artist on Penmaenmawr, The.

Sequoia Trees
Reader. When Paul Bunyan was ill we sent.
Simpson, L. Redwoods, The.
Wright, C. Thumbprint.

Serenity
Bible, *O.T.* "All night the cicada chirps."
Coleridge, S. Ode to Tranquillity.
Dickinson, E. After great pain a formal feeling comes—.
Hayden, R. Monet's "Waterlilies."
Holden, J. Falling from Stardom.
Hopkins, G. She schools the flighty pupils of her eyes.
Kipling, R. If you can keep your head when all [about you].
Li Po. On the Mountain: Question and Answer.
Machi. Tanka: "With a serene look."
Meek. Walk Around the Lake, A.
Ortiz. Serenity in Stones, The.
Park, T. Hymn to the Graveyard.
Pau-Llosa. Ostiones Y Cangrejos Moros.
Pierman. Eight Cows.
Shin, S. It is Not Time Yet to Light the Candle.
Tao-chi. Trip to the Village of the River of White Sand, A.
Very. Cottage, The.
Wang Chiu ssu. I love the serenity of living in the woods.
Wigglesworth. Still was the night, serene and bright.
Winchilsea. Enquiry after Peace. A Fragment.
Wright, C. One Summer.
Wu Chia-chi. In the morning they build embankments against floods.
Yang Chi. Wu Shan-yang.
Yang Shih-ch'i. After the rain, the vegetables from your garden.
Yüan Mei. Finding Serenity.
Zukofsky, L. Not much more than being.

Serfs. *See* **Slavery**

Sermons
Borges. Matthew 5:1–12; Seeing the crowds, he went up on the mountain.

Servants
Allen, H. Upstairs Downstairs.
Bishop, E. Cootchie, Miss Lula's servant, lies in marl.
Borges. Matthew 25:14–30; "For it will be as when a man."
Brooks, G. Bronzeville Woman in a Red Hat.
Brown, S. In an Old House.
Cardenal. Luke 16:1–9; He also said to the disciples.
Cave. Written by Desire of a Lady, on an Angry, Petulant Kitchen-Maid.
Clare, J. My Mary.
Cumbo. Domestics.
Cuney. No Images.
De la Mare. Buttons.
Dransfield. War of the Roses, The.
Duffy, C. Warming Her Pearls.
Eliot, T. Aunt Helen.
Evans, M. When in Rome.
Greig, A. Maid and I, The.
Herrick. Upon Prue [or Prew], His Maid.
Hillyer. Familiar Faces, Long Departed.
Howe, F. Scattered Light.
Hughes, L. Madam and Her Madam.
Madam's Past History.
Porter.
Kipling, R. Servant When He Reigneth, A.
Maclaurin. Elegy: "Nor Hammond's love nor Shenstone's was sincere."
Mo Shih-lung. Flower Shadows.
Moos. Sisters?
Muldoon, P. Big House, The.
Munby. Serving Maid, The.
Nobuyuki. In Berlin.
Pan Chieh-yû. Poem in Rhyme-Prose Form.

Popa. Prisoners of the Little Box, The.
Rilke. Luke 15:11–19; And he said, "There was a man."
Ríos, A. Nani.
Ssu-k'ung Shu. In Illness, Dismissing My Singing Girl.
Swift, J. Mrs. Harris's Petition.
To Their Excellencies the Lords Justices of Ireland, the Humble Petition of Frances Harris, Who Must Starve, and Die a Maid if It Miscarries.
Taylor, E. Written by the Barrow Side, Where She Was Sent to Wash Linen.
Turner, F. On the Pains of Translating Miklós Radnóti.
Unknown. How Is the Night?
Walcott. Midsummer: XXX.
Wilbur. Summer Morning, A.
Winchilsea. Reformation.
Wyatt, T. Heart and service to you proffered, The.

Service Stations. *See* **Gasoline Stations**

Service (botany)
Davie. Life of Service, The.

Sestina (form)
Anderson, P. Sestina in Time of Winter.
Ansen. Fit of Something against Something, A.
Bishop, E. Sestina: "September rain falls on the house."
Cooper, J. Morning on the St. John's.
Gioia. My Confessional Sestina.
Hecht, A. Sestina d'Inverno.
Jacobsen, J. Limbo Dancer, The.
Justice, D. Here in Katmandu.
Nims, J. Tide Turning.
Porter, F. Island in the Evening, The.
Pound, E. Sestina: Altaforte.
Ríos, A. Nani.
Shapcott, T. Sestina with Refrain.
Wallace, R. Grandmother Grace.
Walsh, C. Quintina of Crosses, A.
Watkins, E. Figures of Authority.
Webb, P. Imperfect Sestina.

See also **Sestina in Title and First Line Index**

Seven Deadly Sins
Dunbar, W. Dance of the Sevin Deidly Synnis, The.

Severn River, England
Evans, S. Seven Fiddlers, The.
Tennyson, A. Hushing of the Wye, The.

Sewall, Samuel
Hecht, A. Samuel Sewall.

Sewers
Kipling, R. Municipal.

Sewing
Acosta. My Mother Pieced Quilts.
Alvarez, J. Naming the Fabrics.
Bell, A. This is my work so.
Bishop, E. House Guest.
Cornford, F. Peasant Woman, A.
Crystal. Embroidery.
Dunbar-Nelson. I sit and sew—a useless task it seems.
Ford-Smith. Lala: The Dressmaker.
Gray, F. With cheerful mind we yield to men.
Hall, H. For a Broken Needle.
Instruction.
Late Sewing.
Listening Macaws, The.
Inez. Absolving You.
Lilley. Sewing Lesson, The.
Mar, L. My Mother, Who Came from China, Where She Never Saw Snow.
Peirce. Quilts.
Pelham. When i was young.
Taylor, E. Huswifery.
Unknown. Balgu Song.
Delia Very Angry.
Ode to the Sewing Needle.
Oh, the Funniest Thing.
Ward, J. Comfort-Maker.
Zhao. Needle and Thread.

See also **Seamstresses; Tailoring and Tailors**

Sex
Acklais. Give me your silver knife, right here.

Adcock, F. Against Coupling.
Happy Ending.
Adisa. Discover Me.
Ai. Before You Leave.
Why Can't I Leave You?
Alici. What She Said ("Like milk").
"Alta." Bitter Herbs.
Euch, are you having your period?
First Pregnancy.
Penus envy, they call it.
Amichai. Quick And Bitter.
3.
We did it in front of the mirror.
Amis, K. Aberdarcy: The Chaucer Road.
Ammons. Their Sex Life.
Ammuvanar. What He Said ("My love whose bangles").
Andrade, E. Fable.
Music.
Antipater of Thessalonica. Phoebus was a herdsman.
Antiphanes. When Cytherea slipped her wily sash off.
Antiphilus. Even then I said.
Antistius Vetus. Priapus the Scarecrow.
"Antler." What Every Boy Knows.
Argentarius. About Menophila's morals there are strange rumours.
Come, Gobrys, there are other gods besides the Muses.
Dead, you will lie under a yard of earth.
Epigram: "Hetero-sex is best for the man of a serious turn of mind."
Her perfect naked breast.
I can't bear to watch your hips.
Take off those flimsy nets, Lysidice.
Your kink, Heraclea, is sucking off.
Asclepiades. Arkheanassa.
Didyme waved her wand at me.
Great is a drink of snow.
I touched up sexy Hermione.
Once I lay down with Hermione.
Swearing an oath to Demeter.
To you, Kypris, Lysidike.
You're saving it? What for?
Automedon. Gymnastics Teacher, The.
That Asiatic striptease girl / who goes in for those.
Barker, G. O Golden Fleece ("O Golden Fleece she is where she lies tonight").
Barrax. Adagio.
Bass, E. To Praise.
Bassus. I refuse to turn into gold.
I'll never have a river of gold.
Your flatteries are boring.
Bateman, C. Beatitude.
Baudelaire. She Is Not Satisfied.
Baxter, J. Bar Room Conversation.
Behn, A. Disappointment, The.
Willing Mistriss, The.
Behn, R. French Horn.
Beresford. Courtship, The.
Berggolts. You took me, hostile, sullen—.
Bernstein, O. Her Words from the Corner.
Blake, W. Little Girl Lost, A.
Long John Brown & Little Mary Bell.
Sick Rose, The.
Bold, A. Special Theory of Relativity, A.
Bond, S. Tuesday Night Affair.
Borson. Lust.
Bowman, C. Demographics.
Mr. X.
Brecht, S. Here then is the life-giving activity given to every man: the sexual / act, vivificator.
Bromige. Logical Positivist, The.
Brooks, G. Ballad of Edie Barrow, The.
Burns, R. I Once was a maid, tho' I cannot tell when.
Patriarch, The.
Byrkit. Only Dance There Is, The.
Cable, G. Criole Candjo.
Carew, T. On the Marriage of T. K. and C. C.: The Morning Stormy.
Rapture, A.
Cartwright, W. No Platonic [or Platonique] Love.

Cassian. Blood, The.
Catullus. Carmen 10 ("Varus, whom I chanced to meet").
Carmen 61 ("Guardian of Helicon, Urania's son").
Carmen 69 ("That no fair woman will, wonder not why").
Carmina, LV.
Carmina, XIII.
Less pub than brothel, and you, the regulars.
Cavafy. Days of 1901.
Celan. When you lie in.
Cendrars. Great Fetishes, The.
Cherry, K. Going Down on America.
Chigetsu. Propriety.
Child, A. Squeeze.
Chu Shu-chen. Spring Joy.
Ciardi. Censorship.
Cillactor. Young lady may increase her stock, A.
Cleveland, J. To the State of Love or The Senses' Festival.
Clifton, H. Monsoon Girl.
Coleman, W. African Sleeping Sickness.
At the Record Hop.
Breast Examination.
Mastectomy.
Congreve. Song: "Pious Selinda goes to prayers."
Conoley. I'd like a little love in the wine-red Afternoon.
Cooley. Loom, The.
Cooper, J. Circle, a Square, a Triangle and a Ripple of Water, A.
Corbière. To the Eternal Feminine.
Cornish, S. Generations 1.
Cortez. So Long.
Suppression.
Couzyn. Way towards each other is through our bodies, The.
Creeley. Way, The.
Crozier, L. Poem for Sigmund.
Cruceius. Fair Ursly, in a merry mood.
Cummings, E. I like my body when it is with your.
I will be / M o ving in the Street of her.
May i feel said he.
O by the by / has anybody seen.
Raise the shade.
She being Brand.
Who's most afraid of death?thou.
Cummins, J. Sestina.
Cunningham, J. Epigram: "And now you're ready while she was here."
Dali. Great Masturbator, The.
Daumal. Persephone That Is to Say Double Issue.
Davies, S. Faith (wench) I cannot court thy sprightly eyes.
Deutsch. Solitude.
Di Prima. Ave.
Dickey, J. Sheep Child, The.
Djogo. Wooden Handle, The.
Dobyns. Desire.
Dorcey. Sea Flower.
Dove, R. Adolescence—II.
Dowson. Non Sum Qualis Eram Bonae sub Regno Cynara[e].
Drayton. To His Coy Love, A Canzonet.
Du Bellay. To Venus.
Duesing. Reprieve.
Duffy, C. Oppenheim's Cup and Saucer.
Dunn, S. Let's See If I Have It Right.
Man Who Closed Shop, The.
Vanishings, The.
Edson, R. Conjugal.
Elliott, A. Angel.
Here Today.
Love Poem, The.
Ellis, T. Kiss in the Dark, A.
Elmslie, K. One Night Stand.
Ennis. Alice of Daphne, 1799.
"Ern Malley." Boult to Marina.
Erucius of Cyzicus. How massively, with what a fine stiff rise.
Ewart. Creation Myth Haiku.
Office Friendships.

Fell, A. And Again.
Fields, D. Fine romance! with no kisses!, A.
Flaccus. Flaccus gave me, the silver lamp.
Flanders, M. Have Some Madeira, M'dear?
Flatman. Appeal to Cats in the Business of Love, An.
Foley, M. Middle Manager in Paradise, The.
Forbes, D. Politics of Envy.
Freeman, J. Fifteen.
García Lorca. Unfaithful Wife, The.
Gerstler. BZZZZZZZ.
Gibbons, R. White Beach.
Ginsberg, A. Change: Kyoto-Tokyo Express, The.
End, The.
Kaddish.
Pull my daisy.
Glatstein. Ruth.
Glück, L. Labor Day.
Mock Orange.
Song of Obstacles.
Wound, The.
Godfrey. Bath.
Goethe. Roman Elegy Ia.
Gogarty. On First Looking into Krafft-Ebing's Psychopathosexualis [or Psychopathia Sexualis].
Goldbarth. World of Expectations, The.
Gorham. White Tiger Leaps, The.
Gouri. And this happened in Prague many years ago?
Graham, W. Lying Dear, The.
Graves, R. Death Grapple, The.
Glutton, The.
Metaphor, The.
Quiet Glades of Eden, The.
Thieves, The.
Griffin, P. To His Importunate Mistress.
Gunn, T. Carnal Knowledge.
Modes of Pleasure.
Hacker, M. Future Conditional.
Saturday Morning.
Wagers.
Halliday, M. Population.
Hammial. Jane.
Handy, W. Yellow Dog Blues.
Harper, M. Elvin's Blues.
Harwood, G. Carnal Knowledge.
Hass, R. Privilege of Being.
Heaney, S. Rite of Spring.
Hecht, A. End of the Weekend, The.
Heffernan, M. Message, The.
Heine. Morning After, The.
Hejinian. Solitude flared out, The.
Helwig. Words from Hell.
Hemphill. Where Seed Falls.
Heredia. Antony and Cleopatra.
Herrick. Epithalamy to Sir Thomas Southwell and His Lady, An.
Good-Night, or Blessing, The.
Poet Loves a Mistress, but Not to Marry, The.
To Anthea ("Ah my Anthea! must my heart still break?")
To Electra ("I'll [or Ile] come to thee in all those shapes").
Vision to Electra, The.
Ho Xuan Huong. Man-and-Wife Mountain, The.
Ode to the Fan.
Scolding Some Dunces.
Holan. From Untitled.
Meeting in a Lift.
Hope, A. Fafnir.
Imperial Adam, naked in the dew.
Lingam and the Yoni, The.
Lot and His Daughters I.
Horovitz, F. Night-Piece.
Howe, M. Death, the Last Visit.
Hsiao-Wei. For My Wife.
Huelsenbeck, R. We hardly had gotten the man's pants down.
Hull, L. Frugal Repasts.
Love Song During Riot with Many Voices.
Inez. Warrior Daughters.
Irenaeus Referendarius. Why do you stare at the floor, Chrysilla.
Jarman, M. Los Angeles.

Jarrell. In Nature There Is Neither Right nor Left nor Wrong.
Johnson, G. I Want to Die While You Love Me.
Jones, R. Shakti.
Jones, R. Wan Chu's Wife in Bed.
Jong. Colder.
Jonson, B. Now, bride and bridegroom, help to sing.
To Pertinax Cob.
Kahn, G. Makin' Whoopee.
Kantaris. Airing the Chapel.
Keats. Sharing Eve's Apple.
Kennelly. Bread.
Kicknosway. Mr. Muscle-On.
King, J. Hymn: "For you I would put on embroidered robes."
Kinnell. After Making Love We Hear Footsteps.
When one has lived a long time alone.
Kirsch, S. Don Juan is coming in the morning.
Kirstein. Double Date.
Koestenbaum, P. Sonnet 37: "I'd decided I initiate most."
Koestenbaum, W. 1975.
Komunyakaa. Sunday Afternoons.
Kovner. How Many Poems Were Lost.
Kowit. When he pressed his lips to my mouth.
Kumin, M. After Love.
Kunio. Tanka: "Woman."
Kwon, I. Apocalypse, The.
Laforgue. For the Book of Love.
Lane, P. If.
Laux. China.
Lawrence, D. Love On the Farm.
Lehman. Guilt Trip.
Leithauser. Post-Coitum Tristesse: A Sonnet.
Leonidas of Tarentum. Antiginides' two daughters, Melo.
Levertov. Ache of marriage, The.
Wife, The.
Lewis, L. Urinating Man, The.
Lifshin. Fitzi in the Yearbook.
Midwest is Full of Vibrators, The.
Lochhead, L. Dreaming Frankenstein.
Lovelace, R. On Sanazar's being honoured with six hundred Duckets by the Clarissimi of Venice, for composing an Elegiack Hexastick of The City. A Satyre.
To Amarantha, That She Would Dishevel[l] Her Hair[e].
Lowry, M. Volcano is dark and suddenly thunder, The.
Lucilius. Cleombrotus the bruiser.
Zenonis has a splendid tutor for her son—.
Lucretius. Posture, The.
Macedonius. You ask me, girl, why I withdraw my sword.
Mackenzie, K. Fool, The.
Ginger-flowers.
Searchlights.
MacLeish. You Also, Gaius Valerius Catullus.
MacNeice. And love hung still as crystal over the bed.
Major, C. Inside Diameter.
On Trying to Imagine the Kiwi Pregnant.
Mallarmé. Another Fan.
Marichiko. I cannot forget.
I hold your head tight.
Marie-Madeleine. Crucifixa.
Sappho.
Vagabonds.
Words of Old Age*.
Marlowe. Elegies.
Men of wealthy Sestos, every year, The.
Martial. Either get out of the [my] house or conform to my tastes, woman.
Epigram 34: "Lesbia, why are your amours."
What'mmmIdoin'? slurs Lyris, feigning shock.
Martin, C. Satyr, Cunnilinguent: To Herman Melville.
Victoria's Secret.
Masters, E. Margaret Fuller Slack.
Mayer, B. First turn to me after a shower.
Work in Progress.
McCarriston. Castle in Lynn, A.

McClintock, M. She leaves.
McClure, M. (Fuck Ode).
McHugh, H. Note Delivered by a Female Impersonator.
McNaughton. Balls.
Meinke. Helen.
Meleager. By Timo's locks.
  Epigram: "I was thirsty."
  Love cast!
Michaux. Simplicity.
Middleton, C. Adelaide's Dream.
Mihalic. Approaching Storm.
Mikata Shami. Bound up it always.
Milan, J. Woman, 2.
Millay, E. I, being born a woman and distressed.
Miller, E. She is flat on her back.
Miller, L. Substitute, The.
Milosz, C. Earth.
Montagu, L. Between your sheets you soundly sleep.
  Receipt to Cure [or for] the Vapours, A.
Montague, J. Tracks.
Moore, H. First Time: 1950.
  Green Place, A.
Moore, T. Did Not.
Musaeus. Consummation.
Musgrave. Exchange of Fire.
Nashe. Choise of valentines, The.
Neruda. Sexual Water.
Nichols, G. Configurations.
Nordbrandt. Sailing.
Oates. Growing Together.
O'Hara, F. Ave Maria.
  Cornkind.
  Easter.
  Mary Desti's Ass.
Olds, S. First Sex.
  For My Daughter.
  Knowing, The.
  Monarchs.
  New Mother.
  Sex without Love.
  Sisters of Sexual Treasure, The.
Olson, C. Song of Ullikummi, The.
Oppian. Loves of the Eel, The.
Orampokiyar. What She Said ("In his country").
Orban, O. Summer on the Lake, A.
Ovid. 1.5.
Padgett, R. First Drift.
  Tell Us, Josephine.
Palladas. Women.
Palmer, M. Or maybe this / is the sacred.
Paquet. Basket Case.
Parker, P. For Willyce.
Parmenion of Macedon. You poured down like gold, / Olympian Zeus.
  Zeus paid Danaé in gold:/ thus I pay you.
Pasolini. Sex, consolation for misery!
Pasternak, B. Hops.
Paulus Silentiarius. Gold cut the knot of otherwise.
  I saw them, caught them in the act.
  Our kisses / Rhodope.
  Our kisses / Rhodope / let us steal.
  She lay all night beside me.
  Slip off that gown.
Paz. Counterparts.
  Key of Water, The.
Peacock, M. Have You Ever Faked an Orgasm?
  Return, The.
  She Lays ("She lays each beautifully mooned finger").
  Surge, The.
Pennant. Wildebeest of Carmine Street, The.
Peskett. Window Dressing.
Petri. Gratitude.
Petronius Arbiter. Fornication is a filthy business.
  Fragment of Petronius, A.
  Good God, what a night that was.
Philetas. Past fifty and cloyed at last.
Phillips, D. Five.
Philodemus. —"Hello there.—"Hello there yourself.

"I know, fair lady, how to love the lover well."
I, who used to score five, even nine times.
Naked warmth of you is still, The.
That silent publicizer of unheard-of news.
Picabia. Spermal Chimney.
Piercy. Crabs.
Pilkington, L. Fair and Softly goes far or, The Wary Physician.
Plato. Sokrates to Xanthippé.
Porter, P. Now it's in all the novels, what's pornography to do?
Sex and the Over Forties.
Poseidippus. Don't tell lies with your tears.
  If someone's with her.
Pound, E. Ballatetta.
  Temperaments, The.
Price, R. Twenty-One Years.
Rabbitt. Over All.
Raine, C. Sexual Couplets.
Redmond. My tongue paints a path of fire.
Rexroth, K. As I came from the.
  I cannot forget / The perfumed dusk inside the.
  I hold your head tight between.
  I scream as you bite.
  Lying in the meadow, open to you.
  You wake me, / Part my thighs, and kiss me.
  Your tongue thrums and moves.
Rich, A. My mouth hovers across your breasts.
  That "old last act"! / And yet sometimes.
  Two Songs.
  Waking in the Dark.
Rivard. Naive Invocation.
Rochester, J. Song of a Young Lady to Her Ancient Lover, A.
  Twelve months must pass ere you can yet arrive.
Roethke. Mistake, The.
  Moment, The.
  Partner, The.
  Sensualists, The.
Rotella, A. Lying in the wet grass.
Rothenberg, J. Song of Quavering, A.
Rufinus. Europa's kiss / even if.
  I do not enjoy.
  I hate an easy woman.
  If girls were nice.
  Leaving the Boys Behind.
  Let us wash each other's body.
  Melissias denies she's in love.
  Prodike.
  Rhodope, Melite and Rhodoklea / contested.
Rukeyser, M. Rondel: "Now that I am fifty-six."
  Speed of Darkness, The.
Rumens. Double Bed.
Rutsala. Lovers in Summer.
Ryan, G. In the Purple Bar.
St. John, D. My friend, a man I love as wholly.
Sanchez, S. Haiku.
  Prelude to Nothing.
Sappho. All the stars turn away their faces.
Scalapino. Floating Series 1.
  Floating Series 2.
  How can I help myself, as one woman said to me about wanting.
  Third Part.
Schwerner. Tablet V.
Scott, J. Changing Room.
Sedley. On the Happy Corydon and Phyllis.
Seifert. Fingerprints.
  Garland on the Wrist, A.
Selman, R. And so I went forth in uniform.
  I licked and kissed her in a bathroom stall.
  What did sex have to do with politics?
Sexton. Farmer's Wife, The.
  From the Garden.
Shakespeare, W. Sonnet 135.
Shapiro, K. First Time, The.
Sherwood, G. Song of a Young Lady to Her Ancient Lover, A.
Sholl. Midnight Vapor Light Breakdown.
Shurin. City of Men.
  Forward or Back.

Shuttle. Old Man, The.
  Passion.
Simmons, J. Honeymoon, The.
  Rogation Day: Portrush.
Slessor. Sleep.
Smith, P. Dylan, Two Days.
Smith, S. Conviction IV.
Soutar. Tryst [or Trysting Place], The.
Spivack, K. Love U.S.A.
Stallworthy, J. Source, The.
Stanescu. Winter Ritual.
Stein, D. Heat.
Stein, G. Lifting belly. Are you. Lifting.
Steinmar. Farmhand lay all hidden, A.
Stevenson, A. Daughter's Difficulties as a Wife, A: Mrs. Reuben Chandler to Her Mother in New Orleans.
Strato. Epigram: "Long hair, endless curls trained by the devoted."
  Give, and take the cash.
  He's a dragon, see.
  I swore to you, son of Kronos, never.
  Off with you, boy! Pretended prude!
  Two Plus Two.
Swede. One button undone.
Swenson, M. Riding the "A."
  Trellis for R, A.
Swirszczynska. First Madrigal, The.
  When We Wake Up in the Morning.
Symons, A. Bianca.
Taylor, J. Epigram: "Lusty wench as nimble as an eel, A."
  Virgo, August.
Teika. From the beginning.
Tessimond. Heaven.
Theocritus. Idyll.
  Wedding Song: Lullaby for Sleepy Lovers.
Tolson. Lena Lovelace.
Tonks. Story of a Hotel Room.
Tsvetayeva. Poem of the End, The.
Tysh, G. Genitalia.
Unknown. Bridegroom, beloved of my heart.
  Chalcan Female Song.
  Hogyn cam to bowers dore.
  I do not care if.
  I have a newe gardin.
  Knight and Shepherd's Daughter, The.
  Lady T-rc----l's Ring.
  Late last night, a girl came.
  On Komochi Mountain.
  One Writing against His Prick.
  Poetess's Bouts-Rimés, The.
  Prayer yo Hymen.
  Shall we stay in the.
  Songs of Courtship.
  Sthenelais.
  Till the good morning star.
  Uguisu on the flowering plum, The.
  What Her Girl Friend Asked and What She Replied Regarding His Return.
Valentine, J. Sex.
Vallejo. Trilce.
Vas. Just This.
Verlaine. Anointed Vessel.
  In that café crowded with fools we stood.
  Thousand and Three, A.
Vidyakara. Four Poems.
Vidyapati. New Love.
Villiers. Cabin-Boy, The.
Villon. Ballad of Villon and Fat Madge, The.
Virgil. Love and the Creatures.
Vivien. Undine.
Wagoner, D. Loons Mating.
Walker, A. She said: "When I was with him."
Wallace, R. Facts of Life, The.
Walwicz. Wonderful.
Waters, M. Hoochie Coochie.
Wayman. Wayman in Love.
Weatherly, T. Blues for Franks Wooten.
Weaver, M. Message on Cape Cod, The.
Weiners. Act #2.
Whitman, W. Dalliance of the Eagles, The.
  From pent-up aching rivers.
  I believe in you my soul, the other I am must not abase itself to you.
  This is the female form.

Woman waits for me, she contains all, nothing is lacking, A.
Wickham. Fired Pot, The.
Wieners. Acceptance.
Doll.
Loneliness, The.
Long Nook.
Suck, The.
To H.
What Happened?
Wilbur. Late Aubade, A.
Williams, J. Little Tumescence, A.
Williams, P. In the Dark.
Williams, S. This Is a Sad-Ass Poem for a Black Woman to Be Writing.
Wollach. Preannual Poem.
Splitting the Infinite.
Wood, V. Saturday Night.
Woods, J. Lie closed, my lately loved, in the far bed.
Wright, K. Underneath the Archers *or* What's All This about Walter's Willy?
Yamanaka. Kala: Saturday Night at the Pahala Theatre.
Yosano. Hair unbound, in this.
Tanka: "Pressing my breasts."
This autumn will end.
Young, A. Conjugal Visits.
Zeidner. Transvestite.
Zonas. Pomegranate just splitting, a peach just furry, A.
Zwicky. Jack Frost.

See also Erotic Love; Homosexuality and Homosexuals

Sexism
Ai. Mother's Tale, The.
"Alta." Penus envy, they call it.
Barbauld. Rights of Woman, The.
Browne, F. Australian Emigrant, The.
Browning, E. Lord Walter's Wife.
Chudleigh. To the Ladies.
Clarke, C. Hair: A Narrative.
Coleman, W. Women of my Color.
Egerton, S. Emulation, The.
Fu Hsüan. Woman.
Gallagher, T. Conversation with a Fireman from Brooklyn.
Griffin, S. Answer to a Man's Question, "What Can I Do About Women's Liberation?", An.
Hope, A. Advice to Young Ladies.
Huxley, A. Second Philosopher's Song.
Jiles. Paper Matches.
Jordan, J. Poem About My Rights.
Kendall, M. Woman's Future.
Koch, K. Sleeping with Women.
Lorde. Revolution Is One Form of Social Change.
Millay, E. I, being born a woman and distressed.
Mitchison. Dick and Colin at the Salmon Nets.
Momoi. Portrait.
Piercy. Barbie Doll.
Reeve, C. Sacred Heliconian spring, The.
Rich, A. Snapshots of a Daughter-in-Law.
Rilke. Someday there will be girls and women whose name will no longer mean.
Shange. It's Not so Good to be Born a Girl/ Sometimes.
Thomas, E. On Sir J—— S—— Saying in a Sarcastic Manner, My Books Would Make Me Mad; an Ode.
Tollet. What cruel laws depress the female kind.
Unknown. Folk Song.
Poem for Jacqueline Hill.
Wakoski. Poet Recognizing the Echo of the Voice, A.
Wickham. Affinity, The.
Winchilsea. Introduction, The: "Did I, my lines intend for public[k] view."

Sexton, Anne
Sexton. January 1st.

Sexual Abuse
Bevington, L. One more bruised heart laid bare! one victim more!

Bridges. Lisa's Ritual, Age 10.
Clifton, L. Shapeshifter Poems.
To my Friend, Jerina.
Dobyns. Gun, The.
Emanuel, L. Silence. She Is Six Years Old.
Frost, R. Subverted Flower, The.
McCarriston. Castle in Lynn, A.
Selman, R. What did sex have to do with politics?

Sexual Exploitation
Cooper, D. Being Aware.
Ho Xuan Huong. Snail.
Kunitz, S. She wept, she railed, she spurned the meat.
Moreton. Ballad: "Altho' a slave me is born and bred."
Swenson, M. James Bond Movie, The.
Women / should be / pedestals / moving.

Sexuality
Adcock, F. Against Coupling.
Al-Harizi. Secret Kept, A.
Allen, P. Eve the fox swung.
Ameen. Monologue of a Dying Beast.
Sonnet No. 22.
Asclepiades. Although she's a girl, Dorkion.
Bass, E. For Barbara, who said She Couldn't Visualize Two Women Together.
In Celebration.
Vaginas of women, all the clusters.
Baudelaire. Femmes Damnées.
Brant, B. Her name is Helen.
Broumas, O. Rapunzel.
Snow White.
Buchanan, G. Theatrical Venus.
Burns, R. Green grow the rashes, O.
Green grow the rashes, O; / Green grow the rashes, O; / The lasses they hae wimble bores.
Catullus. Carmen 45 ("Phyllis Corydon clutched to him").
Chaucer. Experience, though noon auctoritee.
Creeley. Hole, The.
Dickinson, E. Wild Nights—Wild Nights!
Donne. To His Mistress Going To Bed.
Dove, R. After Reading *Mickey in the Night Kitchen* for the Third Time Before Bed.
Ewart. Semantic Limerick According to Dr. Johnson's Dictionary (Edition of 1765), The.
Semantic Limerick According to the Shorter Oxford English Dictionary (1933), The.
Farewell. Quaerè.
Ferlinghetti, L. Dark Portrait, A.
Frightened / by the sound of my own voice.
Fox, S. Grandmother.
Giovanni. Seduction.
Gogarty. On First Looking into Krafft-Ebing's *Psychopathosexualis* [*or* Psychopathia Sexualis].
González, A. Inventory of Places Propitious for Love.
Graves, R. Cry Faugh!
Gunn, T. Courage, a Tale.
Hacker, M. February 25.
If we talk, we're too tired to make love; if we.
Hamer. Getting Happy.
Ho Xuan Huong. Funny Grotto, The.
Girl Without a Sex, The.
Threefold Pass, The.
Hoover, P. Baseball.
Hope, A. Flower Poem.
Ignatow, Y. Androgeny is the universe.
Joyce, W. My Daughter's Pundalunda.
Kariara. Leopard lives in a Muu tree, A.
Komunyakaa. Thorn Merchant's Mistress, The.
Kumin, M. Louise Bourgeois Exhibit.
Rendezvous, The.
Larkin, P. Annus Mirabilis.
Levertov. Mutes, The.
Lorde. Meet.
Marlatt, D. Trying. a trying child. trying it on for size. the role.
McElroy, C. In My Mother's Room.
McFadden, R. Contemplations of Mary.
Melville, H. After the Pleasure Party.
Mouré. Aspen.
Niger. What?/ a rhythm.

Olds, S. Connoisseuse of Slugs, The.
First Boyfriend.
Olsen, W. Oasis Motel, The.
Orampokiyar. What She Said ("Like the high fanning tufts on swift horses").
Owen, M. Urban Cowboy Hat.
Parker, P. For Willyce.
Philodemus. Sixty sun-decked years Charito has gotten to.
Porter, C. I'm a Gigolo.
Rabbitt. Bernadette Murphy, 1943-1955.
Rich, A. Dialogue.
Rukeyser, M. Along history, forever.
St. John, D. Quote Me Wrong Again and I'll Slit the Throat of Your Pet Iguana.
Schorr. Amusement.
Schuyler, J. Tom.
Trinidad. C'est Plus Qu'en Crime, C'est une Faute.
Unknown. Marvelous Encounter at Blue Creek, The.
Vivien. Roses Rising.
Your strange hair, cold light.
Wendt. Newest Banana Plant Leaf, The.
Whitman, W. As Adam early in the morning.
Behold this swarthy face, these gray eyes.
From pent-up aching rivers.
Spontaneous me, Nature.
To the garden the world anew ascending.
Walt Whitman, a kosmos, of Manhattan the son.
Wilbur. Catch, The.
Yeats. Whence Had They Come?

Seymour, Jane
Unknown. Death of Queen Jane, The.

Shadbush. *See* Service (botany)

Shadows
Alexander, L. Nocturne Varial.
Alver. Fragment.
Angelou. Life Doesn't Frighten Me.
Apollinaire. Shadow.
Atkins. Dark Area.
Balmont. Vanishing Shadows.
Bateson. I Heard a Noise and Wishèd for a Sight.
Bernstein, O. What She Wanted to Be.
Boldman. I end in shadow.
Priest, The.
Booth, P. Countershadow, The.
Bowes-Lyon. Refugee, A.
Campion, T. Follow thy fair sun unhappy shadow.
Ceravolo. Dangers of the Journey to the Happy Land.
Chang Heng. Dancers of Huai-nan, The.
Ch'ien T'ao. Shady, shady the wood in front of the Hall;.
Substance, Shadow, and Spirit.
Coleridge, M. Shadow.
Crane, H. At Melville's Tomb.
Garden Abstract.
Cuney. Death Bed, The.
Daniel, S. Shadows.
De la Mare. Love Lies Here.
De' Medici. (To the Virgin).
Del Renzio. Can You Change a Shilling?
Donne. Lecture upon the Shadow, A.
Duchamp. Cast Shadows.
Empson. Legal Fiction.
"Field." Beloved, my glory in thee is not ceased.
Fitzgerald, E. 68.
Fulton, R. Stopping by Shadows.
Gates, L. Silent Buddha, The.
Gorman, L. Down the billboard girl's bare belly.
Grimké, A. Tenebris.
Hayden, R. Broken Dark, The.
Hearne, V. Riding a Nervous Horse.
Heidbreder. Copycat, copycat / Shadow's a copycat!
Hewitt, J. Substance and Shadow.
Hollander, J. Swan and Shadow.
Holtby, W. Resurrection.
Howe, S. He plodded away through drifts of i / ce.
Hubbell, P. Shadows.

Jaccottet. Serenity.
These wood-shadows, timid, patient.
Jewell. Mountain shadow.
Johnson, G. Escape.
Johnston, E. Mother's Love, A.
Juarroz. Prompting of my shadow, The.
Kassiane. Troparion.
Kovner. What's Not in the Heart.
Lamb, E. Lizard inching, A.
Landon. Farewell!
Laughlin, J. Step on His Head.
Levertov. Scenes from the Life of the
Peppertrees.
Levin, P. Shadow Returns, The.
Lyles. Summer stillness.
Madhubuti. After Her Man Had Left Her for
the Sixth Time That Year / (An Uncommon
Occurrence).
Maiden. Climbing.
McClintock, M. Across the sands.
Small girl, A.
Merwin, W. Door, A.
Last One, The.
Mew. Shade-Catchers, The.
Mo Shih-lung. Flower Shadows.
Montgomery, S. Evening lecture.
With the last lamp.
Pagis. Testimony.
Piatt, J. My Shadow's Stature.
Pinkerton, H. On Dorothea Lange's
Photograph "Migrant Mother" (1936).
Pizzarelli. Brim-shadow, The.
Just before the storm.
Plarr. Shadows.
Popa. Adventure of the Quartz Pebble, The.
Porumbacu. Anesthesia.
Roethke. In a dark time, the eye begins to
see.
Roseliep. Black hen, The.
Rotella, A. Not speaking.
Sheck. White Noise.
Shūji. Tanka: "Out of the shade."
Shurin. Blue Shade.
Siddal. Silent Wood, A.
Southard. Gleaming—sunken stones.
Stevens, W. Rabbit Is King of the Ghosts, A.
Stevenson, R. Armies in the Fire.
My Shadow.
Stoutenburg. Cat at Night.
Su Tung-p'o. Shadow of Flowers, The.
Swede. One by one to the floor all of her
shadows.
Passport check.
Symonds. Lux Est Umbra Dei[1].
Symons, A. La Mélinite: Moulin-Rouge.
T'ang Yin. Inscribed on a Painting of
Bamboo.
T'ao Ch'ien. Substance, Shadow, and Spirit.
Troupe. Sense of Coolness, A.
Unknown. Water Bug and the Shadows, The.
Van den Heuvel. From behind me.
Shadow in the folded napkin, The.
Volkow. Washerwoman, The.
Walcott. Season of Phantasmal° Peace, The.
Wen Cheng-ming. Recording My Happiness
upon Returning Home.
Wilde, O. Harlot's House, The.
Willmot. Breathing.
Wills, J. Coolness.
Yau. Radiant Silhouette I.
Yeats. New Faces, The.
Yoshimi. Tanka: "Casting shadows."
Yü Chi. When I Was Young, I Stopped by a
Wine Shop in Chi-men and Wrote This
Poem, Inscribed It and Signed It, "Written by
Lien the Eighteenth." The People of That
District Have Since Taken It To Be a Poem
of [the God] Lü Tung-pin! I Have Recorded
It Here as an Amusement.
Yüan Mei. Night of the Fifteenth, Second
Month.
Zach. Death Came for Michael Rockinghorse
early one morning.
Zanzotto. How long between the grain and the
wind.

**Shaftesbury, Anthony Ashley Cooper, 1st Earl
of**
Dryden, J. Achitophel: The Earl of Shaftsbury.
In pious times ere [or e'r] priest-craft did
begin.
Shaka
Mtshali. Birth of Shaka, The.
Shakers (First Church of The Millennium)
McMahon, L. Ann Lee.
Unknown. Simple Gifts.
Shakespeare, William
Arnold, M. Shakespeare.
Bogan, L. To an Artist, to Take Heart.
Brettell. African Student.
Coleridge, H. To Shakespeare.
Crane, H. To Shakespeare.
Drayton. And be it said of thee.
Edwards, T. To Shakespeare.
"Field." Prologue.
Hayes, A. Much Ado About Nothing,
Thanksgiving, 1972.
Holland, H. Upon the Lines and Life of the
Famous Scenic Poet, Master William
Shakespeare.
Keats. On Sitting Down to Read "King Lear"
Once Again.
Kemble. To Shakespeare.
Lalic. First Actor to Hamlet.
Lawrence, D. When I read Shakespeare I am
struck with wonder.
Lloyd, R. True Genius.
Melville, H. Coming Storm, The.
Milton. On Shakespear[e].
Plutzik. Dream about Our Master, William
Shakespeare, The.
Porter, C. Brush Up Your Shakespeare.
Ray, H. Shakespeare.
Robinson, E. Ben Jonson Entertains a Man
from Stratford.
Schwartz, D. Dogs Are Shakespearean,
Children Are Strangers.
Shakespeare, W. Sonnet 135.
Simmons, J. Stephano Remembers.
Sorescu. Shakespeare created the world in
seven days.
Suckling, J. Supplement of an Imperfect Copy
of Verses of Mr. Will. Shakespeare's, by the
Author, A.
Weöres. To the Spirits of Shakespeare and
Velázquez.
Zeidner. Transvestite.
Shamans
Kao Ch'i. Ballad of the Neighborhood
Shaman.
Li Tung-yang. To Yung-erh—Imitating a
Work by Master Jade Stream.
Shame
Ayton. To an Inconstant One.
Bentley, E. When their lordships asked Bacon.
Breton, N. Cradle Song: "Come, little babe."
Bromley, A. My Mother's Face Never Moved.
Browning, E. Sonnet: "Can it be right to give
what I can give?"
Burns, R. Rantin Laddie, The.
Byron, G. When we two parted.
Cavafy. In Despair.
Dafydd ap Gwilym. Rattle Bag, The.
Damas. Reality.
Dharker. Purdah, 1.
Donne. Flea, The.
Triple Fool[e], The.
Fumiko. Tanka: "Although blooming."
Goldsmith, O. Song: "When lovely woman
stoops to folly."
Grimké, A. Triolet, A.
Hacker, M. Mother II.
Han Yü. Flowering Plums.
Hughes, L. I too, sing America.
Inez. Warrior Daughters.
Jana Bai. Cast off all shame.
Johnson, L. Decadent's Lyric, A.
Justice, D. In Bertram's Garden.
Kao Ch'i. Passing By the Battlefield at Feng-
k'ou.
Klepfisz. Dinosaurs and Larger Issues.
Ku. Shame.
Levertov. In California During the Gulf War.

Lucie-Smith. Lesson, The.
MacKay, C. Only a Thought.
Meredith, G. 'Tis Christmas weather, and a
country house.
Mora. Cortez's Horse.
Nash, O. Say About Seven or Seven-Fifteen.
Nemerov. Fall Again, The.
Oliver, M. Strawberry Moon.
Orampokiyar. What Her Girl Friend Said,
When the Woman Was About to Take Back
Her Unfaithful Husband.
Paranar. What Her Friend Said to Her, within
the Lover's Hearing.
Po Chü-i. Bitter Cold, Living in the Village.
Sick Leave.
Polkowski. I Don't Know That Man.
Ramanujan. At Forty.
Schorr. Amusement.
Seneca. Senec. Traged. ex Thyeste Chor. 2.
Shakespeare, W. Sonnet 72.
Sonnet 129.
Shepard, O. It's a Low Down Dirty Shame.
Stevenson, R. Time to Rise.
Tomkiw. Last Night in Elvisville.
Unknown. Ichthyosaurus, The.
Viscusi. Autobiography.
Wilbur. Shame.
Wratislaw. Sonnet Macabre.
Wright, J. In Shame and Humiliation.
Yukitsuna. Tanka: "With a hangover."
Shannon (river), Ireland
Kennelly. Swimmer, The.
Ni Dhomhnaill. Feeding a Child.
Parthenogenesis.
Race, The.
Shannon Estuary Welcoming the Fish, The.
Shaped Poetry
Apollinaire. It's Raining.
Little Car, The.
Burford, W. Christmas Tree, A.
"Carroll." Lobster Quadrille, A.
Long Tale, A.
Charles, D. Concrete Cat.
Coffey. Headrock.
Cummings, E. I / never / guessed any.
R-p-o-p-h-e-s-s-a-g-r.
Dauenhauer. Tlingit Concrete Poem.
Francescato. Semen.
Herbert, G. Our Life Is Hid with Christ in
God.
Herrick. Pillar of Fame, The.
Hollander, J. State of Nature, A.
Swan and Shadow.
Hollander, R. You Too? Me Too—Why Not?
Soda Pop.
Inman, P. XX.
Madeleva. O / Holy / Wood.
Mayer, H. Oil.
Morgan, E. Computer's First Christmas Card,
The.
Solt. Forsythia.
Marriage.
Moonshot Sonnet.
Rain Down.
Wild Crab.
Swenson, M. Women.
Towne, A. Dead of Winter.
Unknown. Hang Up the Baby's Stocking!
Owl / whose home was in the hemlock, The.
Virgil. Grass path lasts.
Webb, C. Shape of History, The.
Weiman. Andy-Diana DNA Letter.
Williams, E. Like Attracts Like.
Sharecroppers
Hughes, L. Share-Croppers.
Sharks
"Carroll." Lobster, The.
Ciardi. About the Teeth of Sharks.
Dickey, J. Shark's Parlor, The.
Gunn, T. Cannibal.
Heyen. Spirit of Wrath, The.
Hood, T. Sally Simpkin's Lament, [or John
Jones's Kit-Cat-astrophe].
Hood, T. Ballad of the Basking Shark, The.
MacCaig. Basking Shark.
Martin, C. Sharks at the New York Aquarium.
Melville, H. Maldive Shark, The.

Orban, O. Snowfall in Boston.
Pratt, E. Shark, The.
Wevill. Birth of a Shark, The.

Shaving
Unknown. Burma-Shave Roadside Signs.
Updike. Upon Shaving Off One's Beard.
Yukitsuna. Tanka: "Changing."

Shaw, George Bernard
Beerbohm, M. Epitaph for G. B. Shaw.

Shaw, Robert Gould
Dunbar, P. Robert Gould Shaw.
Lowell, J. Memoriae Positum R. G. Shaw.
Lowell, R. For the Union Dead.
Ray, H. Robert G. Shaw.

Sheep
Atwood. November.
Baca. Mantanza to Welcome Spring.
Blake, W. Shepherd, The.
Bonnefoy. Top of the World, The.
Campbell, D. Ariel.
Davies, W. Child's Pet, A.
    Sheep.
Djogo. Black Sheep, The.
Djurdjic. I carry my black sheep back to her
    herd.
Francis, R. Sheep.
Gay, J. Wild Boar and the Ram, The.
Hall, D. Ruminant pillows! Gregarious soft
    boulders!
Hoffenstein. Sheep.
Hsü Ling. Teleg Song.
Kelly, R. Tune.
Lansing. Gold in the Mud, The.
Meynell, A. Shepherdress, The.
Morgenstern. Moonsheep stands on the huge
    lawn, The.
Mother Goose. Baa, baa, black sheep, have
    you any wool?
    Little Bo-Peep has lost her sheep.
Ni Tsan. Waking from a Nap.
Rossetti, C. Blessed that flock safe penned in
    Paradise.
Sappho. Evening Star who gathers everything.
Sedulius Scottus. Death of a Ram.
Sidney, P. My sheep are thoughts, which I
    both guide and serve.
Taylor, A. Sheep, The.
Thorley. Happy Sheep, The.
Tsvetayeva. Slope like a path for, A.
Unknown. Derby Ram, The.
    Herdsman's Song.
    Shearing, The.
    Sky is strewn with stars, The.
See also **Lambs**

Sheepshearing and Sheepshearers
Morgenstern. Moonsheep stands on the huge
    lawn, The.
Unknown. Banks of the Condamine, The.
    Click Go the Shears.

Sheets
Dickey, W. January White Sale.
Unknown. Song of the Sheet.

Shelley, Percy Bysshe
Beddoes. Lines Written in a Blank Leaf of the
    Prometheus Unbound.
Browning, R. Memorabilia.
    Sun-treader, life and light be thine for ever!
Corso. I Held a Shelley Manuscript.
Hardy, T. Shelley's Skylark.
Hood, T. False Poets and True.
Hunt, L. To Percy Shelley.
    To the Same.
Monroe, A. To W. S. M.
Parker, D. Lives and Times of John Keats,
    Percy Bysshe Shelley, and George Gordon
    Noel, Lord Byron, The.
Rossetti, D. Percy Bysshe Shelley: Inscription
    for the Couch, Still Preserved, on which He
    Passed the Last NIght of His Life.
Simic. Shelley.
Thomson, J. Voice of right amidst a world
    gone wrong, A.
Wade, T. Shelley.

Shells
Armour. Covering the Subject.
Cooper, G. Only One Mother.

Gascoyne. Cage, The.
Holmes, O. Chambered Nautilus, The.
Keller, D. Mussels.
Lovelace, R. Snail [or Snayl], The.
Lowell, A. Sea Shell.
McDonald, E. Itherness.
Moore, M. Paper Nautilus, The.
Ray, H. Enchanted Shell, The.
Root, J. Naming the Shells.
Scott, G. Frutta di Mare.
Sobin, G. Notes on Sound, Speech, Speech-
    Crystals and the Celestial Echo.
Stephens, J. Shell, The.
Stickney, T. On Some Shells Found Inland.
Swenson, M. Some Small Shells from the
    Windward Islands.
Tennyson, A. Minnie and Winnie.
Todd, R. Mantelpiece of Shells, A.
Unknown. Dark young pine, at the center of
    the earth originating.
    She sells sea-shells on the sea shore.
    Shell Secrets.
Walpole, H. To Lady Anne Fitzpatrick, When
    about Five Years Old, with a Present of
    Shells, 1772.
White, E. Conch.
Wright, K. Let's Hear it for the Limpet.
See also **Snails; Clams and Clamming; Oysters**

Shellshock
Owen, W. Chances, The.
    Conscious.
    Dead-Beat, The.
    Dulce Et Decorum Est.
    Mental Cases.

Shenandoah River and Shenandoah Valley
Melville, H. Portent, The.

Shepherds and Shepherdesses
Barnes, W. Shep'erd Bwoy, The.
Barnfield. Affectionate Shepherd, The.
Behn, A. Disappointment, The.
Benton, P. Psalm 23: "Lord is my shepherd; I
    shall not want, The."
Bible, O.T. Psalm 23.
    Psalm 023: "Lord is my shepherd; I shall not,
    The."
    There were some shepherds living in the same
    part of the country.
Blake, W. Shepherd, The.
Bloomfield. Moonlight. . . Scattered Clouds.
Bobrowski. Wild Swan, The.
Breton, N. Merry Country Lad, The.
Carew, T. Pastoral[1] Dialogue, A.
Cavalcanti. Ballata: Concerning a Shepherd-
    Maid.
Clare, J. Shepherd Boy, The.
Clarke, P. Young Shepherd Bathing His Feet.
Coleridge, S. Hunting Song.
Crashaw. Hymne of the Nativity, Sung by the
    Shepheards, A.
De la Mare. Nod.
Drayton. Daffodil Song, The.
    Roundelay Between Two Shepherds, A.
    Roundelay: "Motto Tell me, thou skilful
    shepherd's swain."
"Ephelia." On a Bashful Shepherd.
Erskine, J. Shepherd Speaks, The.
Fitts. Ya Se Van Los Pastores.
Fletcher, J. Folding the Flocks.
Garrison, T. Shepherd Who Stayed, The.
Gay, J. Tuesday; or, the Ditty.
Greene, R. Description of the Shepherd and
    His Wife, The.
    Phillis and Coridon.
    Shepherd's Wife's Song, The.
Hall, D. Ruminant pillows! Gregarious soft
    boulders!
Heine. Shepherd Boy, The.
Hennell. Shepherd and Shepherdess.
Hopkins, G. Sonnet: "Shepherd's brow,
    fronting forked lightning, owns, The."
Hughes, L. Shepherd's Song at Christmas.
Ivask, I. I am the shepherd of the heavenly
    flock.
Jones, M. Lass of the Hill, The.
Kirkup. Shepherd's Tale, The.
Leonidas of Tarentum. You shepherds who
    wander this lonely mountainside.

Lodge, T. Shepherd's Sorrow, Being
    Disdained in Love, The.
Lu Yu. Herd-Boy, The.
MacNeice. Nuts in May.
Marlowe. Passionate Shepherd [or Sheepheard]
    To His Love, The.
Marvell. Clorinda and Damon.
Meigs, M. Shepherd Left Behind, The.
Mew. Old Shepherd's Prayer.
Meynell, A. Shepherdress, The.
Mother Goose. Little Bo-Peep has lost her
    sheep.
    Little Boy Blue, come blow [up] your horn[!].
Nicholson, N. Shepherds' Carol.
Parker, K. Long, Long Ago.
Ralegh, W. Nimphs [or Nymph's] Reply to
    the Sheepheard [or Shepherd], The.
Raleigh. Nymph's Reply to the Shepherd, The.
Ravikovitch. Hovering at a Low Altitude.
Schwartz, D. Passionate Shepherd to His
    Love, The.
Shlonsky. Shepherd.
Sidney, P. Double Sestine [or Sestina].
    Lord, the Lord my shepherd is, The.
    My sheep are thoughts, which I both guide
    and serve.
Simpson, L. Green Shepherd, The.
Spenser. Is not thilke the mery moneth of
    May.
    Shepherd's Calendar, 'June', The.
Tate, N. While shepherds watched their flocks
    by night.
Thiele, C. Tom Farley.
Unknown. Herdsman's Song.
    Long, Long Ago.
    Red sky at night.
Vaughan, H. Shepherds [or Shepheards], The.
Verlaine. L'Allée.
Weöres. Saturn Sinking.
Wickham. Song of the Lonely Shepherd.
Wordsworth, W. Last of the Flock, The.
    Michael [A Pastoral Poem].
Yang Shih-ch'i. Herdboy returns, none too
    early, The.
Yeats. Song of the Happy Shepherd, The.
Young, A. Shepherd's Hut, The.

Sheppard, W. H.
Johnson, M. Dedicated to Dr. W. H.
    Sheppard.

Sheridan, Philip Henry
Melville, H. Sheridan at Cedar Creek.
Read, T. Sheridan's Ride.

Sherman, William Tecumseh, Union general
Bentley, E. "No, sir," said General Sherman.
Melville, H. Iris.
Work. Marching through Georgia.

Shields
Archilochus. Shield, The.
    That good shield I threw away.
Robinson, E. Beauty as a Shield.
Unknown. Riddles.

Shiloh, Battle of (1862)
Melville, H. Shiloh [A Requiem].
Unknown. Battle of Shiloh, The.
    Drummer Boy of Shiloh, The.

Ships and Shipbuilding
Abbey, H. What do we plant when we plant
    the tree?
Argentarius. Trader, untie the long stern-
    cables.
Bell, J. Ships, The.
Bierds. Off the Aleutian Chain.
Bishop, E. Casabianca.
    Large Bad Picture.
Blight. Into the Ark.
Bontemps. Nocturne of the Wharves.
Bridges, R. Passer-by, A.
Brown, G. Press-Gang.
Brownell, H. Burial of the Dane, The.
Carew, T. To Her in Absence; a Ship.
Cassity. Epigoni Go French Line.
Cendrars. Frisco-City.
Cervantes. Refugee Ship.
Clough. Qua Cursum Ventus.
Crane, S. I explain the silvered passing of a
    ship at night.
Dawe, G. Question of Covenants, A.

Dickinson, E.   There is no Frigate like a Book.
Dunbar, P.   Ships That Pass in the Night.
Eimers.   History of Navigation, A.
Emerson, R.   Letters.
Flecker.   Old Ships, The.
Haines, J.   Mothball Fleet: Benicia, California.
Holmes, O.   Chambered Nautilus, The.
Howard, R.   Seeing Cousin Phyllis Off.
Johnson, L.   Troopship, The.
Kelly, B.   Courting the Famous Figures at the
   Grotto of Improbable Thought.
Kipling, R.   Derelict, The.
King, The.
   McAndrew's Hymn.
Kooser.   Afterlife, The.
Larkin, P.   North Ship, The.
Lawrence, D.   Argonauts, The.
   Build then the ship of death, for you must
   take.
   Ship of Death, The.
Lear, E.   Jumblies, The.
Longfellow, H.   Building of the Ship, The.
   Cumberland, The.
Lorde.   Fishing the White Water.
Lowell, A.   Camouflaged Troop-Ship.
MacLeish.   Steamboat Whistle, The.
Masefield.   Cargoes.
   Sea-Fever.
Mayer, B.   Port, The.
McCaig.   Poem: "There is a wailing baby
   under every stone and you walk."
McNeill, A.   Straight Seeking.
Melville, H.   Berg, The.
   Man-of-War Hawk, The.
   Temeraire, The.
Mitchell, W.   Tacking Ship Off Shore.
Morris, G.   Main-Truck; or, A Leap for Life,
   The.
Morton, D.   Old Ships.
Mother Goose.   I saw a ship a-sailing.
   I saw three ships come sailing by.
   Three wise men of Gotham.
Newcastle, M.   Sea Similized to Meadows and
   Pastures: the Mariners, to Shepherds: the
   Mast, to a May-Pole: the Fish, to Beasts,
   The.
Nicholls, J.   Mary Celeste.
Ologoudou.   Liberty.
Oppen.   Taste, The.
Pagis.   Logbook.
Po Chü-i.   Spring River, The.
Rakosi.   Unswerving Marine.
Ransom, J.   Good Ships.
Rossetti, C.   Rainbow, The.
Scott, W.   Gallant Ship, The.
Shalom.   Stoker, The.
Singer, B.   SOS Lifescene.
Smith, A.   Steamer left he black and oozy
   wharves, The.
Squire.   Ship, The.
Stevenson, R.   Rain is raining all around, The.
   Where Go the Boats?
Stewart, D.   Garden of Ships, The.
Strnisa.   Ship, A.
Supervielle.   Like an ox streaming saliva,
   yoked to the plough.
Transtromer.   Syros.
Unknown.   Blow, Boys, Blow [*or* Blow,
   Bullies, Blow].
   Golden Vanity, The.
   Sir Andrew Barton.
   When I went with you.
Whitman, W.   Aboard at a ship's helm.
   After the sea-ship, after the whistling winds.
   Battle of the *Bonhomme Richard* and the
   Serapis.
   Dismantled Ship, The.
   Patrolling Barnegat.
   Song for All Seas, All Ships.
Wordsworth, W.   Where lies the Land to
   which yon Ship must go?
   With Ships the sea was sprinkled far and nigh.
Work.   Ship That Never Returned, The.
Yün Shou-p'ing.   War ships, cold tides.
Zhenkai.   Evening Scene, An.

See also **Boats; Freighters; Yachts**
Shipwrecks
   "Bagritzky."   Watermelon.
   Césaire, A.   Ex-Voto for a Shipwreck.
   Chiang Lu.   Wrecked Boat on the River Shore.
   Colvin, J.   Flying Dutchman, The.
   Cowper, W.   Castaway, The.
      On the Loss of the *Royal George.*
   Craveirinha.   Ode to a Lost Cargo in a Ship
      Called *Save.*
   Dickinson, E.   Glee—The great storm is over.
   Dobell, S.   "How's My Boy?"
   Falconer, W.   "All hands unmoor!" proclaims a
      boisterous cry.
   Fordham.   Shipwreck.
      Tribute to a Lost Steamer.
   Gilbert, S.   Etiquette.
   Gu Cheng.   Ark.
   Hardy, T.   Convergence of the Twain, The.
   Henry.   Verses.
   Ho Sun.   At Parting.
   Hollander, J.   Last Words.
   Homer.   Great wave drove at him with
      toppling crest, A.
   Horace.   4.7.
   Hughes, T.   I can understand the haggard eyes.
   Kingsley, C.   Three Fishers [Went Sailing],
      The.
   Lattimore.   RMS Lusitania.
   Lee-Hamilton.   Sunken Gold.
   Leopardi.   Infinite, The.
   Lightfoot.   Wreck of the Edmund Fitzgerald,
      The.
   Longfellow, H.   Wreck of the *Hesperus*, The.
   Masefield.   Posted.
   Maunick.   Further off is the measured force the
      word of the sea.
   McGrath, T.   Offering.
   Melville, H.   Aeolian Harp, The.
      Berg, The.
      Far Off-Shore.
      Haglets, The.
   Menken.   Ship That Went Down, The.
   Pratt, E.   Final Moments, The.
   Rich, A.   Diving into the Wreck.
   Rossetti, D.   White Ship, The.
   Shakespeare, W.   Ariel's Song ("Full fathom
      [*or* fadom] five thy father lies").
   Southey, R.   Inchcape Rock, The.
   Stead, C.   Rain, and a flurry of wind shaking
      the pear's white blossom.
   Tsvetayeva.   Slope like a path   for, A.
   Unknown.   Golden Vanity, The.
      Isle of Man Shore, The.
      Loss of the *Due Dispatch*, The.
      Picking Rushes.
      Sir Patrick Spens [*or* Spence].
   Vaiiunaite.   Nausicaa.
   Valéry.   Crusoe had provided all the
      necessaries and was more or less at leisure
      in.
   Waller, E.   Upon his Majesties repairing of
      Pauls.
   Whitman, W.   To the Man-of-War Bird.
   Whittier.   Skipper Ireson's Ride.
   Yosano.   Tanka: "Sea inside my heart, The."
Shirts
   Pinsky.   Shirt.
   Sandburg, C.   Shirt.
   Shapcott, T.   Blue Paisley Shirt, The.
   Simic.   Shirt.
Shiva
   Jeffers, R.   Shiva.
   Mahadevi.   I do not call it his sign.
      It was like a stream.
      Vein of sapphires, A.
      When I am hungry.
      When the body becomes Your mirror.
   Meenakshi.   If Hot Flowers Come to the
      Street.
   Munivar.   On the marriage platform made of
      gold.
Shoes and Shoemakers
   Agard, J.   New Shoes.
   Barnes, W.   Grammer's Shoes.
   Benedikt.   European Shoe is constructed of
      grass and reed, [bound,] The.

Bernstein, C.   Loose Shoes.
Cohen, E.   #2, Shoes.
Dunbar, W.   Amendis to the Telyouris and
   Sowtaris for the Turnament Maid on Thame,
   The.
Gillilan, P.   Alien goes Shopping.
Herford.   There was a young lady of
   Twickenham.
Herrick.   Sho[o]e Tying, The.
Hotham.   Night comes.
Hughes, L.   Bad Morning.
Kramer, L.   Shoemaker's Wife, The.
Lear, E.   Limericks, II (iii).
   O dear! How disgusting is life!
McCrea.   Boots and Shoes.
McElroy, C.   For Want of a Male a Shoe Was
   Lost.
Miles, J.   Sale.
Mitchell, K.   Black Patent Leather Shoes.
Mother Goose.   Cobbler, cobbler, mend my
   shoe.
Ormond.   At His Father's Grave.
Perreault, J.   Shoe.
Petri.   To Be Said Over and Over Again.
Po Chü-i.   Sentimental Poem.
Simic.   My Shoes.
Smith, W.   Said Dorothy Hughes to Helen
   Hocking.
Sutskever.   Cartload of Shoes, A.
Sutter.   Shoe Shop.
Swirszczynska.   White Wedding Slippers.
Unknown.   Cobbler, The.
   Cobbler, cobbler, mend my shoe.
   Jeremy Hobbler.
   Limerick: "There was an archdeacon who
      said."
   Limerick: "There was an old man of [*or* from]
      Peru / Who dreamt [*or* dreamed] he was
      eating his shoe."
   Lost Shoe, The.
Vallejo.   Poem to Be Read and Sung.
Virgilio.   Alone on the road.
Wolfe, F.   Choosing Shoes.
Wylie.   Velvet Shoes.
See also **Galoshes**
Shoplifting and Shoplifters
   Seaton, M.   Fear of Shoplifting.
   Stanton, M.   Shoplifters.
Shopping Malls
   Disch.   Garage Sale as a Spiritual Exercise,
      The.
   Gilmore, B.   Bow to Allah.
   Giscombe.   All (Facts, Stories, Chance).
   Stokesbury.   Day Begins at Governor's Square
      Mall.
Shopping and Shops
   Atkins.   New Storefront.
   Bialoszewski.   Ballad of Going Down to the
      Store, A.
   Cornish, S.   Your Mother.
   Coulette.   Junk Shop, The.
   Desnos.   St Merri district, The.
   Disch.   Rapist's Villanelle, The.
   Field, R.   General Store.
   Follain.   Buying.
   Gillilan, P.   Alien goes Shopping.
   Ginsberg, A.   Supermarket in California, A.
   Hongo.   Winnings.
   Jennings, E.   My Grandmother.
   Jones, M.   Soliloquy on an Empty Purse.
   Longley, M.   Greengrocer, The.
   MacNeice.   Christmas Shopping.
   McOrlan.   Accessories shop, The.
      Hairdresser's, The.
   Mother Goose.   To market, to market / To buy
      a plum bun.
   Peacock, M.   How I Had to Act.
   Roberts, L.   Gift Shop in Pecs.
   Shapiro, K.   Garage Sale.
   Simic.   Grocery.
   Thompson, C.   Christmas Rush, The.
   Tolson.   African China.
   Unknown.   Country Store, The.
      Old woman was sweeping her house, and she
         found, An.
      To market, to market, to buy a fat pig.
   Voznesensky.   Chorus of Nymphs, A.

Wright, J. To a Salesgirl, Weary of Artificial Holiday Trees.

Shores
Ammons. Corsons Inlet.
  So I Said I Am Ezra.
Arendt. Lost Bay.
Barnard, M. Shoreline.
Barrington, J. Villanelle VI.
Bishop, E. Little Exercise.
Blight. Landfall, The.
Bridges, R. Cliff-Top, The.
Browning, R. Meeting At Night.
Campbell, W. Morning on the Shore.
"Carroll." Lobster Quadrille, A.
Cowley, H. Blank Verse Written on the Sea Shore.
Cranch. Pines and the Sea, The.
Croly. Aestuary, An.
Deutsch. Earliness at the Cape.
Duggan, L. Five. One.
  One. One.
Eliot, T. Cape Ann.
Emerson, R. Sea-Shore.
Feinstein, E. Coastline.
Frost, R. Once by the Pacific.
Ghiselin. Headland.
Grosholz. Outer Banks, The.
Hadas, R. Sentimental Education.
Harwood, G. Clair de Lune.
Hughes, L. Moonlight Night: Carmel.
Joyce, J. On the Beach at Fontana.
Kinnell. Spindrift.
Lamb, E. Far shore, The.
Larkin, P. To the Sea.
Lewis, J. At Carmel Highlands.
McPherson, S. Seaweeds.
Meredith, G. Love's Grave.
  Orchard and the Heath, The.
Merwin, W. Low Fields and Light.
Millay, E. I shall go back again to the bleak shore.
Miyazawa Kenji. Tanka: "Left alone."
Momaday. Winter Holding off the Coast of North America.
Moore, T. I pray you, let us roam no more.
Nims, J. Tide Turning.
O'Loughlin. Bunkers, The.
Oppen. Book of Job and a Draft of a Poem to Praise the Paths of the Living, The.
  Little Pin: Fragment, The.
  O withering seas.
  Taste, The.
Pizzarelli. Bright awning is cranked, A.
Revard. "But Still in Israel's Paths They Shine."
Roethke. Meditation at Oyster River.
  Rose, The.
Rose, P. Anglo-Saxon Comedy.
Roseliep. Pacing.
Shapiro, H. Provincetown, Mass.
Singer, B. Peterhead in May.
Smith, C. On Being Cautioned against Walking on a Headland Overlooking the Sea, because It Was Frequented by a Lunatic.
  Written near a Port on a Dark Evening.
Smith, W. Abruptly all the palm trees rose like parasols.
Södergran. Forest Lake.
Stafford, W. Address to the Vacationers at Cape Lookout, An.
Stevenson, R. At the Seaside [or Sea-Side].
Swenson, M. Morning at Point Dume.
Thomas, D. We lying by seasand, watching yellow.
Tu Fu. Midnight.
Turner, C. Seaside: In and Out of the Season, The.
Turner, J. Foam's Frail Power.
Wade, T. Winter Shore, The.
Walker, T. By the Saltings.
Webb, F. End of the Picnic.
Whitman, W. As I ebb'd with the ocean of life.
  Patrolling Barnegat.
Whittier. Burning Drift-Wood.

See also **Beaches**

Shorter, James A.
Heard, J. Bishop James A. Shorter.

Show Business
Ibrahim, A. Africa, Music and Show Business.
March, J. Queenie was a blonde, and her age stood still.
Thribb. In Memoriam Larry Parnes ("Mr Parnes Shillings and Pence").

See also **Acting and Actors; Motion Pictures; Theater and Theaters**

Shrews
Burns, R. Kellyburnbraes.
Hoban. Small, Smaller.

Shrimp
Browne, M. Shrimp, A! Black thing as widow's crape.

Shrines
Cavalcanti. Sonetto XXXV: To Guido Orlando.
Chu Yün-ming. Shrine of General Pien, The.
Fuller, M. Freedom and Truth.
Ho Xuan Huong. Shrine of Ts'en Yi-tung, The.
McCarthy, T. Party Shrine.
Sanchez, S. Haiku: "Your voice unwrapping."
Virgil. It is I, lads, who look after this place.
Yüan Mei. On the Way to Pa-ling.

See also **Mausoleums; Monuments**

Shropshire, England
Housman, A. On Wenlock Edge the wood's in trouble.

Shrouds
Brown, G. Shroud.
De la Mare. Snow.
Donne. Funeral[l], The.
Sackville-West. Dream, A.
Schnackenberg. Angels Grieving over the Dead Christ.

Siberia
Bienek. Vorkuta.
Mangan, J. Siberia.
Pushkin. Message to Siberia.

Sibyl
Hopkins, G. Spelt from Sibyl's Leaves.

Sicily
Demodocus. All the Cilicians are bad.
Lawrence, D. Bare Almond-Trees.
  Hibiscus and Salvia Flowers.
Seward. On Catania and Syracuse Swallowed Up by an Earthquake, from the Italian of Filicaja.

Sickness. *See* **Illness**

Siddons, Mrs. Sarah
Lamb, C. As When a Child.

Sideshows
Williams, M. Firebreathers at the Café Deux Magots, The.

Sidmouth, Henry Addington, Viscount
Shelley, P. Similes for Two Political Characters of 1819.

Sidney, Sir Philip
Donne. Upon the Translation of the Psalms by Sir Philip Sidney, and the Countess of Pembroke His Sister.
Drayton. Noble Sidney with this last arose, The.
James I, King of England. Epitaph on Sir Philip Sidney, An.
Jonson, B. To Elizabeth, Countess of Rutland.
Ralegh, W. Epitaph on Sir Philip Sidney.
Spenser. Such skill, match't with such courage as he had.
Wilson, E. Scène de Boudoir.

Siena, Italy
Bernstein, O. In a Park, in Siena, at Twilight.

Sierra Leone
Cheney-Coker. On Being a Poet in Sierra Leone.
  Road to Exile Thinking of Vallejo, The.

Sierra Nevada Mountains
Jeffers, R. Ascent to the Sierras.
Miller, J. Sierras.
Rexroth, K. Strength through Joy.

Siestas
Coward. Mad Dogs and Englishmen.

Sight
Aristophanes. Good morrow to the morn next to my gold.
Carrier, C. Perspective.
Cary, P. True Love.
Chang, E. Near-Sightedness.
Creeley. Statue, The.
  Window, The.
Gibson, W. Sight.
Graves, R. Gift of Sight.
Lowell, R. Eye and Tooth.
Rajeevan. Pair of Glasses, A.
Sidney, P. Sapphics.
Traherne. Preparative, The.
Whisenand Open your eyes that you may see.
Zukofsky, L. In Arizona / (how many years in the mountains).

Signorelli, Luca
Graham, J. At Luca Signorelli's Resurrection of the Body.

Silence
Amichai. If I forget thee, Jerusalem.
Ammons. Unsaid.
Andrade, E. Silence.
Angel. As It Is.
Angelou. On Aging.
Bachmann. Psalm: "Be still with me, as all bells are still!"
Baugh, E. Getting There.
Beddoes. To Silence.
Berg, S. Answer, The.
Berry, W. Except.
Bevington, L. With the Tide: A Cry of Weakness.
Bogan, L. Train Tune.
Borkhuis. Inside Language.
Braithwaite. Quiet has a hidden sound.
Brecht, B. When Evil-Doing Comes Like Falling Rain.
Brecht, B. Silence.
  Silence, 2.
Brett, L. La Pathétique.
Brontë, E. How still, how happy! These [or Those] are words.
Byron, G. When we two parted.
Cage. Lecture on Nothing.
Cain, J. Empty room.
Castillo, O. Apolitical Intellectuals.
Celan. Alchemical.
  Language Mesh.
Chin Nung. In the silences between peals of the bell.
Chōkū. Tanka: "After enduring."
  Tanka: "Bulky oil lamp, A."
  Tanka: "New Year's temple bells."
Clare, J. July.
Codrescu. Poetry Paper.
Cofer. Fever.
Coleridge, H. On the Death of Echo, A Favourite Beagle.
Creeley. Waiting.
Cruz Varela. Invocation.
Cummings, E. Silence / .is / a / looking.
Day Lewis. Two Songs.
De la Mare. Autumn.
  Faint Music.
  Listeners, The.
  Love Lies Here.
  Myself.
  Stranger, The.
Del Renzio. Can You Change a Shilling?
Dickinson, E. There is no Silence in the Earth—so silent.
Doinas, S. Words, The.
Dowson. O Mors! Quam Amara Est Memoria Tua Homini Pacem Habenti In Substantiis Suis.
Drummond de Andrade. Looking for Poetry.
Emerson, R. Merops.
Ficowski. Girl of Six from the Ghetto Begging in Smolna Street in 1942, A.
Foster, E. Hermetic Silence.
Galich. Prospectors' Little Waltz, The.
Gallagher, T. Deaf Poem.
Gergely. Silences.

Glatstein. Lost.
Glück, L. Horse.
Gouri. You're no king.
Grunthal. I broke the second part of the First Commandment.
Gurney, I. Silent One, The.
Hacker, M. Against Silence.
Hadas, R. Three Silences.
Hall, D. Je Suis une Table.
Herlin. Light brush of dawn, A.
Hirsch, E. Watcher, The.
Hitchcock. Song of Expectancy.
Holtby, W. Trains in France.
Holub. Silence.
Hood, T. Silence.
Jewell. Cliff dweller ruins.
Finding this cavern.
Somewhere behind me.
Where the coyote called.
Johnson, L. Precept of Silence, The.
Karpowicz. Silence is sucking the earth dry.
King, H. Silence: A Sonnet.
Kinzie. Canicula.
Kizer, C. Antique Father.
Knott. Sonnet: "Way the world is not, The."
Kovner. Lord of Dreams.
What's Not in the Heart.
Lane, P. Wind Thoughts.
Larkin, P. If grief could burn out.
Myxomatosis.
Talking in bed ought to be easiest.
Lavrov. Farewell, I say, farewell to the incomplete.
Lear, E. Limerick: "There was an Old Man who said, 'Hush!'."
Levertov. What Were They Like?
Levi, P. Voices mute for ever, or since yesterday, or just stilled;.
Levine, P. Waking in March.
Longfellow, H. Curfew.
Lovelace, R. To Elinda.
Mangan, G. Nights in Black Valley.
Martin, C. Speech Against Stone.
Martynov. River Silence, The.
Masters, E. Silence.
Matthews, J. Cheerleaders, The.
Merwin, W. For the Anniversary of My Death.
"Prodigal Son," The.
Utterance.
Mey. Quiet Days.
Meynell, A. To Silence.
To the Beloved.
Mo Shih-lung. On a Cold Day I Climbed Tiger Hill With Professor Ho. At the Time, the Local Prefect Had Prohibited Pleasure Excursions and Feasts, But the Mountain Was Quiet and Tranquil, So We Stayed All Day.
Montgomery, S. Her silence at dinner.
Moore, L. Eternal Landscape, The.
Silent deer the sound of a waterfall.
Moore, M. Silence.
Moore, T. Harp That Once through Tara's Halls, The.
Myers, G. Talking to God.
Nobuyuki. Third-Class Car on a Night Train (three poems).
Ōshima Ryōta. No one spoke.
Ou-yang Hsiu. Cicada, The.
Padilla. In Trying Times.
Pagis. Words.
Palinskaite. Silence.
Perry, N. Too Late.
Pilinszky. On the Wall of a KZ-Lager.
Passion of Ravensbrück.
Piombino. Frozen Witness, The.
Po Chü-i. Lao Tzŭ.
Philosophers: Lao-Tzu, The.
Poems in Depression, at Wei Village.
To a Talkative Guest.
Poe. Silence.
Pratt, E. Silences.
Pritchard, N. Cloak, The.
Rannit. Jaan Oks.
So I See You Still.
Wiiralt Drawing in Chartres.

Rich, A. That conversation we were always on the edge.
Richards, E. Wise old owl lived in an oak, A.
Riley, J. Silence.
Ritsos. Distant, The.
Requiem on Poros.
Rossetti, C. Aloof.
Introspective.
Rossetti, D. Severed Selves.
Silent Noon.
Rózewicz. Voice, A.
Rutsala. Silence, The.
Sandburg, C. Aprons of Silence.
Sandhill People.
Sassoon. Elected Silence.
Savard. Descent of Fire, The.
Scovel. Silence, The.
Sepamla. Silence: 2.
Simon, P. Sound of Silence, The.
Smith, S. Portrait, A.
Two Friends.
Via Media Via Dolorosa.
Word, The.
Sobin, G. Premises.
Southerland. Recitation.
Stafford, W. Lost in the Centuries.
Stevens, W. Less and Less Human, O Savage Spirit.
Stevenson, R. Gardener does not love to talk, The.
Stickney, T. In the Past.
Suckling, J. Song: "Why so pale and wan, fond lover?"
Szymborska. Unexpected Meeting.
Tahmisic. Stone and Ashes.
Tasso. "Woods and the rivers are silent," The.
Teasdale. Night Song at Amalfi.
Those who love the most.
Thomas, L. Onion Bucket.
Tsvetkov. What remained of our meetings?
Tu Fu. Dawn Over the Mountains.
Turner, W. Silence.
Unknown. Get Up and Bar the Door.
Raid of the Reidswire, The.
Silent Snake, The.
Success is speaking words of praise.
When I went with you.
Very. Silent, The.
Wain. Apology for Understatement.
Waters, M. Miles Weeping.
Wei Ying-wu. On Sound.
Whitman, W. When I heard the learn'd astronomer.
Whittemore, R. Still Life.
Wickham. Silent Singer, The.
Williams, W. Silence.
Willmot. Small noise, A.
Wright, J. Sparrows in a Hillside Drift.
Wroth. From Pamphilia to Amphilanthus.
Wylie. Velvet Shoes.
Yeats. After Long Silence.
Yoshimi. Tanka: "Gloomy rain."
Tanka: "Street, The."
Young, A. Curative Powers of Silence, The.
Yün Shou-p'ing. Through the windy valley.
Zenmaro. Tanka: "In sullen silence."

Silk
Chin Nung. Evening Scene at Twin Forests.
Foster, E. Poetry and Joy.
Herrick. Upon Julia's Clothes.
Horovitz, F. Loving You.
Po Chü-i. Liao-ling[, sheer patterned silk—what is it like?].
Pound, E. Garden, The.
Shange. Elegance in the extreme.
Unknown. Ballad of the Western Island in the North Country.
Old and New ("She went up the mountain to pluck wild herbs").
Wu Chia-chi. To Ch'eng Fei-t'ao.
Yang Wei-chen. Song of the Waterfall at Mount Lu.
Yün Shou-p'ing. Essence of ink, The.
Zhao. Needle and Thread.

Silkworms
Bourne, V. Silkworm, The.
Okamoto. Tanka: "Innately reserved."

Saitō Mokichi. Tanka: "Self-portrait, A."
Stewart, D. Silkworms, The.
Silva, Antonio José da
Blumenthal, W. Da Silva Gives the Cue.
Silver
De la Mare. Silver.
Herbert, Z. Hakeldama.
Simhath Torah
Gordon, J. Simhat Torah.
Rosenfeld, M. Simchas Torah.
Unknown. This Feast of the Law.
Similes. *See* **Metaphor**
Simon of Cyrene
Auden. Luke 23:26–38; And as they led him away.
Cullen, C. Simon the Cyrenian Speaks.
Simplicity
Boethius. Lib. 2. Metrum 5.
Campion, T. Jack and Joan they think no ill.
Chao Meng-fu. Living in Retirement at Te-ch'ing.
Child, A. Wishes.
Claudian. Felix, qui patriis. . . and c.: Imitated from Claudian.
Collins, W. Ode to Simplicity.
Crowell, G. I have found such joy in simple things.
Emerson, R. Poet ("To clothe the fiery thought").
Glazkov. Simple Man, A.
There are actually people who revel.
Gregg. My Father and God.
Hall, D. Clown, The.
Hartman, M. Life's made up of little things.
Herbert, G. Wreathèd garland of deservèd praise, A.
Hoffenstein. Your little hands.
Hopkins, G. Sonnet: "Shepherd's brow, fronting forked lightning, owns, The."
Horace. Ad Ministram.
Boy, I hate their empty shows.
Simplicity.
Isidorus. On a Fowler.
Jonson, B. Simplex Munditiis.
Juan Chi. Tung-ling melons—men say that long ago.
Kendall, M. Lay of the Trilobite, The.
Khlebnikov, V. I need but little! A crust of bread.
Lipkin, S. Conjunction.
Lu Yu. Snug—the robe sewn from coarse cotton.
Lux. Amiel's Leg.
Murry, A. Familiar Epistle, A.
Nash, O. Reflection on Ingenuity.
Newcastle, M. Claspe, The.
P'an Yüeh. Rhyme-Prose on the Idle Life.
Po Chü-i. New thatched hall, five spans by three, A.
Writing Again on the Same Theme.
Prigov. Whenever I live, like simple.
Ransom, J. Captain Carpenter rose up in his prime.
Shelton, M. When Jesus walked upon the earth.
Sidney, P. Sonnet 28: "You that with allegory's curious frame."
Strand. Out here, dwarfed by mountains and a sky of fires.
T'ao Ch'ien. Moving House ("In spring and fall there are many fine days").
Moving House ("Long time I've wanted to live in the southern village, A").
Poem without a Category ("Brave man has ambitions wide as the four seas, The").
Unknown. Han-shan.
Simple Gifts.
Yes, there are stingy people.
Whittemore, R. Clamming.
Wilbur. Baroque Wall-Fountain in the Villa Sciarra, A.
Wordsworth, W. Farmer of Tilsbury Vale, The.
Wright, J. Birds.
Sin
Addison, J. When rising from the bed of death.

Allingham. Girl's Lamentation, The.
Behn, A. And Forgive Us Our Trespasses.
Bernstein, O. Games.
Berryman. Gislebertus' Eve.
Betjeman. Huxley Hall.
Bible, *N.T.* John 3; But Men Loved Darknesse
     Rather than Light.
Blake, W. Was Jesus Chaste? or did he.
Borges. Luke XXIII.
Bradstreet, A. Flesh and the Spirit, The.
Brooks, P. Christmas Everywhere.
Carney. (Little Things).
Carter, M. After One Year.
Chaucer. Pardoner's Tale, The.
Chesterton, G. Ballade D'une Grande Dame.
Clare, J. Sonnet: "Ere I had known the world
     and understood."
Coleridge, S. Spots in the Sun.
Congreve. Song: "Pious Selinda goes to
     prayers."
Coverdale. Let go the whore of Babylon.
Crane, S. From The Black Riders and Other
     Lines.
     I stood upon a high place.
     There Was One I Met [upon the Road].
     You say you are holy.
Crashaw. But Men loved Darknesse[e] Rather
     Than [*or* Then] Light.
Creeley. Kind of Act Of, The.
Cullen, C. For Daughters of Magdalen.
Donne. Flea, The.
     Licentious Person, A.
     Spit in my face ye [*or* you] Jew[e]s, and
     pierce my side.
Drayton. To My Noble Friend Master William
     Browne: Of the Evil Time.
Drummond de Andrade. Dirty Hand, The.
Fumi Saito. Tanka: "Sweeter than a song."
Gergely. Upon a Renaissance Carving.
Gorey. Limerick: "To his club-footed child
     said Lord Stipple."
Gower, J. Among these othre of Slouthes
     kinde.
Greville, F. 99.
Greville, F. Sonnet: "Down[e] in the depth of
     mine iniquity."
Gwynn, R. Snow White and the Seven Deadly
     Sins.
Hecht, A. Pig.
Herbert, G. Agony [*or* Agonie], The.
     Church-Lock and Key.
     Confession.
     Good Friday.
     Judgement.
     Love bade me welcome[: yet my soul drew
     back].
     Sin: "O that I could a sin once see!"
     Sin (1).
     Sin's Round.
     Storm, The.
Herrick. Bell-Man, The.
     Nothing New.
     To God: an Anthem, Sung in the Chapel at
     White-Hall, Before the King.
     To His Conscience.
Hildegard von Bingen. Antiphon for the Holy
     Spirit.
Hine. Destruction of Sodom, The.
Holst-Warhaft. Matthew 5:27–30; You have
     heard that it was said.
Hong, Y. Thunder.
Hughes, L. Madam and the Minister.
Jeffers, R. Original Sin.
Jonson, B. Epode: "Not to know vice at all,
     and keep[e] true state."
     Hymn[e] to God the Father, A.
     Song. To Celia ("Come my Celia, let us
     prove").
Kennedy, X. First Confession.
Kinnell. Last Songs.
Kocan. AIDS, Among Other Things.
Lanier. Now Pontius Pilate is to judge the
     cause.
Lanyer. Our Mother *Eve*, who tasted of the
     Tree.
Larkin, P. High Windows.
Lee-Hamilton. Ipsissimus.

Lindsay, V. Unpardonable Sin, The.
Locke, A. Sin and despair have so possess'd
     my heart.
     So foul is sin and loathsome in thy sight.
Lovelace, R. Mock Charon, A.
Lowell, R. Katherine's Dream.
Lyon, G. Inventing Sin.
MacKay, C. Only a Thought.
Marie-Madeleine. Crucifixa.
     Sappho.
Marvell. Coronet, The.
     Mower Against Gardens, The.
Meynell, A. Two Questions, The.
Miller, V. Adam's Footprint.
Milton. Book IX.
     Higher Argument.
Montale. Precautions.
Moore, M. To a Giraffe.
Moore, T. Argument, An.
     Did Not.
Mullen, H. Muse & Drudge.
Nash, O. Ha! Original Sin!
     Portrait of the Artist as a Prematurely Old
     Man.
     So That's Who I Remind Me Of.
Nemerov. Historical Judas, The.
Niedecker. Museum Man! / I wish he'd take
     Pa's spitbox!, The.
Oliver, M. Old Whorehouse, An.
O'Reilly, J. Lure, The.
Ovid. 'Twas now the mid of Night, when
     Slumbers close.
Pasternak, B. Mary Magdalene (I).
Pembroke, M. Psalm 57: Miserere Mei, Deus.
Philips, K. To the Queen of Inconstancy,
     Regina Collier, in Antwerp.
Pound, E. Canto XLV.
     Semi-private inducement.
Quarles. On Dinah.
     What is the *World?* A great *Exchange* of
     ware.
Rilke. Luke 15:11–19; And he said, "There
     was a man."
Robinson, A. Scape-Goat, The.
Robinson, E. Children of the Night, The.
     Luke 15:20–32; And he arose and came.
     Tavern, The.
Rodgers, W. Lent.
Roseliep. Brushing my sins.
Rossetti, C. Amor Mundi.
     Ash Wednesday.
     World, The.
Sangster, M. Sin of Omission, The.
Saunders, N. Cinderella.
Shakespeare, W. Sonnet 35.
     Sonnet 94.
     Sonnet 119.
Sidney, P. Sonnet 14: "Alas, have I not pain
     enough, my friend."
Skelton, J. So many cloisters closed.
Sorescu. Fresco.
Southwell. Man's Civil[l] War[re].
     Sinnes Heavie Loade.
Spenser. Bower of Bliss, The.
Stanley, T. Ode XV.
Stanley-Wrench. Man in the Moon, The.
Tate, A. Ah, Christ, I love you rings to the
     wild sky.
Tate, N. Lord, Have Mercy.
Taylor, E. Accusation of the Inward Man,
     The.
     State, a state, oh! dungeon state indeed, A.
Tennyson, A. St. Simeon Stylites.
Terapiano. Lights shining above the Neva.
Thomas, D. Incarnate devil in a talking snake.
Thompson, F. To the Dead Cardinal of
     Westminster.
Thomson, J. Once in a saintly passion.
Unknown. Adam Lay Bound.
     Attend, Young Friends, While I Relate.
     Be sure your sin will find you out.
     Elinor Glyn.
     Gospel train is moving, The.
     If I Could Shut the Gate against My Thoughts.
     In *Bath* a wanton wife did dwell.
     Potato Peel.
     Psalm 58.

     Undo!
     Young People Who Delight in Sin.
Vaughan, H. Corruption.
     Idle Verse.
     Rainbow, The.
Very. Robe, The.
     Serpent, The.
Walcott. Crusoe's Island.
Warren, R. Original Sin.
Westmorland. Man Leavens the Batch.
Wilcox, E. Mistakes.
Wilde, O. Ballad of Reading Gaol, The.
     E Tenebris.
     Hélas!
Wratislaw. Orchids.
     White Lilies.
Yosano. Tanka: "Camellias."
     Tanka: "Clear spring, A."

See also **Original Sin; Seven Deadly Sins**

Singing and Singers

Andal. O you who guard over.
Auden. As I walked out one evening.
Bertrand. Mason Abraham Knupfer is singing,
     trowel in hand, scaffolded, The.
Bible, *O.T.* Psalm 100.
Blake, W. Lark's Song, The.
     Laughing Song.
Blok. Girl was singing in the choir with
     fervor, A.
Boccaccio. I am a young maiden, and I
     willingly.
Bogan, L. M., Singing.
Brennen. Spring.
Brooks, G. Kitchenette Building.
Browning, E. Casa Guidi Windows.
Bunting. Brag, sweet tenor bull.
Burns, R. Of a' the airts the wind can blaw.
Campbell, J. I Am the Mountainy Singer.
Campion, T. Laura.
Catullus. Roman Epithalamion.
Chesterton, G. Christmas Carol, A: "God rest
     you merry gentlemen."
Coffin, F. Mother's Songs.
Colonna, V. As a hungry fledgling, who sees
     and hears.
Cook, E. On Seeing a Bird-Catcher.
     Song of the Imprisoned Bird.
Corbière. Toad, The.
Crane, S. Each small gleam was a voice.
Crashaw. Epithalamion.
Creeley. Air: "The Love of a Woman."
Cummings, E. All which isn't singing is mere
     talking.
Davis, D. Linin' ub De Hymns, De.
Davis, T. Zoom (The Commodores).
Day Lewis. Conflict, The.
Di Prima. For the Dead Lecturer.
Dickey, J. Buckdancer's Choice.
     Folk Singer of the Thirties, A.
Dickinson, E. "Hope" is the thing with
     feathers.
     I shall keep singing!
     To hear an Oriole sing.
Dove, R. Canary.
Dunbar, P. Deacon Jones' Grievance.
     Sympathy.
     When Malindy Sings.
Eady. Young Elvis.
"Eliot." Armgart, to many minds the first
     success.
Emerson, R. Saadi.
Evans, M. And the Old Women Gathered.
Fallis. Wise Johnny.
"Fane." Siren, The.
Ferry. Unawkward Singer, The.
Field, E. Christmas Song: "Why do the bells
     for Christmas ring?"
"Field." Fellowship.
     Fifty Quatrains.
     I sing thee with the stock-dove's throat.
     She is singing to Thee, *Domine!*.
Fields, J. Alabama.
Frost, R. Aim Was Song, The.
     Oven Bird, The.
Gibbons, O. Silver swan, who living had no
     note, The.
Gilbert, S. Ko-Ko's Song.

Graves, R. Love without hope, as when the young bird-catcher.

Gray, J. Poem: "Geranium, houseleek, laid in oblong beds."

Grimald. Garden, The.

Hall, D. Blue Wing, The.

Halpern, M. That's Our Lot.

Hardy, T. During Wind and Rain.

Harris, P. Some Songs Women Sing.

Heaney, S. Singer's House, The.

Hemans. To a Wandering Female Singer.

Henderson, D. Song of Devotion to the Forest.

Henley, W. Margaritæ Sorori [I. M.].

Henson, L. I Am Singing the Cold Rain.

Herbert of Cherbury. To a Lady Who Did Sing Excellently.

Herrick. Againe.
 Upon Her Voice.
 Upon Julia's Voice.

Heywood, T. Matin Song.

Hughes, L. I too, sing America.
 Song for Billie Holiday.
 Weary Blues, The.

Hugo, V. Be like the bird, who.

Jackson, A. Billie in Silk.

Jackson, R. Lady's Way.

Jeffers, L. Nina Simone.

Johnson, J. Lift every [or ev'ry] voice and sing.
 O Black and unknown bards of long ago.

Johnson, R. Beam 7.

Jonson, B. And must I sing? What subject shall I choose?
 Musical Strife: in a Pastoral Dialogue, The.

Kinnell. Last Songs.

Kitahara Hakushū. At a hospital in Tokyo during the summer of 1911.

Lalic. King and the Singer, The.

Lawrence, D. Piano.

Le Gallienne. To the Reader.

Lee, L. I Ask My Mother to Sing.

Lewis, R. Mocking Bird, The.

Li K'ai-hsien. On the Cold Food Festival, Entertaining at the Southern Estate—the Guests Were Li Chiu-ho, Ma Nan-yeh, Wei Tung-kao, Li Hu-ch'uan, Huang K'ung-ts'un, Li Lung-t'ang, and Hu Hu-shan.

Livesay, D. Uninvited, The.

Lo Fu. Song of the Cricket.

Lucilius. Eutychides, who wrote the songs.

Luther. In the bonds of Death He lay.

"MacDiarmid." Empty Vessel.
 Water Music.

Marvell. Fair Singer, The.

Mathews, H. At Night, Hearing Someone Singing in the House Next Door.

McCord, D. Blessèd Lord, What It Is to Be Young.

McGirt. Born like the pines to sing.
 My Song.

McPherson, S. Ability to Make a Face Like a Spider While Singing Blues: Junior Wells, The.

Mechthild von Magdeburg. I cannot dance, O Lord.

Meynell, A. Singers to Come.

Miller, V. Dirge in Jazz Time.

Mistral, G. Song.
 Those Who Do Not Dance.

Moore, L. Bluesman's Blues, A.

Moore, L. Spectacular.

Moore, T. Echo.

Morley, T. Sing we and chant it.

Morris, W. Apology, An.

Mother Goose. Tommy Tucker.

Neal, L. Lady's Days.

Nicarchus of Alexandria. Listen! The night-raven's song.

Norris, K. Mrs. Schneider in Church.

Nye, N. Hugging the Jukebox.

O'Hara, F. Day Lady Died, The.

Ono no Komachi. Cicadas sing, The.

O'Shaughnessy, A. Ode: "We are the music-makers."

Ou-yang Hsiu. East Wind.

Parkes, B. For Adelaide.

Pavic. Song: "Rejoice singer of songs for the deaf."

Penny, R. I Remember How She Sang.

Peyanar. Minstrels sing the jasmine songs.

Po Chü-i. Five-string[1], The.
 Hearing the Early Oriole.
 Madly Singing in the Mountains.
 On Hearing Someone Sing a Poem by Yüan Chên.

Pound, E. Cino.

Ramkissoon-Chen. When the Hindu Woman Sings Calypso.

Ravenscroft, T. Sing we now merily.

Reese, L. Singer, The.

Reeves, J. My Singing Aunt.

Robinson, A. Personality.
 Search for Apollo, A.

Rose. Throat Song: The Whirling Earth.

Rosen, K. Castrato.

Rossetti, C. Birthday, A.

Rossetti, D. Willowwood ("I sat with Love upon a woodside well").

Sandburg, C. Splinter.

Sassoon. Everyone Sang.

Schuyler, J. Let's All Hear It for Mildred Bailey!

Schwartz, D. Small Score, A.

Shelley, M. Oh listen while I sing to thee.

Shelley, P. To Jane ("Keen stars were twinkling, The").

Sidney, P. Song: "O fair! O sweet! when I do look on thee."

Skinner, J. Tullochgorum.

Sloan, M. Eccentricity of the Middle Ground.

Smith, I. Gaelic Songs.

Smith, S. Singing Cat, The.

Spenser. Now is this love already forth to come.

Spires. Apology.
 Interrogations of the Sparrow.

Stanley, T. Celia Singing.

Stein, G. I Am Rose [my eyes are blue].

Stevens, W. Idea of Order at Key West, The.

Stevenson, R. Bright is the ring of words.

Sub-ok. Spring at Yesan Station.

Teasdale. Song Making.

Telestes. It was a Phrygian, Pelops.

Thomas, D. In my craft or sullen art.

Tu Fu. Coming Home Late at Night.

Unknown. Silver swan, who living had no note, The.
 Small bird, forgive me.
 Tongue of Wood, The.
 We are a people who love to sing.
 Young Girl in the Choir, The.

Van Vliet. Courtyard, The.

Very. Song, The: "When I would sing of crooked streams and fields."

Wagoner, D. Singing Lesson, The.

Wakoski. Singer, The.

Walker, M. Since 1619.

Wang Chiu-ssu. Chanting Poems.

Whitman, W. Chanting the square deific, out of the One advancing, out of the sides.
 I hear America singing, the varied carols I hear.

Wickham. Silent Singer, The.

Williams, W. Late Singer, The.

Wordsworth, W. Solitary Reaper, The.

Wyatt, T. Fortune.
 Lover Complaineth the Unkindness of His Love, The.

Young, A. Dance For Ma Rainey, A.

Sioux, The

Anderson, J. Rosebud.

Field, E. Sioux, The.

Oliver, M. Ghosts.

Taylor, R. Dakota: October, 1822, Hunkpapa Warrior.

Sirens (mythology)

Atwood. Siren Song.

Browne, W. Sirens' Song, The.

Daniel, S. Ulysses and the Siren [or Syren].

Darley. Mermaidens' Vesper-Hymn, The.

Day Lewis. Nearing Again the Legendary Isle.

"Fane." Siren, The.

Killigrew, A. Farewel to Worldly Joyes, A ("Farewel to unsubstantial joyes").

Manifold. Sirens, The.

Wilbur. Merlin Enthralled.

Sirens (warning devices)

Ackland. Winter.

Le Bel. Foot Fire Burn Dance.

Wilbur. Fire-Truck, A.

Sisera

Gouri. His Mother.

Guri. His Mother.

Sisters

Aldis, D. Little.

Anderson, L. Red Hot.

Barker, G. My sister Clarissa spits twice if I kiss her.

Belševica. That was a very polite fish.

Bogan, L. Sleeping Fury, The.

Bruce, D. Sonnet 2: "Deep in her seventh month, my sister dozes."

Byron, G. Epistle to Augusta.

Campbell, R. Sisters, The.

"Carroll." Brother and Sister.

Causley. What has happened to Lulu, mother?

Doty, M. Bill's Story.

"Eliot." Long years have left their writing on my brow.

Fisher, R. Funny Folk.

Glück, L. Descending Figure.

Grogan. Elizabeth, Listening.

Howe, M. Split, The.

Jacobsen, J. Sisters, The.

Kamienska. Saint Martha.

Kinnell. Two Set Out on Their Journey.

Leib. In little hands she holds an open book.

Lochhead, L. Grim Sisters, The.

McCullers. Slumber Party.

McGinley. Triolet Against Sisters.

McGuckian. Sitting, The.

McPherson, S. Sisters.

Millay, E. Night is my sister, and how deep in love.

Montale. Eel, the siren, The.

Nastasijevic. To My Dead Sister.

Olds, S. Elder Sister, The.
 Indictment of Senior Officers.
 Sisters of Sexual Treasure, The.

Peeradina, S. Sisters.

Rich, A. Women.

Rossetti, C. Noble Sisters.

Sachs, N. O sister, / where do you pitch your tent?

Sherman, C. Roots.

Sitwell, D. Waltz.

Song. Lost Sister.

Szymborska. In Praise of My Sister.

Tu Fu. I have a sister, little sister, living in Chung-li.

Unknown. Brotherless Sisters.
 Down to the Mire.
 Folk Song.
 Riddling Knight, The.
 Two Sisters, The.

Verlaine. Pensionnaires.

Whittier. Sisters, The.

Williams, S. I never thought to see us.

Wood, R. Cabbages.

Wright, J. Sisters, The.

Yüan Mei. Returning Home.

Sistine Chapel

Michelangelo Buonarroti. To Giovanni da Pistoia When the Author Was Painting the Vault of the Sistine Chapel, 1509.

Sisyphus

Glück, L. Mountain, The.

Mahon. Death and the Sun.

Miles, J. Sisyphus.

Sitting Bull (Sioux Chief)

Neihardt. III. THE COUNCIL ON THE POWDER.

Sitwell, Dame Edith

Brinnin. Thin Façade for Edith Sitwell, A.

Coward. Contours.

Skateboarding and Skateboarders

Morrison, L. Sidewalk Racer Or, On the Skateboard, The.

See also **Roller-Skating and Roller-Skaters**

Skating and Skaters
Atwood. Woman Skating.
Berssenbrugge. Swan, The.
Blunden. Midnight Skaters, The.
Conn. Under the Ice.
Daiches. To Kate, Skating Better than Her Date.
Fletcher, J. Skaters, The.
Livingston, M. 74th Street.
Mother Goose. Three children sliding on the ice.
Roberts, S. Skater, The.
Rukeyser, M. Boys of These Men Full Speed.
Rutsala. Skaters.
Unknown. Three children sliding on the ice.
Wordsworth, W. Skating.

See also **Roller-Skating and Roller-Skating; Skateboarding and Skateboarding**

Skeletons
Alexie. Evolution.
Hartnett. All that is left and definite.
Longfellow, H. Skeleton in Armor [*or* Armour], The.
Lovelace, R. La Bella Bona-Roba.
Samio. Tanka: "Fish skeleton, A."
Shorter. Skeleton in the Cupboard, The.
Smith, L. Skeleton House.
Turner, C. Lion's Skeleton, The.
Unknown. Thin Flynn.
Vardhill. To a Skeleton.
Wright, J. On the Skeleton of a Hound.

See also **Bones**

Skepticism. *See* **Doubt**

Skiing and Skiers
Logan, J. White Pass Ski Patrol.
Merrill, J. Up and Down.
Page, P. T-Bar.
Wrigley, R. Ravens at Deer Creek.

Skin
Brown, R. This is no baby skin—.
Dransfield. Epiderm.
Eimers. Night Without Stars, A.
Ellis, S. Weathered Ides Grant Young Flesh.
Lorde. Hanging Fire.
Mudrooroo. Song Thirty-Four.
Perillo. Skin.
Rosenberg, L. In the End We Are All Light.
Sadoff. Bath, The.
Strong, G. Modern Hiawatha, The.
T'ang Hsien-tsu. Inspector Hsü Claims He Has Found the Secret of Youth.
Thomas, L. Subway Witnesses, The.
Waldman, A. Skin / Meat / BONES.
Welish. Skin.
Wratislaw. Frangipani.
Wright, J. Skins.
Yukitsuna. Tanka: "Changing."
Zimmer. Failings, The.

Skulls
Bancquart. Baroque.
Chế Lan Viên. Human Skull, The.
Dodson, O. Yardbird's Skull.
Fumi Saito. Tanka: "Water streams."
"MacDiarmid." Perfect.
Pitter. Sparrow's Skull, The.
Scott, W. U. S. Sailor with the Japanese Skull, The.
Tollet. On a Death's Head.

Skunks
Dow, P. Skunk, The.
Heaney, S. Skunk, The.
Lowell, R. Skunk Hour.
Miles, J. Bureau 2.

Sky
Aborigine Oral Tradition. Tongues of the lightning Snakes flicker and twist, one to the other, The.
Addison, J. Ode: "Spacious firmament on high, The."
Alexander, E. Ode.
Ashbery. Poem: "While we were walking under the top."
Bazil. Uncertain Admission.
Bevington, L. Measurements.
Bobrowski. Place of Fire.

Bognini. Earth and sky are infinities / Where our cries cannot venture.
Bonnefoy. Top of the World, The.
Bostok. Foetus kicks.
Bridges, R. Sky's unresting cloudland, that with varying play, The.
Byron, G. She walks in Beauty like the night.
Carrier, C. Prospect Before Us, The.
"Carroll." Mad Hatter's Song, The.
Chōkū. Tanka: "Which child."
Vultures—in the midst of war.
Cole, W. Back Yard, July Night.
Crawford, I. Battle, A.
Cummings, E. If up's the word;and a world grows greener.
Daive. Space instead of furniture.
Under the wind I saw.
De la Mare. Rainbow, The.
De Mello Breyner. Day of sea in the sky, made.
Dickinson, E. Brain—is wider than the Sky, The.
Lightly stepped a yellow star.
Of Bronze—and Blaze.
Dorn, E. Song, A.
Dove, R. Teach Us to Number Our Days.
Eigner. Back to it.
In Imitation.
Elmusa. Little Piece of Sky, A.
Fisher, A. Moles.
Fitzgerald, E. 72.
Fumiko. Tanka: "With a thunderous crack."
Galvin, B. Green Evening, A.
García Lorca. Below.
Swath.
Gardner, D. Fire Music.
Gilbert, C. Directions, The.
Grimké, A. For the Candle Light.
Harries, N. Dog-watch.
Harwood, L. Final Painting, The.
Words, The.
Henderson, D. Horizon Blues.
Herlin. Morning space expands the building's.
Red round sun, The.
Sky has recovered its haze-blue tints, The.
Higginson, W. Summer moon.
Holub. On the Origin of the Contrary.
Howe, F. Scattered Light.
Hsieh Chin. Poem on a Little Pine, A.
Ignatow, D. Sky Is Blue, The.
Ivask, Y. Shall we forget the shiver.
Kaplinski, J. We started home, my son and I.
Kenward. Technicians.
Kinnell. Daybreak.
Kitching. No need to scan the skies.
Kizer, C. On a Line from Valéry.
Lauterbach. Subject to Change.
Letts. Irish Skies.
Levchev. Appassionato.
Levertov. Clouds as I see them, rising, The.
Li Ch'ing-chao. "Fisherman's Honor," The.
Lion-Face. KYE HO! Wonderful!
Liu E. On the Night of the Sixteenth of the Eighth Month: Watching the Moon from the Deck of the Ship, Aimo-maru in the Black Water Sea.
Lloyd, D. Duck feathers.
Madge. On One Condition.
Mansour, J. Beyond the breakers.
Masaoka Shiki. Tanka: "Peacefully."
Merrill, J. Upward Look, An.
Miyazawa Kenji. Tanka: "At last."
Tanka: "Like cracks."
Tanka: "Plucked, The."
Tanka: "Silver greeting."
Tanka: "Unsettled."
Mori Ōgai. Tanka: "Under the blue sky."
Nagy, A. Between.
Four-Light Window, A.
Neruda. Ode to the Watermelon.
Nichol. Monotones.
Nichols, G. Sky.
Norris, K. Sky Is Full of Blue and Full of the Mind of God, The.
Petrarch. Now that the sky and earth and wind are still.
Pien Kung. Song of the Boat-Pullers.

Popa. Burning Shewolf.
Posey, A. Nightfall.
Rabéarivelo. Black glassmaker, The.
Hide of the black cow is stretched, The.
Radauskas. Arrow in the Sky.
Star, Sun, Moon.
Radnóti. Clouded Sky.
Ray, H. Sky Picture.
Reavey. How many fires.
Rilke. Once the realization is accepted that even between the closest people.
Roberts, E. Sky, The.
Roberts, G. Night Sky, The.
Robinson, K. Nursery Rhyme.
Root, J. Small Differences.
Roseliep. Sky.
Rummo. Sky bends over the earth, The.
Sandburg, C. Be Ready.
Love in Labrador.
People, Yes, The.
Shapiro, D. Commentary Text Commentary Text Commentary Text.
Shelton, R. Because the Moon Comes.
Shen Chou. Moon in a Winecup, The.
So Chong-ju. Winter Sky.
Stevens, W. Candle a Saint, The.
Stevenson, R. Swing, The.
Wind, The.
Strnisa. Ship, A.
Tadamichi. As I row over the plain.
Taylor, J. Star, The.
Tewa Oral Tradition. Song of the Sky Loom.
Traherne. To the same purpose: he, not long before.
Turberville. Lover to His Lady, The.
Turner, F. Spring Evening.
Unknown. I'm glad the sky is painted blue.
International Chainpoem.
Red sky at night.
Warren, R. Sky.
Timeless, Twinned.
Welish. Within This Book, Called Marguerite.
Whitman, W. On the beach at night.
On the beach at night alone.
Wilson, R. Davy by Starlight.
Yang Chi. Pitch-Ball.
Yau. Engines of Gloom and Affection.
Yü Chi. When I Was Young, I Stopped by a Wine Shop in Chi-men and Wrote This Poem, Inscribed It and Signed It, "Written by Lien the Eighteenth." The People of That District Have Since Taken It To Be a Poem of [the God] Lü Tung-pin! I Have Recorded It Here as an Amusement.
Zach. Problem, The.
Zhenkai. Collection, The.

See also **Constellations; Stars**

Sky Diving and Sky Divers
Anderson, J. Parachutist, The.

Skye, Isle of, Scotland
Revard. October, Isle of Skye.

Skylarks. *See* **Larks**

Skyscrapers
Corso. Ode to Coit Tower.
Field, R. Skyscrapers.
Fletcher, J. Monadnock, The.
Glanz-Leyeles. Madison Square.
Hirsch, E. For the New World.
When Skyscrapers Were Invented in Chicago.
Lee, D. Skyscraper, skyscraper.
Sandburg, C. Prayers of Steel.
Skyscraper.
Yolen. Sky scrape, / City scape.

Slander
"Akhmatova." Slander.
Shakespeare, W. Sonnet 70.
Sonnet 140.
Yeats. He Thinks of Those Who Have Spoken Evil of His Beloved.

Slaughter of the Innocents. *See* **Massacre of the Innocents**

Slaughterhouses
Alexander, M. Chicago.
Hayes, A. Slaughter-House, The.
Kinsella, T. Point, greatly enlarged, The.
Troupe. River Town Packin House Blues.

Slavery
Abu Dulama. Traders in Beauty and Delight.
"Ada." Lines: "From fair Jamaica's fertile plains."
Agard, J. Pan Recipe.
Alexander, E. Passage.
Ba. Nobility.
Baraka. Wise 5.
Barbauld. Epistle to William Wilberforce, Esq., on the Rejection of the Bill for Abolishing the Slave Trade.
Barlow, J. Columbiad, The.
Bennett, G. To a Dark Girl.
Bierce. Hesitating Veteran, The.
Bland, J. Carry me back to old Virginny.
Bly, R. Hearing Men Shout at Night on MacDougal Street.
Brathwaite, E. New World A-Comin'.
Brown, S. Bitter Fruit of the Tree.
Strong Men.
Browning, E. Hiram Powers' "Greek Slave."
Runaway Slave at Pilgrim's Point, The.
Brutus. There was a time when the only worth.
Bryant, W. African Chief, The.
Death of Slavery, The.
Cable, G. Dirge of St. Malo, The.
English muskets went bim! bim!, The.
Campbell, A. Lines: "Wake not again the cannon's thundrous voice."
Campbell, R. Serf, The.
Campbell, T. On Slavery.
Carey, H. Sally in Our Alley.
Chapman, M. African Dirge.
Clifton, L. At the Cemetery, Walnut Grove Plantation, South Carolina, 1989.
Slave Cabin, Sotterly Plantation, Maryland, 1989.
Coicou. Slave's Lament, The.
Cornish, S. Cross Over the River.
Cowper, W. Negro's Complaint, The.
Sweet Meat Has Sour Sauce.
To William Wilberforce, Esq.
Crouch, S. Chops Are Flyin.
Dabydeen, D. Slave Song.
Damas. Black Man's Lament, The.
Shine.
They came that night as the.
Whitewash.
Daryush. Invalid Dawn.
Davidson, D. Sequel of Appomattox.
Dent. Return to English Turn.
Depestre. Black Ore.
Dickey, J. Slave Quarters.
Diop, D. Africa my Africa.
Suffer, Poor Negro!
Those Who Lost Everything.
Vultures, The.
Douglass, F. Middle Passage.
Dove, R. Adolescence—I.
House Slave, The.
Dunbar, P. Ante-Bellum Sermon, An.
Old Cabin, The.
Sympathy.
Emerson, R. Boston Hymn.
Faleti. Independence.
Freneau. To Sir Toby.
Fyodorov. Servile Blood.
Glissant. Child climbs to the island's highest point, The.
One of them, taking advantage of the crew's momentary carelessness.
They fastened a people to merchant ships.
Grainger, J. On festal days; or when their work is done.
Slaves.
Greenwell, D. Broken Chain, The.
Greville, F. Sonnet 78: "Little Hearts, where light-wing'd Passion raignes, The."
Griffin, S. I like to think of Harriet Tubman.
Hacker, M. Part of a True Story.
Hamilton, M. For My Father's Mother Who Has Alzheimer's.
Harper, F. Bible Defence of Slavery.
Bury Me in a Free Land.
Free Labor.
Lines: "At the Portals of the Future."

She's Free!
Slave Auction, The.
Slave Mother, The.
Harper, M. American History.
Makin' Jump Shots.
Harris, J. Aphorisms.
Plantation Proverbs.
Hayden, R. Ballad of Nat Turner, The.
Frederick Douglass.
Middle Passage.
Runagate Runagate.
Henry, P. Is life so dear, or peace so sweet.
Hoagland, E. Gorée ten miles offshore beckons.
Holly. Patriot's Lament, The.
Horton, G. Division of an Estate.
On Hearing of the Intention of a Gentleman to Purchase the Poet's Freedom.
On Liberty and Slavery.
Slave's Complaint, The.
Hsü Chung-hsing. How brave the peasant who lives beside the lake.
Hughes, L. Aunt Sue's Stories.
Iman. Love Your Enemy.
Jeffers, L. Nina Simone.
On Listening to the Spirituals.
Trellie.
Johnson, J. Brothers.
Jolobe. Making of a Servant, The.
Jordan, J. Speculations on the Present through the Prism of the Past.
Kendrick, D. Sidney, Looking for her Mother.
Kgositsile. To Mother.
Kipling, R. Galley-Slave, The.
Song of the Galley-Slaves.
Komunyakaa. Back Then.
Ku K'uang. Sonny grows up in Fukien.
Leadbelly. Take this hammer, (huh!) carry it to the captain, (huh!).
Lindsay, V. Simon Legree—A Negro Sermon.
Longfellow, H. Slave's Dream, The.
Warning, The.
Lorde. Between Ourselves.
Madhubuti. Long Reality, The.
Primitive, The.
Marino. Beautiful Slave, The.
McElroy, C. Gra'ma was a little bit of a thing.
Woman's Song, A.
McKay, C. Enslaved.
In Bondage.
Melville, H. Formerly a Slave.
Misgivings.
Miller, E. Tomorrow.
Moorer. Emancipation Day.
Must Be Freed.
Peonage System, The.
More, H. From The Slave Trade.
Perish th' illiberal thought which would debase.
Slavery.
Sorrows of Yamba, or the Negro Woman's Lamentation, The.
Moreton. Ballad: "Altho' a slave me is born and bred."
Morris, M. House-Slave, The.
Nesbit, E. Wife of All Ages, The.
Neto. Grieved lands of Africa, The.
Niedecker. Will You Write Me a Christmas Poem?
Nobuyuki. Humans Bought and Sold (two poems).
Oppenheim. Slave, The.
Patterson, R. Black Power.
Pereira. Mother Dark.
Pfeiffer, E. Peace to the odalisque, the facile slave.
Pheraios. War Hymn.
Pierpont, J. Fugitive Slave's Apostrophe to the North Star, The.
Plato. To the First of August.
Plumpp. Remembered.
Turf Song.
Po Chü-i. Losing a Slave-Girl.
Randall, D. Southern Road, The.
Robinson, E. Sonnet: "Master and the slave go hand in hand, The."

Rochester, J. To My More Than Meritorious Wife.
Rogers, E. Law! what is law? The wise and sage.
Roumain. Negro peddler of revolt.
Rowe, G. His Ancestry.
Sandburg, C. Osawatomie.
Schwartz, D. Winter Twilight, Glowing Black and Gold, The.
Scott, D. Epitaph: "They hanged him on a clement morning, swung."
Seymour, A. First of August.
Slaves / Humming in the twilight by the shanty door.
Sigourney. To the First Slave Ship.
Simpson, J. To the White People of America.
Skeeter. California, 1852.
Smith, G. Penitential Cries of Jupiter Hammond, The.
Tate, A. Times have changed, there is not left to us, The.
Tati-Loutard. Pilgrimage to Loango Strand.
Voices, The.
Thompson, P. Address to Ethiopia.
Favorite Slave's Story, The.
Fugitive, The.
Husband's Return, The.
Prayer, A: "Oh, Lord! I lift my heart."
Tindal. Cry of the Oppressed, The.
Tirolien. Marie Galante.
Tolson. Dark Symphony.
Toomer. Song of the Son.
Unknown. And can the muse reflect her tear-stain'd eye.
Flying Cloud, The.
Go down, Moses.
Jack and Dinah Want Freedom.
Johnny come down de hollow.
Let My People Go.
Many Thousand Gone.
Me and My Captain.
No more auction block for me.
Pick a Bale of Cotton.
Promises of Freedom.
Run, Nigger, Run!
Slavery chain done broke at last, broke at last, broke at last.
Song to the Runaway Slave.
Song: "We raise de wheat."
Steal Away to Jesus.
Take this hammer—huh!
Wild Negro Bill.
Very. Fugitive Slaves, The.
Slavery.
Walker, A. Early Losses: a Requiem.
Walker, M. Since 1619.
Wang Chiu-ssu. Ballad of Selling a Child.
Waniek. Chosen.
Wheatley, P. No more, America, in mournful strain.
On Being Brought from Africa to America.
To the Right Honourable William, Earl of Dartmouth[, His Majesty's Principal Secretary of State for North America].
Whitfield. From America.
Whitman, A. I never was a slave—a robber took.
In the House of the Aylors.
Lute of Afric's Tribe, The.
Whittier. Clerical Oppressors.
Farewell, The: "Gone, gone,—sold and gone."
For Rightcousness' Sake.
Haschish, The.
Hunters of Men, The.
Ichabod[!].
Official Piety.
Song of Slaves in the Desert.
Williams, S. I Sing This Song for Our Mothers: Ruise.
Work. Kingdom Coming.
Wright, J. Sketch for an Aesthetic Project.
Yearsley. Poem on the Inhumanity of the Slave Trade, A.

Sleds. See **Sleighs**

Sleep
Ackland. Fanny Brawne's Letter Put

Unopened In Keats's Coffin.
When I have said 'I love you' I have said.
Al-Harizi. Lightning, The.
"Aleichem." Sleep, My Child.
Alexie. Reservation Love Song.
Allott. Statue, The.
Alma-Tadema, L. Bed-Time.
Amann. Quietly dozing.
Ames, B. Country of Water.
Ammuvanar. What She Said ("Friend, listen").
Atwood. Variation on the Word *Sleep*.
Auden. Lullaby: "Din of work is subdued, The."
Awoonor. Song of War.
Songs of Sorrow.
Bekederemo. Child Asleep, A.
Bernstein, O. Nocturnal Journey.
What She Didn't Say.
Berrigan, T. Things To Do in Providence.
Bible, *O.T.* Song: "Come, my beloved."
Song: "I was asleep but my heart stayed awake."
Bishop, E. Lullaby for the Cat.
Sleeping on the Ceiling.
Unbeliever, The.
Blair, R. New Dawn, A.
Blake, W. Cradle Song, A: "Sweet dreams form a shade."
Little Girl Found, The.
Bly, R. Waking from Sleep.
Breytenbach. Sleep my little love.
Brontë, C. Is this my tomb, this humble stone.
Brontë, E. Song: "Linnet in the rocky dells, The."
Broumas, O. Sleeping Beauty.
Browning, E. Sleep, The.
Browning, R. Bad Dreams.
Brush. Waiting for the End of the War.
Bunin. It was near midnight when I entered.
Burns, R. Flow gently, sweet Afton, among thy green braes.
Simmer's a pleasant time.
Campion, T. Come, Cheerful Day!
It fell on a summer's [*or* sommers'] day.
Sleep, angry beauty, sleep, and fear[e] not me.
Carmi. She sleeps: yet is her hand awake.
Carryl, C. Sleepy Giant, The.
Causley. Tom Bone.
Celan. All those sleep shapes, crystalline.
Chang Yü. Reading the Poetry Collection of Lü Fang-ch'ing.
Ch'ien T'ao. Shady, shady the wood in front of the Hall;.
Chikako. On this summer night.
Chivers. To Isa Sleeping.
Clifton, L. Women You Are Accustomed To, The.
Clouts. Sleeper, The.
Coleridge, M. 'But in that Sleep of Death what Dreams may Come?'.
Coleridge, S. If I had but two little wings.
Pains of Sleep, The.
Cooper, J. My young mother, her face narrow.
Cornford, F. At Night.
Cox, M. Sleep Apnea.
Word, The.
Crinagoras. Left and right, I toss about my bed.
Cuddihy. This Body.
Cullen, C. Night Rain.
Cummings, E. If you can't eat you got to.
White guardians of the universe of sleep.
Daniel, S. Sonnet: "Care-charmer Sleep[e], son[ne] of the sable night."
De la Mare. Galliass, The.
Nod.
Sleeper, The.
Derricotte. Touching/Not Touching: My Mother.
Djagarov. Night.
Donne. Good-Morrow, The.
Song: "Sweetest love, I do not go[e]."
Dor. Before sleep Baba arranges extra.
Douglas, L. To Sleep.
Dowson. Spleen.
Drayton. Night and Day.
Drummond, W. Sonet to Sleepe.

Dudley, M. Lulling me to sleep.
Dufault. First Night, A.
Dunbar, P. Ere sleep comes down to soothe the weary eyes.
Duncan, R. Sleep is a Deep and Many Voiced Flood.
Eigner. For Sleep.
Ellis, R. Hour of Sleep, The.
Éluard, P. To Her of Whom They Dream.
Elytis. Sleep of the Brave, The.
Erdrich. I Was Sleeping Where the Black Oaks Move.
Espada. Sleeping on the Bus.
Farjeon, E. Good Night.
Ned.
Fearing. Evening Song.
Field, E. Rock-a-by Lady, The.
Sugar-Plum Tree, The.
Wynken, Blynken and Nod one night.
"Field." And on My Eyes Dark Sleep by Night.
Finch, A. For Grizzel McNaught (1709–1792).
Fletcher, J. Sleep Song.
Foix. When I Sleep, Then I See Clearly.
Forbes, C. Dark Mirror.
Picture of a Man.
Ford, C. Desire to be in Two Places at Once, The.
Foscolo. To Evening.
Francis, R. While I slept, while I slept and the night grew colder.
František. Honeycomb of Bees, The.
Frost, R. Stopping by Woods on a Snowy Evening.
Fumi Saito. Tanka: "In my possession."
Fumiko. Tanka: "For this."
Tanka: "In search of a shore."
Gallagher, T. Under Stars.
Galvin, B. Old Trip by Dream Train, The.
Garland, H. Boyish sleep.
Gates, E. Sleep Sweet.
Goethe. To Belinda.
Goll, I. Your sleep is a closed almond.
Graham, J. In the Hotel.
Grass. Music for Brass.
Graves, R. Death Grapple, The.
She tells her love while half asleep.
Griffin, B. Sleep.
Gunn, T. For Signs.
Touch.
Hadas, R. Mars and Venus.
Haines, J. Sleep.
Harrison, J. Lullaby for a Daughter.
Harryman. That Can Not Be Taken Away From It.
Hasford. Bedtime Story.
Hawaiian Oral Tradition. Here all seeking is over.
Henson, L. Sleep Watch.
Herrick. Bellman, The.
Epitaph upon a Virgin, An.
To Daisies, Not to Shut So Soon[e].
Upon a child.
Upon Mistress Elizabeth Wheeler under the Name of Amarillis.
Hogan, L. Our Houses.
Holan. From Untitled.
Hollo. On the occasion of becoming an echo.
Hood, T. Good Night.
Housman, A. When the Eye of Day Is Shut.
Howe, S. Bride's Day.
Hughes, L. Morning After.
Weary Blues, The.
Hughes, T. Bear, The.
Roger the Dog.
Hummer, T. Where You Go When She Sleeps.
Ichijitsu. Snow falls and falls, The.
Imbs. Sleep.
Issa. Cat, The.
Jenner, H. My Savior, hear my prayer.
Joyce, J. I hear an army charging upon the land.
Juana Inés de la Cruz. Because my Lord was born to suffer.
Kanemasa. Guardian of the gate.
K'ang Hai. Listening to the Rain.

Kannan. What Her Girl Friend Said to Him.
Kao Ch'i. Going Out to the Country on a Boat Trip, Sheltering from Rain Beneath a Tree.
Nodding Off.
Keats. Then by the bed-side, where the faded moon.
To Sleep.
Kenyon, J. 4 Often.
Kinnell. After Making Love We Hear Footsteps.
Little Sleep's-Head Sprouting Hair in the Moonlight.
Kinsella, T. Endymion.
Kinzie. Want, predation, sleep.
Kipling, R. City of Sleep, The.
Knott. Death.
Kocbek. Dialectics.
Koch, K. Sleeping with Women.
Kooser. Child Frightened by a Thunderstorm.
Kumin, M. After Love.
Kunitz, S. Science of the Night, The.
Kushner, A. And if you sleep, and if the sheets are clean.
Lauterbach. Boy Sleeping.
Lear, E. Limerick: "There was an Old Man who supposed."
Levertov. Cat as Cat, The.
Luther. Cradle Hymn.
Ma Chih-yüan. To the Tune "Shui hsien-tzu."
MacLeish. Words in Time.
MacNeice. Cradle Song: "Clock's untiring fingers wind the wool of darkness, The."
Madhubuti. Coming of Teddy Bears, The.
You Too Lie down.
Masaoka Shiki. All the hot night.
Tanka: "Peacefully."
Masefield. Sea-Fever.
Matthews, M. Realarro.
Maxton. Elegies.
Mayer, B. Sonnet: "Beauty of songs your absence I should not show."
McCullers. Slumber Party.
McDaniel, J. Following Her to Sleep.
Melville, H. Bench of Boors, The.
Meredith, G. Modern Love.
Merrill, J. About the Phoenix.
Mew. Not for that city of the level sun.
Mihalic. Morning Roar of the City, The.
Miller, V. Aubade: "I press against the emptiness."
Mourning, A.
Miller, W. Willie Winkie.
Mirabai. O friends, I am mad.
Miyazawa Kenji. Siwashing it out once in Siuslaw Forest.
Mole, J. Trick, The.
Monsour. Dream of Dying, A.
Moore, L. Again.
Moore, M. Peter.
Moore, T. Oft in the stilly night.
Mori Ōgai. Tanka: "Frolicking."
Morley, C. Plumpuppets, The.
Mother Goose. Come, let's to bed.
Diddle, diddle, dumpling, my son John.
To sleep easy at night.
Nash, O. Sweet Dreams.
Neruda. Cat's Dream.
Niedecker. Subliminal.
O'Hara, F. Sleeping on the Wing.
Oliver, M. Sleeping in the Forest.
Ondaatje. For you I have slept.
Owen, G. Half asleep.
Oxenham. Sacrament of Sleep, The.
Padgett, R. December.
Parun. Sleeping Youth.
Paschen. Litany.
Pastan. At the Train Museum.
Patchen. Naked Land, The.
Patmore, C. Across the sky the daylight crept.
Paz. Last Dawn.
Philips, A. To Miss Charlotte Pulteney in Her Mother's Arms.
Pinkney, E. Serenade: "Look out upon the stars, my love."
Piombino. My Lady Carries Stones.
Po Chü-i. After Getting Drunk, Becoming

Sober in the Night.
Dreaming of Yüan Chên.
Last Poem.
On the Way to Hangchow: Anchored on the River at Night.
Sleeping on Horseback.
Poole, E. Last Prayer.
Popa. Yawn of Yawns, The.
Porumbacu. Farther Away.
Prudentius. Hymn Before Sleep.
Rabéarivelo. Here is.
   There you are.
Rakovszky. Difficulties of Falling Asleep.
Ransom, J. Janet Waking.
Ratcliffe, S. Beginning in the light as heard, wheel on stone.
Ravenscroft, T. Belmans Song, A.
Reid, A. Spell for Sleeping, A.
Rochester, J. Song: "Absent from thee, I languish still."
Roethke. Root Cellar.
   Waking, The.
Ronsard. Time to be up, Marie, young sleepyhead!
Rossetti, C. Chill, A.
Rossetti, D. Nuptial Sleep.
Rotella, A. In the guest room.
Sanchez, S. Poem at Thirty.
Sandburg, C. Wind Song.
   Work Gangs.
Sappho. Cool Retreat, A.
Sassoon. Falling Asleep.
Saxe, J. Early Rising.
Schwartz, D. O Child, Do Not Fear the Dark and Sleep's Dark Possession.
Seeger, A. Rendezvous, The.
Seth. All you who sleep tonight.
Seward. Invocation, To the Genius of Slumber Written Oct. 1787.
Sonnet 13.
Sexton. Three Green Windows.
Sidney, P. Second Song: "Have I caught my heav'nly jewel."
Sleep.
   Sonnet 39: "Come Sleep, O Sleep."
Smith, C. To Sleep.
Smith, I. Towards the Stars.
Smith, M. Asleep in the City.
Smith, S. Goodnight.
Smith, W. Moon.
Sorescu. Historiotherapy.
Soupault. You Who Sleep.
Spender, S. Daybreak.
Stevenson, A. Marriage, The.
Stevenson, R. Bed in Summer.
   Escape at Bedtime.
   Good Boy, A.
   Land of Nod, The.
   My Bed Is a Boat.
   Time to Rise.
   Young Night Thought.
Stillman, M. Lullaby for Suzanne.
Swenson, M. Sand, The.
   Sleeping with Boa.
Swinburne. Garden of Proserpine, The.
   Love And Sleep.
Tennyson, A. Lullaby: "Sweet and low, sweet and low."
Thelwall. To the Infant Hampden. Written during a Sleepless Night.
Thomas, E. Lights Out.
Toomer. Evening Song.
Tranter. Moment of Waking, The.
Unknown. All Through the Night.
   Chinese Sandmen.
   Early to bed and early to rise.
   Evening Prayer, An.
   Go to bed late.
   How They Sleep.
   I sleep alone.
   Lullaby: "My little baby sleeps, the little birds sleep."
   Lullaby: "Sleep, baby, sleep."
   Now I lay me down to sleep.
   Sleep, baby, sleep.
   Song: "Let not the sluggish sleep."

Ti-ch'ü Song Words.
   Weep you no more, sad fountains.
Valentine, J. After Elegies.
Van Doren. Sleep, grandmother, sleep.
Vaughan, H. Evening-Watch, The.
Virgil. Sleep.
Voznesensky. Dead Still.
Wallace, R. 1001 Nights.
Wang Chiu-ssu. Recording My Happiness.
Wang Yen-Shou. Nightmare, The.
Warner, S. Drawing you, heavy with sleep to lie closer.
Warren, R. Better Than Counting Sheep.
Warton, T. Come, gentle sleep, death's image though thou art.
Watson, R. Nirvana.
Webb, F. Gunner, The.
   Port Phillip Night.
Weigl. Confusion of Planes We Must Wander in Sleep, The.
Wen Cheng-ming. Evening Bell from a Misty Temple.
Whitlow. Book of Routh.
Wigglesworth. Wallowing in all kind of sin.
Wilbur. After the last bulletins the windows darken.
   Beasts in their major freedom / Slumber in peace tonight.
   In Limbo.
   In the Smoking-Car.
   Walking to Sleep.
Willard, E. Rocked in the Cradle of the Deep.
Williams, W. Goodnight, A.
Winters, Y. Precision, The.
Wordsworth, D. Cottager to Her Infant, (By My Sister), The.
Wordsworth, W. Slumber *did* my spirit *seal,* A.
   To Sleep ("Flock of sheep that leisurely pass by, A").
   To Sleep ("Fond words have oft been spoken to thee, sleep!")
   To Sleep ("O gentle Sleep! do they belong to thee").
Wu Wei-yeh. Song to the Tune "Perching Crows."
Ye. All night I could not sleep.
Yeats. Lullaby: "Beloved, may your sleep be sound."
Yevtushenko. Sleep, My Beloved.
Yolen. Troll to her Children, The.
Yondo. Lullaby.
Yosano. Uguisu has not come, The.
Yün Shou-p'ing. In a hidden spot on the northern mountain.

Sleeping Beauty
Unknown. Fair Rosa was a lovely child.

Sleepwalking and Sleepwalkers. *See*
   Somnambulism and Somnambulists

Sleet
MacCaig. Sleet.
Tate, J. Dear Reader.

Sleighs
Haines, J. Snowbound City, The.
Rogers, P. Possible Salvation of Continuous Motion, The.

Slides
Farber. For a Quick Exit.

Sligo. *See* **County Sligo, Ireland**

Sloth
Roethke. Sloth, The.
Watts, I. Sluggard, The.

Sloths
Adcock, F. Three-toed sloth is the slowest creature we know, The.
Roethke. Sloth, The.

Slough, England
Betjeman. Slough.

Slugs
Birney. Slug in Woods.
Clarke, P. My name is Sluggery-wuggery.
Olds, S. Connoisseuse of Slugs, The.
Redgrove, P. Negotium Perambulans.
Roethke. Slug.
Willard, N. Speckled Hen's Morning Song to Biddy Early, The.

See also **Snails**

Slums
Acorn. On Saint-Urbain Street.
Brooks, G. Lovers of the Poor, The.
Campbell, G. In the Slums.
Daryush. You should at times go out.
Davies, W. Rat, The.
Dove, R. Teach Us to Number Our Days.
Goulbourne. This Is the Place Where.
Hayden, R. Summertime and the Living.
Ignatow, D. East Bronx.
   Get the Gasworks.
Joans. Scenery.
Johnson, J. Judeebug's Country.
Jordan, N. Feeding the Lions.
"MacDiarmid." Reflections in a Slum.
Olson, E. Plot Improbable, Character Unsympathetic.
Onuora Oku. Pressure Drop.
Patterson, R. Letter in Winter.
Sepamla. When I Lost Slum Life.
Spender, S. Elementary School Classroom in a Slum, An.
Thomas, R. To the New Annex to the Detroit County Jail.
Wright, J. Neighborhood House, The.

Smallpox
Cordle. Lizzie Discourses on the Small-Pox.
Jones, M. After the Small Pox.
Jonson, B. Epigram. To the Small-Pox, An.
Montagu, L. Saturday: The Small-Pox.
Muldoon, P. Meeting the British.

Smalls, Robert
Heard, J. General Robert Smalls.

Smart, Christopher
Shaw, S. Christopher Smart.

Smells
Baudelaire. Exotic Scent.
Bishop, E. Prodigal, The.
Cameron, E. To David—At Six Months.
Chang Yü. Pavilion for Listening to Fragrance, The.
Chōkū. Tanka: "Nowhere on the leaves."
Coleridge, S. Cologne.
   On My Joyful Departure from the Same City.
Dennis, N. Maltese Goat.
Donne. Perfume, The.
Fainlight, R. Handbag.
Fumiko. Tanka: "Since that evening."
Herbert, G. Odour. 2. Cor. 2, The.
Herrick. Perfume, The.
   To the Most Fair and Lovely Mistress Anne Soame, Now Lady Abdie.
Hoskyns. Epitaph on the Fart in the Parliament House.
Ignatow, D. Refuse Man, The.
Kitahara Hakushū. Tanka: "Gasoline."
   Tanka: "Strong scent, The."
Kleinzahler. East of the Library, Across from the Odd Fellows Building.
Lux. History Books.
MacNeice. Sense of Smell, The.
Matthews, M. Realarro.
McGuckian. Orchid House, The.
McKay, C. Jasmine.
Miyazawa Kenji. Tanka: "At dawn."
   Tanka: "In the blue rays."
Probyn. Changes.
Rapin. Of Roses and Hyacinths.
Shafarman. Russia 1914/Bolinas 1988.
Shchapova. Smells.
Smith, K. Possessions.
Stevenson, A. Himalayan Balsam.
Supervielle. Sphere.
Swift, J. Lady's Dressing Room, The.
Thomas, E. Digging.
Wen Cheng-ming. Around the temple, pines and cedars.
Williams, W. Smell.
Wilson, R. Never since Eden.
Worth, K. Smells.
Yosano. He tempted me to.
Yoshimi. Tanka: "Dream, A."
Yüan Mei. Night of the Fifteenth, Second Month.
Yukitsuna. Tanka: "Always loving."

Smiles
Barlow, G. Nook.
Blake, W. Smile, The.
Browning, E. Sonnet: "If thou must love me, let it be for nought."
Byron, G. I saw thee weep—the big bright tear.
Catullus. Carmen 39.
Coleridge, M. True to myself am I, and false to all.
Creeley. Oh No.
Dickinson, E. They might not need me—yet they might.
Dugan, M. Herbaceous Plodd.
Dunbar, P. Made to Order Smile, The.
Philosophy.
We wear the mask that grins and lies.
"Field." La Gioconda.
Graves, R. One Hard Look.
Hardy, T. Neutral Tones.
Hartman, M. Life's made up of little things.
Herford. Smile of the Goat has a meaning that few, The.
Smile of the Walrus is wild and distraught, The.
Hollo. Mescalito.
Hughes, L. Me and the Mule.
Isler. Little Things, The.
Landor, W. You smiled, you spoke, and I believed.
Li Po. On the Mountain: Question and Answer.
Madhubuti. Judy-One.
Rodgers, C. Poem No. 1.
Shange. You are sucha fool / i haveta love you.
Unknown. Burglar Bill.
Courtesy Tips.
Day began with dismal dougt, The.
Growing Smiles.
Smile, A.
Smile costs nothing but gives much—, A.
Try Smiling.
Wen Cheng-ming. Staying Overnight at Spirit-Source Temple.
Wickham. Silent Singer, The.
Wilbur. Simile for Her Smile, A.
Wylie. Let No Charitable Hope.
Smith, Bessie
Aubert, A. Bessie.
Bessie Smith's Funeral.
Baker, H. Of Walter White's Father in the Rain.
Harper, M. Last Affair: Bessie's Blues Song.
Hayden, R. Homage to the Empress of the Blues.
Smith, John (1580–1631)
Bibb. Capt. Smith and Pocahontas.
Marquis. Noah an' Jonah an' Cap'n John Smith.
Smith, Joseph
Taylor, B. Nauvoo.
Smoke
Barlas. Oblivion! is it not one name of death?
Bennett, R. Smoke Animals.
Borowski. Farewell to Maria.
Ceravolo. Data.
DuBois, W. Song of the Smoke, The.
Forché. Elegy.
Gorman, L. Loud wind.
Hill, G. September Song.
Jaccottet. Serenity.
Lee, L. Interrogation, The.
Montale. House of the Customs-Men, The.
Morgan, R. Phobiphilia.
Mountain, M. Smoke from a neighbor's chimney loneliness.
Nicholson, N. On the Closing of Millom Ironworks.
Pagis. Testimony.
Palmer, M. Notes for Echo Lake 2.
Sachs, N. O the Chimneys.
Thoreau. Smoke.
Tranter. Backyard.
Unknown. Riddle: "Chip chip cherry."
There smoke, sooty smoke.
Williams, W. Classic Scene.

Ya'oz-kest. Smoke Rose.
Yosano. Tanka: "Aster, The."
Smoking and Smokers
Avidan. Burying Uncle Salomon.
Christopher. 5°.
Dunbar, P. Companion's Progress, A.
Harter. Mattress Fire.
Rucker. Swallow Creek.
Seferis. Mathios Paskalis among the Roses.
Spooner. On Giving Up Smoking.
Thribb. Lines on the Award "Pipe Man of the Year" to Magnus Magnusson.
Smuggling and Smugglers
"Bagritzky." Smugglers.
Mei Yao Ch'en. On Hearing that Holders of the *Chin-shih* Degree Are Dealing in Tea.
Snails
Bourne, V. Housekeeper, The.
Snail, The.
Bunyan. Upon the [*or* a] Snail.
Buson. That snail.
"Carroll." Lobster Quadrille, A.
Eybers. Snail.
Gardner, I. Widow's Yard, The.
Gunn, T. Considering the Snail.
Herford. Snail's Dream, The.
Ho Xuan Huong. Snail.
Issahakian. Climb Mount Fuji.
Under the evening moon.
Levine, P. Snails.
Lewis, J. Snail Garden.
Liagarang. Snails.
Lovelace, R. Another ("Centaur, siren [*or* syren], I forgo[e], The").
Snail [*or* Snayl], The.
MacKaye. After Tempest.
Moore, M. To a Snail.
Mother Goose. Snail, The.
Piercy. Spring Offensive of the Snail, The.
Prévert. Song of the snails on their way to a funeral.
Root, J. Snail Winter.
Sarton. Eine Kleine Snailmusik.
Su Shih. On a Snail.
Thompson, P. Snail's Lesson, The.
Unknown. Four-and-twenty tailors went to kill a snail.
Westrup. Poor Snail, The.
See also **Shells; Slugs**
Snakebites
Dickey, J. Venom.
Snakes
Abse. Snake.
Belloc. Python I should not advise, A.
Viper, The.
Bethune, L. Today Tutu Is Beating the Same Burru As Me.
Blake, W. I saw a chapel all of gold.
Bynner. Snake Dance.
Catti Natanar. What He Said ("As a little white snake").
Cheng Hsieh. Contest Snake, The.
Dickey, J. Goodbye to Serpents.
Venom.
Dickinson, E. In Winter in my Room.
Narrow Fellow in the Grass, A.
Dumas, H. Island within Island.
"Field." Dying Viper, A.
Foxton. On a Little Boy's Endeavouring to Catch a Snake.
Ghiselin. Rattler, Alert.
Gotlieb. Cocker of Snooks, A.
Gregg. Copperhead, The.
Guillén, N. Sensemayá.
Harper, M. Alice.
Hecht, A. Lizards and Snakes.
Herrick. Silken Snake, The.
Hughes, T. Cleopatra to the Asp.
Hummer, T. Rural Carrier Stops to Kill a Nine-Foot Cottonmouth, The.
Justice, D. Variations on Southern Themes.
Keats. Palpitating snake, A.
Kunitz, S. Snakes of September, The.
Lamb, C. *et al.* Boy and the Snake, The.
Levertov. Closed World, The.
To the Snake.
Maksimovic. Snake.

Marvell. Coronet, The.
McClatchy. Snake.
Milton. Behold alone / The Woman, opportune to all attempts.
Momaday. Pit Viper.
Montale. To rest at noon, pale and absorbed.
Morgan, R. Mountain Bride.
Nash, O. Experiment Degustatory.
O'Hara, F. In Memory of My Feelings.
Oliver, L. Horned Snake, The.
Ondaatje. Breaking Green.
Palmer, V. Snake, The.
Patchen. Deer and the Snake, The.
Pinsky. Serpent Knowledge.
Pitter. Viper, The.
Plath. Medallion.
Snakecharmer.
Plomer. In the Snake Park.
Ramanujan. Snakes.
Rankin, J. Forever the Snake.
Rao, B. Green Snake.
Raut. Snake.
Roethke. Serpent, The.
Snake.
Ross, W. Snake Trying, The.
Sacchetti. Catch: On a Wet Day.
Sadoleto. Poem of Jacobus Sadoletus on the Statue of Laocoon, The.
Sampson. Anaconda, The.
Seferis. Cats of St. Nicholas, The.
Shelley, P. Fragment: "Wake the serpent not—lest he."
Silko. Time We Climbed Snake Mountain, The.
Sissoko. Meeting Bida.
So Chong-Ju. Flower-Patterned Snake.
Sobiloff. Snake's Destiny, The.
Starbuck, G. Pit Viper.
Su Shih. On A Toad.
Swenson, M. Sleeping with Boa.
Waterbird.
Tadic. Laocoon/Serpent.
Thomas, D. Incarnate devil in a talking snake.
Tsaloumas. Grudge, The.
Unknown. Long ago there was a mighty snake, and beings evil to men.
Origin of the Snake, The.
Silent Snake, The.
Springfield Mountain.
Very. Serpent, The.
Virgil. Snakes.
Wadsworth, W. Snake in the Garden Considers Daphne, The.
Wakoski. Girls, The.
Summer.
Waller, E. To a Fair Lady Playing with a Snake.
Walwicz. Tattoo, The.
Warburton, N. Snake on D. H. Lawrence, The.
Williams, W. Sort of a Song, A.
Winchilsea. Song of the Cannibals, A.
Wright, J. Killer, The.
Sneezing
"Carroll." Duchess's Lullaby, The.
Cassian. Performances.
Te Whetu. Sound of My Sneezing Nose, The.
Unknown. On Proclus's Great Nose.
Sneezing.
Snipes
Clare, J. To the Snipe.
Snobbery and Snobs
Baillie, L. Werena My Heart Licht I Wad Dee.
Bentley, N. Londonderry Air, The.
Bossidy. Boston.
Canning, G. *et al.* Friend of Humanity and the Knife Grinder, The.
Glück, L. My Neighbor in the Mirror.
Hughes, L. High to Low.
Mackail, J. *et al.* On the Hon. George Nathaniel Curzon, Commoner of Balliol.
Moore, M. Labors of Hercules, The.
Sandburg, C. Balloon Faces.
Stephen, J. On a Rhine Steamer.
See also **Social Class**
Snoring
Fatchen. Be Quiet!

Hughes, L.   Morning After.
Nash, O.   Arthur.
Unknown.   Snoring Bedmate, The.

Snorkeling and Snorkelers
Lieberman, L.   Coral Reef, The.

Snow
Adams, E.   Snowman, The.
"Adunis."   Passage, The.
Aichinger.   Glimpse from the Past.
Akahito.   I passed by the beach.
On Fujiyama / Under the midsummer moon.
Tomorrow I was.
Akhmadulina.   Snowfall began its thing, The.
Aldington.   Faun Sees Snow for the First
    Time, The.
Ali, A.   Snowmen.
Allard.   Snow by the window paper flowers
    gathering dust.
Thawing ice the garbage blooming out of it.
Amabile.   Snowfall: Four Variations.
Amann.   Snow falling.
Annensky.   Snow.
Avis.   Evening star, The.
Freshly fallen snow.
Barclay, A.   Winter snowes, all covered is the
    grounde, The.
Berg, S.   To My Friends.
Bernard, A.   Snowfall.
Bethell.   Spring Snow and Tui.
Blake, W.   Soft Snow.
Blok.   Winter day is cold and snowy, The.
Bly, R.   Looking at New-Fallen Snow from a
    Train.
Sleet Storm on the Merritt Parkway.
Snowfall in the Afternoon.
Bold, A.   Auld Symie, The.
Bonnefoy.   All, the Nothing, The.
De Natura Rerum.
Summer Again.
Brickley.   Few flakes appear, A.
Slipping in the snow.
Bridges, R.   London Snow.
Brontë, A.   Song.
Brooks, G.   Cynthia in the Snow.
Brown, L.   Winter Sonnet.
Brownjohn.   Explorer.
Burris.   Strong's Winter.
Buson.   Tethered horse, A.
Buxton.   Putting the World to Bed.
Cain, J.   Someone's newspaper.
Waiting.
Carducci.   Snowfall.
Carew, T.   To My Mistress [*or* Mistris], I
    Burning in Love.
Carson, C.   Slate Street School.
Cheng Hsieh.   On a Painting of a Knight-
    Errant.
Ciardi.   First Snow on an Airfield.
Coatsworth.   On a Night of Snow.
Collins, M.   To F. C.
Conforti.   On the mountain slope.
Creeley.   To and / back and forth.
Crow, S.   Revival.
Cummings, E.   I was sitting in
    mcsoreley's.   outside it was New York
    and beauti- / fully snowing.
Daive.   Nomad, A.
Davidson, J.   Snow.
Davison, P.   Vanishing Point, The.
Day Lewis.   Snowfall on a College Garden.
De la Mare.   Snow.
There blooms no bud in May.
Winter.
Dickinson, E.   After great pain a formal feeling
    comes—.
Safe in their Alabaster Chambers.
Snow, The.
Djanikian.   When I First Saw Snow.
Dobbie.   Things Grow Up out of the Dark.
Dove, O.   Snowing. Snowing. Snowing.
Drevniok.   Deep snow.
Snow at dusk.
Dufault.   First Night, A.
Dunbar-Nelson.   Snow in October.
Earley, J.   One Thousand Nine Hundred and
    Sixty-Eight Winters.
Ehrhart.   Blizzard of Sixty-Six, The.

Emerson, R.   Snow-Storm, The.
Farjeon, E.   For Snow.
Ficowski.   Assumption of Miriam from the
    Street in the Winter of 1942, The.
"Field."   Cyclamens.
Finkel.   Metaphysic of Snow.
Fisher, A.   Snowy Benches.
Forché.   On Returning to Detroit.
Fordham.   Snow Storm, The.
Snowdrop, The.
Frost, F.   Snow-Stars.
Frost, R.   Desert Places.
Dust of Snow.
Onset, The.
Patch of Old Snow, A.
Stopping by Woods on a Snowy Evening.
Storm Fear.
Fumi Saito.   Tanka: "Snow seeping."
García Lorca.   Little Infinite Poem.
Gascoyne.   Rex Mundi.
Gibson, W.   Drove-Road, The.
Giovanni.   Winter Poem.
Goodman, P.   Long Lines.
Gorman, L.   For the smell.
Graham, J.   San Sepolcro.
Graves, R.   She tells her love while half
    asleep.
Gustafson, R.   Wednesday at North Hatley.
Gwerfyl Mechain.   Snowfall, The.
Haas, R.   Rain mixed with sleet.
Hardy, T.   Snow in the Suburbs.
Harr, L.   After the snowfall.
Late snowfall;.
Time it takes, The.
Harter.   On the padlock.
Snowflakes.
White flowers.
Heitzman.   Spaces.
Higginson, W.   More intricate.
Robin listens, A.
Hikmet.   Cucumber, The.
Hotham.   Library book, The.
Morning quiet.
Stalled car.
Housman, A.   Eight O'Clock.
Loveliest of trees, the cherry now.
Howe, S.   He plodded away through drifts of i
    / ce.
Hsieh Hui-lien.   Rhyme-Prose on the Snow.
Hughes, G.   Snow Falling.
Humphries, R.   Dafydd ap Gwilym Resents the
    Winter.
Ichijitsu.   Snow falls and falls, The.
Inez.   Instructions for the Erection of a Statue
    to Myself in Central Park.
Ivask, I.   I am the shepherd of the heavenly
    flock.
Jacob, M.   War.
Jennings, H.   Prose Poem.
Johnson, J.   Renewal.
Juarroz.   To die, but far away.
Justice, D.   Snowfall, The.
Kanemori.   In the mountain village.
Kim, K.   Snowy Night.
Kōkō Emperor.   When I went out in.
Kornilov, V.   Snow.
Kunio.   Tanka: "On the snow."
Levine, P.   Snow.
Levis.   Cocoon, The.
Li Ch'ing-chao.   Tune: "Pure Serene Music."
Li K'ai-hsien.   Crossing the ridge, the
    woodcutter loses his way.
Meeting Trappers on the Road in Heavy
    Snow.
Liu E.   House of Red Leaves, The.
Longfellow, H.   Cross of Snow, The.
Excelsior.
Fragment: December 18, 1847.
Snow-Flakes.
Lorde.   Woman Thing, The.
Lowell, A.   Falling Snow.
Lowell, J.   First Snowfall [*or* Snow-Fall], The.
MacCaig.   Explicit Snow.
"MacDiarmid."   Lourd on my hert as winter
    lies.
MacLeish.   Snowflake Which Is Now and
    Hence Forever, The.

MacNeice.   Snow.
Malouf.   Snow.
Mark, R.   Snow in Town.
Masaoka Shiki.   Frozen in the ice.
Mayer, B.   End of Human Reign on Bashan
    Hill, The.
Generic Elbows.
McClintock, M.   Hearing.
McGough, R.   Snow Poem.
Mechain.   In the Snowfall.
Millay, E.   Buck in the Snow, The.
Snow Storm, The.
Milne, A.   More It Snows, The.
Mitchison.   Tennessee Snow.
Mitsune.   Ceaseless snow.
Miyazawa Kenji.   Tanka: "Snow has fallen."
Monk, M.   Fire Us with Ice, Burn Us with
    Snow.
Moore, L.   Stars.
Mountain, M.   Sn wfl k s.
Murray, L.   Once in a Lifetime, Snow.
Naito Joso.   Fields and mountains.
Nash, O.   Winter Morning.
Nemerov.   Because You Asked about the Line
    between Prose and Poetry.
Ni Tsan.   You ask when I will go back home.
Niedecker.   Element Mother, The.
Okara.   Snowflakes Sail Gently Down, The.
Ou-yang Hsiu.   In the Evening I Walk by the
    River.
Page, P.   Stories of Snow.
Palmer, M.   Letter 5.
Pasternak, B.   Snow is falling, snow is falling.
Pizzarelli.   Snow falls from trees.
Sun brightens.
With no money.
Po Chü-i.   Early Levée, An.
Night Snow.
Passing T'ien-mên Street in Ch'ang-an and
    Seeing a Distant View of Chung-nan
    Mountains.
Releasing a Migrant 'Yen' (Wild Goose).
Pomeroy, R.   Snow.
Preil, G.   Lines on the Rambam.
Rakosi.   January of a Gnat, The.
Ratushinskaya.   Why is the snow pale blue?
Ray, H.   Snow Song.
Richards, L.   Why Does It Snow?
Riley, D.   Poor Snow.
Robinson, F.   Today too.
Rossetti, C.   I dug and dug amongst the snow.
There's snow on the fields.
Rotella, A.   Against his coat.
Saitō Mokichi.   Tanka: "Snowflakes."
Sakanoe No Korenori.   In the dawn.
Schneour.   Song of the Snow.
Shapiro, D.   Taking a Look.
Snodgrass, W.   Snow Songs.
Southard.   Snow-laden bushes.
Steadily it snows.
Southwell.   Burning Babe, The.
Spiess.   Patches of snow.
Winter moon.
Stafford, W.   Holding the Sky.
Near.
One of the Years.
Stephens, J.   White Fields.
Stevens, W.   Snow Man, The.
Stone, R.   Snow.
Su Tung-p'o.   Terrace in the Snow, The.
Tate, J.   Dear Reader.
Storm.
Teika.   I rein in my horse.
Thomas, E.   Snow.
Thaw.
Thompson, F.   To a Snowflake.
Thompson, P.   Snow-Flakes, The.
Thoreau.   When Winter fringes every bough.
Tomlinson, C.   Snow Signs.
Ts'en Shen.   Replying to "On the Occasion of
    Morning Audience after Snow" Poem by
    Assistant Secretary Wang of the Board of
    Sacrifices.
Tsung Ch'en.   Snowstorm: At a Gathering at
    Chang Chu-fu's House, with Tzu-yeh
    Attending, We All Wrote Poems on This
    Subject—I Got the Ryhme-Word, "Hu."

Snowy Mountains.
Song of Meeting.
Tu Mu. Egrets.
Tuckerman, F. Rhotruda.
Unknown. Falling Snow.
Riddle: "Round the house and round the house / and there lies a white glove in the window."
Riddle: "White bird featherless / Flew from Paradise."
Snow, snow faster.
Vallejo. I have a terrible fear of being an animal.
Virgil. Awakening.
Walking the snow-crust.
Virgilio. Crow in the snowy pine, A.
Warren, R. Garden.
Washbourne. Upon a Great Shower of Snow That Fell on May-Day, 1654.
Watkins, V. Fire in the Snow, The.
Snow Curlew, The.
Watson, F. Calendar Rhyme.
Watson, J. Beautiful Snow, The.
Wayman. Despair.
Weigl. Mercy.
White, E. Chairs in Snow.
Wiggin. Scouring pans.
Wilbur. First Snow in Alsace.
Willard, N. Angels in Winter.
Cat to His Dinner, The.
Williams, C. Snow: II.
Wojahn. Photo of My Father in a Snowbound Train.
Riding the Empire Builder, 1948.
Wright, J. Sparrows in a Hillside Drift.
Wylie. Velvet Shoes.
Yang Chi. Studio for Listening to the Snow, The.
Yang Shen. To the Tune "Flowers in the Rain."
Yang Shih-ch'i. Dawn: Clear Skies.
Yosano. At the beginning.
Tanka: "Earth looks, The."
Yoshimi. Tanka: "Streetcar, A."
Young Bear. From the Spotted Night.
Yü Chi. After Snow—Impromptu.
Traveling Early through a Snowy Valley.
Yün Shou-p'ing. Painting of Yams, A.
See also **Snowflakes; Snowmen**

Snow White
Jarrell. Ways and the Peoples, The.
Sexton. Snow White and the Seven Dwarfs.

Snowdrops
Alma-Tadema, L. Snowdrops.
DeBary. Snowdrop, The.
Evans, M. Snowdrops.
Fordham. Snowdrop, The.
Hughes, T. Snowdrop.
MacBeth. Snowdrops.
Rossetti, C. Baby lies so fast asleep.
Vivian. Snowdrops.

Snowflakes
Aiken, C. Snowflake on asphodel, clear ice on rose.
Bodecker. First Snowflake.
Ceravolo. Migratory Noon.
Nemerov. Snowflakes.
Sansom, C. Snowflakes.
See also **Snow**

Snowmen
Ali, A. Snowmen.
Bodecker. Snowman Sniffles.
McGough, R. Snowman, The.
Snowman in a field.
Page, P. Snowman, The.
Schwartz, D. Poem: "Old man in the crystal morning after snow."
Smith, B. Mister Snow Man.
Unknown. Snowman, The.
Urriola. Mister Snowman.
Wilbur. Boy at the Window.

Soap
Johnson, B. Soap, the Oppressor.
MacNeice. Soap Suds.
Muldoon, P. Soap-Pig, The.
Silverstein, S. Dirtiest Man in the World, The.

Sobriety
Keats. Portrait, A.
Po Chü-i. After Getting Drunk, Becoming Sober in the Night.

Soccer
"Otrada." Football.
Ross, A. Stanley Matthews.
Unknown. Bewteis of the Fute-Ball, The.
Zabolotsky. Soccer.

Social Class
Angelou. Sepia Fashion Show.
Bayly. Novel of High Life, A.
Belloc. Lord Heygate had a troubled face.
Bentley, N. Londonderry Air, The.
Bersohn. Dignity of Labor, The.
Betjeman. False Security.
Brooks, G. Beverly Hills, Chicago.
Burns, R. No more of your titled acquaintances boast.
Canning, G. *et al.* Friend of Humanity and the Knife Grinder, The.
Cawein. On Reading the Life of Haroun Er Reshid.
Chimombo. Of Promises and Prophecy.
"Chorny." Kreutzer Sonata, A.
Clare, J. My Mary.
"Cornwall." Leveller, The.
Coward. Stately Homes of England, The.
Cullen, C. For a Lady I Know.
Cummings, E. Come,gaze with me upon this dome.
Little joe gould has lost his teeth and doesn't know where.
Dunn, S. Truck Stop: Minnesota.
Emanuel, L. Patient.
Fenton, J. This Octopus Exploits Women.
Field, E. Lower East Side: The George Bernstein Story.
Hamill, G. Limerick: "'If you're aristocratic,' said Nietzsche."
Hands, E. Poem on the Supposition of an Advertisement, A; Appearing in a Morning Paper, of the Publication of a Volume of Poems, by a Servant-Maid.
Poem on the Supposition of the Book Having Been Published and Read, A.
Hargreaves, W. Burlington Bertie from Bow.
Hernandez, D. Pigeons are the spiks of Birdland.
Hill, G. He adored the desk, its brown-oak inlaid with ebony.
Horace. Such is the worlde, who beares the swey.
Keats. Pensive they sit, and roll their languid eyes.
Khodasevich. Amidst a smoking desolation.
Knight, E. WASP Woman Visits a Black Junkie in Prison, A.
Knott. Funny Poem.
Lawrence, D. O! start a revolution, somebody!
Lê Thánh–tông. Merchants.
"MacDiarmid." Ah, Lenin, you were richt. But I'm a poet.
MacNeice. Under the surface of flux and of fear there is an underground movement.
Masefield. Consecration, A.
Melville, H. Rose Farmer, The.
Nguyễn Bỉnh Khiêm. Clouds float through dreams, are nowhere to be seen.
Three Ranks of Men, Three Grades of Things.
Nguyễn Công Trứ. Scholars and soldiers marshaled in two files!
Nguyễn Trãi. How blessed is a middle rank in life!
Old Banyan Tree, The.
Tired legs won't climb the high road of blue clouds.
Ogundipe-Leslie. Song at the African Middle Class.
Osborn, S. Modest Wit, A.
Pound, E. Garden, The.
Praed. Arrivals at a Watering-Place.
Goodnight to the Season!
"Severyanin." Lilac ice cream! Lilac ice cream!
Stickney, T. Six o'Clock.

Strong, L. Old Woman, Outside the Abbey Theater, An.
Tennyson, A. Lady Clare.
Unknown. Bot then kerpe the king, said, "Kithe what ye hatten".
One Little Boy.
Quarrel of the Six Beasts, The.
Vicar of Bray, The.
Wallace, E. Song of the Bounder, The.
Warr, B. Working Class.
Wilcox, E. No classes here! Why, that is idle talk.
See also **Snobbery**

Social Protest. *See* **Protest, Social**

Social Work and Social Workers
Jordan, N. Feeding the Lions.

Socialism
"Ansky." Emigrant Song.
Conquest. Progress.
Duffy, C. Politico.
Lawrence, D. Hibiscus and Salvia Flowers.
Lindsay, V. Net to Snare the Moonlight, A.
Why I Voted the Socialist Ticket.
"MacDiarmid." First Hymn to Lenin.
Mitchison. To Some Young Communists from an Older Socialist.
Mukhopadhyay, S. Task, The.

Socrates
Jackson, M. Socrates' Death.

Sodom
"Akhmatova." Lot's Wife.
Appleman, P. Waiting for the Fire.
Bible, *O.T.* And there came two angels to Sodom at even.
Duncan, R. This Place Rumord to Have Been Sodom.
Grade. Sodom.
Nemerov. Lot Later.
Whittier. Cities of the Plain, The.

Solace
Bonnefoy. Tree, the Lamp, The.
Churchyard. That humor now, declines for age drawes on.
Daniel, S. Sonnet: "Care-charmer Sleep[e], son[ne] of the sable night."
Harris, W. Samantha Is My Negro Cat.
Herrick. Ode to Master Endymion Porter, upon His Brother's Death, An.
To the Willow-Tree.
Hölderlin. Patmos.
Hopkins, G. Sonnet: "No worst, there is none. Pitched past pitch of grief."
Montagu, L. Receipt to Cure [*or* for] the Vapours, A.
Opie. Stanzas Written under Aeolus' Harp.
Ōshima Ryōta. And Then.
Ransom, J. Winter Remembered.
Surrey. In Windsor Castle.
Wat. Before Breughel the Elder.
Winchilsea. Nocturnal Reverie, A.

Soldiers
Albizzi. Prolonged Sonnet: When the Troops Were Returning from Milan.
Aldington. Field Manoeuvres.
Alegría. Nocturnal Visits.
Allpass. Afterwards.
Apollinaire. Shadow.
Ashbery. Grand Abacus.
Askew. Ballad Which Anne Askew[e] Made and Sang When She Was in Newgate, The.
Asquith. Volunteer, The.
Auden. Ballad: "O what is that sound [which so thrills the ear]."
Ode: To My Pupils.
Roman Wall Blues.
"B., H. d'A." No-Man's-Land.
Ba. Ox-Soldier, The.
Bacheller. Whisperin' Bill.
Balaban. Guard at the Binh Thuy Bridge, The.
Barry, J. In the Footsteps of Genghis Khan.
Barth, R. Insert, The.
Letter from An Hoc (4), by a Seedbed.
Beadle. Lines: "How I love country you have heard."
Beckh. Soldier's Cigarette, The.
Begbie, H. Fall In.

Bierce. Corporal.
To E. S. Salomon.
Blunden. Watchers, The.
Bly, R. Teeth Mother Naked at Last, The.
Boker. Oh! craven, craven! while my brothers fall.
Boyle, K. Invitation in It, from American Citizen, The.
Brooke, R. Soldier, The.
Brown, D. Eating the Forest.
I Was Dancing Alone in Binh Dinh Province.
Returning Fire.
When I Am 19 I Was a Medic.
Brown, F. Veteran, The.
Brown, S. Sam Smiley.
Bùi Khải Nguyên. Man Who Sleeps Out in the Fields, The.
Burns, R. Charlie He's My Darling.
Farewell, A [or The]: "It was a' for our rightfu' king."
I Once was a maid, tho' I cannot tell when.
Byron, G. Eve of Waterloo, The.
Cameron, N. Forgive me, Sire, for cheating your intent.
Campbell, D. Men in Green.
Campbell, T. Soldier's Dream, The.
Catina. Negotiations.
Philosophy.
Causley. Recruiting Drive.
Song of the Dying Gunner A.A.1.
Claudian. Her longer head like a swines snowt doth show.
Coffey. Cold.
Coleman, H. In Ca Mau.
Night Flare Drop, Tan Son Nhut.
OK Corral East Brothers in the Nam.
Collins, W. Ode Written in the Beginning of the Year 1746.
Cooley. Zouave, The.
Cowley, M. Danny.
Cox, D. Song of the Happy Warrior, The.
Crane, S. War Is Kind.
Crewe, R. Harrow and Flanders.
Dana, R. At the Vietnam War Memorial, Washington, D. C.
Đng Trần Côn et al. Song of a Soldier's Wife, The.
Davenant. Soldier Going to the Field, The.
Davison, E. Nocturne: "Be thou at peace this night."
Di Piero. San Antonio de Padua.
Djabali. For My Torturer, Lieutenant D——.
Đỗ Tấn Xuân. Peace! Peace!
Dobyns. Favorite Iraqi Soldier.
Donne. Canonization, The.
Donnelly, C. Poem: "Between rebellion as a private study and the public."
Douglas, K. Aristocrats.
Vergissmeinnicht.
Dove, R. Alfonzo Prepares to Go Over the Top.
Doyle, S. Private of the Buffs; or, The British Soldier in China.
Duchamp. Deferment.
Dugan, A. Portrait from the Infantry.
Dunbar, P. Black Samson of Brandywine.
Colored Soldiers, The.
When Dey 'Listed Colored Soldiers.
Dunn, D. War Blinded.
Duoduo. When the People Stand Up out of the Hard Cheese.
Ehrhart. Blizzard of Sixty-Six, The.
Hunting.
Making the Children Behave.
Relative Thing, A.
Time on Target.
Elliot, E. Battle Song.
Elliot, J. Flowers of the Forest, The.
Emerson, R. In an age of fops and toys.
Evans, G. Horse on a Fence.
Evans, M. I Am a Black Woman.
Fallon, P. Dardanelles 1916.
Feldman, I. Se Aprovechan.
Fiacc. Enemy Encounter.
Fitzgerald, Z. Over the Top with Pershing.
Flecker. War Song of the Saracens.
Fletcher, J. Rebel, A.

Floyd. Lance Corporal Purdue Grace, U. S. M. C.
Private Ian Godwin, U. S. M. C.
Private Jack Smith, U. S. M. C.
Foley, M. Sword is a cold bride. Yuk!, The.
Ford, F. That Exploit of Yours.
Frank, F. Jewish Conscript, The.
Frankau. Deserter, The.
Gun Teams.
Freneau. American Soldier, The.
Frost, R. Not to Keep.
Fuller, R. Spring 1942.
Gardner, I. Cock-a-Hoop.
Garrick. Heart of Oak.
Gellert, L. Before Action.
Gibson, W. Breakfast.
Question, The.
Troopship: Mid-Atlantic.
Gifford, H. For Soldiers.
Gilbert, S. I Am the Very Model [or Pattern] of a Modern Major-General.
Gilmore, P. When Johnny comes marching home again.
"Golodny." Stallion, The.
Graves, R. Sergeant-Major Money.
Two Fusiliers.
Grenfell, J. Into Battle.
Grimke, C. Gathering of the Grand Army, The.
Gudzenko. Ballad about Friendship, A.
I fought on foot in every quarter.
Not from old age our death will come.
Gunn, T. As Expected.
Innocence.
Gurney, I. Canadians.
Farewell.
La Gorgue.
Gwynn, R. Body Bags.
Haines, J. Flight, The.
Hall, D. Disgrace.
How is it the stomach knows first.
There is no place to hide.
Hardy, T. Budmouth Dears.
Colonel's Soliloquy, The.
Departure.
Drummer Hodge.
Man He Killed, The.
Men Who March Away.
Often when warring for he wist not what.
Subalterns, The.
Harper, M. Guerrilla-Cong, The.
Hart, K. Story, The.
Hassett. Armed Forces Day.
Patriot's Day.
Thanksgiving.
Hayden, R. Dream, The.
Hemingway. Champs d'Honneur.
Herbert, S. Cookers, The: A Song of the Transport.
Herschell. Kid Has Gone to the Colors, The.
Hind bint Utba. Tambourine song for Soldiers Going into Battle.
Hodgson, W. Before Action.
Glimpse.
Hood, T. Faithless Nelly Gray.
Horgan. Tintype of a Private in the Fifteenth Georgia Infantry.
Housman, A. Deserter, The.
Epitaph on an Army of Mercenaries.
Grenadier.
Here dead lie we because we did not choose.
I did not lose my heart in summer's even.
In valleys green and still
Lancer.
New Mistress, The.
Recruit, The.
Soldier from the Wars Returning.
Huddle. Cousin.
Vermont.
Hudgins. Serenades in Virginia.
Soldier on the Marsh, A.
Hughes, T. Six Young Men.
Huỳnh Mẫn Đạt. Old Hound, The.
Irby. Heredom.
Ivanov, G. Tune becomes a flower, The.
Jacob, M. War.
Jarmain. Embarkation, 1942.

Jarrell. Description of Some Confederate Soldiers, A.
Eighth Air Force.
Lullaby, A: "For wars his life and half a world away."
Prisoners.
Sick Nought, The.
Soldier Walks under the Trees of the University, The.
Jonas, G. Portrait: The Freedom Fighter.
Jones, D. And to Private Ball it came.
Jonson, B. To Sir Horace Vere.
Kao Ch'i. Lament of a Soldier's Wife.
Kao Shih. Song of Yen.
Kapilar. What Her Friend Said.
Kaplinski, J. White clover will not ask anything.
Kennedy, B. Bad luck to this marching.
Kinnell. Vapor Trail Reflected in the Frog Pond.
Kipling, R. Arithmetic on the Frontier.
Ballad of East and West, The.
Boots.
Bridge-Guard in the Karroo.
Chant-Pagan.
Danny Deever.
'Eathen in 'is blindness bows down to wood an' stone, The.
For all we have and are.
Fuzzy-Wuzzy.
Gentlemen-Rankers.
Gunga Din.
Recessional.
Return, The.
Shillin' a Day.
Tommy.
Widow at Windsor, The.
Kirstein. Foresight.
Rank.
Komunyakaa. Break from the Bush, A.
Somewhere Near Phu Bai.
Kornilov, B. Continuation of Life.
Kornilov, V. Sky, The.
Krige. Soldier, The.
Krohn. Can Tho, favela of crowing cocks.
Larkin, P. Homage to a Government.
MCMXIV.
Lawrence, D. Tommies in the Train.
Layne, M. Beautiful Ladies.
Collect Call.
Gettin' Straight.
Mob, The.
On Hats and Things.
On the Yellow Footprints.
Letts. Spires of Oxford, The.
Leveridge, L. Cry from the Canadian Hills, A.
Lewis, A. All day it has rained, and we on the edge of the moors.
Dawn on the East Coast.
Infantry.
Peasants, The.
Sentry, The.
To a Comrade in Arms.
Unknown Soldier, The.
Li Po. Moon over Mountain Pass.
They Fought South of the Walls.
Longfellow, H. Killed at the Ford.
Lovelace, R. Song: To Lucasta, Going to the War[re]s.
To a Lady with Child that Asked [or Ask'd] an Old Shirt.
Lu Yu. Tune: "Telling of Innermost Feelings."
Lý Thưởng Kiệt. Southern emperor rules the Southern land, The.
"MacDiarmid." Another Epitaph on an Army of Mercenaries.
MacGill. Star-shell holds the sky beyond, A.
Mackintosh, E. Farewell: "Well, you have gone now, comrades."
In Memoriam[, Private D. Sutherland].
MacLean, S. Going Westwards.
Heroes.
MacLeish. Lines for an Interment.
Memorial Rain.
Manifold. Fife Tune.
Manning, F. Grotesque.
Masefield. To-morrow.

Mastoraki. Death of a Warrior, The.
Maturaittamilkkuttan Katuvan Mallanar. What the Servants Said to Him, as He Returned Home.
Mayer, B. Aeschyleans, The.
McCarthy, G. Hooded Legion, The.
Med Building.
McCrae, J. In Flanders Fields the poppies blow.
McGrath, T. Blues for Warren.
Go Ask the Dead.
Nocturne Militaire.
Ode for the American Dead in Asia.
Mei Yao Ch'en. Meeting the Herdsmen.
Melville, H. Ball's Bluff.
March into Virginia, The.
Meredith, G. Flat as to an eagle's eye.
Merwin, W. When the War Is Over.
Mezhirov. Troop Train.
Miller, E. What the Women Told Me.
Milne, A. Buckingham Palace.
Milton. When the Assault Was Intended to the City.
Moffi. Putting an End to the War Stories.
Mộng Tuyết. Red Cross, The.
Moody, W. Harmonics.
On a Soldier Fallen in the Philippines.
Muldoon, P. Truce.
Mura. Natives, The.
Murray, L. Drugs of War, The.
Lament for the Country Soldiers.
Nemerov. Fable of the War, A.
Nguyễn Công Trú'. Scholars and soldiers marshaled in two files!
Nguyễn Đình Thi. Yearning.
Nguyễn Tất Nhiên. Folk Songs For Today.
Nguyễn Ý Thuần. Homecoming.
Ni Tsan. Following the Rhymes of the Six Poems "Thinking of the Past at Ku-Su and Ch'ien-t'ang."
Nichols, R. Comrades: an Episode.
Nikolov, L. What the Servants Said to him, as he returned home.
Nims, J. Trainwrecked Soldiers.
"Nogar." Poem of the Conscripted Warrior.
Nortje. At Rest from the Grim Place.
Norton, C. Bingen on the Rhine.
Odoyevtseva. Ground Glass.
O'Hara, T. Bivouac of the Dead, The.
Okudzhava. Paper Soldier.
Soldier's Ditty, A.
O'Loughlin. Elegy for the Unknown Soldier.
Orwell. Italian soldier shook my hand, The.
Owen, W. Anthem for Doomed Youth.
Apologia Pro Poemate Meo.
Arms and the Boy.
At a Calvary near the Ancre.
Disabled.
Dulce Et Decorum Est.
Exposure.
Futility.
Insensibility.
Mental Cases.
Send-Off, The.
Show, The.
Spring Offensive.
Strange Meeting.
Terre, A.
Oxenham. Where are you sleeping to-night, My Lad.
Pack, R. Epistle from a Half-Pay Officer in the Country to His Friend in London, An.
Pain, B. Army of the Dead, The.
Paine, T. These are the times that try men's.
Pao Chao. Going Out Through the North Gate of Chi.
Paquet. Morning—A Death.
Patchen. Body Beside the Ties, The.
Constant Bridegrooms, The.
Peacock, T. War Song of Dinas Vawr, The.
Phạm Hổ. Hand, The.
Sea, The.
Phan Văn Trị. Grains of Rice.
Piatt, S. Army of Occupation.
Pickering. Haltersick's Song.
Pierpont, J. Warren's Address at Bunker Hill [or to the American Soldiers].

Piontek. In the Woods.
Ponmutiyar. Mother's List of Duties, A.
Young Warrior, A.
Prévert. Familial.
Prince, F. Soldiers Bathing.
Ravikovitch. You Can't Kill a Baby Twice.
Read, S. Happy Warrior, The.
To a Conscript of 1940.
Reed, H. Judging Distances.
Naming Of Parts.
Rickword. Soldier Addresses his Body, The.
Ridler. Prayer in a Pestilent Time.
Robinson, E. Field of Glory, The.
Rooney. Men behind the Guns, The.
Rose, B. Unknown Soldier, The.
Rosenberg, I. Break of Day in the Trenches.
Louse Hunting.
Marching.
Soldier: Twentieth Century.
Troop ship, The.
Rottman. APO 96225.
Ruark. Sleeping Out with My Father.
Sandburg, C. Buttons.
Little girl saw her first troop parade and asked, "What are those?", The.
Old Timers.
Sassoon. Aftermath.
Attack.
Base Details.
Christ and the Soldier.
Does It Matter?[—losing your legs?].
Dreamers.
Dug-Out, The.
Everyone Sang.
Fathers, The.
Foot Inspection.
General, The.
Glory of Women.
In Barracks.
Night on the Conroy.
Redeemer, The.
Repression of War Experience.
Suicide in [the] Trenches.
"They."
Troops, The.
Working Party, A.
Saunders, M. Remembering Day.
Scannell. Great War, The.
Scott of Amwell. Ode: "I hate that drum's discordant sound."
Scott, W. Blue Bonnets over the Border.
Soldier Rest! [Thy Warfare O'er].
Seeger, P. Where have all the flowers gone?—long time passing.
Senghor. After this day's hope—see how the Somme, the Seine, and the wild Slav.
Taga for Mbaye Dyôb.
Service. Pot of Tea, A.
Sexton. I'm dreaming the My Lai soldier again.
Shapiro, K. Nostalgia.
Troop Train.
Simonov. Lieutenant, The.
Wait for me, and I'll come back.
Simpson, L. Ash and the Oak, The.
Back in the States.
Battle, The.
It Was the Last of the Parades.
Runner, The.
Slutsky. Pit of Cologne, The.
Smelyakov. Blind Man, The.
Smith, A. Political Intelligence.
Smith, S. Private Means is dead.
Snodgrass, W. Ten Days Leave.
Sorley. All the Hills and Vales Along.
Soyinka. Civilian and Soldier.
Spender, S. Two Armies.
Stephen, J. Malines.
Stevenson, R. Ticonderoga: A Legend of the West Highlands.
Suckling, J. Soldier, A.
Surrey. Epitaph on Thomas Clere.
Swirszczynska. Conversation Through the Door, A.
He Was Lucky.
Taggard. To the Veterans of the Abraham Lincoln Brigade.

Thomas, E. Owl, The.
Private, A.
Tears.
Thomas, L. Wonders.
Thompson, M. Address by an Ex-Confederate Soldier to the Grand Army of the Republic, An.
Ticknor. Little Giffen.
Trần Huiền Ân. My Mother's Son.
Old Vow, The.
Trench, H. I Heard a Soldier.
Ts'en Shen. Song of the Running Horse River, A: Presented on Seeing General Feng Off on a Campaign to the West.
Tso Yen-nien. Call to Arms.
Tsung Ch'en. Snowstorm: At a Gathering at Chang Chu-fu's House, with Tzu-yeh Attending, We All Wrote Poems on This Subject—I Got the Ryhme-Word, "Hu."
Tsvetayeva. White low sun, low thunderclouds; and back, A.
Tu Fu. Recruiting Officer of Shih-hao.
Sharpen the sword in the Sobbing Waters.
We recruits have our commanders to send us off.
Tucker, M. Soldier Boy's Dream, The.
Tvardovsky. Crossing, The.
Tynan. Joining the Colours.
Ungaretti. Soldiers.
Unknown. At Fifteen I Went Off to the Army;.
Ballad of Mulan, The.
Banks of Claudy, The.
British Grenadiers, The.
Enlisted Today.
Fight at Finnsburg, The.
Girl I Left behind Me, The.
I Climb That Barren Ridge.
I don't want to be a soldier.
Infantryman, The.
Jimmy's Enlisted; or, The Recruited Collier.
Johnny, I Hardly Knew Ye.
Little Jock Elliot.
My Lord's Gone to Service.
My Pretty [Little] Pink.
New Army Education.
Sir Dilberry Diddle, Captain of Militia.
Soldier That Has Seen Service, The.
Soldier's Song.
Soldiers who wish to be a hero.
There Was an Old Soldier.
Two Soldier's Songs.
Volunteer, The.
Wanderer, The ("Who liveth alone longeth for mercy").
We Pick Ferns, We Pick Ferns.
Where are our uniforms?
Voznesensky. Old Song.
Wang Ch'ang-ling. At Jad Gate Pass mountain ridges several thousand-fold.
Wang Chien. Hearing That His Friend Was Coming Back from the War.
Weigl. Girl at the Chu Lai Laundry.
Wen T'ing-yün. Song of Distant Waters, A.
Whistler. Portrait in the Guards, A.
Whitman, W. Army Corps on the March, An.
Artilleryman's Vision, The.
As toilsome I wander'd Virginia's woods.
By the bivouac's fitful flame.
Cavalry Crossing a Ford.
Centenarian's Story, A.
Hush'd be the camps to-day.
March in the ranks hard-prest, and the road unknown, A.
O tan-faced prairie-boy.
Sight in camp in the daybreak gray and dim, A.
Spirit whose work is done—spirit of dreadful hours!
Vigil strange I kept on the field one night;.
Wound-Dresser, The.
Whittemore, R. Day with the Foreign Legion, A.
Recall.
Whittier. Lost Occasion, The.
Wieseltier. Saul Re-enthroned.
Song of the last soldier, A.

Wilbur. Place Pigalle.

Winchilsea. Trail all your pikes, dispirit every drum.

Wordsworth, W. Character of the Happy Warrior.

Wright, J. Confession to J. Edgar Hoover.

Speak.

Yang Chi. Reviewing the Troops at Kuei-lin with Military Inspectors Chiang And Chang.

Yeats. Irish Airman Foresees His Death, An.

Yosano. Tanka: "White tower, A."

Yoshimi. Tanka: "Soldiers on the ground."

Young, S. Epitaph for a Concord Boy.

Zenmaro. Tanka: "No news of him."

Tanka: "Old soldier, An."

Žukauskas. Midwinter Tourists.

See also **War**

Solipsism

Blake, H. Argent Solipsism.

Brontë, E. It's over now; I've known it all.

Cranch. Pines and the Sea, The.

Housman, A. I Counsel You Beware.

Lu Yün. Valley Wind, The.

'Marnia. Accoutrement.

I must be able to protect you.

I want to love you very much.

Solitude

Ai. Man with the Saxophone, The.

Aiken, C. Solitaire.

"Akhmatova." Alone.

Amichai. My Mother Once Told Me.

Arnold, M. To Marguerite.

Auden. Lauds.

Awoonor. Songs of Sorrow.

Berry, W. Except.

Berryman. Huffy Henry hid the day.

When by me in the dusk my child sits down.

Bly, R. After Long Busyness.

Solitude Late at Night in the Woods.

Sunday in Glastonbury.

Boland, E. Woman in Kitchen.

Brontë, A. Captive Dove, The.

Brontë, C. Again I find myself alone, and ever.

Autumn day its course has run—The Autumn evening falls, The.

Obscure and little seen my way.

Brontë, E. I am the only being whose doom.

Little while, a little while.

When weary with the long day's care.

Browning, E. Sonnet: "I lived with visions for my company."

Sonnet: "Thou hast thy calling to some palace-floor."

Bunin. High up on a snowy peak.

Caraion. Bits of Silk.

Cary, A. To Solitude.

Cavafy. As Much As You Can.

Chao Yi. In Search of Solitude.

Ch'en Yü-yi. Sitting on a Rock by Mountain Stream.

Cheney-Coker. Poem for a Guerrilla Leader.

Ch'ien T'ao. I BUILT my hut in a zone of human habitation.

Chin Nung. Traveler, I've been through a thousand changes, A.

Cho, C. Falling Petals.

Chōkū. Tanka: "After enduring."

Tanka: "Late at night in the kitchen."

Chu Yi-tsun. Inscribed on the Painting of "Garden for Retirement": Pavilion of Sincerity, on Rocky Mountain.

Ch'u Yüan. Spirit of the Mountain, The.

Chukhonstev. With your name, I shall name this homeless year.

Cisneros, S. Poet Reflects On Her Solitary Fate, The.

Clare, J. I am: yet what I am none cares or knows.

Solitude.

Song: "I peeled bits of straw and I got switches too."

Clark, L. Fog in November, trees have no heads.

Coleridge, M. Solo.

Cowper, W. Inscription.

Crabbe. Peter Grimes at Aldeburgh.

Creeley. Flower, The.

Crozier, A. Humiliation in Its Disguises.

Cruz Varela. Invocation.

Cruz, V. ALONE/december/night.

Cummings, E. No Thanks, No. 70.

Daive. Woman measures, A.

De la Mare. Solitude.

DeBary. Under a Wiltshire Apple Tree.

Dickinson, E. This is my letter to the World.

Diop, D. Renegade, The.

Dove, R. Daystar.

Weathering Out.

Duffy, C. Plainsong.

Duncan, R. Passage Over Water.

Eliot, T. Gerontion.

Elytis. Anniversary.

Fenton, J. Pitt-Rivers Museum, Oxford, The.

"Field." Eros.

Frost, R. Acquainted with the Night.

Desert Places.

Most of It, The.

Fulton, R. Travelling Alone.

Fumiko. Tanka: "Boxes of sleeping pills."

Gallagher, T. On Your Own.

García Lorca. Poem of Solitude at Columbia University.

González, A. Inventory of Places Propitious for Love.

Graham, W. Malcolm Mooney's Land.

Gurney, I. Walking Song.

Hall, J. St. Peregrinus' Cancer.

Han-shan. Clambering up the Cold Mountain path.

Cold Mountain Poems.

Harrison, G. Alone in the Grange.

Hayden, R. Road in Kentucky, A.

Hejinian. Solitude flared out, The.

Herrick. Not To Love.

Upon the Loss[e] of His Mistresses.

Hewitt, J. Father's Death, A.

Ho Ching-ming. Alone I stand, facing the flowers' shade.

Holden, J. Alone is delicious.

Hopkins, G. Heaven-Haven.

Horovitz, F. Rain—Birdoswald.

Hsieh Ling-yün. Leaving West Archery Hall at Dusk.

Replying to a Poem from My Cousin Hui-lien.

Hsü Pen. To a Hermit in the Mountains.

Huang Tsun-hsien. Spending the Night in an Inn at Swatow and Writing about My Feelings, Sent to Liang Shih-wu.

Huchel. Ammonite, The.

Hugo, R. Letter to Bell from Missoula.

Salt Water Story.

Ivanov, G. I walk and think of various things.

Jarrell. 90 North.

Jeffers, R. Compensation.

Joseph, J. Back to Base.

Joyce, J. I hear an army charging upon the land.

Juan Chi. Autumn's onset means cooling breezes.

Long ago there was an immortal man.

Juarroz. Emptiness of the day, The.

Justice, D. Another Song.

Kao Ch'i. Where Does My Sadness Come From?

Kavanagh, P. Inniskeen Road: July Evening.

Keats. Bright star[, would I were stedfast as thou art—].

Kenyon, J. Portrait of a Figure near Water.

Kim, H. Absolute Solitude, The.

Prayer in Autumn.

Kim, K. Pathos.

Kinnell. When one has lived a long time alone.

Kipling, R. For to Admire.

Klepfisz. They did not build wings for them.

Ku K'uang. Written upon Returning to the Mountains.

Kumin, M. Living Alone with Jesus—.

Kung Tzu-chen. Tune: "Decorous and Pretty."

Kunitz, S. River Road.

Kuppner. Passing Through Doorways.

Lampman. In November.

Larkin, P. Best Society.

Reasons for Attendance.

Vers de Société.

Wants.

Lawrence, D. Desire.

Lee, L. Eating Alone.

Levertov. Losing Track.

Woman Alone, A.

Li Po. Calling on a Taoist Priest in Tai-t'ien Mountain but Failing to See Him.

Drinking Alone in the Moonlight.

Pot of wine among the flowers, A.

Sitting Alone in Ching-t'ing Mountain.

To Amuse Myself.

Li Shang-yin. East wind sighs, the fine rains come, The.

First Month: at Ch'ung-jang House.

Lorde. Hanging Fire.

Lovelace, R. Song: "In mine one [or own] monument I lie [or lye]."

"Lu Hsün." Hesitation.

Lu Yu. Lazy.

Lynd. Solitary, The.

MacDonald, C. Instruction from Bly.

Maclean, A. Death of an Old Woman.

Madhubuti. Loneliness, A.

Mahapatra, J. Monsoon Day Fable, A.

Maran. Silence.

March, A. Not so with me as with the little page.

Marichiko. Every morning.

Marvell. Garden, The.

Masaoka Shiki. Tanka: "Nobody with me."

McClintock, M. I eat alone.

McGrath, T. Letter for Marian, A.

McKuen. Voyeur, The.

Miles, J. Travelers.

Mishra. Robinson Crusoe.

Mitchison. Woman Alone.

Mollineux. Solitude.

Mother Goose. Little Jumping Joan.

Mudrooroo. Hide and Seek.

Nokan. My head is immense.

Nortje. Up Late.

Nye, N. Art of Disappearing, The.

O'Hara, F. Autobiographia Literaria.

1951.

Poem: "Eager note on my door said 'Call me', The."

Okigbo. From flesh into phantom.

Oodgeroo of the tribe Noonuccal. Last of His Tribe.

Oppen. Myself I Sing.

Ou-yang Hsiu. Answer to Ting Yuan Ch'en, An.

Pace, R. This Is English and I Am Speaking It No Matter What.

Padilla. Self-Portrait of the Other.

Pagis. Epilogue to Robinson Crusoe.

Park, M. April.

Pasolini. Lines from the Testament.

Petrarch. Alone and pensive, the most deserted fields.

Petri. To S.V.

Pickthall, M. Quiet.

Piercy. Death of the small commune, The.

Pilinszky. Passion of Ravensbrück.

Pinkerton, H. On Vermeer's "Young Woman with a Water Jug" (1658) in the Metropolitan Museum.

Pitter. Old, childless, husbandless, bereaved, alone.

Po Chü-i. Going Alone to Spend a Night at the Hsien-Yu Temple.

Madly Singing in the Mountains.

On being Removed from Hsün-yang and Sent to Chung-chou.

Poe. "Alone."

Pommy-Vega. Here before the sunrise blue and in this solitude.

Pope, A. Ode on Solitude.

Pyon. Spring Rain.

Ralegh, W. Like to a hermit[e] poor[e][,] in place obscure.

LIKEs to a hermit poor in place obscure.

Ravikovitch. Surely You Remember.

Replansky. I Met My Solitude[. We two stood glaring].

Rexroth, K. Night without end. Loneliness.
Once I shone afar like a.
Two flowers in a letter.
Rilke. Ah, not to be cut off.
Solitude is like rain.
Ritsos. Afternoon is all fallen plaster, black stones, dry thorns, The.
Wreath, A.
Robinson, A. Personality.
Robinson, E. Aaron Stark.
Rossetti, C. Autumn.
L.E.L. E. L.
Verse II.
Sackville-West. Spinster.
To Any M.F.H F. H.
Santayana. Cape Cod.
Sassoon. Elected Silence.
Schwartz, L. Exiles: Ends.
Seferis. Word for Summer, A.
Senghor. I am alone in the plains.
Serge. Hands.
Shakespeare, W. Sonnet 29.
Shelley, P. Invocation: "Earth, ocean, air, belovèd brotherhood!"
Stanzas—April, 1814.
There was a poet whose untimely tomb.
Shelton, R. Alone.
Shih Te. Far, faraway, steep mountain paths.
Sidney, P. Solitariness.
Simic. This Morning.
Simmons, J. Pleasant Joys of Brotherhood, The.
West Strand Visions.
Simpson, L. After Midnight.
Smith, C. On Passing Over a Dreary Tract of Country, and Near the Ruins of a Deserted Chapel, During a Tempest.
Snodgrass, W. Song: "Sweet beast, I have gone prowling."
Snyder, G. Mid-August at Sourdough Mountain Lookout.
Soyinka. Hunchback of Dugbe, The.
Speer. Mama Rosanna's Last Bead-Clack.
Stephens, J. Goat Paths, The.
Stevens, W. Anglais Mort à Florence.
Re-statement of Romance.
Stevenson, A. Willow Song.
Stevenson, R. I saw red evening through the rain.
Translations from Martial.
Stickney, T. In Ampezzo.
Strand. Garden, The.
Morning, A.
Sun Yün-feng. Starting at Dawn.
Sykes, B. One Day.
Synge. Prelude: "Still south I went and west and south again."
T'ai-shang. In Reply to Questions.
T'ang Yen-ch'ien. Walk in the Country, A.
T'ang Yin. Inscribed on a Painting ("On the mountain, old trees, still green in autumn").
T'ao Ch'ien. I built my hut in a place where people live.
In the morning and at night.
In the Year with the Cyclical Sign Mou-shen.
Motionless Clouds.
Teasdale. Open Windows.
Over the Roofs.
Solitary, The.
Weariness.
Tennyson, A. Go By.
Thomas, D. Ears in the turrets hear.
Hunchback in the park, The.
Thomas, E. Rain, midnight rain, nothing but the wild rain.
Thomson, J. Hymn on Solitude.
Tố Hữu. Song on the River of Perfumes, The.
Trần Tế Xu'o'ng. Man Has Lost His Way, A.
Transtrthat Nöer. Solitude.
Tremayne. Legend.
Tu Fu. At the Corner of the World.
Climbing the Heights.
Yangtse and Han.
Tuckerman, F. Sometimes I walk where the deep water dips.
Turner, A. Red Flower.
Under. Alone with the Sea.

Unknown. I look far off at T'ien-t'ai's summit.
I sleep alone.
Little Lady of Ch'ing-ch'i, The.
Loon upon the Lake, The.
Place where I spend my days, The.
Seafarer, The.
There is a mystery in human hearts.
Very. I Was Sick and in Prison.
Vogel, D. How Can I See You, Love.
Voznesensky. Two Poems.
Walcott. Letter from Brooklyn, A.
Winding Up.
Walker, A. Outcast.
Wang I. Lychee-tree, The.
Wang Wei. Deep in the mountain wilderness.
Warren, R. Better Than Counting Sheep.
Wen Cheng-ming. At the lacquered table—my recent calligraphy.
Floating threads of spider webs hang.
Wen T'ing-yün. Tune: "River Messages."
Wheeler, S. Filial Republic, A.
Whitman, W. I saw in Louisiana a live-oak growing.
Wilcox, E. Solitude.
Wilde, R. Lament of the Captive, The.
Williams, W. Danse Russe.
Wilson, J. Sonnet III. Written at Midnight, on Helm Crag.
Winchilsea. Give me, O indulgent fate!
Wither. Sonnet: "I that erstwhile the world's sweet air did draw."
Wollach. At Sea.
Wordsworth, W. Solitary Reaper, The.
These Chairs they have no words to utter.
Wright, C. Sitting at Night on the Front Porch.
Wright, J. Two Postures beside a Fire.
Wu Wei-yeh. Garden Living.
Wylie. Eagle and the Mole, The.
Little Eclogue.
Xuân Diệu. Casting Fragrance to the Winds.
Yang Chi. On Seeing a Firefly in My Room.
Yang Wan-li. Cold Lantern, The.
Yeats. Apparitions, The.
Lake-Isle of Innisfree, The.
Yi, S. Flower-tree.
Yondo. Love.
Yü Chi. Sitting Alone in the Courtyard.
Yün Shou-p'ing. Autumn Plants, Flowers, Bamboo, Rocks.
Zanzotto. Distance.

Solomon (Bible)
Bible, O.T. Song: "I am dark, daughters of Jerusalem."
Browning, R. Solomon and Balkis.
Heine. Solomon.
Herbert, G. Sion.
Moore, M. O To Be A Dragon.
Naden. Solomon Redivivus, 1886.
Rakosi. Sandlewood comes to my mind.
Surrey. I, Solomon, David's son, King of Jerusalem.
Wellesley. Avebury.
Whittier. King Solomon and the Ants.
Yeats. On Woman.
Solomon and the Witch.
Solomon to Sheba.

Somersaults
Harris, W. Historic Moment, An.

Somerset, England
Coleridge, S. This Lime-Tree Bower My Prison.

Somnambulism and Somnambulists
Hirsch, E. For the Sleepwalkers.

Son
Coleridge, H. To Wordsworth.
Cullen, C. Fruit of the Flower.
Harper, M. Nightmare Begins Responsibility.
We Assume: On the Death of Our Son, Reuben Masai Harper.
Hunt, L. To John Keats.
Levine, P. 1933.
Shelley, P. England in 1819.
Smith, B. American Lunch.

Songs
Andal. We rose before dawn.

Anderson, S. Evening Song.
Annand. Mavis, mavis.
Ashbery. Hotel Lautréamont.
Baraka. Alba.
Barbu. Counter Play.
Timbre.
Barrax. There was a song.
Benét, S. Nonsense Song, A.
Bobrowski. Wild Swan, The.
Brecht, B. Three Fragments.
Browning, E. Deserted Garden, The.
Part I.
Calverley. Ballad: "Auld wife sat at her ivied door, The."
Campbell, R. Choosing a Mast.
Celan. Thread suns / above the gray-black [or grey-black] wasteland [or wilderness].
Ceravolo. Sunset.
Chang Yü. Hearing a Song from My Boat.
Ch'ien Ch'ien-i. Pavilions of dance, terraces of song.
Ch'in Kuan. Along the Grand Canal.
Chiricahua Apache Oral Tradition. Song for Girls' Puberty Rites.
Churchyard. That humor now, declines for age drawes on.
Clark, L. There was a man whose nose was long.
Clifton, L. Crazy Horse Names His Daughter.
Cornish, S. Cross Over the River.
Creeley. House, The.
Daniel, S. 46.
Dante Alighieri. Song, 'tis my will that thou do seek out Love.
Darwish, M. Earth Poem.
Psalm 2.
De Mello Breyner. Muse teach me the song.
Dickey, J. Buckdancer's Choice.
Donne. Triple Fool[e], The.
Dowson. Dregs.
Dunbar, P. Compensation.
Emerson, R. Music.
Espada. When Songs Become Water.
Fenton, J. Nothing.
Foster, E. In Your Words.
Fumi Saito. Tanka: "Sweeter than a song."
Gilbo'a. Ancient Song.
Graham, J. Of Forced Sightes and Trusty Ferefulness.
Grahame, K. Duck''s Ditty.
Song of Mr Toad, The.
Gregg. Dark Thing Inside the Day, A.
Gregory. Christmas Lullaby for a New-Born Child.
Grenfell, J. First To Go, The.
Harris, P. Some Songs Women Sing.
Hejinian. Mask of Anger, A.
Hemans. Song of Emigration.
Higo. Hidesong.
Holmes, O. Prologue.
Hooks. Woman's Mourning Song, The.
Howe, J. Battle Hymn [or Battle-Hymn] of the Republic, The.
Howe, S. Say that a ballad.
Hughes, T. I suppose you just gape and let your gaspings.
Hugo, R. My Buddy.
Issa. From the bough / floating down river.
Izumi. Cricket Heard.
Jaccottet. Wishes.
Jackson, A. Ohnedaruth.
Johnson, J. Lift every [or ev'ry] voice and sing.
Joron, A. Birdsongs are aging, The.
Keats. On the Grasshopper and [the] Cricket.
Kelly, B. Song: "Listen: there was a goat's head hanging by ropes in a tree."
Kgositsile. Song for Ilva Mackay and Mongane.
Kitahara Hakushū. Tanka: "Spring bird."
Kunio. Tanka: "Only when."
Ledwidge. Lament for the Poets: 1916.
Lee, L. I Ask My Mother to Sing.
Longfellow, H. Day is done, and the darkness, The.
Lönnrot. It is my desire, it is my wish.
Lowry, M. Joseph Conrad.

Macdonald, G. Shortest and Sweetest of Songs, The.
Meek. Vienna in the Rain.
Meynell, A. To Silence.
Mo Shih-lung. Gathering Lotus with Singing Girls.
Montale. Lemon Trees, The.
Moss, H. Persistence of Song, The.
Nezahualcoyotl. Flower Songs.
O'Connor, P. Raspberry in the Pudding, The.
O'odham. Healing Songs.
Orpingalik. Songs are thoughts, sung out with the breath when people are moved by great forces and ordinary speech no longer suffices.
Padilla. Song of the Juggler.
Pembroke, M. Psalm 100: "O all you lands, the treasures of your joy."
Pettet. Rose Garland Sonnet.
Piatt, S. Sad Spring-Song.
Pindar. Oh! Sovereign of the willing soul.
Plumly. Cedar Waxwing on Scarlet Firethorn.
Probyn. Song Out of Season, A.
Rakosi. Sandlewood comes to my mind.
Reznikoff. I Will Write Songs against You.
Riley, J. Nonsense Rhyme, A.
Roberson. Aerialist Narratives, Chapter Three, The.
Roethke. Light Listened.
Reply, The.
Voice, The.
Rothenberg, J. Song of Quavering, A.
Rukeyser, M. This Place in the Ways.
Salis. Song.
Sanchez, S. For Our Lady.
Sandburg, C. Evening Waterfall.
Work Gangs.
Scott, W. Hunting Song.
Senghor. Be not amazed beloved, if sometimes my song grows dark.
Shelley, P. To a Skylark.
Sherry, J. She'll be comin' 'round the mountain when the shell sometimes is empty.
Shibafune. In the spring ravine.
Sidney, P. First Song: "Doubt you to whom my Muse these notes intendeth [or entendeth]."
Third Song: "If Orpheus' voice had force to breathe music's love."
Snodgrass, W. Song: "Sweet beast, I have gone prowling."
Stafford, K. Feather Bag, Stick Bag.
Stevens, W. Of Mere Being.
Svetlov. Grenada.
Tai Piao-yüan. South of the house, north of the house.
Tapahonso. Listen.
Tekkan. Tanka: "Let those grasses."
Tennyson, A. Brook, The.
Dying Swan, The.
Thaxter. Sandpiper, The.
Theocritus. We had not got half way, nor yet discerned.
Toomer. Song of the Son.
Unknown. Chinese Sandmen.
It's a funny thing, but true.
Love me little, love me long!
Northwest the tall tower stands.
Of this day's glorious feast and revel.
Upon a Maid That Died the Day She Was Married.
Very. Song, The: "When I would sing of crooked streams and fields."
Viiding. I am a serf. I work in the sweat of my brow.
Virgil. Silenus sings.
Virgil. Holding you.
Voigt. Song and Story.
Walker, M. For my people [everywhere singing their slave songs repeatedly: their].
Warner, S. Song for a Street-Song.
Welburn. Gonsalves.
Yellow Wolf Spirit.
Wen Cheng-ming. Hearing a Flute on the River Chi.
Whitman, W. Chanting the square deific, out of the One advancing, out of the sides.
Out of the cradle endlessly rocking.

Whittier. Tent on the Beach: [The Dreamer].
Wilbur. Cicadas.
Plain Song for Comadre, A.
Williams, W. Botticellian Trees, The.
Wong, N. Grandmothers' Song.
Wordsworth, W. Reverie of Poor Susan, The.
Wright, J. Written in a Copy of Swift's Poems, for Wayne Burns.
Xue Tao. Cicadas.
Yang Chi. Describing My Feelings While Living in Retirement by the Riverside: Seven Poems to the Tune "Ch'ing-p'ing-yüeh."
Yang Shen. To the Tune "Stopping My Horse to Listen."
Yeats. Coat, A.
Yi, T. Gang-gang-suwole.
Zarin. Song.
Zealand. Passion at the Chat 'n Chew Diner.

Sonnets
Bogan, L. Single Sonnet.
Botsford. Sonneteering Made Easy.
Burns, R. Sonnet upon Sonnets, A.
Donne. Canonization, The.
Gilder, R. Sonnet, The.
Goethe. Sonnet: "To work away in art's traditional measure."
Keats. On the Sonnet.
Koestenbaum, P. Sonnet 37: "I'd decided I initiate most."
Lee-Hamilton. What the Sonnet Is.
Loines. On a Magazine Sonnet.
Lope de Vega Carpio. Sonnet Right off the Bat.
Moore, M. In Magic Words.
Poe. Enigma, An.
Rossetti, D. Sonnet, A [or The: "Sonnet is a moment's monument"].
Symonds. Sonnet (III), The.
Watts-Dunton. Sonnet's Voice, The.
Wilcox, E. Sonnet, The.
Wordsworth, W. Nuns fret not at their convent's narrow room;.
Sonnet: "Scorn not the sonnet; critic, you have frowned."

Sonora Desert
Shelton, R. Requiem for Sonora.

Sons
Amichai. I Am a Live Man.
My son, in whose face there is already a sign.
Applewhite. Prayer for My Son.
Arghezi. Testament.
Arnold, M. Then Sohrab with his sword smote Rustum's helm.
Bàng Bá Lâ. Mother, I Am Still Here With You.
Baraka. Wise 3.
Barber, M. Written for My Son, and Spoken by Him at His First Putting on Breeches.
Bell, M. Gemwood.
Berryman. Sympathy, A Welcome, A.
Bly, R. Prodigal Son is kneeling in the husks, The.
Bowers, E. Prince, The.
Brodsky, J. Odysseus to Telemachus.
Brooks, G. Big Bessie Throws Her Son into the Street.
Cameron, E. To David—At Six Months.
Ch'ien Ch'ien-i. Rebuttal of Tung-p'o's Poem on "Bathing the Infant," A.
Ch'ien T'ao. Blaming Sons.
Clifton, L. Admonitions.
Wishes for Sons.
Cokinos. Short-Wave.
Coleman, A. Black Baby.
Comfort, A. Notes for My Son.
Corbet. To His Son [or Sonne], Vincent Corbet[t].
Cronin, A. For a Father.
Davidson, D. Randall, my son, before you came just now.
DeFrees. Letter to an Absent Son.
Dhasal. Stone-masons, My Father, and Me.
Dickey, J. Birth, A.
Drayton. To nothing fitter can I Thee compare.
Drummond de Andrade. Travelling in the Family.

Duncan, R. My mother would be a falconress.
Edson, R. Having to Love Something Else, The.
Fitzgerald, R. Figlio Maggiore.
Fordham. Sonnet to My First Born.
Gallagher, T. Each Bird Walking.
García Lorca. Rundown Church (Ballad of the First World War).
Geier. On Your Twenty-First Birthday.
Gillies, A. Two Prayers.
Goethe. Erl-King, The.
Grafflin. To My Son.
Gregory, H. For You, My Son.
Gunn, T. Butcher's Son, The.
Hall, D. My son, my executioner.
Harper, M. Mama's Report.
Heaney, S. Mother of the Groom.
When all the others were away at Mass.
Hernández, M. Lullaby of the Onion.
Hoffman, D. Special Train, A.
Hood, T. World Is with Me, The.
Howes, B. 2nd Wind.
Hsü Pen. To the Filial Son, Ts'ui.
Huang T'ing-chien. Teasing Hsiao-te, My Son.
Hughes, L. Letter.
Humphreys, E. From Father to Son.
Hunt, S. Birth of a Son.
Johnson, D. Home Game.
Jonson, B. On My First Son [or Sonne].
Kaplinski, J. We started home, my son and I.
Kim, J. Mother-thought.
Kinnell. After Making Love We Hear Footsteps.
Kipling, R. My Boy Jack.
Son, A.
Sons of Martha, The.
Kooser. At the End of the Weekend.
Kurup. Master Carpenter, The.
Lamkin. Golden Season.
Lee, L. Final Thing, A.
Weight of Sweetness, The.
Lesser. Woman from Chianciano.
Levertov. Son, The.
Li Po. Sent to My Two Little Children in the East of Lu.
Li Shang-yin. Poem for My Little Boy.
Linden, M. Wayward Son, The.
Lorde. Child Shall Lead, A.
Lu Yu. I Walk Out into the Country at Night.
Macdonagh, T. Wishes for My Son.
Mason, R. Young Man Thinks of Sons, The.
McNair. My Brother Inside the Revolving Doors.
McNeill, L. Hill Daughter.
Meinke. Advice to My Son.
This is a poem to my son Peter.
Meng Chiao. When my son was born, the moon was not bright.
Merwin, W. Yesterday.
Meynell, A. Father of Women, A [Ad Sororem E. B.].
Milne, A. Disobedience.
Morgan, R. Little heart, little heart.
Mother Goose. Old Mother Goose.
Mungoshi. Letter to a Son, A.
Myers, J. Visitation Rites.
Nichols, R. 1.
Nizami Arudi. Calling the Doctor (1000 A.D.)
Nowlan. Mother and Son.
Only when my heart freezes.
Olds, S. Latest Injury, The.
Mother, The.
Oppen. Daedalus: The Dirge.
Ortiz. What I Tell Him.
Ostriker. Leaf Pile, The.
Pastan. Letter to a Son at Exam Time.
Pearse, P. Mother, The.
Penna. Lady on Streetcar.
Peyanar. Embracing the young mother from behind.
Pien Kung. At the Lake—Remembering My Dead Son, Yü.
Potts. For My Father.
Pratt, M. Poem for my Sons.
Publius Terentius Afer. CHREMES. Pese anger not thyself so I thee pray.
Rabbitt. My Father's Watch.

Reid, A. Daedalus.

Rich, A. Jerusalem.

Rilke. Luke 15:11–19; And he said, "There was a man."

Ritsos. Day in May you left me, a day in May I lose you, A.

Roethke. Flight, The.

Rudman, M. Nowhere Water, The.

St. John, P. Reading a Story to My Child.

Saunders, L. Mothers of Sons.

Schultz, P. For My Mother.

Schwartz, D. Young Child and His Pregnant Mother, A.

Sexton. Two Sons.

Shelton, R. Letter to a Dead Father.

Shen Chou. Consoling Wu Te-cheng on the Death of His Son.

Silkin. Death of a Son.

Simic. Spoons with Realistic Dead Flies on Them.

Smith, D. August, on the Rented Farm.

Smith, S. Correspondence between Mr. Harrison in Newcastle and Mr. Sholto Peach Harrison in Hull.

Stallworthy, J. Almond Tree, The.

Stanford, F. Terrorism.

Stevens, W. John Smith and his son, John Smith.

World Without Peculiarity.

Su Shih. Bathing the Infant.

Su Tung-p'o. At the Washing of My Son.

On the Birth of His Son.

T'ang Hsien-tsu. My son, you loved telling the story of Prince Nata.

On the Day of Washing the Buddha in the Year Ting-wei (1607), I Dreamed That My Late Son Shih-ch'ü Was Holding a Book, and Appeared To Be Quite Happy. He Said That He Had Earned His Chin-shih Degree in the Underworld. After We Sighed and Laughed Together for a Long Time, I Woke Up and Wrote This Poem.

T'ao Ch'ien. Blaming Sons.

Tate, A. Mother and Son.

Tate, J. Distance from Loved Ones.

For Mother on Father's Day.

Taylor, E. Few Days in the South in February, A.

Thorne, C. To My Unborn Son.

Tynan. Joining the Colours.

Unknown. Enlisted Today.

Somebody's Mother.

To a New Daughter-in-Law.

Wife of Usher's Well, The.

Vallejo. Right Meaning, The.

Van Doren. Ancient Couple on Lu Mountain, The.

Wen Cheng-ming. Smiling, we set the testing tray before the hall.

Wesley, C. On the Death of His Son.

Westmorland. Dedication of My First Son, A.

Whitman, W. Dirge for Two Veterans.

I knew a man, a common farmer, the father of five sons.

Vigil strange I kept on the field one night;.

Wordsworth, W. Affliction of Margaret—The The.

Wright, J. Having Lost My Sons, I Confront the Wreckage of the Moon: Christmas, 1960.

Two Postures beside a Fire.

Yang Wei-chen. Tu-lu Poem ("Tu-lu, Tu-lu, evil waters running muddy").

Yeats. Prayer for My Son, A.

Yüan Chen. Mourning My Son.

Yukitsuna. Tanka: "Since puberty."

Zenmaro. On the birth of my son.

Sophocles

Arnold, M. Dover Beach.

To a Friend.

Sorcery and Sorcerers

Blok. Sorcerer sang the spring to sleep, The.

Sorrow

Abu Nuwas. Rake, The.

"Adunis." Song of a Man in the Dark.

Aeschylus. Bright light, swift-winged winds, springs of the rivers, numberless.

"Akhmatova." Railings of iron.

Aklais. Woman in Mourning.

Alexander, M. People of Unrest.

Alver. Tailor Called Sorrow, A.

Amichai. Is all this sorrow? I don't know.

Quick And Bitter.

Anacreon. Ode of Anacreon, An.

Anderson, T. Kneading Bread.

Apollonius Rhodius. Now rising shades a solemn scene display.

Arghezi. Testament.

Ashe. To Two Bereaved.

Awoonor. First Circle, The.

Songs of Sorrow.

Bagryana. Only One, The.

Beckett, S. Enueg II.

I would like my love to die.

Beedome. Question and Answer, The.

Berryman. Sometimes the night echoes to prideless wailing.

Blaga. Psalm.

Blake, W. Infant Sorrow.

On Another's Sorrow.

Blok. Girl was singing in the choir with fervor, A.

Braithwaite. House of Falling Leaves, The.

Brodsky, J. To Urania.

Brontë, E. I am the only being whose doom.

She dried her tears, and they did smile.

Spellbound.

Browning, E. Mask, The.

My Heart and I.

Sonnet: "My letters! all dead paper, mute and white."

Year's Spinning, A.

Brutus. They hanged him, I said dismissively.

Burns, R. Banks O' Doon, The.

Bonie Doon.

Cares o' love are sweeter far, The.

Red, Red Rose, A.

Song: "Ae fond kiss, and then we sever."

Ye flowery banks o' bonie Doon.

Byron, G. By the Rivers of Babylon We Sat Down and Wept.

Oh! weep for those that wept by Babel's stream.

Campion, T. When to Her Lute Corinna [or Corinna] Sings.

Carew, T. Epitaph on the Lady Mary Vill[i]ers.

Lover, upon an Accident Necessitating His Departure, Consults with Reason, A.

To Celia, upon Love's Ubiquity.

Castellanos. Hecuba's Testament.

Catullus. Carm. II.

There on th'extreamest Beach, and farthest Sand.

Cavalcanti. Ballata: Of His Lady among Other Ladies.

Chao Luan-luan. Willow Eyebrows.

Chatterton. Mynstrelle's Songe ("O! synge untoe mie roundelaie").

Ch'en Shih-tao. Cold Night.

Chong, H. Late Autumn.

Chou Pang-yen. Tune: "Prince of Lan-ling" (Lan-ling Wang)—on Willows.

Chu Shu-chen. Hysteria.

Old Anguish, The.

Stormy Night in Autumn.

Ch'u Yüan. Spirit of the Mountain, The.

Clampitt. Procession at Candlemas, A.

Coleridge, S. On a Discovery Made Too Late.

"Coolidge." New Every Morning.

Cowper, W. Shrubbery, The.

Cresson. Cloak of Laughter.

Crowell, A. Joy of Incompleteness, The.

Cullen, C. Saturday's Child.

Cummings, E. Always before your voice my soul.

Dante Alighieri. Day agone, as I rode sullenly, A.

Eyes that weep for pity of the heart, The.

That lady of all gentle memories.

De la Mare. At Ease.

Ghost, The.

Old Summerhouse, The.

Di Prima. For H.D.

Dickinson, E. One need not be a Chamber—to be Haunted.

Dimitrova. Woman Pregnant, A.

Dipoko. Our Life.

Dobson, A. Before Sedan.

Dowson. O Mors! Quam Amara Est Memoria Tua Homini Pacem Habenti In Substantiis Suis.

Spleen.

Drummond de Andrade. Dead in Frock Coats, THe.

Dunbar, P. We wear the mask that grins and lies.

Duncan, R. Among my friends love is a great sorrow.

Turning into a restful roomfull.

Dyer, S. I would it were not as it is.

Eisner. Autumn nears. The branches yellow.

Elliot, J. Flowers of the Forest, The.

Euripides. Friends, I account the fortune of my wife.

Ilion, o my city.

Evans, M. If there be sorrow.

Feng Yen-ssu. Tune: "Magpie on the Branch."

"Field." Picture, A.

Figueroa, J. Epitaph: "Old man is gone, The."

Fraser, G. Lament: "In a dismal air; a light of breaking summer."

Frost, R. Love and a Question.

My November Guest.

Fujiwara no Kiyosuke. I may live on until.

Fumiko. Tanka: "My arms."

Tanka: "With sorrow I recall."

Gallagher, T. Stepping Outside.

García Lorca. At the Poorhouse.

Glück, L. Elms.

Gorham. Princess Parade.

Gouri. In the Amorite city spared for my sake from the sword of Joshua.

Graves, R. Lost Love.

Günther. Departure Aria.

Hacker, M. Conclusion: "Did you love well what very soon you left?"

Hall, D. Another Elegy.

Hammond, W. To the Same [My Dear Sister, Mrs S.]: The Tears.

Han-shan. Man lives his life in a dust bowl.

Hardy, T. Going, The.

Heinrich von Morungen. I believe there is no one alive who weeps for my sorrow.

Herbert, G. Joseph's Coat.

Herrick. Bad Season Makes the Poet Sad, The.

On Himselfe ("I fear no earthly powers").

To the Willow-Tree.

Hesiod. Iron Age, The.

Laertes.

Housman, A. They Say My Verse Is Sad: No Wonder.

Howells, W. Forlorn.

Hsin Ch'i-chi. Tune: "Full River Red."

Tune: "Groping for Fish."

Hsü Kan. Deepening shadows bring on sorrow, The.

Ingelow. Story, A.

Ise Tayu. Today is the anniversary of our parting.

Ishikawa Takuboku. Tanka: "As if in water."

Tanka: "Like a white lotus."

Tanka: "Sorrow."

Tanka: "What always seemed."

Izumi. In the dusk the path.

Joyce, J. I hear an army charging upon the land.

Kasa no Iratsume. Evening comes and sorrow crowds my mind.

Gods of heaven are irrational, The.

When evening comes.

Keats. What the Thrush Said.

Kemble. Impromptu.

Kim, H. Tears.

Kim, S. Gift of Love.

Kim, Y. Till The Peonies Bloom.

Kinnell. Burn, The.

Kipling, R. Power of the Dog, The.

Landon. Child Screening a Dove from a

Hawk, A.
Small Miseries.
Lanier, S.   Raven Days, The.
Lerman.   Margaret Whiting Tearfully Sings.
Levine, P.   Red Dust.
Leyvik.   Open up, gate.
Li Ch'ing-chao.   P'u-Shen Sheng Man.
Tune: "Spring at Wu-ling."
Li Ho.   New Bamboo in the North Garden at
Ch'ang-ku.
Li K'ai-hsien.   Compassion for the Farmers.
Li Po.   Moon over the Mountain Pass, The.
Li Shang-yin.   Fallen Flowers.
For ever hard to meet, and as hard to part.
Li Yü.   Tune: "Crows Crying at Nighit."
Tune: Gazing at the South.
Tune: Ripples Sifting Sand.
Tune: Song of Tzu-yeh.
Liu E.   Poem on Falling Leaves.
Liu Yu Hsi.   Bamboo Branch Song.
Sorrowing for the Past at Western Pass
Mountain.
Logan, J.   Braes of Yarrow, The.
Longfellow, H.   Bridge, The.
Rainy Day, The.
Lovelace, R.   Dialogue.
Lu Yu.   Phoenix Hairpins.
MacKay, C.   Only a Thought.
Magrelli.   Especially in weeping.
Massey.   Desolate.
McMullen, A.   By the River.
Mei Yao Ch'en.   In Broad Daylight I Dream
of My Dead Wife.
On the Night of the Fifteenth Day of the First
Month I Go Out and Return.
Sorrow.
Melvill.   Upon one day as I did mourn full
sore.
Meng Chiao.   Don't let freezing hands play
with these pearls.
Failing the Examination.
It must have been a single thread of tears.
Meredith, G.   Dusty Answer, A.
Modern Love.
Mihalic.   Autumn.
Miles, J.   Sorrow.
Mimnermus.   There Is No Joy Without
Aphrodite.
Mitsune.   Ceaseless snow.
Moore, T.   Oft in the stilly night.
Morris, M.   Day my father died, The.
Na-lan Hsing-te.   Tune: "Partridge Sky"—
Parting Sorrows.
Nesbit, E.   Love's Guerdons.
Ni Tsan.   Inscribed on a Painting.
Ofeimun.   How Can I Sing.
Oodgeroo of the tribe Noonuccal.   Song: "Life
is ours in vain."
Orampokiyar.   What Her Girl Friend Said to
the foster-mother ("If you think, mother").
What She Said ("In his place, mother / field-
crabs cut into the pink").
Ovid.   When night falls here, I think of that
other night.
Owen, W.   Roads also have their wistful rest,
The.
Park, Y.   Departing Boat, The.
Philips, K.   Lucasia, Rosania and Orinda
Parting at a Fountain, July 1663.
Pien Kung.   Song of the Boat-Pullers.
Pilkington, L.   Sorrow.
Po Chü-i.   Chu Ch'ên Village.
To Li Chien.
Poe.   Haunted Palace, The.
Valley of Unrest, The.
Pound, E.   Song of the Bowmen of Shu.
Propertius.   Ghosts do exist; death does not
finish everything.
Me happy, night, night full of brightness.
Publius Papinius Statius.   And so Death took
him. Yet be comforted.
Radnóti.   Letter to My Wife.
Raine, K.   Spell Against Sorrow.
Ralegh, W.   Like to a hermit[e] poor[e][,] in
place obscure.
Ocean's Love to Cynthia, The.
Poem Entreating of Sorrow, A.

Rexroth, K.   As the wheel follows the hoof.
Half in a dream.
In the park a crow awakes.
Ridler.   At Parting.
Robinson, A.   Stornelli and Strambotti.
Robinson, E.   Walt Whitman.
Rossetti, C.   Luscious and Sorrowful.
Remember me when I am gone away.
Shut Out.
Saigyo.   Woman Forsaken in Love, A.
Saitō Mokichi.   Tanka: "Yolk, The."
Sappho.   Pain penetrates.
Sassoon.   Lamentations.
Scott, L.   Ettrick.
Seward.   Sonnet 12.
Sonnet 31.
Shelley, P.   To————: "One word is too
often profaned."
Shen Chou.   Lady Picking Flowers, A.
Shen Yüeh.   Song of Woe.
Shūji.   Tanka: "As if it came."
Tanka: "Flowering poppies."
Tanka: "My body."
Siddal.   Dead Love.
Sidney, P.   Sonnet 104: "Envious wits, what
hath been mine offence."
Sidney, R.   Sonnet 25: "Yow that take pleasure
in yowr cruelty."
Smedley, M.   Sorrowful Sea-Gull, The.
Smith, C.   On the Departure of the
Nightingale.
Verses Intended to Have Been Prefixed to the
Novel of Emmeline, but Then Suppressed.
Smith, S.   Satin-clad, with many a pearl.
Sophocles.   Do not you mark how *passionate,*
how *wild.*
Sorescu.   With a green scarf I blindfolded.
Southwell.   Vale of Tear[e]s, A.
Soyinka.   I think it rains.
Stern, G.   Behaving Like a Jew.
Stickney, T.   Here in the North I chase an old
despair.
Sir, say no more.
Surrey.   Description of Spring, Wherein Each
Thing Renews Save Only the Lover.
Swinburne.   Anactoria.
In The Orchard.
Match, A.
Symons, A.   When you were here, ah foolish
then!
Tai Shu-lun.   Wang Chao-chün.
T'ao Ch'ien.   In the morning and at night.
Tennyson, A.   27.
Thomas, E.   When I first came here I had
hope.
Thoreau.   Brother where dost thou dwell?
Ts'ai Yen.   Lamentation, The.
Ts'ao Chih.   Ruins of Lo-yang, The.
Tu Fu.   Loneliness.
Recruiting Officer of Shih-hao.
Tuckerman, F.   Coralie.
Morning comes; not slow, with reddening
gold, The.
Tuqan, F.   Face Lost in the Wilderness.
Unknown.   Aurora and Tithonus.
Bible, Matthew 5:3–12, Phillips, The.
Big Chariot, The.
Bright moon white and silver, The.
Cloudy morning.
Crow caws in the moonlight, A.
First dawn comes, The.
Fowls [or Foweles or Fowles] in the frith.
Lady Greensleeves.
Lament, The: "What shall I send you, my dear
one, there in the underworld?"
My Choice.
My Lady's Tears.
Perle, plesaunte to prynces paye.
Song of Sorrow.
That Cypress Boat Is Drifting.
This world of ours.
When I pick up my koto.
years of a lifetime do not reach a hundred,
The.
Van Vliet.   Coastline never alters for the
fisherman, The.

Venkorran.   What She Said ("Are there others
too").
Villon.   Complaint of the Fair Armoress [or
Armouress], The.
Virgil.   Aeneas sees his wife.
Dido's last night.
Whyles in this sorte he dyd hys tale
pronounce.
Wang An-shih.   Written for My Own
Amusement.
Wang Ch'ang-ling.   Sorrow in the Harem, A.
Wang Kuo-wei.   Tune: "Immortal at the
River."
Wang Wei.   Red Peonies.
Warton, T.   Ode on the Passion.
Wei Wên-Ti.   On the Death of his Father.
Whitman, W.   Hours continuing long, sore and
heavy-hearted.
I sit and look out upon all the sorrows of the
world, and upon all oppression and shame.
O Captain! my Captain! our fearful trip is
done.
Spring.
Wilcox, E.   Way of It, The.
Williams, W.   Waiting.
Widow's Lament in Springtime, The.
Wolfe, C.   To Mary.
Wollach.   House is empty and the trough is
broken, The.
Wordsworth, W.   Excursion, The.
Wroth.   Song 2: "All night I weep[e], all day I
cry, Ay me[e]."
Sonnet 9: "Be[e] you all pleased [or pleas'd]?
your pleasures grieve not[t] me[e]."
Wu Chia-chi.   Woman Tung.
Wyatt, T.   Joy so short alas, the pain so near,
The.
Wylie.   "Desolation Is a Delicate Thing."
Yakamochi.   Better never to have met you.
Yang Shen.   To the Tune "Heavenly
Immortal."
To the Tune "Yellow Oriole" ("Willows
weave spring sorrow").
Yosami, the wife of Hitomaro.   Day after day
I've longed for my husband.
Yosano.   Swifter than hail.
Yoshimi.   Trip to Berlin.
Yü Hsüan-chi.   To Tzu-an.
Yüan Mei.   Ma-wei.
Yukitsuna.   Tanka: "Plaintive, A."
Zimmer.   Father Animus and Zimmer.

See also **Funerals; Grief; Mourning and
Mourners**

Soul

Akers.   Night: Volcano, California.
Amis, K.   Nothing to Fear.
Ammons.   Terrain.
Arghezi.   Gulf.
Arnold, M.   Palladium.
Augustine.   Half Of Me.
Baraka.   Invention of Comics, The.
Barlas.   Cat-Lady, The.
Bekederemo.   Cry of Birth.
Bernstein, C.   From Lines of Swinburne.
Bevington, L.   'Egoisme à Deux'.
Wrestling.
Bialik.   And If the Angel Should Ask.
Bible, *O.T.*   They go down to the sea in.
Blaga.   Soul of the Village, The.
Blake, W.   Introduction: "Hear the voice of the
Bard!"
Blumenthal, M.   Man Lost by a River, A.
Bonar.   Be True [or Be True Thyself].
Bradstreet, A.   There is a path no vulture's eye
hath seen.
Braithwaite.   Rye Bread.
Brontë, A.   Lines Composed in a Wood on a
Windy Day.
Brontë, E.   My Comforter.
No coward soul is mine.
Brooke, R.   Doubts.
Browning, E.   Felicia Hemans.
Fifth Book.
Sonnet: "How do I love thee? Let me count
the ways."
Brownstein.   Last spell cast came late one

afternoon in a brown study. I was studying my-, The.

Campion, T. Are you what your faire lookes expresse?

Laura.

Carney. (Little Things).

Celan. Language Mesh.

Clifton, L. Crazy Horse Instructs the Young Men But In Their Grief They Forget.

Cohen, L. Suzanne takes you down to her place near the river.

Coleridge, M. Friends—With a Difference.

Wilderspin.

Coleridge, S. Psyche.

Constable, H. To St Mary Magdalen.

Cook, E. Old Arm-Chair, The.

Cooke, E. How Did You Die?

Costello, L. Spirit's Song.

Cowley, A. Platonic[k] Love.

Cummings, E. Cambridge ladies who live in furnished souls, The.

Dacre, C. Kiss, The.

Dante Alighieri. Gentle thought there is will often start, A.

My lady looks so gentle and so pure.

So gentle and so virtuous she appears.

That lady of all gentle memories.

Dash. Me Again.

Davenant. There, when they thought they saw in well sought Books.

De la Mare. Love Lies Here.

Ded. I drag a boat over the ocean.

Soul, like the moon, The.

Dementyev, A. It's all over...

Di Piero. Near Damascus.

Dickinson, E. Dare you see a Soul *at the White Heat?*.

Death is a Dialogue between.

Difference between Despair, The.

Faith—is the Pierless Bridge.

Go slow, my soul, to feed thyself.

He fumbles at your Soul.

"Hope" is the thing with feathers.

No Rack can torture me.

Of all the Souls that stand create—.

Of nearness to her sundered Things.

Props assist the House, The.

Single Screw of Flesh, A.

Soul has Bandaged moments, The.

Soul selects her own Society—The The.

Soul that hath a Guest, The.

Soul's distinct connection, The.

Spirit lasts, but in what mode, The.

Donne. Air[e] and Angels.

Ecstasy, The.

Funeral[l], The.

Good-Morrow, The.

Resurrection, Imperfect.

Soules Ignorance in This Life and Knowledge in the Next, The.

To the Countess of Salisbury.

To the Countesse of Bedford ("Honour is so sublime perfection").

Valediction, A: Forbidding Mourning.

What if this present were the world's last night?

Doolittle, H. At least I have the flowers of myself.

Douglas, L. Green River, The.

Ode to My Soul.

Dove, R. History.

Drayton. To the Senses.

Dunbar, P. Ere sleep comes down to soothe the weary eyes.

"Eliot." Felix Holt, the Radical.

Eliot, T. Animula.

Elizabeth I. Written in Her French Psalter.

Emerson, R. World-Soul, The.

Espaillat. Metrics.

"Field." Mummy Invokes his Soul, The.

Fitzgerald, E. I sent my Soul through the Invisible.

Follain. Face the Animal.

Fraser, K. Your sky against my starfish I know how big.

Fullerton. Poetry.

Gilbo'a. My Soul Wanders About.

Ginsberg, A. After Lalon.

Glatstein. I still remember the half-lit meaning.

If you should be surprised, Nathan.

Goldberg, L. On this day they break bread.

Goodison. Always homing now soul toward light.

Graham, J. Soul Says.

Greer, J. Rodin's "Gates of Hell."

Grosholz. Back Trouble.

Gumilyov. Memory.

Hadrian. Adriani Morientis ad Animam Suam.

Adrian's Address to His Soul When Dying.

Animula, vagula, blandula: The Emperor Hadrian to his soul.

My little wandring sportful Soule.

My soul, my pleasant soul and witty.

Halkin, S. Seventy-five are my abyssed forests.

Hayati. Before there was a trace of this world of men.

Is this darkness the night of Power, or the black falling of your hair?

Hemans. Indian Woman's Death-Song, The.

Henley, W. Invictus.

Herbert, G. Our Life Is Hid with Christ in God.

Virtue [or Vertue].

Herrick. Love Palpable.

Hildegard von Bingen. Soul is kissed by God, The.

Holmes, J. Love of the Flesh, The.

Holmes, O. Chambered Nautilus, The.

Tartarus.

Hopkins, G. Caged Skylark, The.

Housman, A. Be still, my soul, be still; the arms you bear are brittle.

Howe, S. He plodded away through drifts of i / ce.

Huxley, A. Two Realities.

Imre. So, then, the soul craves an earthly body.

Jiménez, J. I unpetalled you, like a rose.

John of the Cross. Commentary Applied to Spiritual Things.

Song of the Soul That Knows God by Faith.

Johnson, L. Destroyer of a Soul, The.

Jones, M. After the Small Pox.

József. Attila József.

Kabir. Guest is inside you, and also inside me, The.

Kendrick, D. Note to the Ophthalmologist.

Kgositsile. Mirrors, Without Song.

Kovner. Lord of Dreams.

Kowit. What chord did she pluck in my soul.

Kunio. Tanka: "Standing still."

Lamb, M. What is Love?

Lanier, S. To Beethoven.

Lawrence, D. Healing.

Shadows.

Le Gallienne. Décadent to His Soul, The.

Levertov. Eye Mask.

Weeping Woman.

What It Could Be.

Levy, A. Twilight.

Lewis, C. Impression, An.

Lindsay, C. To My Own Face.

Longfellow, H. Sound of the Sea, The.

Lovelace, R. To Althea, from Prison.

Lowell, A. Behind a Wall.

Lowell, J. Sonnet.

Lowell, R. We imitate, oh horror! tops and bowls.

Lowry, M. Joseph Conrad.

Lucretius. Epicurus praised.

Macdonald, G. Here lie I, Martin Elginbrodde.

Machado Ruiz. But look in your mirror for the other one,.

In our souls everything.

Look for your other half.

Wind, one brilliant day, called, The.

Mackey, N. Slipped Quadrant.

MacLeish. What the Serpent Said to Adam.

Madge. Landscape I.

Marston, P. Inseparable.

Marvell. Dialogue Between The Resolved Soul and Created Pleasure, A.

Dialogue between the Soul and [the] Body, A.

Gallery, The.

see also Ros.

Masaoka Shiki. Having molded clay in the shape of my ailing form.

Masefield. Sea Change.

McGrath, C. Wheatfield Under Clouded Sky.

McKay, C. I Know My Soul.

To the White Fiends.

Mechthild von Magdeburg. God Speaks to the Soul.

How God Comes to the Soul.

Melo Neto. Education by stone: through lessons, An.

Emptiness of man is not like, The.

Mew. Forest road, The.

Millay, E. Above these cares my spirit in calm abiding.

Monkhouse. Any Soul to Any Body.

Moore, M. What Are Years?

Moorsom. Company of the Birds, The.

Nemerov. Speculation.

Neruda. Sonnet XVII.

Newcastle, M. Dialogue betwixt Man, and Nature, A.

Dialogue betwixt the Body and the Mind, A.

Soul and Body.

Okamoto. Tanka: "My mind shattered."

Olds, S. Dead Body Itself, The.

Oliver, M. Some Questions You Might Ask.

Olson, C. Chain of memory is resurrection I am a vain man, The.

What soul / isn't in default?

Owen, W. Show, The.

Patterson, R. Harlem Suite.

Paulinus of Nola. To Ausonius.

Pembroke, M. O Lord, Thou Hast Searched and Known Me.

Philips, K. To My Excellent Lucasia, On Our Friendship.

Po Chü-i. Immeasurable pain!

Poe. Silence.

To One in Paradise.

Ulalume [or Ulalume—a Ballad].

Pope, A. Dull, Sullen Prisoners.

Price, S. Edge, The.

Ralegh, W. Lie, The.

Rankin, J. Tale.

Ray, H. Soul's Courts, The.

Robinson, A. Oasis, An.

Rochester, J. Mistress, The: A Song.

Roethke. Her Reticence.

Journey to the Interior.

Renewal, The.

Rossetti, C. Introspective.

Pause, A.

Study AA Soul), A.

Rumi. Daylight, full of small dancing particles.

Out beyond ideas of wrongdoing and rightdoing.

Rummo. World did not force itself into my soul, it seeped into it, The.

Sachs, N. Rushing at Times Like Flames.

Samio. Tanka: "In the evening wind."

Sarton. All Souls.

Seferis. And if the soul.

Shakespeare, W. Beshrew me but I love her heartily;.

Sonnet 26.

Sonnet 74.

Sonnet 146.

Shchirovsky. Dance of the Soul.

Sholl. Catechism.

Siddal. Lust of the Eyes, The.

Sidney, P. Song: "O fair! O sweet! when I do look on thee."

Sikelianos. Rehearsing for Death.

Smith, S. Animula, Vagula, Blandula.

Childe Rolandine.

Lord Barrenstock and Epicene.

Man is a spirit. This the poor flesh knows.

Scorpion.

Sorescu. Carbon Paper.

Map.

Spenser. Sonnet 79: "Men call you fair [or fayre], and you do[e] credit it."

Sonnet 81: "Fair [*or* Fayre] is my love, when her fair [*or* fayre] golden heares."
Stanescu. Homo Plangens.
Supervielle. Early in the morning.
Traveller, traveller, accept you must go back.
Swenson, M. In Love Made Visible.
Swinburne. Lake of Gaube, The.
Swirszczynska. Troubles with the Soul at Morning Calisthenics.
Szymborska. Preparing a Curriculum Vitae.
T'ao Ch'ien. Substance, Shadow, and Spirit.
Taylor, E. Accusation of the Inward Man, The.
Address to the Soul Occasioned by a Rain, An.
Meditation 8 (First Series).
Teasdale. Weariness.
Tekkan. Tanka: "Faintly white."
Tanka: "Not unlike a fish."
Theresa. Soul, thou must seek thyself in Me.
Thomas, D. Turning of the Year, The.
Toomer. Prayer.
Traherne. My Spirit.
Preparative, The.
Tsung Ch'en. Rebels' cavalry are everywhere, The.
Tsvetayeva. Blatant as factory buildings.
If the soul was born with pinions.
Unknown. Fairest Lord Jesus.
Great Summons, The.
Have I a body or have I none?
I know moon-rise, I know star-rise.
Lyke-Wake Dirge, The [*or* A].
Songs of the Sacred Mysteries.
Soul's Desire, The.
This Little Light of Mine.
Vaughan, H. Peace.
Resurrection and Immortality.
Very. Slowness of Belief in a Spiritual World, The.
Waldrop, R. Lawn of Excluded Middle.
Walsh, O. At length my soul the fatal union finds.
Weatherly, T. Mud Water Shango.
Wen Cheng-ming. For three years I sadly listened.
Weöres. Ecce Homo.
Wheatley, P. On Being Brought from Africa to America.
Whitfield. Yes! strike again that sounding string.
Whitman, W. Come, said my soul.
I believe in you my soul, the other I am must not abase itself to you.
Last Invocation, The.
Noiseless patient spider, A.
Song of Myself.
Wieseltier. Saul Re-enthroned.
Wilbur. Love Calls Us to the Things of This World.
Wilcox, E. Nothing New.
Wilde, O. Hélas!
Winchilsea. Nocturnal Reverie, A.
On Myself.
Yeats. Dialogue of Self and Soul, A.
Lady's Third Song, The.
Yosano. Tanka: "Clear spring, A."
Yoshimi. Tanka: "Casting shadows."
Yukitsuna. Tanka: "Amid the waves of time."
Zanzotto. Campèa.
Zhenkai. Evening Scene, An.
Requiem: "Not the living but the dead."
Ziedonis. How the candle burns.

Sound
Basho. Ancient pool. Sound.
Behrens. Trees are rustling outside the open window, The.
Brecht, S. Silence, 2.
Cherry, K. Pines without peer, The.
Clampitt. Syrinx.
Clare, J. Pleasant Sounds.
Cumbo. Nocturnal Sounds.
Dickinson, E. Of all the Sounds despatched abroad.
DiPalma. Rebus Tact.
Fatchen. Be Quiet!
Felltham. Upon a Rare Voice.

Garland, H. In August.
Hughes, T. Howling of Wolves, The.
Inada. Kicking the Habit.
Jacobsen, J. Bush.
Jones, R. Caught.
Joyce, J. All day I hear the noise of waters.
Kumin, M. Hermit Wakes to Bird Sounds, The.
Sound of Night, The.
Lavrov. Farewell, I say, farewell to the incomplete.
Levertov. Overheard.
Lindsay, M. Hurlygush.
Liu Yu Hsi. Gorges of Wu are hoary and im in the season of mist and rain, The.
Longfellow, H. Spirit of Poetry, The.
Lovelace, R. To a Lady That Desired Me I Would Bear My Part with Her in a Song.
Lowell, J. What [*or* And what] Is So Rare as a Day in June?
Lucretius. How They Communicate.
MacCaig. Blue Tit on a String of Peanuts.
MacNeice. Ear, The.
Magee, K. Tedium Drum, Part IV.
Mahon. Ford Manor.
Mayer, B. Midwinter Day.
McDonald, E. Itherness.
Nims, J. Philosopher.
Nye, N. What Brings Us Out.
Rossetti, C. Wind has such a rainy sound, The.
Shange. I live in music.
Sherman, F. Waterfall, The.
Stevens, W. Continual Conversation with a Silent Man.
No Possum, No Sop, No Taters.
Two Figures in Dense Violet Night.
Strand. I recall that I stood before the breaking waves.
Tabb. Whisper.
Thoreau. Dong, sounds the brass in the east.
They who prepare my evening meal below.
Tremblay, G. Not Sense.
Whitman, W. Proud music of the storm.
Wright, J. Depressed by a Book of Bad Poetry, I Walk toward an Unused Pasture and Invite the Insects to Join Me.
Yang Wan-li. Staying Overnight at the Temple of the Holy Vulture.

Soup
"Carroll." Song of the Mock Turtle, The.
Hilberry. Spoon.
Sandburg, C. Soup.

South Africa
Bereng. Birth of Moshesh, The.
Breytenbach. Dar es-Salaam: Harbour of Peace.
Firewing.
Journey.
Brutus. Clammy cement, The.
On the Island.
Robben Island Sequence.
Campbell, R. Attend my fable if your ears be clean.
On Some South African Novelists.
Césaire, A. Ex-Voto for a Shipwreck.
Cronin, J. Group Photo from Pretoria Local on the Occasion of a Fourth Anniversary (Never Taken).
Naval Base (Part III), The.
Fairbridge, K. South African Exhibition, 1907.
Hope, C. Flight of the White South Africans, The.
Jordan, J. Poem About My Rights.
Poem for South AFrican Women.
Kearney, L. After the Interrogation.
Kipling, R. Chant-Pagan.
Leipoldt. Oom Gert's Story.
Lorde. Evening News, The.
Sisters in Arms.
Mphahlele. Poem, A: "What is there that we can do or say."
Nortje. Letter from Pretoria Central Prison.
Plumpp. Poet.
Runcie. Slumber Song of the Gardens, A.
Sepamla. I Remember Sharpeville.
Measure for Measure.

Odyssey, The.
Silence: 2.
Small, J. Eating the Elephant Whole.
Unknown. Pass Office Song.
Vilakazi. In the Gold Mines.
South African War. *See* Boer War
South Carolina (state)
Moorer. Crum Appointment, The.
Timrod. Carolina.
Charleston.
Ode: "Sleep sweetly in your humble graves."
South Dakota (state)
Boyle, K. Thunderstorm in South Dakota.
Wright, J. Having Lost My Sons, I Confront the Wreckage of the Moon: Christmas, 1960.
South, The, United States
Adcock, B. Southbound.
Alexander, E. Letter: Blues.
Bontemps. Southern Mansion.
Cendrars. South.
Chambers, J. Why Are Daddies So Mean?
Coogler. Alas! for the South.
Crouch, S. Blackie Thinks of His Brothers.
Davis, F. Snapshots of the Cotton South.
Depestre. Prelude.
Emmett. Dixie [*or* Dixie's Land].
Foster, S. Oh! Susanna.
Old Folks at Home[, The].
Giscombe. (1978, Remembering 1962).
(1962 at the edge of town).
(The Recent Past).
Harper, F. Appeal to My Countrywomen, An.
Hayden, R. Runagate Runagate.
Hill, L. Tuskegee.
Hudgins. Saints and Strangers.
Jeffers, L. Tuskegee, Tuskegee!
Justice, D. Variations on Southern Themes.
Kumin, M. Chain, The.
Lazarus, E. South, The.
Lorde. Afterimages.
Melville, H. Iris.
Ousley. When the Mint Is in the Liquor.
Randall, D. Legacy: My South.
Southern Road, The.
Randolph, I. Rebel, The.
Sadoff. Civil Rights.
Shapiro, K. Southerner, The.
Thompson, M. To the South.
Toomer. Georgia Dusk.
Unknown. Confederate Memorial Day.
Walcott. Arkansas Testament, The.
Walker, A. It is true--/ I've always loved.
Walker, M. Childhood.
Weaver, M. Borders.
Wright, J. Invitation to Madison County, An.
South Wind
Lindsay, V. Moon's the North Wind's cooky, The.
Southey, Robert
Byron, G. Dedication: "Bob Southey! You're a poet—poet-laureate."
Don Juan.
"Carroll." Father William.
Unknown. Rebuke to Robert Southey, A.
Soviet Union. *See* Russia
Soweto, South Africa
Soyinka. Funeral Sermon, Soweto.
Space and Space Travel
Auden. Moon Landing.
Barrax. Christmas 1959 et Cetera.
Bold, A. Last Men on Mars.
Bruchac. Let the Midnight Special.
Connell, C. Space Men.
Cook, S. APOLLO.
Ark, The.
Eberhart, R. Dam Neck, Virginia.
On Shooting Particles beyond the World.
Fatchen. 'Jump over the moon?' the cow declared.
Harmer. Space Explorer's Story, The.
Heyen. Steadying, The.
Hubbell, P. Travelers, The.
Kendall, M. Ether Insatiable.
Kirkup. Questions and Answers (a ballad).
Space Trip.
Kitching. Swirling world stands still, The.
Within the space.

Kupriyanov. There is life on other planets.
Magee, W. Giant Rocket.
   How to Reach the Sun. . . on a Piece of
   Paper.
Mitchell, A. Song In Space.
Momaday. Walk on the Moon.
Morgan, E. First Men on Mercury, The.
   Spacepoem 3: Off Course.
Nicholls, J. Space-Shuttle.
Nicholson, N. Off to Outer Space Tomorrow
   Morning.
Owen, G. Space Shot.
Patmore, C. Two Deserts, The.
Plomer. To the Moon and Back.
Pugh. Craft I left in was called Esau, The.
Rice, J. Rockets and quasars.
Rogers, P. Achieving Perspective.
Rosen, M. Aldrin Collins and Armstrong.
   Humpty Dumpty went to the moon.
Rowe, A. Space Settlement.
Russell, S. Poem: "I keep feeling all space as
   my image."
Saitō Mokichi. Tanka: "Infinitely far."
Seaton, M. Wings.
Sharah. Package for Another World.
Smith, I. Children, The.
   Retired.
   Towards the Stars.
Smith, P. Annie Pearl Smith Discovers
   Moonlight.
Södergran. On Foot I Had to Walk Through
   the Solar Systems.
Summerfield. Sci-fi Horrorscopes.
Swenson, M. First Walk on the Moon.
Taylor, B. Canopus.
Walker, T. Doomed Spaceman, The.
Wilson, R. Space Walk.

Spain
Ackland. Instructions From England 1936.
Belloc. Tarantella.
Crane, H. Imperator Victus.
Levine, P. Midget, The.
   Salami.
Machado Ruiz. Here's another Spaniard!
   Welcome!
   Meditation for this Day.
   On the Banks of the Duero.
   Rainbow at Night.
   Today's Meditation.
MacNeice. And I remember Spain.
Marlowe. This said, the restles generall
   through the darke.
O'Hara, F. Madrid.
Ravikovitch. Marionette.
Salazar. Taking It Back.
Spender, S. Port Bou.
Warner, R. Port Bou.
Woodcock. Poem for Garcia Lorca.
Wright, J. Eisenhower's Visit to Franco, 1959.
Young, A. Topsy: Part 2.

Spanish-American War
Kipling, R. White Man's Burden, The.
Moody, W. On a Soldier Fallen in the
   Philippines.

Spanish Armada
Unknown. Sir Francis Drake; or, Eighty-eight.
Wilson, J. Armada, 1588, The.

Spanish Civil War. *See* **Civil War, Spain**

Spanish Succession, War of the
Addison, J. Poem to His Grace the Duke of
   Marlborough, A.
Defoe, D. Word's gone out, and now they
   spread the main, The.
Southey, R. Battle of Blenheim, The.

See also **Blenheim, Battle of**

Spankings
Hayden, R. Whipping, The.
Herrick. Upon Pagget.

Sparrows
Barker, G. Sparrow's Feather, A.
Bible, *O.T.* Psalm 84.
Cartwright, W. Dead Sparrow, The.
Catullus. Death of Lesbia's Bird, The.
Cheney, E. Overheard in an Orchard.
Cotton, N. Bee, the Ant, and the Sparrow,
   The.

Dunn, D. France.
Hackett, J. Bitter morning, A.
Harper, F. Sparrow's Fall, The.
Jarrell. Augsburg Adoration, The.
Johnston, B. Did You Ever Hear an English
   Sparrow Sing?
Kitahara Hakushū. Tanka: "Autumn
   bellflower."
Lear, E. Mr. and Mrs. Spikky Sparrow.
"MacDiarmid." Ho, my little sparrow! For
   well I know.
Mayhall. City Sparrow.
Miles, J. When Sanders brings feed to his
   chickens, some sparrows.
Nemerov. Because You Asked about the Line
   between Prose and Poetry.
Odarchenko. On Red Square, on the chopping
   block.
Savage, M. Disaster, The.
Shea, M. Sparrows sunning.
Sidney, P. Sonnet 83: "Good brother *Philip,* I
   have borne you long."
Skelton, J. Phillip Sparow.
Southard. On the top fence-rail.
Spires. Apology.
   Interrogations of the Sparrow.
Unknown. Little cock sparrow sat on a tree,
   A.
   Song of the Reed Sparrow, The.
Williams, W. Breakfast.
   Pastoral: "Little sparrows, The."
   Sparrow, The.
   Sparrows among Dry Leaves.
Wright, J. Sparrows in a Hillside Drift.

Sparta, Greece
Simonides. For the Spartan Dead at
   Thermopylai (480 B.C.).

Spas
Rochester, J. Tunbridge Wells.

Spastics
Miller, V. Subterfuge.

Speech
Barlow, G. Nook.
Bible, *O.T.* Bible, Proverbs 11:13, The.
   Words of a wise man's mouth are, The.
Bogan, L. Henceforth, from the mind.
"Carroll." Fit the Second: The Bellman's
   Speech.
Chukhonstev. Parrot, The.
Dante Alighieri. Ladies that have intelligence
   in love.
Emerson, R. Merops.
Franklin, B. Bits of Wisdom.
Graves, R. Cool Web, The.
Lipska. That Moment.
MacLeish. Speech to a Crowd.
McElroy, C. You will learn to speak.
Rukeyser, M. Effort at Speech between Two
   People.
Sandburg, C. Languages.
Stickney, T. And the last day being come,
   Man stood alone.
Unknown. Why English Is So Hard!
Wells, C. Overworked Elocutionist, An.
Williams, C. My Mother's Lips.
Williams, S. This Is a Sad-Ass Poem for a
   Black Woman to Be Writing.

See also **Screams; Talk**

Speed
Coatsworth. Swift things are beautiful.
Dufault. Driving Home.
Franklin, B. Bits of Wisdom.
Frost, R. Master Speed, The.
Herford. Snail's Dream, The.
Kandinsky. Chalk and Soot.
MacCaig. Ringed Plover by a Water's Edge.
Mori Ōgai. Tanka: "Never have I."
Pope, A. *et al.* On Riding to See Dean Swift
   in the Mist of the Morning.
Preil, G. How to Read the First Line.
Unknown. However they talk, whatever they.
   Railroad Man for Me, A.

Spelling
Bierce. Orthography.
Lee, L. Persimmons.
Robinson, E. Mortar.

Unknown. Jack Jelf.

Spenser, Edmund ("Colin Clout")
Beaumont, F. Upon Master Edmund Spenser.
Bentley, E. How vigilant was Spenser.
Crabbe. Muse of my Spenser, who so well
   could sing.
Drayton. Grave moral Spenser after these
   came on.
Keats. Spenser! a jealous honourer of thine.
Kennelly. Master.
Ralegh, W. Vision upon This Concei[p]t of
   the Faerie [*or* Faery] Queen[e], A.
Reynolds, J. To Spenser.
Smith, W. To the Most Excellent and Learned
   Shepherd, Colin Clout.
Southey, R. Sweet Spenser, sweetest bard; yet
   not more sweet.
Wordsworth, W. In trellised shed with
   clustering roses gay.

Sphinx
Emerson, R. Sphinx is drowsy, The.
Engonopoulos. On Boetian Roads.
Hayden, R. Sphinx.
MacLeish. What Riddle Asked the Sphinx.
Rukeyser, M. Myth.
Stewart, S. Mouth of the Wolf.

Spider Webs
Cooke, R. Arachne.
De Tabley. Study of a Spider, The.
Eberhart, R. Spider expects the cold of winter,
   The.
Hackett, J. Long line of web, A.
Miles, J. Fields of Learning.
Pitter. Maternal Love Triumphant or Song of
   the Virtuous Female Spider.
Van Doren. Gardener.
Wen Cheng-ming. Floating threads of spider
   webs hang.
Whitman, W. Noiseless patient spider, A.

Spiders
Basho. Spider.
Cooke, R. Arachne.
De Tabley. Study of a Spider, The.
Dickinson, E. Spider holds a Silver Ball, The.
   Spider sewed at Night, A.
Dizhur. With tender back glistening.
Druk. Communal Krakovyak.
Eberhart, R. Spider expects the cold of winter,
   The.
Empson. Arachne.
Farber. Spider.
Frost, R. Design.
   In White.
Fuller, R. Image, The.
Golding, A. . . . This Damsell was not
   famous for the place.
Graham, J. Geese, The.
Hackett, J. Old spider web, An.
Higgs, B. Parson's Pleasure.
Howitt, M. Spider and the Fly, The.
Issa. Don't worry, spiders.
Jackson, L. Elegy in a Spider's Web.
Lindsay, V. Spider and the Ghost of the Fly,
   The.
Little, G. White spider, The.
Littleton. Spider, The.
Lowell, R. Mr. Edwards and the Spider.
McPherson, S. Ability to Make a Face Like a
   Spider While Singing Blues: Junior Wells,
   The.
Merwin, W. Broken, The.
Mother Goose. Little Miss Muffet / Sat on a
   tuffet.
Newcastle, M. Common Fate of Books, The.
Pitter. Maternal Love Triumphant or Song of
   the Virtuous Female Spider.
Rabéarivelo. Slowly / like a crippled cow.
Richards, M. Christmas Spider, The.
Russell, T. To the Spider.
Spenser. Sonnet 71: "I joy to see how in your
   drawen work."
Taylor, E. Upon a Spider Catching a Fly.
Unknown. Inky, dinky spider.
Vallejo. Spider, The.
Whitman, W. Noiseless patient spider, A.
Wratislaw. Orchids.

Spies. *See* **Spying and Spies**
Spinning and Spinners
Huchel. Spindle, The.
Olds, P. My Mother Spinning.
Unknown. Cross-Patch.
Factory Workers' Song.
You might easy know a doffer.
Spinoza, Baruch
Herbert, Z. Mr. Cogito Tells about the
Temptation of Spinoza.
Spinsters
Auden. Miss Gee.
Blamire. O Jenny dear, lay by your pride.
Chudleigh. To the Ladies.
Couto. Lizzie.
Day Lewis. My Mother's Sister.
De la Mare. Three Sisters.
Ellis, C. Old Ladies, The.
Herrick. Upon Himself ("Mop-eyed I am, as
some have said").
Ho Xuan Huong. Confession.
Holmes, O. My aunt! my dear unmarried aunt!
Kasdorf. Leftover Blessings.
Klepfisz. They did not build wings for them.
Lochhead, L. Grim Sisters, The.
Miller, V. Spinster's Lullaby.
Pitter. Old, childless, husbandless, bereaved,
alone.
Plath. Spinster.
Pollitt. Turning Thirty.
Sackville-West. Spinster.
Unknown. I'll Marry Not at All.
Little Lady of Ch'ing-ch'i, The.
Old Maid's Song.
Spiritualism and Spiritualists
Amergin. Amergin's Charm.
Berry, J. It's Me Man.
Brathwaite, E. Xango.
Brontë, E. I'm happiest when most away.
Browning, E. Sleep, The.
King, J. Hymn: "For you I would put on
embroidered robes."
Kipling, R. En-Dor.
Lorde. Winds of Orisha, The.
Mirabai. All I Was Doing Was Breathing.
Why Mira Can't Go Back to Her Old House.
O'Hara, F. Ode to Tanaquil Leclercq:
"Smiling through my own memories of
painful excitement your wide eyes."
Patchen. In the footsteps of the walking air.
Temple, A.
Raine, C. Plain Song.
Smith, S. Mrs Simpkins never had very much
to do.
Wright, J. On the Skeleton of a Hound.
Spirituals
Hughes, L. Notes on the Broadway Theatre.
Tambourines! / Tambourines! / Tambourines!
Johnson, J. O Black and unknown bards of
long ago.
Unknown. Get on Board, Little Children.
Go down, Moses.
I Thank God I'm Free at Las'.
Spittoons
Hughes, L. Brass Spittoons.
Sports
Alexander, E. Today's News.
Armour. Good sportsmanship we hail, we
sing.
Betjeman. Subaltern's Love-Song, A.
Booth, P. Game.
Brooke, R. New Boy's View of Rugger.
Gildner. First Practice.
Jonson, B. To Sir Henry Goodyere.
Sidney, P. Sonnet 53: "In martial sports I had
my cunning tried."
Somervile. Where fair Sabrina's wand'ring
currents flow.
Welch, D. We Used to Play.
Wright, J. Mad Fight Song for William S.
Carpenter, 1966, A.
Wrigley, A. Owdham Footbo'.
See also **Athletics and Athletes; Games;** *names
of specific sports (e.g.,* **Baseball***).*
Spring
Acton, H. Beads of spring rain.

Akahito. Tomorrow I was.
When I went out.
Amann. Billboards.
Ammons. Spring Coming.
Anacreon. Ode 46: "See—the young, the rosy
Spring."
Antipater of Sidon. Priapos of the Harbor.
Argentarius. Trader, untie the long stern-
cables.
Ariosto. Orlando's Madness.
Ashbery. Spring Day.
"Bagritzky." Till Eulenspiegel.
Barbauld. Ode to Spring.
Basho. Village where they ring, A.
Berryman. I wished, all the mild days of
middle March.
Bertrans de Born. Song of Battle.
Bethell. Response.
Bibb. Early spring's sweet blush, The.
Bible, *O.T.* Lo, the Winter Is Past.
Bishop, E. Cold spring, A.
Blake, W. Echoing [*or* Ecchoing] Green, The.
Lark's Song, The.
Laughing Song.
Spring.
To Spring.
Bloomfield. Spring.
Blue Cloud. Spring Equinox.
Bly, R. Sleet Storm on the Merritt Parkway.
Bonnefoy. All, the Nothing, The.
Bontemps. My Heart has Known its Winter.
Bottomley. Eager Spring.
Bradstreet, A. As Spring the Winter Doth
Succeed.
Brickley. Spring evening.
Bridges, R. April, 1885.
First Spring Morning.
Spring Goeth All in White.
While yet we wait for spring, and from the
dry.
Brown, S. After Winter.
Browne, W. Signs of Spring.
Brownell, H. Lawyer's Invocation to Spring,
The.
Browning, R. Home-Thoughts, From Abroad.
Pippa's Song.
Bryant, W. Yellow Violet, The.
Buchanan, G. May Morning.
Bunting. Weeping oaks grieve, chestnuts raise.
Burns, R. Gardener wi' His Paidle; or, The
Gardener's March, The.
Buson. Spring rain! And as yet.
Bye. Spring.
Campbell, R. Georgian Spring.
Carew, T. Spring, The.
Cather, W. Prairie Spring.
Cawein. Purple Valleys, The.
Ceravolo. Spring in This World of Poor
Mutts.
Chao Yi. Spring Sentiments.
Chaucer. Canterbury Tales, The.
General Prologue, The.
Ch'en Liang. Tune: "Beautiful Lady Yü,
The"—Spring Sorrow.
Tune: "Water Dragon's Chant"—Loathsome
Spring.
Ch'en Tzu-lung. Tune: "Telling of Innermost
Feelings"—Wandering in Spring.
Ch'en Yü-yi. Spring Morning.
Chesterman. Outside.
Chia Tao. Last Night of the Third Moon, The.
Ch'in Kuan. Spring Rain.
Tune: "Happy Events Approaching."
Chu Hsi. Spring Sun.
Chu Shu-chen. Hysteria.
Spring has come. I try to forget.
Spring Joy.
Clare, J. February.
Spring Morning, A.
Written in Prison.
Clifton, L. Spring Song.
Coatsworth. March.
Coleridge, S. Answer to a Child's Question.
Collins, A. Another Song.
Song.
Conyus. Upon Leaving the Parole Board
Hearing.

Cook, S. Spring Flower, The.
Cornford, F. Spring Morning.
Cowley, A. Spring, The.
Cristall. Song: "Through springtime walks,
with flowers perfumed."
Cullen, C. To John Keats, Poet, at Spring
Time.
Cummings, E. Darling!because my blood can
sing.
Greedy the people, The.
In Just- / spring when the world is mud-.
O sweet spontaneous.
Spring is like a perhaps hand.
Spring omnipotent goddess thou dost.
Dafydd ap Gwilym. Duw gwyddiad mai da y
gweddai.
Davies, W. Days Too Short.
DeCormier-Shekejian. This Spring.
Dickinson, E. Before you thought of Spring.
Dear March, Come in.
I dreaded that first Robin, so.
Letter to Bee.
Light exists in Spring, A.
Little Madness in the Spring, A.
Spring is the Period.
Dobell, S. Chanted Calendar, A.
Donne. Love's Growth.
Eglitis. Winter has already shriveled—spring
rushes in with / black burial steeds.
Elliot, E. Spring.
Ellis, S. Your Poems at Daybreak, the
Destruction of Knossos by Afternoon.
Elytis. Psalm and Mosaic for a Springtime in
Athens.
Emerson, R. Musketaquid.
Ennis. Drink of Spring, A.
Fainlight, R. Spring in the City.
Fallis. Wise Johnny.
Fallon, P. Spring Song.
Fan Ch'eng-ta. Late Spring.
Farjeon, E. First Gathering.
Fichman. Abishag.
"Field." Goad, The.
Fletcher, J. Love's Emblems.
Fraser, M. Spring.
Frost, R. Prayer in Spring, A.
Spring Pools.
Fumi Saito. Tanka: "This huge pile."
Gibbon, P. Answer, An.
Gibson, M. Beginner's Mind.
Gilbo'a. Death in Spring, A.
Ginsberg, A. Easter Sunday.
Giovanni. Springtime.
Glück, L. For Jane Myers.
Gray, T. Ode on the Spring.
Gregg. To Be Here.
Grigson. In the Spring Garden.
Grimké, A. At April.
When the green lies over the earth, my dear.
Grimke, C. Parting Hymn, A.
Hagiwara Sakutaro. Spring Night.
Haines, J. And When the Green Man Comes.
Halevi. Earth in Spring, A.
Letter to His Friend Isaac, A.
Hardy, T. If it's ever spring again.
Year's Awakening, The.
Harry, J. Walking, when the Lake of the Air
is Blue with Spring.
Harte, B. California Madrigal.
Hass, R. Spring Rain.
Hawker. Are They Not All Ministering
Spirits?
Heaney, S. Rite of Spring.
Henri, A. Early Spring.
Herrick. Apron of Flowers, The.
Farewell Frost; or, Welcome the Spring.
Four Sweet Months, The.
Higginson, W. This spring rain.
Ho Hsun. Spring Breeze.
Hogan, M. Spring.
Holtby, W. Man who hated the spring was
cold and narrow, The.
Hong, Y. Spring Fever.
Hope, A. Return of Persephone, The.
Hopkins, G. May Magnificat, The.
Spring.
Spring and Fall.

Housman, A. Loveliest of trees, the cherry now.

Oh see how thick the goldcup flowers.
Howells, W. In Earliest Spring.
Howitt, M. Spring Song, A.
Hsiao Yen. Spring Song of Tzu-yeh, A.
Hsieh Shang. Song of the Thoroughfare.
Hsin Ch'i-chi. Tune: "Slow Song of Chu Ying-t'ai"—Late Spring.
Hsü Chün-ch'ien. Beginning of Spring—A Stroll with My Wife.
Hsü Pen. In Harmony with Kao "The Second" Ch'i's Poem "On Hearing a P'i-p'a Played Next Door."
Hsü Wei. To Hsü Shih-t'ing.
Huang T'ing-chien. Tune: "Pure Serene Music."
Hughes, L. April Rain Song.
Humphries, R. Heresy for a Class-Room.
Ibycus. In Spring, quince trees.
Ivanov, G. Spring said nothing to me—it couldn't.
Ivaska. To the Memory of a Poet.
Jacobsen, J. Hourglass.
James I, King of Scotland. Spring Song of the Birds.
Johnston, M. Vernal Equinox.
Jones, B. Spring at Nant Dywelan.
Jones, D. For Spring.
Jones, J. We have tulips in our flower bed.
Jones, R. Revelations, First Time.
K'ang Hai. When I have chanted my new poems.
Kao Ch'i. Moss below the Stairs.

Seeking out Hermit Hu.

Spring Day—Remembering Living on the River, A.
Kaplinski, J. In spring during spring.
Katz, B. Spring is when.
Keats. Song of Spring.

Sonnet: "After dark vapours have oppress'd our plains."
Kennedy, X. B Negative.
Keyes, S. Early Spring.
Ki no Tomonori. In the eternal / Light of the spring day.
Kim, K. Spring.
Kim, Y. Till The Peonies Bloom.
King, H. Summer Lost.
Kipling, R. Cuckoo Song.
Kitahara Hakushū. Tanka: "After lunch."

Tanka: "Gasoline."

Tanka: "My uncle."
Knister. February's Forgotten Mitts.
Kōkō Emperor. When I went out in.
Kuan Han-ch'ing. Tune: "Song of Great Virtue"—Spring.
Kuan Yun She. Sending Off Spring.
Kumin, M. May 10th.
Kunio. Tanka: "Standing still."
Kunze, R. Almost a Spring Poem.
Lalic. Tree in the wind remembered like a letter.
Lane, P. Spring.
Larkin, P. Coming.

First Sight.

Spring.
Lawrence, D. Drained Cup, The.

Enkindled Spring, The.

Spring Morning.
Ledwidge. June.

Twilight in Middle March, A.
Lee, J. Spring is a Cat, The.
Leonidas of Tarentum. Spring on the Coast.
Letts. Spring, the Travelling Man.
Levertov. Earliest Spring.

Springtime, The.
Levine, P. Sleepless Night, A.
Li Ch'ing-chao. Mild and peaceful spring glow, Cold Food Day.

Mist.

To the Tune "A Hilly Garden."

Tune: "Charm of Nien-nu, The."

Tune: "Manifold Little Hills."

Two Springs.
Li Po. Awakening from Drunkenness on a Spring Day.

Conversations in the Mountains.

To Tan-Ch'iu.
Li Shang-yin. Day after day spring's glory vies with the glorious sun.

Exile.
Libbey. Spring And.
Liessin. Spring Nocturne.
Liu Yu Hsi. Song of Spring Replying to a Poem by Po Chü-yi, A.
Locke, M. Sonnet: "I hate the Spring in parti-coloured vest."
Longley, M. Freeze-up annexes the sea even, The.
Lowell, J. May is a pious fraud of the almanac.
Lu Yu. Lazy.
Lyly, J. Trico's Song.
Ma Chih-yüan. To the Tune "Shui hsien-tzu."
MacNeice. Spring Voices.
Majer. Spring / slips / silent / snowdrops.
Mao Tse-tung. Tune: "Song of Divination"—On the Plum Tree, after a Poem by Lu Yu.
Marsh, E. Magic Piper, The.
Masaoka Shiki. During an illness.

Spring night.

Tanka: "Nobody with me."
McClintock, M. While we wait.
McGough, R. Fight of the Year, The.
McGrath, T. Black Train, The.
McKay, C. Spring in New Hampshire.
Millay, E. Spring.

Spring in the Garden.
Miller, D. Primavera.
Milton. Eden.

Spring Song.

Spring Time.
Miyazawa Kenji. Spring and the Ashura.
Moore, A. Girls' School.
Moorer. Easter; or, Spring-Time.
Morrison, L. Rural Recreation.
Morton, J. Spring in London.
Mother Goose. Spring is showery, flowery, bowery;.
Mountain, M. On this cold.

Pig and i spring rain.
Murray, P. Returning Spring.
Nahum. Spring Song.
Nashe. Spring.
Nesbit, E. Child's Song in Spring.
Ni Tsan. Inscribed on a Painting.
Nicias. Spring blossoms, honey-bee, in the colours you parade.
Noin. As I approach / The mountain village.
Nukada. When, loosened from the winter's bonds.
O'Hara, F. Easter.
Okamoto. Tanka: "Insect, An."
Oliver, M. May, and among the miles of leafing.
Olson, C. Variations Done for Gerald Van De Wiele.
O'Sullivan, V. To be in a place for spring and not have lived its winter.
Osundare. Eyeful Glances.
Ou-yang Hsiu. Answer to Ting Yuan Ch'en, An.

Green Jade Plum Trees in Spring.

Song of Spring at West Lake, A, Sent to Circuit Officer Hsieh.

Spring Day on West Lake.

Spring Walk to the Pavilion of Good Crops and Peace.

When the Moon is in the River of Heaven.
Overbury. Springtime it brings on the shearing, The.
Overton, R. Blues in "C."
Owen, W. Spring Offensive.
Paley, G. Love.
Pant. Almora Spring.
Pasternak, B. From Superstition.
Peretz. Hope and Faith.
Perry, N. Coming of Spring, The.
Peyanar. What Her Girl Friend Said ("As the cassias blossom").
Piatt, S. Sad Spring-Song.
Pien Kung. First Day of Spring, The.

Walking Outside the City Walls on the Day of the Cold Food Festival.
Po Chü-i. At the End of Spring.

Flower Market, The.

Getting Up Early on a Spring Morning.

Grand Houses at Lo-yang, The.

Parting from the Winter Stove.

Passing T'ien-mên Street in Ch'ang-an and Seeing a Distant View of Chung-nan Mountains.

Since I lay ill, how long has passed?
Poliziano. Welcome to May.
Pommy-Vega. Ah certainty of love in the hand.
Pratt, E. Come Not the Seasons Here.
Pritchard, N. Springtime.
Prudentius. Easter Eve.
Quigless. Spring.
Ransom, J. Miss Euphemia.
Ray, H. Coming of Spring, The.

Idyl of Spring, An.
Reese, L. April in Town.
Rexroth, K. Spring is early this year.
Ridge, L. Spring wind on the Bowery, A.
Ridler. Lumber of Spring.
Rilke. Gently gripped by the.
Rodgers, W. Winter's Cold.
Roethke. Bring the Day!
Rokeah. Hands full of sun are in spring's longing for you.
Rossetti, C. Amen.

First Spring Day, The.

L.E.L E. L.

May.

Spring.

What's in a Name?

Winter: My Secret.
Rossetti, D. Barren Spring.

For Spring By Sandro Botticelli.
Ryokan. First days of spring—the sky.
Saitō Mokichi. Tanka: "Frog."
Samio. Tanka: "On occasion."
Sandburg, C. Lines Written for Gene Kelly to Dance To.

Population Drifts.

Three Spring Notations on Bipeds.
Schneour. Fruited Month, The.
Schuyler, J. Spring.
Scriven, R. Cricketer.
Scully, J. Late Spring, A.
Seeger, A. Rendezvous, The.
"Severyanin." Spring Day.
Seward. On the fleet streams, the Sun, that late arose.
Shakespeare, W. Blossom, The.

Pedlar's Song, The.

Song: "Hark! hark! the lark at heaven's gate sings."

Spring.
Shelley, P. Cloud, The.

Question, The.

Question, The ("I dream'd that, as I wander'd by the way").
Shen Chou. Lady Picking Flowers, A.

To the Tune "Bamboo at West Lake."
Shepherd, R. Where When Was.

White Days.
Shibafune. In the spring ravine.
Sholl. Dogwood blossoms, lovely and full—.
Simic. Spring.
Sitwell, D. Green Song.

How Many Heavens.
Smart, C. On a Bed of Guernsey Lilies.
Smith, C. Sonnet Written at the Close of Spring [or Elegiac Sonnet].

To Spring.
Smith, D. Spring Poem, The.
Snyder, G. Sixth-Month Song in the Foothills.

What have I learned but.
Southard. Mirrored by the spring.
Spenser. Sonnet 70: "Fresh Spring the herald of love's mighty king."
Stevens, W. Depression before Spring.
Stevenson, A. Suburb, The.
Stickney, T. Age in Youth.

On Sandro's Flora.
Still. Spring.

Stilwell. Lyric to Spring.

"Struther." Lament in Spring.

Su Shih. Since coming to Huang-chou. Spring Day.

Su Tung-p'o. Rhyming with Tzu-yu's "Treading the Green."

Spring.

Spring night—one hour worth a thousand gold coins.

Spring Scene.

Summers, H. April Fool.

Surrey. Description of Spring, Wherein Each Thing Renews Save Only the Lover.

When Windsor Walls.

Swinburne. Hounds of Spring, The.

T'ang Hsien-tsu. Hsiu-chou.

T'ang Yin. Fog of night envelops the flowering trees, The.

Tao-chi. Inscribed on a Painting ("Little boat floats by the dock, The").

Tate, A. Seasons of the Soul.

Teika. Spring night's, The.

Theaitetus. Already the field, fair with leaves, in her fruitful bringing to birth.

Thomas, D. I, in my intricate image, stride on two levels.

Thomas, E. Thaw.

Thompson, I. Welcome to Spring.

Thompson, S. April.

Thomson, J. Late Spring.

Thoreau. Winter and Spring Scene, A.

Thyillos. Already swallows build their homes of mud.

Thymocles. Remember, do you remember those solemn words.

Tsung Ch'en. On the spring river, you depart.

Tsurayuki. I went out in the Spring.

Tu Fu. Another Spring.

By the Winding River II.

Chüeh-chü.

Song of the Beautiful Ladies.

Spring.

Spring Rain.

Written on the Wall at Chang's Hermitage.

Tu Mu. Spring in Chiang-nan.

Tucker, M. Spring.

Turner, F. Spring Evening.

Turner, N. God's Plan for Spring.

Ungar. Common Prayer.

Unknown. Before jade pavilions the new moon dims.

Bewwitching the blossoms of the spring grove.

Here we come a-piping.

It's Spring Returning, It's Spring and Love.

Last year in the spring when the birds were calling.

Lenten Is Come with Love to Toune.

Loosed from Winter's prison.

Luminous winds flicker in the moonrise.

March winds and April showers.

May Day.

May-Time.

Now is the month of maying.

Plum flowers all fallen and gone.

Sadness in Spring.

Spring breeze stirs a springtime heart.

Spring garlands the earth with leaves.

Spring Has Come.

Spring in the Bronx.

Spring Song, A.

Sumer is icumen in.

Tune: "Red Embroidered Slippers"—Spring Night.

Voice of my beloved! behold, he cometh leaping, The.

Waking Up.

Young swallows trill their new tune.

Untermeyer, L. Scarcely Spring.

Updike. May.

Vanhomrigh. Hail, blushing goddess, beauteous Spring!

Vaughan, H. Unprofitableness.

Veneris. *Spring,* the new, the warb'ling Spring appears, The.

Very. Spirit, The.

Winter Rain, The.

Virgil. Dark, The.

Wallace, R. In a Spring Still Not Written Of.

Wang T'ing-hsiang. Don't ask about the Six Dynasties of the Sui Palace.

Written in the Office Precincts.

Wang Wei. Composed on a Spring Day on the Farm.

Wang Ya. Song of Spring Journeying.

Wen Cheng-ming. Painting a Picture, The Tranquil Boat—Sent to Ko Ju-ching.

Quiet courtyard fills with greenery, The.

Wen-Ti Chien. Lo-yang.

Wen T'ing-yün. Spring Day in the Countryside, A.

Whitehead, J. Natural Theology, A.

Whitman, A. When genial Spring first bears the mating thrush.

Whitman, W. Spring.

Wilbur. April 5, 1974.

Cicadas.

Seed Leaves.

Wilde, O. Magdalen Walks.

Williams, W. Bird Song.

Late Singer, The.

Spring and All.

Wilson, R. Spring at Fort Okanogan.

Spring in Virginia.

Winters, Y. Time and the Garden.

Woods, J. What Do You Do When It's Spring?

Wordsworth, D. After-recollection at Sight of the Same Cottage.

Wordsworth, W. Change in the Year, A.

Composed at Rydal on May Morning, 1838.

Lines Written in Early Spring.

Written in March [While Resting on the Bridge at the Foot of Brother's Water].

Wotton, S. On a Bank [*or* Banck] asl I Sat [*or* Sate] a-Fishing; a Description of the Spring.

Wright, C. April.

Wright, J. Child, The.

Wu Chün. Song of Spring.

Yakamochi. Over the Spring fields.

Yang Chi. Eastern neighbor, western neighbor.

Five-color robe of embroidered silk, A.

Spring dreams, more spring dreams.

Springtime Embroidery.

Up at the prow, I wash my mouth, dripping water on my robe.

Yang of Sui. Spring River Flowers Moon Night.

Yang Shen. To the Tune "Chao-chün's Sorrow."

To the Tune "Chiang ch'eng tzu."

To the Tune "Flowers in the Rain."

To the Tune "Spring in Tien Is Fine."

To the Tune "Yellow Oriole" ("Willows weave spring sorrow").

Yang Wei-chen. Horseman at the Roadside, The.

Song of a Dream Journey over the Vast Sea.

Yi, S. Does Spring Come to These Forfeited Fields?

Yosano. Tanka: "Two chilly."

Young, A. Last Snow.

Stay, Spring.

Sudden Thaw.

Young, V. On the first day of spring.

Yüan Mei. Ballad of Peach Blossom Spring.

Finding Serenity.

Things Seen on Spring Days.

Yukitsuna. Tanka: "During a trip."

Zukofsky, L. I walk in the old street.

Springfield, Ohio

Linden, M. Riot, A.

Springs

Bryant, W. Fountain, that springest on this grassy slope.

Machej. Orchards in July.

Spruce Trees

George, P. Spruce.

Kirby, J. Proud Little Spruce Fir.

Schuyler, J. Buried at Springs.

Spying and Spies

Bowers, E. Prince, The.

Davis, D. Childhood of a Spy.

Dunn, S. What They Wanted.

Jonson, B. On Spies.

Kowit. Lurid Confessions.

Lehman. Perfidia.

Miller, V. Light Reading.

Petri. Night Song of the Personal Shadow.

Squash (botany)

Francis, R. Squash in Blossom.

Squash (sport)

Lattimore. Game Resumed.

Squid

Chin. Floral Apron, The.

Squirrels

Cowper, W. Squirrel, flippant, pert and full of play, The.

Eberhart, R. On a Squirrel Crossing the Road in Autumn, in New England.

Emerson, R. Fable: "Mountain and the squirrel, The."

Gilbert, C. Glimpses.

Howitt, M. Squirrel, The.

Howitt, W. Migration of the Grey Squirrels, The.

Julian. Mr. Squirrel.

Langland, J. Sacrifice of a Red Squirrel.

Long, R. Found and Lost.

Miller, J. Squirrel Stand.

Taggard. Squirrel near Library.

Unknown. Curliest Thing, The.

Squirrel, The.

Whisky Frisky.

Van Duyn. Sonnet for Minimalists.

Wolfe, H. Gray Squirrel, The.

Yeats. To a Squirrel at Kyle-Na-No.

Sri Lanka

Ondaatje. Letters and Other Worlds.

Stables

Herrick. Another Charme for Stables.

Morgan, R. Hay Scuttle.

Stained Glass

Hardy, T. Young Glass-Stainer, The.

Worth, V. Door.

Stairs

Bernstein, O. Don't Count.

Gibbs, M. On the Banisters.

Hughes, L. Mother to Son.

Levertov. Jacob's Ladder, The.

Li Po. Jade Stairs Resentment.

Slessor. Up in Mabel's Room.

Stalin, Joseph

Aleshkovsky. Comrade Stalin, you are a great scholar.

Herbert, S. Less Nonsense.

Kibirov. Year 1937, The.

Lowell, R. Stalin.

Mandelstam. Poem No. 286 (On Stalin).

Stalin Epigram, The.

You took away all the oceans and all the room.

"Sagittarius." Stalin Moy Golubchik.

Smith, S. Slugabed.

Yevtushenko. Heirs of Stalin, The.

Stamp Collecting. *See* **Philately and Philatelists**

Stanley, Sir Henry Morton

Rubadiri. Stanley Meets Mutesa.

Starfish

Kinnell. Daybreak.

Ormsby, E. Starfish.

Starlings

Hayden, R. Plague of Starlings, A.

Morgan, E. Starlings in George Square, The.

Wilbur. Writer, The.

Stars

Allen, S. If the Stars Should Fall.

To Satch.

Auden. More Loving One, The.

Avis. Evening star, The.

Barnes, J. La Plata, Missouri: Clear November Night.

Battiss. Limpopo.

Bensko. Elk Uncovers the Heavens, The.

Blake, W. Prince of Love, The.

To the Evening Star.

Bold, A. Stars.

Boldman. Fin, A.

Bonnefoy. Top of the World, The.

Well, The.

Bourdillon.　When Love Is Done.
Brontë, E.　Stars.
Bryant, W.　Hymn to the North Star.
Butler, J.　One Reason for Stars.
Byron, G.　She walks in Beauty like the night.
Campbell, J.　Darkness.
Campbell, T.　To the Evening Star.
Cavalcanti.　Ballata: Concerning a Shepherd-Maid.
Cawein.　Stars, The.
Chivers.　Apollo.
Cohen, E.　Drive-By Shooting.
Cole, W.　Back Yard, July Night.
Cooper, G.　Only One Mother.
Coslett.　Pole Star, The.
Daive.　Space instead of furniture.
Dante Alighieri.　To every heart which the sweet pain doth move.
Darley.　Fallen Star, The.
Davidson, L.　Beyond stars.
Di Prima.　Notes on the Art of Memory.
Dickinson, E.　Moon upon her fluent Route, The.
Outer—from the Inner, The.
Doolittle, H.　Sirius: / what mystery is this?
Dove, R.　Planning the Perfect Evening.
Duncan, R.　Passages 37.
Echeruo.　Man and God Distinguished.
Eimers.　Night Without Stars, A.
Espada.　Music of Astronomy, The.
Farber.　Taking Turns.
Fatchen.　Space Spot.
"Field."　Constancy.
Frost, F.　Snow-Stars.
Frost, R.　Canis Major.
Choose Something like a Star.
Come In.
Fuller, R.　Suns in a skein, the uncut stones of night.
Gangnus.　Firing back at my heavy heart.
García Lorca.　In a Corner of the Sky.
One.
Star, A.
Ursa Major.
Giovanni.　Stars.
Graves, R.　By this exchange of eyes, this encirclement.
Star-Talk.
Greville, F.　From Caelica.
Grunthal.　Constant starburst showers us, A.
Gryphius.　To Himself.
Gunn, T.　Blackie, The Electric Rembrandt.
My Sad Captains.
Guthrie, R.　Magi, The.
Haas, R.　Autumn evening.
Habington.　"Nox Nocti Indicat Scientiam."
Han Yü.　Pond shine and sky glow, blue matching blue.
Hardy, T.　Waiting Both.
Harjo, J.　Petroglyph.
Harter.　Clouds.
Only letting in the cat.
Hays, H.　Sacred Children, The.
Heavysege.　Winter Galaxy.
Heine.　Es Stehen Unbeweglich.
Hemans.　Lost Pleiad, The.
Herbert, G.　Artillery [or Artillerie].
Star[re], The.
Higginson, W.　Evening star.
Hollander, J.　Great Bear, The.
Hopkins, G.　How looks the night? There does not miss a star.
Starlight Night, The.
Hotham.　Letting.
Housman, A.　Stars, I Have Seen Them Fall.
Hugo, R.　Elegy: "I expected him to look dead in the casket."
Inada.　Concentration Constellation.
Jaccottet.　Distances.
Jeffers, R.　Nova.
Johnson, J.　Sence You Went Away.
Keats.　Bright star[, would I were stedfast as thou art—].
Kinnell.　Daybreak.
Kipling, R.　Astrologer's Song, An.
Kirschner.　Blueness of Stars, The.
Kogan.　Star.

Kolmar.　Toad, The.
Kunitz, S.　He runs before the wise men: He.
Li Ho.　For the Examination at Ho-nan-fu: Songs of the Twelve Months.
Lloyd, D.　Longest night, The.
Lowell, A.　Hora Stellatrix.
MacCaig.　Blue Tit on a String of Peanuts.
Stars and Planets.
MacLeish.　Epistle to Be Left in the Earth.
Pole Star for This Year.
MacNeice.　Star-Gazer.
Magee, M.　It Is the Stars That Govern Us.
Manilius.　What Constellations rise with the Lion. The great Dog.
Mayakovsky.　Listen.
Now listen! / If the stars shine.
Meredith, G.　Lucifer in Starlight.
Meredith, W.　Country Stars.
Miller, M.　Universe, The.
Moore, L.　Stars.
Morley, T.　You black bright stars, that shine while daylight lasteth.
Morris-Jones.　North Star, The.
Moses ibn Ezra.　Beauty of the Stars, The.
Nemerov.　Speculation.
Newcastle, M.　Of Stars.
Nicholls, J.　Andromeda.
Okigbo.　Eyes Watch the Stars.
Perlman, A.　Survival.
Plath.　Stars over the Dordogne.
Po Chü-i.　Climbing the Terrace of Kuan-yin and Looking at the City of Ch'ang-an.
Popa.　Ashes.
Heaven's Ring.
Ptolemy.　From the Greek.
Star-Gazing.
Rabi'a al-Adawiyya.　O my Lord.
Ray, H.　Star Song.
Rexroth, K.　Heart of Herakles, The.
Rice, J.　I am. . . Star Counting.
Rich, A.　Planetarium.
Rifat.　Stars.
Robinson, A.　Idea, The.
Unum est Necessarium.
Robinson, E.　Credo.
Roseliep.　Birthcry!
Campfire Extinguished.
He removes his glove.
Rossetti, C.　Where innocent bright-eyed daisies are.
Roth, H.　Evening star.
Rukeyser, M.　Darkness Music.
Sachs, N.　Chorus of the Stars.
Sandburg, C.　Stars are too many to count, The.
There Are Different Gardens.
Sappho.　Stars around the luminous moon— how soon they.
Shaw, L.　Stars in Apple Cores.
Sherman, F.　Daisies.
Sidney, P.　Sonnet 26: "Though dusty wits dare scorn astrology."
Sonnet 48: "Soul's joy, bend not those morning stars from me."
Sigourney.　Stars, The.
Simms, W.　Lost Pleiad, The.
Simovic.　Traveling Star.
Smith, I.　Towards the Stars.
Stevenson, R.　Escape at Bedtime.
Strand.　Man in Black, The.
Swede.　Frozen breaths, The.
Stars crickets.
Tanikawa Shuntaro.　Concerning a Girl.
Taylor, B.　Canopus.
Taylor, J.　Star, The.
Teasdale.　Falling Star, The.
Thomas, E.　Shooting Star, A.
Thoreau.　On Ponkawtasset, since, we took our way.
Tico.　After gazing at stars.
Toomer.　Face.
Tranströmer.　Track.
Tu Fu.　Stars and Moon on the Yangtse.
Winter Dawn.
Tuckerman, F.　Roll on, sad world! Not Mercury or Mars.
Some truths may pierce the spirit's deeper

gloom.
Sonnets: "Starry flower, the flower-like stars that fade, The."
Turner, C.　Orion.
Under.　And a Star Fell.
Unknown.　Cicada sings, The.
Song of the Stars, The.
Stars stand up in the air, The.
Wishing Poem.
Vaughan, H.　Friends Departed.
Joy of My Life! While Left Me Here.
To Amoret, of the Difference 'twixt Him and Other Lovers, and What True Love Is.
To Amoret, Walking in a Starry Evening.
Very.　Spheres, The.
Virgil.　Black spaces, The.
Walcott.　Star.
Wang Chiu-ssu.　Song of the Painting of the Long-Life Star.
Warren, R.　Notes on a Life to Be Lived.
Wellesley.　Lost Lane.
Wen Cheng-ming.　Mooring My Boat on the Ssu River and Watching the Moon.
Whitman, W.　On the beach at night.
On the beach at night alone.
When I heard the learn'd astronomer.
Wilbur.　In the Field.
Williams, R.　When Sun Doth Rise.
Williams, W.　El Hombre.
Wills, J.　Another bend.
Wilson, R.　Davy by Starlight.
Wordsworth, W.　I watch, and long have watched, with calm regret.
Yeats.　Sorrow of Love, The ("Quarrel of the sparrows in the eaves, The").
Yosano.　Over the old honeymoon cottage.
Tanka: "Into a pair of stars."
Yun.　Counting the Stars.
Zach.　Like Sand.

See also **Astronomy and Astronomers**

Statistics
Brett, L.　I keep forgetting.
Cunningham, J.　Meditation on Statistical Method.

Statue of Liberty. *See* **Liberty, Statue of**

Statues
Allott.　Statue, The.
Allston.　On the Statue of an Angel, by Bienaimé, in the Possession of J.S. Copley Greene, Esq.
Amann.　Winter burial.
Berryman.　Boston Common.
Bogan, L.　Statue and Birds.
Campana.　Autumn Garden.
Clark, T.　Statue.
Creeley.　Figures, The.
Statue, The.
Custance.　Statues.
White Statue, The.
Daniel, S.　Behold what hap *Pigmalion* had to frame.
Davidson, D.　Twilight on Union Street.
Druce.　Apropos of Garden Statuary: A Disquisition upon a Minor Genre.
Drummond, W.　Statue of Medusa, The.
Elenkov.　Stone.
Ford, C.　Bad Habit, The.
Guest, B.　Walking Buddha.
Handlin.　Cold winter morning.
Inez.　Instructions for the Erection of a Statue to Myself in Central Park.
Johnson, L.　By the Statue of King Charles [or I] at Charing Cross.
Justice, D.　Mrs. Snow.
Landor, W.　Duke of York's Statue, The.
Lesser.　Woman from Chianciano.
Lindsay, V.　Statue of Old Andrew Jackson, The.
Lowell, R.　Christmas Eve under Hooker's Statue.
Marston, J.　*Pigmalion,* whose hie love-hating minde.
Masaoka Shiki.　Having molded clay in the shape of my ailing form.
Mathews, C.　Sculptor, The.
McGinley.　Spanish Lions, The.
Mesens.　Arid Husband, The.

Muir, E. Rider Victory, The.
Nagy, A. I Carried Statues.
Nemerov. Statues in the Public Gardens, The.
Phillips, C. Toys.
Piatt, J. To the Statue on the Capitol.
Piatt, S. Stone For A Statue.
Plath. Colossus, The.
Raine, K. Statues.
Ray, H. Venus of Milo, The.
Rilke. Archaic Torso of Apollo.
Ritsos. Return.
Robinson, F. Brief day ending.
Rossetti, C. Study AA Soul), A.
Santayana. Before a Statue of Achilles.
  On an Unfinished Statue.
Seifert. Fingerprints.
Shelley, P. Ozymandias [of Egypt].
Stafford, W. After Plotinus.
Stern, G. Founder, The.
Stevens, W. Dance of the Macabre Mice.
Thomas, D. Walking in gardens by the sides.
Unknown. Epigram: "Says a Reverend Priest
  to a less Rev'rend friend."
Vance. Frozen Hero, The.
Virgil. It is I, lads, who look after this place.
Watson, R. White Lady, The.
Yeats. Statues, The.
Zagajewski. On the Escalator.
Zenodotus. Statue Of Eros, A.

Steak
Creeley. Naughty Boy.

Steam Baths. *See* **Baths and Bathing**

Steam Rollers and Steam Rolling
Moore, M. To a Steam Roller.

Steam Shovels
Malam. Steam Shovel.

Steamers. *See* **Ships and Shipbuilding**

Steel
Conyus. Six Ten Sixty-Nine.
Sandburg, C. Bar of steel--it is only, A.
  Prayers of Steel.
Wagoner, D. My Father's Garden.

See also **Iron**

Steel Bands
Beissel, H. Pans at Carnival.

Steeples
Moore, M. Steeple-Jack, The.
Williams, W. To a Solitary Disciple.

Steers. *See* **Oxen**

Stein, Gertrude
Nash, O. They Don't Speak English in Paris.

Stenographers
Page, P. Stenographers, The.

See also **Scribes; Secretaries**

Stepfathers and Stepmothers
Smith, S. Papa Love Baby.
Swirszczynska. Second Madrigal, The.
  She Does Not Remember.

Stephen, Saint
Dickinson, P. St. Stephen's Day.
Nichols, K. Feast of Stephen, The.
Sawyer, R. Feast o' Saint [*or* St.] Stephen,
  The.
Suckling, J. Upon Stephen Stoned.

Stepmothers. *See* **Stepfathers and Stepmothers**

Sterne, Laurence
Garrick. Epitaph on Laurence Sterne.
Muldoon, P. Yggdrasill.

Stevedores. *See* **Longshoremen**

Stevens, Wallace
Berryman. So Long? Stevens.
Lim, S. I defy you Wallace Stevens.
Roethke. Rouse for Stevens, A.

Still Lifes
Atwood. Against Still Life.
Tomlinson, C. Paring the Apple.

Stockholm, Sweden
Fulton, R. Remembering an Island.
Van Vliet. Old Champagne Glass.

Stockmen
Gordon, A. Sick Stockrider, The.
Paterson, A. Man from Snowy River, The.

Stoicism
Brontë, E. Old Stoic, The.
Dickinson, E. It might be lonelier.

Durrell. Stoic.
Hodgson, W. Glimpse.
Rossetti, C. Study AA Soul), A.
Sadi. Great Physician, The.

Stonecutting and Stonecutters
Fields, J. Mr. Tut's House A Recollection.
Hernández, M. Tomb of the Imagination.
Jeffers, R. To the Stone-Cutters.

Stonehenge, England
Johnson, R. William Stukeley made his own
  Stonehenge.
Rich, A. Dark lintels, the blue and foreign
  stones, The.
Warton, T. Written at Stonehenge.

Stones and Rocks
Allard. Silence a droplet of water trickles
  down a stone, The.
Ammons. Apologia pro Vita Sua.
Blackburn, P. Stone found me in bright
  sunlight, The.
Blake, W. Clod and [*or &*] the Pebble, The.
Corn. Naskeag.
Creeley. "I Keep to Myself Such Measures."
Davies, H. Poem: "It doesn't look like a
  finger it looks like a feather of broken glass."
Dickinson, E. How happy is the little Stone.
  Soul selects her own Society—The The.
Doolittle, H. Or is it a great tide that covers
  the rock-pool.
Dove, R. Fish in the Stone, The.
Drummond de Andrade. In the middle of the
  road there was a stone.
Dufault. Burden.
Dutton, G. Clach Eanchainn.
Elenkov. Stone.
Ford, C. Desire to be in Two Places at Once,
  The.
Goethe. Symbolum.
Haines, J. Eye in the Rock, The.
Hall, D. Granite and Grass.
Hecht, A. Giant Tortoise.
Herbert, Z. Sense of Identity.
Hughes, T. Still-Life.
Jaccottet. Weight of stones, of thoughts.
Jeffers, R. Rock and Hawk.
  To the Stone-Cutters.
Johnson, R. Beam 7.
Justice, D. Stone.
Kinnell. Path among the Stones, The.
Knight, E. He sees through stone.
Levine, P. Cutting Edge, The.
"MacDiarmid." Crystals like Blood.
  On a Raised Beach.
MacNeice. Death of a Cat, The.
Macpherson, J. Garden shut, a fountain sealed,
  A.
Magowan. Days of 1956.
Mahadevi. Vein of sapphires, A.
Mandel, T. Prospect of Release.
Masaoka Shiki. I can see the stones.
McCaig. Poem: "There is a wailing baby
  under every stone and you walk."
McCarthy, T. Phenomenology of Stones, The.
McClure, M. Moiré.
McCord, D. This Is My Rock.
McGinley. Choice of Weapons, A.
Melly. Homage to René Magritte.
Melo Neto. Education by stone: through
  lessons, An.
Merrill, J. Pyroxenes, The.
Millay, E. Second Fig.
Mo Shih-lung. Meditation Rock, The.
Molodovsky. Prayers: I.
Mountain, M. Beneath / leaf mold.
Okai. 999 Smiles.
Ortiz. Serenity in Stones, The.
Patterson, R. I've Got a Home in That Rock.
Peacock, M. How I Come to You.
Piatt, S. Stone For A Statue.
Piombino. My Lady Carries Stones.
Popa. Adventure of the Quartz Pebble, The.
  Dream of the Quartz Pebble, The.
Porter, P. What I Have Written I Have
  Written.
Pound, E. Ts'ai Chi'h.
Pratt, E. Come Not the Seasons Here.

Pritchard, N. Cassandra and Friend.
  Narrow Path, The.
Ratcliffe, S. Beginning in the light as heard,
  wheel on stone.
Redgrove, P. Minerals of Cornwall, Stones of
  Cornwall.
Reeves, J. Black Pebble, The.
Sartarelli. Early Spring, An.
Simic. Stone.
Skelton, J. Knowledge, Acquaintance.
So Chong-Ju. If I Became a Stone.
Sobin, G. Eleven Rock Poems.
T'ang Hsien-tsu. Cave of Gold Essence—in
  Ning-tu, The.
Tanikawa Shuntaro. Stone and Light.
Tekkan. Tanka: "Except the rare time."
Tomlinson, C. In Defence of Metaphysics.
Ungaretti. You Were Shattered.
Vaughan. Stone, The.
Walcott. Ruins of a Great House.
Wilbur. On the Marginal Way.
  Thyme Flowering among Rocks.
  Two Voices in a Meadow.
Wills, J. Water pools.
Young, A. Black Rock of Kiltearn.
Yu. Rock.
Yüan Chieh. Palace of Rocks, THe.
Yün Shou-p'ing. Brush in rocks, draw a
  stream.
Zealand. Still Life, Untitled, A.
Zenmaro. On Mumonkan[6].
Tanka: "On the road."

Storms
Aiken, C. Hatteras Calling.
Alver. Stellar Hour.
Amichai. Now, in the storm before the calm.
Asclepiades. Snow! Hail! Lower! Lightning!
  Thunder!
Ashbery. Morning Jitters.
Auden. First Things First.
Bachmann. In the Storm of Roses.
Barbauld. Summer Evening's Meditation, A.
Berryman. Your shining—where?—rays my
  wide room with gold.
Bishop, E. Little Exercise.
Blaser. Finder, The.
Blunden. Eastern Tempest.
  Late Light.
Blunt, W. Storm in Summer, A.
Braithwaite. Watchers, The.
Bridges, R. Low Barometer.
  Storm is over, the land hushes to rest, The.
Brontë, A. Lines Composed in a Wood on a
  Windy Day.
Brontë, E. High waving heather'neath stormy
  blasts bending.
Brooks, G. Michael Is Afraid of the Storm.
Brown, R. Storm high.
Bryant, W. After a Tempest.
Burns, R. Tam o' Shanter. [A Tale].
Campbell, D. Windy Gap.
Campbell, T. Lord Ullin's Daughter.
Carver, R. Window, The.
Césaire, A. Ex-Voto for a Shipwreck.
Chu Shu-chen. Stormy Night in Autumn.
Clampitt. Meridian.
Clare, J. Thunder mutters louder and more
  loud, The.
Coleridge, S. Storm, The.
Davenant. Winter Storms, The.
Davie. Remembering the 'Thirties.
Davies, W. Black Cloud, The.
Dawe, G. Sheltering Places.
De la Mare. Silver Penny, The.
Dickinson, E. Glee—The great storm is over.
  It sounded as if the Streets were running.
  These are the Nights that Beetles love.
  Wind begun to knead the Grass, The.
  Wind begun to rock the Grass, The.
  Wind took up the Northern Things, The.
Dipoko. Pain.
Eberhart, R. Youth and Age.
Emerson, R. Snow-Storm, The.
Falconer, W. "All hands unmoor!" proclaims a
  boisterous cry.
Fields, J. Ballad of the Tempest.
Fordham. Snow Storm, The.

Francis, R. Reading of the Psalm, The.
Freneau. Hurricane, The.
Frost, R. Line-Storm Song, A.
Once by the Pacific.
Storm Fear.
Garland, H. Boyish sleep.
Gioia. Summer Storm.
Hadewijch. Knowing Love in Herself.
Hall, D. Granite and Grass.
Sudden Things.
Hardy, T. She Hears The Storm.
Thunderstorm in Town, A.
Heifetz-Tussman. Thunder My Brother.
Heinze. Storm.
Herbert, G. Storm, The.
Herrick. His Hope or Sheet-Anchor.
Hewitt, J. Calling on Peadar O'Donnell at
Dungloe.
Heyward, D. Equinox, The.
Holmes, T. Room for All.
Hooper, V. Deep Season.
Hopkins, G. Hailstorm in May.
Howe, F. Torn Parts: the story.
Howe, J. Wild Night, A.
Hughes, T. Wind.
Jacob, M. 1914.
Jeffers, R. Gale in April.
Jewell. Thunder storm passing.
Johnson, D. Home Game.
Jones, H. On a Fine Crop of Peas Being
Spoiled by a Storm.
Kastelan. Blood and the Storm.
Kennelly. Island, The.
Kipling, R. Storm Cone, The.
Kogan. Thunderstorm.
Kyger. Caption for a Miniature.
Lake, P. In Rough Weather.
Lampman. Thunderstorm, A.
Lawrence, D. Lightning.
Storm in the Black Forest.
Lear, E. Jumblies, The.
Leopardi. Calm after the Storm, The.
Lima, J. Enormous Hand, The.
Lowry, M. Lighthouse invites the storm and
lights it, The.
McGough, R. Storm.
Melville, H. Enviable Isles, The.
Misgivings.
Mihalic. Approaching Storm.
Millay, E. Hearing your words, and not a
word among them.
Mitchell, K. Tree Stillness.
Mitchell, S. Thunderstorm.
Monro. City-Storm.
Montale. Fan, The.
Storm splattering the tough magnolia, The.
Moody, W. Bracelet of Grass, The.
Love in a Storm.
Moore, T. Golden Hour, The.
Morgan, E. Strawberries.
Morton, D. Old Ships.
Murford. Storm and Calm: Sent from Embden
to M. Edw. Ma. and M. Tho. Ly, The.
Nagy, A. Storm.
Nemerov. Brainstorm.
Storm Windows.
Sunday at the End of Summer.
Oliver, M. Lightning.
Padgett, R. After the Broken Arm.
Pagis. Footprints.
Patmore, C. Storm, The.
Pizzarelli. Just before the storm.
Rich, A. Attention.
Storm Warnings.
Ridge, J. Rainy Season in California, The.
Rubadiri. African Thunderstorm, An.
Ryan, R. Wet Night, A.
Schuyler, J. Crocus Night.
Seferis. Last Day, The.
Shakespeare, W. Blow, winds, and crack your
cheeks! Rage.
Shen Chou. On the Fifteenth Day of the
Seventh Month I Came Home Late from the
City.
Silko. In Cold Storm Light.
Singer, B. SOS Lifescene.
Smith, B. Backwater Blues.

Smith, C. Sonnet Written in the Church-Yard
at Middleton in Sussex.
Smith, W. Tempest, The.
Snyder, G. It.
Soyinka. Prisoner.
Stafford, W. Epitaph Ending in And, The.
Steere. On a Sea-Storm nigh the Coast.
Stevenson, R. Last night we had a
thunderstorm in style.
Su Tung-p'o. New Year's Blizzard, The.
Swift, J. Description of a City Shower, A.
Tate, J. Storm.
Thomson, J. Signs of Storm.
Tien Ch'ien. Freedom is Walking toward Us.
Unknown. Approach of the Storm, The.
Been in the Storm So Long.
Far off brough, A.
Lengthening Days.
Ode on a Storm.
Peace Be Still.
Stand by Me.
Summer Niight.
Tempest, The.
West Palm Beach Storm, The.
Virgilio. Heat before the storm.
Walker, J. Safe.
Wallace, R. Storm, The.
Weigl. Song of Napalm.
Whitman, W. Patrolling Barnegat.
Proud music of the storm.
Whittemore, R. Storm from the East, A.
Whittier. Sisters, The.
Wilson, J. Sonnet III. Written at Midnight, on
Helm Crag.
Sonnet VII. Written on Skiddaw, during a
Tempest.
Wright, J. At Thomas Hardy's Birthplace,
1953.
Wright, J. Storm.
Yeats. Mad as the Mist and Snow.
Pity of Love, The.
"Yehoash." That Is All I Heard.
Zanzotto. Behold the thin green.
Zaturenska. Tempest, The.

See also **Blizzards; Tornadoes; Hurricanes**

Storytelling and Storytellers
Armantrout. Generation.
Atwood. It's the story that counts.
Brown, D. When I Am 19 I Was a Medic.
Carson, C. Cocktails.
Chaucer. Franklin's Prologue, The.
Introduction to the Pardoner's Prologue and
Tale.
Nun's Priest's Prologue, The.
Prologue to Sir Thopas.
Coleridge, S. Love.
Davie. Remembering the 'Thirties.
De la Mare. Martha.
Dickinson, E. Ended, ere it begun.
Djanikian. Agami Beach.
Dove, R. Roast Possum.
Dunbar, P. Cabin Tale, A.
Harriet Beecher Stowe.
Fogarty. Remember Something Like This.
Frost, R. Girl's Garden, A.
Giscombe. Bro Duncanson.
(1978, Remembering 1962).
Gorbanevskaya. And where am I from? From
an anecdote.
Graves, R. Devil's Advice to Story-Tellers,
The.
To Juan at the Winter Solstice.
Hamburger, M. Treblinka.
Hankey. I Love to Tell the Story.
Hart, K. Story, The.
Hudgins. Telling, The.
Hughes, L. Aunt Sue's Stories.
Ingelow. Story, A.
Jaccottet. Letter of the 26th June.
Justice, D. But That Is Another Story.
Levi, P. Reveille.
Longfellow, H. Prelude: The Wayside Inn.
Lorde. Teacher.
Madhubuti. Union of Two, The.
McElroy, C. Griots Who Know Brer Fox,
The.

Tapestries.
Under the Oak Table.
Mitchell, S. Good Samaritan et Al, The.
Mother Goose. I'll tell you a story / About
Jack a Nory.
Oldham, P. War Stories.
"Pindar." Town Eclogue, A.
Po Chü-i. Rejoicing at the Arrival of Chi'en
Hsiung.
Reid, A. Spell for Sleeping, A.
Riley, J. Little Orphant Annie's come to our
house to stay.
Robinson, E. Lost Anchors.
Rumi. Minute I heard my first love story,
The.
St. John, P. We Are Going to Be Here Now.
Sandburg, C. They have yarns / Of a
skyscraper so tall they had to put hinges.
Sexton. Cinderella.
Rowing.
Shurin. Blue Shade.
Sidney, P. Sonnet 45: "Stella oft sees the very
face of woe."
Smith, I. Gaelic Stories.
Sprod. Request Number.
Stephens, J. Seumas Beg.
Stevenson, R. Land of Story-Books, The.
Stewart, P. Singing down the Breadfruit.
T'ang Hsien-tsu. My son, you loved telling
the story of Prince Nata.
Thompson, E. Mythology.
Unknown. True storyteller is a, The.
Walcott. Man Who Loved Islands, The.
Wallace, R. 1001 Nights.
Wang Chiu-ssu. Ballad of the Fatherless Boy.
Waniek. Sleepless Nights.
Warren, R. Tell Me a Story.
Waters, M. Mystery of the Caves, The.
Zenmaro. Tanka: "Old soldier, An."

Stowe, Harriet Beecher
Dunbar, P. Harriet Beecher Stowe.
Parker, D. Harriet Beecher Stowe.
Ray, H. Greeting.

Strafford, Thomas Wentworth, 1st Earl of
Cleveland, J. Epitaph on the Earl of Strafford.

Strangers
Arnold, M. Absence.
Barrax. Strangers Like Us: Pittsburgh, Raleigh,
1945–1985.
Bateman, C. Childhood of a Stranger.
Berryman. Dream Song 45.
Bialoszewski. Ballad of Going Down to the
Store, A.
Brown, H. Misguided.
Brown, W. Song For a Tourist.
Bruner. Casual Meeting.
Buchanan, G. Conversations with Strangers.
Bunting. Orotava Road, The.
"Carroll." Visitor, A.
Clifton, L. C. C. Rider.
Coolidge, C. Book of During, IV, The.
Crane, H. Tunnel, The.
Csoori. Stranger, A.
De la Mare. Galliass, The.
Stranger, The.
Ferlinghetti, L. Ladakh Buddhess Biker.
Frost, R. Love and a Question.
Gallagher, T. Hug, The.
Gardner, I. Loud Song, Mother, A.
Garrigue. Stranger, The.
Glazkov. Subject for a Story.
Halliday, M. Vegetable Wisdom.
Hemans. Stranger's heart! Oh! wound it not!,
The.
Hewitt, J. Search, The.
Hongo. Stay with Me.
Hope, A. Inscription for a War.
Housman, A. Shades of night were falling
fast, The.
Hoyt, C. Down from the bridge rail.
Kirchwey. Ambulance.
Levertov. People at Night.
Levin, P. Meeting of Friends, A.
Marinoni. Who Are My People?
McKuen. Voyeur, The.
Muir, E. Killing, The.
Olofsson. Autobiography.

Pizzarelli. Stranger passing, A.
Po Chü-i. Rain.
Rilke. Stranger, The.
Robinson, E. Flammonde.
   Fleming Helphenstine.
Saigyo. Woman Forsaken in Love, A.
Scovell. Stranger, A.
Shange. Elegance in the extreme.
Tadic. Nobody.
Thwaite. Great Foreign Writer Visits Age-Old
   Temple, Greeted by Venerable Abbess, 1955.
Unknown. Turkish Bakery, The.
Very. Strangers, The.
   Yourself.
Wallace, R. Riding in a Stranger's Funeral.
Whitman, W. This moment yearning and
   thoughtful sitting alone.
   To a Stranger.
Wilbur. Caserta Garden.
   Transit.
Woo, D. Habit of staring, The.

Strathclyde (region), Scotland
Reid, A. Isle of Arran.

Strawberries
Graves, R. Wild Strawberries.
Johnson, M. Strawberry, The.
Kenny, M. Wild Strawberry.
Logue, C. Good Taste.
Merwin, W. Strawberries.
Millay, E. Strawberry Shrub, old-fashioned,
   quaint as quinces.
Morgan, E. Strawberries.
Swenson, M. Strawberrying.
Taggard. Millions of Strawberries.
Unknown. Man in the wilderness asked of me,
   The.
Wallace, R. Wild Strawberries.
Willard, N. Original Strawberry.

Streams. *See* **Brooks and Streams**

Street People. *See* **Homeless, The**

Street Performers
Ashbery. Street Musicians.
Mole, J. Musical monkey is dressed like a
   flunkey, The.

Streetcars
Hare, M. Determinism.
Larkin, M. Riding on a Streetcar with My
   Father.
Sandburg, C. Halsted Street Car.
Stone, R. Burned Bridge, The.

Streets
Bachmann. Paris.
Banus. Eighteen.
Baro. Street climbs upward steeply, The.
Barrax. Strangers Like Us: Pittsburgh, Raleigh,
   1945–1985.
Bialoszewski. Ballad of Going Down to the
   Store, A.
Bryant, W. Crowded Street, The.
Desnos. St Merri district, The.
Dutton, G. Street.
Faiz. Vista.
Hardy, T. In a Cathedral City.
Harris, W. Samantha Is My Negro Cat.
Ingelow. Winding-up Time.
Jarman, M. Grid.
Lauterbach. For Example (1): Stepping Out.
Levy, A. Sequel to 'A Reminiscence," The.
   Straw in the street where I pass to-day.
Martinez, D. Necessary Story.
Moss, T. Fisher Street.
Nekrasova. Street perturbs my mind somehow,
   The.
Nordbrandt. Streets.
Nye, N. New Year.
O'Hara, F. Step Away from Them, A.
Paz. Along Galeana Street.
Po Chü-i. Climbing the Terrace of Kuan-yin
   and Looking at the City of Ch'ang-an.
St. John, D. Avenues, The.
Salom. Walking at Night.
Salter. Rebirth of Venus, The.
Scovell. City Worker, The.
Shapiro, K. Manhole Covers.
Shwarts. What that street is called—you can
   read it on the sign.

Simic. Read Your Fate.
Simpson, L. After Midnight.
Slessor. Choker's Lane.
   William Street.
Welish. Crossing Disappearing behind Them.
See also **Roads**

Strength
Aldington. Resentment.
Allison, D. To the Bone.
Arnold, M. Growing Old.
Babcock, M. Be Strong!
Berggolts. Conversation with a Neighbor.
Bible, *O.T.* Bible, Isaiah 40:31, The.
Bible, Proverbs 16:32, The.
   Psalm 62.
Bogan, L. Single Sonnet.
Brant, B. Her name is Helen.
Brooks, G. Strong Men, riding horses. In the
   West.
Brown, S. Strong Men.
Dickinson, E. Banish Air from Air.
"Eliot." Felix Holt, the Radical.
Emerson, R. Compensation ("Wings of Time
   are black and white, The").
Evans, M. I Am a Black Woman.
Galindo. Short Story, A.
Gilbert, C. Beginning by Value.
Grosholz. Eden.
Hadewijch. Love has subjugated me.
Henley, W. Invictus.
Howard, W. Young men!
Hughes, T. Lark begins to go up, The.
Jeffers, R. Rock and Hawk.
Jennings, E. Letter to Peter Levi, A.
Kuan Han-ch'ing. Tune: "Sprig of Flowers,
   A"—Not Bowing to Old Age.
Lincoln, A. Ten Rules of Conduct for
   Individuals and Nations.
Lipkin, S. When I was arranging letters into
   words.
Lovelace, R. Valiant Love.
Martynov. Be kind / Be iron—.
Moore, M. Peter.
Myers, G. Dear God.
Okamoto. Tanka: "Cherry blossoms."
Orban, O. That strength, which behind the
   tongue.
Pfeiffer, E. Lost Light, The.
Piercy. Woman in the ordinary pudgy
   downcast girl, The.
Plath. Mushrooms.
Ransom, J. Agitato Ma Non Troppo ("I have
   a grief").
   Spiel of [the] Three Mountebanks.
Rich, A. Phantasia for Elvira Shatayev.
   Power.
Rossetti, C. Study AA Soul), A.
Sandburg, C. Upstream.
Smart, C. Strength.
Stafford, K. Walking to the Mailbox.
Stern, G. Power of Maples, The.
Tennyson, A. Oak, The.
Unknown. Freedom in the Air.
   Ode to the Betel Palm.
   Strength for To-Day.
   Take My Hand, Precious Lord.
Very. Monument, The.
Webb, T. Ancient Prayer, An.
Whitfield. Self-Reliance.
Whittier. Help.
Wickham. Sportsman, The.
Yeats. Wild Old Wicked Man, The.
Zamora, D. Mother's Day.

Strikes and Strikers
Guiney. Strikers in Hyde Park.
Hayes, A. Joe Hill.
Unknown. Glorious Strike of the Builders,
   The.

String
Belloc. Henry King, Who Chewed Bits of
   String, and Was Early Cut Off in Dreadful
   Agonies.
Brown, G. Shroud.
Gildner. String.
See also **Rope**

Striptease
Durrell. Strip-tease.

Endrezze-Danielson. Stripper, The.

Strokes
Ammons. Parting.
Kitahara Hakushū. Tanka: "My uncle."
Lowery. Stroke.
Plath. Paralytic.
Rukeyser, M. Resurrection of the Right Side.
Stafford, W. Strokes.
Wagoner, D. Walt Whitman Bathing.

Struwwelpeter
Kumin, M. Fräulein Reads Instructive
   Rhymes.

Stuart, Charles Edward (The Young Pretender)
Burns, R. O'er the Water to Charlie.
Unknown. Will He No Come Back Again?

Stuart, James Ewell Brown ("Jeb")
Preston, M. Grave in Hollywood Cemetery,
   Richmond, A.
Thompson, J. Obsequies of Stuart.

Students
Blake, W. School-Boy, The.
Blind. Russian Student's Tale, The.
Brereton, J. You, friend, who whilom tossed
   the ball.
"Chorny." Life.
Clarke, A. Straying Student, The.
Enright, D. University Examinations in Egypt.
Freneau. Indian Student; or, Force of Nature,
   The.
Giovanni. Alabama Poem.
Gorey. Limerick: "Some Harvard men,
   stalwart and hairy."
Hilton, A. Heathen Pass-ee, The.
Hughes, L. Theme for English B.
Kabir. Simple Purification, The.
Kinnell. Correspondence School Instructor
   Says Goodbye to His Poetry Students, The.
Lewis, L. My Students.
Martin, C. E. S. L.
Moore, M. Student, The.
Naden. Scientific Wooing.
Nemerov. September, the First Day of School.
Nguyễn Khuyến. To Some Students Caught
   Nodding in Class.
Po Chü-i. After Passing the Examination.
Savage, M. To a School-Boy at Eton, Yes and
   No.
Snodgrass, W. Campus on the Hill, The.
Spacks. Freshmen.
Tollet. To My Brother at St. John's College in
   Cambridge.
Tucker, S. Discontented Student, The.
Unknown. Student's life is pleasant, The.
   Tutor who tooted the flute, A.
Wallace, R. In a Spring Still Not Written Of.
Wheatley, P. To the University of Cambridge,
   in New-England.
Whitman, W. To a Western Boy.
Wilbur. For the Student Strikers.

Stupidity
Armour. Pachycephalosaurus.
Cheng Hsieh. Collecting Antiques.
"MacDiarmid." Lourd on my hert as winter
   lies.
Samio. Tanka: "Monumental."
Wilkins, M. Ostrich *is a silly bird*, The.
Williams, W. These Purists.

Stuttering and Stutterers
Dugan, A. Stutterer.

Submarines
Cassity. U-24 Anchors off New Orleans.
"Klaxon." Submarines.
Wilkes, H. Q-Boat, The.

Submission
Bateman, E. It's a Great Big Shame.
Cunningham, N. Giving.
Davies, M. Love Song: "There is a strong
   wall about me to protect me."
Dickey, J. Leap, The.
Donne. Why are we[e] by all creatures waited
   on?
Frost, R. Reluctance.
Gunn, T. In Santa Maria del Popolo.
Herrick. To Anthea, Who May Command Him
   Anything.
Killigrew, A. Pastoral Dialogue.

Kizer, C. Bitch.
M–rt–n. Humble Wish, The.
Mirabai. O my friends.
Mitchison. My True Love Hath My Heart.
Murray, P. Conquest.
Nash, O. Tweedledee and Tweedledoom.
Piercy. Friend, The.
Stevenson, A. Suburb, The.
Swenson, M. Women / should be / pedestals / moving.
Teasdale. I would live in your love as the sea-grasses live in the sea.
Tomlinson, C. Oxen: Ploughing at Fiesole.
Trefusis. Valentine, A.
Unknown. Thy heart is like some icy lake.
Wickham. Slighted Lady, The.

Suburbs and Suburban Life
Bawer. Grand Central Station, 20 December 1987.
Behm. Message for Summer in the Suburbs, A.
Betjeman. Middlesex.
  Slough.
Bond, F. Pity Wasted.
Ciardi. Suburban.
Davidson, J. Northern Suburb, A.
Derricotte. Blackbottom.
Dickey, W. Suburban.
Eigner. Trees green the quiet sun.
Elmslie, K. Marbled Chuckle in the Savannahs.
Ewart. Nursery Rhyme.
Gotlieb. Three-handed Fugue.
Gwynn, R. Classroom at the Mall, The.
Hardy, T. Snow in the Suburbs.
Harwood, G. Suburban Sonnet.
Hutchinson, R. Suburban Wife's Song.
James, D. Blind Man Who Sells Brushes, The.
Jeffers, R. Carmel Point.
Jenner, C. Soliloquy in the Suburbs, A.
Kleinzahler. Lunatic of Lindley Meadow, The.
Lawrence, D. Suburbs on a Hazy Day.
Lomax, M. Other Woman, The.
Moss, H. Long Island Springs.
Nathan, L. Answer of Sorts, An.
Piercy. Development, The.
Riddell, E. Suburban Song.
Schuyler, J. Man in Blue, A.
Simpson, L. In the Suburbs.
Stevenson, A. Suburb, The.
Tennyson, A. Suburban Garden.
Upton, L. Lost Child.
Wallace, R. Driving By.
Wilbur. To an American Poet Just Dead.

Subways
Agee. Rapid Transit.
Betjeman. Metropolitan Railway, The.
Blackburn, P. Once-over, The.
Cohen, E. #2, Shoes.
Crane, H. Tunnel, The.
Cruz, V. Going Uptown to Visit Miriam.
Doty, M. Broadway.
Esteves. South Bronx Testimonial.
Fawcett, S. Subway.
Ferlinghetti, L. Reading Yeats.
Hollander, J. Curse, The.
Hughes, L. Subway Rush Hour.
Jacobs, L. Subway train, the / subway train, The.
Jordan, J. All the world moved next to me strange.
Logan, J. Brothers: Two Saltimbanques, The.
McKay, C. Subway Wind.
Merriam, E. Sing a Song of Subways.
Olds, S. On The Subway.
Orlovsky. Poems from Subway to Work.
Pitchford. Queen, The.
Pound, E. In A Station of the Metro.
Virginal, A.
Reznikoff. If there is a scheme.
Seaton, M. Fear of Subways.
Swenson, M. Riding the "A."
Tate, A. Subway, The.
Walcott. Village Life, A.
Warr, M. Brain on Ice.
Weiners. My Mother.

Success
Braley, B. Success ("If you want a thing bad enough").
  That's Success!
Cameron, C. Don't Give Up.
  Success.
Cole, H. Thy Best.
Davis, F. Robert Whitmore.
Dickinson, E. Success is counted sweetest.
  We grow accustomed to the Dark.
Eady. Success.
Erwin. For Someone Temporizing.
Forbes, J. Death, an Ode.
Fort, C. Worker (We Own Two Houses), The.
Garioch. In Princes Street Gairdens.
Gilder, R. Failure and Success.
Guest, E. It Couldn't Be Done.
Hardy, T. Ruined Maid, The.
Hendriks. Where It's At.
Herrick. Wassaile, The.
Ignatow, D. Fisherwoman, The.
Jenkins, J. *et al.* In Ferrara.
Kipling, R. If you can keep your head when all [about you].
  Winners, The.
Lanier. To you I dedicate this work of grace.
Lincoln, A. I Am Not Bound to Win.
Lowry, M. After Publication of Under the Volcano.
Procter, A. Envy.
Riley, J. Back to Griggsby's Station.
Saxe, J. Game of Life, The.
Smith, C. To a Querulous Acquaintance.
Strand. Coming to This.
Trowbridge, J. Farmer John.
Tu Fu. Traveler at Night Writes His Thoughts, A.
Unknown. Always Finish.
  Don't Quit.
  In everything you do.
  Success is speaking words of praise.
  Winner never quits, A.
Whitman, W. When I heard at the close of the day how my name had been receiv'd with plaudits in the capitol, still it was not a happy night for me that follow'd.
Wilcox, E. Will.
Wu Wei-yeh. Seeing Off Sun Ling-hsiu on His Journey to Chen-ting.
Yeats. To a Friend Whose Work Has Come to Nothing.

Sudan
Bekederemo. New from Ethiopia and the Sudan, The.
Kipling, R. Fuzzy-Wuzzy.

Suez Canal
Nemerov. Reflexions on the Seizure of the Suez, and on a Proposal to Line the Banks of That Canal with Billboard Advertisements.

Suffering
Aeschylus. Beseech you, think not I am silent thus.
Afterman. Pietà.
"Akhmatova." Everything Is Plundered[, betrayed, sold].
Alexander, M. Memory.
Alexander, W. Explosive Decibel Journeys.
Aristophanes. Suffering of the gods, The.
Auden. Musée des Beaux Arts.
Bevington, L. One more bruised heart laid bare! one victim more!
Bontemps. My Heart has Known its Winter.
Brainard, E. Compensation.
Brontë, E. Stars.
Brooks, G. My Dreams, My Works Must Wait Till after Hell.
Bruner. Gift, The.
  Rebirth.
Castillo, O. Before the Scales, Tomorrow.
Cheney-Coker. Hunger of the Suffering Man, The.
Chichibabin. Camel.
Ch'ien T'ao. Chill and harsh the year draws to its close;.
Chinnov. Sometimes, you give way to sickness.
Chipasula. Because the Wind Remembers.

Manifesto on Ars Poetica.
  Ritual Girl.
  Talking of Sharp Things.
Clifton, L. Prayer.
Crabbe. Peter Grimes.
Crane, S. Ah, God, the way your little finger moved.
Cullen, C. Magnets.
  Shroud of Color, The.
Dach. Lamentation during His Most Painful Illness.
Daniel, S. If this be love, to draw[e] a weary [or wearie] breath.
  Sonnet: "Care-charmer Sleep[e], son[ne] of the sable night."
Daniel, Y. Sentence, The.
Daniels, K. Lying Down.
Davie. Across the Bay.
Davies, A. New Sentience, The.
Dickinson, E. For each ecstatic instant.
  Through the strait pass of suffering.
  To know just how He suffered—would be dear.
Diop, D. With you I have refound my name.
Dowson. Benedictio Domini.
Drayton. Cryer, The.
Dunbar, P. We wear the mask that grins and lies.
"Field." Maids, not to you my mind doth change.
Friedrich von Hausen. Help! How Minne has deserted me.
Fu Hsüan. Woman.
Glück, L. Elms.
  Poem: "In the early evening, as now, a man is bending."
Goedicke. Without Looking.
Gryphius. Human Misery.
Gumilyov. I, who could have been the best of poems.
  Sixth Sense, The.
Hadewijch. Knowing Love in Herself.
Haines, J. House of the Injured, The.
Hardy, T. Hap.
Hayden, R. Soledad.
Hayes, A. Slaughter-House, The.
Herbert, G. Dialogue, A.
Herbert, Z. Mr. Cogito Meditates on Suffering.
Herrick. His Saviour[']s Words, Going to the Cross[e].
Howard, A. Good Shepherd's Sorrow for the Death of His Beloved Son, The.
Hughes, L. High to Low.
  Strange Hurt.
Hughes, T. God, A.
Jackson, L. Wind Suffers of Blowing, The.
Jouve. We have amazed by our great sufferings.
Juana Inés de la Cruz. Because my Lord was born to suffer.
Kaufman, B. Would You Wear My Eyes?
Kelly, I. To an Unborn Infant.
Kendall, M. Failures.
Knevet. Bottle, The.
Kogan. Star.
Krandievskaya. Those who would not accept went past.
Ku K'uang. Sonny grows up in Fukien.
Kunitz, S. Welcome the Wrath.
Kuzmina-Karavayeva. Who am I, Lord? Just an impostor.
Lane, P. Midnight Song.
Levy, A. Epitaph: "This is the end of him, here he lies."
  Felo de Se.
  Minor Poet, A.
Li K'ai-hsien. In the Second Month of Summer, Taking My Family to the Villages East of the City.
March, A. Out scouting for sound counsels? How to prosper?
Melville, H. Pebbles.
Meredith, G. 30.
Meredith, W. Korean Woman Seated by a Wall, A.
Millay, E. Ancient Gesture, An.
  Pity me not because the light of day.

Mueller, M.   Evolution: A Science Fiction.
Mura.   Argument: On 1942, An.
Neidhart von Reuental.   There is pain in my heart.
Ojaide.   Ward 6.
Olds, S.   I Go Back to May 1937.
Pratt, M.   All the Women Caught in Flaring Light.
Preygel.   Hospital, The.
Ransom, J.   Lady Lost.
  Necrological.
Reeves, J.   Doze, The.
Rilke.   Sonnets to Orpheus, The.
Rossetti, C.   Endure Hardness.
  Sappho.
Sonnet 26: "This Life is full of numbness and of balk."
  There's snow on the fields.
Scott, W.   Hour with thee! When earliest day, An.
Sheck.   White Noise.
"Shu Ting."   Perhaps our cares.
Sidney, P.   Sonnet 2: "Not at [the] first sight, nor with a dribbed shot."
  Sonnet 47: "What, have I thus betrayed my liberty?"
Simic.   Great Infirmities.
Sokolov.   Recollections of the Cross.
Sophocles.   Think on thy father in the vale of years.
Spender, S.   Epilogue to a Human Drama.
Spires.   Good Friday. Driving Weekend.
Unknown.   Boat of Cypress Wood, The.
  Orphan, The.
Very.   My People Are Destroyed for Lack of Knowledge.
Vinokurov.   Every store keeps a book for complaints.
Voznesensky.   Autumn.
Wang Chiu-ssu.   You think I am happy.
Wang Ts'an.   Western Capital is in turmoil, The.
Warren, R.   Riddle in the Garden.
  There once, on that goat island, I.
Wilde, L.   Who Will Show Us Any Good?
Wilde, O.   Ballad of Reading Gaol, The.
Williams, W.   Complaint.
Wroth.   Song: "O[h] me[e], the time is [or has] come to part."
  Sonnet 6: "Ô[h] strive not[t] still to heap[e] disdain[e] on me[e]."
  Sonnet 28: "Griefe, killing griefe: have nott my torments binn."
Wyatt, T.   At last withdraw your cruelty.
  Farewell, all my welfare.
  I love, loved, and so doth she.
  O miserable sorrow withouten cure!
  With serving still.
  Ye know my heart, my lady dear.
Yeats.   Fascination of what's difficult, The.
Yesenin.   From the start, each living thing's.
Zamora, D.   Loyal Housewife.
Zimunya.   Arrivants.

See also **Pain**

Suffern, New York
Kilmer, J.   House with Nobody in It, The.

Suffolk, England
Crabbe.   Peter Grimes at Aldeburgh.

Suffrage. *See* **Voting and Voters**

Sugar
Charles, F.   Sugar Cane.
Dabydeen, C.   Rehearsal.
Wallenstein.   Blues 1.

Suibhne [or Sweeney], King of Ireland
Heaney, S.   I stirred wet sand and gathered myself.
Unknown.   Sweetness of Nature, The.

Suicide
Abse.   Footnote Extended, A.
Aiken, C.   Solitaire.
"Alta."   3 : 1.
Ashbery.   Illustration.
Avidan.   Moment Ago, A.
  Two Memorial Poems.
Azevedo.   Suicide, The.
Balaban.   Story.

Banning, L.   Epitaph for a Scientist.
Barry, J.   Nun in Ninh Hoa, A.
Beer, P.   Lemmings die every year. Over the cliff.
Berryman.   Also I love him: me he's done no wrong.
  Henry's Understanding.
  I've found out why, that day, that suicide. Of Suicide.
Beshenkovskaya.   Old Russia's slavery rights.
  Boiler room. Night.
Bidart.   Sacrifice, The.
Blackburn, T.   Felo de Se.
Brett, L.   My Mother's Friend.
Brontë, E.   F. de Samara to A. G. A.
Broughton, T.   Serenade for Winds.
Bùi Công Trù'ng.   Fallen Fruit, A.
Callimachus.   "Goodbye Sun!" said the Ambracian.
Chatterton.   Sentiment.
Chesterton, G.   Ballade of Suicide, A.
Couani.   What a man, what a moon, what a fish, what a chip, what a block.
Crozier, L.   Last Testaments.
Dacre, C.   Power of Love, The.
Dawe, B.   Family Man, The.
Di Prima.   To the Unnamed Buddhist Nun Who Burned Herself to Death on the Night of June 3, 1966.
Dickey, J.   Leap, The.
Dickinson, E.   He scanned it—staggered.
Duggin.   For My Mother, Who Lives.
Eberhart, R.   Hardy Perennial.
Enzensberger, H.   Poison, The.
Foster, J. Lynn.
Gatty.   Three Little Pigs, The.
Ginsberg, A.   To Lindsay.
Graves, R.   Call it a good marriage—.
  Song: Lift-Boy.
Gregerson.   Salt.
Hale, J.   Six Feet Under.
Hardy, T.   Newcomer's Wife, The.
Harjo, J.   Woman Hanging from the Thirteenth Floor Window, the.
Hewett, D.   This Version of Love.
Ho Ching-ming.   Ballad of Yi River.
Hoffman, D.   Center of Attention, The.
Hood, T.   Bridge of Sighs, The.
  Faithless Nelly Gray.
Hotchkiss.   My Grandfather.
Housman, A.   I Counsel You Beware.
  It nods and curtseys and recovers.
  Sinner's Rue.
Huchel.   Psalm.
Hughes, L.   Bad Luck Card.
  Lament over Love.
  Suicide's Note.
Huxley, A.   Second Philosopher's Song.
Jarman, M.   Questions for Ecclesiastes.
Jones, R.   Trouble in mind, I'm blue.
Justice, D.   Suicides, The.
Kearney, J.   After the Interrogation.
Klappert.   Ellie Mae Leaves in a Hurry.
Knight, E.   For Black Poets Who Think of Suicide.
Knott.   Ant Dodger.
  Goodbye.
  Shorts / Excerpts ("I keep a TV monitor on my chest").
Kumin, M.   How It Is.
Kunitz, S.   Portrait, The.
Levy, A.   Cross-Road Epitaph, A.
  Felo de Se.
  Minor Poet, A.
Lorde.   Between Ourselves.
Lovelace, R.   Dialogue.
Lowell, R.   After the Surprising Conversions.
  Suicide.
Maclean, A.   Death of an Old Woman.
MacNeice.   Springboard, The.
Mahon.   Antarctica.
Mandel, T.   Shade, The.
Miller, E.   Mississippi.
Mirikitani.   Suicide Note.
Montgomery, N.   Eyewash.
Nemerov.   To D———, Dead by Her Own Hand.

Oates.   Suicide, The.
Olds, S.   Summer Solstice, New York City.
Oppen.   In Alsace, during the war.
O'Sullivan, V.   Elegy for a Schoolmate.
Parker, D.   Résumé.
Pfeiffer, E.   So the river—yes, the river; I have come to that at last.
Piercy.   My Rich Uncle, Whom I Only Met Three Times.
Plath.   Ariel.
  Edge.
  Lady Lazarus.
Reznikoff.   When the Second World War began.
Rich, A.   From a Survivor.
  Tattered Kaddish.
  Whatever it was: the grains of the glacier caked in the boot-cleats.
Ritsos.   Requiem on Poros.
Rivard.   Earth to Tell of the Beasts.
Robinson, E.   Miller's wife had waited long, The.
  Richard Cory.
Rodriguez, A.   Heavy blue veins streaked across my mother's legs, some of them bunched up into dark lumps at her ankles.
Roethke.   Kitty-Cat Bird, he sat on a fence, The.
Rukeyser, M.   Power of Suicide, The.
Sackville-West.   Tess.
Sandeen.   Way Down, The.
Sarton.   "Yes," you say, "of course at Christmas".
Sassoon.   Suicide in [the] Trenches.
Scovell.   Suicide, The.
Seward.   Sonnet: "From a rived tree, that stands beside the grave."
Sexton.   Risk, The.
  Wanting to Die.
Shakespeare, W.   Hamlet's Soliloquy.
  Sonnet 66.
Shapcott, T.   Autumn.
Sholl.   Girl Named Spring, A.
Simon, P.   Richard Cory.
Smith, S.   Exeat.
Snodgrass, W.   Magda Goebbels ("This is the needle that we give").
Sorescu.   Start.
Spender, S.   History and Reality.
Spenser.   Who travels [or trauels] by the wearie wandring way.
Starbuck, G.   Of Late.
Stevenson, A.   Suicide.
Stevenson, R.   Celestial Surgeon, The.
Stockenström.   On the Suicide of Young Writers.
Stone, R.   Turn Your Eyes Away.
Storni.   I Am Going to Sleep (Suicide Poem).
Swede.   At the edge of the precipice I become logical.
Symons, J.   Hart Crane.
Tennyson, A.   Lucretius.
Thomson, J.   In the Room.
Unknown.   Caroline of Edinboro' Town.
  Dispute over Suicide, A.
  On the Threshold.
  Poor But Honest.
  Willy Drowned in Yarrow.
Wakoski.   For Craig Who Leapt Off a Cliff in to Hummingbird Light.
  Justice Is Reason Enough.
Walker, A.   Suicide.
Walsh, W.   Despairing Lover, The.
Warren, R.   Confederate Veteran Tries to Explain the Event, A.
Wat.   Joke, A.
Webb, P.   To Friends Who Have Also Considered Suicide.
Whittemore, R.   On the Suicide of a Friend.
Willis, N.   To Helen in a Huff.
Wollach.   Splitting the Infinite.
Wright, C.   Scratch Music.
Wright, F.   Certain Tall Buildings.
Wright, J.   Minneapolis Poem, The.
Wright, J.   Precipice, The.
Wu Chia-chi.   Grain-Barge Wife, The.
  Woman Née Wu, The.

Wyatt, T. Absence! Absenting causeth me to complain.
"Yashin." I am fated to perform a heroic deed.
Young, A. Advice of an Efficiency Expert, The.

Sullivan, John L.
Frost, R. John L. Sullivan Enters Heaven.

Sumac
Very. Sumach Leaves, The.

Summer
Adams, L. Country Summer.
Alexander, E. Nineteen.
Aliger. Summer days are noticeably shortening, The.
Asch. Summer.
Ashbery. Summer.
Baillie, J. Summer's Day, A.
Bampfylde. On a Wet Summer.
Barker, G. Summer Idyll.
Barnes, J. Dog Days 1978.
Barnes, W. Musings.
Basho. Summer grasses grow, The.
Behm. Message for Summer in the Suburbs, A.
Benson, S. Beaten Track, The.
Bernstein, O. Time to Leave.
Berry, J. Pods Pop and Grin.
Bishop, E. Summer's Dream, A.
Blake, W. Prince of Love, The.
School-Boy, The.
Bloomfield. Summer.
Bogan, L. Roman Fountain.
Bonnefoy. Stone, A.
Summer Again.
Braithwaite. Quiet has a hidden sound.
Brickley. Summer evening.
Brodsky, J. Roman Elegies.
Brooks, G. Ballad of Edie Barrow, The.
Bryant, W. Midsummer.
Summer Wind.
Bu-er. Late Indian summer's.
Burns, R. Birks of Aberfeldy, The [Composed on the Spot].
Simmer's a pleasant time.
Call, W. Summer Days.
Canton. Day-Dreams.
Ch'ien T'ao. Matching a Poem by Secretary Kuo.
Shady, shady the wood in front of the Hall;.
Chiyojo. Grazing.
Clampitt. Meridian.
Clare, J. Secret Love.
Summer Images.
Clark, T. You (III).
Coatsworth. What Could Be Lovelier than to Hear.
Corbin, A. Harvest, The.
Cornford, F. Grand Ballet.
Cornish, S. Generations 1.
Cristall. Song: "Through springtime walks, with flowers perfumed."
Cummings, E. Out of midsummer's blazing most not night.
Davies, I. High Summer on the Mountains.
De la Mare. Summer Evening.
Dickinson, E. As imperceptibly as Grief.
Bee is not afraid of me, The.
Consulting summer's clock.
Further in Summer than the Birds.
Indian Summer.
Renunciation.
Soft Sea washed around the House, A.
Some one prepared this mighty show.
'Twas here my summer paused.
Doolittle, H. Blue-geese, white-geese, you may say.
Dumbrveanu. Seeds of Flight.
Dunbar, P. Lover's Lane.
Song of Summer.
Summer in the South.
Summer's Night, A.
Eliot, T. New Hampshire.
Fan Ch'eng-ta. Summer.
"Field." O Wind, thou hast thy kingdom in the trees.
Unbosoming.

Field, R. Summer Morning, A.
Flynn, M. Sandlot Days.
Garner. Summer Solstice.
Gerhardt. Go out in this dear summertide.
Gilbert, C. Now.
Giovanni. Knoxville, Tennessee.
Graves, R. Blue-Fly, The.
Hadas, R. Moments of Summer.
Hardy, T. This Summer and Last.
When Oats Were Reaped.
Harr, L. Hot summer wind, A.
Indian summer.
Hass, R. Bashō, A Departure.
Tahoe in August.
Hayden, R. Summertime and the Living.
Heaney, S. Summer Home.
Henderson-Holmes. Friendly Town #1.
Herrick. Four Sweet Months, The.
Hesiod. Summer.
Higginson, W. Summer moon.
Hoban. Summer goes, summer goes.
Hopkins, G. Summer Malison, The.
Horton, G. On Summer.
Hotham. Unsnapping.
Hristic. Sentimental Voyage Around My Room, A.
HSü Ling. Waters of Lung-t'ou, The.
Hume, A. Summer's Day, A.
Jackson, R. Sunday Brunch.
Jensen, L. To a Stranger (At the End of a Caboose).
Johnson, H. Summer Matures.
Jones, E. High Summer.
Jonson, B. Epithalamion: or, a Song.
Keyser. Rainy summer night.
King, H. Summer Lost.
Kinnell. In Fields of Summer.
Kirattanar. What Her Girl Friend Said before the elopement.
Kitahara Hakushū. Tanka: "Almost invisible."
Kulbak. Summer.
Kunio. Tanka: "Late summer day."
Kunitz, S. End of Summer.
Touch Me.
Lampman. Heat.
Lazarus, E. Long Island Sound.
Li Po. In the Mountains on a Summer Day.
Summer Day in the Mountains.
Llwyd, M. 1. What? summer now? divisions ring.
Lux. There Were Some Summers.
Lyles. Summer night.
Summer stillness.
MacCaig. Looking Down on Glen Canisp.
Summer Farm.
Macdonald, G. Sweet Peril.
Machado Ruiz. Summer Night.
MacLeish. Long Hot Summer.
Magrelli. In summer, like the theaters, I close up.
Mahapatra, J. Summer Poem, A.
Masaoka Shiki. Tanka: "Tree with lush leaves."
Mathews, A. Woodniche.
McClatchy. Grasshopper.
McClintock, M. Long summer day.
McGirt. When the Sun Shines Hot.
McGrath, T. Black Train, The.
Mead, M. Misericordia.
Meredith, G. It is the season of the sweet wild rose.
Out in the yellow meadows, where the bee.
Merrill, J. To a Butterfly.
Meynell, A. Rainy Summer, The.
Summer in England, 1914.
Miller, V. On Approaching My Birthday.
Mitchison. Midsummer Apple Tree, The.
Moore, L. Indian Girl.
Summer noon.
Moore, T. 'Tis the Last Rose of Summer.
Morris, W. Summer Dawn.
Mother Goose. Spring is showery, flowery, bowery;.
Mountain, M. Summer night clothes whirling in a dryer.
Myers, W. Summer.
Nashe. Baning Summer.

Nicholson, N. For Hokey and Henrietta.
O'Hara, F. Summer Breezes.
Orban, O. Summer on the Lake, A.
Ovid. 1.5.
Owen, W. From My Diary, July 1914.
Pagis. Words.
Peele. Song: "When as [or whenas] the rye [or rie] reach to the chin."
Perlman, A. Summer Adjustments.
Plath. Frog Autumn.
Po Chü-i. Beginning of Summer, The.
In Early Summer Lodging in a Temple to Enjoy the Moonlight.
Posey, A. Midsummer.
Power, K. Sestina for Jaime.
Probyn. Song Out of Season, A.
Quigless. Summer.
Rago. Summer Countries, The.
Rexroth, K. Heart of Herakles, The.
Ridlon. That Was Summer.
Robinson, M. London's Summer Morning.
Rossetti, C. Bitter for Sweet.
Fly away, fly away over the sea.
October Garden, An.
Summer.
Summer Is Ended.
Summer Wish, A.
Sampter. Summer Sabbath.
Sarton. Small Joys.
Schuyler, J. Buried at Springs.
I Think.
Shimmer.
Scully, J. Midsummer.
Sexton. I Remember.
Shakespeare, W. Flowers of Perdita, The.
Sonnet 18.
Shelley, P. Summer and Winter.
Simic. Summer Morning.
Simmons, J. For Imelda.
Sloan, M. Eccentricity of the Middle Ground.
So Chong-Ju. Fresh Green, The.
Södergran. Forest Lake.
Soutar. Summer is by.
Spark. Kensington Gardens.
Spiess. Dry, summer day.
Stein, D. Heat.
Stern, G. What It Is Like.
Stevens, W. Banal Sojourn.
Beginning, The.
Credences of Summer.
Stickney, T. I heard a river thro' the valley wander.
Strand. Man in Black, The.
Strange. Childhood.
Stuart, D. River, The.
Su Shun-ch'in. Summertime.
Surrey. Description of Spring, Wherein Each Thing Renews Save Only the Lover.
Love's Rebel.
Swede. Windless summer day.
Swenson, M. Centaur, The.
Tablada. Red cold / guffaw of summer.
Tao-chi. Inscribed on My Large Landscape Hanging Scroll "Listening to a Waterfall."
Tate, A. Seasons of the Soul.
Teasdale. August Night.
Tennyson, A. Dualisms.
Throstle, The.
Thaxter. August.
Trakl. Summer.
Tranströmer. It's been a hard winter, but summer is here and the fields.
Tranter. Backyard.
Treece. That summer, the red may and the white may made.
Tu Fu. South Wind.
Summer Night.
Tuckerman, F. Cricket, The.
Ulinover. In the Courtyard.
Unknown. First of summer, lovely sight.
Full early in the morning.
In the hottest time, when all is still and windless.
Sumer is icumen in.
Summer Song.
Swarm of bees in May, A.
Updike. August.

Virgil. Bitterness.
Trickling.
Wade, B. Summer School.
Walcott. Midsummer LIV.
Midsummer, Tobago.
Midsummer: XXXI.
Rest, Christ! from tireless war. See, it's midsummer.
Wilbur. Exeunt.
My Father Paints the Summer.
Praise in Summer.
Williams, W. Botticellian Trees, The.
Ivy Crown, The.
Wills, J. Summer drizzle.
Wilson, R. Summer.
Wood, S. Witness.
Woty. Lines Written in the Dog-Days.
Young, D. Lace.
Young, K. Preserving, The.
Zach. Soft Warm Breeze, A.
Zanzotto. Campèa.
Ziedonis. That was a beautiful summer.

Sumner, Charles
Ray, H. Charles Sumner.

Sun
Adams, J. Dream, or the Type of the Rising Sun, A.
Al-Harizi. Sun, The.
Alexander, M. People of Unrest.
Ancient Egyptian Oral Tradition. Poem to the Sun ("All the cattle are resting in the fields").
Poem to the Sun ("Boats sail upstream and downstream alike, The").
Aristophanes. Song of the Clouds.
Bacharach. Poem for the Sefirot as a Wheel of Light, A.
Ball, H. Sun, The.
Bartusek. Heliotropism / of branches, now darkened.
Behn, H. Circles.
Berry, J. Pods Pop and Grin.
Bibb. Ode to the Sun.
Blake, W. Ah Sun-flower.
Blight. Sun.
Borowski. Sun of Auschwitz, The.
Brickley. Few flakes appear, A.
Brontë, A. Home.
Brontë, E. It will not shine again.
Brooks, G. Boy Breaking Glass.
Browning, R. Parting at Morning.
Brutus. This sun on this rubble after rain.
Buckley, C. Sun Spots.
Campion, T. Follow thy fair sun unhappy shadow.
Catullus. Lines from Catullus.
Celan. Thread suns / above the gray-black [*or* grey-black] wasteland [*or* wilderness].
Ceravolo. Invisible Autumn.
Charles, F. Omens of the Morning.
Ch'ien T'ao. Chill and harsh the year draws to its close;.
Chu Hsi. Spring Sun.
Clampitt. Sun Underfoot Among the Sundews, The.
Collins, M. To F. C.
Constable, H. Diaphenia like the daffadowndilly.
Dickey, J. Sun.
Dickinson, E. Alter! When the Hills do—.
Blazing in Gold and quenching in Purple.
Presentiment—is that long Shadow—on the Lawn.
Sun and Fog contested, The.
Yellow Man, Purple Man.
Diop, B. Diptych.
Omen.
DiPalma. Fragment.
Donne. Resurrection, Imperfect.
Sun[ne] Rising, The.
Drinkwater. Sun, The.
Drummond, W. Invocation: "Pheobus, arise! / And paint the sable skies."
Euripides. Delphic Dawn.
Ewart. Creation Myth Haiku.
"Field." Ebbtide at Sundown.
Fitzgerald, E. 68.

Fletcher, G. As when the cheerfull Sunne, elamping wide.
Fumiko. Tanka: "Sharing the gentleness."
Gaffarel. Celestial Alphabet Event.
Gates, L. At the river-bend.
Gilbo'a. I love this sunlight cold in spaces transparent turning blue.
Glissant. O Sun! O age-old labor mutely mixed with ocean.
Goodison. Keith Jarrett—Rainmaker.
Gorman, L. Beyond the laughing billboard girl.
Graves, R. Lament for Pasiphaë.
Problems Of Gender.
Greenwell, D. Sun-Flower, The.
Gregor, A. Sunbather in Late October, A.
Harington. Thus all that day, they spent in divers talke.
Harjo, J. Early morning woman.
Harvey, F. November.
Hayati. Before there was a trace of this world of men.
Henderson, D. Horizon Blues.
Hendriks. Recollections of the Sun.
Herbert, G. Son[ne], The.
Herbert, Z. Two Drops.
Herlin. Red round sun, The.
Sky has recovered its haze-blue tints, The.
Hillel. Sun.
Hogan, L. Seeing through the Sun.
Hood, T. No sun—no moon!
Hotham. Sun and moon.
Hottentot Oral Tradition. Song for the Sun That Disappeared behind the Rainclouds.
Hsü Wei. Fifth day of the fifth month.
Hughes, L. Sun Song.
Jackson, L. All things that wake enjoy the sun.
Jeffers, R. Nova.
Jennings, H. Prose Poem.
Joron, A. Shade of a Grammarian.
Kao Ch'i. Walk to the Eastern River Bank, A.
Karpowicz. Artistic Copy.
Kaufman, B. Untitled.
Kazantzakis. O sun, great Oriental, my proud mind's golden cap.
Kenward. Sun.
Kinzie. In air hard as sand.
Knott. Feeding the Sun.
Kovner. Sun-Watchers.
Leonard, T. Miracle of the Burd and the Fishes, The.
Lovelace, R. Lucasta's Fan[ne], with a Looking-Glass[e] in It.
Macdonald, G. Things We Can Depend On.
MacLeish. You, Andrew Marvell.
MacNeice. Morning Sun.
Sunlight on the garden, The.
Madge. On One Condition.
Solar Creation.
Magee, W. How to Reach the Sun. . . on a Piece of Paper.
What is the Sun?
Major, C. Lost in the Desert.
Mansel. Sun's Perpendicular Rays, The.
Marvell. *see also* Ros.
McClellan. Sun went down in beauty, The.
Michie. Arizona Nature Myth.
Miles, J. Forecast.
Miljkovic. Sun.
Miller, M. Universe, The.
Milosz, C. Sun, The.
Morgan, E. Strawberries.
Nemerov. Blue Swallows, The.
Neruda. Ode to the Watermelon.
Nikolov, N. Window, The.
O'Brien, G. Theory of Climate.
O'Hara, F. True Account of Talking to the Sun at Fire Island, A.
Ortiz. Bend in the River.
Owen, M. Narcolepsy.
Owen, W. Futility.
Pape. Making a Great Space Small.
Park, T. Sun, The.
Patterson, R. Glory, Glory. . . .
Sundown Blues.
Perlman, A. Summer Adjustments.

Philips, K. Answer to Another Persuading a Lady to Marriage, An.
Piercy. Noon of the Sunbather.
Sun, The.
Pindar. Pindar on the Eclipse of the Sun.
Pizzarelli. Sun brightens.
Po Chü-i. Early Levée, An.
Getting Up Early on a Spring Morning.
Hearing the Early Oriole.
Ponge. Sun as a Spinning Top (I), The.
Popa. In the Ashtray.
Probyn. End of the Journey, The.
Reese, D. Ol' Hannah.
Rice, J. Sun stuff, star fluff.
Rosen, M. Giant Jojo.
Rosenberg, S. In the laundermat.
Rossetti, D. Hill Summit, The.
Roy, L. Bread Man, The.
Rózewicz. Talent.
Seferis. Our Sun.
Senior. Hill Country.
Sexton. Sun, The.
Shakespeare, W. Sonnet 33.
Sonnet 34.
Shelley, P. Hymn of Apollo.
Shenstone. Hint from Voiture.
Shūji. Tanka: "Out of the shade."
Tanka: "Slanted."
Sidney, P. Sonnet 22: "In highest way of heav'n the sun did ride."
Sidney, R. Songe 17: "Sun is set, and masked night, The."
Smith, B. Mister Snow Man.
Smith, J. Have You Heard the Sun Singing?
Sorescu. With a green scarf I blindfolded.
Southwick. Sun Speaks, The.
Stevens, W. Brave Man, The.
Sense of the Sleight-of-Hand Man, The.
Waving Adieu, Adieu, Adieu.
Stevenson, R. Summer Sun.
Tchernichowsky. I have been to my God like the iris and the anemore.
Tennyson, A. Eagle, The.
Thompson, F. Sun, The.
Trainin. Sunbeams.
Travis, N. Sunbathing.
Trinidad. Hockney: Blue Pool.
Ts'ao Chih. Song of Heavenly Ascent.
Tsvetayeva. White low sun, low thunderclouds; and back, A.
Turner, W. Sun has come, I know, The.
Ungaretti. You Were Shattered.
Unknown. Dawn, The.
Go Down, Old Hannah.
International Chainpoem.
Little wind, blow on the hilltop.
Now Goeth Sun under Wood.
On Francis Drake.
Riddle: "Hickamore hackamore."
Song for Fine Weather.
Song for the Sun That Disappeared behind the Rainclouds.
Song of Lo-fu, The.
To the Sun.
Urriola. Mister Snowman.
Van den Heuvel. Sun goes down, The.
Vaughan, H. Cock-crowing.
Very. Spheres, The.
Virgil. Over and over.
Virgilio. Into the blinding sun.
"W., A." In Praise of the Sun.
Wallace, R. Fresco of Swans and Bears, A.
Waller, E. Song: "Stay Phoebus, stay."
Wang Shih-chieng. After Rain, Visiting the Temple of Heavenly Peace.
Warren, R. Garden, The.
Welish. Scalpel in Hand.
Whitman, W. Give me the splendid silent sun with all his beams full-dazzling.
Wieseltier. Site.
Wilbur. Black November Turkey, A.
Grasse: The Olive Trees.
Williams, W. Metric Figure.
Willmot. Weak sun.
Wills, J. Evening sun, The.
Sun lights up a distant ridge another, The.
Worth, V. Sun, The.

Wu Wei-yeh. Feelings Come As I Pass through Wu-chiang.
Reading the Annals of Emperor Wu of the Han Dynasy.
Yü Chi. Going to the Ministry with Chao Tzu-ch'i.
Yungman. Melons.

Sunburn
Sidney, P. Sonnet 22: "In highest way of heav'n the sun did ride."

Sunday
Brooks, G. Sunday Chicken.
Sundays of Satin-Legs Smith, The.
When You Have Forgotten Sunday: The Love Story.
Dugan, A. Aside.
Grenier. Sunday Morning.
Griffin, S. Sunday Morning.
Hayden, R. Mourning Poem for the Queen of Sunday.
Those Winter Sundays.
Heard, J. Sabbath Bells.
Hemans. Sabbath Sonnet.
Hernandez. Sunday morning.
Hollander, J. Sunday Evenings.
Jenkins, C. Sunday Morning.
Jewett, S. At Home from Church.
Kefala. Sunday Visit.
Levertov. Sunday Afternoon.
MacKay, C. Poor Man's Sunday Walk, The.
MacNeice. Sunday Morning.
Mahon. Another Sunday Morning.
McAuley, J. World on Sunday.
Miles, J. Sunday.
Nemerov. Sunday at the End of Summer.
Rich, A. Mother-in-Law.
Soupault. Sunday.
Stevens, W. Sunday Morning.
Troupe. In Jimmy's Garden.
Vacietis. Sunday.
Vaughan, H. Son-Days [dayes].

See also **Sabbath**

Sundews
Swinburne. Sundew, The.

Sundials
Belloc. I am a sundial. Ordinary words.
I am a sundial, turned the wrong way round.
On a Sundial.
Cunningham, J. Epigram: "I who by day am function of the light."
Dobson, A. Sundial, The.
Quarles. Behold this needle; when the *Arctick* stone.
Scott, W. Rhyme of the Sun-Dial, A.
Unknown. Motto for a Sundial.

Sunflowers
Blake, W. Ah Sun-flower.
Chang Yü. Yellow Sunflower of Szechwan.
Ginsberg, A. Sunflower Sutra.
Greenwell, D. Sun-Flower, The.
Kao Ch'i. Sunflower.
Okamoto. Tanka: "It stands."
Rivner. Sunflower.
Rózewicz. Roots.
Shūji. Tanka: "Its bloom finished."
Su Shih. Sunflower.
Swinburne. Mill Garden, The.
Yang Shih-ch'i. After the rain, the vegetables from your garden.

Sunrise
Auslander, J. Sunrise Trumpets.
Crawford, I. Dark Stag, The.
Daryush. Still-Life.
Deutsch. Earliness at the Cape.
Dickinson, E. I'll tell you how the Sun rose.
Donne. Sun[ne] Rising, The.
Elytis. In the beginning the light And the first hour.
Housman, A. Reveille.
La Grone. Suncoming.
Lowry, M. Sestina in a Cantina.
Momaday. Plainview: 3.
Oliver, M. Sunrise.
Ray, H. Sunrise.
Unknown. East Gate Willows.
Hymn to the Sun.

Song of the Rising Sun Dance.
Sunrise Sequence.
Watkins, V. Fingernail Sunrise.
Wheatley, P. Hymn to the Morning, An.
Zeidner. Kafka Poem.

Sunset
Adams, L. Sundown.
"Æ." Great Breath, The.
Bialik. Sunset.
Bly, R. Sunset at a Lake.
Boldman. Just past sunset.
Borges. Afterglow.
Brontë, E. Evening sun was sinking down, The.
Fair sinks the summer evening now.
Bunyan. Of the Going Down of the Sun.
Buson. Over the vast field of mustard flowers.
Byron, G. Sunset over the Aegean.
Coleridge, M. Moment, A.
Coleridge, S. Sunset, A.
Cummings, E. Who are you,little i.
Curnow. You Will Know When You Get There.
Dickinson, E. How the old Mountains drip with Sunset.
I'll tell you how the Sun rose.
Dowson. Villanelle of Sunset.
Fitzgerald, R. Mise en Scène.
Ford, C. January wraps up the wound of his arm.
Fordham. Sunset.
Frost, R. Acceptance.
Graves, R. Allie, call the birds in.
Land of Whipperginny, The.
Handlin. Sunset.
Herlin. Red round sun, The.
Hotham. Sunset dying.
Kinnell. Daybreak.
Lane, P. Lake Murry.
Lawrence, D. In Trouble and Shame.
Love On the Farm.
Longfellow, H. Sunset.
Lowry, M. Sestina in a Cantina.
MacLeish. Genius, The.
Preil, G. Yellow sunset splashes in the window, A.
Ray, H. Afterglow, The.
At Sunset.
Sunset.
Sunset Picture.
Robinson, E. Dark hills at evening in the west.
Sandburg, C. Flash Crimson.
Mist Forms.
Sunset from Omaha Hotel Window.
Sunsets.
Sappho. Hesperos, you bring home all the bright dawn disperses.
Schuyler, J. Poem: "This beauty that I see."
Scott, W. Datur Hora Quieti.
Dreary Change, The.
Sidney, P. Madrigal.
Stern, G. On the Far Edge of Kilmer.
Stevenson, R. I saw red evening through the rain.
Stickney, T. In Ampezzo.
Swenson, M. On Its Way.
Tennyson, A. Crossing the Bar.
Tu Fu. Sunset glitters on the beads.
Tu Mu. Setting sun is two rods high on the bridge over the brook, The.
Unknown. Song of the Rising Sun Dance.
Van den Heuvel. Stick goes over the falls at sunset, A.
Wharton, E. Autumn Sunset, An.
Whitman, S. November Landscape, A.
Wright, C. Dog Day Vespers.
Yosano. Like tiny golden.

Superior, Lake
Niedecker. Lake Superior.

Superiority
Wotton, S. On His Mistress [*or* Mistris], the Queen of Bohemia.

Supermarkets
Gildner. High-Class Bananas, The.
Ginsberg, A. Supermarket in California, A.
Holman, F. Supermarket.

Meinke. Supermarket.
Nemerov. Grace to Be Said at the Supermarket.
Pape. In Line at the Supermarket.
Wayman. Picketing Supermarkets.

Supernatural
Bridges, R. Low Barometer.
Burns, R. Tam o' Shanter. [A Tale].
Collins, W. Ode on the Poetical Character.
Colman, G. Cold blows the blast--the night's obscure.
Cooke, P. Orthone.
Davidson, J. Ballad of Hell, A.
Ewart. Sonnet: Supernatural Beings.
Hippolyte. Caribbean Exorcism Poem, A.
Hogg, J. Kilmeny.
Keats. La Belle Dame Sans Merci.
Longfellow, H. Skeleton in Armor [*or* Armour], The.
Louis, A. Wakinyan.
Momaday. Headwaters.
Poe. City in the Sea, The.
Raven, The.
Ulalume [*or* Ulalume—a Ballad].
Rabéarivelo. Here is.
Roseliep. Seance.
Service. Cremation of Sam McGee, The.
Shakespeare, W. Hamlet.
Henry IV.
Sherlock. Pocomania.
Strand. Prediction, The.
Thompson, F. In No Strange Land.
Traherne. Shadows in the Water.
Unknown. Tam Lin.
Wolfe, H. Green Candles.
Yeats. Leda and the Swan.

Superstition
Alvarez, J. Sonnet 1: "Everything that happens to me these days."
Angira. If.
Burns, R. Halloween.
Holy Fair, The.
Ciardi. Evil Eye, The.
D'Aguiar. Airy Hall's Exits.
Escoffery. Mother Jackson Murders the Moon.
Hays, H. Sacred Children, The.
Herrick. Charme, or an Allay for Love, A.
Holan. Chicken, The.
Johnson, M. Superstitions.
Kambar. Pond Named Ganga, A.
Karibo. Superstition.
Oppen. Occurrences, The.
Pavic. Flying Temple.
Thompson, C. Johnny's Pet Superstition.
Troupe. Conjuring Against Alien Spirits.
Unknown. Pins.

Supper
Hoffmann, H. Story of Fidgety Philip, The.
Hood, T. Public Dinner, A.
Howes, B. Early Supper.
Morley, C. Animal crackers, and cocoa to drink.
Roethke. Supper with Lindsay.
Taylor, E. Reflexion, The.
Voigt. O mild Christ.

Supplication
Atwood. People come from all over to consult me, bringing their limbs.
Bible, *O.T.* Psalm 130.
Gershon. Uphold Me.
Justice, D. Invitation to a Ghost.

Surfing and Surfers
Cheng Hsieh. Song of Surfing on the Bore.
Gunn, T. From the Wave.
Jarman, M. Supremes, The.
McGough, R. Cousin Reggie.
Wright, J. Surfer, The.

See also **Swimming and Swimmers**

Surgery
Becker, R. Medical Science.
Catina. Negotiations.
Cook, E. Surgeon's Knife, The.
Frost, C. Apple Rind.
Graves, R. Surgical Ward: Men.
Harper, M. Deathwatch.
Henley, W. Before.

Keane, E. Week Seven.
Kirkup. Correct Compassion, A.
Knight, E. Hard Rock Returns to Prison from the Hospital for the Criminal Insane.
MacDonald, C. Objets D'Art.
Nowlan. In the Operating Room.
Shapcott, T. Post Operative.
Stallworthy, J. Letter from Berlin, A.
Young, D. Threshold.
See also **Hospitals; Medicine; Physicians**

Surprise
Brautigan. Surprise.
Creeley. People, The.
Warning, The.
Dickinson, E. As if some little Arctic flower.
Gildner. String.
Graves, R. At First Sight.
Grotesques.
Knott. Sonnet: "Way the world is not, The."
Meinke. Poet, Trying to Surprise God, The.
Rózewicz. I Build.
Smith, D. March Storm, Poquoson, Virginia, 1963.
Swir. Astonishment.
Unknown. Surprise, Surprise.

Surrealism and Surrealists
Breton, A. Three Excerpts.
Césaire, A. First Problem.
Magic.
Wheel is the most beautiful discovery of man and the only one, The.
Crosby, H. Firebrand.
Éluard, P. Lady Love.
Olson, C. Chockablock Once a man was traveling through the woods, and.
Senghor. "African Image Is Not An Image by Equation. . . , The."
Speech and Image: An African Tradition of the Surreal.
Sorescu. Adam paced the footpaths of paradise in a.

Survival
Akhmadulina. Incantation.
Aliger. I live / with a bullet in my heart.
Berryman. Huffy Henry hid the day.
Brecht, B. I, the Survivor.
Brett, L. My Mother's Friend.
Burich. Citizen's Way, The.
Chichibabin. I'll be finished, if I'll survive—.
Ciardi. Gift, The.
Cliff. Within the Veil.
Clifton, L. She Lived.
Cullen, C. Only the Polished Skeleton.
Di Prima. Narrow Path into the Back Country.
Donne. Prohibition, The.
Dove, R. Zeppelin factory, The.
Floyd. Private First Class Brooks Morgenstein, U. S. M. C.
Fort, C. How Old Are the People of the World.
Fuentes. In This Place.
Gaspar. Kapital.
Gershon. I Was Not There.
Gilbert, S. Yarn of the *Nancy Bell*, The.
Glazkov. Declaration.
Glück, L. Phenomenal Survivals of Death in Nantucket.
Graves, R. Survivor, The.
Hacker, M. Cancer Winter.
Hardy, T. Heredity.
Harjo, J. Anchorage.
Harris, R. Riding Over Belmore Park.
Herbert, Z. Abandoned, The.
Hooper, V. Seven Doors Away.
Huddle. Theory.
Kharms. There I was sitting on one leg.
Kinnell. Bear, The.
Under the Maud Moon.
Krichevsky. Refugees.
Kunze, R. Aerial, The.
Reply.
Levi, P. Survivor, The.
Levine, P. Survivor, The.
Lewis, J. Stories.
Libbey. Come Into the Night Grove.
Lorde. Litany for Survival, A.
Mahon. Disused Shed in Co. Wexford, A.

Malouf. Judas Touch, The.
McCarthy, G. Finding the Way Back.
McDougall, J. Reporting Back.
Milosz, C. Child of Europe.
Muir, E. Difficult Land, The.
Horses, The ("Barely a twelvemonth after").
Nekipelov. Alabushevo.
Nemerov. To My Least Favorite Reviewer.
Olds, S. Girl, The.
Oliver, M. Rabbit, The.
Pagis. Ararat.
Peele. Write write yow Croniclers of Tyme and Fame.
Perlman, A. Survival.
Pierman. Pilgrims.
Popa. In the Village of My Forefathers.
Pratt, M. Waulking Song: Two.
Ratushinskaya. But only not to think about the journey.
No, I'm not afraid: after a year.
Rózewicz. Survivor, The.
Rutsala. American Dream.
Simmons, J. In the Wilderness.
Song. Poem: "Water wears away a rock."
Stafford, W. Thinking for Berky.
Stevens, W. Sense of the Sleight-of-Hand Man, The.
Swirszczynska. Good Lord Saved Her, The.
We Survived Them.
TallMountain. Good Grease.
Tennyson, A. Voyage, The.
Turnbull. They have taken my father.
Unknown. Medicine Formula.
Renaud the Woman-killer.
Vysotsky. And ice below, and above—I toil somewhere in between.
Wagoner, D. Staying Alive.
Wickham. Song of Ophelia the Survivor.
Wieseltier. Song of the last soldier, A.
Wright, C. On the Eve of Our Mutually Assured Destruction.
Wright, F. Entry in an Unknown Hand.
Yi, S. Paddies lean against each other.
Young, A. Heap of Faggots, A.
Young, K. Casting.
Zabolotsky. Soccer.
Zach. Be careful. Open your life.

Susanna (Bible)
Crapsey. Susanna and the Elders.
Stevens, W. Peter Quince at the Clavier.
Unknown. Susannah and the Elders.

Sussex, England
Belloc. South Country, The.
West Sussex Drinking Song.
Kipling, R. Puck's Song.

Sutter, John
Winters, Y. John Sutter.

Swallows
Bishop, J. To a Swallow.
Bunyan. Upon the Swallow.
Cibulka. Sky Full of Swallows.
Coatsworth. Swallows, The.
Cowley, A. Swallow, The.
Dowden, E. In the Cathedral Close.
Euenus. To the Swallow.
Fletcher, J. Skaters, The.
Issa. Flying out from.
Jewell. Cliff dweller ruins.
Kao Ch'i. Lying at Leisure during Rain.
Krige. Swallows over the Camp.
Levy, L. Swallow's Flight, The.
Nemerov. Blue Swallows, The.
Rossetti, C. Fly away, fly away over the sea.
Snyder, G. Sixth-Month Song in the Foothills
Swinburne. Itylus.
Thoreau. What's the Railroad to Me?
Toller. O Master Masons.
O My Swallows!
Turner, C. On Shooting a Swallow in Early Youth.
Wang Shih-chieng. Crossing the Yangtze in a Strong Wind.
Yeats. Coole Park, 1929.

Swamps
Bertolino. Frog Voices.
"Ern Malley." Culture as Exhibit.
Frost, R. Wood-Pile, The.

Gray, R. Flames and Dangling Wire.
Heaney, S. Bogland.
Komunyakaa. Landscape for the Disappeared.
Moore, M. I May, I Might, I Must.
Ravenel. Alligator, The.
Wagoner, D. Walking in a Swamp.
Walcott. Swamp, The.

Swans
Aesop. Swan and the Goose, The.
Berssenbrugge. Swan, The.
Bobrowski. Wild Swan, The.
Bogan, L. Winter Swan.
Browning, E. Romance of the Swan's Nest, The.
Cynewulf. Swan, The.
Swan, The: "Silent is my dress when I step across the earth."
Doolittle, H. Leda.
Durrell. Swans.
"Ern Malley." Sweet William.
Ewart. Semantic Limerick According to the Shorter Oxford English Dictionary (1933), The.
Ferry. Unawkward Singer, The.
Fishback. Sitting Pretty.
Gibbons, O. Silver swan, who living had no note, The.
Glanz-Leyeles. White Swan.
Glück, L. Palais des Arts.
Gogarty. Leda and the Swan.
Graves, R. Leda.
Hollander, J. Swan and Shadow.
Jarrell. Black Swan, The.
Jeffers, R. Love the Wild Swan.
Kabir. Swan, tell my your old story.
Key 0or. In the wake.
Kirschner. Two Blue Swans.
Lawrence, D. Swan.
Longley, M. Swans Mating.
Lowbury. Swan.
MacCaig. Intruder in a Set Scene.
Macpherson, J. Swan, The.
Martial. Swan her sweetest Notes sings as she dies, The.
Millay, E. Wild Swans.
Moore, M. No Swan So Fine.
Morgan, E. Siesta of a Hungarian Snake.
Mori Ōgai. Tanka: "White swan."
Pitter. Swan Bathing, The.
Rilke. Swan, The.
Rodgers, W. Swan, The.
Roethke. Swan, The.
Rotella, A. Swans stir of his breath against my hair.
Scovell. Swan's Feet, The.
Sitwell, D. Swans, The.
Smith, S. Bereaved Swan, The.
Speyer. Swans.
Spicer, J. Transformations.
Su Shih. Tune: "Song of Divination."
Tekkan. Tanka: "Plucking feathers."
Tennyson, A. Dying Swan, The.
Unknown. My dress is silent when I tread the ground.
Silver swan, who living had no note, The.
Swan swam [or swan] over the sea.
Van Duyn. Leda.
Leda Reconsidered.
Virgil. Swan's head, The.
Wilson, E. Lakeside.
Wright, J. Three Sentences for a Dead Swan.
Yeats. Among School Children.
Leda and the Swan.
Wild Swans at Coole, The.

Swansea, Wales
Watkins, V. Ode to Swansea.

Sweatshops
Altizer. Sonnet 5: "No, I'll not, carrion, comfort you. Comfort."

Sweden
[dA]kesson. Autobiography.
Evening Walk.
Gouri. Window-Dreaming with SAS.
Koch, K. Energy in Sweden.
Moore, M. Carriage from Sweden, A.
Stewart, F. Black Winter.
Swift, J. On the Göta Canal, 1986.

Sweeney, King of Ireland. *See* **Suibhne, King of Ireland**

Swift, Jonathan
Bogan, L. Hypocrite Swift now takes an eldest daughter.
Clarke, A. Sermon on Swift, A.
Pope, A. Happy Life of a Country Parson, The.
Rich, A. Tryst in Brobdingnag, A.
Schwartz, D. Swift.
Swift, J. Day will come, when't shall be said, The.
Wright, J. Written in a Copy of Swift's Poems, for Wayne Burns.
Yeats. Swift's Epitaph.

Swimming and Swimmers
Avison. Swimmer's Moment, The.
Bloch, J. Idea of a Swimmer.
Booth, P. First Lesson.
Bottoms. Under the Boathouse.
Byron, G. Written After Swimming from Sestos to Abydos.
Cave. Written the First Morning of the Author's Bathing at Teignmouth for the Head-Ache.
Davison, P. Questions of Swimming, 1935.
Dickey, J. Lifeguard, The.
Dunbar, P. Boy's Summer, A.
Fisher, A. Benjamin Jones Goes Swimming.
Foxton. Upon Boys Diverting Themselves in the River.
Francis, R. Swimmer.
Goedicke. In the Ocean.
Greger. Frog in the Swimming Pool, The.
Gregg. Esta.
Hill, S. Voice in the Garden, A.
Karp. Consequences of Waking, The.
Klein, A. Lone Bather.
Kumin, M. Morning Swim.
Lacina. Red Cross Lessons at City Park Pool.
Lane, P. Rain Ditch.
Levine, P. Belle Isle, 1949.
Livingston, M. Swimming Pool.
MacCaig. Kingfisher.
Maguire, S. Perfect Timing.
McElroy, C. Learning to Swim at Forty-Five.
Melville, H. Song from *Mardi*.
Merrill, J. Swimming By Night.
Millay, E. Above these cares my spirit in calm abiding.
Mitchell, K. Night Rain.
Olds, S. One Girl at the Boys Party, The.
Ondaatje. Inner Tube.
Ostriker. Exchange, The.
Peacock, M. So, When I Swim to the Shore.
Pizzarelli. Just before dawn.
Ridler. Bathing Song.
Riley, J. Old Swimmin'-Hole, The.
Rilke. Gazelle, The.
　　　Swan, The.
Sackville-West. Sissinghurst.
Satyamurti. Day Trip.
Scollard. Swimming.
Scott, F. Lakeshore.
Seifert. It was afternoon or later.
Sexton. Nude Swim, The.
Skinner, J. Ballad of the Swimming Angel.
Stuart, D. Rescue.
　　　River, The.
Swenson, M. Morning at Point Dume.
Tomlinson, C. Swimming Chenango Lake.
Tranter. Debbie and Co.
Trinidad. Hockney: Blue Pool.
Unknown. Prayer to the Sockeye Salmon.
　　　Yellow-belly, yellow-belly, come and take a swim.
Warren, R. Red Mullet, The.
Wilson, R. Space Walk.
See also **Surfing and Surfers**

Swinburne, Algernon Charles
Collins, M. If life were never bitter.
Cotter, J. Algernon Charles Swinburne.
Holtby, M. Sister Swallow to Swinburne.

Swings
Allingham. Swing Song, A.
Kuan Yun She. Sending Off Spring.
Li K'ai-hsien. Colorful frames are erected

beside the Yellow River, The.
On the Cold Food Festival, Entertaining at the Southern Estate—the Guests Were Li Chiu-ho, Ma Nan-yeh, Wei Tung-kao, Li Hu-ch'uan, Huang K'ung-ts'un, Li Lung-t'ang, and Hu Hu-shan.
McCord, D. Walnut Tree, The.
Osborn, M. Swing, The.
Stafford, W. At the Playground.
Stevenson, R. Swing, The.
Thompson, I. Swinging.

Switzerland
Arnold, M. Terrace at Berne, The.
Beddoes. Alpine Spirit's Song.
Dickinson, E. Our lives are Swiss.
Hardy, T. Lausanne: In Gibbon's Old Garden: 11–12 p.m.
Klopstock. Lake of Zurich, The.
Merrill, J. Country of a Thousand Years of Peace, The.
Schiff, H. German Frontier at Basel: 1942 and 1992, The.
Shelley, P. Mont Blanc.
Tzara. Zurich Chronicle February 1916.
Wordsworth, W. Thought[s] of a Briton on the Subjugation of Switzerland.

Swordfish
Douglas, K. Marvel, The.

Swords
Chesterman. Sir Nicketty Nox.
Chōkū. Tanka: "Town children."
Davie. Gardens No Emblems.
Herrick. Upon Pagget.
Hill, G. Clash of salutation. As keels thrust into shingle.
Kim, M. Bounty, II, The.
Kipling, R. Runes on Weland's Sword, The.
Sill. Opportunity.
Unknown. End of Clonmacnois, The.
Wilde, O. Ballad of Reading Gaol, The.
Yü Chi. Inscribed on a Painting.

Sydney, Australia
Beveridge. In the Park.
Darwin. Visit of Hope to Sydney Cove, near Botany-Bay.
Dransfield. Flying.
Murray, L. Flight from Manhattan, The.
　　　Sydney and the Bush.

Symbols
Doolittle, H. Sheltered Garden.
Guillén, N. Madrigal.
Herbert, G. Church-Floor[e], The.
Herrick. Primrose, The.
MacCaig. Celtic Cross.
MacNeice. In Lieu.
Merrill, J. Body.
　　　To a Butterfly.
Piatt, J. To the Statue on the Capitol.
Rich, A. Design in Living Colors.
Sandburg, C. Shirt.
Stevens, W. Thirteen Ways of Looking at a Blackbird.
Wright, F. Joseph Come Back as the Dusk.
See also **Metaphor**

Sympathy
Auden. Cats and Dog.
Brontë, E. Sympathy.
Crowell, G. Prayer for a Day's Walk.
Cuddihy. Steps.
Cullen, C. Magnets.
Czerkawska. Thread.
Gardner, I. That "Craning of the Neck."
Hagedorn, J. Solea.
Hardy, T. Often when warring for he wist not what.
Hikmet. Angina Pectoris.
Holmes, O. Sympathies.
Hongo. Underworld, The.
King, H. If we give love and sympathy.
Landon. Poor, The.
Levine, P. Angel Butcher.
Metcalf, R. These Are Not Lost.
Meynell, V. Sympathy.
Mills, W. Pity.
Moorer. Sympathy.
Mordecai. Easy Life.

Pinsky. Questions, The.
Rich, A. For the Dead.
Sandburg, C. Choose.
Sidney, P. Sonnet 31: "With how sad steps, O Moon, thou climb'st the skies!"
Whitman, W. Wild gander leads his flock through the cool night, The.
Williams, B. Friend Who Just Stands By, The.
Woroszylski. Early Chaplin, The.

Synagogues
Shapiro, D. Dead Will Not Praise You, The.
Sillitoe. Synagogue in Prague.

Synge, John Millington
O Direain. Homage to John Millington Synge.
Strong, L. Memory, A.
Yeats. Coole Park, 1929.
　　　In Memory of Major Robert Gregory.
　　　Municipal Gallery Revisited, The.

Syphilis
Sadiq. Tuskegee Experiment.
Wilbur. Pangloss's Song: A Comic-Opera Lyric.
See also **Venereal Disease**

Syria
Brownstein. Stepping Out.

Syrinx. *See* **Pan (god)**

T

Tadpoles
Gould, E. Tadpole, The.
Kusano Shimpei. 4 Or 5 Tadpoles.
Wade, B. Tadpoles.

Tagore, Sir Rabindranath
Tagore. Flute-music.

Tagus River, Spain and Portugal
Wyatt, T. In Spayn.

Tailoring and Tailors
"Ansky." Tailor, The.
Beddoes. Oviparous Tailor, The.
Dunbar, W. Amendis to the Telyouris and Sowtaris for the Turnament Maid on Thame, The.
Farjeon, E. Tailor.
Leftwich. Tailor, The.
Mother Goose. Snail, The.
Shakespeare, W. Thy gown? Why, ay. Come, tailor, let us see't.
Unknown. Four-and-twenty tailors went to kill a snail.
　　　Ode to the Sewing Needle.
Whitney, I. For Women shall you Taylors have.
Zach. Against Parting.

Takatur Erinta Perunceral Irumporai
Kilār, A. Battle Scene.

Taliesin
Unknown. I Am Taliesin. I Sing Perfect Metre.
Williams, C. Taliessin's Song of the Unicorn.

Talk
Betjeman. Reproof Deserved; or After the Lecture.
Cummings, E. All which isn't singing is mere talking.
Davidson, M. Et in Leucadia Ego.
Green, M. Sometimes I dress, with women sit.
Kinnell. For Robert Frost.
McHugh, H. Spilled.
Unknown. Keep this in mind, and all will go.
See also **Speech**

Talmage, S. K.
Tucker, M. Lines on the Death of the Rev. S. K. Talmage.

Talmud, The
Bialik. Talmud Student, The.
Frug. Talmud, The.

Tammuz
Tchernichowsky. Death of Tammuz, The.

Tanguy, Yves
Gascoyne. Yves Tanguy.

Tanks (vehicle)
Weigl. Sharing, The.

Tannhäuser
Levy, N. Tannhauser.

Taos, New Mexico
Hughes, L. House in Taos, A.
Jeffers, R. New Mexican Mountain.

Tapestries
Garrigue. Unicorn and the Lady, The.
Humphries, R. Offering of the Heart Tapestry from Arras, XV Century, The.
Moore, M. Charity Overcoming Envy.
Rich, A. Aunt Jennifer's tigers prance across a screen.
Design in Living Colors.
Ridler. Now as Then.
Santayana. On a Piece of Tapestry.
Simic. Tapestry.

Tara, Ireland
Moore, T. Harp That Once through Tara's Halls, The.

Tarantulas
Lux. Tarantulas on the Lifebuoy.

Tasman, Abel
Curnow. Landfall in Unknown Seas.

Tasmania
Afterman. Van Diemen's Land.
Meredith, L. Tasmanian Scenes.
Porter, H. Hobart Town, Van Diemen's Land (11th June, 1837).
Rose. Truganinny.
Smith, V. Tasmania.
Unknown. Van Dieman's Land.

Taste
DuPlessis, R. Back arched like a bow.
Hacker, M. Canzone: "Consider the three functions of the tongue."
Hall, D. Mangosteens.
Holst-Warhaft. Matthew 5:13; You are the salt of the earth.
Levertov. O Taste and See.
Mirabai. Wild woman of the forests, The.
"Severyanin." Lilac ice cream! Lilac ice cream!
Su Tung-p'o. I planted rice before Spring Festival.
Supervielle. Return to Paris.

Tate, Allen
Davidson, D. Lines Written for Allen Tate on His Sixtieth Anniversary.

Tattoos (skin markings)
Gunn, T. Blackie, The Electric Rembrandt.
Hayden, R. Tattooed Man, The.
Jenkins, L. Confessional Poem.
O'Hara, F. Easter.
Walwicz. Tattoo, The.

Taverns
Graves, R. General Elliott, The.
Keats. Lines on the Mermaid Tavern.
Kirstein. Rank.
Lowry, M. Xochitepec.
"MacDiarmid." Old Wife in High Spirits.
Mechain. Lady of the Ferry Inn.
Robinson, E. Tavern, The.
Stephens, J. Glass of Beer, A.
Wagoner, D. Closing Time.

Taxes
Bierce. To the Bartholdi Statue.
Brown, G. Taxman.
Burns, R. De'il's [*or* Deil's] Awa wi' th' [*or* the] Exciseman, The.
On Mr. Pitt's [*or* Pit's] Hair-Powder Tax.
Elliot, E. Caged Rats.
Harkness, I. New Song on the Birth of the Prince of Wales, A.
Hsü Pen. Ballad of the Merchant.
Lowell, J. Letter Six—The Pious Editors' Creed.
Maksimovic. Matthew 22:15–22; Then the Pharisees went and.
Shen Chou. Painting of Peach Blossom Spring, A.
Steptoe. O' yes.
Ward, E. Ballad on the Taxes, A.

Taxidermy
Fields, J. Owl-Critic, The.
Follain. Taxidermist is sitting / before the russet breasts, A.

Schoenberger. Taxidermist's Daughter, The.

Taxis
Hemphill. Family Jewels.
Kästner. Moral Taxi Ride, The.
Lowell, A. Taxi, The.
MacNeice. Taxis, The.
Slessor. All-night Taxi Stand, The.
Unknown. We four lads from Liverpool are.
Webb, F. Tip for Saturday, A.
Welch, L. After Anacreon.

Tea
Betjeman. Death in Leamington.
How to Get On in Society.
Bynner. What though they conquer us?
"Carroll." Welcome Queen Alice.
Drevniok. Snow at dusk.
Gorham. Princess Parade.
Harter. Bitter tea.
Higginson, W. Writing again.
Hsieh Chin. To Hsiao Shih-ying.
Hurley, M. Tea Party.
Johnson, S. Ballad: "I therefore pray thee, Renny dear."
Kao Ch'i. Picking Tea: A Ballad.
Lear, E. There was an Old Man who forgot.
Mei Yao Ch'en. On Hearing that Holders of the *Chin-shih* Degree Are Dealing in Tea.
Moffett. Twinings Orange Pekoe.
Monro. Milk for the Cat.
Mother Goose. Polly and Sukey.
Po Chü-i. After Eating.
Richards, L. (Bibbily Boo and Wollypotump).
Rilke. Going Blind.
Ritsos. Miniature.
Service. Pot of Tea, A.
Seward. Verses Inviting Stella to Tea on the Public Fast-Day.
Taylor, J. Recreation.
Unknown. Betty.
Virgil. First hot night, The.
Welch, L. Empress herself served tea to Su Tung-po, The.
Wen Cheng-ming. Tea bowls, incense burning—a good feeling here!
This little courtyard—mdash;the wind is pure.
Volumes of books, tea and incense.
Wu Wei-yeh. Garden Living.
See also **Teahouses**

Teaching and Teachers
Anderton. Marking of Folders.
Barolini. Having the Wrong Name for Mr. Wright.
Berryman. Professor's Song, A.
Brook, D. School of Pain, The.
Brown, G. Books.
Burns, R. Epitaph on a Schoolmaster.
Calverley. Schoolmaster Abroad with His Son, The.
Chin. Floral Apron, The.
Colum, P. Poor Scholar of the 'Forties, A.
Davie. To a Teacher of French.
Ded. Soul, like the moon, The.
Di Prima. I Fail as a Dharma Teacher.
Dickey, W. Teaching Swift to Young Ladies.
Eberhart, R. I went to see Irving Babbitt.
Engman. Mushroom Clouds.
Fallon, P. Hedge Schoolmaster, A.
Fitzgerald, R. Figlio Maggiore.
Foster, M. Recruiting Song.
Garioch. Elegy: "They are lang deid, folk that I used to ken."
Gildner. Letter to a Substitute Teacher.
Glück, L. Mountain, The.
Goldsmith, O. Village Schoolmaster, The.
Graham, W. Johann Joachim Quantz's Five Lessons.
Gunn, T. Autumn Chapter in a Novel.
Hadas, R. Pass it on, II.
Hecht, A. Mysteries of Caesar, The.
Herbert, Z. Biology Teacher.
Herodas. Schoolmaster, The.
Hood, T. Irish Schoolmaster, The.
Huddle. Miss Florence Jackson.
Izumi. In the Autumn, on Retreat at a Mountain Temple.
Johnson, E. To Dr. Swift on His Birthday, 30th November 1721.

Jonson, B. To William Camden.
Kamienska. Luke 10:38–42; Now as they went on their way.
Kaneko. Bailey Gatzert: The First Grade, 1945.
Kennedy, X. Golgotha.
Hummingbird.
Kinnell. Correspondence School Instructor Says Goodbye to His Poetry Students, The.
Kinzie. Ringing Words.
Knight, D. "When the Students Resisted, a Minor Clash Ensued."
Lorde. Teacher.
Lucilius. Zenonis has a splendid tutor for her son—.
Markham, E. Prayer, A: "Teach me, Father, how to go."
Martial. To a Schoolmaster.
McCord, D. History of Education.
McElroy, C. Learning to Swim at Forty-Five.
McPherson, S. At the Grave of Hazel Hall.
For Elizabeth Bishop.
Miller, L. Substitute, The.
Nash, O. Purist, The.
Nguyên Khuyên. To Some Students Caught Nodding in Class.
O'Brien, S. In Residence: A Worst Case View.
Patten, B. How the New Teacher Got Her Nickname.
What Happened to Miss Frugle.
Pauker. Grouchy Good Night to the Academic Year, A.
Randall, J. To William Wordsworth from Virginia.
Seymour-Smith. What Schoolmasters Say.
Sholl. This old woman.
Simmons, J. In the Wilderness.
Snodgrass, W. April Inventory.
Campus on the Hill, The.
Snyder, G. Axe Handles.
Song. Out of Our Hands.
Spacks. Freshmen.
Stein, G. Teachers taught her, The.
Strato. Epigram: "There was this gym-teacher."
Tuckerman, F. And two I knew, an old man and a boy.
Unknown. He Who Knows ("He who knows not and knows not [that he knows not]").
Portrait of a Stupid Teacher of Rhetoric.
Tutor who tooted the flute, A.
Who Taught Them?
Wagner, M. Miss Clement's Second Grade.
Walker, T. Owl.
Waniek. Bali Hai Calls Mama.
Weiss, T. Off to Patagonia.
Wendt. Teacher I Wanted to Be, The.
Whitman, W. I am the teacher of athletes.
Whittier. To My Old Schoolmaster.
Zolynas. Love in the Classroom.
See also **Scholarhip and Scholars**

Teahouses
Woty. White Conduit House.
See also **Tea**

Team Spirit
Newbolt. Vitaï Lampada.

Teamsters. *See* **Trucks and Truckers**

Tears
Aeschylus. For me, the tears that welled.
Auden. Embassy.
Bennett, G. Sonnet—2: "Some things are very dear to me—."
Berryman. There sat down, once, a thing on Henry's heart.
Blunt, W. On Her Vanity.
Brontë, C. What does she dream of, lingering all alone.
Brontë, E. If grief for grief can touch thee.
She dried her tears, and they did smile.
Brooke, R. Hill, The.
Brown, S. Chillen Get Shoes.
Browning, E. Flush or Faunus.
Tears.
Byron, G. I saw thee weep—the big bright tear.
When we two parted.

Cavalcanti. Ballata: Of His Lady among Other Ladies.
Chao Meng-fu. Inscribed on Sun An-chih's "Painting of Pines and Catalpas."
Ch'en Tzu-lung. Little cart jolting and banging through the yellow haze of dusk, The.
Clarke, C. What Goes Around Comes Around, or The Proof is in the Pudding.
Coleridge, M. Solo.
Crane, H. To Emily Dickinson.
Crashaw. Tear[e], The.
  Weeper, The.
Dante Alighieri. Eyes that weep for pity of the heart, The.
  Love's pallor and the semblance of deep ruth.
  Mine eyes beheld the blessed pity spring.
  Stay now with me, and listen to my sighs.
  That lady of all gentle memories.
  Very bitter weeping that ye made, The.
De la Mare. TO E. T.: 1917.
Dickinson, E. It's such a little thing to weep.
Dobson, A. Wanderer, The.
Donne. Twicknam [or Twickenham] Garden.
  Valediction: Of Weeping, A.
Eigner. If you weep, I think that.
Ficowski. Girl of Six from the Ghetto Begging in Smolna Street in 1942, A.
Field, E. Journey, A.
"Field." Already to mine eyelids' shore.
Fletcher, P. Hymn: "Drop, drop, slow tears."
Harper, F. Slave Auction, The.
Hawley, B. Bad Mother, The.
Herbert of Cherbury. Tears, Flow No More.
Herder. Esthonian Bridal Song.
Herrick. Hour-Glass, The.
  Seest thou those diamonds which she wears.
  Upon Julia Weeping.
Homer. Thus, many tales Ulysses told his wife.
Ishikawa Takuboku. Tanka: "Mirror in hand."
Jarrell. On the Railway Platform.
Johnson, J. Sence You Went Away.
Jonson, B. Song: "Slow, slow fresh fount, keep time with my salt tears."
Kinnell. Crying only a little bit.
Kipling, R. Recall, The.
Kitahara Hakushū. Tanka: "Today too."
Kitching. If he cried, he cried in private.
Kovner. Voice of My White City, The.
Landor, W. Foreign Ruler, A.
Lehmann, J. No Easy Answer.
Levertov. Weeping Woman.
Lindsay, V. Rain.
Liu Ling-hsien. Inscribed on a Plantain Leaf To Show to a Certain Person.
Marston, P. Inseparable.
Marvell. Eyes and Tears.
Masaoka Shiki. Among the poems I wrote with many pictures spread out before me[2].
Melo Neto. Daily Space.
Meredith, G. Modern Love.
Meynell, A. Maternity.
Mirabai. Heat of Midnight Tears, The.
Mitchell, A. Song In Space.
Mitsune. Ceaseless snow.
Montgomery, S. Crying.
Morris, M. Day my father died, The.
Morris, W. Garden By The Sea, A.
Murray, L. Absolutely Ordinary Rainbow, An.
Nahuatl Oral Tradition. Song for the Festival of Tlaloc, the Rain God.
Nathan, L. Toast.
Neruda. Dictators, The.
  Walking [or Walkin'] Around.
Nobuyuki. Humans Bought and Sold (two poems).
Otomo no Tabito. Better get drunk and cry.
Pasternak, B. Weeping Garden, The.
Pfeiffer, E. Any Husband to Many a Wife.
Po Chü-i. Dreaming of Yüan Chên.
  Good-bye to the People of Hangchow.
  Letter, The.
Ponge. Water of Tears, The.
Porter, P. Non Piangere, Liù.
Pratt, J. Words and Thoughts.
Radauskas. Salesgirl.
Rands. Winifred Waters.

Reese, L. Tears.
Rich, A. Peeling Onions.
Saitō Mokichi. Tanka: "Ever so close."
Samio. Tanka: "Reverently."
Sandburg, C. Bundles.
Shapiro, D. Lateness.
Shea, M. Through the wall.
Sitwell, D. Tears.
Smedley, M. Cavour.
Smith, S. Death Sentence, The.
  Satin-clad, with many a pearl.
  Sigh no more ladies nor gentlemen at all.
Sorescu. Tear, The.
Southwell. Vale of Tear[e]s, A.
Stickney, T. Athenian Garden, An.
Symons, A. Maquillage.
Tasso. What dew or what weeping.
Tati-Loutard. News of My Mother.
Tekkan. Tanka: "Let those grasses."
Tennyson, A. Go By.
Thomas, D. Hand that signed the paper felled a city, The.
Tsvetayeva. Slope like a path for, A.
  This is how they sharpen knives on a.
Unknown. bright moon, oh how white it shines, The.
  Farewell Folk Song.
  I sleep alone.
  Maxim Revised, A.
  Me and My Captain.
  My Lady's Tears.
  This world of ours.
  Weep you no more, sad fountains.
  When I went with you.
Voigt. Woman Who Weeps.
Walker, A. S M.
Wen Cheng-ming. In the past when I saw friends off.
Whitman, W. Tears! tears! tears! / In the night, in solitude, tears.
Woods, M. Tears and Joys.
Yang Shen. To the Tune "Chiang ch'eng tzu."
Yoshimi. Tanka: "Dream, A."
Yüan Mei. Ma-wei.
Yün Shou-p'ing. Green Banana Leaves.
Zach. Poem Too Late, A.
Zenmaro. Tanka: "Nothing."
  Tanka: "Tears, tears."

Technology and Technologists
Algarin. At the Electronic Frontier.
Blanco. Music in the Age of Iron.
Cornford, A. And it came to pass just as they had foretold.
Cummings, E. In heavenly realms of hellas dwelt.
Dyson, E. Old Whim Horse, The.
Fletcher, J. Song of the Moderns.
Halliday, M. Population.
Iwaszkiewicz. How Does the Negative Look. . . .
Kirchwey. Sonogram.
Rice, J. Man and Height.
Updike. Telephone Poles.

Teenagers
Alexander, E. Zodiac.
Brooks, G. We real cool. We.
Dove, R. Adolescence—I.
  Adolescence—II.
  Adolescence—III.
Fraser, K. Dresses.
Gibbons, R. White Beach.
Glenn. José Cruz.
Johnson, J. Girl of fifteen.
Logan, J. Brothers: Two Saltimbanques, The.
McKean. After Listening to Jack Teagarden. . . .
Smith, P. Biting Back.
Stafford, W. Runaway Teen.

Teeth
Berni. Hair of fine silver, shaggy and twisted.
Blyton, C. Night Starvation or The Biter Bit.
Carmichael, R. Tooth, The.
Catullus. Carmen 39.
Chao Meng-fu. Admonition to Myself, An.
Chu Yün-ming. Too Lazy to Write Poetry.
Dickey, W. Poet's Farewell to His Teeth, The.
Gray, J. On A Picture.

Han Yü. Poem on Losing One's Teeth.
Hopkins, L. This Tooth.
Lamb, C. et al. First Tooth, The.
Lux. Little Tooth, A.
McClintock, M. Pushing.
Melville, H. Maldive Shark, The.
Milligan, S. Teeth.
Mother Goose. Teeth and Gums.
"W., C. A." To have it out or not? that is the question.
Yambo. When Negro Teeth Speak.
See also **Dentistry and Dentists**

Telegrams
Frym. Manifesto.
Kramer, L. Red Cross telegram, The.

Telegraph
Joseph, J. Lost Continent, The.
Murray, L. Morse.
Untermeyer, L. To a Vine-clad Telegraph Pole.
Very. First Atlantic Telegraph, The.
  On the Completion of the Pacific Telegraph.

Telemachus
Brodsky, J. Odysseus to Telemachus.

Telephones and Telephoning
Bolton, K. Nonplussed.
Cisneros, S. You Called Me Corazón.
Crosby, H. Telephone Directory.
Dorfman, A. Vocabulary.
Duffy, C. Telephoning Home.
Gardner, I. Telephone rang / in my dream Long Distance from, The.
Ginsberg, A. I Am a Victim of Telephone.
Hacker, M. Rondeau after a Transatlantic Telephone Call.
Ignatow, D. Business Life, The.
  In the Dark.
  Simultaneously, five thousand miles apart.
Karp. Still-Life in the Coat Factory Office.
Kooser. Central.
Mastin. From the Telephone.
Mayer, G. 529 1983.
Miller, J. Plague of Telephones, A.
Nathan, L. Breathing Exercises.
Nemerov. Dial Tone, The.
  Primer of the Daily Round, A.
Palmer, O. Wasting Time.
Piercy. Hand Games.
Porter, D. Lollies Noir.
Richards, L. Eletelephony.
Sheck. Return, The.
Skwirz. Long Distance Calls.
Soyinka. Telephone Conversation.
Stafford, W. Farm on the Great Plains, The.
Toomer. Her Lips Are Copper Wire.
Updike. Telephone Poles.
Wright, C. Legend of Hell, The.

Television
Alexander, J. Winning of the TV West, The.
Alvarez, J. How I Learned to Sweep.
Baraka. In the Tradition / (Not a White Shadow but Black People Will Be Victorious).
Bly, R. Watching Television.
Bruck. Pretty soon / when people hear a quiz show expert.
Codrescu. Telyric.
Cruz, V. Electric Cop, The.
Dawe, B. Not-so-good Earth, The.
Dubie. Radio Sky.
Durcan. Going Home to Mayo, Winter, 1949.
  Wife Who Smashed Television Gets Jail.
Espy. My TV came down with a chill.
Forbes, J. TV.
Hawley, B. Bad Mother, The.
Inez. Old Lady Across the Hall Has Gone to Live Behind the Door, The.
Kelen. Gods Ash Their Cigarettes, The.
Kornilov, V. Announcer, The.
Lalic. Broadcast.
Leto. Mary Morelle Show, The.
McGinley. Death at Suppertime.
  Robin Hood.
Merriam, E. Tube Time.
Moore, L. Spectacular.
Nemerov. Media.
  Mousemeal.

Singular Metamorphosis, A.
Way of Life, A.
O'Hara, F. Poem: "O solo mio, hot diggety, nix 'I wather think I can'."
Scott-Heron. Revolution Will Not Be Televised!, The.
Shange. Different Love Poem / We Need a Change, A.
Sheck. White Noise.
Silverstein, S. Clarence Lee from Tennessee.
Jimmy Jet and His TV Set.
Unknown. Tommy.

Temperance
Adams, C. John Barley-Corn, My Foe.
McLachlan. We Live in a Rickety House.

Temptation
Agard, J. English Girl Eats Her First Mango.
Allen, P. Eve the fox swung.
Auden. From "The Prolific and the Devourer."
Ayton. To His Forsaken Mistress.
Bible, *O.T.* Now the serpent was more subtil than any beast of the field.
Brooks, G. Song in the Front Yard, A.
Byron, G. Ah! didst *thou* tempt my mother?
Carew, T. Song: The Willing Prisoner to His Mistress.
Donne. From Holy Sonnets.
Goethe. Death of a Fly.
Hall, D. Small Fig Tree, A.
Herbert, G. Quip, The.
Sin (1).
Herbert, Z. Mr. Cogito Tells about the Temptation of Spinoza.
Holmes, O. Living Temple, The.
Hughes, T. Theology.
Iskander. Devil and the Shepherd, The.
Lorde. Generation.
MacLeish. What the Serpent Said to Adam.
Mapanje. We Wondered about the Mellow Peaches.
Marlowe. Now, Faustus, what wouldst thou have me do?
Marvell. Dialogue Between The Resolved Soul and Created Pleasure, A.
Milosz, C. Matthew 4:1–11; Then Jesus was led up by the spirit.
Temptation.
Milton. As when of old some orator renowed.
Book IX.
Eve tempts Adam.
Satan tempts Eve.
Temptation of Eve, The.
Tempter Disarmed, The.
Montale. Precautions.
Nasrin. Eve Oh Eve.
O'Reilly, J. Lure, The.
Ovid. O! Love! how cold, and slow to take my part!
Owens, R. Devils Clowns and Women.
Ransom, J. Tall Girl, The.
Rossetti, C. World, The.
Worrying Fruit.
Shakespeare, W. Sonnet 144.
'Tis one thing to be tempted, Escalus.
Solomos, D. Temptation.
Spenser. Bower of Bliss, The.
Tsvetayeva. Fatal volume, The.
Yeats. All things can tempt me from this craft of verse.

Ten Commandments
Clough. Latest Decalogue, The.
Taylor, J. 10 Commandments, are the Law Divine.
Unknown. Ten Commandments, The.
Watts, I. Law Given at Sinai, The.

Tenby, Wales
Unknown. Gereint ab Erbin.
In Praise of Tenby.
Never Tell.

Tennessee (state)
Davidson, D. Descending Chestnut Ridge.
Giovanni. Knoxville, Tennessee.
Jackson, R. Homeric.
Melville, H. Shiloh [A Requiem].
Mitchison. Tennessee Snow.
Reed, I. Chattanooga.
Stevens, W. Anecdote of the Jar.

Tennis
Avison. Tennis.
Heath-Stubbs. Watching Tennis.
Kumin, M. Prothalamion.
Lux. Midnight Tennis Match, The.
Petrie. Old Pro's Lament, The.

Tennyson, Alfred Tennyson, 1st Baron
Bullett. Footnote to Tennyson.
Heard, J. Tennyson's Poems.
Hecht, A. Still Life.
Lawrence, D. Lord Tennyson and Lord Melchett.
Parker, D. Alfred, Lord Tennyson.

Tents
Frost, R. Silken Tent, The.
Kumin, M. Despair.
Whittemore, R. Thinking of Tents.

Termites
Nash, O. Termite, The.

Terns
Eberhart, R. Seals, Terns, Time.
Piercy. Gracious Goodness.

Terror
"Akhmatova." Introduction.
Requiem: "No foreign sky protected me."
Kastelan. As if it resembled your hair.
Levis. For Zbigniew Herbert, Summer, 1971, Los Angeles.
Lowell, R. Fall 1961.
Mori Ōgai. Tanka: "Some medals."
Pasternak, B. Hamlet.
Ratushinskaya. Try to cover your shivering shoulders in rags of the oldest.
Sachs, N. Someone.
Selby, S. Spread, The.
Serge. Dialectic.
Todd, R. Paul Klee.
Warren, R. Terror.
Yeats. Mother of God, The.

Terrorism and Terrorists
Hitchcock. United States Prepare for the Permanent Revolution, The.
Ishikawa Takuboku. Tanka: "What always seemed."
Merrill, J. Casual Wear.
Szymborska. Terrorist, He Watches, The.

Texas Revolution. *See* **Alamo**

Texas (state)
Boswell, M. Texas Ranger, The.
Bowman, C. Mr. X.
Desprez. Lasca.
Fericano. Poem for William Rummel Serving a Life Sentence in a Texas Prison for Not Fixing an Air Conditioner.
Fowler, R. In Blanco County.
Kennedy, X. Down in Dallas, down in Dallas.
Troupe. In Texas Grass.
Unknown. Devil in Texas, The.
El Corrido de Gregorio Cortez.
Hell in Texas.
Villanueva, T. Haciendo Apenas la Recolección.
Williams, W. Desert Music, The.

Thames (river), England
Blake, W. London ("I wander through [*or* thro'] each chartered [*or* charter'd] street").
De la Mare. Old Summerhouse, The.
Denham. Thames from Cooper's Hill, The.
Dunbar, W. To the City of London [*or* In Honour of the City of London].
Herrick. His Tears to Thamesis [*or* Thamasis].
Hutchinson, M. Thames, The.
Sidney, P. Sonnet 103: "O happy Thames, that didst my Stella bear."
Storer. Rivers.
Tollet. On the Prospect from Westminster Bridge.
Wordsworth, W. Lines Written near Richmond, upon the Thames, at Evening.
Remembrance of Collins, Composed upon the Thames near Richmond.

Thankfulness
Burns, R. Grace at Kirkudbright.
Gray, C. Misses Norman lived on Marine Square, The.
Gunn, T. Lines for a Book.

Herbert, G. Antiphon: "Let all the world in ev'ry corner sing / *My God and King.*"
Marvell. Bermudas.
Merwin, W. For the Anniversary of My Death.
"O'Neill." Grace for Light.
Sappho. Thank you, my dear.
Stevenson, R. System.
Thought, A.
Unknown. Give Thanks.
Thanks.
Wilcox, E. Accept My Full Heart's Thanks.
See also **Gratitude**

Thanksgiving
Alford, H. Come, ye thankful people, come.
Alford, J. Thanks Be to God.
Angelou. Thank You, Lord.
Bible, *O.T.* Psalm 95.
Psalm 118.
Psalm 136.
Cummings, E. I thank You God for most this amazing.
Drinkwater. Morning Thanksgiving.
Driscoll, L. Thanksgiving.
Emerson, R. Grace.
Gould, E. Grace and Thanksgiving.
Herrick. Grace for a Child.
Thanksgiving to God for His House, A.
Koch, K. Thanksgiving.
Merrill, W. Not Alone for Mighty Empire.
Moorer. Thanksgiving.
Ochester. Canaries in Uncle Arthur's Basement, The.
Sarson, H. Lovely Things.
Snyder, G. Prayer for the Great Family.
Turner, N. First Thanksgiving of All.
Unknown. Child's Prayer, A.
Thanksgivings, The.

Thanksgiving Day
Child, L. Thanksgiving Day.
Cummings, E. Thanksgiving (1956).
"Douglas." Good Thanksgiving, A.
Dunbar, P. Signs of the Times.
Fisher, A. Thanksgiving Dinner.
Gallagher, T. Strange Thanksgiving.
Johnson, M. Day befo' Thanksgibin', De.
Story of Lovers Leap, The.
Larcom. Volunteer's Thanksgiving, The.
Prelutsky. First Thanksgiving, The.
Weiner, J. Who They Were.
Whittier. Pumpkin, The.
Wier. Holidays.
Woodward, K. Thanksgiving Prayer, A.

Theater and Theaters
Addison, J. Playhouse, The.
Blunden. Concert Party: Busseboom.
Brecht, B. Friends, The.
Cook, E. To Charlotte Cushman.
Dent. Dream Orpheum Balcony.
Doty, M. Adonis Theater.
Fearing. Elegy in a Theatrical Warehouse.
Field, R. Playhouse Key, The.
Gregory, H. Rehearsal, The.
Hecht, A. Peripeteia.
Herbert, Z. What I Saw.
Hirsch, E. Skokie Theatre, The.
Hongo. Underworld, The.
Hooper, V. Drawing Room Drama.
Hughes, L. Notes on the Broadway Theatre.
Inoue. Get Angry, Compass.
Jackson, R. Tee.
Janowitz, P. Necessary Angel, The.
Jonson, B. Ode to Himself.
Kollar. Sunday Matinee.
Lukonin. Stalingrad Theater.
Marinetti. Futurism Wants to Transform the Variety Theater into a Theater of Amazement, Record-setting, and Body-madness.
Morley, H. Epidaurus: / you loved it.
O'Hara, F. Ave Maria.
Pasternak, B. Hamlet.
Phillips, J. Sweethearts.
Pope, A. On a Lady Who P-ssed [*or* P———st] at the Tragedy of Cato.
Rothenberg, J. Realtheater Piece Two.
Sassoon. Blighters.

Shurin. Continuous Thunder.
Smith, J. Playhouse Musings.
Sorescu. Shakespeare created the world in seven days.
Spenser. Sonnet 54: "Of this world's Theatre in which we stay."
Stevens, W. Of Modern Poetry.
Strong, L. Old Woman, Outside the Abbey Theater, An.
Symons, A. Prologue: Before the Curtain.
Szymborska. Theater Impressions.
Taylor, J. As Gold is better that's in fire tride.
Updike. Movie House.
Vinokurov. Hamlet.
Warton, J. Prologue on the Old Winchester Playhouse over the Old Butchers' Shambles.
Weaver, M. Imitation of Life.
Yeats. Fascination of what's difficult, The.
See also **Show Business**

Theft. *See* **Crime and Criminals; Thieves**

Theocritus
Wilde, O. Theocritus.

Theology
Cowper, W. Man on the dubious waves of error toss'd.
Dickinson, E. He preached upon "Breadth" till it argued him narrow.
Dwight. Here stood Hypocrisy, in sober brown.
Hardy, T. Respectable Burgher, The.
Hughes, T. Crow's Theology.
Wordsworth, W. Sonnet: "World is too much with us; late and soon, The."

Thera (island), Greece
Flecker. Santorin.

Theresa, Saint, of Avila
Clemo. Mould of Castile.
Crashaw. Hymn to Saint Teresa.
Wilbur. Teresa.

Thermopylae, Battle of (480 B.C.)
Cameron, N. Thespians at Thermopylae, The.
Cavafy. Thermopylae.
Simonides. For the Spartan Dead at Thermopylai (480 B.C.).

Theseus
Catullus. Carmen 64 ("In old days / driving through soft waters").
Graves, R. Theseus and Ariadne.
Muir, E. Labyrinth, The.
Winters, Y. Theseus: A Trilogy.
See also **Minotaur**

Thieves
Anyidoho. Hero and Thief.
Ba. Familiar Oxen.
Baxter, J. Wild Bees.
Burns, R. Hughie Graham.
Corrothers. Indignation Dinner, An.
De la Mare. Five Eyes.
Dombrovsky. I'm at the bottom again. The baron's there.
Drayton. If he, from heaven that filched the living fire.
Gay, J. Air: "Fox may steal your hens, sir, A."
Graves, R. Thieves, The.
Gunn, T. Idea of trust, or, The.
Harington. Of honest Theft. To my good friend Master Samuel Daniel.
Higginson, W. This spring rain.
Jones, R. Romance of the Poor.
Kapilar. What She Said ("Only the thief was there, no one else").
Khodasevich. Through the Window.
Kipling, R. Ballad of Fisher's Boardinghouse, The.
Kunitz, S. Thief, The.
Leonard, T. Six Glasgow Poems.
Lovelace, R. Mock Charon, A.
Lugovskoy. Bandit, The.
Martial. My Lord, th' Indictment do's not run.
McGough, R. Kleptomaniac, The.
Melville, H. By the Jordan.
Mitchell, S. Good Samaritan et Al, The.
Prunty. Note of Thanks, A.
Reznikoff. Testimony: The United States (1901–1910) Recitative/The South.

Ridge, J. Stolen White Girl, The.
Rieu. Lost Cat, The.
Rothenberg, J. Structural Study of Myth, The.
Shange. Somebody almost walked off wid alla my stuff.
Shea, M. Caught shoplifting.
Shurin. Agora.
Smith, S. Bag-Snatching in Dublin.
Swift, J. Mrs. Harris's Petition.
Unknown. Burglar Bill.
O, let not e'er this quarrel be averred!
Peter hath lost his purse, but will conceal it.
Very. Indian's Retort, The.
Wang Chiu-ssu. Today I am a farmer in the fields.
Wright, J. Gesture by a Lady with an Assumed Name, A.
See also **Crime and Criminals**

Thinness
Lipsitz. Skinny / poem, / all / your / ribs.
Lorde. Song for a Thin Sister.
Nash, O. Curl Up and Diet.
Plath. Frog Autumn.
Po Chü-i. Illness.
Unknown. There was a young lady from Lynn. Thin Flynn.

Thirst
"Asya." Deer, The.
Bishop, J. Hunger and Thirst.
Cameron, N. Green, Green Is El Aghir.
Cowley, A. Drinking.
Dickinson, E. Let me not thirst with this Hock at my Lip.
Kinzie. Orchard dying, The.
Kirchwey. Rogue Hydrant, August.
Leonidas of Tarentum. Cold water falling out of the split rock.
Mahadevi. When I am hungry.
Orban, O. Gypsy Christmas.
Rumi. We can't help being thirsty.
Su Tung-p'o. Tune: Sand of Silk-washing Stream ("Flutter, flutter, on clothes and cap, jujube flowers fall").
Yüan Chen. Pitcher, The.
See also **Hunger**

Thistles
Basho. Roadside thistle, eager, The.
Bly, R. Looking at a Dry Canadian Thistle Brought In from the Snow.
Dixon, R. Song: "Feathers of the willow, The."
Hughes, T. Thistles.
"MacDiarmid." Black leaf owre a white leaf twirls, A.
Thistle's Characteristics, The.
Monro. Thistledown.
Unknown. Theophilus Thistledown, the successful thistle sifter.
Zabolotsky. Thistle.

Thomas Aquinas, Saint
Madeleva. Dumb Oxen.
Moyles. Thomas in the Fields.

Thomas, Dylan
Baxter, J. Obsequy for Dylan Thomas.
Sitwell, D. Elegy for Dylan Thomas.
Watkins, V. Cwmrhydyceirw Elegiacs.

Thomas, Edward ("Edward Eastaway")
Lewis, A. All day it has rained, and we on the edge of the moors.
To Edward Thomas.

Thomas More, Saint. *See* **More, Sir Thomas**

Thomas, Saint
Crashaw. Hymn in Adoration of the Blessed Sacrament.
Görgey. Thomas.
Hill, G. Canticle for Good Friday.
Smart, C. St. Thomas.

Thomas the Rhymer (Thomas of Erceldoune)
Unknown. Thomas the Rhymer [*or* Rimer].

Thomson, James (1700–1748)
Collins, W. Ode Occasioned by the Death of Mr. Thomson.

Thoreau, Henry David
Goldbarth. Letter, A.
Hillman. Thoreau's Fossil Lilies.

Ray, H. Thought at Walden, A.
Very. On Visiting the Graves of Hawthorne and Thoreau.

Thought
Ackerman, D. Rumored Conversation with Oneself Continues in Pittsburgh, The.
Amichai. Look, thoughts and dreams weave over us.
Ammons. Corsons Inlet.
Berssenbrugge. Texas.
Blake, W. Fly, The.
Bogan, L. Henceforth, from the mind.
Boldman. Walking with the river.
Bridges, R. In autumn moonlight, when the white air wan.
Chōkū. Tanka: "Oddly shaped."
Chu Hsi. Thoughts While Reading.
Clare, J. I wish I was where I would be.
Codrescu. Against Meaning.
Coleman, W. ISM, The.
Coleridge, S. Constancy to an Ideal Object.
Coolidge, C. Crack, The.
What is Thought but Won't Hold Still.
Cranch. Gnosis.
Creeley. Fancy.
"I Keep to Myself Such Measures."
Cruz, V. Essay on William Carlos Williams, An.
Dana, R. Chanting Cherubs, The [A Group by Greenough].
Davie. Gardens No Emblems.
Davies, S. Cosmus hath more discoursing in his head.
Davis, D. 6 A.M. Thoughts.
Dickinson, E. I felt a cleavage in my mind.
One need not be a Chamber—to be Haunted.
DiPalma. Rumor's rooster / halloos the distorted.
Drayton. To the Reader of These Sonnets.
Ehrmann. I ponder on life.
Eliot, T. Gerontion.
Freeman, C. Do Not Think.
Graves, R. Thieves, The.
Gunn, T. Confessions of the Life Artist.
Lines for a Book.
Han Yü. Leaves fall turning turning to the ground.
Herford. Smile of the Walrus is wild and distraught, The.
Hewitt, J. Because I paced my thought by the natural world.
I write for my own kind.
Holan. Between the idea and the word.
Hsieh Ling-yün. Climbing the Tower by the Pond.
Hunt, L. Nile, The.
Ishikawa Takuboku. Tanka: "Somehow."
James, J. Side Window.
Jones, L. *et al.* Look for You Yesterday, Here You Come Today.
Juan Chi. Deep in the night and unable to sleep.
Kerouac. 211th Chorus.
Lawrence, D. Demiurge.
Red Geranium and Godly Mignonette.
Lazarus, E. Echoes.
Lee, D. Awareness.
Li Po. Thoughts While Studying at Hanlin Academy Sent to My Colleagues at the Chi-hsien Academy.
Lovelace, R. Song: "Strive not, vain Lover, to be fine."
Lu Kuei Meng. Replying to Hsi-mei's "Thoughts in Early Autumn."
Lu Yu. Night Thoughts.
Tune: "Immortal at the Magpie Bridge"—On Hearing the Cuckoo at Night.
"MacDiarmid." At My Father's Grave.
Mackey, N. Shower of Secret Things, The.
MacNeice. Turf-Stacks.
Mathews, H. Histoire.
Meredith, W. Recollection of Bellagio.
Miyazawa Kenji. "Steel pen."
Tanka: "With red eyes."
Moore, M. Mind Is an Enchanting Thing, The.
Moore, N. Patient, The.
Olson, C. Moon Is the Number 18, The.

Palmer, M. Voice and Address.
Pasternak, B. Cape Mootch.
Ponsot. La Une, A.
Reverdy. Inn.
Rexroth, K. You ask me what I thought about.
Robinson, E. Garden, The.
Rodefer. My mind to me mangles iron. An error is mirror to the truth.
Roethke. Genesis.
  Give Way, Ye Gates.
Samio. Tanka: "With each quiver."
Sandburg, C. Aprons of Silence.
  Bundles.
  Caboose Thoughts.
  Sandhill People.
Shakespeare, W. Sonnet 85.
Sidney, P. My sheep are thoughts, which I both guide and serve.
Smith, S. After-Thought, The.
  White Thought, The.
Sorescu. Carbon Paper.
  Carnival.
Stein, G. I think very well of Susan but I do not know her name.
Stevens, W. Crude Foyer.
  Epilogue: "Soldier, there is a war between the mind."
  Quiet Normal Life, A.
Tahmisic. Letter to a Friend.
Toomer. People.
Traherne. Dreams.
Tu Fu. Night Thoughts While Travelling.
  Quatrain: "I lounge on the jetty in the fragrance of catalpa."
Tuckerman, F. Let me give something!— though my spring be done.
  Nor strange it is, to us who walk in bonds.
Unknown. On the Flightiness of Thought.
Van den Heuvel. My mind takes a leap.
Waldrop, K. Will to Will.
Ward, D. Shakeout.
Whitman, W. Aboard at a ship's helm.
  By the bivouac's fitful flame.
Wilbur. Event, An.
  Fire-Truck, A.
  Mind in its [*or* the] purest play is like some bat.
  Praise in Summer.
Williams, W. There is neither beginning nor end to the imagination.
Wright, J. Breath of Air, A.
Yeats. Meru.

See also **Intellect and Intellectuals; Reason**

Thousand Islands, New York and Ontario
Sangster, C. Thousand Islands, The.

Three Kings. *See* **Magi**

Three Mile Island, Pennsylvania
Williams, C. Tar.

Three Wisemen. *See* **Magi**

Thrushes
Browning, E. Deserted Garden, The.
Clare, J. Thrush's Nest, The.
Frost, R. Come In.
Hardy, T. Darkling Thrush, The.
  Proud Songsters.
  Reminder, The.
Hughes, T. Thrushes.
Larcom. Brown Thrush, The.
Meredith, G. Thrush in February, The.
Meynell, A. Thrush before Dawn, A.
Rossetti, C. Last Rites.
Scott-Hopper. What the Thrush Says.
Tennyson, A. Throstle, The.
Unknown. Thrush's Song, The.
Williams, H. Elegy on a Young Thrush Which Escaped from the Writer's Hand.

Thumbs
Dacey, P. Thumb.

Thunder
Alexander, W. Lightning.
Austin, M. Song of a Man About to Die in a Strange Land.
Ch'u Yüan. Spirit of the Mountain, The.
Clare, J. Thunder mutters louder and more loud, The.
  Written in a Thunder Storm July 15th, 1841.

Davies, W. Black Cloud, The.
Dickinson, E. Farthest Thunder that I heard, The.
Eady. My Mother is a God Fearing Woman.
Fu Hsüan. Thunder. My heart trembles.
Heifetz-Tussman. Thunder My Brother.
Homer. Clash in Arms of the Achaians and Trojans.
Hong, Y. Thunder.
Hotham. Distant thunder.
Hsü Wei. Inscribed on a Painting.
Jewell. Thunder storm passing.
Kinnell. Another Night in the Ruins.
Kitahara Hakushū. Tanka: "Magnolia."
Kogan. Thunderstorm.
Kooser. Child Frightened by a Thunderstorm.
Lawrence, D. Trees in the Garden.
Lowry, M. Volcano is dark and suddenly thunder, The.
Macdonald, G. Baby-Sermon, A.
MacNeice. June Thunder.
McAuley, J. One Tuesday in Summer.
McClintock, M. Tonight. . . wishing.
Morris, W. Thunder in the Garden.
Okigbo. Come Thunder.
  Thunder Can Break.
Pope, A. Gulliver in Lilliput.
Reeves, J. Giant Thunder[, striding home].
Spiess. Muttering thunder.
Stevenson, R. Last night we had a thunderstorm in style.
Tennyson, A. Eagle, The.
  Kraken, The.
Unknown. Dream Song.
  First Song of the Thunder.
  Song of the Thunder.
  Twelfth Song of the Thunder.
  Winter's thunder.
Wang Chiu-ssu. Thunder in the southern mountains, the third month of the year.

Thyme
Sambrook. Wild Thyme.
Wilbur. Thyme Flowering among Rocks.

Tides
Bevington, L. With the Tide: A Cry of Weakness.
Brooke, R. Fish, The.
Bryant, W. Tides, The.
Carman, B. Low Tide on Grand Pré.
Cheng Hsieh. Song of Surfing on the Bore.
DuPlessis, R. She will lie naked.
Farjeon, E. Tide in the river, The.
Fuller, R. Tides, The.
Higginson, W. High tide.
Hill, G. Wreaths.
Ingelow. High Tide on the Coast of Lincolnshire, 1571, The.
Jackson, H. Tides.
Longfellow, H. Tide rises, the tide falls, The.
McCaig. Betweens.
Mew. Sea Love.
Nims, J. Tide Turning.
Root, J. Naming the Shells.
Slessor. Five Bells.
Spenser. Sonnet 75: "One day I wrote her name upon the strand."
Unknown. Wag ballock wag.
Virgil. Low tide.

Tigers
Allur Nanmullai. What He Said ("Heart, knowing, The").
Belloc. Tiger, on the other hand, is kittenish and mild, The.
Blake, W. Tyger, The.
Bunting. Fearful Symmetry.
Chao Meng-fu. In the Ancient Manner.
Dickinson, E. Dying Tiger—moaned for Drink, A.
Goodison. On Becoming a Tiger.
Hope, A. Tiger.
Housman, A. O Have You Caught the Tiger?
Hsü Chung-hsing. How brave the peasant who lives beside the lake.
Hsü Pen. Ballad of the Ferocious Tiger.
Kao Ch'i. Ballad of a Ferocious Tiger.
Leithauser. Tigers of Nanzen-ji, The.
Marquis. Tom-Cat, The.

Milton. Tenants of Paradise.
Monkhouse. There Was a Young Lady of Niger.
Niblett. Tiger behind the bars of his cage growls, The.
Norris, L. Tiger in the Zoo, A.
O'Hara, F. Chez Jane.
Rich, A. Aunt Jennifer's tigers prance across a screen.
Sackville-West. Greater cats with golden eyes, The.
Tao-chi. Searching for Herb Brazier and Cinnabar Well, I Also Saw the Waterfall of Singing Strings. Alongside Was the Cliff of the Lord of the Mountain.
Unknown. There was a young lady of Riga.
  Young Lady of Niger, The.
Yang Shih-ch'i. Inscribed on the Painting, Stabbing a Tiger, by Chao Tzu-ang, in the Collection of Scholar Yang.
Yü Chi. Traveling Early through a Snowy Valley.
Yukitsuna. Tanka: "Child in my arms."

Tightropes and Tightrope Walkers. *See* **Acrobatics and Acrobats**

Till, Emmett
Brooks, G. Last Quatrain of the Ballad of Emmett Till, The.
Emanuel, J. Emmett Till.
Lorde. Afterimages.
Su Man-shu. Addressed to a Koto-player.
Wang Kuo-wei. Tune: "Song of Picking Mulberry."

Time
Adams, J. To the Sun-Dial.
Aiken, C. Prelude LVI: "Rimbaud and Verlaine, precious pair of poets."
Alberti. Angels of the Ruins, The.
Alcuin. These days are too full fraught with diverse dangers.
Alexander, A. This, Too, Shall Pass Away.
Ali, A. History of Paisley, A.
Allen, S. Moment Please, A.
Alterman. Red Ridinghood.
Alver. Stellar Hour.
Amichai. Man in his life has no time to have, A.
Anacreon. Beneath this fragrant myrtle shade.
Ashbery. As You Came from the Holy Land.
  Saying It to Keep It from Happening.
  Wind thrashes the maple seed-pods, The.
Atwood. There Is Only One of Everything.
Auden. As I walked out one evening.
  Fish in the unruffled lakes.
Bailey, P. We live in deeds, not years; in thoughts, not breaths.
Bateman, C. Distances.
Baumel. Doing Time in Baltimore.
Beam. Time is.
Beaumont, J. Hourglass, The.
Beckett, S. My way is in the sand flowing.
Bede. Sparrow's Flight, A.
Bell, M. Mystery of Emily Dickinson, The.
Bennett, J. In a Rose Garden.
Bentley, N. On Lady A——.
Berkson, B. Melting Milk.
Bernstein, O. All this is my time. No time to seek disguise. There'll be.
Berry, W. Dance, The.
Bevington, L. Twilight.
Bible, O.T. Time for Everything, A.
Bishop, E. Anaphora.
  Two Mornings and Two Evenings.
Blok. Before the Court.
Bodecker. Garden Calendar.
Bogan, L. Come, break with time.
Boland, E. Anna Liffey.
Boldman. Moment in the box of jade, A.
Bonnefoy. Tree, the Lamp, The.
Bontemps. To a Young Girl Leaving the Hill Country.
Bower, R. On Door Jambs.
Bowles, W. Time and Grief.
Braithwaite. Quiet has a hidden sound.
Brew. Search, The.
Brodsky, J. Café Trieste: San Francisco.

Brontë, C. Autumn day its course has run—
  The Autumn evening falls, The.
Brontë, E. Self-Interrogation.
  Tell me, tell me, smiling child.
Brooks, G. Marie Lucille.
  Old Mary.
Brown, L. Green arbor that I once knew, A.
Browning, E. Sonnet: "I thought once how
  Theocritus had sung."
Browning, R. Love.
  Prologue: "Poet's age is sad: for why?, The."
Bruner. Time's Hand Is Kind.
Bryant, W. Ages, The.
  Fountain, that springest on this grassy slope.
  Rivulet, The.
Buckley, C. Playing for Time.
Buckley, V. Child is Revenant to the Man,
  The.
Burleigh. Weaver, The.
Byron, G. So we'll go no more a-roving.
  Stanzas for Music ("There's not a joy the
  world can give like that it takes away").
Campbell, T. River of Life, The.
Cane. Harvest to Seduce, A.
Caraion. Ultimate Argument.
Carew, T. Persuasions to Enjoy.
Carroll, J. Heroin.
Carter, M. Being, always to arrange.
Cassity. Chronology.
Cavalli. I pretend to wait for you to enlarge
  the minutes.
  Now that the time seems all mine.
Celan. When you lie in.
Chesterman. Yesterday.
Ch'ien Ch'ien-i. Must I lament the time that's
  gone because I've been cast aside?
Cibulka. Kuks.
Clampitt. Catalpa Tree on West Twelfth
  Street, A.
Clare, J. Ballad: The Sun Had Grown on
  Lessening Day.
Cokinos. Short-Wave.
Cole, N. Saturn.
Cole, T. Dial, The.
Coleridge, S. Time, Real and Imaginary.
Cook, E. Song of the Modern Time.
Cope, W. Bloody men are like bloody buses.
Cornford, F. Unbeseechable, The.
Cowper, W. Comparison, A.
  Work of Gardening, The.
Cranch. December.
  My Old Palette.
  Spirit of the Age, The.
Crane, H. My Grandmother's Love Letters.
  Reliquary.
Creeley. Again.
  Rescue, The.
  River wandering down.
  Sitting Here.
  They.
  Time.
Crompton. Epigram LXVII: Time, the
  Interpreter.
Cuadra, A. In Brief.
Cuddihy. This Body.
Cummings, E. All ignorance toboggans into
  know.
  Anyone lived in a pretty how town.
  Being to timelessness as it's to time.
  Faithfully tinying at twilight voice.
  How many moments must(amazing each).
  If everything happens that can't be done.
  If(touched by love's own secret)we,like
  homing.
  Impression.
  Now is a ship / which captain am.
  Ponder,darling,these busted statues.
  Sonnet IV.
  Stand with your lover on the ending earth.
  Whatever's merely wilful, / and not
  miraculous.
  Wherelings whenlings / (daughters of if but
  offspring of hopefear).
Daniel, S. 46.
  Time, cruel time, come and subdue that brow.
Dao. Accomplices.
Daryush. How on Solemn Fields of Space.

Davidson, M. Thinking the Alps.
Davie. Time Passing, Beloved.
Davies, W. Leisure.
Davison, P. Vanishing Point, The.
Day Lewis. Poem for an Anniversary.
DeClue. Ijajee's Story.
Dekker, T. et al. Folly's Song.
Desnos. If, like winds semaphored by a rose.
  Midway.
Dickinson, E. Clock strikes one that just
  struck two, The.
  Great Streets of silence led away.
  They say that "Time assuages."
  Too happy Time dissolves itself.
Disch. Convalescing in London.
Dobson, A. Sundial, The.
Đông Hồ. River, The.
Donne. Anniversary [or Anniversarie], The.
  Computation, The.
  Our Love Hath No Decay.
Dove, R. Lost Brilliance.
Dransfield. Visiting Hour (Repatriation
  Hospital).
Drayton. To My Noble Friend Master William
  Browne: Of the Evil Time.
Drinkwater. Birthright.
Dugan, A. On Trading Time for Life by
  Work.
Dutton, G. Street.
Eady. Supremes, The.
Eberhart, R. Garden God, The.
  Human Being Is a Lonely Creature, The.
Edson, R. Tearing and Merging of Clouds,
  The.
Ehrenburg. Trumpet, The.
Eliot, T. Burnt Norton.
  East Coker.
  Little Gidding.
Emerson, R. Awed I behold once more.
  Compensation ("Wings of Time are black and
  white, The").
  Days.
  Past, The.
  Test, The.
  Two Rivers.
  Waves.
Farjeon, E. There Isn't Time.
Fazli. Page from the New Diary, A.
Finch, A. Reply From His Coy Mistress, A.
Fitzgerald, E. Life's Chequer-Board.
  Rubáiyát of Omar Khayyám of Naishápúr,
  The.
  74.
  Some We Loved.
Flecker. Stillness.
Florian. First things first.
Forbes, D. Recension Day.
Forché. Burning the Tomato Worms.
Fort, C. Town Clock Burning, The.
Francis, R. Coming and Going.
  Mouse whose name is Time, The.
Frost, R. Nothing Gold Can Stay.
Fulton, R. Stopping by Shadows.
Gardner, D. Fire Music.
Gascoyne. Cage, The.
Ginsberg, A. Caw caw caw crows shriek in
  the white sun over grave stones.
Glover, D. Thistledown.
Glück, L. For My Mother.
  Magi, The.
Goethe. We always have time enough, if we.
Gould, A. Observed Observer, The.
Gouri. Age is ended, another kingdom's
  ended, An.
Graham, J. What the Instant Contains.
Graves, R. Counting the Beats.
  In time all undertakings are made good.
  Lost World, A.
  Love Story, A.
  Time.
Greville, F. 87.
Gwynn, R. Release.
Habington. Recogitabo Tibi Omnes Annos
  Meos.
Hackett, J. Time after time.
Hailsham. If Grief Could Burn Out.
Hall, D. Shudder [, The].

Hardy, T. Anniversary, An.
  Commonplace Day, A.
  During Wind and Rain.
  In a Eweleaze near Weatherbury.
  Long Plighted.
  Old Furniture.
  Second Attempt, A.
  Sunshade, The.
  This Summer and Last.
Harjo, J. Santa Fe.
Hatsui Shizue. Silently / time passes.
Heard, J. Birth of Time, The.
Heine. Who Was It, Tell Me.
Hemensley. Sulking in the Seventies.
Henjō Abbot. If the winds of heaven.
Herbert, G. Life.
  Time.
Herbert of Cherbury. To His Watch, When He
  Could Not Sleep.
Herbert, Z. Wall, The.
Hernández, M. July 18, 1936–July 18, 1938.
Herrick. His Poetry His Pillar.
  Hour-Glass, The.
  Present Time Best Pleaseth, The.
  To [the] Virgins, to Make Much of Time.
  Upon Time.
Hesketh. Love's Advocate.
Hewitt, J. Whit Monday.
Higo. Hidesong.
Hikmet. Letters from Chankiri Prison.
  Since I was thrown inside.
Hippius. L'Imprévisibilité.
Hồ Dzếnh. Shilly-Shally.
Hodgson, R. Time.
  Time, You Old Gypsy Man.
Hölderlin. In the Days of Socrates.
Holmes, O. Last Leaf, The.
Hope, A. Observation Car.
Hopkins, G. To His Watch.
Horace. Aequam Memento.
  Ne'er fash your *thumb* what *gods* decree.
Housman, A. On Wenlock Edge the wood's in
  trouble.
Howe, F. Set golden butter out in a dish.
Hubbell, P. Travelers, The.
Huchel. Poplars, The.
Hughes, L. Negro Speaks of Rivers, The.
Hughes, R. On Time.
Humphries, R. Polo Grounds.
Hunt, L. Rondeau: Jenny Kiss'd [or Kissed]
  Me.
Huy Cận. Talking With the Pyramid.
Ignatow, D. White-haired, I walk in on my
  parents.
Inez. Old Lady Across the Hall Has Gone to
  Live Behind the Door, The.
  Slumnight.
Jaccottet. Don't worry, you'll get there!
  You're close.
Jeffers, R. Carmel Point.
  Gray Weather.
Jefferys. We have lived and loved together.
Jennings, E. Delay.
Jewell. Nearing the mountain.
Johnson, H. Remember not the promises we
  made.
Johnson, L. New Guinea Time.
  Tahiti.
Jonson, B. Hour-Glass [or Houre-Glasse], The.
  Song. To Celia ("Come my Celia, let us
  prove").
Jordan, N. August 8.
Justice, D. Houses.
Juvenal. Client, the patron, the age, The.
Kalász. Time's No Grammar.
Kavanagh, P. Gold Watch.
Keats. To Ailsa Rock.
Kendall, M. Pure Hypothesis, A.
Kennedy, X. In a Prominent Bar in Secaucus
  [One Day].
Kgositsile. In the Mourning.
Khlebnikov, V. Persons, people, and the years.
  Suppose I make a timepiece of humanity.
Kim, Y. Message.
  Years.
Kinnell. Tragedy of Bricks, The.
  Two Set Out on Their Journey.

Knight, E. He sees through stone.
Koertge. Thing Is to Not Let Go of the Vine, The.
Komunyakaa. Way the Cards Fall, The.
Kooser. Year's End.
Kopland. Thanks to the Things.
Korvin-Piotrovsky. Farewell, Captain. In bygone days.
Kowit. Notice.
Kraus. Express Train.
Kunert. Every Day.
Kunitz, S. River Road.
Kushner, A. We don't get to choose our century.
Lalic. Inscribed in the Silver of the Sea.
Landor, W. Love and Age.
Larkin, P. Days.
Lauterbach. Clamor.
Lawrence, D. Humming-Bird.
Song of a Man Who Has Come Through.
Lea, S. Telescope.
Lee, D. There was a man who never was.
Levin, P. Dark Horse.
Meeting of Friends, A.
Levine, P. Ordinary Morning, An.
Sweet Will.
Lewis, A. Mahratta Ghats, The.
Lewis, J. Time and Music.
Li Ho. Lamentations of the Bronze Camels.
Li Yü. Tune: "Ripples Sifting Sand: A Song."
Linden, M. Scraps of Time.
Lipkin, S. In the Desert.
Lister, R. Time Passes.
Toast to 2,000, A.
Longfellow, H. Old Clock on the Stairs, The.
Sand of the Desert in an Hour-Glass.
Tide rises, the tide falls, The.
Longley, M. Gorse Fires.
Lorde. Time of lamentation and curses is passing, The.
Lowell, J. Birthday Verses Written in a Child's Album.
Lowell, R. Difficulties, the impossibilities, The.
Lu Yu. Autumn Thoughts.
I Get Up at Dawn.
Stone on the Hilltop, The.
Lucretius. Threshold Of The New, The.
Machi. Tanka: "From the moment."
MacLeish. Farm, The.
Grazing Locomotives.
Signature for Tempo.
Snowflake Which Is Now and Hence Forever, The.
Words in Time.
You, Andrew Marvell.
MacNeice. August.
Brandy Glass, The.
Cradle Song: "Clock's untiring fingers wind the wool of darkness, The."
Fanfare for the Makers, A.
Meeting Point.
Perdita.
Star-Gazer.
Sunday Morning.
Mahon. Dog Days.
Majumdar, B. Time Wins.
Mandelstam. Finder of a Horseshoe, The.
Mangan, J. Gone in the Wind.
Twenty Golden Years Ago.
Marsden. What Is Time?
Marvell. To His Coy Mistress.
McHugh, H. In Light of Time.
Melville, H. Enthusiast, The.
Meng Chiao. Stones Where the Haft Rotted, The.
Merwin, W. Another Year Come.
For the Anniversary of My Death.
Night Singing.
Mezey. Stream Flowing, The.
Millay, E. Time does not bring relief; you all have lied.
Milosz, C. And yet the books will be there on the shelves, separate beings.
On the Book.
Milosz, O. Bridge, The.
Milton. On Time.

Sonnet: "How soon hath Time the suttle [or subtle] theef [or thief] of youth."
To Mr. Lawrence.
Mole, J. Song of the Hat-Raising Doll.
Momaday. Two Figures.
Moore, H. Green Place, A.
Moore, M. Four Quartz Crystal Clocks.
Moore, M. Noise That Time Makes, The.
Moore, T. I Saw from the Beach.
Moraes, D. Kanheri Caves.
Morgenstern. Korf's Clock.
Moriarty, L. Rondeaux: "Each page a day."
Mother Goose. Ten O'Clock Scholar, [The].
Mueller, L. Palindrome.
Muir, E. Road, The.
Myrinos. Time topples Statyllios like a doddery oak.
Nash, O. Mr. Artesian's Conscientiousness.
Nemerov. Remorse for Time, The.
Neruda. Stone within stone, and man, where was he?
Nezval. Clock in the Old Jewish Ghetto, The.
Nguyễn Bỉnh Khiêm. Rich look grand, the poor seem cheap and mean, The.
Nicholls, J. Timeless.
O'Hara, F. Poetry.
Okigbo. Hurrah for Thunder.
Olson, C. Chockablock Once a man was traveling through the woods, and.
Kingfishers, The.
Maximus, to Gloucester, Letter 27.
Omar Khayyám. Awake! for morning in the bowl of night.
Oppen. To insist that what is true is good, no matter, no matter.
Orban, O. Certain Years.
Peace Pillar.
Owen, G. Gathering in the Days.
Pack, R. Proton Decay.
Pagis. Letter, A.
Palmer, M. Letter 5.
Paquet. Group Shot.
Pastan. After Reading Nelly Sachs.
Pasternak, B. I too have been in love, and my sleepless.
Snow is falling, snow is falling.
Patchen. State of the Nation, The.
Patmore, C. Too soon, too soon comes Death to show.
Peacock, T. Love and Age.
Sun-Dial, The.
Peele. Farewell to Arms, A.
Peskett. Star and Sea.
Pettet. Rose Garland Sonnet.
Phillips, D. Five.
From Arena.
Piatt, S. Lesson in a Picture, A.
Piombino. Frozen Witness, The.
Time Travel.
Po Chü-i. Kept Waiting in the Boat at Chiu-K'ou Ten Days by an Adverse Wind.
Spring River, The.
Poe. Coliseum, The.
Pratt, M. Poem for my Sons.
Price, R. Twenty-One Years.
Pritchard, N. Cloak, The.
Quarles. I saw him dead; I saw his Body fall.
On the Life of Man.
Queneau. If You Imagine.
Radnóti. Clouded Sky.
Ralegh, W. Love and Time.
Nature, that washed her hands in milk.
Nimphs [or Nymph's] Reply to the Sheepheard [or Shepherd], The.
Verses Made the Night before He Died [or Dyed].
Verses Made the Night before His Beheading.
Raleigh. Nymph's Reply to the Shepherd, The.
Rannit. Wiiralt Drawing in Chartres.
Ravikovitch. Time Caught in a Net.
Reed, H. Judging Distances.
Reeves, J. Slowly the tide creeps up the sand.
Reid, A. James Bottle's Year.
Rexroth, K. Time Is the Mercy of Eternity.
Ridler. At Christmas.
Rilke. Sonnets to Orpheus I, 12, The.
Robinson, E. Three Quatrains.

Rosenberg, I. Garden of Joy, The.
Rossetti, C. Amen.
Bride Song.
Life's Parallels, A.
One Certainty, The.
Rukeyser, M. Time Exposures.
Sandburg, C. Four Preludes on Playthings of the Wind.
Languages.
Limited.
People, Yes, The.
Sunset from Omaha Hotel Window.
Sarton. Now I become myself. It's taken.
Schwartz, D. Time's Dedication.
Scott, D. Uncle Time is a ole, ole man.
Scott, W. Hour with thee! When earliest day, An.
Servasius. Rivers level granite mountains.
Seward. Elegy.
Sexton. Road Back, The.
Shakespeare, W. Motley's the Only Wear.
Seven Ages of Man, The.
Sonnet 12.
Sonnet 19.
Sonnet 55.
Sonnet 60.
Sonnet 64.
Sonnet 65.
Sonnet 77.
Sonnet 106.
Sonnet 116.
Sonnet 123.
Sonnet 124.
Sonnet 126.
Shalom. All Is Not So Simple.
Shapiro, K. Drug Store.
Shelley, P. Ozymandias [of Egypt].
Time.
Shen Chou. Drinking at Night with Yen Kung-mou.
Sidney, R. Forsaken woods, trees with sharp storms opressed.
Slessor. Five Bells.
Smith, S. Grange, The.
Holiday, The.
Smith, S. Time be brief.
Smith, W. Abruptly all the palm trees rose like parasols.
Snyder, G. Four Poems for Robin.
Milton by Firelight.
Södergran. There is no one in this world who has time.
Sorescu. Question.
Southey, R. Scholar, The.
Spark. Litany of Time Past.
Spencer, T. Day was a year at first, The.
Spender, S. Epilogue: "Time is a thing."
In railway halls, on pavements near the traffic.
Spenser. Ruines of Time, The.
Whilom, as antique stories tellen us.
Stafford, W. Gift, The.
Montana Eclogue.
Starr, J. Flight.
Stern, G. I Hate My Moaning.
Stevens, W. Martial Cadenza.
This Solitude of Cataracts.
Stillman, M. Song: "Love is a green girl."
Su Tung-p'o. End of the Year, The.
Last Day of the Year, The.
To a Traveler.
Suckling, J. Constant Lover, A [or The].
Love's Clock.
Swan, J. Father Father Son and Son.
Swift, J. Power of Time, The.
Sylvester, J. Rome, Conqueror, Conquered.
Szymborska. View with a Grain of Sand.
T'ai-shang. In Reply to Questions.
Tati-Loutard. Noonday in Immaturity.
Taylor, B. Long Ago, The.
Taylor, H. Flying Change, The.
Teasdale. Song: "Let it be forgotten, as a flower is forgotten."
Tennyson, A. Break, break, break.
Dedication, A: "Dear, near and true—no truer Time himself."
Thomas, D. Force that through the green fuse drives the flower, The.

When, like a running grave, time tracks you down.
Thomas, E. Gone, gone again.
Thomas, R. Centuries.
Thompson, P. Adown the heights of Ages.
Toller. O Heavy Step of Slow Monotony.
Tóth, J. Two Cities.
Trần Gia Thoại. Falling Leaf, A.
Tu Fu. Jade Flower Palace.
Unknown. Deor.
Footprints made on the sands of.
Minutes of Gold.
Thus Passeth.
Tune: "Willow Branches."
Van Duyn. Homework.
Vaughan, H. As time one day by me did pass.
Venclova. Night descended on us with a chill.
Very. Lost, The.
One Generation Passeth Away.
Virgil. Another year!
Vogel, D. There is a last, solitary coach about to leave.
Voznesensky. Somewhere a man puts on his shorts.
Walcott. In a Green Night.
Waniek. House on Moscow Street, The.
Warren, R. Bearded Oaks.
Natural History.
There's a grandfather's clock in the hall, watch it closely. The.
Watkins, V. Old Triton Time.
Wearne. Go on, tell me the season is over.
Webster, A. Faded.
Welish. Within This Book, Called Marguerite.
Wen Cheng-ming. Day drags on, as long as a year!, The.
Wevill. Namelessness.
Wheelock, J. Dear Men and Women.
Whitman, W. Hours continuing long, sore and heavy-hearted.
Leaves of Grass (1855).
To think of time—of all that retrospection.
Whitney, I. And (though I am perswade) that I.
Wilbur. Mill, The.
On the Marginal Way.
Year's End.
Willis, I. Time's Whirligig, Or, The Blue-New-Made-Gentleman Mounted.
Wither. *Sun* hath run his course through all the Signes, The.
Wood, S. Witness.
Wordsworth, W. Mutability.
Wright, C. March Journal.
Wroth. Sonnet 32: "How fast thou fliest, O Time, on loves swift wings."
Wu of Han. From the Most Distant Time.
Wylie. Let No Charitable Hope.
Wynne, J. Time's an hand's-breadth; 'tis a tale.
Xuân Diệu. Come on, make haste—please, won't you hurry up?
Forever, yes, forever I'll love you.
In a Hurry.
Nothingness.
Spring Out of Season.
Yeats. Brown Penny.
Folly Of Being Comforted, The.
Gyres! the gyres! Old Rocky Face look forth, The.
Lamentation of the Old Pensioner, The.
Moods, The.
Yesenin. Rowan Tree Fire, The.
Yi, K. Certain Year, A.
Yoshimi. White sky, The.
Young, A. California Peninsula: El Camino Real.
Yukitsuna. Tanka: "Amid the waves of time."
Tanka: "Overtaken by time."
Zach. How the Days Passed. Who'd have believed they'd.
In the Course of Time the original.
Zweig, P. Poem: "I don't know if I can bear this suddenly."

Timoshenko, Semyon Konstantinovich
Keyes, S. Timoshenko.

Tinkers
Unknown. If "ifs" and "ans" [*or* If ifs and ands were pots and pans].
Tinter Abbey
Stevenson, R. Fragment, A: "Thou strainest through the mountain fern."
Tiresias
Basho. Many, many things.
Clarke, A. My mother wept loudly.
Homer. Here open'd Hell, all Hell I here implor'd.
Jacob, H. Judgement of Tiresias, The.
Unknown. Worldes blisse, have good day!
Yen Chi-tao. Tune: "Mountain Hawthorns."
Tisha Ba'Ab
Unknown. Dirge for the Ninth of Ab.
Titanic (ship)
Dickey, W. Arrival of the Titanic, The.
Hardy, T. Convergence of the Twain, The.
Knight, E. Dark Prophecy: I Sing of Shine.
Pratt, E. Final Moments, The.
Unknown. Great *Titanic.*
Shine and the *Titanic.*
Titanic, a Toast.
Tithonus
Tennyson, A. Tithonus.
Titian (Tiziano Vecellio)
Aretino. If famous Apelles with his hand of art.
Bridges, R. Art is the true and happy science of the soul.
Titus (Roman Emperor)
Heath-Stubbs. Titus and Berenice.
Toads
Allen, E. Toad, A.
Corbière. Toad, The.
Crane, S. "Think as I think," said a man.
Dyer, J. Tenants of an Abandoned Castle.
Ewing, J. Friend in the Garden, A.
Finkel. Spring Song.
Grahame, K. Song of Mr Toad, The.
Grass. Gasco.
Kolmar. Toad, The.
Miyazawa Kenji. Tanka: "At last."
Patterson, R. Hopping Toad Blues.
Rogers, P. Power of Toads, The.
Rosen, M. Teasing Toads, The.
Rossetti, C. Hopping frog, hop here and be seen.
Rotella, A. In the Queen Anne's lace a toad.
Su Shih. On A Toad.
Tekkan. Tanka: "With warts and all."
Unknown. Catfish and Toad.
"Croak!" said the Toad, "I'm hungry, I think."
Ode to the Toad.
Wilbur. Death of a Toad, The.
Zipper. Football, The.
Toadstools. *See* **Mushrooms**
Toasters
Smith, W. Toaster, The.
Tobacco
Browne, I. Blest leaf! whose aromatic gales dispense.
Cotton, C. On Tobacco.
Freneau. Tobacco.
Gurney, I. Tobacco Plant.
Hemminger. Tobacco ("Tobacco is a dirty weed").
Melville, H. Herba Santa.
Miller, J. Hanging Burley.
Moore, L. From the Field.
Unknown. Make three fourths of a cross, and a circle complete.
Says the Miner to the Mucker.
Tobacco is a filthy weed.
Wisdome. Religious Use of [Taking] Tobacco, A.
Tobago. *See* **Trinidad and Tobago**
Toes
Unknown. Hairy Toe, The.
Moses supposes his toeses are roses.
Updike. In Extremis.
See also **Feet**
Tokyo, Japan
Engle, P. Ending, The.

Toledo, Spain
Campbell, R. Toledo.
Williams, W. High Bridge above the Tagus River at Toledo, The.
Tolerance
Bruner. Plea for Tolerance.
Dunbar, P. Accountability.
Toller, Ernst
Auden. In Memoriam: Ernst Toller.
Tollund Man
Heaney, S. Tollund Man, The.
Tombs
Abdullah. Tombs, The.
Bast. Frost Eyebrows was the favorite cat.
Brontë, C. This is my tomb, this humble stone.
Carew, T. Another [Epitaph on Lady Mary Villiers] ("This little vault, this narrow room").
Chao Meng-fu. Inscribed on Sun An-chih's "Painting of Pines and Catalpas."
Clare, J. Loves Lives Beyond the Tomb.
Collins, W. Dirge in "Cymbeline."
De la Mare. Stranger, The.
Dickinson, E. Admirations—and Contempts—of time, The.
After great pain a formal feeling comes—.
"Field." Embalmment.
From Baudelaire.
Herbert, G. Church Monuments.
Herrick. His Winding-Sheet.
To Robin Redbreast.
Hsü Pen. Tomb of the Singing Girl Ch'iung-i, The.
Jacobsen, R. Catacombs in San Callisto, The.
Jonson, B. Little Shrub Growing By, A.
Keats. To Fanny Brawne.
Landor, W. Torch of Love dispels the gloom, The.
Larkin, P. Arundel Tomb, An.
Monsour. Sweeping.
Paulus Silentiarius. Epitaph, An: "My name—my country—what are they to thee."
Poe. Annabel Lee.
Rochester, J. Mistress, The: A Song.
Rossetti, C. Last Rites.
Sandburg, C. Cool Tombs.
Smith, C. Sonnet Written in the Church-Yard at Middleton in Sussex.
Sparrow, J. Epitaph: "This stone, with not unpardonable pride."
Stevens, W. Worms at Heaven's Gate, The.
Unknown. Spirit of Plato.
Vas. Catacombs.
Wharton, E. Tomb of Ilaria Giunigi, The.
Wordsworth, W. Surprised by Joy—impatient as the Wind.
Yüan Hung-tao. Pei-mang Cemetery.
Yüan Mei. Arriving at Hangchou.
See also **Cemeteries; Graves; Monuments; Mausoleums**
Tone, Wolfe
Clarke, A. Wolfe Tone.
Tongues
Dante Alighieri. So gentle and so virtuous she appears.
Dove, R. Adolescence—II.
Franklin, B. Bits of Wisdom.
Hacker, M. Canzone: "Consider the three functions of the tongue."
Lorde. Echoes.
Mackey, N. John Coltrane Arrived with An Egyptian Lady.
McClintock, M. Letting my tongue.
Redmond. My tongue paints a path of fire.
Strong, P. Tongue, The.
Tate, G. Tonguing.
Unknown. One reason a dog is such a lovable.
Theophilus Thistledown, the successful thistle sifter.
Tongue of Wood, The.
Tools
Ormsby, F. Under the Stairs.
O'Sullivan, O. His Request.
Unknown. Ch'ing-yang Ford.
Toothaches. *See* **Teeth**
Torah, The
Bialik. Talmud Student, The.

Ficowski. Both Your Mothers.
Gordon, J. Simhat Torah.
Unknown. Angels Came a-Mustering, The.
  This Feast of the Law.

Tories
Moore, T. Tory Pledges.

Tornadoes
Fulton, A. News of the Occluded Cyclone.
McHugh, H. Tornado Survivor.
Moss, T. Tornados.
Olsen, W. Storm Chasers, The.
Sine. Tornado Warning.
Spaziani. If it were a sea, this immense wind.
Unknown. Sherman Cyclone, The.
  Tupelo Destruction, The.

Toronto, Ontario
Lee, D. Often I sit in the sun and brooding
  over the city, always.

Tortoises
Atwood. Elegy for the Giant Tortoises.
Clarke, C. Tortoise and Badger.
Hecht, A. Giant Tortoise.
Hsü Chung-hsing. I shake my robe—and mists
  disperse, leaving clear autumn sky.
Lawrence, D. Baby Tortoise.
  Lui et Elle.
  Tortoise Gallantry.
  Tortoise-Shell.
  Tortoise Shout.
Oppian. Loves of the Tortoise, The.
Patten, B. Complacent Tortoise, The.
Smith, S. My Tortoise.
Unknown. Out of the lofty cavern wandering.
Zhenkai. Old Temple, The.

Torture
Atwood. Torture.
Balaban. Opening Le Ba Khon's Dictionary.
Bampfylde. On Hearing That Torture Was
  Suppressed throughout the Austrian
  Dominions.
Beer, P. Footbinding.
Berryman. Song of the Tortured Girl, The.
Bly, R. Romans Angry about the Inner World.
Cohen, L. Heirloom.
Daniel, Y. You stand beside me here, each
  day and every hour.
de Jesús. Curfew.
Djabali. For My Torturer, Lieutenant D——.
Dorfman, A. Last Waltz in Santiago.
Drayton. To His Coy Love, A Canzonet.
Ekelof. Hangman / what will you do with my
  arms?
Faiz. Prison Daybreak, A.
Hamburger, M. Between the Lines.
Hart, H. Prisoner of Camau, The.
Hayes, A. Slaughter-House, The.
Herbert, Z. What I Saw.
Hetherington, G. Man from Changi, The.
Hughes, J. Respect for Law and Order, A.
Ignatow. Ritual Three.
Jamison, B. Ask This of a Mother Whose
  Daughter Has Been Tortured.
Kearney, L. After the Interrogation.
Kilar, K. Poet's Counsel, A ("You come from
  the line of a Cŏla King").
Kovur Kilar. Poet's Counsel, A ("You come
  from the line of a Cola king").
Kunert. Vain Attempt.
Levchev. Confession and Salute to the Fire.
Oden. Riven Quarry, The.
Plath. Hanging Man, The.
Rózewicz. Voice, A.
Rukeyser, M. Rational Man.
Sadi. Great Physician, The.
Smith, S. My Cats.
Sorescu. Fresco.
Tadic. Antipsalm.
Unknown. Sweet, sweet, sweet, let me go.
Tom, Jill and Bob.
Utkin. Komsomol Song.

Touch
Glück, L. Song of Obstacles.
Gray, J. Mishka [is poet among the beasts].
Gunn, T. Touch.
Horovitz, F. Do you not know that I need to
  touch you.
Kinzie. Glinting like water.

Mew. Ne Me Tangito.
Mouré. She Touched Me.
O'Neill, M. My fingers are antennae.
Paranar. What She Said ("Like moss on
  water").
Raine, K. Love-Poem: "Yours is the face that
  the earth turns to me."
Rossetti, C. First Day, The.
Sackville-West. Valediction.
Swenson, M. Blindman placed, The.
"Feel me to do right," our father said on his
  deathbed.

Toulouse-Lautrec, Henri de
Justice, D. Mule Team and Poster.

Tourism and Tourists
Adisa. Cultural Trip, A.
Amichai. Tourists.
Atwood. At the Tourist Centre in Boston.
Birney. Toronto Board of Trade Goes Abroad.
Bishop, E. Arrival at Santos.
Bromige. Edible World, The.
Brown, G. Trout Fisher.
Brown, W. Song For a Tourist.
Dove, R. Sightseeing.
Dugan, A. Memorial Service for the Invasion
  Beach Where the Vacation in the Flesh Is
  Over.
  Niagara Falls.
Duggan, L. Qantas Bags.
Garioch. Embro to the Ploy.
Grosholz. Outer Banks, The.
Hall, D. Christ Church Meadows, [Oxford].
Hoagland, E. Gorée ten miles offshore
  beckons.
Kunitz, S. Thief, The.
Melville, H. Attic Landscape, The.
Merrill, J. Casual Wear.
Moss, H. Tourists.
Page, P. Permanent Tourists, The.
Phillips, C. You Are Here.
Rathenow. Prague.
Rose, P. Anglo-Saxon Comedy.
Sharma. American Tourist.
Shiffert. Manners.
Stafford, W. Preservation.
Szymborska. Pietà.
Tibble. Trials of a Tourist.
Tsaloumas. Progressive Man's Indignation, A.
Tuwhare. Friend.
Walcott. Virgins, The.
Weaver, M. Message on Cape Cod, The.
Yambo. When Negro Teeth Speak.
Yenser, S. Blue Guide.
Zagajewski. Auto Mirror.
Žukauskas. Midwinter Tourists.

Toussaint L'Ouverture, François Dominique
Goodison. Kenscoff.
Ray, H. Toussaint L'Ouverture.
Wordsworth, W. To Toussaint L'Ouverture.

Towns
Auden. Who will endure.
Barnes, W. Be'mi'ster.
Browning, R. Up at a Villa—Down in the
  City.
Cervantes. Poema para los Californios
  Muertos.
Cummings, E. Anyone lived in a pretty how
  town.
Dove, R. Small Town.
Fraser, G. Home Town Elegy.
Graham, W. Children of Greenock, The.
Greenaway. Which Is the Way to Somewhere
  Town?
Hall, D. Town of Hill, The.
Larkin, P. Here.
Lawrence, D. End of Another Home Holiday.
  Whether or Not.
Lux. Grim Town in a Steep Valley.
Moore, M. Steeple-Jack, The.
Muir, E. Good Town, The.
Po Chü-i. After Collecting the Autumn Taxes.
Reese, L. April in Town.
Rukeyser, M. Gauley Bridge.
Sandburg, C. Gone.
Schuyler, J. Elizabethans Called It Dying, The.
Shin, K. Visiting a Rural Town.
Suckling, J. Summons to Town, A.

Tomlinson, C. Two Views of Two Ghost
  Towns.
Wallace, R. Driving By.
Wallace, R. State Poetry Day.
Wickham. Fired Pot, The.
Wright, K. Unlikely Obbligato of
  Andersonstown.

See also **Cities; Villages**

Toys
Bishop, E. Cirque d'Hiver.
Carter, D. Mistress Indiarubber Duck.
Ceravolo. Crocus Turn and Gods, The.
Clark, T. Daily News.
Davies, W. To W.S.—On his Wonderful Toys.
Edson, R. Toy-maker made a toy wife and a
  toy child. He made a toy house and some toy
  years, A.
Field, E. Duel, The.
  Little Boy Blue.
Fisher, R. Incredible Henry McHugh, The.
Hardy, T. New Toy, The.
Hoban. Tin Frog, The.
Jennings, E. My animals are made of wool
  and glass.
Johnson, M. Lost Teddy Bear, The.
Kinzie. Boy.
Leonidas. Philokles offers his bouncing.
McCrea. My Toys.
Mole, J. Jack-in-the-Box is faithful.
Nemerov. Models.
Okudzhava. Paper Soldier.
Patmore, C. Toys, The.
Pyle. Toys Talk of the World, The.
Shapiro, K. Terminal.
Simic. Toy Factory.
Stevenson, R. Block City.
  Dumb Soldier, The.
  Land of Counterpane, The.
  Song of a Traveller, The.
  Travel.
Sutskever. Toys.
Thomas, C. Treasures.
Unknown. My Pet Koala.
Ushida. Deep in the rippling spring.
Worth, V. Magnet.

Track Athletics
Crinagoras. From the Greek Anthology.
Robinson, E. Mighty Runner, A.
Sorescu. Start.
Whitman, W. Runner, The.

Tractors
Hughes, T. Tractor stands frozen—an agony,
  The.
Mountain, M. Quiet day, A.
Unknown. Drive a Tractor.

Tradition
Fuller, R. Translation.
Hewitt, J. From the Tibetan.
Kipling, R. Land, The.
Klepfisz. My Mother's Sabbath Days.
Lorde. Generation.
Lovelace, R. To a Lady with Child that Asked
  [*or* Ask'd] an Old Shirt.
Mahon. Last of the Fire Kings, The.
McElroy, C. This Is the Poem I Never Meant
  to Write.
Olds, S. For My Daughter.
Senior. Birdshooting season the men.
Shapiro, K. Necropolis.
Stafford, W. At the Klamath Berry Festival.

Trafalgar, Battle of (1805)
Hardy, T. Night of Trafalgar, The.
Palgrave. Trafalgar

Traffic
Agard, J. Lollipop lady.
Bond, C. What You Want Means What You
  Can Afford.
Haines, J. Snowbound City, The.
Kharms. Event on the Street, An.
Le Gallienne. Sunset in the City.
Livingston, M. 4-Way Stop.
Sandburg, C. Blue Island Intersection.
Sanders, T. Transit Authority.
Sheck. Rush Hour.
Wilbur. Simile for Her Smile, A.
Winters, Y. Before Disaster.

Traffic Accidents. *See* **Automobile Accidents**

Traherne, Thomas
Wilbur. 'World Without Objects Is a Sensible Emptiness," A."

Trains
Alexander, E. Farewell to You.
Alexie. On the Amtrak from Boston to New York City.
Amann. Night train passes, A.
Anderson, S. Evening Song.
Ashbery. Leaving the Atocha Station.
  Melodic Trains.
Baro. Travelling Backward.
Berryman. Traveller, The.
Betjeman. Parliament Hill Fields.
Bly, R. In a Train.
  Looking at New-Fallen Snow from a Train.
Bogan, L. Train Tune.
Booth, P. Crossing.
  Stations.
Broonzy. Southern Blues, The.
Brown, S. Call Boy.
  Long Track Blues.
  Sister Lou.
Brownjohn. Train will come tomorrow year, The.
Bruchac. Let the Midnight Special.
Buckley, C. Train in the Desert—1916.
Bursk. Tearing Up the Tracks.
Carver, R. Walk, A.
Casey, T. Drill, Ye Tarriers, Drill.
Cendrars. South.
Chōkū. Tanka: "Train speeds on, The."
Cholmondeley-Pennell. Night Mail North, The.
Clark, T. Superballs.
  You (I).
Clarke, A. Journey, The.
Coleridge, M. Train, The.
Collier, M. North Corridor.
Cranch. Locomotive, The.
Crane, H. River, The.
Cummings, E. One Fine Day.
Dawe, B. Renewal Notice.
Delmore Brothers. Wabash Cannonball, The.
Dent. Dream Orpheum Balcony.
Dickey, J. Folk Singer of the Thirties, A.
Dickinson, E. I like to see it lap the Miles.
Dobyns. Freight Cars.
Durcan. Tullynoe: Tête-à-Tête in the Parish Priest's Parlour.
Eberhart, R. Analogue of Unity in Multeity.
Eiseley. And as for Man.
Eliot, T. Skimbleshanks: The Railway Cat.
Emanuel, L. Film Noir: Train Trip Out.
Empson. Beautiful Train, The.
Etter. Great Northern.
  Riding the Rock Island Through Kansas.
Ferlinghetti, L. Starting from San Francisco.
Field, E. Journey, A.
Forché. On Returning to Detroit.
Francis, R. Night Train.
Frost, R. On the Heart's Beginning to Cloud the Mind.
Gallagher, T. Not There.
Galvin, B. For a Daughter Gone Away.
  Old Trip by Dream Train, The.
George, D. Wreck of the Old 97.
Gibbons, R. American Trains.
Giles, B. Late Express, The.
Gioia. In Cheever Country.
Gouri. At the Train Station.
Greenberg, A. Freight Train, Freight Train.
Haines, J. Train Stops at Healy Fork, The.
Hall, D. Sister on the Tracks, A.
Hanzlicek, C. Last Trains, The.
Hanzlik. Cottage Behind the Railway, The.
Hardy, T. Faintheart in a Railway Train.
  Midnight on the Great Western.
Hart-Smith. Nullarbor.
Harte, B. What the Engines Said.
Hayden, R. Runagate Runagate.
Hedin, R. Wreck of the Great Northern, The.
Herlin. Light brush of dawn, A.
Hewitt, J. Frontier, The.
Heyen. Tie, The.
Hikmet. Things I Didn't Know I Loved.

Hilberry. Body and mind, we used to think, were two.
Hoffman, D. Special Train, A.
Hope, A. Observation Car.
Hughes, L. Freedom Train.
  Homesick Blues.
  Jim Crow Car.
  Pennsylvania Station in New York, The.
  Porter.
Hugo, R. Elegy: "I expected him to look dead in the casket."
  Yards of Sarajevo, The.
Jacobsen, J. Reindeer and Engine.
Jacobsen, R. Express train 1256 races alongside hidden, remote villages. House.
Jarrell. On the Railway Platform.
  Orient Express, The.
Jefferson, B. Easy Rider Blues.
Jensen, L. To a Stranger (At the End of a Caboose).
József. Freight trains are pulling in.
Justice, D. Train.
Kendall, M. Underground.
Kennelly. Limerick Train, The.
Kinnell. Lackawanna.
Kooser. City Limits.
Lattimore. North Philadelphia, Trenton, and New York.
  Note on the L and N.
Laux. Children's Train, The.
Lawrence, D. Tommies in the Train.
Leadbelly. Midnight Special, The.
Levertov. By Rail through the Earthly Paradise, Perhaps Bedfordshire.
  Don't You Hear that Whistle Blowin'.
Levin, P. Night Coach.
Levine, P. And the Trains Go On.
Lindsay, V. Flower-fed buffaloes of the spring, The.
Machado Ruiz. Rainbow at Night.
MacLeish. Burying Ground by the Ties.
  Empire Builders.
  Grazing Locomotives.
MacNeice. Figure of Eight.
  Slow Movement.
Martinez, D. Fuego.
Marty. In the Dome Car of the "Canadian."
McBride, M. Red Letters.
McCord, D. Song of the Train.
McGrath, T. Black Train, The.
  End of the Line, The.
Merwin, W. Wheels of the Trains, The.
Millay, E. From a Train Window.
  Travel.
Miller, V. How far is it to you by foot?
Mizejewski. Parents Sleeping.
Monroe, B. In the Pines.
Moorer. Jim Crow Cars.
Mueller, L. Commuter.
Neihardt. Summer turned.
Nemerov. Low-Level Cross-Country.
Nichols, R. 1.
Nims, J. Freight.
Nobuyuki. Third-Class Car on a Night Train (three poems).
"O." Engine Driver, The.
Ochester. Penn Central Station at Beacon, N.Y, The.
Parini. Coal Train.
Pastan. At the Train Museum.
  Last Train, The.
Perlman, A. Summer Adjustments.
Pettit. Self-Portrait Approaching Promontory, Utah.
Pizzarelli. Bending back.
  Snow falls from trees.
Plath. Getting There.
Plumly. For Esther.
Ponciano. Empties Coming Back.
Randall, D. Southern Road, The.
Reiter, T. Rights of Way.
Rich, A. Lucifer in the Train.
Roberson. True we are two grown men.
Roethke. Night Journey.
Rose, P. Terminus.
Rukeyser, M. Campaign.
St. John, D. Iris.

Sandburg, C. Limited.
  Southern Pacific.
  Window.
  Work Gangs.
Sarton. After a Train Journey.
Saxe, J. Rhyme of the Rail[s].
Segooa. Praises of the Train.
Seibert. Casey Jones.
Shapiro, K. Terminal.
  Western Town.
Shepherd, H. Trains.
Sissman. Big Rock-Candy Mountain, The.
Slessor. Night-Ride, The.
Smelyakov. Locomotives' graveyard, The.
Smith, D. Roundhouse Voices, The.
Smith, W. Jittery Jim.
Soto. Who Will Know Us?
Spender, S. Express, The.
Stafford, W. Both Ways.
  Vacation.
Sternlieb. Right of Way.
Stevenson, R. From a Railway Carriage.
Sub-ok. Spring at Yesan Station.
Swenson, M. Riding the "A."
  Written While Riding the Long Island Rail Road.
Taggard. Train: Abstraction.
Tate, J. Manna.
Thompson, I. Holiday Train, The.
Thomson, J. In the Train.
Thoreau. What's the Railroad to Me?
Tranströmer. Below Freezing.
  Track.
Tsvetaeva. You, walking past me.
Unknown. Casey Jones.
  Goat, The.
  Gospel train is moving, The.
  Hallelujah, I'm a Bum.
  Little Black Train Is A-Comin'.
  Poor Paddy Works on the Railway.
  Railroad Bill, Railroad Bill.
  Railroad Blues, The.
  Railroad Cars Are Coming, The.
  Song: The Railway Train.
  Southern Blues, The.
  This Train ("This train is bound for glory, this train").
  Train, The.
  Train is a-comin', oh yes.
Van Doren. Dream of Trains, A.
Veenendaal. On My Fourteenth Wedding Anniversary I Ride on Trains.
Virgil. Coal train, The.
Warner, S. Journey To Barcelona.
Warren, R. Ballad: Between the Boxcars.
Webb, F. Laid Off.
West, K. On Track.
Weston, M. Departure.
Whitman, W. To a Locomotive in Winter.
Wilbur. In the Smoking-Car.
Williams, W. Overture to a Dance of Locomotives.
  To freight cars in the air.
Wojahn. "Mystery Train" Janis Joplin Leaves Port Arthur for Points West, 1964.
  Photo of My Father in a Snowbound Train.
Worsley-Benison. Song of the Engine, The.
Wright, J. Outside Fargo, North Dakota.
Wright, J. Train Journey.
Young, D. Boxcar Poem, The ("Boxcars drift by / clanking, The").
  Project for Freight Trains, A.
Yukitsuna. Tanka: "Overtaken by time."
Zagajewski. At Daybreak.
See also **Railroads; Locomotives**

Traitors. *See* **Treason and Traitors**

Trakl, Georg
Dubie. Trakl.
Lasker-Schüler. Georg Trakl.

Tramps. *See* **Vagabonds**

Transformation
Ai. Man with the Saxophone, The.
Cassian. Equality.
  Temptation.
Cherry, K. Going Down on America.
Chin. Song of the Sad Guitar.
Christopher. 5°.

Clifton, L. Turning into my own.
Coleridge, H. Prayer.
Creeley. Statue, The.
Cullen, C. Protest.
Ded. I was passionate.
Dennis, C. Nuts and Raisins.
Dickinson, E. He touched me, so I live to know.
Drummond, W. Statue of Medusa, The.
Eady. Thrift.
  Young Elvis.
Emerson, R. Character.
Espada. When Songs Become Water.
Field, E. Curse of the Cat Woman.
Glück, L. Undertaking, The.
Goodison. On Becoming a Tiger.
Hall, D. Je Suis une Table.
Hardy, T. Transformations.
Hart-Smith. Nullarbor.
Henson, L. I Am Singing the Cold Rain.
Karp. Taxi to the Flame, A.
Kipling, R. 'Eathen in 'is blindness bows down to wood an' stone, The.
Kunert. Every Day.
Levis. Cocoon, The.
Marippittiyar. Hunter Once, Now an Ascetic, A.
Mayer, B. We've solved the problem, the problem is solved.
McNair. House in Spring.
Mihalic. Metamorphosis.
Mirabai. It's True I Went to the Market.
Mother Goose. Old Woman and the Pedlar, The.
Nemerov. Singular Metamorphosis, A.
Padgett, R. Symbols of Transformation.
Parun. Open Door.
Phylip, S. Seagull, The.
Piercy. Woman in the ordinary pudgy downcast girl, The.
Plath. Love Letter.
Ravikovitch. War's End.
Rilke. Silent friend of many distances, feel.
Rodgers, C. Some Me of Beauty.
Różewicz. Transformations.
Rukeyser, M. Hostages, The.
Rumi. New Rule, The.
  We can't help being thirsty.
Sarton. In Time Like Air.
Shapiro, K. Haircut.
Sitwell, D. Song: "We are the darkness in the heat of the day."
Smith, S. Frog Prince, The.
So Chong-Ju. If I Became a Stone.
Spicer, J. Transformations.
Swenson, C. Line.
Tanikawa Shuntaro. Request.
Tomlinson, C. Door, The.
Turberville. Lover Whose Mistress Feared a Mouse, The.
Untermeyer, L. To a Vine-clad Telegraph Pole.
Van Duyn. Leda Reconsidered.
Warsh. Gout.
Wilbur. Beautiful Changes, The.
Wonodi. Salute to Icheke.
Wright, C. October.
Wylie. Little Eclogue.

Transience

"Akhmatova." Instead of wisdom—experience, a flat.
Auden. As I walked out one evening.
Banning, L. Romancero.
Baranczak, S. If china, then only the kind.
Bede. Sparrow's Flight, A.
Bernstein, O. Of All the Splendor.
Bethell. Response.
  Time.
Bolton, E. Palinode, A.
Browning, R. Prologue: "Poet's age is sad: for why?, The."
Burns, R. Lo worms enjoy the seat of bliss.
Campion, T. To music bent is my retired mind.
  What if a day, or a month, or a year[e].
  Where are all thy beauties now, all hearts enchaining? [or harts enchayning?].

Carew, T. Song, [A]: "Ask me no more where Jove bestows."
Catullus. Carmen 70 ("Lesbia says she'ld rather marry me").
  Lines from Catullus.
Cibulka. Kuks.
Coleridge, S. Egypt's might is tumbled down.
Crane, H. Passage.
Daniel, S. But love whilst that thou mayst be loved again.
  Half-blown Rose, The.
  Sonnet 33: 'When men shall find thy flower'.
Donne. Anniversary [or Anniversarie], The.
Drayton. Sonnet 6: 'How many paltry, foolish, painted things'.
Drummond, W. I know that all beneath the moon decays.
Dryden, J. Song from The Indian Emperor.
Eberhart, R. Groundhog, The.
Eigner. Back to it.
Eliot, T. Burnt Norton.
  Dry Salvages, The.
  East Coker.
Essex, R. Change thy minde since she doth change.
Fitzgerald, E. Some We Loved.
Frost, R. Nothing Gold Can Stay.
Garrigue. From Venice was that afternoon.
Gay, J. Cotillion.
Gouri. Age is ended, another kingdom's ended, An.
Grainger, J. What is fame? An empty bubble.
Guiterman. On the Vanity of Earthly Greatness.
Gustafson, R. Of Green Steps and Laundry.
Habib. Ancestors.
Habington. "Nox Nocti Indicat Scientiam."
Hardy, T. Sunshade, The.
Hass, R. Late Spring.
Herbert, G. Virtue [or Vertue].
Herrick. Corinna's Going A-Maying.
  Putrefaction is the end.
  To a Bed of Tulips.
  To Blossoms.
  To Daffodils [or Daffadills].
  To Dianeme ("Sweet, be not proud of those two eyes").
Holub. Gila Desert in Arizona, The.
"Hope." Request.
Horace. 4.7.
Housman, A. Along the field as we came by.
Izumi. Come quickly—as soon as.
Jeffers, R. To the Stone-Cutters.
King, H. Sic Vita.
Kitahara Hakushū. Tanka: "In the daytime."
Kunze, R. Almost a Spring Poem.
Lalic. Inscribed in the Silver of the Sea.
Lao Tzu. All things pass.
Levertov. Living.
Levine, P. Sweet Will.
Li Po. Song of a Dream Visit to T'ien-mu.
Lowell, A. Falling Snow.
Lucretius. Threshold Of The New, The.
MacNeice. Sunlight on the garden, The.
McOrlan. Wood merchant's parlour, The.
Melville, H. Malvern Hill.
Meredith, G. I play for Seasons; not Eternities!
Merwin, W. Grandmother Watching at Her Window.
Milosz, C. Encounter.
Montagu, L. Lover, The; a Ballad.
Moore, T. 'Tis the Last Rose of Summer.
Muir, E. Road, The.
Nashe. Litany in Time of Plague, A.
Olson, C. La Chute.
Ono no Komachi. As certain as color.
  Imperceptible / It withers in the world.
Peacock, T. Love and Age.
Plato. Apple, The.
Po Chü-i. At the End of Spring.
Ralegh, W. Nature, that washed her hands in milk.
  Nimphs [or Nymph's] Reply to the Sheepheard [or Shepherd], The.
  Verses Made the Night before He Died [or Dyed].

Raleigh. Nymph's Reply to the Shepherd, The.
Ransom, J. Blue Girls.
Reeves, W. Passing of the Forest, The.
Rexroth, K. Half in a dream.
  Some day in six inches of.
  This flesh you have loved.
Robinson, E. Man against the Sky, The.
Rossetti, C. Bed of Forget-Me-Nots, A.
  May.
Sackville, T. Midnight ("Midnight was come, when every vital thing").
Sandburg, C. Caboose Thoughts.
  Flash Crimson.
  Languages.
Shakespeare, W. "Be cheerful, sir."
  Epilogue.
  Song: "Fear no more the heat o' the Sun."
  Sonnet 1.
  Sonnet 3.
  Sonnet 5: 'Those hours that with gentle work'.
  Sonnet 18.
  Sonnet 19.
Shao Yung. Thoughts on T'ien-chin Bridge.
Shelley, P. Hymn to Intellectual Beauty.
  Ozymandias [of Egypt].
Shirley, J. Death the Leveller.
Sidney, P. Splendidis longum valedico nugis.
Sidney, R. Songe 17: "Sun is set, and masked night, The."
Spenser. Sonnet 79: "Men call you fair [or fayre], and you do[e] credit it."
Suckling, J. Constant Lover, A [or The].
Tennyson, A. Break, break, break.
Thompson, F. Too Soon.
Tranströmer. Breathing Space July.
Turberville. To His Friend.
Unknown. I came once to sit on Cold Mountain.
  Ruin, The.
  Ubi Sunt Qui ante Nos Fuerunt? [or Contempt of the World].
Unknown, sometimes at. to Sir Walter Ralegh. Holy Land of Walsingham, The.
Waller, E. Song: "Go[e], lovely rose[—ous sweet and fair]."
Walters, M. Haka: The Feathered Albatross.
Whitman, W. As if a phantom caress'd me.
Wilbur. Looking into History.
  To the Etruscan Poets.
  Transit.
  Two Voices in a Meadow.
Williams, M. After the Revolution for Jesus the Associate Professor [or a Secular Man] Prepares His Final Remarks.
Wordsworth, W. Most alluring clouds that mount the sky, The.
Wright, C. March Journal.
  Snow.
Wright, J. To a Troubled Friend.
Wyatt, T. Is it possible.
  Sonnet: 'Each man me telleth'.
Yeats. Get all the gold and silver that you can.
Yosano. Tanka: "Evanescent."
Zukofsky, L. Cars once steel and green, now old.

See also **Change**

Translation and Translators

Burns, R. On Elphinston's Translation of Martial.
Donne. Upon the Translation of the Psalms by Sir Philip Sidney, and the Countess of Pembroke His Sister.
Erskine, T. On Tom Moore's Translation of Anacreon.
Fenton, J. Lines for Translation into Any Language.
Horace. 'Tis hard, to speake things common, properly.
Jonson, B. To Clement Edmonds, on His *Caesar's Commentaries* Observed, and Translated.
  To My Worthy and Honoured Friend, Mr George Chapman, on His Translation of Hesiod's *Works and Days.*

Keats. On First Looking into Chapman's Homer.
Lesser. Translation.
Merrill, J. Lost in Translation.
Nemerov. Translation.
Pound, E. Translator to Translated.
Ralegh, W. To the Translator of Lucan [or Lucan's Pharsalia, 1614].
Rich, A. Translations.
Roscommon, W. Each poet with a different talent writes.
Walpole, H. On the Translation of Anacreon.
Whitman, W. Out of the cradle endlessly rocking.

Transportation, Penal
Unknown. Moreton Bay.

Trapezes and Trapeze Artists
Morgan, E. Cinquevalli is falling, falling.
Prelutsky. Man on the Flying Trapeze, The.
Unknown. Man on the Flying Trapeze, The.

Trapping and Trappers
Cook, E. On Seeing a Bird-Catcher.
Larkin, P. Myxomatosis.
Li K'ai-hsien. Meeting Trappers on the Road in Heavy Snow.
Staying Overnight on the Banks of Embroidered River.
Moore, M. New York.
Spenser. Sonnet 37: "What guile [or guyle] is this, that those her golden tresses."
Stephens, J. Snare, The.
Unknown. Little Random Creatures, The.

Trash. *See* **Garbage and Garbage Men**

Traveling and Travelers
Adcock, A. Travellers.
Alexander, E. Passage.
Alexander, M. October Journey.
Allen, S. Harriet Tubman aka Moses.
Arabov. Walking the Places I've Never Been.
Armantrout. Leaving.
Ashbery. Lament Upon the Waters, The.
Melodic Trains.
Wind thrashes the maple seed-pods, The.
Auden. On the Circuit.
Barras, J. Peace.
Basho. On this road / no one will follow me.
Baugh, E. Getting There.
Beeks. Parker's Mood.
Bell, M. Gemwood.
Benn. Bunch of drifter sons hollered, A.
Bernstein, O. Nocturnal Journey.
Berrigan, D. Prayer: "I left Cornell / with half a wit; six mismated socks."
Berryman. Traveller, The.
Bishop, E. Arrival at Santos.
Moose, The.
Over 2000 Illustrations and a Complete Concordance.
Questions of Travel.
Bly, R. Driving toward the Lac Qui Parle River.
Bobrowsky. Journey, The.
Bontemps. Nocturne of the Wharves.
Brew. Lonely Traveller, The.
Breytenbach. Asylum.
Journey.
Brock-Broido. Carrowmore.
Brown, G. Five Voyages of Arnor, The.
Brown, S. Tin Roof Blues.
Browning, R. Home-Thoughts, from the Sea.
Byron, G. He who, grown aged in this world of woe.
Lines to Mr Hodgson.
Carew, T. Upon Master Walter Montagu's Return from Travel.
Catullus. Attis.
Cendrars. South.
Chang Chi. Coming at Night to a Fisherman's Hut.
Chang Yü. Merchant's Joy, The.
Chao Meng-fu. In the Ancient Manner.
Chaucer. In May, that moder is of monthes glade.
Ch'en Yü-yi. Journeying to Hsiang-yi.
Chia Tao. Passing by a Mountain Village: Evening.
Ch'ien Ch'ien-i. No Flowers.

Ch'ien T'ao. LONG time ago, A.
Child, L. Thanksgiving Day.
Chin Nung. I remember when he took me on a trip to this place.
Mooring in the Rain at Sung-ling.
Traveler, I've been through a thousand changes, A.
Chong, H. Going by far.
Ch'u Yüan. Lament for Ying, A.
Oftentimes, I grew dejected and sobbed.
Yüan, Ch'ü.
Cohen, L. Suzanne takes you down to her place near the river.
Crane, H. River, The.
Crane, S. Wayfarer / Perceiving the pathway to truth, The.
Crinagoras. Sailing to Italy—fitting out / commissioning—to see the friends.
Cristofor. Night Traveller.
Dame. On the road to Damascus, Maryland.
Darwish, M. We travel like other people, but we return to nowhere. As if travelling.
Davison, P. Where the Sun Ends.
De la Mare. Listeners, The.
Railway Junction, The.
Deane, S. Return.
DeClue. Ijajee's Story.
Dennis, C. Traveller, The.
Dickinson, E. Caterpillar.
I like to see it lap the Miles.
I watched the Moon around the House.
DiPalma. Wrong Side of the Door, The.
Dixon, M. Place, Places.
Doinas, S. Ascent, The.
Donne. On His Mistress [or Mistris].
Song: "Sweetest love, I do not go[e]."
Dorn, E. Geranium.
Drayton. To the Virginian Voyage.
Drummond de Andrade. Travelling in the Family.
Duffy, C. In Your Mind.
Eliot, T. Journey of the Magi.
"Eliza." Epistle to John Walker, Esq., An.
Emanuel, L. Film Noir: Train Trip Out.
Euripides. Chorus sing of escape, The.
Ferlinghetti, L. Starting from San Francisco.
Field, E. Journey, A.
Field, E. Wynken, Blynken and Nod one night.
Fulton, R. Travelling Alone.
Galvin, B. Old Trip by Dream Train, The.
Gander. Table Laid with Horrors, A.
Garioch. Property.
Gay, J. *et al.* Mary Gulliver to Capt. Lemuel Gulliver.
Ginsberg, A. So I dream nightly of an embarkation.
Giovanni. They Clapped.
Glück, L. Magi, The.
Goethe. Diary, The.
Song of the Traveler at Evening.
Goodison. Road of the Dread, The.
Görgey. Folkway.
Gossett. On the Question of Fans/ The Slave Quarters Are Never Air Conditioned.
Graddon. Travelling.
Graves, R. Legs, The.
Travel[l]er's Curse after Misdirection[, The].
Gray, J. Le Voyage À Cythère.
Gray, J. Journey: the North Coast.
Greenaway. When You and I Grow Up. Which Is the Way to Somewhere Town?
Grosholz. Life of a Salesman.
Gunn, T. Discovery of the Pacific, The.
Gurney, I. Walking Song.
Guthrie, R. Magi, The.
Hadas, R. Journey Out.
Haines, J. There Are No Such Trees in Alpine, California.
Han Yü. Officer at the Rapids, The.
Harington. Thus all that day, they spent in divers ways.
Hecht, A. Prospects.
Herrick. Salutation.
Hewitt, J. Frontier, The.
Hikmet. Things I Didn't Know I Loved.

Ho Ching-ming. Bamboo Branch Song.
Presented to Wang Wen-hsi.
Ho Hsun. Traveler with his heavy heart, The.
Ho Sun. At Parting.
Howes, B. Home Leave.
Hsieh Ling-yün. Climbing Stone Drum Mountain Above the Shores of Shang-shu.
Entering the Mouth of P'eng-li Lake.
Journeying by Stream: Following Chin-chu Torrent I Cross the Mountains.
Hsü Chung-hsing. Traveling by Boat at Shun-ch'ang.
Hsü Pen. Saying Goodbye to a Monk from Japan.
Tomb of the Singing Girl Ch'iung-i, The.
Huang Ching-jen. Traveling at Break of Day.
Huang T'ing-chien. Climbing K'uai Pavilion.
Huchel. On the Way.
Imr el Kais. Ode: "Weep, ah weep love's losing, love's with its dwelling place."
Jackson, A. Love of Travellers, The.
Jamie. Way We Live, The.
Jarrell. On the Railway Platform.
Jenkins, J. *et al.* In Ferrara.
Jordan, J. Roman Poem Number Nine.
K'ang Hai. Dreaming of Master Chung-lu.
Kao Ch'i. Mooring Our Boat at Tan-yang Harbor.
Kapilar. What She Said ("Forest animals walk there").
Kazantzis. Frightened Flier Goes North, The.
Keats. Keen, fitful gusts are whispering here and there.
Naughty Boy, The.
Kenyon, J. Here.
Kipling, R. Gipsy Trail, The.
Sestina of the Tramp-Royal.
Kitahara Hakushū. Tanka: "Today too."
Kloefkorn. On the Road.
Knox, C. Rune, A.
Larbaud. Images.
Larkin, P. Arrivals, Departures.
Lattimore. North Philadelphia, Trenton, and New York.
Lear, E. Jumblies, The.
Lee, L. Home From Abroad.
Levis. Widening Spell of the Leaves, The.
Li Ho. Bronze Immortal Takes Leave of Han, A.
Li Hsün. Tune: "Stretch of Cloud over Mount Wu, A."
Li K'ai-hsien. In the Second Month of Summer, Taking My Family to the Villages East of the City.
Trip to a Mountain Village, A.
Li Ling. Parting from Su Wu.
Li Meng-yang. Autumn Vista.
Li Po. Road to Shu Is Hard, The.
Li Tung. For the Monk San-tsang on His Return to the Western Regions.
Li Tung-yang. Following the Rhymes of Yang T'ing-ho's Poem, "On the Road Back, Accompanying the Imperial Retinue on a Visit to the Tombs of Former Emperors."
Liu E. Poem on Falling Leaves.
Liu Yung. Tune: "Prelude to Allure Goddesses."
Logan, J. Trip to Four or Five Towns, A.
Longfellow, H. Excelsior.
Tide rises, the tide falls, The.
Lu Yu. Blue Rapids.
I Had Occasion to Tell a Visitor about an Old Trip I Took.
Leaving the Monastery Early in the Morning.
Long Sigh.
Sending Tzu-lung Off to a Post in Chi-chou.
Ma Chih-yüan. Tune: "Sky-clear Sand"— Autumn Thoughts.
Machado Ruiz. Rainbow at Night.
MacLeish. Immortal Helix.
Tourist Death.
Madhubuti. Poet: What Ever Happened to Luther?
Markham, E. Her story.
Martial. De Hortis Julii Martialis.
Masefield. Sea-Fever.
McGrath, T. Epitaph: "Again, traveller you

have come a long way led by that star."
Long Way Outside Yellowstone, A.
McGuckian. To a Cuckoo at Coolanlough.
Mei Yao Ch'en. I Remember the Blue River.
Melville, H. Return of the Sire de Nesle A.D. 16, The.
Meng Chiao. Ballad of Ching Mountain.
On Mount Ching.
Stopping on a Journey at the East Water Pavilion at Lo-ch'eng.
Meng Hao Jan. Crossing the Hsiang River at Night.
Merrill, J. Family Week at Oracle Ranch.
Friend of the Fourth Decade, The.
Thousand and Second Night, The.
Merwin, W. Wheels of the Trains, The.
Miles, J. Travelers.
Millay, E. Travel.
Unexplorer, The.
Miller, E. Tomorrow.
Miller, J. Countryside.
Miller, M. Not That Far.
Monkhouse. To a New-Born Child.
Moore, J. Astronauts.
Moss, H. Movies for the Home.
Tourists.
Mother Goose. To Babylon.
Mueller, L. Commuter.
Muldoon, P. Making the Move.
Nguyễn Chí Thiện. Travel with grief—goodbye to joy!
Ni Tsan. You ask when I will go back home.
Nichol. Ferry Me Across.
Nichols, G. Epilogue: "I have crossed an ocean."
Nortje. Native's Letter.
O'Hara, F. Mary Desti's Ass.
Terrestrial Cuckoo, A.
You Are Gorgeous and I'm Coming.
Ortiz. Travels in the South.
Upstate.
Otalantaiyar. Six on the Desert Ways.
Padilla. Nuclear Umbrella.
Park, M. Traveler, The.
Pastan. Last Train, The.
Pasternak, B. On Early Trains.
Peskett. From Belfast to Suffolk.
Phillips, D. Hounds are either the work of wind, The.
Pien Kung. New Year's Day—Following the Rhymes of Inspector Luan-chiang.
Paintings of Various Subjects by Fang Jih-sheng: Baby Chicks Following Their Mother.
Song of the Transport Workers—Seeing Off Fang Wen-yü on His Way to His Post as Inspector of Transportation.
Piombino. Time Travel.
Plath. Getting There.
Plumly. For Esther.
Po Chü-i. Arriving at Hsün-yang.
Dream of Mountaineering, A.
On the Way to Hangchow: Anchored on the River at Night.
Sleeping on Horseback.
Starting Early from the Ch'u-ch'êng Inn.
Taoism and Buddhism.
Traveler's Moon, The.
Popa. Journey.
Price, L. Maidens of London's Brave Adventures, Or, a Boon Voyage Intended for the Sea, The.
Probyn. End of the Journey, The.
Purdy, A. Blue City, The.
Quarles. Stay My Steps in Thy Paths, That My Feet Do Not Slide.
Ralegh, W. 'As ye came from the holy land'.
Ravikovitch. Tirzah and the Wide World.
Reeves, J. Mr Kartoffel's a whimsical man.
Rilke. Stranger, The.
Robinson, E. John Evereldown.
Robinson, M. Stanzas Written between Dover and Calais, in July, 1792.
Roditi. Seance.
Roethke. Night Journey.
Rosen, M. Night Before His Parents' First Trip to Europe His Mother Writes a Letter "To Our Children", The.

Rossetti, C. Old-World Thicket, An.
Uphill [or Up-Hill].
Rossetti, D. Constant keeping-past of shaken trees.
Rukeyser, M. Ajanta.
Rumi. That Journeys Are Good.
Sanders, T. Transit Authority.
Sarton. After a Train Journey.
Shelley, P. Ozymandias [of Egypt].
World's Wanderers, The.
Sherman, F. Kite, A.
Sidney, P. Sonnet 84: "Highway, since you my chief Parnassus be."
Sloan, M. Eccentricity of the Middle Ground.
Soyinka. Death in the Dawn.
Spence, L. Prows O' Reekie, The.
Stevenson, R. Far-Farers, The.
From a Railway Carriage.
Land of Nod, The.
My Bed Is a Boat.
Travel.
Tropics vanish, and meseems that I, The.
Vagabond, The.
Stow. Landfall.
Su Man-shu. Chanting These Verses on My Way to Yodoe.
Su Tung-p'o. I travel day and night toward the Yangtze and the sea.
New Year's Eve blizzard kept me from leaving, The.
On the Siu Cheng Road.
Summers, H. Report.
Sun Yün-feng. On the Road through Chang-te.
Supervielle. Traveller, traveller, accept you must go back.
Sylvester, J. Modern Times.
Symons, A. Wanderer's Song.
Tai Shu-lun. Accidental Meeting with an Old Friend While Traveling at Night, An.
Tao-chi. Inscribed on the Wall at the Temple of the Auspicious Talisman.
Mood comes on—I want to cross Hsi-ling, The.
T'ao Ch'ien. Passing Ch'ien-hsi as Military Adviser in the Third Month of the Year Yi-ssu.
Taylor, A. Goethe and Brentano.
Taylor, H. Somewhere along the Way.
Thomas, E. Good-Night.
Thoreau. For though the eaves were rabbeted.
Thwaite. At Birth.
Trakl. Revelation and Decline.
Tranter. Moment of Waking, The.
Treece. Horror.
Ts'ao Chih. Roaming Immortal.
Tsung Ch'en. Side by side, we ride out of the city.
Tu Fu. Chengtu.
From the jagged edges of purple clouds to the west.
Journey North.
To Wei Pa, a Retired Scholar.
Traveler, a traveler, Tzu-mei his name, A.
Traveler at Night Writes His Thoughts, A.
Tu Hsün-ho. Traveler's Thoughts.
Tu Mu. Climbing to Lo-yu Plateau, before Leaving for Wu-hsing.
Easing My Heart.
Li Po put it in a poem, this West-of-the-Waters Abbey.
On the Road.
Travelling in the Mountains.
Whirled ten years beyond all bounds.
Uloccanar. What Her Girl Friend Said, Consoling Her when She Was Distressed by the Town's Gossip.
Unknown. Donkey Riding.
Going on always on and on.
"How many miles is it to Babylon?"
Let me gallop, let me go.
Meeting in the Road.
My Pretty [Little] Pink.
What Her Girl Friend Said to Him, Trying to Dissuade Him from His Long Journey.
Urdang. Evening of Home Movies, An.
Van Duyn. Into Mexico.
Viidikas. Future.

Vysotsky. Unruly Horses.
Wagoner, D. Breaking Camp.
Walcott. Fortunate Traveller, The.
Walker, M. October Journey.
Wang An-shih. At the Chiang-ning River Mouth.
Wang Shih-chieng. Seeing Off Editor Wang Chou-tz'u and Secretary Lin Shih-lai on Their Mission as Envoys to the Ryūkyū Islands.
Thinking of the Past on an Autumn Night at Tz'u-jen Temple.
Written beneath Hui Mountain, When Tsou Liu-yi Comes by for a Visit.
Wang T'ing-hsiang. At Arrow Rapids, the water splashes foam.
Song of the Wanderer.
Wang Ts'an. Occasional Verse.
Wang Wei. Seeking a Mooring.
Wang Yü-ch'eng. Journey to a Village.
Journeying to the Village.
Warner, S. Journey To Barcelona.
Warsh. Precious Mettle.
Weaver, M. My Father's Geography.
Wei Chuang. Lament of the Lady of Ch'in, The.
Wen Cheng-ming. On First Returning from Taking the Examinations: Feelings at Cloud-Stop Pavilion.
Weston, M. Departure.
Whitbread. To My Fellow-Mariners, March, '53.
Whitman, W. Promise to California, A.
Wickham. Dilemma, The.
Wier. Daytrip to Paradox.
Willard, N. One for the Road.
Woo, D. Expatriates.
Wordsworth, W. I traveled [or travell'd] among unknown men.
Inner Vision, The.
Stepping Westward.
Wright, C. Spread Rhythm.
Woman Looking Through a Viewmaster.
Wright, J. Stages on a Journey Westward.
Wright, J. Sketch for an Aesthetic Project.
Wright, J. Train Journey.
Wu Wei-yeh. On the Twenty-fourth of the Third Month, in the Year Ting-wei Sailed across Lake T'ai from Behind the Mountain.
Xuân Diệu. It's All in the Heart.
Yang Chi. After my illness, so hard to be a traveler.
Yang Shen. To the Tune "Song of the Plum Blossom at the River Town."
Yang Shih-ch'i. Song of the Merchant's Wife.
Yen Yü. My Boat Moored on a River.
Yü Chi. Traveling Early through a Snowy Valley.
Yüan Mei. On the Twenty-First Day of the Fifth Month, I Reached Home.
On the Way to Pa-ling.
Yün Shou-p'ing. Inscribed on a Painting ("Who needs a raft that can invade the stars?")
Zeidner. Kafka Poem.
Zepeda, O. People on Wayward Journeys.
Zuni Oral Tradition. Following their road of exit, they stooped over and came out.

Treason and Traitors
Burns, R. Such a Parcel of Rogues in a Nation.
Campbell, A. Warning.
Cunningham, J. Epigram: "This Humanist Whom No Beliefs Constrained."
De la Mare. Ballad of Christmas, A.
Elizabeth I. Doubt of future foes exiles my present joy, The.
Hammial. Treason's Choice.
Harington. Of Treason.
Neruda. They Receive Instructions Against Chile.
Petronius Arbiter. Chorus: "Can nothing great, and at the height."
Po Chü-i. Everlasting Sorrow, The.
Thelwall. Stanzas on Hearing for Certainty that we were to be Tried for High Treason.

Unknown. Golden Vanity, The.
Sir Mordred, traitor false and vile.

Treasures
Bible, *O.T.* Lay not up for yourselves
treasures.
Brown, G. Beachcomber.
Cooke, R. Blue-Beard's Closet.
DeLeeuw. Auction Sale—Household
Furnishings.
Doolittle, H. In no wise is the pillar-of-fire.
Lee-Hamilton. Sunken Gold.
Leland, C. Ballad: "Der noble Ritter Hugo."
Mistral, G. Rose, The.
Pound, E. Seafarer, The.
Thomas, C. Treasures.
Unknown. Anglo-American Chainpoem.

Treaties
Lipska. When our enemies fall asleep.
Pagis. Draft of a Reparations Agreement.
Thomas, D. Hand that signed the paper felled
a city, The.

Tree Toads. See Toads

Tree of Life
Byron, G. Ah! didst *thou* tempt my mother?
Dugan, A. Last Statement for a Last Oracle.
Rukeyser, M. Speaking Tree, The.

Trees
Abbey, H. What do we plant when we plant
the tree?
Ackland. Blossom into a rose as you are
bidden.
Adamson. Elm Tree in Paddington, An.
Adcock, F. Trees.
Adisa. Rainbow, The.
"Adunis." Tree of Fire.
Akahito. Black jewel like, The.
Al-Harizi. Sun, The.
Allard. Passing clouds only a stand of aspens
is in light.
Andreyev, V. Deep scar engraved in the
bark's dark silver, A.
Armantrout. Necromance.
Ashbery. Some Trees.
Barrax. There was a song.
Bartusek. Heliotropism / of branches, now
darkened.
Belševica. Don't be oversure of your cherry-
tree.
Bhartrihari. Three Poems.
Bible, *O.T.* Bible, Psalm 1:1–3, The.
Psalm 1.
Birney. Poet-Tree.
Blake, W. In a Myrtle [*or* Mirtle] Shade.
Bloze. Leaves have yellowed like, The.
Bodenheim. Advice to a Forest.
Bognini. Suddenly an old man on the
threshold of the age.
We are men of the new world a tree prompts
us to harmony.
Bontemps. Blight.
Breton, A. More than Suspect.
Brooks, G. Birth in a Narrow Room, The.
Brown, K. Five-Fingered Maple, The.
Brown, L. Green arbor that I once knew, A.
Burns, R. Tree of Liberty, The.
Butler, J. Stranger to Europe, waiting release.
Campbell, D. Here, under pear-trees, on the
broad verandahs.
Caraion. Always, In March.
Carstairs. Addressed to a Beech Tree.
Carter, M. Bitter Wood.
Cendrars. Great Fetishes, The.
Chalmers, P. When Mary Goes Walking.
Chandler, C. Tree in the Garden, The.
Chang Yü. Song of the Old Oak.
Clare, J. Fallen Elm, The.
Coleridge, S. Trees.
Cooper, J. Long, Disconsolate Lines.
Cowper, W. On Pruning.
Crane, H. Mango Tree, The.
Creeley. Turn, The.
Dao. Stretch out your hands to me.
Davies, H. Poem: "In the stump of the old
tree, where the heart has rotted out."
Davison, P. Cross Cut.
Dawe, B. Renewal Notice.
De la Mare. Me.

Three Cherry Trees, The.
Two gardens see!—this, of enchanted flowers.
Deutsch. Paradigm.
Dickinson, E. Not at Home to Callers.
Doolittle, H. *Amen.*
Dove, R. Dusting.
Horse and Tree.
Dugan, A. On Trees.
Duggan, E. Juniper.
Dumas, H. Root Song.
Dunbar, P. Haunted Oak, The.
Ehrenburg. Tree, The.
Evans, P. Ode: "Trees have their doubts but
we have ours."
Everson, R. Injured Maple.
Ewing, J. Willow-Man, The.
Field, E. Sugar-Plum Tree, The.
"Field." Nests in Elms.
O Wind, thou hast thy kingdom in the trees.
Figueroa, J. This tree my time keeper.
Finney, N. Uncles.
Fletcher, J. Trees, like great jade elephants,
The.
Ford, C. Plaint.
Frost, R. Axe-Helve, The.
Birches.
On a Tree Fallen across the Road.
Sound of Trees, The.
Spring Pools.
Tree at my window, window tree.
Fumi Saito. Tanka: "Wood borers."
Fumiko. Tanka: "One day I saw."
Gallagher, T. Woodcutting on Lost Mountain.
Garrigue. Country Villa.
Gilbo'a. Watchful Wakeful.
Ginsberg, L. Roots.
Giovanni. Alabama Poem.
Godfrey. Unholy Spring.
Gorham. Empress Receives the Head of a
Taiping Rebel, The.
Graves, R. Hide and Seek.
Grimké, A. Tenebris.
Grunthal. I broke the second part of the First
Commandment.
Gurney, I. Felling a Tree.
Hackett, J. Wind sounds through the trees.
Hagiwara Sakutaro. Lover of Love.
So Terrifyingly Melancholy.
Haines, J. And When the Green Man Comes.
Hajnal. Felled Plane Tree, The.
Han Yü. Withered Tree, A.
Hardy, T. Tree and the Lady, The.
Hazo. Yellow Delicious.
Heaney, S. Sweeney Praises the Trees.
Hemans. Yes! I have seen the ancient oak.
Herrick. All Things Decay and Die.
To Blossoms.
To Groves.
To Sycamores.
Hildegard von Bingen. Alleluia-verse for the
Virgin.
Hogan, L. Thought, A.
Holan. Memory II.
Honig, E. November through a Giant Copper
Beech.
Hope, A. Australia.
Hopkins, G. Binsey Poplars (Felled 1879).
Hsü Chung-hsing. Trees are ancient, thick
with patterns of moss, The.
Huchel. Psalm.
Hughes, T. Trees.
Ignatow, D. Simultaneously, five thousand
miles apart.
Iskander. Overtired branches are fragile.
Ivask, I. Foliage foliage.
Jacobsen, R. Catacombs in San Callisto, The.
Janevski. Song of the Eternal Sailor, The.
Johnson, H. Trees at Night.
Jones, D. These Trees Are No Forest of
Mourners.
Jones, J. I can climb our apple tree.
Joyce, J. Twilight turns from amethyst, The.
Juarroz. Lamp lit, A.
Kangro. Trees Walk Farther Away, The.
Kariara. Leopard lives in a Muu tree, A.
Kavanagh, P. Sometimes.

Keats. Garden-Dream, A.
In drear-nighted December.
Kees. Heat in the Room, The.
Kenney. Sawmill.
Kilmer, J. Trees.
Kinsella, T. In the Ringwood.
Kirsch, S. Mail.
Knott. Poem: "At your light side trees shy."
Kunitz, S. War against the Trees, The.
La Grone. Lines to the Black Oak.
Larkin, P. Trees are coming into leaf, The.
Lawrence, D. Trees in the Garden.
Lear, E. Limerick: "There was an Old Man in
a tree."
Limerick: "There was an Old Man who said,
'Hush!'."
Quangle Wangle's Hat, The.
Levertov. Contraband.
Gathered at the River.
Tree Telling of Orpheus, A.
Levine, P. Sleepless Night, A.
Levy, A. London Plane-Tree, A.
Li Meng-yang. Oriole at Dawn, An.
Li Shang-yin. Willow.
Libbey. Come Into the Night Grove.
Locker-Lampson. Old Oak Tree at Hatfield
Broadoak, The.
Lovelace, R. Orpheus to Woods.
Ma Chih-yüan. Autumn Thoughts.
"MacDiarmid." Sunny Gale.
MacLean, S. Hallaig.
MacLeish. Farm, The.
MacNeice. Tree Party.
Macpherson, J. Garden of the Sexes, The.
Madge. Poem: "Walls of the maelstrom are
painted with trees, The."
Makidemewabe. Tree Old Woman.
Mandelstam. Shy speechless sound, The.
Mapanje. Before Chilembwe Tree.
Masaoka Shiki. Tanka: "Tree with lush
leaves."
Mathias, E. Tall Trees.
McAuley, J. Tomb of Heracles, The.
McClintock, M. Merry-go-round, The.
McCord, D. Every Time I Climb a Tree.
Melville, H. Time's Betrayal.
Mew. Forest road, The.
Trees Are Down, The.
Meyers, B. Daybreak.
Millay, E. Counting-out Rhyme.
Milne, E. Diamond Cut Diamond.
Miyazawa Kenji. Spring and the Ashura.
Tanka: "Like cracks."
Momaday. Trees and Evening Sky.
Montale. Lemon Trees, The.
Storm splattering the tough magnolia, The.
Moore, L. From the Field.
Mordecai. Starapple Tree.
Morris, G. Woodman, spare that tree!
Moss, H. Pruned Tree, The.
Mother Goose. Diddlety, diddlety, dumpty.
Nut Tree, A.
Mountain, M. In / the / woods.
Nagy, A. Figtrees.
Trees.
Nash, O. Song of the Open Road.
Nastasijevic. Still Trees.
Nemerov. Learning by Doing.
Learning the Trees.
Trees.
Nesbit, E. Child's Song in Spring.
Netherclift. London Trees.
Neto. African Poem.
Newcastle, M. Of the Theme of Love.
Nguyễn Trãi. Old Banyan Tree, The.
Ni Tsan. Woodpecker, The.
Okamoto. Tanka: "Twenty days."
Oldham, P. Noon.
Olson, C. Merce of Egypt.
Ortiz. What I Tell Him.
Ou-yang Hsiu. Green Jade Plum Trees in
Spring.
Ovid. Nux (The Walnut Tree).
Pasternak, B. Miracle, The.
Peake. Conceit.
Pettet. Annul.
Phạm Hồ. Tall Trees.

Philips, K. Upon the graving of her Name upon a Tree in Barnelmes Walks.
Pizzarelli. Flinging the frisbee.
Snow falls from trees.
Plath. I Am Vertical.
Winter Trees.
Words.
Po Chü-i. Planting Flowers on the Eastern Embankment.
Pruning Trees.
Radauskas. Hot Day.
Randolph, T. On Grafting.
Ransom, J. Dead Boy.
Rich, A. Trees inside are moving out into the forest, The.
Robinson, E. New Language, The.
Roethke. Bound.
Second Shadow.
Rossetti, C. Autumn.
Dumb Friend, A.
Who has seen the wind? / Neither I nor you.
Rózewicz. Moment.
Sackville-West. Beechwoods at Knole.
Scott, W. Flowers and Trees.
Seferis. Poplar Leaf, The.
Sepamla. Talk to the Peach Tree.
Serote. Growing, The.
Shchipachov. Little Birch Tree, The.
Shen Yüeh. Fragrant Tree, The.
Shepherd, R. What Cannot Be Kept.
Shūji. Tanka: "My body."
Siddal. Silent Wood, A.
Simpson, L. Ash and the Oak, The.
Laurel Tree, The.
Sitwell, S. Tulip Tree.
Snodgrass, W. These trees stand very tall under the heavens.
Sone Yoshitada. Lower leaves of the trees, The.
Sorescu. Carnival.
Spiess. Ostrich fern on shore.
Tar paper cabin.
Stafford, W. Twelfth Birthday.
Stephens, J. Seumas Beg.
Wind stood up, and gave a shout.
Stern, G. Power of Maples, The.
Stevenson, A. Hemlock at Sunset, A.
Stevenson, R. Foreign Lands.
Strand. Keeping Things Whole.
Man in the Tree, The.
Prediction, The.
Sze. Shapes of Leaves, The.
Tagliabue. Bare Arms of Trees, The.
Tai Piao-yüan. Painting, *Mist and Rain on the Spring River,* by Hsiao Chao, The.
Tao-chi. Inscribed on a Painting of a Wu-t'ung Tree by Myself.
Tasso. Now the waves murmur.
Tati-Loutard. Memory of My Mother.
Teller. Lines to a Tree.
Teodorescu. Goodbye.
Thomas, E. Aspens.
Tomlinson, C. Poem: "Upended, it crouches on broken limbs."
Tóth, J. Murmuring.
Turner, W. Music of a Tree, The.
Tuwhare. No Ordinary Sun.
Ungaretti. Soldiers.
Unknown. Anglo-American Chainpoem.
Catkin.
Come the oak before the ash.
Falling Snow.
He Praises the Trees.
If all the seas were one sea.
Nut Tree, A.
On Asuka River.
Rain Song of the Shu'-wi Chai' än (Snake Society), A.
Song to the Trees and Streams.
St. Paul's Steeple.
To a Firefly.
Whango Tree, The.
Virgil. Laughing softly.
Twilight.
Wadsworth, W. Snake in the Garden Considers Daphne, The.
Wallace, R. In One Place.

Walsh, J. Christmas Tree, The.
Wang An-shih. Autumn sun over the *t'ung* tree.
Wang I. Lychee-tree, The.
Wang T'ing-hsiang. Flowering tree does not spare itself, The.
Wen Cheng-ming. Recording My Happiness upon Returning Home.
Whitman, W. I saw in Louisiana a live-oak growing.
Wieseltier. Columns.
Williams, W. Locust Tree in Flower, The.
To Waken an Old Lady.
Young Sycamore.
Williamson, G. Annual Returns.
Willis, P. Meeting Like This.
Wilson, M. Jungle Trees, The.
Wood, W. Trees both in hills and plaines, in plenty be.
Wordsworth, W. Nutting.
Yew-Trees.
Wright, J. Camphor Laurel.
Gum-trees Stripping.
Wu Wei-yeh. Seeing Off Wang Yüan-chao—Reprise.
Yasuda. Shadow of the trees, The.
Yeats. Ragged Wood, The.
Yesenin. My leafless maple tree, your icy coating.
Yukitsuna. Tanka: "Bloom finished, The."
Zach. Give Me What the Tree Has [and what it won't lose].
Zukofsky, L. In Arizona / (how many years in the mountains).
See also names of *individual species of trees.*

Trelawny, Sir Jonathan, Bishop
Hawker. Song of the Western Men, The.

Trench Warfare
Graves, R. It's a Queer Time.
Manning, F. Trenches, The.
Nichols, R. Noon.
Owen, W. Anthem for Doomed Youth.
Exposure.
Rickword. Winter Warfare.
Rosenberg, I. Break of Day in the Trenches.
Rutter, O. Trenches.
Sassoon. Aftermath.
Attack.
Counter-Attack.
Dreamers.
Dug-Out, The.
Rear-Guard, The.
Redeemer, The.
Working Party, A.
Scannell. Great War, The.
West, A. Night Patrol, The.

Trilobites
Kendall, M. Lay of the Trilobite, The.

Trinidad and Tobago
Howes, B. Returning to Store Bay.
Keens-Douglas. Tell Me Again.
Trinidad If Ah Let You.
"Mighty Chalkdust." Brain Drain.
"Mighty Sparrow." Yankees Back, The.
Roach. Piarco.
Walcott. Midsummer, Tobago.
Port of Spain.
Spoiler's Return, The.

Trinity, The
De Vere, A. Feast of the Most Holy Trinity.
"Field." Trinity.

Triolet (form)
Bridges, R. Triolet: "When first we met we did not guess."
Cornford, F. To a Fat Lady Seen from the Train.
Henley, W. Easy is the triolet.
McGinley. Triolet Against Sisters.
See also **Triolet in Title and First Line Index**

Tristan da Cunha (islands)
Campbell, R. Tristan da Cunha.

Tristram and Isolde
Binyon. Tristram's End.
Unknown. Trystan and Esyllt.

Triviality
Atkinson. Same Trouble with Beauty You've Always Had, The.

Bhatt. What Is Worth Knowing?
Hartnett. Enamoured of the miniscule / of the careful and compact.
Sandburg, C. Aprons of Silence.
Unknown. Fascinating Poet's Dream, A.
Wilbur. What's Good for the Soul is Good for Sales.

Trojan War
Arnold, M. Palladium.
Bishop, J. Why They Waged War.
Chapman, G. . . . Through the wall, uprore.
Drummond, W. Trojan Horse, The.
Homer. Achilles Over the Trench.
Achilles sets out.
Apollo Defeats Patroclus.
Clash in Arms of the Achaians and Trojans.
First to the Corse the weeping Consort flew.
Hector's flight.
Menelaus wounded.
Night Piece: the Trojans outside Troy.
Priam and Achilles.
Specimen of a Translation of the Iliad in Blank Verse.
Muir, E. Return of the Greeks, The.
Pound, E. Canto 1.
Sadoleto. Poem of Jacobus Sadoletus on the Statue of Laocoon, The.
Shakespeare, W. Troy Depicted.
Simpson, L. Aegean.
Vigny. Helena.
Virgil. Aeolus looses the winds.
Cupid at work.
Dido's death.
He many waies his labouring thoughts revolves.
Turnus' retreat.
Wright, K. Fortunes of War.
Yeats. Leda and the Swan.

Trolleys. *See* **Streetcars**

Trossachs, The, Scotland
Wordsworth, W. Trosachs, The.

Trout
Brown, G. Trout Fisher.
Hugo, R. Skykomish River Running.
Montague, J. Trout, The.
Todd, R. Trout Flies.
Wilbur. Hamlen Brook.

Troy
Homer. Demodocus sings the fall of Troy.
Specimen of a Translation of the Iliad in Blank Verse.
Hugh, Primate of Orleans. Lament for Troy.
Muir, E. Troy.
Nash, O. First Limick.
Shakespeare, W. Troy Depicted.
Virgil. House of Fame, The.
See also **Trojan War**

Truancy
Graves, R. Death Room, The.

Trucks and Truckers
Dyson, W. Trucker, The.
Ignatow, D. I see a truck mowing down a parade.
Mountain, M. Pick-up truck.
Paquet. Graves Registration.
Schonborg. Rumble, A.
Snyder, G. Why Log Truck Drivers Rise Earlier Than Students of Zen.
Tomlinson, C. At Barstow.
Willis, P. Meeting Like This.

Trujillo Molina, Rafael Leonidas
Dove, R. Parsley.

Trumpets
Grass. Music for Brass.
Jeffers, L. How High the Moon.
Larkin, P. Reasons for Attendance.
McGinley. Women of Jericho, The.
Turner, J. Rhapsodies.

Trust
Baird, M. Do not make things too easy.
Benton, P. Psalm 23: "Lord is my shepherd; I shall not want, The."
Berggolts. My Country.
Bible, *O.T.* Psalm 23.
Creeley. For friendship / make a chain that holds.

Doolittle, H. Now let the cycle sweep us here and there.
Gunn, T. Idea of trust, or, The.
Hewitt, J. Ram's Horn, The.
Horovitz, F. Do you not know that I need to touch you.
Lee, L. Gift, The.
Lopate. Once a long time ago, you remember.
Meynell, A. After a Parting.
Philips, K. EPITAPH. On her Son H. P. at St. Syth's Church where her body also lies Interred.
Pritchard, N. Burnt Sienna.
Raab, L. For You.
Seng-ts'an. Mind of Absolute Trust, The.
Spenser. Sonnet 65.": "Doubt which ye misdeeme, fayre love, is vaine, The."
Tennyson, A. 54.
Thomas, D. Ears in the turrets hear.
Unknown. How terrible it is to trust no one.
Walter, H. I would be true, for there are those [who trust me].
Whitney, I. Rejoice in God that I am gon.
Ye virgins that from Cupid's tents.

Truth
"Æ." Truth.
Argentarius. Love is not just a function of the eyes.
Ashbery. Rain Moving In.
Auden. He watched the stars and noted birds in flight.
History of Truth, The.
Bible, *O.T.* My son, forget not my law; but let thine heart keep my commandments.
Boland, E. Oral Tradition, The.
Bonar. Be True [*or* Be True Thyself].
Borges. John 1:14; And the Word became flesh and dwelt among us.
Brontë, E. Stanzas: "Often rebuked, yet always back returning."
Browning, E. Best Thing in the World, The.
Carew, T. Disdain Returned.
Chao Meng-fu. Pavilion-Where-the-Crane-Came, The.
Chaucer. Lak of Stedfastnesse.
Truth.
Chipasula. Manifesto on Ars Poetica.
Chukhonstev. In the Menagerie.
Clarke, C. What Goes Around Comes Around, or The Proof is in the Pudding.
Cole, P. Where the Honey Speech's Hedge.
Coleridge, M. Contents of an Ink-bottle, The.
Insincere Wish Addressed to a Beggar, An.
True to myself am I, and false to all.
Crane, S. Wayfarer / Perceiving the pathway to truth, The.
Creeley. Bresson's Movies.
Fancy.
Cullen, C. To Certain Critics.
Cummings, E. As freedom is a breakfastfood.
Dacey, P. Porno Love.
Dickinson, E. I died for Beauty—but was scarce.
Opinion is a flitting thing.
Tell all the Truth but tell it slant.
Truth—is as old as God.
Donne. Satire 3.
Duggan, E. Truth.
Dunn, S. What They Wanted.
Eliot, T. Hippopotamus, The.
Emerson, R. Harp, The.
Uriel.
Everson, W. Narrows of Birth, The.
Fuller, M. In the chamber.
Gascoigne. Gascoigne's Woodmanship.
Gascoyne. Truth is Blind, The.
Graves, R. End of Play.
Pier-Glass, The.
Whole Love.
Hacker, M. We may be learning how to tell the truth.
Hanzlik. Variation VI.
Harper, M. Alice.
Heard, J. Truth.
Herbert, G. Courage.
Jordan.
Holmes, O. Our Limitations.

Holst-Warhaft. John 1:1 and 14.
Holub. Garden of Old People, The.
Hughes, L. Theme for English B.
Jackson, L. Helen's Burning.
Jeffers, R. Cassandra.
Joans. Truth, The.
Johnson, G. Lost Illusions.
Jordan, F. I love America where truth can be shouted from the housetops.
Khlebnikov, V. Lone Performer, The.
Kinsella, T. Another September.
Kooser. Gilbert Stuart Portrait of Washington, The.
Landon. Stern Truth.
Lanier, S. To Beethoven.
Lawrence, D. Elemental.
Lehman. Moment of Truth, The.
Levertov. Goddess, The.
Illustration [—a Footnote], The.
Levine, P. Simple Truth, The.
Lincoln, A. I Am Not Bound to Win.
Lipkin, S. When I was arranging letters into words.
Mac Low. Pieces O'six—XVIII.
Macpherson, J. Well, The.
Martinez, D. Necessary Story.
Mathams. Jesus, friend of little children.
McKay, C. Truth.
Meinke. Supermarket.
Melville, H. Enthusiast, The.
Mendelssohn, F. Every Day.
Meredith, G. Dusty Answer, A.
Moorer. Duty, or Truth at Work.
Truth Suppressed, The.
Ofeimun. How Can I Sing.
Prologue: "I have come down."
Olson, C. Kingfishers, The.
Oppen. To insist that what is true is good, no matter, no matter.
Osundare. Sand Seer, The.
Ovid. Golden Age, The.
Padilla. In Trying Times.
Parkes, B. To an Author who Loved Truth More than Fame.
Patmore, C. Magna Est Veritas.
Perelman. Things.
Phùng Quán. What Mother Told Me Once.
"Platonov." Wanderer, The.
Ralegh, W. Lie, The.
Reavey. Dismissing Progress and Its Progenitors.
Revell. Muse.
Rexroth, K. Buddha took some Autumn leaves.
Rich, A. 5:30 A.M.
Frame.
Rodgers, C. Feminism.
Roethke. Open House.
Rossetti, C. My Dream.
Rukeyser, M. All the Little Animals.
Ballad of Orange and Grape.
Believing in those inexorable laws.
Poem as Mask, The.
Ryokan. In all ten directions of the universe.
Sexton. Truth the Dead Know, The.
Shakespeare, W. Phoenix and the Turtle, The.
Sonnet 14.
Sonnet 54.
Shelley, P. Sonnet: "Lift not the painted veil which those who live."
Siddal. Dead Love.
Sidney, P. Sonnet 1: "Loving in truth, and fain[e] in verse my love to show."
Smelyakov. Earth.
Smith, S. Magna Est Veritas.
Spires. Woman on the Dump, The.
Stanton, M. Ballad of the Magic Glasses.
Stevens, W. American Sublime, The.
Man on the Dump, The.
Stevenson, R. Whole Duty of Children.
Swenson, M. In Love Made Visible.
Tate, J. Deaf Girl Playing.
Tennyson, A. Higher Pantheism, The.
Thomas, E. Glory of the beauty of the morning, The.
Torlino. Therefore I Must Tell the Truth.

Tsvetaeva. I know the truth—give up all other truths!
Tung-shan. If you look for the truth outside yourself.
Unknown. Two little eyes to look to God.
Whatsoever things are true.
Very. On Finding the Truth.
Serpent, The.
Whateley. Ode to Truth.
Whitman, W. All truths wait in all things.
Dazzling and tremendous how quick the sunrise would kill me.
Whittier. Brown of Ossawatomie.
Wilbur. Lying.
Williams, W. Hard Listener, The.
Wordsworth, W. Where lies the truth? has man, in wisdom's creed.
Wyatt, T. Farewell: "What should I say."
Mistrustful minds be moved.
Take heed betime, lest ye be spied.
To cause accord or to ag[g]re[e].
What should I say.
Yeats. Leaders of the Crowd, The.
Song of the Happy Shepherd, The.
Zenmaro. At the Van Gogh exibition.

Truth, Sojourner
Fauset. Oriflamme.
Truth. Ain't I a Woman?

Tuberculosis
Chōkū. Tanka: "Among the hundreds."
Ponsot. "Love is not Love."
Thompson, P. Consumptive, The.

Tubman, Harriet
Allen, S. Harriet Tubman aka Moses.
Cornish, S. Cross Over the River.
Griffin, S. I like to think of Harriet Tubman.
Hacker, M. Part of a True Story.
Hayden, R. Runagate Runagate.

Tulip Trees
Sitwell, S. Tulip Tree.

Tulips
Field, E. Tulips and Addresses.
Herrick. Meditation for His Mistress[e], A.
To a Bed of Tulips.
Jones, J. We have tulips in our flower bed.
McClintock, M. Single tulip!, A.
Plath. Tulips are too excitable, it is winter here, too.
Roseliep. In white tulips.
Sandstrom. Stately Lady, The.
Schuyler, J. February.
Symons, A. Hallucination.
Williams, W. Tulip Bed, The.

Tumbleweeds
Clampitt. Amaranth and Moly.
Holden, J. Tumbleweed.

Turkey
Hikmet. Evening Walk, The.
Things I Didn't Know I Loved.
Iwaszkiewicz. Pope in Ancona, The.
Merrill, J. Thousand and Second Night, The.

Turkeys
Dunbar, P. Soliloquy of a Turkey.
Etter. Stuffy Turkey.
Gumilyov. Turkey, The.
Guthrie, W. Turkey in the Corn.
Kelly, B. Wild Turkeys; The Dignity of the Damned.
Mackenzie, K. Table-Birds.
Unknown. Turkey is dancing near the rocks, A.
Wilbur. Black November Turkey, A.

Turner, Mrs. Bishop
Heard, J. Resting.

Turner, Dennis
Hirsch, E. Fast Break.

Turner, Lana
O'Hara, F. Poem: "Lana Turner has collapsed!"

Turner, Nat
Brown, S. Remembering Nat Turner.
Hayden, R. Ballad of Nat Turner, The.

Turnips
Mother Goose. If wishes were horses.
Thomas, E. Swedes.

Unknown. Mr. Finney's Turnip.
Turtle Doves
Unknown. Turtle-Doves' Nest, The.
See also **Doves**
Turtles
Armour. Covering the Subject.
Bible, *O.T.* Lo, the Winter Is Past.
"Carroll." Lobster Quadrille, A.
  Song of the Mock Turtle, The.
Chin. Turtle Soup.
Corman. Tortoise, The.
Heyen. Snapper, The.
Jackson, L. Fun.
Lindsay, V. Little Turtle, The.
Lowell, R. Neo-Classical Urn, The.
McClure, M. From the Window of the
  Beverly Wilshire Hotel.
Nash, O. Turtle lives 'twixt plated decks, The.
Nemerov. Mud Turtle, The.
O'Connor, M. Turtles Hatching.
Rabbitt. Tortoise.
Shakespeare, W. Phoenix and the Turtle, The.
Stafford, K. Walking to the Mailbox.
Swenson, M. Living Tenderly.
Unknown. Long ago there was a mighty
  snake, and beings evil to men.
  Turtle's Song, The.
Willard, N. Feast of St. Tortoise, The.
Williams, W. Turtle, The.
Wu Chen. Fantastic Rock, The.
Zimmer. Zimmer and His Turtle Sink the
  House.
See also **Tortoises**
Tuscany
Wright, J. Journey, The.
Tuskegee Institute
Hill, L. Tuskegee.
"Twain, Mark" (Samuel Langhorne Clemens)
Warren, R. Last Laugh.
Tweed (river), Scotland and England
Bowles, W. Tweed Visited, The.
Twelfth Night
Helton. Old Christmas Morning.
Wadding. For Twelfth Day.
Twickenham, England
Donne. Twicknam [*or* Twickenham] Garden.
Twilight
Adams, L. Home-coming.
"Æ." By the Margin of the Great Deep.
Alexander, J. Winning of the TV West, The.
Bevington, L. Twilight.
Boker. Leaden eyelids of wan twilight close,
  The.
Borkhuis. Inside Language.
Brooke, R. Day That I Have Loved.
Buson. Over the vast field of mustard flowers.
Carruth, H. Twilight comes to the little farm.
Carter, M. In a small city at dusk.
Cummings, E. If in beginning twilight of
  winter will stand.
  Nine birds(rising / through a gold
  moment)climb.
De la Mare. Voices.
Dickey, J. Dusk of Horses, The.
Drevniok. Snow at dusk.
Engle, P. Twilight.
Gouri. Window-Dreaming with SAS.
Gray, R. Dusk, The.
Grimké, A. Winter Twilight, A.
Guest, B. Twilight Polka Dots.
Guggenberger. Twilight.
Hajnal. Half Past Four, October.
Herrick. To Anthea Lying in Bed.
Hirsch, E. Man on a Fire Escape.
Illyés. Deep Dusk.
Izumi. In the dusk the path.
Jakuren. Hanging raindrops, The.
Joyce, J. Twilight turns from amethyst, The.
Komunyakaa. Boat People.
Kunio. Tanka: "Standing still."
Lang, A. Twilight on Tweed.
Lawrence, D. Twilight.
Ledwidge. Twilight in Middle March, A.
Li Ho. Song of the Sacred Strings.
Li Po. Self-abandonment.

Longfellow, H. Afternoon in February.
  Children's Hour, The.
Lopez-Penha. Dusk.
Lyles. Doe's leap, A.
Ma Chih-yüan. Autumn Thoughts.
Martinson. Dusk in the Country.
McBride, M. Going Under of the Evening
  Land, The.
McClintock, M. Grasshopper, A.
Meredith, G. Along the garden terrace, under
  which.
  Ballad of Past Meridian, A.
Merwin, W. Dusk in Winter.
Miyazawa Kenji. Tanka: "Unsettled."
Moore, L. Farther and farther.
Mountain, M. At dusk hot water from the
  hose.
  Quiet day, A.
Noin. Spring twilight.
Owen, W. Anthem for Doomed Youth.
Po Chü-i. Arriving at Hsün-yang.
Pritchard, N. Burnt Sienna.
Ritsos. Not Even Mythology.
Robinson, E. Dark hills at evening in the
  west.
Rossetti, C. Twilight Calm.
Ryozan. When I am lonely.
Smith, C. Written near a Port on a Dark
  Evening.
Sone Yoshitada. Lower leaves of the trees,
  The.
Spiess. Becoming dusk,—.
Teika. I gaze far and long.
Teller. To the Divine Neighbor.
Todorovski. Peaceful Step, A.
Tomlinson, C. Tramontana at Lerici.
Toomer. Georgia Dusk.
Toshinari. Twilight.
Tu Fu. Sunset glitters on the beads.
Unknown. Over the reeds the.
Van den Heuvel. Autumn twilight.
  Twilight.
Voznesensky. Give Me Peace.
Wang Wei. Twilight comes over the
  monastery Garden.
Warren, R. Sky.
  What Voice at Moth-Hour did I hear calling.
Whitman, W. Hours continuing long, sore and
  heavy-hearted.
Wieseltier. Site.
Williams, H. Sonnet to Twilight.
Wills, J. Dusk from rock to rock a
  waterthrush.
Wright, J. Twilights.
Yakamochi. Wind rustles the bamboos, The.
Young, D. Twilight with Xs.
See also **Evening; Sunset**
Twins
Broumas, O. Landscape with Next of Kin.
Escoffery. Twins.
Graves, R. Twins.
Leigh, H. Twins, The.
Leonidas. Eileithyia, brought safe.
Rice, J. On some other planet.
Rumble. Unique?
Shapiro, K. Twins, The.
Unknown. Hymn to Castor and Pollux.
  Twa Brothers, The.
Van Duyn. Twins, The.
Twist, Oliver. *See* **Oliver Twist**
Typing and Typists
Blumenthal, M. Back from the Word-
  Processing Course, I Say to My Old
  Typewriter.
Hewitt, G. Typographical Errors.
Page, P. Typists.
Sexton. That Day.
Tyranny
Auden. Epitaph on a Tyrant.
Blake, W. Grey Monk, The.
Browning, R. Instans Tyrannus.
Brutus. At a Funeral.
Carey, H. Maid's Husband, The.
Chao Meng-fu. Eulogy of the Sagely Virtue of
  His Imperial Majesty Emperor Shih-tsu, A.
Chaucer. Monk's Tale, The.
Cook, E. Idiot-Born, The.

Drofenko. Sketches from History.
Egerton, S. Emulation, The.
Faiz. Prison Evening, A.
Forster, W. In New South Wales, as I plainly
  see.
Gray, T. Tophet.
Greville, F. Chorus Sacerdotum.
Hall, H. Upon the King's Return from
  Flanders, 1695.
Hartwig. Who Says.
Jarrell. State, The.
Jeffers, R. Ave Caesar.
Kipling, R. Ode to Liberty.
Landor, W. Foreign Ruler, A.
Martin, C. Easter Sunday, 1985.
Melville, H. Timoleon.
Mphahlele. Poem, A: "What is there that we
  can do or say."
Neruda. Dictators, The.
Okudzhava. As I Sat in the Armchair of the
  Tsar.
Pembroke, M. Quid gloriaris? Psalm 52.
Pilkington, L. Wish, By a Young Lady, The.
Rushton. Human Debasement; a Fragment.
Saarikoski. No, Quetzalcoatl, don't come back.
Seidel. Pol Pot.
Selby, S. Spread, The.
Shelley, P. Song to the Men of England.
Sousa, N. Poem of João, The.
Supervielle. Rain and the Tyrants.
Thelwall. Stanzas on Hearing for Certainty
  that we were to be Tried for High Treason.
Thomas à Becket. Columbia, the Gem of the
  Ocean.
Thomas, D. Hand that signed the paper felled
  a city, The.
Tryapkin. We banished the tyrant-tsars.
Unknown. Humble Petition of the British
  Jacobins to their Brethren of France, The.
  Trumpet of Liberty sounds through the World,
  The.
Vysotsky. I never believed in mirages.
Warren, R. Apology for Domitian.

U

U.S.S.R. *See* **Russia**
Uccello, Paolo
Corso. Uccello.
Uganda
Walker, A. In Uganda an early king chose.
Ugliness
Antipater of Thessalonica. That dried-up arse,
  Lykainis.
Browning, R. And were I not, as a man may
  say, cautious.
Burns, R. How daur ye ca' me "Howlet-face."
Cook, E. Song of the Ugly Maiden.
Donne. Comparison, The.
Han-shan. Swine gobble dead men's flesh.
Herrick. Upon Blanche.
Jeffers, R. Carmel Point.
Jennings, E. Ugly Child, The.
Lucianus. Artificial Beauty.
"Monty Python." All things dull and ugly.
Moss, T. Owl In Daytime, The.
Notley. One of the Longest Times.
Revell. Muse.
Rich, A. Wherever in this city, screens flicker.
Ross, C. John, Tom, and James.
Sanchez, S. Song No. 3: "Cain't nobody tell
  me any different."
Shakespeare, W. Sonnet 130.
Sidney, P. What length of verse can serve
  brave *Mopsa'*'s good to show?
Soto. Brown Girl, Blonde Okie.
Suckling, J. Deformed Mistress, The.
Swift, J. Progress of Beauty, The.
Welch, L. Chicago Poem.
Wyatt, T. Ye old mule, that thin[c]k your self
  so fair [*or* fayre].
Ukraine
Pasternak, B. You're here. We breathe the
  selfsame air.
Ulysses
Brodsky, J. Odysseus to Telemachus.
Daniel, S. Ulysses and the Siren [*or* Syren].

Doolittle, H. At Ithaca.
Fallon, P. Odysseus.
Flecker. Old Ships, The.
Graves, R. Ulysses.
Hesiod. Laertes.
Hoagland, T. In the Land of the Lotus Eaters.
Holloway, J. Ulysses.
Homer. Circe.
  Landfall.
  Penelope hesitates.
  Suitors watch Ulysses string the bow, The.
  Thus, many tales *Ulysses* told his wife.
  Ulysses Insults over the Cyclops.
  Ulysses Invokes the Dead.
  Ulysses Reunited with Penelope.
Howard, R. Last Words.
Kyger. Maze, The.
Lang, A. Odyssey II.
Lovelace, R. To a Lady That Desired Me I Would Bear My Part with Her in a Song.
Merwin, W. Odysseus.
Muldoon, P. Making the Move.
Pope, A. Argus.
Pound, E. Canto 1.
Stevens, W. World as Meditation, The.
Tennyson, A. Ulysses.

Umbrellas
Dickinson, E. Bat is dun with wrinkled Wings, The.
Harasymowicz. Old Age.
Herford. Elf and the Dormouse, The.
Hutchinson, M. My New Umbrella.
Lauterbach. For Example (1): Stepping Out.
Rossetti, C. When fishes set umbrellas up.
Samio. Tanka: "Monumental."
Stanford, A. Umbrella, The.
Wesley-Smith. Cavendish McKellar.

Uncertainty
Auden. September 1, 1939.
Beckett, S. Enueg II.
Bernstein, O. All this is my time. No time to seek disguise. There'll be.
Bertolino. Landscape, The.
Bolton, K. Nonplussed.
Burrell. Chloe and Myra.
Cassian. Orbits.
Cavafy. Waiting for the Barbarians.
Corbin, A. Love me at last, or if you will not.
Cummins, J. Sestina.
De la Mare. Dear Sir.
Dickinson, E. If you were coming in the Fall.
  Wonder—is not precisely Knowing.
Dimitrova. Steady.
Donne. Satire 3.
Doolittle, H. Fragment 36: "I know not what to do."
Dunn, S. Let's See If I Have It Right.
Etherege. To a Lady Asking Him How Long He Would Love Her.
"Field." Second Thoughts.
Foix. I Arrived in that Town, Everyone Greeted Me and I Recognized no One. When I Was Going to Read My Verses, the Devil, Hidden Behind a Tree, Called Out to Me Sarcastically and Filled My Hands with Newspaper Clippings.
Gouri. If a flame has fallen among the cedars.
Horikawa. Will he always love me?
Jennings, K. Just the Two of Us.
King, J. Moments.
Lea, S. Insomnia: The Distances.
Lowell, J. In a Copy of Omar Khayyám.
Mackey, W. Kama Sutra of Kindness: Position No. 2, The.
MacNeice. Entirely.
  Les Sylphides.
Melville, H. Arch, The.
Merrill, J. About the Phoenix.
Muir, E. In Love For Long.
North, C. Leap Year.
O'Hara, F. Cornkind.
  Meditations in an Emergency.
Oppen. Department of Plants and Structures—obsolete, the old name.
Palmer, M. Who is to say.
Ponsot. Old Mama Saturday.
Ritsos. End of Dodona II, The.

Shapiro, A. Letter said you had to speak to me, The.
Shepherd, R. Brotherhood.
Simic. Clouds Gathering.
Speght. *Disswasion* hearing her assigne my helpe.
Strand. Is it you standing amoung the olive trees.
Sweeney, M. Couple Waiting, A.
Symons, A. And yet, there was a hunger in your eyes.
Teasdale. Flight, The.
Treece. Magic Wood, The.
Van Vliet. Coastline never alters for the fisherman, The.
Warren, R. Mango on the mango tree, The.
Whitman, W. As I lay with my head in your lap camerado.
Whittier. Song of Slaves in the Desert.
Woods, J. What Do You Do When It's Spring?

Uncle Tom's Cabin
Bibb. Eliza in Uncle Tom's Cabin.
Harper, F. She's Free!

Uncles
Avidan. Burying Uncle Salomon.
Barlow, G. Salt.
Blyton, C. Night Starvation or The Biter Bit.
Carson, C. Asylum.
Conn. Todd.
Cullen, C. Uncle Jim.
Cummings, E. Nobody loses all the time.
Etter. Well You Needn't.
Harrison, T. Study.
Hughes, T. My Uncle Dan's an inventor, you may think.
Kasdorf. Uncle.
Kim, Y. Labyrinth.
Kitahara Hakushū. Tanka: "My uncle."
Lear, E. Incidents in the Life of My Uncle Arly.
Levine, P. Uncle.
Mahon. My Wicked Uncle.
Ochester. Canaries in Uncle Arthur's Basement, The.
Piercy. Landed Fish.
  My Rich Uncle, Whom I Only Met Three Times.
Ramke. How Light Is Spent.
Smith, D. Roundhouse Voices, The.
Wright, J. Willy Lyons.

Underground Railroad
Hayden, R. Runagate Runagate.

Undertakers
Moss, T. Owl In Daytime, The.
Nash, O. Tweedledee and Tweedledoom.

Underwear
Ferlinghetti, L. Underwear.
Maitre. Woman Underneath, The.
Weigl. Black Hose, The.

Unemployment
Ackerly. Prayer of an Unemployed Man.
Cavafy. Days of 1908.
  Days of 1908.
Craig, C. City Blues.
Davis, C. Out of Work, Out of Touch, Out of Sorts.
Dugan, A. Prayer: "God, I need a job because I need money."
Espada. Toolmaker Unemployed, The.
Hopkins, G. Tom's Garland: Upon the Unemployed.
Jordan, J. Unemployment/Monologue.
McGinley. Trinity Place.
Small, J. Pig-Sticking Season, The.
Spender, S. Unemployed.
Unknown. Between an Unemployed Artist and His Wife.
Webb, F. Laid Off.

Unicorns
Darley. Unicorn, The.
Garrigue. Unicorn and the Lady, The.
Housman, A. Inhuman Henry.
Lewis, C. Late Passenger, The.
Macpherson, J. Garden shut, a fountain sealed, A.

Moore, M. Sea Unicorns and Land Unicorns.
Mother Goose. Lion and the unicorn, The.
Pitter. Unicorn, The.
Randall, D. Black Poet, White Critic.
Rieu. Unicorn stood, like a king in a dream, The.
Rilke. Oh this is the animal that never was.
T'ang Hsien-tsu. Paintings on My Wall Have Been Damaged by the Weather, The.
Unknown. Dance Song.
  I Stood in the Maytime Meadows.
Webb, P. Days of the Unicorns, The.
Williams, C. Taliessin's Song of the Unicorn.

Union of Soviet Socialist Republics. *See* **Russia**

Unions. *See* **Labor Unions**

United Nations. *See* **World Feredation**

United States
"Aleichem." Sleep, My Child.
Baraka. Das Kapital.
  I don't love you.
Bates, K. America the Beautiful.
Benét, S. American Names.
Berkeley, G. On the Prospect of Planting Arts and Learning in America.
Berryman. American Lights, Seen from Off Abroad.
Bevington, H. Mrs. Trollope in America.
Bly, R. Great Society, The.
Bryant, W. Oh mother of a mighty race.
Césaire, A. State of the Union.
Chin. Portrait of the Self as Nation, 1990–1991, A.
"Chrystos." I Have Not Signed a Treaty with the United States Government.
Cohan. Over There.
Creeley. America, you ode for reality!
Cummings, E. Next to of course god america i.
  Poem, or Beauty Hurts Mr. Vinal.
  Season 'tis,my lovely lambs, The.
Daly, J. Toast to the Flag, A.
Davidson, L. America.
Dickey, J. Coming Back to America.
Dickinson, E. Union.
Evans, M. Status Symbol.
Frost, R. Gift Outright, The.
Ginsberg, A. America I've given you all and now I'm nothing.
  Vow, A.
  Who Runs America?
Goethe. United States, The.
Hardy, T. On an Invitation to the United States.
Harper, F. Then and Now.
Harper, M. Goin' to the Territory.
Hitchcock. United States Prepare for the Permanent Revolution, The.
Holmes, J. Map of My Country, A.
Hopkinson, J. Hail, Columbia.
Hosking. Land of the Free.
Hosmer, F. O Beautiful, My Country.
Hughes, L. I too, sing America.
Huntington, G. International Hymn.
Jeffers, L. My Blackness Is the Beauty of This Land.
Jeffers, R. Eagle Valor, Chicken Mind.
  Shine, Perishing Republic.
Joyce, J. Crazy Quilt.
Kaufman, B. To My Son Parker, Asleep in the Next Room.
Kipling, R. American Spirit speaks, The.
  White Man's Burden, The.
Koch, K. Poem of the Forty-eight States, A.
Lawrence, D. American Eagle, The.
  Evening Land, The.
Lazarus, E. 1492.
  New Colossus, The.
Lewis, A. America Bleeds.
Liddy. Voice of America, 1961, The.
MacLeish. American Letter.
  Empire Builders.
McKay, C. America.
Newlove. America.
Pinsky. Serpent Knowledge.
Randall, D. Melting Pot, The.
Roethke. Night Journey.

Unity

Ryan, R. From My Lai the Thunder Went West.
Shapiro, H. National Cold Storage Company contains, The.
Simpson, L. American Poetry.
Inner Part, The.
To the Western World.
Smith, S. America.
Stephen, J. On a Rhine Steamer.
Stevenson, R. In the States.
Tate, A. Aeneas at Washington.
Ode to the Confederate Dead.
Tillinghast, R. Our Flag Was Still There.
Unknown. Columbia.
Preamble to the Constitution of the United States.
State Quiz.
Van Dyke. America for Me.
Peace Hymn of the Republic.
Wain. Brooklyn Heights.
Whitman, W. America.
For You O Democracy.
I hear America singing, the varied carols I hear.
To the States, To Identify the 16th, 17th, or 18th Presidentiad.
Williams, T. My Country, to Thy Shore.

Unity

Amichai. In My Time, at Your Place.
Lovers in Fall.
Bevington, L. Wrestling.
Bible, *O.T.* Psalm 133.
Borowski. Sun of Auschwitz, The.
Bradstreet, A. Another.
Letter to Her Husband, Absent upon Public[k] Employment, A.
To My Dear and Loving Husband.
Brodsky, J. Six Years Later.
Butler, M. Listen.
Clifton, L. Cutting Greens.
Coleridge, M. We Never Said Farewell[, nor even looked].
Czerkawska. Thread.
Daglarca. Unity.
Daive. She does not move. Takes the man's.
Dao. Stretch out your hands to me.
Dickinson, E. Love—thou art high.
Donne. Ecstasy, The.
Flea, The.
Good-Morrow, The.
Drayton. Heart, The.
Duhamel. Feminism.
Emerson, R. Each and All.
Music.
Nature [1844].
Xenophanes.
Empson. Invitation To Juno.
Flanders, J. House That Fear Built: Warsaw, 1943, The.
Gardner, I. Loud Song, Mother, A.
Ginsberg, A. Change: *Kyoto-Tokyo Express,* The.
Glück, L. Pond, The.
Hadewijch. Madness of love, The.
Harjo, J. Sonata for the Invisible.
Herbert, G. Clasping of Hands.
Herbert of Cherbury. One Another's Mystery.
Hernández, M. Waltz Poem of Those in Love and Inseparable Forever.
Herrick. Power and Peace.
Izumi. I cannot say.
Jonson, B. On the Union.
Julian of Norwich. God wants to be thought of.
Kalvos. Altar of the Fatherland, The.
Khlebnikov, V. Suppose I make a timepiece of humanity.
Komunyakaa. "Everybody's Reading Li Po" Silkscreened on a Purple T-Shirt.
Kovner. Dimmed Observation.
Hour's Late, The.
Vow.
Kunitz, S. Prophecy on Lethe.
Levertov. Ache of marriage, The.
"MacDiarmid." With the Herring Fishers.
Mahadevi. I do not call it his sign.
Manaka. Chorus: "Babylon, I did not come to

you for the sake of coming."
Chorus: "In the name of the people."
Marichiko. Who is there? Me.
Maunick. Further off is the measured force the word of the sea.
I love to encounter you in strange cities.
Melville, H. Art.
Little Good Fellows, The.
Montoya. Just the other day.
Mori Ōgai. Tanka: "Should I stroke it."
Nesbit, E. Song: "Oh, baby, baby, baby dear."
Niemoller. First they came for the Jews.
Nikolov, N. Don't Move Away.
Nordbrandt. Sailing.
Olds, S. Knowing, The.
Olson, C. Celestial Evening, October 1967.
Maximus, to Gloucester, Letter 27.
Poem 143.
Pagis. Tropical Greenhouse.
Palamas. In the sun-glad nakedness.
Parker, P. There Is a Woman in This Town.
Philips, K. Friendship's Mystery, To My Dearest Lucasia.
Piercy. Low Road, The.
Ponsot. Analogue.
Porter, P. Don't Be Afraid, I Am With You.
Ransom, J. Two in August.
Rich, A. Diving into the Wreck.
Hunger.
Phantasia for Elvira Shatayev.
Wherever in this city, screens flicker.
Rivner. Fire in the Stone, The.
Rossetti, C. I loved you first: but afterwards your love.
Rukeyser, M. Conjugation of the Paramecium, The.
Poem as Mask, The.
Rumi. Out beyond ideas of wrongdoing and rightdoing.
We can't help being thirsty.
Skelton, J. Rose both white and Rede, The.
Slessor. Sleep.
Stevens, W. Final Soliloquy of the Interior Paramour.
Stryker. Almighty Lord, with one accord.
Tate, A. Near to me as my flesh, my flesh and blood.
Tsvetayeva. . . . In my melodious city cupolas burn.
Unknown. I have thee, thou hast me.
'One with this world'.
We are, you and me.
Vaughan, H. Knot, The.
Vogel, D. How Can I See You, Love.
Wang T'ing-hsiang. Miscellaneous Poems Written in the Snow.
Whitman, W. One's-Self I sing, a simple separate person.
Wild gander leads his flock through the cool night, The.
You sea! I resign myself to you also—I guess what you mean.
Whittier. Word for the Hour, A.
Williams, W. Mists Over the River.
Winchilsea. Letter to Daphnis, A.
Wright, C. Self-Portrait ("Someday they'll find me out, and my lavish hands").
Yang Fang. Joy of Union, The.

Universe

Blake, W. And every Space that a Man views around his dwelling-place.
Blandiana. Links.
Blaser. Universe is Part of Ourselves, The.
Borges. Everness.
Browning, R. Pisgah-Sights. I.
Pisgah-Sights. II.
Buckley, C. Apologues of Winter Light.
Crane, S. Man said to the universe, A.
Dickinson, E. Bees are Black, with Gilt Surcingles—.
Follain. Music of Spheres.
Fumi Saito. Tanka: "Snow seeping."
Johnson, R. Beam 30, The Garden.
Kelly, R. Looking.
Kenward. What's out there?
Kovner. Scientists Are Mistaken, The.

McGough, R. Phew.
Meynell, A. Christ in the Universe.
Miller, M. Universe, The.
Nahman of Bratzlav. From "The Torah of the Void."
Nemerov. Angel and Stone.
Neruda. Poetry.
Olson, C. Across Space and Time.
Pack, R. Proton Decay.
Pettingell. Ode on Zero.
Popa. Last News about the Little Box.
Raine, K. Scala Coeli.
Rumi. Little by little, wean yourself.
Simpson, L. Physical Universe.
Springer, T. Harmony.
Tada. Universe of the Rose.
Towle. North.
Tuckerman, F. Sonnet: "And so, as this great sphere (now turning slow)."
Valek. Hearing.
Virgil. Anchises to Aeneas.
Whitman, W. Leaves of Grass (1855).

Universities. *See* **Colleges and Universities**

Unknown Soldier

Chesterton, G. Elegy in a Country Churchyard.
Laughlin, E. Unknown, The.
Masters, E. Unknown Soldiers.
Rose, B. Unknown Soldier, The.

Uriel

Emerson, R. Uriel.

Urns

Cullen, C. Uncle Jim.
Lowell, R. Neo-Classical Urn, The.

Ursa Major

Hollander, J. Great Bear, The.

Usury

Campbell, J. Gombeen, The.
Guillén, N. Usurers, The.
Pound, E. Canto 45.
Canto 51.
Canto XLV.

Utah (state)

Frost, R. On the Heart's Beginning to Cloud the Mind.
Stevenson, A. Utah.
Unknown. Marching to Utah.

Ute, The

Tomlinson, C. Ute Mountain.

Utopia

Auden. Vespers.
Beerbohm, M. In a Copy of More's (or Shaw's or Wells's or Plato's or Anybody's) Utopia.
Coleridge, S. Kubla Khan; or, A Vision in a Dream.
Duncan, A. In the Red Grove.
Gilbert, S. Utopia Anglicized.
Ransom, J. Somewhere Is Such a Kingdom.
Unknown. Big Rock Candy Mountains, The.

V

Vacation

Davidson, J. Crystal Palace, The.
Enzensberger, H. Holiday, The.
Hutt. Vacation Time.
Jackson, R. Sunday Brunch.
Leonard, T. Simple Simon.
Merrill, J. Up and Down.
Moss, H. Movies for the Home.
O'Hara, F. Summer Breezes.
Rowe, J. Lake Chemo.
Stafford, W. Vacation.
Stevens, W. Gray Stones and Gray Pigeons.
Twichell. Chanel No. 5.
Unknown. I'm Going to Rocky Island.

Vacuum Cleaners and Vacuum Cleaning

Nemerov. Vacuum, The.

Vagabonds

Bates, K. Despised and Rejected.
Brennan, C. When window-lamps had dwindled, then I rose.
Burnet, D. Road to Vagabondia, The.

Campbell, J. Every Shuiler Is Christ.
Catacalos. One Man's Family.
Colum, P. Old Woman of the Roads, The.
Crane, H. River, The.
Dawe, B. Drifters.
Delmore Brothers. Wabash Cannonball, The.
Dobyns. Freight Cars.
Frost, R. Two Tramps in Mud Time.
Hardy, T. Trampwoman's Tragedy, A.
Haresnape. African Tramp, The.
Hughes, T. November.
Kipling, R. Sestina of the Tramp-Royal.
Leonidas. Wallet, a rawhide goatskin, a cane, A.
Leonidas of Tarentum. Don't waste yourself, dragging out the life of a vagrant.
Levine, P. And the Trains Go On.
Masefield. Wanderer's Song, A.
McGrath, T. Long Way Outside Yellowstone, A.
Neilson, J. Sundowner, The.
Ponsot. Communion of Saints: The Poor Bastard under the Bridge.
Riley, J. Raggedy Man, The.
Stevenson, R. Vagabond, The.
Tate, A. Traveller, The.
Trowbridge, J. Vagabonds, The.
Unknown. Dying Hobo, The.
Jay Gould's Daughter.

Valentine's Day
Drayton. To His Valentine.
Duffy, C. Valentine.
Hall, D. Valentine.
Hemingway. Valentine.
Holt, J. To Mr. Wren, My Valentine Six Year Old.
Moore, M. St. Valentine.
Poe. Valentine, A.
Schuyler, J. Sleep.
Shakespeare, W. Song: "Tomorrow is saint valentine's day."
Spicer, J. Valentine, A.
Stein, G. Very Valentine, A.
Thompson, P. Valentine, A.
Welles. White Valentine.

Valentino, Rudolph
Sapia. Valentino's Hair.

Valleys
Ashbery. Grand Abacus.
Byron, G. Lachin y Gair.
Mistral, G. Song.
Sandburg, C. Mist Forms.
Moist Moon People.
Wordsworth, D. Cottage in Grasmere Vale, A.

Value
Bast. Hywell the Good Weighs the Worth of a Cat.
Dickinson, E. I took one Draught of Life.
Giscombe. Bro Duncanson.
Nathan, L. Bladder Song.
So you aren't Tolstoy or Saint Francis.
Shakespeare, W. Sonnet 52.
Skelton, J. For though my rhyme be ragged.
Smith, S. Valuable.

Vampires
Cassian. Young Vampire, The.
Glaser, E. Undead White European Male.
Guillén, N. Usurers, The.
Kipling, R. Vampire, The.
McDonald, R. Incident in Transylvania.
Raab, L. Voices Answering Back: The Vampires.
Shwarts. Remembrance of Strange Hospitality.
Smith, S. Great Unaffected Vampires and the Moon.
Wilbur. Undead, The.
Yeats. Oil and Blood.

Van Doren, Mark
Hayden, R. Ballad of Remembrance, A.

Van Gogh, Vincent
Cooley. Self-Portrait as Van Gogh.
Różewicz. Roots.
Tomlinson, C. Farewell to Van Gogh.
Zenmaro. At the Van Gogh exibition.

Vancouver, British Columbia
Lowry, M. Christ Walks in This Infernal District Too.

Shiraishi. I Fire at the Face of the Country Where I Was Born.

Vandalism
Beaver. Drummer, The.
Bottoms. Desk, The.

Vanderbilt, Gloria
Cole, W. Poor Kid.

Vane, Sir Henry (1613-62)
Milton. To Sir Henry Vane the Younger.

Vanity
Blunt, W. On Her Vanity.
Bolton, E. Palinode, A.
Bradstreet, A. Flesh and the Spirit, The.
Here Follows Some Verses upon the Burning of Our House [July 10th, 1966. Copied Out of a Loose Paper].
Vanity of All Worldly Things, The.
Byron, G. 'All Is Vanity, Saith the Preacher'.
Carew, T. Ingrateful[l] Beauty Threatened.
Cummings, E. Cambridge ladies who live in furnished souls, The.
Du Bellay. It was the time, when rest, soft sliding downe.
"Ephelia." To a Proud Beauty.
Ferry. Unawkward Singer, The.
Graves, R. Vain and Careless.
Vanity.
Gryphius. All Is Vanity.
Guiterman. On the Vanity of Earthly Greatness.
Gunn, T. Lines for a Book.
Hall, J. Even as the wandering traveler doth stray.
Herbert, G. Vanity [or Vanitie] (1).
Herrick. Upon Rook: Epigram.
Hewitt, J. Ireland.
Howitt, M. Spider and the Fly, The.
Juvenal. Woman stops at nothing, when she wears, A.
Kizer, C. Through a Glass Eye, Lightly.
La Fontaine. Man and His Image, The.
Lawrence, D. Intimates.
True Love at Last.
Le Gallienne. Beauty Accurst.
Leigh, H. Lady and the Doctor, The.
Lucianus. Artificial Beauty.
Machado Ruiz. Don't trace out your profile.
Narcissism / is an ugly fault.
Mayer, G. Narcissus.
McFarlane, J. On National Vanity.
Melville, H. Camoëns.
Nash, O. Evening Out, The.
Piercy. Barbie Doll.
Prior. Oft have I said, the praise of doing well.
Ransom, J. Vanity of the Bright Young Men, The.
Rodgers, C. Feminism.
Rossetti, C. One Certainty, The.
Soeur Louise de la Miséricorde (1674).
Rossetti, D. One Hope, The.
Rufinus Domesticus. I wove this garland, Rodokleia.
Sampson. Anaconda, The.
Scott, W. Madge Wildfire Sings.
Scovell. Vain Girl Jilted, The.
Sexton. Snow White and the Seven Dwarfs.
Shakespeare, W. Sonnet 1.
Shelley, P. Ozymandias [of Egypt].
"Struther." Lament in Spring.
Swift, J. Lady's Dressing Room, The.
Progress of Beauty, The.
T'ao Ch'ien. Imitating the Old Poems.
Tennyson, A. Character, A.
Vaughan, H. Vanity of Spirit.
Watts, I. Man Frail, and God Eternal.
Wen T'ing-yün. Tune: Deva-like Barbarian ("On the many-leafed bedscreens, gold flickers and fades").
Whateley. Vanity of External Accomplishments, The.
Wigglesworth. Song of Emptiness to Fill up the Empty Pages Following, A.
Williams, M. Love and How It Becomes Important in Our Day to Day Lives.
Yeats. Two Trees, The.

See also **Pride**
Variety
Lovelace, R. Scrutiny [or Scrutinie], The.
Ravikovitch. Poem of Explanations.

Vashti
Harper, F. Vashti.
Spencer, A. Before the Feast of Shushan.

Vaudeville
Kirstein. Vaudeville.

Vaughan, Henry
Sassoon. At the Grave of Henry Vaughan.

Vaughn, Robert Boardman
Justice, D. In Memory of the Unknown Poet, Robert Boardman Vaughn.

Vegetables
Ammianus. Supper at Apelles'/ was a garden-butcher's work.
Baca. Green Chile.
Clifton, L. Cutting Greens.
Dove, R. Sunday Greens.
Duncan, R. Turning into a restful roomfull.
Florian. Send my spinach.
Forbes, C. Potlicker Blues.
Gladding. Asparagus.
Hsü Wei. To Hsü Shih-t'ing.
Kumin, M. Mummies, The.
McAlmon. For Instance.
McClintock, M. Hungry / without money—.
Messerli. Angry with China.
Miyazawa Kenji. Tanka: "At dawn."
Mole, J. Trick, The.
Nash, O. Parsnip, children, I repeat, The.
Ormsby, E. Skunk cabbage with its smug and opulent smell, The.
Rotella, A. Asparagus I bite off their heads.
Trying to forget him.
Saitō Mokichi. Tanka: "From where."
Shange. Different Love Poem / We Need a Change, A.
Shūji. Tanka: "On the way home."
Thomas, E. Swedes.
Thomas, L. Onion Bucket.
Unik. Manless Society, The.
Unknown. Do you carrot all for me?
Virgil. Emerging hot and rosy.
Willard, N. How to Stuff a Pepper.
Wu Chia-chi. My hut, beside the crystal stream.
Yün Shou-p'ing. Painting of Yams, A.
See also names of specific vegetables (e.g., Corn).

Vegetarians
Li K'ai-hsien. Prosperous Villager, The.
Yambo. When Negro Teeth Speak.

Velázquez, Diego Rodríguez de Silva y
Conquest. Rokeby Venus, The.
Weöres. To the Spirits of Shakespeare and Velázquez.
Wylie. Castilian.
Zivancevic. Poem with a Tilde in the Title, A.

Venereal Disease
Catina. Negotiations.

Vengeance
Bible, *O.T.* Heathen Are Come into Thine Inheritance, The.
Psalm 55.
Psalm 58.
Psalm 83.
Bruner. Prayer for Strength.
Cortez. Rape.
Guiterman. Ancient History.
Hughes, L. Hard Daddy.
Paulin. Impossible Pictures, The.
Whittier. Cities of the Plain, The.
Wilde, L. Famine Year, The.

Venice, Italy
Beer, P. Birthday Poem from Venice.
Betjeman. Longfellow's Visit to Venice.
Browning, R. Toccata of Galuppi's, A.
Durrell. Water-Colour of Venice, A.
Garrigue. From Venice was that afternoon.
Krustev. Nostalgia for Titian.
Longfellow, H. Venice.
Melville, H. In a Bye-Canal.
Venice.
Naudé. From a Venetian Sequence.
Simpson, L. Music in Venice.

Symons, A. Venice.
Wordsworth, W. On the Extinction of the
   Venetian Republic.

Venus (goddess)
Anacreon. Wounded Cupid. Song, The.
Carew, T. On Sight of a Gentlewoman's Face
   in the Water.
Conquest. Rokeby Venus, The.
Devlin, D. Venus of the Salty Shell.
Gray, J. Le Voyage À Cythère.
Hadas, R. Mars and Venus.
Herrick. How Lillies Came White.
   How Violets Came Blue.
   Wounded Cupid, The.
Leonidas of Alexandria. Upon Venus Putting
   on Mars His Armes.
Lowell, A. Venus Transiens.
Lucretius. Address to Venus.
Moschus. Idyll 1.
Olson, C. Ring of, The.
Ovid. Elegy 9b: "If I heard a voice from
   heaven say 'Live without'."
Peele. Love.
Prior. Ode, An: "Merchant, to secure his
   treasure, The."
Rossetti, C. Venus's Looking-Glass.
Rukeyser, M. Birth of Venus, The.
Salter. Rebirth of Venus, The.
Shakespeare, W. Even as the sun with purple-
   colour'd face.
Unknown. Epigram out of Plato To Madam
   Amara, An.
   Queen of Paphos, Erycine, The.
   Sing, Muse, the Force, and all-informing Fire.
   Spoken by Venus on Seeing Her Statue Done
   by Praxiteles.
Urdang. Birth of Venus.
Veneris. Over sky and land and down under
   the sea.
Spring, the new, the warb'ling Spring appears,
   The.
Watson, W. Invocation: "Appear, O Mother,
   was the perpetual cry."
Wickham. Boor's Wooing, The.
Willis, N. Psyche, Before the Tribunal of
   Venus.

See also **Aphrodite**

Venus of Milo (statue)
Gilder, R. Two Worlds.
Lazarus, E. Venus of the Louvre.
Leconte de Lisle, C. Venus de Milo.

Venus (planet)
Clare, J. Hesperus! the day is gone.
García Lorca. Venus.
Holmes, O. Flaneur, The.
Juana Inés de la Cruz. But Venus first.
Patmore, C. Perspective.
Rice, J. Sky Seasons.

Verdi, Giuseppe
Noyes, A. Barrel-Organ, The.

Verdun, Battle of (1916)
Dugan, A. Memories of Verdun.

Vergil. *See* **Virgil**

Verlaine, Paul
Aiken, C. Prelude LVI: "Rimbaud and
   Verlaine, precious pair of poets."
Hovey. Verlaine.
Robinson, E. Verlaine.

Vermont (state)
Barnstone, A. Mating the Goats.
Corbett, W. Vermont Apollinaire.
Frost, R. "Out, Out—."
Hummer, T. Austerity in Vermont.
Rich, A. Living Memory.
Stone, R. Pokeberries.
Taggard. Poem to Explain Everything about a
   Certain Day in Vermont, A.
Warren, R. Vermont Ballad: Change of
   Season.

Verona, Italy
Claudian. Old Man of Verona, The.

Versailles, France
Moore, M. No Swan So Fine.
Rich, A. Versailles.
Warton, J. Wild, The.

Veterans
Aldington. Proem: "Sixty years after the fall
   of Troy."
Barry, J. Lessons.
Brown, F. Veteran, The.
Chipasula. Tramp.
Cross, Jr. When Chicken Man Came Home to
   Roost.
Dugan, A. Portrait from the Infantry.
Ehrhart. Invasion of Grenada, The.
Fenton, J. German Requiem, A.
Herbert, A. Beaucourt Revisited.
Hughes, S. Walt.
Kipling, R. Chant-Pagan.
Komunyakaa. Report from the Skull's
   Diorama.
McDonald, W. Veteran.
Péret. Hymn of the Patriotic War Veterans.
Sassoon. Does It Matter?[—losing your legs?].
   Fight to a Finish.
   Memorial Tablet.
Sitwell, S. Next War, The.
Waring, B. Refuge at the One Step Down.
Weigl. Anna Grasa.
Wilson, T. Sportsmen in Paradise.
Young Bear. Wadasa Nakamoon, Vietnam
   Memorial.

See also **Soldiers**

Veterans Day. *See* **Armistice**

Vice. *See* **Sin**

Victoria, Queen of England
Ford, F. Sidera Cadentia.
French, W. Queen's After-Dinner Speech, The.
Housman, A. 1887.
Kipling, R. Widow at Windsor, The.
Linden, M. To the Queen of the British
   Government.
Tennyson, A. On the Jubilee of Queen
   Victoria.
Unknown. Much Distressed.
   Queen's Dream, The.

Victory
Behn, A. Song: Love Armed.
   Thousand Martyrs I Have Made, A.
Dickinson, E. Success is counted sweetest.
   Victory comes late.
Donne. Holy Sonnet.
Gordon, A. How We Beat the Favourite.
Hardy, T. Men Who March Away.
Herrick. To the King.
Jonson, B. Her Triumph.
Marvell. Fair Singer, The.
Miller, J. At Our Golden Gate.
Pope, A. Reign of Chaos, The.
Ransom, J. Judith of Bethulia.
Sill. Opportunity.
Treece. Conquerors.
Unknown. Agincourt Carol, The.
   Bạch-đằng River, The.
   Joshua fit de battle of Jericho [*or* ob Jerico].

Vienna, Austria
Howard, R. Lost Art, A.
Meek. Vienna in the Rain.

Vietnam
Ái Lan. Deathless Autumn, A.
Alexander, E. Nineteen.
Allen, D. Short History of the Vietnam War
   Years, A.
Alvarez, J. How I Learned to Sweep.
Anderson, S. Junglegrave.
Appleman, P. Waiting for the Fire.
Balaban. Along the Mekong.
   April 30, 1975.
   Dead for Two Years, Erhart Arranges to Meet
   Me in a Dream.
   Dragonfish, The.
   For Miss Tin in Hue.
   For Mrs. Cam, Whose Name Means "Printed
   Silk."
   Guard at the Binh Thuy Bridge, The.
   In Celebration of Spring.
   News Update.
   Opening Le Ba Khon's Dictionary.
   Story.
   Than, Mau.
   Thoughts Before Dawn.

Bàng Bá Lâ. They Starved, They Starved.
Barry, J. Floating Petals.
   In the Footsteps of Genghis Khan.
   Nights in Nha Trang.
   Nun in Ninh Hoa, A.
Barth, R. Letter from An Hoc (4), by a
   Seedbed.
Berry, D. Sun goes.
Bly, R. Asian Peace Offers Rejected without
   Publication.
   At a March against the Vietnam War.
   Counting Small-Boned Bodies.
   Driving through Minnesota during the Hanoi
   Bombings.
   Teeth Mother Naked at Last, The.
Brown, D. I Was Dancing Alone in Binh
   Dinh Province.
   Illumination.
Brown, S. After the Vietnam War.
Cao Tần. Booby had a little sack, The.
   Five crackpots got together, talked big things.
   Our friend would board the *Thư'o'ng-Tín* and
   go home.
Catina. Philosophy.
Clifton, H. Death of Thomas Merton.
Cobb, C. "Containing Communism."
Coleman, H. Black Soldier Remembers, A.
   Downed Black Pilot Learns How to Fly, A.
   In Ca Mau.
   Night Flare Drop, Tan Son Nhut.
   OK Corral East Brothers in the Nam.
   Remembrance of Things Past.
Cross, Jr. Gliding Baskets.
Dana, R. At the Vietnam War Memorial,
   Washington, D. C.
Đằng Phu'o'ng. Day of Mourning at Yên-Báy,
   The.
Đng Trần Côn *et al.* Song of a Soldier's
   Wife, The.
Dawe, B. Homecoming.
Denning. Fire Support Burk.
   Kim-San.
   Movie, The.
   Night on the Kho Bha Dinh.
   This Time.
Đồng Hồ. War.
Du Tử Lê. Dawn of a New Humankind, The.
Duncan, R. Up Rising.
Ehrhart. Blizzard of Sixty-Six, The.
   Farmer Nguyen.
   Guerrilla War.
   Invasion of Grenada, The.
   Letter.
   Relative Thing, A.
   ". . . the light that cannot fade. . . ."
   Time on Target.
Evans, G. Eye Blade.
   Revelation in the Mother Lode.
Fernandez, R. Legacy of a Brother.
Floyd. Captain James Leson, U. S. M. C.
   Corporal Charles Chungtu, U. S. M. C.
   Lance Corporal Purdue Grace, U. S. M. C.
   Private First Class Brooks Morgenstein, U. S.
   M. C.
   Private Jack Smith, U. S. M. C.
   Sergeant Brandon Just, U. S. M. C.
Fried, E. What Things Are Called.
Ginsberg, A. Vow, A.
   Wichita Vortex Sutra, Part I.
Griffin, S. Song My.
Gwynn, R. Body Bags.
Hà Huyền Chi. Sea, the World, and the Boat
   People, The.
Hải Âu Tử'. Zoo Cages.
Hall, D. Disgrace.
   How is it the stomach knows first.
   There is no place to hide.
Harper, M. Mama's Report.
Hassett. Armed Forces Day.
   Christmas.
   Mother's Day.
   Patriot's Day.
   Thanksgiving.
Hậu Điền. Biding Our Time.
Hayden, R. In the Mourning Time.
Hazo. Battle News.
Hitchcock. Scattering Flowers.

Ho Chi Minh. Song of a Cotton Yarn, The.
Hồ Văn Hảo. Revolutionary Youth.
Ho Xuan Huong. Shrine of Ts'en Yi-tung, The.
Hollenbeck. Anorexia.
Hồng Chu'o'ng. It's Me, Your Son.
Howell, C. Memories of Mess Duty and the War.
Reminder to the Current President, A.
Huddle. Bac Ha.
Nerves.
Theory.
Vermont.
Words.
Huy Cận. Two Wooden Men, The.
Huỳnh Phú Sổ. Bread.
Huỳnh Thúc Kháng. Comedy of the World, The.
Ignatow, D. All Quiet.
James, A. Honor (1969).
Jones, R. Contempt.
Jordan, J. Poem to My Sister, Ethel Ennis, Who Sang "The Star-spangled Banner" at the Second Inauguration of Richard Milhous Nixon.
Kiên Giang. Hero of Our Times, The.
Kinnell. Vapor Trail Reflected in the Frog Pond.
Knott. Two Vietnam Poems: (1966).
Komunyakaa. After the Fall of Saigon.
Boat People.
Break from the Bush, A.
Camouflaging the Chimera.
Dead at Quang Tri, The.
Facing It.
Ia Drang Valley.
Report from the Skull's Diorama.
Somewhere Near Phu Bai.
Starlight Scope Myopia.
Tiger Lady.
Tu Do Street.
Krohn. Can Tho, *favela* of crowing cocks.
Farmer's Song at Can Tho.
Ferryman's Song at Binh Minh.
Layne, M. Collect Call.
Gettin' Straight.
Intersection in the Sky.
Lê Đù'c Thọ. Fighter's Thoughts of Spring, A.
Lehman. Operation Memory.
Levertov. Advent 1966.
Fragrance of Life, Odor of Death.
In Thai Binh (Peace) Province.
Tenebrae.
Weeping Woman.
What Were They Like?
Livesay, D. Waking in the Dark.
Lourie. For All My Brothers and Sisters.
Lowery. Nam.
Luân Hoán. Washing My Wife's Clothes.
Lu'u Văn Vong. Paradise.
Run! Run!
Lý Thu'o'ng Kiệt. Southern emperor rules the Southern land, The.
Lynch, C. Memo.
Madhubuti. Long Reality, The.
Mai Thảo. Island.
Major, C. Vietnam.
Vietnam #4.
Martin, H. Negro Soldier's Viet Nam Diary, A.
McCarthy, E. Kilroy is gone.
McCarthy, G. Arrival.
Fall of Da Nang, The.
Finding the Way Back.
Med Building.
Sound of Guns, The.
McClintock, M. Hamburger Hill.
McClure, M. Song: "Platinum fur and brass revolver shine."
McDonald, W. Caliban in Blue.
Children of Saigon, The.
Christmas Bells, Saigon.
Faraway Places.
For Harper, Killed in Action.
For Kelly, Missing in Action.
Hauling Over Wolf Creek Pass in Winter.

Interview with a Guy Named Fawkes, U.S. Army.
Last Still Days in a Bunker, The.
Rocket Attack.
Veteran.
McGrath, T. Reading the Names of the Vietnam War Dead.
Merwin, W. Asians Dying, The.
Mezey. How Much Longer?
Mishler. Ceremony.
Mitchell, A. To Whom It May Concern.
Moore, J. For You.
Moore, L. Winter 1967.
Mura. Huy Nguyen: Brothers, Drowning Cries.
Natives, The.
Nam Xuyên. Bamboo hedgerow cut a dark-green swath, The.
Nguyễn Chí Thiện. Party holds you down and you lie still, The.
This land's no joy.
Nguyễn Đình Chiểu. Blind Poet Looks at the World Outside, A.
Fisherman Speaks His Mind, A.
Fleeing From Bandits.
Waiting for the East Wind.
Nguyễn Duy Nhuệ. Bamboos of Vietnam.
Nguyễn Khuyến. At an Exposition.
Comedian Gets a Curtain Lecture, The.
On Hearing the Rail Cry.
To a Discarded Fan.
To a Statue.
Nguyễn Tất Nhiên. Folk Songs For Today.
Nguyễn Trãi. Among the great, no smooth and open world.
Womb's own flesh and bone—strong brotherhood, A.
Nguyễn Ý Thuần. Homecoming.
Nhật Tiến. Two Eyes.
Nhu'o'ng Tổng. Sense of History, A.
Notley. White Phosphorus.
Oldham, P. Noon.
War Stories.
Oppenheimer, J. Poem in Defense of Children.
Ormsby, F. Home.
Osaki. Amnesiac.
Paley, G. Women in Vietnam, The.
Paquet. Graves Registration.
It Is Monsoon at Last.
Mourning the Death, by Hemorrhage, of a Child from Honai.
Phạm Hổ. Sea, The.
Phan Bội Châu. Alarm Clock, The.
Mourning Nguyễn Thái Học and Nguyễn Thị Giang.
My Shadow and I.
To a Cuckoo.
Phan chu Trinh. Game of Chess, A.
Impromptu.
Opera Actors.
Phan Trọng Quảng. Independence Day.
Ricksha Man's Impromptu, A.
Phan Văn Hy. Ricksha man does quite a simple job, The.
Phan Văn Trị. Mosquito, you are blessed with all nice things!
Opera Actors.
Phổ Đú'c. Buffalo Boy On a Field of Corpses, The.
Pinsky. Serpent Knowledge.
Pratt, J. Words and Thoughts.
Receveur. August 17, 1970.
Redmond. Gods in Vietnam.
Rich, A. Newsreel.
Ritterbusch. Search and Destroy.
Rottman. APO 96225.
Ryan, R. From My Lai the Thunder Went West.
Schafer. Battle Lines.
Sexton. I'm dreaming the My Lai soldier again.
Shelton, R. Eden After Dark.
Stephens, M. After Asia.
Stewart, F. To a Friend.
T. P. Verses for the End of an Era.
Tạ Hữu Thiện. Looking For Her.
Tản Đà. Ship An-Nam, The.
Troth Between the Hill and the Stream, The.

Thanh Quan. Remembering the Past in the City of the Soaring Dragon.
Thomas, L. Wonders.
Tố Hữu. Elephants.
Trần Cao Vân. It's mere child's play to die—who'd care to try?
Trần Dạ Tù'. Gifts as Tokens of Love.
Trần Huiên Ân. Old Vow, The.
Tran Minh-tong (King). Bạch-đằng River, The.
Farewell to two envoys from the Yüan court.
Trần Mộng Tú. New Year's Wish for a Little Refugee, A.
Trần Tế Xu'o'ng. New-Style Examinations.
No, Thank You!
What earthly use are these Confucian graphs?
Trần Tuấn Khải. Our Land, Our Home.
Tremblay, B. Home Front.
Mayday.
Trinh Tiên. Woman Writes to Her Daughter Who's Studying Overseas, A.
Tru'o'ng Anh Thụy. First Day of School, The.
Unknown. Fourteenth of July, The.
Lake of the Returned Sword, The.
Viên Linh. Cold season—birds all head for warmer climes.
Virgilio. Viet Nam Monument.
Weber, R. Concise History of the Vietnam War: 1965–1968, A.
Webster, E. San Joaquin Valley Poems: 1969.
Weigl. Ambassador, The.
Amnesia.
Anna Grasa.
Burning Shit at An Khe.
Girl at the Chu Lai Laundry.
Her Life Runs Like a Red Silk Flag.
Him, on the Bicycle.
Last Lie, The.
Mines.
Monkey.
Sailing to Bien Hoa.
Song for the Lost Private.
Song of Napalm.
Surrounding Blues on the Way Down.
Temple Near Quang Tri, Not on the Map.
Way of Tet, The.
Whalen. Regalia in Immediate Demand!
Wong, N. Relining Shelves.
Woodard. Tower.
Xuân Thủy. You Cannot Lock Up the Mind.
Yên Ba. Twenty-Eight Lines for My Wife.
Yên Thao. My Home.
Yoshimi. Tanka: "White jet clouds."
Young Bear. Wadasa Nakamoon, Vietnam Memorial.

Vietnam War. *See* **Vietnam; War**

Vikings
Feirstein. Rune-Maker, The.
Kipling, R. Dane-Geld.
Longfellow, H. Skeleton in Armor [*or* Armour], The.
Unknown. Battle of Maldon, The.
Viking Terror, The.
Vikings, The ("Bitter the wind tonight").

Village Idiots
Kapilar. What She Said to Her Girl Friend, after a Tryst at Night (Which Turned Out to Be a Fiasco).

Villages
Blaga. Soul of the Village, The.
Blandiana. From a Village.
Cho, C. At Toriwon.
Cibulka. Kremenez.
Crabbe. Letter I.
Das, M. Horses.
Dove, R. Sightseeing.
Eisenhuth. Night in the Village.
Goldsmith, O. Deserted Village, The.
Village, The ("Sweet was the sound, when oft at evening's close").
Hood, T. Our Village—by a Villager.
Huchel. Melpomene.
Hurdis. Village Fair, The.
Jacobsen, R. Express train 1256 races alongside hidden, remote villages. House.
Kanemori. In the mountain village.
Kim, K. Home.

Longfellow, H. From Evangeline.
  Golden Mile-Stone, The.
  Ropewalk, The.
  Tale of Acadie, A.
  Village Blacksmith, The.
Lu Yu. Evening in the Village.
Machado Ruiz. Summer Night.
Masaoka Shiki. Tanka: "Peacefully."
Mattawa. Watermelon Tales.
Minamoto no Morotada. In the mountain village.
Muneyuki. I can feel the loneliness.
Noin. Spring twilight.
Nowak, T. Psalm of the Field.
Ono no Komachi. Cicadas sing, The.
Ozog. Village for a Wedding.
Pagis. Needless Return.
Patchen. Village Tudda, The.
Peterson, R. Midwest Town.
Po Chü-i. Chu Ch'ên Village.
  Stopping the Night at Jung-yang.
  Village Night.
Raworth. My Face Is My Own, I Thought.
Sakanoe No Korenori. In the dawn.
Smith, I. Listen, I have flown through darkness towards joy.
Somervile. On the Village Green.
Southerland. Two Fishing Villages.
T'ao Ch'ien. Returning to My Home in the Country ("Out here in the fields, few social affairs").
Toshinari. Twilight.
Vayilanrevan. What She Said ("In the tiny village").
Yau. Radiant Silhouette V.

See also **Cities; Towns**
Villanelle (form)
Bishop, E. One Art.
Collins, M. Story We Know, The.
Davidson, J. Unknown, The.
Dowson. Villanelle of Marguerites.
  Villanelle of Sunset.
Empson. Missing Dates.
  Villanelle.
Hugo, R. Freaks at Spurgin Road Field, The.
Humphries, R. Runes for an Old Believer.
Klappert. Ellie Mae Leaves in a Hurry.
Lehman. Amnesia.
Levertov. Obsessions.
Pinsky. Want Bone, The.
Yau. Chinese Villanelle.

See also **Villanelle in Title and First Line Index**
Villon, François, the Virgin
MacDonagh, D. Ballade which Villon Made.
Okudzhava. François Villon.
Swinburne. Ballad of François Villon, A.

Vilna, Poland
Glick. We Survive!
Sutskever. Cartload of Shoes, A.
  Like Groping Fingers.
  Secret Town, The.

Vinci, Leonardo da. *See* **Leonardo da Vinci**
Vines
Chiyojo. From the mind.
Unknown. Old *Chüeh-chü.*

Violence
Acholonu. Other Forms of Slaughter.
Armitage, S. Poem.
Atwood. You fit into me.
Avidan. Some Futureplans.
Ba. Justice is Done.
Balaban. April 30, 1975.
Baraka. Poem Some People Will Have to Understand, A.
Barrax. King: April 4, 1968.
Beaver. Drummer, The.
Berry, J. New Speaker.
Booth, P. Game.
Boyle, K. Poem for February First 1975, A.
Breckenridge. Unlocking the Doors.
Brutus. Robben Island Sequence.
Bukowski. Me against the world.
Butler, S. Arms and the Man.
Cady. Starting 1973: What to Do Now that Peace Has Been Announced.
Carruth, H. Mountain, The.

Cassian. Like Gulliver pulling a hundred ships.
Chipasula. Because the Wind Remembers.
  Dusk.
  Talking of Sharp Things.
Coleman, W. Brute Strength.
Connolly, C. Something is going to go, baby.
Crane, S. From The Black Riders and Other Lines.
Daniels, J. Day of the Two Bodies.
Dao. Résumé.
Derricotte. Poem for My Father.
Dipoko. Pain.
Doyle, S. Some Girls.
Drummond, W. Content and Resolute.
Espada. Waiting for the Cops.
Feirstein. Rune-Maker, The.
Fumi Saito. Turbid current.
Glazkov. Bast shoe idly on the road, A.
Grandmaster Flash *and* the Furious Five. Message, The.
Gregg. Night Music.
Gunn, T. Mirror for Poets, A.
Hacker, M. Sonnet for Iva.
Hayden, R. &[;American Journal&];.
  Locus.
Hecht, A. Third Avenue in Sunlight.
Hewitt, J. Postscript, 1984.
Hongo. Legend, The.
Howe, F. What We Learned.
Hudgins. Around the campfire we sang hymns.
Hughes, L. Bad Man.
  Third Degree.
Hull, L. Fiat Lux.
Jeffers, R. Bloody Sire, The.
Joans. .38, The.
Jones, P. Day of the Dead.
Jordan, J. Female and the Silence of a Man, The.
  I Must Become a Menace to My Enemies.
Joseph, L. Sand Nigger.
Kasischke. Woman Kills Sweetheart with Bowling Ball.
Kaufman, B. Geneology.
Kay, J. Dressing Up.
Kharms. Beginning of a Beautiful Day (A Symphony), The.
Komunyakaa. My Father's Love Letters [*or* Loveletters].
Levertov. Triple Feature.
Lewis, L. Bridget.
Lilley. Sewing Lesson, The.
Lorde. For the Record.
Mapanje. On Being Asked to Write a Poem for 1979.
Mayer, B. Sonnet: Kamikaze: "Dawn and night of fighting, lovers like actual wars."
McCarriston. Castle in Lynn, A.
  Hotel Nights with My Mother.
  To Judge Faolain, Dead Long Enough: A Summons.
McKay, C. To the White Fiends.
Merwin, W. Grandfather in the Old Men's Home.
Miliauskaite. Temporary City.
Monro. Street Fight.
Montagu, L. Epitaph: "Here lies John Hughes and Sarah Drew."
Moore, H. First Time: 1950.
Muske. Field Trip.
Nash, O. Lady from near Rising Sun, A.
Nathan, L. Body Count.
Newcastle, M. Some with sharp swords, to tell O most accursed!
Olds, S. Rites of Passage.
  That Year.
Olson, C. Anecdotes of the Late War.
Oppenheimer, J. Poem in Defense of Children.
Ortleb. Militerotics.
Parker, M. Whither away good neighbour.
Parra, N. Tablets, The.
Peacock, M. Say You Love Me.
  Those Paperweights with Snow Inside.
Pratt, M. Waulking Song: Two.
Redmond. Love Necessitates.

Rich, A. 5:30 A.M.
  Your small hands, precisely equal to my own.
Rodgers, C. Slave Ritual.
Rukeyser, M. This Morning.
Shapiro, K. Fly, The.
Shinder. Prayer.
Sholl. Outside the Depot.
Simon, L. Hattie Went to Market.
Stanford, A. Beating, The.
Swirszczynska. He Was Lucky.
Synge. Danny.
Tekkan. Tanka: "Their father."
Thorpe, A. Against the bolts and welder's bloom of rhetoric.
Unknown. Be punctual then to know.
  Cats of Kilkenny, The.
  Get Up and Bar the Door.
  I had a little pony.
  Lion and the unicorn, The.
  Little cock sparrow sat on a tree, A.
  Railroad Bill, Railroad Bill.
  Stackolee.
Vallejo. Black Riders, The.
Voloshin. In the Bottomless Pit.
  Red Guard.
Voznesensky. Someone is beating a woman.
Walcott. Blues.
Walker, M. Poppa Chicken.
Weaver, M. Beginnings.
  Missing Patriarch, The.
Weigl. Last Lie, The.
  One, The.
Whalen. International Date Line, Monday/ Monday 27:XI:67.
Wickham. Sick Assailant, The.
Wilbur. Tywater.
Williams, W. Mezzo Forte.
Wojahn. Homage to Ryszard Kapuściński.
Yamada. Club, The.
Zenmaro. New York.

Violets
Akahito. When I went out.
Bryant, W. Yellow Violet, The.
Doolittle, H. Sea Violet.
Dunbar-Nelson. Sonnet: "I had no thought of violets of late."
Goethe. Violet in the deepest green, A.
Herrick. How Violets Came Blue.
  Meditation for His Mistress[e], A.
  To Violets.
Moultrie. Violets.
Ropes. Violets.
Rumi. What the Flowers Said.
Shelley, P. On a Faded Violet.
Stanley, T. On a Violet in Her Breast.
Symons, A. Violet.
Taylor, J. Violet, The.
Unknown. Violets.
Young, V. Violets.

Violins
Annensky. Violin Bow and Strings.
Ford, C. Bad Habit, The.
Plumly. Out-of-the-Body Travel.
Rilke. Everything that touches us, me and you.
Welch, M. Touch of the Master's Hand, The.

Virgil [*or*** Vergil]**
Creeley. Heroes.
Tennyson, A. Poets and Their Bibliographies.
  To Virgil [*or* Vergil].

Virgin Islands
Brinnin. Skin Diving in the Virgins.
Walcott. Virgins, The.

Virgin Mary. *See* **Mary, the Virgin**
Virginia (state)
Bland, J. Carry me back to old Virginny.
Brown, S. Virginia Portrait.
Drayton. To the Virginian Voyage.
Eady. Sherbet.
Eliot, T. Virginia.
Frost, R. Gift Outright, The.
Merwin, W. Low Fields and Light.
Randall, J. To William Wordsworth from Virginia.
Smith, D. On a Field Trip at Fredericksburg.
Stone, R. Pokeberries.

Whitman, W.　As toilsome I wander'd Virginia's woods.
Whittier.　Farewell, The: "Gone, gone,—sold and gone."

Virginity and Virgins
Armstrong, J.　Advice to Lovers.
Asclepiades.　What are you saving it for?
Barker, J.　Virgin Life, A.
Baudelaire.　Femmes Damnées.
Beaumont, J.　Whiteness, or Chastity.
Blunt, W.　As To His Choice of Her.
Carew, T.　Maria Wentworth.
Cassian.　Blood, The.
Catullus.　Carmen 61 ("Guardian of Helicon, Urania's son").
Cockburn, C.　Caution, The.
Cowley, A.　Dialogue after Enjoyment.
Honour.
Cummings, E.　She being Brand.
Donne.　Flea, The.
Dryden, J.　Song: "SYLVIA the fair, in the bloom of fifteen."
Egerton, S.　Repulse to Alcander, The.
"Ephelia."　Maidenhead.
Ewart.　To the Virgins, to Make the Most of Time.
Gergely.　Magdalene.
Goldsmith, O.　Song: "When lovely woman stoops to folly."
Goodison.　Wedding in Hanover.
Greene, C.　Something Old, Something New.
Herrick.　Dirge of Jephthah's Daughter, The.
To a Bed of Tulips.
To Anthea ("Let's call for Hymen if agreed thou art").
To Violets.
To Virgins.
To [the] Virgins, to Make Much of Time.
Why Flowers Change Color.
Horace.　Ode.
Hroswitha von Gandersheim.　In Praise of Virginity.
Jackson, L.　Virgin, The.
Jamal, M.　Deflowering.
Justice, D.　In Bertram's Garden.
Killigrew, A.　On a Picture Painted by Herself[, Representing Two Nimphs of Diana's].
Laforgue.　For the Book of Love.
Lifshin.　Fitzi in the Yearbook.
Lima, J.　Poem of any Virgin.
Lluellyn.　Epithalamium: To Mistress M. A.
Lovelace, R.　To Lucasta.
"MacDiarmid."　O wha's the bride that carries the bunch.
Middleton, T.　Changeling, The.
Milton.　Chastity ("I Mean That Too, But Yet a Hidden Strength").
Montagu, L.　Lover, The; a Ballad.
Nobuyuki.　Ashtray (two poems).
Olds, S.　For My Daughter.
Paraske.　My Little Love Lies on the Ground.
Philips, K.　Answer to Another Persuading a Lady to Marriage, An.
Ping.　Of Flesh and Spirit.
Prior.　True Maid, A.
Randolph, T.　On a Maid of Honour Seen by a Scholar in Somerset Garden.
Ransom, J.　Her Eyes.
Rutter, J.　Epithalamium: "Hymen, god of marriage bed."
Sackville-West.　Absence.
Shapiro, K.　First Time, The.
Sikelianos.　Village Wedding, The.
Smart, C.　Song: "Where shall Celia fly for shelter."
Symons, A.　I. Hérodiade.
Taylor, J.　Virgo, August.
Thomas, D.　On the Marriage of a Virgin.
Unknown.　Broomfield Hill, The.
Epitaph of a Girl.
LIKE to a ring without a finger.
Twa Magicians, The.
Whistle, Daughter, Whistle.
Virgil.　How hard a fate enthrals the wretched maid.

Whitney, I.　Ye virgins that from Cupid's tents.

Virtue
Aldrich, T.　Fannie has the sweetest foot.
Armour.　Good sportsmanship we hail, we sing.
Behn, A.　Angellica's Lament.
Browne, W.　Shall I tell you whom I love?
Byron, G.　Sketch from Private Life, A.
Campion, T.　Man of life upright, The.
Carew, T.　Complement, The.
Divine Mistress, A.
Ingrateful[l] Beauty Threatened.
Carter, E.　Ode to Wisdom.
Cavalcanti.　Sonnet: A Rapture Concerning His Lady.
Chaucer.　Complaint unto Pity, The.
Lak of Stedfastnesse.
Constable, H.　Of his Mistress, upon Occasion of her Walking in a Garden.
Daniel, S.　To The Lady Lucie, Countesse of Bedford.
Donne.　Undertaking, The.
Dowriche.　So him at first De Nance commanded was to kill;.
Drayton.　To My Noble Friend Master William Browne: Of the Evil Time.
Egerton, S.　Repulse to Alcander, The.
Goldsmith, O.　Song: "When lovely woman stoops to folly."
Graves, R.　Young Cordwainer, The.
Herbert, G.　Charms and Knots.
Virtue [or Vertue].
Herrick.　King and No King, A.
Hesiod.　When first Both Gods and Men had one Times Birth.
Hopkins, G.　Of virtues I most warmly bless.
Horace.　Conclusion. After the Manner of Horace, ad librum suum, The.
Hunt, L.　Abou Ben Adhem (may his tribe increase!).
Jonson, B.　Elegy, An: "Though beauty be the mark of praise."
Epitaph on Elizabeth, L. H.
Epode: "Not to know vice at all, and keep[e] true state."
Ode. To Sir William Sydney, on His Birthday.
To Sir Henry Cary.
Landor, W.　Rose Aylmer.
Lanier.　To you I dedicate this work of grace.
Locke, M.　Sonnet: "'Tis dead of night; storms rend the troubled air."
Lucretius.　Felicitie of a mind imbracing vertue, that beholdeth the wretched desyres of the worlde, The.
Martial.　In Ponticum.
Moore, M.　Blessed Is the Man.
To a Snail.
Ovid.　If in this Town an unflusht Puny be.
Pembroke, M.　To the Thrice-Sacred Queen Elizabeth.
Puttenham.　Her Majestie resembled to the crowned piller. Ye must read upward.
Rowe, E.　To Celinda.
Shakespeare, W.　When I would pray and think, I think and pray.
Shirley, J.　Would you know what's soft? I dare.
Sidney, P.　Sonnet 25: "Wisest scholar of the wight most wise, The."
Sonnet 31: "With how sad steps, O Moon, thou climb'st the skies!"
Sonnet 52: "Strife is grown between Virtue and Love, A."
Sonnet 71: "Who will in fairest book of Nature know."
Simonides.　There is one story.
Smith, S.　Exeat.
Sophocles.　Colonus' Praise.
Spenser.　Sonnet 79: "Men call you fair [or fayre], and you do[e] credit it."
Taylor, H.　Virtue alone can never die. but lives to.
Thoreau.　Rumors from an Aeolian Harp.
Ts'ao Chih.　Rhyme-Prose on the Goddess of the Lo.
Unknown.　Perle, pleasanter to prynces paye.

Thus Passeth.
Under this plaque I lie, the famous woman.
Uticensis.　What Men in private whisper, never mind.
Wotton, S.　Upon the Sudden Restraint of the Earl[e] of Somerset, Then Falling from Favor [or Favour].
Wyatt, T.　Myn owne John poyntz sins ye delight to know.

Vishnu
Bhavani.　Avatars.
Kirantaiyar.　Hymn to Tirumāl (Viṣṇu).
Mirabai.　All I Was Doing Was Breathing.
It's True I Went to the Market.
Love has stained my body.
O friends, I am mad.
O my friends.
Why Mira Can't Go Back to Her Old House.

Vision
Bond, E.　How We See.
Browning, E.　Poet hath the child's sight in his breast, The.
Brush.　Again.
Carew, T.　On Sight of a Gentlewoman's Face in the Water.
Ceravolo.　Geological Hymn.
Clifton, L.　11/10 Again.
Crane, H.　Wine Menagerie, The.
Crosby, H.　Vision.
Dickinson, E.　Mine—by the Right of the White Election!
Eberhart, R.　In a hard intellectual light / I will kill all delight.
Vision.
Edson, R.　Optical Prodigal, The.
Fincke.　Era of the Vari-Vue, The.
Frost, R.　Neither Out Far Nor In Deep.
Gascoyne.　Cubical Domes, The.
End Is Near the Beginning, The.
Salvador Dali.
Gunn, T.　Unsettled Motorcyclist's Vision of His Death, The.
Hall, D.　Apples.
Hecht, A.　Hill, A.
Hirsch, E.　Man on a Fire Escape.
Jackson, L.　Grandpa dropped his glasses once.
Jarrell.　Orient Express, The.
Kendrick, D.　Note to the Ophthalmologist.
Lauterbach.　Mimetic.
Lawrence, D.　Go deeper than love, for the soul has greater depths.
Lowell, A.　Preparation.
Macklin.　Nearsighted, The.
Merkel, B.　Owls.
Merrill, J.　Octopus, The.
Remora.
Nemerov.　I Only Am Escaped Alone to Tell Thee.
Palmer, M.　Project of Linear Inquiry, The.
Rein.　Glimpsed through a Lens.
Rossetti, C.　Later Life: A Double Sonnet of Sonnets.
Who has seen the wind? / Neither I nor you.
Sachs, N.　In the evening your vision widens.
Saxe, J.　Blind Men and the Elephant, The.
Shapiro, K.　Dome of Sunday, The [or A].
Sillitoe.　Optics.
Sorrentino.　Handbook of Versification.
Stanton, M.　Ballad of the Magic Glasses.
Stern, G.　Coleman Valley Road.
Tomlinson, C.　Through Binoculars.
Towle.　Painting the Eaves.
Van Duyn.　Vision Test, The.
Walcott.　Hotel Normandie Pool, The.
Wroth.　Sonnet 24.

Visiting and Visitors
"Akhmatova."　Guest, The.
Ammons.　Visit.
Becker, C.　Door-Bell, The.
Beerbohm, M.　Chorus of a Song That Might Have Been Written by Albert Chevalier.
Bishop, E.　Faustina, or Rock Roses.
Brown, B.　Jonathan Bing.
Chiao-jan.　Looking for Lu Hung-chien but Failing To Find Him.
Child, L.　Thanksgiving Day.
De la Mare.　Some One.

Dickinson, E. Infinite a sudden Guest, The.
Frost, R. Time to Talk, A.
Garioch. Heard in the Cougate.
Herrick. Night-Piece, to Julia, The.
Panegyric to Sir Lewis Pemberton, A.
Hsieh Ling-yün. Replying to a Poem from My Cousin Hui-lien.
Leapor. Visit, The.
Liu Ch'ang-ch'ing. Rejoicing That the Zen Master Pao Has Arrived from Dragon Mountain.
Lu Yu. Trip to Mountain West Village, A.
Metcalfe. Visit the Sick.
Mother Goose. Nut Tree, A.
Murry, A. Tête à Tête; or, Fashionable Pair: an Eclogue, The.
O'Hara, F. Poem: "Eager note on my door said 'Call me', The."
Pope, A. *et al.* On Riding to See Dean Swift in the Mist of the Morning.
Rossetti, C. Echo.
Enrica, 1865.
Shin, K. Visiting a Rural Town.
Snodgrass, W. Vuillard: "The Mother and Sister of the Artist."
Wen I-to. Last Day, The.

Vivaldi, Antonio
Schwartz, D. Vivaldi.

Vocations. See **Occupations**

Vogler, Georg Joseph
Browning, R. Abt Vogler.

Voices
Baudelaire. Cat, The.
Blake, W. London ("I wander through [*or* thro'] each chartered [*or* charter'd] street").
Bogan, L. Song for the Last Act.
Broughton, T. Lyric.
Browning, R. Meeting At Night.
Chōkū. Tanka: "New Year's temple bells."
Clare, J. Secret, The.
Dauenhauer. Voices.
Finch, A. Dickinson.
Hall, D. White Apples.
Herrick. Againe.
Upon Her Voice.
Upon Julia's Voice.
Johnson, J. Lift every [*or* ev'ry] voice and sing.
Kinnell. Lastness.
Komunyakaa. Twilight Seduction.
Levi, P. Voices mute for ever, or since yesterday, or just stilled;.
Lorde. Echoes.
Lovelace, R. To a Lady That Desired Me I Would Bear My Part with Her in a Song.
Meynell, A. To the Beloved.
Milosz, C. On Angels.
Morley, H. Epidaurus: / you loved it.
Naden. Sister of Mercy, The.
Orban, O. That strength, which behind the tongue.
Samio. Tanka: "Loud voice, A."
Sanchez, S. Haiku: "Your voice unwrapping."
Schubert, D. Successful Summer, A.
Sergeant. Man Meeting Himself.
Shelley, P. To————: "Music, when soft voices die."
Smith, S. Singing Cat, The.
Sobin, G. Violet City: Aspects of the Transitive.
What the music.
Southerland. Recitation.
Stephen, J. Sonnet, A: "Two voices are there: one is of the deep."
Tennyson, A. Break, break, break.
Unknown. Tone of Voice, The.
Young Girl in the Choir, The.
Warren, R. What Voice at Moth-Hour did I hear calling.
Wier. Barely There.
Wordsworth, W. Thought[s] of a Briton on the Subjugation of Switzerland.
Wright, J. For the Marsh's Birthday.
Speak.
To the Poets in New York.
Yau. Angel Atrapado VIII.
Yeats. Everlasting Voices, The.

Yoshimi. White sky, The.
Yukitsuna. Tanka: "Since puberty."

See also **Screams; Speech; Talk**

Volcanoes
Akhmadulina. Volcanoes.
Bishop, E. Crusoe in England.
Daniel, J. To Mt. St. Helens.
Day Lewis. Poem for an Anniversary.
Dickinson, E. I have never seen volcanoes.
Volcanoes be in Sicily.
Fumi Saito. Tanka: "Cluster, A."
Grainger, J. Then earthquakes, nature's agonizing pangs.
Hemans. Image in Lava, The.
Hongo. Eruption: Pu'u Ō'ō.
Hongo Store 29 Miles Volcano Hilo, Hawaii, The.
Lear, E. Limerick: "There was an old person of Gretna."
Lowry, M. Volcano is dark and suddenly thunder, The.
Melville, H. Apparition, The.
Ray, H. Listening Nydia.
Rich, A. Every peak is a crater. This is the law of volcanoes.
Rose. Loo-wit.
Salkey. Soufrière.
Snyder, G. Burning Island.
Turner, W. Romance.
Van Sertima. Volcano.
Walcott. Volcano.

Voltaire, François Marie Arouet de
Auden. Voltaire at Ferney.
Blake, W. Mock on, Mock on Voltaire, Rousseau.

Voodoo
Depestre. Prelude.
Durand, O. Francie-the-Possessed.
Laleau. Voodoo.
Pressoir. Country Graveyard.
Waniek. Women's Locker Room.

Voting and Voters
Chudleigh. To the Ladies.
Cornish, S. Fannie / lou / hamer / never / heard / of.
Dickinson, E. Mine—by the Right of the White Election!
Graves, R. Whole Love.
Harper, F. Deliverance.
Lindsay, V. Why I Voted the Socialist Ticket.
Moorer. Negro Ballot, The.
Nathan, L. Election, The.
Pierpont, J. Ballot, The.
Roberson. Poll.
Unknown. Vote for Lunn.

See also **Woman Suffrage**

Vowels
Swift, J. E I O U, A.

Voyages
Brown, G. Five Voyages of Arnor, The.
Carruth, H. Death, The.
Crane, H. Above the fresh ruffles of the surf.
De la Mare. Galliass, The.
Drayton. To the Virginian Voyage.
Emerson, R. Thine eyes still shined for me, though far.
Ferry. Cythera.
Embarkation for Cythera, The.
Garnet. Bound on a voyage of awful length.
Gould, A. Ice.
Herrick. His Sailing from Julia.
Plaudite, or End of Life, The.
Ho Sun. At Parting.
Jackson, H. My Lighthouses.
Larkin, P. North Ship, The.
Merwin, W. Voyage to Labrador.
Murphy, R. Pat Cloherty's Version of *The Maisie.*
Pound, E. Canto 1.
Sexton. Crossing the Atlantic.
Spender, S. Marston, dropping it in the grate, broke his pipe.
Stevenson, R. Christmas at Sea.
T'ao Ch'ien. On Being Assigned as Military Adviser to the Garrison Army.
Tennyson, A. Voyage, The.

Unknown. Seafarer, The.
St. Andrew's Voyage to Mermedonia.
Walcott. In idle August, while the sea soft.
Whittier. Godspeed.
Wilner, E. Emigration.
Yin Shih. Parting from the Courtier Sung.

Voyeurism and Voyeurs
Coleridge, S. Picture; or, The Lover's Resolution, The.
Dove, R. Small Town.
Heath, R. Seeing Her Dancing.
"Hyde." Close under here, I watched two lovers once.
Lawrence, D. Gloire de Dijon.
Martial. Epigram 34: "Lesbia, why are your amours."
Ristovic. Outhouse.
Shapiro, K. Dome of Sunday, The [*or* A].
Waller, E. Song: "Go[e], lovely rose[—ous sweet and fair]."
Whitman, W. Twenty-eight young men bathe by the shore.

Vuillard, Edouard
Snodgrass, W. Vuillard: "The Mother and Sister of the Artist."

Vulcan
Auden. Shield of Achilles, The.
Herrick. To Vulcan.
Jonson, B. Execration upon Vulcan, An.
Russell, T. Sonnet: Suppos'd to Be Written at Lemnos.

Vulnerability
Dacey, P. Porno Love.
"Eliot." Felix Holt: The Radical.
Koertge. Thing Is to Not Let Go of the Vine, The.
Peacock, M. How I Come to You.
Piercy. Rape Poem.
Ransom, J. Winter Remembered.
Rich, A. Storm Warnings.
Shapiro, K. First Time, The.
Wright, C. Dead are a cadmium blue, The.
Zealand. Primitives Knew How Defenseless, The.

Vultures
Atwood. Vultures.
Belloc. Vulture eats between his meals, The.
Blok. Vulture, The.
Bottoms. Under the Vulture-Tree.
Chōkū. Vultures—in the midst of war.
Diop, D. Vultures, The.
Fumiko. Tanka: "Since that evening."
Jeffers, R. Vulture.
Little, G. Fallen horse.
Muir, E. Mythical Journey, The.
Page, G. Elegist, The.
Rexroth, K. Vulture.
Wilbur. Still, citizen sparrow, this vulture which you call.
Yau. We Are All Vultures.

See also **Buzzards**

W

Wagner, Richard
Brooke, R. Wagner.
Duncan, R. Structure of Rime XVIII.
Hugo, R. December 24 and George McBride Is Dead.
Lanier, S. To Richard Wagner.
Levy, N. Tannhauser.

Wagon Trains
Ferril. Empire Sofa, The.
Guest, B. Santa Fe Trail.
Miller, J. Pilgrims of the Plains.

Wagtails
Clare, J. Little trotty wagtail [he went in the rain].

Wailing Wall, The
Mathews, A. At the Wailing Wall.

Waiters and Waitresses
Amichai. Instructions for the Waitress.
Clarke, M. Wail of the Waiter, The.
Doubiago. From the Waitress Papers.

Dugan, A. To a Red-headed Do-good Waitress.
Dunn, S. Truck Stop: Minnesota.
Eady. Sherbet.
Grahn. Ella, in a Square Apron, Along Highway 80.
McCord, D. Epitaph on a Waiter.
Waring, B. Tip, The.
Zealand. Passion at the Chat 'n Chew Diner.

Waiting Rooms
Bishop, E. In the Waiting Room.
Fulton, R. Waiting-Room, The.
Nemerov. Waiting Rooms.
Sellers, B. In the Counselor's Waiting Room.

Wakes
Unknown. Finnegan's Wake.
Willie's Lyke Wake.

Waking
Andal. O sister of wealth.
Atwood. Up.
Baillie, J. Up! quit thy bower.
Bly, R. Awakening.
Poem in Three Parts.
Waking from Sleep.
Ch'ien Wen-Ti. Getting Up in Winter.
Coleridge, S. If I had but two little wings.
Cummings, E. Raise the shade.
Ded. At the end of a crazy-moon night.
To learn the scriptures is easy.
Donne. Good-Morrow, The.
Duncan, R. Song of the Borderguard, The.
Earley, J. One Thousand Nine Hundred and Sixty-Eight Winters.
"Field." Love rises up some days.
Gascoigne. Gascoigne's Good-Morrow.
Geda. Repentance: The Devil's Blossom.
Gunn, T. Apartment Cats.
Harasymowicz. Waking Up.
Ingelow. Winding-up Time.
Issa. Cat, The.
Keats. Bright star[, would I were stedfast as thou art—].
Kuo Mo-jo. Impressions of Shanghai.
Lawrence, D. Quite Forsaken.
Lee, L. Early in the Morning.
Levine, P. I Remember Clifford.
Lowell, R. Waking Early Sunday Morning.
Mạc Thiên Tích. Morning Bell at Tiêu Monastery, The.
Mackey, N. Phantom Light of All Our Day, The.
MacNeice. September has come and I wake.
Marichiko. Every morning.
Merwin, W. Rain Travel.
Meynell, A. Study, A.
Ni Tsan. Waking from a Nap.
Ojibway Oral Tradition. Calling-One's-Own.
Pagis. Plans.
Pinsky. First Early Mornings Together.
Po Chü-i. Dreaming that I went with Li and Yü to Visit Yüan Chên.
Getting Up Early on a Spring Morning.
My servant wakes me: 'Master, it is broad day'.
Rising Late, and Playing with A-ts'ui, Aged Two.
Roethke. Waking, The.
Shakespeare, W. Song: "Hark! hark! the lark at heaven's gate sings."
Shao Yung. Song on Being Too Lazy to Get Up.
Simic. Poem: "Every morning I forget how it is."
So Chong-Ju. Peony Afternoon.
Steele, T. Joseph.
Stevenson, R. Time to Rise.
Swirszczynska. When We Wake Up in the Morning.
Thaxter. Chanticleer.
Unknown. Aubade: "O, Lady, awake! The azure moon."
Cock-crow Song.
Cock Robin got up early.
Donkey, donkey, old and gray.
Early to bed and early to rise.
Evening Prayer, An.
Get up, get up, you lazy-head.

He Who Knows ("He who knows not and knows not [that he knows not]").
Whitman, W. Day when I rose at dawn from the bed of perfect health, refresh'd, The.
Wilbur. Love Calls Us to the Things of This World.
Williams, W. Spring and All.
Wyatt, T. Lover Showeth How He Is Forsaken of Such as He Sometime Enjoyed, The.

Walden Pond, Massachusetts
Channing. Walden.
Emerson, R. In my garden three ways meet.
Junkins. Walden in July.

Waldenses
Zimmer. Day Zimmer Lost Religion, The.

Wales
Boyce. Ballad of Morgan the Moon, The.
Clarke, G. Taid's Grave.
Ginsberg, A. Wales Visitation.
Graves, R. Welsh Incident.
Humphries, R. Dafydd ap Gwilym Resents the Winter.
For My Ancestors.
Philips, K. On the Welsh Language.
Stone, W. On the Welsh Marches.
Thomas, D. Author's Prologue.
Fern Hill.
When I was a boy.
Thomas, R. Ancients of the World, The.
Welsh History.
Welsh Landscape.
Thrale. Winter in Wales, A.
Turner, C. Artist on Penmaenmawr, The.
Vaughan-Thomas. Hiraeth in N.W.3.
Watkins, V. Peace in the Welsh Hills.
Williams, H. To Dr. Moore, in Anser to a Poetical Epistle Written by Him in Wales.
See also **Welsh, The**

Walking and Walkers
Akers. Night: Volcano, California.
Ammons. Corsons Inlet.
Apollinaire. Crayfish, The.
Auden. As I walked out one evening.
Barker, G. Section VI.
Beckett, S. Enueg I.
Berlin. Couple of Swells, A.
Bethune, L. Harlem Freeze Frame.
Blake, W. London ("I wander through [or thro'] each chartered [or charter'd] street").
Bontemps. "Close Your Eyes!"
Brown, L. Winter Sonnet.
Browning, R. Flower's Name, The.
Bryant, W. To A Waterfowl.
Buckley, C. Playing for Time.
Buson. Sound of a Rat, The.
Byron, G. She walks in Beauty like the night.
So we'll go no more a-roving.
Carver, R. Walk, A.
Cervantes. Colorado Blvd.
Chang Yü. In the Evening, Walking in the Western Fields.
Retreat of Sun Ching-hsiang, The.
Clare, J. To Mary: 'It Is the Evening Hour'.
Coleridge. Witch, The.
Cornish, S. Generations 2.
Crane, H. In Shadow.
Creeley. Place.
Somebody Died.
Dennis, J. Maltese Goat.
Edey *et al.* Trot Along, Pony.
Farjeon, E. Jenny White and Johnny Black.
Frost, R. Acquainted with the Night.
Meeting and Passing.
Gibson, M. Long Walks in the Afternoon.
Gillan. In memory we are walking.
Graham, W. Stepping Stones, The.
Graves, R. Legs, The.
Gurney, I. If I walked straight slap.
Hall, D. Second Stanza for Dr. Johnson, A.
Herford. There was a young lady of Twickenham.
Hollander, J. Effet de Neige.
One of Our Walks.
Howe, F. Torn Parts: the story.
Hsü Pen. Mountain of green trees and orioles everywhere!
Jordan, J. Poem About My Rights.

Kao Ch'i. Walk to the Eastern River Bank, A.
Katrovas. Sky.
Knight, E. Green Grass and Yellow Balloons.
Layton. Cold Green Element, The.
Levy, A. March Day in London, A.
To Vernon Lee.
Li K'ai-hsien. Sent to the Master Physician, "Almond Orchard" Shih.
MacCaig. Shore Road, The.
McKay, L. Night.
McKuen. Voyeur, The.
Meek. Walk Around the Lake, A.
Mezey. Confession, A.
Miller, V. How far is it to you by foot?
Nerval. Girl Cousin, The.
Nesbit, E. Vies Manquées.
Nezval. Trap Door.
O'Hussey. O'Hussey's Ode to the Maguire.
Osgood, F. Ellen Learning to Walk.
Ou-yang Hsiu. Song of "Hand-in-Hand", A.
Plath. Night Walk.
Plumpp. Poems are not places.
Po Chü-i. Illness.
Revell. Other the Wings, The.
Rilke. Gently gripped by the.
Sonnets to Orpheus, The.
Swan, The.
Robinson, A. Tuscan Olives.
Venetian Nocturne.
Rózewicz. I Build.
Sacchetti. Catch: On a Wet Day.
Samio. Tanka: "On a starry night."
Sanchez, S. To Anita.
Sarton. Prothalamion for an Autumn Wedding.
Schwartz, D. Heavy Bear, The.
Scott, W. Madge Wildfire Sings.
Sexton. Noon Walk on the Asylum Lawn.
Shelton, M. When Jesus walked upon the earth.
Smith, S. Bag-Snatching in Dublin.
Södergran. On Foot I Had to Walk Through the Solar Systems.
Stafford, W. Walking West.
Stevenson, R. In autumn when the woods are red.
Strand. Keeping Things Whole.
Su Tung-p'o. Rhyming with Tzu-yu's "Treading the Green."
Tao-chi. Trip to the Village of the River of White Sand, A.
Thomas, E. Sun used to shine while we two walked, The.
Unknown. Footprints made on the sands of.
One of the Awl Songs.
Walk Together Children.
Wakoski. Hummingbird Light.
Whitman, W. Dalliance of the Eagles, The.
Whittier. Forgiveness.
Williams, W. Poem: "As the cat / climbed over."
Wordsworth, W. Daffodils.
Stepping Westward.
Wright, C. Legend of Hell, The.
Wright, F. Joseph Come Back as the Dusk.
Wylie. Velvet Shoes.
Yang Chi. Walking in the Country outside T'ai-yüan on a Spring Day.
Yang Shih-ch'i. Forty *li* through Chü-yang Pass.
Yang Wan-li. Trip to Stone Man Peak, A.
Young, A. Ponce de León: A Morning Walk.
Yü Chi. Late in the Year K'uei-yu (1333), Staying at the Temple of the Upper Regions.
Little Landscape by Yen Wen-kuei, A.
Yüan Mei. Rough Ridge.
Zabolotsky. Walk, A.
Zukofsky, L. I walk in the old street.

Wall Street, New York City
Rukeyser, M. Paper Anniversary.
Yoshimi. Tanka: "Street, The."

Wallace, Sir William
Burns, R. Scots, wha hae wi' Wallace bled.
Unknown. Gude Wallace.

Wallflowers
Wergeland. Wall-Flower, The.

Walls
Bartsch. Still Life with Cleaning Lady.

Brodsky, J. Berlin Wall Tune, The.
Brooks, G. Chicago Picasso, The.
Cavafy. Walls.
Coleridge, M. Gone.
  Impromptu.
Colonna, V. I see in my mind, surrounding
  God.
Dev Sen. Yellow River, The.
Doolittle, H. From The Walls Do Not Fall.
Eigner. Wholes.
Frost, R. Mending Wall.
Fuentes. In This Place.
Fulton, R. Remembering Walls.
Garcia. Salmo: Para El.
Gouri. Jericho unknowing.
Herbert, Z. Wall, The.
Herlin. Warmth of the wind-break wall, The.
Ho Ching-ming. Ballad of the Government
  Granary Clerk.
Hsü Pen. In Harmony with Kao "The Second"
  Ch'i's Poem "On Hearing a P'i-p'a Played
  Next Door."
Ismail. Wall, The.
Kalász. Up against That Wall Everywhere.
Kees. Conversation in the Drawingroom, The.
Kendrick, D. We are the writing on the wall.
Kinzie. Ringing Words.
Kraujiete. In Chalk Rooms.
Le Bel. Boxing the Female.
Mistral, G. Wall.
Montale. To rest at noon, pale and absorbed.
Mori Ōgai. Tanka: "Without incident."
Palmer, M. Notes for Echo Lake 2.
Plumpp. Another mule kicking.
Po Chü-i. After Collecting the Autumn Taxes.
  Losing a Slave-Girl.
  Poem on the Wall, The.
Ralegh, W. My Body in the Walls Captived.
Robinson, A. Personality.
Simic. Wall, A.
Simko. Three Songs.
Spellman. Twist, The.
Spenser. For round about, the wals yclothed
  were.
Surrey. When Windsor Walls.
Swenson, M. Garden at St. John's, The.
Tennyson, A. Blow, Bugle, Blow.
  Flower in the crannied wall.
Tsaloumas. Old Friend.
Unknown. Bridge instead of a Wall, A.
  Eastern Wall stands high and long;, The.
  Wide Walls.
Valentine, J. Tell Me, What Is the Soul.
Warner, S. Port Bou.
Wen Cheng-ming. While It Was Raining.
Wen I-to. Last Day, The.
Wilbur. Caserta Garden.
Williams, W. On Gay Wallpaper.
See also **Fences**

Walnuts
Ovid. Nux (The Walnut Tree).

Walpole, Robert, 1st Earl of Orford
Swift, J. Character of Sir Robert Walpole,
  The.

Walruses
"Carroll." "Time has come," the Walrus, The.
  Walrus and the Carpenter, The.
Herford. Smile of the Walrus is wild and
  distraught, The.

Waltzes and Waltzing
Leland, C. Hans Breitmann's Party [*or* Barty].
Roethke. My Papa's Waltz.
Stevens, W. Sad Strains of a Gay Waltz.
Wilde, O. Harlot's House, The.
Wright, S. Out of the Wailing.

Wanderlust
"Akhmatova." One man follows a straight
  path.
Auden. Wanderer, The.
Baraka. Legacy.
Brown, S. Long Gone.
Di Prima. Ave.
Holloway, J. Ulysses.
Holub. Fairy Tale.
Hovey. Sea Gypsy, The.
Kipling, R. Sestina of the Tramp-Royal.
Masefield. Sea-Fever.

Ponsot. Among Women.
Riddell, E. Wakeful in the Township.
Smith, S. Lightly Bound.
  Wanderer, The.
Stickney, T. Age in Youth.
Tennyson, A. Ulysses.

Wang Wei
Berryman. Note to Wang Wei.
Meng Hao Jan. Parting from Wang Wei.

War
Ai. I Can't Get Started.
Alberti. Warlike Angels, The.
Aldington. Proem: "Sixty years after the fall
  of Troy."
Aldrich, T. Memory.
Amichai. Anniversaries of War.
  I have nothing to say about the war.
  My father was four years at their war.
Amis, K. A. E. H.
  Last War, The.
Anderson, M. Spitting in the Leaves.
Antipater of Sidon. Who hung these shields
  here still all shiny.
Antipater of Thessalonica. Where is your
  famous beauty.
Appleman, P. Peace with Honor.
Archilochus. I don't give a damn if some
  Thracian ape strut.
  That good shield I threw away.
Arnold, M. Dover Beach.
  Last Word, The.
Ashbery. Rivers and Mountains.
Auvaiyar. Chariot Wheel, A.
Awoonor. At the Gates.
  Song of War.
  Songs of Sorrow.
"B., H. d'A." No-Man's-Land.
Bachmann. Every Day.
Balaban. Dragonfish, The.
  For Mrs. Cam, Whose Name Means "Printed
  Silk."
  News Update.
  Than, Mau.
  Thoughts Before Dawn.
  Words for My Daughter.
Barbauld. On the Expected General Rising of
  the French Nation.
Barker, G. Song: "Now this bloody war is
  over."
  To My Mother.
Barks. Becoming Milton.
Barlow, J. Advice to a Raven in Russia
  [December, 1812].
Barry, J. Floating Petals.
  Green Hell, Green Death.
Barth, R. Insert, The.
  Letter from An Hoc (4), by a Seedbed.
  P.O.W.s.
  Postscript.
Bashlachov. Griboyedov's Waltz.
Bass, E. I Didn't Know.
Bayliss. Reported Missing.
Beers, E. All quiet along the Potomac tonight.
Begbie, J. I shouted for blood as I ran,
  brother.
Bekederemo. Casualties are not only those
  who are dead.
  Epilogue to Casualties.
Benét, S. 1935.
Bergman. A. Chronicler, The.
Berryman. Moon and the Night and the Men,
  The.
Bertolino. Frog Voices.
Betjeman. Invasion Exercise on the Poultry
  Farm.
Bible, *O.T.* David's Lament.
Bickerstaffe. What a charming thing's a battle!
Binyon. Unreturning Spring, The.
Bishop, J. In the Dordogne.
Blake, W. War Song [to Englishmen], A.
Blunden. Escape.
  1916 Seen from 1921.
  Preparations for Victory.
Bly, R. At a March against the Vietnam War.
  Counting Small-Boned Bodies.
  Driving through Minnesota during the Hanoi
  Bombings.

Teeth Mother Naked at Last, The.
To President bush at the Start of the Gulf
  War.
War and Silence.
Bobrowsky. Free Fire Zone.
Boker. Brave comrade, answer! When you
  joined the war.
Bond, F. 'After the war,' they used to say,
  and pictured.
Bowers, E. Stoic: for Laura von Courten, The.
Brecht, B. Friends, The.
  From a German War Primer.
  God of War, The.
  This Summer's Sky.
  War Has Been Given a Bad Name.
Breton, A. More than Suspect.
  War.
Brodsky, J. Elegy.
Brontë, E. Loud without the wind was roaring.
Brooke, R. Soldier, The.
Brooks, G. First fight. Then fiddle. Ply the
  slipping string.
  White Troops Had Their Orders but the
  Negroes Looked Like Men.
Brown, D. Eating the Forest.
  I Was Dancing Alone in Binh Dinh Province.
  Patrols.
  Returning Fire.
Brown, G. Press-Gang.
Brownstein. War.
Bruner. Midwinter.
Brush. Again.
Brutus. There was a time when the only
  worth.
Bryant, W. Battle-Field, The.
  Conjunction of Jupiter and Venus, The.
Buchanan, G. War-and-Peace.
Bùi Khải Nguyễn. Man Who Sleeps Out in
  the Fields, The.
Bunting. Vestiges.
Burns, R. Scots, wha hae wi' Wallace bled.
  Silver Tassie, The.
Butler, S. Arms and the Man.
Byron, G. By the Rivers of Babylon We Sat
  Down and Wept.
  Song of Saul before His Last Battle.
Campbell, D. Men in Green.
Campbell, T. Hohenlinden.
Campion, T. Raving warre, begot / In the
  thirstye sands.
Carruth, H. On Being Asked to Write a Poem
  Against the War in Vietnam.
  When howitzers began.
Carson, C. Cocktails.
  Hamlet.
  Mouth, The.
Carter, R. Vietnam Dream.
Causley. Armistice Day.
  Song of the Dying Gunner A.A.1.
Cervantes. Poem for the Young White Man
  Who Asked Me How I, An Intelligent, Well-
  Read Person Could Believe in the War
  Between Races.
Chao Meng-fu. To a Pyrotechnist.
Chaucer. Tale of Sir Thopas, The.
Chế Lan Viên. War Elephant, The.
Chin. Barbarians Are Coming, The.
Chipasula. Tramp.
Chōkū. Tanka: "Imagining."
  Vultures—in the midst of war.
Christopher. Terminus.
Clampitt. Amherst.
Claudian. For France.
Cleveland, J. How? "Providence", and yet a
  Scottish crew?
Cole, N. Saturn.
Coleman, H. Downed Black Pilot Learns How
  to Fly, A.
  In Ca Mau.
Comfort, A. Letter to an American Visitor.
Cornford, F. Grand Ballet.
Cortez. Rape.
Couzyn. World War II.
Cox, D. To My Mother—1916.
Crane, S. There Was a Crimson Clash of War.
  War Is Kind.
Crewe, R. Harrow and Flanders.

Cross, Jr. Gliding Baskets.
Crowe, W. In evil hour, and with unhallow'd voice.
Csoori. We were good, good and obedient.
Cummings, E. I sing of Olaf glad and big.
My sweet old etcetera.
Next to of course god america i.
Cunningham, A. Hame, Hame, Hame.
Currey. Burial Flags.
Unseen Fire.
Đng Trần Côn et al. Song of a Soldier's Wife, The.
Davidson, J. Battle.
War Song.
Dawe, G. Question of Covenants, A.
Day, J. North Sea.
Day Lewis. Where Are the War Poets?
De la Mare. Motley.
Deane, S. History Lessons.
Denning. Fire Support Burk.
Movie, The.
This Time.
Derwood. Elegy: "When in the mirror of a permanent tear."
Đỗ Tấn Xuân. Peace! Peace!
Đông Hồ. String of Pearls, The.
War.
Dorfman, A. I Just Missed the Bus and I'll Be Late for Work.
Douglas, K. Aristocrats.
Enfidaville.
Gallantry.
How to Kill.
Offensive, The.
Vergissmeinnicht.
Dove, R. Alfonzo Prepares to Go Over the Top.
Doyle, S. Some Girls.
Drainac. Classic Verses.
Drummond, W. Trojan Horse, The.
Drunina. So many times I've seen hand-to-hand combat.
Dryden, J. Song: "All, all of a piece throughout."
Dufault. Letter for Allhallows, A.
Dugan, A. On an East Wind from the Wars.
Dunbar-Nelson. I sit and sew—a useless task it seems.
Duncan, R. Fire, The.
Up Rising.
Duoduo. When the People Stand Up out of the Hard Cheese.
Eberhart, R. Fury of Aerial Bombardment, The.
Ehrenburg. January 1939.
"Reconnaissance in force"—just three brief words.
Retribution.
Sons of Our Sons, The.
Ehrenstein. Ares.
Ehrhart. Guerrilla War.
Invasion of Grenada, The.
Relative Thing, A.
Elliot, J. Flowers of the Forest, The.
Elytis. March toward the Front, The.
Empson. Just a Smack at Auden.
Engman. Mushroom Clouds.
Euripides. Against the wittie gifte of shotinge in a bowe.
I crossed sand-hills.
Evans, G. Eye Blade.
Revelation in the Mother Lode.
Fawcett, J. Feast of Blood, The.
Fenton, J. Cambodia.
Dead Soldiers.
German Requiem, A.
Wind.
Fiacc. Enemy Encounter.
Intimate Letter 1973.
Soldiers.
Flecker. War Song of the Saracens.
Floyd. Private First Class Brooks Morgenstein, U. S. M. C.
Foley, M. Ah no, ah no, they weren't all gross and slow.
Ford, F. What the Orderly Dog Saw.
Fort, C. Town Clock Burning, The.

Fosdick, H. Prince of Peace His Banner Spreads, The.
Francis, R. Blood stains how to remove from cotton.
Frank, F. Jewish Conscript, The.
Frankau. Gun Teams.
Headquarters.
Fraser, G. Christmas Letter Home.
Lament: "In a dismal air; a light of breaking summer."
Fuller, R. Autumn 1942.
During a Bombardmant by V-Weapons.
In Africa.
Spring 1942.
Galsworthy. Youth's Own.
García Lorca. Rundown Church (Ballad of the First World War).
Gascoyne. De Profundis.
Uncertain Battle, The.
Gibbons, S. Continuity.
Gibson, M. Wars.
Gibson, W. Breakfast.
Gifford, H. For Soldiers.
Gilbo'a. Kingdom of Silence.
Gloria. Milkfish.
Golding, L. Women at the Corners Stand, The.
Graham, H. Englishman's Home, The.
Graham, M. After the War; When Coltrane Only Wanted to Play Dance Tunes.
Grant, E. War Party.
Graves, R. Escape.
It's a Queer Time.
Recalling War.
Spoils.
Gray, T. Death of Hoel, The.
Triumphs of Owen, The.
Greene, C. Excuse, The.
Grenfell, J. Into Battle.
Grennan. Soul Music: The Derry Air.
Griffin, S. Song My.
Grimke, C. Gathering of the Grand Army, The.
Guest, B. Otranto.
Gunn, T. Last Man, The.
Guri. But We Shall Bloom.
Gurney, I. First Time In.
Silent One, The.
Strange Hells.
War Books.
Gwynn, R. Body Bags.
Hacker, M. Before the War.
Hall, D. How is it the stomach knows first.
There is no place to hide.
Hall, D. Sister on the Tracks, A.
Hardy, T. Channel Firing.
In Time of "The Breaking of Nations."
Man He Killed, The.
Night of Trafalgar, The.
Often when warring for he wist not what.
Harper, M. Guerrilla-Cong, The.
Harry, J. Shot of War, A.
Hart, H. Prisoner of Camau, The.
Hassett. Armed Forces Day.
Mother's Day.
Hawthorne, N. I Left My Low amd Humble Home.
Hay, G. Bizerta.
Hayden, R. Monet's "Waterlilies."
Hazo. Battle News.
Hecht, A. Dover Bitch, The.
Still Life.
Henderson, H. End of a Campaign.
Heóghusa. On Maguire's Winter Campaign.
Winter Campaign, A.
Herbert, S. After the Battle.
Herbert, Z. Abandoned, The.
Report from the Besieged City.
To Marcus Aurelius.
Hernández, M. War.
Heym. War.
Hodgson, W. Back to Rest.
England to Her Sons.
Hollenbeck. Anorexia.
Holub. Corporal Who Killed Archimedes, The.
History Lesson, A.
Lesson, THe.

Homer. Clash in Arms of the Achaians and Trojans.
Mars and Venus.
Sarpedon's Speech.
Hopkinson, A. Chord, The.
Housman, A. Deserter, The.
Recruit, The.
Howe, J. Battle Hymn [or Battle-Hymn] of the Republic, The.
Howell, C. Reminder to the Current President, A.
Hristic. Barbarians.
Huddle. Nerves.
Words.
Hughes, L. Without Benefit of Declaration.
Hughes, T. Thistles.
Hulme, T. Trenches: St Eloi.
"Hyde." Deserted Village, The.
Ilanakanar, M. Mothers.
Isakovsky. Enemy had burned his cottage home, The.
Ivanov, G. I walk and think of various things.
Iverem. Time #2, The.
James, A. Honor (1969).
Jarrell. Come to the Stone.
Eighth Air Force.
Lullaby, A: "For wars his life and half a world away."
Pilot from the Carrier, A.
Sick Nought, The.
War, A.
Jebeleanu. Hannibal.
Jeffers, R. Antrim.
Bloody Sire, The.
Eagle Valor, Chicken Mind.
Eye, The.
Rearmament.
Jefferys. Jeannette and Jeannot.
Johnson, J. Color Sergeant, The.
Jonas, G. Portrait: The Freedom Fighter.
Jones, D. And to Private Ball it came.
Kākkai Pāṭiṉiyār Naccellaiyār. King's Double Nature, A.
Kāmakkaṇṇiyār. Leaf in Love and War, A.
Kandel. First they slaughtered the angels.
Kao Shih. Song of Yen.
Kappiyarrukkappiyanar. Harvest of War.
Kayo. War.
Kennedy, B. Bad luck to this marching.
Kennedy, X. Joshua.
Keyes, S. Europe's Prisoners.
Moon is a poor woman, The.
War Poet.
Khlebnikov, V. Suppose I make a timepiece of humanity.
Khodasevich. Amidst a smoking desolation.
Kiḻār, A. Battle Scene.
Kilar, K. Poet's Counsel, A ("Your enemy is not the kind who wears").
Killigrew, A. Alexandreis.
Kiḻr. Parade, A.
Kinnell. Vapor Trail Reflected in the Frog Pond.
Kipling, R. Boots.
Dane-Geld.
For all we have and are.
Ford o' Kabul River.
Fuzzy-Wuzzy.
Gunga Din.
Storm Cone, The.
Kirstein. P.O.E.
Kiss, A. Emperor Butterfly.
Knott. Two Vietnam Poems: (1966).
Komunyakaa. Camouflaging the Chimera.
Dead at Quang Tri, The.
Starlight Scope Myopia.
Kornilov, B. Continuation of Life.
Krige. Taking of the Koppie, The.
Ku. War Poems 1.
Kulchitsky. Dreamer, visionary, green-eyed sluggard!
Kunitz, S. Foreign Affairs.
Last Picnic, The.
Kunze, R. Hymn To a Woman Under Interrogation.
Kwakiutl Oral Tradition. Warsong of the Kwakiutl.

Langland, J. War.
Larkin, P. Homage to a Government.
MCMXIV.
Lawrence, D. Song of a Man Who Has Come Through.
Lee, L. Moment of War, A.
Lee, L. Furious Versions.
Levertov. Advent 1966.
Christmas 1944.
In California During the Gulf War.
In Thai Binh (Peace) Province.
Life at War.
Tenebrae.
Levine, P. And the Trains Go On.
Baby Villon.
Death of Saul, The.
Heaven.
Lewis, A. All day it has rained, and we on the edge of the moors.
Autumn, 1939.
Christmas Holiday.
Easter at Christmas.
Goodbye.
Peasants, The.
Li Po. Ancient Airs.
Fighting on the South Frontier.
Lament of the Frontier Guard.
Song of War, A.
Li Yü. Tune: "Dance of the Cavalry."
Lindsay, V. Unpardonable Sin, The.
Lipska. When our enemies fall asleep.
Long, R. Refuge.
Longley, M. Ghetto.
Wounds.
Lovelace, R. Song: To Lucasta, Going to the War[re]s.
Lowell, A. Patterns.
Lucan. Cato in the desert.
Lydgate. Henry before Agincourt: October 25, 1415.
Macaulay, R. Many Sisters to Many Brothers.
Macaulay, T. Battle of Naseby, The.
Night sank upon the dusky beach, and on the purple sea.
MacDonagh, D. Just an Old Sweet Song.
Macgoye. Mathenge.
Machado Ruiz. On the Banks of the Duero.
Mackey, N. Phantom Light of All Our Day, The.
MacLean, S. Going Westwards.
MacLeish. Invocation to the Social Muse.
Too-Late Born, The.
MacNeice. Carrickfergus.
Mixer, The.
Makabo. Desert Conflict.
Malouf. Year of the Foxes, The.
Manifold. Fife Tune.
Manning, F. Leaves.
Mansour, J. Regulation equipment.
Mao Tse-tung. Tune: "Deva-like Barbarian"— Ta-po-ti.
Markov. Stendhal.
Marlowe. This said, the restles generall through the darke.
Matshoba. Mantatee Horde, The.
Mayakovsky. You, who live just for orgiastic feasts.
McCarthy, G. Fall of Da Nang, The.
Finding the Way Back.
Med Building.
Sound of Guns, The.
McCarthy, T. Claud Cockburn.
Wisdom of AE, The.
McClure, M. Song: "Platinum fur and brass revolver shine."
McDonald, W. Caliban in Blue.
For Harper, Killed in Action.
Interview with a Guy Named Fawkes, U.S. Army.
Last Still Days in a Bunker, The.
Retired Pilot to Himself, The.
Rocket Attack.
War Games.
Winter Before the War, The.
McGinley. Conquerors, The.
How to Start a War.
Women of Jericho, The.

McGrath, T. Fresco: Departure for an Imperialist War.
Nocturne Militaire.
Melville, H. Conflict of Convictions, The.
Utilitarian View of the Monitor's Fight, A.
Mercer, J. Jubilation T. Cornpone.
Meredith, G. Square along the couch, and stark.
Merton. Lent in a Year of War.
Meynell, A. Summer in England, 1914.
Mezhirov. Ice of Ladoga, The.
We are huddled in a crowd before Kolpino.
Miidhu. War Dance.
Millay, E. Apostrophe to Man.
Milosz, C. On the Book.
Milton. On the Late Massacre [or Massacher] in Piedmont [or Piemont].
Mishler. Ceremony.
Mitchison. Hartmanswillerkopf.
Thinking of War.
Mnasalces. My fighting days are done.
Setting their country free.
Montale. Fan, The.
Montgomerie, W. Edge of the War (1939–), The.
Moore, M. In Distrust of Merits.
Moraga. Loving in the War Years.
More, S. Minstrel Boy to the war is gone, The.
Morris, W. Judgement of God, The.
Mothibi. Speech.
Muir, E. Horses, The ("Barely a twelvemonth after").
Scotland 1941.
Town Betrayed, The.
Muldoon, P. Brock.
Meeting the British.
Mumford, L. Consolation in War.
Mure. O Heavens! O Earth! heer I must pause a space.
Murray, L. Drugs of War, The.
Muske. To the Muse.
Nagy, A. Storm.
Ndlovu. Elegy for the Dead of Soweto.
Ndu. Evacuation.
Neihardt. III. THE COUNCIL ON THE POWDER.
Nemerov. Fable of the War, A.
Redeployment.
Ultima Ratio Reagan.
Newbolt. Gillespie.
Vitaï Lampada.
Newcastle, W. Some with sharp swords, to tell O most accursed!
Nguyễn Đình Chiểu. Fleeing From Bandits.
Nhật Tiến. Two Eyes.
Ní Chuilleanáin. At alarming bell daybreak, before.
Niedecker. War.
Niles, N. Why Should Vain Mortals Tremble.
Nortje. Autopsy.
O'Hara, T. Bivouac of the Dead, The.
Okigbo. Elegy for Alto.
Oldham, P. War Stories.
O'Loughlin. Bunkers, The.
O'odham. War Songs.
Oppen. In Alsace, during the war.
Survival: Infantry.
Wars that are just? A simpler question: In the event.
Ormsby, F. Apples, Normandy, 1944.
Soldier Bathing.
War Photographers, The.
Ortiz. War Poem.
Orwell. As One Non-Combatant to Another.
Osgood, K. Driving Home the Cows.
Owen, G. Message Understood.
Owen, W. Apologia Pro Poemate Meo.
Arms and the Boy.
At a Calvary near the Ancre.
Chances, The.
Conscious.
Disabled.
Dulce Et Decorum Est.
Exposure.
Futility.
Insensibility.
It was a navy boy, so prim, so trim.

Mental Cases.
Next War, The.
On Seeing a Piece of Our Artillery Brought into Action.
Parable of the Old Man and the Young, The.
Send-Off, The.
Sentry, The.
Show, The.
Smile, Smile, Smile.
Spring Offensive.
Strange Meeting.
Terre, A.
Padilla. Song of the Juggler.
Paine, T. These are the times that try men's.
Paley, G. People in My Family.
Paquet. It Is Monsoon at Last.
Mourning the Death, by Hemorrhage, of a Child from Honai.
They Do Not Go Gentle.
Parun. Ballad of the Deceived Flowers.
Peabody, R. Burning the Dolls.
Peacock, T. War Song of Dinas Vawr, The.
Pembroke, M. Psalm 84: "How lovely is thy dwelling."
Penrose, R. Road is Wider Than Long: An Image Diary from the Balkans, July–August 1938, The.
Péret. Nungesser und Coli Sind Verreckt.
Perunkunrur Kilar. Parade, A.
Phạm Hổ. Hand, The.
Sea, The.
Pheraios. War Hymn.
Philips, J. War Poetry.
Phổ Đức. Buffalo Boy On a Field of Corpses, The.
Picasso. Bottle of Suze, A.
Piercy. Peaceable Kingdom, The.
Pierpont, J. Fourth of July, The.
Pitter. 1938.
Po Chü-i. Old Man with the Broken Arm, The.
Prisoner, The.
To his Brother Hsing-chien, Who was Serving in Tung-ch'uan.
Pound, E. Sestina: Altaforte.
Pratt, J. Words and Thoughts.
Prévert. Barbara.
Discourse on Peace, The.
Familial.
Prince, F. Soldiers Bathing.
Pringle. Caffer Commando, The.
Publius Papinius Status. Tisiphone responds.
Radnóti. Postcard (Found on His body after He Was Killed by the Nazis).
"Rayevsky." War.
Read, S. My Company.
To a Conscript of 1940.
Rebelo. Poem for a Militant.
Reed, H. Judging Distances.
Naming Of Parts.
Reitz, F. Proclamation, or Paper Bomb, The.
Rexroth, K. Strength through Joy.
Rich, A. Memory lifts her smoky mirror: 1943.
Richards, I. Warhead Wakes.
Rickword. Soldier Addresses his Body, The.
Winter Warfare.
Ridler. At Parting.
Now as Then.
Prayer in a Pestilent Time.
Ritterbusch. Search and Destroy.
Robinson, E. Field of Glory, The.
Rodgers, W. Sing, Brothers, Sing!
Rolfe, E. No Man Knows War.
Rolls. Dog Fight.
Rose-Troup. What is war?
Rosenberg, I. August 1914.
Break of Day in the Trenches.
Daughters of War.
Louse Hunting.
Marching.
Ross, A. Night Patrol.
Rosten. Out of Our Shame.
Roughton. Building Society Blues.
Rowbotham. Prey to Prey.
Rowe, G. Reason Why, The.

Rozhdestvensky. You Live on a Drifting Road.
Ruark. Sleeping Out with My Father.
Rukeyser, M. Don Baty, the Draft Resister.
Käthe Kollwitz.
Poem: "I lived in the first century of world wars."
Poem Out of Childhood.
Who in one lifetime sees all causes lost.
Sackville-West. September 1939.
"Saki." Carol: "While shepherds watched their flocks by night."
Sandburg, C. Bas-Relief.
Buttons.
Little girl saw her first troop parade and asked, "What are those?", The.
Prayer after World War.
Threes.
Santos, S. Air Base at Châteauroux, France, The.
Sappho. Some say nothing on earth excels in beauty.
Sassoon. Aftermath.
Attack.
Does It Matter?[—losing your legs?].
Everyone Sang.
General, The.
Glory of Women.
Repression of War Experience.
"They."
Scannell. Great War, The.
Schneour. War Comes.
Scott, A. Coronach.
Scott of Amwell. Ode: "I hate that drum's discordant sound."
Scott, W. Lochinvar.
Seeger, A. Rendezvous, The.
Seeger, P. Where have all the flowers gone?—long time passing.
Seifert. Candlestick, The.
Sergeant. Inundation, The.
Shaka, King of the Zulus. Battle Song.
Shakespeare, W. Henry V at the Siege of Harfleur.
Shapiro, K. Conscientious Objector, The.
Quintana lay in the shallow grave of coral.
Scyros.
Troop Train.
Shelton, R. Eden After Dark.
Silius Italicus. Again she Arms prepares: One Captain may.
Simic. Empire of Dreams.
Simmons, J. From the Irish.
Simonides. Because of these men's courage, no smoke rose.
Simonov. Blind Man, The.
Cricket, The.
Simpson, L. Battle, The.
Early in the Morning.
I dreamed that in a city dark as Paris.
Memories of a Lost War.
On the lawn at the villa.
Sissoko. Bombax Tree, The.
Sitwell, D. Lullaby: "Though the world has slipped and gone."
Sitwell, S. Next War, The.
Slutsky. Clerks.
Smith, C. Fragment Descriptive of the Miseries of War.
Smith, I. Chinese Poem.
Smith, S. War in Fife, The.
Snodgrass, W. After experience taught me that all the ordinary.
Sorley. Hundred thousand million mites we go, A.
To Germany.
Soupault. You Who Sleep.
Soutar. Permanence of the Young Men, The.
Southerland. Two Fishing Villages.
Southey, R. Battle of Blenheim, The.
Southwell. New Heaven, New War[re].
Spender, S. Epilogue to a Human Drama.
Two Armies.
Spenser. Tho when they came to the sea coast, they found.
Stadler. Decampment.
Stevens, W. Dry Loaf.

Stramm. Battlefield.
Guard-Duty.
Su Wu. To His Wife.
Surkov. Tenderness.
Svetlov. Grenada.
On Reconnaissance.
Two.
Szymborska. End and the Beginning, The.
Taylor, A. Clearing Away.
Tennyson, A. Blow, Bugle, Blow.
Terry, L. Bar[']s Fight[, August 28, 1746].
Thomas, D. Hand that signed the paper felled a city, The.
Thomas, E. As the team's head-brass flashed out on the turn.
Owl, The.
This is no case of petty right or wrong.
Tô Hữu. Elephants.
Todd, R. Joan Miró ("After that war, when death had gone away").
Joan Miró ("Once there were peasant pots and a dry brown hare").
Poem: "I walk at dawn across the hollow hills."
Toller. To the Mothers.
Trần Dạ Từ. Drinking Song, A.
Gifts as Tokens of Love.
New Lullaby, The.
Trần Huiền Ấn. My Mother's Son.
Old Vow, The.
Trinh Tiên. Woman Writes to Her Daughter Who's Studying Overseas, A.
Ts'ai Yen. Lamentation, The.
Ts'ao Chih. Ruins of Lo-yang, The.
Ts'ao Sung. Protest in the Sixth Year of Ch'ien Fu, A.
Tsung Ch'en. On Hearing That the Sea-Barbarians Are About To Attack Hu-chou—Expressing My Feelings to Tzu-yü.
Rebels' cavalry are everywhere, The.
Tu Fu. City of White Emperor, The.
Man with No Family to Take Leave of, The.
Moon Festival.
Restless Night in Camp, A.
Travelling Northward.
Tu'ơng Phố. Who is that soldier, hero of my heart?
Ungaretti. Rivers, The.
Unknown. Achaian Invasion of Sparta, The.
Age of War, The.
Battle of Brunanburh.
Canadian Song.
Cause of War, The.
Fare Thee Well.
Fight at Finnsburg, The.
Fighting South of the Ramparts.
Fortunes of War, I Tell You Plain, The.
Grain for Emperor Huan.
Graves the rain makes wet and sleek, The.
Ha-Kon-E-Crase, the Eagle Dance.
Hēr Æ???oelstān cyning, eorla drihten.
Hymn: "O God of Hosts, thine Ear incline."
Hymn to the Fallen.
Johnny, I Hardly Knew Ye.
Montcalm and Wolfe.
Oh, It's Nine Years Ago I Was Digging in the Land.
Ojibwa War Songs.
One-and-Twenty.
Raid of the Reidswire, The.
Return from Battle.
Song of the Freedman.
Song of the Lenape Warriors Going against the Enemy, The.
Sweetness of Nature, The.
Ten Thousand Miles.
Tewa Song of War.
Translation of "Pax Bello Potior."
Wanderer, The ("Who liveth alone longeth for mercy").
War Songs.
War the Source of Riches.
Warsong of the Kwakiutl.
We mean to thrash these Prussian Pups.
Well, the war is done.
Utkin. Komsomol Song.
Letter.

Uyematsu. Same Month They Bombed Cambodia, The.
Viên Linh. Hundred Tongues, A.
Viereck, P. Kilroy.
Vildrac. Relief.
Vinkenoog. ((((((Hollanditis)))))).
Virgil. Camilla goes to war.
End.
Turnus kills Pallasy.
Voloshin. Civil War.
Red Guard.
Voznesensky. I am Goya.
War.
Walden. Nation's Friend, The.
Waley. Censorship.
Walker, A. Enemy, The.
Wallace, R. Nightline: An Interview with the General.
Wang Chien. Hearing That His Friend Was Coming Back from the War.
Wang Ts'an. Western Capital is in turmoil, The.
Ware, E. Manila Bay.
Waring, B. Refuge at the One Step Down.
Warner, S. Song for a Street-Song.
Warren, R. Sirocco.
Waxman. War Rug.
Weber, R. Concise History of the Vietnam War: 1965–1968, A.
Weigl. Burning Shit at An Khe.
Him, on the Bicycle.
Monkey.
Wendel. We Shall Return, Luanda.
West, A. Night Patrol, The.
Whalen. Regalia in Immediate Demand!
Whitman, W. Beat! beat! drums!—blow! bugles! blow!
Old War-Dreams.
Respondez! Respondez! / (The war is completed—the price is paid—the title is settled beyond recall).
Whittemore, R. Walk Home, The.
Wilbur. First Snow in Alsace.
Looking into History.
Place Pigalle.
Williams, C. Last Deaths, The.
Williams, W. Are the desolate, dark weeks.
Illegitimate Things.
Wilner, E. Coda, Overture.
Winters, Y. Summer Noon: 1941.
Wolfe, C. Burial of Sir John Moore [after [*or* at] Corunna], The.
Wolff, D. While We Slept.
Wright, J. Mad Fight Song for William S. Carpenter, 1966, A.
Distant roads in the aftermath of war.
Wu Wei-yeh. Ballad of Yüan-yüan.
Yamada. Night Before Good-Bye, The.
Yeats. Ancestral Houses.
Irish Airman Foresees His Death, An.
On Being Asked for a War Poem.
Yên Ba. Twenty-Eight Lines for My Wife.
Yoshimi. Tanka: "Gloomy rain."
Tanka: "Having grown up."
Tanka: "Scissors."
Tanka: "Soldiers on the ground."
Yün Shou-p'ing. War ships, cold tides.
Zabolotsky. Somewhere in a field near Magadan.
Zach. Prologue to a Poem.
Zenmaro. Tanka: "Old soldier, An."
Zuma. Praises of Field-marshal J. C. Smuts, The.

See also **Soldiers; War Casualties; War Dead; Listings for specific Wars and Battles**

War Casualties
Abid ibn al-Abras. Lament for an Arab Encampment.
Balaban. For the Missing in Action.
Bly, R. Driving through Minnesota during the Hanoi Bombings.
Carruth, H. Song: So Often, So Long I Have Thought.
Carson, C. Bloody Hand.
Cole, M. Veteran, The.
Dove, R. Bird Frau, The.
Dunn, D. War Blinded.

Fenton, J. Dead Soldiers.
Ferlinghetti, L. Third World Calling.
Galloway, G. To the Memory of Gavin Wilson (Boot, Leg and Arm Maker).
Garioch. Wire, The.
Gibson, W. Ambulance Train.
Gutteridge. Enemy Dead, The.
Hacker, M. Before the War.
Hood, T. Faithless Nelly Gray.
Jarrell. Field Hospital, A.
  Sick Nought, The.
Keyes, S. Europe's Prisoners.
Longley, M. Wounds.
Lukonin. My Friends.
Magrelli. Each photographed face.
Matthews, H. Women Are Not Gentlemen.
McElroy, D. Nocturn at the Institute.
Montgomerie, W. Edge of the War (1939–), The.
Muir, E. Town Betrayed, The.
Muldoon, P. Field Hospital, The.
Neilson, J. Soldier Is Home, The.
Owen, W. Chances, The.
  Conscious.
  Dead-Beat, The.
  Disabled.
  Dulce Et Decorum Est.
  Futility.
  Mental Cases.
  Sentry, The.
  Terre, A.
  Yes, there's the orderly. He'll change the sheets.
Plowman. Dead Soldiers, The.
Rukeyser, M. Leg in a Plaster Cast, A.
Sassoon. Does It Matter?[— losing your legs?].
  Stretcher Case.
  "They."
Service. Grand-Père.
Shapcott, T. Sestina with Refrain.
Simmons, J. From the Irish.
Simpson, L. Carentan O Carentan.
Sitwell, S. Next War, The.
Slutsky. Filled with the final weariness.
  Hospital.
Smelyakov. From My Diary.
Unknown. Death Song.
  Sure, a little bit of shrapnel fell from out the sky one day.
Vopiscus. Thousand, a thousand, a thousand, A.
Whitman, W. March in the ranks hard-prest, and the road unknown, A.
  Vigil strange I kept on the field one night;.
  Wound-Dresser, The.

See also **Soldiers; War Dead**

War Dead
Aeschylus. On the Thessalians Who Fought at Marathon.
Alcaeus. Philip at Kynoskephalai.
Aldington. Soliloquy 2.
  Trench Idyll.
Allison, D. Funeral Oration, A.
Amichai. Diameter of the bomb was thirty centimeters, The.
  Is all this sorrow? I don't know.
Antipater of Sidon. This piece of Lydian earth holds Amyntor.
Apollinaire. Stanzas Against Forgetting.
Arcos. Dead, The.
Asquith. Volunteer, The.
"B., H. d'A." Givenchy Field.
Balaban. After our war, the dismembered bits.
  In Celebration of Spring.
  Than, Mau.
Betjeman. In Memory of Basil, Marquess of Dufferin and Ava.
Binyon. For the Fallen.
Bly, R. War and Silence.
Bogan, L. To My Brother: Killed: Hammont Wood: October, 1918.
Brooke, R. Dead, The ("These hearts were woven").
Brooks, G. Appendix to the Anniad.
Browning, E. Mother and Poet.
Browning, R. Incident of the French Camp.

Bùi Khải Nguyễn. Man Who Sleeps Out in the Fields, The.
Burns, R. Farewell, A [*or* The]: "It was a' for our rightfu' king."
  Lovely lass o' Inverness, The.
Cannan. Lamplight.
Carrier, C. Pro Patria.
"Caudwell." Classic Encounter.
Causley. At the British War Cemetery, Bayeux.
Ch'en Tao. Song of Lung-hsi.
Chesterton, G. English Graves, The.
Ciardi. Elegy Just in Case.
Clarke, J. Fighting Race, The.
Clifton, L. Death of Thomas Merton.
Collins, W. Ode Written in the Beginning of the Year 1746.
Cox, D. To My Mother—1916.
Crane, S. War Is Kind.
Crosland. Slain.
Dawe, B. Homecoming.
Day, J. North Sea.
Degen. My comrade is in the final agony before death.
Dehn, P. Armistice.
Dickey, J. Hunting Civil War Relics at Nimblewill Creek.
  Performance, The.
Dickinson, E. My Triumph lasted till the Drums.
Douglas, K. Gallantry.
  Vergissmeinnicht.
Dudin. Nightingales.
Dunbar, P. Unsung Heroes, The.
Elmusa. Little Piece of Sky, A.
Emerson, R. Concord Hymn.
Fairfax, J. Forest of the Dead, The.
Feldman, I. Se Aprovechan.
Finch, F. Blue and the Gray, The.
Ford, F. That Exploit of Yours.
Fried, E. What Things Are Called.
Galich. Mistake, A.
García Lorca. Rundown Church (Ballad of the First World War).
Gilbo'a. Death in Spring, A.
Golding, L. In The Gallery Where the Fat Men Go.
Graves, R. Dead Foxhunter, The.
  Devil's Advice to Story-Tellers, The.
Gray, T. Death of Hoel, The.
Greenberg, U. Naming Souls.
Gudzenko. Before the Attack.
Gurney, I. To His Love.
Gutteridge. Enemy Dead, The.
Hardy, T. Drummer Hodge.
  I looked up from my writing.
  Man He Killed, The.
  Souls of the Slain, The.
  Wife in London, A.
Harper, M. Photographs: A Vision of Massacre.
Harry, J. Shot of War, A.
Harte, B. Second Review of the Grand Army, A.
Heaney, S. In Memoriam Francis Ledwidge.
Heard, J. Decoration Day.
  National Cemetery, Beaufort, South Carolina, The.
Hemans. Effigies, The.
Henderson, H. End of a Campaign.
Herbert, S. German Graves, The.
Hill, G. Dear lords of life, stump-toothed, with ragged breath.
Homer. Achilles kills Lycaon.
  Equity in death.
Hope, A. Inscription for a War.
Housman, A. Astronomy.
  Epitaph on an Army of Mercenaries.
  Here dead lie we because we did not choose.
  On the idle hill of summer.
  Recruit, The.
Howell, C. Reminder to the Current President, A.
Hughes, T. Six Young Men.
Jarrell. Burning the Letters.
  Come to the Stone.
  Dead Wingman, The.

  Death of the Ball Turret Gunner, The.
  Losses.
  Protocols.
  Second Air Force.
Kākkai Pāṭiniyār Nacceḷḷaiyār. Mothers.
Kao Ch'i. Passing By the Battlefield at Feng-k'ou.
Keyes, S. Expected Guest, The.
Kipling, R. American Spirit speaks, The.
  Death-Bed, A.
  Gethsemane [1914–18].
  Hyænas [*or* Hyenas], The.
  Mesopotamia.
  My Boy Jack.
Knight, E. Poem for Black Relocation Centers, A.
Komunyakaa. Facing It.
  We Never Know.
Ku. War Poems 7.
Langland, J. War.
Lanier, S. Dying Words of Stonewall Jackson, The.
Larkin, P. MCMXIV.
Lasker-Schüler. Georg Trakl.
Leftwich. Killed in Action.
Letts. Spires of Oxford, The.
Levin, K. Artillery was burying us.
Lewis, A. Unknown Soldier, The.
Longfellow, H. Killed at the Ford.
Lowell, R. For the Union Dead.
  Holy Innocents, The.
Lynch, C. Memo.
"MacDiarmid." Another Epitaph on an Army of Mercenaries.
MacDonagh, D. Of what a quality is courage made.
MacGill. Matey.
Mackintosh, E. Farewell: "Well, you have gone now, comrades."
  In Memoriam[, Private D. Sutherland].
MacLeish. Lines for an Interment.
  Memorial Rain.
MacNeice. Troll's Courtship.
Manifold. Tomb of Lt. John Learmonth, A.I.F, The.
Masters, E. Unknown Soldiers.
McCrae, J. In Flanders Fields the poppies blow.
McDonald, D. Song of Those Who Died, A.
McGrath, T. Ode for the American Dead in Asia.
  Reading the Names of the Vietnam War Dead.
Melville, H. Inscription: "To them who crossed the Flood."
  Memorial on the Slain at Chickamauga.
  Requiem[:] for Soldiers Lost in Ocean Transports, A.
Mew. Cenotaph, The.
Mezhirov. Farewell to Arms, A.
  Lines about a Little Boy.
Moody, W. On a Soldier Fallen in the Philippines.
Moore, T. Minstrel Boy, The.
Nemerov. War in the Air, The.
Newbolt. Messmates.
Newcastle, M. Some with sharp swords, to tell O most accursed!
Okkūr Mācāttaṉar. Widows' Rice.
Olds, S. Leningrad Cemetery, Winter of 1941.
O'Loughlin. Elegy for the Unknown Soldier.
Orlov. They buried him in the terrestrial globe.
Owen, W. Anthem for Doomed Youth.
  Dulce Et Decorum Est.
  Fragment: "I saw his round mouth's crimson deepen as it fell."
  Futility.
  Greater Love.
  Miners.
  Next War, The.
  Send-Off, The.
  Strange Meeting.
Page, G. Smalltown Memorials.
Pagis. November '73.
Pain, B. Army of the Dead, The.
Parry, R. On a Soldier Killed in the Great War.

Phổ Đứ'c. Buffalo Boy On a Field of Corpses, The.
Punkanuttiraiyar. Mothers.
Quasimodo. To the Fifteen of Piazzale Loreto.
Randall, D. Memorial Wreath.
Ransom, J. Necrological.
Rickword. Moonrise Over Battlefield.
Riddell, E. Soldier in the Park, The.
Ronald. In Memoriam J.H.H.
Rose, B. Unknown Soldier, The.
Rozhdestvensky. You Live on a Drifting Road.
Ryan, A. Lines: "Gather the sacred dust."
Sandburg, C. Grass.
Sassoon. Base Details.
Death-Bed, The.
Hero, The.
On Passing the New Menin Gate.
Rank stench of those bodies haunts me still, The.
To Any Dead Officer.
Scott, W. Soldier Rest! [Thy Warfare O'er].
Shakespeare, W. Sonnet 25.
Shin, T. Land of Flowering Azaleas, The.
Simmons, J. From the Irish.
Simonides. For the Spartan Dead at Plataia.
For the Spartan Dead at Thermopylai (480 B.C.).
Simpson, L. Arm in Arm.
Ash and the Oak, The.
Slessor. Beach Burial.
Smelyakov. Judge, The.
Smith, D. On a Field Trip at Fredericksburg.
Snodgrass, W. Flat One, A.
Sorley. Sonnet: "When you see millions of the mouthless dead."
Spender, S. Ultima Ratio Regum.
Stevens, W. Death of a Soldier, The.
Tate, A. Ode to the Confederate Dead.
Tate, J. Lost Pilot, The.
Tennyson, A. Blow, Bugle, Blow.
Thackeray. Due of the Dead, The.
Thomas, E. As the team's head-brass flashed out on the turn.
In Memoriam (Easter, 1915).
Private, A.
Thompson, J. Burial of Latané, The.
Timrod. Christmas.
Ode: "Sleep sweetly in your humble graves."
Toller. Corpses in the Wood.
Tomoana. Full Tide.
Trakl. Grodek.
Tran Minh-tong (King). Bạch-đằng River, The.
Tvardovsky. From a crumpled wartime diary.
Unknown. Bạch-đằng River, The.
Hymn to the Fallen.
Johnny, I Hardly Knew Ye.
Lay of the Last Survivor, The.
My Luve's in Germany.
Song for a Fallen Warrior.
They fought south of the walls.
Those Who Died for Their Country.
Vanparanar. Woman and Her Dying Warrior, A.
Veliyanar Erumai. Horse Did Not Come Back, The.
Viereck, P. Vale from Carthage.
Warren, R. History among the Rocks.
Whitman, W. As toilsome I wander'd Virginia's woods.
Come up from the fields father, here's a letter from our Pete.
Dirge for Two Veterans.
Pensive on her dead gazing I heard the Mother of All.
Reconciliation.
Sight in camp in the daybreak gray and dim, A.
Vigil strange I kept on the field one night;.
Wojahn. Armageddon: Private Gabriel Calvin Wojahn 1900–18.
Wolfe, C. Burial of Sir John Moore &[;after [or at] Corunna&];, The.
Yeats. Irish Airman Foresees His Death, An.
Yoshimi. Tanka: "White jet clouds."
Young, S. Epitaph for a Concord Boy.

Zenmaro. Evidence.
See also Soldiers
War of 1812
Cable, G. English muskets went bim! bim!, The.
Freneau. On the Conflagrations at Washington.
Key. Star-Spangled Banner, The.
Unknown. Banks of Champlain, The.
Battle of New Orleans, The.
James Bird.
Ye Parliament of England.
War of the Grand Alliance
Browning, R. Hervé Riel.
Warblers
Kunio. Tanka: "On the water."
Warburton, William
Edwards, T. Tongue-Doughty Pedant.
Ward, John
Unknown. Captain Ward and the Rainbow.
Warning
Carew, T. Deposition from Love, A.
Herrick. Bellman, The.
Hitomaro. May the men who are born.
Mutukorran. What the Passersby Said to the lover eloping with the girl.
Parra, N. Warnings.
Ralegh, W. Sir Walter Ra[u]le[i]gh to His Son[ne].
Revell. Hotel Sander, The.
Turner, C. Buoy-Bell, The.
Warren, R. Pondy Woods.
Yeats. Never give all the heart, for love.
Warren, Robert Penn
Lawrence, A. Robert Penn Warren's book.
Warsaw Ghetto
Milosz, C. Poor Christian Looks at the Ghetto, A.
Slonimski. Elegy: "No more, no more Jewish townships in Poland."
Valentine, J. Forgiveness Dream.
Warsaw, Poland
Davie. Meeting of Cultures, A.
Flanders, J. House That Fear Built: Warsaw, 1943, The.
Milosz, C. Campo dei Fiori.
Warts
Tekkan. Tanka: "With warts and all."
Washing
Bishop, E. Under the Window: Ouro Prêto.
Herrick. Another Charme (variant).
Kassiane. Troparion.
Lyon, G. Foot-Washing, The.
Moeller. Domestic Poem.
Mother Goose. They that wash on Monday.
Rilke. Pietà.
Volkow. Washerwoman, The.
See also Baths and Bathing
Washing Machines. See Laundry and Laundering
Washington, Booker Taliaferro
Cotter, J. Dr. Booker T. Washington to the National Negro Business League.
Johnson, M. To See Ol' Booker T.
Linden, M. Our Noble Booker T. Washington.
Moorer. Notable Dinner, A.
Randall, D. Booker T. and W. E. B.
Stafford, W. Monuments for a Friendly Girl at a Tenth Grade Party.
Washington (state)
Hugo, R. White Center.
Jensen, L. Age, An.
Snyder, G. Mid-August at Sourdough Mountain Lookout.
Text, The.
Washington, D.C
Cardenal. Tahirassawichi in Washington.
Davis, C. Out of Work, Out of Touch, Out of Sorts.
Dove, R. Banneker.
Hemphill. Family Jewels.
Heyen. Steadying, The.
Iverem. Keeper.
Lowell, R. July in Washington.
March 1, The.

Tate, A. Aeneas at Washington.
Welch, J. Man from Washington, The.
Washington, George
Barlow, J. Advice to a Raven in Russia [December, 1812].
Berryman. Washington in Love.
Hill, B. Tribute to Robert E. Lee.
Jordan, J. Cameo No. II.
Kooser. Gilbert Stuart Portrait of Washington, The.
MacLow. 1789.
Merriam, E. Which Washington?
Monroe, H. Washington.
Turner, N. Washington.
Unknown. George Washington.
Mount Vernon.
Thirty days hath September.
Wakoski. Patriotic Poem.
Wheatley, P. To His Excellency General Washington.
Washington Monument
Sandburg, C. Washington Monument by Night.
Washington Square, New York City
Livingston, M. Envoi: Washington Square Park.
Wasps
Eberhart, R. New Hampshire, February.
Fisher, A. Fair Exchange.
Hine. Wasp, The.
Jarman, M. Children are hiding among the raspberry canes, The.
Little, G. Now ice-covered.
MacBeth. Wasps' Nest, The.
"Macleod." Wasp, The.
Taylor, E. Upon a Wasp Chilled [or Child] with Cold.
Watches
Cornford, F. Watch, The.
Gallagher, T. Kidnap[p]er.
Herbert of Cherbury. To His Watch, When He Could Not Sleep.
Kavanagh, P. Gold Watch.
Lucas, E. Mr. Coggs.
Maguire, S. Perfect Timing.
Rabbitt. My Father's Watch.
Simic. Watch Repair.
Stone, J. Girl in the Hall, The.
Swenson, M. Watch, The.
Tadic. Pocket Watch.
Unknown. Watchmaker's Shop, The.
See also Clocks
Water
Allard. Silence a droplet of water trickles down a stone, The.
Auden. In Praise of Limestone.
Awoonor. So the World Changes.
Basho. Ancient pool. Sound.
Basho et al. Call of Two Birds, The.
Bell, M. Stars Which See, Stars Which Do Not See.
Bernstein, O. Imagined Description of Myself, in Another Scene, An.
Berry, J. Spirits of Movement.
Betjeman. East Anglian Bathe.
Bishop, E. Under the Window: Ouro Prêto.
Bly, R. Awakening.
Blyton, C. Plug-hole Man, The.
Bogan, L. To Be Sung on the Water.
Brathwaite, E. Red Rising.
Brontë, C. Diving.
Brooke, R. Fish, The.
Brooks, G. Kitchenette Building.
Bùi Du'o'ng Lịch. To a Watering Scoop.
Cameron, N. Green, Green Is El Aghir.
Carew, T. To My Mistress Sitting by a River's Side; an Eddy.
Carney. (Little Things).
Carroll, J. Distances, The.
Cecco Angiolieri, da Siena. Sonnet: Of All He Would Do.
Chang Yü. In the Evening, Walking in the Western Fields.
Chiyojo. Morning glory!, The.
Chōkū. Tanka: "From the water's depth."

Codrescu. Imagination of Necessity, The.
Cornford, F. Inscription for a Wayside Spring.
Crashaw. To Our Lord, upon the Water Made Wine.
Creeley. Act of Love, The.
Just Friends.
Pool, The.
Croly. Aestuary, An.
Crossland. Water.
Daive. Lost in contemplation of its end.
Di Prima. Paracelsus.
Dickinson, E. I think that the Root of the Wind is Water.
Doolittle, H. Pool, The.
Dowson. Exile.
Eberhart, R. Garden God, The.
Loon Call, A.
Elenkov. Sauna.
Emerson, R. Water understands / Civilization well, The.
Ennis. Drink of Spring, A.
Espada. When Songs Become Water.
Ford, C. Overturned Lake, The.
Frost, R. West-Running Brook.
Galvin, J. Western Civilization.
Hadewijch. Love's Constancy.
Heaney, S. Cana Revisited.
Drink of Water, A.
Rite of Spring.
Hermocreon. Nymphs of the surface, whom Hermokreon gave.
Herrick. Another Charme (variant).
To the Water Nymphs, Drinking at the Fountain.
Upon Julia's Haire Fill'd with Dew.
Higginson, W. Holding the water.
Howard, R. Waste not, want not, is a maxim I.
HSü Ling. Waters of Lung-t'ou, The.
Hsü Wei. Painting of People Strolling through a Pine Forest, A.
Returning from the Seventy-Two Mountains.
Hughes, T. Man Seeking Experience Enquires His Way of a Drop of Water, The.
Ishikawa Takuboku. Tanka: "As if in water."
Jarman, M. Desire of Water, The.
Jarrell. Well Water.
Jiménez, J. To the bridge of love.
Jordan, J. October 23, 1983.
Joyce, J. All day I hear the noise of waters.
Juana Inés de la Cruz. Since Love is shivering.
Kabir. I have been thinking of the difference between water.
Kambar. Pond Named Ganga, A.
Kao Ch'i. Spring Day—Remembering Living on the River, A.
Kapilar. What She Said to Her Girl Friend When She Returned from the Hills.
Keats. Bright star[, would I were stedfast as thou art—].
Kim, S. Waterfall, A.
Kinzie. Glinting like water.
Kirchwey. Rogue Hydrant, August.
Kitahara Hakushū. Tanka: "Almost invisible."
Kizer, C. Muse of Water, A.
Kusano Shimpei. 4 Or 5 Tadpoles.
Lamb, E. Far back under a ledge.
Larkin, P. Water.
Lawrence, D. Wild Common, The.
Leithauser. Buried Graves, The.
Levertov. Fountain, The.
Wavering.
Levine, P. Belief.
Li Ho. Liang Terrace, The.
Livingston, M. Swimming Pool.
Lorde. Fishing the White Water.
Lowell, R. Water.
Lu Yu. How I Sailed on the Lake till I Came to the Eastern Stream.
MacCaig. Loch Sionascaig.
"MacDiarmid." Water Music.
MacLeish. What Any Lover Learns.
Mahadevi. It was like a stream.
Manger. Rachel Goes to the Well for Water ("Rachel stands by the mirror and plaits").
Masaoka Shiki. I can see the stones.

Mayo, E. Word of Water, The.
McCaig. Betweens.
McCord, D. Perambulator Poem.
McGuckian. Sea or Sky?
McNeill, A. Hello Ungod.
Meng Chiao. Above the gorges, one thread of sky.
Merwin, W. Glass.
Mihalic. Metamorphosis.
Mirabai. I was going to the river for water.
Mitchell, K. Night Rain.
Tree Stillness.
Moore, T. Meeting of the Waters, The.
Morgan, E. Dowser, The.
Morley, H. Curve of the Water.
Mountain, M. At dusk hot water from the hose.
Narasimhaswami. Consolation to Empty Pitchers.
Neruda. Sexual Water.
Nguyễn Thiên Túng. Well, The.
Nikolov, N. Water Outside the Window.
Norris, L. Water.
Okigbo. Bridge.
Oliver, M. At Blackwater Pond the tossed waters have settled.
Diviners, The.
O'Neill, J. Sound of Water.
Padilla. Daily Habits.
Pastan. Erosion.
Love Poem.
Persand. Rain Storm.
Pound, E. Bathtub [or Bath Tub], The.
Ransom, J. Persistent Explorer.
Reid, A. Glass Town, The.
Rilke. Swan, The.
Ross, A. Night Patrol.
Rossetti, C. Echo from Willow-Wood, An.
Roy, L. Suffering The Sea Change: All My Pretty Ones.
Samio. Tanka: "When the gardener."
Sandburg, C. Prairie Waters by Night.
Sarton. In Time Like Air.
Schneour. Like Water down a Slope.
Shapiro, D. To an Idea.
Shūji. Tanka: "On the way home."
Tanka: "To do away with anger."
Silverstein, S. Dirtiest Man in the World, The.
Simko. Three Songs.
Smith, I. Glass of Water, The.
Smith, W. Brooklyn Bridge, Brooklyn Bridge.
Sobin, G. Notes on Sound, Speech, Speech-Crystals and the Celestial Echo.
Solomon ibn Gabirol. Water Song.
Sorescu. Fountains in the Sea.
Southey, R. Cataract of Lodore, The.
Stevens, W. Poems of Our Climate, The.
Su Tung-p'o. White Crane Hill.
Suckling, J. Upon Sir John Lawrence's Bringing Water over the Hills [to My L. Middlesex His House at Witten].
Tadic. Laocoon/Serpent.
Tao-chi. Bend after bend, the long embankment.
Taylor, A. Water.
Thoreau. Fog.
Tomlinson, C. On Water.
Traherne. Shadows in the Water.
Tu Mu. Pool behind Ch'i-an, The.
Unknown. Come, Happy Children,.
God's A-Gonna Trouble the Water.
Lyric by Nine.
Medicine Songs.
Song of the Prophet.
Water Bug and the Shadows, The.
Woes of the Crab, The.
Zuni Derivations.
Ushida. Deep in the rippling spring.
Wang Shih-chieng. Mooring at Night at the River Mouth, I Heard a Flute—Sent to My Elder Brother Hsi-ch'iao.
Wang T'ing-hsiang. At Arrow Rapids, the water splashes foam.
Wen Cheng-ming. Around the temple, pines and cedars.
Wen Yi-tuo. Dead Water.

Winstanley, J. To the Revd. Mr. ——— on His Drinking Sea-Water.
Wollach. Gentle as moon on water and not like the cherry tree that said.
Wright, J. To Flood Stage Again.
Wright, J. Journey to the Place of Ghosts.
Lake in Central Park, The.
Wu Chen. Inscribed on a Painting of Bamboo.
Wu Wei-yeh. Song to the Tune "Perching Crows."
Yang Wan-li. Staying Overnight at the Temple of the Holy Vulture.
Yevtushenko. Siberian Wooing.
Yü Chi. Hearing Loom and Shuttle.
Yüan Chen. To the Waters of the Chia-ling.
Zenodotus. Statue Of Eros, A.
Zukofsky, L. Ways, The.

Water Lilies
Barnes, W. Clote (Water-Lily), The.
Ferlinghetti, L. Monet's Lilies Shuddering.
Hughes, T. To Paint a Water Lily.
Scalapino. Third Part.
Teasdale. Water-Lilies.
Voigt. Lotus Flowers, The.
Wakoski. Light.
Wu of Liang. Water lilies bloom on the Great River.

Water Ouzels
Matchett. Water Ouzel.

Waterbeds
Updike. Insomnia the Gem of the Ocean.

Watercolors
Plath. Watercolor of Grantchester Meadows.

Waterfalls
Adler, F. By the Waterfall.
Annensky. It happened in Vallen-Koski.
Hardy, T. Under the Waterfall.
Heaney, S. Waterfall.
Hopkins, G. It was a hard thing to undo this knot.
Kapilar. Waterfalls and Liquor ("Waterfalls sounded").
Kim, S. Waterfall, A.
Li Po. Viewing the Waterfall at Mount Lu.
Liu Ya-tzu. Cataracts flying down a thousand fathoms roll up a raging billow.
Owen, G. Waterfall.
Ray, H. At the Cascade.
Sherman, F. Waterfall, The.
Snyder, G. By Frazier Creek Falls.
Southey, R. Cataract of Lodore, The.
Tai Piao-yüan. Cheng-tao Temple.
Vaughan, H. Waterfall [or Water-Fall], The.
Welsh, A. Waterfall.
Williams, W. Paterson: The Falls.
Williamson, G. Waterfall.
Wordsworth, W. Louisa; After Accompanying Her on a Mountain Excursion.
Young, A. Falls of Glomach, The.
Yozei Emperor. Falling from the ridge.

Waterford. *See* **County Waterford, Ireland**

Waterfowl
Bryant, W. To A Waterfowl.
Dow, P. Duck Pond at Mini's Pasture, a Dozen Years Later, The.
Swenson, M. Willets, The.
Wordsworth, W. Water Fowl.
See also **Ducks; Geese; Swans**

Watergate
Allen, D. Short History of the Vietnam War Years, A.
Woddis. Final Curtain.
See also **Nixon, Richard Milhous**

Waterloo, Battle of (1815)
Byron, G. Eve of Waterloo, The.

Watermelons
Mattawa. Watermelon Tales.
Neruda. Ode to the Watermelon.
Rowan. Prometheus at Coney Island.
Simic. Watermelons.
Tablada. Red cold / guffaw of summer.
Unknown. Ode to the Watermelon.

Watertowers
Auden. Watertowers, The.

Waterwheels
Finlay, I. Waterwheels·in.

Rumi. Turn me like a waterwheel turning a millstone.

Watts, Isaac
"Carroll." Crocodile, The.
Rodriguez, L. Speaking with Hands.

Watts, Los Angeles, California
Rivers, C. Watts.
Rodriguez, L. Heavy blue veins streaked across my mother's legs, some of them bunched up into dark lumps at her ankles.

Waugh, Evelyn
Connolly, C. On Himself.
Sissman. Elegy: E. W.

Waves
Barrington, J. Villanelle VI.
Borkhuis. Quartet.
Chin Nung. I remember when he took me on a trip to this place.
Curnow. You Will Know When You Get There.
Emerson, R. Waves.
Farjeon, E. There Are Big Waves.
Graham, J. Soul Says.
Greer, J. Rodin's "Gates of Hell."
Gunn, T. From the Wave.
Hadas, R. Sentimental Education.
Haines, J. Awakening.
Hanzlik. Cottage Behind the Railway, The.
Higginson, W. Interstices.
Ho Ching-ming. Presented to Wang Wen-hsi.
Hughes, L. Moonlight Night: Carmel.
Kasa. I love and fear him.
Liu E. On the Night of the Sixteenth of the Eighth Month: Watching the Moon from the Deck of the Ship, Aimo-maru in the Black Water Sea.
McGuckian. Sea or Sky?
Miyazawa Kenji. Tanka: "Left alone."
Morrison, L. Surf.
Okamoto. Tanka: "It stands."
Pawsey. White Horses.
Roditi. Aurora Borealis.
Rossetti, C. Horses of the sea, The.
Shakespeare, W. Sonnet 60.
Southard. Waves now fall short, The.
Spicer, J. Lament for the Makers: "No call upon anyone but the timber drifting in the waves."
Stephens, J. Main-Deep, The.
Swenson, M. How Everything Happens.
Tai Piao-yüan. Painting, *"Mist and Rain on the Spring River,"* by Hsiao Chao, The.
Tasso. Now the waves murmur.
Unknown. Waves.
Van den Heuvel. Starting to rise.
Wang Shih-chieng. Bamboo Branch Song of Han-chia.
Seeing Off Editor Wang Chou-tz'u and Secretary Lin Shih-lai on Their Mission as Envoys to the Ryūkyū Islands.
Wang T'ing-hsiang. Climbing to the Top of the City Walls at Kan-yü.
Whitman, W. By that long scan of waves, myself call'd back, resumed upon myself.
Wordsworth, D. Lake was covered all over, The.
Wu Chen. Level forest stretching far and wide, A.
Ni Tsan Poem Following Rhyme-Words of Wu Chen.
Yang Shen. To the Tune "Heavenly Immortal" ("Waves wash off the peach blossoms").
Yeats. Nineteenth Century and After, The.
Yü Chi. Little Landscape by Yen Wen-kuei, A.

Wayne, John
Denning. Movie, The.
Erdrich. Dear John Wayne.

Wealth
Argentarius. Old Story, The.
Aristophanes. Good morrow to the morn next to my gold.
Barber, M. Unanswerable Apology for the Rich, An.
Belloc. Lord Finchley tried to mend the Electric Light.

Borges. Matthew 25:14–30; "For it will be as when a man."
Brennan, G. Mornin's Mornin, The.
Brontë, E. Old Stoic, The.
Brooks, G. Beverly Hills, Chicago.
Campbell, A. To My Friend.
Cendrars. White Suit.
Chaucer. Miller's [*or* Milleres] Tale, The.
Chin Nung. Who bought a mountain and became a hermit there?
Ch'u Ch'uang I. Country House.
Clark, T. I am still rich.
Coleridge, M. Insincere Wish Addressed to a Beggar, An.
Coward. Stately Homes of England, The.
Crowley, R. Of unsaciable purchasers.
Daryush. Children of wealth in your warm nursery.
Davies, W. No Man's Wood.
Dickey, J. Folk Singer of the Thirties, A.
Donne. Poet Turned Lawyer, The.
Drayton. To nothing fitter can I Thee compare.
Dunbar, P. Common Things.
Place Where the Rainbow Ends, The.
Emerson, R. Chartist's Complaint, The.
Compensation ("Wings of Time are black and white, The").
Fletcher, P. Against a Rich Man Despising Poverty.
Frost, R. In Divés' Dive.
Lovely Shall Be Choosers, The.
"There was a rich man."
Fu Hsüan. Gentle Wind [fans the calm night], A.
Fuller, E. What the king has.
Fulton, A. My Diamond Stud.
Galich. Prospectors' Little Waltz, The.
Gumilyov. Plague, The.
Hall, D. One Day, The.
Hardy, T. Ruined Maid, The.
Hernton. Poem.
Herrick. Amber Bead, The.
His Grange, or Private Wealth.
Horace. Conservation.
I often wish'd, that I had clear.
Hughes, L. Cross.
Hybrias The Cretan. Song of Hybrias the Cretan.
Johnson, S. Short Song of Congratulation [*or* To a Young Heir], A.
Juan Chi. Tung-ling melons—men say that long ago.
Kamienska. And behold, one came up to him.
Kennedy, X. In a Prominent Bar in Secaucus [One Day].
Knott. Funny Poem.
Kuzmina-Karavayeva. I still kept thinking that I was rich.
Lampman. To a Millionaire.
Landon. Poor, The.
Leapor. Strephon to Celia.
Li K'ai-hsien. Commiserating with the Poor.
Jade trees from the rear courtyard of the empire of Ch'en.
Mandelstam. I drink to military asters, to all that I'm censured about.
Martial. There's none, that dwell about them, wish them downe.
Mason, W. Against Formal Gardens.
McGuckian. Waterford.
Melville, H. In a Garret.
Murphy, R. Elixir.
Newcastle, M. Her Descending Down.
Pao Chao. Rhyme-Prose on the Desolate City.
Parrott. More Bagpipe Music.
Peacock, T. Rich and Poor; or, Saint and Sinner.
Po Chü-i. Fifteenth Volume, The.
Grand Houses at Lo-yang, The.
Half-recluse, The.
Light Furs, Fat Horses.
Probyn. Love in Mayfair.
Riley, J. Back to Griggsby's Station.
Robinson, E. Bewick Finzer.
Richard Cory.
Rossetti, C. There's snow on the fields.

Sandburg, C. Child of the Romans.
Seneca. 'Tis not wealth that makes a king.
Sidney, P. Sonnet 37: "My mouth doth water, and my breast doth swell."
Simon, P. Richard Cory.
Smith, C. To a Querulous Acquaintance.
Smith, S. Satin-clad, with many a pearl.
Villains.
Soyinka. After the Deluge.
Stevens, W. Good Man Has No Shape, The.
Stevenson, R. System.
To A Gardener.
Tsvetayeva. If the soul was born with pinions.
Praise to the Rich.
Tu Fu. Elegant Women, The.
To Li Po at the Sky's End.
Unknown. Early to bed and early to rise.
In the house east of here lives an old woman.
May Colven [*or* May Colvin].
Meeting in the Road.
On Late-acquired Wealth *or* Riches.
On the Funeral of a Rich Miser.
One Little Boy.
Virgil. Young *Corydon* (hard Fate) an humble Swain.
Watkyns. Worldly Wealth.
Wilbur. Summer Morning, A.
Wylie. Full Moon.
Yoshimi. Tanka: "Street, The."

Weapons
Behn, A. Song: Love Armed.
Cangiullo. Detonation.
Césaire, A. Miraculous Weapons, The.
Coleridge, M. "He Knoweth Not That the Dead Are Thine."
Cross, Jr. Fifty Gunner, The.
Dickinson, E. My Life Had Stood—A Loaded Gun.
Ehrhart. Hunting.
Time on Target.
Floyd. Private Ian Godwin, U. S. M. C.
Haines, J. Poem Like a Grenade, A.
Hughes, T. Crow's Theology.
Knevet. Vote, The.
Komunyakaa. Somewhere Near Phu Bai.
Starlight Scope Myopia.
Layne, M. Guns.
On Hats and Things.
Leonidas of Tarentum. Eurotas said to the goddess of love.
Ndu. Evacuation.
Owen, W. Arms and the Boy.
Paquet. In a Plantation.
Rebelo. Poem for a Militant.
Reed, H. Naming Of Parts.
Ryan, G. If I Had a Gun.
Spender, S. Ultima Ratio Regum.
Webb, F. Gunner, The.
Weigl. Mines.
Yü Chi. Little Landscape by Chao Ch'ien-li, A.

Weariness
Allen, P. Los Angeles, 1980.
Apollinaire. Zone.
Beckett, S. Enueg I.
Enueg II.
Bradstreet, A. As weary pilgrim, now at rest.
Brodsky, J. Eclogue IV: Winter.
Browning, E. My Heart and I.
Byron, G. So we'll go no more a-roving.
Caraion. Deornamentation.
Chōkū. Tanka: "Somewhere around."
Corso. Zizi's Lament.
Daniel, S. If this be love, to draw[e] a weary [*or* wearie] breath.
De la Mare. Tired Tim.
Dove, R. Lost Brilliance.
Du Maurier. Music.
Grimké, A. Butterflies, white butterflies, in the sunshine.
Hall, H. Walkers at Dusk.
Herrick. To Sycamores.
Hollenbeck. Anorexia.
Hughes, L. Weary Blues, The.
Hull, L. Address.
Iskander. Overtired branches are fragile.
Jastrun, T. Seed, The.

Kazarnovsky. Chinese Laundry.
Kornilov, V. Johnny.
Lewis, L. My Students.
Lu Yu. Third Month, Night of the
  Seventeenth, Written While Drunk.
McDonald, R. Incident in Transylvania.
Neruda. Walking [*or* Walkin'] Around.
Nye, N. New Year.
Paquet. Morning—A Death.
Pasolini. Lines from the Testament.
Petri. Once again.
Radnóti. Clouded Sky.
Rossetti, C. From the Antique.
  In Progress.
  Is the moon tired? she looks so pale.
  Sleeping at last, the trouble and tumult over.
Ryan, G. Orbit.
"Severyanin." Minor Elegy, A.
Shakespeare, W. Sonnet 27.
  Sonnet 50.
Todorovski. Peaceful Step, A.
Tucker, M. I am Weary, Mother.
  Weariness.
Ungaretti. Christmas.
Unknown. Lord Randal[l].
Wylie. Nebuchadnezzar.

Weasels
Helwig. Dead Weasel, A.
Masing. To Every Believer.
Moore, M. Wood Weasel, The.
Unknown. Pop Goes the Weasel.
  Song of the Weasel.

Weather
Ackland. Whether a dove or a seagull lighted
  there.
Alexander, W. Lightning.
Ashbery. Crazy Weather.
Breit. Sacramento.
Brooke, H. While ocean thus the latent store
  bequeaths.
Bryant, W. After a Tempest.
Chu Yi-tsun. Tune: "Song of Divination."
Clark, T. Greeks, The.
Cohen, R. Bones of Incontention, The.
Curnow. Wild Iron.
De la Mare. Scarecrow, The.
Dickinson, E. Sun and Fog contested, The.
Eberhart, R. Flux.
Ewart. Weather, The.
Graves, R. Love Story, A.
  Weather of Olympus, The.
Hardy, T. Weathers [*or* Weather].
Herrick. Fair[e] Days; or, Dawn[e]s
  Deceitful[l].
Hoban. Pedalling Man, The.
Hooper, V. Reading, A.
Horan. By Hallucination Visited.
Hughes, L. Strange Hurt.
Joron, A. Zirkus.
Kenyon, J. Coats.
Kirchwey. He Considers the Birds of the Air.
Libbey. Come Into the Night Grove.
Machi. Tanka: "On a day."
Mahon. Kinsale.
Meredith, W. Weather.
Merriam, E. Spell of Weather, A.
  Weather.
  Windshield Wiper.
Miller, L. Weather of Invention, The.
Momaday. Headwaters.
Roethke. Dinky.
Sine. Tornado Warning.
Skinner, J. Rolling in Clover.
Smith, T. Two Poems on the Fear of Love.
Sobin, G. Towards the Blanched Alphabets.
Swenson, M. Cat and the Weather.
  Weather.
T'ang Hsien-tsu. Paintings on My Wall Have
  Been Damaged by the Weather, The.
Unknown. If bees stay at home.
  Imploration for Clear Weather.
  Song for Fine Weather.
  Sunshiny shower, A.
  Weather.
Virgil. Signs of Rain.
Yang Shih-ch'i. Night Rain beneath the City
  Walls of P'i-chou.

Weathervanes
Bunyan. Upon the Weathercock.
Cynewulf. Weathercock, The: "I puff my
  breast out, my neck swells."
Hine. Riddle: "Invisible, chimerical."
Hoban. Pedalling Man, The.

Weaving and Weavers
Alterman. Maid, The.
Cherry, K. Raiment We Put On, The.
Chester, A. Tapestry Weavers, The.
Coleridge, M. Wilderspin.
Deloney. Weavers Song, The.
Doolittle, H. At Ithaca.
Leonidas. Evening and morning old Platthis
  kept.
Po Chü-i. Liao-ling[, sheer patterned silk—
  what is it like?].
  Red embroidered carpet.
Smith, R. Making the Snowshoes.
Unknown. Factory Workers' Song.
  Linen Weaver, The.
  Old and New ("She went up the mountain to
  pluck wild herbs;").
  Poverty Knock.
  You might easy know a doffer.
Wang Chien. Weaving at the Window.
Wu Wei-yeh. Ancient Feeling.
Yeats. Fragments: "Locke sank into a swoon."
Yüan Chen. Song of the Weaving Woman.

Webster, Daniel
Coatsworth. Daniel Webster's Horses.
Whittier. Ichabod[!].

Webster, John
Eliot, T. Whispers of Immortality.

Wedding Songs
Beaumont, F. *et al.* Bridal Song: "Cynthia, to
  thy power."
  Song: "Hold back thy hours, dark night, till
  we have done."
Chapman, G. Bridal Song: "Now sleep, bind
  fast the flood of air."
Crashaw. Epithalamium: "Come, virgin tapers
  of pure wax."
Herrick. Nuptiall Song, or Epithalamie, on Sir
  Clipseby Crew and His Lady, A.
Hopkins, G. At the Wedding March.
Meleager. Upon a Maid That Died [*or* Dyed]
  the Day She Was Married [*or* Marryed].
Sidney, P. Long Their Coupled Joys Maintain.
Udall. I Mun Be Married a Sunday.
Unknown. Gwan! Gwan! Cry the Fish Hawks.
Warner, F. Epithalamium: "This girl all in
  white is my crystal of light."

Weddings
Adisa. Rainbow, The.
Akhmadulina. Bride, The.
Aristophanes. Peace: A Wedding Song, The.
Baillie, J. Song: Woo'd and married and a'.
Bloch, C. White Petticoats.
Bly, R. My Father's Wedding.
Browne, M. Epithalamion/Wedding Dawn.
Catullus. O divine Urania's son.
Chapman, G. New light gives new directions,
  Fortunes new.
Chicken. At last the beef appears in sight.
Corso. Marriage.
Cummings, E. This little bride & groom are.
Dybek. Cherry.
Fennelly. Poem Not to Be Read at Your
  Wedding.
Goodison. Wedding in Hanover.
Gregory, H. To the Last Wedding Guest.
Hall, D. Wedding Party.
Hardy, T. Country Wedding, The.
Hawaiian Oral Tradition. Here all seeking is
  over.
Heaney, S. Wedding Day.
Heywood, J. Egles byrde hath spred his
  wings, The.
Hopkins, G. At the Wedding March.
Howe, S. Bride's Day.
Jonson, B. Epithalamion: or, a Song.
  Now, bride and bridegroom, help to sing.
Killigrew, T. Epilogue to "The Parson's
  Wedding."
Larkin, P. Waiting For Breakfast, While She
  Brushed Her Hair.

  Wedding-Wind.
  Whitsun Weddings, The.
Leithauser. Old Bachelor Brother.
Levis. Story.
Mapanje. *From Florrie Abraham Witness,
  December 1972.*
Masters, E. Wedding Feast, The.
Mother Goose. I saw three ships come sailing
  by.
Nastasijevic. Roadside Fountain.
Norris, K. Wedding in the Courthouse, The.
Pankcy. Reason, The.
Pasternak, B. Into the enormous sky flew.
Patchen. Temple, A.
Pennecuik. Below fair Peebles, on the river's
  side.
Plath. Wreath for a Bridal.
Pointon. In a post-coach and four, with
  postillions as fine.
Robinson, E. Matthew 22:1–14; And again
  Jesus spoke to them.
Rossetti, C. Love from The North.
Rothenberg, J. Poland / 1931 "The Wedding."
St. John, D. Wedding Preparations in the
  Country.
Salter. What Do Women Want?
Scott, W. Lochinvar.
Sikelianos. Village Wedding, The.
Steele, P. Cana.
Storace. Wedding Song.
Thatcher, C. Moggy's Wedding.
Thompson, P. Tribute to the Bride and
  Groom, A.
Unknown. Bridegroom, beloved of my heart.
  My Lord Summons Me.
  Weddings.
Valentine, J. Bride's Hours, A.
Whitney, I. I.W. To her unconstant Lover.
Wilbur. Wedding Toast, A.
Willard, N. Feast of St. Tortoise, The.
Zabolotsky. Wedding.
Zipper. Wedding over, The.
See also **Marriage**

Weeds
Ammons. Reflective.
Clark, L. Ground Elder.
Glück, L. Witchgrass.
Hamburger, M. Weeding.
Han-shan. In an Abandoned Garden.
Hughes, T. Thistles.
Layzer. Lawn Roller, The.
Lofting. Mister Beers.
McClatchy. Weeds.
Okamoto. Tanka: "Selfish woman."
Roethke. Long live the weeds that overwhelm.
  Weed Puller.
Shakespeare, W. Richard II.
T'ao Ch'ien. Returning to My Home in the
  Country.
Virgil. Weeds.

Weeping. *See* **Tears**

Weissmuller, Johnny
James, C. Johnny Weissmuller Dead in
  Acapulco.

Welcome
Bruner. There is a loneliness on city streets.
Herrick. To His Kinsman, Master Thomas
  Herrick, Who Desired to Be in His Book.

Welfare
Angelou. Momma Welfare Roll.
Bird, D. Can I Say.
Jordan, N. Feeding the Lions.
Lane, P. Sexual Privacy of Women on
  Welfare.

Wellington, Arthur Wellesley, 1st Duke of
Harpur, C. Wellington.
Tennyson, A. Bury the Great Duke.

Wells
Bates, C. At Grandfather's.
Bonnefoy. Well, The.
Brown, T. Well, The.
Chappell, F. Cleaning the Well.
Chiyojo. Morning glory!, The.
Chu Yün-ming. Making Fun of the Well at
  the Inn below the Mountain.
Dickey, J. Underground Stream, The.

Dickinson, E.   What mystery pervades a well!
Frost, R.   For Once, Then, Something.
Graham, H.   Aunt Eliza.
Guobin.   My poem is a bridge, silent, lonely;.
Jarrell.   Well Water.
Macpherson, J.   Well, The.
Manger.   Rachel Goes to the Well for Water ("Rachel stands by the mirror and plaits").
Nguyễn Thiên Túng.   Well, The.
Rilke.   Departure of the Prodigal Son*, The.
Sachdev.   Well, The.
Salom.   Well, The.
Seymour, A.   Well, The.
Tao-chi.   Searching for Herb Brazier and Cinnabar Well, I Also Saw the Waterfall of Singing Strings. Alongside Was the Cliff of the Lord of the Mountain.
Yashashchandra.   Drought.
Yüan Chen.   Pitcher, The.

Welsh, The
Housman, A.   Welsh Marches, The.
Philips, K.   On the Welsh Language.
Thomas, R.   Welsh History.
Unknown.   There were three jovial Welshmen.
See also Wales

Wentworth, Thomas, Earl of Strafford
Cleveland, J.   Epitaph on the Earl of Strafford.

Werewolves
Brautigan.   Boat, A.
Tomson.   Gudewife sits i' the chimney-neuk, The.
Walcott.   Le loupgarou.
Watson, R.   Ballad of the Were-Wolf, A.
Wilbur.   Beasts in their major freedom / Slumber in peace tonight.

Wessex, England
Hardy, T.   Wessex Heights.

West Indies
Crane, H.   O Carib Isle!
Dabydeen, C.   Patriot.
Melville, P.   Honor Maria, I see you.
Tessimond.   Jamaican Bus Ride.
Walcott.   Tales of the Islands.

West, Mae
Field, E.   Mae West.

West, Richard
Gray, T.   Sonnet [on the Death of Mr. Richard West].

West, The, United States
Alexander, J.   Winning of the TV West, The.
Andrews, B.   West West.
Benét, R. et al.   Western Wagons.
Benét, W.   Horse Thief, The.
Boswell, M.   Texas Ranger, The.
Brennan, J.   Let the Rest of the World Go By.
Brooks, G.   Strong Men, riding horses. In the West.
Bryant, W.   Prairies, The.
Cary, A.   West Country, The.
Cather, W.   Spanish Johnny.
Chapman, A.   Out Where the West Begins ("Out where the hand-clasp's a little stronger").
Freneau.   On the Emigration to America [and Peopling the Western Country].
Galvin, J.   Western Civilization.
Garland, H.   Goin' Back T'morrer.
Guest, B.   Santa Fe Trail.
Hall, S.   Boot Hill.
Hollo.   Wild West Workshop Poem.
Keithley.   From Land Logic.
Levertov.   Settling.
Linderman.   Cabins.
McGrath, C.   Wheatfield Under Clouded Sky.
McGrath, T.   . . . All that winter, in the black cold, the buzz-saw screamed and whistled.
Michie.   Arizona Nature Myth.
Miller, J.   Westward Ho!
Neihardt.   One more rendezvous.
Ortiz.   Canyon de Chelly.
Padgett, R.   After the Broken Arm.
Pape.   Making a Great Space Small.
Snyder, G.   Milton by Firelight.
Stephen, J.   On a Rhine Steamer.
Unknown.   California Trail.
"Vestal."   Kit Carson's Last Smoke ("Kit Carson came to old Fort Lyons").

Vinz.   Wild West.
Whitman, W.   Pioneers! O Pioneers!
  Promise to California, A.
Wright, J.   Stages on a Journey Westward.

West Virginia (state)
Atkins.   Narrative.
Burgess, F.   Trapping fairies in West Virginia.
Key.   Written at the White Sulphur Springs.
McKinney, I.   Twilight in West Virginia: Six O'Clock Mine Report.
Wright, J.   Mad Fight Song for William S. Carpenter, 1966, A.

West Wind
Burns, R.   Of a' the airts the wind can blaw.
Cheng Hsieh.   West wind has come again to the "tower of makeup," The.
Halevi.   To the Western Wind.
Herrick.   To the Western Wind.
Mao Tse-tung.   Loushan Pass.
Masefield.   West Wind, The.
Shelley, P.   Ode to the West Wind.
Tsung Ch'en.   Snowstorm: At a Gathering at Chang Chu-fu's House, with Tzu-yeh Attending, We All Wrote Poems on This Subject—I Got the Ryhme-Word, "Hu."
Unknown.   Lover in Winter Plaineth for the Spring, The.
Warren, R.   Blow, West Wind.
Yang Shih-ch'i.   Red Heart Station.

Westminster Abbey
Beaumont, F.   Lines on the Tombs in Westminster.
Betjeman.   In Westminster Abbey.
Cope, W.   Engineers' Corner.

Weston, Louise B.
Fordham.   Mrs. Louise B. Weston.

Weston, Rebecca
Fordham.   Mrs. Rebecca Weston.

Weston, Samuel
Fordham.   Rev. Samuel Weston.

Whales and Whaling
Bancquart.   Portrait of Jonah with woman.
Benét, W.   Whale.
Blight.   Death of a Whale.
Booth, P.   Species.
Carpenter, W.   Autumn.
Dutton, G.   Stranded Whales, The.
Hugo, R.   Lady in Kicking Horse Reservoir, The.
Kennedy, X.   Whales off Wales, The.
Kunitz, S.   Abduction, The.
  Wellfleet Whale, The.
Lawrence, D.   Whales Weep Not!
McClure, M.   For the Death of 100 Whales.
McGonagall.   Famous Tay Whale, The.
Meinke.   Death of the Pilot Whales, The.
Melville, H.   Whale, The.
Merwin, W.   For a Coming Extinction.
  Leviathan.
Mori Ōgai.   Tanka: "Far and near."
Pound, E.   Seafarer, The.
Prévert.   Whale hunt, The.
Sexton.   Whale on the beach, you dinosaur.
Shapiro, D.   In a Blind Garden.
Strand.   Shooting Whales.
Unknown.   Blow Ye Winds in the Morning. Whale, The.
Walcott.   Whale, His Bulwark, The.
Young, M.   Whales, The.

Wharton, Anne
Behn, A.   To Mrs. W. on Her Excellent Verses.

Wharves
Bishop, E.   Bight, The.
  Summer's Dream, A.
Bontemps.   Nocturne of the Wharves.
Booth, P.   Jake's Wharf.

Wheat
Alexander, M.   Iowa Farmer.
Auden.   As I walked out one evening.
Bunting.   Brag, sweet tenor bull.
Clare, J.   Wheat Ripening, The.
Glancy.   Wheat.
Greville, F.   Sonnet: "Nurse-life wheat within his green husk growing, The."
Heaney, S.   Harvest Bow, The.

Jackson, H.   Poppies on the Wheat.
Koneski.   Wheat, The.
Li K'ai-hsien.   Compassion for the Farmers.
McCaig.   Betweens.
Merrill, J.   Upward Look, An.
Pasolini.   John 12:24–25; Truly, truly, I say to you.
Robinson, E.   Sheaves, The.
Rossetti, C.   Amen.
Stafford, K.   Proposal.

Wheatley, Phillis
Hayden, R.   Letter from Phillis Wheatley, A.

Wheelbarrows
Unknown.   When I was a bachelor, I lived by myself.
Williams, W.   Red Wheelbarrow, The.

Wheelchairs
Fiser.   Wheelchairs That Kneel Down Like Elephants.
Owen, W.   Disabled.

Wheeling, West Virginia
Wright, J.   In Response to a Rumor that the Oldest Whorehouse in Wheeling, West Virginia, Has Been Condemned.

Wheelock, Eleazar
Hovey.   Eleazar Wheelock.

Wheels
Blamire.   I've gotten a rock, I've gotten a reel.
Buckley, C.   Train in the Desert—1916.
Césaire, A.   Wheel is the most beautiful discovery of man and the only one, The.
Gunn, T.   Wheel of Fortune, The.
Hildegard von Bingen.   Song to the Creator.
Justice, D.   Train.
Kane, M.   Soap Box Derby, The.
Kinzie.   But her arm—damp, small.
Lattimore.   Note on the L and N.
Le Gallienne.   Sunset in the City.
Levy, A.   March Day in London, A.
Morrison, L.   Surf.
Nemerov.   Extract from Memoirs.
Pinsky.   Figured Wheel, The.
Prunty.   Ferris Wheel, The.
Spenser.   Amoretti, Sonnet 18.
Swenson, M.   Riding the "A."
Wojahn.   "Mystery Train" Janis Joplin Leaves Port Arthur for Points West, 1964.

Whirlpools
Gu Cheng.   Epigraph: "In the sea of life."

Whiskey
Brecht, B.   Alabama Song.
Burns, R.   John Barleycorn [a Ballad].
  Scotch Drink.
  Willie Brew'd [or Brewed] a Peck o' Maut.
Hazard, J.   Whiskey in Whiting, Indiana.
Hughes, L.   Bar.
Unknown.   Rye Whiskey.
  Rye Whisky.

Whistler, James Abbott McNeill
Plumly.   After Whistler.
Pound, E.   To Whistler, American.
Rossetti, D.   Limerick: "There's a combative artist named Whistler."

Whistling and Whistlers
Aldis, D.   Whistles.
Baxter, J.   Twenty little engines.
McGough, R.   He Who Owns the Whistle Rules the World.
T'ang Hsien-tsu.   Descending the Ridge of Flying Clouds.
Unknown.   Wonders of Nature.

White (color)
"Akhmatova."   Along the hard crest of the snowdrift.
Alexander, E.   Nineteen.
Coleridge, M.   White Women, The.
Creeley.   Gift, The.
Dickey, W.   January White Sale.
Donne.   Oh my black[e] soul[e]! now thou art summoned!
"Field."   Cyclamens.
Levertov.   Wings, The.
Senghor.   Pearls.

White, Peregrine
Benét, R. et al.   Peregrine White and Virginia Dare.

White Sulphur Springs, West Virginia
Key. Written at the White Sulphur Springs.
Whitefield, George
Wheatley, P. On the Death of the Rev. Mr.
George Whitefield, 1770.
Thoughts on the Works of Providence.
Whitman, Walt
Borges. Matthew XXV:30.
Carnevali. Walt Whitman.
Crane, H. Cape Hatteras.
Forbes, C. Reading Walt Whitman.
García Lorca. Ode for Walt Whitman.
Ginsberg, A. Supermarket in California, A.
Honig, E. Walt Whitman.
Hughes, L. Old Walt Whitman.
Ignatow, D. Walt Whitman in the Civil War
Hospitals.
McMahon, L. Hopkins and Whitman.
Pound, E. Pact, A.
Robinson, E. Walt Whitman.
Simpson, L. Walt Whitman at Bear Mountain.
Spicer, J. Book of Galahad, The.
Taylor, B. Night the Eighth: Camerados.
Wagoner, D. Walt Whitman Bathing.
Whitman, W. Now precedent songs,
farewell—by every name farewell.
Song of Myself.
Walt Whitman, a kosmos, of Manhattan the
son.
Williams, J. Adhesive Autopsy of Walt
Whitman, The.
Whitsunday. *See* Pentecost
Whittier, John Greenleaf
Heard, J. To Whittier.
Koch, K. You were wearing your Edgar Allan
Poe printed cotton blouse.
Lowell, J. Whittier.
Scott, W. Mr. Whittier.
Widecombe Fair
Unknown. Widdecombe [*or* Widdicombe] Fair.
Widows and Widowers
Atwood. At first I was given centuries.
Barber, M. On Seeing an Officer's Widow
Distracted.
Bible, Apocrypha. Widower.
Chaucer. Experience, though noon auctoritee.
Christine de Pisan. I am a widow, robed in
black, alone.
Clifton, L. She Lived.
Craik. Douglas, Douglas, Tender and True.
Daglarca. Cats.
Davies, S. Contention betwixt a Wife, a
Widow, and a Maid, A.
De la Mare. Widow, The.
Dudley, M. At the backyard fence.
Dunbar, W. Translation by Mark Willhardt.
Widow Has Buried Her Second Husband, The.
Dyer, L. Epitaph on the Monument of Sir
William Dyer at Colmworth, 1641.
"Eliza." To My Husband.
Fanning, R. Shoelace.
Fields, J. Jolly fat widows, The.
Glück, L. Racer's Widow, The.
Hands, L. Widower's Courtship, The.
Hardy, T. At the Draper's.
Herrick. Widow's Tears [*or* Widdowes
Teares]: or, Dirge of Dorcas, The.
Homer. Andromache's Lament for Hector.
Jarrell. Burning the Letters.
Jewett, S. Widows' House, The.
Kipling, R. Widower, The.
Kizer, C. Widow in Wintertime, A.
Kooser. Widow, A.
Livesay, D. Widow.
Lowell, R. For Sale.
Masters, E. Veterans of the Wars.
Widows.
Mathews, H. Out and Back on the Fifteenth
Night of the First Month.
Sad Remembrance.
McNair. Minister's Death, The.
Mei Yao Ch'en. In Broad Daylight I Dream
of My Dead Wife.
On the Death of His Wife.
Middleton, T. Song: "In a maiden-time
professed."
Milton. On His Deceased Wife.

Moffat. Widow's Supper.
Nguyễn Khuyến. Widow's Reply to a
Matchmaker, The.
P'an Yüeh. Lamenting the Dead.
Poe. Annabel Lee.
Roberson. Aerialist Narratives, Chapter Three,
The.
Selyns. Reasons for and against Marrying
Widows.
Smith, S. Autumn.
Southey, R. Widow, The.
Su Tung-p'o. Tune. Song of River City.
Sumangala. Free woman, A. At last free!
Tyler, R. Widower, The.
Unknown. Lament of the Border Widow, The.
Widow's Lament.
Wheatley, P. To a Lady on the Death of Her
Husband.
Whitman, W. Out of the cradle endlessly
rocking.
Williams, W. Widow's Lament in Springtime,
The.
Wilson, R. Rejoicing That Attend the Murder
of Famous Men, The.
Wordsworth, W. *see also* The Wanderer, *Book
1 of* The Excursion.
Wotton, S. Upon the Death of Sir Albert [*or
us*] Morton's Wife.
Wight, Isle of, England
Swinburne. Forsaken Garden, A.
Wigs
Cowper, W. On an Old Woman.
Hemphill. Homicide.
Lucilius. On an Old Woman.
Rossetti, C. If a pig wore a wig.
Unknown. Bald Cavalier, The.
Wilberforce University
Heard, J. Wilberforce.
Linden, M. Golden Jubilee of Wilberforce.
To the Conference.
Wilberforce, William
Cowper, W. To William Wilberforce, Esq.
Wilde, Oscar
Betjeman. Arrest of Oscar Wilde at the
Cadogan Hotel, The.
Douglas, L. Dead Poet, The.
Johnson, L. In Honorem Doriani Creatorisque
Eius.
In Honour of Dorian and his Creator.
Parker, D. Oscar Wilde.
Swinburne. Oscar Wilde.
Wilderness
Berry, W. Peace of Wild Things, The.
Birney. Bushed.
Carruth, H. Loon on Forrester's Pond, The.
Davidson, D. Sanctuary.
Dickson, S. Song—Written at the North.
Graves, R. In the Wilderness.
Rocky Acres.
Hecht, A. Alceste in the Wilderness.
Hopkins, G. Inversnaid.
Kinnell. Lastness.
Under the Maud Moon.
Kipling, R. Pelicans in the Wilderness (A
Grave near Halfa).
MacDermot. Dark foreboding haunts me lest I
die, A.
Machado Ruiz. Coplas.
Mair, C. There was a time on this fair
continent.
McKinnon. North, The.
Milosz, C. Matthew 4:1–11; Then Jesus was
led up by the spirit.
Miyazawa Kenji. Tanka: "Steel pen."
Mother Goose. Man in the wilderness asked
[of] me [*or* said to me], The [*or* A].
Peruṅkaṭuṅkō. What Her Girl Friend Said to
her ("Not happy with what he has").
Pratt, E. Precambrian [*or* Pre-Cambrian]
Shield, The.
Rexroth, K. Living Pearl, A.
Sandburg, C. Wilderness.
Scott, D. En Route.
Scott, F. Laurentian Shield.
Shelton, R. Requiem for Sonora.
Simmons, J. In the Wilderness.
Smith, A. Lonely Land, The.

Snyder, G. Above Pate Valley.
Stevens, W. Anecdote of the Jar.
Symons, A. I. Hérodiade.
Tekkan. Tanka: "Vast wilderness."
Wagoner, D. Staying Alive.
Whitman, W. Italian Music in Dakota.
Yi, Y. Wilderness.
Wildflowers
Blake, W. Wild Flower's Song, The.
Howitt, M. Buttercups and Daisies.
Plumly. Peppergrass.
Wildflower.
Rossetti, D. Woodspurge, The.
Williams, W. Queen-Anne's-Lace.
William II, Emperor of Germany
Unknown. Kaiser Bill went up the hill.
**William III, King of England (William of
Orange)**
Hall, H. Upon the King's Return from
Flanders, 1695.
Unknown. Maria to Henric.
William of Orange. *See* **William III, King of
England**
Williams, Arthur Clement
Bibb. In Memory of Arthur Clement Williams.
Williams, Theodore Samuel ("Ted")
Corso. Dream of a Baseball Star.
Williams, William Carlos
Berryman. 324. An Elegy for W.C.W., The
Lovely Man.
Blackburn, P. Phone Call to Rutherford.
Boyle, K. For Marianne Moore's Birthday.
Creeley. For W.C.W ("Rhyme is after, The").
Cruz, V. Essay on William Carlos Williams,
An.
Eady. William Carlos Williams.
Ginsberg, A. Death News.
Kinnell. To William Carlos Williams.
Koch, K. Variations on a Theme by William
Carlos Williams.
Levertov. Williams: An Essay.
Rexroth, K. Letter to William Carlos
Williams, A.
Scott, J. Typing the Letters.
Shapiro, H. For W C W.
Zukofsky, L. William / Carlos / Williams /
alive!
Willow Trees
Bly, R. Hunting Pheasants in a Cornfield.
Ch'ien Ch'ien-i. Willow catkins beyond the
garden wait for evening tides.
Chu Yün-ming. For Several Years I Have
Wanted To Grow a Garden, But Have Never
Finished One. This Year It Is Already
Halfway Through Summer, and This Has
Made Me Despondent.
Crane, H. Repose of Rivers.
Dixon, R. Song: "Feathers of the willow,
The."
Herrick. To the Willow-Tree.
Hsü Wei. Two Fish by a Willow
Embankment.
Levertov. Willows of Massachusetts, The.
Li Meng-yang. Spring Vista from the Tower
of Illuminated Distance.
Li Shang-yin. Willow.
Liu Yu Hsi. Willow Branch Song.
"MacDiarmid." Sauchs in the Reuch Heuch
Hauch, The.
Ni Tsan. To the Retired Scholar Chang.
Ōshima Ryōta. And Then.
Pack, R. Thrasher in the Willow by the Lake,
The.
Rossetti, C. Under willows among the graves.
Sandburg, C. Prairie Waters by Night.
Tsung Ch'en. Side by side, we ride out of the
city.
Tu Fu. Willow, The.
Unknown. East Gate Willows.
Song, A: "My head on moss reclining."
Wang Shih-chieng. Echoing Old Man Mu's
Poem, "Inscribed on Shen Lang-ch'ien's
Little Landscape, Autumn Willows at Stone
Cliff."
Williams, W. Willow Poem.
Yang Shen. To the Tune "Yellow Oriole"
("Willows weave spring sorrow").

Yü Hsüan-chi. Composed on the Theme "Willows by the Riverside."

Wills
Arghezi. Testament.
Donne. Disinherited.
Will, The.
Fogel, A. Printer's Error, The.
Leapor. Mira's Will.
Rossetti, C. Bruised Reed Shall He Not Break, A.
Schuyler, J. Earth's Holocaust.
Unknown. Lord Randal[l].
My father died a month ago.
Whitney, I. And now let mee dispose such things.
And (though I am perswade) that I.
Aucthour Maketh Her Wyll and Testament, The.
I whole in body and in minde.
Now London have I (for thy sake).
Rejoice in God that I am gon.
Wilcox, E. Will.
Winstanley, J. Last Will and Testament, A.
Wilmot, John, 2d Earl of Rochester. *See* **Rochester, John Wilmot, 2d Earl of**
Wilson, John. *See* **"North, Christopher"**
Wilson, Woodrow
Jeffers, R. Woodrow Wilson.
Wiltshire, England
Sassoon. Prehistoric Burials.
Young, A. Wiltshire Downs.
Winchester, England
Betjeman. Hike on the Downs, A.
Warton, T. On King Arthur's Round Table, at Winchester.
Winchester, Virginia
Read, T. Sheridan's Ride.
Wind
Acton, H. Beads of spring rain.
Alakoye. Eshu.
Alberti. Warlike Angels, The.
Amichai. Elegy: "Wind won't come to draw smiles in dream sand, The."
Ammons. Small Song.
Anthony, G. Autumn Evening.
Austin, M. Song of a Man About to Die in a Strange Land.
Avidan. Minor Mythology.
Barnes, W. Brisk Wind, A.
Jenny out from Hwome.
Wind at the Door, The.
Beckett, S. Enueg I.
Bennett, R. Windy Nights.
Bernstein, O. Wind, That Comes on Suddenly, A.
Berry, J. Spirits of Movement.
Bharati. Wind, 9.
Blake, W. Crystal Cabinet, The.
Bly, R. Poem Against the British.
Bogan, L. Zone.
Boldman. Sitting.
Brand, D. Wind.
Brontë, A. Lines Composed in a Wood on a Windy Day.
Brontë, E. Loud without the wind was roaring.
Night Wind, The.
Sun has set, and the long grass now, The.
Wind, I hear it sighing, The.
Brooke, R. Sonnet: "Oh! Death will find me, long before I tire."
Brown, G. Haddock Fishermen.
Bryant, W. Summer Wind.
Bunya no Asayasu. In a gust of wind the white dew.
Burns, R. O [*or* Oh] wert thou in the cauld blast.
Of a' the airts the wind can blaw.
Carew, T. Prayer to the Wind, A.
Cecco Angiolieri, da Siena. Sonnet: Of All He Would Do.
Chang Yü. Song of the Old Oak.
Chao Yi. Strolling in the Countryside.
Ch'en Tzu-lung. Little cart jolting and banging through the yellow haze of dusk, The.
Chivers. Wind, The.
Chu Yi-tsun. Written at Mauve Garden: Pine Wind Terrace.

Chu Yün-ming. As I Looked at a Lake, My Thoughts Turned to a Certain Friend.
Clampitt. Beach Glass.
Clare, J. Wind That Shakes the Rushes, The.
Clarke, A. Strong Wind, A.
Coleridge, S. Homeric Hexameter, The.
Cook, S. Wind is a wolf, The.
Cummings, E. What if a much of a which of a wind.
Wind has blown the rain away and blown, A.
Dacey, P. Small Dark Song.
Dafydd ap Gwilym. Wind, The.
Daive. Under the wind I saw.
Davie. Wind at Penistone, The.
Davies, W. Villain, The.
Day Lewis. Stand-To, The.
Desnos. If, like winds semaphored by a rose.
Dickinson, E. I think that the Root of the Wind is Water.
There came a Wind like a Bugle.
Wild Nights—Wild Nights!
Wind begun to knead the Grass, The.
Wind—tapped like a tired man, The.
Wind that rose, A.
Wind took up the Northern Things, The.
Wind's Visit, The.
Doolittle, H. Heat.
Sea Rose.
Wind Sleepers, The.
Dugan, A. On an East Wind from the Wars.
"Dylan." Blowin' in the Wind.
Eady. Success.
Eliot, T. Wind sprang up at four o'clock, The.
Emerson, R. Snow-Storm, The.
"Field." O Wind, thou hast thy kingdom in the trees.
Frost, R. Aim Was Song, The.
Bereft.
Brown's Descent; or, The Willy-Nilly.
To the Thawing Wind.
Fu Hsüan. Gentle Wind [fans the calm night], A.
García Lorca. Whole Works, The.
Gascoyne. Yves Tanguy.
Gorman, L. Loud wind.
Graddon. North Wind, The.
Wind, The.
Graham, J. Of Forced Sightes and Trusty Ferefulness.
Graves, R. Weather of Olympus, The.
Gunn, T. Elegy on the Dust.
Gurney, I. April Gale.
Hacker, M. Languedocienne.
Hackett, J. Long line of web, A.
Searching on the wind.
Wind gives way to calm.
Wind sounds through the trees.
Harjo, J. Santa Fe.
Harr, L. Hot summer wind, A.
Harter. In the mirror.
Haste. Wind, The.
Henderson, E. March Wind, The.
Hesiod. Winter.
Heywood, T. Finnes and Laplands are acquainted, The.
Higginson, W. Ducks land, The.
Hine. Riddle: "Invisible, chimerical."
Hoban. Pedalling Man, The.
What the Wind Said.
Hollander, J. Grounds of Winter.
Horan. By Hallucination Visited.
Howes, B. Mistral.
Howitt, W. Wind in a Frolic, The.
Hsü Wei. Fifth day of the fifth month.
Hughes, T. Moon-wind.
Wind.
Imbs. Wind Was There, The.
Izumi. Although the wind.
Jaccottet. Right at the end of night.
Jackson, L. Wind Suffers of Blowing, The.
Jeffers, R. Gale in April.
Jewell. Fall wind in pinyons.
That breeze brought it.
Joron, A. Zirkus.
Kangro. Late Flowers, Wind, Sea, Sand and Fish.

Kao Ch'i. Seeing Flowers I Remember My Late Daughter, Shu.
Keane, S. Once the wind.
Kgositsile. Gods Wrote, The.
Kingsley, C. Ode to the Northeast Wind.
Kleinzahler. San Francisco/New York.
Lane, P. Wind Thoughts.
Larkin, P. Wedding-Wind.
Lawrence, D. Butterfly, the wind blows seaward[, strong beyond the garden wall!].
Suspense.
Le Guin. Child on the Shore, The.
Levis. For Zbigniew Herbert, Summer, 1971, Los Angeles.
Li Meng-yang. Seeing Off Commander In Chief Li to Yün-chung.
Wild Wind.
Lindsay, V. Moon's the North Wind's cooky, The.
Liu E. House of Red Leaves, The.
Liu Pang. Song of the Great Wind.
Lloyd, D. Over dried grass.
Ma Chih-yüan. To the Tune "Shui hsien-tzu."
Macdonald, G. Wind and the Moon, The.
Machado Ruiz. Wind, one brilliant day, called, The.
"Macleod." Unknown Wind, The.
Mar, Y. Handfuls of Wind.
Masaoka Shiki. Tanka: "In the house."
Masefield. West Wind, The.
Masing. Only the Mists are Real.
McCrae, H. Winds.
Merton. Lent in a Year of War.
Merwin, W. Utterance.
Meynell, A. To the Beloved.
Wind Is Blind, The.
Milligan, S. Granny.
Moore, L. Homeplace, The.
Morris-Jones. Wind's Lament, The.
Mother Goose. When the wind is in the east.
Nystrom. Prairie Wind.
O'Hara, F. To Hell with It.
Osundare. Eyeful Glances.
Ou-yang Hsiu. East Wind.
Pagis. Words.
Pasternak, B. Into the enormous sky flew.
Wind, The.
Perlman, A. At Fifty in the Crystal-Dead Eye of the Center.
Petrarch. Now that the sky and earth and wind are still.
Phillips, D. Hounds are either the work of wind, The.
Pien Kung. Song of the Boat-Pullers.
Po Chü-i. Cranes, The.
Kept Waiting in the Boat at Chiu-K'ou Ten Days by an Adverse Wind.
Planting Bamboos.
Pomeroy, R. High Wind at the Battery.
Porter, H. Four Winds.
Probyn. Rondelet: "Say what you please."
Raworth. Collapsible.
Rendall, E. Wind, The.
Rilke. Sonnets to Orpheus, The.
Walk, A.
Robinson, E. New England.
Robinson, F. Down rippling, The.
Roethke. Big Wind.
Child on Top of a Greenhouse.
Words for the Wind.
Rose, P. Wind Debates Asian Immigration, The.
Rosen, M. From the winter wind.
Rossetti, C. Who has seen the wind? / Neither I nor you.
Wind has such a rainy sound, The.
Saitō Mokichi. Tanka: "Infinitely far."
Samio. Tanka: "In the evening wind."
Sandburg, C. Four Preludes on Playthings of the Wind.
Wind Song.
Sargent, E. Sea-Breeze at Matanzas, The.
Sassoon. South Wind.
Shakespeare, W. Song: "Blow, blow, thou winter wind."
Song: "When that I was and a little tiny boy."
Shea, M. Moving.

Shelley, P. Dirge, A: "Rough wind, that moanest loud."
Simic. Windy Evening.
Simms, C. ARCS above OXUS.
Sissoko. Whirlwinds / nearly always.
Southern Bushmen Oral Tradition. Day we die, The.
Spiess. Winter wind.
Steele, T. Library, The.
Stephens, J. Wind stood up, and gave a shout.
Stevens, W. Room on a Garden, A.
  Valley Candle.
Stevenson, A. Gales.
Stevenson, R. Wind, The.
  Windy Nights.
Strand. Man in the Tree, The.
  Marriage, The.
Su Shun-ch'in. Commandeering the Wind.
Su Tung-p'o. Begonias.
  Lotus Viewing.
Sub-ok. Spring at Yesan Station.
Supervielle. Missing France.
Tada. Wind invites wind.
Tagami Kikusha-Ni. Wind From Mt. Fuji, The.
Tahmisic. Limbo.
Taliesin. Song to the Wind, A.
Taylor, A. Air.
Teasdale. Wind, The.
Thurman. Rags.
Tu Fu. Overlooking the Desert.
  South Wind.
  To Li Po at the Sky's End.
Turner, F. April Wind.
Unknown. At the beginning of winter a cold spirit comes.
  Baby Seeds.
  Cool breezes—I sleep by the open window.
  I Have a Young Sister.
  Little wind, blow on the hilltop.
  Lover in Winter Plaineth for the Spring, The.
  No weather is ill.
  O western wind when wilt thou blow.
  Riddle: "High as the sky it flies."
  Song of the Trees.
  Stiff winds blow.
  Summer Breeze.
  Wind and the Bird, The.
  Wind is wild tonight, The.
  Winds, The.
Wakoski. Wind Secrets.
Wang Chiu-ssu. I love the serenity of living in the woods.
Wang T'ing-hsiang. Don't ask about the Six Dynasties of the Sui Palace.
Warner, S. El Heroe.
Warren, R. Blow, West Wind.
Weil, Z. October wind, An.
Wiggin. Wind.
Wilbur. After the last bulletins the windows darken.
  Sleepless at Crown Point.
Williams, W. January.
  Porous.
  Wind Increases, The.
Wordsworth, D. Address to a Child during a Boisterous Winter Evening.
Wu of Han. Autumn wind rises; white clouds fly.
Wu Wei-yeh. At the River Tower Parting from My Younger Brother, Fu-ling.
  Climbing P'iao-miao Peak.
Xuân Diệu. Casting Fragrance to the Winds.
Yang Chi. Pitch-Ball.
  Spring dreams, more spring dreams.
  Springtime Embroidery.
  Studio for Listening to the Snow, The.
Yeats. Wind Blows out of the Gates of the Day, The.
Yü Chi. Going to the Ministry with Chao Tzu-ch'i.
Yu Xuanji At Home in the Summer Mountains.
Yüan Hung-tao. Pei-mang Cemetery.
Yüan Mei. Things Seen.
Yün Shou-p'ing. For a hundred miles the west wind carries the fragrance of millet.

  Green Banana Leaves.
  On a Landscape by Myself.
  Sadness in the Autumn Chambers.
Zach. I Hear Something Falling, said the wind.
Zukofsky, L. Cars once steel and green, now old.
See also North Wind; Tornadoes; West Wind
Windflowers. *See* Anemones
Windhovers. *See* Falcons
Windmills
Lucas, E. Windmill, The.
Windows
Aichinger. Glimpse from the Past.
Aiken, C. Window, The.
Allard. Snow by the window paper flowers gathering dust.
Barnstone, A. Windows in Providence.
Bostok. Pregnant again.
Bowes-Lyon. Refugee, A.
Breton, A. Spectral Attitudes, The.
Brodsky, J. I Sit by the Window.
Brooks, G. Boy Breaking Glass.
Browning, E. Casa Guidi Windows.
Cardenal. Vision from the Blue Window.
Clark, T. Eyeglasses.
Corbet. Upon Fairford Windows.
Cowper, W. Lines Written upon a Window-Shutter at Weston.
Cummings, E. Spring is like a perhaps hand.
Daryush. Still-Life.
Dickinson, E. I had been hungry, all the Years.
Fatchen. Be Quiet!
"Field." Nightfall.
Fleming, E. Window cleaner's life is grand!, A.
Grennan. Woman at Lit Window.
Gunn, T. Monster, The.
Haas, R. Moon at the window.
Herbert, G. Windows, The.
Hoban. Windows.
Hoyt, C. In that empty house.
Ismail. Wall, The.
Jackson, L. Prisms.
Lane, P. Girl at the Window.
Larkin, P. Aubade: "I work all day, and get half-drunk at night."
Levertov. Crack, The.
Lindsay, V. Factory windows are always broken.
Longfellow, H. Ropewalk, The.
Lysohorsky. At a Sunlit Window.
Madhubuti. After Her Man Had Left Her for the Sixth Time That Year / (An Uncommon Occurrence).
McClintock, M. Broken window, A.
Mew. On the Asylum Road.
Millay, E. From a Train Window.
Mountain, M. Pick-up truck.
Nagy, A. Four-Light Window, A.
Nemerov. Storm Windows.
Palmer, M. Theory of the Flower, The.
Raab, L. Sudden Appearance of a Monster at a Window.
Rankine. New Windows.
Ratcliffe, S. Space in the light said to be where one / comes from.
Revell. Sirius.
Roseliep. Child.
Rossetti, C. Reflection.
Rotella, A. From her neon window.
  From the window.
Shange. Tango.
Southard. At the window, sleet.
Synge. Dread.
Taggart, J. Sainte-Chapelle.
Tao-chi. Bend after bend, the long embankment.
Teller. Minor Key.
Thomas, R. View from the Window, The.
Unknown. Green, green
  Optimist fell ten stories, The.
Van den Heuvel. Branch, A.
Wallace-Crabbe. Windows, The.
Yang Shen. To the Tune "New Moon."
Yoshimi. Tanka: "Moment, The."

Zagajewski. Moths watched us through.
Zhenkai. Collection, The.
Windsor Castle
Surrey. In Windsor Castle.
  When Windsor Walls.
Windsor Forest, England
Pope, A. Hymn Written in Windsor Forest, A.
Wine
Abu Zakariya. Bubbling Wine.
Agathias. It is not wine that makes me reel / Not juice of grape I crave.
Al-Harizi. Under Leafy Bowers.
Alcaeus. Evening Song, An.
Aldrich, H. Catch, A.
Antipater of Sidon. This is the grave of grey-haired Maronis.
Argentarius. Welcome, old friend, long-necked bottle.
Ayres. Fly, The.
Barlas. Dancing Girl, The.
Berrigan, T. Certain Slant of Sunlight, A.
Campbell, A. Song of the Decanter.
Cao Bá Quát. Drink and Drown Your Cares.
Cheng Hsieh. On a Painting of a Knight-Errant.
Ch'ien Ch'ien-i. Drinking Wine.
  Poem on Drinking Wine with the Degree-Holder Ku.
Ch'ien T'ao. In the quiet of the morning I heard a knock at my door;.
Chu Yün-ming. Drinking.
  Too Lazy to Write Poetry.
Clements, A. Elegy.
Cowley, A. Epicure, The ("Fill the bowl with rosie [or rosy] wine").
Crashaw. To Our Lord, upon the Water Made Wine.
Dickinson, E. Let me not thirst with this Hock at my Lip.
Dioscorides. Thracian page-boy / mastered, A.
Dioscorides. Hiero's former Nurse.
Doolittle, H. Wine Bowl.
Emerson, R. Bacchus.
Eratosthenes. Bacchus, receive my offering, not.
Fitzgerald, E. 12.
Ghalib, A. Colors of tulips and roses are not the same, The.
Hafiz. Ode 44: "Last night, as half asleep I dreaming lay."
  Ode 487: "With last night's wine still singing in my head."
Heaney, S. Cana Revisited.
Hedylos. From dawn to dark, and back from dark to dawn.
  Let's drink up: with wine, what original.
Herrick. Anacreontic[k] Verse.
  His Farewell [or Fare-well] to Sack.
  To Live Merrily, and To Trust to Good Verses.
  Welcome to Sack, The.
Hofmannsthal. Two of Them, The.
Hsieh Chin. Government wine of Peking is sweeter than honey, The.
Hsü Chün-ch'ien. Sitting Out New Year With My Wife.
Hsü Pen. Following the Rhymes of Kao Chi-ti's Poem: "We Had Planned to Travel to Cloud Cliff But Couldn't Because of Rain."
Japanese Oral Tradition. Butterfly Wine.
Jonson, B. Epigram. To the Household. 1630, An.
  Swell me a bowl with lusty wine.
K'ang Hai. Sitting by Myself.
Kao Ch'i. Mooring Our Boat at Tan-yang Harbor.
Kooser. How to Make Rhubarb Wine.
Lebensohn. Wine.
Li Ch'ing-chao. Quail Sky.
Li Ho. Bring in the Wine.
Li Po. Bring the Wine!
  Drinking Alone in the Moonlight.
  If Heaven weren't fond of wine.
Liu E. Pleasures of Shinbashi.
Lovelace, R. Fly about a Glass[e] of Burnt Claret, A.
  Loose Saraband, A ("Nay, prethee [or prithee]

   dear, draw nigher").
Vintage to the Dungeon, The.
Lu Yu. Boating in Autumn.
   Idleness.
   Pedlar of Spells, The.
   Trip to Mountain West Village, A.
Martial. How he would drinke his Wine.
   You Serve the Best Wines Always, My Dear
      Sir.
Masaoka Shiki. Tanka: "Dipped."
Mo Shih-lung. Drinking Wine.
Moiro. Now you lie—a grape-offering.
Montgomery, S. Her silence at dinner.
Ni Tsan. On the Twentieth Day.
Page, G. In Dante's Hell.
Pankey. Reason, The.
Philip of Thessalonica. I am a plane-tree. I
   was sound and strong when the blasts.
Pien Kung. On Hearing That San-p'ing's
   Newly Brewed Chrysanthemum Wine Is
   Ready to Drink—Investigating with a Poem.
Po Chü-i. Fishing in the Wei River.
   Good-bye to the People of Hangchow.
   Lodging with the Old Man of the Stream.
   My servant wakes me: 'Master, it is broad
      day'.
   Thinking of the Past.
   To his Brother Hsing-chien.
Redi. Bacchus's Opinion of Wine, and Other
   Beverages.
Rilke. John 2:1–12; On the third day there
   was a marriage.
   On the Marriage at Cana.
Ristovic. Old Motif.
Roseliep. Brushing my sins.
Rotella, A. With wine glasses.
Rufinus. I have armoured my feelings.
Rumi. This marriage be wine with halvah,
   honey dissolving in milk.
   When grapes turn.
Shen Chou. Drinking at Night with Yen
   Kung-mou.
   Moon in a Winecup, The.
   Sent in Parting to Yen Kung-su.
   Taoist Huang Has Died of Alcoholism, The.
   To the Tune "Bamboo at West Lake."
   Wine Cup and Bright Moon.
Shirley, J. Two Gentlemen That Broke Their
   Promise of a Meeting.
Steele, P. Cana.
Su Tung-p'o. Rhyming with Tzu-yu's
   "Treading the Green."
   Weaker the wine, The.
T'ang Yin. Song of Peach Blossom Retreat.
T'ao Ch'ien. Stopping Wine.
Thomas, D. This bread I break was once the
   oat.
Ulinover. Havdolah Wine.
Unknown. Bakchos the wine-god / dissolver of
   limbs.
   Five Arabic Verses in Praise of Wine.
   How was I born? Where from? Why did I
   come.
   In Praise of Wine.
Ushakov. Wine.
Wang Chi. 'TELL me now, what should a man
   want'.
Wen Cheng-ming. All of you are seeing me
   off, east of the Emperor's city.
   Mooring My Boat on the Ssu River and
   Watching the Moon.
   Wine of parting flowed and flowed, The.
   Year *Chi-wei* (Fifteen Fifty Nine), New Year's
   Day, The.
Wilbur. Wedding Toast, A.
Wu Wei-yeh. Feelings Come As I Pass
   through Wu-chiang.
Yang Chi. Meeting My Fellow Countryman,
   Yü Wu-chung.
Yang Shen. To the Tune "Stopping My Horse
   to Listen."
Yang Shih-ch'i. Not sobered up from my
   muddy Kao-yang drunk.
Yeats. Drinking Song, A.
Yüan Chieh. Stone Fish Lake.
Yün Shou-p'ing. As we say farewell to
   autumn.

Wings
Brontë, C. Like wolf—and black bull or
   goblin hound.
Day Lewis. Conflict, The.
Dickinson, E. Bat is dun with wrinkled
   Wings, The.
Dove, R. Wingfoot Lake.
Field, E. Icarus.
Herbert, G. Easter-Wings.
Hildegard von Bingen. Antiphon for Divine
   Wisdom.
Hopkins, G. God's Grandeur.
Levertov. Dead Butterfly, The.
Mataka. Ornithology.
Pettet. Annul.
Robinson, A. Song: "Oh for the wings of a
   dove."
Rossetti, C. On the Wing.
Sartarelli. That Land (3).
Sexton. To a Friend Whose Work Has Come
   to Triumph.
Smith, C. On the Aphorism "L'Amitié est
   l'Amour sans Ailes."
Thomson, J. Migrating Birds.
Unknown. In the north-west there is a high
   house.
   Wings.
Warren, R. Evening Hawk.
Watson, R. Cage, The.
Yeats. Mother of God, The.
Yün Shou-p'ing. On a Painting of Mushrooms.

Winter
Ackland. Winter.
Aichinger. Enumeration.
Akhmadulina. Winter.
Alegría. We Were Three.
Aliger. Blue Hour, The.
Amann. Winter burial.
Austin, M. Grass on the Mountain, The.
Bachmann. Days in White.
Barclay, A. Winter snowes, all covered is the
   grounde, The.
Barnes, W. Winter Night, A.
Bartošová. And That Is Why. . . .
Belševica. Willow-catkins threw off their
   narrow shoes.
Berryman. Winter Landscape.
   Winter-Piece to a Friend Away, A.
Bethell. Warning of Winter.
Bible, *O.T.* Lo, the Winter Is Past.
Bishop, E. Two Mornings and Two Evenings.
Blaga. Anno Domini.
Blake, W. Song By an Old Shepherd.
Blok. Winter day is cold and snowy, The.
Bly, R. Three Kinds of Pleasures.
Blyton, E. Winter.
Bobrowski. Shadowland.
Boland, E. Pomegranate, The.
Bold, A. Auld Symie, The.
Boldman. JANUARY FIRST.
Borisov. Untitled.
Bourne, V. Silkworm, The.
Breit. Sacramento.
Brickley. Few flakes appear, A.
Brodsky, J. Eclogue IV: Winter.
Brontë, E. Upon her soothing breast.
Brooks, G. Cynthia in the Snow.
Brown, L. Winter Sonnet.
Brown, S. Virginia Portrait.
Bruner. Midwinter.
Bryant, W. Death of the Flowers, The.
   Winter Piece, A.
Bu-er. Late Indian summer's.
Burke, M. Rainy winter evening.
Burns, R. Up in the Morning Early.
Buxton. Putting the World to Bed.
Bynner. Wintry Mind, The.
Campbell, T. Ode to Winter.
Campbell, W. How One Winter Came in the
   Lake Region.
   Winter Lakes, The.
Campion, T. Now winter nights enlarge.
Caraion. Winter.
Carruth, H. Twilight comes to the little farm.
Chesterman. Outside.
Ch'ien Wen-Ti. Getting Up in Winter.
Ch'in Kuan. Along the Grand Canal.

Chōkū. Tanka: "Train speeds on, The."
Christopher. 5°.
Clare, J. Emmonsail's Heath in Winter.
   Schoolboys in Winter.
   Winter Fields.
   Winter in the Fens.
Clark, L. Singing in the Streets.
Coleridge, M. Witch, The.
Cook, S. Robin in December, The.
Corben. After Christmas.
   Before Christmas.
Corke. Calm Winter Sleep.
Corpi. Winter Song.
Cranch. December.
Cristall. Song: "Through springtime walks,
   with flowers perfumed."
Cummings, E. I was sitting in
   mcsoreley's.   outside it was New York
   and beauti- / fully snowing.
Cunningham, A. Gone Were but the Winter
   Cold.
Daiches. Winter Song.
Daniel, S. When winter snows upon thy sable
   hairs.
Davie. Winter Talent, A.
De la Mare. Alone.
   Winter.
Dickinson, E. I think the Hemlock likes to
   stand.
   Not at Home to Callers.
   There's a certain Slant of light.
   'Twas here my summer paused.
Donaghy, J. Winter.
Donne. Nocturnal[l] upon Saint Lucy's [*or* S.
   Lucies] Day, Being the Shortest Day, A.
Doolittle, H. Blue-geese, white-geese, you may
   say.
Driscoll, L. Thanksgiving.
Eberhart, R. Spider expects the cold of winter,
   The.
Eglitis. Winter has already shriveled—spring
   rushes in with / black burial steeds.
Eigner. Open Air Where.
Eklund. Boyhood Winter.
Eliot, T. Journey of the Magi.
   Little Gidding.
Fallon, P. Winter Work.
Fan Ch'eng-ta. Winter.
Farrar, J. Comparison, A.
Fell, A. Freeze-Frame.
"Field." Sullenness.
   To the Winter Aphrodite.
Field, R. Something told the wild geese.
Finch, R. Turning.
Fisher, A. Snowy Benches.
Flynn, F. Winter Morning.
Follain. Music of Spheres.
Fort, C. How Old Are the People of the
   World.
Francis, R. Blue Winter.
Frost, R. Birches.
   Hillside Thaw, A.
   Old Man's Winter Night, An.
   Onset, The.
   Reluctance.
   Stopping by Woods on a Snowy Evening.
   Winter Eden, A.
"Gander." (The Twelve Months).
Gascoyne. Winter Garden.
Gates, L. Winter dawn;.
Glück, L. Illuminations.
Graddon. Winter Joys.
Graves, R. Frosty Night, A.
   Star-Talk.
Greig, A. Winter Climbing, The.
Grier. My Winter Past.
Grimké, A. Winter Twilight, A.
Grimke, C. Parting Hymn, A.
Hamilton, J. Cold Blows the Wind.
Handlin. Cold winter morning.
Hardy, T. Birds at Winter Nightfall.
   Frozen Greenhouse, The.
   I need not go.
   Neutral Tones.
   Winter in Durnover Field.
Harjo, J. Blue Elliptic.
   Skeleton of Winter.

Harper, M.   Drive In, The.
Harr, L.   Pale dawn moon, A.
Harter.   Winter rain.
Harwood, L.   Animal Days.
Hayden, R.   Those Winter Sundays.
Hayne, P.   On the Occurrence of a Spell of Arctic Weather in May, 1858.
Hecht, A.   Sestina d'Inverno.
Henson, L.   I Am Singing the Cold Rain.
Herlin.   Warmth of the wind-break wall, The.
Hesiod.   Anatomy of Winter, The.
Winter.
Higginson, W.   More intricate.
Hoban.   October Tuesday.
Hollander, J.   Effet de Neige.
Grounds of Winter.
Hood, T.   No sun—no moon!
Hooper, V.   Deep Season.
Hopkins, G.   Winter with the Gulf Stream.
Horan.   By Hallucination Visited.
Housman, A.   In midnights of November.
Night Is Freezing Fast, The.
Winter.
Hsieh Hui-lien.   Rhyme-Prose on the Snow.
Huchel.   Landscape Beyond Warsaw.
On the Way.
Hughes, G.   Snow Falling.
Hughes, L.   Winter Moon.
Hughes, R.   Winter.
Hughes, T.   New Year's [or Year] Song.
Roe-Deer.
Snowdrop.
Hugo, R.   Letter to Scanlon from Whitehall.
Hull, L.   Letter, The.
Hummer, T.   Apocatastasis Foretold in the Shape of a Canvas of Smoke.
Hwang Chin-i.   I cut in two / A long November night.
Izumi.   It is the time of rain and snow.
Jennings, E.   Winter Love.
Jewett, S.   Country Boy in Winter, A.
John.   Child's Winter Evening, A.
Jones, P.   Christmas, Boston Nineteen Eighty Nine.
Juan Chi.   Singing of Thoughts.
Kantaris.   Awakening to Snow.
Stocking Up.
Kao Ch'i.   On a Painting by Hsia Kuei Entitled "Returning in Wind and Snow to a Village Home."
Kaplinski, J.   We started home, my son and I.
Keats.   In drear-nighted December.
Kelly, B.   Silver Lake.
Kenny, M.   December.
Kenyon, J.   Depression in Winter.
February: Thinking of Flowers.
Kinnell.   Bear, The.
Kirsch, S.   Air already smells like snow, my lover, The.
Date.
Kitahara Hakushū.   Tanka: "Winter day."
Komunyakaa.   Smokehouse, The.
Kopland.   Breughel's Winter.
Kuan Han-ch'ing.   Snow powder, flowery.
Lampman.   Winter Evening.
Landor, W.   Winter.
Lawrence, D.   Drained Cup, The.
Levertov.   Crack, The.
Lewis, J.   Stories.
Li Ho.   Northland in Cold, The.
Li K'ai-hsien.   Commiserating with the Poor.
Liu Tsung-yüan.   River Snow.
Locke, M.   Sonnet: "I hate the Spring in parti-coloured vest."
Longenbach.   What You Find in the Woods.
Longfellow, H.   Afternoon in February.
Fragment: December 18, 1847.
Snow-Flakes.
Longley, M.   Remembering Carrigskeewaun.
Lorde.   Teacher.
Woman Thing, The.
Lovelace, R.   Grasshopper, The.
Lowell, R.   New Year's Day.
Lucie-Smith.   Poet in Winter.
MacCaig.   Sleet.
"MacDiarmid."   Lourd on my hert as winter lies.

Macdonald, G.   Sweet Peril.
Machado Ruiz.   Coplas.
Machi.   Tanka: "With a serene look."
Majer.   On my winter walk.
Marcinkevičius.   Father's Winter.
Mathias, E.   In the Wood.
McAuley, J.   Winter Drive.
McClatchy.   Winter without Snow, A.
McCosker.   Full Moon that Strikes the Earth Cold.
McDonald, W.   Winter Before the War, The.
McGrath, T.   Black Train, The.
Merwin, W.   Dusk in Winter.
Mezhirov.   From the War.
Miles, S.   Plumbers.
Miliauskaite.   On winter nights, when my grandmother.
Millay, E.   Spring in the Garden.
Miller, L.   Weather of Invention, The.
Milosz, C.   It Was Winter.
Momaday.   Winter Holding off the Coast of North America.
Moriarty, L.   Rondeaux: "Each page a day."
Morris, L.   Poem of the Frost and Snow.
Morse, S.   Song in the Cold Season.
Mother Goose.   Winter.
Na-lan Hsing-te.   Tune: "Immortal at the River"—Winter Willow.
Nagys.   Laterna Obscura.
Nash, O.   Winter Morning.
Nemerov.   Spell before Winter, A.
Nerval.   Girl Cousin, The.
Nicholls, J.   Winter crept.
Niedecker.   Margaret Fuller.
O'Grady, S.   Winter in Lower Canada.
Oppen.   From a Photograph.
Osgood, F.   Winter Fairyland in Vermont.
Otsuji.   Winter midnight.
Ou-yang Hsiu.   Answer to Ting Yuan Ch'en, An
Owen, G.   Winter Days.
Owen, W.   Exposure.
Padgett, R.   December.
Pasternak, B.   February. Get your ink and weep.
Winter Night.
Paz.   Solo for Two Voices.
Peake.   Conceit.
Pfeiffer, E.   Song of Winter, A.
Plath.   Wintering.
Po Chü-i.   Parting from the Winter Stove.
Sitting at Night.
Winter Night.
Pound, E.   Ancient Music.
Quigless.   Winter.
Rakosi.   Fluteplayers from Finmarken.
Ramler.   Yearning for Winter.
Ramsay, A.   Up in the Air.
Rathenow.   Prague.
Rein.   Calendar of the Air.
Rickword.   Winter Warfare.
Roberson.   Blue Horses.
Roberts, E.   Cold Fear.
Roberts, M.   Demeter Grieving.
Robinson, M.   January, 1795.
Rochester, J.   Mistress, The: A Song.
Roethke.   Coming of the Cold, The.
Ronsard.   Sonnet For Helen.
Root, J.   Snail Winter.
Rossetti, C.   Amen.
Bread and milk for breakfast.
Endure Hardness.
Grown and Flown.
I dug and dug amongst the snow.
Summer.
There's snow on the fields.
Winter.
Winter: My Secret.
Rotella, A.   From her neon window.
Ryan, R.   Lake of the Woods, The.
Winter in Minneapolis.
Saarikoski.   Winter solstice.
Sackville-West.   Persia.
Saigyo.   In Winter.
Scott-Heron.   Winter in America.
Seward.   December Morning.

While one sere leaf, that parting autumn yields.
Shakespeare, W.   Song: "Under the greenwood tree."
Sonnet 97.
Winter.
Shelley, P.   Summer and Winter.
Shumaker.   First Winter: Joy.
Simic.   Winter Night.
Simmons, J.   Archæologist, The.
Simovic.   Breakfast.
Simpson, L.   Landscape with Barns.
Sirr.   Collector's Marginalia, The.
Smith, M.   Stopping to Take Notes.
Snyder, G.   Dragonfly / Dead on the snow.
So Chong-Ju.   Winter Sky.
Southey, R.   Winter.
Spender, S.   Ice.
Spiess.   Chain saw stops, The.
Spivack, K.   March 1st.
Standish.   New Year's Days.
Stanescu.   Winter Ritual.
"Stephany."   What marked the river's flow.
Stephens, J.   White Fields.
Stevens, W.   No Possum, No Sop, No Taters.
Snow Man, The.
Stevenson, R.   Ille Terrarum.
Winter Time [or Winter-Time].
Summers, H.   Cold February.
Synge.   Winter.
Tabb.   Winter Twilight, A.
Tate, A.   Seasons of the Soul.
Taylor, A.   Fire.
Teasdale.   February Twilight.
Night.
Tennyson, A.   Song: "Spirit haunts the year's last hours, A."
Thaxter.   Chanticleer.
Thomas, D.   Winter's Tale, A.
Thomas, E.   Thaw.
Thompson, P.   Winter Night, A.
Thoreau.   Pray to What Earth Does This Sweet Cold Belong.
To the Maiden in the East.
When Winter fringes every bough.
Winter and Spring Scene, A.
Winter Memories.
Thrale.   Winter in Wales, A.
Tomlinson, C.   Winter Encounters.
Tremayne.   Wanting News.
Ts'en Shen.   Song of the White Snow: Saying Farewell to Supervisor Wu Returning to the Capital.
Tso Ssu.   Scholar in the Narrow Street, The.
Tsung Ch'en.   Snowstorm: At a Gathering at Chang Chu-fu's House, with Tzu-yeh Attending, We All Wrote Poems on This Subject—I Got the Ryhme-Word, "Hu."
Tsurayuki.   When.
Tu Fu.   Deep in Winter.
Turner, W.   Song: "Lovely hill-torrents are."
Ungaretti.   Christmas.
Unknown.   At the beginning of winter a cold spirit comes.
Christmas Song ("Trees are all bare not a leaf to be seen, The").
Clear moon brightly shining in the night.
Cold Is the North Wind.
First month of winter: cold air comes.
I bring you news.
Night was growing cold, The.
Snowy Day, A.
Song of Winter, A.
When ice on the pond is three feet thick.
When the Snow is on the Ground.
Wind piercing, hill bare, hard to find shelter.
Winter [or Wynter] Wakeneth All [or Al] My Care.
Winter Wise.
Updike.   Winter Ocean.
Valentine, J.   Snow Landscape, in a Glass Globe.
Valéry.   Helen.
Vallejo.   Our Daily Bread.
Vaughan, H.   I walked [or walkt] the other day to spend my hour.
Venclova.   Dialogue in Winter.

Very. Robe, The.
Spirit, The.
Winter Rain, The.
Viên Linh. Cold season—birds all head for warmer climes.
Virgil. Scythian winters.
When from the palid Sky the Sun descends.
Wade, T. Winter Shore, The.
Wagoner, D. Walking in the Snow.
Walcott. Village Life, A.
Wen-Ti Chien. Winter Night.
White, G. On the Dark, Still, Dry, Warm Weather Occasionally Happening in the Winter Months.
Whiteman. Winter Burn.
Whitman, W. To a Locomotive in Winter.
Wieseltier. On Guard.
Wilbur. April 5, 1974.
Winter Deepening, The.
Year's End.
Wilde, O. Le Jardin des Tuileries.
Williams, W. Are the desolate, dark weeks.
These are the desolate, dark weeks.
Willis, N. January 1, 1829.
Wills, J. Winter again.
Wingfield. Winter.
Wollach. This Poem Should Have Etc.
Wordsworth, D. Address to a Child during a Boisterous Winter Evening.
After-recollection at Sight of the Same Cottage.
O thought I!
Wordsworth, W. Composed Near Calais on the Road Leading to Ardres, August 7, 1802.
Wright, J. Late November in a Field.
Sparrows in a Hillside Drift.
Wright, J. Sonnet for Christmas.
Wright, K. Frozen Man, The.
Red Boots On.
Wylie. Puritan Sonnet, IV.
Velvet Shoes.
Yi, K. Winter Vision, The.
Yorie. Cat's Eye, The.
Young, M. Winter Scene.
Zanzotto. Epiphany.
Zenmaro. Tanka: "All the young men I know."
Žukauskas. Midwinter Tourists.

Winters, Yvor
Gunn, T. To Yvor Winters, 1955.

Wisconsin (state)
Bly, R. Three Kinds of Pleasures.
Booth, P. He was fifteen. And she, Wisconsin.
Wallace, R. Makings of Happiness, The.

Wisdom
Arnold, M. Shakespeare.
Atwood. Procedures for Underground.
Balmont. I don't know the wisdom others seem to need.
Baudelaire. Anywhere Out of the World.
Bible, O.T. Happy Is the Man.
Words of a wise man's mouth are, The.
Blake, W. Voice of the Ancient Bard, The.
Bogan, L. Men loved wholly beyond wisdom.
Bozhilov. Wise Ones, The.
Brecht, B. Three Fragments.
Brew. Search, The.
Carter, E. Ode to Wisdom.
Ch'iao Chi. Tune: "Sheep on Mountain Slope."
Chimombo. Messengers, The.
Ch'iu Wei. Visiting a Recluse on West Mountain and Not Finding Him In.
Cowper, W. Wisdom.
Crane, H. Praise for an Urn.
Crashaw. Neither Durst Any Man From That Day Ask Him Any More Questions.
Cummings, E. If up's the word;and a world grows greener.
May my heart always be open to little.
You shall above all things be glad and young.
Davenant. Lover and Philosopher.
De la Mare. Moonlight.
Ded. On the way to God the difficulties.
Dickinson, E. We learned the Whole of Love.
"Why do I love" You, Sir?
Duggan, L. Eight xx.

Emerson, R. Limits.
Prudence.
Euripides. What is wisdom: What gift of the gods.
Fitzgerald, E. 27.
Hacker, M. Rune of the Finland Woman.
Harris, J. Aphorisms.
Plantation Proverbs.
Herbert, G. Elixir [or Elixer], The.
Hewitt, J. Once alien here my fathers built their house.
Hildegard von Bingen. Antiphon for Divine Wisdom.
Hölderlin. In the Days of Socrates.
"Hope." For This Is Wisdom.
Hsi K'ang. Taoist Song.
Huang T'ing-chien. Once More Following the Rhymes of Pin-lao's Poem "Getting Up After Illness."
Jeffers, R. Prescription of Painful Ends.
Jones, R. Revelations, First Time.
Jonson, B. Ode, An: "High-spirited friend, / I send not balms, nor corsives to your wound."
Juvenal. Fortune a Goddess is to Fools alone.
Kavanagh, P. To Hell with Commonsense.
Lawrence, D. Race and Battle.
Li Shang-yin. Double curtains hang deep in the room of Never Grieve.
Macdonald, G. Baby-Sermon, A.
Makeda (Queen of Sheba). I fell.
Wisdom is.
Martial. Allusion to Martial, An.
Meredith, G. All other joys of life he strove to warm.
Mirabai. Wild woman of the forests, The.
Montagu, L. Lover, The; a Ballad.
Nesbit, E. Things That Matter, The.
Nguyễn Bỉnh Khiêm. Before the world of power you'll fold your arms.
Nguyễn Đình Chiểu. Fisherman Speaks His Mind, A.
Oppen. Quotations.
Owen, G. Prudent Simplicity.
Owen, M. African Sunday.
Philips, A. Wit and Wisdom.
Philodemus. Once I was in love. Who's been exempted?
Pindar. Pindar on the Eclipse of the Sun.
Ransom, J. Address to the Scholars of New England.
Tall Girl, The.
Rexroth, K. Without me you can only.
Richards, E. Wise old owl lived in an oak, A.
Robinson, A. Wise-Woman, The.
Robinson, E. Master, The.
Rossetti, C. God Is Everywhere.
Passing and Glassing.
Rossetti, D. Woodspurge, The.
Shakespeare, W. Beshrew me but I love her heartily;.
Sill. Truth at Last.
Singer, B. For Josef Herman.
Smith, C. Thirty-eight: Addressed to Mrs H—y.
Smith, S. Is it wise.
Portrait.
Snyder, G. Path to Han-shan's place is laughable, The.
Sobiloff. Wisdom has nothing to do with age.
Sokolov. Snow's white pencil outlining the buildings...
Spender, S. Auden at Milwaukee.
Ssu-k'ung Shu. Exhorting Myself.
Stevenson, A. He Who Loved Beauty.
Swift, J. Stella's Birthday ([March 13,] 1727).
Tartler. Sighioara 1982.
Tennyson, A. 108.
Dedication, A: "Dear, near and true—no truer Time himself."
Thackeray. Tragic Story, A.
Thomas, E. Glory of the beauty of the morning, The.
Tolson. African China.
Ts'en Shen. On Climbing the Pagoda of the Temple of Gracious Benevolence with Kao Shih and Hsüeh Chü.
Tsogyel. Listen.

Tu Fu. If you draw a bow, draw the strongest.
Unknown. Man in Our Town.
Sunshiny shower, A.
Voice, A.
When people see the man of Cold Mountain.
Wise men, you have cast me aside.
Vrettakos. Poet, The.
Wang An-shih. Had I been an ox or horse.
Wind blew, a tile fell from the roof, The.
Wellesley. Avebury.
Whalen. Sourdough Mountain Lookout.
Wheatley, P. Thoughts on the Works of Providence.
Whitman, W. When I heard the learn'd astronomer.
Williams, M. Ruby Tells All.
Winner, R. Segregated Railway Diner—1946.
Wordsworth, W. Lines Left upon a Seat in a Yew-Tree which Stands near the Lake of Esthwaite, on a Desolate Part of the Shore, yet Commanding a Beautiful Prospect.
Wright, J. Gum-trees Stripping.
Yeats. Brown Penny.
Coming of Wisdom with Time, The.
Yüan Hao-wen. Croaking frog in a well sees the sky from end to end, A.
Yüan Mei. Words from the Goblet of Wisdom.

See also **Reason; Libraries and Librarians**

Wisemen. *See* **Magi**

Wishes
Allingham. Wishing.
Auden. Song of the Beggars.
Behrens. Someone Else.
Catullus. Carmen 31 ("Apple of islands, Sirmio, & bright peninsulas, set").
Child, A. Wishes.
Chudleigh. Wishes.
Clare, J. I wish I was where I would be.
Clifton, L. Wishes for Sons.
Coleridge, M. Insincere Wish Addressed to a Beggar, An.
Coward. Room with a View, A.
Cowley, A. Wish, The.
Cummings, E. O by the by / has anybody seen.
Dante Alighieri. Sonnet: "Guido, I wish that you and Lapo and I."
Darwish, M. On Wishes.
De la Mare. Bunches of Grapes.
Kiph.
Galvin, B. Willow, Wishbone, Warblers.
Graves, R. Richard Roe and John Doe.
Greenwell, D. Scherzo, A.
Herrick. Upon Batt.
Jarrell. Man Meets a Woman in the Street, A.
Komey. Oblivion.
Lamantia. Time Traveler's Potlatch.
Lu Yu. To Show My Sons.
Manger. Rachel Goes to the Well for Water ("Rachel stands by the mirror and plaits").
Marston, P. Vain Wish, A.
McDonald, D. Birthday Wish, A.
McGinley. Reflections at Dawn.
Mother Goose. If wishes were horses.
Neruda. Ode to the Cat.
Padilla. Self-Portrait of the Other.
Pilkington, L. Wish, By a Young Lady, The.
Poe. Stanzas.
Rogers, F. Wishes.
Rogers, S. Wish, A.
Salter. What Do Women Want?
Sandburg, C. Mag.
Seifert. Candlestick, The.
Shakespeare, W. Blossom, The.
Tanikawa Shuntaro. Request.
Thompson, D. Wish.
Thompson, I. Penny Wish, A.
Trần Tế Xu'o'ng. Best Wishes for the New Year.
Unknown. Five Little Chickens.
Wishing Poem.
Vvedensky. I wish I were a wild beast.
Ward, E. Extravagant Drunkard's Wish, The.
Yeats. He Wishes for the Cloths of Heaven.

Wisteria

Masaoka Shiki. Tanka: "Dipped."
Tanka: "In the vase."
Mori Ōgai. Tanka: "But for the dew."
Shūji. Tanka: "At a corner."

Wit

Behn, A. Rover or The Banished Cavaliers, The.
Calverley. Flight.
"Carroll." Father William.
Cowley, A. Ode: Of Wit.
Martial. Out of an Epigram of Martial.
Pope, A. Impromptu.
Vaughan, H. To the Most Excellently Accomplished Mrs. Katherine Philips.
Winchilsea. Introduction, The: "Did I, my lines intend for public[k] view."

Witchcraft and Witches

Abercrombie. Witchcraft: New Style.
Allingham. Witch-Bride, The.
Alvarez, J. Sonnet 1: "Everything that happens to me these days."
Bennett, R. Witch of Willowby Wood, The.
Bishop, E. Riverman, The.
Bishop, M. Witch of East Seventy-second Street, The.
Burns, R. Tam o' Shanter. [A Tale].
Clarke, C. Wearing My Cap Backwards.
Clifton, L. In Salem.
Coleridge, M. Witch, The.
Witches' Wood, The.
Cummings, E. Hist whist / little ghostthings.
De la Mare. As Lucy came a-walking one morning cold and fine.
Ride-by-Nights, The.
Dekker, T. et al. And why on me? why should the envious world.
Gowar. Annabell and the Witches.
Graves, R. Hag-Ridden.
Herrick. Hag, The ("Hag is astride, The").
Hag, The ("Staff[e] is now greased [or greas'd], The").
Hogg, J. Witch of Fife, The.
Witch's Chant, A.
Housman, A. Her strong enchantments failing.
Ilott. Witch, The.
Kuskin. Knitted Things.
Witches' Ride, The.
Livingston, M. Lazy Witch.
Milton. Castle.
Mó. Wizards.
Raab, L. Witch's Story, The.
Reed, I. Black Cock, The.
Reznikoff. Two Witches.
Robinson, A. Wise-Woman, The.
Santal. Witch, The.
Scott, W. Witch's Ballad, The.
Sexton. Her Kind.
Shakespeare, W. Jesu preserve your royal Majesty!
Thrice the Brinded Cat Hath Mewed.
Thunder. Enter the three Witches.
Shorter. Wind on the Hills, The.
Silko. Invention of White People, The.
Smith, S. Little Boy Lost.
Tynan. Witch, The.
Unknown. Hey-How for Hallowe'en.
Queen Nefertiti.
To lay the lorn spirit, you o'er it must pray.
Walker, M. Ballad of the Hoppy-Toad.
Molly Means.
Yeats. Song Of Wandering Aengus, The.

Wittgenstein, Ludwig Josef Johann

Murphy, R. Philosopher and the Birds, The.

Wives

Ausonius. To His Wife.
Baillie, J. Hooly and Fairly.
Baraka. For Hettie.
Barber, M. Conclusion of a Letter to the Rev. Mr. C——, The.
Barnes, W. Wife A-Lost, The.
Wife a Praïs'd, A.
Woak Hill.
"Bendo." Dream, The.
Blamire. O Donald! ye are just the man.
Bloom, V. Sun-a-shine, Rain-a-fall.

Boyle, K. Invitation in It, from American Citizen, The.
Breton, A. Free Union.
Brontë, C. Pilate's Wife's Dream.
Browning, R. Any Wife to Any Husband.
Burns, R. Kellyburnbraes.
"Carroll." "You are old," said the youth, "and your jaws are too weak."
Caruthers. Prayer of Any Husband.
Catullus. To A Friend.
Cave. Elegy on a Maiden Name, An.
Cheng Hsieh. Mother-in-Law Is Cruel.
Chu Yün-ming. Remembering My Late Wife.
Chudleigh. To the Ladies.
Cowper, W. To Mary.
Đng Trần Côn et al. Song of a Soldier's Wife, The.
Davies, S. Contention betwixt a Wife, a Widow, and a Maid, A.
Day, C. Who Drags the Fiery Artist Down?
Donne. Since she whome I lovd, hath payd her last debt.
Dove, R. Daystar.
Dudley, M. At the backyard fence.
Egerton, S. Emulation, The.
To Marina.
Eliot, T. Dedication to My Wife, A.
Ezekiel. Song to be Shouted Out.
Frost, R. Paul's Wife.
Galassi. Our Wives.
George, D. Asenath.
Gilbert, S. Parachutist's Wife, The.
Gilligan. Bathsheba in mourning.
Gioia. Country Wife, The.
Goldbarth. Lot's Wife.
Goldsmith, O. Double Transformation, The.
Greene, R. Shepherd's Wife's Song, The.
"H., H. E." Riddle, The.
Hardy, T. Wife Waits, A.
Wives in the Sere.
Hartnett. Retreat of Ita Cagney, The.
Haynes, C. Any Wife or Husband.
Hofmannsthal. Emperor of China Speaks, The.
Holst-Warhaft. Old Men of Athens, The.
Homer. Ulysses Reunited with Penelope.
Hotham. My wife still asleep.
Sun and moon.
Ibaragi. What a little girl had on her mind was.
Jarrell. Next Day.
Johnson, S. Empty Heart, An.
Jonson, B. Epistle. To Katharine, Lady Aubigny.
Kavanagh, P. Tinker's Wife.
Kim, K. Conflict.
Kitahara Hakushū. Tanka: "After letting my wife."
Kossman. Pilate's Wife.
Layton. Berry Picking.
Le Gallienne. Décadent to His Soul, The.
Lewis, E. Advice to a Young Lady Lately Married.
Li K'ai-hsien. Parable, A.
Poem Expressing My Wife's Response to One I Sent Her, A.
Lindsay, L. Auld Robin Gray.
Lorde. Evening News, The.
Lowell, R. Old Flame, The.
MacLeish. Poem in Prose.
Martial. Out of an Epigram of Martial.
Mathews, H. Aboard a Boat at Night, Drinking with My Wife.
Marrying Again.
Sad Remembrance.
Mei Yao Ch'en. I Remember the River at Wu Sung.
Mourning for My Wife.
Sad Remembrance.
Menard. To My Wife.
Middleton, T. Song: "In a maiden-time professed."
Milton. On His Deceased Wife.
Monk, M. Verses Written on Her Death-Bed at Bath to Her Husband in London.
Mother Goose. Pumpkin-Eater, The.
Nesbit, E. Wife of All Ages, The.
O'Dalaigh, M. On the Death of His Wife.

Ondaatje. Cinnamon Peeler, The.
Patmore, C. She Was Mine.
Phocylides. On the Problem of Choosing a Wife.
Prior. Fable, A: "In Æsop's tales an honest wretch we find."
Purdy, A. Alive or Not.
Rabéarivelo. Wife is like a blade of grass, A.
Radnóti. Letter to My Wife.
Ramanujan. Love Poem for a Wife, 2.
Ravenscroft, T. Hey ho, what shall I say?
Ríos, A. Teodoro Luna's Two Kisses.
Rochester, J. To My More Than Meritorious Wife.
Roethke. Wish for a Young Wife.
Rogetsu. Roasting chestnuts.
Rossetti, C. I caught a little ladybird / That flies far away.
Schwartz, D. Passionate Shepherd to His Love, The.
Selyns. Of Scolding Wives and the Third Day Ague.
Sexton. For My Lover, Returning to His Wife.
Sholl. Farmwife.
Sims. Garden Song, A.
Smedley, M. Contrast, A.
Smith, S. Be Off!
Smith, W. There was an Old Woman named Piper.
Spacks. October.
Spencer, B. Part of Plenty.
Stevenson, A. By the Boat House, Oxford.
Stevenson, R. So live, so love, so use that fragile hour.
Strong, L. Brewer's Man, The.
Swede. Unhappy wife.
Tai Piao-yüan. Supervisor, Han Chün-mei, Has Shown Me Five Poems He Has Written Called, The Trees Flourish in Early Summer. I Have Therefore Written Down My Own Ignoble Feelings and Sent Them Via Inspector Juan. At This Time, Chün-mei Is Lecturing to the Various Scholars on the I-ching, The.
Tennyson, A. June Bracken and Heather.
Thomas, E. Forsaken Wife, The.
New Litany, Occasioned by an Invitation to a Wedding, A.
Unknown. Did you eever, iver, over.
I Am Your Wife.
In Bath a wanton wife did dwell.
Johnny Sands ("There was a man named Johnny Sands, who married Betty Hague").
Maxims (Exeter Book).
Old and New ("She went up the mountain to pluck wild herbs;").
Old Poem.
Shady grove, my true love.
Tell Her So.
When I pick up my koto.
When I was a bachelor, I lived by myself.
Wife's Lament, The.
Vinokurov. She sits down to eat, breaks off a piece.
Viorst. Honeymoon is over, The.
Virgil. Aeneas sees his wife.
Voigt. Farm Wife.
Jug Brook.
Walden. One to Love.
Walker, A. In Uganda an early king chose.
Wang Chien. Words of the Newly Wed Wife.
Wang Shih-chieng. Lamenting for My Wife.
Webster, A. Love's Mourner.
West, J. Married, poor soul! your empire's over.
Willard, N. King of Cats Sends a Postcard to His Wife, The.
Williams, C. Alzheimer's: The Wife.
Williams, W. Mezzo Forte.
Young Housewife, The.
Winchilsea. Letter to Daphnis, A.
Reformation.
Winstanley, I. Last Will and Testament, A.
Wotton, S. Upon the Death of Sir Albert [or us] Morton's Wife.
Wright, J. Complaint.
Wright, M. Address to Her Husband.

Wu Chia-chi. Woman Née Wu, The.
Yakamochi. When evening comes.
Yang Shih-ch'i. Song of the Merchant's Wife.
Yang Wei-chen. Song of the Merchant's Wife.
Young, D. For a Wife in Jizzen.
Yüan Mei. On the Twenty-First Day of the Fifth Month, I Reached Home.

See also **Marriage**

Wolsey, Thomas, Cardinal

Skelton, J. Such a prelate, I trow.

Wolves

Blue Cloud. Wolf.
Borisov. Untitled.
Brontë, C. Like wolf—and black bull or goblin hound.
Di Prima. If he did not come apart in her hands, he fell.
Durston. Wolf, The.
Eastwick. Wolf and the Lambs, The.
Gildner. Life of the Wolf, The.
Gunn, T. Allegory of the Wolf Boy, The.
Hogan, L. Bear Fat.
Hughes, T. Amulet.
Howling of Wolves, The.
Modest Proposal, A.
Klee. Wolf speaks, while chewing, The.
La Fontaine. Wolf and the Stork, The.
Lillard. Lobo.
MacNeice. Wolves.
McClure, M. From the Window of the Beverly Wilshire Hotel.
McDonald, W. Hauling Over Wolf Creek Pass in Winter.
More, S. De Principe Bono et Malo.
Nemerov. Wolves in the Zoo.
Popa. Burning Shewolf.
Eyes of a Wolf.
Rexroth, K. Wolf.
Silko. Four Mountain Wolves.
Tada. Wind invites wind.
TallMountain. Last wolf hurried toward me, The.
Tate, A. Wolves, The.
Teton Sioux Oral Tradition. Wolf Song.
Unknown. Poem about a Wolf Maybe Two Wolves, A.
Song of an Old Gray Wolf.
Walwicz. Little Red Riding Hood.
Webster, J. Dirge, A: "Call for the robin-redbreast and the wren."
Welburn. Yellow Wolf Spirit.

Woman Suffrage

Cary, P. Advice Gratis to Certain Women.
Jonas, R. Brother Baptis' on Woman Suffrage.

See also **Voting and Voters**

Wombats

Nash, O. Wombat lives across the seas, The.

Women

Ackland. Blossom into a rose as you are bidden.
Lonely Woman, The.
Adcock, F. Soho Hospital for Women, The.
Adisa. Discover Me.
Ai. Mother's Tale, The.
"Akhmatova." Epigram: "Could Beatrice have written like Dante."
Aklais. Woman in Mourning.
Alexander, L. Negro Woman.
Allen, P. Dear World.
Allison, D. Women Who Hate Me, The.
Allnutt. Alien.
Alvarez, J. He: Age doesn't matter when you're both in love.
Woman's Work.
Amaru. Though she's the girl, I am the one who's shy.
Amichai. Clouds have come up from the south, the Nile's.
Amis, K. Bookshop Idyll, A.
Anacreon. Beauty.
Mother Nature gave bulls horns.
Angelou. Momma Welfare Roll.
Phenomenal Woman.
Woman Me.
Appleton, E. Woman Who Understands, The.
Armantrout. Getting Warm.

Arnot. Woman at Home.
Arp. Man. The Woman, The.
Atwood. At first I was given centuries.
Marrying the Hangman.
This story was told to me by another traveller.
Torture.
Ausonius. Mistresse, A.
Averill. Bad for You.
Ayres. Epigram on Woman, An.
Baker, H. Declaimer, The.
Bancquart. Curriculum vitae.
Woman asleep.
Bansode. Woman.
Baraka. Beautiful Black Women.
Barbauld. Rights of Woman, The.
Barber, M. Conclusion of a Letter to the Rev. Mr. C——, The.
Barlas. Cat-Lady, The.
My Lady's Bath.
Barnes, J. Hot Dog Poem, The.
Barrett, E. Woman.
Bass, E. For Barbara, who said She Couldn't Visualize Two Women Together.
Vaginas of women, all the clusters.
Baudelaire. Giantess, The.
Beer, P. Footbinding.
Jane Austen.
Behn, A. To the Fair Clarinda, Who Made Love to Me, Imagin'd More Than Woman.
Behn, R. French Horn.
Benn. Night Café.
Bennett, G. To a Dark Girl.
Bennett, L. Jamaica oman cunny sah!
Bernard. Lark, The.
Berry, J. Girls Can We Educate We Dads?
Betham-Edwards. Power of Women, THe.
Betjeman. Business Girls.
Bialik. Young Acacia, The.
Bissert. Most Beautiful Woman at My Highschool Reunion, The.
Blake, F. Woman's Answer to "The Vampire," A.
Bogan, L. Evening in the Sanitarium.
Women have no wilderness in them.
Bond, F. Pity Wasted.
Bradstreet, A. In Honour of That High and Mighty Princess Queen Elizabeth of Happy Memory.
Prologue, The: "To sing of wars, of captain[e]s, and of kings."
Braithwaite. Watchers, The.
Breton, A. Free Union.
Postman Cheval.
Brontë, C. Lonely Lady, The.
Brooks, G. Mrs. Small went to the kitchen for her pocketbook.
Sadie and Maud.
Sunset of the City, A.
Broumas, O. Rapunzel.
Snow White.
Browne, F. Australian Emigrant, The.
Browning, E. Lord Walter's Wife.
To George Sand / A Desire.
To George Sand: A Recognition.
Bryll. In a Fever.
Burns, R. Bonnie Lesley.
Green grow the rashes, O.
Green grow the rashes, O; / Green grow the rashes, O; / The lasses they hae wimble bores.
Byron, G. She walks in Beauty like the night.
Cable, G. Belle Layotte.
Campbell, J. Old Woman, The.
Campion, T. I care not for these ladies.
Caraion. Enveloping Echo, The.
Cardiff. Combing.
Carew, T. Rapture, A.
Song, [A]: "Ask me no more where Jove bestows."
To My Mistress Sitting by a River's Side; an Eddy.
Carolan. Mabel Kelly.
Peggy Browne.
Cartwright, W. Women.
Cary, P. Advice Gratis to Certain Women.
Cassells. Women, The.

Cataldi. It's Easy.
We Could Have Met.
Catullus. Carmen 70 ("Lesbia says she'ld rather marry me").
Cavalcanti. Ballata: Of His Lady among Other Ladies.
Ceravolo. Women, The.
Cervantes. Beneath the Shadow of the Freeway.
Chatterton. Mynstrelles Songe: "Angelles bee wrogte to bee of neidher kynde."
There Lackethe Somethynge Style.
Chaucer. Wife of Bath's Prologue, The.
Wife of Bath's Tale, The.
Chesterton, G. Ballade D'une Grande Dame.
Chevalier. My Old Dutch.
Ch'ien Wen-Ti. Getting Up in Winter.
Chipasula. Ritual Girl.
Those Rainy Mornings.
"Chrystos." Wings of a Wild Goose, The.
Chudleigh. 'Tis hard we should be by the men despised.
To the Ladies.
Unhappy they, who by their duty led.
Ciardi. To Judith Asleep.
Clampitt. Amaranth and Moly.
Written in Water.
Clarke, A. Subjection of Women, The.
Claudian. Her longer head like a swines snowt doth show.
Clemmons. Freedom Song for the Black Woman, A.
Cleveland, J. Antiplatonic[k], The.
Clifton, L. Crazy Horse Names His Daughter.
For de Lawd.
Song at Midnight.
There Is a Girl Inside.
Thirty-eighth year, The.
Way It Was, The.
Wishes for Sons.
Woman who loves, A.
Women You Are Accustomed To, The.
Clinton. Tantrum Girl Responds to Death.
Cohen, L. Suzanne takes you down to her place near the river.
Coleman, W. American Sonnet (35).
Coleridge, M. Clever Woman, A.
Marriage.
Other Side of a Mirror, The.
White Women, The.
Coleridge, S. Hunting Song.
Collier, M. Womans Labour, an epistle, The.
Congreve. Semele to Jupiter.
Cook, E. Song of the Ugly Maiden.
Corbett, E. Three wise old women were they, were they.
Cortez. Grinding Vibrato.
Couzyn. Message of the men is linear, The.
Coward. Fortitude.
Cowley, A. To His Mistress.
Crawford, V. Pioneer Woman.
Creeley. Air: "The Love of a Woman."
All That Is Lovely in Men.
Memory, The.
Son: "What I took in my hand."
Three Ladies, The.
Whip, The.
Crompton. Epigram VII: Winifred.
Crow, S. They say a man dies.
Cuddihy. Pendulum, The.
Cumbo. Black Sister.
Cummings, E. If i have made, my lady, intricate.
Pretty a day, A.
Cuney. No Images.
Dacre, C. Female Philosopher, The.
Similie.
Daiches. To Kate, Skating Better than Her Date.
Daive. She does not move. Takes the man's.
Woman measures, A.
Daniel, S. To The Lady Lucie, Countesse of Bedford.
Daniels, K. Women's Room in Pennsylvania Station, The.
Dante Alighieri. To waning day, to the wide round of shadow.

Davidson, J. Labourer's Wife, A.
Davies, S. In Librum.
Davies, M. Man's Woman, A.
Day Lewis. My Mother's Sister.
Den Sute-Jo. Woman.
Derricotte. Hamtramck: The Polish Women.
  Touching/Not Touching: My Mother.
Desmond, G. Against Blame of Woman.
Dharker. Purdah, 1.
Di Prima. Ave.
  If he did not come apart in her hands, he fell.
  Practice of Magical Evocation, The.
Dickinson, E. Her breast is fit for pearls.
  Title divine—is mine!
  What Soft—Cherubic Creatures.
Dimitrova. Woman Pregnant, A.
Dioscorides. My downfall: those pink
  articulate lips.
DiPalma. Fragment.
Doinas, S. Woman in the Mirror, The.
Donald. Eye for an Eye, An.
Donne. Indifferent, The.
  Love's Alchemy [or Alchemie].
  Love's Progress.
  Primrose[, Being at Montgomery Castle, upon
    the Hill, on Which It Is Situate], The.
  Song: "Go and catch a falling star."
  Twicknam [or Twickenham] Garden.
  Woman's Constancy.
D'Orleans. Oft in my thought full busily have
    I sought.
  Smiling mouth and laughing eyen° gray, The.
Dorn, E. On the Debt My Mother Owed to
    Sears Roebuck.
Dove, R. Great Palaces of Versailles, The.
  Used.
Doyle, S. Some Girls.
Drummond, W. Madrigal: "Like the Idalian
    Queen[e]."
Dryden, J. To the Pious Memory of the
    Accomplished [or Accomplisht] Young Lady,
    Mrs. Anne Killigrew, [Excellent in the Two
    Sister-Arts of Poesie and Painting].
Dufferin. Charming Woman, The.
Duffy, C. Dolphins, The.
Dumbrveanu. Genesis.
Dunbar, P. Made to Order Smile, The.
Dunbar, W. In Prais of Wemen.
  In Praise of Women.
Duncan, R. Bending the Bow.
  Dancing Concerning a Form of Women, A.
  Tribal Memories.
Dunn, S. Routine Things Around the House,
    The.
DuPlessis, R. Mirror Poem.
Durcan. She Mends an Ancient Wireless.
Eberhart, R. Marrakech.
Egerton, S. Blasphemous wretch! How canst
    thou think or say.
  Emulation, The.
  Liberty, The.
Elenkov. Sauna.
"Eliot." Felix Holt, the Radical.
Eliot, T. Cousin Nancy.
Erdrich. Butcher's Wife, The.
Espada. Secret of the Legal Secretary's
    Cigarette Smoke, The.
Etherege. Song: "Ladies, though to your
    conquering eyes."
Euripides. Of all things which are living and
    can form a judgment.
Evans, M. I Am a Black Woman.
Ewart. Great Women Composers, The.
Fairbridge, K. Magwere, Who Waits
    Wondering.
Ferriter. Lay Your Arms Aside.
"Field." Fifty Quatrains.
  To Christina Rossetti.
Finch, A. For Grizzel McNaught (1709–1792).
Fischerova. Who Knows Something About
    Women?
Foley, M. Brothers and Sisters.
Follain Mirror, A
Fu Hsüan. Woman.
Fujiwara no Atsutada. I think of the days.
Fuller, R. Metamorphoses.
Fulton, A. Cherry Bombs.

Fumi Saito. Tanka: "Don't resemble me."
Fumiko. Tanka: "For this."
Gallagher, T. Breasts.
  Conversation with a Fireman from Brooklyn.
  I Stop Writing the Poem.
  Instructions to the Double.
  On Your Own.
García Lorca. Ballad of Black Grief.
Gascoigne. Sonet Written in Prayse of the
    Browne Beautie, A.
Gay, J. 'Tis woman that seduces all mankind!
  Woman's like the flatt'ring ocean.
  Would You Have a Young Virgin?
Gidlow. I know myself linked by chains of
    fire.
Gilmore, M. Eve-Song.
Giovanni. Life I Led, The.
  Woman Poem.
Glück, L. Palais des Arts.
Godfrey. So Let's Look at It Another Way.
Goedicke. Serious Merriment of Women, The.
Goldbarth. Hey Sweetie.
Golding, L. Women at the Corners Stand,
    The.
Goldsmith, O. Song: "When lovely woman
    stoops to folly."
Goodison. From the Garden of the Women
    Once Fallen.
Gorges. Her [or hir] face her [or hir] tongue
    [or tong] her [or hir] wit.
Grahn. My name is Judith meaning.
  Woman Is Talking to Death, A.
Graves, R. In Her Praise.
  Portrait, The.
  She is no liar, yet she will wash away.
  Three-Faced, The.
  White Goddess, The.
Gray, J. Les Demoiselles de Sauve.
Greenwell, D. Fidelity Rewarded.
Gregg. Lies and Longing.
Grennan. Woman at Lit Window.
Griffin, S. Answer to a Man's Question,
    "What Can I Do About Women's
    Liberation?", An.
Grimké, A. Caprichosa.
Guillén, N. Madrigal.
"H., H. E." Riddle, The.
Habington. Pretty Sport.
Hacker, M. Ballad of Ladies Lost and Found.
  Mother II.
  Rune of the Finland Woman.
Hafiz. Ode 147: "Beauty alone will not
    account for her."
  Ode 44: "Last night, as half asleep I dreaming
    lay."
Hall, D. Blue Wing, The.
Hallack. Divine Office of the Kitchen, The.
Halley. Housewife's Letter: To Mary.
  I'd Rather See than be One, but.
Hampton. Women who Speak with Steak
    Knives.
Hardy, T. Epitaph on a Pessimist.
Harjo, J. Early morning woman.
  Woman Hanging from the Thirteenth Floor
    Window, The.
Harper, F. She's Free!
Harrington, J. Inconstancy.
Harris, P. Some Songs Women Sing.
Hartnett. Sonnet: "I saw magic on a green
    country road."
Hawthorne, N. Oh, Man can seek the
    downward glance.
Hayden, R. Sphinx.
Heaney, S. Wife's Tale, The.
Heath, -. Women.
Hecht, A. Dover Bitch, The.
Hemans. Grave of a Poetess, The.
  Indian Woman's Death-Song, The.
  To a Wandering Female Singer.
  Woman and Fame.
Hemphill. To Some Supposed Brothers.
Henjō Abbot. If the windo of heaven.
Herrick. On Himselfe ("Let me not live, if I
    not love").
  Request to the Graces, An.
  To Meadows [or Meddowes].

Upon Some Women.
Upon the Loss[e] of His Mistresses.
Hirshfield, J. For the Women of Poland:
    December 1981.
Ho Xuan Huong. Cake-That-Drifts-in-Water,
    The.
  Funny Grotto, The.
  Girl Without a Sex, The.
  Man-and-Wife Mountain, The.
  Ode to the Fan.
  Scolding Some Dunces.
  Swinging.
  Threefold Pass, The.
  Woman Lies Alone, A.
Hodgson, R. Gipsy Girl, The.
Hogan, L. Lost Girls, The.
Hollander, J. Lady's-Maid's Song, The.
Hong, Y. On Ornament.
Hope, A. Beyond Phigalia.
  Möbius Strip-Tease.
Horace. Paynter if he shoulde adjoyne, A.
  Tibullus, pull yourself together!
Horovitz, F. Women.
Houston, L. House, A.
Howe, J. Mother's Day Proclamation of 1870.
Hughes, L. As Befits a Man.
  Gypsy Man.
  Harlem Sweeties.
  Jazzonia.
  Preference.
  When Sue Wears Red.
Hugo, R. To Women.
Hull, A. Another Rhythm.
Ignatow, D. Lunchtime.
Ilankiranar. What He Said to His Heart,
    Arguing against Further Ambition and Travel.
Ingram, A. Female mind like a rude fallow
    lies, A.
Jackson, L. Prima Donna Poet Replies, A.
Jackson, R. 1973.
Jacobs, H. On Growing Up the Darker Berry.
Jarrell. In Nature There Is Neither Right nor
    Left nor Wrong.
  Next Day.
Jayaprabha. Burn this Sari.
Jenyns. Choice, The.
  For love no time has she, or inclination.
Johnson, G. Heart of a woman [goes forth
    with the dawn], The.
  Smothered Fires.
Johnston, E. Lines to Ellen, the Factory Girl.
Jones, P. Song: "I have so little sorrow."
Jonson, B. Another. In Defense of Their
    Inconstancy [or Inconstancie]. A Song.
  In the Person of Womankind [A Song
    Apologetic].
  So White, So Soft, So Sweet.
  Song. That Women Are But Men's Shadows.
Jordan, J. Female and the Silence of a Man,
    The.
  Poem About My Rights.
  Poem for South AFrican Women.
Jordan, N. When A Woman Gets Blue.
Kākkai Pāṭiṇiyār Naccellaiyār. King's Double
    Nature, A.
Kang. Rotation (1).
Karni. Woman's Prayer, A.
Karp. Still-Life in the Coat Factory Office.
Kasdorf. When our women go crazy, they're
    scared there won't be.
Kasischke. Woman Kills Sweetheart with
    Bowling Ball.
Kay, J. Photo in the Locket.
Keats. Song.
Keller, D. In the Middle of the Journey.
Kendall, M. Lower Life, The.
  Woman's Future.
Kennedy, X. Nude Descending a Staircase.
Keyes, S. Moon is a poor woman, The.
Killigrew, A. Upon the Saying That My
    Verses Were Made by Another.
Kinsella, J. Sick Woman.
Kinsella, T. Ancestor.
Kipling, R. Female of the Species, The.
  Ladies, The.
  Vampire, The.
Kizer, C. Hera, Hung from the Sky.

One.
Three.
Two.
Klepfisz. Few Words in the Mother Tongue, A.
From the Monkey House and Other Cages: Monkey II.
They did not build wings for them.
Koch, K. Energy in Sweden.
Sleeping with Women.
Talking to Patrizia.
Kolatkar. Old woman grabs, An.
Kooser. Onion Woman, The.
Kora. Woman.
Kowit. In the morning.
What chord did she pluck in my soul.
Kunio. Tanka: "Woman."
La Fontaine. Cat Changed to a Woman, The.
Landon. History of the Lyre, A.
Marriage Vow, The.
Lanyer. Our Mother *Eve,* who tasted of the Tree.
Larkin, J. Rhyme of My Inheritance.
Laughton. Woman with Child, The.
Lawrence, D. Energetic Women.
It's no good, the women are in eruption.
Peacock.
To Women, as Far as I'm Concerned.
Volcanic Venus.
Layne, M. Beautiful Ladies.
Le Bel. Boxing the Female.
Leapor. Essay on Woman, An.
To Artemisia.—'Tis to her we sing.
Lee, L. I Ask My Mother to Sing.
Irises.
Leithauser. Old Bachelor Brother.
Lenngren. Other Fabrics, Other Mores!
Lerner, L. Wish, A.
Leto. Mary Morelle Show, The.
Levertov. Abel's Bride.
Hypocrite women, how seldom we speak.
In Mind.
Mutes, The.
Stepping Westward.
Woman Alone, A.
Lewis, E. Mirror for Detractors, A.
Li Ch'ing-chao. To the Tune "A Hilly Garden."
Lihn. Of all despondencies, death-despair must be the worst.
Six Poems of Loneliness.
Lindsay, C. Love or Fame.
Liu E. Teahouse at Hoshioka, A.
Lochhead, L. Mirror's Song.
Loftin. Weeksville Women.
Logau. Women's Rule.
Lorde. Woman Thing, The.
Women of Dan Dance with Swords in Their Hands to Mark the Time When They Were Warriors, The.
Lovelace, R. Gratiana Dancing [*or* Dauncing] and [*or* &] Singing.
Lowell, A. Patterns.
Sisters, The.
Loy. Three Moments in Paris.
Lu Yu. In a Boat on a Summer Evening, I Heard the Cry of a Water Bird.
Lucan. Since heaven helpes not, deepest hell weele try.
Lum. Riding the North Point Ferry.
Lyly, J. Serving Men's Song, A.
M–rt–n. Humble Wish, The.
"MacDiarmid." One of the Principal Causes of War.
Two Parents, The.
MacDonogh. She Walked Unaware.
Mackey, N. Song of the Andoumboulou.
MacLean, S. Highland Woman, A.
MacLeish. Steamboat Whistle, The.
Madgett. Black Woman.
Woman with Flower.
Madhubuti. Soft: the way her eyes view her children.
Mahapatra, A. Spell.
Maiden. Green Side, The.
Major, C. Balance and Beauty.
Giant Red Woman.

Maksimovic. For the Barren Woman.
Malangatana. Woman.
Mapanje. Cheerful Girls at Smiller's Bar, The.
Marston, J. *Pigmalion,* whose hie love-hating minde.
Martin, C. Victoria's Secret.
Martinez, D. Room itself. The women. The absence of women, The.
Martinez, V. It Is Not.
Masefield. Her heart is always doing lovely things.
McClaurin. I, Woman.
McElroy, C. Illusion.
In My Mother's Room.
Woman's Song, A.
McGinley. Trial and Error.
Why, Some of My Best Friends Are Women.
Women of Jericho, The.
McGuckian. Dream-Language of Fergus, The.
Mast Year, The.
Mr. McGregor's Garden.
Orchid House, The.
Sitting, The.
McKay, C. Wild Goat, The.
McOrlan. Battery woman.
Meleager. Something in my soul.
Meredith, G. My lady unto Madam makes her bow.
This golden head has wit in it. I live.
"Meredith." Changes.
Meredith, W. Korean Woman Seated by a Wall, A.
Merton. There Has to Be a Jail for Ladies.
Meynell, A. Father of Women, A [Ad Sororem E. B.].
Letter from a Girl to Her Own Old Age, A.
Michaux. Simplicity.
Miliauskaite. These are lilacs.
Millay, E. I, being born a woman and distressed.
Oh, Oh, you will be sorry for that word!
Mirikitani. Breaking Tradition.
Mitchell, E. Thoughts after Ruskin.
Mitchison. Woman Alone.
Montagu, L. Lover, The; a Ballad.
Moore, M. Sojourn in the Whale.
Moraga. Loving in the War Years.
Mordecai. Tell Me.
Morgan, R. And blessed be the women who get you through.
On the Watergate Women.
Phobiphilia.
Mori. Speaking Through White: For My Mother.
Moss, T. Dennis's Sky Leopard.
Raising a Humid Flag.
Mouré. She Touched Me.
Mphande. Why the Old Woman Limps.
Mullen, H. Roadmap.
Naden. Two Artists, The.
Nash, O. I Never Even Suggested It.
Nasrin. Another Life.
At the Back of Progress. . . .
Border.
Character.
Nathan, L. Body Count.
Toast.
Neruda. In my sky at twilight you are like a cloud.
Nesbit, E. Wife of All Ages, The.
Newcastle, M. Woman drest by Age, A.
Nezval. Lilac by the Museum on St. Wenceslas Square, The.
Nguyễn Công Trú'. Ode to All Flowers.
Ngwenya. Woman.
Nicarchus of Alexandria. I like a lot of woman, full grown.
I like a woman built on ample lines.
Niconoë has just inched past her prime.
Nichols, G. Tropical Death.
Nikolov, N. Window, The.
Norris, K. Poem about Faith, A.
Norton, C. Obscurity of Woman's Worth.
Picture of Sappho, The.
Notley. White Peacock, The.
O Direain. That Face.

Ogundipe-Leslie. On Reading an Archeological Article.
Oliver, M. Strawberry Moon.
Ombres. Morning Hours.
"O'Neill." Her Sister.
O'Neill, R. Dream of Sappho, A.
Lee.
Sister, The.
Oppen. Morality Play: Preface, A.
Orampokiyar. What She Said ("In his place, mother / field-crabs cut into the pink").
What She Said ("In the full river").
O'Reilly, J. Lure, The.
Osgood, F. Ah! woman still.
Woman.
Ostriker. Propaganda Poem: Maybe for Some Young Mamas.
Ou-yang Hsiu. Song of Liang Chou.
Ovid. O! Love! how cold, and slow to take my part!
Owen, M. "Assholes!" her eyes seem grey in this soup the hangars.
Owens, R. Devils Clowns and Women.
Pace, R. Tingel-Tangel.
Paley, G. Women in Vietnam, The.
Palladas. Cuckolded husbands have no certain sign.
Theft of fire, The. Man's worst bargain yet.
Women.
Women all / cause rue.
Pande, M. Two Women Knitting.
Parker, D. On Being a Woman.
Parker, M. Whither away good neighbour.
Parker, P. For Willyce.
There Is a Woman in This Town.
Parkes, B. Lilian's Second Letter.
Patmore, C. Tribute, A.
Pattanshetti. Woman / is a problem negative.
Penfold, N. Woman with the Wild-Grown Hair Relaxes after Another Long Day, The.
Pereira. Two Strange Worlds.
Pfeiffer, E. Peace to the odalisque, the facile slave.
Philips, K. Answer to Another Persuading a Lady to Marriage, An.
Friendship in Emblem, or the Seal, to my Dearest Lucasia.
Friendship in Embleme, or the Seal. To my dearest Lucasia.
Friendship's Mystery, To My Dearest Lucasia.
To My Excellent Lucasia, On Our Friendship.
Phocylides. On the Problem of Choosing a Wife.
Piatt, S. Pique at Parting, A.
Piercy. Book of Ruth and Naomi, The.
Sabbath of Mutual Respect, The.
Unlearning to Not Speak.
Woman in the ordinary pudgy downcast girl, The.
Pilkington, L. Wish, By a Young Lady, The.
Pinkney, E. Health, A.
Pitter. Old, childless, husbandless, bereaved, alone.
Plath. Ariel.
Edge.
Poe. Stanzas.
Valentine, A.
Polwhele. Alas! in every aspiration bold.
Ponsot. Among Women.
Pope, A. Epistle [II,] to a Lady[: Of the Characters of Women].
Impromptu.
On a Certain Lady at Court.
Pound, E. Bathtub [*or* Bath Tub], The.
Portrait d'une Femme.
Tame Cat.
Pratt, M. All the Women Caught in Flaring Light.
Waulking Song: Two.
Prescod. Women Are Different.
Prestwich. How to Choose a Mistress.
Probyn. Ballade of Lovers.
Frustrated.
Masquerading.
Procter, A. Woman's Answer, A.
Woman's Question, A.
Prunty. Elderly Lady Crossing on Green.

Queen Latifah. Evil That Men Do, The.
Randall, D. Blackberry Sweet.
Randolph, T. In Praise of Women in General.
Rankin, R. Women of Maine, The.
Ransom, J. Lady Lost.
Ravikovitch. Portrait.
Reeve, C. Sacred Heliconian spring, The.
Reid, A. Lesson for Beautiful Women, A.
Replansky. Two Women.
Rich, A. After Twenty Years.
Blood-Sister.
Culture and Anarchy.
Dark lintels, the blue and foreign stones, The.
Every peak is a crater. This is the law of volcanoes.
Floating Poem, Unnumbered, The.
From a Survivor.
From an Old House in America.
Hunger.
I come home from you through the early light of spring.
Mirror in Which Two Are Seen as One, The.
Paula Becker to Clara Westhoff.
Phantasia for Elvira Shatayev.
Phenomenology of Anger, The.
Planetarium.
Re-forming the Crystal.
Sleeping, turning in turn like planets.
Snapshots of a Daughter-in-Law.
Suppose you want to write.
That conversation we were always on the edge.
Translations.
Waking in the Dark.
Women.
Your small hands, precisely equal to my own.
Rilke. Someday there will be girls and women whose name will no longer mean.
Ríos, A. Inquietude of a Particular Matter, The.
Ristovic. Maids.
Robinson, A. Wise-Woman, The.
Robinson, M. Modern Female Fashions.
Rochester, J. Song: "Love a woman? You're [or Y'are] an ass."
Rodgers, C. Poem for Some Black Women.
Rodgers, W. Stormy Night.
Rodney. Anywoman's Lyric.
Rodriguez, J. About this Woman.
Roethke. I knew a woman, lovely in her bones.
She.
Romano, R. So I Lost My Temper.
Roseliep. Campfire Extinguished.
Rosenberg, I. Female God, The.
Rossetti, C. From the Antique.
Passing and Glassing.
Rowe, E. To Celinda.
Rowe, N. Epigram: "Whilst maudlin Whigs deplore their Cato's fate."
Rózewicz. Pigtail.
Rufinus. I hate an easy woman.
Rufinus Domesticus. We who find no joy in celebrity.
Rukeyser, M. Cries From Chiapas.
Käthe Kollwitz.
More of a Corpse Than a Woman.
Myth.
Rushing. Sent for You Yesterday.
Sabina. Midnight Velada, The.
Salamun. Clumsy Guys.
Salkey. Inside.
Salter. What Do Women Want?
Sanchez, S. Present.
Sarton. My Sisters, O My Sisters.
Sassoon. Glory of Women.
Saunders, R. Hush Honey.
Scarfe. Ode in Honour.
Schwartz, D. Sonnet on Famous and Familiar Sonnets and Experiences.
Scott, M. Women of the Future.
Scovell. Vain Girl Jilted, The.
Seiblee. Wind.
Senghor. Before night comes I think of you and for you before I fall.
Senior. To the Madwoman in My Yard.
Sexton. Consorting with Angels.

Her Kind.
In Celebration of My Uterus.
Shakespeare, W. Sea Song, A: "Master, the swabber, the boatswain and I, The."
Shapiro, K. Buick.
Dome of Sunday, The [or A].
Recognition of Eve, The.
Shelley, P. She met me, Stranger, upon life's rough way.
Sheridan, H. Charming Woman, The.
Sheridan, R. Song: "Here's to the maiden [or maid] of bashful fifteen."
Sidney, P. What tongue can her perfections tell.
Simon, L. Hattie Went to Market.
Simonov. Remember, Alyosha, the roads of Smolensk.
Singh, K. On Reading a Love Poem.
Skeen. Women Who Cook.
Skelton, J. To Mistress [or Maystres] Margaret Hussey.
Smedley, M. Cavour.
Contrast, A.
Smith, P. Blonde White Women.
Smith, S. Celts, The.
Dear Female Heart, I am sorry for you.
House of Mercy, A.
Marriage I think.
Snodgrass, W. Vuillard: "The Mother and Sister of the Artist."
Södergran. Vierge Moderne.
Sölle. He needs you.
Song. Girl Powdering Her Neck.
Mehinaku Girl in Seclusion, A.
Sorescu. Adam paced the footpaths of paradise in a.
Souza. Women in Dutch Painting.
Speght. *Disswasion* hearing her assigne my helpe.
Spencer, A. Lady, Lady, I saw your face.
Letter to My Sister.
Wife-Woman, The.
Spenser. Sonnet 1: "Happy ye leaves! whenas those lily hands."
Sonnet 8: "More than most fair [or fayre], full of the living fire [or fyre]."
Sonnet 10: 'Unrighteous Lord of Love'.
Sonnet 15: "Ye tradeful merchants that, with weary toil."
Sonnet 54: "Of this world's Theatre in which we stay."
Sonnet 67: "Like a huntsman after weary chase."
Sonnet 70: "Fresh Spring the herald of love's mighty king."
Sonnet 81: "Fair [or Fayre] is my love, when her fair [or fayre] golden heares."
Stanley, T. Changed, Yet Constant.
Stephens, J. Glass of Beer, A.
Stevens, W. Ordinary Women, The.
Strand. Prediction, The.
Strickland. Diringer's *The Alphabet: A Key to the History of Mankind.*
Suckling, J. Constant Lover, A [or The].
Woman's Constancy.
Sumangalamata. At last free.
Supervielle. Voyages.
Swenson, M. Women.
Women / should be / pedestals / moving.
Swift, J. Cassinus and Peter.
Gentle Echo on Woman, A.
Lady's Dressing Room, The.
Swirszczynska. Greatest Love, The.
Szymborska. Women of Rubens, The.
Taggard. At Last the Women are Moving.
Taylor, S. Elena's Song.
Thesen. Mean Drunk Poem.
Thomas, E. On Sir J―― S―― Saying in a Sarcastic Manner, My Books Would Make Me Mad; an Ode.
Thomas, L. Electricity of Blossoms.
Tipper. To a Young Lady that Desired a Verse of My Being Servant One Day, and Mistress Another.
Tollet. What cruel laws depress the female kind.
Tomioka. Girlfriend.

Tsvetayeva. Fatal volume, The.
We shall not escape Hell, my passionate.
Yesterday he could still look in my eyes, yet.
Ufland. It has for ages been observed.
Ullman. Mauve.
Unknown. Alison.
Around the green gravel the grass grows green.
Bear's Song, The.
Chalcan Female Song.
Cloe to Artimesa.
Dispraise of Absalom, The.
Female Wits, The: A Song by a Lady of Quality.
Girl.
Her bracelets tinkle.
How to Choose a Mistress.
Impossible to Trust Women.
Little Lady of Ch'ing-ch'i, The.
Lords of Creation, The.
Love Song: "Beautiful is she, this woman."
Lovely the young peach tree.
Marvelous Encounter at Blue Creek, The.
Maxim Revised, A.
Maxims (Exeter Book).
My Lady Carenza of the lovely body.
O Woman, Shapely as the Swan.
One of the Awl Songs.
Sally, Sally Waters, sprinkle in the pan.
Song of Lo-fu, The.
To Caelia.
Twelfth Song of the Thunder.
When I look at her.
Woman is by aptitude.
Woman of Three Cows, The.
Women, women, love of women.
Vas. Just This.
Vaughan, H. To the Most Excellently Accomplished Mrs. Katherine Philips.
Verlaine. Femme et Chatte.
Vice. Pants.
Vidyapati. Twin Hills.
Villanueva, A. Witches' Blood.
Villon. Ballad[e] of Dead Ladies.
Virgil. Camilla goes to war.
Vizenor. Raising the Flag.
Voigt. Woman Who Weeps.
Voznesensky. Darkmotherscream is a Siberian dance.
Someone is beating a woman.
Waddington, M. Old Women of Toronto.
Wakoski. Belly Dancer.
Waldman, A. Because I don't have spit.
Waldrop, R. Lawn of Excluded Middle.
Walker, A. Women.
Wallace, W. Hand That Rocks the Cradle Is the Hand That Rules the World, The.
Waller, E. To a Fair Lady Playing with a Snake.
Wandor. Eve to Lilith.
Eve's Commentary.
Lilith to Eve.
Ruth's Story, As Told to Lilith.
Wang Chien. Words of the Newly Wed Wife.
Waniek. Ballad of Aunt Geneva, The.
Ward, N. Mercury shew'd Apollo, Bartas Book.
Waring, B. When a Beautiful Woman Gets on the Jutiapa Bus.
Watson, R. Ballad of the Bird-Bride.
Wayman. Another Poem about the Madness of Women.
Webster, A. Love's Mourner.
Whitman, A. "Come now, my love, the moon is on the lake;."
If it be shame to love a pretty woman.
These creatures of the languid Orient.
Whitman, S. Morning-Glory, The.
Whitman, W. This is the female form.
Woman waits for me, she contains all, nothing is lacking, A.
Wickham. Creatrix.
Dedication of the Cook.
Friend Cato.
Meditation at Kew.
Wilbur. Catch, The.
She.

Willard, N.　Cat's Second Song, The.
Williams, C.　Gulf Coast Blues.
Williams, S.　I Want Aretha to Set This to Music.
She Had Known Brothers.
Straight Talk from Plain Women.
You Were Never Miss Brown to Me.
Williams, W.　Marriage.
Portrait of a Lady.
Proletarian Portrait.
Queen-Anne's-Lace.
To a Friend Concerning Several Ladies.
Woman Walking.
Willis, N.　Unseen Spirits.
Winchilsea.　Answer, The.
Circuit of Apollo, The.
Friendship Between Ephelia and Ardelia.
On Myself.
Wither.　Author's Resolution, The.
I loved a lass, a fair one.
Wollach.　Body, The.
Preannual Poem.
Wordsworth, W.　She was a Phantom of delight.
Solitary Reaper, The.
Wu Wei-yeh.　Ballad of Yüan-yüan.
Wyatt, T.　Lover Showeth How He Is Forsaken of Such as He Sometime Enjoyed, The.
Yamada.　Club, The.
Yau.　Radiant Silhouette II.
Yeats.　Crazy Jane Talks with the Bishop.
Friends.
Lapis Lazuli.
Michael Robartes and the Dancer.
No Second Troy.
On Woman.
Prayer for My Daughter, A.
Thought from Propertius, A.
To an Isle in the Water.
Yosano.　Tanka: "Agonizing beyond words."
Tanka: "But for women."
Tanka: "Peony in her hair, The."
Young, E.　On Women ("Lavinia is polite").
Yukitsuna.　Tanka: "Changing."
Tanka: "During a trip."
Zach.　Poem Too Late, A.
Zamora, D.　To Be a Woman.
Zangwill.　To a Pretty Girl.
Zimmer.　Queen, The.

Wood
Bernstein, C.　Take then these nail and boards.
Bly, R.　Old Boards.
Carter, M.　Bitter Wood.
Dorn, E.　Rick of Green Wood, The.
Frost, R.　Wood-Pile, The.
Hardy, T.　Workbox, The.
Harris, M.　Physics One.
Hart-Smith.　Boomerang.
Kocbek.　Stick, The.
Koch, K.　Down at the docks.
Kunitz, S.　Knot, The.
Lowell, R.　Soft Wood.
Martin, A.　Forest.
Matveyeva.　Wood.
McGrath, C.　Dialectical Poem #1.
Mountain, M.　Wood pile.
Nash, O.　Termite, The.
Palmer, H.　Woodworker's Ballad.
Pien Kung.　Song of the Woodcutter of the Sea.
Spicer, J.　Lament for the Makers: "No call upon anyone but the timber drifting in the waves."
Unknown.　Tongue of Wood, The.
Walker, T.　Owl.
Welch, L.　He Thanks His Woodpile.
Young, A.　Heap of Faggots, A.

Woodpeckers
Cary, P.　Legend of the Northland, A.
Clare, J.　Green Woodpecker's Nest, The.
Creeley.　Like They Say.
Ni Tsan.　Woodpecker, The.
Roberts, E.　Woodpecker pecked out a little round hole, The.
Sambrook.　Woodpecker, The.
Weatherly, T.　Blues for Franks Wooten.

Woods. *See* **Forests**

Wool
Bowes-Lyon.　Woman Knitting, A.
Fergusson.　Braid Claith.
Yang Chi.　Springtime Embroidery.

Words
Agard, J.　Poetry Jump-Up.
Alvarez, J.　Bilingual Sestina.
He: Age doesn't matter when you're both in love.
Sonnet 42: "Sometimes the words are so close I am."
Ammons.　Triphammer Bridge.
Andrade, E.　Silence.
Atwood.　Variations on the Word *Love.*
Aubert, A.　When the Wine Was Gone.
Auden.　Words.
Bachmann.　You words, come, after me!
Baraka.　Ka 'Ba.
Bast.　Body of the Great Cat, The.
Beadle.　Words are but leaves to the tree of mind.
Behn, A.　Love's Witness.
Bernstein, C.　Kiwi Bird in the Kiwi Tree, The.
Virtual Reality.
Berryman.　To My Father.
Bible, *O.T.*　Bible, Proverbs 15:1, The.
Blokh.　Random talk has blown in.
Bozhilov.　Lilies.
Bromige.　Lines: "Repressive desublimation."
Brooke, R.　Fragment: "Isn't ligature—or is it ligament?—a lovely word?"
Brown, D.　Coming Home.
Brown, R.　Fry says a word.
Browning, E.　Sonnet: "And wilt thou have me fashion into speech."
Brutus.　Sometimes a mesh of ideas.
Causley.　Old Mrs Thing-um-e-bob.
Ceravolo.　Data.
Césaire, A.　Lagoonal Calendar.
Macumba Word.
Ch'ien T'ao.　I BUILT my hut in a zone of human habitation.
Clark, T.　You (IV).
Codrescu.　Imagination of Necessity, The.
Coleridge, M.　"He Knoweth Not That the Dead Are Thine."
Only a little shall we speak of thee.
Colesworthy.　Little word in kindness spoken, A.
Coolidge, C.　Hand Further, The.
Leaving Rattle Bar.
Manlius to Coeymans.
Tab, The.
This Garden Being: The Hanging of Books.
Cortez.　No Simple Explanations.
Creeley.　Language, The.
Token, A.
Waiting.
Cullen, C.　Incident.
Cummings, E.　Little joe gould has lost his teeth and doesn't know where.
Darwish, M.　Words.
Davidson, J.　Battle.
Davidson, M.　Form of Chiasmus; The Chiasmus of Forms, The.
Davies, A.　Outer Layers of Nervousness, The.
Ded.　To learn the scriptures is easy.
Desnos.　Like.
Dharmaraj.　Full of rain, the word.
Dickinson, E.　Could mortal lip divine.
Man may make a Remark, A.
Word is dead, A.
DiPalma.　Poem for Claude.
Dissanayake.　Freedom.
Doinas, S.　Words, The.
Donahue, J.　Desire's green / and gold corona / in the wavering branch.
Dove, R.　Ö.
Drummond de Andrade.　Looking for Poetry.
Du Maurier.　Music.
Dunn, S.　He/She.
Eady.　Sherbet.
Why Do So Few Blacks Study Creative Writing?
Elwell.　Important Words.

Ewart.　Word-Bird knows that everybody in Britain is frightened to death of *words,* The.
Faiz.　Once Again the Mind.
Francis, R.　Like Ghosts of Eagles.
Frost, R.　Beyond Words.
Ends.
Gibson, M.　Learning a New Language.
Gilbert, C.　Kite-Flying.
Gilbo'a.　I've Come to the Simplest Words.
Glatstein.　I still remember the half-lit meaning.
Gloria.　In Language.
Gouri.　And of all that was theirs only the letters were left.
Graham, W.　Malcolm Mooney's Land.
Graves, R.　Never Such Love.
Tilth.
Greenwald, T.　Privets Come into Season at High Tide.
Grenier.　Open the door Oakland.
Gumilyov.　Words.
Hadas, R.　Winged Words.
Hanlon, G.　Plainsong.
Hass, R.　Meditation at Lagunitas.
Hathaway, W.　My Words.
Hejinian.　Tree rows in orchards are capable of patterns. What, The.
Herlin.　So many traces, fragile monuments.
Hippolyte.　Air between Us (for an Expatriate), The.
Hoagland, E.　Anti-Semanticist, The.
Holan.　Cave of Words, The.
Holst-Warhaft.　John 1:1 and 14.
Howe, S.　Right or ruth.
Howell, T.　Acre of performance is worth a, An.
Hughes, L.　Sweet Words on Race.
Words Like Freedom.
Izumi.　Cricket Heard.
Jabès.　Book, The.
Jaccottet.　Reason.
Jackson, L.　World and I, The.
Jacobsen, R.　Cobalt.
Jarrell.　Islands, The.
Jones, P.　Prayer.
Jordan, N.　August 8.
Joron, A.　Baring the Device.
Shade of a Grammarian.
Kgositsile.　To Mother.
To My Daughter.
Klepfisz.　Few Words in the Mother Tongue, A.
Koch, K.　Permanently.
Kolatkar.　Alphabet, The.
Korn.　Put Your Word to My Lips.
Kruchyonykh.　Declaration of the Word as Such.
Kunert.　News from Behind the Seven Hills.
Vain Attempt.
Kunitz, S.　Touch Me.
Kuzminsky.　I'm cold. I'm destitute and absurd.
Landon.　Power of Words, The.
Landor, W.　Idle Words.
Larkin, P.　Talking in bed ought to be easiest.
Lee, L.　Persimmons.
Levi, P.　Voices mute for ever, or since yesterday, or just stilled;.
Lipsitz.　Skinny / poem, / all / your / ribs.
Longfellow, H.　Day is done, and the darkness, The.
Lorde.　Coal.
Lowry, M.　Strange Type.
MacLeish.　Reproach to Dead Poets.
Magee, K.　Tedium Drum, Part IV.
Major, C.　Swallow the Lake.
Mandelstam.　By denying me the seas, the right to run and fly.
Martin, A.　Malcolm MacKerral.
Mayakovsky.　I know the force of words, I know their clarion call.
McCarthy, G.　Hooded Legion, The.
McClure, M.　Rant Block.
McDonald, R.　Hollow Thesaurus, The.
McGinley.　Choice of Weapons, A.
McHugh, H.　And What Do You Get.
I Knew I'd Sing.

Mechthild von Magdeburg. Of all that God has shown me.
Meredith, W. Illiterate, The.
Merriam, E. How to Eat a Poem.
Merwin, W. Unwritten, The.
Utterance.
Millay, E. It is the fashion now to wave aside.
Mo Shih-lung. To the Monk Wu-hsia on the Occasion of His Editing the Lotus Sutra.
Mobilio. Third Kind of Interior Word, The.
Muldoon, P. Quoof.
Mullen, H. Momma Sayings.
Neal, L. Don't say goodbye to the Porkpie Hat that rolled.
Nichol. Two Words; a Wedding.
Noguere. Scribes, The.
Notley. Jack Would Speak Through the Imperfect Medium of Alice.
Ormsby, E. Origins.
Padgett, R. Louisiana Perch.
Who and Each.
Pagis. Words.
Palmer, M. Fifth Prose.
Notes for Echo Lake 3.
Sun.
Voice and Address.
Parkes, B. For Adelaide.
Patchen. Moon, Sun, Sleep, Birds, Live.
Patterson, R. "Word to the Wise Is Enough, A."
Peacock, M. Anger Sweetened.
Piombino. Pyramids, The.
Plath. Poems, Potatoes.
Words.
Po Chü-i. Lao Tzŭ.
Poe. Valentine, A.
Polkowski. World is only air / shining, granular, transparent things, The.
Probyn. Rondelet: "Say what you please."
Questel. Judge Dreadword.
Ramke. Buchenwald.
Reed, H. Naming Of Parts.
Reed, I. Beware: Do Not Read This Poem.
Robinson, K. Nesting of Layer Protocols.
Rosen, M. Night Before His Parents' First Trip to Europe His Mother Writes a Letter "To Our Children", The.
Rózewicz. Voice, A.
Rukeyser, M. Ballad of Orange and Grape.
Rutsala. Words.
Ryuichi. Human House.
Salamun. Clumsy Guys.
"Samoylov." Words.
Sandburg, C. Languages.
Little girl, be careful what you say.
Precious Moments.
Threes.
Scannell. Protest Poem.
Schnackenberg. Supernatural Love.
Schuyler, J. Freely Espousing.
Sepamla. Talk to the Peach Tree.
Shelley, P. To———: "One word is too often profaned."
Sidney, P. Sonnet 1: "Loving in truth, and fain[e] in verse my love to show."
Singer, B. Sort of Language, A.
Smith, S. Portrait, A.
Pretty.
Revenge, Timotheus cries, and in that shout.
Word, The.
Snyder, G. Riprap.
So Chong-Ju. Sneeze, A.
Sobin, G. Premises.
Spender, S. Word bites like a fish, The.
Staff. Speech.
Swinburne. Match, A.
Taggart, J. Never Too Late.
Twenty One Times.
Tate, J. Missed Opportunity, A.
Thomas, D. Especially when the October wind.
Tikhonov. Fire, the rope, the bullet, and the ax, The.
Unknown. Man of Words [and not of deeds], A.
Success is speaking words of praise.
Today I lost my temper.

What a to-do to die today.
Why English Is So Hard!
Ushakov. Wine.
Vaginov. Song of Words.
Violi. Rifacimento.
Wade, B. Truth.
Wain. Apology for Understatement.
Waldrop, R. To explore the nature of rain I opened the door because inside the workings of language clear vision is impossible.
Wallace-Crabbe. Double Dactyl.
Wasserman, R. Putting in a Word.
Watten. Radio.
Weaver, M. Borders.
Weekend Equestrian, The.
Weiner, H. From *Spoke / Aug 19.*
Remembered Sequel.
Seen Words.
Wheeler, S. Run on a Warehouse.
Whitman, W. Leaves of Grass (1855).
Williams, C. My Mother's Lips.
Williams, W. Fragment: "As for him who."
Sort of a Song, A.
Wilson, E. Nursery Vignette.
Wright, J. In Shame and Humiliation.
Yau. We Are All Vultures.
Yeats. Song of the Happy Shepherd, The.
Young, D. Project for Freight Trains, A.
Zamora, D. Precisely because I do not have.
Zarin. Song.
Zukofsky, L. Non Ti Fidar.
See also **Language**

Wordsworth, William
Arnold, M. And Wordsworth! Ah, pale ghosts, rejoice!
Barker, G. Resolution of Dependence.
Browning, E. On a Portrait of Wordsworth by B. R. Haydon.
Browning, R. Lost Leader, The.
Byron, G. Dedication: "Bob Southey! You're a poet—poet-laureate."
Don Juan.
"Carroll." White Knight's Song, The.
Clare, J. To Wordsworth.
Coleridge, H. He Lived amidst th' Untrodden Ways.
To Wordsworth.
Coleridge, S. To William Wordsworth.
De la Mare. Bards, The.
Ewart. William Wordsworth (1770-1850).
Ferlinghetti, L. I am waiting for my case to come up.
Grimke, C. Wordsworth.
Harrison, T. Remains.
Hemans. To the Poet Wordsworth.
Hopkins, G. Triolet.
Keyes, S. William Wordsworth.
Landon. On Wordsworth's Cottage, near Grasmere Lake.
Landor, W. To Wordsworth.
Nicholson, N. To the River Duddon.
Randall, J. To William Wordsworth from Virginia.
Shelley, M. On Reading Wordsworth's Lines on Peele Castle.
Shelley, P. All things that Peter saw and felt.
To Wordsworth.
Stephen, J. Sonnet, A: "Two voices are there: one is of the deep."
Stevenson, R. Fragment, A: "Thou strainest through the mountain fern."
Watson, S. Wordsworth's Grave.

Work and Workers. *See* **Labor and Laborers**
World. *See* **Earth**
World Federation
Tennyson, A. For I Dipped [*or* Dipt] into the Future.
World War I
Aldington. Field Manoeuvres.
Proem: "Sixty years after the fall of Troy."
Soliloquy 2.
Apollinaire. Calligram, 15 May 1915.
Little Car, The.
Post Card.
Stanzas Against Forgetting.
Armstrong, J. Another Reply to "In Flanders Fields."

"B., H. d'A." No-Man's-Land.
Binyon. For the Fallen.
Bishop, J. In the Dordogne.
Blunden. Concert Party: Busseboom.
Vlamertinghe.
Watchers, The.
Zonnebeke Road, The.
Brooke, R. Peace.
Soldier, The.
Cannan. Rouen.
Chesterton, G. Elegy in a Country Churchyard.
Coffey. Cold.
Cohan. Over There.
Crewe, R. Harrow and Flanders.
Cummings, E. Bigness of cannon, The.
Come, gaze with me upon this dome.
My sweet old etcetera.
Douglas, K. Soissons.
Dove, R. Alfonzo Prepares to Go Over the Top.
Fallon, P. Dardanelles 1916.
Fitzgerald, Z. Over the Top with Pershing.
Frankau. Deserter, The.
Gun Teams.
García Lorca. Rundown Church (Ballad of the First World War).
Gibson, W. Back.
Breakfast.
Conscript, The.
Golding, L. In The Gallery Where the Fat Men Go.
Graves, R. Dead Foxhunter, The.
Goliath and David.
Recalling War.
Sergeant-Major Money.
Two Fusiliers.
Grenfell, J. Into Battle.
Prayer for Those on the Staff.
Griffith, L. Silver Jubilee.
Gurney, I. Ballad of the Three Spectres.
Silent One, The.
Target, The.
Towards Lillers.
Hardy, T. And There Was a Great Calm.
Channel Firing.
In Time of "The Breaking of Nations."
Men Who March Away.
Often when warring for he wist not what.
Pity of It, The.
Heaney, S. In Memoriam Francis Ledwidge.
Herbert, A. After the Battle.
Beaucourt Revisited.
Hillyer. Eternal Return, The.
Hodgson, W. Back to Rest.
Before Action.
England to Her Sons.
Glimpse.
Housman, A. Here dead lie we because we did not choose.
Hughes, T. Walt.
Hugo, R. Yards of Sarajevo, The.
Hulme, T. Trenches: St Eloi.
Johnstone, P. High Wood.
Jones, D. But sweet sister death has gone debauched today and stalks.
Kipling, R. Death-Bed, A.
For all we have and are.
Gethsemane [1914–18].
Mesopotamia.
My Boy Jack.
Nativity, A.
Larkin, P. MCMXIV.
Lawrence, D. Song of a Man Who Has Come Through.
Tommies in the Train.
Lilliard. America's Answer.
Longley, M. Wounds.
Lowell, A. Camouflaged Troop-Ship.
McCrae, J. In Flanders Fields the poppies blow.
Meynell, A. Summer in England, 1914.
Mezhirov. Troop Train.
Mitchell, J. Reply to "In Flanders Fields."
Nichols, R. Noon.
Owen, W. Anthem for Doomed Youth.
Apologia Pro Poemate Meo.

Chances, The.
Conscious.
Disabled.
Dulce Et Decorum Est.
Exposure.
Futility.
Greater Love.
Next War, The.
Parable of the Old Man and the Young, The.
Send-Off, The.
Sentry, The.
Show, The.
Smile, Smile, Smile.
Spring Offensive.
Strange Meeting.
Terre, A.
Palmer, V.   Farmer Remembers the Somme, The.
Péret.   Hymn of the Patriotic War Veterans.
Little Song of the Maimed.
Pound, E.   Coming of War, The; Actaeon.
There died a myriad.
These fought in any case.
Read, S.   My men go wearily.
To a Conscript of 1940.
Rickword.   Soldier Addresses his Body, The.
Winter Warfare.
Rosenberg, I.   August 1914.
Break of Day in the Trenches.
Marching.
"Saki."   Carol: "While shepherds watched their flocks by night."
Sassoon.   Aftermath.
Attack.
Base Details.
Blighters.
Counter-Attack.
Death-Bed, The.
Does It Matter?[—losing your legs?].
Dreamers.
Dug-Out, The.
Everyone Sang.
Fight to a Finish.
General, The.
Glory of Women.
On Passing the New Menin Gate.
Rear-Guard, The.
Redeemer, The.
Repression of War Experience.
Suicide in [the] Trenches.
To Any Dead Officer.
Working Party, A.
Scannell.   Great War, The.
Seeger, A.   Rendezvous, The.
Simpson, L.   I dreamed that in a city dark as Paris.
Sorley.   Sonnet: "When you see millions of the mouthless dead."
Squire.   Dilemma, The.
Stallworthy, J.   War Story.
Thomas, E.   As the team's head-brass flashed out on the turn.
In Memoriam (Easter, 1915).
Private, A.
This is no case of petty right or wrong.
Toller.   Corpses in the Wood.
Trakl.   Grodek.
In the East.
Unknown.   Cricketers of Flanders, The.
I don't want to be a soldier.
We are Fred Karno's army.
We mean to thrash these Prussian Pups.
Van Dyke.   America's Welcome Home.
West, A.   Night Patrol, The.
Whitmell.   Christ in Flanders.
Wilson, T.   Magpies in Picardy, The.
Sportsmen in Paradise.
Yeats.   On Being Asked for a War Poem.
Reprisals.

World War II
"Agyeya."   Hiroshima.
Andreyev, D.   Night winds! Dark mountainous skies.
Aragon.   Lilacs and the Roses, The.
Auden.   Here war is harmless like a monument.
September 1, 1939.

Barker, G.   To Any Member of My Generation.
Bell, M.   Footnote to Enright's "Apocalypse."
Berggolts.   Conversation with a Neighbor.
Berryman.   Moon and the Night and the Men, The.
Betjeman.   In Westminster Abbey.
Bobrowski.   Kaunas 1941.
Borowski.   Two Countries.
Bowers, E.   Stoic: for Laura von Courten, The.
Brecht, B.   Children's Crusade 1939.
War Has Been Given a Bad Name.
Brown, H.   Incident on a Front Not Far from Castel di Sangro.
Caraion.   Song from the Occupation Time.
Carruth, H.   Mountain, The.
Causley.   Conversation in Gibraltar 1943.
Death of an Aircraft.
Chin.   American Rain.
Chukhonstev.   In the Menagerie.
Ciardi.   Elegy Just in Case.
Corwin, N.   Man unto His Fellow Man.
Crow, S.   El Alamein.
Cummings, E.   YgUDuh / ydoan / yunnuhstan.
Daniels, K.   For Miklos Radnóti: 1909-1944.
Desnos.   Letter to Youki.
Night Watchman of Pont-au-Change, The.
Dickey, J.   Firebombing, The.
Doolittle, H.   From The Walls Do Not Fall.
Douglas, K.   Aristocrats.
Vergissmeinnicht.
Dove, R.   Aircraft.
Sightseeing.
Dudin.   Nightingales.
Dugan, A.   Memorial Service for the Invasion Beach Where the Vacation in the Flesh Is Over.
Eich.   Old Postcards.
Eimers.   Another Kimono.
Éluard, P.   Nazi Song.
Elytis.   March toward the Front, The.
Fenton, J.   German Requiem, A.
Field, E.   World War II.
Fuller, R.   Spring 1942.
Gascoyne.   Wartime Dawn, A.
Glazkov.   Prayer: "Lord, stand up for the Soviets."
Gudzenko.   Before the Attack.
Hecht, A.   'More Light! More Light!'.
Henderson, H.   Seven Good Germans.
Herbert, S.   Less Nonsense.
Herbert, Z.   Painter.
Holan.   Children at Christmas in 1945.
Holman, M.   Notes for a Movie Script.
Hongo.   O-Bon: Dance for the Dead.
Huchel.   Landscape Beyond Warsaw.
Roads.
Hughes, L.   World War II.
Hugo, R.   Napoli Again.
View from Cortona, A.
Inada.   From Our Album.
Jarrell.   Burning the Letters.
Camp in the Prussian Forest, A.
Dead Wingman, The.
Death of the Ball Turret Gunner, The.
Eighth Air Force.
Field Hospital, A.
For an Emigrant.
Front, A.
Losses.
Lullaby, A: "For wars his life and half a world away."
Pilot from the Carrier, A.
Pilots, Man Your Planes.
Range in the Desert, The.
Second Air Force.
Sick Nought, The.
Truth, The.
Jeffers, R.   Black-out.
May-June, 1940.
Kaufman, B.   War Memoir: Jazz, Don't Listen to It at Your Own Risk.
Keesing.   Reverie of a Mum.
Keyes, S.   Timoshenko.
Klepfisz.   Death Camp.
Perspectives on the Second World War.
Krynicki.   By entering the grand lottery.

Laing, A.   New Jerusalem, The.
Langland, J.   War.
Levin, K.   Artillery was burying us.
Lewis, A.   Peasants, The.
Lewis, S.   Deluge 1939, The.
Liu Ya-tzu.   On Hearing the News of the Japanese Surrender.
Overjoyed at Soviet Russia's Entry into the War.
Lochhead, L.   My Mother's Suitors.
Lowell, R.   Exile's Return, The.
Holy Innocents, The.
Mad Negro Soldier Confined at Munich, A.
Lukonin.   To Kolya Otrada.
MacLean, S.   Death Valley.
Going Westwards.
Macnab.   El Alamein Revisited.
MacNeice.   Streets of Laredo, The.
McElroy, C.   For Want of a Male a Shoe Was Lost.
McGrath, T.   Blues for Warren.
Milosz, C.   Dedication: "You whom I could not save / Listen to me."
Mitsui.   Photograph of a Child, Japanese-American Evacuation, Bainbridge Island, Washington, March 30, 1942.
Montague, J.   Welcoming Party, A.
Montgomerie, W.   Edge of the War (1939–), The.
Moore, M.   In Distrust of Merits.
Keeping Their World Large.
Morgan, E.   Cinquevalli is falling, falling.
Mura.   Argument: on 1942, An.
Narovchatov.   Wolf Cub.
Nemerov.   War in the Air, The.
Olds, S.   Leningrad Cemetery, Winter of 1941.
Oppen.   In Alsace, during the war.
Route.
Panchenko.   Ballad of the Shot Heart.
Pasternak, B.   Fresco Come to Life.
Perelman.   Broken Mirror, The.
Porter, P.   May, 1945.
Quasimodo.   19 January 1944.
Read, S.   To a Conscript of 1940.
Reed, H.   Chard Whitlow.
Rukeyser, M.   Breaking Open.
"Sagittarius."   Croaked the Eagle: "Nevermore."
Nerves.
"Samoylov."   Forties, fateful forties, The.
Schmitz.   Picture of Okinawa, A.
Schuyler, J.   Let's All Hear It for Mildred Bailey!
Scott, W.   U. S. Sailor with the Japanese Skull, The.
Shapcott, T.   Shadow of War, 1941.
Shapiro, K.   Progress of Faust, The.
Quintana lay in the shallow grave of coral.
Shepherd, R.   Lucky One, The.
Simic.   Begotten of the Spleen.
Simonov.   Remember, Alyosha, the roads of Smolensk.
Simpson, L.   Carentan O Carentan.
Runner, The.
Sitwell, D.   Still falls the Rain—.
Slessor.   Beach Burial.
Slutsky.   Pit of Cologne, The.
Smith, S.   I Remember.
Soupault.   You Who Sleep.
Stern, G.   Dancing, The.
Stone, R.   That Winter.
Svetlov.   Italian, The.
Swirszczynska.   Conversation Through the Door, A.
I Am Afraid of Fire.
White Wedding Slippers.
Tate, J.   Lost Pilot, The.
Tillinghast, R.   Our Flag Was Still There.
Tvardovsky.   Crossing, The.
Urin.   Oh, Maika in a maika, there's the smell of summer.
Viereck, P.   Kilroy.
Vale from Carthage.
Waniek.   Lonely Eagles.
Tuskegee Airfield.
Winters, Y.   Night of Battle.
Summer Noon: 1941.

Wong, N. Can't Tell.
Yevtushenko. Babii Yar.
Zach. War Confession.
Zhigulin. Campfireburners.
Žukauskas. Midwinter Tourists.

Worldliness
Brooks, G. Mrs. Small went to the kitchen for her pocketbook.
Donne. London Street, A.
Since she whome I lovd, hath payd her last debt.
Herbert, Z. Mr. Cogito Tells about the Temptation of Spinoza.
Killigrew, A. Farewell to Worldly Joyes, A ("Farewel to unsubstantial joyes").
Wordsworth, W. Sonnet: "World is too much with us; late and soon, The."
See also **Libraries and Librarians**

Worms
Allen, M. Angleworms.
Bakken. How to Eat Corn.
Blake, W. Sick Rose, The.
Clarke, P. My name is Sluggery-wuggery.
Cobbing. Worm.
Cole, W. Two Sad.
Danner. This Is an African Worm.
De la Mare. Old Shellover.
Fuller, R. Autobiography of a Lungworm.
Inez. Woman Who Loved Worms, The.
Jones, J. I can climb our apple tree.
Lawrence, D. Worm Either Way.
Levertov. Earth Worm, The.
"MacDiarmid." Ex Vermibus.
Martinson. Earthworm, The.
Marvell. Mower to the Glow-Worms [or Glowworms or Glo-Worms], The.
Nobuyuki. Returning from Abroad.
Riley, J. Wee little worm in a hickory-nut, A.
Rosen, M. Christmas Dinner.
Rossetti, C. Handy Mole who plied no shovel, A.
Sexton. Fury of Flowers and Worms, The.
Smith, S. Reversionary.
Stevens, W. Worms at Heaven's Gate, The.
Toomer. Face.
Unknown. Maggot Song.

Wormwood
Thoreau. Tall Ambrosia.

Worry
Apollonius Rhodius. Now rising shades a solemn scene display.
Bruner. Dreaded Task, The.
Chuang Tzu. Need to Win, The.
Chung-ch'ang T'ung. Speaking My Mind.
Davies, W. Leisure.
Frost, R. Armful, The.
Hall, D. Jealous Lovers, The.
Holtby, W. Boats in the Bay.
Roberson. Sonnet.
Schuyler, J. Letter to a Friend: Who Is Nancy Daum?
Silverstein, S. Whatif.
T'ao Ch'ien. Substance, Shadow, and Spirit.
Unknown. Worries.
Worry—is like a distant hill.
Wordsworth, W. Affliction of Margaret—The The.
Yang Shih-ch'i. Night Rain: A Wall Collapses—Sent To My Neighbors.
Yosano. She who carries / in her heart a love.

Worship and Worshipers
Aristophanes. CHORUS. Ye Children of Man! whose life is a span.
Avison. Water and Worship: An Open-Air Service on the Gatineau River.
Awoonor. At the Gates.
Baxter, R. Ye holy Angels bright.
Bible, *O.T.* Bible, Isaiah 40:31, The.
Bless the Lord, O my soul.
Psalm 29.
Psalm 98.
Psalm 100.
Psalm 134.
Psalm 147: "Praise ye the Lord."
Psalm 148.
Bradstreet, A. As Spring the Winter Doth Succeed.

Cannon, N. Ark, The.
Carew, T. New Year's Sacrifice: To Lucinda, A.
Carhart. Saturday Night Worship.
Cheng Hsieh. Girl from Ch'ang-kan is just fourteen years old, The.
Coleridge, S. Eolian Harp, The.
Colonna, V. As a hungry fledgling, who sees and hears.
Dante Alighieri. I felt a spirit of love begin to stir.
Dickinson, E. Some keep the Sabbath going to Church.
Doolittle, H. Hippolytus Temporizes.
Emerson, R. Sursum Corda.
Enheduanna. From The Hymn to Inanna.
Gascoigne. Gascoigne's Good-Morrow.
Gay, J. Molly Mog [or The Fair Maid of the Inn].
Ghalib, A. Let the ascetics sing of the garden of Paradise.
World is no more than the Beloved's single face, The.
Godolphin. Hymn: "Lord, when the wise men came from far[r]."
Han Yü. Girl of Mt. Hua, The.
Hardy, T. Afternoon Service at Mellstock.
Henderson, D. Song of Devotion to the Forest.
Herbert, G. Altar, The.
Christmas.
Love (2).
Misery [*or* Miserie].
Praise (2).
Prayer (I).
Sunday.
Temper (1), The.
Temper (2), The.
True Hymn, A.
Hill, G. Eia, with handbells, jews' harps, risible.
Hopkins, G. Pied Beauty.
Kabir. Inside this clay jar there are meadows and groves and the One who made them.
Kākkai Pāṭiṇiyār Nacceḷḷaiyār. What Her Girl Friend Said to her lover on his return.
Keats. Fragment of an Ode to Maia Written on May Day, 1818.
Kendall, M. Education's Martyr.
Kyger. Every day I burn a stick of incense.
Leonidas of Tarentum. Silver Love, an anklet, A.
Lindsay, V. At Mass.
Longfellow, S. Again as evening's shadow falls.
Mahadevi. I do not call it his sign.
McNeill, A. Hello Ungod.
Mechthild von Magdeburg. True love in every moment praises God.
Mirabai. Heat of Midnight Tears, The.
I was going to the river for water.
Love has stained my body.
O my friends.
Okudzhava. I need to worship someone.
Pembroke, M. Laudate Dominum.
Psalm 100: "O all you lands, the treasures of your joy."
Penstone. Praise to God for things we see.
Perronet. All hail the Power of Jesus' name!
Popa. Admirers of the Little Box, The.
Rabi'a al-Adawiyya. O my Lord.
O my Lord, if I worship you from fear of Hell.
Robbins, H. And have the bright immensities.
Sappho. As the full moon slowly rose.
At last, on delicate feet.
Smart, C. My Cat Jeoffry.
Southwell. Child[e] My Choice [*or* Choyse], A.
Stanley, T. Paraphrase Upon Part of the CXXXIX Psalm, A.
Sylvester, J. Sweet mouth, that send'st a musky-rosed breath;.
Traherne. On Christmas-Day
Unknown. Go, Hart.
Lord among the Clouds, The.
Lord of the River.
Virgil. It is I, lads, who look after this place.

Watts, I. Flying Fowl, and Creeping Things, Praise Ye the Lord.
Hosanna to Christ.
Whittier. First-Day Thoughts.
Worship.
Winchilsea. Hymn, The: "To the Almighty on his radiant throne."
Yu Xuanji. At Home in the Summer Mountains.
See also **Churches; Prayer; Religion**

Wounded Knee, Battle of (1890)
Rose. I Expected My Skin and My Blood to Ripen.

Wreaths
"MacDiarmid." One of the Principal Causes of War.
Ritsos. Wreath, A.

Wrecks
Hall, D. Blue Wing, The.
Merwin, W. Bones, The.

Wren, Sir Christopher
Bentley, E. Clerihew: "Savonarola."
Sir Christopher Wren.

Wrens
Bennett, R. Mistress Jenny Wren.
Bly, R. Looking at a Dead Wren in My Hand.
Davies, W. Jenny Wren.
Levis. To a Wren on Calvary.
Mother Goose. Dove and the Wren, The.
Thompson, P. Little Wren, A.
Unknown. Hunting the Wren.
Warning, A.
Wee jenny wren she lays sixteen, The.
Wren, The.
Wills, J. Larger.

Wrestling and Wrestlers
Bekederemo. Leader, The.
Bevington, L. Wrestling.
Ramanujan. At Forty.
Soto. Wrestler's Heart, The.

Wright, James
Cooper, J. Hotel De Dream.
Orr, G. Elegy: "Not only doesn't the Ohio."

Wright, Richard
Madgett. Images.
Rivers, C. Mourning Letter from Paris, A.
To Richard Wright.

Writing and Writers
Adamson. Home, The Spare Room, The.
Adcock, F. Future Work.
Agard, J. Poetry Jump-Up.
Aiken, J. Do It Yourself.
"Akhmatova." Epigram: "Could Beatrice have written like Dante."
I care nothing for battle odes.
Alcock. Receipt for Writing a Novel, A.
Ali, A. Homage to Faiz Ahmed Faiz.
Allison, D. When I drink I become / the joy of faggots.
Alvarez, J. Bilingual Sestina.
Sonnet 42: "Sometimes the words are so close I am."
Woman's Work.
Alver. Iron Nerves.
"Amorous Lady." On Being Charged with Writing Incorrectly.
Andrews, T. Cinema Vérité: The Death of Alfred, Lord Tennyson.
Andreyev, D. For the Unveiling of a Memorial.
Antin. David ross called up from syracuse and wanted to know if.
Private Occasion in a Public Place, A.
Artaud. All Writing Is Garbage.
Ashbery. And "Ut Pictura Poesis" Is Her Name.
Auden. Novelist, The.
Baca. It Started.
Bachmann. No Delicacies.
Bàng Bá Lâ. If in a Future Life We Meet Again.
Barber, M. Conclusion of a Letter to the Rev. Mr. C——, The.
How I succeed, you kindly ask.
Beckovic. Yevtushenko.
Beer, P. Jane Austen.

Behn, A. Rover or The Banished Cavaliers, The.
Benedikt. Events by Moonlight.
Bernstein, C. Klupzy Girl, The.
Wait.
Berrigan, T. Final Sonnet, A.
Personal Poem #9.
Sonnet LV: "Grace to be born and live as variously as possible."
Words for Love.
Berryman. Henry's Fate.
I can't get him out of my mind, out of my mind.
Of Suicide.
Sonnet 115: "All we were going strong last night this time."
Winters close, Springs open, no child stirs, The.
Betjeman. Ballad of George R. Sims, The.
Reproof Deserved; or After the Lecture.
Blagden. To George Sand on her Interview with Elizabeth Barrett Browning.
Blake, W. When Klopstock England defied.
Blamire. Epistle to Her Friends at Gartmore.
Blok. Poets, The.
Blount, A. Cure for Poetry, A.
Blumenthal, M. I Have Lived This Way for Years and Do Not Wish to Change.
Bly, R. After Drinking All Night with a Friend, We Go Out in a Boat at Dawn to See Who Can Write the Best Poem.
Boileau-Despéaux. Garden of Writing, The.
Borges. Matthew XXV:30.
Bradstreet, A. Prologue, The: "To sing of wars, of captain[e]s, and of kings."
Brecht, B. Bad Time for Poetry.
Breytenbach. Out There.
Bristol. Crime of the Ages, The.
Brodsky, J. York: In Memoriam W. H. Auden.
Brontë, E. Alone I sat; the summer day.
Aye, there it is! It wakes to-night.
Night Wind, The.
O thy bright eyes must answer now.
Brown, W. Rilke.
Browne, W. On the Countess Dowager of Pembroke.
Browning, E. Curse for a Nation, A.
Felicia Hemans.
Fifth Book.
Sonnet: "My poet, thou canst touch on all the notes."
Sonnet: "Thou hast thy calling to some palace-floor."
To George Sand / A Desire.
To George Sand: A Recognition.
Bryant, W. Poet, The.
Buchanan, G. Lyle Donaghy, Poet, 1902-1949.
Budenz. Poeta Fui.
Bukowski. Black poets / young, The.
Bunimovich. Explanatory Note.
Bunin. High up on a snowy peak.
Bunting. What the Chairman Told Tom.
Burgess, F. Cinq Ans Après.
Burns, R. Epistle to J. Lapraik, an Old Scotch Bard.
On Elphinston's Translation of Martial.
Byrom. Passive Participle's Petition, The.
Byron, G. Byron on Southey.
Canto the Eleventh.
Epistle from Mr Murray to Dr Polidori.
Next comes the dull disciple of thy school.
Campbell, R. On Professor Drennan's Verse.
On Some South African Novelists.
Caraion. Memory.
Carew, T. Fancy, A.
To Ben Jonson.
Carey, H. Author's Quietus, The.
Carruth, H. Freedom and Discipline.
On Being Asked to Write a Poem Against the War in Vietnam.
Cassian. Other Life, the.
Catullus. Carmen 65 ("Grief reached across the world to get me").
To Varus.
Cavafy. And I Lounged and Lay on Their Beds.

Cavalli. Someone told me.
Cawein. Poetry.
Cervantes. Poem for the Young White Man Who Asked Me How I, An Intelligent, Well-Read Person Could Believe in the War Between Races.
Chakravarty, A. Fire.
Chan Fang-sheng. Sailing Homeward.
Chang Yü. In a Book-Box I Found the Lost Manuscript of a Poem Sent to Me by the Late Kao [Ch'i].
Reading the Poetry Collection of Lü Fang-ch'ing.
Retreat of Liu Kuo-pao, The.
To the Innkeeper at Five Rivers, Sun Pen.
Channing. Poet's Hope, A.
Chao Meng-fu. Living in Retirement at Te-ch'ing.
Chapman, G. Homer and the Brazen Head of Rumour.
Chaucer. To His Scribe Adam.
Chế Lan Viên. More Thoughts on Nguyễn.
Ch'en Shih-tao. Cold Night.
Cheney-Coker. Letter to a Tormented Playwright.
On Being a Poet in Sierra Leone.
Road to Exile Thinking of Vallejo, The.
Cheng Hsieh. Twenty-eight Characters Sent to Tung-ts'un on the Subject of the Poems He Burned.
Cherry, K. History.
Ch'in Chia. To His Wife.
Chin. Exile's Letter: After the Failed Revolution.
Chin Nung. Written at the End of Master Ho-ching's Collected Works.
Chong, H. Miserable.
"Chorny." Stylized Donkey, A.
Chu Yün-ming. Painting of the Butterfly Dream by the Master Artist Li Tsai, A.
Too Lazy to Write Poetry.
Ciardi. Gift, The.
Cisneros, S. Poet Reflects On Her Solitary Fate, The.
Clarke, C. Wearing My Cap Backwards.
Clewell. This Book Belongs to Susan Someone.
Clough. If to write, rewrite, and write again.
Codrescu. Paper on Humor.
Coffin, F. Harriet Beecher Stowe's Works.
Coleridge, H. He Lived amidst th' Untrodden Ways.
Coleridge, S. On Donne's Poetry.
Collins, B. Tuesday, June 4th, 1991.
Columcille. Invocation, An: "My claw is tired of scribing!"
Cook, E. Lines / Suggested by the Song of a Nightingale.
To the Late William Jerdan.
Coolidge, C. Crystal Text, The.
Noon Point.
On Induction of the Hand.
Cooper, J. Poem with Capital Letters, A.
Cope, W. Engineers' Corner.
Exchange of Letters.
Serious Concerns.
Triolet.
"Cornwall." Poet's Thought, A.
Corrothers. Me 'n' Dunbar.
Cortez. No Simple Explanations.
Cowley, A. Muse, The.
Written in Juice of Lem[m]on.
Cowley, H. Ode to Della Crusca.
To Della Crusca. The Pen.
Cowper, W. To Mary Unwin.
To William Hayley, Esq.: In Reply to His Solicitation to Write with Him in a Literary Work.
Crane, H. Passage.
Crane, S. Little ink more or less!, A.
Crashaw. On Mr. G. Herberts Booke, The Temple.
Creeley. Waiting.
Cronin, A. Lines for a Painter.
Crsnaru. Lions of Babylon, The.
Cruz, V. Today Is a Day of Great Joy.

Cullen, C. To Certain Critics.
Yet Do I Marvel.
Cummings, E. It was a goodly co.
Dacey, P. Porno Love.
Dacre, C. Sappho; or, The Resolve.
Đặng Phu'o'ng. To Nguyễn Du.
Daniels, K. For Miklos Radnóti: 1909-1944.
Darley. Pass of Death, The.
Dash. Me Again.
Davenant. There, when they thought they saw in well sought Books.
Davie. Rejoinder to a Critic.
Davys. Behind the moth-eaten curtain, 'stead of press.
Day Lewis. Where Are the War Poets?
De la Mare. Moonshine.
Scribe, The.
Di Prima. Loba Addresses the Goddess, The / or The Poet as Priestess Addresses the Loba-Goddess.
On Sitting Down to Write, I Decide Instead to Go to Fred Herko's Concert.
Dickey, J. False Youth: Autumn: Clothes of the Age.
Dickinson, E. I reckon—when I count at all.
Missing All—prevented Me, The.
Publication—is the Auction.
Tell all the Truth but tell it slant.
This is my letter to the World.
This was a Poet—It is That.
Doinas, S. Pythia.
Đông Hồ. Buying a Dress for My Love.
Poem of Humankind, The.
Donne. Canonization, The.
Poet Turned Lawyer, The.
Sapho To Philaenis.
To Mr. R. W ("Kindly I envy thy song's [or songs] perfection").
Triple Fool[e], The.
Valediction of the Book, A.
Donnell. Canadian Prairies View of Literature, The.
Dooley, D. How I Wrote It.
Doolittle, H. Fragment 36: "I know not what to do."
Douglas, L. Dead Poet, The.
Dransfield. Day at a Time.
Endsight.
Drayton. First Steps Up Parnassus.
Drummond, W. I know that all beneath the moon decays.
Dryden, J. To the Pious Memory of the Accomplished [or Accomplist] Young Lady, Mrs. Anne Killigrew, [Excellent in the Two Sister-Arts of Poesie and Painting].
Dunbar, P. Misapprehension.
Poet, The.
Then and Now.
Dunbar, W. Lament for the Makaris.
Duncan, R. Bending the Bow.
Dancing Concerning a Form of Women, A.
Poetry, a Natural Thing.
Eady. Why Do So Few Blacks Study Creative Writing?
"Elagin." Come now, my friend, you must not say.
Has my life been a failure? I wonder—.
Eliot, T. Whispers of Immortality.
Ellis, S. Your Poems at Daybreak, the Destruction of Knossos by Afternoon.
Ellis, T. View of the Library of Congress from Paul Laurence Dunbar High School.
Engman. Another Word for Blue.
Enright, D. Evil Days, The.
Equi. Date with Robbe-Grillet, A.
Evans, P. Ode to Tennis.
Ewart. Black Box, The.
Fennelly. Poem Not to Be Read at Your Wedding.
Ferlinghetti, L. Constantly risking absurdity.
Sea and Ourselves at Cape Ann, The.
World is a beautiful place, The.
Ferry. Rereading Old Writing.
"Field." To Christina Rossetti.
Finch, A. Dickinson.
Reply From His Coy Mistress, A.
Fitzgerald, E. 71.

Forbes, C. Poet's Shuffle, The.
Forbes, J. Monkey's Pride.
Fordham. Pen, The.
Frere. I've often wish'd that I could write a book.
Frost, R. It takes all sorts of in- and outdoor schooling.
Gabai. For the Last Time on My Native Estate...
Gallagher, T. I Stop Writing the Poem.
Garrigue. Cortège for Colette.
Gifford, W. Lo, Della Crusca! In his closet pent.
Gilbert, S. Ferdinando and Elvira; or, The Gentle Pieman.
Gilbo'a. I'll grab hold of a butt of dream.
Ginsberg, A. Howl.
  On Burroughs' Work.
  Poem Rocket.
Gioia. My Confessional Sestina.
  Next Poem, The.
Glazkov. Boyarina Morozova, The.
  Introduction to a Poem.
  Khikhimora.
  Poetograd.
Glück, L. Mountain, The.
  Poem: "In the early evening, as now, a man is bending."
Gogarty. To a Friend.
Gorbanevskaya. Like a soldier from Anders's army.
Gorham. Empress Receives the Head of a Taiping Rebel, The.
Grabill. Ars Poetica.
Graham, W. Malcolm Mooney's Land.
  Night City, The.
Graves, R. Laureate, The.
  Plea to Boys and Girls, A.
  Reader over My Shoulder, The.
Gray, J. Mishka [is poet among the beasts].
Gray, T. Progress of Poesy, The.
Greenwell, D. To Christina Rossetti.
  To Elizabeth Barrett Browning, in 1851.
  To Elizabeth Barrett Browning, in 1861.
Griffin, S. Stories and Poems.
Grossman, A. Dust.
Gudzenko. I fought on foot in every quarter.
Gunn, T. Expression.
  Mirror for Poets, A.
Guobin. My poem is a bridge, silent, lonely;.
Hacker, M. Feeling and Form.
Hadas, R. Winged Words.
Hall, D. Another Elegy.
  Poet at Twenty, A.
  To a Waterfowl.
Han Yü. Leaves fall turning turning to the ground.
  This morning I can't seem to get out of bed.
Hands, E. Poem on the Supposition of an Advertisement, A; Appearing in a Morning Paper, of the Publication of a Volume of Poems, by a Servant-Maid.
  Poem on the Supposition of the Book Having Been Published and Read, A.
Hardy, T. Epitaph for George Moore.
  George Meredith (1828-1909).
  I looked up from my writing.
Harington. Of honest Theft. To my good friend Master Samuel Daniel.
Harjo, J. Bird.
  Strange Fruit.
Harper, M. In Hayden's Collage.
Harris, W. Historic Moment, An.
Harrison, T. Heartless Art, The.
  On Not Being Milton.
Harte, B. Miss Edith's Modest Request.
Hartnett. Enamoured of the miniscule / of the careful and compact.
  I have exhausted the delighted range.
Hayden, R. Paul Laurence Dunbar.
Heaney, S. Digging.
  From the Frontier of Writing.
Heine. To a Political Poet.
Hejinian. Can one take captives by writing.
Hemans. Grave of a Poetess, The.
Hemensley. Look! she said you can see.
  My poem's in the oven where it.

Place was famed for, The.
Poem by John Thorpe, A.
Hendriks. Where It's At.
Henley, W. Easy is the triolet.
Herbert, G. Jordan (2)(II): "When first my lines [or verse] of heavenly [or heav'nly] joy[e]s made mention."
  Posy [or Posie], The.
  Sonnet: "My God, where is that ancient heat towards Thee."
  Sonnet: "Sure Lord, there is enough in thee to dry."
Herbert, Z. Five Men.
Hen is the best example of what living constantly with humans, The.
Knocker, A.
Hernton. Distant Drum, The.
Herrick. Argument of His Book, The.
  His Desire.
  His Poetry His Pillar.
  His Prayer to Ben[.] Jo[h]nson.
  His Request to Julia.
  Not Every Day Fit for Verse.
  Ode for Ben Jonson, An.
  To God ("Do with me, God! as Thou didst deal with John").
  To His Book ("Before the Press scarce one co'd see").
  To M. Denham, on His Prospective Poem.
  To the Generous Reader.
  To the Reverend Shade of His Religious Father.
  Upon His Verses.
  When He Would Have His Verses Read.
Hewitt, J. I write for my own kind.
  Local Poet, A.
Higginson, W. I look up.
  Writing again.
Hilton, D. Finding a Chet Baker Album in the Dimestore 2-for-$1 Pile.
Hirschman, J. Transfiguration.
Holmes, O. At the "Atlantic" Dinner, December 15, 1874.
Hood, T. First Attempt in Rhyme, A.
Hoover, P. Poems We Can Understand.
Horace. Our rural Ancestors, with little blest.
  Paynter if he shoulde adjoyne, A.
Horton, G. On Hearing of the Intention of a Gentleman to Purchase the Poet's Freedom.
Housman, A. Terence, this is stupid stuff.
Howe, S. Right or ruth.
Hsieh Chin. I still remember Conch-Shell Slope, west of the River Tzu.
Hsü Wei. From Chekiang I Went to Hsin-an and Climbed Even-with-the-Clouds Mountain. On the Way Back There Were Many Beautiful Sights at the Inns Where I Stayed and Yet I Could Not Write One Word of Poetry. When I Got Back to the Main Road I Wrote These Four Lines to Make Fun of Myself.
Hs'üan-Chi. On a Visit to Ch'ung Chen Taoist Temple.
Hughes, L. Theme for English B.
Hughes, T. Famous Poet.
Hugo, R. Letter to Logan from Milltown.
  Letter to Reed from Lolo.
Hunt, L. But now came the men of right visiting claims;.
  'Twas in eighteen eleven those bards came to dine;.
Inada. Wintersong.
Iskander. Overtired branches are fragile.
Ivanov, G. Fog. The road I usually wander down.
Ivaska. That which has remained unlived.
  To the Memory of a Poet.
Jaccottet. I rise with an effort and look out.
Jackson, L. Poet's Corner, The.
Jackson, L. Prima Donna Poet Replies, A.
Jackson, R. After the Dance.
  1973.
Jacobs, H. It is not just.
James, C. Book of my enemy has been remaindered, The.
Jarman, M. Unholy Sonnets.
Jarrell. Author to the Reader, The.

Jeffers, R. But I Am Growing Old and Indolent.
  Love the Wild Swan.
Jemie. Toward a Poetics.
Johnson, J. O Black and unknown bards of long ago.
Johnson, L. In Honorem Doriani Creatorisque Eius.
  In Honour of Dorian and his Creator.
Johnson, S. Prologue to Garrick's *Lethe*.
Johnston, E. Address to Nature on its Cruelty, An.
Jones, M. Epistle to Lady Bowyer, An.
Jong. Castration of the Pen.
Jonson, B. Ode to Himself.
  On Playwright ("Playwright convict of public wrongs to men").
  On Poet-Ape.
  Sonnet to the Noble Lady, the Lady Mary Wroth, A.
  To Francis Beaumont.
  To Thomas Palmer [on His Book "The Sprite of Trees and Herbs"].
Justice, D. Variations on a Text by Vallejo.
Kalász. Impromptu.
K'ang Hai. When I have chanted my new poems.
Kao Ch'i. Song of the Man of Green Hill, The.
Kaufman, B. Unhistorical Events.
Kavanagh, P. Sanctity.
Keats. All These Are Vile.
  Ode: "Bards of passion and of mirth."
Kelly, R. Newark.
  Rainmakers, The.
Kemble. Impromptu.
  Lines.
Kendall, M. Failures.
Kendrick, D. We are the writing on the wall.
Kennelly. Master.
Keyes, S. War Poet.
Killigrew, A. Upon the Saying That My Verses Were Made by Another.
Kilmer, J. Trees.
Kim, K. Pathos.
Kinsella, T. Route of the Táin, The.
Kirsanov. Lyric Poem.
Kirsch, S. Stopover.
Kizer, C. Two.
Kleinzahler. Case in Point, A.
Knight, E. For Black Poets Who Think of Suicide.
  Green Grass and Yellow Balloons.
  Poem to Galway Kinnell, A.
Koch, K. Circus, The.
Komunyakaa. My Father's Love Letters [or Loveletters].
Kornilov, B. Drawer of My Writing Desk, The.
"Korzhavin." I was never an ascetic.
Kovner. While at Prayer.
Kung Tzu-chen. My neighbor's child cries in the middle of the night.
"Kusikov." Mountain Forest.
Lamb, L. New Canto, A.
Landon. Stanzas on the Death of Mrs Hemans.
Landor, W. Proud word you never spoke, but you will speak.
Lane, P. Midnight Song.
Larkin, P. Limerick: "There was an old fellow of Kaber."
Lawrence, D. Fate and the Younger Generation.
  I Am in a Novel.
Layton. Berry Picking.
  Birth of Tragedy, The.
Lazarus, E. Echoes.
Leapor. Headache, The.
  Upon Her Play Being Returned to Her, Stained with Claret.
Lear, E. Self-Portrait of the Laureate of Nonsense.
Leonard, T. Fathers and Sons.
  Good Style.
Levertov. Caedmon.
  Common Ground, A.
  Secret, The.

Levine, P.   On the Edge.
Levy, A.   London Poets.
Lewis, A.   To Edward Thomas.
Lewis, E.   Mirror for Detractors, A.
Li Ho.   My Man Pa Replies.
Li K'ai-hsien.   Poem Expressing My Wife's Response to One I Sent Her, A.
Wei-ch'i Chess.
Li Tung-yang.   To Yung-erh—Imitating a Work by Master Jade Stream.
Lipsitz.   Skinny / poem, / all / your / ribs.
Little, J.   Given to a Lady Who Asked Me to Write a Poem.
Lochhead, L.   Mad Meg on my mantelpiece.
Longfellow, H.   Picture-Writing.
Poets, The.
Longley, M.   Freeze-up annexes the sea even, The.
Lorde.   Learning to Write.
Paperweight.
Lowell, A.   Sisters, The.
Lowell, J.   Emerson.
Lowell, R.   Epilogue: "Those blessèd structures, plot and rhyme."
For John Berryman.
Ford Madox Ford ("Lobbed ball plops, then dribbles to the cup, The").
Lowry, M.   After Publication of Under the Volcano.
Epitaph: "Malcolm Lowry."
Joseph Conrad.
Strange Type.
Lu Yu.   After Getting Drunk, I Scribble Songs and Poems.
Inscribed on My Grass-script Calligraphy Written While Drunk.
Shown to My Son Yü.
Lukonin.   My Friends.
MacBeth.   Orange Poem, The.
"MacDiarmid."   Ah, Lenin, you were richt. But I'm a poet.
Jean! Jean! Gin she's no' here it's no' oor bed.
Machi.   Tanka: "From the moment."
MacLeish.   Ars Poetica.
Critical Observations.
Reasons for Music.
Reproach to Dead Poets.
MacNeice.   Elegy for Minor Poets.
Madhubuti.   Poet: What Ever Happened to Luther?
Magee, K.   Instrumentum Vocale.
Magrelli.   I look for a way of writing.
Pen slides, The.
Ten poems written in one month.
Mahon.   Table Talk.
Mandelstam.   Enough of snivelling! Shove our papers in the desk.
Manilius.   From whose large mouth for verse all that since live.
Marston, J.   Fy Satyre fie, shall each mechanick slave.
Martial.   Ad Sabellum.
Post-Obits and the Poets.
To my ill Reader.
Your bookcases are crammed with manuscripts.
Marvell.   On Mr Milton's "Paradise Lost."
Masters, E.   Margaret Fuller Slack.
Petit, the Poet.
Matthews, W.   Cat, The.
Dream, The.
Mingus at the Showplace.
Matuzeviius.   Writing in the Fire, The.
Maunick.   This Strange Calculation of Roots.
Maxton.   Ode.
Mayakovsky.   No matter how much more waiting I'll have to do.
Mayer, B.   Sonnet: "Beauty of songs your absence I should not show."
McCarriston.   Revision.
McClatchy.   At a Reading.
McElroy, C.   Learning to Swim at Forty-Five.
McGrath, C.   James Wright, Richard Hugo, the Vanishing Forests of the Pacific Northwest.
McMahon, L.   Hopkins and Whitman.
McOrlan.   Modern circus, The.

Meinke.   Poet, Trying to Surprise God, The.
Melville, H.   Camoëns.
Melville, P.   Honor Maria, I see you.
Meng Chiao.   Lament for Lu Yin.
Seeing Off Master Tan.
Merrill, J.   Angel.
Merry.   Genius, or Muse, whate'er thou art! whose thrill.
To Anna Matilda.
Merwin, W.   One of the Lives.
Unwritten, The.
Miller, E.   Another Love Affair/Another Poem.
Miller, V.   Subterfuge.
Milne, E.   Diamond Cut Diamond.
Milton.   On Shakespear[e].
Mnthali.   To the Writers' Worship in Zomba.
Montagu, L.   Verses Addressed to the Imitator of the First Satire of the Second Book of Horace: An Attack on Pope.
Moore, M.   Baseball and Writing.
Poetry.
Moore, M.   Literature: The God, Its Ritual.
Moore, T.   Announcement of a New Grand Acceleration Company for the Promotion of the Speed of Literature.
Moorsom.   Don't be literary, darling, don't be literary.
Morgan, E.   After a Death.
Morton, J.   Someone asked the publisher.
Muir, E.   To Franz Kafka.
Mukhopadhyay, S.   Task, The.
Muldoon, P.   Briefcase, The.
Mura.   Grandfather-in-law.
Myers, J.   Experts, The.
Nabokov.   Fame.
What is the evil deed I have committed?
Naden.   Moonlight and Gas.
Poet and Botanist.
Nagy, A.   To a Poet.
Nam Trân.   Beauty and the Poet.
Narayana Rao, V.   White Paper.
Nekrasova.   Rublyov XVth Century.
Nemerov.   Makers, The.
Media.
Style.
Newcastle, M.   Claspe, The.
'Poet I am neither born, nor bred," A.
Poetresses Hasty Resolution, The.
Poetresses Petition, The.
Nguyễn Chí Thiện.   My poetry is no poetry, no.
Nguyễn Nhu'o'c Pháp.   In a Garret.
Ni Tsan.   Man in Hangchou Spread Word that I Had Died. Chen-chü Heard of This and Was Upset, So I Have Written This To Send Him, A.
Nicholson, N.   To the River Duddon.
Niedecker.   Element Mother, The.
Noguere.   Scribes, The.
Secret, The.
Norris, L.   Thin Prison, The.
Norse.   Believing in the Absurd.
Business of poetry, The.
Norton, C.   Obscurity of Woman's Worth.
Notley.   Jack Would Speak Through the Imperfect Medium of Alice.
O'Grady, D.   Reading the Unpublished Manuscripts of Louis MacNeice at Kinsale Harbour.
O'Hara, F.   Answer to Voznesensky and Evtushenko.
Day Lady Died, The.
Les Luths.
My Heart.
Ode: Salute to the French Negro Poets.
Personal Poem.
Poetry.
To Hell with It.
Today.
Why I Am Not a Painter.
Okudzhava.   Reflections Near the House Where Titian Tabidze Lived.
They exterminate poets.
Oldham, J.   One night, as I was pondering of late.
Ondaatje.   Burning Hills.

Oppen.   Silver as / The needle's eye.
Taste, The.
Orlovsky.   Collaboration: Letter to Charlie Chaplin.
Ovid.   1.15.
Conclusion.
Elegies 3.1: "Old wood stands uncut, of long years' space, An."
Padgett, R.   Advice to Young Writers.
Page, G.   Elegist, The.
Jerry's Plains, 1848.
Late Night Radio.
Pagis.   Houses.
Palmer, M.   Eighth Sky.
Fifth Prose.
Notes for Echo Lake 3.
Sun.
Park, H.   Ode to Merciful Bodhisattva.
Parkes, B.   For Adelaide.
To an Author who Loved Truth More than Fame.
To Elizabeth Barrett Browning.
Parshchikov.   Prelude, Spoken to My Work Tools.
Pasolini.   Day of My Death, The.
Pastan.   Ars Poetica.
Elegy.
Pasternak, B.   Darling, it's frightening! When a poet loves.
Feasts, The.
Peake.   I cannot give the reasons.
Perelman.   Chronic Meanings.
Let's Say.
Money.
Things.
Petrov, A.   Poetry in the Underground Passage.
Philips, K.   To her royall highnesse the Dutchesse of Yorke.
Phillips, C.   Passing.
Phùng Quán.   What Mother Told Me Once.
Pindar.   Oh! Sovereign of the willing soul.
Pizzarelli.   Tonite.
Plumly.   Reading with the Poets.
Plumpp.   Poems are not places.
Po Chü-i.   Fifteenth Volume, The.
Idle Droning.
Illness and idleness give me much leisure.
Mad Poem Addressed to My Nephews and Nieces, A.
Madly Singing in the Mountains.
On a Box Containing his Own Works.
On Board Ship: Reading Yüan Chên's Poems.
Poem on the Wall, The.
Polwhele.   Thou, who with all the poet's genuine rage.
Pope, A.   Epigram from the French: "Sir, I admit your general [or gen'ral] Rule."
Epistle to Dr Arbuthnot, An: "There are, who to my person pay their court."
Epitaph for One Who Would Not Be Buried in Westminster Abbey ("Heroes, and Kings! your distance keep").
Essay on Criticism.
Impromptu.
Porter, P.   On This Day I Complete My Fortieth Year.
Pound, E.   E. P. Ode Pour l'Election de Son Sepulchre.
Soirée.
Tea-rose tea-gown, etc.
Pratt, M.   Poem for My Sons.
Prayton.   Paradice on earth is found, A.
Pritam, A.   Creative Process, The.
Quiller-Couch.   Harbour of Fowey, The.
Quillinan.   Hour Glass, The.
Rabéarivelo.   One day some young poet.
Reading.
You delude yourself.
Your Work.
Ralegh, W.   Epitaph on Sir Philip Sidney.
If Cynthia be a queen, a princess, and supreme.
In Commendation of George Gascoigne's Steel Glass.
To the Translator of Lucan [or Lucan's Pharsalia, 1614].

Ransom, J. Conrad in Twilight.
Survey of Literature.
Rashidi Samarqandi. Complaint to a Court
Poet.
Redmond. Parapoetics.
Reese, L. Lyric on the Lyric, A.
Reeves, J. W.
Rich, A. Focus.
Upper Broadway.
Robinson, E. Sonnet: "Master and the slave go
hand in hand, The."
Sonnet: "Oh for a poet—for a beacon bright."
Roethke. Supper with Lindsay.
Rossetti, C. L.E.L E. L.
Rossetti, D. On the Poet, Arthur
O'Shaughnessy—.
Rothenberg, J. Portrait of Myself with Arshile
Gorky and Gertrude Stein.
Rowe, E. Forgo the charming Muses! No, in
spite.
Rowe, G. Mrs. Francis Ellen Harper.
Rowlands. Prologue: "Under the shadow of
the gloomy night."
Roy, L. Bread Man, The.
Rózewicz. Memory of a Dream From the
Year 1963.
Poem of Pathos.
Who Is a Poet.
"Samoylov." Old Derzhavin.
Sanchez, S. To P. J. (2 Yrs Old Who Sed
Write a Poem for Me in Portland, Oregon).
Sandburg, C. One Modern Poet.
Ten Definitions of Poetry.
Sansom, M. It was not that I lost direction.
Sarton. My Sisters, O My Sisters.
Scannell. Poem on Bread.
Schwartz, D. Baudelaire.
Scott, A. Coronach.
Selvinsky. Sebastopol.
"Severyanin." Epilogue: "I, the genius
Severyanin."
Sexton. Black Art, The.
Obsessive Combination of Ontological Inscape,
Trickery and Love, An.
Seymour, A. Millionaire.
Shakespeare, W. Post Mortem.
Sonnet 21.
Sonnet 23.
Sonnet 76.
Sonnet 78.
Sonnet 80.
Sonnet 86.
Sonnet 106.
Sonnet 110.
Sonnet 116.
Sonnet: "What's in the braine that Inck may
character."
Shange. Oh, I'm 10 Months Pregnant.
You are sucha fool / i haveta love you.
Shapiro, D. Archaic Torsos.
Realistic Bar and Grill, A.
Shapiro, H. Hello There!
Shen Chou. Bamboo Villa, The.
Consoling Wu Te-cheng on the Death of His
Son.
To the Tune "Nan-hsiang-tzu."
Sidney, P. Sonnet 1: "Loving in truth, and
fain[e] in verse my love to show."
Sonnet 3: "Let dainty wits cry on the sisters
nine."
Sonnet 15: "You that do search for every
purling spring."
Sonnet 27: "Because I oft, in dark abstracted
guise."
Sonnet 90: "Stella, think not that I by verse
seek fame."
Simmons, J. Written, Directed by and Starring.
Simpson, L. American Poetry.
Suddenly.
Singh, K. On Reading a Love Poem.
Sirr. Beginnings.
Skelton, J. Phillip Sparow.
Slingeland. About Writing Poetry.
Slutsky. Prosaics.
Smith, C. Partial Muse, has from my earliest
hours, The.
Smith, D. Reading the Books Our Children

Have Written.
Spring Poem, The.
Smith, I. Oban 1955–82.
Smith, S. Lads of the village, we read in the
lay, The.
Portrait.
Souvenir de Monsieur Poop.
Sterilization.
To School!
Voice from the Tomb (1).
Snyder, G. As for Poets.
Axe Handles.
How Poetry Comes to Me.
Riprap.
Sóng Hồng. To be a poet—if it means to hum
with winds.
Sorrentino. September in Kittery.
Soutar. Makar, The.
Southey, R. Cataract of Lodore, The.
Scholar, The.
Southwick. Horse on the Wall.
Spark. Against the Transcendentalists.
Going up to Sotheby's.
Spaziani. Merciful Shore, The.
Spenser.
Sonnet 1: "Happy ye leaves! whenas those lily
hands."
Sonnet 75: "One day I wrote her name upon
the strand."
Sonnet 80: "After so long a race as I have run."
Starbuck, G. Said / Agatha Christie to.
Stedman, E. Prelude to *An American
Anthology.*
Stein, G. Patriarchal poetry their origin their
history their origin.
Stephen, J. Sonnet, A: "Two voices are there:
one is of the deep."
Stern, G. Romance.
Stevens, W. Bantams in Pine-Woods.
Epilogue: "Soldier, there is a war between the
mind."
Of Modern Poetry.
Planet on the Table, The.
Ultimate Poem Is Abstract, The.
Stevenson, A. Fiction-Makers, The.
Making Poetry.
Re-reading Jane.
Stevenson, R. Fragment, A: "Thou strainest
through the mountain fern."
Henry James.
To the Muse.
Stokesbury. To His Book.
Strand. Eating Poetry.
Szymborska. Starvation Camp near Jaslo.
Tada. Poetry Calendar, A.
Taggart, J. Pen Vine and Scroll.
Tai Piao-yüan. Returning to Yin-ch'eng Early
in the Year *Ting-ch'ou* (1277).
T'ang Yin. Inscribed on a Painting ("At the
country inn, thousands of peach trees").
Ten days of wind and rain, depressing
darkness!
Tarkovsky. Poet, The.
Sight grows dim—my power.
Tate, A. Non Omnis Moriar.
Tate, G. Last Instructions.
Tate, J. Teaching the Ape to Write Poems.
Tekkan. Tanka: "Too emotional."
Tennyson, A. What hope is here for modern
rhyme.
Thomas, D. Author's Prologue.
Especially when the October wind.
In my craft or sullen art.
On no work of words now for three lean
months in the bloody.
Thomas, L. Marvelous Land of Indefinitions,
The.
Thompson, F. From stones and poets you may
know.
Thribb. Lines on the Hundredth Anniversary
of the Birth of W. Somerset Maugham.
Thù'a Phong. Mother's Faith.
Thwaite. Great Foreign Writer Visits Age-Old
Temple, Greeted by Venerable Abbess, 1955.
Tipping. Poet at Work.
Tomlinson, C. Macduff.
Trinh Tiên. Woman Writes to Her Daughter

Who's Studying Overseas, A.
Troupe. In Jimmy's Garden.
Ts'ao P'i. Lotus Lake.
Tu Fu. Snow Storm.
To Li Po at the Sky's End.
To Pi Ssu Yao.
Traveler at Night Writes His Thoughts, A.
Tuckerman, F. As sometimes in a grove at
morning chime.
But war his overturning trumpet blew.
His heart was in his garden; but his brain.
Turner, F. On the Pains of Translating Miklós
Radnóti.
Unknown. Certain scholar named Mr. Wang,
A.
China has many people and many heroes.
Fascinating Poet's Dream, A.
Limerick: "Well, it's partly the shape of the
thing."
Riddle: "Land was white, The."
Tune: "Celebration in the Eastern Plain"—
Replying to a Lyric Song by the Senior Poet
Ma Chih-yüan.
Van Duyn. Moose in the Morning, Northern
Maine.
Vision Test, The.
Vaughan, H. To the Most Excellently
Accomplished Mrs. Katherine Philips.
Vinokurov. Poetry Editor.
Voigt. Dancing with Poets.
Voznesensky. Dogalypse.
Two Poems.
Vrettakos. Poet, The.
Vũ Hoàng Chu'o'ng. Beau Ideal, The.
Wagoner, D. Walking in the Snow.
Wakoski. Hummingbird Light.
Walcott. Codicil.
Hotel Normandie Pool, The.
Man Who Loved Islands, The.
Volcano.
Waldman, A. Evangelle.
Two Men.
Wallace, R. Double-Play, The.
Waller, E. Of English Verse.
Wang Chiu-ssu. Chanting Poems.
Quiet Sitting.
Total failure—mdash;Master Han Shan, A.
Wang T'ing-hsiang. Written in the Office
Precincts.
Warren, R. Flaubert in Egypt.
Watson, S. To Lord Tennyson.
Watten. Statistics.
Wayman. Despair.
Welch, L. In Answer to a Question From P.
W.
Whenever I make a new poem.
Welish. Blood or Color.
Kiss Tomorrow Goodbye.
Wen Cheng-ming. Where among the blue
clouds.
While It Was Raining.
Whalen. Walking beside the Kamogawa,
Remembering Nansen and Fudo and Gary's
Poem.
Whateley. On the Author's Husband Desiring
Her to Write Some Verses.
Wheatley, P. To Mæcenas.
Whitman, A. Poet hath a realm within, and
throne, The.
Whitman, W. As I lay with my head in your
lap camerado.
As I sit writing here, sick and grown old.
Excelsior.
Here the frailest leaves of me and yet my
strongest lasting.
I am the poet of reality.
Now precedent songs, farewell—by every
name farewell.
To a Certain Civilian.
Whittier. Proem: "I love the old melodious
lays."
Wilbur. Beasts in their major freedom /
Slumber in peace tonight.
Cottage Street, 1953.
Digression, A.
To an American Poet Just Dead.
To the Etruscan Poets.

Writer, The.
Wilde, L. Désillusion.
Poet's Destiny, The.
Willard, N. One for the Road.
Why I Never Answered Your Letter.
William of Aquitaine. I will write a poem about nothing.
Williams, W. Apology.
Sort of a Song, A.
To an Elder Poet.
Wind Increases, The.
Wilson, E. Enemies of Promise.
Wilson, T. Magpies in Picardy, The.
Winchilsea. Answer, The.
Circuit of Apollo, The.
Introduction, The: "Did I, my lines intend for public[k] view."
Wither. For a Poet.
Woodbridge. Upon the Author. By a Known Friend
Wordsworth, W. London 1802.
Poet!—He Hath Put His Heart to School, A.
Sonnet: "Scorn not the sonnet; critic, you have frowned."
Woroszylski. Franz Kafka (II).
Wright, C. Dog Day Vespers.
Wright, J. To the Poets in New York.
Wyat. What makes me write my dearest Freind you aske.
Wyatt, T. My pen, take pain a little space.
Xuân Diệu. Feelings and Emotions.
Foreword to a Book of Poems.
Yang Chi. On Seeing a Firefly in My Room.
Submitting a Memorial Requesting Permission to Return Home and Care for My Parents.
Walking in the Country outside T'ai-yüan on a Spring Day.
Yang Shih-ch'i. Inscribed on the Painting, Stabbing a Tiger, by Chao Tzu-ang, in the Collection of Scholar Yang.
Not sobered up from my muddy Kao-yang drunk.
Yeats. Coole Park, 1929.
Ego Dominus Tuus.
Model for the Laureate, A.
On Being Asked for a War Poem.
Pardon, old fathers, if you still remain.
To a Poet, Who Would Have Me Praise Certain Bad Poets, Imitators of His and Mine.
Yesenin. From the start, each living thing's.
Yevtushenko. From a Talk.
Yosano. Tanka: "Writes poetry."
That evening when.
Young, A. Loneliness.
Prestidigitator 1, The.
Studio Up Over In Your Ear.
Yes, the Secret Mind Whispers.
Yukitsuna. Tanka: "Bloom finished, The."
Yün Shou-p'ing. As old age approaches.
Zephaniah. According to my Mood.
See also **Handwriting**

Wyatt, Sir Thomas
Amis, K. Note on Wyatt, A.
Surrey. Another Tribute to Wyatt.
Death of Wyatt, The.
In Praise of Wyatt's Psalms.
Tribute to Wyatt.

Wyoming (state)
Major, C. I Was Looking for the University.
Stafford, W. Accountability.

X

X-Rays
Eybers. Röntgen Photograph.
Goedicke. One More Time.
Plomer. Walk in Würzburg, A.

Xantippe
Levy, A. Xantippe.

Xenophanes
Emerson, R. Xenophanes.

Y

Yachts
Spencer, B. Yachts on the Nile.

Williams, W. Yachts, The.
See also **Boats; Sailing and Sailors**

Yaks
Belloc. Yak, The.
Corso. Mad Yak, The.

Yangtze River
Li Meng-yang. Mooring at Hsia-k'ou at Night.
Lu Yu. I Had Occasion to Tell a Visitor about an Old Trip I Took.
Merchant's Joy, The.
Ni Tsan. Inscribed on the Painting, "River in Autumn."
Po Chü-i. Alarm at First Entering the Yangtze Gorges.
Wang An-shih. On the Yangtze.
Wang Shih-chieng. Crossing the Yangtze in a Strong Wind.
Wang T'ing-hsiang. Song of the Wanderer.
Wen Cheng-ming. I sit on horseback at Twin Bridges.
Yang Wei-chen. Song of the Merchant's Wife.
Yu Kuang-chung. When I am dead, lay me down between the Yangtze.

Yankees (New York baseball team)
Moore, M. Baseball and Writing.
Petersen. Ballad of Dead Yankees, The.

Yarrow [*or* Yarrow Water], Scotland
Logan, J. Braes of Yarrow, The.
Unknown. Willy Drowned in Yarrow.
Wordsworth, W. Yarrow Unvisited [1803].
Yarrow Visited [September, 1814].

Years
Haavikko. Days become years. Years.
One who writes us is now doing four plays a year, The.
Landor, W. Love and Age.
Lister, R. Toast to 2,000, A.
Longfellow, H. Poet's Calendar, The.
Moore, M. What Are Years?
Orban, O. Certain Years.
Pagis. Wall Calendar.
Probyn. Anniversaries.
Shelley, P. Time.
Spencer, T. Day was a year at first, The.
Tada. Poetry Calendar, A.

Yeats, John Butler
Ferlinghetti, L. 26.

Yeats, William Butler
Auden. Earth, receive an honoured guest.
Chesterton, G. After W. B. Yeats.
Ferlinghetti, L. Reading Yeats.
French, W. Queen's After-Dinner Speech, The.
Ginsberg, A. After Yeats.
Keyes, S. William Yeats in Limbo.
Stuart, F. Remembering Yeats.
Tate, A. Winter Mask.
Yeats. Circus Animals' Desertion, The.

Yellow (color)
Collop. Praise of a Yellow Skin, The, or An Elizabeth in Gold.
Herrick. How Marigolds Came Yellow.
Hongo. Yellow Light.
Preil, G. Yellow sunset splashes in the window, A.
Wilde, O. Symphony in Yellow.

Yew Trees
Boker. Leaden eyelids of wan twilight close, The.
Plath. Moon and the Yew Tree, The.
Tennyson, A. Old yew, which graspest at the stones.
Thompson, F. Fallen Yew, A.
Wordsworth, W. Yew-Trees.

Yiddish
Glatstein. Where the Cedars.

Ying Yao
Wang Wei. Weeping for Ying Yao.

Yom Kippur
Amichai. On the Day of Atonement.
Bloch, C. Yom Kippur.
Leiser, J. Kol Nidra.
Milosz, C. To Raja Rao.
Zangwill. Yom Kippur.

York, Anne Hyde, Duchess of
Philips, K. To her royall highnesse the Dutchesse of Yorke.

Yorkshire, England
"Ophelia." Snaith Marsh; a Yorkshire Pastoral.
Young, A. In Teesdale.

Yoruba
Lorde. Winds of Orisha, The.

Young, Brigham
Taylor, B. Nauvoo.

Young, Lester
Berrigan, T. String of Pearls.
Eshleman, C. Foo to the Infinite.
Young, A. Lester Leaps In.
Zimmer. Sitting with Lester Young.

Young Men's Christian Association
Linden, M. Y. M. C. A, The.

Youth
Adams, A. Her Dancing Days.
Akhmadulina. Fairy Tale about Rain, A.
Alcaeus. O frail flower.
Allen, E. Rock Me to Sleep[, Mother].
Arnold, M. Youth and Calm.
Ashbery. Other Tradition, The.
Our Youth.
Barker, J. To My Young Lover.
Baumel. Thirty-Six Poets.
Bawer. Grand Central Station, 20 December 1987.
Beauvais. Furniture.
Beckett, S. Gnome.
Betjeman. Youth and Age on Beaulieu River, Hants.
Bialik. Talmud Student, The.
Blake, W. Ah Sun-flower.
School-Boy, The.
Voice of the Ancient Bard, The.
Bly, R. For My Son Noah, Ten Years Old.
Brome. Epithalamy.
Brooke, R. Sonnet: In Time of Revolt.
Brooks, G. We real cool. We.
Browning, R. Youth and Art.
Bynner. Lines to Do with Youth.
Byron, G. 'All Is Vanity, Saith the Preacher'.
Stanzas Written on the Road between Florence and Pisa.
Campion, T. First Love.
There is a Garden in her face.
What fair pomp have I spied of glittering ladies.
Carew, T. To My Cousin (C.R.) Marrying My Lady (A.)
"Carroll." Father William.
Cervantes. Meeting Mescalito at Oak Hill Cemetery.
Ch'u Yüan. Yüan, Ch'ü.
Clare, J. To a Bower.
When I was young I fell in love and got but little good on't.
Clark, T. You (II).
Clifton, L. There Is a Girl Inside.
Clive. Old Age.
Coleman, W. At the Record Hop.
Coleridge, M. Unwelcome.
Coleridge, S. Youth and Age.
Cowley, H. Departed Youth.
Crane, H. Legend.
Cullen, C. Uncle Jim.
Youth Sings a Song of Rosebuds.
Cummings, E. Old age sticks / up Keep.
One Fine Day.
You shall above all things be glad and young.
Custance. Peacocks: A Mood.
Dao. Résumé.
Darr. At Sixteen.
"Der Nistor." At the Doors.
Dickey, J. Leap, The.
Dove, R. Flash Cards.
Dunn, S. Tenderness.
Vanishings, The.
Eberhart, R. Youth and Age.
Ehrhart. ". . . the light that cannot fade. . . ."
Elizabeth I. When I was fair and young, then [*or* and] favour graced me;.
Elovic. Brooklyn Bound.
Embiricos. Caryatids, The.
Emerson, R. I Can.
In an age of fops and toys.

Fanshawe, C. When last we parted, thou wert young and fair.
Felltham. On a Hopeful Youth.
Ferlinghetti, L. Pennycandystore beyond the El, The.
Fitzgerald, E. 27.
Frost, R. Birches.
Gay, J. Cotillion.
Youth and Love.
Gibbs, B. "What You See Is Me."
Glazkov. Poetograd.
Gluck, L. Garden, The.
Goldberg, L. Remembrance of Beginnings of Things.
Gray, J. Parsifal Imitated from the French of Paul Verlaine.
Gray, T. Ode on a Distant Prospect of Eton College.
Greville, F. Sonnet: "Nurse-life wheat within his green husk growing, The."
Grimké, A. When the green lies over the earth, my dear.
Hardy, T. Superseded, The.
Hayden, R. Paul Laurence Dunbar.
Hays, H. For One Who Died Young.
Heaney, S. Guttural Muse, The.
Heard, J. To Youth.
Herbert, G. Answer, The.
Herrick. To [the] Virgins, to Make Much of Time.
Hine. Côte de Liesse.
Hogg, J. Boy's Song, A.
Holan. Cave of Words, The.
Holden, J. Seventeen.
"Hope." Youth.
Horace. 1.25: Ribald Romeos Less and Less Berattle ("Parcius iunctas quatiunt fenestras").
Odes 1.9.
Odes 4.7.
Horat. Carm. lib. 4. Ode 13.
Soracte.
To his Friend in Love with a young Girl.
Housman, A. Here dead lie we because we did not choose.
Lads in their hundreds to Ludlow come in for the fair, The.
Loitering with a vacant eye.
Think no more, lad; laugh, be jolly.
When I was one-and-twenty.
Howard, W. Young men!
Huch. Young Girl.
Hull, L. Holy City, City of Night.
Irvine, W. To be Young, Gifted, and Black.
Jarman, M. Los Angeles.
Jeffers, R. Age in Prospect.
Jiménez, J. Green was the maiden, green, green!
Johnson, G. Lost Illusions.
Youth.
Johnson, S. Short Song of Congratulation [or To a Young Heir], A.
Jonson, B. Death and Love.
Song. To Celia ("Come my Celia, let us prove").
Jordan, J. Unemployment/Monologue.
Kerouac. My Gang.
127th Chorus.
Kingsley, C. Young and Old.
Kinzie. Glinting like water.
Kipling, R. My Rival.
R.A.F. (Aged Eighteen).
Knight, E. For Freckle-Faced Gerald.
Korkiya. Stanzas: "With youthful loss of memory, in my voiceless land."
Kunio. Tanka: "Stalwartly."
Larkin, P. Sad Steps.
Wild Oats.
Lawrence, D. White Horse, The.
Youth Mowing, A.
Lazarus, E. Youth.
Le Gallienne. To the Reader.
Le Pan. Incident, An.
Levine, P. You Can Have It.
Li Po. River Merchant's Wife, The; a Letter.
Lindsay, V. Leaden-eyed, The.
Lindsay, V. Leaden-Eyed, The.
Liu Yung. Tune: "Wanderings of a Youth."

Llywelyn-Williams. When I Was Young.
Longfellow, H. My Lost Youth.
Lorde. Generation.
Major, C. My Seasonal Body, My Ears.
Mapanje. On African Writing.
Mazur. Lilacs on Brattle Street.
McCord, D. Blesséd Lord, What It Is to Be Young.
McGinley. Ballade of Lost Objects.
Portrait of Girl with Comic Book.
Village Spa.
Mei Yao Ch'en. Next Door.
Merrill, J. Watching the Dance.
Merwin, W. Lament for the Makers.
Meynell, A. October Redbreast, The.
Mezey. If I Should Die Before I Wake.
Miles, J. Album.
Milosz, C. Bypassing rue Descartes.
Milton. Fifth Ode of Horace. Lib. I, The.
Sonnet: "How soon hath Time the suttle [or subtle] theef [or thief] of youth."
Moore, T. I Saw from the Beach.
Moritz. In that town I was twenty. Snow there lay.
Murphy, R. Morning Call.
Nemerov. Blue Suburban.
Boy with Book of Knowledge.
O'Hara, F. Blocks.
Olds, S. 35/10.
Ovid. Elegies 3.6.
Come then sick youth unto my sacred skill.
Owen, W. Anthem for Doomed Youth.
Parable of the Old Man and the Young, The.
Sonnet, to a Child.
Patchen. Street Corner College.
Petri. Christmas 1956.
Pilinszky. On the Back of a Photograph.
Pinkney, E. Voyager's Song, The.
Po Chü-i. At the End of Spring.
Going to the Mountains with a Little Dancing Girl, Aged Fifteen.
Poe. Happiest day—the happiest hour, The.
Lake: To———, The.
Pound, E. River-Merchant's Wife: A Letter, The.
Praed. School and Schoolfellows.
Prior. Phillis's Age.
Ralegh, W. Nature, that washed her hands in milk.
Ranaivo. Distress.
Ransom, J. Piazza Piece.
Vision by Sweetwater.
Reid, A. Daedalus.
Rich, A. Middle-Aged, The.
Riley, J. Old Swimmin'-Hole, The.
Robinson, A. Sibyl, The.
Robinson, R. Creek, The.
Rochester, J. Against Constancy.
Roethke. Her Words.
Wish for a Young Wife.
Rossetti, C. Dream-Love.
Rowe, G. His Boyhood.
Rukeyser, M. Poem Out of Childhood.
Rutsala. Lovers in Summer.
"Samoylov." Forties, fateful forties, The.
Sappho. These are the ashes of Timas.
Satyamurti. Day Trip.
Schneour. Cherries.
Senghor. Luxembourg 1939.
Shakespeare, W. Madrigal, A: "Crabbed age and youth cannot live together."
Sonnet 3.
Sonnet 126.
Sweet-and-Twenty.
Shaoxuan. Black hair and red cheeks: for how long?
Sherwood, G. Song of a Young Lady to Her Ancient Lover, A.
Shūji. Tanka: "Like a long."
Sidney, P. Sonnet 21: "Your words my friend (right healthful caustics) blame."
Simmons, J. One of the Boys.
Smelyakov. Lovely Leda.
Sokolov. Snow's white pencil outlining the buildings...
Sorrentino. Razzmatazz.

Southey, R. Old Man's Comforts and How He Gained Them, The.
Stevenson, R. In the States.
Sing me a song of a lad that is gone.
Stoddard, R. Never Again.
Stone, R. How to Catch Aunt Harriette.
Suckling, J. Against Fruition ("Stay here, fond youth, and ask no more").
Surrey. Laid in my quiet bed, in study as I were.
Swenson, M. How to Be Old.
Symons, A. Emmy ("Emmy's exquisite youth and her virginal air").
Faint Love.
Thymocles. Remember now? Do you.
Toomer. Delivered at the Knighting of Lord Durgling by Great Bruce-Jean.
Troupe. Reflections on Growing Older.
Turner, N. Washington.
Unknown. Milla, the glory of whose beauteous rays.
On a Female Rope-Dancer.
Van Duyn. What the Motorcycle Said.
Vaux. Age Looks Back at Youth.
Verlaine. L'Allée.
Vinokurov. Shows.
Vũ Hoàng Chu'o'ng. To the Black Nymph.
Wain. When It Comes.
Walcott. Glory Trumpeter, The.
Wallace, R. In a Spring Still Not Written Of.
Wever. In Youth Is Pleasure.
Whitman, W. We two boys together clinging.
Wickham. Pilgrimage.
Wilbur. Star System, The.
Williams, C. World's greatest tricycle rider, The.
Williams, J. On Reading Aloud My Early Poems.
Williams, W. Deceptrices, The.
Winchilsea. Upon My Lord Winchilsea's Converting the Mount in His Garden to a Terrace.
Wordsworth, W. Edward VI.
Foster-Mother's Tale.
Wright, J. Child, The.
Wyatt, T. Lament my loss[e], my labo[u]r, and my pain [or payne].
Since love is such that, as ye wot.
Yeats. Brown Penny.
Crazy Jane Grown Old Looks at the Dancers.
Down by the salley gardens my love and I did meet;.
On Hearing That the Students of Our New University Have Joined the Agitation against Immoral Literature.
Politics.
To a Young Girl.
Whence Had They Come?
Who Goes with Fergus?
Youth and Age.
Young, D. Twilight with Xs.
Yuan Chi. Regret.
Zabolotsky. Ivanovs, The.
Ugly Girl, The.

Yugoslavia

Christopher. Terminus.
Durrell. Sarajevo.
Hampton. Yugoslav Story.
Hugo, R. Yards of Sarajevo, The.
Radnóti. Seventh Eclogue.
Scully, J. Crew Practice on Lake Bled, in Jugoslavia.

Yukio Mishima. *See* **Mishima, Yukio**

Yukon Territory

Service. Cremation of Sam McGee, The.
Spell of the Yukon, The.

Z

Zacchaeus

Quarles. On Zacchaeus [or Zachens].

Zambia

Livesay, D. Leader, The.

Zebras

Campbell, R. Zebras, The.

Unknown. Zebra.
  Zebra Stallion.

Zen Buddhism
  Allen, P. Zen Americana.
  Chia Tao. Weeping for the Zen Master Po-
    yen.
  Dunn, S. Something Like Happiness.
  Equi. Sometimes I Get Distracted.
  Kyger. Philip Whalen's Hat.
  Liu Ch'ang-ch'ing. Rejoicing That the Zen
    Master Pao Has Arrived from Dragon
    Mountain.
  Pritchard, N. Love Poem.
  Snyder, G. December.
  Yüan Hung-tao. On Receiving My Letter of
    Termination.
  Record of My Trip to Mount She, A.
See also **Buddha and Buddhism**

Zeppelins. *See* **Dirigibles**

Zeus
  Aeschylus. Zeus, whoever Zeus may be, if he.
  Avianus. Monkey, The.
  Bowes-Lyon. Leda.
  Calas. Columns of the Temple of Olympian
    Zeus.
  "Field." Come, Gorgo, put the rug in place.
  Greenwell, D. Demeter and Cora.
  Hesiod. Bronze Age, The.
    Iron Age, The.
  Homer. Juno seduces Jove.
    Thetis Asks Jove to Revenge Her Son
    Achilles.
  Moschus. Into the Mead he comes, nor (seen)
    doth fright.
  Plomer. Europa.
  Spenser. Therein was writ, how often
    thundering Jove.

Unknown. But *Jove* at length with just
    Resentment fir'd.
  Yeats. Leda and the Swan.

Zinnias
  Worth, V. Zinnias, stout and stiff.

Zion
  Halevi. My Heart Is in the East.
    Ode to Zion.
    To the Western Wind.
  Heine. By the Waters of Babylon.
    Song: "There stands a lonely pine-tree."
  Kovner. I Don't Know if Mount Zion would
    recognize itself.
  Lazarus, E. New Ezekiel, The.
  Reznikoff. Hebrew of your poets, Zion, The.
  Rosenberg, I. Through These Pale Cold Days.
  Sampter. Kadia the Young Mother Speaks.
    Promised Land, The.
  Schneour. Last Words of Don Henriquez, The.
  Unknown. Light and Rejoicing to Israel.

Zionism
  Imber. Hatikvah—a Song of Hope.
    Zionist Marching Song.
  Schneour. Road, The.
  Zangwill. Theodor Herzl.

Zodiac
  Farjeon, E. Zodiac.
  Ruskin. Zodiac Song, The.
  Yeats. Chosen.
  Zabolotsky. Signs of the Zodiac are fading,
    The.

Zola, Émile
  Robinson, E. Zola.

Zoos
  Banker, I. Lion Thoughts.

Dickey, J. Encounter in the Cage Country.
  Edgar, M. Lion and Albert, The.
  Garrigue. False Country of the Zoo.
  Gillilan, P. Alien at the Zoo.
  Hughes, T. Jaguar, The.
  Jarrell. Woman at the Washington Zoo, The.
  Kavanagh, P. Goldie Sapiens.
  Ku. Shame.
  Kunio. Tanka: "All the way."
  Plomer. In the Snake Park.
  Ramanujan. In the Zoo.
  Sandburg, C. Elephants Are Different to
    Different People.
  Swenson, M. Lion.
  Thackeray. At the Zoo.
  Unknown. Cheerful old bear at the zoo, A.
  Van Amburgh's Menagerie ("Van Amburgh is
    the man that goes with all the shows").
  Wain. Au Jardin des Plantes.
  Williams, O. Picture Postcard of a Zoo.
  Wright, D. On the Death of an Emperor
    Penguin in Regent's Park, London.
  Yukitsuna. At the zoo (two poems).

Zulus
  Adisa. Women at the Crossroad / (May
    Elegba Forever Guard the Right Doors).
  Campbell, R. Zulu Girl, The.
  Kunene. Meeting with Vilakazi, the Great
    Zulu Poet, A.
  Mtshali. Birth of Shaka, The.
    Inside My Zulu Hut.
  Shapiro, H. National Cold Storage Company
    contains, The.
  Unknown. Lalela Zulu.
  Van den Heever. Fallen Zulu Commander,
    The.